1997

# Encyclopedia
## of
# Human Rights

# Encyclopedia
## of
# Human Rights

### Second Edition

## Edward Lawson

**With a Foreword by**

*José Ayala-Lasso*
**United Nations High Commissioner for Human Rights**

**Introductory Essay by**

*Laurie S. Wiseberg*
**Executive Director, Human Rights Internet**

**Research and Contributing Editor**
*Jan K. Dargel*
**University of Tampa, FL**

**Editor**
*Mary Lou Bertucci*
**Melrose Park, PA**

Taylor & Francis
*Publishers since 1798*

Published with the cooperation of the United Nations High Commissioner for Human Rights/Centre for Human Rights, as a contribution to the United Nations Decade on Human Rights Education, 1995–2005.

| USA | Publishing Office: | Taylor & Francis |
|-----|--------------------|------------------|
| | | 1101 Vermont Avenue, NW, Suite 200 |
| | | Washington, DC 20005-3521 |
| | | Tel: (202) 289-2174 |
| | | Fax: (202) 289-3665 |
| | Distribution Center: | Taylor & Francis |
| | | 1900 Frost Road, Suite 101 |
| | | Bristol, PA 19007-1598 |
| | | Tel: (215) 785-5800 |
| | | Fax: (215) 785-5515 |
| UK | | Taylor & Francis Ltd. |
| | | 1 Gunpowder Square |
| | | London EC4A 3DE |
| | | Tel: 0171 583 0490 |
| | | Fax: 0171 583 0581 |

**ENCYCLOPEDIA OF HUMAN RIGHTS, Second Edition**

1 2 3 4 5 6 7 8 9 0    E B E B    9 8 7 6

This book was set in Baskerville by Impressions Book and Journal Services, Inc. The editors were Mary Lou Bertucci, Christine Winter, and Catherine Simon. Technical development by Bernadette Capelle. Cover design by Michelle Fleitz. Printing and binding by Edwards Brothers, Inc.

A CIP catalog record for this book is available from the British Library.
♾ The paper in this publication meets the requirements of the ANSI Standard Z39.48-1984 (Permanence of Paper)

**Library of Congress Cataloging-in-Publication Data**

Encyclopedia of human rights / [compiled by] Edward Lawson : with a foreword by José Ayala-Lasso : introductory essay by Laurie S. Wiseberg : research and contributing editor, Jan K. Dargel : editor, Mary Lou Bertucci.—2nd ed.
    p.   cm.
   Includes index.

    1. Human rights—Encyclopedias.  2. Civil rights—Encyclopedias.
I. Lawson, Edward (Edward H.)  II. Bertucci, Mary Lou.
JC571.E67  1996             96-21852
323.4'03—dc20           CIP
ISBN 1-56032-362-0

# CONTENTS

# FOREWORD

In December 1994, the United Nations General Assembly proclaimed the period 1995–2005 "United Nations Decade for Human Rights Education" (Resolution 49/184 of 23 December 1994). The General Assembly also welcomed the Plan of Action for the Decade, as contained in the report of the United Nations Secretary-General.

This decision was taken pursuant to a recommendation of the World Conference on Human Rights (Vienna, June 1993) in the Vienna Declaration and Programme of Action, which stated that human rights education, training, and public information were essential for the promotion and achievement of stable and harmonious relations among communities and for fostering mutual understanding, tolerance, and peace. Education is a basic human right and a crucial tool for the promotion and protection of all human rights and fundamental freedoms.

Education must be directed, among other objectives, toward the strengthening of respect for human rights; the full development of the human personality and the sense of its dignity; the promotion of understanding, tolerance, gender equality, and friendship among all nations, indigenous peoples, racial, ethnic, and religious groups; the enabling of all persons to participate effectively in a free society and the furtherance of the activities of the United Nations for maintenance of peace.

The Decade for Human Rights Education focuses on stimulating and supporting local, national, and international initiatives and activities in human rights education and information.

Promoting human rights education is one of my major responsibilities as High Commissioner for Human Rights. Success in this common endeavour will depend upon the strength of the partnership we are able to build between Governments, international organizations, professional associations, academic institutions, and large segments of civil society.

At a time when human rights occupy a central position in all United Nations activities and are so closely linked to peace, democracy, and development, human rights education and information provide the best means of reaching the minds of all human beings, making everyone a direct participant in this cooperative effort.

The first edition of the *Encyclopedia of Human Rights* met with great success, particularly in the libraries of graduate and law schools of universities all over the world. This valuable initiative is a timely means of drawing attention to the distance already traveled and the progress that remains to be achieved toward universal respect for, and observance of, human rights for all—because human rights and fundamental freedoms are the birthright of all human beings.

This second edition, enriched with new texts of human rights international instruments and documents, is an important contribution to the United Nations Decade on Human Rights Education.

I would like to commend the author and the publishers for their forward-looking initiative as well as their dedication in fostering increased awareness and wider knowledge of human rights. I am convinced that this new edition will prove to be of value to all those interested in the promotion and protection of human rights and actively contribute to the building of a universal culture of human rights.

JOSÉ AYALA-LASSO
United Nations High Commissioner for Human Rights

# PREFACE

Five years have passed since the first edition of the *Encyclopedia of Human Rights* was published and offered to the general public. In that time it has established itself as a standard reference work on UN-related human rights activities and programs, and it is used daily by students of this and many related fields, by high officials of the UN's nearly 200 Member States, and by organizations that share in relevant activities.

But the landscape of human rights has changed between the first and this second edition. And it continues to change. Human rights are more accepted now than ever as basic entitlements. This is recognized in international law, the drafting of which as it relates to human rights is now nearly complete. Yet we have far to go in enforcing these rights. We have seen progress in the past 5 years, in the dismantling of apartheid in South Africa, the devolution of political rights to the former Soviet republics, and free elections in Haiti and Sierra Leone. We have also seen atrocities in Bosnia-Herzegovina, genocide in Rwanda and Burundi, and continued repression of the rights of women and children the world over.

The second edition of the *Encyclopedia of Human Rights* is both an updated edition and an expansion of the first. Errors have been corrected wherever found, and a few innovations have been made. It has been revised to include new documents and reports of recent events. Out-of-date information has been deleted except in cases where it appears to be of critical historical importance. Government-supplied information has been reproduced sparingly because of the possibility of self-interest in its selection or interpretation. Instead, this edition relies primarily on the reports of competent but substantially disinterested "Special Rapporteurs." Consultants and "treaty-monitoring" bodies have been officially designated to explore the most serious human rights problems— sometimes existing in a single country but frequently in a large area of the world.

In the increasingly numerous instances where reports are submitted to particular UN bodies in compliance with the requirements of international conventions that they have ratified, their reports are not only examined in public meetings of treaty-monitoring bodies, but the conclusions and recommendations of those bodies are made public. The States concerned have begun to find it helpful to report back to the UN the action they have taken to implement particular suggestions.

To make this *Encyclopedia* convenient and satisfactory in its field, various means have been employed. In physical details the book is compact and as nearly exhaustive as possible (although at nearly 5 pounds it is perhaps a bit on the heavy side). Because space is at a premium, every effort has been made to avoid duplication, particularly through the provision of numerous cross-references and a comprehensive index designed to link up entries on particular aspects of a single subject. The substance of the entries provides essential information in language intelligible to the ordinary reader.

The *Encyclopedia* is in no sense an official publication of the United Nations. It is rather only one of many answers to appeals for help in disseminating and explaining the human rights program of the United Nations to peoples everywhere. The appeal in this case was voiced by the UN General Assembly, which in resolution 49/184 of 23 December 1994 proclaimed the 10-year period beginning on 1 January 1995 the United Nations Decade for Human Rights Education. In that resolution, the General Assembly appealed to all Governments to contribute to the implementation of the Plan of Action for the Decade proposed by the Secretary-General (UN Doc. A/49/261/Add. 1, annex), and to governmental and non-governmental educational agencies to intensify their efforts to establish and implement programs of human rights education, as recommended in the Plan of Action, in particular by adopting and implementing their own national plans. Implementation of the international Plan of Action is to be coordinated by the United Nations High Commissioner for Human Rights.

This second edition of the *Encyclopedia of Human Rights* is offered to readers with the hope that it will be found to be comprehensive and complete, and that it will stimulate interest in establishing a climate favoring the full enjoyment of every human right and fundamental freedom by every inhabitant of this world.

Finally, I should like once again to thank all those who contributed to the timely publication of the second edition of the *Encyclopedia*, including, in particular, those whose names are set out on the copyright page. And once again, thanks to my wife Irene, who provided endless personal help and encouragement during the lengthy period of preparing this volume.

EDWARD LAWSON
Tampa, Florida

# PREFACE TO THE FIRST EDITION

Half a century ago, in 1941, President Franklin D. Roosevelt of the United States of America and Prime Minister Winston Churchill of the United Kingdom expressed, in the Atlantic Charter, their fervent hope "to see established a peace which will afford to all nations the means of dwelling in safety within their own boundaries, and which will afford assurance that all the men in all the lands may live out their lives in freedom from want and fear."

One year later, 26 allied nations expressed, in the Declaration by United Nations, their firm conviction "that complete victory over their enemies is essential to defend life, liberty, independence and religious freedom, and to preserve human rights and justice in their own lands as well as in other lands." In so doing, they were the first to use the term "human rights" in an international instrument. Later, 21 additional nations joined in adherence to the declaration.

The United Nations Charter, which entered into force in 1945, provides that the UN promote (article 55) "universal respect for, and observance of, human rights and fundamental freedoms for all without distinction as to race, sex, language or religion," and that (article 56) "all Members pledge themselves to take joint and separate action in cooperation with the Organization for the achievement of the purposes set forth in Article 55."

In 1946, the Division of Human Rights was established as part of the United Nations Secretariat, then housed at Hunter College in the Bronx, New York; and I was one of the first to join its staff. I was then in no sense an expert on human rights—actually, there was none in those days because the term was new and undefined—but I had acquired a good record of success in placing members of various minorities in training programs and in employment, and in combatting prejudice and discrimination against them, first in the American federal emergency relief programs of the late 1930s and later in the employment programs of the War Production Board and the War Manpower Commission of the early 1940s.

The division's first assignment was to assist the newly established UN Commission on Human Rights—composed of the representatives of 18 UN member States under the chairmanship of Mrs. Franklin D. Roosevelt—to prepare an "international bill of rights." We did that primarily by studying the various draft bills which had been submitted by the delegations of Chile, Cuba, and Panama; by the American Federation of Labor; and by private individuals, including Dr. Lauterpacht of Cambridge University, Dr. Alvarez of the American Institute of International Law, the Rev. Parsons of the Catholic Association for International Peace, Mr. McNitt of the Faculty of Law of Southwestern University, and Mr. H.G. Wells. We prepared a mammoth analytical compilation of all the rights and freedoms mentioned in those draft bills, as well as those protected by the constitutions of UN member States; and on that basis formulated the "Secretariat Draft Outline of an International Bill of Human Rights" (UN Doc. E/CN.4/AC.1/3 and Add. 1). That draft outline, together with a few United States' proposals for the rewording of some of its items and a new draft International Bill of Human Rights submitted by the United Kingdom, provided the basis for the commission's work in this field.

It was at the second session of the commission, held at the European office of the United Nations in Geneva from 2 to 17 December 1947, that the conception of an international bill of human rights composed of three parts—a declaration, a convention, and measures for implementation—began to crystallize, as it became evident that many governments were prepared to support a declaration if it were to precede and not to replace a convention. The commission included in its report on that session (UN Doc. E/600) its views on measures of implementation, which served as a basis for all subsequent study in that field.

At its third session, held at Lake Success, New York, from 24 May to 18 June 1948, the commission redrafted the declaration, taking into account suggestions made by its drafting committee; by its Sub-Commission on Prevention of Discrimination and Protection of Minorities; by the Commission on the Status of Women; and by the United Nations Conference on Freedom of Information, which had met in Geneva in March 1948. It also took into account some provisions of the American Declaration of the Rights and Duties of Man which had been adopted by the Ninth International Conference of American States convened at Bogota in May 1948.

The UN General Assembly met in Paris that year and, after a general debate on the commission's draft declaration, referred it to its Third (Social, Humanitarian and Cultural) Committee for detailed consideration. The committee, composed then of the representatives of 56 member States, devoted 81 meetings to considering the draft and, in the process, examined and disposed of 168 proposals for amendments. As a result, the General Assembly was able to adopt and proclaim the Universal Declaration of Human Rights on 10 December 1948 by 48 votes in favor, none against, and eight abstentions.

Thus was born what Mrs. Roosevelt called the "Magna Carta of Mankind" and others termed the lodestar of the international community: a document that set out simply and clearly what was later described in the 1968 Proclamation of Teheran as "a common understanding of the peoples of the world concerning the inalienable and inviolable rights of all members of the human family."

Having lived through these eventful days, and having served as secretary of the Commission on Human Rights and of its Sub-Commission on Prevention of Discrimination and Protection of Minorities, and as deputy secretary of the United Nations Conference on Freedom of Information, I looked forward to a further whirlwind of activity which would rapidly make the enjoyment of human rights and fundamental freedoms a reality for all the peoples of the world. In particular, I hoped for the quick adoption of the remainder of the International Bill of Human Rights, for the preparation of some realistic measures which would protect suffering minorities throughout the world, and for the completion of a declaration or convention on freedom of information, which the General Assembly had designated as "a fundamental human right and the touchstone of all the freedoms to which the United Nations is consecrated."

But for many reasons—including political shifts which started when the change of government in Czechoslovakia in February 1948 cast its shadow over the Conference on Freedom of Information, intensified with the blockade of Berlin later the same year, and escalated finally into the long Cold War—my dreams were not fulfilled for many years, and then only in part.

The International Covenants on Human Rights were concluded only in 1966 and entered into force some ten years later. One of them—the Covenant on Civil and Political Rights—contains provisions on minorities (article 27) and on freedom of information (article 19). But the minorities provisions are so unsatisfactory that, in 1978, the Commission on Human Rights established an openended working group to draft a declaration on minority rights. That and similar working groups, established annually, were unable to produce a text suitable for consideration by the commission up to 1990. And the freedom of information provisions of the covenant clearly lack the precise definitions and the provisions for international supervision which had marked the draft convention prepared by the conference.

Another serious enthusiasm-damper stemmed from the curiously self-denying statement which the Commission on Human Rights adopted at its first session, in January 1947, to the effect that "the Commission recognizes that it has no power to take any action in regard to complaints concerning human rights." Such a statement had been formulated by some members who argued that, by drawing attention to the serious gap resulting from the absence of such power, the commission could stimulate its parent bodies to correct the situation; joined by other members who maintained that the commission should not be unduly taken up with the consideration of letters from individuals and organizations, and that, above all, it should not be turned into the "complaints bureau" of the United Nations. But, in practice, the statement, once approved by the Economic and Social Council, prevented the commission from dealing with the thousands of petitions, complaints, and other communications that flooded in to it from all parts of the world.

This incredible arrangement, almost impossible to explain to suffering victims of human rights violations, was maintained until 1970, when the council adopted a "Procedure for Dealing with Communications relating to Violations of Human Rights and Fundamental Freedoms" (resolution 1503 [XLVIII]).Many thousands of complaints have since been handled in accordance with that procedure, which authorizes the Sub-Commission on Prevention of Discrimination and Protection of Minorities to consider them together with other relevant information and to refer to the commission "particular situations which appear to reveal a consistent pattern of gross and reliably attested violations of human rights requiring attention by the Commission."

Earlier, the United Nations itself had undergone a slow but notable change; by the end of 1965, its original membership of 51 States had swelled to 119 with the addition of 68 new members: 36 from Africa, 16 from Asia, ten from western Europe, five from eastern Europe, and one from Latin America. The new majority, largely from the non-aligned third world, moved resolutely to put a stop to a broad range of violations of human rights:

—On 21 December 1965, the General Assembly concluded the International Convention on the Elimination of all Forms of Racial Discrimination, creating the first human rights monitoring machinery of global scope in the form of the Committee on the Elimination of Racial Discrimination;

—On 16 December 1966, the General Assembly adopted and opened for ratification or accession the International Covenant on Economic, Social and Cultural Rights; the International Covenant on Civil and Political Rights; and the Optional Protocol to the latter, creating additional monitoring machinery of global scope in the form of the Committee on Economic, Social and Cultural Rights and the Human Rights Committee; and

—On 13 May 1968, the International Conference on Human Rights consolidated a truly global concept by declaring, in the above-mentioned Proclamation of Teheran, that "the Universal Declaration of Human Rights states a common understanding of the peoples of the world concerning the inalienable and inviolable rights of all members of the human family and constitutes an obligation for the members of the international community."

The conference also gave new directions to the international human rights program. It observed, for example, that armed conflicts (resolution XXIII) continued to plague humanity; that the widespread violence and brutality of the times—including massacres, summary executions, tortures, inhuman treatment of prisoners, killing of civilians in armed conflicts, and the use of chemical and biological means of warfare—eroded human rights and engendered counter-brutality; and the conference expressed the conviction that humanitarian principles must prevail even during periods of armed conflict. It also pointed out in the Proclamation of Teheran (para. 18) that "while recent scientific discoveries and technological advances have opened vast prospects for economic, social and cultural progress, such developments may nevertheless endanger the rights and freedoms of individuals and will require continuing attention."

Thereafter, for some years, the Division of Human Rights prepared a series of studies, in consultation with the International Committee of the Red Cross, on steps which could be taken to secure the better application of existing humanitarian international conventions and rules in all armed conflicts and to address the need for additional instruments to ensure the better protection of civilians, prisoners, and combatants in such conflicts and to prohibit and limit the use of certain methods and means of warfare.

After examining the first and second of these reports, in 1969 and 1970, the General Assembly adopted (resolution 2675 [XXV]) a series of "Basic Principles for the Protection of Civilian Populations in Armed Conflicts." Seven further reports, prepared between 1971 and 1977, enabled the concerned United Nations organs to follow and to comment on the work of the Diplomatic Conference on the Reaffirmation and Development of International Humanitarian Law Applicable in Armed Conflicts, which had been convened by the Swiss Federal Council to consider draft additional protocols to the Geneva Conventions of 1949 prepared by the International Committee of the Red Cross. At its fourth and final session, held in Geneva in 1977, the diplomatic conference adopted and opened for ratification or accession two additional protocols to the Geneva Conventions, namely, Protocol I relating to the Protection of Victims of International Armed Conflicts and Protocol II relating to the Protection of Victims of Non-international Armed Conflicts. In addition, it proposed that a special conference be held to consider the prohibition of the use of certain conventional weapons for humanitarian reasons.

The Division of Human Rights also prepared a series of studies on the effect of various scientific and technological developments upon the enjoyment of human rights, dealing with such matters as the protection of the human personality and its physical and intellectual integrity in the light of advances in biology, medicine, and biochemistry (UN Docs. E/CN.4/1172 and Corr. 1 and Add. 1–3, and E/CN.4/1173); the balance which should be established between scientific and technological progress and the intellectual, spiritual, cultural, and moral advancement of humanity (UN Doc. E/CN.4/1199 and Add. 1); and the human rights implications of the genetic manipulation of microbes (UN Doc. E/CN.4/1235).

After examination of the studies, the General Assembly solemnly proclaimed, on 10 November 1975, the "Declaration on the Use of Scientific and Technological Progress in the Interests of Peace and for the Benefit of Mankind," which calls upon all States to ensure that the results of scientific and technological developments are used in the interests of strengthening international peace and security, freedom, and independence; for the economic and social development of peoples; and for the realization of human rights and fundamental freedoms in accordance with the United Nations Charter.

In 1974, the Division of Human Rights was transferred, except for a small liaison office, from the United Nations headquarters building in New York to its European office in Geneva, Switzerland, located in the Palais des Nations, which once had housed the League of Nations. While the shift may have been fully justified by those who proposed and supported it, its practical results were not always positive. For example, neither the Commission on Human Rights nor its sub-commission—nor any of their sessional working groups—has since been convened in any city but Geneva. And Geneva—despite its beauty and charm, its inspiring history and perpetual neutrality, and its central location in the heart of Europe—still lacks the stimulating dynamism, the active information media, and the far-reaching communications networks of a city like New York. Getting the message of human rights out to all the peoples of the world is a bit more complicated from Geneva, and those of us who live in North America, for example, find it much harder to follow in detail significant human rights developments within the United Nations system.

The Division of Human Rights has since been strengthened and restructured into what is now known as the Centre for Human Rights. Its direction has been placed in the hands of the Under-Secretary-General for Human Rights, its mandate has been broadened to include new functions of coordination, its workload has increased tremendously, and its hard-working staff is being augmented.

Since 1977 activities of the Centre for Human Rights—and indeed all human rights activities within the United Nations system—have been based on a series of concepts formulated by the General Assembly as it prepared to commemorate the 30th anniversary (1978) of the Universal Declaration of Human Rights. These concepts, re-affirmed by the assembly at ten subsequent sessions, are as follows (resolution 32/130, para. 1 [a] to [h]:

The General Assembly. . . .

1. Decides that the approach to the future work within the United Nations system with respect to human rights questions should take into account the following concepts:

(a)  All human rights and fundamental freedoms are indivisible and interdependent; equal attention and urgent consideration should be given to the implementation, promotion and protection of both civil and political, and economic, social and cultural rights;

(b)  "The full realization of civil and political rights without the enjoyment of economic, social and cultural rights is impossible; the achievement of lasting progress in the implementation of human rights is dependent upon sound and effective national and international policies of economic and social development" as recognized by the Proclamation of Teheran of 1968;

(c)  All human rights and fundamental freedoms of the human person and of peoples are inalienable;

(d)  Consequently, human rights questions should be examined globally, taking into account both the overall context of the various societies in which they present themselves, as well as the need for the promotion of the full dignity of the human person and the development and well-being of the society;

(e)  In approaching human rights questions within the United Nations system, the international community should accord, or continue to accord, priority to the search for solutions to the mass and flagrant violations of human rights of peoples and persons affected by situations such as those resulting from *apartheid*, from all forms of racial discrimination, from colonialism, from foreign domination and occupation, from aggression and threats against national sovereignty, national unity and territorial integrity, as well as from the refusal to recognize the fundamental rights of peoples to self-determination and of every nation to the exercise of full sovereignty over its wealth and natural resources;

(f)  The realization of the new international economic order is an essential element for the effective promotion of human rights and fundamental freedoms and should also be accorded priority;

(g)  It is of paramount importance for the promotion of human rights and fundamental freedoms that Member States undertake specific obligations through accession to or ratification of international instruments in this field; consequently, the standard-setting work within the United Nations system in the field of human rights and the universal acceptance and implementation of the relevant international instruments should be encouraged;

(h)  The experience and contribution of both developed and developing countries should be taken into account by all organs of the United Nations system in their work related to human rights and fundamental freedoms. . . .

Taking these directives into account, the work of the United Nations human rights organs has since expanded rapidly. Both the Commission on Human Rights and its sub-commission have learned to make the best use of qualified members either by appointing them as special rapporteurs to survey and report on situations existing in particular countries or to study controversial subjects such as religious intolerance, the use of torture, or the use of mercenaries as a means of violating human rights and impeding the exercise of the right of people to self-determination; or by assigning them to small working groups which handle complaints, seek to define the rights of minorities or indigenous peoples, endeavor to end slavery and other forms of servitude, or prepare the drafts of new international instruments. The result has been an incredibly rapid outpouring of resolutions, decisions, and instruments setting out new standards and rules designed to ensure to everyone on earth the full enjoyment of his human rights and fundamental freedoms.

Moreover, within the UN system, six independent treaty-monitoring bodies have become active and effective in their work: the Committee on the Elimination of Racial Discrimination; the Human Rights Committee; the Committee on Economic, Social and Cultural Rights; the Committee on the Elimination of Discrimination against Women; the Committee against Torture, and the Commission against *Apartheid* in Sports. A seventh, the Committee on the Rights of the Child, has been authorized by the Convention on the Rights of the Child, which entered into force on 2 September 1990.

In addition, several highly specialized organs are also active in the field, including the Special Committee to Investigate Israeli Practices Affecting the Human Rights of the Population of the Occupied Territories and the Committee on the Exercise of the Inalienable Rights of the Palestinian People, both of which report to the General Assembly; the *Ad Hoc* Working Group of Experts on Southern Africa, which reports to the Commission on Human Rights; and the Group of Three, composed of members of that commission, which monitors the implementation of the International Convention on the Suppression and Punishment of the Crime of *Apartheid.*

While most of these activities are funded out of the normal United Nations budget, several of the treaty-monitoring bodies are supported mainly by contributions assessed against the States parties to the conventions under which they were established. Some other work is financed, at least in part, by voluntary funds—for the victims of torture, for indigenous peoples, and for advisory services and technical assistance, for example—to which interested States, organizations, and individuals contribute.

Further intensive international activities to promote and protect the enjoyment of human rights are being carried on simultaneously by four of the specialized agencies within the United Nations system—the International Labor Organization; the United Nations Educational, Scientific and Cultural Organization; the Food and Agriculture Organization; and the World Health Organization—and by three major regional intergovernmental organizations outside the UN system—the Council of Europe, the Organization of African Unity, and the Organization of American States—as well as by specialized groups such as the International Committee of the Red Cross and the signers of the Helsinki Accord. Only by assessing all these efforts together can we see how widespread and intensive is the current World Campaign for Human Rights. Add on the thousands of active national and local campaigns directed to the same end, and it becomes all but impossible to keep track of them. All of these efforts inspire great hope for the future.

As a member of the UN Secretariat, one of my tasks was to organize and direct seminars and study groups on various aspects of human rights in such far-flung cities as Bangkok, Thailand; Bogota, Colombia; Budapest, Hungary; Dar-es-Salaam, Tanzania; Kandy, Sri Lanka; Lome, Togo; and Warsaw, Poland. After retiring in 1975, I taught courses in human rights to American undergraduate university students of political science and international affairs. These experiences made me realize that human rights had rapidly developed into a vast and important new subject—almost a new discipline—in which there was tremendous interest but a surprising paucity of relevant information available for intensive study or instruction.

That is why, several years ago, I set out to prepare a basic textbook for the teaching of human rights—a much-needed item which, although discussed in theory at great length in international conferences of educational experts, has yet to be produced.

At an early stage in that work I realized two things. First, there was an immediate prior need to identify and bring together in convenient form the unbelievably large bulk of documentation concerning human rights, including the 40-odd-year backlog and the continuing sizable output of the United Nations system and the equally large, if not larger, production of the regional intergovernmental and non-governmental organizations. Secondly, the ultimate requirement was not so much a single basic textbook suitable for use at every level and in every conceivable situation as a media blitz directed at a number of constituencies and designed to meet the unique human rights concerns of each: one campaign, for example, aimed at political leaders and legislators, another at religious leaders, and still another at students and teachers at various levels and in different disciplines. This trend of thought was confirmed by discussions, in the United Nations Seminar on the Teaching of Human Rights, held at Geneva from 5 to 9 December 1989. At its final meeting, the chairman summed up the major results of those discussions as follows (UN Doc. E/CN.4/1989/68, para. 121):

(b) What to teach? Human rights teaching should generally take a multidisciplinary approach in order to introduce different dimensions and perspectives of human life: historical, philosophical, religious, legal, social, cultural, political and economic. The main aim [is] to make known the basic facts about the universally accepted international human rights standards, including their intercultural background. The interrelationship between human rights and peace, development, environment and other international issues should also be emphasized in the process of human rights teaching.

(c) Whom to teach? It [is] very important to confirm that everyone [is] aware of his or her own rights, as human rights and fundamental freedoms should be guaranteed to everyone. Human rights teaching should thus be directed to every quarter. First of all, those in a position to directly affect the basic human rights of the individual, such as law enforcement personnel, lawyers and judges, as well as the military men when at war or when called upon to maintain security in times of emergency internal situations, should be well taught as regards human rights. It [is] also vital that legislators who are in charge of drafting laws should be educated about international human rights standards so that their legislation would be in conformity with their country's international obligations. Persons, be they in medicine, engineering, technology, media, data processing, political parties, civil service, municipalities and other centers of power, such as village councils, trade unions, etc., also [need] to be aware of human rights. Teaching and training of professionals should consist of not only the basic rules of the organization of their prospective profession, but also an ethical and legal code of conduct taking into account the impact of their activities on the basic human rights of others. School children and students at all institutions, be they civil, police or military, should also be the target of this process. . . .

With these views in mind, I temporarily put aside my plan for preparing a single basic human rights textbook, usable at all levels and in any circumstance, in favor of doing the necessary groundwork first. That groundwork is to be found in this encyclopedia, intended to serve as a standard reference work bringing together in a single volume everything important to know about the international, regional, and national activities so far undertaken with a view to promoting the enjoyment by everyone of his human rights and fundamental freedoms.

As will be seen, the encyclopedia deals with important developments in the field of human rights that occurred between 1945, when the United Nations Charter entered into force, and 30 June 1990, when the manuscript went to press. A few important instruments in force before 1945—for example, the Slavery Convention of 25 September 1926 and the ILO Forced Labor Convention of 28 June 1930—are included because they protected human rights both before and after 1945. And, in a few exceptional instances, it was possible to insert information concerning events which occurred after 30 June 1990 in the proofreading process, as for example in the case of the UN Security Council action immediately following the invasion of Kuwait by Iraq.

However, generally speaking, it was not possible to include in the body of the encyclopedia international decisions taken after mid-1990. I regret this shortcoming in the published edition, although it was beyond my control. It is due to the continuous and open-ended activity of the United Nations and other international organizations in the field of human rights. By its very nature, no encyclopedia can ever be totally up-to-date; and I hope to reduce the unavoidable time lag in subsequent editions.

These materials have been carefully selected and are presented objectively and with a minimum of editorial comment. They are arranged by title in letter-by-letter alphabetical sequence and are thoroughly cross-referenced and indexed. The entries include the complete official texts of some 200 international standard-setting instruments dealing with various aspects of human rights—covenants, conventions, protocols, agreements, declarations, recommendations, and statements of principle—of which 105 were prepared by organs of the United Nations; 34 by organs of the Council of Europe; 13 by organs of the Organization of American States; five by organs of the Organization of African Unity; four by diplomatic conferences convened by the Swiss Federal Council in cooperation with the International Committee of the Red Cross; and three by signers of the Helsinki Accord.

The material includes also information about the mandates and the work of 78 of the international governmental organs that normally deal with human rights questions, and about the activities of more than 125 international non-governmental organizations that participate actively in their proceedings. Information also is presented on the situation of human rights in each of 165 countries and territories, including all United Nations member States; and the human rights provisions of the constitutions of 25 of those countries are reproduced in full.

More than 200 entries deal with various aspects of particular rights and freedoms; they explain the concepts involved and indicate how the competent international organs have interpreted the scope and meaning of the relevant provisions. Others reproduce landmark international court decisions or provide information about studies, reports, or procedures still in the preliminary stages. Appendices include an extensive bibliography, compiled by Human Rights Internet, lists of the States that have ratified or acceded to major human rights conventions; a chronological list of international human rights instruments; a catalog of the numerous studies and reports on human rights prepared by or for United Nations bodies; and a list of the conventions adopted by the International Labor Conference between 1919 and 1989—sometimes referred to as the International Labor Code—each of which promotes the realization by working men and women of certain human rights and fundamental freedoms.

This mass of materials presents an impressive picture—particularly the numerous treaties, conventions, protocols, declarations, and statements of principle which set lofty standards with a view to protecting the status of the individual throughout the world. Their very existence has already brought about a radical change in the nature and the structure of world order: whereas the law of nations once regulated only the intercourse of independent States in peace and war, the new world order affirms that a primary aim of international cooperation in the field of human rights is for a life of freedom, dignity, and peace for all peoples and for every human being.

Formal international implementation of human rights standards, unfortunately, has not kept pace with the promulgation and acceptance of these standards. Treaty-monitoring bodies such as the Human Rights Committee, the Committee on Economic, Social and Cultural Rights, the Committee on the Elimination of Racial Discrimination, the Committee on the Elimination of Discrimination against Women, and the Committee against Torture are just beginning to make progress in their work; and their functioning is hampered by a continuing backlog of reports on implementation from States parties to the relevant conventions, by a shortage of financial resources, and by some overlapping of the issues dealt with in those conventions. These problems have been studied by an independent expert, whose recommendations on reporting and monitoring procedures, on servicing and financing of the supervisory bodies, and on long-term approaches to human rights standard-setting and implementation mechanisms are scheduled for early consideration by the General Assembly.

Meanwhile, the informal day-to-day realization of human rights proceeds irresistibly and independently of such formal measures. Who would have thought, early in 1989, that revolutionary demands for civil and political rights, for free multi-party elections, and for free-market economics would have swept across such countries as Bulgaria, Czechoslovakia, East Germany, Hungary, Poland, Romania, and even portions of the Union of Soviet Socialist Republics; that the cold war would have ended; that the Berlin Wall would have come down; or that Germany would have been reunited, all within two years? And who would have imagined, early in 1990, that even these developments affecting the human rights and fundamental freedoms of millions of Europeans would so soon have been overshadowed by threats of war in the Middle East and the worldwide surge of concern about protection of the human rights and fundamental freedoms of civilians, hostages, prisoners of war, refugees, displaced persons, and women and children trapped in the areas of armed conflict?

However, intensification of international measures of implementation—primarily by treaty bodies competent to monitor applicable standards and to expose all who fail to live up to them—still appears to offer the most realistic possibility that, in due time, everyone will be able fully to enjoy his human rights and fundamental freedoms. The existing treaty-monitoring bodies should become increasingly effective as their problems are resolved, and new bodies undoubtedly will be added. At the same time, the Commission on Human Rights will be alerted whenever necessary to the existence of gross and systematic violations of human rights requiring urgent corrective action by its special rapporteurs and working groups which study and report on country-oriented and subject-oriented topics and on the complaints and other communications received.

Of course, if there ever is to develop a full balance between the lofty standards of the human rights instruments and their practical results, some more effective measures of enforcement eventually will be required. One possibility is the establishment of an international court of human rights, performing on a worldwide basis functions similar to those already performed in western Europe by the European Court of Human Rights and to those already performed in Latin America by the Inter-American Court of Human Rights. Another is the establishment of an international criminal court for the trial of persons charged with crimes against humanity and other crimes involving gross violations of human rights. A draft statute for such a court was prepared by two Committees on International Criminal Jurisdiction appointed by the General Assembly in 1951 and 1953, respectively; but such a statute was never concluded by the assembly.

As may be realized, the encyclopedia's substantive contents range well beyond the somewhat limited original concept of human rights and include a wide variety of closely interlinked social, humanitarian, and disarmament issues such as the advancement of women; the prevention of crime and the establishment of standards in criminal justice; the protection of refugees and displaced or stateless persons; the protection of civilians in time of armed conflict; the treatment of prisoners of war; and the prohibition of nuclear, chemical, bacteriological, or biological weapons.

Its basic function is to provide to all concerned—governments, regional and national organizations, research institutions, the media, public officials at all levels, students and interested individuals and groups throughout the world—easy access to the impressive wealth of documentation on human rights issues which the international community has developed and accumulated. A secondary aim is to make all those materials available also to those who teach and those who study in related disciplines such as political science and international affairs, as well as to those who provide and those who receive specialized training in such areas as law enforcement, military law, diplomacy, and medicine.

A third and most important goal is to distribute to all who suffer violations of their human rights or fundamental freedoms information on the scope and content of those rights and on the procedures available to them to put a stop to such violations and to remedy the wrongs that have been committed.

With a view to achieving these objectives, the encyclopedia is issued as a single, self-contained volume which does not require the use of any other publication. The selection of materials to be included has been impartial and objective in the sense that no single individual or national point of view; no social, economic, cultural or political system; and no academic discipline are stressed; and references to existing situations are always drawn from sources least likely to be biased: studies and reports prepared under the auspices of the competent international organizations and agencies.

Thus, while essentially a reference tool prepared to provide a factual and theoretical basis for serious high-level study of human rights principles and issues on a global scale, the encyclopedia may also appropriately serve as an interim manual for the teaching of those principles and issues. And hopefully it may contribute in some measure to eventual solution of some of the most pressing problems of the ongoing revolution for democracy and human rights that marks the 1990s as the "Decade for Democratization."

Unfortunately, even as that decade progresses, scourges such as foreign occupation and domination, racial and religious intolerance and discrimination, "disappearances," torture and mass poverty remain in place and must be extirpated. The spread of information and education about human rights principles and procedures is an imperative first step, and the uncompromising application of those principles and use of those procedures must immediately follow. For this to happen, both the past and future victims of human rights violations, as well as all entrusted with protecting the enjoyment of those rights, must become aware of the content and applicability of local, national and international human rights policies and procedures, and must not hesitate to use them.

The challenge of this decade is to realize by the year 2000, if not sooner, the full enjoyment by every living individual of his human rights and fundamental freedoms, guaranteed by a political order motivated by the conscience of the world. To promote and to assist in the achievement of that goal is the ultimate objective of this encyclopedia.

Finally, a personal word about the many individuals and organizations whose cooperation and contributions have helped to make *Encyclopedia of Human Rights* a compendium of basic knowledge and information on the subject of human rights and fundamental freedoms.

I am especially indebted to Jan Martenson, Under-Secretary-General for Human Rights of the United Nations, for his continuing encouragement and for his "Foreword" to this publication; and to all the staff of the Centre for Human Rights in Geneva and its Liaison Office at the UN headquarters in New York for the time and effort they have devoted to providing me with the voluminous but essential documentation which I have presented, summarized, or quoted here.

I am particularly grateful for the kind cooperation of so many governments for making available information on the human rights situation in their respective countries, either directly in response to my requests or indirectly through their reports to the competent treaty-monitoring bodies.

I am also grateful for the assistance provided by so many concerned international organizations, including such specialized agencies of the United Nations as the International Labor Organization; the United Nations Educational, Scientific and Cultural Organization; the Food and Agriculture Organization; and the World Health Organization; such regional bodies as the Council of Europe, the Organization of African Unity, and the Organization of American States; and such non-governmental bodies as the International Committee of the Red Cross and Amnesty International.

My sincere thanks go to Kate McKay, former president and publisher of Taylor and Francis, Inc., who first understood the need for such an encyclopedia; to Ted Crane who succeeded her; to Sharon Spina and Jung Ra who handled the production details; and to Human Rights Internet, which prepared the extensive bibliography, found in Appendix A.

And my very special thanks must go to Mary Lou Bertucci, the talented editor and human rights enthusiast who has, for several years, relieved me of the hardest part of my job—the organizing, the revising, the proofreading, the correcting, the ungarbling, the indexing, and the otherwise nursemaiding of a constantly expanding compilation of information—from her home in Philadelphia; and to my wife, Irene, without whose patience, understanding, and good humor I would not have finally been able to send this encyclopedia to press.

EDWARD LAWSON
Tampa, Florida

# INTRODUCTORY ESSAY

Human rights are entitlements due to every man, woman, and child because they are human. They include rights pertaining to the security of the person, including the right not to be deprived of life or liberty without due process of law; the right not to be tortured or subjected to cruel, inhuman, or degrading treatment or punishment; and the right not to be held in slavery or servitude. They are nonderogable rights: Their violation can never by justified, even by a state of national emergency. Human rights also include civil and political rights, among them the right to freedom of thought, conscience, and religion; the right to freedom of opinion and expression; the right to freedom of peaceful assembly and association; the right to freedom of movement; and the right to take part in the government of one's own country, directly or through freely chosen representatives. There are also economic, social, and cultural rights to which everyone is entitled. These include basic survival rights to food, shelter, health care, and social services; the right to work; the right to education; and the right to participate in the cultural life of one's community. The premise of current international law is that these rights are inherent in the human person: They are not *given* to people by the State, and the State cannot deprive people of their rights. The reality, of course, is that throughout history, people have had to fight to win their rights, because power holders are rarely magnanimous in granting them.

In the early 1970s, when I first began doing research in international human rights, political scientists like myself who considered this an important field of study and advocacy were considered idealists. The model of Realpolitik still dominated international relations theory, and the Cold War dominated strategic thinking. It was easy to dismiss as dreamers those misguided enough to think that they could hold governments accountable to the standards that had been articulated in the 1948 Universal Declaration of Human Rights. The United Nations Charter, adopted in 1945, may have spoken of "We the peoples of the United Nations," but the world in the 1970s was still one in which States were considered *the key* (if not the only significant) actors. Some political scientists grudgingly acknowledged a modest role for organizations like the United Nations (which, after all, was composed of States, not "peoples"), but almost no attention was paid to the role of non-governmental organizations (NGOs).

As we approach the end of this century, there has been a significant paradigm shift. Human rights now has a prominent place on the international agenda; the United Nations has been entrusted with enormous responsibilities for managing global problems, including human rights; and the importance of NGOs as international actors is now widely recognized. Human rights is now a respected area of study in its own right, and treated in such disciplines as international law, political science, sociology, anthropology, history, and philosophy. There is also a large and burgeoning academic human rights literature as well as a plethora of studies by NGOs and intergovernmental organizations (IGOs), as illustrated by the bibliographies in this *Encyclopedia*. What has produced so dramatic a change?

The paradigm shift has been occasioned by at least five significant developments. First has been the erosion of the concept of State sovereignty. In the context of human rights, this has meant that States can no longer hide behind the shield of "domestic jurisdiction" as they abuse the rights of their citizens.

Fifty years after the adoption of the Universal Declaration of Human Rights—that is, after a half century of persistent lobbying and pressure by human rights advocates—there now exists a substantial corpus of international human rights law[1] and a large number of arenas and mechanisms for dealing with human rights violations, at both the international and regional levels.

At the UN World Conference on Human Rights in Vienna in June 1993, States reaffirmed their "solemn commitment . . . to fulfil their obligations to promote universal respect for, and observance and protection of, all human rights and fundamental freedoms in accordance with the Charter of the United Nations, other instruments relating to human rights, and international law."[2] They agreed that, in the framework of the purposes and principles of the United Nations, "the promotion and protection of all human rights is a legitimate concern of the international community."[3] And they further agreed that all human rights derive from the dignity and worth inherent in the human person, and that the human person is the central subject of human rights and fundamental freedoms, and consequently should be the principal beneficiary and should participate actively in the realization of these rights and freedoms.[4]

The second and related development leading to the paradigm shift has been the phenomenon of "globalization"—the fact that key issues and problems that once were national now defy national solutions. This includes concerns such as poverty, environmental degradation, population explosion, the regulation of multinational corporations, the control of the drug trade and criminal syndicates, and the need for humanitarian responses to natural disasters or civil wars. Together with the third development—the shrinkage of the globe brought about by the technological revolution in communications—and the fourth development—the end of the Cold War—this has caused States to turn increasingly to the United Nations for solutions to planetary crises. Whether the United Nations is capable of responding to these challenges, crippled as it is by lack of financial resources, overwhelmed as it is by the multiplicity of simultaneous demands on it, and hampered as it is by its traditional interstate structures, remains an open question.

What, however, is clear is that the United Nations, which remains an inter-governmental, not supranational, actor, cannot do it alone. Not only does it need the power and resources of the one remaining superpower and other key States, it increasingly needs the ideas, the dynamism, and the expertise of NGOs. As the Secretary-General of the United Nations recently wrote, "The activity of non-state actors has today become an essential dimension of public life at all levels and in all parts of the world."[5] Indeed, in the human rights field, it has been the unrelenting pressure of NGOs that has largely been responsible for the evolution of the international human rights system to its current state. Thus the fifth development, and a critical one, has been the development of a worldwide and vibrant human rights movement, exposing and denouncing human rights violations, lobbying governments and IGOs, extending legal and humanitarian aid to victims, helping to draft protective legislation, devising legal remedies, educating government and civil society about human rights standards, and building links of solidarity across the globe.

If the progress made has been far beyond what might have been expected in the 1970s, and certainly far beyond the expectations of the 1950s and 1960s, it is nonetheless sobering to consider the enormous gap between the ideals of international human rights law and the reality of continuing gross human rights violations. We see these violations over and over again, now in technicolor on our TVs. In just the past few years, we have witnessed the carnage in Rwanda, where more than a half million people were slaughtered in the space of a few weeks; the "ethnic cleansing" and rape in Bosnia-Herzegovina; the ferocity of the Russian response to the secession of Chechnya, with massive, indiscriminate shelling of Chechnyan towns; and the complete disintegration of social order in Somalia and Liberia, which has exposed individuals to the brutality of bandits and warlords.

The report of a recent conference noted that, between 1989 and 1992, there were 83 armed conflicts (all but three were civil conflicts), in which more than 90% of the casualties were civilians.[6] A 1988 study on genocide estimated that between 7 and 16 million people have perished since 1945 in genocidal conflict.[7] A 1995 report of the International Federation of Red Cross and Red Crescent Societies asserted that there are 42 million displaced people, 160 million people affected by disasters, and 2 billion people whom the United Nations Development Programme (UNDP) estimates live in a state of vulnerability and poverty.[8]

At the same time, highly repressive and frequently corrupt governments remain in power in many regions, imprisoning, torturing, and "disappearing" those who dare to speak out against their tyranny or their plunder. Thus, in November 1995, we witnessed the audacity with which the Nigerian regime of General Sani Abacha executed Ken Saro Wiwa and eight other Ogoni activists for protesting against the environmental degradation of their delta homeland by multinational oil companies. Thus we watch as China, wooed by Western leaders in search of business opportunities, arrogantly continues to crack down on all dissidents, practices torture and forced labor in its prisons and "re-education camps," squashes all signs of a Tibetan independence movement, and tightens its control over the media and unofficial churches. Burma, Cuba, Indonesia, Iran, Iraq, North Korea, Saudi Arabia, Sudan, Syria, Vietnam, and Zaire, to name only a few of the offenders, remain under authoritarian, or totalitarian, rule.[9]

The gap between ideal and reality is also stark when considering women's human rights. At the Fourth World Conference on Women's Rights held in Beijing in September 1995, governments committed themselves to "ensure the full implementation of the human rights of women and of the girl child as an inalienable, integral and indivisible part of all human rights and fundamental freedoms."[10] The situation of women raises questions about the sincerity of this commitment. In a 1995 report, Amnesty International described that situation in the following terms:

In 1994 women suffered every known abuse and violation of fundamental human rights. Torturers, executioners, jailers and killers did not discriminate on grounds of sex, unless it was to subject women to abuses to which they are particularly vulnerable.[11]

Discrimination against women is a deadly disease. More women and girls die every day from various forms of gender-based discrimination and violence than from any other type of human rights abuse. Every year, according to the UN Children's Fund (UNICEF), more than a million infant girls die because they are born female. Every year, because of discrimination, countless women are battered to death by their husbands, burned alive for bringing "disgrace" on the family, killed for non-payment of dowries, bought and sold in unacknowledged slave markets for domestic or sexual purposes, or have their genitals mutilated in the name of tradition.[12]

For all the noble statements of governments professing their commitment to international human rights standards, less than 1% of the United Nations budget is devoted to human rights. Although new institutions have been created—the Office of the UN High Commissioner for Human Rights, more than a dozen thematic human rights mechanisms, modalities for UN human rights monitoring, and a large technical assistance program—the funding to ensure the effectiveness of these mechanisms has not been forthcoming. Therefore, as we move toward the next millennium and approach the 50th anniversary of the Universal Declaration of Human Rights, it is important to see how far we have come, and how far we still must go to attain a world order in which the dignity of every woman, man, and child is respected as a matter of right.

## The International Bill of Human Rights: A Framework for Human Rights Protection

Prior to World War II, there existed no international human rights law binding on nation States. Two social movements were, however, important antecedents to the current human rights regime.

The first was the movement to abolish slavery and the slave trade, which began in Britain in the 18th century, gave birth to the Anti-Slavery Society (an NGO that still exists today to fight modern forms of slavery), and whose lobbying culminated in the first antislavery treaties.[13] The second was the Red Cross movement, which originated during the Crimean War in the revulsion of a Swiss businessman, Henri Dunant, to the immeasurable suffering of wounded soldiers during the 1859 Battle of Solferino. Dunant founded the International Committee of the Red Cross (ICRC), which was the catalyst for a diplomatic conference in Geneva in 1864 that elaborated the first Geneva Convention for the Amelioration of the Condition of the Wounded in Armies in the Field.[14] This was the antecedent to international humanitarian law (the Geneva Conventions and Protocols) and the laws of war, as well as to national Red Cross Societies and the International Federation that joins them into the Red Cross movement.

In the period between the World Wars I and II, there were other significant beginnings. Efforts were made to offer protection to individuals by means of the "minorities treaties," whereby the States concerned agreed not only to provide certain rights and minimal levels of treatment to minorities within their territories, but also to accept a degree of international supervision by the League of Nations over their compliance with these obligations.[15] Economic and social rights began to receive international recognition with the founding of the International Labor Organization (ILO) in 1919,[16] and assistance to refugees was first organized under international auspices in 1921 with the appointment of a League of Nations High Commissioner for Refugees.[17]

It was, however, in response to the horrors of the Nazi Holocaust that NGOs began pressuring States to lay the conceptual and legal foundations for international human rights law. The United Nations, initially conceived narrowly as a security agency, emerged from the San Francisco conference in 1945 as "an organization concerned with justice, international law, trusteeship for dependent peoples, education, human rights, and the economic and social well-being of peoples everywhere."[18] It was NGOs that were largely responsible for inserting human rights into the Preamble and six different articles of the UN Charter. It was NGOs that convinced the U.S. government that human rights should become one of the central pillars of the United Nations system, both a goal in its own right and a crucial instrument for achieving the other UN goals of international peace and security.[19]

This is set out in Article 1 of the UN Charter, which lists among the UN's purposes to develop "friendly relations among nations based on respect for the principle of equal rights and self-determination of peoples" and achieve "international cooperation . . . in promoting and encouraging respect for human rights and for fundamental freedoms for all, without distinction as to race, sex, language, or religion." This is restated in Article 55, under the heading of International Economic and Social Cooperation, which calls on the UN to promote "universal respect for, and observance of, human rights and fundamental freedoms for all without distinction as to race, sex, language, or religion."

To this end, in 1946, a Commission on Human Rights (CHR) was constituted as one of the functional commissions of the UN Economic and Social Council (ECOSOC)–the only functional commission specifically mentioned in the Charter. A Division of Human Rights was established as part of the UN Secretariat to support the work of the CHR. The following year, the Commission, then composed of 18 member States (with the U.S. representative, Eleanor Roosevelt, as Chair), established a Sub-Commission on Prevention of Discrimination and Protection of Minorities. This was a body of independent human rights experts (initially 12, but increased to 18 by 1965), who were to assist the CHR.

The first task of the Commission was to prepare an "international bill of human rights." The Sub-Commission was to examine the "provisions that should be adopted in defining the principles to be applied in the field of prevention of discrimination on grounds of race, sex, language or religion, and in the field of the protection of minorities." In 1947, the CHR decided that, because of the complexities involved in drafting a legally binding document, the international bill of human rights should not be crafted as a single comprehensive act, but should consist of two documents, a declaration, and a covenant, plus measures of implementation.[20]

The first fruits of the Commission were reaped on 10 December 1948, with the adoption by the United Nations of the Universal Declaration of Human Rights (UDHR). The vote in the General Assembly, then composed of 56 member States, was 48 in favor, 8 abstaining (the socialist States, Saudi Arabia, and South Africa), and none against. The UDHR, proclaimed as "a common standard of achievement for all peoples and all nations," addressed itself to the right of individuals "to life, liberty and security of person" as well as to their civil and political, economic, social, and cultural rights.

One day earlier, on 9 December, the UN General Assembly had adopted the first multilateral human rights treaty, the Convention on the Prevention and Punishment of the Crime of Genocide. The Convention condemned genocide as a crime under international law and, "to liberate mankind from such an odious scourge," provided for the punishment of those found guilty of the crime, "whether they are constitutionally responsible rulers, public officials or private individuals." Although the treaty received enough ratifications to enter into force on 12 January 1951, the international criminal court envisaged in the Genocide Convention has yet to be established.

In 1948, the hope of the CHR was that the Universal Declaration, which was not really law but a statement of principles, would rapidly be codified into an international convention, with enforcement mechanisms to hold States accountable for violations. Indeed, in 1947, Australia went so far as to advocate the establishment of an international court of human rights, empowered to hear appeals of decisions of national courts "in which any question arises as to the rights of citizenship or the enjoyment of human rights and fundamental freedoms"; to hear and determine human rights disputes referred to it by the CHR; and to hear "disputes arising out of Articles affecting human rights in any treaty or convention between States referred to it by parties to the treaty or convention."[21] However, by the end of 1948, the international consensus that this would have required had already evaporated with the onset of the Cold War. Not until December 1966 were the remaining portions of the International Bill of Human Rights adopted, containing no provisions as radical as those in the Australian proposal.

Moreover, because the Western and the Socialist States had different ideas about the importance of civil and political rights on the one hand and economic, social, and cultural rights on the other, three separate instruments emerged: (1) the International Covenant on Economic, Social and Cultural Rights, under which a State party agrees "to take steps . . . to the maximum of its available resources, with a view to achieving progressively the full realization of the rights recognized in the present Covenant . . ."; (2) the International Covenant on Civil and Political Rights, under which each State party undertakes "to respect and to ensure to all individuals within its territory and subject to its jurisdiction the rights recognized in the present Covenant . . ."; and (3) the Optional Protocol to the latter Covenant, whereby any State that becomes party to the Protocol recognizes the competence of the Human Rights Committee (created to monitor the Covenant) to receive and consider "communications from individuals claiming to be victims of violations of any of the rights set forth in the Covenant." Another 10 years passed before these three instruments garnered sufficient ratifications to enter into force, in 1976.

Indeed, for nearly two decades, from 1947 to 1967, States were permitted to violate the rights of their people with impunity because, notwithstanding the lofty words of the UDHR or the Genocide Convention, there was insufficient political will among nations to hold each other accountable to international standards. At its first meeting, in January 1947, the CHR adopted a resolution effectively denying itself the mandate to enforce internationally recognized human rights: "The Commission recognizes that it has no power to take any action in regard to any complaints concerning human rights."[22] This "no power to act" doctrine[23] was promptly approved by the Economic and Social Council. Thus, until 1970, when the ECOSOC adopted Resolution 1503 (a "Procedure for Dealing with Communications relating to Violations of Human Rights and Fundamental Freedoms"), the thousands of complaints sent to the UN concerning human rights violations were sent into limbo. The UN Secretariat drew up confidential lists of the complaints, with names deleted to protect those who wrote them, but when the lists were considered in private meetings of the CHR, there was never any debate on the substance of the allegations. "The Commission closed its doors to decide that, in accordance with its 1947 decision, it was not competent to investigate or take action on any of these complaints."[24]

What the UN concentrated on during these decades was "promotion" rather than protection. In addition to its work on the International Bill of Human Rights, the UN drafted and subsequently adopted the International Convention on the Elimination of All Forms of Racial Discrimination in December 1965. This was the first international human rights instrument with an oversight mechanism—a Committee of experts, serving in their personal capacities, which would consider reports from States parties "on the legislative, judicial, administrative or other measures adopted by them" to "give effect to the provisions of the Convention." The Convention also provided for the Committee to receive and consider communications from individuals or groups claiming to be victims of a violation of any of the rights set forth in the Convention, provided that the State party had made a declaration recognizing the competence of the Committee to do so.

By the mid-1960s, the composition of the United Nations had changed dramatically. Its membership 51 States (originally) had more than doubled, to 119 member States, with the admission of 68 new members: 36 from Africa, 16 from Asia, 10 from Western Europe, five from Eastern Europe, and one from Latin America.[25] It was largely under pressure from the nonaligned States, especially the African ones, that the UN moved to abrogate the self-denying rule of the CHR. The catalyst was the *apartheid* system in South Africa, and racial discrimination elsewhere on the continent, which had become increasingly repugnant to the UN membership. In March 1966, under pressure from African governments, ECOSOC requested that the Commission expand its terms of reference to allow consideration of violations of human rights and fundamental freedoms, "including policies of racial discrimination and segregation and of *apartheid* in all countries, with particular reference to colonial and other dependent countries and territories."

The following year, the Commission took up the challenge, requesting from ECOSOC the authority to make a thorough study and investigation of situations that reveal a "consistent pattern" of violations of human rights so it could report, with recommendations to ECOSOC. It also requested that ECOSOC authorize the CHR and the Sub-Commission on Prevention of Discrimination and Protection of Minorities to examine communications received by the United nations for information relevant to "gross" violations of human rights and fundamental freedoms. ECOSOC acceded by adopting Resolution 1235 (XLII) on 6 June 1967. What occurred thereafter was a schizophrenic reaction, with the United Nations manifesting a blatant double standard: It issued a resounding condemnation of *apartheid*, paralleled by a complete refusal to consider gross violations elsewhere in the world.

In 1967, the CHR decided to create an *Ad Hoc* Group of Experts to investigate charges of torture and ill-treatment of prisoners, detainees, and persons in police custody in South Africa,[26] with the purpose of giving maximum exposure to these violations by the white apartheid regime. Information was to be gathered from all sources, especially nongovernmental ones: The Group was to "receive communications and hear witnesses and use such modalities of procedure as it may deem appropriate" and "recommend action to be taken in concrete cases."[27] Over the course of the next year, the mandate was expanded to cover prisoners in most of Southern Africa, and the Group was given the additional task of looking into trade union rights, first in South Africa, and then in Southern Rhodesia and Southwest Africa.[28] Also in 1967, the Commission appointed a Special Rapporteur to survey past UN action in its efforts to eliminate the policies and practices of *apartheid*, to study relevant legislation and practice, and to report and make recommendations on measures that might be taken by the General Assembly.[29] With these investigations, the "no power to act" doctrine of the CHR appeared to have had become a dead letter. The reality was more complex.

With the passage of ECOSOC Resolution 1235, the Sub-Commission on Prevention of Discrimination and Protection of Minorities of independent experts, taking seriously the authority it had received to make a thorough study and investigation of situations that reveal a "consistent pattern" of violations of human rights, decided to do just that, but with respect to Greece, where in April 1967 a right-wing military junta had seized power, and with respect to Haiti, where the Duvalier regime was engaged in brutal repression.[30] In preparing its report, it drew heavily on information supplied by Amnesty International, an NGO launched in 1961 that had already acquired a considerable reputation for the reliability of its information.[31] At the February–March 1968 session of the CHR, the Greek and Haitian representatives counterattacked, denying all charges against them, accusing the Sub-Commission of attempting to divert attention from *apartheid*, and warning that no State would be immune to condemnation if the CHR permitted itself to condemn governments on the basis of unofficial communications received by the United Nations. One or the other representative intimated that a certain power had been accused of genocide in Vietnam, that a European country had been accused of denying religious freedom to Jews, and that Biafra (which was waging a war of secession from Nigeria) was alleging atrocities.[32] These darts aimed at the West, the East, and the non-aligned, respectively, were effective in neutralizing the Sub-Commission, and the CHR decided to take no action on its recommendation. To make certain that the Sub-Commission would not in future deviate from the sanctioned narrow focus on Southern Africa, the CHR increased the membership of the Sub-Commission from 18 to 26, the additions coming primarily from Asia and Africa to reflect "equitable geographic representation."[33] Nonetheless, the dam shielding States from international scrutiny had been breached, and the many fingers plugging the holes would not be able to stem the flow of condemnation for longer than a decade.

For one thing, Resolution 1235 meant that the CHR would give annual consideration to the question of violations of human rights and fundamental freedoms. Although members of the Commission were reluctant to discuss the transgressions of other member States of the United Nations and frequently gave this agenda item short shrift, after the 1967 Israeli occupation of the West Bank and Gaza, the policies of Israel (along with those of South Africa, Southern Rhodesia, and Namibia) became fair game in the CHR,[34] and by 1974 one other pariah state—General Pinochet's Chile—became a subject of the CHR's scrutiny.[35]

In addition, from 1967 to 1970, the CHR and Sub-Commission, turning their attention to how best to handle communications relating to violations of human rights, devised the confidential "1503 procedure." So named after ECOSOC Resolution 1503 (XLVIII) of 1970, the procedure provides that a working group on communications of the Sub-Commission annually screen communications and refer to the Sub-Commission those that appear to reveal a consistent pattern of gross and reliably attested violations of human rights. The Sub-Commission considers these, along with replies, if any, from governments, considering also all "other relevant information," then determines which situations it will refer to the CHR.[36] For its part, the CHR may decide to take no action, to discontinue consideration under the 1503 procedure and consider the situation under another procedure, to make a thorough study of the situation, or to call for an investigation by an *ad hoc* committee. Although this entire procedure is confidential and its effectiveness has thus been questioned, since 1978, the Chair of the CHR has each year publicly announced the names of the countries on this confidential or "black list" prior to the CHR's public debate on violations.[37] Governments are known to go to great lengths to avoid being "black-listed," although frequently this is through lobbying, "politicking," or public relations work rather than by moderating repressive behavior.[38]

## The Emergence of the Human Rights Movement

It is now widely recognized that it was largely as a result of pressure from human rights NGOs that, in the late 1970s, States reluctantly moved from promotion of human rights, and a concentration on the drafting of international instruments and standards, to the protection of human rights, with an emphasis on implementation and enforcement. As late as October 1980, Theo van Boven (Director of the UN Centre for Human Rights from 1977 to 1982) and Bertie Ramcharan (Special Adviser to three directors of the Human Rights Centre) observed, "notwithstanding their commitment in the Charter to achieve international cooperation in promoting and protecting human rights and fundamental freedoms, and notwithstanding, in many instances, their subsequent acceptance of other instruments . . . there is still in practice a visibly discernible lack of commitment on the part of many governments either to protect human rights in their own countries, or to act for their protection at the international level."[39]

Throughout the 1970s and for much of the 1980s, an important consequence of this lack of commitment was the unwillingness of governments to monitor and to speak out against the human rights violations of other governments, unless there was a specific ideological, economic, or military advantage to doing so. As Felice Gaer points out,

> Early subjects of scrutiny were comparatively small countries, often reflecting the cold war ideological divide, with each side sponsoring criticism of some countries and shielding "their own." Thus, after Chile came under scrutiny, three more rightist authoritarian Latin American States were cited publicly: Guatemala (1980), El Salvador (1981), and Bolivia (1981). Others, such as Argentina and Uruguay were discussed only in confidential session, under the "1503" procedures. In response to public citation of so many Latin States, the Commission was pressed to add Poland (1982), Afghanistan (1984), and Iran

(1984). In each case, a single individual (alternatively called an "expert," "special representative," or "special rapporteur") was appointed to investigate the facts and report back. . . . And in virtually every instance, NGOs have been a factor in documenting the human rights situation, thus confronting abusive governments and their sponsors at the Commission on Human Rights sessions."[40]

Professor Louis Henkin of Columbia University made the same point in 1978 when he observed, "the early assumption that States might be prepared to scrutinize other States and be scrutinized by them" has not stood up, and there has been little "horizontal" enforcement.[41] Indeed, it has become clear that, to the extent that national governments or IGOs were moved to express genuine concern for human rights, this was largely the result of pressures exerted upon them by the human rights community.

The human rights community is, admittedly, a nebulous concept. It includes legislators and executive policy-makers, journalists and opinion leaders, foundations, academics, and others. However, the core of this community is a mixture of "pure type" nongovernmental human rights organizations (local or grassroots, national, regional, or international) and a multitude of other private associations (including trade unions, churches, professional associations, and "peoples' organizations") that have exhibited active concern for, and involvement in, the human rights struggle.[42]

More formally, a human rights NGO is a private association whose raison d'être derives from the promotion and/or protection of one or more internationally recognized human rights. To a large extent, an NGO is defined by what it is not: It is not governmental, that is, it is not controlled by government. Stated positively, an NGO is autonomous or independent of government.[43]

Such organizations are typically led by human rights activists or human rights defenders, that is, individuals who make a major commitment to, and openly take up, the defense and protection of the human rights of others. Human rights defenders need not, however, be formally associated with an organization: They may be lawyers, journalists, writers, religious leaders, trade unionists, health workers, or teachers; frequently, they are associated with broad-based "peoples' organizations" of peasants, workers, slum dwellers, indigenous peoples, or women. They are individuals who champion the human rights of others, often at great risk to their own lives and safety. These human rights NGOs and human rights defenders have been the spearhead of the human rights movement that began to coalesce into a significant force in the late 1970s.[44]

Although, as discussed above, there were NGOs concerned with human rights at the founding of the United Nations, in the 1950s and 1960s, they were still few in number and their influence was limited. Prominent in the early years were NGOs like B'nai B'rith International, the World Conference on Religion and Peace, the World Young Women's Christian Association, or the Friends Peace and International Relations Committee. There were also a few international NGOs with a specific human rights concern: the International League for the Rights of Man (created in 1942, now called the International League for Human Rights),[45] the International Commission of Jurists (established in 1951),[46] and Amnesty International (created in 1961).[47] In the 1970s, there was, however, an enormous expansion in the number of NGOs concerned with human rights and in the diversity of these organizations. In addition, many social sector organizations, including trade unions, churches, and professional associations, began to devote significant attention to human rights issues. Although some groups were country specific and some issue specific, and not all shared the same vision of a human rights regime, what gave this new universe of NGOs the characteristics of a movement is that they all appealed to the same set of international standards—the International Bill of Human Rights—in trying to hold States accountable for their behavior.

A number of factors contributed to this coalescence. The coup against the Allende government in Chile in 1973 and the solidification of military dictatorships throughout the southern Cone in South America gave rise to human rights organizations throughout the continent, and to numerous human rights and solidarity groups in Europe and North America.[48] Dissidents in Eastern Europe and the USSR were given an enormous boost by the signing and subsequent dissemination of the Helsinki Final Act of the Conference on Security and Cooperation in Europe in 1975, and by the "Helsinki watch" committees and Soviet Jewry groups that emerged in the West to support them.[49] The development of a social justice agenda and a liberation theology by elements in the Catholic Church in the wake of Pope John's Vatican II (1961) and the Medellín Conference (1968), and the move from study to action programs in the Fourth Assembly of the World Council of Churches in 1968[50] meant that religious communities were predisposed to "witnessing" and to the development of justice and peace programs. The development of a human rights program by the Ford Foundation in the mid-1970s, which made resources available to human rights NGOs;[51] the awarding of the Nobel Peace Prize to Amnesty International in 1977; the end of the Vietnam War, which meant that progressive Americans could redirect their energies to a broader range of concerns;[52] and the coming into force of the human rights covenants in 1976 all contributed to the coalescence of the movement. Thus, in 1977, when U.S. President Carter took up the banner of human rights as his own, and got human rights inscribed as an enduring item on the international political agenda, he was less a leader than a follower of a trail already blazed by NGOs. Nonetheless, the fact that a superpower legitimated the human rights struggle was of enormous importance to the role human rights NGOs were able to play on the world stage.

In the context of the United Nations, it is important to note that Article 71 of the Charter acknowledged the potential contribution that NGOs could make to the work of the organization in the areas of concern to the ESOSOC, that is, international economic, social, cultural, educational, health, and related matters (including human rights). It did this by providing that the ECOSOC "may make suitable arrangements for consultation" with international NGOs, and it could make such arrangements "where appropriate, with national organizations after consultation with the Member of the United Nations concerned." The purposes of the consultation, later articulated in ECOSOC Resolution 2/3 (1946), were two: "to enable the Council . . . to secure expert information and advice" and "to enable organizations which represent important elements of public opinion to express their views."

Article 71 of the UN Charter was not so much breaking new ground as it was formalizing a relationship that had already emerged during the League of Nations era. Although the Covenant of the League did not contain provisions for a formal link with international NGOs, under the League it had become normal practice to consult with such organizations.[53] Chiang Pei-heng, quoting Bertram Pickard,[54] writes,

> participation without vote" was "normal practice" for NGOs, with "little if any distinction . . . made between IGOs and NGOs, both of which, when consulted, were placed upon an equal footing with government representatives in all but voting."[55]

Chiang notes further,

> NGO representatives to the various committees of the League . . . although not able to vote, were allowed to speak, present reports, initiate discussions, propose resolutions and amendments, and be assigned to subcommitees.[56]

The relationship that the ECOSOC established with NGOs did not go nearly so far. The UN clearly distinguishes between "consultation" with NGOs in Article 71 and "participation without vote" granted to specialized agencies in Article 70. ECOSOC Resolution 1296 (which, since 1968, has defined how NGOs relate to ECOSOC and its subsidiary bodies) specifically notes (in paragraph 12) that: "[t]his distinction . . . is fundamental and arrangements for consultation should not be such as to accord to non-governmental organizations the same rights of participation as accorded to States not members of the Council and to the specialized agencies brought into relationship with the United Nations." This is underlined in the next paragraph (paragraph 13): "The arrangements should not be such as to overburden the Council or transform it from a body for coordination of policy and action, as contemplated in the Charter, into a general forum for discussion."

Moreover, as ECOSOC elaborated its rules for working with NGOs (in Resolutions 2/3 of 1946, 288B (X) of 1950, and 1296 (XLIV) of 1968), it progressively tightened control over NGOs, so that Resolution 1296 provides for the suspension or withdrawal of status "if the organization clearly abuses its consultative status by systematically engaging in unsubstantiated or politically motivated acts against States Members of the United Nations contrary to and incompatible with the principles of the Charter." Although in the early years, it was the U.S. government that was concerned with keeping NGOs in check, especially those sympathetic to the Eastern bloc,[57] by the late 1960s, a very different situation prevailed. The impetus for the 1968 review came from two sources: the growth in UN membership, which led to the enlargement of the ECOSOC by the addition of African and Asian countries with little understanding of the NGO concept, and a February 1967 exposé by *Ramparts* magazine and the *New York Times* that the CIA was clandestinely funding many NGOs.[58] Sidney Liskofsky, of the American Jewish Committee, published the following analysis in 1970:

> During the 1960s, Afro-Asian membership in the U.N. increased greatly, depriving the West of its majority and its dominant position in the organization. With this change came increasing expressions of hostility, and even challenges, to the NGO system by Communist and Afro-Asian States. This culminated in a decision to investigate the entire system and re-examine the status assigned to NGOs. The two-year review which followed became deeply enmeshed in the rivalries and conflicts that beset the U.N., espe-

cially those concerning the Middle East. Finally, the Arab-Soviet bloc mounted a virtual assault against organizations specializing in the U.N.'s human rights program, particularly Jewish ones. . . .

As originally proposed by Tanzania, the chief purpose of the review was to determine the truth of widely bruited charges regarding C.I.A. infiltration of NGOs, through subsidies and otherwise, which, if proven, might negate claims to non-governmental status. However, among Communist and certain Afro-Asian governments, chiefly the Arab, which endorsed the review, general hostility to the NGO system, and even the NGO concept, was a more fundamental motivation.[59]

This was only the prelude to what was, several years later, to be a highly targeted campaign to silence human rights NGOs. In the mid-1970s, as the UN CHR began to address seriously human rights violations in the context of protection, human rights NGOs began to address their information and concerns to these bodies. As I wrote in 1977,

At that time the ECOSOC did not clearly enunciate its rules of parliamentary order, but convention and habit ensured that NGOs would ''address'' the issues of violations of human rights and their violators with circumlocutions, euphemisms, and evasions. In February 1974, however, the unwritten rule against ''naming names'' was broken when Mrs. Salvadore Allende, widow of the slain Chilean President, was invited to address the United Nations Commission. . . . No one interrupted Mrs. Allende to object or invoke a Roberts-type ruling calling her to order. Observing this, Dr. Homer A. Jack, representing the World Conference on Religion and Peace (WCRP), seized upon the opportunity to present a ''state of the world'' human rights status report, with empirical detail about victims and violators. The following day, Professor Frank C. Newman from Amnesty International made very detailed charges about torture in Chile.

Moreover, a few months later—in May 1974—the executive director of yet another human rights organization, Niall MacDermot of the International Commission of Jurists, wrote an article for a special human rights section of the *London Times* in which he similarly violated the nation-protecting diplomatic protocol. Specifically, MacDermot dealt with real-world, real-time events, regimes and peoples by discussing the eight cases of consistent patterns of gross violations then under investigation by the [Communications] Working Group of the Commission. The culmination of this series of NGO ''indiscretions'' came at the 31st session of the U.N. Commission on Human Rights in Geneva in February 1975. At that meeting, Dr. Homer Jack of the WCRP spoke out forcefully once again, this time addressing the question of religious persecution. . . .[60]

States were furious. Egypt, Pakistan, the Soviet Union, Turkey, Zaire, the Philippines, and Syria all took the floor to protest that Jack's statements were untrue, slanderous, or biased. ''We are extremely concerned about the abuse of freedom of speech practiced by some representatives of nongovernmental organizations,'' said the Egyptian delegate.[61] Then, in private session, the CHR

requested ECOSOC to take measures that would impose severe restrictions on the nature of NGO communications about human rights violations, whether those communications were to the U.N. or in the form of public statements. . . . [ECOSOC then decided] ''that any non-governmental organization failing to show proper discretion in an oral or written statement may render itself subject to suspension of its consultative status . . .[62]

This threat, like the sword of Damocles, was to hang over the head of NGOs for many years, even though, over time and through persistent efforts, the NGOs were able to force the UN publicly to confront governments engaged in gross violations of human rights.

## The Functions of Human Rights NGOs[63]

Precisely what is it that human rights NGOs do that has made States perceive them as such a threat? A short answer is that they ''speak truth to power.'' If a government is repressive and violative of international human rights norms, the power elite has every reason to view human rights NGOs as a threat to their legitimacy. More analytically, human rights NGOs have performed at least six distinctive functions.

*Fact-Finding or Information Gathering, Analysis, and Dissemination.* The first is information gathering, evaluation, and dissemination. It is common knowledge that the intergovernmental human rights machinery would grind to a halt were it not fed by the fact-finding of human rights NGOs. Diego Garcia-Sayan puts it as follows:

> The United Nations Working Group on Forced Disappearances . . . along with many intergovernmental organizations, relies basically upon NGOs and not the Governments themselves. The NGOs provide the Group with information, pressure it to act, and clamour for results. This is true of all the United Nations specialized groups.
>
> Anyone who has ever attended a session of the United Nations Commission on Human Rights has seen the caution—to say the least—with which the government representatives act. Except in extreme cases or when dealing with countries which few or no Governments defend . . . it would seem that there exists a policy of not criticizing neighbouring countries directly or harshly. Strange but notorious silences can be understood simply as indicating geopolitical interests. The "prosecutors" in these circumstances, that is to say those who hold human rights concerns above others, are the NGOs. They are the fuel and the lubricant which allow the machine to function and speed the working up. . . . [T]he NGOs contribute greatly to upholding the international community's ethics. If it were not for their efforts, this system of ethics would have been eroded a long time ago.[64]

Felice Gaer notes that

> . . . the Working Group on Arbitrary Detentions reported in 1995 that 74% of the cases it took up in 1994 were brought by international NGOs, and another 23% came from national NGOs . . . The Special Rapporteur on Arbitrary Executions acknowledges the "important" role of NGOs in alerting the international community about summary executions, and the Rapporteur on freedom of expression describes the NGO contribution as "primordial."[65]

At the national level, although governments are charged with investigating allegations of human rights abuses, there are only a handful of countries where the system for the administration of justice, together with national institutions (i.e., governmental human rights commissions or ombudsmen), can be relied on to gather, analyze, and act impartially on "the facts." Even in the societies that profess to be the most democratic, private associations and the media frequently first expose abuses of power.

Accurate and timely information is the main currency of human rights NGOs and the basis for their legitimacy. Amnesty International led the way by developing a research department to underpin all campaign work. When NGO information was challenged as being one-sided, a charge that was often leveled in the mid-1980s in the context of the civil war in El Salvador, NGOs took up the gauntlet. They broadened their fact-finding to cover not only violations committed by government forces, but also violations committed by insurgents. They also began to document violations of humanitarian law as well as international human rights law.[66]

Over the course of two decades, such fact-finding has become the work of professionals rather than amateurs. It has developed its own methodology and has evidenced a strong concern for protecting those who provide the information. More recently, NGOs have begun to use video cameras as well as written affidavits to document abuses. They have begun to standardize data so that it can be computerized and/or statistically analyzed[67] and have developed specialized techniques for dealing with certain types of evidence (as with the application of forensic anthropology to mass graves, genetic matching to identify disappeared grandchildren, and techniques to confirm the application of torture).

*Denunciation of the Violations.* In dealing with human rights violators, denunciation is an important strategy. Many tactics can and have been employed in different situations: issuing press releases and mounting press campaigns; publishing reports and disseminating these widely, especially to policymakers; using the pulpit and the religious network for "witnessing"; holding demonstrations, rallies, and sit-ins; organizing peoples' tribunals at which witnesses testify to the violations; denouncing through videos, films, popular music, or theater; testifying before governmental or inter-governmental bodies; and most recently, using fax networks, electronic mail, and the Internet (increasingly, World Wide Web sites) to disseminate information globally.

Informing all these tactics is the hope that by exposing the violations to the harsh glare of public opinion, one can achieve one of several ends. A dictatorship can be shamed into putting a halt to violations; domestic opposition can be mobilized to destabilize a dictatorial regime; and/or international opposition can be generated, leading to pressure and possibly open sanctions against an offending government.

Experience has shown that no regime, except the most insular, wishes to be branded as a human rights violator. Hence, governments engage in a whole host of tactics to counter such denunciations. These have ranged from blatant denial of the facts to impugning the reputation of the fact-finders (e.g., labeling human rights NGOs as subversive, terrorist, or antinationalistic), pleading that special circumstances (i.e., a threat to the nation) require special measures (e.g., national security legislation), hiring high-powered public relations firms to give a dictatorship a different image, and creating their own government-organized non-governmental organizations (GON-GOs) or national institutions to produce counterreports.

***Lobbying in Governmental and Inter-Governmental Arenas.*** Human rights NGOs, recognizing the limitations of their own power, have lobbied governments at the national, regional, and international levels to take action to halt gross violations. Thus, NGOs have been active before the Inter-American Commission and Court of Human Rights, the European Commission and Court of Human Rights, the African Commission on Human Rights, the Organization on Security and Cooperation in Europe, the European Parliament, the Commonwealth, and Le Francophonie. In recent years, such lobbying has also targeted international financial institutions like the International Monetary Fund (IMF), the World Bank, and the World Trade Organization (WTO). With respect to the violations of dictatorial regimes, the objective of the lobbying has usually been the application of negative sanctions against the offending regime, but occasionally also State intervention in the form of private diplomacy.

Within the context of the United Nations, such lobbying has led to the development of a new set of mechanisms for the protection of human rights. One of the most important lobbying exercises in which the human rights NGOs engaged was in the context of disappearances during the "dirty war" in Argentina and the repression in Chile, which led in 1980 to the establishment of the first thematic mechanism of the CHR: a five-person expert Working Group on forced or involuntary disappearances.[68] Since that time, more than a dozen thematic mechanisms have been created, enabling the Commission to monitor the behavior of governments worldwide and, in some cases, to request information as a matter of urgency when there was an imminent threat to the life, liberty, or physical integrity of individuals.[69]

Of particular note is the lobbying and mobilization in which NGOs engaged prior to the World Conference on Human Rights in 1993, which resulted in a recommendation in the Vienna Declaration and Plan of Action to consider the establishment of a High Commissioner for Human Rights. Although the idea of a High Commissioner dates back to a December 1947 French proposal for an Attorney-General of human rights and reemerged in various forms over the years,[70] in 1993 Amnesty International took it up as part of an entire package of reforms of the UN's Human Rights Program[71] and was supported by NGOs in all regions. After the World Conference, the General Assembly, acting on the Vienna Declaration, created a working group to debate the specifics of the post and mandate. In February 1994, José Ayala-Lasso, Ecuador's UN envoy, was appointed as the first High Commissioner. Less successful was the pre-Conference lobbying spearheaded by the International Commission of Jurists for the establishment of an International Criminal Court,[72] as the Vienna Declaration merely "encourages the International Law Commission to continue its work on an international criminal court" (paragraph 92). Since the U.S. government has strongly resisted progress on this front, NGO lobbying has not been able to move the issue forward.

Perhaps the most successful NGO lobbying effort of the 1990s was the lobbying of the women's human rights movement prior to the 1993 World Conference, to get women's rights recognized as human rights, not only in the Vienna Declaration, but throughout the entire United Nations system. When the Commission on Human Rights was created in February 1946, its mandate extended to preventing all forms of discrimination, including discrimination on the basis of sex, and it was to elaborate declarations or conventions on all human rights, including those on the status of women.[73] However, in June 1946, ECOSOC created a Commission on the Status of Women (CSW) to promote women's rights. Although the intention behind the CSW was to give greater emphasis to women's rights than they would receive if subsumed under the CHR, instead women's rights were "ghettoized," at least until the 1990s. For example, the Committee on the Elimination of All Forms of Discrimination against Women (CEDAW), which monitored the implementation of the 1979 CEDAW Convention, was the only treaty body not serviced by the UN Center for Human Rights in Geneva. Questions relating to women were relegated to structures endowed with less power and resources than the general human rights bodies.[74]

Moreover, the women's rights movement and the human rights movement developed on their own separate trajectories, rarely intersecting. At the World Conferences on Women (Mexico 1975, Copenhagen 1980, and Nairobi 1985), few human rights NGOs were visible participants. International human rights NGOs rarely disaggregated their data on the basis of gender or gave particular attention to violations of women's human rights. Women's issues were not discussed in the CHR or the Sub-Commission; none of the special rapporteurs or working groups focused on gender-based violence or discrimination. This began to change in 1990. As described by Wendy Parker and Pauline Comeau,

> When the World Conference was announced in 1990, women's organizations detected a vacuum in the agenda and decided they would fill it. But they knew it would be an uphill battle. Women's rights are so far outside the mainstream in the UN that, when the themes for the world event were first proposed, women's issues were not even on the list.
>
> The women's effort began at the grassroots to determine key issues. These efforts at the local level were essential. . . .
>
> The result? A united message that violations against women—be it female infanticide, mass rape in armed conflict, sex tourism, circumcision practices, or domestic violence—are universal and such gender-based violence must be considered a matter of fundamental rights at the universal level.
>
> Women's caucuses then carried this message to three regional meetings (Tunisia, Costa Rica, and Thailand) held in preparation for the Vienna conference, and then through four UN preparatory meetings (PrepComs) in Geneva. By the time women reached Vienna, the groups had amassed a petition with a half a million names from 124 countries demanding that "gender violence be recognized as a violations of human rights."[75]

In this case, lobbying targeted not only governments, but other (human rights) NGOs as well. Sustained follow-up after Vienna led to the appointment of a Special Rapporteur on Violence against Women, instructions that all UN mechanisms and bodies begin considering women's human rights as part of their mandates, a strong human rights dimension to the Beijing Declaration and Plan of Action, and much greater gender sensitivity in reporting by human rights NGOs.

*International Solidarity and Humanitarian Relief.* A strategy of international solidarity and humanitarian relief evolved to provide protection to victims and potential victims under dictatorial regimes. This has included the following, *inter alia*. The "adoption" tactic of Amnesty International involves its groups adopting specific political prisoners and campaigning for their release, sometimes for years. Urgent Action (UA) Networks, also introduced by Amnesty, are now widely used by many NGOs (including churches, trade unions, and professional associations). Such networks organize hundreds of people around the world, who are poised to respond immediately (by telegram or fax) to prevent torture, disappearance, the application of the death penalty, or most recently, violence against women. Some of the UN special rapporteurs take action on the basis of these UA Network initiatives, immediately contacting governments to request information about cases. In particularly dangerous situations, NGOs have used the tactic of "accompaniment," whereby a human rights activist (or a trade unionist or peasant leader) at risk is "body-guarded" 24 hours a day by a foreign companion armed only with a camera. Pioneering efforts in El Salvador and Sri Lanka have substantiated that dictators are less likely to kill or disappear an activist under such protection.

International NGOs have also provided money, and in some cases legal advice and or lawyers, to defend political prisoners on trial for their life or liberty. They have also provided material and/or moral support to the families of the detainees. Of course, it was NGOs that were behind the establishment in the early 1980s of the UN Voluntary Fund for Torture, to support programs that provide direct medical, psychological, social, or other assistance to torture victims and their families. NGOs have also assisted victims or their friends and relatives in preparing cases brought before inter-governmental human rights bodies (such as the Inter-American and European Commissions and Courts and the Human Rights Committee) as well as preparing counterreports to the States parties reports considered by the UN treaty bodies (e.g., the Committee on Economic, Social and Cultural Rights and the Committee on the Rights of the Child).

Particularly innovative has been the strategy of using international standards in domestic courts to sue human rights violators. The 1988 decision of the U.S. Court of Appeals for the Second Circuit, in the case of *Filartiga v Peña-Irala*, was a landmark victory. The Center for Constitutional Rights (CRC) in New York filed the case in New York in 1984 on behalf of the Paraguayan activist and physician, Joel Filartiga, accusing the Inspector General of Police of Asunsion (who was then residing in the U.S.) in the torture death of Filartiga's 17-year-old son. This involved the use of the Alien Tort Act as the basis for bringing a federal action for an alleged human rights violation of internationally recognized human rights law. Although the District Court initially refused to hear the case, on appeal the case was both heard and decided in favor of Filartiga. The Court awarded him a judgment of $10.3 million. Filartiga would never see the $10.3 million, but the case sent a clear message that human rights torturers could not find safe haven in the U.S.

Subsequent to that case, U.S. human rights groups lobbied for and saw a new law enacted, the *Torture Victim Protection Act.* This Act permits anyone to sue any person living in the United States for torture committed anywhere in the world. In April 1995, another landmark victory was registered in the case brought against Guatemalan General Hector Alejandro Gramajo, responsible for the torture and murder of thousands of Guatemalans while he was Vice-Chief of Staff in the early 1980s and Defense Minister from 1987 to 1990. Gramajo was served with two law suits in 1991, as he was graduating from the John F. Kennedy School of Government at Harvard University. He left the country and refused to contest the case. Nonetheless, a judgment of $47.5 million was made in favor of eight Guatemalans and an American nun on whose behalf the suits were filed. "In this case, plaintiffs have convincingly demonstrated that, at a minimum, Gramajo was aware of and supported widespread acts of brutality committed by personnel under his command resulting in thousands of civilian deaths," wrote Judge Woodlock.[76]

*Human Rights Education.* A fifth function, which has become particularly relevant to societies in transition from dictatorial to democratic rule, is human rights education. Individuals and communities cannot adequately protect their rights if they do not know their rights. Human rights education tends to be primarily the responsibility of national NGOs, because they can best interpret international standards in the local context; however, international and regional NGOs have also mounted educational campaigns and are likely to be instrumental in implementing the United Nations Decade on Human Rights Education (1995–2005).[77]

*Providing Expertise to the United Nations in Implementing Its Programs.* A final function is one that has only recently become evident in the human rights sphere, although NGOs have been quietly performing it for years: namely, providing expertise to the UN to enable it to implement its programs. This role was evident much earlier in other areas of the ECOSOC's competence, for example, in development or environmental protection. In human rights, one tended to talk and think in terms of NGOs providing information rather than expertise.

Over the last several decades, NGOs have assisted the UN in drafting international legislation, as, for example, with the Convention against Torture,[78] the Convention on the Rights of the Child,[79] the Convention on the Protection of the Rights of All Migrant Workers and Members of Their Families, and the draft Universal Declaration on the Rights of Indigenous People. In the latter case, it has been representatives of indigenous peoples and groups who have contributed most to the elaboration of the document.[80] As LeBlanc has written,

> NGOs can participate in the human rights norm-creation process in a variety of ways, including attending conferences, suggesting draft articles for inclusion in norm-creating instruments, criticizing articles in draft stage, doing research, providing advice and assistance . . . and offering legal expertise and advice.[81]

However, in recent years, there have been some new departures. Many of the special rapporteurs selected to monitor violations are individuals who have received their training and experience in the NGO movement, and additionally, each of these individuals has come out of the non-governmental human rights movement and received their training in that movement.

In a similar vein, to implement its program of technical assistance to governments in the area of human rights, the UN Centre for Human Rights has increasingly employed experts from the human rights community to conduct needs assessments, to train judges or the police, to establish human rights documentation centers, and to develop programs and manuals in human rights education.[82] More recently, as the UN Centre for Human Rights has dispatched human rights monitors to countries such as Guatemala, Haiti, Rwanda, and Burundi, individual monitors have been recruited (by UN Volunteers) through non-governmental human rights organizations. The non-governmental human rights movement, now some 20 years old (if one dates its origin as a movement to the mid-1970s), has trained a professional cadre and equipped them with skills that are vitally important as the UN attempts to confront the new challenges of humanitarian intervention, conflict management, and democratization.

This places human rights NGOs in a somewhat novel situation. Because the NGOs have been the primary source of information on human rights violations committed by governments, they are frequently perceived—especially by rights-violating regimes—as hostile antagonists of governments. Now, human rights NGOs—or at least some of them—are being cast in the role of implementing UN policies to assist governments. This is a fairly significant shift in perspective, with considerable implications for both the United Nations and for human rights NGOs.

## UN–NGO Relations: The Consultative Status Review

Over the past three years, a Working Group of ECOSOC has been engaged in a process of reassessing how it relates to NGOs. Mandated by the ECOSOC under Resolutions 1993/80 and 1993/214, this review marks the first time in 27 years that the rules governing NGO relations with the United Nations—ECOSOC Resolution 1296 (XLIV) of 23 February 1968—were to be revised. Specifically, the mandate of the Working Group is to undertake a general review with a view to (1) updating, if necessary, Resolution 1296; (2) introducing coherence in the rules governing the participation of NGOs in international conferences convened by the United Nations; and (3) examining ways and means of improving practical arrangements for the work of the Committee on Non-Governmental Organizations and the NGO Unit of the UN Secretariat.

Such a review was clearly necessitated by the reality that, in all areas of the world and in all spheres of activity, there has been a mushrooming of NGOs, including international and regional NGOs and networks, and national and local NGOs. And inasmuch as the United Nations is the most important universal arena for discussing and devising strategies to confront global problems, these NGOs have increasingly been drawn into UN debates and fora. The Earth Summit (officially the UN Conference on Environment and Development) in Rio in June 1992 was not only "the biggest ever gathering of heads of state in history,"[83] but

> At the Earth Summit in Rio, and at the four PrepCom sessions, the UN granted NGOs unprecedented access to the process and therefore to the delegates themselves. Instead of limiting access to those NGOs in consultative status, NGOs who could prove "particular competence" in the issues of environment and development were also given accreditation.[84]

This precedent was subsequently followed at the World Conference on Human Rights (Vienna, 1993), the World Conference on Population and Development (Cairo, 1994), the Social Development Summit (Copenhagen, 1995), the World Conference on Women (Beijing, 1995), and Habitat (to be held in Istanbul in 1996), although the conference accreditation procedure has been ad hoc and somewhat different in each case. Moreover, many of the NGOs accredited to these international UN meetings have expressed a strong interest in participating in the follow-up. For example, some 500 NGOs have been concerned with participating in the new UN Commission on Sustainable Development (CSD), created to implement the commitments made at the Earth Summit. As it stands at present, NGOs accredited to world conferences do not get any form of automatic accreditation to the ECOSOC (i.e., consultative status), although, in the case of NGOs following the work of the CSD, the UN Secretary-General asked that they all be placed on the ECOSOC Roster, pending a final decision about their status after the ECOSOC NGO review. Thus, the impetus to revise Resolution 1296 was the desire to facilitate NGO access to UN processes and arenas, to permit national NGOs (largely excluded from consultative status under Resolution 1296) access to the UN, and to bring UN regulations and procedures into line with current reality—a reality that recognizes the important contribution NGOs make, or can make, to the work of the United Nations.

Although many governments know the value and importance of NGOs, "their capacity to mobilize resources, play an advocacy role, provide policy analysis, plan and carry out projects and programmes, deliver emergency assistance and monitor and participate in the implementation of international agreements and programmes of action,"[85] others still regard NGOs with suspicion, and often with hostility, particularly when it comes to human rights NGOs. Thus, whereas the Vienna Declaration made advances on many fronts, especially by affirming the universality of human rights, the interdependence of all human rights, and the integration of women's rights into human rights, paragraph 38 is ambivalent, at best, on the question of NGOs. After lauding the important role of NGOs in the promotion of all human rights and humanitarian activities at national, regional, and international levels, it states as follows:

> The World Conference on Human Rights emphasizes the importance of continued dialogue and cooperation between Governments and non-governmental organizations. Non-governmental organizations and their members *genuinely* involved in the field of human rights should enjoy the rights and freedoms recognized in the Universal Declaration of Human Rights, and the protection of national law.

These rights and freedoms may not be exercised contrary to the purposes and principles of the United Nations. Non-governmental organizations should be free to carry out their human rights activities, without interference, *within the framework of national law* and the Universal Declaration of Human Rights. [Emphasis added.]

By qualifying the activities of NGOs with the phrase "genuinely involved in the field of human rights," and circumscribing NGO activities with national law—often far more restrictive than international norms—States are still flexing their sovereign muscles to keep NGOs in check.

One must note that NGOs themselves were not united in what they hoped to achieve through this review process. One key issue, whether to open consultative status to a much broader range of NGOs, especially national NGOs and networks, including affiliates of international NGOs, was highly divisive. On the one side were those NGOs (and governments) arguing for a democratization of the relationship between NGOs and ECOSOC by allowing political space for new actors (especially from the south) to participate more fully. On the other side were NGOs concerned that opening the UN so broadly would erode the rights and privileges they (largely northern-based NGOs) had worked so hard to achieve. These include, for example, the right to make oral and written interventions at meetings of ECOSOC's subsidiary bodies and, in some cases, to propose items for the agenda. Many of the G77 States, although committed at the level of rhetoric to welcoming national, especially southern, NGOs into a relationship with the United Nations, want nonetheless to ensure that this would not include national human rights NGOs that might criticize their human rights records. Thus, the G77 has been standing firmly behind a paragraph that states,

> Organizations accorded special consultative status because of their interest in the field of human rights and humanitarian assistance should have a general international concern with this matter, not restricted to the interests of a particular group of persons, a single nationality or the situation in a single State or restricted group of States. . . .[86]

At the time of this writing, the issue remains a major point of contention. Together with other sections which remain in square brackets, it may have to be resolved by ECOSOC in July 1996.

## Conclusion

However the consultative status review ends, I suggest that this is only the beginning, not the culmination, of a process of determining how NGOs, IGOs, and governments will relate to one another in the coming years in the face of the multiplicity of global challenges. There will have to be new and innovative ways for sharing ideas and expertise, including, for example, electronic conferencing and communications. The "best practices" that have evolved over time will need to be studied carefully as the United Nations is reformed and made more responsive and relevant to the problems of the next century. It will be necessary to determine how responsibilities can most effectively be shared in the face of the complex emergencies that will, more than likely, continue to plague the world. And these groups will have to find ways and means of addressing root causes of violations, rather than treating only their symptoms.

Although the task of developing a corpus of international human rights law—a task which the CHR set for itself in 1946—is largely completed, there are still some areas where work remains to be done. For example, there is the draft Declaration on the Rights of Human Rights Defenders,[87] which has been on the table since 1984, when the CHR established a working group to deal with the rights of people, individually and in association with each other, to promote and protect human rights and fundamental freedoms.[88] Although the term *human rights defenders* is not specifically mentioned in the Defenders' Declaration (as it has come to be called), its intended purpose is to reaffirm that human rights advocates will enjoy such basic internationally recognized human rights as freedom of association, expression, movement, speech, and conscience, and not be denied these rights because they are defending the rights of others. That the draft Defenders' Declaration has not yet been finalized must be attributed to the animosity that some States, most recently Cuba, China, Syria, and Nigeria, still have toward human rights NGOs. These States have actively supported language that would constitute an erosion, not a reaffirmation, of their rights.[89]

Undoubtedly, there will also be new issues and areas that will require the elaboration of international standards (for example, genetic engineering, *in vitro* fertilization, or "the right to die," which have all just begun to come under national regulation). However, the issue of the next century will clearly be how to monitor and enforce international standards. In this context, one key concern is the issue of "impunity" for gross violators of human rights, and hence the question of an international criminal court. Another concern is streamlining and improving on the effectiveness of current human rights machinery. This has been a subject of intense discussion by the chairpersons of the committees dealing with treaty bodies, the special mechanisms (i.e., the working groups and special rapporteurs), and the technical assistance program of the UN Centre for Human Rights. Among other things, it is clear that attention must be given to computerizing the information on which all depend for their oversight and finding ways of sharing this information, as for example by developing relevant databases on the World Wide Web or Gopher sites on the Internet. The UN Centre is currently being restructured to better integrate the Office of the High Commissioner into the human rights program and to make it possible for the Centre to respond more effectively to "early warnings" and complex emergencies. Thought is also being given to bringing a human rights perspective to all of the work of the United Nations, including development, peace making, and peace building.

Two things are central to the success of these operations: the political will to implement the changes and the financial and human resources needed to do so. The goal toward which all strive was clearly articulated in the Vienna Declaration—a world where "all human rights are universal, indivisible and interdependent and inter-related." To get there,

> The international community must treat human rights globally in a fair and equal manner, on the same footing, and with the same emphasis. While the significance of national and regional particularities and various historical, cultural and religious backgrounds must be borne in mind, it is the duty of States, regardless of their political, economic and cultural systems, to promote and protect all human rights and fundamental freedoms.[90]

Stated differently, the challenge is to develop a global culture anchored in this human rights framework, and institutions at the local, national, regional, and international levels that support it.

LAURIE S. WISEBERG
Executive Director, Human Rights Internet

## Notes

1. There are 94 instruments listed in *Human Rights: A Compilation of International Instruments,* Vol. I, Universal Instruments, New York: United Nations, 1993. Vol. II, Regional Instruments (not yet published) will contain the regional human rights instruments of the Organization of American States, Council of Europe, Organization of African Unity, and Conference on Security and Cooperation in Europe.
2. Vienna Declaration and Programme of Action adopted at the World Conference on Human Rights, A/CONF.157/24/25 June 1993, para. 1.
3. Ibid., para. 4.
4. Ibid., second paragraph of the preamble.
5. *General Review of Arrangements for Consultations with Non-Governmental Organizations. Report of the Secretary-General.* Document prepared for the ECOSOC Open-Ended Working Group on the Review of Arrangements for Consultations with Non-Governmental Organizations. A/AC.70/1994/5, 26 May 1994, p. 3–4.
6. Ad Hoc Working Group on NGOs and Peacebuilding, *NGOs and Peacebuilding: Lessons Learned and the Next Steps. Conference Report, November 21–23, 1995, Ottawa, Ontario, Canada,* written by Peggy Teagle, 1996.
7. Barbara Harff and Ted Robert Gurr, "Towards Empirical Theories of Genocides and Politicides: Identification and Measurement of Cases Since 1945," *International Studies Quarterly,* Vol. 32, No. 3, p. 359–371, cited in Samuel Totten, "Non-Governmental Organizations Working on Genocide," *The Widening Circle of Genocide. Genocide: A Critical Bibliographic Review* (Israel W. Charney, ed.). Transaction Publishers: New Brunswick (USA) and London (UK), 1994, pp. 325–357 at 325.
8. International Federation of Red Cross and Red Crescent Societies, "Introduction," *World Disasters Report 1995.*
9. For a useful overview of the status of human rights in 1995, see the "Introduction to Human Rights Watch," *World Report 1996.* New York, NY: 1996.
10. "Beijing Declaration and Platform for Action," adopted by the Fourth World Conference on Women: Action for Equality, Development, and Peace, Beijing, 15 September 1995, para. 9 of the Declaration.
11. *Amnesty International Report 1995.* London, UK: 1995, p. 1.
12. Ibid., p. 5.

13. See Peter Archer, "Action by Unofficial Organizations on Human Rights," in *The International Protection of Human Rights*, (Evan Luard, ed.). London: Thames and Hudson, 1967, pp. 160–182, at 162–164. For an accounting of the history of the Anti-Slavery Society, today called Anti-Slavery International for the Protection of Human Rights, see C.W.W. Greenidge, *Slavery*. London, 1958.

14. Archer, op.cit., pp. 165-166; and, George Willemin and Roger Heacock, *The International Committee of the Red Cross*. International Organization and the Evolution of World Society, Vol. 2. Boston/The Hague/Dordrecht/Lancaster: Martinus Nijhoff, 1984, pp. 19–20. The ICRC was originally called the International and Permanent Committee for Relief to Wounded Military Personnel.

15. Richard B. Bilder, "Can Minorities Treaties Work?", in *The Protection of Minorities and Human Rights*, Yoram Dinstein and Mala Tabory (eds.). Dordrectht/Boston/London: Martinus Nijhoff, 1992, pp. 59–82, at 60. For the texts of these treaties, see: Hurst Hannum, ed., *Documents on Autonomy and Minority Rights*, Dordrecht/Boston/London: Martinus Nijhoff, 1993.

16. See, e.g., International Labour Office, *International Labour Standards: A Workers' Education Manual*, 3rd ed., Geneva: 1990, Chapter 1.

17. Leon Gordenker, *Refugees in International Politics*. New York: Columbia University Press, 1987, p. 20–21.

18. Dorothy B. Robins, *U.S. Non-Governmental Organizations and the Educational Campaign from Dumbarton Oaks, 1944, through the San Francisco Conference, 1945*. Ph.D. Dissertation, New York University, 1960, p. 186; cited in Chiang Pei-heng, *Non-Governmental Organizations at the United Nations: Identity, Role and Function*. New York: Praeger, 1981, p. 5.

19. Felice D. Gaer, "Reality Check: Human Rights Non-Governmental Organizations Confront Governments at the United Nations," draft paper prepared for a meeting of the Academic Council on the United Nations System, April 1995, 19 pp. at p. 2–3.

20. William Korey, "The Key to Human Rights Implementation," *International Conciliation*, November 1968, No. 570, p. 11.

21. Ibid., p. 12.

22. ESCOR: 4th Sess., 1947, Suppl. No. 3 (E/259), p. 6; cited by Korey, op.cit., p. 17.

23. Egon Schwelb and Philip Alston, "The Principal Institutions and Other Bodies Founded Under the Charter," in *The International Dimensions of Human Rights*, (Karel Vasak, gen. ed., revised and edited by Philip Alston), Vol. 1. Westport, CT: Greenwood Press, 1982, pp. 231–301, at 271.

24. Warren Weinstein, "Africa's Approach to Human Rights at the United Nations," *Issue: A Quarterly Journal of Opinion*, Vol. VI, No. 4 (Winter 1976), pp.14–22, at 15.

25. Edward Lawson, "Preface," *Encyclopedia of Human Rights*, (1st ed.) New York: Taylor & Francis, 1991, p. x.

26. John Carey, *The UN Protection of Civil and Political Rights*. New York, NY: Syracuse University Press for the Procedural Aspects of International Law Institute, 1970, p. 95.

27. Ibid., p. 96.

28. Ibid., p. 95.

29. Schwelb and Alston, op.cit., p. 291.

30. Korey, op.cit., p. 21-22.

31. On Amnesty International's reporting on the violations in Greece and Haiti during this period, see: Egon Larsen, *A Flame in Barbed Wire: The Story of Amnesty International*. New York: W.W. Norton & Company, 1979, pp. 42–46, and pp. 25–27.

32. Korey, op.cit., p. 22.

33. Ibid., p. 23.

34. See, e.g., "New Working Methods of the U.N. Human Rights Commission," *The Review of the International Commission of Jurists*, No. 2 (June 1969), pp. 27–32, especially p. 32.

35. See, e.g., "Human Rights Commission," *The Review of the International Commission of Jurists*, No. 12 (June 1974), pp. 19-20, at 20..

36. Schwelb and Alston, op.cit., p. 274.

37. Ibid., p. 275.

38. See, e.g., one journalist's account of the lengths to which Argentina's Ambassador, Gabriel Martínez, went to keep Argentina's military junta off the blacklist in the late 1970s. Iain Guest, *Behind the Disappearances: Argentina's Dirty War Against Human Rights and the United Nations*. Philadelphia: University of Pennsylvania Press, 1990, especially Part II.

39. Theo C. van Boven and B.G. Ramcharan, "Problems in the Protection of Human Rights at the International Level," *Human Rights Internet Reporter*, Vol. 6, no. 1 (September–October 1980), pp. 10–12 at 10.

40. Gaer, op.cit., p. 5.

41. Louis Henkin, *The Rights of Man Today*. Boulder, CO: Westview Press, 1978, especially footnote on p. 108.

42. A "pure type" human rights NGO is one established specifically to do human rights work. Such groups may have a universal focus, like Amnesty International or Human Rights Internet (HRI) in Canada, or a regional or country-specific one, like the Inter-American Institute for Human Rights (IIDH) in Costa Rico or the Peoples' Union for Civil Liberties (PUCL) in India. It may have a mandate that is broad, like that of the Human Rights Watch Committees in New York, or narrowly focused on one issue, like the Minority Rights Group (MRG) in the UK or Defense for Children International (DCI) in Switzerland. All of these groups exist solely to do human rights work. By way of contrast, trade unions, churches or professional associations were created for other purposes, although they may devote substantial resources to the defense of human rights.

43. The question of what is non-governmental is not as straightforward as it appears at first sight, since organizations can be controlled to a greater or lesser degree by governments. For some useful insights into this problem, see: Henry J. Steiner, *Diverse Partners: Non-Governmental Organizations in the Human Rights Movement.* Cambridge, MA: Harvard Law School Human Rights Program and Human Rights Internet, 1991, pp. 70–74.

44. For a more detailed discussion of human rights defenders, see: Laurie S. Wiseberg, ''Protecting Human Rights Activists and NGOs: What More Can Be Done?'' *Human Rights Quarterly*, Vol. 13, no. 4 (November 1991), pp. 525–544; Laurie S. Wiseberg, *The Importance of Freedom of Association for Human Rights NGOs.* Essays on Human Rights and Democratic Development No. 3. Montreal, Quebec, Canada: International Centre for Human Rights and Democratic Development, 1993; and Lawyers Committee for Human Rights, *Shackling the Defenders.* New York: March 1994.

45. Laurie S. Wiseberg and Harry M. Scoble, ''The International League for Human Rights: The Strategy of a Human Rights NGO,'' *Georgia Journal of International and Comparative Law*, Vol. 7 (1977), p. 289–313.

46. Howard B. Tolley, Jr., *The International Commission of Jurists: Global Advocates for Human Rights.* Philadelphia: University of Pennsylvania Press, 1994.

47. Larson, op.cit., and Jonathan Power, *Against Oblivion: Amnesty International's Fight for Human Rights.* U.K.: Fontana Paperbacks, 1981.

48. The scope of the Latin American human rights movement is captured in the *Human Rights Directory: Latin America and the Caribbean*, published as a special issue of the *Human Rights Internet Reporter*, Vol. 13, Nos. 2 & 3 (January 1990).

49. *Human Rights Internet Directory: Eastern Europe and the USSR.* Boston, MA.: Human Rights Internet, 1987.

50. Donal Dorr, *The Social Justice Agenda: Justice, Ecology, Power and the Church.* Maryknoll, NY: Orbis Books, 1991, Chapters 2 and 3.

51. While I know of no study of the impact of the Ford Foundation's program on the human rights movement, I do know that the foundation's support was critical in 1970s, when it was the only serious human rights funder. Groups like Helsinki Watch (and subsequently, all the Human Rights Watch Committees), the Lawyers Committee for Human Rights, the International League for Human Rights, the International Commission of Jurists, the Clearinghouse on Human Rights of the American Association for the Advancement of Science, Human Rights Internet, and numerous human rights groups in Latin America and Asia got significant funding, and in many cases their first serious funding, through that program.

52. The Coalition for a New Foreign and Military Policy, formed in Washington, DC in 1976, emerged from the anti-Vietnam war movement; it created a Human Rights Working Group which was the major human rights lobby in the United States in the late 1970s.

53. Chiang Pei-heng, *Non-Governmental Organizations at the United Nations: Identity, Role and Function.* New York: Praeger Publishers, 1981, p. 34–39. This is the best (and possibly the only serious) historical treatment of NGO consultative relations with the United Nations.

54. Bertram Pickard, *The Greater United Nations.* New York: Carnegie Endowment for International Peace, [1956], p. 26.

55. Chiang, op.cit., p. 35.

56. Ibid.

57. There was no such provision in the earlier resolutions, although in 1950, two NGOs were expelled—the International Association of Democratic Lawyers (IADL) and the International Organization of Journalists (IOJ); and one was demoted from Category B to Roster–the World Federation of Democratic Youth (WFDY). In 1954, Category B status was also withdrawn from the Women's International Democratic Federation (WIDF). All four were NGOs with strong ties to the Soviet Union and the Eastern bloc, and all had been vocal in criticizing the US-led UN intervention in Korea. Thus, the first sanctioning of the NGOs was clearly orchestrated by the US, which at that time controlled the votes in both ECOSOC and its NGO Committee. Chiang, op.cit., p. 104–106.

58. The list included the National Student Association, the International Confederation of Free Trade Unions, the International Commission of Jurists, and Pax Romana. Ibid., p. 107–108 and especially footnote 85 on p. 120–121.

59. Sidney Liskofsky, ''The U.N. Reviews its NGO System,'' *Reports on the Foreign Scene*, No. 10 (January 1970). New York: American Jewish Committee, p. 1–2.

60. Laurie S. Wiseberg and Harry M. Scoble, ''The International League for Human Rights: The Strategy of a Human Rights NGO,'' *Georgia Journal of International & Comparative Law*, Vol. 7 (1977), p. 303–304.

61. Ibid., p. 304.

62. Ibid., p. 304–305.

63. This section draws on and develops several of my earlier treatments of this subject, notably: ''The Role of Non-Governmental Organizations,'' in *Put Our World to Rights: Towards a Commonwealth Human Rights Policy*, (Flora MacDonald, ed.). Commonwealth Human Rights Initiative: London, 1991, pp. 149–174. For two recent treatments of this subject, see: Michael H. Posner and Candy Whittome, ''The Status of Human Rights NGOs,'' in *Columbia Human Rights Law Review*, Vol. 25, 1994, p. 269–290; and Gaer, op.cit. For an earlier examination, see: David Weissbrodt, ''The Contribution of International Nongovernmental Organizations to the Protection of Human Rights,'' in *Human Rights in International Law: Legal and Policy Issues* (Theodor Meron, ed.), Clarendon Press, Oxford, 1984, p. 403–438.

64. Diego Garcia-Sayan, ''Non-Governmental Organizations and the Human Rights Movement in Latin America,'' *Bulletin of Human Rights*, No. 90/1, 1991 (New York, NY: United Nations), pp. 31–41 at pp. 38–39.

65. Gaer, op.cit., p. 8.

66. For an elaboration on this, see: Laurie S. Wiseberg, ''Human Rights Reporting,'' *Human Rights Internet Reporter*, Vol. 11, no. 4 (September 1986), p. 3–6.

67. Much of the information on the basis of which Truth Commissions have written their reports, or the basis on which prosecutions have been prepared against gross violators—e.g., in Argentina, Brazil, Chile or El Salvador and currently in Ethiopia, Haiti, and South Africa—has been NGO data, increasingly computerized in highly sophisticated databases. Such information has also been placed at the disposal of the International War Crimes Tribunals on the former Yugoslavia and Rwanda.

68. David Kramer and David Weissbrodt, ''The 1980 U.N. Commission on Human Rights and the Disappeared,'' *Human Rights Quarterly*, Vol. 3, No. 1 (February 1981), pp. 18-33; and Nigel Rodley, *The Treatment of Prisoners Under International Law.* Oxford: Clarendon Press for UNESCO: 1987, pp.193–199.

69. Currently, in addition to the Working Group on Disappearances, there is a Working Group on Arbitrary Detention and one on the Right to Development. There are also Special Rapporteurs on Contemporary Forms of Racism, Summary and Arbitrary Executions, Torture, Religious Intolerance, Mercenaries, Freedom of Opinion and Expression, the Sale of Children, the Independence of Judges and Lawyers, Violence against Women, and Illicit Dumping of Toxic Waste. There is a Representative of the Secretary-General on Internally Displaced Persons; and there is a Special Process for dealing with missing persons in the former Yugoslavia.

70. Roger Stenson Clark, *A United Nations High Commissioner for Human Rights.* The Hague: Martinus Nijhoff, 1972, Chapter 3.

71. ''Amnesty International: A Special Commissioner could move quickly on urgent human rights situations,'' *Human Rights Tribune*, Vol. 2, No. 1 (June 1993), p. 18.

72. ''International Commission on Jurists: A permanent penal court is central to ICJ Agenda,'' *Human Rights Tribune*, Vol. 2, No. 1 (June 1993), p. 24.

73. Lawson, *Encyclopedia*, op.cit., p. 213.

74. Laura Reanda, ''Human Rights and Women's Rights: The United Nations Approach,'' *Human Rights Quarterly*, Vol. 3, No. 2 (Spring 1981), pp. 11–31, at 12.

75. Wendy Parker & Pauline Comeau, ''Women succeed in Vienna where others fail,'' *Human Rights Tribune*, Vol. 2, No. 2 (November 1993), pp. 22–25 at 22.

76. *Globe and Mail*, April 13, 1995, p. A2.

77. The Decade was proclaimed by the General Assembly on December 23, 1994 by Resolution 49/184. See, also, *Preparation of a Plan of Action for a United Nations Decade for Human Rights Education. Report of the Secretary-General.* A/49/261/Add.1, 14 November 1994.

78. Peter Baehr, ''The General Assembly: Negotiating the Convention on Torture,'' in *The United Nations in the World Political Economy.* (David Forsythe, ed.). New York: St. Martin's Press, 1989, pp. 36–53, on the role of Amnesty International and the International Commission of Jurists.

79. Cynthia Price Cohen, ''The Role of Nongovernmental Organizations in the Drafting of the Convention on the Rights of the Child,'' Human Rights Quarterly, Vol. 12, No. 1 (February 1990), pp.137–147; and Lawrence J. LeBlanc, *The Convention on the Rights of the Child: United Nations Lawmaking on Human Rights.* Lincoln and London: University of Nebraska Press, 1995, pp. 40–45.

80. Elsa Stamatopoulou, ''Indigenous Peoples and the United Nations: Human Rights as a Developing Dynamic,'' *Human Rights Quarterly*, Vol. 16, No. 1, pp. 58–81.

81. LeBlanc, op.cit., p. 41.

82. Consider the following: The UN Rapporteur on Torture is Nigel Rodley, who for some 15 years was head of the legal office of Amnesty International; the UN Rapporteur on Extra-Legal Executions is Waly Bacré Ndiaye, formerly head of the Senegalese section of Amnesty International; Thomas Hammarberg, Chair of the Committee on the Rights of the Child, was Secretary-General of Amnesty International; so, too, was Ian Martin, who currently heads the UN's human rights mission to Rwanda and formerly headed the Haiti human rights mission; in 1994–1995, the Human Rights Director of the UN's mission to El Salvador (ONUSAL) was Reed Brody, formerly Executive Director of the International Commission of Jurists and Executive Director of the Human Rights Law Group; Radhika Coomaraswamy, UN Rapporteur on Violence against Women, is Director of the International Centre for Ethnic Studies in Sri Lanka; the Special Representative of the Secretary General on Haiti is Adama Dieng, Secretary-General of the International Commission of Jurists; and the Rapporteur for the special process dealing with missing persons in the former Yugoslavia is Manfred Novak, Director of the Boltzmann Institute for Human Rights.

83. Michael McCoy and Patrick McCully, *The Road from Rio: An NGO Guide to Environment and Development.* Urtecht, The Netherlands: International Books for World Information Service on Energy (WISE), 1993, p. 9.

84. Ibid., p. 11.

85. This is wording that was used in the preamble of the draft document prepared for the May 1995 review session, E/AC/70/1995/CRP.1, which was rejected by that meeting.

86. Open-ended Working Group on the Review of Arrangements for Consultations with Non-Governmental Organizations, Non-Paper No. 11 (Status of negotiations as of 23 January 1996), para. 17.

87. This is officially the ''Draft Declaration on the Rights and Responsibility of Individuals, Groups and Organs of Society to Promote and Protect Universally Recognized Human Rights and Fundamental Freedoms.''

88.  Pauline Comeau, "Defending the Defenders: Interview with Nigel Rodley," *Human Rights Tribune*, Vol. 1, No. 2 (Summer 1992), pp. 5–6.

89.  Memorandum on the UN Draft Declaration on Human Rights Defenders, March 14, 1996, prepared by Harry Barnes and Karin Ryan for U.S. President Carter.

90.  Vienna Declaration, para. 5.

# USER'S GUIDE

As detailed by the author in his preface, this second edition of the *Encyclopedia of Human Rights* is a unique compendium that brings together material about international, regional, and national activities undertaken between the years 1945 and 1996 to promote and protect the enjoyment of human rights and fundamental freedoms by everyone without distinction. In its objective presentation of basic human rights documentation, the *Encyclopedia* is comprehensive and carefully designed to make available in clear and accessible form a wealth of data that has not been adequately used and is already in danger of being neglected or lost.

*Contents.* Produced as a contribution to the United Nations Decade for Human Rights Education (1995–2005) initiated by the UN General Assembly, this reference work includes a central core of information on:
—international instruments having a bearing on the enjoyment of human rights and fundamental freedoms;
—international organizations (both governmental and non-governmental) established to promote and protect those rights and freedoms;
—practical ways by which international, regional, and national bodies promote, monitor, and supervise the implementation of those rights and freedoms;
—the state of human rights in 186 countries and territories around the globe;
—biographical information on Nobel Peace Prize winners and their contributions to human rights;
—information about the composition, functions, and accomplishments of each of the many international organizations, agencies, and bodies that deal with various aspects of human rights.

In regard to continuing human rights situations in 186 countries and territories, reviews of existing conditions are presented in entries bearing the names of those States and areas. The information cited—culled from reports made available to the United Nations and other inter-governmental bodies by a variety of sources, including reports submitted to treaty-monitoring bodies by the individual governments; studies prepared by special rapporteurs, working groups, and experts; communications received from non-governmental organizations and interested individuals; and data available from previously published materials, including current periodicals—provides an indication of prevailing conditions that may promote or inhibit the full enjoyment of rights and freedoms.

*Alphabetical Order.* The entries are presented in letter-by-letter alphabetical order. General human rights documents are presented under their full official title (e.g., "Universal Declaration of Human Rights" is alphabetized by *Universal*). Documents dealing with specific aspects of human rights are presented under the subject with which they are concerned (e.g., the Declaration on Territorial Asylum is listed under *Asylum: Declaration on Territorial Asylum*). Internal and external cross references, as explained further on, are used throughout the book to provide the reader with additional information on any subject.

In addition to UN conventions and declarations, a number of documents concluded by other intergovernmental organizations are included. Those concluded by the Organization of American States are preceded by the term *Inter-American*, those concluded by the Organization of African Unity by *African*, and those concluded by the Council of Europe by *European*. The current status of many of these instruments is set out in Appendix B.

Finally, the runners indicating the last entry to be found on the page repeat the full title of the entry, as often as possible. However, due to the length of some official document titles, the runners for these entries have been shortened for convenience. These abbreviations do not break the alphabetical order of the entries.

*Cross-References.* Entries may contain internal and external cross-references to other entries within the *Encyclopedia*. Internal cross-references are set in boldface type and indicate a related entry elsewhere in the *Encyclopedia*. Where there is an internal cross-reference to a subject-specific document for which there is a full entry elsewhere, the full official title of the document is given, followed by the subject heading under which it can be found, in parentheses. External cross references are set in italic type at the end of the entry, preceded by the words *SEE ALSO* and indicate material that supplements the primary entry. An example follows:

> **ANTI-SEMITISM.** Anti-Semitism is a term that refers to hostility toward the Jewish people.
>
> The United Nations has been concerned about the effects of this form of intolerance for many years. As early as 1948, for example, the UN General Assembly adopted and opened for signature and ratification the Convention on the Prevention and Punishment of the Crime of Genocide (see **GENOCIDE**), which proceeded, in large measure, out of the horrors of the Holocaust perpetrated by the Nazis in World War II. In 1960, the Sub-Commission on Prevention of Discrimination and Protection of Minorities indicated its concern about "the manifestations of anti-Semitism and other forms of racial and national hatred and religious and national prejudices of a similar nature" that had occurred late in 1959 in various countries, which the Sub-Commission characterized as "reminiscent of the crimes and outrages committed by the Nazis prior to and during the Second World War." The Sub-Commission indicated that "it is the responsibility of the United Nations to speak out against these manifestations, to ascertain the underlying facts and causes, and to recommend the most effective measures which can be taken against them."
>
> The consensus that had originally characterized the international campaign to combat racism and racial discrimination in all its forms was, however, seriously set back in 1975 when the UN General Assembly adopted resolution 3379 (XXX) of 10 November, which equated Zionism with racism. Only in 1991 did the Assembly decide (resolution 46/86 of 16 December) to revoke this determination.
>
> ***SEE ALSO*** *Xenophobia.*

*Citations.* Many international instruments, national constitutions, official studies, and special rapporteur reports are reproduced, in full or in part. In all cases, the sources of these official documents are set directly in the body of the entry, as follows:

> . . . Such a text was adopted by the congress in Milan, Italy, on 5 September 1985. It was later endorsed by the UN General Assembly on 29 November 1985 (resolution 40/32) and on 13 December 1985 (resolution 40/146). The text (UN Doc. A/CONF.121/22, chap. I, sect. D.2) is as follows: . . .

Citations of documents issued by international organizations follow the system in use by those agencies. UN human rights documents, for example, usually bear symbols which indicate (1) the main issuing organ, for example, the General Assembly (A/), the Security Council (S/), the Economic and Social Council (E/), or the Secretariat (ST/); (2) the subsidiary organ, for example, the Commission on Human Rights (CN.4/), the Commission on the Status of Women (CN.6/), or the Sub-Commission on Prevention of Discrimination and Protection of Minorities (CN.4/Sub.2), or a specially convened conference (CONF.); (3) the year of issue (1990/); and (4) the number of the document in the year's series. Thus, a typical document numbered E/CN.4/Sub.2/1990/36 would be the 36th document issued for use by the Sub-Commission in 1990. The symbols are useful mainly in making a quick but precise reference to a particular document or in ordering copies of it from a source of supply, such as a UN repository library or Human Rights Internet.

*Bibliographies.* Most entries contain an extensive selected bibliography, prepared by Human Rights Internet (HRI), intended to supplement the information cited within the entry. HRI has provided references from independent, non-governmental studies as well as scholarly works published between 1985 and 1995.

*Glossary.* There is a glossary of terms often used in referring to human rights situations. These terms are defined in their international usage, irrespective of their applications in national laws or cultures. The glossary also includes selected Latin terms.

*Appendices.* There are two appendices in this work.

Appendix A offers a chronological list of the documents contained in this work. It is presented so that the student may see quickly and easily how human rights developed as an international field and how treaties address the changing nature of society and world concerns.

Appendix B lists the statuses (ratifying countries) of all major UN human rights treaties and conventions.

*Index.* A subject index, the most expeditious method to provide access to the wealth of information contained in the *Encyclopedia*, will be found at the end of the book.

The method follows, as closely as possible, the subject-indexing terms employed by Human Rights Internet in its periodic comprehensive indexes, a method which will be familiar to students in the human rights field.

> Armed Conflict, **103–104.** *See also* Conscientious objection; Geneva
> Red Cross conventions and Protocols; Mercenarism
> civilian population in, 103
> protection principles for, 103, **104**, 114
> combatants, legal status of, **104–105**
> Declaration on the Protection of Women and Children in Emergency and Armed Conflict, **114**
> Geneva Convention protocols, 103–104
> Hague Convention. *See* Convention for the Protection of Cultural Property in Event of Armed Conflict

In addition, boldface numbers indicate a reference to a full entry within the *Encyclopedia*.

# A

**ABORTION.** Abortion is defined as the intentional removal of a fetus from the mother's womb other than for the purpose of producing a live birth or removing a dead fetus. Neither accidental premature birth nor spontaneous expulsion of the fetus due to disease, malfunction, or trauma of the mother is normally considered as abortion. The **WORLD HEALTH ORGANIZATION** places abortion within the category of "fertility regulation."

Issues concerning the right to life of the mother and that of the unborn child were debated repeatedly in the course of the preparation of the **INTERNATIONAL BILL OF HUMAN RIGHTS.** When article 3 of the **UNIVERSAL DECLARATION OF HUMAN RIGHTS** was being drafted by the UN Commission on Human Rights and its drafting committee, it was proposed that the life of the unborn child should be specifically protected by insertion of the words "from the moment of conception." The proposal was rejected after the representative of the **COMMISSION ON THE STATUS OF WOMEN** pointed out that this qualification of the right to life could not be reconciled with the legislation of many States which provides for abortion in cases specified by law, notably in order to preserve the life of a woman. The vote in each body was preceded by a discussion on the question as to whether or not the term "right to life" implied or contained the idea of life "from the moment of conception." While some participants in the drafting process considered the idea to be implicit in the term, others maintained that this was not necessarily the case.

Article 3 of the Universal Declaration of Human Rights, and later article 6(1) of the **INTERNATIONAL COVENANT ON CIVIL AND POLITICAL RIGHTS,** was subsequently adopted by the General Assembly without the phrase "from the moment of conception."

In modern practice, abortion is prohibited in some countries and territories while available upon request in others. In a large number of countries, medical termination of pregnancy is permissible but only under specified conditions: for example, if continuation of the pregnancy would involve risk to the life of the pregnant woman or if there is a substantial risk that, if the child were born, it would suffer from such physical or mental abnormalities as to be seriously handi-

capped. In recent years, concern for the mental health of the prospective mother has begun to gain acceptance in national legislation as a justification for abortion, as in cases where pregnancy is the result of rape.

*INTERNATIONAL CONFERENCE ON POPULATION AND DEVELOPMENT.* In an attempt to chart world population strategy for the next 20 years, the United Nations sponsored an International Conference on Population and Development, held in Cairo, Egypt, Sept. 5–13, 1994. Similar conferences had been held in 1974 and 1984, but with little resulting success in curbing worldwide population growth. The 1994 conference differed significantly from the efforts of the previous 20 years, which had concentrated on promoting birth control, by adopting a unique position that holds that population and development demands should be seen as allied to improving the status of women. More than 150 nations attended the Conference; but, even before its opening, there were problems with States whose predominant religion is either Catholicism or Islam, over language that was interpreted as condoning abortion, sexual promiscuity, and homosexuality.

Anti-abortion forces were led by the Vatican delegation, which objected, in particular, to the original language contained in paragraph 8.25. The Vatican argued that the original language could be interpreted as encouraging abortion as a form of birth control, and demanded that abortion be banned altogether and not be asserted as a fundamental part of women's rights. After several days of intense negotiation, the Vatican and its allies agreed to the rewording of the controversial paragraph as follows:

In no case should abortion be promoted as a method of family planning. All governments and relevant intergovernmental and nongovernmental organizations are urged to strengthen their commitment to women's health, to deal with the health impact of unsafe abortion as a major public health concern and to reduce the recourse to abortion through expanded and improved family planning services. Women who have unwanted pregnancies should have ready access to reliable information and compassionate counseling.

Prevention of unwanted pregnancies must always be given the highest priority, and all attempts should be made to eliminate the need for abortion. In circumstances in which abor-

1

tion is legal, such abortion should be safe. Any measures or changes related to abortion within the health system can only be determined at the national or local level according to the national legislative process. In all cases, women should have access to quality services for the management of complications arising from abortion. Post-abortion counseling, education and family planning services should be offered promptly, which will also help to avoid repeat abortions.

The Conference approved the final 113-page "Programme of Action" on its last day. Though the agreement is nonbinding and does not supersede national legislation on any matters contained therein, it represents a general agreement in recognizing the importance of population control and development of nations as being tied to the reproductive health-care services, especially to women.

*SEE ALSO* Right to Life.

**BIBLIOGRAPHY.** Brooks, J. E. "Abortion Policy in Western Democracies: A Cross-National Analysis," *Governance* 5, no. 3 (July 1992): 342–357. Scholarly article, in English; bibliography, pp. 356–357.

Frankowski, S. J., and G. F. Cole. *Abortion and Protection of the Human Fetus.* Dordrecht, the Netherlands: Martinus Nijhoff, 1987. Scholarly collection, in English; bibliography, pp. 332–334.

*Harvard Women's Law Journal* (Spring 1987). Scholarly articles in special issue, in English.

Sheeran, Patrick J. *Women, Society, the State, and Abortion: A Structuralist Analysis.* New York: Praeger, 1987. Scholarly monograph, in English.

Szumski, Bonnie, ed. *Abortion: Opposing Viewpoints.* St. Paul, MN, USA: Greenhaven Press, 1986. Edited collection, in English; bibliography, pp. 49, 81, 106, 145, 169, and 200 (for periodical literature) and an annotated list of monographs, pp. 207–210.

**ACCEPTANCE OF HUMAN RIGHTS INSTRUMENTS.** See **HUMAN RIGHTS.**

**ACCESS OF NEWS PERSONNEL TO UN MEETINGS.** See **MEDIA.**

**ACCESS TO UN HUMAN RIGHTS PROCEDURES.** See **HUMAN RIGHTS.**

**ACQUIRED IMMUNE DEFICIENCY SYNDROME.** See **AIDS.**

**ACTION-AID.** A non-governmental organization in consultative status (Category II) with the UN **ECONOMIC AND SOCIAL COUNCIL,** Action-Aid was founded in 1972, under its former title of "Action in Distress." Its primary contact is with members of the European Community, with a network of organizations in four European countries. Action-Aid is an international charity organization, whose work includes the Action-Aid Education Programme.

Action-Aid. Contact: Ana Toni, Tapstone Rd., Chard, Somerset, UK. Telephone: (44-460) 62972. Fax: (44-460) 67191.

**ADDAMS, LAURA JANE (1860–1935).** This American social reformer and pacifist was awarded the Nobel Peace Prize in 1931 (a joint recipient with Nicholas Murray Butler). Born in Cedarville, IL, Addams was graduated from Rockford College in Illinois and also studied at Philadelphia University and the Toynbee Hall Settlement, an experimental school dedicated to the development of adult education, the collection of social data, and the improvement of social conditions.

Based on her experiences at Toynbee Hall, Addams founded Hull House in 1889 in a lower class neighborhood in Chicago. Under her leadership, Hull House became a leading voice in progressive welfare programs, including the first juvenile court law, tenement-house regulations, and an eight-hour working day for women.

In addition, Addams was the first woman president of the National Conference of Social Work and was chair of the Women's Peace Party (USA) and the International Congress of Women at the Hague. When the International Congress founded the Women's International League for Peace and Freedom, Addams became its first president, a position she held until 1929. Among her writings are *Democracy and Social Ethics, Newer Ideas of Peace,* and *Twenty Years at Hull House.*

In citing her for the Prize, the Nobel Committee paid homage to "the work which women can do for the cause of peace and fraternity among nations."

**BIBLIOGRAPHY.** Farrell, John C. *Beloved Lady.* Baltimore, MD, USA: Johns Hopkins Press, 1967.

Gray, Tony. *Champions of Peace.* London: Paddington Press, 1976.

Schlessinger, Bernard S., and June H. Schlessinger, eds. *Who's Who of Nobel Prize Winners.* Phoenix, AZ, USA: Oryx Press, 1991.

**ADMINISTRATION OF JUSTICE.** As the UN Secretary-General stated in his report to the 1993 session of the General Assembly (UN Doc. A/48/575, para. 57), "human rights in the administration of justice continues to be a primary focus of the United Nations human rights program, including technical assistance, standard-setting, and dissemination of information. Effective coordination of activities in this field, within the United Nations system and with non-governmental organizations, intergovernmental organizations and Governments, is crucial to the continued success of these efforts. The numerous existing United Nations standards relative to human rights in the administration of justice provide a strong substantive framework for protection, and thus should remain the focus of sustained and effective dissemination and technical assistance efforts aimed at their implementation at the national level, in particular through the program of advisory services and technical assistance of the Center for Human Rights."

***INTERNATIONAL INSTRUMENTS CONCERNING THE ADMINISTRATION OF JUSTICE.*** The promotion and protection of human rights in the administration of justice has indeed been a subject of primary concern to a number of UN human rights bodies over a period of nearly 50 years. Principles relating to the subject first were set out in the Universal Declaration of Human Rights of 10 December 1948, and were subsequently elaborated in the International Convention on the Elimination of All Forms of Racial Discrimination, and the Convention on the Elimination of All Forms of Discrimination Against Women. Free access to courts of law is provided to refugees, on a basis of equality with citizens, by the Convention Relating to the Status of Refugees (article 16), and to stateless persons by the Convention Relating to the Status of Stateless Persons (article 16).

In addition, worldwide standards relating to the administration of justice are established in a number of international instruments, among them:

(1) Standard Minimum Rules for the Treatment of Prisoners

(2) Basic Principles for the Treatment of Prisoners

(3) Body of Principles for the Protection of all Persons under any Form of Detention or Imprisonment

(4) United Nations Rules for the Protection of Juveniles Deprived of Their Liberty

(5) Declaration on the Protection of All Persons from Being Subjected to Torture and Other Cruel, Inhuman or Degrading Treatment or Punishment

(6) Convention Against Torture and Other Cruel, Inhuman or Degrading Treatment or Punishment

(7) Principles of Medical Ethics Relevant to the Role of Health Personnel, Particularly Physicians, in the Protection of Prisoners and Detainees Against Torture and Other Cruel, Inhuman or Degrading Treatment or Punishment

(8) Safeguards Guaranteeing Protection of the Rights of Those Facing the Death Penalty

(9) Code of Conduct for Law Enforcement Officials

(10) Basic Principles on the Use of Force and Firearms by Law Enforcement Officials

(11) Basic Principles on the Role of Lawyers

(12) Guidelines on the Role of Prosecutors

(13) United Nations Standard Minimum Rules for Non-Custodial Measures (The Tokyo Rules)

(14) United Nations Guidelines for the Prevention of Juvenile Delinquency (The Riyadh Guidelines)

(15) United Nations Standard Minimum Rules for the Administration of Juvenile Justice (The Beijing Rules)

(16) Declaration of Basic Principles of Justice for Victims of Crime and Abuse of Power

(17) Basic Principles on the Independence of the Judiciary

(18) Model Treaty on the Transfer of Proceedings in Criminal Matters

(19) Model Treaty on the Transfer of Supervision of Offenders Conditionally Sentenced or Conditionally Released

(20) Declaration on the Protection of All Persons from Enforced Disappearances

(21) Principles on the Effective Prevention and Investigation of Extra-Legal, Arbitrary and Summary Executions.

The UN General Assembly has repeatedly affirmed the importance of full implementation of international standards in the administration of justice, including those set out in the instruments mentioned above, and has urged Member States to develop strategies for the practical application of those standards. It has stressed the significant role to be played by the specialized agencies, the regional commissions concerned, and international institutes and other governmental and non-governmental organizations within the UN system. In resolution 48/137 of 20 December 1993, the General Assembly welcomed especially "the important work of the Commission on Human Rights and of the Sub-Commission on Prevention of Discrimination and Protection of Minorities in the field of human rights and the administration of justice, in particular regarding the independence of the judiciary, the independence of judges and lawyers, the right to a fair trial, habeas corpus, human rights and states of emergency, the question of arbitrary detention, the privatization of prisons and the question of the impunity of perpetrators of violations of human rights." It also welcomed "the important work of the Commission on Crime Prevention and Criminal Justice" in this field.

In this same resolution, the Assembly acknowledged that "the administration of justice, including law enforcement and prosecutorial agencies and, especially, an independent judiciary and legal profession, in full conformance with applicable standards contained in international human rights instruments, are essential to the full and non-discriminatory realization of human rights and indispensable to the processes of democracy and sustainable development."

Further, the General Assembly appealed to governments to include in their national development plans the administration of justice as an integral part of the development process and to allocate adequate resources for the provision of legal-aid services with a view to the protection and promotion of human rights, and urged the Secretary-General "to consider favourably requests for assistance by States in the field of the administration of justice within the framework of the United Nations programme of advisory services and technical co-operation in the field of human rights, and to strengthen coordination of activities in this field."

***ADMINISTRATION OF JUSTICE IN LABOR MATTERS.***
The International Labor Organization is frequently concerned, in the course of its activities aimed at advancing the economic and social welfare of working people, with problems related to the administration of justice. As described by the ILO in a background paper prepared for the Preparatory Committee of the World Conference on Human Rights (UN Doc. A/CONF. 157/PC 61/Add. 10, Annex II):

First of all is the principle that human rights are unitary. As the ILO's supervisory bodies have said many times, the human rights protected by the ILO cannot be adequately implemented in a climate which does not respect the rule of law and ensure the protection of human rights generally.

In this context, the independence and impartiality of the judicial authorities is primordial. One basic provision which contributes to this may be found in the ILO Discrimination (Employment and Occupation) Convention, 1958 (No. 111), which has been ratified by more than 100 countries. This Convention prohibits any discrimination, exclusion or preference based on race, colour, sex, religion, political opinion and national or social origin. It applies, first of all, to employment under the direct control of a governmental authority, and therefore necessarily to the recruitment and appointment of judicial personnel and of others involved in the administration of justice. The ILO Committee of Experts had indeed explicitly held that this instrument applies to the appointment of judges.

The applicability of this principle is evident: If the judicial authorities are chosen on the basis of a discriminatory approach—or in the most extreme case are selected only from one ethnic group or shade of political opinion—the effect on the administration of justice in a pluralistic culture can be disastrous.

The same considerations apply, of course, to lawyers. There are, unfortunately, many cases in which judges and lawyers who do not share the opinions of the dominant political power are subject to dismissal and even arrest, with consequences for the administration of justice which are not difficult to imagine.

Apart from protection of the personnel involved in the administration of justice, more general principles laid down in ILO standards are also relevant to the administration of justice. The two ILO Forced Labour Conventions cover one aspect of this question. The Forced Labour Convention, 1930 (No. 29), ratified by most States, prohibits all forced or compulsory labour, [and] provides that this shall not include " . . . any work of service carried out . . . as a consequence of a conviction in a court of law." This means that forced labour may not be imposed on detainees, accused persons and the like. This corresponds to the presumption of innocence before conviction that is contained in the International Covenant on Civil and Political Rights and most national legislations.

Another aspect of the question under the same Convention is that compulsory labour by convicted prisoners is allowed, provided that it is carried out under the supervision of the public authorities and does not include hiring out prisoners to private individuals, companies or associations. This is a particularly difficult problem. The real problem in practice might be said to consist not so much of the hiring out as the conditions under which these persons are often obliged to work. This can, in extreme cases, amount almost to slave labour; and prisoners may be made to work under conditions that would be unacceptable for any other workers: little or no compensation, very long hours, unacceptable conditions of safety and health. There may also be an element of corruption here. It should be remembered that prisoners have the same human rights as everyone else, except for those which may have been explicitly removed as a consequence of their conviction.

The Abolition of Forced Labour Convention, 1957 (No. 105), covers another aspect of this question. While convention No. 29 prohibits forced labour except under defined conditions, Convention No. 105 prohibits its imposition for defined reasons. It refines the permission given in Convention No. 29 for convicted prisoners to work, by defining certain offenses for which forced labour is not allowed. These include forced or compulsory labour imposed as a means of political coercion of education or as a punishment for holding or expressing political views opposed to those of the established political, economic, or social system; as a means of labour discipline; as a punishment for having participated in strikes; and as a means of racial, social, national or religious discrimination.

The problem here consists of the criminalisation of "political" offenses in many countries. Simply put, in many countries, those who criticise the President are not political opponents: they are criminals. Or those who go on strike when the government does not want them to—a strongly protected right of workers in most circumstances—are not seen as trade unionists protecting the rights of their colleagues but, again, as criminals. And as criminals, once convicted, they are subject to the same regime as all prisoners.

The final aspect of labour and the administration of justice is found in the field of labour administration. The administration of justice is not confined to criminal law. It extends also to drafting and implementing the laws and regulations governing the rights of workers. It includes such obvious human rights subjects as the working of human rights commissions, which are established to prevent or correct discrimination in employment, through such work-a-day matters as ensuring that workers receive the wages to which they are entitled, that they work in safe and healthy conditions, or that they are free from being made to work as children. And, of course, it covers the fundamental right of organisation, the rights of employers and of workers to join in organisations of their choosing to defend their rights. These are all rights that are protected under the International Covenant on Economic, Social and Cultural Rights; in some cases, also by the International Covenant on Civil and Political Rights; and by a large number of ILO conventions.

Here again, the administration of justice and the correct working of the courts and legal systems play a major role in assuring the protection of these human rights. Whether through the regular courts or through special tribunals, all the factors cited above for the protection of the ability of the judiciary to function under proper conditions are equally relevant here.

*RACISM IN THE ADMINISTRATION OF JUSTICE.* At its 1979 session, the **SUB-COMMISSION ON PREVENTION OF DISCRIMINATION AND PROTECTION OF MINORITIES** examined a preliminary study on the independence and impartiality of the judiciary, jurors, and assessors, prepared by the Secretary-General (UN Doc. E/CN.4/Sub.2/428), and decided (resolution 4 A [XXXIII]) to appoint one of its members, Mr. Justice Abu Sayeed Chowdhury (Bangladesh) as its special rapporteur to study the subject further.

The special rapporteur's final report (UN Doc. CN.4/Sub.2/1982/7) was considered by the Sub-Commission at its 1982 session. Entitled "Study on discriminatory treatment of members of racial, ethnic, religious or linguistic groups at the various levels in the administration of criminal justice, such as police, military, administrative and judicial investigations, arrest, detention, trial and execution of sentences, including the ideologies or beliefs which contribute or lead to racism in the administration of criminal justice," it set out the following conclusions and recommendations:

*Conclusions.* Discriminatory treatment against members of racial, ethnic, religious or linguistic groups at the various levels in the administration of justice is, in a number of jurisdictions, a fact of current life. It would seem that as politically and economically subordinate minority groups seek to achieve self-determination and rise in the social structure, they are continually confronted by the legal structure. Many minority group members feel that the criminal legal system is heavily weighted against them and that the police represent a foreign, alien power.

If legal systems are to deal effectively with mounting attacks from minority group members, the issues and allegations at hand will have to be frankly discussed. The Special Rapporteur has attempted to address the relationship between the structure of the criminal justice system and minority groups. Rather than looking at one phase of this relationship, he has included the issues of police conduct, police and the community, factors of arrest and detention, the question of violence by the police, the factor of judicial proceedings, and finally, military justice.

The use of force by the police, causing great bodily harm and even death, figures prominently in complaints of minority groups against the police. That some policemen are killed is sufficiently impressive to underscore what might be termed the "dangerous" nature of the job, although the public image and the image of the police themselves have been known to exaggerate the real danger considerably. At any rate, society equips the policeman with instruments of vio-

lence for his own protection, because it is in society's interest that he be able to protect himself.

On the basis of certain statistics, it would appear that many more people are killed by the police than there are police killed in the line of duty. Homicides committed by police officers are of particular concern to certain minority groups since they continue to be the victims of these killings at a very disproportionate rate.

There is little indication, if any, that the norms which define the permissible use of violence by the police have, as a general rule, been internalized. Given the wide discretion and the absence of effective sanctions the police are apt to conform not to the requirements of due process of law, but rather to the pressures of the politically powerful.

Much of the friction between law officers and minority communities might be said to stem from the under-representation of members of minority groups in the police force of many communities.

The quality of the relationship between the police and the community is of utmost importance. How a policeman handles day-to-day contacts with citizens and minority groups in particular will, to a large extent, shape the relationship between the police and community.

The criminal court is one of the most crucial institutions in the criminal justice system. It is expected to meet society's demands to convict and punish serious offenders while at the same time ensuring that the innocent and unfortunate are not oppressed. The administration of criminal justice is an issue of great public concern; particularly as it relates to members of minority groups. The pervasive mistrust of such groups of the criminal justice system is said to be an important contributing factor to social discontent and upheaval; the police and the courts have been identified as sources of conflict between the dominant and non-dominant groups.

During periods when we are witnessing what might be termed a proliferation of military hostilities, one can see the need for adopting, subscribing to and adhering to rules and regulations pertaining to the conduct of such hostilities among civilized nations. During these periods, certain rights of combatants and non-combatants must be observed. Perhaps, in the light of today's advanced war technology, new rules and regulations of an international character might be called for.

*Recommendations.* (1) Legislative provisions generally provide important safeguards to supplement the ordinary law, where ordinary law guarantees do not exist or do not operate satisfactorily. It is suggested that national legislation should recognize the need for special protection to ensure that the basic rights of minorities are observed.

(2) Provision should be made for effective and enforceable remedies, reporting procedures, complaint and investigative procedures and conciliation machinery and processes. In this connection, complementary action should be taken by administrative and executive authorities concurrent with action taken by legislative and judicial authorities.

(3) It is recognized that the *Principles on Equality in the Administration of Justice* formulated by Mr. Mohammed A. Abu Rannat in his *Study* on that subject [UN Doc. E/CN.4/Sub.2/296] apply to all groups of society in general. It is suggested that in the administration of criminal justice the special needs and circumstances of minority groups should be given consideration in the interest of equity and justice. Courts should be relatively free and should have discretionary powers to interpret the law to fit situations not foreseen by the legal draughtsman.

(4) Efforts should be made to bring minority groups into

the various processes of government and administration so that their views can be adequately represented and also to enable them to identify with these processes.

(5) Criminal justice services should have officers recruited among minorities.

(6) Affirmative action where deemed necessary would induce confidence and provide the services with personnel capable of understanding problems of minority groups.

**SEE ALSO** *Judiciary; Juvenile Justice.*

**BIBLIOGRAPHY.** Centre for the Independence of Judges and Lawyers (CIJL). "The Independence of Judges and Lawyers: A Compilation of International Standards," *CIJL Bulletin* no. 25–26 (April–October 1990): 1–123. Special issue, in English.

United Nations. *Study of Equality in the Administration of Justice.* Prepared by Mohammed Ahmed Abu Ranat, Special Rapporteur. 1969. UN Doc. E/CN.4/Sub.2/296/Rev. 1; Sales no. E.71.XIV.3.

———. *Study of the Right of Arrested Persons to Communicate with Those Whom It Is Necessary for Them to Consult in Order to Ensure Their Defence or to Protect Their Essential Interests.* Prepared by the Committee on the Right of Everyone to be Free from Arbitrary Arrest, Detention and Exile. 1969. UN Doc. E/CN.4/996.

———. *Study of the Right of Everyone to be Free from Arbitrary Arrest, Detention and Exile.* Prepared by the Committee on the Right of Everyone to be Free from Arbitrary Arrest, Detention and Exile. 1962. UN Doc. E/CN.4/826/Rev. 1; Sales no. 65.XIV.2.

———. *Study on the Independence and Impartiality of the Judiciary, Jurors and Assessors and the Independence of Lawyers.* Prepared by L.M. Singhvi, Special Rapporteur. 1985 and 1988. UN Docs. E/CN.4/Sub.2/1985/18 and Add. 1–6; E/CN.4/Sub.2/1988/20 and Add. 1 and Add. 1/Corr. 1.

**ADMINISTRATIVE DETENTION.** This practice, whereby individuals may be detained or interned by the administrative authorities, without charge or trial by an independent judicial body and without any protection for their human rights, is in wide use in many countries, including some which regard themselves as democratic.

A preliminary examination of the situation relating to administrative detention was undertaken by the Sub-Commission on Prevention of Discrimination and Protection of Minorities at its 1985 session. At that time, it requested (decision 1985/110) one of its members, Mr. Louis Joinet (France), to prepare an explanatory paper on the subject. That paper (UN Doc. E/CN.4/Sub.2/1987/16) and an analysis of the legal features of administrative detention prepared later (UN Doc. E/CN.4/Sub.2/1988/12) were considered by the Sub-Commission at its 1988 session.

In the explanatory paper, Mr. Joinet listed the primary purposes of administrative detention as follows: (1) prevention (or suppression) of serious disturbances of public order and security of the State;

(2) immigration control and expulsion of foreigners and surveillance of their political activities; (3) disciplinary measures; (4) medical-social measures (against drug addicts, the insane, etc.); (5) measures to combat social adjustment; and (6) measures to protect civilian populations in time of war.

**DETENTION OF UN STAFF MEMBERS, EXPERTS, AND THEIR FAMILIES.** At its 1980 session, the UN commission on human rights expressed concern (resolution 31/XXXVI) about reports of infringements of the human rights of United Nations staff members and the abrogation of the rights conveyed to them under the Convention on the Privileges and Immunities of the United Nations. It appealed to Member States to respect their obligations under that convention and under the United Nations Charter, the Universal Declaration of Human Rights and the International Covenant on Civil and Political Rights; and requested the Secretary-General to use his good offices to ensure the full enjoyment of human rights and the enjoyment of the rights conveyed under the Convention on Privileges and Immunities, by United Nations staff members.

In 1986, the General Assembly deplored (resolution 41/205) the growing number of cases where the functioning, safety, and well-being of officials had been adversely affected, including cases of detention in Member States and abduction by armed groups and individuals, and the increasing number of cases in which the lives and well-being of officials had been placed in jeopardy during the exercise of their official functions.

In 1987, the Sub-Commission on Prevention of Discrimination and Protection of Minorities requested the Secretary-General (resolution 1987/21) to submit to it in 1988 "a detailed report on the situation of international civil servants and their families detained, imprisoned, missing or held in a country against their will, in order to enable the Sub-Commission to consider these cases in the light of the international instruments relating to human rights."

In response, the Secretary-General submitted to the Sub-Commission at its 1988 session a report (UN Doc. E/CN.4/Sub. 2/1988/17) in which he placed at the disposal of members of the Sub-Commission his most recent report on the subject to the General Assembly (UN Doc. A/C.5/42/14), provided some additional information on recent developments, and analyzed the types of violations of human rights suffered by international civil servants. The analysis (Section III, para. 17–29) was as follows:

Types of Violations of Human Rights Suffered by International Civil Servants

## A. Arbitrary Arrest and Detention

Most of the cases reported to the Secretary-General concern violations caused by the arrest and detention of staff members.

(a) Legal Aspects. When a staff member of the United Nations—whether internationally or locally recruited—is arrested or detained by government authorities, the Secretary-General has the right and the duty to find out the reasons for the arrest. Under the terms of the Charter of the United Nations (article 105) and the Convention on the Privileges and Immunities of the United Nations (articles V and VI), all staff members are immune from legal process in respect of words spoken or written and all acts performed by them in their official capacity. As the Administrative Committee on Co-ordination pointed out in its report of 15 April 1980 (E/1980/34), on international cooperation and coordination in the United Nations system, "International organizations, which are the instrument of international co-operation, cannot fully discharge their duties unless they can count on a completely independent international civil service".

It follows that the United Nations is entitled to functional protection of its staff members. It is for the Secretary-General alone, and not for Member States, to determine whether or not an act by a staff member has been performed in his official capacity. To that end, he needs to learn the facts. He must be in a position to visit the staff member under arrest, to converse with him, to be apprised of the grounds for the arrest and the formal charges. He is entitled to assist the staff member in arranging legal counsel for his or her defence and to appear in legal proceedings to defend any United Nations interest affected by the arrest or detention. All these provisions are contained in a Memorandum on the United Nations legal rights when a staff member or other agent of the United Nations, or a member of their family, is arrested or detained (ST/AI/299, of 10 December 1982).

If it is established that the arrest or detention of a staff member is connected with his official duties, his right to immunity is invoked. If, on the other hand, it is found that the case is not connected with the person's official duties, the Secretary-General can and should waive immunity so that justice may take its course. In that case, the Secretary-General none the less ensures that the staff member under arrest and in detention is equitably treated and that due and proper procedures are followed.

(b) Present Situation. At the present time, for approximately 90 cases of detention the Secretary-General has still not been able fully to exercise his right of protection.

(c) Conditions of Detention. The Secretary-General's previous report (A/C.5/42/14) describes the ill-treatment inflicted on some staff members in the course of detention and the fact that, despite the Secretary-General's appeals, the authorities in the countries concerned have refused to allow the staff members to receive the necessary care.

All too often, the visiting rights, both of representatives of the Secretary-General and of the families, are refused, trials, if any, are held in camera and counsel appointed by the United Nations cannot take part in them. The report in question also states that "in many of the cases reported by UNRWA and UNIFIL, the staff members concerned are being detained not for the alleged commission of any offence but merely as part of large groups of persons who happen to live in a particular locality or village".

## B. Killings, Executions, Deaths in Detention

Over the past 15 years, according to the report submitted by the staff representatives to the Fifth Committee of the General Assembly in 1987 (A/C.5/42/37), 10 staff members have been killed, executed, assassinated, have died—or are presumed to have died—in detention in conditions that have never been clarified.

## C. Disappearances

According to report A/C.5/42/37 by the staff representatives, 11 staff members are still reported missing. The oldest case dates back to 1976.

## D. Ban on Leaving a Country

Sometimes, officials sent on mission or coming back from home leave are no longer authorized to return to their duty station. In most cases, after some time a letter of resignation—signed or unsigned by the staff member—reaches the Secretary-General, who has no assurance that the resignation is an act freely decided on by the staff member, since he cannot talk openly and directly with the staff member.

## E. Violation of the Rights of the Families

The arbitrary arrest, death or disappearance of a staff member, in itself means that the human rights of the families are violated. Moreover, the person in question is often the one who supports the family and therefore the families may experience serious financial difficulties. In cases of arbitrary arrest, the United Nations generally continues to pay the staff member's salary. . . .

The Sub-Commission was influenced by data submitted by international non-governmental organizations that indicated that hundreds of UN staff members had been detained, imprisoned, or "disappeared" since the UN was formed, and that 120 staff members were at that time in this category.

The Secretary-General submitted an updated version of his report on this subject to the Sub-Commission to the 1989 session of the Commission on Human Rights, following consideration by the 1988 General Assembly of the question of respect for the privileges and immunities of officials of the United Nations and its specialized agencies and related organizations. After examining the report, the Commission, on 6 March 1989 (resolution 1989/28), appealed to Member States (a) to allow medical teams to investigate cases in which the health of staff members, experts, and their families who are being detained reportedly has suffered, and to permit the necessary medical treatment to be made available, and (b) to provide adequate and prompt information concerning the arrest or detention of United Nations staff members and their families, and to grant the representative of the competent international organizations access to them without delay.

A preliminary report entitled "Protection of the Human Rights of United Nations Staff Members, Experts and Their Families," prepared by the Special Rapporteur (UN Doc. E/CN.4/Sub.2/1989/28) was presented to the Sub-Commission at its 1989 session. A final report (E/CN.4/Sub.2/1992/19) was examined by the Commission on Human Rights at its 1993 session, together with an updated report by the Secretary-General on the detention of international civil servants and their families (E/CN.4/1993/22).

**BIBLIOGRAPHY.** Amnesty International. *Administrative Detention.* London: 1988. NGO report, in English.

————. *South Korea: Administrative Detention.* London: 1989. NGO report, in English.

Birzeit University, Public Relations Office. *The Twentieth Year: A Report on the Status of Academic Freedom and Human Rights at Birzeit University in the Twentieth Year of Israeli Military Occupation.* Jerusalem, Occupied Territories: 1988. Conference report, in English.

Halabi, Usama R. "The Legality of Utilizing Administrative Detention in the Israeli Occupied Territories," *Netherlands Quarterly of Human Rights* 9, no. 4 (1991): 398–417. Scholarly article, in English.

Harding, Andrew, and John Hatchard, eds. *Preventive Detention and Security Law: A Comparative Survey.* Dordrecht, the Netherlands: Martinus Nijhoff, 1993. Collection of scholarly contributions, in English.

Law in the Service of Man/Al-Haq. *Administrative Detention in the Occupied West Bank.* Ramallah, Occupied Territories: 1986. NGO report, in English.

————. *Ansar 3: A Case for Closure.* Ramallah, Occupied Territories: 1988. NGO mission report, in English.

————. *Briefing Papers on Twenty Years of Israeli Occupation of the West Bank and Gaza.* Ramallah, Occupied Territories: 1987. NGO briefing paper collection, in English.

————. *Punishing a Nation: Human Rights Violations during the Palestinian Uprising, Dec. 1987–Dec. 1988.* Ramallah, Occupied Territories: 1988. NGO report, in English.

Merrett, Christopher. "Detention Without Trial in South Africa: The Abuse of Human Rights as State Strategy in the Late 1980s." *Africa Today* 37, no. 2 (1990): 53–66. Scholarly article, in English.

Middle East Watch. *Prison Conditions in Israel and the Occupied Territories.* New York: Human Rights Watch, 1991. NGO factfinding report, in English.

Pacheco, Allegra A. "Occupying an Uprising: The Geneva Convention and the Israeli Administrative Detention Policy during the First Year of the Palestinian General Uprising: December 1987–December 1988," *Columbia Human Rights Law Review* 21, no. 2 (Spring 1990): 515–563. Scholarly article, in English.

Playfair, Emma. *Administrative Detention in the Occupied West Bank.* Ramallah, Occupied Territories: Law in the Service of Man/Al-Haq, 1986. NGO occasional paper, in English.

Rishmawi, Mona. "Administrative Detention in International Law: The Case of the Israeli Occupied West Bank and Gaza," *The Palestine Yearbook of International Law* 5 (1989): 83–128. Scholarly article, in English.

Rodley, Nigel S. *The Treatment of Prisoners under International Law.* Paris: Clarendon Press, 1987. Scholarly monograph, in English.

Shalev, Carmel. *The Price of Insurgency: Civil Rights in the Occupied Territories.* Jerusalem, Israel: West Bank Database Project, 1988. NGO report, in English.

Stavros, Stephanos. "The Right to a Fair Trial in Emergency Situations," *International and Comparative Law Quarterly* 41 (April 1992): 343–365. Scholarly article, in English.

Sullivan, Kerry S. "Pre-Trial Detention of Suspects in Northern Ireland: A Violation of Fundamental Human Rights," *Journal of International Comparative Law* 11, no. 1 & 2 (1990): 297–322. Scholarly article, in English.

Tomasevski, Katarina. *Prison Health: International Standards and National Practices in Europe.* Helsinki, Finland: Helsinki Institute for Crime Prevention and Control, 1992. Report, in English.

United Nations. Centre for Human Rights, Crime Prevention and Criminal Justice Branch. *Human Rights and Pre-Trial Detention: A Handbook of International Standards relating to Pre-Trial Detention.* New York: 1994. Professional Training Series, No. 3 United Nations, Sub-Commission on Prevention of Discrimination and Protection of Minorities. Report on the Practice of Administrative Detention, Submitted by Mr. Louis Joinet. Geneva, Switzerland: 1990. Intergovernmental study, in English and French.

————. *The Right to a Fair Trial: Current Recognition and Measures Necessary for Its Strengthening.* Second Report Prepared by Mr. Stanislav Chernichenko and Mr. William Treat in Accordance With Resolution 1990/18 of the Sub-Commission and Resolution 1991/43 of the Commission on Human Rights. Geneva, Switzerland: 1991. Intergovernmental document, in English and French.

United Nations, Sub-Commission on Prevention of Discrimination and Protection of Minorities. *Report on the Practice of Administrative Detention.* Submitted by Mr. Louis Joinet. Geneva, Switzerland: 1990. Intergovernmental report, in English and French.

Vitullo, Anita. *Ansar 2: Detention, Humiliation, and Intimidation.* Chicago, IL, USA: Palestine Human Rights Information Center and Human Rights Research and Education Foundation/Database Project, 1987. NGO report, in English.

Zucker, Dedi. "Droits de l'Homme et Repression de l'Intifada" (Human Rights and Repression of the Intifadah). *Revue d'Etudes Palestiniennes* 29 (Oct. 1988): 75–91. NGO article, in French.

**ADVANCEMENT OF WOMEN DIVISION, UN.** The UN Division for the Advancement of Women, which forms part of the Center for Social Development and Humanitarian Affairs of the United Nations Secretariat, is located at the Vienna International Center, Austria. It provides executive direction, management, administrative and substantive services to all United Nations organs when they deal with questions relating to the advancement of women, including the GENERAL ASSEMBLY, the ECONOMIC AND SOCIAL COUNCIL, the COMMISSION ON THE STATUS OF WOMEN, the COMMITTEE ON THE ELIMINATION OF DISCRIMINATION AGAINST WOMEN, and their subsidiary bodies. In close collaboration with the Crime Prevention and Criminal Justice Branch of the Center, and with the intergovernmental and non-governmental organizations and research institutions concerned, it carries out research and prepares studies, reports, and other documentation at the request of these organs; assists in the implementation of their recommendations; and collects and disseminates information on their activities.

*SEE ALSO Women's Rights.*

**AFFIRMATIVE ACTION.** Several international instruments provide for action to be taken by States parties in order to remedy the effects of past discrimination on grounds such as race, sex, language, or religion. For example, the International Covenant on Civil and Political Rights provides:

*Article 27.* In those States in which ethnic, religious or linguistic minorities exist, persons belonging to such minorities shall not be denied the right, in community with the other members of their group, to enjoy their own culture, to profess and practice their own religion, or to use their own language.

The International Convention on the Elimination of All Forms of Racial Discrimination contains the following provision:

*Article 1 (4).* Special measures taken for the sole purpose of securing adequate advancement of certain racial or ethnic groups or individuals requiring such protection as may be necessary to ensure such groups or individuals equal enjoyment or exercise of human rights and fundamental freedoms shall not be deemed racial discrimination, provided, however, that such measures do not, as a consequence, lead to the maintenance of separate rights for different racial groups and that they shall not be continued after the objectives for which they were taken have been achieved.

The Convention on the Elimination of All Forms of Discrimination Against Women provides that:

*Article 4.* 1. Adoption by States Parties of temporary special measures aimed at accelerating de facto equality between men and women shall not be considered discrimination as defined in the present Convention, but shall in no way entail as a consequence the maintenance of unequal or separate standards; these measures shall be discontinued when the objectives of equality of opportunity and treatment have been achieved.
2. Adoption by States Parties of special measures, including those measures contained in the present Convention, aimed at protecting maternity, shall not be considered discriminatory.

The Commission on the Status of Women has from time to time called for affirmative action to improve the status of women. On its recommendation, the UN Economic and Social Council, at its first 1989 session, urged governments (resolution 1989/36) "to give high priority to measures and temporary affirmative action programs that will more rapidly bring about equality in women's economic participation, in particular to programs that will ensure the following:

(a) women's access to the labor market and to education and training;
(b) elimination of sex segregation in the labor market and in education;
(c) women's participation in trade unions;
(d) equal pay for equal work;
(e) equal access to economic resources, including credit and membership in cooperatives; and
(f) improved conditions in the informal sector including, where desirable, the application of labor standards, and the development or improvement of sex-disaggregated statistics that accurately reflect women's work in the informal economic sector.

*SEE ALSO Racial Discrimination.*

**BIBLIOGRAPHY.** Bayefsky, Anne F. "The Principle of Equality or Non-Discrimination in International Law," *Human Rights Law Journal* 11, no. 1–2 (1990): 1–34. Scholarly article, in English.
Hepple, Bob. "Discrimination and Equality of Opportunity: Northern Irish Lessons," *Oxford Journal of Legal Studies* 10, no. 3 (Autumn 1990): 408–421. Scholarly article, in English.
Ong Puay Liu. "Ethnic Quotas in Malaysia: Affirmative Action or indigenous Right?" *Asian Profile* 18, no. 4 (August 1990): 325–334. Scholarly article, in English.
Scutt, Jocelynne A. *Women and the Law: Commentary and Materials.* Melbourne, Victoria, Australia: The Law Book Company, 1990. Educational material, in English; bibliography, pp. xxxi–lii.
Smith, Nicolas. "Affirmative Action: Its Origin and Point," *South African Journal on Human Rights* 8, no. 2 (1992): 234–248. Scholarly article, in English.
Wyzan, Michael L. (ed.). *The Political Economy of Ethnic Discrimination and Affirmative Action: A Comparative Perspective.* New York: Praeger, 1990. Collection of scholarly articles, in English; bibliography, pp. 217–231.

**AFGHANISTAN.** The Democratic Republic of Afghanistan is a country in Southern Asia. It has borders with Iran, Pakistan, Tajikistan, and Turkmenistan. It achieved independence from Great Britain by the Treaty of Rawalpindi of 1919 and became a member of the United Nations in 1946. The population is estimated to be 16,290,000. Ethnic groups include Pathans, Hazaras, Tajiks, Turkomens, and Uzbeks. Languages commonly used include Dari and Pushtu. Islam (Sunni, 74%; Shi'ite, 25%) is the predominant religion. The courts follow the Hanafi jurisprudence of Islamic law in the absence of conflicting constitutional provisions.

The government (1994) took the form of an Islamic republic. Between 1964 and 1973, it had been governed in accordance with a constitution under which King Zahir Shah appointed one-third of the deputies, the people elected one-third, and one-third was chosen by the provincial assemblies. However, on 17 July 1973, Prime Minister Sardar Mohammed Daoud seized power, abrogated the constitution, and declared himself President and Prime Minister of the new republic.

In 1977, two factions of the People's Democratic Party of Afghanistan ended a 10-year disagreement, united, and organized a coup that overthrew Daoud and established the Democratic Republic of Afghanistan. The Secretary-General of the People's Democratic Party (PDPA), Nur Mohammed Taraki, became President of the pro-Soviet Revolutionary Council, installed as the country's supreme governing body, and initiated a "reform" program that ran counter to many long-held traditions of the Afghan people. The dispute between the two factions of the PDPA led to further disagreement between two leaders: Taraki and Hafizullah Amin. In a September 1979 coup, Amin took over from Taraki.

*SOVIET INVASION.* On 24 December 1979, troops of the Union of Soviet Socialist Republics entered Afghanistan on the invitation of Hafizullah Amin and the Revolutionary Council under a "Treaty of Friendship, Good Neighborliness and Co-operation," which had been negotiated during the presidency of Nur Mohammed Taraki. Amin died a few days later under mysterious circumstances; Pakistan later charged that he had been executed on 27 December by Soviet troops stationed in Kabul. He was replaced by Babrak Karmal, who, in turn, was succeeded in November 1986 by Lt. Gen. Mohammed Najibullah, a former head of the secret police who, since May of that year, had served as general secretary of the Central Committee of the People's Democratic Party.

*UN REACTION TO SOVIET INVASION.* In January 1980, with Soviet troop strength in Afghanistan reaching 85,000, the UN Security Council held an urgent meeting with a view to calling for the immediate withdrawal of Soviet troops but was unable to issue the call because of the negative vote cast by the Union of Soviet Socialist Republics. It then called for a special session of the General Assembly to consider the problem.

On 14 January 1980, the UN General Assembly (resolution ES-6-1) expressed its grave concern about the developments in Afghanistan and their implications for international peace and security and called for the immediate, unconditional, and total withdrawal of foreign troops from that country in order to enable its people to determine their own form of government and to choose their economic, political, and social systems free from outside intervention, coercion, or restraint of any kind.

The UN COMMISSION ON HUMAN RIGHTS, in February 1980, condemned the Soviet military aggression against the Afghan people; denounced and deplored it as a flagrant violation of international laws, cove-

nants, and norms; and called upon all peoples and governments to persist in condemning this aggression and denouncing it as a violation of human rights and of the freedoms of peoples.

For several years thereafter, the Commission and the General Assembly repeatedly expressed the view that the withdrawal of foreign forces from Afghanistan was essential for restoring the enjoyment of human rights in that country and expressed their concern and anxiety at the continuing presence of the foreign troops and the reports of extensive human rights violations. On 15 March 1984, the Commission on Human Rights proposed that the Economic and Social Council authorize the appointment of a Special Rapporteur to examine the human rights situation in Afghanistan, with a view to formulating proposals that could contribute to ensuring full protection of the human rights of all residents of the country before, during, and after the withdrawal of all foreign forces.

With the approval of the Council, Mr. Felix Ermacora (Austria) was appointed as the Commission's Special Rapporteur to examine the human rights situation in Afghanistan. In this capacity, he later submitted five reports to the Commission (UN Docs. E/CN.4/1985/21, E/CN.4/1986/2, E/CN.4/1987/22, E/CN.4/1988/25, and E/CN.4/1990/25) and five to the General Assembly (UN Docs. A/40/843, A/41/778, A/42/667 and Corr. 1, A/43/742, and A/44/669). These reports were based upon his own observations following contacts and discussions with senior government officials, leaders of opposition movements, and other well-informed persons, the collection of a substantial body of documentation, and several visits to areas in Afghanistan and Pakistan.

*PEACE TALKS.* In December 1987, the Secretary-General's personal representative, Diego Cordovez, visited Washington, D.C., and Moscow, where he held a number of meetings with senior officials of the United States of America and the Union of Soviet Socialist Republics. In Moscow, Soviet Foreign Minister Eduard Shevardnadze gave him assurance of his government's determination that negotiations towards the achievement of a comprehensive settlement of the situation relating to Afghanistan could be concluded. On the basis of these consultations, it was agreed that a round of talks would be held in Geneva beginning on 1 March 1988.

Following extended and intensive consultations in Geneva over a period of six weeks, it was possible to announce on 8 April 1988 that the instruments which would comprise the settlement were in final form and ready for signature. The "Agreements on the Settlement of the Situation Relating to Afghanistan" were signed on 14 April 1988 at the European office of the

United Nations in Geneva. They comprised the following four instruments (the texts were issued as UN Doc. S/19835, annex):

(1) Bilateral Agreement between the Republic of Afghanistan and the Islamic Republic of Pakistan on the Principles of Mutual Relations, in Particular on Non-Interference and Non-Intervention;

(2) Declaration on International Guarantees;

(3) Bilateral Agreement between the Republic of Afghanistan and the Islamic Republic of Pakistan on the Voluntary Return of Refugees; and

(4) Agreement on the Interrelationships for the Settlement of the Situation Relating to Afghanistan (including the annexed Memorandum of Understanding on the monitoring arrangements to be provided by the United Nations).

The instruments were signed by Foreign Minister Abdul Wakil of Afghanistan and the Minister of State for Foreign Affairs Zain Noorani of the Islamic Republic of Pakistan on behalf of their respective governments as parties to the settlement, and by Foreign Minister Eduard Shevardnadze of the U.S.S.R. and Secretary of State George Shultz of the United States of America on behalf of their respective governments as States guarantors. At the signing ceremony, the UN Secretary-General noted that the arrangements laid the basis for the exercise by all Afghans of their right to self-determination and that the challenges facing the people of Afghanistan could and must be met by them alone. Later, he appointed Mr. Diego Cordovez as his representative on the Settlement of the Situation Relating to Afghanistan and established the Good Offices Mission, composed of 50 military officers temporarily detached from other United Nations operations, to monitor the implementation of the agreements, which called for the withdrawal of one-half of the foreign troops from Afghanistan by 15 August 1988 and the withdrawal of all troops within nine months.

The Special Rapporteur of the Commission on Human Rights, Felix Ermacora, welcomed signature of the so-called Geneva Agreements and agreed with the Secretary-General's statement that they represented "a major stride in the effort to bring peace to Afghanistan and to assure a reprieve for its people." However, he was not able to report any immediate improvement in the human rights situation within the country. "Acts of war are continuing," he stated in his report to the 1988 session of the General Assembly. "Violations of human rights are at least as frequent as in the past, affecting particularly the civilian population and endangering the lives and security of innocent men, women and children."

In this connection, he pointed out that the Geneva Agreements stipulated only the conditions for the exercise of the right of self-determination of the Afghan people; they were still to be implemented fully. The United Nations had established its Good Offices Mission, which had observed the withdrawal of Soviet troops and had set up the Office of the Coordinator for United Nations Humanitarian and Economic Assistance Programs Relating to Afghanistan—both linked closely with human rights and humanitarian issues. However, the agreements were silent on several important human rights questions, such as the treatment of amnestied persons, investigation of the fate of persons who had "disappeared," the release of prisoners, and the dismantling of revolutionary or special tribunals, revolutionary or special prosecutors, and the special police.

Moreover, he recalled that at the conclusion of the Geneva Agreements, the Alliance of the Opposition had indicated that its members did not feel bound by them because they had not been consulted or involved in the negotiations which produced the agreements.

*SOVIET WITHDRAWAL AND ITS AFTERMATH.* In accordance with provisions of the Geneva Agreements, the Union of Soviet Socialist Republics began to withdraw its estimated 115,000 troops from Afghanistan on 15 May 1988. The withdrawal was completed on 15 February 1989.

After examining the report that the Special Rapporteur presented to its 1989 session (UN Doc. A/44/669, annex), the Assembly recognized (resolution 44/161) that a situation of armed conflict continued to exist in Afghanistan, leaving large numbers of victims and causing enormous human suffering to the civilian population, that the treatment of prisoners detained in connection with that conflict did not conform to the internationally recognized principles of humanitarian law, and that more than five million refugees were living outside Afghanistan, with many others displaced within the country. The Assembly noted that the main reasons given by the refugees for not returning to Afghanistan, pending the achievement of a comprehensive political solution, were the continued fighting in some provinces, the use of very destructive arms in the conflict, and the minefields that had been laid in many parts of the country. It also noted that acts of terrorism had significantly increased.

The General Assembly, welcoming the cooperation which the Afghan authorities had accorded to the Special Rapporteur, urged all parties concerned to work for the achievement of a comprehensive political solution based on the right of self-determination and for the creation of a situation that would permit the return of refugees and the full enjoyment of human rights by all Afghans. It called upon all parties to the conflict, in order to alleviate the serious suffering of the Afghan people, strictly to respect human life and the principles and provisions of international humanitarian law and to cooperate fully and effectively with international humanitarian institutions, especially with the **INTERNATIONAL COMMITTEE OF THE RED CROSS,** in particular by granting it unrestricted access to all parts of the country.

At the same time, the Assembly noted reports of the interrogation practices of the Afghan authorities, the large number of political prisoners, and the conditions of prisoners awaiting trial. It called upon the Afghan authorities to investigate thoroughly the fate of disappeared persons, to apply amnesty decrees equally to foreign detainees, to reduce the period during which prisoners await trial, to treat all prisoners—especially those awaiting trial or in custody in juvenile rehabilitation centers—in accordance with the Standard Minimum Rules for the Treatment of Prisoners, and to allow the International Committee of the Red Cross to visit them regularly in accordance with its established criteria.

*PROBLEMS WITH A COALITION GOVERNMENT.* In April/May 1992, however, there was a dramatic change in the political situation in Afghanistan: the former government peacefully handed over power to a coalition composed of numerous political factions, and a Shura Ahl-e-Hal Wa Aqd (conference) was convened to reach agreement on the distribution of power. However, as the Special Rapporteur noted in his report to the 1993 session of the Commission on Human Rights (E/CN.4/1993/42, para. 52–53):

Not all groups were represented nor were they in favour of this gathering and its decisions have not been generally recognized. The Shura appointed Mr. Burhanuddin Rabbani as President of the Islamic State of Afghanistan. The parliamentary assembly which was created from among the members of the Shura has been entrusted with the drafting of the constitution. The legitimacy of the Shura and its procedures have been contested. In the absence of a written constitution, the legitimacy of the Shura and its political validity may only be judged against the rules contained in the Koran. It would appear that the perception of the Shura as a fait accompli has divided the country, giving rise to a new wave of violence and is hampering the attainment of a peaceful political solution.

Military factions and factions formed along tribal and religious lines are currently struggling to gain political power, which has led to untold loss of life and property. Even United Nations premises in Kabul have been badly damaged, and it has been reported that the damage incurred in the third week of January 1993 has exceeded that incurred in the course of the past 13 years. Staff of the United Nations and of nongovernmental organizations who were providing humanitarian assistance to the Afghan people have been brutally murdered. Political power in the provinces is held by different groups and does not necessarily correspond to or is in agreement with the government decisions taken in Kabul. The danger exists that the armed struggle currently taking place in Kabul does not remain limited to the capital. Fighting which began in

January 1994 left 2,500 people dead over the following six months. Another 200 civilians died in the April 1995 Russian airstrikes against Islamic rebels fighting the Tajikistan government from northern Afghani villages.

In her 1993 yearly report, the United Nations **HIGH COMMISSIONER FOR REFUGEES** indicated that out of a total of 19.7 million refugees world wide, there were an estimated 4.5 million Afghan refugees, more than from any other country.

In a subsequent report to the 1993 session of the General Assembly, the Special Rapporteur put forward his conclusions and recommendations in the following terms (A/48/584, para. 102–142):

### A. Conclusions

After the holding of the Shura Ahl-e-Hal Wa Aqd, the Special Rapporteur expressed doubts whether the circumstances in which it was held, the participation and the decisions taken would be accepted as a valid basis for normal and peaceful political development in Afghanistan. Indeed, the power struggle continued after the shura, which prompted the convening of a gathering of the political parties initiated by the leaders of Saudi Arabia and Pakistan and attended by a representative of the Islamic Republic of Iran, to discuss and adopt guidelines for a political solution. All party leaders with whom the Special Rapporteur met during his last visit to the region agreed that it was necessary to find a solution to the power struggle. The Special Rapporteur has concluded that among the principal causes of dissent are differences of opinion concerning the approach to a political solution.

The political situation in Afghanistan is characterized by political agreements adopted by the coalition of leaders of nine former opposition parties. The Afghan Peace Accord concluded at Islamabad in March 1993 provided for the formation of a Government for a period of 18 months in which Mr. Rabbani would remain President and Mr. Hekmatyar would assume the office of Prime Minister. Agreement was also reached on an electoral process and the formation of an independent Election Commission.

The Peace Accord also contained the text of the Division of Powers. The Cabinet established thereby would work on the principle of collective responsibility.

Under the Jalalabad Accord of May 1993, it was decided, inter alia, to establish a Supreme Council which would provide guidance concerning policy-making and whose aims would be to stop the war throughout Afghanistan, establish an Islamic army and form a cabinet "with the consent of the majority of the Jehadi leaders and approval of the President."

Having concluded the Islamabad and Jalalabad accords, which could represent a point of departure for the day-to-day functioning of a government, the country's political leaders are not in a position to implement them. The envisaged organs and commissions are not working and no time-frame concerning their programmes has been respected. On the contrary, the different political groups terrorize each other. For example, political enemies are the targets of mine or bomb explosions and differences concerning relatively minor issues may result in massive killing. In addition, the lives of certain members of private organizations which are independent from the Afghan political forces have been threatened.

Kabul is a decentralized area in which no government can

really exercise power. Power is shared principally between groups loyal to President Rabbani and those loyal to Prime Minister Hekmatyar. The airport is currently controlled by forces over which the President has authority. Flights into and out of the capital and travel are possible only when there is a common understanding on the use of the airport.

There is no central power which exercises control over the provinces. Provinces are mostly governed by shuras, which are often headed by prominent field commanders and do not reflect the composition or alliances of the so-called coalition in Kabul, as is the case in Nangarhar Province in the east. In the northern and western parts of the country, authority is exercised by persons whose authority extends beyond a single province and who have so far been able to guarantee law and order in their zones of influence. The infighting in Kabul may have repercussions in the provinces. The conflict can also be more or less specific to a given province, as was the case with the assassination in September 1993 of the Deputy Governor of Nangarhar Province, which has given rise to general instability in the area. The current conflict in Kandahar Province does not follow the pattern of the alliances that have been formed elsewhere. (For more detailed information concerning local administrations set up by mujahideen commanders, see appendix 2 to the Amnesty International report of September 1993 entitled "Afghanistan: Political Crisis and the Refugees," AI INDEX: ASA 11/01/93.)

Kabul is governed by groups that are partners in the coalition and by those created along tribal and other lines. They control different sectors of the city, without any coordination, which accounts for a general lack of safety in the city. The Mayor's office is located in an area where a certain amount of governmental authority and infrastructure may be observed, but beyond that relatively small area, control is exercised by armed groups, at times in a manner that can hardly be described as being in conformity with human rights standards.

The most badly damaged area in Kabul is that of the University with which the Special Rapporteur was well acquainted from earlier visits to the city. He was shocked to see houses, buildings, institutions and university premises and facilities either destroyed or heavily damaged and visibly looted.

In Kabul, some 36,000 houses have been partly or fully destroyed and more than 30,000 damaged. Approximately 110,000 families have been displaced and thousands of persons have been killed or wounded during the battles in and around the city. Numerous cases of rape and ill-treatment by armed persons have been reported. A reliable source told the Special Rapporteur that women have never been treated in Afghanistan with such a lack of respect as in recent months.

Contrary to expectations, the massive repatriation of refugees, which began after the breakdown of the former Government when more than 1.3 million persons returned from Pakistan alone, has not continued. In 1993, a relatively small number of refugees chose to return from Pakistan. The Pakistani authorities, who have continued to provide assistance to Afghan refugees in conjunction with UNHCR and a number of nongovernmental organizations, have closed more than 120 administrative units within refugee camps, principally in the Baluchistan and North West Frontier provinces. An estimated 2 million refugees remain in Pakistan, and approximately 2.15 million are still in the Islamic Republic of Iran. Written reports and oral testimony have been received concerning the harassment in northern Afghanistan of refugees returning from the Islamic Republic of Iran, especially from Khorasan Province.

More than 90,000 new refugees have arrived in Pakistan since April 1992. they are mostly unregistered refugees from urban areas who have not been placed in camps and do not receive any assistance. Most live in appalling conditions, some of them in squatters' camps with no facilities.

The Special Rapporteur was informed about the situation of members of the Afghan Sikh and Hindu communities who have fled Kabul. Numerous families from those communities were able to find shelter in India, but some faced administrative difficulties when crossing borders on the way, mostly through the North West Frontier and Baluchistan provinces. It would appear that many are now willing to return. Members of those communities who spoke with the Special Rapporteur told him that they did not leave Afghanistan because of racial hatred but owing to the insecurity caused by shelling and looting.

The continuous serious threat to the right to life has been characterized by massacres such as the one perpetrated in an area of Kabul controlled by members of the Afghan Shia community. The armed groups which participated in the massacre also raped women and girls and ill-treated children. All Afghans, regardless of their ethnic background, were subject to atrocities. Despite the gravity of the offences, no thorough investigation into the matter has reportedly been undertaken.

A mass grave was discovered in 1992 near the city of Herat. Many of the dead were killed by shots in the head. It would appear that the killing dates back to 1978–79 when the first uprising against the communist Government started in and around Herat. The Special Rapporteur was informed that this was not the only mass grave discovered in the country. He is of the opinion that the discovery of mass graves will help to elucidate the fate of persons who disappeared in Afghanistan in the late 1970s.

Death sentences continue to be pronounced and are reportedly carried out in conformity with the Shariah. The Special Rapporteur was informed that the death sentences which were passed and carried out in public in 1992 were exceptional measures taken under specific circumstances and in view of the situation prevailing at the time.

The governmental authorities in Kabul have stated that there are no political prisoners in detention centres under their control. However, they have indicated that investigation procedures are conducted by the police, under the control of the Attorney-General, and are transferred to courts after the completion of the files. As regards torture, the Special Rapporteur was informed that the Islamic rules and regulations enshrined in the Koran forbid such practice.

It has been admitted that prisons controlled by political parties and other groups exist in Afghanistan. Not all parties have prisons. The Special Rapporteur was not able to obtain information concerning the number of prisoners detained in such prisons, their location or how they were treated. It would appear that they are often held as hostages. The International Committee of the Red Cross has tried to obtain permission to visit those prisoners. The Special Rapporteur is of the view that the existence of a central government would preclude the creation of prisons controlled by parties.

The fate of former Soviet prisoners has remained unresolved. Afghan groups which have such prisoners in their custody are reluctant to release them unconditionally. It would appear that they are considered an element for bargaining, which is unequivocally prohibited by humanitarian law. Negotiations concerning the release of a number of the prisoners coincided with the Special Rapporteur's visit to Afghanistan. However, peace in the country and the establishment of normal international relations warrant a final step such as the release of those prisoners, whose number is estimated at between 80 and 235. They should be allowed to decide where they want to go: remain in Afghanistan integrated into the Afghan society, go to a third country, or return to their homes.

Fortunately, after the Islamic Government took office, there were no massive or systematic acts of revenge against persons who occupied prominent positions in the previous Government. However, individual acts of revenge have been reported.

As concerns the amnesty which was proclaimed after the establishment of an Islamic Government, it would appear that problems have arisen with regard to the interpretation of the general amnesty decree which was adopted unanimously under former President Mojjadidi and which principally concerns high-ranking officials of the former Government. As he has indicated in his reports to the General Assembly and the Commission on Human Rights, the Special Rapporteur is of the opinion that even former President Najibullah should be granted amnesty since the amnesty decree of the Government did not provide for any exceptions.

The Special Rapporteur was able to obtain special information about education from persons who exercise authority in a number of provinces located in the western, northern and eastern parts of the country. The Special Rapporteur sees no possibility for the revival of the university life in Kabul, especially in the scientific and technical fields which require fully equipped institutes and laboratories.

The situation of Afghan refugees in both Pakistan and the Islamic Republic of Iran has been regulated by agreements concluded between UNHCR, the Government of Afghanistan and the Governments of the Islamic Republic of Iran and Pakistan, which resulted in the establishment of Tripartite Commissions. Reference is made in the agreements to the human rights enshrined in the Universal Declaration of Human Rights and the International Covenant on Civil and Political Rights. It has been reported, however, that Afghan refugees have recently been repatriated forcibly from the Islamic Republic of Iran, in particular from Khorasan Province. The Special Rapporteur received detailed testimony from reliable sources concerning this practice of expulsion.

The economic and social situation in Afghanistan is far from satisfactory. Basic commodities are not always available on the market, and prices are high in comparison with the average income. A number of areas have been affected by epidemics of diseases such as cholera. Although the UN has made considerable efforts with regard to mine clearing, the process cannot advance rapidly for lack of funds and equipment.

It has been reported that the National Museum in Kabul has been partly destroyed and looted. The Special Rapporteur is aware that heavy fighting has taken place in the area where the museum is located but was unable to ascertain the veracity of the reports.

The Special Rapporteur has finally come to the conclusion that the situation of human rights in Afghanistan is far from being satisfactory. Owing to the absence of an effective central government, the existing authorities are unable to govern the provinces, and not even all areas in Kabul are under their control. Only a democratic understanding between the representatives of the political parties can solve the conflict, which could escalate into a total war with repercussions for the security of the whole region. The conflict in neighbouring Tajikistan, for example, has spilled over into Afghanistan and created a new problem of Tajik refugees and internally displaced Afghans. The respect of the human rights enshrined in the Universal Declaration and the International Covenant on Civil and Political Rights and the International Covenant on Economic, Social and Cultural Rights, to which Afghanistan is a party and which it has pledged to implement, is not guaranteed. This is also one of the reasons for the absence of a "pull factor" that would prompt Afghan refugees to return to their country. It would appear that the "push factors" that keep the refugees away continue to prevail, among them insecurity, unrest, mines and the problems that the international community faces in rendering assistance. The Afghan people have been overwhelmed by large amounts of sophisticated weapons, which were helpful in waging the war against foreign occupation but whose existence is disastrous for peace, if anyone can command a situation by use of weapons. The people are victims of a situation that, after the victory of the liberation struggle, has rendered the whole country helpless.

### B. Recommendations

The Special Rapporteur wishes to reiterate the recommendations contained in his report to the General Assembly at its 47th session (A/47/656), namely that humanitarian law must be respected scrupulously (para. 130); that the Government should issue a declaration on the basis of article 4 of the International Covenant on Civil and Political Rights (para. 131); the International Committee of the Red Cross should be allowed to visit places of detention organized by combatants or governmental authorities wherever they may be (para. 133). He also reiterates his recommendations on the administration of justice (para. 134) and on non-discriminatory application of the amnesty decree (para. 140).

The Government of Afghanistan should implement the provisions of the Islamabad and Jalalabad accords, which provide for the establishment of an Election Commission and a Supreme Council mandated to draft the Constitution.

The United Nations should offer advisory services and technical assistance concerning the drafting of the constitution and holding direct elections or a Loya Jirga in keeping with Afghan tradition. The new Constitution should embody human rights principles that are in conformity with the Shariah and with those enshrined in UN instruments.

Since it is possible for the UN to provide advisory services and technical assistance only when there is peace, security and a functioning central government, the weapons currently in the possession of unauthorized organized armed groups should be handed over, under the supervision of the United Nations, and used for the creation of a central governmental army or destroyed.

The former Soviet prisoners of war should be released unconditionally, in conformity with the Geneva Conventions of August 1949. Since the amnesty decree of the Government did not provide for any exceptions, former Pres. Najibullah should be granted amnesty. In view of his state of health, he should be released promptly on humanitarian grounds.

Prisons run by political parties should be abolished and their prisoners released, or, if a case exists, given a fair trial. The International Committee of the Red Cross and the Special Rapporteur should be allowed to monitor the implementation of this recommendation.

Every effort should be made to broaden and accelerate the process of mine clearing.

Every effort should be made to enable displaced persons to return safely to their homes and to rebuild them.

Respect for women and their honour and dignity should be ensured in accordance with the provisions of international human rights instruments and the Geneva Conventions.

Political conflicts should be solved by peaceful and democratic means. The use of weapons to gain power or achieve political goals should be declared unlawful unanimously.

As the Special Rapporteur has been asked on several occasions to mobilize the United Nations to assist once again in reaching a political solution to the power struggle, he recommends the political organs of the United Nations at least to attempt to bring the conflicted groups to the negotiation table.

The Special Rapporteur appeals to the international community to continue its efforts in favour of mine-clearing and provide financial and other contributions for that process, so that the reconstruction of the villages and cities in Afghanistan can advance and refugees may return to a safe environment.

UNESCO should be invited to study the situation of the cultural heritage of the country, in particular that of the Kabul Museum. Efforts should be made to reconstruct the University of Kabul and revive the educational process.

In addition to continuing its humanitarian activities, the United Nations should continue to monitor the developments concerning the situation of human rights in Afghanistan.

The Special Rapporteur recommends that his report should also be translated into the Dari and Pashtu languages, which would help reflect the interest of the international community in the fate of Afghanistan so that the Afghan people and conflict are not forgotten.

Pointing out that "peace and security in Afghanistan are prerequisite for the successful repatriation of about four million refugees, in particular the achievement of a comprehensive political solution and the establishment of a freely and democratically elected government, the end of armed confrontation in Kabul and in some provinces, the clearance of the minefields that have been laid in many parts of the country, the restoration of an effective authority in the whole country and the reconstruction of the economy," the UN General Assembly, in resolution 48/152 of 20 December 1993, urged, among other things:

(a) disarmament of all parties (para. 5);

(b) respect for the honor and dignity of women (para. 9);

(c) abolition of prisons run by political parties (para. 11); and

(d) investigations into disappearances and the equal application of amnesty to all detainees (para. 12).

**BIBLIOGRAPHY.** Amnesty International. *Afghanistan: Unlawful Killings and Torture.* London: 1988. NGO report, in English.

Center on War and the Child. *Afghanistan: The War against Children, a Summary Report.* Eureka Springs, AR: 1987. NGO report, in English.

Ermacora, Felix. "Afghanistan and the Conscience of the World." *SIM Newsletter* 17 (March 1987): 3–12. NGO article, in English.

Heinz, Wolfgang S. *Ursachen und Folgen von Menschenrechtsverletzungen in der Dritten Welt* (Causes and Consequences of Human Rights Violations in Third World Countries). Saarbrucken, FRG: Verlag Breitenbach, 1986. Scholarly monograph, in German; bibliography on Afghanistan, pp. 357–360. Also, 20 pages of bibliography on human rights and development at end of volume.

Human Rights Watch. *Afghanistan: The Forgotten War—Human Rights Abuses and Violations of the Laws of War Since the Soviet Withdrawal.* New York: 1991. NGO factfinding report, in English.

Jawad, Nassim. *Afghanistan: A Nation of Minorities.* London: Minority Rights Group, 1992. NGO report, in English.

Maley, William. "Social Dynamics and the Disutility of Terror: Afghanistan, 1978–1989," in *State Organized Terror: The Case of Violent Internal Repression,* eds. P. Timothy Bushnell et al., pp. 113–131. Boulder, CO, USA: Westview Press, 1991. Scholarly article, in English; bibliography, pp. 126–131.

Rubin, B.B. *To Die in Afghanistan.* New York: Asia Watch Committee, 1985. NGO mission report, in English.

UN High Commissioner for Refugees. "Afghanistan: A Sad Legacy of the Cold War" (Afghanistan: triste legs de la guerre froide), *Refugees* no. 88 (January 1992): 16–20. Article, in English and French.

Wirsing, Robert. *The Baluchis and Pathans.* London: Minority Rights Group, 1987. NGO report, in English.

**AFRICA WATCH.** See **HUMAN RIGHTS WATCH.**

**AFRICAN ASSOCIATION OF EDUCATION FOR DEVELOPMENT.** A non-governmental organization in consultative status (Category II) with the UN Economic and Social Council, this organization was founded in June 1978, in Dakar, Senegal. It promotes "conscientization" of African populations so that they rely upon their own forces for an endogenous and self-centered development. It has members in 18 countries.

Among its publications are *Famille et Développement* (quarterly) and educational pamphlets on various topics.

African Association of Education for Development. Address: BP 3907, Lomé, Togo. Telephone: (228) 21-63-16. Fax: (228) 21-63-16. Telex: 5131 Tg. President: Koffi Attignon.

**AFRICAN CHARTER ON HUMAN AND PEOPLES' RIGHTS (1981).** The charter—which may be cited as the Banjul Charter on Human and Peoples' Rights because it was drafted in Banjul, Gambia—is unique in several ways: (1) it deals with civil and political rights as well as with economic, social, and cultural rights in a single document; (2) it sets out the obligations of human beings as well as their rights; and (3) it deals with the rights of peoples as well as those of individuals.

The Charter was adopted on 28 June 1981 by the Heads of State and Government of the Organization of African Unity (18th assembly) in Nairobi, Kenya, and entered into force on 21 October 1986 after being ratified by a majority of the OAU member States. The text (OAU Doc. CAB/LEG/67/3/Rev. 5) is as follows:

### Preamble

The African States members of the Organization of African Unity, parties to the present convention entitled "African Charter on Human and Peoples' Rights",

Recalling Decision 115 (XVI) of the Assembly of Heads of State and Government at its Sixteenth Ordinary Session held in Monrovia, Liberia, from 17 to 20 July 1979 on the preparation of a "preliminary draft on an African Charter on Human and Peoples' Rights providing inter alia for the establishment of bodies to promote and protect human and peoples' rights";

Considering the Charter of the Organization of African Unity, which stipulates that "freedom, equality, justice and dignity are essential objectives for the achievement of the legitimate aspirations of the African peoples";

Reaffirming the pledge they solemnly made in Article 2 of the said Charter to eradicate all forms of colonialism from Africa, to coordinate and intensify their cooperation and efforts to achieve a better life for the peoples of Africa and to promote international cooperation having due regard to the Charter of the United Nations and the Universal Declaration of Human Rights;

Taking into consideration the virtues of their historical tradition and the values of African civilization which should inspire and characterize their reflection on the concept of human and peoples' rights;

Recognizing on the one hand, that fundamental human rights stem from the attributes of human beings, which justifies their national and international protection and on the other hand that the reality and respect of peoples rights should necessarily guarantee human rights;

Considering that the enjoyment of rights and freedoms also implies the performance of duties on the part of everyone;

Convinced that it is henceforth essential to pay a particular attention to the right to development and that civil and political rights cannot be dissociated from economic, social and cultural rights in their conception as well as universality and that the satisfaction of economic, social and cultural rights is a guarantee for the enjoyment of civil and political rights;

Conscious of their duty to achieve the total liberation of Africa, the peoples of which are still struggling for their dignity and genuine independence, and undertaking to eliminate colonialism, neo-colonialism, apartheid, zionism and to dismantle aggressive foreign military bases and all forms of discrimination, particularly those based on race, ethnic group, color, sex, language, religion or political opinions;

Reaffirming their adherence to the principles of human and peoples' rights and freedoms contained in the declarations, conventions and other instruments adopted by the Organization of African Unity, the Movement of Non-Aligned Countries and the United Nations;

Firmly convinced of their duty to promote and protect human and peoples' rights and freedoms taking into account the importance traditionally attached to these rights and freedoms in Africa;

Have agreed as follows:

### Part I: Rights and Duties
### Chapter I Human and Peoples' Rights

*Article 1.* The Member States of the Organization of African Unity parties to the present Charter shall recognize the rights, duties and freedoms enshrined in this Charter and shall undertake to adopt legislative or other measures to give effect to them.

*Article 2.* Every individual shall be entitled to the enjoyment of the rights and freedoms recognized and guaranteed in the present Charter without distinction of any kind such as race, ethnic group, color, sex, language, religion, political or any other opinion, national and social origin, fortune, birth or other status.

*Article 3.* 1. Every individual shall be equal before the law.

2. Every individual shall be entitled to equal protection of the law.

*Article 4.* Human beings are inviolable. Every human being shall be entitled to respect for his life and the integrity of his person. No one may be arbitrarily deprived of this right.

*Article 5.* Every individual shall have the right to the respect of the dignity inherent in a human being and to the recognition of his legal status. All forms of exploitation and degradation of man particularly slavery, slave trade, torture, cruel, inhuman or degrading punishment and treatment shall be prohibited.

*Article 6.* Every individual shall have the right to liberty and to the security of his person. No one may be deprived of his freedom except for reasons and conditions previously laid down by law. In particular, no one may be arbitrarily arrested or detained.

*Article 7.* 1. Every individual shall have the right to have his cause heard. This comprises: a) the right to an appeal to competent national organs against acts of violating his fundamental rights as recognized and guaranteed by conventions, laws, regulations and customs in force; b) the right to be presumed innocent until proved guilty by a competent court or tribunal; c) the right to defence, including the right to be defended by counsel of his choice; d) the right to be tried within a reasonable time by an impartial court or tribunal.

2. No one may be condemned for an act or omission which did not constitute a legally punishable offence at the time it was committed. No penalty may be inflicted for an offence for which no provision was made at the time it was committed. Punishment is personal and can be imposed only on the offender.

*Article 8.* Freedom of conscience, the profession and free practice of religion shall be guaranteed. No one may, subject to law and order, be submitted to measures restricting the exercise of these freedoms.

*Article 9.* 1. Every individual shall have the right to receive information.

2. Every individual shall have the right to express and disseminate his opinions within the law.

*Article 10.* 1. Every individual shall have the right to free association provided that he abides by the law.

2. Subject to the obligation of solidarity provided for in Article 29 no one may be compelled to join an association.

*Article 11.* Every individual shall have the right to assemble freely with others. The exercise of this right shall be subject only to necessary restrictions provided for by law in particular those enacted in the interest of national security, the safety, health, ethics and rights and freedoms of others.

*Article 12.* 1. Every individual shall have the right to freedom of movement and residence within the borders of a State provided he abides by the law.

2. Every individual shall have the right to leave any country including his own, and to return to his country. This right may only be subject to restrictions provided for by law for the protection of national security, law and order, public health or morality.

3. Every individual shall have the right, when persecuted, to seek and obtain asylum in other countries in accordance with laws of those countries and international conventions.

4. A non-national legally admitted in a territory of a State Party to the present Charter, may only be expelled from it by virtue of a decision taken in accordance with the law.

5. The mass expulsion of non-nationals shall be prohibited. Mass expulsion shall be that which is aimed at national, racial, ethnic or religious groups.

*Article 13.* 1. Every citizen shall have the right to participate freely in the government of his country, either directly or through freely chosen representatives in accordance with the provisions of the law.

2. Every citizen shall have the right of equal access to the public service of his country.

3. Every individual shall have the right of access to public property and services in strict equality of all persons before the law.

*Article 14.* The right to property shall be guaranteed. It may only be encroached upon in the interest of public need or in the general interest of the community and in accordance with the provisions of appropriate laws.

*Article 15.* Every individual shall have the right to work under equitable and satisfactory conditions, and shall receive equal pay for equal work.

*Article 16.* 1. Every individual shall have the right to enjoy the best attainable state of physical and mental health.

2. States parties to the present Charter shall take the necessary measures to protect the health of their people and to ensure that they receive medical attention when they are sick.

*Article 17.* 1. Every individual shall have the right to education.

2. Every individual may freely take part in the cultural life of his community.

3. The promotion and protection of morals and traditional values recognized by the community shall be the duty of the State.

*Article 18.* 1. The family shall be the natural unit and basis of society. It shall be protected by the State which shall take care of its physical health and morals.

2. The State shall have the duty to assist the family which is the custodian of morals and traditional values recognized by the community.

3. The State shall ensure the elimination of every discrimination against women and also ensure the protection of the rights of the woman and the child as stipulated in international declarations and conventions.

4. The aged and the disabled shall also have the right to special measures of protection in keeping with their physical or moral needs.

*Article 19.* All peoples shall be equal; they shall enjoy the same respect and shall have the same rights. Nothing shall justify the domination of a people by another.

*Article 20.* 1. All peoples shall have the right to existence. They shall have the unquestionable and inalienable right to self-determination. They shall freely determine their political status and shall pursue their economic and social development according to the policy they have freely chosen.

2. Colonized or oppressed peoples shall have the right to free themselves from the bonds of domination by resorting to any means recognized by the international community.

3. All peoples shall have the right to the assistance of the States parties to the present Charter in their liberation struggle against foreign domination, be it political, economic or cultural.

*Article 21.* 1. All peoples shall freely dispose of their wealth and natural resources. This right shall be exercised in the exclusive interest of the people. In no case shall a people be deprived of it.

2. In case of spoliation the dispossessed people shall have the right to the lawful recovery of its property as well as to an adequate compensation.

3. The free disposal of wealth and natural resources shall be exercised without the prejudice to the obligation of promoting international economic cooperation based on mutual respect, equitable exchange and the principles of international law.

4. States parties to the present Charter shall individually and collectively exercise the right to free disposal of their wealth and natural resources with a view to strengthening African unity and solidarity.

5. States parties to the present Charter shall undertake to eliminate all forms of foreign economic exploitation particularly that practiced by international monopolies so as to enable their peoples to fully benefit from the advantages derived from their national resources.

*Article 22.* 1. All peoples shall have the right to their economic, social and cultural development with due regard to their freedom and identity and in the equal enjoyment of the common heritage of mankind.

2. States shall have the duty, individually or collectively, to ensure the exercise of the right to development.

*Article 23.* 1. All peoples shall have the right to national and international peace and security. The principles of solidarity and friendly relations implicitly affirmed by the Charter of the United Nations and reaffirmed by that of the Organization of African Unity shall govern relations between States.

2. For the purpose of strengthening peace, solidarity and friendly relations, States parties to the present Charter shall ensure that:

(a) any individual enjoying the right of asylum under Article 12 of the present Charter shall not engage in subversive activities against his country of origin or any other State party to the present Charter;

(b) their territories shall not be used as bases for subversive or terrorist activities against the people of any other State party to the present Charter.

*Article 24.* All peoples shall have the right to a general satisfactory environment favorable to their development.

*Article 25.* States parties to the present Charter shall have the duty to promote and ensure through teaching, education and publication, the respect of the rights and freedoms contained in the present Charter and to see to it that these freedoms and rights as well as corresponding obligations and duties are understood.

*Article 26.* States parties to the present Charter shall have the duty to guarantee the independence of the Courts and shall allow the establishment and improvement of appropriate national institutions entrusted with the promotion and protection of the rights and freedoms guaranteed by the present Charter.

### Chapter II Duties

*Article 27.* 1. Every individual shall have duties towards his family and society, the State and other legally recognized communities and the international community.

2. The rights and freedoms of each individual shall be exercised with due regard to the rights of others, collective security, morality and common interest.

*Article 28.* Every individual shall have the duty to respect and consider his fellow beings without discrimination, and to maintain relations aimed at promoting, safeguarding and reinforcing mutual respect and tolerance.

*Article 29.* The individual shall also have the duty:

1. To preserve the harmonious development of the family and to work for the cohesion and respect of the family; to respect his parents at all times, to maintain them in case of need;

2. To serve his national community by placing his physical and intellectual abilities at its service;

3. Not to compromise the security of the State whose national or resident he is;

4. To preserve and strengthen social and national solidarity, particularly when the latter is threatened;

5. To preserve and strengthen the national independence and the territorial integrity of his country and to contribute to its defence in accordance with the law;

6. To work to the best of his abilities and competence, and to pay taxes imposed by law in the interest of the society;

7. To preserve and strengthen positive African cultural values in his relations with other members of the society, in the spirit of tolerance, dialogue and consultation and, in general, to contribute to the promotion of the moral well-being of society;

8. To contribute to the best of his abilities, at all times and at all levels, to the promotion and achievement of African unity.

### Part II: Measures of Safeguard

### Chapter I Establishment and Organization of the African Commission on Human and Peoples' Rights

*Article 30.* An African Commission on Human and Peoples' Rights, hereinafter called "the Commission", shall be established within the Organization of African Unity to promote human and peoples' rights and ensure their protection in Africa.

*Article 31.* 1. The Commission shall consist of eleven members chosen from amongst African personalities of the highest reputation, known for their high morality, integrity, impartiality and competence in matters of human and peoples' rights; particular consideration being given to persons having legal experience.

2. The members of the Commission shall serve in their personal capacity.

*Article 32.* The Commission shall not include more than one national of the same State.

*Article 33.* The members of the Commission shall be elected by secret ballot by the Assembly of Heads of State and Government, from a list of persons nominated by the States parties to the present Charter.

*Article 34.* Each State party to the present Charter may not nominate more than two candidates. The candidates must have the nationality of one of the States parties to the present Charter. When two candidates are nominated by a State, one of them may not be a national of that State.

*Article 35.* 1. The Secretary General of the Organization of African Unity shall invite States parties to the present Charter at least four months before the elections to nominate candidates;

2. The Secretary General of the Organization of African Unity shall make an alphabetical list of the persons thus nominated and communicate it to the Heads of State and Government at least one month before the elections.

*Article 36.* The members of the Commission shall be elected for a six year period and shall be eligible for re-election. However, the term of office of four of the members elected at the first election shall terminate after two years and the term of office of the three others, at the end of four years.

*Article 37.* Immediately after the first election, the Chairman of the Assembly of Heads of State and Government of the Organization of African Unity shall draw lots to decide the names of those members referred to in Article 36.

*Article 38.* After their election, the members of the Commission shall make a solemn declaration to discharge their duties impartially and faithfully.

*Article 39.* 1. In case of death or resignation of a member of the Commission, the Chairman of the Commission shall immediately inform the Secretary General of the Organization of African Unity, who shall declare the seat vacant from the date of death or from the date on which the resignation takes effect.

2. If, in the unanimous opinion of other members of the Commission, a member has stopped discharging his duties for any reason other than a temporary absence, the Chairman of the Commission shall inform the Secretary General of the Organization of African Unity, who shall then declare the seat vacant.

3. In each of the cases anticipated above, the Assembly of Heads of State and Government shall replace the member whose seat became vacant for the remaining period of his term unless the period is less than six months.

*Article 40.* Every member of the Commission shall be in office until the date his successor assumes office.

*Article 41.* The Secretary General of the Organization of African Unity shall appoint the Secretary of the Commission. He shall also provide the staff and services necessary for the effective discharge of the duties of the Commission. The Organization of African Unity shall bear the costs of the staff and services.

*Article 42.* 1. The Commission shall elect its Chairman and Vice Chairman for a two year period. They shall be eligible for re-election.

2. The Commission shall lay down its rules of procedure.

3. Seven members shall form a quorum.

4. In case of an equality of votes, the Chairman shall have a casting vote.

5. The Secretary General may attend the meetings of the Commission. He shall neither participate in deliberations nor shall he be entitled to vote. The Chairman of the Commission may, however, invite him to speak.

*Article 43.* In discharging their duties, members of the Commission shall enjoy diplomatic privileges and immunities provided for in the General Convention on the Privileges and Immunities of the Organization of African Unity.

*Article 44.* Provision shall be made for the emoluments and allowances of the members of the Commission in the Regular Budget of the Organization of African Unity.

## Chapter II Mandate of the Commission

*Article 45.* The functions of the Commission shall be:

1. To promote Human and Peoples' Rights and in particular:

   a) to collect documents, undertake studies and researches on African problems in the field of human and peoples' rights, organize seminars, symposia and conferences, disseminate information, encourage national and local institutions concerned with human and peoples' rights, and should the case arise, give its views or make recommendations to Governments.

   b) to formulate and lay down, principles and rules aimed at solving legal problems relating to human and peoples' rights and fundamental freedoms upon which African Governments may base their legislations.

   c) to co-operate with other African and international institutions concerned with the promotion and protection of human and peoples' rights.

2. Ensure the protection of human and peoples' rights under conditions laid down by the present Charter.

3. Interpret all the provisions of the present Charter at the request of a State party, an institution of the OAU or an African Organization recognized by the OAU.

4. Perform any other tasks which may be entrusted to it by the Assembly of Heads of State and Government.

## Chapter III Procedure of the Commission

*Article 46.* The Commission may resort to any appropriate method of investigation; it may hear from the Secretary General of the Organization of African Unity or any other person capable of enlightening it.

*Communication From States*

*Article 47.* If a State party to the present Charter has good reasons to believe that another State party to this Charter has violated the provisions of the Charter, it may draw, by written communication, the attention of that State to the matter. This communication shall also be addressed to the Secretary General of the OAU and to the Chairman of the Commission. Within three months of the receipt of the communication, the State to which the communication is addressed shall give the enquiring State, written explanation or statement elucidating the matter. This should include as much as possible relevant information relating to the laws and rules of procedure applied and applicable, and the redress already given or course of action available.

*Article 48.* If within three months from the date on which the original communication is received by the State to which it is addressed, the issue is not settled to the satisfaction of the two States involved through bilateral negotiation or by any other peaceful procedure, either State shall have the right to submit the matter to the Commission through the Chairman and shall notify the other States involved.

*Article 49.* Notwithstanding the provisions of Article 47, if a State party to the present Charter considers that another State party has violated the provisions of the Charter, it may refer the matter directly to the Commission by addressing a communication to the Chairman, to the Secretary General

of the Organization of African Unity and the State concerned.

*Article 50.* The Commission can only deal with a matter submitted to it after making sure that all local remedies, if they exist, have been exhausted, unless it is obvious to the Commission that the procedure of achieving these remedies would be unduly prolonged.

*Article 51.* 1. The Commission may ask the States concerned to provide it with all relevant information.

2. When the Commission is considering the matter, States concerned may be represented before it and submit written or oral representation.

*Article 52.* After having obtained from the States concerned and from other sources all the information it deems necessary and after having tried all appropriate means to reach an amicable solution based on the respect of Human and Peoples' Rights, the Commission shall prepare, within a reasonable period of time from the notification referred to in Article 48, a report stating the facts and its findings. This report shall be sent to the States concerned and communicated to the Assembly of Heads of States and Government.

*Article 53.* While transmitting its report, the Commission may make to the Assembly of Heads of State and Government such recommendations as it deems useful.

*Article 54.* The Commission shall submit to each ordinary Session of the Assembly of Heads of State and Government a report on its activities.

*Other Communications*

*Article 55.* 1. Before each Session, the Secretary of the Commission shall make a list of the communications other than those of States parties to the present Charter and transmit them to the members of the Commission, who shall indicate which communications should be considered by the Commission.

2. A communication shall be considered by the Commission if a simple majority of its members so decide.

*Article 56.* Communications relating to human and peoples' rights referred to in Article 55 received by the Commission, shall be considered if they:

1. indicate their authors even if the latter request anonymity;

2. are compatible with the Charter of the Organization of African Unity or with the present Charter;

3. are not written in disparaging or insulting language directed against the State concerned and its institutions or to the Organization of African Unity;

4. are not based exclusively on news discriminated through the mass media;

5. are sent after exhausting local remedies, if any, unless it is obvious that this procedure is unduly prolonged;

6. are submitted within a reasonable period from the time local remedies are exhausted or from the date the Commission is seized of the matter; and

7. do not deal with cases which have been settled by these States involved in accordance with the principles of the Charter of the United Nations, or the Charter of the Organization of African Unity or the provisions of the present Charter.

*Article 57.* Prior to any substantive consideration, all communications shall be brought to the knowledge of the State concerned by the Chairman of the Commission.

*Article 58.* 1. When it appears after deliberations of the Commission that one or more communications apparently relate to special cases which reveal the existence of a series of serious or massive violations of human and peoples' rights, the Commission shall draw the attention of the Assembly of Heads of State and Government to these special cases.

2. The Assembly of Heads of State and Government may then request the Commission to undertake an in-depth study of these cases and make a factual report, accompanied by its findings and recommendations.

3. A case of emergency duly noticed by the Commission shall be submitted by the latter to the Chairman of the Assembly of Heads of State and Government who may request an in-depth study.

*Article 59.* 1. All measures taken within the provisions of the present Chapter shall remain confidential until such a time as the Assembly of Heads of State and Government shall otherwise decide.

2. However, the report shall be published by the Chairman of the Commission upon the decision of the Assembly of Heads of State and Government.

3. The report on the activities of the Commission shall be published by its Chairman after it has been considered by the Assembly of Heads of State and Government.

### Chapter IV Applicable Principles

*Article 60.* The Commission shall draw inspiration from international law on human and peoples' rights, particularly from the provisions of various African instruments on human and peoples' rights, the Charter of the United Nations, the Charter of the Organization of African Unity, the Universal Declaration of Human Rights, other instruments adopted by the United Nations and by African countries in the field of human and peoples' rights as well as from the provisions of various instruments adopted within the Specialized Agencies of the United Nations of which the parties to the present Charter are members.

*Article 61.* The Commission shall also take into consideration, as subsidiary measures to determine the principles of law, other general or special international conventions, laying down rules expressly recognized by member states of the Organization of African Unity, African practices consistent with international norms on human and peoples' rights, customs generally accepted as law, general principles of law recognized by African states as well as legal precedents and doctrine.

*Article 62.* Each state party shall undertake to submit every two years, from the date the present Charter comes into force, a report on the legislative or other measures taken with a view to giving effect to the rights and freedoms recognized and guaranteed by the present Charter.

*Article 63.* 1. The present Charter shall be open to signature, ratification or adherence of the member states of the Organization of African Unity.

2. The instruments of ratification or adherence to the present Charter shall be deposited with the Secretary General of the Organization of African Unity.

3. The present Charter shall come into force three months after the reception by the Secretary General of the instruments of ratification or adherence of a simple majority of the member states of the Organization of African Unity.

### Part III: General Provisions

*Article 64.* 1. After the coming into force of the present Charter, members of the Commission shall be elected in accordance with the relevant Articles of the present Charter.

2. The Secretary General of the Organization of African Unity shall convene the first meeting of the Commission at the Headquarters of the Organization within three months of the constitution of the Commission. Thereafter, the Commission shall be convened by its Chairman whenever necessary but at least once a year.

*Article 65.* For each of the States that will ratify or adhere to the present Charter after its coming into force, the Charter shall take effect three months after the date of the deposit by that State of its instrument of ratification or adherence.

*Article 66.* Special protocols or agreements may, if necessary, supplement the provisions of the present Charter.

*Article 67.* The Secretary General of the Organization of African Unity shall inform member states of the Organization of the deposit of each instrument of ratification or adherence.

*Article 68.* The present Charter may be amended if a State party makes a written request to that effect to the Secretary General of the Organization of African Unity. The Assembly of Heads of State and Government may only consider the draft amendment after all the States parties have been duly informed of it and the Commission has given its opinion on it at the request of the sponsoring State. The amendment shall be approved by a simple majority of the States parties. It shall come into force for each State which has accepted it in accordance with its constitutional procedure three months after the Secretary General has received notice of the acceptance.

***NATIONAL IMPLEMENTATION OF THE CHARTER IN THE INTERNAL LEGAL SYSTEMS OF AFRICA.*** A seminar on national implementation of the Charter, organized by the African Commission on Human and Peoples' Rights in cooperation with the Raoul Wallenberg Institute of the University of Lund, Sweden, was convened at Banjul, Gambia, 26–30 October 1992. The conclusions and recommendations of the seminar, as summarized by Mr. Ibrahim Ali Badawi El-Sheikh, Chairman of the Commission, and made available to the Preparatory Committee of the World Conference on Human Rights (1993) (UN Doc. A/CONF. 157/PC/62/Add. 8) are as follows:

1. The Seminar notes the following in relation to the status of the Charter:

(a) States party to the African Charter shall accord the Charter a definitive legal status in their national legal systems.

(b) In the event of a conflict involving a provision of the Charter and national legislation, the Charter provision shall prevail.

(c) The African Charter is a treaty within the definition of the Vienna Convention on the Law of Treaties. It enshrines the fundamental principle pact sunt servanda and an obligation is imposed on parties thereto not to invoke their municipal laws as an excuse for failure to perform an obligation imposed by the Charter.

(d) The provisions of the African Charter as are in force shall not be repealed, amended or suspended save in accordance with general principles of international law.

The Seminar considers that:

2. The following points should be observed in relation to the incorporation of the African Charter into internal legal systems:

(a) The automatic incorporation of the African Charter into the internal legal system of the parties thereto could be advantageous to the States Parties to the Charter in the sense of sparing them the difficulties of reviewing their present legislation so as to conform to the African charter.

(b) Whatever means a State Party to the African Charter may choose in order to make the Charter applicable in its internal legal system, the provisions of the Charter are nevertheless to be fully observed in accordance with the requirements of international law.

3. The Seminar believes that human rights must primarily be secured within the national legal system of each State Party to the Charter. In this regard, it is vital that:

(a) The Rule of Law is strictly respected in all activities of the State and all branches of public administration.

(b) The judiciary is guaranteed full independence. In this regard, States Party to the Charter are requested to facilitate the establishment and improvement of appropriate national institutions for the promotion and protection of the rights and freedoms guaranteed by the Charter in accordance with Article 26 of the Charter.

(c) Access to courts of law is secured to all individuals, regardless of their financial means.

4. The Seminar is of the view that:

(a) The African Charter should be interpreted in the light of the impressive body of jurisprudence which has developed on similar provisions in other universal and regional instruments on human rights and related matters. Such instruments could be of practical relevance and value to judges and counsel and should as often as possible be referred to.

(b) It is within the proper nature of the judicial process and well established judicial functions for national courts to have regard to international obligations which a country undertakes whether or not they have been incorporated into domestic law–for the purpose of removing ambiguity or uncertainty from national constitutions and laws written or unwritten.

(c) Judges and lawyers have a special contribution to make in administration of justice in fostering universal respect for fundamental rights and freedoms.

(d) It is particularly important to ensure that all persons including judges, lawyers, litigants and others are made aware of applicable human rights norms wherever they may be stated and particularly those in the Charter. In this respect, the Seminar underlines the importance of Article 25 of the African Charter which obligates States party to the Charter to promote and ensure through teaching, education and publication, respect for the rights and freedoms expressed in the Charter.

5. The Seminar welcomes the fact that 47 African States have ratified the Charter. It is hoped that such ratification is followed by compliance by the States of their obligation to submit reports under Article 62 of the Charter on the measures taken with a view to implementing the African Charter.

6. The Seminar notes with interest the activities undertaken so far by the African Commission on Human and Peoples' Rights and expresses the views that:

(a) It is important that a State's report submitted to the African Commission should indicate:

(i) Whether the rights, fundamental freedoms and duties expressed in the Charter are protected by the Constitution of that State or by a "Bill of Rights," and whether there are provisions for derogations and in what circumstances;

(ii) Whether the provisions of the Charter can be invoked before the courts, other tribunals or administrative authorities for direct implementation or application, or whether they have to be incorporated into internal laws or regulations before they are enforceable by the authorities;

(iii) What judicial, administrative or other authorities have jurisdiction affecting human rights;

(iv) What remedies are available to an individual whose rights are violated;

(v) Non-legislative measures adopted to implement the Charter;

(vi) Difficulties encountered in the process of implementing the Charter.

(b) It would facilitate the work of the Commission and that of the OAU Member States if the States designate high-ranking officials to act as focal points in the relations between the Commission and the States. Such focal points would facilitate the follow-up on the Commission's recommendations and contact between States and the Commission.

(c) It is noted that the lack of legal aid services in Africa precludes the majority of the African population from asserting their human rights. It is recommended that the question of legal aid and recourse procedures should be accorded greater attention in the work of the African Commission and that States and NGOs should take the initiative to promote the establishment of legal aid services.

(d) The Commission should find ways to provide advisory services upon request to States, in relation to the incorporation of the African Charter in their internal legal systems, preparation of their reports and other matters relating to the implementation of the Charter.

(e) The resources and time allocated for the work of the Commission are inadequate. In this regard, the Assembly of Heads of State and Government of the OAU is requested to provide the Commission with full political, financial and administrative support with a view to enabling the Commission to properly carry out its mandate in accordance with the Charter, which is vital for ensuring promotion of respect and protection of the rights expressed in the Charter and thus securing peace, stability and development in Africa.

7. The Seminar considers it advisable that the OAU take initiatives to revise the Charter, including the possibility of creating an African Human Rights Court. Such revision should be carried out by the adoption of additional protocols under Article 66 of the Charter. The Seminar looks upon such a revision as a move towards strengthening the work of the Commission as well as a response to developments occurring since the adoption of the Charter.

8. The Seminar presumes that, after adopting the African Charter and creating an independent Commission, the Assembly of the Heads of State and Government of the OAU shall see to it that the Commission's recommendations are responded to, that they are published, and that just satisfaction is afforded to injured parties.

9. The Seminar underlines the importance of the African Commission's taking advantage, as it shall consider appropriate, of relevant universal and regional mechanisms established to promote and protect human rights.

10. The Seminar, aware of the links existing between human rights and international humanitarian law, wishes to underscore the need to disseminate and implement the provisions of international humanitarian law applicable in time of armed conflicts.

11. The Seminar calls upon all contracting parties to instruments relating to international humanitarian law to adopt adequate measures at the national level to ensure the implementation of the provisions of international humani-

tarian law. Such measures are necessary for the protection of the human being in time of armed conflicts.

*SEE ALSO* American Convention on Human Rights and Protocols; American Declaration of the Rights and Duties of Man; European Convention on Human Rights and Protocols; International Covenant on Economic, Social and Cultural Rights; Universal Declaration of Human Rights.

**BIBLIOGRAPHY.** *The African Charter and Human Rights.* Geneva: UN Center for Human Rights, 1990, pub. HR/PUB/90/1. Intergovernment document, in English.

Amnesty International. *A Guide to the African Charter on Human and Peoples' Rights.* London: 1991. NGO document, in English, French, Portuguese, and Arabic.

Amoah, Philip. "The African Charter on Human and Peoples' Rights: An Effective Weapon for Human Rights?" *Revue africaine de droit international et comparé* 4, no. 1 (1992): 226–240. Scholarly article, in English.

Carver, Richard. "Called to Account: How African Governments Investigate Human Rights Violations," *African Affairs* 89, no. 356 (July 1990): 391–415. Scholarly article, in English.

Gaer, Felice D. "First Fruits: Reporting by States under the African Charter on Human and Peoples' Rights," *Netherlands Quarterly of Human Rights* 10, no. 1 (1992): 29–42. Scholarly article, in English.

Gye-Wado, Onje. "The Rule of Admissibility under the African Charter on Human and Peoples' Rights," *African Journal of International and Comparative Law* 3 (1991): 742–755. Scholarly article, in English.

Kodjo, Edem. "The African Charter on Human and Peoples' Rights," *Human Rights Law Journal* 11, no. 3–4 (1990): 271–283. Scholarly article, in English.

Mahmud, Sakah Saidu. "The State and Human Rights in Africa in the 1990s: Perspectives and Prospects," *Human Rights Quarterly* 15, no. 3 (August 1993): 485–498. Scholarly article, in English.

Ouguergouz, Fatsah. *La Charte africaine des droits de l'homme et des peuples: Une approche juridique des droits de l'homme entre tradition et modernité* (The African Charter of Human and Peoples' Rights: A Legal Approach to Human Rights between Tradition and Modernity). Geneva, Switzerland: Institut Universitaire de Hautes Etudes Internationales, 1993. Scholarly monograph, in French; bibliography, pp. 395–420.

Peter, Chris Maina. *Human Rights in Africa: A Comparative Study of the African Human and People's Rights Charter and the New Tanzanian Bill of Rights.* New York: Greenwood Press for the Consortium on Human Rights Development, 1990. Scholarly monograph, in English.

Theodoropoulos, Christos, ed. *Human Rights in Europe and in Africa: A Comparative Analysis.* Athens, Greece: Hellenic University Press, 1992. Scholarly monograph, in English and Greek.

## AFRICAN COMMISSION ON HUMAN AND PEOPLES' RIGHTS.

The Commission was established in accordance with Part II, chap. I, article 30 of the African Charter on Human and Peoples' Rights (Banjul Charter), which provides that the purpose of the Commission is "to promote human and peoples' rights and ensure their protection in Africa." The functions of the Commission, as set out in article 45, are:

1. To promote Human and Peoples' Rights and in particular:

a) to collect documents, undertake studies and researches on African problems in the field of human and peoples' rights, organize seminars, symposia and conferences, disseminate information, encourage national and local institutions concerned with human and peoples' rights, and, should the case arise, give its views or make recommendations to Governments;

b) to formulate and lay down principles and rules aimed at solving legal problems relating to human and peoples' rights and fundamental freedoms upon which African Governments may base their legislations;

c) co-operate with other African and international institutions concerned with the promotion and protection of human and peoples' rights;

2. ensure the protection of human and peoples' rights under conditions laid down by the present Charter;

3. interpret all the provisions of the present Charter at the request of a State Party, an institution of the OAU or an African organization recognized by the OAU;

4. perform any other tasks which may be entrusted to it by the Assembly of Heads of State and Government.

***CONSIDERATION OF COMMUNICATIONS FROM STATES MEMBERS.*** Under articles 47–49, a State party which believes that another State party has violated a provision of the charter may submit a written communication to that effect either to the State concerned or directly to the Commission; in either case, the State concerned, the Chairman of the Commission and the Secretary-General of the OAU are notified. If the issue is not settled within three months to the satisfaction of the two States involved, either State may submit it to the Commission. After ascertaining that all domestic remedies have been exhausted, the Commission examines such submissions with a view to securing a friendly settlement. If it fails to do so, it submits a report to the States concerned and to the OAU Assembly of Heads of State and Government stating the facts, its findings, and its recommendations if any.

***CONSIDERATION OF OTHER COMMUNICATIONS.*** Under articles 55–59 of the charter, the Commission receives before each session a list of communications other than those from States parties and decides which of them to consider. Such communications are considered if a simple majority of members of the Commission decide to do so. Any communication to be considered is first brought to the knowledge of the State concerned. The procedure then followed is set out in articles 58 and 59 as follows:

*Article 58.* 1. When it appears after deliberations of the Commission that one or more communications apparently relate to special cases which reveal the existence of a series of serious or massive violations of human and peoples' rights, the Commission shall draw the attention of the Assembly of Heads of State and Government to these special cases.

2. The Assembly of Heads of State and Government may then request the Commission to undertake an in-depth study of these cases and make a factual report, accompanied by its findings and recommendations.

3. A case of emergency duly noticed by the Commission shall be submitted by the latter to the Chairman of the Assembly of Heads of State and Government, who may request an in-depth study;

*Article 59.* 1. All measures taken within the provisions of the present Chapter shall remain confidential until such a time as the Assembly of Heads of State and Government shall otherwise decide.

2. However, the report shall be published by the Chairman of the Commission upon the decision of the Assembly of Heads of State and Government.

3. The report on the activities of the Commission shall be published by its Chairman after it has been considered by the Assembly of Heads of State and Government.

In addition to the reports mentioned above, the Commission submits a report on its activities to each ordinary session of the Assembly of Heads of State and Government, in accordance with article 54 of the charter.

Under articles 31–35 of the charter, the Commission consists of 11 members "chosen from among African personalities of the highest reputation, known for their high morality, integrity, impartiality and competence in matters of human and peoples' rights, particular consideration being given to persons having legal experience." The members of the Commission serve in their personal capacity (they are in no way representatives of a State and cannot designate anyone else to act for them). They are elected by secret ballot by the Assembly of Heads of State and Government from a list of persons nominated by the States parties to the charter.

Under article 64 of the charter, the Commission is convened by its chairman whenever necessary, but at least once a year.

**BIBLIOGRAPHY.** African Commission on Human and Peoples' Rights. "2nd Activity Report of the African Commission on Human and Peoples' Rights adopted on 14 June 1989" and "3rd Activity Report of the Africa Commission on Human and Peoples' Rights, adopted on 28 April 1990," *Human Rights Law Journal* 11, no. 3–4 (1990): 390–429 & 432–440. Intergovernmental report, in English.

Benedek, Wolfgang. "The African Charter and Commission on Human and Peoples' Right: How to Make it More Effective," *Netherlands Quarterly of Human Rights* 11, no. 1 (1993): 25–40. Scholarly article, in English; bibliography, pp. 39–40.

International Commission of Jurists (ICJ). *How to Address a Communication to the African Commission on Human and Peoples' Rights.* Geneva, Switzerland: 1992. NGO document, in English, French, and Arabic.

Kufuor, Kofi Otneng. "Safeguarding Human Rights: A Critique of the African Commission on Human and Peoples' Rights," *Afrique et développement* 18, no. 2 (1993): 65–77. Scholarly article, in English; bibliography, p. 77.

Omozurike, U. O. "The African Commission on Human and Peoples' Rights: An Introduction," *Review of the African Commission on Human and Peoples' Rights* 1 (1991): 5–15. Scholarly article, in English.

Welch, Claude E. "The African Commission on Human and Peoples' Rights: A Five-Year Report and Assessment," *Human Rights Quarterly* 14, no. 1 (1992): 43–61. Report, in English.

———. "The Organization of African Unity and the Promotion of Human Rights," *Journal of Modern African Studies* 29, no. 4 (1991): 535–555. Scholarly article, in English.

**AFRICAN NATIONAL CONGRESS OF SOUTH AFRICA.** A former liberation movement recognized by the Organization of African Unity and invited by the UN General Assembly to participate in the work of UN bodies as an observer, the ANC is the largest and most powerful of several anti-apartheid organizations that represented the bulk of South Africa's 68% black majority. Founded in 1912 to work for improvement in race relations in South Africa, the ANC in 1944 established its Youth League directed by three young men, Nelson Mandela, Walter Sisulu, and Oliver Tambo. By 1949, when the Africaner-dominated National Party came into power and introduced apartheid into the country's legal system, these three controlled the ANC. In 1952, as strict apartheid was extended into nearly every phase of daily life, Mandela, Sisulu, and Tambo organized a defiance campaign of civil disobedience. Despite the arrest of 8,500 of their supporters, they intensified the struggle; and in 1955, the ANC issued its "Freedom Charter," calling for a non-racial democratic organization of society, as follows:

### Preamble

We, the people of South Africa, declare for all our country and the world to know:

That South Africa belongs to all who live in it, black and white, and that no government can justly claim authority unless it is based on the will of the people;

That our people have been robbed of their birthright to land, liberty and peace by a form of government founded on injustice and inequality;

That our country will never be prosperous or free until all our people live in brotherhood, enjoying equal rights and opportunities;

That only a democratic state, based on the will of the people can secure to all their birthright without distinction of colour, race, sex, or belief;

And therefore, we, the people of South Africa, black and white together—equals, countrymen and brothers—adopt this Freedom Charter. And we pledge ourselves to strive together, sparing nothing of our strength and courage, until the democratic changes here set out have been won.

## The People Shall Govern!

Every man and woman shall have the right to vote for and stand as a candidate for all bodies which make laws.

All the people shall be entitled to take part in administration of the country.

The rights of the people shall be the same regardless of race, colour or sex.

All bodies of minority rule, advisory boards, councils and authorities shall be replaced by democratic organs of self-government.

## All National Groups Shall Have Equal Rights!

There shall be equal status in the bodies of state, in the courts and in the schools for all national groups and races;

All national groups shall be protected by law against insults to their race and national pride;

All people shall have equal rights to use their own language and to develop their own folk culture and customs;

The preaching and practice of national, race, or colour discrimination and contempt shall be a punishable crime;

All apartheid laws and practices shall be set aside.

## The People Shall Share in the Country's Wealth!

The national wealth of our country, the heritage of all South Africans, shall be restored to the people;

The mineral wealth beneath the soil, the banks and monopoly industry shall be transferred to the ownership of the people as a whole;

All other industries and trade shall be controlled to assist the well-being of the people;

All people shall have equal rights to trade where they choose, to manufacture and to enter all trades, crafts and professions.

## The Land Shall be Shared among Those Who Work It!

Restriction of land ownership on a racial basis shall be ended and all the land re-divided amongst those who work it, to banish famine and land hunger;

The state shall help the peasants with implements, seed, tractors and dams to save the soil and assist the tillers;

Freedom of movement shall be guaranteed to all who work on the land;

All shall have the right to occupy land wherever they choose;

People shall not be robbed of their cattle, and forced labour and farm prisons shall be abolished.

## All Shall be Equal before the Law!

No one shall be imprisoned, deported or restricted without a fair trial;

No one shall be condemned by the order of any Government official;

The courts shall be representative of all the people;

Imprisonment shall be only for serious crimes against the people, and shall aim at re-education, not vengeance;

The police force and army shall be open to all on an equal basis and shall be the helpers and protectors of the people;

All laws which discriminate on grounds of race, colour or belief shall be repealed.

## All Shall Enjoy Equal Human Rights!

The law shall guarantee to all their right to speak, to organise, to meet together, to publish, to preach, to worship, and to educate their children;

The privacy of the house from police raids shall be protected by law;

All shall be free to travel without restriction from countryside to town, from province to province and from South Africa abroad;

Pass laws, permits and all other laws restricting these freedoms shall be abolished.

## There Shall be Work and Security!

All who work shall be free to form trade unions, to elect their officers and to make wage agreements with their employers;

The state shall recognise the right and duty of all to work, and to draw full unemployment benefits;

Men and women of all races shall receive equal pay for equal work;

There shall be a forty-hour working week, a national minimum wage, paid annual leave and sick leave for all workers and maternity leave on full pay for all working mothers;

Miners, domestic workers, farm workers and civil servants shall have the same rights as all others who work;

Child labour, compound labour, the tot system and contract labour shall be abolished.

## The Doors of Learning and of Culture Shall be Opened!

The government shall discover, develop and encourage national talent for the enhancement of our cultural life;

All the cultural treasures of mankind shall be open to all, by free exchange of books, ideas, and contact with other lands;

The aim of education shall be to teach the youth to love their people and their culture, to honour human brotherhood, liberty and peace;

Education shall be free, compulsory, universal and equal for all children;

Higher education and technical training shall be opened to all by means of state allowances and scholarships awarded on the basis of merit;

Adult illiteracy shall be ended by a mass state education plan;

Teachers shall have all the rights of other citizens;

The colour bar in cultural life, in sport and in education shall be abolished.

## There Shall be Houses, Security and Comfort!

All people shall have the right to live where they choose, to be decently housed, and to bring up their families in comfort and security;

Unused housing space is to be made available to the people;

Rent and prices shall be lowered, food plentiful and no one shall go hungry;

A preventive health scheme shall be run by the state;

Free medical care and hospitalisation shall be provided for all, with special care for mothers and young children;

Slums shall be demolished and new suburbs built where all have transport, roads, lighting, playing fields, creches and social centres;

The aged, the orphans, the disabled and the sick shall be cared for by the state;

Rest, leisure and recreation shall be the right of all;

Fenced locations and ghettos shall be abolished, and laws which break up families shall be repealed.

### There Shall be Peace and Friendship!

South Africa shall be a fully independent state, which respects the rights and sovereignty of all nations;

South Africa shall strive to maintain world peace and the settlement of all international disputes by negotiation—not war;

Peace and friendship amongst all our people shall be secured by upholding the equal rights, opportunities and status of all;

The people of the protectorates—Basutoland, Bechuanaland and Swaziland—shall be free to decide for themselves their own future;

The right of all the peoples of Africa to independence and self-government shall be recognised, and shall be the basis of close cooperation.

Let all who love their people and their country now say, as we say here:

"These Freedoms We Will Fight for, Side by Side, Throughout Our Lives, until We Have Won Our Liberty."

In 1959, some ANC members, advocating greater militance, formed the rival Pan-Africanist Congress (PAC). Following the Sharpeville massacre of 21 March 1960—in which South African police killed 69 unarmed blacks—a state of emergency was declared by the government, and both the ANC and PAC were outlawed. Nevertheless, both launched guerilla movements in 1961. Nelson Mandela, who organized and commanded the ANC's new military wing, known as Umkonto we Sizwe (Spear of the People), was arrested in 1962 after returning from a trip abroad and charged with leaving the country illegally. In November of that year, he was convicted and sentenced to five years in prison.

While Mandela was in prison, the police raided the ANC's underground headquarters in Rivonia, outside Johannesburg, and seized documents setting out plans for the proposed guerilla campaign. Accused of sabotage and conspiracy to overthrow the government, Mandela and eight co-defendants were convicted and sentenced to life imprisonment. Mandela spent the next 18 years in notorious Robben Island Prison, although the UN Security Council issued a call for his release in June 1980.

In 1985, South African President P. W. Botha offered to free Mandela if he would renounce violence. Mandela responded that he would not do so before the government took the initiative in dismantling apartheid and granting full political rights to black South Africans.

By 1986, a new wave of black unrest had swept over the country and had become so violent that the gov-

ernment declared a nationwide state of emergency. However, by 1989, sanctions imposed by individual governments, and by the international community, began to take effect. In August 1989, Botha was replaced as president by F. W. de Klerk, a leader of the governing National Party who realized that white and black South Africans would have to share a single country, which he called "a new South Africa." Before the end of the year, President de Klerk had freed Mandela's colleagues and had conferred with Mandela at the presidential office in Cape Town.

On 2 February 1990, both the African National Congress and the Pan-Africanist Congress were legalized, and the government announced that those who had been imprisoned merely for belonging to those groups, or for other purely political reasons, would be released. At the same time, it put an end to the state of emergency in all but a small area of the country.

Nine days later, after 27 years in prison, Nelson Mandela was released and immediately began discussions, aimed at putting an end to apartheid, with President de Klerk. Visiting ANC headquarters-in-exile in Lusaka, Zambia, Mandela was designated as the organization's deputy president (President Oliver Tambo, seriously ill, was confined to a hospital in Sweden at the time), and discussed the ANC's approach to its first formal talks with government officials.

These talks, aimed at clearing the way for substantive future negotiations on ending white minority rule and abolishing the apartheid system, were held at Cape Town from 2 to 4 May 1990. When they concluded, the following joint communique was issued:

The government and the ANC agree on a common commitment toward the resolution of the existing climate of violence and intimidation from whatever quarter as well as a commitment to stability and to a peaceful process of negotiations. Flowing from this commitment, the following was agreed upon:

1. The establishment of a working group to make recommendations on a definition of political offenses in the South African situation; to discuss, in this regard, time scales; and to advise on norms and mechanisms for dealing with the release of political prisoners and the granting of immunity in respect of political offenses to those inside and outside South Africa. All persons who may be affected will be considered.

The working group will bear in mind experiences in Namibia and elsewhere. The working group will aim to complete its work before 21 May 1990. It is understood that the South African government, in its discretion, may consult other political parties and movements and other relevant bodies. The proceedings of the working group will be confidential.

In the meantime the following offenses will receive attention immediately: (a) The leaving of the country without a valid travel document. (b) Any offenses related merely to organizations which were previously prohibited.

2. In addition to the arrangements mentioned in Para-

25

graph 1, temporary immunity from prosecution for political offenses committed before today will be considered on an urgent basis for members of the National Executive Committee and selected other members of the ANC from outside the country, to enable them to return and help with the establishment and management of political activities, to assist in bringing violence to an end and to take part in peaceful political negotiations.

3. The government undertakes to review existing security legislation to bring it into line with the new dynamic situation developing in South Africa in order to insure normal and free political activities.

4. The government reiterates its commitment to work toward the lifting of the state of emergency. In this context the ANC will exert itself to fulfill the objectives contained in the preamble.

5. Efficient channels of communication between the government and the ANC will be established in order to curb violence and intimidation from whatever quarter immediately.

The government and ANC agree that the objectives contained in this minute should be achieved as early as possible.

On 6 May 1990, Nelson Mandela and other ANC leaders briefed the heads of South Africa's black tribal "homelands" on the outcome of the Cape Town talks and sought to enlist them as allies. Chief Mangosuthu Gatsha Buthelezi of KwaZulu, whose Inkatha followers were at the time engaged in pitched battles with ANC supporters in Natal Province, was conspicuously absent. The ANC's problems with Inkatha continued throughout the next four years, resulting in bloodshed between warring factions.

In July 1991, President de Klerk and ANC President Mandela announced, while on a joint visit to Washington, D.C., that a decision had been made in Johannesburg, with the agreement of a majority of concerned parties (the most notable dissenting parties being the black Inkatha Freedom Party and the white Conservative Party), that South Africa's first election open to black voters would be held on 27 April 1994. Mandela immediately opened an international drive to raise funds to enable the ANC to participate in the political process (up to that time, financial aid had been provided by the Swedish government).

In November 1993, the leaders of the ANC joined with representatives of 20 other South African parties in approving a new Constitution, to take effect immediately after the first universal elections. Aimed at establishing a government of national unity, the new Constitution guarantees fundamental rights to all citizens of South Africa, including freedom of speech, movement, religion and political activity, and fair trials. It also prohibits discrimination based on race, gender, sexual orientation, physical disability or age; and prohibits torture and forced labor.

In welcoming the new Constitution, Mandela said, "We have reached the end of an era. . . . Millions who were not allowed to vote will do so now. I, too, for the first time in my life, will vote."

Nelson Mandela was elected South Africa's first black president in the April 1994 elections. He and F. W. de Klerk were jointly awarded the 1993 Nobel Peace Prize.

**SEE ALSO** *Apartheid; Mandela, Nelson; South Africa.*

**AFRO-ASIAN PEOPLES' SOLIDARITY ORGANIZATION.** An international non-governmental organization in consultative status (Category II) with the UN Economic and Social Council and UNESCO, and observer status with the Non-Aligned Movement, AAPSO is composed of affiliated organizations located in approximately 67 countries of Africa, Asia, Europe, and Latin and North America.

Founded in Egypt in 1957, and first known as the Organization for Afro-Asian Peoples' Solidarity, AAPSO endeavors to unite, coordinate and strengthen the struggle of the African and Asian people against imperialism and colonialism, to accelerate the independence of those peoples and to ensure their economic, social, and cultural development. It is mandated by its constitution "to safeguard, respect and uphold human rights and to support the struggle for democracy." It supports national liberation movements and cooperates with progressive and democratic organizations as part of the worldwide, anti-imperialist front of peoples.

AAPSO publishes *Development and Socio-Economic Progress* (quarterly); the monthly political magazine *Solidarity*; and *Afro-Asian Publications,* a series on issues of topical interest. All books and pamphlets are published in English, French, and Arabic.

Afro-Asian Peoples' Solidarity Organization. Address: 89 Abdel Aziz al-Saoud Street, Manial, Cairo, Egypt. Telephone: (20-2) 362-2946 or 363-6081. Fax: (20-2) 363-7361. Cable: AFROASIATICO Cairo. Telex: 92627 AAPSO UN. Secretary-General: Nouri Abdul Razzak.

**AGE OF CONSENT.** The age at which persons are legally permitted to perform acts and undertake responsibilities prohibited to them earlier in life. Internationally, the Convention on Consent to Marriage, Minimum Age for Marriage and Registration of Marriages, which is accepted as legally binding by States which have ratified or acceded to it, provides (in article 2) that:

States parties to the present Convention shall take legislative action to specify a minimum age for marriage. No marriage shall be legally entered into by any person under this age, except where a competent authority has granted a dispensation as to age, for serious reasons, in the interest of the intending spouses.

The Recommendation on Consent to Marriage, Minimum Age for Marriage and Registration of Marriages, which applies to all States, proposes a minimum age of 15 in Principle II, which provides that:

Member States shall take legislative action to specify a minimum age for marriage, which in any case shall not be less than fifteen years of age; no marriage shall be legally entered into by any person under this age, except where a competent authority has granted a dispensation as to age, for serious reasons, in the interest of the intending spouses.

*SEE ALSO* *Marriage and the Family.*

**AGGRESSION.** The League of Nations attempted to define the term "aggression" in 1923 and 1924 but was unable to reach an agreement. The UN General Assembly assumed the task in 1950 and was able to complete it only in 1974, after numerous texts had been considered by the **INTERNATIONAL LAW COMMISSION,** the Sixth (Legal) Committee of the Assembly, and three special committees established by the Assembly in 1953, 1956, and 1967, respectively.

The definition was finalized by the third of the special committees and was adopted by the Assembly on 14 December 1974 (resolution 3314 [XXIX]). Its acceptance represented a resolution of many difficulties which had divided member States up to that time, particularly regarding the meanings of the right to self-determination, freedom, and independence.

The text of the "Definition of Aggression," annexed to resolution 3314 (XXIX), is as follows:

The General Assembly,

Basing itself on the fact that one of the fundamental purposes of the United Nations is to maintain international peace and security and to take effective collective measures for the prevention and removal of threats to the peace, and for the suppression of acts of aggression or other breaches of the peace,

Recalling that the Security Council, in accordance with Article 39 of the Charter of the United Nations, shall determine the existence of any threat to the peace, breach of the peace or act of aggression and shall make recommendations, or decide what measures shall be taken in accordance with Articles 41 and 42, to maintain or restore international peace and security,

Recalling also the duty of States under the Charter to settle their international disputes by peaceful means in order not to endanger international peace, security and justice,

Bearing in mind that nothing in this Definition shall be interpreted as in any way affecting the scope of the provisions of the Charter with respect to the functions and powers of the organs of the United Nations,

Considering also that, since aggression is the most serious and dangerous form of the illegal use of force, being fraught, in the conditions created by the existence of all types of weapons of mass destruction, with the possible threat of a world conflict and all its catastrophic consequences, aggression should be defined at the present stage,

Reaffirming the duty of States not to use armed force to deprive peoples of their right to self-determination, freedom and independence, or to disrupt territorial integrity,

Reaffirming also that the territory of a State shall not be violated by being the object, even temporarily, of military occupation or of other measures of force taken by another State in contravention of the Charter, and that it shall not be the object of acquisition by another State resulting from such measures or the threat thereof,

Reaffirming also the provisions of the Declaration of Principles of International Law concerning Friendly Relations and Co-operation among States in accordance with the Charter of the United Nations,

Convinced that the adoption of a definition of aggression ought to have the effect of deterring a potential aggressor, would simplify the determination of acts of aggression and the implementation of measures to suppress them and would also facilitate the protection of the rights and lawful interests of, and the rendering of assistance to, the victim,

Believing that, although the question whether an act of aggression has been committed must be considered in the light of all the circumstances of each particular case, it is nevertheless desirable to formulate basic principles as guidance for such determination,

Adopts the following Definition of Aggression:

*Article 1.* Aggression is the use of armed force by a State against the sovereignty, territorial integrity or political independence of another State, or in any other manner inconsistent with the Charter of the United Nations, as set out in this Definition.

Explanatory note: In this Definition the term "State":

(a) Is used without prejudice to questions of recognition or to whether a State is a member of the United Nations;

(b) Includes the concept of a "group of States" where appropriate.

*Article 2.* The first use of armed force by a State in contravention of the Charter shall constitute prima facie evidence of an act of aggression although the Security Council may, in conformity with the Charter, conclude that a determination that an act of aggression has been committed would not be justified in the light of other relevant circumstances, including the fact that the acts concerned or their consequences are not of sufficient gravity.

*Article 3.* Any of the following acts, regardless of a declaration of war, shall, subject to and in accordance with the provisions of article 2, qualify as an act of aggression:

(a) The invasion or attack by the armed forces of a State of the territory of another State, or any military occupation, however temporary, resulting from such invasion or attack, or any annexation by the use of force of the territory of another State or part thereof;

(b) Bombardment by the armed forces of a State against the territory of another State or the use of any weapons by a State against the territory of another State;

(c) The blockade of the ports or coasts of a State by the armed forces of another State;

(d) An attack by the armed forces of a State on the land, sea or air forces, or marine and air fleets of another State;

(e) The use of armed forces of one State which are within the territory of another State with the agreement of the receiving State, in contravention of the conditions provided for in the agreement or any extension of their presence in such territory beyond the termination of the agreement;

(f) The action of a State in allowing its territory, which it has placed at the disposal of another State, to be used by that other State for perpetrating an act of aggression against a third State;

(g) The sending by or on behalf of a State of armed bands, groups, irregulars or mercenaries, which carry out acts of armed force against another State of such gravity as to amount to the acts listed above, or its substantial involvement therein.

*Article 4.* The acts enumerated above are not exhaustive and the Security Council may determine that other acts constitute aggression under the provisions of the Charter.

*Article 5.* 1. No consideration of whatever nature, whether political, economic, military or otherwise, may serve as a justification for aggression.

2. A war of aggression is a crime against international peace. Aggression gives rise to international responsibility.

3. No territorial acquisition or special advantage resulting from aggression is or shall be recognized as lawful.

*Article 6.* Nothing in this Definition shall be construed as in any way enlarging or diminishing the scope of the Charter, including its provisions concerning cases in which the use of force is lawful.

*Article 7.* Nothing in this Definition, and in particular article 3, could in any way prejudice the right to self- determination, freedom and independence, as derived from the Charter, of peoples forcibly deprived of that right and referred to in the Declaration on Principles of International Law concerning Friendly Relations and Co-operation among States in accordance with the Charter of the United Nations, particularly peoples under colonial and racist régimes or other forms of alien domination; nor the right of these peoples to struggle to that end and to seek and receive support, in accordance with the principles of the Charter and in conformity with the above-mentioned Declaration.

*Article 8.* In their interpretation and application the above provisions are interrelated and each provision should be construed in the context of the other provisions.

**BIBLIOGRAPHY.** Bresheeth, Haim, and Nira Yuval-Davis, eds. *The Gulf War and the New World Order.* London: Zed Books, 1991. Monograph, in English.

Fisler, Lori, and David J. Scheffer, eds. *Law and Force in the New International Order.* Boulder, CO, USA: Westview Press for the American Society of International Law, 1991. Scholarly collection of articles, in English.

Mapel, David R. "Military Intervention and Rights," *Millenium—Journal of International Studies* 20, no. 1 (1991): 41–55. Scholarly article, in English.

Paust, Jordan J. "Aggression against Authority: The Crime of Oppression, Politicide and Other Crimes against Human Rights," *Case Western Reserve Journal of International Law* 18, no. 2 (Spring 1986): 283–306. Scholarly article, in English.

Servicio Paz y Justicia, Argentina (Service for Peace and Justice, Argentina). *Centroamerica: Efectos de Una Agresion Regional* (Central America: Effects of a Regional Aggression). Buenos Aires, Argentina: 1987. NGO report, in Spanish.

Vincent-Daviss, Diana, and Radu Popa. "The International Legal Implications of Iraq's Invasion of Kuwait: A Research Guide," *New York University Journal of International Law and Politics* 23 (1990): 231–321. Scholarly article, with bibliography, in English.

**AGING.** In 1948, Argentina submitted a draft Declaration of Old Age Rights to the UN General Assembly. The draft was referred to the Economic and Social Council, which called upon the Commission on Human Rights and the Social Commission to study the question. No definitive action resulted; and, in 1969, an item entitled "Question of the elderly and the aged" was put on the Assembly's agenda at the request of Malta.

In 1970 the Secretary-General issued a preliminary report (UN Doc. A/8364) to assist the Assembly in its discussion. The report pointed out that "the world is faced today with a paradoxical situation in which society is doing everything possible to increase the absolute and relative numbers of old people (through efforts to reduce death rates and birth rates respectively), but at the same time society is neglecting to utilize their vast potentials and very often creating socio-economic conditions which place a handicap on their physical and psycho-social adjustment."

The Assembly was unable to discuss the question at its 1970 session; but, on 18 December 1971, it requested the Secretary-General (resolution 2842 [XXVI]) to continue his study and to suggest guidelines for national policies and international action related to the needs and the role of the elderly and the aged in society.

In a further report on the subject presented to the General Assembly in 1973 (UN Doc. A/9126), the Secretary-General pointed out (paras. 183–186) that:

In all areas of the world, but in particular in the more developed areas, major conditions of the aged, such as age discrimination, economic insecurity and the lack of the right to work, and failure of those responsible to provide for an equitable distribution of national income and wealth, require major redefinition of existing policies, such as social security, the right to work, the right to needed social and health services, housing, and educational and cultural and recreational opportunities. A policy on aging, therefore, is essential, as the world approaches the twenty-first century, in order to assure the increasing numbers and proportions of older persons their basic human rights–full participation and contribution to, as well as protection in, the society of which they are a part.

The report noted the demographic increase in the absolute and relative size of the aging populations of the world, a trend that was expected to continue because of medical advances, and the decrease in birth and death rates. It states that, whereas in 1970 there were approximately 291 million persons 60 years of age or over throughout the world, this number was expected to increase to nearly 585 million by the year 2000, or by more than 100 percent, whereas the world's population as a whole would increase from 3.6 to 6.5 billion, or by approximately 80 percent. It was anticipated that the increase of the older populations would be proportionately higher in the less-developed regions, where persons over age 60 had numbered 5.4% of the total population in 1970, as compared with 14.1% in the more developed regions.

In 1978, the General Assembly decided (resolution 33/52) to organize a World Assembly on Aging in 1982 as a forum to launch an international program of action aimed at guaranteeing economic and social security to older persons, as well as opportunities for them to contribute to national development. In 1982, the World Assembly on Aging, held in Vienna, adopted by consensus the Vienna International Plan of Action on Aging, which the General Assembly subsequently endorsed (resolution 37/51). The endorsement was reaffirmed in 1987 (resolution 42/51), at which time the Assembly requested the Secretary-General, through the Commission for Social Development, to continue to monitor progress in the implementation of the plan of action and welcomed the establishment, in Malta, of the International Institute on Aging, in pursuance of a recommendation made in the plan of action.

The Secretary-General has since submitted annual reports to the UN General Assembly reviewing and appraising the implementation of the International Plan of Action on Aging, as manifested in a variety of activities that address aging in the context of human rights, development, population, employment, education, health, housing, family, disability, and the advancement of women.

Recognizing the complexity and rapidity of the aging of the world's population and the need to have a common basis for the promotion and protection of the rights of the elderly, the General Assembly adopted on 16 December 1991 (resolution 46/91) the "United Nations Principles for Older Persons," based on the International Plan of Action on Aging, as follows:

The General Assembly
Appreciating the contribution that older persons make to their societies,
Recognizing that, in the Charter of the United Nations, the peoples of the United Nations declare, inter alia, their determination to reaffirm faith in fundamental human rights, in the dignity and worth of the human person, in the equal rights of men and women and of nations large and small and to promote social progress and better standards of life in larger freedom,
Noting the elaboration of those rights in the Universal Declaration of Human Rights, the International Covenant on Economic, Social and Cultural Rights, and the International Covenant on Civil and Political Rights and other dec-

larations to ensure the application of universal standards to particular groups,
In pursuance of the International Plan of Action on Aging, adopted by the World Assembly on Aging and endorsed by the General Assembly in its resolution 37/51 of 3 December 1982,
Appreciating the tremendous diversity in the situation of older persons, not only between countries but within countries and between individuals, which requires a variety of policy responses,
Aware that in all countries, individuals are reaching an advanced age in greater numbers and in better health than ever before,
Aware of the scientific research disproving many stereotypes about inevitable and irreversible declines with age,
Convinced that in a world characterized by an increasing number and proportion of older persons, opportunities must be provided for willing and capable older persons to participate in and contribute to the ongoing activities of society,
Mindful that the strains on family life in both developed and developing countries require support for those providing care to frail older persons,
Bearing in mind the standards already set by the International Plan of Action on Aging and the conventions, recommendations and resolutions of the International Labor Organization, the World Health Organization, and other United Nations entities,
Encourages Governments to incorporate the following principles into their national programmes whenever possible:

### Independence

1. Older persons should have access to adequate food, water, shelter, clothing and health care through the provision of income, family and community support and self-help.
2. Older persons should have the opportunity to work or to have access to other income-generating opportunities.
3. Older persons should be able to participate in determining when and at what pace withdrawal from the labor force takes place.
4. Older persons should have access to appropriate educational and training programmes.
5. Older persons should be able to live in environments that are safe and adaptable to personal preferences and changing capacities.
6. Older persons should be able to reside at home for as long as possible.

### Participation

7. Older persons should remain integrated in society, participate actively in the formulation and implementation of policies that directly affect their well-being, and share their knowledge and skills with younger generations.
8. Older persons should be able to seek and develop opportunities for service to the community and to serve as volunteers in positions appropriate to their interests and capabilities.
9. Older persons should be able to form movements or associations of older persons.

### Care

10. Older persons should benefit from family and community care and protection in accordance with each society's system of cultural values.

11. Older persons should have access to health care to help them to maintain or regain the optimum level of physical, mental and emotional well-being and to prevent or delay the onset of illness.

12. Older persons should have access to social and legal services to enhance their autonomy, protection and care.

13. Older persons should be able to utilize appropriate levels of institutional care providing protection, rehabilitation, and social and mental stimulation in a humane and secure environment.

14. Older persons should be able to enjoy human rights and fundamental freedoms when residing in any shelter, care or treatment facility, including full respect for their dignity, beliefs, needs, and privacy and for the right to make decisions about their care and the quality of their lives.

### Self-fulfilment

15. Older persons should be able to pursue opportunities for the full development of their potential.

16. Older persons should have access to the educational, cultural, spiritual and recreational resources of society.

### Dignity

17. Older persons should be able to live in dignity and security and be free of exploitation and physical or mental abuse.

18. Older persons should be treated fairly regardless of age, gender, racial or ethnic background, disability or other status, and be valued independently of their economic contribution.

*YEAR OF THE ELDERLY.* In 1992 the UN General Assembly designated the year 1999 the International Year of Older Persons (resolution 47/5 of 16 October 1992). At its 1993 session, the Assembly redesignated the International Year of Older Persons (1999) as the International Year of the Elderly (resolution 48/433 of 20 December 1993).

**AGUDATH ISRAEL WORLD ORGANIZATION.** An international non-governmental organization in consultative status (Category II) with the Economic and Social Council and with UNESCO and UNICEF, AIWO was founded in 1912 at a congress of orthodox Jewry convened in Katowice, Poland. Before World War II, it was represented in the parliaments of Poland, Romania, and Lithuania; in recent years, it has been represented in the Parliament of Israel.

Composed of national organizations in 18 countries, with a total membership of 500,000, Agudath Israel's function is to solve, by coordination of orthodox Jewish effort throughout the world, problems which periodically confront the Jewish people as a whole. To this end, it organizes frequent international conferences, furthers religious education, stimulates the development of a Jewish press and literature, and represents and protects the rights and interests of Jewish

communities all over the world. It also contributes funds to a number of charities and provides funds for scholarships and religious activities.

AIWO publishes the daily *Hamodia* in Jerusalem; the weekly *Jewish Tribune* in London; and monthlies in Antwerp, Buenos Aires, New York, Zurich, and Buenos Aires.

Agudath Israel World Organization. Address: Hacherut Square, P.O. Box 326, Jerusalem, Israel. Telephone: (972-2) 384357. Fax: (972-2) 383-634. Cable: Worldaguda, Jerusalem. Secretary-General: Abraham Hirsch.

**AIDS.** Acquired immune deficiency syndrome (AIDS), caused by one or more naturally occurring retro-viruses of undetermined origin, has assumed pandemic proportions, affecting all regions of the world, and represents a threat to the attainment of health for all.

On 26 October 1987, the UN General Assembly expressed deep concern (resolution 42/8) about this global health problem. The assembly commended the World Health Organization (WHO) for its efforts towards global AIDS prevention and control, confirmed that WHO should continue to direct and coordinate the global battle against AIDS, and invited that organization to facilitate the exchange of information on and the promotion of national and international research for the prevention and control of AIDS. The Assembly, further, invited the Secretary-General of WHO to report to it in 1988, through the Economic and Social Council, on new developments in the global AIDS pandemic.

Report of the Secretary-General on international and domestic measures taken to protect human rights and prevent discrimination in the context of HIV/AIDS.

### Introduction

This report has been prepared in accordance with Commission on Human Rights resolution 1994/49, entitled "The protection of human rights in the context of human immunodeficiency virus (HIV) and acquired immune deficiency syndrome (AIDS)", of 4 March 1994, in which the Commission requested the Secretary-General to prepare, for its consideration at its fifty-first session, a report on international and domestic measures taken to protect human rights and prevent discrimination in the context of HIV/AIDS and to make recommendations thereon.

In the same resolution, the Commission on Human Rights called upon all States to:

(a) Ensure that their laws, policies and practices, including those introduced in the context of HIV/AIDS, respected human rights standards and did not have the effect of inhibiting programmes for the prevention of HIV/AIDS and for the care of persons infected with HIV/AIDS (para. 1);

(b) Take all the necessary steps, including appropriate and speedy redress procedures, to ensure the full enjoyment of civil, political, economic, social and cultural rights by people with HIV/AIDS, their families and those in any way associated with them, and people presumed to be at risk of infection, with particular attention to women, children and vulnerable groups, in order to prevent discriminatory action against them or their social stigmatization, and to ensure their access to the necessary care and support (para. 2).

In addition, the Commission urged all States to:

(a) Include in their AIDS programmes measures to combat social stigmatization, discrimination and violence directed against persons with HIV/AIDS, and to take the necessary steps to develop the supportive social environment necessary for the effective prevention and care of AIDS (para. 3);

(b) Review their legislation and practice to ensure the right to privacy and integrity of persons with HIV/AIDS and those presumed to be at risk of infection (para. 4).

In accordance with the above, the Secretary-General sent out a note verbale, dated 22 July 1994, to Governments, requesting information with regard to international and domestic measures taken to protect human rights in the context of HIV/AIDS. Replies were received from the Governments of Angola, Australia, Bangladesh, Chile, China, Croatia, the Islamic Republic of Iran, Iraq, Luxembourg, Mauritius, Mexico, Morocco, New Zealand, the Republic of Korea, Slovenia, Switzerland, Turkey, Yugoslavia and Zimbabwe.

The Secretary-General also sent out a communication with a similar request for information, and drawing attention to the preliminary, progress and final reports of Mr. Luis Varela Quirós, Special Rapporteur of the Sub-Commission on Prevention of Discrimination and Protection of Minorities on discrimination against HIV-infected people or people with AIDS (E/CN.4/Sub.2/1990/9, E/CN.4/Sub.2/1991/10, E/CN.4/Sub.2/1992/10 and E/CN.4/1995/45 page 4 E/CN.4/Sub.2/1993/9), to relevant bodies of the United Nations system, specialized agencies, working groups and special rapporteurs, the human rights treaty bodies, the World Bank and other relevant financial institutions, and those concerned with the status of women, as well as non-governmental organizations.

Replies were received from the Department for Humanitarian Affairs, the Division for the Advancement of Women, the General Assembly and Trusteeship Council Affairs Division, the Economic Commission for Latin America and the Caribbean, the Economic and Social Commission for Western Asia, the United Nations Environment Programme, the United Nations Population Fund, the Office of the United Nations High Commissioner for Refugees, the United Nations Interregional Crime and Justice Research Institute, the International Labour Organisation, the United Nations Educational, Scientific and Cultural Organization, the World Health Organization (Global Management Committee Task Force on HIV/AIDS Coordination and Global Programme on AIDS) and the International Monetary Fund.

Replies were also received from the Inter-American Court of Human Rights, Interpol, the Inter-Parliamentary Union and the Organization of African Unity, as well as the following non-governmental organizations: Caritas Internationalis, International Confederation of Midwives, International Council of Nurses, International Fellowship of Reconciliation, International Institute of Humanitarian Law, International Lesbian and Gay Association, Soroptimist International, World Education Fellowship and World Organization against Torture.

In order to set the framework for discussion, this report first outlines those human rights concerns relevant in the context of HIV/AIDS and recalls the links between the mutually reinforcing public health and human rights rationales which are often invoked in the context of the epidemic.

## Human Rights and HIV/AIDS

It is within the context of what is called the "third epidemic" of HIV/AIDS, namely the social, cultural and economic reactions to the HIV/AIDS epidemic, that the issue of protection of human rights and fundamental freedoms of persons infected with HIV and persons with AIDS, as well as all concerned persons, arises.

Indeed, a strong and clear public health rationale exists for the protection of human rights and the dignity of infected persons. For example, if it is the common practice that HIV infection, or simply suspicion of infection, leads to a stigmatization of the person or group, or to discrimination *vis-à-vis* the concerned (such as loss of employment or obstacles to access to education), these persons will undoubtedly actively try to avoid detection and, as a result, lose contact with health and social services. This reluctance to seek assistance out of fear of stigmatization and discrimination in turn not only exacerbates the difficulty of preventing infection but also runs counter to any educational and outreach efforts in this context.

It is, therefore, evident that practices of discrimination and stigmatization of infected persons are to be considered hazardous to public health. Consequently, the protection of human rights and the prevention of discrimination in the context of HIV/AIDS should constitute an integral part of public health policies for the prevention and control of HIV/AIDS.

Human rights have been a part of the debate on a common global response to AIDS at the United Nations from the very beginning. It has also long been the position of the World Health Organization (WHO), as the monitoring and implementing agency of the Global AIDS Strategy, that human rights must form an integral component of any response to the HIV/AIDS pandemic that is ravaging the globe. This is because human rights interface with HIV/AIDS in a number of critical ways. In the first instance, failure to protect human rights increases the risk of transmission of the disease. Prevention of transmission is a complex and delicate process of education and behaviour change regarding intimate and sometimes illicit behaviour. Prevention of transmission depends on people coming forward to learn how to avoid infection, how to practice safe sex, and how and why they should act responsibly. Coercive measures, such as mandatory testing, lack of confidentiality and segregation, drive people away from prevention education and health-care services and subvert this process of behavioural change.

Secondly, individuals and groups in society who are disadvantaged and/or do not enjoy the full exercise of their rights are particularly vulnerable to infection as they have limited or no access to HIV/AIDS-related education, prevention and health-care programmes. Such groups include women, children, minorities, migrants, indigenous peoples, men having sex with men, commercial sex workers and injecting drug users. These groups may have neither the information they need nor the ability to act on it so as to avoid infection. Infection among such groups rapidly diffuses to society at large.

Finally, discrimination against and stigmatization of persons already affected by HIV/AIDS (those infected, suspected of infection and their families and associates) greatly magnifies the tragic impact the disease has on their lives. Such discrimination is widespread. It not only violates the rights of those affected but also further disables them by limiting their access to employment, housing, health care and vitally needed social support systems.

Thus, the discrimination and stigma associated with HIV/AIDS both infringe on the rights and dignity of those affected and pose a serious public health threat to society. Since the late 1970s, over 17 million people have become infected with the HIV virus. By the year 2000, it is estimated that 40 million will be infected.

Until there is awareness of the importance of the connection between successful HIV/AIDS prevention and human rights, it is likely that Governments will continue to employ discriminatory laws and policies, and that third-party discrimination and stigmatization will also continue. Such awareness can only be created through monitoring, advocacy and education. At present, there is no systematic monitoring of HIV/AIDS-related human rights violations, as the major human rights monitoring groups have yet to include the issue as part of their ongoing reporting.

Furthermore, it is emphasized that beyond the rather limited concept of non-discrimination, there exists an inherently more positive obligation on the part of the international community and national Governments to ensure the respect and dignity of all human beings, including the enabling and creation of a supportive environment for HIV-infected persons and persons with AIDS, their families and relatives, fostering a spirit of tolerance and solidarity.

The human rights rationale advanced in the context of HIV/AIDS concerns some of the most basic provisions of international human rights standards. The right to life, which has been recognized to entail positive obligations on the part of the international community and Governments actively and effectively to protect human lives, is known to have been restricted on the grounds of public health considerations. In fact, the protection of public health has also been recognized as legitimate grounds for the restriction of human rights. Similarly, measures which limit privacy, the freedom of movement or individual liberty have also been dictated by needs to protect public health. In this connection, however, it is important to note that any kind of derogation from existing human rights standards may only be applied in situations where a specific law spells out the nature of the derogation, where the derogation is considered strictly necessary for the fulfilment of a strictly proportional (to the nature of the measure) and pressing objective. This is to say that the State would in effect have to prove public health justifications before it could derogate from any human rights standards.

In accordance with the mandate contained in Commission resolution 1994/49, this report outlines, in chapter II, the measures taken at the international level to protect human rights and prevent discrimination, including the existing international and regional legal standards, as well as the work done by international organizations. In this connection, it should be noted that, as far as existing international human rights standards are concerned, this report is limited to an overview of a wide variety of existing literature in this area. Secondly, the measures taken by international organizations to protect human rights and prevent discrimination

which are referred to in this report are largely based on information received by the Secretary-General in response to his request for contributions and are, therefore, not exhaustive. It should be noted, however, that the Secretary-General has chosen to focus only on positive measures undertaken in the context of human rights and HIV/AIDS, so as to remain within the limits of the mandate. Furthermore, these measures are intended to serve as an inspiration to Governments and activists in the area and to show that even with small means and small-scale projects much can be achieved in the context of raising awareness and empowering the individual to fight for his or her rights.

In chapter III, examples of such positive measures undertaken at the national level are provided, based mainly on the responses to the Secretary-General's request for information.

In his conclusions and recommendations, as contained in number of measures actively promoting the protection of the human rights of HIV/AIDS-infected persons or persons with AIDS, especially as compared to existing legislation and other measures which actively restrict or in some cases deny, not in accordance with recognized criteria for exceptional circumstances, the human rights and fundamental freedoms of concerned persons.

## Measures Taken to Protect Human Rights in the Context of HIV/AIDS at the International Level

*International and regional human rights instruments*

Human rights in relation to health are covered by a wide spectrum of international instruments. In addition to the most basic provision contained in article 12 of the International Covenant on Economic, Social and Cultural Rights, which provides for the right of everyone to the enjoyment of the highest attainable standard of physical and mental health and requests States Parties to the Covenant to undertake steps to achieve the full realization of this right, including the prevention and control of epidemic diseases and the creation of conditions which would assure medical service and medical attention to all in the event of sickness, other international human rights instruments cover the prevention of discrimination, human rights in the administration of justice, employment and social welfare, progress and development, all of which relate to concerns raised by HIV/AIDS. Although there do not at present exist any international legal instruments dealing exclusively with HIV/AIDS, it is important to point out that the general guarantees concerning health and the other above-mentioned rights can be applied in the context of HIV/AIDS on the basis of the universally recognized non-discrimination principle. The Sub-Commission on Prevention of Discrimination and Protection of Minorities, in its resolution 1994/29, confirmed that "discrimination on the basis of AIDS or HIV status, actual or presumed, is prohibited by existing international human rights standards and that the term 'or other status' in non-discrimination provisions in international human rights texts should be interpreted to cover health status, including HIV/AIDS".

Furthermore, international human rights treaty bodies, responsible for the supervision and monitoring of these instruments through periodic reviews of States parties' report, are developing case law or jurisprudence in the interpretation of their respective instruments. These opinions and recommendations are important in the context of HIV/AIDS, because they define the application of human rights of a general nature within the particular context of HIV/AIDS.

The following analysis, although by no means exhaustive, highlights some examples of the links between internationally guaranteed human rights and the application of these rights in the particular context of the HIV/AIDS epidemic.

The right to privacy is widely provided for in international and regional human rights instruments. However, there exist several possible measures that would necessarily entail interferences with the individual's right to privacy, which the State concerned would need to justify under the established criteria. These measures include mandatory testing for HIV infection; compulsory registration of persons considered likely to be infected with HIV, but who have not been tested; mandatory collection, storage and processing by public authorities of personal information about those who are suspected of being infected or have been tested; making AIDS or HIV a notifiable disease; disclosure of test results or of other personal information to third parties; criminalization of behaviour thought to be conducive to the spread of AIDS.

The right to liberty and security of person is unfortunately also often affected by national legislation, policies and directives in the context of HIV/AIDS. In order to determine whether the protection of the international human rights instruments applies to the deprivation of liberty, the types of measures taken and their implementation must be taken into account. For example, a lawful deprivation of liberty and a possible isolation imposed on a prisoner as a disciplinary measure will not be regarded as constituting independent deprivations of liberty. This type of measure might, however, raise questions with regard to the right not to be subjected to inhuman or degrading treatment. On the other hand, measures justified on the grounds of public health, such as compulsory quarantine or compulsory internment, would appear to involve a deprivation of liberty. Such measures would not only have to satisfy the test that they are not arbitrary but are taken on reasonable grounds and in accordance with a procedure established by law. Moreover, the State would have to establish, in the case of detention, that the individual concerned had the infection and that her or his detention was necessary for the prevention of its spread.

In this connection, WHO has repeatedly stressed that detention or segregation of any kind is not warranted for the prevention and control of the spread of AIDS. Furthermore, WHO recommends, within its strategy for the prevention of the spread of HIV, that persons suspected or known to be HIV-infected should remain integrated within society to the maximum possible extent and be helped to assume responsibility for preventing HIV transmission to others.

The right to freedom of movement, comprising various issues such as entry into a country, abode and movement within a territory, expulsion from a country and leaving a country, is provided for in article 13 of the Universal Declaration of Human Rights.

There are, in international law, some basic considerations in connection with this right: the right to enter a country is confined to nationals of the States concerned; there is no express obligation upon States to let aliens enter their territory. However, in particular on the basis of the principle of non-discrimination and possible treaty obligations, some controls and restrictions are posed on States' ability to control entry for purposes of work, travel and immigration. The question that arises, therefore, is to what extent, if at all, a State might legitimately impose controls on entry into its territory of those who are HIV-infected, restrict their movement within the country or permit or require their expulsion from it.

For nationals, the right to enter is absolute and not subject to any restrictions. Consequently, a State cannot legitimately make entry into its territory of its own returning nationals subject to their taking an HIV test. It is also not the case that the State may impose compulsory HIV testing on all aliens as a condition for entering the country. Such a requirement could only be imposed in cases where the State could establish that it was necessary for the protection of public health.

In this context, the Secretary-General has recently received information concerning draft legislation in Russia which would indeed be in contravention of existing international human rights standards and, in particular, constitute an arbitrary interference with the right to privacy and the right to freedom of movement. On 11 November 1994, the Duma, the lower house of the Russian Parliament, passed draft federal legislation "On the prevention of the spread in the Russian Federation of disease caused by the human immunodeficiency virus (HIV infection)", which provides for compulsory testing of all foreigners and stateless citizens coming to or located in Russia, as well as of Russian citizens working in "certain" professions and for receiving "certain" types of medical assistance. Furthermore, the word "certain" is as of yet not precisely defined and, therefore, leaves a rather wide margin of interpretation.

In this respect, attention is drawn to the above arguments on the basis of which the State concerned is required to establish that these measures are taken on reasonable grounds for the protection of public health. Furthermore, it appears questionable whether the passing of such legislation would be in conformity with existing obligations of the State concerned undertaken through the ratification of international human rights instruments.

In addition, WHO has stated that since HIV infection is already present in every region and in virtually every major city in the world, even total exclusion of all travellers (foreigners and citizens travelling abroad) cannot prevent the introduction and spread of HIV.

The protection against expulsion from a country afforded by international human rights law is more limited and differs in certain significant aspects between the various instruments. As regards the protection afforded to aliens, most provide that an alien lawfully in the territory of a State may be expelled only in pursuance of a decision reached in accordance with the law. Furthermore, the International Covenant on Civil and Political Rights provides for the alien to be given the opportunity to submit reasons against her or his expulsion and to have the case completely reviewed, the public health exception not being a reason for the non-application of the safeguards.

According to information submitted to the Secretary-General by one Government, out of 27 HIV-positive cases so far detected in that country, "one of them was an expatriate and sent back to his home country, two others have already died. There is no report of human rights violations in any one of these cases". According to the argument reported in the preceding paragraph, however, the expulsion of expatriates on the grounds of seropositivity must occur in accordance with a decision reached by law. It is clearly evident from this example that human rights considerations simply are not taken into account in many countries when, for example, a person is expelled on the grounds of protecting public health.

In connection with travel restrictions and HIV/AIDS, WHO has promulgated a policy of non-sponsorship of international conferences in countries which impose short-term travel restrictions. This policy has been adopted throughout the United Nations system. Furthermore, WHO is at present developing policy on long-term travel restrictions.

As far as the human right to marry and found a family is concerned, a policy of mandatory premarital HIV testing, coupled with the denial of a marriage licence if either person prove to be infected, would be a measure interfering with human rights as protected by the international human rights instruments. The same applies to the prohibition of the marriage of persons known, or suspected, to be infected with HIV. Furthermore, owing to the increase in sexual activity outside of marriage, the argument that prohibiting marriage would be an effective means of preventing either sexual or perinatal transmission of the HIV virus is not sustainable.

International human rights instruments provide that everyone has the right to work, to free choice of employment, to just and favourable conditions of work and to protection against unemployment. ILO Convention No. 111, entitled Convention concerning Discrimination in Respect of Employment and Occupation (1958), in its article 1 (a), defines the term discrimination in respect of employment and occupation as "any distinction, exclusion or preference made on the basis of race, colour, sex, religion, political opinion, national extraction or social origin, which has the effect of nullifying or impairing equality of opportunity or treatment in employment or occupation". States parties have, however, the possibility, after consultations with representative employers' and workers' organizations, to add to the list enumerated in article 1 (a) any other grounds on which discrimination is prohibited, such as, for example, seropositive status.

In addition, the Committee on Economic, Social and Cultural Rights has interpreted the relevant provisions of the Covenant to include an effective guarantee against arbitrary dismissal as an integral element of the right to work.

Unfortunately, misconceptions about HIV and the groundless fear of contagion often give rise to discrimination against workers infected or suspected of being infected with HIV. Indeed, it could be said that most of the crises relating to AIDS in the workplace are an invasion of workers' privacy. The employer has no reason to require staff or job applicants to undergo HIV screening, and even less to divulge anyone's HIV status or take it into account in decisions concerning employment.

The activities conducted by the International Labour Office (ILO) over the last 10 years to promote and protect human rights and prevent HIV/AIDS-related discrimination are based on a number of international labour conventions and recommendations, in particular the ILO Convention (No. 111) mentioned above; the Convention concerning Termination of Employment at the Initiative of the Employer (No. 158), 1982; the Convention concerning Vocational Rehabilitation and Employment (Disabled Persons) (No. 159), 1983; the Occupational Health Services Convention (No. 161) and Recommendation (No. 171), 1985; and the Convention concerning Employment and Conditions of Work and Life of Nursing Personnel (No. 149), 1977.

While no international labour convention or recommendation at present deals expressly with HIV/AIDS, the provisions of some of these instruments can be applied to the problem and suggest both the preferable way of reaching consensus on an HIV/AIDS policy (the instruments aimed at promoting consultations and negotiations) and the scope of such a policy (the provisions of the above-mentioned conventions and recommendations; ILO instruments on social insurance and social security are also relevant to the HIV/AIDS problem).

Applied judiciously, the principles stated in a number of international labour conventions and recommendations and in the WHO/ILO Joint Declaration on AIDS and the Work-place afford broad protection of HIV-infected people and people with AIDS against discrimination and the violation of their fundamental rights in regard to employment and occupation. Respect for human rights and an effective strategy to combat AIDS are two inseparable concepts.

There is nothing, therefore, to prevent the criteria applicable to HIV infection and AIDS from being added to the list of prohibited reasons for discrimination in employment and occupation. A more rational approach might be to include among the prohibited reasons for discrimination a provision broad enough to encompass HIV and AIDS without implying privileged treatment for the victims compared with people with other infections which likewise often allow an occupational activity to be continued for a certain time before causing incapacity and premature death at a point that is impossible to predict. Thus, a person's physical or mental health, disabilities in the broad sense of the term, deficiencies and medical history have been included as prohibited criteria for discrimination in the laws and collective agreements of several countries.

Furthermore, in the context of ILO Convention No. 158, if an HIV-infected worker remains capable of performing his work and his conduct at work is irreproachable, the presence of the virus should not in itself constitute a "valid reason" for termination in the meaning of article 4 of the Convention, which provides that "the employment of a worker shall not be terminated unless there is a valid reason for such termination connected with the capacity or conduct of the worker or based on the operational requirements of the undertaking, establishment or service". Similarly, the groundless fears to which the presence of such a person at the workplace may give rise among colleagues or customers cannot be regarded as a reason for termination either on personal grounds or with reference to the "operational requirements of the undertaking".

Another example is article 2 of ILO Convention No. 159, which requires the Member State ratifying the Convention to implement and periodically review a national policy on vocational rehabilitation and employment of disabled persons. The periodic review clause is relevant to HIV/AIDS by virtue of the need to consider these new phenomena from the perspective of incapacity for work. The policy which Member States are required to formulate and implement under article 2 must be "based on the principle of equal opportunity between disabled workers and workers generally"; at the same time, "special positive measures aimed at effective equality of opportunity and treatment between disabled workers and other workers shall not be regarded as discriminating against other workers" (art. 4).

Certain provisions of these instruments are also intended to protect workers' privacy. The Occupational Health Services Recommendation (No. 171) states that provisions should be adopted "to protect the privacy of the workers and to ensure that health surveillance is not used for discriminatory purposes or in any other manner prejudicial to their interests" (para. 11 (2)).

In that regard, the WHO/ILO Joint Declaration on AIDS and the Workplace protects the right of employees to confidentiality regarding all medical information, including HIV/AIDS status (item 2). The fears of their colleagues and discrimination by their employers prevent a large number of HIV-infected people from seeking the information, treatment and assistance they need. It is also significant that the WHO/ILO Joint Declaration states that HIV/AIDS screening as part of the assessment of fitness to work should not be required (para. 1 and item 1).

Furthermore, in accordance with ILO standards and international human rights instruments, the United Nations Secretariat has prepared a document analysing the impact of HIV/AIDS on United Nations personnel and operational policy (ACC/1991/DEC/10 and ACC/1993/PER/R.6, annex III). This document encourages all United Nations bodies to, inter alia, develop and implement an active staff education strategy for HIV/AIDS and to make available voluntary testing with pre- and post-counselling and assured confidentiality to all United Nations staff members and their families. These guidelines indicate that no testing for HIV infection should be permitted with respect to any health insurance scheme. Furthermore, with regard to terms of appointment and service, HIV infection is not taken in itself to constitute a lack of fitness to work and no HIV screening of candidates is required for recruitment. Similarly, HIV infection or AIDS should not in itself be considered a basis for termination of employment, and should fitness to work be impaired by HIV-related illness, then reasonable alternative working arrangements should be made.

Furthermore, in the context of HIV/AIDS respect for the right to education; the right to an adequate standard of living, including housing; and the right to social security, assistance and welfare, should be particularly carefully considered.

For example, a health policy prohibiting children infected with HIV from attending school not only cannot be justified on public health grounds but also may run counter to information and education efforts on HIV/AIDS which are integrated into school curricula. With regard to the right to adequate housing and to social security, assistance and welfare, the right to equal protection of the law, derived from the principle of non-discrimination, is a powerful complement to the protection of the human rights of people with HIV/AIDS. It follows that an individual with HIV/AIDS may only be subjected to differential treatment in any field regulated and protected by law if it can be established that the distinction has a legitimate aim and reasonable justification and that the means employed are proportionate to that aim.

In addition to the international and regional standards, as well as their monitoring bodies, that provide for the protection of the human rights of persons with AIDS, the Commission on Human Rights and its Sub-Commission have been concerned with the issue of prevention of discrimination in the context of HIV/AIDS. Since 1988, the Commission has regularly adopted resolutions on HIV/AIDS-related discrimination. In 1990, it approved the recommendation of the Sub-Commission to appoint Mr. Luis Varela Quirós, for a period of three years, as Special Rapporteur on discrimination against HIV-infected people or people with AIDS.

The Special Rapporteur submitted his preliminary report to the Sub-Commission in 1990 (E/CN.4/Sub.2/1990/9), his progress report in 1991 (E/CN.4/Sub.2/1991/10), as well as another report in 1992 (E/CN.4/Sub.2/1992/10).

In his final report to the Sub-Commission in 1994 (E/CN.4/Sub.2/1994/9), the Special Rapporteur described the global AIDS situation, the importance of preventing HIV/AIDS-related discrimination, discriminatory practices and legal policy frameworks for protection against discrimination. He provided a synopsis of replies received from Governments, United Nations specialized agencies and bodies, intergovernmental and non-governmental organizations, containing information on legal and policy framework introduced in response to AIDS. The Special Rapporteur concluded that strategies to prevent HIV/AIDS-related discrimination needed to combine education with legal protection against discrimination.

In his conclusions and recommendations the Special Rapporteur emphasized that discrimination against HIV-infected people or people with AIDS is neither admissible under international human rights instruments nor justified as an appropriate means of policy for controlling the AIDS pandemic. In fact, discriminatory practices can be eradicated only by means of national and international education programmes that create a genuine climate of respect for human rights and reject any discriminatory policy against socially vulnerable groups.

At its forty-sixth session, in August 1994, the Sub-Commission had before it a report of the Secretary-General (E/CN.4/Sub.2/1994/8), which briefly outlines the progress made within the United Nations system with regard to a joint and cosponsored United Nations programme on HIV/AIDS.

This joint United Nations programme, which is expected to become functional in January 1996, is aimed at eliminating duplication of efforts by the United Nations system in the field of HIV/AIDS; ensuring day-to-day interaction and the integration of ideas and approaches systemwide and beyond; assisting Governments in coordinating the efforts of various external support agencies; joint and coordinated fund-raising at global and national levels; and achieving consistency with the coordination mechanisms adopted by the General Assembly in line with the reform of the United Nations system in that regard.

Concerning the particularly vulnerable status of women in the context of HIV/AIDS, the Committee on the Elimination of Discrimination against Women (CEDAW) adopted, in 1990, general recommendation No. 15, which recommends, inter alia, that programmes to combat AIDS should give special attention to the rights and needs of women and children, and to the factors relating to the reproductive role of women and their subordinate position in some societies which make them especially vulnerable to HIV infection; and that States parties ensure the active participation of women in primary health care and take measures to enhance their role as care providers, health workers and educators in the prevention of infection with HIV.

In 1990 also, the Commission on the Status of Women adopted its resolution 35/5, entitled "Women and the prevention and control of acquired immunodeficiency syndrome (AIDS)", in which it invited member States to evaluate and strengthen their policies and programmes for the control of AIDS for the benefit of women through, inter alia, the coordination of such programmes with other programmes for women, in particular, programmes for family planning, maternal and child health, school education and the control of sexually transmitted diseases.

*The work of international and regional organizations*

In view of the World Health Organization's numerous activities in the promotion and protection of human rights and prevention of discrimination in the field of HIV/AIDS, and its role as the implementing and coordinating agency for the Global Strategy on AIDS, the World Health Organization Global Programme on AIDS (WHO/GPA) and the Global Management Committee Task Force on HIV/AIDS Coordination (WHO/GMC Task Force), have contributed extensively to the present report.

The Global AIDS Strategy has achieved a precedent in the history of responding to disease by incorporating the consideration of human rights. The World Health Assembly has affirmed that human rights standards fully apply in the context of HIV/AIDS, stressing:

(a) The responsibility of the State to safeguard the health of everyone;

(b) The vital importance of respect for the human rights and dignity of HIV-infected people and people with AIDS to the success of AIDS prevention and control;

(c) The avoidance of discriminatory action against and stigmatization of HIV-infected people and people with AIDS.

WHO/GPA has promoted HIV/AIDS-related human rights through standard-setting, monitoring, advocacy, training and research, and the provision of technical and legal advice to States with regard to their national AIDS programmes and HIV/AIDS-related legislation. In terms of standard-setting, WHO/GPA has issued, after various consultations, policies and guidelines concerning human rights and HIV/AIDS, HIV testing, partner notification and HIV/AIDS in the workplace, sports and prisons. In 1995, the following issues and their human rights components will be considered further: HIV testing and HIV in the workplace, in migration and in the military.

WHO/GPA also monitors discriminatory legislation, policies and practices at the national level, by using a variety of sources such as medium-term plans for national AIDS programmes, external national AIDS programme reviews, staff missions, the media and reports from regional offices, country staff, community-based organizations and non-governmental organizations and persons living with HIV/AIDS. Furthermore, WHO/GPA is currently developing indicators which will make possible the measuring of progress in reducing HIV/AIDS-related discrimination at the national and local levels. WHO/GPA is also establishing a country-specific human rights database, comprising information from various sources to indicate actual or potential areas of concern, including information on positive and negative measures taken in the area of human rights. Subsequently, those areas of concern will be addressed by intervention and/or advocacy through various channels, such as regional offices and missions.

WHO/GPA is also initiating a research project on the determinants of HIV/AIDS-related discrimination, stigmatization and denial, focusing on the nature and process of HIV/AIDS-related stigmatization in developing countries and the implications of these prevention and care programmes.

Legal advice is also given to Governments on those aspects of their legislation and practice which constitute areas of concern. WHO/GPA reviews draft and implemented HIV/AIDS-specific legislation or health legislation which includes HIV/AIDS-related provisions and provides comments and recommendations when appropriate. Information on legislation comes from a number of sources, including Governments, WHO regional offices, non-governmental organizations and individuals.

Furthermore, the WHO Health Legislation Unit has produced and regularly updates the "Tabular information on legal instruments dealing with HIV infection and AIDS". This compilation is distributed widely to Governments, universities, institutions, academics and non-governmental organizations. In this connection, WHO/GPA intends to develop HIV/AIDS-specific model legislation based on non-discrimination and respect and promotion of relevant human rights principles, which may serve as a basic legal framework for Governments seeking to adapt existing legislation or implement new legislation aimed at the prevention of HIV/AIDS.

WHO/GPA also supports national and regional legal and ethical networks sponsored by UNDP, as well as networks of persons living with HIV/AIDS and recognizes, in accordance with WHO resolution 42.34 of 1989, the importance of involving non-governmental organizations and persons living with HIV/AIDS in the design and implementation of HIV/AIDS responses, including responses against discrimination. It has become increasingly apparent that action and advocacy on issues of law, ethics and human rights at local and national levels by institutions, individuals, non-governmental and community-based organizations and persons living with HIV/AIDS is essential to change attitudes and address stigmatization, discrimination and intolerance. It is hoped that such networks will be able to provide the international community with continuous and updated information on the extent and content of HIV/AIDS-related discrimination, as well as examples of concrete means by which to address it.

Recognizing the importance of basic human rights knowledge among all those active in the field of HIV/AIDS, WHO/GPA has conducted a number of human rights training seminars at WHO headquarters to enable its staff to identify areas of concern within their activities. WHO/GPA intends to continue this activity and further aims at developing human rights training materials and training programmes for staff, national AIDS programme managers, relevant ministries (for example, of health, the interior and justice), law enforcement officers, immigration officials, health-care workers and non-governmental and community-based organizations. In order to enable reviewers and others involved in national AIDS programmes to integrate human rights concerns into their programmes, WHO/GPA is developing a human rights check-list and aide-mémoire which will be circulated for use by AIDS programme planners and reviewers.

Finally, WHO/GPA has established contacts with United Nations human rights treaty bodies, such as the Committee on the Rights of the Child and the Committee on Economic, Social and Cultural Rights so as to bring HIV/AIDS-related human rights issues to the attention of all experts and Governments in the context of reporting procedures.

The WHO/GMC Task Force on HIV/AIDS Coordination was established in 1993 to examine ways and means to improve collaboration and coordination between different types of organizations involved in HIV/AIDS work, both at the international and national levels. On the basis of information collected on obstacles to collaboration and coordination, the GMC Task Force has produced guiding principles which describes conditions that should be fulfilled to provide a good basis for collaboration and coordination.

In addition, the GMC Task Force is currently developing an information system on HIV/AIDS activities supported by external development assistance. Data has been provided by organizations of the United Nations system, bilateral donors and a limited number of non-governmental organizations and national AIDS programmes. The information which is available at present in the database shows that external assistance to HIV/AIDS work executed by Governments, non-governmental organizations or other institutions is often provided in a broad context and the different HIV/AIDS components are not specified. The policies and programmes for the protection of human rights and prevention of discrimination of the executing agency are important elements for consideration in external assistance programmes Yet it has not been possible to document principles and processes within development assistance agencies aimed at protecting human rights in the fight against the HIV/AIDS epidemic.

With a view to capacity building in the area of law, ethics and HIV in developing countries, the United Nations Development Programme, in collaboration with national Governments, has sponsored intercountry consultations, with participants from Governments, public authorities, the legal community and non-governmental organizations. These consultations have formed national and regional ethical, legal and human rights networks.

One of the principles underpinning these networks is that, unless there exists a firm commitment within each country to integrate ethical, legal and human rights considerations into the overall response to the HIV/AIDS epidemic, then compliance with international standards risks being token at best. It is also argued by some that human rights monitoring is an inadequate framework for dealing with an epidemic that requires change in the behaviour of individuals and communities. The UNDP networks, therefore, work on the basis of a compelling need to find ways of engendering such an approach from within communities. The objective of the initiative is to make the critical links between people and organizations within and between countries, so as to act as a catalyst for sound ethical policies on HIV/AIDS and to generate advocacy by and on behalf of people affected in different countries.

These regional networks reflect the objectives of the national networks of which they are composed, working in partnership with already existing national, regional and international groups and organizations in related areas. Network members include lawyers, ethicists, people living with HIV/AIDS, representatives of national AIDS programmes, Governments, non-governmental and community-based organizations and women's groups. Regional networks reinforce national networks and provide a forum for discussion and exchange of experience. At present, there are three such networks, the Latin America/Caribbean network and the Asian and African networks.

Most recently, UNDP organized an African Inter-Country Consultation on Ethics, Law and HIV, which, in the Declaration at Dakar, of 1 July 1994, affirmed that any action, whether personal, institutional, professional or governmental, in response to the HIV epidemic, should be guided by the principles of, inter alia, non-discrimination, confidentiality and privacy, ethics in research and prohibition of mandatory HIV testing.

Some other examples of measures taken by GMC Task Force constituencies which target the building of a supportive environment in the area of ethics, human rights and HIV within affected communities are the following:

(a) An AIDS Consortium in South Africa focuses on legal and human rights issues and promotes the principles of non-discrimination against people living with HIV/AIDS through policy, advocacy, lobbying, information exchange and networking. Financial support is received from donor agencies in the Netherlands and in the United States;

(b) The Humanistic Institute for Cooperation with Developing Countries (HIVOS) is funding activities, including information dissemination on HIV/AIDS, counselling, human rights protection and network development, carried out by the non-governmental organization called "Positive People" in Goa, India. HIVOS is also extending financial support to a non-governmental organization in Kuala Lumpur, "Pink Triangle", which has created an AIDS hotline, and a documentation centre including information on the protection of human rights in the context of HIV/AIDS;

(c) The Interchurch Agency for Development Cooperation (ICCO) has supported the "Comité d'action pour les droits des femmes et des enfants" in Mali in carrying out educational activities regarding human rights and HIV/AIDS.

ILO policy on HIV/AIDS and the workplace forms an integral part of the ILO mission to promote social justice and protect workers against violations of their rights and fundamental freedoms in the field of employment. The protection of HIV-infected people and people with AIDS against discrimination in employment is a very important component of the ILO programme of action on HIV/AIDS. The other components of this programme are: protection of the health of workers in areas of employment particularly exposed to AIDS, such as health professionals and maritime workers, the promotion of public information and awareness concerning HIV/AIDS through the working environment, i.e. undertakings and employers' and workers' associations and, lastly, study of the impact of HIV/AIDS on the labour market and social security costs.

This policy was defined in consultation with WHO following the international meeting on AIDS and the workplace organized jointly by WHO and ILO at Geneva in 1988. The conclusions and recommendations of an international meeting on AIDS were set out in a consensus statement on AIDS and the workplace.

This document, entitled "WHO/ILO Joint Declaration on AIDS and the Workplace" states, inter alia, that pre-employment HIV/AIDS screening as part of the assessment of fitness to work is unnecessary and should not be required. Pre-employment screening for insurance or other purposes raises serious concerns about discrimination and merits closer and further study. The Declaration further stipulates that, in order to maintain a mutually understanding climate to protect persons affected by, or perceived to be affected by HIV/AIDS from stigmatization and all forms of discrimination in the workplace, information and education are essential. It should be recognized that the workplace can play a decisive role in the prevention of the spread of HIV by providing information and relevant assistance which might be needed by workers, for example when taking conscious decisions concerning their sex life or how to show solidarity and respect vis-à-vis their colleagues, neighbours and friends affected by HIV/AIDS.

Indeed, ILO notes that work in the great majority of occupations and occupational situations presents no risk of the contraction or transmission of HIV, either between workers, from workers to customers or from customers to workers. However, for a minority of workers—personnel whose task is to provide health care—the risk of contracting or transmitting HIV infection may well be inherent to the occupational activity. Such workers will therefore have to take precautions for their safety and health. It is important to assess carefully the risks associated with certain functions in order to identify those which are at risk and those which are not, and to define clearly those for which precautions must be taken.

The general machinery for supervising and monitoring international labour standards comprises two main bodies: the Committee on the Application of Standards of the International Labour Conference and the Committee of Experts on the Application of Conventions and Recommendations. The latter, with technical support from the International Labour Standards Department, has the task of considering government reports and, where appropriate, comments by employers' and workers' organizations from the legal standpoint.

The regular activities of monitoring the relevant international instruments to protect HIV-infected people and people with AIDS against discrimination in employment are supplemented and reinforced by practical action to provide information and education concerning HIV/AIDS prevention and by studies and research on the impact of AIDS on workers' rights and on employment and economic and social development.

Information and education activities relating to the prevention of AIDS and its adverse effects on the enjoyment of human rights in employment are organized by various ILO services within periodic seminars and technical cooperation programmes in several fields, particularly workers' education, women and development, population and social and family welfare, equality of opportunity and treatment, and working conditions and the working environment.

The United Nations Population Fund (UNFPA) provides support for HIV/AIDS prevention and care activities in line with national AIDS control policies and programmes, within the scope of the WHO/GPA global strategy for HIV/AIDS prevention and control. These activities are integrated into ongoing programmes and projects in the population sector, particularly maternal and child health service delivery and information, education and communication programmes and projects. UNFPA specifically recognizes that it is essential that development and health strategies ensure that women have more control over their lives, their reproductive and sexual health and their fertility.

Furthermore, UNFPA actively supports and participates in an inter-agency venture, namely the ongoing series of regional HIV/AIDS workshops of the Joint Consultative Group on Policy (UNDP, UNICEF, WFP, IFAD and UNFPA), which focuses on the training of trainers in the workplace. The workshops cover basically three areas, namely technical, medical information, training of trainers and United Nations personnel policy on HIV/AIDS. The purpose of the workshops is to extend awareness and knowledge of HIV/AIDS to country-level staff members of the five organizations through trainers' workshops and informal staff networks of support, so that the participants, upon return to their duty station, run workshops and act as information focal points on HIV/AIDS to United Nations staff and their families in the field. Three such workshops have been held so far: in Harare (March 1993), Dakar (January 1994) and Bogota (July 1994).

The Office of the United Nations High Commissioner for Refugees (UNHCR) has established a working group on AIDS, which has formulated "Policy and Guidelines regarding Refugee Protection and Assistance and Acquired Immune Deficiency Syndrome (AIDS)", and keeps the issue under continuous review. The Policy and Guidelines were drawn up in response to cases where Governments started to consider the need for testing for AIDS and screening for purposes of admission of asylum seekers and resettlement of refugees. In this context, the UNHCR Policy and Guidelines take as their basis the argument that refugees are not a group especially at risk for HIV infection/AIDS and should therefore not be subjected to specific measures unless these are applied to all residents, citizens and refugees alike, in the country concerned. Mandatory mass screening of refugees and asylum seekers in the context of admission, asylum, resettlement and voluntary repatriation are, therefore, not applicable. UNHCR further advocates that screening just in no cases lead to refoulement or denial of voluntary repatriation. In addition, national measures carried out to combat AIDS and to prevent the spread of the HIV virus, in so far as they have an impact on refugees and asylum seekers, must only be applied in the context of the overall objectives of the international system with regard to this group of people, namely protection and solutions. The UNHCR policy, therefore, is to ensure that local refugee populations, where necessary, benefit from national AIDS programmes and contribute to the refugee component of those programmes.

UNHCR has also pointed out that in every refugee situation in which AIDS or HIV infection is an issue, both human rights and protection principles oblige States and UNHCR to cooperate in order to avoid individual tragedy. This involves recognition of the fact that exclusion is no solution, and that responses must be geared to the dual objectives of combating the disease and protecting the refugee and his or her rights. These objectives also entail the highest degree of inter-State and inter-agency cooperation.

The United Nations Educational, Scientific and Cultural Organization (UNESCO) has, since 1988, undertaken activities in the field of HIV/AIDS, through its Programme of Education for the Prevention of AIDS. The Programme is based on the notion that preventative education against AIDS, not only by imparting knowledge but as a means of changing attitudes and behaviour concerning HIV/AIDS, goes hand in hand with the ethics of human relations and with the struggle for human rights.

The current approach of UNESCO in education for the prevention of AIDS is the initiation and organization of a series of high-level Regional Planning Seminars on AIDS and Education within the School System to encourage education and training policies to take into account the impact of HIV/AIDS and the vital role of school-based preventative education. This approach includes capacity-building in the areas of educational planning, curriculum development and teacher training, facilitating collaboration between education and health sectors and fostering the development and implementation of national action plans in the field of school-based AIDS education.

According to information received, the United Nations Interregional Crime and Justice Research Institute (UNICRI), within its Drug Abuse Comprehensive Project, collects and disseminates scientific and legislative documentation in the area of prevention and control of drug abuse and related phenomena, including AIDS. Scientific articles, national and international legislation, as well as tools for prevention campaigns, videos and posters on HIV/AIDS prevention are collected in the UNICRI library database and are available for consultation on site.

The Inter-Parliamentary Union, at its 87th Inter-Parliamentary Conference (Yaoundé, April 1992) adopted a resolution entitled "The pandemic nature of acquired immune deficiency syndrome (AIDS)", which urged all Governments to ensure protection of the human rights and civil liberties of people infected, or believed likely to be infected.

The member States of the Organization of African Unity (OAU), in July 1992, adopted the Dakar Declaration on the AIDS Epidemic in Africa, which identifies prevention as the key to slowing the spread of AIDS in Africa and containing its ultimate impact as a national responsibility and international challenge. Whereas the Declaration refers to a number of measures to be taken in the context of the epidemic, such as increased budgetary allocations, political commitment to mobilizing society and planning for the care of people with HIV infection and AIDS, it should be mentioned that no specific reference is made to the protection of all human rights and fundamental freedoms of the individual.

## Measures Taken to Protect Human Rights in the Context of HIV/AIDS at the National Level

At the outset, it is notable that many of the replies received in response to the Secretary-General's note verbale simply indicated that the Government in question fully agreed with the contents of Commission resolution 1994/49 and applied no discriminatory measures violating the human rights of the persons concerned. However, references to positive measures undertaken to protect these rights were generally not made and, therefore, are presumed not to exist.

*National policy and legislation*

One Government indicated that the legislation in force in the country in regard to HIV/AIDS prohibits defamation or discrimination against persons infected with HIV/AIDS, and that deterrent measures are taken to prevent practices likely to bring them and their families into social disrepute. However, no further details were provided.

Other replies indicated that, although the concept of non-discrimination may be recognized in the national AIDS programmes, no specific national legislation has been adopted to actively safeguard the human rights of infected individuals.

The Government of Zimbabwe informed the Secretary-General that the AIDS Coordination Programme under the Ministry of Health and Child Welfare has adopted a policy of non-discrimination, non-stigmatization and respect for human rights in relation to HIV/AIDS. Consistent with this policy, a team of consultants comprising a legal expert, a medical practitioner, a communications expert, a sociologist and an economist has been engaged to assist in compiling comprehensive policies on HIV/AIDS and to make recommendations on areas for requisite legislation. The Zimbabwean policy conceptual framework outlines a set of principles which will guide the formulation of policy and programme responses in the current environment. These principles stipulate, inter alia, that "coping strategies of communities must be central to the national response and community-based organisations need to be instrumental in ensuring human survival and development", and that "people infected with HIV retain the right to participate in society without discrimination, and have the same right to comprehensive and appropriate health care, income support and community services as other members of the community". The Zimbabwean experience is an example of applying a multidisciplinary approach to the issue of HIV/AIDS. Not only does the complex nature of the problem require a public health response but law and ethics are important influences to be considered in order to effectively control and prevent the epidemic, whilst at the same time being able to guarantee the human rights and fundamental freedoms of the infected individuals and their families.

In the Netherlands, after a significant political debate on whether, in certain cases, people should be tested for HIV infection, focusing mainly on policies regarding admitting people with HIV infection to life insurance and employment disability insurance schemes and policies regarding job appointments, the Government is in favour of establishing a "code of conduct" which would include a number of provisions to protect the legal position of the applicant and a complaints procedure. This "code" is to be drawn up by insurance companies themselves, for approval by the Government.

However, with regard to national legislation, as well as to international standards, it should be borne in mind that although one country might not yet have HIV/AIDS specific legislation in force, the protection granted under health legislation in general also applies to the particular instance of HIV/AIDS. In Slovenia, for example, the Law of Health Care provides for equality in access to health care (not HIV specific), obligatory consent before any medical procedure is undertaken (not HIV specific) and confidentiality (not HIV

specific), which are all relevant principles to be safeguarded in connection with the epidemic.

*Institutional structures*

According to information received, in many countries national committees have been established to implement relevant legislation and directives which are designed to safeguard the right to privacy and integrity of the persons concerned. In many cases, however, these national committees are barely functional owing to inadequate financing.

In Canada, as part of the national AIDS strategy, an initiative was taken to establish a Federal Interdepartmental Committee on Human Rights and AIDS, with the Department of Justice as chair and the centre of responsibility lying with the Public Law Branch, Human Rights Law Section. The Committee draws on the expertise of all federal departments and monitors the evolution of public health policy in relation to HIV/AIDS and human rights. The Committee has already undertaken various studies on complex human rights issues relating to HIV/AIDS, such as the revision of the Treasury Board policy on HIV/AIDS in the workplace, the question of HIV-antibody testing of persons accused or convicted of sexual assault and the human rights issues relating to the use of criminal law to deal with HIV/AIDS-related actions.

In Mexico, the National Human Rights Commission, set up in June 1990, acts as a body to which persons considering themselves to be discriminated against because they are seropositive or have AIDS may have recourse. The National Human Rights Commission is also currently conducting a study for the period May 1994 to May 1995 with a view to identifying the various types of discrimination committed against people with HIV/AIDS. In addition, a brochure has been prepared by the National Commission entitled "Human rights of people with HIV or AIDS who are deprived of their freedom". This leaflet gives general information on the epidemic, its prevention and control, as well as listing the rights of the individual with HIV/AIDS, such as the right to be free from discrimination, the right to privacy and confidentiality, the right to freedom of movement, etc.

The measures taken by the Croatian Commission for the Prevention of HIV/AIDS, within the Ministry of Health, in implementing certain provisions of the national programme on AIDS have been made subject to approval by a so-called "ethics commission" of the Ministry of Health, so as to ensure the effective protection of human rights within the context of preventative measures to fight the epidemic.

*Education and information programmes*

Frequently, in the context of HIV/AIDS, so-called "high-risk groups" are identified, generally on the basis of sexual preference, lifestyle and racial or national origin, whose individual rights and freedoms may be affected on a large scale by virtue of their denial or discriminatory application (such as imposed testing or restriction of movement or activities) due to their apparent high-risk contamination factor. Unfortunately, most measures taken with regard to these identified groups are restrictive or discriminating in nature and generally do not focus on the prevention and protection needed to make these groups "lower risk" (through changes in behaviour, for example).

One positive example is that of prison training schemes undertaken in New Zealand, where the prevention of the transmission of HIV poses a particular challenge to the managers of penal institutions. The Government has a two-pronged approach. Firstly, special sessions on HIV/AIDS for all prison officers are part of staff education programmes; HIV infection guidelines have been transmitted to each institution along with a training video. Secondly, inmates are offered health education on a voluntary basis, which includes information about HIV/AIDS. Prisoners are informed about the needle exchange scheme which operates outside prisons and the techniques of cleaning drug injecting equipment.

The Government of Australia has implemented the broad principles of its national HIV/AIDS strategy that the law should complement and assist education and other public health measures through a recent community anti-discrimination campaign called "HIV doesn't discriminate . . . people do", which was launched in 1993 and updated in June 1994. This campaign aims to reduce discriminatory attitudes and behaviour towards people living with HIV/AIDS. It consists of television advertisements and print commercials, also translated for use in the ethnic press, reinforcing the safety of everyday social contact, using affected people instead of actors to destigmatize people living with HIV/AIDS, by showing them as, inter alia, someone's friend, relation, neighbour or partner.

Two other information dissemination projects funded by the Government of Australia are also of interest. The first informs people living with HIV/AIDS of what constitutes discrimination, their rights and responsibilities and available avenues of redress. The second targets health workers to assist them in better understanding what constitutes discrimination and in developing appropriate policies and practices which enhance quality of care.

In Brazil the Candido Mendes College in Rio de Janeiro introduced, in August 1992, a voluntary course entitled "AIDS–legal approaches" into their law curriculum. The course aims to help influence public policy by sensitizing students to the legal problems encountered by persons living with HIV/AIDS, as well as to teach students how to defend the rights of people in need. The course curriculum covers issues such as civil law, involving the possibility of civil liabilities (for example, civil suits against blood banks); contract law (for example, action against private health insurance companies refusing to cover HIV/AIDS-related treatment expenses); family law; inheritance law; labour law (for example, cases involving dismissal on the grounds of HIV/AIDS infection); criminal law (cases involving intentional transmission of HIV); as well as violations of basic human rights law. In addition, law students opting for this course gain practical experience in providing legal assistance in lawsuits.

Soroptimist International, a non-governmental organization in consultative status with the Economic and Social Council, reported on the various activities undertaken by its national affiliates in two programme areas, "Health and human rights" and "Status of women", which include the promotion of education, information and research with regard to HIV/AIDS, the support of human rights of patients and families affected by HIV/AIDS, as well as advocacy of the participation of women in prevention and control of HIV/AIDS. More specifically, Soroptimist International is currently drafting its next quadrennial project (1995–1999), entitled "AIDS education and alternatives to prostitution for women in northern Thailand", which would entail the provision of AIDS education and training for northern Thai women in income-generating pursuits in order to improve their status as women and increase their awareness of their human rights and thereby to decrease their vulnerability to HIV/AIDS infection.

*Other measures*

The Government of Iraq, in its response, indicated that special care is made available to persons with HIV/AIDS, as well as their families. They are provided with financial, social

and educational support and periodic meetings are organized for such persons and their families in order to discuss and help to solve their problems and avoid any measure that might lead to social discrimination against them and their families.

The Government of China reported that, in June 1994, the Ministries concerned organized a symposium in Beijing on the right way to prevent and control AIDS in China. At this symposium, experts and academics called upon society to do more to protect the rights of people living with HIV/AIDS. The Government was also called upon, through legislative and other administrative steps, to protect, inter alia, the human rights to life, privacy, work, social welfare and medical treatment of individuals concerned. "These appeals and suggestions came to the attention of the Ministries concerned and are by degrees being implemented and put into practice."

A conference of health ministers of the Latin American countries on the subject "Health and development: AIDS, a social and economic question" was held at Brasilia in May 1993. The Conference adopted many conclusions and recommendations, including some interesting ones made in connection with the prevention of discriminatory restrictions on international travel. The Conference recommended, inter alia:

(a) The elimination of any requirement regarding serological tests for HIV infection as a condition for obtaining any type of visa (work, temporary residence, transit, tourist and student visas);

(b) Development of research into population movement patterns, epidemiological studies of behaviour and social studies designed to establish HIV/AIDS/STD transmission patterns, and identification of community support mechanisms and social impact in communities marked by substantial movements of persons and in frontier areas;

(c) The conclusion of bilateral and/or multilateral agreements between countries in the Latin American region which guarantee medical assistance for persons coming from other countries in the region, to the extent consistent with the laws and assistance facilities of each country;

(d) Development and implementation of information, education and communication activities to prevent infection by HIV and other sexually transmitted diseases (STDs), for the benefit of travellers, tourists, persons in transit, immigrants and host populations.

In December 1994, the Government of France, in cooperation with WHO, organized a summit of Heads of State and Government, called the "Paris AIDS Summit". In preparation for this summit, strategic meetings were organized at which issues such as blood safety, the development and accessibility of preventative technology, care and support of people affected by HIV/AIDS and prevention of and vulnerability to HIV/AIDS were addressed. The report of the strategic meeting on vulnerability to HIV/AIDS addressed the relationship between HIV/AIDS-related discrimination, human rights and ethics in particular and identified women and children as especially vulnerable groups.

In the final document of the Paris AIDS Summit, the Paris Final Declaration, of 1 December 1994, 42 heads of State solemnly declared to, inter alia, undertake in their national policies the protection and promotion of the rights of individuals, in particular those living with or most vulnerable to HIV/AIDS, through the legal and social environment and to ensure equal protection under the law for persons living with HIV/AIDS with regard to access to health care, employment, education, travel, housing and social welfare and to improve women's status, education and living conditions.

Another constructive example of promotion of the dignity and rights of people living with HIV/AIDS is the work of the Grupo Pela Vida ("Group for Life"), a loosely-linked network of non-governmental organizations in Brazil. This activist movement, run mainly by volunteers, helps towards the creation of a supportive environment and the strengthening of community action by defining the right to life as the right to complete citizenship. The methods of work of the Group for Life are various. They include outreach through meetings and discussion groups on topics of interest to the participants, which at the same time raise awareness and provide an opportunity for social contacts and solidarity. Workshops to develop personal coping skills, as well as special groups for women, homosexuals and those living in extreme poverty have been created to break through the social barriers and prejudices creating feelings of isolation, fear, clandestinity and loneliness in persons infected with HIV/AIDS.

The Group for Life provides a free legal service to individuals who wish to take legal action against institutions which have violated the human rights of persons living with HIV/AIDS, and also gives free legal advice to public hospitals, labour unions and other institutions on the matter. In addition, besides producing oriented information in the form of brochures and a bulletin, the Group for Life has placed a telephone hot-line at the disposal of the general public. In 1993, the Group successfully launched a nation-wide radio campaign for the prevention of HIV/AIDS, which received wide media coverage.

The Group for Life has also established an international outlet by being a constituent of the WHO Global Management Committee Task Force on HIV/AIDS. This is a practical way to be regularly informed of the latest developments in research and policy in the field of HIV/AIDS at the international level.

The International Confederation of Midwives, a non-governmental organization in consultative status with the Economic and Social Council, in May 1993, adopted a policy/position statement on HIV/AIDS, which recognized that "midwives, by virtue of their close professional relationship with women and their families, are in a unique position to influence changes in lifestyles which may assist in containing the spread of this disease. In keeping with this belief, the midwife should, inter alia, provide education regarding the spread of HIV and ensure that women who are HIV positive or have AIDS have access to non-discriminatory midwifery care in pregnancy, childbirth and the puerperium". This is an example of action taken by a professional interest group in an area of specific concern to promote the human rights and non-discrimination of people living with HIV/AIDS.

## Conclusions and Recommendations

*At the national level*

In conclusion, it is noted with satisfaction that the protection of human rights and the prevention of discrimination have been accepted in principle in the context of many national AIDS programmes. General principles such as the rejection of screening of the whole population, voluntary and informed consent for HIV testing, anonymity and confidentiality of testing and test results and the rejection of mandatory treatment and isolation, as well as the obligation to ensure the safety of blood transfusions, are contained in most of these programmes. Yet a dramatic gap seems to exist

between national policies and legislation and their implementation. What is more, many national policies in effect actively interfere with the human rights of the individual and are generally carried out without legal justification.

It is strongly urged that all government action which might interfere with internationally respected human rights standards must be provided for and carried out in accordance with the law, and only when the measures taken are proportional with a pressing objective. In the context of HIV/AIDS, coercive policies, such as testing, public disclosure of status, segregation and the discriminatory denial of employment, housing, education and travel have no public health rationale.

All Governments that replied reiterated their commitment to the protection of human rights and the prevention of discrimination in the context of HIV/AIDS. Many also stated that measures are being taken at the national level to implement this commitment. However, it is regrettable that only a few replies provided more details concerning these measures, because the present report was intended to highlight the various types of positive measures that may be taken at the national, regional and international levels to ensure the protection of human rights in the context of HIV/AIDS.

Since most national AIDS programmes generally do not contain specific measures for the protection of human rights and prevention of discrimination, Governments are requested, in accordance with Commission on Human Rights resolution 1994/49, to include in their national AIDS programmes specific measures to combat social stigmatization, discrimination and violence directed against persons with HIV/AIDS and to develop a supportive legal and social environment necessary for the effective prevention and care of AIDS.

Furthermore, it is recommended that all Governments engage in a careful study of their existing legal systems with a view to identifying and developing the legal instruments necessary for the protection of people infected by HIV/AIDS and their families and associates, for the reduction in vulnerability to infection of certain disadvantaged groups in society and for the implementation of national AIDS programmes, in conformity with national health and development policies and on the basis of respect for human rights.

In the context of the effective implementation of national AIDS programmes and the review of legislation and administrative policies, it is recommended that national machinery be established to monitor these processes. This may be done by extending the mandate and responsibilities of existing machinery, such as national human rights commissions, or by setting up new structures. Those States that have already established such bodies are to be commended. It is urged that additional resources be allocated to ensure their effective functioning.

Education, outreach and the dissemination of information are generally considered to be the most effective means for preventing and controlling the disease, especially because it is mostly fear and ignorance that result in the ostracism and stigmatization of, and discrimination against, HIV-infected people and people with AIDS. In fact, it has been agreed that "HIV transmission can be prevented through informed and responsible behaviour", so that it becomes the responsibility of individuals not to put themselves or others at risk of HIV infection, thereby generating a need for self-protection as well as a moral obligation to protect others through behaviour modification. It is, therefore, satisfying to note that in the domain of education and information in particular the efforts of Governments and non-governmental organizations are increasing.

It has been has observed, however, that although many information and education campaigns inform the public on the nature, spread and prevention of the disease from a public health perspective, often the human rights and fundamental freedoms of the individual are not sufficiently addressed. Concepts such as confidentiality and informed consent, non-discrimination and freedom from stigmatization and marginalization should be set in the legal context of existing international and national standards and the Government's obligation to ensure these rights for all human beings needs to be highlighted.

It has been noted that already disadvantaged groups or those whose human rights are already not respected are increasingly vulnerable to infection and to the impact of AIDS through diminished access to prevention information, education programmes and health care, and social and legal services and support. Governments should, therefore, take special measures to reach these groups with prevention information and education and with care programmes. Furthermore, the Secretary-General strongly advocates for this reason, a participatory and democratic approach with regard to measures protecting human rights and preventing discrimination in the context of HIV/AIDS is strongly advocated. Persons living with HIV/AIDS should be perceived as an integral part of the solution to the problem and, therefore, be involved in the formulation, planning and execution of such measures, wherever possible. It is only through this participatory approach that a certain acceptability of AIDS prevention and control programmes for most affected groups can be achieved, which in turn results in voluntary behaviour modifications which are essential for effective and durable change.

Furthermore, Governments are urged to give increased support to action-oriented social and behavioral research, based on community priorities, that can lead to the development and implementation of improved strategies for reducing people's vulnerability to the risks and consequences of HIV/AIDS.

In this connection, increased focus on women and children is recommended, as the consequences of HIV/AIDS not only threaten women's health but also burden their role as caretakers of the sick and destitute. The social, developmental and health consequences of AIDS need to be seen from the perspective of gender, yet this is not always the case. The abolition of the sexual, legal, social and economic subordination of women should be made a human rights imperative, essential for reducing their own and their children's susceptibility to HIV/AIDS and enabling them to respond effectively to the epidemic.

In this context, the following suggestions made by the Commission on the Status of Women at its thirty-eighth session in March 1994 are highlighted: a comprehensive, integrated model of health services for women should be applied, adequately funded and available to all at affordable cost; gender-sensitive research and training for health workers and greater participation and effective representation of women, especially female health-care workers, in planning and programme delivery, including training of women doctors and health technicians, should be supported; efforts should be made to combat HIV/AIDS through a recognition of gender factors and their specific and growing impact on women.

The development and support are encouraged of national networks of non-governmental organizations and commu-nity-based organizations and people living with HIV/AIDS, which engage in advocacy, action, human resources development, consensus-building and legal support for those affected by HIV/AIDS, both those vulnerable to infection and those already infected. These networks should be linked at the regional level and advise the joint and co-sponsored United Nations programme at the international level.

*At the international level*

The developments and the progress achieved towards the establishment of a joint and co-sponsored United Nations programme on HIV/AIDS are welcomed. In this connection it is recommended that the six co-sponsoring agencies take urgent steps to incorporate a clear and effective human rights component in the proposed programme, which at present is lacking.

Furthermore, in accordance with the Paris Declaration of 1 December 1994, the joint and co-sponsored programme is called upon to strengthen national and international mechanisms that are concerned with HIV/AIDS-related human rights and ethics, including the use of an advisory council and national and regional networks to provide leadership, advocacy and guidance in order to ensure that non-discrimination, human rights and ethical principles form an integral part of the response to the pandemic.

Support is expressed for the proposals for global and national initiatives, put forward by the strategic meeting on vulnerability in preparation for the Paris AIDS Summit, which call for the fostering of a supportive climate through a global campaign for tolerance and understanding of people living with HIV/AIDS, spearheaded by the co-sponsoring agencies of the joint and co-sponsored United Nations programme on HIV/AIDS in the context of the International Year of Tolerance in 1995.

Bearing in mind the various practices of States with regard to persons infected with HIV or persons with AIDS, as well as the urgent necessity to provide proper protection of the rights and freedoms of these persons and to ensure the application of non-discrimination in all areas of life, the need is recognized for joint effort and action on the part of the international community. As stated by WHO, although there are sufficient general human rights standards that could be applied to HIV/AIDS issues, there is little understanding of how these specifically apply in this area. Therefore, more needs to be done to encourage and guide States to abandon discriminatory and coercive policy and to guide them in the implementation of protective legislation and practice.

In this connection, it is recommended that the Commission on Human Rights consider the elaboration of a set of guidelines or principles to assist Governments in shaping their national policies in regard to the human rights dimension of HIV/AIDS. The development of such guidelines or principles could provide an international framework for discussion of human rights considerations at the national, regional and international levels in order to arrive at a more comprehensive understanding of the complex relationship between the public health rationale and the human rights rationale of HIV/AIDS. In particular, Governments could benefit from guidelines that outline clearly how human rights standards apply in the area of HIV/AIDS and indicate concrete and specific measures, both in terms of legislation and practice, that should be undertaken. Given the rapid spread of the disease and its devastating personal, economic and social impact, time is of the essence in this regard.

In this context, the recommendation of the Sub-Commission, contained in its resolution 1994/29 of 26 August 1994, that the present report consider the development of a declaration on respect for human rights in the response to AIDS and guidelines for the prevention of AIDS-related discrimination is particularly welcome.

Also welcome is the request of the Sub-Commission, contained in the same resolution, that the Commission on Human Rights consider recommending the organization by the Centre for Human Rights of a second international expert consultation on human rights and AIDS, with particular emphasis on the prevention of AIDS-related discrimination and stigma. This second international consultation may wish to consider preparing a contribution to the drafting of the international guidelines or principles, referred to above.

Finally, it is noted with interest that the Sub-Commission, in the same resolution, requested the Commission on Human Rights to consider the appropriate methods by which to keep under continuous review the protection of the rights of people affected by AIDS-related discrimination. It is recommended to the Commission that it consider this question in greater detail at its present session.

In its resolution 1995/44 concerning the protection of human rights in the context of human immunodeficiency virus (HIV) and acquired immune deficiency syndrome (AIDS), the Commission on Human Rights,

Recognizing that the increasing challenges presented by HIV/AIDS require renewed efforts to ensure universal respect for and observance of human rights and fundamental freedoms for all, as well as the avoidance of HIV/AIDS-related discrimination and stigma,

Mindful that respect for the principle of non-discrimination is the key to the protection and realization of human rights and fundamental freedoms as recognized in international instruments,

Recalling General Assembly resolutions 45/187 of 21 December 1990 and 46/203 of 20 December 1991, Economic and Social Council resolution 1990/86 of 27 July 1990, World Health Assembly resolutions WHA41.24 of 13 May 1988, WHA43.10 of 16 May 1990, WHA45.35 of 14 May 1992 and WHA46.37 of 14 May 1993, general recommendation 15 of the Committee on the Elimination of Discrimination against Women and other relevant resolutions and decisions adopted by organizations of the United Nations system, as well as by other competent forums,

Welcomes the Final Declaration of the Paris AIDS Summit, of 1 December 1994, in which the participants pledged to promote and protect the rights of people infected and affected by HIV/AIDS,

Also welcomes the progress made in the establishment of a joint and co-sponsored United Nations programme on HIV/AIDS,

Recalling its resolutions 1992/56 of 3 March 1992, 1993/53 of 9 March 1993 and 1994/49 of 4 March 1994 concerning discrimination against people with HIV infection or AIDS,

Acknowledging the significant role of the World Health Organization, and other bodies of the United Nations system, and the major contribution made by national and international non-governmental organizations, in particular organizations of people living with HIV/AIDS, and the International Federation of Red Cross and Red Crescent Societies, in fighting discrimination against and advocating the rights of people living with HIV/AIDS,

Noting with appreciation the Rights and Humanity Declaration and Charter on HIV and AIDS transmitted to the Commission at its forty-eighth session by the Permanent Mission of the Gambia to the United Nations (E/CN.4/1992/82),

Concerned that lack of full enjoyment of their fundamental rights by persons suffering from economic, social or legal disadvantage heightens their vulnerability to the risk of HIV infection,

Noting that, according to a report submitted to the Commission on the Status of Women at its thirty-third session (E/CN.6/1989/6/Add.1), women are especially vulnerable to the risk of HIV infection and to the economic and social impact of AIDS as a result of their disadvantageous legal, social and economic status, and concerned at the increasing rate of HIV infection among women and girls,

Expressing its grave concern that the continuing exploitation of children, including child prostitution, poses the risk of transmission of HIV,

Concerned at evidence indicating that groups in society suffering discrimination in the enjoyment of their fundamental rights, and disadvantage with respect to their access to education, health care and social services, are as a result more vulnerable to the risk of infection and to the personal and social impact of the pandemic,

Alarmed at discriminatory laws and policies and the emergence of new forms of discriminatory practices which deny people living with HIV/AIDS, their families and associates, as well as high-risk groups, enjoyment of their fundamental rights and freedoms,

Concerned that the fear and ignorance surrounding HIV/AIDS are leading to increased stigmatization of and prejudice against people living with HIV/AIDS or presumed to be at risk of infection, sometimes resulting in intimidation, harassment or violence against such individuals, as well as to arbitrary detention and deportation,

Bearing in mind that, as recognized by the World Health Assembly in its resolution WHA45.35, there is no public health rationale for any measures that limit the rights of the individual, notably measures establishing mandatory screening,

Stressing that discrimination and stigmatization are counterproductive to measures to prevent and control HIV/AIDS, and that anti-discrimination measures form a component part of an effective public health strategy,

Emphasizing the responsibility of Governments to take measures to counter social stigmatization of and discrimination against those affected by HIV/AIDS, and their commitment to strengthen national and international mechanisms that are concerned with HIV/AIDS-related human rights and ethics,

Recognizing that HIV transmission can be prevented through informed and responsible behaviour, and emphasizing the role and responsibility of individuals, groups and organs of society aimed at promoting, in a spirit of human solidarity and tolerance, a social environment supportive of the effective prevention and eradication of the root causes of the HIV/AIDS pandemic,

Welcoming the report by the Secretary-General on international and domestic measures taken to protect human rights and prevent discrimination in the context of HIV/AIDS (E/CN.4/1995/45) and his recommendations therein, but noting with concern that there is insufficient information about successful strategies for protecting human rights in the context of HIV/AIDS,

1. Confirms that discrimination on the basis of AIDS or HIV status, actual or presumed, is prohibited by existing international human rights standards, and that the term "or

other status" in non-discrimination provisions in international human rights texts can be interpreted to cover health status, including HIV/AIDS;

2. Calls upon all States to ensure, where necessary, that their laws, policies and practices, including those introduced in the context of HIV/AIDS, respect human rights standards, including the right to privacy and integrity of people living with HIV/AIDS, prohibit HIV/AIDS-related discrimination and do not have the effect of inhibiting programmes for the prevention of HIV/AIDS and for the care of persons infected with HIV/AIDS;

3. Also calls upon all States to take all the necessary steps, including appropriate and speedy redress procedures, and the introduction of protective legislation and appropriate education to combat discrimination, prejudice and stigma, to ensure the full enjoyment of civil, political, economic, social and cultural rights by people living with HIV/AIDS, their families and associates, and people presumed to be at risk of infection, with particular attention to women, children and vulnerable groups, and to address such concerns within their activities in the context of the United Nations Year for Tolerance, 1995;

4. Further calls upon all States to strengthen their efforts to advance the legal, economic and social status of women, children and vulnerable groups in order to render them less vulnerable to the risk of HIV infection and to the adverse socio-economic consequences of the AIDS pandemic;

5. Recognizes the need to protect women and girls from sexual abuse and violence and calls upon the Special Rapporteur on the sale of children, child prostitution and child pornography, the Committee on the Rights of the Child, the Commission on the Status of Women and the Working Group on Contemporary Forms of Slavery to pay sustained attention to the risk which the continuing exploitation of children, including child prostitution, poses for the transmission of HIV;

6. Invites States to involve non-governmental and community-based organizations and people living with HIV/AIDS in the formulation and implementation of public policies, including the support of participatory programmes for prevention, care and social support among vulnerable and marginalized populations;

7. Calls upon States to take all necessary steps, in particular appropriate education and information measures, to facilitate informed and responsible behaviour;

8. Invites the Human Rights Committee, the Committee on Economic, Social and Cultural Rights and other similar bodies to give full attention to monitoring States parties' compliance with their commitments under the relevant human rights instruments regarding the rights of people living with HIV/AIDS, their families and associates, or people presumed to be at risk of infection;

9. Calls upon the Subcommission on Prevention of Discrimination and Protection of Minorities to keep the issue of AIDS-related discrimination under continuous review under all relevant agenda items, as well as within the work of its relevant working groups and special rapporteurs;

10. Calls upon relevant professional bodies to re-examine their codes of professional practice with a view to strengthening respect for human rights and dignity in the context of HIV/AIDS, and calls upon the relevant authorities to develop training in this regard;

11. Requests the co-sponsors of the joint and co-sponsored United Nations programme on HIV/AIDS to integrate a strong human rights component throughout the strategies and work of the future programme;

12. Requests the High Commissioner for Human Rights to consider appropriate methods by which to keep under continuous review the protection of human rights in the context of the HIV/AIDS pandemic and to undertake with the Centre for Human Rights, in cooperation with the joint and co-sponsored United Nations programme on HIV/AIDS, non-governmental agencies and other actors in the field, the task of elaborating guidelines on promoting and protecting respect for human rights in the context of HIV/AIDS, and to reflect in this regard on the possibility of organizing a second international expert consultation on human rights and AIDS;

13. Requests the Secretary-General to consult with Governments, relevant United Nations bodies, specialized agencies and non-governmental organizations with a view to keeping under review the protection of human rights in the context of the HIV/AIDS pandemic and to prepare for the consideration of the Commission at its fifty-second session a progress report on the development of a human rights component in the joint and co-sponsored United Nations programme on HIV/AIDS and on the status of the guidelines mentioned in paragraph 12.

***SEE ALSO*** *Health as a Human Right.*

***BIBLIOGRAPHY.*** Bayer, Ronald, and D. L. Kirp, eds. *AIDS in the Industrialized Democracies: Passions, Politics, and Policies.* Montreal, Canada: McGill-Queen's University Press, 1992. Scholarly monograph, in English.

Bernstein, David. "From Pesthouses to AIDS Hospices: Neighbors' Irrational Fears of Treatment Facilities for Contagious Diseases," *Columbia Human Rights Law Review* 22, no. 1 (Fall 1990): 1–20. Scholarly article, in English.

Breum, M., and A. Hendriks, eds. *AIDS and Human Rights: An International Perspective.* Copenhagen: Danish Center of Human Rights, 1988. Edited collection, in English.

Carlé, Pia, Aart Hendriks, and Dineke Zeegers. *AIDS and Human Rights in the European Communities.* Utrecht, the Netherlands: Netherlands Institute of Human Rights 1991. Research report, in English.

Cohen, Roberta, and Laurie Wiseberg. *Double Jeopardy–Threat to Life and Human Rights: Discrimination against Persons with AIDS.* Cambridge, MA, USA: Human Rights Internet, 1990. NGO report, in English.

Fuss, Sev S., and Dineke Zeegers. "Reporting of AIDS and Human Immunodeficiency Virus (HIV) Infection: A Worldwide Review of Legislative and Regulatory Patterns and Issues," *AIDS & Public Policy Journal* 5, no. 1 (Winter 1990): 32–36. Scholarly article, in English.

Gostin, L., and W. J. Curran, guest eds. "AIDS, Law and Policy," *Law, Medicine and Health Care* 15, no. 1–2 (Summer 1987). Scholarly article, in English; bibliography, organized by such headings as "antidiscrimination," "criminal law," "education," "employment," "homosexuals," "immigration," "insurance," "law and policy," "prison," and "privacy," pp. 86–89.

Guest, Iain. "Special Report: The World Health Organization and AIDS," *UN Watch* 2 (Spring/Summer 1988): 2–11. IGO report, in English.

Malinowsky, H. Robert, and G. J. Perry. *AIDS information Sourcebook: Third Edition 1991–92.* Phoenix, AZ, USA: Oryx Press, 1991. Reference material, in English.

Mariasy, Judith. *Triple Jeopardy: Women & AIDS.* London: Panos Institute, 1990. Research report, in English.

Panos Institute. *AIDS and the Third World.* 2d ed. London: 1987. NGO report, in English.

————. *The Third Epidemic: Repercussions of the Fear of AIDS.* London: 1990. Research report, in English.

Parts, Mark. "The Eighth Amendment and the Requirement of Active Measures to Prevent the Spread of AIDS in Prisons," *Columbia Human Rights Law Review* 22, no. 2 (Spring 1991): 217–249. Scholarly article, in English.

Sabatier, Renee. *Blaming Others: Prejudice, Race and Worldwide AIDS.* London: Panos Institute and the Norwegian Red Cross, 1988. Monograph, in English.

Shilts, Randy. *And the Band Played On: Politics, People and the AIDS Epidemic.* New York: St. Martin's Press, 1987. Journalistic monograph, in English.

Swiss Institute of Comparative Law. *Comparative Study on Discrimination against Persons with HIV or AIDS.* Strasbourg, France: Council of Europe, 1993. Intergovernmental report, in English.

UN Center for Human Rights. *Report of an International Consultation on AIDS and Human Rights.* Geneva, Switzerland: 26–28 July 1989. World Campaign for Human Rights Series; Doc. No. HR/PUB/90/2 (1991).

UN Sub-Commission on Prevention of Discrimination and Protection of Minorities. *Discrimination against HIV-Infected People or People with AIDS: Final Report Submitted by Mr. Varela Quirós, Special Rapporteur.* Geneva, Switzerland: 1992. Intergovernmental document, in English and French.

Watstein, S. B., and R. A. Laurich. *AIDS and Women: A Sourcebook.* Phoenix, AZ, USA: Oryx Press, 1991. Reference material, in English.

World Health Organization. Global Programme on AIDS. *International Conference on the Implications of AIDS for Mothers and Children: Technical Statements and Selected Presentations.* Geneva, Switzerland: 1991. Intergovernmental conference report, in English.

————. *Inventory of Non-Governmental Organizations Working on AIDS in Countries that Receive Development Cooperation or Assistance.* Geneva, Switzerland: United Nations, 1991. Directory, in English.

World Health Organization. Regional Conference on AIDS and Human Rights. Brazzaville, People's Republic of the Congo, 12–14 March 1990. WHO Regional Office for Africa.

————. Regional Workshop on Legal and Ethical Aspects of AIDS and HIV Infection. Seoul, Republic of Korea, 23–25 April 1990. WHO Report Series 1.

**ALBANIA.** The Republic of Albania is a country in southern Europe, on the Adriatic Sea. It has borders with Greece and the former Yugoslavia. It achieved independence from Turkey in 1944 and became a member of the United Nations in 1955. Its population is estimated to be 3,305,000, with an annual growth of 1.8%. Ethnic groups include Greeks, Vlachs, Bulgars, Serbs, and Gypsies. Languages commonly used include Albanian (official), Gheg in the north, and Tosk in the south. In 1967, the government closed all churches and mosques and declared Albania to be an atheist State. Religions practiced up to that time included Christianity (Albanian Orthodox, 20%; Roman Catholic, 10%) and Islam (70%). Literacy is estimated at 75%.

After World War II, a communist dictatorship was established in Albania under the leadership of hardliner Enver Hoxha, who ruled until his death in 1985. Under its former title, the People's Socialist Republic of Albania, the Council of Ministers was its executive organ. However, policy decisions were taken by the Albanian Workers' (Communist) Party and its Politburo. The First Secretary of the Party was President of the Presidium and Head of State.

As the former Socialist Republic, Albania was cited repeatedly by the UN Commission on Human Rights and the Sub-Commission on Prevention of Discrimination and Protection of Minorities for its treatment of minority citizens, particularly the Greeks, its largest minority, and for its stringent anti-religious policies. Albania outlawed religion in 1967 when it became the world's first atheist country.

After the fall of the communist dictatorship in 1990, restrictions on religious worship were relaxed. A new government, elected in 1992, completely altered the national approach to human rights in the country. The sweeping changes are described in a communication to the United Nations, dated 28 January 1993, from the charge d'affaires of the Permanent Mission of the Republic of Albania, reading in part as follows (E/CN.4/1993/43):

### The Democratic Processes

The important democratic movements and, more particularly, the student movements in 1990 in Albania led to the fall of the communist dictatorship, which had ruled for 45 years. The collapse of communism in Albania marked the beginning of a broad process of construction of a genuinely democratic society, based on free competition and respect for human rights. It should be noted that several political, economic and social changes have taken place in Albanian society since 1990. Albania has already shown its political orientation towards democracy; its increasingly active commitment to international processes; far-reaching political, economic, and social reforms; its determination to respect and fulfil its commitments under the International Covenants; and, more particularly, its determination to respect international human rights standards constitute genuine evidence of this orientation.

It is possible to gain a more precise idea of the results achieved by Albania since 1990 by taking account of what it inherited from communist rule. The communist regime in Albania, one of the harshest in eastern and central Europe, was characterized by flagrant and massive violations of human rights. The suppression of freedom of conscience, and refusal of the right to freedom of expression and organization assumed broad proportions. Albania has inherited a very weak economy from the old regime, which makes it difficult to implement reforms and, more particularly, to undertake economic reforms. However, Albania has now totally abandoned the communist path of development and has committed itself with determination to the building of a modern democracy.

The new society that Albania wishes to build is based on the democratic principles of respect for human rights, respect for the primacy of law, and multi-party democracy.

Respect for human rights has been, and still remains, one of the chief concerns of the Albanian Government since its establishment following the elections of 22 March 1992, which brought to power the democratic forces of society. The problems relating to human rights are regarded as forming an integral part of the ongoing political, economic and social reforms. In the new legislative context that has been formulated and continues to be put in place, it is stated that respect for human rights constitutes one of the fundamental principles of political and social organization in Albania. The legislative context that protects these rights and condemnation of violations of these rights constitute a valuable achievement that creates the possibility of making further progress. Article 2 of Constitutional Act No. 7,491 of 29 April 1992, relating to the principal provisions of the Constitution, which is in force until enactment of the new Constitution–a draft of which has been submitted to Parliament for consideration–states: "The dignity of man, his rights and freedoms, the free development of his personality, the constitutional order, equality before the law, social justice, and the multiparty system constitute the foundations of this State, which has an obligation to respect them and to protect them." This new legal instrument affirms that the primacy of law constitutes one of the fundamental principles of the organization of society, which is a further guarantee for the building of an advanced democratic society based on respect for the law. After affirming the principle of the separation of powers, this Act stipulates that: "the activity of the State shall be exercised by the organs of the State recognized by the law," while article 6 of the Act provides that the political parties "shall be completely independent of the State." This will help to eliminate the possibility of usurpation of power by a State-sponsored party, as occurred under the communist regime.

It is further stated that the form of government in Albania is parliamentary democracy. The multi-party system is regarded as a fundamental condition for democracy and the will of the people constitutes the foundations of power. Thus, article 1 of the Act, relating to the principal provisions of the Constitution, states: "Albania is a parliamentary republic. National sovereignty originates from the people and is vested in the people." Article 3 of the Act provides that the referendum is one of the means by which the people participate in the political life of the country, stipulating specifically that: "the people shall exercise its power by means of its representative organs, and through the exercise of the referendum."

It should be noted that considerable efforts have been made to put these principles into practice.

### Results of the Reforms

(a) The Primacy of Law

*Development of the Legislative Framework.* The process of reform of social organization in Albania and the construction of a democratic society could not be achieved within the context of the old legislative structure. For this reason, the building and establishment of a new legislative structure capable of supporting the process of reform constitute an important achievement in the construction of a democratic and pluralist society.

Many laws have been amended and several others have been formulated and ratified. Thus, several amendments have been made to the legislation concerning the death penalty, which has been abolished for women and persons under the age of 18, and concerning the reintroduction of reha-

bilitation, conditional release, and many other criminal procedures.

The text of the new constitution has been prepared in accordance with the principles of a democratic society and with the assistance of many foreign experts. A special chapter of the text deals with human rights and fundamental freedoms. Ratification of the text will undoubtedly create an essential, adequate and important framework for the development of the democratic process and respect for human rights.

Other draft legislation, such as the Status of Journalists Bill and the Religious Communities Bill, is in the course of preparation and will shortly be submitted to Parliament for consideration.

*Reorganization of the Judiciary.* The reform of the system of judicial institutions has constituted an important element of the State's activity in restructuring the national institutional framework. The efforts made to this end have already yielded good results, such as the overall reorganization of the existing judicial institutions, the re-establishment and functioning of the Ministry of Science (whose activity was suspended from 1963–1990), progress in the area of impartiality and the independence of the organs of justice, etc. Act No. 7,574 of 24 June 1992 relating to the organization of justice and amendments to the Codes of Penal and Civil Procedure clearly determines the competence of judges, prosecutors and pre-trial bodies, thereby conferring a legitimate character on their activities. Article 5 of the Constitutional Act states: "Judicial authority shall be exercised by the organs of justice, which shall be independent and refer only to the authority of the law."

It should, however, be noted that, in its efforts to permit the independent functioning of the organs of justice, our country has encountered certain difficulties and a number of serious obstacles, such as the non-existence of properly qualified personnel to ensure the functioning of the organs of justice, the inexperience of recently employed personnel, and the absence of a tradition of impartiality among the judiciary. These difficulties are having an adverse effect on the restructuring of the organs of justice and their independent functioning. It should, however, be stated that the reorganization of the system of organs of justice is already at an acceptable level.

Improvement of the Administration of the State. Another important aspect of the reform of the institutional structures has been the establishment of a new administration whose activity is based on the relevant laws. To this end, the Act on the depoliticization of certain organs of the State gives effect to article 6 of the Act relating to the principal provisions of the Constitution, which forbids political party activity in the organs of the State administration and in the organs of justice. More precisely, this Act prohibits activity by the parties or political organizations or associations in the departments, enterprises or military institutions of the Ministry of Defence and the Ministry of Public Order, in the Ministry of Foreign Affairs and in diplomatic missions abroad, in the Ministry of Justice, in the organs of the administration of justice, in the Albanian news agency and radio and television stations, and in the organs of power and local administration. The enforcement of this Act was of particular importance in the context of the activity of the organs of justice and the organs of public order.

The restructuring of the organs for the maintenance of public order has been another subject of concern of the Albanian Government in the context of the reorganization of the administration of the State. The main objective of the efforts made in this area has been the introduction of legislation aimed at governing the activity of these organs with due concern for observance of the law and respect for human dignity. The Forces of Law and Order Act aims precisely at this end. It should be added that this new organization of the forces of law and order has been of particular importance in the maintenance of public order. However, it should also be noted that there have been a number of difficulties and obstacles to overcome, such as the absence of qualified personnel and facilities. Albania has declared its willingness to accept any technical assistance in this area. With this in mind, it has already greatly expanded its contacts with many international organizations and is maintaining increasingly close relations with them by organizing a growing number of exchanges of experience, seminars, etc.

*Democratic Institutions.* The process of establishing democratic institutions has been a difficult one, but some success is being achieved at the present time.

The elections held on 22 March 1992, the first genuinely free elections, led to the establishment of a multi-party Parliament, with seats held by five parties: the Democratic Party (the majority party), the Socialist Party, the Social Democrat Party, the Republican Party, and the Union for Human Rights Party. This multi-party system means that Parliament has become a major instrument in furthering the new democracy.

In regard to the organization and establishment of democratic institutions, the separation of powers has been yet another major achievement in the functioning of a State governed by the rule of law. This separation is set out in the Constitutional Act, in which art 3 affirms that "the fundamental principle of the organization of the State is the separation of the Legislature, Executive and Judiciary."

The establishment of the Constitutional Court of the Republic is another important advance, as it guarantees strict observance of the law and lawful activity by the State. Ever since its establishment, the Constitutional Court has considered a number of issues and played an important role in interpreting the law and eliminating violations of the Constitutional Act.

Progress has also been made in creating a system of institutions and organizations for the protection of human rights. The Parliamentary Human Rights Commission and the Albanian Helsinki Committee are undoubtedly notable achievements, particularly since the democratic process in Albania has been under way for only a short period. The Albanian Government is now making efforts to set up the institution of an ombudsman, which it regards as an important part of the requisite means for protecting human rights.

The reorganization of the local authorities is a special factor in the process of democratizing institutions. The local authorities, established after free elections and on the basis of democratic principles, have replaced the previous local authorities, which simply existed as a matter of form and were wholly dependent on the central authorities. The law containing some amendments to Act No. 4,791 laid the foundations for the new local authorities. Article 3 of the Act states that "the local authorities shall be organized and shall operate in accordance with the principles of self-government, independence and decentralization." Article 4 of Act No. 7,572 states that "problems of special importance to a particular administrative unit may be solved by a referendum in which all inhabitants of that unit entitled to vote may participate."

(b) Multi-Party Democracy

*The Multi-Party System and Non-Governmental Organizations.*
The introduction of multi-party politics in 1990 was an im-

portant victory for the forces of democracy in Albania. This method of organizing political life is now safeguarded by the Constitutional Act, which states that "multi-party politics is one of the prerequisites of democracy in Albania," and is regarded as the most suitable way of building a genuinely democratic society.

It should be emphasized that a large number of political, religious and cultural organizations and associations operate in Albania. They can be established by a simple procedure, provided their programme is lawful and their activities do not conflict with the Constitution and the law. It should be noted that this is not a restriction on freedom of association, for registration of parties and organizations is a straightforward procedure that consists in verifying whether the by-laws are in conformity with the laws and the Constitution. There are approximately 26 political parties in Albania, and they freely participate in the country's political life.

Free, democratic elections are a constant safeguard of democracy. The Constitutional Act guarantees free elections by universal and equal suffrage and direct, secret ballot.

The elections held on 22 March 1990 marked a victory for the forces of democracy and a decisive move by Albania on the path to democracy. The elections in July 1992 led to the establishment of pluralist local authorities.

Since 1990, when a multi-party political system was introduced in Albania, great strides have been taken in regard to human rights. Human dignity, the rights and freedoms of the individual, the development of his personality and equality before the law are viewed as the basic principles of the State, which is required to observe and foster them. The law guarantees equality for all. Legislation has been amended and is being further supplemented in keeping with international human rights standards.

*The Situation of Minorities in Albania.* The establishment of democratic processes in Albania has created favourable conditions for closer examination of the problems of its minorities. Since the fall of communism in 1990, Albania has declared its determination to move towards construction of a democratic society based on respect for human rights, and in this connection, it has undertaken to observe and implement the international standards relating to the rights of members of national minorities.

Albania has also stated its intention to do its utmost to meet, without any form of discrimination, all its commitments deriving from the International Human Rights Covenants. This also applies to members of the minorities living in Albania. The Constitutional Act states that Albania recognizes and respects the international standards relating to the rights of members of minorities and places all Albanian citizens, including members of minorities, on an equal footing. Thus, the members of minorities now enjoy the same rights as other Albanian citizens.

They are free to practice their religion, to have their own religious articles, to impart or receive information, and to receive a religious education.

They may also freely use their mother tongue, and are given every possibility of maintaining, preserving, and developing their ethnic, linguistic, cultural, and religious identity. The State has undertaken to establish favourable conditions for them fully to enjoy their rights. There are now many cultural institutions, libraries, and information centres in Albania where members of minorities may use and develop their mother tongue. In addition, they have the right to be educated in their mother tongue. There is already such a pre-school and junior school educational system. For example, in the district of Gjirokastra, a region where a number of villages are inhabited by members of the Greek minority, 964 pupils are currently receiving primary education in Greek; there are 67 teachers, 54 of whom have completed a Greek-speaking teacher-training course, and six senior teachers who have completed their studies at the Pedagogical Training Institute for junior school teachers. It should also be mentioned that there is a professorship in Greek at the University of Gjirokastra.

Members of minorities enjoy full political and civil rights. They take an active and direct part in Albanian politics by means of free elections, referenda, and the political parties. They have their own political associations and organizations, such as, for example, the Omonia association, which is active throughout virtually the whole country. The Union for Human Rights Party represents a majority of the Greek minorities; and, at the most recent parliamentary elections, it won two seats. Minorities are also involved in a number of cultural associations currently in existence in Albania.

Another feature of the realization of the rights of members of minorities is their representation in local bodies and institutions, where they are able to express their wishes through their representatives. They are thus able to play a considerable part in organizing social and economic life, especially in the regions where they live.

The members of minorities in Albania enjoy economic and social rights without discrimination. Like all other Albanian citizens, they enjoy the right to work and to fair remuneration, and the right of access to public services and health services. And like other Albanian citizens, they enjoy the State-guaranteed right to welfare and social security.

Naturally, Albania's very low level of development does not enable members of minorities to enjoy their economic and social rights to the full; however, it should be pointed out that no discrimination is practiced against them on account of their ethnic, linguistic, or religious identity.

Albania is determined to fulfil its commitments under the International Covenants to which it has acceded, and is prepared to accede to the other principal international human rights instruments. This is clearly demonstrated by its openness towards the outside world and by the intensification of its human rights activities over the past two years. More particularly, it has established closer relations with the United Nations Centre for Human Rights, the Council of Europe, and the organs that deal with the human dimension within the Conference on Security and Cooperation in Europe.

Clearly, during this period of political and economic transition, Albania is encountering difficulties and obstacles to the building of democracy and the realization of human rights. The absence of a democratic tradition of respect for human rights, the lack of experience and of qualified personnel capable of developing modern legislation, and the difficult economic circumstances are some of the main problems and obstacles facing Albania in its efforts to build a genuinely democratic society. For this reason, cooperation between Albania and the international community in this sphere is of unquestionable importance.

Having considered this communication at its 1993 session, the UN Commission on Human Rights, in resolution 1993/65 of 10 March 1993, welcomed the positive steps taken by the Albanian Government and called upon the Government to continue to adopt legislative and administrative measures to meet all requirements under the International Bill of Human Rights and other relevant international instruments, by which freedom, democracy, and the rule of law would be further consolidated and the human rights and fundamental freedoms of all Albanian citizens, including minorities, would be effectively promoted and guaranteed. Further, the Commission encouraged technical cooperation between the Center for Human Rights and the Voluntary Fund for Technical Cooperation in the Field of Human Rights, on the one hand, and the Albanian Government, on the other, on the basis of an agreement concluded on 13 February 1992.

Under that agreement, the Center organized in Tirana, from 2–6 November 1992, an intensive training course for 60 Albanian police, prison, and military officers. During the course, international experts discussed international human rights standards in the sphere of the administration of justice and a number of practical techniques for law enforcement in accordance with human rights. In addition, from 2–12 November 1992, the Center carried out a human rights assessment mission in Albania.

Despite the sweeping changes described by Government officials, Albania remains Europe's poorest country, the only one meeting the UN criteria for classification among the world's "least developed." Many buildings that had been collectively used under the communist regime, such as schools, cultural centers, agricultural storage houses, health stations, and even stables, were destroyed during the transition period; and crops have been reduced through the privatization of land, the withdrawal of tractors from central stations, and the high cost of fertilizers and insecticides. Nevertheless, in 1993, most Albanian voters supported the Democratic Party of President Sali Berisha.

A Report by the UN Secretary General on the situation of human rights in Albania was issued in December 1994:

At its fiftieth session, the Commission on Human Rights adopted resolution 1994/57 entitled "Situation of human rights in Albania", in which it called upon the Government of Albania to pursue its positive steps towards meeting the requirements under the International Bill of Human Rights and other relevant international instruments, by which the human rights and fundamental freedoms of all Albanian citizens, including the rights of persons belonging to minorities, would be effectively promoted and guaranteed; encouraged technical cooperation between the Centre for Human Rights and the Voluntary Fund for Technical Cooperation in the Field of Human Rights, on the one hand, and the Government of Albania, on the other, on the basis of the Agreement concluded on 13 February 1992; requested the Secretary-General (a) to bring the resolution to the attention of the Government of Albania and to invite it to provide information regarding its implementation and (b) to report to the Commission at its fifty-first session on the implementation of the resolution.

On 2 November 1994 the Under-Secretary-General for Human Rights addressed a note verbale to the Permanent Representative of Albania to the United Nations Office at Geneva in which he requested the Government of that country to communicate to him any information or observation it might wish to present in accordance with resolution 1994/57.

At the time the present report was being prepared, no response had been received by the Centre for Human Rights from the Government of Albania.

### Advisory Services and Technical Assistance

The United Nations Centre for Human Rights and the Government of Albania agreed to cooperate on a programme of technical assistance for Albania on the basis of an agreement signed in February 1992. In May 1992 a staff member of the Centre for Human Rights engaged in informal consultations with the Government of Albania regarding the implementation of the Agreement. On 8 September 1992, the Government of Albania officially requested that the Centre for Human Rights conduct a mission to assess Albania's needs for technical assistance in the human rights field. The needs assessment mission was conducted from 4 to 12 November 1992 by two staff members of the Centre for Human Rights, assisted by a consultant from the University of Minnesota Law School. As a result of this mission a country programme of assistance for Albania was prepared.

The first component of the programme was a training course, organized by the Centre for Human Rights, for Albanian law enforcement officials, police, military and prison personnel on human rights in the administration of justice, which was held at Tirana from 2 to 6 November 1992.

Another component of the programme was a training seminar, Human Rights in the Administration of Justice, organized by the Centre for Human Rights for Albanian judges and lawyers, held at Tirana from 12 to 15 April 1993; some 70 judges and lawyers participated. As part of the training seminar, the centre financed the translation into Albanian and the printing of the following international human rights instruments: (i) Universal Declaration of Human Rights; (ii) International Covenant on Civil and Political Rights; (iii) International Covenant on Economic, Social and Cultural Rights; (iv) Standard Minimum Rules for the Treatment of Prisoners; (v) Convention against Torture and Other Cruel, Inhuman or Degrading Treatment or Punishment; (vi) Code of Conduct for Law Enforcement Officials; (vii) United Nations Standard Minimum Rules for the Administration of Juvenile Justice ("The Beijing Rules"); (viii) Basic Principles on the Independence of the Judiciary; (ix) Basic Principles on the Role of Lawyers and (x) Guidelines on the Role of Prosecutors.

Two government officials, one from the Ministry of Foreign Affairs and a judge from the Tirana Court of Justice, were chosen by the Government of Albania to participate in the fellowship programme in the field of human rights, conducted at Geneva and at Strasbourg in collaboration with the International Institute of Human Rights.

Under the advisory services programme, three other government officials, one from the Ministry of Foreign Affairs, one from the Ministry of Justice and one from the Ministry of Education, received fellowships to participate in the training course on the preparation of reports required under the United Nations human rights treaties, held at Geneva in November 1993.

In cooperation with the Ministry of Justice, the Centre for Human Rights sent two experts to Albania in January 1994. The two experts, one from the University of Gent (Belgium) and another from the Cour de Cassation in Paris (France), provided legal assistance to the Ministry in the drafting of legislation on the administration of juvenile justice and the legal regulation of acts of civil registration.

The Centre for Human Rights sent an expert, Ms. Laurie Wiseberg, Executive Director of Human Rights Internet (Canada), to Albania from 18 to 22 July 1994 to determine the feasibility of establishing a documentation and research centre on human rights, as envisaged in component IV, "Basic library and documentation unit on human rights", of the February 1992 Agreement.

Based on the expert's recommendations, officials of the Centre for Human Rights have discussed informally with the Permanent Representative of Albania to the United Nations Office at Geneva the possibility of redeploying the budget allocations and establishing the documentation and research centre on human rights as early as possible in 1995.

***BIBLIOGRAPHY.*** Ceka, Neritan. "Albania: Democracy or Anarchy?" *East European Reporter* 5, no. 1 (Jan.–Feb. 1992): 50–54. News article, in English.

Commission on Security and Cooperation in Europe (CSCE). *Human Rights and Democratization in Albania.* Washington, DC, USA: 1994. Government report, in English.

Human Rights Watch. "Albania," *Human Rights Watch World Report 1995* pp. 186–188. New York: 1995. NGO report, in English.

Iliopoulos-Strangas, Julia, ed. *Human Rights in Occupied Cyprus and in Albania.* Athens, Greece: Ant. N. Sakkoulas Publications for the Marangopoulos Foundation for Human Rights (MFHR), 1990. NGO report, in English and Greek.

Johannes Wier Foundation for Health and Human Rights. *Albania, Health and Human Rights: An Inventory of Pressing Issues: Report of Five Missions in 1991–1992.* Amersfoort, the Netherlands: 1992. NGO factfinding report, in English; bibliography, pp. 19–21.

Minnesota Lawyers International Human Rights Committee. *Human Rights in the People's Socialist Republic of Albania.* Minneapolis, MN, USA: 1990. NGO report, in English.

**ALGERIA.** The Democratic People's Republic of Algeria is a country in north Africa, on the Mediterranean Sea. It has borders with Libya, Mali, Mauritania, Morocco, Niger, Tunisia, and Western Sahara. It achieved independence from France in 1962 and became a member of the United Nations the same year. Its total population is estimated by the UN to be 26,925,000. Ethnic groups include Arabs and Berbers, but national censuses have never indicated the ethnic or racial origin of inhabitants. Languages commonly used include Arabic (official), French, and Berber. Religions practiced include Islam (Sunni), the State religion, 99%; and Christianity (Roman Catholic), 1%. Literacy is estimated at about 52%.

The government (1994) took the form of a republic. Under its National Charter and Constitution of 1976, socialism is the political philosophy of the country. The president, elected for a five-year term, is Head of

State; the prime minister, representing the party or coalition given the majority in a popular election, is head of government. Legislative authority is in the hands of the 281-member National Popular Assembly, members of which are elected for five-year terms. The only political party is the National Liberation Front.

The National Commission of Legislation has conducted an extensive review of civil, criminal, public, commercial and family legislation that remained from the French colonial system. New codes have been, or are being, prepared, in many areas, and all French laws still on the books have been declared invalid. The new code that deals with family and personal status continues to be based on Muslim law but will be administered by the civil courts.

It is estimated that two-thirds of Algeria's population is under 30 years old. The government devotes more than half its budget to education and programs for young people, regarding them as a huge human potential. At independence, there were only 2,725 Algerian college students; in 1987, there were more than 100,000. Concerned about the lure of Islamic fundamentalism among the young, the government has tried to channel religious activity through State-supported mosques overseen by the Ministry of Religious Affairs.

Algeria played a key role in the release, on 20 January 1981, of 52 Americans who had been held captive for 444 days in the U.S. embassy in Teheran. Chosen by Iran to represent it in negotiations with the U.S. government, the Algerian Government turned the hostages over to American authorities in Algiers.

*CIVIL UNREST.* In October 1988, economic and political unrest in Algeria gave rise to a series of riots that ended when President Chadli Benjedid announced a series of political changes, which included increasing the powers of the prime minister and broadening the base of representation by making changes in the ruling political party, the National Liberation Front, which has governed Algeria without interruption since the end of the war of independence. However, demands for the institution of a multi-party system, and for putting an end to alleged official use of torture, have not produced the desired results.

In recent years, Algeria has been disturbed by violence that began after the country's first multi-party general election was canceled in January 1992 because the Islamic Salvation Front, which was later banned, won over 80% of the parliamentary seats in the first round of that election and appeared to be headed for victory. President Chadli Benjedid stepped down as the election process ended. His successor, Mohammed Boudiaf, was assassinated five months later. Thereafter, the country remained in an indefinite

state of emergency because of violent conflicts between Muslim militants and security forces.

In January 1994, Liamine Zeroual, a former general, was appointed as President by the army-backed leadership of the country, replacing a five-member collective presidency headed by Ali Kafi. The new President, scheduled to hold office during a three-year transition period to enable the nation to hold new elections, is considered to be strong enough to put an end to the violence that has taken 10,000 lives (an official government estimate) between 1992 and September 1994, whether he does so by a negotiated settlement with the Islamic militants—a well-armed movement that seeks Islamist rule—or by a military crackdown. Early in 1995, street fighting broke out between police and civilians over repression by the government.

As a State Party to the International Covenant on Civil and Political Rights, Algeria submitted its initial report to the UN Human Rights Committee pursuant to article 40 of the Covenant (CCPR/C/62/Add. 1) on 15 April 1991, during the presidency of Chadli Benjedid. The Committee adopted the following comments on the report on 9 April 1992 (CCPR/C/79/Add. 1):

Introduction. The Committee notes that the dialogue with the Algerian delegation was particularly constructive, because the delegation endeavoured to answer members' questions candidly without trying to conceal the difficulties. It thanks the State Party through the latter's representative for its good report, which was submitted within the specified period. The report contains detailed information on the laws and regulations relating to the application of the provisions of the Covenant. The Committee regrets, however, that the report includes little information concerning the actual application of human rights standards. It also regrets the failure of the report to indicate the factors and difficulties that are impeding the application of those standards. Lastly, it notes with regret that the report, having been submitted on 5 April 1991, could make no reference to the states of emergency, notification of which reached the Secretary-General on 19 June and 13 February 1992, respectively.

Positive Aspect. The Committee notes with satisfaction that Algeria has ratified or acceded to a number of international human rights instruments, in particular the Covenant and the first Optional Protocol thereto, and has made the declaration provided for in article 41 of the Covenant. In addition, Algeria has included in its Constitution various provisions relating to human rights and has amended a number of legislative texts in order to reflect international human rights standards. The Committee also notes with satisfaction the establishment of a Ministry of Human Rights, later replaced by a national human rights monitoring body.

Factors and Difficulties Impeding the Application of the Covenant. The Committee notes that, at the time of the submission of the report, Algeria was in a process of transition to democracy. Since that time, Algeria has been faced with substantial difficulties that have brought this process to a standstill. The Algerian authorities therefore considered such ways and means as seemed to them appropriate in order to prevent forces that they considered hostile to democracy from taking advantage of democratic procedure in order to harm democracy. Among the measures adopted in this respect are the proclamation of the two states of emergency and the interruption of the electoral process.

Principal Subjects of Concern. The Committee expresses its concern regarding the suspension of the democratic process and, in general, regarding the blocking of democratic mechanisms. It is concerned about the high number of arrests (8,800) and the abusive use of firearms by members of the police in order to disperse demonstrations. The Committee expresses doubts about respect for due process, especially before military tribunals, about the real possibilities for implementing the right to a fair trial, about the numerous cases of torture and ill-treatment that have been brought to its attention, and about the restrictions on rights to freedom of opinion and expression and freedom of the press. The Committee further considers that, in the light of the provision of article 6 requiring States Parties that have not abolished the death penalty to reserve it for the most serious crimes, it is contrary to the Covenant to impose the death penalty for crimes that are of an economic nature.

The Committee also regrets the many cases of discrimination against women and the non-recognition of minorities, especially the Berbers.

Suggestions and Recommendations. The Committee recommends that Algeria put an end as promptly as possible to the exceptional situation that prevails within its borders and allow all the democratic mechanisms to resume their functioning under fair and free conditions. It draws the attention of the State Party to the fact that the Covenant does not permit derogation from certain rights even in times of emergency and that, therefore, any excesses relating to, inter alia, the right to life, torture, and the right to freedom of conscience and expression are violations of the Covenant that should not be allowed to continue. The Committee hopes that the State Party will make an evaluation of the application of the provisions of the Covenant after the report was written and would like to be kept informed of any changes in the situation and of all future developments.

The following year the UN Committee on the Elimination of Racial Discrimination reported the following:

The Committee considered the tenth periodic report of Algeria (CERD/C/209/Add.4) at its 962nd, 963rd and 983rd meetings, held on 4 and 18 March 1993 (see CERD/C/SR.962, 963 and 983).

The report was introduced by the representative of the State party who underlined his country's support for the fight against racism and racial discrimination and, in particular, against apartheid.

He stated that the Constitution adopted by referendum on 23 February 1989 contained new provisions providing for political pluralism, an independent judiciary and voting by secret ballot. It also prohibited all forms of racial discrimination, for which sanctions were foreseen in legislation. Although the current state of emergency represented a difficult period for Algeria, it in no way affected the country's traditional struggle against racial discrimination, nor the determination of the Algerian people to defend the cause of liberty, justice and equality.

Members of the Committee welcomed the report of the State party, which contained useful information on the constitutional and legislative basis for the implementation of the Convention. Members noted, however, that more informa-

tion was needed on the actual application of the Convention, particularly in the courts, and on economic, social and demographic developments which had occurred in the country. Further information was needed on factors and difficulties encountered in the application of the Convention. Further information was also required regarding the composition of the population with regard to minorities, most notably Berbers, Tuaregs, Jews and the black population that inhabited the southern region of Algeria. With respect to the last-named group, it was pointed out that black Algerians appeared to be particularly disadvantaged in terms of access to housing and education. Members of the Committee also wished to know which minorities the Government recognized as such.

It was noted that important progress had been achieved in the application of the Convention since Algeria last presented a report in 1987, particularly as a result of the new Constitution adopted in 1989. In connection with the Constitution and national legislation in general, members wished to know what was the status of the Convention in the legal system. It was emphasized that the Convention should be accorded a status in Algerian domestic law superior to that of domestic legislation. Concern was expressed that the present state of emergency affected the exercise of fundamental rights.

With respect to article 2 of the Convention, members of the Committee wanted to know whether Algeria had adopted legislation expressly prohibiting racial discrimination and, if not, whether the Government was planning to do so. In that connection, members pointed out that the population in Algeria was sufficiently varied that special legislation on racial discrimination was necessary.

In regard to article 4, members of the Committee wished to know whether there had been acts of violence, or incitement to violence, directed against any particular racial or ethnic group; and whether racist organizations or propaganda had been declared illegal.

With regard to article 5 of the Convention, members wished to know whether there was discrimination in the field of employment. It was emphasized that statistical indicators on problems such as unemployment, delinquency and illiteracy were needed in order to determine the degree to which minorities had been socially integrated. Particular concern was expressed over the situation of the Berber minority and, in that connection, further information was requested on the extent to which they enjoyed the rights enumerated in article 5 of the Convention. Members expressed interest in the new national commission for human rights and wished to know how its members were appointed, how its independence was ensured and what role it played in addition to monitoring respect for human rights.

Concerning article 6 of the Convention, members of the Committee wished to know how many complaints of racial discrimination had been received by the competent authorities and how many sentences had been handed down for acts of racism. More complete information was required in general on the application of the Convention in the courts and the jurisprudence that had developed as a result, and on the independence of the judiciary. Members emphasized the importance of ensuring that lawyers and judges were well acquainted with the provisions of the Convention.

With respect to article 7, members of the Committee wished to have further information on the availability of instruction in their language for linguistic minorities at the primary and secondary school levels. In particular, members wished to know whether the Berber language was taught in such schools.

Members of the Committee commended Algeria as one of the States parties that had made the declaration under article 14 of the Convention recognizing the competence of the Committee to receive communications from individuals and groups of individuals alleging that their rights under the Convention had been violated. However, in view of the fact that the Committee had as yet received no communications concerning Algeria, members of the Committee wished to know what steps had been taken to make known that article of the Convention to the general public.

Replying to the questions raised by members of the Committee, the representative of the State party stated that the Algerian population was composed of Arabs, Berbers, Mozabites and Tuaregs. The Berbers lived essentially in three regions: Kabylie, a region near Algiers, where around 4 million Berbers lived; Aures, in the eastern part of the country, where there were 8 to 9 million; and in the south, where there were an additional 1 million. In view of the fact that the total population of Algeria was 23 million, it was difficult to consider the Berbers as a minority. They participated fully and on a basis of equality in Algerian life and were in no sense marginalized. With respect to their language, there was no discrimination. The Berber language, amazigh, was widely spoken in the regions where the Berbers lived, particularly in Kabylie. At the present time, however, the written language was not sufficiently structured for it to be taught in schools. There was ongoing research, particularly at the University of Tizi-Ouzou, in that regard, which would ultimately make such instruction possible. The nomads of the south, who were now often sedentary, were totally integrated and were in no way repressed. Refugees in southern Algeria were neither Algerian nor were they persecuted.

With respect to freedom of association, the prohibition by law of regionalist political parties needed to be understood within the context of conditions in Algeria at the time of independence: the end of colonial rule had been achieved with difficulty and there had been threats of secession and dismemberment of the nation when independence was achieved. In order to counter that tendency, regionalism was encouraged in terms of culture, but was discouraged as a platform for politics. There were currently 67 political parties in Algeria and over 20,000 associations of various kinds, which had full freedom to pursue their activities.

Concerning the monitoring of human rights, the Minister of Human Rights had taken office in 1992 but had subsequently been replaced by the National Commission on Human Rights (Observatoire national des droits de l'homme). The Commission was under the direct authority of the President and its administrative and financial independence were guaranteed. Non-governmental organizations were represented on the Commission, as were the Ministers of Justice and Education and representatives of the bar. Its task was to protect the fundamental human rights of citizens and provide information about human rights. It submitted an annual report on the human rights situation to the President of the National People's Assembly, which was made public two months afterwards.

With respect to education, the representative stated that it had not yet been possible to provide school courses that familiarized students with the provisions of the Convention. At present, the State was more immediately concerned with the problem of simply providing education. He expressed surprise at the mention of discrimination allegedly encountered by five black foreign students at the University of Oran.

That university, like others in Algeria, had trained many black African students, including diplomats, from other countries in the region. With regard to black Algerians, their numbers were limited and they encountered no racial discrimination, including at the university.

Many young Algerians living in France had acquired French nationality in addition to Algerian nationality. An intergovernmental accord permitted them to choose in which country they preferred to perform their military service. With regard to the request that the next report of Algeria include statistical indicators and other detailed information on the situation of minorities, the representative assured the Committee that he would forward that request to his Government.

## Concluding Observations

The Committee noted with interest the legislative and institutional changes that had occurred in Algeria in recent years, which created the framework necessary for the respect of human rights in general and for preventing and combating racial discrimination.

The Committee expressed its appreciation of the spirit of openness and cooperation that characterized the report, as well as the dialogue with the representative of the Government, while expressing its concern at the difficulties of the current situation in Algeria.

Taking into account the fact that the report was oriented especially towards legislative texts, the Committee considered that the next report should contain more demographic and statistical information on social indicators reflecting, in particular, the situation of ethnic and racial groups, in particular Berbers and blacks, as well as on judicial or administrative decisions taken to give effect to the Convention. It was also considered necessary to clarify the effect of emergency measures taken by the Government with regard to the application of the Convention.

The Committee considered, in particular, that the next report should clarify the place of the Berber population in Algerian society with respect to identity, language, participation in public life and the social benefits provided for in article 5 of the Convention.

***BIBLIOGRAPHY***. *Article 19. Algeria: Assassination in the Name of Religion.* London, UK: 1993. NGO report, in English.

Bekhechi, M.A. "Human Rights in Algeria: A Legal Analysis." Paper presented at the Workshop on Human Rights Documentation, Maseru, Lesotho, 24–28 August 1987. Scholarly conference paper, in French.

————. "Souverainete, Developpement et Droits de l'Homme dans la Constitution Algerienne et en Droit International" (Sovereignty, Development and Human Rights in the Algerian Constitution and International Law). Paper delivered at a colloquium on "The Constitution and Constitutionalism in Algeria," University of Annaba, 26–28 April 1987. Scholarly conference paper, in French.

Human Rights Watch. "Algeria," *Human Rights Watch Report 1995*, pp. 256–261. New York: 1995. NGO report, in English.

Mahiou, Ahmed. "La constitution algérienne et le droit international" (Algerian Constitution and International Law), *Revue générale de droit international public* 94, no. 2 (1990): 419–454. Scholarly article, in French.

Melasuo, Tuomo. "Culture and Minorities in the Arabo-Islamic Identity of Algeria," in *Islam: State and Society,* eds.

Klaus Ferdinand and Mehdi Mozaffari, pp. 183–194. Curzon Press, 1990. Scholarly article, in English.

Middle East Research and Information Project (MERIP). "Europe's Other Frontier: North Africa Faces the 1990s," *Middle East Report* no. 163 (March–April 1990): 46 pp. NGO special issue, in English.

Middle East Watch (MEW). *Human Rights Abuses in Algeria: No One Is Spared.* New York: Human Rights Watch, 1994. NGO report, in English.

Sivan, Emmanuel. "The Kabyls: An Oppressed Minority in North Africa," in *Case Studies on Human Rights and Fundamental Freedoms: A World Survey,* Vol. 1, ed. Willem A. Veenhoven, pp. 261–279. The Hague: Martinus Nijhoff, 1975. Edited collection, in English.

**ALIENS.** In 1973, the UN Economic and Social Council requested that the Commission on Human Rights and its Sub-Commission on Prevention of Discrimination and Protection of Minorities "consider as a matter of priority the problem of the applicability of existing international provisions for the protection of human rights to individuals who are not citizens of the country in which they live" and to suggest viable measures, including drafting a declaration, that would alleviate the situation of this special group. In 1974, the Sub-Commission appointed Baroness Elles as special rapporteur (resolution 10 [XXVII]) to report to the Secretary-General on the subject. The Special Rapporteur's report was considered by the Sub-Commission in 1977, at its thirtieth session. That report (UN publication No. E.80.XIV.2) contained, *inter alia,* (a) a brief historical outline of the development of the protection granted to aliens; (b) consideration of international protection of the human rights of aliens, including the stateless and refugees; (c) an analysis of the restrictions, reservations, limitations, and derogations that may be made on human rights on the ground of nationality; and (d) a review and evaluation of the machinery available to non-citizens for redress of injuries and other remedies for the enforcement of their human rights. The report also annexed a draft declaration on the human rights of aliens.

The Sub-Commission transmitted the study and a revised draft declaration to the Commission of Human Rights (resolution 9 [XXXI]) in 1979, which subsequently passed on an again-revised draft declaration and comments from Governments to the UN General Assembly. In 1980, the General Assembly decided to establish an open-ended working group to elaborate a final version of the draft declaration. The final declaration (reprinted below) was adopted by the Assembly in resolution 40/144 of 13 December 1985.

*Equality with Citizens.* After examining reports submitted by States Parties to the International Covenant on Civil and Political Rights in accordance with article 40 of that instrument, the UN Human Rights Committee in 1986 adopted a general comment setting out its view on the question of equality of aliens and citizens, as follows (UN Doc. A/41/40, Annex VI, para. 1–10):

Reports from States parties have often failed to take into account that each State party must ensure the rights in the Covenant to "all individuals within its territory and subject to its jurisdiction" (art. 2, para. 1). In general, the rights set forth in the Covenant apply to everyone, irrespective of reciprocity, and irrespective of his or her nationality or statelessness.

Thus, the general rule is that each one of the rights of the Covenant must be guaranteed without discrimination between citizens and aliens. Aliens receive the benefit of the general requirement of non-discrimination in respect of the rights guaranteed in the Covenant, as provided for in article 2 thereof. This guarantee applies to aliens and citizens alike. Exceptionally, some of the rights recognized in the Covenant are expressly applicable only to citizens (article 25), while article 13 applies only to aliens. However, the Committee's experience in examining reports shows that in a number of countries other rights that aliens should enjoy under the Covenant are denied to them or are subject to limitations that cannot always be justified under the Covenant.

A few constitutions provide for equality of aliens with citizens. Some constitutions adopted more recently carefully distinguish fundamental rights that apply to all and those granted to citizens only, and deal with each in detail. In many States, however, the constitutions are drafted in terms of citizens only when granting relevant rights. Legislation and case law may also play an important part in providing for the rights of aliens. The Committee has been informed that in some States fundamental rights, though not guaranteed to aliens by the Constitution or other legislation, will also be extended to them as required by the Covenant. In certain cases, however, there has clearly been a failure to implement Covenant rights without discrimination in respect of aliens.

The Committee considers that in their reports States parties should give attention to the position of aliens, both under their law and in actual practice. The Covenant gives aliens all the protection regarding rights guaranteed therein, and its requirements should be observed by States parties in their legislation and in practice as appropriate. The position of aliens would thus be considerably improved. States parties should ensure that the provisions of the Covenant and the rights under it are made known to aliens within their jurisdiction.

The Covenant does not recognize the right of aliens to enter or reside in the territory of a State party. It is in principle a matter for the State to decide who it will admit to its territory. However, in certain circumstances an alien may enjoy the protection of the Covenant even in relation to entry or residence, for example, when considerations of non-discrimination, prohibition of inhuman treatment and respect for family life arise.

Consent for entry may be given subject to conditions relating, for example, to movement, residence and employment. A State may also impose general conditions upon an alien who is in transit. However, once aliens are allowed to enter the territory of a State party they are entitled to the rights set out in the Covenant.

Aliens thus have an inherent right to life, protected by law, and may not be arbitrarily deprived of life. They must not be subjected to torture or to cruel, inhuman or degrading treatment or punishment; nor may they be held in slavery or servitude. Aliens have the full right to liberty and security of the person. If lawfully deprived of their liberty, they shall be treated with humanity and with respect for the inherent dignity of their person. Aliens may not be imprisoned for failure to fulfil a contractual obligation. They have the right to liberty of movement and free choice of residence; they shall be free to leave the country. Aliens shall be equal before the courts and tribunals, and shall be entitled to a fair and public hearing by a competent, independent and impartial tribunal established by law in the determination of any criminal charge or of rights and obligations in a suit at law. Aliens shall not be subjected to retrospective penal legislation, and are entitled to recognition before the law. They may not be subjected to arbitrary or unlawful interference with their privacy, family, home or correspondence. They have the right to freedom of thought, conscience and religion, and the right to hold opinions and to express them. Aliens receive the benefit of the right of peaceful Assembly and of freedom of association. They may marry when at marriageable age. Their children are entitled to those measures of protection required by their status as minors. In those cases where aliens constitute a minority within the meaning of article 27, they shall not be denied the right, in community with other members of their group, to enjoy their own culture, to profess and practise their own religion and to use their own language. Aliens are entitled to equal protection by the law. There shall be no discrimination between aliens and citizens in the application of these rights. These rights of aliens may be qualified only by such limitations as may be lawfully imposed under the Covenant.

Once an alien is lawfully within a territory, his freedom of movement within the territory and his right to leave that territory may only be restricted in accordance with article 12, paragraph 3. Differences in treatment in this regard between aliens and nationals, or between different categories of aliens, need to be justified under article 12, paragraph 3. Since such restrictions must, inter alia, be consistent with the other rights recognized in the Covenant, a State party cannot, by restraining an alien or deporting him to a third country, arbitrarily prevent his return to his own country (art. 12, para. 4).

Many reports have given insufficient information on matters relevant to article 13. That article is applicable to all procedures aimed at the obligatory departure of an alien, whether described in national law as expulsion or otherwise. If such procedures entail arrest, the safeguards of the Covenant relating to deprivation of liberty (arts. 9 and 10) may also be applicable. If the arrest is for the particular purpose of extradition, other provisions of national and international law may apply. Normally an alien who is expelled must be allowed to leave for any country that agrees to take him. The particular rights of article 13 only protect those aliens who are lawfully in the territory of a State party. This means that national law concerning the requirements for entry and stay must be taken into account in determining the scope of that protection, and that illegal entrants and aliens who have stayed longer than the law or their permits allow, in particular, are not covered by its provisions. However, if the legality of an alien's entry or stay is in dispute, any decision on this point leading to his expulsion or deportation ought to be taken in accordance with article 13. It is for the competent authorities of the State party, in good faith and in the exercise of their powers, to apply and interpret the domestic law, observing, however, such requirements under the Covenant as equality before the law (art. 26).

Article 13 directly regulates only the procedure and not the substantive grounds for expulsion. However, by allowing only those carried out "in pursuance of a decision reached in accordance with law", its purpose is clearly to prevent arbitrary expulsions. On the other hand, it entitles each alien to a decision in his own case and, hence, article 13 would not be satisfied with laws or decisions providing for collective or mass expulsions. This understanding, in the opinion of the Committee, is confirmed by further provisions concerning the right to submit reasons against expulsion and to have the decision reviewed by and to be represented before the competent authority or someone designated by it. An alien must be given full facilities for pursuing his remedy against expulsion so that this right will in all the circumstances of his case be an effective one. The principles of article 13 relating to appeal against expulsion and the entitlement to review by a competent authority may only be departed from when "compelling reasons of national security" so require. Discrimination may not be made between different categories of aliens in the application of article 13.

*Smuggling of Aliens.* At its 1993 session, the UN General Assembly took up, for the first time, the problems raised by the activities of criminal organizations that illicitly profit by convincing individuals to migrate illegally, forcing them into forms of debt, bondage, or servitude in order to pay for their passage; endangering their lives; and imposing severe costs on States that have been called upon to rescue the aliens and to provide for their medical care, food, housing, and transportation.

Noting that the smuggling of aliens, whether by ship, air, or ground transportation, can involve criminal elements in many States—including those where the smuggling scheme was planned, the State of nationality of the aliens, the State where the means of transport was prepared, the flag State of any vessels or aircraft that transport them, and the States through which they transit—the Assembly, in resolution 48/102 of 20 December 1993, condemned the practice of alien smuggling in violation of international and national law and without regard for the safety, well-being, and human rights of the migrants.

The Assembly then urged States to take appropriate steps to frustrate these illegal activities and thus to protect would-be migrants from exploitation and loss of life, inter alia, by amending criminal laws, if necessary, to encompass alien smuggling and by establishing and improving procedures to permit the immediate discovery of false travel documents supplied by smugglers. While emphasizing that international efforts to prevent alien smuggling should not inhibit legal migration or freedom of travel, or undercut the protection provided by international law to refugees, the Assembly reaffirmed the need to observe fully international and national law in dealing with alien smuggling, including the provision of humane treatment and strict observance of all human rights of migrants.

**SEE ALSO** *Refugees; Statelessness.*

**BIBLIOGRAPHY.** Australian Human Rights Commission. *Human Rights and the Migration Act 1958.* Canberra, Australia: 1985. Government report, in English.

Bauman, Christopher P. "An International Standard of Partial Compensation upon the Expropriation of an Alien's Property," *Case Western Reserve Journal of International Law* 19, no. 1 (Winter 1987): 103–119. Scholarly article, in English.

Blackburn, Robert, ed. *Rights of Citizenship.* London: Mansell, 1993. Scholarly monograph, in English.

Brubaker, W. Rogers. "Citizenship Struggles in Soviet Successor States," *International Migration Review* 26, no. 2 (Summer 1992): 269–291. Scholarly article, in English; bibliography, pp. 289–291.

Council of Europe, Directorate of Human Rights. *Human Rights of Aliens in Europe.* Dordrecht, the Netherlands: Martinus Nijhoff, 1985. IGO conference proceedings, in English.

Ferris, Elizabeth G. *The Central American Refugees.* New York: Praeger Publishers, 1987. Scholarly report, in English.

Frelick, Bill. *The Back of the Hand: Bias and Restrictionism towards Central American Asylum Seekers in North America.* Washington, D.C.: U.S. Committee for Refugees, 1988. NGO monograph, in English.

Gibney, Mark. *Strangers or Friends.* Westport, CT, USA: Greenwood Press, 1986. Scholarly monograph, in English.

Hull, Elizabeth. *Without Justice for All: The Constitutional Rights of Aliens.* Westport, CT, USA: Greenwood Press, 1985. Scholarly monograph, in English.

Komitee fur Grundrechte und Demokratie (Committee for Basic Rights and Democracy). *Auswirkungen des Auslanderrechts auf die Situation der Migrantinen, Inbesondere Turkischer Frauen* (Consequences of Laws concerning Aliens on the Situation of Migrants, especially Turkish Women). Senbachstal, FRG: 1987. NGO report, in German.

Moore, Jennifer. "Simple Justice: Humanitarian Law as a Defense against Deportation," *Harvard Human Rights Journal* 4 (Spring 1991): 11–46. Scholarly article, in English.

Peuchot, Éric. "Droit de vote et condition de nationalité" (Right to Vote and the Nationality Requirement), *Revue de droit public et de science politique en France et à l'étranger* 107, no. 2 (1991): 481–524. Scholarly article, in French.

Plender, Richard, ed. *International Migration Law.* rev. 2d ed. Dordrecht, the Netherlands: Martinus Nijhoff, 1988. Scholarly edited collection, in English.

United Nations Commission on Human Rights. *Further Promotion and Encouragement of Human Rights and Fundamental Freedoms . . . National Institutions for the Protection of Human Rights: Report of the Secretary General, E/CN.4/1987/37.* 1986. IGO document, in English.

White, P., and C. Kesteloot, eds. "Les communautés étrangères en Europe" (Foreign Communities in Europe), *Espace, populations, sociétés* no. 2 (1990). Special issue, in English and French.

Yothment, Nivita Riley. *The Undocumented: Victims of Oppression.* Tucson, AZ, USA: ACCORD, 1979. NGO report, in English; bibliography, pp. 28–29.

## ALIENS' RIGHTS: DECLARATION ON THE HUMAN RIGHTS OF INDIVIDUALS WHO ARE NOT NATIONALS OF THE COUNTRY IN WHICH THEY LIVE, UN (1985).

The Declaration was the result of an extensive study of the applicability of existing international provisions on the protection of the human rights of aliens prepared by the Baroness Elles, a Special Rapporteur of the UN SUB-COMMISSION ON PREVENTION OF DISCRIMINATION AND PROTECTION OF MINORITIES. A draft declaration on aliens' rights was presented as part of the study and was considered in detail by the Sub-Commission and later by the Third Committee of the General Assembly.

The Declaration was adopted by the UN General Assembly on 13 December 1985 (resolution 40/144). The text, annexed to that resolution, is as follows:

*Article 1.* For the purposes of this Declaration, the term "alien" shall apply, with due regard to qualifications made in subsequent articles, to any individual who is not a national of the State in which he or she is present.

*Article 2.* 1. Nothing in this Declaration shall be interpreted as legitimizing the illegal entry into and presence in a State of any alien, nor shall any provision be interpreted as restricting the right of any state to promulgate laws and regulations concerning the entry of aliens and the terms and conditions of their stay or to establish differences between nationals and aliens. However, such laws and regulations shall not be incompatible with the international legal obligations of that State, including those in the field of human rights.

2. This Declaration shall not prejudice the enjoyment of the rights accorded by domestic law and of the rights which under international law a State is obliged to accord to aliens, even where this Declaration does not recognize such rights or recognizes them to a lesser extent.

*Article 3.* Every State shall make public its national legislation or regulations affecting aliens.

*Article 4.* Aliens shall observe the laws of the State in which they reside or are present and regard with respect the customs and traditions of the people of that State.

*Article 5.* 1. Aliens shall enjoy, in accordance with domestic law and subject to the relevant international obligations of the State in which they are present, in particular the following rights:

(a) The right to life and security of person; no alien shall be subjected to arbitrary arrest or detention; no alien shall be deprived of his or her liberty except on such grounds and in accordance with such procedures as are established by law;

(b) The right to protection against arbitrary or unlawful interference with privacy, family, home or correspondence;

(c) The right to be equal before the courts, tribunals and all other organs and authorities administering justice and, when necessary, to free assistance of an interpreter in criminal proceedings and, when prescribed by law, other proceedings;

(d) The right to choose a spouse, to marry, to found a family;

(e) The right to freedom of thought, opinion, conscience and religion; the right to manifest their religion or beliefs, subject only to such limitations as are prescribed by law and are necessary to protect public safety, order, health or morals or the fundamental rights and freedoms of others;

(f) The right to retain their own language, culture and tradition;

(g) The right to transfer abroad earnings, savings or

other personal monetary assets, subject to domestic currency regulations.

2. Subject to such restrictions as are prescribed by law and which are necessary in a democratic society to protect national security, public safety, public order, public health or morals or the rights and freedoms of others, and which are consistent with the other rights recognized in the relevant international instruments and those set forth in this Declaration, aliens shall enjoy the following rights:

(a) The right to leave the country;

(b) The right to freedom of expression;

(c) The right to peaceful assembly;

(d) The right to own property alone as well as in association with others, subject to domestic law.

3. Subject to the provisions referred to in paragraph 2, aliens lawfully in the territory of a State shall enjoy the right to liberty of movement and freedom to choose their residence within the borders of the State.

4. Subject to national legislation and due authorization, the spouse and minor or dependent children of an alien lawfully residing in the territory of a State shall be admitted to accompany, join and stay with the alien.

*Article 6.* No alien shall be subjected to torture or to cruel, inhuman or degrading treatment or punishment and, in particular, no alien shall be subjected without his or her free consent to medical or scientific experimentation.

*Article 7.* An alien lawfully in the territory of a State may be expelled therefrom only in pursuance of a decision reached in accordance with law and shall, except where compelling reasons of national security otherwise require, be allowed to submit the reasons why he or she should not be expelled and to have the case reviewed by, and be represented for the purpose before, the competent authority or a person or persons specially designated by the competent authority. Individual or collective expulsion of such aliens on grounds of race, colour, religion, culture, descent or national or ethnic origin is prohibited.

*Article 8.* 1. Aliens lawfully residing in the territory of a State shall also enjoy, in accordance with the national laws, the following rights, subject to their obligations under article 4:

(a) The right to safe and healthy working conditions, to fair wages and equal remuneration for work of equal value without distinction of any kind, in particular, women being guaranteed conditions of work not inferior to those enjoyed by men, with equal pay for equal work;

(b) The right to join trade unions and other organizations or associations of their choice and to participate in their activities. No restrictions may be placed on the exercise of this right other than those prescribed by law and which are necessary, in a democratic society, in the interests of national security or public order or for the protection of the rights and freedoms of others;

(c) The right to health protection, medical care, social security, social services, education, rest and leisure, provided that they fulfil the requirements under the relevant regulations for participation and that undue strain is not placed on the resources of the State.

2. With a view to protecting the rights of aliens carrying on lawful paid activities in the country in which they are present, such rights may be specified by the Governments concerned in multilateral or bilateral conventions.

*Article 9.* No alien shall be arbitrarily deprived of his or her lawfully acquired assets.

*Article 10.* Any alien shall be free at any time to communicate with the consulate or diplomatic mission of the State of which he or she is a national or, in the absence thereof, with the consulate or diplomatic mission of any other State entrusted with the protection of the interests of the State of which he or she is a national in the State where he or she resides.

**ALL INDIA WOMEN'S CONFERENCE.** An international non-governmental organization in consultative status with the UN Economic and Social Council (Category II), the All India Women's Conference is the largest women's organization in Southeast Asia, with over 500 branches in India and abroad and an individual membership of over one million.

Founded in 1926, AIWC works for a society based on the principles of social justice, personal integrity, and equal rights, and specifically for the progress and welfare of women and children. AIWC manages a number of projects for women and children in rural and urban areas throughout its Indian branches, such as short stay homes, "old stay" homes, family counseling centers, a blind girls' training project, working women's hostels, and schools for tribal children.

AIWC publishes the quarterly journal *Roshni* (in English).

All India Women's Conference. Address: Sarojini House, 6 Bhaghwandas Road, New Delhi 110001, India. Telephone: (61-11) 38-96-80. Cable: Hindmahlia. President: Shobhane Ranade.

**AMERICAN ASSOCIATION FOR THE ADVANCEMENT OF SCIENCE AND HUMAN RIGHTS PROGRAMS.** A non-governmental organization dedicated to aiding scientists whose internationally recognized human rights have been violated, the Association advances the use of scientific methods and procedures in the documentation and prevention of human rights violations, promotes international human rights within the scientific community, and addresses the conceptual and measurement issues of human rights.

The Association has available four-month volunteer internships and publishes the *Directory of Persecuted Scientists, Engineers, and Health Professionals* and *The Report on Science and Human Rights,* both of which are distributed free.

*AAAS SCIENTIFIC FREEDOM AND RESPONSIBILITY AWARD.* Established in 1980, this annual award for human rights activity honors scientists and engineers whose exemplary actions have served to foster scientific freedom and responsibility. The Award recognizes those who have acted to protect the public's health, safety, or welfare; have focused public attention on the potential impact of science and technology on society by participating in public policy debates; or have established precedents in social responsibility or in defending the professional freedom of scientists and engineers. The recipient receives $2,500 and a commemorative plaque.

The AAAS Award is open to individuals or organizations in the scientific or engineering fields. Nominations from the public are submitted to a Selection Committee drawn from the AAAS Standing Committee. The Board of Directors chooses the recipients on the recommendation of the Selection Committee. Past recipients include Inez Austin (1991) and Robert Watson and Daniel Albritton (1992).

*AAAS SCIENCE AND HUMAN RIGHTS PROGRAM.* Since its inception in 1976, the Science and Human Rights Program has taken action on behalf of some 2,000 scientists, engineers, and health professionals. The Program is based on the premise that scientific societies should encourage international respect for accepted human rights standards. The Program has five major purposes: (1) to document human rights violations affecting the scientific community worldwide and to bring effective aid to foreign scientists, health professionals, engineers, teachers, and students; (2) to advance the use of scientific methods and procedures in the documentation and prevention of human rights abuses, through work in the forensic sciences, genetics, statistics and information management, and medicine, particularly in the treatment of torture victims; (3) to develop scientific methods for monitoring implementation of human rights; (4) to promote greater understanding and support for human rights within the scientific community; and (5) to support the right of academic freedom and the ability of scientists, teachers, and students to pursue their work without interference.

*AAAS SCIENCE AND HUMAN RIGHTS ACTION NETWORK (AAASHRAN).* Begun in 1993, the Human Rights Action Network uses electronic mail to inform AAAS members and others of cases deserving special attention and to coordinate efforts to send appeals to governments on behalf of colleagues experiencing human rights violations.

American Association for the Advancement of Science and Human Rights Programs. Address: 1333 H St., NW, Washington, DC, 20005. Telephone: (202) 362-6797. Fax: (202) 289-4950. Contact: Elisa Muñoz.

## AMERICAN ASSOCIATION OF JURISTS. A non-governmental organization in consultative status (Category II) with the UN Economic and Social Council, the American Association of Jurists was founded in

Panama in 1975. The Association currently has national branches in 27 countries and territories in the Americas.

American Association of Jurists. Address: Paranà 257, 1017 Buenos Aires, Argentina. Telephone: (54-1) 40-2724. Fax: (54-1) 325-6454. Administrative Secretary: Nora Morales.

## AMERICAN CONVENTION ON HUMAN RIGHTS (1969) AND PROTOCOLS (1988).
The Convention, also known as the Pact of San Jose, Costa Rica, provides protection of human rights on a regional basis by countries in North, Central, and South America, roughly comparable to that provided by countries in western Europe by the European Convention on Human Rights. It establishes two organs for this purpose: the **INTER-AMERICAN COMMISSION ON HUMAN RIGHTS** and the **INTER-AMERICAN COURT OF HUMAN RIGHTS.** The functions of the Commission include investigation, conciliation, the making of recommendations, and the issuance of reports setting out its findings and conclusions. The Court, if its jurisdiction is accepted by the State concerned, may make definitive determinations of human rights violations by a State, award damages for the violations, and arrange for the consequences of the violations to be remedied.

The Convention was adopted at San Jose on 22 November 1969 by the Inter-American Specialized Conference on Human Rights and entered into force on 18 July 1978.

Provisions adding certain economic, social, and cultural rights to the catalogue of matters with which the convention is concerned are set out in the Additional Protocol, also known as the Protocol of San Salvador, which will enter into force, in accordance with its article 74, "as soon as eleven States have deposited their instruments of ratification or accession." The Additional Protocol was approved unanimously by the OAS General Assembly on 17 November 1988 on the basis of a draft prepared by the Inter-American Commission on Human Rights.

The text of the Convention, as adopted at San Jose in 1969, (OAS Treaty Series 36), is as follows:

### Preamble

The American states signatory to the present Convention,

Reaffirming their intention to consolidate in this hemisphere, within the framework of democratic institutions, a system of personal liberty and social justice based on respect for the essential rights of man;

Recognizing that the essential rights of man are not derived from one's being a national of a certain state, but are based upon attributes of the human personality, and that they therefore justify international protection in the form of a convention reinforcing or complementing the protection provided by the domestic law of the American states;

Considering that these principles have been set forth in the Charter of the Organization of American States, in the American Declaration of the Rights and Duties of Man, and in the Universal Declaration of Human Rights, and that they have been reaffirmed and refined in other international instruments, worldwide as well as regional in scope;

Reiterating that, in accordance with the Universal Declaration of Human Rights, the ideal of free men enjoying freedom from fear and want can be achieved only if conditions are created whereby everyone may enjoy his economic, social, and cultural rights, as well as his civil and political rights; and

Considering that the Third Special Inter-American Conference (Buenos Aires, 1967) approved the incorporation into the Charter of the Organization itself of broader standards with respect to economic, social, and educational rights and resolved that an inter-American convention on human rights should determine the structure, competence, and procedure of the organs responsible for these matters,

Have agreed upon the following:

**Part I State Obligations and Rights Protected**

Chapter I—General Obligations

*Article 1.* Obligation to Respect Rights. 1. The States Parties to this Convention undertake to respect the rights and freedoms recognized herein and to ensure to all persons subject to their jurisdiction the free and full exercise of those rights and freedoms, without any discrimination for reasons of race, color, sex, language, religion, political or other opinion, national or social origin, economic status, birth, or any other social condition.

2. For the purposes of this Convention, "person" means every human being.

*Article 2.* Domestic Legal Effects. Where the exercise of any of the rights or freedoms referred to in Article 1 is not already ensured by legislative or other provisions, the States Parties undertake to adopt, in accordance with their constitutional processes and the provisions of this Convention, such legislative or other measures as may be necessary to give effect to those rights or freedoms.

Chapter II—Civil and Political Rights

*Article 3.* Right to Juridical Personality. Every person has the right to recognition as a person before the law.

*Article 4.* Right to Life. 1. Every person has the right to have his life respected. This right shall be protected by law and, in general, from the moment of conception. No one shall be arbitrarily deprived of his life.

2. In countries that have not abolished the death penalty, it may be imposed only for the most serious crimes and pursuant to a final judgment rendered by a competent court and in accordance with a law establishing such punishment, enacted prior to the commission of the crime. The application of such punishment shall not be extended to crimes to which it does not presently apply.

3. The death penalty shall not be reestablished in states that have abolished it.

4. In no case shall capital punishment be inflicted for political offenses or related common crimes.

5. Capital punishment shall not be imposed upon persons who, at the time the crime was committed, were under 18 years of age or over 70 years of age; nor shall it be applied to pregnant women.

6. Every person condemned to death shall have the right to apply for amnesty, pardon, or commutation of sentence, which may be granted in all cases. Capital punishment shall not be imposed while such a petition is pending decision by the competent authority.

*Article 5.* Right to Humane Treatment. 1. Every person has the right to have his physical, mental, and moral integrity respected.

2. No one shall be subjected to torture or to cruel, inhuman, or degrading punishment or treatment. All persons deprived of their liberty shall be treated with respect for the inherent dignity of the human person.

3. Punishment shall not be extended to any person other than the criminal.

4. Accused persons shall, save in exceptional circumstances, be segregated from convicted persons, and shall be subject to separate treatment appropriate to their status as unconvicted persons.

5. Minors while subject to criminal proceedings shall be separated from adults and brought before specialized tribunals, as speedily as possible, so that they may be treated in accordance with their status as minors.

6. Punishments consisting of deprivation of liberty shall have as an essential aim the reform and social readaptation of the prisoners.

*Article 6.* Freedom from Slavery. 1. No one shall be subject to slavery or to involuntary servitude, which are prohibited in all their forms, as are the slave trade and traffic in women.

2. No one shall be required to perform forced or compulsory labor. This provision shall not be interpreted to mean that, in those countries in which the penalty established for certain crimes is deprivation of liberty at forced labor, the carrying out of such a sentence imposed by a competent court is prohibited. Forced labor shall not adversely affect the dignity or the physical or intellectual capacity of the prisoner.

3. For the purposes of this article, the following do not constitute forced or compulsory labor:

a) work or service normally required of a person imprisoned in execution of a sentence or formal decision passed by the competent judicial authority. Such work or service shall be carried out under the supervision and control of public authorities, and any persons performing such work or service shall not be placed at the disposal of any private party, company, or juridical person;

b) military service and, in countries in which conscientious objectors are recognized, national service that the law may provide for in lieu of military service;

c) service exacted in time of danger or calamity that threatens the existence or the well-being of the community; or

d) work or service that forms part of normal civic obligations.

*Article 7.* Right to Personal Liberty. 1. Every person has the right to personal liberty and security.

2. No one shall be deprived of his physical liberty except for the reasons and under the conditions established beforehand by the constitution of the State Party concerned or by a law established pursuant thereto.

3. No one shall be subject to arbitrary arrest or imprisonment.

4. Anyone who is detained shall be informed of the reasons for his detention and shall be promptly notified of the charge or charges against him.

5. Any person detained shall be brought promptly before a judge or other officer authorized by law to exercise judicial

power and shall be entitled to trial within a reasonable time or to be released without prejudice to the continuation of the proceedings. His release may be subject to guarantees to assure his appearance for trial.

6. Anyone who is deprived of his liberty shall be entitled to recourse to a competent court, in order that the court may decide without delay on the lawfulness of his arrest or detention and order his release if the arrest or detention is unlawful. In States Parties whose laws provide that anyone who believes himself to be threatened with deprivation of his liberty is entitled to recourse to a competent court in order that it may decide on the lawfulness of such threat, this remedy may not be restricted or abolished. The interested party or another person in his behalf is entitled to seek these remedies.

7. No one shall be detained for debt. This principle shall not limit the orders of a competent judicial authority issued for nonfulfillment of duties of support.

*Article 8.* Right to a Fair Trial. 1. Every person has the right to a hearing, with due guarantees and within a reasonable time, by a competent, independent, and impartial tribunal, previously established by law, in the substantiation of any accusation of a criminal nature made against him or for the determination of his rights and obligations of a civil, labor, fiscal, or any other nature.

2. Every person accused of a criminal offense has the right to be presumed innocent so long as his guilt has not been proven according to law. During the proceedings, every person is entitled, with full equality, to the following minimum guarantees:

a) the right of the accused to be assisted without charge by a translator or interpreter, if he does not understand or does not speak the language of the tribunal or court;

b) prior notification in detail to the accused of the charges against him;

c) adequate time and means for the preparation of his defense;

d) the right of the accused to defend himself personally or to be assisted by legal counsel of his own choosing, and to communicate freely and privately with his counsel;

e) the inalienable right to be assisted by counsel provided by the state, paid or not as the domestic law provides, if the accused does not defend himself personally or engage his own counsel within the time period established by law;

f) the right of the defense to examine witnesses present in the court and to obtain the appearance, as witnesses, of experts or other persons who may throw light on the facts;

g) the right not to be compelled to be a witness against himself or to plead guilty; and

h) the right to appeal the judgment to a higher court.

3. A confession of guilt by the accused shall be valid only if it is made without coercion of any kind.

4. An accused person acquitted by a nonappealable judgment shall not be subjected to a new trial for the same cause.

5. Criminal proceedings shall be public, except insofar as may be necessary to protect the interests of justice.

*Article 9.* Freedom from Ex Post Facto Laws. No one shall be convicted of any act or omission that did not constitute a criminal offense, under the applicable law, at the time it was committed. A heavier penalty shall not be imposed than the one that was applicable at the time the criminal offense was committed. If subsequent to the commission of the offense the law provides for the imposition of a lighter punishment, the guilty person shall benefit therefrom.

*Article 10.* Right to Compensation. Every person has the right to be compensated in accordance with the law in the event he has been sentenced by a final judgment through a miscarriage of justice.

*Article 11.* Right to Privacy. 1. Everyone has the right to have his honor respected and his dignity recognized.

2. No one may be the object of arbitrary or abusive interference with his private life, his family, his home, or his correspondence, or of unlawful attacks on his honor or reputation.

3. Everyone has the right to the protection of the law against such interference or attacks.

*Article 12.* Freedom of Conscience and Religion. 1. Everyone has the right to freedom of conscience and of religion. This right includes freedom to maintain or to change one's religion or beliefs, and freedom to profess or disseminate one's religion or beliefs, either individually or together with others, in public or in private.

2. No one shall be subject to restrictions that might impair his freedom to maintain or to change his religion or beliefs.

3. Freedom to manifest one's religion and beliefs may be subject only to the limitations prescribed by law that are necessary to protect public safety, order, health, or morals, or the rights or freedoms of others.

4. Parents or guardians, as the case may be, have the right to provide for the religious and moral education of their children or wards that is in accord with their own convictions.

*Article 13.* Freedom of Thought and Expression. 1. Everyone has the right to freedom of thought and expression. This right includes freedom to seek, receive, and impart information and ideas of all kinds, regardless of frontiers, either orally, in writing, in print, in the form of art, or through any other medium of one's choice.

2. The exercise of the right provided for in the foregoing paragraph shall not be subject to prior censorship but shall be subject to subsequent imposition of liability, which shall be expressly established by law to the extent necessary to ensure:

a) respect for the rights or reputations of others; or

b) the protection of national security, public order, or public health or morals.

3. The right of expression may not be restricted by indirect methods or means, such as the abuse of government or private controls over newsprint, radio broadcasting frequencies, or equipment used in the dissemination of information, or by any other means tending to impede the communication and circulation of ideas and opinions.

4. Notwithstanding the provisions of paragraph 2 above, public entertainments may be subject by law to prior censorship for the sole purpose of regulating access to them for the moral protection of childhood and adolescence.

5. Any propaganda for war and any advocacy of national, racial, or religious hatred that constitute incitements to lawless violence or to any other similar action against any person or group of persons on any grounds including those of race, color, religion, language, or national origin shall be considered as offenses punishable by law.

*Article 14.* Right of Reply. 1. Anyone injured by inaccurate or offensive statements or ideas disseminated to the public in general by a legally regulated medium of communication has the right to reply or to make a correction using the same communications outlet, under such conditions as the law may establish.

2. The correction or reply shall not in any case remit other legal liabilities that may have been incurred.

3. For the effective protection of honor and reputation, every publisher, and every newspaper, motion picture, radio, and television company, shall have a person responsible who is not protected by immunities or special privileges.

*Article 15.* Right of Assembly. The right of peaceful Assembly, without arms, is recognized. No restrictions may be placed on the exercise of this right other than those imposed in conformity with the law and necessary in a democratic society in the interest of national security, public safety or public order, or to protect public health or morals or the rights or freedom of others.

*Article 16.* Freedom of Association. 1. Everyone has the right to associate freely for ideological, religious, political, economic, labor, social, cultural, sports, or other purposes.

2. The exercise of this right shall be subject only to such restrictions established by law as may be necessary in a democratic society, in the interest of national security, public safety or public order, or to protect public health or morals or the rights and freedoms of others.

3. The provisions of this article do not bar the imposition of legal restrictions, including even deprivation of the exercise of the right of association, on members of the armed forces and the police.

*Article 17.* Rights of the Family. 1. The family is the natural and fundamental group unit of society and is entitled to protection by society and the state.

2. The right of men and women of marriageable age to marry and to raise a family shall be recognized, if they meet the conditions required by domestic law, insofar as such conditions do not affect the principle of nondiscrimination established in this Convention.

3. No marriage shall be entered into without the free and full consent of the intending spouses.

4. The States Parties shall take appropriate steps to ensure the equality of rights and the adequate balancing of responsibilities of the spouses as to marriage, during marriage, and in the event of its dissolution. In case of dissolution, provision shall be made for the necessary protection of any children solely on the basis of their own best interests.

5. The law shall recognize equal rights for children born out of wedlock and those born in wedlock.

*Article 18.* Right to a Name. Every person has the right to a given name and to the surnames of his parents or that of one of them. The law shall regulate the manner in which this right shall be ensured for all, by the use of assumed names if necessary.

*Article 19.* Rights of the Child. Every minor child has the right to the measures of protection required by his condition as a minor on the part of his family, society, and the state.

*Article 20.* Right to Nationality. 1. Every person has the right to a nationality.

2. Every person has the right to the nationality of the state in whose territory he was born if he does not have the right to any other nationality.

3. No one shall be arbitrarily deprived of his nationality or of the right to change it.

*Article 21.* Right to Property. 1. Everyone has the right to the use and enjoyment of his property. The law may subordinate such use and enjoyment to the interest of society.

2. No one shall be deprived of his property except upon payment of just compensation, for reasons of public utility or social interest, and in the cases and according to the forms established by law.

3. Usury and any other form of exploitation of man by man shall be prohibited by law.

*Article 22.* Freedom of Movement and Residence.

1. Every person lawfully in the territory of a State Party has the right to move about in it, and to reside in it subject to the provisions of the law.

2. Every person has the right to leave any country freely, including his own.

3. The exercise of the foregoing rights may be restricted only pursuant to a law to the extent necessary in a democratic society to prevent crime or to protect national security, public safety, public order, public morals, public health, or the rights or freedoms of others.

4. The exercise of the rights recognized in paragraph 1 may also be restricted by law in designated zones for reasons of public interest.

5. No one can be expelled from the territory of the state of which he is a national or be deprived of the right to enter it.

6. An alien lawfully in the territory of a State Party to this Convention may be expelled from it only pursuant to a decision reached in accordance with law.

7. Every person has the right to seek and be granted asylum in a foreign territory, in accordance with the legislation of the state and international conventions, in the event he is being pursued for political offenses or related common crimes.

8. In no case may an alien be deported or returned to a country, regardless of whether or not it is his country of origin, if in that country his right to life or personal freedom is in danger of being violated because of his race, nationality, religion, social status, or political opinions.

9. The collective expulsion of aliens is prohibited.

*Article 23.* Right to Participate in Government. 1. Every citizen shall enjoy the following rights and opportunities:

a) to take part in the conduct of public affairs, directly or through freely chosen representatives;

b) to vote and to be elected in genuine periodic elections, which shall be by universal and equal suffrage and by secret ballot that guarantees the free expression of the will of the voters; and

c) to have access, under general conditions of equality, to the public service of his country.

2. The law may regulate the exercise of the rights and opportunities referred to in the preceding paragraph only on the basis of age, nationality, residence, language, education, civil and mental capacity, or sentencing by a competent court in criminal proceedings.

*Article 24.* Right to Equal Protection. All persons are equal before the law. Consequently, they are entitled, without discrimination, to equal protection of the law.

*Article 25.* Right to Judicial Protection. 1. Everyone has the right to simple and prompt recourse, or any other effective recourse, to a competent court or tribunal for protection against acts that violate his fundamental rights recognized by the constitution or laws of the state concerned or by this Convention, even though such violation may have been committed by persons acting in the course of their official duties.

2. The States Parties undertake:

a) to ensure that any person claiming such remedy shall have his rights determined by the competent authority provided for by the legal system of the state;

b) to develop the possibilities of judicial remedy; and

c) to ensure that the competent authorities shall enforce such remedies when granted.

Chapter III—Economic, Social, and Cultural Rights

*Article 26.* Progressive Development. The States Parties undertake to adopt measures, both internally and through international cooperation, especially those of an economic and technical nature, with a view to achieving progressively, by legislation or other appropriate means, the full realization of the rights implicit in the economic, social, educational, scientific, and cultural standards set forth in the Charter of the Organization of American States as amended by the Protocol of Buenos Aires.

Chapter IV—Suspension of Guarantees, Interpretation, and Application

*Article 27.* Suspension of Guarantees. 1. In time of war, public danger, or other emergency that threatens the independence or security of a State Party, it may take measures derogating from its obligations under the present Convention to the extent and for the period of time strictly required by the exigencies of the situation, provided that such measures are not inconsistent with its other obligations under international law and do not involve discrimination on the ground of race, color, sex, language, religion, or social origin.

2. The foregoing provision does not authorize any suspension of the following articles: Article 3 (Right to Juridical Personality), Article 4 (Right to Life), Article 5 (Right to Humane Treatment), Article 6 (Freedom from Slavery), Article 9 (Freedom from Ex Post Facto Laws), Article 12 (Freedom of Conscience and Religion), Article 17 (Rights of the Family), Article 18 (Right to a Name), Article 19 (Rights of the Child), Article 20 (Right to Nationality), and Article 23 (Right to Participate in Government), or of the judicial guarantees essential for the protection of such rights.

3. Any State Party availing itself of the right of suspension shall immediately inform the other States Parties, through the Secretary General of the Organization of American States, of the provisions the application of which it has suspended, the reasons that gave rise to the suspension, and the date set for the termination of such suspension.

*Article 28.* Federal Clause. 1. Where a State Party is constituted as a federal state, the national government of such State Party shall implement all the provisions of the Convention over whose subject matter it exercises legislative and judicial jurisdiction.

2. With respect to the provisions over whose subject matter the constituent units of the federal state have jurisdiction, the national government shall immediately take suitable measures, in accordance with its constitution and its laws, to the end that the competent authorities of the constituent units may adopt appropriate provisions for the fulfillment of this Convention.

3. Whenever two or more States Parties agree to form a federation or other type of association, they shall take care that the resulting federal or other compact contains the provisions necessary for continuing and rendering effective the standards of this Convention in the new state that is organized.

*Article 29.* Restrictions Regarding Interpretation. No provision of this Convention shall be interpreted as:

a) permitting any State Party, group, or person to suppress the enjoyment or exercise of the rights and freedoms recognized in this Convention or to restrict them to a greater extent than is provided for herein;

b) restricting the enjoyment or exercise of any right or freedom recognized by virtue of the laws of any State Party or by virtue of another convention to which one of the said states is a party;

c) precluding other rights or guarantees that are inherent in the human personality or derived from representative democracy as a form of government; or

d) excluding or limiting the effect that the American Declaration of the Rights and Duties of Man and other international acts of the same nature may have.

*Article 30.* Scope of Restrictions. The restrictions that, pursuant to this Convention, may be placed on the enjoyment or exercise of the rights or freedoms recognized herein may not be applied except in accordance with laws enacted for reasons of general interest and in accordance with the purpose for which such restrictions have been established.

*Article 31.* Recognition of Other Rights. Other rights and freedoms recognized in accordance with the procedures established in Articles 76 and 77 may be included in the system of protection of this Convention.

Chapter V—Personal Responsibilities

*Article 32.* Relationship between Duties and Rights. 1. Every person has responsibilities to his family, his community, and mankind.

2. The rights of each person are limited by the rights of others, by the security of all, and by the just demands of the general welfare, in a democratic society.

**Part II Means of Protection**

Chapter VI—Competent Organs

*Article 33.* The following organs shall have competence with respect to matters relating to the fulfillment of the commitments made by the States Parties to this Convention:

a) the Inter-American Commission on Human Rights, referred to as "The Commission;" and

b) the Inter-American Court of Human Rights, referred to as "The Court."

Chapter VII—Inter-American Commission on Human Rights

Section 1. Organization

*Article 34.* The Inter-American Commission on Human Rights shall be composed of seven members, who shall be persons of high moral character and recognized competence in the field of human rights.

*Article 35.* The Commission shall represent all the member countries of the Organization of American States.

*Article 36.* 1. The members of the Commission shall be elected in a personal capacity by the General Assembly of the Organization from a list of candidates proposed by the governments of the member states.

2. Each of those governments may propose up to three candidates, who may be nationals of the states proposing them or of any other member state of the Organization of American States. When a slate of three is proposed, at least one of the candidates shall be a national of a state other than the one proposing the slate.

*Article 37.* 1. The members of the Commission shall be elected for a term of four years and may be reelected only once, but the terms of three of the members chosen in the first election shall expire at the end of two years. Immediately following that election the General Assembly shall determine the names of those three members by lot.

2. No two nationals of the same state may be members of the Commission.

*Article 38.* Vacancies that may occur on the Commission for reasons other than the normal expiration of term shall be filled by the Permanent Council of the Organization in accordance with the provisions of the Statute of the Commission.

*Article 39.* The Commission shall prepare its Statute, which it shall submit to the General Assembly for approval. It shall establish its own Regulations.

*Article 40.* Secretariat services for the Commission shall be furnished by the appropriate specialized unit of the General Secretariat of the Organization. This unit shall be provided with the resources required to accomplish the tasks assigned to it by the Commission.

Section 2. Functions

*Article 41.* The main function of the Commission shall be to promote respect for and defense of human rights. In the exercise of its mandate, it shall have the following functions and powers:

a) to develop an awareness of human rights among the peoples of America;

b) to make recommendations to the governments of the member states, when it considers such action advisable, for the adoption of progressive measures in favor of human rights within the framework of their domestic law and constitutional provisions as well as appropriate measures to further the observance of those rights;

c) to prepare such studies or reports as it considers advisable in the performance of its duties;

d) to request the governments of the member states to supply it with information on the measures adopted by them in matters of human rights;

e) to respond, through the General Secretariat of the Organization of American States, to inquiries made by the member states on matters related to human rights and, within the limits of its possibilities, to provide those states with the advisory services they request;

f) to take action on petitions and other communications pursuant to its authority under the provisions of Articles 44 through 51 of this Convention; and

g) to submit an annual report to the General Assembly of the Organization of American States.

*Article 42.* The States Parties shall transmit to the Commission a copy of each of the reports and studies that they submit annually to the Executive Committees of the Inter-American Economic and Social Council and the Inter-American Council for Education, Science, and Culture, in their respective fields, so that the Commission may watch over the promotion of the rights implicit in the economic, social, educational, scientific, and cultural standards set forth in the Charter of the Organization of American States as amended by the Protocol of Buenos Aires.

*Article 43.* The States Parties undertake to provide the Commission with such information as it may request of them as to the manner in which their domestic law ensures the effective application of any provisions of this Convention.

Section 3. Competence

*Article 44.* Any person or group of persons, or any nongovernmental entity legally recognized in one or more member states of the Organization, may lodge petitions with the Commission containing denunciations or complaints of violation of this Convention by a State Party.

*Article 45.* 1. Any State Party may, when it deposits its instrument of ratification of or adherence to this Convention, or at any later time, declare that it recognizes the competence of the Commission to receive and examine communications in which a State Party alleges that another State Party has committed a violation of a human right set forth in this Convention.

2. Communications presented by virtue of this article may be admitted and examined only if they are presented by a State Party that has made a declaration recognizing the aforementioned competence of the Commission. The Commission shall not admit any communication against a State Party that has not made such a declaration.

3. A declaration concerning recognition of competence may be made to be valid for an indefinite time, for a specified period, or for a specific case.

4. Declarations shall be deposited with the General Secretariat of the Organization of American States, which shall transmit copies thereof to the member states of that Organization.

*Article 46.* 1. Admission by the Commission of a petition or communication lodged in accordance with Articles 44 or 45 shall be subject to the following requirements:

a) that the remedies under domestic law have been pursued and exhausted in accordance with generally recognized principles of international law;

b) that the petition or communication is lodged within a period of six months from the date on which the party alleging violation of his rights was notified of the final judgment;

c) that the subject of the petition or communication is not pending in another international proceeding for settlement; and

d) that, in the case of Article 44, the petition contains the name, nationality, profession, domicile, and signature of the person or persons or of the legal representative of the entity lodging the petition.

2. The provisions of paragraphs 1.a and 1.b of this article shall not be applicable when:

a) the domestic legislation of the state concerned does not afford due process of law for the protection of the right or rights that have allegedly been violated;

b) the party alleging violation of his rights has been denied access to the remedies under domestic law or has been prevented from exhausting them; or

c) there has been unwarranted delay in rendering a final judgment under the aforementioned remedies.

*Article 47.* The Commission shall consider inadmissible any petition or communication submitted under Articles 44 or 45 if:

a) any of the requirements indicated in Article 46 has not been met;

b) the petition or communication does not state facts that tend to establish a violation of the rights guaranteed by this Convention;

c) the statements of the petitioner or of the state indicate that the petition or communication is manifestly groundless or obviously out of order; or

d) the petition or communication is substantially the same as one previously studied by the Commission or by another international organization.

Section 4. Procedure

*Article 48.* 1. When the Commission receives a petition or communication alleging violation of any of the rights protected by this Convention, it shall proceed as follows:

a) If it considers the petition or communication admissible, it shall request information from the government of the state indicated as being responsible for the alleged violations and shall furnish that government a transcript of the pertinent portions of the petition or communication. This information shall be submitted within a reasonable period to be determined by the Commission in accordance with the circumstances of each case.

b) After the information has been received, or after the period established has elapsed and the information has not been received, the Commission shall ascertain whether the grounds for the petition or communication still exist. If they do not, the Commission shall order the record to be closed.

c) The Commission may also declare the petition or communication inadmissible or out of order on the basis of information or evidence subsequently received.

d) If the record has not been closed, the Commission shall, with the knowledge of the parties, examine the matter set forth in the petition or communication in order to verify the facts. If necessary and advisable, the Commission shall carry out an investigation, for the effective conduct of which it shall request, and the states concerned shall furnish to it, all necessary facilities.

e) The Commission may request the states concerned to furnish any pertinent information and, if so requested, shall hear oral statements or receive written statements from the parties concerned.

f) The Commission shall place itself at the disposal of the parties concerned with a view to reaching a friendly settlement of the matter on the basis of respect for the human rights recognized in this Convention.

2. However, in serious and urgent cases, only the presentation of a petition or communication that fulfills all the formal requirements of admissibility shall be necessary in order for the Commission to conduct an investigation with the prior consent of the state in whose territory a violation has allegedly been committed.

*Article 49.* If a friendly settlement has been reached in accordance with paragraph 1.f of Article 48, the Commission shall draw up a report, which shall be transmitted to the petitioner and to the States Parties to this Convention, and shall then be communicated to the Secretary General of the Organization of American States for publication. This report shall contain a brief statement of the facts and of the solution reached. If any party in the case so requests, the fullest possible information shall be provided to it.

*Article 50.* 1. If a settlement is not reached, the Commission shall, within the time limit established by its Statute, draw up a report setting forth the facts and stating its conclusions. If the report, in whole or in part, does not represent the unanimous agreement of the members of the Commission, any member may attach to it a separate opinion. The written and oral statements made by the parties in accordance with paragraph 1.e of Article 48 shall also be attached to the report.

2. The report shall be transmitted to the states concerned, which shall not be at liberty to publish it.

3. In transmitting the report, the Commission may make such proposals and recommendations as it sees fit.

*Article 51.* 1. If, within a period of three months from the date of the transmittal of the report of the Commission to the states concerned, the matter has not either been settled or submitted by the Commission or by the state concerned to the Court and its jurisdiction accepted, the Commission may, by the vote of an absolute majority of its members, set forth its opinion and conclusions concerning the question submitted for its consideration.

2. Where appropriate, the Commission shall make pertinent recommendations and shall prescribe a period within which the state is to take the measures that are incumbent upon it to remedy the situation examined.

3. When the prescribed period has expired, the Commission shall decide by the vote of an absolute majority of its members whether the state has taken adequate measures and whether to publish its report.

Chapter VIII—Inter-American Court of Human Rights
Section 1. Organization
*Article 52.* 1. The Court shall consist of seven judges, nationals of the member states of the Organization, elected in an individual capacity from among jurists of the highest moral authority and of recognized competence in the field of human rights, who possess the qualifications required for the exercise of the highest judicial functions in conformity with the law of the state of which they are nationals or of the state that proposes them as candidates.

2. No two judges may be nationals of the same state.

*Article 53.* 1. The judges of the Court shall be elected by secret ballot by an absolute majority vote of the States Parties to the Convention, in the General Assembly of the Organization, from a panel of candidates proposed by those states.

2. Each of the States Parties may propose up to three candidates, nationals of the state that proposes them or of any other member state of the Organization of American States. When a slate of three is proposed, at least one of the candidates shall be a national of a state other than the one proposing the slate.

*Article 54.* 1. The judges of the Court shall be elected for a term of six years and may be reelected only once. The term of three of the judges chosen in the first election shall expire at the end of three years. Immediately after the election, the names of the three judges shall be determined by lot in the General Assembly.

2. A judge elected to replace a judge whose term has not expired shall complete the term of the latter.

3. The judges shall continue in office until the expiration of their term. However, they shall continue to serve with regard to cases that they have begun to hear and that are still pending, for which purposes they shall not be replaced by the newly elected judges.

*Article 55.* 1. If a judge is a national of any of the States Parties to a case submitted to the Court, he shall retain his right to hear that case.

2. If one of the judges called upon to hear a case should be a national of one of the States Parties to the case, any other State Party in the case may appoint a person of its choice to serve on the Court as an ad hoc judge.

3. If among the judges called upon to hear a case none is a national of any of the States Parties to the case, each of the latter may appoint an ad hoc judge.

4. An ad hoc judge shall possess the qualifications indicated in Article 52.

5. If several States Parties to the Convention should have the same interest in a case, they shall be considered as a single party for purposes of the above provisions. In case of doubt, the Court shall decide.

*Article 56.* Five judges shall constitute a quorum for the transaction of business by the Court.

*Article 57.* The Commission shall appear in all cases before the Court.

*Article 58.* 1. The Court shall have its seat at the place determined by the States Parties to the Convention in the General Assembly of the Organization; however, it may convene in the territory of any member state of the Organization of American States when a majority of the Court considers it desirable, and with the prior consent of the state concerned. The seat of the Court may be changed by the States Parties to the Convention in the General Assembly by a two-thirds vote.

2. The Court shall appoint its own Secretary.

3. The Secretary shall have his office at the place where the Court has its seat and shall attend the meetings that the Court may hold away from its seat.

*Article 59.* The Court shall establish its Secretariat, which shall function under the direction of the Secretary of the Court, in accordance with the administrative standards of the General Secretariat of the Organization in all respects not incompatible with the independence of the Court. The staff of the Court's Secretariat shall be appointed by the Secretary General of the Organization, in consultation with the Secretary of the Court.

*Article 60.* The Court shall draw up its Statute which it shall submit to the General Assembly for approval. It shall adopt its own Rules of Procedure.

Section 2. Jurisdiction and Functions

*Article 61.* 1. Only the States Parties and the Commission shall have the right to submit a case to the Court.

2. In order for the Court to hear a case, it is necessary that the procedures set forth in Articles 48 and 50 shall have been completed.

*Article 62.* 1. A State Party may, upon depositing its instrument of ratification or adherence to this Convention, or at any subsequent time, declare that it recognizes as binding, ipso facto, and not requiring special agreement, the jurisdiction of the Court on all matters relating to the interpretation or application of this Convention.

2. Such declaration may be made unconditionally, on the condition of reciprocity, for a specified period, or for specific cases. It shall be presented to the Secretary General of the Organization, who shall transmit copies thereof to the other member states of the Organization and to the Secretary of the Court.

3. The jurisdiction of the Court shall comprise all cases concerning the interpretation and application of the provisions of this Convention that are submitted to it, provided that the States Parties to the case recognize or have recognized such jurisdiction, whether by special declaration pursuant to the preceding paragraphs, or by a special agreement.

*Article 63.* 1. If the Court finds that there has been a violation of a right or freedom protected by this Convention, the Court shall rule that the injured party be ensured the enjoyment of his right or freedom that was violated. It shall also rule, if appropriate, that the consequences of the measure or situation that constituted the breach of such right or freedom be remedied and that fair compensation be paid to the injured party.

2. In cases of extreme gravity and urgency, and when necessary to avoid irreparable damage to persons, the Court shall adopt such provisional measures as it deems pertinent in matters it has under consideration. With respect to a case not yet submitted to the Court, it may act at the request of the Commission.

*Article 64.* 1. The member states of the Organization may consult the Court regarding the interpretation of this Convention or of other treaties concerning the protection of human rights in the American states. Within their spheres of competence, the organs listed in Chapter X of the Charter of the Organization of American States, as amended by the Protocol of Buenos Aires, may in like manner consult the Court.

2. The Court, at the request of a member state of the Organization, may provide that state with opinions regarding the compatibility of any of its domestic laws with the aforesaid international instruments.

*Article 65.* To each regular session of the General Assembly of the Organization of American States the Court shall submit, for the Assembly's consideration, a report on its work during the previous year. It shall specify, in particular, the cases in which a state has not complied with its judgments, making any pertinent recommendations.

Section 3. Procedure

*Article 66.* 1. Reasons shall be given for the judgment of the Court.

2. If the judgment does not represent in whole or in part the unanimous opinion of the judges, any judge shall be entitled to have his dissenting or separate opinion attached to the judgment.

*Article 67.* The judgment of the Court shall be final and not subject to appeal. In case of disagreement as to the meaning or scope of the judgment, the Court shall interpret it at the request of any of the parties, provided the request is made within ninety days from the date of notification of the judgment.

*Article 68.* 1. The States Parties to the Convention undertake to comply with the judgment of the Court in any case to which they are parties.

2. That part of a judgment that stipulates compensatory damages may be executed in the country concerned in accordance with domestic procedure governing the execution of judgments against the state.

*Article 69.* The parties to the case shall be notified of the judgment of the Court and it shall be transmitted to the States Parties to the Convention.

Chapter IX—Common Provisions

*Article 70.* 1. The judges of the Court and the members of the Commission shall enjoy, from the moment of their election and throughout their term of office, the immunities extended to diplomatic agents in accordance with international law. During the exercise of their official function they shall, in addition, enjoy the diplomatic privileges necessary for the performance of their duties.

2. At no time shall the judges of the Court or the members of the Commission be held liable for any decisions or opinions issued in the exercise of their functions.

*Article 71.* The position of judge of the Court or member of the Commission is incompatible with any other activity that might affect the independence or impartiality of such judge or member, as determined in the respective statutes.

*Article 72.* The judges of the Court and the members of the Commission shall receive emoluments and travel allowances in the form and under the conditions set forth in their statutes, with due regard for the importance and independence of their office. Such emoluments and travel allowances shall be determined in the budget of the Organization of American States, which shall also include the expenses of the Court and its Secretariat. To this end, the Court shall draw up its own budget and submit it for approval to the General Assembly through the General Secretariat. The latter may not introduce any changes in it.

*Article 73.* The General Assembly may, only at the request of the Commission or the Court, as the case may be, determine sanctions to be applied against members of the Commission or judges of the Court when there are justifiable grounds for such action as set forth in the respective statutes. A vote of a two-thirds majority of the member states of the Organization shall be required for a decision in the case of members of the Commission and, in the case of judges of the Court, a two-thirds majority vote of the States Parties to the Convention shall also be required.

**Part III General and Transitory Provisions**

Chapter X—Signature, Ratification, Reservations, Amentments, Protocols, and Denunciation

*Article 74.* This Convention shall be open for signature and ratification by or adherence of any member state of the Organization of American States.

2. Ratification of or adherence to this Convention shall be made by the deposit of an instrument of ratification or adherence with the General Secretariat of the Organization of American States. As soon as eleven States have deposited their instruments of ratification or adherence, the Convention shall enter into force. With respect to any state that ratifies or adheres thereafter, the Convention shall enter into force on the date of the deposit of its instrument of ratification or adherence.

3. The Secretary General shall inform all member states of the Organization of the entry into force of the Convention.

*Article 75.* This Convention shall be subject to reservations only in conformity with the provisions of the Vienna Convention on the Law of Treaties signed on May 23, 1969.

*Article 76.* 1. Proposals to amend this Convention may be submitted to the General Assembly for the action it deems appropriate by any State Party directly, and by the Commission or the Court through the Secretary General.

2. Amendments shall enter into force for the state ratifying them on the date when two-thirds of the States Parties to this Convention have deposited their respective instruments of ratification. With respect to the other States Parties, the amendments shall enter into force on the dates on which they deposit their respective instruments of ratification.

*Article 77.* 1. In accordance with Article 31, any State Party and the Commission may submit proposed protocols to this Convention for consideration by the States Parties at the General Assembly with a view to gradually including other rights and freedoms within its system of protection.

2. Each protocol shall determine the manner of its entry into force and shall be applied only among the States Parties to it.

*Article 78.* 1. The States Parties may denounce this Convention at the expiration of a five-year period from the date of its entry into force and by means of notice given one year in advance. Notice of the denunciation shall be addressed to the Secretary General of the Organization, who shall inform the other States Parties.

2. Such a denunciation shall not have the effect of releasing the State Party concerned from the obligations contained in this Convention with respect to any act that may constitute a violation of those obligations and that has been taken by that state prior to the effective date of denunciation.

Chapter XI—Transitory Provisions

Section 1. Inter-American Commission on Human Rights

*Article 79.* Upon the entry into force of this Convention, the Secretary General shall, in writing, request each member state of the Organization to present, within ninety days, its candidates for membership on the Inter-American Commission on Human Rights. The Secretary General shall prepare a list in alphabetical order of the candidates presented, and transmit it to the member states of the Organization at least thirty days prior to the next session of the General Assembly.

*Article 80.* The members of the Commission shall be elected by secret ballot of the General Assembly from the list of candidates referred to in Article 79. The candidates who obtain the largest number of votes and an absolute majority of the votes of the representatives of the member states shall be declared elected. Should it become necessary to have several ballots in order to elect all the members of the Commission, the candidates who receive the smallest number of votes shall be eliminated successively, in the manner determined by the General Assembly.

Section 2. Inter-American Court of Human Rights

*Article 81.* Upon the entry into force of this Convention, the Secretary General shall, in writing, request each State Party to present, within ninety days, its candidates for membership on the Inter-American Court of Human Rights. The Secretary General shall prepare a list in alphabetical order of the candidates presented and transmit it to the States Parties at least thirty days prior to the next session of the General Assembly.

*Article 82.* The judges of the Court shall be elected from the list of candidates referred to in Article 81, by secret ballot of the States Parties to the Convention in the General Assembly. The candidates who obtain the largest number of votes and an absolute majority of the votes of the representatives of the States Parties shall be declared elected. Should it become necessary to have several ballots in order to elect all the judges of the Court, the candidates who receive the smallest number of votes shall be eliminated successively, in the manner determined by the States Parties.

*ADDITIONAL PROTOCOL.* In its annual reports to the OAS General Assembly, the Inter-American Commission on Human Rights highlighted, for a number of years, the importance of economic, social, and cultural rights and the need to establish institutional mechanisms to protect such rights effectively. Between 1980 and 1985, the Commission–convinced that, as an organization specifically entrusted with the promotion and protection of human rights, it had the obligation to play as active a role in the protection of economic, social, and cultural rights as it was playing with regard to civil and political rights–studied all aspects of the subject.

In 1985, the OAS General Assembly requested the Commission (resolution 778 [XV-]/85) to submit to it a draft additional protocol to the American Convention on Human Rights with regard to economic, social, and cultural rights. The Assembly also directed the OAS Permanent Council to inform it of the views of member States and of the agencies and organizations interested in the content of the draft additional protocol, with respect to the rights to be protected and the institutional mechanisms that should be established for the appropriate protection of such rights.

In preparing the Additional Protocol, the Commission coordinated its efforts with those of a working group established for that purpose by the Committee on Juridical and Political Affairs of the OAS Permanent Council. It sent its draft to the Permanent Council and submitted it to the OAS General Assembly.

The Additional Protocol, also known as the Protocol of San Salvador, was approved unanimously by the OAS General Assembly on 17 November 1988. It will enter into force, in accordance with its article 74, "as soon as eleven States have deposited their instruments of ratification or accession." The text is as follows:

### Preamble

The States Parties to this Protocol Additional to the American Convention on Human Rights,

Reaffirming their intention to consolidate in this hemisphere, within the framework of democratic institutions, a system of personal liberty and social justice based on respect for the essential rights of man;

Recognizing that the essential rights of man are not derived from one's being a national of a certain State, but are based upon attributes of the human person, for which reason they merit international protection in the form of a convention reinforcing or complementing the protection provided by the domestic law of the American States;

Considering the close relationship that exists between economic, social, and cultural rights and civil and political rights, in that the two categories of rights constitute an indivisible whole based on the recognition of the dignity of the human person for which reason both require permanent protection and promotion if they are to be fully realized, although the violation of one group of rights in favor of the realization of the other group can never be justified;

Recognizing that, in accordance with the Universal Declaration of Human Rights and the American Convention on Human Rights, the ideal of free human beings enjoying freedom from fear and want can only be achieved if conditions are created whereby everyone may enjoy his economic, social and cultural rights as well as his civil and political rights;

Bearing in mind that, although fundamental economic, social and cultural rights have been embodied in earlier international instruments of both world and regional scope, it is essential that those rights be reaffirmed, developed and perfected in order to consolidate in America, on the basis of full respect for the rights of the individual, the democratic representative form of government as well as the right to its peoples to development, self-determination, and the free disposal, in accordance with international law, of their wealth and natural resources; and

Considering that the General Assembly of the Organization has repeatedly expressed its wish to draw up a protocol additional to the American Convention on Human Rights for the purpose of defining the economic, social, and cultural rights to be protected and to establish institutional arrangements for ensuring the appropriate protection of such rights; and

Considering that the American Convention on Human Rights provides that draft protocols additional to that Convention may be submitted for consideration to the States Parties, meeting together on the occasion of the General Assembly of the Organization of American States, for the purpose of gradually incorporating other rights and freedoms into the system for the protection thereof;

Have agreed upon the following Protocol Additional to the American Convention on Human Rights:

*Article 1.* Obligation to Adopt Measures. The States Parties to this Protocol Additional to the American Convention on Human Rights (Pact of San José, Costa Rica, 1969) undertake to adopt all the necessary measures within the extent of the resources available to them, to achieve the progressive realization of the rights recognized in this Protocol.

*Article 2.* Obligation of Non-discrimination. 1. The States Parties to this Protocol undertake to guarantee the exercise of the rights set forth herein without discrimination of any kind.

2. The States Parties to this Protocol undertake to invest men and women with equal title to the enjoyment of all the economic, social and cultural rights set forth in this Protocol.

*Article 3.* Obligation to Enact Domestic Legislation. If the exercise of the rights set forth in this Protocol is not already guaranteed by legislative or other provisions, the States Par-

ties undertake to adopt, in accordance with their constitutional processes and the provisions of this Protocol, such legislative or other measures as may be necessary for making those rights a reality.

*Article 4.* Inadmissibility of Restrictions. Prohibited if any restriction or diminution of a right recognized or guaranteed in a state's internal legislation or by means of international treaties, on the pretext that the present Protocol does not recognize the right or recognizes it to a lesser degree.

*Article 5.* Scope of Restrictions and Limitations. The States Parties may only establish restrictions and limitations on the enjoyment and exercise of the rights established in the present Protocol by means of laws promulgated with the purpose of preserving the general welfare in a democratic society, to the extent that they are compatible with these rights, public health and morality.

*Article 6.* Right to Work. Everyone shall have the right to work, which includes the right of opportunity to lead a decent life by carrying out an activity which one freely chooses or accepts.

*Article 7.* Just and Satisfactory Conditions of Work. The right to work defined in the foregoing article presupposes that the same is carried out in just and satisfactory conditions, which the States Parties to the Present Protocol undertake to guarantee in their internal legislation:

a. Remuneration which guarantees, at a minimum, to all workers decent living conditions for them and their families and just and equal wages for work of equal value, without distinction. Women must be guaranteed working conditions equal to those of men.

b. Freedom to change employment, opportunities of promotion and mobility, work stability and the corresponding indemnization in the case of unjustified dismissal.

c. Safety and hygiene at work.

d. The prohibition of night work or unhealthy or dangerous working conditions for persons under the age of 18 and, in general, all work which could place in danger the youth's health, safety or morals. As regards minors under the age of 16, the work day will be subordinated to the provisions regarding compulsory education and in no case will it constitute an excused absence from classes or a limitation on benefitting from education received.

e. The limitation on the hours of work, both daily and weekly. The days will be of shorter duration if the work is dangerous or unhealthy.

f. Rest, leisure, reasonable limitation of working hours and paid vacations as well as remuneration for public holidays.

*Article 8.* Trade Union Rights. 1. The States Parties undertake to ensure the right of everyone to form trade unions and to join the trade union of his choice for the promotion and protection of his economic and social interests. As an extension of that right, the States Parties shall permit trade unions to establish national federations or confederations, or to join those that already exist, as well as to form international trade union organizations and to join that of their choice. The States Parties shall also permit trade unions, federations and confederations to function freely.

2. The exercise of the rights set forth above may be subject only to the restrictions stipulated by the law, provided that they are characteristic of a democratic society and necessary for safeguarding public order and protecting public health or morals and the rights and freedoms of other persons.

*Article 9.* Right to Strike. 1. The States Parties to the present Protocol recognize the right to strike of trade union organizations.

2. The right to strike recognized in the present Protocol must be exercised in conformity with the laws of the corresponding State.

3. The provision of the present article shall not prevent States from imposing legal restrictions on the right to strike as regards members of the armed forces, the police or other public service agents of the State.

*Article 10.* Right to Social Security. 1. Everyone shall have the right to social security that protects him against the consequences of unemployment, old age, and disability which, being the result of causes beyond his control, prevent him physically or mentally from earning the means for a decent living.

2. In the case of persons who are employed, the right to social security shall cover at least medical care and an allowance or retirement benefit in the case of occupational accidents or occupational disease and, in the case of women, paid maternity leave before and after childbirth.

*Article 11.* Right to Health. 1. Everyone shall have the right to health, which is understood to mean the enjoyment of the highest degree of physical, mental and social wellbeing.

2. To that end, the States Parties undertake to recognize health as a public good and in particular to guarantee this right by means of the following:

a. Primary health care, that is, essential health care made available to all individuals and families in the community;

b. To extend the benefits of health services to all individuals subject to the State's jurisdiction;

c. Universal immunization against the principal infectious diseases;

d. The prevention and treatment of endemic diseases;

e. The education of the population concerning the prevention and treatment of health problems;

f. The satisfaction of health needs of the highest risk groups, who because of their poverty are the most vulnerable.

*Article 12.* Right to a Healthy Environment. Everyone shall have the right to live in an environment free of pollution and to have access to basic urban services, especially a safe water supply and sewerage services.

*Article 13.* Right to Food. Everyone has the right to adequate nutrition which guarantees the possibility of enjoying the highest level of physical, emotional and intellectual development.

*Article 14.* Right to Education. 1. Everyone has the right to education.

2. The State Parties to the present Protocol agree that, in general, education should be directed towards the full development of the human personality and human dignity, and ought to strengthen respect for human rights, fundamental freedoms and peace. They agree, also, that education ought to equip all persons in the task of achieving a decent existence and enabling one to participate effectively in a democratic society.

3. The States Parties to the present Protocol recognize that, in order to achieve the complete exercise of the right to education:

a. Primary education shall be compulsory and accessible to all without cost;

b. Secondary education in its different forms, including technical and professional secondary education, shall be made generally available and accessible to all by every appropriate means, and in particular, by the progressive introduction of free education;

c. Higher education shall be made equally accessible to all, on the basis of capacity, by every appropriate means, and in particular, by the progressive introduction of free education;

d. Basic education shall be encouraged or intensified as far as possible for those persons who have not received or completed the whole cycle of primary instruction;

e. Programs of special education shall be established for the handicapped, so as to provide special instruction and training for persons with physical disabilities or mental deficiencies.

*Article 15.* Right to Freedom of Education. 1. The States Parties to this Protocol undertake to respect the liberty of parents and, where applicable, legal guardians to choose for their children schools other than those established by the public authorities, provided they conform to such minimum educational standards as which may be laid down or approved by the State, and to ensure the religious and moral education of their children in conformity with their own convictions.

2. No provision of this Article shall be construed so as to interfere with the freedom of individuals and organizations from establishing and directing educational institutions, subject to the observance of the principles set forth above and to the requirement that the education given in such institutions shall conform to such minimum standards as may be laid down by the State.

*Article 16.* Rights to the Benefits of Culture. 1. The States Parties to this Protocol recognize the right of everyone:

a. To take part in the cultural and artistic life of the community.

b. To enjoy the benefits of scientific progress and its applications.

2. The steps to be taken by the States Parties to this Protocol to ensure the full exercise of this right shall include those necessary for the conservation, the development and the diffusion of science, culture and art.

3. The States Parties to the present Protocol undertake to respect the freedom indispensable for scientific research and creative activity.

4. The States Parties to this Protocol recognize the benefits to be derived from the encouragement and development of international contacts and cooperation in the scientific and cultural fields.

*Article 17.* Right to the Founding and the Protection of Families. 1. The family is the natural and fundamental element of society and ought to be protected by the society and the State.

2. Everyone shall have the right to found a family, which he shall exercise in accordance with the provisions of the pertinent domestic legislation.

3. Without prejudice to the provisions of article 17 of the American Convention on Human Rights, the States Parties undertake, pursuant to the present Protocol, to accord special protection to the family group and in particular:

a. To accord special attention and assistance to mothers during a reasonable period before and after childbirth.

b. To guarantee children adequate nutrition both during nursing and while attending school.

c. To adopt special measures for the protection of adolescents in order to guarantee the full development of their physical, intellectual and moral capacities.

d. To undertake special programs of family training so as to help create a stable and positive environment in which children will receive and develop the values of understanding, solidarity, respect and responsibility.

*Article 18.* Rights of the Child. Every child has the right to the protection which the conditions of childhood requires as regards the family, society and the State. Every child has the right to grow under the protection and responsibility of its parents; except in exceptional circumstances, as defined by the courts, a child of young age ought not to be separated from its mother. Every child has the right to free and compulsory education, at least in its basic phase, and to continue at higher levels of the educational system.

*Article 19.* Protection of the Aged. Everyone shall have the right to special protection during his old age. To that end, the States Parties undertake to adopt the necessary measures for ensuring the realization of this right, and, in particular:

a. To provide appropriate facilities, such as specialized food and medical attention for persons of an advanced age who lack it and are unable to provide for themselves.

b. To undertake specific employment programs for providing the aged with an opportunity to engage in a productive activity appropriate to their ability and respectful of their vocation or wishes.

c. To promote the formation of social organizations designed to improve the quality of life of the aged.

*Article 20.* Protection of Disabled Persons. Everyone affected by a reduction in physical or mental capabilities shall have the right to receive special care to enable them to fully develop their personality. To that end, the States Parties undertake to adopt such measures as may be necessary for that purpose, and, in particular:

a. To undertake specific programs for providing disabled persons with the resources and necessary environment for achieving that objective, including employment programs adequate to their possibilities and which they shall be free to accept.

b. To include in urban development guidelines consideration of ways of solving the specific requirements generated by the necessities of this special group.

c. To promote the formation of social organizations in which disabled persons can develop a full life.

*Article 21.* Means of Protection. 1. The Inter-American Commission on Human Rights will monitor the observance of the economic, social and cultural rights set forth in the present Protocol by means of the preparation of special reports. The Commission's Regulations shall determine the nature of these reports.

2. The Commission shall take into consideration the progressive nature of the observance of the rights subject to protection by this Protocol.

3. The States Parties to the present Protocol undertake to supply the Inter-American Commission on Human Rights, at its request, with information on the measures which they have adopted at their own initiative or at the request of the latter and on the progress achieved as regards the goal of ensuring the observance of the rights recognized in this Protocol.

4. In the exercise of the function set forth in the above paragraphs, the Commission shall be able to count on the advice of experts and to establish the relations it considers appropriate with the organs and agencies of the Inter-American and the UN systems.

5. Without prejudice to the above, in the case of the rights set forth in Articles 8, 9 and 15 of this Protocol, in the case of a violation of these rights directly imputable to a State Party to this Protocol, such a situation shall give rise to the application of the individual petition procedure set forth in Articles 44 to 51 and 61 to 69 of the American Convention on Human Rights and the corresponding involvement of the Commission and where applicable, the Inter-American Court of Human Rights.

*Article 22.* Signature and Ratification or Accession Entry into Force. 1. This Protocol shall be open for signature and ratification or accession by any State Party to the American Convention on Human Rights.

2. Ratification or accession to this Protocol shall be effected through the deposit of an instrument of ratification or accession with the General Secretariat of the Organization of American States.

3. As soon as seven States have deposited their instruments of ratification or accession, the Protocol shall enter into force.

4. The Secretary General shall inform all the member States of the Organization of the entry into force of the Protocol.

### Recommendations

On the basis of the background information and considerations set forth, the Commission requests the General Assembly of the Organization of American States, meeting at its sixteenth regular session, to adopt the following decisions:

1. That it reaffirm the urgent need for governments that have not yet reestablished representative democracy as their system of government to put in place the relevant institutional mechanisms for restoring that system in as short a period of time as possible free, secret and by means of informed elections, since democracy is the best guarantee for the observance of human rights and the basis of solidarity among the States of the Hemisphere.

2. That it recommend to the Member States that they provide all necessary guarantees to non-governmental human rights organizations so that they may continue to contribute to the promotion and defense of human rights and that the Member States respect the freedom and integrity of the leaders of said organizations.

3. That, with respect to the Additional Protocol to the American Convention on Human Rights on economic, social and cultural rights, it transmit the draft prepared by the Inter-American Commission on Human Rights to the Governments of the Member States so that they may make observations or comments on the draft and transmit them to the Permanent Council, which will enable the Council to submit them to the States Parties to the American Convention on Human Rights which will meet on the occasion of the seventeenth regular session of the General Assembly at which time they will be in a position to adopt the new version of the draft Protocol.

4. That it reiterate to the Member States which are not Parties to the American Convention on Human Rights (the 1969 Pact of San José, Costa Rica) that they ratify, or adhere to, said instrument, and in case they have not done so, to recognize the competence of the Inter-American Commission on Human Rights to receive and examine inter-State communications in accordance with Article 45, paragraph 3 of the Convention as well as to accept the obligatory jurisdiction of the Inter-American Court on Human Rights, in conformity with Article 62, paragraph 2 of said Convention.

***DRAFT OF AN ADDITIONAL PROTOCOL REGARDING THE DEATH PENALTY.*** The Inter-American Commission on Human Rights, in its 1986–1987 annual report, proposed to the States Parties to the American Convention on Human Rights, under the authority given it by article 77 of that convention, the following draft additional protocol to the convention (OAS Doc. OEA/Ser. L/V/II.71 Doc. 9/rev. 1, chap. V [I]):

*Article 1.* The States Parties to this Protocol shall not impose the death penalty on any person under their jurisdiction. Accordingly, no one may be punished by the death penalty nor executed.

*Article 2.* 1. Reservations may not be made to this Protocol except for the sole purpose of excluding from application of the Protocol especially severe military offenses that were committed during a foreign war.

2. A State making the reservation authorized by the previous paragraph may, at the time of deposition of its instrument of ratification or adhesion, inform the Secretary General of the Organization of American States as to what military offenses are subject to the death penalty under that country's domestic law.

*Article 3.* 1. This Protocol shall be open to the signature and to the ratification or adhesion of any State Party to the American Convention on Human Rights.

2. Ratification of this Protocol or adhesion to it shall be made through deposit of an instrument of ratification or adhesion at the General Secretariat of the Organization of American States.

In explanation of its proposal, the Commission included the following statement in the report:

The Inter-American Commission on Human Rights, concerned about the behavior of some States in extending the death penalty or applying it in a generalized manner, has appealed, on previous occasions, to all governments of the Americas to abolish the death penalty, in keeping with the spirit of Article 4 of the American Convention on Human Rights and in line with the universal trend toward abolition of the death penalty.

As is widely known, in order to facilitate adoption by the largest number of states, the American Convention on Human Rights did not abolish the death penalty but only restricted its application. Specifically, Article 4 of the Convention in five of its six paragraphs established various limitations on the imposition of the death penalty. These limitations are as follows: (1) the death penalty may be imposed only for the most serious crimes; (2) it may be imposed only pursuant to a sentence handed down by a court of competent jurisdiction; (3) also it may be imposed only under a law providing for such punishment, enacted prior to the commission of the crime; (4) it may not be re-established in States that have abolished it; (5) in no case shall capital punishment be inflicted for political offenses or related common crimes; (6) it may not be imposed upon persons who, at the time the crime was committed, were under 18 years of age or over 70 years of age; (7) nor may it be applied to pregnant women; and (8) every person condemned to death shall have the right to appeal for amnesty, pardon or commutation of sentence, which may be granted in all cases. Capital punishment shall not be imposed while such an appeal is pending decision by the authority of competent jurisdiction.

Although the Commission understands that in 1969, when the American Convention on Human Rights was adopted, prevailing conditions would have not permitted abolishing the death penalty through a convention, experience in the almost two decades since and the trend in the vast majority of the countries of the Americas to amend their criminal codes or even their constitutional provisions, as has occurred with Haiti and Nicaragua, in order to ban the death penalty, cause the Commission to consider that conditions are now ripe for adopting an instrument to abolish the death penalty.

In recent years, the Commission has observed that the purported purpose of capital punishment—that is, by imposing it, the State helps to save the lives of others by preventing the commission of the crimes for which the death penalty has been established—has not been achieved in practice, and on the contrary, the death penalty often has had a counterproductive effect by generating greater violence. In that regard, the Commission can only share the views set forth in numerous studies according to which it has not yet been shown that capital punishment has any impact on reducing criminality.

Moreover, there are a great many ethical and legal reasons and even reasons of civic harmony, which the Commission shares, requiring the abolition of the death penalty. From the ethical standpoint, one cannot justify defending an absolute value like human life by resorting to a strict application of the talionic principle of "an eye for an eye," which in this case becomes, "a life for a life." The foregoing involves a concept of law and punishment that is purely retributive, that is, one evil must be answered by another of a similar kind. In that sense, the State's right to punish certain criminal behavior cannot be absolute and must surely be limited by those rights of the human person that are inalienable, foremost among them being the right to life.

From the standpoint of criminal policy, the death penalty violates the principle of special prevention by denying the possibility of rehabilitation or reform of the offender, a rationale that constitutes one of the fundamental purposes of punishment.

The irreparable nature of the death penalty must also be kept in mind, that is, it does not admit of judicial errors. However, as unfortunately has occurred in the past, it has in hundreds of cases been shown later that the death penalty was imposed as a result of a judicial error.

It is also necessary to point out, as the Commission has, that the death penalty has been used by totalitarian regimes and military dictators as an instrument to eliminate dissidents or even to hide those really guilty of other crimes.

Finally, the Commission considers that the right to life, as has occurred with the right to humane treatment, should be protected in the most absolute manner possible under international law.

It is now possible to state that, thanks to the fact that the international community has become mindful of how intolerable the practice of torture is under any circumstances, the right not to suffer physical torment has become absolute. Consequently, how could it be accepted that the right to life, which is at the very basis of the other human rights, does not have similar protection? In this regard, the Commission considers that the death penalty is one of the most serious offenses against a human being that can be conceived of, because it terminates the person's very existence.

The above reasons, as well as the repugnance produced by the cruel, inhumane and degrading nature of this punishment, has led most American countries to abolish the death penalty, at least for common crimes. Thus, of the 19 countries that today are parties to the American Convention on Human Rights, only four retain the death penalty. It is also significant that those countries are not parties to the Pact of San José, Costa Rica—that is, they are States that have not shown an interest in undertaking international commitments to respect human rights. With the sole exception of Brazil, which is in the process of completing its internal procedures to be party to that instrument, all of them maintain the death penalty for all types of crimes.

Of the States that are parties to the American Convention on Human Rights, Bolivia, Colombia, Costa Rica, Dominican Republic, Ecuador, Haiti, Honduras, Nicaragua, Panama, Uruguay and Venezuela, have abolished the death penalty for all kinds of crimes. The domestic law of Argentina, El Salvador, Mexico, and Peru does not impose the death penalty for common crimes, and maintains it only for serious military offenses committed under exceptional circumstances, such as in time of war.

This trend to abolish the death penalty can also be seen in other regions. Thus, in April 1983, several States Parties to the European Convention for the Protection of Human Rights and Fundamental Liberties—which, like the American Convention, allows the death penalty, under certain restrictions—adopted Protocol 6 to that Convention, abolishing the death penalty. Likewise, the United Nations is now considering, as a result of successive General Assembly resolutions, an Optional Protocol to the International Covenant on Civil and Political Rights, which declares the death penalty to be abolished.

All of these antecedents confirm to the Commission the desirability of proposing to the States Parties to the American Convention on Human Rights that they take another step forward with respect to current Article 4 of that Convention, so that capital punishment will be banned through a new instrument.

The American Convention provides two possible ways to amend its provisions. Under Article 76, any State Party to the Convention, the Commission or the Court can, through the OAS Secretary General, submit to the General Assembly proposed amendments to the Convention. Also, Article 77 empowers any State Party and the Commission to submit "proposed protocols to this Convention for consideration by the States Parties at the General Assembly with a view to gradually including other rights and freedoms within its system of protection."

Which would be best—amending Article 4 or including the Additional Protocol to the Convention—should be carefully studied.

In the Commission's view, while the amendment to the current provision governing the right to life could be the best way to take a categorical stand against the death penalty, and, from the legal standpoint, regulate one subject under a single instrument, it might have the disadvantage that those States that are now parties to the Pact of San José, Costa Rica, or that in the future might become parties to it, and that still maintain the death penalty, would have to make an express reservation to that provision, if it is authorized, or if they do not accept the possibility of making a reservation, they would be prevented from participating in the Convention, which could cause even more difficulties from the standpoint of protecting human rights. In these circumstances, it would appear preferable to have on this topic two coexisting rules established by two successive treaties, a possibility allowed by the American Convention on Human Rights and authorized by general international law, as shown in Article 30 of the 1969 Vienna Convention on the Law of Treaties.

Thus the present Article 4 will remain in effect for countries that do not become parties to the Additional Protocol or that ratify it in the future or that are parties to the American Convention on Human Rights but not to the Additional Protocol on the Abolition of the Death Penalty.

Since the current Article 4 of the Convention coexists with the Additional Protocol, that will make it possible for the Convention to provide that reservations may not be made to the Protocol or that they will have a very limited and specific scope.

Another important problem to consider is whether the obligation the States Parties to the Additional Protocol will acquire not to impose the death penalty will be absolute, that is, that under no circumstances may the death penalty be imposed, regardless of the offense committed, or, whether some exceptions might be accepted, particularly those that would make it possible to impose the death penalty for serious military crimes committed under exceptional circumstances, such as during a foreign war, a situation that the laws of a large number of States that are now parties to the Pact of San José, Costa Rica, now provide for. If what is desired is to make, as the Commission seeks, significant progress regarding the present Article 4 of the American Convention on Human Rights, and also, to enable the new protocol to have the largest number of ratifications or adhesions possible, it would appear desirable that, as established in Protocol 6 of the European Convention on Human Rights and Basic Freedoms and provided for in the draft of the United Nations Special Rapporteur on abolition of the death penalty, the States might be authorized to impose the death penalty for specified military offenses committed in wartime.

Because of the exceptional character of such authorization, any statement made by a country on becoming party to the Protocol must expressly specify how it would be an express reservation to the general rule abolishing the death penalty.

Based on the above considerations, the Commission, under the authority given it by Article 77 of the American Convention on Human Rights, proposes to the States parties to the American Convention on Human Rights meeting on the occasion of the OAS General Assembly, the . . . draft additional protocol to the Convention.

***SEE ALSO*** *African Charter on Human and Peoples' Rights; American Declaration of the Rights and Duties of Man; European Convention on Human Rights and Protocols; Universal Declaration of Human Rights.*

***BIBLIOGRAPHY.*** Gros Espiel, Hector. *Los Derechos Económicos, Sociales y Culturales en el Sístema Interamericano* (Economic, Social and Cultural Rights in the Interamerican System). San Jose, Costa Rica: Libro Libre, 1986. Monograph, in Spanish.

Inter-American Commission on Human Rights. *Annual Report of the Inter-American Commission on Human Rights.* Washington, D.C., USA: Organization of American States, various years. Intergovernmental annual report, in English.

Kokott, Juliane. "No Impunity for Human Rights Violations in the Americas," *Human Rights Law Journal* 14, no. 5–6 (1993): 153–159. Scholarly article, in English.

LeBlanc, Larry. "The Economic, Social and Cultural Rights Protocol to the American Convention and Its Background," *Netherlands Quarterly of Human Rights* 10, no. 2 (1992): 130–154. Scholarly article, in English.

Medina, Cecilia. "The Inter-American Commission on Human Rights and the Inter-American Court of Human

Rights: Reflections on a Joint Venture," *Human Rights Quarterly* 12, no. 4 (1990): 439–464. Scholarly article, in English.

Mower, A. Glenn, Jr. *Regional Human Rights: A Comparative Study of the West European and Inter-American Systems.* Westport, CT, USA: Greenwood Press, 1991. Scholarly monograph, in English; bibliography, pp. 171–174.

## AMERICAN DECLARATION OF THE RIGHTS AND DUTIES OF MAN (1948).

The Declaration, drafted by the Inter-American Juridical Committee and completed and adopted by the Ninth International Conference of American States at Bogota, Colombia, on 2 May 1948, is unique in that it first recognized that States do not create or concede rights but only recognize rights that have always existed and that are inherent in the very nature of the individual human being. Adoption of the American Declaration preceded by only a few months the adoption of the **UNIVERSAL DECLARATION OF HUMAN RIGHTS,** based on the same principle. The text of the Declaration of the Rights and Duties of Man (OAS Doc. OEA/Ser. L/V/II.65, Doc. 6, pp. 19–25) is as follows:

Whereas:

The American peoples have acknowledged the dignity of the individual, and their national constitutions recognize that juridical and political institutions, which regulate life in human society, have as their principal aim the protection of the essential rights of man and the creation of circumstances that will permit him to achieve spiritual and material progress and attain happiness;

The American States have on repeated occasions recognized that the essential rights of man are not derived from the fact that he is a national of a certain state, but are based upon attributes of his human personality;

The international protection of the rights of man should be the principal guide of an evolving American law;

The affirmation of essential human rights by the American States together with the guarantees given by the internal regimes of the states establish the initial system of protection considered by the American States as being suited to the present social and juridical conditions, not without a recognition on their part that they should increasingly strengthen that system in the international field as conditions become more favorable,

The Ninth International Conference of American States agrees

To adopt the following:

### Preamble

All men are born free and equal, in dignity and in rights, and, being endowed by nature with reason and conscience, they should conduct themselves as brothers one to another.

The fulfillment of duty by each individual is a prerequisite to the rights of all. Rights and duties are interrelated in every social and political activity of man. While rights exalt individual liberty, duties express the dignity of that liberty.

Duties of a juridical nature presuppose others of a moral nature which support them in principle and constitute their basis.

Inasmuch as spiritual development is the supreme end of human existence and the highest expression thereof, it is the duty of man to serve that end with all his strength and resources.

Since culture is the highest social and historical expression of that spiritual development, it is the duty of man to preserve, practice and foster culture by every means within his power.

And, since moral conduct constitutes the noblest flowering of culture, it is the duty of every man always to hold it in high respect.

### Chapter One: Rights

*Article 1.* Right to Life, Liberty and Personal Security. Every human being has the right to life, liberty and the security of his person.

*Article 2.* Right to Equality Before the Law. All persons are equal before the law and have the rights and duties established in this Declaration, without distinction as to race, sex, language, creed or any other factor.

*Article 3.* Right to Religious Freedom and Worship. Every person has the right freely to profess a religious faith, and to manifest and practice it both in public and in private.

*Article 4.* Right to Freedom of Investigation, Opinion, Expression and Dissemination. Every person has the right to freedom of investigation, of opinion, and of the expression and dissemination of ideas, by any medium whatsoever.

*Article 5.* Right to Protection of Honor, Personal Reputation and Private and Family Life. Every person has the right to the protection of the law and against abusive attacks upon his honor, his reputation, and his private and family life.

*Article 6.* Rights to a Family and to Protection thereof. Every person has the the right to establish a family, the basic element of society, and to receive protection therefor.

*Article 7.* Right to Protection for Mothers and Children. All women, during pregnancy and the nursing period, and all children have the right to special protection, care and aid.

*Article 8.* Right to Residence and Movement. Every person has the right to fix his residence within the territory of the state of which he is a national, to move about freely within such territory, and not to leave it except by his own will.

*Article 9.* Right to Inviolability of Home. Every person has the right to the inviolability of his home.

*Article 10.* Right to the Inviolability and Transmission of Correspondence. Every person has the right to the inviolability and transmission of his correspondence.

*Article 11.* Right to the Preservation of Health and to Well-being. Every person has the right to the preservation of his health through sanitary and social measures relating to food, clothing, housing and medical care, to the extent permitted by public and community resources.

*Article 12.* Right to Education. Every person has the right to an education, which should be based on the principles of liberty, morality and human solidarity.

Likewise every person has the right to an education that will prepare him to attain a decent life, to raise his standard of living, and to be a useful member of society.

The right to an education includes the right to equality of opportunity in every case, in accordance with natural talents, merit and the desire to utilize the resources that the state or the community is in a position to provide.

Every person has the right to receive, free, at least a primary education.

*Article 13.* Right to the Benefits of Culture. Every person has the right to take part in the cultural life of the community, to enjoy the arts, and to participate in the benefits that result from intellectual progress, especially scientific discoveries.

He likewise has the right to the protection of his moral and material interests as regards his inventions or any literary, scientific or artistic works of which he is the author.

*Article 14.* Right to Work and to Fair Remuneration. Every person has the right to work, under proper conditions, and to follow his vocation freely, in so far as existing conditions of employment permit.

Every person who works has the right to receive such remuneration as will, in proportion to his capacity and skill, assure him a standard of living suitable for himself and for his family.

*Article 15.* Right to Leisure Time and to the Use thereof. Every person has the right to leisure time, to wholesome recreation, and to the opportunity for advantageous use of his free time to his spiritual, cultural and physical benefit.

*Article 16.* Right to Social Security. Every person has the right to social security which will protect him from the consequences of unemployment, old age, and disabilities arising from causes beyond his control that make it physically or mentally impossible for him to earn a living.

*Article 17.* Right to Recognition of Juridical Personality and of Civil Rights. Every person has the right to be recognized everywhere as a person having rights and obligations, and to enjoy the basic civil rights.

*Article 18.* Right to a Fair Trial. Every person may resort to the courts to ensure respect for his legal rights. There should likewise be available to him a simple, brief procedure whereby the courts will protect him from acts of authority that, to his prejudice, violate any fundamental constitutional rights.

*Article 19.* Right to Nationality. Every person has the right to the nationality to which he is entitled by law and to change it, if he so wishes, for the nationality of any other country that is willing to grant it to him.

*Article 20.* Right to Vote and to Participate in Government. Every person having legal capacity is entitled to participate in the government of his country, directly or through his representatives, and to take part in popular elections, which shall be by secret ballot, and shall be honest, periodic and free.

*Article 21.* Right of Assembly. Every person has the right to assemble peaceably with others in a formal public meeting or an informal gathering, in connection with matters of common interest of any nature.

*Article 22.* Right of Association. Every person has the right to associate with others to promote, exercise and protect his legitimate interests of a political, economic, religious, social, cultural, professional, labor union or other nature.

*Article 23.* Right to Property. Every person has a right to own such private property as meets the essential needs of decent living and helps to maintain the dignity of the individual and of the home.

*Article 24.* Right of Petition. Every person has the right to submit respectful petitions to any competent authority, for reasons of either general or private interest, and the right to obtain a prompt decision thereon.

*Article 25.* Right of Protection from Arbitrary Arrest. No person may be deprived of his liberty except in the cases and according to the procedures established by pre-existing law.

No person may be deprived of liberty for nonfulfillment of obligations of a purely civil character.

Every individual who has been deprived of his liberty has the right to have the legality of his detention ascertained without delay by a court, and the right to be tried without due delay or, otherwise, to be released. He also has the right to humane treatment during the time he is in custody.

*Article 26.* Right to Due Process of Law. Every accused person is presumed to be innocent until proved guilty.

Every person accused of an offense has the right to be given an impartial and public hearing, and to be tried by courts previously established in accordance with pre-existing laws, and not to receive cruel, infamous or unusual punishment.

*Article 27.* Right of Asylum. Every person has the right, in case of pursuit not resulting from ordinary crimes, to seek and receive asylum in foreign territory, in accordance with the laws of each country and with international agreements.

*Article 28.* Scope of the Rights of Man. The rights of man are limited by the rights of others, by the security of all, and by the just demands of the general welfare and the advancement of democracy.

## Chapter Two: Duties

*Article 29.* Duties to Society. It is the duty of the individual so to conduct himself in relation to others that each and every one man fully form and develop his personality.

*Article 30.* Duties toward Children and Parents. It is the duty of every person to aid, support, educate and protect his minor children, and it is the duty of children to honor their parents always and to aid, support and protect them when they need it.

*Article 31.* Duty to Receive Instructions. It is the duty of every person to acquire at least an elementary education.

*Article 32.* Duty to Vote. It is the duty of every person to vote in the popular elections of the country of which he is a national, when he is legally capable of doing so.

*Article 33.* Duty to Obey the Law. It is the duty of every person to obey the law and other legitimate commands of the authorities of his country and those of the country in which he may be.

*Article 34.* Duty to Serve the Community and the Nation. It is the duty of every able-bodied person to render whatever civil and military service his country may require for its defense and preservation, and, in case of public disaster, to render such services as may be in his power.

It is likewise his duty to hold any public office to which he may be elected by popular vote in the state of which he is a national.

*Article 35.* Duties with Respect to Social Security and Welfare. It is the duty of every person to cooperate with the state and the community with respect to social security and welfare, in accordance with his ability and with existing circumstances.

*Article 36.* Duty to Pay Taxes. It is the duty of every person to pay the taxes established by law for the support of public services.

*Article 37.* Duty to Work. It is the duty of every person to work, as far as his capacity and possibilities permit, in order to obtain the means of livelihood or to benefit his community.

*Article 38.* Duty to Refrain from Political Activities in a Foreign Country. It is the duty of every person to refrain from taking part in political activities that, according to law, are reserved exclusively to the citizens of the state in which he is an alien.

*SEE ALSO* *African Charter on Human and Peoples' Rights; American Convention on Human Rights and Protocols; European Convention on Human Rights and Protocols.*

*BIBLIOGRAPHY.* Cohen, Marcelo G. "The Universal Declaration of Human Rights and Latin America," *ICJ Review* no. 41 (December 1988): 44–47. NGO article, in English.

**AMERICAN FRIENDS SERVICE COMMITTEE.** An international non-governmental organization that seeks to implement the Quaker concens for peace, social justice, and humanitarian service, AFSC provides refugee relief, resettlement, social and technical assistance outside of the United States, and works through action programs within the U.S. to provide a voice for the oppressed and to educate the public on issues of racism, sexism, prisoners' rights, and community relations. In its long history, this organization has provided relief to civilians and combatants during World War II, the Korean War, the Vietnam War, and other international crises.

Founded in 1917 in the United States, the American Friends Service Committee emerged from a long history of pacifism in America. The Quakers, a religious community opposed to violence in any form, first came to America to escape religious persecution in England. Led by William Penn, they founded the city of Philadelphia in Pennsylvania, then an unarmed colony. From the beginning of their existence in America, the Quakers served social causes, such as the anti-slavery movement and prison reform.

During World War I, many Quakers were imprisoned because of their conscientious objection to war; others started relief work on the battlefields. After the war, the Friends Service Committee coordinated relief efforts to Germany. Their relief corps also worked in Poland and Serbia; and during the Spanish Civil War, it rendered aid to both sides.

During World War II, the American Friends Service Committee went to the aid of Japanese-Americans, who had been summarily evacuated from their homes and placed in resettlement camps along the West Coast.

For its efforts during World War II and for providing an opportunity for conscientious objectors to perform a "service of love" during wartime, the American Friends Service Committee was awarded the 1947 Nobel Peace Prize, along with the British Friends Service Council.

American Friends Service Committee. Address (national office): 1501 Cherry Street, Philadelphia, PA, USA 19102-1479. Telephone: (215) 241-7048. Fax: (215) 241-7275.

**AMERICAN UNIVERSITY, CENTER FOR CIVIL AND HUMAN RIGHTS.** Established in 1990, the Center for Human Rights and Humanitarian Law at the Washington School of Law of American University sponsors conferences with international organizations and NGOs, assists in developing human rights and humanitarian materials, and trains lawyers in the theory and practice of human rights and humanitarian law. The Center is also a home for American and foreign human rights monitors and scholars to study and pursue research in these areas.

In addition, the Washington School of Law conducts the International Human Rights Clinic. A total of eight third-year law students and LL.M. candidates are enrolled in the clinic each semester to study doctrine and lawyering skills through a combination of supervised advocacy in actual cases and projects, case and project review meetings, and a weekly seminar. Students in the clinic practice in both international and domestic forums. In litigation, students represent individuals or groups, usually from outside of the United States, through petitions using the mechanisms of the UN and the OAS. In domestic cases, students represent aliens seeking political asylum in the United States through the processes of the Immigration and Naturalization Service, the Board of Immigration Appeals, and U.S. courts. Students also prepare legal memoranda or reports for international NGOs in the Washington, D.C., area. Clinic director: Prof. Rick Wilson.

Center for Civil and Human Rights. Address: Washington School of Law, American University, 4400 Massachusetts Avenue, Washington, D.C., USA 20016. Telephone: (202) 885-2612. Fax: (202) 885-3601. Directors: Prof. C. Grossman, Prof. R. Goldman, and Prof. H. Schwartz.

**AMERICAS WATCH.** See **HUMAN RIGHTS WATCH.**

**AMNESTY.** Amnesty refers to the abolition, or overlooking, by a government of an offense of a political nature, such as treason or rebellion, frequently on condition that the offender resume his or her duties as a citizen within a prescribed period of time.

At its 1983 session, the UN Sub-Commission on Prevention of Discrimination and Protection of Minorities approved (resolution 1983/34) the preparation of a study of amnesty laws and their role in the safeguard and promotion of human rights and appointed one of its members, Mr. Louis Joinet (France) as Special Rapporteur for the study.

The Study on Amnesty Laws and their Role in the

Safeguard and Promotion of Human Rights (UN Doc. E/CN.4/Sub.2/1985/16) was presented to the Sub-Commission at its 1985 session. In the study, the Special Rapporteur reviewed the principal elements of amnesty laws, taking into account the specific characteristics of various legal systems, and explained the importance that the promulgation of such laws could have for the safeguard and promotion of human rights and fundamental freedoms.

In particular, the Special Rapporteur analyzed in some detail (para. 22–46) the various purposes of amnesty in the modern world, as follows:

### 1. Amnesty for Ordinary Offences

Amnesties covering ordinary offences must be clearly distinguished in their purposes from amnesties covering political offences.

In the field of human rights, amnesty for ordinary offences is an expression of the relatively broad power of civil society to grant every citizen the right of oblivion, if only to facilitate his reintegration into society.

Moreover, the constantly renewed hope of a future amnesty is a substantial contribution to the reduction of tension in prisons, especially when amnesty laws are promulgated at regular intervals.

Subsidiarily the authorities sometimes see in amnesty laws a means of dealing with the overcrowding of prisons, a situation which may prejudice the human rights of prisoners. The preambles of some amnesty laws explicitly refer to this consideration (e.g., Portugal, Decree Law No. 259/74 of 15 June 1974, providing for an amnesty for ordinary offences. See also the amnesty recently granted in the United Kingdom to reduce prison overcrowding).

In some cases, the purpose of an amnesty is strictly humanitarian. In Zaire, the act of 17 November 1981 covers disabled persons. In Syria, Act No. 26 of 12 March 1978 covers incurable or chronically ill prisoners. In the Eastern European countries, such humanitarian measures appear to be traditional, particularly in respect of children, women, the aged and the sick. In the USSR (Decrees of 19 October 1979 and 14 October 1981), in Bulgaria (1979) and in Hungary (Acts of 29 March 1975), measures of this kind have been adopted—in particular, to mark the International Year of the Child—for the benefit of minors, pregnant women and mothers of very young children.

### 2. Amnesty for Political Offences

As the aim of the authorities is directly linked to the current political situation, every amnesty can be described as being a "variable geometry measure." An analysis of the documents provided to the Rapporteur, shows that the goals most frequently sought are:

(a) Amnesty and the Control of Tensions. This is the role assigned to traditional amnesties granted at regular intervals to mark anniversaries, national holidays or elections. They are based largely on custom and are repetitive in nature, and their effectiveness lies in their regularity.

By the same token, as pointed out by the Inter-American Commission on Human Rights (IACHR), the use of amnesty laws as a method of alleviating the consequences of emergency measures following the lifting of a state of emergency serves the same purpose. This point was highlighted in the Commission's report on Nicaragua (1981). (Doc. OEA/Ser. L/7/II/53, doc. 25, recommendations 3–5).

(b) Amnesty and Transition to Democracy. During the transition from an authoritarian régime to democracy, the scope of the amnesty is the tangible sign of the extent of the desire to open up the political process.

As the deadline for the establishment of democracy approaches, authoritarian régimes are tempted to grant themselves amnesty in order to escape the future rigours of democratic legislation. What is sought is not so much reconciliation as impunity. By promulgating an amnesty law known as the "pacification law" on 25 September 1983, the Argentine military junta attempted to obviate any possibility of criminal or civil proceedings being constituted against those responsible for serious violations of human rights committed during operations designed to restore public order. This law was based directly on Chilean Decree-Law No. 2191 of 18 April 1978, which benefited principally "those responsible for assassinations, torture and other offences committed during the administration of the Junta, rather than to grant a genuine amnesty to political opponents." (UN Doc. A/33/331, para. 273 and Annex XXVIII).

Like any amnesty granted unilaterally, the "de facto" Argentine law merely caused feelings to run higher. Consequently, one of the first acts of the new democratic régime was to repeal it and subsequently to introduce amendments to the criminal procedure enabling numerous persons detained on political grounds to be released. One example of a law which played a major role in the restoration and consolidation of democracy was the Uruguayan amnesty law of 8 March 1985. The reasons for this were both political and legal. Politically, it had been preceded by a large-scale propaganda campaign, even before the initiation of the democratic process. That campaign had facilitated the unification of the opposition—it is difficult to oppose a demand for a genuine amnesty—and enabled it to be used as a test of the political desire for openness. This was, so to speak, a "hard won" amnesty, which was ratified, after a broad exchange of views, by the newly elected parliament in a vote reflecting the diversity of opinions. A consensus, the prerequisite for the desired reconciliation, was thus achieved. Juridically, the amnesty enabled all political prisoners to be released, without granting impunity to those guilty of serious violations of human rights.

(c) Amnesty and the Neutralization of Opposition Groups. Here, the purpose of amnesty is to seek social tranquility less by consensus than by a reduction of tensions, and thus of the opposition's scope for action by forcing it to adopt a passive role. The aim is normalization rather than reconciliation through both persuasion and dissuasion.

Such was the aim of the Polish amnesty law of 20 September 1984, enacted after the lifting of martial law, whose effects it was designed to alleviate. The goal of reducing tensions was achieved given the large number of individuals benefiting from the amnesty. (According to the report submitted to Parliament by the Minister for Justice on 20 September 1984, 630 prisoners guilty of non-criminal offences against the State and public order were released, out of a total of 652 detainees. Proceedings against persons at liberty were discontinued in 1916 cases, of which 347 concerned social conflicts. Two hundred and twenty-five persons against whom action had not been taken presented themselves to the authorities to acknowledge their "anti-government acts" so as to benefit from the amnesty.) From this standpoint, it was an excellent law, subsequently amended by two provisions which illustrate the exhortative approach involving the alternate use of persuasion and dissuasion. Persuasion: in order to benefit from the amnesty, offenders who have not been identified or against whom proceedings have not yet been taken, are encouraged under article 2 to present themselves within three months to the authorities to sign an undertaking to discontinue their activities and to disclose the nature, place and date of the reprehensible acts. Article 7 provides that, in the event of recidivism, any amnestied person forfeits entitlement to benefit from that measure. The sentence must be served or the proceedings re-opened. From this standpoint, it is not so much a law of amnesty as a measure employing the device of suspension.

In some cases, persuasion involves the reduction of sentences. In Syria, Act No. 49 of 17 July 1980 adopts this exhortative method in respect of a religious opposition group. As members of the group are liable to the death penalty the law provides that any convicted member who dissociates himself from the group in writing shall have his sentence commuted to forced labour or life imprisonment, with the possibility of a maximum reduction of five years. Other penalties may be reduced by from one to three years.

(d) Amnesty, Guerrillas and Dissociation. Clemency is used in anti-guerrilla campaigns to encourage combatants to leave their organizations.

Recent Guatemalan legislation provides a clear illustration of this method. Impunity is granted to guerrillas who give themselves up to the authorities, lay down their arms and sign a sworn undertaking to take no further part in guerrilla activities. The initial law of 27 March 1982, under which guerrillas were allowed 30 days "repentance period", has been extended by an impressive number of decree-laws with progressively longer time-limits—27 April 1983 (30 days), 11 August 1983 (90 days), 17 November 1983 (60 days), 17 January 1984 (60 days), 16 March 1984 (90 days), 15 June 1984 (90 days), 10 September 1984 (180 days) and 11 March 1985 (300 days).

(e) Amnesty, Guerrillas and Peace Strategies. In the case of international conflicts, the question of amnesty, when it arises, is in theory dealt with by peace agreements.

On the other hand, in the case of non-international armed conflicts governed by common article 3 of the 1949 Geneva Conventions and by the Additional Protocol II, peace agreements, which are by nature intergovernmental, are not applicable. The promulgation of an amnesty law designed to facilitate or confirm the cessation of the state of belligerence or rebellion, can to some extent play the role of an armistice.

The law may even be negotiated through neutral persons or institutions, or by means of any other mediation or good offices procedure, without the laying down of arms being a prerequisite, and with the promulgation of the amnesty law confirming the cessation of hostilities or the beginning of a truce. This is true of the talks currently being held in El Salvador between the Government and FDR-FMLN, with the help of the good offices of the Catholic Church. The first of the two proposals presented by the Government involves "a general and unconditional amnesty for all those who have participated directly or indirectly in offences related to the situation of political violence".

In the course of negotiations to end the Biafran war, item 11 of the negotiation plan provided for an amnesty of the same kind for participants in the rebellion. This law was finally promulgated on 14 January 1970.

Throughout the negotiations which preceded the Camp David accords, the Egyptian representatives continually urged upon the American and Israeli delegates the "adoption of a new policy which could create a climate of confidence in the occupied territories". To this end, on 18 October 1978, the Minister for Foreign Affairs of Egypt sent a memorandum to the United States Secretary of State proposing, inter alia, "granting an amnesty to Palestinian political prisoners."

Colombian law No. 35 of 19 November 1982 "decreeing an amnesty and enacting other provisions for the restoration and preservation of peace" is a particularly good example of such measures. Firstly, the law was the mainspring of the "peace strategy" which was to culminate, initially, in the current truce. Secondly, taking into account the deep-rooted causes of the conflict, particularly the poverty of the most underprivileged segments, article 8 of the law provides that "the Government shall be authorized to make the necessary budgetary appropriations and transfers and to contract the domestic and external loans required to organize and carry out programmes of rehabilitation, land distribution, rural housing, credit, education, health and job creation for those who, under the amnesty granted by this act, become reintegrated in peaceful life under the protection of the institutions, together with all inhabitants of regions affected by the armed conflict."

It will be recalled that, in its resolution 1984/16, the Sub-Commission enthusiastically encouraged this initiative, considering that it constituted a valuable precedent "since it progressively transforms a process of conflict into a momentum for peace, creating conditions for national reconciliation, inasmuch as it takes into account not only the facts but also the economic and social causes of the situation." (UN Doc. E/CN.4/Sub.2/1984/43, p. 90).

(f) Amnesty and Return of Exiles. "Return of exiles" and "amnesty" are closely linked. A comparative study of the 19 pieces of legislation intended specifically to encourage return which were communicated to the Rapporteur reveals the following characteristics:

The amnesty frequently becomes void if there is no actual return (or submission of applications) within a period determined by the law, and varying from one month (Zaire) to two years (Romania);

Either a limitative list of the beneficiaries is set forth in the act, or the text sets out a general measure (Ethiopia, with regard to the return of refugees from Djibouti), and, in some cases, lists the persons excluded from the scope of the amnesty (Chad). Perpetrators of war crimes are generally excluded (Hungary and Yugoslavia);

In some cases, exiles must confirm in writing that they wish to benefit from the amnesty (Hungary, Lesotho and Somalia);

Occasionally, provision is made for a monitoring authority (Chad and Somalia) or for a guaranteed appeal procedure (Yugoslavia).

In many cases, efforts to implement such legislation come up against three obstacles:

The obligation to return by, for example, imposing a time-limit, appears inconsistent with article 13 of the Universal Declaration of Human Rights and with article 12 of the International Covenant on Civil and Political Rights which guarantee the right of freedom of movement of individuals. The amnesty should be limited to restoring to the exile his full right to freedom of movement, without obliging him to exercise it;

The amnesty should lay down strict guarantees in order to ensure the safety of those benefiting from it. The effectiveness of such legislation is inversely proportional to the scope of the guarantees afforded. In the absence of such guarantees, the only effect of such legislation is to lend credence to the idea in world public opinion that a process of liberalization is in progress. In the case of Paraguay, for example, the authorization to return is based on a simple public statement by the authorities, and is not covered by the minimum guarantee afforded by the promulgation of a law. This omission, in addition to the continued state of siege, has deterred most of the very large number of exiles from returning;

The exercise of the right to return creates major reception and integration problems. Some laws contain provisions on that question. In Ghana, the amnesty law of 6 May 1962 provides for facilities for return and for reintegration procedures. The Uruguayan law referred to above contains a provision (article 24) setting up a national repatriation commission to assist refugees.

The conclusions of the Special Rapporteur, as set out in the final paragraphs (82–84) of the study, were as follows:

Amnesty deals only with the effects and not with the causes of national dissension, especially when article 21 of the Universal Declaration of Human Rights, which spells out the foundations of a democratic régime, is not respected and a state of emergency is instituted.

The same is true when serious and manifest violations of the most rudimentary cultural, social or economic rights are at the root of civil conflicts or dissension.

In such situations, the amnesty process can only be effective if it is coupled with social, economic or political measures permitting action to deal with the causes, viz.:

(a) In the short term, the repeal of emergency laws as a corollary of the amnesty: since like causes produce like effects, the release of political prisoners may come to nothing if the emergency laws which permitted massive arrests in violation of human rights subsist;

(b) In the medium term, the holding of elections in accordance with the stipulations of article 21 of the Universal Declaration of Human Rights;

(c) In the long term the implementation of economic and social measures attacking the root causes of national dissension.

After examining the study at its 1985 session, the Sub-Commission expressed its appreciation to the Special Rapporteur and recommended that the study should be published and disseminated as widely as possible, in all the official languages of the United Nations. The Commission on Human Rights and the Economic and Social Council approved this recommendation (Commission resolution 1986/51 and Council resolution 1986/38, respectively).

**SEE ALSO** *Impunity.*

**BIBLIOGRAPHY.** Africa Watch. *South Africa: Accounting for the Past—The Lessons for South Africa from Latin America.* New York: Human Rights Watch, 1992. NGO report, in English.

Americas Watch. *Truth and Partial Justice in Argentina: An Update.* New York: Human Rights Watch, 1991. NGO fact-finding report, in English.

———. *Chile: The Struggle for Truth and Justice for Past Human Rights Violations.* New York: Human Rights Watch, 1992. NGO report, in English.

Amnesty International. *Argentina: The Military Juntas and Human Rights–Report of the Trial of the Former Junta Members.* London: 1987. NGO report, in English.

———. "GDR Announces Amnesty and Abolishes Death Penalty," 24 July 1987. NGO press release, in English.

———. "Taiwan: Amnesty of 22 April 1988," 24 March 1988. NGO urgent action bulletin, in English.

———. *Viet Nam: Thousands Released in National Day Amnesty.* London: 1987. NGO report, in English.

Aspen Institute for Humanistic Studies. *State Crimes: Punishment or Pardon.* Aspen, CO, USA: 1988. NGO conference papers, in English.

Esponda, Jaime. *La Dimension Educative del Hacer Justicia en la Transicion Democratica* (The Educative Dimension of Doing Justice in the Democratic Tradition). Montevideo, Uruguay: Consejo de Education de Adultos de America Latina, 1986. NGO monograph, in Spanish.

Garro, A. M., and H. Dahl. "Legal Accountability for Human Rights Violations in Argentina: One Step Forward and Two Steps Back," *Human Rights Law Journal* 8, pts. 2–4 (1987): 283–344. Scholarly article, in English.

Kokott, Juliane. "No Impunity for Human Rights Violations in the Americas," *Human Rights Law Journal* 14, no. 5–6 (1993): 153–159. Scholarly article, in English.

Paulette, D.A. "Penales: ¿indulto, amnistia . . . ? Urgen soluciones, pero . . . ¡ya!" (Prisons: Pardons or Amnesty? Solutions Are Necessary . . . Right Now!), *Informe Mensual* 18 (1990): 19–28. NGO article, in Spanish.

Poland Watch Center. "Political Prisoners Released," *Poland Watch Digest* 7–8 (Aug.–Sept. 1986): 1–5. NGO article, in English.

Roht-Arriaza, Naomi. "State Responsibility to Investigate and Prosecute Grave Human Rights Violations in International Law," *California Law Review* 78, no. 2 (March 1990): 449–513. Scholarly article, in English.

Umana Luna, Eduardo. *Hacia La Paz? (Los Ilicitos y Los Presos Politicos: Las Amnistias y Los Indultos)* (Towards Peace? [Illicit Behavior and Political Prisoners: Amnesties and Pardons]). Bogota, Colombia: Comite de Solidaridad con los Presos Politicos, 1985. Monograph, in Spanish.

**AMNESTY INTERNATIONAL.** An international non-governmental organization in consultative status with the UN Economic and Social Council (Category II), and with UNESCO, OAS, OAU, and the Council of Europe, Amnesty International (AI) has affiliated sections in 47 countries and territories.

Amnesty International began in 1961 with a newspaper article by British lawyer Peter Benenson, who urged people everywhere to begin working impartially and peacefully for the release of prisoners of conscience. Within months, thousands of people from various countries sent in offers of practical help—many were prepared to help collect information on cases, publicize them, and approach governments—and what started as a brief publicity effort has become one of the most influential and highly respected human rights organizations in the world.

As its primary mandate, AI seeks to release prisoners of conscience—those detained for their beliefs, color, sex, ethnic origin, language, or religion, who have not used or advocated violence. It works for fair and prompt trials for political prisoners and opposes the death penalty and torture of prisoners. Through its network of members and supporters, AI takes up individual cases, mobilizes public opinion, and seeks improved international standards for treatment of prisoners. AI observers are sent to observe trials, and delegates visit countries to interview prisoners and speak with government officials. AI organizes "Amnesty International Week" each October and publicizes three "Prisoners of the Month" awards. In 1977, for its contributions "to securing the ground for freedom, for justice and thereby for peace in the world," Amnesty International received the Nobel Peace Prize. On the occasion of the 30th anniversary of the Universal Declaration of Human Rights (1978), AI was awarded the UN Human Rights Prize.

*PUBLICATIONS.* To publicize its concerns and activities, Amnesty International supports a large-scale publication program. The most influential and widely disseminated of its many reports is the annually published *Amnesty International Report,* which provides a country-by-country survey of AI's work. The *Amnesty International Newsletter,* a bulletin issued monthly, updates reports of factfinding missions, details of the arrest and release of political prisoners, and reliable reports of torture and executions. In addition, AI publishes *Amnesty International* (on microfiche), a collection of published and unpublished research materials, updated annually; *Voices for Freedom,* an anthology that relates the stories of AI prisoners of conscience; *Torture in the Eighties*; *Against Torture*; *Political Killings by Governments*; and numerous leaflets, booklets, individual accounts, and briefings on human rights situations in countries in regions all over the world.

Amnesty International. Address: International Secretariat, 1 Easton Street, London WC1X 8DJ, UK. Telephone: (44-71) 413-5500. Fax: (44-71) 956-1157. Cable: Amnesty London WC1. Telex: 28502. Secretary-General: Pierre Sané.

## ANDEAN COMMISSION OF JURISTS. An international non-governmental organization in consultative status with the UN Economic and Social Council (Category II), and in cooperative status with the Organization of American States, the Commission has individual members in six South American countries.

Founded in 1980 in Bogota, Colombia, the Com-

mission promotes, defends, and publicizes the principles that constitute civilian society and the rule of law and works for the protection of human rights in the Andean sub-region.

The Commission publishes the monthly *Andean Newsletter,* the monthly *Drug Trafficking Update,* the quarterly *Boletin de la Comisión Andina de Juristas*; and the bi-annual *Lecturas sobre Temas Constitucionales.*

Andean Commission of Jurists. Address: Los Sauces 285, San Isidro, Lima 27, Peru. Telephone: (51-14) 40-7907. Fax: (51-14) 42-6468. Executive Secretary: Dr. Diego Garcia-Sayán.

## ANDORRA. The Co-Principality of Andorra (under French and Spanish rule) is a country in western Europe and is not a member of the United Nations. It is situated in the eastern Pyrenees, on the border between France and Spain. One of the smallest countries in the world, it occupies a mountainous territory of only 185 square miles. Its total population is estimated at 56,000, scattered in seven villages. Ethnic groups include Catalan, Spanish, French, and Portuguese. Languages commonly used include Catalan (official), Spanish, and French. Literacy is estimated at 100%.

Andorra came into existence in 1278 when the French Count of Foix and the Spanish Bishop of Seo de Urgel agreed to recognize each other as co-princes of the Andorran valleys. Under this agreement, sovereignty is now exercised jointly by the president of the French Republic and the bishop of Urgel, who are charged with the conduct of foreign affairs, defense, and the judicial system. Every second year, the valleys pay the sum of 960 francs to France and 460 pesetas to the bishop.

The government (1994) took the form of a co-principality, ruled under the jurisdiction of the co-princes and their representatives by an Executive Council of 28 members, four from each of the seven parishes, elected for terms of four years. Since 1970, women have had equal suffrage with men. The council elects a syndic and a sub-syndic (managers) to implement its decisions.

The judicial system is handled jointly by the co-princes, who appoint two civil judges and alternately appoint an appeals judge. There are two supreme courts, the Perpignan Superior Court at Perpignan, France, and the Episcopal Superior Court of Seo de Urgel, Spain. Criminal law is administered by the Tribunal de Corts, consisting of two designated representatives of the co-princes and the judge of appeals.

There are no political parties in Andorra, and candidates for election run as independents.

**ANGELL, NORMAN (1872–1967).** Sir Ralph Norman Angell, British author and pacifist, was awarded the 1933 Nobel Peace Prize. His major work is *The Grand Illusion,* which showed the economic futility of war, even for the victors.

Born in Holbeach, Lincolnshire, England, he studied at elementary schools in England and in advanced schools in France and Switzerland. After emigrating to the United States, he began a career as a journalist, working at the *St. Louis Globe-Democrat* and the *San Francisco Chronicle.* On his return to Europe, he continued as a journalist; his dispatches to American newspapers on the Dreyfus case made him famous.

His first book was published in 1903; *Patriotism under Three Flags: A Plea for Rationalism in Politics* set the tone for Angell's universalism and pacifism, themes later developed in his remarkably successful *The Grand Illusion,* a work that sold over two million copies and was translated into 25 languages. Over a 41-year period, Angell published 41 books. He also invented a card game, contributed to newspapers and journals, edited the journal *Foreign Affairs* from 1928 to 1931, and served as a Labor MP from 1929 to 1931. For his services to the British nation, he was knighted in 1931.

In his Nobel acceptance speech, Angell stated, "The force that makes war does not derive its strength from the interested motives of evil men; it derives its strength from the disinterested motives of good men. . . . It is made, not usually by evil men knowing themselves to be wrong but is the outcome of policies pursued by good men usually passionately convinced that they are right."

***BIBLIOGRAPHY.*** Gray, Tony. *Champions of Peace.* London: Paddington Press, 1976.

Schlessinger, Bernard S., and June H. Schlessinger, eds. *Who's Who of Nobel Prize Winners.* Phoenix, AZ, USA: Oryx Press, 1991.

**ANGOLA.** The People's Republic of Angola is a country in middle Africa, on the Atlantic Ocean. It has borders with Congo, Namibia, Zaire, and Zambia. It achieved independence from Portugal in 1975 and became a member of the United Nations in 1976. Its population is estimated to be 10,735,000. Ethnic groups include the Ovimbundu (37%), Kimbundu (25%), Bakongo (13%), Chokwe and Lunda (8%), Ganguela (8%), and others (9%). Languages in common use include Bantu, Portuguese (official), and a number of African vernaculars. Religions practiced include Christianity (Roman Catholic, 70%; Protestant denominations, 20%) and Animism (10%). Angola is a secular State; its constitution calls for complete separation of religion and State and respect for all religious beliefs. Literacy is estimated at 25%.

The government (1994) took the form of a republic. However, elections called for by the constitution have not taken place and the officially recognized political party, the Popular Movement for the Liberation of Angola–Labor Party (MPLA), makes most decisions concerning national policy. The head of that party is president of the country. After independence, certain portions of Angola, in the east and south, were controlled by the National Movement for the Total Independence of Angola, which sought to replace the existing government.

When Angola was granted independence by Portugal in 1974, it was understood that a constituent Assembly would be elected immediately and that the differences between the three major political groups would be settled amicably. But after a brief period of conflict, the MPLA overrode its rivals, the National Front for the Liberation of Angola (FNLA) and the National Union for the Total Independence of Angola and an MPLA government was recognized by the Organization of African States. The struggle for political power did not end, however; and, late in 1987, some areas of Angola were not in the control of the government.

A one-party State ruled by the MPLA, Angola's political power is concentrated in the hands of its President , who is head of government and of the party. He is assisted by an 11-member Political Bureau, a 65-member Central Committee, and a Council of Ministers. There is a People's Assembly which meets annually, but policy decisions are normally made by the party. The constitution sets out the rights and duties of the citizen and provides for free elections and an independent judiciary. However, in practice, opposition views and political parties are not tolerated, and all branches of the government tend to follow guidelines established by the party.

UNITA, led by Jonas Savimbi, established itself in the southeastern corner of Angola and, with assistance from the United States of America, steadily increased its area of influence. However, its activities were confined to low-level guerrilla operations in the central highlands and eastern areas of the country. FNLA was less effective and its leader, Holden Roberto, left the country.

On 22 December 1988, after months of negotiation with the assistance of American mediators, two agreements were signed at UN headquarters in New York, the first a tri-partite agreement between Angola, Cuba, and South Africa providing for the independence of Namibia and the second an agreement between Angola and Cuba providing for the phased withdrawal of about 50,000 Cuban troops from Angola. The Cuban pullout was scheduled to begin on 1 April 1989 and to be completed by 1 July 1991. Earlier, toward the end of August 1988, South Africa had pulled its troops out of Angola after a 13-month offensive that had reached more than 180 miles into the country.

Angola's economic rehabilitation has since been a matter of concern for the international community. On 15 December 1989, the UN General Assembly, noting that the country's economy had been adversely affected by the acts of aggression and destabilization perpetrated by South Africa and expressing deep concern about the human suffering and the destruction of property that had resulted from those acts, expressed its solidarity with and support for the efforts of Angola to lessen those adverse effects and to cope with the economic and social problems, and appealed to the international community to render its substantial financial, material, and technical assistance necessary for the economic rehabilitation of Angola.

After the pullout of foreign troops, a Peace Accord was signed by the warring Angolan factions on May 31, 1991, and democratic elections were held, under UN auspices, on September 28 and 30, 1992. International observers, including the Special Representative of the Secretary-General, certified the elections as being generally free and fair, and steps were then taken to set up a Government of National Unity, which would reflect the election results. However, UNITA refused to take part in the political process, and the civil war erupted anew. The resulting situation of civil strife caused more than three million Angolans to become refugees in neighboring countries or to become internally displaced persons. The situation worsened in mid-1993, despite three UN Security Council demands for an end to the hostility. In September 1994, the UN Secretary-General reported a 10% increase in the number of people severely affected by the war since the beginning of the year. NGO reports have stated that both the Government and UNITA have been responsible for widespread and systematic violations of the laws of war. UNITA, in particular, was responsible for the indiscriminate shelling of besieged cities, resulting in the death of thousands of civilians and in the indiscriminate destruction of property. After 19 years of civil war in which at least a half million people died, the Angolan government and UNITA signed a peace accord in November 1994. A plan to send 7,000 UN peace-keeping troops was approved in early 1995.

**SPECIAL DECLARATION ON ANGOLA.** With this background, the World Conference on Human Rights, held in Vienna, Austria, in 1993, adopted, without a vote, the following "Special Declaration on Angola":

The World Conference on Human Rights,

Mindful of its objective to uphold and promote full respect for an effective promotion of human rights,

Recalling the signing of the Peace Accords for Angola on 31 May 1991,

Recalling that democratic elections were held on 28 and 30 September 1992, which the Special Representative of the Secretary-General and other international observers certified as being generally free and fair, and that steps have been taken to set up a Government of National Unity which would reflect the results of the legislative elections, and deeply regretting the failure of UNITA to take part in the political institutions thus established,

Alarmed at the continuing and unnecessary loss of innocent lives resulting from the resumption of war,

Alarmed also at the deliberate targeting of the civilian population and economic and social structures, in total disregard of international humanitarian law and internationally recognized human rights standards and norms,

Disturbed by the current situation of civil strife which has resulted in more than 3 million refugees and internally displaced persons,

Recalling Security Council resolutions 804 (1993) of 29 January 1993; 811 (1993) of 12 March 1993; and 834 (1993) of 1 June 1993,

Urges the international community and all international bodies, in particular the Security Council, to take forceful and decisive steps with a view to:

(a) Immediately implementing an effective cease-fire and restoring peace and security in the Republic of Angola;

(b) Calling upon the Security Council to implement rapidly its resolutions 804 (1993), 811 (1993), and 834 (1993),

(c) Applying pressure on UNITA to accept unreservedly the results of the democratic elections of 1992 and abide fully by the Peace Accords;

(d) Urging all States to refrain from any action which directly or indirectly could jeopardize the implementation of the Peace Accords, and in this context urges all States to refrain from providing any form of direct or indirect military assistance or other support to UNITA inconsistent with the peace process;

(e) Extending immediate humanitarian assistance to the millions of refugees and internally displaced persons;

(f) Effectively eradicating the consequences of the resumption of war and the human rights violations arising therefrom by way of joint international efforts for the reconstruction of the political, economic and social institutions of the Republic of Angola;

(g) Reaffirming the commitment of the international community to the preservation of the unity and territorial integrity of Angola.

**BIBLIOGRAPHY.** Africa Watch. *Angola: Civilians Devastated by 15-Year War.* New York: Human Rights Watch, 1991. NGO factfinding report, in English.

Amnesty International. *Angola: Human Rights Guarantees in the Revised Constitution.* London: 1991. NGO factfinding report, in English.

Brennan, T. O. *Uprooted Angolans: From Crisis to Catastrophe.* Washington, D.C.: U.S. Committee for Refugees, 1987. NGO report, in English.

Human Rights Watch. "Angola," *Human Rights Watch World Report 1995,* pp. 9–12. New York: 1995. NGO report, in English.

**ANKARA UNIVERSITY, HUMAN RIGHTS CENTER.** Established in 1978, the Center grew out of a longstanding interest of the Faculty of Political Sciences to teach courses on human rights and civil liberties. The Center contributes to UN activities, cooperates with scientific and other organizations in Turkey and throughout the region, strives to ensure that human rights teaching is placed in the curricula of Turkish schools and in the codes of conduct for various professional organizations, and organizes meetings and symposia at the national and international level. In addition, since its inception the Center has published numerous texts on the subject of human rights, among them *The Rights to Life* (1981) and *Textes de bases des droit de l'homme* (1991). The Center also publishes the *Revue des Droits de l'Homme,* a journal published three times a year in Turkish, English, and French.

Human Rights Center. Address: Ankara University, Faculty of Political Sciences, Cebeci, Ankara 06590, Turkey. Telephone: (90-4) 319-13-96. Fax: (90-4) 319-77-36. Directors: Prof. Feyyaz Golcuklu and Prof. Tekin Akilioglu.

**ANTIGUA AND BARBUDA.** A country in the Caribbean comprising three islands of the Lesser Antilles—Antigua, Barbuda, and Redonda—it achieved independence from Great Britain in 1981 and became a member of the United Nations the same year. Its population is estimated to be 77,000. The bulk of the people are of African origin; the remainder are descendants of British, Portuguese, Lebanese, and Syrian settlers. The predominant religion is Christianity (Anglican and Roman Catholic). Literacy is estimated at 90%.

The government (1994) took the form of a parliamentary state and member of the Commonwealth of Nations, of which the British sovereign is the symbolic head. Executive power is vested in the governor-general, representing the crown, and a Cabinet headed by the prime minister, representing the party or coalition given a majority in popular elections. Legislation is prepared by the 17-member Parliament. The predominant political party is the Antigua Labour Party.

Originally inhabited by the "stone people," estimated to have lived there since 1775 B.C., Antigua became a slave-plantation colony after coming under British control in 1632, its trees being stripped away to permit sugarcane production. Although emancipated in 1934, the slaves—brought from the west coast of Africa—remained bound to their plantation owners until they formed trade unions in the early 1940s. The Antigua Trades and Labor Union (ALP) has dominated the political scene since that time and won its most recent victory in the general elections of 1994. For the fifth consecutive time, the Antigua Labour Party won and Lester Bird succeeded his father as Prime Minister.

Antigua and Barbuda has an outstanding record in the field of human rights and a long history of fair elections, peaceful changes of government, and constitutional protection of freedom of opinion and expression and freedom from intolerance and discrimination on the ground of religion or belief. Antigua agreed to establish a safe haven for 2,000 Haitian refugees in mid-1994.

**ANTI-SEMITISM.** Anti-Semitism is a term that refers to hostility towards the Jewish people.

The United Nations has been concerned about the effects of this form of intolerance for many years. As early as 1948, for example, the UN General Assembly adopted and opened for signature and ratification the Convention on the Prevention and Punishment of the Crime of Genocide, which proceeded, in large measure, out of the horrors of the Holocaust perpetrated by the Nazis in World War II. In 1960, the Sub-Commission on Prevention of Discrimination and Protection of Minorities indicated its concern about "the manifestations of anti-Semitism and other forms of racial and national hatred and religious and national prejudices of a similar nature" that had occurred late in 1959 in various countries, which the Sub-Commission characterized as "reminiscent of the crimes and outrages committed by the Nazis prior to and during the Second World War." The Sub-Commission indicated that "it is the responsibility of the United Nations to speak out against these manifestations, to ascertain the underlying facts and causes, and to recommend the most effective measures which can be taken against them."

The consensus that had originally characterized the international campaign to combat racism and racial discrimination in all its forms was, however, seriously set back in 1975 when the UN General Assembly adopted resolution 3379 (XXX) of 10 November, which equated Zionism with racism. Only in 1991 did the Assembly decide (resolution 46/86 of 16 December) to revoke this determination.

*SEE ALSO* Genocide; Xenophobia.

*BIBLIOGRAPHY.* Association for the Study of the Nationalities of the USSR and Eastern Europe. "Pamyat," *Nationalities Papers* 19, no. 2 (Fall 1991): 134–250. Collection of scholarly articles, in English.

Bauman, Zygmut. *Modernity and the Holocaust.* Ithaca, NY, USA: Cornell University Press, 1991. Scholarly monograph, in English.

Dinstein, Yoram, ed. "International Legal Colloquium on Racial and Religious Hatred and Group Libel," *Israel Yearbook on Human Rights.* Dordrecht, the Netherlands: Martinus Nijhoff, 1993. Scholarly collection of articles, in English.

Fein, Helen, ed. *Genocide Watch.* New Haven, CT, USA: Yale University Press, 1992. Scholarly monograph, in English.

Gitelman, Zvi. "Glasnost, Perestroika and Antisemitism," *Foreign Affairs* 70, no. 2 (Spring 1991): 141–159. Scholarly article, in English.

Institute of Jewish Affairs. "Special Issue: Government Nationalities and the Jews of Russia, 1772–1990—Proceedings of a Conference Convened by the institute of Jewish Studies, University College, London, 26 and 27 March 1990," *East European Jewish Affairs* 21, no. 1 (Summer 1991). Collection of scholarly articles, in English.

Lerner, Natan. *Group Rights and Discrimination in International Law.* Dordrecht, the Netherlands: Martinus Nijhoff, 1991. Scholarly monograph, in English.

Shafir, Michael. "Anti-Semitism without Jews in Romania," *Report on Eastern Europe* 2, no. 26 (1991): 20–32. Article, in English.

## ANTI-SLAVERY INTERNATIONAL FOR THE PROTECTION OF HUMAN RIGHTS.

An international non-governmental organization in consultative status with the UN Economic and Social Council (Category II), ILO, UNESCO, and UNICEF, the organization is also known as the Anti-Slavery Society and has 1,800 individual members in 43 countries.

Founded in 1839 as the British and Foreign Anti-Slavery Society, the organization was amalgamated in 1909 with the Aborigines Protection Society. The Society works to eliminate all forms of slavery, including forced labor; to promote the well-being and defend the interests of oppressed and threatened indigenous and other peoples; and to promote human rights in accordance with the principles of the Universal Declaration of Human Rights. The society participated in activities that led to the adoption of the League of Nations Convention on Slavery (1926) and the UN Convention on Slavery (1956) and in the appointment of the Working Group on Contemporary Forms of Slavery.

At its 1989 session, the UN Sub-Commission on Prevention of Discrimination and Protection of Minorities (resolution 1989/1940) congratulated the Anti-Slavery Society, "the oldest human rights organization in the world," on the occasion of its 150th anniversary, noting "the great contribution that the Anti-Slavery Society has made to the cause of human rights over the last century-and-a-half by its tireless advocacy, research and concern for indigenous peoples as well as those suffering from the abuses of slavery and slavery-like practices," . . . "the important and continuing vital work the Society does in maintaining its global programs and providing information to the Sub-Commis-

sion," . . . and "the need for these valuable sources to be maintained."

### ANTI-SLAVERY MEDAL.

Established in 1991, the Anti-Slavery Medal is an honorary award presented annually to the person or organization deemed to perform outstanding service in the campaign against slavery or slave-like practices.

The 1994 recipient of the Anti-Slavery Medal was Fr. Edwin Paraison, an Episcopalian priest from Haiti who works with Haitian cane cutters enslaved on sugar cane plantations (bateyes) in the Dominican Republic. An ongoing part of Fr. Paraison's work is to encourage more cohesion among the Haitian community in the Dominican Republic by setting up links between the groups on different bateyes. He has also successfully publicized the working conditions for children on the plantations that produce sugar for export to the United States, resulting in pressure from the US Government to stop the exploitation of child labor or risk losing preferential customs duty status on sugar exports. Among other medal recipients are the Bonded Liberation Front of India (1991), for its support of those trapped in debt bondage in India, and Fr. Richardo Rezende Figueira (1992), a parish priest in Rio Mari, Para State, Brazil, who also is a representative of the Pastoral Land Commission. Fr. Figueira was cited for his advocacy of land reform and defense of rural laborers, rubber tappers, riverside communities, and migrant squatters; and ECPAT (End Child Prostitution in Asian Tourism).

### PUBLICATIONS.

The Anti-Slavery Society publishes the annual *Anti-Slavery Reporter,* a bi-annual newsletter, and an annual report, as well as periodic research reports. The group has also issued special information series: Child Labour Series; Human Rights Series; Indigenous Peoples Series.

Anti-Slavery International for the Protection of Human Rights. Address: Unit 4 Stableyard, Broomgrove Road, London, SW9 9 TL, UK. Telephone: (44-71) 924-9555. Fax: (44-71) 738-4110.

## APARTHEID.

The first volume of the dictionary of the Afrikaans language, *Woordeboek van die Afrikaans Taal,* compiled under official auspices by a group of philologists and published in Pretoria, South Africa, in 1950, defines *apartheid* as

a political tendency or trend in South Africa based on the general principles (a) of a differentiation corresponding to differences of race and/or color and/or level of civilization, as opposed to assimilation; (b) of the maintenance and perpetuation of the individuality (identity) of the different color groups of which the population is composed, and of the separate development of these groups in accordance with their individual nature, traditions and capabilities, as opposed to integration. In its practical application this policy involves arrangements and endeavors including, inter alia, measures to effect a degree of purely local or spacial separation, e.g., with respect to residential zones, public utilities, transport, entertainments, etc.; measures concerning political rights, e.g., separate electoral lists, separate representation in Parliament and in the Provincial Councils; also a territorial segregation, e.g., the fact of reserving fairly extensive territories for the exclusive use of one population group, e.g., the Native territories.

When South Africa achieved independence in 1910, within the British Empire, it was composed of two formerly independent republics, Orange and Transvaal, and two former British colonies, Cape and Natal. A multi-ethnic State, it had a population of about 6,000,000 persons divided by the union authorities into four main groups: "Europeans," or persons of pure European descent; "natives," or persons of the Bantu race; "Asiatics," or natives of Asia and their descendants, mainly Indians; and "mixed or other coloured," or persons of mixed race, mainly Cape Coloured, Cape Malays, Bushmen, and Hottentots. People in the latter three groups were referred to collectively as "non-Europeans" and were generally relegated to an inferior position politically, economically, socially, and culturally.

The "Europeans" had two different origins. Some were descendants of Dutch colonists, speaking Afrikaans, whose families had lived in the country more than three centuries and who were concentrated in the rural agricultural areas; others were descendants of English-speaking immigrants whose families had lived in the country less than a century and who were concentrated in the cities of the Cape and Natal Province.

Even before independence, the Act of 1909, under which the Union of South Africa was organized, denied to non-Europeans the basic right of direct representation in Parliament, although they constituted more than three-quarters of the population. Discriminatory legislation adopted between 1910 and 1948 further limited their role in South African life but did not cut it off completely.

However, in 1948, the United Party, dominated by the English-speaking population, lost control of the government to the National Party of the Africaners, and policies of racial segregation and discrimination—apartheid—were installed. The new system effectively ensured Europeans a monopoly of economic power, while preventing non-Europeans from acquiring land in certain areas, reducing their productive capacity and earning ability, and training them, in segregated schools, to accept their inferior position.

The basic racist doctrine of apartheid, as expressed by South Africa's Prime Minister and Minister of Native Affairs in the early 1950s, was summed up in a comprehensive Report of the United Nations Commission on the Racial Situation in the Union of South Africa, submitted to the UN General Assembly in 1953 (UN Doc. A/2505 and Add. 1, Chap. V, para. 402–406) in the following terms:

One of the most striking phenomena of the world in which we live is the diversity of human races. They were created separate. This separation must be maintained even when economic or other circumstances have brought about a certain mingling of racial groups. With this aim in view, the sense of colour must be fostered and developed amongst the whites in such a way that the purity of the race is maintained.

As the heir to Western Christian civilization, the white race in South Africa has a twofold mission to fulfil: one with respect to the other members of the community of nations of Western Christian civilization, the other with respect to the coloured races with which events have brought it in contact and which are at a primitive or very backward stage of civilization.

Towards the former it owes a duty to maintain fully and to perpetuate its "character as a partner in the Western Christian civilization". It is the mission of the white race living in South Africa to protect that civilization "against attacks from outside and subversion from within". In other words, though representing a numerical minority, it must at any cost safeguard its position of domination over the coloured races. Naturally therefore it looks askance at any dogma of civic equality. This is why it cannot grant to the Natives, any more than to the Cape Coloured or the Indians, the same political rights which it itself enjoys. If the latter exercise the franchise as they do, for example, in Cape Province, they must vote on separate electoral lists and their representatives in Parliament and in the Provincial Councils must continue to be Europeans.

This position of domination imposes as a corollary a strict duty of justice and Christian "trusteeship" towards the non-White. This trusteeship must continue until the latter have reached a stage of maturity and responsibility that will justify an eventual process of emancipation.

On either side of the deep, wide gulf which, because of the difference in cultural levels, separates the White from the non-White, each race stands separated by characteristics which are permanent because they are hereditary. A race can only "fulfill itself" if it remains faithful to its inner law. This is especially true of the Bantu who have languages and their own distinct customs, rites and institutions. Mix them with the descendants of Europeans and they will be only pitiful imitators. They will lose the original qualities proper to their race without acquiring those of the superior group.

The best service, therefore, that the Whites can render to the non-Whites is to separate them from the white population, to consider them as distinct social and economic groups, and to see that, as far as possible, they live in territories, zones, or "locations" assigned to them as their own. In this way in their own communities they will enjoy all the rights of citizens for chief among those rights is the opportunity to develop to the maximum the distinct aptitudes of each member of the community.

Although aimed primarily at safeguarding the purity and the tutelary mission of the white race, apartheid is not in any way a negative policy of oppression or exploitation of the non-White by the White. On the contrary, it is a constructive policy, a policy of benevolence, protection and co-operation. In fact, according to this policy, "the supremacy (baaskap) of the European in his sphere" has a counterpart in the supremacy of the Bantu, the Cape Coloured or the Indian each in his own sphere.

The ideal situation for the apartheid policy would clearly have been that "the course of history had been different", that "there had arisen in South Africa a state in which only Bantu lived and worked, and another in which only Europeans lived and worked. This is not the situation today, however". As the result either of negligence or of a deliberate policy of laissez-faire, previous Governments have tolerated a sort of racial chaos in the country in which points and areas of contact and entanglement between different races have multiplied. The more numerous those points and areas of contact, however, the more chances are there of incidents, conflicts and outbursts. And unless energetic and concerted steps are taken to reverse the present trend towards a mixed development of races in the large urban centres, we may expect fearful clashes of interests and great suffering and bloodshed affecting all sections of the population.

The racist oppression of apartheid has caused enormous suffering among the non-European populations of South Africa by such devices as depriving them of rights of citizenship in their own country, crowding them into small barren areas where they cannot earn a living or practice a trade or profession, detaining them indefinitely without trial and torturing detainees held for interrogation, "banning" those who oppose the system, and even killing unarmed men, women, and children, as happened in Sharpeville in 1960 and Soweto in 1976.

In 1968 the **TEHERAN INTERNATIONAL CONFERENCE ON HUMAN RIGHTS,** in the Proclamation of Teheran, declared that:

Gross denials of human rights under the repugnant policy of apartheid are a matter of gravest concern to the international community. This policy of apartheid, condemned as a crime against humanity, continues seriously to disturb international peace and security. It is therefore imperative for the international community to use every possible means to eradicate this evil. The struggle against apartheid is recognized as legitimate.

In 1977, the World Conference against Apartheid, held at Lagos from 22 to 26 August, adopted the Lagos Declaration for Action Against Apartheid, in which it set out its conclusion that:

Apartheid, the policy of institutionalized racist domination and exploitation, imposed by a minority regime in South Africa, is a flagrant violation of the Charter of the United Nations and the Universal Declaration of Human Rights. It rests on the dispossession, plunder, exploitation and social deprivation of the African people since 1652 by colonial settlers and their descendants. It is a crime against the conscience and dignity of mankind. It has resulted in immense suffering and involved the forcible moving of mil-

lions of Africans under special laws restricting their freedom of movement; and the denial of elementary human rights to the great majority of the population as well as the violation of the inalienable right to self-determination of all of the people of South Africa. This inhuman policy has been enforced by ruthless measures of repression and has led to escalating tension and conflict.

*A COLLECTIVE FORM OF SLAVERY.* In 1980, the UN Secretary-General prepared and submitted to the Sub-Commission on Prevention of Discrimination and Protection of Minorities, at its request, a report entitled "Apartheid as a Collective Form of Slavery," in which he noted (UN Doc. E/CN.4/Sub.2/449, para. 231) that:

the international community has recognized that the apartheid system in South Africa is not simply a racial discrimination problem to be solved through education and political and social reforms. Rather, it has been increasingly understood that the essence of apartheid lies in the dispossession of the black population through the imposition of quasi-colonial rule, and in the harnessing of the labor of the vanquished indigenous people through a variety of coercive measures for the benefit of white investors, both South African and foreign. The international community has therefore described the apartheid system as a slavery-like practice imposed on an entire collectivity, which can be eradicated only through a complete restructuring of the existing political and economic relationships.

After examining the report, the Sub-Commission referred it to the Ad Hoc Working Group of Experts on Southern Africa, the Special Committee Against Apartheid, and the Director-General of the International Labor Organization for their consideration and such action as they may deem appropriate (resolution 8 [XXXIII]). At the same time, the Sub-Commission strongly rejected the labor practices of the Government of South Africa as constituting "a modern form of slavery."

*AN INTERNATIONAL CRIME.* In a number of resolutions and decisions adopted by the UN General Assembly between 1966 and 1970, the South African policy of apartheid was condemned as constituting a crime against humanity. In 1968, the International Conference on Human Rights declared, in resolution III, that "the policy of apartheid or other similar evils are a crime against humanity punishable in accordance with the provisions of relevant international instruments dealing with such crimes."

On 18 March 1970, the Commission on Human Rights called upon its Ad Hoc Working Group of Experts on Southern Africa "to study, from the point of view of international penal law, the question of apartheid, which has been declared a crime against humanity" (resolution 8 [XXVI]). In 1972, the Working

Group presented a "Study Concerning the Question of Apartheid from the Point of View of International Penal Law" (UN Doc. E/CN.4/1075) to the Commission.

In the Study, the Working Group analyzed the concept of international penal law in doctrine, then reviewed elements of the policy of apartheid brought to light in the work of the United Nations to which international penal law might be applied. The conclusions of the group were: (1) that ill-treatment of political prisoners and the like on racial grounds, the extermination of, or the attempt to exterminate, members of a racial group, the killing of persons, deportations, slavery-like practices and the ill-treatment inflicted upon freedom-fighters are acts resulting from the policies of apartheid and must be considered crimes under international law; (2) that South Africa is responsible for these acts either under international public law or under the Geneva Conventions and the peace treaties concluded at the end of the World War II to which South Africa is a party; (3) that no effective international machinery exists, however, for the judicial determination of the penal responsibility of States and individuals; and (4) that, besides alarming world public opinion regarding the fact that South Africa, by certain elements of its apartheid policies, is continuously committing crimes under international law, nothing can be done at this time to bring the State authorities in question to book.

The International Convention on the Suppression and Punishment of the Crime of Apartheid, adopted by the General Assembly on 30 November 1973, opens with the statement that "the States parties to the present Convention declare that apartheid is a crime against humanity and that inhuman acts resulting from the policies and practices of apartheid and similar policies and practices of racial segregation and discrimination . . . are crimes violating the principles of international law." After defining the term "the policy of apartheid," in article II, the Convention provides (article III) that

International criminal responsibility shall apply, irrespective of the motive involved, to individuals, members of organizations and institutions and representatives of the State, whether residing in the territory of the State in which the acts are perpetrated or in some other State, whenever they: (a) Commit, participate in, directly incite or conspire in the commission of the acts mentioned in article II of the Convention; (b) Directly abet, encourage or co-operate in the commission of the crime of apartheid.

Under article V of the Convention, "persons charged with the acts enumerated in article II . . . may be tried by a competent tribunal of any State party to the Convention which may acquire jurisdiction over the person of the accused or by an international penal tribunal having jurisdiction with respect to those States parties which shall have accepted its jurisdiction." It does not, however, go so far as to establish effective international machinery for the judicial determination of the States' penal responsibility toward individuals alleged to have committed the crime of apartheid.

*UN GENERAL ASSEMBLY ACTIONS.* Throughout the years of the practice of apartheid in South Africa, the UN General Assembly has denounced this racist policy in numerous ways.

In 1962, the Assembly set up (resolution 1761 [XVII]) the Special Committee Against Apartheid, first known as the Special Committee on the Policies of Apartheid of the Government of the Republic of South Africa, to review the racial policies of that Government. In 1965, the Assembly established (resolution 2054 B [XX]) the United Nations Trust Fund for South Africa to provide humanitarian assistance to victims of apartheid and racial discrimination in South Africa and Namibia.

In 1967, the Assembly set up the UN Educational and Training Programme for Southern Africa to provide scholarships for nationals of South Africa and Namibia for study and training abroad.

In 1970, the Assembly singled out the policy in its Declaration on the Occasion of the Twenty-Fifth Anniversary of the United Nations, adopted on 24 October 1970 (resolution 2627 [XXV]), calling apartheid "an evil policy . . . which is a crime against the conscience and dignity of mankind and, like Nazism, is contrary to the principles of the Charter."

In 1973, the General Assembly adopted and opened for ratification and accession (resolution 3068 [XXVIII]) the International Convention on the Suppression and Punishment of the Crime of Apartheid, which entered into force on 18 July 1976. In accordance with article IX of this Convention, the Chairman of the Commission on Human Rights appointed a "Group of Three" members of the Commission, who are also representatives of States party to the Convention, to meet immediately prior to each annual session of the Commission to consider and to adopt conclusions and recommendations concerning reports submitted by States parties on the legislative, judicial, administrative, or other measures that they have adopted to give effect to the provisions of the Convention. The Group of Three subsequently examined the nature and extent of the responsibility of transnational corporations for the continued existence of the apartheid system, including legal actions that may be taken under the Convention against such corporations whose operations in South Africa fall within the definition of the crime of apartheid.

In 1974, the Assembly invited representatives of the South African liberation movements—the African National Congress and the Pan Africanist Congress of Azania—to participate as observers in the debates on apartheid, which were then held in its Special Political Committee.

In 1976, the Assembly began discussing apartheid in plenary rather than in committee meetings and again invited the two liberation movements to participate.

Also in 1976, the Assembly prepared and adopted (resolution 31/6J) a comprehensive "Program of Action against Apartheid," which was to be implemented by "Governments, intergovernmental organizations, trade unions, churches, anti-apartheid and solidarity movements, and other non-governmental organizations in order to assist the people of South Africa in their struggle for the total eradication of apartheid and the exercise of the right of self-determination by all the people of South Africa irrespective of race, color and creed."

In 1977, the Assembly adopted and proclaimed (resolution 32/105 M) the International Declaration Against Apartheid in Sports.

In 1985, the Assembly adopted and opened for ratification and acceptance the International Convention Against Apartheid in Sports. The Convention entered into force on 3 April 1985. To monitor compliance with the Convention, article 11 provides for the establishment of the Commission Against Apartheid in Sports to review reports from States parties on the legislative, judicial, administrative, or other measures which they have adopted to give effect to provisions of the Convention.

In 1988, the General Assembly adopted resolution 43/50 A of 5 December, in which it demanded, as it had on past occasions: (a) the lifting of the state of emergency; (b) the immediate and unconditional release of Nelson Mandela and all other political prisoners and detainees; (c) the lifting of the ban on all political organizations and opponents of apartheid; (d) the safe return of all political exiles; (e) the withdrawal of the regime's troops from black townships; (f) the repeal of restrictions on the freedom of the press; (g) the end of the policy of bantustanization and forced population removals; and (h) the end of military and paramilitary activities aimed at neighboring countries.

In 1989, the UN General Assembly held a special session on the question of apartheid at UN headquarters in New York, at which it reviewed developments relating to that question and unanimously adopted, on 14 December 1989, the Declaration on Apartheid and its Destructive Consequences in Southern Africa (UN Doc. A/RES/S-16-1), in which the Assembly once again urged that serious efforts be made to end apartheid through negotiations based on the principle of justice and peace for all.

However, following adoption by the General Assembly of the Declaration on Apartheid and its Destructive Consequences in Southern Africa, the situation in that country changed considerably.

As steps to remove the legal and social barriers imposed by apartheid were adopted by the South African Government, the General Assembly noted on 8 October 1993 (resolution 48/1) "that the transition to democracy has now been enshrined in the law of South Africa."

On that basis, the Assembly decided that all the provisions that it had adopted "relating to prohibitions or restriction on economic relations with South Africa and its nationals, whether corporate or natural, including the areas of trade, investment, finance, travel and transportation, shall cease to have effect as of the date of the adoption of the present resolution." It further decided "that all provisions adopted by the General Assembly relating to the imposition of an embargo on the supply of petroleum and petroleum products to South Africa, and on investment in the petroleum industry there, shall cease to have effect as of the date that the Transitional Executive Council becomes operational."

On 20 December 1993, the General Assembly, in resolution 48/159, recognized the responsibility of the United Nations and the international community to help the South African people in their legitimate struggle for the elimination of apartheid through peaceful means and, inter alia, welcomed the agreements reached within the framework of the multiparty negotiations on holding elections on 27 April 1994; the establishment of the Transitional Executive Council; the independent Electoral and Media Commissions; the independent Broadcasting Authority; the Constitution for the Transitional Period; and the Electoral Bill.

*UN SECURITY COUNCIL ACTIONS.* The UN Security Council took up the question of race conflict in South Africa in 1960 and recognized (resolution 134 [1960]) that the situation, if it continued, might endanger international peace and security. In 1963, the council instituted a voluntary embargo against the supply of arms to South Africa, calling upon all States (resolution 181 [1963]) to end the sale and shipment of arms, ammunition, and military vehicles to that country. This ban was reiterated and strengthened to include the sale of equipment and material for the maintenance and manufacture of arms and ammunition, in 1964, 1970, and 1972.

In 1974, the Security Council considered, at the request of the General Assembly, the relationship between the United Nations and South Africa "in the light of the constant violation by South Africa of the Charter and the Universal Declaration of Human Rights." A proposal for immediate expulsion of South Africa from the UN was considered but not adopted because of the negative vote—"veto"—of three permanent members: France, the United Kingdom, and the United States. Although it continued to be a UN member, South Africa was not represented at assembly sessions held in 1975, 1976, and 1977.

In 1975, the Council considered a proposal to make the arms embargo mandatory but was unable to do so because of the negative votes of the same permanent members: France, the United Kingdom, and the United States. The General Assembly, which for ten years had been calling upon the council to take action against South Africa under chapter 7 of the UN Charter, expressed regret at its failure to do so and called the action of the permanent members "an abuse of their veto." Another attempt to make the embargo mandatory failed in 1976. However, in 1977, after a lengthy debate sparked by South Africa's use of massive violence against African people, including the shooting of demonstrators at Soweto in June 1976, the Council decided unanimously (resolution 418 [1977]) to impose a mandatory arms embargo. Its decision was that all States should cease any provision to South Africa of arms and related material of all types, including the sale or transfer of weapons and ammunition, military vehicles and equipment, paramilitary police equipment, and spare parts for them; and that all States should refrain from any cooperation with South Africa in the manufacture and development of nuclear weapons. The Council further established a committee to monitor the progress of the implementation of the resolution and to study ways and means of making the embargo more effective.

In March 1985, the Council called upon the South African authorities (resolution 560 [1985]) to release unconditionally and immediately all political prisoners and detainees, including Nelson Mandela and all other black leaders with whom it must deal in any meaningful discussion of the future of the country. In July of that year, it strongly condemned (resolution 569 [1985]) the apartheid system, the mass arrests and detentions carried out by the Pretoria government, and the murders that had been committed, as well as the establishment of a "state of emergency" in 36 districts. It demanded the immediate lifting of the state of emergency and reaffirmed its view that only the total elimination of apartheid and the establishment in South Africa of a free, united, and democratic society on the basis of universal suffrage could lead to a solution of the country's problems.

The Council was unable, up to the end of 1988, to impose comprehensive and mandatory sanctions against South Africa as provided in chapter 7 of the UN Charter. In this connection, the General Assembly has for a number of years adopted resolutions (for example, resolutions 38/39 D, 39/72 A, 40/64 A, 41/35 B, and 42/23 C) urging the Council to take such action and urging the governments of the United Kingdom, the United States of America, and others that are opposed to the application of such sanctions to reassess their policies and cease their opposition.

However, by the 1990s, the South African situation had changed considerably. As steps to remove the legal and social barriers imposed by apartheid were adopted by the South African Government, the Security Council found it possible to authorize, in 1992, the deployment of a UN Observer Mission in that country (resolutions 765 and 792 [1992]).

***SOLIDARITY OBSERVANCES.*** For many years, opponents of apartheid throughout the world have observed four "international days of solidarity" with victims of this crime.

March 21 is observed as the International Day for the Elimination of Racial Discrimination, to commemorate the massacre in Sharpeville, South Africa, in which scores of unarmed people were killed while staging a peaceful demonstration of protest against the "pass laws" on 21 March 1960.

June 16 is observed as the International Day of Solidarity with the Struggling People of South Africa, to commemorate the massacre in Soweto, South Africa, on 16 June 1976, when hundreds of unarmed school children were brutalized and killed by the police as they demonstrated against the imposition of the Afrikaans language and the Bantu system of education.

August 9 is observed as the International Day of Solidarity with the Struggle of Women in South Africa and Namibia, to commemorate the demonstration by South African women on 9 August 1956, in Pretoria, to protest the extension of the "pass laws" to women.

October 11 is observed as the Day of Solidarity with South African Political Prisoners (all those imprisoned, interned, or otherwise restricted for opposing apartheid), to publicize their plight and to help bring about compliance by South Africa with United Nations decisions on the question.

In addition, many governments and organizations observe the anniversary of the death of Steve Biko, 12 September, to pay tribute to him and to all other martyrs in the struggle to end apartheid, including those killed while in prison; and the birthday of Nelson Mandela, 18 July, to pay tribute to him for his outstanding contribution to the struggle for liberation in South Africa as leader of the African National Congress and to publicize the heroic struggle of the liberation movement to which he dedicated his life.

**SEE ALSO**  *African National Congress; Apartheid entries; Mandela, Nelson; Race; Racial Discrimination; Self-Determination; South Africa.*

**BIBLIOGRAPHY.**  African Commission on Human and Peoples' Rights and UNESCO Division of Human Rights and Peace. *Human Rights Issues for a Post-Apartheid South Africa: Final Report of Banjul, The Gambia, Workshop 18–21 June 1991.* Geneva, Switzerland: June 1991. Conference report, in English.

Barratt, John. *Transition in South Africa: The Global Context and the International Role.* Johannesburg, South Africa: South African institute of International Affairs, 1992. Scholarly monograph, in English.

Centre for Applied Legal Studies, University of the Witwatersrand. "Focus on Socio-Economic Rights," *South African Journal on Human Rights* 8, no. 4 (1992): 451–490. Collection of articles, in English.

———. "Land and Property Rights," *South African Journal on Human Rights* 8, no. 3 (1992): 295–450. Special issue, in English.

Collins, Richard. "Broadcasting Policy for a Post Apartheid South Africa," *Critical Arts: A Journal for Cultural Studies* 6, no. 1 (1992): 26–51. Scholarly article, in English.

Corrigall, Jim, Elaine Unterhalter, and Gillian Slovo. *Subverting Apartheid: Education, Information and Culture under Emergency Rule.* London: IDAF Publications, 1990. Monograph, in English.

Egero, Bertil. *South Africa's Bantustans: From Dumping Grounds to Battlefronts.* Uppsala, Sweden: Scandinavian Institute of African Studies, 1991. Scholarly monograph, in English.

Frederikse, Julie. *The Unbreakable Thread: Non-Racialism in South Africa.* Bloomington, IN, USA: Indiana University Press, 1990. Scholarly monograph, in English.

International Defence and Aid Fund for South Africa. *Apartheid: The Facts.* London: 1991. Monograph, in English.

Penna, David R. "Apartheid, the Law and Reform in South Africa," *Africa Today* 37, no. 2 (2nd Quarter 1990): 5–21. Scholarly article, in English.

"Racial Divisions, Skills Divisions," *South African Labour Bulletin* 17, no. 2 (March/April 1993): 23–55. Collection of articles, in English.

"Racism and Repression in South Africa: The Two Faces of Apartheid," *Harvard Human Rights Yearbook* 2 (Spring 1989): 97–124. Scholarly article, in English.

Taylor, Rupert. "The Myth of Ethnic Division: Township Conflict on the Reef," *Race & Class: A Journal for Black and Third World Liberation* 33, no. 2 (Oct.–Dec. 1991): 1–14. Scholarly article, in English.

Truluck, Anne. *No Blood on Our Hands: Political Violence in the Natal Midlands; 1987 to mid-1992, and the Role of the State, "White" Political Parties and Business.* Pietermaritzburg, South Africa: Black Sash, 1992. Scholarly monograph, in English.

Tsotsi, W. M. *Human Rights in the Homelands of South Africa.* Roma, Lesotho: Institute of Southern African Studies, National University of Lesotho, 1992. Scholarly monograph, in English.

United Nations Economic and Social Council. *Violations of Human Rights in South Africa: Report of the Ad Hoc Working Group of Experts—Final Report of the Ad Hoc Working Group of Experts on Southern Africa prepared in accordance with Commission on Human Rights resolutions 1991/21 and 1992/19 and Economic and Social Council decision 1991/237.* New York: United Nations, 1993. IGO report, in English.

United Nations Human Rights Commission. *Checkmate for Apartheid? Special Report on Two Years of Destabilisation—July 1990 to June 1992.* Braamfontein, South Africa: HRC, n.d. NGO special report, in English.

Van Nieuwkerk, Anthoni. *Transitional Politics in South Africa: From Confrontation to Democracy.* Johannesburg, South Africa: The South African Institute of International Affairs, 1992. Scholarly monograph, in English.

**APARTHEID: INTERNATIONAL CONVENTION AGAINST APARTHEID IN SPORTS (1985).**  The Convention defines "apartheid" as meaning "a system of institutionalized racial segregation and discrimination for the purpose of establishing and maintaining domination by one racial group of persons over another racial group of persons and systematically oppressing them, such as that pursued by South Africa," and "apartheid in sports" as meaning "the application of the policies and practices of such a system in sports activities, whether organized on a professional or an amateur basis." States which ratify or accede to the Convention strongly condemn apartheid and undertake to pursue the policy of eliminating the practice of apartheid in all its forms from sports. The International Convention grew out of the earlier "International Declaration Against Apartheid in Sports," adopted by the UN General Assembly on 14 December 1977 (resolution 32/105).

To monitor implementation of the Convention, article 11 authorizes the establishment of a Commission Against Apartheid in Sports, consisting of 15 members of high moral character and committed to the struggle against apartheid. Members are to be elected by States parties from among their nationals, having regard to the most equitable geographical distribution and the representation of the principal legal systems, with particular attention being paid to the participation of persons having experience in sports administration.

States parties to the Convention undertake (article 12) to submit to the UN Secretary-General, for consideration by the Commission, reports on the legislative, judicial, administrative, or other measures which they have adopted to give effect to the provisions of the Convention. The Commission reports annually to the UN General Assembly on its activities and may make suggestions and general recommendations based on its examination of the reports and information received from the States parties, together with comments, if any, from States parties concerned.

Under article 13, a State party may at any time declare that it recognizes the competence of the Commission to receive and examine complaints concerning breaches of the Convention submitted by States parties which have also made such a declaration. The Commission is authorized to decide on the appropriate measures to be taken in respect of such breaches.

The Convention, adopted by the UN General Assembly on 10 December 1985 (resolution 40/64), is as follows:

The States Parties to the present Convention,

Recalling the provisions of the Charter of the United Nations, in which all Members pledged themselves to take joint and separate action, in co-operation with the Organization, for the achievement of universal respect for, and observance of, human rights and fundamental freedoms for all without distinction as to race, sex, language or religion,

Considering that the Universal Declaration of Human Rights proclaims that all human beings are born free and equal in dignity and rights and that everyone is entitled to all the rights and freedoms set forth in the Declaration without distinction of any kind, particularly in regard to race, colour or national origin,

Observing that, in accordance with the International Convention on the Elimination of All Forms of Racial Discrimination, States Parties to that Convention particularly condemn racial segregation and apartheid and undertake to prevent, prohibit and eradicate all practices of this nature in all fields,

Observing that the General Assembly of the United Nations has adopted a number of resolutions condemning the practice of apartheid in sports and has affirmed its unqualified support for the Olympic principle that no discrimination be allowed on the grounds of race, religion, or political affiliation and that merit should be the sole criterion for participation in sports activities,

Considering that the International Declaration Against Apartheid in Sports, which was adopted by the General Assembly on 14 December 1977, solemnly affirms the necessity for the speedy elimination of apartheid in sports,

Recalling the provisions of the International Convention on the Suppression and Punishment of the Crime of Apartheid and recognizing, in particular, that participation in sports exchanges with teams selected on the basis of apartheid directly abets and encourages the commission of the crime of apartheid, as defined in that Convention,

Resolved to adopt all necessary measures to eradicate the practice of apartheid in sports and to promote international sports contacts based on the Olympic principle,

Recognizing that sports contact with any country practising apartheid in sports condones and strengthens apartheid in violation of the Olympic principle and thereby becomes the legitimate concern of all Governments,

Desiring to implement the principles embodied in the International Declaration Against Apartheid in Sports and to secure the earliest adoption of practical measures to that end,

Convinced that the adoption of an International Convention Against Apartheid in Sports would result in more effective measures at the international and national levels, with a view to eliminating apartheid in sports,

Have agreed as follows:

*Article 1.* For the purposes of the present Convention:

(a) The expression "apartheid" shall mean a system of institutionalized racial segregation and discrimination for the purpose of establishing and maintaining domination by one racial group of persons over another racial group of persons and systematically oppressing them, such as that pursued by South Africa, and "apartheid in sports" shall mean the application of the policies and practices of such a system in sports activities, whether organized on a professional or an amateur basis;

(b) The expression "national sports facilities" shall mean any sports facility operated within the framework of a sports programme conducted under the auspices of a national government;

(c) The expression "Olympic principle" shall mean the principle that no discrimination be allowed on the grounds of race, religion or political affiliation;

(d) The expression "sports contracts" shall mean any contract concluded for the organization, promotion, performance or derivative rights, including servicing, of any sports activity;

(e) The expression "sports bodies" shall mean any organization constituted to organize sports activities at the national level, including national Olympic committees, national sports federations or national governing sports committees;

(f) The expression "team" shall mean a group of sportsmen organized for the purpose of participating in sports activities in competition with other such organized groups;

(g) The expression "sportsmen" shall mean men and women who participate in sports activities on an individual or team basis, as well as managers, coaches, trainers and other officials whose functions are essential for the operation of a team.

*Article 2.* States Parties strongly condemn apartheid and undertake to pursue immediately by all appropriate means the policy of eliminating the practice of apartheid in all its forms from sports.

*Article 3.* States Parties shall not permit sports contact with a country practising apartheid and shall take appropriate action to ensure that their sports bodies, teams, and individual sportsmen do not have such contact.

*Article 4.* States Parties shall take all possible measures to prevent sports contact with a country practising apartheid and shall ensure that effective means exist for bringing about compliance with such measures.

*Article 5.* States Parties shall refuse to provide financial or other assistance to enable their sports bodies, teams and individual sportsmen to participate in sports activities in a country practising apartheid or with teams or individual sportsmen selected on the basis of apartheid.

*Article 6.* Each State Party shall take appropriate action against its sports bodies, teams and individual sportsmen that participate in sports activities in a country practising apartheid or with teams representing a country practising apartheid, which in particular shall include:

(a) Refusal to provide financial or other assistance for any purpose to such sports bodies, teams and individual sportsmen;

(b) Restriction of access to national sports facilities by such sports bodies, teams and individual sportsmen;

(c) Non-enforceability of all sports contracts which involve sports activities in a country practising apartheid or with teams or individual sportsmen selected on the basis of apartheid;

(d) Denial and withdrawal of national honours or awards in sports to such teams and individual sportsmen;

(e) Denial of official receptions in honour of such teams or sportsmen.

*Article 7.* States Parties shall deny visas and/or entry to representatives of sports bodies, teams and individual sportsmen representing a country practising apartheid.

*Article 8.* States Parties shall take all appropriate action to secure the expulsion of a country practising apartheid from international and regional sports bodies.

*Article 9.* States Parties shall take all appropriate measures to prevent international sports bodies from imposing financial or other penalties on affiliated bodies which, in accordance with United Nations resolutions, the provisions of the present Convention and the spirit of the Olympic principle, refuse to participate in sports with a country practising apartheid.

*Article 10.* 1. States Parties shall use their best endeavours to ensure universal compliance with the Olympic principles of non-discrimination and the provisions of the present Convention.

2. Towards this end, States Parties shall prohibit entry into their countries of members of teams and individual sportsmen participating or who have participated in sports competitions in South Africa and shall prohibit entry into their countries of representatives of sports bodies, members of teams and individual sportsmen who invite on their own initiative sports bodies, teams and sportsmen officially representing a country practising apartheid and participating under its flag. States Parties may also prohibit entry of representatives of sports bodies, members of teams or individual sportsmen who maintain sports contacts with sports bodies, teams or sportsmen representing a country practising apartheid and participating under its flag. Prohibition of entry should not violate the regulations of the relevant sports federations which support the elimination of apartheid in sports and shall apply only to participation in sports activities.

3. States Parties shall advise their national representatives to international sports federations to take all possible and practical steps to prevent the participation of the sports bodies, teams and sportsmen referred to in paragraph 2 above in international sports competitions and shall, through their representatives in international sports organizations, take every possible measure:

(a) To ensure the expulsion of South Africa from all federations in which it still holds membership as well as to deny South Africa reinstatement to membership in any federation from which it has been expelled;

(b) In case of national federations condoning sports exchanges with a country practising apartheid, to impose sanctions against such national federations including, if necessary, expulsion from the relevant international sports organization and exclusion of their representatives from participation in international sports competitions.

4. In cases of flagrant violations of the provisions of the present Convention, States Parties shall take appropriate action as they deem fit, including, where necessary, steps aimed at the exclusion of the responsible national sports governing bodies, national sports federations or sportsmen of the countries concerned from international sports competition.

5. The provisions of the present article relating specifically to South Africa shall cease to apply when the system of apartheid is abolished in that country.

*Article 11.* 1. There shall be established a Commission Against Apartheid in Sports (hereinafter referred to as "the Commission") consisting of fifteen members of high moral character and committed to the struggle against apartheid, particular attention being paid to participation of persons having experience in sports administration, elected by the States Parties from among their nationals, having regard to the most equitable geographical distribution and the representation of the principal legal systems.

2. The members of the Commission shall be elected by secret ballot from a list of persons nominated by the States Parties. Each State Party may nominate one person from among its own nationals.

3. The initial election shall be held six months after the date of the entry into force of the present Convention. At least three months before the date of each election, the Secretary-General of the United Nations shall address a letter to the States Parties inviting them to submit their nominations within two months. The Secretary-General shall prepare a list in alphabetical order of all persons thus nominated, indicating the States Parties which have nominated them, and shall submit it to the States Parties.

4. Elections of the members of the Commission shall be held at a meeting of States Parties convened by the Secretary-General at United Nations Headquarters. At that meeting, for which two thirds of the States Parties shall constitute a quorum, the persons elected to the Commission shall be those nominees who obtain the largest number of votes and an absolute majority of the votes of the representatives of States Parties present and voting.

5. The members of the Commission shall be elected for a term of four years. However, the terms of nine of the members elected at the first election shall expire at the end of two years; immediately after the first election, the names of these nine members shall be chosen by lot by the Chairman of the Commission.

6. For the filling of casual vacancies, the State Party whose national has ceased to function as a member of the Commission shall appoint another person from among its nationals, subject to the approval of the Commission.

7. States Parties shall be responsible for the expenses of the members of the Commission while they are in performance of Commission duties.

*Article 12.* 1. States Parties undertake to submit to the Secretary-General of the United Nations, for consideration by the Commission, a report on the legislative, judicial, administrative or other measures which they have adopted to give effect to the provisions of the present Convention within one year of its entry into force and thereafter every two years. The Commission may request further information from the States Parties.

2. The Commission shall report annually through the Secretary-General to the General Assembly of the United Nations on its activities and may make suggestions and general recommendations based on the examination of the reports and information received from the States Parties. Such suggestions and recommendations shall be reported to the General Assembly together with comments, if any, from States Parties concerned.

3. The Commission shall examine, in particular, the implementation of the provisions of article 10 of the present Convention and make recommendations on action to be undertaken.

4. A meeting of States Parties shall be convened by the Secretary-General at the request of a majority of the States Parties to consider further action with respect to the implementation of the provisions of article 10 of the present Convention. In cases of flagrant violation of the provisions of the present Convention, a meeting of States Parties shall be convened by the Secretary-General at the request of the Commission.

*Article 13*. 1. Any State Party may at any time declare that it recognizes the competence of the Commission to receive and examine complaints concerning breaches of the provisions of the present Convention submitted by States Parties which have also made such a declaration. The Commission may decide on the appropriate measures to be taken in respect of breaches.

2. States Parties against which a complaint has been made, in accordance with paragraph 1 of the present article, shall be entitled to be represented and take part in the proceedings of the Commission.

*Article 14*. 1. The Commission shall meet at least once a year.

2. The Commission shall adopt its own rules of procedure.

3. The secretariat of the Commission shall be provided by the Secretary-General of the United Nations.

4. The meetings of the Commission shall normally be held at United Nations Headquarters.

5. The Secretary-General shall convene the initial meeting of the Commission.

*Article 15*. The Secretary-General of the United Nations shall be the depositary of the present Convention.

*Article 16*. 1. The present Convention shall be open for signature at United Nations Headquarters by all States until its entry into force.

2. The present Convention shall be subject to ratification, acceptance or approval by the signatory States.

*Article 17*. The present Convention shall be open for accession by all States.

*Article 18*. 1. The present Convention shall enter into force on the thirtieth day after the date of deposit with the Secretary-General of the United Nations of the twenty-seventh instrument of ratification, acceptance, approval or accession.

2. For each State ratifying, accepting, approving or acceding to the present Convention after its entry into force, the Convention shall enter into force on the thirtieth day after the date of deposit of the relevant instrument.

*Article 19*. Any dispute between States Parties arising out of the interpretation, application or implementation of the present Convention which is not settled by negotiation shall be brought before the International Court of Justice at the request and with the mutual consent of the States Parties to the dispute, save where the Parties to the dispute have agreed on some other form of settlement.

*Article 20*. 1. Any State Party may propose an amendment or revision to the present Convention and file it with the depositary. The Secretary-General of the United Nations shall thereupon communicate the proposed amendment or revision to the States Parties with a request that they notify him whether they favour a conference of States Parties for the purpose of considering and voting upon the proposal. In the event that at least one third of the States Parties favour such a conference, the Secretary-General shall convene the conference under the auspices of the United Nations. Any amendment or revision adopted by the majority of the States Parties present and voting at the conference shall be submitted to the General Assembly of the United Nations for approval.

2. Amendments or revisions shall come into force when they have been approved by the General Assembly and accepted by a two-thirds majority of the States Parties, in accordance with their respective constitutional processes.

3. When amendments or revisions come into force, they shall be binding on those States Parties which have accepted them, other States Parties still being bound by the provisions of the present Convention and any earlier amendment or revision which they have accepted.

*Article 21*. A State Party may withdraw from the present Convention by written notification to the depositary. Such withdrawal shall take effect one year after the date of receipt of the notification by the depositary.

*Article 22*. The present Convention has been concluded in Arabic, Chinese, English, French, Russian and Spanish, all texts being equally authentic.

## APARTHEID: INTERNATIONAL CONVENTION ON THE SUPPRESSION AND PUNISHMENT OF THE CRIME OF APARTHEID (1976).

For many years, the UN General Assembly and Security Council have periodically drawn attention to the inalienable right of the people of South Africa to self-determination and freedom and have affirmed that the practice of apartheid—the policy of racial segregation and discrimination imposed by the government upon the inhabitants of that country and, before its independence in 1989, on those of Namibia—constitutes a crime against humanity and a total negation of the purposes and principles of the United Nations Charter.

On 30 November 1973, the General Assembly adopted and opened for signature, ratification, or accession (resolution 3068 [XXVIII]) the International Convention on the Suppression and Punishment of the Crime of Apartheid, modeled after the Convention on the Prevention and Punishment of the Crime of Genocide, and urged that it be accepted and implemented without delay. The Convention entered into force on 18 July 1976.

Article 7 of the Convention calls for reports to be submitted periodically by the States parties on the legislative, administrative, or other measures that they have adopted and that give effect to the provisions of the Convention. Article 9 authorizes the appointment, by the Chairman of the UN Commission on Human Rights, of the Group of Three, consisting of three members of the Commission who are also representatives of States parties to the Convention. The Group of Three is established at each annual session of the Commission and examines and reports on the periodic reports of States parties.

The text of the Convention (annexed to General Assembly resolution 3068 [XXVIII]) is as follows:

The States Parties to the present Convention,
Recalling the provisions of the Charter of the United Nations, in which all Members pledged themselves to take joint and separate action in co-operation with the Organization for the achievement of universal respect for, and observance of, human rights and fundamental freedoms for all without distinction as to race, sex, language or religion,
Considering the Universal Declaration of Human Rights, which states that all human beings are born free and equal

in dignity and rights and that everyone is entitled to all the rights and freedoms set forth in the Declaration, without distinction of any kind, such as race, colour or national origin,

Considering the Declaration on the Granting of Independence to Colonial Countries and Peoples, in which the General Assembly stated that the process of liberation is irresistible and irreversible and that, in the interests of human dignity, progress and justice, an end must be put to colonialism and all practises of segregation and discrimination associated therewith,

Observing that, in accordance with the International Convention on the Elimination of All Forms of Racial Discrimination, States particularly condemn racial segregation and apartheid and undertake to prevent, prohibit and eradicate all practices of this nature in territories under their jurisdiction,

Observing that, in the Convention on the Prevention and Punishment of the Crime of Genocide, certain acts which may also be qualified as acts of apartheid constitute a crime under international law,

Observing that, in the Convention on the Non-Applicability of Statutory Limitations to War Crimes and Crimes Against Humanity, "inhuman acts resulting from the policy of apartheid" are qualified as crimes against humanity,

Observing that the General Assembly of the United Nations has adopted a number of resolutions in which the policies and practices of apartheid are condemned as a crime against humanity,

Observing that the Security Council has emphasized that apartheid and its continued intensification and expansion seriously disturb and threaten international peace and security,

Convinced that an International Convention on the Suppression and Punishment of the Crime of Apartheid would make it possible to take more effective measures at the international and national levels with a view to the suppression and punishment of the crime of apartheid,

Have agreed as follows:

*Article 1.* 1. The States Parties to the present Convention declare that apartheid is a crime against humanity and that inhuman acts resulting from the policies and practices of apartheid and similar policies and practices of racial segregation and discrimination, as defined in article 2 of the Convention, are crimes violating the principles of international law, in particular the purposes and principles of the Charter of the United Nations, and constituting a serious threat to international peace and security.

2. The States Parties to the present Convention declare criminal those organizations, institutions and individuals committing the crime of apartheid.

*Article 2.* For the purpose of the present Convention, the term "the crime of apartheid", which shall include similar policies and practices of racial segregation and discrimination as practised in southern Africa, shall apply to the following inhuman acts committed for the purpose of establishing and maintaining domination by one racial group of persons over any other racial group of persons and systematically oppressing them:

(a) Denial to a member or members of a racial group or groups of the right to life and liberty of person:

(i) By murder of members of a racial group or groups;

(ii) By the infliction upon the members of a racial group or groups of serious bodily or mental harm, by the infringement of their freedom or dignity, or by subjecting

them to torture or to cruel, inhuman or degrading treatment or punishment;

(iii) By arbitrary arrest and illegal imprisonment of the members of a racial group or groups;

(b) Deliberate imposition on a racial group or groups of living conditions calculated to cause its or their physical destruction in whole or in part;

(c) Any legislative measures and other measures calculated to prevent a racial group or groups from participation in the political, social, economic and cultural life of the country and the deliberate creation of conditions preventing the full development of such a group or groups, in particular by denying to members of a racial group or groups basic human rights and freedoms, including the right to work, the right to form recognized trade unions, the right to education, the right to leave and to return to their country, the right to a nationality, the right to freedom of movement and residence, the right to freedom of opinion and expression, and the right to freedom of peaceful assembly and association;

(d) Any measures, including legislative measures, designed to divide the population along racial lines by the creation of separate reserves and ghettos for the members of a racial group or groups, the prohibition of mixed marriages among members of various racial groups, the expropriation of landed property belonging to a racial group or groups or to members thereof;

(e) Exploitation of the labour of the members of a racial group or groups, in particular by submitting them to forced labour;

(f) Persecution of organizations and persons, by depriving them of fundamental rights and freedoms, because they oppose apartheid.

*Article 3.* International criminal responsibility shall apply, irrespective of the motive involved, to individuals, members of organizations and institutions and representatives of the State, whether residing in the territory of the State in which the acts are perpetrated or in some other State, whenever they:

(a) Commit, participate in, directly incite or conspire in the commission of the acts mentioned in article II of the present Convention;

(b) Directly abet, encourage or co-operate in the commission of the crime of apartheid.

*Article 4.* The States Parties to the present Convention undertake:

(a) To adopt any legislative or other measures necessary to suppress as well as to prevent any encouragement of the crime of apartheid and similar segregationist policies or their manifestations and to punish persons guilty of that crime;

(b) To adopt legislative, judicial and administrative measures to prosecute, bring to trial and punish in accordance with their jurisdiction persons responsible for, or accused of, the acts defined in article 2 of the present Convention, whether or not such persons reside in the territory of the State in which the acts are committed or are nationals of that State or of some other State or are stateless persons.

*Article 5.* Persons charged with the acts enumerated in article II of the present Convention may be tried by a competent tribunal of any State Party to the Convention which may acquire jurisdiction over the person of the accused or by an international penal tribunal having jurisdiction with respect to those States Parties which shall have accepted its jurisdiction.

*Article 6.* The States Parties to the present Convention undertake to accept and carry out in accordance with the Charter of the United Nations the decisions taken by the Security Council aimed at the prevention, suppression and punishment of the crime of apartheid, and to co-operate in the implementation of decisions adopted by other competent organs of the United Nations with a view to achieving the purposes of the Convention.

*Article 7.* 1. The States Parties to the present Convention undertake to submit periodic reports to the group established under article 9 on the legislative, judicial, administrative or other measures that they have adopted and that give effect to the provisions of the Convention.

2. Copies of the reports shall be transmitted through the Secretary-General of the United Nations to the Special Committee on Apartheid.

*Article 8.* Any State Party to the present Convention may call upon any competent organ of the United Nations to take such action under the Charter of the United Nations as it considers appropriate for the prevention and suppression of the crime of apartheid.

*Article 9.* 1. The Chairman of the Commission on Human Rights shall appoint a group consisting of three members of the Commission on Human Rights, who are also representatives of States Parties to the present Convention, to consider reports submitted by States Parties in accordance with article 7.

2. If, among the members of the Commission on Human Rights, there are no representatives of States Parties to the present Convention or if there are fewer than three such representatives, the Secretary-General of the United Nations shall, after consulting all States Parties to the Convention, designate a representative of the State Party or representatives of the States Parties which are not members of the Commission on Human Rights to take part in the work of the group established in accordance with paragraph 1 of this article, until such time as representatives of the States Parties to the Convention are elected to the Commission on Human Rights.

3. The group may meet for a period of not more than five days, either before the opening or after the closing of the session of the Commission on Human Rights, to consider the reports submitted in accordance with article 7.

*Article 10.* 1. The States Parties to the present Convention empower the Commission on Human Rights:

(a) To request United Nations organs, when transmitting copies of petitions under article 15 of the International Convention on the Elimination of All Forms of Racial Discrimination, to draw its attention to complaints concerning acts which are enumerated in article 2 of the present Convention;

(b) To prepare, on the basis of reports from competent organs of the United Nations and periodic reports from States Parties to the present Convention, a list of individuals, organizations, institutions and representatives of States which are alleged to be responsible for the crimes enumerated in article 2 of the Convention, as well as those against whom legal proceedings have been undertaken by States Parties to the Convention;

(c) To request information from the competent United Nations organs concerning measures taken by the authorities responsible for the administration of Trust and Non-Self-Governing Territories, and all other Territories to which General Assembly resolution 1514 (XV) of 14 December 1960 applies, with regard to such individuals alleged to be responsible for crimes under article 2 of the Convention

who are believed to be under their territorial and administrative jurisdiction.

2. Pending the achievement of the objectives of the Declaration on the Granting of Independence to Colonial Countries and Peoples, contained in General Assembly resolution 1514 (XV), the provisions of the present Convention shall in no way limit the right of petition granted to those peoples by other international instruments or by the United Nations and its specialized agencies.

*Article 11.* 1. Acts enumerated in article 2 of the present Convention shall not be considered political crimes for the purpose of extradition.

2. The States Parties to the present Convention undertake in such cases to grant extradition in accordance with their legislation and with the treaties in force.

*Article 12.* Disputes between States Parties arising out of the interpretation, application or implementation of the present Convention which have not been settled by negotiation shall, at the request of the States Parties to the dispute, be brought before the International Court of Justice, save where the parties to the dispute have agreed on some other form of settlement.

*Article 13.* The present Convention is open for signature by all States. Any State which does not sign the Convention before its entry into force may accede to it.

*Article 14.* 1. The present Convention is subject to ratification. Instruments of ratification shall be deposited with the Secretary-General of the United Nations.

2. Accession shall be effected by the deposit of an instrument of accession with the Secretary-General of the United Nations.

*Article 15.* 1. The present Convention shall enter into force on the thirtieth day after the date of the deposit with the Secretary-General of the United Nations of the twentieth instrument of ratification or accession.

2. For each State ratifying the present Convention or acceding to it after the deposit of the twentieth instrument of ratification or instrument of accession, the Convention shall enter into force on the thirtieth day after the date of the deposit of its own instrument of ratification or instrument of accession.

*Article 16.* A State Party may denounce the present Convention by written notification to the Secretary-General of the United Nations. Denunciation shall take effect one year after the date of receipt of the notification by the Secretary-General.

*Article 17.* 1. A request for the revision of the present Convention may be made at any time by any State Party by means of a notification in writing addressed to the Secretary-General of the United Nations.

2. The General Assembly of the United Nations shall decide upon the steps, if any, to be taken in respect of such request.

*Article 18.* The Secretary-General of the United Nations shall inform all States of the following particulars:

(a) Signatures, ratifications and accessions under articles 13 and 14;

(b) The date of entry into force of the present Convention under article 15;

(c) Denunciations under article 16;

(d) Notifications under article 17.

*Article 19.* 1. The present Convention, of which the Chinese, English, French, Russian and Spanish texts are equally authentic, shall be deposited in the archives of the United Nations.

2. The Secretary-General of the United Nations shall

transmit certified copies of the present Convention to all States.

The following year the UN Committee on the Elimination of Racial Discrimination reported the following:

The Committee considered the tenth periodic report of Algeria (CERD/C/209/Add.4) at its 962nd, 963rd and 983rd meetings, held on 4 and 18 March 1993 (see CERD/C/SR.962, 963 and 983).

The report was introduced by the representative of the State party who underlined his country's support for the fight against racism and racial discrimination and, in particular, against apartheid.

He stated that the Constitution adopted by referendum on 23 February 1989 contained new provisions providing for political pluralism, an independent judiciary and voting by secret ballot. It also prohibited all forms of racial discrimination, for which sanctions were foreseen in legislation. Although the current state of emergency represented a difficult period for Algeria, it in no way affected the country's traditional struggle against racial discrimination, nor the determination of the Algerian people to defend the cause of liberty, justice and equality.

Members of the Committee welcomed the report of the State party, which contained useful information on the constitutional and legislative basis for the implementation of the Convention. Members noted, however, that more information was needed on the actual application of the Convention, particularly in the courts, and on economic, social and demographic developments which had occurred in the country. Further information was needed on factors and difficulties encountered in the application of the Convention. Further information was also required regarding the composition of the population with regard to minorities, most notably Berbers, Tuaregs, Jews and the black population that inhabited the southern region of Algeria. With respect to the last-named group, it was pointed out that black Algerians appeared to be particularly disadvantaged in terms of access to housing and education. Members of the Committee also wished to know which minorities the Government recognized as such.

It was noted that important progress had been achieved in the application of the Convention since Algeria last presented a report in 1987, particularly as a result of the new Constitution adopted in 1989. In connection with the Constitution and national legislation in general, members wished to know what was the status of the Convention in the legal system. It was emphasized that the Convention should be accorded a status in Algerian domestic law superior to that of domestic legislation. Concern was expressed that the present state of emergency affected the exercise of fundamental rights.

With respect to article 2 of the Convention, members of the Committee wanted to know whether Algeria had adopted legislation expressly prohibiting racial discrimination and, if not, whether the Government was planning to do so. In that connection, members pointed out that the population in Algeria was sufficiently varied that special legislation on racial discrimination was necessary.

In regard to article 4, members of the Committee wished to know whether there had been acts of violence, or incitement to violence, directed against any particular racial or ethnic group; and whether racist organizations or propaganda had been declared illegal.

With regard to article 5 of the Convention, members wished to know whether there was discrimination in the field of employment. It was emphasized that statistical indicators on problems such as unemployment, delinquency and illiteracy were needed in order to determine the degree to which minorities had been socially integrated. Particular concern was expressed over the situation of the Berber minority and, in that connection, further information was requested on the extent to which they enjoyed the rights enumerated in article 5 of the Convention. Members expressed interest in the new national commission for human rights and wished to know how its members were appointed, how its independence was ensured and what role it played in addition to monitoring respect for human rights.

Concerning article 6 of the Convention, members of the Committee wished to know how many complaints of racial discrimination had been received by the competent authorities and how many sentences had been handed down for acts of racism. More complete information was required in general on the application of the Convention in the courts and the jurisprudence that had developed as a result, and on the independence of the judiciary. Members emphasized the importance of ensuring that lawyers and judges were well acquainted with the provisions of the Convention.

With respect to article 7, members of the Committee wished to have further information on the availability of instruction in their language for linguistic minorities at the primary and secondary school levels. In particular, members wished to know whether the Berber language was taught in such schools.

Members of the Committee commended Algeria as one of the States parties that had made the declaration under article 14 of the Convention recognizing the competence of the Committee to receive communications from individuals and groups of individuals alleging that their rights under the Convention had been violated. However, in view of the fact that the Committee had as yet received no communications concerning Algeria, members of the Committee wished to know what steps had been taken to make known that article of the Convention to the general public.

Replying to the questions raised by members of the Committee, the representative of the State party stated that the Algerian population was composed of Arabs, Berbers, Mozabites and Tuaregs. The Berbers lived essentially in three regions: Kabylie, a region near Algiers, where around 4 million Berbers lived; Aures, in the eastern part of the country, where there were 8 to 9 million; and in the south, where there were an additional 1 million. In view of the fact that the total population of Algeria was 23 million, it was difficult to consider the Berbers as a minority. They participated fully and on a basis of equality in Algerian life and were in no sense marginalized. With respect to their language, there was no discrimination. The Berber language, amazigh, was widely spoken in the regions where the Berbers lived, particularly in Kabylie. At the present time, however, the written language was not sufficiently structured for it to be taught in schools. There was ongoing research, particularly at the University of Tizi-Ouzou, in that regard, which would ultimately make such instruction possible. The nomads of the south, who were now often sedentary, were totally integrated and were in no way repressed. Refugees in southern Algeria were neither Algerian nor were they persecuted.

With respect to freedom of association, the prohibition by law of regionalist political parties needed to be understood within the context of conditions in Algeria at the time of independence: the end of colonial rule had been achieved with difficulty and there had been threats of secession and dismemberment of the nation when independence was achieved. In order to counter that tendency, regionalism was encouraged in terms of culture, but was discouraged as a platform for politics. There were currently 67 political parties in Algeria and over 20,000 associations of various kinds, which had full freedom to pursue their activities.

Concerning the monitoring of human rights, the Minister of Human Rights had taken office in 1992 but had subsequently been replaced by the National Commission on Human Rights (Observatoire national des droits de l'homme). The Commission was under the direct authority of the President and its administrative and financial independence were guaranteed. Non-governmental organizations were represented on the Commission, as were the Ministers of Justice and Education and representatives of the bar. Its task was to protect the fundamental human rights of citizens and provide information about human rights. It submitted an annual report on the human rights situation to the President of the National People's Assembly, which was made public two months afterwards.

With respect to education, the representative stated that it had not yet been possible to provide school courses that familiarized students with the provisions of the Convention. At present, the State was more immediately concerned with the problem of simply providing education. He expressed surprise at the mention of discrimination allegedly encountered by five black foreign students at the University of Oran. That university, like others in Algeria, had trained many black African students, including diplomats, from other countries in the region. With regard to black Algerians, their numbers were limited and they encountered no racial discrimination, including at the university.

Many young Algerians living in France had acquired French nationality in addition to Algerian nationality. An intergovernmental accord permitted them to choose in which country they preferred to perform their military service. With regard to the request that the next report of Algeria include statistical indicators and other detailed information on the situation of minorities, the representative assured the Committee that he would forward that request to his Government.

### Concluding Observations

The Committee noted with interest the legislative and institutional changes that had occurred in Algeria in recent years, which created the framework necessary for the respect of human rights in general and for preventing and combating racial discrimination.

The Committee expressed its appreciation of the spirit of openness and cooperation that characterized the report, as well as the dialogue with the representative of the Government, while expressing its concern at the difficulties of the current situation in Algeria.

Taking into account the fact that the report was oriented especially towards legislative texts, the Committee considered that the next report should contain more demographic and statistical information on social indicators reflecting, in particular, the situation of ethnic and racial groups, in particular Berbers and blacks, as well as on judicial or administrative decisions taken to give effect to the Convention. It was also considered necessary to clarify the effect of emergency measures taken by the Government with regard to the application of the Convention.

The Committee considered, in particular, that the next report should clarify the place of the Berber population in Algerian society with respect to identity, language, participation in public life and the social benefits provided for in article 5 of the Convention.

**ARAB LAWYERS' UNION.** An international nongovernmental organization in consultative status with the UN Economic and Social Council (Category II), and with UNESCO, the Union is affiliated with Bar associations in 15 countries.

Founded in Cairo in 1958, the Arab Lawyers' Union works to facilitate contacts between Arab lawyers, to assure the freedom of lawyers in their work and the independence of magistrates, and to allow all Arab lawyers to take cases in any Arab country. The Union also seeks to safeguard and develop legislative and judiciary language and to harmonize the conditions of the legal profession. The union supports the Palestine Liberation Movement and the Defence of Palestinian Resistance Workers and is engaged in founding an Arab Organization for Human Rights.

The Union publishes *Al Hakk* (The Law) in Arabic with French and English sections.

Arab Lawyers' Union. Address: 13 Ittlehad El-Mouhameen El-Arab St., Garden City, Cairo, Egypt. Telephone: (20-2) 355-71-32. Fax: (20-2) 354-77-19. Cable: UNAVAR CAIRO. Secretary-General: Farouk Mustafa Abu Eissa.

**ARAB ORGANIZATION FOR HUMAN RIGHTS.** The AOHR is a non-governmental organization in consultative status with the UN Economic and Social Council (Category II) and in observer status with the OAU's African Commission on Human and Peoples' Rights. Founded in December 1983 in Limassol, Cyprus, the AOHR calls for respect of human rights and fundamental freedoms of all citizens and individuals in Arab countries and defends those whose rights have been violated, while also providing financial assistance to the victims' families. It attempts, regardless of political considerations, to obtain the release of detained or imprisoned persons and provides legal assistance where necessary and possible. Also among AOHR's goals are improved conditions for prisoners of conscience and amnesty of persons sentenced for political reasons. In coordination with the Arab Lawyers' Union, the AOHR has launched a campaign for "Freedom for Prisoners of Conscience in the Arab World."

The Organization has members in 31 countries.

The AOHR publishes the monthly newsletters *Al-monaz-zama Alarabiya Lihoqouq Alinsan-Nashra Ikhbariya* and *Arab Organization for Human Rights Newsletter*; the quarterly *Hoquoq Alinsan Filwatan Alarabi*; and the annual *Alkitab Alsanaoui Lihoquoq Alinsan Filwatan Alarabi*.

Arab Organization for Human Rights. Address: 17 Midan Aswan, Mohandesseen, Giza 12311, Cairo, Egypt. Telephone: (20-2) 346- 6582. Fax: (20-2) 344-8166. Cable: Bassioman. Secretary-General: Mohammed Fayek.

**ARAFAT, YASSAR (1929–).** Born in Jerusalem, this Palestinian leader shared the 1994 Nobel Peace Prize with Israeli President Itzshak Rabin and Foreign Minister Shimon Perez for their peace initiative in the Middle East. Regarded by many as a terrorist, Arafat was not a universally popular choice for the Prize, even within Palestinian circles, where he is sometimes regarded as a failed leader of his people. Indeed, one member of the Nobel Committee resigned in protest over Arafat's award, citing the Palestinian's past actions as being irreconcilable with the philosophy of the Peace Prize.

Yassar Arafat was educated at Cairo University, where he led the Palestinian Students' Union and co-founded the Fatah, a Palestinian resistance group. In 1964, the Palestinian Liberation Organization (PLO) was founded; Fatah gained control of the PLO, and Arafat became the PLO's acknowledged leader. He established headquarters in Lebanon but was forced to leave in 1983, when his policies fell out of favor with the majority of the PLO. He then moved his base to Tunis. In 1988, Arafat recognized the State of Israel and renounced terrorism as a weapon in the fight for a Palestinian homeland, steps that led eventually to the opening of the peace process.

After years of Israeli occupation in the Gaza Strip and greater Jericho area, Palestinians in these areas, some 800,000 inhabitants, were granted limited self-rule in May 1994. Arafat became leader of the Palestinian Authority, which assumed control of these areas.

In citing Arafat and his co-winners for the 1994 Peace Prize, the Nobel Committee stated that "by concluding the Oslo Accords and subsequently following them up, Arafat, Perez and Rabin made substantial contributions to a historic process through which peace and cooperation can replace war and hate." When notified of his Prize, Arafat stated, "The prize is . . . for my people who have suffered much, for our martyrs, for our prisoners, for our children, so we can have a lasting peace." In accepting the Peace Prize at the December 1994 ceremonies in Oslo, Norway, Arafat stated that the negotiations between the PLO and Israel were the "first glance of the crescent moon of

peace." He called for the peace talks to be accelerated, for donor countries to make good on their financial help to the newly autonomous Gaza Strip and Jericho, and for the future of Jerusalem and of Israeli settlements on the West Bank to be settled.

**ARBITRARY ARREST, DETENTION, OR EXILE.** Freedom from arbitrary arrest, detention, or exile is a fundamental freedom proclaimed in article 9 of the **UNIVERSAL DECLARATION OF HUMAN RIGHTS.** The meaning and scope of this freedom is clarified in the **INTERNATIONAL COVENANT ON CIVIL AND POLITICAL RIGHTS** in the following provision:

*Article 9.* 1. Everyone has the right to liberty and security of person. No one shall be subjected to arbitrary arrest or detention. No one shall be deprived of his liberty except on such grounds and in accordance with such procedures as are established by law.

2. Anyone who is arrested shall be informed, at the time of arrest, of the reasons for his arrest and shall be promptly informed of any charges against him.

3. Anyone arrested or detained on a criminal charge shall be brought promptly before a judge or other officer authorized by law to exercise judicial power and shall be entitled to trial within a reasonable time or to release. It shall not be the general rule that persons awaiting trial shall be detained in custody, but release may be subject to guarantees to appear for trial, at any other stage of the judicial proceedings, and, should occasion arise, for execution of the judgement.

4. Anyone who is deprived of his liberty by arrest or detention shall be entitled to take proceedings before a court, in order that that court may decide without delay on the lawfulness of his detention and order his release if the detention is not lawful.

5. Anyone who has been the victim of unlawful arrest or detention shall have an enforceable right to compensation.

The **AMERICAN CONVENTION ON HUMAN RIGHTS,** open for acceptance by member States of the **ORGANIZATION OF AMERICAN STATES,** provides that:

1. Every person has the right to personal liberty and security.

2. No one shall be deprived of his physical liberty except for the reasons and under the conditions established beforehand by the constitution of the State Party concerned or by a law established pursuant thereto.

3. No one shall be subject to arbitrary arrest or imprisonment.

4. Anyone who is detained shall be informed of the reasons for his detention and shall be promptly notified of the charge or charges against him.

5. Any person detained shall be brought promptly before a judge or other officer authorized by law to exercise judicial power and shall be entitled to trial within a reasonable time or to be released without prejudice to the continuation of the proceedings. His release may be subject to guarantees to assure his appearance for trial.

6. Anyone who is deprived of his liberty shall be entitled to recourse to a competent court, in order that the court

may decide without delay on the lawfulness of his arrest or detention and order his release if the arrest or detention is unlawful. In State Parties whose laws provide that anyone who believes himself to be threatened with deprivation of his liberty is entitled to recourse to a competent court in order that it may decide on the lawfulness of such threat, this remedy may not be restricted or abolished. The interested party or another person in his behalf is entitled to seek these remedies.

7. No one shall be detained for debt. This principle shall not limit the orders of a competent judicial authority issued for nonfulfillment of duties of support.

The **AFRICAN CHARTER ON HUMAN AND PEOPLES' RIGHTS,** open for acceptance by member States of the **ORGANIZATION OF AFRICAN UNITY,** provides that:

Every individual shall have the right to liberty and to the security of his person. No one may be deprived of his freedom except for reasons and conditions previously laid down by law. In particular, no one may be arbitrarily arrested or detained.

The **EUROPEAN CONVENTION ON HUMAN RIGHTS,** open for acceptance by members of the Council of Europe, provides that:

1. Everyone has the right to liberty and security of person. No one shall be deprived of his liberty save in the following cases and in accordance with a procedure prescribed by law;
   a. the lawful detention of a person after conviction by a competent court;
   b. the lawful arrest or detention of a person for non-compliance with the lawful order of a court or in order to secure the fulfilment of any obligation prescribed by law;
   c. the lawful arrest or detention of a person effected for the purpose of bringing him before the competent legal authority on reasonable suspicion of having committed an offence or when it is reasonably considered necessary to prevent his committing an offence or fleeing after having done so;
   d. the detention of a minor by lawful order for the purpose of educational supervision or his lawful detention for the purpose of bringing him before the competent legal authority;
   e. the lawful detention of persons for the prevention of the spreading of infectious diseases, of persons of unsound mind, alcoholics or drug addicts or vagrants;
   f. the unlawful arrest or detention of a person to prevent his effecting an unauthorised entry into the country or of a person against whom action is being taken with a view to deportation or extradition.

2. Everyone who is arrested shall be informed promptly, in a language which he understands, of the reasons for his arrest and of any charge against him.

3. Everyone arrested or detained in accordance with the provisions of paragraph 1(c) of this Article shall be brought promptly before a judge or other officer authorised by law to exercise judicial power and shall be entitled to trial within a reasonable time or to release pending trial. Release may be conditioned by guarantees to appear for trial.

4. Everyone who is deprived of his liberty by arrest or detention shall be entitled to take proceedings by which the lawfulness of his detention shall be decided speedily by a court and his release ordered if the detention is not lawful.

5. Everyone who has been the victim of arrest or detention in contravention of the provisions of this Article shall have an enforceable right to compensation.

***COMMENTS ON ARTICLE 9 OF THE INTERNATIONAL COVENANT ON CIVIL AND POLITICAL RIGHTS.*** In 1982, after examining reports submitted by States parties to the International Covenant on Civil and Political Rights in accordance with its article 40, the UN **HUMAN RIGHTS COMMITTEE** adopted the following general comments on article 9 (UN Doc. A/37/40, Annex V, para. 1 and 2):

Article 9, which deals with the right to liberty and security of persons, has often been somewhat narrowly understood in reports by States parties, and they have therefore given incomplete information. The Committee points out that paragraph 1 is applicable to all deprivations of liberty, whether in criminal cases or in other cases such as, for example, mental illness, vagrancy, drug addiction, educational purposes, immigration control, etc. It is true that some of the provisions of article 9 (part of paragraph 2 and the whole of paragraph 3) are only applicable to persons against whom criminal charges are brought. But the rest, and in particular the important guarantees laid down in paragraph 4, i.e. the right to control by a court of the legality of the detention, applies to all persons deprived of their liberty by arrest or detention. Furthermore, States parties have in accordance with article 2 (3) also to ensure that an effective remedy is provided in other cases in which an individual claims to be deprived of his liberty in violation of the Covenant.

Paragraph 3 of article 9 requires that in criminal cases any person arrested or detained has to be brought "promptly" before a judge or other officer authorized by law to exercise judicial power. More precise time limits are fixed by law in most States parties and, in the view of the Committee, delays must not exceed a few days. Many States have given insufficient information about the actual practices in this respect.

***STUDY OF THE RIGHT TO LIBERTY.*** In 1956, eight years after the Universal Declaration of Human Rights had proclaimed the right of everyone to liberty and ten years before the International Covenant on Civil and Political Rights had been adopted, the UN Commission on Human Rights determined that no study of the practical effects of denial of the right to liberty had been undertaken on an international scale and decided that such a study was justified and necessary. It appointed a committee, composed of four of its members, to prepare the study.

The Committee carried out its task on the basis of information provided by the Secretary-General, the governments of member States, and the competent intergovernmental and non-governmental organizations. It submitted the Study of the Right of Everyone to be Free from Arbitrary Arrest, Detention and Exile (UN publication, Sales no. 65.XIV.2) to the Commission on Human Rights in 1962.

The Study concentrates largely on procedural laws governing deprivation of liberty prior to, or other than by, a final court sentence in criminal proceedings. For purposes of the Study, the Committee defined "arrest" to mean the act of taking a person into custody under the authority of the law or by compulsion of another kind and to include the period from the moment he is placed under restraint up to the time he is brought before an authority competent to order his continued custody or to release him. It defined "detention" to mean the act of confining a person to a certain place, whether or not in continuation of arrest, and under restraints which prevent him from living with his family or carrying out his normal occupational or social activities. "Exile" was applied to (a) the expulsion or exclusion of a person from the country of which he is a national and (b) the banishment of a person within the country by way of forcible removal from the place of residence.

Regarding the word "arbitrary," it was understood that one of the results of the study would be a definition of that word. For the purpose of the study, however, the Committee adopted the following definition: An arrest or detention is arbitrary if it is (a) on grounds or in accordance with procedures other than those established by law or (b) under the provisions of a law the purpose of which is incompatible with respect for the right to liberty and security of person.

As requested by the Commission on Human Rights (resolution 2 [XVII]), the Committee formulated its conclusions as a series of draft principles on freedom from arbitrary arrest and detention. Because exile as a form of punishment appeared at that time to have virtually disappeared, the Committee did not consider it necessary to include provisions regulating that situation; however, the Committee refrained from proposing the complete abolition of exile on the ground that, in certain cases (e.g., voluntary exile in lieu of incarceration for political offenses), it may be more humane than incarceration or other more severe measures.

The Commission on Human Rights decided, at its 1962 session (resolution 2 [XVIII]), to transmit the draft principles to member States and to the specialized agencies for their comments. At the same time, it called upon the Committee to proceed with a closely related study of the right of arrested persons to communicate with those whom it is necessary for them to consult in order to ensure their defense or to protect their essential interests.

Both studies were considered by the Commission at its 1969 session. Noting that the second study (UN Doc. E/CN.4/996) proposed that certain modifications be made in the draft principles set out in the first, the Commission again sought the comments of the governments and agencies concerned.

The Commission did not consider the subject further until 1975, when it called upon the UN SUB-COM-MISSION ON PREVENTION OF DISCRIMINATION AND PROTECTION OF MINORITIES (resolution 10 [XXXII]) to examine the relevant documentation and to draw up a body of principles for the protection of all persons under any form of detention or imprisonment.

The Sub-Commission completed the draft of such a body of principles in 1978, and the UN Economic and Social Council requested the Secretary-General (resolution 1979/34) to forward it to the General Assembly, together with the comments of governments thereon.

In 1980 the UN General Assembly referred the question to its Third (Social, Humanitarian and Cultural) Committee, in which an open-ended working group was set up to elaborate a final version of the principles. The working group was unable to complete its work in 1980; and, since 1981, the Assembly has referred the question to its Sixth (Legal) Committee, where similar open-ended working groups were set up annually until 1988.

The working group that met during the 43d session (1988) of the Assembly completed the elaboration of the draft Body of Principles for the Protection of All Persons Under Any Form of Detention or Imprisonment. On its recommendation, and that of the Sixth Committee, the Assembly approved on 9 December 1988 (resolution 43/173) the Body of Principles for the Protection of All Persons Under Any Form of Detention or Imprisonment. It requested the Secretary-General to inform the members of the United Nations or members of specialized agencies of the adoption of the Body of Principles and urged that all efforts be made so that the Principles become generally known and respected.

Meanwhile, the Sub-Commission on Prevention of Discrimination and Protection of Minorities continues the annual review of developments relating to the human rights of persons subjected to any form of detention or imprisonment, initiated in 1974 (resolution 7 [XXVII]). The review is conducted at each session of the Sub-Commission by its Working Group on Detention. Issues given particular attention include (a) prolonged or indefinite detention of large numbers of unconvicted persons without formal charges brought against them; (b) the necessity of impartial judicial control over arrest and detention practices; (c) the lack of, or ineffectiveness of, judicial control over arrest and detention practices; (d) the role of secret police and paramilitary organizations; and (e) the position of the family and relatives of arrested and detained persons.

**A**

*SEE ALSO* Disappearances; Law Enforcement; Prisoners.

**BIBLIOGRAPHY.** United Nations Committee on the Right of Everyone to Be Free from Arbitrary Arrest, Detention and Exile. *Study of the Right of Arrested Persons to Communicate with Those Whom It Is Necessary for Them to Consult in Order to Ensure Their Defence or to Protect Their Essential Interests.* UN Doc. E/CN.4/996). UN report, available in official languages.

————. *Study of the Right of Everyone to Be Free from Arbitrary Arrest, Detention and Exile.* New York: 1962. UN publication, Sales no. E.65.XIV.2. UN report, available in official languages.

United Nations Sub-Commission on Prevention of Discrimination and Protection of Minorities. *Application of International Standards Concerning the Human Rights of Detained Juveniles: Report Prepared by the Special Rapporteur, Mrs. Mary Concepción Bautista, Pursuant to Sub-Commission Resolution 1990/21.* Geneva, Switzerland: 1991. IGO document, in English and French.

————. *Report on the Practice of Administrative Detention, Submitted by Mr. Louis Joinet.* Geneva, Switzerland: 1990. IGO document, in English and French.

————. *The Right to a Fair Trial: Current Recognition and Measures Necessary for Its Strengthening: Second Report Prepared by Mr. Stanislav Chernichenko and Mr. William Treat in Accordance With Resolution 1990/18 of the Sub-Commission and Resolution 1991/43 of the Commission on Human Rights.* Geneva, Switzerland: 1991. IGO document, in English and French.

**ARGENTINA.** The Argentine Republic is a country in temperate South America, on the Atlantic Ocean. It has borders with Bolivia, Brazil, Chile, Paraguay, and Uruguay. It achieved independence from Spain in 1816 and became a member of the United Nations in 1945. Its population is estimated to be 32,950,000. Ethnic groups include persons of Spanish, Italian, Lebanese, Syrian, and South American origin, and an indigenous population of about 50,000. Languages in common use include Spanish (official), English, Italian, Portuguese, and German. Religions practiced include Christianity (Roman Catholic, 92%; Protestant denominations, 2%), Judaism (2%), and others (2%). Under article 2 of the national constitution, the federal government supports the Roman Catholic Apostolic Church. Literacy is estimated at 95%.

The government (1994) took the form of a republic. It is a federal union of 22 provinces, one national territory, and one federal district. Under the constitution of 1994, the president and vice-president are elected by popular vote through an electoral college, each for a term of four years. The president and his cabinet together exercise executive authority. Legislation is prepared by the 254-member Chamber of Deputies and the 46-member Senate. Active political parties include the Radical Civic Union and the Justicialista (Peronist) Party. The 1994 Constitution, which replaced that of 1853, also granted greater independence to the judiciary.

Argentina experienced an extended period of violations of human rights under Juan Peron, the military dictator who absorbed many fascist ideas in the Italy of Mussolini and who collaborated with Germany through most of World War II. Overwhelmingly victorious in the election of February 1946, shortly after Argentina had belatedly entered the war on the side of the allies and had become a member of the United Nations, Peron established a regime based on the support of reactionaries, the army, nationalists, and clerical groups which curtailed all political and civil rights and created concentration camps for dissenters.

In 1960, Adolf Eichman was taken from Argentina, where he had found asylum, to Israel where he was put on trial for war crimes. At a meeting of the UN Security Council on 22 June, the Foreign Minister of Israel recognized that the persons who had captured Eichman had broken the laws of Argentina and apologized for this act, which Israel believed should be seen in the light of the "exceptional and unique character of the crimes attributed to Eichman." The Council called for "appropriate reparation" on the part of Israel, to which the Foreign Minister replied that, in the view of his government, its expression of regret constituted adequate reparation.

*"THE DIRTY WAR."* During the period between 1976 and 1983, military regimes were responsible for a "dirty war" within the country that took the lives of nearly 9,000 people and included the torture of many more. Military rule was discredited and collapsed after an unsuccessful campaign to seize the Falkland Islands (Malvinas) from Great Britain.

The civilian government that replaced the junta on 12 December 1983 has experienced difficulties in establishing and maintaining firm control over "the colonels" and in adopting the measures necessary to promote and protect the enjoyment of civil, political, economic, social and cultural rights. Shortly after he assumed the presidency, in 1983, Raul Alfonsin defied the military to support the trial and conviction of five former armed forces commanders, two of them former presidents, on charges of human rights violations during the "dirty war." After these trials were over, however, the military and other elements called for a general amnesty, which would prevent the trials from going deeper into the officer ranks. In December 1986, President Alfonsin, citing a desire for national reconciliation and a "military threat" to resume control of the country, supported passage of a law that set tight timetables for thousands of cases which had not reached the courts. The result was that fewer than 150 cases could be brought to trial, and no further charges or investigations were permitted.

***DISAPPEARANCES AND AMNESTY.*** In explanation of the policy followed during the past decade with respect to the tracing of persons who had disappeared under the military regime (1976–1983) and bringing to justice those responsible for those disappearances, the Government of Argentina pointed out, in a note verbale dated 22 January 1993 (E/CN.4/1994/26), that two main factors had influenced its actions: political considerations and legal considerations:

[Political Considerations.] At the outset, it should be recalled that Dr. Raúl Alfonsín assumed leadership of the government in December 1983 after eight years of de facto governments. Through his election, one demand came to the fore, which was that the penal mechanisms provided by a State governed by the rule of law should be reinstituted.

The citizens regained control of the institutions of the Republic, but at a time of deep political, social and economic crisis, and they had no choice but to live side by side in the State with representatives of a regime that had given its stamp of approval to impunity. Consequently, the civil authorities, bound by the legal constraints of a State subject to the rule of law, which by definition gives full scope to pluralism and all kinds of power struggles, had to confront major political dilemmas whenever decisions were to be taken.

The Alfonsín Government helped to ensure that formal standards and institutions took precedence over the operative rules and machinery of social conflict. The members of the judiciary—who had also occupied the same positions under the military regime—were made responsible for healing—in their own way—the wounds inflicted on Argentine society by the military governments. Consequently, when the time came to apportion blame, political concerns took second place to legal ones.

But, in fact, the determining factor where justice was concerned proved to be the actual relationship between the political, economic and social forces.

In 1983, the democratic Government was faced with a dilemma in the form of, on the one hand, the self-amnesty law that had been enacted by the last government of the dictatorship, and on the other, the electoral campaign promise that the guilty would be tried and punished. It was, thus, torn between the claim to total impunity and a desire to apply the Penal Act to the fullest extent in order to punish the crimes committed by the political repression. That dilemma was not to be settled in the lawcourts alone.

As early as January 1984, through a legislative amendment to the Code of Military Justice, the civilian Government had been obliged to resort to the expedient of having the persons responsible for State terrorism tried by the military courts, in an attempt to set in motion a purge of the armed forces from within, thereby sparing the incipient democracy traumatic situations later on. The prosecutions ordered by the President of the Nation in his capacity as Commander-in-Chief, based on the irrefutable evidence brought by CONADEP, led to attempted insubordination on the part of the leaders and to deliberate delays by the military courts designed to thwart the process of reconciliation.

The cases had to be referred to the ordinary lawcourts:

they were brought successively before the Federal Court of Appeals and the Supreme Court of Justice.

Even before the trial of the commanding officers, it had become clear how far the prevailing political situation would allow opposing views to be reconciled and a firm and lasting peace to be built that would entail the unconditional application of justice.

Subsequently, there were acts of insubordination and threats against the institutional order and disturbing expressions of disagreement among the officers of the armed forces, which often had the approval of the spokesmen of the establishment, who then, as now, controlled the mass media and the mainsprings of economic power. The riots and armed rebellions came later, centering chiefly on Monte Caseros and Villa Martelli.

The State was also subjected to pressure from the World Bank, which demanded solutions to the formidable external debt problem that the democratic regime had inherited from the administration of the dictatorship, while the national economic groups refused to submit to the discipline needed to execute the Government's internal adjustment programmes. This led to the so-called golpes blancos, which triggered burst of runaway inflation.

The Punto Final (General Amnesty) and Obediencia Debida (Due Obedience) laws were enacted against this background of conflict. The first law granted a fixed-term amnesty to the soldiers who had not yet been tried; the second wiped out crimes committed by junior officers of all the armed and security forces whether they had been tried or not.

The relationship between the social forces was such that it considerably lessened the possibility of imposing justice, and the people became less insistent in their demands, having become resigned to the need to avoid putting any pressure on the Government that might endanger democratic stability.

The full price of peace and of the maintenance of the rule of law had not yet been paid when Raúl Alfonsín had to hand over the presidency to the newly elected Carlos Menem.

Although justice continued to be a legitimate aspiration, along with suitable punishment for those found guilty of human rights violations, by the time the situation became settled, the goals originally pursued had been considerably debased.

The pardon granted to the commanding officers was an inevitable consequence of previous legal and political developments and grew out of the national and international context in which the Government was working where the balance of social forces left no room for intransigence. Sorrowfully, the Peronists and indeed society as a whole accepted it, because they were aware of the difficulties involved in reconciling peace and justice after the bloody carapintada (painted faces) uprising of 1990. In that situation, Dr. Menem, in the exercise of his leadership and of his constitutional powers, chose to establish priorities and to stem the conflict.

The price to be paid for resolving a contradiction fraught with risks for the rule of law was, however, the lowest possible one: the President assumed sole responsibility for pardoning and releasing from prison the agents of repression who had been brought to justice and who remained guilty and convicted of their crimes. . . .

[Legal Considerations.] In order to be consistent with the theory that the guilty should stand trial, it would have been necessary to place in an infinite number of docks the direct and indirect perpetrators and their necessary co-perpetrators and partners, accomplices and accessories. Within these categories, the weight of the law would have had to be brought to bear upon the majority of the officers and non-commissioned officers of the three armed and security forces, and even the recruits involved in the illegal acts. Furthermore, the investigations would have revealed the full extent of responsibility of thousands of civil servants in the central government, the prison, municipal and hospital administration, and of all the institutions that had been involved in the repression, in addition to thousands of civilian accessories. To have met the demand would have triggered chaos.

The first step taken by the government to avoid this was the enactment of the General Amnesty Law. Its effect was to stem the avalanche of complaints concerning all kinds of illegal acts, which threatened to obstruct the work that society wanted the judiciary to perform. In this way, the political authorities managed to extricate themselves from an awkward situation, but at a price: the objective limitations of the judicial system were exposed to view, and it became clear that it was a mistake to make the criminal courts responsible for settling a political and social conflict.

The other decision that paved the way for impunity was the Due Obedience Law. The mass of suspects was, thus, reduced to the commanding officers of the government Juntas, and a host of guilty persons was, thus, spared having to appear before the lawcourts.

The trial of the nine commanding officers put an end to the idea that all those responsible should be punished. Reason and the bare facts showed that this was unreasonable and indeed physically impracticable. No one today can demand the impossible.

It did not require extraordinary imagination to foresee the consequences of the election promise to have all the guilty tried and punished, but when the time came to carry it out, there was no escaping the conclusion that such a procedure was not feasible, with the result that the disappointment and discontent of the multitudes who had been living in the false hope of an unattainable utopia would not have been long in erupting.

Regarding the fate of the persons who "disappeared" between 1976 and 1993, the UN Working Group on Enforced or Involuntary Disappearances reported to the 1994 session of the UN Commission on Human Rights (UN Doc. E/CN.4/1994/26) that, since 1981, the Working Group had transmitted 3,462 cases to the Government of Argentina and had received 2,947 responses. It considered only 43 of the cases to have been clarified by the Government's response (13 persons arrested and released, 19 children located, and 11 bodies located and identified). Thirty-three (33) other cases had been clarified by non-governmental sources (seven persons released from detention, nine children located, and 13 bodies located and identified). One new case of a disappeared person, however, was reported to have occurred in 1993.

***DISAPPEARANCE OF CHILDREN.*** The special situation of children who "disappeared" in Argentina during the period from 1974 to 1981 was drawn to the attention of the UN Commission on Human Rights by its Working Group on Enforced or Involuntary Disappearances in the Working Group's first report, submitted to the Commission in 1981 (UN Doc. E/CN.4/1435 and Add. 1) in the following terms (para. 171):

Most of the cases of the reported disappearance of children in Argentina relate to children born or presumed to be born of mothers who were themselves missing and reportedly held in secret detention centres at the time of their delivery. In a number of cases, information about the fact of delivery is provided by people who report having been themselves detained in such centres and to have direct knowledge of the birth. According to the information received, a large number of women—many of them pregnant—were held in one particular detention centre which reportedly had some facilities to attend to women in childbirth. In other cases, it is reported that women were taken to a military hospital for the birth. The reports in a number of cases, indicate that children born in the above circumstances were handed over to relatives, generally their grandparents. This information coincides with that provided by relatives of pregnant women reported missing to the effect that they were given new-born babies by members of the security forces or civilians who informed them that the person reported missing had given birth to the child; the relatives were warned not to make any inquiries or comments on the matter. . . . The Group also received reports relating to children who were abducted together with the parents and are still missing. Reports of cases of disappearance of minors who were reportedly arrested on their own were also received.

In 1984, the Argentine National Commission on the Disappearances of Persons, following its investigation into thousands of disappearances that had occurred in Argentina between 1974 and 1981, reported that:

(1) the forcible removal of a child from his legitimate family and his placement in another family environment chosen according to an ideological view of "what is needed to save him" is a treacherous usurpation of roles;
(2) the oppressors who removed the children from their homes or from their mothers at the time of birth decided the fate of those babies as coldly as someone dispensing of the spoils of war;
(3) the missing children, who have been stripped of their identity and taken away from their relatives, are, and will continue for a long time to be, a deep open wound in our society. A blow has been struck at the helpless, vulnerable and innocent, thus creating a new type of torture.

At the time the report was issued, the "Grandmothers of the Plaza de Mayo" (Abuelas de Plaza de Mayo) an organization established by the grandmothers of the missing children, knew of 172 children who had been detained together with their parents, or born during their mothers' captivity, and had not been returned to their families. A number of the children were later located in Paraguay, Uruguay, Chile, and other South American countries, their identity being confirmed by hemogenetic tests.

In 1987, the SUB-COMMISSION ON PREVENTION OF DISCRIMINATION AND PROTECTION OF MINORITIES expressed deep concern (decision 1987/107) over reports concerning the critical situation of disappeared children in Argentina who had been located in Paraguay, sometimes living in the homes of military officers who had been involved in the torture or murder of their parents, and requested its chairman to appoint one of its members to establish and maintain contact with the competent authorities and institutions, including humanitarian organizations, which would report to him on the situation and ensure that there are no further risks of disappearances; and to request the authorities concerned to facilitate his task.

The Commission on Human Rights endorsed this request (resolution 1988/76) and Mr. Theo van Boven (Netherlands) was appointed to carry out the mandate of the Sub-Commission. He visited Argentina in July 1988 and received the cooperation of the authorities concerned and of the many interested organizations and individuals. He was unable, however, to visit Paraguay at that time because the Paraguayan government indicated that the question of the children was under examination by the courts and that, under these circumstances, such a visit could be considered as interference in the judicial process. In this connection, the Government of Paraguay stated that, in all those cases in which extradition had been requested by the Argentine Government, there had been a ruling by the courts of first and second instance agreeing to the request. However, the cases had still to be examined by the supreme court.

In his report to the Sub-Commission (UN Doc./ CN.4/Sub.2/1988/19), Mr. van Boven described a number of cases of disappearance of children, and indicates how they were kidnapped, sometimes as a result of the collaboration and complicity of the security forces of more than one country. In this connection, he reported that:

During the proceedings instituted by the current Government of Argentina against the members of the three military juntas during whose term of office most of the 8,961 disappearances recorded by the National Commission on the Disappearance of Persons occurred, specific and concordant evidence was brought to the attention of the population of Argentina and of the world concerning the existence of repressive machinery operated by the military and designed systematically to eliminate not only the members of armed organizations, but also members of the opposition and their families and relatives, inasmuch as they might carry the possible seeds of the opposition's continuity. The eradication of a certain type of opposition in Argentine society was the objective that led to repressive practices of a genocidal nature based on the political ideas of the victims and on those of their families and close relatives.

The disappearances of very young children and of children born during their mothers' captivity was [sic] part of this scheme. The children of "subversive elements" should not be returned to their families, since they might then grow up in the same moral and political environment that had made their parents "subversive elements." It was therefore necessary "to hand them over" to other persons who would offer them an environment in keeping with the oppressors' ideology.

*THE GRANDMOTHERS OF THE PLAZA DE MAYO.* Mr. van Boven also described (para. 17–23) the activities of the group of Argentine women known as the Grandmothers of the Plaza de Mayo (Abuelas de Plaza de Mayo), organized to locate and facilitate the return of the "disappeared" children:

Like the Mothers of the Plaza de Mayo, the Grandmothers started looking for their children and grandchildren as soon as the disappearances began. Some of them knew that their children had been murdered and that only their grandchildren could give them back something of the lives that had been taken away from them. Others have so far been unable to find out exactly what happened to their children, but they do know that their grandchildren are in the hands of the persons responsible for the murder or disappearance of the parents or in the hands of officials, former officials and other persons involved in crimes connected with enforced or involuntary disappearances.

From the very beginning, the Grandmothers of the Plaza de Mayo worked with persistence and courage to find their grandchildren. Over the years and, as a result of their untiring efforts and appeals for national and international solidarity, the Grandmothers managed to set up an organization that has a computer system for the processing of information which is received from all types of sources inside and outside the country. The Grandmothers also have teams of legal advisers, as well as teams of doctors and psychologists, which perform specific functions in connection with the search and recovery of missing children and the medical and psychological treatment required by the children who are returned to their legitimate families. The author of this report met during his mission with members of these teams and discussed with them the nature and the results of their work. He was also deeply moved by his meeting with some of the now eleven and twelve year old children who after their disappearance are reunited with their legitimate families.

With the assistance of the American Association for the Advancement of the Sciences, the Grandmothers of the Plaza de Mayo succeeded in introducing in Argentina the use of genetic analyses to determine kinship with the highest degree of certainty. This method, which was already being used in other countries to establish kinship, was used for the first time in Argentina to determine a child's relationship with its biological family in the absence of the parents. A team of Argentine doctors was trained to conduct genetic analyses to determine a child's real family.

As a result of their painstaking and untiring efforts, the Grandmothers of the Plaza de Mayo have acquired quite rightly considerable national and international prestige and have been able to find 42 children. The finding of the children is, however, not, as it should be, always the happy outcome of a difficult search; in some cases, as is also evident from the mandate given to the author of the present report, it marks the beginning of the arduous task of ensuring that the children are returned to their legitimate families.

The families of the children who were located had to institute and endure lengthy judicial proceedings during which they could not always count on the determination of the judges, some of whom were far too slow and did not use all the legal remedies available for the children's prompt return.

According to the Grandmothers of the Plaza de Mayo, delays in proceedings and the failure by the competent State agencies to keep watch on those who had appropriated the children enabled some of them to leave the country and take away the children being sought by their legitimate families.

**BIBLIOGRAPHY.** Abuelas de Plaza de Mayo (Grandmothers of Plaza de Mayo). *Information* 10 (September 1986): 1–15. NGO bulletin, in Spanish.

Academia de Humanismo Cristiano (Academy of Christian Humanism). "Violacion de Derechos Humanos y Democratization en Argentina" (Violation of Human Rights and Democratization in Argentina), *Chilean Review of Human Rights* 2, no. 4 (1985): 14–27. Journal article, in Spanish.

Agosin, Majorie. "A Visit to the Mothers of the Plaza de Mayo," *Human Rights Quarterly* 9, no. 3 (August 1987): 426–435. Scholarly article, in English.

Americas Watch. *Truth and Partial Justice in Argentina: An Update.* New York: Human Rights Watch, 1991. NGO factfinding report, in English.

Americas Watch and Centro de Estudios Legales y Sociales (Centre for Legal and Social Studies). *Police Violence in Argentina: Torture and Police Killings in Buenos Aires.* New York: Human Rights Watch, 1991. NGO factfinding report, in English.

Amnesty International. *Argentina: The Military Juntas and Human Rights, Report of the Trial of the Former Junta Members.* London: 1987. NGO report, in English.

Anderson, Martin Edwin. *Dossier Secreto: Argentina's Desaparecidos and the Myth of the "Dirty War."* Boulder, CO, USA: Westview Press, 1993. Scholarly monograph, in English; bibliography, pp. 376–386.

Comision Nacional sobre la Desaparicion de Personas (National Commission on the Disappeared). *Nunca Mas: The Report of the Argentine National Commission on the Disappeared.* New York: Farrar Straus Giroux and Index on Censorship, 1986. Government report, in English.

Crawford, Kathryn Lee. "Due Obedience and the Rights of Victims: Argentina's Transition to Democracy," *Human Rights Quarterly* 12, no. 1 (Feb. 1990): 17–52. Scholarly article, in English.

Frühling E., Hugo. *El Movimiento de Derechos Humanos y la Transición Democrática en Chile y Argentina* (The Human Rights Movement and the Democratic Transition in Chile and Argentina). Santiago, Chile: Programa de Derechos Humanos, Universidad Academia de Humanismo Cristiano, 1990. Scholarly article, in Spanish.

Garro, A. M., and H. Dahl. "Legal Accountability for Human Rights Violations in Argentina: One Step Forward and Two Steps Back," *Human Rights Law Journal* 8, pts. 2–4 (1987): 283–344. Scholarly article, in English.

Giorgi, Alicia. *Caso Giorgi: A los Hijos de un Detenido-Desaparecido* (The Giorgi Case: To the Children of a Detained-Disappeared Person). Buenos Aires, Argentina: 1990. Monograph, in Spanish.

Oficina de Solidaridad para Exiliados Argentinos (Office of Solidarity for Argentine Exiles). *Reencuentro.* Buenos Aires, Argentina: 1986. NGO bulletin, in Spanish.

Partnoy, Alicia. *The Little School: Tales of Disappearance and Survival in Argentina.* Pittsburgh, PA, USA: Cleis Press, 1986. Collection of essays, in English.

Pion-Berlin, David. "The Ideological Governance of Perception in the Use of State Terror in Latin America: The Case of Argentina," in *State-Organized Terror: The Case of Violent Internal Repression,* ed. P. T. Bushnell et al., pp. 135–152. Boulder, CO, USA: Westview Press, 1991. Scholarly article, in English; bibliography, pp. 150–152.

Poneman, Daniel. *Argentina: Democracy on Trial.* New York: Paragon House, 1987. Scholarly monograph, in English.

Servicio Paz y Justicia—Argentina (Service for Peace and Justice—Argentina). *The Argentine Military Crisis: A Preliminary Balance.* Buenos Aires, Argentina: 1988. NGO report, in English.

Simpson, John, and Jana Bennett. *The Disappeared and the Mothers of the Plaza.* New York: St. Martin's Press, 1985. Scholarly monograph, in English.

**ARIAS SÀNCHEZ, OSCAR (1941–).** This former president of Costa Rica won the 1987 Nobel Peace Prize for his work in arbitrating a longstanding dispute between Central American neighboring states. Arias Sànchez was born in Heredia, Costa Rica; and was educated at the Colegio Saint Francis in Moravia, Boston University in the United States (medicine), University of Costa Rica (law), the London School of Economics, and the University of Essex in Great Britain (doctorate in economics). He was a professor at the University of Costa Rica from 1969 to 1972. From 1972 to 1977, he was Costa Rica's minister of planning; he later served as general secretary of his National Liberation Party. In addition, throughout the 1970s and 1980s, Arias Sànchez served in many other national and academic positions. He is also the author of many books, including *Grupos de Presión en Costa Rica* (1970); *Democracia, Independencia y Sociedad Latinoamericana* (1977); and *Nuevos Rumbos para el Desarrollo Costarricense* (1980).

In Costa Rica, Arias Sànchez worked for a socialistic program of distribution of wealth, which included government-sponsored education, health, and housing programs and consumer and producer cooperatives. He also maintained the policy of neutrality that his presidential predecessor Luis Alberto Monge had forged in relation to Costa Rica's Central American neighbors, especially the strife-torn El Salvador and Nicaragua. Regarding the situation in Nicaragua, in particular, Arias Sànchez felt that then-president Daniel Ortega Saavedra led a repressive regime that had not been democratically elected, yet he also felt that the United States should not be funding the "Contra" rebels in that country.

Two months after his election as president, Arias Sànchez brought together the presidents of Guatemala, El Salvador, Honduras, and Nicaragua in a Central American summit conference to discuss the so-called Contadora Peace Accord. No official agreement was ever reached, largely because of disagreements regarding arms control and limits on international military maneuvers in the region, but the declaration called for continued dialogue to enhance democracy and pluralism in Central America, to promote regional cooperation for social and economic development, and to establish means for resolving neighboring tensions without outside interference.

In February 1987, Arias Sànchez proposed a new ten-point peace plan, based on the Contadora Accord but broader in scope, to the presidents of Honduras, Guatemala, and El Salvador. Described as a "risk for peace," the plan called for immediate cease-fires in all guerrilla wars in the region, the suspension of all outside military aid, a general amnesty, and the initiation of peace negotiations. These initial actions would be followed by free elections in the region, guarantees for improved human and civil rights, and a general reduction in military forces. After months of debate, muddied by the interference of the United States, in August 1987, five Central American heads of state signed a regional peace plan modified from the original Arias Sànchez plan. The plan ultimately proved unsuccessful, but Arias Sànchez's efforts for a diplomatic settlement of regional conflicts earned him the Nobel Peace Prize. In citing him for the award, the Nobel Committee stated that Arias Sànchez made an "outstanding contribution to the possible return of stability and peace to a region long torn by strife and civil war."

**BIBLIOGRAPHY.** Current Biography 1987, 13–17. New York: W. H. Wilson.

Schlessinger, Bernard S., and June H. Schlessinger, eds. *Who's Who of Nobel Prize Winners.* Phoenix, AZ, USA: Oryx Press, 1991.

**ARMED CONFLICT.** The protection of the human rights of civilians, prisoners, and combatants in international and non-international armed conflicts has been an important issue on the agenda of several United Nations organs since the TEHERAN INTERNATIONAL CONFERENCE ON HUMAN RIGHTS pointed out on 12 May 1968 (resolution XXIII) "that the widespread violence and brutality of our times, including massacres, summary executions, tortures, inhuman treatment of prisoners, killing of civilians in armed conflicts and the use of chemical and biological means of warfare, including napalm bombing, erode human rights and engender counter-brutality." The Conference called upon the UN Secretary-General to study "(a) the steps which could be taken to secure the better application of existing humanitarian conventions and rules in all armed conflicts and (b) the need for additional humanitarian international conventions or

for possible revision of existing conventions to ensure the better protection of civilians, prisoners and combatants in all armed conflicts and the prohibition and limitation of the use of certain methods and means of warfare."

Later in 1968, the General Assembly affirmed (resolution 2444 [XXIII]) three basic principles to be observed by all governmental and other authorities responsible for action in armed conflicts which had been formulated by the International Conference of the Red Cross held in Vienna in 1965: "(a) that the right of the parties to a conflict to adopt means of injuring the enemy is not unlimited; (b) that it is prohibited to launch attacks against the civilian populations as such; and (c) that distinction must be made at all times between persons taking part in the hostilities and members of the civilian population to the effect that the latter be spared as much as possible."

In 1973, the General Assembly, noting that the Diplomatic Conference on the Reaffirmation and Development of International Humanitarian Law Applicable in Armed Conflicts was to be convened at Geneva in 1974 on the invitation of the Swiss Federal Council, invited the Conference to examine the question of the use of napalm and other incendiary weapons, as well as other specific conventional weapons which may be deemed to cause unnecessary suffering or to have indiscriminate effects and to seek agreement on rules prohibiting or restricting the use of such weapons.

In 1974, the Assembly expressed its deep concern over the sufferings of women and children belonging to the civilian population who, in periods of emergency and armed conflict, are too often the victims of inhuman acts and suffer serious harm and proclaimed (resolution 3318 [XXIX]) the Declaration on the Protection of Women and Children in Emergency and Armed Conflict. The Declaration calls for special efforts to be made by States involved in armed conflicts, military operations in foreign territories, or military operations in territories still under colonial domination to spare women and children from the ravages of war and to ensure that they not be deprived of food, shelter, medical care, and other inalienable rights.

The Diplomatic Conference on Reaffirmation and Development of International Humanitarian Law Applicable to Armed Conflicts met in Geneva in 1974, 1975, 1976, and 1977 and examined all of the questions mentioned above in the course of revising two draft additional protocols to the Geneva Conventions of 12 August 1949 submitted by the INTERNATIONAL COMMITTEE OF THE RED CROSS. Both additional protocols were adopted by the Conference on 8 June 1977.

Protocol I, Additional to the Geneva Conventions of 12 August 1949, relating to the protection of victims of international armed conflicts, has six main parts. Part I sets out general principles and the scope of their application. Part II deals with the problems of the wounded, sick, and shipwrecked, with medical transportation and with missing or dead persons. Part III relates to methods and means of warfare and the status of combatants and prisoners of war. Part IV sets out methods for protection of the civilian population against the effects of hostilities and rules for the treatment of persons in the power of a party to the conflict. Part V contains provisions for the execution of the Geneva Conventions and of the Protocol, and Part VI sets out provisions for signature, ratification, acceptance, and amendment of the Protocol.

Protocol II, Additional to the Geneva Conventions of 12 August 1949, relating to the protection of victims of non-international armed conflicts, has five parts. Part I indicates the scope of the instrument, which is limited to conflicts that take place in the territory of a contracting party between its armed forces and dissident armed forces or other organized armed groups. Part II sets out rules for the humane treatment of all persons who do not take a direct part or who have ceased to take part in hostilities, whether or not their liberty has been restricted. Part III provides for the protection and care of the wounded, sick and shipwrecked, and Part IV provides for the protection of the civilian population in general. Part V contains provisions for signature, ratification, and amendment of the Protocol.

Among the acts prohibited by the protocols are violence to the life, health, and physical or mental well-being of persons; collective punishments; the taking of hostages; acts of terrorism; outrages upon personal dignity; slavery and the slave trade in all their forms; pillage; and threats to commit any of these acts.

**SEE ALSO** *Conscientious Objection to Military Service; Geneva Red Cross Conventions and Protocols; Mercenarism.*

**BIBLIOGRAPHY.** Bothe, Michael, Thomas Kurzidem, and Peter Macalister-Smith, eds. *National Implementation of International Humanitarian Law. Proceedings of an International Colloquium held at Bad Homburg, June 17–19, 1988.* Dordrecht, the Netherlands: Martinus Nijhoff, 1990. Conference report, in English; bibliography, pp. 275–286, by country, of military and Red Cross manuals on International law.

Bouvier, Antoine. "Protection of the Natural Environment in Time of Armed Conflict," *International Review of the Red Cross* no. 285 (1991): 567–578 (English); no. 792 (1991): 599–611 (French). Scholarly article, in English and French.

Fisler, Lori, and David J. Scheffer, eds. *Law and Force in the New International Order.* Boulder, CO, USA: Westview Press for the American Society of International Law, 1991. Scholarly collection of articles, in English.

Gardam, Judith Gail. *Non-Combatant Immunity as a Norm of International Humanitarian Law.* Dordrecht, the Netherlands: Martinus Nijhoff, 1993. Scholarly monograph, in English; bibliography, pp. 183–193.

Meron, Theodor, and Allen Rosas. "A Declaration of Minimum Humanitarian Standards," *American Journal of International Law* 85, no. 2 (April 1991): 375–381. Scholarly article, in English.

Myers, Roger. "A New Remedy for Northern Ireland: The Case for United Nations Peacekeeping Intervention in an Internal Conflict," *New York Law School Journal of International and Comparative Law* 11, no. 1 & 2 (1990): 1–166. Scholarly article, in English.

Niyugenko, Gérard. "The Implementation of International Humanitarian Law and the Principle of State Sovereignty," *International Review of the Red Cross* no. 281 (March–April 1991): 105–133. Scholarly article, in English and French.

Plattner, Denise. "The Penal Repression of Violations of International Humanitarian Law Applicable in Non-International Armed Conflicts," *International Review of the Red Cross* no. 278 (Sept.–Oct. 1990): 409–420 (English); no. 785: 443-455 (French). Scholarly article, in English and French.

Ramcharan, B. G. "The Security Council and Humanitarian Emergencies," *Netherlands Quarterly of Human Rights* 9, no. 1 (1991): 19–35. Scholarly article, in English.

**ARMED CONFLICT: BASIC PRINCIPLES FOR THE PROTECTION OF CIVILIAN POPULATION IN ARMED CONFLICTS.** In 1970, the UN General Assembly, while noting (resolution 2675 [XXV]) that a series of international instruments had been adopted for the alleviation of human suffering in any form and in particular in armed conflicts, including the Geneva Conventions of 1949, concluded that, nevertheless, there was a need for better protection of human rights in armed conflicts and that civilian populations were in special need of increased protection. The Assembly accordingly affirmed eight basic principles for the protection of civilian populations in armed conflicts, without prejudice to their future elaboration within the framework of progressive development of the international law of armed conflict:

1. Fundamental human rights, as accepted in international law and laid down in international instruments, continue to apply fully in situations of armed conflict.

2. In the conduct of military operations during armed conflicts, a distinction must be made at all times between persons actively taking part in the hostilities and civilian populations.

3. In the conduct of military operations, every effort should be made to spare civilian populations from the ravages of war, and all necessary precautions should be taken to avoid injury, loss or damage to civilian populations.

4. Civilian populations as such should not be the object of military operations.

5. Dwellings and other installations that are used only by civilian populations should not be the object of military operations.

6. Places or areas designated for the sole protection of civilians, such as hospital zones or similar refuges, should not be the object of military operations.

7. Civilian populations, or individual members thereof, should not be the object of reprisals, forcible transfers or other assaults on their integrity.

8. The provision of international relief to civilian populations is in conformity with the humanitarian principles of the Charter of the United Nations, the Universal Declaration of Human Rights and other international instruments in the field of human rights. The Declaration of Principles for International Humanitarian Relief to the Civilian Population in Disaster Situations, as laid down in resolution XXVI adopted by the twenty-first International Conference of the Red Cross, shall apply in situations of armed conflict, and all parties to a conflict should make every effort to facilitate this application.

## ARMED CONFLICT: BASIC PRINCIPLES OF THE LEGAL STATUS OF COMBATANTS STRUGGLING AGAINST COLONIAL AND ALIEN DOMINATION AND RACIST REGIMES.

In 1973, the Assembly considered another aspect of the question: the legal status of the combatants in an armed struggle against colonial and alien domination and racist regimes. It noted that, despite its numerous appeals, compliance with universally recognized norms of modern international law had not yet been ensured and that the treatment of combatants struggling against colonial and alien domination and racist regimes remained inhuman. As an interim measure it proclaimed (resolution 3103 [XXVIII]) six basic principles of the legal status of such combatants, again without prejudice to their elaboration in the future within the framework of the development of international law applying to the protection of human rights in armed conflicts:

1. The struggle of peoples under colonial and alien domination and racist régimes for the implementation of their right to self-determination and independence is legitimate and in full accordance with the principles of international law.

2. Any attempt to suppress the struggle against colonial and alien domination and racist régimes is incompatible with the Charter of the United Nations, the Declaration on Principles of International Law concerning Friendly Relations with Co-operation among States in accordance with the Charter of the United Nations, the Universal Declaration of Human Rights and the Declaration on the Granting of Independence to Colonial Countries and Peoples and constitutes a threat to international peace and security.

3. The armed conflicts involving the struggle of peoples against colonial and alien domination and racist régimes are to be regarded as international armed conflicts in the sense of 1949 Geneva Conventions, and the legal status envisaged to apply to the combatants in the 1949 Geneva Conventions and other international instruments is to apply to the persons engaged in armed struggle against colonial and alien domination and racist régimes.

4. The combatants struggling against colonial and alien domination and racist régimes captured as prisoners are to be accorded the status of prisoners of war and their treatment should be in accordance with the provisions of the Geneva Convention relative to the Treatment of Prisoners of War, of 12 August 1949.

5. The use of mercenaries by colonial and racist régimes against the national liberation movements struggling for their freedom and independence from the yoke of colonialism and alien domination is considered to be a criminal act and the mercenaries should accordingly be punished as criminals.

6. The violation of the legal status of the combatants struggling against colonial and alien domination and racist régimes in the course of armed conflicts entails full responsibility in accordance with the norms of international law.

## ARMED CONFLICT: CONVENTION FOR THE PROTECTION OF CULTURAL PROPERTY IN THE EVENT OF ARMED CONFLICT, UNESCO (1954).

The Convention, also known as the Hague Convention, together with the UNESCO Protocol to the Convention for the Protection of Cultural Property in the Event of Armed Conflict, was adopted at the Hague on 14 May 1954 by an international conference of States convened by UNESCO. It entered into force on 7 August 1956.

Under the Convention, the contracting parties undertake to safeguard cultural property of great importance to the cultural heritage of peoples, irrespective of its origin or ownership, in the event of armed conflict; and also to provide special protection for the refuges intended to shelter such property. The procedures for application of the Convention are set out in a series of regulations for its execution.

The text of the Convention, and of the regulations for its execution (*UNESCO's Standard-Setting Instruments*, No. IV.A.3, pp. 3–17 and 18–33, respectively), are as follows:

The High Contracting Parties,
Recognizing that cultural property has suffered grave damage during recent armed conflicts and that, by reason of the developments in the technique of warfare, it is in increasing danger of destruction;
Being convinced that damage to cultural property belonging to any people whatsoever means damage to the cultural heritage of all mankind, since each people makes its contribution to the culture of the world;
Considering that the preservation of the cultural heritage is of great importance for all peoples of the world and that it is important that this heritage should receive international protection;
Guided by the principles concerning the protection of cultural property during armed conflict, as established in the Conventions of The Hague of 1899 and of 1907 and in the Washington Pact of 15 April, 1935;
Being of the opinion that such protection cannot be effective unless both national and international measures have been taken to organize it in time of peace;
Being determined to take all possible steps to protect cultural property;
Have agreed upon the following provisions:

### Chapter I: General Provisions regarding Protection

*Article 1. Definition of Cultural Property.* For the purposes of the present Convention, the term 'cultural property' shall cover, irrespective of origin or ownership:

(a) movable or immovable property of great importance to the cultural heritage of every people, such as monuments of architecture, art or history, whether religious or secular; archaeological sites; groups of buildings which, as a whole, are of historical or artistic interest; works of art; manuscripts, books and other objects of artistic, historical or archaeological interest; as well as scientific collections and important collections of books or archives or of reproductions of the property defined above;

(b) buildings whose main and effective purpose is to preserve or exhibit the movable cultural property defined in sub-paragraph (a) such as museums, large libraries and depositories of archives, and refuges intended to shelter, in the event of armed conflict, the movable cultural property defined in sub-paragraph (a);

(c) centres containing a large amount of cultural property as defined in sub-paragraphs (a) and (b), to be known as 'centres containing monuments'.

*Article 2. Protection of Cultural Property.* For the purposes of the present Convention, the protection of cultural property shall comprise the safeguarding of and respect for such property.

*Article 3. Safeguarding of Cultural Property.* The High Contracting Parties undertake to prepare in time of peace for the safeguarding of cultural property situated within their own territory against the foreseeable effects of an armed conflict, by taking such measures as they consider appropriate.

*Article 4. Respect for Cultural Property.* 1. The High Contracting Parties undertake to respect cultural property situated within their own territory as well as within the territory of other High Contracting Parties by refraining from any use of the property and its immediate surroundings or of the appliances in use for its protection for purposes which are likely to expose it to destruction or damage in the event of armed conflict; and by refraining from any act of hostility directed against such property.

2. The obligations mentioned in paragraph 1 of the present Article may be waived only in cases where military necessity imperatively requires such a waiver.

3. The High Contracting Parties further undertake to prohibit, prevent and, if necessary, put a stop to any form of theft, pillage, or misappropriation of, and any acts of vandalism directed against, cultural property. They shall refrain from requisitioning movable cultural property situated in the territory of another High Contracting Party.

4. They shall refrain from any act directed by way of reprisals against cultural property.

5. No High Contracting Party may evade the obligations incumbent upon it under the present Article, in respect of another High Contracting Party, by reason of the fact that the latter has not applied the measures of safeguard referred to in Article 3.

*Article 5. Occupation.* 1. Any High Contracting Party in occupation of the whole or part of the territory of another High Contracting Party shall as far as possible support the competent national authorities of the occupied country in safeguarding and preserving its cultural property.

2. Should it prove necessary to take measures to preserve cultural property situated in occupied territory and damaged by military operations, and should the competent national authorities be unable to take such measures, the Occupying Power shall, as far as possible, and in close co-operation with such authorities, take the most necessary measures of preservation.

3. Any High Contracting Party whose government is considered their legitimate government by members of a resistance movement, shall, if possible, draw their attention to the obligation to comply with those provisions of the Convention dealing with respect for cultural property.

*Article 6. Distinctive Marking of Cultural Property.* In accordance with the provisions of Article 16, cultural property may bear a distinctive emblem so as to facilitate its recognition.

*Article 7. Military Measures.* 1. The High Contracting Parties undertake to introduce in time of peace into their military regulations or instructions such provisions as may ensure observance of the present Convention, and to foster in the members of their armed forces a spirit of respect for the culture and cultural property of all peoples.

2. The High Contracting Parties undertake to plan or establish in peace-time, within their armed forces, services or specialist personnel whose purpose will be to secure respect for cultural property and to co-operate with the civilian authorities responsible for safeguarding it.

### Chapter II: Special Protection

*Article 8. Granting of Special Protection.* 1. There may be placed under special protection a limited number of refuges intended to shelter movable cultural property in the event of armed conflict, of centres containing monuments and other immovable cultural property of very great importance, provided that they:

(a) are situated at an adequate distance from any large industrial centre or from any important military objective constituting a vulnerable point, such as, for example, an aerodrome, broadcasting station, establishment engaged upon work of national defence, a port or railway station of relative importance or a main line of communication;

(b) are not used for military purposes.

2. A refuge for movable cultural property may also be placed under special protection, whatever its location, if it is so constructed that, in all probability, it will not be damaged by bombs.

3. A centre containing monuments shall be deemed to be used for military purposes whenever it is used for the movement of military personnel or material, even in transit. The same shall apply whenever activities directly connected with military operations, the stationing of military personnel, or the production of war material are carried on within the centre.

4. The guarding of cultural property mentioned in paragraph 1 above by armed custodians specially empowered to do so, or the presence, in the vicinity of such cultural property, of police forces normally responsible for the maintenance of public order shall not be deemed to be used for military purposes.

5. If any cultural property mentioned in paragraph 1 of the present Article is situated near an important military objective as defined in the said paragraph, it may nevertheless by placed under special protection if the High Contracting Party asking for that protection undertakes, in the event of armed conflict, to make no use of the objective and particularly, in the case of a port, railway station or aerodrome, to divert all traffic therefrom. In that event, such diversion shall be prepared in time of peace.

6. Special protection is granted to cultural property by its entry in the 'International Register of Cultural Property un-

der Special Protection.' This entry shall only be made, in accordance with the provisions of the present Convention and under the conditions provided for in the Regulations for the execution of the Convention.

*Article 9. Immunity of Cultural Property under Special Protection.* The High Contracting Parties undertake to ensure the immunity of cultural property under special protection by refraining, from the time of entry in the International Register, from any act of hostility directed against such property and, except for the cases provided for in paragraph 5 of Article 8, from any use of such property or its surroundings for military purposes.

*Article 10. Identification and Control.* During an armed conflict, cultural property under special protection shall be marked with the distinctive emblem described in Article 16, and shall be open to international control as provided for in the Regulations for the execution of the Convention.

*Article 11. Withdrawal of Immunity.* 1. If one of the High Contracting Parties commits, in respect of any item of cultural property under special protection, a violation of the obligations under Article 9, the opposing Party shall, so long as this violation persists, be released from the obligation to ensure the immunity of the property concerned. Nevertheless, whenever possible, the latter Party shall first request the cessation of such violation within a reasonable time.

2. Apart from the case provided for in paragraph 1 of the present Article, immunity shall be withdrawn from cultural property under special protection only in exceptional cases of unavoidable military necessity, and only for such time as that necessity continues. Such necessity can be established only by the officer commanding a force the equivalent of a division in size or larger. Whenever circumstances permit, the opposing Party shall be notified, a reasonable time in advance, of the decision to withdraw immunity.

3. The Party withdrawing immunity shall, as soon as possible, so inform the Commissioner-General for cultural property provided for in the Regulations for the execution of the Convention, in writing, stating the reasons.

### Chapter III: Transport of Cultural Property

*Article 12. Transport under Special Protection.* 1. Transport exclusively engaged in the transfer of cultural property, whether within a territory or to another territory, may, at the request of the High Contracting Party concerned, take place under special protection in accordance with the conditions specified in the Regulations for the execution of the Convention.

2. Transport under special protection shall take place under the international supervision provided for in the aforesaid Regulations and shall display the distinctive emblem described in Article 16.

3. The High Contracting Parties shall refrain from any act of hostility directed against transport under special protection.

*Article 13. Transport in Urgent Cases.* 1. If a High Contracting Party considers that the safety of certain cultural property requires its transfer and that the matter is of such urgency that the procedure laid down in Article 12 cannot be followed, especially at the beginning of an armed conflict, the transport may display the distinctive emblem described in Article 16, provided that an application for immunity referred to in Article 12 has not already been made and refused. As far as possible, notification of transfer should be made to the opposing Parties. Nevertheless, transport con-

veying cultural property to the territory of another country may not display the distinctive emblem unless immunity has been expressly granted to it.

2. The High Contracting Parties shall take, so far as possible, the necessary precautions to avoid acts of hostility directed against the transport described in paragraph 1 of the present Article and displaying the distinctive emblem.

*Article 14. Immunity from Seizure, Capture and Prize.* 1. Immunity from seizure, placing in prize, or capture shall be granted to:

(a) cultural property enjoying the protection provided for in Article 12 or that provided for in Article 13;

(b) the means of transport exclusively engaged in the transfer of such cultural property.

2. Nothing in the present Article shall limit the right of visit and search.

### Chapter IV: Personnel

*Article 15. Personnel.* As far as is consistent with the interests of security, personnel engaged in the protection of cultural property shall, in the interests of such property, be respected and, if they fall into the hands of the opposing Party, shall be allowed to continue to carry out their duties whenever the cultural property for which they are responsible has also fallen into the hands of the opposing Party.

### Chapter V: The Distinctive Emblem

*Article 16. Emblem of the Convention.* 1. The distinctive emblem of the Convention shall take the form of a shield, pointed below, per saltire blue and white (a shield consisting of a royal-blue square, one of the angles of which forms the point of the shield, and of a royal-blue triangle above the square, the space on either side being taken up by a white triangle).

2. The emblem shall be used alone, or repeated three times in a triangular formation (one shield below), under the conditions provided for in Article 17.

*Article 17. Use of the Emblem.* 1. The distinctive emblem repeated three times may be used only as a means of identification of:

(a) immovable cultural property under special protection;

(b) the transport of cultural property under the conditions provided for in Articles 12 and 13;

(c) improvised refuges, under the conditions provided for in the Regulations for the execution of the Convention.

2. The distinctive emblem may be used alone only as a means of identification of:

(a) cultural property not under special protection;

(b) the persons responsible for the duties of control in accordance with the Regulations for the execution of the Convention;

(c) the personnel engaged in the protection of cultural property;

(d) the identity cards mentioned in the Regulations for the execution of the Convention.

3. During an armed conflict, the use of the distinctive emblem in any other cases than those mentions in the preceding paragraphs of the present Article, and the use for any purpose whatever of a sign resembling the distinctive emblem, shall be forbidden.

4. The distinctive emblem may not be placed on any immovable cultural property unless at the same time there is

displayed an authorization duly dated and signed by the competent authority of the High Contracting Party.

## Chapter VI: Scope of Application of the Convention

*Article 18. Application of the Convention.* 1. Apart from the provisions which shall take effect in time of peace, the present Convention shall apply in the event of declared war or of any other armed conflict which may arise between two or more of the High Contracting Parties, even if the state of war is not recognized by one or more of them.

2. The Convention shall also apply to all cases of partial or total occupation of the territory of a High Contracting Party, even if the said occupation meets with no armed resistance.

3. If one of the Powers in conflict is not a Party to the present Convention, the Powers which are Parties thereto shall nevertheless remain bound by it in their mutual relations. They shall furthermore be bound by the Convention, in relation to the said Power, if the latter has declared that it accepts the provisions thereof and so long as it applies them.

*Article 19. Conflicts not of an International Character.* 1. In the event of an armed conflict not of an international character occurring within the territory of one of the High Contracting Parties, each party to the conflict shall be bound to apply, as a minimum, the provisions of the present Convention which relate to respect for cultural property.

2. The parties to the conflict shall endeavour to bring into force, by means of special agreements, all or part of the other provisions of the present Convention.

3. The United Nations Educational, Scientific and Cultural Organization may offer its services to the parties to the conflict.

4. The application of the preceding provisions shall not affect the legal status of the parties to the conflict.

## Chapter VII: Execution of the Convention

*Article 20. Regulations for the Execution of the Convention.* The procedure by which the present Convention is to be applied is defined in the Regulations for its execution, which constitute an integral part thereof.

*Article 21. Protecting Powers.* The present Convention and the Regulations for its execution shall be applied with the co-operation of the Protecting Powers responsible for safeguarding the interests of the Parties to the conflict.

*Article 22. Conciliation Procedure.* 1. The Protecting Powers shall lend their good offices in all cases where they may deem it useful in the interests of cultural property, particularly if there is disagreement between the Parties to the conflict as to the application or interpretation of the provisions of the present Convention or the Regulations for its execution.

2. For this purpose, each of the Protecting Powers may, either at the invitation of one Party, of the Director-General of the United Nations Educational, Scientific and Cultural Organization, or on its own initiative, propose to the Parties to the conflict a meeting of their representatives, and in particular of the authorities responsible for the protection of cultural property, if considered appropriate on suitably chosen neutral territory. The Parties to the conflict shall be bound to give effect to the proposals for meeting made to them. The Protecting Powers shall propose for approval by the Parties to the conflict a person belonging to a neutral Power or a person presented by the Director-General of the United Nations Educational, Scientific and Cultural Organization, which person shall be invited to take part in such a meeting in the capacity of Chairman.

*Article 23. Assistance of Unesco.* 1. The High Contracting Parties may call upon the United Nations Educational, Scientific and Cultural Organization for technical assistance in organizing the protection of their cultural property, or in connexion with any other problem arising out of the application of the present Convention or the Regulations for its execution. The Organization shall accord such assistance within the limits fixed by its programme and by its resources.

2. The Organization is authorized to make, on its own initiative, proposals on this matter to the High Contracting Parties.

*Article 24. Special Agreements.* 1. The High Contracting Parties may conclude special agreements for all matters concerning which they deem it suitable to make separate provision.

2. No special agreement may be concluded which would diminish the protection afforded by the present Convention to cultural property and to the personnel engaged in its protection.

*Article 25. Dissemination of the Convention.* The High Contracting Parties undertake, in time of peace as in time of armed conflict, to disseminate the text of the present Convention and the Regulations for its execution as widely as possible in their respective countries. They undertake, in particular, to include the study thereof in their programmes of military and, if possible, civilian training, so that its principles are made known to the whole population, especially the armed forces and personnel engaged in the protection of cultural property.

*Article 26. Translations Reports.* 1. The High Contracting Parties shall communicate to one another, through the Director-General of the United Nations Educational, Scientific and Cultural Organization, the official translations of the present Convention and of the Regulations for its execution.

2. Furthermore, at least once every four years, they shall forward to the Director-General a report giving whatever information they think suitable concerning any measures being taken, prepared or contemplated by their respective administrations in fulfilment of the present Convention and of the Regulations for its execution.

*Article 27. Meetings.* 1. The Director-General of the United Nations Educational, Scientific and Cultural Organization may, with the approval of the Executive Board, convene meetings of representatives of the High Contracting Parties. He must convene such a meeting if at least one-fifth of the High Contracting Parties so request.

2. Without prejudice to any other functions which have been conferred on it by the present Convention or the Regulations for its execution, the purpose of the meeting will be to study problems concerning the application of the Convention and of the Regulations for its execution, and to formulate recommendations in respect thereof.

3. The meeting may further undertake a revision of the Convention or the Regulations for its execution if the majority of the High Contracting Parties are represented, and in accordance with the provisions of Article 39.

*Article 28. Sanctions.* The High Contracting Parties undertake to take, within the framework of their ordinary criminal jurisdiction, all necessary steps to prosecute and impose penal or disciplinary sanctions upon those persons, of whatever nationality, who commit or order to be committed a breach of the present Convention.

## Final Provisions

*Article 29. Languages.* 1. The present Convention is drawn up in English, French, Russian and Spanish, the four texts being equally authoritative.

2. The United Nations Educational, Scientific and Cultural Organization shall arrange for translations of the Convention into the other official languages of its General Conference.

*Article 30. Signature.* The present Convention shall bear the date of 14 May, 1954 and, until the date of 31 December, 1954, shall remain open for signature by all States invited to the Conference which met at The Hague from 21 April, 1954 to 14 May, 1954.

*Article 31. Ratification.* 1. The present Convention shall be subject to ratification by signatory States in accordance with their respective constitutional procedures.

2. The instruments of ratification shall be deposited with the Director-General of the United Nations Educational, Scientific and Cultural Organization.

*Article 32. Accession.* From the date of its entry into force, the present Convention shall be open for accession by all States mentioned in Article 30 which have not signed it, as well as any other State invited to accede by the Executive Board of the United Nations Educational, Scientific and Cultural Organization. Accession shall be effected by the deposit of an instrument of accession with the Director-General of the United Nations Educational, Scientific and Cultural Organization.

*Article 33. Entry into Force.* 1. The present Convention shall enter into force three months after five instruments of ratification have been deposited.

2. Thereafter, it shall enter into force, for each High Contracting Party, three months after the deposit of its instrument of ratification or accession.

3. The situations referred to in Articles 18 and 19 shall give immediate effect to ratifications or accessions deposited by the Parties to the conflict either before or after the beginning of hostilities or occupation. In such cases the Director-General of the United Nations Educational, Scientific and Cultural Organization shall transmit the communications referred to in Article 38 by the speediest method.

*Article 34. Effective Application.* 1. Each State Party to the Convention on the date of its entry into force shall take all necessary measures to ensure its effective application within a period of six months after such entry into force.

2. This period shall be six months from the date of deposit of the instruments or ratification or accession for any State which deposits its instrument of ratification or accession after the date of the entry into force of the Convention.

*Article 35. Territorial Extension of the Convention.* Any High Contracting Party may, at the time of ratification or accession, or at any time thereafter, declare by notification addressed to the Director-General of the United Nations Educational, Scientific and Cultural Organization, that the present Convention shall extend to all or any of the territories for whose international relations it is responsible. The said notification shall take effect three months after the date of its receipt.

*Article 36. Relation to Previous Conventions.* 1. In the relations between Powers which are bound by the Conventions of The Hague concerning the Laws and Customs of War on Land (IV) and concerning Naval Bombardment in Time of War (IX), whether those of 29 July, 1899 or those of 18 October, 1907, and which are Parties to the present Convention, this last Convention shall be supplementary to the aforementioned Convention (IX) and to the Regulations annexed to the aforementioned Convention (IV) and shall substitute for the emblem described in Article 5 of the aforementioned Convention (IX) the emblem described in Article 16 of the present Convention, in cases in which the present Convention and the Regulations for its execution provide for the use of this distinctive emblem.

2. In the relations between Powers which are bound by the Washington Pact of 15 April, 1935 for the Protection of Artistic and Scientific Institutions and of Historic Monuments (Roerich Pact) and which are Parties to the present Convention, the latter Convention shall be supplementary to the Roerich Pact and shall substitute for the distinguishing flag described in Article III of the Pact the emblem defined in Article 16 of the present Convention, in cases in which the present Convention and the Regulations for its execution provide for the use of this distinctive emblem.

*Article 37. Denunciation.* 1. Each High Contracting Party may denounce the present Convention, on its own behalf, or on behalf of any territory for whose international relations it is responsible.

2. The denunciation shall be notified by an instrument in writing, deposited with the Director-General of the United Nations Educational, Scientific and Cultural Organization.

3. The denunciation shall take effect one year after the receipt of the instrument of denunciation. However, if, on the expiry of this period, the denouncing Party is involved in an armed conflict, the denunciation shall not take effect until the end of hostilities, or until the operations of repatriating cultural property are completed, whichever is the later.

*Article 38. Notifications.* The Director-General of the United Nations Educational, Scientific and Cultural Organization shall inform the States referred to in Articles 30 and 32, as well as the United Nations, of the deposit of all the instruments of ratification, accession or acceptance provided for in Articles 31, 32 and 39 and of the notifications and denunciations provided for respectively in Articles 35, 37 and 39.

*Article 39. Revision of the Convention and of the Regulations for its Execution.* 1. Any High Contracting Party may propose amendments to the present Convention or the Regulations for its execution. The text of any proposed amendment shall be communicated to the Director-General of the United Nations Educational, Scientific and Cultural Organization who shall transmit it to each High Contracting Party with the request that such Party reply within four months stating whether it:

(a) desires that a Conference be convened to consider the proposed amendment;

(b) favours the acceptance of the proposed amendment without a Conference; or

(c) favours the rejection of the proposed amendment without a Conference.

2. The Director-General shall transmit the replies, received under paragraph 1 of the present Article, to all High Contracting Parties.

3. If all the High Contracting Parties which have, within the prescribed time-limit, stated their views to the Director-General of the United Nations Educational, Scientific and Cultural Organization, pursuant to paragraph 1(b) of this Article, inform him that they favour acceptance of the amendment without a Conference, notification of their decision shall be made by the Director-General in accordance with Article 38. The amendment shall become effective for

all the High Contracting Parties on the expiry of ninety days from the date of such notification.

4. The Director-General shall convene a Conference of the High Contracting Parties to consider the proposed amendment if requested to do so by more than one-third of the High Contracting Parties.

5. Amendments to the Convention or to the Regulations for its execution, dealt with under the provisions of the preceding paragraph, shall enter into force only after they have been unanimously adopted by the High Contracting Parties represented at the Conference and accepted by each of the High Contracting Parties.

6. Acceptance by the High Contracting Parties of amendments to the Convention or to the Regulations for its execution, which have been adopted by the Conference mentioned in paragraphs 4 and 5, shall be effected by the deposit of a formal instrument with the Director-General of the United Nations Educational, Scientific and Cultural Organization.

7. After the entry into force of amendments to the present Convention or to the Regulations for its execution, only the text of the Convention or of the Regulations for its execution thus amended shall remain open for ratification or accession.

*Article 40. Registration.* In accordance with Article 102 of the Charter of the United Nations, the present Convention shall be registered with the Secretariat of the United Nations at the request of the Director-General of the United Nations Educational, Scientific and Cultural Organization.

In faith whereof the undersigned, duly authorized, have signed the present Convention.

Done at The Hague, this fourteenth day of May, 1954, in a single copy which shall be deposited in the archives of the United Nations Educational, Scientific and Cultural Organization, and certified true copies of which shall be delivered to all the States referred to in Articles 30 and 32 as well as to the United Nations.

## Regulations for the Execution of the Convention for the Protection of Cultural Property in the Event of Armed Conflict

### Chapter I: Control

*Article 1. International List of Persons.* On the entry into force of the Convention, the Director-General of the United Nations Educational, Scientific and Cultural Organization shall compile an international list consisting of all persons nominated by the High Contracting Parties as qualified to carry out the functions of the Commissioner-General for Cultural Property. On the initiative of the Director-General of the United Nations Educational, Scientific and Cultural Organization, this list shall be periodically revised on the basis of requests formulated by the High Contracting Parties.

*Article 2. Organization of Control.* As soon as any High Contracting Party is engaged in an armed conflict to which Article 18 of the Convention applies:

(a) It shall appoint a representative for cultural property situated in its territory; if it is in occupation of another territory, it shall appoint a special representative for cultural property situated in that territory;

(b) The Protecting Power acting for each of the Parties in conflict with such High Contracting Party shall appoint delegates accredited to the latter in conformity with Article 3 below;

(c) A Commissioner-General for Cultural Property shall be appointed to such High Contracting Party in accordance with Article 4.

*Article 3. Appointment of Delegates of Protecting Powers.* The Protecting Power shall appoint its delegates from among the members of its diplomatic or consular staff or, with the approval of the Party to which they will be accredited, from among other persons.

*Article 4. Appointment of Commissioner-General.* 1. The Commissioner-General for Cultural Property shall be chosen from the international list of persons by joint agreement between the Party to which he will be accredited and the Protecting Powers acting on behalf of the opposing Parties.

2. Should the Parties fail to reach agreement within three weeks from the beginning of their discussions on this point, they shall request the President of the International Court of Justice to appoint the Commissioner-General, who shall not take up his duties until the Party to which he is accredited has approved his appointment.

*Article 5. Functions of Delegates.* The delegates of the Protecting Powers shall take note of violations of the Convention, investigate, with the approval of the Party to which they are accredited, the circumstances in which they have occurred, make representations locally to secure their cessation and, if necessary, notify the Commissioner-General of such violations. They shall keep him informed of their activities.

*Article 6. Functions of the Commissioner-General.* 1. The Commissioner-General for Cultural Property shall deal with all matters referred to him in connexion with the application of the Convention, in conjunction with the representative of the Party to which he is accredited and with the delegates concerned.

2. He shall have powers of decision and appointment in the cases specified in the present Regulations.

3. With the agreement of the Party to which he is accredited, he shall have the right to order an investigation or to conduct it himself.

4. He shall make any representations to the Parties to the conflict or to their Protecting Powers which he deems useful for the application of the Convention.

5. He shall draw up such reports as may be necessary on the application of the Convention and communicate them to the Parties concerned and to their Protecting Powers. He shall send copies to the Director-General of the United Nations Educational, Scientific and Cultural Organization, who may make use only of their technical contents.

6. If there is no Protecting Power, the Commissioner-General shall exercise the functions of the Protecting Power as laid down in Articles 21 and 22 of the Convention.

*Article 7. Inspectors and Experts.* 1. Whenever the Commissioner-General for Cultural Property considers it necessary, either at the request of the delegates concerned or after consultation with them, he shall propose, for the approval of the Party to which he is accredited, an inspector of cultural property to be charged with a specific mission. An inspector shall be responsible only to the Commissioner-General.

2. The Commissioner-General, delegates and inspectors may have recourse to the services of experts, who will also be proposed for the approval of the Party mentioned in the preceding paragraph.

*Article 8. Discharge of the Mission of Control.* The Commissioners-General for Cultural Property, delegates of the Protecting Powers, inspectors and experts shall in no case exceed their mandates. In particular, they shall take account of the security needs of the High Contracting Party to which they are accredited and shall in all circumstances act in accordance with the requirements of the military situations as communicated to them by that High Contracting Party.

*Article 9. Substitutes for Protecting Powers.* If a Party to the conflict does not benefit or ceases to benefit from the activities of a Protecting Power, a neutral State may be asked to undertake those functions of a Protecting Power which concern the appointment of a Commissioner-General for Cultural Property in accordance with the procedure laid down in Article 4 above. The Commissioner-General thus appointed shall, if need be, entrust to inspectors the functions of delegates of Protecting Powers as specified in the present Regulations.

*Article 10. Expenses.* The remuneration and expenses of the Commissioner-General for Cultural Property, inspectors and experts shall be met by the Party to which they are accredited. Remuneration and expenses of delegates of the Protecting Powers shall be subject to agreement between those Powers and the States whose interests they are safeguarding.

## Chapter II: Special Protection

*Article 11. Improvised Refuges.* 1. If, during an armed conflict, any High Contracting Party is induced by unforeseen circumstances to set up an improvised refuge and desires that it should be placed under special protection, it shall communicate this fact forthwith to the Commissioner-General accredited to that Party.

2. If the Commissioner-General considers that such a measure is justified by the circumstances and by the importance of the cultural property sheltered in this improvised refuge, he may authorize the High Contracting Party to display on such refuge the distinctive emblem defined in Article 16 of the Convention. He shall communicate his decision without delay to the delegates of the Protecting Powers who are concerned, each of whom may, within a time-limit of 30 days, order the immediate withdrawal of the emblem.

3. As soon as such delegates have signified their agreement or if the time-limit of 30 days has passed without any of the delegates concerned having made an objection, and if, in the view of the Commissioner-General, the refuge fulfils the conditions laid down in Article 8 of the Convention, the Commissioner-General shall request the Director-General of the United Nations Educational, Scientific and Cultural Organization to enter the refuge in the Register of Cultural Property under Special Protection.

*Article 12. International Register of Cultural Property under Special Protection.* 1. An "International Register of Cultural Property under Special Protection" shall be prepared.

2. The Director-General of the United Nations Educational, Scientific and Cultural Organization shall maintain this Register. He shall furnish copies to the Secretary-General of the United Nations and to the High Contracting Parties.

3. The Register shall be divided into sections, each in the name of a High Contracting Party. Each section shall be subdivided into three paragraphs, headed: Refuges, Centres containing Monuments, Other Immovable Cultural Property. The Director-General shall determine what details each section shall contain.

*Article 13. Requests for Registration.* 1. Any High Contracting Party may submit to the Director-General of the United Nations Educational, Scientific and Cultural Organization an application for the entry in the Register of certain refuges, centres containing monuments or other immovable cultural property situated within its territory. Such applica-

tion shall contain a description of the location of such property and shall certify that the property complies with the provisions of Article 8 of the Convention.

2. In the event of occupation, the Occupying Power shall be competent to make such application.

3. The Director-General of the United Nations Educational, Scientific and Cultural Organization shall, without delay, send copies of applications for registration to each of the High Contracting Parties.

*Article 14. Objections.* 1. Any High Contracting Party may, by letter addressed to the Director-General of the United Nations Educational, Scientific and Cultural Organization, lodge an objection to the registration of cultural property. This letter must be received by him within four months of the day on which he sent a copy of the application for registration.

2. Such objection shall state the reasons giving rise to it, the only valid grounds being that:

    (a) the property is not cultural property;

    (b) the property does not comply with the conditions mentioned in Article 8 of the Convention.

3. The Director-General shall send a copy of the letter of objection to the High Contracting Parties without delay. He shall, if necessary, seek the advice of the International Committee on Monuments, Artistic and Historical Sites and Archaeological Excavations and also, if he thinks fit, of any other competent organization or person.

4. The Director-General, or the High Contracting Party requesting registration, may make whatever representations they deem necessary to the High Contracting Parties which lodged the objection, with a view to causing the objection to be withdrawn.

5. If a High Contracting Party which has made an application for registration in time of peace becomes involved in an armed conflict before the entry has been made, the cultural property concerned shall at once be provisionally entered in the Register, by the Director-General, pending the confirmation, withdrawal or cancellation of any objection that may be, or may have been, made.

6. If, within a period of six months from the date of receipt of the letter of objection, the Director-General has not received from the High Contracting Party lodging the objection a communication stating that it has been withdrawn, the High Contracting Party applying for registration may request arbitration in accordance with the procedure in the following paragraph.

7. The request for arbitration shall not be made more than one year after the date of receipt by the Director-General of the letter of objection. Each of the two Parties to the dispute shall appoint an arbitrator. When more than one objection has been lodged against an application for registration, the High Contracting Parties which have lodged the objections shall, by common consent, appoint a single arbitrator. These two arbitrators shall select a chief arbitrator from the international list mentioned in Article 1 of the present Regulations. If such arbitrators cannot agree upon their choice, they shall ask the President of the International Court of Justice to appoint a chief arbitrator who need not necessarily be chosen from the international list. The arbitral tribunal thus constituted shall fix its own procedure. There shall be no appeal from its decisions.

8. Each of the High Contracting Parties may declare, whenever a dispute to which it is a Party arises, that it does not wish to apply the arbitration procedure provided for in the preceding paragraph. In such cases, the objection to an application for registration shall be submitted by the Direc-

tor-General to the High Contracting Parties. The objection will be confirmed only if the High Contracting Parties so decide by a two-third majority of the High Contracting Parties voting. The vote shall be taken by correspondence, unless the Director-General of the United Nations Educational, Scientific and Cultural Organization deems it essential to convene a meeting under the powers conferred upon him by Article 27 of the Convention. If the Director-General decides to proceed with the vote by correspondence, he shall invite the High Contracting Parties to transmit their votes by sealed letter within six months from the day on which they were invited to do so.

*Article 15. Registration.* 1. The Director-General of the United Nations Educational, Scientific and Cultural Organization shall cause to be entered in the Register, under a serial number, each item of property for which application for registration is made, provided that he has not received an objection within the time-limit prescribed in paragraph 1 of Article 14.

2. If an objection has been lodged, and without prejudice to the provision of paragraph 5 of Article 14, the Director-General shall enter property in the Register only if the objection has been withdrawn or has failed to be confirmed following the procedures laid down in either paragraph 7 or paragraph 8 of Article 14.

3. Whenever paragraph 3 of Article 11 applies, the Director-General shall enter property in the Register if so requested by the Commissioner-General for Cultural Property.

4. The Director-General shall send without delay to the Secretary-General of the United Nations, to the High Contracting Parties, and, at the request of the Party applying for registration, to all other States referred to in Articles 30 and 32 of the Convention, a certified copy of each entry in the Register. Entries shall become effective thirty days after despatch of such copies.

*Article 16. Cancellation.* 1. The Director-General of the United Nations Educational, Scientific and Cultural Organization shall cause the registration of any property to be cancelled:

(a) at the request of the High Contracting Party within whose territory the cultural property is situated;

(b) if the High Contracting Party with requested registration has denounced the Convention, and when that denunciation has taken effect;

(c) in the special case provided for in Article 14, paragraph 5, when an objection has been confirmed following the procedures mentioned either in paragraph 7 or in paragraph 8 or Article 14.

2. The Director-General shall send without delay, to the Secretary-General of the United Nations and to all States which received a copy of the entry in the Register, a certified copy of its cancellation. Cancellation shall take effect thirty days after the despatch of such copies.

## Chapter III: Transport of Cultural Property

*Article 17. Procedure to Obtain Immunity.* 1. The request mentioned in paragraph 1 of Article 12 of the Convention shall be addressed to the Commissioner-General for Cultural Property. It shall mention the reasons on which it is based and specify the approximate number and the importance of the objects to be transferred, their present location, the location now envisaged, the means of transport to be used, the route to be followed, the date proposed for the transfer and any other relevant information.

2. If the Commissioner-General, after taking such opinions as he deems fit, considers that such transfer is justified, he shall consult those delegates of the Protecting Powers who are concerned, on the measures proposed for carrying it out. Following such consultation, he shall notify the Parties to the conflict concerned of the transfer, including in such notification all useful information.

3. The Commissioner-General shall appoint one or more inspectors, who shall satisfy themselves that only the property stated in the request is to be transferred and that the transport is to be by the approved methods and bears the distinctive emblem. The inspector or inspectors shall accompany the property to its destination.

*Article 18. Transport Abroad.* Where the transfer under special protection is to the territory of another country, it shall be governed not only by Article 12 of the Convention and by Article 17 of the present Regulations, but by the following further provisions:

(a) while the cultural property remains on the territory of another State, that State shall be its depositary and shall extend to it as great a measure of care as that which it bestows upon its own cultural property of comparable importance;

(b) the depositary State shall return the property only on the cessation of the conflict; such return shall be effected within six months from the date on which it was requested;

(c) during the various transfer operations, and while it remains on the territory of another State, the cultural property shall be exempt from confiscation and may not be disposed of either by the depositor or by the depositary. Nevertheless, when the safety of the property requires it, the depositary may, with the assent of the depositor, have the property transported to the territory of a third country, under the conditions laid down in the present article;

(d) the request for special protection shall indicate that the State to whose territory the property is to be transferred accepts the provisions of the present Article.

*Article 19. Occupied Territory.* Whenever a High Contracting Party occupying territory of another High Contracting Party transfers cultural property to a refuge situated elsewhere in that territory, without being able to follow the procedure provided for in Article 17 of the Regulations, the transfer in question shall not be regarded as misappropriation within the meaning of Article 4 of the Convention, provided that the Commissioner-General for Cultural Property certifies in writing, after having consulted the usual custodians, that such transfer was rendered necessary by circumstances.

## Chapter IV: The Distinctive Emblem

*Article 20. Affixing of the Emblem.* 1. The placing of the distinctive emblem and its degree of visibility shall be left to the discretion of the competent authorities of each High Contracting Party. It may be displayed on flags or armlets; it may be painted on an object or represented in any other appropriate form.

2. However, without prejudice to any possible fuller markings, the emblem shall, in the event of armed conflict and in the cases mentioned in Articles 12 and 13 of the Convention, be placed on the vehicles of transport so as to be clearly visible in daylight from the air as well as from the ground. The emblem shall be visible from the ground:

(a) at regular intervals sufficient to indicate clearly the perimeter of a centre containing monuments under special protection;

(b) at the entrance to other immovable cultural property under special protection.

*Article 21. Identification of Persons.* 1. The persons mentioned in Article 17, paragraph 2(b) and (c) of the Convention may wear an armlet bearing the distinctive emblem, issued and stamped by the competent authorities.

2. Such persons shall carry a special identity card bearing the distinctive emblem. This card shall mention at least the surname and first names, the date of birth, the title or rank, and the function of the holder. The card shall bear the photograph of the holder as well as his signature or his fingerprints, or both. It shall bear the embossed stamp of the competent authorities.

3. Each High Contracting Party shall make out its own type of identity card, guided by the model annexed, by way of example, to the present Regulations. The High Contracting Parties shall transmit to each other a specimen of the model they are using. Identity cards shall be made out, if possible, at least in duplicate, one copy being kept by the issuing Power.

4. The said persons may not, without legitimate reason, be deprived of their identity card or of the right to wear the armlet.

***PROTOCOL TO THE UNESCO CONVENTION FOR THE PROTECTION OF CULTURAL PROPERTY IN THE EVENT OF ARMED CONFLICT (1954).*** The Protocol, like the parent Convention, was adopted on 14 May 1954 by an intergovernmental conference convened at the Hague under the auspices of the United Nations Educational, Scientific and Cultural Organization on the invitation of the Government of the Netherlands. Under the Protocol, contracting states undertake not to export cultural property displaced in the event of an armed conflict, or if they do export cultural property, to return it. The text of the protocol is as follows:

The High Contracting Parties are agreed as follows:

**Part I**

1. Each High Contracting Party undertakes to prevent the exportation, from a territory occupies by it during an armed conflict, of cultural property as defined in article 1 of the Convention for the Protection of Cultural Property in the Event of Armed Conflict signed at The Hague on 14 May 1954.

2. Each High Contracting Party undertakes to take into its custody cultural property imported into its territory either directly or indirectly from any occupied territory. This shall either be effected automatically upon the importation of the property or, failing this, at the request of the authorities of that territory.

3. Each High Contracting Party undertakes to return, at the close of hostilities, to the competent authorities of the territory previously occupied, cultural property which is in its territory, if such property has been exported in contravention of the principle laid down in the first paragraph. Such property shall never be retained as war reparations.

4. The High Contracting Party whose obligation it was to prevent the exportation of cultural property from the territory occupied by it, shall pay an indemnity to the holders in good faith of any cultural property which has to be returned in accordance with the preceding paragraph.

**Part II**

5. Cultural property coming from the territory of a High Contracting Party and deposited by it in the territory of another High Contracting Party for the purpose of protecting such property against the dangers of an armed conflict, shall be returned by the latter, at the end of hostilities, to the competent authorities of the territory from which it came.

**Part III**

6. The present Protocol shall bear the date of 14 May 1954 and, until the date of 31 December 1954, shall remain open for signature by all States invited to the Conference which met at The Hague from 21 April 1954 to 14 May 1954.

7. (a) The present Protocol shall be subject to ratification by signatory States in accordance with their respective constitutional procedures.

(b) The instruments of ratification shall be deposited with the Director-General of the United Nations Educational, Scientific and Cultural Organization.

8. From the date of its entry into force, the present Protocol shall be open for accession by all States mentioned in paragraph 6 which have not signed it as well as any other State invited to accede by the Executive Board of the United Nations Educational, Scientific and Cultural Organization. Accession shall be effected by the deposit of an instrument of accession with the Director-General of the United Nations Educational, Scientific and Cultural Organization.

9. The States referred to in paragraphs 6 and 8 may declare, at the time of signature, ratification or accession, that they will not be bound by the provision of section I or by those of section II of the present Protocol.

10. (a) The present Protocol shall enter into force three months after five instruments of ratification have been deposited.

(b) Thereafter, it shall enter into force, for each High Contracting Party, three months after the deposit of its instrument of ratification or accession.

(c) The situations referred to in articles 18 and 19 of the Convention for the Protection of Cultural Property in the Event of Armed Conflict, signed at The Hague on 14 May 1954, shall give immediate effect to ratifications and accession deposited by the parties to the conflict either before or after the beginning of hostilities or occupation. In such cases, the Director-General of the United Nations Educational, Scientific and Cultural Organization shall transmit the communications referred to in paragraph 14 by the speediest method.

11. (a) Each State party to the protocol on the date of its entry into force shall take all necessary measures to ensure its effective application within a period of six months after such entry into force.

(b) This period shall be six months from the date of deposit of the instruments of ratification or accession for any State which deposits its instrument of ratification or accession after the date of the entry into force of the protocol.

12. Any High Contracting Party may, at the time of ratification or accession, or at any time thereafter, declare by notification addressed to the Director-General of the United Nations Educational, Scientific and Cultural Organization, that the present Protocol shall extend to all or any of the

territories for whose international relations it is responsible. The said notification shall take effect three months after the date of its receipt.

13. (a) Each High Contracting Party may denounce the present protocol, on its own behalf, or on behalf of any territory for whose international relations it is responsible.

(b) The denunciation shall be notified by an instrument in writing, deposited with the Director-General of the United Nations Educational, Scientific and Cultural Organization.

(c) The denunciation shall take effect one year after receipt of the instrument of denunciation. However, if, on the expiry of this period, the denouncing Party is involved in an armed conflict, the denunciation shall not take effect until the end of hostilities, or until the operations of repatriating cultural property are completed, whichever is the later.

14. The Director-General of the United Nations Educational, Scientific and Cultural Organization shall inform the States referred to in paragraphs 6 and 8, as well as the United Nations, of the deposit of all the instruments of ratification, accession or acceptance provided for in paragraph 7, 8 and 15 and the notifications and denunciations provided for respectively in paragraphs 12 and 13.

15. (a) The present protocol may be revised if revision is requested by more than one-third of the High Contracting Parties.

(b) The Director-General of the United Nations Educational, Scientific and Cultural Organization shall convene a Conference for this purpose.

(c) Amendments to the present protocol shall enter into force only after they have been unanimously adopted by the High Contracting Parties represented at the Conference and accepted by each of the High Contracting Parties.

(d) Acceptance by the High Contracting Parties of amendments to the present Protocol, which have been adopted by the Conference mentioned in sub- paragraphs (b) and (c), shall be effected by the deposit of a formal instrument with the Director-General of the United Nations Educational, Scientific and Cultural Organization.

(e) After the entry into force of amendments to the present protocol, only the text of the said protocol thus amended shall remain open for ratification or accession.

In accordance with Article 102 of the Charter of the United Nations, the present protocol shall be registered with the Secretariat of the United Nations at the request of the Director-General of the United Nations Educational, Scientific and Cultural Organization.

In faith whereof the undersigned, duly authorized, have signed the present protocol.

Done at the The Hague, this fourteenth day of May 1954, in English, French, Russian and Spanish, the four texts being equally authoritative, in a single copy which shall be deposited in the archives of the United Nations Educational, Scientific and Cultural Organization, and certified true copies of which shall be delivered to all the States referred to in paragraphs 6 and 8 as well as to the United Nations.

## ARMED CONFLICT: DECLARATION ON THE PROTECTION OF WOMEN AND CHILDREN IN EMERGENCY AND ARMED CONFLICT (1974).

In 1974, the UN General Assembly expressed concern over the suffering of women and children in periods of emergency and armed conflict. Aware that they too often were the victims of inhuman acts from which they suffered serious harm, and conscious of its responsibility for the destiny of the rising generation, the Assembly adopted this Declaration and called for its strict observance by all member States.

The Declaration was adopted by the General Assembly on 14 December 1974 (resolution 3318 [XXIX]). The text, annexed to the resolution, is as follows:

The General Assembly,

Having considered the recommendation of the Economic and Social Council contained in its resolution 1861 (LVI) of 16 May 1974,

Expressing its deep concern over the sufferings of women and children belonging to the civilian population who in periods of emergency and armed conflict in the struggle for peace, self-determination, national liberation and independence are too often the victims of inhuman acts and consequently suffer serious harm,

Aware of the suffering of women and children in many areas of the world, especially in those areas subject to suppression, aggression, colonialism, racism, alien domination and foreign subjugation,

Deeply concerned by the fact that, despite general and unequivocal condemnation, colonialism, racism and alien and foreign domination continue to subject many peoples under their yoke, cruelly suppressing the national liberation movements and inflicting heavy losses and incalculable sufferings on the populations under their domination, including women and children,

Deploring the fact that grave attacks are still being made on fundamental freedoms and the dignity of the human person and that colonial and racist foreign domination Powers continue to violate international humanitarian law, . . .

Solemnly proclaims this Declaration on the Protection of Women and Children in Emergency and Armed Conflict and calls for the strict observance of the Declaration by all Member States:

1. Attacks and bombings on the civilian population, inflicting incalculable suffering, especially on women and children, who are the most vulnerable members of the population, shall be prohibited, and such acts shall be condemned.

2. The use of chemical and bacteriological weapons in the course of military operations constitutes one of the most flagrant violations of the Geneva Protocol of 1925, the Geneva Conventions of 1949 and the principles of international humanitarian law and inflicts heavy losses on civilian populations, including defenceless women and children, and shall be severely condemned.

3. All States shall abide fully by their obligations under the Geneva Protocol of 1925 and the Geneva Conventions of 1949, as well as other instruments of international law relative to respect for human rights in armed conflicts, which offer important guarantees for the protection of women and children.

4. All efforts shall be made by States involved in armed conflicts, military operations in foreign territories or military operations in territories still under colonial domination to spare women and children from the ravages of war. All the necessary steps shall be taken to ensure the prohibition of measures such as persecution, torture, punitive measures, degrading treatment and violence, particularly against that

part of the civilian population that consists of women and children.

5. All forms of repression and cruel and inhuman treatment of women and children, including imprisonment, torture, shooting, mass arrests, collective punishment, destruction of dwellings and forcible eviction, committed by belligerents in the course of military operations or in occupied territories shall be considered criminal.

6. Women and children belonging to the civilian population and finding themselves in circumstances of emergency and armed conflict in the struggle for peace, self-determination, national liberation and independence, or who live in occupied territories, shall not be deprived of shelter, food, medical aid or other inalienable rights, in accordance with the provisions of the Universal Declaration of Human Rights, the International Covenant on Civil and Political Rights, the International Covenant on Economic, Social and Cultural Rights, the Declaration of the Rights of the Child or other instruments of international law.

## ARMENIA.

**ARMENIA.** The Republic of Armenia, formerly the Armenian Soviet Socialist Republic of the U.S.S.R., declared its independence in 1991 and was admitted to membership in the United Nations in March of 1992. It is a member of the Commonwealth of Independent States. In 1994, the country failed to ratify a new constitution.

Bounded on the north by Georgia, on the west by Turkey, on the south by Iran, and on the east by Azerbaijan, Armenia is a tableland south of the Caucasus Mountains, lying at an altitude of about 6,000 feet.

Reputed to have been the first country to make Christianity its State religion, Armenia's population, estimated at about 3,429,000, is composed largely of Armenian-speaking Christians. For many years, a feud has existed between Armenia and neighboring Azerbaijan, which has a population consisting largely of ethnic Turks. The dislike of Armenians for Turks is fed by memories of World War I, when the Ottoman Empire carried out mass deportations of its Armenian population.

Recently, over a period of more than five years, small armies have fought to seize and hold the disputed territory of Nagorno-Karabakh, a part of Azerbaijan inhabited by Armenians. Armenia contends that the fighting is being done by Armenian residents of Nagorno-Karabakh, while Azerbaijan contends that national Armenian forces are directly involved. In 1994, the region remained under an Azerbaijani trade embargo that reduced energy and food supplies to the country, forcing the government to reopen the troubled Metzamor nuclear reactor. It has been reported by the NGO Human Rights Watch that Armenia has forcibly drafted conscripts into the army in raids using press-gang tactics to fight in this region and other areas of Azerbaijan.

In August 1993, the UN Security Council issued a statement condemning "the attack on the Fuzuli region from the Nagorno-Karabakh region just as it has previously condemned the invasion and seizure of the districts of Kelbadjar and Agdam in the Azerbaijani Republic." The Council demanded "a stop to all attacks and an immediate cessation of the hostilities and bombardments."

**BIBLIOGRAPHY.** Human Rights Watch. "Armenia," *Human Rights Watch World Report* 1995, pp. 188–190. New York: 1995. NGO report, in English.

U.S. Committee for Refugees. *Faultlines of National Conflict: Refugees and Displaced Persons from Armenia and Azerbaijan.* Washington, D.C.: Immigration and Refugee Services of America, 1994. NGO report, in English.

**ARMS EXPORTS.** The Parliamentary Assembly of the Council of Europe, in a resolution adopted on 27 September 1989 (resolution 928 [1989]), stated its conviction that then-existing levels of arms exports, while declining, clearly went beyond that required for legitimate self-defense and security purposes of many recipient nations and that purchases of arms often were pursued at the expense of the economic and social development of countries in the so-called third-world countries. It also set out its view that many arms exports may be used for violations of human rights over which the exporting country has no control, except to refuse to export arms that could be used for domestic repression.

Concerned that the full facts and figures of international arms sales are not always revealed to parliaments or to the public of member countries and that the final destination of arms can be concealed, the Parliamentary Assembly called upon member States of the Council:

a. to work in favor of reduced, better-controlled arms exports to third world countries, and to create, as a first step, control mechanisms, including at parliamentary level, to oversee hardware arms exports in particular;

b. to initiate the setting up of an open register on the production of and trade in conventional weapons, to which all members of the United Nations will be invited to adhere, such a register to be organized in co-operation with existing specialist organizations such as the Stockholm International Peace Research Institute (SIPRI) and the London International Institute for Strategic Studies (IISS);

c. to establish common criteria and definitions for arms sales, including modernisation and maintenance of equipment already supplied, to draw attention to the risk of armed conflict in the regions of recipient states, and to pay particular regard to international obligations in the field of human rights;

d. to incorporate, where this is not already the case, such criteria in their national legislation while ensuring that they are scrupulously adhered to, and to establish parliamentary control bodies to this end;

e. to use their best endeavours to promote an international conference under the auspices of the United Nations, with the active participation of all the major arms-exporting countries, with a view to limiting, monitoring and controlling arms exports, bearing especially in mind the dangers to world peace of third world conflicts, and to create towards this end a co-ordinating body on North-South arms trade policies;

f. to promote, using where possible existing regional organisations, confidence-building and enhanced security measures for recipient countries consistent with programmes reducing levels of arms exports;

g. to urge third world countries to devote scarce resources primarily to civilian investment, rather than excessive armament, making this one of the factors to be considered when granting official development assistance and debt relief, and to promote democracy in third world societies aimed at the realisation of human rights and socially and environmentally sound policies, and hence help avoid their militarisation;

h. to build upon the 1982 United Nations' proposals and encourage national studies on the economics and practicalities of disarmament and development that can be implemented by exporting and recipient states alike;

i. to ask the Organisation for Economic Co-operation and Development (OECD) to study the problems, possibilities and consequences related to the conversion from military to civilian production, building on past experiences;

j. to give high priority to encouraging a level of harmonisation of national legislation controlling and licensing arms exports, and to take urgent steps to ensure the credibility of and compliance with end-user certificates for arms export sales with the maximum possible parliamentary scrutiny and contact.

***ILLICIT ARMS TRAFFIC.*** In resolution 48/75 F of 16 December 1993, the UN General Assembly recognized that the illicit arms traffic is a disturbing, dangerous, and increasingly common phenomenon and that, with the technical sophistication and destructive capability of conventional weapons, the destabilizing effects of that traffic increase. Accordingly, it called upon all Member States to give priority to eradicating the illicit arms traffic associated with destabilizing activities such as terrorism, drug trafficking, and common criminal acts, and urged them to monitor arms transfers effectively and to adopt strict measures to prevent arms from falling into the hands of parties engaged in the illicit traffic in arms.

***SEE ALSO*** *Chemical Weapons; Conventional Weapons; Nuclear Weapons.*

**ARNOLDSON, KLAS (1844–1916).** In 1908, Klas Pontus Arnoldson, Swedish journalist and pacifist, shared the Nobel Peace Prize with Frederik Bajer. Arnoldson's pacifism was concentrated within the Scandinavian countries; his Peace Prize was awarded primarily because of his support of Norwegian claims to independence at the time of the dissolution of the

Swedish-Norwegian Union in 1905. The choice of Arnoldson was unpopular in Sweden.

Born in Göteborg, Sweden, Arnoldson was a self-educated man who read widely in history, religion, and philosophy. His tolerant religious views were published in *Nordiska Dagbladet,* a daily he edited in the 1870s; in *Sanningssokaren,* a monthly journal devoted to "practical Christianity"; and in many books and pamphlets. In 1883, he co-founded the Swedish Peace and Arbitration Association. In his Nobel lecture, Arnoldson suggested a worldwide referendum on peace: "In all countries, an appeal should be issued for every adult man and woman to sign the following declaration: If other nations will abolish their armed forces and be content with a joint police force for the whole world, then I, the undersigned, wish my own nation to do the same."

***BIBLIOGRAPHY.*** Gray, Tony. *Champions of Peace.* London: Paddington Press, 1976.

Schlessinger, Bernard S., and June H. Schlessinger, eds. *Who's Who of Nobel Prize Winners.* Phoenix, AZ, USA: Oryx Press, 1991.

**ARTICLE 19.** A non-governmental organization in consultative status (roster) with the UN **ECONOMIC AND SOCIAL COUNCIL** and observer status with the **AFRICAN COMMISSION ON HUMAN AND PEOPLES' RIGHTS,** Article 19 takes its name from the 19th article of the Universal Declaration of Human Rights, which states that everyone has the right to freedom of opinion and expression; its major focus is one of strengthening this freedom worldwide.

Article 19 publishes *Article 19 Bulletin, Censorship News, Censorship Reports, Commentaries on Freedom of Expression and Information,* and *Country Studies.*

Article 19. Address: 90 Borough Street, London SE1 1LL, UK. Telephone: (44-71) 403-4822. Fax: (44-71) 403-1943. Director: Frances D'Souza.

**ASIA WATCH.** See **HUMAN RIGHTS WATCH.**

**ASSEMBLY AND ASSOCIATION.** See **FREEDOM OF ASSEMBLY AND ASSOCIATION.**

**ASSER, TOBIAS MICHAEL CAREL (1838–1913).** Two years before his death, Tobias Asser of the Netherlands shared the Nobel Peace Prize with Albert Hermann Fried. Asser, an authority on international law, had a long and distinguished career as an educator and arbitrator. He was cited by the Nobel Prize Committee as a "practical legal statesman" and a "pioneer in the field of international legal relations."

Born in Amsterdam, Asser studied law at the Athenaeum in his home city, received his doctorate in 1860, and taught law at the Athenaeum (later called the University of Amsterdam), resigning his professorship in 1893. Asser firmly believed that legal conflicts between nations should be settled through international arbitration; in 1893, he persuaded the Dutch government to call a conference at The Hague to establish a uniform international procedure for conducting trials. He served as president of the four Hague Conferences on International Law (1893, 1894, 1900, and 1901). Later, in 1907, he was instrumental in organizing the Permanent Court of Arbitration. He also founded the Review of International Law and Comparative Legislation. Among his arbitration successes were the Bering Straits dispute between the United States and Russia and the so-called "Pious Fund" dispute between the United States and Mexico. However, his greatest achievement in the field of international law was his negotiations concerning the neutralization of the Suez Canal; because of his efforts, Spain and Holland were elected to the Suez Canal Commission as representatives of smaller nations, along with Great Britain, France, the United States, and Turkey.

**BIBLIOGRAPHY.** Gray, Tony. *Champions of Peace.* London: Paddington Press, 1976.

Schlessinger, Bernard S., and June H. Schlessinger, eds. *Who's Who of Nobel Prize Winners.* Phoenix, AZ, USA: Oryx Press, 1991.

**ASSOCIATED COUNTRY WOMEN OF THE WORLD.** An international non-governmental organization in consultative status (Category II) with the UN Economic and Social Council, UNESCO, UNICEF, and the FAO, the ACWW has a total membership of 9 million in 65 countries and territories.

Founded in 1930 in Vienna as the "Liaison Committee of Rural Women's and Homemakers' Organizations," the ACWW promotes friendly relations and understanding among rural women and works to raise their standard of living. The group maintains a clearinghouse for information and collects information and compiles reports at the request of UN bodies, including the Commission on the Status of Women. The group has also established trust funds, such as the "Lady Aberdeen Scholarship Fund," the "Elsi Zimmern Memorial Fund" for leadership and organizational training, and the "Nutrition Education Fund" for aid to developing countries.

ACWW publishes the quarterly *The Countrywoman,* conference reports, pamphlets, and a 3H series of booklets for developing countries. It has also published *ACWW 40 Years and More* by Mariann Meier.

Associated Country Women of the World. Address: Vincent House, Vincent Square, London SW1P 2NB, UK. Telephone: (44-71) 834-8635. Fax: (44-71) 233-6205. Cable: Ascoworld London. Secretary-General: Jennifer Pearce.

**ASYLUM: DECLARATION ON TERRITORIAL ASYLUM, UN (1967).** Drawn up by the Sixth (Legal) Committee of the UN General Assembly, the Declaration sets out principles relating to the granting or refusal of asylum by States and makes clear the continuing interest of the international community in the question of asylum. The declaration was adopted by the UN General Assembly on 14 December 1967 (resolution 2312 [XXII]). The text, annexed to that resolution, is as follows:

The General Assembly,

Noting that the purposes proclaimed in the Charter of the United Nations are to maintain international peace and security, to develop friendly relations among all nations and to achieve international co-operation in solving international problems of an economic, social, cultural or humanitarian character and in promoting and encouraging respect for human rights and for fundamental freedoms for all without distinction as to race, sex, language or religion,

Mindful of the Universal Declaration of Human Rights, which declares in article 14 that:

"1. Everyone has the right to seek and to enjoy in other countries asylum from persecution.

2. This right may not be invoked in the case of prosecutions genuinely arising from non-political crimes or from acts contrary to the purposes and principles of the United Nations",

Recalling also article 13, paragraph 2, of the Universal Declaration of Human Rights, which states:

"Everyone has the right to leave any country, including his own, and to return to his country",

Recognizing that the grant of asylum by a State to persons entitled to invoke article 14 of the Universal Declaration of Human Rights is a peaceful and humanitarian act and that, as such, it cannot be regarded as unfriendly by any other State,

Recommends that, without prejudice to existing instruments dealing with asylum and the status of refugees and stateless persons, States should base themselves in their practices relating to territorial asylum on the following principles:

*Article 1.* 1. Asylum granted by a State, in the exercise of its sovereignty, to persons entitled to invoke article 14 of the Universal Declaration of Human Rights, including persons struggling against colonialism, shall be respected by all other States.

2. The right to seek and to enjoy asylum may not be invoked by any person with respect to whom there are serious reasons for considering that he has committed a crime against peace, a war crime or a crime against humanity, as

defined in the international instruments drawn up to make provision in respect of such crimes.

3. It shall rest with the State granting asylum to evaluate the grounds for the grant of asylum.

*Article 2.* 1. The situation of persons referred to in article 1, paragraph 1, is, without prejudice to the sovereignty of States and the purposes and principles of the United Nations, of concern to the international community.

2. Where a State finds difficulty in granting or continuing to grant asylum, States individually or jointly or through the United Nations shall consider, in a spirit of international solidarity, appropriate measures to lighten the burden on that State.

*Article 3.* 1. No person referred to in article 1, paragraph 1, shall be subjected to measures such as rejection at the frontier or, if he has already entered the territory in which he seeks asylum, expulsion or compulsory return to any State where he may be subjected to persecution.

2. Exception may be made to the foregoing principle only for overriding reasons of national security or in order to safeguard the population, as in the case of a mass influx of persons.

3. Should a State decide in any case that exception to the principle stated in paragraph 1 of this article would be justified, it shall consider the possibility of granting to the person concerned, under such conditions as it may deem appropriate, an opportunity, whether by way of provisional asylum or otherwise, of going to another State.

*Article 4.* States granting asylum shall not permit persons who have received asylum to engage in activities contrary to the purposes and principles of the United Nations.

## ASYLUM: INTER-AMERICAN CONVENTION ON DIPLOMATIC ASYLUM (1954).

Under the Convention, States parties may grant asylum to persons being sought for political reasons or political offenses in its legations, war vessels, or military camps or aircraft located in the territory of another State until that territorial State permits the asylee to depart from the country under government guarantees ensuring his safety. The Convention was adopted by the Tenth Inter-American Conference of American States, convened at Caracas, on 28 March 1954 and entered into force on 29 December 1954. The text of the convention (OAS Treaty Series 18) is as follows:

The governments of the Member States of the Organization of American States, desirous of concluding a convention on diplomatic asylum, have agreed to the following articles:

*Article 1.* Asylum granted in legations, war vessels, and military camps or aircraft, to persons being sought for political reasons or for political offences, shall be respected by the territorial State in accordance with the provisions of this convention.

For the purposes of this convention, a legation is any seat of a regular diplomatic mission, the residence of chiefs of mission, and the premises provided by them for the dwelling places of asylees when the number of the latter exceeds the normal capacity of the buildings.

War vessels or military aircraft that may be temporarily in shipyards, arsenals, or shops for repair may not constitute a place of asylum.

*Article 2.* Every State has the right to grant asylum; but it is not obligated to do so or to state its reasons for refusing it.

*Article 3.* It is not lawful to grant asylum to persons who, at the time of requesting it, are under indictment or on trial for common offences or have been convicted by competent regular courts and have not served the respective sentence, nor to deserters from land, sea, and air forces, save when the acts giving rise to the request for asylum, whatever the case may be, are clearly of a political nature.

Persons included in the foregoing paragraph who de facto enter a place that is suitable as an asylum shall be invited to leave or, as the case may be, shall be surrendered to the local authorities, who may not try them for political offences committed prior to the time of the surrender.

*Article 4.* It shall rest with the State granting asylum to determine the nature of the offence or the motives for the persecution.

*Article 5.* Asylum may not be granted except in urgent cases and for the period of time strictly necessary for the asylee to depart from the country with the guarantees granted by the government of the territorial State, to the end that his life, liberty, or personal integrity may not be endangered, or that the asylee's safety is ensured in some other way.

*Article 6.* Urgent cases are understood to be those, among others, in which the individual is being sought by persons or mobs over whom the authorities have lost control, or by the authorities themselves, and is in danger of being deprived of his life or liberty because of political persecution and cannot, without risk, ensure his safety in any other way.

*Article 7.* If a case of urgency is involved, it shall rest with the State granting asylum to determine the degree of urgency of the case.

*Article 8.* The diplomatic representative, commander of a warship, military camp, or military airship, shall, as soon as possible after asylum has been granted, report the fact to the Minister of Foreign Affairs of the territorial State, or to the local administrative authority if the case arose outside the capital.

*Article 9.* The official furnishing asylum shall take into account the information furnished to him by the territorial government in forming his judgement as to the nature of the offence or the existence of related common crimes; but his decision to continue the asylum or to demand a safe-conduct for the asylee shall be respected.

*Article 10.* The fact that the government of the territorial State is not recognized by the State granting asylum shall not prejudice the application of the present convention, and no act carried out by virtue of this convention shall imply recognition.

*Article 11.* The government of the territorial State may, at any time, demand that the asylee be withdrawn from the country, for which purpose the said State shall grant a safe-conduct and the guarantees stipulated in article 5.

*Article 12.* Once asylum has been granted, the State granting asylum may request that the asylee be allowed to depart for foreign territory, and the territorial State is under obligation to grant immediately, except in case of force majeure, the necessary guarantees, referred to in article 5, as well as the corresponding safe-conduct.

*Article 13.* In the cases referred to in the preceding articles, the State granting asylum may require that the guarantees be given in writing, and may take into account, in determining the rapidity of the journey, the actual conditions of danger involved in the departure of the asylee.

The State granting asylum has the right to transfer the asylee out of the country. The territorial State may point out the preferable route for the departure of the asylee, but this does not imply determining the country of destination.

If the asylum is granted on board a warship or military airship, departure may be made therein, but complying with the previous requisite of obtaining the appropriate safe-conduct.

*Article 14*. The State granting asylum cannot be held responsible for the prolongation of asylum caused by the need for obtaining the information required to determine whether or not the said asylum is proper, or whether there are circumstances that might endanger the safety of the asylee during the journey to a foreign country.

*Article 15*. When, in order to transfer an asylee to another country, it may be necessary to traverse the territory of a State that is a party to this convention, transit shall be authorized by the latter, the only requisite being the presentation, through diplomatic channels, of a safe-conduct, duly countersigned and bearing a notation of his status as asylee by the diplomatic mission that granted asylum.

En route, the asylee shall be considered under the protection of the State granting asylum.

*Article 16*. Asylees may not be landed at any point in the territorial State or at any place near thereto, except for exigencies of transportation.

*Article 17*. Once the departure of the asylee has been carried out, the State granting asylum is not bound to settle him in its territory; but it may not return him to his country of origin, unless this is the express wish of the asylee.

If the territorial State informs the official granting asylum of its intention to request the subsequent extradition of the asylee, this shall not prejudice the application of any provision of the present convention. In that event, the asylee shall remain in the territory of the State granting asylum until such time as the formal request for extradition is received, in accordance with the juridical principles governing that institution in the State granting asylum. Preventive surveillance over the asylee may not exceed thirty days.

Payment of the expenses incurred by such transfer and of preventive control shall devolve upon the requesting State.

*Article 18*. The official furnishing asylum may not allow the asylee to perform acts contrary to the public peace or to interfere in the internal politics of the territorial State.

*Article 19*. If as a consequence of a rupture of diplomatic relations the diplomatic representative who granted asylum must leave the territorial State, he shall abandon it with the asylees.

If this is not possible for reasons independent of the wish of the asylee or the diplomatic representative, he must surrender them to the diplomatic mission of a third State, which is a party to this convention, under the guarantees established in the convention.

If this is also not possible, he shall surrender them to a state that is not a party to this convention and that agrees to maintain the asylum. The territorial State is to respect the said asylum.

*Article 20*. Diplomatic asylum shall not be subject to reciprocity. Every person is under its protection, whatever his nationality.

*Article 21*. The present convention shall be open for signature by the Member States of the Organization of American States and shall be ratified by the signatory States in accordance with their respective constitutional procedures.

*Article 22*. The original instrument, whose texts in the English, French, Portuguese, and Spanish languages are equally authentic, shall be deposited in the Pan American Union, which shall send certified copies to the governments for the purpose of ratification. The instruments of ratification shall be deposited in the Pan American Union, and the said organization shall notify the signatory governments of the said deposit.

*Article 23*. The present convention shall enter into force among the States that ratify it in the order in which their respective ratifications are deposited.

*Article 24*. The present convention shall remain in force indefinitely, but may be denounced by any of the signatory States by giving advance notice of one year, at the end of which period it shall cease to have effect for the denouncing State, remaining in force, however, among the remaining signatory States. The denunciation shall be transmitted to the Pan American Union, which shall inform the other signatory States thereof.

## ASYLUM: INTER-AMERICAN CONVENTION ON TERRITORIAL ASYLUM (1954).

Under the Convention, States parties undertake to recognize and respect the right of every State to admit into its territory such persons as it deems advisable without, by so doing, giving rise to a complaint by any other State, as well as the right of every State to refuse to expel or extradite from its territory persons persecuted for political reasons or offenses elsewhere. The Convention was adopted by the Tenth Inter-American Conference of American States, convened at Caracas, on 28 March 1954 and entered into force on 29 December 1954. The text of the convention (OAS Treaty Series 19), is as follows:

The governments of the Member States of the Organization of American States, desirous of concluding a convention regarding territorial asylum, have agreed to the following articles:

*Article 1*. Every State has the right, in the exercise of its sovereignty, to admit into its territory such persons as it deems advisable, without, through the exercise of this right, giving rise to complaint by any other State.

*Article 2*. The respect which, according to international law, is due the jurisdictional right of each State over the inhabitants in its territory, is equally due, without any restriction whatsoever, to that which it has over persons who enter it proceeding from a State in which they are persecuted for their beliefs, opinions, or political affiliations, or for acts which may be considered as political offences.

Any violation of sovereignty that consists of acts committed by a government or its agents in another State against the life or security of an individual, carried out on the territory of another State, may not be considered attenuated because the persecution began outside its boundaries or is due to political considerations or reasons of state.

*Article 3*. No State is under the obligation to surrender to another State, or to expel from its own territory, persons persecuted for political reasons or offences.

*Article 4*. The right of extradition is not applicable in connexion with persons who, in accordance with the qualification of the solicited State, are sought for political offences, or for common offences committed for political ends, or when extradition is solicited for predominantly political motives.

*Article 5.* The fact that a person has entered into the territorial jurisdiction of a State surreptitiously or irregularly does not affect the provisions of this convention.

*Article 6.* Without prejudice to the provisions of the following articles, no State is under the obligation to establish any distinction in its legislation, or in its regulations or administrative acts applicable to aliens, solely because of the fact that they are political asylees or refugees.

*Article 7.* Freedom of expression of thought, recognized by domestic law for all inhabitants of a State, may not be ground of complaint by a third State on the basis of opinions expressed publicly against it or its government by asylees or refugees, except when these concepts constitute systematic propaganda through which they incite to the use of force or violence against the government of the complaining State.

*Article 8.* No State has the right to request that another State restrict for the political asylees or refugees the freedom of assembly or association which the latter State's internal legislation grants to all aliens within its territory, unless such assembly or association has as its purpose fomenting the use of force or violence against the government of the soliciting State.

*Article 9.* At the request of the interested State, the State that has granted refuge or asylum shall take steps to keep watch over, or to intern at a reasonable distance from its border, those political refugees or asylees who are notorious leaders of a subversive movement, as well as those against whom there is evidence that they are disposed to join it.

Determination of the reasonable distance from the border, for the purpose of internment, shall depend upon the judgment of the authorities of the State of refuge.

All expenses incurred as a result of the internment of political asylees and refugees shall be chargeable to the State that makes the request.

*Article 10.* The political internees referred to in the preceding article shall advise the government of the host State whenever they wish to leave its territory. Departure therefrom will be granted, under the condition that they are not to go to the country from which they came; and the interested government is to be notified.

*Article 11.* In all cases in which a complaint or request is permissible in accordance with this convention, the admissibility of evidence presented by the demanding State shall depend on the judgement of the solicited State.

*Article 12.* This convention remains open to the signature of the Member States of the Organization of American States, and shall be ratified by the signatory States in accordance with their respective constitutional procedures.

*Article 13.* The original instrument, whose texts in the English, French, Portuguese, and Spanish languages are equally authentic, shall be deposited in the Pan American Union, which shall send certified copies to the governments for the purpose of ratification. The instruments of ratification shall be deposited in the Pan American Union; this organization shall notify the signatory governments of said deposit.

*Article 14.* This convention shall take effect among the States that ratify it in the order in which their respective ratifications are deposited.

*Article 15.* This convention shall remain effective indefinitely, but may be denounced by any of the signatory States by giving advance notice of one year, at the end of which period it shall cease to have effect for the denouncing State, remaining, however, in force among the remaining signatory States. The denunciation shall be forwarded to the Pan American Union, which shall notify the other signatory States thereof.

**AUNG SAN SUU KYI (1945– ).** The daughter of a Burmese revolutionary, Aung San Suu Kyi was awarded the 1991 Nobel Peace Prize for being "the leader of a democratic opposition which employs nonviolent means to resist a regime characterized by brutality." The Nobel Peace Prize Committee also called her "one of the most extraordinary examples of civil courage in Asia in recent decades."

Born in Yangon, Aung San Suu Kyi is the daughter of "the father of modern Burma," Aung San, who was assassinated in 1947, less than six months before Burma became independent. She lived much of her life abroad, receiving her education in India and Great Britain. While studying political science, philosophy, and economics at Oxford University, she became strongly influenced by a sense of duty toward her native country, in particular to learn more about her father. In intervening years, she researched as much as she could about him, as well as studying the history of Burma and its people. However, it was years later—after her marriage and the birth of two sons—that she returned to Burma, now Myanmar, to care for her dying mother.

On returning to Myanmar in 1988, Aung San Suu Kyi found a country in turmoil, with people demonstrating for democratic reform after years of autocratic and xenophobic rule by General Ne Win. Armed soldiers patroled the streets, and several hundred demonstrators, mostly students, were killed. In August 1988, an estimated 3,000 demonstrators were killed by soldiers firing indiscriminately into crowds. She made her first public appearance in late August, emerging as a hope for reconciliation between the army and the people, since she viewed the armed forces as a necessary part of a nation. She soon became the leader of the democratic movement, establishing the National League for Democracy, which won a landslide victory in 1989 elections. The government, however, refused to recognize the election results.

In July 1989, Aung San Suu Kyi was placed under house arrest. For the next five years, she lived in a two-story house, owned by her family, overlooking Inya Lake in Yangon, never leaving the compound. In January 1995, after many international appeals, especially a UN resolution that called for her unconditional release, the government released Aung San Suu Kyi from house arrest.

**BIBLIOGRAPHY.** Aung San Suu Kyi. *Freedom from Fear and Other Writings.* Oxford, UK: Oxford University Press, 1991.

*Current Biography Yearbook 1992.* New York: W.H. Wilson.

**AUSTRALIA.** The Commonwealth of Australia occupies an island continent in Oceania, between the Indian Ocean and the Coral and Tasmanian Seas. It includes five continental States and the island State of Tasmania and has jurisdiction over a number of island territories in the Indian Ocean and the sub-Antarctic, including the Australia Antarctic territory. It achieved independence from Great Britain in 1901, and became a member of the United Nations in 1945. Its population is estimated to be 16,965,000. The 1986 census counted 3,477,400 (22%) overseas-born persons, of whom approximately 50% were born in non-English-speaking countries. In that census about 1.5% of the respondents identified themselves as Aboriginals or Torres Strait Islanders. Members of these groups are entitled by law to the full range of fundamental rights and freedoms of other Australians but, in practice, remain in a disadvantaged position. English is the official language; aboriginal vernaculars are used by some of the indigenous peoples. Christianity (Anglican, 30%; Roman Catholic, 30%; Methodist/Presbyterian, 15%; and others, 25%) is the predominant religion. Literacy is estimated at 99%.

The government (1992) took the form of a federal parliamentary state and member of the Commonwealth of Nations, of which the British sovereign is the symbolic head. Executive power is exercised by the governor-general, representing the crown, and a cabinet headed by the prime minister, representing the party or coalition given the majority in a popular election. The federal Parliament consists of a 76-member Senate, members of which are elected for terms of six years, and a 148-member House of Representatives, members of which serve for terms of three years. Voting is compulsory for those 18 or over. Judicial authority is exercised by the High Court of Australia, federal courts, and state courts, each state having its own judicial system. Political parties include the Australian Labor Party, the Liberal Party, and the National Party.

Australia's federal and legal systems were described by the Government in its eighth periodic report submitted in 1991 to the Committee on the Elimination of Racial Discrimination (CERD/C/194/Add. 2) as follows:

### Federal System

Australia is a federation in which legislative, executive and judicial powers are shared between the federal Parliament, the executive and the judiciary and the corresponding organs of the six States: New South Wales, Victoria, Queensland, Western Australia, South Australia, and Tasmania. In each of these political units, there is a parliament elected by the people, an executive responsible to that parliament, formed by the majority party or parties in parliament, and an independent judiciary.

In addition to the States, there are also a number of Australian Territories, which are those parts of Australia not part of a State. Australia has ten territories in all. The inhabited territories are:

(a) Territories internal to the mainland: the Australian Capital Territory (which includes Canberra, the capital city of Australia and seat of the federal Government), the Northern Territory, and the Jervis Bay Territory;

(b) Territories external to the mainland: The Australian Antarctic Territory, Norfolk Island, Cocos (Keeling Islands), and Christmas Island.

The uninhabited Territories, which are all external to the mainland are: the Territory of Ashmore and Cartier Islands, the Coral Sea Islands Territory, and the Territory of Heard Island and McDonald Islands.

Two of the Territories—the Australian Capital Territory and the Northern Territory—are self-governing and may be regarded, for the purposes of this report, as standing in the same position as a State of Australia. A third Territory—Norfolk Island—has more limited legislative and executive government to enable it to run its own affairs to the greatest practicable extent. The federal Government is responsible for the administration of the remaining territories.

### Legal System

The laws applying in Australia fall into two broad categories:

(a) Legislation in the form of statutes passed by a parliament or subordinate legislation made by the executive which is subject to disallowance by Parliament; and

(b) Rules derived from decisions of courts, being:

(i) the common law proper (i.e., laws developed through judicial recognition, independent of any legislative enactment; and

(ii) judicial interpretation of legislation.

In the Australian legal system, every person, whether private citizen or government official, is equally subject to the law. Governments must operate through and within the law. Government officials must have legal authority for their actions and are subject to legal sanctions if they contravene the law, including sanctions for breach of the criminal law. Disciplinary proceedings may also be brought against government officials.

Under the Constitution, the federal Parliament is granted specified legislative powers. Most of those powers are possessed concurrently with the States while a smaller number are vested exclusively in the Commonwealth. Each State has power, which it exercises subject to the Constitution, to make laws for the peace, order and good government of the State. Where legislative power is possessed concurrently by the Commonwealth and the States, the Constitution provides that federal laws prevail over inconsistent State laws.

The Constitution confers on the federal Parliament the power to make laws with respect of external affairs. . . . The Constitution also confers on the federal Parliament the power to make laws with respect to the people of any "race" for whom it is deemed necessary to make special laws. This confers plenary power on the federal Parliament to legislate with respect to Australia's indigenous peoples–Aboriginal and Torres Strait Islander people. . . .

From the early years of its independence, Australia

has been noted for its legislation promoting the enjoyment of certain human rights: political rights for women were recognized in 1902, old-age pensions initiated in 1910, maternity allowances in 1912, subsidies to parents of more than one child in 1941, and unemployment and sickness benefits in 1944. At the same time, however, its "white Australia" immigration policy was known and condemned in most parts of the world. Although the policy was publicly discarded in 1973, European migrants are still favored; the criteria that prospective migrants must be "economically viable" and "have personal qualities that would enable them to fit into the Australian community" have been used to exclude millions of Asian and African candidates.

**ABORIGINES.** As regards Aboriginals, the Australian public was largely unaware of their condition until the Queen of England arrived in Canberra in 1974 to open Parliament and was confronted with an impressive demonstration protesting their deplorable situation. The resulting increased awareness of the problems that they faced led to the adoption on 10 December 1981 of the Human Rights Commission Act and the development of an attitude of "multiculturalism" in the country.

However, the situation of the aboriginal people was drawn to public attention forcibly in January 1988, when thousands of them gathered in Sydney to protest, rather than to join in, Australia's celebration of the bicentennial of the arrival of its first white settlers. Boycotting the festivities, the aboriginals pointed out that for them the two- century period had been one of annihilation, dispossession, and increasing poverty. Their population had been reduced to about 160,000—about half its total before the advent of the settlers—and they had become outcasts in their own land, living on reservations or in urban slums, suffering infant mortality three times the national rate and earning half the national average wage.

The Australian Government has taken a number of steps over the years to provide protection of the Aboriginal heritage. The Australian Heritage Commission Act has special provisions to protect places associated with Aboriginal history, culture or beliefs. About 3,000 Aboriginal sites are included on the Register of the National Estate. Among other acts are the Aboriginal and Torres Strait Islander Heritage Protection Act of 1984 and the Protection of Movable Cultural Heritage Act of 1986. In addition, The Museum of Australia Act provides that one of the Museum's three major components shall be a Gallery of Aboriginal Australia. Along with the growing interest in preserving and diffusing Aboriginal culture is an acknowledgment that the Aboriginals have contributed much to the culture and science. The Australian Institute of Aboriginal

Studies is constituted by an Act of Parliament to promote Aboriginal studies; to publish or assist in the publication of the results of these studies; and to encourage and assist co-operation among universities, museums, and other institutions concerned with such studies.

In the area of education, the federal government mandates that full educational opportunities must be available to all persons of Aboriginal and Torres Strait Islander decent and that they receive an education in harmony with their cultural values and chosen lifestyle. The Government stated in its 1991 report to the UN Committee on the Elimination of Racial Discrimination that

Aboriginal and Torres Strait Islander Australians are entitled by law to the full range of fundamental rights and freedoms of other Australians, but in practice many remain in a disadvantaged situation. The Australian government recognizes that these citizens constitute a group for whom special measures are required and has developed a range of programmes to address the continuing effects of disadvantage. It is worth emphasizing, however, that the problems confronting Aboriginal and Torres Strait Islander peoples—just as those confronting migrants—should not be seen exclusively in terms of racial discrimination. Clashes of value systems and cultures are frequently at issue.

**MULTICULTURALISM.** According to the 1986 census, 22% of the Australian population was born overseas and approximately 50% of this figure was born in a non-English-speaking country. Because of its immigration statistics, as well as its indigenous population, Australia is faced with the question of multiculturalism. As regards multiculturalism, the Australian Government stated, in the aforementioned 1991 report, that it

is firmly committed to a policy of multiculturalism, which assures the right of all individuals to retain and develop their culture, language and lifestyle and to participate fully in all aspects of diverse cultures, and aims to ensure that full use is made of the skills and abilities of all Australian residents regardless of cultural background or country of origin.

In defining multiculturalism—as opposed to the use of the term as simply a description of Australia's irreversible cultural and ethnic diversity—the federal Government has emphasized that its multicultural policy is quite distinct from immigration policy. It plays no part in migrant selection.

The Government's definition of multicultural policy has three dimensions:
(a) Cultural identity: the right of all Australians, within carefully defined limits, to express and share their individual cultural heritage, including their language and religion;
(b) Social justice: the right of all Australians to equality of treatment and opportunity, including the removal of bar-

riers of race, ethnicity, culture, religion, language, gender, or place of birth; and

(c) Economic efficiency: the need to maintain, develop and utilize effectively the skills and talents of all Australians, regardless of background.

There are also limits to multiculturalism, and these have been made explicit:

(a) Multicultural policies are based upon the premise that all Australians should have an overriding and unifying commitment to Australia, to its interests and future, first and foremost;

(b) Multicultural policies require all Australians to accept the basic structures and principles of Australian society—the Constitution and the rule of law, tolerance and equality, parliamentary democracy, freedom of speech and religion, English as the national language, and equality of the sexes; and

(c) Multiculturalism policies impose obligations as well as confer rights: the right to express one's own culture and beliefs involves a reciprocal responsibility to accept the right of others to express their views and values.

In July 1989, the federal Government released the National Agenda for Multicultural Australia, the most comprehensive and forward-looking statement of multicultural policy ever endorsed by an Australian Government, federal or State.

The significance of the National Agenda is threefold:

(a) It clearly defined the policy of multiculturalism, articulating the long-term goals and objectives that underpin the policy;

(b) It set in [motion] a series of enduring structural and institutional changes; and

(c) It included a broad package of immediate programme initiatives.

**HUMAN RIGHTS AND EQUAL OPPORTUNITY COMMISSION.** The Australian Government established the Human Rights and Equal Opportunity Commission on 10 December 1986 (Human Rights Day), when its predecessor, the Human Rights Commission, completed its five-year term. The Government explained the scope and function of the new Commission to the United Nations (E/1990/7/Add. 13):

The Commission presently has responsibilities under four Acts of the Australian Parliament: (a) the Racial Discrimination Act of 1975; (b) The Sex Discrimination Act of 1984; (c) The Human Rights and Equal Opportunity Commission of 1986; and (d) The Privacy Act of 1988.

Under these Acts of Parliament, the Commission has particular responsibilities in relation to seven international instruments: (a) The International Covenant on Civil and Political Rights; (b) the UN Declaration of the Rights of the Child; (c) the Declaration on the Rights of Mentally Retarded Persons; (d) the Declaration on the Rights of Disabled Persons; (e) the Convention concerning Discrimination in Respect of Employment and Occupation (ILO Convention 111); (f) the Convention on the Elimination of All Forms of Racial Discrimination; and (g) the Convention on the Elimination of All Forms of Discrimination against Women.

The functions of the Commission include the following:

(a) To examine legislation and, in certain cases, proposed legislation, to determine whether it conforms with Australia's obligations under the various international instruments within the Commission's jurisdiction;

(b) To inquire into acts or practices in Australia that may be inconsistent with any rights established by these instruments;

(c) Where the Commission and the court consider it appropriate, to intervene in private litigation when issues of human rights arise;

(d) To coordinate research, educational, and other programmes for the purposes of promoting human rights;

(e) To report to the Federal Government on its own initiative or when requested by the Federal Government, on any action that should be taken by Australia on matters relating to human rights or to comply with Australia's obligations under these international instruments or other instruments declared by the Attorney-General to be "relevant international instruments" for the Commission's purposes; and

(f) In certain circumstances, to receive and conciliate individual complaints of human rights infringements.

It may be observed generally that three important principles have emerged in Australia in the development of legislative measures concerning human rights. These are:

(a) That legislation may be required in particular areas to supplement common law guarantees of human rights, and selective remedies may need to be developed for the enforcement of specific human rights;

(b) That formal administrative machinery needs to be established to investigate infringements of human rights and to attempt to achieve a settlement of issues of conciliation; and

(c) That facilities need to be established, on a systematic basis, that foster programmes of education and research and other programmes to promote human rights.

**UN OBSERVATIONS.** From 24 to 28 May 1993, the UN Committee on Economic, Social and Cultural Rights examined a report from the Australian Government on its efforts to comply with the Covenant and observed the following (E/C.12/1993/9):

### Positive Aspects

The Committee notes with satisfaction the efforts made within the federal structure of Australia to establish machinery to ensure compliance with the education-related provisions of the Covenant. The Committee also notes with satisfaction that the State party, since the submission of its previous report to the Committee, has undertaken various initiatives and measures designed to redress imbalances in the provision of education for identified disadvantaged groups in Australia, including the Aboriginal and Torres Strait Islander populations, girls, persons with disabilities and minority groups. The Committee welcomes the fact that numerous studies or reviews have been undertaken or are in preparation on education-related matters and that the findings of these studies are taken into account in the determination of educational policy and national action plans. The Committee finds of particular importance the development of a national strategy for equity in schooling, the impact on the teaching profession of the National Project on the Quality of Teaching and Learning, and the initiatives being taken concerning human rights education in curriculum development. The Committee also welcomes the development of appropriate indicators to monitor progress in the achievement of set objectives of national policy on education.

The Committee is encouraged by the development of programmes to promote multiculturalism and the recognition being placed on the racial and cultural differences in Australia.

### Factors and Difficulties Impeding the Implementation of the Covenant

The Committee notes that differences exist in legislation concerning education within the federal system of Australia. The Committee also notes that the State party has identified several groups as being disadvantaged with regard to the participation in education. In particular, the Committee notes that socio-economic factors and the isolation of certain Aboriginal and Torres Strait Islander communities constitute major difficulties in the implementation of the Covenant.

The Committee recognizes that limited resources and the geographic isolation of certain aboriginal communities have been the principal impediments in furthering cultural development and international contacts.

### Principal Subjects of Concern

The Committee considers the situation of disadvantaged groups in the educational system to be of particular concern. The Committee specifically notes the situation of the Aboriginals and Torres Strait Islanders in education that affects their prospects for future employment, as well as the problems of illiteracy among the adults of this group, the majority of which did not have primary and secondary education.

The Committee is also concerned about the lack of opportunities available to persons with disabilities to fully enjoy their rights to education.

The Committee is concerned about the effects of funding accorded to non-government schools on the quality of education in government schools.

As regards the implementation of Article 15 of the Covenant, the Committee expresses its particular concern that Aboriginals and Torres Strait Islanders do not have sufficient opportunities to fully involve themselves in creating awareness of their cultural heritage.

The Committee expresses concern over provisions of the Federal Customs Regulations that prohibit the importation of certain materials as referred to in paragraph 310 of the report. The practical application of these provisions could run counter to freedom of artistic creation and performance.

### Suggestions and Recommendations

The Committee underlines the importance, in the context of federalism in Australia, of close cooperation and coordination between different authorities and organizations for the effective implementation of the provisions contained in Articles 13–15 of the Covenant.

The Committee suggests that activities be undertaken throughout the federal structure of Australia to sensitize society to the situation and different needs of persons with disabilities and other groups. As part of the efforts to be undertaken to change and influence attitudes towards vulnerable groups, the Committee recommends that further measures be taken to strengthen the human rights education component in formal and non-formal curricula.

The Committee considers it important that the State party take particular measures to involve different groups in the process of preparing reports for the Committee and in making these reports widely known and available to the public as well as to make available the summary records and concluding observations following the Committee's consideration of the report.

The Committee recommends that due attention be given to the development of indicators for measuring progress in the implementation of the rights covered by Articles 13–15 of the Covenant. Information on the results and progress made in this area should be provided when the State party next reports to the Committee. In addition, the Committee emphasizes the importance of taking steps to monitor more closely the general situation of Aboriginals and Torres Strait Islanders and other disadvantaged groups particularly in education and culture. The Committee, therefore, appreciates that the government of Australia is fully aware of the difficulties impeding the implementation of the Covenant.

The Committee emphasizes the appropriateness of the efforts being undertaken by the Government to identify the needs of disadvantaged groups and to continue to draw on the results of studies and reviews in the development of policy initiatives to respond to the needs of such groups. The Committee underscores the importance that it attaches to the economic, social and cultural rights of persons with disabilities and of the elderly and therefore urges the Government to direct major efforts towards assessing and addressing the needs of these groups in relation to their rights under Articles 13–15 of the Covenant.

The Committee appreciates the expression of commitment by the Government to implement equity in schooling as a matter of public responsibility, and thus recommends that legislative efforts be undertaken to eliminate remaining obstacles in the equitable access to educational establishments . . .

The Committee recommends that action be taken to provide Aboriginal artists with opportunities to participate in international fora in order to promote awareness in their indigenous culture.

***SPECIAL PROBLEMS OF CHILDREN.*** The problem of the sale of children, child pornography, and child prostitution in Australia was addressed by a UN Special Rapporteur on a two-week visit to that country (at the invitation of the Australian Government) beginning on 18 October 1992. The Special Rapporteur, Vitit Muntarbhorn, visited various parts of the country including Cairns, Alice Springs, Darwin, Perth, Sydney, Melbourne, Canberra, and Brisbane and also visited various projects at the field level to speak with children and youths in a number of communities in order to reflect their views in his report. He also consulted governmental and non-governmental organizations, as well as concerned individuals. The report (E/CN.4/1993/67/Add. 1) recommends the following:

## A. General

More attention should be paid to the need to prevent the sale of children, child prostitution, and child pornography and to address their root causes. On the one hand, this depends upon integrated and interdisciplinary action to tackle economic deprivations, cultural alienation, and family breakup and breakdown. The measures to be maximized include proactive human development activities and support facilities, such as access to education and training, income generating occupations, availability of loans and credit for self-employment, support for self-management, child and family subsidies, and maximization of their participation at all stages of the development process.

There is a close relationship between the above and the need to return land to the Aboriginal and Torres Strait Islander peoples so that they can use it to regenerate community participation. However, prevention calls for more effective monitoring and law enforcement against criminal elements seeking to exploit children nationally and internationally.

Both the supply and demand sides of child exploitation need to be dealt with in a more coordinated manner. Of particular concern is the responsibility of the customers of child exploitation, as well as that of intermediaries and suppliers. There is a need to encourage private sector participation so as to exert pressure on industries to safeguard against child exploitation.

Information gathering on issues of child exploitation should be improved continually, especially as much of this work is not publicized. The catalytic Australian report Our Homeless Children should be updated. Statistics should be collected more extensively on the issues of the sale of children, child prostitution, and child pornography. Data need to be disaggregated so as to highlight gender variations and the problems relating to different groups in Australia.

The interrelationship between laws, policies, and practices relating to children's rights in the federal, state and customary settings should be analyzed more closely, and a compendium on these matters should be compiled.

The multicultural nature of Australian society attests to the need for greater participation from all sectors of the community in preventing and remedying the problems of concern to this study. The issues of child abuse and exploitation should be raised more visibly in all communities and in the educational process so as to improve public awareness of the dangers that may lurk for children. Multilingualism in collecting and disseminating relevant information, and training on the different cultures existing in Australia should also be promoted.

Comprehensive policies, laws and mechanisms on child protection at the federal, state and local levels are desirable. The possibility of a federal code on youth and children's rights and related federal policy and the appointment of a federal minister on child and youth affairs may be explored. The mechanisms that may be tendered for the future include children's ombudspersons, interstate consultative forums, youth/child participatory councils, local committees on children's rights, neighbourhood watch, and cross-cultural watchdogs for child protection.

Law enforcement authorities should establish specific child protection units. They should be trained to respond to the range of the rights of the child espoused by the Convention on the Rights of the Child and the various cultures that interplay with these rights. The participation of the Aboriginal and Torres Strait Islander peoples, migrant groups, and women in the police force should be encouraged. Dialogues between the police and representatives of community groups and the children themselves should be enhanced.

Interaction between government authorities, community leaders, and non-governmental organizations should be promoted to prevent and remedy the negative situations covered in this report. This includes the need to maximize the role of elders in the Aboriginal and Torres Strait Islander communities. The fact that many grandparents are now looking after their grandchildren, where the parents are absent or unable to do so, invites further cooperation with and support for grandparents to assist and protect their grandchildren.

Protection of children from exploitation is closely associated with respect for women's rights. Stronger measures are desired to counter the vestiges of gender discrimination that are detrimental to both women and children. These include action against domestic violence and alcoholism, the need for responsible parenting, and sharing by both parents in looking after children.

Cooperation with the mass media should be maximized, especially as they may assist in identifying cases of child exploitation and in mobilizing the community against the perpetrators. The potential of multilingualism in relation to use of the mass media in order to reach out to the different sectors of the community may also be explored.

## B. Sale of Children

The possibility of enacting new laws, or including new provisions in existing laws, against the sale and trafficking of children should be considered at the federal and state levels.

Measures should be taken to remedy the consequences of forced transfers of Aboriginal children from their families. These include support for children to trace their families and facilities to enhance family reunification. Aboriginal attitudes towards adoptions should be borne in mind and child placement principles reflecting Aboriginal cultures should be recognized by all states.

The federal and state systems should ensure that private adoption agencies are registered and that effective procedures are in place against commercialization of intercountry adoptions. They should bear in mind international developments, particularly under the auspices of the Hague Conference on Private International Law, to finalize an international convention on intercountry adoptions. They should promote bilateral and other arrangements with the source countries so as to prevent the sale of children through intercountry adoptions. Development aid may also be given to families in the source countries so as to enable them to retain their children.

States should endeavour to harmonize their adoption laws and policies in keeping with the standards set by the Convention on the Rights of the Child. Cooperation with the federal authorities and foreign counterparts should be improved so as to ensure that malpractices do not take place when Australians complete the adoption process abroad and seek to have it recognized in Australia.

Precautions to prevent abuses that may arise from guardianship orders and sponsorships are required, as these are sometimes used to circumvent adoption laws and procedures. More study of "adoption-like" practices is recommended.

States should pass anti-surrogacy legislation. They should liaise with the federal authorities to prevent Australians from entering into surrogacy arrangements overseas. This is an area where extra-territorial application of laws may be recognized in the context of Australians seeking to bypass local jurisdiction.

The possibility of acceding to the ILO Minimum Age Convention, 1973 (No. 138), concerning child labour should be canvassed. This should be coupled with the adoption of comprehensive laws and policies in all States to prohibit the exploitation of child labour. The provisions should include minimum age, classification of prohibited work, work conditions, and remedies for violations by employers. More preventive, remedial and integrated measures are required to protect children from being used in criminal activities, such as burglaries and the sale of drugs. A study on the employment of children in family businesses among migrant groups is also recommended.

States should adopt effective laws and policies on organ transplantation with specific provisions to protect children from exploitation. The guidelines established by the World Health Organization on this matter should be taken into account.

### C. Child Prostitution

States should ensure that they address the root causes of child prostitution by means of the integrated and interdisciplinary measures noted above, as well as provide redress through appropriate sanctions, legal aid and assistance.

States should harmonize their laws and policies on child prostitution so as to be consistent with each other. The possibility of protecting children from prostitution until the age of 18 may be explored, and this would be in keeping with the definition of "child" offered by the Convention on the Rights of the Child.

Improved law enforcement against the customers of child prostitution is advocated as is the need to apprehend the intermediaries. In the context of transnational sexual exploitation, the possibility of incriminating the acts of Australians overseas is proposed.

Greater cooperation and information exchange through formal and informal channels between the receiving countries and sending countries are required.

The recommendations of the recent National Conference on Child Prostitution in Asian Tourism, held in Melbourne in November 1992, should be supported as follows:

(a) In the receiving countries: Establishment of specialist law-enforcement units; Scrutiny of sponsorships of children which may lead to child exploitation; Prosecution of sex offenders of children; Monitoring and tracing of pedophiles; Visits by law-enforcement personnel from sending countries to receiving countries so as to improve coordination with law-enforcement personnel, and vice versa.

(b) In the sending countries: Identification of those involved in organising sex tours; Maintenance of files on pedophiles; Establishment of specialized units to collect information; Vigilance by customs officials where nationals return from abroad under suspicion of carrying child pornography.

There should be mandatory reporting of child-abuse cases, and the rules of evidence may need to be liberalized so as not to require corroboration in these instances.

More education on safe sex techniques to protect young people from the threat of AIDS is called for. Support facilities such as counselling, hospices and subsidies are also needed for those with AIDS.

Rehabilitation measures should be promoted to assist children in prostitution to return to the community and adopt other lifestyles. This entails appropriate accommodation, counselling and psychological support, flexible schooling, and occupational activities that can provide for livelihood needs. The emphasis should be on development of the child, bearing in mind cultural sensitivity, rather than welfare for the child. The role of community organizations and cooperation with community networks should be maximized in this regard.

### D. Child Pornography

State laws should prohibit the possession of child pornography, as well as their production, sale, distribution and exhibition. They should bear in mind technological advancements that may need to be tackled to prevent child pornography. The current age threshold of 16 for the protection of children from exploitation may also need to be reconsidered in light of the Convention on the Rights of the Child, which uses 18 as the age threshold between childhood and adulthood.

States should require mandatory reporting by film processors where they come across child pornography.

The recommendations concerning child prostitution referred to above, particularly in regard to receiving and sending countries, also apply to child pornography, as the two types of exploitation are often interrelated. In this context, the possibility of extending national jurisdiction to cover the deeds of Australians overseas deserves serious consideration.

***BIBLIOGRAPHY.*** Amnesty International. *Australia: A Criminal Justice System Weighted Against Aboriginal People.* London: 1993. NGO report, in English.

Australia Human Rights and Equal Opportunity Commission. *Racist Violence: Report of National Inquiry into Racist Violence in Australia.* Sydney, Australia: Australian Government Publishing Service, 1991. Government report, in English.

Bailey, Peter. "The Australian Human Rights Commission." Paper presented at the LAWASIA Conference on . . . South Pacific, 12–14 April 1985. Conference paper, in English.

Castles, Stephen. "The Australian Model of Immigration and Multiculturalism: Is It Applicable to Europe?" *International Migration Review* 26, no. 2 (Summer 1992): 549–567. Scholarly article, in English; bibliography, pp. 565–567.

Crawford, James. "Australian Immigration Law and Refugees: The 1989 Amendments," *International Journal of Refugee Law* 2, no. 4 (1990): 627–635. Scholarly article, in English.

Dilton, Pamela. "Self Determination or Self Management?" *Australian International Law News* (1990): 3–13. Scholarly article, in English.

Edwards, Judy. *Prostitution and Human Rights: A Western Australian Case Study.* Discussion Paper No. 8. Canberra, Australia: Human Rights Commission (Australia), 1986. NGO occasional paper, in English.

Einfeld, Marcus. *Bicentennial Oration: Human Rights and Constitutional Entrenchment, Statement by . . . President of the Australian Human Rights and Equal Opportunity Commission on the Presentation of the Report of the Commission's Inquiry into the Social and Material Needs of the Residents of Toomelah, Boggabilla and Goondiwindi.* Sydney, Australia: 1988. Collection of speeches, in English.

Fonteyne, Jean-Pierre. "Overview of Refugee Determination Procedures in Australia," *International Journal of Refugee Law* 6, no. 2 (1994): 253–264. Scholarly article, in English.

Freedom of Information and Expression in Australia. *Com-*

*mentaries on Freedom of Information and Expression No. 11.* London: Article 19, 1988. NGO report, in English.

Gaze, Beth, and Melinda Jones. *Law, Liberty and Australian Democracy.* Melbourne, Victoria, Australia: The Law Book Company, 1990. Educational material, in English; bibliography, pp. xxii–xxxvi.

International Work Group for Indigenous Affairs. *Land Rights Now: The Aboriginal Fight for Land in Australia.* IWGIA Document 54. Copenhagen: 1985. NGO report, in English.

Levi, Margaret, and Sara Singleton. "Women in 'The Working Man's Paradise': Sole Parents, the Women's Movement, and the Social Policy Bargain in Australia," *Social Research—International Quarterly of Social Sciences* 58, no. 3 (Fall 1991): 627–651. Scholarly article, in English.

MacAllister, Ian, and Rhonda Moore. "The Development of Ethnic Prejudice: An Analysis of Australian Immigrants," *Ethnic Racial Studies* 14, no. 2 (1991): 127–151. Scholarly article, in English.

McRae, H., G. Nettheim, and L. Beacroft. *Aboriginal Legal Issues: Commentary and Materials.* Melbourne, Victoria, Australia: The Law Book Company, 1991. Educational material, in English; bibliography, pp. xxi–xxxvii.

Nettheim, Garth. "Indigenous Rights, Human Rights with Reference to Australia." Paper presented at a seminar on "The Rights of Indigenous Peoples," organized by the Australian National Commission for UNESCO, 1 May 1986. Conference paper, in English.

———. "The Aborigine in Comparative Law." Paper presented at the 12th International Congress on Comparative Law, Sydney, 19 August 1986. Conference paper, in English.

Scutt, Jocelynne A. *Women and the Law: Commentary and Materials.* Melbourne, Victoria, Australia: The Law Book Company, 1990. Educational material, in English; bibliography, pp. xxxi–lii.

"Special Issue: Human Rights," *Melbourne University Law Review* 18, no. 2 (1991). Scholarly articles, in English.

Survival International. "Sympathy Abroad, Backlash at Home," *Survival International News* 21 (1988): 6. NGO article, in English.

Tay, Alice Erh-Soon. *Human Rights for Australia.* Discussion Paper No. 1. Canberra, Australia: Human Rights Commission (Australia), 1986. Bibliography, in English.

Thornton, Margaret. *The Liberal Promise: Anti-Discrimination Legislation in Australia.* Melbourne, Victoria, Australia: Oxford University Press, 1990. Scholarly monograph, in English; bibliography, pp. 350–383.

Whitlam, Gough. "Australia and the UN Commission on Human Rights," *Australian Journal of International Affairs* 45, no. 1 (1991): 51–59. Scholarly article, in English.

Wilcox, Murray R. *An Australian Charter of Rights?* Sydney, Australia: The Law Book Company, 1993. Scholarly monograph, in English.

Witton, Ron. "Australia: Post-War Immigration and the Development of Legal Rights," *Human Rights Forum* 1, no. 5 (January–March 1986): 3–9. NGO article, in English.

**AUSTRIA.** The Republic of Austria is a country in western Europe that has borders with Czechoslovakia, the Federal Republic of Germany, Hungary, Italy, Liechtenstein, Switzerland, and Yugoslavia. After occupation by German troops in 1938, it regained its independence in 1955 and became a member of the United Nations the same year. Its population is estimated by the UN to be 7,899,000. Austria, along with Finland and Sweden, became a member of the European Union in January 1995. Shortly thereafter it also joined NATO's partnership for peace program.

The government (1990) took the form of a republic composed of nine provinces (Bundesländer). The president is elected by popular vote for a term of six years and acts as head of State. The chancellor, representing the party or coalition given the majority in a popular election, is head of government. Legislation is prepared by the 58-member Bundesrat, members of which are elected by provincial assemblies, and the 183-member Nationalrat, members of which are elected by popular vote. The predominant political parties are the Social Democratic Party, the People's Party, and the Freiheitliche Party.

In a "core" document prepared in March 1992, the Government of Austria provided the following information concerning the land and the people (HRI/CORE/1/Add. 8):

The federal territory covers an area of 83,855 square kilometres. The area of permanent settlement accounts for 32,900 square kilometres. The area used for agriculture amounts to 35,480 square kilometres; and for forestry, 31,910 square kilometres.

Austria has a residential population of 7.5 million, living in 2.7 million households. On average, there are 230 persons per square metre of the permanently settled area. The most densely populated areas are the big cities. Vienna, which accounts for 329.17 square kilometres of the area of permanent settlement, has a population of 1.5 million, i.e., 4,652 people per square kilometre. Densely populated cities (with a population of more than 1,000 per square kilometre of the permanently settled area) are Linz, Steyr, Wels, Salzburg, Graz, Innsbruck, Klagenfurt, and Villach.

With respect to the general legal framework within which human rights are protected, the core document points out that the Austrian constitutional system guarantees respect for human rights essentially through the 1867 Basic Law of the State concerning the general rights of citizens and the European Convention for the Protection of Human Rights and Fundamental Freedoms. The fundamental rights that are guaranteed, therefore, have the status of directly applicable law, which is binding on the legislature, the executive, and court practice. It goes on to state the following:

Fundamental rights should be regarded primarily as civil liberties that protect all citizens against illegal interference by the authorities. Fundamental rights must also be respected by public servants and by the courts when applying the law. Whenever the laws to be applied by public servants or the courts need to be interpreted, this must be done with full respect for fundamental rights. It is a generally accepted principle that all legal provisions must be interpreted in a manner not incompatible with fundamental rights.

As regards the interrelation between domestic law and international law, the Austrian Federal Constitution offers two possibilities. The first one, which is generally applied, is to the so-called "general transformation" of international law into domestic law. This means that an international treaty, after having been approved by the Nationalrat and ratified by the Federal President, is promulgated in the Federal Law Gazette and thus transformed into domestic law without restriction. The second possibility under the Federal Constitution is that an international treaty is approved by the Nationalrat with the reservation that the requisite laws for its application in Austria will be adopted. In such case, the international treaty is also promulgated in the Federal Law Gazette but does not become effective domestically, which means that it is binding upon the Republic of Austria only in relation to other States. Obligations arising from this international treaty must be fulfilled by the legislature adopting the requisite legislation.

Only the European Convention for the Protection of Human Rights and Fundamental Freedoms was converted into domestic law and was given constitutional law status in 1964.

What has been said above provides an answer to the question whether the provisions of international instruments for the protection of human rights may be invoked directly before Austrian authorities. This applies only to the provisions of the European Convention for the Protection of Human Rights and Fundamental Freedoms.

The wording of all international instruments for the protection of human rights is promulgated in the Federal Law Gazette and, therefore, is accessible to everybody at almost no cost. In addition, there are several publications of law texts that also contain the wording of these instruments. A translation into languages other than German has proved unnecessary.

The reports required under the international instruments for the protection of human rights are collectively prepared by the Federal Chancellery with the assistance, as a rule, of other federal ministries. They are not the subject of public discussion.

*OMBUDSMAN.* Austria has also established the institution of ombudsman, called the Volksanwaltschaft, similar to that functioning in a number of countries, for dealing with acts of maladministration by public authorities. Anyone may complain to the ombudsman regarding such acts, provided that the person is affected by the acts and has exhausted other legal remedies against them. The ombudsman is authorized to examine pertinent complaints and, if he considers them to be justified, to try to change the administrative measure in question. He may also recommend specific action in a certain case, or as a result of a certain case, to the competent federal minister. In addition, he is entitled to draw attention, in his annual reports, to grievances he has ascertained and, if necessary, to suggest changes in legal provisions.

*ETHNIC MINORITIES.* With regard to the treatment of ethnic groups in particular, the Austrian Parliament on 7 July 1976 adopted the Act of Ethnic Groups (Bundesgesetzblatt, No. 396/1976) providing for the preservation, where warranted, of special assistance to such groups with a view to ensuring their continued existence and the preservation of their national characteristics. The Act provides for the establishment of an Ethnic Group Advisory Board to propose methods of organizing assistance to such groups.

*BIBLIOGRAPHY.* Amnesty International (AI). *Austria: The Alleged Ill-Treatment of Foreigners: A Summary of Concern.* London: 1994. NGO report, in English.

———. *Austria: Torture and Ill-Treatment.* London: 1990. NGO report, in English.

Kussbach, Erich. "The 1991 Austrian Asylum Law," *International Journal of Refugee Law* 6, no. 2 (1994): 227–243. Scholarly article, in English.

Nowak, Manfred. *Politische Grundrechte* (Political Rights). Vienna, Austria: Springer-Verlag, 1988. Scholarly monograph, in German; bibliography, pp. 542–572.

Nowak, M., D. Steurer, and H. Tretter, eds. *Fortschritt im Bewustsein der Grund–und Menschenrechte: Festschrift fur Felix Ermacora* (Progress in the Spirit of Human Rights: Essays in Honor of Felix Ermacora). Kehl am Rhein, FRG: N.P. Engel Verlag, 1988. Scholarly edited collection, in English and German.

World Jewish Congress, Commission on the Holocaust and Crimes of the Nazis. *Waldheim's Nazi Past: The Dossier.* Geneva: 1988. NGO report, in English.

**AZANIA.** South Africa's name before its colonization, Azania is still used by many of its people and by one of its liberation movements, the Pan Africanist Congress of Azania.

**AZERBAIJAN.** The independent Republic of Azerbaijan, formerly the Azerbaijan Soviet Socialist Republic of the U.S.S.R., is located in southwest Asia and bounded on the north by Georgia, on the west by Armenia, on the south by Iran, and on the east by the Caspian Sea. Its population, estimated at 7,510,000, consists primarily of Shi'ite Moslems, speaking Azen Turkish, but also includes Mongols, Turks, and a large Armenian Christian minority. In recent years, the population of the country has been swelled by thousands of refugees driven out of the disputed area of Nagorno-Karabakh, which lies between this State and Armenia.

In an election held in June 1992, Abulfez Eichibey was elected President of Azerbaijan with almost 60% of the vote. However, his popularity waned with the country's defeat in the war with Armenia over the territory of Nagorno-Karabakh. It further waned when Mr. Eichibey fled from Baku to Nakhichevan, a small area separated from the rest of Azerbaijan by Armenia. Shortly thereafter, a non-binding referendum on public confidence in the president produced a humiliating rejection of his administration and paved the way for Heydar Aliyev, a former Soviet KGB general and Politburo member who had been elected chairman of Azerbaijan's parliament and, thus, vice-president, to assume effective executive authority.

In June 1993, the United Nations, noting the rapidly deteriorating humanitarian situation in Azerbaijan, set up an interagency humanitarian program for the country; and shortly thereafter, the number of refugees and displaced persons there was found to exceed one million. The UN General Assembly, in resolution 48/114 of 20 December 1993, appealed to all States and agencies to supply assistance to those persons.

In 1994, when Armenian forces from Karabakh seized more Azeri territory, the offensive resulted in more than 50,000 Azeri displaced. By the end of 1994, more than 800,000 Azeri refugees and displaced persons from Armenia and Nagorno-Karabakh and its environs were unable to return to their homes.

As reported by the NGO Human Rights Watch, political chaos, internal revolt, and political assassinations disastrously affected human rights in Azerbaijan in 1994. In September, gunmen assassinated the deputy speaker of Azerbaijan's parliament, and also the President's security chief. Shortly thereafter, police units whose members had been charged in the assassinations seized the general prosecutor and held him hostage. This situation prompted, on October 3, a 60-day state of emergency in Baku, Azerbaijan's capital, and, a few days later, in Ganje, the second largest city. In addition, treason charges were brought against the prime minister and several other ministers. In addition, it was reported that the government of Heydar Aliyev intimidated other political parties, harassed the press, and prevented political demonstrations.

On 3 August 1994, the Human Rights Committee issued the following response to a report by Azerbaijan on the International Covenant on Civil and Political Rights:

The Human Rights Committee considered the initial report of Azerbaijan (CCPR/C/81/Add.2) at its 1332nd and 1336th meetings, on 12 and 14 July 1994, and adopted the following comments on 27 July 1994:

## Introduction

The Committee thanks Azerbaijan for its initial report and welcomes the presence of a high-level delegation before the Committee. It notes the timely submission of the report and thanks the State Party for the core document (HRI/CORE/1/Add.41/Rev.1). The Committee notes with regret however that, while providing detailed information on prevailing legislation in Azerbaijan, the report does not contain enough information on the way in which the Covenant is implemented in practice or on the factors and difficulties affecting the implementation of the Covenant throughout the area under the jurisdiction of Azerbaijan. The information provided orally by the delegation made good these deficiencies to some extent and provided the Committee with a better insight into the human rights situation in Azerbaijan.

## Factors and Difficulties Affecting the Implementation of the Covenant

The situation of armed conflict with a neighbouring country and the recurrent internal unrest are affecting the exercise of human rights in Azerbaijan and have given rise to a pattern of gross human rights violations. Recognized obstacles arising out of the transition from the legal order inherited from the past to a democratic system must be addressed to in a manner compatible with respect to the Covenant.

## Positive Aspects

The Committee notes that Azerbaijan has declared that it is bound by the Covenant through a declaration of accession, though it would have been correct for it to have regarded itself as succeeding to the obligations of the Covenant as a member State of the former Soviet Union. Nonetheless, the Committee notes with appreciation that the delegation, addressing questions raised by members of the Committee, did not deny accountability for events occurred in the country after the date of independence but before the date of accession. It also takes note of the efforts of the Government of Azerbaijan to include human rights in its new Constitution, to adopt new human rights legislation and to ensure the rule of law. It also notes that the Government has demonstrated the will to initiate far-reaching structural reforms, particularly with regard to the judiciary.

## Principal Subjects of Concern

The Committee is concerned by the status of the Covenant within the Azerbaijani legal system and by the lack of clarity regarding the resolution of possible conflicts between the Covenant and national law. Furthermore, it does not seem possible for an individual to invoke the Covenant before the courts.

The Committee regrets the position adopted in the report regarding the principle of self-determination. In that connection, it recalls that, under article 1 of the Covenant, that principle applies to all peoples and not merely to colonized peoples.

The Committee notes that the state of emergency was declared in 1993 and is concerned by the lack of clarity in the law governing the conditions in which the state of emergency can be implemented.

The Committee deeply deplores the events which have occurred recently in Azerbaijan in the context of the armed conflict and have involved numerous violations of the rights guaranteed by the Covenant. There have been reports of cases of summary execution, enforced or involuntary disappearance, torture and other acts of violence against the person, as well as arbitrary detention. The practice of hostage-taking as a retaliatory measure or for bargaining purposes also seems widespread. Such violations have not been investigated and the persons responsible for them have therefore not been punished. Nor have the victims or their families been compensated.

The Committee is disturbed at the number of death sentences pronounced and at the lack of any appeal procedure for persons under sentence of death.

The Committee was disturbed by the obstacles which have thus far prevented the implementation of article 12 of the Covenant. Passport applications seem to have been rejected without proper justification. The visa requirement for some categories of persons wishing to leave the country is an unacceptable restriction on the liberty of movement and the requirement of a visa to return to Azerbaijan is contrary to article 12 of the Covenant.

The Committee has doubts regarding the independence and impartiality of the judiciary in Azerbaijan and deplores the fact that the "Procuratura" still exists.

The Committee notes with concern the lack of laws guaranteeing the right of information and the fact that the laws inherited from the former regime have not been amended to guarantee the rights provided for in article 19 of the Covenant.

The Committee is concerned by the power of the Ministry of Justice to refuse to register a political party or an association, which is an obstacle to the pluralism of political parties as provided for in article 25 of the Covenant.

### Suggestions and Recommendations

The Committee recommends that the State Party should revise the former legislation as soon as possible, in order to introduce a democratic system more in keeping with the requirements of the covenant.

The Committee urges the Azerbaijani Government to put an end to the gross violations of human rights which have occurred, and continue to occur, in Azerbaijan, to conduct investigations into them, to punish the persons guilty of such acts and to compensate the victims.

The Committee recommends that the use of the death penalty should be reduced and that provision should be made for the right to appeal against a death sentence.

The Committee invites the Azerbaijani Government to amend its judicial system as quickly as possible and abolish the old "Procuratura".

The Committee suggests that the authorities of the State Party should introduce legislation guaranteeing freedom of information and of the press and, in general, freedom of expression and opinion.

The Committee recommends that the Azerbaijani Government should ensure the pluralism of political parties and remove obstacles to their registration.

The Committee recommends that the Government should take account of the Committee's general comment No. 23 (50), concerning article 27 of the Covenant, in drafting legislative or regulatory texts for the full protection of the rights of individuals belonging to minorities.

The Committee stresses the need to improve information and education regarding human rights so as to make the public more familiar with the provisions of the Covenant. It also recommends that the authorities should consider the possibility of acceding to the first optional protocol to the Covenant.

**BIBLIOGRAPHY.** Amnesty International. *Azerbaijan: Hostages in the Context of the Karabakh Conflict: An Update.* London: 1994. NGO report, in English.

————. *Azerbaydzhan: Hostages in the Karabakh Conflict: Civilians Continue to Pay the Price.* London: 1993. NGO report, in English.

Commission on Security and Cooperation. *Implementation of the Helsinki Accords: Hearing before the Commission on Security and Cooperation in Europe: The Nagorno-Karabakh Crisis — Prospects for Resolution.* Washington, D.C.: U.S. Government Printing Office, 1991. Government hearings, in English.

Helsinki Watch. *Bloodshed in the Caucasus: Escalation of the Armed Conflict in Nagorno Karabakh.* New York: 1992. NGO report, in English.

————. *Bloodshed in the Caucasus: Indiscriminate Bombing and Shelling by Azerbaijani Forces in Nagorno Karabakh.* New York: 1993. NGO Report, in English.

————. *Prison Conditions in the Soviet Union: A Report of Facilities in Russia and Azerbaidzan.* New York: Human Rights Watch, 1991. NGO factfinding report, in English.

Helsinki Watch and the Inter-Republic Memorial Society. *Conflict in the Soviet Union: Black January in Azerbaidzhan.* New York: Human Rights Watch, 1991. NGO factfinding report, in English.

Human Rights Watch. "Azerbaijan," *Human Rights Watch World Report 1995* pp. 190–192. NGO report, in English.

Roy, Olivier, ed. "Des ethnies aux nations en Asie centrale" (From Ethnics to Nations in Central Asia), *Revue du monde musulman et de la Méditerranée.* no. 59–60 (1991): 15–162. Special issue, in French.

U.S. Committee for Refugees. *Faultlines of National Conflict: Refugees and Displaced Persons from Armenia and Azerbaijan.* Washington, D.C.: Immigration and Refugee Services of America, 1994. NGO report, in English.

U.S. Immigration and Naturalization Service, Resource Information Centre. *Azerbaijan: The Status of Armenians, Russians, Jews, and Other Minorities.* Washington, D.C.: U.S. Department of Justice, 1993. Government report, in English.

# B

**BACTERIOLOGICAL WARFARE.** See **CHEMICAL WEAPONS.**

**BAHÁ'Í INTERNATIONAL COMMUNITY.** An international non-governmental organization in consultative status (Category II) with the UN **ECONOMIC AND SOCIAL COUNCIL** and **UNICEF,** the Bahá'í community has members in 167 countries and 47 territories, with National Spiritual Assemblies (national or regional governing bodies of Bahá'í communities) in 166 countries and territories.

Founded in 1844, the Community is a cross-section of peoples of the world, including almost all nationalities, classes, trades, and professions, representing more than 1,600 ethnic groups. It comprises members of the Bahá'í faith, an independent world religion, founded in Persia (now Iran) by Mirzá Husayn-'Alí, known as Bahá'u'lláh, the Glory of God. The group participates in all UN activities related to human rights and strives, in particular, to eliminate prejudice and discrimination, based on the faith's fundamental belief in the organic oneness of humanity. The community also promotes the teachings of the Bahá'í religion and advocates equality of men and women, universal compulsory education, an international auxiliary language, a just solution to world economic problems, a universal tribunal, and a world commonwealth.

The community has an extensive publication program, including religious and children's publications and the annual *Bahá'í World,* the monthly *Bahá'í News,* and the quarterlies *La pensee Baha'ie, Opinioni Bahá'í,* and *One Country.*

Bahá'í International Community. Address: Bahá'í World Centre, P.O. Box 155, 31001 Haifa, Israel. Telephone: (972-4) 372-433. Fax: (972-4) 372-425. Cable: BAHAIFAITH,HAIFA. Telex: 46626 BAYT IL. Secretary-General: Paul Reynolds.

**BAHAMAS.** The Bahamas Islands occupies an archipelago in the Caribbean consisting of more than 700 islands and islets, beginning 50 miles off the southeastern coast of the United States and extending 700 miles, almost to Haiti. The principal islands are New Providence, Grand Bahamas, Eleuthera, and Long Island. The Bahamas achieved independence from Great Britain in 1973 and became a member of the United Nations the same year. Its population is estimated to be 265,000. Ethnically, 85% of the population is descended from Africans imported as slaves and emancipated in 1838; the remainder are descendants of British and American residents. English is the only language in common use. Christianity (Anglican, 25%; Baptist, 30%; Methodist, 7%; and Roman Catholic, 22%) is the predominant religion. Literacy is estimated at 90%.

The government (1990) took the form of a parliamentary State and member of the Commonwealth of Nations, of which the British sovereign is the symbolic head. Executive power is exercised by the governor-general, representing the crown, and the prime minister, representing the party or coalition given a majority in a popular election. There is a bicameral legislature consisting of the Senate, appointed by the governor-general on advice of the prime minister and opposition party leader, and an Assembly elected by popular vote. The judiciary is organized along British lines. Political parties include the Progressive Liberal Party and the Free National Movement.

Up to 1968, the Bahamas were controlled by the predominantly white United Bahamians. The majority population has since retained full control by overwhelming victories in general elections. In 1987, the Progressive Liberal Party won 31 of the 49 seats in Parliament.

The rights of trade unions have occasionally been the subject of inquiry by international organizations. Allegations concerning the infringement of such rights were submitted to the UN Economic and Social Council in 1976 by unions in the Bahamas. Rejected as unfounded by the Government, the allegations were forwarded to the International Labor Organization for consideration by its Fact-finding and Conciliation Commission on Freedom of Association.

***BIBLIOGRAPHY.*** Grand Bahama Human Rights Association. *Bahama Watch* (1989 ff). NGO newspaper, in English.

# B

**BAHRAIN.** The State of Bahrain is an Arab country in western Asia that occupies an archipelago consisting of 33 islands in the Persian Gulf, off the coast of Saudi Arabia. It achieved independence from Great Britain in 1971 and became a member of the United Nations the same year. Its population is estimated to be 561,000. Ethnic groups include Arabs, Iranians, Pakistanis, and Hindus. Arabic is the official language; Farsi and Urdu are commonly used. Islam (Shi'ite, 70%; Sunni, 30%) is the predominant religion. Literacy is estimated at 75%.

The government (1994) took the form of a monarchy. The emir is ruler and head of State; the prime minister, appointed by the emir, is head of government. There is a Council of Ministers, members of which are appointed by the emir. Judges are also appointed by the emir. The National Council, established by the constitution of 1973, was dissolved by the emir in 1975. In exercising his constitutional authority to close down the assembly, he reported to the people of Bahrain on the danger to national security stemming from the alleged subversive activity of some assembly members.

While it existed, the National Assembly, consisting of male citizens elected for four-year terms and about 16 Cabinet ministers, was the first elected Parliament in the country's history. Violent demonstrations by Shi'ite Moslems seeking equal rights swept through the country at the end of 1994 and into 1995. Commercial and government buildings were set on fire and hundreds of demonstrators were arrested.

*BIBLIOGRAPHY.* Amnesty International. *Bahrain: Concerns in the State of Bahrain.* London: 1989. NGO report, in English.

————. *Bahrain: Conviction of Nine Political Prisoners.* London: 1988. NGO report, in English.

————. *Bahrain: Incommunicado Detention and Unfair Trial.* London: 1988. NGO report, in English.

————. "Bahrain: Torture of Prisoners," *Amnesty International Newsletter* 16, no. 11 (November 1986): 7. NGO newsletter article, in English.

————. *Bahrain: Violations of Human Rights.* London: 1991. NGO factfinding report, in English and French.

————. *Reports of Torture of Political Prisoners in Bahrain.* London: 1986. NGO report, in English.

Committee for the Defence of Human Rights in Bahrain. "Statement on the Bahraini Government Repressive Acts." Damascus, Syria: 8 October 1988. NGO urgent action statement, in English.

Federation Internationale des Droits de l'Homme (International Federation of Human Rights). "Bahrain: Greve de la faim des prisonniers politique" (Bahrain: Hunger Strike by Political Prisoners), *Lettre de la FIDH* 214 (22 September 1987): 2. NGO article, in French.

Institute for Women's Studies in the Arab World. "Women of Bahrain," *AL-RAIDA* 8, no. 37 (1 August 1986): 1–16. NGO bulletin, in English.

**BAJER, FREDERIK (1837–1922).** This Danish journalist and pacifist shared the **NOBEL PEACE PRIZE** for 1908 with **KLAS PONTUS ARNOLDSON.** In 1872, Bajer, was elected to the Danish House of Representatives (the Folketing), where he advocated the emancipation of women, international peace, and Danish neutrality. He was one of the founders of the Dansk Kvindesamfund (Danish Women's Society) and of the Nordisk Fristats Samfund (Society of Nordic Free States). His efforts on behalf of pacifism and Danish neutrality led him to establish in 1882 the Foreningen til Danmarks Neutralisering (Society for the Promotion of Danish Neutrality), later known simply as the Danish Peace Society. He was also a leader in arranging the first Scandinavian Peace Conference in 1885. At the second World Peace Conference, held in London in 1890, Bajer suggested a special bureau that would distribute pacifist literature. From this suggestion, the International Peace Bureau was established, and Bajer served as president of its governing board until 1907. The Bureau itself was a recipient of the Peace Prize in 1910. In 1891, he founded the Danish Interparliamentary Union and contributed to the creation of the Scandinavian Interparliamentary Union in 1908.

*BIBLIOGRAPHY.* Gray, Tony. *Champions of Peace.* London: Paddington Press, 1976.

Schlessinger, Bernard S., and June H. Schlessinger, eds. *Who's Who of Nobel Prize Winners.* Phoenix, AZ, USA: Oryx Press, 1991.

**BALCH, EMILY GREENE (1867–1961).** This American social reformer shared the 1946 **NOBEL PEACE PRIZE** with **JOHN RALEIGH MOTT,** also an American. Balch was born in Boston, MA, and was educated at Bryn Mawr College, Harvard University, and the University of Chicago. In 1896, she accepted a professorship in economics and sociology at Wellesley College. Among her political causes were women's suffrage, racial justice, and control of child labor.

At the outbreak of World War I, she became a pacifist and helped to found the Women's International Committee for Permanent Peace, later renamed the **WOMEN'S INTERNATIONAL LEAGUE FOR PEACE AND FREEDOM.** Balch later donated her Nobel Peace Prize money to this organization and worked for it without salary. She actively campaigned against the United States' entry into the war and wrote a successful pacifist book, *Approaches to the Great Settlement.*

Between the two world wars, Balch worked with the **LEAGUE OF NATIONS** on projects such as disarmament, the internationalization of aviation, and drug control.

During World War II, Balch abandoned her former pacifist and isolationist stance and actively worked for American involvement in the conflict. After the war, she supported the work of the United Nations.

**BIBLIOGRAPHY.** Gray, Tony. *Champions of Peace.* London: Paddington Press, 1976.

Schlessinger, Bernard S., and June H. Schlessinger, eds. *Who's Who of Nobel Prize Winners.* Phoenix, AZ, USA: Oryx Press, 1991.

## BALDWIN (ROGER) MEDAL OF LIBERTY AWARD.

Established in 1989, the Roger Baldwin Award is presented biennially by the Lawyers Committee for Human Rights to an organization or individual making a significant contribution to human rights anywhere outside of the United States of America. (In alternating years, it is presented by the American Civil Liberties Union for human rights contributions within the USA.) The award carries a $25,000 prize.

For more information, contact: Lawyers Committee for Human Rights, 330 Seventh Avenue, 10th Fl., New York, NY 10001, USA. Telephone: (212) 629-6170. Fax: (212) 967-0916.

## BALLUET, PAUL HENRI BENJAMIN (1852–1924).

Paul Balluet was the family name of the Baron d'Estournelles de Constant de Rebecque, co-recipient of the 1909 **NOBEL PEACE PRIZE.** After serving in diplomatic missions for France to Turkey and the Netherlands, he was dispatched to England, where he mediated a dispute between France and England over a blockade during the French-Siamese border disputes of 1893. In 1895, he was elected deputy for Sarthe in the Loire district and in 1904 was elected senator for that same district.

Balluet believed in European consolidation. Until a European Union could be formed, however, Balluet worked for improvement in France's relations with England and Germany. In 1899, he was the French representative at the first Hague Peace Conference and supported arbitration throughout his career. Indeed, in 1905, he founded the Association for International Conciliation in an effort to spread his belief in the power of mediation.

**BIBLIOGRAPHY.** Gray, Tony. *Champions of Peace.* London: Paddington Press, 1976.

Schlessinger, Bernard S., and June H. Schlessinger, eds. *Who's Who of Nobel Prize Winners.* Phoenix, AZ, USA: Oryx Press, 1991.

**BANGLADESH.** The People's Republic of Bangladesh is a country in southern Asia, located on the Bay of Bengal. It borders on India and Myanmar. Known as East Bengal until the British withdrew from the Indian sub-continent in 1947, and as East Pakistan for almost 25 years until the occupying Pakistani forces were driven out by Indian army units in 1971, Bangladesh achieved independence from Pakistan in 1974 and became a member of the United Nations the same year. Its population is estimated to be 120,850,000. Ethnic groups include the Bengalis (98%) and the Biharis (2%), the latter consisting of the descendants of about one million persons who migrated to East Bengal when the sub-continent was partitioned. Languages commonly used include Bengali (official), English, and Urdu. Religions practiced include Islam (83%) and Hinduism (17%). Literacy is estimated at 28%.

The government (1994) took the form of an Islamic Republic and member of the Commonwealth of Nations, of which the British sovereign is the symbolic head. Political parties include the Jatita Party, the Awami League, the Jamaat-i-Islami, and the Bangladesh Nationalist Party.

Bangladesh was born of civil strife, which broke out in East Pakistan in March 1971 and resulted in the death of more than one million Bengalis and the flight to India of about 10 million Bengali refugees. The Secretary-General of the United Nations notified the Security Council that the situation constituted a threat to international peace and security, but the Council was unable to act because of the negative vote of the Union of Soviet Socialist Republics. The General Assembly then called for a ceasefire and the withdrawal of troops.

In December 1971, India moved troops into East Pakistan and routed the West Pakistani occupation forces. A provisional government was formed in January 1972, with Justice Abu Sayeed Choudhury as president and Sheikh Mujibur Rahman as prime minister. Between 1975 and 1981, Bangladesh had four presidents: Kondakar Mushtaque Ahmed, founder of the Awami League, installed after the assassination of Mujibur by young army officers in a coup of 15 August 1975; Abu Sadat Mohammed Sayem, installed after a military coup had forced Ahmed from power on 6 November 1975; General Ziaur Rahman, army chief of staff, installed after Sayem's resignation on 21 April 1977; Vice President Abdus Sattar, installed after army officers had killed Ziaur in an attempted coup on 30 May 1981; and General Hossein Mohammed Ershad, army chief of staff, who took control after a bloodless coup of 24 March 1982 and assumed the office of president in 1983.

President Ershad committed himself to lifting martial law and restoring constitutional government. National elections were held in May 1986, filling the 300 elected seats of the National Assembly, and Ershad was elected president in October of that year, with 84% of the vote. Because the opposition contended that the election had been rigged, President Ershad dissolved Parliament and called for fresh elections to be held in March 1988. His party was again the overwhelming winner, but the elections were marred by widespread violence.

The President resigned from office late in 1990; and in the elections that followed early in 1992, Mrs. Khaleda Zia, widow of former President Ziaur Rahman, won a decisive victory and was named Prime Minister.

In her new capacity, Zia has aggressively promoted education and vocational training for women and girls, has successfully introduced family planning, and has set up cooperatives to protect the health of mothers and their children. She has seldom met with resistance from the men of the country, and her relations with the armed forces are unusually good because of her late husband's long military service. In early 1994, however, opposition parties staged a boycott of Parliament that effectively halted governmental activity for many months and weakened the authority of the Prime Minister's government, raising doubts about its ability to survive until the next scheduled elections.

The country remains confronted with serious human rights problems, including the situation of the Biharis, who consider themselves to be unwanted by India, Pakistan, or Bangladesh. To protect the rights and freedoms of this and other disadvantaged groups, the Bangladesh constitution aims at realizing, through democratic process, a society in which the rule of law, human rights, fundamental freedoms, and equality and justice is secured for all citizens without discrimination.

In addition, an international furor was raised over the case of feminist writer Taslima Nasrin, who has been accused of insulting the Koran. Nasrin, who has received death threats from Muslim clerics, was officially charged by the government with insulting the Muslim religion, prompting her to go into hiding and seek asylum in Sweden. If brought to trial, she faces a maximum penalty of two years' imprisonment under a little-used section of the Bangladesh penal code that proscribes statements or writings "intended to outrage the religious feeling of any class by insulting its religion or religious believers." In July 1994, Attorney General Aminul Huq warned that the enactment of a "blasphemy law" would constitute a contradiction of fundamental human rights and Islam. Draft resolutions to enact such a law remained pending at the end of 1994.

**BIBLIOGRAPHY.** Amnesty International. *Bangladesh: Large-Scale Detention without Trial of Opposition Members, July 1987–February 1988.* London: 1988. NGO report, in English.

————. "File on Torture: Bangladesh," *Amnesty International Bulletin (Ottawa, Canada)* 13, no. 5 (July–August 1986): 9–10. NGO bulletin article, in English.

Andreassen, Bard-Anders, and Asbjorn Eide, eds. *Human Rights in Developing Countries 1987/88: A Yearbook on Human Rights in Countries Receiving Nordic Aid.* Copenhagen: Christian Michelsen Institute, 1988. NGO report, in English; bibliography, classified by country, pp. 357–372.

Chittagong Hill Tracts Commission. *"Life Is Not Ours": Land and Human Rights in the Chittagong Hill Tracts, Bangladesh.* Amsterdam, the Netherlands: 1991. NGO report, in English.

Commission for Justice and Peace of the Catholic Bishops' Conference. "All BAVS Clinics Closed after Forced Sterilization Incident," *Hotline Newsletter* 10 (August–September 1987): 8. NGO news article, in English.

————. "CCHRB Expresses Concern over Land-Grabbing," *Hotline Newsletter* 26 (January 1987): 3. NGO article, in English.

————. "Hardship Encourages Sterilization: A Survey of 950 Sterilized Persons in Bangladesh," *Hotline Newsletter* 22 (May 1986): 1, 4–5. NGO article, in English.

Cooper, Jeremy. "The Garo of Bangladesh: A Forest People's Struggle to Survive," *Ethnic and Racial Studies* 15, no. 1 (January 1992): 85–100. Scholarly article, in English.

Coordinating Council for Human Rights in Bangladesh. *Election Observation Report: Election to 5th Parliament, 1991.* Dhaka, Bangladesh: 1991. NGO Report, in English.

————. *Upazila Election 1990 Observation.* Dhaka, Bangladesh: 1990. NGO factfinding mission, in English.

Human Rights Watch. *Bangladesh. Human Rights Watch World Report 1995* pp. 130–132. New York: 1995. NGO report, in English.

Immigration and Refugee Board Documentation Centre. *Bangladesh: Country Profile.* Ottawa, Ontario, Canada: 1990. Government briefing paper, in English and French.

"Index on Censorship. Bangladesh Detains Opposition Leaders and Censors the Press." Briefing Paper 289 (18 November 1987): NGO briefing paper, in English.

International Work Group for Indigenous Affairs. "Bangladesh: Garo Lands Taken with Government Support," *IWGIA Newsletter* 50 (July 1987): 33–34. NGO article, in English.

————. "Bangladesh: Three Massacres in the Chittagong Hill Tracts and Violent Attacks on Tribal Peoples in Dighinala," *IWGIA Newsletter* 47 (October 1986): 7–11. NGO article, in English.

Liberty International. *Human Rights Report on Bangladesh (January 1985–July 1985).* Mymensingh, Bangladesh: 1985. NGO bulletin, in English.

Martuza, Ghulam, and M. A. Momen. *Trade Unionism and Trade Union Laws in Bangladesh.* Dhaka, Bangladesh: Bangladesh Society for the Enforcement of Human Rights, 1986. NGO monograph, in English.

Mey, Wolfgang. *Wir Wollen Nicht Euch—Wir Wollen Eurer Land* (We Don't Want You—We Want Your Land). Goettingen, FRG: Gesellschaft fur Bedrohte Volker (Society for Endangered Peoples), 1988. NGO report, in German.

Minority Rights Group International and Coordinating Council for Human Rights in Bangladesh. *The Adivasis of Bangladesh.* London: 1991. NGO report, in English.

Ram, Mohan. "Bangladesh: The Tribal Turmoil," *Far Eastern Economic Review* (26 June 1986): 21–22. Journal article, in English.

Shamin, Ishrat. *Trafficking of Asian Women: A Case Study of*

*Bangladesh, July 1987.* Scholarly conference paper, in English; bibliography, p. 12.

Society for Environment and Human Development. *Indigenous Peoples of Bangladesh.* Dhaka, Bangladesh: 1993. NGO report, in English.

Survival International. *Bangladesh: Genocide in the Chittagong Hill Tracts—New Evidence.* London: 2 May 1985. NGO bulletin, in English.

U.S. Committee for Refugees. *From Isolation to Exile: Refugees from the Chittagong Hill Tracts of Bangladesh.* Washington, D.C.: 1988. NGO report, in English.

**BAPTIST WORLD ALLIANCE.** A non-governmental organization in consultative status (Category II) with the UN ECONOMIC AND SOCIAL COUNCIL and **UNICEF,** the BWA was founded in London in 1905. It acts as a voluntary and fraternal organization for promoting fellowship and cooperation among Baptists.

The BWA publishes *The Baptist World* quarterly and operates the BWA Information Service.

Baptist World Alliance. Address: 6733 Curran St., McLean, VA 22101, USA. Telephone: (703) 790-8980. Fax: (703) 893-5160. Secretary-General: Dr. Denton Lotz.

**BARBADOS.** Barbados is a country that occupies an island in the Caribbean, east of the Windward Islands. It achieved independence from Great Britain in 1966 and became a member of the United Nations the same year. Its population is estimated to be 258,000. Ethnic groups include blacks (92%), whites (3%), East Indians (0.5%), and others (Chinese, Amerindians, Portuguese, and Syrian/Lebanese, 1.5%). The language in common use is English. Christianity (Anglican, 70%; Roman Catholic, 4%; Methodist, 9%) is the predominant religion; 17% of the population profess other faiths or none at all. Literacy is estimated at 97%.

The government (1994) took the form of a parliamentary State and member of the Commonwealth of Nations, of which the British sovereign is the symbolic head. Executive power is exercised by the governor-general, representing the crown, and the prime minister, representing the party or coalition given the majority in a popular election. Legislation is prepared by a bicameral legislature consisting of a 21-member Senate appointed by the governor-general after consultation with the prime minister, and a 27-member Assembly elected by the people. Political parties include the Barbados Labour Party and the Democratic Labour Party.

In Barbados, the population lives and co-exists in a liberal atmosphere generally free of the tensions that characterize race relations in some other parts of the world. Within the ethnic groups, there are cultural/religious associations, such as the Syrian Women's Association, the American Women's Group, and the Canadian Women's Group, the major aim of which is protection of the cultural traditions of their respective countries of origin.

In a report presented to the UN Human Rights Committee on 25 November 1987, the Government of Barbados supplied the following information (UN Doc. CCPR/C/42/Add. 3, para. 1–9):

Barbados conforms to the Westminster model of a parliamentary democracy. It has adopted a written Constitution which is the supreme law of the land. The Constitution has incorporated a Bill of Rights which generally, and most times specifically, embodies the principles of the Covenant on Civil and Political Rights.

It is within this legal framework that the rights expressed in the Covenant are given effect or supported as the case may be.

Barbados subscribes to and supports the principles of the right of self-determination and free disposal of wealth and resources as embodied in article 1 of the Covenant. A review of Barbados' history at the United Nations will lend evidence of this.

Section 23 of the Constitution guarantees to a substantial degree protection against discrimination. The Barbados Constitution does not protect against discrimination based on the ground of sex. However, the general laws do not embody the principle of sex discrimination and have progressively been updated to obviate any hardship which may previously have existed in common law. In this regard the Succession Act of 1975 makes it impossible for a husband to disinherit his wife. Women in Barbados have the same rights as men in respect of property, contracts and the family and this is supported by legislation, namely the Married Persons (formerly Married Women) Act, 1896, succeeded in some respects by the Property Act, 1979 and the Family Law Act, 1981.

Barbados recognizes that the problem is not simply one of legislation and has established a Women's Affairs Bureau further to advance the cause of women.

The Constitution does not provide for nondiscrimination on the basis of language. The reason for its omission would seem to be that Barbados is essentially monocultural. This was so at the drafting of the Constitution and remains so today. A small section of the population comprises persons of Asian descent but there have been no expressions of having borne hardship on account of language.

The Constitution does provide for protection from discrimination on grounds of national origin though not social origin. The former would fall under the rubric of "place of origin" as provided in section 23. As regards social origin the area in which discrimination on this ground would be more operative would be in respect of children born out of wedlock. This problem has now been overcome by the Status of Children Reform Act, 1979, which equalizes the status of children born in Barbados and abolished the former common law distinctions of legitimate and illegitimate children.

The Constitution does not guarantee protection from discrimination to non-citizens of Barbados. In reality, however, there are no laws which impose restrictions on non-citizens in their enjoyment of the fundamental rights and freedoms guaranteed by the Constitution to citizens of Barbados. The exception is the protection of freedom of movement afforded by section 22 of the Constitution in so far as that section guarantees the right to enter Barbados and immunity from expulsion from Barbados. Restrictions are thought necessary in this regard to safeguard the integrity of its borders and immigration laws.

The Constitution excepts from its nondiscrimination provision any law dealing with adoption, marriage, divorce, burial, devolution of property on death or other matters of personal law. It is unclear what type of exceptions this provision of the Constitution anticipated. However, it is not possible to point to any rule or provision of personal law which but for this provision would have infringed the Constitution.

Ten years of Democratic Labour Party rule were ended as the Barbados Labour Party won 19 of the 28 seats in the House of Assembly in elections held two years early due to a vote of no confidence in the previous administration.

Examination of Report by Treaty-Monitoring Body:

Information was requested concerning the rate of divorce, the reasons for changes and whether procedures for reconciliation achieved the desired goal. In reply, it was noted that there was no evidence on the question but that it merited further study.

Concluding comments of the Committee on Human Rights

### Positive Aspects

The Committee particularly noted positive features in the reports of Barbados:

(a) That Barbados had ratified the Convention without reservation demonstrated the Government's commitment to achieving equality for women in public and private life;

(b) The Committee welcomed the fact that the Government had continued with its plans of action to improve the status of women in Barbados in spite of economic problems encountered during the reporting period. The Committee was pleased that the Government had recognized the need to cushion the impact on women of its structural adjustments;

(c) The Committee noted that Barbados had enacted most, if not all, the national legislation required to give effect to the Convention in Barbados;

(d) The Committee praised the Government for its emphasis on education as the key factor in advancing the status of women in that country;

(e) The Committee also applauded the continued operation of government machinery which had the responsibility to collect information about the status of women in Barbados, cooperate with non-governmental organizations in improving the lot of women, provide programmes designed to assist and support women in the community and disseminate information designed to improve women's status.

### Principal Subjects of Concern

The Committee expressed concern at the serious lack of female participation in politics and in the representation of Barbados at the international level and in other decision-making positions. The Committee considered that to be of

such importance that it wished Barbados to consider enhanced campaigns to involve women in those positions by applying article 4 of the Convention.

The Committee was also concerned, given the importance of tourism to the Barbados economy, to ensure that the Government was aware of the potential for an increase in prostitution. More detailed information about the incidence of prostitution, its control and the provision of health care for prostitutes should be included in the next report.

Finally, the Committee wished to encourage the Government of Barbados to consult with non-governmental organizations when preparing its next report and to obtain their assistance in achieving the Convention's objective of improving the status of women in its country.

### Suggestions and Recommendations

The Committee expressed the wish that in future reports Barbados would provide more information:

(a) Evaluating the impact of programmes designed to enhance the status of women and legislation granting women equal status with men;

(b) Evaluating the outcome of the latest plan of action of the Bureau of Women's Affairs and the educational programmes in schools and tertiary institutions;

(c) Setting out whether there had been any noticeable improvements in the status of women such as improved educational standards, decrease in prostitution, reduction of violence against women and greater participation in decision-making roles in public life;

(d) Stating whether the Bureau's educational programmes had resulted in an improved commitment to the equal status of women by both men and women;

(e) Giving more information about women in the workforce, for example their pay and terms of employment, their participation in trade unions and what obstacles they faced in employment in such areas as achieving equal pay with men.

**BIBLIOGRAPHY.** Article 19. *Freedom of Information and Expression in Barbados.* London: 1989. NGO report, in English.

Stern, Vivien. *Deprived of their Liberty.* Belleville, Barbados: Caribbean Rights, 1990. NGO research report, in English.

## BASIC PRINCIPLES FOR THE PROTECTION OF CIVILIANS IN ARMED CONFLICTS. See ARMED CONFLICT.

## BASIC PRINCIPLES FOR THE TREATMENT OF PRISONERS. See PRISONERS.

## BASIC PRINCIPLES FOR THE USE OF FORCE AND FIREARMS BY LAW ENFORCEMENT OFFICIALS. See LAW ENFORCEMENT.

## BASIC PRINCIPLES OF THE LEGAL STATUS OF COMBATANTS STRUGGLING AGAINST COLONIAL AND ALIEN DOMINATION AND RACIST REGIMES. See ARMED CONFLICT.

**BASIC PRINCIPLES ON THE INDEPENDENCE OF THE JUDICIARY (1985).** See **JUDICIARY.**

**BASIC PRINCIPLES ON THE ROLE OF LAWYERS.** See **LAWYERS.**

**BEERNAERT, AUGUSTE MARIE FRANÇOIS (1829–1912).** Beernaert, a Belgian prime minister, shared the 1909 **NOBEL PEACE PRIZE** with **PAUL HENRI BENJAMIN BALLUET.** Beernaert was born in Ostend and received a doctorate in law from the University of Louvain. In 1873, he was appointed Belgium's minister of public work; in 1884, he served briefly as minister of agriculture but was then appointed prime minister. Under his administration the Belgian state of the Congo was created in 1885 with King Leopold as sovereign and general suffrage was introduced in Belgium.

After his cabinet fell, Beernaert became active in the Interparliamentary Union, presiding over several of its conferences and serving as president of its council and its executive committee. At the Peace Conference at The Hague, he presided over the first Commission on Arms Limitations; indeed, Beernaert was a prominent figure in all peace conferences from 1889 to 1912. He was also a member of the **PERMANENT COURT OF ARBITRATION** and mediated many international quarrels.

*BIBLIOGRAPHY.* Gray, Tony. *Champions of Peace.* London: Paddington Press, 1976.
Schlessinger, Bernard S., and June H. Schlessinger, eds. *Who's Who of Nobel Prize Winners.* Phoenix, AZ, USA: Oryx Press, 1991.

**BEGIN, MENACHEM (1913–1992).** In 1978, Menachem Begin and **ANWAR SADAT** were jointly awarded the **NOBEL PEACE PRIZE** for their work on the Camp David Accords, which ended years of enmity between the States of Israel and Egypt. Born and educated in Brest-Litovsk, Poland (now Russia), Begin studied law at Warsaw University. He was an active Zionist, becoming head of the Polish Zionist movement in 1931.

With the advent of Nazism, Begin fled to Russia in 1939, enlisted in the Free Polish Army in 1941, and was sent to British-mandated Palestine, where he later commanded the Irgun-Zvai Lemui movement, a commando group that advocated the establishment of the State of Israel by any means. Under Begin's leadership, the Irgun was responsible for the execution of British Mandatory soldiers and of the villagers of Deir Yassin.

When the State of Israel was established in 1948, the conservative Herut Party was formed from the Irgun, with Begin as leader of the newly established political party. In 1973, Begin became of the Likud Party, a coalition of three political parties. In 1977, he formed a coalition government and served as Israeli prime minister from that year until his resignation in 1983.

In December 1977, Begin and Anwar Sadat of Egypt opened negotiations to ease Middle East tensions. The Camp David Accords, signed in September 1978, established diplomatic relations between the two countries for the first time in 30 years.

*BIBLIOGRAPHY.* Schlessinger, Bernard S., and June H. Schlessinger, eds. *Who's Who of Nobel Prize Winners.* Phoenix, AZ, USA: Oryx Press, 1991.
Silver, Eric. *Begin: A Biography.* London: Weidenfeld and Nicolson, 1984.

**BEIJING RULES.** A term applied to the United Nations Standard Minimum Rules for the Administration of Juvenile Justice. See **JUVENILE JUSTICE** for the complete text.

**BELARUS.** Formerly the Byellorussian Soviet Socialist Republic of the Union of Soviet Socialist Republics, Belarus became an independent republic and member of the Commonwealth of Independent States in 1991. These major developments were described by the Government in its initial report to the UN Committee on the Rights of the Child, submitted in February 1993 (UN Doc. CRC/C/3/Add. 14):

*Land and People.* The Republic of Belarus is situated in the central part of Europe and borders on Lithuania, Latvia, Russia, Ukraine, and Poland. It covers an area of 207,600 sq. km. and is divided into six regions (oblast). Its capital is Minsk.

In the early 20th century, Belarus, which had been part of the Russian Empire, enjoyed a brief period of independence. This lasted from 1 January 1919 until 30 December 1922, after which Belarus became a Republic of the Soviet Union.

A crucial political and economic event in the country's history was the adoption on 25 August 1991 of the Act conferring the status of constitutional law on the Declaration by the Byelorussian Supreme Council of State Sovereignty of the Byelorussian Soviet Socialist Republic and of the Ordinance on safeguarding the political and economic independence of the Byelorussian SSR. In December 1991, the Agreement establishing the Commonwealth of Independent States was signed, the 1922 treaty on the establishment of the Union of Soviet Socialist Republics was denounced, and the Constitution of the USSR was declared null and void in the territory of Belarus.

The population of Belarus is estimated to be 10,280,800. Of this number 4,827,900 are men and 5,452,900 are women. The urban population is 6,952,100 and the rural population [is] 3,328,700.

Overall, the mean lifespan is 70.7 years (65.5 years for men and 75.5 years for women). In the urban population, mean lifespan is 71.3 years (66.5 years for men, 75.7 years for women); among the rural population it is 68.7 years (63.2 years for men, 74.7 years for women). Speakers of the mother tongue comprise 77.7% of the total population. The composition of the population by nationality is as follows: Belarusians, 1,151,800; Russians, 342,000; Ukrainians, 291,000; Poles, 417,700. Other nationalities are also represented.

*Social and Economic Development.* The basic indicators of social and economic development for the Republic are as follows: gross national product at current prices amounted to 30 billion roubles in 1985, 40.4 billion roubles in 1990, and 71.8 billion roubles in 1991. Growth by comparison with 1985 was 124% in 1990 and 122% in 1991.

The weakening, and in some cases breakdown, of the economic relationships that characterized the industrial and intersectoral specialization and cooperation in the economy of the former Soviet Union, have been detrimental to the overall economic and social situation in Belarus and are making the current transitional period more difficult for the Republic. According to the State Committee for Statistics (GOSKOMSTAT), between January and September 1992, national income fell by 15%; manufacturing output fell by 785 enterprises (58.1% of the total number); meat production fell by 135,200 tonnes (23.2%); butter production by 30,100 tonnes (27.8%); and production of whole milk products by 134,800 tonnes (10.7%). The only production rises concerned cereals (+665,000 tonnes) and, consequently, bread and bakery products (+13,000 tonnes or 1.3%).

Over the same nine months in 1992, personal monetary income rose by a factor of 6.5 compared to the period from January to September 1991. Average monthly pay for industrial and white-collar workers were 3,373 roubles. Retail prices for consumer goods and services rose by a factor of 9.3.

The deterioration in the economic situation in Belarus and the fall in living standards have had undesirable social consequences, including a worsening in the country's demographic trends.

In 1992, the number of births (135,000) was 29,900 fewer than in 1985. Births during the first nine months of 1992 were 7,500 fewer than during the same period of 1991. The mortality rate per thousand children below the age of 15 was 10.6 in 1985, 10.7 in 1990, and 11.2 in 1991. The infant mortality rate (deaths before the first birthday per 1,000 live births) was 14.5 (number of deaths 2,439) in 1985, 11.9 (1.732) in 1990, and 12.1 (1.616) in 1991. In 1991, the population of the Republic grew by 0.2%, while the urban and rural populations grew by 0.1% and 0.15%, respectively.

*Health Effects of Chernobyl Incident.* A major factor in the deterioration in the health of the population has been the accident at the Chernobyl nuclear power station, the worst effects of which were felt in the territory of Belarus.

In contaminated areas, there has been an increase in anaemia among expectant mothers and the number of premature births. In the Mogilev region, for example, the incidence of perinatal anaemia was 9.4%, a figure five times higher than before the accident. Children have still not been evacuated from the danger zone. According to GOSKOMSTAT, there are 485,900 children below the age of 14 and 129,200 young people above the age of 14 living in the contaminated areas.

Studies of the health of children living in the contaminated areas have shown a significant increase in the incidence of diseases affecting the ear, nose, and throat; bile ducts; and digestive organs (between 40% and 80% above the incidence in unaffected areas). There has also been an increase in chronic diseases of the haematopoietic and lymphatic systems. Between 40% and 60% of school children exposed to radiation show signs of cardiovascular dysfunction. The number of children born with congenital deformities has increased by between 15% and 20% in the contaminated areas. Congenital anomalies account for 20% of child mortality. The increase in the incidence of thyroid disorders has been particularly marked, and exceeds the maximum levels noted elsewhere in the world.

*Juvenile Delinquency.* Apart from physical health problems, the moral and mental health of children is a major problem facing Belarus in the changed economic and social conditions. The number of offenses committed by minors is increasing. During a seven-month period in 1992, 3,273 offenses were committed by minors, which marks a 19% increase over the same period in 1991. The nature of prostitution is also changing, and there are now 45 registered underage prostitutes. The growing wave of drug and toxic substance abuse, which affects principally young people, is a serious threat.

The level of criminality among minors is being affected by phenomena that are new to Belarus. The number of young people who are neither undergoing education nor in employment is rising at a disastrous rate, and this problem is compounded by the lack of structured leisure activities and the fall in living standards.

At the beginning of October 1992, 14,900 persons were registered with the Employment Centre as unemployed; and 12,600 were receiving unemployment benefits. To date during 1992, 3,600 secondary-school leavers have asked for assistance in finding employment. Of that number, 1,700 have been found employment and 110 have been registered as unemployed.

*Basic Rights.* The rights and freedoms of citizens of Belarus and of foreigners and stateless persons are guaranteed by the Constitution (the Basic Law, December 1978), by the Declaration of State Sovereignty of the Republic of Belarus (August 1991), and by other legislative instruments. The standards that these documents put into effect correspond to the provisions of the Universal Declaration of Human Rights and international treaties. Under Belarusian law, all citizens, irrespective of national and social origin, sex, language, political or other convictions, religion, place of residence, property status, or other circumstances, are equally entitled to protection of their rights and freedoms. Judicial protection of rights and freedoms is guaranteed, so that any citizen who believes that his rights have been infringed is entitled to seek redress in the courts.

Special protection is provided for the victims of political repression from the 1920s to the 1980s. The Supreme Council of the Republic has approved regulations on the restoration of these persons' rights (December 1990), procedures have been established for the rehabilitation of the victims of political repression (June 1991), and a Commission has been created under the Supreme Council to assist in securing the rights and perpetuating the memory of the victims of political repression from the 1920s to 1980s (November 1991).

However, it must be admitted that no definitive mechanism for monitoring the implementation of human rights has yet been devised or embodied in law in Belarus. Prevailing legislative practice is such that the provisions of international human rights instruments are not incorporated directly in domestic law. We need to convert the relevant provisions of international law into domestic law or to adopt rules that refer back to international instruments. . . .

***UN REACTION.*** Earlier, in 1992, reports submitted by the Government of Belarus were submitted to the

UN **Committee Against Torture** (UN Doc. CAT/C/17/Add. 6) and to the UN **Human Rights Committee** (UN Doc. CCPR/C.52/Add. 8), and were considered by those bodies. After considering the latter report, the Human Rights Committee adopted the following comments (UN Doc. CCPR/C/79/Add. 5):

### A. Introduction

The [Human Rights] Committee expresses its appreciation to the State party for its report and for engaging through a high-ranking delegation in a constructive and frank dialogue with the Committee. The wealth of additional information provided in the introductory statement and in the replies given by the delegation of Belarus to the questions raised by the Committee and by individual members has allowed the Committee to have a clearer picture of the overall situation in the country at a turning point in its history as it makes the transition toward multi-party democracy. The report, and the additional information that was subsequently provided, have enabled the Committee to obtain a comprehensive view of the State party's compliance with the obligations undertaken under the International Covenant on Civil and Political Rights and human rights standards set forth therein.

### B. Positive Aspects

The Committee notes with satisfaction that there has been clean progress in securing civil and political rights in Belarus since the consideration of the second periodic report, and especially since the submission of the third periodic report in July 1990. It is particularly noteworthy that the reforms in Belarus are being handled in a manner that allows a propitious social and political environment for the further protection and promotion of human rights.

The Committee also notes with satisfaction that recently enacted laws, notably the Law on Citizenship, are of a liberal character, demonstrating the Government's intention to restructure society in accordance with basic democratic principles. Existing laws, for example those relating to national minorities, are also generally being applied in a manner compatible with the Covenant. Additionally, it welcomes the readiness of the Government of Belarus to make use of the experiences of established democracies with respect to the promotion and protection of human rights.

### C. Factors and Difficulties Impeding the Implementation of the Covenant

The Committee notes that the heritage of the negative aspects of the past could not be rectified overnight and that much remains to be done to make irreversible the process of introducing multi-party democracy and strengthening the rule of law. The Committee also notes that Belarus continues to face various problems during the present period of transition that make the task of implementing civil and political rights particularly difficult. In this connection, it also notes that the Government's efforts in restructuring the existing legal system have at times been hampered by certain lacunae in national legislation as well as by continuing resort to legislation of the former regime.

### D. Principal Subjects of Concern

The Committee expresses concern about the fact that certain drafts, pending before the legislature, are not fully in conformity with the provisions of the Covenant, particularly in respect of freedom of movement. Problems in this regard relate in particular to grounds on which passports may be issued and to clauses dealing with exit visas, particularly in respect of holders of State secrets—which are incompatible with article 12, paragraph 3, of the Covenant. The Committee is also concerned as to the planned retention of the internal residence permit ("propiska") system. The retention of the death penalty for many offences, even though limited in application, is also of concern to the Committee. The retention of the classification of persons belonging to any religion, in particular the Jewish faith, as a distinct nationality is also without justification. In many areas not covered by new legislation, much depends on the good will of the authorities, with the danger still present that the latter would be unduly influenced by certain attitudes inherited from the past.

### E. Suggestions and Recommendations

The Committee considers it to be particularly important that constitutional and legislative reforms should be expedited and that they should be in full conformity with the existing international standards enshrined in the International Covenant on Civil and Political Rights. In drafting new legislation affecting human rights, special attention should be paid to the establishment of effective judicial guarantees for the safeguard of civil and political rights. Attention should be paid in all legislation to ensure that any limitations on human rights are in strict conformity with the limitations to those rights permitted in the Covenant. Existing provisions limiting or restricting freedom of movement, including the requirement for exit visas and the clause relating to holders of State secrets, should be eliminated from pending legislation to bring it fully into conformity with article 12, paragraph 3, of the Covenant.

*1994 PRESIDENTIAL ELECTION.* In July 1994, the voters in Belarus gave a remarkable mandate to Aleksandr Lukashenko, a crusader against corruption who comes to the position of President with no significant domestic or international political experience. Receiving more than 80% of the vote (more than 70% of the country's 7.4 million eligible voters participated in the election), Lukashenko defeated former Prime Minister Vyacheslav Kebich. Lukashenko, a former Communist party member, rose to fame in 1993 as the head of a parliamentary commission investigating official corruption. He campaigned on the platform of dismissing virtually all of the allegedly corrupt government and also of linking Belarus more closely with Russia in both political and economic matters. Despite the landslide vote, Lukashenko's election might plunge the country into more instability because, as of the end of 1994, it was not clear who would help Lukashenko run his government. Under Belarus law, parliament retains the right to vote on the choice of candidates for Prime Minister and other top ministers.

The entire Belarus political establishment supported former Prime Minister Kebich against Lukashenko in the presidential election.

**BELGIUM.** The kingdom of Belgium is a country in western Europe, on the North Sea. It has borders with the Federal Republic of Germany, France, and the Netherlands. It achieved independence from the Netherlands in 1830 and became a member of the United Nations in 1945. Its population is estimated to be 10,030,000. Ethnic groups include persons of Italian, Moroccan, French, Dutch, Turkish, and Spanish origin. Languages spoken include Dutch (57%), French (32%), bilingual Dutch-French (9%), and others (2%). Dutch-speaking Belgians are commonly referred to as "Flemings"; French-speaking Belgians as "Walloons." Religions practiced include Christianity (mostly Roman Catholic), 98%; Islam, 1%; and others, 1%. Literacy is estimated at 98%.

The government (1994) took the form of a constitutional monarchy. The king is head of State. When King Baudoin died in 1993, his brother, King Albert II, took the throne. The prime minister, representing the party or coalition given the majority in a popular election, is head of government. The legislature consists of a 181-member Senate and a 150-member Chamber of Deputies. Of the Senate's members, 106 are chosen by popular vote, 50 by provincial authorities, and 25 by the Senate itself. Representatives are elected by proportional representation. Members of both houses serve for terms of four years. Suffrage is universal and those who fail to vote are fined. Political parties include Flemish-speaking Social Christians, French-speaking Social Christians, Flemish-speaking Socialists, French-speaking Socialists, French-speaking Liberals, Flemish-speaking Liberals, and the Flemish Peoples' Party.

Disagreement between French-speaking Walloons in the south and Dutch-speaking Flemish in the north has been a perennial source of controversy and almost resulted in the downfall of the coalition government in 1985, 1986, and 1987. However, the coalition was retained by a small majority in elections held in 1987, 1991, and 1995. Parliament has since passed measures aimed at transferring power from the central government to three regions: Wallonia, Flanders, and Brussels.

In its second periodic report on the implementation of the **INTERNATIONAL COVENANT ON CIVIL AND POLITICAL RIGHTS,** submitted in 1991, the Belgium Government included the following general comments concerning the place of the Covenant in Belgium's internal law (CCPR/C/57/Add. 3):

In Belgium, in order for the provisions of an international treaty to be incorporated in internal law, the treaty must be approved by the legislative chambers, in accordance with article 68 of the Constitution, ratified by the Crown as a branch of the Executive and brought to the attention of the citizens by its publication in the *Moniteur belge.*

The International Covenant on Civil and Political Rights was approved by Parliament on 15 May 1981, ratified by the Crown on 21 April 1983, and published in the *Moniteur belge* on 6 July 1983. Its provisions, therefore, form part of internal law and are binding. Once the provisions of an international treaty have been incorporated into internal law, the question arises of their legal effects and, in particular, whether they may be invoked directly by individuals in national courts. The problem is that of the direct applicability of the provisions of an international treaty.

When no provision of an international treaty determines expressis verbis whether all or part of its provisions have a direct effect in the internal law of the contracting States, under Belgian law, it is for the court to decide whether a treaty provision is directly applicable. The problem is one of interpretation which the court must resolve, mainly in the light of articles 31 to 33 of the Vienna Convention on the Law of Treaties, of 23 May 1969. In Belgium, it is generally recognized that an international provision produces direct effects when it is clear and comprehensive, when it requires the Belgian State either to refrain from action or to act in a specific manner, and when it may be invoked as a source of law by individuals without need for any additional internal legislation for the purpose of implementation.

The International Covenant on Civil and Political Rights does not determine specifically whether its provisions are directly applicable. Consequently, in accordance with the principles mentioned above, direct applicability is a matter that must be settled by the court. This is what the Court of Cassation of Belgium did in a decision of 17 January 1984 by affirming that article 9, paragraph 2, of the Covenant produced direct effects in internal law for individuals. Since then, the Court of Cassation has confirmed such direct applicability in the case of other provisions of the Covenant.

The legal effect of the provisions of an international treaty also depends on their recognized place in the hierarchy of internal law in the event of conflict with national provisions. In Belgium, several attempts have been made, in the course of constitutional review procedures, to incorporate into law a general principle designed to bring the authority of treaties into line with that of the provisions of internal law. Thus far, all those attempts have failed. Consequently, the Court of Cassation provided the solution, in a decision on 27 May 1971 in the case of S.A. Fromagerie Franco-Suisse Le Ski. The Court affirmed the primacy of provisions of international treaties having direct effects in internal law over provisions of national origin, even subsequent ones. A Belgian court may, therefore, apply national provisions only if they are compatible with those of international treaties directly applicable in internal law. It verifies, inter alia, the conformity of national law with the directly applicable provisions of the Covenant. This had been done in the case of the aforementioned decision of 17 January 1984 by the Court of Cassation.

*UN REACTION.* After considering the above report from the Belgian Government, on 7 April 1992, the UN **HUMAN RIGHTS COMMITTEE** adopted the following comments (UN Doc. CCPR/C/79/Add.3):

*Positive Aspects.* The Committee notes with satisfaction the changes in law and in practice during the period under review, in particular, the several decisions of the Court of Cassation affirming the applicability of certain provisions of the Covenant; the law on economic reorientation prohibiting any discrimination based on sex; the law abolishing all discrimination between children born in and out of wedlock; the draft law permitting immediate communication between the accused and his lawyer; the bill proposing to abolish the death penalty; and the planned accession to the Second Optional Protocol to the Covenant.

*Factors and Difficulties Impeding the Application of the Covenant.* The Committee notes some of the major difficulties experienced by Belgium, such as the centrifugal character of Belgian federalism, the bipolar nature of the legal system, and the language differences among the population. The complexity of the Belgian legal framework seems to have impeded a direct reference to the Covenant to a certain extent.

*Principal Subjects of Concern.* Although noting the direct applicability of several provisions of the Covenant which form part of Belgian domestic law, the Committee is concerned about the difference between civil rights enjoyed by citizens and those enjoyed by aliens, which may lead to discrimination against aliens. Other areas of concern include the scope of interpretation given to article 6 of the Covenant; the adequacy of monitoring pre-trial detention as well as the impartiality of the authorities who examine those arrested; the adequacy of remedies for wrongful detention; the adequacy of information on freedom of expression especially in relation to television broadcasting; and arrangements as to freedom of assembly in open air.

*Suggestions and Recommendations.* The Committee recommends to the State party more adequately to reflect in internal administrative practice the provisions of the Covenant which are not reflected in the European Convention for the Protection of Human Rights and Fundamental Freedoms (e.g., arts. 25, 26, and 27); and to ensure that the laws regarding restrictions on freedom of expression and assembly are compatible with those provided for in the Covenant. The Committee also recommends that the State party further improve the effectiveness of the protection granted to minority rights at the communal level. The Committee further recommends that the State party reconsider its reservations so as to withdraw as many as possible.

**BIBLIOGRAPHY.** Batselé, Didier, Michel Hanotiau, and Odile Daurmont. "La lutte contre le racisme et la xénophobie: mythe ou réalité?" (Fighting Back Racism and Xenophobia: A Myth or Reality?), *Revue trimestrielle des droits de l'homme* 2, no. 7 & 8 (July 1991): 319–346, 435–471. Scholarly article, in French; bibliography in detailed footnotes within text.

Index on Censorship. "Censorship in Belgium," *Index on Censorship* 16, no. 3 (March 1987): 39. NGO article, in English.

Manço, Altay, and Ural Manço. *Les Turcs de Belgique: identités et trajectoires d'une minorité* (The Turks of Belgium: Identities and Trajectories of a Minority). Brussels, Belgium: Info-Türk, 1992. Scholarly monograph, in French.

Médiathèque de la Communauté française de Belgique. *Droits de l'homme, droits des peuples: guide pour l'information et l'éducation* (Human and Peoples' Rights: A Guide for Information and Education). Brussels, Belgium: 1989. NGO bibliography, in French

Minority Rights Group. *Co-Existence in Some Plural European Societies.* London: 1986. NGO report, in English.

Royal Commission for Immigration Policy. *L'Intégration: une politique de longue haleine–Vol. 1: Repères et premières propositions/Vol. 2: Philosophies, politiques et opinions/Vol. 3: Données argumentaires* (Integration: A Long Term Policy–Vol. 1: References and Initial Propositions/Vol. 2: Philosophies, Policies, and Opinions/Vol. 3: Argumentative Facts). Brussels, Belgium: 1989. Government report, in French.

White, P., and C. Kesteloot, eds. "Les communautés étrangères en Europe" (Foreign Communities in Europe), *Espace, populations, sociétés* no. 2 (1990). Special issue, in English and French.

**BELIZE.** A small country in central America, on the Caribbean Sea, formerly known as British Honduras, Belize achieved independence from Great Britain in 1974 and became a member of the United Nations in 1981. Its population is estimated to be 186,000. Ethnic groups include persons of African origin, Mestizos (mixed), and Amerindian Creoles. Languages commonly used include English (official), Spanish, and Mayan. Religions practiced include Christianity (Roman Catholic, 62%; Anglican, 12%; Methodist, 6%; and others, including Seventh Day Adventists, Mennonites, Jehovah's Witnesses, and Baptists (17%) and the Bahá'í faith (3%).

The government (1992) took the form of a parliamentary State and member of the British Commonwealth. Executive authority is exercised by the Governor and the Prime Minister. The members of Parliament are elected by popular vote. The judiciary is organized along British lines. Political parties include the United Democratic Party, the People's United Party, and the Christian Democratic Party.

Belize is sparsely settled; and, up to 1972, its population diminished as workers migrated to the United States of America. However, since 1972, the population has grown because of an influx of settlers and refugees from neighboring Central American countries.

***THE QUESTION OF TORTURE.*** Belize is a party to the Convention against Torture and Other Cruel, Inhuman or Degrading Treatment or Punishment. In a note dated 18 April 1991 (UN Doc. CAT/C/5/Add. 25) to the UN Committee against Torture, the government informed the Committee of the following:

"Torture" as defined in article 1 of the Convention is prohibited by the Constitution of Belize. Section 7 of the Belize Constitution enjoins that "no person shall be subjected to torture or to inhuman or degrading punishment or other treatment." Further, under section 8 of the Constitution, no person shall be required to perform forced labour, nor held in slavery or servitude.

The various acts constituting torture are offences under the criminal laws of Belize. For example, intentional infliction of pain or suffering will amount to the offences of assault, harm, wounding, etc. Similarly, the use of unwarrantable violence by a police officer against a person in custody is an offence under the Police Act of Belize.

Judicial corporal punishment was abolished in Belize by the Abolition of Judicial Corporal Punishment Act, 1978. No person in prison can be obliged to do hard labour.

Adequate provisions exist in Belize to ensure that confessional statements taken by the police or other persons in authority from accused persons by the use of torture are not admitted in evidence. According to the Evidence Act of Belize, before any such statement is received in evidence, the prosecution must prove to the satisfaction of the judge that it was not induced by any promise of favour or advantage or by use of fear, threat or pressure by or on behalf of a person in authority. The police authorities must also follow "judges' rules," which lay down guidelines as to the treatment of persons in custody. To ensure the observance of these rules, a judge is required to hold a "trial within a trial" to satisfy himself that a statement sought to be admitted in evidence was given by the accused person freely and voluntarily.

The provisions of the Convention can be invoked by the courts only through their transformation into specific internal laws and administrative regulations. However, as the main ingredients of the Convention are already incorporated in our laws, no further enabling legislation is absolutely necessary.

Any person who alleges that his constitutional right not to be subjected to torture has been breached can apply to the Supreme Court for redress. Where any act of torture amounts to an offence, criminal proceedings may be instituted.

The Human Rights Commission of Belize acts as a watchdog in the matter of torture and brings any such cases to the notice of the authorities. Recently, at the insistence of the Human Rights Commission, an independent Commission of Inquiry was set up by the Prime Minister of Belize under the Commissions of Inquiry Act, to investigate a case of alleged torture of an alien by police authorities.

It is not the practice in Belize to extradite any person who there is reason to believe may be subjected to torture in the requesting State. Extradition is normally granted according to bilateral extradition treaties which, as a rule, exclude the extradition of offenders accused of political offences.

Any person in Belize who is arrested or detained has a constitutional right to be informed promptly, and in any case no later than 48 hours, of the reasons for his arrest or detention, and to communicate without delay in private with a lawyer of his own choice. He is also entitled to the remedy by way of habeas corpus for determining the validity of his detention.

In Belize, unlike several other countries, there are no preventive detention laws and no special courts to try special offences. All persons are equal before the law and are entitled without any discrimination to the equal protection of the law. All courts sit in public to try cases according to the ordinary law of the land.

No difficulties have arisen in Belize in regard to the fulfilment of obligations under the Convention. This is because the main provisions of the Convention are already incorporated in our laws and are habitually followed by all concerned.

***BIBLIOGRAPHY.*** "Belize," *Mesoamerica* 6, no. 12 (December 1987): 2–3. News article, in English.

**BENIN.** The Republic of Benin is a country in western Africa, on the Gulf of Guinea. Formerly known as Dahomey, it has borders with Burkina Faso, Niger, Nigeria, and Togo. It achieved independence from France in 1960 and became a member of the United Nations the same year. Its population is estimated to be 5,083,000. Ethnic groups include the Fons, Adjas, Baribas, Yorubas, and Mahis. Languages commonly used include French (official) and several African vernaculars. Religions practiced include Animism (65%), Christianity (17%), and Islam (18%). Literacy is estimated at 20%.

The government (1994) took the form of a republic. However, since 1973, Benin has been under military rule, with all power in the hands of the president, a National Executive Council, a National Revolutionary Assembly, and a variety of People's Courts. Decisions relating to national policy are taken by the Party of the People's Revolution of Benin, the only political party.

During the 18th and 19th centuries, the kings of Dahomey sold thousands of slaves—mostly prisoners whom they had taken in local warfare—to traders who shipped them to markets in Brazil and the Caribbean. France, which led the efforts to suppress the slave trade in west Africa, assumed control of the country in 1892 and organized it as a protectorate. It remained a French colony until 1960, when it became the independent Republic of Dahomey. Its name was changed to the People's Republic of Benin in 1975.

Since it achieved independence, Benin has been unstable politically and economically. There have been numerous coups, attempted coups, and governments. In the absence of exploitable natural resources, its economy has stagnated, and the gross national product has been only slightly more than $300 per person.

On 8 December 1989 President Mathieu Kerekou announced on national radio, after meetings of the government, of Parliament, and of the Central Committee of the Popular Revolution of Benin, that Marxism-Leninism no longer would be Benin's official ideology and that steps would be taken soon to introduce "a healthy political climate" in the country. Shortly thereafter, however, some 20,000 protesters demanded his resignation.

In March 1991, elections resulted in the first popularly elected President in 30 years, Nicephore Soglo, but there has been no economic improvement to date resulting from the move away from socialism and toward private enterprise.

***BIBLIOGRAPHY.*** Amnesty International. "Benin: Fear of Torture/Legal Concern," *Urgent Action* (15 November 1985): 1. NGO bulletin, in English.

———. *Benin: Human Rights Violations*. London: 1987. NGO report, in English.

———. *Benin: Political Imprisonment and Torture*. London: 1988. NGO report, in English.

————. *Benin: Recent Arrest of Students and Other Individuals.* London: 1985. NGO report, in English.

## BERKELEY HUMAN RIGHTS PROGRAM. See UNIVERSITY OF CALIFORNIA, HUMAN RIGHTS PROGRAM.

## BETHEL COLLEGE, DEPARTMENT OF GLOBAL STUDIES.

Bethel College offers an undergraduate degree in Global Studies that combines a concentration in environmental studies, international development, or peace studies, with an integrative core of studies in political science, economics, environmental biology, and ethics. In addition to his or her specific area of concentration, the student takes courses in the other two areas to develop skills in thinking coherently and systematically about the links between environment, development, and conflict.

The goal of Global Studies is to prepare graduates for work in fields related to (1) stewardship of the planet (environment); (2) assistance of the poor in developing countries (international development); and (3) the resolution of human conflict within a framework of social justice (peace studies). Among the courses offered are "Relief, Development, and Social Justice," "Global Issues in Environment, Human Conflict, and Development," "Peacemaking and International Conflict," and "Nonviolence Theory and Practice." In addition, the College also offers a Summer Peace Institute for Teachers at the elementary, secondary, and post-secondary levels and internships with organizations that specialize in conflict resolution, development, or environmental issues.

Global Studies Program. Address: Bethel College, North Newton, KS 67117, USA. Telephone: (316) 283-2500. Fax: (316) 284-5286. Chair: Prof. P. McKay.

## BHUTAN.

The Kingdom of Bhutan is a country in southern Asia. It has borders with China and India. Always independent, Bhutan was occupied by the British and subsidized by them from 1910 until 1949, when India assumed control of its foreign affairs. Bhutan became a member of the United Nations in 1971. Its population is estimated to be 1,680,000. Ethnic groups include Nepalese (25%), Bhote (60%), and indigenous populations (15%). Languages in common use include Dzongkha, a Tibetan dialect (official), Nepali, and English. Religions practiced include Buddhism (70%), Hinduism (25%), and Islam (5%). Literacy is estimated at 15%.

The government (1994) took the form of a monarchy. The king is ruler, head of State and of government. He is advised by a Council of Ministers and a Royal Advisory Council. In addition, there is a National Assembly (Tsongdu), composed of not more than 150 members, 100 of whom are elected by the people, 10 by the organizations of lamas, and 40 appointed by the king. Heads of all government departments are required to subject themselves and their policies to the scrutiny of the National Assembly at least once a year. There are no political parties and suffrage, in voting for members of the National Assembly, is on the basis of one vote per family. Each family has a "headman," who either votes or designates someone to cast the family ballot.

***BIBLIOGRAPHY.*** Amnesty International. *Bhutan: Forcible Exile.* London: 1994. NGO report, in English.

Institute for Human Rights, Environment and Development. *Bhutanese Refugees: Destitutes without Destination: A Documentation of Human Rights Violations in the Kingdom of Bhutan.* Kathmandu, Nepal: 1993. NGO report, in English.

Institute for Human Rights, Environment and Development, and the Human Rights Organisation of Bhutan. *Bhutan in Turmoil: Documentation of Human Rights Violations in Bhutan—Submitted to the UN Sub-Commission on Human Rights.* Kathmandu, Nepal: INHURED, 1992. NGO report, in English.

International Centre for Law in Development and the Informal Sector Service Centre. *The Bhutan Tragedy—When Will It End?: First Report of the SAARC Jurists Mission on Bhutan.* Kathmandu, Nepal: 1992. NGO factfinding report, in English.

Rose, Carol. *Flight for the Thundering Dragon.* Kathmandu, Nepal: Institute of Current World Affairs, 1991. Factfinding report, in English.

Third World Studies Centre. *Bhutan: Violations of Human Rights.* New Delhi, India: Anand Swaroop Verma, 1992. NGO report, in English.

Thronson, David B. *Cultural Cleansing: A Distinct National Identity and the Refugees from Southern Bhutan.* Kathmandu, Nepal: International Institute for Human Rights, Environment and Development, 1993. Monograph, in English.

## B'NAI B'RITH INTERNATIONAL.

A non-governmental organization in consultative status (roster) with the UN **ECONOMIC AND SOCIAL COUNCIL, UNESCO,** and the **COUNCIL OF EUROPE,** the B'nai B'rith International was established in Jerusalem in May 1959, growing out of the much-older B'nai B'rith, which was founded in New York City in 1843 to serve as a service agency within the American Jewish community. Now, with approximately 450,000 members in more than 47 countries and territories, BBI's activities are directed mainly toward uniting persons of the Jewish faith in the work of promoting the highest interests of humanity and in particular toward combating discrimination on such grounds as race, religion, or origin. It also seeks to integrate refugees and migrants and to develop Jewish culture in youth and student groups and through adult education.

Directed by a board of governors elected by its delegate conference, BBI is organized into lodges, chapters, and smaller units, most of which meet on a monthly basis. Among its constituent organizations are the Anti-Defamation League of B'nai B'rith, which serves as a "watchdog" for Jewish people and acts to improve intergroup relations; B'nai B'rith International Commission on Continuing Jewish Education; B'nai B'rith Women; and the B'nai B'rith Youth Organization. Its main publication is the *BBI Jewish Monthly*.

B'nai B'rith International Council. Address: 1640 Rhode Island Ave., NW, Washington, D.C., 20036. Telephone: (202) 857-6582. Fax: (202) 857-1099. Telex: 710-822-0068. Director: Seymour Cohen.

**BIOETHICS.** Because of scientific breakthroughs in creating life forms, the question of bioethics to protect the rights of mankind—or the possibility of the rights of new life forms—has been debated in human rights forums.

At its 1992 session, the UN **SUB-COMMISSION ON PREVENTION OF DISCRIMINATION AND PROTECTION OF MINORITIES** decided to consider at a later session the possibility of elaborating new human rights standards relating to scientific developments that can affect the mental condition or the genetic structure of human beings.

Noting this decision, the UN **COMMISSION ON HUMAN RIGHTS,** at its 1993 session, recognized in resolution 1993/91 "the need for international cooperation in order to ensure that mankind as a whole benefits from the life sciences and to prevent them from being used for any purpose other than the good of mankind," and indicated that it was convinced of the necessity of developing life science ethics at the national and international levels. Accordingly, it invited governments and agencies and organizations within the UN system to inform the Secretary-General of activities being carried out to ensure that the life sciences develop in a manner respectful of human rights.

**BIOLOGICAL WARFARE.** See **CHEMICAL WEAPONS.**

**BODY OF PRINCIPLES FOR THE PROTECTION OF ALL PERSONS UNDER ANY FORM OF DETENTION OR IMPRISONMENT (1988).** See **PRISONERS.**

**BOJAXHIU, AGNES GONXHA.** See **TERESA, MOTHER.**

**BOLIVAR (SIMON) PRIZE.** Sponsored by **UNESCO,** the Prize was established in accordance with the ideals of Simon Bolivar, to reward individuals and institutions whose activities—whether in the form of intellectual or artistic creation, social achievement, or mobilization of public opinion—promote freedom, independence, and dignity of peoples and the strengthening of international solidarity. The 1992 recipients were Aung San Suu Kyi of Myanmar and Julius K. Nyerere of Tanzania.

For more information, contact: UNESCO, 7 Place de Fonteroy, 75700 Paris, France. Telephone: (33-1) 45-68-38-14. Fax: (33-1) 40-65-98-71.

**BOLIVIA.** The Republic of Bolivia is a landlocked country in tropical South America. It has borders with Argentina, Brazil, Chile, Paraguay, and Peru. It achieved independence from Spain in 1825 and became a member of the United Nations in 1945. Its population is estimated to be 7,411,000. Ethnic groups include the Aymara (25%) and Quechua (30%)—descendants of survivors of the once-predominant Amerindian population which was reduced to slavery by the Spanish colonists—European (20%), and mixed (25%). Languages commonly used include Spanish (official), Aymara, and Quechua. Religions practiced include Christianity (mostly Roman Catholic), 95%; the Bahá'í faith, 4%; and others, 1%. Literacy is estimated at 75%.

The government (1994) took the form of a republic. Under the 1967 constitution, the president is elected by popular vote and acts as Head of State and Government. However, in the event that no candidate receives 50% of the vote, the Congress chooses between the two top candidates. This, in fact, occurred in 1985, when the Nationalist Democratic Action Party (ADN), headed by General Hugo Banzer Suarez, won a narrow plurality of the popular vote (32.8%). The National Revolutionary Movement (MNR) came in second because its leader, former President Victor Paz Estenssoro, polled 30.4% of the vote, and the Movement of the Revolutionary Left (MIR) placed third with 10.2% of the vote for its candidate, Jaime Paz Zamora. In spite of the ADN plurality of some 37,000 votes—and because of the preference given to rural over urban votes in the apportionment of seats in Congress—the MNR won more legislative seats than the ADN. When, in the congressional run-off, the MIR cast its lot with the MNR, former President Victor Paz Estenssoro was elected to a fourth term in office.

A country naturally rich in minerals, the indifference of Bolivia's colonizers to the development of other resources gave rise in the 19th century to a system of social inequality in which the Amerindian indigenous peoples, although they constitute more than half the total population, were forced to work the mines and till the fields under duress and were ignored in society and in government.

In 1826, Simon Bolivar, then the most powerful man in South America after leading several successful revolutions, drew up a constitution for Bolivia. However, from that time onward, conflicting personal, military, and political aspirations plagued the country. Only in recent years did it begin to use its vast oil and mineral revenues to promote development. Frequent strikes have drawn attention to the lot of the Bolivian worker, while frequent revolts have dramatized the situation of the surviving Amerindian population. In mid-1994 the government signed a pact with the Bolivian Workers' Confederation, bringing a 23-year general strike to an end and increasing salaries, including the monthly minimum wage. However, conflict arose again in mid-1995 when the government incarcerated hundreds of union members, imposed a curfew, and revoked a variety of constitutional rights, including the right to assemble, the right to bear arms, and the right to free travel within the country.

Rich in natural resources but plagued by internal conflicts, strikes, inflation, and a wide variety of economic and social problems, Bolivia endured some 60 revolutions in 160 years and revised its Constitution more than 10 times. In one of the conflicts, which began in 1965, a Cuban-based revolutionary movement led by Major Ernesto (Che) Guevara was put down on 8 October 1967 by the Bolivian army with strong assistance from Bolivian peasants and U.S. military advisors, Guevara dying in the process.

On 17 July 1980, the government was taken over by Bolivian General Luis Garcia Tejada, and almost immediately rumors of serious violations of human rights began to circulate. In September 1980, the UN **SUB-COMMISSION ON PREVENTION OF DISCRIMINATION AND PROTECTION OF MINORITIES,** meeting in Geneva, called upon the **COMMISSION ON HUMAN RIGHTS** to study the situation and to take urgent steps to correct it.

The Commission appointed one of its members, Professor Hector Gros Espiell, as its special envoy for this purpose; and, in the three following years, he made three factfinding trips to Bolivia.

After the first trip, in 1981, he reported that he was convinced that, following 17 July 1980, grave, massive, and persistent violations of human rights were committed in Bolivia. He added, however, that "the situation has improved in recent months and the most serious and grave violations committed following 17 July 1980 have not recurred with the same intensity. It is

to be hoped that the positive trend will continue, intensify and succeed in overcoming the obvious difficulties which restrict, hinder and affect it."

After the second trip, in 1982, he reported that he had found "an auspicious and positive situation of full respect for human rights and a total identification of the authorities with the idea that it is necessary to ensure, uphold and increase the promotion, defence and guarantee of those rights, and that their protection should be free from any kind of discrimination. This situation—which contrasts radically with that which existed after 17 July 1980—is however limited by the adverse economic and social conditions, which can only be overcome by political stability and economic and social development."

After the third trip, in 1983, he reported that "since 10 October 1982, when the constitutional government of President Hernan Siles Zuazo was established, the situation of human rights in Bolivia has improved notably. Not only have provisions which inherently affected the recognition and legal guarantees of human rights been repealed: there have, in actual fact, been no serious violations of human rights. . . . This assertion is based on and supported by the absence of fresh complaints and the direct personal conviction reached by the Special Envoy as a result of his visit."

The special envoy recommended that the United Nations should continue, "through advisory services and assistance, to support and promote the local effort—which is the irreplaceable and determining factor—to ensure the full observance of human rights and fundamental freedoms in Bolivia."

The Commission on Human Rights, at its 1983 session, noted the determination of the Bolivian government to ensure that a thorough investigation of all past violations of human rights would be undertaken with a view to establishing responsibility through due process or law, welcomed the accession by Bolivia to the International Covenants on Human Rights and the Optional Protocol to the **INTERNATIONAL COVENANT ON CIVIL AND POLITICAL RIGHTS,** and concluded its consideration of the matter. Bolivia's progress in the field of human rights has since been monitored by the UN **HUMAN RIGHTS COMMITTEE.**

**BIBLIOGRAPHY.** Americas Watch. *Bolivia: The Trial of Responsibilities: The Garcia Meza Tejada Trial.* New York: Human Rights Watch, 1993. NGO report, in English.

Andean Commission of Jurists. *Bolivia: Administración de Justicia y Derechos Humanos* (Bolivia: Administration of Justice and Human Rights). Lima, Peru: 1993. NGO monograph, in Spanish; bibliography, pp. 187–189.

Asociation de Familiares de Detenidos, Desaparecidos y Martires por la Liberacion Nacional (Association of Relatives of the Detained, Disappeared, and Martyrs of National Liberation). "Logros de ASOFAMD" (Achievements of ASO-

FAMD), *Boletin* 2, no. 10 (1985): 3–5. NGO bulletin, in Spanish.

————. *Parotani: Informe sobre la Represion a los Campesinos* (Parotani: Report on the Repression of Peasants). La Paz, Bolivia: 1987. NGO mission report, in Spanish.

Del Granado, Juan. *Juicio a la Dictadura de Luis Garcia Meza: Contra la Impunidad* (Bring Luis Garcia Meza's Dictatorship to Justice: Against Impunity). La Paz, Bolivia: Asamblea Permanente de los Derechos Humanos de Bolivia, 1987. NGO report, in Spanish.

North American Congress on Latin America. "Bolivia: The Poverty of Progress," *Report on the Americas* 25, no. 1 (July 1991): 9–36. NGO article, in English.

Pettersson, Bjorn, and Lesley Mackay. *Human Rights Violations Stemming from the "War on Drugs" in Bolivia.* Cochabamba, Bolivia: Andean Information Network, 1993. NGO report, in English.

**BONDED LABOR.** See **DEBT BONDAGE.**

**BORLAUG, NORMAN ERNEST (1914–).** Norman Borlaug, an American geneticist and plant pathologist, was the recipient of the 1970 **NOBEL PEACE PRIZE.** Although a scientist, Borlaug received the Peace Prize because of his work in feeding developing nations. His work is often characterized as the "green revolution," a description for the phenomenal increase in grain production in the 1960s and 1970s due to Borlaug's plant research in Mexico that resulted in a high-yielding, fungus-resistant, dwarf wheat.

Born in Cresco, IA, USA, and educated at the University of Minnesota, Borlaug began working in 1944 with the Rockefeller Foundation on an agricultural program in Mexico aimed at increasing and improving that country's food supply. It was during this time that Borlaug and his scientific team developed the new strain of wheat. In later years, Borlaug refined and adapted his dwarf wheat to fit the agricultural needs of such countries as Pakistan, Turkey, Afghanistan, Iran, Iraq, Tunisia, Morocco, Lebanon, and the former Soviet Union.

In his Nobel lecture, Borlaug stated, "For the underprivileged billions . . . , hunger has been a constant companion, and starvation has all too often lurked in the nearby shadows. . . . Never before in the history of agriculture has a transplantation of high-yielding varieties coupled with an entirely new technology and strategy been used on such a massive scale, in so short a period of time, and with such great success."

**BIBLIOGRAPHY.** Gray, Tony. *Champions of Peace.* London: Paddington Press, 1976.

Paarlberg, Don. *Norman Borlaug: Hunger Fighter.* Washington, D.C.: Foreign Economic Development Service, 1970.

Schlessinger, Bernard S., and June H. Schlessinger, eds. *Who's Who of Nobel Prize Winners.* Phoenix, AZ, USA: Oryx Press, 1991.

**BOSNIA AND HERZEGOVINA.** Formerly one of the six republics of Yugoslavia, Bosnia and Herzegovina became an independent republic in 1991 with the collapse of its mother country. In 1992, however, it was invaded by Serbian militia and terrorists, the violent conflict resulting in thousands of deaths and widespread devastation of the land. With a population estimated at about 4,375,000, composed of a large Muslim majority (43%) and minorities of Serbs (31%) and Croats (17%), Bosnia and Herzegovina had existed for many years as a quiet agricultural and mining community, first as part of the Ottoman Empire, then under Austria-Hungarian occupation, and subsequently as a part of Yugoslavia. Its most important city, Sarajevo, had been brought to world attention by the assassination there of Archduke Francis Ferdinand of Austria, an event that precipitated World War I.

*ETHNIC CLEANSING.* With the invasion of the Serbs in 1992, the situation in Bosnia and Herzegovina escalated rapidly, despite a long series of efforts by the UN **SECURITY COUNCIL** to put an end to the conflict. On 4 August 1992, the Council's President issued a statement referring to reports of imprisonment and abuse of civilians in camps, prisons, and detention centers within the territory of the former Yugoslavia, and especially in Bosnia-Herzegovina, which, in his view, demanded that international organizations—in particular, the International Committee of the Red Cross—be granted immediate, unimpeded, and continued access to all such places.

On 13 August 1992, the UN **SUB-COMMISSION ON PREVENTION OF DISCRIMINATION AND PROTECTION OF MINORITIES,** meeting in Geneva, expressed its horror at, and its total and unqualified condemnation of, policies of so-called "ethnic cleansing," which had generated vast displacement of people and large flows of refugees of the different groups in the region. In Bosnia and Herzegovina, the ethnic cleansing affected the Muslim people in particular.

One day later, on 14 August 1992, the UN **COMMISSION ON HUMAN RIGHTS,** meeting for its first special session at the request of the Government of the United States of America, stated unanimously that it was

appalled at the continuing reports of widespread, massive and grave violations of human rights perpetrated within the territory of the former Yugoslavia and especially in Bosnia and Herzegovina, including reports of summary and arbitrary executions; enforced disappearances, torture, and other cruel, inhuman or degrading treatment; arbitrary arrest and detention; hostage-taking; lack of due process and lack of respect for the rule of law; restrictions on freedom of thought, expression, and association; deliberate attacks on non-combatants, hospitals, and ambulances; restrictions on access to food and health care; wanton devastation and destruction of property; and serious violations of human rights in places of detention.

[The Commission also expresses its particular abhorrence] at the concept and practice of "ethnic cleansing"... which, at a minimum, entails deportations and forcible mass removal or expulsion of persons from their homes in flagrant violation of their human rights, and which is aimed at the dislocation or destruction of national, ethnic, racial, or religious groups.

In resolution 1992/S-1/1, adopted that day without vote, the Commission on Human Rights condemned "in the strongest terms all violations of human rights within the territory of the former Yugoslavia, and especially in Bosnia and Herzegovina," and condemned absolutely "the concept and practice of 'ethnic cleansing.' " Further, it requested its Chairman "to appoint a Special Rapporteur to investigate first-hand the human rights situation in the territory of the former Yugoslavia, in particular within Bosnia and Herzegovina, and to receive relevant, credible information on the human rights situation there from Governments, individuals, and intergovernmental and non-governmental organizations."

In the same resolution, the Commission welcomed the establishment, pursuant to Security Council resolution 780 (1992) of 6 October 1992, of a Commission of Experts to examine and analyze information relating to violations of international humanitarian law, and reaffirmed "that all persons who perpetrate or authorize crimes against humanity or other grave breaches of international humanitarian law are individually responsible for those breaches and that the international community will exert every effort to bring them to justice." In this connection, the Commission called upon all States "to consider the extent to which the acts committed in Bosnia and Herzegovina and in Croatia constitute genocide."

*REPORTS OF THE UN SPECIAL RAPPORTEUR.* In a second report to the Commission on Human Rights, the Special Rapporteur reported on continuing open hostilities in the former Yugoslavia. "It has been conservatively estimated," he wrote, "that 5,000 people were displaced in central Bosnia in one week in early May. However, figures are very difficult to confirm because people are hiding, afraid of both the actual fighting and of ethnic persecution. Looting, rape, executions and intimidation are reported to be commonplace." The conclusions that he formulated at the end of the report are as follows (E/CN.4/1994/4):

The information gathered in the preparation of this report demonstrates that the recent eruption of hostilities between Croat and government forces in Central Bosnia and Herzegovina involved massive and systematic violations of human rights and international humanitarian law.

The forced displacement and detention of civilians, arbitrary executions, attacks on towns as well as the destruction of villages and religious sites have become part of a deliberate and systematic policy of ethnic cleansing conducted by Croat forces in that region. The fate of the civilian population of Ahmici is a particularly shocking application of this policy.

Arbitrary executions and torture have been carried out by government forces. The danger of retaliation for ethnic cleansing committed by Croat forces against Croat civilians in towns such as Zenica is a real one.

The credibility of the parties' commitment to human rights will be tested by their willingness to bring to justice the perpetrators of such atrocities as are outlined in this report.

Commitments that all parties to the conflicts in Bosnia and Herzegovina have repeatedly entered into to respect human rights and international humanitarian law, including written agreements concluded upon international mediation, have been systematically violated.

The peace plan, according to which Bosnia and Herzegovina would be divided along ethnic lines, has been used in order to create ethnically homogenous areas. The lack of an effective international response to counter the policy of ethnic cleansing perpetrated by Serb forces from the beginning of the war created the precedent of impunity that has allowed them to continue and that has encouraged Croat forces to adopt the same policy.

Without stopping the war and without applying sufficient pressure to force an end to human rights violations any attempts to find a just and lasting political solution will be doomed to fail.

In his third report, made to the 1994 session of the Commission on Human Rights, the Special Rapporteur summarized the then-existing situation in Bosnia and Herzegovina as follows:

### A. Introductory Remarks

The Special Rapporteur is concerned by the continuation of "ethnic cleansing" in all its forms. He draws particular attention to mass expulsions of peoples, military attacks on civilians, abuse of women, and assaults on "safe areas." Attacks on aid convoys as well as attempts to impose tasks also give cause for serious concern. There have been direct attacks, resulting in the death of aid workers and the temporary suspension of delivery. At the time of writing of [this] report, all convoys have been suspended.

These violations are the subject of this chapter, which is based on information gathered from a variety of reliable sources, and on-site investigations made by the Special Rapporteur's field staff in eastern Bosnia, western Herzegovina and central Bosnia, and in Sarajevo by the Special Rapporteur himself and the field staff assisting him. Bosnian Serb authorities have not yet permitted an investigation of the human rights situation in the territories under their control.

### B. "Ethnic Cleansing"

The dynamic of destruction set in motion by "ethnic cleansing" has affected almost every area of Bosnia and Herzegovina. Much of the country is under arms and the population is increasingly polarized. The war has exhausted stocks of food and timber and seriously damaged supplies of water, energy and medicines. The onset of a second winter in such conditions threatens the lives of many thousands of civilians, especially those who have lost their homes. Food, fuel, clothing, construction materials and medicine are in urgent need.

Over 2.1 million people have been displaced from their homes since the war in Bosnia and Herzegovina began—nearly 50% of the population recorded in the census of 1991. Some 800,000 of them are estimated to have sought refuge outside Bosnia and Herzegovina; the rest are seeking refuge inside the country. Tens of thousands have gone to the "safe areas," such as Gorazde, Zepa, Srebrenica, Tuzla, Bihac and Sarajevo.

The purpose of the "safe areas" was to provide people with the food and medicines they needed in places where their security was guaranteed. Relentless military action by Bosnian Serb forces, however, has turned them into areas under siege. In Sarajevo on 9 and 10 November 1993, mortar attacks killed 12 people. In the incident on 9 November, two shells hit a school building in the densely populated district of Alipasno Polje, killing three children and their teacher and wounding 40 other people, most of them children. Gorazde, Bihac and Zepa have also been shelled. In Srebrenica and Tuzla in particular, supplies of food, water and fuel have been the prime objects of attack. In September 1993, fighting broke out in the Bihac "safe area" between the army and separatists who announced the formation of an "Autonomous Province of Western Bosnia."

Sometimes the parties to the conflict instigate or use movements of large numbers of peoples in order to achieve "ethnic cleansing." The movement of large numbers of displaced persons inside the country has been used by some parties as a pretext for further "ethnic cleansing."

In other areas, the arrival of displaced people en masse has changed the composition of populations and sometimes heightened tension that the war had already created between local Muslim, Croat and Serb civilians.

Food shortages and other hardships have put added strains on the relationship between local civilians and refugees. Some local residents resent what they see as "preferential" treatment given to displaced people by aid agencies, and this has sparked conflict in Tuzla, Travnik and other major receiving centres for refugees.

By October 1993, the vast majority of Muslims and Croats had been driven out of Banja Luka and Doboj in the north of the country, and measures to expel them from the northeast were intensifying. In the west, most non-Croats were expelled en masse from the lower Neretva valley after the alliance between Bosnian Croat forces and the Government collapsed in April 1993. Fighting has continued in central and northeast Bosnia since the Special Rapporteur's last report.

The process of "ethnic cleansing" taking place in parts of Bosnia and Herzegovina is inextricably linked with violations of fundamental human rights. Summary executions and arbitrary arrests and detention have continued unabated on a wide scale and rapes have been reported.

## C. Rape

The Special Rapporteur continues to be disturbed by reports of rape and other sexual abuses. Pursuant to the Commission on Human Rights resolution 1993/8 on 23 February 1993, the Special Rapporteur reports as follows.

At least 100 women were reported to have been raped by Bosnian Croat (HVO) soldiers between April and October 1993. This is probably an incomplete figure, because limited access to Mostar and the dispersal of refugees from western Herzegovina made it difficult to obtain information. No HVO soldier is known to have been punished for this crime.

Evictions from Mostar are said to have been accompanied by gratuitous sexual abuse, including rape. Typically, Muslim women have been strip-searched by male HVO soldiers before being forced across the confrontation line. On 29 September 1993, two Muslim women were allegedly raped by HVO soldiers after being strip-searched at a former tuberculosis clinic in Mostar called "the Dispensary."

A Muslim woman is reported to have been raped by uniformed HVO soldiers who broke into her home in Mostar in mid-July 1993, after she and her Croat husband had hidden Muslim neighbours in their appartment and helped them to escape from the city. Two Muslim women who escaped from the village of Stupni Do on 23 October 1993, alleged that they had been raped by HVO soldiers who massacred other villagers.

There were continuing reports from many places that women had been raped by Bosnian Serb civil and military police, as well as soldiers, but the difficulty of gaining access to Serb-held territories prevented the collection of comprehensive information.

On 8 May 1993, three men in military police uniforms were reported to have broken into a Muslim home in Doboj and put guns to the mouths of a seven-year-old boy and his father, while one of them raped the mother at gunpoint in the next room. He is alleged to have said that because she was a Muslim, he had come "to cool her down." Similar rapes have been reported from Bijeljina, Liskovac, and Brcko.

In Trebinje on 20 July 1993, three soldiers are said to have entered the home of one of the few remaining Muslim families, forced them at gunpoint to strip naked and tied the wife's hands behind her back. They then raped her. She remained in hospital with broken ribs, a damaged lung, and other internal injuries until 27 August 1993, when the family was evacuated from Trebinje.

Since February 1993, it is alleged that in areas of fighting Bosnian Muslim paramilitaries have raped Bosnian Croat women, apparently on the grounds of their ethnic origin. Reports of this have come from Mostar and Bugojno. It is not yet possible to estimate the full scale of sexual abuse that may have taken place, however, because access to conflict zones is limited and the refugee population has dispersed.

Young women have been detained for the purpose of sexual abuse by Bosnian Serb Army soldiers. In July 1993, it was reported that around 30 Muslim women were being detained for these purposes in BSA barracks in Nerici. Another 100 women, aged between 15 and 17, were said to be detained in this way in the "Westphalia" coffeehouse near Stolina, a coffeehouse near Skijana, and a private house in Grcica until August 1993. Recent reports suggest that detention at the "Westphalia" coffeehouse may have stopped.

## D. Human Rights Violations by Forces under the Control of the Government of Bosnia and Herzegovina

*Summary Executions.* Massacres of civilians were reported to the Special Rapporteur, allegedly committed by soldiers acting for the Government. The reports referred to killings in the villages of Trusine on 17 April 1993; Mileteci on 24 April 1993; Maljine on 8 June 1993; Doljani on 27 and 28 June 1993; Bistrica in August 1993; Kriz and Uzdol on 14 September 1993; and Kopijari on 21 October 1993. The overall number of victims was conservatively estimated to be 120, but an exact total was not possible to verify.

All the victims were Bosnian Croats, and none was reported to have offered armed resistance. In many cases there is evidence that the killings were accompanied by protracted cruelty and mutilation of corpses. Eyewitnesses to the atrocities at Maljine, Doljani, and Kopijari claimed that foreign irregular soldiers—so-called "Mojahedin"—affiliated to the 7th Brigade of the Army of Bosnia and Herzegovina were responsible.

On 16 September 1993 the Army issued a condemnation of the killings in Kriz and Uzdol and promised to punish the individuals responsible. The Special Rapporteur wrote to President Izetbegovic on 15 October 1993, welcoming this investigation. He also asked to be told precisely what procedures were in force to subordinate irregular troops to the Army command structure and what measures were used to enforce discipline. On 22 October 1993 President Izetbegovic sent a letter in which he condemned the killings and gave assurances that an investigation had been instigated.

The Special Rapporteur also received allegations of individual murders inspired by ethnic revenge. One concerned Radislav and Marina Komjenac, two elderly civilians—said to be Bosnian Serbs—who were taken from their homes in Sarajevo and summarily executed on 26 June 1993. The killings appear to have been in retaliation for a mortar attack that killed seven Muslim civilians in the old town. Government militia were alleged to be responsible. The Special Rapporteur wrote to the Government on 14 August 1993 expressing concern about the report and asking what steps had been taken to punish the perpetrators.

In a reply dated 23 September 1993, the acting Prime Minister, Mr. Hadzo Efendic, denied there was any ethnic motivation in the killing of the couple—whom he said were of Serb and Croat origin—and said that an investigation of the crime was underway. The Special Rapporteur will follow this case and others that have been brought to his attention.

The Special Rapporteur found a report in the Croatian newspaper *Vjesnik* on 9 August 1993 that 35 Bosnian Croats had been hanged by government forces outside a Roman Catholic Church in Zenica to be untrue.

*Arbitrary Arrests and Detention and Violations of the Rights of Detainees.* In an agreement brokered by the International Committee of the Red Cross (ICRC), the Government released 309 Bosnian Croats from Konjic detention centre on 19 October 1993. At the end of October 1993, it was holding around 1,100 detainees in 24 registered detention centres, and an unknown number of others elsewhere. The largest registered detention centres were in Tarcin and Pazaric, on the road west from Sarajevo, and in Zenica, central Bosnia.

Only a small proportion of the registered detainees were believed to be prisoners-of-war. The others were civilians of Bosnian Serb or Bosnian Croat origin, detained in order to provide a pool of prisoners to exchange for Bosnian Muslims held as prisoners-of-war, or for use on the frontline as forced labour, or to protect the army's advance as "human shields." During the Special Rapporteur's mission to Sarajevo in August 1993 the Minister of the Interior admitted that civilians had been arrested, but claimed they had all signed statements volunteering to be exchanged for other detainees. The Special Rapporteur stressed at the meeting that statements made in such circumstances could not be regarded as voluntary.

Testimony from Banovici in northeast Bosnia illustrates how civilian detainees have been used as "human shields."

Between 12 and 30 May 1993, around 80 Bosnian Serbs and Bosnian Croats were arrested or drafted into the army and immediately taken to Podobala village, where they were divided into detachments and forced to dig shelters on the confrontation line between government and Bosnian Serb forces. As the shelters were dug, the government forces advanced.

There is no right to conscientious objection under the law of Bosnia and Herzegovina, and individuals who refused the draft in Banovici were arrested and also sent to the frontline. On 7 June 1993 five of them were injured during shelling. Detainees have also been reported killed doing forced labour on confrontation lines at Gornij Vakuf, Hranici, Bugojno and Travnik, among other places.

On 14 August 1993 the Special Rapporteur wrote to the Government to express his abhorrence of this practice. He urged the authorities to ensure that everyone under arrest had effective recourse to a court and that independent agencies be immediately informed of their case and given access to them.

There were allegations that some Bosnian Croat prisoners-of-war in government detention centres in Mostar and Konjic had been forced to give blood. These allegations, however, did not receive independent confirmation.

To date international agencies have been granted only very limited access to the "music school" detention centre at Zenica. A Bosnian Croat who was held there between April and September 1993, together with 46 others, all unregistered, alleges that he was kept without food for the first week, held in a cellar with no light for 45 days and beaten during interrogation on the legs and kidneys with telephone cables, batons and shovel handles.

*Restrictions on Freedom of Movement.* In August 1993 the city War Presidency announced that Croats were forbidden to leave Bugojno, a town contested by government and Bosnian Croat troops. Only 2,500 Croats remain in Bugojno since government troops defeated Bosnian Croat forces there in July 1993. Since then ethnic tension has been high. Apart from the rape incidents already noted, 16 other serious crimes against the Croat minority are under investigation. Looting and harassment of Croat civilians is reported to be commonplace, especially in the villages near Bugojno.

In Zenica, the authorities formally announced in September 1993 that its 23,000 Croats were forbidden to leave the city, although in practice they had been prevented from doing so since June 1993. Periodically the authorities have organized exchanges of local Croats for Muslims from the Vitez pocket and Vares. Croats have been issued false identity documents with Muslim names and driven out of the city in coaches with a military police escort. The average cost for each person is said to be DM 250, paid to city officials, military police and private entrepreneurs running the exchanges. In known cases Croat men of fighting age have been prevented from leaving with their families.

In Sarajevo, which is under siege by Bosnian Serb forces, most Serbs who have applied for permission to leave have been refused by the government Secretariat for Evacuations. Around 700 sick and elderly Serbs who were given permission to leave in December 1992 were allowed to go only on 8 November 1993. Fifty-nine of them are said to have died while waiting for the opportunity to leave.

*Military Attacks on Civilians.* Civilians in the western part of Mostar have been subjected to attack from government-held positions in the east.

*Other Violations of Human Rights and Humanitarian Law.* In central Bosnia, Roman Catholic sources have alleged that

**B**

church buildings in 66 parishes have been deliberately damaged or destroyed by either Government or Serb soldiers.

### E. Human Rights Violations by Bosnian Croat Forces

*Summary Executions.* On 18 April 1993, at least 89 Muslim civilians in the village of Ahmici in central Bosnia were summarily executed, allegedly by HVO soldiers. The village contained no legitimate military target and there was reported to be no organized resistance to the attack. The Special Rapporteur issued a report on this atrocity in May 1993, based on an investigation carried out by his field staff.

In western Herzegovina the Special Rapporteur is investigating reports that nine Muslim civilians—five men and four women—were taken from their homes in Mokronoge by HVO soldiers on 9 August 1993 and shot dead at close range with machine guns.

On 23 August 1993 HVO soldiers opened fire on two families of Muslim civilians they were forcing across the Mostar bridge, killing one man in front of his wife.

The bodies of at least 15 Muslim civilians have been recovered in the village of Stupni Do in central Bosnia, where they were massacred on 23 October 1993, reportedly by HVO troops. They had either been shot at close range or burned to death and included a group of women, found still clutching each other's arms. HVO representatives denied that a massacre had taken place, and for three days prevented international observers from visiting the village.

*Mass Deportations and Violations of Human Rights by Means of Administrative Measures in Western Herzegovina.* The Neretva valley south of Mostar has traditionally been predominantly populated by Croats. By April 1993 an estimated 16,000 Muslims had come to Mostar from other parts of Bosnia and Herzegovina and at least 12,000 to other towns in the area.

On 15 April 1993 the Mostar city authorities adopted Statute No. 266/93, which severely restricted the provision of humanitarian relief to displaced people. An estimated 10,000 Muslims were disqualified from assistance and those living in abandoned flats were given a deadline by HVO forces to leave by 9 May 1993. In some cases the deadline was enforced with arson and threats of death.

The eviction of Muslim residents in Mostar began in June 1993. On 14 and 15 June 1993 alone several thousand Muslims living in west Mostar were rounded up and their personal papers—including leases for their apartments—were burned in the street. They were then forced across the bridge, under a hail of gunfire from HVO soldiers, to the eastern part of the city, which is under Government control. They were told they were being evicted to make room for Croats coming from Travnik. Forced evictions and transfers of the Muslim population in Mostar were still being reported in October 1993.

Deportations of Muslims from other parts of western Herzegovina began on 13 July 1993, when around 500 civilians were collected up from villages between Stolac and Capljina and forced to walk across the confrontation line with government forces between Buna and Blagaj. HVO soldiers threatened to shoot any who returned. By late August 1993, 20,000 Muslims had been forced across the line.

Before the expulsions took place, Croat authorities had used administrative powers to harass Muslim residents and progressively curtail their rights. These measures included widespread job dismissals from late 1992; house searches by civilian and military police in April 1993; the house arrest of

Muslim men in Stolac in April 1993; the disconnection of telephones in Capljina and the requisitioning of cars by HVO soldiers on 4 July 1993. Similar activities occurred at the same time at Tomislavgrad and Livno.

On 13 June 1993 the Croat mayor of Capljina broadcast a radio statement saying that the lives and security of local Muslims could "no longer be guaranteed." After that, normal life for them reportedly became impossible: it was dangerous for Muslims to appear in the street, and they could obtain food only with the help of Croat neighbours, friends, or spouses. Muslim families became targets of nighttime looting by masked thugs, their property was damaged, and the Capljina police provided little protection. Similar attacks were reported in the village of Gradska from mid-August 1993. The homes of Muslim families were routinely looted by night, and by day military police prevented them from reporting these incidents to United Nations Civilian Police patrols.

*Arbitrary Arrests and Detention and Violations of the Rights of Detainees.* The systematic arrest of Muslim men began in May 1993 and reached a peak at the end of July 1993 when an estimated 15,000 were in detention. During this period male Serbs and Roma (gypsies) living in western Herzegovina were also detained. Six hundred Muslims were freed on 19 October 1993 under the agreement brokered by ICRC. At the end of October 1993 HVO was holding 4,200 detainees in eight registered detention centres, one of the largest being Rodoc heliodrome outside Mostar.

Most arrestees were civilian men of fighting age, although some young boys and men over 60 were also detained. Around 6,300 Muslims were arrested in Mostar on 30 June 1993; 5,500 in Capljina between May and July 1993; 1,350 in Stolac in July 1993; and 92 in Gradska in August 1993.

It appeared that the arrests were part of a deliberate policy to rid western Herzegovina of non-Croats. Muslim former detainees from Capljina, arrested without a warrant in late June 1993, were forced to sign a statement saying that they would "voluntarily" leave Capljina on their release.

On 17 July 1993, detainees in Rodoc heliodrome who had letters guaranteeing their entry to third countries were told to sign papers from the HVO Office for Displaced Persons and Refugees in Mostar saying that they wanted to leave Bosnia and Herzegovina. Even detainees without letters of guarantee were told that they should leave, on the false promise that when they arrived in the Republic of Croatia, they would be resettled in a third country. Within a matter of hours, during which detainees had to see their families and pack their belongings, several hundred detainees were deported to the Republic of Croatia.

It was alleged that Croatian border police who stopped one convoy on 18 July 1993 took note of the number of detainees and their identity documents, if any. However, another convoy was apparently allowed to cross the border near Vrgorac unhindered. Detainees in a third convoy were allegedly transferred to Croatian vehicles at the border and given a Croatian police escort to Gasinci. These alleged incidents would indicate that authorities in the Republic of Croatia were actively involved in this deportation.

Muslim and Serb civilians were also detained so that they could be exchanged for Bosnian Croats held as prisoners-of-war. Detainees with a high "exchange value," because they had relatives in the Army of Bosnia and Herzegovina, were reportedly not deported to the Republic of Croatia. Detainees were used to do forced labour in dangerous conditions, such as digging trenches and filling sandbags near confrontation zones. A number was reported killed doing this work.

When international agencies obtained access to HVO detention centres, they found conditions of appalling brutality and degradation. Broken ribs, broken fingers, bruising, and heart dysfunction were common among detainees as a result of beatings they had received from guards. A more detailed picture of conditions in these centres was given in the Special Rapporteur's report on Mostar.

The release of all detainees was said to be one of the aims of the Commission on Human Rights and Humanitarian Issues established within the administration of the so-called "Croatian Republic of Herzeg-Bosnia" in September 1993. Ostensibly through its good offices, the detention centre at Dretelj was partly closed down at the beginning of October and a number of prisoners were released. By that time, however, the homes of most detainees from western Herzegovina had been occupied by Bosnian Croats.

*Military Attacks on Civilians.* The largely Muslim population held in eastern Mostar has been shelled from Bosnian Croat positions in the west of the city since August 1993, up to 400 times in one day. Also, international observers have confirmed that Bosnian Croat snipers in Mostar and western Herzegovina used against civilians especially deadly 12.7 calibre rifles with an effective range of up to one km. and equipped for night firing. On 18 April, a truck loaded with explosives and driven by a Muslim driver, whose family was reportedly kept hostage, was exploded in the centre of Stari Vitez, a Muslim enclave within the Lasva valley HVO pocket. The explosion killed five civilians.

The mainly Muslim town of Maglaj has been up to 90% destroyed by Croat and Serb artillery, and both forces have prevented the town from receiving deliveries of humanitarian aid for four months. Civilians have been killed when attempting to retrieve aid dropped from the air.

There have been direct attacks on aid workers. At least eight Muslim drivers were shot dead by Bosnian Croat soldiers or their supporters near Novi Travnik on 11 and 12 June 1993. On 14 August, a UNHCR driver was killed by an HVO sniper in Stari Vitez while driving a clearly marked armoured vehicle.

*Other Violations of Human Rights and Humanitarian Law.* In early July 1993, Bosnian Croat forces imposed exorbitant taxes on foreign-aid convoys. In September 1993, the Commission on Human Rights and Humanitarian Issues promised to help reopen a relief route inland through western Herzegovina. No improvement in the situation has been noted since then, however; and, as of 25 October 1993, 400 tons of international aid remained blocked at Metkovic by Bosnian Croat authorities. Bosnian Croat forces have imposed such narrow definitions on "relief" that many essential items, such as shoes, clothing, engineering parts, and emergency construction materials for winter have not been allowed through to central Bosnia.

The drive to eliminate ethnic diversity has in some areas been accompanied by efforts to obliterate all traces of minority culture. In Stolac in western Herzegovina, for instance, when major expulsions of non-Croats began on 1 August 1993, four mosques were reportedly blown up. A famous 16th century mosque was destroyed in Croat-held Pocitelj on 23 August 1993, after the last Muslims had been deported from the village. On 9 November 1993, the historical Ottoman bridge in Mostar was destroyed by military action. It had been registered with UNESCO as a monument of major cultural importance and was also the only means by which water could be obtained by people in the eastern part of the town.

## F. Human Rights Violations by Bosnian Serb Forces

*Expulsions and Restrictions on Freedom of Movement.* The expulsion of non-Serbs from Serb-held territories is in some areas nearly complete. Only 1,000 Muslims remain in Doboj, for instance, out of the 43,000 recorded in the 1993 census. In Bosanski Novi, only 800 remain of the 15,000 Muslims registered there in April 1993. All non-Serbs have been expelled from villages such as Bukovica, Mala Vukovica, Tombak and Zajir.

Control over the movement of non-Serbs is exercised by "Commissions for Exchange," assisted in some documented cases by local Red Cross officials. Non-Serbs wishing to leave must apply to be "exchanged" for Serbs outside the area, or to be reunited with family members in other countries.

Non-Serbs who have a male relative in detention, or who are themselves "under a working obligation" to the authorities, may not apply to leave.

Since March 1993, the procedure for leaving has been regulated by instructions issued in Pale, the administrative centre of the so-called "Republic of Srpska." These prevent non-Serbs from leaving by car or taking valuables with them and require them to pay for a bus seat and to renounce their citizenship. They must also pay a tax to each municipality they cross in transit.

The "tax" appears to have fluctuated from area to area. In June 1993, for instance, a bus seat cost non-Serbs DM 40 in Doboj and between DM 200–300 in Bijeljina. Transit taxes have ranged from DM 30 per municipality to DM 60 in Bijeljina. The average cost of surrendering a passport was DM 10. These sums have been paid to officials of the Commissions for Exchange and, in some identifiable cases, to representatives of the local Red Cross. Some individuals have been forced to leave behind close relatives because they could not afford the cost of leaving.

The procedure has typically been applied in an arbitrary and brutal manner. Non-Serbs from Brcko, Bijeljina, Banja Luka and other places have told how commission officials put them on a bus at short notice with a minimum of personal belongings and forced them to surrender their house keys. The military police searched them and confiscated valuable items, sometimes with beatings. They were then driven to points on the confrontation line and forced to walk across minefields to positions held by the Government, for instance at Satorovici and in the Tuzla region. In some cases, this was the fate of non-Serbs who believed they were being taken abroad to be reunited with their families. Hundreds of non-Serbs from Bijeljina and Doboj who had not even applied to leave have also been deported across the confrontation line.

Reports implicated authorities of the Federal Republic of Yugoslavia (FRY) in helping to expel some non-Serbs abroad. On 24 August 1993, a group of 17 Muslims was allegedly driven by bus from Bijeljina through FRY territory to the Hungarian border. A group of 33 was then reportedly taken from Bijeljina through FRY territory to the Hungarian border at Backi Breg on 29 August 1993. This report was confirmed in September 1993 by a senior member of the FRY border police. Since then FRY involvement in expulsions from Bijeljina appears to have ceased. The Special Rapporteur does not know if FRY authorities assisted in the expulsions of non-Serbs from other towns.

*Summary Executions, "Disappearances," and Other Acts of Violence against the Person.* Several incidents of summary execution have been of concern to the Special Rapporteur.

In Doboj, for instance, on 22 March 1993, BSA soldiers

are said to have killed three Muslims and one Croat in Rad-nicka Street, shooting them first and then cutting their throats.

Since the Special Rapporteur's last report, numerous non-Serbs are known to have "disappeared" from their homes. Commonly their "disappearance" followed confrontations with uniformed men and within days their homes were occupied by Serbs. The corpses of relatively few have been located subsequently. One of these was a Muslim found in Banja Luka morgue on 30 March 1993, with his arms and lower lip cut, three days after he had been taken from his home by uniformed men.

Non-Serbs appear to have lost any claim to protection. This was illustrated on 1 August 1993, when civilian police who were called out to protect Muslim families during an attack in Liskovac, Gradiska municipality, only arrived three hours after it was over.

The attack lasted 90 minutes; during it, eyewitnesses report, 12 men, some in uniform, broke into a Muslim home, beat the residents and destroyed their belongings. An 80-year-old grandmother who protested was shot through the head, as were two men of the family. The 18-year-old grand-daughter was then repeatedly raped. At a neighbouring house, the 12 men beat and shot the Muslim owner, beat and raped his 27-year-old wife and shot her mother dead and threw her into the street. They then set fire to two more houses before leaving at 5 a.m.

A military exercise on 19 April 1993 by BSA forces with heavy calibre weapons was the culmination of 13 days of attacks against non-Serbs in the Banja Luka suburb of Vrbanja. These attacks included: the fatal knifing of a Muslim man (6 April 1993); the burning of seven Muslim homes and looting of others (11 April 1993); the shooting dead of two Muslim women bystanders by BSA soldiers returning from the frontline (12 April 1993); the shooting dead of a Muslim civilian by a man in military uniform (12 April 1993); an axe attack on a Muslim man (14 April 1993); and sniping at several Muslim homes by military personnel (19 April 1993).

*Arbitrary Arrests and Detention and the Ill-Treatment of Detainees.* By the end of October 1993, Bosnian Serb forces were holding around 500 detainees, including women, in 22 registered detention centres and an unknown number of others elsewhere. The largest number was held in the Batkovici complex.

Most detainees were civilians. Some had been arrested when they were on the point of leaving the territory with their families, like some 60 Muslim and Croat men detained as they were about to cross the confrontation line near Bijeljina between 4 and 11 September 1993 and sent to Batkovici detention centre. It appeared they were detained so that they could be exchanged for Bosnian Serbs held elsewhere as prisoners-of-war. Other Muslims, Croats, and Roma (gypsies) have been arrested to provide a labour force in conflict zones, or to act as "human shields." In late June 1993, for instance, non-Serb men and women were arrested in their homes and on the street in the Milkovac suburb of Doboj and forced to stand as a "living wall" on the confrontation line at Putnikovo Brdo.

Note has already been made . . . of the practice of detaining women for the purpose of sexual abuse by BSA soldiers.

The Special Rapporteur continues to be concerned by reports of the mistreatment of detainees in registered detention centres and camps. According to testimonies of people released from Batkovici detention centre, conditions for both men and women were harsh and degrading, with constant beatings, sometimes resulting in deaths.

*Violations of Human Rights by Means of Administrative Measures.* Using administrative measures alone, Bosnian Serb authorities have stripped non-Serbs of many basic human rights since 1992.

The right to paid employment has been made dependent on willingness to be drafted into the BSA. Those who refuse military call-up have been dismissed from their jobs and detained for up to 20 days, during which they have often been forced to work in conflict zones. Since March 1993, under instructions issued from Pale, the families of men refusing the draft have also been dismissed from their work. People without paid work automatically lose the right to housing, health insurance, and a pension.

The instructions issued in March 1993 have made people dismissed from their jobs liable to perform unpaid labour at so-called Public Service Offices. Individuals performing a "work obligation to the authorities," as this is called, are forbidden to apply to leave the area. According to numerous testimonies, "work obligation" has involved long hours of heavy physical labour, often at confrontation lines digging shelters, or in the fields or cleaning the streets. Forced labourers from Doboj reported that they were fed only if they were made to do jobs away from their home town. Otherwise, they were expected to provide their own food.

In Banja Luka, Doboj and other towns, civilian and military police have subjected people living in non-Serb districts to constant document checks, identifying their ethnic origin and employment status. In many cases, they have been instantaneously drafted for forced labour, often without the opportunity even to contact their families first.

Since 1992 Muslims and Croats have also been systematically evicted from their homes, ostensibly to make room for Serbs displaced from other areas. Those serving in the BSA were largely excepted. According to testimonies of people who have left the area, since March 1993, the practice has developed of telephones of non-Serbs in Banja Luka being cut off and of their private shops being closed down. Vehicles belonging to non-Serbs in Bijeljina have been requisitioned by the BSA and farming equipment has been confiscated. Ration cards have also been withheld from non-Serbs in Doboj and Grbavica, preventing them from collecting food relief.

*Military Attacks on Civilians.* The shelling of Sarajevo, begun by Bosnian Serb forces 18 months ago, escalated in October 1993. As of August 1993, 264 shells had hit the central civilian hospital at Kosevo, which lies within 300 metres of the confrontation line, killing staff and patients alike. As the hospital is clearly visible from Bosnian Serb positions, at least some of those impacts must be considered intentional. On 25 October, a four-month-old baby in its pram was seriously wounded by a sniper's bullet fired from a Serb-held position.

As has already been noted, Serb and Croatian forces have largely destroyed the town of Maglaj and have both prevented the delivery of humanitarian aid and killed civilians attempting to retrieve air-dropped parcels.

In towns and cities, where high buildings have offered them protection and anonymity, snipers have claimed the lives of civilians as they queued for food or water, or waited at military checkpoints.

In May 1993, the Special Rapporteur reported on the ambush of Muslim refugees in the Cerska valley by Bosnian Serb forces. On 6 July 1993, a group of 76 Muslim civilians fleeing from Srebrenica on foot to Kladanj were reportedly ambushed twice by Bosnian Serb troops. When the 10 survivors reached the village of Turalic, they were discovered by a Bosnian Serb tank patrol. They were then allegedly fired on by the tank.

In Maglaj on 1 June 1993, a UNHCR convoy was deliberately shelled from the Serbian positions. Two drivers and one staff member were killed.

*Other Violations of Human Rights and Humanitarian Law.* Bosnian Serbs have imposed taxes on foreign aid convoys in the same manner as the Bosnian Croat forces.

Five out of six mosques in Serb-held Bijeljina and almost all mosques in Banja Luka were reportedly blown up in 1993. Eyewitnesses claimed that the demolition was systematic, and the sites were quickly replanted with trees.

### SPECIAL DECLARATION ON BOSNIA AND HERZEGOVINA.

At its 20th plenary meeting, on 15 June 1993, the World Conference on Human Rights, held in Vienna, Austria, adopted (88 votes for, 1 against, 54 abstentions) the following declaration:

The World Conference on Human Rights adopts the following special declaration on Bosnia and Herzegovina:

The United Nations World Conference on Human Rights, mindful of its objective to uphold and promote full respect for and effective promotion of human rights, and bearing in mind its appeal made to the Security Council on the tragedy in the Republic of Bosnia and Herzegovina, declares that,

The tragedy in the Republic of Bosnia and Herzegovina, characterized by naked Serbian aggression, unprecedented violations of human rights and genocide, is an affront to the collective conscience of mankind. Hundreds and thousands of innocent civilians have been slaughtered, incarcerated and forced to flee their homes because of the reprehensible policy of ethnic cleansing. Over 40,000 Bosnian women have been subjected to the gruesome crime of rape,

At present, over 70% of the territory of a State Member of the United Nations, the Republic of Bosnia and Herzegovina, is under Serbian occupation, the remaining few towns under Bosnian control are under constant siege and their residents are being deliberately starved,

This situation calls for urgent and resolute action by the international community,

Therefore,

The United Nations World Conference on Human Rights categorically condemns the ongoing aggression against the Republic of Bosnia and Herzegovina, the heinous practice of ethnic cleansing, war crimes and crimes against humanity, particularly the extermination of its Muslim population.

The World Conference believes that the practice of ethnic cleansing resulting from Serbian aggression against the Muslim and Croat population in the Republic of Bosnia and Herzegovina constitutes genocide in violation of the Convention on the Prevention and Punishment of the Crime of Genocide.

The World Conference affirms that the failure of the international community to prevent and punish genocide and redress atrocities in the Republic of Bosnia and Herzegovina calls into question the commitment of the international community to the protection of fundamental human rights and freedoms all over the world.

The World Conference strongly condemns Serbia-Montenegro, the Yugoslave National Army, the Serbian militia and the extremist elements in the Bosnian Croatian militia forces as perpetrators of these crimes.

The World Conference, in order to restore the credibility of and the trust in the United Nations as the custodian of international law and human rights, gives the highest priority to addressing the tragic situation in the Republic of Bosnia and Herzegovina and urges the international community to assume full responsibility to restore peace and stability in the Republic of Bosnia and Herzegovina based on the principles of justice, independence, sovereignty, unity and territorial integrity, including the inviolability of its internationally recognized borders.

The World Conference categorically rejects the aggressor plan to partition the Republic of Bosnia and Herzegovina.

The World Conference urges the world community and all international bodies, in particular the Security Council, to take forceful and decisive steps for effective measures of peacemaking in the Republic of Bosnia and Herzegovina with a view to:

1. Preventing and punishing genocide in the Republic of Bosnia and Herzegovina.

2. Rejecting any acquisition of territory in the Republic of Bosnia and Herzegovina by the use of force, and calling upon all occupying forces to withdraw immediately from those territories.

3. Calling upon the Security Council to implement the Vance-Owen Peace Plan under Chapter VII of the Charter of the United Nations.

4. Immediately implementing an effective cease-fire, accompanied by the neutralization of all heavy weaponry, which should be placed under the control of the United Nations Protection Force, and the interdiction of all arms supplies to Serbian forces operating in the Republic of Bosnia and Herzegovina.

5. Simultaneously implementing effective measures to secure the roll-back of invasion unless the invading forces voluntarily withdraw.

6. Lifting the arms embargo against the Republic of Bosnia and Herzegovina in order to enable it to exercise its right to self-defense in accordance with Article 51 of the Charter and implementing all necessary measures under the Charter in order to reverse the aggression perpetrated by Serbian forces.

7. Extending immediate humanitarian help for the relief of persons in besieged towns and cities as well as other victims.

8. Restoring the sovereignty, independence and territorial integrity of the Republic of Bosnia and Herzegovina.

9. Implementing speedily Security Council resolution 808 (1993) of 22 February 1993, which established an international tribunal for the prosecution of persons responsible for serious violations of international humanitarian law committed in the territory of the former Yugoslavia since 1991, and bringing immediately to trial all persons suspected of committing crimes against humanity, including war crimes.

10. Effectively eradicating the tragic consequences of the aggression and the human rights violations in the Republic of Bosnia and Herzegovina, by way of joint international efforts for the reconstruction of the political and physical institutions of the Republic of Bosnia and Herzegovina.

11. Enabling all refugees, deportees and displaced persons to return safely to their homes in the Republic of Bosnia and Herzegovina and restoring their properties, hence rejecting any documents signed by them under duress.

12. Strongly warning against and rejecting any intention to use the safe-haven areas in the Republic of Bosnia and Herzegovina as permanent refugee camps which would perpetuate the fruits of aggression, occupation and territorial gains.

The World Conference, on behalf of the international

community, pledges its solidarity with the people and the Government of the Republic of Bosnia and Herzegovina, and urges the Security Council to fulfill its responsibilities under the Charter of the United Nations, particularly under Article 24, by taking all prompt and effective measures in order to restore peace and affirm the independence, sovereignty and territorial integrity of the Republic of Bosnia and Herzegovina and uphold the human rights of its people.

In February 1994, NATO issued an ultimatum that forced Bosnian Serb forces to pull back their weaponry around Sarajevo or place it under UN supervision. A "weapons exclusion" zone was established around the city, and the cease-fire remained in place in that area until July when fighting erupted on Mount Igman, an area just outside of Sarajevo that had been demilitarized by the UN in 1993. Another "protected" area, Gorazde, was the site of shelling in the fall of 1994, including attacks on humanitarian aid convoys.

The United Nations protection force (UNPROFOR) in Bosnia-Herzegovina was under increasing attacks from Bosnian Serbs in 1994. In February, the UN Secretary-General formally opposed NATO air strikes in the area, even though existing Security Council resolutions mandated the use of force to protect peacekeepers and to ensure the delivery of humanitarian aid. NATO was more willing to use air strikes when UN troops or safe areas were under attack, but the Russians and UN field commanders were opposed to expanding NATO intervention. On 27 October 1994, NATO and the UN reached a draft compromise that would allow unannounced air strikes when there is little danger of civilian casualties and that would require warnings if the strikes could endanger civilians.

***WAR CRIMES TRIBUNAL.*** On 15 August 1994, South African Judge Richard Goldstone became prosecutor for the first international war crimes tribunal since the Nuremburg trials. The tribunal was established by the United Nations. The first indictments were handed down in November 1994. In February 1995, the tribunal indicted 39 individuals for atrocities in Bosnia-Herzegovina.

***DAYTON AGREEMENT.*** In November 1995, representatives from the warring factions in Bosnia and American diplomats met in Dayton, OH (USA), for intensive negotiating sessions, aimed at reaching a peace treaty to bring the horrific civil war in Bosnia-Herzegovina to an end. On 21 November 1995, the so-called "Dayton Agreement" was reached. Under the Agreement, the following was cited:

1. Bosnia will be preserved as a single nation, within the borders maintained as of the date of the Agreement. The nation will consist of two parts: a Muslim-Croat federation that will control 51% of the territory and a Serb republic that will hold the remaining 49%.

2. The capital Sarajevo will no longer be divided by checkpoints and closed bridges. The city will come under the control of the Muslim-Croat federation.

3. The eastern and western parts of the Serb republic will be attached by a portion of land in the country's northeast corner; the size of this corridor, known as the Posavina Corridor, will be determined by binding arbitration. A second land corridor will link the Muslim-held town of Gorazde in the east with the rest of the Muslim-Croat federation.

4. All citizens of Bosnia will be able to move freely between the Serb and Muslim-Croat territories.

5. The Serbs will retain the towns of Srebrenica and Zepa, two Muslim enclaves that were overrun by the Serbs in 1995, despite the presence of UN peacekeeping forces.

6. Bosnia's central government will be responsible for foreign policy, foreign trade, monetary policy, citizenship, immigration, and other national functions. A president and national parliament will be chosen in 1996; the elections will be supervised by international monitors.

7. Those charged with war crimes will be excluded from holding political or military office. At the time of the signing, the war crimes tribunal at The Hague had indicted more than 50 Serbs and Croats, including Radovan Karadzic and Gen. Ratko Mladic, who had been the political and military leaders of the Bosnian Serbs during the hostilities.

8. War refugees will be allowed to return to their homes.

9. The human rights of Bosnian citizens will be monitored by an independent commission and protected by an internationally trained civilian police force.

10. A NATO peacekeeping force will be deployed in Bosnia early in 1996 to prevent new outbreaks of violence.

**BIBLIOGRAPHY.** Amnesty International. *Bosnia-Herzegovina: Rape and Sexual Abuse by Armed Forces.* London: 1993. NGO report, in English.

———. *Bosnia-Herzegovina: "You Have No Place Here": Abuses in Bosnian Serb-Controlled Areas.* London: 1994. NGO report, in English.

Helsinki Watch. *Bosnia-Hercegovina: Abuses by Bosnian Croat and Muslim Forces in Central and Southwestern Bosnia-Hercegovina.* New York: Human Rights Watch, 1993. NGO report, in English.

———. *War Crimes in Bosnia-Hercegovina: Volume I.* New York: Human Rights Watch, 1992; Volume II (1993). NGO reports, in English.

Human Rights Watch. "Bosnia-Hercegovina," in *Human Rights Watch World Report 1995*, pp. 192–198. New York: 1995. NGO report, in English.

Immigration and Refugee Board Documentation Centre. *Yugoslavia: Chronology of Events September 1991–July 1992.* Ottawa, Canada: 1992. Government briefing paper, in English and French.

International Court of Justice. *Reports of Judgments, Advisory Opinions and Orders : Case concerning Application of the Convention on the Prevention and Punishment of the Crime of Genocide: (Bosnia and Herzegovina v. Yugoslavia): Further Requests for the Indication of Provisional Measures: Order of 13 September 1993.* The Hague, the Netherlands: 1993. IGO court decision, in English and French.

International Human Rights Law Group. *No Justice, No Peace: Accountability for Rape and Gender-Based Violence in the Former Yugoslavia.* Washington, D.C.: 1993. NGO factfinding report, in English.

Stigmayer, Alexandra, ed. *Mass Rape: The War against Women in Bosnia-Herzegovina.* Lincoln, NE, USA: University of Nebraska Press, 1994. Collection of articles, in English.

U.S. Committee for Refugees (USCR). *Croatia's Crucible: Providing Asylum for Refugees from Bosnia and Hercegovina.* Washington, D.C.: American Council for Nationalities Service, 1992. NGO factfinding report, in English.

United States Commission on Security and Cooperation in Europe. *The Crisis in Bosnia and Herzegovina.* Hearings before the Commission on Security and Cooperation in Europe, 102nd Congress, 2nd Session, May 12, 1992. Washington, D.C.: 1992. Government report, in English.

———. *The Referendum on Independence in Bosnia-Hercegovina, February 29–March 1, 1992.* Washington, D.C.: 1992. Government factfinding report, in English.

United States Senate, Committee on Foreign Relations. *The Ethnic Cleansing of Bosnia-Hercegovina: A Staff Report.* Washington, D.C.: 1992. Government report, in English.

Women Living under Muslim Laws. *Dossier d'information sur les crimes de guerre contre les femmes en ex-Yougoslavie: actions et initiatives pour les défendre, mise à jour no. 3* (Compilation of Informations on Crimes of War against Women in Ex-Yugoslavia: Actions and Initiatives in Their Defence, Update No. 3). Montpellier, France: 1994. Topical issue, in English and French.

**BOTSWANA.** The Republic of Botswana is a country in southern Africa. It has borders with Namibia, South Africa, Zambia, and Zimbabwe. Formerly known as the Bechuanaland Protectorate, it achieved independence from Great Britain in 1966 and became a member of the United Nations the same year. Its population is estimated to be 1,379,000. The Batswana tribe, which makes up about 95% of the population, is divided into eight sub-groups: Bamangwato, Bakwena, Batawana, Bang-waktse, Bakgatla, Bamalete, Barolong, and Batlokwa. Bushmen (Basarwa) and Kgalagadi constitute small minorities. In addition, there are about 5,500 British citizens and an increasingly large number of student refugees from South Africa and Namibia. The UN Secretary-General, in cooperation with the UN High Commissioner for Refugees, has organized programs of assistance for such refugees, and the UN **GENERAL ASSEMBLY** has appealed to all States to contribute to such programs. Languages commonly spoken include English and Setswana. Religions practiced include Christianity (50%) and Animism (50%). Literacy is estimated at 24% (in English) and 35% (in Setswana).

The government (1994) took the form of a republic and member of the Commonwealth of Nations. The president is head of State and government. There is a unicameral National Assembly consisting of 34 elected and six appointed members, which meets at least once every five years. There is also an advisory House of Chiefs, which considers any bill relating to a matter of tribal concern. Political parties include the Democratic Party, the National Front, the People's Party, and the Progressive Union.

Because of economic conditions in Botswana, about 40,000 residents are forced to work in neighboring African countries, mainly South Africa. Problems arise because wives and children normally are not allowed to accompany men to work areas in those countries.

Nevertheless, Botswana has progressed from being one of the least developed African nations at the time of independence to one of the richest ex-colonies, mainly because it has effectively exploited its vast natural mineral resources, including diamonds, and has used the income wisely to provide roads, education, and health services. Moreover, because it has maintained good race relations, even though it borders with and is partly dependent upon South Africa, it has won broad political, economic, and moral support from democratic countries throughout the world.

**BIBLIOGRAPHY.** Andreassen, Bard-Anders, and Asjborn Eide, eds. "Botswana," in *Human Rights in Developing Countries 1987–88: A Yearbook on Human Rights in Countries Receiving Nordic Aid,* pp. 26–39. Copenhagen: Akademisk Forlag, 1988. NGO report, in English; bibliography, pp. 357–358.

Maluwa, Tiyanjana. "The Concept of Asylum and the Protection of Refugees in Botswana: Some Legal and Political Aspects," *International Journal of Refugee Law* 2, no. 4 (1990): 587–610. Scholarly article, in English.

Maope, K. A. *Human Rights in Botswana, Lesotho and Swaziland: A Survey of the BOLESWA Countries.* Human and People's Rights Monograph Series No.1. Roma, Lesotho: Institute of Southern African Studies, 1986. NGO scholarly monograph, in English.

Molutsi, Patrick P., and John D. Holm. "Developing Democracy When Civil Society Is Weak: The Case of Botswana," *African Affairs* 89, no. 356 (1990): 323–340. Scholarly article, in English.

Neff, Stephen C. "Human Rights in Africa: Thoughts on the African Charter on Human and Peoples' Rights in the Light of Case Law from Botswana, Lesotho, and Swaziland," *International and Comparative Law Quarterly* 33 (1984): 331–347. Scholarly article, in English.

———. *Human Rights in Botswana, Lesotho and Swaziland: Implications of Adherence to International Human Rights Treaties.* Human and Peoples' Rights Monograph Series No. 2. Roma, Lesotho: Institute of Southern African Studies, 1986. Scholarly monograph, in English.

Parson, Jack. "The Peasantariat, Politics, and Democracy in Botswana," in *Democracy and Socialism in Africa*, eds. Robin Cohen and Harry Goulbourne, pp. 180–198. Boulder, CO, USA: Westview Press, 1991. Scholarly article, in English.

Southall, R. J. "Botswana as a Host Country for Refugees." Journal of Commonwealth and Comparative Politics 12, no. 2 (1984): 151–179. Scholarly article, in English.

Stephen, David. *The San of the Kalahari*. London: Minority Rights Group, 1982. NGO report, in English; selective bibliography, p. 16.

Swedish International Development Assistance. *Country Report: Botswana*. Stockholm, Sweden: 1990. NGO briefing paper, in English.

## BOURGEOIS, LÉON VICTOR AUGUSTE (1851–1925).

Léon Bourgeois received the 1920 **NOBEL PEACE PRIZE** based largely on his work on behalf of the **LEAGUE OF NATIONS.** Born in Dura, France, Bourgeois was a lawyer, but he left the practice of law for that of politics, serving in many governmental posts, including briefly as France's prime minister (1895–1896) and as president of its senate (1920–1923).

Bourgeois worked on a commission that developed principles for a League of Nations, propositions that Bourgeois submitted to the Paris Peace Conference in 1919. Bourgeois envisioned the League as a juridical military organization, to be called into action only when needed, whose purpose was to preserve peace. He also believed that the League should confine its work to arbitration and the enforcement of international justice. He supported the use of diplomatic, economic, or military sanctions as a League weapon. While his views were not adopted in the actual formation of the League of Nations, his influence was felt and he served as France's principal representative to the League.

***BIBLIOGRAPHY.*** Gray, Tony. *Champions of Peace*. London: Paddington Press, 1976.

Schlessinger, Bernard S., and June H. Schlessinger, eds. *Who's Who of Nobel Prize Winners*. Phoenix, AZ, USA: Oryx Press, 1991.

## BOYD ORR, JOHN (1880–1971).

John Boyd Orr was awarded the 1949 **NOBEL PEACE PRIZE** for his efforts to "find ways of making men healthier and happier so as to secure peace." It was one of the few times that the Peace Prize went to a scientist in the field of world hunger (in 1970 **NORMAN BORLAUG** was to be cited for his work in agriculture).

Born in Ayrshire, Scotland, Boyd Orr received his medical degree from Glasgow University. He established a nutrition institute in Aberdeen, Scotland. Because of his publicized views on the importance of a healthy diet, he was appointed as to an international committee established by the League of Nations to es-
tablish food guidelines for the world. After World War II, Boyd Orr was instrumental in the establishment of the Food and Agricultural Organization (FAO) of the United Nations and was appointed the organization's first Director-General. In this capacity, Boyd Orr championed the idea of a "World Food Board," which would create reserves of food, counteract price increases in the event of crop failure, and raise capital to finance the sale of surplus food to needy countries. The plan never reached fruition.

In addition to his scientific research, Boyd Orr served as president of the National Peace Council and as president of the World Union of Peace Organizations, to which bodies he donated his Peace Prize money.

As a world-renowned scientist and nutritionist, Boyd Orr published many books, among them the influential *Food, Health and Income* (London: Macmillan, 1936); *Food and the People* (London: Pilot Press, 1943); and *Feast and Famine* (London: Rathbone Books, 1957). In addition to the Peace Prize, his work to eliminate hunger and malnutrition was recognized with the French Legion D'Honneur (1949), the Gold Medal of the International Federation of Agricultural Producers (1949), and the Bordon Gold Medal (1958). He was knighted by Great Britain in 1935 and raised to a peerage in 1948, when he became Lord Boyd Orr of Brechin.

***BIBLIOGRAPHY.*** *Current Biography Yearbook 1946*. New York: H. W. Wilson, 1947.

Gray, Tony. *Champions of Peace*. London: Paddington Press, 1976.

Schlessinger, Bernard S., and June H. Schlessinger, ed. *Who's Who of Nobel Prize Winners*. Phoenix, AZ, USA: Oryx Press, 1991.

## BRANDT, WILLY (1913–1992).

Born Karl Herbert Frahm in Lübeck, Germany, West German statesman Willy Brandt received the 1971 **NOBEL PEACE PRIZE.** In a political life filled with accomplishments, Brandt's greatest achievement may have come as chancellor of West Germany, when he instituted a policy of ostpolitik, resulting in a détente between West Germany, East Germany, and the Soviet Union.

Brandt fled from his German homeland in 1933 due to the rising tide of Nazism, settling in Norway first and then, after Norway's invasion by Germany in 1940, in Sweden. He returned to Berlin after the war and began working for his native country. He was a member of the Bundestag from 1949 to 1957 and was mayor of Berlin from 1957 to 1966, during which time the Berlin Wall was erected (1961), separating West and East Berlin. Brandt also became chairman of the Social Democratic Party in 1964; from 1966 to 1969, he served as vice-chancellor and minister for foreign affairs in a coalition government between the Christian Democrats and the Social Democrats. In 1969, he became chancellor in a coalition government between his party and the Free Democrats, resigning that post in 1974. He later chaired a commission on the world economy, resulting in the Brandt Commission Report of 1980.

As mayor of Berlin and chancellor of West Germany, Brandt worked for peaceful collaboration between West and East Europe; in 1970, he signed a non-aggression pact with the Soviet Union. In that same year, he regularized relations between West Germany and Poland. He also, throughout his career, stressed the importance of a pan-Europe federation, a concept that may see fruition in the near future with the European Union. In choosing Brandt for the Prize, the Nobel Committee cited his "efforts to obtain for the people of West Berlin the fundamental human rights of personal security and full freedom of movement" and his "outstanding efforts to create conditions of peace in Europe."

**BIBLIOGRAPHY.** Gray, Tony. *Champions of Peace.* London: Paddington Press, 1976.

Schlessinger, Bernard S., and June H. Schlessinger, eds. *Who's Who of Nobel Prize Winners.* Phoenix, AZ, USA: Oryx Press, 1991.

## BRANTING, KARL HJALMAR (1860–1925).

Often called the "father of Swedish socialism," Karl H. Branting shared the 1921 **NOBEL PEACE PRIZE** with **CHRISTIAN LOUIS LANGE.** Born in Stockholm, Branting studied mathematics and astronomy at the University of Uppsala. However, he abandoned his scientific career in 1884 and became a journalist. In 1886, Branting became editor of *Socialdemokraten* (The Social Democrat) and was among the founding members of the Social Democratic Labor party, formed in Sweden in 1889. In later years, he served as party president.

Branting first entered public politics in 1896, when he was elected to the Swedish parliament. Over the next 20 years, he served in various capacities, including minister of finance in a Liberal-Socialist coalition government. He served as Swedish prime minister three times between 1919 and 1925. Under his first government, Swedish women gained the vote.

Like other early Nobel Peace Prize recipients, Branting worked for the peaceful dissolution of the union between Sweden and Norway in 1905. He also led the movement to bring Sweden into the **LEAGUE OF NATIONS,** becoming the League's first Swedish representative in 1923. Throughout his political career, Branting had been opposed to armed conflict and defense expenditures at the expense of social services. As League representative, he ardently advocated disarmament and mediated such problems as the Greek-Italian conflict of 1923 and the British-Turkish dispute of 1924. Branting also helped in drafting the Geneva Protocol for International Security.

**BIBLIOGRAPHY.** Gray, Tony. *Champions of Peace.* London: Paddington Press, 1976.

Schlessinger, Bernard S., and June H. Schlessinger, eds. *Who's Who of Nobel Prize Winners.* Phoenix, AZ, USA: Oryx Press, 1991.

**BRAZIL.** The Federative Republic of Brazil is the largest country in tropical South America, occupying nearly half the continent and having borders with every South American country except Chile and Ecuador. It achieved independence from Portugal in 1822 and became a member of the United Nations in 1945. Its population is estimated to be 159,630,000. Ethnic groups include descendants of slaves imported from Africa before 1888, as well as descendants of immigrants from Italy, Germany, Japan, Portugal, and Spain. Religions practiced include Christianity (Roman Catholic, 88%; Protestant, 6%) and others; social evolution in Brazil has been marked by the influence of many different religions and beliefs, which have often interchanged some of their elements and practices. Literacy is estimated at 75%.

The government (1994) took the form of a republic, consisting of 22 states, one federal district, and four territories. It is headed by the president, elected by the National Congress acting as an electoral college. That congress is composed of the Senate and the Chamber of Deputies. The president serves for a term of six years, members of the Senate for eight years, and members of the Chamber of Deputies for four years. Congressional elections are by equal, direct, and compulsory suffrage, and by proportional representation. The election of a civilian president under this procedure in 1985 ended 19 years of rule by military junta. Political parties include the Party of the Brazilian Democratic Movement, the Democratic Social Party, the Liberal Front Party, the Democratic Workers' Party, the Workers' Party, and the Brazilian Labor Party.

Slavery supported the Portuguese plantation structure until the slave trade was abolished in 1850; the slaves, of African origin, were emancipated gradually, with complete abolition of slavery only in 1888. The modern population of Brazil is composed of three main racial elements—whites, blacks, and Amerindians—each made up of many ethnic groups. In recent years, a fourth element has been added: the largest community of Japanese immigrants outside Japan itself, clustered in Sao Paulo.

To deal with violations of human rights, the government in December 1985 re-organized the Brazilian Council for the Defence of Human Rights, which had been established in 1964, by creating within the council four sections, each placed under the responsibility of a "defender." These sections investigate, respectively, alleged abuses in respect of (1) electoral frauds, (2) violence resulting from land disputes in the countryside, (3) acts of discrimination on all grounds, and (4) abuse of power. The council's sessions, formerly closed, have been opened to the general public since it convened in its new form early in 1986.

As regards the Indian people who comprise about 1% of the total population, the main thrust of modern Brazilian policy is to preserve their culture while assuring their progressive integration into national life. A staff body within the Ministry of Culture coordinates and supports activities and initiatives of non-governmental organizations, private institutions, and individuals striving to enhance the Indians' role in national life by making their presence more visible while respecting their cultural identity. The new body plans to preserve Indian languages by printing books and preparing tapes in those languages, and, in general, to promote indigenous culture through all the media of communication.

In January 1985, after 21 years of military rule, Tancredo Neves, a civilian, was elected president by the 686-member electoral college. However, his untimely death just prior to the date on which he was to assume office led to the inauguration of his running mate, Jose Sarney, as president.

In the arrangement through which the military yielded power to a civilian government, military leaders extracted promises that human rights abuses committed while they were in office would be overlooked. Accordingly, no investigations were made of a number of terrorist attacks or of many "disappearances" which had occurred between 1979 and 1985, in which the military were said to have been involved. President Sarney identified himself closely with the armed forces, which, in turn, supported his decision to serve for at least five years of the six-year term given him by the electoral college.

In Brazil's first direct presidential election since 1960, held in 1989, Fernando Collor de Mello, a free-market advocate, was chosen to serve for a term of five years. In 1994, a candidate with strong democratic values and a broad popular mandate, Fernando Henrique Cardoso was elected president.

**YANOMAMI INDIANS.** A serious problem confronting the new president is the plight of Brazil's Yano-
mami Indians, described in a statement circulated to the 1990 session of the UN **COMMISSION ON HUMAN RIGHTS** by Survival International, a non-governmental organization in consultative status, as follows (UN Doc. E/CN.4/1990/NGO 63, paras. 1–11):

Survival International, an organization for the protection of the rights of threatened tribal peoples in all regions of the world, has worked with and on behalf of the Yanomami in the Amazon Basin since Survival's establishment 20 years ago. We submit this statement to update the Commission on the urgent situation of the Yanomami in Brazil, who are faced with wholesale invasion of their land and their own physical destruction.

In the past several years, an estimated 45,000 Brazilian gold miners have invaded Yanomami territory, bringing with them disease, environmental degradation, and massive disruption of traditional Yanomami life. This invasion has been facilitated or tolerated by the Brazilian Government, despite domestic and international outcries.

The Brazilian Constitution states that Indians have a right to "their social organization customs, languages, beliefs and traditions, and aboriginal rights to the lands they traditionally occupy, it being the responsibility of the Union [the Brazilian federal government] to demarcate them, protect and guarantee respect for all their property". Traditional lands are defined as "those inhabited by them on a permanent basis, those utilized for their productive activities, those absolutely necessary for the preservation of environmental resources necessary to their well-being, and those necessary for their physical and cultural reproduction, according to their usages, customs and traditions".

While the Yanomami traditionally occupy and use 9.4 million hectares of land in Brazil, a presidential decree issued in February 1989 demarcated only 2.4 million hectares—in 19 separate and discontinuous areas—as Yanomami territory. The more than two-thirds of the Yanomami territory not demarcated is now considered "national forest" and is open to economic exploitation, including gold prospecting and mining.

There are numerous reports of armed confrontations between the 45,000 miners and the 10,000 Yanomami, and miners have also unwittingly brought in much disease. A medical team comprised of human rights groups and the government Indian agency, FUNAI, completed a preliminary examination of the Yanomami in January 1990 and noted an alarming spread of a frequently fatal and resistant strain of malaria, falciparum. Of the Yanomami tested, almost one in four showed the presence of malaria and two-thirds of the malaria cases are of the falciparum type. In addition to malaria, 80 per cent of those examined were suffering from intestinal parasites, 20 per cent from severe malnutrition, and 12 per cent from respiratory infections. There were also numerous cases of conjunctivitis, gastroenteritis, hepatitis and tuberculosis.

In October 1989, a judge from the 7th Federal Court in Brasilia issued an injunction requiring the Government to evict the miners from all territory traditionally occupied by the Yanomami. However, on 11 January 1990, the Government issued a ruling effectively reversing the court order and halting the evictions.

In addition, Brazilian President Jose Sarney signed a decree on 25 January 1990 creating a "garimpeiro reserve" to house miners removed from Yanomami territory. The reserve is illegal under the terms of the October 1989 court injunction as some of the area lies within Yanomami territory.

Despite press reports that as many as 10,000 of the gold miners have left Yanomami territory for other areas in Brazil and Guyana, other observers have reported that any so-called evacuation of miners is proceeding at a "snail's pace". There are also reports that the miners will not move to the new reserve area as they claim its gold reserves are almost exhausted.

There has been much discussion within United Nations human rights bodies about the need for "early warning" systems which could alert bodies such as the Commission on Human Rights to situations in which action is urgently required. Such warnings of the possible destruction of the Yanomami as a people have been made to the Commission for years, yet no effective action has yet been taken.

Survival International recognizes that the Brazilian Government has taken some steps to protect the Yanomami, but developments in the past few months indicate that these measures are wholly inadequate and that the Yanomami are at even greater risk today that at this time last year. Survival understands the competing demands and desperate economic situation of many non-Indian Brazilians and is sympathetic to the Government's efforts to deal with this situation. However, economic development cannot be built upon the corpses of the Yanomami.

Survival International respectfully urges the Commission to request additional information from the Government of Brazil regarding the situation of the Yanomami and the guarantees promised them under the Brazilian Constitution and fundamental international human rights norms. In addition, we appeal to the Government of Brazil to abide by the decisions of its own courts and to demarcate and protect all the Yanomami lands from destructive exploitation and invasion.

***EXPLOITATION OF CHILDREN.*** The UN Commission on Human Rights decided, in resolution 1990/68 of 7 March 1990, to appoint a Special Rapporteur to consider matters relating to the sale of children, child prostitution, and child pornography. The Special Rapporteur, Mr. Vitit Muntarbhorn, presented reports to the 1992 and 1993 sessions of the Commission (E/CN.4/1992/55 and E/CN.4/1993/67), and in an addendum to the first report (E/CN.4/1992/55/Add. 1) summarized the results of a visit to Brazil in January 1992, undertaken at the invitation of the Government of Brazil. The Special Rapporteur described the situation that he investigated on that visit in the addendum (paras. 4–10) as follows:

The issue of sale of children, child prostitution, and child pornography in Brazil can only be truly understood if one bears in mind the broad array of political, socioeconomic, and cultural problems facing the country. No less important are the historical antecedents, including a long period of colonization and slavery (particularly the movement of slaves from Africa to Brazil until the end of the nineteenth century), which has shaped much of the contemporary scenario relevant to the fate of children and their families.

The country has a huge land mass and a population of nearly 150 million people. There is a mosaic of different peoples who trace their ancestry to the different phases of development in Brazil. These include the indigenous group,

namely the Indians who inhabit mainly the Amazonian region; those of European descent, including immigrants from Portugal and other Western European countries (many of whom are to be found in the southeastern part of the country); those of Asian descent, primarily Japanese; and a large mass of those of African origin (many of whom are to be found in the northeastern part of the country). The last group in particular traces its roots in Brazil to the time when there was close trade between Brazil and West Africa, accentuated by the fact that Brazil and various African nations were previously Portuguese colonies.

Until the mid-1980s, the country was under military rule for two decades. This inevitably had substantial impact on the types of laws and policies concerning children and their families. The current Government under President Collor is part of a more recent process towards democratization. This bodes well for the official attitude toward laws and policies concerning children and their families. In terms of political will, the more democratic tenets of government in present-day Brazil reflect a welcome orientation toward democracy and popular participation, not least in regard to child development.

On the socioeconomic front, the vestiges of the past indicate broad disparities between the haves and have-nots, which ultimately have repercussions for children. As noted by the 1991 World Development Report: "In 1980 the southeastern region of Brazil (with about 40% of the people) had an estimated per capita nominal income more than three times that of the northeastern region (30% of the people)." The 1991 Human Development Report adds the following: "The top fifth of the population in Brazil earns 26 times more than the bottom fifth." This is aggravated by a great concentration of land holdings in the hands of the very few, coupled with a high birthrate and increasing marginalization of rural groups. This has led to an extensive influx of rural people to urban areas in search of employment. One consequence is the large number of people in slums on the periphery of major cities and a multitude of homeless people inhabiting the streets, particularly street children of Afro-Brazilian origin.

Externally, the country is faced with an enormous debt incurred by previous administrations and a concentration of power and decisionmaking in the big cities. The scenario is encapsulated as follows [Human Development Report 1991, p. 34]: "The economic problems of the 1980s have hit this (Latin American) region very hard. The debt crisis, high interest rates, barriers raised against Latin American exports and low commodity prices—all wrought havoc with some of the region's past achievements in human development. Average inflation rates soared above 100% during the 1980s in Brazil . . . eroding real wages and discouraging investment."

This has been compounded by the structural adjustment policies imposed by world financial institutions that have curtailed national allocations for social development expenditure, particularly in relation to child and family subsidies. Together with the current recession, including a high level of unemployment and pervasive social inequality, it is not difficult to conclude that both external and internal socioeconomic difficulties pose major obstacles to the governmental and nongovernmental sectors dealing with children. These impediments take their toll in regard to the children of concern to the Special Rapporteur's mandate.

The most tragic consequences are to be found in relation to the violence suffered by children at three levels: first, social violence that is a consequence of societal defects affecting the livelihood of children, e.g., poverty, infant and child mortality, and unfulfilled needs such as access to education and health facilities; second, domestic violence that entails the physical and mental disintegration of families due to economic and other pressures; third, personal violence that includes physical and mental harm suffered by individuals. All three forms of violence are particularly pertinent in view of injuries inflicted upon many street children. They have been highlighted both nationally and internationally by the killings of street children in various parts of the country in recent years. The fact that these killings persist today and that many of the perpetrators remain at large is a most disquieting sign of the times. As the sale of children, child prostitution, and child pornography are often linked to life in the streets, the menace faced by street children requires urgent action to deal with the issue.

*Recommendations of the Special Rapporteur.* After describing in the same report a number of innovative laws and policies responsive to the needs of children and their families that have been adopted since the advent of the Collor Government, the Special Rapporteur summarized the findings of his visit and submitted to the Commission on Human Rights the following recommendations (para. 24):

### (a) General

1. More emphasis should be placed on interdisciplinary action to tackle the root causes of child exploitation. This includes socioeconomic measures, coupled with appropriate budgetary allocations for child and family development to satisfy basic needs and elevate their quality of life.

2. At the national level, the priority of child development and protection raises fundamental issues of social justice and equity, including the need for better income distribution, child and family subsidies, access to education, family planning and health facilities, occupational means, and reallocation of land holdings and other resources to reduce the gap between the rich and the poor.

3. At the international level, debt servicing and structural adjustment measures should respond more concretely to the plight of children and their families at the local level. World financial institutions and development agencies need to address the paradox whereby conditions are imposed upon Brazil with a view to macroeconomic adjustment that concomitantly impede the measures required to promote child and family development at the microeconomic level.

4. More emphasis should be placed upon preventive action that is interrelated with the variety of measures already noted in the interdisciplinary setting. From the perspective of remedial action, easier access to courts and other places providing help should be ensured along with the provision of legal aid and other assistance. This should be coupled with counselling and occupational and other measures to help children and their families return to a normal life.

5. Law enforcement should be improved with more training of law enforcement personnel, including police, judges and lawyers. Measures should be taken against law-enforcement personnel who abuse the law for their own ends. This should entail the identification or establishment of an independent entity (e.g., an ombudsman) who would hear the grievances of the public against such persons. More incentives (e.g., higher pay and rewards for exemplary conduct) should be provided to promote better performance. More specifically concerning the plethora of police categories

found in Brazil, attention should be paid to the need to democratize the police force and to convert military elements into civilian elements, as well as to increase the number of women on the force.

6. More forums for police and other personnel should be established to exchange ideas and information between different states in the federal system, as this may facilitate cooperation in regard to transfrontier cases. A similar approach may be used for the police forces of different countries and for Interpol.

7. The role of nongovernmental organizations and community initiatives is already recognized and should be maximized in partnership with governmental organizations. The business sector should be encouraged to become more involved in assisting child-related activities. Tax deductions and other incentives should be promoted for both the nongovernmental and private sectors.

8. There should be local and national databases in the areas of concern to this mandate. The governmental and nongovernmental sectors are encouraged to collect data on the issues dealt with in this report. This should lead to an annual national report on the sale of children, child prostitution, and child pornography that would be made available to the Special Rapporteur and the world community.

9. Although the issue of killings and other assaults on street children per se is beyond the purview of this study, the linkage between these children and the three sectors of this mandate raises legitimate concerns for their safety. National agencies are invited to take more effective action to protect these children. At the international level, international organizations, including the various human rights organs of the United Nations, should take greater interest in the issue and promote correlative action to protect this group of children. A disquieting feature of attacks against street children is that the majority is directed against those of Afro-Brazilian origin. The marginalisation of this group calls for more measures to help the children and families of this category, which tends to be relegated to the lower socioeconomic stratum of Brazilian society.

### (b) Sale of Children

10. Registries of children and families involved in adoptions should be established at the municipal, national, and international levels.

11. Monitoring and tracing of adoptions should be promoted at all levels both before and after the adoption procedure is completed. At the national and local levels, the establishment of various councils to protect children, as envisaged by the Statute of the Child and Adolescent, can be utilized in this respect. At the transnational level, more multilateral and bilateral agreements to ensure follow-up evaluation are required in regard to intercountry adoptions.

12. Supervision of the intermediaries and prevention of abuses by these entities should be promoted. This should be seen in the light of the draft international convention on intercountry adoptions that seeks to compel the accreditation of intermediaries and the monitoring of their operations through central agencies in each country as part of the supervisory process.

13. Intercountry adoptions should only be explored after local adoption possibilities are exhausted. Where possible, measures should be promoted to assist families to exercise the option of retaining their children without resorting to giving them up for adoption; this entails more socioeco-

nomic assistance and sponsorship by private individuals and other entities, both nationally and internationally.

14. In regard to the exploitation of child labour, more attention should be paid to children working in various agricultural and industrial sectors, including sugar cane plantations and small-scale factories. The plight of children used as domestics deserves more attention. The close relationship between the multitude of street children and various forms of work (and related exploitation) needs further scrutiny.

15. As part of the social security framework, more child and family subsidies are required to alleviate the economic burden imposed on child labourers and to facilitate their access to education. Educational programmes need to be made more flexible and occupation-related so as to respond to the socioeconomic needs of children and their families.

16. More vigorous action to prevent the sale of children for organ transplantation is required. This should incorporate the guidelines enunciated by the World Health Organization concerning human organ transplantation.

17. At the municipal, state, and federal levels, registries to document disappeared children should be established and assistance provided to their families.

### (c) Child Prostitution

18. Stronger measures are needed to implement the existing law and policy to protect children in this group. This entails the prosecution of intermediaries, on the one hand, and the need to discourage customers from using the services of child prostitutes, on the other hand. Rehabilitation measures, coupled with longterm monitoring, should take the form of community participation and assistance rather than institutionalization in state or federal institutions.

19. Tourist agencies should be called upon to exert pressure against sex tourism. This should involve world tourist organisations so as to mobilize travel agents and the service sector to counter the transnationalization of child prostitution.

20. Monitoring of child prostitution requires more effective cooperation between local and federal police in internal cases and between the police forces of different countries in external cases. The cooperation of Interpol is also crucial in this respect.

21. Dissemination of information on AIDS should be maximized. For those who have tested HIV positive, antidiscrimination measures need to be implemented, coupled with assistance measures in the form of hospices and occupational activities.

22. The responsibility of the customer, whether through legal sanctions or incentives for behavioural change, should be promoted. The notion of "consumer liability" should be propagated more broadly through the use of the mass media.

### (d) Child Pornography

23. More effective law enforcement calls for more community vigilance in this field. This includes raising of community consciousness and involvement of the mass media in identifying abuses.

24. Laws and policies should prepare for the advent of new forms of technology that may result in child pornography, e.g., computers used for such purposes.

25. The responsibility of the customer should be enhanced, as already indicated above.

After considering the Special Rapporteur's report, the Commission on Human Rights endorsed his conclusions and recommendations concerning the strengthening of preventive strategies to tackle the root causes of the sale of children, child prostitution, and child pornography, and stressed the need for an effective multidisciplinary approach on the national and international level.

**BIBLIOGRAPHY.** Adorno, Sergio. "Sistema penitenciario no Brasil" (Brazilian Penitentiary System). *Revista Direitos Humanos GAJOP* 6, no. 9 (January 1991): 23–32. NGO article, in Portuguese.

Alvim, M. *Da Violencia contra o Menor Extermino de Criancas e Adolescentes* (The Killings of Children and Adolescents in Brazil). Rio de Janeiro: Centre for the Mobilization of Marginalized Populations, 1991. NGO study, in Portuguese. Published in English in 1988.

Americas Watch. *Criminal Injustice: Violence against Women in Brazil.* New York: Human Rights Watch, 1991. NGO report, in English.

―――. *Forced Labor in Brazil.* New York: Human Rights Watch, 1990. NGO factfinding report, in English.

―――. *Rural Violence in Brazil.* New York: Human Rights Watch, 1991. NGO factfinding report, in English.

Americas Watch, Physicians for Human Rights (PHR), and American Association for the Advancement of Science. *The Search for Brazil's Disappeared: The Mass Grave at Dom Bosco Cemetery.* Washington, D.C.: Human Rights Watch, 1991. NGO factfinding report, in English.

Amnesty International. *Brazil: Authorized Violence in Rural Areas.* London: 1988. NGO report, in English.

―――. *Brazil: "We Are the Land": Indigenous Peoples' Struggle for Human Rights.* London: 1992. NGO report, in English.

―――. *Torture and Extrajudicial Executions in Urban Brazil.* London: 1990. NGO report, in English.

Archdiocese of Sao Paulo. *Brazil: Nunca Mais* (Brazil: Never Again). 3d ed. Petropolis, Brazil: Editora Vozes, Ltda., 1985. Research project report, in Portuguese.

Barros Laraia, Roque de. *New Trends in Brazilian Indian Affairs.* London: International Organisation for the Elimination of All Forms of Racial Discrimination, 1985. NGO report, in English.

Benzi Grupioni, Luis Donisete. "Derechos Indígenas en la Nueva Constitución Brasileña" (Indigenous Rights in the New Brazilian Constitution), *Hombre y Ambiente: El Punto de Vista Indígena* 5, no. 20 (December 1991): 53–64. Scholarly article, in Spanish; bibliography, p. 59.

Branford, Sue, and Oriel Glock. *The Last Frontier: Fighting over Land in the Amazon.* London: Zed Press, 1985. Scholarly monograph, in English.

Bridel, Renee, and Jean-Paul Collomp. *The Sexual Exploitation and Abuse of Children in Brazil: 13 November–2 December 1986.* Paris: Federation Internationale des Droits de l'Homme, 1987. NGO mission report, in English.

Catholic Institute for International Relations. *Liberate the Land: A Statement by the Bishops of Brazil.* Third World Theology Series. London: 1986. NGO monograph, in English.

Chevigny, Paul G. "Police Deadly Force as Social Control: Jamaica, Argentina, and Brazil," *Criminal Law Forum* 1, no. 3 (Spring 1990): 389–425. Scholarly article, in English.

Comissao Pro-Indio de Sao Paulo (Pro-Indian Commission of Sao Paulo). *A Questao da Mineracao em Terra Indigena*

(The Issue of Mining on Indian Land). Sao Paulo: 1985. NGO monograph, in Portuguese.

de O. Santos, Leinad Ayer, and Lúcia M.M. de Andrade, eds. *Hydroelectric Dams on Brazil's Xingu River and Indigenous Peoples.* Cambridge, MA, USA: Cultural Survival, 1990. NGO research report, in English.

de Souza Filho, C.F. Marés. "O Direito Envergonhado (O Direito e os Indios No Brasil)" (The Shameful Law [The Law and Indians in Brazil]), *Revista IIDH* no. 15 (June 1992): 145–164. Scholarly article, in Portuguese.

de Souza Martins, Jose. "A Escravidao Hoje no Brasil" (Slavery Today in Brazil), *Cadernos Do CEAS* 104 (July–August 1986): 52–54. NGO article, in Portuguese.

Gomes de Costa, A., and B. Schmidt-Rahmer. "Brazil Children Spearhead a Movement for Change," in *The Convention: Child Rights and UNICEF Experience at the Country Level*, pp. 35–45. Florence, Italy: UNICEF/Innocenti, 1992. IGO study.

Guerra, A. *Combating Violence against Children and Adolescents in Brazil Today.* Brasilia, Brazil: Ministry of the Child, 1991. NGO study, in English and Portuguese.

Human Rights Watch. "Brazil," in *Human Rights Watch World Report 1995*, pp. 71–76. New York: 1995. NGO report, in English.

———. *Final Justice: Police and Death Squad Homicides of Adolescents in Brazil.* New York: 1994. NGO report, in English.

International Federation of Human Rights. *Brésil: rapport d'enquête sur les assassinats d'enfants* (Brazil: Factfinding Report on Child Assassinations). Paris: 1991. NGO factfinding report, in French.

Junqueira, Carmen, and Betty Mindlin. *The Aripuana Park and the Polonoroeste Programme.* Translated by Sheila Aikman. Cophenhagen: International Work Group for Indigenous Affairs, 1987. NGO monograph, in English.

Lemineur, M. "Child Prostitution in Brazil." Unpublished LLM dissertation, 1991.

Leonel, Mauro, Betty Mindlin, and Carmen Junqueira. "The Joint Responsibility of the International Community in the Indigenous and Environmental Issues of the Brazilian Amazon." *IWGIA Newsletter* no. 3 (August/September 1992): 6–19. NGO article, in English; bibliography, p. 19.

Pope, Clara Amanda. *Human Rights and the Catholic Church in Brazil, 1970–1983: The Pontifical Justice and Peace Commission of the Sao Paulo Archdiocese—A Case Study.* 25 March 1984. Unpublished scholarly paper, in English.

Sakek, M. T., and J. A. Borges. *Educacion y Ciudadnia: La Exclusion Politica de los Analfabetos en el Brazil* (Education and Citizenship: The Political Exclusion of Illiterates in Brazil). San Jose, Costa Rica: Instituto Interamericano de Derechos Humanos, Centro de Asesoria y Promocion Electoral, Inter-American Institute of Human Rights, and Center for Electoral Counseling and Promotion, 1985. IGO monograph, in Spanish.

Sutton, Alison. *Slavery in Brazil: A Link in the Chain of Modernisation: The Case of Amazonia.* London: Anti-Slavery International, 1994. NGO report, in English; bibliography, pp. 148–150.

Swift, Anthony. *Brazil: The Fight for Childhood in the City.* Florence, Italy: UNICEF International Child Development Centre, 1991. IGO monograph, in English.

World Council of Churches, Commission on the Churches' Participation in Development. *The Debt Crisis and Brazil: A Case Study.* Geneva: 1987. NGO monograph, in English; bibliography, p. 45.

**BRIAND, ARISTIDE P. H. (1862–1932).** This remarkable Frenchman was a co-recipient of the 1926

**NOBEL PEACE PRIZE.** In his long career, Briand served as France's foreign minister and 11 times as its premier. Born in Brittany, he studied law in Paris and became a strident advocate of the syndicalist doctrine of revolution by strike. He also advocated the armed insubordination of soldiers called out to suppress strikes or to fight for their country.

With René Viviani and Jean Jaurès, he founded the French Socialist party; and in 1904, the group established the newspaper *L'Humanité*. It was two years earlier, in 1902, that Briand was first elected to public office; while in office, the fiery socialist began to move toward the right of the political spectrum and eventually, in his long political career, came to the middle ground, renouncing war as an instrument of national policy (the Kellog-Briand Pact of 1928 between the United States of America and France) and working for European consolidation.

Briand was awarded the 1926 Nobel Peace Prize principally for his efforts on the Locarno Pacts of October 1925, which consisted of a number of separate agreements that secured frontiers in Western Europe and opened the way for Germany's entry into the League of Nations (the previous year, British statesman **JOSEPH AUSTEN CHAMBERLAIN** was awarded the Prize also because of the Pacts).

*BIBLIOGRAPHY.* Gray, Tony. *Champions of Peace.* London: Paddington Press, 1976.

Schlessinger, Bernard S., and June H. Schlessinger, eds. *Who's Who of Nobel Prize Winners.* Phoenix, AZ, USA: Oryx Press, 1991.

**BRUNEI DARUSSALAM.** The State of Brunei Darussalam is a country in southeastern Asia, on the northwest coast of the island of Borneo, facing the South China Sea. It is split into two parts by the East Malaysian State of Sarawak. Formerly known as Brunei, it achieved independence from Great Britain on 1 January 1984 and became a member of the United Nations the same year. Its population is estimated to be 273,000. Ethnic groups include Malays (65%), Chinese (20%), indigenous populations, mainly Ibans (8%), and others (7%). Languages in common use include Malay and English (both official), Chinese, Iban, and other indigenous vernaculars. Religions practiced include Islam (official), 66%; Buddhism, 14%; Christianity, 10%; and others, 10%. Literacy is estimated at 45% overall, 95% among the young.

The government (1994) took the form of a monarchy. The sultan rules, under a 1965 constitution, with the assistance of a six-member cabinet and a Council of Ministers, all appointed by himself. The constitution provides for an elected Legislative Council of 20 members; however, no elections were held after 1965. There is one political party: the Brunei National Democratic Party.

Because of its oil wealth, the people of Brunei Darussalam enjoy first-class schools and health systems. There are no universities in the country, but qualified students are given government scholarships to study in British institutions.

**BIBLIOGRAPHY.** Amnesty International. *Administrative Detention.* London: 1988. NGO report, in English.
————. *Southeast Asia: Human Rights Violations in Brunei, Indonesia, Malaysia, Philippines.* London: 1987. NGO report, in English.
Malaysia-Singapore-Brunei Studies Group. *Berita* 12, no. 3 (Fall 1986): 1–17. NGO articles, in English.

**BUISSON, FERDINAND EDOUARD (1841–1932).** F. E. Buisson was born in Paris and educated at the Lycée Bonaparte. He was forced into political exile in 1866 when he refused to take an oath of allegiance to the emperor Napoleon III. In 1867 he took part in the first Geneva peace conference, advocating European consolidation. For the next two decades, he worked on education reform, publishing his *Dictionnaire de Pédagogie* and becoming a professor of education at the Sorbonne. He was awarded the **NOBEL PEACE PRIZE** in 1927 jointly with the German pacifist Ludwig Quidde. In citing Buisson for the Prize, the Nobel Committee recognized his commitment to education and commented that "great original work for peace must be preceded by the education of the people." In the late 1890s, he campaigned for the reversal of the Dreyfus conviction and founded the Ligue des Droits de l'Homme, becoming president of the League in 1913.

Although fundamentally opposed to war, he supported French efforts in World War I because of German militarism. After the war, he worked for reconciliation between the two countries. He donated the proceeds of his Nobel Peace Prize to various pacifist organizations.

**BIBLIOGRAPHY.** Gray, Tony. *Champions of Peace.* London: Paddington Press, 1976.
Schlessinger, Bernard S., and June H. Schlessinger, eds. *Who's Who of Nobel Prize Winners.* Phoenix, AZ, USA: Oryx Press, 1991.

**BULGARIA.** Bulgaria is a country in eastern Europe, on the Black Sea. It has borders with Greece, Romania, Turkey, and Yugoslavia. It achieved independence from Turkey in 1908 and became a member of the United Nations in 1955. Its population is estimated to be 8,842,000. Minority ethnic and national groups include persons of Armenian, Greek, Gypsy, Jewish, and Turkish descent, together making up about 9% of the population. Bulgarian is the only language in common use. Literacy is estimated at 95%.

The government (1994) took the form of a republic. However, for many years, starting in 1944, Bulgaria was under the rule of a coalition known as the Fatherland Front, after Soviet troops had marched into the country without opposition. In 1971, its constitution was revised to stipulate, in article 1, that "the leading force in society and in the State is the Bulgarian Communist Party." During this period, Todor Zhivkov, as head of that party, was the country's hardline leader.

Although the Bulgarian people were repeatedly subjected to discrimination and forced assimilation during periods of colonial occupation by the Ottoman Turks and although Bulgaria was an ally of Germany during the World Wars I and II, all strata of Bulgarian society firmly resisted attempts to hand over Bulgarian Jews to Nazi occupation forces during World War II, saving the lives of tens of thousands of people.

In recent years, Bulgaria adopted measures to overcome the social disadvantages of its Gypsy population, to improve their way of life and to raise their standard of living. These measures include the construction of housing, the establishment of children's homes, and the integration of Gypsy children into public educational institutions. Despite these steps forward, the Gypsy population in Bulgaria, according to reports of non-governmental organizations, continues to be harassed, often by police officers and private security guards.

Relations between Bulgaria's slavic majority and its large ethnic Turkish minority have been strained for many years. In 1985, ethnic rivalries in Bulgaria began to intensify; and in the three years that followed, some 310,000 Bulgarian Muslims of Turkish descent fled into Turkey to escape what they described as religious and ethnic repression. In particular, the refugees charged that Bulgarian authorities had forced them to take Slavic names, had banned their use of the Turkish language in public, and prohibited various practices prescribed by their religion. Until Turkey closed its borders with Bulgaria, the migration escalated into one of the most serious and abrupt shifts of population in Europe since World War II.

At the Sixteenth Islamic Conference of Foreign Ministers, held at Fez, Morocco, from 6 to 10 January 1986, a resolution on the plight of the Turkish-Muslim minority in Bulgaria was adopted, under which the Secretary-General of the Organization of the Islamic Conference was entrusted with the task of appointing a three-member contact group composed of eminent personalities to examine the condition of the Muslim minority in Bulgaria. The contact group visited Bulgaria for this purpose in June 1987. In its report, submitted to the Seventeenth Islamic Conference of Foreign Ministers convened at Amman, Jordan, from 21 to 25 March 1988, the group summarized its conclusions as follows (UN Doc. A/ 43/230):

That the Muslims in Bulgaria have been subjected to official pressure and coercion in changing their Islamic names into Bulgarian/Slavic ones, which has the effect of destroying their Islamic identity;

That the Muslims in Bulgaria have been denied the right to follow their religion freely and that some of their religious rituals/rites, such as circumcision of young children, have been prohibited on pain of criminal prosecution;

That the Muslims in Bulgaria have been denied free use of their places of worship (mosques), and the restrictions on their use on a particular day in a week or on a particular time only is a negation of a basic religious right of Muslims;

That the Muslims in Bulgaria, the majority of whom are of Turkish origin, have been prohibited and denied the right to use their own language and to protect and preserve their cultural heritage, on pain of criminal prosecution and punishment for violation of such prohibition; and

That there are several cases of split families because of the migration of Muslims from Bulgaria to Turkey and that in some such cases, very close relations such as fathers, mothers, sons and daughters were separated from each other.

Between 1985 and 1989, the worsening situation of Bulgaria's Turkish minority was the subject of frequent discussions in the Parliamentary Assembly of the Council of Europe. On 26 September 1989, the Assembly adopted resolution 927 (1989), as follows:

The Assembly,
Considering in Resolution 846 (1985) on the situation of ethnic and Muslim minorities in Bulgaria, its Recommendation 1109 (1989) on the situation of refugees of Bulgarian nationality in Turkey, and the report on the situation of the ethnic and Muslim minority in Bulgaria presented by its Committee on Relations with European Non-Member Countries (Doc. 6106);

Noting with satisfaction that the Bulgarian authorities finally received a subcommittee of the Assembly from 13 to 19 July 1989 under the required conditions, namely that it should be able to choose where it went and with whom it spoke and use its own interpreters;

Regretting, however, that it did not have the opportunity of meeting all the "dissidents" mentioned in the programme;

Taking note of the following information brought back by the subcommittee:

(i) a major human tragedy is taking place in Bulgaria, with hundreds of thousands of Bulgarian Muslims leaving for Turkey;

(ii) these Muslims are leaving the country both because of the serious denial of their rights—name-changing, ban on speaking Turkish, and restrictions on the practice of their religion—and because they are encouraged by offers of resettlement through the Turkish media;

(iii) although there were a number of expulsions in May 1989, since then departures, although nominally voluntary, have constituted a mass exodus;

(iv) quite apart from the human tragedy they represent, these departures are not a lasting solution, particularly in view of their consequences both for Bulgaria—loss of manpower and disorganisation of rural life—and for Turkey—reception, accommodation, and labour-market problems;

Noting that the number of immigrants has reached over 300,000; that, as from 22 August 1989, the Turkish Government decided to reestablish the entrance visa obligation for Bulgarian citizens; and that about 20,000 of them have already returned to Bulgaria;

Observing that there is disagreement as to the ethnic identity of the majority of the Muslim community; the Bulgarians say that it is composed of Bulgarians islamised during Ottoman rule and the Turks that it consists of Muslims of Turkish ethnic origin undergoing forced assimilation;

Recognising that the amendments to the legislation on nationality and passports adopted by the Bulgarian National Assembly on 8 and 9 May 1989 represent a step forward in terms of the provisions of the instruments adopted within the CSCE and United Nations framework and should help to satisfy Turkey's demands aimed at securing a free choice of homeland for the Bulgarian ethnic and Muslim community and guaranteeing that families are reunited;

Welcoming the resolution adopted on 21 September 1989 by the relevant committee of Bulgaria's National Assembly stressing the need that the authorities implement the freedom of religion that is guaranteed by the Constitution as well as the free use of different languages in everyday contacts between citizens, and hoping for an immediate application of this resolution by the Bulgarian Government;

Observing that dialogue between the Bulgarian and Turkish Governments is currently at a standstill and that the protocol that they signed in Belgrade on 23 February 1988 has not been implemented; and encouraging the Council of Europe and its member states to contribute to the opening of a constructive dialogue between the Bulgarian and the Turkish Governments with a view to establishing more satisfactory neighbourly relations that will lead to a migration agreement between the two countries;

Noting, moreover, that several countries have already put into practice with regard to Bulgaria the control mechanism relating to the human dimension of the CSCE provided for in the concluding document of the January 1989 Vienna Conference;

Recalling that, in its Recommendation 1109, adopted on 6 July 1989, the Assembly recommends that the Committee of Ministers "appeal to the governments of member states so that they provide, as a matter of urgency, concrete and coordinated aid to Turkey in order that these exiles be accorded a decent reception corresponding to standards of human dignity,"

Urges the Bulgarian Government:
(i) to end immediately its policy of forced assimilation, which is to be regarded as the main cause of the present exodus, with a view to allowing its ethnic and Muslim minority to resume the practical use of their original names, together with the unrestricted use of the Turkish language and of Muslim religious practices;

(ii) to grant its ethnic and Muslim minority the rights of a minority in the spirit of the concluding document adopted by the Vienna CSCE review meeting of January 1989;

Also urges the Turkish authorities:
(i) as a gesture of goodwill, to avoid any propaganda element in its information services to the ethnic and Muslim minority in Bulgaria;

(ii) to take the necessary steps to enable separated families to reunite in accordance with their wishes;

Demands that both governments examine together what

each country can do to help solve the concrete problems of the ethnic and Muslim minority in Bulgaria in order to avoid the mass exodus;

Asks the member states of the Council of Europe to promote the opening of negotiations between Bulgaria and Turkey with a view to easing the tension between the two countries, which could have dangerous political and economic consequences for the whole of the continent;

Instructs its Committee on Migration, Refugees and Demography to examine on the spot the conditions under which Muslims from Bulgaria are received and settled in Turkey, to check that compliance with Assembly Recommendation 1056 on national refugees and missing persons in Cyprus is observed, and report back to it in due course, with proposals, in the light of Recommendation 1109, on the level of assistance the member states of the Council of Europe should supply to the Turkish Government to carry out its resettlement programme.

***THE END OF COMMUNIST RULE.*** The process of democratic reform proceeded at a slower pace in Bulgaria than in some other eastern European countries, reflecting perhaps Bulgaria's long history of Turkish domination and its 35 years of hardline Stalinist rule by Todor I. Zhivkov. On 10 November 1989, Zhivkov was ousted after a sudden Politburo coup; and on 13 December, he was summarily expelled from the Communist Party following a call by a new leader, Peter Mladenov, for the Party to give up its monopoly on political power. Shortly thereafter, the Party's Central Committee acted on Mladenov's suggestion by calling on the Parliament to repeal article 1 of the Constitution so that it might prove itself against competitive opposition in free elections. Zhivkov was later convicted of embezzling an estimated $24 million and sentenced to seven years in prison.

In the first election open to all parties, unions, and other groups, the Communists won control of Parliament. Later, the Party invited growing elements of opposition to join a "government of national consensus." However, thirteen major opposition groups, drawn into a coalition, rejected the offer because they realized that, in such a government, Communist elements would continue to be dominant. Their insistence on another election, under rules ensuring fairness to all participants, won widespread support, shown in an unprecedented number of strikes and public demonstrations. Soon, deep splits became evident within the Communist hierarchy.

In the first truly free elections, held in 1992, Zhelyu Zhelev, leader of the opposition Union of Democratic Forces, was chosen as president, in a forced coalition with the minority Turkish Muslims. A long era of Communist domination in Bulgaria came to an end. However, the Bulgarian Socialist Party (former Communists) took 125 of the 240 contested parliamentary seats, while the Union of Democratic Forces took 68 seats in elections in December 1994.

***BIBLIOGRAPHY.*** Amnesty International. *Bulgaria: Continuing Human Rights Abuses against Ethnic Turks.* London: 1987. NGO report, in English.

"Bulgaria—No Relaxation for Muslims," *Impact International* 16, no. 20 (November 1986): 2. NGO article, in English.

"Bulgaria's Turks Tell of Terror in Forced Assimilation Drive," *Washington Post,* 8 April 1986. In English.

Commission on Security and Cooperation in Europe. *Basket I—Implementation of the Final Act of the Conference on Security and Cooperation in Europe: Findings Eleven Years after Helsinki.* Washington, D.C.: Government Printing Office, 1987. Government report, 1987, in English.

———. *National Minorities in Eastern Europe: The Turkish Minority in Bulgaria.* Washington, D.C.: Government Printing Office, 1987. Government report, in English.

Helsinki Watch. *Bulgaria: Police Violence against Gypsies.* New York: Human Rights Watch, 1993. NGO report, in English.

———. *Decommunization in Bulgaria.* New York: Human Rights Watch, 1993. NGO report, in English.

———. *Destroying Ethnic Identity: Selective Persecution of Macedonians in Bulgaria.* New York: Human Rights Watch, 1991. NGO factfinding report, in English.

Human Rights Watch. "Bulgaria," in *Human Rights Watch World Report 1995,* pp. 198–201. New York: 1995. NGO report, in English.

Immigration and Refugee Board Documentation Centre. *Bulgaria: The Impact of Reform.* Ottawa, Canada: 1991. NGO report, in English and French.

International Commission of Jurists. "Bulgaria/Turkey," *The ICJ Review* 38 (June 1987): 1–3. NGO article, in English.

Internationale Gesellschaft fur Menschenrechte (International Society for Human Rights). *CSCE and Human Rights: Divided Families and the Denial of Freedom of Movement (Documentation).* Frankfurt/Main, FRG: 1987. NGO document collection, in English.

Korkud, Refik. *Bulgaria Carries on Chauvinistic Policies.* Ankara, Turkey: Turkiye Fikir Ajansi, 1986. Situation report, in English.

Pashovski, Slavi. "Minorities in Bulgaria," in *The Protection of Ethnic and Linguistic Minorities in Europe,* eds. John Packer and Kristian Myntti, pp. 67–78. Turku/Abo, Finland: Abo Akademi Institute for Human Rights, 1993. Scholarly article, in English; bibliography, p. 78.

"The Position of the Turks in Bulgaria," *Review of International Affairs* 36, no. 837 (February 1985). Journal article, in English.

Research Center for Religion and Human Rights in Closed Societies. *Bulgaria: Imprisonment of Ethnic Turks: Human Rights Abuses during the Forced Assimilation of the Ethnic Turkish Minority.* London: 1988. NGO report, in English.

**BUNCHE, RALPH JOHNSON (1904–1971).** The first black Nobel Peace laureate and the grandson of a former slave, Ralph Bunche was born in Detroit, MI, USA, and lived in poverty throughout his youth. To help his family, he worked at various jobs from the age of seven and supported himself at the University of California from the proceeds of an athletic scholarship and a janitor's job. He received his master's degree from Harvard University in 1928 and later was to receive a doctorate from the same university. In 1932–33, as a Rosenwald Fellow at Harvard, he researched colonial and racial problems in Togoland and Dahomey. Throughout the rest of the decade, he continued his work on colonial policy, including doing field research among African tribes.

In 1941, under the Roosevelt administration, he entered the Office of Strategic Services as a colonial-affairs expert. In 1944, he was appointed territorial specialist in colonial affairs under the U.S. State Department, becoming the first black director in an American administration. During the Roosevelt administration, he was part of the so-called "Black Cabinet," which informally counseled the president on minority problems. In 1945 and 1946, Bunche participated as a member of the U.S. delegation in the London UN conferences and was a representative to the 1946 ILO conference in Paris. Bunche had a long and distinguished career as a UN diplomat: he was appointed director of the Trusteeship Department of the UN Secretariat, serving in that capacity from 1947 to 1954. He served as UN Under-Secretary for Special Political Affairs (1954–1967) and ended his career as Under-Secretary-General (1968–1971).

Bunche received the 1950 **NOBEL PEACE PRIZE** because of his work in the Middle East from June 1947 to August 1949, when open warfare broke out between Arabs and Jews in Palestine. The United Nations appointed Count Folke Bernadotte of Sweden as mediator; Bunche was his chief aide. When the Count was assassinated on September 17, 1948, Bunche became the UN's acting mediator and obtained an armistice after 11 months of intensive negotiation. Bunche continued his career of international diplomacy throughout the 1950s and early 1960s.

In the United States, Bunche tackled the problem of racial discrimination. He declined an appointment by the Truman administration because of segregated housing in Washington, D.C. In 1956, he helped to lead the civil rights march in Montgomery, AL, and supported the National Association for the Advancement of Colored People (NAACP).

In addition to the Nobel Peace Prize, Bunche also received the Springarm Medal of the NAACP (1949) and the Medal of Freedom (1963).

***BIBLIOGRAPHY.*** Gray, Tony. *Champions of Peace.* London: Paddington Press, 1976.

Mann, Peggy. *Ralph Bunche: UN Peacemaker.* New York: Coward, McCann and Geoghegan, 1975.

Schlessinger, Bernard S., and June H. Schlessinger, eds. *Who's Who of Nobel Prize Winners.* Phoenix, AZ, USA: Oryx Press, 1991.

**BURKINA FASO.** A country in western Africa, formerly known as Upper Volta. It has borders with Benin, Ghana, Mali, Niger, and Togo. It achieved independence from France in 1960 and became a member of the United Nations the same year. Its population is estimated to be 9,808,000.

The Upper Volta, as it is still popularly called despite the official change of name in 1984, is a multinational State and a melting pot of peoples; more than 60 ethnic groups of varying size are included in its population. Among these groups are the Mossi, 48%; the Peul, 10%, the Lobi-Dagarai, 7%; the Mandé, 6.9%; the Bobo, 6.7%; the Sénoufo, 5.4%; the Gourounsi, 5.3%; the Bissa, 4.7%; and the Gourmantché, 4.5%. Each ethnic group has its own spoken language more or less widely used; the Mooré language, spoken by the Mossi, covers almost the entire central plateau of the Upper Volta and is increasingly spreading into many regions of the country. Bambara or Jula is widely spoken in large towns and other urban areas. The western Atlantic groups understand Poulon or Fulfuldé, a language spoken in the Sahel and by a few scattered groups of Peul. Religions practiced include Animism (67.8%), Islam (27.5%), and Christianity (Roman Catholic, 3.7%; Protestant, 1%). Literacy is estimated at 10%.

In 1994, the Government was a provisional military one.

Labor unrest and repeated allegations of government inefficiency have been major destabilizing factors in Burkina Faso since 1960, when the first constitution provided for the election of a president and members of a National Assembly by universal suffrage, for terms of five years.

A general strike and series of violent street demonstrations, organized by labor unions, forced the first president, Maurice Yameogo, to resign on 3 January 1966. The presidency was taken over by Lt. Col. Aboubakar Sangoule Lamizana, chief of staff of the army, who suspended the constitution but announced that he intended to restore civilian rule after four years.

On 14 June 1970, the second constitution was adopted, establishing the four-year transition period. However, the government found itself paralyzed by a dispute between the prime minister and the National Assembly early in 1974, whereupon President Lamizana suspended the second constitution, dismissed the Cabinet and National Assembly, and postponed the return to civilian control.

A third constitution was adopted and a complete return to civilian government was carried out by late November 1977, and elections were held in April and May 1978. President Lamizana, who had directed the transition, was returned to office. However, he found himself unable to resolve major differences with several labor unions; and, after a two-month teachers' strike, he was overthrown in a bloodless coup on 25

November 1980. Colonel Saye Zerbo, leader of the Military Committee for Reform and National Progress, assumed the presidency, suspended the third constitution, and dissolved the National Assembly.

A two-year period elapsed before still another coup ousted Col. Zerbo and established the People's Salvation Council, headed by Maj.-Dr. Jean-Baptiste Ouedraogo, as the supreme governing authority. The council, composed of 117 military personnel of various ranks and services, guaranteed the enjoyment of human rights so long as they did not threaten national security or public order, and promised a return to democratically elected civilian government by November 1984.

The People's Salvation Council was ousted, in turn, by a coup organized by Capt. Thomas Sankara—a follower of Libya's Muammar Qadhafi—who had once served as prime minister in the Ouedraogo government, had been dismissed and imprisoned, and eventually had been released in an effort to end discord within the army leadership. Upon taking office, Sankara formed the National Council for the Revolution with himself as president, established a number of committees for the "Defense of the Revolution" to mobilize the masses and to carry out political education and restructuring functions, and announced the goal of the revolution to be a national, independent, self-sufficient planned economy. To signal the absence of any tie to its colonial past, the name of the country was changed to Burkina Faso ("Land of the Upright Men").

The National Council did not hesitate to discharge teachers who went on strike in March 1984, to imprison the leaders of the largest radical trade union, and to continue the ban on political activity. Its Popular Revolutionary Tribunals tried and sentenced a number of former government officials. Its policies with reference to human rights were announced on 2 October 1983 by President Sankara as follows:

One of the essential concerns of the National Revolutionary Council is to unite the various nationalities in the Upper Volta in the common struggle against the enemies of our revolution. In our country, there is a multitude of ethnic groups differing from one another in language and customs. All these groups together make up the Upper Voltan nation. Imperialism, with its policy of divide and rule, has done its utmost to exacerbate the differences between them to set them against each other. CNR policy will aim at joining together these different nationalities so that they can live in equality and enjoy the same opportunities. For this purpose, special stress will be laid on economic development of the various regions, the promotion of trade between them, combatting prejudices among ethnic groups and settling differences between them in a spirit of unity, and punishing those who sow dissension.

However, on 15 October 1989, President Sankara was overthrown by his second-in-command, Capt. Blaise Compaore. A unit of Capt. Compaore's commandos shot Sankara and twelve aides and buried their bodies in a common grave, supposedly to prevent President Sankara from carrying out a plot to kill Capt. Compaore. The new government, known as the Popular Front, has not been able to win either widespread civilian support or strong military backing.

As a result of the civil war in Liberia, it was estimated that more Liberians inhabited the Burkina Faso refugee camps than any city in Liberia, with the possible exception of Monrovia. More than half of Liberia's 2.3 million population had dispersed, mainly to Burkina Faso or Guinea.

***BIBLIOGRAPHY.*** Amnesty International. *Burkina Faso: Political Imprisonment and the Use of Torture from 1983 to 1988.* London: 1988. NGO report, in English.

Jaudel, Etienne. *Rapport de Mission: Burkina Faso (Mission Report: Burkina Faso).* Paris: Federation Internationale des Droits de l'Homme, 1988. NGO report, in French.

Muase, Charles Kabeya. *Syndicalisme et démocratie en Afrique noire: l'expérience du Burkina Faso* (Syndicalism and Democracy in Black Africa: The Experience of Burkina Faso). France: Karthala, 1989. Scholarly monograph, in French.

Sandwidi, Kourita. "La Protection des droits de l'homme au Burkina Faso" (The Protection of Human Rights in Burkina Faso), in *Les Droits de l'homme en Afrique*, pp. 19–133. Dakar, Senegal: Institut des droits de l'homme et de la paix, Université Cheikh Anta Diop de Dakar, 1991. Scholarly article, in French.

Women's International Network. "Female Circumcision: Genital and Sexual Mutilation." *WIN News* 14, no. 3 (Summer 1988): 24–27; 14, no. 4 (Autumn 1988): 21–26; 15, no. 1 (Winter 1989): 28–29. NGO edited collection, in English.

## BURMA. See MYANMAR.

**BURUNDI.** The Republic of Burundi is a country in eastern Africa. It has borders with Rwanda, the United Republic of Tanzania, and Zaire. Burundi was originally part of a single United Nations trust territory known as Rwanda-Urundi, which was under Belgian administration. Its first national elections were held in January 1961 under UN supervision. On 1 July 1962, the UN General Assembly, in cooperation with Belgium, terminated the trusteeship agreement and recognized two independent States: Burundi and Rwanda. Burundi became a member of the United Nations the same year. Its population is estimated to be 6,118,000. Ethnic groups include the Hutu (85%), the Tutsi (14%), and the Twa (1%). Languages commonly used include Kirundi (official), French, and Swahili. Religions practiced include Christianity (Roman Catholic, 78%; Protestant denominations, 5%), Animism (17%), and Islam (1%). Literacy is estimated at 25%.

Although the Hutu tribesmen, who are farmers of Bantu origin, comprise 85% of the country's population, and the Tutsi tribesmen, who are warrior-pastoralists of Nilotic origin, comprise less than 15%—and although both speak the same language and frequently intermarry—the minority Tutsis have controlled the government of Burundi since the day of independence. Their domination has deep roots but appears to be based, at least in part, on size: they are noticeably taller than the Hutus, and tower over the pygmy Twa (who average 5 feet, 1 inch, in height).

Serious intertribal conflicts broke out soon after independence. In 1965, and again in 1969, the Tutsis prevailed after killing hundreds of Hutus. Early in 1972, the Hutus attacked and killed about 2,000 Tutsis. The government retaliated with a countrywide massacre in which members of the police force and youth organizations methodically slaughtered some 150,000 Hutus, including most of that group's educated elite. About 100,000 more were forced to seek refuge in neighboring Rwanda, Tanzania, and Zaire.

A United Nations mission visited Burundi between 22 and 28 June 1972 and confirmed reports that between 80,000 and 200,000 had died in Burundi, that approximately 500,000 people were in need of assistance, that 40,000 refugees in Rwanda, Tanzania, and Zaire were also in need of assistance, and that a great number of houses, schools, hospitals, and other public buildings had been destroyed by the conflict.

New violence erupted in mid-May 1973 and continued through July of that year, in which further mass killings of Hutus were reported to be comparable in number to those of 1972. In this case, the ORGANIZATION OF AFRICAN UNITY assumed responsibility for dealing with the conflict, considering it a possible threat to African peace.

In their efforts to avoid involvement in the internal affairs of Burundi, the United Nations and most of its members dealt with the crisis in Burundi as a "humanitarian disaster" and a refugee problem, rather than as a series of gross violations of human rights or as a case of genocide. Their activities were confined for the most part to factfinding and to providing assistance to refugees and other displaced persons.

The Burundi Government headed by Col. Jean-Baptiste Bagaza—in which three-quarters of the Cabinet and the National Assembly and nearly all army officers were Tutsis—called for tribal reconciliation and national unity and arranged for many refugees to return to Burundi and to regain the possessions left behind when they fled from the country. Hutus, for their part, did not raise the issue of majority rule again. In 1984, President Bagaza was re-elected, receiving 99.63% of the vote; however, he was deposed on 3 September 1987, while attending a conference in Quebec, Canada. His successor, Maj. Pierre Buyoya, is also a member of the Tutsi tribe.

The tribal situation in Burundi erupted again in mid-1988 and was such that large numbers of people were forced to flee the country. Ethnic violence which erupted in mid-August between the ruling Tutsi tribe and the majority Hutus resulted in the massacre of more than 5,000 persons. Most of the deaths were attributed to Tutsi soldiers who turned their arms against the unarmed Hutu people. As a consequence, more than 35,000 Hutu refugees fled to nearby Rwanda.

The government (1994) is a provisional military one, following a series of rapid changes during which the country was plunged into violence with great loss of life and mass displacement of the population. In 1993, President Melchoir Ndadaye, a Hutu who had won office as Burundi's first elected leader and who had briefly initiated human rights reforms (described in a report to the UN Human Rights Committee [CCPR/C/68/Add. 2]), was assassinated in an attack led by former President Jean Baptiste Bagaza. The coup marked the resumption of the ethnic feuding because his assailants were Tutsi. It has been estimated that between 30,000 and 50,000 people were killed in late 1993, while hundreds of thousands of people fled to Tanzania, Rwanda, or Zaire. Then, on 6 April 1994, a new president of Burundi, Cyprian Ntaryamira, who had been appointed by the National Assembly to serve out Ndadaye's term, died when the plane in which he was returning from a peace mission in Tanzania crashed as the result of an attack while approaching the airport at Kigali, Rwanda. The Burundian and Rwandan presidents had tried, with other Central and East African leaders, to mediate an end to the ethnic warfare that disrupted both countries. By the end of 1994, Sylvestre Ntibatunganya, former president of the National Assembly, was installed to serve out the remainder of the five-year term originally won by Ndadaye in June 1993. Although ethnic clashes continued in 1994 and hundreds of people were killed, Burundi did not experience the wholesale slaughter that marked its neighbor, Rwanda.

In July 1994 the Human Rights Committee responded to a report by Burundi on the International Covenant on Civil and Political Rights:

In the light of past and continuing events in Burundi affecting the human rights guaranteed by the International Covenant on Civil and Political Rights, and in accordance with article 40, paragraph 1 (b), of the Covenant, the Committee requested the Government of Burundi on 29 October 1993 to submit a report, not later than 31 January 1994, if necessary in summary form, describing in particular the implementation of articles 4, 6, 7, 9, 12 and 25 of the Covenant during the current period, for consideration by the Committee at its fiftieth session.

At its fiftieth session, the Committee noted that the

report requested had not been submitted by the Government of Burundi and, through its Chairman, asked for it to be submitted to the Committee for consideration at its fifty-first session. In response to this request, the Government of Burundi submitted a report on 12 July 1994 (CCPR/C/98) which was considered by the Committee at its 1349th and 1350th meetings on 25 July 1994. The Committee adopted the following comments on 28 July 1994:

### Introduction

The Committee thanks the State Party for its report and welcomes the presence before the Committee of a high-level delegation. The Committee notes with regret, however, that while providing some information on the implementation of articles 4, 6, 7, 9, 12 and 25 of the Covenant, the report does not contain enough information on the situation obtaining in the country and the difficulties affecting the application of the Covenant. The information provided orally by the delegation made good those deficiencies and provided the Committee with a better insight into the human rights situation in Burundi.

### Factors and Difficulties Affecting the Application of the Covenant

The Committee notes that, since its accession to independence, Burundi has regularly had to contend with serious conflicts between the Hutu majority and the Tutsi minority, largely attributable to socio-political difficulties inherited from the past. Those conflicts, particularly the most recent one in autumn 1993, following the assassination of the President of the Republic, have been marked by gross violations of human rights. The lack of effective measures following such events, as well as the de facto impunity enjoyed, regardless of rank, by members of the army, police, gendarmerie, security forces or administration responsible for serious violations of human rights, are obstacles to the restoration of lasting peace and to the halting of the cycle of violence between the Hutu majority and the Tutsi minority.

The dominance in the army, the police, the gendarmerie, the security forces, the judicial system and, generally, in the most senior civil-service posts of persons belonging to a minority group is a factor constantly and seriously affecting the application of the Covenant and one which continually arouses the fears of the majority of the population. The recent unrest on an unprecedented scale in a neighbouring country (Rwanda), which has resulted in a massive influx of refugees into Burundi, is a further difficulty likely to have extremely negative effects on the application of the Covenant in that country.

### Positive Aspects

The authorities have made an effort to consider a number of measures to restore civil peace and harmony among the various elements of the Burundi population, although those efforts do not for the time being seem to have had concrete effects.

The Committee also notes that foreign non-governmental organizations have been allowed to conduct inquiries into human rights violations in Burundi without hindrance.

### Principal Subjects of Concern

The Committee deplores the massacres following clashes between Hutu and Tutsi that have occurred in Burundi since its consideration of the initial report in October 1992, and the increasingly serious obstacles to the peaceful coexistence of the various elements of the Burundi population. The attempts to restore civil peace, to assuage the tensions of daily life in society and to redress the balance in the various State institutions, particularly the army, the police, the gendarmerie, the security forces and the judiciary, so as to make them more representative of the various elements of the population, have clearly failed.

The Committee deplores the pattern of gross violations of human rights in the form of numerous summary executions, disappearances and instances of torture which occurred following the events of autumn 1993. The army, the police, the gendarmerie and the security forces have continued to be responsible for many violations of human rights. The civilian population continues to be armed and further violations of human rights are to be feared.

The Committee deplores the lack of any inquiry into the above-mentioned violations. As a result, the perpetrators have remained unpunished and continue to perform, and sometimes to abuse, their functions in the army, police, gendarmerie or security forces. The victims or their families have received no compensation of any kind. The judiciary has shown itself incapable of carrying out its duties independently and impartially and has been unable to initiate the necessary investigations or bring those responsible to trial. Furthermore, the fact that the commissions of inquiry recently set up to identify those responsible for human rights violations consist of individuals belonging to only one of the country's population groups is a source of serious concern and has served only to shake the population's confidence in the authorities and exacerbate strife and violence between the various population groups.

The Committee deplores the fact that the provisions of the Covenant not referred to in the Committee's decision have also been the subject of serious violations. In particular, the use of the media to incite hostility and violence among the various population groups constitutes a clear violation of the provisions of article 20 of the Covenant.

### Suggestions and Recommendations

The Committee urges the State party to initiate without delay a process of national reconciliation. This process should be accompanied by various specific measures, such as the establishment of commissions of inquiry made up of members of each of the country's population groups. Impartial foreign observers could participate in the inquiries in order to identify those responsible for gross violations of human rights in the autumn of 1993, to bring them to trial and punish them, and to remove all persons involved in such crimes from the various State bodies, particularly the army, the police, the gendarmerie and the security forces. The victims and their families should also be compensated.

The Committee suggests using the media to promote national reconciliation and harmony among Burundi's various population groups. Strenuous efforts should be made to educate and inform the whole of Burundi society regarding human rights. This campaign should take account of Burundi's traditions and customs, including the role of mothers in educating their children.

The Committee believes that it is essential to take urgent measures to reorganize public institutions, so as to ensure balanced participation by all population groups in the conduct of public affairs and to permit all citizens, without distinction, to have access to public service, in the administration, the army, the police, the gendarmerie, the security forces and the judiciary. In addition, the Committee considers that the army should be brought under the effective control of the civilian authorities. The judiciary and the civil service should also be opened immediately to those groups, so that they can be seen by the population to be impartial and representative of the population as a whole and in order to restore some degree of public confidence in national institutions.

In view of the considerable difficulties encountered by the State party in implementing the Covenant, the gross violations of human rights which occurred in autumn 1993, and the serious danger of a recurrence of such violations, the Committee is of the view that, in its efforts at internal pacification and national reconciliation, Burundi should receive the resolute support of the international community.

The Committee recommends that the High Commissioner for Human Rights should continue to make strenuous efforts to help Burundi avoid any future recurrence of gross violations of human rights, for example, by encouraging the establishment of international investigation machinery.

The Committee encourages the High Commissioner for Human Rights and the United Nations Centre for Human Rights in their efforts to provide advisory services and technical assistance in the field of human rights.

The Committee, for its part, is ready to respond constructively to any appropriate request for assistance by the Government of Burundi, provided that it is clear and accompanied by a firm resolve on the part of the Government to adopt the measures necessary for the effective implementation of the Covenant.

## Conclusions and Recommendations

*The problem and prospects for solutions.* The problems of internal displacement in Burundi emanate from the ethnic conflict, mostly between the Tutsi and the Hutu, largely orchestrated by their political elites. Durable solutions, therefore, have to be political with respect for fundamental human rights principles. Finding a formula that is mutually agreeable has proved exceedingly difficult as the conflict has come to assume a zero-sum nature.

The main elements of the confrontation between Hutu and Tutsi are closely correlated to the history of the nation, as described above. With remarkable consistency, this history was recounted over and over, during the Representative's mission, highlighting in particular instances of ethnically motivated assassinations of political leaders and the intercommunal violence and massacres that followed them. The Burundian especially lamented the demise of the monarchy which had symbolized the nation and maintained the unity of the country through a complex system of patron-client favours and obligations. Closely associated with the demise of the monarchy is a virtual collapse of the traditional system of social administration and leadership at all levels, leaving an open field for political entrepreneurs for whom there appeared to be a generalized mistrust throughout the country.

The nature of the ethnic composition of the country and the lopsided manner in which power is ethnically distributed seems to define the options available to the Burundians. As noted earlier, since the two major ethnic groups are intricately interwoven, partitioning the country along ethnic lines would be out of the question. And although the Hutu are an overwhelming majority favoured by electoral democracy, real power of the State in terms of the military and the economy remains firmly entrenched with the Tutsi. Short of a self-destructive violence which cannot leave either side victorious, functional compromise appears to be an imperative, with a view to long-term reform and emphasis on education in the meantime. This seems to centre on three major areas: land, the military, and the judiciary. The peace test has already failed once. It cannot fail for a second time.

Even in the case that peace is achieved, it can be expected that certain elements will continue to foment insecurity through terrorist actions and armed attacks. Disarmament of militias must therefore become a priority for the Government. Spontaneous violence between Tutsi and Hutu will also probably continue. The risk that these events will degenerate largely depends on the role and the attitude of the army. For this reason, it is important that the leadership of the forces of law and order maintain control of the armed forces, lest anarchy result. At the same time, the military must become more representative of the entire population.

Land issues will continue to have an impact on politics and stability. The management of land vacated by returning Rwandan refugees to Rwanda (of the old, mostly Tutsi, caseload) will be part of the political debate: tensions could rise with regard to whether this land should be allocated to Burundian returnees (Hutu) or to displaced persons (Tutsi). The issue of land and the position of returnees and displaced persons need to be addressed, with recommendations on what legal reforms may be necessary and what administrative structures should be put in place to ensure impartial solutions to this intricate problem. Given the political implications any action in this field will have, assistance should be sought from United Nations agencies and other relevant expertise.

In terms of patterns of displacement Burundi presents an anomalous picture. In most other countries visited by the Representative the displaced tend to be members of disadvantaged groups and in general do not enjoy a special favour from the system. In the case of Burundi, however, the reverse is often true. The fact that Tutsi were in camps, rather than being evidence of their disfavour, was because they needed protection by the army. Paradoxically, however, being favoured has often been a source of misery for the displaced Tutsi. This is a fact that those in charge of the affairs of the country should realize and take responsibility for. On the other hand, politicians of all sides need to unequivocally support peace in place of hatred, and endeavour to liberate politics from ethnic cleavages and divisiveness.

If political stability holds, displaced populations will have more assurances to return home and start planting again, in which case assistance will be necessary for the reconstruction of destroyed houses and the planting of seeds and food crops. Any further psycho-social assistance will depend on such stability, since it requires a certain amount of hope for a better future, and the existence of an environment in which confidence in oneself and in one's neighbour can be rebuilt.

At the same time, reconstruction is inconceivable in a hostile environment. For that reason projects of pacification, recohabitation and reconciliation which have already been initiated warrant more support and involvement by the international community, as well as frequent assessments and evaluations to ensure that their objectives are being met. Other peace initiatives should be actively explored, for instance, the possibility of promoting ethnic reconciliation through radio programmes, since the "rumour machine" is extremely powerful. How life in the communes can again be organized and whether the institution of ubusingantahe can be resurrected are at this stage difficult to judge. The need for a profound research in the area of community building in Burundi would seem indispensable. Non-governmental organizations could play an important role in promoting inter-ethnic dialogue at all levels.

A peculiarity of current social life in Burundi is the almost complete absence of social projects or plans for such projects. This will have to be changed, especially as far as the youth is concerned. In the words of one minister, the Burundian rarely take an initiative on their own, but as members of a group they can be very energetic. This should be channelled through the creation of grass-roots organizations to support the justice system or for purposes of economic rehabilitation and development.

*International human rights standards.* There can be no doubt that the civilian Government is positively disposed towards the protection of human rights. In 1994, it sponsored a resolution on the human rights situation in Burundi and also acceded to seven human rights instruments. On the other hand, lack of progress in investigations and hostilities towards international missions of inquiry can be taken to mean that it also opposes a full disclosure of facts related to violence and human rights violations.

The analysis under chapter II.B shows that respect for human rights is especially vulnerable in Burundi. In addition, according to the Committee on the Elimination of Racial Discrimination no effective remedy for human rights violations exists and there is no effective prohibition of incitement to violence either in the armed forces and the police or among the general public. Strengthening human rights law and its implementation should be a central element in the new Government's policies.

For the reasons stated above, derogations from international human rights obligations, where permissible, should be resorted to only in extreme cases; the principle of proportionality should, in such cases of absolute necessity, be strictly observed and procedural requirement for such derogations should be followed meticulously.

Burundi should also accede to the Genocide Convention as a matter of priority. The concept of individual responsibility as enshrined in the Genocide Convention and further elaborated in connection with the notion of "crimes against humanity", could become an effective deterrent.

*Women and children.* Investing in the social and psychological rehabilitation of the women affected by the crisis is an important factor to be taken into account by the international relief and development agencies. For instance, women have rarely participated in the perpetration of massacres and have been targets of killings less often; for these reasons they remain the stable element of the nuclear family and the society. Women are furthermore the centre of subsistence activity in the camps and are playing a major role in the reconstruction of their homes. Since many women have become widows as a result of the violence, and displaced women heads-of-household are particularly numerous, their economic survival, and that of their children, will depend on their being able to earn a living and receive education and training if needed. Their being able to own and inherit land should also become a priority. Investment in the youth, which consists of over 50 per cent of the country, and not just the educated youth, appears to be a priority, if, for example, the formation of militias and guerrillas is to be curbed.

The role that education of women and children can play in this domain cannot be overemphasized. Notably, the adult literacy rate in 1990 was 50 per cent, with twice as many women as men being illiterate. Peace education projects, such as the ones undertaken by UNICEF, merit further support and follow-up. Those "women's groups for peace" which are already operational should be supported. Legal measures to improve the status of women especially as far as property and inheritance rights are concerned are urgently needed. Support in needs assessment and project implementation for any of the above could be provided by the AFWIC programme of UNIFEM, which is based in Nairobi, and which has gained expertise, over the last few years, in the protection and empowerment of African women who have been displaced by crises. The World Bank and development agencies should be engaged as well.

*Human rights activities.* Education in human rights at all levels of the civil and military administration is crucial at this point in the history of the country. The project administered by the Advisory Services Branch of the Centre for Human Rights must be given more international staff to fulfill its stated goals in the promotion and protection of human rights. The project should be implemented in close cooperation with the international agencies in the country, in particular with UNHCR and UNICEF, and should be coordinated with the various activities undertaken by the office of the Special Representative of the Secretary-General. It should aim at capacity building within the Government and the provision of assistance with administration of resources and sound governance. Needs assessment missions such as the one undertaken by the Centre for Human Rights in September 1994 for the provision of technical assistance for the strengthening of law enforcement must be welcomed and encouraged and their recommendations must be given serious consideration.

In addition to this project there is also a need for a small-scale international presence which will monitor the humanitarian and human rights situation in the country, especially the situation of the internally displaced, liaise with the other international agencies and advise both the Special Representative of the Secretary-General and the Representative on internally displaced persons on the situation pertaining to their respective mandates, and maintain open channels of communication between these actors. Such an office could provide the necessary information to the Secretary-General for his annual reports to the Commission on Human Rights on the human rights situation in Burundi as well as the Representative on internally displaced persons and maintain links with other international and regional human rights forums.

Apart from the proposed small-scale presence, a monitoring mission has been called for by international NGOs and by the Special Representative of the Secretary-General on Burundi, which would coordinate the responses of the United Nations and the OAU, supplement the OAU mission in the country and act as a dissuasive presence, through reporting and intervention with the authorities to protect individuals and to prevent a deterioration of the human rights situation, and to facilitate by international observers in the country the process of national reconciliation. Questions were raised, however, about the deployment of an extensive monitoring mission at this time. Some felt that large numbers of international "witnesses" would be received with hostility and could jeopardize the presence of international agencies in the country.

At the same time there seems to be widespread agreement on the need for a formal investigation into the coup d'état, and the ensuing massacres, of October 1993, so that perpetrators can be identified and punished. This, however, poses a dilemma. On the one hand, the cause of peace requires broadening the bases of national consensus and reconciliation. On the other hand, identifying and punishing those responsible for the massacres seem to be necessary for the restoration of confidence in the rule of law and the judicial system. Chronic feelings of revenge and a deeply entrenched tradition of killing as the only way of dealing with the "enemy" could best be addressed after such measures. The "Convention of Government" requires that no one who is implicated in any way whatsoever in these events could be a member of the Government or the National Assembly or hold a high-level position in Government, a requirement which cannot be fully satisfied without establishing the facts and allocating responsibility. In addressing this issue, the need for action should be balanced with the sensitivities involved and the serious political repercussions that such inquiries could have, even before any conclusions have been reached or made public. In this connection, the South African Truth Commission and the Tribunal on Rwanda provide models worth considering. One could also envisage a national judicial investigation made up of members of each of the country's population groups, with the assistance and collaboration of international experts/consultants.

In these human rights activities, it is important to bear in mind that the internally displaced and dispersed populations are particularly vulnerable, being virtual hostages in the conflict. Whether they are the displaced Tutsis threatened by the majority Hutu, or the dispersed Hutu threatened by the minority Tutsis with the power of the military behind them, both groups fall into a vacuum of State responsibility. The precariousness of the situation is compounded by the cleavage within the State between the elected Government and the army, which is normally the arm of the Government. This is a situation which clearly calls for international attention, protection, and assistance. Indeed, the need goes beyond the normal human rights procedures and may warrant a more assertive international action in cooperation with all the pivotal actors.

*International humanitarian, peace-making and peace-keeping operations.* Resources for humanitarian aid and for other emergency responses in Burundi will have to be strengthened in order to meet ongoing needs, which for the moment are not expected to diminish. Since reductions in emergency aid can have serious political repercussions, they have to be avoided. Assistance will be required for the reactivation of the regular marketing channels for seeds and other farm inputs, detailed assessments of the affected populations, and with the resettlement of the displaced, where possible. International presence and aid are not evenly distributed throughout the country; Muramvya, for instance, seems to have been neglected by the agencies. Increased assistance must be connected to assurance of security for the humanitarian agencies both by the Government and the military.

It is important to caution that international humanitarian aid issues are being exploited by political parties for political ends. Reductions in food aid to displaced persons or reluctance on the part of international agencies to become involved with assistance to them is seen through ethnic lenses and criticized. International agencies find themselves struggling to avoid becoming pawns in the political game. In doing so they risk allowing the situation to distort their own assessment of humanitarian needs. In other words, while it

is often true that the Tutsi displaced may be less needy in terms of food and security, and that their fears may be exaggerated, it cannot be excluded that in certain cases there will be serious and real problems. The Representative fully appreciates the dilemmas frequently facing the agencies. But whatever the difficulties and shortcomings, it is worth noting that all government officials expressed appreciation for the increased international attention the country had been receiving lately.

It has to be noted also that the international agencies appeared to have been caught somewhat by surprise by the crisis of internal displacement in Burundi. This is understandable in a situation where competing needs are enormous and increasing in the region as a whole. Resources were directed towards addressing the needs in Goma and other camps for Rwandan refugees. Agencies in Burundi were left with fewer stocks and less means to address the humanitarian situation there and the dilemmas of how to prioritize the needs and which persons to care for first.

This is where the issue of mandate becomes crucial. With no one agency specifically mandated to cater for the internally displaced, comprehensiveness in addressing their needs in cases such as Burundi will remain elusive. It is not only a matter of allocating resources but also of assessing the true nature of the problem in the country. For this reason, it was suggested to the Representative that he dispatch a delegate to "advocate for the displaced", in other words, to pool information on needs assessments and current activities undertaken by the international agencies and the NGOs. The Representative considers this proposal as meriting serious consideration by the Commission.

In any event, representatives of the agencies suggested on various occasions that inter-agency cooperation could be strengthened to achieve at least a better assessment of needs, in particular in health and sanitation. There could also be a geographic distribution of responsibilities. International presence could become more visible in the camps of the displaced, while a meeting could be called with the participation of the Minister of Social Action, the agencies and the donors, to discuss possible ways of addressing these needs. Assistance to and protection for the internally displaced should be increased, while at the same time the authorities, in coordination with humanitarian agencies, should take the primary responsibility for placing administrative structures in the camps and for organizing the distribution of relief assistance. Humanitarian agencies should nevertheless supervise these arrangements and the deployment of monitors to encourage return, as in Rwanda, should also be considered. The agencies could help with the provision of technical expertise and know-how, not only for providing protection and assistance during the emergency phase, but also for facilitating reintegration, rehabilitation, and the resumption of normal life. While the creation of local NGOs should be encouraged and supported, international NGOs should also be urged to become involved in all these phases.

The various problems mentioned earlier with regard to the inevitable "politicization" of the provision of humanitarian assistance imply that such assistance has to be linked with sufficient international presence. The fear was, however, expressed that large-scale international military escorts would not be welcome and could heighten tensions and expose expatriate and local staff, unless it was decisive, well coordinated, and adequate to meet the need for effective humanitarian action.

Indeed, one heavily debated issue in Burundi is that of international military intervention to prevent another massacre or genocide similar to the one experienced in Rwanda. Whereas the parties of the majority have favoured such an intervention as a means to protect themselves, the army vehemently opposes it because it would mean loss of military power (the only way the Tutsi minority feels they can protect themselves). There is no easy answer to this question, although international observers have pointed out that peace solutions have to be found within the country and that no amount of outside force will have any impact in the long-term search for peace. Such military action is in any case very unlikely in the present international climate. Nevertheless, the potential for such action can have a persuasive force that should not be underestimated, if only as a last resort.

The international community must retain its unified approach to the problems currently facing the country. Until now several declarations by the Security Council, the European Union and the OAU have expressed their support for the moderate forces and have called for an early resumption and conclusion of the negotiations. A peaceful settlement and the re-establishment of peace have also been posed as the condition for the approval of loans and other development aid. Donors and other countries, as well as the international organizations, must continue to emphasize that the international community will simply not sit by and watch another tragedy of the magnitude of the massacres in Rwanda. Any number of legal and political options, ranging from individual sanctions to outright military intervention, are available to the Security Council and the General Assembly, which have already been seized with the situation in the country and are watching developments closely.

In addition to emergency preparedness and relief assistance, international agencies are already considering how to resume more long-term development work. Donors will have to consider that rapid economic development to counter unemployment and other economic hardships will be an important factor in the maintenance of peace.

It has been suggested that a comprehensive approach is one in which a variety of different but concerted measures are brought to bear in the effort to break the cycle of exile, return, internal displacement and exile. The ultimate goal of such an approach is to promote the overall stability of the society and respect for the rights of its citizens, and thus to remedy the factors causing displacement. The maintenance of peace and security, the promotion of economic and social development and respect for human rights must be considered essential elements of any fully comprehensive humanitarian approach. For this reason an analysis of the precise functions of all the components of the United Nations activities mentioned above (political, humanitarian, human rights, developmental) would seem indispensable. Actors in those sectors should benefit from the presence of the Special Representative of the Secretary-General for Burundi and his coordinating capacity.

*Regional approaches.* Burundi forms part of an entire region affected by a common problem of displacement, to which a solution also implies the need for a subregional approach. For this reason it has been recommended that a broader approach to the question of national reconciliation should be strengthened and that a subregional conference to that effect should be convened. This initiative should be fully supported. The issue of displacement should form part and parcel of any such conference, as well as other measures or activities undertaken by the United Nations since refugees are threatening to become one of the most critical and complicated problems in Central Africa.

Regional approaches on the part of the United Nations should be further developed. At the moment, separate structures have been put in place in each of the countries to deal with the respective situations. In this connection, it could be useful to evaluate the role of the Special Envoys for Rwanda and Burundi of the Secretary-General and of the High Commissioner for Refugees in order to design ways of promoting comprehensive regional approaches.

The Organization of African Unity should also be urged to explore appropriate regional initiatives.

*Concluding comment.* The case of Burundi provides significant insights into the generic problem of internal displacement and the diverse ways in which it is manifested. When viewed comparatively with the situation in the other countries visited by the Representative of the Secretary-General, insights from the Burundi case become particularly instructive and useful in developing approaches to the problems in their appropriate national contexts.

In several of the countries visited—for instance, Somalia, Sudan, Sri Lanka, and the former Yugoslavia—the displaced were identifiable as large clusters of people in camps, uprooted from their homes, and divested of all their resource-base, as a result of which they were entirely dependent on humanitarian assistance and uncertain protection from the controlling authorities. In El Salvador, on the other hand, in the aftermath of the peace agreement, the internally displaced were largely villagers living in rural areas where they were still constrained by lack of land and vital services and under precarious security conditions. In Colombia, the displaced found their security in merging into the community to avoid being clearly identified. But since the communities into which they merged were equally poor and inadequately protected, the plight of the internally displaced and that of their host communities did not differ much. In a way, Burundi brought these various forms of internal displacement together. The displaced in the army-protected camps represented the typical form seen in many countries, while the dispersed were somewhat comparable to the displaced of El Salvador and Colombia.

There were, however, distinctive features to the situation of both the displaced and the dispersed in Burundi. Unlike the displaced in other countries whose source of insecurity was often both the military and the rebel forces in conflict situations, the displaced in Burundi were protected by the army. The dispersed, on the other hand, avoided the security forces for their own protection. But unlike the displaced of El Salvador or Colombia, they did not disappear into the rural villages or communities; instead, they disappeared into the hills, the marshes, and the valleys, away from the roads.

What accounts for the distinctive features in the Burundi case is the division between the Government, which is identified with the majority Hutu, and the army, which is identified with the minority Tutsi. Since the effective tool of control is the army, the Tutsi displaced depended on it for protection while the Hutus hid from it. The military is normally the effective arm of the Government; in Burundi, the two were on opposite sides.

This cleavage between the elected Government of the majority and the army representing the minority made Burundi a good example of the vacuum of responsibility normally associated with a national identity crisis. While this vacuum usually means that the Government or any other controlling authority fails to provide adequate protection and assistance for those under its sovereignty, in the case of Burundi, the crisis is a dual one because of the division between the Government and the army, with each providing protection and assistance to its group, while constituting a threat to the other group.

Ironically, both sides feel sufficiently threatened by the other and look to the international community for protection, although their precise needs, requests, and expectations differ with their particular circumstances. The Government and therefore the majority Hutu would go beyond assistance to emphasize protection, if need be through international military intervention, while the army and therefore the Tutsi would be content with material assistance and be strongly opposed to military presence.

Burundi thus represents a situation which needs international involvement to help both sides of a divided nation to provide protection and assistance to all its citizens and to help the country restore peace, harmony, a sense of collective belonging to the nation, and a common purpose in nation-building. It is a country where, despite the zero-sum character of the conflict, there is room for considerable creativity in addressing the national crisis. But this creativity has to be stimulated or facilitated by the mediatory role of outsiders.

It is noteworthy that these cleavages, though deeply entrenched, are more fictional or mythical than real, if physical or cultural characteristics are the determining factors. Besides, considerable intermarriage is said to have taken place. Whenever the Representative questioned the Burundians whether they could distinguish between the Tutsis and the Hutus, the answer was always highly qualified: Yes, but with a significant margin of error, sometimes specified as between 30–35 per cent. And as pointed out earlier, all Burundians speak the same language and are residentially intermingled. When the Representative asked whether there was an intellectual movement in the country to explode the divisive myths of ethnic identity, the answer was in the negative. The explanation given was that the genocidal massacres had deprived the nation of at least a generation of educated men and women who could have provided intellectual leadership in this area. As a result, the present leadership was said to be unusually young, and of course overburdened with pressing political problems and crises. Nevertheless, when pointed out to them, the Burundians easily recognize that much of what divides them is a function of perceptions that only partially reflect or explain their complex reality.

Perceptions are, however, real and often provide a compelling basis for action. Nevertheless, perceptions change with time and contexts. What the international community can do to assist Burundi is to redefine and restructure the context to allow alternative visions for the nation to come into focus. In many ways, the challenge for the people of Burundi is to restructure previously stratified power relationships to foster equity among ethnic groups while also building on the constructive aspects of their past. A salient aspect of this past is that Tutsis and Hutus lived together as neighbours, intermarried, and saw themselves first and foremost as Burundians, bound together by common history, language, culture, and now the challenge of nationhood. Protecting and assisting the internally displaced is only a microcosm of the challenge. Burundians need to feel that their Government and its army will protect them all equally and provide them with assistance without discrimination on any ground, not least ethnicity, and that the international community stands ready and willing to cooperate towards that common goal.

In his report prepared for the 1996 session of the General Assembly (E/CN.4/1996/16), the Sprecial Rapporteur outlines the overall situation of human rights in Burundi and provides some keys to understanding the concept of "ethnic racism" and the policies deriving from it.

His recommendations include (1) consolidation of democratic institutions in order to eradicate impunity; (2) measures to put an end to insecurity; (3) the strengthening of civil society; and (4) the promotion of the enjoyment of human rights. In particular he proposes that the work of the Centre for Human Rights office in Bujumbura should be considerably strengthened, not only with a view to increasing the number of persons or groups in Burundi that are protected or covered by its programs but also to prevent possible human rights abuses.

***BIBLIOGRAPHY.*** Amnesty International. *Burundi: Killings of Children by Government Troops.* London: 1988. NGO report, in English.

————. *Religious Intolerance.* London: 1986. NGO report, in English.

Breytenbach, W. J. "Inter-Ethnic Conflict in Africa," in *Case Studies on Human Rights and Fundamental Freedoms: A World Survey,* vol. 1, ed. W. A. Veenhoven, pp. 309–331. The Hague, the Netherlands: Martinus Nijhoff: 1975. Collection of articles, in English.

Human Rights Watch. "Burundi," in *Human Rights Watch World Report, 1995* pp. 12–16. New York: 1995. NGO report, in English.

International Federation of Human Rights. *Burundi Rapport: Commission internationale d'enquête sur les violations des droits de l'homme depuis le 21 octobre 1993* (Burundi: Report of an International Investigation on Human Rights Violations since October 21, 1993). Paris: 1994. NGO factfinding report, in French.

U.S. Department of State. *Country Reports on Human Rights Practices for 1988.* Washington, D.C.: Government Printing Office, 1989. Government report, in English.

**BUTLER, NICHOLAS MURRAY (1862–1947).** Nicholas Butler was co-winner of the 1931 **NOBEL PEACE PRIZE.** Born in New Jersey, he received a doctorate in 1884 from Columbia College (later University); in 1902, he became president of that university and remained in that position until his death. Throughout his long public career, he worked to reform the American educational system. Among his accomplishments were the establishment of the Teachers' College; the founding and editing of *The Educational Review,* and reports on state and local educational systems. He published *Education in the United States* in 1910.

Butler was responsible for persuading Andrew Carnegie to establish the Carnegie Endowment for International Peace with a gift of $10 million. During his

35-year association with the endowment, Butler served as head of its section on international education and communication, founded the European branch of the endowment, and was its president from 1925 to 1945.

***BIBLIOGRAPHY.*** Gray, Tony. *Champions of Peace.* London: Paddington Press, 1976.

Schlessinger, Bernard S., and June H. Schlessinger, eds. *Who's Who of Nobel Prize Winners.* Phoenix, AZ, USA: Oryx Press, 1991.

# C

**CAIRO DECLARATION ON HUMAN RIGHTS IN ISLAM (1990).** On 5 August 1990, Member States of the Islamic Conference, meeting in Cairo, Egypt, adopted the Cairo Declaration on Human Rights in Islam, the text of which was later circulated as a document of the UN **GENERAL ASSEMBLY** (A/45/421) and of the World Conference on Human Rights (A/CONF.157/PC/35), which met in Vienna, Austria, in 1993. The text underscores the central role that the concepts of fundamental rights and universal freedoms play in the Islamic religion.

The Member States of the Organization of the Islamic Conference,

Reaffirming the civilizing and historical role of the Islamic Ummah which God made the best nation that has given mankind a universal and well-balanced civilization in which harmony is established between this life and the hereafter and knowledge is combined with faith; and the role that this Ummah should play to guide a humanity confused by competing trends and ideologies and to provide solutions to the chronic problems of this materialistic civilization,

Wishing to contribute to the efforts of mankind to assert human rights, to protect man from exploitation and persecution, and to affirm his freedom and right to a dignified life in accordance with the Islamic Shari'ah,

Convinced that mankind which has reached an advanced stage in materialistic science is still, and shall remain, in dire need of faith to support its civilization and of a self-motivating force to guard its rights,

Believing that fundamental rights and universal freedoms in Islam are an integral part of the Islamic religion and that no one as a matter of principle has the right to suspend them in whole or in part or violate or ignore them in as much as they are binding divine commandments, which are contained in the Revealed Books of God and were sent through the last of His Prophets to complete the preceding divine messages thereby making their observance an act of worship and their neglect or violation an abominable sin, and accordingly every person is individually responsible—and the Ummah collectively responsible—for their safeguard,

Proceeding from the above-mentioned principles,

Declare the following:

*Article 1.* (a) All human beings form one family whose members are united by submission to God and descent from Adam. All men are equal in terms of basic human dignity and basic obligations and responsibilities, without any discrimination on the grounds of race, colour, language, sex, religious belief, political affiliation, social status or other considerations. True faith is the guarantee for enhancing such dignity along the path to human perfection.

(b) All human beings are God's subjects, and the most loved by Him are those who are most useful to the rest of His subjects, and no one has superiority over another except on the basis of piety and good deeds.

*Article 2.* (a) Life is a God-given gift and the right to life is guaranteed to every human being. It is the duty of individuals, societies and States to protect this right from any violation, and it is prohibited to take away life except for a Shari'ah-prescribed reason.

(b) It is forbidden to resort to such means as may result in the genocidal annihilation of mankind.

(c) The preservation of human life throughout the term of time willed by God is a duty prescribed by Shari'ah.

(d) Safety from bodily harm is a guaranteed right. It is the duty of the State to safeguard it, and it is prohibited to breach it without a Shari'ah-prescribed reason.

*Article 3.* (a) In the event of the use of force and in case of armed conflict, it is not permissible to kill non-belligerents such as old men, women and children. The wounded and the sick shall have the right to medical treatment; and prisoners of war shall have the right to be fed, sheltered and clothed. It is prohibited to mutilate dead bodies. It is a duty to exchange prisoners of war and to arrange visits or reunions of the families separated by the circumstances of war.

(b) It is prohibited to fell trees, to damage crops or livestock, and to destroy the enemy's civilian buildings and installations by shelling, blasting or any other means.

*Article 4.* Every human being is entitled to inviolability and the protection of his good name and honour during his life and after his death. The State and society shall protect his remains and burial place.

*Article 5.* (a) The family is the foundation of society, and marriage is the basis of its formation. Men and women have the right to marriage, and no restrictions stemming from race, colour or nationality shall prevent them from enjoying this right.

(b) Society and the State shall remove all obstacles to marriage and shall facilitate marital procedure. They shall ensure family protection and welfare.

*Article 6.* (a) Woman is equal to man in human dignity, and has rights to enjoy as well as duties to perform; she has her own civil entity and financial independence, and the right to retain her name and lineage.

(b) The husband is responsible for the support and welfare of the family.

*Article 7.* (a) As of the moment of birth, every child has rights due from the parents, society and the State to be accorded proper nursing, education and material, hygienic and moral care. Both the fetus and the mother must be protected and accorded special care.

(b) Parents and those in such like capacity have the right to choose the type of education they desire for their children, provided they take into consideration the interest and future of the children in accordance with ethical values and the principles of the Shari'ah.

(c) Both parents are entitled to certain rights from their children, and relatives are entitled to rights from their kin, in accordance with the tenets of the Shari'ah.

*Article 8.* Every human being has the right to enjoy his legal capacity in terms of both obligation and commitment. Should this capacity be lost or impaired, he shall be represented by his guardian.

*Article 9.* (a) The quest for knowledge is an obligation, and the provision of education is a duty for society and the State. The State shall ensure the availability of ways and means to acquire education and shall guarantee educational diversity in the interest of society so as to enable man to be acquainted with the religion of Islam and the facts of the universe for the benefit of mankind.

(b) Every human being has the right to receive both religious and worldly education from the various institutions of education and guidance, including the family, the school, the university, the media, etc., and in such an integrated and balanced manner as to develop his personality, strengthen his faith in God and promote his respect for and defence of both rights and obligations.

*Article 10.* Islam is the religion of unspoiled nature. It is prohibited to exercise any form of compulsion on man or to exploit his poverty or ignorance in order to convert him to another religion or to atheism.

*Article 11.* (a) Human beings are born free, and no one has the right to enslave, humiliate, oppress or exploit them, and there can be no subjugation but to God the Most-High.

(b) Colonialism of all types being one of the most evil forms of enslavement is totally prohibited. Peoples suffering from colonialism have the full right to freedom and self-determination. It is the duty of all States and peoples to support the struggle of colonized peoples for the liquidation of all forms of colonialism and occupation, and all States and peoples have the right to preserve their independent identity and exercise control over their wealth and natural resources.

*Article 12.* Every man shall have the right, within the framework of Shari'ah, to free movement and to select his place of residence whether inside or outside his country and, if persecuted, is entitled to seek asylum in another country. The country of refuge shall ensure his protection until he reaches safety, unless asylum is motivated by an act which Shari'ah regards as a crime.

*Article 13.* Work is a right guaranteed by the State and society for each person able to work. Everyone shall be free to choose the work that suits him best and which serves his interests and those of society. The employee shall have the right to safety and security as well as to all other social guarantees. He may neither be assigned work beyond his capacity nor be subjected to compulsion or exploited or harmed in any way. He shall be entitled—without any discrimination between males and females—to fair wages for his work without delay, as well as to the holidays, allowances and promotions which he deserves. For his part, he shall be required to be dedicated and meticulous in his work. Should workers and employers disagree on any matter, the State shall intervene to settle the dispute and have the grievances redressed, the rights confirmed and justice enforced without bias.

*Article 14.* Everyone shall have the right to legitimate gains without monopolization, deceit or harm to oneself or to others. Usury (riba) is absolutely prohibited.

*Article 15.* (a) Everyone shall have the right to own property acquired in a legitimate way, and shall be entitled to the rights of ownership, without prejudice to oneself, others or

to society in general. Expropriation is not permissible except for the requirements of public interest and upon payment of immediate and fair compensation.

(b) Confiscation and seizure of property is prohibited except for a necessity dictated by law.

*Article 16.* Everyone shall have the right to enjoy the fruits of his scientific, literary, artistic or technical production and the right to protect the moral and material interests stemming therefrom, provided that such production is not contrary to the principles of Shari'ah.

*Article 17.* (a) Everyone shall have the right to live in a clean environment, away from vice and moral corruption, an environment that would foster his self-development; and it is incumbent upon the State and society in general to afford that right.

(b) Everyone shall have the right to medical and social care, and to all public amenities provided by society and the State within the limits of their available resources.

(c) The State shall ensure the right of the individual to a decent living which will enable him to meet all his requirements and those of his dependents, including food, clothing, housing, education, medical care and all other basic needs.

*Article 18.* (a) Everyone shall have the right to live in security for himself, his religion, his dependents, his honour and his property.

(b) Everyone shall have the right to privacy in the conduct of his private affairs, in his home, among his family, with regard to his property and his relationships. It is not permitted to spy on him, to place him under surveillance or to besmirch his good name. The State shall protect him from arbitrary interference.

(c) A private residence is inviolable in all cases. It will not be entered without permission from its inhabitants or in any unlawful manner, nor shall it be demolished or confiscated and its dwellers evicted.

*Article 19.* (a) All individuals are equal before the law, without distinction between the ruler and the ruled.

(b) The right to resort to justice is guaranteed to everyone.

(c) Liability is in essence personal.

(d) There shall be no crime or punishment except as provided for in the Shari'ah.

(e) A defendant is innocent until his guilt is proven in a fair trial in which he shall be given all the guarantees of defence.

*Article 20.* It is not permitted without legitimate reason to arrest an individual, or restrict his freedom, to exile or to punish him. It is not permitted to subject him to physical or psychological torture or to any form of humiliation, cruelty or indignity. Nor is it permitted to subject an individual to medical or scientific experimentation without his consent or at the risk of his health or of his life. Nor is it permitted to promulgate emergency laws that would provide executive authority for such actions.

*Article 21.* Taking hostages under any form or for any purpose is expressly forbidden.

*Article 22.* (a) Everyone shall have the right to express his opinion freely in such manner as would not be contrary to the principles of the Shari'ah.

(b) Everyone shall have the right to advocate what is right, and propagate what is good, and warn against what is wrong and evil according to the norms of Islamic Shari'ah.

(c) Information is a vital necessity to society. It may not be exploited or misused in such a way as may violate sanctities and the dignity of Prophets, undermine moral and ethical values or disintegrate, corrupt or harm society or weaken its faith.

(d) It is not permitted to arouse nationalistic or doctrinal hatred or to do anything that may be an incitement to any form of racial discrimination.

*Article 23.* (a) Authority is a trust; and abuse or malicious exploitation thereof is absolutely prohibited, so that fundamental human rights may be guaranteed.

(b) Everyone shall have the right to participate, directly or indirectly, in the administration of his country's public affairs. He shall also have the right to assume public office in accordance with the provisions of Shari'ah.

*Article 24.* All the rights and freedoms stipulated in this Declaration are subject to the Islamic Shari'ah.

*Article 25.* The Islamic Shari'ah is the only source of reference for the explanation or clarification of any of the articles of this Declaration.

**CAMBODIA.** The kingdom of Cambodia is located in southeastern Asia, situated on the Indochinese Peninsula, facing the Gulf of Thailand. It has borders with Laos, Thailand, and Vietnam. It achieved independence from France in 1949 and became a member of the United Nations in 1955 as Democratic Kampuchea. Its population is estimated to be 8,928,000. Ethnic groups include the Khmer (90%), Chinese (5%), and others including Chams, Vietnamese, and Burmese (5%). Languages commonly in use include Khmer (official), Chinese, French, and Vietnamese. Religions practiced include Buddhism (Theravada), Islam, and Animism. Literacy is estimated at 48%.

Once a part of the extensive Khmer Kingdom, which covered nearly all of Southeast Asia, Cambodia was in danger of being overrun by the neighboring Vietnamese until the French combined it with Laos and Vietnam to form French Indochina. After occupation by the Japanese during World War II, Cambodia achieved independence within the French Union in 1949. As a result of the French–Indochinese war, the Cambodians, under Prince Sihanouk, won full military control of their country in 1953.

Incursions of Vietnamese into Cambodian territory and anti-Vietnamese riots provoked a coup that ended the Sihanouk regime in 1970. As the Vietnamese moved deeper into the country, the new government, headed by Lon Nol, was threatened until U.S. President Richard Nixon sent Vietnamese and American troops to clear them from the border areas. The Vietnam peace agreement of 1973 provided for the withdrawal of all foreign forces from Cambodia; however, sporadic fighting continued until 1975, when the Cambodian government collapsed.

In December 1975, The People's Republic of Kampuchea was established under a new constitution, under a State presidium headed by Pol Pot. Within the next two years, more than two million Cambodians

died as a result of the brutality and other human rights violations of the new regime.

On Christmas Day 1978, Vietnamese forces launched a full invasion of Cambodia, capturing Phnom Penh on 7 January and driving the remnants of Cambodia's army toward the Thai borders. Constitutional political processes were suspended in 1978, when the country was occupied by Vietnamese troops and a pro-Vietnamese government was installed.

Between 1975 and 1980, thousands of Khmer fled first the terror of Pol Pot and then the attack and occupation by Vietnamese military forces. More than 200,000 were admitted to Thailand as refugees before the border was closed in 1980, more than 205,000 were accepted by other countries, and about 140,000 were admitted to the United States.

Beginning in 1980, fleeing Cambodians lived in camps along the Thai–Cambodian border. In 1984–85, a Vietnamese attack forced 225,000 of them into Thailand, where they were granted temporary asylum. Food, shelter, and medical care are provided to this population by joint efforts of the Royal Thai Government, the United Nations Border Relief Operation, the **INTERNATIONAL COMMITTEE OF THE RED CROSS,** and private voluntary agencies.

From 1978 to 1991, no single government controlled all of Cambodia. A coalition government in exile, formed in June 1982 and headed by Prince Samdech Norodom Sihanouk, was recognized by the United Nations; it represented an alliance that ex-President Sihanouk formed with his former Prime Minister Son Sann and Pol Pot's representative Khieu Samphan to oppose the regime installed in Phnom Penh by the Vietnamese. That regime, headed by President Heng Samrin, General Secretary of the Kampuchean People's Revolutionary Party, administered the machinery of government and controlled most of the territory of the country.

In January 1990, a two-day meeting of the five permanent members of the UN **SECURITY COUNCIL**—China, France, the United Kingdom of Great Britain and Northern Ireland, the United States of America, and the Union of Soviet Socialist Republics—was held in Paris to consider the situation in Cambodia. On 16 June 1990, they agreed that they would be guided by the following principles in working for a resolution of the problem:

No acceptable solution can be achieved by force of arms.

An enduring peace can only be achieved through a comprehensive political settlement including the verified withdrawal of foreign forces, a cease-fire and the cessation of outside military assistance.

The goal should be self-determination for the Cambodian people through free, fair and democratic elections.

All accept an enhanced U.N. role in the resolution of the Cambodian problem.

There is an urgent need to speed up diplomatic efforts to achieve a settlement.

The complete withdrawal of foreign forces must be verified by the United Nations.

The five would welcome an early resumption of a constructive dialogue among the Cambodian factions which is essential to facilitating the transition process and which should not be dominated by any one of them.

An effective U.N. presence will be required during the transition period in order to assure internal security.

A special representative of the U.N. Secretary General is needed in Cambodia to supervise U.N. activities during a transition period culminating in the inauguration of a democratically elected government.

The scale of the U.N. operation should be consistent with the successful implementation of a Cambodian settlement and its planning and execution should take account of the heavy financial burden that may be placed on member states.

Free and fair elections must be conducted under direct U.N. administration.

The elections must be conducted in a neutral political environment in which no party would be advantaged.

The five permanent members commit themselves to honouring the results of free and fair elections.

All Cambodians should enjoy the same rights, freedoms and opportunities to participate in the election process.

A supreme National Council might be the repository of Cambodian sovereignty during the transition process.

Questions involving Cambodian sovereignty should be resolved with the agreement of the Cambodian parties.

The five support all responsible efforts by regional parties to achieve a comprehensive political settlement and will remain in close touch with them, with the view to reconvening the Paris conference at an appropriate time.

In February 1990, the 12 countries of the European Community passed a warning to the six countries of the South East Asian Nations Association that they would oppose what had become the normal practice of seating the coalition government headed by Prince Norodom Sihanouk at the September 1990 session of the UN General Assembly on the ground that it includes representatives of the Khmer Rouge. The United States of America and the European Community countries never recognized the coalition as the legitimate government of Cambodia but did not object to its participation in the work of the General Assembly while the country was occupied by the Vietnamese. Withdrawal of the Vietnamese in September 1989, in their view, changed the conflict in Cambodia into a civil war in which the United Nations could not take sides.

The civil war was brought to an end only after the Paris Conference on Cambodia adopted, late in 1991, a series of three UN-brokered agreements designed "to achieve an internationally guaranteed comprehensive settlement" of the problem.

In accordance with these agreements, Cambodians elected a new National Assembly in May 1993; that

Assembly approved a new constitution that made possible the return of Prince Norodom Sihanouk as King of Cambodia. First elected as King in 1941 when the country was a French colony, he took office as King for the second time on 24 September 1993, twenty-three years after having been overthrown in a coup while on a trip to Moscow.

One of the three Paris Conference agreements, the Agreement on a Comprehensive Political Settlement of the Cambodia Conflict, includes a Part III devoted to human rights matters. In article 15, Cambodia undertakes "to ensure respect for an observance of human rights and fundamental freedoms in Cambodia; to support the right of all Cambodian citizens to undertake activities which would promote and protect human rights and fundamental freedoms; to take effective measures to ensure that the policies and practices of the past shall never be allowed to return; and to adhere to relevant international human rights instruments." Under article 17, "the United Nations Commission on Human Rights should continue to monitor closely the human rights situation in Cambodia, including, if necessary, by the appointment of a Special Rapporteur who would report his findings annually to the Commission and to the General Assembly."

The UN Secretary-General submitted a detailed report on the situation in Cambodia to the **COMMISSION ON HUMAN RIGHTS** at its 1993 session (UN Doc. E/CN.4/1993/19) in which he described in detail the numerous activities of the human rights component of the United Nations Transitional Authority in Cambodia, which had been established in accordance with the Paris Conference agreements. These activities included investigations of complaints concerning violations of human rights and adoption of corrective measures; reviews of prison conditions; distribution of educational and training information; presentation of international human rights instruments to the Supreme National Council with a view to accession; and reviews of the judicial and penal system in the light of human rights standards. In addition, the Center for Human Rights designed and implemented a long-term program of technical assistance and advisory services aimed at contributing to a lasting improvement in human rights in the country. In light of these developments, the Secretary-General put forward a number of proposals for further action leading to a permanent and comprehensive approach to the promotion and protection of human rights in Cambodia. The Commission noted the report with appreciation and requested the Secretary-General (resolution 1993/6 of 19 February 1993) to ensure a continued United Nations presence in Cambodia through, among other things, the operations of the Center for Human Rights. The Commission also requested that the Secretary-General appoint a Special Representative to guide and coordinate UN human rights presence in that country.

The UN General Assembly, on 20 December 1993, recognized (resolution 48/154) "that Cambodia's tragic recent history requires special measures to ensure the protection of the human rights of all people in Cambodia and the non-return to the policies and practices of the past, as stipulated in the Paris Agreements."

In 1994, the first full year of the democratically elected government, there were some changes for the better. Past atrocities were being investigated for accountability, and the government was cooperating with international human rights organizations. There also was, however, the continued civil war against the Khmer Rouge, thousands of displaced civilians, and problems of citizenship and terrorist attacks against ethnic Vietnamese. Parliament voted overwhelmingly to ban the Khmer Rouge and to encourage other countries to arrest any Khmer rebels within their borders.

Conflict between King Sihanouk and his son, Prince Ranaiddh, who had become Cambodia's first Prime Minister following the UN-supervised elections of 1993, continued to prevail. Several Thais were found guilty of involvement in an attempted coup in early 1994.

The UN Commission on Human Rights, recalling the Agreement on a Comprehensive Political Settlement of the Cambodia Conflict signed in Paris on 23 October 1991, including part III relating to human rights, its own requests to the Secretary-General to appoint a special representative in Cambodia, and the Secretary-General's subsequent appointment of a special representative, welcomed in resolution 1995/55 of 5 March 1995 the establishment in Cambodia of the office of the Centre for Human Rights. It took note of the report of the Special Representative of the Secretary-General on the situation of human rights in Cambodia (E/CN.4/1995/87 and Add 1), and endorsed his recommendations and conclusions, including those aimed at ensuring the independence of the judiciary and the establishment of the rule of law, good governance, and freedom of expression.

In the same resolution the Commission expressed grave concern about the atrocities committed by the Khmer Rouge, including the massacre of approximately 50 villagers in Battambang Province in October 1994, the numerous incidents of kidnapping of villagers, attacks on tourists, including the taking and killing of foreign hostages, and other deplorable incidents detailed in the reports of the Special Represetative.

***BIBLIOGRAPHY.*** Abrams, F., D. Orentlicher, and S. Heder. *Kampuchea: After the Worst.* New York: Lawyers Committee for Human Rights, 1985. NGO mission report, in English.

Amnesty International. *Cambodia: Arbitrary Killings of Ethnic Vietnamese.* London: 1993. NGO report, in English.

————. *Cambodia: Recent Human Rights Developments.* London: 1990. NGO factfinding report, in English.

————. *Kampuchea: Political Imprisonment and Torture.* London: 1987. NGO report, in English.

————. *Kampuchea: Officially Reported Political Arrests and Allegations of Torture and Arbitrary Detention.* London: 1988. NGO report, in English.

Asia Watch. *An Exchange on Human Rights and Peace-keeping in Cambodia.* New York: Human Rights Watch, 1993. NGO issue paper, in English.

————. *Human Rights in Cambodia: Testimony of Kenneth Roth, Deputy Director of Human Rights Watch before the Senate Foreign Relations Committee.* New York: Human Rights Watch, 1990. NGO report, in English.

————. *Violations of the Rules of War by the Khmer Rouge.* New York: Human Rights Watch, 1990. NGO report, in English.

Burns, Cynthia, Anne Campbell, and Yos Hut Khemacaro. *A Human Rights Teaching Curriculum for Cambodians.* Aranyaprathet, Thailand: UNBRO, 1991. Educational material, in English.

Cambodia Documentation Commission. *The Khmer Rouge Genocide: Accountability and Response.* New York: 1987. NGO report, in English.

Chanda, Nayan. *Brother Enemy: The War after the War.* New York: Harcourt Brace Jovanovich, 1986. Scholarly monograph, in English.

Hannum, Hurst. "International Law and Cambodian Genocide: The Sounds of Silence," *Human Rights Quarterly* 11, no. 1 (February 1989): 82–138. Scholarly article, in English.

Hannum, H., and D. Hawk. *The Case against the Standing Committee of the Communist Party of Kampuchea.* New York: Cambodia Documentation Commission, 1986. NGO legal brief, in English.

Hawk, David. *Human Rights: Aspects of a Comprehensive Solution to the Conflict in Cambodia.* New York: Cambodia Documentation Commission, 1990. NGO report, in English.

Horizons Khmers. *Bottin khmer 1992: répertoire des organismes oeuvrant pour la communauté cambodgienne en France, en Thailande et au Cambodge* (Bottin Khmer 1992: A Directory of Active Organizations for the Cambodian Community in France, Thailand, and Cambodia). Paris: Horizons Khmers, 1992. NGO directory, in French.

Indochina Policy Forum. *Recommendation for the New Administration on U.S. Policy toward Indochina.* Queenstown, MD, USA: Aspen Institute, 1988. NGO report, in English.

Jennar, Raoul M. "UNTAC: 'International Triumph' in Cambodia?" *Security Dialogue* 25, no. 2 (June 1994): 145–156. Scholarly article, in English.

Kiernan, Ben. *Cambodia: The Eastern Zone Massacres.* New York: Center for the Study of Human Rights, Columbia University, 1987. Scholarly study, in English.

————. "The Cambodian Crisis, 1990–1992: The UN Plan, the Khmer Rouge, and the State of Cambodia," *Bulletin of Concerned Asian Scholars* 24, no.2 (April 1992): 3–24. Scholarly article, in English.

————. "The Genocide in Cambodia, 1975–79," *Bulletin of Concerned Asian Scholars* 22, no. 2 (April–June 1990): 35–40. Scholarly article, in English.

Tarr, Chou Meng. "The Vietnamese Minority in Cambodia," *Race & Class* 34, no. 2 (Dec. 1992): 33–47. Scholarly article, in English.

U.S. Committee for Refugees. *"Something Like Home Again": The Repatriation of Cambodian Refugees.* Washington, D.C.: Immigration and Refugee Services of America, 1994. NGO report, in English.

Volkman, Toby Alice, ed. "Cambodia 1990," *Cultural Survival Quarterly* 14, no. 3 (1990): 1–85. Article, in English.

**CAMEROON.** The Republic of Cameroon is a country in middle Africa, on the Gulf of Guinea. It has borders with Chad, the Central African Republic, the Congo, Equatorial Guinea, and Gabon. It achieved independence from France in 1960 and became a member of the United Nations the same year. Its population is estimated to be 12,875,000. The northern part of the country is inhabited by Sahelian nomadic peoples such as the Peul and the Fulbe, while the Bantu and Pygmies live in the south. Languages commonly used include English and French (both official) and more than 80 African vernaculars. Religions practiced include Christianity (Roman Catholic, 35%; Protestant, 18%), Islam (35%), and Animism (12%). Literacy is estimated at 65%.

Unification of ethnic groups and harmonization of their development have always been among the priorities of the government. This desire to ensure national concord is clearly proclaimed in the preamble to the 1972 constitution, which reads:

Proud of its cultural and linguistic diversity, a feature of its national personality which it is helping to enrich, but profoundly aware of the imperative need to achieve complete unity, solemnly declares that it constitutes one and the same nation, committed to the same destiny, and affirms its unshakeable determination to construct the Cameroonian fatherland on the basis of the idea of fraternity, justice and progress.

The government (1994) took the form of a republic, uniting what were formerly East and West Cameroon. Under the 1972 constitution, executive power is vested in the President, elected by popular vote with universal adult suffrage for a term of five years. There is no Vice President or Prime Minister; should the presidency become vacant, its powers are assumed, until the election of a new President, by the President of the General Assembly. The President is assisted by a cabinet of 26 ministers whom he appoints. Legislation is handled by the 150-member National Assembly, the members of which are elected for five-year terms which can be extended or shortened by the President. The only political party is the Cameroon National Union.

Once a German colony, the Cameroons were occupied by French and British troops during World War I. In 1919, the French and British zones became mandates under the **LEAGUE OF NATIONS.** In 1946, they were made trust territories of the United Nations.

The territory administered by France became an autonomous State in 1957 and an independent country three years later.

Between 1955 and the mid-1960s, Cameroon suffered recurring waves of terrorist activity initiated by the outlawed Union of Cameroon Peoples and supported by radical regimes of nearby countries. Political conciliation was effected only after the last important rebel leader was captured in 1970. Since that time, the Cameroon People's Democratic Movement has dominated the political scene, with the cooperation of a unified labor movement and a variety of associations of women and youth. Traditional kingdoms and tribal organizations are permitted to exercise their customary functions of government among their followers, and the formal court system honors tribal laws and customs when they do not conflict with national law.

After serving four full five-year terms of office, President Ahmadou Ahidjo resigned in November 1982 and was succeeded by Prime Minister Paul Biya. After Biya had received his own mandate as President on 25 January 1984, the position of Prime Minister was abolished. In 1984, the presidential security force attempted to overthrow the government, but the army remained loyal and ended the coup attempt. In March 1985, Biya presided at the Fourth Party Congress at which the party changed its name to the Cameroon People's Democratic Movement. Biya was re-elected in 1988.

An act adopted by the National Assembly and promulgated by the President on 4 February 1984 modified the constitution, changing the name of the country from "United Republic of Cameroon" to "Republic of Cameroon," and providing that it be a unitary State, "one and indivisible, secular and devoted to social service."

All governments of the Cameroons have endeavored to re-educate Cameroonians in a spirit of ethnic co-existence so as to enable them to transcend the tribal framework and adjust to the new national dimension. Special social measures have been taken to protect women, youth, and the handicapped in recent years, and a program has been initiated to settle the Pygmies of the country's southeastern forests, an ethnic group estimated to number about 50,000, by regrouping them in village communities and establishing health centers and pilot schools.

In March 1994 the **HUMAN RIGHTS COMMITTEE** responded to a report by Cameroon relating to the International Covenant on Civil and Political Rights:

The Committee considered the second periodic report of Cameroon (CCPR/C/63/Add. 1) at its 1306th to 1308th meetings, held on 30 and 31 March 1994 (see CCPR/C/SR.1306–1308), and adopted the following observations:

## Introduction

The Committee thanks Cameroon for its report and welcomes the Government's willingness to pursue the dialogue entered into with the Committee. The report, although a summary and rather theoretical, otherwise conforms to the Committee's guidelines regarding the form and contents of periodic reports (CCPR/C/20/Rev. 1), and the oral comments were a valuable complement to the information given in writing. The replies to the questions of Committee members by a competent high-level delegation helped to make the dialogue between the delegation and the Committee frank and fruitful.

## Factors and Difficulties Impeding the Application of the Covenant

The ignorance of individuals as to their rights impedes the enjoyment thereof and contributes to their failure to provide remedies for violation of those rights. Accordingly, there remain many unaddressed human rights violations. The survival of certain traditions and customs sometimes constitutes an obstacle to the application of the Covenant, particularly with regard to equality of men and women.

## Positive Aspects

The establishment of the National Committee for Human Rights and Freedoms represents a notable advance in the promotion of human rights in Cameroon.

The acts passed in 1990, in particular Act No. 90-56 of 19 December 1990 concerning political parties, establishing a multiparty system, constitute an encouraging factor for the implementation of the Covenant.

The detailed information given orally by the delegation on the situation of minorities in Cameroon is indicative of the positive approach of the country's authorities to the implementation of article 27 of the Covenant.

## Principal Subjects of Concern

The Committee regrets the fact that the Secretary-General was not notified in the correct manner, in accordance with the requirements of article 4 of the Covenant, of the proclamation of a state of emergency at the time of the events that took place in the country's Nord-Ouest province in 1992.

The Committee deplores the fact that the State party has not embarked on all the necessary reforms to combat the factors still impeding equality of men and women.

The Committee is concerned that, in spite of a recent reduction, the number of offences punishable by the death penalty in the Criminal Code is still excessive, in particular aggravated theft or traffic in toxic or dangerous wastes, and at the number of death sentences handed down by the courts.

It deplores the infringements of the right to life by representatives of the security forces, the Army and even paramilitary groups in respect of civilians, not only during the events of 1992 but also in March 1993 and, more recently, in March 1994.

The Committee deplores the multiple cases of torture, ill-treatment, extrajudicial execution and illegal detention, suffered in particular by journalists and political opponents. Torture and ill-treatment seem to be practised systematically by the security forces, and on several occasions their brutality has caused the death of the victims.

It also deplores the fact that such brutality is practiced in prisons, as well as non-respect for the provisions of article 10 of the Covenant in detention centres where men and women, convicted and unconvicted prisoners, adult and juvenile offenders are held in the same, generally insalubrious, cells.

The Committee notes that freedom of expression is not guaranteed, owing to the requirement of prior deposit of all publications, censorship and the control exercised by the authorities over the press, radio and television.

The Committee questions the independence of the judiciary; in particular, the composition of the Supreme Council of Justice does not seem such as to guarantee respect for this principle.

The Committee expresses its regret at the difficulties encountered by workers in exercising freely and peacefully their rights under articles 21 and 22 of the Covenant.

The Committee is concerned about the conditions in which the presidential elections of 11 October 1992 were held, and, in particular, it expresses its concern at the numerous allegations of fraud made during the different ballots.

## Suggestions and Recommendations

The Committee recommends that the Cameroonian authorities avail themselves of the constitutional reform to incorporate in the national legal system all the rights guaranteed by the Covenant, and that each article of the draft be systematically checked against the provisions of the Covenant.

Measures should be taken to organize free, equitable and transparent elections.

The Committee invites the Government to disseminate the Covenant by culturally appropriate means, so that everyone has a knowledge of his rights, whatever his place of residence and his situation in Cameroonian society.

The Committee urges the authorities of Cameroon to revise the Criminal Code with a view to restricting the number of offences carrying the death penalty.

The Committee strongly recommends that the Government take all necessary measures to prevent summary executions, torture, ill-treatment and illegal detention, that all such cases be investigated in order to bring those suspected of having committed such acts before the courts, that those found guilty be punished and that the victims be compensated.

The Committee invites the Cameroonian authorities to modify their legislation applicable to administrative detention so as to make it limited in time and subject to appeal in accordance with article 9, paragraph 4, of the Covenant. The Committee urges the Cameroonian authorities to require law-enforcement officers to have a strict respect for the provisions of article 9 of the Covenant, in order to put an end to arbitrary or illegal detention, by organizing specific training for them if necessary.

The Committee invites the Cameroonian authorities to adopt as a matter of urgency the measures necessary to ensure that in prisons and detention centres all the provisions of article 10 of the Covenant are fully respected.

Measures should be taken, if necessary in the form of constitutional reform, to guarantee the independence and impartiality of the judiciary, in accordance with article 14, paragraph 1, of the Covenant.

The Committee invites the Government to improve the situation of women, with a view to achieving the effective application of article 3 of the Covenant, in particular by adopting the necessary educational and other measures to overcome the weight of certain customs and traditions and by proceeding as soon as possible with its plan to amend the Family Code.

The Committee recommends that the Cameroonian authorities remove censorship once and for all and amend the Act of 19 December 1990, with a view to ensuring its conformity with article 19 of the Covenant.

**BIBLIOGRAPHY.** Africa Watch. *Cameroon: Attacks against Independent Press.* New York: Human Rights Watch, 1991. NGO factfinding report, in English.

Amnesty International. *Cameroon: Amnesty International's Concerns Arising from the April 1984 Coup Attempt.* London: 1987. NGO report, in English.

———. *Cameroon: Imprisoned for Advocating a Multi-party System: The Yondo Black Affair.* London: 1990. NGO factfinding report, in English.

———. *Cameroon: The Imprisonment of Jehovah's Witnesses.* London: 1985. NGO report, in English.

———. *Religious Intolerance.* London: 1986. NGO report, in English.

———. *Summary Trials and Secret Executions in the Republic of Cameroon.* London: 1984. NGO report, in English.

Ankomah, Baffour. "Cameroon's Forbidden Topics," *Index on Censorship* 17, no. 2 (February 1988): 22–24. NGO article, in English.

Baudelot, Yves, and Alfred Pognon. *Rapport de Mission d'Observation Judiciare: Proces de Monsier Ahidjo et de ses Deux Aides de Camp* (Trial Observer Mission Report: The Trial of Mr Ahidjo and his Two Aides). Paris: Federation Internationale des Droits de l'Homme, 1984. NGO mission report, in French.

Baudouin, Patrick. "Intervention de la FIDH au Cameroun" (FIDH Intervention in Cameroon), *La Lettre de la FIDH* 173 (25 November 1986): 3–4. NGO case note, in French.

Beti, Mongo. "Biya or Botha—What's the Difference?" *Index on Censorship* 16, no. 9 (October 1987): 40, 42. NGO article, in English.

Bipoun-Woum, Joseph-Marie. "Cameroon," in *Individual Rights and the State in Foreign Affairs,* eds. Elihu Lauterpacht and J. G. Collier, pp. 77–93. New York: Praeger, 1977. Collection of scholarly articles, in English.

Eteki-Otabela, Marie-Louise. "Dix ans de luttes du Collectif des femmes pour le renouveau: quelques réflexions sur le mouvement féministe camerounais" (The Women's Collective for Renewal—Ten Years of Struggle. Reflections on the Feminist Movement in Cameroon), *Recherches féministes* 5, no. 1 (1992): 125–134. Special issue, in French.

Hodges, Tony. *Jehovah's Witnesses in Africa.* London: Minority Rights Group, 1985. NGO report, in English; bibliography, p. 14.

Nwosu, Humphrey N. "The Concepts of Nationalism and Right in Self-Determination: Cameroon as a Case Study," *Africa Quarterly* 16, no. 2 (1976): 256–273. NGO article, in English.

**CANADA.** One of the largest countries in the world, Canada occupies the northern part of the North American continent. It has a border on the south with the United States of America, marked in part by the Great Lakes, and in the far northwest with the state of Alaska. It fronts on the Atlantic, the Pacific, and the Arctic oceans. Canada achieved independence from Great Britain in 1867 and became a member of the United Nations in 1945. Its population is estimated to be 30,530,000.

The official census of Canada conducted in 1986 demonstrated that a wide range of ethnic groups make up the Canadian mosaic. Of the then-total of over 24,000,000 Canadians, 8.4 million (33.6%) were of British origin, 6.1 million (24.4%) of French origin, 6.2 million (24.8%) of origins neither British nor French, and 4.3 million (17.1%) of a multiple origin that included either British or French. Nearly three quarters of a million Canadians reported an aboriginal origin. Of all Canadians who reported having neither British nor French origins, 63% were of European background; 10%, Asian; 6%, South- or West-Asian (Middle Eastern); 6%, aboriginal; 3%, black; and 2%, other. Christianity is the religion practiced by the majority of the Canadian people (Roman Catholic, 46%; United Church, 18%; Anglican, 12%; and Eastern Orthodox, 1.5%). Many of the remainder report that they adhere to no religion.

The government (1994) took the form of a federal state comprised of ten provinces (Alberta, British Columbia, Manitoba, New Brunswick, Newfoundland, Nova Scotia, Ontario, Prince Edward Island, Quebec, and Saskatchewan) and two territories (Northwest Territories and Yukon). (It is also a member of the British Commonwealth, of which the British Queen is the symbolic head. All official acts of the sovereign and her representative, the Governor-General, are determined by the Canadian authorities, who are responsible to the Canadian Parliament.) The Governor-General acts only with the agreement of the Prime Minister and his cabinet. The Prime Minister is the leader of the party or coalition holding the majority of seats in the House of Commons. Elections are normally held every five years but may be called earlier if the House of Commons so decides. Parliament is composed of a 104-member Senate, members of which are appointed for life, and a 282-member elected House of Commons, apportioned according to the provincial population. Political parties include the Progressive Conservative Party, the Liberal Party, and the New Democratic Party. While the ratification of international treaties is the prerogative of the Government of Canada, the implementation of those treaties is shared by the Government, the provincial governments, and, following a delegation of authority by the Parliament of Canada, the territorial governments.

***CONCERNS OF MINORITIES.*** In December 1982, the Canadian House of Commons created a Special Committee on Indian Self-Government to review all legal and related institutional factors affecting the status, development, and responsibilities of tribal governments on Indian reserves. This Committee was also to make recommendations with regard particularly to possible provisions of new legislation and improved administrative arrangements to apply to some or all of those governments, taking into account the various social, economic, administrative, political, and demographic situations of Indian bands and their views in regard to administrative or legal change. In its report, submitted to Parliament in November 1983, the Committee recommended that the federal government establish a new relationship with Indian First Nations and that an essential element of this relationship be recognition of Indian self-government. The Committee recommended that the right of the Indian people to self-government be explicitly stated and entrenched in the constitution of Canada. Indian First Nation governments would form a distinct order of government in Canada, with their jurisdiction being defined. Proposals to achieve such self-government were outlined in the report.

In June 1983, the Parliament established a special Parliamentary Committee to examine the problems related to the participation of "visible minorities" in Canadian society and to propose measures to increase such participation—"visible minorities" being defined as non-whites who are not participating fully in Canadian society. The Committee's report, issued in March 1984 and entitled "Equality Now!", included 80 recommendations designed to increase the participation of such minorities in Canadian life and to facilitate their enjoyment of human rights and fundamental freedoms. The government has since been working on the implementation of those recommendations.

Also in June 1983, the Royal Commission of Inquiry on Equality in Employment was set up, by order-in-council. The Commission was authorized to explore the most efficient, effective, and equitable means of promoting employment opportunities, eliminating systemic discrimination, and assisting all individuals to compete for employment opportunities on an equal basis. Four target groups were identified: women, native people, disabled persons, and "visible minorities." As the same time, the Commission was requested to examine the employment practices of 11 designated crown and government-owned corporations. The Commission's report, submitted in October 1984, contained 117 recommendations addressed to the Government of Canada.

In March 1985, the Government announced measures in response to the report, measures that touch the working lives of more than one million Canadians. They include mandatory employment equity reporting requirements in the private sector, an equity compliance policy for federal contractors, the integration of employment equity into all federal training and job development programs, and increased equity measures within the public service and federal crown corporations.

***FRENCH-SPEAKING MINORITY.*** The question of discrimination on the ground of language arose frequently in Canada because of the size and concentration of English-speaking and French-speaking elements of the population. In colonial days, the settlers, who were largely of French background, resented the influx of thousands of English-speaking immigrants from England and the United States, and had frequent disputes with them over the valuable fisheries and the fur trade. Gradually outnumbered, French-speaking Canadians began to fear that they had become second-class citizens and clashed with the newcomers over the issue of bilingualism in government, the courts, and the schools. This eventually led to the formation in the 1960s of a separatist movement in the predominantly French province of Quebec. However, Pierre Elliot Trudeau, a French Canadian who became Prime Minister in 1968, refused the idea of separation, although he supported programs for increased bilingualism and greater provincial autonomy. Separatism remains a national issue, especially in Quebec.

***CANADIAN HUMAN RIGHTS ACT.*** Changes were also made in the procedures for handling complaints under the Canadian Human Rights Act. A revamped complaints process, streamlining the system, has been adopted by the Canadian Human Rights Commission. The Human Rights Act, adopted in 1977, prohibits discrimination in employment and in the provision of goods, services, and accommodation on numerous grounds including race, color, and national or ethnic origin. As amended in 1983, it also prohibits harassment on any of those grounds and discrimination on the part of unions or employer's organizations.

***POVERTY.*** In 1991 the Government of Canada submitted to the UN Secretary-General its second report concerning the implementation of articles 10–15 of the **INTERNATIONAL COVENANT ON ECONOMIC, SOCIAL AND CULTURAL RIGHTS** (UN Doc. E/1990/6/Add. 3). After considering the report at meetings held on 17 and 18 May 1993, the UN **COMMITTEE ON ECONOMIC, SOCIAL AND CULTURAL RIGHTS** adopted the following concluding observations (E/C.12/1993/5):

### A. Introduction

. . . The Committee commends the State party on its excellent report which contains detailed and complete information on the legal framework for the implementation of the rights under consideration, on the manner of interpretation and application of many of the respective laws by the Canadian courts, as well as on the programmes and initiatives designed to realize economic, social and cultural rights. The Committee welcomes the extensive statistical data provided by the Government and appreciates the considerable efforts made to provide further information in reply to the questions submitted in writing. The Committee notes with satisfaction the detailed explanation given by the delegation of Canada to all questions raised by the Committee, as well as the fact that several ministries, departments, and agencies had been consulted in the course of the preparation of the report.

Finally the Committee is very appreciative of the constructive manner in which the delegation referred to the contributions of Canadian non-governmental organizations to the Committee's review of the implementation of the Covenant in Canada.

## B. Positive Aspects

The Committee notes with satisfaction the general strengthening of the protection of human rights in Canada through the Canadian Charter of Rights and Freedoms and through improvements of other human rights legislation. The Committee was informed that the Charter of Rights and Freedoms guarantees, in section 7, the right to security of the person and in section 15, the equal benefit and protection of the law. It notes with satisfaction that Canadian courts have applied these provisions to cover certain economic and social rights, and that the Supreme Court of Canada has, on occasion, turned to the International Covenant on Economic, Social and Cultural Rights for guidance as to the meaning of provisions of the Charter.

The Committee notes, in particular, that the courts have applied section 15 to the Charter to extend parental benefits and security of tenure in the field of housing. The Committee was informed that the process of interpretation of the Charter is still in its early stages, but that its provisions and the interpretations adopted by the Supreme Court in early cases suggest that the Canadian courts will give full consideration to the rights in the Covenant when interpreting and applying the Canadian Charter of Rights and Freedoms.

The Committee received information on the Court Challenges Programme which has, in the past, enabled disadvantaged groups or individuals to take important test cases before the courts. Recognizing the importance of effective legal remedies against violations of social, economic and cultural rights, and of remedying the conditions of social and economic disadvantage of the most vulnerable groups and individuals, the Committee highly commends the State party for having developed such a programme.

The Committee notes with satisfaction that the State party has made significant progress in many areas covered by articles 10–15. It notes improvements to maternity and parental benefits and important initiatives to prevent child abuse and neglect and address domestic violence. It notes that a child tax credit has been introduced to assist low-income families.

The Committee notes with satisfaction that the poverty rate among elderly couples has declined significantly over the last decade, primarily because of the positive effect of the Old Age Security Programme and the Guaranteed Income Supplement.

The Committee notes with satisfaction that Canadians as a whole enjoy a high standard of health care, with a health-care system which is based on universality and accessibility. The Committee notes that infant mortality rates among Ca-

nadians have declined, particularly among aboriginal Canadians, a group which previously had extremely high infant-mortality rates.

## C. Factors and Difficulties Impeding the Application of the Covenant

The State party reported no fundamental difficulties impeding the application of the Covenant, although it was noted that Canada has been affected by the recent recession. By the same token, it enjoyed one of the highest rates of economic growth during the 1980s.

On a technical level, the State party reported that it takes considerable time to compile information requested by the Committee because of the involvement of ten provinces and two territories in most of the areas covered by the Covenant.

## D. Principal Subjects of Concern

In view of the obligation arising out of article 2 of the Covenant to apply the maximum of available resources to the progressive realization of the rights recognized in the treaty, and considering Canada's enviable situation with regard to such resources, the Committee expresses concern about the persistence of poverty in Canada. There seems to have been no measurable progress in alleviating poverty over the last decade, nor in alleviating the severity of poverty among a number of particularly vulnerable groups.

In particular, the Committee is concerned about the fact that, according to information available to it, more than half of the single mothers in Canada, as well as a large number of children, live in poverty. The State party has not outlined any new or planned measures to remedy this situation. Of particular concern to the Committee is the fact that the federal Government appears to have reduced the ratio of its contributions to cost-sharing agreements for social assistance.

The Committee received information from nongovernmental organizations about families being forced to relinquish their children to foster care because of inability to provide adequate housing or other necessities.

The Committee is concerned that there seems to exist no procedure to ensure that those who must depend entirely on welfare payments do thereby derive an income that is at or above the poverty line.

A further subject of concern for the Committee is the evidence of hunger in Canada and the reliance on food banks operated by charitable organizations.

The Committee is concerned that the right to security of tenure is not enjoyed by all tenants in Canada.

The Committee learned from nongovernmental organizations of widespread discrimination in housing against people with children, people on social assistance, people with low incomes, and people who are indebted. Although prohibited by law in many of Canada's provinces, these forms of discrimination are apparently common. A more concerted effort to eliminate such practices would, therefore, seem to be in order.

The Committee notes the omission from the Government's written report and oral presentation of any mention of the problems of homelessness. The Committee regretted that there were no figures available from the Government on the extent of homelessness, on the numbers of persons evicted annually throughout the country, on the lengths of waiting lists or the percentage of houses accessible to people with disabilities.

Given the evidence of homelessness and inadequate living conditions, the Committee is surprised that expenditures on social housing are as low as 1.3% of Government expenditures.

The Committee is concerned that, in some court decisions and in recent constitutional discussions, social and economic rights have been described as mere "policy objectives" of governments rather than as fundamental human rights. The Committee was also concerned to receive evidence that some provincial governments in Canada appear to take the position in courts that the rights in article 11 of the Covenant are not protected, or only minimally protected, by the Charter of Rights and Freedoms. The Committee would like to have heard of some measures being undertaken by provincial governments in Canada to provide for more effective legal remedies against violations of each of the rights contained in the Covenant.

The Committee was very concerned to learn that the "Court Challenges Programme" has been cancelled.

The Committee is concerned to learn that in a few cases, courts have ruled that the right to security of the person in the Charter does not protect Canadians from social and economic deprivation or from infringements of their rights to adequate food, clothing, and housing.

The Committee is concerned that provincial human rights legislation has not always been applied in a manner that would provide improved remedies against violations of social and economic rights, particularly concerning the rights of families with children and the right to an adequate standard of living, including food and housing.

### E. Suggestions and Recommendations

The Committee recommends the incorporation in human-rights legislation of more explicit reference to social, economic, and cultural rights.

The Committee recommends a concerted Government action to eliminate the need for food banks.

The Committee recommends the extension of security of tenure to all tenants and draws the attention of the State party to its General Comment No. 4 on the Right to Adequate Housing (article 11-1 of the Covenant), in particular paragraph 8.

The Committee recommends that the federal Government implement the recommendations of the Standing Committee on Human Rights and the Status of Disabled Persons, of June 1992, to restore the "Court Challenges Programme" and that funding also be provided for Charter challenges by disadvantaged Canadians to provincial legislation.

In recognition of the increasingly important role played by the courts in ordering remedial action against violations of social and economic rights, the Committee recommends that the Canadian judiciary be provided with training courses on Canada's obligations under the Covenant and on their effect on the interpretation and application of Canadian law.

The Committee encourages the Canadian courts to continue to adopt a broad and purposive approach to the interpretation of the Charter of Rights and Freedoms and of human rights legislation so as to provide appropriate remedies against violations of social and economic rights in Canada.

The Committee recommends that the key governmental bodies concerned enter into a dialogue at the domestic level with the representatives of the Canadian nongovernmental organizations that have presented information to the Committee.

Finally, the Committee requests the Canadian Government to inform the Committee of any developments and measures taken with regard to the issues raised and recommendations made in paragraphs 14 to 32 of the present concluding observations.

**BIBLIOGRAPHY.** Adelman, Howard, ed. *Refugee Policy: Canada and the United States.* Toronto, Canada: York Lanes Press for the Centre for Refugee Studies, 1991. Conference papers, in English.

Adelman, Howard, and C. Michael Lanphier, eds. *Refuge or Asylum? A Choice for Canada.* Toronto, Canada: York Lanes Press for the Centre for Refugee Studies, 1990. Conference papers, in English.

Article 19. *Freedom of Information and Expression in Canada.* London: 1990. NGO factfinding report, in English.

Association Henri-Capitant (Section québécoise). *Droit civil et droits autochtones: confrontation ou complémentarité? Recueil des textes présentés à la conférence Henri-Capitant du 12 avril 1991 à la Faculté de droit de l'Université de Montréal* (Civil Law and Indigenous Rights: Papers Presented at Henri-Capitant Conference held on 12 April 1991 at the Faculty of Law, University of Montreal). Outremont, Quebec, Canada: 1992. Scholarly conference report, in French.

Baker, David. "An Overview of Human Rights for Disabled People in Canada." Paper presented at the International Experts Meeting on Ways and Means to Ensure Effective Exercise of Human Rights by Disadvantaged Groups, Quebec, Canada, 18 September 1985. In English.

Bayefsky, A. F., and M. Eberts, eds. *Equality Rights and the Canadian Charter of Rights and Freedoms.* Canadian Legal Classic Series. Toronto: Carswell, 1985. Scholarly edited collection, in English.

Boldt, M., and J. A. Long, eds. *The Quest for Justice: Aboriginal Peoples and Aboriginal Rights.* Toronto: University of Toronto Press, 1985. Scholarly edited collection, in English.

British Columbia Council of Human Rights. *Human Rights: A Responsibility We All Share.* Vancouver, Canada: 1986. Government bulletin, in English.

Canada (Government of). *Implementation of the International Covenant on Economic, Social and Cultural Rights, Initial Reports Concerning Rights Covered by Articles 13 to 15.* Canada: 7 May 1985, E/1982/3/Add. 34. IGO document, in English.

*Canadian Charter of Rights: Annotated.* Aurora, Ontario: Canada Law Book, 1987. Reference book, in English and French.

Canadian Council on Social Development, Court Challenges Program. *A Guide to the Charter for Equality-Seeking Groups.* Ottawa, Canada: 1987. Government manual, in English and French.

Comeau, Pauline, and Aldo Santin. *The First Canadians: A Profile of Canada's Native People Today.* Toronto, Canada: James Lorimer, 1990. Scholarly monograph, in English.

Gesellschaft fur Bedrohte Volker (Association for Endangered Peoples). "Inuit in Kanada," *Pogrom* 119 (16 January 1986): 46–56. NGO article, in German.

Gillies, David. "Canada and International Human Rights: The Road Ahead," *Netherlands Quarterly of Human Rights* 8, no. 4 (1990): 361–370. Scholarly article, in English.

Hathaway, James C. *The Law of Refugee Status.* Toronto, Canada: Butterworths, 1991. Scholarly monograph, in English; bibliography, pp. 235–242.

Howard, Rhoda E. "The National Question in Canada: Quebec," *Human Rights Quarterly* 13, no. 3 (August 1991): 412–419. Scholarly article, in English.

Human Rights Research and Education Centre, University of Ottawa. *Human Rights in Canada: Into the 1990s and Beyond*. Ottawa, Canada: 1990. Collective papers, in English.

International Federation of Human Rights. *Labrador and Northeastern Quebec*. Paris: 1986. NGO mission report, in English.

—————. *Rapport de mission: crise d'Oka. Mission d'enquête et d'observation sur les événements survenus à Kanesatake, Oka et Kahnawake (Québec, Canada) été 1990* (Mission Report: The Oka Crisis. Fact-finding Mission to Kanesatake, Oka and Kahnawake, Quebec, Canada in Summer 1990). Paris: FIDH, 1990. NGO factfinding report, in French.

Jones, Camille. "Toward Equal Rights and Amendment of Section 12(1)(b) of the Indian Act: A Postscript to Lovelace v. Canada," *Harvard Women's Law Journal* 8 (Spring 1985): 195–213. Scholarly article, in English.

Latin American Working Group. *An Anti-Intervention Handbook: Canadians and the Crisis in Central America*. Toronto, Canada: 1985. Handbook, in English.

Marcus, Alan R. *Out in the Cold: The Legacy of Canada's Inuit Relocation Experiment in the High Arctic*. Document 71. Copenhagen, Denmark: International Work Group for Indigenous Affairs, 1992. NGO monograph, in English; bibliography, pp. 91–102.

Matas, David. *Domestic Implementation of International Human Rights Agreements*. 12 January 1987. Unpublished scholarly article, in English.

Mathews, R., and C. Pratt. "Human Rights and Foreign Policy: Principles and Canadian Practice," *Human Rights Quarterly* 7, no. 2 (May 1985): 159–188. Scholarly article, in English.

Nolan, C. J. "The Influence of Parliament on Human Rights in Canadian Foreign Policy," *Human Rights Quarterly* 7, no. 3 (August 1985): 373–390. Scholarly article, in English.

Refugee Documentation Project (York University). "Beyond the Plaut Report: Toward a Truly Humanitarian Refugee Policy for Canada," *Refuge* 5, no. 1 (October 1985): 6–9. NGO article, in English.

Schabas, William A. *International Human Rights Law and the Canadian Charter: A Manual for the Practitioner*. Toronto, Canada: Carswell, 1991. Scholarly monograph, in English; bibliography, pp. 317–338.

Schelew, Michael. "The New Refugee Measures—The End of Canada's Humanitarian Tradition," *Amnesty International Bulletin* 13, no. 5 (July–August 1986): 14–15. NGO article, in English.

Schneiderman, David, ed. "Language and the State: The Law and Politics of Identity," *Proceedings of the Second National Conference on Constitutional Affairs*. Cowansville, Quebec, Canada: Éditions Yvon Blais & Centre for Constitutional Studies, 1991. Conference report, in English and French.

Smith, James G. E. "Canada—The Lubicon Lake Cree," *Cultural Survival Quarterly* 11, no. 3 (1987): 61–62. NGO article, in English.

Turpel, M. E., R. Jones, and P. File. "Aboriginal Peoples: A Human Rights Perspective," *Rights and Freedoms* 59 (February 1987): 3–4. NGO article, in English.

Vries, Gijs de. "Report: Broken Promises: Canada and its Aboriginal Peoples," *Netherlands Quarterly of Human Rights* 10, no. 2 (1992): 166–183. Scholarly article, in English.

**CANADIAN HUMAN RIGHTS FOUNDATION, INTERNATIONAL HUMAN RIGHTS TRAINING PROGRAM.** Held annually, the International Human Rights Training Program is a two-week, intensive summer course that brings together more than 100 participants from over 34 countries. The program provides training by leading human rights experts in a practical yet academic atmosphere. The curriculum is action-oriented and open to educators and students of human rights, representatives of development agencies and NGOs, representatives of grassroots organizations, members of government agencies, and any individual with a serious interest in human rights issues.

Participants learn about key philosophies, institutions, and current practices in human rights; explore the social, economic, and political context of major issues; and employ innovative and practical working methods. There are compulsory sessions on international human rights protection, the philosophy of human rights, and women and human rights. Participants also choose from lecture series that explore such topics as international law and minority rights, the rights of indigenous peoples, and building democratic institutions. Hands-on workshops address topics such as protecting civilian populations in times of crisis, election monitoring, and building human rights networks. Participants from outside of Canada may attend a third week of the training program to develop working strategies for specific human rights problems in their home countries.

International Human Rights Training Program. Address: Canadian Human Rights Foundation, 1425 boulevard René-Lévesque West, Suite 307, Montreal, Quebec, Canada H3G 1T7. Telephone: (514) 954-0382. Fax: (514) 954-0659.

**CANADIAN HUMAN RIGHTS YEARBOOK.** Established in 1983, this annual publication is divided into two parts: one part concentrates on international human rights developments in the preceding year; the other, on Canadian developments. It is published in French as *Annuaire canadien des droits de la personne*. Contributors include experts in various fields, including law, philosophy, and sociology. The Yearbook also presents the most comprehensive Charter of Rights bibliography currently available.

Past issues have included articles on the right to equality of aboriginal peoples, the criminality of racial harassment, the right to food, and involuntary sterilization of the mentally handicapped. The 1991–92 Yearbook was devoted to papers presented at a workshop organized jointly by the UN Center for Human Rights and the Canadian Department of Justice.

*Canadian Human Rights Yearbook.* Address: University of Ottawa Press, 542 King Edward, Ottawa, ON,

# C

Canada K1N 6N5. Telephone: (613) 564-2270. Fax: (613) 564-9284. Editor: Suzanne Bossé.

**CAPE VERDE.** The Republic of Cape Verde is an archipelago in the Atlantic Ocean west of Dakar, Senegal; it consists of ten islands divided into two groups: Barlavento in the north and Sotavento in the south. It achieved independence from Portugal in 1975 and became a member of the United Nations the same year. Its population is estimated to be 404,000. A majority of its population is of mixed African and Portuguese origin. Languages commonly used include Portuguese (official) and Crioulo. Christianity (Roman Catholic, 80%; Protestant denominations, 20%) is the predominant religion. Literacy is estimated at 37%.

The government (1994) took the form of a republic, headed by a President and Prime Minister, both elected by the 56-member National Assembly. The President, as head of State, exercises executive authority in the country with the assistance of an appointed Council of Ministers.

One of the first acts of the National Assembly, after Cape Verde became independent, was to revoke and replace legislation inherited from the Portuguese occupation that was felt to be inconsistent with the real interests of the people. Besides replacing the colonial judicial system, it revised most of the laws regulating marriage, affiliation, and paternal-filial relations. Under the new laws, the exploitation of contradados—a form of forced labor—is forbidden, discrimination against persons born out of wedlock is abolished, and a network of people's tribunals is established to give the population greater facility of access to the organs of the judiciary and, incidentally, to open all positions in the judiciary to women.

Suffrage is universal. There is a single political party, the African Party for the Independence of Cape Verde. However, multi-party elections were initiated in 1990.

**CAPITAL PUNISHMENT.** Capital punishment, or the death penalty, has been a subject of international concern since the second half of the 18th century, when it was drawn to public attention by Cesare Beccaria, the noted Italian jurist and criminologist, who in his *Essay on Crimes and Punishment* put forward a series of convincing arguments against capital punishment and the inhuman treatment of criminals.

In 1959, the UN **GENERAL ASSEMBLY** (resolution 1396 [XIV]) invited the Economic and Social Council to initiate a study of the question of capital punishment, of the laws and practices relating to it, and of the effects of capital punishment, and its abolition, on the rate of criminality. The resulting study, entitled "Capital Punishment" (UN publication, Sales no. 62.IV.2), was prepared by Mr. Marc Ancel, a justice of the French Supreme Court and Director of the Criminal Science Section of the Institute of Comparative Law in Paris.

In the study, the author summarized the two opposing views then being put forward for retaining or abolishing capital punishment, as follows (paras. 213–230):

A theoretical controversy on the problem of capital punishment has been going on at least since Beccaria. George Fox had raised the issue as early as 1651 in his letters to the judges and in particular in his pamphlet *To the Parliament and Commonwealth of England* published in 1659, submitting 59 proposals for reforms, one of which was the proposal, then a very bold one, that henceforth the penalty of death should be applied only to murder. The British colonies of America had, before their independence, accepted the same ideas. There is no need to recall here the opinions expressed at the end of the eighteenth century and during the humanitarian and liberal period of the twentieth century. Whether one desires it or not, the controversy has once more become very topical in the last twenty years. Accordingly, in a comprehensive report on the problem as it stands today, one can hardly avoid giving an account of the two opposing views in the matter.

It is not the intention of the author to repeat here the reasons that were officially given in each of the countries concerned at the time of abolition or to analyse the respective positions of the various countries and national schools of thought; rather, he means to catalogue and briefly describe the reasons usually put forward today, for the guidance of public opinion, for retaining and for abolishing capital punishment.

In favour of the death penalty, the idea most commonly accepted is that of its deterrent effect—i.e., the protection of society from the risk of a second offence by a criminal who is not executed and who may subsequently be released or who may escape. Similarly, it is argued, the State has the right to protect itself. Many speak of the concept of self-defence and some even regard the death penalty as a necessity and the public authority as the representative in this regard of God on earth.

A related argument that is often advanced is that based on the idea of atonement: the death penalty (it is said) is the only just punishment for the gravest of crimes, or the only one capable of effacing an unpardonable crime. Some add that even if, from the philosophical point of view, the death penalty may be of doubtful legitimacy, it represents a political necessity for the protection not merely of society but of the social order itself. Similarly, it is contended that, since the death penalty is the only means of eliminating the offender altogether, this penalty is necessary, at least provisionally, when the public peace is endangered by certain particularly dangerous forms of crime. This view is based on concepts largely derived from the doctrine of pericolosità and of the irredeemability of certain offenders; on the basis of these ideas, capital punishment represents the extreme security measure of elimination. Some claim that, on this basis, it is legitimate to do away with "social monsters". This purely utilitarian idea is sometimes linked with the other idea that the State has a duty to impose inflexible rules of social conduct.

An analogous notion is that based on what is sometimes termed realism in the prevention of crime. The supporters of this view argue that a particularly potent weapon is needed for dealing with dangerous criminals and individuals. This is the reasoning of those who say that capital punishment is needed not only for the protection of human life and of certain cultural values but even to safeguard certain social property which is placed under the protection of the law.

Yet others argue that public opinion remains generally favourable to the death penalty and that the public as a whole, and particularly the police and prison officials, believe in its effectiveness. It is urged that this sincere belief should be respected and also that possible victims should be protected by maintaining the penalty of death. In the Middle East and in Africa, its value as a deterrent appears to be recognized in principle; even if its deterrent effect should be debatable, many claim that it ought to be regarded as genuine, or that, for reasons of public safety, those concerned ought to be encouraged to believe in it.

A somewhat similar idea is put forward by many who claim that the death penalty should be retained because it is virtually impossible to find another penalty to replace it; imprisonment, even for a long term, is said to be inadequate and its effects are moreover minimized by the practice of anticipated release. It is further argued that, if imprisonment in these cases were really to be a solitary confinement for life, it would be more cruel than death; and besides, imprisonment in perpetuity leaves no hope to the offender and does not encourage him to repentance in the same way as the immediate prospect of the supreme penalty.

Another, equally very utilitarian, view held in some countries is that the execution of the condemned person represents a saving of public funds and hence a saving for the taxpayer, who is not called upon to pay for the maintenance of anti-social criminals for an indefinite, or at least very long, period. And it is further said that an execution avoids certain popular reactions which must be expected in cases of heinous crimes if an over-excited public opinion were not aware that the criminal can be sentenced to death.

Against these arguments for the retention of the death penalty, the abolitionists advance the following considerations.

Their main argument is that based on the sanctity of human life; since it is wrong to kill, the State should set the example and should be the first to respect human life. Some go as far as to say that an execution is a self-mutilation of the State: though the State has admittedly the capacity to defend itself and to command, it is not empowered to eliminate a citizen, and in doing so the State does not erase the crime but repeats it.

It is further argued that the penalty of death can only be justified under the aspect of collective vengeance, of atonement, or of absolute retribution. But the modern tendency is to regard penalties as having no object other than prevention and punishment, and this object can be achieved by means other than the taking of life. The abolitionists refer in this connexion to the abuses frequently committed in the past, even in a recent past, when the death penalty was applied frequently and indiscriminately, and point out that its retention involves dangers of this kind. In Latin America, in particular, it is stressed that capital punishment might be used for political purposes.

Furthermore, it is said, the lex talionis is obsolete and hence an execution is a sort of judicial or legal murder; also, the existence of the penalty of death debases justice. For some years now, in America and Europe, it has been stren-

uously contended that the mere presence of capital punishment in the catalogue of penalties falsifies criminal proceedings, which take on the character of a sinister tragi-comedy; the existence of this penalty renders criminal justice uncertain. Recent works on sociology and judicial psychology indicate the extreme relativity of capital sentences.

Another argument used by the abolitionists is that the penalty of death rests in reality on a somewhat metaphysical concept of human freedom, whereas the social sciences show that an offender does not generally enjoy complete freedom. Absolute justice is therefore an illusion, and full atonement a fiction. Besides, how can human justice evaluate individual responsibility in absolute terms? The condemned person is in reality paying for other people or suffering for the sake of the example. His execution then appears to have no moral foundation.

Nor does the death penalty have the deterrent effect attributed to it: indeed, it is said, the statistics of crime show that its abolition does not lead to any increase in crime, and consequently capital punishment loses its basic traditional justification.

Moreover, the penalty of death is a form of cruelty and inhumanity unworthy of a civilization which claims to be humane; doctors report that even the most efficient methods do not result in instantaneous and painless death. Above all, the chief defect of the death penalty is that it is irrevocable, and in spite of all the official statements, sometimes repeated with complacency, judicial error is always possible, and a few have certainly occurred recently. In such cases, the penalty of death appears as an unpardonable crime committed by society.

In any event, society can protect itself by other means, and the death penalty is no more than a lazy answer, which hinders the search for effective means of curbing crime and for a rational system of prevention. In addition, the death penalty is unjust in that, whatever may be claimed to the contrary, it affects not only the criminal himself but also his close relatives and brands the whole family with the mark of infamy. It is, moreover, paradoxical to claim that the death penalty alone makes repentance possible; it certainly totally precludes the rehabilitation of the human being concerned. The finality of the death penalty makes it impossible to adapt it to the gravity of the offence committed; all the attempts to draw a distinction between capital murder and other forms of homicide have proved arbitrary. In a progressive society, the death penalty appears on reflection as being the opposite of true atonement.

A further argument advanced by the abolitionists is that there is a contradiction in claiming that the death penalty has a deterrent effect and, at the same time, surrounding the execution with secrecy. The curiosity aroused by an execution is notoriously morbid, and it is increasingly realized that the penalty of death may itself have criminogenous effects, particularly upon those abnormal individuals who, in spite of all legal and judicial precautions, are often executed. And in some countries (it is added) the death penalty is applied most unequally, both from the social and from the radical points of view; some persons have not sufficient financial means to defend themselves or are morally unable to do so. The conclusion reached is, therefore, that this penalty, which should be the expression of absolute justice, often leads in practice to injustices against individuals.

These are the reasons generally given for and against capital punishment. Most of them have no doubt been stated over and over again. However, since the controversy has recently been revived and has even become heated, the author felt that he could hardly refrain from mentioning the arguments briefly in the present report.

In 1963, the study was examined by the Ad Hoc Committee of Experts on the Prevention of Crime and the Treatment of Offenders, the Economic and Social Council, and the General Assembly. The Council and the Assembly called upon the Commission on Human Rights to consider it from the point of view of human rights and requested the Secretary-General to submit a report on new developments with respect to the law and practice concerning the death penalty and new contributions of the criminal sciences in the matter. This report, entitled "Capital Punishment—Developments 1961–1965" (UN publication, Sales no. E.67.IV.15, part II), was subsequently prepared by Mr. Norval Morris, an expert appointed by the Secretary-General.

After examining all the available information in 1968, the United Nations Consultative Group on the Prevention of Crime and the Treatment of Offenders summarized the situation then existing, with respect to capital punishment, in the following terms (UN Doc. A/7243, paras. 11–14):

The Consultative Group, from the information made available to it and from experience of members with crime and its treatment in their own countries, was of the view that there is a strong trend in most countries towards the abolition of capital punishment or at least towards fewer executions. This tendency is particularly strong in relation to capital punishment for murder. This trend has legislative, judicial and executive aspects. A growing number of offenders who are sentenced to death is spared through processes of appeal or by executive clemency. Where it is used, capital punishment is increasingly a discretionary rather than a mandatory sanction. The Consultative Group also noted that a number of countries had abolished capital punishment for humanitarian reasons irrespective of any possible deterrent effect it might be thought to have.

There is a perceptible tendency in some countries, running contrary to what was noted in the previous paragraph, towards the legislative provision for, and actual application of, capital punishment for certain political and economic crimes. Times of political insecurity and attack have resulted, in some countries, in a larger recourse to capital punishment for statutory offences related to political or racial issues. The Consultative Group was of the view that in such cases it is of importance that if such a punishment is thought to be essential by the State it should not be mandatory.

Almost all countries provide for the exclusion of certain offenders from capital punishment because of their mental and physical condition, age, sex and extenuating circumstances. These exemptions are being gradually broadened at the legislative, judicial and executive levels.

The disparity between the legal provisions for capital punishment and the actual application of those provisions grows greater in those countries that have capital punishment in their laws.

At its 1982 session, the UN General Assembly requested the Commission on Human Rights (resolution 37/192) to consider the idea of elaborating a draft of a second optional protocol to the **INTERNATIONAL COVENANT ON CIVIL AND POLITICAL RIGHTS,** aimed at the abolition of the death penalty, taking into account the available documentation on the subject. The request was passed on to the **SUB-COMMISSION ON PREVENTION OF DISCRIMINATION AND PROTECTION OF MINORITIES,** which in 1984 (resolution 1984/7) appointed one of its members, Mr. Marc Bossuyt, as Special Rapporteur and entrusted him with the preparation of a comparative analysis concerning the proposal to elaborate such an optional protocol. The report prepared by the Special Rapporteur (E/CN.4/Sub.2/1987/20) was examined by the Sub-Commission in 1988 and transmitted to the Commission on Human Rights (resolution 1988/22).

The report analyzed the available information concerning the death penalty and the views on the subject expressed in the competent international bodies and presented the draft of a second optional protocol that envisaged the abolition of the death penalty for ordinary crimes with the possibility of retaining it for crimes under military law or crimes committed in exceptional circumstances such as in wartime.

The Commission on Human Rights forwarded the Special Rapporteur's report and the draft protocol to the General Assembly, which considered them in 1989 and adopted, on 15 December of that year, the International Covenant on Civil and Political Rights: Second Optional Protocol, Aiming at Abolition of the Death Penalty. Article 1 of this Protocol provides that "no one under the jurisdiction of a State Party to the present Optional Protocol shall be executed," and that "each State Party shall take all necessary measures to abolish the death penalty within its jurisdiction." Article 5 provides for international monitoring of these provisions by the UN Human Rights Committee.

***CAPITAL PUNISHMENT APPLIED TO PERSONS UNDER THE AGE OF 18.*** The UN Sub-Commission on Prevention of Discrimination and Protection of Minorities at its 1989 session, on recommendation of its Working Group on Detention, urgently appealed (resolution 1989/32) to all member States that apply the death penalty to persons under the age of 18 to take the necessary legislative and administrative measures with a view to stopping this practice forthwith and requested States in which the death penalty is applicable to consider the possibility of enacting legislation specifically prohibiting its application to persons under 18 years of age, in accordance with existing international standards.

In support of this decision, the Sub-Commission pointed out that the nonapplicability of the death penalty to persons under the age of 18 is stipulated by the International Covenant on Civil and Political Rights (article 6 [5]), the American Convention on Human Rights (article 4 [5]), the Convention on the Rights of the Child (article 37 [a]), and the Geneva Conventions and their Protocols I and II. It also recalled that the UN General Assembly had opposed the imposition of the death penalty on persons under the age of 18 (for example, in resolutions 35/172 of 15 December 1980 and 40/143 of 13 December 1985), indicating that the application of the death penalty for crimes committed by persons below that age violates minimum international standards for the protection of human rights applicable to all member States.

In a report on extrajudicial, summary, or arbitrary executions (UN Doc. E/CN.4/1994.7) presented to the 1994 session of the UN Commission on Human Rights, Special Rapporteur Bacre Waly Ndiaye indicated that he had received reports during his investigation concerning the imposition and execution of death sentences on minors in Pakistan and the United States of America, and that he was concerned about legislation in Algeria, China, and Peru that allows for the execution of minors. In addition, the Special Rapporteur reported allegations that he had received concerning executions of mentally retarded persons in the United States of America.

### SAFEGUARDS FOR THOSE FACING CAPITAL PUNISHMENT.

The following safeguards, guaranteeing protection of the rights of those facing the death penalty, were approved by the UN Economic and Social Council on 25 May 1984 (resolution 1984/50):

1. In countries which have not abolished the death penalty, capital punishment may be imposed only for the most serious crimes, it being understood that their scope should not go beyond intentional crimes with lethal or other extremely grave consequences.

2. Capital punishment may be imposed only for a crime for which the death penalty is prescribed by law at the time of its commission, it being understood that if, subsequent to the commission of the crime, provision is made by law for the imposition of a lighter penalty, the offender shall benefit thereby.

3. Persons below 18 years of age at the time of the commission of the crime shall not be sentenced to death, nor shall the death sentence be carried out on pregnant women, or on new mothers, or on persons who have become insane.

4. Capital punishment may be imposed only when the guilt of the person charged is based upon clear and convincing evidence leaving no room for an alternative explanation of the facts.

5. Capital punishment may only be carried out pursuant to a final judgement rendered by a competent court after legal process which gives all possible safeguards to ensure a fair trial, at least equal to those contained in article 14 of the International Covenant on Civil and Political Rights, including the right of anyone suspected of or charged with a crime for which capital punishment may be imposed to adequate legal assistance at all stages of the proceedings.

6. Anyone sentenced to death shall have the right to appeal to a court of higher jurisdiction, and steps should be taken to ensure that such appeals shall become mandatory.

7. Anyone sentenced to death shall have the right to seek pardon, or commutation of sentence; pardon or commutation of sentence may be granted in all cases of capital punishment.

8. Capital punishment shall not be carried out pending any appeal or other recourse procedure or other proceeding relating to pardon or commutation of the sentence.

9. Where capital punishment occurs, it shall be carried out so as to inflict the minimum possible suffering.

### CAPITAL PUNISHMENT IN ARMED CONFLICTS.

The Geneva Convention Relative to the Treatment of Prisoners of War of 12 August 1949 provides safeguards against the arbitrary imposition of the death penalty on such prisoners in the following terms:

*Article 100.* Prisoners of war and the Protecting Powers shall be informed, as soon as possible, of the offences which are punishable by the death sentence under the laws of the Detaining Power.

Other offences shall not thereafter be made punishable by the death penalty without concurrence of the Power upon which the prisoners of war depend.

The death sentence cannot be pronounced on a prisoner of war unless the attention of the court has, in accordance with article 87, second paragraph been particularly called to the fact since the accused is not a national of the Detaining Power, he is not bound to it by any duty of allegiance, and that he is in its power as the result of circumstances independent of his own will.

*Article 101.* If the death penalty is pronounced on a prisoner of war, the sentence shall not be executed before the expiration of a period of at least six months from the date when the Protecting Power receives, at an indicated address, the detailed communication provided for in article 107.

Similarly, the Geneva Convention Relative to the Protection of Civilian Persons in Time of War of 12 August 1949 restricts the freedom of the occupying power to impose capital punishment upon such persons, in the following terms:

*Article 68.* (2) The penal provisions promulgated by the Occupying Power in accordance with articles 64 and 65 may impose the death penalty on a protected person only in cases where the person is guilty of espionage, of serious acts of sabotage against the military installations of the Occupying Power or of international offences which caused the death of one or more persons, provided that such offences were punishable by death under the law of the occupied territory in force before the occupation began.

(3) The death penalty may not be pronounced on a protected person unless the attention of the court has been particularly called to the fact that since the accused is not a national of the Occupying Power, he is not bound to it by any duty of allegiance.

(4) In any case, the death penalty may not be pro-

nounced on a protected person who was under 18 years of age at the time of the offence.

The same Convention sets out procedural requirements to be met before the death penalty may be carried out, as follows:

In no case shall persons condemned to death be deprived of the right to petition for pardon or reprieve.

No death sentence shall be carried out before the expiration of a period of at least six months from the date of receipt by the Protecting Power of the notification of the final judgment confirming such death sentence, or of an order denying pardon or reprieve.

The six months' period of suspension of the death sentence herein prescribed may be reduced in individual cases in circumstances of grave emergency involving an organized threat to the security of the Occupying Power or its forces, provided always that the Protecting Power is notified of such reduction and is given reasonable time and opportunity to make representations to the competent occupying authorities in respect of such death sentences.

Further, Protocol I, Additional to the Geneva Conventions of 12 August 1949, provides (article 76) that pregnant women shall not be executed and (article 77) that no one may be executed who was under 18 when the offense was committed.

**EXECUTIONS.** In 1981, the General Assembly expressed (resolution 37/182) its alarm at the occurrence on a large scale of summary or arbitrary executions, including extralegal executions, condemned that practice, and welcomed the appointment by the Economic and Social Council of a Special Rapporteur to examine the question and to report to the Commission on Human Rights.

In his 1983 report to the Commission, Special Rapporteur S. A. Wako (Kenya) examined in some detail the basic concepts underlying his study, bearing in mind the fact that no international instrument defines either "summary" or "arbitrary" executions. For the purpose of his work, he adopted the following tentative definitions (UN Doc. E/CN.4/1983/16, para. 66):

"Summary execution" is the arbitrary deprivation of life as a result of a sentence imposed by the means of summary procedure in which the due process of law and in particular the minimum procedural guarantees as set out in article 14 of the International Covenant on Civil and Political Rights are either curtailed, distorted, or not followed;

"Arbitrary execution" is the arbitrary deprivation of life as the result of the killing of persons carried out by the order of a government or with its complicity or tolerance or acquiescence without any judicial or legal process;

"Extralegal execution" refers to killings committed outside the judicial or legal process, and at the time illegal under relevant national or international laws. Accordingly, in certain circumstances, an "arbitrary execution," as defined above, can be an extralegal execution.

In this connection, he pointed out that the types of executions enumerated above do not include deaths resulting from the use of reasonable force in law enforcement or permitted under relevant national or international legal standards; nor do they include killings in armed conflict not forbidden under international humanitarian law. Further, he added that "although the resolutions leading to the mandate of the present study limit the concept of summary or arbitrary executions to acts of omissions attributable to governments or government agents, the Special Rapporteur considers that further thought should be given to responsibility of nongovernmental groups for acts of omissions leading to the deprivation of life in a manner equivalent to that resulting from summary or arbitrary execution."

In subsequent reports, the Special Rapporteur analyzed the information that reached him from various sources concerning a considerable number of alleged summary or arbitrary executions, while realizing that that information represented only a small part of the entire phenomenon of this violation of the right to life. He concluded that a considerable number of summary or arbitrary executions remained undetected or unknown, not only by the international community but also by the population in the countries concerned, and called for suggestions as to how the phenomenon might be more accurately monitored.

In these reports, he also indicated that summary or arbitrary executions take place in all parts of the world, most frequently as a result of internal armed conflict but also as the result of excessive or illegal use of force by law enforcement agencies in arresting or detaining suspects. In some cases, individuals were simply executed without a trial, or after a trial which lacked the safeguards to protect the rights of the defendant prescribed in article 14 of the International Covenant on Civil and Political Rights.

In the report covering his activities in 1988, the Special Rapporteur summarized his correspondence with 36 governments concerning alleged summary or arbitrary executions in their countries: Bangladesh, Benin, Brazil, Burma, Chad, China, Colombia, Czechoslovakia, the former Democratic Yemen, El Salvador, Ethiopia, Guatemala, Haiti, Honduras, India, Indonesia, Iran, Iraq, Israel, Mauritania, Nepal, Nicaragua, Nigeria, Pakistan, Peru, Philippines, Somalia, South Africa, Sri Lanka, Sudan, Syria, Thailand, Uganda, United Kingdom of Great Britain and Northern Ireland, Yemen, and Zaire. In addition, he held meetings with representatives of nine governments in connection with alleged summary or arbitrary executions in their countries: Algeria, Benin, Burma, China, Indonesia, Iraq, Nigeria, and Sri Lanka.

In this report, the Special Rapporteur stated the following (UN Doc. E/CN.4/1989/25, paras. 314–316):

In the period under review, the Special Rapporteur has received more reports than at any time during the period of his mandate, alleging increased use of chemical weapons. In at least three areas, there were allegations that chemical weapons had been used and that they had resulted in thousands of deaths. In this regard, the Special Rapporteur welcomes the determination of the international community as reflected in the Final Declaration of the representatives of States participating in the Conference on the Prohibition of Chemical Weapons which met in Paris from 7 to 11 January 1989 when they resolved to prevent any recourse to chemical weapons by completely eliminating them, and solemnly affirmed their commitment not to use chemical weapons and condemned such use.

A disturbing feature of the period under review is the increasing number of allegations which the Special Rapporteur has received to the effect that thousands of people have lost their lives at the hands of police or other law enforcement officials in demonstrations. It would appear that the law enforcement officials did not act with the restraint required in such cases according to the Code of Conduct for Law Enforcement Officials. The Special Rapporteur would therefore strongly reiterate the recommendation he made in his last report that the United Nations Centre for Human Rights should organize seminars or workshops for law enforcement officials to train them and inculcate in them the principle that they should carry out their work with due respect for the human rights of the individual, and to familiarize them with various international human rights instruments which are directly related to their work. There is also room for bilateral and multilateral technical assistance in this regard.

One of the problematic issues that has faced the Special Rapporteur is how to determine whether a "death squad" or an extreme right- or left-wing group which is responsible for killing people is acting independently or with the support, tolerance, connivance or encouragement of the Government. In some countries it is alleged that, although such groups are ostensibly independent, they are sponsored by the Government or the Government tolerates them or in fact they include police and military personnel in plain clothes and under orders from their superiors. The Governments have said that such groups act independently of them. The Special Rapporteur would welcome the Commission's views on how to deal with this problem. Whatever the position, it is the primary duty and responsibility of the Government to ensure that the right to life is guaranteed and protected from anyone who attempts to violate it.

In the report covering his activities in 1989, the Special Rapporteur set out the following recommendations (UN Doc. E/CN.4/1990/22, chap. IV, para. 477):

(a) Governments:
(i) Review national laws and regulations, as well as the practice of the judicial and law enforcement authorities, with a view to securing effective implementation of the standards set by Economic and Social Council resolution 1989/65 of 24 May 1989;
(ii) As a matter of priority, take measures to ensure the effective protection of persons who play key roles in defending human rights and promoting social justice from death threats and assassination attempts;
(iii) Include a thorough curriculum of human rights in the training of all law enforcement and military personnel;
(iv) Establish an office within the Government in order to improve co-operation with the United Nations and other international organizations in human rights matters.
(b) International organizations:
(i) Emphasize the importance of the implementation of international human rights norms and principles as set forth in international human rights instruments and resolutions, in particular by the General Assembly and the Economic and Social Council;
(ii) Organize at the regional and national levels human rights seminars and training courses, utilizing the manual on the effective prevention and investigation of extralegal, arbitrary and summary executions;
(iii) Strengthen the United Nations Centre for Human Rights with a view to meeting the ever-growing requirements in the monitoring of human rights protection and advisory services;
(iv) Promote information activities in order to disseminate as widely as possible the latest achievements in the field of human rights, so that the international community may be aware of the ways in which human rights can be protected and promoted.

In his report to the 1994 session of the Commission on Human Rights, the Special Rapporteur, Bacre Waly Ndiaye, summarized his activities involving the receipt and handling of allegations on the threat or use of the death penalty (E/CN.4/1994/7, paras. 700–711):

*Death Threats.* The Special Rapporteur received allegations concerning death threats or fear for the lives and physical security of more than 380 persons. He continues to view urgent appeals on behalf of those under threat as an essential part of his mandate. In the past year, he has transmitted urgent appeals with the aim of preventing loss of life to the Governments of: Argentina, Bangladesh, Brazil, Burundi, Chad, Ecuador, El Salvador, India, Indonesia, Iran, Panama, Papua New Guinea, Paraguay, Peru, Philippines, Rwanda, South Africa, Sri Lanka, Togo, Turkey, Venezuela, and Zaire. In almost all of these countries, the lives of human rights activists, members of the political opposition, trade unions, community workers, writers, and journalists were reported to be at serious risk. The Special Rapporteur is particularly concerned about Colombia, where he intervened by sending 26 urgent appeals, and Guatemala, where he sent 25 urgent appeals. Furthermore, the Special Rapporteur noted with deep concern reports about the alleged execution, while in custody, of a prisoner in Azerbaijan, and the killing of two mothers of disappeared children in Brazil. In both cases, he had urged the authorities to ensure their protection. It is also most disturbing that in countries such as Brazil, Colombia, Guatemala, South Africa, and Turkey, patterns of intimidation and threats seem to persist for years.

The Special Rapporteur urges all governments to adopt effective measures, in accordance with the requirements of each particular case, to ensure full protection of those who are at risk of extrajudicial, summary, or arbitrary execution. The Special Rapporteur calls on the authorities to conduct investigations into all instances of death threats or attempts against lives that are brought to their attention, regardless of whether or not any judicial or other procedures have been activated by those under threat.

*Deaths in Custody.* The Special Rapporteur received numerous reports concerning deaths in custody in Azerbaijan, Cambodia, and Sierra Leone. Such deaths were alleged to be the result of torture or other cruel, inhuman, and degrading treatment in Bangladesh, Cuba, Ecuador, India, Indonesia, Israel, Mexico, Nepal, Peru, South Africa, Turkey, and Yugoslavia. The Special Rapporteur also received allegations of deaths in custody due to medical neglect or otherwise untenable prison conditions in Cuba, Morocco, and Togo. A particular form of death while in detention was reported, as in former years, in Myanmar, where Muslim villagers continue to be forced by the military to serve as porters and die after torture or simply because they are too weak to carry on.

The Special Rapporteur appeals to all governments to ensure that conditions of detention in their countries conform to the Standard Minimum Rules for the Treatment of Prisoners and other pertinent international instruments. He also urges them to make efforts to ensure full respect of the international norms and principles prohibiting any form of torture or other cruel, inhuman, or degrading treatment. Prison guards and other law-enforcement personnel should receive training so as to be familiar with these norms as well as the rules and regulations concerning the use of force and firearms to prevent escape or control disturbances. The Special Rapporteur also calls on the competent authorities to prosecute and punish all those who, through action or omission, are found responsible for the death of any person held in custody, in breach of the aforementioned international instruments.

*Deaths due to Abuse of Force by Law-Enforcement Officials.* The Special Rapporteur received a considerable number of allegations concerning violations of the right to life as a consequence of excessive or arbitrary use of force. Cases in this category were reported in Brazil, Cameroon, Chad, Chile, the Comoros, Egypt, Honduras, Israel, and Venezuela. In Bangladesh, Cameroon, Chad, Chile, the Central African Republic, El Salvador, India, Lebanon, Malawi, Nepal, South Africa, and Zaire, hundreds of people were reportedly killed by security forces using excessive force against participants in demonstrations and other manifestations. The Special Rapporteur was particularly shocked by reports about deliberate use of firearms against young children by Israeli security forces and Brazilian military police.

The Special Rapporteur calls on all governments to ensure that the security forces receive thorough training in human rights matters and, in particular, with regard to the restrictions on the use of force and firearms in the discharge of their duties. Such training should include methods of keeping crowds of people under control without resorting to excessive force. Full and independent investigations must be carried out into alleged deaths due to abuse of force, and all law-enforcement officials responsible for violations of the right to life must be held accountable.

*Violations of the Right to Life during Armed Conflicts.* The Special Rapporteur received increasing numbers of reports concerning deaths as a consequence of armed conflicts, both international and internal, in various parts of the world. Massive violations of the right to life were said to have been committed against combatants who had been captured, or after they had laid down their arms, and particularly civilians. This was reported, for example, in Angola, Azerbaijan, Cam-

bodia, Chad, Djibouti, Liberia, Papua New Guinea, Sierra Leone, Somalia, Sri Lanka, the Sudan, Tajikistan, Turkey, and the conflict areas in the former Yugoslavia. Thousands of people were reportedly killed, either as a direct consequence of the hostilities—through deliberate and indiscriminate shelling of residential areas, often with heavy weaponry including aerial bombardments, and deliberate executions—or indirectly, as a result of sieges; blocking off water, food, and medical supplies; or refusal to evacuate sick or wounded persons. Children, elderly, and those in poor health are particularly affected by such measures.

The Special Rapporteur calls on all parties to conflicts, international or internal, to respect the norms and standards of international human rights and humanitarian law that protect the lives of the civilian population and those combatants who are captured or lay down their arms. He also appeals to all those involved in armed conflicts to allow convoys of humanitarian aid to reach their destinations as well as to allow the evacuation of the wounded, elderly persons, and children. All those responsible for violations of the right to life in situations of armed conflicts must be held accountable. In this context, the Special Rapporteur particularly wishes to endorse the appeals for respect for the right to life made by the Special Rapporteurs on the situation of human rights in the Sudan and, on repeated occasions, by the Special Rapporteur on the human rights situation in the territory of the former Yugoslavia.

In this context, the Special Rapporteur wishes to refer to the role of the United Nations in situations of armed conflict. Increasingly often called upon to exercise peacekeeping tasks, UN personnel in many countries are operating under very difficult and often dangerous conditions. A high number of UN staff has on many occasions risked, and lost, their lives. However, in the recent past, reports have been received indicating that members of UN forces were themselves involved in extrajudicial, summary, or arbitrary killings in Somalia. The Special Rapporteur is of the view that, as each State is bound under international law to respect these standards, an organ representing States in their collectivity has at least the same degree of responsibility. A human rights component should be an integral part of all peacekeeping and observer missions. As such missions under the auspices of the United Nations multiply, it may be desirable to envisage the institution of an organ within the United Nations, or within each peacekeeping or observer mission, to investigate human rights abuses by members of such missions and hold their authors responsible. Provisions should also be made to grant compensation to the victims of such abuses or, in the case of extrajudicial killings, their families. With a view to preventing such incidents, all members of peacekeeping and observer missions should receive thorough training in human rights matters as well as in mediation and conflict resolution.

*Violations of the Right to Life in the Context of Communal Violence.* The Special Rapporteur would once again like to draw the attention of the international community to the problem of communal violence, understood as acts of violence committed by groups of citizens of a country against other groups. In Burundi, Nigeria, Rwanda, and Zaire, where violent confrontations were reported between different ethnic groups, government forces allegedly not only did not intervene to stop the violence but actively supported one side in the conflict, or even began it. In other instances, governments, for example those of Bangladesh and Sri Lanka, denied their responsibility for killings, asserting that they occurred in the context of communal violence. Such conflicts, if allowed to continue, may degenerate into genocide. Effective steps should, therefore, be taken by governments of countries where acts of communal violence occur to curb such disturbances at an early stage. The Special Rapporteur also strongly appeals to all governments to refrain from supporting groups, on ethnic or other grounds, either actively or by simply tolerating acts of violence committed by them. On the contrary, efforts should be made toward reconciliation and peaceful coexistence of all parts of the population, regardless of ethnic origin, religion, or any other distinction. Mass communication media and campaigns of education and information promoting mutual respect should be used in this regard. Furthermore, all acts of incitement to hatred or violence must be punished.

*Expulsion of Persons to a Country Where Their Life Is in Danger.* The Special Rapporteur received reports about the imminent extradition of one or more persons to countries where their lives might be at risk. All governments should take due notice of the norms and principles contained in international instruments that refer to this particular question. They should refrain from extraditing a person in circumstances where his or her safety is not fully guaranteed.

*Rights of the Victims.* As stated earlier, the recognition of the right of victims or their families to receive adequate compensation is both a recognition of the State's responsibility for the acts of its organs and an expression of respect for the human being. Granting compensation presupposes compliance with the obligation to carry out an investigation into allegations of human rights abuses with a view to identifying and prosecuting their perpetrators. Financial or other compensation provided to the victims or their families before such investigations are initiated or concluded, however, does not exempt governments from this obligation. The Special Rapporteur notes with concern that, with the exception of Nepal, no government provided him with information about any such compensation provided to victims or their dependents. The Special Rapporteur urges States to make pertinent provisions under national legislation and set up funds for those who have suffered damage as a consequence of extrajudicial, summary, or arbitrary execution or attempted execution.

**SEE ALSO** *American Convention on Human Rights: Additional Protocol on the Death Penalty (Draft); European Convention on Human Rights: Protocol VI; Executions; Executions: Principles on the Effective Prevention and Investigation of Extra-Legal, Arbitrary and Summary Executions; Prisoners' Rights; Right to Life.*

**BIBLIOGRAPHY.** Amnesty International. *Africa: Towards Abolition of the Death Penalty.* London: 1991. NGO factfinding report, in English.

————. *USA: Death Penalty in the United States of America: Developments from 1 September 1989 to 31 December 1990.* London: 1991. NGO factfinding report, in English.

Boxman, Renee E. "The Road to Soering and Beyond: Will the United States Recognize the 'Death Row Phenomenon'?" *Houston Journal of International Law* 14, no. 1 (Fall 1991): 1–84. Scholarly article, in English.

Hintze, Michael D. "Attacking the Death Penalty: Toward a Renewed Strategy Twenty Years after Furman," *Columbia Human Rights Law Review* 24, no. 2 (Summer 1993): 395–433. Scholarly article, in English.

Hood, Roger. *The Death Penalty: A World-Wide Perspective: A Report to the United Nations Committee on Crime Prevention and Control.* Oxford, UK, and New York: Clarendon Press & Oxford University Press, 1991. Monograph, in English.

**CARITAS INTERNATIONALIS.** An international non-governmental organization in consultative status with the UN ECONOMIC AND SOCIAL COUNCIL (Category II) and with ILO, UNESCO, FAO, UNICEF, and the COUNCIL OF EUROPE, Caritas Internationalis is a member of the Conference of International Catholic Organizations and of the Pontifical Council CO-RUNUM.

Founded in 1950, CI is a confederation of 122 autonomous national Catholic organizations in 145 countries and territories directed by its statutes "to spread charity and social justice in the world." Each national Caritas organization is independent, and its program differs according to local needs and conditions. CI aims to coordinate, inform, and represent the many charitable and social welfare efforts of the Catholic Church and works in particular for the powerless, refugees and exiles, and the homeless and hungry.

CI regularly publishes the periodical *Intercaritas* and the monthly *Information Flyer* in English, French, and Spanish.

Caritas Internationalis. Address: Palazzo San Calisto 16, I-00120 Vatican City. Telephone: (39-6) 698-7197. Fax: (39-6) 6988-7237. Cable: INTERCARITAS ROMA. Secretary-General: Gerhard Meier.

**CARTER-MENIL HUMAN RIGHTS AWARD.** This annual award was established in 1986 by former U.S. President Jimmy Carter and Mrs. Dominique de Menil to honor individuals or organizations that promote the protection of human rights. The recipients receive $100,000. The awards are announced on December 10, the anniversary of the Universal Declaration of Human Rights.

Among past winners are al Haq and B'Tselem, two organizations working for human rights in the Israeli Occupied Territories (1989); Consejo de Comunidades Etnicas Runujel Junam of Guatemala and the Civil Rights Movement of Sri Lanka (1990); and six Jesuit priests murdered at the University of Central America (1991). In 1992, two organizations shared the award: the Native American Rights Fund of Boulder, CO, and the Haitian Refugee Center of Miami, FL. The Native American Rights Fund was founded in 1970 and is concerned with issues of religious freedom, the preservation of tribal existence and self-determination, the protection of natural resources, the development of Indian law, and governmental accountability. The Haitian Refugee Center was formed in 1980 and provides free legal support to Haitian refugees, including assis-

C

tance preparing asylum claims. No award was given in 1993 or 1994.

In October 1993, however, a special peace award was announced by the Carter-Menil Human Rights Foundation to the people of Norway for their efforts in resolving the Israeli-Palestinian conflict and for promoting peace worldwide. The award included the dedication of the Tony Smith sculpture "Marriage" to the people of Norway and a $100,000 Foundation prize to the Institute of Applied Social Sciences for its work in brokering the September 1993 declaration of principles between the Palestine Liberation Organization and the State of Israel.

Nominations for the Carter-Menil Human Rights Prize are submitted by human rights organizations around the world and are evaluated by an advisory committee appointed by the Carter Center. The final decision is made by President Carter and Mrs. de Menil, based on the committee's recommendation.

Carter-Menil Human Rights Prize. Address: The Carter Center, One Copenhill, Atlanta, GA 30307, USA. Telephone: (404) 420-5108. Fax: (404) 420-5145. Telex: 543236.

**CASSIN, RENÉ-SAMUEL (1887–1976).** René-Samuel Cassin, career diplomat and "author" of the Universal Declaration of Human Rights, received the **NOBEL PEACE PRIZE** in 1968, at the age of 81. Born in Bayonne, France, he received a degree in humanities and a law degree and doctorate from the University of Aix-en-Provence. In 1914 he became a doctor in juridical, economic, and political sciences, but had to forgo his burgeoning career when World War I broke out.

Profoundly affected by his wartime experiences, Cassin began campaigning after the war for compensation to war veterans, including pensions and professional retraining programs; he extended his campaign for veterans' compensation to other European countries. He also worked for disarmament.

During World War II, he left France with Gen. Charles de Gaulle, serving as his minister of justice in exile. After the war, Cassin served in many public capacities: as president of the Council of the National School of Administration; president of the French National Overseas Center of Advanced Studies; president of the French branch of the World Federation of Democratic Jurists; president of the Society of Comparative Legislation; and president of the International Institute of Diplomatic Studies and Research. He was a jurist of the Court of Arbitration at The Hague (1950–1960) and president of the European Court of Human Rights (1965–1968). With his Nobel Peace Prize money, Cassin founded the International Institute of Human Rights, which offers a specialized study sum-

mer session that provides advanced courses on international and comparative law of human rights.

Indeed, Cassin's Peace Prize was awarded precisely for his lifelong dedication to human rights. From 1945 to 1947, Cassin served as Eleanor Roosevelt's vice-chairman on the UN Commission on Human Rights. It was the Commission's task to prepare a document that specified what rights and freedoms should be guaranteed to all people in every country and under every legal system. Cassin helped draft the actual document—the Universal Declaration of Human Rights (1948)—which has served as the cornerstone of the human rights movement for 50 years. Years later, Cassin also prepared the International Covenant on Civil and Political Rights and the International Covenant on Economic, Social and Cultural Rights.

In his long and illustrious career, Cassin received many other awards, among them UN's Human Rights Prize (1968); the Goethe Prize (1973); and the French Grand Croix Legion d'Honneur and Croix de Guerre.

**BIBLIOGRAPHY.** Gray, Tony. *Champions of Peace.* London: Paddington Press, 1976.
Schlessinger, Bernard S., and June H. Schlessinger, eds. *Who's Who of Nobel Prize Winners.* Phoenix, AZ, USA: Oryx Press, 1991.

**CATHOLIC UNIVERSITY OF LYON, HUMAN RIGHTS INSTITUTE.** Established in 1985, the Human Rights Institute offers an undergraduate certificate in human rights, a master's in human rights, and a D.E.A. (Ph.D.). The Institute also maintains an Eastern European and an African human rights monitoring project. Students travel on observer missions, collection data on human rights situations, and carry out research. In addition, the Center publishes the quarterly *Revue de l'Institute des droits de l'homme de Lyon.*

Human Rights Institute. Address: Catholic University of Lyon, 10-12, one Alphonse Fochier, 69002 Lyon, France. Telephone: (33) 72-32-50-50. Fax: (33) 72-32-50-19. Director: Pascale Boucaud.

**CECIL, EDGAR ALGERNON ROBERT (1864–1958).** Lord Robert Cecil was awarded the **NOBEL PEACE PRIZE** for 1937. An aristocrat by birth, a lawyer by education, Lord Cecil was an ardent supporter of the **LEAGUE OF NATIONS** and was instrumental in drafting the Covenant of the League.

After World War I, well into his middle age, Cecil became convinced that human survival lay in ensuring world peace; and he believed that world peace could be ensured through an international diplomatic organization: the League of Nations. At the Paris Peace

Conference, he served as the British representative for negotiations for a League of Nations; between 1920 and 1922, he represented South Africa in the League Assembly; and from 1927 until the League's collapse in 1946, Lord Cecil was responsible for British activities in the League.

In addition to the Nobel Peace Prize, Lord Cecil received the Woodrow Wilson Foundation Peace Award in 1924.

**BIBLIOGRAPHY.** Gray, Tony. *Champions of Peace.* London: Paddington Press, 1976.

Schlessinger, Bernard S., and June H. Schlessinger, eds. *Who's Who of Nobel Prize Winners.* Phoenix, AZ, USA: Oryx Press, 1991.

**CENTER FOR HUMAN RIGHTS, UN.** A United Nations division, formerly known as the Division of Human Rights, the Center, which is the unit of the United Nations Secretariat most directly concerned with human rights, is a part of the United Nations office in Geneva. UN High Commissioner for Human Rights José Ayala Lasso is responsible for the Center's overall supervision.

The Center provides executive direction, management, and administrative and substantive services to a number of United Nations organs when they deal with human rights matters, including the **GENERAL ASSEMBLY,** the **ECONOMIC AND SOCIAL COUNCIL,** the **COMMISSION ON HUMAN RIGHTS,** its **SUB-COMMISSION ON PREVENTION OF DISCRIMINATION AND PROTECTION OF MINORITIES,** the **COMMITTEE ON THE ELIMINATION OF RACIAL DISCRIMINATION,** the **HUMAN RIGHTS COMMITTEE,** the **COMMITTEE ON ECONOMIC, SOCIAL AND CULTURAL RIGHTS,** the **COMMITTEE AGAINST TORTURE,** and their subsidiary bodies. It carries out research and prepares studies at the request of these bodies, administers the program of advisory services in the field of human rights, collects and disseminates information on questions related to human rights, and prepares publications on the subject.

The Center includes the office of the High Commissioner, within which there is an administrative support unit, a liaison office in New York, and four sections: the International Instrument Section; the Research, Studies and Prevention of Discrimination Section; the Advisory Services Section; and the External Relations, Publication and Documentation Section.

The Center endeavors to maintain and strengthen coordination with specialized agencies that are concerned with human rights questions, such as the **INTERNATIONAL LABOR ORGANIZATION,** the United Nations Educational, Scientific and Cultural Organization, the **WORLD HEALTH ORGANIZATION,** and the

**FOOD AND AGRICULTURAL ORGANIZATION** of the United Nations. Meetings to review ongoing programs and to explore cooperative endeavors are held at least once a year.

The Center also cooperates closely with the human rights organs of regional intergovernmental organizations, such as those of the **ORGANIZATION OF AMERICAN STATES,** the **ORGANIZATION OF AFRICAN UNITY,** and the **COUNCIL OF EUROPE.** In addition, the Center maintains contact with interested governments in order to work out the details of advisory services and technical assistance projects for the promotion and protection of human rights. Such arrangements vary widely from country to country and include the training of officials, judges, police, and military officers; the setting up of law faculties; the organization of law libraries; the drafting of legal texts in keeping with the provisions of international human rights instruments; the collection and circulation of relevant information and reference materials; and the publication of law journals.

On 7 March 1989, the Commission on Human Rights adopted without a vote a resolution entitled "Co-ordinating Role of the Center for Human Rights" (resolution 1989/54), in which it supported the efforts of the UN Secretary-General to enhance the role and importance of the Center for Human Rights as a co-ordinating unit in the system of bodies dealing with the promotion and protection of human rights, and expressed the hope that the steps being taken in that direction, including the measures to promote the settlement of regional conflicts, would foster cooperation in upholding and protecting human rights and fundamental freedoms, better understanding, mutual respect, trust, and tolerance in relations between States and peoples.

The General Assembly, in resolution 47/127 of 18 December 1992, recognized "the important role of the Center for Human Rights in the promotion, protection and implementation of human rights and the need to provide sufficient human resources to the Center, particularly in view of the fact that its workload has dramatically increased while resources have failed to keep pace with the expansion of its responsibilities." The Assembly supported the efforts of the Secretary-General to enhance the role and importance of the Center as the coordinating unit within the United Nations system of bodies dealing with human rights.

**BIBLIOGRAPHY.** Cohen, Roberta. *Human Rights and Humanitarian Emergencies: New Roles for UN Human Rights Bodies.* Washington, D.C.: Center for Policy Analysis and Research on Refugee Issues, 1992. NGO discussion paper, in English.

Schmidt, Markus G. "Achieving Much with Little: The Work of the United Nations Centre for Human Rights," *Neth-*

C

*erlands Quarterly of Human Rights* 8, no. 4 (1990): 371–380.
Scholarly article, in English.

United Nations. *Coordinating Role of the Center for Human
Rights within the United Nations Bodies and Machinery Dealing
with the Promotion and Protection of Human Rights.* UN Doc. E/
CN.4/1992/21; Add. 1 and 2.

————. *Developments Relating to the Activities of the
Center for Human Rights.* UN Doc. E/CN.4/1992/75 and
1993/87.

**CENTER FOR SOCIAL DEVELOPMENT AND HU-
MANITARIAN AFFAIRS, UN.** Part of the UN office
at Vienna, the Center is responsible for four major
programs closely related to the promotion and protection of human rights, and works closely with the
Center for Human Rights:

1. The program on the advancement of women began in
the United Nations as part of the human rights program and
involves the technical and substantive servicing of the UN
Commission on the Status of Women and the UN Committee on the Elimination of Discrimination against Women.

2. The program on crime prevention and criminal justice
began, in part, through the acquisition of the mandate of
the Penal Commission of the League of Nations. This program has had a long relationship with the human rights program in terms of the rights of those accused or convicted of
a crime.

3. The program on global social issues and policies has
included concern with the general enjoyment of economic
and social rights, including analysis in terms of social institutions like the family.

4. The program on the integration of social groups has
included concern for the enjoyment of human rights by specific groups of the population, including the development
of international policy norms to protect the rights of disadvantaged groups.

**CENTRAL AFRICAN REPUBLIC.** The Central African Republic, formerly part of the colony of French
Equatorial Africa, is a landlocked State in central Africa. It has borders with Cameroon, Chad (also formerly part of French Equatorial Africa), Congo, Sudan, and Zaire. It achieved independence from France
in 1960 and became a member of the United Nations
the same year. Its population is estimated to be
3,068,000. The population of the Central African Republic includes a large number of ethnic communities
that form part of the following major ethnic groups:
Banda, Baya, Mandjia, Yakoma, Ngbaka, Ali, Kaba,
Karé, Baminga (Pygmies), Gbanou, Sango, Zandé,
Nzakara, Mbati, Gbougou, Ngbakamandjia, Mboroco
(Peuls), Hausa (of Arabized origin), etc. There are
also groups from other African countries (Cameroon,
Chad, Congo, Senegal, Sudan, and Zaire), as well as
naturalized groups of French, Portuguese, and Leba-

nese origin. Languages commonly used include Sango
and French (official) and a wide variety of African languages. Religions practiced include Christianity (Protestant faiths, 50%; Roman Catholic, 33%), Islam (5%),
and Animism (12%). Literacy is estimated at 35%.

The government (1990) took the form of a republic
under a constitution approved by more than 97% of
the population on 5 February 1981, which guarantees
the fundamental rights and freedoms of the people,
the multiparty system, and the existence of trade unions. However, the constitution was suspended with
the coming into power on 1 September 1981 of the
Military Committee for National Recovery. The Committee indicated that it would continue to respect and
apply the provisions concerning the basic rights of citizens. Under Committee rule, only its President, who
is head of State, has discretionary power in the administrative sphere. The judicial system operates in a normal manner.

During the 14-year period between 1965 and 1979,
the Central African Republic was ruled by an authoritarian and dictatorial regime headed by Jean-Bedel
Bokassa, the army Chief of Staff who seized power in
a military coup on 31 December 1965 and declared
himself, successively, Field Marshal; President for Life;
and, on 4 December 1976, Emperor Bokassa I of the
Central African Empire.

Although the constitution of the empire guaranteed
the basic human rights and fundamental freedoms, it
was ignored by the Bokassa regime, which became
known for its gross violations of human rights, including arbitrary arrests, executions, and "disappearances"; a massacre of schoolchildren; and the establishment of a military court system in which the
accused had no right to a defense and no means of
appeal.

Bokassa's initiatives and personal ambitions led him
to spend more than $100 million on his coronation as
emperor at a time when many of the country's three
million people were without food or shelter. He
sought and obtained assistance from the government
of South Africa to build the "200-villas" complex in
Bangui which he then used as his private property.
And he ordered at least 20 of his real or imagined
opponents to be put to death in Bangui's Ngaragba
Prison. In 1979, he ordered the arrest of more than
100 schoolchildren when they protested against being
forced to buy uniforms made in a factory owned by his
wife; soldiers called to quiet the disturbance opened
fire and killed many of the children.

A French-backed coup under the leadership of former President David Dacko deposed Bokassa on 20
September 1979. A new constitution was prepared and
was approved by 97% of the electorate on 5 February
1981. This constitution contained provisions guaran-

teeing fundamental human rights, including freedom of thought, freedom of expression, freedom to vote, and freedom of movement; established a multi-party system; and provided for the existence of trade unions. Unfortunately, serious differences soon arose based on varying interpretations of the idea of a multiparty system. As a result, the political, economic, and social life of the country was paralyzed. The army once again stepped in, on 1 September 1981, and assumed power under army General Andre Kolingba. The new regime suspended the constitution immediately but stated that it would respect and apply the provisions concerning the basic rights of citizens.

On 21 November 1986, a new constitution was enacted that provided for parliamentary elections to be held, in which only one party—the Centrafrican Democratic Assembly—would be eligible to participate. The new constitution also prolonged the term of office of President Kolingba by six years. In 1992, multiparty legislative and presidential elections were held in October but were canceled when it became obvious that Kolingba was losing.

Jean-Bedel Bokassa, who had taken refuge in France, was sentenced to death in absentia in 1980. Nevertheless, he returned voluntarily to the Central African Republic in October 1986, saying he wanted to clear himself of all charges against him. He was tried by a nine-member court—three judges and six jurors—and found guilty of having ordered prisoners put to death by brutal means. He was also found guilty of the massacre of schoolchildren in September 1979. Acquitted on several of 14 charges, including cannibalism, he was sentenced to death in July 1987; however, in March 1988, his sentence was commuted to life in prison.

From 1980 to the present, the UN General Assembly has affirmed the need for international action to assist the Government of the Central African Republic in its efforts to reconstruct, rehabilitate, and develop the country. The Assembly continues to monitor the situation; but, in resolution 47/159 of 18 December 1992, it was only able to note "the grave difficulties that the Government of the Central African Republic has continued to face since 1982 in achieving the objectives of its development programme, owing to the harmful effects of the international economic situation, and the need to provide it with supplementary resources so as to enable it to achieve those objectives."

At its 972nd and 983rd meetings, held on 11 and 18 March 1993 (see CERD/C/SR.972 and 983), the Committee on the Elimination of Racial Discrimination reviewed the implementation of the Convention by the Central African Republic, based on its previous report (CERD/C/117/Add. 5) and its consideration by the Committee (see CERD/C/SR.751 and 752). The Committee noted that no report had been received since 1984.

Members of the Committee observed that approximately 80 ethnic groups made up the population of the Central African Republic, but it primarily comprised the Baya, Banda, Babinga, Baka, and Zanda groups. However, members of the Yakoma group dominated the administration even though they accounted for less than 5 percent of the population. In particular, the forest-dwelling Bayaka, or Pygmies, were often victims of discrimination and exploitation. The Government had done little to correct that situation.

The revised Constitution should ensure respect for human rights and the principle of equality before the law. More information was needed as to how legislation implemented the provisions of the Convention. Additional information was also required as to the social and economic situation of the various ethnic groups. Members of the Committee wished to know whether there were any integrationist or multiracial organizations; whether there were any human rights organizations actively combating racism and racial discrimination; what measures had been taken to criminalize racial discrimination and provide appropriate punishment under the law; what measures had been taken to protect refugees in the country; and what mechanisms existed to ensure the right to recourse under article 6 of the Convention. Members also wished to have information on recent developments concerning the evolution toward pluralist democracy, including the scheduling of elections and the modification of the Constitution.

In concluding the review, the Committee expressed its regret that the Central African Republic had not submitted a report since 1984 and had not responded to its invitation to participate in the meeting and to furnish the relevant information. The Committee wished to draw the attention of the State party to the possibility of requesting technical assistance from the United Nations Center for Human Rights in the preparation of its report.

The Committee hoped to receive a new report shortly. This was particularly important in view of the changes that had taken place in the Central African Republic since 1984.

**BIBLIOGRAPHY.** Amnesty International. *Arrests and Cases of Political Imprisonment Reported to Amnesty International in the Central African Republic during the First Half of 1985.* London: 1985. NGO bulletin, in English.

Article 19. *Freedom of Information and Expression in the Central African Republic.* London: 1989. NGO report, in English.

Azonga, Tikum Mbah. "Central African Republic: Kolingba's Promises," *West Africa* (30 June 1986): 1356–1357. Magazine article, in English.

Bayalama, Sylvain. "Pluralism and Political Change in

# C

Central Africa," *Africa Today* 38, no. 3 (1991): 66–71. Article, in English.

Brody, Reed. *"Où est l'honneur?" Le procès disciplinaire de Maître Nicolas Tiangaye, Bangui, République centrafricaine, 9–10 octobre 1990* ("Where is the Honor?" The Disciplinary Trial of the Lawyer Nicolas Tiangaye, Bangui, Central African Republic, October 9–10, 1990). Geneva, Switzerland: Center for the Independence of Judges and Lawyers and the International Commission of Jurists, 1990. NGO factfinding report, in French.

"CAR: Clemency for Political Detainees," *West Africa* (15 September 1986): 1947. Magazine article, in English.

Demafouth, Jean-Jacques. "Landlocked and Uninformed," *Index on Censorship* 14, no. 5 (October 1985): 22–24. NGO article, in English.

**CENTRAL AMERICAN UNIVERSITY, INSTITUTE FOR HUMAN RIGHTS.** Founded in 1985, the Institute studies human rights from a theoretical perspective, documents the human rights situation in El Salvador, and works with the Faculty of Law to provide a legal-aid program and to study ways of improving existing legislation. The Institute coordinates seminars and workshops on human rights for university employees, and for church and human rights groups and lawyers. In addition, the Institute has a well-established publishing program; among its publications are the five-volume *Documentos sobre los Derechos Humanos* (1986) and *Democracy, Liberalism and Human Rights* (1987).

Institute for Human Rights. Address: Central American University "Jose Simeon Canas," P.O. (01) 168, Autopista Sur, San Salvador, El Salvador. Telephone: (503) 240-011. Fax: (503) 731-010. Director: Dr. Segundo Montes, SJ.

**CHAD.** The Republic of Chad, formerly part of the colony of French Equatorial Africa, is a landlocked State in central Africa. It has borders with Cameroon, the Central African Republic (also formerly part of French Equatorial Africa), Libya, Niger, Nigeria, and Sudan. It achieved independence from France in 1960 and became a member of the United Nations the same year. Its population is estimated to be 5,297,000.

About 200 ethnic groups are included in the population. In the north the following groups may be distinguished: the Bouiala, the Arabs, the Khozam, the Djatne, the Kareda, the Amakaza, the Toubou, the Gorane, the Hadjarai, the Zakawa, the Kanembou, the Bornou, the Ouaddaiens, the Boudouna, the Niergue, the Kouka, the Dadjo, the Baguirmiens, and the Kotoko. This list is far from exhaustive. In the south the main groups are the Mboum, the Laka, the Kaba, the Soumou, the Gor, the Mongo, the Ngambave, the Goulaye, the Mbaye, the Sara, the Daye, the Ngama, the Sara-Kaba, the Boua, the Nyelim, the Mouroum, the Mberi, the Gabri, the Kabalaye, the Soumouraye, the Nanichere, the Marba, the Kim, the Karo, the Massa, the Moudang, the Toupouri, the Falata, and the Goula. These are the principal ethnic groups of southern Chad. It should be noted that there is interpenetration between the different ethnic groups.

Languages commonly used include French and Arabic (both official) and Sara; in addition, more than 100 African languages and dialects are spoken. Religions practiced include Islam (45%), Christianity (30%), and Animism (25%). For the most part, Muslim groups, whose main activity is livestock breeding, live in the northern areas of the country, while Christian and animist groups, who engage in farming, live in the southern areas. Literacy is estimated at 20%.

The government (1994) took the form of a republic. However, the 1962 constitution, which provided an intrinsic guarantee of the human rights and public freedoms, as well as a guarantee of the rights of the citizen based on the principles of liberty, humanity, and equality, has been repealed. The Fundamental Act of the Third Republic, which replaced the constitution, provides, in article 18, for "the establishment of a political democracy which guarantees the fundamental freedoms and rights of the individual, of associations and of communities and the effective participation of all levels of society in the conduct of public affairs."

The President is head of State and of government and exercises administrative authority in the country. Legislation is dealt with by the National Consultative Assembly, constituted in 1982.

*CONFLICT BETWEEN CHAD AND LIBYA.* A Libyan-financed rebel movement, the Chadian National Liberation Front, fomented and encouraged civil strife in northern Chad between 1975 and 1979. In March 1979, a number of rebel groups met at Lagos and formed a "provisional government" headed by Goukouni Oueddi. That government was challenged, after being in power for one year, by its own Defense Minister Hissèn Habré, who ousted Goukouni Oueddi and set up a government of reconciliation with a cabinet that included the leaders of several earlier conflicts. His offer of a cabinet post to Goukouni Oueddi, who took refuge in Algiers, was turned down.

Libyan troops occupied much of northern Chad between 1980 and 1986. However, in March 1987, Hissèn Habré's Chadian forces took Libyan bases in Gouro and Ounianga, capturing an estimated half-billion dollars worth of weapons and supplies, including planes, tanks, artillery pieces, rocket launchers, trucks, and jeeps. As a result, Chad found itself with one of the best-equipped armies in Africa.

On 24 September 1987, Libya and Chad agreed to

let the **ORGANIZATION OF AFRICAN UNITY** mediate their territorial conflict over the Aozou border strip. However, it was only in February 1994 that the dispute was settled by the International Court of Justice, which rejected Libya's claims to the strip.

*EFFECTS OF NATURAL DISASTERS.* Tens of thousands of Chadians, who had been displaced in neighboring countries by drought and warfare, returned to Chad between 1986 and 1989. By the end of 1989, the United Nations High Commissioner for Refugees had assisted the reintegration of several hundred thousand Chadian returnees who had repatriated mainly from the Central African Republic, Nigeria, and the Sudan.

On 15 December 1989, the UN General Assembly expressed (resolution 44/153) concern about the persistence of the harmful effects of the drought, desertification, floods, and infestations of locusts and grasshoppers—problems compounding the already precarious food and health situation in Chad—and concluded that the large mass of voluntary returnees and displaced persons would pose serious social and economic problems for the government of that country. It reiterated its earlier appeals to all States and intergovernmental and non-governmental organizations to support the efforts of the government of Chad to assist and resettle the returnees and displaced persons and again called upon the Secretary-General and the United Nations High Commissioner for Refugees to mobilize emergency humanitarian assistance for this purpose.

*CIVIL WAR.* In December 1990, the pro-Western government fell to rebel forces, the Libyan-supported Patriotic Salvation Movement; its leader, Idriss Deby assumed the presidency. The new government promised to introduce multiparty democracy. Unfortunately, civil strife continued. Not until April 1993 could all the concerned forces be brought together. The Sovereign National Conference, convened at N'Djamena from 15 January to 7 April 1993, succeeded in initiating a process of democratization. But even this important accomplishment was not enough to avert massacres of Chadians by rebel groups that occurred on 4 and 8 August 1993 in the cities of Chokoyam and N'Djamena.

Meeting in Geneva, the UN **SUB-COMMISSION ON PREVENTION OF DISCRIMINATION AND PROTECTION OF MINORITIES,** in resolution 1993/10 of 20 August 1993, strongly condemned the gross and continuing violations of human rights in Chad, called upon the Chadian authorities to implement the decisions of the Sovereign National Conference, and appealed to the international community to contribute by the appro-

priate means and by taking positive measures to enhance the promotion and protection of human rights and fundamental freedoms in the country.

Various UN committees have reviewed the situation of Discrimination in Chad, one such report in early 1993 by the UN Committee on the Elimination of Racial Discrimination contained the following:

At its 980th and 983rd meetings, held on 17 and 18 March 1993 (see CERD/C/SR.980 and 983), the Committee reviewed the implementation of the Convention by Chad based on its previous report (CERD/C/114/Add. 2) and its consideration by the Committee (see CERD/C/SR.838). The Committee noted that no report had been received since 1986.

The representative of the State party explained that, during the previous dictatorial regime of President Hissène Habré, there had been many discriminatory policies in favour of the Goranes, the tribe of the President. During the years of dictatorship, 1982 to 1990, more than 40,000 persons had been killed, more than 80,000 children orphaned, more than 30,000 women widowed, and more than 20,000 persons deprived of material and moral support. The new democratic government had initiated a number of steps in an effort to establish the rule of law and guarantee respect for human rights. Among the measures adopted were the establishment, by Decree 14/P-CE/CJ/90, of a commission to investigate crimes committed under the dictatorship. The post of Minister of Humanitarian Affairs had recently been established with a view to creating the conditions necessary for the exercise of human rights, coordinating humanitarian undertakings, monitoring respect for human rights and educating the general public in that regard, and providing a mechanism for reparations to victims of human rights abuses. Additionally, the newly created National Human Rights Commission investigated reports of human rights abuses, including torture, disappearances and arbitrary detention, and promoted human rights education. Fundamental human rights were now guaranteed in the Charter of the Republic, which had been adopted in March 1991 under Decree No. 001/PR/91. Lastly, the Government has taken the necessary steps to ratify the International Covenant on Civil and Political Rights, the International Covenant on Economic, Social, and Cultural Rights, and the Convention against Torture and Other Cruel, Inhuman, or Degrading Treatment or Punishment.

The representative of the State party assured the Committee that there were no political prisoners in Chad and no journalists in detention. There had not been a state of emergency since 1 December 1992. The present Government was doing everything possible to restore peace in the country following 30 years of civil war. Although Chad had not been represented at the deliberations of the Committee since 1986, it would be in the future.

Members of the Committee welcomed the presence of the representative of Chad and expressed their satisfaction with the re-establishment of a dialogue with that State party. The representative had provided the Committee with much useful information. However, there were still many areas that required further clarification. In particular, members of the Committee wished to have more information regarding the size of the various ethnic groups in Chad and the extent to which their economic, social, and cultural rights were respected. In that connection, the results of the 1993 census should be communicated to the Committee by the Government. Members of the Committee stated that steps needed to be taken to assist the various ethnic groups with regard to culture, education, and social welfare. Members of the Committee expressed their concern over the reported persecution of the Hajerai ethnic group, which had been closely associated with the previous regime. Information was also needed on whether vulnerable ethnic groups were adequately represented in the new National Human Rights Commission.

Members of the Committee invited the State party to follow up the dialogue by submitting a new report that would conform to the Committee's revised general guidelines for the submission of reports.

In his reply, the representative of the State party stated that Chad counted among its population no less than 110 tribes. He assured members of the Committee that racial discrimination was not a tradition in Chad. During the previous regime, an attempt had been made to create divisions in the country between north and south, between Christians and Muslims and between French speakers and Arabic speakers. All of those discriminatory practices had since been terminated. At present, there were 33 political parties in Chad. In order to prevent the rise of tribalism, each party was required by law to have membership in at least 10 of the country's 14 regions. The Hajerai ethnic group had been reintegrated; those persons who had been arrested in the clashes of October 1991 had been released.

Further responses to the questions posed by members of the Committee would be contained in the next report submitted by Chad.

### Provisional Concluding Observations

The Committee welcomed the presence of the Minister of Humanitarian Affairs of Chad, who had come to present his Government's point of view, thus demonstrating Chad's willingness to reopen the dialogue with the Committee after many years of silence.

The Committee took note with satisfaction of the commitment made by the representative of Chad to submit the written periodic report in the prescribed manner at the next session and reiterated its offer to the advisory services of the Centre for Human Rights to assist Chad in preparing the report, if it so wished.

The Committee emphasized the particular importance it attached, during the country's present transition period, to the measures taken by the Government of Chad to consolidate the rule of law and to prevent the return of any dictatorial regime or of any policies of discrimination or repression against particular ethnic groups.

***BIBLIOGRAPHY.*** Amnesty International. *Appeal to Chad's National Conference and Political Leaders for Action to Protect Human Rights.* London: 1993. NGO report, in English.

————. *Chad: Arrests of Members of the Hadjerai Ethnic Group.* London: 1988. NGO report, in English.

————. *Chad: Chadian National Conference Adopts Resolutions to Prevent Human Rights Violations.* London: 1993. NGO report, in English.

————. *Chad Campaign 21 April to end August 1993: Never Again? Killings Continue into the 1990s.* London: 1993. NGO report, in English.

————. *Republique du Tchad: "Disparitions," Executions, Extrajudiciares et Detention Secrete* (Republic of Chad: "Disappearances," Extrajudicial Executions and Secret Detention). London: 1987. NGO report, in French.

Whiteman, Kaye. *Chad.* London: Minority Rights Group, 1988. NGO report, in English.

## CHAMBERLAIN, JOSEPH AUSTEN (1863–1937).

Sir Joseph Austen Chamberlain was co-recipient of the 1925 **NOBEL PEACE PRIZE.** Born in Birmingham, England, Chamberlain first entered the British parliament in 1899 and remained an MP all his life. He also served as civil lord of the admiralty, financial secretary to the Treasury, postmaster general, chancellor of the Exchequer (under three administrations), secretary of state for India, foreign secretary, and first lord of the admiralty.

Chamberlain received his Nobel Peace Prize, as did his co-recipient **CHARLES GATES DAWES** and the next year's recipient **ARISTIDE BRIAND,** for his work in securing the Locarno Pacts of 1925, by which Germany's western frontiers were mutually agreed upon by Great Britain, France, Italy, Belgium, and Germany.

***BIBLIOGRAPHY.*** Dutton, David. *Austen Chamberlain: Gentleman in Politics.* London: Transaction Books, 1987.

Gray, Tony. *Champions of Peace.* London: Paddington Press, 1976.

Schlessinger, Bernard S., and June H. Schlessinger, eds. *Who's Who of Nobel Prize Winners.* Phoenix, AZ, USA: Oryx Press, 1991.

## CHARTER OF PARIS FOR A NEW EUROPE (1990).

In 1973 the Conference on Security and Cooperation in Europe (renamed in 1994 the **ORGANIZATION ON SECURITY AND COOPERATION IN EUROPE**) was convened among 32 European States and the United States and Canada in Helsinki, Finland. From that Conference emerged the Helsinki Process, the function of which was to establish a framework for ensuring peace and security in Europe as well as the protection of human rights. The 1990 meeting of the CSCE, held in Paris, France, culminated in the adoption of the Charter of Paris for a New Europe by the 34 participating States. Although not a legally binding document, the Charter establishes the States' commitments to, and reaffirms the juridical significance of, certain political and human rights. The text of the Charter is as follows:

Meeting of the Heads of State or Government of the participating States of the Conference on Security and Co-operation in Europe (CSCE): Austria, Belgium, Bulgaria, Canada, Cyprus, Czech and Slovak Federal Republic, Denmark, Finland, France, Germany, Greece, Holy See, Hungary, Iceland, Ireland, Italy-European Community, Liechtenstein, Luxembourg, Malta, Monaco, Netherlands, Norway, Poland, Portugal, Romania, San Marino, Spain, Sweden,

Switzerland, Turkey, Union of Soviet Socialist Republics, United Kingdom, United States of America and Yugoslavia (Paris, 19–21 November 1990).

## A New Era of Democracy, Peace and Unity

We, the Heads of State or Government of the States participating in the Conference on Security and Co-operation in Europe, have assembled in Paris at a time of profound change and historic expectations. The era of confrontation and division of Europe has ended. We declare that henceforth our relations will be founded on respect and co-operation.

Europe is liberating itself from the legacy of the past. The courage of men and women, the strength of the will of the peoples and the power of the ideas of the Helsinki Final Act have opened a new era of democracy, peace and unity in Europe.

Ours is a time for fulfilling the hopes and expectations our peoples have cherished for decades: steadfast commitment to democracy based on human rights and fundamental freedoms; prosperity through economic liberty and social justice; and equal security for all our countries.

The Ten Principles of the Final Act will guide us towards this ambitious future, just as they have lighted our way towards better relations for the past fifteen years. Full implementation of all CSCE commitments must form the basis for the initiatives we are now taking to enable our nations to live in accordance with their aspirations.

## Human Rights, Democracy and Rule of Law

We undertake to build, consolidate and strengthen democracy as the only system of government of our nations. In this endeavour, we will abide by the following:

Human rights and fundamental freedoms are the birthright of all human beings, are inalienable and are guaranteed by law. Their protection and promotion is the first responsibility of government. Respect for them is an essential safeguard against an over-mighty State. Their observance and full exercise are the foundation of freedom, justice and peace.

Democratic government is based on the will of the people, expressed regularly through free and fair elections. Democracy has as its foundation respect for the human person and the rule of law. Democracy is the best safeguard of freedom of expression, tolerance of all groups of society, and equality of opportunity for each person.

Democracy, with its representative and pluralist character, entails accountability to the electorate, the obligation of public authorities to comply with the law and justice administered impartially. No one will be above the law.

We affirm that, without discrimination, every individual has the right to: freedom of thought, conscience and religion or belief, freedom of expression, freedom of association and peaceful assembly, freedom of movement; no one will be: subject to arbitrary arrest or detention, subject to torture or other cruel, inhuman or degrading treatment or punishment; everyone also has the right: to know and act upon his rights, to participate in free and fair elections, to fair and public trial if charged with an offence, to own property alone or in association and to exercise individual enterprise, to enjoy his economic, social and cultural rights.

We affirm that the ethnic, cultural, linguistic and religious identity of national minorities will be protected and that persons belonging to national minorities have the right freely to express, preserve and develop that identity without any discrimination and in full equality before the law.

We will ensure that everyone will enjoy recourse to effective remedies, national or international, against any violation of his rights.

Full respect for these precepts is the bedrock on which we will seek to construct the new Europe.

Our States will co-operate and support each other with the aim of making democratic gains irreversible.

## Economic Liberty and Responsibility

Economic liberty, social justice and environmental responsibility are indispensable for prosperity.

The free will of the individual, exercised in democracy and protected by the rule of law, forms the necessary basis for successful economic and social development. We will promote economic activity which respects and upholds human dignity.

Freedom and political pluralism are necessary elements in our common objective of developing market economies towards sustainable economic growth, prosperity, social justice, expanding employment and efficient use of economic resources. The success of the transition to market economy by countries making efforts to this effect is important and in the interest of us all. It will enable us to share a higher level of prosperity which is our common objective. We will co-operate to this end.

Preservation of the environment is a shared responsibility of all our nations. While supporting national and regional efforts in this field, we must also look to the pressing need for joint action on a wider scale.

## Friendly Relations among Participating States

Now that a new era is dawning in Europe, we are determined to expand and strengthen friendly relations and co-operation among the States of Europe, the United States of America and Canada, and to promote friendship among our peoples.

To uphold and promote democracy, peace and unity in Europe, we solemnly pledge our full commitment to the Ten Principles of the Helsinki Final Act. We affirm the continuing validity of the Ten Principles and our determination to put them into practice. All the Principles apply equally and unreservedly, each of them being interpreted taking into account the others. They form the basis for our relations.

In accordance with our obligations under the Charter of the United Nations and commitments under the Helsinki Final Act, we renew our pledge to refrain from the threat or use of force against the territorial integrity or political independence of any State, or from acting in any other manner inconsistent with the principles or purposes of those documents. We recall that non-compliance with obligations under the Charter of the United Nations constitutes a violation of international law.

We reaffirm our commitment to settle disputes by peaceful means. We decide to develop mechanisms for the prevention and resolution of conflicts among the participating States.

With the ending of the division of Europe, we will strive for a new quality in our security relations while fully respecting each other's freedom of choice in that respect. Security is indivisible and the security of every participating State is inseparably linked to that of all the others. We therefore pledge to co-operate in strengthening confidence and security among us and in promoting arms control and disarmament.

We welcome the Joint Declaration of Twenty-Two States on the improvement of their relations.

Our relations will rest on our common adherence to democratic values and to human rights and fundamental freedoms. We are convinced that in order to strengthen peace and security among our States, the advancement of democracy, and respect for and effective exercise of human rights, are indispensable. We reaffirm the equal rights of peoples and their right to self-determination in conformity with the Charter of the United Nations and with the relevant norms of international law, including those relating to territorial integrity of States.

We are determined to enhance political consultation and to widen co-operation to solve economic, social, environmental, cultural and humanitarian problems. This common resolve and our growing interdependence will help to overcome the mistrust of decades, to increase stability and to build a united Europe.

We want Europe to be a source of peace, open to dialogue and to co-operation with other countries, welcoming exchanges and involved in the search for common responses to the challenges of the future.

### Security

Friendly relations among us will benefit from the consolidation of democracy and improved security.

We welcome the signature of the Treaty on Conventional Armed Forces in Europe by twenty-two participating States, which will lead to lower levels of armed forces. We endorse the adoption of a substantial new set of Confidence- and Security-building Measures which will lead to increased transparency and confidence among all participating States. These are important steps towards enhanced stability and security in Europe.

The unprecedented reduction in armed forces resulting from the Treaty on Conventional Armed Forces in Europe, together with new approaches to security and co-operation within the CSCE process, will lead to a new perception of security in Europe and a new dimension in our relations. In this context we fully recognize the freedom of States to choose their own security arrangements.

### Unity

Europe whole and free is calling for a new beginning. We invite our peoples to join in this great endeavour.

We note with great satisfaction the Treaty on the Final Settlement with respect to Germany signed in Moscow on 12 September 1990 and sincerely welcome the fact that the German people have united to become one State in accordance with the principles of the Final Act of the Conference on Security and Co-operation in Europe and in full accord with their neighbours. The establishment of the national unity of Germany is an important contribution to a just and lasting order of peace for a united, democratic Europe aware of its responsibility for stability, peace and co-operation.

The participation of both North American and European States is a fundamental characteristic of the CSCE; it underlies its past achievements and is essential to the future of the CSCE process. An abiding adherence to shared values and our common heritage are the ties which bind us together. With all the rich diversity of our nations, we are united in our commitment to expand our co-operation in all fields. The challenges confronting us can only be met by common action, co-operation and solidarity.

### The CSCE and the World

The destiny of our nations is linked to that of all other nations. We support fully the United Nations and the enhancement of its role in promoting international peace, security and justice. We reaffirm our commitment to the principles and purposes of the United Nations as enshrined in the Charter and condemn all violations of these principles. We recognize with satisfaction the growing role of the United Nations in world affairs and its increasing effectiveness, fostered by the improvement in relations among our States.

Aware of the dire needs of a great part of the world, we commit ourselves to solidarity with all other countries. Therefore, we issue a call from Paris today to all the nations of the world. We stand ready to join with any and all States in common efforts to protect and advance the community of fundamental human values.

### Guidelines for the Future

Proceeding from our firm commitment to the full implementation of all CSCE principles and provisions, we now resolve to give a new impetus to a balanced and comprehensive development of our co-operation in order to address the needs and aspirations of our peoples.

### Human Dimension

We declare our respect for human rights and fundamental freedoms to be irrevocable. We will fully implement and build upon the provisions relating to the human dimension of the CSCE.

Proceeding from the Document of the Copenhagen Meeting of the Conference on the Human Dimension, we will cooperate to strengthen democratic institutions and to promote the application of the rule of law. To that end, we decide to convene a seminar of experts in Oslo from 4 to 15 November 1991.

Determined to foster the rich contribution of national minorities to the life of our societies, we undertake further to improve their situation. We reaffirm our deep conviction that friendly relations among our peoples, as well as peace, justice, stability and democracy, require that the ethnic, cultural, linguistic and religious identity of national minorities be protected and conditions for the promotion of that identity be created. We declare that questions related to national minorities can only be satisfactorily resolved in a democratic political framework. We further acknowledge that the rights of persons belonging to national minorities must be fully respected as part of universal human rights. Being aware of the urgent need for increased cooperation on, as well as better protection of, national minorities, we decide to convene a meeting of experts on national minorities to be held in Geneva from 1 to 19 July 1991.

We express our determination to combat all forms of racial and ethnic hatred, antisemitism, xenophobia and discrimination against anyone as well as persecution on religious and ideological grounds.

In accordance with our CSCE commitments, we stress that free movement and contacts among our citizens as well as the free flow of information and ideas are crucial for the maintenance and development of free societies and flourishing cultures. We welcome increased tourism and visits among our countries.

The human dimension mechanism has proved its usefulness, and we are consequently determined to expand it to include new procedures involving, inter alia, the services of experts or a roster of eminent persons experienced in human rights issues which could be raised under the mechanism. We shall provide, in the context of the mechanism, for individuals to be involved in the protection of their rights. Therefore, we undertake to develop further our commitments in this respect, in particular at the Moscow Meeting of the Conference on the Human Dimension, without prejudice to obligations under existing international instruments to which our States may be parties.

We recognize the important contribution of the Council of Europe to the promotion of human rights and the principles of democracy and the rule of law as well as to the development of cultural co-operation. We welcome moves by several participating States to join the Council of Europe and adhere to its European Convention on Human Rights. We welcome as well the readiness of the Council of Europe to make its experience available to the CSCE.

### Security

The changing political and military environment in Europe opens new possibilities for common efforts in the field of military security. We will build on the important achievements attained in the Treaty on Conventional Armed Forces in Europe and in the Negotiations on Confidence- and Security-building Measures. We undertake to continue the CSBM negotiations under the same mandate, and to seek to conclude them no later than the Follow-up Meeting of the CSCE to be held in Helsinki in 1992. We also welcome the decision of the participating States concerned to continue the CFE negotiation under the same mandate and to seek to conclude it no later than the Helsinki Follow-up Meeting. Following a period for national preparations, we look forward to a more structured co-operation among all participating States on security matters, and to discussions and consultations among the thirty-four participating States aimed at establishing by 1992, from the conclusion of the Helsinki Follow-up Meeting, new negotiations on disarmament and confidence and security building open to all participating States.

We call for the earliest possible conclusion of the Convention on an effectively verifiable, global and comprehensive ban on chemical weapons, and we intend to be original signatories to it.

We reaffirm the importance of the Open Skies initiative and call for the successful conclusion of the negotiations as soon as possible.

Although the threat of conflict in Europe has diminished, other dangers threaten the stability of our societies. We are determined to co-operate in defending democratic institutions against activities which violate the independence, sovereign equality or territorial integrity of the participating States. These include illegal activities involving outside pressure, coercion and subversion.

We unreservedly condemn, as criminal, all acts, methods and practices of terrorism and express our determination to work for its eradication both bilaterally and through multilateral co-operation. We will also join together in combating illicit trafficking in drugs.

Being aware that an essential complement to the duty of States to refrain from the threat or use of force is the peaceful settlement of disputes, both being essential factors for the maintenance and consolidation of international peace and security, we will not only seek effective ways of preventing, through political means, conflicts which may yet emerge, but also define, in conformity with international law, appropriate mechanisms for the peaceful resolution of any disputes which may arise. Accordingly, we undertake to seek new forms of co-operation in this area, in particular a range of methods for the peaceful settlement of disputes, including mandatory third-party involvement. We stress that full use should be made in this context of the opportunity of the Meeting on the Peaceful Settlement of Disputes which will be convened in Valletta at the beginning of 1991. The Council of Ministers for Foreign Affairs will take into account the Report of the Valletta Meeting.

### Economic Co-operation

We stress that economic co-operation based on market economy constitutes an essential element of our relations and will be instrumental in the construction of a prosperous and united Europe. Democratic institutions and economic liberty foster economic and social progress, as recognized in the Document of the Bonn Conference on Economic Co-operation, the results of which we strongly support.

We underline that co-operation in the economic field, science and technology is now an important pillar of the CSCE. The participating States should periodically review progress and give new impulses in these fields.

We are convinced that our overall economic co-operation should be expanded, free enterprise encouraged and trade increased and diversified according to GATT rules. We will promote social justice and progress and further the welfare of our peoples. We recognize in this context the importance of effective policies to address the problem of unemployment.

We reaffirm the need to continue to support democratic countries in transition towards the establishment of market economy and the creation of the basis for self-sustained economic and social growth, as already undertaken by the Group of twenty-four countries. We further underline the necessity of their increased integration, involving the acceptance of disciplines as well as benefits, into the international economic and financial system.

We consider that increased emphasis on economic co-operation within the CSCE process should take into account the interests of developing participating States.

We recall the link between respect for and promotion of human rights and fundamental freedoms and scientific progress. Co-operation in the field of science and technology will play an essential role in economic and social development. Therefore, it must evolve towards a greater sharing of appropriate scientific and technological information and knowledge with a view to overcoming the technological gap which exists among the participating States. We further encourage the participating States to work together in order to develop human potential and the spirit of free enterprise.

We are determined to give the necessary impetus to co-operation among our States in the fields of energy, transport and tourism for economic and social development. We welcome, in particular, practical steps to create optimal conditions for the economic and rational development of energy resources, with due regard for environmental considerations.

We recognize the important role of the European Community in the political and economic development of Europe. International economic organizations such as the United Nations Economic Commission for Europe (ECE), the Bretton Woods Institutions, the Organisation for Economic Co-operation and Development (ECD), the European Free Trade Association (EFTA) and the International Chamber of Commerce (ICC) also have a significant task in promoting economic co-operation, which will be further enhanced by the establishment of the European Bank for Reconstruction and Development (EBRD). In order to pursue our objectives, we stress the necessity for effective co-ordination of the activities of these organizations and emphasize the need to find methods for all our States to take part in these activities.

### Environment

We recognize the urgent need to tackle the problems of the environment and the importance of individual and co-operative efforts in this area. We pledge to intensify our endeavours to protect and improve our environment in order to restore and maintain a sound ecological balance in air, water and soil. Therefore, we are determined to make full use of the CSCE as a framework for the formulation of common environmental commitments and objectives, and thus to pursue the work reflected in the Report of the Sofia Meeting on the Protection of the Environment.

We emphasize the significant role of a well-informed society in enabling the public and individuals to take initiatives to improve the environment. To this end, we commit ourselves to promoting public awareness and education on the environment as well as the public reporting of the environmental impact of policies, projects and programmes.

We attach priority to the introduction of clean and low-waste technology, being aware of the need to support countries which do not yet have their own means for appropriate measures.

We underline that environmental policies should be supported by appropriate legislative measures and administrative structures to ensure their effective implementation.

We stress the need for new measures providing for the systematic evaluation of compliance with the existing commitments and, moreover, for the development of more ambitious commitments with regard to notification and exchange of information about the state of the environment and potential environmental hazards. We also welcome the creation of the European Environment Agency (EEA).

We welcome the operational activities, problem-oriented studies and policy reviews in various existing international organizations engaged in the protection of the environment, such as the United Nations Environment Programme (UNEP), the United Nations Economic Commission for Europe (ECE) and the Organisation for Economic Co-operation and Development (OECD). We emphasize the need for strengthening their co-operation and for their efficient co-ordination.

### Culture

We recognize the essential contribution of our common European culture and our shared values in overcoming the division of the continent. Therefore, we underline our attachment to creative freedom and to the protection and promotion of our cultural and spiritual heritage, in all its richness and diversity.

In view of the recent changes in Europe, we stress the increased importance of the Cracow Symposium and we look forward to its consideration of guidelines for intensified co-operation in the field of culture. We invite the Council of Europe to contribute to this Symposium.

In order to promote greater familiarity amongst our peoples, we favour the establishment of cultural centres in cities of other participating States as well as increased co-operation in the audio-visual field and wider exchange in music, theatre, literature and the arts.

We resolve to make special efforts in our national policies to promote better understanding, in particular among young people, through cultural exchanges, co-operation in all fields of education and, more specifically, through teaching and training in the languages of other participating States. We intend to consider first results of this action at the Helsinki Follow-up Meeting in 1992.

### Migrant Workers

We recognize that the issues of migrant workers and their families legally residing in host countries have economic, cultural and social aspects as well as their human dimension. We reaffirm that the protection and promotion of their rights, as well as the implementation of relevant international obligations, is our common concern.

### Mediterranean

We consider that the fundamental political changes that have occurred in Europe have a positive relevance to the Mediterranean region. Thus, we will continue efforts to strengthen security and co-operation in the Mediterranean as an important factor for stability in Europe. We welcome the Report of the Palma de Mallorca Meeting on the Mediterranean, the results of which we all support.

We are concerned with the continuing tensions in the region, and renew our determination to intensify efforts towards finding just, viable and lasting solutions, through peaceful means, to outstanding crucial problems, based on respect for the principles of the Final Act.

We wish to promote favourable conditions for a harmonious development and diversification of relations with the non-participating Mediterranean States. Enhanced co-operation with these States will be pursued with the aim of promoting economic and social development and thereby enhancing stability in the region. To this end, we will strive together with these countries towards a substantial narrowing of the prosperity gap between Europe and its Mediterranean neighbours.

### Non-governmental Organizations

We recall the major role that non-governmental organizations, religious and other groups and individuals have played in the achievement of the objectives of the CSCE and will further facilitate their activities for the implementation of the CSCE commitments by the participating States. These organizations, groups and individuals must be involved in an appropriate way in the activities and new structures of the CSCE in order to fulfil their important tasks.

### New Structures and Institutions of the CSCE Process

Our common efforts to consolidate respect for human rights, democracy and the rule of law, to strengthen peace and to promote unity in Europe require a new quality of political dialogue and co-operation and thus development of the structures of the CSCE.

The intensification of our consultations at all levels is of prime importance in shaping our future relations. To this end, we decide on the following:

We, the Heads of State or Government, shall meet next time in Helsinki on the occasion of the CSCE Follow-up Meeting 1992. Thereafter, we will meet on the occasion of subsequent follow-up meetings.

Our Ministers for Foreign Affairs will meet, as a Council, regularly and at least once a year. These meetings will provide the central forum for political consultations within the CSCE process. The Council will consider issues relevant to the Conference on Security and Co-operation in Europe and take appropriate decisions. The first meeting of the Council will take place in Berlin.

A Committee of Senior Officials will prepare the meetings of the Council and carry out its decisions. The Committee will review current issues and may take appropriate decisions, including in the form of recommendations to the Council. Additional meetings of the representatives of the participating States may be agreed upon to discuss questions of urgent concern.

The Council will examine the development of provisions for convening meetings of the Committee of Senior Officials in emergency situations.

Meetings of other Ministers may also be agreed by the participating States.

In order to provide administrative support for these consultations we establish a Secretariat in Prague.

Follow-up meetings of the participating States will be held, as a rule, every two years to allow the participating States to take stock of developments, review the implementation of their commitments and consider further steps in the CSCE process.

We decide to create a Conflict Prevention Centre in Vienna to assist the Council in reducing the risk of conflict.

We decide to establish an Office for Free Elections in Warsaw to facilitate contacts and the exchange of information on elections within participating States.

Recognizing the important role parliamentarians can play in the CSCE process, we call for greater parliamentary involvement in the CSCE, in particular through the creation of a CSCE parliamentary assembly, involving members of parliaments from all participating States. To this end, we urge that contacts be pursued at parliamentary level to discuss the field of activities, working methods and rules of procedure of such a CSCE parliamentary structure, drawing on existing experience and work already undertaken in this field.

We ask our Ministers for Foreign Affairs to review this matter on the occasion of their first meeting as a Council.

Procedural and organizational modalities relating to certain provisions contained in the Charter of Paris for a New Europe are set out in the Supplementary Document which is adopted together with the Charter of Paris.

We entrust to the Council the further steps which may be required to ensure the implementation of decisions contained in the present document, as well as in the Supplementary Document, and to consider further efforts for the strengthening of security and co-operation in Europe. The

Council may adopt any amendment to the supplementary document which it may deem appropriate.

The original of the Charter of Paris for a New Europe, drawn up in English, French, German, Italian, Russian and Spanish, will be transmitted to the Government of the French Republic, which will retain it in its archives. Each of the participating States will receive from the Government of the French Republic a true copy of the Charter of Paris.

The text of the Charter of Paris will be published in each participating State, which will disseminate it and make it known as widely as possible.

The Government of the French Republic is requested to transmit to the Secretary-General of the United Nations the text of the Charter of Paris for a New Europe which is not eligible for registration under Article 102 of the Charter of the United Nations, with a view to its circulation to all the members of the Organization as an official document of the United Nations.

The Government of the French Republic is also requested to transmit the text of the Charter of Paris to all the other international organizations mentioned in the text.

**CHEMICAL WEAPONS.** On 1 September 1988, the UN Sᴜʙ-Cᴏᴍᴍɪssɪᴏɴ ᴏɴ Pʀᴇᴠᴇɴᴛɪᴏɴ ᴏꜰ Dɪsᴄʀɪᴍɪ-ɴᴀᴛɪᴏɴ ᴀɴᴅ Pʀᴏᴛᴇᴄᴛɪᴏɴ ᴏꜰ Mɪɴᴏʀɪᴛɪᴇs, referring to the Protocol for the Prohibition of the Use of Asphyxiating, Poisonous or Other Gases, and of Bacteriological Methods of Warfare, expressed deep concern (resolution 1988/27) about reports of the increased use of chemical weapons, especially against civilian populations, and stated that it was deeply shocked and saddened by the destruction of human life, lifelong disabilities, and great suffering caused by such weapons.

Noting that negotiations were then under way, in the Conference on Disarmament, on the complete, effective, and verifiable prohibition of the development, production, stockpiling, and use of all chemical weapons and of their destruction, the Sub-Commission called upon all States that had not then done so to consider on a priority basis acceding to the Protocol, and to observe strictly its principles and objectives. The Sub-Commission decided to study the subject further, and requested the Secretary-General to collect information on the use of chemical weapons and on the danger they represent to life, physical security, and other human rights; and to submit a report to it at its 1989 session.

On 7 December 1988, the UN General Assembly called upon all States (resolution 43/74 A) to be guided by the need to curb the spread of chemical weapons pending the conclusion of a convention on the prohibition of all chemical weapons and on their destruction, and also requested the Secretary-General to investigate reports of the use of such weapons.

The Secretary-General's report to the 1989 session of the Sub-Commission (UN Doc. E/CN.4/Sub.2/

1989/4) dealt with such issues as definition and description of chemical weapons; the use and allegations of the use of chemical weapons; the danger they represent to life, physical security, and other human rights; the importance and continuing validity of the Geneva Protocol of 1925; and relevant aspects of multilateral and national activities relating to the ban of chemical weapons. The Secretary-General then presented the following conclusions (paras. 109–112):

(a) recognizing that the use of chemical weapons agents may destroy human life and cause lifelong disability and great suffering, the use of such weapons constitutes a violation of basic human rights, in particular the right to life and the right to liberty and security of person. Therefore, urgent and effective measures should be undertaken by the international community to prevent the future use of those kinds of weapons;

(b) efforts to achieve the complete and effective prohibition of the development, production and stockpiling of all chemical weapons and their destruction are of crucial importance and should be pursued by the international community as a matter of continuing urgency;

(c) the strict observance by all States of the principles and objectives of the 1925 Geneva Protocol could prevent the further use in military conflicts of asphyxiating, poisonous or other gases. The Secretary-General, in his statement at the Paris Conference, declared that "Sans respect du Protocole de Genève, il n'y aura pas d'élimination définitive de l'arme chimique";

(d) the mobilization of the public opinion in favour of banning chemical weapons would also represent an important factor in that regard.

In almost all replies received the conviction was expressed that the only reliable and true way to eliminate the danger of future chemical war was the finalization and setting into force of a universal convention banning the development, production, stockpiling and use of chemical weapons, and obliging States parties to destroy their stockpiles of chemical weapons and their production facilities for these weapons.

Support was expressed for appropriate and effective steps taken by the United Nations in this field. It was affirmed that the United Nations provided a framework and an instrument enabling the international community to exercise vigilance with respect to the prohibition of the use of chemical weapons.

The initiative of the Sub-Commission in its resolution 1988/27 and its consideration of that issue were generally considered helpful in sensitizing public opinion for the work of the Conference on Disarmament towards the early conclusion of a global, universally adhered to chemical weapons ban, thereby eliminating any future use of chemical weapons.

Having examined the report, the Sub-Commission on 1 September 1989 took note of it (resolution 1989/39) and called upon all States to abide strictly by their international obligations in this field. In doing so, it

endorsed Security Council resolutions 612 (1988) of 9 May 1988 and 620 (1988) of 26 August 1988, both on the need to consider appropriate and effective measures for eliminating the use of chemical weapons; and General Assembly resolution 43/74 A of 7 December 1988, in which the assembly called upon all States to be guided by the need to curb the spread of chemical weapons pending the conclusion of a convention on the complete, effective, and verifiable prohibition of the development, production, stockpiling, and use of all chemical weapons and on their destruction.

On 15 December 1989, the General Assembly renewed its call to all States (resolution 44/115 B) to observe strictly the principles and objectives of the Protocol for the Prohibition of the use in war of Asphyxiating, Poisonous or Other Gases, and of Bacteriological Methods of Warfare, and condemned vigorously all actions that violate that obligation. In that same resolution, the Assembly requested the Secretary-General to carry out promptly investigations in response to reports that may be brought to his attention by any member State concerning the possible use of chemical and bacteriological (biological) or toxic weapons that may constitute a violation of the 1925 general protocol or other relevant rules of customary international law in order to ascertain the facts of the matter, and to report promptly the results of any such investigation to all member States.

While continuing its support for measures to uphold the authority of the Protocol and of a Declaration on the Prohibition of Chemical Weapons adopted on 11 January 1989 by a consensus of 149 States participating in the Conference on the Prohibition of Chemical Weapons, convened at Paris, UN organs persisted in their efforts to achieve the effective prohibition and elimination of all types of weapons of mass destruction and stressed the need to prevent any recourse to chemical weapons by eliminating them completely.

In 1992, after many years of intensive negotiations, the UN Conference on Disarmament was able to complete the draft of a comprehensive Convention on the Prohibition of the Development, Production, Stockpiling and Use of Chemical Weapons and on Their Destruction (UN Doc. A/47/27, appendix 1).

Commending the Convention, the General Assembly requested the Secretary-General to open it for signature in Paris on 30 November 1992 (resolution 47/39 of 30 November 1992) and called upon all States to accept it at the earliest possible date and "to ensure the effective implementation of this unprecedented, global, comprehensive and verifiable multilateral disarmament agreement, thereby enhancing cooperative multilateralism as a basis for international peace and security."

SEE ALSO *Arms Exports; Conventional Weapons; Nuclear Weapons.*

**BIBLIOGRAPHY.** Committee against Repression and for Democratic Rights in Iraq. *Chemical Weapons: UN Report Brands Iraq as a Violator of the 1925 Geneva Protocol.* March 1986. NGO flier, in English.

————. "Cyanide Massacre at Halabja," *Iraq Solidarity Voice* 19 (April 1988). NGO article, in English.

"Corporate Crime and Violence," *Multinational Monitor* 8, no. 4 (April 1987): 4–25. Article in special issue, in English.

Cultural Survival. "Militarization and Indigenous Peoples: Part I—The Americas and the Pacific," *Cultural Survival Quarterly* 11, no. 3 (1987). NGO special issue, in English.

Ermacora, Felix. "Afghanistan and the Conscience of the World," *SIM Newsletter* 17 (March 1987): 3–12. NGO article, in English.

Federation Internationale des Droits de l'Homme (International Federation of Human Rights). "Le Martyr du Peuple Kurde" (The Martyrdom of the Kurdish People), *La Lettre de la FIDH* 241 (22 March 1988). NGO newsletter, in French.

"Fumigaciones e incendios: efectos devastadores" (Chemical Fumigations and Forest Fires: Devastating Effects), *Noticias de Guatemala* 9, no. 142 (July 1987): 3–6. News article, in Spanish.

International Association of Political Scientists for the United Nations. *United Nations Middle East Brief.* Vienna, Austria: 1988. NGO document collection, in English.

International Working Group for Indigenous Affairs. "Burma: Human Rights in Burma," *IWGIA Newsletter* 50 (July 1987): 35–45. NGO article, in English.

"Kurdistan: A Homeland Besieged," *Toward Freedom: Report on Non-Alignment in the Developing Countries* 37, no. 5 (Oct.–Nov. 1988): 57, 60. News article, in English.

Physicians for Human Rights. *Winds of Death: Iraq's Use of Poison Gas against its Kurdish Population.* Somerville, MA, USA: 1989. NGO report, in English.

Ramshaw, P., and T. Steers. *Intervention on Trial: The New York War Crimes Tribunal on Central America and the Caribbean.* New York: Praeger Publishers and National Lawyers Guild, 1987. NGO study, in English.

Robinson, J., J. Guillemin, and M. Meselson. "Yellow Rain: The Story Collapses," *Foreign Policy* 68 (Fall 1987): 100–117. Scholarly article, in English.

Saeedpour, Vera Beaudin. *Information Packet.* New York: Kurdish Program, Cultural Survival, 1988. NGO press release, in English.

## CHEMICAL WEAPONS: CONVENTION ON THE PROHIBITION OF THE DEVELOPMENT, PRODUCTION AND STOCKPILING OF BACTERIOLOGICAL (BIOLOGICAL) AND TOXIN WEAPONS AND ON THEIR DESTRUCTION (1972).

Under the Convention, States Parties undertake never to develop bacteriological or toxin weapons, to destroy or divert to peaceful uses all such weapons in their possession, and not to transfer such weapons to other States. A State party may, however, withdraw from the convention (article 13) "if it decides that extraordinary events, related to the subject matter of the Convention, have jeopardized the supreme interests of its country."

Opened for signature and ratification or accession simultaneously in London, Moscow, and Washington on 10 April 1972, the Convention designates three depository governments: the United Kingdom of Great Britain and Northern Ireland, the United States of America, and the Union of Soviet Socialist Republics. It entered into force on 26 March 1975. The text of the Convention (United Nations, "Juridical Yearbook," 1971, p. 118) is as follows:

The States Parties to this Convention,

Determined to act with a view to achieving effective progress towards general and complete disarmament, including the prohibition and elimination of all types of weapons of mass destruction, and convinced that the prohibition of the development, production and stockpiling of chemical and bacteriological (biological) weapons and their elimination, through effective measures, will facilitate the achievement of general and complete disarmament under strict and effective international control,

Recognizing the important significance of the Protocol for the Prohibition of the Use in War of Asphyxiating, Poisonous or Other Gases, and of Bacteriological Methods of Warfare, signed at Geneva on June 17, 1925, and conscious also of the contribution which the said Protocol has already made, and continues to make, to mitigating the horrors of war,

Reaffirming their adherence to the principles and objectives of that Protocol and calling upon all States to comply strictly with them,

Recalling that the General Assembly of the United Nations has repeatedly condemned all actions contrary to the principles and objectives of the Geneva Protocol of June 17, 1925,

Desiring to contribute to the strengthening of confidence between peoples and the general improvement of the international atmosphere,

Desiring also to contribute to the realization of the purposes and principles of the Charter of the United Nations,

Convinced of the importance and urgency of eliminating from the arsenals of States, through effective measures, such dangerous weapons of mass destruction as those using chemical or bacteriological (biological) agents,

Recognizing that an agreement on the prohibition of bacteriological (biological) and toxin weapons represents a first possible step towards the achievement of agreement on effective measures also for the prohibition of the development, production and stockpiling of chemical weapons, and determined to continue negotiations to that end,

Determined, for the sake of all mankind, to exclude completely the possibility of bacteriological (biological) agents and toxins being used as weapons,

Convinced that such use would be repugnant to the conscience of mankind and that no effort should be spared to minimize this risk,

Have agreed as follows:

*Article 1.* Each State Party to this Convention undertakes never in any circumstances to develop, produce, stockpile or otherwise acquire or retain:

(1) Microbial or other biological agents, or toxins whatever their origin or method of production, of types and in

quantities that have no justification for prophylactic, protective or other peaceful purposes;

(2) Weapons, equipment or means of delivery designed to use such agents or toxins for hostile purposes or in armed conflict.

*Article 2.* Each State Party to this Convention undertakes to destroy, or to divert to peaceful purposes, as soon as possible but not later than nine months after the entry into force of the Convention, all agents, toxins, weapons, equipment and means of delivery specified in article 1 of the Convention, which are in its possession or under its jurisdiction or control. In implementing the provisions of this article all necessary safety precautions shall be observed to protect populations and the environment.

*Article 3.* Each State Party to this Convention undertakes not to transfer to any recipient whatsoever, directly or indirectly, and not in any way to assist, encourage, or induce any State, group of States or international organizations to manufacture or otherwise acquire any of the agents, toxins, weapons, equipment or means of delivery specified in article 1 of the Convention.

*Article 4.* Each State Party to this Convention shall, in accordance with its constitutional processes, take any necessary measures to prohibit and prevent the development, production, stockpiling, acquisition or retention of the agents, toxins, weapons, equipment and means of delivery specified in article 1 of the Convention, within the territory of such State, under its jurisdiction or under its control anywhere.

*Article 5.* The States Parties to this Convention undertake to consult one another and to cooperate in solving any problems which may arise in relation to the objective of, or in the application of the provisions of, the Convention. Consultation and cooperation pursuant to this article may also be undertaken through appropriate international procedures within the framework of the United Nations and in accordance with its Charter.

*Article 6.* (1) Any State Party to this Convention which finds that any other State Party is acting in breach of obligations deriving from the provisions of the Convention may lodge a complaint with the Security Council of the United Nations. Such a complaint should include all possible evidence confirming its validity, as well as a request for its consideration by the Security Council.

(2) Each State Party to this Convention undertakes to cooperate in carrying out any investigation which the Security Council may initiate, in accordance with the provisions of the Charter of the United Nations, on the basis of the complaint received by the Council. The Security Council shall inform the States Parties to the Convention of the results of the investigation.

*Article 7.* Each State Party to this Convention undertakes to provide or support assistance, in accordance with the United Nations Charter, to any Party to the Convention which so requests, if the Security Council decides that such Party has been exposed to danger as a result of violation of the Convention.

*Article 8.* Nothing in this Convention shall be interpreted as in any way limiting or detracting from the obligations assumed by any State under the Protocol for the Prohibition of the Use in War of Asphyxiating, Poisonous or Other Gases, and of Bacteriological Methods of Warfare, signed at Geneva on June 17, 1925.

*Article 9.* Each State Party to this Convention affirms the recognized objective of effective prohibition of chemical weapons and, to this end, undertakes to continue negotiations in good faith with a view to reaching early agreement on effective measures for the prohibition of their development, production and stockpiling and for their destruction, and on appropriate measures concerning equipment and means of delivery specifically designed for the production or use of chemical agents for weapons purposes.

*Article 10.* (1) The States Parties to this Convention undertake to facilitate, and have the right to participate in, the fullest possible exchange of equipment, materials and scientific and technological information for the use of bacteriological (biological) agents and toxins for peaceful purposes. Parties to the Convention in a position to do so shall also cooperate in contributing individually or together with other States or international organizations to the further development and application of scientific discoveries in the field of bacteriology (biology) for prevention of disease, or for other peaceful purposes.

(2) This Convention shall be implemented in a manner designed to avoid hampering the economic or technological development of States Parties to the Convention or international cooperation in the field of peaceful bacteriological (biological) activities, including the international exchange of bacteriological (biological) agents and toxins and equipment for the processing, use or production of bacteriological (biological) agents and toxins for peaceful purposes in accordance with the provisions of the Convention.

*Article 11.* Any State Party may propose amendments to this Convention. Amendments shall enter into force for each State Party accepting the amendments upon their acceptance by a majority of the States Parties to the Convention and thereafter for each remaining State Party on the date of acceptance by it.

*Article 12.* Five years after the entry into force of this Convention, or earlier if it is requested by a majority of Parties to the Convention by submitting a proposal to this effect to the Depositary Governments, a conference of States Parties to the Convention shall be held at Geneva, Switzerland, to review the operation of the Convention, with a view to assuring that the purposes of the preamble and the provisions of the Convention, including the provisions concerning negotiations on chemical weapons, are being realized. Such review shall take into account any new scientific and technological developments relevant to the Convention.

*Article 13.* (1) This Convention shall be of unlimited duration.

(2) Each State Party to this Convention shall in exercising its national sovereignty have the right to withdraw from the Convention if it decides that extraordinary events, related to the subject matter of the Convention, have jeopardized the supreme interests of its country. It shall give notice of such withdrawal to all other States Parties to the Convention and to the United Nations Security Council three months in advance. Such notice shall include a statement of the extraordinary events it regards as having jeopardized its supreme interests.

*Article 14.* (1) This Convention shall be open to all States for signature. Any State which does not sign the Convention before its entry into force in accordance with paragraph (3) of this Article may accede to it at any time.

(2) This Convention shall be subject to ratification by Signatory States. Instruments of ratification and instruments of accession shall be deposited with the Governments of the United States of America, the United Kingdom of Great Britain and Northern Ireland and the Union of Soviet Socialist Republics, which are hereby designated the Depositary Governments.

(3) This Convention shall enter into force after the de-

posit of instruments of ratification by twenty-two Governments, including the Governments designated as Depositaries of the Convention.

(4) For States whose instruments of ratification or accession are deposited subsequent to the entry into force of this Convention, it shall enter into force on the date of the deposit of their instruments of ratification or accession.

(5) The Depositary Governments shall promptly inform all signatory and acceding States of the date of each signature, the date of deposit of each instrument of ratification or of accession and the date of the entry into force of this Convention, and of the receipt of other notices.

(6) This Convention shall be registered by the Depositary Governments pursuant to Article 102 of the Charter of the United Nations.

*Article 15.* This Convention, the English, Russian, French, Spanish and Chinese texts of which are equally authentic, shall be deposited in the archives of the Depositary Governments. Duly certified copies of the Convention shall be transmitted by the Depositary Governments to the Governments of the signatory and acceding States.

## CHEMICAL WEAPONS: DECLARATION ON THEIR PROHIBITION (1989).

The Conference on the Prohibition of Chemical Weapons, convened in Paris from 7 to 11 January 1989, adopted by consensus of the 149 participating States, on 11 January 1989, the following final declaration (UN Doc. A/44/88, Annex):

The Representatives of States participating in the Conference on the Prohibition of Chemical Weapons, bringing together States Parties to the Geneva Protocol of 1925 and other interested States in Paris from 7 to 11 January 1989, solemnly declare the following:

1. The participating States are determined to promote international peace and security throughout the world in accordance with the Charter of the United Nations and to pursue effective disarmament measures. In this context, they are determined to prevent any recourse to chemical weapons by completely eliminating them. They solemnly affirm their commitments not to use chemical weapons and condemn such use. They recall their serious concern at recent violations as established and condemned by the competent organs of the United Nations. They support the humanitarian assistance given to the victims affected by chemical weapons.

2. The participating States recognize the importance and continuing validity of the Protocol for the prohibition of the use in war of asphyxiating, poisonous or other gases and bacteriological methods of warfare, signed on 17 June 1925 in Geneva. The States Parties to the Protocol solemnly reaffirm the prohibition as established in it. They call upon all States which have not yet done so to accede to the Protocol.

3. The participating States stress the necessity of concluding, at an early date, a Convention on the prohibition of the development, production, stockpiling and use of all chemical weapons, and on their destruction. This Convention shall be global and comprehensive and effectively verifiable. It should be of unlimited duration. To this end, they call on the Conference on Disarmament in Geneva to redouble its efforts, as a matter of urgency, to resolve expeditiously the remaining issues and to conclude the Convention at the earliest date. All States are requested to make, in an appropriate

way, a significant contribution to the negotiations in Geneva by undertaking efforts in the relevant fields. The participating States therefore believe that any State wishing to contribute to these negotiations should be able to do so. In addition, in order to achieve as soon as possible the indispensable universal character of the Convention, they call upon all States to become parties thereto as soon as it is concluded.

4. The participating States are gravely concerned by the growing danger posed to international peace and security by the risk of the use of chemical weapons as long as such weapons remain and are spread. In this context, they stress the need for the early conclusion and entry into force of the Convention, which will be established on a non-discriminatory basis. They deem it necessary, in the meantime, for each State to exercise restraint and to act responsibly in accordance with the purpose of the present declaration.

5. The participating States confirm their full support for the United Nations in the discharge of its indispensable role, in conformity with its Charter. They affirm that the United Nations provide a framework and an instrument enabling the international community to exercise vigilance with respect to the prohibition of the use of chemical weapons. They confirm their support for appropriate and effective steps taken by the United Nations in this respect in conformity with its Charter. They further reaffirm their full support for the Secretary-General in carrying out his responsibilities for investigations in the event of alleged violations of the Geneva Protocol. They express their wish for early completion of the work undertaken to strengthen the efficiency of existing procedures and call for the co-operation of all States, in order to facilitate the action of the Secretary-General.

6. The participating States, recalling the Final Document of the first Special Session of the United Nations General Assembly devoted to Disarmament in 1978, underline the need to pursue with determination their efforts to secure general and complete disarmament under effective international control, so as to ensure the right of all States to peace and security.

## CHEMICAL WEAPONS: PROTOCOL FOR THE PROHIBITION OF THE USE OF ASPHYXIATING, POISONOUS OR OTHER GASES, AND OF BACTERIOLOGICAL METHODS OF WARFARE (1925).

The Protocol, concluded and signed in Geneva on 17 June 1925, was the first international instrument of universal scope to prohibit the use in war of poisonous and other gases, and of bacteriological methods of warfare. The subject, however, had been mentioned earlier in several peace treaties concluded at the close of World War I, including the Treaty of Versailles.

The Protocol entered into force for each signatory power as from the date of deposit of its instrument of ratification. The text (94 LNTS 65) is as follows:

The Undersigned Plenipotentiaries, in the name of their respective Governments:

Whereas the use in war of asphyxiating, poisonous or other gases, and of all analogous liquids, materials or devices, has been justly condemned by the general opinion of the civilized world; and

Whereas the prohibition of such use has been declared in Treaties to which the majority of Powers of the world are Parties; and

To the end that this prohibition shall be universally accepted as a part of International Law, binding alike the conscience and the practice of nations;

Declare:

That the High Contracting Parties, so far as they are not already Parties to Treaties prohibiting such use, accept this prohibition, agree to extend this prohibition to the use of bacteriological methods of warfare and agree to be bound as between themselves according to the terms of this declaration.

The High Contracting Parties will exert every effort to induce other States to accede to the present Protocol. Such accession will be notified to the Government of the French Republic, and by the latter to all signatory and acceding Powers, and will take effect on the date of the notification by the Government of the French Republic.

The present Protocol, of which the French and English texts are both authentic, shall be ratified as soon as possible. It shall bear to-day's date.

The ratifications of the present Protocol shall be addressed to the Government of the French Republic, which will at once notify the deposit of such ratification to each of the signatory and acceding Powers.

The instruments of ratification of and accession to the present Protocol will remain deposited in the archives of the Government of the French Republic.

The present Protocol will come into force for each signatory Power as from the date of deposit of its ratification, and, from that moment, each Power will be bound as regards other Powers which have already deposited their ratifications.

In witness whereof the Plenipotentiaries have signed the present Protocol.

Done at Geneva in a single copy, the seventeenth day of June, One Thousand Nine Hundred and Twenty-Five.

**CHILDREN'S RIGHTS.** Promotion and protection of the rights of children have long been a major concern of the international community. In 1924, long before the United Nations was established, the **LEAGUE OF NATIONS** adopted the Geneva Declaration of the Rights of the Child. The need to extend international protection to children was first recognized by the United Nations in 1948, in article 25 (2) of the **UNIVERSAL DECLARATION OF HUMAN RIGHTS.** Protection of children was further elaborated in the Declaration of the Rights of the Child of 1959. Later the concept was spelled out in two parts of the International Bill of Human Rights: the **INTERNATIONAL COVENANT ON CIVIL AND POLITICAL RIGHTS** (articles 23 and 24) and the **INTERNATIONAL COVENANT ON ECONOMIC, SOCIAL AND CULTURAL RIGHTS** (article 10). The Convention on the Rights of the Child was concluded by the UN **GENERAL ASSEMBLY** on 28 November 1989 (resolution 44/25), and the UN **COMMITTEE ON THE RIGHTS OF THE CHILD** was convened in Geneva for its opening session on 3 September 1991.

Particular problems related to children's rights are dealt with in a number of international instruments, some of universal application (such as the Declaration of Social and Legal Principles relating to the Protection and Welfare of Children, with Special Reference to Foster Placement and Adoption Nationally and Internationally; the United Nations Standard Minimum Rules for the Administration of Juvenile Justice [also known as the Beijing Rules]; and the Declaration on the Protection of Women and Children in Emergency and Armed Conflict) and others of regional application (such as the European Convention on the Adoption of Children, the European Convention on Recognition and Enforcement of Decisions concerning the Custody of Children and on Restoration of the Custody of Children, and the Inter-American Convention on Conflict of Laws governing the Adoption of Minors).

On 30 September 1990, the World Summit for Children, meeting in New York, prepared and adopted the World Declaration on the Survival, Protection and Development of Children in the 1990s, which committed national political leaders to prioritizing children's rights. In June 1993, the World Conference on Human Rights, meeting in Vienna, Austria, adopted the Vienna Declaration and Program of Action, which called for, *inter alia,* effective measures against female infanticide; harmful child labor; sale of children and their organs; and child prostitution, child pornography, and other forms of sexual abuse.

At its 1992 session, the UN Commission on Human Rights adopted a comprehensive Program of Action for the Prevention of the Sale of Children, Child Prostitution and Child Pornography. Later in 1992, the UN General Assembly requested the Commission (resolution 48/159) to create a working group to study "the elaboration of guidelines, in close contact with the Special Rapporteur, of a possible draft convention on the issues related to the sale of children, child prostitution and child pornography, as well as the basic measures required for preventing and eradicating these serious problems."

*RIGHT TO PROTECTION.* Children's rights were first set out in precise legal form in article 24 of the International Covenant on Civil and Political Rights, which provides that:

1. Every child shall have, without any discrimination as to race, color, sex, language, religion, national or social origin, property, or birth, the right to such measures of protection as are required by his status as a minor, on the part of his family, society and the State.
2. Every child shall be registered immediately after birth and shall have a name.
3. Every child has the right to acquire a nationality.

With regard to article 24, the UN Human Rights Committee, at its 35th session, held at United Nations headquarters, New York, from 20 March to 7 April 1989, adopted the following comment (UN Doc. A/44/40, Annex VI, general comment 17 [35]):

1. Article 24 of the International Covenant on Civil and Political Rights recognizes the right of every child, without any discrimination, to receive from his family, society and the State the protection required by his status as a minor. Consequently, the implementation of this provision entails the adoption of special measures to protect children, in addition to the measures that States are required to take under article 2 to ensure that everyone enjoys the rights provided for in the Covenant. The reports submitted by States parties often seem to underestimate this obligation and supply inadequate information on the way in which children are afforded enjoyment of their right to a special protection.

2. In this connection, the Committee points out that the rights provided for in article 24 are not the only ones that the Covenant recognizes for children and that, as individuals, children benefit from all of the civil rights enunciated in the Covenant. In enunciating a right, some provisions of the Covenant expressly indicate to States measures to be adopted with a view to affording minors greater protection than adults. Thus, as far as the right to life is concerned, the death penalty cannot be imposed for crimes committed by persons under 18 years of age. Similarly, if lawfully deprived of their liberty, accused juvenile persons shall be separated from adults and are entitled to be brought as speedily as possible for adjudication; in turn, convicted juvenile offenders shall be subject to a penitentiary system that involves segregation from adults and is appropriate to their age and legal status, the aim being to foster reformation and social rehabilitation. In other instances, children are protected by the possibility of the restriction—provided that such restriction is warranted—of a right recognized by the Covenant, such as the right to publicize a judgement in a suit at law or a criminal case, from which an exception may be made when the interest of the minor so requires.

3. In most cases, however, the measures to be adopted are not specified in the Covenant and it is for each State to determine them in the light of the protection needs of children in its territory and within its jurisdiction. The Committee notes in this regard that such measures, although intended primarily to ensure that children fully enjoy the other rights enunciated in the Covenant, may also be economic, social and cultural. For example, every possible economic and social measure should be taken to reduce infant mortality and to eradicate malnutrition among children and to prevent them from being subjected to acts of violence and cruel and inhuman treatment or from being exploited by means of forced labour or prostitution, or by their use in the illicit trafficking of narcotic drugs, or by any other means. In the cultural field, every possible measure should be taken to foster the development of their personality and to provide them with a level of education that will enable them to enjoy the rights recognized in the Covenant, particularly the right to freedom of opinion and expression. Moreover, the Committee wishes to draw the attention of States parties to the need to include in their reports information on measures adopted to ensure that children do not take a direct part in armed conflicts.

4. The right to special measures of protection belongs to every child because of his status as a minor. Nevertheless, the Covenant does not indicate the age at which he attains his majority. This is to be determined by each State party in the light of the relevant social and cultural conditions. In this respect, States should indicate in their reports the age at which the child attains his majority in civil matters and assumes criminal responsibility. States should also indicate the age at which a child is legally entitled to work and the age at which he is treated as an adult under labour law. States should further indicate the age at which a child is considered adult for the purposes of article 10, paragraphs 2 and 3. However, the Committee notes that the age for the above purposes should not be set unreasonably low and that in any case a State party cannot absolve itself from its obligations under the Covenant regarding persons under the age of 18, notwithstanding that they have reached the age of majority under domestic law.

5. The Covenant requires that children should be protected against discrimination on any grounds such as race, colour, sex, language, religion, national or social origin, property or birth. In this connection, the Committee notes that, whereas non-discrimination in the enjoyment of the rights provided for in the Covenant also stems, in the case of children, from article 2 and their equality before the law from article 26, the non-discrimination clause contained in article 24 relates specifically to the measures of protection referred to in that provision. Reports by States parties should indicate how legislation and practice ensure that measures of protection are aimed at removing all discrimination in every field, including inheritance, particularly as between children who are nationals and children who are aliens or as between legitimate children and children born out of wedlock.

6. Responsibility for guaranteeing children the necessary protection lies with the family, society and the State. Although the Covenant does not indicate how such responsibility is to be apportioned, it is primarily incumbent on the family, which is interpreted broadly to include all persons composing it in the society of the State party concerned, and particularly on the parents, to create conditions to promote the harmonious development of the child's personality and his enjoyment of the rights recognized in the Covenant. However, since it is quite common for the father and mother to be gainfully employed outside the home, reports by States parties should indicate how society, social institutions and the State are discharging their responsibility to assist the family in ensuring the protection of the child. Moreover, in cases where the parents and the family seriously fail in their duties, ill-treat or neglect the child, the State should intervene to restrict parental authority and the child may be separated from his family when circumstances so require. If the marriage is dissolved, steps should be taken, keeping in view the paramount interest of the children, to give them necessary protection and, so far as is possible, to guarantee personal relations with both parents. The Committee considers it useful that reports by States parties should provide information on the special measures of protection adopted to protect children who are abandoned or deprived of their family environment in order to enable them to develop in conditions that most closely resemble those characterizing the family environment.

7. Under article 24, paragraph 2, every child has the right to be registered immediately after birth and to have a name. In the Committee's opinion, this provision should be interpreted as being closely linked to the provision concerning the right to special measures of protection and it is designed

to promote recognition of the child's legal personality. Providing for the right to have a name is of special importance in the case of children born out of wedlock. The main purpose of the obligation to register children after birth is to deduce the danger of abduction, sale of or traffic in children, or of other types of treatment that are incompatible with the enjoyment of the rights provided for in the Covenant. Reports by States parties should indicate in detail the measures that ensure the immediate registration of children born in their territory.

8. Special attention should also be paid, in the context of the protection to be granted to children, to the right of every child to acquire a nationality, as provided for in article 24, paragraph 3. While the purpose of this provision is to prevent a child from being afforded less protection by society and the State because he is stateless, it does not necessarily make it an obligation for States to give their nationality to every child born in their territory. However, States are required to adopt every appropriate measure, both internally and in co-operation with other States, to ensure that every child has a nationality when he is born. In this connection, no discrimination with regard to the acquisition of nationality should be admissible under internal law as between legitimate children and children born out of wedlock or of stateless parents or based on the nationality status of one or both of the parents. The measures adopted to ensure that children have a nationality should always be referred to in reports by States parties.

*CHILD LABOR.* The exploitation of child labor is a practice that frequently gives rise to effects similar to those of slavery. The exploitation of child labor was one of the first preoccupations of the **INTERNATIONAL LABOR ORGANIZATION** (ILO). In 1919, the International Labor Conference adopted at its first session several conventions on the subject, including the Minimum Age (Industry) Convention (No. 5) and the Night Work of Young Persons (Industry) Convention (No. 6). In 1920, the ILO adopted the Minimum Age (Sea) Convention (No. 7) and in 1921, the Minimum Age (Agriculture) Convention (No. 10). The most recent ILO convention on the subject is the Minimum Age Convention, 1973 (No. 138), which revises a number of earlier conventions on the same subject and is, in turn, complemented by other ILO conventions that contain provisions on minimum age in specialized areas or that deal with other aspects of the work of young people.

In a contribution prepared by the International Labor Office for the World Conference on Human Rights in 1993 (A/CONF. 157/PC/61/Add. 10, Annex III), the basic requirements of Convention No. 138 are summarized:

The minimum age for employment or work (i.e., not only work within an employment relationship) shall be not less than 15 years, or the end of compulsory schooling, whichever is higher. In developing countries, the minimum age may be declared at 14 years. Light work may be performed from the age of 13 years (or 12 if the basic minimum is set at 14), if it is unlikely to harm the child's health or development, and if it will not prejudice school or vocational training. A minimum age of 18 years shall be set for employment or work likely to jeopardise the health, safety or morals of a young person; but it may be set at 16 if health, safety and morals are fully protected and adequate specific instruction or vocational training has been provided. The competent authority must define the dangerous work referred to. Work done by children in the context of properly supervised vocational training is excluded. It is also possible to exclude various categories of employment or sectors of the economy, and to limit the application of the Convention to specified areas of the country, but regular information has to be provided on the situation in sectors or areas thus excluded, and the exclusions and exceptions may be withdrawn at any time.

In addition to instruments on minimum age for employment, a number of ILO instruments prescribe the conditions under which young people are allowed to work. Hours of work for young workers are regulated by three ILO conventions: Night Work of Young Persons (Industry), 1919 (No. 6), mentioned above; Night Work of Young Persons (Non-Industrial Occupations), 1946 (No. 79); and Night Work of Young Persons (Industry) (Revised), 1948 (No. 90). All of these conventions prohibit night work by persons younger than 18 years old.

As concerns conditions of employment, the following ILO conventions prohibit work in particular situations for persons under the age of 18: the White Lead (Painting) Convention, 1921 (No. 13), the Radiation Protection Convention, 1960 (No. 115), the Maximum Weight Convention, 1967 (No. 127), the Benzene Convention, 1971 (No. 136), and the Occupational Safety and Health (Dock Work) Convention, 1979 (No. 152).

Another series of conventions requires that persons under 18 years of age not be admitted to employment unless found fit for the work by a thorough medical examination: at sea (No. 16 of 1921), in industry (No. 77 of 1946), in nonindustrial occupations (No. 78 of 1946) and in underground work (No. 124 of 1965).

Finally, the ILO has two fundamental conventions on forced or compulsory labor: the Forced Labor Convention, 1930 (No. 29) and the Abolition of Forced Labor Convention, 1957 (No. 105). Even though these instruments do not refer to children explicitly, they have been invoked frequently to criticize forced child labor. Under these instruments, the ILO Committee of Experts on the Applications of Conventions and Recommendations frequently examines cases of bonded child labor, sale of children, and other abuses.

Because it has long been recognized that law is not sufficient in itself to combat child labor, nor even to correct its worst abuses, and that the roots of the phenomenon lie in causes that the law cannot reach—poverty, deprivation, and exclusion—the ILO supplements its standard-setting work with research, information dissemination, and direct technical assistance to help countries to understand the nature, extent, and consequences of child labor and to formulate and implement corrective policies and programs.

***Seminar on Child Labor, 1984.*** The problem of child labor continues to draw international attention. At the request of the UN Commission on Human Rights, a "Seminar on Ways and Means of Achieving the Elimination of the Exploitation of Child Labor in All Parts of the World" was held at the European office of the United Nations, Geneva, from 28 October to 8 November 1984. Organized by the Center for Human Rights in close cooperation with the International Labor Office, under the program of Advisory Services in the Field of Human Rights, the Seminar was attended by experts nominated by the governments of 24 States and by the representatives of a number of intergovernmental and non-governmental organizations.

The conclusions of the Seminar, as summarized in its report (UN Doc. ST/HR/SER. A/18, chap. VI), are as follows:

(a) The exploitation of child labour is an intolerable evil which must be eliminated as a matter of the greatest urgency;

(b) The exact extent of the exploitation of child labour is not known, but it takes place in a very large number of countries throughout the world, and very many children, possibly over 100 million, are the victims of such exploitation;

(c) The exploitation of child labour takes many forms, and certain types of exploitation, for example, child prostitution and the employment of children in hazardous occupations including armed conflict, are particularly abhorrent;

(d) Certain categories of children, for example, refugee or migrant children or children in countries with an apartheid régime, or territories under foreign occupation are particularly vulnerable to exploitation;

(e) The factors leading to the exploitation of child labour vary very widely, and include economic, social, cultural and other factors. Probably the most important causes of such exploitation are poverty and underdevelopment. For some children, work is at present an absolute necessity in order to survive;

(f) Other factors which have a bearing on the number of children at work include the general level of employment, the educational system of a country, and in particular whether, and up to what age school attendance is free and compulsory; the existence within a country of vocational training schemes, and of comprehensive legislation on the subject of child labour and the effectiveness of its enforcement; and the scope and adequacy for the needs of families of a country's social welfare and social security systems; the cultural changes that many countries are undergoing also constitute a factor influencing the number of children at work;

(g) The total elimination of all forms of exploitation of child labour throughout the world is endorsed unanimously as a long term objective. However, it will take many years to achieve. Success will depend on gradual progress in the achievement of a number of distinct short-term and medium-term programmes aimed at specific, clearly defined, and realistic objectives;

(h) No one organization acting in isolation could hope to solve a problem of such magnitude. The elimination of the exploitation of child labour will require economic reforms aimed at a more equitable distribution of the world resources as well as the active co-operation of all those concerned with the problem, including international organizations, national Governments, local authorities, nongovernmental organizations at international, national and local levels, trade unions, employers, and the children themselves. Such co-operation is likely to depend on the effective mobilization of public opinion worldwide.

***Program of Action, 1993.*** At its 1993 session, the UN Commission on Human Rights expressed its concern at the widespread abuse of child labor, based on information it had received from the Working Group on Contemporary Forms of Slavery, the Special Rapporteur on the sale of children, the ILO, **UNICEF,** and other sources. The Commission adopted the Progamme of Action for the Elimination of the Exploitation of Child Labor (resolution 1993/79, Annex), as follows:

### General

1. In spite of the progress made in combating the exploitation of child labour, in particular through the development of national and international norms which have defined the bases of legal protection, and of mechanisms for monitoring their application, the exploitation of child labour still remains a current and widespread phenomenon of a serious nature in various parts of the world.

2. This phenomenon, which is both complex and worldwide, varies from one country to another. Although the industrialized countries are not spared, it affects the developing countries more particularly, and within each country the more vulnerable groups of the population. Poverty is often the main cause of child labour, but generations of children should not be condemned, until poverty is overcome, to exploitation. Underdevelopment cannot justify exploitation of which children are the victims. The Governments concerned and the international community as a whole must not wait for development problems to be adequately solved before attacking the phenomenon of the exploitation of child labour. Besides the long-term action which should be initiated with a view to treating the deep causes underlying the exploitation of child labour, it is essential that urgent measures and medium- and short-term action be taken to meet the immediate needs of the children who are exposed to the gravest dangers, while making sure that such action is integrated into economic and social development strategies.

3. High priority should be given to the elimination of the most odious or degrading forms of child exploitation, in particular child prostitution, pornography, the sale of children, the employment of children in dangerous occupations or for enforced begging and debt bondage.

4. The international community should place particular emphasis on the new phenomena of the exploitation of child labour, such as the use of children for illegal, clandestine or criminal purposes, including their implication in the narcotic drugs traffic or in armed conflicts or military activities.

5. Action should be directed, first, towards the most dangerous forms of child labour and the elimination of work by children under 10 years of age, with a view to the total elimination of child labour as prohibited by the provisions of the relevant international instruments.

6. Special attention should be paid to the most vulnerable categories of children: children of immigrants, street children, children of minority groups, indigenous children, refugee children, children in occupied territories and those under the apartheid regime.

7. In order to reach the core of one of the prime causes of exploitation of child labour, which is poverty, increased resources should be made available through bilateral and multilateral channels for the elimination of the exploitation of child labour. Elimination of the phenomena linked with the exploitation of child labour calls for social measures and development assistance. Their prevention will require deep structural reforms in the economic, social and cultural spheres.

8. Particular attentions should also be given to social rehabilitation, education and information. It is important that the means of protecting children should be strengthened by development, the reinforcement of legislation and proper application of the relevant laws.

9. Adequate means and concerted measures are necessary at the local, national, regional and international levels.

### Information

10. The public could be made aware of the problem and the different aspects of the exploitation of child labour by national and international information campaigns. The extent of the problem cannot be accurately defined by reference to the statistics from various sources. The sectors favouring the exploitation of child labour should be specially targeted (agriculture, non-structured urban sector and domestic service). It is important to reach he children who are the invisible victims of parallel employment networks. At the national level it is necessary to develop means of investigation and supervision by labour inspectors in order to detect and prosecute cases of exploitation of child labour, so as to break up the clandestine employment networks. Public and private institutions and agencies dealing with children who have been victims of labour exploitation should be encouraged to keep appropriate statistical information for scientific purposes, while respecting anonymity and confidentiality. The information campaign should also be able to reach children directly, in order to inform them of their rights and make them aware of the risks they run.

### Education and Vocational Training

11. There is undoubtedly a link between child labour, illiteracy, school failure and the lack of vocational training. Education is one of the most effective measures to prevent child labour. Massive literacy programmes combined with legislation making basic training obligatory and free, as well as measures to combat school wastage and to develop vocational training in the form, for example, of a system of apprenticeship, are extremely necessary. Such programmes could be supported by community campaigns to increase the awareness and motivation of families, and in particular of women.

### Social Action

12. The economic and social causes of the persistence of child labour, including the fact that it is seen in many cases as a means of survival for the children and their families, should be taken up in order to offer an alternative that will take the children out of the circle of poverty and exploitation. Urgent measures could be taken on behalf of children who are subjected to high physical and moral risks. It is important to give them protection and assistance, including social and medical assistance, while at the same time pursuing the objective of the elimination of child labour. These urgent measures should be backed up by programmes of social rehabilitation.

### Development Aid

13. For many countries, the implementation of local, regional and national programmes on behalf of children requires appropriate international aid and a deeper commitment by the international community, whether through specific projects or through development assistance.

### Labour Standards and Their Application

14. States should adhere to the international standards in force and ensure that they are rigorously applied. It is important that, in accordance with article 1 of the Minimum Age Convention, 1973 (No. 138) of the International Labour Organisation, States should undertake "to pursue a national policy designed to ensure the effective abolition of child labour and to raise progressively the minimum age for admission to employment or work to a level consistent with the fullest physical and mental development of young persons." National legislation should explicitly prohibit dangerous or high-risk employment and prescribe penalties for employers who break this law, as well as providing for the establishment of an effective labour inspection system. In at least three cases, the exploitation of child labour is no less than a flagrant crime which violates the Charter of the United Nations, the principles of the Charter and the Universal Declaration of Human Rights, the most elementary principles of morality and all positive laws. Energetic repressive action is called for in these cases, namely:

(a) Sale and similar practices (serfdom, bond service, fake adoption, abandonment);

(b) Child prostitution, trafficking in pornography involving the sexuality of children, and international traffic in girls and boys for immoral purposes;

(c) Underage maidservants in a position of servitude.

### Duties of States

15. States should fully apply the provisions of the Declaration on the Rights of the Child proclaimed by the General Assembly in its resolution 1386 (XIV) of 20 November 1959, and more particularly:

(a) Principle 2, according to which "The child shall enjoy special protection, and shall be given opportunities and facilities, by law and by other means, to enable him to develop physically, mentally, morally, spiritually and socially in a healthy and normal manner and in conditions of freedom and dignity. . . ."

(b) Principle 9, according to which "The child shall be

protected against all forms of neglect, cruelty and exploitation. He shall not be the subject of traffic, in any form. . . . "

16. States should consider the possibility of ratifying, as soon as possible, the Convention on the Rights of the Child adopted by the General Assembly in its resolution 44/25 of 20 November 1989, and in this context should fully implement, in particular, article 32, which reads as follows:

"1. States Parties recognize the right of the child to be protected from economic exploitation and from performing any work that is likely to be hazardous or to interfere with the child's education, or to be harmful to the child's health or physical, mental, spiritual, moral or social development.

"2. States Parties shall take legislative, administrative, social and educational measures to ensure the implementation of the present article. To this end, and having regard to the relevant provisions of other international instruments, States Parties shall in particular:

"(a) Provide for a minimum age or minimum ages for admission to employment;

"(b) Provide for appropriate regulation of the hours and conditions of employment;

"(c) Provide for appropriate penalties or other sanctions to ensure the effective enforcement of the present article."

17. Over forty countries have ratified the Minimum Age Convention, 1973 (No. 138), of the International Labour Organisation. Those that have not done so should take appropriate steps to ratify that Convention. In this connection, greater assistance from the International Labour Organisation should be extended to the developing countries to facilitate their increased participation in standard-setting activities and in the implementation of ratified conventions.

18. States should adopt and implement policies and programmes to narrow the gap between legislation and its implementation in practice.

19. States should, until such time as child labour is eliminated, pay specific attention to the issue of protection of working children and make recommendations on ways and means to ensure that their working conditions are kept under scrutiny and control.

20. States which have not already done so should review their legislation in the field of child labour with a view to the absolute prohibition of the employment of children in the following cases:

(a) Employment before the normal age of completion of primary schooling in the country concerned;

(b) Underage maid service;

(c) Night work;

(d) Work in dangerous or unhealthy conditions;

(e) Activities linked with prostitution, pornography and other forms of sexual trade and exploitation;

(f) Work concerned with trafficking in and production of illicit drugs;

(g) Work involving degrading or cruel treatment.

21. States should take preventive and curative measures, including the strengthening of their legislation, to combat the phenomena of the exploitation of child labour, such as the use of children for illegal, clandestine or criminal pruposes, including the traffic in narcotic drugs, or in armed conflicts or military activities, or any other form of conflict.

22. Member States should be encouraged to strengthen cooperation between police and all public and private organizations which deal with cases of exploitation of child labour either within or outside the family, to facilitate identification of cases of exploitation of chld labour and to take measures necessary to eliminate it.

23. States should, where necessary, undertake development programmes with a view to:

(a) Making primary education compulsory and available free to all;

(b) Assisting and encouraging families in order that their children may continue their education, in order to combat illiteracy and the phenomenon of school dropouts; and, until such time as primary education is compulsory and available free to all, developing school programmes, including part-time education programmes, adapted to the needs of children who are not in school;

(c) Adapting school curricula to the preparation of a child for a career;

(d) Improving the training programmes of professional workers dealing with child labour, in particular labour inspectors, social workers and magistrates, with a view, in particular, to making them more sensitive to the needs of children;

(e) Establishing or improving medical services for children.

24. States should ensure the availability of a sufficient number of work inspectors and train them systematically to deal with cases of exploitationof child labour. Particular attention should be given in national and regional plans for economic and social development to the occupational training of young people. National development plans should also include a section ensuring that the most deprived have sufficient resources to be able to protect themselves from conditions leading to exploitation.

25. All Member States should endeavour to establish national agencies or institutions to promote the rights of children and to protect them from any form of exploitation. Particular efforts should be made to stress the importance of family values.

**Role of UN Bodies and Specialized Agencies**

26. The Internatinal Labour Organisation should be encouraged in its activities within the framework of its work programme relating to child labour. Other United Nations bodies and specialized agencies, in particular, UNICEF, UNESCO, and WHO, should develop and/or reinforce their activities in the field of child labour.

27. All competent UN bodies and specialized agencies, development banks and intergovernmental bodies involved in development projects should ensure that no child is employed either directly or through local subcontractors.

28. The United Nations and the specialized agencies, having regard to their special responsibilities in the field of child labour, should pay special attention to the situation of children in South Africa and in the occupied Arab territories.

29. While the question of exploitation of child labour should primarily be dealt with by the International Labour Organisation, the United Nations human rights bodies should continue to be concerned with this question in the framework of the rights of the child in general. The Sub-Commission on Prevention of Discrimination and Protection of Minorities and its Working Group on Contemporary Forms of Slavery should continue to have responsibility in this field.

30. The United Nations and the specialized agencies, including the United Nations University, should continue to incorporate in their programmes a series of interdisciplinary and multinational projects for comparative research on the various aspects of the exploitation of child labour through-

out the world and in particular in the countries of Africa, Asia and Latin America.

31. The United Nations and the specialized agencies should reinforce their programmes related to the elimination of the exploitation of child labour, and in particular to the study of the economic, social, legal and cultural factors which give rise for it.

32. The Secretary-General should invite all United Nations bodies and special agencies to attach greater importance to eliminating the exploitation of child labour and to study and discuss this issue at forthcoming international conferences, with special emphasis being placed on it at major conferences.

33. An international child welfare fund should be established. The resources of the fund would be allocated to combat violations of the rights provided for in the Convention on the Rights of the Child, particularly the rights of those children living in especially difficult circumstances, such as orphans and street children, refugees or displaced persons, victims of war and of natural and man-made disasters, including such perils as exposure to radiation and dangerous chemicals, children of migrant workers and other socially disadvantaged groups, child workers or youth trapped in the bondage of prostitution, sexual abuse and other forms of exploitation, disabled children and juvenile delinquents and victims of apartheid and foreign occupation. Such children deserve special attention, protection and asistance from their families and communities and as part of national efforts and international cooperation.

### Cooperation at the Local, National and International Levels

34. Major steps should be taken by Governments, international organizations and nongovernmental organizations to increase awareness amongst children, parents, workers, trade unions and employers of the causes and the adverse effects of child labour and measures to combat its exploitation. Such steps could include wider dissemination of relevant international instruments translated, where appropriate, into languages other than the official languages of the United Nations, as well as the development and strengthening of existing norms.

35. Support should be given to nongovernmental organizations concerned with the problem of child labour, particularly at the community level, and a constructive partnership should be evolved between Governments and nongovernmental organizations.

36. The United Nations bodies and the specialized agencies dealing with the problem of child labour should seek the cooperation of national and international trade unions.

37. Appropriate and necessary forms of support should be given to nongovernmental organizations at all levels, especially community organizations, concerned with the problem of child labour.

38. Concerned United Nations bodies and specialized agencies should examine the possibility of promoting an information campaign among villagers, employers, parents, children and other groups in countries where child labour exists.

39. Members of the international commuity should cooperate in order to assist developing countries in creating conditions under which child labour could be entirely eliminated.

*CHILDREN AND DRUGS.* Alarmed by the fact that drug dealers' organizations are making use of children in their illicit production of and trafficking in drugs and by the increase in the number of drug-addicted children, and conscious of the physical and psychological damage inflicted on children by the illicit use of narcotic drugs and of its serious effects both on their potential for development and their relationships with their families and society, the UN General Assembly on 8 December 1988 (resolution 43/121) strongly condemned drug trafficking in all its forms, particularly those criminal activities that involve children in the use, production, and illicit sale of narcotic drugs and psychotropic substances; and urged all States to join together to promote the establishment of national and international programs to protect children from the illicit consumption of drugs and psychotropic substances and from involvement in illicit production and trafficking.

The Assembly invited the governments of those States most affected by drug use among their child population to adopt urgent additional measures, as part of their national strategies, to prevent, reduce, and eliminate drug use by children, with the aim of ensuring for children a social and family environment that will preserve their health, physical fitness, and well-being. It also called upon all States to promote the adoption, by their legislative authorities, of measures providing for suitably severe punishment of drug-trafficking crimes that involve children.

Later, the Economic and Social Council, on 22 May 1989, appealed (resolution 1989/123) to the competent international agencies and the United Nations Fund for Drug Abuse Control to assign high priority to financial support for prevention campaigns and programs designed to rehabilitate drug-addicted minors and conducted by government bodies.

*DETENTION OF CHILDREN.* At its 1985 session, the UN Sub-Commission on Prevention of Discrimination and Protection of Minorities requested the Secretary-General (resolution 1985/19) to invite governments, United Nations organs, specialized agencies, intergovernmental organizations, the **INTERNATIONAL COMMITTEE OF THE RED CROSS,** and other non-governmental organizations to submit information concerning the incarceration of children under the age of 18 with adult prisoners, and to solicit their views on ways and means of preventing this practice. The Secretary-General was asked to compile the information received and to submit it in a report to the Sub-Commission at its 1986 session.

The information compiled by the Secretary-General (UN Doc. E/CN.4/Sub.2/1987/30 and Add. 1) was drawn to the attention of the Sub-Commission at its

1987 session, and was considered as background documentation by the Sub-Commission's Working Group on Contemporary Forms of Slavery and its Working Group on Detention. However, it was not examined in detail by the Sub-Commission or by either working group.

At its 1989 session, the Sub-Commission requested the Secretary-General (resolution 1989/31) to update his report by including in it further information made available to him on the question of children deprived of their liberty and to submit the new version to the Sub-Commission's 1990 session for consideration. At the same time, it appointed one of its members, Mrs. Mary Concepcion Bautista (Philippines), to prepare a report on the application of international standards concerning the human rights of detained juveniles, in particular the separation of juvenile and adult offenders in penal institutions, detention pending trial, least possible use of institutionalization, and the objectives of institutional treatment.

***CHILDREN IN MILITARY SERVICE.*** The UN Sub-Commission on Prevention of Discrimination and Protection of Minorities at its 1989 session expressed deep concern (resolution 1989/41) that, in many parts of the world, children continue to take part in hostilities and are recruited into the armed forces. It recognized that children who have been trained to hate and have participated in war are often mentally and morally crippled for life and deplored the fact that many child soldiers have been killed or seriously injured, while others languish as prisoners of war.

The Sub-Commission decided to pursue the subject in subsequent sessions and called upon the Secretary-General to prepare for its examination a report dealing with the recruitment of children into government and non-governmental armed forces and their participation in hostilities.

***CHILDREN AND ARMED CONFLICTS.*** At its second session, in 1992, the UN Committee on the Rights of the Child discussed the situation of children in armed conflicts and prepared a series of recommendations on the subject, which were later strongly supported by the World Conference on Human Rights.

Noting this development, the Commission on Human Rights, at its 1993 session, deplored the continued practice of enlisting children in the armed forces and expressed its deep concern at the alarming figures for deaths and serious injuries entailing lifelong disability among children in areas of conflict. Alarmed by information drawn to its attention that some particularly injurious weapons, especially antipersonnel mines, continue to strike long after conflicts have ended, and noting that children are often among the main victims of such weapons, the Commission requested all States to render full support to prevent the indiscriminate use of antipersonnel mines and to protect and assist victims. It invited all international and intergovernmental organizations concerned to ensure that all possible assistance is given to child victims of antipersonnel mines, who are often disabled for life, with a view to their physical and psychological recovery and social reintegration.

The General Assembly, meeting later in 1993, expressed concern about the tragic situation of children caught in armed conflicts in many parts of the world, and called upon States to respect fully the dispositions contained in the Geneva Conventions of 1949 and the two additional Protocols of 1977, as well as the Convention on the Rights of the Child, which accord children affected by armed conflicts special protection and treatment.

***CHILD REFUGEES.*** The particular problems experienced by children who are refugees, which often exposes them to practices having effects similar to those of slavery, have for some time been a matter of special concern to the Office of the United Nations High Commissioner for Refugees (UNHCR). A standing Working Group on Refugee Children At Risk was established in that office early in 1987 to monitor those problems and to suggest ways of ameliorating or remedying them.

In October 1987, the High Commissioner presented a paper to his executive committee (UN Doc. EC/SCP/46) enumerating the problems and the possible solutions. After examining the subject, the executive committee adopted a series of conclusions on refugee children, in which it:

(a) Expressed appreciation to the High Commissioner for his Report on Refugee Children (EC/SCP/46) and noted with serious concern the violations of their human rights in different areas of the world and their special needs and vulnerability within the broader refugee population;

(b) Recognized that refugee children constitute approximately one half of the world's refugee population and that the situation in which they live often gives rise to special protection and assistance problems as well as to problems in the area of durable solutions;

(c) Reiterated the widely recognized principle that children must be among the first to receive protection and assistance;

(d) Stressed that all action taken on behalf of refugee children must be guided by the principle of the best interests of the child as well as by the principle of family unity;

(e) Condemned the exposure of refugee children to physical violence and other violations of their basic rights, including through sexual abuse, trade in children, acts of piracy, military or armed attacks, forced recruitment, political exploitation or arbitrary detention, and called for national and international action to prevent such violations and assist the victims;

(f) Urged States to take appropriate measures to register the births of refugee children born in countries of asylum;

(g) Expressed its concern over the increasing number of cases of statelessness among refugee children;

(h) Recommended that children who are accompanied by their parents should be treated as refugees if either of the parents is determined to be a refugee;

(i) Underlined the special situation of unaccompanied children and children separated from their parents, who are in the care of other families, including their needs as regards determination of their status, provision for their physical and emotional support and efforts to trace parents or relatives; and in this connection, recalled the relevant paragraphs of Conclusion No. 24 (XXXII) on Family Reunification;

(j) Called upon the High Commissioner to ensure that individual assessments are conducted and adequate social histories prepared for unaccompanied children and children separated from their parents, who are in the care of other families, to facilitate provision for their immediate needs, the analysis of the longterm as well as immediate viability of existing foster arrangements, and the planning and implementation of appropriate durable solutions;

(k) Noted that while the best durable solution for an unaccompanied refugee child will depend on the particular circumstances of the case, the possibility of voluntary repatriation should at all times be kept under review, keeping in mind the best interests of the child and the possible difficulties of determining the voluntary character of repatriation;

(l) Stressed the need for internationally and nationally supported programmes geared to preventive action, special assistance and rehabilitation for disabled refugee children and encouraged States to participate in the "Twenty or More" Plan providing for the resettlement of disabled refugee children;

(m) Noted with serious concern the detrimental effects that extended stays in camps have on the development of refugee children and called for international action to mitigate such effects and provide durable sessions as soon as possible;

(n) Recognized the importance of meeting the special psychological, religious, cultural and recreational needs of refugee children in order to ensure their emotional stability and development;

(o) Reaffirmed the fundamental right of refugee children to education and called upon all States, individually and collectively, to intensify their efforts, in co-operation with the High Commissioner, to ensure that all refugee children benefit from primary education of a satisfactory quality, that respects their cultural identity and is oriented towards an understanding of the country of asylum;

(p) Recognized the need of refugee children to pursue further levels of education and recommended that the High Commissioner consider the provision of post-primary education within the general programme of assistance;

(q) Called upon all States, in co-operation with UNHCR and concerned agencies, to develop and/or support programmes to address nutritional and health risks faced by refugee children, including programmes to ensure an adequate, well-balanced and safe diet, general immunization and primary health care;

(r) Recommended regular and timely assessment and review of the needs of refugee children, either on an individual basis or through sample surveys, prepared in cooperation with the country of asylum, taking into account all relevant factors such as age, sex, personality, family, religion, social and cultural background and the situation of the local population, and benefiting from the active involvement of the refugee community itself;

(s) Reaffirmed the need to promote continuing and expanded cooperation between UNHCR and other concerned agencies and bodies active in the fields of assistance to refugee children and protection, including through the development of legal and social standards;

(t) Noted the importance of further study of the needs of refugee children by UNHCR, other intergovernmental and nongovernmental agencies and national authorities, with a view to identification of additional support programs and reorientation as necessary of existing ones;

(u) Called upon the High Commissioner to develop further, in consultation with concerned organizations, guidelines to promote co-operation between UNHCR and these organizations to improve the international protection, physical security, well-being and normal psychosocial development of refugee children;

(v) Called upon the High Commissioner to maintain the UNHCR Working Group on Refugee Children at Risk as his focal point on refugee children, to strengthen the Working Group and to inform the members of the executive committee, on a regular basis, of its work.

*STREET CHILDREN.* Children who literally live on the streets of large cities, whether because they have been abandoned by their families or have run away from home, have become a tragic problem in recent years. The UN General Assembly, in resolution 47/126 of 18 December 1992, and the Commission on Human Rights, in resolution 1993/81 of 10 March 1993, expressed grave concern at the growing number of worldwide reports of street children being involved in and affected by serious crime, drug abuse, violence, and prostitution; and urged governments (a) to seek comprehensive ways to prevent the marginalization of children and the phenomenon of street children and (b) to restore street children's full participation in society; to involve these children in the development of such programs; and to provide adequate nutrition, shelter, health care, and education.

Both the Assembly and the Commission invited governments, UN bodies and organizations, and intergovernmental and non-governmental agencies to cooperate with each other and to ensure greater awareness and more effective action to solve this problem.

At its 1993 session, the General Assembly welcomed (resolution 48/136 of 20 December 1993) the special attention given to the rights of children by the World Conference on Human Rights, citing particularly part 1, paragraph 21, of the Vienna Declaration and Program of Action; and welcomed the work of UNICEF and its National Committee in reducing the suffering of street children, as well as the work of the Committee on the Rights of the Child; the Special Rapporteur of the Commission on Human Rights on the Sale of Children, Child Prostitution and Child Pornography; and the UN International Drug Control Program.

*Sale of Children, Child Prostitution, and Child Pornography.* In 1983, the UN Economic and Social Council requested the **CENTER FOR HUMAN RIGHTS** (resolution 1983/30) to prepare, in liaison with other UN agencies and with the competent non-governmental organizations, a study on the sale of children. The study (UN Doc. E/CN.4/Sub.2/28) was presented to the Sub-Commission on the Prevention of Discrimination and Protection of Minorities at its 1987 session; but the Sub-Commission (resolution 1987/32) requested that it be put back on the drawing board and, with the help of United Nations agencies and non-governmental organizations, be given a deeper and broader accent, introducing matters relating to organ transplants and the fetus trade. The revised report on the sale of children (UN Doc. E/CN.4/Sub.2/1988/30) was submitted to the Sub-Commission at its 1988 session. Also, at that session, the UN Working Group on Contemporary Forms of Slavery reviewed in detail developments relating to slavery and the slave trade. Its examination of the question of the sale of children was summarized in its report to the Sub-Commission (UN Doc. E/CN.4/Sub.2/1988/32, chap. III B, paras. 17–28).

At its 1989 session, the Sub-Commission, on recommendation of its Working Group on Contemporary Forms of Slavery, proposed (resolution 1989/42) the appointment of such a Special Rapporteur "to consider matters relating to the sale of children, child prostitution and child pornography, including the problem of the adoption of children for commercial purposes" and suggested that a person of international reputation should be appointed as Special Rapporteur by the Chairman of the Commission on Human Rights following consultations with other officers of the Commission. The Commission appointed Mr. Vitit Muntarbhorn as Special Rapporteur.

At its 1991 session, the Sub-Commission on the Prevention of Discrimination and Protection of Minorities considered a preliminary report by the Special Rapporteur of the Commission on Human Rights on the sale of children, child prostitution, and child pornography (E/CN.4/1991/51), and a report prepared by its Working Group on Contemporary Forms of Slavery (E/CN.4/1991/41 and Corr. 1) that contained information relating to the same subject and included information on child soldiers.

*Program of Action.* On the basis of these reports, the Sub-Commission sent a draft program of action to combat these evils to the Commission on Human Rights (decision 1991/113), which then adopted (resolution 1992/74) the following Program of Action for

the Prevention of the Sale of Children, Child Prostitution, and Child Pornography:

### General

1. Child victims of trafficking and sale, child prostitution and child pornography are children in especially difficult circumstances, as indicated in the World Declaration on the Survival, Protection and Development of Children, adopted in New York on 30 September 1990 for the World Summit for Children.

2. The trafficking in and sale of children, child prostitution and child pornography constitute modern forms of slavery that are incompatible with human rights, human dignity and values and jeopardize the welfare of individuals, families and society as a whole.

3. To prevent the trafficking in and sale of children, child prostitution and child pornography, concerted measures are called for at the national, regional and international levels, including information, education, assistance and rehabilitation, legislative measures and a strengthening of law enforcement in this field. Coordinating agencies should be appointed or established at the national, regional and global levels.

4. At the global level, coordination of the Program of Action should be carried out by the Center for Human Rights in cooperation with other sections of the United Nations Secretariat, the Center for Social Development and Humanitarian Affairs of the Secretariat, the United Nations Development Program, the United Nations High Commissioner for Refugees, UNICEF, the ILO, UNESCO, and WHO. Cooperation should also be established with regional bodies, the World Tourism Organization, INTERPOL and nongovernmental organizations.

5. Economic conditions will continue to have considerable influence over the destiny of children, particularly in the developing countries. For the future of all children, it is absolutely essential to ensure or revive sustained and sustainable economic growth and development in all countries.

6. The best interests of the child should govern every decision and guide all efforts undertaken to implement this Program of Action.

7. The measures contained within this Program of Action should be implemented bearing in mind the economic imbalance that exists between industrialized States and the developing nations and the need to support the efforts of developing countries in this regard.

8. States are required to accord a clear high level of commitment and priority to combat and eliminate the trafficking in, sale and sexual exploitation of children.

9. States should systematically discourage the exercise of all customs, traditions and practices that encourage the trafficking in and sale or sexual exploitation of children.

10. The sale of children, child prostitution and child pornography cannot be justified by reason of poverty or underdevelopment. Besides the longterm action required to treat the underlying causes and thus prevent these phenomena from occurring in the future, it is essential that States take urgent and immediate measures to reduce the dangers that children face.

11. In situations of emergency, national or international conflicts, or disasters, when communities and normal patterns of life break down, children are especially vulnerable. In such circumstances, States should take all necessary mea-

sures to protect children from trafficking, sale and sexual exploitation.

## Information

12. International, regional and national information campaigns are required to raise public awareness at all levels of the grave problems of trafficking in, and sale of children, child prostitution and child pornography by:

(a) Warning and informing people about these grave abuses;

(b) Informing them about prevention programs;

(c) Publicizing ways of reporting these abuses;

(d) Publicizing services for victims;

(e) Making known the penalties for the perpetrators;

(f) Teaching that culture and traditions that encourage these forms of child abuse are contrary to international norms for the protection of children.

13. In order to increase the availability and to improve the quality of information, investigation of abuses should be undertaken by public and private institutions. The results should, wherever possible, be made public and exchanged between governmental and nongovernmental organizations at the local, national and international levels. Due regard should be paid to the need for confidentiality with regard to the identity of victims.

14. It is imperative that information programs be carried out on a continuous basis. Nevertheless, to provide a focus for the campaigns, States should consider the possibility of proclaiming a world day for the abolition of contemporary forms of slavery. The anniversary of the adoption of the Convention for the Suppression of the Traffic in Persons and of the Exploitation of the Prostitution of Others, 2 December, might be an appropriate date. Alternatively, an international children's day already established in a State's calendar might be used for this purpose.

15. Media should contribute fully to these information efforts with a view to ending the silence surrounding these forms of child exploitation.

16. Nongovernmental organizations and associations should be encouraged to lend their full support to these efforts.

17. Law enforcement agencies should be given a significant role in these information campaigns.

## Education

18. The following educational goals are central to this Program of Action:

(a) Universal primary education for all, with special emphasis on girls;

(b) Accelerated literacy programs for women and girls;

(c) Vocation-oriented formal and/or nonformal education curricula.

19. Preventive educational programs could usefully be integrated into primary and secondary school curricula. Similar programs should be designed for out-of-school children and particularly vulnerable groups, for example, street children, adolescent mothers and single and abandoned mothers.

20. Specific educational measures and training should be directed towards professionals who work with children, including teachers, social workers, health workers, members of the police, members of the judiciary and religious personnel.

Special educational measures should be directed towards the general public, especially men and parents, and to particular groups, such as travel agencies, tourists and the military.

21. All educational efforts should be based on universal ethical principles including the recognition of the integrity of the family and of every child's fundamental rights to the integrity of his or her own body and the protection of his or her identity. Such educational programs should include:

(a) The rights of the child and the respect due to all children by all;

(b) The inculcation of values such as self-esteem;

(c) The transmission of universal ethical principles;

(d) Making the child understand the dangers of trafficking and sale, child prostitution and pornography, including health risks such as AIDS and of drug and alcohol consumption and their damaging effects;

(e) Ways to prevent, identify and expose such abuses and to help child victims;

(f) Education in fatherhood and motherhood, including the need to create a family atmosphere of trust and communication within which a child can expose these issues;

(g) The principle of equality between men and women.

22. Innovative methods, including the use of the mass media, and grassroot community-based methods reaching the widest possible public, including potential victims, should be encouraged.

23. In all educational measures, care should be taken to avoid both underplaying and sensationalizing these issues. Account should be taken of the sociocultural characteristics and economic conditions of each country and, where children are involved, of the age of the child.

## Legal Measures and Law Enforcement

24. Preventive legislation aimed at protecting children should be promulgated, strengthened and better enforced. Police, courts, and treatment and support systems should focus on the welfare and protection of children. Legal aid should be made available to those who claim to have been sexually violated and to parents or legal guardians in cases of trafficking in and sale of children. Methods should be developed to obtain evidence from the child without further traumatization, and witnesses should be afforded protection.

25. Trafficking in, sale or sexual exploitation of children are serious crimes and must be treated as such. Efforts should be made to detect, arrest and convict clients, consumers, procurers, intermediaries and accomplices, and provision made for sanctions that take into account the grave nature of these offences.

26. Effective legislative and enforcement measures must also be directed against the intermediaries and others who encourage and make profits from the trafficking in, sale and sexual exploitation of children, such as agents, dealers, brothel-owners, policemen, and others involved. The proceeds from such activities should be seized and confiscated.

27. The Convention on the Rights of the Child provides protection against trafficking in, sale and sexual exploitation of children. States are encouraged to become parties to the Convention at the earliest possible date. For its implementation within States, national institutions composed of representatives of public agencies, nongovernmental organizations and associations should be established to coordinate action and to protect children and their rights.

28. States are urged to become parties to the ILO con-

ventions pertaining to the employment of children, in particular the Minimum Age Convention, 1973 (No. 138), and effectively to enforce laws that prohibit the employment of children in work likely to endanger their morals and physical health.

29. States are urged to ratify and effectively implement the Supplementary Convention on the Abolition of Slavery, the Slave Trade, and Institutions and Practices Similar to Slavery of 1956, and the Convention for the Suppression of the Traffic in Persons and of the Exploitation of the Prostitution of Others of 1949, and, furthermore, to submit reports regularly to the Secretary-General of the United Nations on their implementation.

30. States are urged to take all necessary measures to ensure that persons involved in trafficking in, sale or sexual exploitation of children are punished or extradited to other countries.

31. States should keep under review all new forms of technology that could be used for trafficking in, sale or sexual exploitation of children, and adopt appropriate legislation.

## Social Measures and Development Assistance

32. These abuses are often linked with poverty. Their prevention and elimination require long-range structural reforms in the social and economic fields. In the short term, development activities of UN agencies, especially the World Bank and the International Monetary Fund, and of other international and national agencies should have a substantive and positive impact on children and promote appropriate development strategies and policies. Priority should be given to formulating a family policy to prevent abuse and to policies aimed at improving the social, economic and working conditions of girls and women in general, and of the poorest girls and women in particular. Local community-based projects, including collective self-help projects should also be encouraged.

33. The needs of children who have been victims of trafficking, sale or sexual exploitation should be taken into account in development plans and assistance. Special attention should be given to certain groups of children at risk, for example, street children, teenage single mothers, children of broken homes or those whose mothers are in prostitution and other children in especially difficult circumstances. Governments, specialized agencies, UN bodies and nongovernmental organizations should be encouraged to initiate projects designed to protect street children from sexual abuse (mobile units to offer social and medical aid, small-scale enterprise projects for children, "safe houses," emergency centers, etc.). Efforts should be made to reunite street children in cities with their families in rural areas and in general to improve the social, economic and working conditions of parents whose children are victims of sexual exploitation or are at high risk.

## Rehabilitation and Reintegration

34. Rehabilitation and reintegration programs using an interdisciplinary approach should be established to assist children who have been victims of trafficking, sale or sexual exploitation and their families. Agencies implementing such programs, whether public or nongovernmental, should be established, or strengthened by being provided with the necessary support and funding. They should be encouraged to request technical assistance, evaluational assistance, infor-

mation on new methods of self-funding schemes, etc., from the United Nations bodies and from public or private, national or international sources with relevant competence.

## International Coordination

35. Bilateral and multilateral cooperation among law enforcement agencies is essential. States should establish their own data bases, improve their reporting at all levels, exchange information and report to the International Criminal Police Organization to enable a special data bank on suspects involved in crossborder trafficking, sale or sexual exploitation of children to be set up. The experience gained in international police cooperation in combating drug traffic should be used to prevent international traffic in and sexual exploitation of children.

36. A special intergovernmental task force should be set up at the regional level to assist Governments in devising ways and means of checking the phenomena of the trafficking in, sale and sexual exploitation of children; national-level commissions should plan new measures to address these problems in cooperation with concerned nongovernmental organizations.

## Trafficking in and Sale of Children

37. The measures mentioned in the following paragraphs specific to the trafficking in and sale of children are required.

38. States should take effective legal and administrative measures to prevent the abduction and sale of children for whatever purpose (sexual exploitation, any form of labour, adoption, criminal activities, trafficking in organs, etc.). Laws should be adopted or strengthened that impose penalties on parents and on all others knowingly involved in the trafficking in and sale of children.

39. States should pay special attention to preventing and severely punishing any case of sale, abduction or traffic of children for transplantation of organs, particularly from developing to developed countries. They should cooperate with each other and with intergovernmental and nongovernmental organizations to these ends.

40. States should adopt urgent and effective procedures at the national level and through bilateral and international cooperation to find abducted, unlawfully removed or disappeared children and to trace families and reunite such children with their families. In this regard, special attention should be given to the situation of refugee children and their need for protection from trafficking, sale and sexual exploitation.

41. Measures should be taken to ensure that international adoptions do not involve the sale of children by their parents or their illicit removal. Procedures for this purpose should be based on the Declaration on Social and Legal Principles relating to the Protection and Welfare of Children, with Special Reference to Foster Placement and Adoption Nationally and Internationally of 1986, and the Convention on the Rights of the Child . Under no circumstances must adoption be allowed to involve financial gain for any of the parties involved. The commercialization of adoption procedures should be prohibited.

42. Intercountry adoptions, where permitted by national law, should only take place through competent, professional and authorized agencies in both the country of origin and the receiving country of the children.

43. The procedures for child birth registration, renunciation of parental rights and consent to adoption by a parent should be strictly regulated by law and adequate counselling offered to the biological parents.

44. Governmental and nongovernmental bodies should cooperate at the national and international levels in order to promote and develop local and national alternatives to intercountry adoptions, such as child-care facilities, including day care and other support services for parents, care by relatives, foster-family care and domestic adoptions. Special efforts should be made to ensure that parents are not incited to part with their children for socioeconomic reasons.

### Child Prostitution

45. The measures mentioned in the following paragraphs specific to child prostitution, independently of whether the clients are locals or foreigners, should be taken.

46. Incest and sexual abuse within the family or by the child's employers may lead to child prostitution. States therefore should take all apropriate legislative, administrative, social and educational measures to protect children against all forms of abuse while in the care of parents, family or legal guardians or any other person.

47. Special attention should be paid to the problem of sex tourism. Legislative and other measures should be taken to prevent and combat sex tourism, both in the countries from which the customers come and those to which they go. Marketing tourism through the enticement of sex with children should be penalized on the same level as procurement.

48. The World Tourism Organization should be encouraged to convene an expert meeting designed to offer practical measures to combat sex tourism.

49. States with military bases or troops, stationed on foreign territory or not, should take all the necessary measures to prevent such military personnel from being involved in child prostitution. The same applies to other categories of public servants who for professional reasons are posted abroad.

50. Legislation should be adopted to prevent new forms of technology from being used for soliciting for child prostitution.

### Child Pornography

51. The measures mentioned in the following paragraphs specific to child pornography are required.

52. Law enforcement agencies and social and other services should place a higher priority on the investigation of child pornography in order to prevent and eliminate any exploitation of children.

53. States that have not yet done so are urged to enact legislation making it a crime to produce, distribute or possess pornographic material involving children.

54. Where required, new legislation and penalties should be introduced to the mass media that broadcast or publish material threatening the psychic or moral integrity of children or containing unhealthy or pornographic descriptions and to prevent new technology being used to produce pornography, including video films and pornographic computer games.

**INTERNATIONAL YEAR OF THE CHILD.** In General Assembly resolutions 31/169, 32/109, and 33/83, the United Nations designated the year 1979 as the International Year of the Child. At the conclusion of that year, the General Assembly declared UNICEF as the United Nations' lead agency for the concerns of children worldwide.

***SEE ALSO*** *Committee on the Rights of the Child, UN; Juvenile Justice; Youth.*

**BIBLIOGRAPHY. 1. General.** Alston, P., S. Parker, and J. Seymour, eds. *Children, Rights and the Law.* Oxford, UK: Clarendon Press, 1992. Collection of scholarly articles, in English; bibliography, pp. 236–244.

Flekkoy, Malfrid Grude. *A Voice for Children: Speaking Out as their Ombudsman.* London, UK: UNICEF & Jessica Kingsley, 1991. Scholarly monograph, in English; bibliography, pp. 230–231.

Freeman, Michael, and Philip Veerman, eds. *The Ideologies of Children's Rights.* Dordrecht, the Netherlands: Martinus Nijhoff, 1992. Scholarly collection of articles, in English.

Nurkse, Dennis, and Kay Castelle, eds. *Children's Rights: Crisis and Challenge.* New York: Defense for Children International—USA, 1990. NGO monograph, in English.

Smyke, Patricia. *Caught in the Cross Currents: What's Happened to Children and People Who Work for Children in the Ten Years Since the International Year of the Child.* New York: NGO Committee on UNICEF, 1989. NGO report, in English.

United Nations Children's Fund (UNICEF). *The Rights of the World's Children: A Development Education Kit.* New York: 1989. IGO monograph, in English.

**2. Right to Protection.** France, Council of State. *Statut et Protection de l'Enfant* (Status and Protection of Children). Paris: Documentation Française, 1991. Goverment research report, in French.

Trinidad and Tobago, Ministry of Social Development and Family Services and UNICEF. *Caribbean Regional Conference on Child Abuse and Neglect.* Port of Spain, Trinidad and Tobago: 1990. Conference report, in English.

**3. Child Labor.** *Action for Children.* Published in New York by NGO Committee on UNICEF and UNICEF, this journal is an excellent source of information on children's rights.

Albright, J., M. Kunstel, and R. McKay. *Stolen Childhood: A Global Report on the Exploitation of Children.* New York: Defense for Children International—USA, 1987. News articles and photographs, in English.

Anderson, Leslie, E. J. Kelley, and Zarakivi Kinnunen. *Restavek: Child Domestic Labor in Haiti.* Minneapolis, MN, USA: Minnesota Lawyers International Human Rights Committee, 1990. NGO factfinding report, in English.

Bequele, A., and J. Boyden, eds. *Combating Child Labour.* Geneva: International Labor Office, 1988. IGO monograph, in English.

Boudhdiba, A. *Study on the Exploitation of Child Labor.* New York: United Nations, 1981. UN Sales no. E.82.XIV.2.

Child Workers in Asia and International Labour Office. *Child Labour: Law and Practice* 10, no. 1 (1991). IGO topical issue, in English.

Child Workers in Asia Support Group. *Child Workers in Asia* 1–5 (1985–1989). This NGO journal, published in Bangkok, Thailand, deals entirely with child labor and is an excellent source of information.

*Children's Rights Monitor.* This journal, published in Geneva, Switzerland, focuses entirely on children's rights and is an excellent source for all children's issues.

Coordinating Group for Religion in Society. "Facing Up to Child Defence for Children International." *1987 Activity Report of the International Secretariat of DCI.* Geneva: 1988. NGO annual report, in English.

Cross, Peter. *Kashmiri Carpet Children: Exploited Village Weavers.* London, UK: Anti-Slavery International, 1991. NGO monograph, in English.

Defense for Children International—USA. *Database on the Rights of the Child.* New York: 1987. Abstracts, in English.

Lapierre, Dominique. *The City of Joy.* Trans. Kathryn Spink. Garden City, NY, USA: Doubleday & Company, 1985. Novel, in English; originally published in French as *La Cite de la Joie* (Paris: Editions Robert Laffont).

Lawyer's Committee for Human Rights. *A Childhood Abducted: Children Cutting Sugar Cane in the Dominican Republic.* New York: 1991. NGO factfinding report, in English.

Lorenzo, Ray. *Italy: Too Little Time and Space for Childhood.* Florence, Italy: UNICEF International Child Development Centre, 1991. IGO monograph, in English.

United Nations, Commission on Human Rights. *Draft Programme of Action for the Elimination of the Exploitation of Child Labour: Report of the Secretary General Prepared Pursuant to Commission on Human Rights Resolutions 1991/54 and 1991/55.* Geneva, Switzerland: 1991. IGO document, in English and French.

"The Vast Green Fields: Plantation Children," *Child Workers in Asia* 7, no. 1 (Jan. 1991): NGO special issue, in English.

Williams, Suzanne. *Child Workers in Portugal: A Report on Child Labour in Portugal for Anti-Slavery International.* London, UK: Anti-Slavery International, 1992. NGO report, in English.

**4. Children and Drugs.** International Catholic Child Bureau (ICCB). *Children and Drug Abuse.* Geneva, Switzerland: August 1988. NGO manual, in English.

Lorenzo, Ray. *Italy: Too Little Time and Space for Childhood.* Florence, Italy: UNICEF International Child Development Centre, 1991. IGO monograph, in English.

**5. Detention.** American-Arab Anti-Discrimination Committee. *Children of the Stones.* Washington, D.C.: 1988. NGO report, in English.

Amnesty International. *Children: The Youngest Victims.* London: 1987. NGO report, in English.

Cook, Helena. *The War against Children: South Africa's Younger Victims.* New York: Lawyers Committee for Human Rights, 1986. NGO mission report, in English.

Defense for Children International. "Apartheid's Children," *International Children's Rights Monitor* 4, no. 2 (2nd quarter 1987). NGO article, in English.

————. *Children in Prison in Turkey.* Geneva: 1988. NGO report, in English.

Detainees' Parents Support Committee. *A Memorandum on Children under Repression.* Johannesburg, South Africa: 1986. NGO report, in English.

Jupp, Michael. *Children under Apartheid.* Brooklyn, NY, USA: Defense for Children International—USA, 1987. NGO report, in English; bibliography, pp. 187–191.

Sopher, Sharon. *Witness to Apartheid.* San Francisco, CA, USA: Southern Africa Media Center/California Newsreel, 1986. Documentary film, in English.

Streib, Victor L. *Death Penalty for Juveniles.* Bloomington, IN, USA: Indiana University Press, 1987. Scholarly report, in English; classified bibliography, pp. 237–250.

Tomasevski, Katarina. *Children in Adult Prisons: An International Perspective.* New York: St. Martin's Press, 1986. NGO report, in English.

————. "The Placement of Children in Institutions: Deprivation of Liberty . . . or Not?" *International Children's Rights Monitor* 3, no. 3 (Nov. 1986): 7–10. NGO article, in English.

United Nations. *Application of International Standards concerning the Human Rights of Detained Juveniles.* New York: 1990 and 1991 (E/CN.4/Sub.2/1990/25 Add. 1 and 2; E/CN.4/Sub.2/1991/24).

————. *Application of the Death Penalty to Persons under Eighteen Years of Age.* New York: 1990 (E/CN.4/Sub.2/1990/26).

United Nations Centre for Social Development and Humanitarian Affairs. "Juvenile Justice in International Perspective: Special Double Volume," *International Review of Criminal Policy* no. 39–40 (1990). Special issue, in English.

United Nations Sub-Commission on Prevention of Discrimination and Protection of Minorities. *Application of International Standards concerning the Human Rights of Detained Juveniles: Report Prepared by the Special Rapporteur, Mrs. Mary Concepción Bautista, Pursuant to Sub-Commission Resolution 1990/21.* Geneva, Switzerland: 1991. IGO document, in English and French.

**6. Military Service.** Dodge, Cole P., and Magne Raundalen. *Reaching Children in War: Sudan, Uganda and Mozambique.* Bergen, Norway & Uppsala, Sweden: Scandinavian Institute of African Studies, 1991. Collective works, in English.

Elahi, Maryam. "The Rights of the Child Under Islamic Law: Prohibition of the Child Soldier," *Columbia Human Rights Law Review* 19, no. 2 (Spring 1988): 259–279. Scholarly article, in English.

Plattner, Denise. "Protection of Children in International Humanitarian Law," *International Review of the Red Cross* 24, no. 240 (n.d.): 140–152. Scholarly article, in English.

United Nations Sub-Commission on Prevention of Discrimination and Protection of Minorities. *The Adoption of Children for Commercial Purposes and the Recruitment of Children into Government and Non-Governmental Armed Forces: Report of the Secretary-General.* Geneva, Switzerland: 1990. IGO document, in English and French.

————. *Report of the Working Group on Contemporary Forms of Slavery on Its Sixteenth Session.* Chairman/Rapporteur: Mrs. F. Z. Ksentini. Geneva, Switzerland: 1991. IGO document, in English and French.

**7. Children in Armed Conflicts.** Berman, Nina. "Project Launched in Mozambique to Aid Children 'Instrumentalized' by War," *Action for Children* 3, no. 4 (1988): 1, 8. NGO article, in English.

Center on War and the Child. *Uganda: Land of the Child Soldier—A Summary Report.* Eureka Springs, AR, USA: 1987. NGO report, in English.

Cultural Survival. "Children: The Battleground of Change," *Cultural Survival Quarterly* 10, no. 4 (1986). NGO article, in English.

Dutli, Maria Teresa. "Captured Child Combatants," *International Review of the Red Cross* no. 278 (Sept.–Oct. 1990): 421–434 (English); "Enfants—combattants prisonniers," *Revue internationale de la Croix-Rouge* no. 785: (Sept.–Oct. 1990): 456–470 (French). Scholarly article, in English and French.

Elahi, Maryam. "The Rights of the Child under Islamic Law: Prohibition of the Child Soldier," *Columbia Human Rights Law Review* 19, no. 2 (Spring 1988): 259–279. Scholarly article, in English.

Ennew, Judith. "Child Soldiers: Serving or Working?" *International Children's Rights Monitor* 2, no. 2 (2nd quarter 1985): 18–19. NGO article, in English.

Estrada-Claudio, Sylvia, José F. Bartolome, and Grace Aguiling-Dalisay. "Children's Stories: New Psychological Models Are Needed to Help Children Caught in Counter-

Insurgency," *Solidaridad II* 13, no. 4 (1990): 15–18. Research report, in English.

Monzon, Vivian. *Filipino Children in Situations of Armed Conflicts*. Kensington, Australia: Law Association for Asia and the Pacific, 1990. NGO research report, in English.

NGO Committee on UNICEF and UNICEF. "Child Soldiers of Uganda," *Action for Children* 1, no. 5 (1986): 6. IGO article, in English.

Pompey, Carmen. "The Military Training of the Young," *Radio Free Europe Research* 11, no. 46 (14 November 1986): 25–26. Government bulletin article, in English.

Radda Barnen and Swedish Save the Children. *A Humanitarian Appeal for Children in Armed Conflicts*. Stockholm: 1987. NGO appeal, in English.

U.S. Helsinki Watch Committee and Asia Watch Committee. *To Win the Children: Afghanistan's Other War*. New York: 1986. NGO report, in English.

United Nations. *The Adoption of Children for Commercial Purposes and the Recruitment of Children into Government and Nongovernmental Armed Forces*. New York: 1990 (E/CN.4/Sub.2/1990/43).

Walker, J. "Boy Soldiers in a Grown-Up's War," *Child Workers in Asia* 3, no. 1 (Jan.–March 1987): 1–2. NGO article, in English.

**8. Child Refugees.** Center for Documentation on Refugees and Save the Children Alliance. *A Selected and Annotated Bibliography on Refugee Children*. Geneva, Switzerland: 1988. NGO bibliography, in English.

Pask, E. Diane. "Unaccompanied Refugee and Displaced Children: Jurisdiction, Decision-Making and Representation," *International Journal of Refugee Law* 1, no. 2 (April 1989): 199–219. Scholarly article, in English.

Price Cohen, Cynthia. "The Rights of the Child: Implications for Change in the Care and Protection of Refugee Children," *International Journal of Refugee Law* 3, no. 4 (Oct. 1991): 675–691. Scholarly article, in English.

Women's Commission for Refugee Women and Children. *Going Home: The Prospect of Repatriation for Refugee Women and Children*. Washington, D.C.: 1992. Conference papers, in English.

**9. Street Children.** Agnelli, Susanna. *Street Children: A Growing Urban Tragedy*. London: Independent Commission on International Humanitarian Issues and Weidenfield and Nicolson, 1986. NGO monograph, in English.

Amnesty International. *Guatemala: Extrajudicial Executions and Human Rights Violations against Street Children*. London: 1990. NGO factfinding report, in English and French.

Black, Maggie. *Philippines: Children of the Runaway Cities*. Florence, Italy: UNICEF International Child Development Centre, 1991. IGO monograph, in English.

Chatterjee, Amrita. *India: The Forgotten Children of the Cities*. Florence, Italy: UNICEF International Child Development Centre, 1992. IGO monograph, in English.

Child Workers in Nepal Concerned Center. *Lost Childhood: Survey Research on Street Children of Kathmandu*. Kathmandu, Nepal: 1990. NGO factfinding report, in English.

"Child Workers on the Street," *Child Workers in Asia* 5, no. 2 (April–June 1989). Special issue, in English.

Defense for Children International. *International Investigation into the Rights of Abandoned Children*. Geneva, Switzerland: 1989. NGO report, in English.

Swift, Anthony. *Brazil: The Fight for Childhood in the City*. Florence, Italy: UNICEF International Child Development Centre, 1991. IGO monograph, in English.

**10. Sale of Children, Child Prostitution, and Child Pornography.** Asian Center for the Progress of Peoples. "What Has Become of Our Children?" *Asia Link* 12, no. 4 (July–Aug. 1990). Special issue, in English.

Fernand-Laurent, J. *Suppression of the Traffic in Persons and the Exploitation of the Prostitution of Others*. New York: United Nations, 1983 (E/1983/7).

International Catholic Child Bureau. *The Sexual Exploitation of Children: Field Responses*. Geneva, Switzerland: 1991. NGO directory, in English and French.

Muntarbhorn, V. *Sale of Children*. New York: United Nations, 1992 (E/CN.4/1991/51 and 1992/55).

Narvasen, Ove. *The Sexual Exploitation of Children in Developing Countries*. Oslo, Norway: Redd Barna—Norwegian Save the Children, 1989. NGO factfinding report, in English; bibliography, pp. 70–75.

O'Grady, Ron. *The Child and the Tourist: The Story behind the Escalation of Child Prostitution in Asia*. Bangkok, Thailand: End Child Prostitution in Asian Tourism, 1992. NGO monograph, in English.

"Say NO! to Child Prostitution," *Child Workers in Asia* 6, no. 2 (April–June 1990). NGO Special issue, in English.

United Nations Sub-Commission on Prevention of Discrimination and Protection of Minorities. *The Adoption of Children for Commercial Purposes and the Recruitment of Children Into Government and Non-Governmental Armed Forces: Report of the Secretary-General*. Geneva, Switzerland: 1990. IGO document, in English and French.

————. *Report of the Working Group on Contemporary Forms of Slavery on Its Sixteenth Session*. Chairman/Rapporteur: Mrs. F. Z. Ksentini. Geneva, Switzerland: 1991. IGO document, in English and French.

**CHILDREN'S RIGHTS: CONVENTION ON THE RIGHTS OF THE CHILD (1989).** The Convention, concluded by the UN **GENERAL ASSEMBLY** on 20 November 1989 (resolution 44/25), affirms that children's rights require special protection and aims not only to provide such protection but also to ensure the continuous improvement in the situation of children all over the world, as well as their development and education in conditions of peace and security.

The Convention establishes (article 43) a ten-member Committee of Experts on the Rights of the Child to examine the progress made by States parties in achieving its objectives. The experts are to be selected by the States parties from among their nationals.

A draft of the Convention was submitted to the UN Commission on Human Rights, at its 1978 session, by Poland. Between 1979 and 1989, the Commission elaborated the draft with the assistance of an open-ended working group. In 1988, the General Assembly requested the Commission to give the highest priority to this task and to make every effort to complete the text in 1989, the year marking the 30th anniversary of the Declaration of the Rights of the Child and the 10th anniversary of the International Year of the Child (1979).

The Commission concluded its work on the Convention at its 1989 session and forwarded it to the General Assembly through the Economic and Social Council. The Assembly adopted it without a recorded vote and opened it for signature, ratification, and accession. The text of the Convention on the Rights of the Child, annexed to resolution 44/25, is as follows:

### Preamble

The States Parties to the present Convention,

Considering that, in accordance with the principles proclaimed in the Charter of the United Nations, recognition of the inherent dignity and of the equal and inalienable rights of all members of the human family is the foundation of freedom, justice and peace in the world,

Bearing in mind that the peoples of the United Nations have, in the Charter, reaffirmed their faith in fundamental human rights and in the dignity and worth of the human person, and have determined to promote social progress and better standards of life in larger freedom,

Recognizing that the United Nations has, in the Universal Declaration of Human Rights and in the International Covenants on Human Rights, proclaimed and agreed that everyone is entitled to all the rights and freedoms set forth therein, without distinction of any kind, such as race, colour, sex, language, religion, political or other opinion, national or social origin, property, birth or other status,

Recalling that, in the Universal Declaration of Human Rights, the United Nations has proclaimed that childhood is entitled to special care and assistance,

Convinced that the family, as the fundamental group of society and the natural environment for the growth and well-being of all its members and particularly children, should be afforded the necessary protection and assistance so that it can fully assume its responsibilities within the community,

Recognizing that the child, for the full and harmonious development of his or her personality, should grow up in a family environment, in an atmosphere of happiness, love and understanding,

Considering that the child should be fully prepared to live an individual life in society, and brought up in the spirit of the ideals proclaimed in the Charter of the United Nations, and in particular in the spirit of peace, dignity, tolerance, freedom, equality and solidarity,

Bearing in mind that the need to extend particular care to the child has been stated in the Geneva Declaration of the Rights of the Child of 1924 and in the Declaration of the Rights of the Child adopted by the General Assembly on 20 November 1959 and recognized in the Universal Declaration of Human Rights, in the International Covenant on Civil and Political Rights (in particular in articles 23 and 24), in the International Covenant on Economic, Social and Cultural Rights (in particular in article 10) and in the statutes and relevant instruments of specialized agencies and international organizations concerned with the welfare of children,

Bearing in mind that, as indicated in the Declaration of the Rights of the Child, "the child, by reason of his physical and mental immaturity, needs special safeguards and care, including appropriate legal protection, before as well as after birth",

Recalling the provisions of the Declaration on Social and Legal Principles relating to the Protection and Welfare of Children, with Special Reference to Foster Placement and Adoption Nationally and Internationally; the United Nations Standard Minimum Rules for the Administration of Juvenile Justice (The Beijing Rules); and the Declaration on the Protection of Women and Children in Emergency and Armed Conflict,

Recognizing that, in all countries in the world, there are children living in exceptionally difficult conditions, and that such children need special consideration,

Taking due account of the importance of the traditions and cultural values of each people for the protection and harmonious development of the child,

Recognizing the importance of international cooperation for improving the living conditions of children in every country, in particular in the developing countries,

Have agreed as follows:

### Part I

*Article 1.* For the purposes of the present Convention, a child means every human being below the age of eighteen years unless, under the law applicable to the child, majority is attained earlier.

*Article 2.* 1. States Parties shall respect and ensure the rights set forth in the present Convention to each child within their jurisdiction without discrimination of any kind, irrespective of the child's or his or her parent's or legal guardian's race, colour, sex, language, religion, political or other opinion, national, ethnic or social origin, property, disability, birth or other status.

2. States Parties shall take all appropriate measures to ensure that the child is protected against all forms of discrimination or punishment on the basis of the status, activities, expressed opinions, or beliefs of the child's parents, legal guardians, or family members.

*Article 3.* 1. In all actions concerning children, whether undertaken by public or private social welfare institutions, courts of law, administrative authorities or legislative bodies, the best interests of the child shall be a primary consideration.

2. States Parties undertake to ensure the child such protection and care as is necessary for his or her well-being, taking into account the rights and duties of his or her parents, legal guardians, or other individuals legally responsible for him or her, and, to this end, shall take all appropriate legislative and administrative measures.

3. States Parties shall ensure that the institutions, services and facilities responsible for the care or protection of children shall conform with the standards established by competent authorities, particularly in the areas of safety, health, in the number and suitability of their staff, as well as competent supervision.

*Article 4.* States Parties shall undertake all appropriate legislative, administrative, and other measures for the implementation of the rights recognized in the present Convention. With regard to economic, social and cultural rights, States Parties shall undertake such measures to the maximum extent of their available resources and, where needed, within the framework of international cooperation.

*Article 5.* States Parties shall respect the responsibilities, rights and duties of parents or, where applicable, the members of the extended family or community as provided for by local custom, legal guardians or other persons legally responsible for the child, to provide, in a manner consistent with the evolving capacities of the child, appropriate direction and guidance in the exercise by the child of the rights recognized in the present Convention.

*Article 6.* 1. States Parties recognize that every child has the inherent right to life.

2. States Parties shall ensure to the maximum extent possible the survival and development of the child.

*Article 7.* 1. The child shall be registered immediately after birth and shall have the right from birth to a name, the right to acquire a nationality and, as far as possible, the right to know and be cared for by his or her parents.

2. States Parties shall ensure the implementation of these rights in accordance with their national law and their obligations under the relevant international instruments in this field, in particular where the child would otherwise be stateless.

*Article 8.* 1. States Parties undertake to respect the right of the child to preserve his or her identity, including nationality, name and family relations as recognized by law without unlawful interference.

2. Where a child is illegally deprived of some or all of the elements of his or her identity, States Parties shall provide appropriate assistance and protection, with a view to speedily re-establishing his or her identity.

*Article 9.* 1. States Parties shall ensure that a child shall not be separated from his or her parents against their will, except when competent authorities subject to judicial review determine, in accordance with applicable law and procedures, that such separation is necessary for the best interests of the child. Such determination may be necessary in a particular case such as one involving abuse or neglect of the child by the parents, or one where the parents are living separately and a decision must be made as to the child's place of residence.

2. In any proceedings pursuant to paragraph 1 of the present article, all interested parties shall be given an opportunity to participate in the proceedings and make their views known.

3. States Parties shall respect the right of the child who is separated from one or both parents to maintain personal relations and direct contact with both parents on a regular basis, except if it is contrary to the child's best interests.

4. Where such separation results from any action initiated by a State Party, such as the detention, imprisonment, exile, deportation or death (including death arising from any cause while the person is in the custody of the State) of one or both parents or of the child, that State Party shall, upon request, provide the parents, the child or, if appropriate, another member of the family with the essential information concerning the whereabouts of the absent member(s) of the family unless the provision of the information would be detrimental to the well-being of the child. States Parties shall further ensure that the submission of such a request shall of itself entail no adverse consequences for the person(s) concerned.

*Article 10.* 1. In accordance with the obligation of States Parties under article 9, paragraph 1, applications by a child or his or her parents to enter or leave a State Party for the purpose of family reunification shall be dealt with by States Parties in a positive, humane and expeditious manner. States Parties shall further ensure that the submission of such a request shall entail no adverse consequences for the applicants and for the members of their family.

2. A child whose parents reside in different States shall have the right to maintain on a regular basis, save in exceptional circumstances, personal relations and direct contacts with both parents. Towards that end and in accordance with the obligation of States Parties under article 9, paragraph 2, States Parties shall respect the right of the child and his or her parents to leave any country, including their own, and to enter their own country. The right to leave any country shall be subject only to such restrictions as are prescribed by law and which are necessary to protect the national security, public order (*ordre public*), public health or morals or the rights and freedoms of others and are consistent with the other rights recognized in the present Convention.

*Article 11.* 1. States Parties shall take measures to combat the illicit transfer and non-return of children abroad.

2. To this end, States Parties shall promote the conclusion of bilateral or multilateral agreements or accession to existing agreements.

*Article 12.* 1. States Parties shall assure to the child who is capable of forming his or her own views the right to express those views freely in all matters affecting the child, the views of the child being given due weight in accordance with the age and maturity of the child.

2. For this purpose, the child shall in particular be provided the opportunity to be heard in any judicial and administrative proceedings affecting the child, either directly, or through a representative or an appropriate body, in a manner consistent with the procedural rules of national law.

*Article 13.* 1. The child shall have the right to freedom of expression; this right shall include freedom to seek, receive and impart information and ideas of all kinds, regardless of frontiers, either orally, in writing or in print, in the form of art, or through any other media of the child's choice.

2. The exercise of this right may be subject to certain restrictions, but these shall only be such as are provided by law and are necessary:

(a) For respect of the rights or reputations of others; or

(b) For the protection of national security or of public order (*ordre public*), or of public health or morals.

*Article 14.* 1. States Parties shall respect the right of the child to freedom of thought, conscience and religion.

2. States Parties shall respect the rights and duties of the parents and, when applicable, legal guardians, to provide direction to the child in the exercise of his or her right in a manner consistent with the evolving capacities of the child.

3. Freedom to manifest one's religion or beliefs may be subject only to such limitations as are prescribed by law and are necessary to protect public safety, order, health or morals, or the fundamental rights and freedoms of others.

*Article 15.* 1. States Parties recognize the rights of the child to freedom of association and to freedom of peaceful assembly.

2. No restrictions may be placed on the exercise of these rights other than those imposed in conformity with the law and which are necessary in a democratic society in the interests of national security or public safety, public order (*ordre public*), the protection of public health or morals or the protection of the rights and freedoms of others.

*Article 16.* 1. No child shall be subjected to arbitrary or unlawful interference with his or her privacy, family, home or correspondence, nor to unlawful attacks on his or her honour and reputation.

2. The child has the right to the protection of the law against such interference or attacks.

*Article 17.* States Parties recognize the important function performed by the mass media and shall ensure that the child has access to information and material from a diversity of national and international sources, especially those aimed at the promotion of his or her social, spiritual and moral well-being and physical and mental health. To this end, States Parties shall:

(a) Encourage the mass media to disseminate information and material of social and cultural benefit to the child and in accordance with the spirit of article 29;

(b) Encourage international co-operation in the production, exchange and dissemination of such information and material from a diversity of cultural, national and international sources;

(c) Encourage the production and dissemination of children's books;

(d) Encourage the mass media to have particular regard to the linguistic needs of the child who belongs to a minority group or who is indigenous;

(e) Encourage the development of appropriate guidelines for the protection of the child from information and material injurious to his or her well-being, bearing in mind the provisions of articles 13 and 18.

*Article 18.* 1. States Parties shall use their best efforts to ensure recognition of the principle that both parents have common responsibilities for the upbringing and development of the child. Parents or, as the case may be, legal guardians, have the primary responsibility for the upbringing and development of the child. The best interests of the child will be their basic concern.

2. For the purpose of guaranteeing and promoting the rights set forth in the present Convention, States Parties shall render appropriate assistance to parents and legal guardians in the performance of their child-rearing responsibilities and shall ensure the development of institutions, facilities and services for the care of children.

3. States Parties shall take all appropriate measures to ensure that children of working parents have the right to benefit from child-care services and facilities for which they are eligible.

*Article 19.* 1. States Parties shall take all appropriate legislative, administrative, social and educational measures to protect the child from all forms of physical or mental violence, injury or abuse, neglect or negligent treatment, maltreatment or exploitation, including sexual abuse, while in the care of parent(s), legal guardian(s), or any other person who has the care of the child.

2. Such protective measures should, as appropriate, include effective procedures for the establishment of social programmes to provide necessary support for the child and for those who have the care of the child, as well as for other forms of prevention and for identification, reporting, referral, investigation, treatment and follow-up of instances of child maltreatment described heretofore, and, as appropriate, for judicial involvement.

*Article 20.* 1. A child temporarily or permanently deprived of his or her family environment, or in whose own best interests cannot be allowed to remain in that environment, shall be entitled to special protection and assistance provided by the State.

2. States Parties shall in accordance with their national laws ensure alternative care for such a child.

3. Such care could include, *inter alia,* foster placement, kafalah of Islamic law, adoption or if necessary placement in suitable institutions for the care of children. When considering solutions, due regard shall be paid to the desirability of continuity in a child's upbringing and to the child's ethnic, religious, cultural and linguistic background.

*Article 21.* States Parties that recognize and/or permit the system of adoption shall ensure that the best interests of the child shall be the paramount consideration and they shall:

(a) Ensure that the adoption of a child is authorized only by competent authorities who determine, in accordance with applicable law and procedures and on the basis of all pertinent and reliable information, that the adoption is permissible in view of the child's status concerning parents, relatives and legal guardians and that, if required, the persons concerned have given their informed consent to the adoption on the basis of such counselling as may be necessary;

(b) Recognize that intercountry adoption may be considered as an alternative means of child's care, if the child cannot be placed in a foster or an adoptive family or cannot in any suitable manner be cared for in the child's country of origin;

(c) Ensure that the child concerned by intercountry adoption enjoys safeguards and standards equivalent to those existing in the case of national adoption;

(d) Take all appropriate measures to ensure that, in intercountry adoption, the placement does not result in improper financial gain for those involved in it;

(e) Promote, where appropriate, the objectives of the present article by concluding bilateral or multilateral arrangements or agreements, and endeavour, within this framework, to ensure that the placement of the child in another country is carried out by competent authorities or organs.

*Article 22.* 1. States Parties shall take appropriate measures to ensure that a child who is seeking refugee status or who is considered a refugee in accordance with applicable international or domestic law and procedures shall, whether unaccompanied or accompanied by his or her parents or by any other person, receive appropriate protection and humanitarian assistance in the enjoyment of applicable rights set forth in the present Convention and in other international human rights or humanitarian instruments to which the said States are Parties.

2. For this purpose, States Parties shall provide, as they consider appropriate, co-operation in any efforts by the United Nations and other competent intergovernmental organizations or non-governmental organizations cooperating with the United Nations to protect and assist such a child and to trace the parents or other members of the family of any refugee child in order to obtain information necessary for reunification with his or her family. In cases where no parents or other members of the family can be found, the child shall be accorded the same protection as any other child permanently or temporarily deprived of his or her family environment for any reason, as set forth in the present Convention.

*Article 23.* 1. States Parties recognize that a mentally or physically disabled child should enjoy a full and decent life, in conditions which ensure dignity, promote self-reliance and facilitate the child's active participation in the community.

2. States Parties recognize the right of the disabled child to special care and shall encourage and ensure the extension, subject to available resources, to the eligible child and those responsible for his or her care, of assistance for which application is made and which is appropriate to the child's condition and to the circumstances of the parents or others caring for the child.

3. Recognizing the special needs of a disabled child, assistance extended in accordance with paragraph 2 of the present article shall be provided free of charge, whenever possible, taking into account the financial resources of the parents or others caring for the child, and shall be designed to ensure that the disabled child has effective access to and receives education, training, health care services, rehabilitation services, preparation for employment and recreation opportunities in a manner conducive to the child's achieving the fullest possible social integration and individual development, including his or her cultural and spiritual development.

4. States Parties shall promote, in the spirit of international cooperation, the exchange of appropriate information in the field of preventive health care and of medical, psychological and functional treatment of disabled children,

including dissemination of and access to information concerning methods of rehabilitation, education and vocational services, with the aim of enabling States Parties to improve their capabilities and skills and to widen their experience in these areas. In this regard, particular account shall be taken of the needs of developing countries.

*Article 24.* 1. States Parties recognize the right of the child to the enjoyment of the highest attainable standard of health and to facilities for the treatment of illness and rehabilitation of health. States Parties shall strive to ensure that no child is deprived of his or her right of access to such health care services.

2. States Parties shall pursue full implementation of this right and, in particular, shall take appropriate measures:

(a) To diminish infant and child mortality;

(b) To ensure the provision of necessary medical assistance and health care to all children with emphasis on the development of primary health care;

(c) To combat disease and malnutrition, including within the framework of primary health care, through, *inter alia,* the application of readily available technology and through the provision of adequate nutritious foods and clean drinking-water, taking into consideration the dangers and risks of environmental pollution;

(d) To ensure appropriate prenatal and postnatal health care for mothers;

(e) To ensure that all segments of society, in particular parents and children, are informed, have access to education and are supported in the use of basic knowledge of child health and nutrition, the advantages of breast-feeding, hygiene and environmental sanitation and the prevention of accidents;

(f) To develop preventive health care, guidance for parents and family planning education and services.

3. States Parties shall take all effective and appropriate measures with a view to abolishing traditional practices prejudicial to the health of children.

4. States Parties undertake to promote and encourage international cooperation with a view to achieving progressively the full realization of the right recognized in the present article. In this regard, particular account shall be taken of the needs of developing countries.

*Article 25.* States Parties recognize the right of a child who has been placed by the competent authorities for the purposes of care, protection or treatment of his or her physical or mental health, to a periodic review of the treatment provided to the child and all other circumstances relevant to his or her placement.

*Article 26.* 1. States Parties shall recognize for every child the right to benefit from social security, including social insurance, and shall take the necessary measures to achieve the full realization of this right in accordance with their national law.

2. The benefits should, where appropriate, be granted, taking into account the resources and the circumstances of the child and persons having responsibility for the maintenance of the child, as well as any other consideration relevant to an application for benefits made by or on behalf of the child.

*Article 27.* 1. States Parties recognize the right of every child to a standard of living adequate for the child's physical, mental, spiritual, moral and social development.

2. The parent(s) or others responsible for the child have the primary responsibility to secure, within their abilities and financial capacities, the conditions of living necessary for the child's development.

3. States Parties, in accordance with national conditions and within their means, shall take appropriate measures to assist parents and others responsible for the child to implement this right and shall in case of need provide material assistance and support programmes, particularly with regard to nutrition, clothing and housing.

4. States Parties shall take all appropriate measures to secure the recovery of maintenance for the child from the parents or other persons having financial responsibility for the child, both within the State Party and from abroad. In particular, where the person having financial responsibility for the child lives in a State different from that of the child, States Parties shall promote the accession to international agreements or the conclusion of such agreements, as well as the making of other appropriate arrangements.

*Article 28.* 1. States Parties recognize the right of the child to education, and with a view to achieving this right progressively and on the basis of equal opportunity, they shall, in particular:

(a) Make primary education compulsory and available free to all;

(b) Encourage the development of different forms of secondary education, including general and vocational education, make them available and accessible to every child, and take appropriate measures such as the introduction of free education and offering financial assistance in case of need;

(c) Make higher education accessible to all on the basis of capacity by every appropriate means;

(d) Make educational and vocational information and guidance available and accessible to all children;

(e) Take measures to encourage regular attendance at schools and the reduction of drop-out rates.

2. States Parties shall take all appropriate measures to ensure that school discipline is administered in a manner consistent with the child's human dignity and in conformity with the present Convention.

3. States Parties shall promote and encourage international co-operation in matters relating to education, in particular with a view to contributing to the elimination of ignorance and illiteracy throughout the world and facilitating access to scientific and technical knowledge and modern teaching methods. In this regard, particular account shall be taken of the needs of developing countries.

*Article 29.* 1. States Parties agree that the education of the child shall be directed to:

(a) The development of the child's personality, talents and mental and physical abilities to their fullest potential;

(b) The development of respect for human rights and fundamental freedoms, and for the principle enshrined in the Charter of the United Nations;

(c) The development of respect for the child's parents, his or her own cultural identity, language and values, for the national values of the country in which the child is living, the country from which he or she may originate, and for civilizations different from his or her own;

(d) The preparation of the child for responsible life in a free society, in the spirit of understanding, peace, tolerance, equality of sexes, and friendship among all peoples, ethnic, national and religious groups and persons of indigenous origin;

(e) The development of respect for the natural environment.

2. No part of the present article or article 28 shall be construed so as to interfere with the liberty of individuals and bodies to establish and direct educational institutions, sub-

ject always to the observance of the principles set forth in paragraph 1 of the present article and to the requirements that the education given in such institutions shall conform to such minimum standards as may be laid down by the State.

*Article 30.* In those States in which ethnic, religious or linguistic minorities or persons of indigenous origin exist, a child belonging to such a minority or who is indigenous shall not be denied the right, in community with other members of his or her group, to enjoy his or her own culture, to profess and practise his or her own religion, or to use his or her own language.

*Article 31.* 1. States Parties recognize the right of the child to rest and leisure, to engage in play and recreational activities appropriate to the age of the child and to participate freely in cultural life and the arts.

2. States Parties shall respect and promote the right of the child to participate fully in cultural and artistic life and shall encourage the provision of appropriate and equal opportunities for cultural, artistic, recreational and leisure activity.

*Article 32.* 1. States Parties recognize the right of the child to be protected from economic exploitation and from performing any work that is likely to be hazardous or to interfere with the child's education, or to be harmful to the child's health or physical, mental, spiritual, moral or social development.

2. States Parties shall take legislative, administrative, social and educational measures to ensure the implementation of the present article. To this end, and having regard to the relevant provisions of other international instruments, States Parties shall in particular:

(a) Provide for a minimum age or minimum ages for admission to employment;

(b) Provide for appropriate regulation of the hours and conditions of employment;

(c) Provide for appropriate penalties or other sanctions to ensure the effective enforcement of the present article.

*Article 33.* States Parties shall take all appropriate measures, including legislative, administrative, social and educational measures, to protect children from the illicit use of narcotic drugs and psychotropic substances as defined in the relevant international treaties, and to prevent the use of children in the illicit production and trafficking of such substances.

*Article 34.* States Parties undertake to protect the child from all forms of sexual exploitation and sexual abuse. For these purposes, States Parties shall in particular take all appropriate national, bilateral and multilateral measures to prevent:

(a) The inducement or coercion of a child to engage in any unlawful sexual activity;

(b) The exploitative use of children in prostitution or other unlawful sexual practices;

(c) The exploitative use of children in pornographic performances and materials.

*Article 35.* States Parties shall take all appropriate national,

bilateral and multilateral measures to prevent the abduction of, the sale of or traffic in children for any purpose or in any form.

*Article 36.* States Parties shall protect the child against all other forms of exploitation prejudicial to any aspects of the child's welfare.

*Article 37.* States Parties shall ensure that:

(a) No child shall be subjected to torture or other cruel, inhuman or degrading treatment or punishment. Neither capital punishment nor life imprisonment without possibility of release shall be imposed for offences committed by persons below eighteen years of age;

(b) No child shall be deprived of his or her liberty unlawfully or arbitrarily. The arrest, detention or imprisonment of a child shall be in conformity with the law and shall be used only as a measure of last resort and for the shortest appropriate period of time;

(c) Every child deprived of liberty shall be treated with humanity and respect for the inherent dignity of the human person, and in a manner which takes into account the needs of persons of his or her age. In particular, every child deprived of liberty shall be separated from adults unless it is considered in the child's best interest not to do so and shall have the right to maintain contact with his or her family through correspondence and visits, save in exceptional circumstances;

(d) Every child deprived of his or her liberty shall have the right to prompt access to legal and other appropriate assistance, as well as the right to challenge the legality of the deprivation of his or her liberty before a court or other competent, independent and impartial authority, and to a prompt decision on any such action.

*Article 38.* 1. States Parties undertake to respect and to ensure respect for rules of international humanitarian law applicable to them in armed conflicts which are relevant to the child.

2. States Parties shall take all feasible measures to ensure that persons who have not attained the age of fifteen years do not take a direct part in hostilities.

3. States Parties shall refrain from recruiting any person who has not attained the age of fifteen years into their armed forces. In recruiting among those persons who have attained the age of fifteen years but who have not attained the age of eighteen years, States Parties shall endeavour to give priority to those who are oldest.

4. In accordance with their obligations under international humanitarian law to protect the civilian population in armed conflicts, States Parties shall take all feasible measures to ensure protection and care of children who are affected by an armed conflict.

*Article 39.* States Parties shall take all appropriate measures to promote physical and psychological recovery and social reintegration of a child victim of: any form of neglect, exploitation, or abuse; torture or any other form of cruel, inhuman or degrading treatment or punishment; or armed conflicts. Such recovery and reintegration shall take place in an environment which fosters the health, self-respect and dignity of the child.

*Article 40.* 1. States Parties recognize the right of every child alleged as, accused of, or recognized as having infringed the penal law to be treated in a manner consistent with the promotion of the child's sense of dignity and worth, which reinforces the child's respect for the human rights and fundamental freedoms of others and which takes into account the child's age and the desirability of promoting the child's reintegration and the child's assuming a constructive role in society.

2. To this end, and having regard to the relevant provisions of international instruments, States Parties shall, in particular, ensure that:

(a) No child shall be alleged as, be accused of, or recognized as having infringed the penal law by reason of acts or omissions that were not prohibited by national or international law at the time they were committed;

(b) Every child alleged as or accused of having infringed the penal law has at least the following guarantees:

(i) To be presumed innocent until proven guilty according to law;

(ii) To be informed promptly and directly of the charges against him or her, and, if appropriate, through his or her parents or legal guardians, and to have legal or other appropriate assistance in the preparation and presentation of his or her defence;

(iii) To have the matter determined without delay by a competent, independent and impartial authority or judicial body in a fair hearing according to law, in the presence of legal or other appropriate assistance and, unless it is considered not to be in the best interest of the child, in particular, taking into account his or her age or situation, his or her parents or legal guardians;

(iv) Not to be compelled to give testimony or to confess guilt; to examine or have examined adverse witnesses and to obtain the participation and examination of witnesses on his or her behalf under conditions of equality;

(v) If considered to have infringed the penal law, to have this decision and any measures imposed in consequence thereof reviewed by a higher competent, independent and impartial authority or judicial body according to law;

(vi) To have the free assistance of an interpreter if the child cannot understand or speak the language used;

(vii) To have his or her privacy fully respected at all stages of the proceedings.

3. States Parties shall seek to promote the establishment of laws, procedures, authorities and institutions specifically applicable to children alleged as, accused of, or recognized as having infringed the penal law, and, in particular:

(a) The establishment of a minimum age below which children shall be presumed not to have the capacity to infringe the penal law;

(b) Whenever appropriate and desirable, measures for dealing with such children without resorting to judicial proceedings, providing that human rights and legal safeguards are fully respected.

4. A variety of dispositions, such as care, guidance and supervision orders; counselling; probation; foster care; education and vocational training programmes and other alternatives to institutional care shall be available to ensure that children are dealt with in a manner appropriate to their well-being and proportionate both to their circumstances and the offence.

*Article 41.* Nothing in the present Convention shall affect any provisions which are more conducive to the realization of the rights of the child and which may be contained in:

(a) The law of a State Party; or

(b) International law in force for that State.

### Part II

*Article 42.* States Parties undertake to make the principles and provisions of the Convention widely known, by appropriate and active means, to adults and children alike.

*Article 43.* 1. For the purpose of examining the progress made by States Parties in achieving the realization of the obligations undertaken in the present Convention, there shall be established a Committee on the Rights of the Child, which shall carry out the functions hereinafter provided.

2. The Committee shall consist of ten experts of high moral standing and recognized competence in the field covered by this Convention. The members of the Committee shall be elected by States Parties from among their nationals and shall serve in their personal capacity, consideration being given to equitable geographical distribution, as well as to the principal legal systems.

3. The members of the Committee shall be elected by secret ballot from a list of persons nominated by States Parties. Each State Party may nominate one person from among its own nationals.

4. The initial election to the Committee shall be held no later than six months after the date of the entry into force of the present Convention and thereafter every second year. At least four months before the date of each election, the Secretary-General of the United Nations shall address a letter to States Parties inviting them to submit their nominations within two months. The Secretary-General shall subsequently prepare a list in alphabetical order of all persons thus nominated, indicating States Parties which have nominated them, and shall submit it to the States Parties to the present Convention.

5. The elections shall be held at meetings of States Parties convened by the Secretary-General at United Nations Headquarters. At those meetings, for which two thirds of States Parties shall constitute a quorum, the persons elected to the Committee shall be those who obtain the largest number of votes and an absolute majority of the votes of the representatives of States Parties present and voting.

6. The members of the Committee shall be elected for a term of four years. They shall be eligible for re-election if renominated. The term of five of the members elected at the first election shall expire at the end of two years; immediately after the first election, the names of these five members shall be chosen by lot by the Chairman of the meeting.

7. If a member of the Committee dies or resigns or declares that for any other cause he or she can no longer perform the duties of the Committee, the State Party which nominated the member shall appoint another expert from among its nationals to serve for the remainder of the term, subject to the approval of the Committee.

8. The Committee shall establish its own rules of procedure.

9. The Committee shall elect its officers for a period of two years.

10. The meetings of the Committee shall normally be held at United Nations Headquarters or at any other convenient place as determined by the Committee. The Committee shall normally meet annually. The duration of the meetings of the Committee shall be determined, and reviewed, if necessary, by a meeting of the States Parties to the present Convention, subject to the approval of the General Assembly.

11. The Secretary-General of the United Nations shall provide the necessary staff and facilities for the effective performance of the functions of the Committee under the present Convention.

12. With the approval of the General Assembly, the members of the Committee established under the present Convention shall receive emoluments from United Nations resources on such terms and conditions as the Assembly may decide.

*Article 44.* 1. States Parties undertake to submit to the Committee, through the Secretary-General of the United Nations, reports on the measures they have adopted which give effect to the rights recognized herein and on the progress made on the enjoyment of those rights:

(a) Within two years of the entry into force of the Convention for the State Party concerned;

(b) Thereafter every five years.

2. Reports made under the present article shall indicate factors and difficulties, if any, affecting the degree of fulfillment of the obligations under the present Convention. Reports shall also contain sufficient information to provide the Committee with a comprehensive understanding of the implementation of the Convention in the country concerned.

3. A State Party which has submitted a comprehensive initial report to the Committee need not, in its subsequent reports submitted in accordance with paragraph 1 (b) of the present article, repeat basic information previously provided.

4. The Committee may request from States Parties further information relevant to the implementation of the Convention.

5. The Committee shall submit to the General Assembly, through the Economic and Social Council, every two years, reports on its activities.

6. States Parties shall make their reports widely available to the public in their own countries.

*Article 45.* In order to foster the effective implementation of the Convention and to encourage international cooperation in the field covered by the Convention:

(a) The specialized agencies, the United Nations Children's Fund, and other United Nations organs shall be entitled to be represented at the consideration of the implementation of such provisions of the present Convention as fall within the scope of their mandate. The Committee may invite the specialized agencies, the United Nations Children's Fund and other competent bodies as it may consider appropriate to provide expert advice on the implementation of the Convention in areas falling within the scope of their respective mandates. The Committee may invite the specialized agencies, the United Nations Children's Fund, and other United Nations organs to submit reports on the implementation of the Convention in areas falling within the scope of their activities;

(b) The Committee shall transmit, as it may consider appropriate, to the specialized agencies, the United Nations Children's Fund and other competent bodies, any reports from States Parties that contain a request, or indicate a need, for technical advice or assistance, along with the Committee's observations and suggestions, if any, on these requests or indications;

(c) The Committee may recommend to the General Assembly to request the Secretary-General to undertake on its behalf studies on specific issues relating to the rights of the child;

(d) The Committee may make suggestions and general recommendations based on information received pursuant to articles 44 and 45 of the present Convention. Such suggestions and general recommendations shall be transmitted to any State Party concerned and reported to the General Assembly, together with comments, if any, from States Parties.

## Part III

*Article 46.* The present Convention shall be open for signature by all States.

*Article 47.* The present Convention is subject to ratification. Instruments of ratification shall be deposited with the Secretary-General of the United Nations.

*Article 48.* The present Convention shall remain open for accession by any State. The instruments of accession shall be deposited with the Secretary-General of the United Nations.

*Article 49.* 1. The present Convention shall enter into force on the thirtieth day following the date of deposit with the Secretary-General of the United Nations of the twentieth instrument of ratification or accession.

2. For each State ratifying or acceding to the Convention after the deposit of the twentieth instrument of ratification or accession, the Convention shall enter into force on the thirtieth day after the deposit by such State of its instrument of ratification or accession.

*Article 50.* 1. Any State Party may propose an amendment and file it with the Secretary-General of the United Nations. The Secretary-General shall thereupon communicate the proposed amendment to States Parties, with a request that they indicate whether they favour a conference of States Parties for the purpose of considering and voting upon the proposals. In the event that, within four months from the date of such communication, at least one third of the States Parties favour such a conference, the Secretary-General shall convene the conference under the auspices of the United Nations. Any amendment adopted by a majority of States Parties present and voting at the conference shall be submitted to the General Assembly for approval.

2. An amendment adopted in accordance with paragraph 1 of the present article shall enter into force when it has been approved by the General Assembly of the United Nations and accepted by a two-thirds majority of States Parties.

3. When an amendment enters into force, it shall be binding on those States Parties which have accepted it, other States Parties still being bound by the provisions of the present Convention and any earlier amendments which they have accepted.

*Article 51.* 1. The Secretary-General of the United Nations shall receive and circulate to all States the text of reservations made by States at the time of ratification or accession.

2. A reservation incompatible with the object and purpose of the present Convention shall not be permitted.

3. Reservations may be withdrawn at any time by notification to that effect addressed to the Secretary-General of the United Nations, who shall then inform all States . Such notification shall take effect on the date on which it is received by the Secretary-General.

*Article 52.* A State Party may denounce the present Convention by written notification to the Secretary-General of the United Nations. Denunciation becomes effective one year after the date of receipt of the notification by the Secretary-General.

*Article 53.* The Secretary-General of the United Nations is designated as the depositary of the present Convention.

*Article 54.* The original of the present Convention, of which the Arabic, Chinese, English, French, Russian and Spanish texts are equally authentic, shall be deposited with the Secretary-General of the United Nations.

In witness thereof the undersigned plenipotentiaries, being duly authorized thereto by their respective Governments, have signed the present Convention.

**BIBLIOGRAPHY.** "Article Series: The Draft United Nations Convention on the Rights of the Child," *New York Law School Journal of Human Rights* 7, Part 1 (Fall 1989). Scholarly articles in a special issue, in English.

Clergerie, Jean-Louis. "L'adoption d'une convention internationale sur les droits de l'enfant" (The Adoption of an International Convention on the Rights of the Child), *Revue du droit public et de la science politique en France et à l'étranger* 106, no. 2 (1990): 435–510. Scholarly article, in French.

Cohen, Cynthia Price. "United Nations Convention on the Rights of the Child: Introductory Note," *The Review—International Commission of Jurists* no. 44 (June 1990): 36–41. NGO article, in English.

Cohen, Cynthia Price, and Howard A. Davidson, eds. *Children's Rights in America: U.N. Convention on the Rights of the Child Compared with United States Law.* Washington, D.C.: American Bar Association, Center on Children and the Law & Defense for Children International—USA, 1990. Scholarly monograph, in English.

Cohen, Cynthia Price, and Per Miljeteig-Olssen. "Status Report: United Nations Convention on the Rights of the Child," *New York Law School Journal of Human Rights* 8, Part 2 (Spring 1991): 367–382. Scholarly article, in English.

France, Council of State. *Statut et Protection de l'Enfant* (Status and Protection of Children). Paris: Documentation Française, 1991. Government research report, in French.

Freeman, Michael, and Philip Veerman, eds. *The Ideologies of Children's Rights.* Dordrecht, the Netherlands: Martinus Nijhoff, 1992. Scholarly collection of articles, in English.

Ledogar, Robert J. "Implementing the Convention on the Rights of the Child through National Programmes of Action for Children," *International Journal of Children's Rights* 1, no. 1 (1993): 99–113. Scholarly article, in English; bibliography, p. 113.

"Symposium: UN Convention on Children's Rights," *Human Rights Quarterly* 12, no. 1 (Feb. 1990): pp. 94–178. Scholarly articles, in English.

UNICEF International Child Development Centre. *The Convention: Child Rights and UNICEF Experience at the Country Level.* Florence, Italy: 1991. IGO monograph, in English.

*Working Paper on the Drafting of the Convention on the Rights of the Child.* Geneva, Switzerland: Defense for Children International; International Catholic Child Bureau; and Radda Barnen International, n.d. In English.

## CHILDREN'S RIGHTS: DECLARATION OF THE RIGHTS OF THE CHILD (1959).

The Declaration was adopted on 20 November 1959 by the UN General Assembly (resolution 1386 [XIV]). When it was under preparation, it was pointed out that many of the rights and freedoms which it dealt with had already been proclaimed for everyone, including children, in the Universal Declaration of Human Rights. The Assembly decided, nevertheless, that the special needs of children justified a separate international instrument. The text of the declaration is as follows:

### Preamble

Whereas the peoples of the United Nations have, in the Charter, reaffirmed their faith in fundamental human rights and in the dignity and worth of the human person, and have determined to promote social progress and better standards of life in larger freedom,

Whereas the United Nations has, in the Universal Declaration of Human Rights, proclaimed that everyone is entitled to all the rights and freedoms set forth therein, without distinction of any kind, such as race, colour, sex, language, religion, political or other opinion, national or social origin, property, birth or other status,

Whereas the child, by reason of his physical and mental immaturity, needs special safeguards and care, including appropriate legal protection, before as well as after birth,

Whereas the need for such special safeguards has been stated in the Geneva Declaration of the Rights of the Child of 1924, and recognized in the Universal Declaration of Human Rights and in the statutes of specialized agencies and international organizations concerned with the welfare of children,

Whereas mankind owes to the child the best it has to give,

Now therefore,

The General Assembly

Proclaims this Declaration of the Rights of the Child to the end that he may have a happy childhood and enjoy for his own good and for the good of society the rights and freedoms herein set forth, and calls upon parents, upon men and women as individuals, and upon voluntary organizations, local authorities and national Governments to recognize these rights and strive for their observance by legislative and other measures progressively taken in accordance with the following principles:

Principle 1. The child shall enjoy all the rights set forth in this Declaration. Every child, without any exception whatsoever, shall be entitled to these rights, without distinction or discrimination on account of race, colour, sex, language, religion, political or other opinion, national or social origin, property, birth or other status, whether of himself or of his family.

Principle 2. The child shall enjoy special protection, and shall be given opportunities and facilities, by law and by other means, to enable him to develop physically, mentally, morally, spiritually and socially in a healthy and normal manner and in conditions of freedom and dignity. In the enactment of laws for this purpose, the best interests of the child shall be the paramount consideration.

Principle 3. The child shall be entitled from his birth to a name and a nationality.

Principle 4. The child shall enjoy the benefits of social security. He shall be entitled to grow and develop in health; to this end, special care and protection shall be provided both to him and to his mother, including adequate prenatal and post-natal care. The child shall have the right to adequate nutrition, housing, recreation and medical services.

Principle 5. The child who is physically, mentally or socially handicapped shall be given the special treatment, education and care required by his particular condition.

Principle 6. The child, for the full and harmonious development of his personality, needs love and understanding. He shall, wherever possible, grow up in the care and under the responsibility of his parents, and, in any case, in an atmosphere of affection and of moral and material security; a child of tender years shall not, save in exceptional circumstances, be separated from his mother. Society and the public authorities shall have the duty to extend particular care to children without a family and to those without adequate means of support. Payment of State and other assistance towards the maintenance of children of large families is desirable.

Principle 7. The child is entitled to receive education, which shall be free and compulsory, at least in the elementary stages. He shall be given an education which will promote his general culture and enable him, on a basis of equal opportunity, to develop his abilities, his individual judgement, and his sense of moral and social responsibility, and to become a useful member of society.

The best interests of the child shall be the guiding principle of those responsible for his education and guidance; that responsibility lies in the first place with his parents.

The child shall have full opportunity for play and recreation, which should be directed to the same purposes as education; society and the public authorities shall endeavour to promote the enjoyment of this right.

Principle 8. The child shall in all circumstances be among the first to receive protection and relief.

Principle 9. The child shall be protected against all forms of neglect, cruelty and exploitation. He shall not be the subject of traffic, in any form.

The child shall not be admitted to employment before an appropriate minimum age; he shall in no case be caused or permitted to engage in any occupation or employment which would prejudice his health or education, or interfere with his physical, mental or moral development.

Principle 10. The child shall be protected from practices, which may foster racial, religious and any other form of discrimination. He shall be brought up in a spirit of understanding, tolerance, friendship among peoples, peace and universal brotherhood, and in full consciousness that his energy and talents should be devoted to the service of his fellow men.

## CHILDREN'S RIGHTS: WORLD DECLARATION ON THE SURVIVAL, PROTECTION, AND DEVELOPMENT OF CHILDREN (1990).

The World Declaration, adopted by the World Summit for Children, which met in New York on 30 September 1990, aims at providing a better future for every child. It was accompanied by a Plan of Action for Implementing the World Declaration, calling for specific action to be taken with respect to the Convention on the Rights of the Child and on such questions as child health, food and nutrition, the role of women, maternal health and family planning, the role of the family, basic education and literacy, children in especially difficult circumstances, protection of children during armed conflicts, children and the environment, and the alleviation of poverty and revitalization of economic growth.

The UN GENERAL ASSEMBLY examined both the World Declaration and the Program of Action at its 1990 session, and on 21 December 1990 urged all States and other members of the international community to work toward achieving the goals and objectives endorsed in these documents as an integral part of their national plans and international cooperation (resolution 45/217). It especially urged donor countries to assist developing countries in achieving these goals by increasing their contributions to programs targeted for the special needs of children.

The World Declaration and the Plan of Action, adopted unanimously by the political leaders of virtually all governments, is as follows:

1. We have gathered at the World Summit for Children to undertake a joint commitment and to make an urgent universal appeal—to give every child a better future.

2. The children of the world are innocent, vulnerable, and dependent. They are also curious, active, and full of hope. Their time should be one of joy and peace, of playing, learning, and growing. Their future should be shaped in harmony and cooperation. Their lives should mature, as they broaden their perspectives and gain new experiences.

3. But for many children, the reality of childhood is altogether different.

### The Challenge

4. Each day, countless children around the world are exposed to dangers that hamper their growth and development. They suffer immensely as casualties of war and violence; as victims of racial discrimination, apartheid, aggression, foreign occupation, and annexation; as refugees and displaced children, forced to abandon their homes and their roots; as disabled; or as victims of neglect, cruelty, and exploitation.

5. Each day, millions of children suffer from the scourges of poverty and economic crisis—from hunger and homelessness, from epidemics and illiteracy, from degradation of the environment. They suffer from the grave effects of the problems of external indebtedness and also from the lack of sustained and sustainable growth in many developing countries, particularly the least-developed ones.

6. Each day, 40,000 children die from malnutrition and disease, including acquired immunodeficiency syndrome (AIDS), from the lack of clean water and inadequate sanitation and from the effects of the drug problem.

7. These are challenges that we, as political leaders, must meet.

### The Opportunity

8. Together, our nations have the means and the knowledge to protect the lives and to diminish enormously the suffering of children, to promote the full development of their human potential and to make them aware of their needs, rights, and opportunities. The Convention on the Rights of the Child provides a new opportunity to make respect for children's rights and welfare truly universal.

9. Recent improvements in the international political climate can facilitate this task. Through international cooperation and solidarity it should now be possible to achieve concrete results in many fields—to revitalize economic growth and development, to protect the environment, to prevent the spread of fatal and crippling diseases, and to achieve greater social and economic justice. The current moves toward disarmament also mean that significant resources could be released for purposes other than military ones. Improving the well-being of children must be a very high priority when these resources are reallocated.

### The Task

10. Enhancement of children's health and nutrition is a first duty and also a task for which solutions are now within reach. The lives of tens of thousands of boys and girls can be saved every day because the causes of their death are readily preventable. Child and infant mortality is unacceptably high in many parts of the world but can be lowered dramatically with means that are already known and easily accessible.

11. Further attention, care, and support should be ac-

corded to disabled children, as well as to other children in very difficult circumstances.

12. Strengthening the role of women in general and ensuring their equal rights will be to the advantage of the world's children. Girls must be given equal treatment and opportunities from the very beginning.

13. At present, over 100 million children are without basic schooling, and two-thirds of them are girls. The provision of basic education and literacy for all are among the most important contribution that can be made to the development of the world's children.

14. Half a million mothers die each year from causes related to childbirth. Safe motherhood must be promoted in all possible ways. Emphasis must be placed on responsible planning of family size and on child spacing. The family, as a fundamental group and natural environment for the growth and well-being of children, should be given all necessary protection and assistance.

15. All children must be given the chance to find their identity and realize their worth in a safe and supportive environment, through families and other caregivers committed to their welfare. They must be prepared for responsible life in a free society. They should, from their early years, be encouraged to participate in the cultural life of their societies.

16. Economic conditions will continue to influence greatly the fate of children, especially in developing nations. For the sake of the future of all children, it is urgently necessary to ensure or reactivate sustained and sustainable economic growth and development in all countries and also to continue to give urgent attention to an early, broad, and durable solution to the external debt problems facing developing debtor countries.

17. These tasks require a continued and concerted effort by all nations, through national action and international cooperation.

### The Commitment

18. The well-being of children requires political action at the highest level. We are determined to take that action.

19. We ourselves hereby make a solemn commitment to give high priority to the rights of children, to their survival, and to their protection and development. This will also ensure the well-being of all societies.

20. We have agreed that we will act together, in international cooperation, as well as in our respective countries. We now commit ourselves to the following ten-point program to protect the rights of children and to improve their lives:

(1) We will work to promote earliest possible ratification and implementation of the Convention on the Rights of the Child. Programs to encourage information about children's rights should be launched worldwide, taking into account the distinct cultural and social values in different countries.

(2) We will work for a solid effort of national and international action to enhance children's health, to promote prenatal care, and to lower infant and child mortality in all countries and among all peoples. We will promote the provision of clean water in all communities for all their children, as well as universal access to sanitation.

(3) We will work for optimal growth and development in childhood, through measures to eradicate hunger, malnutrition, and famine and thus to relieve millions of children of tragic sufferings in a world that has the means to feed all its citizens.

(4) We will work to strengthen the role and status of women. We will promote responsible planning of family size, child spacing, breastfeeding, and safe motherhood.

(5) We will work for respect for the role of the family in providing for children and will support the efforts of parents, other caregivers, and communities to nurture and care for children, from the earliest stages of childhood through adolescence. We also recognize the special needs of children who are separated from their families.

(6) We will work for programs that reduce illiteracy and provide educational opportunities for all children, irrespective of their background and gender; that prepare children for productive employment and lifelong learning opportunities, i.e, through vocational training; and that enable children to grow to adulthood within a supportive and nurturing cultural and social context.

(7) We will work to ameliorate the plight of millions of children who live under especially difficult circumstances—as victims of apartheid and foreign occupation; orphans and street children and children of migrant workers; the displaced children and victims of natural and manmade disasters; the disabled and the abused, the socially disadvantaged and the exploited. Refugee children must be helped to find new roots in life. We will work for special protection of the working child and the abolition of illegal child labour. We will do our best to ensure that children are not drawn into becoming victims of the scourge of illicit drugs.

(8) We will work carefully to protect children from the scourge of war and to take measures to prevent further armed conflicts, in order to give children everywhere a peaceful and secure future. We will promote the values of peace, understanding, and dialogue in the education of children. The essential needs of children and families must be protected even in times of war and in violence-ridden areas. We ask that periods of tranquility and special relief corridors be observed for the benefit of children, where war and violence are still taking place.

(9) We will work for common measures for the protection of the environment at all levels, so that all children can enjoy a safer and healthier future.

(10) We will work for a global attack on poverty, which would have immediate benefits for children's welfare. The vulnerability and special needs of the children of the developing countries, and in particular the least-developed ones, deserve priority. But growth and development need promotion in all States, through national action and international cooperation. That calls for transfers of appropriate additional resources to developing countries as well as improved terms of trade, further trade liberalization, and measures for debt relief. It also implies structural adjustments that promote world economic growth, particularly in developing countries, while ensuring the well-being of the most vulnerable sectors of the populations, in particular the children.

### The Next Steps

21. The World Summit for Children has presented us with a challenge to take action. We have agreed to take up that challenge.

22. Among the partnerships we seek, we turn especially to children themselves. We appeal to them to participate in this effort.

23. We also seek the support of the United Nations system, as well as other international and regional organizations, in the universal effort to promote the well-being of

children. We ask for greater involvement on the part of nongovernmental organizations in complementing national efforts and joint international action in this field.

24. We have decided to adopt and implement a Plan of Action, as a framework for more specific national and international undertakings. We appeal to all our colleagues to endorse that Plan. We are prepared to make available the resources to meet these commitments, as part of the priorities of our national plans.

25. We do this not only for the present generation, but for all generations to come. There can be no task nobler than giving every child a better future.

## Plan of Action for Implementing the World Declaration

### I. Introduction

1. This Plan of Action is intended as a guide for national Governments, international organizations, bilateral aid agencies, nongovernmental organizations (NGO), and all other sectors of society in formulating their own programs of action for ensuring the implementation of the Declaration of the World Summit for Children.

2. The needs and problems of children vary from country to country, and indeed from community to community. Individual countries and groups of countries, as well as international, regional, national, and local organizations, may use this Plan of Action to develop their own specific programs in line with their needs, capacity, and mandates. However, parents, elders, and leaders at all levels throughout the world have certain common aspirations for the well-being of their children. This Plan of Action deals with these common aspirations, suggesting a set of goals and targets for children in the 1990s, strategies for reaching those goals, and commitments for action and followup measures at various levels.

3. Progress for children should be a key goal of overall national development. It should also form an integral part of the broader international development strategy for the Fourth United Nations Development Decade. As today's children are the citizens of tomorrow's world, their survival, protection, and development are prerequisites for the future development of humanity. Empowerment of the younger generation with knowledge and resources to meet their basic human needs and to grow to their full potential should be a primary goal of national development. As their individual development and social contribution will shape the future of the world, investment in children's health, nutrition, and education is the foundation for national development.

4. The aspirations of the international community for the well-being of children are best reflected in the Convention on the Rights of the Child unanimously adopted by the General Assembly of the United Nations in 1989. This Convention sets universal legal standards for the protection of children against neglect, abuse, and exploitation, as well as guaranteeing to them their basic human rights, including survival, development, and full participation in social, cultural, educational, and other endeavours necessary for their individual growth and well-being. The Declaration of the World Summit calls on all Governments to promote earliest possible ratification and implementation of the Convention.

5. In the past two years, a set of goals for children and development in the 1990s has been formulated in several international forums attended by virtually all Governments, relevant UN agencies, and major NGOs. In support of these goals and in line with the growing international consensus in favor of greater attention to the human dimension of de-

velopment in the 1990s, this Plan of Action calls for concerted national action and international cooperation to strive for the achievement, in all countries, of the following major goals for the survival, protection, and development of children by the year 2000.

(a) Reduction of 1990 under-5 child mortality rates by one-third or to a level of 70 per 1,000 live births, whichever is the greater reduction;

(b) Reducation of maternal mortality rates by half of 1990 levels;

(c) Reduction of severe and moderate malnutrition among under-5 children by one-half of 1990 levels;

(d) Universal access to safe drinking water and to sanitary means of excreta disposal;

(e) Universal access to basic education and completion of primary education by at least 80% of primary-school-age children;

(f) Reduction of the adult illiteracy rate to at least half its 1990 level (the appropriate age group to be determined in each country), with emphasis on female literacy;

(g) Protection of children in especially difficult circumstances, particularly in situations of armed conflicts.

6. A list of more detailed sectoral goals and specific actions that would enable the attainment of the above-stated major goals can be found in the appendix to this Plan of Action. These goals will first need to be adapted to the specific realities of each country in terms of phasing, priorities, standards, and availability of resources. The strategies for the achievement of the goals may also vary from country to country. Some countries may wish to add other development goals that are uniquely important and relevant for their specific country situation. Such adaptation of the goals is of crucial importance to ensure their technical validity, logistical feasibility, and financial affordability, and to secure political commitment and broad public support for their achievement.

### II. Specific Actions for Child Survival, Protection and Development

7. Within the context of these overall goals, there are promising opportunities for eradicating or virtually eliminating age-old diseases that have afflicted tens of millions of children for centuries and for improving the quality of life of generations to come. Achievement of these goals would also contribute to lowering population growth, as sustained decline in child death rates toward the level at which parents become confident that their first children will survive is, with some time lag, followed by even greater reduction in child births. To seize these opportunities, the Declaration of the World Summit for Children calls for specific actions in the following areas:

Convention on the Rights of the Child: 8. The Convention on the Rights of the Child, unanimously adopted by the UN General Assembly, contains a comprehensive set of international legal norms for the protection and well-being of children. All governments are urged to promote earliest possible ratification of the Convention, where it has not already been ratified. Every possible effort should be made in all countries to disseminate the Convention and, wherever it has already been ratified, to promote its implementation and monitoring.

Child Health: 9. Preventable childhood diseases—such as measles, polio, tetanus, tuberculosis, whooping cough, and diphtheria, against which there are effective vaccines, and diarrhoeal diseases, pneumonia, and other acute respiratory infections that can be prevented or effectively treated through relatively low-cost remedies—are currently responsible for the great majority of the world's 14 million deaths of children under five years and disability of millions more every year. Effective action can and must be taken to combat these diseases by strengthening primary health care and basic health services in all countries.

10. Besides these readily preventable or treatable diseases and some others, such as malaria, which have proved more difficult to combat, children today are faced with the new spectre of the AIDS pandemic. In the most seriously affected countries, HIV/AIDS threatens to offset the gains of child-survival programs. It is already a major drain on limited public-health resources needed to support other priority health services. The consequences of HIV/AIDS go well beyond the suffering and death of the infected child and include risks and stigmas that affect parents and siblings and the tragedy of "AIDS orphans." There is an urgent need to ensure that programs for the prevention and treatment of AIDS, including research on possible vaccines and cures that can be applicable in all countries and situations, and massive information and education campaigns, receive a high priority for both national action and international cooperation.

11. A major factor affecting the health of children as well as adults is the availability of clean water and safe sanitation. These are not only essential for human health and well-being but also contribute greatly to the emancipation of women from the drudgery that has a pernicious impact on children, especially girls. Progress in child health is unlikely to be sustained if one-third of the developing world's children remain without access to clean drinking water and half of them without adequate sanitary facilities.

12. Based on the experience of the past decade, including the many inovations in simple, low-cost techniques and technologies to provide clean water and safe sanitary facilities in rural areas and urban shanty towns, it is now desirable as well as feasible, through concerted national action and international cooperation, to aim at providing all the world's children with universal access to safe drinking water and sanitary means of excreta disposal by the year 2000. An important related benefit of universal access to water and sanitation combined with health education will be the control of many waterborne diseases, among them elimination of guinea-worm disease (dracunculiasis), which currently afflicts some 10 million children in parts of Africa and Asia.

Food and Nutrition: 13. Hunger and malnutrition in their different forms contribute to about half of the deaths of young children. More than 20 million children suffer from severe malnutrition, 150 million are underweight, and 350 million women suffer from nutritional anaemia. Improved nutrition requires (a) adequate household food security, (b) healthy environment and control of infections, and (c) adequate maternal and child care. With the right policies, appropriate institutional arrangements, and political priority, the world is now in a position to feed all the world's children and to overcome the worst forms of malnutrition, i.e., drastically to reduce diseases that contribute to malnutrition, to halve protein-energy malnutrition, virtually to eliminate vitamin A deficiency and iodine deficiency disorders, and to reduce nutritional anaemia significantly.

14. For the young child and the pregnant woman, provision of adequate food during pregnancy and lactation; promotion, protection, and support of breastfeeding and complementary feeding practices, including frequent feeding; growth monitoring with appropriate follow-up actions; and nutritional surveillance are the most essential needs. As the child grows older, and for the adult population as a whole, an adequate diet is an obvious human priority. Meeting this need requires employment and income-generating opportunities, dissemination of knowledge, and supporting services to increase food production and distribution. These are key actions within broader national strategies to combat hunger and malnutrition.

Role of Women, Maternal Health, and Family Planning: 15. Women in their various roles play a critical part in the well-being of children. The enhancement of the status of women and their equal access to education, training, credit, and other extension services constitute a valuable contribution to a nation's social and economic development. Efforts for the enhancement of women's status and their role in development must begin with the girl child. Equal opportunity should be provided for the girl child to benefit from the health, nutrition, education, and other basic services to enable her to grow to her full potential.

16. Maternal health, nutrition, and education are important for the survival and well-being of women in their own right and are key determinants of the health and well-being of the child in early infancy. The causes of the high rates of infant mortality, especially neonatal mortality, are linked to untimely pregnancies, low birth weight and preterm births, unsafe delivery, neonatal tetanus, high fertility rates, etc. These are also major risk factors for maternal mortality claiming the lives of 500,000 young women each year and resulting in ill-health and suffering for many millions more. To redress this tragedy, special attention should be given to health, nutrition, and education of women.

17. All couples should have access to information on the importance of responsible planning of family size and the many advantages of child spacing to avoid pregnancies that are too early, too late, too many, or too frequent. Prenatal care, clean delivery, access to referral facilities in complicated cases, tetanus toxoid vaccination, and prevention of anaemia and other nutritional deficiencies during pregnancy are other important interventions to ensure safe motherhood and a healthy start in life for the newborn. There is an added benefit of promoting maternal and child health programs and family planning together in that, acting synergistically, these activities help accelerate the reduction of both mortality and fertility rates, and contribute more to lowering rates of population growth than either type of activity alone.

Role of the Family: 18. The family has the primary responsibility for the nurturing and protection of children from infancy to adolescence. Introduction of children to the culture, values, and norms of their society begins in the family. For the full and harmonious development of their personality, children should grow up in a family environment, in an atmosphere of happiness, love, and understanding. Accordingly, all institutions of society should respect and support the efforts of parents and other caregivers to nurture and care for children in a family environment.

19. Every effort should be made to prevent the separation of children from their families. Whenever children are separated from their family owing to *force majeure* or in their own best interest, arrangements should be made for appropriate alternative family care or institutional placement, due regard being paid to the desirability of continuity in a child's upbringing in his or her own cultural milieu. Extended families, relatives, and community institutions should be given support to help to meet the special needs of orphaned, displaced, and abandoned children. Efforts must be made to ensure that no child is treated as an outcast from society.

Basic Education and Literacy: 20. The international community, including virtually all the governments of the world, have undertaken a commitment at the World Conference on Education for All at Jomtien, Thailand, to increase significantly educational opportunity for over 100 million children and nearly one billion adults, two-thirds of them girls and women, who at present have no access to basic education and literacy. In fulfillment of that commitment, specific measures must be adopted for (a) the expansion of early childhood development activities, (b) universal access to basic education, including completion of primary education or equivalent learning achievement by at least 80% of the relevant school-age children with emphasis on reducing the current disparities between boys and girls, (c) the reduction of adult illiteracy by half, with emphasis on female literacy, (d) vocational training and preparation for employment, and (e) increased acquisition of knowledge, skills, and values through all educational channels, including modern and traditional communication media, to improve the quality of life of children and families.

21. Besides its intrinsic value for human development and improving the quality of life, progress in education and literacy can contribute significantly to improvement in maternal and child health, in protection of the environment and in sustainable development. As such, investment in basic education must be accorded a high priority in national action as well as international cooperation.

Children in Especially Difficult Situations: 22. Millions of children around the world live under especially difficult circumstances—as orphans and street children; as refugees or displaced persons; as victims of war and natural and man-made disasters, including such perils as exposure to radiation and dangerous chemicals; as children of migrant workers and other socially disadvantaged groups; as child workers or youth trapped in the bondage of prostitution, sexual abuse, and other forms of exploitation; as disabled children; as juvenile delinquents; and as victims of apartheid and foreign occupation. Such children deserve special attention, protection, and assistance from their families and communities and as part of national efforts and international cooperation.

23. More than 100 million children are engaged in employment, often heavy and hazardous and in contravention of international conventions that provide for their protection from economic exploitation and from performing work that interferes with their education and is harmful to their health and full development. With this in mind, all States should work to end such child-labor practices and see how the conditions and circumstances of children in legitimate employment can be protected to provide adequate opportunity for their healthy upbringing and development.

24. Drug abuse has emerged as a global menace to very large numbers of young people and, increasingly, children—including permanent damage incurred in the prenatal stages of life. Concerted action is needed by governments and intergovernmental agencies to combat illicit production, supply, demand, trafficking, and distribution of narcotic drugs and psychotropic substances to counter this tragedy. Equally important is community action and education, which are vitally needed to curb both the supply of and the demand for illicit drugs. Tobacco and alcohol abuse are also problems requirng action, especially preventive measures and education among young people.

Protection of Children during Armed Conflicts: 25. Children need special protection in situations of armed conflict. Recent examples in which countries and opposing factions have agreed to suspend hostilities and adopt special mea-

sures such as "corridors of peace" to allow relief supplies to reach women and children and "days of tranquility" to vaccinate and to provide other health services for children and their families in areas of conflict need to be applied in all such situations. Resolution of a conflict need not be a prerequisite for measures explicitly to protect children and their families to ensure their continuing access to food, medical care, and basic services; to deal with trauma resulting from violence; and to exempt them from other direct consequences of violence and hostilities. To build the foundation for a peaceful world where violence and war will cease to be acceptable means for settling disputes and conflicts, children's education should inculcate the values of peace, tolerance, understanding, and dialogue.

Children and the Environment: 26. Children have the greatest stake in the preservation of the environment and its judicious management for sustainable development as their survival and development depends on it. The child survival and development goals proposed for the 1990s in this Plan of Action seek to improve the environment by combating disease and malnutrition and promoting education. These contribute to lowering death rates as well as birth rates, improved social services, better use of natural resources, and, ultimately, to the breaking of the vicious cycle of poverty and environmental degradation.

27. With their relatively low use of capital resources and high reliance on social mobilization, community participation, and appropriate technology, the progams designed to reach the child-related goals of the 1990s are highly compatible with and supportive of environmental protection. The goals for the survival, protection, and development of children as enunciated in this Plan of Action should, therefore, be seen as helping to protect and preserve the environment. Still more action is needed, of course, to prevent the degradation of the environment in both the industrialized and the developing countries, through changes in the wasteful consumption patterns of the affluent, and by helping to meet the necessities of survival and development of the poor. Programs for children that not only help to meet their basic needs but that inculcate in them respect for the natural environment with the diversity of life that it sustains and its beauty and resourcefulness that enhance the quality of human life must figure prominently in the world's environmental agenda.

Alleviation of Poverty and Revitalization of Economic Growth: 28. Achievement of child-related goals in the areas of health, nutrition, education, etc., will contribute much to alleviating the worst manifestations of poverty. But much more will need to be done to ensure that a solid economic base is established to meet and sustain the goals for long-term child survival, protection, and development.

29. As affirmed by the international community at the eighteenth special session of the UN General Assembly (April 1990), a most important challenge for the 1990s is the need for revitalization of economic growth and social development in the developing countries and to address together the problems of abject poverty and hunger that continue to afflict far too many people in the world. As the most vulnerable segment of human society, children have a particular stake in sustained economic growth and alleviation of poverty, without which their well-being cannot be secured.

30. To foster a favourable international economic environment, it is essential to continue to give urgent attention to an early, broad, and durable solution to the external debt problems facing developing debtor countries; to mobilize external and domestic countries; to take steps to ensure that

the problem of the net transfer of resources from developing to developed countries does not continue in the 1990s and that its impact is effectively addressed; to create a more open and equitable trading system to facilitate the diversification and modernization of the economies of developing countries, particularly those that are commodity-dependent; and to make available substantial concessional resources, particularly for the least-developed countries.

31. In all of these efforts, the fulfillment of the basic needs of children must receive a high priority. Every possible opportunity should be explored to ensure that programs benefiting children, women, and other vulnerable groups are protected in times of structural adjustments and other economic restructuring. For example, as countries reduce military expenditures, part of the resources released should be channelled to programs for social and economic development, including those benefiting children. Debt-relief schemes could be formulated in ways that the budget reallocations and renewed economic growth made possible through such schemes would benefit programs for children. Debt relief for children, including debt swaps for investment in social development programs, should be considered by debtors and creditors. The international community, including private-sector creditors, are urged to work with developing countries and relevant agencies to support debt relief for children. To match increased efforts by developing countries themselves, the donor countries and international institutions should consider targeting more development assistance to primary health care, basic education, low-cost water and sanitation programs, and other interventions specifically endorsed in the Summit Declaration and this Plan of Action.

32. The international community has recognized the need to stop and reverse the increasing marginalization of the least-developed nations, including most countries of sub-Saharan Africa and many landlocked and island countries that face special development problems. These countries will require additional long-term international support to complement their own national efforts to meet the pressing needs of children over the 1990s.

## Follow-up Actions and Monitoring

33. Effective implementation of this Plan of Action will require concerted national action and international cooperation. As affirmed in the Declaration, such action and cooperation must be guided by the principle of a "first call for children"—a principle that the essential needs of children should be given high priority in the allocation of resources, in bad times as well as in good times, at national and international as well as at family levels.

34. It is particularly important that the child-specific actions proposed must be pursued as part of strengthening broader national development programs combining revitalized economic growth, poverty reduction, human-resource development, and environmental protection. Such programs must also strengthen community organizations, inculcate civic responsibility, and be sensitive to the cultural heritage and social values that support progress without alienation of the younger generation. With these broad objectives in mind, we commit ourselves and our governments to the following actions:

Action at the National Level: (i) All governments are urged to prepare, before the end of 1991, national programs of actions to implement the commitments undertaken in the World Summit Declaration and this Plan of Action. National governments should encourage and assist provincial and local governments as well as NGOs, the private sector, and civic groups to prepare their own programs of action to help to implement the goals and objectives included in the Declaration and this Plan of Action;

(ii) Each country is encouraged to reexamine in the context of its national plans, programs, and policies, how it might accord higher priority to programs for the well-being of children in general, and for meeting over the 1990s the major goals for child survival, development, and protection as enumerated in the World Summit Declaration and this Plan of Action;

(iii) Each country is urged to reexamine in the context of its particular national situation; its current national budget; and in the case of donor countries, its development-assistance budget to ensure that programs aimed at the achievement of goals for the survival, protection, and development of children will have a priority when resources are allocated. Every efforts should be made to ensure that such programs are protected in times of economic austerity and structural adjustments;

(iv) Families; communities; local governments; NGOs; social, cultural, religious, business, and other institutions, including the mass media, are encouraged to play an active role in support of the goals enunciated in this Plan of Action. The experience of the 1980s shows that it is only through the mobilization of all sectors of society, including those that traditionally did not consider child survival, protection, and development as their major focus, that significant progress can be achieved in these area. All forms of social mobilization, including the effective use of the great potential of new information and communication capacity of the world, should be marshalled to convey to all families the knowledge and skills required for dramatically improving the situation of children;

(v) Each country should establish appropriate mechanisms for the regular and timely collection, analysis, and publication of data required to monitor relevant social indicators relating to the well-being of children—such as neonatal, infant, and under-five mortality rates; maternal mortality and fertility rates; nutritional levels; immunization coverage; morbidity rates of diseases of public-health importance; school enrollment and achievement and literacy rates—which record the progress being made towards the goals set forth in this Plan of Action and corresponding national plans of action. Statistics should be disaggregated by gender to ensure that any inequitable impact of programs on girls and women can be monitored and corrected. It is particularly important that mechanisms be established to alert policymakers quickly to any adverse trends to enable timely corrective action. Indicators of human development should be periodically reviewed by national leaders and decisionmakers, as is currently done with indicators of economic development.

(vi) Each country is urged to reexamine its current arrangements for responding to natural disasters and manmade calamities that often afflict women and children the hardest. Countries that do not have adequate contingency planning for disaster preparedness are urged to establish such plans, seeking support from appropriate international institutions where necessary;

(vii) Progress toward the goals endorsed in the Summit Declaration and this Plan of Action could be further accelerated, and solutions to many other major problems confronting children and families greatly facilitated, through further research and development. Governments, industry, and academic institutions are requested to increase their efforts in both the basic and operational research, aimed at new technical and technological breakthroughs, more effective social mobilization, and better delivery of existing social services. Prime examples of the area in which research is urgently needed include, in the field of health, improved vaccination technologies, malaria, AIDS, respiratory infections, diarrhoeal diseases, nutritional deficiences, tuberculosis, family planning, and care of the newborn. Similarly there are important research needs in the area of early child development, basic education, hygiene and sanitation, and in coping with the trauma facing children who are uprooted from their families and face other particularly difficult circumstances. Such research should involve collaboration among institutions in both the developing and the industrialized countries of the world.

Action at the International Level: 35. Action at the community and national levels is, of course, of critical importance in meeting the goals and aspirations for children and development. However, many developing countries, particularly the least-developed and indebted ones, will need substantial international cooperation to enable them to participate effectively in the worldwide effort for child survival, protection, and development. Accordingly, the following specific actions are proposed to create an enabling international environment for the implementation of this Plan of Action.

(i) All international development agencies—multilateral, bilateral, and nongovernmental—are urged to examine how they can contribute to the achievement of the goals and strategies enunciated in the Declaration and this Plan of Action as part of more general attention to human development in the 1990s. They are requested to report their plans and programs to their respective governing bodies before the end of 1991 and periodically thereafter;

(ii) All regional institutions, including regional political and economic organizations, are requested to include consideration of the Declaration and this Plan of Action on the agenda of their meetings, including at the highest political level, with a view to developing agreements for mutual collaboration for implementation and ongoing monitoring;

(iii) Full cooperation and collaboration of all relevant UN agencies and organs as well as other international institutions are requested in ensuring the achievement of the goals and objectives of the national plans envisaged in the World Summit Declaration and Plan of Action. The governing bodies of all concerned agencies are requested to ensure that, within their mandates, the fullest possible support is given by these agencies for the achievement of these goals;

(iv) the assistance of the United Nations is requested to institute appropriate mechanisms for monitoring the implementation of this Plan of Action, using existing expertise of the relevant UN statistical offices, the specialized agencies, UNICEF, and other UN organs. Furthermore, the Secretary-General of the United Nations is requested to arrange for a mid-decade review, at all appropriate levels, of the progress being made toward implementing the commitments of the Declaration and Plan of Action;

(v) As the world's lead agency for children, the United Nations Children's Fund (UNICEF) is requested to prepare, in close collaboration with the relevant specialized agencies and other UN organs, a consolidated analysis of the plans and actions undertaken by individual countries and the international community in support of the child-related development goals for the 1990s. The governing bodies of the relevant specialized agencies and UN organs are requested to include a periodic review of the implementation of the Declaration and this Plan of Action at their regular sessions and to keep the General Assembly of the United Nations, through the Economic and Social Council, fully informed of progress to date and additional action required during the decade ahead.

36. The goals enunciated in the Declaration and this Plan of Action are ambitious and the commitments required to implement them will demand consistent and extraordinary effort on the part of all concerned. Fortunately, the necessary knowledge and techniques for reaching most of the goals already exist. The financial resources required are modest in relation to the great achievements that beckon. And the most essential factor—the provision to families of the information and services necessary to protect their children—is now within reach in every country and for virtually every community. There is no cause that merits a higher priority than the protection and development of children, on whom the survival, stability, and advancement of all nations—and, indeed, of human civilization—depends. Full implementation of the Declaration and this Plan of Action must, therefore, be accorded a high priority for national action and international cooperation.

**CHILE.** The Republic of Chile is a country in temperate South America, on the Pacific Ocean. It has borders with Argentina, Bolivia, and Peru; and a number of offshore islands are included in its territories. It achieved independence from Spain in 1818 and became a member of the United Nations in 1945. Its population is estimated to be 13,635,000. The indigenous population is estimated by the government as: Mapuches, between 500,000 and 600,000; Aymaras, 35,000; Atacamena Indians, 3,000; Alacalufes, 100; Kawashkar, 50; Yagan, 4; and Rapanui (Easter Islanders), 3,090. Religions practiced include Christianity (Roman Catholic, 89%; Protestant denominations, 10%) and Judaism (1%). Spanish is the official language, but a number of indigenous languages are also recognized as official within the indigenous development areas. Literacy is estimated at 94%.

The government (1994) took the form of a republic. The 1925 constitution provides for three branches of government: the executive under the President, the legislative in the form of a Congress, and the judicial with the Supreme Court as its authority. Under that constitution, the President is elected every five years. In 1970, President Salvador Allende Gossens was elected with 36% of the votes, defeating two other candidates, with the support of Unidad Popular, a combination of Socialists, Communists, and other leftist groups. His election was accepted in the international community as an example of a Marxist elected to high office by the democratic process. However, the control of Congress remained in the hands of parties opposed to Unidad Popular. Although, in 1972, Unidad Popular won 44% of the popular vote, there was strong opposition to some parts of its program, which included nationalization of the banks and copper mines and acceleration of land reform.

On 11 September 1973, the government of President Allende was ousted by a coup d'etat engineered by a military junta, in which the President lost his life. The military chief, General Augusto Pinochet Ugarte, assumed the office of President on 17 December 1974. In the 16 years between that date and 15 December 1989–when Chile's voters elected Christian Democrat Patricio Aylwin Azócar to lead them back to civilian government—the situation in that country provoked innumerable complaints of gross violations of human rights, many of which proved valid upon investigation. President Aylwin was succeeded on 11 March 1994 by Eduardo Frei Ruiz-Tagle, elected to serve for a six-year term.

On 1 March 1974, the **COMMISSION ON HUMAN RIGHTS** received information alleging that violations of human rights had taken place in Chile and that the lives of many political, social, and educational figures were in danger. At that time, it called upon the government junta, for the first time, to cease activities contrary to the **UNITED NATIONS CHARTER** and the International Covenants on Human Rights. Later, after receiving detailed and alarming studies of continuing widespread violations of human rights in Chile from such non-governmental organizations as **AMNESTY INTERNATIONAL,** the **INTERNATIONAL COMMISSION OF JURISTS,** and the **WORLD CONFEDERATION OF ORGANIZATIONS OF THE TEACHING PROFESSION,** the Commission established a working group to keep the situation under review. The working group was later replaced by a Special Rapporteur.

Several Special Rapporteurs have since kept the Commission on Human Rights informed about the situation of human rights in Chile; they have been, successively, Judge Abdoulaye Dieye (Senegal), Judge Rajsoomer Lallah (Mauritius), and, most recently, Prof. Fernando Volio Jiminez (Costa Rica), who assumed his mandate on 1 February 1985. Each report of each Special Rapporteur clearly indicated the broad extent and serious nature of the violations of human rights which took place in Chile under the military regime of General Augusto Pinochet.

Prof. Fernando Volio Jiminez submitted ten reports on the subject either to the UN General Assembly or to the Commission on Human Rights between 1985 and 1990. The ninth report (UN Doc. A/44/635), submitted to the Assembly's 1989 session, was a preliminary summary on the evolution of the human rights situation in Chile throughout 1989. The tenth report (UN Doc. E/CN.4/1990/5), submitted to the Commission's 1990 session, covered the most significant developments during the second half of 1989.

The General Assembly took note of the ninth report and invited the Commission (resolution 44/166) "to evaluate . . . the situation of human rights in Chile, bearing in mind the reports presented by the Special Rapporteur, to consider the mandate of the Special Rapporteur and also how the item is to be dealt with on the agenda in the light of developments in the situation, and to report to the General Assembly at its forty-fifth [1990] session."

The tenth report (UN Doc. E/CN.4/1990/5) was examined in detail by the Commission on Human Rights at its 1990 session. In the report, the Special Rapporteur indicated that, while preparing it, he had not received any information from the Chilean government, as had been the case in the past, that government having decided not to accept the renewal of his mandate due to the politically and ideologically based attitude that the Commission on Human Rights had maintained with respect to Chile. The report, accordingly, was based on information from other interested parties, which had provided him with testimony and documents of relevance to his mandate and which he had analyzed in the light of the norms set forth in the international treaties ratified by Chile and other norms of international human rights law recognized as universally applicable. The Special Rapporteur indicated that individuals and groups had emerged from all sectors and had engaged in a quest for solutions, with the establishment of a democratic regime as their overriding objective. In particular, he reported that

The 1985 picture gradually changed. That of 1990 is very different. On two memorable occasions, principally, in October 1988 and December 1989, the Chilen people were able to exercise their right to decide on Chile's political future by means of elections carried out in a conducive atmosphere since the obstacles . . . had been removed, and the way was open for representative democracy, the guardian of freedom.

In addition to the elections in December 1989, the following developments contributed to improve the human rights situation during the period covered in this report: (a) The adoption by the Government Junta (the current Legislative Power), of the National Congress Act, regulating the composition and powers of the Chamber of Deputies and the Senate, whose members were chosen in the aforementioned elections and who will take up their duties on 14 March 1990. This law has constitutional status and is the last of those laws which the Special Rapporteur worked to promote during his mandate, all of which were designed to protect fundamental rights, as a component of the new democratic structure; (b) The administrative internal banishment of two important trade-union leaders was ended; (c) The Government Junta adopted various amendments to the Penal Code and to the Code of Penal Procedure, to ensure better protection for the rights of persons facing trial in the civil courts; (d) The civil courts took a major step in the right direction when Judge Dobra Lusic of the Santiago Third Criminal Court sentenced four CNI agents, who had been among a group of 40 organized civilians who had attacked demonstrators on 1 May 1983 in the Plaza

Venezuela in Santiago. The judgement observed that the attackers' purpose had been to "employ violence in order to repress acts through which the demonstrators indicated moral dissent"; (e) On 11 January 1990 the dissolution was announced of the CNI (the secret police). . . .

The task of continuing to restore the system of human rights protection will devolve upon the new Government of Chile, chosen in the December 1989 elections, to ensure that redress is made for the wrongs suffered by many individuals until March 1990, when the democratic Government will take office. That responsibility will obviously be an inherent component of the new political régime. Representative democracy was conceived in order to promote and ensure universal respect for freedom, and to use that essential and irreplaceable tool to make room for any activity that dignifies the human condition. The Special Rapporteur also feels that in those circumstances, the activities of a Special Rapporteur will not be necessary, although it might be desirable to have a new and specific form of international cooperation for the protection of human rights on the part of the United Nations. That would, of course, be left to the discretion of the Government of Chile and of the Commission on Human Rights.

Nevertheless, much remains to be done to ensure that Chilean society enjoys a reliable system of legal protection for freedom. The representative democracy that will take its place in March 1990 is without doubt an extraordinarily important starting-point from which to pursue the combat to ensure that freedom prevails in its manifold and prolific guises. However, this in no way overlooks the major obstacles that the men and institutions of the new régime will face in that sphere, as a result of the very nature of the system of Government and of democratic life, and on account of the deep rifts created within Chilean society over many years of acute political conflict, exacerbated by violence.

The Commission on Human Rights examined the Special Rapporteur's tenth report on the situation of human rights in Chile at its 1990 session. The Commission noted the improvement in the situation of human rights in that country, as described by the Special Rapporteur, but regretted that, despite the many recommendations by the international community to the military government of Chile, the following were still pending:

(a) judicial and administrative identification and punishment of the persons responsible for crimes, disappearances, torture, persecution, intimidation and other forms of cruel, inhuman and degrading treatment, as well as the situation of persons in custody on political grounds;

(b) a return to normal of the administration of justice, especially in regard to a reform of the system of military justice and a review of the decision by the military courts; and

(c) a review of the rules whereby persons committing serious violations of human rights are granted impunity.

The Commission took note of the decision adopted by the military government junta to disband the National Information Agency and expressed its trust that the agency's archives will be kept at the disposal of the courts of justice and the authorities of the government-elect.

In addition, the Commission noted the commitment made by the government-elect of Patricio Aylwin Azócar to carry out the efforts necessary to secure a full return to normal of the traditional democratic legal system that was affected, from 1973 onwards, as a result of an enforced system of institutions that made for more than 16 years of serious and systematic infringements of national and international standards on human rights. It also welcomed the Aylwin government's commitment to bring Chile fully into the international human rights system established by the United Nations and thus to continue to follow up known unresolved cases and many others that emerge from inquiries conducted by bodies in the system.

In the belief that the Chilean democratic process and management by the then-government-elect would restore the rule of law based on full enjoyment of human rights and fundamental freedoms, the Commission decided not to renew the mandate of the Special Rapporteur, as from the time President Aylwin took office, and requested the government of Chile to report to it, at its 1991 session, on the follow-up to the recommendations adopted by the United Nations up to 11 March 1990.

After the installation of President Aylwin in 1990, General Pinochet refused to step aside as commander of the army; and it was assumed he felt he must retain that position in order to protect members of the armed forces from prosecution for the killings, "disappearances," and torture that had occurred during the period of his presidency.

For his part, President Aylwin indicated that he would not intentionally set out to prosecute General Pinochet or anyone who had served under him but that he would not block any congressional or judicial investigations that might lead to charges. On 12 March 1990, he announced that he had signed a decree freeing a number of political prisoners and would resolve other cases in a spirit of justice, with the exception of those accused of acts of violence. He also indicated that he would propose, as soon as possible, abolition of the death penalty in Chile.

In a report submitted to the UN Committee against Torture and Other Cruel, Inhuman or Degrading Treatment or Punishment on 16 February 1994, just a month prior to the end of the Aylwin government, representatives of Chile described that country's new legal and political framework (UN Doc. CAT/C/20/Add. 3, paras. 5–7):

After being democratically elected in December 1989, the Government of President Aylwin took office in Chile on 11

March 1990 and the Parliament was formally installed, initiating a process of restoration of the democratic institutional system interrupted by the military regime. Since that date, Chile has functioned normally under the rule of law, with State bodies, the armed forces, the police, political parties, and trade union and social organizations performing their appointed functions under the law and the Constitution. It should be emphasized that no "states of constitutional exception" have been declared by the Government and that, consequently, the rights and freedoms guaranteed to all persons by the Constitution have not been restricted in any way.

Habeas corpus is once again applicable in the normal manner. The termination of permanent "states of constitutional exception," the institutional framework that made torture possible under the previous regime, has contributed to a change of attitude on the part of the courts, regarding their duty to watch over the lawfulness of detention through the due processing of habeas corpus applications. This is demonstrated, for instance, by decisions of the Military Appeal Court accepting such applications, remedying arbitrary acts committed in the course of detention, and instructing police officers and the military tribunals to rectify procedural errors occurring during such detention.

The political and legal normality described above has substantially changed the situation regarding fundamental rights and freedoms in the country as compared with the 1973–1990 period. The democratic government has put an end to what the National Commission for the Truth and Reconciliation, after carrying out an investigation, described as a situation of systematic violation of human rights by the military regime. During that period, the report of the National Commission expressly states, " . . . torture was a daily occurrence. . . . Ill-treatment and torture were inflicted systematically at secret places of detention belonging to DINA and other intelligence services . . ." and there was ". . . an undeniable reality of torture, as evidenced by the vast number and virtual uniformity of such acts. . . ."

Regarding compensation for acts of torture, the report states (paras. 39–41):

In response to the recommendations made by the National Commission for the Truth and Reconciliation in regard to compensation for victims of human rights violations during the military regime, and as a contribution of the State to this endeavour and a specific form of reparation designed to confer legal recognition on a problem experienced in Chile by a significant segment of the population, the Program of Compensation and Full Health Care for Victims of Human Rights Violations (PRAIS) was introduced in 1991. At present, seven PRAIS teams are functioning as part of state health services in different areas of the country, financed by contributions from those services and international cooperation. Apart from torture victims, beneficiaries of PRAIS include family members of missing detainees, persons executed for political reasons, and exiles.

From the time it was launched until the first quarter of 1993, this Program provided coverage to 8,029 persons. . . .

PRAIS defines its central objective as being the provision of comprehensive physical and psychological health care to persons whose fundamental rights have been violated, which means that, in addition to the above-mentioned situations relating to repression during the previous period, the Program is now handling cases of victims of ill-treatment occur-

ring after 1990. This has happened in specific cases on which no statistics have been compiled.

On 6 March 1994, the Commission for Reconciliation, a Chilean human rights organization, revised its estimate of the number of people killed by government agents during the years from 1973 to 1989, from an earlier figure of 2,297 to a total of 3,129.

In May 1995 the Supreme Court of Chile upheld the convictions and prison sentences of the former head of the military secret police and his deputy for directing the assassination of opposition leader Orlando Letelier in Washington, D.C., in 1976. These marked the first prison sentences for high-ranking military officials from the government of General Pinochet.

**BIBLIOGRAPHY.** American Association for the Advancement of Science, Committee on Scientific Freedom and Responsibility. *The Open Secret: Torture and the Medical Profession in Chile.* Washington, D.C.: 1987. NGO report, in English.

Americas Watch. *Chile: The Struggle for Truth and Justice for Past Human Rights Violations.* New York: Human Rights Watch, 1992. NGO report, in English.

————. *Human Rights and the 'Politics of Agreements': Chile During President Aylwin's First Year.* New York: Human Rights Watch, 1991. NGO factfinding report, in English.

Ampuero, R., M. Calamai, V. Murillo, and R. Sandri, eds. *Cile: Fra Dittatura E Democrazia* (Chile: Dictatorship and Democracy). Milan: Franco Angeli Libri, 1985. Collection of scholarly articles, in Italian.

Anderson, F. R., W. W. Falsgraf, F. S. Moran, Jr., R. J. Woolsey, and A. Young. *Chile at the Crossroads: A Report of the Delegation of the American Bar Association to Chile, April 18–22, 1988.* Chicago, IL, USA: American Bar Association, 1988. NGO mission report, in English.

Aylwin, José, and J. E. Besnier. *Demandas de los Pueblos Indígenas de Chile en la Transición Democrática* (Demands of the Chilean Indigenous Peoples as Part of the Democratic Transition Process). Santiago, Chile: Chilean Commission of Human Rights, 1990. Issue paper, in Spanish.

Aylwin, José, and Eduardo V. Castillo. *Legislación sobre Indígenas en Chile a través de la Historia* (A Historical Survey of Chilean Legislation concerning Indigenous Peoples). Santiago, Chile: Chilean Commission of Human Rights, 1990. Research report, in Spanish.

Chilean Commission for Human Rights. *Pueblo, Tierra, Desarrollo: Conceptos Fundamentales Para una Nueva Ley Indígena* (People, Earth, Development: Fundamental Concepts for a New Indigenous Law). Santiago, Chile: 1992. NGO report, in Spanish.

Chilean Commission for Human Rights, National Education Campaign for Truth and Human Rights. *"To Believe in Chile." Sintesis del Informe de la Comisión de Verdad y Reconciliación* (Summary of the Truth and Reconciliation Commission Report). Santiago, Chile: 1991 NGO report, in English and Spanish.

Christian Churches' Social Assistance Foundation. *Programa de Reunificación Familiar: Reencuentro en el Exilio* (Family Reunification Program: Meeting in Exile). Santiago, Chile: 1991. Research paper, in Spanish; bibliography, pp. 97–98.

Detzner, J. A. *Tribunales Chilenos y Derecho Internacional de Derechos Humanos: La Recepcion del Derecho Internacional de Derechos Humanos en el Derecho Interno Chileno* (Chilean Courts and

International Human Rights Law: The Reception of International Human Rights Law in Chilean National Law). Santiago, Chile: Comision Chilena de Derechos Humanos, 1988. NGO monograph, in Spanish; bibliography, pp. 161–182.

Freedom House. *A Mission to Chile.* New York: 1988. NGO mission report, in English.

Frülhing E., Hugo. *El Movimiento de Derechos Humanos y la Transición Democrática en Chile y Argentina* (The Human Rights Movement and the Democratic Transition in Chile and Argentina). Santiago, Chile: Human Rights Program, University Academy of Christian Humanism, 1990. Scholarly article, in Spanish.

———. *Nonprofit Organization as Opposition to Authoritarian Rule: The Case of Human Rights Organizations and Private Research Centers in Chile.* New Haven, CT, USA: Program on Non-Profit Organizations and Institute for Social and Policy Studies (Yale University), n.d. Scholarly research paper, in English.

———, ed. *Represion Politica y Defensa de los Derechos Humanos* (Political Repression and the Defense of Human Rights). Santiago, Chile: Centro de Estudios Sociales, 1986. NGO edited collection, in Spanish.

German Justice and Peace Commission. *Ley, Justicia y Represion en Chile* (Law, Justice and Repression in Chile). Bonn, FRG: 1987. Mission report, in Spanish.

Human Rights Program, University Academy of Christian Humanism. "El Caso Chileno en la Comunidad Internacional" (The Chilean Case before the International Community), *Revista Chilena de Derechos Humanos* 12 (April 1990). Special issue, in Spanish.

Human Rights Watch. *Chile: Unsettled Business: Human Rights in Chile at the Start of the Frei Presidency.* New York: 1994. NGO report, in English.

———. "Chile," in *Human Rights Watch World Report 1995,* pp. 76–79. New York: 1995. NGO report, in English.

Inter-American Commission on Human Rights. *Report on the Situation of Human Rights in Chile.* Doc. 17. Washington, D.C.: 1985. IGO mission report, in English.

International Commission of Jurists and the Centre for the Independence of Judges and Lawyers. *Chile: A Time of Reckoning—Human Rights and the Judiciary.* Geneva, Switzerland: 1992. NGO report, in English.

International Federation of Human Rights. *Rapport de mission: l'élection du 14 décembre 1989 au Chili. Rapport final de la délégation pan-canadienne d'observation* (Mission Report: Elections of December 14, 1989 in Chile. Final Report of a Canadian Delegation of Election Observers). Paris: 1990. NGO factfinding report, in French.

International League for Human Rights. *The Long Road to Justice: A Report on the Letelier-Moffitt Case.* New York: 1991. NGO factfinding report, in English.

Medina Quiroga, Cecilia. *The Battle of Human Rights: Gross, Systematic Violations and the Inter-American System.* Dordrecht, the Netherlands: Martinus Nijhoff, 1986. Scholarly monograph, in English.

———. "Chile: Obstacles and Challenges for Human Rights," *Netherlands Quarterly of Human Rights* 10, no. 2 (1992). Scholarly article, in English.

National Commission for Truth and Reconciliation. *Informe Rettig: Informe de la Comisión Nacional de Verdad y Reconciliación—Febrero de 1991* (The Rettig Report: Report of the National Commission for Truth and Reconciliation, February 1991). Santiago, Chile: La Nación & Les Ediciones del Ornitorrinco, 1991. 2 vols. Government report, in Spanish.

Oppenheim, Lois H. *Politics in Chile: Democracy, Authoritarianism, and the Search for Development.* Boulder, CO, USA:

Westview Press, 1993. Monograph, in English; bibliography, pp. 241–247.

Orellana, P. V. *Algunos Aspectos Cuantitativos de la Situacion de los Presos Politicos en Chile* (Some Quantitative Aspects of the Political Prisoner Situation in Chile). Santiago, Chile: Fundacion de Ayuda Social de las Iglesias Cristianas, 1988. Scholarly monograph, in Spanish.

Orellana, Patricio, and Elizabeth Quay Hutchinson. *El Movimiento de Derechos Humanos en Chile, 1973–1990* (The Human Rights Movement in Chile, 1973–1990). Santiago, Chile: Centro de Estudios Políticos Latinoamericanos Simón Bolívar, 1991. Scholarly monograph, in Spanish; bibliography, pp. 195–198.

Physicians for Human Rights. *Sowing Fear: The Uses of Torture and Psychological Abuse in Chile.* Somerville, MA, USA: 1988. NGO report, in English.

Thome, Joseph R. "People Versus the Authoritarians: Grass Root Organizations and Chile's Transition to Democracy," *Beyond Law: Stories of Law and Social Change from Latin America and around the World* 1, no. 2 (July 1991): 85–109. Scholarly article, in English; bibliography, pp. 107–109.

UN Commission on Human Rights. *Question of Human Rights in Chile: Report.* Prepared by Special Rapporteur F. V. Jimenez, E/CN.4/1987/7. 1987. IGO document, in English.

———. *Question of Human Rights in Chile.* Prepared by Special Rapporteur F. V. Jimenez, E/CN.4/1986/2. 1986. IGO document, in English.

U.S. House of Representatives, Subcommittee on Human Rights and International Relations and Subcommittee on Western Hemisphere Relations. *US Policy, Human Rights and the Prospects for Democracy in Chile.* Washington, D.C.: Government Printing Office, 1988. Government hearings, in English.

Vicaria de la Solidaridad (Vicariate of Solidarity). *Vicaria de la Solidaridad Duodecimo Año de Labor 1987* (Vicariate of Solidarity 1987, 12th Year of Activity). Santiago, Chile: 1988. NGO report (issued annually), in Spanish.

Washington Office on Latin America. *Chile, the Multilateral Development Banks and U.S. Human Rights Law: A Delegation Report.* Washington, D.C.: 1986. NGO mission report, in English.

Zabel, W. D., D. Orentlicher, and D. E. Nachman. *Human Rights and the Administration of Justice in Chile: Report of a Delegation of the Association of the Bar of the City of New York and of the International Bar Association.* London: International Bar Association, 1987. NGO mission report, in English.

**CHINA.** The People's Republic of China is a country in east Asia, on the Yellow Sea, the East China Sea, and the South China Sea. It has borders with Afghanistan, Bhutan, India, Korea, the Kyrgyz Republic, Laos, Mongolia, Myanmar, Nepal, Pakistan, the Russian Federation, and Tadzhikistan. Always independent, China became a member of the United Nations in 1945 and is one of the permanent members of the UN **SECURITY COUNCIL.** Its population is estimated to be 1,179,030,000—the largest in the world.

China is a multinational country; 56 nationalities live on its 9.6 million sq. km. of land. All nationalities other than the Han, which has the largest population, are customarily called minority nationalities; however, in China the word "minority" does not have a political meaning. The census of 1982 showed a total of over 67,230,000 minority people, with 15 nationalities having populations of over one million each, 31 nationalities having populations of between 10,000 and one million each, and nine having populations of less than 10,000 each. The majority Han nationality accounts for 92% of the nation's total population, while the 55 minorities constitute 8%. The Zhuang are the largest minority with a population of 13 million, while the Hezhen are the smallest with only 1,400 people.

Languages in common use include modern standard Chinese (official), Mandarin, Cantonese, and many local languages and dialects. Although the practice of religion is discouraged, Confucianism, Buddhism, Christianity, and Islam are widely practiced. Literacy is estimated at 76.5%.

The government (1994) took the form of a republic. Under the 1982 constitution, China is governed by a State Council headed by the premier, who is elected by the main legislative organ, the 2,978-member National People's Congress. Deputies to the Congress are elected by popular vote, with universal suffrage. The only political party is the Communist Party.

China has a long history of suffering, similar to that of other developing countries. Like them, China was the victim of colonialist aggression and oppression over a period of many years. Internally, it also was the victim of national oppression and discrimination.

By the end of the 19th century, Great Britain, France, Germany, and Russia had established "zones of influence" in China and had obtained valuable commercial "concessions." The United States government tried to initiate an "open door" policy, under which all nations would enjoy equal access to China's trade; but Chinese fear and resentment of foreigners stood in the way, and the Boxer Rebellion of 1900 was aimed at expelling all foreign influence.

In 1911, Sun Yat-sen led a republican revolution that forced the abdication of China's emperor. Sun Yat-sen became China's first President but resigned within a year in favor of a military ruler who established a repressive regime. After World War I, which China entered on the Allied side, the Nine-Power Treaty signed at the Washington Conference (1921–1922) guaranteed Chinese territorial integrity and the open door policy.

Civil war raged for some years between Sun Yat-sen's party, the Kuomintang, based in the south, and the "war lords" (semi-independent military commanders), based in the north. In 1928, the Kuomintang was able to establish a government in Nanking which won some foreign recognition. The Japanese, taking advantage of the dissention, occupied Manchuria in 1932. By 1937, the Kuomintang and the communists had reached a shaky agreement to cooperate against the Japanese.

While World War II eliminated the Japanese threat, the rift between the nationalists and the Communists in China widened. After a period of civil war, a national assembly, boycotted by the Communists, adopted a democratic constitution, under which the first elected legislature—composed largely of Kuomintang members and including no Communists—met early in 1948 and selected Chiang Kai-shek as China's first constitutional President. Chiang's Executive Yuan (Cabinet) included Minority party members.

However, the Communists gained the upper hand in renewed internal warfare and, in August 1949, founded "New China" from their capital in Beijing (formerly Peking). They proceeded immediately to reorganize the country and to consolidate its territory; and, by April 1950, followers of Chiang Kai-shek were forced to retreat to the offshore island of Formosa, which they renamed Taiwan.

The government of the United States refused to recognize the People's Republic of China for nearly 30 years. In the United Nations, China continued to be represented by the Chiang Kai-shek authorities for more than 20 years. However, the UN General Assembly, on 25 October 1971, decided "to restore all its rights to the People's Republic of China and to recognize the representatives of its Government as the only legitimate representatives of China to the United Nations, and to expel forthwith the representatives of Chiang Kai-shek from the place which they unlawfully occupy at the United Nations and in all the organizations related to it." Chiang Kai-shek died of a heart attack on 5 April 1975, and the United States government recognized the People's Republic of China as of 1 January 1979.

In 1958, Mao Zedong, the Communist party leader, organized the "Great Leap Forward" campaign of village industrialization and the establishment of rural communes. The campaign failed, and Mao and his supporters moved to Shanghai, from which they organized a "Cultural Revolution" in which Red Guard Units—composed mostly of students freed from the schools—campaigned against "old ideas, old culture, old habits and old customs." The campaign often involved mass brutality and gross violations of human rights by uncontrolled mobs of armed young people. Efforts to bring it under control were ineffective for several years.

Early in 1972 U.S. President Richard Nixon visited China and met with Mao as well as with President Zhou Enlai. This brought about a movement toward reconciliation. Mao died in 1976, after which his widow and three colleagues—known as the "Gang of Four"—were accused of having undermined the party, the government, and the economy. Later the Central Committee of the Communist party found Mao Zedong responsible for the "grave blunders" of the Cultural Revolution.

On 5 October 1967, three major human rights instruments—the International Covenant on Economic, Social and Cultural Rights, the International Covenant on Civil and Political Rights, and the First Optional Protocol to the latter Covenant, were signed on behalf of the "Republic of China" by the Taiwanese authorities representing China in the United Nations at that time. However, on 29 September 1972, the UN Secretary-General received a communication from the Minister of Foreign Affairs of the People's Republic of China stating that:

1. With regard to the multilateral treaties signed, ratified, or acceded to by the defunct Chinese Government before the establishment of the Government of the People's Republic of China, my Government will examine their contents before making a decision in the light of the circumstances as to whether or not they should be recognized.
2. As from 1 October 1949, the day of the founding of the People's Republic of China, the Chiang Kai-shek clique has no right at all to represent China. Its signature and ratification, or accession to, any multilateral treaties by usurping the name of "China" are all illegal and null and void. My Government will study these multilateral treaties before making a decision in the light of the circumstances as to whether or not they should be acceded to.

By the end of 1993, the Government of the People's Republic of China had not ratified any of the above-mentioned instruments. It had, however, become a party to the International Convention on the Suppression and Punishment of the Crime of Apartheid, the Convention on the Prevention and Punishment of the Crime of Genocide, the Convention on the Rights of the Child, the Convention on the Elimination of All Forms of Discrimination against Women, the Convention against Torture and Other Cruel, Inhuman or Degrading Treatment or Punishment, the Convention relating to the Status of Refugees, and the Protocol relating to the Status of Refugees.

In September 1992, the UN Secretary-General transmitted to all Member States a decision of the UN Commission on Human Rights welcoming "the organization of regional workshops on various human rights issues" and encouraging all States in each region of the world "to consider further the establishment of regional arrangements for the promotion and protection of human rights in the region." In reply, the Government of China observed that:

Full enjoyment of human rights has long been mankind's ideal. Every country is making its own efforts to promote the general enjoyment of human rights. The Chinese Government considers that different countries' differing views on human rights and choices of measures to protect them in the light of the individual circumstances and special features of each need to be acknowledged and respected. A pattern of human rights safeguards evolved in any one region will only suit that region, and cannot be treated as a standard to be imposed on other countries and regions.

The Asian region has its own characteristics. Hence the Asian region neither should nor can slavishly imitate the regional human rights protection mechanisms of other regions. Asian countries can, by means of increased contacts and interchanges, increase their mutual understanding, and, subject to equality, reciprocal respect and noninterference in one another's internal affairs, together explore the implications of and channels for increasing international cooperation in human rights, in order to contribute to the promotion and protection of human rights in the region.

In May 1994, United States President Bill Clinton announced that he would extend China's Most Favored Nation trading status despite widespread criticism and, further, that he planned to review the policy of tying trading status to a nation's human rights record.

***PROTECTION OF MINORITIES.*** For many years, the Government of China has endeavored to eliminate the discrimination and oppression on the ground of "nationality" that has persistently divided the Chinese people. In a report presented to the UN **COMMITTEE ON THE ELIMINATION OF RACIAL DISCRIMINATION** on 7 March 1988, the Chinese Government summarized its recent efforts in this field (UN Doc. CERD/C.153/Add. 2, paras. 3–22):

The People's Republic of China has always persisted in a policy of equality of all its nationalities and engaged in helping the minority nationalities develop their economy and culture. China has made new efforts in promoting national unity and common prosperity and has thereby achieved new results.

In the Seventh Five-Year Plan of the People's Republic of China for Economic and Social Development (1986–1990) there is a special provision on the development of areas inhabited by minority nationalities, "We should take full advantage of the abundant natural resources in these areas. We shall improve conditions for farming and animal husbandry, increase grain output, step up the development of pasture land by planting trees and grass, and gradually create a balanced ecological environment. We shall push forward the development of the energy and raw and semi-finished materials industries and improve transport facilities. We shall promote trade among different nationalities and encourage the production of articles of daily use to meet the special needs of minority peoples and accelerate the construction of culture in these areas."

The Chinese Government has adopted a series of economic, legal and administrative measures which are practical and effective to implement the economic and social development programme for the minority nationality areas and has scored notable results.

The central Government gives favourable consideration and assistance to the autonomous areas in finance. It is stipulated that revenues belonging to the autonomous areas in accordance with the State financial system can be disposed of by the autonomous organs. The State will also provide financial subsidies for their economic development when necessary. In 1985 and 1986 there is a 10% increase over the previous year in financial subsidy by the central Government to the five autonomous regions and Yunnan, Guizhou and Qinhai provinces where many minority nationalities inhabit. The central Government has given Tibet a total of more than 10 billion yuan RMB in the form of financial subsidy since 1952.

A somewhat different aspect of the question of minorities was, however, revealed in a dispatch dated February 1990, stating that, according to the official New China News Agency, Prime Minister Li Peng had warned against independence movements among China's ethnic minorities in a speech delivered a few days earlier and had warned that independence efforts would be crushed immediately. "We must not relax our vigilance," Mr. Li was quoted as saying. "We should wipe out all separatist activities while they are still in the embryonic stage."

In a report to the Commission on Human Rights, dated 13 December 1993, the Government of China provided the following information on its efforts to protection the human rights of minorities (E/CN.4/1994/72):

China played an active part in the formulation of the Declaration on the Rights of Persons Belonging to National or Ethnic, Religious and Linguistic Minorities, and was pleased to see several suggestions it made accepted into the text.

The Chinese Government believes the Declaration to be a balanced document emphasizing peaceful and constructive ways and means of upholding the rights of persons belonging to minorities. The steps suggested in the Declaration would be of benefit in guaranteeing that such persons enjoyed the same rights and freedoms as other citizens, on an equal footing; they would help to promote joint, harmonious, and common development within every ethnic group in a nation.

Established Chinese policy and action on protecting the rights of persons belonging to national or ethic, religious and linguistic minorities are not only wholly consistent with the Declaration but in practice surpass its stipulations in many respects.

### National or Ethnic Minorities

China has 56 different nationalities. It is a unitary multiethnic State. Han Chinese represent 92% of the total population, and the other 55 nationalities, 8%. The basic principle of the Chinese Government's treatment of interethnic relations is to make all nationalities flourish equally, jointly, and together. The Chinese Constitution states that all nationalities in the People's Republic of China are equal. The State protects the lawful rights and interests of the minority nationalities and upholds and develops the relationship of equality, unity, and mutual assistance among all China's nationalities. Discrimination against and oppression of any nationality are prohibited; any acts that undermine the unity of the nationalities or instigate their secession are prohibited.

The people of minority nationalities, like people of Han nationality, enjoy all the civil rights laid down in the Constitution and the laws on an equal footing; at the same time, again in accordance with the law, they enjoy the special rights belonging to minorities.

In order to ensure that, in politics, the people of every minority nationality can fully enjoy all their rights, China has instituted the system of regional national autonomy. Organs of self-government have been set up in districts where minority nationalities are concentrated; and, run by the local nationalities and taking into consideration the special political, economic, and cultural features of those nationalities, they manage the affairs of the districts and the nationalities that live there. By the end of 1990, China had set up 159 autonomous local governments. In areas inhabited by several nationalities or where nationalities are scattered, it has set up over 1,500 national townships in order to enable scattered nationalities and nationalities living together to enjoy proper equal rights.

Under the electoral law of the People's Republic of China, national minorities are represented at every level of people's congresses throughout the country in proportion to their size vis-à-vis other nationalities. This guarantees that they can participate in the affairs of State directly and through the intermediary of their representatives.

Economically, many minority nationalities inhabit regions in the south and west where natural conditions are poor; and this, combined with historical reasons, means that their level of economic development is often relatively low. For many years now, the Chinese Government has furnished minority areas with extensive financial, material, and technological support, actively reducing the disparities in economic development between them and other regions in order to bring about common development and prosperity for all nationalities.

### Religious Minorities

China has no State religion. All faiths are equal, without distinction.

The Chinese Constitution states that citizens enjoy freedom of religious belief and the freedom to believe in no religion; they are free to believe in any kind of religion; and to cease to believe in a religion they formerly believed in, or vice versa.

The State protects normal religious activities and the lawful interests of religious circles. The Government does have a department of religious affairs, which is responsible for guaranteeing the application of its policy on freedom of religious belief.

China follows a policy of religious independence, autonomy, and self-management, and opposes any foreign influence over, domination of, or interference in its domestic religious affairs in the interests of protecting its citizens' right to true freedom of belief.

The Chinese Government actively supports religious organizations and members of religious circles within the country in establishing friendly contacts with foreign religious organizations and circles on the basis of the principles of sustained independence, autonomy, and self-management, and of reciprocal respect, and looks upon their international links as one element of the Chinese people's relations with the peoples of the rest of the world.

### Linguistic Minorities

Under Chinese legislation, every nationality is at liberty to use and develop its own language and writing system. The

Government assists minorities in arranging cultural education using their own languages and writing systems, and is helping the ten minority nationalities that have no writing systems to devise one.

Under article 6 of the Chinese Code of Criminal Procedure, citizens of every nationality are entitled to use their own languages and writing systems in conducting legal proceedings. The people's courts, peoples, procuratorates, and public security authorities must arrange translation for individuals taking part in legal proceedings who are not proficient in the local language. In areas where minority nationalities are concentrated or where many are mingled, the local language must be used in interrogations, written court decisions, proclamations, and other documents.

With assistance from the Government, many regions have set up minority-language publishing and news agencies that put out newspapers, periodicals, and books in the writing systems used by minority nationalities.

*PRO-DEMOCRACY DEMONSTRATIONS.* In the course of 1989, Chinese authorities had summarily crushed both a major separatist movement and a major movement for democratic participation in government. In March, in Tibet, a peaceful demonstration calling for independence, led by monks and nuns, had led to the imposition of martial law after police had beaten and fired upon the demonstrators. In April, in Beijing, a peaceful demonstration calling for democracy, led by students, had again led to the imposition of martial law after the army had beaten, machine-gunned, and run over the demonstrators with trucks and armored vehicles.

In August 1989, the UN **SUB-COMMISSION ON PREVENTION OF DISCRIMINATION AND PROTECTION OF MINORITIES** placed China on a list of countries accused of seriously violating the human rights of their citizens. By a secret ballot of 15 in favor and 9 against, the Sub-Commission on 31 August expressed its concern (resolution 1989/5) about the events which had taken place in China and about their consequences in the field of human rights and requested the Secretary-General to transmit to the Commission on Human Rights information provided by the government of China and by other reliable sources. At the same time, it made an appeal for clemency, in particular in favor of persons deprived of their liberty as a result of the above-mentioned events.

In accordance with the above-mentioned resolution, the UN Secretary-General sent, on 30 October 1989, a note verbale to the Minister of Foreign Affairs of China in which he referred to the resolution and requested the government of China, should it wish to submit information pursuant to operative paragraph 1, to do so before 1 January 1990.

On 1 December 1989, the Permanent Representative of the People's Republic of China to the United Nations office at Geneva replied as follows:

Last June, there occurred in Beijing a rebellion which was supported by hostile forces abroad and constituted an attempt to overthrow the legitimate Government of the People's Republic of China and subvert the socialist system set forth in the Constitution through violent means. The Chinese Government took resolute measures to quell the rebellion in the interests of the overwhelming majority of the Chinese people. This is entirely China's internal affairs and is a matter different in nature from the question of human rights. However, with the plotting and encouragement of some Western members, the Sub-Commission on Prevention of Discrimination and Protection of Minorities adopted resolution 1989/5 at its forty-first session. This is a brutal interference in China's internal affairs while hurting the feeling of the Chinese people. The Spokesman of the Foreign Ministry of the People's Republic of China issued a statement on 2 September 1989, solemnly declaring the firm objection of the Chinese Government to the resolution and deeming it to be illegal and null and void.

The Secretary-General transmitted information on the 1989 uprising provided by the government of China to the Commission on Human Rights on 23 January 1990. On 30 January 1990, he transmitted to the Commission certain information provided by "other reliable sources": three non-governmental organizations in consultative status with the Economic and Social Council (UN Doc. E/CN.4/1990/52). The organizations were Amnesty International (annex I), the International Commission of Health Professionals for Health and Human Rights (annex II), and the International League for Human Rights (annex III). Only the information provided by Amnesty International is presented here (UN Doc. E/CN.4/1990/52, annex I):

### Violations of Human Rights in China

*Introduction.* In this document Amnesty International describes its concerns about recent human rights violations in China. It believes it important that the recent events be considered in the light of the overall human rights situation in the country.

In August 1989, Amnesty International published a report entitled "Preliminary Findings on Killings of Unarmed Civilians, Arbitrary Arrests and Summary Executions since 3 June 1989," which described Amnesty International's concerns about human rights violations in China since early June 1989, when heavily armed troops moved into the centre of Beijing to suppress pro-democracy protests, killing many unarmed protesters and bystanders.

Serious violations of human rights continue to occur in China and Amnesty International has not recorded any significant improvement since August 1989. Though releases have occurred, thousands of people continue to be imprisoned throughout China for their participation in the pro-democracy protests of 1989. There have been further arbitrary arrests and prisoners continue to be detained incommunicado without charge or trial, imprisoned or executed after unfair trials. Martial law was lifted in Beijing on 10 January 1990, but no measures of clemency or redress have been announced for those imprisoned as prisoners of conscience, subjected to prolonged detention without charge or trial for political reasons, or sentenced to imprisonment or to death after unfair trials. Indeed, the laws which permit such violations to take place remain in force.

Amnesty International estimates that at least 1,000 people were killed and thousands more injured in Beijing in early June 1989 when troops fired into crowds of protesters and bystanders—the vast majority of them unarmed. Amnesty International believes that many of these killings were extrajudicial executions, the result of a deliberate decision by those in authority to suppress the peaceful protests even if this meant widespread killings. The atmosphere of terror which followed the military operation made it impossible to determine the true death toll. Thousands of people were subsequently detained throughout China in connection with the protests, including many prisoners of conscience, and most were held incommunicado for long periods. Some were reported to have been severely beaten or tortured by soldiers or police. Dozens were officially reported to have been sentenced to death or to terms of imprisonment after trials which were summary and unfair, and secret executions were also reported. . . .

*Events in Beijing in Early June 1989.* On 20 May 1989, following five weeks of peaceful student-led demonstrations, martial law was imposed in Beijing. The order was issued in the name of the State Council and signed by Prime Minister Li Peng. Its stated aim was to "firmly stop the unrest", to safeguard public order and to "ensure the normal function" of government.

The student protests, which started in Beijing in mid-April 1989 and soon spread to most major cities, received wide popular support and developed into a pro-democracy movement. On 18 May 1989, an estimated one million people demonstrated in Beijing in support of students on hunger-strike and on 23 May 1989 a similar number again took to the streets to protest the imposition of martial law, the largest known popular demonstration of discontent in the history of the People's Republic of China.

On the night of 3 to 4 June 1989 hundreds of armoured military vehicles escorted by tens of thousands of troops moved into the centre of Beijing to enforce martial law, firing both at random and deliberately into crowds of protesters and bystanders—the vast majority of them unarmed. Further shootings of unarmed civilians occurred in the next few days. The numerous incidents in which civilians were deliberately shot by soldiers or crushed by military vehicles have been amply documented by the eyewitness testimonies and documents published or broadcast since then. Amnesty International described some of these incidents in its August 1989 report "Preliminary Findings on Killings of Unarmed Civilians, Arbitrary Arrests and Summary Executions Since 3 June 1989". Amnesty International concluded in that report that:

(a) From mid-April until the military operations of 3 and 4 June in Beijing, the popular protest movement started by Beijing students was peaceful. There is no indication that leaders of the protest movement at any point advocated violence or attempted to overthrow the Government by violent means.

(b) During the night of 3 to 4 June, some troops opened fire either at random or deliberately at crowds whenever they met obstructions or large groups of people. No warnings were given before troops opened fire. Conventional methods for the dispersal or control of crowds without resort to firearms or other use of lethal force were not used.

(c) The vast majority of civilians were unarmed. Some were killed in residential buildings due to random or intentional shooting by troops. Some were shot in the back among crowds of people running away from troops firing at them;

some were crushed to death by military vehicles. Those killed included children and old people.

(d) After the army took control of central Beijing there were still, for several days, incidents during which troops opened fire on unarmed civilians without warning or provocation.

(e) Many of the killings of unarmed civilians were extrajudicial executions: deliberate killings by government forces acting outside the limits of the law. Troops deliberately shot and killed individuals even when there was no immediate threat of violence by them, in violation of international standards that lethal force should only be used when absolutely necessary and in direct proportion to the legitimate objective it is intended to achieve.

In the past few months, the Chinese authorities have publicized their official version of what happened in Beijing on 3 and 4 June. They have produced videotapes and testimonies from individuals suggesting that the army not only exercised "great restraint", but also that many soldiers were victims of violence provoked by "rioters". Testimonies have been used to support official claims that no one was killed during the final evacuation of Tiananmen Square, but these and other documentation provide only a partial version of what occurred. The authorities have failed to take account of the well-attested incidents in which civilians were deliberately shot by soldiers. They still have not explained why a decision was taken to use lethal force against unarmed civilians, and why conventional crowd-control methods were not used to disperse protesters before 3 June. They continue to maintain that some 200 civilians only, as well as "several dozen" soldiers, were killed during the military operations in Beijing; but this represents a gross underestimate. Information received by Amnesty International indicated that at least a thousand civilians and, according to reports, about 16 soldiers were killed.

Amnesty International has continued to receive reports and eye witness testimonies about events in Beijing during the night of 3 to 4 June, which generally confirm the description given in its August 1989 report. . . .

*Events in Chengdu on 4 and 5 June 1989.* Killings of civilians are also reported to have occurred on 4 and 5 June 1989 in Chengdu, the capital of Sichuan province, where violent confrontations between security forces and protesters took place after news of the Beijing massacre spread. In Chengdu, as in many other cities, students had organized peaceful demonstrations and sit-ins in the centre of the city in May and early June. According to reports, on 4 June, as news of events in Beijing was received, crowds of people converged on the Sichuan Government Offices in central Chengdu and attacked the building with stones. Security forces then attacked the crowds with tear gas and truncheons, reportedly also using knives and bayonets. Gunfire was also heard intermittently during the violent confrontations which continued for two days, resulting in widespread damage to buildings in the centre of the city and many casualties.

According to official sources, eight civilians—including two students—were killed on 4 June during the clashes and 1,800 people were injured, including 700 civilians and 1,100 members of the security forces. Unofficial estimates of the number of civilian casualties are much higher, ranging from about 30 to over 300 for the number of those killed, with many more injured. One source reported that 27 people had died in one of Chengdu's four major hospitals as a result of the 4 June clashes. The total number of casualties recorded in hospitals is not known. Further violent confrontations occurred during the night of 5 and 6 June in various parts of central Chengdu.

While Amnesty International has been unable to ascertain the total number of people killed in Chengdu on 4 and 5 June 1989, it has received detailed testimonies indicating that the security forces used extreme brutality against unarmed protesters and bystanders. . . .

*Human Rights Violations since June 1989.* The Chinese authorities have not disclosed the total number of people detained, tried or executed throughout the country since the June crackdown on pro-democracy protesters. At least 6,000 arrests have been officially reported throughout China; but the real number of those detained is believed to run into tens of thousands. Between 8,000 and 10,000 people are said to have been detained in Beijing alone—the majority in June and July—although some sources suggest that around 4,000 were released after various periods in detention for interrogation. Arbitrary arrests, however, have continued. Since September, Amnesty International has received numerous reports about students, academics and others arrested in various places in China for their alleged activities in connection with the pro-democracy protests. Few such arrests, however, have been confirmed by official sources.

The arbitrary detention or imprisonment of people involved in peaceful political or religious activities is facilitated by a number of provisions in Chinese law and by practices which, while contrary to the letter of the law, have become the norm in the People's Republic of China. It is common, for instance, for people to be detained by police for weeks or months without charge, in breach of the procedures for arrest and detention laid down in China's Criminal Procedure Law. A 1957 law, which was updated with new regulations in November 1979, also permits longterm detention without charge or trial: it provides for the detention of people considered to have "anti-socialist views" or to be "hooligans" in camps or prisons for up to four years for "re-education through labour". Detention orders for those subjected to "re-education through labour" are issued outside the judicial process by Public Security (police) officers. China's Criminal Law (1980) also includes provisions which are used to imprison people for the peaceful exercise of their basic human rights. Articles 98 and 102, in particular, provide punishments ranging from deprivation of political rights to life imprisonment for people charged with organizing or taking part in a "counter-revolutionary" group or with carrying out "counter-revolutionary propaganda and agitation". These two articles, as well as others, have often been used in the past to imprison people whom Amnesty International considers to be prisoners of conscience.

Those detained are believed to be held incommunicado. Chinese law does not permit access to lawyers until a few days before trial—or in some cases until the trial starts. It is also common for prisoners to be denied visits from their family until the trial. Some detainees are reported to have been severely beaten by soldiers or police after arrest, and many are feared to have been tortured or ill-treated to force them to confess to crimes or to denounce others.

Amnesty International has long been concerned about the occurrence of torture in China. In 1987 it published a report entitled "China: Torture and Ill-treatment of Prisoners," which documented the widespread use of torture in China and pointed out that the absence of sufficient safeguards for detainees' rights in Chinese law contributed to a pattern of abuse. It recommended the introduction of several safeguards, in particular that limits be placed on incom-

municado detention, but none of these safeguards have yet been introduced in China.

Some of those arrested since June 1989 were sentenced to death or imprisonment after unfair trials. In June 1989, the Supreme People's Court called on local courts to "try quickly and punish severely" those involved in the "counter-revolutionary rebellion", using 1983 legislation that provides for swift and summary procedures with little opportunity for defence in the trials of "criminals who gravely endanger public security." This legislation allows the courts to bring defendants to trial without giving them a copy of the indictment in advance and without giving advance notice of the trial or issue summons in advance to all parties involved—including defence lawyers. Furthermore, trials are often a mere formality as the verdicts are usually decided in advance. The well-known practice of "verdict first, trial second" has been acknowledged by top Chinese legal officials in late 1988. This practice, as well as the use of torture to induce confessions and the extreme limitations on the role of defence lawyers, have been criticized by members of the Chinese legal profession in numerous articles published in the official legal press since 1987.

The following are a few examples of people officially reported to have been tried and sentenced in connection with the protests.

(a) Xiao Bin, a worker from Dalian in northeast China, was the first person known to be sentenced in connection with the protests for exercising his right to freedom of speech. He was arrested on 11 June 1989 after being shown on Chinese television speaking to an American ABC television crew in Beijing earlier that month: on 13 July 1989 it was announced that he had been found guilty under Article 102 of the Criminal Law of "spreading rumours" and of "vilifying the righteous act of the martial law troops". He was sentenced to 10 years' imprisonment for "counter-revolutionary propaganda and incitement."

(b) In late August 1989 the first student officially reported to have been tried in connection with the demonstrations was sentenced to nine years' imprisonment on the same charge. Zhang Weiping, an art student in Hangzhou, was accused of telling Voice of America radio in June that students in Hangzhou had successfully asked provincial government officials to fly the flag at half mast to mourn those killed in Beijing.

(c) In a recent case, Chen Zhixiang, a 26-year-old teacher in Guangzhou (Canton), was sentenced to 10 years imprisonment on 11 January 1990 for displaying a poster attacking Chinese leaders three days after troops crushed the pro-democracy protests in Beijing on 4 June 1989.

Secret trials of students active in the protest movement were reported to have started in Beijing in November 1989. Four students from the Foreign Affairs college in Beijing were reported to have gone on trial that month for "counter-revolutionary" crimes, but their names and details of their cases were not known. The trials were reportedly held in secret and even the families of the accused were not allowed to attend. Trials of "counter-revolutionaries" are said to have continued, but only a few were officially reported. The fate, whereabouts and conditions of many intellectuals, students and workers involved in the protests remain unknown though they have now been imprisoned for several months. Leaders of the movement are known to be detained in Qincheng prison, north of Beijing, which has traditionally been used to hold prominent political prisoners.

Some of those arrested in connection with the protests were charged with ordinary criminal offences, such as block-

# C

ing traffic, damaging vehicles, attacking soldiers or police, arson or looting—and faced summary trial and possible execution under the 1983 legislation. On 21 June three workers were shot in Shanghai after a "public sentencing rally" for allegedly setting fire to a train after it had ploughed through demonstrators blocking the track and killed at least six people. The next day seven "rioters" were executed in Beijing after being convicted of wounding troops and burning military vehicles in the capital on 4 June. Despite international appeals for clemency, all had their death sentences upheld by the courts.

Though only a few dozen executions have been publicly reported, some sources estimate that in Beijing alone several hundred people were executed secretly between June and August 1989. Various sources have reported that at least two execution grounds were used: one located in the north-west of Beijing, where groups of prisoners were reported to have been shot before dawn in June and July. One source said at least eight groups of up to 20 people had been shot near the bridge by mid-July 1989.

*TIBET.* From time to time, the United Nations bodies have received reports of violations of human rights and fundamental freedoms that are said to threaten the distinct cultural, religious, and national identity of one of China's minority nationalities, the Tibetan people.

In its 1990 report to the UN Commission on Human Rights, cited previously, Amnesty International reported the following concerning the situation in Tibet:

In Tibet, martial law was imposed in the capital, Lhasa, on 7 March 1989 following two days of violent confrontations after police attempted to stop a peaceful demonstration by a small group of Tibetan monks and nuns calling for Tibet's independence. Eye-witnesses described "ill-organized" police savagely beating Tibetans and "firing indiscriminately." By 9 March the official death toll was 16, but unofficial Tibetan sources estimated that over 60 people had died and more than 200 had been injured. Over 1,000 Tibetans were reportedly arrested, though the authorities acknowledged no more than a few hundred arrests, and there were reports of secret summary executions. Further arrests occurred in the following months.

Evidence of persistent human rights violations in Tibet since pro-independence demonstrations started in September 1987 includes reports of numerous arbitrary arrests, longterm detention without charge or trial and torture.

Amnesty International has received reports about the torture and ill-treatment of prisoners which include testimonies from political detainees who were released in late 1988 or early 1989 and others. They allege that many detainees were subjected to torture, including severe beatings, shocks with electric batons and prolonged suspension by the arms. Some detainees are said to have died as a result of torture. One detainee, Tseten Norgye, a married bookkeeper who was arrested in Lhasa in April or May 1989 reportedly suffered a severe eye injury as a result of torture. He was reported to have been arrested after police found a mimeograph machine in his house which they alleged was used to print literature advocating Tibetan independence. He is held in Lhasa's Chakpori detention centre and is not known to have been charged.

To Amnesty International's knowledge, the first trial of Tibetans involved in pro-independence activities since Sep-

tember 1987 took place in Lhasa in January 1989. The official New China News Agency announced at the time that 27 Tibetans had been publicly tried for offences related to demonstrations in 1987 and 1988. One of these—Yulo Dawa Tsering, a senior monk from Ganden monastery detained in December 1987—was sentenced to 10 years' imprisonment and three years' deprivation of political rights on charges of "collaborating with foreign reactionary elements."

In August 1989 the People's Daily announced that 10 Tibetans accused of offences related to the March 1988 protests in Lhasa had been sentenced. Others were tried and sentenced during the following months. One, named as Passang, was sentenced to life imprisonment for taking part in the protests.

Amnesty International has received other reports of arrests and trials of Tibetans in the past few months. At least 16 Tibetan nuns were reported to have been arrested for demonstrating in September and October 1989. Six of the nuns were subsequently sent to labour camps without charge or trial, after receiving administrative sentences of three years' "re-education through labour." Detention orders for "re-education through labour" are issued outside the judicial process by Public Security (police) officers and those thus punished cannot question the grounds for their detention or appeal against it in a court of law. Several other Tibetans, including four monks and one young student, were assigned to terms of up to three years' "re-education through labour" between September and December 1989 for their alleged participation in demonstrations. Others, including 10 monks from Drepung monastery, were tried on "counter-revolutionary" charges for alleged pro-independence activities. Those arrested recently include five students from Lhasa No. 1 Middle School who were arrested on 8 December 1989 for allegedly setting up in March 1989 a "counter-revolutionary" group called the Gangchen (Mountain Range) Youth Association and putting up posters in various places in Lhasa. No punishment against them has yet been announced.

At its 1991 session, in resolution 1991/10, the UN Sub-Commission on Prevention of Discrimination and Protection of Minorities expressed its concern at such reports, and called upon the Government to fully respect the fundamental rights and freedoms of the Tibetan people. It called upon the Secretary-General to transmit information on the situation to the Commission on Human Rights.

Accordingly, the Commission on Human Rights received and considered, at its 1992 session, a document reproducing the reply of the Chinese Government (UN Doc. E/CN.4/1992/37, Part B) and information submitted by seven non-governmental sources. The Government's reply was as follows:

1. In recent years, a handful of Tibetan separatists in exile and some anti-China forces in the world have repeatedly stated that Tibet used to be an "independent State" in history, and it lost its status of independence only after the "armed invasion" and "occupation" of Tibet carried out by China in the early 1950s ... thus "violating" human rights in Tibet. All this is nothing but distorting history and altering facts. It is known to all that the Tibetan nationality is one of the 56 nationalities in China with [a] long history. As early as the 13th century, Tibet, as one of the main concentrated

communities for Tibetans, had become an administrative region of China and inalienable part of the Chinese territory. Over the past 700 years or more, the successive central governments of China exercised effective sovereign control over Tibet. Since the beginning of the contemporary history, though the imperialist and colonial forces adopted political and diplomatic measures or even launched armed invasions against Tibet, imposed pressures on the central governments of China, and drove wedges between local authorities in Tibet and the central governments in an attempt to separate Tibet from China, they never succeeded in changing the fact that China possesses complete sovereignty over Tibet. No country in the world has ever recognized the so-called "independence in Tibet."

After the founding of new China in October 1949, it was the Chinese Government's responsibility as well as the shared demand of all the Chinese nationalities, including the Tibetans, to liberate its own territory, expel the imperialist forces, remove outside obstacles preventing the Tibetan people from enjoying rights of equality and freedom, and safeguard China's sovereignty and territorial integrity. Under such circumstances, through the concerted efforts of the central People's Government and the local Government of Tibet, the two sides sent delegations and conducted friendly negotiations. Agreement was reached on various matters related to the peaceful liberation of Tibet; and the Agreement of the central People's Government and the local Government of Tibet on Measures for the Peaceful Liberation of Tibet was signed on 23 May 1951. This Agreement is an important and legally binding document for the Government of new China to settle its domestic ethnic question.

On 24 October of that same year, the Dalai Lama, as the highest leader of the local government of Tibet at the time, sent a telegram to Chairman Mao Zedong of the central People's Government to express his complete approval of and support to this Agreement. . . . Facts have shown explicitly that the realization of the peaceful liberation of Tibet is a concrete demonstration of the Chinese Government's exercising of sovereignty over Tibet as well as an internal affair of China. . . .

2. The Chinese Government succeeded in abolishing the feudal system of serfdom and establishing a socialist democratic system, making a great historic contribution to ensuring for the Tibetan people human rights and fundamental freedoms. During several hundred years when Tibet was governed by the local government of Tibet led by successive Dalai Lama, a feudal system of serfdom that integrates religion with politics was practised there. . . . Ruled by such a system, the serfs and slaves, accounting for more than 95% of the population, had no political and social rights to speak of, and they were even deprived of their most basic personal freedoms and most fundamental right to subsistence. They possessed no means of production whatsoever; and they themselves and their descendants were part of the property of the slave owners. . . . In 1959, the democratic reform was successfully carried out in Tibet by the Government of China, and the dark feudal system of serfdom abolished. The Tibetan people thus completely freed themselves from their untold sufferings under the slave owners, attained for the first time their human rights and fundamental freedoms, and started to enjoy their citizen's and political rights guaranteed by the constitution of China and all the economic, social, and cultural rights. In the face of all this, a small number of self-exiled Tibetan separatists and certain supporting foreign political forces have called the abolishment of the feudal system . . . deprivation of the Tibetan people's basic human rights and freedoms. This is noting but confusing the rights and wrongs.

3. China is a unified multinational State. In addition to the Han nationality, which accounts for the overwhelming majority of the country's population, there are another 55 minority nationalities, including the Tibetans. In such a multinational State, the proper handling of the ethnic question and relationship is always a major issue concerning the country's stability and development. Therefore, ever since the founding of the People's Republic, the Government of new China has attached great importance to the ethnic question and work. In this connection, its basic lines and policies are designed to promote national equality and unity, practice regional autonomy in the areas of minority nationalities, conduct mutually beneficial cooperation, and achieve common development and prosperity of all nationalities. There are explicit provisions in both China's constitution and the Law on Regional National Autonomy stipulating that different nationalities enjoy completely equal rights in the political, economic, cultural, and other fields. These provisions have been carried out fully in Tibet.

Tibet is one of the autonomous regions of China and an administrative unit at the provincial level. The people's congress and government of the Tibet Autonomous Region not only have the same range of power as enjoyed by the local State organs in other provinces, but also enjoy many special rights for autonomous regions provided for in the Law on Regional National Autonomy. These special rights include: establishing autonomous organizations, exercising regional national autonomy, using and developing the spoken and written Tibetan language, formulating regulations on the exercise of autonomy and separate regulations according to the political, economic, and cultural features of Tibet, implementing State laws and policies in line with the local actual conditions, formulating and implementing special policies, managing and independently arranging projects of local economic development, independently managing educational, cultural, and public health undertakings, protecting and developing traditional culture, protecting local natural environment, and independently exploring and using local natural resources.

The Tibetan people, like other nationalities in China, enjoy all the citizen's rights embodied in the constitution and the State laws, such as freedom of religious belief, and also enjoy other special rights designed by autonomous organizations' rules and regulations to preserve the special interest of the minority nationalities. Over the past 40 years, achievements recognized by the whole world have been achieved in Tibet's economic and cultural development. The splendid traditional culture of Tibet has been inherited and developed with unprecedented progress in such fields as education, science, culture, public health, as well as other social welfare undertakings for the public benefit. The people's living standard has been raised remarkably, and the religious belief of the Tibetan people is fully respected and protected. . . .

4. "To safeguard State unity and national unity" and "to prohibit any act which undermines the unity of the nationalities or instigates national division" are basic principles of China's constitution and basic obligations that should be performed by every Chinese citizen. However, since autumn in 1987, a handful of Tibetan separatists, supported by certain anti-China forces, designed and instigated many rounds of riots in Lhasa, the capital of the Tibet Autonomous Region. Under the pretext of the "independence of Tibet," they engaged in attacking, smashing, looting, and burning many government institutions; breaking into shops; setting

fire to public facilities; damaging schools; and even opening fire on policemen and innocent citizens. Their acts seriously disrupted social order and harmed and threatened the life and property of the Lhasa people and their normal operation of work and living.... It is entirely necessary and justified for the Chinese Government to adopt measures to resolutely suppress such riots. Such measures are not violations of human rights; on the contrary, they are just and indisputable actions indispensable for the maintenance of the legitimate rights of the large number of citizens.

5. During the process of suppressing the riots, the public security and legal departments of the autonomous region, based on law, took away from the rioting places 1,025 people engaged in riots for interrogation, among which 807 were released after interrogation and education within the legal timeframe, 97 received disciplinary sanctions, and only 121 were sentenced according to law. Nobody was executed. The judiciary departments of the autonomous region, strictly observing provisions of prohibiting maltreatment to prisoners, rendered humanitarian treatment to the criminals serving their sentences....

6. For many years, certain international forces have supported and connived at the activities carried out by a handful of separatists to separate Tibet from China. In order to find excuses for such activities, they have used "the human rights question in Tibet" to willfully attack and slander the Chinese Government. This is the background to why some members of the [UN] Sub-Commission [on the Prevention of Discrimination and Protection of Minorities] plotted the adoption of the resolution of the situation in Tibet....

Three items attached to the Chinese Government's reply were reproduced in Annex I of the UN Secretary-General's report: (1) a press release, dated 24 August 1991, setting out the remarks of the spokesman for the Chinese Foreign Ministry; (2) a statement on the social structure and social formation in Tibet before 1959; and (3) a statement on human rights protection in Tibet.

Information from a number of non-governmental organizations was reproduced in Annex II of the report: (1) Amnesty International, "China: Amnesty International's Concerns in Tibet"; (2) Disabled People's International, Human Rights Advocates, International Federation of Human Rights, et al., "The Situation in Tibet: A Survey of Current Human Rights Violations, including Denial of the Right to Self-Determination"; (3) Habitat International Coalition, "Analysis of the Situation regarding the Rights to Adequate Housing in Tibet"; (4) International Fellowship of Reconciliation, "Violations of Human Rights in Tibet: A Social and Cultural Perspective"; (5) International League for Human Rights, "Human Rights Violations in Tibet"; (6) Law Association for Asia and the Western Pacific, "Extrajudicial Forms of Political Control in Tibet"; (7) Minority Rights Group, "The Exercise of Economic, Social, and Cultural Rights in China: A Tibetan Perspective."

The Secretary-General also drew attention, in Part C of the report, to other relevant UN documentation, as follows:

In the report submitted by the Special Rapporteur on summary or arbitrary executions to the Commission at its 48th session (E/CN.4/1992/30), paragraphs 91 to 98 contain relevant communications of the Special Rapporteur to the Government of China, as well as the Government's reply thereto. The report of the Special Rapporteur on the question of torture (E/CN.4/1992/17) also reflects, in paragraphs 41 to 43, relevant appeals.... The Working Group on Enforced or Involuntary Disappearances also reports in paragraphs 83 to 88 of document E/CN.4/1992/18, on communications transmitted to the Government of China, as well as on the Government's replies. Finally, the report of the Special Rapporteur on Religious Intolerance (E/CN.4/1992/52) also contains, in paragraphs 20 to 22, relevant communications....

**BIBLIOGRAPHY.** Amnesty International. *China: The Massacre of June 1989 and its Aftermath.* London: 1990. NGO factfinding report, in English.

—————. *China: Prisoners of Conscience in the People's Republic of China.* London: 1987. NGO report, in English.

—————. *China: Torture and Ill-Treatment of Prisoners.* London: 1987. NGO report, in English.

—————. *People's Republic of China: Summary of Amnesty International's Concerns, January 1987–April 1988.* London: 1988. NGO report, in English.

Asia Watch. *Anthems of Defeat: Crackdown in Hunan Province 1989–1992.* New York: 1992. NGO factfinding report, in English.

—————. *Detained in China and Tibet: A Directory of Political and Religious Prisoners.* New York: Human Rights Watch, 1994. NGO report, in English.

—————. *Economic Reform, Political Repression*, vol. 5, no. 4. New York: Human Rights Watch, 1993. NGO report, in English.

—————. *Prison Labor in China.* New York: Human Rights Watch, 1991. NGO factfinding report, in English.

—————. *Punishment Season: Human Rights in China after Martial Law.* New York: Human Rights Watch, 1990. NGO factfinding report, in English.

—————. *Rough Justice in Beijing: Punishing the "Black Hands" of Tiananmen Square.* New York: Human Rights Watch, 1991. NGO factfinding report, in English.

Asia Watch and Human Rights in China. *The Price of Obscurity in China: Revelations about Prisoners Arrested after June 4, 1989.* New York: Human Rights Watch, 1994. NGO report, in English.

Cheng, Chu-yuang. *Behind the Tiananmen Massacre: Social, Political, and Economic Ferment in China.* Boulder, CO, USA: Westview Press, 1990. Scholarly monograph, in English.

Cohen, Roberta. "People's Republic of China: The Human Rights Exception," *Human Rights Quarterly* 9, no. 4 (November 1987): 447–549. Scholarly article, in English.

Donnelly, J., and R. E. Howard, eds. *International Handbook on Human Rights.* Westport, CT, USA: Greenwood Press, 1987. Scholarly edited collection, in English.

Edwards, R. R., L. Henkin, and A. J. Nathan. *Human Rights in Contemporary China.* New York: Columbia University Press, 1986. Scholarly essays, in English.

Gap Min, Pyong. "A Comparison of the Korean Minorities in China and Japan," *International Migration Review* 26, no. 1

(Spring 1992): 4–21. Scholarly article, in English; bibliography, pp. 20–21.

Hong Kong Trade Union Education Centre. *A Moment of Truth: Workers' Participation in China's 1989 Democracy Movement and the Emergence of Independent Unions.* Hong Kong: Asia Monitor Resource Center, 1991. NGO monograph, in English.

Hsiung, James C. *Human Rights in East Asia: A Cultural Perspective.* New York: Pergamon House, 1985. Scholarly edited collection, in English.

Human Rights Watch. "China and Tibet," in *Human Rights Watch World Report 1995*, pp. 142–149. NGO report, in English.

International League for Human Rights. *Getting Down to Business: The Human Rights Responsibilities of China's Investors and Trade Partners.* New York: 1992. NGO report, in English.

International League for Human Rights and the Ad Hoc Study Group on Human Rights in China. *Winter in Beijing: Continuing Repression since the Beijing Massacre.* New York: 1990. NGO report, in English.

Kent, Ann E. *Human Rights in the People's Republic of China: National and International Dimensions.* Canberra, Australia: Peace Research Centre, Australian National University, 1990. Scholarly monograph, in English; bibliography, pp. 83–90.

Khu, Josephine M. T. "Selected Bibliography of English-Language Materials on the Law of the People's Republic of China," *Columbia Journal of Transnational Law* 28, no. 2 (1990): 531–575. Bibliography, in English.

Koch-Miramond, L., et al. *La Chine et les droits de l'homme* (China and Human Rights). Paris: Harmattan, 1991. NGO monograph, in French.

Kolodner, Eric. "Religious Rights in China: A Comparison of International Human Rights Law and Chinese Domestic Legislation," *Human Rights Quarterly* 16, no. 3 (August 1994): 455–490. Scholarly article, in English.

Mok Chiu Yu, and J. Frank Harrison. *Voices from Tiananmen Square: Beijing Spring and the Democracy Movement.* Montreal, Canada: Black Rose Books, 1990. Monograph, in English.

Oksenberg, Michel, L. R. Sullivan, and Marc Lambert, eds. *Beijing Spring, 1989: Confrontation and Conflict. The Basic Documents.* Armonk, NY, USA: M.E. Sharpe, 1990. Collective works, in English.

Schacht, Chris. *Report of the Australian Human Rights Delegation to China.* Canberra, Australia: Australian Government Publishing Service, 1991. Government factfinding report, in English.

Whitfield, Susan, ed. *After the Event: Human Rights and their Future in China.* London: Wellsweep Press, 1993. Conference report, in English.

Wing-yue, Leung. *Smashing the Iron Rice Pot: Workers and Unions in China's Market Socialism.* Kowloon, Hong Kong: Asia Monitor Resource Center, 1988. NGO report, in English.

Wu, Hongda Harry. *Laogai: The Chinese Gulag.* Boulder, CO, USA: Westview Press, 1992. Monograph, in English.

Wu, Y., F. Michael, J. F. Copper, T. Lee, M. Hsia Chang, and A. J. Gregor. *Human Rights in the People's Republic of China.* Boulder, CO, USA: Westview Press, 1988. Scholarly study, in English.

*Tibet.* Amnesty International. *China: No Progress on Human Rights: Update No. 1 to "Detained in China and Tibet."* New York: Human Rights Watch, 1994. NGO report, in English.

Asia Watch. *Human Rights in Tibet.* New York: Human Rights Watch, 1988. NGO report, in English.

————. *Merciless Repression: Human Rights in Tibet.* New York: Human Rights Watch, 1990. NGO factfinding report, in English.

Donnet, Pierre-Antoine. *Tibet mort ou vif* (Tibet Dead or Alive). Paris: Gallimard, 1990. Monograph, in French; bibliography, pp. 351–354.

Donnet, Pierre-Antoine, Guy Privat, and Jean-Paul Ribes, eds. *Tibet: des journalistes témoignent* (Tibet: Journalists Testify). Paris: Harmattan, 1992. Report, in French.

Forbes, Ann, and Carole McGranahan. *Developing Tibet?: A Survey of International Development Projects.* Washington, D.C.: Cultural Survival & International Campaign for Tibet, 1992. Report, in English.

Gesellschaft fur Bedrohte Volker und Verein der Tibetaner in Deutschland (Association for Endangered Peoples and Association of Tibetans in Germany). *Tibet: Traum oder Trauma?* (Tibet: Dream or Trauma?). Göttingen, FRG: 1987. NGO report, in German.

International Alert. *Tibet: An International Consultation, 6–8 July 1990, London.* London: 1990. Conference report, in English.

International Campaign for Tibet. *Forbidden Freedoms: Beijing's Control of Religion in Tibet.* Washington, D.C.: 1990. NGO factfinding report, in English; bibliography, pp. 97–100.

Kelly, Petra K., Gert Bastian, and Pat Aiello, eds. *The Anguish of Tibet.* Berkeley, CA, USA: Parallax Press, 1991. Monograph, in English; bibliography, pp. 378–382.

Law Association for Asia and the Pacific and Tibet Information Network. *Defying the Dragon: China and Human Rights in Tibet.* London: 1991. NGO factfinding report, in English.

Leckie, Scott. *Destruction by Design: Housing Rights Violations in Tibet.* Utrecht, the Netherlands: Centre on Housing Rights and Evictions, 1994. NGO monograph, in English.

Ledger, W. P. *The Chinese and Human Rights in Tibet.* London: Parliamentary Human Rights Group, 1988. NGO report, in English.

Moquette, Marc. "Tibet, the Right to Self-Determination and Territorial Integrity," *Netherlands Quarterly of Human Rights* 8, no. 3 (1990): 261–274. Scholarly article, in English.

Ruiz, Hiram A. *Tibetan Refugees: Still at Risk.* Washington, D.C.: US Committee for Refugees, 1990. NGO factfinding report, in English.

Van Walt Van Praag, Michael C. "Population Transfer and Survival of the Tibetan Identity," *Interculture* 23, no. 1 (Winter 1990): 8–23. Article, in English and French.

————. *The Status of Tibet: History, Rights, and Prospects in International Law.* Boulder, CO, USA: Westview Press, 1987. Scholarly monograph, in English.

**CHRISTIAN DEMOCRAT INTERNATIONAL.** An international non-governmental organization in consultative status with the UN ECONOMIC AND SOCIAL COUNCIL (Category II) and with UNESCO and UNCTAD, the Council draws together 55 national Christian Democratic organizations in 50 countries and territories.

CDI conducts seminars on Christian Democratic ideology and has a Permanent Committee on Human Rights. It strives for world coordination of Christian Democratic organizations in the promotion of humanist values aimed at a communitarian, participatory, and pluralist society. One of its primary goals, as formulated in a resolution on human rights issued by its

International Political Bureau in 1988, is "to work for the democratization of those countries where people are submitted to regimes which deny political, social, economic and cultural pluralism and are not generated by free elections." The resolution adds that "a respect for human rights means [1] a condition for citizens' participation . . . in their country's affairs, [2] a guarantee for peace, as important as disarmament, [and 3] an assurance that the benefits of development will not be used by rulers . . . to strengthen their position, but will be shared by all citizens in the framework of social justice."

CDI publishes *Khristianskaya Demokratia* six times a year; *Human Rights* five times a year; and *DC-Info* and *Documents* four times a year, all in English, French, and Spanish. In addition, *DC-Info* also is sometimes published in German, Dutch, Hungarian, Polish, Italian, and Russian.

Christian Democrat International. Address: Rue de la Victoire 16, Boite 1, B-1060 Brussels, Belgium. Telephone: (32-2) 537-13-22. Fax: (32-2) 537-93-48. Telex: 61118 IDC. Secretary-General: André Louis.

**CHRISTIAN PEACE CONFERENCE.** An international non-governmental organization in consultative status (Category II) with the UN ECONOMIC AND SOCIAL COUNCIL, the COMMISSION ON HUMAN RIGHTS, and UNESCO, CPC is also a member of the CONGO Committee on Human Rights.

CPC was founded in 1958 as an international movement of theologians, clergy, and laymen and grew out of their conviction of faith in a time of rising international tension. CPC aims to be a forum in which Christians from all over the world can meet together and search for solutions to political, social, and economic problems. Through regional Committees and member churches in 80 countries and territories, CPC works for world peace through disarmament, human rights, international cooperation, and peaceful coexistence efforts. The Conference promotes social and economic structures aimed toward eliminating oppression, exploitation, racial discrimination, hunger, and illiteracy and opposes imperialism.

The Christian Peace Conference publishes *CPC Information* ten times a year in English and German.

Christian Peace Conference. Address: Prokopova 4, 130 00 Prague, Czech Republic. Telephone: (42-2) 27-97-22. Fax: (42-2) 27-68-53. Coordinating Secretary: Kenyon E. Wright.

**CITY UNIVERSITY OF NEW YORK, INTERNATIONAL WOMEN'S HUMAN RIGHTS LAW CLINIC.** Established in 1992, the Clinic is an advocacy program with two objectives: (1) to assist women in developing and pursuing international, regional, and local strategies to advance the human rights of women, with a focus on gender violence, reproductive and sexual rights, health, and the indivisibility of social and economic rights; and (2) to educate future lawyers, as well as visiting legal scholars and activists, in developing their ability to use the international system to advance women's human rights. The program consists of a seminar in human rights law from a gender perspective and engagements in legal advocacy projects, such as interventions in the international and regional systems and applying international human rights concepts in domestic initiatives.

International Women's Human Rights Law Clinic. Address: City University of New York Law School, 65-21 Main Street, Flushing, NY 11367, USA. Telephone: (718) 575-4300. Fax: (718) 575-4478. Directors: Prof. Rhonda Copelon and Prof. Celina Romany.

**CIVIL AND POLITICAL RIGHTS: SIRACUSA PRINCIPLES.** The "Siracusa Principles on the Limitation and Derogation Provisions of the International Covenant on Civil and Political Rights," set out below, were formulated by a group of 31 distinguished experts in international law, convened by the International Commission of Jurists, its American Association, the International Association of Penal Law, the Urban Morgan Institute of Human Rights, and the International Institute of Higher Studies in Criminal Sciences, meeting at Siracusa, Italy, from 30 April to 4 May 1984. Experts who participated came from Brazil, Canada, Chile, Egypt, France, Greece, Hungary, India, Ireland, Kuwait, the Netherlands, Norway, Poland, Switzerland, Turkey, the United Kingdom, the United States, the UN Center for Human Rights, the INTERNATIONAL LABOR ORGANIZATION, and the sponsoring organizations.

The participants agreed upon the need for a close examination of the conditions and grounds for permissible limitations and derogations enunciated in the Covenant in order to achieve an effective implementation of the rule of law. As frequently emphasized by the UN General Assembly, a uniform interpretation of limitations on rights in the Covenant is of great importance.

In examining these limitations and derogations, the participants sought to identify their legitimate objectives, the general principles of interpretation that govern their imposition and application, and some of the main features of the grounds for limitation or derogation. It was recognized that other criteria determined the scope of the rights in the Covenant, e.g., the concept of arbitrariness, but time was not available to examine them.

Participants in the conference agreed that (a) there is a close relationship between respect for human rights and the maintenance of international peace and security; indeed, the systematic violation of human rights undermines national security and public order and may constitute a threat to international peace; and (b) notwithstanding the different stages of economic development reached in different States, the implementation of human rights is an essential requirement for development in the broadest sense.

The principles set out below were considered by participants in the conference to reflect the present state of international law, with the exception of certain recommendations indicated by the use of the verb "should," instead of "shall."

The principles, drawn to the attention of the Commission on Human Rights at its 1985 session by the permanent representative of the Netherlands to the UN office at Geneva, are as follows (UN Doc. E/CN.4/1985/4):

### Part I. The Limitation Clauses in the Covenant

A. General Interpretative Principles relating to the Justification of Limitations. (The term "limitations" in these principles includes the term "restrictions" as used in the Covenant.)

1. No limitations or grounds for applying them to rights guaranteed by the Covenant are permitted other than those contained in the terms of the Covenant itself.

2. The scope of a limitation referred to in the Covenant shall not be interpreted so as to jeopardize the essence of the right concerned.

3. All limitation clauses shall be interpreted strictly and in favour of the rights at issue.

4. All limitations shall be interpreted in the light and context of the particular right concerned.

5. All limitations on a right recognized by the Covenant shall be provided for by law and be compatible with the objects and purposes of the Covenant.

6. No limitation referred to in the Covenant shall be applied for any purpose other than that for which it has been prescribed.

7. No limitation shall be applied in an arbitrary manner.

8. Every limitation imposed shall be subject to the possibility of challenge to and remedy against its abusive application.

9. No limitation on a right recognized by the Covenant shall discriminate contrary to article 2, paragraph 1.

10. Whenever a limitation is required in the terms of the Covenant to be "necessary", this term implies that the limitation:

    (a) Is based on one of the grounds justifying limitations recognized by the relevant article of the Covenant,

    (b) Responds to a pressing public or social need,

    (c) Pursues a legitimate aim, and

    (d) Is proportionate to that aim.

Any assessment as to the necessity of a limitation shall be made on objective considerations.

11. In applying a limitation, a State shall use no more restrictive means than are required for the achievement of the purpose of the limitation.

12. The burden of justifying a limitation upon a right guaranteed under the Covenant lies with the State.

13. The requirement expressed in article 12 of the Covenant, that any restrictions be consistent with other rights recognized in the Covenant, is implicit in limitations to the other rights recognized in the Covenant.

14. The limitation clauses of the Covenant shall not be interpreted to restrict the exercise of any human rights protected to a greater extent by other international obligations binding on the State.

B. Interpretative Principles relating to Specific Limitation Clauses.

"Prescribed by law." 15. No limitation on the exercise of human rights shall be made unless provided for by national law of general application which is consistent with the Covenant and is in force at the time the limitation is applied.

16. Laws imposing limitations on the exercise of human rights shall not be arbitrary or unreasonable.

17. Legal rules limiting the exercise of human rights shall be clear and accessible to everyone.

18. Adequate safeguards and effective remedies shall be provided by law against illegal or abusive imposition or application of limitations on human rights.

"In a democratic society." 19. The expression "in a democratic society" shall be interpreted as imposing a further restriction on the limitation clauses it qualifies.

20. The burden is upon a State imposing limitations so qualified to demonstrate that the limitations do not impair the democratic functioning of the society.

21. While there is no single model of a democratic society, a society which recognizes, respects and protects the human rights set forth in the Charter of the United Nations and the Universal Declaration of Human Rights may be viewed as meeting this definition.

"Public order." 22. The expression "public order (ordre public)" as used in the Covenant may be defined as the sum of rules that ensure the functioning of society or the set of fundamental principles on which society is founded. Respect for human rights is part of public order (ordre public).

23. Public order (ordre public) shall be interpreted in the context of the purpose of the particular human right which is limited on this ground.

24. State organs or agents responsible for the maintenance of public order (ordre public) shall be subject to controls in the exercise of their power through the parliament, courts or other competent independent bodies.

"Public health." 25. Public health may be invoked as a ground for limiting certain rights in order to allow a State to take measures dealing with a serious threat to the health of the population or individual members of the population. These measures must be specifically aimed at preventing disease or injury or providing care for the sick and injured.

26. Due regard shall be had to the International Health Regulations of the World Health Organization.

"Public morals." 27. Since public morality varies over time and from one culture to another, a State which invokes public morality as a ground for restricting human rights, while enjoying a certain margin of discretion, shall demonstrate that the limitation in question is essential to the maintenance of respect for fundamental values of the community.

28. The margin of discretion left to States does not apply to the rule of non-discrimination as defined in the Covenant.

"National security." 29. National security may be invoked

to justify measures limiting certain rights only when they are taken to protect the existence of the nation, its territorial integrity or political independence against force or threat of force.

30. National security cannot be invoked as a reason for imposing limitations to prevent merely local or relatively isolated threats to law and order.

31. National security cannot be used as a pretext for imposing vague or arbitrary limitations and may only be invoked when there exist adequate safeguards and effective remedies against abuse.

32. The systematic violation of human rights undermines national security and may jeopardize international peace and security. A State responsible for such violation shall not invoke national security as a justification for measures aimed at suppressing opposition to such violation or at perpetrating repressive practices against its population.

"Public safety." 33. Public safety means protection against danger to the safety of persons, to their life or physical integrity or serious damage to their property.

34. The need to protect public safety can justify limitations provided by law. It cannot be used for imposing vague or arbitrary limitations and may only be invoked when there exist adequate safeguards and effective remedies against abuse.

"Rights and freedoms of others" or the "Rights and reputations of others." 35. The scope of the rights and freedoms of others that may act as a limitation upon rights in the Covenant extends beyond the rights and freedoms recognized in the Covenant.

36. When a conflict exists between a right protected in the Covenant and one which is not, recognition and consideration should be given to the fact that the Covenant seeks to protect the most fundamental rights and freedoms. In this context special weight should be afforded to the rights from which no derogation may be made under article 4 of the Covenant.

37. A limitation to a human right based upon the reputation of others shall not be used to protect the State and its officials from public opinion or criticism.

Restrictions on public trial. 38. All trials shall be public unless the Court determines in accordance with law that:

The press or the public should be excluded from all or part of a trial on the basis of specific findings announced in open court showing that the interest of the private lives of the parties or their families or of juveniles so requires; or

The exclusion is strictly necessary to avoid publicity (a) prejudicial to the fairness of the trial or (b) endangering public morals, public order (ordre public) or national security in a democratic society.

**Part II. Derogations in a Public Emergency**

A. "Public Emergency which Threatens the Life of the Nation."

39. A State party may take measures derogating from its obligations under the International Covenant on Civil and Political Rights pursuant to article 4 (hereinafter called "derogation measures") only when faced with a situation of exceptional and actual or imminent danger which threatens the life of the nation. A threat to the life of the nation is one that:

(a) Affects the whole of the population and either the whole or part of the territory of the State, and

(b) Threatens the physical integrity of the popula-

tion, the political independence or the territorial integrity of the State or the existence or basic functioning of institutions indispensable to ensure and protect the rights recognized in the Covenant.

40. Internal conflict and unrest that do not constitute a grave and imminent threat to the life of the nation cannot justify derogations under article 4.

41. Economic difficulties per se cannot justify derogation measures.

B. Proclamation, Notification and Termination of a Public Emergency.

42. A State party derogating from its obligations under the Covenant shall make an official proclamation of the existence of a public emergency threatening the life of the nation.

43. Procedures under national law for the proclamation of a state of emergency shall be prescribed in advance of the emergency.

44. A State party derogating from its obligations under the Covenant shall immediately notify the other States parties to the Covenant, through the intermediary of the Secretary-General of the United Nations, of the provisions from which it has derogated and the reasons by which it was actuated.

45. The notification shall contain sufficient information to permit the States parties to exercise their rights and discharge their obligations under the Covenant. In particular it shall contain:

(a) The provisions of the Covenant from which it has derogated;

(b) A copy of the proclamation of emergency, together with the constitutional provisions, legislation, or decrees governing the state of emergency in order to assist the States parties to appreciate the scope of the derogation;

(c) The effective date of the imposition of the state of emergency and the period for which it has been proclaimed;

(d) An explanation of the reasons which actuated the Government's decision to derogate, including a brief description of the factual circumstances leading up to the proclamation of the state of emergency;

(e) A brief description of the anticipated effect of the derogation measures on the rights recognized by the Covenant, including copies of decrees derogating from these rights issued prior to the notification.

46. States parties may require that further information necessary to enable them to carry out their role under the Covenant be provided through the intermediary of the Secretary-General.

47. A State party which fails to make an immediate notification in due form of its derogation is in breach of its obligations to other States parties and may be deprived of the defences otherwise available to it in procedures under the Covenant.

48. A State party availing itself of the right of derogation pursuant to article 4 shall terminate such derogation in the shortest time required to bring to an end the public emergency which threatens the life of the nation.

49. The State party shall, on the date on which it terminates such derogation, inform the other States parties, through the intermediary of the Secretary-General of the United Nations, of the fact of the termination.

50. On the termination of a derogation pursuant to article 4, all rights and freedoms protected by the Covenant shall be restored in full. A review of the continuing consequences of derogation measures shall be made as soon as possible.

Steps shall be taken to correct injustices and to compensate those who have suffered injustice during or in consequence of the derogation measures.

C. "Strictly Required by the Exigencies of the Situation."

51. The severity, duration and geographic scope of any derogation measure shall be such only as are strictly necessary to deal with the threat to the life of the nation and are proportionate to its nature and extent.

52. The competent national authorities shall have a duty to assess individually the necessity of any derogation measure taken or proposed to deal with the specific dangers posed by the emergency.

53. A measure is not strictly required by the exigencies of the situation where ordinary measures permissible under the specific limitation clauses of the Covenant would be adequate to deal with the threat to the life of the nation.

54. The principle of strict necessity shall be applied in an objective manner. Each measure shall be directed to an actual, clear, present or imminent danger and may not be imposed merely because of an apprehension of potential danger.

55. The national constitution and laws governing states of emergency shall provide for prompt and periodic independent review by the legislature of the necessity for derogation measures.

56. Effective remedies shall be available to persons claiming that derogation measures affecting them are not strictly required by the exigencies of the situation.

57. In determining whether derogation measures are strictly required by the exigencies of the situation, the judgement of the national authorities cannot be accepted as conclusive.

D. Non-derogable Rights.

58. No State party shall, even in time of emergency threatening the life of the nation, derogate from the Covenant's guarantees of the right to life; freedom from torture, cruel, inhuman or degrading treatment or punishment, and from medical or scientific experimentation without free consent; freedom from slavery or involuntary servitude; the right not to be imprisoned for contractual debt; the right not to be convicted or sentenced to a heavier penalty by virtue of retroactive criminal legislation; the right to recognition as a person before the law; and freedom of thought, conscience and religion. These rights are not derogable under any conditions even for the asserted purpose of preserving the life of the nation.

59. States parties to the Covenant, as part of their obligation to ensure the enjoyment of these rights to all persons within their jurisdiction (article 3, paragraph 1), and to adopt measures to secure an effective remedy for violations (article 2, paragraph 3), shall take special precautions in time of public emergency to ensure that neither official nor semi-official groups engage in a practice of arbitrary and extrajudicial killings or involuntary disappearances, that persons in detention are protected against torture and other forms of cruel, inhuman or degrading treatment or punishment, and that no persons are convicted or punished under laws or decrees with retroactive effect.

60. The ordinary courts should maintain their jurisdiction, even in a time of public emergency, to adjudicate any complaint that a non-derogable right has been violated.

E. Some General Principles on the Introduction and Application of a Public Emergency and Consequent Derogation Measures.

61. Derogation from rights recognized under international law in order to respond to a threat to the life of the nation is not exercised in a legal vacuum. It is authorized by law and as such it is subject to several legal principles of general application.

62. A proclamation of a public emergency shall be made in good faith based upon an objective assessment of the situation in order to determine to what extent, if any, it poses a threat to the life of the nation. A proclamation of a public emergency, and consequent derogations from Covenant obligations that are not made in good faith, are violations of international law.

63. The provisions of the Covenant allowing for certain derogations in a public emergency are to be interpreted restrictively.

64. In a public emergency the rule of law shall still prevail. Derogation is an authorized and limited prerogative to respond adequately to a threat to the life of the nation. The derogating State shall have the burden of justifying its actions under law.

65. The Covenant subordinates all procedures to the basic objectives of human rights. Article 5, paragraph 1, of the Covenant sets definite limits to actions taken under the Covenant:

"Nothing in the present Covenant may be interpreted as implying for any State, group or person any right to engage in any activity or perform any act aimed at the destruction of any of the rights and freedoms recognized herein or at their limitation to a greater extent than is provided for in the present Covenant."

Article 29, paragraph 2, of the Universal Declaration of Human Rights sets out the ultimate purpose of law:

"In the exercise of his rights and freedoms, everyone shall be subject only to such limitations as are determined by law solely for the purpose of securing due recognition and respect for the rights and freedoms of others and of meeting the just requirements of morality, public order and the general welfare in a democratic society."

These provisions apply with full force to claims that a situation constitutes a threat to the life of a nation and hence enables authorities to derogate.

66. A bona fide proclamation of a public emergency permits a derogation from specified obligations in the Covenant, but does not authorize a general departure from international obligations. The Covenant in articles 4, paragraph 1 and 5, paragraph 2, expressly prohibits derogations which are inconsistent with other obligations under international law. In this regard, particular note should be taken of international obligations which apply in a public emergency under the Geneva and ILO Conventions.

67. In a situation of a non-international armed conflict, a State party to the 1949 Geneva Conventions for the protection of war victims may not under any circumstances suspend the right to a trial by a court offering the essential guarantees of independence and impartiality (article 3 common to the 1949 Conventions). Under the 1977 additional Protocol II the following rights with respect to penal prosecution shall be respected under all circumstances by States parties to the Protocol:

(a) The duty to give notice of charges without delay and to grant the necessary rights and means of defence;

(b) Conviction only on the basis of individual penal responsibility;

(c) The right not to be convicted, or sentenced to a heavier penalty, by virtue of retroactive criminal legislation;

(d) Presumption of innocence;

(e) Trial in the presence of the accused;

(f) No obligation on the accused to testify against himself or to confess guilt;

(g) Duty to advise the convicted person on judicial and other remedies.

68. The ILO basic human rights Conventions contain a number of rights dealing with such matters as forced labour, freedom of association, equality in employment and trade-union and workers' rights which are additional to those in the Covenant. Some of these are not subject to derogation during an emergency; others permit derogation, but only to the extent strictly necessary to meet the exigencies of the situation.

69. No State, including those that are not parties to the Covenant, may suspend or violate, even in times of public emergency:

—The right to life;

—Freedom from torture or cruel, inhuman or degrading treatment or punishment and from medical or scientific experimentation;

—The right not to be held in slavery or involuntary servitude; and

—The right not to be subjected to retroactive criminal penalties as defined in the Covenant.

Customary international law prohibits in all circumstances the denial of such fundamental rights.

70. Although protections against arbitrary arrest and detention (article 9) and the right to a fair and public hearing in the determination of a criminal charge (article 14) may be subject to legitimate limitations if strictly required by the exigencies of an emergency situation, the denial of certain rights fundamental to human dignity can never be strictly necessary in any conceivable emergency, and respect for them is essential in order to ensure enjoyment of non-derogable rights and to provide an effective remedy against their violation. In particular:

(a) All arrests and detention and the place of detention shall be recorded, if possible centrally, and made available to the public without delay;

(b) No person shall be detained for an indefinite period of time, whether detained pending judicial investigation or trial or detained without charge;

(c) No person shall be held in isolation without communication with his family, friend or lawyer for longer than a few days, e.g., three to seven days;

(d) Where persons are detained without charge, the need for their continued detention shall be considered periodically by an independent review tribunal;

(e) Any person charged with an offence shall be entitled to a fair trial by a competent, independent and impartial court established by law;

(f) Civilians shall normally be tried by the ordinary courts; where it is found strictly necessary to establish military tribunals or special courts to try civilians, their competence, independence and impartiality shall be ensured and the need for them reviewed periodically by the competent authority;

(g) Any person charged with a criminal offence shall be entitled to the presumption of innocence and to at least the following rights to ensure a fair trial:

—The right to be informed of the charges promptly, in detail and in a language he understands,

—The right to have adequate time and facilities to prepare the defence including the right to communicate confidentially with his lawyer,

—The right to a lawyer of his choice, with free legal assistance if he does not have the means to pay for it and to be informed of this right,

—The right to be present at the trial,

—The right not to be compelled to testify against himself or to make a confession,

—The right to obtain the attendance and examination of defence witnesses,

—The right to be tried in public save where the court orders otherwise on grounds of security with adequate safeguards to prevent abuse,

—The right to appeal to a higher court;

(h) An adequate record of the proceedings shall be kept in all cases;

(i) No person shall be tried or punished again for an offence for which he has already been convicted or acquitted.

F. Recommendations concerning the Functions and Duties of the Human Rights Committee and United Nations Bodies.

71. In the exercise of its power to study, report and make general comments on States parties' reports under article 40 of the Covenant, the Human Rights Committee may and should examine the compliance of States parties with the provisions of article 4. Likewise it may and should do so when exercising its powers in relevant cases under article 41 and the Optional Protocol relating, respectively, to inter-State and individual communications.

72. In order to determine whether the requirements of article 4, paragraphs 1 and 2 have been met and for the purpose of supplementing information in States parties' reports, members of the Human Rights Committee, as persons of recognized competence in the field of human rights, may and should have regard to information they consider to be reliable provided by other intergovernmental bodies, nongovernmental organizations and communications by individuals.

73. The Human Rights Committee should develop a procedure for requesting additional reports under article 40, paragraph 1 (b), from States parties which have given notification of derogation under article 4, paragraph 3, or which are reasonably believed by the Committee to have imposed emergency measures subject to the constraints of article 4. Such additional reports should relate to questions concerning the emergency in so far as it affects the implementation of the Covenant and should be dealt with by the Committee at the earliest possible date.

74. In order to enable the Human Rights Committee to perform its fact-finding functions more effectively it should develop its procedures for the consideration of communications under the Optional Protocol in order to permit the hearing of oral submissions and evidence and visits to States parties alleged to be in violation of the Covenant. If necessary, the States parties to the Optional Protocol should consider amending it to this effect.

75. The United Nations Commission on Human Rights should request its Sub-Commission on Prevention of Discrimination and Protection of Minorities to prepare an annual list of States, whether parties to the Covenant or not, that proclaim, maintain or terminate a public emergency together with:

—In the case of a State party, the proclamation and notification; and

—In the case of other States, any available and apparently reliable information concerning the proclamation, threat to the life of the nation, derogation measures and their proportionality, non-discrimination and respect for non-derogable rights.

76. The United Nations Commission on Human Rights and its Sub-Commission should continue to utilize the technique of appointment of Special Rapporteurs and investi-

gatory and fact-finding bodies in relation to prolonged public emergencies.

**SEE ALSO** *International Covenant on Civil and Political Rights; Women: Inter-American Convention on the Granting of Civil Rights to Women.*

**CIVIL DEFENSE FORCES.** In its 1992 report to the UN **Commission on Human Rights,** the Working Group on Enforced or Involuntary Disappearances drew attention to the worldwide proliferation of so-called "civil-defense forces" not belonging to or accountable to any regular law-enforcement agency, some of which had taken actions seriously jeopardizing the enjoyment of human rights.

At the request of the Commission, the UN Secretary-General collected information on domestic law and practice with regard to such forces and submitted a preliminary report on the subject to the Commission at its 1993 session (E/CN.4/1993/34). A final report (E/CN.4/1994/38) was placed before the Commission at its 1994 session. In that report, the information made available by governments was summarized as follows (section I A, paras. 5–12):

The responses received from States Members of the United Nations may be divided into three groups: (1) those which reported having no such forces; (ii) those which reported having no such forces, but provided legislation relating to law enforcement in general and/or public emergencies and natural disasters affecting the civilian population; and (iii) those which reported on the existence of such forces within their jurisdictions.

The sole exception to the above classificaion of responses was that of India, which reported that civil defence in that country "is not a 'Force' at all [but] is primarily a non-uniform voluntary organization . . . designed to operate during hostile attack with the following aims and objects: (a) to save life, (b) to minimize damage to property, and (c) to maintain continuity of production. In peace time, it generally does not play any role."

In the first group noted above, Nepal and San Marino reported that they had no forces as contemplated in Commission resolution 1993/54. Jordan, the Islamic Republic of Mauritania, Senegal, and Tunisia reported that they had no civil defence forces functioning outside the official organs of the State charged with the responsibility of law enforcement and/or national defence. Nepal and Senegal also reported that they had no laws for the establishment of such forces as those referred to in resolution 1993/54. Cape Verde reported that it had neither forces nor law on the matter, but was in the process of drafting relevant legislation. For its part, Honduras reported that it had neither forces nor law relating to civil defence forces in the sense of resolution 1993/54, but that such forces had once been created in the country during its July 1969 armed conflict with El Salvador; on that occasion, such forces had been created spontaneously in order to protect against attacks or sabotage directed against civil installations of strategic importance. Honduras further reported that a similar system of public

protection had also been improvised in response to the natural disaster caused by Hurricane Fifi in 1974, and that a Permanent Committee for Contingencies now exists to respond to such exceptional circumstances.

In the second group, Botswana reported that it had no such forces as those referred to in resolution 1993/54 and that matters of law enforcement and national defence were regulated, respectively, through police forces operating under the Police Act . . . and defence forces operating under the Defence Force Act. . . . In responding to the Secretary-General's inquiry on the subject of civil defence forces, Cameroon referred to its obligations under the four Geneva Conventions of 12 August 1949, the two Additional Protocols thereto of 8 June 1977, together with Law No. 86/16 of 6 December 1986 . . . concerning the general reorganization of civil protection; with regard to its practice, two principal bodies which were not official organs of State charged with law enforcement were engaged in the protection of human rights and fundamental freedoms: the Cameroon Red Cross and the National Commission on Human Rights and Freedoms. In referring to their laws on natural disasters and public emergencies, Cyprus drew attention to its Civil Defense Law of 1964–1988 and the related General Regulations of 1966–1982; Kazakhstan drew attention to Governmental Decrees of 1991 and 1992 under which the independent State Commission on Emergency Situations was constituted, organized, and functioned in connection with regulations articulated under five Governmental Regulations, one Decree of the Supreme Soviet (Council) of Kazakhstan, and one Presidential Decree; and Ukraine drew attention to its Law on the Civil Defence of Ukraine. Denmark stated that it had adopted a new act, the Preparedness Act, on 23 December 1992 (replacing its previous Civil Defence Act of July 1982), which had regulated matters concerning the protection of the civilian population under emergency situations such as natural disasters. With a similar reference to public emergencies, Croatia reported that it was preparing a law on the system of protection of people, property, and environment.

In the third group noted above, Peru, the Russia Federation, and Saudi Arabia reported as follows.

The Government of Peru emphasized the need to protect the civilian population, particularly in rural and native communities, against terrorist acts. In that context, many communities had organized their own self-defence committees. While serving an important need in the present day, those formations were said to have historical and cultural bases in the mountain and jungle regions of Peru. Similarly, the formation of civil-defence patrols (rondas campesinas) was said not to be a new phenomenon, but had traditionally existed in order to protect the property and population of rural communities; in modern times, the patrols defended their communities against terrorists and also assisted with community development. While the patrols generally concentrated on maters of security and defence, the Self-Defence Committees acted on the political and social levels, emphasizing development. They had enjoyed considerable success in achieving their objectives, primarily because they had a good knowledge of the territory where terrorists were active, they were familiar with local customs, and they spoke the local languages. In addition, the self-defence committees and the patrols had had a positive effect in urban areas where urban patrols (rondas urbanas) had been organized in order to help protect the most vulnerable populations, such as children, in the fight against drug-traffickers and also in order to assist these populations with development activities of a civil and social character. In recognizing and supporting the efforts of those popular organizations, the Government of Peru had promulgated the following laws: (i) Law No. 24571, which provided official recognitionto the rondas campesinas, pacíficas, democràtics y autónomas; (ii) Decree Law 740 on the Possession and Use of Arms by the rondas campesinas, which allowed for the use of arms with the previous authorization of the Joint Command of the Armed Forces; (iii) Decree Law 741, which provided official recognition to the self-defence committees; and (iv) Supreme Decree 077/DE-92, approving the Regulations on the Organization and Functions of the Self-Defence Committees authorized under the Joint Command of the Armed Forces. As a result of that legislation, the Government reported, there were approximately 4,732 such committees recognized in Peru, with about 370,000 members. As for the Montoneros, which Amnesty International mentioned in its report *AI Index: AMR 46/56/91* of November 1991 (see also E/CN.4/1993/34, para. 15), the Government denied completely the existence of such groups.

The Government of the Russian Federation reported that the Russian constitution prohibited "the creation of power structures and illegal armed forces not provided for by the Constitution and laws of the Russian Federation".... Therefore, the formation of civil-defence forces acting independently of State bodies and not under their jurisdiction was illegal under Russian legislation even in extraordinary circumstance. Nevertheless, two groups of the nature of those referred to in Commission resolution 1993/54 existed. The first group was legally formed as part of the restoration of the Cossacks' traditional system of self-administration as a result of the Decision of 16 July 1992 of the Supreme Soviet of the Russian Federation entitled "Rehabilitation of the Cossacks" and the 15 March 1993 Decree of the President of the Russian Federation on the "Reform of military structures and frontier and internal military forces on the territory of the northern Caucasian region of the Russian Federation and State support for the Cossacks." As a result, "voluntary non-military institutions with Cossack territorial communal self-administering bodies" had been created to participate, inter alia, "in civil and territorial defence activities, disasters, and emergency situations." The second group was composed of "illegal armed and paramilitary formations" which had emerged in certain regions, "particularly areas of conflict between various nationalities." Those groups were identified as either "socio-political organizations . . . of an extremist nature" or formations under "individual territorial authorities which exceed their constitutional powers." The Government noted that the "activities of such illegal formations may well threaten—and are indeed threatening—the enjoyment of human rights and fundamental freedoms." In an attempt to respond to that problem, the President of the Russian Federation had promulgated the Decree of 13 January 1993 on measures to exercise greater contorl over the formation and activities of such groups and, in particular, to ensure that unconstitutional "paramilitary groupings and armed formations are brought to justice." In response to the inter-ethnic conflict in North Ossetia and Ingushetiya, the Supreme Soviet of North Ossetia had taken the decision to create its own republican guard and a people's militia; however, in a decision of 13 January 1993 of the Presidium of the Supreme Soviet of the Russian Federation had found those formations unconstitutional and, therefore, invalid. The Government reported that it had as yet been impossible to resolve completely the problem of illegal armed formations acting under the guise of self-defence forces in certain regions of Russia, but the consolidation of democratic Rus-

sian legality following the Russian parliamentary elections of 12 December 1993 and the adoption of the new Russian constitution would help to solve that problem.

The Government of Saudi Arabia reported as follows: "In accordance with article 27 of the Basic Order of the Government of Saudi Arabia, the State protects human rights and the responsibilities of its civilian defence forces are entrusted with the State security institution and in accordance with Islamic legislation."

Information submitted by the Inter-American Commission on Human Rights was summarized as follows (section IB, paras. 13–15):

The Inter-American Commission on HumanRights submitted a copy of its Fourth Report on the Situation of Human Rights in Guatemala (OEA/Ser.L/V/II.83, Doc. 16 rev. of 1 June 1993), and also a copy of its Press Release No. 18/91 of 10 September 1993, issued in Guatemala City upon the conclusion of the Commission's visit to that country. Both the press release and the report address the problem of civilian self-defence patrols (patrullas de autodefensa civil) or, as they are now reported to be called, voluntary civil self-defence committees (comites voluntarios de autodefensa civil).

According to the Fourth Report on the Situation of Human Rights in Guatemala, patterns of violence whereby the right to life and humane treatment are violated may be classified into two major groups, one of which arises from "the illegal action of the self-defence patrols." Chapter VI of that report is devoted to a description of these forces and their evolution over the past dozen years since their creation under "the de facto military regime headed by General Efrain Rios Montt in late 1981" (pp. 53–61). The report also comments on the practice of enforced recruitment into the Civilian Self-Defence Patrols (p. 52), the consequences of refusing participation in such patrols (p. 54), and the remilitariation of the countryside through the reconstitution and expansion of civil-defence forces under the rubric of Voluntary Civilian Self-Defence Committees since August 1992 (pp. 54–60). Several statements and complaints on these issues received by the Inter-American Commission are briefly summarized in the report. In relation to mass graves thought to be the burial sites of some of the 45,000 Guatemalans said to have "disappeared" or the 100,000 said to have been killed by security forces or civil patrols between 1960 and 1991, a testimony is recounted attributing responsibility to a civil patrol for the execution and burial in a mass grave of a dozen civilians from San José Pachoj (p. 45).

By way of conclusions, the Inter-American Commission on Human Rights states in the abovementioned report that, in general, "the creation of unregimented and undisciplined security forces, without the kind of structure, training, and internal and external supervision that all forces of law and order must have, engenders conflict and human rights violations" (p. 60). With respect to the specific situation in Guatemala, the Inter-American Commission made the following observation:

"The tragic and ongoing human rights violations that can be traced to the existence and nature of militarized civilian patrols prompts the Commission to recommend to the Guatemalan Government that they immediately be disbanded and that a fully organized and professional police force be created, one answerable to civilian authorities, reasonably well paid, and trained to perform their duty to protect the security and tranquillity of the people, with full respect for human rights and Guatemalan law" (p. 60).

The UN's Special Rapporteur on Extra-Judicial, Summary or Arbitrary Executions referred to problems related to the existence of civil-defense forces in his report to the 1994 session of the Commission on Human Rights (E/CN.4/1994/7, paras. 719–720):

In several countries, civilians, particularly in rural and/or remote areas, have formed groups of self-defence in situations where they feel that their lives or property are threatened. While such threats may emanate from common criminality, for example, cattle thieves, civil-defence forces are frequent in areas where armed opposition groups operate. Often, they are supported or even set up by the security forces and integrated into the governments' counter-insurgency strategy. This was reported to be the case, for example, with the Bangladesh Rifles and Ansar Guards; the civil self-defence patrols (PAC) in Guatemala, the rondas campesinas and comités de defensa civil in Peru; the Citizen's Armed Forces Geographical Units (CAFGUs) in the Philippines; or the Kontrgerilla and Village Guards in Turkey. The Special Rapporteur received numerous reports about extrajudicial, summary, or arbitrary executions committed by members of such groups, either in cooperation with units of the security forces or with their acquiescence. With very few exceptions, they were said to enjoy impunity for their actions. Often, the victims of such killings were said to be peasants suspected of being members or sympathizers of the armed opposition because they refused to join the, ostensibly voluntary, civil-defence groups.

The Special Rapporteur appeals to the governments of all countries where such civil-defence structures exist to ensure full respect of human rights by the members of these groups. In particular, they should be trained to act in conformity with the restrictions on the use of force and firearms for law-enforcement officials. All arms used by such groups, particularly if provided by the military, should be registered and their use subjected to strict control. All abuses should be punished, and effective measures should be taken to prevent their occurrence. Furthermore, no one should be forced to participate in civilian defence forces against his or her wishes.

***SEE ALSO*** *Impunity; Law Enforcement.*

**COLOMBIA.** The Republic of Colombia is a country in tropical South America, on the Pacific Ocean and the Caribbean Sea. It has borders with Brazil, Ecuador, Panama, Peru, and Venezuela. It achieved independence from Spain in 1919 and became a member of the United Nations in 1945. Its population is estimated to be 34,640,000 including mestizos (57%), whites (20%), blacks (5%), mulattos (14%), and indigenous populations of Amerindian origin (4%). The language in common use is Spanish. The predominant religion is Christianity (Roman Catholic, 96%; Protestant denominations, 4%). Literacy is estimated at 85%.

The government (1994) took the form of a republic.

The president is elected by popular vote, serves a four-year term of office, and appoints his own cabinet. The legislature is bicameral: a 160-member House of Representatives and a 100-member Senate. Members of both houses are elected by popular vote for terms of four years. Political parties include the Liberal Party, the Conservative Party, the National Popular Alliance, the National Opposition Union, the Front for the Unity of the People, the National Independent Labor Movement, the Communist Party, the Socialist Workers' Party, and the Patriotic Union of the Colombian Revolutionary Armed Forces.

In 1994 Ernesto Samper Pizano of the ruling Liberal Party became President in elections in which voters elected a Vice-President for the first time.

Although Colombia has the reputation of being one of the most democratic countries in South America, it has experienced its share of human rights problems, due in large part to continuing rivalry between members of the Conservative Party, who favor centralism and participation by the Catholic Church in government and education, and those of the Liberal Party, who favor federalism, anticlericalism, and social reforms. This rivalry has given rise to serious disturbances, riots, and even civil war.

The country has been experiencing guerrilla and subversive movements since 1948. These forces, operating under various names, have periodically created violence and otherwise demonstrated their rejection of the policies of the government, recently with the support of gangs of drug traffickers.

Following the murder of Minister of Justice Rodrigo Lara Bonilla on 30 April 1984, the government declared a nationwide state of seige under which it assumed special powers authorized by the constitution, including the empowering of military criminal courts to try offenses defined in the "National Statute on Narcotic Drugs" and those relating to the carrying of, or traffic in, weapons exclusively used by the armed forces. During the four-year term of President Belisario Betancur Cuartas (1982–1986), the government made an extraordinary effort to secure peace in the country, including a proclamation of amnesty approved by Law No. 35 of 1982 and the establishment of a "Peace Committee" to mediate differences between the opposing factions.

***CONTROL OF DRUG TRAFFICKING.*** At the time of the state-of-siege declaration, the government promulgated a series of decrees relating to the control of narcotic drugs. The National Statute on Narcotic Drugs was amended to embody these decrees by Law No. 30 of 31 January 1986; these decrees prohibited the unlawful trade in substances used in the production of narcotic drugs and empowered national and local officials to confiscate such substances. Subsequently, with technical assistance provided by the United Nations, the government formulated a national plan to combat the illicit traffic in and consumption of narcotic drugs and psychotropic substances and concluded an agreement under which the United Nations Fund for Drug Abuse finances the establishment of a data bank, a study of alternative possibilities for the treatment and rehabilitation of drug-dependent persons, and a plan whereby the coca lead crop in certain areas of the country is to be replaced by non-narcotic crops. In a number of international forums, Colombia has maintained that traffic in narcotic and psychotropic substances should be declared a crime against humanity.

In 1991, the leader of Colombia's largest cocaine cartel, Pablo Emilio Escobar Gaviria, surrendered to Colombian authorities hours after being barred from extradition. Charged with hundreds of killings, including the deaths of 150 persons in the bombing of an airliner, Escobar negotiated the surrender through a prominent Colombian television minister. Picked up by helicopter and flown to a prison especially built to house him in comfort near his hometown of Envigado, Escobar was protected against any outside attack. He was soon joined in the prison by his brother Roberto and other cartel leaders. Colombian President Gaviria Trujillo predicted that Escobar's imprisonment would mark the end of narcoterrorism in Colombia. Escobar broke out of his comfortable jail in July 1992; and, for 16 months, he eluded more than 1,600 army troops and police deployed in efforts to recapture him. He was finally shot dead by police and soldiers in Medellin.

**FREEDOM OF BELIEF.** As regards religion or belief, in 1973 Colombia signed an agreement with the Holy See, known as the Valez–Palmas Concordat. Its main provisions were summarized by the government as follows:

(a) It does not proclaim an official religion. The State merely declares that it regards the Catholic religion as being of "fundamental importance to the public welfare and the full development of the community";

(b) The new concordat substantially retains the provisions of the 1887 Agreement concerning recognition by the State of the Church's spiritual authority, legal personality and capacity to collect offerings and contributions from its followers;

(c) The State accords Catholic marriage—i.e., "marriage celebrated in accordance with the norms of canonical law"—full recognition for civil purposes, but does not make it obligatory;

(d) Bishops—and persons canonically assimilated to them—are granted an immunity in criminal matters identical in scope to that extended to diplomatic agents;

(e) Members of the clergy and religious orders enjoy a

degree of privilege in criminal proceedings instituted against them by the Commission on Non-Ecclesiastical Offences;

(f) The Church undertakes to give the President of the Republic advance confidential notice of episcopal appointments with a view to ascertaining whether he has "civil or political objections" to the candidates;

(g) The State acknowledges the Church's freedom of instruction and independence to organize and run faculties, institutes, seminaries and a training establishment for religious orders;

(h) The State undertakes to make a reasonable contribution to the maintenance of Catholic educational establishments and to include courses of religious instruction in its primary and secondary school curricula;

(i) Church and State undertake to co-operate in the social advancement of indigenous persons and other inhabitants of what were formerly known as "mission territories";

(j) The financial obligations acquired by the State by virtue of the Núñez Concordat and the Misiones Agreement of 1953 are consolidated."

The concordat regime is not considered to be inconsistent with effective recognition of freedom of conscience since the existence of a treaty between the civil and ecclesiastical authorities is not deemed to be prejudicial to the right of non-Catholic citizens to be exempt from compulsion in religious matters and since its maintenance does not affect adversely the equality of all citizens before the law. However, one effect of the concordat is that, in Colombia, all family law on matters normally within the public domain is in the hands of the Catholic Church.

**INDIGENOUS POPULATION.** The Indians of Colombia are considered to be an indigenous population, not an ethnic minority. The government respects their sociocultural organization and their traditions, and they are considered to be Colombian citizens. They govern themselves in accordance with their own customs and traditions; in some communities, government is in the hands of an indigenous leader, while, in others, it is the responsibility of a governing council or similar body.

Lands originally held by the indigenous populations were plundered by settlers as they became more accessible by improved transport and communications. In an effort to alleviate the serious problem which was developing, the government established, first, a system of reservations and, subsequently, a number of indigenous reserves, designed to protect their land from encroachment. The Colombian Agrarian Reform Institute established 128 such reservations and reserves, on which more than 20,000 indigenous families are settled.

Each indigenous community, and each member who is of full age, has the right to participate actively in the political life of the country, with the corresponding rights and obligations of the exercise of citizenship authorized by the constitution and other legislation, including the right to vote and to stand in elections for all public or representative offices. Bilingual education is directed at providing education to young indigenous people in their own language, simultaneously with the teaching of Spanish; and the government has trained a number of young indigenous persons to promote education, health, etc., within their own communities.

The situation improved early in 1990 when the government recognized Indian land rights to half the Colombian Amazon—home to 55,000 Indians and 200 white settlers—covering 69,000 sq. mi. These traditional Indian lands now belong to the Indian communities in perpetuity and cannot be sold.

*DISAPPEARANCES.* Between 1984 and 1986, a state of siege prevailed in Colombia, and complaints of "disappearances" were reported to international bodies, including the **COMMISSIONS ON HUMAN RIGHTS** of the United Nations and of the **ORGANIZATION OF AMERICAN STATES.** In general, these complaints alleged that official violence was the consequence of a counter-insurgency strategy, in which the armed forces played the leading role. "Disappearances" were said to be a part of that strategy, in which military, security services, and the police were involved. Many of the "missing" persons had been taken to military, security, or police premises before "disappearing," according to a few who succeeded in escaping or were released.

The Colombian government responded by stating that, in fact, human rights violations resulting from excesses of government authorities had been markedly reduced in 1986 and that all complaints were being thoroughly investigated by the country's attorney-general. As of 8 September 1985, a State Human Rights Commission had been established in the attorney-general's office to deal with human rights matters in general and, in particular, such questions as disappearances, allegations of unlawful arrest, treatment of persons held by the authorities, and relations between the indigenous communities and the government.

However, the number of disappearances escalated markedly in 1987 and 1988. On 30 January 1989, the Colombian Government invited the UN Commission on Human Rights' Special Rapporteur on Summary or Arbitrary Executions, S. Amos Wako (Kenya), to visit the country. The Special Rapporteur's report on his visit (UN Doc. C/CN.4/1990/22/Add. 1), threw new light on the subject of disappearances. It read in part (chap. VI):

Colombia has experienced a continuous and protracted period of violence of varying degrees and intensity since April 1948 following the assassination of the liberal leader Jorge Eliecer Gartan. There has been an increase in the type and number of actors in this climate of violence. For a similar period, Colombia has been under a state of siege. During the ten year period between 1948 and 1958, it is estimated that between 200,000 and 300,000 people died as a result of fighting between the supporters of the Liberal and Conservative Parties. The 1958 agreement between the two parties under which they agreed to share power alternatively for the next 16 years brought an end to this type of violence. However, sections of the population particularly those with a different ideology or political thinking from the Conservative and Liberal Parties felt excluded or marginalized from the political process.

A large number of poor Colombians felt excluded from participation in political life. Hence, the seeds of another source of violence, that of guerrilla movements, were planted. The peasant self-defence groups that had been promoted by the Liberal Party evolved into the Revolutionary Army Forces of Colombia (FARC) and the National Liberation Army (ELN). There are currently eight guerrilla movements including the "April 19" movement (M-19) which came into being after allegations of fraud during the 1970 presidential election. The main targets of the guerrilla action have been the armed forces and the police. To combat the guerillas, the civilian population was organized in civilian self-defence groups and this was regulated by Order No. 0005 of the High Command of the Armed Forces, 1969, and the Counter-Insurgency Regulations (Regulation EJC 3-10). As the drug trade became increasingly part of the Colombian society, another very important contribution to violence in Colombia was introduced. The drug barons engaged in wholesale purchasing of land by way of investment, often in guerrilla-controlled areas and this inevitably led to a conflict between them and the guerrillas. A number of killings have also occurred as a result of gang wars between the cartels over control of territory.

To achieve their aims, the drug traffickers set up paramilitary organizations. The first of such groups "Muerte a secuestradores" (M.A.S.) (Death to Kidnappers) was set up following the kidnapping of one of the daughters of a major drug baron by members of M-19. According to a DAS report, the hit men and drug dealers who operate in Puerto Boyaca use the Association of Farmers and Stock-Breeders of Central Magdalena (ACDEGAM) as a front for their illegal activities. In the course of time, many civilian self-defence groups were gradually taken over by the drug barons. It is estimated that there are currently over 140 paramilitary groups operating in Colombia today. The paramilitary groups are trained and financed by drug traffickers and possibly a few landowners. They operate very closely with elements in the armed forces and the police. Most of the killings and massacres carried out by the paramilitary groups occur in areas which are heavily militarized. The paramilitary groups are able to move easily in such areas and commit murders with impunity. As the report shows, in some cases, the military or police either turn a blind eye to what is being done by paramilitary groups or give support by offering safe conduct passes to members of the paramilitary or by impeding investigation. For example, the Director of the National Criminal Investigation Department at the time of the La Rochela massacre said that what worried him most was that inquiries for which he was responsible were turning up more and more evidence of indulgence, tolerance and backing of extreme right-wing groups by members of the police and the army. "We are carrying out very serious investigations and they have been harassing my men, who are being threatened by members of the National Police. The Judicial Technical Police is scared. It would be irresponsible of me to make any claim to the contrary."

Paramilitary groups are the greatest source of violations

to the right to life in Colombian society today. Most of the killings and massacres have not only occurred at their hands but they have contributed to what has come to be known as impunity, that is the knowledge on the part of the perpetrators of these crimes that they will not be subject to the due process of law and punished for their misdeeds. Far reaching steps have to be taken to eliminate the prevailing climate of impunity and to curtail summary or arbitrary executions taking place as if they are part of everyday life. These policies will involve, not only strong political will but resources and technical expertise. It is for the latter, where appropriate and with the agreement of Colombia, that the international community can provide assistance.

Any solution to the problem of violence in Colombian society today has to address itself to the problem posed by the paramilitary groups. The Government is aware of this and has taken steps against them. By Decree 813, an Advisory Commission was set up to combat paramilitary groups. The Commission's mandate is to create a plan of action to combat paramilitary groups. By Decree 814, a special force of up to 1,000 men was set up to combat these groups. The Special Rapporteur was informed that there had been some success in the war against such groups and that 17 of the groups had been disbanded. However, a lot more still needs to be done, bearing in mind that there are still 140 groups in existence. Decree 816 recognizes the role of properly instituted self-defence groups, but only at the initiative of the President by way of a decree which must be countersigned by the Ministers of Defence and the Government. The recruitment of civilians is only for defence purposes. The previous legislation which authorized the armed forces to give restricted weapons to self-defence groups has been revoked.

There should be an all out effort aimed at disbanding all the paramilitary groups not authorized and regulated by the law. The new Decree 1194/89 which aims at punishing those who promote, finance, train or take part in hired assassination (paramilitary) groups should be fully implemented. The enormity of this task should not be underestimated. There is bound to be resistance to such measures not only from within the military and the police but also from within the traditional political and economic élites who would rather have as priority the fight against the guerrillas. However if the violence is to be dealt with successfully then the problem of the existence of paramilitary groups has to be confronted.

Coupled with the disbanding of paramilitary groups, all persons in the armed forces and the police who have corroborated with or given support to such groups, hit men or drug traffickers, should be dismissed. The Government believes that the majority of the police and the military are not linked to the drug traffickers because otherwise the various actions aimed against them would not have been successful. It has been suggested that, through administrative action and the exercise of the constitutional powers vested in the President of the Republic to freely appoint and remove his agents, the Executive could and should remove members of the armed forces involved with such groups. Article 120, Ordinals 1 and 5 of the Constitution give the President power to do so, and Article 125, Ordinal 4 of Decree 095 of 1982, and Article III, Ordinal 4 of Decree 096 of 1989 give power to remove members of the armed forces from duty. Already, the Government has begun to do this. The Executive asserted its authority in the dismissal of four police officials guilty of causing the disappearance of persons and of committing torture and murders. There is also the example of Colonel Luis Bahorquez Montaya, Commander of the Puerto Boyaca who was relieved of his duty for his evident

links with the paramilitary groups in the region. The same could possibly be said for Colonel Diego Hernan Velandia Postrana, Commander of the Santander Batallion of Ocána. However, there needs to be a more determined effort to remove such officers from the armed forces and police.

Another area which needs to be looked into as a matter of urgency is in the administration of justice. As can be seen from the report, very many judges, investigators and witnesses have either lost their lives or been threatened with death in the course of their duties. A climate of genuine fear exists among these groups of peoples which hampers the administration of justice and which contributes to the phenomena known as impunity. Witnesses cannot come forward to give evidence and even if they make statements, they are later retracted because of intimidation and fear of being killed. Proper investigations cannot be carried out and, therefore, many files are closed for lack of evidence. For those few files where there is evidence, a judge may not be able to mete out justice without fear or favour. The end result is that the guilty escape punishment because of lack of evidence. Adequate protection of all those involved in the administration of justice is, therefore, a matter of highest priority.

The Government is aware of this problem and on 18 August 1989, it issued a decree setting up a fund to pay for effective protection of judges and members of their families. Up to the time of the visit of the Special Rapporteur, however, no fund had been established because of lack of resources. Lack of funds is also the reason why witnesses are not given protection. DAS and the Department of Criminal Instruction have tried within their own limited resources to give protection to some of the witnesses but this has not on the whole been successful. The Special Rapporteur was told that in a few cases where the name, identity card and place of residence were changed, the witness was nevertheless killed. A fund for providing adequate security to those involved in the administration of justice is vital at this stage of Colombian history and it is an area in which the international community can assist. . . .

The worst hit groups of people have been peasants and workers. As somebody told the Special Rapporteur, every peasant is considered to be a potential guerrilla. The root causes giving rise to dissatisfaction among the peasants and workers have to be dealt with. It is therefore important that urgent programmes of action be taken to bring about social justice so that the economic and social conditions of peasants and workers can be considerably improved. The democratic reforms should be such that the peasant and the worker will not just be onlookers but active participants in the democratic and decision-making process. The role of groups which operate with peasants and workers, be they political parties, trade-unions, educators, non-governmental organizations dealing with economic, social, cultural and human rights issues, should be given due recognition and in a climate in which they can operate without intimidation from any quarter. There appears to be a systematic campaign by the paramilitary and extreme right-wing groups to eliminate or disrupt those organizations. The Government has already taken some steps to address the root causes: for example, dialogue with the guerrilla movements, programmes to ensure health and basic education for all, more jobs, agrarian reform and improving and rehabilitating substandard human settlement. The struggle against paramilitary groups and drug-traffickers will, it is hoped, eliminate or lessen the danger to these initiatives and thereby promote a healthy and constructive debate and discussion. This will, perhaps, lead to the accommodation of various sectors of the population and a consensus in the society that Colombia should be a society which belongs to all and in which there is peace, democracy, the rule of law, social justice and respect for human rights.

In a society which has been marked by such violence there is a need for a sustained campaign to promote human rights and the value of respecting them. Human rights need to be emphasized in the activities of the armed forces and police and whoever violates them should be disciplined and punished; the teaching of human rights should be compulsory to all public officials and in all educational establishments.

The efforts being made particularly by the Presidential Adviser on Human Rights in this regard are commendable and should be given support. Mention should also be made of the institution of Municipal Ombudsmen. The Special Rapporteur met a few of them. Some of them appeared to know their role but some did not. Some were operating not only under difficult conditions but also under threat to their lives. The Municipal Ombudsmen have a potential of really promoting and protecting human rights at the grass roots level. Their position should be strengthened and resources should be at their disposal so that they can function effectively.

The Commission on Human Rights examined the report of the Special Rapporteur at its 1990 session. On 6 March 1990, it strongly condemned once again (resolution 1990/51) the large number of summary or arbitrary executions, including extra-legal executions, which continue to take place in various parts of the world, and appealed urgently to governments, United Nations bodies, specialized agencies, and regional intergovernmental organizations. The subsequent 1993 "Report of the Working Group on Enforced or Involuntary Disappearances" contained the following update:

### Information Reviewed and Transmitted to the Government

The Working Group's activities in relation to Colombia are recorded in its previous eight reports to the Commission.

During the period under review, the Working Group transmitted 25 newly reported cases of disappearance to the Government of Colombia, of which 15 were reported to have occurred in 1993; 16 of those cases were transmitted under the urgent action procedure (and 2 of them were clarified in 1993). The Group also retransmitted to the Government one case containing additional information submitted by the sources.

By letters dated 15 June, 20 October and 3 December 1993, the Government was notified that 10 cases were now considered clarified, 7 based on its replies and 3 on the basis of further information provided by the source. The Government was also informed that in one case the Group had applied the six-month rule. By letters dated 22 January and 5 July 1993, the Government was reminded of reports of disappearance transmitted during the previous six months under the urgent action procedure. By letter dated 15 June 1993, the Working Group reminded the Government of all outstanding cases.

In a letter dated 20 October 1993, the Working Group informed the Government of allegations of a general nature it had received concerning the phenomenon of disappearance in the country or the solution of the cases not yet clarified.

### Information and Views Received from Relatives of Missing Persons or from Non-governmental Organizations

The majority of the newly reported cases of disappearance, and general information on the human rights situation in Colombia, were submitted by Amnesty International, the Association of Relatives of Disappeared Detainees (ASFAD-DES), the Justice and Peace Commission and the Andean Commission of Jurists. These organizations also provided information on the basis of which three cases have been considered clarified.

Fifteen of the cases transmitted were reported to have occurred in 1993, and 10 cases were reported to have occurred in 1992. The forces alleged to be responsible for the disappearances were the Armed Forces (12 cases), the police (seven cases), the Administrative Department for Security (one case) and armed men in civilian clothes believed to be linked to government forces (five cases).

According to information received, despite the fact that the 1991 Constitution is operative and State institutions have been established and reactivated in order to protect human rights, as in the case of the Defensoréa del Pueblo and the Office of the Attorney-General, the human rights situation in Colombia has not changed substantially as compared with 1992 and is still disturbing. Counter-insurgency and anti-narcotics operations, involving indiscriminate attacks that directly affect the civilian population, human rights violations by members of the Armed Forces and acts of violence by guerrilla or paramilitary groups are still common.

According to information received, the State of Internal Strife has not helped to improve the human rights situation. The Constitutional Court has declared that the numerous decrees issued by the Executive in exercise of its powers under the State of Strife are in conformity with the Constitution. This is the case with most of the provisions contained in Decree No. 1810 of 1992, whereby the Armed Forces are authorized to detain and investigate civilians at military units, in contravention of article 28 of the Constitution, under which "No one may be importuned in his/her person or family, sent to gaol or arrested, nor may his/her home be searched, except pursuant to a written order from a competent legal authority, subject to legal process and for reasons previously established by law". According to information received, this situation makes for excesses against detainees by the Armed Forces that cannot always be kept in check.

Reports received also speak of apparent impunity in connection with cases of forcible disappearances in which State officials are implicated. Such impunity seems to be made easier by the following circumstances.

Both the previous Constitution and the 1991 Constitution establish a special military jurisdiction for members of the forces of law and order who, by act or omission, violate the law or the Constitution while on active service. It was reported that this jurisdiction is in practice ineffectual, for two basic reasons:

(a) The immediate superior of the person carrying out the order, in other words, the one involved in a human rights violation, is the Brigade Commander, who is at the same time a judge of first instance in the military courts, so that he is both the judge and the plaintiff;

(b) The military courts do not allow relatives to bring criminal indemnification proceedings in the trial, thereby

C

making it impossible to submit evidence, object to the evidence produced or appeal against decisions. State officials who have been convicted of human rights violations are not normally dismissed but have been transferred and, in some instances, promoted. In addition, proceedings are initiated only in a few of the large number of complaints against State officials that reach the Office of the Attorney-General.

### Information and Views Provided by the Government

In the course of 1993 the Government provided replies on five cases of disappearance by different notes verbales. In two cases the Government replied that an investigation was being carried out; in another two cases that the persons in question had been detained but were not missing; and in the fifth case that the person had requested the protection of the Army. The Government also sent a reply with respect to one case on which the Working Group had made a prompt intervention in 1992. According to the Government, the person in question had been given protection by the security forces since May 1993.

The Government also provided the Working Group with information about the draft bill in accordance with which it was intended to typify disappearance as a crime in the Colombian Penal Code.

The Government, furthermore, submitted its comments on the implementation of the Declaration on the Protection of all Persons from Enforced Disappearance.

### Statistical Summary

|       |                                                                                              | Total | Females |
|-------|----------------------------------------------------------------------------------------------|-------|---------|
| I.    | Cases reported to have occurred in 1993                                                       | 15    | 0       |
| II.   | Outstanding cases                                                                            | 700   | 61      |
| III.  | Total number of cases transmitted to the Government by the Working Group                      | 895   | 76      |
| IV.   | Government responses (a) Number of cases on which the Government has provided one or more specific responses | 665   | —       |
|       | (b) Cases clarified by the Government's responses                                            | 150   | 9       |
| V.    | Cases clarified by non-governmental sources                                                   | 45    | 6       |

In mid-1991, a constituent assembly, established to reform Colombia's constitution, made a curious decision: it voted, by 51 votes to 13, with 10 abstentions, to ban extraditions from the country. The vote was later recognized as having guaranteed the surrender of Pablo Escobar, the leader of the country's largest cocaine cartel, a criminal empire that had for some years earned upwards of $20 billion a year by supplying 80% of the cocaine sold in the United States of America. Other constitutional reforms were also established: permitting Roman Catholics to obtain civil divorces and eliminating the large sums of government money that members of congress had been allowed to spend within their districts.

**BIBLIOGRAPHY.** Americas Watch. *The Central Americanization of Colombia? Human Rights and the Peace Process.* New York: 1986. NGO report, in English.

———. *The "Drug War" in Colombia: The Neglected Tragedy of Political Violence.* New York: Human Rights Watch, October 1990. NGO factfinding report, in English.

Amnesty International. *Colombia: Children and Minors: Victims of Political Violence.* London: 1994. NGO report, in English.

Asociacion de Familiares de Detenidos Desaparecidos (Association of Families of the Detained-Disappeared). *Informe Colombiano* (Colombian Report). Bogota: 1987. NGO report, in Spanish.

Camargo, Eduardo Matyas. "Narco Paramilitarismo y Derechos Humanos en Colombia" (Narco-Paramilitarism and Human Rights in Colombia), *Boletín—Comisión Andina de Juristas* 25 (June 1990): 9–15. Scholarly article, in Spanish.

Colectivo de Abogados Jose Alvear Restrepo (Jose Alvear Restrepo Lawyers' Collective). *El Camino de la Niebla: La Desaparicion Forzada en Colombia y su Impunidad* (The Foggy Road: Forced Disappearance and Impunity in Colombia). Bogota: 1988. NGO report, in Spanish.

Comision Andina de Juristas (Andean Commission of Jurists). *Colombia: El Derecho a la Justicia* (Colombia: The Right to Justice). Lima, Peru: 1988. NGO report, in Spanish.

———. *Violencia en Colombia* (Violence in Colombia) Lima, Peru: March 1990. NGO mission report, in Spanish.

Comite Permanente por la Defensa de los Derechos Humanos (Permanent Committee for the Defense of Human Rights). *Itinerario de la Represion y la Violencia Institucionalizadas: Colombia 1986* (Itinerary of Institutionalized Violence and Repression: Colombia 1986). Bogota: 1988. NGO report, in Spanish.

———. "La Justicia Colombiana Condena la Utilizacion de la Tortura en los Interrogatorios Judiciales" (The Colombian Judiciary Condemns the Use of Torture in Judicial Inquests), in *Boletin de Prensa.* 10 July 1985. NGO bulletin, in Spanish.

———. *Relacion de Victimas de Desaparicion Forzada en Colombia* (Account of Victims of Forced Disappearances in Colombia). Bogota: 1987. NGO report, in Spanish.

Giraldo, Javier. *Algunos Rasgos de la Situation de Violencia que Vive Hoy Colombia* (Some Features of Violence in Colombia Today). Bogota: Centro de Investigacion y Educacion Popular, 1987. NGO report, in Spanish.

Huggins, Martha K., ed. *Vigilantism and the State in Modern Latin America: Essays on Extralegal Violence.* New York: Praeger, 1991. Scholarly collective works, in English; bibliography, pp. 243–248.

Human Rights Watch. "Colombia," in *Human Rights Watch World Report 1995,* pp. 79–85. New York: 1995. NGO report, in English.

———. *State of War: Political Violence and Counterinsurgency in Colombia.* New York: 1993. NGO report, in English.

International Work Group for Indigenous Affairs. "Colombia: Massacre of Embera Indians Causes International Outcry," *IWGIA Newsletter* 50 (July 1987): 82–86. NGO article, in English.

Liga Internacional por los Derechos y la Liberacion de los Pueblos—Seccion Colombiana (International League for the Rights and the Liberation of Peoples—Colombian Section). *Tribunal Permanente de los Pueblos: Proceso a la Impunidad de Crimenes de Lesa Humanidad* (Permanent Peoples' Tribunal: Trial on Impunity for Crimes against Humanity). Bogota: 1990. NGO report, in Spanish.

Mendex Madrigal, Luis, ed. *Derechos Humanos y Servicios*

*Legales en el Campo: Colombia 1988* (Human Rights and Legal Services in the Countryside: Colombia 1988). Bogota: Instituto Latinoamericano de Servicios Legales Alternativos, Comision Andina de Juristas, and International Commission of Jurists, 1988. NGO conference proceedings, in Spanish.

Pearce, Jenny. *Colombia: Inside the Labyrinth.* London: Monthly Review Press, 1990. Scholarly monograph, in English; bibliography, pp. 294–302.

Peña Díaz, Héctor. "Notas sobre la Convención Americana de Derechos Humanos y la Legislación Colombiana" (Notes on the American Convention on Human Rights and Columbian Legislation), *Derechos Humanos* (March–April 1991): 4–9. Educational material, in Spanish.

Sanchez G., and D. Meertens. *Bandoleros, Gamonales y Campesinos: El Caso de la Violencia en Colombia* (Bandits, Landowners and Peasants: The Case of Violence in Colombia), 3rd ed. Bogota: El Ancora Editores, 1985. NGO report, in Spanish; bibliography, pp. 246–255.

Umana Luna, Eduardo. *Hacia la Peace? (Los Ilicitos y los Presos Politicos: Las Amnistias y los Indultos)* (Towards Peace? [Illicit Behavior and Political Prisoners: Amnesties and Pardons]). Bogota: Comite de Solidaridad con los Presos Politicos, 1985. Scholarly monograph, in Spanish.

———. *La Tramoya Colombiana (Praxis y Derechos Humanos)* (The Colombian "Entanglement" [Practice and Human Rights]). Bogota: Corporacion Colectivo de Abogados, 1988. Scholarly monograph, in Spanish.

United Nations Commission on Human Rights. *Report on the Visit to Colombia by the Special Rapporteur on Summary or Arbitrary Executions [S. Amos Wako] (11–20 October 1990).* Geneva, Switzerland: 1990. IGO document, in English and French.

U.S. Committee for Refugees. *Feeding the Tiger: Colombia's Internally Displaced People.* Washington, D.C.: American Council for Nationalities Service, 1993. NGO issue paper, in English; bibliography, p. 28.

Varon, Miguel. "Colombia: New Government Fails to Halt Multiple Killings," *Latinamerica Press* 18, no. 35 (25 September 1986): 1–2. NGO newsletter article, in English.

Vervaele, John. "Criminal Law and the Protection of Human Rights in Colombia," *SIM Newsletter: Netherlands Quarterly of Human Rights* 6, no.3 (October 1988): 5–27. Scholarly article, in English.

Washington Office on Latin America. *The Colombian National Police, Human Rights and U.S. Drug Policy.* Washington, D.C.: 1993. NGO report, in English.

## COLUMBIA UNIVERSITY, CENTER FOR THE STUDY OF HUMAN RIGHTS.

The Center was founded in 1978 to promote interdisciplinary research and teaching in human rights. A university-wide activity, it promotes research as a primary goal to elucidate the role that human rights considerations play in contemporary civilization. To that end, the Center supports a number of programs, including the University Seminar on Human Rights, begun in 1978; an annual, week-long symposium, begun in 1979; and the Gitleson/Meyerwitz Prize, awarded to a Columbia student for the best composition on human rights; and research projects. At the end of 1994, the Center was sponsoring four research projects: (1) Rights and Constitutionalism in International Affairs; (2) Religious Freedom; (3) Constitutionalism in China; and (4) the African Human Rights Education Project. In addition to its other activities, the Center also sponsors the "Advocates Program," a four-month training program for human rights activists from third-world countries.

The document collection of the Center is housed in Columbia's Human Rights Reading and Resource Room. The collection comprises country-specific files, files on human rights organizations, off-prints and pre-publication articles, human rights organization publications, and reports and bibliographic information.

The Center offers summer internships enabling Columbia students to work with human rights groups in third-world countries and has cooperated in the administration of the Law School's Summer Internship Human Rights Program. It publishes a periodic newsletter and has published Louis Henkin's *The Rights of Man Today,* the monograph *Elements of Constitutionalism,* and *Twenty-Five Human Rights Documents.*

Center for the Study of Human Rights. Address: Columbia University, 1108 International Affairs Building, 420 W. 118th Street, New York, NY 10027, USA. Telephone: (212) 854-2479. Fax: (212) 316-4578. Telex: 220094 COLU UR. Executive Director: Paul Martin.

## COMMISSION FOR SOCIAL DEVELOPMENT, UN.

The Commission, established in 1946 by the UN Economic and Social Council as the Social Commission (resolution 10[II]) and given a new name and broader mandate in 1966 to act as the preparatory and advisory body in the whole range of social development (resolution 1139 [XLI]), is mandated to advise the Council (1) on social policies of a general character, giving particular attention to policies designed to promote social progress, to establish social objectives, program priorities, and social research in areas affecting social and economic development; (2) on practical measures that may be needed in the social field, including questions of social welfare, community development, urbanization, housing, and social defense; (3) on measures needed for the coordination of activities in the social field; and (4) on such international agreements and conventions on any of these matters.

Before its change of name and mandate, the Social Commission, in 1950, prepared the draft of a declaration on the rights of the child, based on the Declaration of Geneva, which had been adopted by the Assembly of the League of Nations in 1924. After the draft had been reviewed by the UN Commission on Human Rights and the Economic and Social Council, it was transmitted to the General Assembly, which adopted and proclaimed the Declaration on the

Rights of the Child on 29 November 1959 (resolution 1386[XIV]).

Later the Commission for Social Development prepared the draft of a declaration on social development, which the General Assembly adopted and proclaimed on 11 December 1969 (resolution 2542 [XXIV]) as the Declaration on Social Progress and Development.

The Declaration states that social progress and development shall aim at the continuous raising of the material and spiritual standards of living of all members of society, with respect for and compliance with human rights and fundamental freedoms, through the attainment of such goals as: (1) the assurance at all levels of the right to work and the right of everyone to form trade unions and workers' associations and to bargain collectively; (2) the elimination of hunger and malnutrition and the guarantee of the right to proper nutrition; (3) the achievement of the highest standards of health and the provision of health protection for all, if possible free of charge; (4) the eradication of illiteracy and the assurance of the right to universal access to culture, to free compulsory education at the elementary level, and to free education at all levels; and (5) the provision for all, particularly persons in low-income groups and large families, of adequate housing and community services. The Declaration also calls for equitable sharing of scientific and technological advances by developed and developing countries and a steady increase in the use of science and technology for the benefit of the social development of society.

Originally set at 18, the membership of the Commission was increased to 21 in 1961 and to 32 in 1966. The Commission consists of one representative of each of the 32 States elected by the Economic and Social Council according to the following patterns: eight members from African states, six from Asian states, six from Latin American states, eight from western European and other states, and four from states of eastern Europe. The States elected to the Commission are expected to nominate as their representatives nationals who hold key positions in the planning or execution of national social development policies or others qualified to discuss the formulation of such policies in more than one sector of development. With a view to securing a balanced representation in the various fields covered by the Commission, the Secretary-General consults with the governments elected before they nominate their representatives. The representatives thus nominated are then confirmed by the Council. They serve for a term of four years.

**COMMISSION FOR THE DEFENSE OF HUMAN RIGHTS IN CENTRAL AMERICA.** A non-governmental organization in consultative status with the UN ECONOMIC AND SOCIAL COUNCIL, the Commission was founded in Costa Rica in 1978 to promote and protect human rights in Central America, and to coordinate and support national non-governmental human rights organizations within their specific countries. Its members are in ten countries. The Commission receives and follows up on allegations of human rights violations; prepares educational materials and organizes workshops; provides legal assistance to national commissions; researches legal aspects on human rights matters; and coordinates a regional information network.

Among the Commission's publications are *Brecha*, published monthly in Spanish and six times a year in English, and *Documentación sobre Derechos Humanos*, a monthly published in Spanish.

Commission for the Defense of Human Rights in Central America. Address: P.O. 189, Paseo de los Estudiantes, San José, Costa Rica. Telephone: (506) 24-59-10. Fax: (506) 34-29-35. Telex: CDHUCA CR. General Coordinator: Silvia Porras.

**COMMISSION OF THE CHURCHES ON INTERNATIONAL AFFAIRS OF THE WORLD COUNCIL OF CHURCHES.** An international non-governmental organization in consultative status with the UN ECONOMIC AND SOCIAL COUNCIL (Category II), and with the ILO and UNESCO, the Commission is an agency of the World Council of Churches and assists the constituency of WCC in dealing with questions of international scope. In this capacity, it studies world problems of international justice and world order, makes known the results of such studies to the churches and organizations affiliated with WCC, and represents WCC in its relations with international organs. The Commission is composed of 30 commissioners and 40 commissioners-at-large, appointed by WCC upon nomination by its Executive Committee.

CCIA's primary human rights concerns are with the development, promotion and protection of religious liberty, the provision of assistance to dependent peoples, indigenous populations, refugees, migrants and other disadvantaged groups, and the operation of a broad program aimed at combating racism and racial discrimination. It also deals with questions related to conscientious objection to military service. In these functions, it is assisted by its Human Rights Advisory Group.

Commission of the Churches on International Affairs of the World Council of Churches. Address: 150 route de Ferney, CH-1211 Geneva, Switzerland. Telephone: (41-22) 791-6111. Fax: (41-22) 791-0361. Cable: OIKOUMENE GENEVA. Telex: 415730 OIK CH. Acting Director: Rev. C. Harper.

**COMMISSION ON HUMAN RIGHTS, UN.** The Commission on Human Rights was established by the UN **ECONOMIC AND SOCIAL COUNCIL** on 16 February 1946 (resolution 5 [I]) in accordance with article 68 of the **UNITED NATIONS CHARTER,** which authorizes the Council to set up "commissions in economic and social fields and for the protection of human rights." The Commission's original mandate was to submit to the Council proposals, recommendations, and reports regarding (1) an international bill of rights; (2) international declarations or conventions on civil liberties, the status of women, freedom of information and similar matters; (3) the protection of minorities; (4) the prevention of discrimination on grounds of race, sex, language, or religion; and (5) any other matter concerning human rights. In 1979, a new function was added: to assist the Economic and Social Council in the coordination of activities concerning human rights in the United Nations system (Council resolution 1979/36, approved in General Assembly resolution 34/25).

Since it first met in 1947, the Commission has been at the forefront of international activity to define, promote, and protect human rights and fundamental freedoms. In addition to preparing a number of international treaties and declarations, the Commission has considered many situations involving violations of those rights and freedoms; has sought, through persuasion and dialogue, to prevent and eliminate human rights violations; has recommended measures to ensure compliance with universally recognized norms of human rights; and has offered and provided, upon request, advisory services and other expert assistance to reduce the incidence of violations of human rights. In addition, it has monitored, through its Group of Three, governments' implementation of the International Convention on the Suppression and Punishment of the Crime of Apartheid (see **APARTHEID**). The Commission's most notable achievements include the initial drafting of the **UNIVERSAL DECLARATION OF HUMAN RIGHTS,** the **INTERNATIONAL COVENANT ON ECONOMIC, SOCIAL AND CULTURAL RIGHTS,** the **INTERNATIONAL COVENANT ON CIVIL AND POLITICAL RIGHTS** and Optional Protocol thereto—instruments which together comprise the International Bill of Human Rights—and many other human rights treaties and declarations, including the International Convention on the Elimination of All Forms of Racial Discrimination (see **RACIAL DISCRIMINATION**), the International Convention on the Suppression and Punishment of the Crime of Apartheid, and the Convention against Torture and Other Cruel, Inhuman or Degrading Treatment or Punishment (see **TORTURE**).

*EXPERTS AND WORKING GROUPS.* In addition to debating and taking action on items on the agenda of its annual sessions, the Commission has developed a variety of mechanisms which enable it to carry out its work effectively. On many occasions, it has called upon one or more of its members, or other qualified experts, to perform fact-finding tasks, designating them as "special rapporteurs," "special representatives," or "special envoys." These experts, acting in their personal capacity, have examined questions relating to thematic human rights issues, such as summary and arbitrary executions, torture, intolerance based on religion or belief, and the use of mercenaries. They have also examined the human rights situations in particular countries. And, in a few cases, they have assisted governments to plan and take action to restore respect for human rights in territories under their jurisdiction. The Commission has also made use of working groups to examine particular situations (such as the Ad Hoc Working Group of Experts on Southern Africa), to consider broad categories of human rights violations (such as the Working Group on Enforced or Involuntary Disappearances), to draft new international instruments (such as the Working Group on a Draft Convention of the Rights of the Child), or to consider the realization of specific rights (such as the Working Group of Governmental Experts on the Right to Development).

*COMMUNICATIONS.* The Commission employs a special procedure, established by the Economic and Social Council in resolution 503 (XLVIII) of 27 May 1970, in examining situations which appear to reveal a consistent pattern of violations of human rights. Under the procedure, communications alleging such situations received by the Center for Human Rights are forwarded first to the governments concerned for their comments, if any. The communications, together with the comments of governments, are first considered by a working group of the Sub-Commission on Prevention of Discrimination and Protection of Minorities. If the Sub-Commission, on recommendation of the working group, considers that a particular situation fulfills the criteria set out in Council resolution 503, it refers it to the Commission, which decides what further action is to be taken. The Commission reports on such action to the Council. All activities under this procedure are confidential, and the results remain confidential, unless the Council decides otherwise.

*COMPOSITION.* The Commission is composed of one representative from each of the UN member States, selected by the Council on the basis of equitable geographical distribution according to the following pattern: eleven members from African States, nine from Asian States, eight from Latin American States, ten from Western European and other States, and five from States of Eastern Europe. With a view to securing a balanced representation in the various fields covered by the Commission, the Secretary-General consults with the governments elected by the Council before those governments nominate their representatives. After nomination, the representatives are confirmed by the Council. The term of office is three years. The Commission meets for one session each year, usually at the United Nations office in Geneva, for a period of about six weeks between mid-February and late March. In recent years, the Economic and Social Council has authorized the Commission to hold additional meetings beyond the period normally allotted, to enable it to complete its work.

*SPECIAL SESSIONS OF THE COMMISSION.* On 25 May 1990, the Economic and Social Council first authorized the Commission on Human Rights to meet exceptionally between its regular annual sessions, provided that a majority of States Members of the Commission agreed, in order to deal expeditiously with urgent human rights situations. The Council set down the following procedure for convening such special sessions:

1. Any State Member of the United Nations may request the Secretary-General to convene a special session of the Commission on Human Rights. Such a request shall be submitted, together with the reason for the request, to the Assistant Secretary-General for Human Rights at Geneva.
2. The following rules shall apply for the consideration of such requests:
   (a) The Assistant Secretary-General shall immediately transmit the request, together with the reasons given, to the States members of the Commission by the most expeditious means of communication available and inquire whether or not they support the request;
   (b) States members of the Commission shall, within four UN working days from the date of the communication from the Assistant Secretary-General, express in writing their views concerning the request;
   (c) The replies from States members of the Commission must reach the office of the Assistant Secretary-General for Human Rights not later than 6 p.m. Geneva time on the fourth day;
   (d) The Assistant Secretary-General shall duly inform the States members of the Commission of the results of the inquiry and, if the majority of States members have expressed support for the convening of a special session of the Commission within the deadline referred to in paragraph 2(c) above, in conformity with Economic and Social Council resolution 1990/48 of 25 May 1990, the Assistant Secretary-General shall communicate the opening date of the special session;
   (e) The special session shall open between the fourth and the sixth UN working day after the deadline referred to in paragraph 2(c) above.
3. In considering the appropriateness of holding a special session, States members of the Commission may take into consideration whether the Economic and Social Council or

the General Assembly is in regular session and is, or is likely to be, seized of the matter concerned;
4. The duration of the special session shall, in principle, not exceed three days;
5. The rules of procedure of such a special session shall be the rules of procedure of the functional commissions of the Economic and Social Council.
6. The Commission on Human Rights meeting in special session may take the same decisions as at its regular sessions.
7. If the Commission in special session requests the submission of a report on the matter under consideration, the report, together with any information provided by the State concerned, shall be distributed promptly by the Assistant Secretary-General to all States members of the Commission.
8. If the report and the information referred to in paragraph 7 above are not considered by the Commission meeting in special session on the issue, they shall be considered at the next regular session of the Commission or the General Assembly or at the next substantive session of the Economic and Social Council, whichever occurs earlier.

*BIBLIOGRAPHY.* Bossuyt, Marc J. "The Development of Special Procedures of the United Nations Commission on Human Rights," *Human Rights Law Journal* 6, no. 2–4: 179–210. Scholarly article, in English.

Brody, Reed, Penny Parker, and David Weissbrodt. "Major Developments in 1990 at the UN Commission on Human Rights," *Human Rights Quarterly* 12, no. 4 (Nov. 1990): 559–588. Scholarly article, in English.

Davidse, Koen M. "The 48th Session of the UN Commission on Human Rights and UN Monitoring of Violations of Civil and Political Rights," *Netherlands Quarterly of Human Rights* 10, no. 3 (1992): 283–302. Scholarly article, in English.

Kamarotos, Alexander S. A *View into NGO Networks in Human Rights Activities: NGO Action with Special Reference to the UN Commission on Human Rights and its Sub-Commission.* Geneva, Switzerland: Graduate Institute of International Studies, 1990. Scholarly monograph, in English.

Lillich, Richard B. *International Human Rights: Law, Policy and Process.* Boston, MA, USA: Little, Brown, 1991. Educational material, in English.

Parker, Penny, and David Weissbrodt. "Major Developments at the UN Commission on Human Rights in 1991," *Human Rights Quarterly* 13, no. 4 (Nov. 1991): 573–613. Scholarly article, in English.

Zoller, Adrien-Claude. "46th Session of the United Nations Commission on Human Rights (Geneva, 29 January–9 March 1990)," *Netherlands Quarterly of Human Rights* 8, No. 2 (1990): 140–175. Report, in English.

**COMMISSIONS ON HUMAN RIGHTS.** In addition to the UN Commission on Human Rights (see above), two other international organs bear the name "Commission on Human Rights." There are the European Commission on Human Rights and **INTER-AMERICAN COMMISSION ON HUMAN RIGHTS.** In addition, the **AFRICAN COMMISSION ON HUMAN AND PEOPLES' RIGHTS** is considered a human rights commission.

**COMMISSION ON THE STATUS OF WOMEN, UN.** The Commission on the Status of Women was established by the UN **ECONOMIC AND SOCIAL COUNCIL** on 21 June 1946 (resolution 11 [II]) and is mandated to prepare reports and recommendations to the Council on promoting women's rights in the political, economic, civic, social, and educational fields and to develop recommendations and proposals for action on urgent problems in the field of women's rights with the object of implementing the principle that men and women shall have equal rights. The Commission also acts from time to time as the preparatory body for international conferences on the rights of women, and recently it has been assigned a major role in reviewing and coordinating all activities of the United Nations system relevant to women's issues.

On 27 July 1988, the Council expressed the view (resolution 1988/60) that the central substantive coordinating role of the Commission in advancing the status of women and integrating women in development has three distinct aspects: (1) intergovernmental cooperation, regional, and sectoral intergovernmental bodies to achieve a coherent and complementary approach to implementing the Nairobi Forward-Looking Strategies for the Advancement of Women within the United Nations; (2) interagency coordination, which relates to measures taken by organizations of the United Nations system to coordinate the implementation of the Forward-Looking Strategies; and (3) legislative linkage, which relates to action taken by the Commission to link the implementation of the Forward-Looking Strategies to all relevant United Nations intergovernmental decisions and other international strategies and plans and programs of action.

*COMPOSITION.* Originally 15, membership in the Commission was increased to 18 in 1951; to 21 in 1961; to 32 in 1966; and, most recently, to 45 by resolution 989/45 adopted by the Economic and Social Council on 24 May 1989. Under that resolution, the Commission consists of one representative of each of the 45 States, elected by the Council on the basis of equitable geographical distribution according to the following pattern: 13 members from African States, 11 members from Asian States, four members from Eastern European States, nine members from Latin American and Caribbean States, and eight members from western European and other States.

The Commission holds one session every two years, either at the International Conference Center in Vienna or at United Nations headquarters in New York.

*COMMUNICATIONS.* The Working Group on Communications, established by the Commission at its 1988 session, examined a list of communications concerning the situation of women in specific countries and the replies received from a number of govern-ments. It analyzed the substance of the communications and agreed that many of them dealt with very serious and extensive violations of human rights, including different forms of discrimination against women. Such discrimination took the form of unequal rights in economic and social life, inequality before the law, and continued physical and sexual violence against women in detention. In addition, reports concerned family relationships, educational rights and participation in political activities.

The Working Group expressed particular concern about sexual harassment of women at the workplace and urged continued monitoring of the problem. It was distressed at the lack of response from several governments to communications regarding violations of the education, employment, and political rights of women, as well as the safety of women in detention. It proposed that the Commission on the Status of Women urge the Economic and Social Council to recommend that member States take legislative and other appropriate measures to halt the current negative trends related to the status of women in their countries.

The General Assembly, in resolutions adopted in 1991, 1992, and 1993 (resolutions 46/98, 47/95, and 48/108), has reaffirmed the central role of the Commission on the Status of Women in matters related to the advancement of women, and has called upon the Commission to promote implementation of the Nairobi Forward-Looking Strategies and its central objectives of equality, development, and peace. The Assembly has also repeatedly requested the Commission to give special attention to women in developing countries, particularly in Africa, and to recommend further measures for equal opportunity and for integration of women into the development process.

The Commission was designated as the preparatory body for the Fourth World Conference on Women, which was held in Beijing, China, in 1995.

**COMMITTEE AGAINST TORTURE, UN.** The Committee against Torture was established in accordance with article 17 of the Convention against Torture and Other Cruel, Inhuman or Degrading Treatment or Punishment, adopted by the UN **GENERAL ASSEMBLY** on 10 December 1984 (resolution 39/46). Opened for signature and ratification or accession on 4 February 1985, the Convention entered into force on 26 June 1987.

Each State party to the Convention undertakes to take effective legislative, administrative, judicial, and other measures to prevent acts of torture in any territory under its jurisdiction, and to submit reports to the Committee against Torture on the measures it has taken to this end. The Committee against Torture is empowered to consider the reports, to make general comments on them which are forwarded to the State concerned, and to include its comments and observations in its annual report to the General Assembly.

States parties may, in addition, make declarations provided for in articles 21 and 22 of the Convention. Under article 21, such a State may declare that it recognizes the competence of the Committee to receive and consider communications to the effect that one State party claims that another is not fulfilling its obligations under the Convention. The Committee is authorized to deal with such a complaint only after it has ascertained that all domestic remedies have been invoked and exhausted. If that is the case, it may try to find a friendly solution, either directly or by setting up a conciliation commission for the purpose.

Under article 22, a State party may declare that it recognizes the competence of the Committee to receive communications from or on behalf of individuals subject to its jurisdiction who claim to be victims of a violation by a State party of the provisions of the Convention. The Committee is authorized to deal with such a complaint after screening out communications which are anonymous or incompatible with the provisions of the Convention. It may bring admissible communications to the State party concerned and consider them in the light of all the information made available by the individual and the State. It then forwards its views to both parties and reports annually on its activities to the General Assembly.

The provisions of articles 21 and 22 entered into force on 26 June 1987 after ten States had made the necessary declarations. At a meeting of the States parties, convened on that day at the United Nations office in Geneva, members of the Committee against Torture were elected.

**COMMUNICATIONS.** At its first and second sessions, held in 1988 and 1989, respectively, the Committee adopted its rules of procedure, including general rules (Part I, rules 1–63), rules relating to the functions of the Committee (Part II, rules 64–112), and rules relating to interpretation and amendments (Part III, rules 113 and 144). The rules relating to the functions of the Committee are as follows (UN Doc. CAT/C/3/ Rev. 1):

### XVI. Reports From States Parties Under Article 19 of the Convention

*Rule 64. Submission of Reports.* 1. The States parties shall submit to the Committee, through the Secretary-General, reports on the measures they have taken to give effect to their undertakings under the Convention, within one year after the entry into force of the Convention for the State party

concerned. Thereafter the States parties shall submit supplementary reports every four years on any new measures taken and such other reports as the Committee may request.

2. The Committee may, through the Secretary-General, inform the States parties of its wishes regarding the form and contents of the reports to be submitted under article 19 of the Convention.

*Rule 65. Non-Submission of Reports.* 1. At each session, the Secretary-General shall notify the Committee of all cases of non-submission of reports under rules 64 and 67 of these rules. In such cases the Committee may transmit to the State party concerned, through the Secretary-General, a reminder concerning the submission of such report or reports.

2. If, after the reminder referred to in paragraph 1 of this rule, the State party does not submit the report required under rules 64 and 67 of these rules, the Committee shall so state in the annual report which it submits to the States parties and to the General Assembly of the United Nations.

*Rule 66. Attendance by States Parties at Examination of Reports.* The Committee shall, through the Secretary-General, notify the States parties, as early as possible, of the opening date, duration and place of the session at which their respective reports will be examined. Representatives of the States parties shall be invited to attend the meetings of the Committee when their reports are examined. The Committee may also inform a State party from which it decides to seek further information that it may authorize its representative to be present at a specified meeting. Such a representative should be able to answer questions which may be put to him by the Committee and make statements on reports already submitted by his State, and may also submit additional information from his State.

*Rule 67. Request for Additional Reports.* 1. When considering a report submitted by a State party under article 19 of the Convention, the Committee shall first determine whether the report provides all the information required under rule 64 of these rules.

2. If a report of a State party to the Convention, in the opinion of the Committee, does not contain sufficient information, the Committee may request that State to furnish an additional report, indicating by what date the said report should be submitted.

*Rule 68. General Comments by the Committee.* 1. After its consideration of each report, the Committee, in accordance with article 19, paragraph 3, of the Convention, may make such general comments on the report as it may consider appropriate and shall forward these, through the Secretary-General, to the State party concerned, which in reply may submit to the Committee any comment that it considers appropriate. The Committee may, in particular, indicate in its general comments whether, on the basis of its examination of the reports and information supplied by the State party, it appears that some of the obligations of that State under the Convention have not been discharged.

2. The Committee may, where necessary, indicate a time-limit within which observations from States parties are to be received.

3. The Committee may, at its discretion, decide to include any comments made by it in accordance with paragraph 1 of this rule, together with any observations thereon received from the State party concerned, in its annual report made in accordance with article 24 of the Convention. If so requested by the State party concerned, the Committee may also include a copy of the report submitted under article 19, paragraph 1, of the Convention.

## XVII. Proceedings Under Article 20 of the Convention

*Rule 69. Transmission of Information to the Committee.* 1. The Secretary-General shall bring to the attention of the Committee, in accordance with the present rules, information which is, or appears to be, submitted for the Committee's consideration under article 20, paragraph 1, of the Convention.

2. No information shall be received by the Committee if it concerns a State party which, in accordance with article 28, paragraph 1, of the Convention, declared at the time of ratification of or accession to the Convention that it did not recognize the competence of the Committee provided for in article 20, unless that State has subsequently withdrawn its reservation in accordance with article 28, paragraph 2, of the Convention.

*Rule 70. Register of Information Submitted.* The Secretary-General shall maintain a permanent register of information brought to the attention of the Committee in accordance with rule 69 above and shall make the information available to any member of the Committee upon request.

*Rule 71. Summary of the Information.* The Secretary-General, when necessary, shall prepare and circulate to the members of the Committee a brief summary of the information submitted in accordance with rule 69 above.

*Rule 72. Confidentiality of Documents and Proceedings.* All documents and proceedings of the Committee relating to its functions under article 20 of the Convention shall be confidential, until such time when the Committee decides, in accordance with the provisions of article 20, paragraph 5, of the Convention, to make them public.

*Rule 73. Meetings.* 1. Meetings of the Committee concerning its proceedings under article 20 of the Convention shall be closed.

2. Meetings during which the Committee considers general issues, such as procedures for the application of artiicle 20 of the Convention, shall be public, unless the Committee decides otherwise.

*Rule 74. Issue of Communiqués concerning Closed Meetings.* The Committee may decide to issue communiqués, through the Secretary-General, for the use of the information media and the general public regarding its activities under article 20 of the Convention.

*Rule 75. Preliminary Consideration of Information by the Committee.* 1. The Committee, when necessary, may ascertain, through the Secretary-General, the reliability of the information and/or of the sources of the information brought to its attention under article 20 of the Convention or obtain additional relevant information substantiating the facts of the situation.

2. The Committee shall determine whether it appears to it that the information received contains well-founded indications that torture, as defined in article 1 of the Convention, is being systematically practised in the territory of the State party concerned.

*Rule 76. Examination of the Information.* 1. If it appears to the Committee that the information received is reliable and contains well-founded indications that torture is being systematically practised in the territory of a State party, the Committee shall invite the State party concerned, through the Secretary-General, to co-operate in its examination of the information and, to this end, to submit observations with regard to that information.

2. The Committee shall indicate a time-limit for the submission of observations by the State party concerned, with a view to avoiding undue delay in its proceedings.

3. In examining the information received, the Committee shall take into account any observations which may have been submitted by the State party concerned, as well as any other relevant information available to it.

4. The Committee may decide, if it deems it appropriate, to obtain from the representatives of the State party concerned, governmental and non-governmental organizations, as well as individuals, additional information or answers to questions relating to the information under examination.

5. The Committee shall decide, on its initiative and on the basis of its rules of procedure, the form and manner in which such additional information may be obtained.

*Rule 77. Documentation from United Nations Bodies and Specialized Agencies.* The Committee may at any time obtain, through the Secretary-General, any relevant documentation from United Nations bodies or specialized agencies that may assist it in the examination of the information received under article 20 of the Convention.

*Rule 78. Establishment of an Inquiry.* 1. The Committee may, if it decides that this is warranted, designate one or more of its members to make a confidential inquiry and to report to it within a time-limit which may be set by the Committee.

2. When the Committee decides to make an inquiry in accordance with paragraph 1 of this rule, it shall establish the modalities of the inquiry as it deems it appropriate.

3. The members designated by the Committee for the confidential inquiry shall determine their own methods of work in conformity with the provisions of the Convention and the rules of procedure of the Committee.

*Rule 79. Co-operation of the State Party Concerned.* The Committee shall invite the State party concerned, through the Secretary-General, to co-operate with it in the conduct of the inquiry. To this end, the Committee may request the State party concerned:

(a) To designate an accredited representative to meet with the members designated by the Committee;

(b) To provide its designated members with any information that they, or the State party, may consider useful for ascertaining the facts relating to the inquiry;

(c) To indicate any other form of co-operation that the State may wish to extend to the Committee and to its designated members with a view to facilitating the conduct of the inquiry.

*Rule 80. Visiting Mission.* If the Committee deems it necessary to include in its inquiry a visit of one or more of its members to the territory of the State party concerned, it shall request, through the Secretary-General, the agreement of that State party and shall inform the State party of its wishes regarding the timing of the mission and the facilities required to allow the designated members of the Committee to carry out their task.

*Rule 81. Hearings in Connection with the Inquiry.* 1. The designated members may decide to conduct hearings in connection with the inquiry as they deem it appropriate.

2. The designated members shall establish, in co-operation with the State party concerned, the conditions and guarantees required for conducting such hearings. They shall request the State party to ensure that no obstacles are placed in the way of witnesses and other individuals wishing to meet with the designated members of the Committee and that no retaliatory measure is taken against those individuals or their families.

3. Every person appearing before the designated members for the purpose of giving testimony shall be requested to take an oath or make a solemn declaration concerning

the veracity of his/her testimony and the respect for confidentiality of the proceedings.

*Rule 82. Assistance during the Inquiry.* 1. In addition to the staff and facilities to be provided by the Secretary-General in connection with the inquiry and/or the visiting mission to the territory of the State party concerned, the designated members may invite, through the Secretary-General, persons with special competence in the medical field or in the treatment of prisoners as well as interpreters to provide assistance at all stages of the inquiry.

2. If the persons providing assistance during the inquiry are not bound by an oath of office to the United Nations, they shall be required to declare solemnly that they will perform their duties honestly, faithfully and impartially, and that they will respect the confidentiality of the proceedings.

3. The persons referred to in paragraphs 1 and 2 of the present rule shall be entitled to the same facilities, privileges and immunities provided for in respect of the members of the Committee, under article 23 of the Convention.

*Rule 83. Transmission of Findings, Comments or Suggestions.* 1. After examining the findings of its designated members submitted to it in accordance with rule 78, paragraph 1, the Committee shall transmit, through the Secretary-General, these findings to the State party concerned, together with any comments or suggestions that it deems appropriate.

2. The State party concerned shall be invited to inform the Committee within a reasonable delay of the action it takes with regard to the Committee's findings and in response to the Committee's comments or suggestions.

*Rule 84. Summary Account of the Results of the Proceedings.* 1. After all the proceedings of the Committee regarding an inquiry made under article 20 of the Convention have been completed, the Committee may decide, after consultations with the State party concerned, to include a summary account of the results of the proceedings in its annual report made in accordance with article 24 of the Convention.

2. The Committee shall invite the State party concerned, through the Secretary-General, to inform the Committee directly or through its designated representative of its view concerning the question referred to in paragraph 1 of this rule, and may indicate a time-limit within which the view of the State party should be communicated to the Committee.

## XVIII. Procedure for the Consideration of Communications Received Under Article 21 of the Convention

*Rule 85. Declarations by States Parties.* 1. The Secretary-General shall transmit to the other States parties copies of the declarations deposited with him by States parties recognizing the competence of the Committee, in accordance with article 21 of the Convention.

2. The withdrawal of a declaration made under article 21 of the Convention shall not prejudice the consideration of any matter that is the subject of a communication already transmitted under that article; no further communication by any State party shall be received under that article after the notification of withdrawal of the declaration has been received by the Secretary-General, unless the State party has made a new declaration.

*Rule 86. Notification by the State Parties Concerned.* 1. A communication under article 21 of the Convention may be referred to the Committee by either State party concerned by notice given in accordance with paragraph 1(b) of that article.

2. The notice referred to in paragraph 1 of this rule shall contain or be accompanied by information regarding:

(a) Steps taken to seek adjustment of the matter in accordance with article 21, paragraphs 1 (a) and (b), of the Convention, including the text of the initial communication and of any subsequent written explanations or statements by the States parties concerned which are pertinent to the matter;

(b) Steps taken to exhaust domestic remedies;

(c) Any other procedure of international investigation or settlement resorted to by the States parties concerned.

*Rule 87. Register of Communications.* The Secretary-General shall maintain a permanent register of all communications received by the Committee under article 21 of the Convention.

*Rule 88. Information to the Members of the Committee.* The Secretary-General shall inform the members of the Committee without delay of any notice given under rule 86 of these rules and shall transmit to them as soon as possible copies of the notice and relevant information.

*Rule 89. Meetings.* The Committee shall examine communications under article 21 of the Convention at closed meetings.

*Rule 90. Issue of Communiqués concerning Closed Meetings.* The Committee may, after consultation with the States parties concerned, issue communiqués, through the Secretary-General, for the use of the information media and the general public regarding the activities of the Committee under article 21 of the Convention.

*Rule 91. Requirements for the Consideration of Communications.* A communication shall not be considered by the Committee unless:

(a) Both States parties concerned have made declarations under article 21, paragraph 1, of the Convention;

(b) The time-limit prescribed in article 21, paragraph 1 (b), of the Convention has expired;

(c) The Committee has ascertained that all available domestic remedies have been invoked and exhausted in the matter, in conformity with the generally recognized principles of international law, or that the application of the remedies is unreasonably prolonged or is unlikely to bring effective relief to the person who is the victim of the violation of the Convention.

*Rule 92. Good Offices.* 1. Subject to the provisions of rule 91 of these rules, the Committee shall proceed to make its good offices available to the States parties concerned with a view to a friendly solution of the matter on the basis of respect for the obligations provided for in the Convention.

2. For the purpose indicated in paragraph 1 of this rule, the Committee may, when appropriate, set up an ad hoc conciliation Commission.

*Rule 93. Request for Information.* The Committee may, through the Secretary-General, request the States parties concerned or either of them to submit additional information or observations orally or in writing. The Committee shall indicate a time-limit for the submission of such written information or observations.

*Rule 94. Attendance by the States Parties Concerned.* 1. The States parties concerned shall have the right to be represented when the matter is being considered in the Committee and to make submissions orally and/or in writing.

2. The Committee shall, through the Secretary-General, notify the States parties concerned as early as possible of the opening date, duration and place of the session at which the matter will be examined.

3. The procedure for making oral and/or written sub-

missions shall be decided by the Committee, after consultation with the States parties concerned.

*Rule 95. Report of the Committee.* 1. Within 12 months after the date on which the Committee received the notice referred to in rule 86 of these rules, the Committee shall adopt a report in accordance with article 21, paragraph 1 (h), of the Convention.

2. The provisions of paragraph 1 of rule 94 of these rules shall not apply to the deliberations of the Committee concerning the adoption of the report.

3. The Committee's report shall be communicated, through the Secretary-General, to the States parties concerned.

## XIX. Procedure for the Consideration of Communications Received Under Article 22 of the Convention

A. General Provisions

*Rule 96. Declarations by States Parties.* 1. The Secretary-General shall transmit to the other States parties copies of the declarations deposited with him by States parties recognizing the competence of the Committee, in accordance with article 22 of the Convention.

2. The withdrawal of a declaration made under article 22 of the Convention shall not prejudice the consideration of any matter which is the subject of a communication already transmitted under that article; no further communication by or on behalf of an individual shall be received under that article after the notification of withdrawal of the declaration has been received by the Secretary-General, unless the State party has made a new declaration.

*Rule 97. Transmission of Communications to the Committee.* 1. The Secretary-General shall bring to the attention of the Committee, in accordance with the present rules, communications which are or appear to be submitted for consideration by the Committee under paragraph 1 of article 22 of the Convention.

2. The Secretary-General, when necessary, may request clarification from the author of a communication as to his wish to have his communication submitted to the Committee for consideration under article 22 of the Convention. In case there is still doubt as to the wish of the author, the Committee shall be seized of the communication.

3. No communication shall be received by the Committee or included in a list under rule 98 if it concerns a State which has not made the declaration provided for in article 22, paragraph 1, of the Convention.

*Rule 98. List and Register of Communications.* 1. The Secretary-General shall prepare lists of the communications brought to the attention of the Committee in accordance with rule 97 above, with a brief summary of their contents, and shall circulate such lists to the members of the Committee at regular intervals. The Secretary-General shall also maintain a permanent register of all such communications.

2. The full text of any communication brought to the attention of the Committee shall be made available to any member of the Committee upon his request.

*Rule 99. Request for Clarification or Additional Information.* 1. The Secretary-General may request clarification from the author of a communication concerning the applicability of article 22 of the Convention to his communication, in particular regarding:

(a) The name, address, age and occupation of the author and the verification of his identity;

(b) The name of the State party against which the communication is directed;

(c) The object of the communication;

(d) The provision or provisions of the Convention alleged to have been violated;

(e) The facts of the claim;

(f) Steps taken by the author to exhaust domestic remedies;

(g) The extent to which the same matter is being examined under another procedure of international investigation or settlement.

2. When requesting clarification or information, the Secretary-General shall indicate an appropriate time-limit to the author of the communication with a view to avoiding undue delays in the procedure under article 22 of the Convention.

3. The Committee may approve a questionnaire for the purpose of requesting the above-mentioned information from the author of the communication.

4. The request for clarification referred to in paragraph 1 of the present rule shall not preclude the inclusion of the communication in the list provided for in rule 98, paragraph 1.

*Rule 100. Summary of the Information.* For each registered communication the Secretary-General shall, as soon as possible, prepare and circulate to the members of the Committee a summary of the relevant information obtained.

*Rule 101. Meetings.* 1. Meetings of the Committee or its subsidiary bodies during which communications under article 22 of the Convention will be examined shall be closed.

2. Meetings during which the Committee may consider general issues, such as procedures for the application of article 22 of the Convention, may be public if the Committee so decides.

*Rule 102. Issue of Communiqués concerning Closed Meetings.* The Committee may issue communiqués, through the Secretary-General, for the use of the information media and the general public regarding the activities of the Committee under article 22 of the Convention.

*Rule 103. Inability of a Member to Take Part in the Examination of a Communication.* 1. A member shall not take part in the examination of a communication by the Committee or its subsidiary body:

(a) If he has any personal interest in the case; or

(b) If he has participated in any capacity in the making of any decision on the case covered by the communication.

2. Any question which may arise under paragraph 1 above shall be decided by the Committee without the participation of the member concerned.

*Rule 104. Withdrawal of a Member.* If, for any reason, a member considers that he should not take part or continue to take part in the examination of a communication, he shall inform the Chairman of his withdrawal.

B. Procedure for Determining Admissibility of Communications

*Rule 105. Method of Dealing with Communications.* 1. In accordance with the following rules, the Committee shall decide as soon as possible whether or not a communication is admissible under article 22 of the Convention.

2. The Committee shall, unless it decides otherwise, deal with communications in the order in which they have been placed before it by the Secretariat.

3. The Committee may, if it deems it appropriate, decide to consider jointly two or more communications.

4. The Committee may, if it deems it appropriate, decide to join the consideration of the question of admissibility of a communication to the consideration of the communication on its merits.

*Rule 106. Establishment of a Working Group.* 1. The Committee may, in accordance with rule 61, set up a Working

Group to meet shortly before its sessions, or at any other convenient time to be decided by the Committee in consultation with the Secretary-General, for the purpose of making recommendations to the Committee regarding the fulfillment of the conditions of admissibility of communications laid down in article 22 of the Convention and assisting the Committee in any manner which the Committee may decide.

2. The Working Group shall not comprise more than five members of the Committee. The Working Group shall elect its own officers, develop its own working methods, and apply as far as possible the rules of procedure of the Committee to its meetings.

*Rule 107. Conditions for Admissibility of Communications.* 1. With a view to reaching a decision on the admissibility of a communication, the Committee or its Working Group shall ascertain:

(a) That the communication is not anonymous and that it emanates from an individual subject to the jurisdiction of a State party recognizing the competence of the Committee under article 22 of the Convention;

(b) That the individual claims to be a victim of a violation by the State party concerned of the provisions of the Convention. The communication should be submitted by the individual himself or by his relatives or designated representatives or by others on behalf of an alleged victim when it appears that the victim is unable to submit the communication himself, and the author of the communication justifies his acting on the victim's behalf;

(c) That the communication is not an abuse of the right to submit a communication under article 22 of the Convention;

(d) That the communication is not incompatible with the provisions of the Convention;

(e) That the same matter has not been and is not being examined under another procedure of international investigation or settlement;

(f) That the individual has exhausted all available domestic remedies. However, this shall not be the rule where the application of the remedies is unreasonably prolonged or is unlikely to bring effective relief to the person who is the victim of the violation of this Convention.

2. The Committee shall consider a communication, which is otherwise admissible, whenever the conditions laid down in article 22, paragraph 5, are met.

*Rule 108. Additional Information, Clarifications and Observations.* 1. The Committee or the Working Group established under rule 106 may request, through the Secretary-General, the State party concerned or the author of the communication to submit additional written information, clarifications or observations relevant to the question of admissibility of the communication.

2. Requests referred to in paragraph 1 of this rule which are addressed to the State party shall be accompanied by the text of the communication.

3. A communication may not be declared admissible unless the State party concerned has received the text of the communication and has been given an opportunity to furnish information or observations as provided in paragraph 1 of this rule, including information relating to the exhaustion of domestic remedies.

4. The Committee or the Working Group may adopt a questionnaire for requesting such additional information or clarifications.

5. The Committee or the Working Group shall indicate a time-limit for the submission of such additional information or clarification with a view to avoiding undue delay.

6. If the time-limit is not respected by the State party concerned or the author of a communication, the Committee or the Working Group may decide to consider the admissibility of the communication in the light of available information.

7. If the State party concerned disputes the contention of the author of a communication that all available domestic remedies have been exhausted, the State party is required to give details of the effective remedies available to the alleged victim in the particular circumstances of the case and in accordance with the provisions of article 22, paragraph 5 (b), of the Convention.

8. Within such time-limit as indicated by the Committee or the Working Group, the State party or the author of a communication may be afforded an opportunity to comment on any submission received from the other party pursuant to a request made under the present rule. Non-receipt of such comments within the established time-limit should, as a rule, not delay the consideration of the admissibility of the communication.

9. In the course of the consideration of the question of the admissibility of a communication, the Committee or the Working Group may request the State party to take steps to avoid a possible irreparable damage to the person or persons who claim to be victim(s) of the alleged violation. Such a request addressed to the State party does not imply that any decision has been reached on the question of the admissibility of the communication.

*Rule 109. Inadmissible Communications.* 1. Where the Committee decides that a communication is inadmissible under article 22 of the Convention, or its consideration is suspended or discontinued, the Committee shall as soon as possible transmit its decision, through the Secretary-General, to the author of the communication and, where the communication has been transmitted to a State party concerned, to that State party.

2. If the Committee has declared a communication inadmissible under article 22, paragraph 5, of the Convention, this decision may be reviewed at a later date by the Committee upon a written request by or on behalf of the individual concerned. Such written request shall contain documentary evidence to the effect that the reasons for inadmissibility referred to in article 22, paragraph 5, of the Convention no longer apply.

C. Consideration of Communications on their Merits

*Rule 110. Method of Dealing with Admissible Communications.* 1. When it has been decided that a communication is admissible under article 22 of the Convention, the Committee shall transmit to the State party, through the Secretary-General, the text of its decision together with any submission received from the author of the communication not already transmitted to the State party under rule 108, paragraph 2. The Committee shall also inform the author of the communication, through the Secretary-General, of its decision.

2. Within six months, the State party concerned shall submit to the Committee written explanations or statements clarifying the case under consideration and the remedy, if any, that may have been taken by it. The Committee may indicate, if it deems it necessary, the type of information it wishes to receive from the State party concerned.

3. In the course of its consideration, the Committee may inform the State party of its views on the desirability, because of urgency, of taking interim measures to avoid possible irreparable damage to the person or persons who claim to be victim(s) of the alleged violation. In doing so, the Committee shall inform the State party concerned that such expression

of its views on interim measures does not prejudice its final views on the merits of the communication.

4. Any explanations or statements submitted by a State party pursuant to this rule shall be transmitted, through the Secretary-General, to the author of the communication who may submit any additional written information or observations within such time-limit as the Committee shall decide.

5. The Committee may invite the author of the communication or his representative and representatives of the State party concerned to be present at specified closed meetings of the Committee in order to provide further clarifications or to answer questions on the merits of the communication.

6. The Committee may revoke its decision that a communication is admissible in the light of any explanations or statements submitted by the State party pursuant to this rule. However, before the Committee considers revoking that decision, the explanations or statements concerned must be transmitted to the author of the communication so that he may submit additional information or observations within a time-limit set by the Committee.

*Rule 111. Views of the Committee on Admissible Communications.* 1. Admissible communications shall be considered by the Committee in the light of all information made available to it by or on behalf of the individual and by the State party concerned. The Committee may refer the communication to the Working Group for assistance in this task.

2. The Committee or the Working Group may at any time, in the course of the examination, obtain through the Secretary-General any documentation that may assist in the disposal of the case from United Nations bodies or the specialized agencies.

3. After consideration of an admissible commuication, the Committee shall formulate its views thereon. The views of the Committee shall be forwarded, through the Secretary-General, to the author of the communication and to the State party concerned.

4. Any member of the Committee may request that a summary of his individual opinion be appended to the views of the Committee when they are forwarded to the author of the communication and to the State party concerned.

5. The State party concerned shall be invited to inform the Committee in due course of the action it takes in conformity with the Committee's views.

*Rule 112. Summaries in the Committee's Annual Report and Inclusion of Texts of Final Decisions.* 1. The Committee shall include in its annual report a summary of the communications examined and, where appropriate, a summary of the explanations and statements of the States parties concerned and of its own views.

2. The Committee may decide to include in its annual report the text of its views under article 22, paragraph 7, of the Convention. It may also decide to include in its annual report the text of any decision declaring a communication inadmissible under article 22 of the Convention.

## COMMITTEE ON CRIME PREVENTION AND CONTROL, UN.

First established as an ad hoc advisory Committee of experts by the UN **GENERAL ASSEMBLY** on 1 December 1950, the Committee was authorized by the UN **ECONOMIC AND SOCIAL COUNCIL** in 1971 (resolution 1584 [L]) to advise the Secretary-General, the Commission for Social Development, the

UN **COMMISSION ON HUMAN RIGHTS,** and other concerned bodies in devising and formulating programs for study on an international basis and policies for international action in the field of crime prevention and criminal justice. The Committee was directed to report to the Commission for Social Development and, as appropriate, to the Commission on Human Rights, and the Commission on Narcotic Drugs.

Since 1978 the primary task of the Committee has been to prepare United Nations Congresses on the Prevention of Crime and Treatment of Offenders, as authorized by the General Assembly (resolution 32/60) by submitting appropriate proposals to the Economic and Social Council concerning, *inter alia*, the place and time of the congresses, the provisional agenda, the participants, and the preparation of the necessary documentation.

Members are elected by the Economic and Social Council for a term of four years, with half the membership being elected every two years, from among experts who possess the necessary qualifications and professional or scientific knowledge in the field and are nominated by member States. The Committee normally meets in March of alternate years for a session of approximately eight days, at the International Conference Center in Vienna.

## COMMITTEE ON ECONOMIC, SOCIAL AND CULTURAL RIGHTS, UN.

The Committee was established by the UN **ECONOMIC AND SOCIAL COUNCIL** on 28 May 1985 (resolution 1985/17) to assist it in implementing the provisions of the International Covenant on Economic, Social and Cultural Rights, which entered into force on 3 January 1976. The Committee replaced the Council's Sessional Working Group of Governmental Experts on the Implementation of the Covenant, which had been established on 3 May 1978 (decision 1978/10).

States parties to the Covenant agree to take steps, individually and through international assistance and cooperation, especially economic and technical, to the maximum of their available resources, with a view to achieving progressively the full realization of the rights recognized in the Covenant by all appropriate means, particularly the adoption of legislative measures. They also undertake to guarantee that these rights will be exercised without discrimination of any kind and to ensure the equal right of men and women to their enjoyment.

***REPORTS BY STATES.*** States parties also undertake to submit to the Secretary-General, for consideration by the Council, reports on the measures they have adopted and the progress made in achieving the observance of the rights recognized in the covenant. The Council may also arrange to receive progress reports from the specialized agencies concerned. After considering all the information available to it, the Council forwards to the General Assembly reports summarizing that information and presenting recommendations of a general character. The Committee on Economic, Social and Cultural Rights assists it in performing these tasks.

*COMPOSITION.* Under Council resolution 1985/17, the Committee consists of "eighteen members who shall be experts with recognized competence in the field of human rights, serving in their personal capacity, due consideration being given to equitable geographical distribution and to the representation of different forms of social and legal systems; to this end, fifteen seats will be equally distributed among the regional groups while the additional three seats will be allocated in accordance with the increase in the total number of States parties per regional group." Members of the Committee are elected by the Council by secret ballot for a term of four years, from a list of persons nominated by States parties to the Covenant.

*SESSIONS.* The Committee holds one session per year, at the United Nations office in Geneva or at the United Nations headquarters in New York. The first session of the Committee was held in Geneva from 9 to 27 March 1987.

As authorized by Economic and Social Council resolution 1988/4, each session is preceded by meetings of a pre-sessional working group composed of five of its members, appointed by the Chairman in consultation with members of the Committee. The principal purpose of the working group is to identify in advance the questions which might most usefully be discussed with representatives of the reporting States, with the aim of improving the efficiency of the system and facilitating the task of States' representatives by providing advance notice of the principal issues which might arise in the examination of the reports. The working group allocates to each of its members initial responsibility for undertaking a detailed review of a specific number of reports and of putting before the group a preliminary list of issues. The lists of issues, revised and supplemented on the basis of observations by the other members of the group, are transmitted to the permanent missions of the States concerned.

*RULES RELATING TO FUNCTIONS OF THE COMMITTEE.* The provisional rules of procedure adopted by the Committee on 21 February 1989 include (Part II) the following rules (58–69) relating to the handling of reports received from States under articles 16 and

17 of the Covenant, reports received from specialized agencies under article 18, and information and documentation received from other sources (UN Doc. E/1989/22, Annex IV):

### XV. Reports from States Parties Under Articles 16 and 17 of the Covenant

*Rule 58. Submission of Reports.* 1. In accordance with article 16 of the Covenant, the States parties shall submit to the Council for consideration by the Committee reports on the measures which they have adopted and progress made in achieving the observance of the rights recognized in the Covenant.

2. In accordance with article 17 of the Covenant and Council resolution 1988/4, the States parties shall submit their initial reports within two years of the entry into force of the Covenant for the State party concerned and thereafter periodic reports at five-year intervals.

*Rule 59. Non-Submission of Reports.* 1. At each session, the Secretary-General shall notify the Committee of all cases of non-submission of reports under rule 58 of these rules. In such cases the Committee may recommend to the Council to transmit to the State party concerned, through the Secretary-General, a reminder concerning the submission of such reports.

2. If, after the reminder referred to in paragraph 1 of this rule, the State party does not submit the report required under rule 58 of these rules, the Committee shall so state in the annual report which it submits to the Council.

*Rule 60. Form and Content of Reports.* 1. Upon approval of the Council, the Committee may inform the States parties, through the Secretary-General, of its wishes regarding the form and contents of the reports to be submitted under article 16 of the Covenant and the programme established by Council resolution 1988/4.

2. The general guidelines for reports by the States parties may, when necessary, be considered by the Committee with a view to making suggestions for their improvement.

*Rule 61. Consideration of Reports.* 1. The Committee shall consider the reports submitted by States parties to the Covenant in accordance with the programme established by Council resolution 1988/4.

2. The Committee shall normally consider the reports submitted by States parties under article 16 of the Covenant in the order in which they have been received by the Secretary-General.

3. Reports of the States parties scheduled for consideration by the Committee shall be made available to the members of the Committee at least six weeks before the opening of the session of the Committee. Any reports by States parties received by the Secretary-General for processing less than 12 weeks before the opening of the session shall be made available to the Committee at its session in the following year.

*Rule 62. Attendance by States Parties at Examination of Reports.* 1. Representatives of the reporting States are entitled to be present at the meetings of the Committee when their reports are examined. Such representatives should be able to make statements on the reports submitted by their States and reply to questions which may be put to them by the members of the Committee.

2. The Secretary-General shall notify the States parties as early as possible of the opening date and duration of the session of the Committee at which their respective reports

are scheduled for consideration. For the meetings referred to in the preceding paragraph, representatives of the States parties concerned shall be specially invited to attend.

*Rule 63. Request for Additional Information.* 1. When considering a report submitted by a State party under article 16 of the Covenant, the Committee shall first satisfy itself that the report provides all the information required under existing guidelines.

2. If a report of a State party to the Covenant, in the opinion of the Committee, does not contain sufficient information, the Committee may request the State concerned to furnish the additional information which is required, indicating the manner as well as the time within which the said information should be submitted.

*Rule 64. Suggestions and Recommendations.* The Committee shall make suggestions and recommendations of a general nature on the basis of its consideration of reports submitted by States parties and of the reports submitted by the specialized agencies in order to assist the Council to fulfill, in particular, its responsibilities under articles 21 and 22 of the Covenant. The Committee may also make suggestions for the consideration by the Council with reference to articles 19 and 23 of the Covenant.

*Rule 65. General Comments.* The Committee may prepare general comments based on the various articles and provisions of the Covenant with a view to assisting States parties in fulfilling their reporting obligations.

## XVI. Reports from Specialized Agencies Under Article 18 of the Covenant

*Rule 66. Submission of Reports.* In accordance with the provisions of article 18 of the Covenant and the arrangements made by the Council thereunder, the specialized agencies are called upon to submit reports on the progress made in achieving the observance of the provisions of the Covenant falling within the scope of their activities. These reports may include particulars of decisions and recommendations on such implementation adopted by their competent organs.

*Rule 67. Consideration of Reports.* The Committee is entrusted with the task of considering the reports of the specialized agencies, submitted to the Council in accordance with article 18 of the Covenant and the programme established under Council resolution 1988 (LX).

*Rule 68. Participation of Specialized Agencies.* The specialized agencies concerned shall be invited to designate representatives to participate at the meetings of the Committee. Such representatives may make general statements on matters falling within the scope of the activities of their respective organizations at the end of the discussion by the Committee of the report of each State party to the Covenant. The representatives of the States parties presenting reports to the Committee shall be free to respond to, or take into account, the statements made by the specialized agencies.

## XVII. Other Sources of Information

*Rule 69. Submission of Information, Documentation and Written Statements.* 1. Non-governmental organizations in consultative status with the Council may submit to the Committee written statements that might contribute to full and universal recognition and realization of the rights contained in the Covenant.

2. The Committee may recommend to the Council to invite United Nations bodies concerned and regional inter-governmental organizations to submit to it information, documentation and written statements, as appropriate, relevant to its activities under the Covenant.

*General Comments of the Committee.* The purpose of the Committee's general comments is explained in the introduction to annex III of its 1989 report to the Economic and Social Council (E/1989/22):

The Committee endeavours, through its general comments, to make the experience gained so far through the examination of these reports available for the benefit of all States parties in order to assist and promote their further implementation of the Covenant; to draw the attention of the States parties to insufficiencies disclosed by a large number of reports; to suggest improvements in the reporting procedures; and to stimulate the activities of the States parties, the international organizations, and the specialized agencies concerned in achieving progressively and effectively the full realization of the rights recognized in the Covenant. Whenever necessary, the Committee may, in the light of the experience of States parties and of the conclusions which it had drawn therefrom, revise and update its general comments.

General Comment 1. At its third session, the Committee adopted its first general comment on the subject of reporting by States:

1. The reporting obligations which are contained in part IV of the Covenant are designed principally to assist each State party in fulfilling its obligations under the Covenant and, in addition, to provide a basis on which the Council, assisted by the Committee, can discharge its responsibilities for monitoring States parties' compliance with their obligations and for facilitating the realization of economic, social and cultural rights in accordance with the provisions of the Covenant. The Committee considers that it would be incorrect to assume that reporting is essentially only a procedural matter designed solely to satisfy each State party's formal obligation to report to the appropriate international monitoring body. On the contrary, in accordance with the letter and spirit of the Covenant, the processes of preparation and submission of reports by States can, and indeed should, serve to achieve a variety of objectives.

2. A first objective, which is of particular relevance to the initial report required to be submitted within two years of the Covenant's entry into force for the State party concerned, is to ensure that a comprehensive review is undertaken with respect to national legislation, administrative rules and procedures, and practices in an effort to ensure the fullest possible conformity with the Covenant. Such a review might, for example, be undertaken in conjunction with each of the relevant national ministries or other authorities responsible for policy-making and implementation in the different fields covered by the Covenant.

3. A second objective is to ensure that the State party monitors the actual situation with respect to each of the rights on a regular basis and is thus aware of the extent to which the various rights are, or are not, being enjoyed by all individuals within its territory or under its jurisdiction. From the Committee's experience to date, it is clear that the fulfillment of this objective cannot be achieved only by the preparation of aggregate national statistics or estimates, but also requires that special attention be given to any worse-off regions or areas and to any specific groups or subgroups that appear to be particularly vulnerable or disadvantaged. Thus, the essential first step toward promoting the realization of economic, social and cultural rights is diagnosis and knowledge of the existing situation. The Committee is aware that this process of monitoring and gathering information is po-

tentially a time-consuming and costly one and that international assistance and cooperation, as provided for in article 2, paragraph 1, and articles 22 and 23 of the Covenant, may well be required in order to enable some States parties to fulfill the relevant obligations. If that is the case, and the State party concludes that it does not have the capacity to undertake the monitoring process which is an integral part of any process designed to promote accepted goals of public policy and is indispensable to the effective implementation of the Covenant, it may note this fact in its report to the Committee and indicate the nature and extent of any international assistance that it may need.

4. While monitoring is designed to give a detailed overview of the existing situation, the principal value of such an overview is to provide the basis for the elaboration of clearly stated and carefully targeted policies, including the establishment of priorities which reflect the provisions of the Covenant. Therefore, a third objective of the reporting process is to enable the Government to demonstrate that such principled policy-making has in fact been undertaken. While the Covenant makes this obligation explicit only in article 14 in cases where "compulsory primary education, free of charge" has not yet been secured for all, a comparable obligation "to work out and adopt a detailed plan of action for the progressive implementation" of each of the rights contained in the Covenant is clearly implied by the obligation in article 2, paragraph 1, "to take steps . . . by all appropriate means. . . ."

5. A fourth objective of the reporting process is to facilitate public scrutiny of government policies with respect to economic, social and cultural rights and to encourage the involvement of the various economic, social and cultural sectors of society in the formulation, implementation, and review of the relevant policies. In examining reports submitted to it to date, the Committee has welcomed the fact that a number of States parties, reflecting different political and economic systems, has encouraged input by such nongovernmental groups into the preparation of their reports under the Covenant. Other States have ensured the widespread dissemination of their reports with a view to enabling comments to be made by the public at large. In these ways, the preparation of the report, and its consideration at the national level can come to be of at least as much value as the constructive dialogue conducted at the international level between the Committee and representatives of the reporting State.

6. A fifth objective is to provide a basis on which the State party itself, as well as the Committee, can effectively evaluate the extent to which progress has been made towards the realization of the obligations contained in the Covenant. For this purpose, it may be useful for States to identify specific benchmarks or goals against which their performance in a given area can be assessed. Thus, for example, it is generally agreed that it is important to set specific goals with respect to the reduction of infant mortality, the extent of vaccination of children, the intake of calories per person, the number of persons per health-care provider, etc. In many of these areas, global benchmarks are of limited use, whereas national or other more specific benchmarks can provide an extremely valuable indication of progress.

7. In this regard, the Committee wishes to note that the Covenant attaches particular importance to the concept of "progressive realization" of the relevant rights and, for that reason, the Committee urges States parties to include in their periodic reports information that shows the progress over time, with respect to the effective realization of the relevant rights. By the same token, it is clear that qualitative, as well as quantitative, data are required in order for an adequate assessment of the situation to be made.

8. A sixth objective is to enable the State party itself to develop a better understanding of the problems and shortcomings encountered in efforts to realize progressively the full range of economic, social, and cultural rights. For this reason, it is essential that States parties report in detail on the "factors and difficulties" inhibiting such realization. This process of identification and recognition of the relevant difficulties then provides the framework within which more appropriate policies can be devised.

9. A seventh objective is to enable the Committee, and the States parties as a whole, to facilitate the exchange of information among States and to develop a better understanding of the common problems faced by States and a fuller appreciation of the type of measures which might be taken to promote effective realization of each of the rights contained in the Covenant. This part of the process also enables the Committee to identify the most appropriate means by which the international community might assist States, in accordance with articles 22 and 23 of the Covenant. In order to underline the importance which the Committee attaches to this objective, a separate general comment on those articles will be discussed by the Committee at its fourth session.

General Comment 2. At its fourth session, the Committee adopted its second general comment on "International technical assistance matters" (art. 22 of the Covenant):

1. Article 22 of the Covenant establishes a mechanism by which the Economic and Social Council may bring to the attention of relevant UN bodies any matters arising out of reports submitted under the Covenant "which may assist such bodies in deciding, each within its field of competence on the advisability of international measures likely to contribute to the effective implementation of the . . . Covenant." While the primary responsibility under Article 22 is vested in the Council, it is clearly appropriate for the Committee on Economic, Social and Cultural Rights to play an active role in advising and assisting the Council in this regard.

2. Recommendations in accordance with Article 22 may be made to any "organs of the United Nations, their subsidiary organs and specialized agencies concerned with furnishing technical assistance." The Committee considers that this provision should be interpreted so as to include virtualy all UN organs and agencies involved in any aspect of international development cooperation. It would, therefore, be appropriate for recommendations in accordance with Article 22 to be addressed, *inter alia,* to the Secretary-General, subsidiary organs of the Council such as the Commission on Human Rights, the Commission on Social Development, and the Commission on the Status of Women; other bodies such as UNDP, UNICEF, AND CDP; agencies such as the World Bank and IMF; and any of the other specialized agencies such as ILO, FAO, UNESCO, and WHO.

3. Article 22 could lead either to recommendations of a general policy nature or to more narrowly focused recommendations relating to a specific situation. In the former context, the principal role of the Committee would seem to be to encourage greater attention to efforts to promote economic, social, and cultural rights within the framework of international development cooperation activities undertaken by, or with the assistance of, the United Natios and its agencies. In this regard, the Committee notes that the Commission on Human Rights, in its resolution 1989/13 of 2 March 1989, invited it "to give consideration to means by which the various UN agencies working in the field of development could best integrate measures designed to pro-

mote full respect for economic, social, and cultural rights in their activities."

4. As a preliminary practical matter, the Committee notes that its own endeavours would be assisted, and the relevant agencies would also be better informed, if they were to take a greater interest in the work of the Committee. While recognizing that such an interest can be demonstrated in a variety of ways, the Committee observes that attendance by representatives of the appropriate UN bodies at its first four sessions has, with the notable exceptions of ILO, UNESCO, and WHO, been very low. Similarly, pertinent materials and written information had been received from only a very limited number of agencies. The Committee considers that a deeper understanding of the relevance of economic, social, and cultural rights in the context of international development cooperation activities would be considerably facilitated through greater interaction between the Committee and the appropriate agencies. At the very least, the day of general discussion on a specific issue, which the Committee undertakes at each of its sessions, provides an ideal context in which a potentially productive exchange of views can be undertaken.

5. On the broader issues of the promotion of respect for human rights in the context of development activities, the Committee has so far seen only rather limited evidence of the specific efforts by UN bodies. It notes with satisfaction in this regard the initiative taken jointly by the Center for Human Rights and UNDP in writing to UN Resident Representatives and other field-based officials, inviting their "suggestions and advice in particular with respect to possible forms of cooperation in ongoing projects [identified] as having a human-rights dimension or in new ones in response to a specific Government's request." The Committee has also been informed of longstanding efforts undertaken by ILO to link its own human rights and other international labour standards to its technical cooperation activities.

6. With respect to such activities, two general principles are important. The first is that the two sets of human rights are indivisible and interdependent. This means that efforts to promote one set of rights should also take full account of the other. UN agencies involved in the promotion of economic, social, and cultural rights should do their utmost to ensure that their activities are fully consistent with the enjoyment of civil and political rights. In negative terms, this means that the international agencies should scrupulously avoid involvement in projects that, for example, involve the use of forced labour in contravention of international standards, or promote or reinforce discrimination against individuals or groups contrary to the provisions of the Covenant, or involve large-scale evictions or displacement of persons without the provision of all appropriate protection and compensation. In positive terms, it means that, wherever possible, the agencies should act as advocates of projects and approaches that contribute not only to economic growth or other broadly defined objectives, but also to enhanced enjoyment of the full range of human rights.

7. The second principle of general relevance is that development cooperation activities do not automatically contribute to the promotion of respect for economic, social, and cultural rights. Many activities undertaken in the name of "development" have subsequently been recognized as ill-conceived and even counter-productive in human-rights terms. In order to reduce the incidence of such problems, the whole range of issues dealt with in the Covenant should, wherever possible and appropriate, be given specific and careful consideration.

8. Despite the importance of seeking to integrate human-rights concerns into development activities, it is true that proposals for such integration can too easily remain at a level of generality. Thus, in an effort to encourage the operationalization of the principle contained in article 22 of the Covenant, the Committee wishes to draw attention to the following specific measures that merit consideration by the relevant bodies:

(a) As a matter of principle, the appropriate UN organs and agencies should specifically recognize the intimate relationship that should be established between development activities and efforts to promote respect for human rights in general, and economic, social, and cultural rights in particular. The Committee notes in this regard the failure of each of the first three UN Development Decade Strategies to recognize that relationship and urges that the fourth such strategy, to be adopted in 1990, should rectify that omission;

(b) Consideration should be given by UN agencies to the proposal, made by the Secretary-General in a report of 1979, that a "human rights impact statement" be required to be prepared in connection with all major development cooperation activities;

(c) The training or briefing given to project and other personnel employed by UN agencies should include a component dealing with human-rights standards and principles;

(d) Every effort should be made, at each phase of a development project, to ensure that the rights contained in the Covenants are duly taken into account. This would apply, for example, in the initial assessment of the priority needs of a particular country, in the identification of particular projects, in project design, in the implementation of the project, and in its final evaluation.

9. A matter that has been of particular concern to the Committee in the examination of the reports of States parties is the adverse impact of the debt burden and of the relevant adjustment measures on the enjoyment of economic, social, and cultural rights in many countries. The Committee recognizes that adjustment programs will often be unavoidable and that these will frequently involve a major element of austerity. Under such circumstances, however, endeavours to protect the most basic economic, social, and cultural rights become more, rather than less, urgent. States parties to the Covenant, as well as the relevant UN agencies, should thus make a particular effort to ensure that such protection is, to the maximum extent possible, built-in to the programs and policies designed to promote adjustment. Such an approach, which is sometimes referred to as "adjustment with a human face" or as promoting "the human dimension of development" requires that the goal of protecting the rights of the poor and vulnerable should become a basic objective of economic adjustment. Similarly, international measures to deal with the debt crisis should take full account of the need to protect economic, social, and cultural rights through, *inter alia*, international cooperation. In many situations, this might point to the need for major debt relief initiatives.

10. Finally, the Committee wishes to draw attention to the important opportunity provided to States parties, in accordance with article 22 of the Covenant, to identify in their reports any particular needs they might have for technical assistance or development cooperation.

General Comment 3. At its fifth session (1990), the Committee adopted its third general comment, on the Nature of States Parties Obligations (article 2, para. 1):

1. Article 2 is of particular importance to a full understanding of the Covenant and must be seen as having a dy-

namic relationship with all of the other provisions of the Covenant. It describes the nature of the general legal obligations undertaken by States parties to the Covenant. Those obligations include both what may be termed (following the work of the International Law Commission) obligations of conduct and obligations of result. While great emphasis has sometimes been placed on the difference between the formulations used in this provision and that contained in the equivalent article 2 of the International Covenant on Civil and Political Rights, it is not always recognized that there are also significant similarities. In particular, while the Covenant provides for progressive realization and acknowledges the constraints due to the limits of available resources, it also imposes various obligations that are of immediate effect. Of these, two are of particular importance in understanding the precise nature of States parties obligations. One of these, which is dealt with in a separate General Comment, and which is to be considered by the Committee at its sixth session, is the "undertaking to guarantee" that relevant rights "will be exercised without discrimination. . . ."

2. The other is the undertaking in article 2(1) "to take steps," which in itself, is not qualified or limited by other considerations. The full meaning of the phrase can also be guaged by noting some of the different language versions. In English the undertaking is "to take steps"; in French it is "to act" (s'engage à agir); and in Spanish it is "to adopt measures" (a adoptar medidas). Thus, while the full realization of the relevant rights may be achieved progressively, steps toward that goal must be taken within a reasonably short time after the Covenant's entry into force for the States concerned. Such steps should be deliberate, concrete, and targeted as clearly as possible towards meeting the obligations recognized in the Covenant.

3. The means that should be used in order to satisfy the obligation to take steps are stated in article 2(1) to be "all appropriate means, including particularly the adoption of legislative measures." The Committee recognizes that, in many instances, legislation is highly desirable and, in some cases, may even be indispensable. For example, it may be difficult to combat discrimination effectively in the absence of a sound legislative foundation for the necessary measures. In fields such as health, the protection of children and mothers, and education, as well as in respect of the matters dealt with in articles 6 to 9, legislation may also be an indispensable element for many purposes.

4. The Committee notes that States parties have generally been conscientious in detailing at least some of the legislative measures that they have taken in this regard. It wishes to emphasize, however, that the adoption of legislative measures, as specifically foreseen by the Covenant, is by no means exhaustive of the obligations of States parties. Rather, the phrase "by all appropriate means" must be given its full and natural meaning. While each State party must decide for itself which means are the most appropriate under the circumstances with respect to each of the rights, the "appropriateness" of the means chosen will not always be self-evident. It is, therefore, desirable that States parties' reports should indicate not only the measures that have been taken but also the basis on which they are considered to be the most "appropriate" under the circumstances. However, the ultimate determination as to whether all appropriate measures have been taken remains one for the Committee to make.

5. Among the measures that might be considered appropriate, in addition to legislation, is the provision of judicial remedies with respect to rights that may, in accordance with the national legal system, be considered justiciable. The

Committee notes, for example, that the enjoyment of the rights recognized, without discrimination, will often be appropriately promoted, in part, through the provision of judicial or other effective remedies. Indeed, those States parties that are also parties to the International Covenant on Civil and Political Rights are already obligated (by virtue of arts. 2 [paras. 1 and 3], 3, and 26) of that Covenant to ensure that any person whose rights or freedoms (including the right to equality and nondiscrimination) recognized in that Covenant are violated, "shall have an effective remedy" (art. 2 [3a]). In addition, there are a number of other provisions in the International Covenant on Economic, Social and Cultural Rights, including articles 3, 7(a)(i), 8, 10(3), 13(2a), 13(3), 13(4), and 15(3), which would seem to be capable of immediate application by judicial and other organs in many national legal systems. Any suggestion that the provisions indicated are inherently non-self-executing would seem to be difficult to sustain.

6. Where specific policies aimed directly at the realization of the rights recognized in the Covenant have been adopted in legislative form, the Committee would wish to be informed, *inter alia*, as to whether such laws create any right of action on behalf of individuals or groups who feel that their rights are not being fully realized. In cases where constitutional recognition has been accorded to specific economic, social, and cultural rights, or where the provisions of the Covenant have been incorporated directly into national law, the Committee would wish to receive information as to the extent to which these rights are considered to be justiciable (i.e., able to be invoked before the courts). The Committee would also wish to receive specific information as to any instances in which existing constitutional provisions relating to economic, social, and cultural rights have been weakened or significantly changed.

7. Other measures that may also be considered "appropriate" for the pruposes of article 2(1) include, but are not limited to, administrative, financial, educational, and social measures.

8. The Committee notes that the undertaking "to take steps . . . by all appropriate means including particularly the adoption of legislative measures" neither requires nor precludes any particular form of government or economic system being used as the vehicle for the steps in question, provided only that it is democratic and that all human rights are thereby respected. Thus, in terms of political and economic systems, the Covenant is neutral and its principles cannot accurately be described as being predicated exclusivey upon the need for, or the desirability of, a socialist or a capitalist system, or a mixed, centrally planned, or laissez-faire economy, or upon any other particular approach. In this regard, the Committee reaffirms that the rights recognized in the Covenant are susceptible of realization within the context of a wide variety of economic and political systems, provided only that the interdependence and indivisibility of the two sets of human rights, as affirmed *inter alia* in the preamble to the Covenant, is recognized and reflected in the system in question. The Committee also notes the relevance in this regard of other human rights and in particular the right to development.

9. The principal obligation of result reflected in article 2(1) is to take steps "with a view to achieving progressively the full realization of the rights recognized" in the Covenant. The term "progressive realization" is often used to describe the intent of this phrase. The concept of progressive realization constitutes a recognition of the fact that full realization of all economic, social, and cultural rights will generally

not be able to be achieved in a short period of time. In this sense, the obligation differs significantly from that contained in article 2 of the International Covenant on Civil and Political Rights, which embodies an immediate obligation to respect and ensure all of the relevant rights. Nevertheless, the fact that realization over time, or in other words progressively, is foreseen under the Covenant should not be misinterpreted as depriving the obligation of all meaningful content. It is on the one hand a necessary flexibility device, reflecting the realities of the real world and the difficulties involved for any country in ensuring full realization of economic, social, and cultural rights. On the other hand, the phrase must be read in the light of the overall objective, indeed the *raison d'être*, of the Covenant, which is to establish clear obligations for States parties in respect of the full realization of the rights in question. It thus imposes an obligation to move as expeditiously and effectively as possible towards that goal. Moreover, any deliberately retrogressive measures in that regard would require the most careful consideration and would need to be fully justified by reference to the totality of the rights provided for in the Covenant and in the context of the full use of the maximum available resources.

10. On the basis of the extensive experience gained by the Committee, as well as by the body that preceded it, over a period of more than a decade of examining States parties reports, the Committee is of the view that a minimum core obligation to ensure the satisfaction of, at the very least, minimum essential levels of each of the rights is incumbent upon every State party. Thus, for example, a State party in which any significant number of individuals is deprived of essential foodstuffs, of essential primary health care, of basic shelter and housing, or of the most basic forms of education is, *prima facie*, failing to discharge its obligations under the Covenant. If the Covenant were to be read in such a way as not to establish such a minimum core obligation, it would be largely deprived of its *raison d'être*. By the same token, it must be noted that any assessment as to whether a State has discharged its minimum core obligation must also take account of resource constraints applying within the country concerned. Article 2(1) obligates each State party to take the necessary steps "to the maximum of its available resources." In order for a State party to be able to attribute its failure to meet at least its minimum core obligations to a lack of available resources, it must demonstrate that every effort has been made to use all resources that are at its disposition in an effort to satisfy, as a matter of priority, those minimum obligations.

11. The Committee wishes to emphasize, however, that even where the available resources are demonstrably inadequate, the obligation remains for a State party to strive to ensure the widest possible enjoyment of the relevant rights under the prevailing circumstances. Moreover, the obligations to monitor the extent of the realization, or more especially of the non-realization, of economic, social, and cultural rights, and to devise strategies and programs for their promotion, are not in any way eliminated as a result of resource constraints. The Committee has already dealt with these issues in its General Comment No. 1 (1989).

12. Similarly, the Committee underlines the fact that, even in times of severe resources constraints, whether caused by a process of adjustment, of economic recession, or by other factors, the vulnerable members of society can and indeed must be protected by the adoption of relatively low-cost targeted programs. In support of this approach, the Committee takes note of the analysis prepared by UNICEF entitled "Adjustment with

a Human Face: Protecting the Vulnerable and Promoting Growth," the analysis by UNDP in its Human Development Report 1990, and the analysis by the World Bank in the World Bank Development Report 1990.

13. A final element of article 2(1), to which attention must be drawn, is that the undertaking given by all States parties is "to take steps, individually and through international assistance and cooperation, especially economic and technical. . . . " The Committee notes that the phrase "to the maximum of its available resources" was intended by the drafters of the Covenant to refer to both the resources existing within a State and those available from the international community through international cooperation and assistance. Moreover, the essential role of such cooperation in facilitating the full realization of the relevant rights is further underlined by the specific provisions contained in articles 11, 15, 22, and 23. With respect to article 22, the Committee has already drawn attention, in General Comment No. 2 (1990), to some of the opportunities and responsibilities that exist in relation to international cooperation. Article 23 also specifically identifies "the furnishing of technical assistance" as well as other activities, as being among the means of "international action for the achievement of the rights recognized. . . ."

14. The Committee wishes to emphasize that, in accordance with articles 55 and 56 of the Charter of the United Nations, with well-established principles of international law, and with the provisions of the Covenant itself, international cooperation for development and, thus, for the realization of economic, social, and cultural rights is an obligation of all States. It is particularly incumbent upon these States that are in a position to assist others in this regard. The Committee notes in particular the importance of the Declaration on the Right to Development, adopted by the General Assembly in its resolution 41/128 of 4 December 1986, and the need for States parties to take full account of all of the principles recognized therein. It emphasizes that, in the absence of an active program of international assistance and cooperation on the part of all those States that are in a position to undertake one, the full realization of economic, social, and cultural rights will remain an unfulfilled aspiration in many countries. In this respect, the Committee also recalls the terms of its General Comment No. 2 (1990).

At its sixth session (1991), the Committee adopted its fourth general comment, on **HOUSING AS A HUMAN RIGHT** (article 11[1] of the Covenant). See entry under that title.

**COMMITTEE ON NON-GOVERNMENTAL ORGANIZATIONS, UN.** The UN **ECONOMIC AND SOCIAL COUNCIL,** as authorized by article 71 of the **UNITED NATIONS CHARTER,** has made arrangements for consultation with non-governmental organizations (NGOs) concerned with matters falling within its competence (Council resolution 1296 [XLIV]). In studying or dealing with human rights problems, UN organs often call upon NGOs in consultative status to supply information concerning situations that exist in various parts of the world. In addition, NGOs also supply information concerning allegations of violations of human rights to bodies authorized to supervise the application of various international instruments in the field. Under these arrangements the Council's Committee on Non-Governmental Organizations divides such organizations into three groups:

Category I, which is made up of NGOs having a basic interest in most of the Council's activities;

Category II, which is made up of those having a special competence but are concerned with only a few of the Council's activities; and

The Roster, which contains the names of NGOs that can make occasional and useful contributions to the Council's work.

All the organizations in "consultative status" may send observers to public meetings of the Council and its subsidiary bodies. They can submit written statements for circulation and present their views orally. As regards human rights, more than 100 NGOs regularly attend and participate in meetings of the COMMISSION ON HUMAN RIGHTS, the SUB-COMMISSION ON PREVENTION OF DISCRIMINATION AND PROTECTION OF MINORITIES, and the COMMISSION ON THE STATUS OF WOMEN. The Council, on 26 May 1987, invited all such organizations to submit to it written statements that might contribute to full and universal recognition and realization of the rights set out in the International Covenant on Economic, Social and Cultural Rights and requested the Secretary-General to make those statements available to the Committee on Economic, Social and Cultural Rights.

## COMMITTEE ON THE ELIMINATION OF DISCRIMINATION AGAINST WOMEN, UN.

The Committee was established in accordance with article 17 of the Convention on the Elimination of All Forms of Discrimination against Women, adopted by the UN GENERAL ASSEMBLY on 18 December 1979 (resolution 34/180). States parties to the Convention agree to pursue, by all appropriate means and without delay, a policy of elimination of discrimination against women, and to this end undertake, in article 2:

(a) to embody the principle of equality of men and women in their national constitutions or other appropriate legislation if not yet incorporated therein and to ensure, through law and other appropriate means, the practical realization of this principle;

(b) to adopt appropriate legislative and other measures, including sanctions where appropriate, prohibiting all discrimination against women;

(c) to establish legal protection of the rights of women on an equal basis with men and to ensure through competent national tribunals and other public institutions the effective protection of women against any act of discrimination;

(d) to refrain from engaging in any practice of discrimi-

nation against women and to ensure that public authorities and institutions shall act in conformity with this obligation;

(e) to take all appropriate measures to eliminate discrimination against women by any person, organization or enterprise;

(f) to take all appropriate measures, including legislation, to modify or abolish existing laws, regulations, customs and practices which constitute discrimination against women; and

(g) to repeal all national penal provisions which constitute discrimination against women.

The Committee on the Elimination of Discrimination against Women was established at a meeting of States parties to the Convention. The Committee consists of 23 members. They are nominated by States parties to the Convention and elected at a meeting of those States, consideration being given to equitable geographical representation and to representation of different forms of civilization and the world's principal legal systems. The term of office is four years. The Committee meets annually for a period of two weeks, normally at the Vienna International Center or at United Nations headquarters in New York.

*RESPONSIBILITIES.* The responsibilities of the Committee, set out in articles 18 to 22 of the Convention, may be summarized as follows:

***Consideration of Reports of States Parties.*** Under article 18(1) of the Convention, States parties undertake to submit to the Secretary-General, for consideration by the Committee, reports on the legislative, judicial, administrative, or other measures which they have adopted to give effect to the provisions of the Convention and on the progress made in this respect. Under article 20, the Committee may consider these reports to monitor the progress made in the implementation of the Convention.

***Making of Suggestions and General Recommendations.*** Under article 21, the Committee may make suggestions and general recommendations based on its examination of the reports and information received from States.

*RULES ON THE FUNCTIONS OF THE COMMITTEE.* The Committee's Rules of Procedure, adopted on 22 October 1982, the closing date of its first session and reproduced in the report of that session (UN Doc. A/35/45, Annex III), include the following provisions relating to the consideration of the periodic reports that the States parties are required to submit under article 18 of the Convention:

*Rule 46. Form of Reports.* 1. The Committee may formulate suggestions and general recommendations as to the form, contents and dates of the periodic reports that the States parties are required to submit under article 18 of the Convention.

2. Such suggestions and general recommendations shall take into account the integrated reporting system on the status of women endorsed by the Economic and Social Council in its resolution 1980/38.

*Rule 47. Non-receipt of Reports.* 1. At each session the Secretary-General shall notify the Committee of the non-receipt of any report required from a State party under article 18 of the Convention.

2. The Committee may, through the Secretary-General, transmit to the States concerned reminders of any overdue reports.

3. If even after a reminder has been transmitted pursuant to paragraph 2 a State concerned does not submit the report required under the Convention, the Committee shall include a reference to this effect in its annual report to the General Assembly.

*Rule 48. Suggestions and General Recommendations.* 1. In case the Committee finds that substantial improvement of its work is likely to be brought about by additional information on the part of a State party, concerning its report, the Committee may invite the State concerned to provide it with such additional information.

2. Suggestions and general recommendations made by the Committee based on the examination of the reports received from States parties under article 18 of the Convention shall be communicated by the Committee, through the Secretary-General, to the States parties for their comments.

3. The Committee may, where necessary, indicate a time-limit within which comments are to be received.

*Rule 49. Attendance by States Parties.* 1. Representatives of States parties shall be present at meetings of the Committee when the State's report is being examined and shall participate in discussions and answer questions concerning the said report.

2. The Committee shall, through the Secretary-General, notify the States parties at least six weeks in advance of the opening date, duration and place of the session at which their respective reports will be examined.

*Rule 50. Working Methods for Examining Reports.* The Committee may elaborate working methods to assist it in performing most efficiently its task of examining the reports of States parties and to consider the progress made since the entry into force of the Convention for them and since the submission of any previous reports.

At its 1988 session, the Committee adopted four general recommendations. The first proposed that States parties to the Convention make greater use of temporary special measures—such as positive action, preferential treatment, or quota systems to advance women's integration into education, the economy, politics, and employment. The second recommended that States parties to the Convention establish and/or strengthen effective national machinery, institutions, and procedures to formulate and monitor the implementation of measures to eliminate discrimination against women. The third called for adequate resources and services to be made available to the Committee to enable it to perform its functions under the Convention. And the fourth proposed that States parties to the Convention should ensure to women, on equal terms with men and without any discrimination, opportunities to represent their governments at the international level and to participate in the work of international organizations.

***VIOLENCE AGAINST WOMEN.*** At its 11th session in 1992, the Committee adopted a general recommendation on violence against women (no. 19):

*Background.* 1. Gender-based violence is a form of discrimination that seriously inhibits women's ability to enjoy rights and freedoms on a basis of equality with men.

2. In 1989, the Committee recommended that States should include in their reports information on violence and on measures introduced to deal with it (General recommendation 12, eighth session).

3. At its tenth session in 1991, it was decided to allocate part of the 11th session to a discussion and study on article 6 and other articles of the Convention relating to violence towards women and the sexual harassment and exploitation of women. That subject was chosen in anticipation of the 1993 World Conference on Human Rights, convened by the General Assembly by its resolution 45/155 of 18 December 1990.

4. The Committee concluded that not all the reports of States parties adequately reflected the close connection between discrimination against women, gender-based violence, and violations of human rights and fundamental freedoms. The full implementation of the Convention required States to take positive measures to eliminate all forms of violence against women.

5. The Committee suggested to States parties that, in reviewing their laws and policies and in reporting under the Convention, they should have regard to the following comments of the Committee concerning gender-based violence.

*General Comments.* 6. The Convention in article 1 defines discrimination against women. The definition of discrimination includes gender-based violence, that is, violence that is directed against a woman because she is a woman or that affects women disproportionately. It includes acts that inflict physical, mental, or sexual harm or suffering, threats of such acts, coercion, and other deprivations of liberty. Gender-based violence may breach specific provisions of the Convention, regardless of whether those provisions expressly mention violence.

7. Gender-based violence, which impairs or nullifies the enjoyment by women of human rights and fundamental freedoms under general international law or under human rights conventions, is discrimination within the meaning of article 1 of the Convention. These rights and freedoms include:

(a) The right to life;

(b) The right not to be subject to torture or to cruel, inhuman or degrading treatment or punishment;

(c) The right to equal protection according to humanitarian norms in time of international or internal armed conflict;

(d) The right to liberty and security of person;

(e) The right to equal protection under the law;

(f) The right to equality in the family;

(g) The right to the highest standard attainable of physical and mental health;

(h) The right to just and favourable conditions of work.

8. The Convention applies to violence perpetrated by public authorities. Such acts of violence may breach that State's obligations under general international human rights law and under other conventions, in addition to breaching this Convention.

9. It is emphasized, however, that discrimination under the Convention is not restricted to action by or on behalf of Governments (see articles 2[e], 2[f], and 5). For example, under article 2(e), the Convention calls on States parties to take all appropriate measures to eliminate discrimination against women by any person, organization, or enterprise. Under general international law and specific human rights covenants, States may also be responsible for private acts if they fail to act with due diligence to prevent violations of rights or to investigate and punish acts of violence, and for providing compensation.

*Comments on Specific Articles of the Convention. Articles 2 and 3.* 10. Articles 2 and 3 establish a comprehensive obligation to eliminate discrimination in all its forms in addition to the specific obligations under articles 5–16.

*Articles 2(f), 5, and 10(c).* 11. Traditional attitudes by which women are regarded as subordinate to men or as having stereotyped roles perpetuate widespread practices involving violence or coercion, such as family violence and abuse, forced marriage, dowry deaths, acid attacks, and female circumcision. Such prejudices and practices may justify gender-based violence as a form of protection or control of women. The effect of such violence on the physical and mental integrity of women is to deprive them of the equal enjoyment, exercise, and knowledge of human rights and fundamental freedoms. While this comment addresses mainly actual or threatened violence, the underlying consequences of these forms of gender-based violence help to maintain women in subordinate roles and contribute to their low level of political participation and to their lower level of education, skills, and work opportunities.

12. These attitudes also contribute to the propagation of pornography and the depiction and other commercial exploitation of women as sexual objects, rather than as individuals. This, in turn, contributes to gender-based violence.

*Article 6.* 13. States parties are required by article 6 to take measures to suppress all forms of traffic in women and exploitation of the prostitution of women.

14. Poverty and unemployment increase opportunities for trafficking in women. In addition to established forms of trafficking, there are new forms of sexual exploitation, such as sex tourism, the recruitment of domestic labour from developing countries to work in developed countries, and organized marriages between women from developing countries and foreign nationals. These practices are incompatible with the equal enjoyment of rights by women and with respect for their rights and dignity. They put women at special risk of violence and abuse.

15. Poverty and unemployment force many women, including young girls, into prostitution. Prostitutes are especially vulnerable to violence because their status, which may be unlawful, tends to marginalize them. They need the equal protection of laws against rape and other forms of violence.

16. Wars, armed conflicts, and the occupation of territories often lead to increased prostitution, trafficking in women, and sexual assault of women, which require specific protective and punitive measures.

*Article 11.* 17. Equality in employment can be seriously impaired when women are subjected to gender-specific violence, such as sexual harassment in the workplace.

18. Sexual harassment includes such unwelcome sexually determined behaviour as physical contact and advances, sexually coloured remarks, showing pornography and sexual demands, whether by words or actions. Such conduct can be humiliating and may constitute a health and safety problem; it is discriminatory when the woman has reasonable grounds to believe that her objection would disadvantage her in connection with her employment, including recruitment or promotion, or when it creates a hostile working environment.

*Article 12.* 19. States parties are required by article 12 to take measures to ensure equal access to health care. Violence against women puts their health and lives at risk.

20. In some States, there are practices perpetuated by culture and tradition that are harmful to the health of women and children. These practices include dietary restrictions for pregnant women, preference for male children, and female circumcision or genital mutilation.

*Article 14.* 21. Rural women are at risk of gender-based violence because traditional attitudes regarding the subordinate role of women persist in many rural communities. Girls from rural communities are at special risk of violence and sexual exploitation when they leave the rural community to seek employment in towns.

*Article 15 (and Article 5).* 22. Compulsory sterilization or abortion adversely affects women's physical and mental health, and infringes on the right of women to decide on the number and spacing of their children.

23. Family violence is one of the most insidious forms of violence against women. It is prevalent in all societies. Within family relationships, women of all ages are subjected to violence of all kinds, including battering, rape, other forms of sexual assault, mental and other forms of violence, which are perpetuated by traditional attitudes. Lack of economic independence forces many women to stay in violent relationships. The abrogation of their family responsibilities by men can be a form of violence and coercion. These forms of violence put women's health at risk and impair their ability to participate in family life and public life on a basis of equality.

*Specific Recommendations.* 24. In light of these comments, the Committee on the Elimination of Discrimination against Women recommends:

(a) States parties should take appropriate and effective measures to overcome all forms of gender-based violence, whether by public or private act;

(b) States parties should ensure that laws against family violence and abuse, rape, sexual assualt, and other gender-based violence give adequate protection to all women and respect their integrity and dignity. Appropriate protective and support services should be provided for victims. Gender-sensitive training of judicial and law-enforcement officers and other public officials is essential for the effective implementation of the Convention:

(c) States parties should encourage the compilation of statistics and research on the extent, causes, and effects of violence and on the effectiveness of measures to prevent and deal with violence;

(d) Effective measures should be taken to ensure that the media respect and promote respect for women;

(e) States parties in their reports should identify the nature and extent of attitudes, customs, and practices that perpetuate violence against women, and the kinds of violence that result. They should report the measures that they have undertaken to overcome violence, and the effects of those measures;

(f) Effective measures should be taken to overcome these attitudes and practices. States should introduce education and public information programmes to help eliminate prejudices which hinder women's equality (recommendation no. 3, 1987);

(g) Specific preventive and punitive measures are necessary to overcome trafficking and sexual exploitation;

(h) States parties in their reports should describe the extent of all these problems and the measures, including penal provisions, preventive and rehabilitiation measures, that have been taken to protect women engaged in prostitution or subject to trafficking and other forms of sexual exploitation. The effectiveness of these measures should also be described;

(i) Effective complaints procedures and remedies, including compensation, should be provided;

(j) States parties should include in their reports information on sexual harassment, and on measures to protect women from sexual harassment and other forms of violence of coercion in the workplace;

(k) States parties should establish or support services for victims of family violence, rape, sexual assualt, and other forms of gender-based violence, including refuges, specially trained health workers, rehabilitation, and counselling;

(l) States parties should take measures to overcome such practices and should take account of the Committee's recommendation on female circumcision (recommendation No. 14) in reporting on health issues;

(m) States parties should ensure that measures are taken to prevent coercion in regard to fertility and reproduction, and to ensure that women are not forced to seek unsafe medical procedures such as illegal abortion because of lack of appropriate services in regard to fertility control;

(n) States parties in their reports should state the extent of these problems and should indicate the measures that have been taken and their effect;

(o) States parties should ensure that services for victims of violence are accessible to rural women and that where necessary special services are provided to isolated communities;

(p) Measures to protect them from violence should include training and employment opportunities and the monitoring of the employment conditions of domestic workers;

(q) States parties should report on the risks to rural women, the extent and nature of violence and abuse to which they are subject, their need for and access to support and other services, and the effectiveness of measures to overcome violence;

(r) Measures that are necessary to overcome family violence should include: (i) criminal penalties where necessary and civil remedies in case of domestic violence; (ii) legislaion to remove the defence of honour in regard to the assault or murder of a female family member; (iii) services to ensure the safety and security of victims of family violence, including refuges, counselling, and rehabilitation programmes; (iv) rehabilitation programmes for perpetrators of domestic violence; and (v) support services for families where incest or sexual abuse has occurred.

(s) States parties should report on the extent of domestic violence and sexual abuse and on the preventive, punitive, and remedial measures that have been taken;

(t) States parties should take all legal and other measures that are necessary to provide effective protection of women against gender-based violence, including, *inter alia*: (i) effective legal measures, including penal sanctions, civil remedies, and compensatory provisions to protect women against all kinds of violence, including violence and abuse in the family, sexual assault, and sexual harassment in the workplace; (ii) preventive measures, including public information and education programmes to change attitudes concerning the roles and status of men and women; (iii) protective measures, including refuges, counselling, rehabilitation, and support services for women who are the victims of violence or who are at risk of violence.

(u) States parties should report on all forms of gender-based violence, and such reports should include all available data on the incidence of each form of violence and on the effects of such violence on the women who are victims;

(v) The reports of States parties should include information on the legal, preventive, and protective measures that have been taken to overcome violence against women and on the effectiveness of such measures.

## COMMITTEE ON THE ELIMINATION OF RACIAL DISCRIMINATION, UN.

The Committee was established in accordance with articles 8 and 9 of the International Convention on the Elimination of All Forms of Racial Discrimination, adopted by the UN **GENERAL ASSEMBLY** on 21 December 1965 (resolution 2106 A [XX]). The Convention entered into force on 4 January 1969.

States parties to the Convention undertake to pursue without delay a policy of eliminating racial discrimination in all its forms and of promoting understanding among races. Further, they undertake to guarantee equality before the law in the enjoyment of human rights, particularly in respect of the right of everyone to equal treatment before all organs administering justice; the right to security of persons and protection by the State against violence or bodily harm; and all the political, civil, economic, social and cultural rights that belong to every person. Racial discrimination is defined in the Convention as "any distinction, exclusion, restriction or preference based on race, colour, descent, or national or ethnic origin which has the purpose or effect of nullifying or impairing the recognition, enjoyment or exercise, on an equal footing, of human rights and fundamental freedoms in the political, economic, social, cultural or any other field of public life."

*RESPONSIBILITIES.* The responsibilities of the Committee on the Elimination of Racial Discrimination, set out in articles 9 and 11–16 of the Convention, include the following:

*1. Consideration of Reports of States.* Under Article 9, paragraph 1, States which have ratified or acceded to the Convention undertake to submit to the Secretary-General for consideration by the Committee reports on the legislative, judicial, administrative, or other measures that they have adopted and that give effect to the provisions of the Convention, including its antidiscrimination provisions. The Committee is empowered to examine these reports, to request further information from the States, to make suggestions and general recommendations based on consideration of the reports and information, and to report on those activities to the UN General Assembly.

2. *Consideration of Complaints of One State against Another.* Under Article 11, if a State party to the Convention considers that another State party is not giving effect to the convention's provisions, it may bring the matter to the attention of the Committee. With respect to such complaints, the Committee is authorized (a) to transmit the communication to the concerned state; (b) to "deal with" the matter, after it has ascertained that all available domestic remedies have been invoked and exhausted, in conformity with the generally recognized principles of international law; (c) to appoint an ad hoc conciliation commission to attempt to find an amicable solution; (d) to communicate the report of the ad hoc commission to each of the disputing parties so that each may indicate whether or not it accepts the commission's recommendations; and (e) to communicate that report, together with the declarations of the concerned parties, to the other States parties to the Convention and to report on the matter to the General Assembly.

3. *Consideration of Communications from Individuals and Groups.* Under article 14, and subject to the conditions and requirements set out there, the Committee may receive and consider communications from individuals or groups of individuals, within its jurisdiction, claiming to be victims of a violation by a State party to the Convention of any of the rights set forth therein. With regard to such communications, the Committee is authorized (a) to bring confidentially to the attention of the State alleged to be violating any provision of the Convention and communication referred to it, but without revealing the identity of the individual or groups concerned without his or their express consent; (b) to consider the communication in light of all information made available to it by the concerned State and the petitioner; (c) to forward its suggestions and recommendations, if any, to the concerned State and the petitioner; and (d) to report on the matter to the General Assembly.

4. *Consideration of Information relating to Trust and Non-Self-Governing Territories.* Regarding racial discrimination in trust and non-self-governing territories, the Committee is authorized, under article 15, (a) to receive from the competent UN bodies reports concerning measures taken by the administering powers within those territories and from the Secretary-General all relevant information available to him regarding those territories; (b) to express opinions and make recommendations addressed to the concerned UN bodies on the petitions and reports transmitted to it; and (c) to report on the matter to the General Assembly.

The Committee submits an annual report to the General Assembly covering the matters mentioned above. If the Committee has dealt with a complaint by one state against another, in accordance with articles 11–13 of the Convention, there is no provision requiring that this be included in the annual report; instead, article 13, para. 3, provides that the Chairman of the Committee shall communicate the report of the ad hoc conciliation commission to the other States parties to the Convention.

*COMPOSITION.* Under article 8 of the Convention, the Committee is composed of "eighteen experts of high moral standing and acknowledged impartiality elected by States Parties from among their nationals, who shall serve in their personal capacity, consideration being given to equitable geographical distribution and to the representation of different forms of civilization as well as of the principal legal systems." The term of office is five years.

*SESSIONS.* The Committee normally holds two sessions each year, lasting from two to three weeks' duration, one at New York and the other at Geneva. However, due to non-payment of contributions by a number of States parties, since 1989 certain sessions have been canceled. In resolutions adopted in 1990, 1991, 1992, and 1993, the General Assembly has appealed to those States parties to honor their financial obligations under the Convention.

In 1992, representatives of the States parties agreed to amend the Convention by revising article 8, para. 6, and adding a new article 8, para. 7, providing that members of the Committee should receive emoluments from UN resources. The General Assembly endorsed these amendments on 16 December 1992 (resolution 47/111) and requested the Secretary-General to provide for the financing of the Committee from the regular budget of the United Nations, beginning with the budget for the biennium 1994–1995, and to ensure that the Committee meets as scheduled until the amendments enter into force.

**COMMITTEE ON THE EXERCISE OF THE INALIENABLE RIGHTS OF THE PALESTINIAN PEOPLE, UN.** Established by the UN **GENERAL ASSEMBLY** on 10 November 1975 (resolution 3376 [XXX]), the Committee's function is to recommend to the Assembly a program designed to enable the Palestinian people to exercise (1) their right to self-determination without outside interference, (2) their right to national independence and sovereignty, and (3) their right to return to their homes and property from which they have been displaced and uprooted.

Originally composed of 20 UN member States, the Committee was enlarged to 23 by the General Assembly (decision 31/318). The term of office of members is indeterminate. The Committee holds one session each year.

The 1993 report of the Committee (UN Doc. A/48/35) was received by the General Assembly (resolution 48/158), which welcomed the signing of the Declaration of Principles on Interim Self-Government Arrangements by the Government of Israel and the Palestine Liberation Organization (A/48/486) on 13 December 1993 in Washington, D.C. The Assembly expressed the view that the Committee could make a valuable contribution to international efforts to promote the implementation of the Declaration and to mobilize international support for and assistance to the Palestinian people during the transitional period.

## COMMITTEE ON THE RIGHTS OF THE CHILD, UN.

The Committee was established, in accordance with article 43 of the Convention on the Rights of the Child, "for the purpose of examining the progress made by States Parties in achieving the realization of the obligations undertaken in the Convention." Its members—"ten experts of high moral standing and recognized competence in the field"—were elected by the States Parties from among their nationals, to serve in their personal capacity.

The Convention, adopted by the UN **GENERAL ASSEMBLY** on 20 November 1989, entered into force on 2 September 1990; and by the close of 1993, it had been ratified or acceded to by 153 States. Reports by States parties on the measures that they had adopted to give effect to the rights set out in the Convention began to reach the Committee's staff as early as September 1992.

The Committee held its first session at Geneva from 30 September to 18 October 1991. At its 1991 and 1992 meetings, it concentrated on organizational matters, determining its methods of work, examining possible sources of information, and working out its relations with other UN human rights bodies.

Having decided in 1992 that it would issue its concluding observations after considering each report of a State party, reflecting the main points of discussion and indicating issues that would require a follow-up, it did so for the first time in mid-January 1993.

*SEE ALSO* Children's Rights.

## COMOROS.

The Federal Islamic Republic of the Comoros is a country that occupies four islands in the Indian Ocean between the east African mainland and the Island of Madagascar; the islands are Grande-Comore, Anjouan, Moheli, and Mayotte. It achieved independence from France in 1975 and became a member of the United Nations the same year. However, Mayotte has since been the subject of contention, France having refused to withdraw from the island. The population of the Comoros is estimated to be 503,000 without Mayotte. Ethnic groups include the Antalote, Cafre, Makoa, and Oimatsaha. Languages in common use include Shaafi Islam (a Swahili dialect), French, and Malagasy. Religions practiced include Islam (Shirazi Muslim), 80%; Christianity (Roman Catholic), 14%; and other faiths, 16%. The island of Mayotte has a Christian majority; the other islands are predominantly Islamic. Literacy is estimated at 15%.

The government (1994) took the form of a federal Islamic republic. The President is head of State; the Premier, head of government. There is a Council of Government composed of nine ministers appointed by the President, on which each island's governor has a non-voting seat. There is also a 39-member unicameral Federal Assembly. Each island is administered by a governor nominated by the President and an elected Legislative Assembly. The judicial code is based on French and traditional Islamic law. The United Progress Party is the only political party.

The sovereignty of Comoros over the island of Mayotte has been repeatedly reaffirmed by the UN General Assembly, the **ORGANIZATION OF AFRICAN UNITY,** the Movement of Non-Aligned Countries, and the **ORGANIZATION OF THE ISLAMIC CONFERENCE** but the Government of France has not honored commitments, made prior to 1975, ensuring respect for the unity and territorial integrity of the Comoros.

In November 1989, President Ahmed Abdallah Abdermane—who had been elected first in 1972 when the Comoros was still a French possession and who had ruled since that time for all but three years—was assassinated by rebels shortly after winning a referendum that would have permitted him to seek another six-year term. He had survived earlier coup attempts in 1983, 1985, and 1987.

Replaced by an interim government headed by Supreme Court Justice Mohammed Djohar, the former President's authority actually was maintained for several weeks by Col. Bob Denard, a mercenary who had for many years controlled the 650-man presidential guard. Reluctant to return to France, where he faced legal action, Denard departed for South Africa on 15 December, together with 21 other mercenaries.

Elections held in February 1990–the first ever in independent Comoros—had to be suspended after widespread voting irregularities were reported and seven presidential candidates charged widespread fraud and demanded the immediate resignation of the interim president.

***BIBLIOGRAPHY.*** Amnesty International. "Campaign for Prisoners of the Month: Comoros," *Amnesty International Newsletter* 16, no. 7 (July 1986): 2. NGO article, in English.

————. *Comoros: The Detention without Trial and Allegations of Torture of Suspected Opponents of the Government.* London: 1985. NGO report, in English.

————. *Comoros: Prisoners of Conscience.* London: 1985. NGO report, in English.

Fagart, Thierry. *Rapport de Mission (4 au 8 mai 1985): La Situation des Droits de l'Homme en Republique Islamique des Comores* (Mission Report [May 4–8 1985]: The Human Rights Situation in the Islamic Republic of the Comoros). Paris:

Federation Internationale des Droits de l'Homme, 1985. NGO mission report, in French.

## CONFERENCE OF EUROPEAN CHURCHES.

A non-governmental organization in consultative status (Category II) with the UN ECONOMIC AND SOCIAL COUNCIL, the Conference was founded in 1964 to establish contacts among Christian churches in all parts of Europe. It has 115 European churches as members (Protestant, Angelican, Catholic, and Orthodox).

The Conference publishes the *CEC Documentation Service* (twice a year) and *CEC News* (irregularly) in English, French, and German.

Conference of European Churches. Address: 150 route de Ferney, P.O. Box 2100, CH-1211 Geneva 2, Switzerland. Telephone: (41-22) 791-62-27. Fax: (41-22) 791-03-61. Cable: OIKOUMENE. Telex: 415730 OIK CH. Secretary-General: Jean Fischer.

## CONGO.

The People's Republic of the Congo is a country in middle Africa, on the Atlantic Ocean. It has borders with Angola, Cameroon, Central African Republic, Gabon, and Zaire. It achieved independence from France in 1960 and became a member of the United Nations the same year. Its population is estimated to be 2,413,000. More than 15 ethnic groups are included in the population, among them the Bacongo, the Bateke, the Bukongui, the M'bochi, and the Sangha. Languages commonly used include French (official), Lingala, and Kikongo. Religions practiced include Christianity (Roman Catholic, 54%); Protestant denominations, 24%; Animism, 19%; and Islam 3%. Literacy is estimated at 56%.

The government (1994) took the form of "a single, indivisible and secular People's Republic." Under article 2 of the constitution of 8 July 1979 as amended in 1984, sovereignty resides in the people, and all authority emanates from the people through a single party, the Congolese Labour Party, "the highest form of political and social organization of the people." The constitution provides, specifically in Title II, entitled "Public Freedoms and the Individual," for the protection of the rights set out in the International Covenant on Civil and Political Rights, including the right to life; the right to freedom of the individual; the right to inviolability of the home; the right not to be subjected to searches, except in conditions laid down by law; the right to inviolability of correspondence; the right not to be imprisoned, except in cases provided for by law; and the right to nondiscrimination. In addition, human rights are protected by provisions of the Penal Code, the Labor Code, the Nationality Code, the Fam-

ily Code, and the Act of April 1983 reorganizing the system of justice.

**BIBLIOGRAPHY.** Amnesty International. *Congo: Background to Political Arrests in 1987 and 1988.* London: 1988. NGO report, in English.
————. *Reports of Torture in the People's Republic of the Congo.* London: 1985. NGO report, in English.
————. *Republic of Congo: Unlawful Political Detentions and Amnesty International's Concern about Unfair Trial.* London: 1990. NGO factfinding report, in English and French.
Federation Internationale des Droits de l'Homme (International Federation of Human Rights). *Congo: 3 au 7 Aout 1986, Me. Henri Choukroun, Proces de Brazzaville* (Congo: August 3–17, 1986, Me. Henri Choukroun, Trial in Brazzaville). Paris: 1986. NGO mission report, in French.
*Freedom of Information and Expression in the Congo: A Commentary by Article 19 on the Report Submitted to the United Nations Human Rights Committee by the Government of the Congo.* London: Article 19, 1987. NGO report, in English.
Menga, Roger-Julien. *La Charte Africaine des Droits de l'Homme et des Peuples et l'Ordre Juridique Congolais* (The African Charter of Human and Peoples' Rights and the Congolese Juridical Order). Geneva: Institut Universitaire de Hautes Etudes Internationales, 1984. Scholarly monograph, in French; bibliography, pp. 148–158.
Tchibinda, J. F., and N. Mayetela. "The Rights of the Child in the People's Republic of the Congo," in *Law and the Status of the Child,* vol. 1, eds. Anna Mamalakis Papas, pp. 183–220. New York: United Nations Institute for Training and Research (UNITAR), 1983. Collection of scholarly articles, in English.

## CONSCIENTIOUS OBJECTION TO MILITARY SERVICE.

The UN COMMISSION ON HUMAN RIGHTS took up the question of conscientious objection to military service, which had become a matter of great concern to young people in a number of countries, at its 1971 session. There was general agreement in the Commission as to the duty of the individual national of a country to defend his family and society when that country was attacked and to contribute to the country's response to treaty obligations arising, for example, under the UNITED NATIONS CHARTER. But there were wide differences of opinion concerning the desirability of permitting any exceptions to bearing arms for active military duty on grounds such as conscientious objection, religious belief, or moral conviction.

To obtain up-to-date information on the subject, the Commission requested the Secretary-General to prepare a report on national legislation and other measures relating to conscientious objection to military service and on alternative service. It received the report (UN Doc. E/CN.4/1118 and Corr. 1 and Add. 1–3) in 1972 but was unable to deal with the question further until 1980, when it authorized the SUB-COMMISSION ON PREVENTION OF DISCRIMINATION AND PROTECTION OF MINORITIES to prepare a comprehensive report. The Sub-Commission designated two of its members, Mr. Asbjørn Eide (Norway) and Mr. Chama Mubanga-Chipoya (Zambia), as Special Rapporteurs, and the report (UN Doc. E/CN.4/ Sub.2/1982/24) was completed in 1982.

Meanwhile, the General Assembly had dealt with a closely related subject, the question of the status of persons refusing service in military or police forces recruited to enforce apartheid. In 1978, it had recognized (resolution 33/165) the right of all such persons to refuse that kind of service and had called upon member States to grant asylum or safe transit to another State to persons compelled to leave their country of nationality solely because of a conscientious objection to assisting in the enforcement of apartheid through service in military or police forces. And, in 1979, it had appealed (resolution 34/93 A) to the youth of South Africa to refrain from enlisting in the South African armed forces "designed to defend the inhuman system of apartheid, to repress the legitimate struggle of the oppressed people and to threaten, and commit, acts of aggression against neighboring States."

The report prepared by the Special Rapporteurs (subsequently issued as United Nations publication, Sales no. E.85.XIV.1) summarizes, in chapter I, the concept and dimensions of conscientious objection, the relevant international standards, and the action taken by international organizations to supervise the implementation of those standards. Chapter II contains an analysis of relevant information received from governments and the intergovernmental and non-governmental organizations. In chapter III, the conclusions and recommendations of the Special Rapporteurs are set out:

It seems appropriate to recall some basic contradictions encountered: on the one hand the need felt by almost every State for some degree of military strength and, on the other, the dual vocation of the United Nations to advance peace and international understanding as well as respect for the human being.

The contradictions reflect some fundamental dilemmas in the world today. One is between the assertion of national community and the search for a global community. Another is between the assertion of national authority and respect for those who dissent on grounds of conscience.

These dilemmas become more serious with the passage of time. The existence and the work of the United Nations and the specialized agencies, such as UNESCO, have provided young people everywhere with a vision of a world based on solidarity, justice and human dignity: 1985 has been declared International Youth Year, to be devoted to "participation, development and peace". In preparation for it, the General Assembly, in its resolution 37/48 of 3 December 1982, on International Youth Year, again considered it necessary to disseminate among youth the ideals of peace, respect for human rights and fundamental freedoms, human solidarity and dedication to the objectives of progress and development. UNESCO has for several years promoted education

for human rights and international understanding, and is also now seeking to promote education on disarmament. These activities influence the thinking of young people and some respect should be shown for the dedication of youth to such ideals.

If the existing material is considered in the light of those dilemmas and the moral imperatives promoted by the United Nations and its specialized agencies, the following picture emerges.

### 1. Voluntarism or Compulsion in Performance of Military Service

State practice varies widely regarding the extent to which military service is voluntary or enforced. States can be divided into categories on this issue, as follows:

(a) A large number of States have no conscription, i.e. no compulsory military service. Available information indicates that 67 countries fall into this category. The problem of conscientious objection is of less significance in such cases. Problems might emerge if objection developed in the mind of an enlisted person after joining the service. Provision should be made, in law or in the contract of enlistment, for withdrawal from service in such cases. Such provisions exist in some countries, but available material makes it difficult to ascertain their extent.

(b) A few countries have conscription in law, but do not enforce it. For practical purposes; the situation of the objector in such circumstances is similar to that under (a). Six countries fall into this category. Legislation should be passed in the countries in this category to provide for recognition of conscientious objection in case conscription is enforced.

(c) The next category includes States which had conscription (compulsory service) and enforce it, but which mitigate that circumstance by formal and genuine recognition of conscientious objection, at least on some grounds. Fifteen countries fall into this category. Taken together, countries and territories belonging to categories (a), (b) and (c) grant freedom to the individual, to a greater or lesser extent, to decide whether or not to join the armed forces. Altogether, 88 countries appear to be included in this larger group.

(d) Then there are the countries which enforce compulsory service in the armed forces, and do not recognize the right of objectors to be exempted from military service, but which allow objectors, in certain circumstances, to be given non-combatant roles in the armed forces. There are two subdivisions in this group: first, countries where the law provides for transfer to non-combatant roles (available material indicates that this is the situation in five countries); secondly, countries which in individual cases have allowed transfer to non-combatant roles on an ad hoc basis (information received indicates that this has happened in seven countries). It is difficult, however, to obtain reliable information on the extent to which this takes places, since it is an ad hoc decision by the relevant authorities to place a person in a non-combatant role and the reasons for it are not necessarily given.

(e) Finally, there is a group of 40 States with conscription which do not recognize conscientious objection in law and where there has been no indication that objectors have been allowed, by administrative decision, to perform unarmed services within the armed forces. It is possible that in some of these countries nobody has actually objected to military service. It should be noted that a few countries have been mentioned twice, for example Israel, which has obligatory military service for both men and women but which follows different practices with regard to the two sexes.

For the countries in category (c) above (those with conscription, which recognize conscientious objection), the
range of grounds on which objection is considered valid requires consideration. Reference is often made to "religious,"
"moral," or "political" objection. The concept of "political"
objection is particularly unfortunate, since it covers a wide
range of different reasons for objecting—some of them laudable from a United Nations perspective, others less laudable.

The relevant distinction is between absolute and partial
objection. Absolute objection is based on the conviction that
it is wrong under all circumstances to take part in the killing
of others. Partial objection is based on the acceptance of the
use of armed force purely for defence, but refusal to serve
in armed actions which are tantamount to aggression, occupation or repression of human rights, or where the means
and methods of armed action are considered unacceptable.
Both forms of objection are normally based on moral convictions of a religious or humanistic inspiration.

In practice, States that recognize conscientious objection
normally do so only for those who hold an absolute, pacifist,
position. In recent years there have been cases where partial
objection has been recognized, in particular when the objection is based on refusal to serve in armed forces when the use
of weapons of mass destruction is envisaged as a possibility.

One important reason why partial objection is not normally recognized is that State authorities probably never
agree with the objector that their actual or contemplated use
of force is or will be in contravention of international law.

... [T]he South African authorities do not agree that their
use of armed force is illegal, even though universal opinion
outside South Africa, as evidenced by decisions of the General Assembly and the Security Council, is that the continued
occupation of Namibia is in contravention of international
law and that armed force to maintain the occupation is
clearly illegal. The fact that Governments will not accept that
their use of force is illegal or illegitimate should not, however, prevent recognition of an objection to serve by individuals who disagree with the authorities. There have been in
the past and will be in the future cases where public opinion
(internationally and nationally) is split regarding the legitimacy of the use of force or the means used. It should be
possible to accept that young persons called up for conscription may hold a justifiable position on a given issue which
differs from that of the authorities. Therefore national authorities might recognize that some individuals, to the best
of their conscience, hold a strong conviction which should
be respected, even when it differs from the official position
of the Government.

Where conscientious objection is recognized, differences
exist regarding the way in which conscientious objector
status can be obtained. Three sets of factors must be considered in this regard:

(a) How impartial are the institutions, or tribunals, which
decide whether or not such status shall be granted? Are the
legal standards applied comparable to those applied in a fair
trial?

(b) At what time must the request for objector status be
made? Is it admitted at the time of call-up only, or also later,
whenever the conscientious conviction develops?

(c) Does the Government disseminate information about
the right to conscientious objection, and does it allow non-
governmental organizations to do so?

The material collected indicates that some countries have
developed impartial institutions or use the regular civilian
courts, with the application of normal legal safeguards, to
determine the issue. In other cases, military tribunals are
used and may not be sufficiently impartial with regard to the
issue of conscientious objection. In still other cases, the decision is left to the discretion of individuals within the military administration, with no possibility of appeal. It seems
reasonable, if conscientious objection is recognized in some
but not all cases, that an impartial tribunal should take the
decision and that information on the right to objection
should be available to all.

## 2. Alternative Service

Where conscientious objection is recognized, provision is
normally made for alternative service, but there are also considerable differences in this connection. In some countries,
the alternative service is such that it corresponds closely to
the ideas expressed in the sixth preambular paragraph of
General Assembly resolution 37/48, which states that the Assembly is

"Convinced of the imperative to harness the energies, en-
thusiasms and creative abilities of youth to the tasks of nation-building, the struggle for self-determination and national independence, in accordance with the Charter of the
United Nations, and against foreign domination and occupation, for the economic, social and cultural advancement
of peoples, the implementation of the new international economic order, the preservation of world peace and the promotion of international cooperation and understanding."

In some cases, therefore, objectors are assigned alternative service related to social improvement, development or
promotion of international peace.

In other cases the alternative service seems to be considered more as a punishment for refusing military service, in
that it consists in hard work without a meaningful content.

Recommendations of the Special Rapporteurs were
presented in the form of a text by which the Sub-Commission would propose to the Commission on Human
Rights the adoption of a resolution along the following lines:

The Commission on Human Rights, recalling its resolution 40 (XXXVII) of 12 March 1981 and General Assembly
resolution 33/165 of 20 December 1978, as well as General
Assembly resolutions 34/151 of 17 December 1979, 35/126
of 11 December 1980, 36/28 of 13 November 1981 and 37/
48 of 3 December 1982 on International Youth Year: Participation, Development, Peace, recommends that the Economic and Social Council should request the General
Assembly to make the following recommendations, preferably in connection with the preparations for International
Youth Year, 1985:

1. *Right to Conscientious Objection.* (a) States should recognize by law the right of persons who, for reasons of conscience or profound conviction arising from religious, ethical, moral, humanitarian or similar motives, refuse to
perform armed service, to be released from the obligation
to perform military service.

(b) States should, as a minimum, extend the right of objection to persons whose conscience forbids them to take
part in armed service under any circumstances (the pacifist
position).

(c) States should recognize by law the right to be released
from service in armed forces which the objector considers
likely to be used to enforce apartheid.

(d) States should recognize by law the right to be released from service in armed forces which the objector considers likely to be used in action amounting to or approaching genocide.

(e) States should recognize by law the right to be released from service in armed forces which the objector considers likely to be used for illegal occupation of foreign territory.

(f) States should recognize the right of persons to be released from service in armed forces which the objector holds to be engaged in, or likely to be engaged in, gross violations of human rights.

(g) States should recognize the right of persons to be released from the obligation to perform service in armed forces which the objector considers likely to resort to the use of weapons of mass destruction or weapons which have been specifically outlawed by international law or to use means and methods which cause unnecessary suffering.

*2. Procedural Aspects.* (a) States should maintain or establish independent decision-making bodies to determine whether a conscientious objection is valid under national law in any specific case. There should always be a right of appeal to an independent, civilian judicial body.

(b) Applicants should be granted a hearing and be entitled to be represented by legal counsel and to call witnesses.

(c) States should disseminate information about the right of objection, and allow non-governmental organizations to do likewise.

*3. Alternative Service.* States should provide alternative service for the objector, which should be at least as long as the military service, but not excessively long so that it becomes in effect a punishment. States should, to the extent possible, seek to give the alternative service a meaningful content, including social work or work for peace, development and international understanding.

*4. Trial and Penalties where the Objection is not Found Valid.* Even when States give effect to the above recommendations, there will be some cases where the objection is not found valid, and where penalties will be imposed on persons who persist in their objection. In such cases:

(a) Imposition of such penalties should be decided upon by an impartial civilian court applying the normal criteria of fair trial;

(b) Penalties should not be excessively severe, and should take due account, as mitigating factors, of the conscience or conviction of the person concerned.

*5. Asylum.* Taking into account the existence of rules of international law, under which an individual retains the right and the duty to refuse illegal orders under national law, and the provisions of General Assembly resolution 33/165 as well as the basic right to freedom of conscience, international standards should be established which will ensure a favourable attitude towards conscientious objectors requesting asylum in conformity with obligations under international law. Furthermore, it appears to be the practice of many countries not to refuse asylum to conscientious objectors to military service. International legislation on this practice might clarify an area of human rights in which there are international and individual obligations.

*6. Recruitment of Children and Minors.* While the question of the use of children in war has not been dealt with as such in this report, it is nevertheless suggested that the Sub-Commission should consider how to follow up the concern expressed on this matter. In this connection, account should be taken of the provisions in Additional Protocol I of June 1977 to the Geneva Convention of 1949, article 77, paragraph 2, in which the parties to a conflict pledge themselves to take all feasible measures in order that children under 15 do not take a direct part in hostilities and, in particular, to refrain from recruiting them into their armed forces. A similar prohibition is found in Protocol II, article 4, paragraph 3 (c).

In 1983, the Sub-Commission on the Prevention of Discrimination and the Protection of Minorities received and examined the report, expressed its deep appreciation to the Special Rapporteurs, and transmitted the report (resolution 1983/22) to the Commission on Human Rights. The Commission examined it in 1984; and, on its recommendation, the Economic and Social Council decided (resolution 1984/27) that it should be printed and given the widest possible distribution. The Council also requested that it be transmitted to governments and to interested international organizations for their comments and that such comments should be drawn to the attention of the Commission.

At its 1985 session, the Commission on Human Rights, after reviewing the comments received by the Secretary-General (E/CN.4/1985/25 and Add. 1–4), considered a draft resolution on conscientious objection to military service (UN Doc. E/CN.4/1985/L.33/Rev. 1) and a number of amendments thereto. Unable to reach agreement in the time available, it adjourned the debate to its 1987 session.

The Commission on Human Rights has since returned periodicially to the subject of conscientious objection to military service, refining its views in resolutions 1987/46, 1989/59, and 1993/84. In resolution 1989/59, adopted on 8 March 1989, the Commission first recognized "the right of everyone to have conscientious objections to military service as a legitimate exercise of the right of freedom of thought, conscience, and religion." In resolution 1993/84, adopted on 10 March 1993, the Commission unanimously put forward its views of the subject:

The Commission on Human Rights . . .

1. Draws attention to the right of everyone to have conscientious objections to military service as a legitimate exercise of the right to freedom of thought, conscience, and religion as laid down in article 18 of the Universal Declaration of Human Rights as well as article 18 of the International Covenant on Civil and Political Rights;

2. Affirms that persons performing compulsory military service should not be excluded from the right to have conscientious objections to military service;

3. Recognizes the fact that there exists various domestic legislation concerning conscientious objection to military service;

4. Appeals to States, if they have not already done so, to enact legislation and to take measures aimed at exemption from military service on the basis of a genuinely held conscientious objection to armed service;

5. Reminds States with a system of compulsory military service where such provision has not already been made of its recommendation that they introduce for conscientious

**C**

objectors various forms of alternative service which are compatible with the reasons for conscientious objection, bearing in mind the experience of some States in this respect, and that they refrain from subjecting conscientious objectors to imprisonment;

6. Emphasizes that such forms of alternative service should be of a noncombatant or civilian character, in the public interest, and not of a punitive nature;

7. Appeals to Member States, if they have not already done so, to establish within the framework of their national legal system independent and impartial decision-making bodies with the task of determining whether a conscientious objection is valid in a specific case;

8. Affirms the importance of the availability of information about the right to conscientious objection to military service and the means of acquiring conscientious objector status to all relevant persons affected by military service;

9. Requests the Secretary-General to transmit the text of the present resolution to all States Members of the United Nations and to include the right of conscientious objection to military service in the public information activities of the United Nations;

10. Also requests the Secretary-General to report to the Commission at its 51st session on the question of conscientious objection to military service, taking into account the comments provided by Governments and further information received by him.

**BIBLIOGRAPHY.** Amnesty International. *Adoption of Prisoner of Conscience—Switzerland.* London: 1986. NGO appeal, in English.

————. *Conscientious Objection to Military Service.* London: 1988. NGO report, in English.

————. *Greece: Conscientious Objection.* London: 1988. NGO report, in English.

Bacon, Margaret Hope. *The Quiet Rebels: The Story of the Quakers in America.* Philadelphia, PA, USA: New Society Publishers, 1985. Scholarly monograph, in English; bibliography, pp. 221–224.

Catholic Institute for International Relations. *Country and Conscience: South African Conscientious Objectors.* London: 1988. NGO report, in English.

Davies, Gareth. "Conscientious Objection and the Freedom and Peace Movement in Poland," *Religion in Communist Lands* 16, no. 1 (Spring 1988): 4–20. NGO article, in English.

Duffar, Jean. "L'objection de conscience en droit français" (Conscientious Objection in French Law), *Revue de droit public et de science politique en France et à l'étranger* 107, no. 3 (1991): 657–695. Scholarly article, in French.

Freedom and Peace Movement. *Documents from the Independent Seminar: "International Peace and the Helsinki Agreements."* Warsaw, Poland: 1987. NGO document collection, in English.

Human Awareness Programme. *Militarisation Dossier.* Johannesburg, South Africa: 1986. NGO dossier, in English.

Information Centre for Polish Affairs. "Keston College on Jehovah's Witnesses Imprisoned for Refusing Military Service," *Uncensored Poland News Bulletin* 5/87 (6 March 1987): 18–19. NGO article, in English.

Kaufman, Edy. "Prisoners of Conscience: The Shaping of a New Human Rights Concept," *Human Rights Quarterly* 13, no. 3 (Aug. 1991): 339–367. Scholarly article, in English.

Keston College. "Conscientious Objection: The Situation in Yugoslavia," *Religion in Communist Lands* 15, no. 3 (Winter 1987): 332–335. NGO article, in English.

Klippenstein, Lawrence. "Exercising a Free Conscience: The Conscientious Objectors of the Soviet Union and the German Democratic Republic," *Religion in Communist Lands* 13, no. 3 (Winter 1985): 282–291. Scholarly article, in English.

Kuzas, Kevin J. "Asylum for Unrecognized Conscientious Objectors to Military Service: Is There a Right Not to Fight?" *Virginia Journal of International Law* 31, no. 3 (Spring 1991): 447–478. Scholarly article, in English.

Lippman, Matthew. "The Recognition of Conscientious Objection to Military Service as an International Human Right," *California Western International Law Journal* 21, no. 1 (1990–1991): 31–66. Scholarly article, in English.

Madrid-Malo Garizabal, Mario. *La Libertad de Rehusar: Estudio sobre el Derecho a la Objeción de Conciencia* (The Freedom to Refuse: A Study on the Right to Conscientious Objection). Bogota, Colombia: Escuela Superior de Administración Pública, Instituto de Derechos Humanos "Guillermo Cano," 1991. Research report, in Spanish; bibliography, pp. 185–209.

Musalo, Karen. "Conscientious Objection to Military Service Accepted as Valid Basis for Claim to Political Asylum for Salvadoran Men," *Immigration Newsletter* 16, no. 3 (May–June 1987): 3–7. NGO article, in English.

Smith-Gordon, Maureen. *Refugee Claims Based on Refusal to Perform Military Service.* North York, Ontario, Canada: York University, 1991. Research paper, in English.

Southern African Catholic Bishops' Conference. *The Things that Make for Peace.* Pretoria, South Africa: 1985. NGO report, in English.

U.S. Helsinki Watch Committee. "Eastern European Appeal on Conscientious Objection," March 1988. NGO press release, in English.

————. *From Below: Independent Peace and Environmental Movements in Eastern Europe and the USSR.* New York: 1987. NGO report, in English.

**CONSTITUTIONAL COUNCILS.** Constitutional Councils are organs established within the framework of the legislative system of many countries, having as one of their functions the protection and promotion of human rights. They are described in the UN Secretary-General's report entitled "National Institutions for the Protection and Promotion of Human Rights" (E/CN.4/1987/37, paras. 16–18), prepared at the request of the General Assembly (resolution 42/123):

In many countries, organs have been established with a view to ensuring that laws adopted by parliament do not violate constitutional norms and principles.

For example, a 1983 amendment to the Hungarian Constitution called for the National Assembly to elect a Constitutional Council to exercise control over the constitutionality of legal rules and legal directives or guidelines. The Constitutional Council is empowered to suspend the enforcement of any legal provisions (except legislative enactments by the National and Presidential Council) and directives and rulings of the Supreme Court. The Constitutional Council also assists in the interpretation of the provisions of the Constitution.

Constitutional Councils similarly charged with determining the constitutionality of legislative acts, may, in some countries, function as independent bodies outside the parliamentary sphere. For instance, in France, the Constitutional Council is neither a legislative nor a judicial organ. However, in accordance with article 61 of the French Constitution of 4 October 1958, the Constitutional Council is empowered to examine the constitutionality of acts referred to it, before they are promulgated. The Council may be seized by the President of the Republic, the Prime Minister, the President of the National Assembly, the President of the Senate or 60 deputies or senators.

**SEE ALSO** *Legislative Bodies and Human Rights.*

**BIBLIOGRAPHY.** Carver, Richard, and Paul Hunt. *National Human Rights Institutions in Africa.* Banjul, Gambia: African Centre for Democracy and Human Rights Studies, 1991. NGO research report, in English.

Commonwealth Secretariat. Human Rights Unit. *National Human Rights Institutions in the Commonwealth: Directory—Survey and Analysis.* London: 1992. Directory, in English.

Turpin, Dominique. "La Commission nationale consultative des droits de l'Homme" (National Consultative Human Rights Commission), *Revue de droit public et de la science politique en France et à l'étranger* 105, no. 1 (1989): 61–90. Scholarly article, in French.

## CONSULTATIVE COUNCIL OF JEWISH ORGANIZATIONS.

An international non-governmental organization in consultative status with the UN **ECONOMIC AND SOCIAL COUNCIL** (Category II), the **ILO, UNESCO,** and the **COUNCIL OF EUROPE.** Founded in 1946 in New York as the Coordinating Board of Jewish Organizations for Consultation with the Economic and Social Council of the United Nations, CCJO promotes respect for human rights and fundamental freedoms and cooperates and consults with the Council and its subsidiary bodies on problems relating to human rights and economic, social, cultural, educational, and related matters. It has established a library in Paris (50,000 volumes).

CCJO publishes *AJA* (quarterly) and *Les nouveaux cahiers* (quarterly).

Consultative Council of Jewish Organizations. Address: 420 Lexington Ave., Suite 1733, New York, NY 10170, USA. Telephone: (212) 808-5437. Fax: (212) 983-0094. Secretary-General: Warren Green.

## CONVENTIONAL WEAPONS: CONVENTION ON PROHIBITIONS OR RESTRICTIONS ON THE USE OF CERTAIN CONVENTIONAL WEAPONS WHICH MAY BE DEEMED TO BE EXCESSIVELY INJURIOUS OR TO HAVE INDISCRIMINATE EFFECTS, AND PROTOCOLS (1981).

This Convention and its annexed protocols I to III are significant recent additions to the body of international humanitarian law applicable in armed conflict, supplementing the Geneva Convention Relative to the Treatment of Prisoners of War, the Geneva Convention Relative to the Protection of Civilian Persons in Time of War, the Protocol Additional to the Geneva Conventions of 12 August 1949, Relating to the Protection of Victims of International Armed Conflicts, and the Protocol Additional to the Geneva Conventions of 12 August 1949, Relating to the Protection of Victims of Non-International Conflicts.

The Convention and annexed protocols are based on the conviction that the suffering of victims of war would be significantly reduced by agreements prohibiting or restricting, on humanitarian grounds, the use of weapons which are excessively dangerous or which have indiscriminate effects. One of their purposes is to protect the right of everyone to live in peace and without being subjected to torture or to cruel, inhuman, or degrading treatment or punishment. Annexed Protocol I prohibits the use of any weapon the primary effect of which is to injure by fragments which, in the human body, escape detection by X-rays. Annexed Protocol II prohibits or restricts the use of mines, booby-traps, and other devices. Annexed Protocol III prohibits or restricts the use of incendiary weapons.

The Convention and its protocols were prepared by the United Nations Conference on Prohibitions or Restrictions of Use of Certain Conventional Weapons Which May Be Deemed to be Excessively Injurious or to Have Indiscriminate Effects, convened at the European office of the United Nations, Geneva, and were adopted by the Conference on 10 October 1980. They were opened for signature and ratification or accession on 10 April 1981 and entered into force on 2 December 1983. The text of the Convention and annexed protocols (UN Doc. A/CONF. 95/15 and Corr. 1, annex I) is as follows:

The High Contracting Parties,

Recalling that every State has the duty, in conformity with the Charter of the United Nations, to refrain in its international relations from the threat or use of force against the sovereignty, territorial integrity or political independence of any State, or in any other manner inconsistent with the purposes of the United Nations,

Further recalling the general principle of the protection of the civilian population against the effects of hostilities,

Basing themselves on the principle of international law that the right of the parties to an armed conflict to choose methods or means of warfare is not unlimited, and on the principle that prohibits the employment in armed conflicts of weapons, projectiles and material and methods of warfare of a nature to cause superfluous injury or unnecessary suffering,

Also recalling that it is prohibited to employ methods or means of warfare which are intended, or may be expected, to cause widespread, long-term and severe damage to the natural environment,

Confirming their determination that in cases not covered

by this Convention and its annexed Protocols or by other international agreements, the civilian population and the combatants shall at all times remain under the protection and authority of the principles of international law derived from established custom, from the principles of humanity and from the dictates of public conscience,

Desiring to contribute to international détente, the ending of the arms race and the building of confidence among States, and hence to the realization of the aspiration of all peoples to live in peace,

Recognizing the importance of pursuing every effort which may contribute to progress towards general and complete disarmament under strict and effective international control,

Reaffirming the need to continue the codification and progressive development of the rules of international law applicable in armed conflict,

Wishing to prohibit or restrict further the use of certain conventional weapons and believing that the positive results achieved in this area may facilitate the main talks on disarmament with a view to putting an end to the production, stockpiling and proliferation of such weapons,

Emphasizing the desirability that all States become parties to this Convention and its annexed Protocols, especially the militarily significant States,

Bearing in mind that the General Assembly of the United Nations and the United Nations Disarmament Commission may decide to examine the question of a possible broadening of the scope of the prohibitions and restrictions contained in this Convention and its annexed Protocols,

Further bearing in mind that the Committee on Disarmament may decide to consider the question of adopting further measures to prohibit or restrict the use of certain conventional weapons,

Have agreed as follows:

*Article 1. Scope of Application.* This Convention and its annexed Protocols shall apply in the situations referred to in Article 2 common to the Geneva Conventions of 12 August 1949 for the Protection of War Victims, including any situation described in paragraph 4 of Article 1 of Additional Protocol I to these Conventions.

*Article 2. Relations With Other International Agreements.* Nothing in this Convention or its annexed Protocols shall be interpreted as detracting from other obligations imposed upon the High Contracting Parties by international humanitarian law applicable in armed conflict.

*Article 3. Signature.* This Convention shall be open for signature by all States at United Nations Headquarters in New York for a period of twelve months from 10 April 1981.

*Article 4. Ratification, Acceptance, Approval or Accession.* 1. This Convention is subject to ratification, acceptance or approval by the Signatories. Any State which has not signed this Convention may accede to it.

2. The instrument of ratification, acceptance, approval or accession shall be deposited with the Depositary.

3. Expressions of consent to be bound by any of the Protocols annexed to this Convention shall be optional for each State, provided that at the time of the deposit of its instrument of ratification, acceptance or approval of this Convention or of accession thereto, that State shall notify the Depositary of its consent to be bound by any two or more of these Protocols.

4. At any time after the deposit of its instrument of ratification, acceptance or approval of this Convention or of accession thereto, a State may notify the Depositary of its consent to be bound by any annexed Protocol by which it is not already bound.

5. Any Protocol by which a High Contracting Party is bound shall for that Party form an integral part of this Convention.

*Article 5. Entry Into Force.* 1. This Convention shall enter into force six months after the date of deposit of the twentieth instrument of ratification, acceptance, approval or accession.

2. For any State which deposits its instrument of ratification, acceptance, approval or accession after the date of the deposit of the twentieth instrument of ratification, acceptance, approval or accession, this Convention shall enter into force six months after the date on which that State has deposited its instrument of ratification, acceptance, approval or accession.

3. Each of the Protocols annexed to this Convention shall enter into force six months after the date by which twenty States have notified their consent to be bound by it in accordance with paragraph 3 or 4 of Article 4 of this Convention.

4. For any State which notifies its consent to be bound by a Protocol, annexed to this Convention after the date by which twenty States have notified their consent to be bound by it, the Protocol shall enter into force six months after the date on which that State has notified its consent so to be bound.

*Article 6. Dissemination.* The High Contracting Parties undertake, in time of peace as in time of armed conflict, to disseminate this Convention and those of its annexed Protocols by which they are bound as widely as possible in their respective countries and, in particular, to include the study thereof in their programmes of military instruction, so that those instruments may become known to their armed forces.

*Article 7. Treaty Relations Upon Entry Into Force of This Convention.* 1. When one of the parties to a conflict is not bound by an annexed Protocol, the parties bound by this Convention and that annexed Protocol shall remain bound by them in their mutual relations.

2. Any High Contracting Party shall be bound by this Convention and any Protocol annexed thereto which is in force for it, in any situation contemplated by Article 1, in relation to any State which is not a party to this Convention or bound by the relevant annexed Protocol, if the latter accepts and applies this Convention or the relevant Protocol, and so notifies the Depositary.

3. The Depositary shall immediately inform the High Contracting Parties concerned of any notification received under paragraph 2 of this Article.

4. This Convention, and the annexed Protocols by which a High Contracting Party is bound, shall apply with respect to an armed conflict against that High Contracting Party of the type referred to in Article 1, paragraph 4, of Additional Protocol I to the Geneva Conventions of 12 August 1949 for the Protection of War Victims:

(a) where the High Contracting Party is also a party to Additional Protocol I and an authority referred to in Article 96, paragraph 3, of that Protocol has undertaken to apply the Geneva Conventions and Additional Protocol I in accordance with Article 96, paragraph 3, of the said Protocol, and undertakes to apply this Convention and the relevant annexed Protocols in relation to that conflict; or

(b) where the High Contracting Party is not a party to Additional Protocol I and an authority of the type referred to in subparagraph (a) above accepts and applies the obligations of the Geneva Conventions and of this Convention and the relevant annexed Protocols in relation to that conflict. Such an acceptance and application shall have in relation to that conflict the following effects:

(i) the Geneva Conventions and this Convention and its relevant annexed Protocols are brought into force for the parties to the conflict with immediate effect;

(ii) the said authority assumes the same rights and obligations as those which have been assumed by a High Contracting Party to the Geneva Conventions, this Convention and its relevant annexed Protocols; and

(iii) the Geneva Conventions, this Convention and its relevant annexed Protocols are equally binding upon all parties to the conflict.

The High Contracting Party and the authority may also agree to accept and apply the obligations of Additional Protocol I to the Geneva Conventions on a reciprocal basis.

*Article 8. Review and Amendments.* 1. (a) At any time after the entry into force of this Convention any High Contracting Party may propose amendments to this Convention or any annexed Protocol by which it is bound. Any proposal for an amendment shall be communicated to the Depositary, who shall notify it to all the High Contracting Parties and shall seek their views on whether a conference should be convened to consider the proposal. If a majority, that shall not be less than eighteen of the High Contracting Parties so agree, he shall promptly convene a conference to which all High Contracting Parties shall be invited. States not parties to this Convention shall be invited to the conference as observers.

(b) Such a conference may agree upon amendments which shall be adopted and shall enter into force in the same manner as this Convention and the annexed Protocols, provided that amendments to this Convention may be adopted only by the High Contracting Parties and that amendments to a specific annexed Protocol may be adopted only by the High Contracting Parties which are bound by that Protocol.

2. (a) At any time after the entry into force of this Convention any High Contracting Party may propose additional protocols relating to other categories of conventional weapons not covered by the existing annexed Protocols. Any such proposal for an additional protocol shall be communicated to the Depositary, who shall notify it to all the High Contracting Parties in accordance with subparagraph 1 (a) of this Article. If a majority, that shall not be less than eighteen of the High Contracting Parties, so agree, the Depositary shall promptly convene a conference to which all States shall be invited.

(b) Such a conference may agree, with the full participation of all States represented at the conference, upon additional protocols which shall be adopted in the same manner as this Convention, shall be annexed thereto and shall enter into force as provided in paragraphs 3 and 4 of Article 5 of this Convention.

3. (a) If, after a period of ten years following the entry into force of this Convention, no conference has been convened in accordance with subparagraph 1 (a) or 2 (a) of this Article, any High Contracting Party may request the Depositary to convene a conference to which all High Contracting Parties shall be invited to review the scope and operation of this Convention and the Protocols annexed thereto and to consider any proposal for amendments of this Convention or of the existing Protocols. States not parties to this Convention shall be invited as observers to the conference. The conference may agree upon amendments which shall be adopted and enter into force in accordance with subparagraph 1 (b) above.

(b) At such conference consideration may also be given to any proposal for additional protocols relating to other categories of conventional weapons not covered by the existing annexed Protocols. All States represented at the conference may participate fully in such consideration. Any additional protocols shall be adopted in the same manner as this Convention, shall be annexed thereto and shall enter into force as provided in paragraphs 3 and 4 of Article 5 of this Convention.

(c) Such a conference may consider whether provision should be made for the convening of a further conference at the request of any High Contracting Party if, after a similar period to that referred to in subparagraph 3 (a) of this Article, no conference has been convened in accordance with subparagraph 1 (a) or 2 (a) of this Article.

*Article 9. Denunciation.* 1. Any High Contracting Party may denounce this Convention or any of its annexed Protocols by so notifying the Depositary.

2. Any such denunciation shall only take effect one year after receipt by the Depositary of the notification of denunciation. If, however, on the expiry of that year the denouncing High Contracting Party is engaged in one of the situations referred to in Article 1, the Party shall continue to be bound by the obligations of this Convention and of the relevant annexed Protocols until the end of the armed conflict or occupation and, in any case, until the termination of operations connected with the final release, repatriation or reestablishment of the person protected by the rules of international law applicable in armed conflict, and in the case of any annexed Protocol containing provisions concerning situations in which peace-keeping, observation or similar functions are performed by United Nations forces or missions in the area concerned, until the termination of those functions.

3. Any denunciation of this Convention shall be considered as also applying to all annexed Protocols by which the denouncing High Contracting Party is bound.

4. Any denunciation shall have effect only in respect of the denouncing High Contracting Party.

5. Any denunciation shall not affect the obligations already incurred, by reason of an armed conflict, under this Convention and its annexed Protocols by such denouncing High Contracting Party in respect of any act committed before this denunciation becomes effective.

*Article 10. Depositary.* 1. The Secretary-General of the United Nations shall be the Depositary of this Convention and of its annexed Protocols.

2. In addition to his usual functions, the Depositary shall inform all States of:

(a) signatures affixed to this Convention under Article 3;

(b) deposits of instruments of ratification, acceptance or approval of or accession to this Convention deposited under Article 4;

(c) notifications of consent to be bound by annexed Protocols under Article 4;

(d) the dates of entry into force of this Convention and of each of its annexed Protocols under Article 5; and

(e) notifications of denunciation received under article 9, and their effective date.

*Article 11. Authentic Texts.* The original of this Convention with the annexed Protocols, of which the Arabic, Chinese, English, French, Russian and Spanish texts are equally authentic, shall be deposited with the Depositary, who shall transmit certified true copies thereof to all States.

## Protocol on Non-Detectable Fragments (Protocol I)

It is prohibited to use any weapon the primary effect of which is to injure by fragments which in the human body escape detection by X-rays.

## Protocol on Prohibitions or Restrictions on the Use of Mines, Booby-Traps and Other Devices (Protocol II)

*Article 1. Material Scope of Application.* This Protocol relates to the use on land of the mines, booby-traps and other devices defined herein, including mines laid to interdict beaches, waterway crossings or river crossings, but does not apply to the use of anti-ship mines at sea or in inland waterways.

*Article 2. Definitions.* For the purpose of this Protocol:

1. "Mine" means any munition placed under, on or near the ground or other surface area and designed to be detonated or exploded by the presence, proximity or contact of a person or vehicle, and "remotely delivered mine" means any mine so defined delivered by artillery, rocket, mortar or similar means or dropped from an aircraft.

2. "Booby-trap" means any device or material which is designed, constructed or adapted to kill or injure and which functions unexpectedly when a person disturbs or approaches an apparently harmless object or performs an apparently safe act.

3. "Other devices" means manually-emplaced munitions and devices designed to kill, injure or damage and which are actuated by remote control or automatically after a lapse of time.

4. "Military objective" means, so far as objects are concerned, any object which by its nature, location, purpose or use makes an effective contribution to military action and whose total or partial destruction, capture or neutralization, in the circumstances ruling at the time, offers a definite military advantage.

5. "Civilian objects" are all objects which are not military objectives as defined in paragraph 4.

6. "Recording" means a physical, administrative and technical operation designed to obtain, for the purpose of registration in the official records, all available information facilitating the location of minefields, mines and booby-traps.

*Article 3. General Restrictions on the Use of Mines, Booby-Traps and Other Devices.* 1. This Article applies to:

    (a) mines;

    (b) booby-traps; and

    (c) other devices.

2. It is prohibited in all circumstances to direct weapons to which this Article applies, either in offence, defence or by way of reprisals, against the civilian population as such or against individual civilians.

3. The indiscriminate use of weapons to which this Article applies is prohibited. Indiscriminate use is any placement of such weapons:

    (a) which is not on, or directed at, a military objective; or

    (b) which employs a method or means of delivery which cannot be directed at a specific military objective; or

    (c) which may be expected to cause incidental loss of civilian life, injury to civilians, damage to civilian objects, or a combination thereof, which would be excessive in relation to the concrete and direct military advantage anticipated.

4. All feasible precautions shall be taken to protect civilians from the effects of weapons to which this Article applies. Feasible precautions are those precautions which are practicable or practically possible taking into account all circumstances ruling at the time, including humanitarian and military considerations.

*Article 4. Restrictions on the Use of Mines Other Than Remotely Delivered Mines, Booby-Traps and Other Devices in Populated Areas.* 1. This Article applies to:

    (a) mines other than remotely delivered mines;

    (b) booby-traps; and

    (c) other devices.

2. It is prohibited to use weapons to which this Article applies in any city, town, village or other area containing a similar concentration of civilians in which combat between ground forces is not taking place or does not appear to be imminent, unless either:

    (a) they are placed on or in the close vicinity of a military objective belonging to or under the control of an adverse party; or

    (b) measures are taken to protect civilians from their effects, for example, the posting of warning signs, the posting of sentries, the issue of warnings or the provision of fences.

*Article 5. Restrictions on the Use of Remotely Delivered Mines.* 1. The use of remotely delivered mines is prohibited unless such mines are only used within an area which is itself a military objective or which contains military objectives, and unless:

    (a) their location can be accurately recorded in accordance with Article 7(1)(a); or

    (b) an effective neutralizing mechanism is used on each such mine, that is to say, a self-actuating mechanism which is designed to render a mine harmless or cause it to destroy itself when it is anticipated that the mine will no longer serve the military purpose for which it was placed in position, or a remotely controlled mechanism which is designed to render harmless or destroy a mine when the mine no longer serves the military purpose for which it was placed in position.

2. Effective advance warning shall be given of any delivery or dropping of remotely delivered mines which may affect the civilian population, unless circumstances do not permit.

*Article 6. Prohibition on the Use of Certain Booby-Traps.* 1. Without prejudice to the rules of international law applicable in armed conflict relating to treachery and perfidy, it is prohibited in all circumstances to use:

    (a) any booby-trap in the form of an apparently harmless portable object which is specifically designed and constructed to contain explosive material and to detonate when it is disturbed or approached; or

    (b) booby-traps which are in any way attached to or associated with:

        (i) internationally recognized protective emblems, signs or signals;

        (ii) sick, wounded or dead persons;

        (iii) burial or cremation sites or graves;

        (iv) medical facilities, medical equipment, medical supplies or medical transportation;

        (v) children's toys or other portable objects or products specially designed for the feeding, health, hygiene, clothing or education of children;

        (vi) food or drink;

        (vii) kitchen utensils or appliances except in military establishments, military locations or military supply depots;

        (viii) objects clearly of a religious nature;

        (ix) historic monuments, works of art or places of

worship which constitute the cultural or spiritual heritage of peoples;

(x) animals or their carcasses.

2. It is prohibited in all circumstances to use any booby-trap which is designed to cause superfluous injury or unnecessary suffering.

*Article 7. Recording and Publication of the Location of Minefields, Mines and Booby-Traps.* 1. The parties to a conflict shall record the location of:

(a) all pre-planned minefields laid by them; and

(b) all areas in which they have made large-scale and pre-planned use of booby-traps.

2. The parties shall endeavour to ensure the recording of the location of all other minefields, mines and booby-traps which they have laid or placed in position.

3. All such records shall be retained by the parties who shall:

(a) immediately after the cessation of active hostilities:

(i) take all necessary and appropriate measures, including the use of such records, to protect civilians from the effects of minefields, mines and booby-traps; and either

(ii) in cases where the forces of neither party are in the territory of the adverse party, make available to each other and to the Secretary-General of the United Nations all information in their possession concerning the location of minefields, mines and booby-traps in the territory of the adverse party; or

(iii) once complete withdrawal of the forces of the parties from the territory of the adverse party has taken place, make available to the adverse party and to the Secretary-General of the United Nations all information in their possession concerning the location of minefields, mines and booby-traps in the territory of the adverse party;

(b) when a United Nations force or mission performs functions in any area, make available to the authority mentioned in Article 8 such information as is required by that Article;

(c) whenever possible, by mutual agreement, provide for the release of information concerning the location of minefields, mines and booby-traps, particularly in agreements governing the cessation of hostilities.

*Article 8. Protection of United Nations Forces and Missions from the Effects of Minefields, Mines and Booby-Traps.* 1. When a United Nations force or mission performs functions of peace-keeping, observation or similar functions in any area, each party to the conflict shall, if requested by the head of the United Nations force or mission in that area, as far as it is able:

(a) remove or render harmless all mines or booby-traps in that area;

(b) take such measures as may be necessary to protect the force or mission from the effects of minefields, mines and booby-traps while carrying out its duties; and

(c) make available to the head of the United Nations force or mission in that area, all information in the party's possession concerning the location of minefields, mines and booby-traps in that area.

2. When a United Nations fact-finding mission performs functions in any area, any party to the conflict concerned shall provide protection to that mission except where, because of the size of such mission, it cannot adequately provide such protection. In that case it shall make available to the head of the mission the information in its possession concerning the location of minefields, mines and booby-traps in that area.

*Article 9. International Co-operation in the Removal of Minefields, Mines and Booby-Traps.* After the cessation of active hostilities, the parties shall endeavour to reach agreement, both among themselves and, where appropriate, with other States and with international organizations, on the provision of information and technical and material assistance—including, in appropriate circumstances, joint operations—necessary to remove or otherwise render ineffective minefields, mines and booby-traps placed in position during the conflict.

**Technical Annex to the Protocol on Prohibitions or Restrictions on the Use of Mines, Booby-Traps and Other Devices (Protocol II)**

*Guidelines on Recording.* Whenever an obligation for the recording of the location of minefields, mines and booby-traps arises under the Protocol, the following guidelines shall be taken into account.

1. With regard to pre-planned minefields and large-scale and pre-planned use of booby-traps:

(a) maps, diagrams or other records should be made in such a way as to indicate the extent of the minefield or booby-trapped area; and

(b) the location of the minefield or booby-trapped area should be specified by relation to the co-ordinates of a single reference point and by the estimated dimensions of the area containing mines and booby-traps in relation to that single reference point.

2. With regard to other minefields, mines and booby-traps laid or placed in position:

In so far as possible, the relevant information specified in paragraph 1 above should be recorded so as to enable the areas containing minefields, mines and booby-traps to be identified.

**Protocol on Prohibitions or Restrictions on the Use of Incendiary Weapons (Protocol III)**

*Article 1. Definitions.* For the purpose of this Protocol:

1. "Incendiary weapon" means any weapon or munition which is primarily designed to set fire to objects or to cause burn injury to persons through the action of flame, heat, or a combination thereof, produced by a chemical reaction of a substance delivered on the target.

(a) Incendiary weapons can take the form of, for example, flame throwers, fougasses, shells, rockets, grenades, mines, bombs and other containers of incendiary substances.

(b) Incendiary weapons do not include:

(i) Munitions which may have incidental incendiary effects, such as illuminants, tracers, smoke or signalling systems;

(ii) Munitions designed to combine penetration, blast or fragmentation effects with an additional incendiary effect, such as armour-piercing projectiles, fragmentation shells, explosive bombs and similar combined-effects munitions in which the incendiary effect is not specifically designed to cause burn injury to persons, but to be used against military objectives, such as armoured vehicles, aircraft and installations or facilities.

2. "Concentration of civilians" means any concentration of civilians, be it permanent or temporary, such as in inhabited parts of cities, or inhabited towns or villages, or as in camps or columns of refugees or evacuees, or groups of nomads.

3. "Military objective" means, so far as objects are concerned, any object which by its nature, location, purpose or use makes an effective contribution to military action and

whose total or partial destruction, capture or neutralization, in the circumstances ruling at the time, offers a definite military advantage.

4. "Civilian objects" are all objects which are not military objectives as defined in paragraph 3.

5. "Feasible precautions" are those precautions which are practicable or practically possible taking into account all circumstances ruling at the time, including humanitarian and military considerations.

*Article 2. Protection of Civilians and Civilian Objects.* 1. It is prohibited in all circumstances to make the civilian population as such, individual civilians or civilian objects the object of attack by incendiary weapons.

2. It is prohibited in all circumstances to make any military objective located within a concentration of civilians the object of attack by air-delivered incendiary weapons.

3. It is further prohibited to make any military objective located within a concentration of civilians the object of attack by means of incendiary weapons other than air-delivered incendiary weapons, except when such military objective is clearly separated from the concentration of civilians and all feasible precautions are taken with a view to limiting the incendiary effects to the military objective and to avoiding, and in any event to minimizing, incidental loss of civilian life, injury to civilians and damage to civilian objects.

4. It is prohibited to make forests or other kinds of plant cover the object of attack by incendiary weapons except when such natural elements are used to cover, conceal or camouflage combatants or other military objectives, or are themselves objectives. . . .

**SEE ALSO** *Arms Exports; Chemical Weapons; Nuclear Weapons.*

## COORDINATING BOARD OF JEWISH ORGANIZATIONS.

An international non-governmental organization in consultative status (Category II) with the UN **ECONOMIC AND SOCIAL COUNCIL,** CBJO was founded in New York in 1947. The Board's function is to coordinate the United Nations work of its constituent organizations—which include the B'nai B'rith International Council and national bodies in South Africa and the United Kingdom—aimed at the promotion and protection of human rights, with special attention directed at combatting persecution and discrimination on grounds such as race, religion, and national or social origin.

CBJO publishes reports on its activities from time to time.

Coordinating Board of Jewish Organizations. Address: 1640 Rhode Island Avenue, N.W., Washington, D.C., 20036, USA. Telephone: (202) 857-6500. Executive Secretary: Thomas Neumann.

## COPYRIGHT: UNIVERSAL COPYRIGHT CONVENTION (REVISED) AND PROTOCOLS.

The Universal Copyright Convention, originally adopted at Geneva on 6 September 1952, was revised by the Conference for the Revision of the Universal Copyright Convention, convened by **UNESCO,** and adopted by that conference, in Paris, on 24 July 1971. The revised convention entered into force on 10 July 1974.

One purpose of the revision was to introduce a preferential system to benefit the developing countries (articles 5bis, 5ter, and 5quater). Another was to establish standard periods and provisions of copyright protection in all the contracting States.

The revised convention covers not only the authors of literary works but also the originators of musical, dramatic and cinematographic productions, paintings, engravings, and sculpture. Article 4bis extends the overall protection of the convention to include the basic rights ensuring the author's economic interests, including the exclusive right to authorize reproduction by any means, public performance, and broadcasting.

Two protocols are annexed to the Universal Copyright Convention as revised at Paris on 24 July 1971. Protocol 1 concerns the application of the convention to works of stateless persons and refugees; Protocol 2 concerns the application of the convention to the works of certain international organizations.

The text of the Convention (UNESCO's Standard-Setting Instruments, No. V.2.A.2) is as follows:

The Contracting States,

Moved by the desire to ensure in all countries copyright protection of literary, scientific and artistic works,

Convinced that a system of copyright protection appropriate to all nations of the world and expressed in a universal convention, additional to, and without impairing international systems already in force, will ensure respect for the rights of the individual and encourage the development of literature, the sciences and the arts.

Persuaded that such a universal copyright system will facilitate a wider dissemination of works of the human mind and increase international understanding,

Have resolved to revise the Universal Copyright Convention as signed at Geneva on 6 September 1952 (hereinafter called 'the 1952 Convention'), and consequently,

Have agreed as follows:

*Article 1.* Each Contracting State undertakes to provide for the adequate and effective protection of the rights of authors and other copyright proprietors in literary, scientific and artistic works, including writings, musical, dramatic and cinematographic works, and paintings, engravings, and sculpture.

*Article 2.* 1. Published works of nationals of any Contracting State and works first published in that State shall enjoy in each other Contracting State the same protection as that other State accords to works of its nationals first published in its own territory, as well as the protection specially granted by this Convention.

2. Unpublished works of nationals of each Contracting State shall enjoy in each other Contracting State the same protection as that other State accords to unpublished works of its own nationals, as well as the protection specially granted by this Convention.

3. For the purpose of this Convention any Contracting State may, by domestic legislation, assimilate to its own nationals any person domiciled in that State.

*Article 3.* 1. Any Contracting State which, under its domestic law, requires as a condition of copyright, compliance with formalities such as deposit, registration, notice, notarial certificates, payment of fees or manufacture or publication in that Contracting State, shall regard these requirements as satisfied with respect to all works protected in accordance with this Convention and first published outside its territory and the author of which is not one of its nationals, if from the time of the first publication all the copies of the work published with the authority of the author or other copyright proprietor bear the symbol accompanied by the name of the copyright proprietor and the year of first publication placed in such manner and location as to give reasonable notice of claim of copyright.

2. The provisions of paragraph 1 shall not preclude any Contracting State from requiring formalities or other conditions for the acquisition and enjoyment of copyright in respect of works first published in its territory or works of its nationals wherever published.

3. The provisions of paragraph 1 shall not preclude any Contracting State from providing that a person seeking judicial relief must, in bringing the action, comply with procedural requirements, such as that the complainant must appear through domestic counsel or that the complainant must deposit with the court or an administrative office, or both, a copy of the work involved in the litigation; provided that failure to comply with such requirements shall not affect the validity of the copyright, nor shall any such requirement be imposed upon a national of another Contracting State if such a requirement is not imposed on nationals of the State in which protection is claimed.

4. In each Contracting State there shall be legal means of protecting without formalities the unpublished works of nationals of other Contracting States.

5. If a Contracting State grants protection for more than one term of copyright and the first term is for a period longer than one of the minimum periods prescribed in Article 4, such State shall not be required to comply with the provisions of paragraph 1 of this Article in respect of the second or any subsequent term of copyright.

*Article 4.* 1. The duration of protection of a work shall be governed, in accordance with the provisions of Article 2 and this Article, by the law of the Contracting State in which protection is claimed.

2. (a) The term of protection for works protected under this Convention shall not be less than the life of the author and twenty-five years after his death. However, any Contracting State which, on the effective date of this Convention in that State, has limited this term for certain classes of works to a period computed from the first publication of the work, shall be entitled to maintain these exceptions and to extend them to other classes of works. For all these classes the term of protection shall not be less than twenty-five years from the date of first publication.

(b) Any Contracting State which, upon the effective date of this Convention in that State, does not compute the term of protection upon the basis of the life of the author, shall be entitled to compute the term of protection from the date of the first publication of the work or from its registration prior to publication, as the case may be, provided the term of protection shall not be less than twenty-five years from the date of first publication or from its registration prior to publication, as the case may be.

(c) If the legislation of a Contracting State grants two or more successive terms of protection, the duration of the first term shall not be less than one of the minimum periods specified in sub-paragraphs (a) and (b).

3. The provisions of paragraph 2 shall not apply to photographic works or to works of applied art; provided, however, that the term of protection in those Contracting States which protect photographic works, or works of applied art in so far as they are protected as artistic works, shall not be less than ten years for each of said classes of works.

4. (a) No Contracting State shall be obliged to grant protection to a work for a period longer than that fixed for the class of works to which the work in question belongs, in the case of unpublished works by the law of the Contracting State of which the author is a national, and in the case of published works by the law of the Contracting State in which the work has been first published.

(b) For the purposes of the application of sub-paragraph (a), if the law of any Contracting State grants two or more successive terms of protection, the period of protection of that State shall be considered to be the aggregate of those terms. However, if a specified work is not protected by such State during the second or any subsequent term for any reason, the other Contracting State shall not be obliged to protect it during the second or any subsequent term.

5. For the purposes of the application of paragraph 4, the work of a national of a Contracting State, first published in a non-Contracting State, shall be treated as though first published in the Contracting State of which the author is a national.

6. For the purposes of the application of paragraph 4, in case of simultaneous publication in two or more Contracting States, the work shall be treated as though first published in the State which affords the shortest term; any work published in two or more Contracting States within thirty days of its first publication shall be considered as having been published simultaneously in said Contracting States.

*Article 4bis.* 1. The rights referred to in Article 1 shall include the basic rights ensuring the author's economic interests, including the exclusive right to authorize reproduction by any means, public performance and broadcasting. The provisions of this Article shall extend to works protected under this Convention either in their original form or in any form recognizably derived from the original.

2. However, any Contracting State may, by its domestic legislation, make exceptions that do not conflict with the spirit and provisions of this Convention, to the rights mentioned in paragraph 1 of this Article. Any State whose legislation so provides, shall nevertheless accord a reasonable degree of effective protection to each of the rights to which exception has been made.

*Article 5.* 1. The rights referred to in Article 1 shall include the exclusive right of the author to make, publish and authorize the making and publication of translations of works protected under this Convention.

2. However, any Contracting State may, by its domestic legislation, restrict the right of translation of writings, but only subject to the following provisions:

(a) If, after the expiration of a period of seven years from the date of the first publication of a writing, a translation of such writing has not been published in a language in general use in the Contracting State, by the owner of the right of translation or with his authorization, any national of such Contracting State may obtain a non-exclusive licence from the competent authority thereof to translate the work into that language and publish the work so translated.

(b) Such national shall in accordance with the proce-

303

dure of the State concerned, establish either that he has re-quested, and been denied, authorization by the proprietor of the right to make and publish the translation, or that, after due diligence on his part, he was unable to find the owner of the right. A licence may also be granted on the same con-ditions if all previous editions of a translation in a language in general use in the Contracting State are out of print.

(c) If the owner of the right of translation cannot be found, then the applicant for a licence shall send copies of his application to the publisher whose name appears on the work and, if the nationality of the owner of the right of trans-lation is known, to the diplomatic or consular representative of the State of which such owner is a national, or to the organization which may have been designated by the gov-ernment of that State. The licence shall not be granted be-fore the expiration of a period of two months from the date of the dispatch of the copies of the application.

(d) Due provision shall be made by domestic legislation to ensure to the owner of the right of translation a compen-sation which is just and conforms to international standards, to ensure payment and transmittal of such compensation, and to ensure a correct translation of the work.

(e) The original title and the name of the author of the work shall be printed on all copies of the published trans-lation. The licence shall be valid only for publication of the translation in the territory of the Contracting State where it has been applied for. Copies so published may be imported and sold in another Contracting State if a language in gen-eral use in such other State is the same language as that into which the work has been so translated, and if the domestic law in such other State makes provision for such licences and does not prohibit such importation and sale. Where the fore-going conditions do not exist, the importation and sale of such copies in a Contracting State shall be governed by its domestic law and its agreements. The licence shall not be transferred by the licensee.

(f) The licence shall not be granted when the author has withdrawn from circulation all copies of the work.

*Article 5bis.* 1. Any Contracting State regarded as a devel-oping country in conformity with the established practice of the General Assembly of the United Nations may, by a no-tification deposited with the Director-General of the United Nations Educational, Scientific and Cultural Organization (hereinafter called "the Director-General") at the time of this ratification, acceptance or accession or thereafter, avail itself of any or all of the exceptions provided for in Articles 5ter and 5quater.

2. Any such notification shall be effective for ten years from the date of coming into force of this Convention, or for such part of that ten-year period as remains at the date of deposit of the notification, and may be renewed in whole or in part for further periods of ten years each if, not more than fifteen or less than three months before the expiration of the relevant ten-year period, the Contracting State depos-its a further notification with the Director-General. Initial notifications may also be made during these further periods of ten years in accordance with the provisions of this Article.

3. Notwithstanding the provisions of paragraph 2, a Con-tracting State that has ceased to be regarded as a developing country as referred to in paragraph 1 shall no longer be entitled to renew its notification made under the provisions of paragraph 1 or 2, and whether or not it formally withdraws the notification such State shall be precluded from availing itself of the exceptions provided for in Articles 5ter and 5quater at the end of the current ten-year period, or at the end of three years after it has ceased to be regarded as a developing country, whichever period expires later.

4. Any copies of a work already made under the excep-tions provided for in Articles 5ter and 5quater may continue to be distributed after the expiration of the period for which notifications under this Article were effective until their stock is exhausted.

5. Any Contracting State that has deposited a notification in accordance with Article 13 with respect to the application of this Convention to a particular country or territory, the situation of which can be regarded as analogous to that of the States referred to in paragraph 1 of this Article, may also deposit notifications and renew them in accordance with the provisions of this Article with respect to any such country or territory. During the effective period of such notifications, the provisions of Articles 5ter and 5quater may be applied with respect to such country or territory. The sending of copies from the country or territory to the Contracting State shall be considered as export within the meaning of Articles 5ter and 5quater.

*Article 5ter.* 1. (a) Any Contracting State to which Article 5bis(1) applies may substitute for the period of seven years provided for in Article 5(2) a period of three years or any longer period prescribed by its legislation. However, in the case of a translation into a language not in general use in one or more developed countries that are party to this Con-vention or only the 1952 Convention, the period shall be one year instead of three.

(b) A Contracting State to which Article 5bis (1) ap-plies may, with the unanimous agreement of the developed countries party to this Convention or only the 1952 Conven-tion and in which the same language is in general use, sub-stitute, in the case of translation into that language, for the period of three years provided for in sub-paragraph (a) an-other period as determined by such agreement but not shorter than one year. However, this sub-paragraph shall not apply where the language in question is English, French or Spanish. Notification of any such agreement shall be made to the Director-General.

(c) The licence may only be granted if the applicant, in accordance with the procedure of the State concerned, establishes either that he has requested, and been denied, authorization by the owner of the right of translation, or that, after due diligence on his part, he was unable to find the owner of the right. At the same time as he makes his request he shall inform either the International Copyright Informa-tion Centre established by the United Nations Educational, Scientific and Cultural Organization or any national or re-gional information centre which may have been designated in a notification to that effect deposited with the Director-General by the government of the State in which the publisher is believed to have his principal place of business.

(d) If the owner of the right of translation cannot be found, the applicant for a licence shall send, by registered airmail, copies of this application to the publisher whose name appears on the work and to any national or regional information centre as mentioned in sub-paragraph (c). If no such centre is notified he shall also send a copy to the inter-national copyright information centre established by the United Nations Educational, Scientific and Cultural Orga-nization.

2. (a) Licences obtainable after three years shall not be granted under this Article until a further period of six months has elapsed and licences obtainable after one year until a fur-ther period of nine months has elapsed. The further period shall begin either from the date of the request for permission

to translate mentioned in paragraph 1(c) or, if the identity or address of the owner of the right of translation is not known, from the date of dispatch of the copies of the application for a licence mentioned in paragraph 1(d).

(b) Licences shall not be granted if a translation has been published by the owner of the right of translation or with his authorization during the said period of six or nine months.

3. Any licence under this Article shall be granted only for the purpose of teaching, scholarship or research.

4. (a) Any licence granted under this Article shall not extend to the export of copies and shall be valid only for publication in the territory of the Contracting State where it has been applied for.

(b) Any copy published in accordance with a licence granted under this Article shall bear a notice in the appropriate language stating that the copy is available for distribution only in the Contracting State granting the licence. If the writing bears the notice specified in Article 3(1) the copies shall bear the same notice.

(c) The prohibition of export provided for in sub-paragraph (a) shall not apply where a governmental or other public entity of a State which has granted a licence under this Article to translate a work into a language other than English, French or Spanish sends copies of a translation prepared under such licence to another country if:

(i) the recipients are individuals who are nationals of the Contracting State granting the licence, or organizations grouping such individuals;

(ii) the copies are to be used only for the purpose of teaching, scholarship or research;

(iii) the sending of the copies and their subsequent distribution to recipients is without the object of commercial purpose; and

(iv) the country to which the copies have been sent has agreed with the Contracting State to allow the receipt, distribution or both and the Director-General has been notified of such agreement by any one of the governments which have concluded it.

5. Due provision shall be made at the national level to ensure:

(a) that the licence provides for just compensation that is consistent with standards of royalties normally operating in the case of licences freely negotiated between persons in the two countries concerned; and

(b) payment and transmittal of the compensation; however, should national currency regulations intervene, the competent authority shall make all efforts, by the use of international machinery, to ensure transmittal in internationally convertible currency or its equivalent.

6. Any licence granted by a Contracting State under this Article shall terminate if a translation of the work in the same language with substantially the same content as the edition in respect of which the licence was granted is published in the said State by the owner of the right of translation or with his authorization, at a price reasonably related to that normally charged in the same State for comparable works. Any copies already made before the licence is terminated may continue to be distributed until their stock is exhausted.

7. For works which are composed mainly of illustrations a licence to translate the text and to reproduce the illustrations may be granted only if the conditions of Article 5quater are also fulfilled.

8. (a) A licence to translate a work protected under this Convention, published in printed or analogous forms of reproduction, may also be granted to a broadcasting organi-

zation having its headquarters in a Contracting State to which Article 5bis (1) applies, upon an application made in that State by the said organization under the following conditions:

(i) the translation is made from a copy made and acquired in accordance with the laws of the Contracting State;

(ii) the translation is for use only in broadcasts intended exclusively for teaching or for the dissemination of the results of specialized technical or scientific research to experts in a particular profession;

(iii) the translation is used exclusively for the purposes set out in condition (ii), through broadcasts lawfully made which are intended for recipients on the territory of the Contracting State, including broadcasts made through the medium of sound or visual recordings lawfully and exclusively made for the purpose of such broadcasts;

(iv) sound or visual recordings of the translation may be exchanged only between broadcasting organizations having their headquarters in the Contracting State granting the licence; and

(v) all uses made of the translation are without any commercial purpose.

(b) Provided all of the criteria and conditions set out in sub-paragraph (a) are met, a licence may also be granted to a broadcasting organization to translate any text incorporated in an audio-visual fixation which was itself prepared and published for the sole purpose of being used in connexion with systematic instructional activities.

(c) Subject to sub-paragraphs (a) and (b), the other provisions of this Article shall apply to the grant and exercise of the licence.

9. Subject to the provisions of this Article, any licence granted under this Article shall be governed by the provisions of Article 5, and shall continue to be governed by the provisions of Article 5 and of this Article, even after the seven-year period provided for in Article 5(2) has expired. However, after the said period has expired, the licensee shall be free to request that the said licence be replaced by a new licence governed exclusively by the provisions of Article 5.

*Article 5quater.* 1. Any Contracting State to which Article 5bis (1) applies may adopt the following provisions:

(a) If, after the expiration of (i) the relevant period specified in sub-paragraph (c) commencing from the date of first publication of a particular edition of a literary, scientific or artistic work referred to in paragraph 3, or (ii) any longer period determined by national legislation of the State, copies of such edition have not been distributed in that State to the general public or in connexion with systematic instructional activities at a price reasonably related to that normally charged in the State for comparable works, by the owner of the right of reproduction or with his authorization, any national of such State may obtain a non-exclusive licence from the competent authority to publish such edition at that or a lower price for use in connexion with systematic instructional activities. The licence may only be granted if such national, in accordance with the procedure of the State concerned, establishes either that he has requested, and been denied, authorization by the proprietor of the right to publish such work, or that, after due diligence on his part, he was unable to find the owner of the right. At the same time as he makes his request he shall inform either the international copyright information centre established by the United Nations Educational, Scientific and Cultural Organization or any national or regional information centre referred to in sub-paragraph (d).

(b) A licence may also be granted on the same conditions if, for a period of six months, no authorized copies of the edition in question have been on sale in the State concerned to the general public or in connexion with systematic instructional activities at a price reasonably related to that normally charged in the State for comparable works.

(c) The period referred to in sub-paragraph (a) shall be five years except that:

(i) for works of the natural and physical sciences, including mathematics, and of technology, the period shall be three years;

(ii) for works of fiction, poetry, drama and music, and for art books, the period shall be seven years.

(d) If the owner of the right of reproduction cannot be found, the applicant for a licence shall send, by registered air mail, copies of his application to the publisher whose name appears on the work and to any national or regional information centre identified as such in a notification deposited with the Director-General by the State in which the publisher is believed to have his principal place of business. In the absence of any such notification, he shall also send a copy to the international copyright information centre established by the United Nations Educational, Scientific and Cultural Organization. The licence shall not be granted before the expiration of a period of three months from the date of dispatch of the copies of the application.

(e) Licences obtainable after three years shall not be granted under this Article:

(i) until a period of six months has elapsed from the date of the request for permission referred to in sub-paragraph (a) or, if the identity or address of the owner of the right of reproduction is unknown, from the date of the dispatch of the copies of the application for a licence referred to in sub-paragraph (d);

(ii) if any such distribution of copies of the edition as is mentioned in sub-paragraph (a) has taken place during that period.

(f) The name of the author and the title of the particular edition of the work shall be printed on all copies of the published reproduction. The licence shall not extend to the export of copies and shall be valid only for publication in the territory of the Contracting State where it has been applied for. The licence shall not be transferable by the licensee.

(g) Due provisions shall be made by domestic legislation to ensure an accurate reproduction of the particular edition in question.

(h) A licence to reproduce and publish a translation of a work shall not be granted under this Article in the following cases:

(i) where the translation was not published by the owner of the right of translation or with his authorization;

(ii) where the translation is not in a language in general use in the State with power to grant the licence.

2. The exceptions provided for in paragraph 1 are subject to the following additional provisions:

(a) Any copy published in accordance with a licence granted under this Article shall bear a notice in the appropriate language stating that the copy is available for distribution only in the Contracting State to which the said licence applies. If the edition bears the notice specified in Article 3 (1), the copies shall bear the same notice.

(b) Due provision shall be made at the national level to ensure:

(i) that the licence provides for just compensation that is consistent with standards of royalties normally operating in the case of licences freely negotiated between persons in the two countries concerned; and

(ii) payment and transmittal of the compensation; however, should national currency regulations intervene, the competent authority shall make all efforts, by the use of international machinery, to ensure transmittal in internationally convertible currency or its equivalent.

(c) Whenever copies of an edition of a work are distributed in the Contracting State to the general public or in connexion with systematic instructional activities, by the owner of the right of reproduction or with his authorization, at a price reasonably related to that normally charged in the State for comparable works, any licence granted under this Article shall terminate if such edition is in the same language and is substantially the same in content as the edition published under the licence. Any copies already made before the licence is terminated may continue to be distributed until their stock is exhausted.

(d) No licence shall be granted when the author has withdrawn from circulation all copies of the edition in question.

3. (a) Subject to sub-paragraph (b), the literary, scientific or artistic works to which this Article applies shall be limited to works published in printed or analogous forms of reproduction.

(b) The provisions of this Article shall also apply to reproduction in audio-visual form of lawfully made audio-visual fixations including any protected works incorporated therein and to the translation of any incorporated text into a language in general use in the State with power to grant the licence; always provided that the audio-visual fixations in question were prepared and published for the sole purpose of being used in connexion with systematic instructional activities.

*Article 6.* "Publication", as used in this Convention, means the reproduction in tangible form and the general distribution to the public of copies of a work from which it can be read or otherwise visually perceived.

*Article 7.* This Convention shall not apply to works or rights in works which, at the effective date of this Convention in a Contracting State where protection is claimed, are permanently in the public domain in the said Contracting State.

*Article 8.* 1. This Convention, which shall bear the date of 24 July 1971, shall be deposited with the Director-General and shall remain open for signature by all States party to the 1952 Convention for a period of 120 days after the date of this Convention. It shall be subject to ratification or acceptance by the signatory States.

2. Any State which has not signed this Convention may accede thereto.

3. Ratification, acceptance or accession shall be effected by the deposit of an instrument to that effect with the Director-General.

*Article 9.* 1. This Convention shall come into force three months after the deposit of twelve instruments of ratification, acceptance or accession.

2. Subsequently, this Convention shall come into force in respect of each State three months after that State has deposited its instrument of ratification, acceptance or accession.

3. Accession to this Convention by a State not party to the 1952 Convention shall also constitute accession to that Convention; however, if its instrument of accession is deposited before this Convention comes into force, such State may make its accession to the 1952 Convention conditional upon the coming into force of this Convention. After the coming

into force of this Convention, no State may accede solely to the 1952 Convention.

4. Relations between States party to this Convention and States that are party only to the 1952 Convention, shall be governed by the 1952 Convention. However, any State party only to the 1952 Convention may, by a notification deposited with the Director-General, declare that it will admit the application of the 1971 Convention to works of its nationals or works first published in its territory by all States party to this Convention.

*Article 10.* 1. Each Contracting State undertakes to adopt, in accordance with its Constitution, such measures as are necessary to ensure the application of this Convention.

2. It is understood that at the date this Convention comes into force in respect of any State, that State must be in a position under its domestic law to give effect to the terms of this Convention.

*Article 11.* 1. An Intergovernmental Committee is hereby established with the following duties:

(a) to study the problems concerning the application and operation of the Universal Copyright Convention;

(b) to make preparation for periodic revisions of this Convention;

(c) to study any other problems concerning the international protection of copyright, in co-operation with the various interested international organizations, such as the United Nations Educational, Scientific and Cultural Organization, the International Union for the Protection of Literary and Artistic Works and the Organization of American States;

(d) to inform States party to the Universal Copyright Convention as to its activities.

2. The Committee shall consist of the representatives of eighteen States party to this Convention or only to the 1952 Convention.

3. The Committee shall be selected with due consideration to a fair balance of national interests on the basis of geographical location, population, languages and stage of development.

4. The Director-General of the United Nations Educational, Scientific and Cultural Organization, the Director-General of the World Intellectual Property Organization and the Secretary-General of the Organization of American States, or their representatives, may attend meetings of the Committee in an advisory capacity.

*Article 12.* The Intergovernmental Committee shall convene a conference for revision whenever it deems necessary, or at the request of at least ten States party to this Convention.

*Article 13.* 1. Any Contracting State may, at the time of deposit of its instrument of ratification, acceptance or accession, or at any time thereafter, declare by notification addressed to the Director-General that this Convention shall apply to all or any of the countries or territories for the international relations of which it is responsible and this Convention shall thereupon apply to the countries or territories named in such notification after the expiration of the term of three months provided for in Article 9. In the absence of such notification, this Convention shall not apply to any such country or territory.

2. However, nothing in this Article shall be understood as implying the recognition or tacit acceptance by a Contracting State of the factual situation concerning a country or territory to which this Convention is made applicable by another Contracting State in accordance with the provisions of this Article.

*Article 14.* 1. Any Contracting State may denounce this Convention in its own name or on behalf of all or any of the countries or territories with respect to which a notification has been given under Articles 13. The denunciation shall be made by notification addressed to the Director-General. Such denunciation shall also constitute denunciation of the 1952 Convention.

2. Such denunciation shall operate only in respect of the State or of the country or territory on whose behalf it was made and shall not take effect until twelve months after the date of receipt of the notification.

*Article 15.* A dispute between two or more Contracting States concerning the interpretation or application of this Convention, not settled by negotiation, shall, unless the States concerned agree on some other method of settlement, be brought before the International Court of Justice for determination by it.

*Article 16.* 1. This Convention shall be established in English, French and Spanish. The three texts shall be signed and shall be equally authoritative.

2. Official texts of this Convention shall be established by the Director-General, after consultation with the governments concerned, in Arabic, German, Italian and Portuguese.

3. Any Contracting State or group of Contracting States shall be entitled to have established by the Director-General other texts in the language of its choice by arrangement with the Director-General.

4. All such texts shall be annexed to the signed texts of this Convention.

*Article 17.* 1. This Convention shall not in any way affect the provisions of the Berne Convention for the Protection of Literary and Artistic Works or membership in the Union created by that Convention.

2. In application of the foregoing paragraph, a declaration has been annexed to the present Article. This declaration is an integral part of this Convention for the States bound by the Berne Convention on 1 January 1951, or which have or may become bound to it at a later date. The signature of this Convention by such States shall also constitute signature of the said declaration, and ratification, acceptance or accession by such States shall include the declaration, as well as this Convention.

*Article 18.* This Convention shall not abrogate multilateral or bilateral copyright conventions or arrangements that are or may be in effect exclusively between two or more American Republics. In the event of any difference either between the provisions of such existing conventions or arrangements and the provisions of this Convention, or between the provisions of this Convention and those of any new convention or arrangement which may be formulated between two or more American Republics after this Convention comes into force, the convention or arrangement most recently formulated shall prevail between the parties thereto. Rights in works acquired in any Contracting State under existing conventions or arrangements before the date this Convention comes into force in such State shall not be affected.

*Article 19.* This Convention shall not abrogate multilateral or bilateral conventions or arrangements in effect between two or more Contracting States. In the event of any difference between the provisions of such existing conventions or arrangements and the provisions of this Convention, the provisions of this Convention shall prevail. Rights in works acquired in any Contracting State under existing conventions or arrangements before the date on which this Convention comes into force in such State shall not be affected. Nothing in this Article shall affect the provisions of Articles 17 and 18.

*Article 20.* Reservations to this Convention shall not be permitted.

*Article 21.* 1. The Director-General shall send duly certified copies of this Convention to the States interested and to the Secretary-General of the United Nations for registration by him.

2. He shall also inform all interested States of the ratifications, acceptances and accessions which have been deposited, the date on which this Convention comes into force, the notification under this Convention and denunciations under Article 14.

*Appendix Declaration relating to Article 17.* The States which are members of the International Union for the Protection of Literary and Artistic Works (hereinafter called "the Berne Union") and which are signatories to this Convention,

Desiring to reinforce their mutual relations on the basis of the said Union and to avoid any conflict which might result from the co-existence of the Berne Convention and the Universal Copyright Convention,

Recognizing the temporary need of some States to adjust their level of copyright protection in accordance with their stage of cultural, social and economic development,

Have, by common agreement, accepted the terms of the following declaration:

(a) Except as provided by paragraph (b), works which, according to the Berne Convention, have as their country of origin a country which has withdrawn from the Berne Union after 1 January 1951, shall not be protected by the Universal Copyright Convention in the countries of the Berne Union;

(b) Where a Contracting State is regarded as a developing country in conformity with the established practice of the General Assembly of the United Nations, and has deposited with the Director-General of the United Nations Educational, Scientific and Cultural Organization, at the time of its withdrawal from the Berne Union, a notification to the effect that it regards itself as a developing country, the provisions of paragraph (a) shall not be applicable as long as such State may avail itself of the exceptions provided for by this Convention in accordance with Article 5bis;

(c) The Universal Copyright Convention shall not be applicable to the relationships among countries of the Berne Union in so far as it relates to the protection of works having as their country of origin, within the meaning of the Berne Convention, a country of the Berne Union.

*Resolution concerning Article 11.* The Conference for Revision of the Universal Copyright Convention,

Having considered the problems relating to the Intergovernmental Committee provided for in Article 11 of this Convention, to which this resolution is annexed,

Resolves that:

1. At its inception, the Committee shall include representatives of the twelve States members of the Intergovernmental Committee established under Article 11 of the 1952 Convention and the resolution annexed to it, and, in addition, representatives of the following States: Algeria, Australia, Japan, Mexico, Senegal and Yugoslavia.

2. Any States that are not party to the 1952 Convention and have not acceded to this Convention before the first ordinary session of the Committee following the entry into force of this Convention shall be replaced by other States to be selected by the Committee at its first ordinary session in conformity with the provisions of Article 11 (2) and (3).

3. As soon as this Convention comes into force the Committee as provided for in paragraph 1 shall be deemed to be constituted in accordance with Article 11 of this Convention.

4. A session of the Committee shall take place within one year after the coming into force of this Convention; thereafter the Committee shall meet in ordinary session at intervals of not more than two years.

5. The Committee shall elect its Chairman and two Vice-Chairmen. It shall establish its Rules of Procedures having regard to the following principles:

(a) The normal duration of the term of office of the members represented on the Committee shall be six years with one-third retiring every two years, it being however understood that, of the original terms of office, one-third shall expire at the end of the Committee's second ordinary session which will follow the entry into force of this Convention, a further third at the end of its third ordinary session, and the remaining third at the end of its fourth ordinary session.

(b) The rules governing the procedure whereby the Committee shall fill vacancies, the order in which terms of membership expire, eligibility for re-election, and election procedures, shall be based upon a balancing of the needs for continuity of membership and rotation of representation, as well as the considerations set out in Article 11 (3).

Expresses the wish that the United Nations Educational, Scientific and Cultural Organization provide its Secretariat.

In faith whereof the undersigned, having deposited their respective full powers, have signed this Convention.

Done at Paris, this twenty-fourth day of July 1971, in a single copy.

***PROTOCOL 1.*** The Protocol provides for application of the Convention to the works of stateless persons and refugees. It was adopted by the Conference for the Revision of the Universal Copyright Convention, in Paris, on 24 July 1971, and entered into force on 10 July 1974. It is subject to ratification, acceptance, or accession by States parties to the Universal Copyright Convention (revised).

The text of the Protocol (UNESCO's Standard-Setting Instruments, No.V.2.A.2) is as follows:

The States party hereto, being also party to the Universal Copyright Convention as revised at Paris on 24 July 1971 (hereinafter called "the 1971 Convention").

Have accepted the following provisions:

1. Stateless persons and refugees who have their habitual residence in a State party to this Protocol shall, for the purposes of the 1971 Convention, be assimilated to the nationals of that State.

2. (a) This Protocol shall be signed and shall be subject to ratification or acceptance, or may be acceded to, as if the provisions of Article 8 of the 1971 Convention applied hereto.

(b) This Protocol shall enter into force in respect of each State, on the date of deposit of the instrument of ratification, acceptance or accession of the State concerned or on the date of entry into force of the 1971 Convention with respect to such State, whichever is the later.

(c) On the entry into force of this Protocol in respect of a State not party to Protocol 1 annexed to the 1951 Convention, the latter Protocol shall be deemed to enter into force in respect of such State.

In faith whereof the undersigned, being duly authorized thereto, have signed this Protocol.

Done at Paris this twenty-fourth day of July 1971, in the English, French and Spanish languages, the three texts being equally authoritative, in a single copy which shall be deposited with the Director-General of the United Nations Educational, Scientific and Cultural Organization. The Director-General shall send certified copies to the signatory States, and to the Secretary-General of the United Nations for registration.

***PROTOCOL 2.*** The Protocol provides for application of the Convention to the works of certain international organizations, in particular to works published for the first time by the United Nations, by the specialized agencies in relationship therewith, or by the Organization of American States. It was adopted by the Conference for the Revision of the Universal Copyright Convention, in Paris, on 24 July 1971, and entered into force on 10 July 1974. It is subject to ratification, acceptance, or accession by States parties to the Universal Copyright Convention (revised).

The text of the Protocol (UNESCO's Standard-Setting Instruments, No.V.2.A.2) is as follows:

The States party hereto, being also party to the Universal Copyright Convention as revised at Paris on 24 July 1971 (hereinafter called "the 1971 Convention"),

Have accepted the following provisions:

1. (a) The protection provided for in Article 2 (1) of the 1971 Convention shall apply to works published for the first time by the United Nations, by the Specialized Agencies in relationship therewith, or by the Organization of American States.

(b) Similarly, Article 2 (2) of the 1971 Convention shall apply to the said organization or agencies.

2. (a) This Protocol shall be signed and shall be subject to ratification or acceptance, or may be acceded to, as if the provisions of Article 8 of the 1971 Convention applied hereto.

(b) This Protocol shall enter into force for each State on the date of deposit of the instrument of ratification, acceptance or accession of the State concerned or on the date of entry into force of the 1971 Convention with respect to such State, whichever is the later.

In faith whereof the undersigned, being duly authorized thereto, have signed this Protocol.

Done at Paris, this twenty-fourth day of July 1971, in the English, French and Spanish languages, the three texts being equally authoritative, in a single copy which shall be deposited with the Director-General of the United Nations Educational, Scientific and Cultural Organization. The Director-General shall send certified copies to the signatory States, and to the Secretary-General of the United Nations for registration.

## CORRIGAN, MAIREAD (1944–).

In 1976, Mairead Corrigan, aunt of nieces and a nephew killed by a runaway car driven by an IRA terrorist in Northern Ireland, shared the **NOBEL PEACE PRIZE** with **BETTY WILLIAMS,** also of Northern Ireland.

Born in Belfast, Corrigan spent an unremarkable life until the "troubles" in Northern Ireland intruded into her own family. Her sister was walking with her children on a public street when a car slammed into them. The driver of the car was an IRA terrorist who had been himself slain behind the wheel by British troops. As a result of her children's death, Corrigan's sister later committed suicide.

In an attempt to have good come from this tragedy, Corrigan, a Catholic, and her co-winner Betty Williams, a Protestant, founded the Peace People, an organization dedicated to bringing together Catholics and Protestants in Northern Ireland who wanted to see an end to the sectarian warfare. They announced that the Peace People opposed "all violence whether it is from the UDA, the IRA, or the British Army." Because of their efforts, the pair were beaten and ridiculed, but they were also rewarded: in addition to the Peace Prize, the two women received the Carl von Ossietzky Medal and the Norwegian People's Peace Prize, the latter awarded by 22 Norwegian newspapers when the Nobel Committee did not award a 1976 Peace Prize (Corrigan and Williams received the award retroactively in 1977).

In announcing Corrigan as the Peace Prize recipient, the Nobel Committee stated that she "acted from a profound conviction that the individual can make a meaningful contribution to peace through constructive reconciliation."

***BIBLIOGRAPHY.*** Schlessinger, Bernard S., and June H. Schlessinger, eds. *Who's Who of Nobel Prize Winners.* Phoenix, AZ, USA: Oryx Press, 1991.

## COSTA RICA.

The Republic of Costa Rica is a country in Central America, between the Pacific Ocean and the Caribbean Sea. It has borders with Nicaragua and Panama. It achieved independence from Spain in 1821 and became a member of the United Nations in 1945. Its population is estimated to be 3,225,000. Ethnic groups include persons of European origin (96%), African origin (3%), and Amerindian origin (1%). Languages commonly used include Spanish and English. Christianity (Roman Catholic) is the State religion and the predominant faith. Literacy is estimated at 90%.

The government (1994) took the form of a republic. Under the 1949 constitution, the president is elected for a four-year term by popular vote and is not eligible for re-election. He exercises executive authority as head of State and government. Legislation is prepared by the 57-member unicameral Legislative Assembly, members of which also are elected for terms of four years. Political parties include the National Liberation Party, the Unity Party, the Communist Party, the Pueblo Unido Party, and the Movimiento Nacional Party.

In February 1994 Jose Maria Figueres Olsen was

C

elected President with 49.7% of the vote. He is the son of Jose ''Pepe'' Figueres Ferrer who had successfully instituted constitutional democracy while bringing and end to the rule of the Costa Rican army during the civil war of 1948.

Before the constitution of 1949 entered into force, an executive decree of 4 April 1942 prohibited entry into the country of aliens arriving as immigrants or temporary residents of "persons of the Negro race, Chinese, Arabs, Syrians, Turks, Armenians, Gypsies, coolies, etc." Restrictions against Chinese were abolished in 1943, and other restrictions were repealed in 1973. Article 33 of the 1949 constitution states: "All persons are equal before the law and no discrimination whatsoever may be practiced contrary to human dignity."

In order to promote the welfare of Costa Rica's indigenous populations, the National Indigenous Affairs Commission was established by Act No. 5251 of 19 June 1971.

*BIBLIOGRAPHY.* Basok, Tanya. "Welcome Some and Reject Others: Constraints and Interests Influencing Costa Rican Policies on Refugees," *International Migration Review* 24, no. 92 (Winter 1990): 722–747. Scholarly article, in English.

Bourgois, Philippe. *Ethnic Diversity on a Corporate Plantation: Guaymi Labor on a United Fruit Brands Subsidiary in Bocas del Toro, Panama, and Talamanca, Costa Rica.* Cambridge, MA, USA: Cultural Survival, 1985. NGO special paper, in English.

Carranza, Elías, Henry Issa El-Khoury, and Maria del Rosario León. *Sistema Penal y Derechos Humanos en Costa Rica: Muertes Violentas en Hechos de Intervención Policial, Muertes Violentas en el Sistema Penitenciario, Muertes en Accidentes de Tránsito* (The Penal System and Human Rights in Costa Rica: Violent Deaths in Cases of Police Intervention, Violent Deaths in the Penitentiary System, Deaths in Transit-Related Accidents). San Jose: Costa Rica: Editorial Universitaria Centroamericana; Instituto Latinoamericano de Naciones Unidas para la Prevención del Delito y Tratamiento del Delincuente; and Instituto Interamericano de Derechos Humanos, 1990. Research report, in Spanish.

Centro de Derechos Humanos. "Fray Francisco de Vitoria, O.P." (Center for Human Rights "Fr. Francisco de Vitoria, O.P.") "Costa Rica," *Justicia y Paz* 2, no. 1 (November 1986): 54–55. NGO article, in Spanish.

Comision Costarricense de Derechos Humanos (Costa Rican Commission for Human Rights). "CODEHU Ante la Situacion de los Reclusos" (CODEHU and the Conditions of Prisoners), *Informativo* 4 (March–April 1986): 16. NGO article, in Spanish.

———. *Consideraciones en Torno a los Derechos Humanos en Costa Rica* (Considerations concerning Human Rights in Costa Rica). San Jose, Costa Rica: 1987. NGO report, in Spanish.

———. *Informe sobre la Situation de los Derechos Humanos en Costa Rica* (Report on the Human Rights Situation in Costa Rica). San Jose, Costa Rica: 1987. NGO report, in Spanish.

———. *Situación de los Derechos Humanos en Costa Rica: 1 de marzo 1989–31 de agosto de 1990* (Human Rights Situation in Costa Rica: March 1, 1989–August 31, 1990). San Jose, Costa Rica: 1991. Annual report, in Spanish.

Comision para la Defensa de los Derechos Humanos (Central American Committee for Defense of Human Rights). *Informe sobre la Situacion de los Derechos Humanos en Centroamerica, 1986* (Report on the Human Rights Situation in Central America, 1986). San Jose, Costa Rica: 1987. NGO monograph, in English.

Fernandez, G., and L. Narvaez. "Refugees and Human Rights in Costa Rica: The Mariel Cubans," *International Migration Review* 21 (Summer 1987): 406–415. Scholarly research note, in English.

Hernadez Valle, Ruben. *Costa Rica: Elecciones de 1986 Analisis de los Resultados* (Costa Rica: 1986 Elections Analysis of the Results). San Jose, Costa Rica: Instituto Interamericano de Derechos Humanos, Centro de Asesoria y Promocion Electoral/Inter-American Institute of Human Rights, and Center for Electoral Counseling and Promotion, 1986. Research paper, in Spanish.

McColm, R. Bruce. *To License a Journalist? A Landmark Decision in the Schmidt Case. The Opinion of the Inter-American Court of Human Rights.* New York: Freedom House, 1986. NGO report, in English.

**COUNCIL OF EUROPE.** A regional intergovernmental organization composed of 32 States of Europe, the Council was established in accordance with the Statute of the Council of Europe. As of 1995, its members are: Austria, Belgium, Bulgaria, Czech Republic, Cyprus, Denmark, Estonia, Finland, France, Germany, Great Britain, Greece, Hungary, Iceland, Ireland, Italy, Liechtenstein, Lithuania, Luxembourg, Malta, the Netherlands, Norway, Poland, Portugal, Romania, San Marino, Slovakia, Slovenia, Spain, Sweden, Switzerland, and Turkey. The Council endeavors to promote unity among its members for the purpose of safeguarding and realizing the ideals and principles that are their common heritage and facilitating their economic and social progress. It also works to improve living conditions and to develop human values; to uphold the principles of parliamentary democracy and human rights; and to demonstrate to Europeans that they live in a framework that goes beyond the individual State and that provides a "European dimension" to their lives.

The Council's organizational structure includes the Committee of Ministers of the Council of Europe, composed of the foreign ministers of each member States or their alternates, which meets twice a year to take action on behalf of the Council; the Consultative Assembly, composed of 170 members elected or appointed by their respective national parliaments, which meets three times a year to debate matters within its competence and to present its conclusions and recommendations to the Committee of Ministers; and the Secretariat, consisting of the Secretary-General, the Deputy Secretary-General, and such staff as may be required. The composition and functions of the Committee of Ministers are set out in detail in chapter IV of the Statute of the Council; those of the

310

Consultative Assembly in chapter V; and those of the Secretariat in chapter VI.

Since 1981, the Council has awarded, every three years, the Council of Europe Human Rights Prize, consisting of a medal and a certificate, for outstanding work in the protection of human rights.

In addition to its human rights activities, the Council is engaged in a broad range of activities, such as problems of the media in a democratic society; social and socio-economic matters; education, culture, and sport; youth; health; heritage and environment; local and regional government; and legal cooperation.

Among the Council's publications are the *Yearbook of the European Convention on Human Rights,* issued annually; the *Human Rights Information Sheet,* issued twice a year; the *Digest of Strasbourg Case-law Relating to the European Convention on Human Rights,* issued annually in two series: *Series A—Judgements and Decisions,* and *Series B—Pleadings, Oral Arguments and Documents*; and the *European Treaty Series,* issued irregularly.

**STATUTE.** Under the Statute, membership of the Council is open to any European State invited to join by the Committee of Ministers of the Council of Europe on the ground that it is considered able and willing to fulfill the obligations set out in article 3 of the statute—i.e., to accept the principles of the rule of law and of the enjoyment by all persons within its jurisdiction of human rights and fundamental freedoms and to collaborate sincerely and effectively in the realization of the aims of the Council. Texts of chapters I, IV, V, and VI of the Statute (European Treaty Series 1) follow:

### Chapter I. Aim of the Council of Europe

*Article 1.* (a) The aim of the Council of Europe is to achieve a greater unity between its Members for the purpose of safeguarding and realising the ideals and principles which are their common heritage and facilitating their economic and social progress.

(b) This aim shall be pursued through the organs of the Council by discussion of questions of common concern and by agreements and common action in economic, social, cultural, scientific, legal and administrative matters and in the maintenance and further realisation of human rights and fundamental freedoms.

(c) Participation in the Council of Europe shall not affect the collaboration of its Members in the work of the United Nations and of other international organisations or unions to which they are parties.

(d) Matters relating to National Defence do not fall within the scope of the Council of Europe. . . .

### Chapter IV. Committee of Ministers

*Article 13.* The Committee of Ministers is the organ which acts on behalf of the Council of Europe in accordance with Articles 15 and 16.

*Article 14.* Each Member shall be entitled to one representative on the Committee of Ministers, and each representative shall be entitled to one vote. Representatives on the Committee shall be the Ministers for Foreign Affairs. When a Minister for Foreign Affairs is unable to be present or in other circumstances where it may be desirable, an alternate may be nominated to act for him, who shall, whenever possible, be a member of his Government.

*Article 15.* (a) On the recommendation of the Consultative Assembly or on its own initiative, the Committee of Ministers shall consider the action required to further the aim of the Council of Europe, including the conclusion of conventions or agreements and the adoption by Governments of a common policy with regard to particular matters. Its conclusions shall be communicated to Members by the Secretary-General.

(b) In appropriate cases, the conclusions of the Committee may take the form of recommendations to the Governments of Members, and the Committee may request the Governments of Members to inform it of the action taken by them with regard to such recommendations.

*Article 16.* The Committee of Ministers shall, subject to the provisions of Articles 24, 28, 30, 32, 33 and 35, relating to the powers of the Consultative Assembly, decide with binding effect all matters relating to the internal organisation and arrangements of the Council of Europe. For this purpose the Committee of Ministers shall adopt such financial and administrative regulations as may be necessary.

*Article 17.* The Committee of Ministers may set up advisory and technical committees or commissions for such specific purposes as it may deem desirable.

*Article 18.* The Committee of Ministers shall adopt its rules of procedure, which shall determine amongst other things:

(i) the quorum;

(ii) the method of appointment and term of office of its President;

(iii) the procedure for the admission of items to its agenda, including the giving of notice of proposals for resolutions; and

(iv) the notifications required for the nomination of alternates under Article 14.

*Article 19.* At each session of the Consultative Assembly the Committee of Ministers shall furnish the Assembly with statements of its activities, accompanied by appropriate documentation.

*Article 20.* (a) Resolutions of the Committee of Ministers relating to the following important matters, namely:

(i) recommendations under Article 15 (b);

(ii) questions under Article 19;

(iii) questions under Article 21 (a) (i) and (b);

(iv) questions under Article 33;

(v) recommendations for the amendment of Articles 1 (d), 7, 15, 20 and 22; and

(vi) any other question which the Committee may, by a resolution passed under (d) below, decide should be subject to a unanimous vote on account of its importance require the unanimous vote of the representatives casting a vote, and of a majority of the representatives entitled to sit on the Committee.

(b) Questions arising under the rules of procedure or under the financial and administrative regulations may be decided by a simple majority vote of the representatives entitled to sit on the Committee.

(c) Resolutions of the Committee under Articles 4 and 5

require a two-thirds majority of all the representatives entitled to sit on the Committee.

(d) All other resolutions of the Committee, including the adoption of the Budget, of rules of procedure and of financial and administrative regulations, recommendations for the amendment of articles of this Statute, other than those mentioned in paragraph (a) (v) above, and deciding in case of doubt which paragraph of this Article applies, require a two-thirds majority of the representatives casting a vote and of a majority of the representatives entitled to sit on the Committee.

*Article 21.* (a) Unless the Committee decides otherwise, meetings of the Committee of Ministers shall be held:

    (i) in private, and

    (ii) at the seat of the Council.

(b) The Committee shall determine what information shall be published regarding the conclusions and discussions of a meeting held in private.

(c) The Committee shall meet before and during the beginning of every session of the Consultative Assembly and at such other times as it may decide.

### Chapter V. Consultative Assembly

*Article 22.* The Consultative Assembly is the deliberative organ of the Council of Europe. It shall debate matters within its competence under this Statute and present its conclusions, in the form of recommendations, to the Committee of Ministers.

*Article 23.* (a) The Consultative Assembly may discuss and make recommendations upon any matter within the aim and scope of the Council of Europe as defined in Chapter I. It shall also discuss and may make recommendations upon any matter referred to it by the Committee of Ministers with a request for its opinion.

(b) The Assembly shall draw up its Agenda in accordance with the provisions of paragraph (a) above. In so doing, it shall have regard to the work of other European intergovernmental organisations to which some or all of the Members of the Council are parties.

(c) The President of the Assembly shall decide, in case of doubt, whether any question raised in the course of the Session is within the Agenda of the Assembly.

*Article 24.* The Consultative Assembly may, with due regard to the provisions of Article 38 (d), establish committees or commissions to consider and report to it on any matter which falls within its competence under Article 23, to examine and prepare questions on its agenda and to advise on all matters of procedure.

*Article 25.* (a) The Consultative Assembly shall consist of Representatives of each Member elected by its Parliament or appointed in such manner as that Parliament shall decide, subject, however, to the right of each Member Government to make any additional appointments necessary when the Parliament is not in session and has not laid down the procedure to be followed in that case. Each Representative must be a national of the Member whom he represents, but shall not at the same time be a member of the Committee of Ministers.

The term of office of Representatives thus appointed will date from the opening of the Ordinary Session following their appointment; it will expire at the opening of the next Ordinary Session except that, in the event of elections to their Parliaments having taken place, Members shall be entitled to make new appointments.

If a Member fills vacancies due to death or resignation, or

proceeds to make new appointments as a result of elections to its Parliament, the term of office of the new Representatives shall date from the first Sitting of the Assembly following their appointment.

(b) No Representative shall be deprived of his position as such during a session of the Assembly without the agreement of the Assembly.

(c) Each Representative may have a substitute who may, in the absence of the Representative, sit, speak and vote in his place. The provisions of paragraph (a) above apply to the appointment of substitutes.

*Article 26.* Members shall be entitled to the number of Representatives given below:

Austria, 6; Belgium, 7; Denmark, 5; France, 18; Germany, 18; Greece, 7; Iceland, 3; Ireland, 4; Italy, 18; Luxembourg, 3; Netherlands, 7; Norway, 5; Sweden, 6; Turkey, 10; United Kingdom of Great Britain and Northern Ireland, 18.

*Article 27.* The conditions under which the Committee of Ministers collectively may be represented in the debates of the Consultative Assembly, or individual representatives on the Committee or their alternates may address the Assembly, shall be determined by such rules of procedure on this subject as may be drawn up by the Committee after consultation with the Assembly.

*Article 28.* (a) The Consultative Assembly shall adopt its rules of procedure and shall elect from its members its President, who shall remain in office until the next ordinary session.

(b) The President shall control the proceedings but shall not take part in the debate or vote. The substitute of the Representative who is President may sit, speak and vote in his place.

(c) The rules of procedure shall determine *inter alia*:

    (i) the quorum;

    (ii) the manner of the election and terms of office of the President and other officers;

    (iii) the manner in which the agenda shall be drawn up and be communicated to Representatives; and

    (iv) the time and manner in which the names of Representatives and their Substitutes shall be notified.

*Article 29.* Subject to the provisions of Article 30, all resolutions of the Consultative Assembly, including resolutions:

    (i) embodying recommendations to the Committee of Ministers;

    (ii) proposing to the Committee matters for discussion in the Assembly;

    (iii) establishing committees or commissions;

    (iv) determining the date of commencement of its sessions;

    (v) determining what majority is required for resolutions in cases not covered by (i) to (iv) above or determining cases of doubt as to what majority is required, shall require a two-thirds majority of the Representatives casting a vote.

*Article 30.* On matters relating to its internal procedure, which includes the election of officers, the nomination of persons to serve on committees and commissions and the adoption of rules of procedure, resolutions of the Consultative Assembly shall be carried by such majorities as the Assembly may determine in accordance with Article 29 (v).

*Article 31.* Debates on proposals to be made to the Committee of Ministers that a matter should be placed on the Agenda of the Consultative Assembly shall be confined to an indication of the proposed subject-matter and the reasons for and against its inclusion in the Agenda.

*Article 32.* The Consultative Assembly shall meet in ordinary session once a year, the date and duration of which shall be determined by the Assembly so as to avoid as far as possible overlapping with parliamentary sessions of Members and with sessions of the General Assembly of the United Nations. In no circumstances shall the duration of an ordinary session exceed one month unless both the Assembly and the Committee of Ministers concur.

*Article 33.* Ordinary sessions of the Consultative Assembly shall be held at the seat of the Council unless both the Assembly and the Committee of Ministers concur that the session should be held elsewhere.

*Article 34.* The Consultative Assembly may be convened in extraordinary session, upon the initiative either of the Committee of Ministers or of the President of the Assembly after agreement between them, such agreement also to determine the date and place of the session.

*Article 35.* Unless the Consultative Assembly decides otherwise, its debates shall be conducted in public.

### Chapter VI. Secretariat

*Article 36.* (a) The Secretariat shall consist of a Secretary-General, a Deputy Secretary-General and such other staff as may be required.

(b) The Secretary-General and Deputy Secretary-General shall be appointed by the Consultative Assembly on the recommendation of the Committee of Ministers.

(c) The remaining staff of the Secretariat shall be appointed by the Secretary-General, in accordance with the administrative regulations.

(d) No members of the Secretariat shall hold any salaried office from any Government or be a member of the Consultative Assembly or of any legislature or engage in any occupation incompatible with his duties.

(e) Every member of the staff of the Secretariat shall make a solemn declaration affirming that his duty is to the Council of Europe and that he will perform his duties conscientiously, uninfluenced by any national considerations, and that he will not seek or receive instructions in connexion with the performance of his duties from any Government or any authority external to the Council and will refrain from any action which might reflect on his position as an international official responsible only to the Council. In the case of the Secretary-General and the Deputy Secretary-General this declaration shall be made before the Committee, and in the case of all other members of the staff, before the Secretary-General.

(f) Every Members shall respect the exclusively international character of the responsibilities of the Secretary-General and the staff of the Secretariat and not seek to influence them in the discharge of their responsibilities.

*Article 37.* (a) The Secretariat shall be located at the seat of the Council.

(b) The Secretary-General is responsible to the Committee of Ministers for the work of the Secretariat. Amongst other things, he shall, subject to Article 38 (d), provide such secretariat and other assistance as the Consultative Assembly may require.

Council of Europe. Address: BP 431 R-6, F-67006 Strasbourg CEDEX, France. Telephone: (33) 88-61-49-61. Cable: EUROPA Strasbourg. Telex: EUR 870-943. Fax: (33) 88-36-70-57. Secretary-General: Marcelino Oreja.

*SEE ALSO* *"European"* entries.

**BIBLIOGRAPHY.** Berger, Vincent. *Case Law of the European Court of Human Rights.* Sarasota, FL, USA: UNIFO Publishers, 1989. Scholarly casebook, in English; bibliography, pp. 447–459.

Council of Europe. *Collection of Recommendations, Resolutions and Declarations of the Committee of Ministers concerning Human Rights, 1949–87.* Strasbourg, France: 1989. IGO document, in English.

———. *European Court of Human Rights: Survey of Activities 1959–1989.* Strasbourg, France: 1990. IGO report, in English.

———. *Yearbook of the European Convention on Human Rights.* Dordrecht, the Netherlands: Martinus Nijhoff. IGO annual report, in English and French; volume 1 (1960) to present.

Danish Center of Human Rights. *The Implementation in National Law of the European Convention on Human Rights. Proceedings of the Fourth Copenhagen Conference on Human Rights, 28 and 29 October 1988.* Copenhagen, Denmark: 1989. NGO conference proceedings, in English.

Drzemczewski, Andrew. "The Council of Europe's Cooperation and Assistance Programmes for Countries of Central and Eastern Europe in the Human Rights Field," *Human Rights Law Journal* 12, no. 8–9 (Sept. 1991): 335–344. Report, in English.

———. "The Council of Europe's Cooperation and Assistance Programmes for Countries of Central and Eastern Europe in the Human Rights Field: 1990 to September 1993," *Human Rights Law Journal* 14, no. 7–8 (Sept. 1993): 229–248. Report, in English.

———. "The Work of the Council of Europe's Directorate of Human Rights," *Human Rights Law Journal* 11, no. 1–2 (1990): 89–117. Scholarly article, in English.

Heffernan, Liz, and James Kingston, eds. *Human Rights: A European Perspective.* Dublin, Ireland: Round Hall Press, 1994. Scholarly collection of articles, in English.

Kedzia, Zdizislaw, Anna Korula, and Manfred Nowak, eds. "Perspectives of an All-European System of Human Rights Protection: The Role of the Council of Europe, the CSCE, and the European Communities—Proceedings and Recommendations of an International Conference, Poznan, Poland, 8–11 October 1990," in *All-European Human Rights Yearbook,* vol. 1. Kehl am Rhein, Germany: N.P. Engel Publisher, 1991. Scholarly collective works, in English.

Macdonald, R. St. J., F. Matscher, and H. Petzold, eds. *The European System for the Protection of Human Rights.* Dordrecht, the Netherlands: Martinus Nijhoff, 1993. Scholarly collective works, in English.

Mahoney, Paul. "Judicial Activism and Judicial Self-Restraint in the European Court of Human Rights: Two Sides of the Same Coin," *Human Rights Law Journal* 11, no. 1–2 (1990): 57–88. Scholarly article, in English.

Mower, A. Glenn, Jr. *Regional Human Rights: A Comparative Study of the West European and Inter-American Systems.* Westport, CT, USA: Greenwood Press, 1991. Scholarly monograph, in English; bibliography, pp. 171–174.

Perotti, Antonio. *Action to Combat Intolerance and Xenophobia in the Activities of the Council of Europe's Council for Cultural Co-Operation 1969–1989.* Strasbourg, France: 1991. Scholarly article, in English; bibliography, pp. 45–47.

**CREMER, WILLIAM RANDAL (1828–1908).** Born in Fareham, Wiltshire, England, William Cremer came from a poor and working-class background to attain a

**C**

British knighthood in 1907 and the NOBEL PEACE PRIZE in 1903. Cremer's career was dedicated to the rights of the working man. He was instrumental in the First International Working Men's Association and founded the Workmen's Peace Association, later renamed the International Arbitration League. It was the League that was to formulate a plan for a high court of nations, which eventually materialized as the Hague Tribunal. Cremer also co-founded the Inter-parliamentary Union in 1889.

**BIBLIOGRAPHY.** Evans, Howard. *Sir Randal Cremer: His Life and Works.* London: T. Fisher Unwin, 1909.

Gray, Tony. *Champions of Peace.* London: Paddington Press, 1976.

Schlessinger, Bernard S., and June H. Schlessinger, eds. *Who's Who of Nobel Prize Winners.* Phoenix, AZ, USA: Oryx Press, 1991.

**CRIME PREVENTION.** The Seventh United Nations Congress on Prevention of Crime and the Treatment of Offenders, which met at Milan from 26 August to 6 September 1985, adopted the "Milan Plan of Action" (UN publication, Sales no. E.86.IV.1), in which it emphasized that basic crime prevention strategy must seek to eliminate the causes and conditions that favor crime, bearing in mind that racial discrimination, including apartheid, unemployment, illiteracy, the deterioration of living conditions in certain regions of the world—in particular regarding the grave economic situation confronting African and many other countries—and any form of violation of human rights and fundamental freedoms constitute especially negative factors in this respect.

The Congress expressed the view that programs of crime prevention and treatment of offenders must be grounded in the political, economic, social, and cultural realities of each country and implemented in a climate of freedom and respect for human rights and that it is essential that UN member States develop an effective capacity for the formulation and planning of crime prevention policies in coordination with their strategies for economic, political, social, and cultural development. Deploring the increase and gravity of crime in different parts of the world, it called upon member States "to take all measures within their power to eliminate conditions of life that degrade human dignity and are factors relevant to crime, including unemployment, poverty, illiteracy, racial discrimination, apartheid and social injustice," and recommended that all States promote the broadest possible participation of the people in political, social, and other measures designed to prevent crime.

*ENVIRONMENTAL AND CULTURAL CRIMES.* On 24 May 1989, the UN ECONOMIC AND SOCIAL COUNCIL received a report prepared by the Secretary-General (UN Doc. E/AC.57/1988/16), which it had requested in 1986, developing a number of proposals for concerted international action against the forms of crime identified in the Milan Plan of Action. The Council expressed its alarm at the marked increased in the transnational dimensions of serious forms of crime and by the comparative immunity enjoyed by the perpetrators of such criminality; the Council also indicated dismay at the shortcomings of existing intlernational cooperation arrangements and instruments for the prevention of transnational criminality. In particular, the Council was concerned at the growing tendency of some governments and transnational corporations to facilitate the dumping of toxic nuclear and industrial waste in developing countries and at the devastating damage to the environment that is the direct outcome of harmful and illicit practices, such as the dumping of toxic waste, the thoughtless depletion of nonrenewable resources, the extermination of animal species, the massive use of herbicides and defoliants, and the release into the atmosphere of harmful gases and radioactive substances. The Council was also concerned about the sustained pillage of archeological sites and the illicit trade in objects belonging to the cultural heritage of nations and the ensuring damage to the national identity of peoples.

Accordingly, the Council invited governments, intergovernmental and non-governmental organizations, and other decisionmaking bodies to examine the Secretary-General's recommendations. In particular, it urged governments to examine existing domestic legislation, for enacting provisions that protect the natural environment and that establish adequate compensation for the victims of toxic waste; and invited the governments to exercise stricter and more effective control over the industrial sectors that could be involved in dumping toxic waste in developing countries. Finally, it called upon the Eighth UN Congress on the Prevention of Crime and the Treatment of Offenders to consider the topic of transnational crimes against the environment and against the cultural patrimony of countries.

*CORRUPTION IN PUBLIC ADMINISTRATION.* The Eighth UN Congress on the Prevention of Crime and the Treatment of Offenders, held at Havana, Cuba, from 27 August to 7 September 1990, noted that the problems of corruption in public administration were universal and that, although they had particularly deleterious effects on nations with vulnerable economies, those effects are felt throughout the world. The Congress stated its conviction that corrupt activities of public officials could destroy the potential effectiveness of all types of government programs, hinder development, and victimize both individuals and groups (UN Doc. A/CONF.144/28/Rev. 1, chap. I, sec. C).

The UN Commission on Human Rights, at its 1991 session, found that, despite progress achieved by the international commmunity respecting standard-setting for realizing economic, social, and cultural rights, the implementation and promotion of these rights had not received sufficient attention within the UN system.

At its 1992 session, the Commission decided that, when discussing the question of economic, social, and cultural rights, it would be mindful of the problem of the fraudulent enrichment of top state officials, prejudicial to the public interest; the factors responsible for this fraud; and the agents involved in all countries involved in such enrichment. In reaching this decision, the Commmission noted that, in some countries, corruption has become systematic; and further that it has acquired a transnational character, in particular as a result of the illicit arms trade, international drug-trafficking, and money laundering. It concluded that "for many peoples who have been the victims of institutionalized corruption and who, at present, are seeking to strengthen their democratic system, a satisfactory solution to these problems is necessary not only from a moral point of view but, above all, in order to ensure reparation of the damage caused to their economic interests as a result of the illicit removal of these resources."

***UN COMMISSION.*** The UN Commission on Crime Prevention and Criminal Justice is a functional commission of the UN Economic and Social Council. The Crime Prevention and Criminal Justice Branch of the Centre for Social Development and Humanitarian Affairs acts as Secretariat for the Commission, which has its headquarters in Vienna, Austria.

***SEE ALSO*** *Committee on Crime Prevention and Control, UN; Drug Abuse.*

***BIBLIOGRAPHY.*** Clark, Roger S. "Human Rights and the UN Committee on Crime Prevention and Control," *The Annals* 506 (Nov. 1989): 68–84. Scholarly article, in English.

Dahl, Henry. "The Influence and Application of the Standard Penal Code for Latin America," *American Journal of Criminal Law* 17 (1990): p. 234–285. Scholarly article, in English.

Stein, Nancy, and Suzie Dod Thomas, eds. "Criminality, Imprisonment & Women's Rights in the 1990's," *Social Justice* 17, no. 2 (Summer 1990). Special issue, in English.

United Nations. *The United Nations and Crime Prevention.* New York: 1991. IGO report, in English.

## CRIMES AGAINST THE PEACE AND SECURITY OF MANKIND.

The UN **GENERAL ASSEMBLY** affirmed, at its 1946 session (resolution 94 [I]) the principles of international law recognized by the charter of the Nurmberg Tribunal and the Judgment of the Tribunal and directed its Committee on the Codification of International Law "to treat as a matter of primary importance plans for the formulation, in the context of a general codification of offenses against the peace and security of mankind, or of an International Criminal Code, of the principles recognized" in that charter and judgment. That committee did not undertake this task itself but recommended to the General Assembly the establishment of an International Law Commission, which the Assembly established on 21 November 1947 (resolution 174 [II]). The Assembly directed the new International Law Commission (resolution 177 [II]) to

(a) formulate the principles of international law recognized in the Charter of the Nurmberg Tribunal and in the Judgment of the Tribunal, and

(b) prepare a draft code of offenses against the peace and security of mankind, indicating clearly the place to be accorded to the principles mentioned in subparagraph (a).

On the basis of a report submitted by a Special Rapporteur, the Law Commission completed its formulation of principles and submitted it to the General Assembly. The principles, in part, are as follows (UN Doc. A/1316, pt. three, paras. 98–127):

*Principle 1.* Any person who commits an act which constitutes a crime under international law is responsible therefor and liable to punishment. . . .

*Principle 6.* The crimes hereinafter set out are punishable as crimes under international law:

(a) Crimes against peace:

(i) planning, preparation, initiation or waging a war of aggression or a war in violation of international treaties, agreements or assurances;

(ii) participation in a common plan or conspiracy for the accomplishment of any of the acts mentioned under (i).

(b) War crimes: Violations of the laws or customs of war which include, but are not limited to, murder, ill-treatment or deportation to slave-labor or for any other purpose of civilian population of or in occupied territory, murder or ill-treatment of prisoners of war, of persons on the seas, killing of hostages, plunder of public or private property, wanton destruction of cities, towns or villages, or devastation not justified by military necessity.

(c) Crimes against humanity: Murder, extermination, enslavement, deportation and other inhuman acts done against any civilian population, or persecutions on political, racial or religious grounds, when such acts are done or such persecutions are carried out in execution of or in connection with any crime against peace or any war crime.

*Principle 7.* Complicity in the commission of a crime against peace, a war crime, or a crime against humanity as set forth in Principle 6 is a crime under international law.

As regards the draft code of offenses, the Commission's drafting Sub-Committee prepared a provisional

# C

draft code that was referred to the Special Rapporteur, who was requested to submit a further report.

The General Assembly, at its 1950 session, invited the governments of member States to furnish their observations on the formulation prepared by the Commission and requested the Commission, in preparing the draft code of offenses against the peace and security of mankind, to take account of any observations made on the formulation.

In 1951, the Commission adopted a draft Code of Offenses against the Peace and Security of Mankind (UN Doc. A/1858, paras. 57–58) and submitted it to the General Assembly. Three years later, in 1954, the Commission made some changes in the previously adopted text and transmitted a revised version of the draft code to the Assembly.

At its 1954 session, the General Assembly examined the draft code, found that it raised a number of problems closely related to the question of the definition of aggression, and decided (resolution 898 [IX]) to postpone further consideration of the code until its Special Committee on the Question of Defining Aggression had submitted its report. There followed a long series of postponements and delays, even after the General Assembly had adopted by consensus the "Definition of Aggression" on 14 December 1974 (resolution 3314 [XXIX, annex]). Finally, in 1981, the Assembly resumed its invitation to the International Law Commission to proceed with its work on the draft Code of Offenses against the Peace and Security of Mankind. The Commission did so; and, as the work progressed, it recommended that the title of the topic be changed to "Draft Code of Crimes against the Peace and Security of Mankind." The Assembly expressed its agreement with this recommendation in 1987.

At the end of 1989, the Commission had not completed the preparation of the draft code. However, in its 1989 annual report to the Assembly, it presented the texts of all the draft articles which it had provisionally adopted up to that time (UN Doc. A/44/10, para. 217), as follows:

**Chapter I—Introduction**

Part I. Definition and Characterization

*Article 1. Definition.* The crimes [under international law] defined in this draft Code constitute crimes against the peace and security of mankind.

*Article 2. Characterization.* The characterization of an act or omission as a crime against the peace and security of mankind is independent of internal law. The fact that an act or omission is or is not punishable under internal law does not affect this characterization.

Part II. General Principles

*Article 3. Responsibility and Punishment.* 1. Any individual who commits a crime against the peace and security of mankind is responsible for such crime irrespective of any motives

invoked by the accused that are not covered by the definition of the offence and is liable to punishment therefor.

2. Prosecution of an individual for a crime against the peace and security of mankind does not relieve a State of any responsibility under international law for an act or omission attributable to it.

*Article 4. Obligation to Try or Extradite.* 1. Any State in whose territory an individual alleged to have committed a crime against the peace and security of mankind is present shall either try or extradite him.

2. If extradition is requested by several States, special consideration shall be given to the request of the States in whose territory the crime was committed.

3. The provisions of paragraphs 1 and 2 of this article do not prejudge the establishment and the jurisdiction of an international criminal court. (This paragraph will be deleted if an international criminal court is established.)

*Article 5. Non-applicability of Statutory Limitations.* No statutory limitation shall apply to crimes against the peace and security of mankind.

*Article 6. Judicial Guarantees.* Any individual charged with a crime against the peace and security of mankind shall be entitled without discrimination to the minimum guarantees due to all human beings with regard to the law and the facts. In particular:

1. He shall have the right to be presumed innocent until proved guilty;

2. He shall have the rights:

(a) In the determination of any charge against him, to have a fair and public hearing by a competent, independent and impartial tribunal duly established by law or by treaty;

(b) To be informed promptly and in detail in a language which he understands of the nature and cause of the charge against him;

(c) To have adequate time and facilities for the preparation of his defence and to communicate with counsel of his own choosing;

(d) To be tried without undue delay;

(e) To be tried in his presence, and to defend himself in person or through legal assistance of his own choosing; to be informed, if he does not have legal assistance, of this right; and to have legal assistance assigned to him and without payment by him in any such case if he does not have sufficient means to pay for it;

(f) To examine, or have examined, the witnesses against him and to obtain the attendance and examination of witnesses on his behalf under the same conditions as witnesses against him;

(g) To have the free assistance of an interpreter if he cannot understand or speak the language used in court;

(h) Not to be compelled to testify against himself or to confess guilt.

*Article 7. Non bis in idem.* [1. No one shall be liable to be tried or punished for a crime under this Code for which he has already been finally convicted or acquitted by an international criminal court.]

2. Subject to paragraphs 3, 4 and 5 of this article, no one shall be liable to be tried or punished for a crime under this Code in respect of an act for which he has already been finally convicted or acquitted by a national court, provided that, if a punishment was imposed, it has been enforced or is in the process of being enforced.

3. Notwithstanding the provisions of paragraph 2, an individual may be tried and punished [by an international criminal court or] by a national court for a crime under this Code if the act which was the subject of a trial and judgement

316

as an ordinary crime corresponds to one of the crimes characterized in this Code.

4. Notwithstanding the provisions of paragraph 2, an individual may be tried and punished by a national court of another State for a crime under this Code:

(a) if the act which was the subject of the previous judgement took place on the territory of that State;

(b) if that State has been the main victim of the crime.

5. In the case of a subsequent conviction under this Code, the court, in passing sentence, shall deduct any penalty imposed and implemented as a result of a previous conviction for the same act.

*Article 8. Non-retroactivity.* 1. No one shall be convicted under this Code for acts committed before its entry into force.

2. Nothing in this article shall preclude the trial and punishment of anyone for any act which, at the time when it was committed, was criminal in accordance with international law or domestic law applicable in conformity with international law. . . .

*Article 10. Responsibility of the Superior.* The fact that a crime against the peace and security of mankind was committed by a subordinate does not relieve his superiors of criminal responsibility, if they knew or had information enabling them to conclude, in the circumstances at the time, that the subordinate was committing or was going to commit such a crime and if they did not take all feasible measures within their power to prevent or repress the crime.

· *Article 11. Official Position and Criminal Responsibility.* The official position of the individual who commits a crime against the peace and security of mankind, and particularly the fact that he acts as Head of State or Government, does not relieve him of criminal responsibility.

### Chapter II—Acts Constituting Crimes Against the Peace and Security of Mankind

Part I. Crimes against Peace

*Article 12. Aggression.* 1. Any individual to whom responsibility for acts constituting aggression is attributed under this Code shall be liable to be tried and punished for a crime against peace.

2. Aggression is the use of armed force by a State against the sovereignty, territorial integrity or political independence of another State, or in any other manner inconsistent with the Charter of the United Nations.

3. The first use of armed force by a State in contravention of the Charter shall constitute prima facie evidence of an act of aggression although the Security Council may, in conformity with the Charter, conclude that a determination that an act of aggression has been committed would not be justified in the light of other relevant circumstances, including the fact that the acts concerned or their consequences are not of sufficient gravity.

4. [In particular] any of the following acts, regardless of a declaration of war, constitutes an act of aggression, due regard being paid to paragraphs 2 and 3 of this article:

(a) The invasion or attack by the armed forces of a State of the territory of another State, or any military occupation, however temporary, resulting from such invasion or attack, or any annexation by the use of force of the territory of another State or part thereof;

(b) Bombardment by the armed forces of a State against the territory of another State or the use of any weapons by a State against the territory of another State;

(c) The blockade of the ports or coasts of a State by the armed forces of another State;

(d) An attack by the armed forces of a State on the land, sea or air forces, or marine and air fleets of another State;

(e) The use of armed forces of one State which are within the territory of another State with the agreement of the receiving State, in contravention of the conditions provided for in the agreement, or any extension of their presence in such territory beyond the termination of the agreement;

(f) The action of a State in allowing its territory, which it has placed at the disposal of another State, to be used by that other State for perpetrating an act of aggression against a third State;

(g) The sending by or on behalf of a State of armed bands, groups, irregulars or mercenaries, which carry out acts of armed force against another State of such gravity as to amount to the acts listed above, or its substantial involvement therein;

(h) Any other acts determined by the Security Council as constituting acts of aggression under the provisions of the Charter.

[5. Any determination by the Security Council as to the existence of an act of aggression is binding on national courts.]

6. Nothing in this article shall be interpreted as in any way enlarging or diminishing the scope of the Charter of the United Nations including its provisions concerning cases in which the use of force is lawful.

7. Nothing in this article could in any way prejudice the right to self-determination, freedom and independence, as derived from the Charter, of peoples forcibly deprived of that right and referred to in the Declaration on Principles of International Law concerning Friendly Relations and Cooperation among States in accordance with the Charter of the United Nations, particularly peoples under colonial and racist regimes or other forms of alien domination; nor the right of these peoples to struggle to that end and to seek and receive support, in accordance with the principles of the Charter and in conformity with the above-mentioned Declaration.

*Article 13. Threat of Aggression.* Threat of aggression consisting of declarations, communications, demonstrations of force or any other measures which would give good reason to the Government of a State to believe that aggression is being seriously contemplated against that State.

*Article 14. Intervention.* 1. Intervention in the internal or external affairs of a State by fomenting [armed] subversive or terrorist activities or by organizing, assisting or financing such activities, or supplying arms for the purpose of such activities, thereby [seriously] undermining the free exercise by that State of its sovereign rights.

2. Nothing in this article shall in any way prejudice the right of peoples to self-determination as enshrined in the Charter of the United Nations.

*Article 15. Colonial Domination and Other Forms of Alien Domination.* Establishment or maintenance by force of colonial domination or any other form of alien domination contrary to the right of peoples to self-determination as enshrined in the Charter of the United Nations.

**SEE ALSO** *War Crimes.*

**BIBLIOGRAPHY.** Bassiouni, M. Cherif. *Crimes against Humanity in International Criminal Law.* Dordrecht, the Netherlands: Martinus Nijhoff, 1992. Scholarly monograph, in English.

Fédération Internationale des Droits de l'Homme. *Rapport de mission: France, 14–19 octobre 1990. État des procédures judiciaires en cours diligentées pour crimes contre l'humanité* (Mission Report: France, October 14–19, 1990. Judicial Procedure for Crimes against Humanity). Paris: 1991. NGO fact-finding report, in French.

Hannum, Hurst. "International Law and Cambodian Genocide: The Sounds of Silence," *Human Rights Quarterly* 11, no. 1 (Feb. 1989): 82–138. Scholarly article, in English.

International League for the Rights and the Liberation of Peoples—Colombian Section. *Tribunal Permanente de los Pueblos: Proceso a la Impunidad de Crimenes de Lesa Humanidad* (Permanent Peoples' Tribunal: Trial on Impunity for Crimes against Humanity). Bogota, Colombia: 1990. NGO report, in Spanish.

Mbemba, Jean-Martin. *L'autre mémoire du crime contre l'humanité* (The Other Memory of Crimes against Humanity). Dakar, Senegal: Présence africaine, 1990. Monograph, in French.

McCormack, T.L.H., and G.J. Simpson. "The International Law Commission's Draft Code against the Peace and Security of Mankind: An Appraisal of the Substantive Provisions," *Criminal Law Forum* 5, no. 1 (1994): 1–55. Scholarly article, in English.

Rosenbaum, Alan S. *Prosecuting Nazi War Criminals*. Boulder, CO, USA: Westview Press, 1993. Scholarly monograph, in English.

Sunga, Lyal S. *Individual Responsibility in International Law for Serious Human Rights Violations*. Dordrecht, the Netherlands: Martinus Nijhoff, 1992. Scholarly monograph, in English.

Teitel, Ruti. "Crime and Punishment: Accountability for State-Sponsored Mass Murder (Dedicated to the Memory of Owen M. Kupferschmid)," *New York Law Journal of International and Comparative Law* 11, no. 3 (1990): 323–432. Scholarly articles, in English.

**CROATIA.** The Republic of Croatia, formerly a part of Yugoslavia, attained statehood after democratic parliamentary elections in 1990 and proclaimed its independence on 8 October 1991. Facing the Adriatic Sea, it is bounded on the northwest by Slovenia, on the north by Hungary, and on the south by Bosnia-Herzegovina. Its population is estimated to be 4,793,000. Ethnic groups include the Croats and Serbs. Religion has long been a source of friction between these two groups: the Croats are Roman Catholic, while the Serbs are mainly Orthodox Christian. Literacy is estimated at 92%.

Although Croatia has been under foreign domination since the 12th century, the country was briefly an independent State during World War II. Allied with the Nazis, the country was responsible at that time for the deaths of thousands of Serbs and Jews. In 1946, Croatia once again became part of Yugoslavia. But the ethnic conflict between Croats and Serbs continued.

*UNITED NATIONS PROTECTION FORCE (UNPRO-FOR).* Established in March 1992 as an interim ar-

rangement to create the conditions of peace and security required for the negotiations of an overall settlement of the Yugoslav crisis, UNPROFOR is deployed in three "United Nations Protected Areas" (UNPAs) in Croatia. UNPROFOR's mandate is to ensure that the UNPAs are demilitarized. There were several enlargements of the mandate in 1992: in June, to include monitoring of certain areas in Croatia (so-called "pink zones") that were outside the agreed UNPA boundaries; in August, to enable UNPROFOR to control the entry of civilians into the UNPAs and to perform immigration and customs functions at the UNPA borders at international frontiers; and in 1992, to include monitoring of the demilitarization of the Prevlaka Peninsula near Dubrovnik and to ensure control of the Peruca Dam, situated in one of the pink zones.

*UN REACTION.* On 6 November 1992, the UN **HUMAN RIGHTS COMMITTEE** adopted the following comments on the situation in Croatia (UN Doc. CCPR/C/79/Add. 15):

### Introduction

1. Deeply concerned by recent and current events in the territory of the former Yugoslavia affecting human rights protected under the International Covenant on Civil and Political Rights; noting that all the peoples within the territory of the former Yugoslavia are entitled to the guarantees of the Covenant; and acting under article 40, paragraph 1 (b) of the Covenant, the Committee, on 7 October 1992, requested the Government of the Republic of Croatia to submit a short report on the following issues in respect of persons and events now coming under its jurisdiction:

(a) measures taken to prevent and combat the policy of "ethnic cleansing" pursued, according to several reports, in the territory of certain parts of the former Yugoslavia, in relation to articles 6 and 12 of the International Covenant on Civil and Political Rights;

(b) measures taken to prevent arbitrary arrests and killings of persons, as well as disappearances, in relation to articles 6 and 9 of the International Covenant on Civil and Political Rights;

(c) measures taken to prevent arbitrary executions, torture, and other inhuman treatment in detention camps, in relation to articles 6, 7, and 10 of the International Covenant on Civil and Political Rights;

(d) measures taken to combat advocacy of national, racial, or religious hatred constituting incitement to discrimination, hostility, or violence, in relation to article 20 of the International Covenant on Civil and Political Rights.

2. Pursuant to that request, Croatia submitted a short special report entitled "Report on measures taken to prevent criminal acts perpetrated in violation of the human rights and freedoms in the Republic of Croatia. . . .

3. On 12 October 1992, the Republic of Croatia notified the Secretary-General of the United Nations that it had succeeded, as from 8 October 1991 (the date of its proclamation of independence), to various human rights treaties, including the International Covenant on Civil and Political Rights.

## Positive Aspects

4. Certain factors encouraging to the guaranteeing of human rights were noted. The Republic of Croatia has attained statehood after democratic parliamentary elections in 1990. The new Constitutional Law of Human Rights and Freedoms and the Rights of Ethnic and National Communities or Minorities, adopted in December 1991 and amended in April 1992, incorporated UN treaty obligations on human rights. An office for interethnic relations had been opened, which would have branches in various districts of Croatia and a wide-reaching mandate. The Croatian delegation confirmed that, in the view of the Government, the only proper use of ethnic identity was to ensure that ethnic minorities received the guarantees to which they are entitled under article 27 of the Covenant. It was also noted that certain charges had been brought in the courts against persons who were accused of crimes against civilians, crimes against prisoners of war, and the crime of genocide. The three prisoners-of-war camps in Croatia were under the control of the Ministry of Defence and open to the International Committee of the Red Cross. The Government had condemned the policies of the ultraright paramilitaries and political parties and was conducting investigations into the activities of certain members of parliament belonging to the Croatian Right Party.

## Factors and Difficulties Impeding the Application of the Covenant

5. Since its independence, the territory of the Republic of Croatia has been subject to large-scale military action. This has resulted in massive violations of human rights, including significant loss of life, torture, disappearances, and summary executions, with entire towns destroyed and populations displaced. Because of the conflict in the neighbouring Bosnia-Herzegovina, Croatia has also received very large numbers of refugees.

6. The representatives also informed the Committee that Croatia controlled only about three-quarters of its territory, the remainder being under the authority of UNPROFOR. The delegation conceded that there had been periods during the hostilities on its territory when public order had broken down and when there had been an inability to control ethnically based violence against Serbs. It accepted legal responsibility for those events.

## Principal Subjects of Concern

7. The Commitee was concerned with the preamble to the constitution whereby the Republic of Croatia is defined as "the national state of the Croat nation and a state of members of other nations and minorities." Concern was expressed about longstanding discrimination against, and harassment of, ethnic Serbs residing within Croatia. In particular, the circulation of lists of persons or groups on the basis of their ethnic origin is to be deplored. Purges have been permitted of the public services, and the police have become identified with ultraright nationalism. Members of the military are often seen in public, including in Bosnia-Herzegovina, wearing fascist emblems. Serbs have been removed from their jobs in the press, and there have been widespread arrests and disappearances. Persons are being held in deplorable conditions in places of detention in Bosnia-Herzegovina, which are under the control of the Croatian army or local Croatian military factions who receive the backing of the Republic of Croatia. The international responsibility of the Republic of Croatia is engaged in relation to these events.

8. The Committee believes that there are in Croatia undesignated places of detention where persons are held, often by private groups. Many persons for whom there is no legitimate cause of detention are unlawfully held. Sometimes they are deprived of their liberty simply in order to be able to effect exchanges for Croatians held as prisoners elsewhere.

## Recommendations

9. The Government of Croatia is urged to act vigorously against all manifestations of racial hatred. Public condemnation should be made of the circulation of lists of persons' names based on ethnicity, and further appropriate action should be taken. Strong efforts should be made to identify undeclared places of detention and to ensure that only bona fide prisoners of war are held in properly notified camps operating in accordance with the Geneva Conventions and the Covenant. Responsibility must be accepted for the acts of the military in other territories as well as in Croatia. Clear instructions should be issued to all military personnel as to their obligations under the Covenant. The foregoing has to be borne in mind in the context of support afforded, directly or indirectly, to local Croatian militia in Bosnia-Herzegovina. Those responsible for violations of human rights should be brought speedily before the courts. In that regard, the existing distinctions between military and civil jurisdictions should be reviewed so that military personnel might be tried and, if found guilty, punished under normal civil jurisdiction.

The UN General Assembly also considered questions relating to Croatia late in 1992. In resolution 47/166 of 18 December, the Assembly noted the efforts of the Croatian Government to solve problems of postwar reconstruction of the national infrastructure and, at the same time, to solve the problems of refugees, displaced persons, and victims of war within the State. The Assembly also expressed concern about the potential effects of the deepening crisis in the former Yugoslavia in the event that no rapid progress in the postwar recovery of Croatia is established.

Recognizing the importance of the relationship between economic recovery and peaceful interethnic relations, the General Assembly appealed to all States and organizations to provide cooperation in various forms, in particular in the most severely affected areas, in order to facilitate the return of refugees and internally displaced persons.

**BIBLIOGRAPHY.** Commission on Security and Cooperation in Europe. *Human Rights and Democratization in Croatia.* Washington, D.C.: 1993. Government report, in English.

———. *Parliamentary and Presidential Elections in an Independent Croatia.* Washington, D.C.: 1992. Government report, in English.

Human Rights Watch. "Croatia," in *Human Rights Watch World Report 1995,* pp. 201–203. New York: 1995. NGO report, in English.

United Nations. *United Nations Peace-Keeping.* New York: UN Dept. of Public Information, 1994. No. DPI/1399–93527.

# C

———. *United Nations Peace-Keeping Update: May 1994.* New York: UN Dept. of Public Information, 1994. No. DPI/1306/Rev. 3.

U.S. Committee for Refugees. *Croatia's Crucible: Providing Asylum for Refugees from Bosnia and Hercegovina.* Washington, D.C.: American Council for Nationalities Service, 1992. NGO factfinding report, in English.

**CUBA.** The Republic of Cuba is a country occupying the largest and westernmost of the West Indian Islands, situated at the point where the Atlantic Ocean, the Caribbean Sea, and the Gulf of Mexico converge. It achieved independence from Spain in 1899 and became a member of the United Nations in 1945. Its population is estimated to be 10,900,000. Ethnic groups include persons of Spanish, African, American, and mixed origins. The language in common use is Spanish. Literacy is estimated at 96%.

The government (1994) took the form of a republic. Executive authority is exercised by the President and a 31-member Council of State, both elected by the National Assembly of People's Power. Members of the Assembly are elected by popular vote, suffrage being universal for all citizens 16 years of age or older who have not applied for permanent emigration, and serve for terms of five years. The Communist Party of Cuba is the only recognized political party; the First Secretary of the party is President of the Council of State and of the country. The judiciary is subordinate to the Council of State.

The Cuban Social Democratic Party is reported to function underground but is not recognized by the government and holds no group meetings. Its founder, Roberto Luque Escalona is its only known member. There, is, however, a small human rights movement, some members of which were reported to have been arrested for applauding international scrutiny of the human rights situation in the country.

Discovered by Columbus in 1492, Cuba served as a base for Spanish exploration of the Americas. The indigenous Arawak Indians were soon decimated by the colonists, who replaced them by slaves imported from Africa. After slavery was abolished in the 1880s, the freed black workers and their offspring contributed much to the social and political development of the island, if only by periodic revolts against their miserable lot. The colonial element was, however, constantly replenished by immigrants from Europe; and a wealthy, well-governed Cuba achieved representation in the Spanish Cortes in 1810. Withdrawal of this representation in 1848 led to a series of revolts against Spanish rule, some of which were supported by the United States of America.

*CUBAN–AMERICAN RELATIONS.* Cuba and the United States of America are separated by only 90 miles and have shared a long history. After the sinking of the Maine in Havana harbor in 1898, the forces of Cuba and the U.S.A. combined against the Spanish. The treaty that ended the Spanish–American War established Cuba as an independent republic but gave the United States government the right to intervene in Cuban affairs—an arrangement that was criticized as imperialism in Latin America and opposed by many in the United States. The United States' right to intervene was abandoned in 1934, when a new era of friendly relations with Cuba was inaugurated under the Franklin Roosevelt administration. This era ended, however, shortly after the government of Fulgencio Batista was overthrown by the revolutionary government headed by Fidel Castro on 1 January 1959, an event that precipitated the flight of thousands of Cubans from their island homeland to refuge in the United States, settling mainly in the state of Florida. A trade boycott of Cuba was imposed by the United States in 1960 and has since been tightened.

In 1961, a band of anti-Castro immigrants, financed, trained, and supported by the U.S.A., attempted to invade Cuba but were routed in Cochinos Bay (Bay of Pigs). In 1962, U.S. President J.F. Kennedy blockaded Cuba and threatened war if the U.S.S.R. did not withdraw missiles from the island, weapons reportedly aimed at strategic U.S. cities. In 1980, when President Jimmy Carter was in office, Castro allowed thousands of Cuban refugees to sail to the United States in the so-called "Mariel boatlift." The refugees overtaxed the U.S. immigration system and added to the deterioration of the Carter administration. Many of these refugees were returned to Cuba under allegations that they were criminals released from Cuban prisons; many others were placed in holding camps within the United States, to the dismay of human rights activists who saw this action as a violation of the Cubans' refugee status.

In August 1994, Cubans once again began fleeing to the United States, this time due to the crushing poverty experienced in their homeland. While the Cuban economy was never a strong one under the Castro regime, the collapse of communism and the refusal of the U.S. Government to lift its three-decade-long trade embargo combined to wreak havoc on Cuba's fragile economy. In 1990, Castro had imposed draconian austerity measures; and, in 1992, the Russian Government stopped sending economic aid to the island. For weeks in the summer of 1994, thousands of Cubans were picked up by the U.S. Coast Guard off the coast of Florida. At first, they were allowed in and once again detained by immigration. Then, U.S. President Bill Clinton attempted to stop the flow by ending the three decades of special status the United States had granted to fleeing Cubans, declaring that they would not be allowed into the U.S.

and instructing the U.S. Coast Guard to return the refugees to the American naval base at Guantánamo Bay. Undeterred, Cubans continued to take to the seas on their rafts. Finally, after weeks of intense negotiations, the United States and Cuba signed an immigration pact on 15 September 1995. Under this agreement, the United States will accept a minimum of 20,000 Cubans a year on regular visas and an unspecified number of close relatives of residents now in the United States. Also eligible, for one year only, would be those Cubans on the visa waiting list in the American diplomatic mission in Havana. The Cubans, for their part, agreed to try to stop the exodus of rafters without using force. The agreement specifically states that "the Republic of Cuba will take effective measures in every way it possibly can to prevent unsafe departures using mainly persuasive methods."

*HUMAN RIGHTS VIOLATIONS.* The nature and extent of human rights violations in Cuba has been difficult to ascertain because of conflicting propaganda claims and the refusal of the Cuban Government to cooperate with international organizations interested in making on-the-spot investigations. However, allegations persist that political prisoners are held in detention after arbitrary or summary trials and that some are subjected to systematic torture.

At its 1991 session, the UN **COMMISSION ON HUMAN RIGHTS** received a report on the human rights situation in Cuba, prepared by the Special Representative of the Secretary-General, Raphael Rivas Posada, who later resigned and was replaced by Carl-Johan Groth, subsequently designated as the Commission's Special Rapporteur.

The Special Rapporteur submitted an interim report to the 1992 session of the General Assembly (A/47/625) and another to the 1993 session of the Commission on Human Rights (E/CN.4/1993/39). The latter contains the following conclusions and recommendations (paras. 58–66):

The Government of Cuba still refuses to accept the Commission on Human Rights' decision to continue monitoring human rights conditions in that country and rejects all cooperation with the Special Rapporteur. The Rapporteur once agains calls upon the Government of Cuba to modify this stance and to enter into open and direct dialogue on the circumstances and specific cases described and presented in his reports and on any other aspect of the human rights issue. He also calls on the Government to afford him the opportunity to visit the country as is customary for those fulfilling the mandates of the Commission on Human Rights.

The Special Rapporteur has, however, recently received communications from organizations and institutions based in Cuba in conformity with the current laws. . . . The statements of these organizations focus on successes achieved in the social and educational sector but also refer to the United States' economic, commercial, and financial embargo of Cuba as the fundamental reason for the economic shortfalls and lack of room for political reforms.

The present report concentrates foremost on analysing reports received concerning conditions in the areas of civil and political rights and comments both on aspects related to the constitutional and legal framework and on specific cases of violations of justice and the way it operates. The report presents in detail the investigation carried out by the Committee of Experts on the Application of Conventions and Recommendations of the International Labour Organization (ILO) and the Committee on Freedom of Association, which examine the implementation of different conventions in Cuba. It does so not only for their fundamental relevance but also because they are a way of involving committees with which the government has maintained a dialogue. In addition, some economic and social development data, based on information supplied to the United Nations by government sources, have been collected: the most recent Human Development Report compiled by the United Nations Development Programme, reports from nongovernmental sources and communications from Cuba transmitted by the abovementioned institutions.

Bearing all this in mind, the Special Rapporteur considers that the recommendations presented in his latest report are, unfortunately, still valid and current, and that is the reason for repeating them as follows:

(a) Ratify the principal human rights instruments to which Cuba is not a part, in particular, the Covenant on Civil and Political Rights with its Optional Protocols and the Covenant on Economic, Social and Cultural Rights;

(b) Cease persecuting and punishing citizens for reasons relating to the freedom of peaceful expression and association;

(c) Permit legalization of independent groups, especially those seeking to carry out human rights or trade-union activities, and allow them to act within the law, but independently;

(d) Respect the guarantees of due process, in accordance with the provisions set forth in international covenants;

(e) Ensure greater transparency and guarantees in the prison system, so as to avoid incidents of excessive violence exercised against prisoners. In this connection, it would be a major achievement to renew the agreement with the International Committee of the Red Cross and to allow independent national groups access to prisons;

(f) Review sentences imposed for offences with political connotations and for trying to leave the country illegally;

(g) Expedite and make more transparent the procedure for applying for permission to leave and enter the country, while, at the same time, avoiding measures of retaliation against the applicants. Family reunification cases should be given priority attention. On this subject, the Special Rapporteur is aware of the need for persons wishing to travel to have visas for entry into other countries.

In early September 1993, the bishops of Cuba published a long pastoral letter analysing different aspects of the country's social, economic, and political conditions. In addition to the letter, the Special Rapporteur received a document signed by several groups, considered dissident within Cuba, that had joined forces. Both the letter and document make a series of proposals, listed below, which were outlined and presented to the Government. The Special Rapporteur felt it was important to take note of these texts since they are the products of real-life experiences and actual day-to-day contact with the realities of Cuban life.

The pastoral letter contains the following passage specifically:

"It seems to us that, concomitant with certain economic changes in the life of the country now beginning to be put into practice, some of the irritating policies should be eradicated because it would generate unquestionable relief and a source of hope in the national soul.

"(1) The exclusive and ubiquitous presence of the official ideology, accompanied by identification of terms that cannot be construed as unambiguous: Fatherland and socialism, State and Government, authority and power, legality and morality, Cuban and revolutionary. This centralist and ideologically all-embracing role of the State generates a feeling of fatigue caused by constant repetition of guidance and instructions;

"(2) Limitations imposed not only on the exercise of certain freedoms, which could be occasionally justifiable, but also on freedom itself. A significant change in this policy would guarantee, *inter alia*, administration of an independent judiciary that would lead us, based on stable foundations, towards consolidation of a state of law;

"(3) Excessive control by the State Security agencies which, at times, reaches even into the strictly private lives of individuals. That explains fear, the origin of which is poorly understood but felt as though it were caused by something ungraspable under a veil;

"(4) The large number of persons imprisoned for activities that might be decriminalized or reconsidered as a way to free many of those serving sentences for economic, political, or other similar reasons;

"(5) Discrimination for philosophical, political, or religious beliefs, the effective elimination of which would encourage participation of all the Cubans, without distinction, in the life of the nation."

The dissident organizations group, for its part, speaks of a common platform: amnesty for political prisoners; vindication for the freedom of association, speech, meeting, and peaceful demonstration; [vindication for] the press, trade unionism, and the right to enter and leave the country; [and] eradication of all forms of social and political discrimination, safeguarding the national identity, independence, and sovereignty. In addition, these organizations, distingushed by their peaceful *modus operandi*, have demonstrated the willingness to begin a dialogue with the authorities within the law.

In the opinion of the Special Rapporteur, the most constructive measures, in an international context, for improving the human rights situation in Cuba should start by eliminating, as soon as possible, the vestiges of the cold war as they relate to Cuba while endeavouring, instead, to promote the country's return to the regional and world system of cooperation and settlement of conflicts. The Rapporteur has the impression that a few timid steps are now starting to be adopted towards greater confidence between Cuba and its neighbours, particularly the United States. This may have a favourable repercussion in the matter of human rights.

Cuba's role in the cold war has vanished along with the economic assistance it received from the former Soviet Union. Fundamental changes in the way the domestic economy operates are more decisive than any other as a way for the nation to provide for its own citizens. To avoid traumatic and costly disruptions, these changes should emerge without delay. The international community must encourage a reform programme designed to improve productivity and efficiency in the economy. Such reforms would naturally assume a greater place for market forces to operate and greater entrepreneurial freedom. The Special Rapporteur considers that incentives or, at the very least, a policy that does not obstruct changes in the current system, rather than pressure or external conditioning are likely to produce reforms tending towards deregulating not only the economy but also political life. This opinion is not shared by all those concerned about Cuba's future, but neither is it isolated. It was also expressed in a different context by the UN General Assembly in resolution 47/19 of 24 November 1992, [entitled] "Necessity of ending the economic, commercial, and financial embargo imposed by the United States of America against Cuba" which states . . . that the Assembly urges States with laws and regulations whose extraterritorial effects affect the sovereignty of other States and the legitimate interests of entities or persons under their jurisdiciton, as well as the freedom of trade and navigation, to take the necessary measures to set them aside or to cancel their effect as quickly as possible in accordance with their own legal system.

After considering the report, the Commission on Human Rights, in resolution 1993/63 of 10 March 1993, endorsed it, and called upon the Government of Cuba to permit the Special Rapporteur the opportunity to carry out his mandate in full, in particular by allowing him to visit Cuba. It expressed particular concern that the Cuban Government had failed to carry out its commitment to cooperate with the Commission in conformity with articles 55 and 56 of the UN Charter and concern at mounting intolerance for freedom of speech and assembly in Cuba.

The UN General Assembly, after examining a further report at its 1993 session, called upon the Cuban Government, in resolution 48/142 of 20 December 1993,

to adopt measures proposed by the Special Rapporteur to ratify international human rights instruments; to cease the persecution and punishment of citizens for reasons related to freedom of expression and peaceful association; to permit legalization of independent groups; to respect guarantees of due process; to permit access to the prisons by national independent groups and international humanitarian agencies; to review sentences for crimes of a political nature; and to cease retaliatory measures toward those seeking permission to leave the country.

In his report to the 1994 session of the Commission on Human Rights (E/CN.4/1994/51, para. 65), the Special Rapporteur indicated that "the government of Cuba still refuses to accept the Commission's decision to continue monitoring human rights conditions in that country and all cooperation with the Special Rapporteur. . . ."

At its fifty-first session, held in March 1995, the UN Commission on Human Rights considered a report on the situation of human rights in Cuba by its Special Rapporteur, prepared in accordance with the mandate which the Commission had given him in resolution 1994/71 of 9 March 1994 "to review and report on the situation of human rights in Cuba and to maintain direct contact with the Government and citizens of Cuba."

Deeply concerned at information in the report on arbitrary arrests, beatings, imprisonment, harassment and threats, including loss of employment against human rights defenders and others who are engaged in the peaceful exercise of their rights, and at continued violations in Cuba of fundamental rights and freedoms enumerated in the Universal Declaration of Human Rights, the Commission ''called upon the government of Cuba to permit the Special Rapporteur the opportunity to carry out his mandate in full, in particular by allowing him to visit Cuba.'' In this connection, however, the Commission endorsed the Special Rapprteur's view that, while positive, the Government of Cuba's decision to invite the High Commissioner for Human Rights to visit the country should be regarded as a point of departure for all mechanisms of the Commission of Human Rights, including the Special Rapporteur.

Extending the mandate of the Special Rapporteur for one year, and again requesting him to maintain direct contacts with the Government and citizens of Cuba, the Commission called upon the Government of Cuba ''to bring the observance of human rights and fundamental freedoms in Cuba up to universally recognized standards, to end all violations of human rights as recommended by the Special Rapporteur, including in particular by permitting freedom of peaceful expression and assembly and by ending immediately the detention and imprisonment of human rights defenders and others, including those deemed to be 'dangerous' and imprisoned without any regard for due process, in contravention of applicable human rights standards.''

**BIBLIOGRAPHY.** Americas Watch. *Cuba: Attacks against Independent Associations March 1990–February 1991.* New York: Human Rights Watch, 25 February 1991. NGO report, in English

————. *Cuba: Behind a Sporting Facade, Stepped-Up Repression.* New York: Human Rights Watch, 11 August 1991. NGO report, in English.

————. ''Cuba: Stifling Dissent in the Midst of Crisis,'' *News From Americas Watch* 6, no. 2 (1994): 1–18. NGO report, in English.

————. *Tightening the Grip: Human Rights Abuses in Cuba—August 1991–February 1992.* New York: Human Rights Watch, 24 February 1992. NGO report, in English.

Amnesty International. *Cuba: The Human Rights Situation* (Cuba: la situation des droits de l'homme). New York: December 1990. NGO factfinding report, in English and French.

————. *Cuba: Recent Developments affecting the Situation of Political Prisoners and the Use of the Death Penalty—An Update.* London: 1989. NGO report, in English.

Association Internationale Contre la Torture (International Association against Torture). *Mission to Cuba: Report.* Milan: 1988. NGO mission report, in Spanish, French, and English.

Bengelsdorf, Carollee. ''On the Problem of Studying Women in Cuba,'' *Race and Class* 27, no. 2 (Autumn 1985): 35–50. Scholarly article, in English.

Bofill Pages, Ricardo, comp. *Cuba 1988: La Situacion de los Derechos Humanos* (Cuba 1988: The Human Rights Situation). Miami, FL, USA: Comite Cubano Por Derechos Humanos, 1989. NGO report, in Spanish.

Brown, Charles J., and Armando M. Lago. *The Politics of Psychiatry in Revolutionary Cuba.* New York: Transaction Publishers for Freedom House and of Human Rights, 1991. Research report, in English; bibliography, pp. 189–198.

Clark, Juan, Angel De Fana, and Amaya Sánchez. *Human Rights in Cuba: An Experiential Perspective.* Miami, FL, USA: SAETA Ediciones for the Research Institute for Cuban Studies, North/South Center, University of Miami, 1991. Scholarly study, in English.

Henkin, A. H., M. J. Camejo, R. J. Hiller, M. H. Posner, S. Ritchin, and K. Roth. *Human Rights in Cuba: Report of a Delegation of the Association of the Bar of the City of New York.* New York: Association of the Bar of the City of New York, 1988. NGO mission report, in English.

Human Rights Watch. ''Cuba,'' in *Human Rights Watch World Report 1995,* pp. 85–89. New York: 1995. NGO report, in English.

Organization of American States. *Informe Anual de la Comision Interamericana de Derechos Humanos 1985–1986* (Annual Report of the Inter-American Commission of Human Rights 1985–1986). Washington, D.C.: 1986. IGO annual report, in Spanish.

Pedraza-Bailey, Sylvia. ''Cuba's Exiles: Portrait of a Refugee Migration,'' *International Migrations Review* 19, no. 1 (Spring 1985): 4–34. Scholarly article, in English; bibliography, pp. 31–34.

UN Commission on Human Rights. *Consideration of the Report of the Mission which Took Place in Cuba in Accordance with Commission Decision 1988/106.* 21 February 1989. 11 bis. IGO document, in English.

**CULTURAL RIGHTS.** The right of everyone to participate in cultural life is proclaimed in the **UNIVERSAL DECLARATION OF HUMAN RIGHTS** in the following terms:

*Article 27.* 1. Everyone has the right freely to participate in the cultural life of the community, to enjoy the arts and to share in scientific advancement and its benefits.

2. Everyone has the right to the protection of the moral and material interests resulting from any scientific, literary or artistic production of which he is the author.

The right is further elaborated in the **INTERNATIONAL COVENANT ON ECONOMIC, SOCIAL AND CULTURAL RIGHTS,** as follows:

*Article 15.* 1. The States Parties to the present Covenant recognize the right of everyone:

(a) To take part in cultural life;

(b) To enjoy the benefits of scientific progress and its applications;

(c) To benefit from the protection of the moral and material interests resulting from any scientific, literary or artistic production of which he is the author.

2. The steps to be taken by the States Parties to the present Covenant to achieve the full realization of this right shall

include those necessary for the conservation, the development and the diffusion of science and culture.

3. The States Parties to the present Covenant undertake to respect the freedom indispensable for scientific research and creative activity.

4. The States Parties to the present Covenant recognize the benefits to be derived from the encouragement and development of international contacts and cooperation in the scientific and cultural fields.

Nondiscrimination on racial grounds in respect of the right to participate in culture is ensured by the International Convention on the Elimination of All Forms of Racial Discrimination (see **RACIAL DISCRIMINATION**) in the following provision:

*Article 5.* In compliance with the fundamental obligations laid down in article 2 of this Convention, States Parties undertake to prohibit and to eliminate racial discrimination in all its forms and to guarantee the right of everyone, without distinction as to race, colour, or national or ethnic origin, to equality before the law, notably in the enjoyment of the following rights: . . .
(e) Economic, social and cultural rights, in particular: . . .
(vi) The right to equal participation in cultural activities.

Non-discrimination on the ground of sex in respect of the right is ensured in the Convention on the Elimination of All Forms of Discrimination against Women in the following provision:

*Article 13.* States Parties shall take all appropriate measures to eliminate discrimination against women in other areas of economic and social life in order to ensure, on a basis of equality of men and women, the same rights, in particular: . . .
(c) The right to participate in recreational activities, sports and all aspects of cultural life.

Within the United Nations system, primary responsibility for the preparation and supervision of international measures to promote and protect enjoyment of the right to culture lies with the **UNITED NATIONS EDUCATIONAL, SCIENTIFIC AND CULTURAL ORGANIZATION.** Its basic tools in this endeavor are the UNESCO Declaration of the Principles of International Cultural Co-operation, of 4 November 1966; the UNESCO Declaration on the Guiding Principles on the Use of Satellite Broadcasting for the Free Flow of Information, the Spread of Education and Greater Cultural Exchange, of 15 November 1972; and the UNESCO Declaration on Fundamental Principles concerning the Contribution of the Mass Media to Strengthening Peace and International Understanding, to the Promotion of Human Rights and to Countering Racialism, apartheid and Incitement to War, of 28 November 1978.

In accordance with the procedures for implementation of the International Covenant on Economic, Social and Cultural Rights adopted by the UN **ECONOMIC AND SOCIAL COUNCIL** on 11 May 1976 (resolution 1988 [LX]), UNESCO submits to the Council, at regular intervals, reports on the progress made in achieving the observance of the provisions of the Covenant falling within the scope of its activities, as provided under article 18 of the Covenant.

*RETURN OR RESTITUTION OF CULTURAL PROPERTY.* Normative instruments relating to the right to cultural property are the UNESCO Convention for the Protection of Cultural Property in the Event of Armed Conflict, with regulations for the execution of the Convention, of 14 May 1954 (known as the Hague Convention); the Protocol of that Convention, also of 14 May 1954; the UNESCO Convention on the Means of Prohibiting and Preventing the Illicit Import, Export and Transfer of Ownership of Cultural Property, of 14 November 1970; the UNESCO Convention concerning the Protection of the World Cultural Heritage, of 16 November 1972; the UNESCO Recommendation concerning the Most Effective Means of Rendering Museums Accessible to Everyone, of 14 December 1960; the UNESCO Recommendation on the Means of Prohibiting and Preventing the Illicit Import, Export, and Transfer of Ownership of Cultural Property, of 19 November 1964; the UNESCO Recommendation concerning the Protection, at the National Level, of the Cultural and Natural Heritage, of 16 November 1972; the UNESCO Recommendation concerning the Safeguarding and Contemporary Role of Historic Areas, of 26 November 1976; the UNESCO Recommendation on the Protection of Moveable Cultural Property, of 28 November 1978; the UNESCO Recommendation concerning the status of the Artist, of 27 October 1980; and the UNESCO Recommendation for the Safeguarding and Preservation of Moving Images, of 27 October 1980.

At its 1993 session, the UN General Assembly received a joint report of the Secretary-General and the UNESCO Director-General on the implementation of the UNESCO Convention on the Means of Prohibiting and Preventing the Illicit Import, Export and Transfer of Ownership of Cultural Property. The Assembly expressed its concern that clandestine excavations and illicit traffic in cultural property continue to impoverish the cultural heritage of all peoples.

In resolution 48/15 of 2 November 1993, the General Assembly recommended that States adopt or strengthen protective legislation regarding their own heritage and that of other peoples and reaffirmed its earlier view

that the restitution to a country of its objects d'art, monuments, museum pieces, archives, manuscripts, documents, and any other cultural or artistic treasures contributes to the strengthening of international cooperation and to the preservation and flowering of universal cultural values through fruitful cooperation between developed and developing countries

*SEE ALSO* Indigenous Peoples.

**BIBLIOGRAPHY.** Appell, G. N. *Our Vision of Human Rights Is Too Small!: Anthropological Perspective on Fundamental Human Rights.* Waltham, MA, USA: Brandeis University, 1992. Scholarly monograph, in English; bibliography, pp. 51–62.

Capotorti, Francesco. *Study on the Rights of Persons belonging to Ethnic, Religious and Linguistic Minorities.* New York: UN Centre for Human Rights, 1991. IGO document, in English.

Centre interdisciplinaire d'éthique et des droits de l'homme à l'Université de Fribourg (Fribourg University Interdisciplinary Centre for Ethics and Human Rights). *Les droits culturels: une catégorie sous-développée de droits de l'homme* (Cultural Rights: An Underdeveloped Human Rights Category), vol. 7, no. 1. Fribourg, Switzerland: 1991. Conference report, in French.

Clinton, Robert N. "The Right of Indigenous Peoples as Collective Group Rights," *Arizona Law Review* 32, no. 4 (1990): 739–747. Scholarly article, in English.

Craven, Matthew, and Caroline Dommen. "Making Room for Substance: Fifth Session of the Committee on Economic, Social and Cultural Rights," *Netherlands Quarterly of Human Rights* 9, no. 1 (1991): 83–95. Report on proceedings, in English.

Leckie, Scott. "An Overview and Appraisal of the Fifth Session of the UN Committee on Economic, Social and Cultural Rights," *Human Rights Quarterly* 13, no. 4 (1991): 545–572. Scholarly article, in English.

Plichtová, Jana, ed. *Minorities in Politics—Cultural and Languages Rights: Proceeding from International Symposium on Minorities in Central Europe.* Bratislava, Czechoslovakia: Czechoslovak Committee in the European Cultural Foundation, 1992. Conference report, in English.

Thomason, Douglas N. "Rolling Back History: The United Nations General Assembly and the Right to Cultural Property," *Case Western Reserve Journal of International Law* 22, no. 1 (Winter 1990): 47–96. Scholarly article, in English.

## CULTURAL RIGHTS: CONVENTION CONCERNING THE PROTECTION OF THE WORLD CULTURAL HERITAGE, UNESCO (1972).

The Convention, adopted on 16 November 1972 by the UNESCO General Conference at its 17th session, held in Paris, entered into force on 17 December 1975. Each State party to the Convention undertakes to ensure conservation of elements of the world cultural heritage situated in its territory, to make an inventory of such elements, and to recognize that it is the duty of the international community as a whole to cooperate in conserving that heritage.

The Convention provides for the establishment of an intergovernmental committee, known as the World Heritage Committee, to supervise protection of items recognized as forming part of the world's cultural and natural heritage which are of universal value from the point of view of history, art, science, or esthetics, and a fund, known as the World Heritage Fund, to finance such activities.

The text of the Convention (*UNESCO's Standard-Setting Instruments*, No. IV.A.5) is as follows:

The General Conference of the United Nations Educational, Scientific and Cultural Organization, meeting in Paris from 17 October to 21 November 1972, at its seventeenth session,

Noting that the cultural heritage and the natural heritage are increasingly threatened with destruction not only by the traditional causes of decay, but also by changing social and economic conditions which aggravate the situation with even more formidable phenomena of damage or destruction,

Considering that deterioration or disappearance of any item of the cultural or natural heritage constitutes a harmful impoverishment of the heritage of all the nations of the world,

Considering that protection of this heritage at the national level often remains incomplete because of the scale of the resources which it requires and of the insufficient economic, scientific and technical resources of the country where the property to be protected is situated,

Recalling that the Constitution of the Organization provides that it will maintain, increase and diffuse knowledge, by assuring the conservation and protection of the world's heritage, and recommending to the nations concerned the necessary international Conventions,

Considering that the existing international Conventions, recommendations and resolutions concerning cultural and natural property demonstrate the importance, for all the peoples of the world, of safeguarding this unique and irreplaceable property, to whatever people it may belong,

Considering that parts of the cultural or natural heritage are of outstanding interest and therefore need to be preserved as part of the world heritage of mankind as a whole,

Considering that, in view of the magnitude and gravity of the new dangers threatening them, it is incumbent on the international community as a whole to participate in the protection of the cultural and natural heritage of outstanding universal value, by the granting of collective assistance which, although not taking the place of action by the State concerned, will serve as an effective complement thereto,

Considering that it is essential for this purpose to adopt new provisions in the form of a Convention establishing an effective system of collective protection of the cultural and natural heritage of outstanding universal value, organized on a permanent basis and in accordance with modern scientific methods,

Having decided, at its sixteenth session, that this question should be made the subject of an international Convention,

Adopts this sixteenth day of November 1972 this Convention.

### I. Definitions of the Cultural and the Natural Heritage

*Article 1.* For the purposes of this Convention, the following shall be considered as "cultural heritage,"

Monuments: architectural works, works of monumental sculpture and painting, elements or structures of an archaeological nature, inscriptions, cave dwellings and combinations of features, which are of outstanding universal value from the point of view of history, art or science;

Groups of buildings: groups of separate or connected buildings which, because of their architecture, their homogeneity or their place in the landscape, are of outstanding universal value from the point of view of history, art or science;

Sites: works of man or the combined works of nature and of man, and areas including archaeological sites which are of outstanding universal value from the historical, aesthetic, ethnological or anthropological points of view.

*Article 2.* For the purposes of this Convention, the following shall be considered as "natural heritage":

Nature features consisting of physical and biological formations or groups of such formations, which are of outstanding universal value from the aesthetic or scientific point of view;

Geological and physiographical formations and precisely delineated areas which constitute the habitat of threatened species of animals and plants of outstanding universal value from the point of view of science or conservation;

Natural sites or precisely delineated natural areas of outstanding universal value from the point of view of science, conservation or natural beauty.

*Article 3.* It is for each State Party to this Convention to identify and delineate the different properties situated on its territory mentioned in Articles 1 and 2 above.

## II. National Protection and International Protection of the Cultural and Natural Heritage

*Article 4.* Each State Party to this Convention recognizes that the duty of ensuring the identification, protection, conservation, presentation and transmission to future generations of the cultural and natural heritage referred to in Articles 1 and 2 and situated on its territory, belongs primarily to that State. It will do all it can to his end, to the utmost of its own resources and, where appropriate, with any international assistance and cooperation, in particular, financial, artistic, scientific and technical, which it may be able to obtain.

*Article 5.* To ensure that effective and active measures are taken for the protection, conservation and presentation of the cultural and natural heritage situated on its territory, each State Party to this Convention shall endeavour, in so far as possible, and as appropriate for each country:

(a) To adopt a general policy which aims to give the cultural and natural heritage a function in the life of the community and to integrate the protection of that heritage into comprehensive planning programmes;

(b) To set up within its territories, where such services do not exist, one or more services for the protection, conservation and presentation of the cultural and natural heritage with an appropriate staff and possessing the means to discharge their functions;

(c) To develop scientific and technical studies and research and to work out such operating methods as will make the State capable of counteracting the dangers that threaten its cultural or natural heritage;

(d) To take the appropriate legal, scientific, technical, administrative and financial measures necessary for the identification, protection, conservation, presentation and rehabilitation of this heritage; and

(e) To foster the establishment or development of national or regional centres for training in the protection, conservation and presentation of the cultural and natural heritage and to encourage scientific research in this field.

*Article 6.* 1. Whilst fully respecting the sovereignty of the States on whose territory the cultural and natural heritage mentioned in Articles 1 and 2 is situated, and without prejudice to property rights provided by national legislation, the States Parties to this Convention recognize that such heritage constitutes a world heritage for whose protection it is the duty of the international community as a whole to co-operate.

2. The States Parties undertake, in accordance with the provisions of this Convention, to give their help in the identification, protection, conservation and preservation of the cultural and natural heritage referred to in paragraphs 2 and 4 of Article 11 if the States on whose territory it is situated so request.

3. Each State Party to this Convention undertakes not to take any deliberate measures which might damage directly or indirectly the cultural and natural heritage referred to in Articles 1 and 2 situated on the territory of other States Parties to this Convention.

*Article 7.* For the purpose of this Convention, international protection of the world cultural and natural heritage shall be understood to mean the establishment of a system of international co-operation and assistance designed to support States Parties to the Convention in their efforts to conserve and identify that heritage.

## III. Intergovernmental Committee for the Protection of the World Cultural and Natural Heritage

*Article 8.* 1. An Intergovernmental Committee for the Protection of the Cultural and Natural Heritage of Outstanding Universal Value, called "the World Heritage Committee", is hereby established within the United Nations Educational, Scientific and Cultural Organization. It shall be composed of 15 States Parties to the Convention, elected by States Parties to the Convention meeting in general assembly during the ordinary session of the General Conference of the United Nations Educational, Scientific and Cultural Organization. The number of States members of the Committee shall be increased to 21 as from the date of the ordinary session of the General Conference following the entry into force of this Convention for at least 40 States.

2. Election of members of the Committee shall ensure an equitable representation of the different regions and cultures of the world.

3. A representative of the International Centre for the Study of the Preservation and Restoration of Cultural Property (Rome Centre), a representative of the International Council of Monuments and Sites (ICOMOS) and a representative of the International Union for Conservation of Nature and Natural Resources (IUCN), to whom may be added, at the request of States Parties to the Convention meeting in general assembly during the ordinary sessions of the General Conference of the United Nations Educational, Scientific and Cultural Organization, representatives of other intergovernmental or non-governmental organizations, with similar objectives, may attend the meetings of the Committee in an advisory capacity.

*Article 9.* 1. The term of office of States members of the World Heritage Committee shall extend from the end of the ordinary session of the General Conference during which they are elected until the end of its third subsequent ordinary session.

2. The term of office of one-third of the members designated at the time of the first election shall, however, cease at the end of the first ordinary session of the General Conference following that at which they were elected; and the term of office, of a further third of the members designated at the same time shall cease at the end of the second ordinary session of the General Conference following that at which they were elected. The names of these members shall be chosen by lot by the President of the General Conference of

the United Nations Educational, Scientific and Cultural Organization after the first election.

3. States members of the Committee shall choose as their representatives persons qualified in the field of the cultural or natural heritage.

*Article 10.* 1. The World Heritage Committee shall adopt its Rules of Procedure.

2. The Committee may at any time invite public or private organizations or individuals to participate in its meetings for consultation on particular problems.

3. The Committee may create such consultative bodies as it deems necessary for the performance of its functions.

*Article 11.* 1. Every State Party to this Convention shall, in so far as possible, submit to the World Heritage Committee an inventory of property forming part of the cultural and natural heritage, situated in its territory and suitable for inclusion in the list provided for in paragraph 2 of this Article. This inventory, which shall not be considered exhaustive, shall include documentation about the location of the property in question and its significance.

2. On the basis of the inventories submitted by States in accordance with paragraph 1, the Committee shall establish, keep up to date and publish, under the title of "World Heritage List", a list of properties forming part of the cultural heritage and natural heritage, as defined in Articles 1 and 2 of this Convention, which it considers as having outstanding universal value in terms of such criteria as it shall have established. An updated list shall be distributed at least every two years.

3. The inclusion of a property in the World Heritage List requires the consent of the State concerned. The inclusion of a property situated in a territory, sovereignty or jurisdiction over which is claimed by more than one State shall in no way prejudice the rights of the parties to the dispute.

4. The Committee shall establish, keep up to date and publish, whenever circumstances shall so require, under the title of "List of World Heritage in Danger", a list of the property appearing in the World Heritage List for the conservation of which major operations are necessary and for which assistance has been requested under this Convention. This list shall contain an estimate of the cost of such operations. The list may include only such property forming part of the cultural and natural heritage as is threatened by serious and specific dangers, such as the threat of disappearance caused by accelerated deterioration, large-scale public or private projects or rapid urban or tourist development projects; destruction caused by changes in the use or ownership of the land; major alterations due to unknown causes; abandonment for any reason whatsoever; the outbreak or the threat of an armed conflict; calamities and cataclysms; serious fires, earthquakes, landslides; volcanic eruptions; changes in water level, floods, and tidal waves. The Committee may at any time, in case of urgent need, make a new entry in the List of World Heritage in Danger and publicize such entry immediately.

5. The Committee shall define the criteria on the basis of which a property belonging to the cultural or natural heritage may be included in either of the lists mentioned in paragraphs 2 and 4 of this article.

6. Before refusing a request for inclusion in one of the two lists mentioned in paragraphs 2 and 4 of this article, the Committee shall consult the State Party in whose territory the cultural or natural property in question is situated.

7. The Committee shall, with the agreement of the States concerned, co-ordinate and encourage the studies and research needed for the drawing up of the lists referred to in paragraphs 2 and 4 of this article.

*Article 12.* The fact that a property belonging to the cultural or natural heritage has not been included in either of the two lists mentioned in paragraphs 2 and 4 of Article 11 shall in no way be construed to mean that it does not have an outstanding universal value for purposes other than those resulting from inclusion in these lists.

*Article 13.* 1. The World Heritage Committee shall receive and study requests for international assistance formulated by States Parties to this Convention with respect to property forming part of the cultural or natural heritage, situated in their territories, and included or potentially suitable for inclusion in the lists referred to in paragraphs 2 and 4 of Article 11. The purpose of such requests may be to secure the protection, conservation, presentation or rehabilitation of such property.

2. Requests for international assistance under paragraph 1 of this article may also be concerned with identification of cultural or natural property defined in Articles 1 and 2, when preliminary investigations have shown that further inquiries would be justified.

3. The Committee shall decide on the action to be taken with regard to these requests, determine where appropriate, the nature and extent of its assistance, and authorize the conclusion, on its behalf, of the necessary arrangements with the government concerned.

4. The Committee shall determine an order of priorities for its operations. It shall in so doing bear in mind the respective importance for the world cultural and natural heritage of the property requiring protection, the need to give international assistance to the property most representative of a natural environment or of the genius and the history of the peoples of the world, the urgency of the work to be done, the resources available to the States on whose territory the threatened property is situated and in particular the extent to which they are able to safeguard such property by their own means.

5. The Committee shall draw up, keep up to date and publicize a list of property for which international assistance has been granted.

6. The Committee shall decide on the use of the resources of the Fund established under Article 15 of this Convention. It shall seek ways of increasing these resources and shall take all useful steps to this end.

7. The Committee shall co-operate with international and national governmental and nongovernmental organizations having objectives similar to those of this Convention. For the implementation of its programmes and projects, the Committee may call on such organizations, particularly the International Centre for the Study of the Preservation and Restoration of Cultural Property (the Rome Centre), the International Council of Monuments and Sites (ICOMOS) and the International Union for Conservation of Nature and Natural Resources (IUCN), as well as on public and private bodies and individuals.

8. Decisions of the Committee shall be taken by a majority of two-thirds of its members present and voting. A majority of the members of the Committee shall constitute a quorum.

*Article 14.* 1. The World Heritage Committee shall be assisted by a Secretariat appointed by the Director-General of the United Nations Educational, Scientific and Cultural Organization.

2. The Director-General of the United Nations Educational, Scientific and Cultural Organization, utilizing to the fullest extent possible the services of the International Centre for the Study of the Preservation and the Restoration of Cultural Property (the Rome Centre), the International

Council of Monuments and Sites (ICOMOS) and the International Union for Conservation of Nature and Natural Resources (IUCN) in their respective areas of competence and capability, shall prepare the Committee's documentation and the agenda of its meetings and shall have the responsibility for the implementation of its decisions.

## IV. Fund for the Protection of the World Cultural and Natural Heritage

*Article 15.* 1. A Fund for the Protection of the World Cultural and Natural Heritage of Outstanding Universal Value, called "the World Heritage Fund", is hereby established.

2. The Fund shall constitute a trust fund, in conformity with the provisions of the Financial Regulations of the United Nations Educational, Scientific and Cultural Organization.

3. The resources of the Fund shall consist of:

(a) Compulsory and voluntary contributions made by the States Parties to this Convention,

(b) Contributions, gifts or bequests which may be made by:

(i) other States;

(ii) the United Nations Educational, Scientific and Cultural Organization, other organizations of the United Nations system, particularly the United Nations Development Programme or other intergovernmental organization;

(iii) public or private bodies or individuals;

(c) Any interest due on the resources of the Fund;

(d) Funds raised by collections and receipts from events organized for the benefit of the Fund; and

(e) All other resources authorized by the Fund's regulations, as drawn up by the World Heritage Committee.

4. Contributions to the Fund and other forms of assistance made available to the Committee may be used only for such purposes as the Committee shall define. The Committee may accept contributions to be used only for a certain programme or project, provided that the Committee shall have decided on the implementation of such programme or project. No political conditions may be attached to contributions made to the Fund.

*Article 16.* 1. Without prejudice to any supplementary voluntary contribution, the States Parties to this Convention undertake to pay regularly, every two years, to the World Heritage Fund, contributions, the amount of which, in the form of a uniform percentage applicable to all States, shall be determined by the General Assembly of States Parties to the Convention, meeting during the sessions of the General Conference of the United Nations Educational, Scientific and Cultural Organization. This decision of the General Assembly requires the majority of the States Parties present and voting, which have not made the declaration referred to in paragraph 2 of this Article. In no case shall the compulsory contribution of States Parties to the Convention exceed 1 per cent of the contribution to the Regular Budget of the United Nations Educational, Scientific and Cultural Organization.

2. However, each State referred to in Article 31 or in Article 32 of this Convention may declare, at the time of the deposit of its instruments of ratification, acceptance or accession, that it shall not be bound by the provisions of paragraph 1 of this Article.

3. A State Party to the Convention which has made the declaration referred to in paragraph 2 of this Article may at any time withdraw the said declaration by notifying the Di-

rector-General of the United Nations Educational, Scientific and Cultural Organization. However, the withdrawal of the declaration shall not take effect in regard to the compulsory contribution due by the State until the date of the subsequent General Assembly of States Parties to the Convention.

4. In order that the Committee may be able to plan its operations effectively, the contributions of States Parties to this Convention which have made the declaration referred to in paragraph 2 of this Article, shall be paid on a regular basis, at least every two years, and should not be less than the contributions which they should have paid if they had been bound by the provisions of paragraph 1 of this Article.

5. Any State Party to the Convention which is in arrears with the payment of its compulsory or voluntary contribution for the current year and the calendar year immediately preceding it shall not be eligible as a Member of the World Heritage Committee, although this provision shall not apply to the first election.

The terms of office of any such State which is already a member of the Committee shall terminate at the time of the elections provided for in Article 8, paragraph 1 of this Convention.

*Article 17.* The States Parties to this Convention shall consider or encourage the establishment of national, public and private foundations or associations whose purpose is to invite donations for the protection of the cultural and natural heritage as defined in Articles 1 and 2 of this Convention.

*Article 18.* The States Parties to this Convention shall give their assistance to international fund-raising campaigns organized for the World Heritage Fund under the auspices of the United Nations Educational, Scientific and Cultural Organization. They shall facilitate collections made by the bodies mentioned in paragraph 3 of Article 15 for this purpose.

## V. Conditions and Arrangements for International Assistance

*Article 19.* Any State Party to this Convention may request international assistance for property forming part of the cultural or natural heritage of outstanding universal value situated within its territory. It shall submit with its request such information and documentation provided for in Article 21 as it has in its possession and as will enable the Committee to come to a decision.

*Article 20.* Subject to the provisions of paragraph 2 of Article 13, sub-paragraph (c) of Article 22 and Article 23, international assistance provided for by this Convention may be granted only to property forming part of the cultural and natural heritage which the World Heritage Committee has decided, or may decide, to enter in one of the lists mentioned in paragraphs 2 and 4 of Article 11.

*Article 21.* 1. The World Heritage Committee shall define the procedure by which requests to it for international assistance shall be considered and shall specify the content of the request, which should define the operation contemplated, the work that is necessary, the expected cost thereof, the degree of urgency and the reasons why the resources of the State requesting assistance do not allow it to meet all the expenses. Such requests must be supported by experts' reports whenever possible.

2. Requests based upon disasters or natural calamities should, by reasons of the urgent work which they may involve, be given immediate, priority consideration by the Committee, which should have a reserve fund at its disposal against such contingencies.

3. Before coming to a decision, the Committee shall carry out such studies and consultations as it deems necessary.

*Article 22.* Assistance granted by the World Heritage Committee may take the following forms:

(a) Studies concerning the artistic, scientific and technical problems raised by the protection, conservation, presentation and rehabilitation of the cultural and natural heritage, as defined in paragraphs 2 and 4 of Article 11 of this Convention;

(b) Provision of experts, technicians and skilled labour to ensure that the approved work is correctly carried out;

(c) Training of staff and specialists at all levels in the field of identification, protection, conservation, presentation and rehabilitation of the cultural and natural heritage;

(d) Supply of equipment which the State concerned does not possess or is not in a position to acquire;

(e) Low-interest or interest-free loans which might be repayable on a long-term basis;

(f) The granting, in exceptional cases and for special reasons, of non-repayable subsidies.

*Article 23.* The World Heritage Committee may also provide international assistance to national or regional centres for the training of staff and specialists at all levels in the field of identification, protection, conservation, presentation and rehabilitation of the cultural and natural heritage.

*Article 24.* International assistance on a large scale shall be preceded by detailed scientific, economic and technical studies. These studies shall draw upon the most advanced techniques for the protection, conservation, presentation and rehabilitation of the natural and cultural heritage and shall be consistent with the objectives of this Convention. The studies shall also seek means of making rational use of the resources available in the State concerned.

*Article 25.* As a general rule, only part of the cost of work necessary shall be borne by the international community. The contribution of the State benefiting from international assistance shall constitute a substantial share of the resources devoted to each programme or project, unless its resources do not permit this.

*Article 26.* The World Heritage Committee and the recipient State shall define in the agreement they conclude the conditions in which a programme or project for which international assistance under the terms of this Convention is provided, shall be carried out. It shall be the responsibility of the State receiving such international assistance to continue to protect, conserve and present the property so safeguarded, in observance of the conditions laid down by the agreement.

## VI. Educational Programmes

*Article 27.* 1. The States Parties to this Convention shall endeavour by all appropriate means, and in particular by educational and information programmes, to strengthen appreciation and respect by their peoples of the cultural and natural heritage defined in Articles 1 and 2 of the Convention.

2. They shall undertake to keep the public broadly informed of the dangers threatening this heritage and of activities carried on in pursuance of this Convention.

*Article 28.* States Parties to this Convention which receive international assistance under the Convention shall take appropriate measures to make known the importance of the property for which assistance has been received and the role played by such assistance.

## VII. Reports

*Article 29.* 1. The States Parties to this Convention shall, in the reports which they submit to the General Conference of the United Nations Educational, Scientific and Cultural Organization on dates and in a manner to be determined by it, give information on the legislative and administrative provisions which they have adopted and other action which they have taken for the application of this Convention, together with details of the experience acquired in this field.

2. These reports shall be brought to the attention of the World Heritage Committee.

3. The Committee shall submit a report on its activities at each of the ordinary sessions of the General Conference of the United Nations Educational, Scientific and Cultural Organization.

## VIII. Final Clauses

*Article 30.* This Convention is drawn up in Arabic, English, French, Russian and Spanish, the five texts being equally authoritative.

*Article 31.* 1. This Convention shall be subject to ratification or acceptance by States members of the United Nations Educational, Scientific and Cultural Organization in accordance with their respective constitutional procedures.

2. The instruments of ratification or acceptance shall be deposited with the Director-General of the United Nations Educational, Scientific and Cultural Organization.

*Article 32.* 1. This Convention shall be open to accession by all States not members of the United Nations Educational, Scientific and Cultural Organization which are invited by the General Conference of the Organization to accede to it.

2. Accession shall be effected by the deposit of an instrument of accession with the Director-General of the United Nations Educational, Scientific and Cultural Organization.

*Article 33.* This Convention shall enter into force three months after the date of the deposit of the twentieth instrument of ratification, acceptance or accession, but only with respect to those States which have deposited their respective instruments of ratification, acceptance or accession on or before that date. It shall enter into force with respect to any other State three months after the deposit of its instrument of ratification, acceptance or accession.

*Article 34.* The following provisions shall apply to those States Parties to this Convention which have a federal or non-unitary constitutional system:

(a) With regard to the provisions of this Convention, the implementation of which comes under the legal jurisdiction of the federal or central legislative power, the obligations of the federal or central government shall be the same as for those States Parties which are not federal States;

(b) With regard to the provisions of this Convention, the implementation of which comes under the legal jurisdiction of individual constituent States, countries, provinces or cantons that are not obliged by the constitutional system of the federation to take legislative measures, the federal government shall inform the competent authorities of such States, countries, provinces or cantons of the said provisions, with its recommendation for their adoption.

*Article 35.* 1. Each State Party to this Convention may denounce the Convention.

2. The denunciation shall be notified by an instrument in writing, deposited with the Director-General of the United Nations Educational, Scientific and Cultural Organization.

3. The denunciation shall take effect twelve months after

the receipt of the instrument of denunciation. It shall not affect the financial obligations of the denouncing State until the date on which the withdrawal takes effect.

*Article 36.* The Director-General of the United Nations Educational, Scientific and Cultural Organization shall inform the States members of the Organization, the States not members of the Organization which are referred to in Article 32, as well as the United Nations, of the deposit of all the instruments of ratification, acceptance, or accession provided for in Articles 31 and 32, and of the denunciations provided for in Article 35.

*Article 37.* 1. This Convention may be revised by the General Conference of the United Nations Educational, Scientific and Cultural Organization. Any such revision shall, however, bind only the States which shall become Parties to the revising Convention.

2. If the General Conference should adopt a new Convention revising this Convention in whole or in part, then, unless the new Convention otherwise provides, this Convention shall cease to be open to ratification, acceptance or accession, as from the date on which the new revising Convention enters into force.

*Article 38.* In conformity with Article 102 of the Charter of the United Nations, this Convention shall be registered with the Secretariat of the United Nations at the request of the Director-General of the United Nations Educational, Scientific and Cultural Organization.

Done in Paris, this twenty-third day of November 1972, in two authentic copies bearing the signature of the President of the seventeenth session of the General Conference and of the Director-General of the United Nations Educational, Scientific and Cultural Organization, which shall be deposited in the archives of the United Nations Educational, Scientific and Cultural Organization, and certified true copies of which shall be delivered to all the States referred to in Articles 31 and 32 as well as to the United Nations.

**SEE ALSO** *Armed Conflict: Convention for the Protection of Cultural Property in the Event of Armed Conflict, UNESCO.*

## CULTURAL RIGHTS: CONVENTION ON THE MEANS OF PROHIBITING AND PREVENTING THE ILLICIT IMPORT, EXPORT AND TRANSFER OF OWNERSHIP OF CULTURAL PROPERTY, UNESCO (1970).

The Convention was adopted by the UNESCO General Conference (16th session), held in Paris, on 14 November 1970. It entered into force on 14 November 1972.

Under the Convention, States parties undertake to prevent museums within their territories from acquiring cultural property which has been illegally exported, to prohibit the import of cultural property stolen from a museum or other public institution, and to recover and return stolen and imported cultural property at the request of the State of origin.

The text of the Convention (*UNESCO's Standard-Setting Instruments,* No. IV.A.4) is as follows:

The General Conference of the United Nations Educational, Scientific and Cultural Organization, meeting in Paris from 12 October to 14 November 1970, at its sixteenth session,

Recalling the importance of the provisions contained in the Declaration of the Principles of International Cultural Co-operation, adopted by the General Conference at its fourteenth session,

Considering that the interchange of cultural property among nations for scientific, cultural and educational purposes increases the knowledge of the civilization of Man, enriches the cultural life of all peoples and inspires mutual respect and appreciation among nations,

Considering that cultural property constitutes one of the basis elements of civilization and national culture, and that its true value can be appreciated only in relation to the fullest possible information regarding is origin, history and traditional setting,

Considering that it is incumbent upon every State to protect the cultural property existing within its territory against the dangers of theft, clandestine excavation, and illicit export,

Considering that, to avert these dangers, it is essential for every State to become increasingly alive to the moral obligations to respect its own cultural heritage and that of all nations,

Considering that, as cultural institutions, museums, libraries and archives should ensure that their collections are built up in accordance with universally recognized moral principles,

Considering that the illicit import, export and transfer of ownership of cultural property is an obstacle to that understanding between nations which it is part of Unesco's mission to promote by recommending to interested States, international Conventions to this end,

Considering that the protection of cultural heritage can be effective only if organized both nationally and internationally among States working in close co-operation,

Considering that the Unesco General Conference adopted a Recommendation to this effect in 1964,

Having before it further proposals on the means of prohibiting and preventing the illicit import, export and transfer of ownership of cultural property, a question which is on the agenda for the session as item 19,

Having decided, at its fifteenth session, that this question should be made the subject of an international convention,

Adopts this Convention on the fourteenth day of November 1970.

*Article 1.* For the purposes of this Convention, the term "cultural property" means property which, on religious or secular grounds, is specifically designated by each State as being of importance for archaeology, prehistory, history, literature, art or science and which belongs to the following categories:

(a) Rare collections and specimens of fauna, flora, minerals and anatomy, and objects of palaeontological interest;

(b) Property relating to history, including the history of science and technology and military and social history, to the life of national leaders, thinkers, scientists and artists and to events of national importance;

(c) Products of archaeological excavations (including regular and clandestine) or of archaeological discoveries;

(d) Elements of artistic or historical monuments or archaeological sites which have been dismembered;

(e) Antiquities more than one hundred years old, such as inscriptions, coins and engraved seals;

(f) Objects of ethnological interest;

(g) Property of artistic interest, such as:

(1) Pictures, paintings and drawings produced entirely by hand on any support and in any material (excluding industrial designs and manufactured articles decorated by hand);

(2) Original works of statuary art and sculpture in any material;

(3) Original engravings, prints and lithographs;

(4) Original artistic assemblages and montages in any material;

(h) Rare manuscripts and incunabula, old books, documents and publications of special interest (historical, artistic, scientific, literary, etc.) singly or in collections;

(i) Postage, revenue and similar stamps, singly or in collections;

(j) Archives, including sound, photographic and cinematographic archives;

(k) Articles of furniture more than one hundred years old and old musical instruments.

*Article 2.* 1. The States Parties to this Convention recognize that the illicit import, export and transfer of ownership of cultural property is one of the main causes of the impoverishment of the cultural heritage of the countries of origin of such property and that international co- operation constitutes one of the most efficient means of protecting each country's cultural property against all the dangers resulting therefrom.

2. To this end, the States Parties undertake to oppose such practices with the means at their disposal, and particularly by removing their causes, putting a stop to current practices, and by helping to make the necessary reparations.

*Article 3.* The import, export or transfer of ownership of cultural property effected contrary to the provisions adopted under this Convention by the States Parties there to, shall be illicit.

*Article 4.* The States Parties to this Convention recognize that for the purpose of the Convention property which belongs to the following categories forms part of the cultural heritage of each State:

(a) Cultural property created by the individual or collective genius of nationals of the State concerned, and cultural property of importance to the State concerned created within the territory of that State by foreign nationals or stateless persons resident within such territory;

(b) Cultural property found within the national territory;

(c) Cultural property acquired by archaeological, ethnological or natural science missions, with the consent of the competent authorities of the country of origin of such property;

(d) Cultural property which has been the subject of a freely agreed exchange;

(e) Cultural property received as a gift or purchased legally with the consent of the competent authorities of the country of origin of such property.

*Article 5.* To ensure the protection of their cultural property against illicit import, export and transfer of ownership, the States Parties to this Convention undertake, as appropriate for each country, to set up within their territories one or more national services, where such services do not already exist, for the protection of the cultural heritage, with a qualified staff sufficient in number for the effective carrying out of the following functions:

(a) Contributing to the formation of draft laws and regulations designed to secure the protection of the cultural heritage and particularly prevention of the illicit import, export and transfer of ownership of important cultural property;

(b) Establishing and keeping up to date, on the basis of a national inventory of protected property, a list of important public and private cultural property whose export would constitute an appreciable impoverishment of the national cultural heritage;

(c) Promoting the development or the establishment of scientific and technical institutions (museums, libraries, ar-

chives, laboratories, workshops . . . ) required to ensure the preservation and presentation of cultural property;

(d) Organizing the supervision of archaeological excavations, ensuring the preservation *in situ* of certain cultural property, and protecting certain areas reserved for future archaeological research;

(e) Establishing, for the benefit of those concerned (curators, collectors, antique dealers, etc.) rules in conformity with the ethical principles set forth in this Convention; and taking steps to ensure the observance of those rules;

(f) Taking educational measures to stimulate and develop respect for the cultural heritage of all States, and spreading knowledge of the provisions of this Convention;

(g) Seeing that appropriate publicity is given to the disappearance of any items of cultural property.

*Article 6.* The States Parties to this Convention undertake:

(a) To introduce an appropriate certificate in which the exporting State would specify that the export of the cultural property in question is authorized. The certificate should accompany all items of cultural property exported in accordance with the regulations;

(b) To prohibit the exportation of cultural property from their territory unless accompanied by the above- mentioned export certificate;

(c) To publicize this prohibition by appropriate means, particularly among persons likely to export or import cultural property.

*Article 7.* The States Parties to this Convention undertake:

(a) To take the necessary measures, consistent with national legislation, to prevent museums and similar institutions within their territories from acquiring cultural property originating in another State Party which has been illegally exported after entry into force of this Convention, in the States concerned. Whenever possible, to inform a State of origin Party to this Convention of an offer of such cultural property illegally removed from that State after the entry into force of this Convention in both States;

(b) (1) to prohibit the import of cultural property stolen from a museum or a religious or secular public monument or similar institution in another State Party to this Convention after the entry into force of this Convention for the States concerned, provided that such property is documented as appertaining to the inventory of that institution;

(2) at the request of the State Party of origin, to take appropriate steps to recover and return any such cultural property imported after the entry into force of this Convention in both States concerned, provided, however, that the requesting State shall pay just compensation to an innocent purchaser or to a person who has valid title to that property. Requests for recovery and return shall be made through diplomatic offices. The requesting Party shall furnish, at its expense, the documentation and other evidence necessary to establish its claim for recovery and return. The Parties shall impose no customs duties or other charges upon cultural property returned pursuant to this Article. All expenses incident to the return and delivery of the cultural property shall be borne by the requesting Party.

*Article 8.* The States Parties to this Convention undertake to impose penalties or administrative sanctions on any person responsible for infringing the prohibitions referred to under Articles 6 (b) and 7 (b) above.

*Article 9.* Any State Party to this Convention whose cultural patrimony is in jeopardy from pillage of archaeological or ethnological materials may call upon other States Parties who are affected. The States Parties to this Convention undertake, in these circumstances, to participate in a concerted international effort to determine and to carry out the necessary concrete measures, including the control of exports and imports and international commerce in the specific materials concerned. Pending agreement each State concerned shall take provisional measures to the extent feasible to prevent irremediable injury to the cultural heritage of the requesting State.

*Article 10.* The States Parties to this Convention undertake:

(a) To restrict by education, information and vigilance, movement of cultural property illegally removed from any State Party to this Convention and, as appropriate for each country, oblige antique dealers, subject to penal or administrative sanctions, to maintain a register recording the origin of each item of cultural property, names and addresses of the supplier, description and price of each item sold and to inform the purchaser of the cultural property of the export prohibition to which such property may be subject;

(b) To endeavour by educational means to create and develop in the public mind a realization of the value of cultural property and the threat to the cultural heritage created by theft, clandestine excavations and illicit exports.

*Article 11.* The export and transfer of ownership of cultural property under compulsion arising directly or indirectly from the occupation of a country by a foreign power shall be regarded as illicit.

*Article 12.* The States Parties to this Convention shall respect the cultural heritage within the territories for the international relations of which they are responsible, and shall take all appropriate measures to prohibit and prevent the illicit import, export and transfer of ownership of cultural property in such territories.

*Article 13.* The States Parties to this Convention also undertake, consistent with the laws of each State:

(a) To prevent by all appropriate means transfers of ownership of cultural property likely to promote the illicit import or export of such property;

(b) To ensure that their competent services co- operate in facilitating the earliest possible restitution of illicitly exported cultural property to its rightful owner;

(c) To admit actions for recovery of lost or stolen items of cultural property brought by or on behalf of the rightful owners;

(d) To recognize the indefeasible right of each State Party to this Convention to classify and declare certain cultural property as inalienable which should therefore *ipso facto* not be exported, and to facilitate recovery of such property by the State concerned in cases where it has been exported.

*Article 14.* In order to prevent illicit export and to meet the obligations arising from the implementation of this Convention, each State Party to the Convention should, as far as it is able, provide the national services responsible for the protection of its cultural heritage with an adequate budget and, if necessary, should set up a fund for this purpose.

*Article 15.* Nothing in this Convention shall prevent States Parties thereto from concluding special agreements among themselves or from continuing to implement agreements already concluded regarding the restitution of cultural property removed, whatever the reason, from its territory of origin, before the entry into force of this Convention for the States concerned.

*Article 16.* The States Parties to this Convention shall in their periodic reports submitted to the General Conference of the United Nations Educational, Scientific and Cultural Organization on dates and in a manner to be determined by it, give information on the legislative and administrative provisions which they have adopted and other action which they have taken for the application of this Convention, together with details of the experience acquired in this field.

*Article 17.* 1. The States Parties to this Convention may call on the technical assistance of the United Nations Educational, Scientific and Cultural Organization, particularly as regards:

(a) Information and education;

(b) Consultation and expert advice;

(c) Co-ordination and good offices.

2. The United Nations Educational, Scientific and Cultural Organization may, on its own initiative conduct research and publish studies on matters relevant to the illicit movement of cultural property.

3. To this end, the United National Educational, Scientific and Cultural Organization may also call on the co-operation of any competent non-governmental organization.

4. The United Nations Educational, Scientific and Cultural Organization may, on its own initiative, make proposals to States Parties to this Convention for its implementation.

5. At the request of at least two States Parties to this Convention which are engaged in a dispute over its implementation, UNESCO may extend its good offices to reach a settlement between them.

*Article 18.* This Convention is drawn up in English, French, Russian and Spanish, the four texts being equally authoritative.

*Article 19.* 1. This Convention shall be subject to ratification or acceptance by States members of the United Nations Educational, Scientific and Cultural Organization in accordance with their respective constitutional procedures.

2. The instruments of ratification or acceptance shall be deposited with the Director-General of the United Nations Educational, Scientific and Cultural Organization.

*Article 20.* 1. This Convention shall be open to accession by all States not members of the United Nations Educational, Scientific and Cultural Organization which are invited to accede to it by the Executive Board of the Organization.

2. Accession shall be effected by the deposit of an instrument of accession with the Director-General of the United Nations Educational, Scientific and Cultural Organization.

*Article 21.* This Convention shall enter into force three months after the date of the deposit of the third instrument of ratification, acceptance or accession, but only with respect to those States which have deposited their respective instruments on or before that date. It shall enter into force with respect to any other State three months after the deposit of its instrument of ratification, acceptance or accession.

*Article 22.* The States Parties to this Convention recognize that the Convention is applicable not only to their metropolitan territories but also to all territories for the international relations of which they are responsible; they undertake to consult, if necessary, the governments or other competent authorities of these territories on or before ratification, acceptance or accession with a view to securing the application of the Convention to those territories, and to notify the Director-General of the United Nations Educational, Scientific and Cultural Organization of the territories to which it is applied, the notification to take effect three months after the date of its receipt.

*Article 23.* 1. Each State Party to this Convention may denounce the Convention on its own behalf or on behalf of any territory for whose international relations it is responsible.

2. The denunciation shall be notified by an instrument in writing, deposited with the Director-General of the United Nations Educational, Scientific and Cultural Organization.

3. The denunciation shall take effect twelve months after the receipt of the instrument of denunciation.

*Article 24.* The Director-General of the United Nations Educational, Scientific and Cultural Organization shall inform the States members of the Organization, the States not members of the Organization which are referred to in Article 20, as well as the United Nations, of the deposit of all the instruments of ratification, acceptance and accession provided for in Articles 19 and 20, and of the notifications and denunciations provided for in Articles 22 and 23 respectively.

*Article 25.* 1. This Convention may be revised by the General Conference of the United Nations Educational, Scientific and Cultural Organization. Any such revision shall, however, bind only the States which shall become Parties to the revising convention.

2. If the General Conference should adopt a new convention revising this Convention in whole or in part, then, unless the new convention otherwise provides, this Convention shall cease to be open to ratification, acceptance or accession, as from the date on which the new revising convention enters into force.

*Article 26.* In conformity with Article 102 of the Charter of the United Nations, this Convention shall be registered with the Secretariat of the United Nations at the request of the Director-General of the United Nations Educational, Scientific and Cultural Organization.

Done in Paris this seventeenth day of November 1970, in two authentic copies bearing the signature of the President of the sixteenth session of the General Conference and of the Director-General of the United Nations Educational, Scientific and Cultural Organization, which shall be deposited in the archives of the United Nations Educational, Scientific and Cultural Organization, and certified true copies of which shall be delivered to all the States referred to in Articles 19 and 20 as well as to the United Nations.

The foregoing is the authentic text of the Convention duly adopted by the General Conference of the United Nations Educational, Scientific and Cultural Organization during its sixteenth session, which was held in Paris and declared closed the fourteenth day of November 1970.

In faith whereof we have appended our signatures this seventeenth day of November 1970.

## CULTURAL RIGHTS: DECLARATION OF THE PRINCIPLES OF INTERNATIONAL CULTURAL CO-OPERATION, UNESCO (1966).

The Declaration, adopted by the UNESCO General Conference (14th session) held in Paris, on 4 November 1966, the 20th anniversary of the founding of UNESCO, sets out principles for the guidance of governments, authorities, organizations, associations, and institutions responsible for cultural activities. Based on a study authorized by the UN Economic and Social Council in 1960 (resolution 803 [XXX]), the principles are designed to serve as guidelines for bilateral, regional, and international action regarding the relations and exchanges in the fields of education, science, and culture.

The text of the Declaration (*UNESCO's Standard-Setting Instruments*, No. IV.C.1) is as follows:

The General Conference of the United Nations Educational, Scientific and Cultural Organization, met in Paris for its fourteenth session, this fourth day of November 1966, being the twentieth anniversary of the foundation of the Organization.

Recalling that the Constitution of the Organization declares that "since wars begin in the minds of men, it is in the minds of men that the defences of peace must be constructed" and that the peace must be founded, if it is not to fail, upon the intellectual and moral solidarity of mankind,

Recalling that the Constitution also states that the wide diffusion of culture and the education of humanity for justice and liberty and peace are indispensable to the dignity of man and constitute a sacred duty which all the nations must fulfill in a spirit of mutual assistance and concern,

Considering that the Organization's Member States, believing in the pursuit of truth and the free exchange of ideas and knowledge, have agreed and determined to develop and to increase the means of communication between their peoples,

Considering that, despite the technical advances which facilitate the development and dissemination of knowledge and ideas, ignorance of the way of life and customs of peoples still presents an obstacle to friendship among the nations, to peaceful co-operation and to the progress of mankind,

Taking account of the Universal Declaration of Human Rights, the Declaration of the Rights of the Child, the Declaration on the Granting of Independence to Colonial Countries and Peoples, the United Nations Declaration on the Elimination of all Forms of Racial Discrimination, the Declaration on the Promotion among Youth of the Ideals of Peace, Mutual Respect and Understanding between Peoples, and the Declaration on the Inadmissibility of Intervention in the Domestic Affairs of States and the Protection of their Independence and Sovereignty, proclaimed successively by the General Assembly of the United Nations,

Convinced by the experience of the Organization's first twenty years that, if international cultural co-operation is to be strengthened, its principles require to be affirmed,

Proclaims this Declaration of the principles of international cultural co-operation, to the end that governments, authorities, organizations, associations and institutions responsible for cultural activities may constantly be guided by these principles; and for the purpose, as set out in the Constitution of the Organization, of advancing, through the educational, scientific and cultural relations of the peoples of the world, the objectives of peace and welfare that are defined in the Charter of the United Nations:

*Article 1.* 1. Each culture has a dignity and value which must be respected and preserved.

2. Every people has the right and the duty to develop its culture.

3. In their rich variety and diversity, and in the reciprocal influences they exert on one another, all cultures form part of the common heritage belonging to all mankind.

*Article 2.* Nations shall endeavour to develop the various branches of culture side by side and, as far as possible, simultaneously, so as to establish a harmonious balance between technical progress and the intellectual and moral advancement of mankind.

*Article 3.* International cultural co-operation shall cover all aspects of intellectual and creative activities relating to education, science and culture.

*Article 4.* The aims of international cultural co-operation in its various forms, bilateral or multilateral, regional or universal, shall be:

1. To spread knowledge, to stimulate talent and to enrich cultures;

2. To develop peaceful relations and friendship among the peoples and bring about a better understanding of each other's way of life;

3. To contribute to the application of the principles set out in the United Nations Declarations that are recalled in the Preamble to this Declaration;

4. To enable everyone to have access to knowledge, to enjoy the arts and literature of all peoples, to share in advances made in science in all parts of the world and in the resulting benefits, and to contribute to the enrichment of cultural life;

5. To raise the level of the spiritual and material life of man in all parts of the world.

*Article 5.* Cultural co-operation is a right and a duty for all peoples and all nations, which should share with one another their knowledge and skills.

*Article 6.* International co-operation, while promoting the enrichment of all cultures through its beneficent action, shall respect the distinctive character of each.

*Article 7.* 1. Broad dissemination of ideas and knowledge, based on the freest exchange and discussion, is essential to creative activity, the pursuit of truth and the development of the personality.

2. In cultural co-operation, stress shall be laid on ideas and values conducive to the creations of a climate of friendship and peace. Any mark of hostility in attitudes and in expression of opinion shall be avoided. Every effort shall be made, in presenting and disseminating information, to ensure its authenticity.

*Article 8.* Cultural co-operation shall be carried on for the mutual benefit of all the nations practising it. Exchanges to which it gives rise shall be arranged in a spirit of broad reciprocity.

*Article 9.* Cultural co-operation shall contribute to the establishment of stable, long-term relations between peoples, which should be subjected as little as possible to the strains which may arise in international life.

*Article 10.* Cultural co-operation shall be specially concerned with the moral and intellectual education of young people in a spirit of friendship, international understanding and peace and shall foster awareness among States of the need to stimulate talent and promote the training of the rising generations in the most varied sectors.

*Article 11.* 1. In their cultural relations, States shall bear in mind the principles of the United Nations. In seeking to achieve international co-operation, they shall respect the sovereign equality of States and shall refrain from intervention in matters which are essentially within the domestic jurisdiction of any State.

2. The principles of this Declaration shall be applied with due regard for human rights and fundamental freedoms.

## CULTURAL RIGHTS: RECOMMENDATION ON PARTICIPATION BY THE PEOPLE AT LARGE IN CULTURAL LIFE AND THEIR CONTRIBUTION TO IT, UNESCO (1976).

This recommendation, which aims at ensuring the promotion and protection of cultural rights as human rights, was adopted by the UNESCO General Conference (19th session), held in Nairobi, Kenya, on 26 November 1976. In scope it concerns, in its own words, "everything that should be done by Member States or the authorities to democratize the means and instruments of cultural activity,

so as to enable all individuals to participate freely and fully in cultural creation and its benefits, in accordance with the requirements of social progress."

The text of the recommendation (*UNESCO's Standard-Setting Instruments,* No. IV.B.7) is as follows:

The General Conference of the United Nations Educational, Scientific and Cultural Organization, meeting in Nairobi from 26 October to 30 November 1976, at its nineteenth session.

Recalling that under the terms of Article 27 of the Universal Declaration of Human Rights, "everyone has the right freely to participate in the cultural life of the community, to enjoy the arts and to share in scientific advancement and its benefits",

Recalling that the Constitution of Unesco states, in its Preamble, that the wide diffusion of culture, and the education of humanity for justice and liberty and peace are indispensable to the dignity of man,

Recalling the provisions of the Declaration of the Principles of International Cultural Co-operation adopted by the General Conference of Unesco on 4 November 1966 at its fourteenth session, and in particular Article 1 which states that "each culture has a dignity and value which must be respected and preserved", and Article IV which stipulates that one of the aims of international cultural co-operation is "to enable everyone to have access to knowledge, to enjoy the arts and literature of all peoples, to share in advances made in science in all parts of the world and in the resulting benefits, and to contribute to the enrichment of cultural life", and also the provisions of the Final Act of the Conference on Security and Co-operation in Europe to the effect that the participating States, "desiring to contribute to the strengthening of peace and understanding among peoples and to the spiritual enrichment of the human personality without distinction as to race, sex, language or religion", will set themselves the objective, amongst others, of promoting access by all to their respective cultural achievements,

Considering that cultural development not only complements and regulates general development but is also a true instrument of progress,

Considering:

(a) that culture is an integral part of social life and that a policy for culture must therefore be seen in the broad context of general State policy, and that culture is, in its very essence, a social phenomenon resulting from individuals joining and co-operating in creative activities,

(b) that culture is today becoming an important element in human life and one of the principal factors in the progress of mankind, and that an essential premise for such progress is to ensure the constant growth of society's spiritual potential, based on the full, harmonious development of all its members and the free play of their creative faculties,

(c) that culture is not merely an accumulation of works and knowledge which an élite produces, collects and conserves in order to place it within reach of all; or that a people rich in its past and its heritage offers to others as a model which their own history has failed to provide for them; that culture is not limited to access to works of art and the humanities, but is at one and the same time the acquisition of knowledge, the demand for a way of life and the need to communicate,

Considering that participation by the greatest possible number of people and associations in a wide variety of cultural activities of their own free choice is essential to the development of the basic human values and dignity of the individual, and that access by the people at large to cultural values can be assured only if social and economic conditions are created that will enable them not only to enjoy the benefits of culture, but also to take an active part in overall cultural life and in the process of cultural development,

Considering that access to culture and participation in cultural life are two complementary aspects of the same thing, as is evident from the way in which one affects the other—access may promote participation in cultural life and participation may broaden access to culture by endowing it with its true meaning—and that without participation, mere access to culture necessarily falls short of the objectives of cultural development,

Noting that cultural action often involves only a minute proportion of the population and that, moreover, existing organizations and the means used do not always meet the needs of those who are in a particularly vulnerable position because of their inadequate education, low standard of living, poor housing conditions and economic and social dependence in general,

Noting that there is often a wide discrepancy between the reality and the proclaimed ideals, declared intentions, programmes or expected results,

Considering that while it is essential and urgent to define objectives, contents and methods for a policy of participation by the people at large in cultural life, the solutions envisaged cannot be identical for all countries, in view of the current differences between the socio- economic and political situations in States,

Reaffirming the principles of respect for the sovereignty of States, non-interference in the internal affairs of other countries, equality of rights and the right of peoples to self-determination,

Aware of the responsibility which devolves upon Member States to implement cultural policies for the purpose of advancing the objectives set forth in the Charter of the United Nations, the Constitution of Unesco, the International Covenant on Economic, Social and Cultural Rights, and the Declaration of the Principles of International Cultural Co-operation,

Bearing in mind that elimination of the economic and social inequality which prevents broad sections of the population from gaining access to knowledge which is the foundation of science and technology, and from becoming aware of their own cultural needs, implies broader participation on their part; that to these obstacles must be added a resistance to change, and barriers of all kinds, whether they are of political or commercial origin or take the form of a reaction by closed communities,

Considering that the problem of access and participation can be solved by collective approaches extending to many sectors and aspects of life; that such approaches should be diversified according to the special characteristics of each community, the whole forming a true design for living calling for basic policy options,

Considering that access to culture and participation in cultural life are essential components of an overall social policy dealing with the condition of the working masses, the organization of labour, leisure time, family life, education and training, town-planning and the environment,

Aware of the important role that can be played in cultural and social life by: young people, whose mission is to contribute to the evolution and progress of society; parents, particularly because of the decisive influence which they exercise on the cultural education of children and the development of their creativity; elderly people who are available to discharge a new social and cultural function; workers, because of the active contribution they make to social changes; artists, as creators and bearers of cultural values; cultural development personnel whose task is to secure the effective participation in cultural life of all sections of the population and to ascertain and express their aspirations, relying for this purpose on the collaboration of the spontaneous leaders of the community,

Considering that access and participation, which should provide everyone with the opportunity not only to receive benefits but also to express himself in all the circumstances of social life, imply the greatest liberty and tolerance in the fields of cultural training and the creation and dissemination of culture,

Considering that participation in cultural life presupposes an affirmation of the personality, its dignity and value, and also the implementation of the fundamental rights and freedoms of man attested by the Charter of the United Nations and international legal instruments concerning human rights, and that the cultural development of the individual is hindered by such phenomena as the policy of aggression, colonialism, neo- colonialism, fascism and racism in all its forms and manifestations, as well as by other causes,

Considering that participation in cultural life takes the form of an assertion of identity, authenticity and dignity; that the integrity of identity is threatened by numerous causes of erosion stemming, in particular, from the prevalence of inappropriate models or of techniques which have not been fully mastered,

Considering that the assertion of cultural identity should not result in the formation of isolated groups but should, on the contrary, go hand in hand with a mutual desire for wide and frequent contacts, and that such contacts are a fundamental requirement without which the objectives of the present recommendation would be unattainable,

Bearing in mind the fundamental part played by general education, cultural education and artistic training, and the use of working time and free time, with a view to full cultural development, in a context of life-long education,

Considering that the mass media can serve as instruments of cultural enrichment, both by opening up unprecedented possibilities of cultural development, in contributing to the liberation of the latent cultural potential of individuals, to the preservation and popularization of traditional forms of culture, and to the creation and dissemination of new forms, and by turning themselves into media for group communication and promoting direct participation by the people,

Considering that the ultimate objective of access and participation is to raise the spiritual and cultural level of society as a whole on the basis of humanistic values and to endow culture with a humanistic and democratic content, and that this in turn implies taking measures against the harmful effect of 'commercial mass culture', which threatens national cultures and the cultural development of mankind, leads to debasement of the personality and exerts a particularly harmful influence on the young generation,

Having before it, as item 28 of the agenda of the session, proposals concerning participation by the people at large in cultural life and their contribution to it,

Having decided at its eighteenth session that this question should be made the subject of an international regulation, to take the form of a recommendation to Member States,

Adopts, this twenty-sixth day of November 1976, the present Recommendation.

The General Conference recommends Member States to

implement the following provisions, taking whatever legislative or other steps may be required—in conformity with the constitutional practice of each State and the nature of the question under consideration—to apply the principles and norms formulated in this Recommendation within their respective territories.

The General Conference recommends Member States to bring this Recommendation to the knowledge of authorities, institutions and organizations which can help to ensure participation by the people at large in cultural life and their contribution to it.

The General Conference recommends Member States to submit to it, at such times and in such manner as it shall determine, reports concerning the action they have taken upon this Recommendation.

## I. Definitions and Scope of the Recommendation

1. This Recommendation concerns everything that should be done by Member States or the authorities to democratize the means and instruments of cultural activity, so as to enable all individuals to participate freely and fully in cultural creation and its benefits, in accordance with the requirements of social progress.

2. For the purposes of the Recommendation:

(a) by access to culture is meant the concrete opportunities available to everyone, in particular through the creation of the appropriate socio-economic conditions, for freely obtaining information, training, knowledge and understanding, and for enjoying cultural values and cultural property;

(b) by participation in cultural life is meant the concrete opportunities guaranteed for all—groups or individuals—to express themselves freely, to communicate, act, and engage in creative activities with a view to the full development of their personalities, a harmonious life and the cultural progress of society;

(c) by communication is meant relations between groups or individuals desirous of freely exchanging or pooling information, ideas and knowledge with a view to promoting dialogue, concerted action, understanding and a sense of community while respecting their originality and their differences, in order to strengthen mutual understanding and peace.

3. For the purposes of the Recommendation:

(a) the concept of culture has been broadened to include all forms of creativity and expression of groups or individuals, both in their ways of life and in their artistic activities;

(b) free democratic access to culture of the people at large presupposes the existence of appropriate economic and social policies;

(c) participation in cultural life presupposes involvement of the different social partners in decision-making related to cultural policy as well as in the conduct and evaluation of activities;

(d) free participation in cultural life is related to:

(1) a development policy for economic growth and social justice;

(2) a policy of life-long education which is geared to the needs and aspirations of all people and makes them aware of their own intellectual potentialities and sensitivity, provides them with cultural education and artistic training, improves their powers of self-expression and stimulates their creativity, thus enabling them more successfully to master social changes and to participate more fully in the community life of society;

(3) a science and technology policy inspired by the resolve to safeguard the cultural identity of the peoples;

(4) a social policy directed towards progress and, more precisely, the attenuation—with a view to their elimination—of the inequalities handicapping certain groups and individuals, especially the least privileged, in regard to their living conditions, their opportunities and the fulfilment of their aspirations;

(5) an environment policy designed, through the planned use of space and the protection of nature, to create a background to living conducive to the full development of individuals and societies;

(6) a communication policy designed to strengthen the free exchange of information, ideas and knowledge, in order to promote mutual understanding, and encouraging to this end the use and extension of both modern and traditional media for cultural purposes;

(7) a policy for international co-operation based on the principle of equality of cultures, mutual respect, understanding and confidence and strengthening of peace.

## II. Legislation and Regulations

4. It is recommended that Member States, if they have not already done so, adopt legislation or regulations in conformity with their national constitutional procedures, or otherwise modify existing practices in order to:

(a) guarantee as human rights those rights bearing on access to and participation in cultural life, in the spirit of the Universal Declaration of Human Rights, of the International Covenant on Economic, Social and Cultural Rights and of the International Covenant on Civil and Political Rights and in accordance with the ideals and objectives set forth in the United Nations Charter and in the Constitution of Unesco;

(b) provide effective safeguards for free access to national and world cultures by all members of society without distinction or discrimination based on race, colour, sex, language, religion, political convictions, national or social origin, financial situation or any other consideration and so to encourage free participation by all sections of the population in the process of creating cultural values;

(c) pay special attention to women's full entitlement to access to culture and to effective participation in cultural life;

(d) promote the development and dissemination of national cultures and the development of international co-operation in order to make the cultural achievements of other peoples better known and to strengthen friendship and mutual understanding;

(e) create appropriate conditions enabling the populations to play an increasingly active part in building the future of their society, to assume responsibilities and duties and exercise rights in that process;

(f) guarantee the recognition of the equality of cultures, including the cultures of national minorities and of foreign minorities if they exist, as forming part of the common heritage of all mankind, and ensure that they are promoted at all levels without discrimination; ensure that national minorities and foreign minorities have full opportunities for gaining access to and participating in the cultural life of the countries in which they find themselves in order to enrich it with their specific contributions, while safeguarding their right to preserve their cultural identity;

(g) protect, safeguard and enhance all forms of cultural expression such as national or regional languages, dialects, folk arts and traditions both past and present, and rural cultures as well as cultures of other social groups;

(h) ensure that the handicapped are integrated in cultural life and have opportunities of contributing to it;

(i) ensure equality of access to education;

(j) guarantee freedom of expression and communication serving to strengthen the ideals of humanism;

(k) bring about conditions conducive to creative work and ensure the freedom of creative artists and the protection of their works and rights;

(l) improve the professional status of the various categories of personnel required for the implementation of cultural policies;

(m) ensure that cultural education and artistic training are given their proper place in the curricula of educational and training establishments, and extend enjoyment of the artistic heritage to the population outside the education system;

(n) multiply opportunities for intellectual, manual or gestural creation and encourage artistic training, experience and expression with a view to bringing about the integration of art and life;

(o) provide the mass media with a status ensuring their independence, due attention being paid to the effective participation of creative artists and the public; these media should not threaten the authenticity of cultures or impair their quality; they ought not to act as instruments of cultural domination but serve mutual understanding and peace;

(p) reconcile the duty to protect and enhance everything connected with the cultural heritage, traditions and the past with the need to allow the endeavours of the present and the modern outlook to find expression;

(q) (1) protect and enhance the heritage of the past, and particularly ancient monuments and traditions which may contribute to the essential equilibrium of societies subject to a rapid process of industrialization and urbanization;

(2) make the public aware of the importance of town-planning and architecture, not only because they are the reflection of cultural and social life, but above all because they condition the very background to living;

(3) associate the population with the conservation and management of the natural environment both at the national and at the international levels, since the quality of the natural environment is essential to the full development of the human personality;

(r) create, through the appropriate bodies, conditions making it possible for work and leisure, each in its own way, to offer opportunities for cultural creation to each and every one, and lay down conditions governing working and leisure hours and the operational organization of cultural institutions which will enable the greatest possible number of people to gain access to culture and participate in cultural life;

(s) reject concepts which, under the guise of cultural action, are based on violence and aggression, domination, contempt and racial prejudice, as well as on debasing ideas or practices;

(t) strengthen their work in support of peace and international understanding, in accordance with the Declaration of the Principles of International Cultural Co-operation and encourage the dissemination of ideas and cultural goods conducive to the strengthening of peace, security and co-operation.

## III. Technical, Administrative, Economic and Financial Measures

5. It is recommended to Member States, if they have not already done so, that they make the necessary technical, administrative and financial resources available to upgrade policies for cultural action from the insignificant position to which they may still be relegated until they reach an operationally effective level enabling them to achieve the goals of life-long education and cultural development and to ensure to the maximum that the people at large have access to culture and participate freely in cultural life. For this purpose Member States should take the following measures:

*A. Ways and Means of Cultural Action. Decentralization of Facilities, Activities and Decisions.* 6. Member States or the appropriate authorities should:

(a) foster decentralization of activities and encourage the development of local centres, special attention being paid to under-populated peripheral or under- privileged areas;

(b) encourage, extend and strengthen the network of cultural and artistic institutions not only in large towns but also in smaller towns, villages and urban neighbourhoods;

(c) encourage the setting up of facilities best suited to the needs of the users and foster the integration of facilities used for cultural activities with those which are designed for social and educational work and which should be mobile to some extent, in order to make available to the widest possible public all the means needed for the heightening of awareness and for cultural development;

(d) encourage the use for cultural purposes of all public facilities that promote communication among groups and individuals;

(e) encourage inter-regional and inter-community exchanges;

(f) stimulate regional or local initiative, both by providing decision-makers with the necessary resources at appropriate levels and by sharing the decision-making function with the representatives of other parties interested in cultural problems; and to this end develop secondary centres for administrative decision-making;

(g) develop methods for the promotion or artistic creation and cultural activity by the people at large, based upon the people's own organizations, in both residential areas and working places;

(h) apply special measures for certain disadvantaged groups and for environments with a poorly developed cultural life. Special attention should be paid to, e.g., children, the handicapped, people living in hospitals and prisons, and people living in remotely situated areas, as well as those in city slums. Decisions and responsibility should, as much as possible, be left with the group participating in the activities.

*Concerted Action.* 7. Member States or the appropriate authorities should encourage concerted action and cooperation both as regards the activities themselves and decision-making:

(a) by paying special attention to creative cultural and artistic non-institutional and non-professional activities and by providing all possible support to amateur activities in all their diversity;

(b) by establishing advisory structures, at the local, regional and national levels, bringing together representatives of the professional and social groups concerned who will participate in determining the objectives and ways and means of cultural action.

*Trade Unions and Other Workers' Organizations.* 8. Member

States or the appropriate authorities should take all such measures as will be of assistance to socio-cultural organizations for the people at large, trade unions and other workers' organizations for wage-earners or the self-employed (farmers, craftsmen, etc.) in freely carrying out their cultural policies or projects so as to enable them to enjoy the whole wealth of cultural values and to take an active part in the cultural life of society.

*"Animation."* 9. Member States or the appropriate authorities should:

(a) contribute to the training of cultural development personnel, in particular of "animateurs", who should act as information, communication and expression intermediaries, by putting people in contact with each other and serving as a connecting link between the public, the work of art, and the artist, and between the public and cultural institutions;

(b) provide such personnel with means of action enabling them, on the one hand, to give support to the spontaneous "animateurs" of local communities and, on the other hand, to stimulate initiative and participation, using the necessary training methods;

(c) encourage the use of instruments and equipment for communication and expression which have education value and offer a potential for creation, by making them available to cultural centres and institutions such as public libraries, museums, etc.

*Artistic Creation.* 10. Member States or other appropriate authorities should:

(a) create social, economic and financial conditions which should provide artists, writers and composers of music with the necessary basis for free creative work;

(b) define, for this purpose, in addition to the legal measures connected with copyright and the protection of works of art:

(1) social measures applying to all professional artists and fiscal measures designed to assist not only collective forms of artistic creation (theatre, cinema, etc.) but also individual artists;

(2) a policy of fellowships, prizes, State commissions, and the engagement of artists, particularly for the construction and decoration of public buildings;

(3) a policy for the dissemination of culture (exhibitions, performances of musical and theatrical works, etc.);

(4) a research policy that offers individual artists, groups and institutions the possibility of carrying out experiments and research in multi-purpose workshops, without feeling obliged to produce successful results, in such a way as to foster an artistic and cultural renewal;

(c) consider establishing funds to provide aid for artistic creation;

(d) encourage the endeavours of all who have a vocation for artistic creation and help young people to develop their talents without any discrimination and strengthen specialized institutions providing professional training in all the arts;

(e) promote opportunities for the publication of high-quality reproductions of artistic works, the publication and translation of literary works and the publication and performance of musical compositions;

(f) associate artists at all levels in the formulation and implementation of cultural policies;

(g) ensure the multiplicity of bodies called upon to assess works of art and the regular renewal of their membership, as well as the multiplicity of sources of finance, so as to safeguard the freedom of creative artists;

(h) give technical, administrative and financial assistance to groups of amateur artists and support co-operation between non-professional and professional artists.

*Cultural Industries.* 11. Member States or the appropriate authorities should make sure that the criterion of profit-making does not exert a decisive influence on cultural activities, and, in drawing up cultural policies, provide for machinery for negotiating with private cultural industries, as well as for supplementary or alternative initiatives.

*Dissemination.* 12. Member States or the appropriate authorities should:

(a) adopt a policy of granting subsidies and awarding prizes for cultural goods and services, and bring about conditions which will ensure that they are disseminated and become accessible to the broadest possible social categories, particularly in cultural fields neglected by commercial enterprises;

(b) take steps by means of a policy of appropriate subsidies and contracts, to further the development of the activities of cultural associations at the national, regional and local levels;

(c) give prominence to a type of dissemination which is conducive to an active frame of mind in the public rather than to passive consumption of cultural products.

*Research.* 13. Member States or the appropriate authorities should foster cultural development research projects which aim, *inter alia,* at evaluating current activities as well as stimulating new experiments and studying their impact on the widest possible audiences, with a view to the possible adoption of fresh measures in connection with cultural policies.

*B. Policies Related to Cultural Action. Communication.* 14. Member States or the appropriate authorities should:

(a) promote all occasions for communication, such as meetings, debates, public performances, group activities, and festivals, for the purpose of encouraging dialogue and a continuous exchange of ideas between individuals, the public, creative artists, "animateurs" and producers;

(b) develop the opportunities for cultural contact and exchange provided by sports events, nature discovery expeditions, art and aesthetic education, current events and tourism;

(c) encourage the usual social intermediaries (communities, institutions, agencies, trade unions, and other groups) to promote information and free cultural expression for their members on the widest possible scale, in order to increase their awareness of and familiarize them with cultural activities;

(d) supply information that is apt to generate feedback and personal initiative;

(e) facilitate access to written works by arranging for mobile and flexible forms of dissemination, and provide for extension work in places such as libraries or reading rooms;

(f) promote extensive use of audio-visual media in order to bring the best of the culture of both past and present within the reach of large sectors of the population, including, where applicable, oral traditions, in the collection of which the media can assuredly assist;

(g) promote the active participation of audiences by enabling them to have a voice in the selection and production of programmes, by fostering the creation of a permanent flow of ideas between the public, artists and producers and by encouraging the establishment of production centres for use by audiences at local and community levels;

(h) encourage the communication media to increase the number and variety of their programmes in order to offer the widest range of choices, bearing in mind the extreme diversity of audiences, to enhance the cultural quality of programmes intended for the public at large, to select spoken and visual languages accessible to all audiences, to give preference to material which serves the purposes of information and education rather than those of propaganda and publicity and to pay special attention to the protection of national cultures from potentially harmful influences of some types of mass production;

(i) promote comparative studies and research on the reciprocal influence as between the artist, the mass media and society and on the relationship between the production and impact of cultural programmes;

(j) provide, with a view to life-long education, an introduction to audio-visual languages as well as to choosing communication media and programmes with discrimination from an early age;

(k) develop, in a general way, forms of education and training which are adapted to the special characteristics of audiences in order to make them capable of receiving, selecting and grasping the mass of information which is put into circulation in modern societies.

*Education.* 15. Member States or the appropriate authorities should:

(a) link cultural plans systematically with educational plans within the context of life-long education embracing the family, the school, community life, vocational training, continuing education and cultural activity;

(b) help people at large to gain access to knowledge, bearing in mind the need to create socio-economic conditions such as will allow them to participate in community life, and make whatever changes may be required in educational systems, content and methods;

(c) develop, in a systematic manner, cultural education and artistic training programmes at all levels by inviting contributions from artists and those responsible for cultural action.

*Youth.* 16. Member States or the appropriate authorities should offer young people a wide range of cultural activities which correspond to their needs and aspirations, encourage them to acquire a sense of social responsibility, awaken their interests in the cultural heritage of their own country and in that of all mankind and, with a view to cultural co-operation in a spirit of friendship, international understanding and peace, promote the ideals of humanism and respect for widely recognized educational and moral principles.

*Environment.* 17. Member States or the appropriate authorities should:

(a) set up machinery for concerted action allowing the inhabitants or their representatives to be closely associated with the preparation and implementation of town- planning projects and changes to the architectural setting in which they live, and also with the safeguarding of historic quarters, towns and sites and their integration into a modern environment;

(b) take into consideration the international instruments adopted on such issues by intergovernmental organizations.

## IV. International Co-operation

18. Member States or the appropriate authorities should:

(a) strengthen bilateral and multilateral, and regional and international cultural co-operation with due regard for the generally recognized principles of international law and the ideals and objectives of the United Nations, sovereignty and independence of States, mutual advantage, and the equality of cultures;

(b) inspire in the people at large respect for other peoples and a refusal to countenance acts of international violence and policies based on force, domination and aggression;

(c) encourage the circulation of ideas and cultural values conducive to better understanding among men;

(d) develop and diversify cultural exchanges with a view to promoting an ever deeper appreciation of the values of each culture and, in particular, draw attention to the cultures of the developing countries as a mark of esteem for their cultural identity;

(e) contribute actively to the implementation of cultural projects and to the production and dissemination of works created by common endeavours, and develop direct contacts and exchanges between institutions and persons active in the cultural field, as well as research on cultural development;

(f) encourage non-governmental organizations, socio-cultural organizations for the people at large, trade unions and social and occupational groups, women's associations, youth movements, co-operatives and other organizations (for instance, artists' associations) to participate in international cultural exchanges and their development;

(g) take account, in exchanges of persons, of the mutual enrichment resulting from co-operation between specialists from different countries;

(h) bear in mind that the need for introductory courses and information on culture is all the greater when the aim is to arouse interest in the civilizations and cultures of other nations in order to open men's minds to the recognition of the plurality and equality of cultures;

(i) ensure that the messages chosen are inserted or reinserted into a universal context so that opportunities for access to culture may have significance for the whole international community;

(j) take account of the important contribution that the press, books, audio-visual media, and in particular television, can make to the mutual understanding of nations and to their knowledge of the cultural achievements of other nations; encourage the use of communication media, including tele-communication satellites, to promote the ideals of peace, human rights and fundamental freedoms, friendship among men and international understanding and co-operation, and thus create the necessary conditions to enable their national cultures to resist ideas of hatred between peoples, war, force and racism, in view of their adverse consequences and their corruptive effect on young people;

(k) provide appropriate financial facilities for activities which aim at promoting international exchanges and cultural co-operation.

## V. Federal or Confederate States

19. In the implementation of this Recommendation, Member States with a federal or confederate constitution shall not be bound to carry the provisions of the Recommendation into effect when competence for the latter is constitutionally vested in each of the constituent states, provinces or cantons; in such a case, the sole obligation of the federal or confederate government concerned shall be to inform the states, provinces or cantons of those provisions and to recommend their adoption.

The foregoing is the authentic text of the Recommendation duly adopted by the General Conference of the United Nations Educational, Scientific and Cultural Organization during its nineteenth session, which was held in Nairobi, and declared closed the thirtieth day of November 1976.

In faith whereof we have appended our signatures.

**CYPRUS.** The Republic of Cyprus is a non-Arab country of western Asia, occupying an island in the eastern Mediterranean, 40 miles south of Turkey and 60 miles west of Syria. It achieved independence from Great Britain in 1960 and became a member of the United Nations the same year. Its population is estimated to be 527,000. Ethnic groups include persons of Greek origin (80%) and of Turkish origin (18%); the remaining 2% includes Armenians, Latins, Maronites, and others. Languages in common use include Greek and Turkish (both official) and English. Religions practiced include Christianity (Greek Orthodox, 75%; Roman Catholic, 3%; other faiths, 2%), and Islam (20%). Literacy is estimated at 90%.

The government (1994) took the form of a republic. Under the 1960 constitution, the President is of Greek origin and the Vice President of Turkish origin; they are elected by the Greek and Turkish communities, respectively. Legislative authority is exercised by the House of Representatives, members of which also are elected by each community separately: 70% Greek Cypriotes and 30% Turkish Cypriotes. Each community is entitled to a communal chamber; however, the Greek communal chamber was abolished in 1965, while the Turkish communal chamber continued to function. Turkish members of the House of Representatives did not attend its sessions after 1974.

*UNITED NATIONS PEACE-KEEPING FORCE IN CYPRUS (UNFICYP).* When Cyprus became independent on 16 August 1960, the Constitution was intended to balance the interests of the island's Greek Cypriot and Turkish Cypriot communities. The application of the provisions of the constitution, however, encountered difficulties from the beginning and led to a succession of constitutional crises and the eventual outbreak of violence between the two communities in December 1963. On 4 March 1964, the UN Security Council established UNFICYP (resolution 186/1964), with a mandate to prevent a recurrence of fighting and, as necessary, to contribute to the maintenance and restoration of law and order. Since that time, the council has extended UNFICYP's mandate, usually for periods of six months at a time.

As of May 1994, UNFICYP was composed of 1,200 troops and support personnel, 12 military observers, and 35 civilian police. The Force has suffered 165 casualties since its inception.

*INVASION BY TURKEY.* Since 1974, when the Cypriot National Guard, favoring a union with Greece, ousted the President, Cyprus has been torn by communal tensions. The invasion of Cyprus by Turkey on 20 July 1974, explained as a necessity to protect the Turkish Cypriot minority, led to Turkish control of 40% of the island. Proclamation by Turkish Cypriot

authorities of a "Turkish Republic of Northern Cyprus" was declared to be invalid by the UN Security Council, which requested the UN Secretary-General to use his good offices to achieve progress towards a settlement of the problem: the UN Peacekeeping Force for Cyprus has been established on the island since 1974. Despite not being internationally recognized, "North Cyprus" maintains a separate government with a Prime Minister and a President. The partition of the island runs east-west, dividing Nicosia, which is considered the capital of both sectors.

In 1975, the UN **COMMISSION ON HUMAN RIGHTS** called on all parties concerned to undertake measures to facilitate the voluntary return of all refugees to their homes in safety and to settle all other aspects of the refugee problem. The UN General Assembly requested the Secretary-General to exert every effort, in cooperation with the International Committee of the Red Cross, to assist in tracing and accounting for missing persons. The Secretary-General accordingly established the Committee on Missing Persons in Cyprus, which has since been engaged in investigating 168 individual cases on which it decided to concentrate its efforts.

In recent years, the Secretary-General has reported annually to the Commission on Human Rights concerning human rights in Cyprus and to the Security Council on the overall situation in that country.

In resolution 1987/50, the Commission on Human Rights again called for the full restoration of all human rights to the populations of Cyprus, in particular to refugees; considered attempts to settle any part of Varosha by people other than its inhabitants as illegal; called for the tracing of and accounting for missing persons without delay; and called for the restoration of all fundamental freedoms to all Cypriots, including the freedom of movement, the freedom of settlement, and the right to property.

The Security Council, for its part, since 1974, has attempted to promote an overall agreement between the Governments of Greece and Turkey, reaffirming its position that the existing status quo is not acceptable. To facilitate such an agreement, the Council urged all concerned to commit themselves to the following "confidence-building" measures:

(a) that, as a first step towards the withdrawal of non-Cypriot forces, the number of foreign troops in Cyprus be reduced significantly and that Cyprus itself reduce its defense-spending;

(b) that the military authorities on each side cooperate with the UN Peacekeeping Force in Cyprus to extend the unmanning agreement of 1989 to all nearby areas;

(c) that, to implement resolution 550 of 1984, the area presently controlled by the UN Peacekeeping Force be extended to include Varosha;

(d) that each side actively promote people-to-people contact between the Greek and Turkish communities by reducing restrictions on the movement of persons across the Buffer Zone;

(e) that restrictions imposed on foreign visitors crossing the Buffer Zone be reduced;

(f) that each side propose bicommunal projects;

(g) that both sides commit themselves to a Cyprus-wide census under the UN auspices;

(h) that both sides cooperate with the United Nations in undertaking feasibility studies (i) regarding resettlement and rehabilitation of persons who would be affected by territorial adjustments as part of the overall agreement, and (ii) regarding the program of economic development to benefit those who would resettle in the area under Turkish Cypriot administration.

**BIBLIOGRAPHY.** Amnesty International. *Cyprus: A Summary of Amnesty International's Concerns.* London: 1994. NGO report, in English.

Iliopoulos-Strangas, Julia, ed. *Human Rights in Occupied Cyprus and in Albania.* Athens, Greece: Ant. N. Sakkoulas Publications for the Marangopoulos Foundation for Human Rights, 1990. NGO report, in English and Greek.

Lassen, Nina, and Jacob Gammelgaard. *Report on the Danish Refugee Council's Mission to Cyprus and Lebanon.* Copenhagen, Denmark: Danish Refugee Council, 1991. Factfinding report, in English.

Rossides, Eugene Y. "Cyprus and the Rule of Law," *Syracuse Journal of International Law and Commerce* 17, no. 1 (1991): 21–90. Scholarly article, in English.

**CZECH REPUBLIC.** The Czech Republic occupies the western two-thirds of the former Czechoslovakia, and came into existence as the result of its separation from Slovakia on 1 January 1993. It is a landlocked country in eastern Europe, having borders with Austria, Germany, Poland, and Slovakia. Its population is estimated to be 10,335,000. Vaclav Havel, who served as president of Czechoslovakia from December 1989 to July 1992 (and who resigned when he became convinced that the country would not continue as a united federal State), was elected president of the Czech Republic on 26 January 1993 by its Parliament.

Although Czechoslovakia prospered after freeing itself from its Austrian rulers and was well-governed by its first presidents, T.G. Masaryk and Eduard Benes, it experienced serious political difficulties because of the presence within its borders of several antagonistic national minorities. A European crisis developed when the German minority, led by Konrad Henlein and backed by Adolph Hitler, demanded union of the country's predominantly German districts with Germany. Under threat of war, Hitler was given the Bohemian borderlands (Sudetenland) by the Munich Pact of September 1938.

During World War II, a provisional Czech government was set up in England, and Czech units fought against Nazi Germany. In April 1944, Russian and American forces moved into Czechoslovakia; and, in May 1945, European military operations ended with the fall of Prague. The Potsdam Conference of 1945 approved the expulsion of 3,000,000 Germans from Czechoslovakia, as well as an exchange of national minorities between Czechoslovakia and Hungary. It was announced in March 1994 that nearly 20,000 Czechs who had been detained or imprisoned during the Nazi occupation will receive $33.7 million in restitution.

In the elections of 1946, the Communist Party emerged as the strongest political group. With Benes as President, a six-party coalition cabinet was formed with Clement Gottwald, head of the party, as Premier. In February 1948, communist elements seized complete control of the State in a coup d'etat. Shortly thereafter, Benes resigned and Gottwald assumed the office of President. A new constitution was adopted which provided a measure of autonomy for Slovakia. Under its provisions, nearly every branch of Czech economic life was nationalized.

*THE PRAGUE SPRING.* In 1968, a liberalization movement spread across Czechoslovakia. Antonin Novotny, the longtime Stalinist ruler of the country, was deposed as party leader and succeeded by Alexander Dubcek, a Slovak, who declared that he intended to make Communism democratic. On 22 March, Novotny resigned as President and was succeeded by Gen. Ludvik Svoboda. On April 6, Premier Joseph Lenart resigned and was succeeded by Oldrich Cernik, who pledged to carry out democratization and economic reforms.

Unfortunately, the movement toward democracy was short-lived. In August 1968, Soviet, Polish, East German, Hungarian, and Bulgarian troops invaded Czechoslovakia to put an end to the reforms. Czech citizens demonstrated and even rioted, but to no avail: press censorship followed and old-line Communists were installed in office.

In April 1969, Dubcek resigned as leader of the Communist Party and was replaced by Gustav Husak. In January 1970, Premier Cernik was ousted. Censorship was tightened, and the Communist Party expelled one-third of its members. The reform movement was dead for all practical purposes, but it was resurrected less than ten years later.

*CHARTER 77.* Czechoslovakia's transition to a multiparty political system may be said to have started in January 1977, when some 1,000 Czech "dissidents" signed a declaration of human rights known as Charter 77, based on provisions of the International Covenants on Human Rights and designed to enable all citizens "to live and work as free people." The text of Charter 77 is as follows:

On 13 October 1976 the Collection of Laws of the C.S.S.R. (No. 120) published the "International Covenant on Civil and Political Rights" and the "International Covenant on Economic, Social and Cultural Rights" which had been signed in the name of our Republic in 1968, confirmed in

Helsinki in 1975, and which acquired validity here on 23 March 1976. From that day our citizens have the right, and our State the duty, to be guided by them.

The rights and freedoms of everyone, which are guaranteed by these Covenants, are important values of civilization for which the efforts of many progressive forces have been directed in history, and their statement in law can significantly assist human development in our society.

We therefore welcome the fact that the Czechoslovak Socialist Republic has ratified these Covenants.

Their publication, however, reminds us with new urgency how many fundamental civil rights remain, unfortunately, only on paper in our country. Countless citizens have to live in fear that, if they were to express themselves in accordance with their convictions, they or their children could be denied the right to education.

Exercising the right "to seek, receive and impart information and ideas of all kinds, regardless of frontiers, either orally, in writing or in print" or "in the form of art" (Article 19 [2] of the Covenant on Civil and Political Rights) is attacked not only extra-judicially, but also judicially, often in the guise of criminal prosecution (witness to this are, for example, the trials of young musicians now proceeding).

Freedom of expression is suppressed by the central control over all communications media and publishing and cultural facilities. No political, philosophical, scientific or artistic expression which however slightly deviates from the official ideological or aesthetic bounds can be published; public criticism of crisis symptoms in society is barred; there is no opportunity for public defense against false and offensive accusations by official propaganda (the legal protection against "attacks on honor and reputation," explicitly guaranteed by article 17 of the Covenant on Civil and Political Rights, does not exist in practice); false accusations cannot be refuted and every attempt to get restitution through the courts is in vain; open debate in the area of intellectual and cultural work is excluded. Many scholars and cultural workers and other citizens are discriminated against merely because in earlier years they legally or openly voiced opinions which are condemned by the present political power.

The right to thought, conscience and religion, explicitly guaranteed by article 18 of the Covenant on Civil and Political Rights, is systematically restricted by arbitrary authority: by curtailing the activities of priests, who are permanently threatened by the possibility that State consent to the performance of their office may be refused or withdrawn; by job or other sanctions against those who express their religious beliefs in word or deed; by suppressing religious teaching, etc.

As an instrument for restricting, and often completely suppressing, many civil rights we have the system whereby, in effect, all institutions and organizations of state are subordinated to the political directives from the apparatus of the ruling party and to the decisions of individuals influential in the power structure. The Constitution of the C.S.S.R. and the other laws and legal norms give no authority either for the content and form, nor for the making and application of such decisions; they are often purely verbal, entirely unknown to citizens, and uncontrollable by them; their originators are responsible to none but themselves and their hierarchy, yet they exert a decisive influence on the legislative and executive organs of state administration, the judiciary, the trade unions, organizations around special interests and other public organizations, other political parties, enterprises, factories institutes, offices, and other establishments, and their orders take precedence over the law. When an organization or individual comes into conflict with such an order in their interpretation of their rights and duties, they cannot turn to an impartial institution. All this gravely limits enjoyment of the rights deriving from articles 21 and 22 of the Covenant (the right to freedom of association and the prohibition of any restriction on the exercise of that right) and from article 25 (the equal right of everyone to take part in the conduct of public affairs), and 26 (prohibiting any discrimination before the law). The present situation also prevents workers and other employees from forming and joining the trade unions of their choice for the promotion and protection of their economic and social interests and from exercising the right to strike (article 8, para. 1 of the International Covenant on Economic, Social and Cultural Rights).

Other civil rights, including the explicit prohibition of "arbitrary or unlawful interference with privacy, family, home or correspondence" (article 17 of the Covenant on Civil and Political Rights), are also gravely infringed by the many ways in which the Ministry of the Interior controls citizens' lives, for instance by tapping telephones, by installing listening devices in homes, by checking on mail, by personal surveillance, by house searches, or by forming a network of informers from among the public (often won over by impermissable threats or promises), etc. The Ministry also frequently intervenes in employers' decisions, inspires discriminatory actions by official bodies and organizations, or campaigns in the media. This activity is not regulated by law; it is secret and the public has no defence against it.

In cases of politically motivated prosecution, the examining and judicial organs infringe the rights of the accused and of their defence, although these are guaranteed by article 14 of the International Covenant on Civil and Political Rights. People convicted in this manner are treated in prison in a way which denies them their human dignity, endangers their health and attempts to break them morally.

There is also a general infringement of paragraph 2 of article 2 of the Covenant on Civil and Political Rights, which guarantees the right of everyone to leave any country, including his own; under the pretext of "national security," mentioned in paragraph 3 of that article, the exercise of this right is tied to various impermissible conditions. Arbitrary procedure is also employed in issuing entry visas to foreign nationals, many of whom are unable to visit Czechoslovakia merely because they have had working or friendly contacts with people who are discriminated against here.

Some citizens call attention to the constant infringement of human rights and democratic freedoms—either privately at their places of work, or publicly, which is possible in practice only through the foreign media—and demand remedy in concrete cases; but their voices usually get no response, or they become the subjects of investigation.

The responsibility for maintaining civil rights in the land belongs, of course, to the political and State power. But not to it alone. Everyone bears his share of responsibility for public matters, and hence also for the observance of treaties valid in law, which are, in any case, binding not only upon governments but also on all citizens.

The sense of this responsibility, the belief in the meaning of citizens' commitment, the will for it, and the common need to seek a new and more effective expression of it, has led us to think of drawing up Charter 77, the origin of which we are publicly announcing today.

Charter 77 is a free, informal and open association of people of varied opinions, varied beliefs and professions, who are united by the will individually and jointly to work for the respecting of civil and human rights in our country and in the world—rights recognized for all men in both International Covenants on Human Rights, in the Final Act of the Helsinki Conference, in various other international documents against war, force and social and spiritual oppression, and which above all are set out in the Universal Declaration of Human Rights.

Charter 77 is rooted in the solidarity and friendship of people who share a concern for the ideals which they have seen, and still see, as part of their lives and work.

Charter 77 is not an organisation, it has no status, no permanent bodies or formally organised membership. Anyone who agrees with its ideas, takes part in its work, and supports it, belongs to it.

Charter 77 is not a basis for activity as a political opposition. It aims to serve the general interest as do many similar initiatives by citizens in various countries in the West and the East. Thus it is not intended to put forward its own programs of political or social reform or changes, but to conduct in its sphere a constructive dialogue with the political and State power, especially by calling attention to various cases where human and civil rights are infringed, to propose solutions, submit more general proposals aimed at strengthening these rights and their guarantees, to act as an intermediary in possible conflict situations which may be caused by the lack of political rights, etc.

By its symbolical name Charter 77 stresses its origin on the threshold of a year declared as the Year of Political Prisoners, and in which the Belgrade conference is to examine how the Helsinki undertakings have been implemented.

As signatories to this declaration, we empower Prof. Dr. Jan Patocka, Dr. H.C. Vaclav Havel and Prof. Jiri Hajek DrSc to be spokesmen for Charter 77. These spokesmen are authorized to represent the Charter both in relation to State and other organisations, and to the public here and abroad, and they guarantee by their signatures the authenticity of the documents. In us, and in other citizens who join in, they will have their associates who will take part with them in any necessary negotiations, will undertake specific tasks and will share all responsibility with them.

We believe that Charter 77 will contribute to enabling all Czechoslovak citizens to live and work as free people.

## RISE OF DEMOCRACY.

Charter 77, and the loose organization that supported it, led the Czech government to tighten restrictions on the exercise of civil and political rights. Nevertheless, it gained strength over the years; and, in October 1989, Milos Jakes, chairman of the Communist Party of Czechoslovakia, found it necessary to send heavily armed police to crush a demonstration by some 10,000 people shouting "Freedom!" and "We want democracy!" after the arrest of Vaclav Havel, one of the originators of Charter 77, and other leading dissidents.

Demonstrators again thronged into the streets of Prague on 17 November after Mr. Jakes had asserted that such protests would not be tolerated and were brutally dispersed by the police. Two days later, they returned to protest the police actions, and elements of opposition formed an organization known as the Civic Forum to demand reforms.

On 24 November, Milos Jakes resigned; and, on 29 November, Parliament stripped the Czech constitution of the provision giving the Communist Party the dominant role in society. On 10 December, Czechoslovakia's first cabinet in 41 years without a Communist majority was sworn in.

On 28 December, Alexander Dubcek, who had led the ill-fated "Prague Spring" liberalization movement of 1968, was elected chairman of the Parliament. And on the next day, Vaclav Havel, playright and spokesman for Charter 77, was elected president of Czechoslovakia.

In the first half of 1994, the Czech Republic requested membership in NATO and became an associate member of the European Union, along with nine other eastern European nations.

**BIBLIOGRAPHY.** Bugajski, Janusz. *Czechoslovakia: Charter 77's Decade of Dissent.* New York: Praeger and the Center for Strategic and International Studies, 1987. Scholarly monograph, in English.

Commission on Security and Cooperation in Europe. *Human Rights in Czechoslovakia: The Documents of Charter 77 (1982–1987).* Washington, D.C.: U.S. Government Printing Office, 1988. Government document collection, in English.

Heneka, A., F. Janouch, V. Precan, and J. Vladislav, eds. *Besieged Culture: Czechoslovakia Ten Years after Helsinki.* Stockholm: Charter 77 Foundation and the International Helsinki Federation for Human Rights, 1985. NGO edited collection, in English.

Human Rights Watch. "The Czech Republic," in *Human Rights Watch World Report 1995*, pp. 203–205. New York: 1995. NGO report, in English.

International League for Human Rights. *Human Rights in Czechoslovakia: Comments on the Czechoslovak Government's Official Report to the Committee on the Elimination of Racial Discrimination.* New York: 1987. NGO report, in English.

Pehe, Jiri. "The Prague Spring—in 1988," *Freedom at Issue* 102 (May–June 1988): 17–23. NGO article, in English.

Plichtová, Jana, ed. *Minorities in Politics—Cultural and Languages Rights: Proceeding from International Symposium on Minorities in Central Europe.* Bratislava, Czechoslovakia: Czechoslovak Committee in the European Cultural Foundation, 1992. Conference report, in English.

Radio Free Europe/Radio Liberty. "Charter 77," *Radio Free Europe Research* Special Report No. 1 (17 January 1987): 1–21. Government report, in English.

———. "Charter 77 Document on Conditions in Prisons," *Radio Free Europe Research* 12, no. 36 (11 September 1987): 31–33. Government article, in English.

———. "Charter 77 on the Federal Assembly Elections," *Radio Free Europe Research* 11, no. 23 (6 June 1986): 21. Government report, in English.

———. "Eastern Europe in 1988," *Radio Free Europe Research* 13, no. 52 (30 December 1988): 1–53. Government background paper, in English.

Ulc, Otto. "Integration of the Gypsies in Czechoslovakia," in *Ethnic Groups*, vol. 9, pp. 107–117. London: Gordon and Breach Science Publishers, 1991. Scholarly article in a collection, in English.

U.S. Helsinki Watch Committee. *Ten Years of Charter 77.* New York: 1986. NGO book, in English.

———. *Struggling for Ethnic Identity: Czechoslovakia's Endangered Gypsies.* New York: 1992. NGO report, in English.

U.S. Helsinki Watch Committee/Physicians for Human Rights. *Medical Mission to Czechoslovakia.* New York: 1988. NGO report, in English.

# D

DALAI LAMA (1935–). Religious leader of the Tibetan people and recipient of the **NOBEL PEACE PRIZE** in 1989, Tensin Gymatsho was born in Taktser, Tibet. He is revered as the 14th reincarnation of the Bodhisattva Avalokiteshavara, the Dalai Lama. The Dalai Lama ruled Tibet as a child, from the age of 5; he fled his native country in 1959 after its invasion by the Chinese. Since his exile, he has traveled throughout the world in an effort to restore self-determination to Tibet.

The Chinese have historically considered Tibet to be a part of their territory and held sway over the province for centuries. However, in 1912, the 13th Dalai Lama declared Tibet independent and expelled all Chinese residents. In 1950, after the Communist victory in the Chinese civil war, Mao Tse-Tung's armies invaded Tibet, resulting in the 17-year-old Dalai Lama's escape into India and the eventual signing of the "Seventeen-Point Peace Treaty," which stated that Tibet was an official province of China. On his return from India, the young leader began years of negotiation with the Chinese to ease the tensions between the two peoples. However, his efforts met with no success. Guerrilla warfare broke out in the late 1950s; and in 1959, the Dalai Lama fled his native land for a second time, at the urging of his people and Tibetan officials who feared for his personal safety. He received diplomatic asylum from India. The Chinese set the Panchen Lama, the second-ranking Tibetan figure, in his place but deposed that rule in 1964 and established the Tibet Autonomous Region, governed by ethnic Chinese.

Since that time, the Dalai Lama has traveled over the world in an effort to make known the trials of the Tibetan people. In 1962, he published *My Land and My People,* which detailed the Tibetan culture and struggle for independence. In addition, in that same year, the Dalai Lama's cabinet-in-exile proclaimed a new Tibetan constitution. In the late 1970s and throughout the 1980s, the Dalai Lama visited both the Union of Soviet Socialist Republics and the United States. With the death of Mao Tse-Tung and the fall of the "Gang of Four" in China, negotiations reopened over the sovereignty of Tibet and the return of the Dalai Lama. He has publicly stated, however, that he will not return to his homeland until his people call him—when they tell him that conditions have improved.

In citing him for the Peace Prize, the Nobel Selection Committee recognized his "nonviolent campaign to end China's long domination of his homeland" and praised his advocacy of "a peaceful solution based upon tolerance and mutual respect to preserve the historical and cultural heritage of his people."

***BIBLIOGRAPHY.*** *Current Biography 1982,* pp. 78–92. New York: W. H. Wilson.

Schlessinger, Bernard S., and June H. Schlessinger, eds. *Who's Who of Nobel Prize Winners.* Phoenix, AZ, USA: Oryx Press, 1991.

DAWES, CHARLES (1865–1951). Co-winner of the 1925 **NOBEL PEACE PRIZE,** this American vice president (under Calvin Coolidge) was born in Marietta; was graduated from Marietta College with a B.A. and an M.A.; and received a law degree from the University of Cincinnati Law School. But his greatest successes came not as a lawyer but as a businessman, banker, and financier. Because of his reputation and business acumen, Dawes was appointed the first director of the U.S. Bureau of the Budget.

After World War I, a continuing international financial problem was that of the monetary reparations owed by Germany. In 1923, Dawes chaired the Allied Reparations Committee, which had the job of solving the reparations problem without endangering European fiscal stability. The solution was the Dawes Plan; this plan combined loans from the allies to restore German industry. Although not a lasting solution, the plan relieved the financial strain under which Germany labored. It was for this resolution that Dawes received the Nobel Peace Prize. He donated his award money to the Johns Hopkins University School of International Relations.

After serving as vice president of the United States, Dawes continued in public office, serving as the American ambassador to Great Britain (1929–1932), and, during the Great Depression, as head of the Reconstruction Finance Corporation.

In addition to the Nobel Peace Prize, Dawes received other international recognition throughout his career: he was awarded the U.S. Distinguished Service Medal; made a Companion of the Bath (England), a Commander of S.S. Maurice and Lazarus (Italy), and a Commander of the Legion d'Honneur (France); and inducted into the Order of Leopold (Belgium).

***BIBLIOGRAPHY.*** Gray, Tony. *Champions of Peace.* London: Paddington Press, 1976.

Schlessinger, Bernard S., and June H. Schlessinger, eds. *Who's Who of Nobel Prize Winners.* Phoenix, AZ, USA: Oryx Press, 1991.

**DEBT BONDAGE.** A practice giving rise to effects similar to those of slavery or the slave trade, defined in the Supplementary Convention on the Abolition of Slavery, the Slave Trade and Institutions and Practices Similar to Slavery (article 1 [a]) as "the status or condition arising from a pledge by a debtor of his personal services or of those of a person under his control as security for debt, if the value of those services as reasonably assessed is not applied towards the liquidation of the debt or the length and nature of those services are not respectively limited and defined."

In 1981 a report entitled "Study on the Exploitation of Child Labor" was prepared by Mr. A. Boudhiba, Special Rapporteur of the UN **SUB-COMMISSION ON PREVENTION OF DISCRIMINATION AND PROTECTION OF MINORITIES** (UN publication, Sales no. E.82.XIV.2), in which the author mentioned debt bondage as one of the principal mechanisms for the exploitation of workers, including children, but did not discuss the question in detail.

However, the attention of the Sub-Commission's Working Group on Contemporary Forms of Slavery was drawn to the continuing existence of debt bondage at its 1993 session by representatives of **ANTI-SLAVERY INTERNATIONAL,** a non-governmental organization. Statements of these representatives are summarized in the Working Group's report as follows (UN Doc. C/EN.4/Sub.2/1993/30, paras. 47, 51–53):

[Brazil] 47. The representative of Anti-Slavery International made a statement concerning debt bondage in Brazil, citing it as the main mechanism of forced labour in that country. The practice was said to be prevalent in certain branches of economic activity in the Amazon region. Many of the labourers were coerced into their situations through fraud, and many of the victims came from areas hit by recession or drought. Intimidation and physical force were used frequently to inhibit workers from leaving. Their wages were often used to pay for transportation, tools, and food. That system left them in a cycle of debt. It was noted that figures regarding the pervasiveness of the practice might be inaccurate owing to the limited number of reported cases and a lack of systematic official monitoring. The following recommendations were proposed by Anti-Slavery International as short-term measures to address that situation:

(a) Enterprises should be held responsible for the conditions and fate of labourers working for them. Enterprises found to have used slave labour should be disqualified from fiscal incentives and government credit schemes; indeed, there are already legal provisions covering expropriation of land under the 1988 [Brazilian] Constitution;

(b) As seasonal labour flows are predictable, considerably more could be done to monitor the exodus of workers from one side of the country to another. In addition to strengthening the resolve of highway police and regional labour inspectorates, trade unions, local councils, human rights organizations, and State representatives could play a role in registering and keeping track of workers migrating for work;

(c) The use of intermediaries in contracting labour is open to abuse and could lead to illegal forms of recruitment. Ways should be found to regulate and control those practices. . . .

[Nepal] 51. A representative of Anti-Slavery International made a statement concerning bonded labour in Nepal, where the organizations's reports estimated that there are as many as 100,000 families of bonded labourers. Bonded labourers with a one-year, verbal contract are known as kamaiyas. A large proportion of these labourers are Tharu, the indigenous people of Nepal. Fifty percent [50%] of all Tharus are kamaiyas. The standard terms of their employment are the following:

(a) A fixed amount of food, land, cash, or other goods is paid to the kamaiya by the employer or master, usually too little for the kamaiya and his family to live on for one year;

(b) The possibility exists for the master to fine the kamaiya up to RS.54 (US$1) per day in the case of absence. He could also be fined for loss or damage of tools;

(c) The wife and children of the kamaiya work for the same master without additional payment; the family is the labour unit.

52. If the master does not fulfil his contractual duties or abuses the kamaiya, the contract could not be ended before the end of the year. Women in kamaiya families are often victims of sexual harassment by the masters. Although kamaiyas are officially able to look for new masters at the end of the year, a system of loans keeps labourers in debt and bondage. Because they borrowed the money from their masters, they must remain in their servitude until the loan is paid back. The bondage to the master could be lifelong and sometimes generations long.

[Pakistan] 53. Another representative of Anti-Slavery International spoke on the subject of bonded labour in Pakistan. He raised the issue of the ongoing system of feudalism and its influence on the Pakistani Government and media. He stated that feudal landlords engage in the purchasing and selling of slaves. [The landlords] are extremely powerful and have the right to rule over their labourers. Bonded labourers are found in such industries and activities as carpet-making, the textile industry, coal mining, brickmaking, and camel racing. The workers are sometimes subjected to sexual abuse as well. The representative stated that the central Government of Pakistan is running carpet and handicraft centres in which children are employed under the same harsh conditions found elsewhere. Regarding that issue, the following recommendations were made:

(a) The United Nations should appoint a special rapporteur on bonded labour and child labour;

(b) The ILO Program of Action against Child Bondage,

adopted at Islamabad in November 1992, should be implemented in South Asia; drastic steps have to be taken;

(c) September 18 should be declared an international day for the abolition/elimination of the bonded labour system, as has already been done in South Asia;

(d) The United Nations should draw up an international syllabus, based on the Human Rights Charter for students of all ages;

(e) Arrangements should be made for legal aid for workers and free and compulsory education for all children up to the age of 18;

(f) There should be an international campaign for consumers not to buy carpet and other articles made by children;

(g) Every country should have a law prohibiting the import of articles made by children or bonded labour.

On the recommendation of the Working Group and of the Sub-Commission, the UN **COMMISSION ON HUMAN RIGHTS** authorized the Sub-Commission to appoint a Special Rapporteur to update the report of Mr. Boudhiba and to extend that study to the problem of debt bondage (decision 1993/112 of 10 March 1993).

**SEE ALSO** *Forced Labor; Slavery and the Slave Trade.*

**BIBLIOGRAPHY.** Cross, Peter. *Kashmiri Carpet Children: Exploited Village Weavers.* London: Anti-Slavery International, 1991. NGO monograph, in English.

Mendelsohn, Oliver. "Life and Struggles in the Stone Quarries of India: A Case-Study," *Journal of Commonwealth & Comparative Politics* 29, no. 1 (1991): 44. Scholarly article, in English.

Sinha, Arun. *Against the Few: Struggles of India's Rural Poor.* London: Zed Books, 1991. Scholarly monograph, in English.

United Nations Sub-Commission on Prevention of Discrimination and Protection of Minorities. *Report of the Working Group on Contemporary Forms of Slavery on Its Sixteenth Session.* Geneva, Switzerland: 1991. Intergovernmental study, in English and French.

## DECLARATION BY UNITED NATIONS (1942).

On 1 January 1942, the representatives of 26 nations fighting against the Axis aggressors signed, in Washington, D.C., a document entitled "Declaration by United Nations." This is the first landmark in the evolution of the United Nations. The text of the declaration (U.S. Department of State Bulletin, 3 January 1942, p. 3) is as follows:

The Governments signatory hereto,

Having subscribed to a common program of purposes and principles embodied in the Joint Declaration of the President of the United States of America and the Prime Minister of the United Kingdom of Great Britain and Northern Ireland dated 14 August, 1941, known as the Atlantic Charter,

Being convinced that complete victory over their enemies is essential to defend life, liberty, independence and religious freedom, and to preserve human rights and justice in their own lands as well as in other lands, and that they are now engaged in a common struggle against savage and brutal forces seeking to subjugate the world,

Declare:

(1) Each Government pledges itself to employ its full resources, military or economic, against those members of the Tripartite Pact and its adherents with which such government is at war.

(2) Each Government pledges itself to co-operate with the Governments signatory hereto and not to make a separate armistice or peace with the enemies.

The foregoing declaration may be adhered to by other nations which are, or which may be, rendering material assistance and contributions in the struggle for victory over Hitlerism.

Done at Washington, January First, 1942.

The original signatories of the Declaration were the United States, United Kingdom, Union of Soviet Socialist Republics, China, Australia, Belgium, Canada, Costa Rica, Cuba, Czechoslovakia, the Dominican Republic, El Salvador, Greece, Guatemala, Haiti, Honduras, India, Luxembourg, the Netherlands, New Zealand, Nicaragua, Norway, Panama, Poland, South Africa, and Yugoslavia. Later, 21 additional nations communicated their adherence to the Declaration.

## DEFENSE FOR CHILDREN INTERNATIONAL.

An international non-governmental organization in consultative status (Roster) with the UN **ECONOMIC AND SOCIAL COUNCIL** and the **COUNCIL OF EUROPE,** Defense for Children International was founded in Geneva, Switzerland, as one of the initiatives of the International Year of the Child (1979). DCI has grown to encompass 38 affiliated national sections, including sections in the United Kingdom, the United States of America, France, Finland, Mexico, Colombia, the Netherlands, Italy, and Argentina. DCI fosters awareness about, and solidarity around, children's rights situations, issues, and initiatives throughout the world; seeks to promote and implement the most effective means of securing the protection of these rights in concrete situations, from both a preventative and a curative standpoint; and is one of the principal advocates of the UN Convention on the Rights of the Child (see **CHILDREN'S RIGHTS**). Members of its staff assisted working groups drafting the standard minimum rules for the protection of juveniles deprived of their liberty. In recent years, DCI has submitted numerous statements on the violations of children's rights to the UN Center for Human Rights, particularly concerning children in prison, child labor, child prostitution, and trafficking and sale of children. It has publicized specific cases of violations; has undertaken action-oriented investigations and taken direct action in situations involving violations of the rights of specific groups of children; has monitored and evaluated the implementation of accepted children's rights; and has worked for improved international standards in this field.

DCI has an extensive publication program, with each national section publishing individual reports and studies on a national and international scope. Among the publications of the parent organization is the monthly *International Children's Rights Monitor,* published in English, French, and Spanish.

Defense for Children International. Address: 1 rue de Varembé, P.O. 88, CH–1211 Geneva 20, Switzerland. Telephone: (41-22) 734-05-58. Fax: (41-22) 740-11-45. Telex: 414 128 dci ch. Secretary-General: Trevor Davies.

**DE KLERK, FREDERIK WILLEM (1936–).** In 1993, the world witnessed the once-thought-impossible combination of South Africans **NELSON MANDELA** and F. W. de Klerk as co-winners of the **NOBEL PEACE PRIZE.** De Klerk, South Africa's last president under the racist regime of apartheid and its first vice-president under the democratic government of Mandela, is credited with helping to end apartheid in his native land.

Born in 1936 in Johannesburg in the Transvaal, de Klerk grew up in an Afrikaner family of politicians (the Afrikaners constitute approximately 60% of South Africa's white populations). He was educated in South Africa and considers English his second language, Afrikaan being his first. His first political experience came when he won a parliamentary seat for Vereeniging for the National party. He later was appointed minister of posts and telecommunications and minister of social welfare and pensions. His predecessor as president, P. W. Botha, appointed de Klerk to many posts, including minister of sports and recreation; minister of mines, energy, and environmental planning; and minister of national education and planning. In 1986, he became the leader of the House of Assembly.

Although considered a conservative, de Klerk recognized the need for reform in the repressive apartheid regime. He was considered a pragmatic and flexible politician. When Botha suffered a series of strokes that necessitated his relinquishing the presidency, de Klerk entered the race with four other candidates. He campaigned on a platform that described his Nationalist party to be a middle-of-the-road between the whites-only Conservatives and the majority-rule (i.e., blacks) Democratic party. His Nationalists stood for "group rights," under a two-tiered system of self-governance and consensus.

At his inauguration, de Klerk stated, "History offers us a unique opportunity for peaceful solutions. I trust the people of South Africa will . . . show the courage and vision required to break the cycle of conflict, tension, and isolation which has gripped us for so long— the courage and vision to work for a new, strong, and just South Africa." But de Klerk had himself been elected under a whites-only mandate. He began a series of meetings with anti-apartheid leaders such as Allan Boesak and 1994 Nobel Prize winner Archbishop Desmond Tutu to discuss the opening of negotiations with the outlawed African National Congress (ANC), of which Nelson Mandela was the internationally revered leader. de Klerk also spoke with other South African black leaders, such as Zulu chief Mangosuthu Gatsha Buthelezi, the leader of the Inkatha movement.

The ANC agreed to talks only if some conditions were met: the lifting of the state of emergency, the ban on outlawed organizations, and the release of Nelson Mandela and other political prisoners. On 2 February 1990, the 30-year ban on the ANC and approximately 60 other political groups was lifted. Mandela was released from prison on 11 February, after serving 27-1/2 years. De Klerk and Mandela began a series of talks between the government and the ANC aimed at overcoming the problems caused by apartheid.

In the first elections open to all citizens of South Africa held in April 1994, de Klerk was elected vice president, serving under the presidency of Nelson Mandela.

***BIBLIOGRAPHY.*** *Current Biography 1990,* pp. 179–182. New York: W. H. Wilson.

**DENMARK.** The Kingdom of Denmark is a country in northern Europe, between the North Sea and the Baltic. Jutland, the peninsular portion of the country, is joined to the European continent by a border with Germany. The country also includes the Faeroe Islands, Greenland, and 406 smaller islands. Invaded and occupied by German forces in 1940, Denmark was liberated by British troops in May 1945 and became a member of the United Nations the same year. Its population is estimated to be 5,169,000. Ethnic groups include Danes, Eskimos, Faeroese, and Germans; however, ethnicity is not registered by the government. Languages commonly used include Danish, English, German, Faeroese, and Greenlandic. Christianity (Evangelical Lutheran, 97%) is the predominant religion. Literacy is estimated at 99%.

The government (1994) took the form of a constitutional monarchy. Under the 1953 constitution, the sovereign presides over the cabinet and appoints the prime minister. Legislative authority is exercised jointly by the sovereign and the 179-member Folketing, or Parliament, members of which are elected by popular vote for terms of four years. Political parties include the Conservative People's Party, the Socialist People's Party, the Liberal Party, the Radical Liberal Party, the Centre Democrats, the Progress Party, Common Cause, the Christian People's Party, and the Left-wing Socialists.

Serfdom was abolished in Denmark in 1788. During the 19th century, Denmark was transformed from a country of poor peasants to a nation of the most prosperous farmers in Europe, mainly because agricultural workers were taught in "folk schools" to specialize in dairy products. Economic recovery was more rapid in Denmark than in the rest of Europe after World War II, and thousands of immigrants flocked to the country in search of employment. By 1973, when a general recession and high unemployment reduced the need for foreign workers, Denmark imposed a ban on immigration. Since then, residence and work permits are issued only to aliens satisfying certain requirements established by law, with priority accorded to nationals of other Nordic countries and to those of member States of the European Economic Community. This practice has been characterized by some as a subtle form of discrimination against would-be immigrants from other countries.

Once admitted, immigrants enjoy largely the same rights as Danish citizens. After three years' residence, they may vote in local government elections. They are not, however, entitled to vote in elections for the Folketing. It is a main principle of immigration policy that problems encountered by immigrants should be dealt with, at both the central and the local government level, by the same authorities as those handling the rest of the population. At the central government level, elements of the immigration policy are coordinated by a special ministerial committee.

Demands for even stricter control of immigration were a factor in the general election held in 1981, which paved the way for Poul Schülter to become premier in 1982. Further disputes over immigration and general economic policies led to elections in 1988 in which Schülter's position was confirmed by a narrow margin. In 1994, Poul Nyrup Rasmussen served as premier. His government coalition was composed of Social Democrats, Centre Democrats, and Radical Democrats.

Long noted for its strict neutrality, Denmark joined the North Atlantic Treaty Organization (NATO) in 1949 and the European Economic Community (ECC) in 1972. In 1993, Denmark ratified the Maastricht Treaty, which would establish a federal Europe, although the Treaty was originally rejected in 1992.

***FAEROE ISLANDS.*** The Faeroe Islands is one of two offshore territories that Denmark administers. This territory consists of 21 islands in the North Atlantic, near the Shetland Islands. They joined Denmark voluntarily in 1386 and, since 1948, have enjoyed home rule and send two members to the Folketing.

***GREENLAND.*** Greenland, which became part of Denmark in 1953, has enjoyed home rule since 1979. However, two human rights problems have caused concern.

Denmark's right to exploit Greenland's vast mineral resources has been challenged on the ground that the right to such exploitation is inherent in the right of the peoples of Greenland to self-determination as formulated in article 1 of both International Covenants on Human Rights. One point of view is that Greenlanders are not "people" in the legal sense of the covenants; another is that they exercised their right to self-determination in 1953 by opting to make the island an integral part of Denmark.

The question of formal recognition by Denmark of the language of Greenland is another item of contention: Greenlanders conceive of their language as an integral part of their unique identity which deserves recognition and preservation; Danish authorities point out that Danish is the only linguistic link between Greenland's population and the rest of the world and that the major part of higher education can take place only in Danish-speaking universities. As a compromise, the Greenlandic Home Rule Act provides for thorough teaching of Danish as well as Greenlandic.

***BIBLIOGRAPHY.*** Amnesty International. *Denmark: Police Ill-Treatment.* London: 1994. NGO report, in English.

**DEROGATION.** Refusal or failure of a State party to a treaty to fulfill an obligation that it has accepted under the treaty.

Article 4 of the **INTERNATIONAL COVENANT ON CIVIL AND POLITICAL RIGHTS** provides that:

1. In time of public emergency which threatens the life of the nation and the existence of which is officially proclaimed, the States Parties to the present Covenant may take measures derogating from their obligations under the present Covenant to the extent strictly required by the exigencies of the situation, provided that such measures are not inconsistent with their other obligations under international law and do not involve discrimination solely on the ground of race, colour, sex, language, religion or social origin.

2. No derogation from articles 6, 7, 8 (paragraphs 1 and 2), 11, 15, 16 and 18 may be made under this provision.

3. Any State Party to the present Covenant availing itself of the right of derogation shall immediately inform the other States Parties to the present Covenant, through the intermediary of the Secretary-General of the United Nations, of the provisions from which it has derogated and of the reasons by which it was actuated. A further communication shall

be made, through the same intermediary, on the date on which it terminates such derogation.

Some provisions of the Covenant (for example, articles 19, 21, and 22) explicitly permit restrictions of particular rights or freedoms to be imposed by law when necessary for such purposes as the protection of national security, public safety, public order, public health or morals, or the rights and freedoms of others.

Under article 4, paragraph 1, the only situation in which a State party may legitimately impose further restrictions on the enjoyment of human rights and fundamental freedoms is the existence of a "state of public emergency which threatens the life of the nation and the existence of which has been publicly proclaimed."

Under article 4, paragraph 2, no derogations whatsoever may be made, even during a period of public emergency, with regard to the rights and freedoms set out in the following articles:

Article 6, on the right to life;
Article 7, on the prohibition of torture and cruel, inhuman or degrading treatment or punishment;
Article 8, para. 1 and 2, on the prohibition of slavery, the slave trade, and other forms of servitude;
Article 11, on contractual obligations;
Article 15, on the prohibition of retroactive application of penal law;
Article 16, on recognition as a person before the law; and
Article 18, on freedom of thought, conscience and religion.

The rights listed above are sometimes referred to as "basic" human rights.

Under article 4, paragraph 3, any State party availing itself of the right of derogation is required to inform other States parties immediately of the provisions from which it has abrogated and the reasons for its action and to inform them later of the date on which it terminates such derogation.

The **HUMAN RIGHTS COMMITTEE** adopted the following comment on article 4 at its 13th session, held at the United Nations office in Geneva from 13 to 31 July 1981 (UN Doc. A/36/40, chap. VII, general comment 5 [13], paras. 1–3):

Article 4 of the Covenant has posed a number of problems for the Committee when considering reports from some States parties. When a public emergency which threatens the life of a nation arises and it is officially proclaimed, a State party may derogate from a number of rights to the extent strictly required by the situation. The State party, however, may not derogate from certain specific rights and may not take discriminatory measures on a number of grounds. The State party is also under no obligation to inform the other States parties immediately, through the Secretary-General, of the derogations it has made including the reasons therefor and the date on which the derogations are terminated.

States parties have generally indicated the mechanism provided in their legal systems for the declaration of a state of emergency and the applicable provisions of the law governing derogations. However, in the case of a few States which had apparently derogated from Covenant rights, it was unclear not only whether a state of emergency had been officially declared but also whether rights from which the Covenant allows no derogation had in fact not been derogated from and further whether the other States parties had been informed of the derogations and of the reasons for the derogations.

The Committee holds the view that measures taken under article 4 are of an exceptional and temporary nature and may only last as long as the life of the nation concerned is threatened and that, in times of emergency, the protection of human rights becomes all the more important, particularly those rights from which no derogations can be made. The Committee also considers that it is equally important for States parties, in times of public emergency, to inform the other States parties of the nature and extent of the derogations they have made and of the reasons therefor and, further, to fulfil their reporting obligations under article 40 of the Covenant by indicating the nature and extent of each right derogated from together with the relevant documentation.

In resolution 43/114 adopted on 8 December 1988, the UN **GENERAL ASSEMBLY** stressed the importance of avoiding the erosion of human rights by derogation and underlined the necessity of strict observance of the agreed conditions and procedures for derogation under article 4 of the International Covenant on Civil and Political Rights, bearing in mind the need for States parties to provide the fullest possible information during states of emergency, so that the justification for and appropriateness of measures taken in these circumstances can be assessed.

**SEE ALSO** *State of Emergency.*

**D'ESTOURNELLES DE CONSTANT, BARON.** See **BALLUET, PAUL HENRI BENJAMIN.**

**DETENTIONS: ARBITRARY.** The Commission on Human Rights, report of the Working Group on Arbitrary Detention, made the following conclusions and recommendations:

### General Conclusions

In its resolution 1994/32, the Commission noted with concern that the practice of arbitrary detention is facilitated and aggravated by several factors such as abuse of states of emergency, exercise of the powers specific to states of emergency without a formal declaration, non-observance of the principle of proportionality between the gravity of the measures taken and the situation concerned, too vague a definition of offences against State security, and the existence of special or emergency jurisdictions (para. 14).

Such concerns had already been expressed by the Group

in its previous reports (E/CN.4/1993/24 and E/CN.4/1994/27). On the basis of the experience gained during its four years of existence, the Group can affirm that the main causes of arbitrary deprivation of liberty are those mentioned in the previous paragraph.

The Group notes that cases of arbitrary detention are not exclusive to repressive regimes—although there they are certainly more numerous and unjust, entail harsher conditions, afford fewer possibilities of obtaining release and carry a higher risk of being subjected to torture or enforced disappearance—but also occur under democratic regimes, especially in connection with the procedures for the admission or expulsion of aliens.

The Working Group therefore accords the greatest importance to all initiatives aimed at strengthening the rule of law, re-enforcing the independence of the judiciary and professionalizing the police, particularly in their knowledge of covenants, declarations and conventions, the Standard Minimum Rules for the Treatment of Prisoners, the Code of Conduct for Law Enforcement Officials and the Body of Principles for the Protection of All Persons under Any Form of Detention or Imprisonment.

The advisory services of the Centre for Human Rights should attach special importance to these matters. Pursuant to the Commission's decision in paragraph 2 of its resolution 1994/69, the Working Group offers the cooperation of its members in elaborating, devising and preparing materials and implementing programmes of this kind.

Eighteen of the cases dealt with resulted from the existence of a state of emergency that had been officially declared, or at any rate invoked by the Government to vindicate its powers to detain individuals. According to the Special Rapporteur of the Sub-Commission on Prevention of Discrimination and Protection of Minorities, a state of emergency was in force in 32 countries in December 1994 (as against 29 countries in 1993), to which should be added—as indicated in the 1993 report—that some countries exercise powers specific to states of emergency without a formal declaration.

The Working Group once again expresses its concern over the existence in many countries of special, ideologically inspired courts, operating under various designations. During 1994 the Group continued to receive communications reporting arrests justified in terms of decisions taken by courts of this kind, such as "people's courts", "revolutionary courts", "Council of War", "Supreme Court of the Armed Forces", "Supreme Court of State Security", as well as, more generally, detentions ordered by military courts which, while they do not appear to be formally prohibited by the Universal Declaration of Human Rights or by the International Covenant on Civil and Political Rights, often fail to meet the "independent and impartial" requirement laid down in article 14 of the Covenant.

The Universal Declaration of Human Rights states that "Everyone has the right to an effective remedy by the competent national tribunals for acts violating the fundamental rights granted him by the constitution or by law" (art. 8), while the International Covenant on Civil and Political Rights provides that "Anyone who is deprived of his liberty by arrest or detention shall be entitled to take proceedings before a court, in order that that court may decide without delay on the lawfulness of his detention and order his release if the detention is not lawful" (art. g (4)). This is the remedy or action of habeas corpus. Unfortunately it does not exist in all countries, thereby depriving citizens of a powerful means of defence against arbitrary detention, or at least a way of promptly remedying injury caused by unlawful or unjust imprisonment. The remedy of habeas corpus, characterized by its non-official character, urgency and ex officio action by the judge, is the best remedy against this kind of human rights violation. The Group reiterates its interest in the preparation of a declaration on the subject by the Sub-Commission on Prevention of Discrimination and Protection of Minorities, particularly regarding the non-derogable nature of habeas corpus as an inherent human right.

In 1994, the Group received complaints concerning 293 persons who, according to the sources, were arbitrarily detained (in 1993, 181 persons). During 1994, the Group adopted 48 decisions regarding the situation of 112 detained persons.

The Group is concerned by the failure of Governments to respond to its requests for information. Out of the 293 individual cases transmitted, it received information from Governments regarding 90 persons, or approximately 31 per cent of the total. The Group also regrets that, in many cases, Governments limit their replies to providing general information or merely affirming the non-existence of arbitrary detention in the country or referring to the constitutional measures preventing it from occurring, without making any direct reference to the case transmitted.

The sources that provided the Group with the most information were the international non-governmental organizations (74 per cent). National non-governmental organizations made submissions to the Group in only 23 per cent of cases, while families did so in 3 per cent of cases. While such intercession means that the Group is informed of the detention with quite some delay, which prevents it from taking more expeditious action, it may be noted that the quality of the information provided has improved.

In any event, and with a view to making the Group, its mandate and its working methods more familiar and helping families and national non-governmental organizations, the Group, under the Human Rights Fact Sheet publications service of the Centre for Human Rights, is preparing a Fact Sheet on arbitrary detention, which is due to appear next year.

The Working Group wishes to remind the Commission of the cases of individuals who have been declared to be unlawfully detained and who have been arbitrarily deprived of their freedom for many years (E/CN.4/1994/27, para. 62). The Group has received no information regarding their release.

The Working Group wishes to reiterate its concern at the imprecision with which legislation in many countries describes the conduct charged. The examples given in earlier reports were again noted in the year covered by this report (acts described by the Governments concerned as "treason", "acts hostile to a foreign State", "enemy propaganda", "terrorism", etc.). During 1994, the Group observed that there are criminal classifications under which it is not even clear whether the perpetrator of an "attack on State security" used violence or merely manifested an opinion. In this connection, the Group believes that consideration should be given to the possibility of suggesting that the competent body (the forthcoming Ninth United Nations Congress on the Prevention of Crime and the Treatment of Offenders) should make recommendations to ensure that criminal classifications established by national law are in conformity with the general principles guaranteeing that the right to the principle of restrictiveness or lawfulness is not arbitrarily disregarded as described.

In 1994, the Group conducted its first two in situ missions.

Their results reinforced the Group's opinion concerning the usefulness of such missions for the performance of its mandate. The Working Group is the only universal international mechanism which can make visits to places of detention in order to concern itself not only with conditions of detention (a matter related to the mandate of the International Committee of the Red Cross), but also the legal status of prisoners (date and circumstances of arrest, officials involved, prisoner's appearance in court, notification of charges, remedies available to challenge detention, etc.). This interest even surprised prison officers and public servants in general in the countries visited, who apparently expected or were prepared to show the Group sanitary facilities, food, etc.

By reason of its mandate of "investigating cases of detention imposed arbitrarily", it was not possible for the Group to have an overall view of the situation regarding deprivation of liberty in a particular country and to make recommendations which it deemed relevant. The visits it conducted enabled it to verify the lawfulness of detentions not only on a case-by-case basis but also from a general standpoint, in relation both to normative aspects and to practical implementation. For this purpose, interviews with prisoners, on the one hand, and judges and police officers, on the other, were enormously important. Had time permitted—and, for future missions, consideration will be given to this possibility—it would also have been interesting to consult case files or attend hearings.

The visits afford the Governments concerned a splendid opportunity to demonstrate both respect for the rights of prisoners and progress made in this area.

The Group notes that, in some countries, the law provides for the possibility of individuals being tried by anonymous, or so-called "faceless", judges. This situation is especially disturbing and may serve to reduce the population's confidence in judges. The Working Group, conscious of the fact that the existence of such courts may seriously affect, inter alia, the right to personal freedom which is the object of its mandate, but at the same time understanding the need to ensure the life and physical integrity of judges and their families, hopes that this issue can be discussed with the Special Rapporteur on the Independence of the Judiciary at the next meeting of special rapporteurs and chairmen of working groups.

### Recommendations

The Working Group reiterates the recommendations made in its previous reports, which remain fully applicable. Without prejudice to this fact, the Group addresses the following recommendations to the Commission on Human Rights:

(a) The Commission should consider the possibility of converting the mandate of the Special Rapporteur of the Sub-Commission on Prevention of Discrimination and Protection of Minorities on the question of states of emergency and respect for human rights into a mandate of the Commission;

(b) The Commission should urge the continuation of the annual meetings of special rapporteurs and chairmen of working groups, whose usefulness was demonstrated both at the World Conference on Human Rights held in Vienna in 1993 and at the first meeting held in May 1994, as provided for by the Commission in paragraph 13 of its resolution 1994/53;

(c) The Commission, when adopting the resolution on the question of arbitrary detention, should approve the procedure for following up decisions declaring a case of detention to be arbitrary. As already explained, the Group, in compliance with the request made in paragraph 19 of resolution 1994/32, drew up a proposal for follow-up on which Governments were consulted. Bearing in mind the Government replies, the Group acknowledged the point made by the Governments of Bahrain and the Netherlands that the proposed deadline for replying to the Group might be regarded as short by some Governments, and therefore modified its original proposal. Consequently, the procedure for following up the Group's decisions which is proposed to the Commission is as follows:

"The Working Group suggests that a Government which has been the subject of a Working Group decision deeming a detention to be arbitrary should be requested to inform the Working Group, within four months from the date of transmittal of the decision, of the measures adopted in compliance with the Group's recommendations. For the time being, it is suggested that this procedure should be applied only in cases in which the prisoner has not been released. Should the Government fail to abide by the Group's recommendations, the Group might proceed to recommend to the Commission on Human Rights that it should request that Government to report to the Commission on the matter, in accordance with the modalities deemed most appropriate by the Commission."

The Group also asks the Commission to make the following requests to Governments:

(a) Long-standing detainees (see para. 50) whose detention has been deemed arbitrary by the Group should be released, not only in compliance with the recommendation made by the Group in its decisions but also for humanitarian reasons;

(b) Governments which have been maintaining states of emergency in force for many years should lift them, limit their effects or review the custodial measures that affect many persons, and in particular should apply the principle of proportionality rigorously.

The Group recommends that the Commission should request the Sub-Commission on Prevention of Discrimination and Protection of Minorities to consider the possibility of initiating a study on the preparation of a declaration or protocol concerning the subject of habeas corpus as a human right and guarantee of the right to personal freedom, as well as respect for its non-derogability.

In the Working Group's opinion, the Commission might request the next meeting of special rapporteurs and chairmen of working groups to study the most appropriate coordination mechanisms for increasing the efficiency of its work and reports and programming in situ visits.

In the Group's view, the Commission might suggest that the competent organ (Ninth United Nations Congress on the Prevention of Crime and the Treatment of Offenders) should study declarations or recommendations designed to ensure that internal national legislation, in describing conduct warranting penal sanctions, should be of a rigour consistent with the requirements of contemporary criminal science regarding the categorization of offences.

The Group suggests that the Commission should request the Special Rapporteur on the independence and impartiality of the judiciary, jurors and assessors and the independence of lawyers to study the possible impact of the existence of anonymous judges on the independence of the judiciary.

In the Group's view the Commission might ask the Centre for Human Rights to study the possibility of including the matters referred to in paragraphs 41 and 42 in advisory services programmes.

### Annex 1: Revised Methods of Work

The methods of work are largely based on those applied, in the light of 11 years' experience, by the Working Group on Enforced or Involuntary Disappearances, with due regard for the specific features of the terms of reference of the Working Group on Arbitrary Detention under Commission on Human Rights resolution 1991/42, whereby it has the duty of informing the Commission by means of a comprehensive report (para. 5), and also of "investigating cases" (para. 2).

The Group takes the view that such investigation should be of an adversarial nature so as to assist it in obtaining the cooperation of the State concerned by the case considered.

In the opinion of the Working Group, situations of arbitrary detention, in the sense of paragraph 2 of resolution 1991/42, are those described in accordance with the principles set out in annex I of document E/CN.4/1992/20.

In the light of resolution 1991/42, the Working Group shall deem admissible communications received from the concerned individuals themselves or their families. Such communications may also be transmitted to the Working Group by representatives of the above-mentioned individuals as well as by Governments and intergovernmental and non-governmental organizations.

The communications must be submitted in writing and addressed to the secretariat giving the family name, first name and address of the sender, and (optionally) his telephone, telex and telefax numbers.

As far as possible, each case shall form the subject of a specific presentation indicating family name, first name and any other information making it possible to identify the person detained and all elements clarifying the legal status of the person concerned, particularly:

(a) The date and place of the arrest or detention and the forces presumed to have carried them out, together with all other information shedding light on the circumstances in which the person was arrested or detained;

(b) The reasons given by the authorities for the arrest or detention or the offences;

(c) The relevant legislation applied to the case in point;

(d) The internal steps taken, including domestic remedies, especially approaches to the administrative and legal authorities, particularly for verification of the detention and, as appropriate, their results or the reasons why such steps were ineffective or were not taken; and

(e) A short account of the reasons why the deprivation of liberty is regarded as arbitrary.

In order to facilitate the Group's work, it is hoped that communications will be submitted taking into account the model questionnaire.

Failure to comply with all formalities set forth in paragraphs 6 and 7 shall not directly or indirectly result in the inadmissibility of the communication.

The cases notified shall be brought to the attention of the Government concerned by the Chairman of the Group or, if he is not available, by the Vice-Chairman, by means of a letter transmitted through the Permanent Representative to the United Nations asking the Government to reply after having carried out the appropriate inquiries so as to provide the Group with the fullest possible information.

The communication shall be transmitted with an indica-tion of the deadline established for receipt of a reply. The deadline may not exceed 90 days. If the reply has not been received by the time the deadline is reached, the Working Group may, on the basis of all data compiled, take a decision.

The procedure known as "urgent action" may be resorted to:

(a) In cases in which there are sufficiently reliable allegations that a person is being detained arbitrarily and that the continuation of the detention constitutes a serious danger to that person's health or even life. In such cases, between the sessions of the Working Group, the Working Group authorizes its Chairman or, in his absence, the Vice-Chairman, to transmit the communication by the most rapid means to the Minister for Foreign Affairs of the country concerned, stating that this urgent action in no way prejudges the Working Group's final assessment of whether the detention is arbitrary or not;

(b) In other cases, where the detention may not constitute a danger to a person's health or life, but where the particular circumstances of the situation warrant urgent action. In such cases, between the sessions of the Working Group, the Chairman or the Vice-Chairman, in consultation with two other members of the Working Group, may also decide to transmit the communication by the most rapid means to the Minister for Foreign Affairs of the country concerned.

However, during sessions, it devolves on the Working Group to take a decision whether to resort to the urgent action procedure.

Between the sessions of the Working Group, the Chairman may, either personally or by delegating any of the members of the Group, request an interview with the Permanent Representative to the United Nations of the country in question in order to facilitate mutual cooperation.

Any information supplied by the Government concerned on specific cases shall be transmitted to the sources from which the communications were received, with a request for comments on the subject or additional information.

In the light of the information examined during its investigation, the Working Group shall take one of the following decisions:

(a) If the person has been released, for whatever reason, since the Working Group took up the case, the case is filed; nevertheless, the Working Group reserves the right to decide, on a case-by-case basis, whether or not the deprivation of liberty was arbitrary, notwithstanding the release of the person concerned;

(b) If the Working Group determines that it is established that the case is not one of arbitrary detention, the case is also filed;

(c) If the Working Group decides that it does not have enough information to take a decision, the case remains pending for further information;

(d) If the Working Group decides that it does not have enough information to keep the case pending, the case may be filed without further action;

(e) If the Working Group decides that the arbitrary nature of the detention is established, it shall make recommendations to the Government concerned. The decisions and recommendations shall also be transmitted three weeks after their transmittal to the Government to the source from which the case was originally received, and be brought to the attention of the Commission on Human Rights in the annual report of the Working Group to the Commission.

When the case under consideration concerns a country of which one of the members of the Working Group is a national, that member shall not, in principle, participate in the discussion because of the possibility of a conflict of interest.

The Working Group will not deal with situations of international armed conflict in so far as they are covered by the Geneva Conventions of 12 August 1949 and their Additional Protocols, particularly when the International Committee of the Red Cross (ICRC) has competence.

In accordance with the provisions of paragraph 4 of resolution 1993/36, the Working Group may, on its own initiative, take up cases which, in the opinion of any one of its members, might constitute arbitrary detention. If the Group is in session, the decision to communicate the case to the Government concerned shall be taken at that session. Outside the session, the Chairman, or in his absence the Vice-Chairman, may decide on transmittal of the case to the Government, provided at least three members of the Group so agree. When acting on its own initiative, the Working Group shall give preferential consideration to the thematic or geographical subjects to which the Commission on Human Rights has requested it to pay special attention.

The Working Group shall also communicate any decision it adopts to the Commission on Human Rights, whether thematic or country-oriented, or to the body set up by the appropriate treaty for the purpose of proper coordination between all organs of the system.

**DEUTSCHER RICHTERBUND (GERMAN ASSOCIATION OF JUDGES) HUMAN RIGHTS PRIZE.** Established in 1991, this prize is awarded every two years to judges, prosecutors, or lawyers who contribute to the defense of human rights in their countries under risk of their lives, health, or freedom. The first recipient of the prize was Peruvian lawyer Augusto Zuniga Paz.

For more information, contact: Deutscher Richterbund, Seufertstrasse 27, D-5300 Bonn 2, Germany. Fax: (49) 228-33-47-23.

**DEVELOPMENT.** In 1981, the Commission on Human Rights established (resolution 36 [XXXVII]) the Working Group of Governmental Experts on the Right to Development composed of 15 governmental experts appointed by its chairman, and instructed it to study "the scope and contents of the right to development and the most effective means to ensure the realization, in all countries, of the economic, social, and cultural rights enshrined in various international instruments, paying particular attention to the obstacles encountered by developing countries in their efforts to secure the enjoyment of human rights."

The final report of the Working Group (UN Doc. E/CN.4/1985/11), containing the draft of a declaration on the right to development, was submitted to the Commission at its 1985 session. The Commission forwarded it to the General Assembly, which on 4 December 1986 was able to adopt and proclaim (resolution 41/128) the *Declaration on the Right to Development*. At the same time, the Assembly welcomed (resolution 41/131) the Commission's decision to entrust further tasks to the working group relating to the realization of the provisions of the Declaration.

In adopting the Declaration, the Assembly confirmed that "the right to development is an inalienable human right and that equality of opportunity for development is a prerogative both of nations and of individuals who make up nations."

The Declaration itself defines the right to development as "an inalienable human right by virtue of which every human person and all peoples are entitled to participate in, contribute to and enjoy economic, social, cultural and political development, in which all human rights and fundamental freedoms can be fully realized." It adds that "the human right to development also implies the full realization of the right of peoples to self-determination, which includes, subject to the relevant provisions of both International Covenants on Human Rights, the exercise of their inalienable right to full sovereignty over all their natural wealth and resources."

After examining the Working Group's 1988 report (UN Doc. E/CN.4/1988/10), which contained a set of recommendations in tentative form, the Commission on Human Rights took note of it with approval (resolution 1988/26), requested the Secretary-General to transmit it to the General Assembly, and agreed that future work on the question of the right to development should proceed step-by-step and in stages. It invited the Secretary-General to obtain further comments and views on the subject and to include them in an expanded analytical compilation which would also include relevant statements made during the discussions in the Commission and the Economic and Social Council; and called upon the working group to prepare final recommendations on how an evaluation system for the implementation and further enhancement of the Declaration could be set up.

The General Assembly on 8 December 1988 endorsed (resolution 43/127) the views expressed, and the requests made, by the Commission. It called upon the Commission to decide at its 1989 session, on the basis of the working group's report and the views expressed by its own members, on the future course of action on the question, in particular on practical measures for the implementation and enhancement of the Declaration.

In a separate resolution on the subject adopted the same day (resolution 43/126), the General Assembly reiterated the importance of the right to development for all countries, particularly developing countries. It stressed that the achievement of that right requires a concerted international and national effort to eliminate economic deprivation, hunger, and disease in all parts of the world without discrimination; and emphasized that, to this end, international cooperation should aim at the maintenance of stable and sustained economic growth with simultaneous action to increase concessional assistance to developing countries, build world food security, resolve the debt burden, eliminate trade barriers, promote stability, and enhance scientific cooperation.

After examining the report of the working group in its 1989 session (UN Doc. E/CN.4/1989/10), which reflected the views expressed during that session on the implementation and further enhancement of the Declaration, the Commission requested the Secretary-General (resolution 1989/45) to circulate it to all governments, United Nations organs and specialized agencies, and other governmental and non- governmental organizations, drawing their attention to the analytical compilation of replies (UN Doc. E/CN.4/AC.39/1989/1). It also called upon the Secretary-General to transmit a questionnaire to governments, United Nations organs and specialized agencies, as well as to other governmental and non-governmental organizations, including those active in development and human rights, in order to elicit from them additional updated and more specific views on the subject of the implementation and further enhancement of the Declaration.

In the same resolution, the Commission invited the Secretary-General to organize, in 1989, a global consultation on the realization of the right to development involving experts with relevant experience gained at the national level and representatives of organizations and agencies within the United Nations system, including those active in development and human rights, to focus on the fundamental problems posed by the implementation of the Declaration, the criteria which might be used to identify progress, and the mechanisms for stimulating and evaluating such progress.

The Global Consultation on the Realization of the Right to Development as a Human Right took place at the United Nations office in Geneva from 8 to 12 January 1990. Leading experts in the various fields were invited to prepare short background papers and to participate in the consultation by introducing their topics and taking part in the ensuing discussions.

In addition to the speakers under each item of the agenda, representatives of specialized agencies; concerned units of the United Nations Secretariat; international trade, development, and financial institutions; and non-governmental organizations participated in the discussions. A special effort was made to ensure the participation of representatives of development-related non-governmental organizations and, in particular, those with direct experience in development projects. The consultation began with a round-table exchange of views on "Development and Human Rights: Global Perspectives and New Policy Directions," which provided a framework for the ensuing debates of the consultation.

In addition to the expert participants, ten United Nations bodies, two intergovernmental organizations, 36 non-governmental organizations, and 53 States were represented at the consultation, with more than 170 persons attending in one capacity or another.

*DEVELOPMENT AND DISARMAMENT.* A total of 150 States and 183 nongovernmental organizations participated in the International Conference on the Relationship between Disarmament and Development, convened by the UN General Assembly (decision 41/422), which met at the headquarters of the United Nations in New York from 24 August to 11 September 1987, and concluded its work by adopting its report (UN publication, Sales No. E.87.IX.8) containing the final document of the conference (chap. II).

Many sections of the final document refer either to human rights in general, to particular rights and freedoms, or to matters bearing upon the realization of economic, social, cultural, civil, or political rights. Excerpts from these sections follow:

The States participating in the International Conference on the Relationship between Disarmament and Development,

Desirous of:

(a) Enhancing and strengthening the commitment of the international community to disarmament and development and giving impetus to renewed efforts in both these fields;

(b) Raising world consciousness that true and lasting peace and security in this interdependent world demands rapid progress in both disarmament and development;

(c) Directing global attention at a high political level on the implications of world-wide military spending against the sombre background of the present world economic situation;

(d) Looking at disarmament, development and security in their relationship in the context of the interdependence of nations, interrelationships among issues and mutuality of interests;

(e) Taking greater account of the relationship between disarmament and development in political decision making;

(f) Furthering the international community's collective knowledge of the military and nonmilitary threats to security;

Adopt the following Final Document:

In the Charter of the United Nations, Member States have undertaken to promote the establishment and maintenance of international peace and security with the least diversion for armaments of the world's human and economic resources. The Member States also express in the Charter their determination to employ international machinery for the promotion of the economic and social advancement of all peoples. The United Nations has thus a central role to play for the promotion of both disarmament and development. Disarmament and development are two of the most urgent challenges facing the world today. They constitute priority concerns of the international community in which all nations—developed and developing, big and small, nuclear and non-nuclear—have a common and equal stake. Disarmament and development are two pillars on which enduring international peace and security can be built.

The continuing arms race is absorbing far too great a proportion of the world's human, financial, natural and technological resources, placing a heavy burden on the economies of all countries and affecting the international flow of trade, finance and technology, in addition to hindering the process of confidence-building among States. The global military expenditures are in dramatic contrast to economic and social underdevelopment and to the misery and poverty afflicting more than two thirds of mankind. Thus, there is a commonality of interests in seeking security at lower levels of armaments and finding ways of reducing these expenditures. The world can either continue to pursue the arms race with characteristic vigour or move consciously and with deliberate speed towards a more stable and balanced social and economic development within a more sustainable international economic and political order; it cannot do both.

Global interest in the relationship between disarmament and development is reflected in proposals by a politically and geographically broad spectrum of States since the early days of the United Nations. There is an increasing understanding of this relationship, in part due to the expert studies and reports prepared by the United Nations. The contrast between the global military expenditures and the unmet socio-economic needs provides a compelling moral appeal for relating disarmament to development. There is also a growing recognition that both overarmament and underdevelopment constitute threats to international peace and security.

The convening under the aegis of the United Nations of the International Conference on the Relationship between Disarmament and Development is a landmark in the process of undertaking, at a political level, the multilateral consideration of the relationship between disarmament and development.

*Relationship Between Disarmament and Development in all its Aspects and Dimensions.* While disarmament and development both strengthen international peace and security and promote prosperity, they are distinct processes. Each should be pursued vigorously regardless of the pace of progress in the other; one should not be made a hostage to the other. Pursuit of development cannot wait for the release of resources from disarmament.

Similarly, disarmament has its own imperative separate from the purpose of releasing resources for development.

However, disarmament and development have a close and multidimensional relationship. Each of them can have an impact at the national, regional and global levels in such a way as to create an environment conducive to the promotion of the other.

The relationship between disarmament and development in part derives from the fact that the continuing global arms race and development compete for the same finite resources at both the national and international levels. The allocation of massive resources for armaments impedes the pursuit of development to its optimal level.

Considering the present resource constraints of both developed and developing countries, reduced world military spending could contribute significantly to development. Disarmament can assist the process of development not only by

releasing additional resources but also by positively affecting the global economy. It can create conditions conducive to promoting equitable economic and technological co-operation and to pursuing the objectives of a new international economic order.

Real economic growth as well as just and equitable development, and particularly the elimination of poverty, are necessary for a secure and stable environment at the national, regional and international levels. They can reduce tensions and conflicts and the need for armament.

In the relationship between disarmament and development, security plays a crucial role. Progress in any of these three areas would have a positive effect on the others.

Security is an overriding priority for all nations. It is also fundamental for both disarmament and development. Security consists of not only military, but also political, economic, social, humanitarian and human rights and ecological aspects.

Enhanced security can, on the one hand, create conditions conducive to disarmament and, on the other, provide the environment and confidence for the successful pursuit of development. The development process, by overcoming nonmilitary threats to security and contributing to a more stable and sustainable international system, can enhance security and thereby promote arms reduction and disarmament. Disarmament would enhance security both directly and indirectly. A process of disarmament that provides for undiminished security at progressively lower levels of armaments could allow additional resources to be devoted to addressing nonmilitary challenges to security, and thus result in enhanced overall security.

An effective implementation of the collective security provisions of the Charter of the United Nations would enhance international peace and security and thus reduce the need of Member States to seek security by exercising their inherent right of individual or collective self-defence, also recognized by the Charter. The judgement as to the level of arms and military expenditures essential for its security rests with each nation. However, the pursuit of national security regardless of its impact on the security of others can create overall international insecurity, thereby undermining the very security it aims at promoting. This is even more so in the context of the catastrophic consequences of a nuclear war.

It is widely accepted that the world is overarmed and that security should be sought at substantially lower levels of armaments. The continued arms race in all its dimensions, and its spreading into new areas, pose a growing threat to international peace and security and even to the very survival of mankind. Moreover, global military spending on nuclear and conventional arms threatens to stall the efforts aimed at reaching the goals of development so necessary to overcome non-military threats to peace and security.

The use or threat of use of force in international relations, external intervention, armed aggression, foreign occupation, colonial domination, policies of *apartheid* and all forms of racial discrimination, violation of territorial integrity, of national sovereignty, of the right to self-determination, and the encroachment of the right of all nations to pursue their economic and social development free from outside interference constitute threats to international peace and security. International security will be guaranteed in turn to the extent that peaceful and negotiated solutions to regional conflicts are promoted.

Recently, nonmilitary threats to security have moved to the forefront of global concern. Underdevelopment and declining prospects for development, as well as mismanagement and waste of resources, constitute challenges to security. The degradation of the environment presents a threat to sustainable development. The world can hardly be regarded as secure so long as there is polarization of wealth and poverty at the national and international levels. Gross and systematic violations of human rights retard genuine socioeconomic development and create tensions which contribute to instability. Mass poverty, illiteracy, disease, squalor and malnutrition afflicting a large proportion of the world's population often become the cause of social strain, tension and strife.

Growing interdependence among nations, interrelationship among global issues, mutuality of interests, collective approach responding to the needs of humanity as a whole and multilateralism provide the international framework within which the relationship between disarmament, development and security should be shaped.

*Implications of the Level and Magnitude of the Continuing Military Expenditures.* The current level of global military spending in pursuit of security interests represents a real increase of between four and five times since the end of the Second World War. It also reflects approximately 6 per cent of the world gross domestic product and has been estimated to be more than 20 times as large as all official development assistance to developing countries. During the 1980s, global military expenditure has grown on an average at a faster rate than during the second half of the 1970s. . . .

In contrast to the current level and trends in global military expenditure, the state of the world economy in the 1980s has been characterized by a slowdown in growth of demand and output compared with the preceding two decades, generally lower rates of inflation, difficulties in many countries in adapting to structural changes, a mounting stock of debt, high real interest rates, inadequate net flows of financial resources, shifts in exchange rates, high and increasing levels of protection, commodity prices depressed to their lowest level in 50 years, terms-of-trade losses sustained by commodity exporting countries, and a generally insecure economic environment in which millions of people still lack the basic conditions for a decent life.

The use of resources for military purposes amounts to a reduction of resources for the civilian sector. Military spending provides little basis for future industrial civilian production. Military goods are generally destroyed or soon used up. While there are some civilian byproducts of military research and training there are better direct, nonmilitary routes to follow.

The opportunity cost of military expenditures over the past 40 years has been and continues to be borne by both developed and developing countries, as there is a pressing need for additional resources for development in both groups of countries. In developing countries, it has been estimated that close to 1 billion people are below the poverty line, 780 million people are undernourished, 850 million are illiterate, 1.5 billion have no access to medical facilities, an equally large number are unemployed, and 1 billion people are inadequately housed. In developed countries, resources are required, *inter alia,* for meeting the priority needs of urban renewal, the restoration of some of the infrastructures, the reduction of unemployment, the protection of the environment, the further development of welfare systems and the development of non-conventional sources of energy. The developing countries are doubly affected: (a) in proportion to the expenditure they incur themselves; and

(b) because of the disturbing effect of military expenditure on the world economy.

The present world economic situation should also be seen in the context of the arms race. For certain countries the high deficits caused by military expenditures as well as the cumulative effect of subsequent rise in the interest rates have the effect of diverting substantial flows of capital away from development activities. In this sense, the whole world is affected by the arms race. . . .

*Ways and Means of Releasing Additional Resources for Development Purposes.* Apart from promoting international peace, security and co-operation, disarmament can improve the environment for the pursuit of development by:

(a) Releasing resources from the military to the civilian sector at the national level;

(b) Removing the distortions in the national and international economy induced by military expenditure;

(c) Creating favourable conditions for international economic, scientific and technological co-operation and for releasing resources for development at the regional and international levels, on both a bilateral and a multilateral basis.

Resources released as a result of disarmament measures should be devoted to the promotion of the wellbeing of all peoples, the improvement of the economic conditions of the developing countries and the bridging of the economic gap between developed and developing countries. These resources should be additional to those otherwise available for assistance to developing countries. . . .

The final document concludes with a comprehensive action program, designed with a view to fostering an interrelated perspective on disarmament, development, and security; to promoting multilateralism as providing the international framework for shaping the relationship between disarmament, development, and security based on interdependence among nations and mutuality of interests; and to strengthening the central role of the United Nations in the interrelated fields of disarmament and development.

In a resolution adopted on 7 December 1988 (resolution 43/75 B), the UN General Assembly requested the Secretary-General to take action through the appropriate organs of the United Nations to implement the action program adopted by the conference. In another resolution, adopted the following day (resolution 43/113), the Assembly reaffirmed that there is a close and multidimensional relationship between disarmament and development, that progress in disarmament would considerably promote progress in development, and that resources released through disarmament measures could contribute to the economic and social development and wellbeing of all peoples; and recognized that the realization of the right to development may help to promote the enjoyment of all human rights and fundamental freedoms.

***INCOME DISTRIBUTION AND HUMAN RIGHTS.*** Disturbed that income distribution, both within and between nations, was becoming increasingly unbalanced according to the Human Development Report of the

United Nations Development Program for 1993, with income concentrated in fewer and fewer hands, the Sub-Commission on Prevention of Discrimination and Protection of Minorities urged all States (resolution 1993/40 of 26 August 1993) "to undertake political, economic, fiscal, social, legal and other necessary measures designed to ensure more equitable access to and control over economic and other resources." It further urged the international community, the bodies and organizations of the United Nations system, the specialized agencies, the international financial institutions and other relevant actors "to undertaken measures designed to close the current widening gap in income distribution, both within and between nations."

The Sub-Commission, in the same resolution, decided to entrust Mr. Asjbørn Eide with the task of preparing a preliminary study on the relationship between the enjoyment of human rights and income distribution at both the national and international levels, with a view to determining how most effectively to strengthen activities in this field. This decision was subsequently endorsed by the Commission on Human Rights (resolution 1994/20 of 1 March 1994).

*SEE ALSO* New International Economic Order; United Nations: Funds.

*BIBLIOGRAPHY.* Barsh, Russel Lawrence. "The Right to Development as a Human Right: Results of the Global Consultation." *Human Rights Quarterly* 13, no. 3 (Aug. 1991): 322–338. Scholarly article, in English.

Gutto, Shadrack B.O. *Human and Peoples' Rights for the Oppressed: Critical Essays on Theory and Practice from Sociology of Law Perspectives.* Lund, Sweden: Lund University Press, 1993. Scholarly collection of essays, in English; bibliography, pp. 422–449.

Lavielle, Jean-Marc. "Les rapports entre les droits de l'homme, le développement et la paix" (Relationship between Human Rights, Development and Peace). *Revue trimestrielle des droits de l'homme* 1, no. 3 (July 1990): 211–229. Scholarly article, in French.

Nanda, Ved P.; George W. Shepherd; and Eileen McCarthy-Arnolds. *World Debt and the Human Condition: Structural Adjustment and the Right to Development.* Westport, CT, USA: Greenwood, 1993. Monograph, in English; bibliography, pp. 233–240.

Nguema, Isaac. "L'Afrique, les droits de L'homme et le développement" (Africa, Human Rights and Development). *Review of the African Commission on Human and Peoples' Rights* 1 (Oct. 1991): 16–50. Scholarly article, in French.

Roy Chowdhury, S.; E. Denters; and P.J.I.M. de Waart, eds. *The Right to Development in International Law.* Dordrecht, The Netherlands: Martinus Nijhoff, 1992. Scholarly collective works, in English.

Shepherd, George W. "The African Right to Development: World Policy and the Debt Crisis." *Africa Today* 37, no. 4 (1990): 5–14. Scholarly article, in English.

Shepherd, George W., and Mark O.C. Anikpo, eds. *Emerging Human Rights: The African Political Economy Context.* Westport, CT, USA: Greenwood Press, 1990. Scholarly collective works, in English; bibliography, pp. 223–235.

Sottas, Eric, et al. *The Least-Developed Countries: Development and Human Rights* Geneva, Switzerland: World Organisation against Torture, 1990. NGO research report, in English and French; bibliography, pp. 149–152.

Tomasevski, Katarina. *Development Aid and Human Rights Revisited.* London: Pinter Publishers, 1993. Scholarly monograph, in English.

United Nations, Sub-Commission on Prevention of Discrimination and Protection of Minorities. *The Realization of Economic, Social and Cultural Rights. Final Report Submitted by Mr. Danilo Türk, Special Rapporteur.* Geneva, Switzerland: 1992. Intergovernmental document, in English and French.

**DEVELOPMENT: DECLARATION ON SOCIAL PROGRESS AND DEVELOPMENT (1969).** The Declaration, drafted by the UN Commission for Social Development, defines the objectives of social development—so necessary for the realization of human rights and social justice—and the means of attaining those objectives. Its message is that social development must aim at the continuous raising of the material and spiritual standards of living of all members of society with full respect for, and compliance with, all human rights and fundamental freedoms.

The Declaration was adopted by the UN **GENERAL ASSEMBLY** on 11 December 1969 (resolution 2542 [XXIV]). The text, annexed to that resolution, is as follows:

The General Assembly,

Mindful of the pledge of Members of the United Nations under the Charter to take joint and separate action in co-operation with the Organization to promote higher standards of living, full employment and conditions of economic and social progress and development,

Reaffirming faith in human rights and fundamental freedoms and in the principles of peace, of the dignity and worth of the human person, and of social justice proclaimed in the Charter,

Recalling the principles of the Universal Declaration of Human Rights, the International Covenants on Human Rights, the Declaration of the Rights of the Child, the Declaration on the Granting of Independence to Colonial Countries and Peoples, the International Convention on the Elimination of All Forms of Racial Discrimination, the United Nations Declaration on the Elimination of All Forms of Racial Discrimination, the Declaration on the Promotion among Youth of the Ideals of Peace, Mutual Respect and Understanding between Peoples, the Declaration on the Elimination of Discrimination against Women and of resolutions of the United Nations,

Bearing in mind the standards already set for social progress in the constitutions, conventions, recommendations and resolutions of the International Labour Organisation, the Food and Agriculture Organization of the United Nations, the United Nations Educational, Scientific and Cultural Organization, the World Health Organization, the United Nations Children's Fund and of other organizations concerned,

Convinced that man can achieve complete fulfilment of his aspirations only within a just social order and that it is consequently of cardinal importance to accelerate social and economic progress everywhere, thus contributing to international peace and solidarity,

Convinced that international peace and security on the one hand, and social progress and economic development on the other, are closely interdependent and influence each other,

Persuaded that social development can be promoted by peaceful coexistence, friendly relations and co-operation among States with different social, economic or political systems,

Emphasizing the interdependence of economic and social development in the wider process of growth and change, as well as the importance of a strategy of integrated development which takes full account at all stages of its social aspects,

Regretting the inadequate progress achieved in the world social situation despite the efforts of States and the international community,

Recognizing that the primary responsibility for the development of the developing countries rests on those countries themselves and acknowledging the pressing need to narrow and eventually close the gap in the standards of living between economically more advanced and developing countries and, to that end, that Member States shall have the responsibility to pursue internal and external policies designed to promote social development throughout the world, and in particular to assist developing countries to accelerate their economic growth,

Recognizing the urgency of devoting to works of peace and social progress resources being expended on armaments and wasted on conflict and destruction,

Conscious of the contribution that science and technology can render towards meeting the needs common to all humanity,

Believing that the primary task of all States and international organizations is to eliminate from the life of society all evils and obstacles to social progress, particularly such evils as inequality, exploitation, war, colonialism and racism,

Desirous of promoting the progress of all mankind towards these goals and of overcoming all obstacles to their realization,

Solemnly proclaims this Declaration on Social Progress and Development and calls for national and international action for its use as a common basis for social development policies:

### Part I—Principles

*Article 1.* All peoples and all human beings, without distinction as to race, colour, sex, language, religion, nationality, ethnic origin, family or social status, or political or other conviction, shall have the right to live in dignity and freedom and to enjoy the fruits of social progress and should, on their part, contribute to it.

*Article 2.* Social progress and development shall be founded on respect for the dignity and value of the human person and shall ensure the promotion of human rights and social justice, which requires:

(a) The immediate and final elimination of all forms of inequality, exploitation of peoples and individuals, colonialism and racism, including nazism and apartheid, and all other policies and ideologies opposed to the purposes and principles of the United Nations;

(b) The recognition and effective implementation of civil and political rights as well as of economic, social and cultural rights without any discrimination.

*Article 3.* The following are considered primary conditions of social progress and development:

(a) National independence based on the right of people to self-determination;

(b) The principle of non-interference in the internal affairs of States;

(c) Respect for the sovereignty and territorial integrity of States;

(d) Permanent sovereignty of each nation over its natural wealth and resources;

(e) The right and responsibility of each State and, as far as they are concerned, each nation and people to determine freely its own objectives of social development, to set its own priorities and to decide in conformity with the principles of the Charter of the United Nations the means and methods of their achievement without any external interference;

(f) Peaceful coexistence, peace, friendly relations and co-operation among States irrespective of differences in their social, economic or political systems.

*Article 4.* The family as a basic unit of society and the natural environment for the growth and well-being of all its members, particularly children and youth, should be assisted and protected so that it may fully assume its responsibilities within the community. Parents have the exclusive right to determine freely and responsibly the number and spacing of their children.

*Article 5.* Social progress and development require the full utilization of human resources, including, in particular:

(a) The encouragement of creative initiative under conditions of enlightened public opinion;

(b) The dissemination of national and international information for the purpose of making individuals aware of changes occurring in society as a whole;

(c) The active participation of all elements of society, individually or through associations, in defining and in achieving the common goals of development with full respect for the fundamental freedoms embodied in the Universal Declaration of Human Rights;

(d) The assurance to disadvantaged or marginal sectors of the population of equal opportunities for social and economic advancement in order to achieve an effectively integrated society.

*Article 6.* Social development requires the assurance to everyone of the right to work and the free choice of employment. Social progress and development require the participation of all members of society in productive and socially useful labour and the establishment, in conformity with human rights and fundamental freedoms and with the principles of justice and the social function of property, of forms of ownership of land and of the means of production which preclude any kind of exploitation of man, ensure equal rights to property for all and create conditions leading to genuine equality among people.

*Article 7.* The rapid expansion of national income and wealth and their equitable distribution among all members of society are fundamental to all social progress, and they should therefore be in the forefront of the preoccupations of every State and Government.

The improvement in the position of the developing countries in international trade resulting among other things from the achievement of favourable terms of trade and of equitable and remunerative prices at which developing countries market their products is necessary in order to make it possible to increase national income and in order to advance social development.

*Article 8.* Each Government has the primary role and ultimate responsibility of ensuring the social progress and well-being of its people, of planning social development measures as part of comprehensive development plans, of encouraging and co-ordinating or integrating all national efforts towards this end and of introducing necessary changes in the social structure. In planning social development measures, the diversity of the needs of developing and developed areas, and of urban and rural areas, within each country, shall be taken into due account.

*Article 9.* Social progress and development are the common concerns of the international community, which shall supplement, by concerted international action, national efforts to raise the living standards of peoples.

Social progress and economic growth require recognition of the common interest of all nations in the exploration, conservation, use and exploitation, exclusively for peaceful purposes and in the interests of all mankind, of those areas of the environment such as outer space and the sea-bed and ocean floor and the subsoil thereof, beyond the limits of national jurisdiction, in accordance with the Purposes and Principles of the Charter of the United Nations.

## Part II—Objectives

Social progress and development shall aim at the continuous raising of the material and spiritual standards of living of all members of society, with respect for and in compliance with human rights and fundamental freedoms, through the attainment of the following main goals:

*Article 10.* (a) The assurance at all levels of the right to work and the right of everyone to form trade unions and workers' associations and to bargain collectively; promotion of full productive employment and elimination of unemployment and under-employment; establishment of equitable and favourable conditions of work for all, including the improvement of health and safety conditions; assurance of just remuneration for labour without any discrimination as well as a sufficiently high minimum wage to ensure a decent standard of living; the protection of the consumer;

(b) The elimination of hunger and malnutrition and the guarantee of the right to proper nutrition;

(c) The elimination of poverty; the assurance of a steady improvement in levels of living and of a just and equitable distribution of income;

(d) The achievement of the highest standards of health and the provision of health protection for the entire population, if possible free of charge;

(e) The eradication of illiteracy and the assurance of the right to universal access to culture, to free compulsory education at the elementary level and to free education at all levels; the raising of the general level of life-long education;

(f) The provision for all, particularly persons in low income groups and large families, of adequate housing and community services.

Social progress and development shall aim equally at the progressive attainment of the following main goals:

*Article 11.* (a) The provision of comprehensive social security schemes and social welfare services; the establishment and improvement of social security and insurance schemes for all persons who, because of illness, disability or old age, are temporarily or permanently unable to earn a living, with a view to ensuring a proper standard of living for such persons and for their families and dependants;

(b) The protection of the rights of the mother and child; concern for the upbringing and health of children; the pro-vision of measures to safeguard the health and welfare of women and particularly of working mothers during pregnancy and the infancy of their children, as well as of mothers whose earnings are the sole source of livelihood for the family; the granting to women of pregnancy and maternity leave and allowances without loss of employment or wages;

(c) The protection of the rights and the assuring of the welfare of children, the aged and the disabled; the provision of protection for the physically or mentally disadvantaged;

(d) The education of youth in, and promotion among them of, the ideals of justice and peace, mutual respect and understanding among peoples; the promotion of full participation of youth in the process of national development;

(e) The provision of social defence measures and the elimination of conditions leading to crime and delinquency, especially juvenile delinquency;

(f) The guarantee that all individuals, without discrimination of any kind, are made aware of their rights and obligations and receive the necessary aid in the exercise and safeguarding of their rights.

Social progress and development shall further aim at achieving the following main objectives:

*Article 12.* (a) The creation of conditions for rapid and sustained social and economic development, particularly in the developing countries; change in international economic relations; new and effective methods of international co-operation in which equality of opportunity should be as much a prerogative of nations as of individuals within a nation;

(b) The elimination of all forms of discrimination and exploitation and all other practices and ideologies contrary to the purposes and principles of the Charter of the United Nations;

(c) The elimination of all forms of foreign economic exploitation, particularly that practised by international monopolies, in order to enable the people of every country to enjoy in full the benefits of their national resources.

Social progress and development shall finally aim at the attainment of the following main goals:

*Article 13.* (a) Equitable sharing of scientific and technological advances by developed and developing countries, and a steady increase in the use of science and technology for the benefit of the social development of society;

(b) The establishment of a harmonious balance between scientific, technological and material progress and the intellectual, spiritual, cultural and moral advancement of humanity;

(c) The protection and improvement of the human environment.

## Part III—Means and Methods

On the basis of the principles set forth in this Declaration, the achievement of the objectives of social progress and development requires the mobilization of the necessary resources by national and international action, with particular attention to such means and methods as:

*Article 14.* (a) Planning for social progress and development, as an integrated part of balanced over-all development planning;

(b) The establishment, where necessary, of national systems for framing and carrying out social policies and programmes, and the promotion by the countries concerned of planned regional development, taking into account differing regional conditions and needs, particularly the development of regions which are less favoured or under-developed by comparison with the rest of the country;

(c) The promotion of basic and applied social research, particularly comparative international research applied to the planning and execution of social development programmes.

*Article 15.* (a) The adoption of measures to ensure the effective participation, as appropriate, of all the elements of society in the preparation and execution of national plans and programmes of economic and social development;

(b) The adoption of measures for an increasing rate of popular participation in the economic, social, cultural and political life of countries through national governmental bodies, non-governmental organizations, cooperatives, rural associations, workers' and employers' organizations and women's and youth organizations, by such methods as national and regional plans for social and economic progress and community development, with a view to achieving a fully integrated national society, accelerating the process of social mobility and consolidating the democratic system;

(c) Mobilization of public opinion, at both national and international levels, in support of the principles and objectives of social progress and development;

(d) The dissemination of social information, at the national and the international level, to make people aware of changing circumstances in society as a whole, and to educate the consumer.

*Article 16.* (a) Maximum mobilization of all national resources and their rational and efficient utilization; promotion of increased and accelerated productive investment in social and economic fields and of employment; orientation of society towards the development process;

(b) Progressively increasing provision of the necessary budgetary and other resources required for financing the social aspects of development;

(c) Achievement of equitable distribution of national income, utilizing, *inter alia,* the fiscal system and government spending as an instrument for the equitable distribution and redistribution of income in order to promote social progress;

(d) The adoption of measures aimed at prevention of such an outflow of capital from developing countries as would be detrimental to their economic and social development.

*Article 17.* (a) The adoption of measures to accelerate the process of industrialization, especially in developing countries, with due regard for its social aspects, in the interests of the entire population; development of an adequate organizational and legal framework conducive to an uninterrupted and diversified growth of the industrial sector; measures to overcome the adverse social effects which may result from urban development and industrialization, including automation; maintenance of a proper balance between rural and urban development, and in particular, measures designed to ensure healthier living conditions, especially in large industrial centres;

(b) Integrated planning to meet the problems of urbanization and urban development;

(c) Comprehensive rural development schemes to raise the levels of living of the rural populations and to facilitate such urban-rural relationships and population distribution as will promote balanced national development and social progress;

(d) Measures for appropriate supervision of the utilization of land in the interests of society.

The achievement of the objectives of social progress and development equally requires the implementation of the following means and methods:

*Article 18.* (a) The adoption of appropriate legislative, administrative and other measures ensuring to everyone not only political and civil rights, but also the full realization of economic, social and cultural rights without any discrimination;

(b) The promotion of democratically based social and institutional reforms and motivation for change basic to the elimination of all forms of discrimination and exploitation and conducive to high rates of economic and social progress, to include land reform, in which the ownership and use of land will be made to serve best the objective of social justice and economic development;

(c) The adoption of measures to boost and diversify agricultural production through, *inter alia,* the implementation of democratic agrarian reforms, to ensure an adequate and well-balanced supply of food, its equitable distribution among the whole population and the improvement of nutritional standards;

(d) The adoption of measures to introduce, with the participation of the Government, low-cost housing programmes in both rural and urban areas;

(e) Development and expansion of the system of transportation and communications, particularly in developing countries.

*Article 19.* (a) The provision of free health services to the whole population and of adequate preventive and curative facilities and welfare medical services accessible to all;

(b) The enactment and establishment of legislative measures and administrative regulations with a view to the implementation of comprehensive programmes of social security schemes and social welfare services and to the improvement and co-ordination of existing services;

(c) The adoption of measures and the provision of social welfare services to migrant workers and their families, in conformity with the provisions of Convention No. 97 of the International Labour Organisation (on migration for employment) and other international instruments relating to migrant workers;

(d) The institution of appropriate measures for the rehabilitation of mentally or physically disabled persons, especially children and youth, so as to enable them to the fullest possible extent to be useful members of society—these measures shall include the provision of treatment and technical appliances, education, vocational and social guidance, training and selective placement, and other assistance required—and the creation of social conditions in which the handicapped are not discriminated against because of their disabilities.

*Article 20.* (a) The provision of full democratic freedoms to trade unions; freedom of association for all workers, including the right to bargain collectively and to strike; recognition of the right to form other organizations of working people; the provision for the growing participation of trade unions in economic and social development; effective participation of all members of trade unions in the deciding of economic and social issues which affect their interests;

(b) The improvement of health and safety conditions for workers, by means of appropriate technological and legislative measures and the provision of the material prerequisites for the implementation of those measures, including the limitation of working hours;

(c) The adoption of appropriate measures for the development of harmonious industrial relations.

*Article 21.* (a) The training of national personnel and cadres, including administrative, executive, professional and technical personnel needed for social development and for over-all development plans and policies;

(b) The adoption of measures to accelerate the extension and improvement of general, vocational and technical education and of training and retraining, which should be provided free at all levels;

(c) Raising the general level of education; development and expansion of national information media, and their rational and full use towards continuing education of the whole population and towards encouraging its participation in social development activities; the constructive use of leisure, particularly that of children and adolescents;

(d) The formulation of national and international policies and measures to avoid the "brain drain" and obviate its adverse effects.

*Article 22.* (a) The development and co-ordination of policies and measures designed to strengthen the essential functions of the family as a basic unit of society;

(b) The formulation and establishment, as needed, of programmes in the field of population, within the framework of national demographic policies and as part of the welfare medical services, including education, training of personnel and the provision to families of the knowledge and means necessary to enable them to exercise their right to determine freely and responsibly the number and spacing of their children;

(c) The establishment of appropriate child-care facilities in the interest of children and working parents.

The achievement of the objectives of social progress and development finally requires the implementation of the following means and methods:

*Article 23.* (a) The laying down of economic growth rate targets for the developing countries within the United Nations policy for development, high enough to lead to a substantial acceleration of their rates of growth;

(b) The provision of greater assistance on better terms; the implementation of the aid volume target of a minimum of 1 per cent of the gross national product at market prices of economically advanced countries; the general easing of the terms of lending to the developing countries through low interest rates on loans and long grace periods for the repayment of loans, and the assurance that the allocation of such loans will be based strictly on socio-economic criteria free of any political considerations;

(c) The provision of technical, financial and material assistance, both bilateral and multilateral, to the fullest possible extent and on favourable terms, and improved co-ordination of international assistance for the achievement of the social objectives of national development plans;

(d) The provision to the developing countries of technical, financial and material assistance and of favourable conditions to facilitate the direct exploitation of their national resources and natural wealth by those countries with a view to enabling the peoples of those countries to benefit fully from their national resources;

(e) The expansion of international trade based on principles of equality and non-discrimination, the rectification of the position of developing countries in international trade by equitable terms of trade, a general non-reciprocal and non-discriminatory system of preferences for the exports of developing countries to the developed countries, the establishment and implementation of general and comprehensive commodity agreements, and the financing of reasonable buffer stocks by international institutions.

*Article 24.* (a) Intensification of international co-operation with a view to ensuring the international exchange of information, knowledge and experience concerning social progress and development;

(b) The broadest possible international technical, scientific and cultural co-operation and reciprocal utilization of the experience of countries with different economic and social systems and different levels of development, on the basis of mutual advantage and strict observance of and respect for national sovereignty;

(c) Increased utilization of science and technology for social and economic development; arrangements for the transfer and exchange of technology, including know-how and patents, to the developing countries.

*Article 25.* (a) The establishment of legal and administrative measures for the protection and improvement of the human environment, at both national and international level;

(b) The use and exploitation, in accordance with the appropriate international régimes, of the resources of areas of the environment such as outer space and the sea-bed and ocean floor and the subsoil thereof, beyond the limits of national jurisdiction, in order to supplement national resources available for the achievement of economic and social progress and development in every country, irrespective of its geographical location, special consideration being given to the interests and needs of the developing countries.

*Article 26.* Compensation for damages, be they social or economic in nature—including restitution and reparations—caused as a result of aggression and of illegal occupation of territory by the aggressor.

*Article 27.* (a) The achievement of general and complete disarmament and the channelling of the progressively released resources to be used for economic and social progress for the welfare of people everywhere and, in particular, for the benefit of developing countries;

(b) The adoption of measures contributing to disarmament, including, *inter alia,* the complete prohibition of tests of nuclear weapons, the prohibition of the development, production and stockpiling of chemical and bacteriological (biological) weapons and the prevention of the pollution of oceans and inland waters by nuclear wastes.

**DEVELOPMENT: DECLARATION ON THE RIGHT TO DEVELOPMENT, UN (1986).** Adopted after long study and some controversy, the Declaration confirms the view of the international community that the right to development is an inalienable human right "by virtue of which every human person and all peoples are entitled to participate in, contribute to and enjoy economic, social, cultural and political development, in which all human rights and fundamental freedoms can be fully realized."

The Declaration was adopted by the UN **GENERAL ASSEMBLY** on 4 December 1986 (resolution 41/128). The text, annexed to that resolution, is as follows:

The General Assembly,

Bearing in mind the purposes and principles of the Charter of the United Nations relating to the achievement of international co-operation in solving international problems of an economic, social, cultural or humanitarian nature, and in promoting and encouraging respect for human rights and fundamental freedoms for all without distinction as to race, sex, language or religion,

Recognizing that development is a comprehensive economic, social, cultural and political process, which aims at the constant improvement of the well-being of the entire population and of all individuals on the basis of their active, free and meaningful participation in development and in the fair distribution of benefits resulting therefrom,

Considering that under the provisions of the Universal Declaration of Human Rights everyone is entitled to a social and international order in which the rights and freedoms set forth in that Declaration can be fully realized,

Recalling the provisions of the International Covenant on Economic, Social and Cultural Rights and the International Covenant on Civil and Political Rights,

Recalling further the relevant agreements, conventions, resolutions, recommendations and other instruments of the United Nations and its specialized agencies concerning the integral development of the human being, economic and social progress and development of all peoples, including those instruments concerning decolonization, the prevention of discrimination, respect for, and observance of, human rights and fundamental freedoms, the maintenance of international peace and security and the further promotion of friendly relations and co-operation among States in accordance with the Charter,

Recalling the right of peoples to self-determination, by virtue of which they have the right freely to determine their political status and to pursue their economic, social and cultural development,

Recalling further the right of peoples to exercise, subject to relevant provisions of both International Convenants on Human Rights, their full and complete sovereignty over all their natural wealth and resources,

Mindful of the obligation of States under the Charter to promote universal respect for, and observance of, human rights and fundamental freedoms for all without distinction of any kind such as race, colour, sex, language, religion, political or other opinion, national or social origin, property, birth or other status,

Considering that the elimination of the massive and flagrant violations of the human rights of the peoples and individuals affected by situations such as those resulting from colonialism, neo-colonialism, apartheid, all forms of racism and racial discrimination, foreign domination and occupation, aggression and threats against national sovereignty, national unity and territorial integrity and threats of war would contribute to the establishment of circumstances propitious to the development of a great part of mankind,

Concerned at the existence of serious obstacles to development, as well as to the complete fulfilment of human beings and of peoples, constituted, *inter alia*, by the denial of civil, political, economic, social and cultural rights, and considering that all human rights and fundamental freedoms are indivisible and interdependent and that, in order to promote development, equal attention and urgent consideration should be given to the implementation, promotion and protection of civil, political, economic, social and cultural rights and that, accordingly, the promotion of, respect for, and enjoyment of certain human rights and fundamental freedoms cannot justify the denial of other human rights and fundamental freedoms,

Considering that international peace and security are essential elements for the realization of the right to development,

Reaffirming that there is a close relationship between dis-

armament and development and that progress in the field of disarmament would considerably promote progress in the field of development and that resources released through disarmament measures should be devoted to the economic and social development and well-being of all peoples and, in particular, those of the developing countries,

Recognizing that the human person is the central subject of the development process and that development policy should therefore make the human being the main participant and beneficiary of development,

Recognizing that the creation of conditions favourable to the development of peoples and individuals is the primary responsibility of their States,

Aware that efforts to promote and protect human rights at the international level should be accompanied by efforts to establish a new international economic order,

Confirming that the right to development is an inalienable human right and that equality of opportunity for development is a prerogative both of nations and of individuals who make up nations,

Proclaims the following Declaration on the right to development:

*Article 1.* 1. The right to development is an inalienable human right by virtue of which every human person and all peoples are entitled to participate in, contribute to and enjoy economic, social, cultural and political development, in which all human rights and fundamental freedoms can be fully realized.

2. The human right to development also implies the full realization of the right of peoples to self-determination, which includes, subject to relevant provisions of both International Covenants on Human Rights, the exercise of their inalienable right to full sovereignty over all their natural wealth and resources.

*Article 2.* 1. The human person is the central subject of development and should be the active participant and beneficiary of the right to development.

2. All human beings have a responsibility for development, individually and collectively, taking into account the need for full respect of their human rights and fundamental freedoms as well as their duties to the community, which alone can ensure the free and complete fulfilment of the human being, and they should therefore promote and protect an appropriate political, social and economic order for development.

3. States have the right and the duty to formulate appropriate national development policies that aim at the constant improvement of the well-being of the entire population and of all individuals, on the basis of their active, free and meaningful participation in development and in the fair distribution of the benefits resulting therefrom.

*Article 3.* 1. States have the primary responsibility for the creation of national and international conditions favourable to the realization of the right to development.

2. The realization of the right to development requires full respect for the principles of international law concerning friendly relations and co-operation among States in accordance with the Charter of the United Nations.

3. States have the duty to co-operate with each other in ensuring development and eliminating obstacles to development. States should fulfil their rights and duties in such a manner as to promote a new international economic order based on sovereign equality, interdependence, mutual interest and cooperation among all States, as well as to encourage the observance and realization of human rights.

*Article 4.* 1. States have the duty to take steps, individually and collectively, to formulate international development policies with a view to facilitating the full realization of the right to development.

2. Sustained action is required to promote more rapid development of developing countries. As a complement to the efforts of developing countries effective international cooperation is essential in providing these countries with appropriate means and facilities to foster their comprehensive development.

*Article 5.* States shall take resolute steps to eliminate the massive and flagrant violations of the human rights of peoples and human beings affected by situations such as those resulting from apartheid, all forms of racism and racial discrimination, colonialism, foreign domination and occupation, aggression, foreign interference and threats against national sovereignty, national unity and territorial integrity, threats of war and refusal to recognize the fundamental right of peoples to self-determination.

*Article 6.* 1. All States should co-operate with a view to promoting, encouraging and strengthening universal respect for and observance of all human rights and fundamental freedoms for all without any distinction as to race, sex, language and religion.

2. All human rights and fundamental freedoms are indivisible and interdependent; equal attention and urgent consideration should be given to the implementation, promotion and protection of civil, political, economic, social and cultural rights.

3. States should take steps to eliminate obstacles to development resulting from failure to observe civil and political rights as well as economic, social and cultural rights.

*Article 7.* All States should promote the establishment, maintenance and strengthening of international peace and security and, to that end, should do their utmost to achieve general and complete disarmament under effective international control as well as to ensure that the resources released by effective disarmament measures are used for comprehensive development, in particular that of the developing countries.

*Article 8.* 1. States should undertake, at the national level, all necessary measures for the realization of the right to development and shall ensure, *inter alia,* equality of opportunity for all in their access to basic resources, education, health services, food, housing, employment and the fair distribution of income. Effective measures should be undertaken to ensure that women have an active role in the development process. Appropriate economic and social reforms should be made with a view to eradicating all social injustices.

2. States should encourage popular participation in all spheres as an important factor in development and in the full realization of all human rights.

*Article 9.* 1. All the aspects of the right to development set forth in this Declaration are indivisible and interdependent and each of them should be considered in the context of the whole.

2. Nothing in this Declaration shall be construed as being contrary to the purposes and principles of the United Nations, or as implying that any State, group or person has a right to engage in any activity or to perform any act aimed at the violation of the rights set forth in the Universal Declaration of Human Rights and in the International Covenants on Human Rights.

*Article 10.* Steps should be taken to ensure the full exercise and progressive enhancement of the right to development, including the formulation, adoption and implementation of policy, legislative and other measures at the national and international levels.

**DEVELOPMENT INNOVATIONS AND NETWORKS.** Founded in Geneva in 1980 under its French name Innovations et réseaux pour le développement (IRED), this non-governmental organization has consultative status with the UN **ECONOMIC AND SOCIAL COUNCIL** (Category II) and **UNESCO.** IRED supports initiatives that can contribute to endogenous, self-reliant development at local, regional, and national levels; and supports and promotes self-reliant development zones. It also encourages cooperation among poor countries and industrialized ones. It publishes the quarterly *IRED Forum* in French, English, and Spanish.

Development Innovations and Networks. Address: 3 rue de Varembé, Case 116, CH-1211 Geneva 20, Switzerland. Telephone: (41-22) 734-1716. Fax: (41-22) 740-0011. Secretary-General: Fernand Vincent.

**DIANA.** A consortium of law librarians, university-based human rights centers, and other non-governmental human rights organizations has undertaken the monumental task of combining the "information highway" and the needs of human rights advocates and researchers around the world for timely, authoritative literature in their discipline. The project—DIANA—will promote the creation, organization, dissemination, and preservation of primary and secondary electronic materials critical to human rights research.

The project is named in honor of Diana Vincent-Daviss (1943–1993), the late librarian of the Yale Law School and the first deputy director of the Schell Center for International Human Rights at Yale Law School. A prototype of DIANA currently exists on the Internet on a World Wide Web server at the University of Cincinnati College of Law (Internet is currently available in about 40 countries). The prototype database contains a small sampling of some basic human rights documents from the United Nations, related U.S. State Department reports, cases from the **INTER-AMERICAN COURT OF HUMAN RIGHTS,** and Diana Vincent-Daviss' bibliography on women's rights. Eventually, the system will include all major international human rights treaties; international, regional, and national court decisions concerning human rights; a legal brief "bank"; and important human rights treatises and journals. Most of these documents will be in full text.

Documents on DIANA will be available in several forms: archival electronic text, optical images, and hypertext markup language (HTML) files. The archival electronic text will be saved in a universally accept format that will allow maximum future electronic use of the data. The word-searchable HTML data files will allow the user to search all documents on DIANA. All information contained on DIANA may be accessed without charge.

It is estimated that DIANA will be completely on-line by the end of the century. Those interested in monitoring the development of DIANA may do so through telnet: Taft.law.uc.edu (enter lynx at log-in); or by connecting via an Internet browser (such as Mosaic or Cello) to the following uniform resource locator (URL) on the Internet: http;//www.law.uc.edu/Diana.

**DISABILITY.** The United Nations has been continuously concerned, since its establishment, with the situation of disabled persons. In 1976, the UN **GENERAL ASSEMBLY** proclaimed (resolution 31/123) the year 1981 to be the International Year of Disabled Persons; and in 1982 it adopted (resolution 37/52) the World Program of Action concerning Disabled Persons and proclaimed (resolution 37/53) the period 1983–1992 the United Nations Decade of Disabled Persons.

*DECLARATION ON THE RIGHTS OF DISABLED PERSONS.* On 9 December 1975, the UN General Assembly adopted the Declaration on the Rights of Disabled Persons (resolution 3447 [XXX]), and recommended that all Member States should bear its principles in mind in establishing their national policies, plans, and programs. The Declaration included the following provisions:

1. The term "disabled person" means any person unable to ensure by himself or herself, wholly or partly, the necessities of a normal individual and/or social life, as a result of a deficiency, either congenital or not, in his or her physical or mental capabilities.

2. Disabled persons shall enjoy all the rights set forth in this Declaration. These rights shall be granted to all disabled persons without any exception whatsoever and without distinction or discrimination on the basis of race, colour, sex, language, religion, political, or other opinions, national or social origin, state of wealth, birth, or any other situation applying either to the disabled person himself or herself or to his or her family.

3. Disabled persons have the inherent right to respect for their human dignity. Disabled persons, whatever the origin, nature, and seriousness of their handicaps and disabilities, have the same fundamental rights as their fellow-citizens of the same age, which implies first and foremost the right to enjoy a decent life, as normal and full as possible.

4. Disabled persons have the same civil and political rights as other human beings; paragraph 7 of the Declaration on the Rights of Mentally Retarded Persons applies to any possible limitation or suppression of those rights for mentally disabled persons.

5. Disabled persons are entitled to the measures designed to enable them to become as self-reliant as possible.

6. Disabled persons have the right to medical, psychological, and functional treatment, including prosthetic and orthetic appliances to medical and social rehabilitation, education, vocational training and rehabilitation, aid, counselling, placement services, and other services that will enable them to develop their capabilities and skills to the maximum and will hasten the process of their social integration or reintegration.

7. Disabled persons have the right to economic and social security and to a decent level of living. They have the right, according to their capabilities, to secure and retain employment or to engage in a useful, productive, and remunerative occupation and to join trade unions.

8. Disabled persons are entitled to have their special needs taken into consideration at all stages of economic and social planning.

*STUDY OF HUMAN RIGHTS AND DISABLED PERSONS.* At the request of the UN **ECONOMIC AND SOCIAL COUNCIL** (resolution 1984/26), the **SUB-COMMISSION ON PREVENTION OF DISCRIMINATION AND PROTECTION OF MINORITIES** (resolution 1984/20) appointed one of its members, Mr. Leandro Despouy (Argentina), to undertake an in-depth study of the relationship between human rights and disability and to include in the study consideration of and recommendations regarding human rights and humanitarian law violations that result in disability or have a particular impact on disabled persons; all forms of discrimination against disabled persons; apartheid as it relates to disability; institutionalization and institutional abuse; and economic, social, and cultural rights as they relate to disability. The Sub-Commission also requested the Special Rapporteur to include, on a preliminary basis, an outline of the topic of scientific experimentation as it relates to disabled persons. The Special Rapporteur submitted his final report (UN publication, Sales no. E.92.XIV.4) to the Sub-Commission at its 1991 session.

*STANDARD RULES ON EQUALIZATION OF OPPORTUNITY.* At its 1992 session, the Commission on Human Rights considered the Special Rapporteur's report (resolution 1992/48 of 3 March 1992) and also welcomed the decision by the Commission for Social Development to elaborate standard rules on the equalization of opportunities for disabled persons, which would be transmitted to the General Assembly.

The Standard Rules were prepared on the basis of experience gained during the UN Decade of Disabled Persons (1983–1992). They also reflect the terms of relevant instruments adopted by the International Labor Organization, particularly regarding the employment of disabled persons without discrimination. The

Rules were adopted without a vote by the General Assembly on 20 December 1993 (resolution 48/96), and read as follows:

## I. Preconditions for Equal Participation

*Rule 1. Awareness-raising.* States should take action to raise awareness in society about persons with disabilities, their rights, their needs, their potential, and their contribution.

1. States should ensure that responsible authorities distribute up-to-date information on available programmes and services to persons with disabilities, their families, professionals in this field, and the general public. Information to persons with disabilities should be presented in accessible form.

2. States should initiate and support information campaigns concerning persons with disabilities and disability policies, conveying the message that persons with disabilities are citizens with the same rights and obligations as others, thus justifying measures to remove all obstacles to full participation.

3. States should encourage the portrayal of persons with disabilities by the mass media in a positive way; organizations of persons with disabilities should be consulted on this matter.

4. States should ensure that public education programmes reflect in all their aspects the principle of full participation and equality.

5. States should invite persons with disabilities and their families and organizations to participate in public education programmes concerning disability matters.

6. States should encourage enterprises in the private sector to include disability issues in all aspects of their activity.

7. States should initiate and promote programmes aimed at raising the level of awareness of persons with disabilities concerning their rights and potential. Increased self-reliance and empowerment will assist persons with disabilities to take advantage of the opportunities available to them.

8. Awareness-raising should be an important part of the education of children with disabilities and in rehabilitation programmes. Persons with disabilities could also assist one another in awareness-raising through the activities of their own organizations.

9. Awareness-raising should be part of the education of all children and should be a component of teacher-training and training of all professionals.

*Rule 2. Medical Care.* States should ensure the provision of effective medical care to persons with disabilities.

1. States should work towards the provision of programmes run by multidisciplinary teams of professionals for early detection, assessment, and treatment of impairment. This could prevent, reduce, or eliminate disabling effects. Such programmes should ensure the full participation of persons with disabilities and their families at the individual level, and of organizations of persons with disabilities at the planning and evaluation level.

2. Local community workers should be trained to participate in areas such as early detection of impairments, the provision of primary assistance, and referral to appropriate services.

3. States should ensure that persons with disabilities, particularly infants and children, are provided with the same level of medical care within the same system as other members of society.

4. States should ensure that all medical and paramedical personnel are adequately trained and equipped to give medical care to persons with disabilities and that they have access to relevant treatment methods and technology.

5. States should ensure that medical, paramedical, and related personnel are adequately trained so that they do not give inappropriate advice to parents, thus restricting options for their children. This training should be an ongoing process and should be based on the latest information available.

6. States should ensure that persons with disabilities are provided with any regular treatment and medicines they may need to preserve or improve their level of functioning.

*Rule 3. Rehabilitation.* States should ensure the provision of rehabilitation services to persons with disabilities in order for them to reach and sustain their optimum level of independence and functioning.

1. States should develop national rehabilitation programmes for all groups of persons with disabilities. Such programmes should be based on the actual individual needs of persons with disabilities and on the principles of full participation and equality.

2. Such programmes should include a wide range of activities, such as basic skills training to improve or compensate for an affected function, counselling of persons with disabilities and their families, developing self-reliance, and occasional services such as assessment and guidance.

3. All persons with disabilities, including persons with severe and/or multiple disabilities, who require rehabilitation should have access to it.

4. Persons with disabilities and their families should be able to participate in the design and organization of rehabilitation services concerning themselves.

5. All rehabilitation services should be available in the local community where the person with disabilities lives. However, in some instances, in order to attain a certain training objective, special time-limited rehabilitation courses may be organized, where appropriate, in residential form.

6. Persons with disabilities and their families should be encouraged to involve themselves in rehabilitation, for instance as trained teachers, instructors, or counsellors.

7. States should draw upon the expertise of organizations of persons with disabilities when formulating or evaluating rehabilitation programmes.

*Rule 4. Support Services.* States should ensure the development and supply of support services, including assistive devices for persons with disabilities, to assist them to increase their level of independence in their daily living and to exercise their rights.

1. States should ensure the provision of assistive devices and equipment, personal assistance, and interpreter services, according to the needs of persons with disabilities, as important measures to achieve the equalization of opportunities.

2. States should support the development, production, distribution, and servicing of assistive devices and equipment and the dissemination of knowledge about them.

3. To achieve this, generally available technical know-how should be utilized. In States where high-technology industry is available, it should be fully utilized to improve the standard and effectiveness of assistive devices and equipment. It is important to stimulate the development and production of simple and inexpensive devices, when possible using local material and local production facilities. Persons with disabilities themselves could be involved in the production of those devices.

4. States should recognize that all persons with disabilities who need assistive devices should have access to them as ap-

propriate, including financial accessibility. This may mean that assistive devices and equipment should be provided free of charge or at such a low price that persons with disabilities or their families can afford to buy them.

5. In rehabilitation programmes for the provision of assistive devices and equipment, States should consider the special requirements of girls and boys with disabilities concerning the design, durability, and age-appropriateness of assistive devices and equipment.

6. States should support the development and provision of personal assistance programmes and interpretation services, especially for persons with severe and/or multiple disabilities. Such programmes would increase the level of participation of persons with disabilities in everyday life, at home, at work, in school, and during leisure-time activities.

7. Personal assistance programmes should be designed in such a way that the persons with disabilities using the programmes have a decisive influence on the way in which the programmes are delivered.

## II. Target Areas for Equal Participation

*Rule 5. Accessibility.* States should recognize the overall importance of accessibility in the process of the equalization of opportunities in all spheres of society. For persons with disabilities of any kind, States should (a) introduce programmes of action to make the physical environment accessible; and (b) undertake measures to provide access to information and communication.

(a) Access to Physical Environment

1. States should initiate measures to remove the obstacles to participation in the physical environment. Such measures should be to develop standards and guidelines and to consider enacting legislation to ensure accessibility to various areas in society, for instance concerning housing, buildings, public transport services, and other means of transportation, streets, and other outdoor environments.

2. States should ensure that architects, construction engineers, and others who are professionally involved in the design and construction of the physical environment have access to adequate information on disability policy and measures to achieve accessibility.

3. Accessibility requirements should be included in the design and construction of the physical environment from the beginning of the designing process.

4. Organizations of persons with disabilities should be consulted when developing standards and norms for accessibility. They should also be involved locally from the initial planning stage when public construction projects are being designed, thus ensuring maximum accessibility.

(b) Access to Information and Communication

5. Persons with disabilities and, where appropriate, their families and advocates should have access to full information on diagnosis, rights, and available services and programmes at all stages. Such information should be presented in forms accessible to people with disabilities.

6. States should develop strategies to make information services and documentation accessible for different groups of people with disabilities. Braille, tape services, large print, and other appropriate technologies should be used to provide access to written information and documentation for persons with visual impairments. Similarly, appropriate technologies should be used to provide access to spoken information for persons with auditory impairments or comprehension difficulties.

7. Consideration should be given to the use of sign language in the education of deaf children, in their families and communities. Sign language interpretation or services should also be provided to facilitate the communication between deaf persons and others.

8. Consideration should also be given to the needs of people with other communication disabilities.

9. States should encourage the media, especially television, radio, and newspapers, to make their services accessible.

10. States should ensure that new computerized information and service systems offered to the general public are either made initially accessible or are adapted to be made accessible to persons with disabilities.

11. Organizations of persons with disabilities should be consulted when developing measures to make information services accessible.

*Rule 6. Education.* States should recognize the principle of equal primary, secondary, and tertiary education opportunities for children, youth, and adults with disabilities in integrated settings. They should ensure that the education of persons with disabilities is an integral part of the educational system.

1. General educational authorities are responsible for the education of persons with disabilities in integrated settings. Education for persons with disabilities should form an integral part of national educational planning, curriculum development, and school organization.

2. Education in mainstream schools presupposes the provision of interpreter and other appropriate support services. Adequate accessibility and support services, designed to meet the needs of persons with different disabilities, should be provided.

3. Parent groups and organizations of persons with disabilities should be involved in the education process at all levels.

4. In States where education is compulsory, it should be provided to girls and boys with all kinds and all levels of disabilities, including the most severe.

5. Special attention should be given in the following areas:

(a) Very young children with disabilities;

(b) Pre-school children with disabilities;

(c) Adults with disabilities, particularly women.

6. To accommodate educational provisions for persons with disabilities in the mainstream, States should:

(a) Have a clearly stated policy, understood and accepted at the school level and by the wider community;

(b) Allow for curriculum flexibility, addition, and adaptation;

(c) Provide for quality materials, ongoing teacher training, and support teachers.

7. Integrated education and community-based programmes should be seen as complementary approaches in providing cost-effective education and training for persons with disabilities. National community-based programmes should encourage communities to use and develop their resources to provide local education to persons with disabilities.

8. In situations where the general school system does not yet adequately meet the needs of all persons with disabilities, special education may be considered. It should be aimed at preparing students for education in the general school system. The quality of such education should reflect the same standards and ambitions as general education and should be closely linked to it. At a minimum, students with disabilities

should be afforded the same portion of educational resources as students without disabilities. States should aim for the gradual integration of special education services with mainstream education. It is acknowledged that in some instances special education may currently be considered to be the most appropriate form of education for some students with disabilities.

9. Owing to the particular communication needs of deaf and deaf/blind persons, their education may be more suitably provided in schools for such persons or special classes and units in mainstream schools. At the initial stage, in particular, special attention needs to be focused on culturally sensitive instruction that will result in effective communication skills and maximum independence for people who are deaf or deaf/blind.

*Rule 7. Employment.* States should recognize the principle that persons with disabilities must be empowered to exercise their human rights, particularly in the field of employment. In both rural and urban areas, they must have equal opportunities for productive and gainful employment in the labour market.

1. Laws and regulations in the employment field must not discriminate against persons with disabilities and must not raise obstacles to their employment.

2. States should actively support the integration of persons with disabilities into open employment. This active support could occur through a variety of measures, such as vocational training, incentive-oriented quota schemes, reserved or designated employment, loans or grants for small business, exclusive contracts or priority production rights, tax concessions, contract compliance, or other technical or financial assistance to enterprises employing workers with disabilities. States should also encourage employers to make reasonable adjustments to accommodate persons with disabilities.

3. States' action programmes should include:

(a) Measures to design and adapt workplaces and work premises in such a way that they become accessible for persons with different disabilities;

(b) Support for the use of new technologies and the development and production of assistive devices, tools, and equipment and measures to facilitate access to such devices and equipment for persons with disabilities, to enable them to gain and maintain employment;

(c) Provision of appropriate training and placement and ongoing support such as personal assistance and interpreter services.

4. States should initiate and support public awareness-raising campaigns designed to overcome negative attitudes and prejudices concerning workers with disabilities.

5. In their capacity as employers, States should create favourable conditions for the employment of persons with disabilities in the public sector.

6. States, workers' organizations, and employers should cooperate to ensure equitable recruitment and promotion policies, employment conditions, rates of pay, measures to improve the work environment in order to prevent injuries and impairments and measures for the rehabilitation of employees who have sustained employment-related injuries.

7. The aim should always be for persons with disabilities to obtain employment in the open labour market. For persons with disabilities whose needs cannot be met in open employment, small units of sheltered or supported employment may be an alternative. It is important that the quality of such programmes be assessed in terms of their relevance

and sufficiency in providing opportunities for persons with disabilities to gain employment in the labour market.

8. Measures should be taken to include persons with disabilities in training and employment programmes in the private and informal sectors.

9. States, workers' organizations, and employers should cooperate with organizations of persons with disabilities concerning all measures to create training and employment opportunities, including flexible hours, part-time work, job-sharing, self-employment, and attendant care for persons with disabilities.

*Rule 8. Income Maintenance and Social Security.* States are responsible for the provision of social security and income maintenance for persons with disabilities.

1. States should ensure the provision of adequate income support to persons with disabilities who, owing to disability or disability-related factors, have temporarily lost or received a reduction in their income or have been denied employment opportunities. States should ensure that the provision of support takes into account the costs frequently incurred by persons with disabilities and their families as a result of the disability.

2. In countries where social security, social insurance, or other social welfare schemes exist or are being developed for the general population, States should ensure that such systems do not exclude or discriminate against persons with disabilities.

3. States should also ensure the provision of income support and social security protection to individuals who undertake the care of a person with a disability.

4. Social security systems should include incentives to restore the income-earning capacity of persons with disabilities. Such systems should provide or contribute to the organization, development, and financing of vocational training. They should also assist with placement services.

5. Social security programmes should also provide incentives for persons with disabilities to seek employment in order to establish or re-establish their income-earning capacity.

6. Income support should be maintained as long as the disabling conditions remain in a manner that does not discourage persons with disabilities from seeking employment. It should only be reduced or terminated when persons with disabilities achieve adequate and secure income.

7. States, in countries where social security is to a large extent provided by the private sector, should encourage local communities, welfare organizations, and families to develop self-help measures and incentives for employment or employment-related activities for persons with disabilities.

*Rule 9. Family Life and Personal Integrity.* States should promote the full participation of persons with disabilities in family life. They should promote their right to personal integrity, and ensure that laws do not discriminate against persons with disabilities with respect to sexual relationships, marriage, and parenthood.

1. Persons with disabilities should be enabled to live with their families. States should encourage the inclusion in family counselling of appropriate modules regarding disability and its effects on family life. Respite-care and attendant-care services should be made available to families which include a person with disabilities. States should remove all unnecessary obstacles to persons who want to foster or adopt a child or adult with disabilities.

2. Persons with disabilities must not be denied the opportunity to experience their sexuality, have sexual relationships, and experience parenthood. Taking into account that persons with disabilities may experience difficulties in get-

ting married and setting up a family, States should encourage the availability of appropriate counselling. Persons with disabilities must have the same access as others to family-planning methods, as well as to information in accessible form on the sexual functioning of their bodies.

3. States should promote measures to change negative attitudes towards marriage, sexuality and parenthood of people with disabilities, especially of girls and women with disabilities, which still prevail in society. The media should be encouraged to play an important role in removing such negative attitudes.

4. Persons with disabilities and their families need to be fully informed about taking precautions against sexual and other forms of abuse. Persons with disabilities are particularly vulnerable to abuse in the family, community, or institutions and need to be educated on how to avoid the occurrence of abuse, recognize when abuse has occurred, and report on such acts.

*Rule 10. Culture.* States will ensure that persons with disabilities are integrated into and can participate in cultural activities on an equal basis.

1. States should ensure that persons with disabilities have the opportunity to utilize their creative, artistic, and intellectual potential, not only for their own benefit, but also for the enrichment of their community, be they in urban or rural areas. Examples of such activities are dance, music, literature, theatre, plastic arts, painting, and sculpture. Particularly in developing countries, emphasis should be placed on traditional and contemporary art forms, such as puppetry, recitation, and storytelling.

2. States should promote the accessibility to and availability of places for cultural performances and services, such as theatres, museums, cinemas, and libraries, to persons with disabilities.

3. States should initiate the development and use of special technical arrangements to make literature, films, and theatre accessible to persons with disabilities.

*Rule 11. Recreation and Sports.* States will take measures to ensure that persons with disabilities have equal opportunities for recreation and sports.

1. States should initiate measures to make places for recreation and sports, hotels, beaches, sports arenas, gym halls, etc., accessible to persons with disabilities. Such measures should encompass support for staff in recreation and sports programmes, including projects to develop methods of accessibility and participation, information, and training programmes.

2. Tourist authorities, travel agencies, hotels, voluntary organizations, and others involved in organizing recreational activities or travel opportunities should offer their services to all, taking into account the special needs of persons with disabilities. Suitable training should be provided to assist that process.

3. Sports organizations should be encouraged to develop opportunities for participation by persons with disabilities in sports activities. In some cases, accessibility measures could be enough to open up opportunities for participation. In other cases, special arrangements or special games would be needed. States should support the participation of persons with disabilities in national and international events.

4. Persons with disabilities participating in sports activities should have access to instruction and training of the same quality as other participants.

5. Organizers of sports and recreation should consult with organizations of persons with disabilities when developing their services for persons with disabilities.

*Rule 12. Religion.* States will encourage measures for equal participation by persons with disabilities in the religious life of their communities.

1. States should encourage, in consultation with religious authorities, measures to eliminate discrimination and make religious activities accessible to persons with disabilities.

2. States should encourage the distribution of information on disability matters to religious institutions and organizations. States should also encourage religious authorities to include information on disability policies in the training for religious professions, as well as in religious education programmes.

3. They should also encourage the accessibility of religious literature to persons with sensory impairments.

4. States and/or religious organizations should consult with organizations of persons with disabilities when developing measures for equal participation in religious activities.

### III. Implementation Measures

*Rule 13. Information and Research.* States assume the ultimate responsibility for the collection and dissemination of information on the living conditions of persons with disabilities and promote comprehensive research on all aspects, including obstacles which affect the lives of persons with disabilities.

1. States should at regular intervals, collect gender-specific statistics and other information concerning the living conditions of persons with disabilities. Such data collection could be conducted in conjunction with national censuses and household surveys and could be undertaken in close collaboration, *inter alia,* with universities, research institutes, and organizations of persons with disabilities. The data collection should include questions on programmes and services and their use.

2. States should consider establishing a data bank on disability, which would include statistics on available services and programmes as well as on the different groups of persons with disabilities. They should bear in mind the need to protect individual privacy and personal integrity.

3. States should initiate and support programmes of research on social, economic, and participation issues that affect the lives of persons with disabilities and their families. Such research should include studies on the causes, types, and frequencies of disabilities, the availability and efficacy of existing programmes and the need for development and evaluation of services and support measures.

4. States should develop and adopt terminology and criteria for the conduct of national surveys, in cooperation with organizations of persons with disabilities.

5. States should facilitate the participation of persons with disabilities in data collection and research. To undertake such research, States should particularly encourage the recruitment of qualified persons with disabilities.

6. States should support the exchange of research findings and experiences.

7. States should take measures to disseminate information and knowledge on disability to all political and administration levels within national, regional, and local spheres.

*Rule 14. Policy-making and Planning.* States will ensure that disability aspects are included in all relevant policy-making and national planning.

1. States should initiate and plan adequate policies for persons with disabilities at the national level and stimulate and support action at regional and local levels.

2. States should involve organizations of persons with disabilities in all decisionmaking relating to plans and programmes concerning persons with disabilities or affecting their economic and social status.

3. The needs and concern of persons with disabilities should be incorporated into general development plans and not be treated separately.

4. The ultimate responsibility of States for the situation of persons with disabilities does not relieve others of their responsibility. Anyone in charge of services, activities, or the provision of information in society should be encouraged to accept responsibility for making such programmes available to persons with disabilities.

5. States should facilitate the development by local communities of programmes and measures for persons with disabilities. One way of doing this could be to develop manuals or checklists and providing training programmes for local staff.

*Rule 15. Legislation.* States have a responsibility to create the legal bases for measures to achieve the objectives of full participation and equality for persons with disabilities.

1. National legislation, embodying the rights and obligations of citizens, should include the rights and obligations of persons with disabilities. States are under an obligation to enable persons with disabilities to exercise their rights, including their human, civil, and political rights, on an equal basis with other citizens. States must ensure that organizations of persons with disabilities are involved in the development of national legislation concerning the rights of persons with disabilities, as well as in the ongoing evaluation of that legislation.

2. Legislative action may be needed to remove conditions which may adversely affect the lives of persons with disabilities, including harassment and victimization. Any discriminatory provisions against persons with disabilities must be eliminated. National legislation should provide for appropriate sanctions in case of violations of the principles of nondiscrimination.

3. National legislation concerning persons with disabilities may appear in two different forms. The rights and obligations may be incorporated in general legislation or contained in special legislation. Special legislation for persons with disabilities may be established in several ways:

(a) By enacting separate legislation, dealing exclusively with disability matters;

(b) By including disability matters within legislation on particular topics;

(c) By mentioning persons with disabilities specifically in the texts that serve to interpret existing legislation.

A combination of those different approaches might be desirable. Affirmative action provisions may also be considered.

4. States may consider establishing formal statutory complaints mechanisms in order to protect the interests of persons with disabilities.

*Rule 16. Economic Policies.* States have the financial responsibility for national programmes and measures to create equal opportunities for persons with disabilities.

1. States should include disability matters in the regular budgets of all national, regional, and local government bodies.

2. States, nongovernmental organizations, and other interested bodies should interact to determine the most effective ways of supporting projects and measures relevant to persons with disabilities.

3. States should consider the use of economic measures (loans, tax exemptions, earmarked grants, special funds, and so on) to stimulate and support equal participation by persons with disabilities in society.

4. In many States, it may be advisable to establish a disability development fund, which could support various pilot projects and self-help programmes at the grassroots level.

*Rule 17. Coordination of Work.* States are responsible for the establishment and strengthening of national coordinating committees, or similar bodies, to serve as a national focal point on disability matters.

1. The national coordinating committee or similar bodies should be permanent and based on legal as well as appropriate administrative regulation.

2. A combination of representatives of private and public organizations is most likely to achieve an intersectoral and multidisciplinary composition. Representatives could be drawn from concerned government ministries, organizations of persons with disabilities and nongovernmental organizations.

3. Organizations of persons with disabilities should have considerable influence in the national coordinating committee in order to ensure proper feedback of their concerns.

4. The national coordinating committee should be provided with sufficient autonomy and resources to fulfill its responsibilities in relation to its decisionmaking capacities. It should report to the highest governmental level.

*Rule 18. Organizations of Persons with Disabilities.* States should recognize the right of the organizations of persons with disabilities to represent persons with disabilities at national, regional, and local levels. States should also recognize the advisory role of organizations of persons with disabilities in decisionmaking on disability matters.

1. States should encourage and support economically and in other ways the formation and strengthening of organizations of persons with disabilities, family members, and/or advocates. States should recognize that those organizations have a role to play in the development of disability policy.

2. States should establish ongoing communication with organizations of persons with disabilities and ensure their participation in the development of government policies.

3. The role of organizations of persons with disabilities could be to identify needs and priorities, to participate in the planning, implementation, and evaluation of services and measures concerning the lives of persons with disabilities and to contribute to public awareness and to advocate change.

4. As instruments of self-help, organizations of persons with disabilities provide and promote opportunities for the development of skills in various fields, mutual support among members, and information sharing.

5. Organizations of persons with disabilities could perform their advisory role in many different ways, such as having permanent representation on boards of government-funded agencies, serving on public commissions, and providing expert knowledge on different projects.

6. The advisory role of organizations of persons with disabilities should be ongoing in order to develop and deepen the exchange of views and information between the State and the organizations.

7. Organizations should be permanently represented on the national coordinating committee or similar bodies.

8. The role of local organizations of persons with disabilities should be developed and strengthened to ensure that they influence matters at the community level.

*Rule 19. Personnel Training.* States are responsible for ensuring the adequate training of personnel, at all levels, involved in the planning and provision of programmes and services concerning persons with disabilities.

1. States should ensure that all authorities providing services in the disability field give adequate training to their personnel.

2. In the training of professionals in the disability field, as well as in the provision of information on disability in general training programmes, the principle of full participation and equality should be appropriately reflected.

3. States should develop training programmes in consultation with organizations of persons with disabilities, and persons with disabilities should be involved as teachers, instructors, or advisors in staff training programmes.

4. The training of community workers is of great strategic importance, particularly in developing countries. It should involve persons with disabilities and include the development of appropriate values, competence and technologies as well as skills which can be practiced by persons with disabilities, their parents, families, and members of the community.

*Rule 20. National Monitoring and Evaluation of Disability Programmes in the Implementation of the Standard Rules.* States are responsible for the continuous monitoring and evaluation of the implementation of national programmes and services concerning the equalization of opportunities for persons with disabilities.

1. States should periodically and systematically evaluate national disability programmes and disseminate both the bases and the results of the evaluations.

2. States should develop and adopt terminology and criteria for the evaluation of disability-related programmes and services.

3. Such criteria and terminology should be developed in close cooperation with organizations of persons with disabilities from the earliest conceptual and planning stages.

4. States should participate in international cooperation in order to develop common standards for national evaluation in the disability field. States should encourage national coordinating committees to participate also.

5. The evaluation of various programmes in the disability field should be built in at the planning stage, so that the overall efficacy in fulfilling their policy objectives can be evaluated.

*Rule 21. Technical and Economic Cooperation.* States, both industrialized and developing, have the responsibility to cooperate in and take measures for the improvement of the living conditions of persons with disabilities in developing countries.

1. Measures to achieve the equalization of opportunities of persons with disabilities, including refugees with disabilities, should be integrated into general development programmes.

2. Such measures must be integrated into all forms of technical and economic cooperation, bilateral and multilateral, governmental and nongovernmental. States should bring up disability issues in discussions on such cooperation with their counterparts.

3. When planning and reviewing programmes of technical and economic cooperation, special attention should be given to the effects of such programmes on the situation of persons with disabilities. It is of the utmost importance that persons with disabilities and their organizations are consulted on any development projects designed for persons with disabilities. They should be directly involved in the development, implementation, and evaluation of such projects.

4. Priority areas for technical and economic cooperation should include:

(a) The development of human resources through the development of skills, abilities, and potentials of persons with disabilities and the initiation of employment-generating activities for and of persons with disabilities;

(b) The development and dissemination of appropriate disability-related technologies and know-how.

5. States are also encouraged to support the formation and strengthening of organizations of persons with disabilities.

6. States should take measures to improve the knowledge of disability issues among staff involved at all levels in the administration of technical and economic cooperation programmes.

*Rule 22. International Cooperation.* States will participate actively in international cooperation concerning policies for the equalization of opportunities for persons with disabilities.

1. Within the United Nations, its specialized agencies, and other concerned intergovernmental organizations, States should participate in the development of disability policy.

2. Whenever appropriate, States should introduce disability aspects in general negotiations concerning standards, information exchange, development programmes, etc.

3. States should encourage and support the exchange of knowledge and experience between:

(a) Nongovernmental organizations concerned with disability issues;

(b) Research institutions and individual researchers involved in disability issues;

(c) Representatives of field programmes and of professional groups in the disability field;

(d) Organizations of persons with disabilities;

(e) National coordinating committees.

4. States should ensure that the United Nations and its specialized agencies, as well as all intergovernmental and interparliamentary bodies, at global and regional levels, include in their work the global and regional organizations of persons with disabilities.

## IV. Monitoring Mechanism

1. The purpose of a monitoring mechanism is to further the effective implementation of the Standard Rules. It will assist each State in assessing its level of implementation of the Rules and in measuring its progress. The monitoring should identify obstacles and suggest suitable measures which would contribute to the successful implementation of the Rules. The monitoring mechanism will recognize the economic, social, and cultural features existing in individual States. An important element should also be the provision of advisory services and the exchange of experience and information between States.

2. The Standard Rules on the Equalization of Opportunities for Persons with Disabilities shall be monitored within the framework of the sessions of the Commission for Social Development. A Special Rapporteur with relevant and extensive experience of disability issues and international organizations shall be appointed, if necessary, funded by extrabudgetary resources, for three years to monitor the implementation of the Standard Rules.

3. International organizations of persons with disabilities having consultative status with the Economic and Social

Council and organizations representing persons with disabilities who have not yet formed their own organizations should be invited to create among themselves a panel of experts, on which organizations of persons with disabilities shall have a majority, taking into account the different kinds of disabilities and necessary equitable geographical distribution, to be consulted by the Special Rapporteur and, when appropriate, by the Secretariat.

4. The panel of experts will be encouraged by the Special Rapporteur to review, advise, and provide feedback and suggestions on the promotion, implementation, and monitoring of the Standard Rules.

5. The Special Rapporteur shall send a set of questions to States, entities within the United Nations system, and intergovernmental and nongovernmental organizations, including organizations of persons with disabilities. The set of questions should address implementation plans for the Standard Rules in States. The questions should be selective in nature and cover a number of specific rules for indepth evaluation. In preparing the questions, the Special Rapporteur should consult with the panel of experts and the Secretariat.

6. The Special Rapporteur shall seek to establish a direct dialogue not only with States but also with local nongovernmental organizations, seeking their views and comments on any information intended to be included in the reports. The Special Rapporteur shall provide advisory services on the implementation and monitoring of the Standard Rules and assistance in the preparation of replies to the sets of questions.

7. The Centre for Social Development and Humanitarian Affairs of the United Nations Office at Vienna, as the UN focal point on disability issues, the United Nations Development Programme, and other entities and mechanisms within the UN system, such as the regional commissions and specialized agencies and interagency meetings, shall cooperate with the Special Rapporteur in the implementation and monitoring of the Standard Rules at the national level.

8. The Special Rapporteur, assisted by the Secretariat, shall prepare reports for submission to the Commission for Social Development, at its thirty-fourth and thirty-fifth sessions. In preparing such reports, the Rapporteur should consult with the panel of experts.

9. States should encourage national coordinating committees or similar bodies to participate in implementation and monitoring. As the focal points on disability matters at the national level, they should be encouraged to establish procedures to coordinate the monitoring of the Standard Rules. Organizations of persons with disabilities should be encouraged to be actively involved in the monitoring of the process at all levels.

10. Should extrabudgetary resources be identified, one or more positions of interregional advisor on the Standard Rules should be created to provide direct services to States, including:

(a) The organization of national and regional training seminars on the content of the Standard Rules;

(b) The development of guidelines to assist in strategies for implementation of the Standard Rules;

(c) Dissemination of information about best practices concerning implementation of the Standard Rules.

11. At its thirty-fourth session, the Commission for Social Development should establish an open-ended working group to examine the Special Rapporteur's report and make recommendations on how to improve the application of the Standard Rules. In examining the Special Rapporteur's report, the Commission, through its open-ended working group, shall consult international organizations of persons with disabilities and specialized agencies, according to rules 71 and 76 of the rules of procedure of the functional commissions of the Economic and Social Council.

12. At its session following the end of the Special Rapporteur's mandate, the Commission should examine the possibility of either renewing that mandate, appointing a new Special Rapporteur or considering another monitoring mechanism, and should make appropriate recommendations to the Economic and Social Council.

13. States should be encouraged to contribute to the United Nations Voluntary Fund on Disability in order to further the implementation of the Standard Rules.

***INTERNATIONAL DAY OF DISABLED PERSONS (3 DECEMBER).*** On 3 December 1982, the UN General Assembly proclaimed the period 1983–1992 the UN Decade of Disabled Persons (resolution 37/53). On 14 October 1992, it proclaimed 3 December as the International Day of Disabled Persons (resolution 47/3). In resolution 48/97 of 20 December 1993, the General Assembly appealed to all governments to observe this day, using it as an opportunity to awaken the consciousness of citizens regarding the gains that society will derive from the integration of disabled persons in every area of social, economic, and political life.

***WORLD PROGRAM OF ACTION CONCERNING DISABLED PERSONS.*** In 1982, the UN General Assembly adopted (resolution 37/52) the World Program of Action concerning Disabled Persons. At its 1993 session, in resolution 48/99, it noted "the importance of developing and carrying out concrete long-term strategies for the full implementation of the World Program, with the aim of achieving a society for all by the year 2000," and requested the Secretary-General to give higher priority and visibility to disability issues within the UN system.

***TALLINN GUIDELINES ON DISABILITY.*** The Guidelines for Action on Human Resources Development in the Field of Disability, which set out a guiding philosophy and a series of strategies to be undertaken to promote the further development and continued progress of disabled persons, were adopted by the International Meeting on Human Resources in the Field of Disability, convened at Tallinn, Estonian Soviet Socialist Republic, in the former USSR, from 14 to 22 August 1989. On 8 December 1989, the UN General Assembly requested the Secretary-General (resolution 44/70) to bring the Guidelines to the attention of member States, national coordinating bodies, and concerned intergovernmental and nongovernmental organizations. The Guidelines, annexed to resolution 44/70, are as follows:

### Introduction

1. The International Meeting on Human Resources in the Field of Disability, convened at Tallinn, Estonian Soviet So-

cialist Republic, Union of the Soviet Socialist Republics, from 14 to 22 August 1989, having considered the situation of human resources development in the field of disability, particularly in developing countries, firmly believes that the reinforcement of existing as well as new and innovative action is required to promote the further development and continued progress of disabled persons.

2. Following the adoption of the World Programme of Action concerning Disabled Persons by the General Assembly, in its resolution 37/52 of 3 December 1982, there has been a growing need for higher priority to be given to the development of the human resources of disabled persons, with specific reference to education and training, employment, and science and technology. In this connection, the General Assembly also, in its resolution 37/53 of 3 December 1982, proclaimed the United Nations Decade of Disabled Persons, 1983–1992, encouraging Member States to utilize that period as one of the means to implement the World Programme of Action.

3. The main objectives of the World Programme of Action are to promote effective measures for the prevention of disability, for rehabilitation and for the realization of the goals of full participation and equality for persons with disabilities. To accomplish these goals, due regard must be paid to education, training and work opportunities.

4. While it is acknowledged that the living conditions of the general population in developing countries urgently need to be improved, the objectives of the World Programme of Action call for the situation of disabled persons to be given special attention during the remainder of the Decade and beyond. Effective implementation of the World Programme of Action will make an important contribution to the development process of societies through the mobilization of more human resources.

5. While it is also acknowledged that a number of countries have already initiated or carried out activities within the framework of the World Programme of Action, further concerted efforts should be made to integrate the human resources development of disabled persons into intersectoral planning at the national level.

### Guiding Philosophy

6. Human resources development is a human-centred process that seeks to realize the full potential and capabilities of human beings. This process is fundamental to the concept of equalization of opportunities, in keeping with the goals of the World Programme of Action.

7. Through human resources development, disabled persons are able effectively to exercise their rights of full citizenship. As full citizens, they have the same rights and responsibilities as other members of society, including the right to life, as declared in international human rights instruments. They also have the same choices as other citizens in the social, cultural, economic and political life of their communities.

8. Because persons with disabilities are agents of their own destiny rather than objects of care, Governments and organizations need to reflect this perception in their policies and programmes. This means that disabled persons, as individuals and as members of organizations, should be involved in the decision-making process as equal partners.

9. The abilities of disabled persons and their families should be strengthened through community-based supplementary services provided by Governments and non-govern-mental organizations. These services should promote self-determination and enable disabled persons to participate in the development of society. Governments should recognize and support the role of disabled persons' organizations in enabling persons with disabilities to take charge of their own lives.

### Strategies

A. *Participation of Persons with Disabilities.* 10. A statutory basis is required to enable disabled persons to participate as full citizens in decision-making at all levels of the planning, implementation, and monitoring and evaluation of policies and programmes.

11. To facilitate the full participation of disabled persons and enable them to exercise their rights as citizens, access to information is essential. To this end, all information has to be adapted to appropriate formats. These information formats may include Braille script, large print, audio-visual media and sign-language interpretation. Information channels should include television, radio, newspapers and postal services. Governments should work with organizations of disabled persons to identify appropriate information formats and channels to reach disabled citizens.

12. Governments should adopt, enforce and fund legally binding standards and regulations to improve access for persons with disabilities, ensuring that buildings, streets, and road, sea and air transport are barrier-free, architecturally and in all other ways. Communication systems and security and safety measures should be developed and adapted to meet the needs of disabled persons.

13. To facilitate the recruitment of disabled persons and to assist private-sector industries in hiring them, organizations at the national, regional and international levels, including the United Nations, should identify and maintain listings of qualified disabled candidates.

B. *Strengthening of Grassroots Initiatives.* 14. Local community initiatives should be especially promoted. Disabled persons and their families should be encouraged to form grass-roots organizations, with governmental recognition of their importance and governmental support in the form of financing and training.

15. Governmental and non-governmental organizations concerned with disability issues should allow disabled persons to participate as equal partners.

16. The efficient functioning of governmental and non-governmental organizations concerned with disability calls for training in organizational and management skills.

C. *Promotion of an Integrated Approach.* 17. Overall national policy frameworks with supporting legislation should be developed.

18. The essence of an integrated approach is the inclusion of disability issues in all ministries and at every level of government policy and planning. National co-ordination bodies, with linkages at the local, regional and interregional levels, should be established or strengthened. The membership of those bodies should include all government ministries, legislative committees and non-governmental organizations, particularly organizations of disabled persons. The co-ordination body should review existing policies, plans and programmes, identify existing and projected resources and monitor and evaluate the implementation of national policies.

19. National development programmes should include disability components.

20. Disabled women should be included in the existing national and regional programmes aimed at women.

21. At the level of service delivery, an integrated approach entails co-operation and referral among professionals working in organizational settings that provide educational, vocational, health and social services.

*D. Promotion of Education and Training.* 22. The early years are critical in the overall development of a disabled child and in fostering positive attitudes towards the child. Specific programmes and training materials should be developed to address these needs during the formative infant and pre-school years.

23. Education at the primary, secondary and higher levels should be available to disabled persons within the regular educational system in regular school settings, as well as in vocational training programmes. When such education is provided to deaf students, teachers and/or interpreters who are proficient in the indigenous sign language must be provided.

24. Special education programmes and schools that promote the indigenous sign language and the indigenous deaf culture must be available to deaf people. Deaf people should be employed in such programmes and schools.

25. Cost-effective alternatives to segregated school facilities should be developed and implemented by Governments at the national and local levels. These alternatives include special education teachers as consultants to regular education teachers, resource rooms with specialized personnel and materials, special classrooms in regular schools and interpreters for deaf students.

26. The education of disabled children should involve the co-operation and concerted efforts of health and social services, as well as teachers and parents. It should provide support measures, such as technical aids, especially adapted pedagogical approaches, and incentives for teachers.

27. The content and quality of education and training should ensure the acquisition of skills that are economically viable and that provide opportunities for work. Career education and vocational training programmes should be available to ensure the transition of disabled students into the economic mainstream.

28. In addition to being offered formal skills training and education, disabled persons should be offered training in social and self-help skills to prepare them for independent living. Special efforts should be made to promote education and skills training for disabled girls and women, in both urban and rural areas.

29. General teacher-training curricula should include a course of study in skills for teaching disabled children and young persons in regular schools.

30. Each Government should have a national plan for training and employing an adequate number of health, education and vocational professionals in rehabilitation. Persons with disabilities should be recruited for such training and employment.

31. In fields such as education, labour, health and social services, law, architecture and technical development, which are often involved in the different aspects of rehabilitation, the professional training should include training on the rights and needs of disabled people. Professionals in these fields should also be made aware of the resources available for disabled persons so that appropriate referrals can be made or services provided.

32. Appropriate technology should be considered essential for the utilization of available resources. This may include simple, universally available equipment, as well as computer technology.

*E. Promotion of Employment.* 33. Disabled persons have the right to be trained for and to work on equal terms in the regular labour force. Community-based rehabilitation programmes should be encouraged to provide better job opportunities in developing countries. Use should be made of the vocational services, guidance and training, placement, employment and related services that already exist for workers in general. On-the-job training may be more effective than conventional training.

34. General development programmes that provide loans, training and equipment for income-generating activities should include disabled persons.

35. Employment opportunities can be promoted primarily by measures relating to employment and salary standards that apply to all workers and secondarily by measures offering special support and incentives. In addition to formal employment, opportunities should be broadened to include self-employment, co-operatives and other group income-generating schemes. Where special national employment drives have been launched for youth and unemployed persons, disabled persons should be included. Disabled persons should be actively recruited, and when a disabled candidate and a non-disabled candidate are equally qualified, the disabled candidate should be chosen.

36. Employers' and workers' organizations should adopt, in co-operation with organizations of disabled persons, policies that promote the training and employment of disabled and non-disabled persons on an equal basis, including disabled women.

37. Policies for affirmative action should be formulated and implemented to increase the employment of disabled women. Governments and non-governmental organizations should support the creation of income-generating projects involving disabled women.

*F. Provisions for Funding.* 38. In general, funding should be allocated through regular sectoral budgeting systems. A national rehabilitation fund may be established to facilitate the employment or self-employment of disabled persons. This fund could be used to cover the costs of training, equipment, and initial capital outlay.

39. Similarly, funds should be established for loans to small-scale pilot projects at the grass-roots level; such funds could be administered locally using simple procedures.

*G. Promotion of Community Awareness.* 40. To increase community understanding of the rights, needs and potentials of disabled persons, collaborative efforts with disabled persons and their organizations are required to develop and promote a flow of information using mass media, especially film, television, radio and print media. In particular, information for disabled persons and their families on all aspects of living with a disability should be as clear and uncomplicated as possible.

41. Community awareness programmes should include specific strategies for the prevention of disability. Government efforts aimed at early identification, intervention and prevention should be strengthened through community awareness and community involvement in programmes on disability.

42. Persons with mental disability (mental retardation or mental illness) or multiple disabilities are among the most stigmatized groups of citizens. They have the right to make choices, take risks, control their own lives and live in the community. Their adult status, abilities and aspirations must be respected and reinforced by their inclusion in decision-

making, although many may need individual advocacy to be clearly understood.

43. It should be acknowledged that people with mental and multiple disabilities benefit from education, skills training and work opportunities. For many of these people, opportunities need to be individualized. Support is required to help them and their families to establish and maintain a positive life-style.

44. The World Programme of Action should be translated into all national languages, through governmental action. Braille, large print and simplified versions should also be made available by the appropriate media to ensure as wide a distribution as possible to all citizens, including disabled persons, their families, and non-governmental and governmental organizations.

*H. Improving the Methodology for Human Resources Development.* 45. Policies and programmes for human resources development concerning disabled persons should be based on an assessment of their needs and resources as well as on the potential of existing development programmes and services to meet those needs. The implementation of such policies and programmes should be periodically monitored, with adjustments made to ensure effective implementation.

46. Evaluation should be built into programmes at the planning stage so that their overall efficacy in fulfilling policy objectives can be assessed. Persons with disabilities should play an active role in developing the criteria for monitoring and evaluation.

47. Increased attention should be given to services for people with hearing, speech, mental, intellectual or multiple disabilities.

48. The requirements of particular groups, such as disabled children, disabled women, the disabled elderly, disabled migrants and refugees, should also be recognized and met.

49. Governmental and non-governmental organizations should utilize recent developments in education through communications media, also known as distance education, which has been found to be an appropriate methodology in human resources development in the field of disability.

50. The local use of appropriate technologies for producing such items as wheel chairs, prosthetic devices and mobility aids, as well as aids for hearing and seeing, should take into account the technical, socio-economic and cultural conditions in the particular society. Each country should have a national system for the delivery of rehabilitation aids.

*I. Regional and International Cooperation.* 51. Training programmes in human resources development in the field of disability should be strengthened by collaborative efforts at the regional and/or subregional levels. Such programmes should be co-ordinated through existing intergovernmental and regional organizations, including those of disabled persons.

52. International development aid projects should include a component specifically aimed at supporting organizations of disabled persons and training their members. In addition, employment opportunities should be made available to disabled individuals within these projects.

53. All international development assistance programmes directed at macro-level planning and development, such as those in agriculture or education, should include a specific component ensuring the participation of disabled persons in such schemes.

54. At both the national and interregional levels, Governments should strongly support collaboration with non-gov-

ernmental agencies in specific areas of disability, to ensure co-ordination and to prevent duplication of services.

55. Linkages between organizations of disabled persons in developed and developing countries should be strengthened. This can be done through the exchange of information, training and meetings to provide forums for disabled persons to share experiences on strategic approaches. Workshops and field studies should be organized to train trainers and the management personnel of organizations of disabled persons.

56. Implementation of these Guidelines relies on effective action at the national level. This action should be supplemented by concerted efforts at the international level, particularly on the part of the United Nations and its focal point for the implementation of the World Programme of Action concerning Disabled Persons, as well as its relevant organizations and specialized agencies. National and international non-governmental organizations, in particular organizations of disabled persons, should be fully involved.

*SEE ALSO* Equality.

**BIBLIOGRAPHY.** Bayefsky, A. F., and M. Eberts, eds. *Equality Rights and the Canadian Charter of Rights and Freedoms.* Toronto, Canada: Carswell, 1985. Edited collection, in English.

Boylan, Esther. *Women and Disability.* London: Zed Books, 1991. Monograph, in English; bibliography, pp. 102–105.

Canadian Council on Social Development, Court Challenges Program. *A Guide to the Charter for Equality-Seeking Groups.* Ottawa, Canada: 1987. Government manual, in English and French.

Daes, Erica-Irene. *Study on Guidelines, Principles, and Guarantees for the Protection of Persons Suffering from Mental Disorder.* New York: United Nations, n.d. Sales no. E.85.XIV.9. Intergovernmental study, in English.

Evans, T., P. Molan, and P. Burgess. *The Treatment of Disabled Persons in Social Security and Taxation Law.* Canberra, Australia: Human Rights Commission, 1986. Government monograph, in English.

Gajerski-Cauley, Anne, ed. *Women, Development and Disability.* Winnipeg, Manitoba, Canada: Coalition of Provincial Organizations of the Handicapped, 1989. NGO discussion paper, in English and French.

Human Rights Research and Education Centre, University of Ottawa (Centre de recherche et d'enseignement sur les droits de la personne, Université d'Ottawa). "Rights of Disabled Persons," in *Human Rights in Canada: Into the 1990s and Beyond,* pp. 31–62. Ottawa, Canada: University of Ottawa, 1990. Scholarly collective papers, in English.

Joneken, Anneli. *Disabled Women: Young, Elderly, Migrants, Heads of Households, and All Other Women and Girls with Disabilities.* New York: UN Committee on the Elimination of Discrimination against Women, 1990. Doc. EGM/VM/1990/WP9. Intergovernmental study, in English.

Poupon, Thérèse. "L'insertion professionnelle des handicapés en France et à l'étranger" (Employment of People with Disabilities in France and Abroad), in *Problèmes économiques,* no. 2.294, pp. 25–32. Paris: Documentation française, 1992. Research report, in French.

Sheehan, R., and J. Jardine. *Epilepsy and Human Rights.* Canberra, Australia: Human Rights Commission, 1984. Government monograph, in English.

Taiwan Church News. "The Continuing Struggle for

Rights of the Disabled," *Occasional Bulletin* 5, no. 1 (Dec. 1987–Jan. 1988): 3. NGO article, in English.

Torelli, Maurice. *The Protection of the Rights of Disabled Persons Afforded under Various International Instruments.* New York: UNESCO, 1981. Doc. SS.81/WS/43. Extracts, in English.

United Nations Commission on Human Rights. *Report of the Working Group on the Principles for the Protection of Persons with Mental Illness and for the Improvement of Mental Health Care.* Geneva, Switzerland: 1991. Intergovernmental study, in English and French.

United Nations Sub-Commission on Prevention of Discrimination and Protection of Minorities. *Human Rights and Disability.* Geneva, Switzerland: 1991. Intergovernmental study, in English and French.

Ware, Helen. *Legal and Ethical Aspects of the Management of Newborns with Severe Disabilities.* Canberra, Australia: Human Rights Commission, 1985. Government monograph, in English.

World Health Organization. *Is the Law Fair to the Disabled? A European Survey.* WHO Regional Publications, European Series, no. 29. Copenhagen, Denmark: WHO Regional Office for Europe, 1990. Intergovernmental study, in English.

**DISABLED PEOPLE'S INTERNATIONAL.** An international non-governmental organization in consultative status with the UN ECONOMIC AND SOCIAL COUNCIL (Category II), and with **ILO, UNESCO,** and the **COUNCIL OF EUROPE,** DPI brings together organizations of disabled persons in 70 countries.

Founded in 1981, Disabled People's International views "Equalization of Opportunities" as one of its fundamental concepts. The "DPI Manifesto" defines equalization of opportunities as full participation for the world's disabled in the rights to education, rehabilitation, employment, economic security, and independent living; to participation in social, cultural, and political activities; and to influence the development of society. DPI pursues its goals principally through its cooperation with other organizations of the disabled and through its world congress (held every three years) and world council meeting (held annually). DPI publishes *Vox Nostra*.

Disabled People's International. Address: 101-7 Evergreen Place, Winnepeg R3L 2T3, Canada. Telephone: (1-204) 287-8010. Fax: (1-204) 287-8157. Development Program Director: Yutta Fricke.

**DISAPPEARANCES.** In December 1978, the UN GENERAL ASSEMBLY first expressed concern (resolution 33/173) about reports reaching it from various parts of the world relating to enforced or involuntary disappearances of persons and requested the Commission on Human Rights to consider the question of "disappeared" persons with a view to making appropriate recommendations. The Assembly called upon governments, in the event of reports of enforced or involuntary disappearances, to devote appropriate resources to searching for such persons and to undertake speedy and impartial investigations; to ensure that law enforcement and security authorities or organizations are fully accountable, especially in law, in the discharge of their duties, such accountability to include legal responsibility for unjustifiable excesses which might lead to enforced or involuntary disappearances and to other violations of human rights; to ensure that the human rights of all persons, including those subjected to any form of detention or imprisonment, are fully respected; and to cooperate with other governments, relevant United Nations organs, specialized agencies, intergovernmental organizations, and humanitarian bodies in a common effort to search for, locate, or account for such persons in the event of reports of enforced or involuntary disappearances.

The Commission on Human Rights, in 1980, decided (resolution 20 [XXVI]) to establish the UN Working Group on Enforced or Involuntary Disappearances, consisting of five of its members serving as experts in their individual capacities, to examine questions relating to the disappearance of persons. The working group has presented reports to each session of the Commission since 1981.

*REPORT OF THE WORKING GROUP (1994).* In its report to the **COMMISSION ON HUMAN RIGHTS** (E/CN.4/1994/26), the Working Group on Enforced or Involuntary Disappearances set out its conclusions and recommendations as follows (paras. 532–540):

Since the Working Group was established, 13 years ago, one event stands out as the single most encouraging achievement in combating disappearances worldwide: the adoption by the General Assembly of the Declaration on the Protection of All Persons from Enforced Disappearance. By proclaiming the Declaration, on 18 December 1992, the international community, more clearly than ever before, expressed its commitment to put an end to perhaps the most comprehensive and pernicious way of violating human rights. Comprehensive, since making people disappear amounts to infringing upon a variety of human rights, including, as the Declaration points out, the right to life, the right to liberty and security of the person and the right not to be subjected to torture. Pernicious, since a disappearance places the victim outside the protection of the law, as the preamble phrases it. Enforced disappearance "undermines the deepest values of any society committed to respect for the rule of law, human rights and fundamental freedoms", the preamble continues. The most striking expression, however, of how the General Assembly views the phenomenon is the stipulation in the Declaration that the systematic practice of disappearance "is of the nature of a crime against humanity".

The past year has shown that the policy and practice of many States run counter to the Declaration. While disappearances continue to be reported to the United Nations, many Governments have not shown any determination to reflect the provisions of the Declaration in their national legislation. In this context, reference may be made to article 4, which provides that "all acts of enforced disappearance shall be offences under the criminal law"; to article 17, positing that such acts "shall be considered a continuing offence"; and to article 18, that perpetrators "shall not benefit from any special amnesty law".

There is every reason for the international community to remain alert, for the phenomenon of disappearances is still rampant. In 1993, over 3,000 cases of enforced disappearance throughout the world were transmitted by the Working Group to a total of 30 Governments. It should be noted, however, that of the cases so transmitted, only 118 were reported as having occurred in 1993. In comparison, during the previous year, 8,000 cases were transmitted to 59 Governments, of which 353 cases were reported to have taken place in 1992. Doubtless, it would be an error to conclude that disappearances worldwide have diminished by more than 50 per cent. The numbers quoted, as the Working Group has stated time and again, do not necessarily reflect the actual incidence of the phenomenon, since the United Nations is dependent on external sources for information on individual cases. The Working Group estimates that the real number of disappearances is higher. Progress in dealing with the problem has not been such that attention could instead be directed to other forms of violation, perceived as more pressing.

The growing commitment of the United Nations to peacemaking is of relevance to the Working Group's mandate as well. Some of these operations, such as the ones in Cambodia and El Salvador, have contained a strong human rights verification component. Thus, depending on the situation concerned, such operations may enhance greater respect for human rights. In El Salvador, for example, no more cases of enforced disappearance are being reported. Wherever appropriate, the United Nations should incorporate such a component in the mandate of such operations.

Of course, in certain situations the difficulties are overwhelming. The situation in Yugoslavia is a case in point. It stands out as an armed conflict of dramatic proportions and has caused thousands of cases of disappearance. Consequently, the Working Group has followed developments in the region with great concern. The fact is, however, that the Working Group's methods of work were not designed to handle situations of the size and nature the world is witnessing in the former Yugoslavia. It was for this reason that the Working Group, in its report last year, drew special attention to the question of how cases of disappearance from that area should be dealt with by the United Nations. At the request of the Special Rapporteur on the situation of human rights in the former Yugoslavia, one of the Group's members carried out a mission to parts of the territory of the former Yugoslavia. On the basis of the report on the mission, and following consultations with the Special Rapporteur and the International Committee of the Red Cross, the Working Group has decided to propose to the Special Rapporteur the establishment of a special procedure by the Commission on Human Rights. All cases of missing persons in any part of the former Yugoslavia should be considered under this "special process", regardless of whether the victim is a non-combatant civilian or a combatant, and irrespective of whether the perpetrators are connected to the Government or not. This special procedure should be implemented as a joint mandate by one member of the Working Group acting in his individual capacity and the Special Rapporteur on the

situation of human rights in the former Yugoslavia, resulting in their submission of joint reports to the Commission on Human Rights.

One of the problems encountered in the former Yugoslavia as regards clarifying cases of missing persons concerns clandestine mass graves. This aspect prompts the Working Group to draw the Commission's attention once again to the wider question of exhumation and identification of possible victims of human rights violations, an important element in the investigation of cases of disappearance in any part of the world. The Working Group has found that in some situations local authorities cooperate with international forensic scientists and implement the standards internationally accepted for this purpose. But it is a matter of concern that in many other situations independent forensic teams are not only denied cooperation but are intimidated and subjected to reprisal. Needless to say, such situations are intolerable.

In connection with the relevance of forensic sciences to the clarification of disappearances, the Working Group continued its contacts with relevant professional organizations. It brought the results of these contacts to the attention of the Secretary-General, pursuant to Commission resolution 1993/33. The Group welcomes establishment by the Secretary-General of a list of forensic experts and experts in related disciplines. Such experts, it is envisaged, can be requested to help in providing technical and advisory services in this field. They can also be of use to international human rights mechanisms, Governments and the Centre for Human Rights in other activities, such as monitoring and training local investigative teams.

As a final observation of a more general nature, the Working Group is pleased to note that more and more people, government officials as well as human rights activists, are becoming increasingly aware of the Group's attempts to achieve positive results in its humanitarian work. Cooperation with most Governments is improving. Nevertheless, the following Governments have failed to extend a minimum of cooperation, for they have not sent even a single reply to the Working Group's communications, despite having received at least one reminder, and in most cases several reminders: Afghanistan, Angola, Bulgaria, Burkina Faso, Burundi, Guinea, Mauritania, Rwanda and Mozambique. The Commission should consider drawing the attention of these Governments to their obligations.

The Working Group remains concerned at the continuing problem of the inadequacy of resources placed at its disposal for the fulfilment of its task. Indeed, the staff servicing the Group was further reduced in 1993 owing to the increase in Special Procedures mandates by the Commission on Human Rights, for which almost no additional human resources were made available and which therefore had to be, to a large extent, accommodated within existing resources. The unfortunate consequence of this situation is that a backlog of some 8,000 cases is being carried over to the year 1994. This number does not include the 11,103 cases that have so far been received from the former Yugoslavia and which the Group estimated to constitute only a portion of the actual number of cases that will be reported in the months to come. The Group has made extensive reference to all the negative consequences this situation entails in the conclusions to its previous report (E/CN.4/1993/25, paras. 522–523). At this juncture it wishes to appeal once again to the Commission as its parent body, as well as to its members individually, to take every possible measure which would increase the staff support which the Working Group urgently requires to carry out its mandate effectively.

The international community, for its part, must also take action in this matter. Concretely, the United Nations should look for more powerful ways of guaranteeing the observance of basic rights in armed conflict situations. Human lives are at stake and so is the cause of human rights as such. Perhaps more important in the long run, the credibility of the United Nations as a monitor of basic rights implementation in general hangs in the balance. Not only the victims themselves, particularly the noncombatants caught in the middle, but the public at large look to the world organization for convincing action—action that makes a difference.

Needless to say, peace provides an environment in which human rights may thrive. Negotiations, then, aimed at re-establishing peace must be further promoted by the international community. An important element in such negotiations, from the outset, should be the establishment of adequate guarantees for human rights enjoyment by the Governments concerned. The prevention of disappearances and—of paramount importance—the clarification of disappearances that have occurred in the course of the conflict should be among the elements. In particular, the tracing of missing persons is not a burden that should be left routinely to the International Committee of the Red Cross on account of its vast experience in the matter. The primary responsibility for ascertaining the fate and whereabouts of the disappeared lies squarely with the Government concerned. By its very nature, UN action to that effect is auxiliary.

The situation in the former Yugoslavia stands out as an armed conflict of dramatic proportions, having produced thousands of refugees and displaced persons, as well as people detained, tortured, killed, and disappeared. Clearly, the international community could not stand idly by in the face of so much human misery and so grave a threat to the peace. Eventually, it will have to become involved in all aspects of the situation, including the question of disappeared people. On this issue, too, it needs to take action that transcends symbolic values alone and merits credibility on the basis of effectiveness. In view of the overwhelming dimensions, the Working Group is urgently seeking the guidance of the Commission on Human Rights, its parent body, on how to approach the matter of the disappeared in the former Yugoslavia.

In 1992, some 8,000 cases of disappearances were transmitted to 59 Governments, while 353 cases were reported to have taken place in the same year, worldwide. Eleven new countries are now on the Working Group's files, and many more cases have been received from an increasing number of sources. The dramatic increase in the number of cases submitted to the Working Group reveals more awareness throughout the world of the existence of the Working Group and its mandate, and an increased confidence on the part of relatives of missing persons and nongovernmental organizations in the action of human rights mechanisms. More clearly than ever, the problem of enforced disappearances is a global concern. Thousands of cases all over the world have not yet been clarified, and many cases continue to occur.

The cooperation extended to the Working Group by the majority of Governments continues to improve. Most of them have responded promptly to the inquiries of the Working Group. . . . However, there are 10 Governments that have never provided replies . . . regarding specific cases of disappearances: Afghanistan, Angola, Burkina Faso, Guinea, Lebanon, Mauritania, Mozambique, Nepal, Seychelles, and Zimbabwe. The continued absence of replies from these Governments should be a matter for serious concern to the Commission.

Enforced disappearances could be significantly reduced with an independent and efficient administration of justice. One of the things it could achieve is to help relatives of missing persons draw the maximum benefit from the habeas corpus procedure, which is still, in relative terms, the most powerful legal remedy to help uncover the fate and whereabouts of a disappeared person. It is essential that legislation and practice provide for an expeditious and easily accessible habeas corpus.

On the matter of clarification, some countries have decided to disclose records of security services containing information on the fate of missing persons. In several countries, relatives have repeatedly requested to be allowed access to the military and police archives and insisted that such documentation be put at the disposal of the public. The Working Group is of the opinion that such disclosure would not only serve the purpose of clarification but would also have an impact on preventing new cases of disappearance from arising as well as on putting an end to the vicious circle of impunity. In its tentative considerations on the question of impunity, the Working Group has stated that the investigation of disappearances and the publication of the results of the investigation are perhaps the most important means of establishing accountability for the Government as such.

On the question of impunity, the Working Group was encouraged by the numerous contributions it received concerning its tentative considerations on the question of impunity. Governments and nongovernmental organizations have replied readily and have provided important insights into the mater. The Working Group will continue to examine the question of impunity next year within the context of its mandate to study the phenomenon of disappearance and how to eliminate this hideous practice.

Exhumation and identification of possible victims of human rights violations have proved to be significant in the investigation of cases of disappearances. In compliance with Commission resolution 1992/24, the Working Group has given special attention to the role of teams of forensic experts in this matter. The Working Group will continue to devote its thinking to the topic and expects to receive comments from the Commission on the preliminary scheme. . . .

In a number of countries, exhumation and identification of corpses is being carried out by local authorities. In some, the authorities cooperate closely with international forensic teams, an example to be emulated elsewhere. In a few instances, however, forensic teams, whether local or international, have been subjected to reprisals and acts of intimidation. The Working Group expresses its deep concern about this. Any such act is reprehensible as a matter of principle, but in addition the effectiveness of the exercise may be frustrated as a result.

The Working Group deeply regrets that behaviour affecting the basic rights of relatives of victims and human rights organizations persists. Particularly, the action of Governments in actually preventing witnesses from having access to representatives of UN human rights bodies in the course of country visits constitutes conduct that adds insult to injury. The Commission on Human Rights has duly paid attention to this over the last several years. While again inviting nongovernmental organizations to devote more attention to the prompt intervention procedure, the Group urges the Governments concerned to adopt special measures to protect individuals and groups involved in the investigation of cases of disappearances and to investigate promptly and thoroughly any act that could affect or have affected them.

Since 1984, the Working Group has insisted that an international instrument be drawn up on enforced or involuntary disappearances. The Group is gratified to note that, at its 48th regular session, the commission, in its resolution 1992/29, approved the text of a draft Declaration on the Protection of All Persons from Enforced Disappearances. By incorporating the standards of the Declaration, domestic legislation should consider all acts oriented towards carrying out or tolerating an enforced disappearance as serious offences under criminal law, punishable with appropriate penalties by the ordinary courts. . . .

During 1992, the Working Group transmitted a number of cases of disappearances twice as high as the number for 1991 and at least four times the number of cases transmitted in previous years. . . . Nevertheless, some 8,000 cases still await consideration at the secretariat level.

Having examined the Working Group's report, the Commission on Human Rights at its 1993 session (resolution 1993/35) invited all Governments to take appropriate legislative or other steps to prevent and punish the practice of enforced disappearances. The Commission also urged Governments to take steps to protect the families of disappeared persons against any intimidation or ill-treatment to which they might be subjected and to ensure that, when a state of emergency is introduced, the protection of human rights is guaranteed.

**SEE ALSO** *Arbitrary Arrest, Detention, or Exile; Law Enforcement; Prisoners; Victims' Rights.*

**BIBLIOGRAPHY.** American Association for the Advancement of Science, Clearinghouse on Science and Human Rights. *Guatemala: Case Reports 1980–1985.* Washington, D.C.: 1986. NGO report, in English.

Amnesty International. *"Disappearances" and Political Killings: Human Rights Crisis of the 1990s—A Manual for Action.* London: 1993. NGO document, in English. Chapter C-1: "Iraq: The World Would not Listen"; chapter C-2: "Sri Lanka: 'Disappearance' and Murder as Techniques of Counterinsurgency"; chapter C-3: "Colombia: Strategies for Evading Accountability"; chapter C-5: "Turkey: Responses to an Emerging Pattern of Extrajudicial Executions."

———. *Getting Away with Murder: Political Killings and "Disappearances" in the 1990s.* London: 1993. NGO report, in English.

———. *Recent Developments in the Investigations into "Disappearances" in Argentina.* London: 1985. NGO report, in English.

———. *Sri Lanka: What Has Happened to the "Disappeared"?* London: 1988. NGO report, in English.

Anderson, Martin Edwin. *Dossier Secreto: Argentina's Desaparecidos and the Myth of the 'Dirty War'.* Boulder, CO, USA: Westview Press, 1993. Scholarly monograph, in English; bibliography, pp. 376–386.

Asociacion Centroamericana de Familiares de Detenidos-Desaparecidos (Central American Association of Families of the Detained-Disappeared). *Honduras: Desaparecidos, Juicio y Condena* (Honduras: Disappearances, Trial and Sentence). San Jose, Costa Rica: 1989. NGO report, in Spanish.

———. *La Practica de la Desaparicion Forzada de Personas en Guatemala* (The Practice of Forced Disappearance of Persons in Guatemala). San Jose, Costa Rica: 1988. NGO report, in Spanish; bibliography, annotated by key words, pp. 297–304.

Brody, Reed. "Commentary on the Draft UN 'Declaration on the Protection of All Persons From Enforced or Involuntary Disappearances,' " *Netherlands Quarterly of Human Rights* 8, no. 4 (1990): 381–394. Scholarly article, in English.

———. "The UN Working Group on Enforced or Involuntary Disappearances," *Peoples for Human Rights: IMADR Yearbook* 3 (1991): 30–38. Scholarly article, in English.

Comisión Nacional de Verdad y Reconciliación (National Commission for Truth and Reconciliation). *Informe Rettig: Informe de la Comisión Nacional de Verdad y Reconciliación—Febrero de 1991* (The Rettig Report: Report of the National Commission for Truth and Reconciliation, February 1991), 2 vols. Santiago, Chile: La Nación & Les Ediciones del Ornitorrinco, 1991. Governmental report, in Spanish.

Giorgi, Alicia. *Caso Giorgi: A los Hijos de un Detenido-Desaparecido* (The Giorgi Case: To the Children of a Detained-Disappeared Person). Buenos Aires, Argentina: 1990. Monograph, in Spanish.

Guest, Iain. *Behind the Disappearances: Argentina's Dirty War against Human Rights and the United Nations.* Philadelphia, PA, USA: University of Pennsylvania Press, 1990. Scholarly monograph, in English.

Liga Colombiana por los Derechos y la Liberacion de los Pueblos y Colectivo de Abogados Jose Alvear Restrepo (Colombian League for the Rights and Liberation of Peoples and Jose Alvear Restrepo Lawyers' Collective). *El Camino de la Niebla: La Desaparicion Forzada en Colombia y su Impunidad* (The Foggy Road: Forced Disappearance and Impunity in Colombia). Bogota, Colombia: 1988. NGO report, in Spanish.

Minnesota Lawyers International Human Rights Committee. *Expectations Denied: Habeas Corpus and the Search for Guatemala's Disappeared.* Minneapolis, MN, USA: 1988. NGO report, in English.

Rodley, Nigel S. "UN Action Procedures against 'Disappearances,' Summary or Arbitrary Executions, and Torture," *Human Rights Quarterly* 8, no. 4 (Nov. 1986): 700–730. Scholarly article, in English.

Roht-Arriaza, Naomi. "State Responsibility to Investigate and Prosecute Grave Human Rights Violations in International Law," *California Law Review* 78, no. 2 (March 1990): 449–513. Scholarly article, in English.

Secretariat International des Juristes pour l'Amnistie en Uruguay (International Secretariat of Lawyers for Amnesty in Uruguay). *Situacion de las Personas Desaparecidas y los Hechos que la Motivaron* (Situation of the Disappeared Persons and the Motivation behind It). Paris: 1985. NGO report, in Spanish.

Simpson, J., and J. Bennett. *The Disappeared and the Mothers of the Plaza.* New York: St. Martin's Press, 1985. Scholarly study, in English.

United Nations Commission on Human Rights. *Report of the Working Group on the Declaration on the Protection of All Persons from Enforced Disappearances.* Geneva, Switzerland: 1992. Intergovernmental report, in English and French.

Wiseberg, L. S., and L. Ocampo. "The Philippines Revisited: Plus ca change, Plus ca reste la meme. Excerpts from a Report by the International League for Human Rights," *Human Rights Internet* 13, no. 1 (Spring 1989). Commentary, NGO report, in English.

## DISAPPEARANCES: DECLARATION ON THE PROTECTION OF PERSONS FROM ENFORCED DISAPPEARANCE, UN (1992).

Adopted by the UN GENERAL ASSEMBLY, without a vote, on 18 December 1992 (resolution 47/133), the Declaration is as follows:

The General Assembly,

Considering that, in accordance with the principles proclaimed in the Charter of the United Nations and other international instruments, recognition of the inherent dignity and of the equal and inalienable rights of all members of the human family is the foundation of freedom, justice and peace in the world,

Bearing in mind the obligation of States under the Charter of the United Nations, in particular Article 55, to promote universal respect for, and observance of, human rights and fundamental freedoms,

Deeply concerned that in many countries, often in a persistent manner, enforced disappearances occur, in the sense that persons are arrested, detained or abducted against their will or otherwise deprived of their liberty by officials of different branches or levels of Government, or by organized groups or private individuals acting on behalf of, or with the support, direct or indirect, consent or acquiescence of the government, followed by a refusal to disclose the fate or whereabouts of the persons concerned or a refusal to acknowledge the deprivation of their liberty, thereby placing such persons outside the protection of the law,

Considering that enforced disappearance undermines the deepest values of any society committed to respect of the rule of law, human rights and fundamental freedoms, and that the systematic practice of such acts is of the nature of a crime against humanity,

Recalling resolution 33/173 of 20 December 1978, by which the General Assembly expressed concern about the reports from various parts of the world relating to enforced or involuntary disappearances, as well as about the anguish and sorrow caused by those disappearances, and called upon Governments to hold law enforcement and security forces legally responsible for excesses which might lead to enforced or involuntary disappearances of persons,

Recalling also the protection afforded to victims of armed conflicts by the Geneva Conventions of 12 August 1949 and the Additional Protocols of 1977,

Having regard in particular to the relevant articles of the Universal Declaration of Human Rights and the International Covenant on Civil and Political Rights, which protect the right to life, the right to liberty and security of the person, the right not to be subjected to torture and the right to recognition as a person before the law,

Having regard further to the Convention against Torture and Other Cruel, Inhuman or Degrading Treatment or Punishment, which provides that States Parties shall take effective measures to prevent and punish acts of torture,

Bearing in mind the Code of Conduct for Law Enforcement Officials, the Basic Principles on the Use of Force and Firearms by Law Enforcement Officials, the Declaration of Basic Principles of Justice for Victims of Crime and Abuse of Power and the Standard Minimum Rules for the Treatment of Prisoners,

Affirming that, in order to prevent enforced disappearances, it is necessary to ensure strict compliance with the Body of Principles for the Protection of All Persons under Any Form of Detention or Imprisonment contained in its

resolution 43/173 of 9 December 1988, and with the Principles on the Effective Prevention and Investigation of Extralegal, Arbitrary and Summary Executions, set forth in the annex to Economic and Social Council resolution 1989/65 of 24 May 1989 and endorsed by the General Assembly in its resolution 44/162 of 15 December 1989,

Bearing in mind that, while the acts which comprise enforced disappearance constitute a violation of the prohibitions found in the aforementioned international instruments, it is nonetheless important to devise an instrument which characterizes all acts of enforced disappearance of persons as very serious offences, setting forth standards designed to punish and prevent their commission,

1. Proclaims the present Declaration on the Protection of All Persons from Enforced Disappearance, as a body of principles for all States;

2. Urges that all efforts be made so that this Declaration becomes generally known and respected.

*Article 1.* 1. Any act of enforced disappearance is an offence to human dignity. It is condemned as a denial of the purposes of the Charter of the United Nations and as a grave and flagrant violation of the human rights and fundamental freedoms proclaimed in the Universal Declaration of Human Rights and reaffirmed and developed in international instruments in this field.

2. Such act of enforced disappearance places the persons subjected thereto outside the protection of the law and inflicts severe suffering on them and their families. It constitutes a violation of the rules of international law guaranteeing, *inter alia*, the right to recognition as a person before the law, the right to liberty and security of the person and the right not to be subjected to torture and other cruel, inhuman or degrading treatment or punishment. It also violates or constitutes a grave threat to the right to life.

*Article 2.* 1. No State shall practise, permit or tolerate enforced disappearances.

2. States shall act at the national and regional levels and in cooperation with the United Nations to contribute by all means to the prevention and eradication of enforced disappearance.

*Article 3.* Each State shall take effective legislative, administrative, judicial or other measures to prevent and terminate acts of enforced disappearance in any territory under its jurisdiction.

*Article 4.* 1. All acts of enforced disappearance shall be offences under the criminal law punishable by appropriate penalties which shall take into account their extreme seriousness.

2. Mitigating circumstances may be established in national legislation for persons who, having participated in enforced disappearances, are instrumental in bringing the victims forward alive or in providing voluntarily information which would contribute to clarifying cases of enforced disappearance.

*Article 5.* In addition to such criminal penalties as are applicable, enforced disappearances render their perpetrators and the State or State authorities which organize, acquiesce in or tolerate such disappearances liable at civil law, without prejudice to the international responsibility of the State concerned in accordance with the principles of international law.

*Article 6.* 1. No order or instruction of any public authority, civilian, military or other, may be invoked to justify an enforced disappearance. Any person receiving such an order or instruction shall have the right and duty not to obey it.

2. Each State shall ensure that orders or instructions di-

recting, authorizing or encouraging any enforced disappearance are prohibited.

3. Training of law enforcement officials shall emphasize the above provisions.

*Article 7.* No circumstances whatsoever, whether a threat of war, a state of war, internal political instability or any other public emergency, may be invoked to justify enforced disappearances.

*Article 8.* 1. No State shall expel, return (refouler) or extradite a person to another State where there are substantial grounds to believe that he would be in danger of enforced disappearance.

2. For the purpose of determining whether there are such grounds, the competent authorities shall take into account all relevant considerations including, where applicable, the existence in the State concerned of a consistent pattern of gross, flagrant or mass violations of human rights.

*Article 9.* 1. The right to a prompt and effective judicial remedy as a means of determining the whereabouts or state of health of persons deprived of their liberty and/or identifying the authority ordering or carrying out the deprivation of liberty is required to prevent enforced disappearances under all circumstances, including those referred to in article 7.

2. In such proceedings, competent national authorities shall have access to all places holding persons deprived of their liberty and to each part thereof, as well as to any place in which there are grounds to believe that such persons may be found.

3. Any other competent authority entitled under the law of the State or by any international legal instruments to which a State is party may also have access to such places.

*Article 10.* 1. Any person deprived of liberty shall be held in an officially recognized place of detention and, in conformity with national law, be brought before a judicial authority promptly after detention.

2. Accurate information on the detention of such persons and their place or places of detention, including transfers, shall be made promptly available to their family members, their counsel or to any other persons having a legitimate interest in the information unless a wish to the contrary has been manifested by the persons concerned.

3. An official up-to-date register of all persons deprived of their liberty shall be maintained in every place of detention. Additionally, each State shall take steps to maintain similar centralized registers. The information contained in these registers shall be made available to the persons mentioned in the paragraph above, to any judicial or other competent and independent national authority and to any other competent authority entitled under the law of the State concerned or any international legal instrument to which a State concerned is a party, seeking to trace the whereabouts of a detained person.

*Article 11.* All persons deprived of liberty must be released in a manner permitting reliable verification that they have actually been released and, further, have been released in conditions in which their physical integrity and ability fully to exercise their rights are assured.

*Article 12.* 1. Each State shall establish rules under its national law indicating those officials authorized to order deprivation of liberty, establishing the conditions under which such orders may be given, and stipulating penalties for officials who, without legal justification, refuse to provide information on any detention.

2. Each State shall likewise ensure strict supervision, including a clear chain of command, of all law enforcement officials responsible for apprehensions, arrests, detentions, custody, transfers and imprisonment, and of other officials authorized by law to use force and firearms.

*Article 13.* 1. Each State shall ensure that any person having knowledge or a legitimate interest who alleges that a person has been subjected to enforced disappearance has the right to complain to a competent and independent State authority and to have that complaint promptly, thoroughly and impartially investigated by that authority. Whenever there are reasonable grounds to believe that an enforced disappearance has been committed, the State shall promptly refer the matter to that authority for such an investigation, even if there has been no formal complaint. No measure shall be taken to curtail or impede the investigation.

2. Each State shall ensure that the competent authority shall have the necessary powers and resources to conduct the investigation effectively, including powers to compel attendance of witnesses and production of relevant documents and to make immediate on-site visits.

3. Steps shall be taken to ensure that all involved in the investigation, including the complainant, counsel, witnesses and those conducting the investigation, are protected against ill-treatment, intimidation or reprisal.

4. The findings of such an investigation shall be made available upon request to all persons concerned, unless doing so would jeopardize an ongoing criminal investigation.

5. Steps shall be taken to ensure that any ill-treatment, intimidation or reprisal or any other form of interference on the occasion of the lodging of a complaint or the investigation procedure is appropriately punished.

6. An investigation, in accordance with the procedures described above, should be able to be conducted for as long as the fate of the victim of enforced disappearance remains unclarified.

*Article 14.* Any person alleged to have perpetrated an act of enforced disappearance in a particular State shall, when the facts disclosed by an official investigation so warrant, be brought before the competent civil authorities of that State for the purpose of prosecution and trial unless he has been extradited to another State wishing to exercise jurisdiction in accordance with the relevant international agreements in force. All States should take any lawful and appropriate action available to them to bring all persons presumed responsible for an act of enforced disappearance, found to be within their jurisdiction or under their control, to justice.

*Article 15.* The fact that there are grounds to believe that a person has participated in acts of an extremely serious nature such as those referred to in article 4, paragraph 1, regardless of the motives, shall be taken into account when the competent authorities of the State decide whether or not to grant asylum.

*Article 16.* 1. Persons alleged to have committed any of the acts referred to in article 4, paragraph 1, shall be suspended from any official duties during the investigation referred to in article 13.

2. They shall be tried only by the competent ordinary courts in each State, and not by any other special tribunal, in particular military courts.

3. No privileges, immunities or special exemptions shall be admitted in such trials, without prejudice to the provisions contained in the Vienna Convention on Diplomatic Relations.

4. The persons presumed responsible for such acts shall be guaranteed fair treatment in accordance with the relevant provisions of the Universal Declaration of Human Rights and

other relevant international agreements in force at all stages of the investigation and eventual prosecution and trial.

*Article 17.* 1. Acts constituting enforced disappearance shall be considered a continuing offence as long as the perpetrators continue to conceal the fate and the whereabouts of persons who have disappeared and these facts remain unclarified.

2. When the remedies provided for in article 2 of the International Covenant on Civil and Political Rights are no longer effective, the statute of limitations relating to acts of enforced disappearance shall be suspended until these remedies are re-established.

3. Statutes of limitations, where they exist, relating to acts of enforced disappearance shall be substantial and commensurate with the extreme seriousness of the offence.

*Article 18.* 1. Persons who have, or are alleged to have, committed offences referred to in article 4, paragraph 1, shall not benefit from any special amnesty law or similar measures that might have the effect of exempting them from any criminal proceedings or sanction.

2. In the exercise of the right of pardon, the extreme seriousness of acts of enforced disappearance shall be taken into account.

*Article 19.* The victims of acts of enforced disappearance and their family shall obtain redress and shall have the right to adequate compensation, including the means for as complete a rehabilitation as possible. In the event of the death of the victim as a result of an act of enforced disappearance, their dependants shall also be entitled to compensation.

*Article 20.* 1. States shall prevent and suppress the abduction of children of parents subjected to enforced disappearance and of children born during their mother's enforced disappearance, and shall devote their efforts to the search for, and identification of, such children and to the restitution of the children to their families of origin.

2. Considering the need to protect the best interests of children referred to in the preceding paragraph, there shall be an opportunity, in States which recognize a system of adoption, for a review of the adoption of such children and, in particular, for annulment of any adoption which originated in enforced disappearance. Such adoption should, however, continue to be in force if consent is given, at the time of the review mentioned above, by the child's closest relative.

3. The abduction of children of parents subjected to enforced disappearance or of children born during their mother's enforced disappearance, and the act of altering or suppressing documents attesting to their true identity, shall constitute an extremely serious offence, which shall be punished as such.

4. For these purposes, States shall, where appropriate, conclude bilateral and multilateral agreements.

*Article 21.* The provisions of the present Declaration are without prejudice to the provisions enunciated in the Universal Declaration of Human Rights or in any other international instrument, and shall not be construed as restricting or derogating from any of the provisions contained therein.

## DIVISION FOR PALESTINIAN RIGHTS, UN.

In 1977, the UN **GENERAL ASSEMBLY** recognized the need for the dissemination of information on the inalienable rights of the Palestinian people and on the efforts of the United Nations to promote those rights.

It requested the Secretary-General to establish a "Special Unit on Palestinian Rights" in the UN Secretariat, which would prepare studies and publications on this issue and provide maximum publicity (resolution 32/ 40 B of 2 December 1977). The unit, later renamed the Division for Palestinian Rights, is currently part of the Department of Political Affairs of the UN Secretariat. Its mandate has been annually extended and expanded several times over the years.

The Division services the UN Committee on the Exercise of the Inalienable Rights of the Palestinian People and carries out its functions in consultation with and under the guidance of the Committee.

## DJIBOUTI.

The Republic of Djibouti is a country in eastern Africa, at the juncture of the Red Sea and the Gulf of Aden. It has borders with Ethiopia and Somalia. Formerly known as the Territory of Afars and Issas, it achieved independence from France in 1977 and became a member of the United Nations the same year. Its population is estimated to be 396,000.

Ethnic groups include Somalis (48%), Afars (38%), Europeans (9%), and Arabs (5%). Languages commonly used include French (official), Somali, Afar, and Arabic. Religions practiced include Islam (94%) and Christianity (Roman Catholic) (6%). Literacy is estimated at 17%.

The government (1994) took the form of a republic. The President is head of State; the Prime Minister is head of government. Legislation is drafted by the 65-member Constituent Assembly. The only recognized political party is the People's Progress Assembly.

Djibouti is important as the terminal of the Djibouti–Addis Ababa railroad, which carries more than half of Ethiopia's foreign trade. It also serves as a base for ships and planes of the United States of America.

In 1988, the UN Secretary-General reported to the **GENERAL ASSEMBLY** on the situation of refugees in Djibouti. As of the end of 1987, 11,356 refugees, mostly from Ethiopia, had entered the country. Approximately 11,000 lived in Dikhil and Ali-Sabieh camps, while the remainder resided in Djibouti-Ville. The voluntary repatriation of refugees to Ethiopia commenced in December 1986; and, by 30 June 1987, more than 3,000 had returned to their homes. However, the plight of the remaining refugees and the constantly increasing inflow of displaced persons severely affected the inadequate social services and the infrastructure of the country.

The refugee problem was still far from solution towards the end of 1989, when the General Assembly expressed its concern (resolution 44/150) about a new inflow of over 35,000 externally displaced persons, which had added considerably to the burden already carried by Djibouti.

Noting with satisfaction that over 6,000 refugees had already been granted settlement and integration in Djibouti, despite the physical, social, and economic obstacles that face the country, the General Assembly welcomed the steps the country had taken, in cooperation with the United Nations High Commissioner for Refugees, and urged the High Commissioner to mobilize, on an emergency basis, the necessary resources to provide assistance.

Subsequently, in resolutions 46/173 of 19 December 1991, 47/155 of 18 December 1992, and 48/198 of 21 December 1993, the General Assembly has noted that the situation in Djibouti has been adversely affected by the evolving situation in the Horn of Africa and that the presence of over 100,000 refugees and persons displaced from their countries has placed serious strains on the country's fragile economic, social, and administrative infrastructure and has raised serious security issues. A critical economic situation of the country has resulted because many priority development projects have been suspended in light of the regional and international situation.

*BIBLIOGRAPHY.* Arab Organization for Human Rights. *Report: Human Rights in the Arab World.* Cairo: 1987. NGO report, in Arabic and English.

Gesellschaft fur Bedrohte Volker (Association for Endangered Peoples). "Horn von Afrika: Nationalitatenkonflikte in Athiopien, Somalia, und Djibouti" (The Horn of Africa: Nationality Conflict in Ethiopia, Somalia, and Djibouti). *Pogrom* 127–128 (February 1987): 13–84. NGO article, in German.

Immigration and Refugee Board Documentation Centre. *The Horn of Africa: Somalis in Djibouti, Ethiopia and Kenya.* Ottawa, Canada: 1991. Government briefing paper, in English and French.

## DOCTORS WITHOUT BORDERS.

**DOCTORS WITHOUT BORDERS.** Created in France in 1971 by a group of doctors who wanted to aid victims of war and natural disaster, Doctors without Borders is a non-governmental organization, the largest private medical disaster relief organization in the world, an international network pooling resources to ease human suffering anywhere it may occur. Each year Doctors without Borders sends some 3,000 volunteer doctors, nurses, and other health-care specialists from 45 nations into some 70 countries to help people in distress.

Doctors without Borders volunteers dedicate six months to two years of service. The teams often are the first to arrive on the scene. Among the countries that Doctors without Borders is helping in the 1990s are Afghanistan, Azerbaijan, Bosnia-Herzegovina, Rwanda, and Sudan. Although this NGO treats all peo-

ple in need, of special importance in these conflicts are the children.

Doctors without Borders (USA). Address: P.O. Box 110, New York, NY 10277, USA.

## DOMESTIC VIOLENCE.

**DOMESTIC VIOLENCE.** At its 1985 session, the UN **GENERAL ASSEMBLY** recognized (resolution 40/36) that abuse and battery in the family are critical problems that have serious physical and psychological effects on individual family members, especially the young, and jeopardize the health and survival of the family unit, and requested the Secretary-General to intensify research on the subject of domestic violence from a criminological perspective and to formulate action-oriented strategies that could serve as a basis for policy formulation. All relevant UN bodies, agencies, and institutes were called upon to collaborate with the Secretary-General in ensuring a concerted and sustained effort to combat this problem, and UN member States were invited to adopt specific measures—including the following—with a view to making the criminal and civil justice system more sensitive in its response to domestic violence:

(a) To introduce, if not already in place, civil and criminal legislation in order to deal with particular problems of domestic violence, and to enact and enforce such laws in order to protect battered family members and punish the offender and to offer alternative ways of treatment for offenders, according to the type of violence;

(b) To respect, in all instances of the criminal proceeding, starting with the police investigation, the special and sometimes delicate position of the victim, in particular in the manner in which the victim is treated;

(c) To initiate preventive measures, such as providing support and counselling to families, in order to improve their ability to create a non-violent environment, emphasizing principles of education, equality of rights and equality of responsibilities between women and men, their partnership and the peaceful resolution of conflicts;

(d) To inform the public, as necessary, through all available channels, about serious acts of violence perpetrated against children, in order to create public awareness of this problem;

(e) To deliver appropriate, specialized assistance to victims of domestic violence, as an integral part of social policy;

(f) To provide, as a temporary solution, shelters and other facilities and services for the safety of victims of domestic violence;

(g) To provide specialized training and units for those who deal in some capacity with victims of domestic violence;

(h) To initiate or intensify research and collect data on the background, extent and types of domestic violence;

(i) To make legal remedies to domestic violence more accessible and, in view of the criminogenic effects of the phenomenon, in particular on young victims, to give due consideration to the interests of society by maintaining a balance between intervention and the protection of privacy;

(j) To ensure that social welfare and health administration systems are more intensely engaged in providing assistance to victims of familial violence and abuses, and to make all efforts to co-ordinate social welfare and criminal justice measures.

Also at its 1985 session, the General Assembly emphasized the need to focus on all victims of domestic violence and to consider common policies and specialized approaches regarding women, children, the elderly, and those especially vulnerable because of disability. The Assembly recognized that domestic violence is prevalent in all segments of society regardless of class, income, culture, gender, age, or religion; and that this complex problem is viewed differently in various cultures and must be addressed on an international level with sensitivity to the diverse cultures. The Assembly urged member States "to begin or continue to explore, develop, and implement multidisciplinary policies, measures, and strategies, within and outside of the criminal justice system, with respect to domestic violence in all its facets, including legal, law enforcement, judicial, societal, educational, psychological, economic, health-related, and correctional aspects, and in particular: (a) to take all possible steps to prevent domestic violence; (b) to ensure fair treatment of and effective assistance to the victims of domestic violence; (c) to increase awareness and sensitivity concerning domestic violence, in particular by fostering the education of criminal justice and other professionals in regard to this issue; and (d) to provide appropriate treatment for the offenders."

*SEE ALSO Marriage and the Family; Women's Rights: Declaration on the Elimination of Violence against Women.*

**DOMINICA.** The Commonwealth of Dominica is a country occupying an island in the Windward Group of the West Indies, between Martinique and Guadeloupe. It achieved independence from Great Britain in 1978 and became a member of the United Nations the same year. Its population is estimated to be 88,000. Languages commonly used include English and a French patois. Christianity (Roman Catholic, 80%; Anglican, Methodist, and other Protestant denominations, 20%) is the predominant religion. Literacy is estimated at 80%.

The government (1994) took the form of a republic and member of the British Commonwealth. The President, elected by the House of Assembly, is head of State; the Prime Minister, appointed by the President on advice of the Assembly, is head of government. Legislation is prepared by the 21-member House of Assembly. Political parties include the Freedom Party, the Opposition United Workers Party, and the United Dominica Labor Party.

Dominica is one of a small number of countries that

has had a woman as Prime Minister. Mary Eugenia Charles became Prime Minister in July 1980 and was returned to office for a second five-year term in 1985. In June 1995 elections, the United Workers Party defeated the Freedom Party, taking 11 of 21 seats in the National Assembly, and Edison James replaced Eugenia Charles as Prime Minister.

*BIBLIOGRAPHY.* Thompson, Robert. *Green Gold: Bananas and Dependency in the Eastern Caribbean.* London: Latin American Bureau, 1987. NGO monograph, in English.

**DOMINICAN REPUBLIC.** The Dominican Republic is a country occupying the eastern two-thirds of the island of Santo Domingo, formerly called Hispaniola, which it shares with Haiti. It achieved independence from Spain in 1844 and became a member of the United Nations in 1945. Its population is estimated by the UN to be 7,267,000. Languages commonly used include Spanish and Quech. Christianity (Roman Catholic) is the predominant religion. Literacy is estimated at 77%.

The government (1994) took the form of a republic. Under the 1966 constitution, the State is composed of three powers: (a) the Executive Power, exercised by the President, who is elected every four years and is advised by a cabinet of 13 Secretaries of State; (b) the legislature, composed of two houses: the Senate, with 30 members, one for each province and the National District; and the Chamber of Deputies or Lower House, with 120 members; and (c) the judiciary, composed of a Supreme Court of Justice made up of 11 judges. The Office of the Procurator-General is the body that has competence to ensure full respect for human rights.

Since 1981, the Dominican Republic has acted as host to the International Research and Training Institute for the Advancement of Women, an autonomous body under the auspices of the United Nations, functioning under guidelines established by the UN **ECONOMIC AND SOCIAL COUNCIL** in resolution 1998 (LX) of 12 May 1976.

Because the part of the island of Santo Domingo now known as the Dominican Republic—the oldest European settlement in the western hemisphere—passed back and forth between Spain and France in the colonial days and was ruled by dictators for many years, its history is one of recurrent disorder and disregard for human rights.

In 1795, Spain ceded the colony to France. However, the area now known as the Dominican Republic was conquered by Haitians twice—once in 1801 by troops under the leadership of Toussaint L'Ouverture and again in 1822 by units commanded by Jean Pierre

Boyer. On both occasions, the occupation was ended by Dominican revolts; the colonists, who were white and whose culture was predominantly Spanish, feared rule by the Haitians, who were black and of African origin. Uprising and disorder persisted under a series of dictators; and, in 1916, the United States Marines intervened to restore quiet, remaining in the country until 1934. They left after a Dominican sergeant who had been trained by the Marines, Rafael Leonides Trujillo, established a dictatorship, which lasted until his assassination in 1961.

After Trujillo's assassination, a new constitution was adopted and free elections were held. Juan Bosch, a leftist leader, was elevated to the presidency. But he was soon replaced by a military coup; and when Bosch's supporters rebelled, American marines and troops were again sent to the island to restore quiet. They were later replaced by a peacekeeping force composed of troops from a number of countries. In 1966, new elections were held, and the presidency was won by Joaquin Balaguer. The peacekeeping force withdrew, and President Balaguer was able to win three subsequent four-year terms in open, honest elections. He was defeated in 1978 by Antonio Guzman, who, in turn, was succeeded in 1982 by Salvador Jorge Blanco. Former President Balaguer was re-elected in 1986 and 1994. However, following allegations of electoral fraud, his term was reduced from four to two years.

**REPORT TO THE UN HUMAN RIGHTS COMMITTEE (1993).** As a State party to the International Covenant on Civil and Political Rights, the Dominican Republic submitted its third periodic report under article 40 of the Covenant (UN Doc. CCPR/C/70/Add. 3) to the **HUMAN RIGHTS COMMITTEE** in 1993. The Committee adopted the following comments on this report on 8 April 1993:

*A. Introduction.* The Committee welcomes the . . . report of the Dominican Republic. . . . The Committee notes, however, that the information provided . . . was in many respects incomplete and did not take into account the dialogue that had taken place during the Committee's consideration of the previous report. The Committee would also have appreciated a more candid appraisal by the State party of existing legislative deficiencies as well as factors and difficulties encountered in the application of the Covenant. . . .

*B. Factors and Difficulties Impeding the Application of the Covenant.* The Committee notes that the Dominican Republic has received large numbers of refugees and foreign workers. It also notes that the State party has had to overcome a legacy of authoritarianism. These and other circumstances may to a certain extent explain why many of the provisions of the Covenant still have not been incorporated into the legal order of the Republic.

*C. Principal Subjects of Concern.* The Committee notes with regret that, in general, there has been a lack of progress in the application of the Covenant since the consideration of the State party's second periodic report. In particular, there remains a significant body of legislation that still is not in conformity with the Covenant despite the fact that more than 15 years have elapsed since the accession of the Dominican Republic to the Covenant. A number of rights contained in the Covenant are not guaranteed in the present legal framework and other rights are being invalidated by domestic legal provisions that are incompatible with the Covenant. The Committee also regrets that it has not been informed in an unequivocal way about the Covenant's de jure and de facto status within the legal system of the Dominican Republic. In addition, the grounds for declaring a state of emergency are too broad, and the range of rights that may be derogated from is too wide to be in conformity with article 4 of the Covenant. The Committee is also concerned over the lack of adequate knowledge of the provisions of the Covenant by the legal profession, judicial officials, and the public at large. Furthermore, the Committee notes that there is no governmental authority specifically responsible for ensuring the observance of human rights standards. In that connection, the Committee notes that there has not been sufficient followup to its views adopted under the Optional Protocol but welcomes the promise of the State party for closer cooperation in this regard in the future.

The Committee expresses its concern over the lack of protection afforded to Haitians living or working in the country from such serious human rights abuses as forced labour and cruel, inhuman, or degrading treatment. The Committee expresses its concern over the fact that the protection of the fundamental human rights of foreigners is subject to reciprocity. The Committee also expresses its concern over the degrading living and working conditions of Haitian labourers and the tolerated practices that effectively restrict their freedom of movement. Although some progress has been made in improving their living and working conditions, particularly with regard to child labour, these remain at an unacceptably low level. Furthermore, while many Haitian workers have been prevented from leaving their place of work, there have also been incidents of mass expulsions from the country. In this regard, the Committee considers that Presidential Decree No. 233-91, which resulted in the mass deportation of Haitian workers under 16 and over 60 years of age, represents a serious violation of several articles of the Covenant.

The Committee expresses its concern over the low level of legal protection and effective remedies available to the public concerning arbitrary arrest and lengthy pretrial detention. The Committee notes with concern the large number of detainees awaiting trial, which is particularly worrisome in view of the high number of cases of alleged police abuse during detention and reports of unhealthy prison conditions. The Committee also underlines that punishment by exile is not compatible with the Covenant. Moreover, the powers and independence of the judiciary do not appear to be sufficiently protected. A judicial order for release should be implemented without question.

The Committee expresses its concern over the inadequate protection of the rights of ethnic, religious, and linguistic minorities in the Dominican Republic. In this regard, the Committee notes that the prohibition of broadcasting in a language other than Spanish is not in conformity with article 19 of the Covenant. The right of peaceful assembly is apparently not adequately respected by the police.

*D. Recommendations.* The Committee recommends that the State party should undertake a major initiative aimed at harmonizing its domestic legislation with the provisions of the Covenant. In this regard, the constitution and the relevant civil and penal codes should be reviewed in order to bring the law and its application into line with the provisions of the Covenant. The State party should also consider the establishment of offices and mechanisms to monitor the application of human rights standards and protect and promote human rights. This could include the designation of an independent office to receive complaints and, where necessary, undertake investigations into abuses. More publicity should be given to the provisions of the Covenant and the Optional Protocol in order to ensure that the legal profession, the judiciary, and the general public are more aware of their contents.

The situation concerning the living and working conditions of Haitian labourers should be addressed as a matter of priority. The State party should ensure the implementation of laws concerning labour standards, including adequate monitoring of working conditions. In this regard, the Committee emphasizes the necessity of strengthening the capacity of the labour inspectorate to monitor effectively the working conditions of Haitian labourers, with a view to ending their slavelike exploitation. Child labourers in particular require a higher level of protection and the relevant international standards should be vigorously applied. There should also be more active enforcement, particularly in the "export zones," of the exercise of trade union rights in conformity with article 22 of the Covenant. Additionally, Presidential Decree No. 233-91 should be abolished rather than merely suspended.

The Committee recommends that measures should be immediately undertaken to reduce the backlog of persons in detention awaiting trial and that the number of exceptions to the 48-hour rule should be significantly reduced. Much more severe sanctions are needed to discourage effectively torture and other abuses by prison and law-enforcement officials. Steps should also be taken to tighten the regulations governing the use of firearms by police. Training courses in international human rights standards should be provided for police and prison officials.

The Committee recommends that the State party take further steps for the elimination of discrimination concerning ethnic, religious, and linguistic minorities and recommends that the relevant legislation be reviewed in order to ensure its conformity with the Covenant.

***BIBLIOGRAPHY.*** Americas Watch, National Coalition for Haitian Refugees, and Caribbean Rights. *Haitian Sugar Cane Cutters in the Dominican Republic.* New York: Human Rights Watch, 1989. NGO report, in English.

―――――. *Harvesting Oppression: Forced Haitian Labor in the Dominican Sugar Industry.* New York: Human Rights Watch, 1990. NGO factfinding report, in English.

―――――. *Half Measures: Reform, Forced Labour and the Dominican Sugar Industry.* New York: Human Rights Watch, 1991. NGO factfinding report, in English.

Ferguson, James. *Dominican Republic: Beyond the Lighthouse.* London: Latin America Bureau, 1992. Monograph, in English; bibliography, pp. 111–113.

Lawyer's Committee for Human Rights. *A Childhood Abducted: Children Cutting Sugar Cane in the Dominican Republic.* New York: 1991. NGO factfinding report, in English.

―――――. *Expulsions of Haitians and Dominico-Haitians from the Dominican Republic.* New York: 1991. NGO factfinding report, in English.

U.S. Congress, House of Representatives Committee on Foreign Affairs. *The Plight of the Haitian Sugarcane Cutters in the Dominican Republic: Hearing before the Subcommittees on Human Rights and International Organizations, and on Western Hemisphere Affairs, June 11, 1991.* Washington, D.C.: U.S. Government Printing Office, 1991. Government report, in English.

**DRUG ABUSE.** In the brief "Survey of Specific Humanitarian Issues in the Contemporary World" presented to the 1986 session of the UN **GENERAL ASSEMBLY,** the Secretary-General included the following remarks on the subject of the drug problem (UN Doc. A/41/472, sect. U, paras. 80–81):

The drug abuse phenomenon is increasingly recognized as having a negative impact in most regions of the world. Drug-related problems affect all social strata and age groups in developing countries as well as in the industrialized world. Despite national and international efforts, the worldwide production of illicit drugs continues to mount with devastating results. The scourge of illicit drug traffic and drug abuse has reached ever more dangerous proportions. The humanitarian dimensions of the drug abuse phenomenon are painfully clear, including the crippling of the drug-dependent person, the burden to family members, and the high social costs in terms of absenteeism, required medical care and, in growing numbers, drug-related deaths reflecting wasted lives. In addition, the siphoning of significant human and financial resources seriously affects economic and social development. One of the most tragic aspects is the devastation brought by drug abuse to the younger generation, as thousands of young lives are irreparably damaged or lost to this terrifying social blight.

In resolution 40/120 of 13 December 1985, the General Assembly expressed its deep concern at the constant upward trend in illicit traffic and drug abuse, which posed serious dangers for individual human rights and for the economic, cultural and political structures of society. In resolution 40/121 of the same date, it reaffirmed that maximum priority must be given to the fight against the illicit production of, demand for and traffic in illicit drugs and related international criminal activities, such as the illegal arms trade and terrorist practices, which also had an adverse effect not only on the well-being of peoples but also on the stability of institutions, as well as posing a threat to the sovereignty of States.

These and similar efforts of UN bodies have continued and intensified in recent years. Unfortunately, as late as 1993, the General Assembly admitted (resolution 48/12 of 28 October 1993) that it was "profoundly alarmed by the magnitude of the rising trend in drug abuse, illicit production and trafficking of narcotics and psychotropic substances that threaten the health and well-being of millions of persons, in particular the youth, in all the countries of the world." The Assembly then renewed its commitment to further strengthen international cooperation against illicit production, sale, demand, traffic, and distribution of narcotics and psychotropic substances.

***DECLARATION ON THE CONTROL OF DRUG TRAFFICKING AND DRUG ABUSE, UN (1984).*** The Declaration reflects the view of the UN General Assembly that drug trafficking and drug abuse have become international criminal problems threatening the efforts of the international community to promote social progress and better standards of life for the peoples of the world. The text of the Declaration, adopted by the Assembly on 14 December 1984 (resolution 39/142), is as follows:

The General Assembly,
Bearing in mind that the purposes and principles of the Charter of the United Nations reaffirm faith in the dignity and worth of the human person and promote social progress and better standards of life in larger freedom and international co-operation in solving problems of an economic, social, cultural or humanitarian character,

Considering that Member States have undertaken in the Universal Declaration of Human Rights to promote social progress and better standards of life for the peoples of the world,

Considering that the international community has expressed grave concern at the fact that trafficking in narcotics and drug abuse constitute an obstacle to the physical and moral well-being of peoples and of youth in particular,

Desiring to heighten the awareness of the international community of the urgency of preventing and punishing the illicit demand for, abuse of and illicit production of and traffic in drugs,

Considering that the Quito Declaration against Traffic in Narcotic Drugs of 11 August 1984 and the New York Declaration against Drug Trafficking and the Illicit Use of Drugs of 1 October 1984 recognize the international nature of this problem and emphasize that it should be solved with the firm support of the entire international community,

Considering that the Commission on Narcotic Drugs, the International Narcotics Control Board and the United Nations Fund for Drug Abuse Control have made valuable contributions to the control and elimination of drug trafficking and drug abuse,

Recognizing that existing international instruments, including the Single Convention on Narcotic Drugs of 1961, as amended by the 1972 Protocol Amending the Single Convention on Narcotic Drugs of 1961, and the Convention on Psychotropic Substances of 1971, have created a legal framework for combating trafficking in narcotic drugs and drug abuse in their specialized fields,

Declares that:
1. Drug trafficking and drug abuse are extremely serious problems which, owing to their magnitude, scope and widespread pernicious effects, have become an international criminal activity demanding urgent attention and maximum priority.

2. The illegal production of, illicit demand for, abuse of and illicit trafficking in drugs impede economic and social progress, constitute a grave threat to the security and development of many countries and peoples and should be combated by all moral, legal and institutional means, at the national, regional and international levels.

3. The eradication of trafficking in narcotic drugs is the collective responsibility of all States, especially those affected by problems relating to illicit production, trafficking or abuse.

4. States Members shall utilize the legal instruments against the illicit production of and demand for, abuse of and illicit traffic in drugs and adopt additional measures to counter new manifestations of this shameful and heinous crime.

5. States Members undertake to intensify efforts and to coordinate strategies aimed at the control and eradication of the complex problem of drug trafficking and drug abuse through programmes including economic, social and cultural alternatives.

***SEE ALSO*** *Crime Prevention.*

**BIBLIOGRAPHY.** Americas Watch. *The "Drug War" in Colombia: The Neglected Tragedy of Political Violence.* New York: Human Rights Watch, 1990. NGO factfinding report, in English.

Camargo, Eduardo Matyas. "Narco Paramilitarismo y Derechos Humanos en Colombia" (Narco-Paramilitarism and Human Rights in Colombia), *Boletín—Comisión Andina de Juristas* 25 (June 1990): 9–15. NGO article, in Spanish.

Chungara, Domitila. "Pueblos Indígenas, Opresión y Coca" (Indigenous Peoples, Oppression and Coca), *Boletín—Comisión Andina de Juristas* 23 (December 1989): 7–12. NGO article, in Spanish.

Garcia-Sayan, Diego, ed. *Coca, Cocaina y Narcotrafico: Laberinto en los Andes* (Coca, Cocaine and Drug Traffic: Labyrinth in the Andes). Lima, Peru: Comisión Andina de Juristas, 1989. NGO monograph, in Spanish.

Holland, Robert. "Criminal Sanctions for Drug Abuse during Pregnancy: The Antithesis of Fetal Health," *New York Law School Journal of Human Rights* 8, Part 2 (Spring 1991): 459. Scholarly article, in English.

Pettersson, Bjorn, and Lesley Mackay. *Human Rights Violations Stemming from the 'War on Drugs' in Bolivia.* Cochabamba, Bolivia: Andean Information Network, 1993. NGO report, in English.

Szasz, Thomas. *Our Right to Drugs: The Case for a Free Market.* Westport, CT, USA: Praeger, 1992. Scholarly monograph, in English; bibliography, pp. 185–189.

**DUCOMMUN, ELIE (1833–1906).** Born in Neuchâtel, Switzerland, Elie Ducommun, co-winner of the 1902 **NOBEL PEACE PRIZE,** began as a teacher in the Geneva public schools but made his mark as a journalist early in his life. He was editor of the political newspaper *Revue de Genéve*, of *Helvétie*, and of *Les États-Unis d'Europe*, and founder of the radical journal *Der Fortschritt*. He also held political offices from 1855–1875 and was Secretary-General of the Jura-Berne-lucern Railroad from 1875–1903.

But Ducommun received the Nobel Peace Prize, the second one ever awarded, not because of his journalistic background but because of his commitment to pacifism. As head of the **INTERNATIONAL PEACE BU-**

REAU in Berne, Ducommun was the "head of the united work of all peace societies in the world" (in the words of the Nobel Committee's citation). He worked tirelessly for the Bureau, taking no money for his efforts. Ducommun was the first of several Bureau leaders to receive the Prize, and the International Peace Bureau itself received the Prize in 1910.

*BIBLIOGRAPHY.* Gray, Tony. *Champions of Peace.* London: Paddington Press, 1976.

Schlessinger, Bernard S., and June H. Schlessinger, eds. *Who's Who of Nobel Prize Winners.* Phoenix, AZ, USA: Oryx Press, 1991.

**DUNANT, HENRI (1828–1910).** The first **NOBEL PEACE PRIZE** recipient, a co-winner with **FREDERICK PASSY,** was a man who witnessed the horrors of war at close range, even though he never served in the armed forces of any country; because of this experience, he founded the **INTERNATIONAL RED CROSS.**

A fervently religious man who traveled as an evangelist, Dunant, through unusual circumstances, happened to be present at the Battle of Solferino in Italy in June 1859, at which the Italians and French lost 15,000 men, and the Austrians, who opposed them, lost 13,000. Dunant immediately recruited help from villagers and soldiers to care for the dying and wounded. He wrote of his experiences in *Un Souvenir de Solferino,* which received international acclaim. The book, in effect, laid the groundwork for the establishment of a society of trained volunteers who could care for the sick in wartime. In October 1863, the **INTERNATIONAL RED CROSS** was established; at the Geneva Convention of 1864, the medical personnel were officially granted neutrality in times of war.

In addition to the Red Cross, Dunant was committed to the abolition of slavery, disarmament, international arbitration of disputes, and a homeland for the Jews.

*BIBLIOGRAPHY.* Gray, Tony. *Champions of Peace.* London: Paddington Press, 1976.

Hart, Ellen. *Man Born to Live: Life and Work of Henri Dunant.* London: Victor Gollancz, 1953.

Schlessinger, Bernard S., and June H. Schlessinger, eds. *Who's Who of Nobel Prize Winners.* Phoenix, AZ, USA: Oryx Press, 1991.

# E

**ECONOMIC AND SOCIAL COUNCIL, UN.** Established in accordance with the **UNITED NATIONS CHARTER** (article 7) as a principal organ of the United Nations, the Council's principal functions and powers are:

(a) to make or initiate studies and reports with respect to international economic, social, cultural, educational, health, and related matters, and to make recommendations with respect to any such matters to the General Assembly, to members of the United Nations and to the specialized agencies concerned;

(b) to make recommendations for the purpose of promoting respect for, and observance of, human rights and fundamental freedoms for all;

(c) to prepare draft Conventions for submission to the General Assembly, with respect to matters falling within its competence; and

(d) to call, in accordance with the rules prescribed by the United Nations, international conferences on matters falling within its competence.

As regards the specialized agencies, the Council may:

(a) enter into agreements with any of the specialized agencies, defining the terms on which the agencies shall be brought into relationship with the United Nations, such agreements being subject to approval by the General Assembly;

(b) coordinate the activities of the specialized agencies through consultation with and recommendations to such agencies and through recommendations to the General Assembly and to the members of the United Nations;

(c) take appropriate steps to obtain regular reports from the specialized agencies, and make arrangements with the members of the United Nations and with the specialized agencies, to obtain reports on the steps taken to give effect to its own recommendations and to recommendations on matters falling within its competence made by the General Assembly; and

(d) communicate its observations on these reports to the General Assembly.

The Economic and Social Council may furnish information to and assist the Security Council upon its request. It performs such functions as fall within its competence in connection with the carrying out of the recommendations of the General Assembly. It may, with the approval of the Assembly, perform services at the request of members of the United Nations and at the request of specialized agencies.

Further, in accordance with the terms of the UN Charter, the Council has been authorized by the General Assembly to request advisory opinions of the **INTERNATIONAL COURT OF JUSTICE** on legal questions arising within the scope of its activities.

As regards human rights, the Council is empowered in article 55 of the UN Charter to promote "universal respect for, and observance of, human rights and fundamental freedoms for all without distinction as to race, sex, language, or religion." States which are members of the United Nations pledge themselves, by article 56, "to take joint and separate action in cooperation with the Organization for the achievement of the purposes set forth in article 55."

Subsidiary organs reporting to the Council include (a) functional commissions and sub-commissions; (b) regional commissions; (c) standing Committees; (d) special bodies; and (e) ad hoc Committees.

Of the Council's functional commissions and sub-commissions, three are concerned exclusively with human rights matters: the **COMMISSION ON HUMAN RIGHTS,** its **SUB-COMMISSION ON PREVENTION OF DISCRIMINATION AND PROTECTION OF MINORITIES,** and the **COMMISSION ON THE STATUS OF WOMEN.** Two others—the **COMMITTEE ON CRIME PREVENTION AND CONTROL** and **COMMISSION FOR SOCIAL DEVELOPMENT**—deal with human rights questions from time to time when considering matters within their respective mandates. All report directly to the Council and, through it, to the General Assembly.

Of the treaty-monitoring bodies, four—the **COMMITTEE ON ECONOMIC, SOCIAL AND CULTURAL RIGHTS,** the **HUMAN RIGHTS COMMITTEE,** the **COMMITTEE ON THE RIGHTS OF THE CHILD,** and the **COMMITTEE ON THE ELIMINATION OF DISCRIMINATION AGAINST WOMEN**—are concerned exclusively with human rights. Two—the **COMMITTEE ON THE ELIMINATION OF RACIAL DISCRIMINATION** and the **COMMITTEE AGAINST TORTURE**—report directly to the General Assembly. One—the Group of Three—reports on implementation of the Convention against

*Apartheid* to the Commission on Human Rights and, through it, to the Council and the General Assembly.

Three special Committees established by the General Assembly report direct to the Assembly: the Committee on the Exercise of the Inalienable Rights of the Palestinian People, the Special Committee against *Apartheid* and the Special Committee to Investigate Israeli Practices Affecting the Human Rights of the Palestinian People and Other Arabs of the Occupied Territories.

The Council was originally composed of 18 members in accordance with article 61 of the UN Charter. The membership was increased to 27 by an amendment to that article which entered into force on 31 August 1965, and to 54 by an amendment which entered into force on 24 September 1973. Members of the Council are elected by the General Assembly according to the following pattern established by Assembly resolution 2847 (XXVI) of 20 December 1971: 14 from African States, 11 from Asian States, 10 from Latin American States, 13 from Western European and other States, and six from States of eastern Europe. Elections are held by secret ballot, and there are no nominations. Members are elected by a two-thirds' majority of the Assembly; their term of office is three years. The Council reports to the General Assembly.

The Council normally holds three sessions each year. The first, an organizational session, is convened on the first Tuesday in February for approximately three days. The second is convened on the first Tuesday in May for approximately three weeks, and the third, on the first Wednesday in July, for approximately three weeks, in Geneva.

## ECONOMIC, SOCIAL, AND CULTURAL RIGHTS.

The enjoyment of certain economic, social, and cultural rights, set out in articles 22 to 28 of the **UNIVERSAL DECLARATION OF HUMAN RIGHTS** and elaborated in the **INTERNATIONAL COVENANT ON ECONOMIC, SOCIAL AND CULTURAL RIGHTS** as well as in a number of international conventions adopted by specialized agencies and other intergovernmental organizations, cannot be adequately ensured merely by the enforcement of existing laws or the passage of new ones but can only be achieved progressively through gradual improvement of the economic, social, and cultural situations in which people live.

Accordingly, the Covenant does not establish a complaint procedure but provides primarily (article 16) for States parties to report periodically on the measures they have adopted and the progress made in achieving the enjoyment of such rights. The rights involved include the right to work; the right to social security; the right to an adequate standard of living; the right to the enjoyment of the highest attainable standards of physical and mental health; the right of the family, motherhood, and childhood to protection and assistance; the right to education; the right to participate freely in cultural life; and the right to development.

The reports of States parties, and reports submitted by the specialized agencies concerned, are directed to the UN Secretary-General, who transmits them to the Economic and Social Council. In monitoring the implementation of the Covenant, the Council is assisted by its **COMMITTEE ON ECONOMIC, SOCIAL AND CULTURAL RIGHTS.** The Committee, established by the Council on 25 May 1985 (resolution 1985/17), took over the functions of the sessional Working Group of Governmental Experts on the Implementation of the International Covenant on Economic, Social and Cultural Rights, which the Council had established on a temporary basis in 1978 (resolution 1978/10).

The Committee on Economic, Social and Cultural Rights held its first annual session at the United Nations office in Geneva from 9 to 27 March 1987, and its second at the same location from 8 to 25 February 1988. The Committee, and the sessional working group which preceded it, examined 124 initial reports and 44 second periodic reports concerning the rights covered by articles 6 to 9, 10 to 12, and 13 to 15 of the Covenant up to the end of 1988. The reports were received from all regions of the world and included countries with widely differing socioeconomic, cultural, political, and legal systems. They touched upon most of the problems which might arise in implementing the Covenant, although they did not provide a reliable or complete picture on a worldwide basis of the situation of the enjoyment of economic, social, and cultural rights.

*ILO ACTIVITIES.* In its 1988 report to the Economic and Social Council under article 18 of the International Covenant on Economic, Social and Cultural Rights (UN Doc. E/1988/6), the **INTERNATIONAL LABOR ORGANIZATION** stated the following (paras. 1–12):

By resolution 1988 (LX) of 11 May 1976, the United Nations Economic and Social Council called upon the specialized agencies to submit to it reports, in accordance with Article 18 of the International Covenant on Economic, Social and Cultural Rights, on the progress made in achieving the observance of the provisions of the Covenant falling within the scope of their activities. In November 1976, the Governing Body of the International Labour Office agreed, in response to this request, that the International Labour Organisation would present such reports to the Economic and Social Council. The Governing Body also decided, for that purpose, to entrust to the Committee of Experts on the Application of Conventions and Recommendations the task of examining reports and other available information on the

# E

implementation of the provisions of the Covenant falling within the scope of the ILO's activities.

In pursuance of the above-mentioned mandate, the Committee of Experts from 1978 to 1987 examined the situation in respect of the implementation of Articles 6 to 9 and of certain provisions of Article 10 of the Covenant by States Parties to the Covenant which have supplied reports in accordance with the reporting programme established by the Economic and Social Council. The Committee of Experts made nine reports on this subject which were transmitted to the Secretary-General of the United Nations and presented to the Council. . . . In its last report in 1987, the Committee of Experts noted with particular interest that, by resolution 1985/17 of 28 May 1985, the United Nations Economic and Social Council had decided to set up a Committee on Economic, Social and Cultural Rights, composed of 18 experts serving in their personal capacity, and that this Committee should succeed in 1987 to the Sessional Working Group of governmental experts that the Council had set up in 1978 in order to assist it in its examination of the reports on the implementation of the Covenant.

Following the creation of the new Committee, the Committee of Experts re-examined the manner in which the ILO could best submit its reports in accordance with Article 18 of the Covenant. The Committee of Experts accordingly recommended that the ILO should no longer seek to evaluate separately the extent to which the Covenant was implemented, but that it should inform the new Committee of the results of the operation of the various ILO supervisory procedures in the fields covered by the Covenant and should entrust to the International Labour Office in future to communicate this information to the United Nations for presentation to the Committee on Economic, Social and Cultural Rights. It should remain open to the Committee of Experts to report on particular situations whenever it deemed this desirable or when specifically requested to do so by the new Committee. The Governing Body of the ILO, at its two hundred and thirty-sixth session (May 1987), approved this recommendation made by the Committee of Experts.

The present report has therefore been drawn up in accordance with the arrangements approved by the above decision of the Governing Body. It contains information concerning countries listed in the table of contents of which reports have been received by 1 December 1987. . . .

In previous rights, the Committee of Experts has commented on several occasions on the relationship between the provisions of the Covenant and the standards laid down in international labour Conventions, the nature of the obligations resulting from them and the way in which the Committee of Experts consequently presented its comments on the implementation of the Covenant. Upon the completion of the first cycle of the reporting programme on the Covenant, the Committee of Experts, in its sixth report (E/1983/40), recalled these general observations which it hoped could be of use to the States Parties and would be of interest to the Economic and Social Council and its Sessional Working Group responsible for examining the implementation of the Covenant. It would therefore appear appropriate to recall briefly the main points of these observations.

The Committee of Experts noted that the provisions of Article 2, paragraph 1, of the Covenant, and the nature of a number of the rights recognized in the Covenant, rather than implying an immediate obligation to achieve a fixed standard, require continuing action for the mobilization of available resources in order to progressively implement and improve the exercise of these rights. This is the case, for example, with the right to work, the right to the enjoyment of just and favourable conditions of work and the right to social security, which the States Parties undertake to recognize in accordance with Articles 6, 7 and 9, respectively, of the Covenant. However, in respect of trade union rights, the States Parties undertake in accordance with Article 8 of the Covenant, not only to recognize, but also to ensure the rights in question. The nature of obligations under Article 8 of the Covenant is therefore similar to those under corresponding ILO Conventions. The Committee of Experts also noted that the achievement of union rights is not dependent on the availability of resources, but should represent an important contribution not only to a basic freedom but also to the effective participation of the productive forces in society in the development process.

With regard to the subjects dealt with in the various Articles of the Covenant, those covered by Articles 6–9 are all within the competence of the ILO. In respect of Articles 10–12, only two questions dealt with in paragraphs 2 and 3 of Article 10 fall directly within the scope of the ILO, namely maternity protection and the protection of children and young persons in relation to employment and work. However, of the matters dealt with within the framework of the application of Articles 6–9 of the Covenant, those in the fields of training and employment, remuneration and social security, affect the right to an adequate standard of living, within the meaning of Article 11. Similarly, questions concerning occupational safety and health and the provision of health care within the framework of social security also affect the right to health within the meaning of Article 12. Articles 13–15 deal with questions which fall principally within the scope of organizations other than the ILO.

Article 23 of the Covenant includes among the methods of international action for the achievement of the rights recognized in the Pact, the conclusion of Conventions and the adoption of Recommendations. In this respect, ILO standards that are relevant to Articles 6–10 of the Covenant, even if they have not been ratified, may provide a useful source of reference and guidance in the fields under consideration.

Mention may be made in this connection of the general surveys of the Committee of Experts that are undertaken each year on the application of instruments selected by the Governing Body of the ILO as the subject of reports on unratified Conventions and Recommendations and under article 19 of the Constitution of the International Labour Organisation. These general surveys in recent years have dealt with questions directly linked to the rights provided for under Articles 6–10 of the Covenant: abolition of forced labour (1979), minimum age (1981), freedom of association and collective bargaining (1983), working time (1984), equal remuneration (1986), protection of the working environment (1987). In 1988, the general survey of the Committee of Experts will be on the Discrimination (Employment and Occupation) Convention (No. 111) and Recommendation (No. 111), 1958. In 1989, the survey will deal with social security standards concerning old-age benefits.

In addition to standard-setting activities, other ILO activities may be of interest in view of their relevance to questions having a general influence on the recognition and achievement of the human rights provided for in the Covenant. Reference may be made by way of illustration to the High-Level Meeting on Employment and Structural Adjustment (Geneva, 23–25 November 1987), attended by representatives of the principal international institutions concerned, which examined the consequences of international trade and financial and monetary practices on employment and poverty. These questions are closely related to issues of the current, international economic situation in respect of which the Committee on Economic, Social and Cultural Rights has expressed its deep concern (Report on the First Session of the Committee, paragraph 302). Similarly, a number of the subjects discussed at the International Labour Conference or examined by the various bodies of the Governing Body of the ILO, would be of interest within the framework of the international measures likely to contribute to the effective implementation of the Covenant referred to under its Articles 22 and 23.

As Part II of the report, the ILO presented a list, for each of articles 6 to 10 of the Covenant, of the principal relevant ILO Conventions, as follows:

### Article 6 of the Covenant

Unemployment Convention, 1919 (No. 2); Forced Labour Convention, 1930 (No. 29); Fee-Charging Employment Agencies Convention, 1933 (No. 34); Employment Service Convention, 1948 (No. 88); Fee-Charging Employment Agencies Convention (Revised), 1949 (No. 96); Abolition of Forced Labour Convention, 1957 (No. 105); Discrimination (Employment and Occupation) Convention, 1958 (No. 111); Social Policy (Basic Aims and Standards) Convention, 1962 (No. 117); Employment Policy Convention, 1964 (No. 122); Paid Educational Leave Convention, 1974 (No. 140); Human Resources Development Convention, 1975 (No. 142); Workers with Family Responsibilities Convention, 1981 (No. 156); Termination of Employment Convention, 1982 (No. 158); Vocational Rehabilitation and Employment (Disabled Persons) Convention, 1983 (No. 159).

### Article 7 of the Covenant

*Remuneration.* Minimum Wage-Fixing Machinery Convention, 1928 (No. 26); Minimum Wage-Fixing Machinery (Agriculture) Convention, 1951 (No. 99); Minimum Wage-Fixing Convention, 1970 (No. 131).
   *Equal Remuneration.* Equal Remuneration Convention, 1951 (No. 100).
   *Rest, Limitation of Working Hours and Holidays with Pay.* Hours of Work (Industry) Convention, 1919 (No. 1); Weekly Rest (Industry) Convention, 1921 (No. 14); Hours of Work (Commerce and Offices) Convention, 1930 (No. 30); Forty-Hour Week Convention, 1935 (No. 47); Holidays with Pay Convention, 1936 (No. 52); Holidays with Pay (Agriculture) Convention, 1952 (No. 101); Weekly Rest (Commerce and Offices) Convention, 1957 (No. 106); Holidays with Pay Convention (Revised), 1970 (No. 132).
   *Safe and Healthy Working Conditions.* White Lead (Painting) Convention, 1921 (No. 13); Marking of Weight (Packages Transported by Vessels) Convention, 1929 (No. 27); Protection against Accidents (Dockers) Convention, 1929 (No. 28); Protection against Accidents (Dockers) Convention (Revised), 1932 (No. 32); Safety Provisions (Building) Convention, 1937 (No. 62); Labour Inspection Convention, 1947 (No. 81); Radiation Protection Convention, 1960 (No. 115); Guarding of Machinery Convention, 1963 (No. 119); Hygiene (Commerce and Offices) Convention, 1964 (No. 120); Maximum Weight Convention, 1967 (No.127); Labour Inspection (Agriculture) Convention, 1969 (No. 129); Benzene Convention, 1971 (No. 136); Occupational Cancer Convention, 1974 (No. 139); Working Environment (Air Pollution, Noise and Vibration) Convention, 1977 (No. 148); Occupational Safety and Health (Dock Work) Convention, 1979 (No. 152); Occupational Safety and Health Convention, 1981 (No. 155); Occupational Health Services Convention, 1985 (No. 161); Asbestos Convention, 1986 (No. 162).

### Article 8 of the Covenant

Right of Association (Agriculture) Convention, 1921 (No.11); Freedom of Association and Protection of the Right to Organise Convention, 1948 (No. 87); Right to Organise and Collective Bargaining Convention, 1949 (No. 98); Workers' Representatives Convention, 1971 (No. 135); Rural Workers' Organisations Convention, 1975 (No. 141); Labour Relations (Public Service) Convention, 1978 (No. 151); Collective Bargaining Convention, 1981 (No. 154).

### Article 9 of the Covenant

Workmen's Compensation (Agriculture) Convention, 1921 (No. 12); Workmen's Compensation (Accidents) Convention, 1925 (No. 17); Workmen's Compensation (Occupational Diseases) Convention, 1925 (No. 18); Equality of Treatment (Accident Compensation) Convention, 1925 (No. 19); Sickness Insurance (Industry) Convention, 1927 (No. 24); Sickness Insurance (Agriculture) Convention, 1927 (No. 25); Old-Age Insurance (Industry, etc.) Convention, 1933 (No. 35); Old-Age Insurance (Agriculture) Convention, 1933 (No. 36); Invalidity Insurance (Industry, etc.) Convention, 1933 (No. 37); Invalidity Insurance (Agriculture) Convention, 1933 (No. 38); Survivors' Insurance (Industry, etc.) Convention, 1933 (No. 39); Survivors' Insurance (Agriculture) Convention, 1933 (No. 40); Workmen's Compensation (Occupational Diseases) Convention (Revised), 1934 (No. 42); Unemployment Provisions Convention, 1934 (No. 44); Maintenance of Migrants' Pension Rights Convention, 1935 (No. 48); Social Security (Minimum Standards) Convention, 1952 (No. 102); Equality of Treatment (Social Security) Convention, 1962 (No. 118); Employment Injury Benefits Convention, 1964 (No. 121); Invalidity, Old-Age and Survivors' Benefits Convention, 1967 (No. 128); Medical Care and Sickness Benefits Convention, 1969 (No. 130); Maintenance of Social Security Rights Convention, 1982 (No. 157).

### Article 10 of the Covenant

*(a) Maternity Protection (re para. 2).* Maternity Protection Convention, 1919 (No. 3); Maternity Protection Convention (Revised), 1952 (No. 103).
   *(b) Protection of Children and Young Persons in Relation to Employment and Work (re para. 3).* Minimum Age (Industry) Convention, 1919 (No. 5); Minimum Age (Sea) Convention, 1920 (No. 7); Minimum Age (Agriculture) Convention, 1921 (No. 10); Minimum Age (Trimmers and Stokers) Convention, 1921 (No. 15); Minimum Age (Non-Industrial Employment) Convention, 1932 (No. 33); Minimum Age (Sea) Convention (Revised), 1936 (No. 58); Minimum Age (Industry) Convention (Revised), 1937 (No. 59); Minimum Age (Non-Industrial Employment) Convention (Revised), 1937 (No. 60); Minimum Age (Fishermen) Convention, 1959 (No. 112); Social Policy (Basic Aims and Standards) Convention, 1952 (No. 117); Minimum Age (Underground Work) Convention, 1965 (No. 123); Minimum Age Convention, 1973 (No. 138); Night Work of Young Persons (Industry) Conven-

tion, 1919 (No. 6); Night Work (Bakeries) Convention, 1925 (No. 20); Night Work of Young Persons (Non-Industrial Occupations) Convention, 1946 (No. 79); Night Work of Young Persons (Industry) Convention (Revised), 1948 (No. 90); White Lead (Painting) Convention, 1921 (No. 13) (Article 3); Radiation Protection Convention, 1960 (No. 115) (Article 7); Maximum Weight Convention, 1967 (No. 127) (Article 7); Benzene Convention, 1971 (No. 136) (Article 11); Medical Examination of Young Persons (Sea) Convention, 1921 (No. 16); Medical Examination (Seafarers) Convention, 1946 (No. 73); Medical Examination of Young Persons (Industry) Convention, 1946 (No. 77); Medical Examination of Young Persons (Non-Industrial Occupations) Convention, 1946 (No. 78); Medical Examination (Fishermen) Convention, 1959 (No. 113); Medical Examination of Young Persons (Underground Work) Convention, 1965 (No. 124)

*UNESCO ACTIVITIES.* In its 1988 report to the Economic and Social Council under article 18 of the International Covenant on Economic, Social and Cultural Rights (UN Doc. E/1988/7), the **UNITED NATIONS EDUCATIONAL, SCIENTIFIC AND CULTURAL ORGANIZATION** stated:

This report contains information on the progress made in achieving observance of the provisions of articles 13 to 15 of the International Covenant on Economic, Social and Cultural Rights. The last report was made in August 1981 in implementation of a decision of the Executive Board (109 EX/Decision 5.4.3) which instructed the Committee on Conventions and Recommendations "to prepare, pursuant to article 18 of the Covenant, a report on progress made in the enforcement of human rights that fall within the context of the Organization's activities, including *inter alia* information on the decisions and recommendations adopted by the General Conference and the Executive Board." Since the reporting period for specialized agencies is six years, this report is tabled for consideration by the Committee on Economic, Social and Cultural Rights at the spring 1988 session.

The normative instruments to which this report refers, and their state of ratification, are set out in annex I. The body of this report will deal with the implementation of some of these as well as, in some cases, programs of relevance to implementation.

Normative instruments, however, by their nature are only illustrative of the work UNESCO has done that is relevant to the subject of this document. Literacy, for example, is of importance not only to the right to education but to rights to culture, while copyright provisions, not mentioned in this document, are nevertheless crucial to the writer, actor or performer. General work on human rights or on discrimination has not been mentioned. This work is nevertheless crucial to the way in which the articles here dealt with are really implemented.

The report then summarizes briefly (paras. 8–10) UNESCO's system involving submission by member States of periodic reports:

Under the terms of Article VIII of UNESCO's Constitution, every Member State is required to submit to the Organization, at the request of the General Conference, a report on the action taken by it to give effect to

recommendations and Conventions it has adopted. In addition, under Article 7 of the Convention, States parties thereto must give information to the General Conference concerning the legislative and administrative provisions which they have adopted for the application of that Convention. A similar provision is included in the Recommendation in respect of all Member States. Moreover, the *Ad Hoc* Committee of Governmental Experts which drew up the Convention and the Recommendation stressed the decisive role that the reports would have to play in the conduct of a positive and continuous policy for which the Convention provides the essential basis. At its thirteenth session, in 1964, the General Conference decided that the time had come to give effect to the provisions of Article 7 of the Convention and to the similar provisions of the Recommendation, and it invited the Executive Board to take the necessary measures to put into effect by 1965 a procedure for the submission and examination of reports from Member States.

By a decision adopted in May 1965 (70 EX/Decision 5.2.1), the Executive Board stipulated that the reports of the Governments should be presented at regular intervals in a standardized form so as to cover all the provisions of both the Convention and the Recommendation and enable the General Conference to make an evaluation of their worth, as well as formulate proposals for new recommendations. The same decision also stated that, to ensure uniformity in the reports, clear, specific and simple questionnaires should be prepared to which Governments would be requested to reply within 10 months.

Lastly, the Executive Board decided that these reports, after analysis by the Secretariat, would be examined by a special Committee of the Executive Board and transmitted with the Board's comments to the General Conference.

*Article 13: Right to Education.* The 1988 report lists eight UNESCO instruments as being of particular relevance to realization of the right to education. It does not, however, provide specific information on the significance of these instruments to the implementation of the provisions of article 13. The eight UNESCO instruments are as follows:

(a), (b), and (c) The Convention and Recommendation against Discrimination in Education, of 14 December 1960 and the Protocol instituting a Conciliation and Good Offices Commission to be responsible for seeking the settlement of any disputes which may arise between States Parties to the Convention against Discrimination in Education, of 10 December 1962;

(d) The Revised Recommendation concerning Technical and Vocational Education, of 19 November 1974;

(e) The Recommendation concerning the Status of Teachers, of 5 October 1966;

(f) The Recommendation concerning Education for International Understanding, Co-operation and Peace and Education Relating to Human Rights and Fundamental Freedoms, of 19 November 1974;

(g) The Recommendation on the Development of Adult Education, of 26 November 1976;

(h) The Declaration on Race and Racial Prejudice, of 27 November 1978;

(i) The International Charter of Physical Education and Sport, of 21 November 1978.

**Implementation of the Convention and Recommendation against Discrimination in Education.** In its 1988 report to the Economic and Social Council, UNESCO quotes, in paras. 16–32, the following extracts from the report submitted to the UNESCO General Conference in Sofia in 1985 on the implementation of the UNESCO Convention against Discrimination in Education and the corresponding recommendation. The report was based on examination, by UNESCO's Committee on Conventions and Recommendations, of information supplied by the governments of 84 countries:

*Discrimination.* The Committee noted that with the sole exception of the report drawn up by the United Nations body responsible for Namibia all the replies received contained the assertion that there are no legal provisions or regulations providing for discrimination in education.

The Committee observed that certain situations described in some of the reports were of a discriminatory nature, although it was not always possible to determine whether such situations result from a deficiency in the law or from specific infringements of it.

Furthermore, the Committee noted that preferential measures were taken for the benefit of underprivileged groups in some countries. As it already indicated in its previous reports, it considers that the differences introduced for the purposes of protection and consisting, for example, in according preferential treatment to children from culturally underprivileged backgrounds are not discriminatory in the sense in which this term is used in the Convention and Recommendation, but on the contrary are some of the legitimate means of promoting equality of opportunity, in the spirit of the relevant provisions of the International Convention on the Elimination of all Forms of Racial Discrimination adopted by the United Nations General Assembly at its twentieth session.

*Separate Educational Systems or Establishments for Students of the Two Sexes.* The Committee was already of the opinion in its third report that it was possible to detect a gradual expansion of co-education, especially at the primary and higher levels. It would seem clear from the fourth consultation that this tendency has increased and that co-education has been introduced in some countries where, for traditional or pedagogical reasons, separate education was the rule. In these countries co-educational institutions have appeared alongside single sex establishments, which have continued in existence mainly at the secondary level.

The Committee has also noted with satisfaction the efforts made by some developing States to achieve not only equal opportunity of access to education for both sexes and an improvement in the enrolment ratio of girls (which nevertheless still remains considerably lower than that of boys), but also equality as regards the courses of study available, the equipment and the qualifications of the staff when education is provided in separate establishments.

*Compulsory and Free Primary Education.* Despite improvements in the enrolment ratios in the vast majority of the countries, primary education has not been made compulsory and provided free of charge in a number of Member States on account of a number of difficulties, which include not only the lack of financial resources, the shortage of teachers, shortages of educational equipment and facilities and the geographically scattered nature of the population, but also in some cases restrictions of a religious or traditional nature and even the opposition of parents who require the assistance of their children for agricultural or domestic work.

*Generalization of Secondary Education.* The Committee is pleased to note the progress which has been achieved by many Member States towards the generalization of secondary education. The extension of compulsory schooling to cover the first phase or all the various phases of such education has been achieved in several countries; such schooling has been provided free of charge and this principle has often been extended to cover textbooks, meals, clothing and even the provision of accommodation for pupils in some States. The considerable increase achieved over 10 years in enrolment ratios for the child population as a whole in the case of Benin or for the culturally underprivileged aboriginal groups in the case of Australia reveal the success of the efforts undertaken by the Governments concerned.

The Committee also noted with interest the attention given by many Member States to achieving a fair balance between general secondary education and vocational and professional training in order to create a better preparation for working life and take into account socio-economic conditions and the needs of the labour market.

The reports of several States mention the difficulties which they have encountered in their efforts to generalize secondary education: inadequacy of financial resources, shortages of teachers, lack of premises and equipment and the scattered nature of the population.

*Access to Higher Education.* New higher education establishments have been set up in several countries and a decentralization effort is under way in certain States with a view to making access to higher education easier for population groups far away from the metropolitan countries and major cities, through improved geographical distribution. The Committee noted with satisfaction that this growth in higher education is accompanied in several countries by better access to this level of education for hitherto disadvantaged population categories. It noted the information contained in certain reports stressing that the proportion of minorities in the student population has improved considerably, or that the number of female students is about to reach, as in Poland, or even overtake, as in the United States, that of male students. The Committee further noted that several Governments which had answered this part of the questionnaire were of the view that equality of access to higher education based on the abilities of each person had been achieved in their territories. Certain reports specify that higher education is in fact open to all according to individual abilities, merits and aptitudes.

The Committee must however observe that the concept of equality of opportunities and treatment is much wider and more complex than that of mere legal equality in the right of access: it also covers the differences existing between *de facto* situations and the resultant material difficulties, which national policies seeking to establish equality of opportunities, which the 1960 instruments require States to develop and implement, must strive to overcome.

Free education is an important factor in equality of opportunity and the Committee noted with satisfaction that it had been extended to higher education in many countries. It also noted, however, that the cost of registration and tuition fees in several States was too high and that it hampered access by many candidates to this level of education.

The granting of fellowships and loans to students offsets

these difficulties to a certain extent and the Committee noted with interest information providing details, in the reports received, of financial assistance and other facilities granted to students in order to meet both their registration and tuition fees and their maintenance expenses.

*Adult Education and Continuing Education.* The Committee was happy to note the interest shown by all the 58 Governments who replied to this part of the questionnaire in the struggle against illiteracy. During the past 12 years, and particularly since the last consultation of Member States, major strides have been made in this field and the illiteracy rate has fallen markedly in many countries.

The Committee further noted that the efforts of the Governments concerned were not limited merely to providing literacy training for persons who had not received any primary education and that craft or vocational training taking employment needs into account had been organized in most cases.

In any case, adult education is not restricted to the primary level. Continuing education leading to or even including higher education has been organized in many countries.

*Implementation of the Revised Recommendation concerning Technical and Vocational Education.* According to the revised recommendation [para. 33–34], adopted by the UNESCO General Conference on 19 November 1974, member States should contribute to the achievement of society's goals of greater democratization and social, cultural, and economic development through technical and vocational education, which should aim at eliminating barriers between levels and areas of education, between education and employment and between school and society. The Revised Recommendation makes specific reference to equality of access for women and men to such education, special forms of education for disadvantaged and handicapped persons, participation of representatives of various segments of society in policy formulation on local and national levels, and equal standards of quality in different educational streams in order to exclude possible discrimination between them.

In accordance with resolution 25 adopted by the General Conference at its twenty-second session, a questionnaire for reporting on the implementation of the Revised Recommendation since its adoption in 1974 was sent to all Member States in December 1985 and a synoptic analysis of the 44 reports received was submitted to the Committee on Conventions and Recommendations of the Executive Board at its one hundred and twenty-second session. Also, in conformity with the above-cited resolution, the Committee's report, which contains the synoptic analysis as well as the Committee's conclusions and recommendations, including a proposed timetable for the second consultation of Member States on the application of the Revised Recommendation, will be submitted to the General Conference at its twenty-fourth session.

*Implementation of the Recommendation concerning the Status of Teachers.* The UNESCO General Conference, on the basis of the report [para. 35–37] on the application of the Recommendation submitted to it by the Joint ILO/UNESCO Committee of Experts on the Application of the Recommendation concerning the Status of Teachers, invited Member States to respond to the next questionnaire to be sent to them on the application of the Recommendation and also invited the Director-General, in consultation with the Director-General of the International Labour Office, to continue to examine the question of a possible revision of the Recommendation.

The fourth questionnaire relating to the implementation of the Recommendation on the Status of Teachers was sent to Member States in January 1987. The replies of Member States will be analysed by the Joint ILO/UNESCO Committee of Experts and a report presented to the General Conference in 1989.

The programme of activities undertaken during the 1984–1985 and 1986–1987 biennia has been based on the conclusions of the 1982 report of the Joint ILO/UNESCO Committee of Experts dealing notably with the need for the improvement of the quality of teachers through training. Studies concerning a possible Convention were carried out in 1987 and consultations with ILO are in progress prior to the preparation of a technical report on the question for submission to the Executive Board and the General Conference.

*Implementation of the Recommendation concerning Education for International Understanding, Co-operation and Peace and Education relating to Human Rights and Fundamental Freedoms [para. 38–39].* The Intergovernmental Conference on Education for International Understanding, Co-operation and Peace and Education relating to Human Rights and Fundamental Freedoms, with a view to Developing a Climate of Opinion Favourable to the Strengthening of Security and Disarmament (April 1983) was convened by the Director-General of UNESCO, in pursuance of resolution 1/01 (paragraph 5 (d)) adopted by the General Conference at its twenty-first session; it took place at UNESCO Headquarters in Paris from 12 to 20 April 1983, and was considered by the speakers to occupy a special place in UNESCO's action in the development of international education, and to reflect increased awareness of the role played by education in the fields covered by the 1974 Recommendation.

The program for 1986–1987 included:

(i) The launching of a Plan for the Development of Education for International Understanding, Co-operation and Peace, which was adopted at the twenty-third session of the General Conference, and executed in 1986, which was proclaimed International Year of Peace by the United Nations General Assembly.

(ii) The establishment of a Consultative Committee on steps to promote the full and comprehensive implementation of the 1974 Recommendation.

(iii) The establishment of a permanent system of reporting on the steps taken by Member States to implement the 1974 Recommendation. . . .

*Implementation of the Declaration on Race and Racial Prejudice [para. 41–42].* In accordance with paragraph 2 (a), (b) and (c) of the resolution for the implementation of that Declaration, the Director-General prepared "a comprehensive report on the world situation in the fields covered by the Declaration", which was submitted to the General Conference at its twenty-first session, held in 1980, in the case of the first report (UNESCO Doc. 21 C/78). The second report (UNESCO Doc. 22 C/86) was submitted to the General Conference in 1983.

In pursuance of resolution 12.2 adopted at that session, which invites the Director-General "to increase to four years the periodicity of his comprehensive reports on the world situation in the fields covered by the Declaration on Race and Racial Prejudice", the third report will be submitted to the General Conference in 1987. . . .

*Implementation of the Recommendation on the Development of Adult Education [para. 47–52].* The fourth International Conference on Adult Education was held in Paris from 19 to 29 March 1985. Among other topics, the Conference discussed the development of adult education as an essential prerequisite for lifelong education and an important factor in the democratization of education. The Conference also considered the contribution adult education could make to the development of active participation in economic, social and cultural life. A declaration on "the right to learn" was unanimously adopted.

The International Congress on Human Rights Teaching, Information and Documentation, nine years after the Vienna International Congress on the Teaching of Human Rights, was held in Malta from 31 August to 5 September 1987.

The programme covered the following themes: human rights education and teaching; human rights research in the social and human sciences, legal and political sciences, history and philosophy; human rights information and documentation.

After recalling the provisions of Article 13 (1) of the International Covenant on Economic, Social and Cultural Rights and Article 7 of the International Convention on the Elimination of all Forms of Racial Discrimination, the Congress recommended that in its periodic reports to the Committee of Experts on the International Covenant on Economic, Social and Cultural Rights and to the Committee on the Elimination of Racial Discrimination (CERD) respectively, UNESCO draw the attention of Member States to their obligation to ensure the human rights education requested in Article 13 (1) of the Covenant and Article 7 of the Convention, and particularly to the efforts made by the States parties to include human rights teaching in school and university curricula.

In the recommendations regarding priorities for research, the main emphasis was placed on economic, social and cultural rights and the exercise of individual rights. In addition, UNESCO was requested to further the debate on collective rights with a view to elucidating their various dimensions. Prominence was thus given to research on the interactions between individual human rights and the rights of ethnic, religious, political or other minorities. Furthermore, the participants in the Congress considered that UNESCO should contribute to analysing the different conceptual approaches to human rights in view of the fact that, despite appearances, they refer at present to different contexts.

In co-operation with the Committee for research on the sociology of education of the International Sociological Association, a series of studies on the right to education were prepared and discussed at the World Congress of Sociology, held in New Delhi (India) in August 1986. The studies, relating in particular to Colombia, Ghana, Guyana, Nigeria, Pakistan and the Philippines, highlight the structural obstacles to the effective exercise of the right to education and the efforts made to overcome them. Special attention is paid to the question of access of girls and women to education.

In addition, in collaboration with the International Association for the Development of Cross-Cultural Communication (AIMAV) and in co-operation with the Faculty of Law of the Federal University of Pernambuco, UNESCO organized an international symposium in Recife (Brazil) from 7 to 9 October 1987 on human rights and cultural rights, particularly linguistic rights.

*Implementation of the International Charter of Physical Education and Sport.* In adopting this Charter on 21 November 1987, the UNESCO General Conference expressed its conviction "that one of the essential conditions for the effective exercise of human [para. 53–60] rights is that everyone should be free to develop and preserve his or her physical, intellectual and moral powers, and that access to physical education and sport should consequently be assured and guaranteed for all human beings". The Preamble also recalls

the United Nations Charter, in which the peoples proclaim their faith in fundamental human rights, and the Universal Declaration of Human Rights. The purpose of the Charter, according to the final paragraph of the Preamble is "placing the development of physical education and sport at the service of human progress, promoting their development, and urging governments, competent non-governmental organizations, educators, families and individuals themselves to be guided thereby, to disseminate it and to put it into practice".

In accordance with Article 1 of the Charter, which stipulates that "every human being has a fundamental right of access to physical education and sport", considerable progress has been noted in respect of the training of personnel, the extension of the practice of sport for all and international co-operation.

With regard to training, concerning which the Charter states in Article 4, paragraph 4.1, that all personnel who assume professional responsibility for physical education and sport must be given preliminary as well as further training, two subregional seminars, one of which was to promote sport for women, and one national seminar were organized in Africa in 1986 and 1987, training courses were provided in Latin America (Brazil and Mexico) and a seminar was held in Asia in 1985 (Republic of Korea).

The practice of physical education and sport for all was in fact extended to girls and women as a result of pilot projects carried out in Egypt, Peru and the Philippines within the framework of the 1986–1987 biennium, along with a national seminar held in Africa.

Millions of people in all population groups participated in the first World Week of Physical Fitness and Sport for All, organized in the context of International Youth Year in 1985. A second such Week is planned during the 1988–1989 biennium.

The rehabilitation of certain traditional sports such as wushu in China has enabled thousands of people to rediscover and practise them. Studies and research have been undertaken on traditional games and dances, thereby opening up the possibility of organizing world traditional games and dance festivals (document 24 C/5).

Agreements and a memorandum on co-operation have been signed with the Supreme Council for Sport in Africa (SCSA), the Conférence des ministres de la jeunesse et des sports des pays d'expression française (CONFEJES) and the International Olympic Committee (IOC).

Lastly, it is noteworthy that since the adoption of a recommendation concerning the difficulties involved in organizing and staging international sports competitions by the Intergovernmental Committee for Physical Education and Sport, which has held five sessions since it was set up (1979, 1981, 1983, 1984 and 1986), the Organization has hosted the second United Nations International Conference on Sports Boycott against South Africa (1986) and contributed to the preparation of the United Nations International Convention against *Apartheid* in Sports.

*Article 14: Principle of Compulsory Education, Free of Charge for All.* The 1988 report lists three UNESCO instruments as being of particular relevance to this principle: the Convention against Discrimination in Education (see **EDUCATION**), the recommendation on the same subject, and the protocol to Convention instituting a Conciliation and Good Offices Commission to be responsible for seeking a settlement of any disputes which may arise between States parties to the

Convention. As regards these instruments, the report states that:

> This Convention and this Recommendation are of particular significance in connection with the implementation of many of the provisions contained in both Articles 13 and 14 of the International Covenant on Economic, Social and Cultural Rights.

The purpose of the Convention and Recommendation is not only to eliminate and to prevent all discrimination, but also to promote equality of opportunity and treatment in education. These instruments thus correspond in two separate but complementary aims contained in UNESCO's Constitution. Indeed, in addition to forms of discrimination which result from legal provisions or administrative practices and thus are a deliberate denial of the right of certain members of the community to education, the injustices to be countered and eradicated include inequalities which are often the consequence not so much of a conscious intention as of a set of social, geographical, human, economic and historical circumstances. These inequalities have sometimes been called "passive" forms of discrimination, the better to distinguish them from "active" and wilful forms.

Under Article 3, States parties to the Convention pledge themselves to take a series of steps immediately. They must *inter alia* abrogate or modify any statutory provisions and discontinue any administrative practices which involve discrimination in education. They must also "not allow differences of treatment by the public authorities between nationals, except on the basis of merit or need, in the matter of school fees and the grant of scholarships or other forms of assistance to pupils. . .".

On the other hand, the measures to be taken to ensure equality of opportunity in education are, in many countries, of a complex character and are not restricted to the field of education. They also call for considerable expenditure which has to be spread out in time.

The Convention therefore stipulates that States undertake to formulate, develop and apply a national policy which, by methods appropriate to the circumstances and to national usage, will tend to promote equality of opportunity and of treatment in the matter of education.

*Article 15. Right to Take Part in Cultural Life and Enjoy the Benefits of Scientific Progress.* The 1988 report lists 15 UNESCO instruments as being of general relevance to realization of the right to take part in cultural life and enjoy the benefits of scientific progress, as follows:

(a) Convention for the Protection of Cultural Property in the Event of Armed Conflict, with Regulations for the Execution of the Convention of 14 May 1954 (Hague Convention);

(b) Protocol for the Protection of Cultural Property in the Event of Armed Conflict, of 14 May 1954;

(c) Recommendation concerning the Most Effective Means of Rendering Museums Accessible to Everyone, of 14 December 1960;

(d) Recommendation on the Means of Prohibiting and Preventing the Illicit Export, Import and Transfer of Ownership of Cultural Property, of 19 November 1964;

(e) Declaration of the Principles of International Cultural Co-operation, of 4 November 1966;

(f) Convention on the Means of Prohibiting and Preventing the Illicit Import, Export and Transfer of Ownership of Cultural Property, of 14 November 1970;

(g) Declaration of Guiding Principles on the Use of Satellite Broadcasting for the Free Flow of Information, the Spread of Education and Greater Cultural Exchange, of 15 November 1972;

(h) Recommendation concerning the Protection, at National Level, of the Cultural and Natural Heritage, of 16 November 1972;

(i) Convention concerning the Protection of the World Cultural Heritage, of 16 November 1972;

(j) Recommendation concerning the Safeguarding and Contemporary Role of Historic Areas, of 26 November 1976;

(k) Recommendation on Participation by the People at Large in Cultural Life and Their Contribution to It, of 26 November 1976;

(l) Declaration on Fundamental Principles concerning the Contribution of the Mass Media to Strengthening Peace and International Understanding, to the Promotion of Human Rights and to Countering Racialism, *Apartheid* and Incitement to War, of 28 November 1978;

(m) Recommendation on the Protection of Movable Cultural Property, of 28 November 1978;

Of these, the report considers in detail only three of the more recently adopted instruments, pointing out that, while this approach is dictated by the need to avoid an unduly long report, the remaining instruments are all of considerable importance in terms of the implementation of the International Covenant on Economic, Social and Cultural Rights.

*Implementation of the Recommendation on Participation by the People at Large in Cultural Life and Their Contribution to It (paras. 62–69).* This recommendation, adopted by the UNESCO General Conference on 26 November 1976, aims to promote cultural rights as human rights and to ensure by appropriate legislation and regulations as well as by technical, administrative, economic, and financial measures, access to culture and participation in cultural life by the population at large.

The recommendation specifies that "culture is an integral part of social life," that it is "at one and the same time the acquisition of knowledge, the demand for a way of life and the need to communicate" and that "participation by the greatest possible number of people and associations in a wide variety of cultural activities of their own free choice is essential to the development of basic human values and dignity of the individual."

In its preamble the recommendation makes reference to the obligations of States under a number of international instruments, including the International Covenant on Economic, Social and Cultural Rights. In addition the preamble notes that cultural action often involves only a minute proportion of the population and that existing organizations and means used do not always meet the needs of those who are in a particularly vulnerable position because of their inadequate education, low standard of living, poor housing conditions and economic and social dependence in general. It also notes that there is often a wide discrepancy between the reality and the proclaimed ideals, declared intentions, programmes, or expected results, but observes that while it is essential and urgent to define objectives, contents, and methods for a policy of participation by the people at large in cultural life, the solutions envisaged cannot be identical for all countries, in view of the current differences between the socioeconomic and political situations in States.

The broad scope of the recommendation is indicated in its first article, which states that it concerns everything that should be done by Member States or the authorities to democratize the means and instruments of cultural activity, so as to enable all individuals to participate freely and fully in cultural creation and its benefits, in accordance with the requirements of social progress.

The recommendation also contains definitions of the phrases "access to culture," "participation in cultural life," and "communication" and provides that free participation in cultural life is related to policy in a wide range of other areas including development in general, lifelong education, science and technology, social progress, environment, communication and international co-operation. In general the recommendation provides, *inter alia*, that States should take appropriate action in order to: guarantee as human rights those rights bearing on access to and participation in cultural life; provide effective safeguards for free access to national and world cultures by all members of society without distinction or discrimination based on race, color, sex, language, religion, political convictions, national or social origin, financial situation, or any other consideration; pay special attention to women's full entitlement to access to culture and of effective participation in cultural life; create appropriate conditions enabling the populations to play an increasingly active part in building the future of their society, to assume responsibilities and duties and exercise rights in that process; and to guarantee the recognition of the equality of cultures, including the cultures of national minorities and of foreign minorities if they exist, as forming part of the common heritage

of all mankind, and ensure that they are promoted at all levels without discrimination.

A World Conference on Cultural Policies (MONDIACULT) was held in Mexico to take stock of the experience gained since the Venice Conference. Its purpose was to stimulate thinking on the fundamental problems of culture in the contemporary world and in the world of tomorrow and to formulate new guidelines (cf. paras. 17–22 of the Mexico City Declaration on Cultural Policies).

In accordance with Recommendation No. 27 adopted by the World Conference on Cultural Policies (MONDIACULT), the United Nations General Assembly, on the proposal of UNESCO, proclaimed, on 8 December 1986, the World Decade for Cultural Development for the period 1988–1997. Two of the four objectives to which the Plan of Action for the Decade are keyed bear explicitly upon (a) broadening participation in culture and (b) promotion of international cultural cooperation.

Mention should also be made of the studies undertaken on the rights and legislative provisions enshrined in the legal systems of some countries in respect of culture, in order to identify those of them that facilitate the application of the measures advocated in the Recommendation on Participation by the People at Large in Cultural Life and Their Contribution to It and the various MONDIACULT recommendations.

***Implementation of the Declaration on Fundamental Principles concerning the Contribution of the Mass Media to Strengthening Peace and International Understanding, to the Promotion of Human Rights and to Countering Racialism, Apartheid and Incitement to War.*** This Declaration, adopted by the UNESCO General Conference on 28 November 1978, is of major importance in the context of UNESCO's efforts to ensure, pursuant to article 2, para. 2, of the Covenant that the rights with which it is concerned will be exercised without discrimination of any kind. The Declaration is of particular relevance in relation to article 15, para. 4, of the Covenant, whereby States parties recognize the benefits to be derived from the encouragement and development of international contacts and cooperation in the scientific and cultural fields (para. 72).

The principles on which the Declaration is based are clearly indicated in Article I, which states that:
"The strengthening of peace and international understanding, the promotion of human rights and the countering of racialism, *apartheid* and incitement to war demand a free flow and a wider and better balanced dissemination of information. To this end, the mass media have a leading contribution to make. This contribution will be the more effective to the extent that the information reflects the different aspects of the subject dealt with. . . ."

***A New World Information and Communication Order (paras. 75–77).*** Resolution 21 C/4.19 states a number of considerations on which a new world information and communication order could be based, including:

a) respect for each people's cultural identity and for the right of each nation to inform the world public about its interests, its aspirations and its social and cultural values;

b) respect for the right of all peoples to participate in international exchanges of information on the basis of equality, justice and mutual benefit; and

c) respect for the right of the public, of ethnic and social groups and of individuals to have access to information sources and to participate actively in the communication process.

UNESCO's efforts in the past few years have concentrated mostly on the further elucidation of the notion of a new world information and communication order. Thus, the first roundtable on this subject was organized jointly with the United Nations Department of Public Information in Igls, Austria, September 1983, followed by a second roundtable, held in Copenhagen, Denmark, April 1986. The reports of both of these roundtables were submitted respectively to the United Nations General Assembly. Parallel to that, the General Conference at its twenty-second session (Paris, 1983) stressed that a new world information and communication order is to be seen as an evolving and continuous process, which has henceforth become part of the official term.

At the more operational level, the International Programme for the Development of Communication, created in 1980 and regarded as an important practical step towards the implementation of a new world information and communication order, seen as an evolving and continuous process, has been carrying out its mandate in assisting the developing countries in their efforts to develop their human and material potential for communication. Since its establishment IPDC has received requests for financing amounting to US$79,210,000. Financing has been ensured through a Special Account amounting to US$11,710,000, which covers only 14.7 percent of expressed needs. In addition to this, it has to date awarded 470 fellowships under its training program. These figures make it clear, however, that the response of the international community to the stated needs has not yet been such as to launch a process which would put an end to the imbalance existing worldwide in respect both of the means of communication and of the flow of information. The Intergovernmental Council asked the secretariat to make a detailed study of ways of improving the mobilization of IPDC's financial resources, and of its procedures and methods of work.

***Implementation of the Recommendation concerning the Status of the Artist.*** In its preamble, the recommen-

dation, adopted by the UNESCO General Conference on 27 October 1980, recalls (paras. 78–82) a number of international instruments, including the International Covenant on Economic, Social and Cultural Rights; it recognizes *inter alia* that the arts in their fullest and broadest definition are and should be an integral part of life and that it is necessary and appropriate for governments to help create and sustain not only a climate encouraging freedom of artistic expression but also the material conditions facilitating the release of this creative talent.

The Recommendation sets forth a number of guiding principles for Member States in this field:

they should ensure that the population as a whole, has access to art and encourage all activities designed to highlight the action of artists for cultural development; they have a duty to protect, defend and assist artists and their freedom of creation, and ensure them of the right to establish trade unions and professional organizations of their choosing; they should make it possible for organizations representing artists to participate in the formulation of cultural policies and employment policies; they should define a policy for providing assistance and material and moral support for artists; they should see that artists are accorded the protection provided for in respect of freedom of expression and communication by international and national legislation concerning human rights; they should ensure that all individuals have the same opportunities to acquire and develop the skills necessary for the complete development and exercise of their artistic talents, to obtain employment and to exercise their profession without discrimination.

The Recommendation further invites Member States to take appropriate measures to encourage the vocation and training of artists; to promote and protect their social status; to improve employment, working and living conditions of artists, so as to enable them to benefit from all the legal, social and economic advantages pertaining to the status of workers; and closely to associate artists with decisions relating to cultural policies and their implementation.

This Recommendation is of particular relevance to Articles 6 and 15 of the Covenant—which are reproduced in the Annex to the Recommendation—whereby the States parties recognize *inter alia* "the right to work, which includes the right of everyone to the opportunity to gain his living by work which he freely chooses or accepts" and "the right of everyone to take part in cultural life" and "to benefit from the protection of the moral and material interests resulting from any scientific, literary or artistic production of which he is the author".

In order to measure the progress made in implementing this Recommendation, in December 1986 UNESCO sent a questionnaire to Member States and to the national Committees of the non-governmental organizations concerned. It emerges from the replies received by August 1987 from 27 Member States representing five regions and 13 NGO national Committees that a number of legislative and/or administrative measures have been adopted to improve the status of artists. These measures relate in particular to the protection of the moral and material rights of performing artists and the improvement of their economic and social status. However, considerable progress still needs to be made to give effect to all the provisions of the Recommendation. It should be noted that, with this in view, UNESCO proposes, during the 1988–1989 biennium, to draw up in consultation with government authorities and artists in different fields a 10-year plan for the systematic implementation of the Recommendation. The 10-year plan forms part of the activities envisaged by UNESCO as its contribution to implementation of the World Decade for Cultural Development.

***Implementation of the Recommendation on the Status of Scientific Researchers.*** The Recommendation, adopted by the UNESCO General Conference on 24 November 1974 (paras. 83–86), is noteworthy because of the wide range of topics with which it deals and the fact that it has been adopted by governments with no votes against and with only four abstentions.

To assist UNESCO Member States in creating national legislation concerning the status of scientific researchers, whether members of the national civil service or personnel assimilated thereto, a model framework-law on the "National Cadre of Scientific Researchers" has been drawn up by the Division of Science and Technology Policies of UNESCO. This model is based on the text of the above-mentioned UNESCO 1974 Recommendation. The framework-law, which scrupulously respects the substance of the Recommendation aims at facilitating the practical application of the principles and norms which that standard-setting text sets forth.

Being aware of the importance of greater public awareness of the indispensable role that science and technology have to play in our contemporary world, and of the social, moral, [and] ethical problems that modern scientific and technological progress has introduced into the life of societies, UNESCO has published a book "Science and scientific researchers in modern society" written by Dr. John P. Dickinson.

It describes the socio-economic and cultural aspects of scientific research as well as the rights and responsibilities inherent in the researcher's work. The work contains examples of codes and standards concerning the ethics of scientific research and established precedents, together with various statements by international non-governmental and intergovernmental organizations. This information appears in an annex to the book, which makes it very useful for a wide readership.

***Implementation of the Recommendation and Convention on the Means of Prohibiting and Preventing the Illicit Import, Export and Transfers of Ownership of Cultural Property.*** One of the major objectives of UNESCO is the promotion of international contacts and cooperation in all the spheres of its organizational competence. In pursuit of this objective, UNESCO has adopted a large range of normative instruments. Among these, the Recommendation (1964) and the Convention (1970) on the Means of Prohibiting and Preventing the Illicit Import, Export and Transfers of Ownership of Cultural Property are of particular importance (paras. 88–94).

Article 1 of the Convention defines the term "cultural property" for the purposes of the Convention and in Article 2 the States Parties to the Convention recognize that the illicit import, export and transfer of ownership of cultural property is one of the main causes of the impoverishment of the cultural heritage of the countries of origin of such

property and that international co-operation constitutes one of the most efficient means of protecting each country's cultural property against all the dangers resulting therefrom. To this end, the States Parties undertake to oppose such practices with the means at their disposal, and particularly by removing their causes, putting a stop to current practices, and by helping to make the necessary reparations.

For the purpose of promoting the attainment of these objectives, the States Parties to the Convention undertake to comply with a range of specific obligations contained in Articles 5 to 14. Article 16 provides that the States Parties shall in their periodic reports submitted to the General Conference of UNESCO, give information on the legislative and administrative provisions which they have adopted and other action which they have taken for the application of the Convention, together with details of the experience acquired in this field. Similarly, paragraph 15 of the Recommendation provides that "Member States should endeavour to assist each other by exchanging the fruits of their experience in the fields covered by (the) Recommendation".

At its twentieth session in 1978, the General Conference of UNESCO examined reports from Member States on measures taken to implement these two instruments. It noted from the report of the Committee on Conventions and Recommendations on this question that certain problems had been raised by some States with respect to the implementation of the Convention which constituted obstacles to the ratification of this instrument (see paras. 204–205 of document 112 EX/CR/SS.1). The General Conference therefore requested the Director-General to seek further information on the problems raised by States as well as on the experience acquired by other States on these issues. It furthermore invited the Executive Board to "instruct its Committee on Conventions and Recommendations to formulate, on the basis of the additional and more comprehensive data referred to above, proposals for the implementation of the Convention, as foreseen in Article 17 thereof, and to submit these proposals in due course to the General Conference". It decided in addition, that Member States would be invited to forward a second report on implementation for examination by the General Conference at its twenty-fourth session.

In pursuance of the above resolution, the Director-General invited Member States to forward to the Secretariat a description of any difficulties that had arisen for the competent authorities in their countries with respect to the implementation of the Convention, asking them to refer not only to the legal but also to the administrative and practical aspects of the question. He also invited Member States to provide information on experience they had acquired in regard to the implementation of the Convention. Since the reports received from States provided very little information on the experience acquired by States concerning the problems of interpretation and implementation referred to by other States, the Director-General convened a group of experts to examine the problems raised by States and to give their views thereon.

The Committee on Convention and Recommendations reviewed in 1983 the information received from States on the problems encountered concerning the implementation of the Convention as well as information received on the experience acquired by other States with respect to these issues. The report of the meeting of experts referred to above was also brought to the attention of the Committee. On the basis of this information the Committee drew up proposals for the implementation of the Convention for consideration by the Executive Board and General Conference.

**E**

At its twenty-second session in 1983, the General Conference endorsed the proposals of the Committee on Conventions and Recommendations and by resolution 11.4 invited States to take a number of measures which, it considered, could improve the implementation of the Convention. In addition to inviting those States which had not already done so to become parties to the Convention, the General Conference invited States to strengthen regional co-operation in the fight against illicit traffic; to draw the attention of all persons benefiting from diplomatic immunities to the need to respect the laws of their host country governing the export of cultural property; to ensure that cultural property which has been the subject of illicit traffic is not provided with services of authentication, evaluation and conservation which may serve to legitimize such traffic; and to adopt the measures advocated in the Recommendation concerning the international exchange of cultural property, in order to develop the circulation of cultural property as a means of discouraging the spread of illicit traffic. The General Conference also called on those States to which illegally exported cultural property is often conveyed to offer assistance to those States which suffer from illicit export of cultural property, in the drawing up of national inventories of cultural property and in the training of specialized personnel.

In accordance with the request of the General Conference at its twentieth session, Member States were invited to submit a second report on action taken to implement the Convention for examination by the General Conference at its twenty-fourth session. Responses received from 25 States Parties to the Convention and 13 States not Parties were examined by the Committee on Conventions and Recommendations meeting during the one hundred and twenty-seventh session of the Executive Board. The reports received from States revealed that considerable importance was attached by States to the system of international co-operation established by the Convention and there was a general recognition that it was only through closer co-operation among States that effective action could be taken to combat the illicit international movement of cultural property and thus protect the cultural heritage of nations from the dangers of theft, clandestine excavations and illicit export of cultural property. The Committee noted that the main problem with respect to the implementation of the Convention stemmed from the fact that, of the 60 States parties to the Convention, most were victims of illicit traffic. To render the instrument more effective, it would be necessary for more States to participate in the system of international co-operation it established and furthermore, for countries victims of illicit traffic to strengthen the protection of their cultural heritage and, in particular, to reinforce export control and for the so-called "importing" countries to take complementary measures, in the name of international solidarity, to regulate the import of cultural property. It would also be necessary to develop a better circulation among States of all useful information which could contribute to the suppression of illicit traffic of cultural property and to strengthen bilateral as well as regional co-operation. The proposals made by the Committee to this end were endorsed by the Executive Board at its one hundred and twenty-seventh session and will be submitted to the General Conference at its twenty-fourth session.

*LIMBURG PRINCIPLES.* The "Limburg Principles on the Implementation of the International Covenant on Economic, Social and Cultural Rights," set out below, were prepared by a group of independent experts in international law convened by the **INTERNATIONAL COMMISSION OF JURISTS,** the Faculty of Law of the University of Limburg (Maastricht, the Netherlands), and the **URBAN MORGAN INSTITUTE FOR HUMAN RIGHTS** of the University of Cincinnati, USA.

The group met in Maastricht from 2 to 6 June 1986 to consider the nature and scope of the obligations of States parties to the Covenant, the consideration of the reports of States parties by the Committee on Economic, Social and Cultural Rights, and international cooperation under Part IV of the Covenant. The principles were drawn to the attention of the UN Commission on Human Rights at its 1987 session at the request of the Permanent Mission of the Kingdom of the Netherlands (UN Doc. E/CN.4/1987/17).

The 29 experts comprising the group came from Australia, the Federal Republic of Germany, Hungary, Ireland, Mexico, the Netherlands, Norway, Senegal, Spain, the United Kingdom, the United States of America, Yugoslavia, the United Nations Centre for Human Rights, the International Labor Organization (ILO), the United Nations Educational, Scientific and Cultural Organization (UNESCO), the World Health Organization (WHO), the Commonwealth Secretariat, and the sponsoring organizations. Four of the participants were members of the Committee on Economic, Social and Cultural Rights.

The participants agreed unanimously on the principles set out below, which in their view reflect the present state of international law, with the exception of certain recommendations indicated by the use of the verb "should" instead of "shall."

The continuing importance of the Limburg Principles on the implementation of the International Covenant on Economic, Social and Cultural Rights was emphasized by the UN Commission on Human Rights in resolution 1993/12 of 26 February 1993.

### Part I: The Nature and Scope of States Parties Obligations

#### A. General Considerations

1. Economic, social and cultural rights are an integral part of international human rights law. They are the subject of specific treaty obligations in various international instruments, notably the International Covenant on Economic, Social and Cultural Rights.
2. The International Covenant on Economic, Social and Cultural Rights, together with the International Covenant on Civil and Political Rights and the Optional Protocol, entered into force in 1976. The Covenants serve to elaborate the Universal Declaration of Human Rights: these instruments constitute the International Bill of Human Rights.
3. As human rights and fundamental freedoms are indi-

visible and interdependent, equal attention and urgent consideration should be given to the implementation, promotion and protection of both civil and political, and economic, social and cultural rights.

4. The International Covenant on Economic, Social and Cultural Rights (hereinafter the Covenant) should, in accordance with the Vienna Convention on the Law of Treaties (Vienna, 1969), be interpreted in good faith, taking into account the object and purpose, the ordinary meaning, the preparatory work and the relevant practice.

5. The experience of the relevant specialized agencies as well as of United Nations bodies and intergovernmental organizations, including the United Nations working groups and special rapporteurs in the field of human rights, should be taken into account in the implementation of the Covenant and in monitoring States parties' achievements.

6. The achievement of economic, social and cultural rights may be realized in a variety of political settings. There is no single road to their full realization. Successes and failures have been registered in both market and non-market economies, in both centralized and decentralized political structures.

7. States parties must at all times act in good faith to fulfil the obligations they have accepted under the Covenant.

8. Although the full realization of the rights recognized in the Covenant is to be attained progressively, the application of some rights can be made justiciable immediately while other rights can become justiciable over time.

9. Non-governmental organizations can play an important role in promoting the implementation of the Covenant. This role should accordingly be facilitated at the national as well as the international level.

10. States parties are accountable both to the international community and to their own people for their compliance with the obligations under the Covenant.

11. A concerted national effort to invoke the full participation of all sectors of society is, therefore, indispensable to achieving progress in realizing economic, social and cultural rights. Popular participation is required at all stages, including the formulation, application and review of national policies.

12. The supervision of compliance with the Covenant should be approached in a spirit of cooperation and dialogue. To this end, in considering the reports of States parties, the Committee on Economic, Social and Cultural Rights, hereinafter called "the Committee", should analyse the causes and factors impeding the realization of the rights covered under the Covenant and, where possible, indicate solutions. This approach should not preclude a finding, where the information available warrants such a conclusion, that a State party has failed to comply with its obligations under the Covenant.

13. All organs monitoring the Covenant should pay special attention to the principles of nondiscrimination and equality before the law when assessing States parties' compliance with the Covenant.

14. Given the significance for development of the progressive realization of the rights set forth in the Covenant, particular attention should be given to measures to improve the standard of living of the poor and other disadvantaged groups, taking into account that special measures may be required to protect cultural rights of indigenous peoples and minorities.

15. Trends in international economic relations should be taken into account in assessing the efforts of the international community to achieve the Covenant's objectives.

## B. Interpretative Principles Specifically Relating to Part II of the Covenant

*Article 2 (1): "To Take Steps . . . by All Appropriate Means, Including Particularly the Adoption of Legislation."* 16. All States parties have an obligation to begin immediately to take steps towards full realization of the rights contained in the Covenant.

17. At the national level States parties shall use all appropriate means, including legislative, administrative, judicial, economic, social and educational measures, consistent with the nature of the rights in order to fulfil their obligations under the Covenant.

18. Legislative measures alone are not sufficient to fulfil the obligations of the Covenant. It should be noted, however, that article 2 (1) would often require legislative action to be taken in cases where existing legislation is in violation of the obligations assumed under the Covenant.

19. States parties shall provide for effective remedies including, where appropriate, judicial remedies.

20. The appropriateness of the means to be applied in a particular State shall be determined by that State party, and shall be subject to review by the United Nations Economic and Social Council, with the assistance of the Committee. Such review shall be without prejudice to the competence of the other organs established pursuant to the Charter of the United Nations.

*"To Achieve Progressively the Full Realization of the Rights."*
21. The obligation "to achieve progressively the full realization of the rights" requires States parties to move as expeditiously as possible towards the realization of the rights. Under no circumstances shall this be interpreted as implying for States the right to defer indefinitely efforts to ensure full realization. On the contrary all States parties have the obligation to begin immediately to take steps to fulfil their obligations under the Covenant.

22. Some obligations under the Covenant require immediate implementation in full by all States parties, such as the prohibition of discrimination in article 2 (2) of the Covenant.

23. The obligation of progressive achievement exists independently of the increase in resources; it requires effective use of resources available.

24. Progressive implementation can be effected not only by increasing resources, but also by the development of societal resources necessary for the realization by everyone of the rights recognized in the Covenant.

*"To the Maximum of Its Available Resources."* 25. States parties are obligated, regardless of the level of economic development, to ensure respect for minimum subsistence rights for all.

26. "Its available resources" refers to both the resources within a State and those available from the international community through international cooperation and assistance.

27. In determining whether adequate measures have been taken for the realization of the rights recognized in the Covenant attention shall be paid to equitable and effective use of and access to the available resources.

28. In the use of the available resources due priority shall be given to the realization of rights recognized in the Covenant, mindful of the need to assure to everyone the satisfaction of subsistence requirements as well as the provision of essential services.

*"Individually and Through International Assistance and Cooperation, Especially Economic and Technical."* 29. International cooperation and assistance pursuant to the Charter of the

United Nations (arts. 55 and 56) and the Covenant shall have in view as a matter of priority the realization of all human rights and fundamental freedoms, economic, social and cultural as well as civil and political.

30. International cooperation and assistance must be directed towards the establishment of a social and international order in which the rights and freedoms set forth in the Covenant can be fully realized (cf. art. 28 Universal Declaration of Human Rights).

31. Irrespective of differences in their political, economic and social systems, States shall cooperate with one another to promote international social, economic and cultural progress, in particular the economic growth of developing countries, free from discrimination based on such differences.

32. States parties shall take steps by international means to assist and cooperate in the realization of the rights recognized by the Covenant.

33. International cooperation and assistance shall be based on the sovereign equality of States and be aimed at the realization of the rights contained in the Covenant.

34. In undertaking international cooperation and assistance pursuant to article 2 (1) the role of international organizations and the contribution of nongovernmental organizations shall be kept in mind.

*Article 2 (2): Nondiscrimination.* 35. Article 2 (2) calls for immediate application and involves an explicit guarantee on behalf of the States parties. It should, therefore, be made subject to judicial review and other recourse procedures.

36. The grounds of discrimination mentioned in article 2 (2) are not exhaustive.

37. Upon becoming a party to the Covenant States shall eliminate *de jure* discrimination by abolishing without delay any discriminatory laws, regulations and practices (including acts of omission as well as commission) affecting the enjoyment of economic, social and cultural rights.

38. *De facto* discrimination occurring as a result of the unequal enjoyment of economic, social and cultural rights, on account of a lack of resources or otherwise, should be brought to an end as speedily as possible.

39. Special measures taken for the sole purpose of securing adequate advancement of certain groups or individuals requiring such protection as may be necessary in order to ensure to such groups or individuals equal enjoyment of economic, social and cultural rights shall not be deemed discrimination, provided, however, that such measures do not, as a consequence, lead to the maintenance of separate rights for different groups and that such measures shall not be continued after their intended objectives have been achieved.

40. Article 2 (2) demands from States parties that they prohibit private persons and bodies from practising discrimination in any field of public life.

41. In the application of article 2 (2) due regard should be paid to all relevant international instruments including the Declaration and Convention on the Elimination of All Forms of Racial Discrimination as well as to the activities of the supervisory Committee (CERD) under the said Convention.

*Article 2 (3): Nonnationals in Developing Countries.* 42. As a general rule the Covenant applies equally to nationals and nonnationals.

43. The purpose of article 2 (3) was to end the domination of certain economic groups of nonnationals during colonial times. In the light of this the exception in article 2 (3) should be interpreted narrowly.

44. This narrow interpretation of article 2 (3) refers in particular to the notion of economic rights and to the notion of developing countries. The latter notion refers to those countries which have gained independence and which fall within the appropriate United Nations classifications of developing countries.

*Article 3: Equal Rights for Men and Women.* 45. In the application of article 3 due regard should be paid to the Declaration and Convention on the Elimination of All Forms of Discrimination against Women and other relevant instruments and the activities of the supervisory Committee (CEDAW) under the said Convention.

*Article 4: Limitations.* 46. Article 4 was primarily intended to be protective of the rights of individuals rather than permissive of the imposition of limitations by the State.

47. The article was not meant to introduce limitations on rights affecting the subsistence or survival of the individual or integrity of the person.

*"Determined by Law."* [The Limburg Principles 48–51 are derived from the Siracusa Principles 15–18, United Nations Doc. E/CN.4/1984/4, 28 September 1984 and 7 Human Rights Quarterly 3 (1985), at p. 5.]

48. No limitation on the exercise of economic, social and cultural rights shall be made unless provided for by national law of general application which is consistent with the Covenant and is in force at the time the limitation is applied.

49. Laws imposing limitations on the exercise of economic, social and cultural rights shall not be arbitrary or unreasonable or discriminatory.

50. Legal rules limiting the exercise of economic, social and cultural rights shall be clear and accessible to everyone.

51. Adequate safeguards and effective remedies shall be provided by law against illegal or abusive imposition on application of limitations on economic, social and cultural rights.

*"Promoting the General Welfare."* 52. This term shall be construed to mean furthering the well-being of the people as a whole.

*"In a Democratic Society."* 53. The expression "in a democratic society" shall be interpreted as imposing a further restriction on the application of limitations.

54. The burden is upon a State imposing limitations to demonstrate that the limitations do not impair the democratic functioning of the society.

55. While there is no single model of a democratic society, a society which recognizes and respects the human rights set forth in the United Nations Charter and the Universal Declaration of Human Rights may be viewed as meeting this definition.

*"Compatible With the Nature of These Rights."* 56. The restriction "compatible with the nature of these rights" requires that a limitation shall not be interpreted or applied so as to jeopardize the essence of the right concerned.

*Article 5.* 57. Article 5 (1) underlines the fact that there is no general, implied or residual right for a State to impose limitations beyond those which are specifically provided for in the law. None of the provisions in the law may be interpreted in such a way as to destroy "any of the rights or freedoms recognized". In addition article 5 is intended to ensure that nothing in the Covenant shall be interpreted as impairing the inherent right of all peoples to enjoy and utilize fully and freely their natural wealth and resources.

58. The purpose of article 5 (2) is to ensure that no provision in the Covenant shall be interpreted to prejudice the provisions of domestic law or any bilateral or multilateral treaties, Conventions or agreements which are already in force, or may come into force, under which more favourable treatment would be accorded to the persons protected. Nei-

ther shall article 5 (2) be interpreted to restrict the exercise of any human right protected to a greater extent by national or international obligations accepted by the State party.

### C. Interpretative Principles Specifically Relating to Part III of the Covenant

*Article 8: "Prescribed by Law."* [The Limburg Principles 59–69 are derived from the Siracusa Principles 10, 15–26, 29–32 and 35–37]

59. See the interpretative principles under the synonymous term "determined by law" in article 4.

*"Necessary in a Democratic Society."* 60. In addition to the interpretative principles listed under article 4 concerning the phrase "in a democratic society", article 8 imposes a greater restraint upon a State party which is exercising limitations on trade union rights. It requires that such a limitation is indeed necessary. The term "necessary" implies that the limitation:

    (a) responds to a pressing public or social need;

    (b) pursues a legitimate aim; and

    (c) is proportional to that aim.

61. Any assessment as to the necessity of a limitation shall be based upon objective considerations.

*"National Security."* 62. National security may be invoked to justify measures limiting certain rights only when they are taken to protect the existence of the nation or its territorial integrity or political independence against force or threat of force.

63. National security cannot be invoked as a reason for imposing limitations to prevent merely local or relatively isolated threats to law and order.

64. National security cannot be used as a pretext for imposing vague or arbitrary limitations and may be invoked only when there exist adequate safeguards and effective remedies against abuse.

65. The systematic violation of economic, social and cultural rights undermines true national security and may jeopardize international peace and security. A State responsible for such violation shall not invoke national security as a justification for measures aimed at suppressing opposition to such violation or at perpetrating repressive practices against its population.

*"Public Order (Ordre Public)."* 66. The expression "public order (*ordre public*)" as used in the Covenant may be defined as the sum of rules which ensures the functioning of society or the set of fundamental principles on which a society is founded. Respect for economic, social and cultural rights is part of public order (*ordre public*).

67. Public order shall be interpreted in the context of the purpose of the particular economic, social and cultural rights which are limited on this ground.

68. State organs or agents responsible for the maintenance of public order shall be subject to controls in the exercise of their power through the parliament, courts, or other competent independent bodies.

*"Rights and Freedoms of Others."* 69. The scope of the rights and freedoms of others that may act as a limitation upon rights in the Covenant extends beyond the rights and freedoms recognized in the Covenant.

### D. Violations of Economic, Social and Cultural Rights

70. A failure by a State party to comply with an obligation contained in the Covenant is, under international law, a violation of the Covenant.

71. In determining what amounts to a failure to comply, it must be borne in mind that the Covenant affords to a State party a margin of discretion in selecting the means for carrying out its objects, and that factors beyond its reasonable control may adversely affect its capacity to implement particular rights.

72. A State party will be in violation of the Covenant, *inter alia*, if:

    —it fails to take a step which it is required to take by the Covenant;

    —it fails to remove promptly obstacles which it is under a duty to remove to permit the immediate fulfilment of a right;

    —it fails to implement without delay a right which it is required by the Covenant to provide immediately;

    —it wilfully fails to meet a generally accepted international minimum standard of achievement, which is within its powers to meet;

    —it applies a limitation to a right recognized in the Covenant other than in accordance with the Covenant;

    —it deliberately retards or halts the progressive realization of a right, unless it is acting within a limitation permitted by the Covenant or it does so due to a lack of available resources or *force majeure*;

    —it fails to submit reports as required under the Covenant.

73. In accordance with international law each State party to the Covenant has the right to express the view that another State party is not complying with its obligations under the Covenant and to bring this to the attention of that State party. Any dispute that may thus arise shall be settled in accordance with the relevant rules of international law relating to the peaceful settlement of disputes.

### Part II. Consideration of States Parties' Reports and International Cooperation Under Part IV of the Covenant

#### A. Preparation and Submission of Reports by States Parties

74. The effectiveness of the supervisory machinery provided in Part IV of the Covenant depends largely upon the quality and timeliness of reports by States parties. Governments are therefore urged to make their reports as meaningful as possible. For this purpose they should develop adequate internal procedures for consultations with the competent government departments and agencies, compilation of relevant data, training of staff, acquisition of background documentation, and consultation with relevant non-governmental and international institutions.

75. The preparation of reports under article 16 of the Covenant could be facilitated by the implementation of elements of the programme of advisory services and technical assistance as proposed by the chairmen of the main human rights supervisory organs in their 1984 report to the General Assembly (United Nations Doc. A39/484).

76. States parties should view their reporting obligations as an opportunity for broad public discussion on goals and policies designed to realize economic, social and cultural rights. For this purpose wide publicity should be given to the reports, if possible in draft. The preparation of reports should also be an occasion to review the extent to which relevant national policies adequately reflect the scope and content of each right, and to specify the means by which it is to be realized.

77. States parties are encouraged to examine the possi-

bility of involving non-governmental organizations in the preparation of their reports.

78. In reporting on legal steps taken to give effect to the Covenant, States parties should not merely describe any relevant legislative provisions. They should specify, as appropriate, the judicial remedies, administrative procedures and other measures they have adopted for enforcing those rights and the practice under those remedies and procedures.

79. Quantitative information should be included in the reports of States parties in order to indicate the extent to which the rights are protected in fact. Statistical information and information on budgetary allocations and expenditures should be presented in such a way as to facilitate the assessment of the compliance with Covenant obligations. States parties should, where possible, adopt clearly defined targets and indicators in implementing the Covenant. Such targets and indicators should, as appropriate, be based on criteria established through international co-operation in order to increase the relevance and comparability of data submitted by States parties in their reports.

80. Where necessary, governments should conduct or commission studies to enable them to fill gaps in information regarding progress made and difficulties encountered in achieving the observance of the Covenant rights.

81. Reports by States parties should indicate the areas where more progress could be achieved through international co-operation and suggest economic and technical co-operation programmes that might be helpful toward that end.

82. In order to ensure a meaningful dialogue between the States parties and the organs assessing their compliance with the provisions of the Covenant, States parties should designate representatives who are fully familiar with the issues raised in the report.

## B. Role of the Committee on Economic, Social and Cultural Rights

83. The Committee has been entrusted with assisting the Economic and Social Council in the substantive tasks assigned to it by the Covenant. In particular, its role is to consider States parties reports and to make suggestions and recommendations of a general nature, including suggestions and recommendations as to fuller compliance with the Covenant by States parties. The decision of the Economic and Social Council to replace its sessional Working Group by a Committee of independent experts should lead to a more effective supervision of the implementation by States parties.

84. In order to enable it to discharge fully its responsibilities the Economic and Social Council should ensure that sufficient sessions are provided to the Committee. It is imperative that the necessary staff and facilities for the effective performance of the Committee's functions be provided, in accordance with ECOSOC resolution 1985/17.

85. In order to address the complexity of the substantive issues covered by the Covenant, the Committee might consider delegating certain tasks to its members. For example, drafting groups could be established to prepare preliminary formulations or recommendations of a general nature or summaries of the information received. Rapporteurs could be appointed to assist the work of the Committee in particular to prepare reports on specific topics and for that purpose consult States parties, specialized agencies and relevant experts and to draw up proposals regarding economic and technical assistance projects that could help overcome difficulties States parties have encountered in fulfilling their Covenant obligations.

86. The Committee should, pursuant to articles 22 and 23 of the Covenant, explore with other organs of the United Nations, specialized agencies and other concerned organizations, the possibilities of taking additional international measures likely to contribute to the progressive implementation of the Covenant.

87. The Committee should reconsider the current six-year cycle of reporting in view of the delays which have led to simultaneous consideration of reports submitted under different phases of the cycle. The Committee should also review the guidelines for States parties to assist them in preparing reports and propose any necessary modifications.

88. The Committee should consider inviting States parties to comment on selected topics leading to a direct and sustained dialogue with the Committee.

89. The Committee should devote adequate attention to the methodological issues involved in assessing compliance with the obligations contained in the Covenant. Reference to indicators, in so far as they may help measure progress made in the achievement of certain rights, may be useful in evaluating reports submitted under the Covenant. The Committee should take due account of the indicators selected by or in the framework of the specialized agencies and draw upon or promote additional research, in consultation with the specialized agencies concerned, where gaps have been identified.

90. Whenever the Committee is not satisfied that the information provided by a State party is adequate for a meaningful assessment of progress achieved and difficulties encountered it should request supplementary information, specifying as necessary the precise issues or questions it would like the State party to address.

91. In preparing its reports under ECOSOC resolution 1985/17, the Committee should consider, in addition to the "summary of its consideration of the reports", highlighting thematic issues raised during its deliberations.

## C. Relations between the Committee and Specialized Agencies, and Other International Organs

92. The establishment of the Committee should be seen as an opportunity to develop a positive and mutually beneficial relationship between the Committee and the specialized agencies and other international organs.

93. New arrangements under article 18 of the Covenant should be considered where they could enhance the contribution of the specialized agencies to the work of the Committee. Given that the working methods with regard to the implementation of economic, social and cultural rights vary from one specialized agency to another, flexibility is appropriate in making such arrangements under article 18.

94. It is essential for the proper supervision of the implementation of the Covenant under Part IV that a dialogue be developed between the specialized agencies and the Committee with respect to matters of common interest. In particular consultations should address the need for developing indicators for assessing compliance with the Covenant; drafting guidelines for the submission of reports by States parties; making arrangements for submission of reports by the specialized agencies under article 18. Consideration should also be given to any relevant procedures adopted in the agencies. Participation of their representatives in meetings of the Committee would be very valuable.

95. It would be useful if Committee members could visit specialized agencies concerned, learn through personal contact about programmes of the agencies relevant to the real-

ization of the rights contained in the Covenant and discuss the possible areas of collaboration with those agencies.

96. Consultations should be initiated between the Committee and international financial institutions and development agencies to exchange information and share ideas on the distribution of available resources in relation to the realization of the rights recognized in the Covenant. These exchanges should consider the impact of international economic assistance on efforts by States parties to implement the Covenant and possibilities of technical and economic cooperation under article 22 of the Covenant.

97. The Commission on Human Rights, in addition to its responsibilities under article 19 of the Covenant, should take into account the work of the Committee in its consideration of items on its agenda relating to economic, social and cultural rights.

98. The Covenant on Economic, Social and Cultural Rights is related to the Covenant on Civil and Political Rights. Although most rights can clearly be delineated as falling within the framework of one or other Covenant, there are several rights and provisions referred to in both instruments which are not susceptible to clear differentiation. Both Covenants moreover share common provisions and articles. It is important that consultative arrangements be established between the Economic, Social and Cultural Rights Committee and the Human Rights Committee.

99. Given the relevance of other international legal instruments to the Covenant, early consideration should be given by the Economic and Social Council to the need for developing effective consultative arrangements between the various supervisory bodies.

100. International and regional intergovernmental organizations concerned with the realization of economic, social and cultural rights are urged to develop measures, as appropriate, to promote the implementation of the Covenant.

101. As the Committee is a subsidiary organ of the Economic and Social Council, non-governmental organizations enjoying consultative status with the Economic and Social Council are urged to attend and follow the meetings of the Committee and, when appropriate, to submit information in accordance with ECOSOC resolution1296 (XLIV).

102. The Committee should develop, in co-operation with intergovernmental organizations and non-governmental organizations as well as research institutes an agreed system for recording, storing and making accessible case law and other interpretative material relating to international instruments on economic, social and cultural rights.

103. As one of the measures recommended in article 23 it is recommended that seminars be held periodically to review the work of the Committee and the progress made in the realization of economic, social and cultural rights by States parties.

***STUDIES.*** An extensive study entitled *The Realization of Economic, Social and Cultural Rights: Problems, Policies, Progress,* prepared by Mr. Manouchehr Ganji (Iran) as Special Rapporteur of the UN Commission on Human Rights, was published by the United Nations in 1975 (United Nations publication, Sales no. E.75.XIV.2). The study reviewed and summarized the situation regarding national norms and standards relating to economic, social, and cultural rights in the less-developed countries, in the then-socialist countries of eastern Europe, and in the developed market-economy countries. It also summarized the international action taken, up to the time of its publication, for the promotion and protection of economic, social, and cultural rights and concluded with a series of observations, conclusions, and recommendations. In 1977, the Commission stressed "the responsibility and duty of all members of the international community to create the necessary conditions for the full realization of economic, social and cultural rights as an essential means of ensuring the real and meaningful enjoyment of civil and political rights and fundamental freedoms," and called upon all States to take national and international measures to remove all obstacles to the full enjoyment of those rights.

The Commission recommended that the Economic and Social Council invite the Secretary-General, in co-operation with UNESCO and other competent specialized agencies, to undertake a study on the subject "The International Dimensions of the Right to Development as a Human Right in Relation with Other Human Rights based on International Co-operation, Taking into Account the Requirements of the New International Economic Order and the Fundamental Human Needs." The Council endorsed this proposal on 13 May 1977 (decision 229 [LXII]). The study prepared by the Secretary-General (UN Doc. E/CN.4/1988/9 and Add. 1 and 2) led eventually to the adoption of the Declaration on the Right to Development (see **DEVELOPMENT**) and to the continuing activity of the Commission's Working Group of Governmental Experts on the Right to Development.

In 1987, the Commission, mindful that the implementation and promotion of economic, social, and cultural rights had not received sufficient attention, requested the Sub-Commission on Prevention of Discrimination and Protection of Minorities (resolution 1987/19) to review the conclusions and recommendations of the 1975 report and to propose a timetable for updating its conclusions and recommendations. The Sub-Commission was also asked to consider the preparation of a study on the impact on human rights of the policies and practices of the major international financial institutions, most notably the International Monetary Fund and the World Bank. In response, the Sub-Commission appointed one of its members as Special Rapporteur to study problems, policies, and progressive measures relating to a more effective realization of economic, social, and cultural rights, which would take into account all available documentation on both subjects suggested by the Commission and would pay special attention to the human rights aspects of such problems as the interrelationship between structural adjustment and food security, employment, health care, education, and cultural development. Mr. Danilo Türk (Yugoslavia) was named Special Rapporteur and called upon to submit a preliminary report at its session in 1989.

A preliminary report entitled "Realization of Economic, Social and Cultural Rights" was presented to the Sub-Commission at its 1989 session (UN Doc. E/CN.4/Sub.2./1989/19). In the report, the Special Rapporteur outlined what he considered to be the main questions to be analyzed in the final version of his study with a view to providing a basis for discussion in the Sub-Commission. He then offered a series of tentative conclusions arising out of his preliminary work, and suggested that the study should be focused on the following problem areas (chap. IV, para. 94):

(a) The question of the evolution of a unified approach to the interpretation and realization of economic, social and cultural rights should be further discussed. This study should contribute to a more balanced approach to both major sets of human rights and to further elaboration of the concept of the interdependence and indivisibility of human rights;

(b) As regards the problem of the realization of economic, social and cultural rights at the national level, the study should focus on two questions: first, the question of extreme poverty and, secondly, the question of the effects of structural adjustment policies on the realization of economic, social and cultural rights. The basic reasons supporting this choice are explained in this preliminary report, while the analytical work will be done at subsequent stages;

(c) International co-operation constitutes a vital element in the realization of economic, social and cultural rights. Further analysis will focus on, first, questions relating to the future work of the specialized agencies which operate in the areas of economic, social and cultural rights (ILO, FAO, UNESCO and WHO) and, secondly, questions relating to the impact of the activities of the international financial institutions (notably IMF and IBRD) on the realization of economic, social and cultural rights;

(d) In the present preliminary report, the question of the possible role of United Nations development agencies, including UNDP, in the realization of economic, social and cultural rights has not been discussed. It is undeniable that this question should be addressed at an appropriate stage. However, it should be dealt with only after completion of the first round of analysis of the problems discussed in the present preliminary report. The same preliminary conclusion applies to the question of strengthening the co-ordinating role of the Economic and Social Council and the Commission on Human Rights in the field of realization of economic, social and cultural rights;

(e) The subsequent phase of preparation of the study on the realization of economic, social and cultural rights will be devoted to an analysis of the problems referred to in this preliminary report. The primary sources of information will be the relevant studies, reports and other documents prepared within the United Nations system as well as the relevant specialized literature and the information provided by non-governmental organizations. A further source of information will be the replies by States on the realization of economic, social and cultural rights under the relevant resolutions of the Commission on Human Rights and the reports of States under article 16 of the International Covenant on Economic, Social and Cultural Rights. The members of the Sub-Commission are invited to make their suggestions to the Special Rapporteur regarding the sources of information to be consulted;

(f) An additional method to be used at subsequent stages might be the attempt to collect information and to study particular experiences in the realization of economic, social and cultural rights in different States, particularly in those States that are experiencing the problems of implementation of structural adjustment programmes. The Special Rapporteur is ready to consult with the Governments that so wish in order to present their experience in subsequent reports on the realization of economic, social and cultural rights;

(g) Finally, the Special Rapporteur would appreciate it if the Sub-Commission would discuss, at its forty-first session, the possibility of considering the question of realization of economic, social and cultural rights under a separate item of its agenda. Consideration and a possible decision on this question will be important for the formulation of the methodology and timing of subsequent reports by the Special Rapporteur on the realization of economic, social and cultural rights.

The final report on the realization of economic, social and cultural rights (UN Doc. E/CN.4/Sub.2/1992/16) was considered by the Sub-Commission at its 1992 session. In resolution 1992/29 of 27 August 1992, the Sub-Commission endorsed the recommendations set out in the report. In particular, it urged the international and financial institutions—in particular the World Bank and the International Monetary Fund—to take greater account of the adverse impacts of their policies and programs of structural adjustment on the realization of economic, social, and cultural rights; encouraged the United Nations Development Program, the World Bank, and other international programs and agencies to cooperate with the UN Center for Human Rights in devising a consistent approach to the election and use of indicators in the field of human rights; and noted with appreciation Commission on Human Rights resolution 1991/18 and Economic and Social Council decision 1991/235 on the convening of a United Nations expert seminar on the use of social and economic indicators in monitoring the realization of economic, social and cultural rights.

***PROPOSED OPTIONAL PROTOCOL TO THE INTERNATIONAL COVENANT.*** The UN Committee on Economic, Social and Cultural Rights, meeting in December 1992, noted that the Special Rapporteur had expressly recommended the preparation of an optional protocol to the International Covenant on Economic, Social and Cultural Rights that would permit communications pertaining to some or all of the rights recognized in the Covenant, and considered this possibility in some detail, as summarized in its report (E/1993/22, paras. 233–234). Discussion in the Committee was based upon an analytical paper prepared by the Special Rapporteur outlining the principal issues that would arise in connection with the drafting of such an optional protocol (E/C.12/1991/WP.2), in which the following conclusions were set out (paras. 93–94):

The overriding argument in favour of developing an optional protocol to the International Covenant on Economic, Social and Cultural Rights is that a system for the examination of individual cases offers the only real hope that the international community will be able to move towards the development of a significant body of jurisprudence in this field. As the experience of the Human Rights Committee demonstrates such a development is essential if economic, social and cultural rights are to be treated as seriously as they deserve to be. Until that happens, efforts by the Commission and the Sub-Commission on Prevention of Discrimination and Protection of Minorities and other bodies to attribute meaningful normative content to those rights shall be doomed to fail.

This is not to say that a petition system should be the only or even the main component in an overall implementation system. It should not. Writing in 1950, Lauterpacht argued for just such an approach. He acknowledged that the "enforcement" of economic and social rights should not be made "primarily judicial in character", although he did not rule out the appropriateness of such an approach in particular instances. He also observed that "[u]nless an effective right of petition . . . is granted to individuals concerned or to bodies acting on their behalf, any international remedy that may be provided will be deficient in its vital aspect."

The analytical paper was adopted by the Committee at its seventh session, on 11 December 1992. Subsequently the Commission on Human Rights, in resolution 1993/14 of 26 February 1993, expressed its conviction "that equal attention and urgent consideration should be given to the implementation, promotion and protection of civil, political, economic, social and cultural rights," and its awareness that "despite progress achieved by the international community with respect to the setting of standards for the realization of the economic, social and cultural rights contained in the International Covenant on Economic, Social and Cultural Rights, the implementation has not received sufficient attention within the framework of the United Nations system."

**SEE ALSO** *Committee on Economic, Social and Cultural Rights, UN; International Covenant on Economic, Social and Cultural Rights; New International Economic Order.*

**BIBLIOGRAPHY.** *Activities of the United Nations and of the Specialized Agencies in the Field of Economic, Social and Cultural Rights.* Report of the Secretary-General, 1952 (UN publication, Sales no. 1952.IV.4).

*The Balance Which Should Be Established Between Scientific and Technological Progress and the Intellectual, Spiritual, Cultural and Moral Advancement of Humanity.* Report of the Secretary-General, 1976 (UN Doc. E/CN.4/1199 and Add. 1).

Cançado Trindade, A.A. "La protection des droits économiques, sociaux et culturels: évolutions et tendances actuelles, particulièrement à l'échelle régionale" (Protection of Economic, Social and Cultural Rights: Evolution and Current Tendencies, Particularly at the Regional Level), *Revue générale de droit international public* 94, no. 4 (1990): 913–946. Scholarly article, in French.

Centre for Applied Legal Studies, University of the Witwatersrand. "Focus on Socio-Economic Rights," *South African Journal on Human Rights* 8, no. 4 (1992): 451–490. Collection of articles, in English.

Common Frontiers Project on Human Rights and Economic Integration. *Economic Integration and Its Impact on Economic, Social and Cultural Rights: The Repercussions of NAFTA as a Case in Point.* Ottawa, Canada: 1993. NGO report, in English.

Craven, Matthew, and Caroline Dommen. "Making Room for Substance: Fifth Session of the Committee on Economic, Social and Cultural Rights," *Netherlands Quarterly of Human Rights* 9, no. 1 (1991): 83–95. Report, in English.

Gomez, Marion. "Social Economic Rights and Human Rights Commissions," *Human Rights Quarterly* (Feb. 1995): 155–169. Scholarly article, in English.

LeBlanc, Larry. "The Economic, Social and Cultural Rights Protocol to the American Convention and Its Background," *Netherlands Quarterly of Human Rights* 10, no. 2 (1992): 130–154. Scholarly article, in English.

*The Realization of Economic, Social and Cultural Rights.* (UN publication, Sales no. 75.XIV/2).

*Study on the Exploitation of Child Labor.* (UN publication, Sales no. E.82.XIV.2).

*Study on the New International Economic Order and the Promotion of Human Rights.* (UN publication, Sales no. E.85.XIV.6).

*Study on the Realization of Economic, Social and Cultural Rights.* (UN Doc. E/CN.4/Sub.2/1992/16).

**ECUADOR.** The Republic of Ecuador is a country in tropical South America, on the Pacific Ocean. It has borders with Colombia and Peru and includes the offshore Galapagos Islands. It achieved independence from Spain in 1822 when it became part of Greater Colombia, a union which dissolved in 1830 with Ecuador becoming an independent State; and became a member of the United Nations in 1945. Its population is to be 11,055,000. Ethnic groups include *mestizos* (36%), whites (26.5%), Amerindians (18.5%), mulattos (14.5%), and Negroes (4.5%). Languages commonly used include Spanish, Quechua, Jibaro, and many Amerindian vernaculars. Christianity (Roman Catholic) is the predominant religion; since the revolution of 1895 replaced conservative by liberal party rule, the Roman Catholic Church is no longer established and freedom of worship is constitutionally guaranteed.

The government (1992) took the form of a republic. Its political history and framework were described in a "core document" which the government submitted to the United Nations on 17 May 1992 (HR/CORE/1/Add. 7) in the following terms:

When Ecuador started out on its independent existence [1822], it was politically linked to Greater Colombia, which comprised what are now the republics of Venezuela, Colombia, Panama and Ecuador. It seceded on 13 May 1830. The first half of the nineteenth century was characterized by conflicts between rival factions, the growth of militarism, increasing political instability and very little economic development. After 1860 there was a marked increase in exports of traditional products, such as coffee, and in particular cocoa, which revolutionized Ecuador's economy and developed the strength of the crop exporters who formed the liberal-minded bourgeoisie. Serious conflicts arose between coastal exporters and highland landowners, most of whom were of a conservative bent. The conservative movement reached its peak under the Government of Gabriel García Moreno, which brought considerable material progress to the country, but at the cost of a total lack of civil liberties.

In 1895 the liberal revolution under the leadership of General Eloy Alfaro rekindled popular hope of far-reaching change. Major works were undertaken: the railway begun by García Moreno was completed; secular education was established; and the growth of exports made economic development possible. However, prosperity did not lead to an improvement in the living conditions of the people. Among the major reforms, mention should be made of the reduction in the power of the Catholic Church, the expropriation of its large estates, the modernization and integration of the economy and the opening-up of the country to foreign markets.

In 1941 Ecuador was attacked by Peru and as a result lost almost half its territory. It was in those circumstances that the Río de Janeiro Protocol was signed on 29 January 1942. On 28 May 1944 a popular uprising throughout Ecuador brought down the Government of Alberto Arroyo del Rio. Doctor José María Velasco Ibarra was declared President.

Between 1948 and 1960 Ecuador experienced a period of democracy, during which it had three Governments. This period was marked by relative economic prosperity, attributable in particular to a large increase in banana exports. An agrarian reform was carried out during the 1960s.

The year 1972 marked the start of a new era. Ecuador began to export oil, which became its main source of income. In the same year, the political situation changed. The leader José María Velasco Ibarra (five times President) was overthrown by the armed forces. In February 1976 General Guillermo Rodríguez Lara was replaced by a Supreme Council of Government.

The country then embarked on the process of restoring a civilian regime with as its first step the organization of a referendum on a new constitution. On 16 June 1978 the candidate of the *Concentración de Fuerzas Populares* party, the lawyer Jaime Roldós Aguilera, won a majority of votes in the presidential elections. His appointment was ratified in a second round of voting.

In 1981 there were armed clashes between Ecuadorian and Peruvian troops in the Condor mountain range. President Roldós was killed in an air crash and replaced as President by Dr. Osvaldo Hurtado Larrea, the Vice-President. In 1983 the Supreme Electoral Council called presidential elections for 1984, which were won by the Social Christian candidate León Febres Cordero. He was succeeded, after new elections in 1992, by Sixto Duran Ballen.

### RECENT DEVELOPMENTS IN CRIMINAL JUSTICE.

Some recent developments relating to the realization of human rights in Ecuador are set out in the Government's report submitted on 21 April 1993 under article 19 of the Convention against Torture and Other Cruel, Inhuman or Degrading Treatment or Punishment (see **TORTURE**) (CAT/C/20/Add. 1), as follows:

Ecuador has taken part in efforts to strengthen an international policy for the protection of human rights by endeavouring to include provisions along these lines in a set of draft laws which are now under consideration. . . .

These documents basically reflect the principles embodied in the Universal Declaration of Human Rights and those provided for in the Convention against Torture and Other Cruel, Inhuman or Degrading Treatment or Punishment. Ecuador has endeavoured to incorporate these universally applicable instruments in its internal legislation. Thus, on 12 November 1991, at the seventh session of the Committee against Torture held at the Palais des Nations in Geneva, my predecessor as Government Procurator submitted, in accordance with article 19 of the Convention, the report supplementing that introduced by the representatives of Ecuador at the fifth session on 14 November 1990.

That report . . . contains an extensive and specific detailed analysis of criminal legislation, criminal procedure and their relationship with various legal provisions entitling certain administrative officials to order coercive measures, detention and penalties and enabling Ecuador's inhabitants to file complaints with the appropriate bodies and claim compensation for loss and injury, [and] also deals with the measures adopted to prevent ill-treatment, torture and other cruel punishment during the investigation of an offence, especially in the first stage, when the possible offence still has not been brought to the attention of the court, whether ordinary or administrative (police court). . . .

The Memorandum of Understanding between the United States International Development Agency, the Supreme Court of Justice, the Government Procurator's Office, the Attorney-General's office, the Office of the Under-Secretary for Justice and the United Nations Latin American Institute for the Prevention of Crime and the Treatment of offenders was signed on 4 June 1992. The purpose of the Memorandum is the preparation of draft texts of the Penal Code, the Code on the Enforcement of Sentences, the Code of Civil Procedure and the Act on the organization of the Public Prosecutor's Office and the Judicial Police, as well as research on the informal settlement of disputes. . . .

Article 19, paragraph 17, of the Political Constitution of Ecuador provides for respect for liberty and security of person and, in referring to the guilt that may be attributed to a person, embodies the basic principle that everyone has the right to be presumed innocent until proved guilty under an enforceable judgement. At the same time, it must be admitted that there has been some moral and psychological ill-treatment in Ecuador as a result of the application of pre-trial detention, in accordance with article 177 of the Code of Penal Procedure, in cases where, in the opinion of the court, there are indications that there has been an offence punishable by imprisonment and that the accused person is the perpetrator of or accessory to the offence. Such imprisonment lasts until the evidence for the prosecution and for the defence has been produced during the first phase of the proceedings, i.e. the pre-trial phase, which ends with an order for a stay or dismissal of proceedings or with an initiating order. As a result of delays in proceedings, this problem has had some negative consequences: (i) prisons are over-crowded; (ii) accused persons are sometimes imprisoned for more time than they would have been if they had been sentenced as guilty of the offence; and (iii) in the event of the dismissal of the proceedings, the right to honour and reputation and the principle of equality before the law are violated.

In view of the seriousness of these problems, an in-depth analysis was made of the consequences of the absence of decisions in criminal cases without an appropriate and effective defence and, on 26 August 1992, the National Congress adopted the Act Amending the Penal Code, considering, in addition to the above-mentioned factors, that these irregularities were a "serious violation of human rights".

The amendments adopted provide that persons who were detained without a stay of proceedings or initiating order for one-third or more of the time provided for by the Penal Code as the maximum penalty for the offence for which they were being prosecuted are to be released immediately. Persons who were not tried within a period of time equal to or greater than half of the maximum penalty provided for by the Penal Code are also to be released immediately. The only exception is for persons accused of offences under the Narcotic Drugs and Psychotropic Substances Act, which provides for harsher treatment.

With a view to the implementation of these rules, prison directors are given administrative power to release a detainee when the court order for his release is not received within the prescribed time limit.

Work is also under way on the amendment of the rules governing criminal procedure. This revision of the procedural system for the administration of criminal justice is designed to eliminate the first phase of the investigation known as the "pre-trial proceedings" and to replace it by oral proceedings and a proper accusation in order to institute a "pre-trial". Contrary to what is provided for in the Political Constitution, the principle of innocence has been violated by the pre-trial detention provided for in article 177 of the Code of Penal Procedure that is still in force. The draft amendment now proposes proceedings conducted in full freedom by competent defence counsel, with a review of the evidence and direct monitoring of the proceedings by the accused.

The Public Prosecutor's office has a leading role to play in the investigation of the offence. This role has been viewed as a better opportunity to ensure full respect for the basic guarantees of the human being and proper law enforcement. The draft amendment regards the Judicial Police as a body under the supervision of the Public Prosecutor's office and as its assistant in the conduct of the pre-trial.

In this new approach to criminal proceedings, account has even been taken of the tricks that may be used to force an accused person to make a statement. Draft article 96 reads: "Methods prohibited for obtaining a statement. The accused person must not be required to make a sworn statement and may not be subjected to any kind of force or coercion. Any method that impairs the accused person's freedom of decision, memory or ability to understand and discern is prohibited; in particular, the following are prohibited: ill-treatment, threats, sleep deprivation, brutality, torture, deceit and the use of narcotic drugs and so-called "truth serums", lie detectors and hypnosis. Article 97 states: "Questioning. Deceitful and suggestive questions are not allowed and answers must not be demanded". Article 99 provides that the statement by the accused must be given freely, without the use of handcuffs or other security devices and only in the presence of authorized persons.

Special emphasis has been placed on the defence of the accused and, in accordance with internationally applicable provisions resulting from the agreement of nations to eliminate all forms of torture and ill-treatment, title III contains rules designed to prevent any type of violation of the personal integrity of the accused. To this end, article 223 provides for proportionality, according to which detention must be commensurate with the expected penalty and may in no case exceed the maximum penalty for the offence; it may not last longer than one year for offences for which the maximum penalty is up to five years or two years for offences for which the penalty is harsher.

The Public Prosecutor's office is vested with authority which, in our system of criminal procedure, always has been and still is, the sole prerogative of the judge, namely, that of ordering pre-trial detention for a period of not more than 24 hours. The principle is established that detention may not be ordered by the police in any case. Pre-trial detention is ordered only to guarantee the appearance of the accused at the trial and to ensure the enforcement of the sentence. Such pre-trial detention cannot be allowed to become an advance penalty. Alternatives have been offered to prevent possible flight. To replace pre-trial detention when it would be afflictive, provision has been made for house arrest, the obligation to submit to the supervision of a particular person or institution, the obligation to report periodically to the judge or court, etc.

One of the concerns that might not have been answered at the seventh session of the Committee against Torture was that of claims for compensation by persons unfairly accused. The draft amendments to the Code of Penal Procedure must take account of Book Seven, title III, stating that a person unfairly convicted or acquitted by dismissal of the proceedings may claim compensation for the days of detention served.

The draft amendments were referred to the National Congress and it is hoped that, with the revisions and changes under consideration by that branch of Government, they will be discussed soon. Ecuador's system of criminal justice requires urgent change in order to meet the objectives not only of universal Conventions and principles, but also the exigencies of its own situation.

*RIGHTS OF INDIGENOUS POPULATIONS.* The indigenous populations of Ecuador, who have preserved their ancient cultural traditions and ways of life for many centuries, have been of concern in recent years to the government and to human rights groups. The Political Constitution of 1978 guarantees equal rights and guarantees for all Eduadorans, but this goal is not easy to attain. Article 1 (3) of the constitution safeguards the linguistic values of the indigenous populations by providing that "the official language is Spanish. Quechua and other indigenous languages are recognized as elements of the national culture." Article 27 (6) provides that "the State shall . . . ensure the preservation of the cultural heritage and the artistic and historical wealth of the Nation," and article 27 (9) provides that " . . . in the schools situated in areas where the population is predominantly indigenous, Quechua or the appropriate indigenous language shall be used in addition to Spanish."

As a step toward meeting these standards, the Ministry of Education and Culture has introduced a system of intercultural bilingual education directed mainly toward the majority indigenous group, the Quechua-speaking population. It has also introduced didactic methods to achieve literacy in the vernacular of each region covered by its "National Literacy Plan." The success of that plan has helped raise the country's literacy rate to about 85%.

In a report presented to the UN COMMITTEE ON THE ELIMINATION OF RACIAL DISCRIMINATION on 5 February 1988, the government of Ecuador provided the following information regarding the participation of the indigenous population in the life of the country (UN Doc. CERD/C/172/Add. 4):

In the 1970s, Ecuador's policy was based on new attitudes which called for revalorization of the national ethnic groups and their cultures. In 1983, the National Office of Indigenous Affairs was established as part of the Ministry of Social Welfare, in order to shape policies on Ecuador's indigenous problems. The Office's functions were, among others, to promote the organization of the indigenous population, to conduct research, to publicize the situation and to co-ordinate activities to assist the indigenous population through other State bodies. At the present time, the unit has been given a higher status as the National Directorate of Indigenous Affairs.

The organization of the indigenous population and the State's new policy concepts have made it possible over the present decade to carry out a number of activities, such as further promotion of the literacy programme, by incorporating indigenous persons as officials of the National Literacy Office, along with the participation of an appreciable number of such persons as literacy instructors; the implementation of various Integral Rural Development programmes for the indigenous inhabitants; the furtherance of initiatives to safeguard, re-enhance and spread the cultures of the various indigenous peoples by means of special institutes, including the Andean Institute of Popular Arts (IADAP) and the Inter-American Centre for Crafts and Popular Arts (CIDAP); and consolidation of the organization of the indigenous peoples.

The ECURANARI (Ecuador Runacapac Riccharimuri) Movement emerged in 1972 and the Napo Indigenous Organizations Federation (FOIN) was established in 1973. Large numbers of the Quechua-speaking population of the Amazon region joined together in the Union of Natives of the Ecuadorian Amazon (UNAE). The Shuar Federation has been strengthened by creating a number of different centres and it is the first indigenous organization to have developed its own system of bilingual education (Spanish-Shuar). In the Amazon the process led to the formation of a regional organization combining the various local organizations (CONFENIAE) and a nationwide co-ordinating body for the indigenous peasant population has also been establishd, namely the Ecuadorian Indigenous Peoples Co-ordinating Council (CONACNIE).

Historically, the indigenous population in the Sierra has consisted of communes with a domestic economy based on socio-productive complementarity. With this situation as the point of departure, co-operatives, associations and community undertakings have been organized as socio-productive alternatives, sponsored by the indigenous federations and by the State. The indigenous population on the Coast and in Oriente have been nomadic, living from hunting, fishing and food gathering. Accordingly, the Ecuadorian State has embarked on the implementation of rural community development projects through the Ministry of Agriculture and the Ministry of Welfare and FODERUMA (Marginalized Rural Areas Development Fund), and their aims are to provide training, financial support for the construction of community works, and supply credit to *de facto* or *de jure* organizations for investment in productive projects. The organizations participate as a factor of paramount importance in these activities. The State allocated $37,600,000 for this purpose in 1986 and 1987.

Under the 1978 Constitution, persons who are illiterate, as are a high proportion of the indigenous inhabitants, may vote. Participation by the indigenous population in political activity is channelled through their organization, both regional and national. These organizations have succeeded in winning a number of demands. Access to land has been achieved in the inter-Andean region through agrarian reform. In the Amazon region, this has been done by granting communal ownership of the land traditionally occupied by the people in the region, and by keeping control over land settlement and the adjudication of land to enterprises. In regard to education and culture, it has been possible to protect indigenous cultures and their values, to respect the unhampered development of those cultures and to foster bilingual and bicultural education.

**BIBLIOGRAPHY.** Americas Watch Committee and Andean Commission of Jurists. *Human Rights in Ecuador.* New York: 1988. NGO report, in English.

Corkill, D., and D. Cubitt. *Ecuador: Fragile Democracy.* London: Latin American Bureau, 1988. NGO report, in English; bibliography of books in English on Ecuador, 1978–1988, p. 113.

**EDUCATION.** The right of everyone to education is proclaimed in the UNIVERSAL DECLARATION OF HUMAN RIGHTS in the following terms:

*Article 26* (1). Everyone has the right to education. Education shall be free, at least in the elementary and fundamental stages. Elementary education shall be compulsory. Technical and professional education shall be made generally available and higher education shall be equally accessible to all on the basis of merit.

(2) Education shall be directed to the full development of the human personality and to the strengthening of respect for human rights and fundamental freedoms. It shall promote understanding, tolerance and friendship among all nations, racial or religious groups, and shall further the activities of the United Nations for the maintenance of peace.

(3) Parents have a prior right to choose the kind of education that shall be given to their children.

The right to education is further elaborated in the INTERNATIONAL COVENANT ON ECONOMIC, SOCIAL AND CULTURAL RIGHTS in the following provisions:

*Article 13.* 1. The States Parties to the present Covenant recognize the right of everyone to education. They agree that education shall be directed to the full development of the human personality and the sense of its dignity, and shall strengthen the respect for human rights and fundamental freedoms. They further agree that education shall enable all persons to participate effectively in a free society, promote understanding, tolerance and friendship among all nations and all racial, ethnic or religious groups, and further the activities of the United Nations for the maintenance of peace.

2. The States Parties to the present Covenant recognize that, with a view to achieving the full realization of this right:

(a) Primary education shall be compulsory and available free to all;

(b) Secondary education in its different forms, including technical and vocational secondary education, shall be made generally available and accessible to all by every appropriate means, and in particular by the progressive introduction of free education;

(c) Higher education shall be made equally accessible to all, on the basis of capacity, by every appropriate means, and in particular by the progressive introduction of free education;

(d) Fundamental education shall be encouraged or intensified as far as possible for those persons who have not received or completed the whole period of their primary education;

(e) The development of a system of schools at all levels shall be actively pursued, an adequate fellowship system shall be established, and the material conditions of teaching staff shall be continuously improved.

3. The States Parties to the present Covenant undertake to have respect for the liberty of parents and, when applicable, legal guardians to choose for their children schools, other than those established by the public authorities, which conform to such minimum educational standards as may be laid down or approved by the State and to ensure the religious and moral education of their children in conformity with their own convictions.

4. No part of this article shall be construed so as to interfere with the liberty of individuals and bodies to establish and direct educational institutions, subject always to the observance of the principles set forth in paragraph 1 of this article and to the requirement that the education given in such institutions shall conform to such minimum standards as may be laid down by the State.

*Article 14.* Each State Party to the present Covenant which, at the time of becoming a Party, has not been able to secure in its metropolitan territory or other territories under its jurisdiction compulsory primary education, free of charge, undertakes, within two years, to work out and adopt a detailed plan of action for the progressive implementation, within a reasonable number of years, to be fixed in the plan, of the principle of compulsory education free of charge for all.

Non-discrimination on racial grounds is ensured by the International Convention on the Elimination of All Forms of Racial Discrimination (see **RACIAL DISCRIMINATION**) in the following provision:

*Article 5.* In compliance with the fundamental obligations laid down in article 2 of this Convention, States parties undertake to prohibit and to eliminate racial discrimination in all its forms and to guarantee the right of everyone, without distinction as to race, colour, or national or ethnic origin, to equality before the law, notably in the enjoyment of the following rights: . . .

(e) Economic, social and cultural rights, in particular: . . .

(vi) The right to education and training.

Non-discrimination on the ground of sex is ensured by the Convention on the Elimination of All Forms of Discrimination Against Women in the following provision:

*Article 10.* States Parties shall take all appropriate measures to eliminate discrimination against women in order to ensure to them equal rights with men in the field of education and in particular to ensure, on a basis of equality of men and women:

(a) The same conditions for career and vocational guidance, for access to studies and for the achievement of diplomas in educational establishments of all categories in rural as well as in urban areas; this equality shall be ensured in pre-school, general, technical, professional and higher technical education, as well as in all types of vocational training;

(b) Access to the same curricula, the same examinations, teaching staff with qualifications of the same standard and school premises and equipment of the same quality;

(c) The elimination of any stereotyped concept of the roles of men and women at all levels and in all forms of education by encouraging coeducation and other types of education which will help to achieve this aim and, in particular, by the revision of textbooks and school programmes and the adaptation of teaching methods;

(d) The same opportunities to benefit from scholarships and other study grants;

(e) The same opportunities for access to programmes of continuing education, including adult and functional literacy programmes, particularly those aimed at reducing, at the earliest possible time, any gap in education existing between men and women;

(f) The reduction of female student drop-out rates and the organization of programmes for girls and women who have left school prematurely;

(g) The same opportunities to participate actively in sports and physical education;

(h) Access to specific educational information to help to ensure the health and well-being of families, including information and advice on family planning.

Finally, the **AFRICAN CHARTER ON HUMAN AND PEOPLES' RIGHTS** provides, in article 17, that every individual shall have the right to education.

Within the United Nations system, primary responsibility for the preparation and supervision of international measures to promote and protect enjoyment of the right to education lies with the **UNITED NATIONS EDUCATIONAL, SCIENTIFIC AND CULTURAL ORGANIZATION.** Its basic tools in this endeavor are the UNESCO Convention against Discrimination in Education, adopted by its General Conference on 14 December 1960; the Protocol instituting a Conciliation and good offices Commission to be responsible for seeking the settlement of any disputes which may arise between States parties to the Convention against

Discrimination in Education, adopted by the conference on 10 December 1962; and the UNESCO Recommendation concerning Education for International Understanding, Co-operation and Peace and Education relating to Human Rights and Fundamental Freedoms, adopted by the conference on 19 November 1974. Other normative UNESCO instruments relating to the right to education include the Recommendation against Discrimination in Education, of 14 December 1960; the UNESCO Recommendation concerning the Status of Teachers, of 5 October 1966; the revised UNESCO Recommendation concerning Technical and Vocational Education, of 19 November 1974; the UNESCO International Charter of Physical Education and Sport, of 21 November 1978; and the UNESCO Declaration on Race and Racial Prejudice (see **RACE**), of 27 November 1978.

In accordance with the procedures for the implementation of the International Covenant on Economic, Social and Cultural Rights adopted by the Economic and Social Council on 11 May 1976 (resolution 1988 [LX]), UNESCO submits to the Council, at regular intervals, reports on the progress made in achieving the observance of the provisions of the Covenant falling within the scope of its activities, as provided under article 18 of the Covenant.

***EDUCATION AND HUMAN RIGHTS.*** Article 26 of the Universal Declaration of Human Rights accurately reflects the consensus of people's concerns about the aims of education, which "shall be directed to the full development of the human personality and to the strengthening of respect for human rights and fundamental freedoms. It shall promote understanding, tolerance, and friendship among all nations, racial or religious groups, and shall further the activities of the United Nations for the maintenance of peace."

Convinced that the promotion of literacy worldwide can contribute to a better understanding of and respect for human rights, and awareness of the fact that human rights education involves more than merely providing information to the recipients but constitutes a comprehensive process depending essentially on respect for the human person, human dignity, and the fostering of attitudes conducive to coexistence, justice and peace, the UN **COMMISSION ON HUMAN RIGHTS,** in resolution 1993/56 of 9 March 1993, recommended "that knowledge of human rights, both in its theoretical dimension and in its practical application, should be established as a priority in educational policies."

In particular, the Commission recommended that the UN General Assembly should declare a decade for human rights education in the light of recommendations that had been adopted by UNESCO's International Congress on Education for Human Rights and Democracy convened at Montreal, Canada, from 8 to 11 March 1993.

The Commission, in resolution 1994/51 of 4 March 1994, called upon the Economic and Social Council "to request the General Assembly to proclaim the 10-year period beginning on 1 January 1995 as the Decade for Human Rights Education." In the resolution the Commission requested the Secretary-General "to consider the establishment of a voluntary fund for human rights education, with special provision for support of the human rights education activities of non-governmental organizations," urged "all Member States, the specialized agencies and the non-governmental organizations to develop plans of work and to consider allocating resources to contribute to the objectives of the Decade," and further urged "all Member States, the specialized agencies and the non-governmental organizations to provide technical and financial cooperation, including measures of support for human rights education programs and the allocation of funds for the attainment of the objectives of the Decade for Human Rights Education.

***Education for Democracy and Human Rights in the Countries of Central and Eastern Europe.*** The General Conference of UNESCO, meeting in Paris on 15 November 1993, adopted a resolution (27 C/Resolution 5.6) entitled "UNESCO's contribution in its fields of competence to the implementation of the democratic reforms and promotion of education for democracy and human rights in the countries of Central and Eastern Europe," which called upon its Director-General:

(a) to continue efforts to support democratic reforms in the countries of Central and Eastern Europe and to contribute to the promotion of a culture of democracy, primarily through the preparation and dissemination in national languages of educational materials and special studies on democracy and human rights and the organization of workshops and seminars on problems related to democracy, designed primarily for educators, young politicians, government officials, local administrators, representatives of mass media, etc.;

(b) to assist in establishing chaos and documentation centres on democracy and human rights in the countries of Central and Eastern Europe;

(c) to undertake efforts to promote knowledge of experience accumulated in long-standing democracies through the organization of special training courses, the granting of fellowships, the provision of special advisers on education for democracy, etc. . . .

***Education and Training Fund for Southern Africa.*** This UN fund, made up of voluntary contributions, was established by the UN General Assembly on 19 December 1967 (resolution 2349 [XXI]). It provides scholarship assistance to inhabitants of South Africa and Namibia for study at senior, secondary, or university level, with preference for study in African institutions. When Angola, Cape Verde, Guinea-Bissau, Mozambique, and Sao Tome and Principe were under Portuguese administration, scholarship assistance was also provided to students of those territories.

The Advisory Committee on the Educational and Training Program for Southern Africa, also established by the General Assembly in 1968, was enlarged from seven to 13 members in 1978 (resolution 33/42). Members are appointed by the Secretary-General and serve for an indeterminate term. Reports of the Advisory Committee are submitted to the Assembly through the Secretary-General. The Advisory Committee meets as required to perform its functions.

*EDUCATION DECADE.* The UN **GENERAL ASSEMBLY,** in resolution 48/127 of 23 December 1993, requested the Commission on Human Rights, in cooperation with Member States, human rights treaty-monitoring bodies, other appropriate bodies, and competent non-governmental organizations, to consider proposals for a United Nations Decade for Human Rights Education. In doing so, the Assembly bore in mind paragraphs 78 to 82 of the Vienna Declaration and Programme of Action, adopted by the World Conference on Human Rights at Vienna on 25 June 1993, the World Plan of Action on Education for Human Rights and Democracy, adopted by the International Congress on Education for Human Rights and Democracy convened by UNESCO at Montreal from 8 to 11 March 1993, according to which "education for human rights and democracy is itself a human right, and a prerequisite for the realization of human rights, democracy and social justice," and Commission on Human Rights resolution 1993/56 of 9 March 1993 in which the Commission recommended that knowledge of human rights, both in its theoretical dimension and in its practical application, should be established as a priority in educational policies.

In its resolution, the Assembly appealed to all governments to step up their efforts to eradicate illiteracy and to direct education toward the full development of the human personality and to the strengthening of respect for human rights and fundamental freedoms, requested the Commission on Human Rights and other competent bodies to consider proposals for a United Nations decade for human rights education, requested the Secretary-General to consider the establishment of a voluntary fund for human rights education, and called upon international, regional and national non-governmental organizations, in particular those concerned with women, labor, development and the environment, as well as all other social justice groups, human rights advocates, educators, religious organizations and the media, to cooperate with the Centre for Human Rights in preparing for the proposed Decade.

After considering the matter further, the Commission on Human Rights proposed (resolution 1994/51 of 4 March 1994) that the ten-year period beginning on 1 January 1995 should be proclaimed as the decade for human rights education, and the General Assembly adopted the proposal (resolution 1994/1994).

*BIBLIOGRAPHY.* Ammoun, Charles D. *Study of Discrimination in Education.* United Nations publication, Sales no. E-57.XIV.3.

Christie, Pam. *The Right to Learn: The Struggle for Education in South Africa.* Braamfontein, South Africa: Ravan Press, 1985. Research study, in English; bibliography at end of each chapter.

*Consultative Meeting to Formulate Suggestions for Educational Action in Favor of Migrant Workers and Their Families.* Paris: UNESCO, 1988 (ED.SS/CCNF. 604/COL. 1).

Dall, Frank. *Education and the United Nations Convention on the Rights of the Child: The Challenge of Implementation.* Florence, Italy: UNICEF and International Child Development Centre, 1993. Scholarly paper, in English.

Drinan, Robert F., ed. *The Right to be Educated.* Washington, D.C.: Corpus, 1986. Edited collection, in English.

Gordon, P., and A. Newnham. *Different Worlds: Racism and Discrimination in Britain,* 2nd rev. ed. London: Runnymede Trust, 1986. NGO report, in English.

Halvorsen, Kate. "Notes on the Realization of the Human Right to Education," *Human Rights Quarterly* 12, no. 3 (Aug. 1990): 341–364. Scholarly article, in English.

*Intergovernmental Conference on Education for International Understanding, Cooperation, Peace and Education Relating to Human Rights and Fundamental Freedoms, with a View to Developing a Climate of Opinion Favourable to the Strengthening of Security and Disarmament.* Paris: UNESCO, 1983 (ED/MD/74).

*International Seminar on the Civic and Political Education of Women (1967).* UN Advisory Services Programme (ST/TAO/HR/30).

Przetacznik, Franciszek. "The Philosophical Concept of the Right to Education as a Basic Human Right," *Revue de droit international, de sciences diplomatiques et politiques* 63, no. 4 (Oct.–Dec. 1985): 257–287. Scholarly article, in English.

UNESCO Regional Office for Education in Africa. *Colloque Regional sur l'Exercise du Droit a l'Education, Dakar 1980* (Regional Colloquium on the Exercise of the Right to Education). Dakar, Senegal: 1980. Conference proceedings, in English.

World Conference on Education for All. *World Declaration on Education for All and Framework for Action to Meet Basic Learning Needs, World Conference on Education for All, Jomtien, Thailand, 5–9 March 1990.* New York: Inter-Agency Commission and WCEFA, 1990. IGO document, in English.

**EDUCATION: CONVENTION AGAINST DISCRIMINATION IN EDUCATION, UNESCO (1960).** The Convention was adopted on 14 December 1960 at UNESCO headquarters in Paris by the UNESCO General Conference (11th session) and entered into force on 22 May 1962. The preparation of such an instrument had been recommended by Mr. Charles D. Ammoun (Lebanon), Special Rapporteur of the **Sub-Commission on Prevention of Discrimination and Protection of Minorities,** in the *Study of Discrimination in Education* (UN publication, Sales no. 1957.XIV.3), and endorsed by the Sub-Commission, the UN **Commission on Human Rights,** and the UN **Economic and Social Council.** The Convention aims at eradicating discrimination based on race, color, sex, language, religion, political or other opinion, national or social origin, nationality or birth, in the field of education, and at ensuring to everyone equality of treatment in this field.

When it adopted the Convention, the UNESCO General Conference also adopted the Recommendation against Discrimination in Education. With the exception of differences in formulation and statutory scope inherent in the nature of these two categories of instrument, the content of the Recommendation is identical to that of the Convention.

Two years later, on 10 December 1962, the UNESCO General Conference (12th session) adopted the Protocol Instituting a Conciliation and Good Offices Commission, which entered into force on 24 October 1968. The UNESCO Conciliation and Good Offices Commission, established in accordance with the protocol, normally holds at least one session each year at the headquarters of UNESCO, in Paris. Its reports are transmitted to the UNESCO General Conference through its executive board.

The text of the Convention against Discrimination in Education (*UNESCO's Standard-Setting Instruments,* No. 1.A.1, p. 3) is as follows:

The General Conference of the United Nations Educational, Scientific and Cultural Organization, meeting in Paris from 14 November to 15 December 1960, at its eleventh session,

Recalling that the Universal Declaration of Human Rights asserts the principle of non-discrimination and

proclaims that every person has the right to education,

Considering that discrimination in education is a violation of rights enunciated in that Declaration,

Considering that, under the terms of its Constitution, the United Nations Educational, Scientific and Cultural Organization has the purpose of instituting collaboration among the nations with a view to furthering for all universal respect for human rights and equality of educational opportunity,

Recognizing that, consequently, the United Nations Educational, Scientific and Cultural Organization, while respecting the diversity of national educational systems, has the duty not only to proscribe any form of discrimination in education but also to promote equality of opportunity and treatment for all in education,

Having before it proposals concerning the different aspects of discrimination in education, constituting item 17.1.4 of the agenda of the session,

Having decided at its tenth session that this question

should be made the subject of an international convention as well as of recommendations to Member States,

Adopts this Convention on the fourteenth day of December 1960.

*Article 1.* 1. For the purpose of this Convention, the term "discrimination" includes any distinction, exclusion, limitation or preference which, being based on race, colour, sex, language, religion, political or other opinion, national or social origin, economic condition or birth, has the purpose or effect of nullifying or impairing equality of treatment in education and in particular:

(a) Of depriving any person or group of persons of access to education of any type or at any level;

(b) Of limiting any person or group of persons to education of an inferior standard;

(c) Subject to the provisions of article 2 of this Convention, of establishing or maintaining separate educational systems or institutions for persons or groups of persons; or

(d) Of inflicting on any person or group of persons conditions which are incompatible with the dignity of man.

2. For the purposes of this Convention, the term "education" refers to all types and levels of education, and includes access to education, the standard and quality of education, and the conditions under which it is given.

*Article 2.* When permitted in a State, the following situations shall not be deemed to constitute discrimination, within the meaning of article 1 of this Convention:

(a) The establishment or maintenance of separate educational systems or institutions for pupils of the two sexes, if these systems or institutions offer equivalent access to education, provide a teaching staff with qualifications of the same standard as well as school premises and equipment of the same quality, and afford the opportunity to take the same or equivalent courses of study;

(b) The establishment or maintenance, for religious or linguistic reasons, of separate educational systems or institutions offering an education which is in keeping with the wishes of the pupil's parents or legal guardians, if participation in such systems or attendance at such institutions is optional and if the education provided conforms to such standards as may be laid down or approved by the competent authorities, in particular for education of the same level;

(c) The establishment or maintenance of private educational institutions, if the object of the institutions is not to secure the exclusion of any group but to provide educational facilities in addition to those provided by the public authorities, if the institutions are conducted in accordance with that object, and if the education provided conforms with such standards as may be laid down or approved by the competent authorities, in particular for education of the same level.

*Article 3.* In order to eliminate and prevent discrimination within the meaning of this Convention, the States Parties thereto undertake:

(a) To abrogate any statutory provisions and any administrative instructions and to discontinue any administrative practices which involve discrimination in education;

(b) To ensure, by legislation where necessary, that there is no discrimination in the admission of pupils to educational institutions;

(c) Not to allow any differences of treatment by the public authorities between nationals, except on the basis of merit or need, in the matter of school fees and the grant of scholarships or other forms of assistance to pupils and necessary permits and facilities for the pursuit of studies in foreign countries;

(d) Not to allow, in any form of assistance granted by the

public authorities to educational institutions, any restrictions or preference based solely on the ground that pupils belong to a particular group;

(e) To give foreign nationals resident within their territory the same access to education as that given to their own nationals.

*Article 4.* The States Parties to this Convention undertake furthermore to formulate, develop and apply a national policy which, by methods appropriate to the circumstances and to national usage, will tend to promote equality of opportunity and of treatment in the matter of education and in particular:

(a) To make primary education free and compulsory; make secondary education in its different forms generally available and accessible to all; make higher education equally accessible to all on the basis of individual capacity; assure compliance by all with the obligation to attend school prescribed by law;

(b) To ensure that the standards of education are equivalent in all public education institutions of the same level, and that the conditions relating to the quality of the education provided are also equivalent;

(c) To encourage and intensify by appropriate methods the education of persons who have not received any primary education or who have not completed the entire primary education course and the continuation of their education on the basis of individual capacity;

(d) To provide training for the teaching profession without discrimination.

*Article 5.* 1. The States Parties to this Convention agree that:

(a) Education shall be directed to the full development of the human personality and to the strengthening of respect for human rights and fundamental freedoms; it shall promote understanding, tolerance and friendship among all nations, racial or religious groups, and shall further the activities of the United Nations for the maintenance of peace;

(b) It is essential to respect the liberty of parents and, where applicable, of legal guardians, firstly to choose for their children institutions other than those maintained by the public authorities but conforming to such minimum educational standards as may be laid down or approved by the competent authorities and, secondly, to ensure in a manner consistent with the procedures followed in the State for the application of its legislation, the religious and moral education of the children in conformity with their own convictions; and no person or group of persons should be compelled to receive religious instruction inconsistent with his or their conviction;

(c) It is essential to recognize the right of members of national minorities to carry on their own educational activities, including the maintenance of schools and, depending on the educational policy of each State, the use or the teaching of their own language, provided however:

(i) That this right is not exercised in a manner which prevents the members of these minorities from understanding the culture and language of the community as a whole and from participating in its activities, or which prejudices national sovereignty;

(ii) That the standard of education is not lower than the general standard laid down or approved by the competent authorities; and

(iii) That attendance at such schools is optional.

2. The States Parties to this Convention undertake to take all necessary measures to ensure the application of the principles enunciated in paragraph 1 of this article.

*Article 6.* In the application of this Convention, the States Parties to it undertake to pay the greatest attention to any recommendations hereafter adopted by the General Conference of the United Nations Educational, Scientific and Cultural Organization defining the measures to be taken against the different forms of discrimination in education and for the purpose of ensuring equality of opportunity and treatment in education.

*Article 7.* The States Parties to this Convention shall in their periodic reports submitted to the General Conference of the United Nations Educational, Scientific and Cultural Organization on dates and in a manner to be determined by it, give information on the legislative and administrative provisions which they have adopted and other action which they have taken for the application of this Convention, including that taken for the formulation and the development of the national policy defined in article 4 as well as the results achieved and the obstacles encountered in the application of that policy.

*Article 8.* Any dispute which may arise between any two or more States Parties to this Convention concerning the interpretation or application of this Convention which is not settled by negotiations shall at the request of the parties to the dispute be referred, failing other means of settling the dispute, to the International Court of Justice for decision.

*Article 9.* Reservations to this Convention shall not be permitted.

*Article 10.* This Convention shall not have the effect of diminishing the rights which individuals or groups may enjoy by virtue of agreements concluded between two or more States, where such rights are not contrary to the letter or spirit of this Convention.

*Article 11.* This Convention is drawn up in English, French, Russian and Spanish, the four texts being equally authoritative.

*Article 12.* 1. This Convention shall be subject to ratification or acceptance by States Members of the United Nations Educational, Scientific and Cultural Organization in accordance with their respective constitutional procedures.

2. The instruments of ratification or acceptance shall be deposited with the Director-General of the United Nations Educational, Scientific and Cultural Organization.

*Article 13.* 1. This Convention shall be open to accession by all States not Members of the United Nations Educational, Scientific and Cultural Organization which are invited to do so by the Executive Board of the Organization.

2. Accession shall be effected by the deposit of an instrument of accession with the Director-General of the United Nations Educational, Scientific and Cultural Organization.

*Article 14.* This Convention shall enter into force three months after the date of the deposit of the third instrument of ratification, acceptance or accession, but only with respect to those States which have deposited their respective instruments on or before that date. It shall enter into force with respect to any other State three months after the deposit of its instrument of ratification, acceptance or accession.

*Article 15.* The States Parties to this Convention recognize that the Convention is applicable not only to their metropolitan territory but also to all non-self-governing, trust, colonial and other territories for the international relations of which they are responsible; they undertake to consult, if necessary, the governments or other competent authorities of these territories on or before ratification, acceptance or accession with a view to securing the application of the Convention to those territories, and to notify the Director-General of the United Nations Educational, Scientific and

Cultural Organization of the territories to which it is accordingly applied, the notification to take effect three months after the date of its receipt.

*Article 16.* 1. Each State Party to this Convention may denounce the Convention on its own behalf or on behalf of any territory for whose international relations it is responsible.

2. The denunciation shall be notified by an instrument in writing, deposited with the Director-General of the United Nations Educational, Scientific and Cultural Organization.

3. The denunciation shall take effect twelve months after the receipt of the instrument of denunciation.

*Article 17.* The Director-General of the United Nations Educational, Scientific and Cultural Organization shall inform the States Members of the Organization, the States not members of the Organization which are referred to in article 13, as well as the United Nations, of the deposit of all the instruments of ratification, acceptance and accession provided for in articles 12 and 13, and of notifications and denunciations provided for in articles 15 and 16, respectively.

*Article 18.* 1. This Convention may be revised by the General Conference of the United Nations Educational, Scientific and Cultural Organization. Any such revision shall, however, bind only the States which shall become Parties to the revising convention.

2. If the General Conference should adopt a new convention revising this Convention in whole or in part, then, unless the new convention otherwise provides, this Convention shall cease to be open to ratification, acceptance or accession as from the date on which the new revising convention enters into force.

*Article 19.* In conformity with Article 102 of the Charter of the United Nations, this Convention shall be registered with the Secretariat of the United Nations at the request of the Director-General of the United Nations Educational, Scientific and Cultural Organization.

Done in Paris, this fifteenth day of December 1960, in two authentic copies bearing the signatures of the President of the eleventh session of the General Conference and of the Director-General of the United Nations Educational, Scientific and Cultural Organization, which shall be deposited in the archives of the United Nations Educational, Scientific and Cultural Organization, and certified true copies of which shall be delivered to all the States referred to in articles 12 and 13 as well as to the United Nations.

The foregoing is the authentic text of the Convention duly adopted by the General Conference of the United Nations Educational, Scientific and Cultural Organization during its eleventh session, which was held in Paris and declared closed the fifteenth day of December 1960.

In faith whereof we have appended our signatures this fifteenth day of December 1960.

## EDUCATION: RECOMMENDATION CONCERNING EDUCATION FOR INTERNATIONAL UNDERSTANDING, CO-OPERATION AND PEACE AND EDUCATION RELATING TO HUMAN RIGHTS AND FUNDAMENTAL FREEDOMS, UNESCO

**(1974).** This milestone recommendation was adopted by the UNESCO General Conference (18th session), held in Paris, on 19 November 1974. Its guiding principle is that all education should be infused with the aims and purposes set forth in the **UNITED NATIONS CHARTER,** the UNESCO constitution, and the **UNIVERSAL DECLARATION OF HUMAN RIGHTS,** particularly article 26, para. 2.

The text of the recommendation (*UNESCO's Standard-Setting Instruments,* No. I.B.3) is as follows:

The General Conference of the United Nations Educational, Scientific and Cultural Organization, meeting in Paris from 17 October to 23 November 1974, at its eighteenth session,

Mindful of the responsibility incumbent on States to achieve through education the aims set forth in the Charter of the United Nations, the Constitution of Unesco, the Universal Declaration of Human Rights and the Geneva Conventions for the Protection of Victims of War of 12 August 1949, in order to promote international understanding, co-operation and peace and respect for human rights and fundamental freedoms,

Reaffirming the responsibility which is incumbent on Unesco to encourage and support in Member States any activity designed to ensure the education of all for the advancement of justice, freedom, human rights and peace,

Noting nevertheless that the activity of Unesco and of its Member States sometimes has an impact only on a small minority of the steadily growing numbers of schoolchildren, students, young people and adults continuing their education, and educators, and that the curricula and methods of international education are not always attuned to the needs and aspirations of the participating young people and adults,

Noting moreover that in a number of cases there is still a wide disparity between proclaimed ideals, declared intentions and the actual situation,

Having decided at its seventeenth session, that this education should be the subject of a recommendation to Member States,

Adopts this nineteenth day of November 1974, the present recommendation.

The General Conference recommends that Member States should apply the following provisions by taking whatever legislative or other steps may be required in conformity with the constitutional practice of each State to give effect within their respective territories to the principles set forth in this recommendation.

The General Conference recommends that Member States bring this recommendation to the attention of the authorities, departments or bodies responsible for school education, higher education and out-of-school education, of the various organizations carrying out educational work among young people and adults such as student and youth movements, associations of pupils' parents, teachers' unions and other interested parties.

The General Conference recommends that Member States submit to it, by dates and in the form to be decided upon by the Conference, reports concerning the action taken by them in pursuance of this recommendation.

### I. Significance of Terms

1. For the purposes of this recommendation:

(a) The word "education" implies the entire process of social life by means of which individuals and social groups learn to develop consciously within, and for the benefit of, the national and international communities, the whole of their personal capacities, attitudes, aptitudes and knowledge. This process is not limited to any specific activities.

(b) The terms "international understanding", "co-operation" and "peace" are to be considered as an indivisible whole based on the principle of friendly relations between peoples and States having different social and political systems and on the respect for human rights and fundamental freedoms. In the text of this recommendation, the different connotations of these terms are sometimes gathered together in a concise expression, "international education".

(c) "Human rights" and "fundamental freedoms" are those defined in the United Nations Charter, the Universal Declaration of Human Rights and the International Covenants on Economic, Social and Cultural Rights, and on Civil and Political Rights.

## II. Scope

2. This recommendation applies to all stages and forms of education.

## III. Guiding Principles

3. Education should be infused with the aims and purposes set forth in the Charter of the United Nations, the Constitution of Unesco and the Universal Declaration of Human Rights, particularly Article 26, paragraph 2, of the last-named, which states: "Education shall be directed to the full development of the human personality and to the strengthening of respect for human rights and fundamental freedoms. It shall promote understanding, tolerance and friendship among all nations, racial or religious groups, and shall further the activities of the United Nations for the maintenance of peace."

4. In order to enable every person to contribute actively to the fulfilment of the aims referred to in paragraph 3, and promote international solidarity and co-operation, which are necessary in solving the world problems affecting the individuals' and communities' life and exercise of fundamental rights and freedoms, the following objectives should be regarded as major guiding principles of educational policy:

(a) an international dimension and a global perspective in education at all levels and in all its forms;

(b) understanding and respect for all peoples, their cultures, civilizations, values and ways of life, including domestic ethnic cultures and cultures of other nations;

(c) awareness of the increasing global interdependence between peoples and nations;

(d) abilities to communicate with others;

(e) awareness not only of the rights but also of the duties incumbent upon individuals, social groups and nations towards each other;

(f) understanding of the necessity for international solidarity and cooperation;

(g) readiness on the part of the individual to participate in solving the problems of his community, his country and the world at large.

5. Combining learning, training, information and action, international education should further the appropriate intellectual and emotional development of the individual. It should develop a sense of social responsibility and of solidarity with less privileged groups and should lead to observance of the principles of equality in everyday conduct. It should also help to develop qualities, aptitudes and abilities which enable the individual to acquire a critical understanding of problems at the national and the international level; to understand and explain facts, opinions and ideas; to work in a group; to accept and participate in free discussions; to observe the elementary rules of procedure applicable to any discussion; and to base value-judgements and decisions on a rational analysis of relevant facts and factors.

6. Education should stress the inadmissibility of recourse to war for purposes of expansion, aggression and domination, or to the use of force and violence for purposes of repression, and should bring every person to understand and assume his or her responsibilities for the maintenance of peace. It should contribute to international understanding and strengthening of world peace and to the activities in the struggle against colonialism and neo-colonialism in all their forms and manifestations, and against all forms and varieties of racialism, fascism, and apartheid as well as other ideologies which breed national and racial hatred and which are contrary to the purposes of this recommendation.

## IV. National Policy, Planning and Administration

7. Each Member State should formulate and apply national policies aimed at increasing the efficacy of education in all its forms and strengthening its contribution to international understanding and co-operation, to the maintenance and development of a just peace, to the establishment of social justice, to respect for and application of human rights and fundamental freedoms, and to the eradication of the prejudices, misconceptions, inequalities and all forms of injustice which hinder the achievement of these aims.

8. Member States should in collaboration with the National Commissions take steps to ensure co-operation between ministries and departments and co-ordination of their efforts to plan and carry out concerted programmes of action in international education.

9. Member States should provide, consistent with their constitutional provisions, the financial, administrative, material and moral support necessary to implement this recommendation.

## V. Particular Aspects of Learning, Training and Action

*Ethical and Civic Aspects.* 10. Member States should take appropriate steps to strengthen and develop in the processes of learning and training, attitudes and behaviour based on recognition of the equality and necessary interdependence of nations and peoples.

11. Member States should take steps to ensure that the principles of the Universal Declaration of Human Rights and of the International Convention on the Elimination of All Forms of Racial Discrimination become an integral part of the developing personality of each child, adolescent, young person or adult by applying these principles in the daily conduct of education at each level and in all its forms, thus enabling each individual to contribute personally to the regeneration and extension of education in the direction indicated.

12. Member States should urge educators, in collaboration with pupils, parents, the organizations concerned and the community, to use methods which appeal to the creative imagination of children and adolescents and to their social activities and thereby to prepare them to exercise their rights and freedoms while recognizing and respecting the rights of others and to perform their social duties.

13. Member States should promote, at every stage of ed-

ucation, an active civic training which will enable every person to gain a knowledge of the method of operation and the work of public institutions, whether local, national or international, to become acquainted with the procedures for solving fundamental problems; and to participate in the cultural life of the community and in public affairs. Wherever possible, this participation should increasingly link education and action to solve problems at the local, national and international levels.

14. Education should include critical analysis of the historical and contemporary factors of an economic and political nature underlying the contradictions and tensions between countries, together with study of ways of overcoming these contradictions, which are the real impediments to understanding, true international co-operation and the development of world peace.

15. Education should emphasize the true interests of peoples and their incompatibility with the interests of monopolistic groups holding economic and political power, which practise exploitation and foment war.

16. Student participation in the organization of studies and of the educational establishment they are attending should itself be considered a factor in civic education and an important element in international education.

*Cultural Aspects.* 17. Member States should promote, at various stages and in various types of education, study of different cultures, their reciprocal influences, their perspectives and ways of life, in order to encourage mutual appreciation of the differences between them. Such study should, among other things, give due importance to the teaching of foreign languages, civilizations and cultural heritage as a means of promoting international and inter-cultural understanding.

*Study of the Major Problems of Mankind.* 18. Education should be directed both towards the eradication of conditions which perpetuate and aggravate major problems affecting human survival and well-being—inequality, injustice, international relations based on the use of force—and towards measures of international co-operation likely to help solve them. Education which in this respect must necessarily be of an interdisciplinary nature should relate to such problems as:

    (a) equality of rights of peoples, and the right of peoples to self-determination;

    (b) the maintenance of peace; different types of war and their causes and effects; disarmament; the inadmissibility of using science and technology for warlike purposes and their use for the purposes of peace and progress; the nature and effect of economic, cultural and political relations between countries and the importance of international law for these relations, particularly for the maintenance of peace;

    (c) action to ensure the exercise and observance of human rights, including those of refugees; racialism and its eradication; the fight against discrimination in its various forms;

    (d) economic growth and social development and their relation to social justice; colonialism and decolonization; ways and means of assisting developing countries; the struggle against illiteracy; the campaign against disease and famine; the fight for a better quality of life and the highest attainable standard of health; population growth and related questions;

    (e) the use, management and conservation of natural resources, pollution of the environment;

    (f) preservation of the cultural heritage of mankind;

    (g) the role and methods of action of the United Nations system in efforts to solve such problems and possibilities for strengthening and furthering its action.

19. Steps should be taken to develop the study of those sciences and disciplines which are directly related to the exercise of the increasingly varied duties and responsibilities involved in international relations.

*Other Aspects.* 20. Member States should encourage educational authorities and educators to give education planned in accordance with this recommendation an interdisciplinary, problem- oriented content adapted to the complexity of the issues involved in the application of human rights and in international co-operation, and in itself illustrating the ideas of reciprocal influence, mutual support and solidarity. Such programmes should be based on adequate research, experimentation and the identification of specific educational objectives.

21. Member States should endeavour to ensure that international educational activity is granted special attention and resources when it is carried out in situations involving particularly delicate or explosive social problems in relations, for example, where there are obvious inequalities in opportunities for access to education.

## VI. Action in Various Sectors of Education

22. Increased efforts should be made to develop and infuse an international and inter-cultural dimension at all stages and in all forms of education.

23. Member States should take advantage of the experience of the Associated Schools which carry out, with Unesco's help, programmes of international education. Those concerned with Associated Schools in Member States should strengthen and renew their efforts to extend the programme to other educational institutions and work towards the general application of its results. In other Member States, similar action should be undertaken as soon as possible. The experience of other educational institutions which have carried out successful programmes of international education should also be studied and disseminated.

24. As pre-school education develops, Member States should encourage in it activities which correspond to the purposes of the recommendation because fundamental attitudes, such as, for example, attitudes on race, are often formed in the pre-school years. In this respect, the attitude of parents should be deemed to be an essential factor for the education of children, and the adult education referred to in paragraph 30 should pay special attention to the preparation of parents for their role in pre-school education. The first school should be designed and organized as a social environment having its own character and value, in which various situations, including games, will enable children to become aware of their rights, to assert themselves freely while accepting their responsibilities, and to improve and extend through direct experience their sense of belonging to larger and larger communities—the family, the school, then the local, national and world communities.

25. Member States should urge the authorities concerned, as well as teachers and students, to re-examine periodically how post-secondary and university education should be improved so that it may contribute more fully to the attainment of the objectives of this recommendation.

26. Higher education should comprise civic training and learning activities for all students that will sharpen their knowledge of the major problems which they should help to solve, provide them with possibilities for direct and contin-

uous action aimed at the solution of those problems, and improve their sense of international co-operation.

27. As post-secondary educational establishments, particularly universities, serve growing numbers of people, they should carry out programmes of international education as part of their broadened function in lifelong education and should in all teaching adopt a global approach. Using all means of communication available to them, they should provide opportunities, facilities for learning and activities adapted to people's real interests, problems and aspirations.

28. In order to develop the study and practice of international co-operation, post-secondary educational establishments should systematically take advantage of the forms of international action inherent in their role, such as visits from foreign professors and students and professional co-operation between professors and research teams in different countries. In particular, studies and experimental work should be carried out on the linguistic, social, emotional and cultural obstacles, tensions, attitudes and actions which affect both foreign students and host establishments.

29. Every stage of specialized vocational training should include training to enable students to understand their role and the role of their professions in developing their society, furthering international co-operation, maintaining and developing peace, and to assume their role actively as early as possible.

30. Whatever the aims and forms of out-of-school education, including adult education, they should be based on the following considerations:

(a) as far as possible a global approach should be applied in all out-of-school education programmes, which should comprise the appropriate moral, civic, cultural, scientific and technical elements of international education;

(b) all the parties concerned should combine efforts to adapt and use the mass media of communication, self-education, and inter-active learning, and such institutions as museums and public libraries to convey relevant knowledge to the individual, to foster in him or her favourable attitudes and a willingness to take positive action, and to spread knowledge and understanding of the educational campaigns and programmes planned in accordance with the objectives of this recommendation;

(c) the parties concerned, whether public or private, should endeavour to take advantage of favourable situations and opportunities, such as the social and cultural activities of youth centres and clubs, cultural centres, community centres or trade unions, youth gatherings and festivals, sporting events, contacts with foreign visitors, students or immigrants and exchanges of persons in general.

31. Steps should be taken to assist the establishment and development of such organizations as student and teacher associations for the United Nations, international relations clubs and Unesco Clubs, which should be associated with the preparation and implementation of co-ordinated programmes of international education.

32. Member States should endeavour to ensure that, at each stage of school and out-of-school education, activities directed towards the objectives of this recommendation be co-ordinated and form a coherent whole within the curricula for the different levels and types of education, learning and training. The principles of co-operation and association which are inherent in this recommendation should be applied in all educational activities.

## VII. Teacher Preparation

33. Member States should constantly improve the ways and means of preparing and certifying teachers and other educational personnel for their role in pursuing the objectives of this recommendation and should, to this end:

(a) provide teachers with motivations for their subsequent work; commitment to the ethics of human rights and to the aim of changing society, so that human rights are applied in practice; a grasp of the fundamental unity of mankind; ability to instill appreciation of the riches which the diversity of cultures can bestow on every individual, group or nation;

(b) provide basic interdisciplinary knowledge of world problems and the problems of international co-operation, through, among other means, work to solve these problems;

(c) prepare teachers themselves to take an active part in devising programmes of international education and educational equipment and materials, taking into account the aspirations of pupils and working in close collaboration with them;

(d) comprise experiments in the use of active methods of education and training in at least elementary techniques of evaluation, particularly those applicable to the social behaviour and attitudes of children, adolescents and adults;

(e) develop aptitudes and skills such as a desire and ability to make educational innovations and to continue his or her training; experience in teamwork and in interdisciplinary studies; knowledge of group dynamics; and the ability to create favourable opportunities and take advantage of them;

(f) include the study of experiments in international education, especially innovative experiments carried out in other countries, and provide those concerned, to the fullest possible extent, with opportunities for making direct contact with foreign teachers.

34. Member States should provide those concerned with direction, supervision or guidance—for instance, inspectors, educational advisers, principals of teacher-training colleges and organizers of educational activities for young people and adults—with training, information and advice enabling them to help teachers work towards the objectives of this recommendation, taking into account the aspirations of young people with regard to international problems and new educational methods that are likely to improve prospects for fulfilling these aspirations. For these purposes, seminars or refresher courses relating to international and inter-cultural education should be organized to bring together authorities and teachers; other seminars or courses might permit supervisory personnel and teachers to meet with other groups concerned such as parent, students, and teachers' associations. Since there must be a gradual but profound change in the role of education, the results of experiments for the remodelling of structures and hierarchical relations in educational establishments should be reflected in training, information and advice.

35. Member States should endeavour to ensure that any programme of further training for teachers in service or for personnel responsible for direction includes components of international education and opportunities to compare the results of their experiences in international education.

36. Member States should encourage and facilitate educational study and refresher courses abroad, particularly by awarding fellowships, and should encourage recognition of such courses as part of the regular process of initial training, appointment, refresher training and promotion of teachers.

37. Member States should organize or assist bilateral exchanges of teachers at all levels of education.

## VIII. Educational Equipment and Materials

38. Member States should increase their efforts to facilitate the renewal, production, dissemination and exchange of equipment and materials for international education, giving special consideration to the fact that in many countries pupils and students receive most of their knowledge about international affairs through the mass media outside the school. To meet the needs expressed by those concerned with international education, efforts should be concentrated on overcoming the lack of teaching aids and on improving their quality. Action should be on the following lines:

(a) appropriate and constructive use should be made of the entire range of equipment and aids available, from textbooks to television, and of the new educational technology;

(b) there should be a component of special mass media education in teaching to help the pupils to select and analyse the information conveyed by mass media;

(c) a global approach, comprising the introduction of international components, serving as a framework for presenting local and national aspects of different subjects and illustrating the scientific and cultural history of mankind, should be employed in textbooks and all other aids to learning, with due regard to the value of the visual arts and music as factors conducive to understanding between different cultures;

(d) written and audio-visual materials of an interdisciplinary nature illustrating the major problems confronting mankind and showing in each case the need for international co- operation and its practical form should be prepared in the language or languages of instruction of the country with the aid of information supplied by the United Nations, Unesco and other Specialized Agencies;

(e) documents and other materials illustrating the culture and the way of life of each country, the chief problems with which it is faced, and its participation in activities of world-wide concern should be prepared and communicated to other countries.

39. Member States should promote appropriate measures to ensure that educational aids, especially textbooks, are free from elements liable to give rise to misunderstanding, mistrust, racialist reactions, contempt or hatred with regard to other groups or peoples. Materials should provide a broad background of knowledge which will help learners to evaluate information and ideas disseminated through the mass media that seem to run counter to the aims of this recommendation.

40. According to its needs and possibilities, each Member State should establish or help to establish one or more documentation centres offering written and audio-visual material devised according to the objectives of this recommendation and adapted to the different forms and stages of education. These centres should be designed to foster the reform of international education, especially by developing and disseminating innovative ideas and materials, and should also organize and facilitate exchanges of information with other countries.

## IX. Research and Experimentation

41. Member States should stimulate and support research on the foundations, guiding principles, means of implementation and effects of international education and on innovations and experimental activities in this field, such as those taking place in the Associated Schools. This action calls for collaboration by universities, research bodies and centres, teacher-training institutions, adult education training centres and appropriate non-governmental organizations.

42. Member States should take appropriate steps to ensure that teachers and the various authorities concerned build international education on a sound psychological and sociological basis by applying the results of research carried out in each country on the formation and development of favourable or unfavourable attitudes and behaviour, on attitude change, on the interaction of personality development and education and on the positive or negative effects of educational activity. A substantial part of this research should be devoted to the aspirations of young people concerning international problems and relations.

## X. International Co-operation

43. Member States should consider international co-operation a responsibility in developing international education. In the implementation of this recommendation they should refrain from intervening in matters which are essentially within the domestic jurisdiction of any State in accordance with the United Nations Charter. By their own actions, they should demonstrate that implementing this recommendation is itself an exercise in international understanding and co-operation. They should, for example, organize, or help the appropriate authorities and non-governmental organizations to organize, an increasing inumber of international meetings and study sessions on international education; strengthen their programmes for the reception of foreign students, research workers, teachers and educators belonging to workers' associations and adult education associations; promote reciprocal visits by schoolchildren, and student and teacher exchanges; extend and intensify exchanges of information on cultures and ways of life; arrange for the translation or adaptation and dissemination of information and suggestions coming from other countries.

44. Member States should encourage the co-operation between their Associated Schools and those of other countries with the help of Unesco in order to promote mutual benefits by expanding their experiences in a wider international perspective.

45. Member States should encourage wider exchanges of textbooks, especially history and geography textbooks, and should, where appropriate, take measures, by concluding, if possible, bilateral and multilateral agreements, for the reciprocal study and revision of textbooks and other educational materials in order to ensure that they are accurate, balanced, up to date and unprejudiced and will enhance mutual knowledge and understanding between different peoples.

The foregoing is the authentic text of the Recommendation duly adopted by the General Conference of the United Nations Educational, Scientific and Cultural Organization during its eighteenth session, which was held in Paris and declared closed the twenty-third day of November 1974.

In faith whereof we have appended our signatures this twenty-fifth day of November 1974.

**EGYPT.** The Arab Republic of Egypt is a country in northern Africa fronting on the Mediterranean (north) and the Red Sea (east). It has borders with· Israel, Libya, and Sudan. It achieved independence from Great Britain in 1922 and became a member of the United Nations in 1945. Its population is estimated to be 57,050,000. A single ethnic group, speaking the same language (Arabic) and professing the same religion (Islam) constitutes the vast majority of the population. However, there are other linguistic and religious groups, including the Copts, who form approximately 7% of the population, the Nubians, and the Bedouins. Languages commonly used include Arabic (official) and English; the Berbers and Nubians use their own language as well as Arabic. Islam is the State religion and the faith of the overwhelming majority of the population. Religious minorities include Christian Copts, a small number of Catholics and Protestants, and a Jewish community whose numbers dwindled after World War II.

The government (1994) took the form of a republic, defined in the 1971 constitution as "an Arab Republic with a democratic, socialist system." Executive authority is exercised by the president as head of State and the premier as head of government. Legislative matters are dealt with by the 448-member Parliament, elected by popular vote with universal suffrage. The president appoints his own cabinet and may appoint one or more vice presidents. Political parties include the National Democratic Party and the *New Wafd*.

There have been four Arab–Israeli wars since 1956. In that year, Egyptian President Gamal Abdel Nasser nationalized the Suez Canal, and Israel invaded the Gaza Strip and the Sinai Peninsula. After the canal had been protected by a United Nations emergency force, all troops were evacuated in 1957. In 1967, Israel invaded the Sinai Peninsula, the east bank of the Jordan River, and the area around the Gulf of Aqaba; and stopped its advance only after the United Nations had arranged a ceasefire and established a peacekeeping force. In 1969, Nasser repudiated the ceasefire and reopened the war but was forced in 1970 to accept an American peace plan under which Egypt recognized Israel's right to secure boundaries and Israel withdrew from part of the occupied Sinai territories.

Nasser died in 1970; and, under his successor, **ANWAR SADAT,** Egypt in 1973 recaptured portions of the Sinai by an attack launched on the eve of Yom Kippur and coordinated with an attack by Syria on the Israeli-held Golan Heights. The 30 years of warfare ended with a truce sponsored by the United Nations in 1974, followed by a peace plan negotiated by U.S. Secretary of State **HENRY KISSINGER.** The Suez Canal was cleared and opened in 1975, and a new UN peacekeeping force was established in the Sinai. Anwar el-Sadat and **MENACHEM BEGIN,** after a series of meetings at Camp David sponsored by American President Jimmy Carter, signed a peace treaty on 26 March 1979 which settled many questions but left unresolved the

problem of Arab autonomy in the Gaza Strip and the West Bank area. Assassinated in 1981, Sadat was succeeded by his vice president, former Air Force Chief of Staff Hosni Mubarak. After completing his first six-year term of office successfully, Mubarak was reelected twice.

*PROBLEMS OF RELIGIOUS FUNDAMENTALISM.* Aside from persistent human rights problems resulting from the poverty of its people and the inability of its economic structure to provide adequate standards of living and health care, Egypt has been torn by disputes between Islamic factions, with Muslim fundamentalists organizing politically to force a return to application of the ancient *Sharia* legal code, while the government responds by increasing its strict control of all religious activities. In 1977, the Political Parties Regulatory Act No. 40 prohibited the exploitation of religion for the establishment of political parties in an effort to prevent the nation from being split into conflicting religious groups organized on political lines. In 1981, Moslem fundamentalists and Christians engaged in streetfighting, which led to a nationwide security crackdown in September of that year; in early October, President Sadat was assassinated in retaliation, resulting in imposition of a state of emergency. The state of emergency has remained in effect since 1981; and, in 1994, was extended until May 31, 1997, by Prime Minister 'Atif Sidqi, who cited as reason for the extension "the regrettable terrorist acts in the country, including attacks on tourists, assassination of officials, bombing of banks, and the treacherous killing of innocent civilians, police officers, and police commanders." In particular, the Islamic Group—a clandestine militant organization that advocates the creation of an Islamic state in Egypt—targeted civilians and tourists for murder in 1994.

*RIGHTS OF THE CHILD.* The initial report of Egypt submitted under article 44 of the Convention on the Rights of the Child (see **CHILDREN'S RIGHTS**) (CRC/C/3 Add. 6; CRC/C/15/Add. 1) was considered by the UN Committee on the Rights of the Child at its 66th to 68th meetings, held on 25 and 26 January 1993. On 28 January 1993, the Committee adopted its concluding observations on the report as follows:

*Positive aspects.* The Committee takes note of efforts made by the Government of Egypt to secure implementation of the Convention's provisions throughout the country. The Committee welcomes the establishment, in January 1989, of the National Council for Childhood and Motherhood. It regards as important features the formulation of a general policy and strategy for the development of Egyptian childhood and the inclusion of the childhood and motherhood components in the five-year State plan 1992/93–1997/98. The Committee also notes with satisfaction the activities of the

Supreme Constitutional Court in so far as the implementation of the Convention is concerned. Furthermore, the Committee notes the intention of the National Council to systematize the collection of statistical and other data as a basis for further efforts in the implementation of the Convention. Indications about research into problems relating to children in especially difficult circumstances are also welcomed. Taken together, these notable developments indicate that the Government of Egypt takes very seriously its obligations under the Convention and is moving toward establishing a firm legal basis for the realization of the rights contained therein.

*Factors and difficulties impeding the implementation of the Convention.* The Committee notes that structural adjustment policies have created difficulties in the full application of the rights guaranteed by the Convention and have had a specific impact on the situation of children, in particular children in low-income categories and in rural areas. The Committee, however, takes this opportunity to recall that, under article 4 of the Convention, States parties are called upon to implement the Convention to the maximum extent of their available resources.

*Principal subjects of concern.* The Committee notes that, although Egyptian laws and regulations guarantee equality between the sexes, there is in reality still a pattern of disparity between boys and girls, in particular as far as access to education is concerned.

Of special concern to the Committee has also been the situation of children in rural areas and of disabled children. In regard to the latter, the Committee expresses concern over the very low number of disabled children who are enrolled in schools, which might reflect an insufficient sensitiveness of the society to the specific needs and situation of those children.

The Committee is concerned about the situation of children in conflict with the law and, in particular, of children serving custodial sentences in social care institutions. Concern is expressed, in general, as to the compatibility with articles 37 and 40 of the Convention of the juvenile justice institutions and the administration of justice system in so far as it relates to juvenile justice.

Specific concern is also expressed regarding the very large number of children between 6 and 14 years of age who are enrolled in the labour force and therefore lack, wholly or partly, the possibility to go to school.

Although children may to a certain extent contribute to seasonal activities, care should always be taken that primary education is available to them and that they are not working in hazardous conditions.

The quality of education in schools also gives cause for concern and may be an explanation for high drop-out rates; the problem relates to pedagogical methods, curricula and the lack of adequate educational material.

The Committee expresses its concern as to the need for measures to improve the health of children, in particular those in the school-age group.

*Suggestions and recommendations.* The Committee emphasizes that the principle of non-discrimination, as provided for under article 2 of the Convention, must be vigorously applied. A more active approach should be taken to eliminating discrimination against certain groups of children, in particular girl children and children in rural areas. With regard to the gap in literacy and school enrolment mentioned in the report, obstacles facing girls should be adequately addressed so that they can enjoy their right to go to school;

further measures might be taken to increase the awareness of parents in this regard.

Steps should be undertaken to afford adequate protection to disabled children, including the possibility, in particular through education, to integrate them into society and to raise the awareness of their families about their specific needs. Efforts for the early detection of the incidence of handicap are important.

Adequate protection should also be afforded to children in conflict with the law. The Committee recommends that the appropriate amendments be made to the Juveniles Act No. 31 of 1974 to adequately reflect the provisions of the Convention as well as other international standards in this field, such as the "Beijing Rules", the "Riyhad Guidelines", and the Rules for the Protection of Juveniles Deprived of their Liberty. In that regard it is suggested that general principles underlying the Convention, such as consideration of the best interest and dignity of the child and its role into society, be taken into account. Deprivation of liberty should always be envisaged as the very last resort, and particular attention should be paid to rehabilitation measures, psychological recovery and social reintegration. Furthermore, deprivation of liberty in social care institutions should be regularly monitored by a judge or an independent body.

The recommendations of the studies on child labour undertaken with the assistance of the International Labour Organisation on the problem of child employment should be implemented and Egyptian legislation on minimum age should be revised. In that regard, consideration should be given to the possibility of acceding to ILO Convention No. 138 and other Conventions on minimum age of employment relating to the protection of children and young persons at work. . . .

**CIVIL AND POLITICAL RIGHTS.** Second periodic report of Egypt submitted under article 40 of the International Covenant on Civil and Political Rights (CCPR/C/51/Add. 71) was considered by the Human Rights Committee at its 1244th to 1247th meetings, held on 19 and 20 July 1993. On 29 July 1993, the Committee adopted its comments on the report as follows:

*Positive aspects.* The Committee welcomes the renewed positive dialogue with the State party, which has helped the Committee to evaluate the situation in Egypt, including compatibility of domestic legislation with the provisions of the Covenant as well as factors and difficulties affecting the implementation of the Covenant in Egypt. The Committee acknowledges the State Party's firm commitment to the principles of the rule of law and democracy.

*Factors and difficulties impeding the application of the Covenant.* The Committee notes that the state of emergency in force in Egypt without interruption since 1981 constitutes one of the main difficulties impeding the full implementation of the Covenant by the State party. In June 1991, the state of emergency was extended until June 1994. In this connection, the Committee regrets that Egypt has not informed the other States parties to the Covenant, through the Secretary-General, of the provisions from which it has derogated and of the reasons by which it was actuated, as specifically required by article 4, paragraph 3, of the Covenant. The delegation, however, assured the Committee that this had happened quite inadvertently.

*Principal subjects of concern.* The Committee expresses concern at the many severe measures taken by the Egyptian Government to combat terrorism in the country. It is aware that the increasing number of terrorist acts especially in the last 12 months have created a dramatic situation in the country. However, recognizing that the Government has a duty to combat terrorism, the Committee considers that the measures taken to do so should not prejudice the enjoyment of the fundamental rights enshrined in the Covenant, in particular, its articles 6, 7 and 9. The Committee is particularly disturbed by the adoption in 1992 of law No. 97 on terrorism, which contains provisions contrary to articles 6 and 15 of the Covenant. The definition of terrorism contained in that law is so broad that it encompasses a wide range of acts of differing gravity. The Committee is of the opinion that the definition in question should be reviewed by the Egyptian authorities and stated much more precisely especially in view of the fact that it enlarges the number of offences which are punishable with the death penalty. The Committee underscores that according to article 6, paragraph 2 of the Covenant, only the most serious crimes may lead to the death penalty.

The Committee also expresses concern at the long duration of the state of emergency in Egypt. Moreover, under the Emergency Act, the President of the Republic is entitled to refer cases to the State security courts, to ratify judgments and to pardon. The President's role as both part of the executive and part of the judiciary system is noted with concern by the Committee, notwithstanding that in the matter of appeal it was explained that it would act only to reduce sentences. On the other hand, military courts should not have the faculty to try cases which do not refer to offences committed by members of the armed forces in the course of their duties.

In addition, concern is expressed by the Committee about the duration and conditions of police custody and administrative detention in Egypt which are likely to expose accused persons to torture and ill-treatment by the police and security forces, as demonstrated by numerous allegations reported by reliable non-governmental sources of information. In this connection, the Committee regrets that Egypt did not provide it with adequate information on investigations made and penalties applied to perpetrators of torture and on compensation and medical rehabilitation of victims of torture, though some additional information was given by the representative of the State party in his final remarks.

The Committee also expresses concern about the multitude of special courts in Egypt. From the point of view of legal consistency in the judicial procedure and procedural guarantees it is important that special courts exist as an exceptional measure, if at all.

Furthermore, the Committee is worried about restrictive legal provisions existing in Egypt with regard to freedom of thought, conscience, religion, association. Restrictions not in conformity with article 18 of regarding various religious communities or sects, such as Baha'is, are a matter of particular concern. Equally, [there is] general concern at the denial by the Egyptian authorities of the country of religious or other minorities as well as the certain laws of provisions concerning penalties of imprisonment with compulsory labour for political offences. There are, in addition, many areas where the law discriminates against women and restricts them in the equal enjoyment of rights and freedoms.

*Suggestions and recommendations.* The Committee recommends that the State party should examine carefully the comments and the observations it has made during the consideration of Egypt's second periodic report in order to consider and adopt legal and practical measures to ensure effective implementation of all the provisions of the Covenant. In addition, many questions and requests for information which have remained unanswered during the debate should find exhaustive replies in the next periodic report. The Committee also recommends that the Egyptian authorities should establish a closer and constructive dialogue with non-governmental organizations active in the field of human rights, and elaborate training programmes on human rights specifically addressed to public officials. The Committee recommends that the State party bring its legislation in conformity with the provisions of article 6 of the Covenant and, in particular, limit the number of crimes punishable by the death penalty. The Committee also recommends that the State party pay particular attention to the protection of the rights of those who are arrested and detained.

***BIBLIOGRAPHY.*** Amnesty International (AI). *Egypt: Human Rights Defenders under Threat.* London: 1994. NGO report, in English.

An-Na'im, Abdullahi Ahmed. "Religious Freedom in Egypt: Under the Shadow of the Islamic 'Dhiman' System," in *Religious Liberty and Human Rights in Nations and in Religion,* ed. Leonard Swindler, pp. 43–59. 1986. Conference paper in edited collection, in English.

Arab Organization for Human Rights. *Report: Human Rights in the Arab World.* Cairo: 1987. NGO report, in Arabic.

Dunn, Michael C. "Fundamentalism in Egypt," *Middle East Policy* 2, no. 3 (1993): 68–77. Scholarly article, in English.

Egyptian Organization for Human Rights (EOHR). *Citizens without Protection: Second Report by the Egyptian Organization for Human Rights on Torture and Ill-Treatment of Citizens in Police Stations.* Cairo, Egypt: 1994. NGO factfinding report, in English.

————. *The Condition of Human Rights in Egypt, 1993.* Cairo, Egypt: 1994. NGO annual report, in English.

————. *Freedom of Opinion and Expression in Egypt.* Giza, Egypt: 1990. NGO factfinding report, in English.

Human Rights Watch. "Egypt," in *Human Rights Watch World Report 1995,* pp. 261–269. New York: 1995. NGO report, in English.

————. *Egypt: Hostage-taking and Intimidation by Security Forces.* New York: 1995. NGO report, in English.

————. *Prison Conditions in Egypt.* New York: 1993. NGO report, in English.

International League for Human Rights. *Human Rights in the Arab Republic of Egypt.* New York: 1985. NGO report, in English.

Karas, Shawky F. *The Copts since the Arab Invasion: Strangers in Their Land.* Jersey City, NJ, USA: American, Canadian and Australian Coptic Association, 1986. NGO report, in English.

# ELECTIONS.

In recent years, the United Nations has provided electoral assistance in many countries and territories. The 1994 UN publication entitled "Human Rights and Elections" presents the following overview of UN involvement in national elections (HR/P/PT/2, chap. I):

The United Nations, through its various subsidiary bodies, has been involved in the conduct of national elections, plebiscites and referenda since its inception. United Nations activity in the field of elections began with the official observation of the Korean elections of 1948. Since then, such activity has continued unabated as a fundamental component of the Organization's decolonization, conflict-resolution and human rights programmes.

The beneficiaries of these efforts have included the peoples of some 30 Trust and Non-Self-Governing Territories, from Togoland in 1956 to the Palau Trust Territory of the Pacific Islands in 1990. They have also included independent States involved in international conflicts, and others seeking to resolve internal strife democratically and to broaden human rights. Thus various levels of United Nations involvement have contributed to the free and fair conduct of popular consultations in Namibia (1989), Nicaragua (1990), Haiti (1990), Cambodia (1991–1993), Angola (1992), Romania (1990–1992), Albania (1991), Lesotho (1991–1992), Malawi (1993), and a host of other countries and territories.

With the end of the cold war and the emergence of a global trend towards democratization, renewed interest in standards for free and fair elections has become evident. Against this background, the international community has increased its efforts to enhance the effectiveness of the principle of free and fair elections and to provide assistance to countries seeking to conduct them,

In order to facilitate the United Nations' increasing involvement in elections, the Secretary-General, pursuant to General Assembly resolution 46/137, designated the Under-Secretary-General, Department of Political Affairs, to be the focal point for electoral assistance. The Electoral Assistance Unit (EAU) was established in order to assist the focal point with the coordination of all United Nations electoral activities. EAU plays a central role in the processing of requests for assistance, and all requests for electoral assistance are channelled through it. When such a request is received, EAU, in conjunction with the United Nations Development Programme (UNDP), the United Nations Centre for Human Rights and other relevant United Nations actors, will usually conduct a needs-assessment mission to determine the type of assistance required and provide support for the initial stages of project development. As soon as a project or mission becomes operational, implementation becomes the full responsibility of the relevant implementing organizations, although EAU support and coordination within the system continues throughout the process.

United Nations involvement in elections begins, in most cases, with a formal request by a Government for assistance. The request will be followed by the fielding of a needs-assessment mission to the country concerned. That mission will carefully examine, in consultation with the Government, political parties, nongovernmental organizations and others, all relevant infrastructural, legal, political, material, financial and human rights needs associated with the conduct of elections. The report emanating from the mission will form the basis for United Nations involvement.

The varying levels of United Nations involvement in elections can be divided into several categories. The first is United Nations organization and conduct of elections. In this situation, the United Nations organizes virtually every aspect of the electoral process. The second category is United Nations supervision of elections. This includes the certification of a Special Representative of the Secretary-General confirming the validity of certain crucial aspects of the electoral process. The third type of United Nations involvement is a verification mission in which the electoral process is organized and administered by a national organ and the United Nations is asked to give its opinion as to the freedom and fairness of the electoral process.

These three types of United Nations involvement are usually undertaken in the context of large-scale peace-keeping missions. All are undertaken only in exceptional circumstances which meet certain strict criteria for United Nations involvement. In particular, all the following five elements must be present:

(a) A formal request has been received from the State concerned;

(b) Broad public support exists for United Nations involvement;

(c) Sufficient advance time remains for comprehensive United Nations involvement;

(d) There exists a clear international dimension to the situation;

(e) A favourable decision has been rendered by an authoritative body of the United Nations (i.e. the General Assembly or the Security Council).

In cases where some of these criteria have not been fulfilled, especially in cases where the missing criterion is the absence of sufficient lead time to undertake a comprehensive mission, the United Nations may decide to respond in one of two ways. The first is to organize a mission to follow the electoral process closely and report to the Secretary-General on its results. In some cases, the Centre for Human Rights or EAU may provide specialized staff to assist in the mission. The second response is to coordinate and support international observers affiliated with other organizations. Neither of these responses can be categorized as a comprehensive supervisory mission and they do not include any express pronouncement on the freedom and fairness of the electoral process. They do, however, provide a certain level of United Nations presence that can strengthen public confidence in the electoral process and enhance the quality of the electoral exercise.

Another type of United Nations involvement is technical assistance with the material, infrastructural, legal and human rights aspects of elections. The provision of technical assistance clearly falls within the existing mandates of UNDP, the Centre for Human Rights and the United Nations Department for Development Support and Management Services. As a result, no new mandate is required for cases involving exclusively technical assistance. Advisory services and technical assistance in the legal, technical and human rights aspects of democratic elections do not include any United Nations involvement in the conduct of elections, nor do they have an observation component. As such, they can often be granted swiftly at a Government's request, without the need for consideration by a political decision-making body of the United Nations.

Thus UNDP, the Centre for Human Rights and the United Nations Department for Development Support and Management Services provide advice and assistance on a wide variety of electoral matters, including advice on crucial issues of human rights, organization of registration processes, identification of citizens through more adequate documentation, computerization of electoral rolls, strengthening of the operation of electoral administration, establishment of institutions for handling adjudications and grievances, electronic electoral data processing, vote-counting technologies, legal and logistic assistance, civic and voter education, radio communications and public information. Finally, if needed, large-scale technical cooperation programmes can be implemented for these purposes.

United Nations human rights standards relating to elections are broad in nature and thus may be achieved through a wide variety of political systems. United Nations electoral assistance does not seek to impose any given political model. Rather, it is based upon a realization that there is no single political system or electoral methodology which is appropriate for all peoples and States. While comparative examples provide useful guidance for the construction of democratic institutions that both respond to domestic concerns and conform to international human rights norms, the best formulation for each jurisdiction will ultimately be that shaped by the particular needs, aspirations and historical realities of the people involved, taken within the framework of international standards.

Finally, United Nations activity in these areas is conducted in conformity with the basic principles of the sovereign equality of States and respect for their territorial integrity and political independence, as enunciated in the Charter of the United Nations. Accordingly, assistance activities are carried out only where requested by the national authorities and supported by the people of the country concerned.

The UN **GENERAL ASSEMBLY** commended (resolution 48/131 of 20 December 1993) the electoral assistance which had been provided to Member States at their request, and proposed that such assistance should continue on a case-by-case basis in accordance with guidelines suggested by the Secretary-General. It recommended that the United Nations, in order to ensure the continuation and consolidation of the democratization process in Member States requesting assistance, provide such assistance both before and after elections have taken place, including needs-assessment missions aimed at recommending programs which might contribute to the consolidation of the democratization process.

***SEE ALSO*** *Political Rights.*

**BIBLIOGRAPHY.** Amin, Kaushika, and Robin Richardson. *Politics for All: Equality, Culture and the General Election 1992.* London: Runnymede Trust, 1992. NGO report, in English; bibliography, pp. 66–67.

Carter Center of Emory University. *Observing Nicaragua's Elections, 1989–1990: Report of the Council of Freely Elected Heads of Government.* Atlanta, GA, USA: 1990. Election observer mission report, in English; bibliography, pp. 119–121.

Commission on Security and Cooperation in Europe. (1) *Report on the Supreme Soviet Elections in Ukraine.* (2) *Report on the Congress of Peoples Deputies Elections in the Russian Republic.* (3) *Report on the April and May 1990 Elections in the Yugoslav Republics of Slovenia and Croatia.* (4) *Report on the Parliamentary Elections in the Republic of Hungary.* (5) *Elections in Central and Eastern Europe: A Compendium of Reports on the Elections held from March to June 1990.* (6) *Elections in the Baltic States and Soviet Republics: A Compendium of Reports on Parliamentary Elections held in 1990.* Washington, D.C.: U.S. Government Printing Office, 1990. Government reports, in English.

————. *Parliamentary and Presidential Elections in an Independent Croatia.* Washington, D.C.: U.S. Government Printing Office, 1992. Government report, in English.

Coordinating Council for Human Rights in Bangladesh.

(1) *Upazila Election 1990 Observation.* (2) *Election Observation Report: Election to 5th Parliament, 1991.* Dhaka, Bangladesh: (1) 1990; (2) 1991. NGO election observer reports, in English.

Election Watch. *Report on the Eighth Malaysian General Elections Held on 20th and 21st October 1990.* Kuala Lumpur, Malaysia: Aliran Kesedaran Negara, 1990. NGO election observer mission report, in English.

Fédération Internationale des Droits de l'Homme and International Federation of Human Rights. *Rapport de Mission: Pakistan. Élections à l'Assemblée nationale et aux assemblées des quatre provinces du Pakistan les 24 et 27 octobre 1990* (Mission Report: Pakistan. Elections to the National Assembly and Four Provincial Assemblies, October 24–27, 1990). Paris: 1990. NGO election observer mission report, in French.

Fédération Internationale des Droits de l'Homme, International Federation of Human Rights, and Comité de solidarité Québec-Chili. *Rapport de mission: l'élection du 14 décembre 1989 au Chili. Rapport final de la délégation pan-canadienne d'observation* (Mission Report: Elections of December 14, 1989 in Chile. Final Report of a Canadian Delegation of Election Observers). Paris: 1990. NGO election observer mission report, in French.

Fox, Gregory H. "The Right to Political Participation in International Law," *Yale Journal of International Law* 17, no. 2 (Summer 1992): 539–608. Scholarly article, in English.

Instituto Historico Centroamericano. "International Election Observers: Nicaragua under a Microscope," *Envio* 9, no. 103 (1990): 20–31. NGO article, in English.

Instituto Interamericano de Derechos Humanos and Centro de Asesoría y Promoción Electoral. (1) *Elecciones Generales—Nicaragua, 25 de Febrero de 1990: Informe de la Misión de Observación* (General Elections in Nicaragua—February 25, 1990: Report of the Observer Mission). (2) *Perú: Elecciones Políticas 8 de Abril y 10 de Junio 1990: Informe de la Misión de Observación* (Peru: Political Elections, April 8 and June 10, 1990: Report of the Observer Mission). San José, Costa Rica: 1990. NGO observer mission reports, in Spanish.

————. *Proceso Electoral y Regimenes Políticos* (Electoral Process and Political Regimes). San José, Costa Rica: 1989. Conference proceedings, in Spanish.

————. *Transición Democrática en América Latina: Reflexiones Sobre el Debate Actual* (Democratic Transition in Latin America: Some Reflections on the Current Debate). San José, Costa Rica: 1990. Scholarly collective works, in Spanish.

Garber, Larry. *Guidelines for International Election Observing.* Washington, D.C.: International Human Rights Law Group, 1984. NGO guidelines, in English.

Garber, Larry, and Eric Bjornlund, eds. *The New Democratic Frontier: A Country-by-Country Report on Elections in Central and Eastern Europe.* Washington, D.C.: National Democratic Institute for International Affairs, 1992. Scholarly collection of articles, in English.

National Democratic Institute for International Affairs. *The October 1990 Elections in Pakistan.* Washington, D.C.: 1991. NGO report, in English.

Shelton, Dinah. "Representative Democracy and Human Rights in the Western Hemisphere," *Human Rights Law Journal* 12, no. 10 (1991): 353–359. Scholarly article, in English.

UN Center for Human Rights. *Human Rights and Elections: A Handbook on the Legal, Technical and Human Rights Aspects of Elections.* Professional Training Series No. 2 (UN Publication HF/P/PT/2).

Washington Office on Latin America. *U.S. Electoral Assistance and Democratic Development.* Washington, D.C.: 1990. NGO report, in English.

# E

**EL SALVADOR.** The Republic of El Salvador is a country in Central America, on the Pacific Ocean. It has borders with Guatemala and Honduras. It achieved independence from Spain in 1838 and became a member of the United Nations in 1945. Its population is estimated to be 5,635,000. Spanish is the official language; Nahua is frequently used. The predominant religion is Christianity (Roman Catholic). Literacy is estimated at 65%.

The government (1994) took the form of a republic. Under the 1983 constitution, executive authority is exercised by the president, elected for a five-year, nonrenewable term. Legislative matters are dealt with by the 60-member National Assembly, elected by popular vote under a proportional representation scheme. There is a Supreme Court, members of which are elected by the Assembly, and a series of lower courts. For detailed information, see UN Doc. HRI/CORE/1/Add. 14.

The UN General Assembly, the UN Commission on Human Rights, the Inter-American Commission on Human Rights, and other international governmental and non-governmental bodies have been deeply concerned about the human rights situation in El Salvador since 1980, when the UN General Assembly requested the Commission to examine that question as soon as possible. A military coup had overthrown the government of Pres. Carolos Humberto Romero in 1979, but the junta couldn't contain a rebellion by the Farabundo Martin National Liberation Front (FMLN). Death squads—organized by right-wing extremists to eliminate suspected leftists and by rebel forces to kill government sympathizers—were blamed for thousands of deaths in the 1980s. Early in 1981, the Commission appointed a special representative to investigate the reports about murders, abductions, disappearances, terrorist acts, and other grave violations of human rights, based on information from all available sources, and to report thereon.

The special representative, Mr. José Antonio Pastor Ridruejo, monitored the situation closely and reported both to the General Assembly and to the Commission for a number of years. His first reports indicated that a state of siege was in effect in El Salvador and that all constitutional safeguards of freedom of movement, freedom of speech, and freedom of correspondence had been suspended.

Later reports indicated that, although serious violations of human rights continued to occur, primarily as a result of the ongoing state of war which persisted in El Salvador, the government had been increasingly effective in its efforts to suppress them.

The 12-year long civil war, responsible for an estimated 75,000 deaths, ended on 16 January 1992, when the government and FMLN signed a peace agreement.

The treaty provided for military and political reforms, in particular, the creation of a UN-sponsored "Truth Commission" and the Ad Hoc Commission to Investigate Human Rights Abuses. However, in May 1993, the National Assembly passed a sweeping amnesty for those who had committed atrocities during the civil war.

In March 1994, former FMLN rebels participated as a legal political party in the presidential, legislative, and municipal elections; this group became the second largest political force in the Legislative Assembly but lost the presidency to Armando Calderón by a 2-to-1 margin. The elections were monitored by the UN Observer Mission to El Salvador (ONUSAL), which declared them "acceptable."

The present government has responded well to correcting the human rights abuses that were rampant on both sides during the civil war. Nevertheless, serious concerns remain, particularly the existence of death squads. Addressing this problem in 1994 was the Joint Group for the Investigation of Illegal Armed Groups for Political Motivation in El Salvador (*Grupo Conjunto*), a committee established in December 1993 in response to the UN-sponsored Truth Commission and the upsurge in death-squad assassinations.

In 1992, the UN Commission on Human Rights requested the Secretary-General (resolution 1992/62) to appoint an independent expert to discharge a new mandate, which consisted initially in providing assistance in human rights matters to the Government of El Salvador, in considering the human rights situation in that country and the effects of the Peace Agreements on the effective enjoyment of human rights. Pedro Nikken (Venezuela) was appointed as the Independent Expert.

In the report which he submitted to the Commission on 3 February 1994, Nikken summarized his conclusions as follows (UN Doc. E/CN.4/1994/11. paras. 134–150):

As the Independent Expert stated in his preceding report, the Peace Agreements are the result of a massive effort by the parties to reach an understanding, an effort that also expressed a profound national aspiration for peace and justice. The form and content of the Agreements are geared not only to ending the armed conflict by political means, but also to the national enterprise of building a new and more democratic society imbued with the spirit of solidarity, in which untrammelled respect for human rights is a fundamental means of State action. The task was not simply to end a war, but to eliminate its causes. The nation is thus offered an extraordinary opportunity for progress. In order to take full advantage of this opportunity, it is imperative that the will which led the parties to reach an understanding and Salvadorian society to encourage them in that objective should be sustained throughout the process of implementation of the Agreements.

Unfortunately, the pace of implementation of the Agreements slowed in 1993. All the important steps took place very slowly and the process seems to be losing its initial momentum as the end of President Cristiani's term of office approaches. This is a development that should put all sectors of Salvadorian society on alert. This process is not one that can be brought to a standstill. The choice is between either moving forwards or moving backwards. Looking back at the horrors of the past must be an incentive for not stopping. It is essential to move forward with renewed vigour.

*Developments in the Human Rights Situation in the Country.* In analysing what happened in 1993, particularly during the second half of the year, it is more obvious that the ending of the conflict would not be enough to establish a climate in which human rights are fully observed and safeguarded, especially when the resources available to civilian society with which to combat violations of these rights are still limited.

There are positive signs that continue to be maintained, such as the eradication of enforced or involuntary disappearances. However, many of the signs of progress which were described in last year's report by the Independent Expert have weakened or been reversed. The number of attempts on human life originating in the practice of extrajudicial or arbitrary executions has increased considerably and the death squads are responsible for intimidating threats for political purposes. Worse still in view of the characteristics of the victims, it is possible to have well-founded suspicions of selective murders committed by criminal organizations. Although torture is not a systematic practice, a larger number of victims was recorded in 1993 and it is not known whether the persons responsible have been punished. Arbitrary detentions continued to be common in 1993, despite the signs of progress which were observed in 1992 and which could not be sustained.

The Joint Group for the Investigation of Illegal Armed Groups, which is coordinated by the Director of the ONUSAL Human Rights Division and has President Cristiani's support, was set up to shed light on the attacks attributed to these groups.

As has been stressed in this report, the structural deficiencies in the judicial system are both a source of violation of the right to due process and an obstacle to the proper safeguarding of human rights. The public cult of violence has also not been overcome and anonymous publications threatening persons and institutions have continued. The armed conflict continues to affect economic, social and cultural rights and the Agreements reached on them in the peace process are only just beginning to have an impact. The noticeable stagnation of the implementation of the Agreements with regard to land is a source of frustration and tension in various sectors of society. The achievement of substantial progress in this area in the shortest possible time is a prerequisite for justice and social stability.

The Independent Expert regrets concluding this report on a less optimistic note than he had hoped and would have liked. In order not to use his own words, he will borrow those which describe the current situation of human rights in the ninth report of the Director of the ONUSAL Human Rights Division: a serious deterioration.

*Implementation of the Peace Agreements.* The Office of the National Counsel for the Defence of Human Rights is called upon to play a central role in the promotion and defence of those rights in the future. Priority must be given to supporting and strengthening it at the levels of domestic action and of international cooperation. It is essential for it to improve its relations and work in close contact with non-governmental organizations.

The National Civil Police is another of the pillars of the Agreements which bolsters the hope that progress will be made in respect for and the safeguarding of human rights. It is an institution conceived in terms of a truly democratic standard: an exclusively civilian body, separate from the armed forces, whose first function is to protect and safeguard the free exercise of the rights and freedoms of individuals. The National Civil Police must not stray from that notion of a democratic, modern police force, integrated into civilian society, rather than engaged in a confrontation with that society.

The organization of the new body reveals some incompatibilities with the contents of the Peace Agreements. In addition to delays in the implementation timetable, there have been disturbing signs of military influence in the police sector. The action by the armed forces in the area of public security took place in 1993 without regard for the requirements of form and of substance provided for in the Constitution. There have been no signs of the actual disbanding of the former National Police, in accordance with the provisions of the Peace Agreements.

To date, the reforms have not been sufficient to overcome the verticality which is a structural defect of the Salvadorian judicial system. Appointment and dismissal of judges, authorization to practise as a lawyer and disqualification therefrom are within the competence of the Supreme Court of Justice. The vertical structure of the administration of justice adversely affects the intellectual freedom of the judge and the independence of lawyers.

The National Council of the Judiciary Act was not amended, despite the recommendations of the Independent Expert and those formulated later by the Commission on the Truth. The Act contains contradictions in that it defines the Council as an independent body, as provided for in the Peace Agreements, but at the same time makes its members liable to dismissal by the Supreme Court of Justice for reasons which include "just cause", thus robbing the judiciary's proclaimed independence of genuine substance.

The discovery of clandestine FMLN arsenals was a serious development that put the peace process to the test. The Independent Expert is confident that the impact of that development within and outside El Salvador and consideration of the effects of such a serious breach will have prompted the FMLN to locate and genuinely destroy all of its weapons.

*Implementation of the Recommendations [of the Truth Commission].* Most of the recommendations contained in this report will be the same as those in the preceding report because, unfortunately, in some cases, the process of implementing them has not been completed and, in others, the recommendations have not been accepted at all.

The military officers on whom the implementation of the recommendations of the Ad Hoc Commission depended have now retired or at least been removed from their posts in the armed forces. In general, however, these retirements have not been the result of the implementation of the Ad Hoc Commission's recommendations, but of the fact that the persons concerned retired after completing the required period of active service in the armed forces. In any event, it is a welcome fact that, in practice, none of the officers referred to in the report of the Ad Hoc Commission is still on active service in the armed forces.

The recommendations of the Commission on the Truth, of which there are about 40, came under different headings. Some of them, which are inferred directly from the results of the investigations and must be acted on most urgently, are aimed at the immediate removal of factors relating directly to the acts investigated or to the fact that they have not been fully cleared up. Of particular significance are the requests that the officers identified as responsible for the crimes should be discharged and that the members of the Supreme Court should resign. The second group of recommendations seeks to find a solution to some structural problems directly linked to the acts examined by the Commission. The third group relates to institutional reforms to prevent the repetition of such acts. Lastly, the Commission formulated its considerations and recommendations with a view to national reconciliation.

In most cases, there has been only preliminary implementation of the recommendations, since Government agencies and legislative bodies are considering draft legislation and the Government is taking preliminary action. However, there are substantive issues on which the recommendations have not been implemented at all. This is the case of the recommendations on the organization and composition of the judicial system; the retirement of the military officers were referred to by the Commission on the Truth and who were not on the Ad Hoc Commission's list and, in general, the dismissal of the persons referred to in the report from their posts; the effectiveness of the remedy of amparo; the recognition of the compulsory jurisdiction of the Inter-American Court of Human Rights; and accession to other international human rights instruments. The victims and their families have also not been compensated. To sum up, the recommendations of the Commission on the Truth have to date not had any practical impact and their partial implementation cannot in general terms be taken as a declaration of intent. . . .

*Recommendations of the Independent Expert.* Government of El Salvador should take maximum advantage of the presence of the ONUSAL Human Rights Division in the country. Its deployment is unprecedented in the history of the international protection of human rights and has brought together highly trained professionals who are in a position to provide the Government with immediate assistance, thereby enabling it to make substantial progress in the observance and safeguarding of human rights.

The Government should endeavour to implement the recommendations it receives, which are intended for the most constructive of purposes. Neither those formulated by the Independent Expert nor most of those by ONUSAL have been given further acceptance. In particular, the implementation of the recommendations of the Commission on the Truth, which are a genuine programme for anchoring El Salvador firmly in the community of democratic societies, should be a priority objective of the Government and of the country as a whole.

It is essential that the criminal practices that were on the increase in 1993 should be eradicated. The Joint Group for the Investigation of Illegal Armed Groups must be given full support so that it may shed light on the truth concerning the macabre death squads. Such support is not limited to the Government of El Salvador, but must come from any Government or democratic police force that is in a position to contribute to a clean-up that the civilized world has resolutely been calling for.

The strengthening of and support for the Office of the National Counsel for the Defence of Human Rights continue to be immediate and priority goals. In order to achieve them, the material, technical and human resources set aside by the State for carrying out its tasks under the Constitution must be concentrated on the Office of the National Counsel. The Government must cooperate with the Office for this purpose. It is essential that relations between the Office and non-governmental organizations should be improved. Through international cooperation, the office of the National Counsel must be provided with the means of holding one or several seminars in the immediate future focusing on the relevant issues, with assistance from persons with expert knowledge of the issues. At least initially, it would also be helpful if one of the experts could act as a full-time consultant to the Office of the National Counsel.

The National Civil Police must be set up and developed in accordance with the model that resulted from the Peace Agreements, as a new force, with a new doctrine, separate from the armed forces. Great care must be taken to ensure that individuals from the armed forces or the former public security forces that were disbanded are not involved in the education of members of the PNC and do not become PNC officers. The Criminal Investigation Division must be retained, as a skilled body, under the functional control of the Attorney-General of the Republic, for investigating criminal acts.

The Independent Expert believes that the separation between the administrative functions of the judicial system and the functions proper of the courts is both beneficial and necessary in order to guarantee the full independence of judges and lawyers. Accordingly, he is of the opinion that the current system, in which the functions in question are concentrated vertically within the Supreme Court of Justice, should be the subject of a careful review. This is a sensitive issue, which has its roots in a number of provisions of the Constitution and which must be dealt with soon as part of the power of Salvadorians to reform their Constitution, bearing in mind above all the harmful consequences of the current system, as well as the results of the investigations and recommendations of the Commission on the Truth.

In any event, the Independent Expert stresses the need to revise the National Council of the Judiciary Act without further delay so as to bring the Council's institutional regime into line with its status as an independent body and "to guarantee its independence from the organs of the State and from political parties", as agreed in the peace negotiations.

The Independent Expert once again strongly urges the Government of El Salvador, in accordance with the recommendations of the Commission on the Truth, to join the rest of the Central American nations and recognize the jurisdiction of the Inter-American Court of Human Rights as a means of providing the Salvadorian people with another instrument for the defence of its fundamental rights and for the strengthening, in a spirit of solidarity, of the system of protection of human rights in the hemisphere.

The unmet needs of the majority of Salvadorians regarding economic, social and cultural rights must be satisfied. In this connection, the implementation of the Peace Agreements provides the initial bases for action; their implementation must be extended with regard to the economic and social programme agreed on and the effective functioning of the Economic and Social Forum as an appropriate mechanism for consultation in this area.

The peace process in El Salvador needs greater support from the international community through the National Reconstruction Plan or any other appropriate means. For various reasons and motives, the international community was interested in seeing an end to the armed conflict in El Salvador. That interest should now be redoubled in order to contribute to the eradication of the causes that gave rise to the conflict.

It now seems clearer than ever that there is an inescapable link between lasting, substantial and irreversible progress in the observance and safeguarding of human rights and the implementation of the Agreements, which must be reflected in the model of society developed during the negotiations. The implementation of the Agreements is not only an obligation involving the honour of the parties, but the very means of achieving such a society. The Government and the FMLN embarked on the negotiations as military adversaries and emerged from them with an achievement and a joint programme on a historic scale. Neither they nor, for that matter, civilian society can agree to or allow the partial implementation of the Agreements without inevitably taking a step backwards. This is a difficult uphill task and one that goes against the current, but, if a person climbing a hill does not keep trying until he reaches the top, he will always run the risk of rolling back down to the bottom. Renewed efforts are thus required to make an irreversible reality of all the projects handed over to the Salvadorian people before the eyes of the world on 16 January 1992.

After considering the report, the Commission on Human Rights adopted on 4 March 1994 a resolution on the situation of human rights in El Salvador (resolution 1994/62), including the following operative paragraphs:

Recognizes that, while there have been improvements in the situation of human rights in El Salvador, some negative circumstances still exist regarding the observance of the right to life and that the capacity of the judicial system to shed light on and punish human rights violations continues to be unsatisfactory;

Urges the Government of El Salvador and the Frente Farabundo Martí para la Liberación Nacional to intensify their efforts to continue and complete the land transfer programme, the programme for the reintegration of former combatants into society, the deployment of the new National Civil Police, the collection of weapons in the private hands of the armed forces and the adoption of the Act on Private Security Services, in accordance with the agreements;

Expresses its belief that it is important to continue strengthening the Office of the National Counsel for the Defence of Human Rights and to carry out the agreed judicial reforms to ensure its independence and impartiality;

Commends the Government of El Salvador on the establishment of the Inter-institutional Investigating Group to investigate human rights violations and punish those responsible, and of the Joint Group for the Investigation of Illegal Armed Groups, set up on the initiative of the Secretary-General and recommended by the Commission on the Truth, and urges all sectors of Salvadorian society to cooperate with that investigation.

**OBSERVATIONS OF THE COMMITTEE ON THE RIGHTS OF THE CHILD.** The Committee considered the initial report of El Salvador (CRC/C/3/Add. 9) at its 85th, 86th, and 87th meetings (CRC/C/SR.85–87), held on 27 and 28 September 1993, and adopted at the 103rd meeting, held on 8 October 1993, the following concluding observations:

*Positive aspects.* The Committee welcomes the frank and critical approach taken by the party in preparing the report and, in particular, the reference therein to the main diffi-

culties encountered by the Government of El Salvador in ensuring the implementation of the Convention.

The Committee notes with satisfaction that public institutions have been established recently for the protection and improvement of living conditions of children. Legal measures adopted or envisaged to better protect the rights of the child, such as the new Family Code pending adoption by Parliament, also appear to be encouraging initiatives. In addition, the Committee appreciates the Government's intention to ratify International Labour Convention No. 138 and other instruments relating to the minimum age for employment.

The Committee welcomes the above initiatives, particularly in view of the fact that measures to protect children are necessary and urgent at the end of a long period of violence and internal conflict in El Salvador, which has caused severe damage to the national economy and deeply affected its society. It hopes that the measures envisaged by the Government will be effectively translated into reality.

*Factors and difficulties impeding the implementation of Convention.* The Committee takes note of the difficult economic and social situation of El Salvador, compounded by persistent poverty and 12 years of internal conflict and violence. The Government recognizes the need for national efforts to solve many of the problems resulting from the conflict and to create guarantees for the full respect of the provisions of the Convention. The Committee hopes that the democratic institutions of the country, as well as its policy of social reconciliation, will be consolidated soon.

*Principal subjects of concern.* The Committee regrets that the Government of El Salvador has not taken due consideration of the provisions of article 4 of the Convention and that restrictions in the national budget affecting social programmes have been detrimental to the protection of the rights of children.

The Committee also notes the lack of coordination between public and private bodies and organizations dealing with the rights of the child.

The Committee expresses concern at the concept of children in "irregular situations" in Salvadorian law. Clarification is needed with regard to the criteria used to define this concept, as well as the possible applicability of penal law to such children.

In addition, the Committee feels that there is a need to consider seriously questions relating to the legal definition of the child, in particular the minimum age for marriage, employment, military service and testimony before a court. It appears that these provisions do not sufficiently take into consideration the principles of the best interest of the child and non-discrimination.

The Committee is alarmed at the large number of children who have been abandoned, displaced or have become orphans as a result of the armed conflict, as well as those who, in order to survive, are forced to live and work in the street.

The Committee is also preoccupied by the widespread discriminatory attitudes towards girls and disabled children, as well as by the existence on a large scale of child abuse and violence within the family.

The Committee notes with concern the lack of training of professional groups working with and for children.

*Suggestions and recommendations.* The Committee recommends that in accordance with article 44, paragraph 4, of the Convention and rule 69 of its provisional rules of procedure, additional information be requested from the Government of El Salvador in order to respond to the questions and concerns expressed by the Committee during its consideration of the initial report. Such information should be submitted by the end of 1994. The Committee also suggests that El Salvador submit its "core document" (see HRI/1991/1) as referred to in paragraph 5 of the Committee's adopted guidelines concerning the initial part of State party reports to be submitted under the various international human rights instruments (CRC/C/5).

The Committee would also like to receive information with regard to the actual implementation of the legislation and the impact of the action planned by the Government to improve respect for the rights of children. The Government should provide, in particular, clarification on the status of the Convention in the domestic legislation of El Salvador and the possibility of invoking the provisions of the Convention directly in court.

In relation to the adverse impact of the internal conflict on children who live in exceptionally difficult situations, the Committee wishes to receive precise information with regard to rehabilitation programmes for affected children and the progress of such programmes, as well as statistical data with regard to displaced children within the country.

The Committee is also interested in being informed about the distribution of child care services in rural and urban areas and the training of relevant personnel.

Strategies and educational programmes along with the adequate dissemination of information should be undertaken in order to counter certain prejudices which affect children negatively, such as gender-based discrimination (known as machismo) and discrimination against disabled children (especially in rural areas), and to enhance the participation of children, in particular within the family.

In the light of the discussions and taking into account the situation of children in El Salvador, the Committee recommends that urgent measures be adopted for the protection of children belonging to vulnerable groups, in particular displaced and refugee children, disabled and homeless children, as well as children subject to abuse or violence within the family. Such measures should encompass social assistance and rehabilitation programmes oriented towards those groups of children and be undertaken, with the cooperation and support of the relevant United Nations agencies and international organizations, in the spirit of article 45 (b) of the Convention.

### COMMENTS OF THE HUMAN RIGHTS COMMITTEE.
On 4 and 5 April 1994, the UN Human Rights Committee considered the second periodic report submitted by the Government of El Salvador in accordance with article 40 of the International Covenant on Civil and Political Rights (UN Doc. CCPR/C/51/Add. 8). After examining the report, the Committee adopted the following comments (CCPR/C/79/Add. 34):

*Introduction.* The Committee welcomes the opportunity to continue its dialogue with the State party following a delay in reporting of over 10 years. The second report contained information about constitutional and legal measures giving effect to the Covenant which was supplemented by the core document. The Committee regrets that the second periodic report neither accurately nor candidly represents the actual human rights situation in El Salvador in the period covered by the report, during which armed conflict and massive violations of human rights have been followed by a peace process supervised by ONUSAL. In particular, it provides little relevant information on such key areas as the protection of the right to life under article 6 of the Covenant, the prohibition of torture under article 7, the right to liberty and security of person under article 9 and the guarantee to due process under the law in accordance with article 14. The Committee regrets, in particular, the complete lack of information regarding either the report of the Truth Commission and the implementation of its recommendations or the Amnesty Law and its impact on the State party's obligations under the Covenant.

The Committee expresses its appreciation to the delegation for the useful information it provided in response to the list of issues as well as to questions and comments of Committee members. However, the Committee regrets that many questions put to the delegation during the discussion remained unanswered.

*Factors and difficulties affecting the application of the Covenant.* The Committee notes that El Salvador has only recently emerged from a long and devastating civil war during which gross and systematic human rights violations occurred and that it is still in the process of recovery and transition to peace.

*Positive aspects.* The Committee notes with satisfaction that the human rights situation has improved in El Salvador and that some progress has been made toward the consolidation of peace and the establishment of the rule of law. In that connection, the Committee notes the signing of the peace accords in 1992 and the creation under that accord of the Truth Commission and the Ad Hoc Commission to investigate past human rights abuses, to recommend action against the perpetrators and to avoid a recurrence of such events. The Committee particularly welcomes the establishment of the Office of the Procurator for the Protection of Human Rights and the Office for Information on Detained Persons as well as the primacy accorded in the Constitution to international human rights instruments over domestic legislation. The Committee also welcomes the legal reform undertaken in some areas, notably with respect to the family code and the establishment of family courts, and the limitation of the jurisdiction of military tribunals.

*Principal subjects of concern.* The Committee is concerned that, despite the signing of the peace accord over two years ago, the rule of law has not yet been effectively reestablished. The Committee expresses concern that human rights violations continue in El Salvador, particularly serious and systematic violations of the right to life carried out by paramilitary groups. In this regard, the Committee notes with alarm that politically-motivated summary and arbitrary executions, death threats and cases of torture have continued to occur since the signing of the peace accord. The Committee also notes that most recommendations of the Truth Commission have still not been implemented. A significant gap persists between constitutional and legal guarantees and the actual application of those legal guarantees. The Committee also notes with concern that the rights and freedoms in the Covenant have not been fully included in the Constitution.

The Committee expresses grave concern over the adoption of the Amnesty Law, which prevents relevant investigation and punishment of perpetrators of past human rights violations and consequently precludes relevant compensation. It also seriously undermines efforts to re-establish respect for human rights in El Salvador and to prevent a recurrence of the massive human rights violations experienced in the past. Furthermore, failure to exclude violators from service in Government, particularly in the military, the National Police and the judiciary, will seriously undermine the transition to peace and democracy.

The Committee expresses concern over continuing human rights abuses by the military and security forces. The Committee notes in this context with particular concern the lack of full and effective control by civilian authorities over the military and the security forces.

The Committee expresses concern over the fact that high officials of the judiciary have been implicated by the Truth Commission in human rights violations. In that connection, the Committee notes with concern that, until serious reform of the judiciary is undertaken, efforts to strengthen the rule of law and to promote respect for human rights will continue to be undermined. The Committee also notes with concern the lack of support and protection given by the civilian authorities to the judiciary in the performance of its duties.

A number of additional concerns remain, including the full and effective application of the Covenant in matters pertaining to the full enjoyment by women of the rights guaranteed under the Covenant and the difficulties encountered in ensuring the full participation of all citizens in the electoral process.

*Suggestions and recommendations.* The Committee endorses the recommendations of the Truth Commission and strongly recommends that the Government take immediate steps to fully implement them.

The Committee emphasizes the obligation of the State party under article 2, paragraph 3, of the Covenant to ensure that victims of past human rights violations have an effective remedy. In order to discharge that obligation, the Committee recommends that the State party review the effect of the Amnesty Law and amend or repeal it as necessary.

The Committee recommends that all necessary measures be urgently taken to combat the continuing human rights violations in El Salvador. All violations should be thoroughly investigated, the offenders punished and the victims compensated. In this connection, the Committee also recommends that the Office of the Procurator for the Protection of Human Rights should be strengthened both with regard to resources and competence in order to ensure that the Procurator may effectively carry out his or her responsibilities.

The Committee recommends that all necessary measures be taken to ensure that human rights are respected by the military. The Committee urges continuing vigorous action to ensure that persons closely associated with human rights abuses do not re-enter the police, army or security forces.

The Committee recommends that major reform of the judiciary be undertaken with a view to establishing an independent and impartial judicial system free from political pressure and intimidation which will safeguard human rights and enforce the rule of law without discrimination.

The Committee urges that respect for human rights be institutionalized at all levels of the Government and recognized as an essential element of the process of national reconciliation and reconstruction. To that end, the Committee recommends that all articles of the Covenant should be fully incorporated into the national legal system; that comprehensive human rights training is provided to judges, the police and the military; and that human rights education be provided in schools at all levels. The active participation of NGOs in the democratization process should also be encouraged.

**BIBLIOGRAPHY.** Americas Watch. *El Salvador: Accountability and Human Rights—The Report of the United Nations Commission on the Truth for El Salvador.* New York: Human Rights Watch, 1993. NGO report, in English.

—————. *El Salvador: Peace and Human Rights—Successes and Shortcomings of the United Nations Observer Mission in El Salvador (ONUSAL).* New York: Human Rights Watch, 2 September 1992. NGO report, in English.

—————. *El Salvador and Human Rights: The Challenge of Reform.* New York: Human Rights Watch, 1991. NGO factfinding report, in English.

—————. *El Salvador's Decade of Terror: Human Rights Since the Assassination of Archbishop Romero.* NGO monograph, in English.

—————. *Labor Rights in El Salvador.* New York: Human Rights Watch, 1988. NGO report, in English.

—————. *Land Mines in El Salvador and Nicaragua: The Civilian Victims.* New York: Human Rights Watch, 1986. NGO report, in English.

—————. *The Massacre at El Mozote: The Need to Remember.* New York: Human Rights Watch, 1992. NGO report, in English.

Amnesty International. *El Salvador: "Death Squads"—A Government Strategy.* London: 1988. NGO report, in English.

—————. *El Salvador: Killings, Torture and "Disappearances."* New York: 1990. NGO factfinding report, in English.

—————. *El Salvador: Peace without Justice.* London: 1993. NGO report, in English.

Comisión de Derechos Humanos de El Salvador. *Situación de los Derechos Humanos y Libertades Fundamentales, en el Primer Año de Gobierno del Lic. Alfredo Cristiani, Presidente de la República de El Salvador* (The Situation of Human Rights and Fundamental Freedoms in the First Year of the Government of the Licentiate Alfredo Cristiani, President of the Republic of El Salvador). San Salvador, El Salvador: 1990. NGO report, in Spanish.

Committee for Peace and Democracy in El Salvador. *One Step Forward: Elections in El Salvador—Report of the Canadian NGO Observer Delegations to the 1994 Salvadoran Elections.* Ottawa, Canada: 1994. NGO report, in English.

Ecumenical Program on Central America and the Caribbean. *Condoning the Killing: Ten Years of Massacres in El Salvador.* Washington, D.C.: 1990. NGO factfinding report, in English.

El Salvador Committee for Human Rights. *Prolonging the Agony: The Human Cost of Low Intensity Warfare in El Salvador.* London: 1987. NGO report, in English.

Human Rights Institute of the Central American University José Simeón Cañas. *The Jesuit Case: A Break with Impunity?* New York: Lawyers Committee for Human Rights, 1991. NGO report, in English.

—————. *Los Derechos Humanos en El Salvador en 1986* (Human Rights in El Salvador 1986). San Salvador: 1987. NGO report, in Spanish.

—————. *Los Derechos Humanos en El Salvador en 1987* (Human Rights in El Salvador in 1987.) San Salvador: 1988. NGO report, in Spanish.

—————. *Los Derechos Humanos y el Decreto 50* (Human Rights and Decree 50). San Salvador: 1986. NGO report, in Spanish.

—————. *Report on Repression against the Salvadoran Labor and Cooperative Movements September 1966–August 1987.* San Salvador: 1987. NGO report, in English.

Human Rights Watch. "El Salvador," in *Human Rights Watch World Report 1995,* pp.90–93. New York: 1995. NGO report, in English.

Inter-Church Committee on Human Rights in Latin America. *Unfulfilled Promises and Growing Fears: Human Rights in El Salvador.* Toronto, Canada: 1994. NGO report, in English.

Kircher, Ingrid. "The Human Rights Work of the United Nations Observer Mission in El Salvador," *Netherlands Quarterly of Human Rights* 10, no. 3 (1992): 303–317. Scholarly article, in English.

Montes, S., F. Melendez, and E. Palacios. *Los Derechos Economicos, Sociales y Culturales en El Salvador* (Economic, Social and Cultural Rights in El Salvador). San Salvador: Instituto de Derechos Humanos Universidad Centroamericana "Jose Simeon Canas," 1988. NGO report, in Spanish.

Organization of American States, Inter-American Commission on Human Rights. *Report on the Situation of Human Rights in El Salvador.* Washington, D.C.: 1994. IGO report, in English.

Physicians for Human Rights. *El Salvador: Health Care under Siege—Violations of Medical Neutrality during the Civil Conflict.* Somerville, MA, USA: 1990. NGO report, in English.

Popkin, Margaret, Jack Spence, and George Vickers. *Justice Delayed: The Slow Pace of Judicial Reform in El Salvador.* Washington, D.C.: Washington Office on Latin America, 1994. NGO report, in English.

Sollis, Peter. "Displaced Persons and Human Rights: The Crisis in El Salvador," *Bulletin of Latin American Research* 11, no. 1 (1992): 49–65. Scholarly article, in English.

United Nations Commission on Human Rights. *Final Report to the Commission on Human Rights on the Situation of Human Rights in El Salvador, prepared by Mr. José Antonio Pastor Ridruejo, in pursuance of the mandate conferred by Commission resolution 1990/77.* Geneva, Switzerland: 1991. IGO document, in English and French.

————. *Final Report on the Situation of Human Rights in El Salvador.* Prepared by Special Rapporteur Jose Antonio Pastor Ridruejo. 3 February 1986. IGO document, in English.

————. *Final Report on the Situation of Human Rights in El Salvador.* Prepared by Special Rapporteur Jose Antonio Pastor Ridruejo, E/CN 4/1987/21. 2 February 1987. IGO report, in English.

## EMPLOYMENT: ANTI-DISCRIMINATION AGENCIES.

Established by national or local governments with a view to eliminating discrimination based on any ground such as race, sex, language, or religion, the role and functions of such agencies are described in the Secretary-General's report entitled *National Institutions for the Protection and Promotion of Human Rights* (UN Doc. E/CN.4/1987/37), prepared at the request of the **GENERAL ASSEMBLY** (resolution 40/123), in the following terms (paras. 91–98):

The importance of fair labour practices and the availability of adequate redress for discrimination in the area of employment has been generally recognized throughout the world as an essential part of any comprehensive human rights protection programme. While Governments frequently include Ministers of Labour in their cabinets to deal with the many issues and problems which characterize the area of employment, an ever-increasing number of States consider that resources of a local and specialized nature are required to address the needs and demands of workers adequately. For instance, labour courts and tribunals, which conciliate, mediate and adjudicate disputes arising under labour agreements, or between workers' unions and employers, have been established in many countries.

States have also created administrative Commissions or agencies, responsible for addressing specific problems in the labour market that may infringe on the rights of some groups and individuals in the community to equal work for fair and equal compensation and adequate working conditions. These Commissions frequently operate under the Ministry of Labour. For example, to assist in eradicating unemployment, the Government of Zimbabwe created the Department of Employment and Employment Promotion, which functions under the Ministry of Labour and Social Services. The primary purpose of this body is to match persons seeking work with existing employment vacancies as quickly as possible, and to work closely with other governmental bodies in an attempt to create productive employment opportunities.

Many of the organizations created by States are established to deal primarily with sexual and racial discrimination in employment. The powers and duties of these Commissions and agencies differ from country to country. Sometimes, they exist solely on the national level, but they are often organized on both the national and local level. For instance, in Australia National and Local Employment Discrimination Committees were established in 1973 to deal with cases of discrimination covered by the International Labour Organisation (ILO) Discrimination (Employment and Occupation) Convention (No. 111), 1958. Basically, the Australian Employment Discrimination Committees consider questions concerning possible discrimination in the remuneration of employees. The National Committee's primary functions are to:

". . . consider allegations of discrimination referred by the State (Local) Committees; consider allegations which involve the Federal Government as an employer and those which are of national significance; to advise the Federal Government on relevant matters of policy; and to develop and promote a community education programme."

The six State (Local) Committees investigate charges of discrimination against employers, and attempt to arrive at amicable settlements through conciliation. The membership of Australia's Employment Discrimination Committees is comprised of representatives of Government, national employers' organizations and the trade-union movement, as well as individuals with special expertise in the problems of employment regarding Aboriginals, migrants and women.

With some modifications, similar powers and duties characterize the United States Equal Employment Opportunity Commission (EEOC). Established by the Civil Rights Act of 1964, EEOC was created to hear and investigate claims of discrimination in employment practices and procedures. When EEOC receives a complaint, it transfers that complaint to the competent State or local agency, which is required to act on the complaint within 60 days. If no such action takes place, EEOC then takes up the claim, investigates the complaint and attempts to arrive at an amicable settlement. If no settlement can be reached, EEOC is empowered to seize the United States District Court (federal court) for adjudication of the matter. This seizure of the court by EEOC does not preclude the victim in the case from initiating his own judicial action as well. Decisions or rulings by the court constitute legally binding precedents, which affect employment policy throughout the nation. Finally, State and local agencies of EEOC which investigate claims of discrimination in employment, are also empowered to investigate charges of unequal access to public facilities and housing as a result of discrimination.

Some equal employment agencies function as "watch-dogs" to ensure that particular pieces of legislation concerning employment and labour are fully complied with. As an example of such an agency, mention may be made of the Vigilance Committees in India. These Committees were created under the Bonded Labour Systems Abolition Act of 1976. Vigilance Committees are comprised of officials, representatives of the locality, social workers and financial and credit institutions. Their basic functions are to advise the district authorities on the implementation of the Act forbidding the practice of bonded labour, to monitor offences under the Act, and to make recommendations on whether action should be taken regarding these offences. The Committee also defends suits instituted against bonded debts.

Often equal employment commissions and agencies also perform advisory services. As previously stated, the Australian National Employment Discrimination Committee advises the Federal Government on employment and labour policy. Similarly, the Tripartite Advisory Committees in India, comprised of government, employer and employee representatives, were established to advise the Government on the formulation of labour policy and to ensure the implementation of labour laws. The French Supreme Council for Professional Equality Between Men and Women, established in 1983 is also an advisory body. The Supreme Council is consulted by the Government on bills and draft decrees designed to ensure professional equality between men and women, as well as on texts dealing with the particular working conditions of the different sexes. The Council may also make proposals designed to improve professional equality between the sexes.

Equal employment agencies are also required, in most cases, to include activities aimed at promoting equality in the employment area as part of their basic functions. For example, both the Danish Equality Council and the Portuguese Commission on Women's Conditions are charged with promoting equality between the sexes in employment and vocational training. The United States EEOC proposes affirmative action hiring plans to employers and industries for voluntary undertaking. Once employers accept such plans, they become binding. In many countries, however, the promotion of equality in employment is the responsibility of human rights and civil rights commissions.

The role of equal employment commissions in safeguarding the workplace from discrimination is clearly an important factor in protecting the human and civil rights of the individual. Although it is often the responsibility of human rights commissions to address issues concerning discrimination in employment, the existence of widespread discrimination in the field of labour relations seems to corroborate the idea that separate agencies, designed to deal solely with employment and labour issues are needed to protect the individual's right to work in an environment free from discrimination. Moreover, agencies comprised of employers and workers play an important role in advising Governments on the needs of the working community. Discrimination in employment is one of the most pernicious violations of human rights, since it undercuts the very livelihood of the individual and frequently triggers a chain reaction of financial and social circumstances which often expose the individual to further exploitation. Therefore, agencies which can address the problem of discrimination in the workplace exclusively, provide an essential service in the protection of human rights.

*BIBLIOGRAPHY.* Ewing, K.D., C.A. Gearty, and B.A. Hepple, eds. *Human Rights and Labour Law: Essays for Paul O'Higgins.* London: Mansell, 1994. Collection of scholarly contributions, in English; bibliography, pp. 344–354.

Fredman, Sandra. "European Community Discrimination Law: A Critique," *Industrial Law Journal* 21, no. 2 (June 1992): 119–134. Scholarly article, in English.

International Labor Organization. *Draft Guide of Practice for Equal Opportunity and Treatment in Employment* (ILO, EGALITE/1985/D.3 [Rev. 1]), 2nd ed., 1986.

————. *International Labor Organization Standards and Action for the Elimination of Discrimination and the Promotion of Equality of Opportunity in Employment* (ILO, EGALITE/1991/D.1).

Maschke, Karen J. *Litigation, Courts, and Women Workers.* Westport, CT, USA: Greenwood Press, 1989. Scholarly monograph, in English; bibliograpy, pp. 107–113.

Siegel, Richard L. *Employment and Human Rights: The International Dimension.* Philadelphia, PA, USA: University of Pennsylvania Press, 1994. Scholarly monograph, in English; bibliography, pp. 255–261.

"Third Comparative Labor Law Roundtable: Unlawful Discrimination in Employment," *Georgia Journal of International and Comparative Law* 20, no. 1 (1990): 1–184. Scholarly article, in English.

## END CHILD PROSTITUTION IN ASIAN TOURISM.

Established in 1990, this non-governmental organization works to protect Asian children from prostitution by taking legal and political action to rt the public to the existence of so-called "sex tours" offered to foreign tourists. It has national committees in 18 countries. ECPAT publishes a quarterly newsletter in English and also has published *Caught in Modern Slavery: Children in Prostitution* and *The Child and the Tourist.*

End Child Prostitution in Asian Tourism. Address: P.O. Box 178, Klong Chan, Bangkok, 10240, Thailand. Telephone: (66-2) 519-2794. Fax: (66-2) 519-2794. Officer: Sudarat Srisang.

## ENVIRONMENT.

In resolutions 1993/90 of 10 March 1993, 1994/65, and 1995/14 of 24 February 1995, the UN **COMMISSION ON HUMAN RIGHTS** pointed out "that the promotion of an environmentally healthy world contributes to the protection of the human rights to life and health of everyone," and called upon States to act "in accordance with their common but differentiated responsibilities and respective capabilities." In the latter resolution, the Commission reaffirmed Principle No. 1 of the Rio Declaration on Environment and Development (reproduced below), which states that human beings are at the center of concerns for sustainable development and that they are entitled to a healthy and productive life in harmony with nature.

The Commission recognized "that illicit dumping of toxic and dangerous substances and waste potentially constitute a serious threat to the human rights to life and health of everyone, bearing especially in mind the vulnerability and concern of developing countries, and that States should adopt and vigorously implement existing Conventions relating to the dumping of toxic and dangerous products and waste, and cooperate in the prevention of illicit dumping." In this connection, it reaffirmed that "States have, in accordance with the Charter of the United Nations and the principles of international law, the sovereign right to exploit their own resources pursuant to their own environmental and developmental policies, and the responsibility to ensure that activities within their jurisdiction or control do not cause damage to the environment of other States or of areas beyond the limits of national jurisdiction."

***RIO DECLARATION.*** The United Nations Conference on Environment and Development, meeting at Rio de Janeiro from 3 to 14 June 1992, prepared and adopted the Rio Declaration on Environment and Development, as follows:

The United Nations Conference on Environment and Development, . . . proclaims that:

*Principle 1.* Human beings are at the centre of concerns for sustainable development. They are entitled to a healthy and productive life in harmony with nature.

*Principle 2.* States have, in accordance with the Charter of the United Nations and the principles of international law, the sovereign right to exploit their own resources pursuant to their own environmental and developmental policies, and the responsibility to ensure that activities within their jurisdiction or control do not cause damage to the environment of other States or of areas beyond the limits of national jurisdiction.

*Principle 3.* The right to development must be fulfilled so as to equitably meet developmental and environmental needs of present and future generations.

*Principle 4.* In order to achieve sustainable development, environmental protection shall constitute an integral part of the development process and cannot be considered in isolation from it.

*Principle 5.* All States and all people shall cooperate in the essential task of eradicating poverty as an indispensable requirement for sustainable development, in order to decrease the disparities in standards of living and better meet the needs of the majority of the people of the world.

*Principle 6.* The special situation and needs of developing countries, particularly the least developed and those most environmentally vulnerable, shall be given special priority. International actions in the field of environment and development should also address the interests and needs of all countries.

*Principle 7.* States shall cooperate in a spirit of global partnership to conserve, protect and restore the health and integrity of the Earth's ecosystem. In view of the different contributions to global environmental degradation, States have common but differentiated responsibilities. The developed countries acknowledge the responsibility that they bear in the international pursuit of sustainable development in view of the pressures their societies place on the global environment and of the technologies and financial resources they command.

*Principle 8.* To achieve sustainable development and a higher quality of life for all people, States should reduce and eliminate unsustainable patterns of production and consumption and promote appropriate demographic policies.

*Principle 9.* States should cooperate to strengthen endogenous capacity-building for sustainable development by improving scientific understanding through exchanges of scientific and technological knowledge, and by enhancing the development, adaptation, diffusion and transfer of technologies, including new and innovative technologies.

*Principle 10.* Environmental issues are best handled with the participation of all concerned citizens, at the relevant level. At the national level, each individual shall have appropriate access to information concerning the environment that is held by public authorities, including information on hazardous materials and activities in their communities, and the opportunity to participate in decision-making processes. States shall facilitate and encourage public awareness and participation by making information widely available. Effective access to judicial and administrative proceedings, including redress and remedy, shall be provided.

*Principle 11.* States shall enact effective environmental legislation. Environmental standards, management objectives and priorities should reflect the environmental and developmental context to which they apply. Standards applied by some countries may be inappropriate and of unwarranted economic and social cost to other countries, in particular developing countries.

*Principle 12.* States should cooperate to promote a supportive and open international economic system that would lead to economic growth and sustainable development in all countries, to better address the problems of environmental degradation. Trade policy measures for environmental purposes should not constitute a means of arbitrary or unjustifiable discrimination or a disguised restriction on international trade. Unilateral actions to deal with environmental challenges outside the jurisdiction of the importing country should be avoided. Environmental measures addressing transboundary or global environmental problems should, as far as possible, be based on an international consensus.

*Principle 13.* States shall develop national law regarding liability and compensation for the victims of pollution and other environmental damage. States shall also cooperate in an expeditious and more determined manner to develop further international law regarding liability and compensation for adverse effects of environmental damage caused by activities within their jurisdiction or control to areas beyond their jurisdiction.

*Principle 14.* States should effectively cooperate to discourage or prevent the relocation and transfer to other States of any activities and substances that cause severe environmental degradation or are found to be harmful to human health.

*Principle 15.* In order to protect the environment, the precautionary approach shall be widely applied by States according to their capabilities. Where there are threats of serious or irreversible damage, lack of full scientific certainty shall not be used as a reason for postponing cost-effective measures to prevent environmental degradation.

*Principle 16.* National authorities should endeavour to promote the internalization of environmental costs and the use of economic instruments, taking into account the approach that the polluter should, in principle, bear the cost of pollution, with due regard to the public interest and without distorting international trade and investment.

*Principle 17.* Environmental impact assessment, as a national instrument, shall be undertaken for proposed activities that are likely to have a significant adverse impact on the environment and are subject to a decision of a competent national authority.

*Principle 18.* States shall immediately notify other States of any natural disasters or other emergencies that are likely to produce sudden harmful effects on the environment of those States. Every effort shall be made by the international community to help States so afflicted.

*Principle 19.* States shall provide prior and timely notification and relevant information to potentially affected States on activities that may have a significant adverse transboundary environmental effect and shall consult with those States at an early stage and in good faith.

*Principle 20.* Women have a vital role in environmental management and development. Their full participation is therefore essential to achieve sustainable development.

*Principle 21.* The creativity, ideals and courage of the youth of the world should be mobilized to forge a global partnership in order to achieve sustainable development and ensure a better future for all.

*Principle 22.* Indigenous people and their communities and other local communities have a vital role in environmental management and development because of their knowledge and traditional practices. States should recognize and duly support their identity, culture and interests and enable their effective participation in the achievement of sustainable development.

*Principle 23.* The environment and natural resources of people under oppression, domination and occupation shall be protected.

*Principle 24.* Warfare is inherently destructive of sustainable development. States shall therefore respect international law providing protection for the environment in times of armed conflict and cooperate in its further development, as necessary.

*Principle 25.* Peace, development and environmental protection are interdependent and indivisible.

*Principle 26.* States shall resolve all their environmental disputes peacefully and by appropriate means in accordance with the Charter of the United Nations.

***TOXIC AND DANGEROUS WASTES.*** Concerned about the increase in illegal international traffic in, and the dumping and resulting accumulation of, toxic and dangerous wastes which jeopardize the right of everyone to a clean environment and adversely affect many countries—in particular, developing countries—the UN GENERAL ASSEMBLY on 20 December 1988 urged all States (resolution 43/212) to take the necessary legal and technical measures in order to halt such illegal traffic in toxic and dangerous products and wastes and, in particular, urged States generating such products and wastes to make every effort to treat and dispose of them in the country of origin to the maximum extent possible, consistent with environmentally sound disposal.

The Assembly called upon all States to prohibit all transboundary movement of toxic and dangerous

wastes carried without prior consent of the competent authorities of the importing country or without full recognition of the sovereign rights of the transit countries and, in this connection, urged them to prohibit such movement without prior notification in writing of the competent authorities of all countries concerned, including the transit countries, and to provide all information required to ensure the proper management of the wastes and full disclosure of the nature of the substances to be received or transported.

***HUMAN RIGHTS AND THE ENVIRONMENT.*** In response to a request by the Sub-Commission on Prevention of Discrimination and Protection of Minorities, endorsed by the Commission on Human Rights, Fatma Zohra Ksentini prepared, as a Special Rapporteur of the Sub-Commission, prepared a note on methods by which a study on the problem of the environment and its relation to human rights could be made. After examining the note, the Sub-Commission requested her to submit a preliminary report on the subject to it at its forty-third session. The preliminary report was examined at the Sub-Commission's 1991 session and a progress report was considered one year later. The latter (UN Doc. E/CN.4/Sub.2/1992/7 and Add. 1) included an analysis of national and international provisions and the decisions and comments of human rights bodies relating to human rights and the environment, as well as information on the results of the Conference on Environment and Development held in Rio de Janeiro from 3 to 14 June 1992 in which the Special Rapporteur had participated as an observer. A second progress report was made available to the Sub-Commission at its 1993 session (E/CN.4/Sub.2/1993/7); it reviewed developments in regard to the recognition and implementation of environmental rights as a human right on the basis of the standards and practices developed at the national, regional and universal levels; and included a number of preliminary conclusions and recommendations:

The problems of the environment are no longer being viewed exclusively from the angle of the pollution affecting the industrialized countries but seen rather as a worldwide hazard threatening the planet and the whole of mankind, as well as future generations. There is now a universal awareness of the widespread, serious and complex character of environmental problems, which call for adequate action at the national, regional and international levels.

The realization of the global character of environmental problems is attested by the progress made in understanding the phenomena that create hazards for the planet, threaten the living conditions of human beings and impair their fundamental rights. These phenomena concern not only the natural environment (the pollution of water, air and atmosphere, seas, oceans and rivers; depletion of the ozone layer; climatic changes) and natural resources (desertification, deforestation, soil erosion, disappearance of certain species;

deterioration of flora and fauna; exhaustion of non-renewable resources, etc.) but also populations and human settlements (housing, town planning, demography, etc.) and the rights of human beings (the human environment, living, working and health conditions; conditions for the exercise and enjoyment of fundamental rights).

By means of a global approach to these phenomena that takes in their multidimensional aspects, including their human aspects, it has become possible to move from environmental law to environmental rights, proclaimed by the 1972 Stockholm Declaration which states in its Principle 1 that "Man has the fundamental right to freedom, equality and adequate conditions of life, in an environment of a quality that permits a life of dignity and well-being, and he bears a solemn responsibility to protect and improve the environment for present and future generations".

Since then, a large number of national, regional and international instruments have been drawn up which have strengthened the legal bases of environmental rights and stressed the intrinsic link that exists between the preservation of the environment and the promotion of human rights.

The Special Rapporteur has endeavoured, within the limits of the means at her disposal, to collect the basic legal instruments underpinning environmental rights and to clarify the relationship existing between the preservation of the environment and human rights. She has received from governments, the United Nations bodies concerned, specialized agencies and intergovernmental and non-governmental organizations, studies, communications, information and comments that have proved very useful for her report. Looking ahead to her final report, she hopes that she will have at her disposal resources that will enable her to make more systematic use of these important sources of information.

This preliminary research has revealed universal acceptance of the environmental rights recognized at the national, regional and international levels.

At the national level, over 60 constitutions brought to the attention of the Special Rapporteur contain specific provisions relating to the protection of the environment; some of them recognize explicitly the right to a satisfactory environment, entailing corresponding duties towards the State and its institutions and rights and/or obligations for individuals and organs of society. An increasing number of national legislations have developed the framework of laws and regulations needed to ensure the right to a satisfactory environment and have spelt out the substantive content of that right and the ways and means whereby it may be exercised, including remedies to safeguard its effective enjoyment and afford guarantees for its implementation. A few constitutions provide in the section dealing with human rights and fundamental freedoms for the right to a healthy environment and the guarantees attaching thereto, including in some cases the right of recourse and petition. Some countries have provided for the punishment of offences against the environment and have introduced into national legislation the principle of compensation for the victims as well as reparation of the damage. There is moreover a trend towards developing and strengthening the means of preventing damage to the environment.

At the regional and universal level, recognition of the right to a satisfactory environment as a human right is reflected both in the related normative developments and in the "environmental" concern that informs the activities of human rights bodies. Although only a few instruments of a binding legal character have established a direct link between the environment and human rights, the regional and international human rights bodies are developing a practice whereby the procedural bases for enforcing the right to a satisfactory environment are becoming more firmly established and the validity of complaints of human rights violations based on ecological considerations is being recognized. These bodies do not dismiss out of hand the idea that ecological factors may hinder the enjoyment of the human rights enshrined in the instruments in their care. On the other hand, those same bodies and more particularly the European Court of Human Rights have, in certain cases, legitimated restrictions on the use of private property in the public interest based on concern for the need to preserve the environment.

Brief though it is, this review of the activities of human rights bodies relevant for the study has made it possible to outline the scope of environmental rights. Many human rights are suited to being applied from an ecological perspective, whether those rights are political, civil, social, economic or cultural, and whether they are exercised individually or collectively. In her previous reports, the Special Rapporteur drew up a list of those rights, albeit a non-exhaustive one.

Her analysis of the ways in which the right to a satisfactory environment relates to other human rights gave the Special Rapporteur occasion to stress the close link existing between that right and the right to development. The fact is that the affirmation of "ecological rights" attaching to recognition of the right to a satisfactory environment cannot be understood if we disregard the problems bound up with development both nationally and internationally. It also rests on the indivisibility and interdependence of all human rights.

The Special Rapporteur noted indigenous peoples, special ties with the land and the environment and their particular vulnerability to ecological hazards. The numerous communications received by the Special Rapporteur on this subject confirm the alarming data reproduced in the reports of the Working Group on Indigenous Populations (see in particular paras. 115 to 120 of document E/CN.4/Sub.2/1992/33).

Environmental damage has direct effects on the enjoyment of a series of human rights such as the right to life, to health, to a satisfactory standard of living, to sufficient food, to housing, to education, to work, to culture, to non-discrimination, to dignity and the harmonious development of one's personality, to security of person and family, to development, to peace, etc.

In this context, it should be stressed how vulnerable certain peoples, populations, groups or categories of persons are to ecological hazards and natural disasters whether caused by man or generated by a state of war and conflict. The Special Rapporteur has pointed out that the poor and disadvantaged, minority groups, women, children, migrant workers and their families, refugees and displaced persons are generally those most affected and least protected.

Conversely, human rights violations in their turn damage the environment. This is true of the right of peoples to self-determination and their right to dispose of their wealth and natural resources, the right to development, to participation, to work and to information, the right of peaceful Assembly, freedom of association, freedom of expression, etc.

In the light of the foregoing, the Special Rapporteur is of the view that effective implementation of the right to a satisfactory environment cannot be dissociated from the twinned efforts to preserve the environment and ensure the right to development. Nor can it be achieved without resolute action to ensure the enjoyment of all human rights.

In order to give practical expression to the right to a satisfactory environment, there is a need for development strategies that are directed towards the implementation of a substantive part of that right (the right to development, to life, to health, to work, etc.). These must go hand in hand with the promotion of the related procedural aspects (due process, right of association and of Assembly, freedom of expression, right of recourse, etc.).

The right to a satisfactory environment is also a right to prevention which gives a new dimension to the right to information, education and participation in decision-making. The right to restitution, indemnification, compensation and rehabilitation for victims must also be seen from the angle of the special responsibility that would follow from the absence of preventive measures.

The right to a satisfactory environment is also a right to the "conservation" of nature for the benefit of future generations. This "futuristic" dimension restores to human rights their original purpose, as embodied in the Charter of the United Nations and the Universal Declaration of 1948. It foreshadows a "new public order" of human rights which would set acceptable limitations on those rights in the general interest while entailing corresponding duties on the part both of the public authorities and of individuals, associations and other components of civil society.

The Special Rapporteur's preliminary recommendations were as follows (UN Doc. E/CN.4/Sub.2/ 1933/7, paras. 134–139):

The Special Rapporteur wishes to leave open the question of the preparation of a new international instrument (Declaration, protocol, etc.) on the right to a satisfactory environment or environmental rights. Since this is a field that is constantly developing, she considers it important to await for practice to crystallize the areas of consensus that might open the way to a possible codification of that right.

The human rights component of the right to a satisfactory environment lends itself, however, to immediate implementation by various bodies, under existing mechanisms for following up regional and international human rights instruments. The practice being developed within those bodies is decisive and should bring into sharper focus the content of the right to a satisfactory environment, the ways and means of implementing it, and the related procedural aspects.

However, it is important to guard against dissimilar practices and ways should therefore be sought of coordinating the work of human rights bodies and of bringing their action into line with a universalistic integrated conception of environmental rights. In this regard, the Special Rapporteur considers it useful:

(a) for guidelines to be drawn up in order to address the environmental aspects of universally recognized human rights;

(b) for a meeting of experts lasting five working days to be organized under the auspices of the Centre for Human Rights with the object of helping to work out a series of practical recommendations on the way in which the right to a satisfactory environment could be rationally incorporated into the activities of human rights bodies, including the working groups, special rapporteurs and bodies established pursuant to international human rights Conventions;

(c) for the Special Rapporteur to participate in the forthcoming meeting of chairmen of human rights bodies or at least for the question of the follow-up and implementation of the right to a satisfactory environment to be included in the agenda of that meeting with a view to recommendations being made on the subject.

The Special Rapporteur recommends that the various human rights bodies should examine, in the various fields of concern to them, the environmental dimension of the human rights under their responsibility. She suggests in particular that the following themes should be regularly examined by the bodies, Committees, working groups and special rapporteurs concerned:

(a) Commission on the Status of Women and Convention on the Elimination of All Forms of Discrimination against Women: rights of women and the environment;

(b) Committee on the Rights of the Child: vulnerability of children in the face of ecological hazards; protection of children against environmental degradation with particular reference to the phenomenon of street children; education of children with a view to the preservation of the environment;

(c) Committee on the Elimination of Racial Discrimination—CERD: racial discrimination and the environment and, more particularly, the tendency for disadvantaged and marginalized groups to be more exposed to environmental hazards. In addition, the Committee could establish appropriate case law for the treatment of complaints addressed to it in conformity with the provisions of the Convention on the Elimination of All Forms of Racial Discrimination;

(d) Committee on Economic, Social and Cultural Rights. The Committee could frame general comments with a view to defining the interaction of the environment with the human rights under its responsibility. It could moreover examine, in the context of ongoing studies, the possibility of including communications on ecological matters in any procedure established by means of a protocol for the treatment of complaints by individuals or States;

(e) Human Rights Committee. The Committee could revise its general comment on the right to life in order to include environmental concerns, frame others with regard to the rights set out in the Covenant and/or, more simply, formulate a general comment defining the links existing between civil and political rights and the environment. Moreover, it should be able, through dealing with complaints, to establish case law that will accommodate environmental concerns;

(f) Working Group on the right to development: environment and development; development and the environment funding institutions; participation by the people in activities for development and the environment, etc.;

(g) Working Group entrusted with the preparation of a draft Declaration on the right and responsibility of individuals, groups and organs of society to promote and protect universally recognized human rights and fundamental freedoms. The group could contemplate the inclusion of specific provisions relating to rights and duties in respect of the preservation of the environment;

(h) Working groups, special rapporteurs for thematic and country studies: conditions of detention and the environment; violations of the human rights of conservationists (tortures, disappearances, right to a fair trial; freedom of expression, etc.); extreme poverty and the environment; right to housing and the environment, in particular squatter settlements, environmental health, town planning; reparation, indemnification, compensation and rehabilitation for environmental victims; expulsions, displacement, forced resettlements with a specific study of the victims of foreign occupation; racism and apartheid; environmental refugees and displaced persons; armed conflicts, observance of humanitarian law, environmental degradation and violation of the rights of civilian populations, rights of indigenous peoples and the environment, etc.

The Centre for Human Rights might consider being represented in the work of the Commission on Sustainable Development.

Having regard to the many communications brought to the attention of the Special Rapporteur expressing serious concern regarding the enjoyment of human rights in relation with ecological factors, the Special Rapporteur considers it desirable for there to be a mechanism for monitoring situations. This might take the form of a thematic special rapporteur in the Commission on Human Rights. The work of the rapporteur could be usefully supplemented by the development of consultative services in this field and by the designation of a mediator. The Special Rapporteur would welcome the advice of the members of the Sub-Commission and other participants in order to formulate more specific proposals in this connection.

*DRAFT PRINCIPLES ON HUMAN RIGHTS AND THE ENVIRONMENT.* At its 1993 session, the Sub-Commission took note of the second progress report with appreciation and endorsed the recommendations it contained. It requested Special Rapporteur Fatma Zohra Ksentini to continue her study and to submit a final report to it at its 1994 session, that report to include a set of conclusions and recommendations aimed at developing basic principles and guidelines with respect to human rights and the environment. In this connection the Sub-Commission invited the Secretary-General to organize an expert meeting prior to the preparation of the final report in order to formulate recommendations on the way in which the right to environment could be incorporated in the activities of human rights bodies. The Special Rapporteur annexed to her report a series of draft principles on Human Rights and Environment, which she recommended for consideration by the Sub-Commission and other competent United Nations bodies, as follows (E/CN.4/Sub.2/1994/9, Annex I):

### Part I

1. Human rights, an ecologically sound environment, sustainable development and peace are interdependent and indivisible.

2. All persons have the right to a secure, healthy and ecologically sound environment. This right and other human rights, including civil, cultural, economic, political and social rights, are universal, interdependent and indivisible.

3. All persons shall be free from any form of discrimination in regard to actions and decisions that affect the environment.

4. All persons have the right to an environment adequate to meet equitably the needs of present generations and that does not impair the rights of future generations to meet equitably their needs.

### Part II

5. All persons have the right to freedom from pollution, environmental degradation and activities that adversely affect the environment, threaten life, health, livelihood, well-being or sustainable development within, across or outside national boundaries.

6. All persons have the right to protection and preservation of the air, soil, water, sea-ice, flora and fauna, and the essential processes and areas necessary to maintain biological diversity and ecosystems.

7. All persons have the right to the highest attainable standard of health free from environmental harm.

8. All persons have the right to safe and healthy food and water adequate to their well-being.

9. All persons have the right to a safe and healthy working environment.

10. All persons have the right to adequate housing, land tenure and living conditions in a secure, healthy and ecologically sound environment.

11. (a) All persons have the right not to be evicted from their homes or land for the purpose of, or as a consequence of, decisions or actions affecting the environment, except in emergencies or due to a compelling purpose benefiting society as a whole and not attainable by other means.

(b) All persons have the right to participate effectively in decisions and to negotiate concerning their eviction and the right, if evicted, to timely and adequate restitution, compensation and/or appropriate and sufficient accommodation or land.

12. All persons have the right to timely assistance in the event of natural or technological or other human-caused catastrophes.

13. Everyone has the right to benefit equitably from the conservation and sustainable use of nature and natural resources for cultural, ecological, educational, health, livelihood, recreational, spiritual and other purposes. This includes ecologically sound access to nature.

Everyone has the right to preservation of unique sites consistent with the fundamental rights of persons or groups living in the area.

14. Indigenous peoples have the right to control their lands, territories and natural resources and to maintain their traditional way of life. This includes the right to security in the enjoyment of their means of subsistence.

Indigenous peoples have the right to protection against any action or course of conduct that may result in the destruction or degradation of their territories, including land, air, water, sea-ice, wildlife or other resources.

15. All persons have the right to information concerning the environment. This includes information, howsoever compiled, on actions or courses of conduct that may affect the environment and information necessary to enable effective public participation in environmental decision-making. The information shall be timely, clear, understandable and available without undue financial burden to the applicant.

16. All persons have the right to hold and express opinions and to disseminate ideas and information regarding the environment.

17. All persons have the right to environmental and human rights education.

18. All persons have the right to active, free and meaningful participation in planning and decision-making activities and processes that may have an impact on the environment and development. This includes the right to a prior

assessment of the environmental, developmental and human rights consequences of proposed actions.

19. All persons have the right to associate freely and peacefully with others for purposes of protecting the environment or the rights of persons affected by environmental harm.

20. All persons have the right to effective remedies and redress in administrative or judicial proceedings for environmental harm or the threat of such harm.

21. All persons, individually and in association with others, have the duty to protect and preserve the environment.

22. All States shall respect and ensure the right to a secure, healthy and ecologically sound environment. Accordingly, they shall adopt administrative, legislative and other measures necessary to effectively implement the rights in this Declaration.

These measures shall aim at the prevention of environmental harm, at the provision of adequate remedies, and at the sustainable use of natural resources and shall include, *inter alia,*

—collection and dissemination of information concerning the environment;

—prior assessment and control, licensing, regulation or prohibition of activities and substances potentially harmful to the environment;

—public participation in environmental decision-making;

—effective administrative and judicial remedies and redress for environmental harm or the threat of such harm;

—monitoring, management and equitable sharing of natural resources;

—measures to reduce wasteful processes of production and patterns of consumption;

—measures aimed at ensuring that transnational corporations, wherever they operate, carry out their duties of environmental protection, sustainable development and respect for human rights; and

—measures aimed at ensuring that the international organizations and agencies to which they belong observe the rights and duties in this Declaration.

23. States and all other parties shall avoid using the environment as a means of war or inflicting significant, long-term or widespread harm on the environment, and shall respect international law providing protection for the environment in times of armed conflict and cooperate in its further development.

24. All international organizations and agencies shall observe the rights and duties in this Declaration.

25. In implementing the rights and duties in this Declaration, special attention shall be given to vulnerable persons and groups.

26. The rights in this Declaration may be subject only to restrictions provided by law and which are necessary to protect public order, health and the fundamental rights and freedoms of others.

27. All persons are entitled to a social and international order in which the rights in this Declaration can be fully realized.

**SEE ALSO** *Standard of Living.*

**BIBLIOGRAPHY.** Barr, Michael S., Robert Honeywell, and Scott A. Stofel. "Labor and Environmental Rights in the Proposed Mexico-United States Free Trade Agreement," *Houston Journal of International Law* 14, no. 1 (Fall 1991): 1–84. Scholarly article, in English.

Bouvier, Antoine. "Protection of the Natural Environment in Time of Armed Conflict," *International Review of the Red Cross* no. 285 (English), no. 792 (French) (Nov.–Dec. 1991): 567–578 (English); 599–611 (French). Scholarly article.

Cobb, John B., Jr. *Sustainability: Economics, Ecology, and Justice.* Maryknoll, NY, USA: Orbis Books, 1992. Scholarly monograph, in English.

Commission on Security and Cooperation in Europe. *Implementation of the Helsinki Accords: Sofia CSCE Meeting on the Protection of the Environment. Hearings before the Commission on Security and Cooperation in Europe. 101st Congress, 1st Session, September 28, 1989.* Washington, D.C.: U.S. Government Printing Office, 1990. Government hearings, in English.

"Corporate Crime and Violence," *Multinational Monitor* 8, no. 4 (April 1987): 4–25. Special issue, in English.

Dommen, Caroline. "Joining Hands for the Future: Human Rights and Environment," *Peoples for Human Rights: IMADR Yearbook* 3 (1991): 7–12. Article, in English.

Gibson, Noralee. "The Right to a Clean Environment," *Saskatchewan Law Review* 54, no. 1 (1990): 5–17. Scholarly article, in English.

Human Rights Watch. *Defending the Earth: Abuses of Human Rights and the Environment.* New York: 1992. NGO report, in English.

Jacobson, Jodi L. *Environmental Refugees: A Yardstick of Habitability.* Washington, D.C.: Worldwatch Institute, 1988. NGO monograph, in English.

Leonel, Mauro, Betty Mindlin, and Carmen Junqueira. "The Joint Responsibility of the International Community in the Indigenous and Environmental Issues of the Brazilian Amazon," *IWGIA Newsletter* no. 3 (Aug./Sept. 1992): 6–19. Article, in English; bibliography, p. 19.

Louka, Elli. *The Transnational Management of Hazardous and Radioactive Wastes.* New Haven, CT, USA: Orville H. Schell, Jr. Center for International Human Rights, Yale Law School, 1992. Scholarly paper, in English.

Moyers, Bill. *Global Dumping Ground: The International Traffic in Hazardous Waste.* Washington, D.C.: Seven Locks Press for the Center for Investigative Reporting, 1990. Research report, in English.

Rao, M., and G. Singh, eds. *The Environmental Activists' Handbook: Environmental Act, Important Judgments, Strategies.* Puntamba, Maharashtra, India: Asha Kendra Documentation Centre, n.d. NGO report, in English.

Shutkin, William Andrew. "International Human Rights Law and the Earth: The Protection of Indigenous Peoples and the Environment," *Virginia Journal of International Law* 31 (Spring 1991): 479–511. Scholarly article, in English.

Third World Network. *Report on Toxic Waste Dumping in Third World Countries.* Penang, Malaysia: 1988. NGO report, in English.

Thorme, Melissa. "Establishing Environment as a Human Right," *Denver Journal of International Law & Policy* 19 (Winter 1991): 301–342. Scholarly article, in English.

United Nations Sub-Commission on Prevention of Discrimination and Protection of Minorities. *Human Rights and the Environment,* by Fatma Zohra Ksentini, Special Rapporteur. New York: 1992 (Progress report: UN Doc. E/CN.4/Sub.2/1992/7).

Weber, Stefan. "Environmental Information and the European Convention on Human Rights," *Human Rights Law Journal* 12, no. 5 (May 1991): 177–185. Scholarly article, in English.

Worldwatch Institute. *State of the World 1993: A Worldwatch Institute Report on Progress Toward a Sustainable Society.* New York: The Institute, 1993. Collection of articles, in English.

**EQUALITY.** A general principle of elementary justice applicable to all human rights, meaning that, whatever level may be reached in the realization of those rights in a particular country or territory, should apply to every individual residing there without discrimination of any kind, the principle is proclaimed in the UNIVERSAL DECLARATION OF HUMAN RIGHTS as follows:

*Article 2.* Everyone is entitled to all the rights and freedoms set forth in this Declaration, without distinction of an kind, such as race, colour, sex, language, religion, political or other opinion, national or social origin, property, birth or other status.

Furthermore, no distinction shall be made on the basis of the political, jurisdictional or international status of the country or territory to which a person belongs, whether it be independent, trust, non-self governing or under any other limitation of sovereignty. . . .

*Article 7.* All are equal before the law and are entitled without any discrimination to equal protection of the law. All are entitled to equal protection against any discrimination in violation of this Declaration and against any incitement to such discrimination.

The INTERNATIONAL COVENANT ON ECONOMIC, SOCIAL AND CULTURAL RIGHTS deals with the principle in the following provisions:

*Article 2.* 2. The States Parties to the present Covenant undertake to guarantee that the rights enunciated in the present Covenant will be exercised without discrimination of any kind as to race, colour, sex, language, religion, political or other opinion, national or social origin, property, birth or other status.

*Article 3.* The States Parties to the present Covenant undertake to ensure the equal right of men and women to the enjoyment of all economic, social and cultural rights set forth in the present Covenant.

The INTERNATIONAL COVENANT ON CIVIL AND POLITICAL RIGHTS contains the following provisions:

*Article 2.* 1. Each State Party to the present Covenant undertakes to respect and to ensure to all individuals within its territory and subject to its jurisdiction the rights recognized in the present Covenant, without distinction of any kind, such as race, colour, sex, language, religion, political or other opinion, national or social origin, property, birth or other status. . . .

*Article 3.* The States Parties to the present Covenant undertake to ensure the equal right of men and women to the enjoyment of all civil and political rights set forth in the present Covenant. . . .

*Article 26.* All persons are equal before the law and are entitled without any discrimination to the equal protection of the law. In this respect, the law shall prohibit any discrimination and guarantee to all persons equal and effective protection against discrimination on any ground such as race, colour, sex, language, religion, political or other opinion, national or social origin, property, birth or other status.

The International Convention on the Elimination of All Forms of Racial Discrimination (see RACIAL DISCRIMINATION) provides that:

*Article 2.* 1. States Parties condemn racial discrimination and undertake to pursue by all appropriate means and without delay a policy of eliminating racial discrimination in all its forms, and promoting understanding among all races, and to this end:

(a) Each State Party undertakes to engage in no act or practise of racial discrimination against persons, groups of persons or institutions and to ensure that all public authorities and public institutions, national and local, shall act in conformity with this obligation;

(b) Each State Party undertakes not to sponsor, defend or support racial discrimination by any persons or organizations;

(c) Each State Party shall take effective measures to review governmental, national and local policies, and to amend, rescind or nullify any laws and regulations which have the effect of creating or perpetuating racial discrimination wherever it exists;

(d) Each State Party shall prohibit and bring to an end, by all appropriate means, including legislation as required by circumstances, racial discrimination by any persons, group or organization;

(e) Each State Party undertakes to encourage, where appropriate, integrationist multi-racial organizations and movements and other means of eliminating barriers between races, and to discourage anything which tends to strengthen racial division.

The Convention of the Elimination of All Forms of Discrimination Against Women contains the following provisions:

*Article 2.* States Parties condemn discrimination against women in all its forms, agree to pursue by all appropriate means and without delay a policy of eliminating discrimination against women and, to this end, undertake:

(a) To embody the principle of the equality of men and women in their national constitutions or other appropriate legislation if not yet incorporated therein and to ensure, through law and other appropriate means, the practical realization of this principle;

(b) To adopt appropriate legislative and other measures, including sanctions where appropriate, prohibiting all discrimination against women;

(c) To establish legal protection of the rights of women on an equal basis with men and to ensure through competent national tribunals and other public institutions the effective protection of women against any act of discrimination;

(d) To refrain from engaging in any act or practice of discrimination against women and to ensure that public authorities and institutions shall act in conformity with this obligation;

(e) To take all appropriate measures to eliminate discrimination against women by any persons, organization or enterprise;

(f) To take all appropriate measures, including legislation, to modify or abolish existing laws, regulations, customs and practices which constitute discrimination against women;

(g) To repeal all national penal provisions which constitute discrimination against women. . . .

*Article 15.* 1. State Parties shall accord to women equality with men before the law.

2. State Parties shall accord to women, in civil matters, a legal capacity identical to that of men and the same opportunities to exercise that capacity. In particular, they shall give women equal rights to conclude contracts and to administer property and shall treat them equally in all stages of procedure in courts and tribunals.

3. States Parties agree that all contracts and all other private instruments of any kind with a legal effect which is directed at restricting the legal capacity of women shall be deemed null and void.

4. States Parties shall accord to men and women the same rights with regard to the law relating to the movement of persons and the freedom to choose their residence and domicile.

The **AMERICAN CONVENTION ON HUMAN RIGHTS,** open for acceptance by member States of the **ORGANIZATION OF AMERICAN STATES,** provides that:

*Article 1.* The States Parties to this Convention undertake to respect the rights and freedoms recognized herein and to ensure to all persons subject to their jurisdiction the free and full exercise of those rights and freedoms, without any discrimination for reasons of race, color, sex, language, religion, political or other opinion, national or social origin, economic status, birth, or any other social condition.

The **AFRICAN CHARTER ON HUMAN AND PEOPLES' RIGHTS,** open for acceptance by member States of the **ORGANIZATION OF AFRICAN UNITY,** contains the following provisions:

*Article 2.* Every individual shall be entitled to the enjoyment of the rights and freedoms recognized and guaranteed in the present Charter without distinction of any kind such as race, ethnic group, colour, sex, language, religion, political or any other opinion, national and social origin, fortune, birth or other status.

*Article 3.* (1) Every individual shall be equal before the law.

(2) Every individual shall be entitled to equal protection of the law.

The **EUROPEAN CONVENTION ON HUMAN RIGHTS,** open for acceptance by member States of the **COUNCIL OF EUROPE,** provides that:

*Article 1.* The High Contracting Parties shall secure to everyone within their jurisdiction the rights and freedoms defined in Section I of this Convention. . . .

*Article 14.* The enjoyment of the rights and freedoms set forth in this Convention shall be secured without discrimination on any ground such as sex, race, colour, language, religion, political or other opinion, national or social origin, association with a nationality minority, property, birth or other status.

*UN RECOMMENDATIONS ON EQUALITY.* After examining reports submitted by States parties to the International Covenant on Civil and Political Rights in accordance with article 40 of that instrument, the UN **HUMAN RIGHTS COMMITTEE** in 1981 adopted a general comment on article 3 setting out its views on the question of the equal right of men and women to the enjoyment of civil and political rights, as follows (UN Doc. A/36/40, Annex VII, paras. 1–5):

Article 3 of the Covenant requiring, as it does, States parties to ensure the equal right of men and women to the enjoyment of all civil and political rights provided for in the Covenant, has been insufficiently dealt with in a considerable number of States reports and has raised a number of concerns, two of which may be highlighted.

First, article 3, as articles 2 (1) and 26 in so far as those articles primarily deal with the prevention of discrimination on a number of grounds, among which sex is one, requires not only measures of protection but also affirmative action designed to ensure the positive enjoyment of rights. This cannot be done simply by enacting laws. Hence more information has generally been required regarding the role of women in practice with a view to ascertaining what measures, in addition to purely legislative measures of protection, have been or are being taken to give effect to the precise and positive obligations under article 3 and to ascertain what progress is being made or what factors or difficulties are being met in this regard.

Secondly, the positive obligation undertaken by States parties under that article may itself have an inevitable impact on legislation or administrative measures specifically designed to regulate matters other than those dealt with in the Covenant but which may adversely affect rights recognized in the Covenant. One example, among others, is the degree to which immigration laws which distinguish between a male and a female citizen may or may not adversely affect the scope of the right of the woman to marriage to non-citizens or to hold public office.

The Committee, therefore, considers that it might assist States parties if special attention were given to a review by specially appointed bodies or institutions of laws or measures which inherently draw a distinction between men and women in so far as those laws or measures adversely affect the rights provided for in the Covenant and, secondly, that States parties should give specific information in their reports about all measures, legislative or otherwise, designed to implement their undertaking under this article.

The Committee considers that it might help the States parties in implementing this obligation, if more use could be made of existing means of international co-operation with a view to exchanging experience and organizing assistance in solving the practical problems connected with the ensurance of equal rights for men and women.

The **COMMITTEE ON THE ELIMINATION OF RACIAL DISCRIMINATION** has adopted several general recommendations to States parties to the International Convention of the Elimination of all Forms of Racial Discrimination after examining periodic reports submitted by those States. In one of these, adopted at its fifth session, held from 14 to 25 February 1972, the

Committee noted that some of the States parties had expressed or implied the belief that certain information on racial discrimination which the Committee had requested in a circular communication need not be supplied by the States on whose territories such discrimination did not exist. The Committee responded (UN Doc. A/8718, chap. IX, General Recommendation I) as follows:

However, inasmuch as, in accordance with article 9, paragraph 1, of the International Convention on the Elimination of All Forms of Racial Discrimination, all States Parties undertake to submit reports on the measures that they have adopted and that give effect to the provisions of the Convention and, since all the categories of information listed in the Committee's communication of 28 January 1970 refer to obligations undertaken by the States Parties under the Convention, that communication is addressed to all States Parties without distinction, whether or not racial discrimination exists in their respective territories. The Committee welcomes the inclusion in the reports from all States Parties, which have not done so, of the necessary information in conformity with all the headings set out in the aforementioned communication of the Committee.

In another general recommendation, approved at its sixth session, held from 7 to 25 August 1972, the Committee indicated a willingness to receive information from States parties to the Convention regarding the status of their relations with racist regimes in southern Africa (UN Doc. A/8718, chap. IX, general recommendation III) as follows:

The Committee has considered some reports from States Parties containing information about measures taken to implement resolutions of United Nations organs concerning relations with the racist régimes in southern Africa.

The Committee notes that, in the tenth paragraph of the preamble to the International Convention on the Elimination of All Forms of Racial Discrimination, States Parties have "resolved", *inter alia*, "to build an international community free from all forms of racial segregation and racial discrimination".

It notes also that, in article 3 of the Convention, "States Parties particularly condemn racial segregation and *apartheid*".

Furthermore, the Committee notes that, in resolution 2784 (XXVI), section III, the General Assembly, immediately after taking note with appreciation of the Committee's second annual report and endorsing certain opinions and recommendations submitted by it, proceeded to call upon "all the trading partners of South Africa to abstain from any action that constitutes an encouragement to the continued violation of the principles and objectives of the International Convention on the Elimination of All Forms of Racial Discrimination by South Africa and the illegal régime in Southern Rhodesia".

The Committee expresses the view that measures adopted on the national level to give effect to the provisions of the Convention are interrelated with measures taken on the international level to encourage respect everywhere for the principles of the Convention.

The Committee welcomes the inclusion in the reports submitted under article 9, paragraph 1, of the Convention, by any State Party which chooses to do so, of information regarding the status of its diplomatic, economic and other relations with the racist régimes in southern Africa.

Similarly, the UN **COMMITTEE ON THE ELIMINATION OF DISCRIMINATION AGAINST WOMEN,** after examining reports submitted by States parties to the Convention on the Elimination of All Forms of Discrimination against Women, adopted at its 1988 session two general recommendations on steps to be taken to give effect to the provisions of that instrument.

In the first (UN Doc. A/43/38, chap. V, general recommendation no. 5), the Committee, noting that, while significant progress had been achieved in regard to repealing or modifying discriminatory laws, there was still a need for action to be taken to implement fully the Convention by introducing measures to promote *de facto* equality between men and women, recommended that States parties make more use of temporary special measures such as positive action, preferential treatment, or quota systems to advance women's integration into education, the economy, politics, and employment.

In the second (Ibid., general recommendation no. 6), the Committee recommended that States parties:

1. Establish and/or strengthen effective national machinery, institutions and procedures, at a high level of Government, and with adequate resources, commitment and authority to:
  (a) Advise on the impact on women of all government policies;
  (b) Monitor the situation of women comprehensively;
  (c) Help formulate new policies and effectively carry out strategies and measures to eliminate discrimination;
2. Take appropriate steps to ensure the dissemination of the Convention, the reports of the States parties under article 18 and the reports of the Committee in the language of the States concerned;
3. Seek the assistance of the Secretary-General and the Department of Public Information in providing translations of the Convention and the reports of the Committee;
4. Include in their initial and periodic reports the action taken in respect of this recommendation.

***NATIONAL CONSTITUTIONAL AND LEGISLATIVE PROVISIONS ON NON-DISCRIMINATION.*** In the Declaration of the Second World Conference to Combat Racism and Racial Discrimination, adopted on 12 August 1983, that conference recognized the central importance of national legislation and judicial and administrative action to combat racial discrimination and the specific value of recourse procedures for the implementation of human rights norms.

In the Program for Action for the Second Decade to Combat Racism and Racial Discrimination, prepared by the conference and approved by the UN

General Assembly on 22 November 1983 (resolution 38/14), the Assembly recommended (para. 50) that:

(a) Governments, where necessary, should guarantee non-discrimination on grounds of race and equal rights for all individuals in their constitutions and legislation;

(b) Governments, where necessary, should undertake to review and update all national legislation and remove all discriminatory provisions;

(c) Legislation should be consistent with international standards embodied in international instruments;

(d) Victims of discrimination should be informed and advised of their rights, by all possible means, and given assistance in securing those rights;

(e) Governments should, where necessary, establish appropriate and effective machinery, including conciliation and mediation procedures and national Commissions to ensure that such legislation is enforced effectively and thereby to promote equality of opportunity and good race relations.

The Program of Action further provided that a system of regular review and appraisal should be continued, to enable member States and all organizations of the United Nations system, including relevant regional bodies and non-governmental organizations, to assess the measures taken towards achieving the aims and objectives of the Second Decade to Combat Racism and Racial Discrimination (1983–1993).

At the request of the UN General Assembly, the Secretary-General submitted to it, in 1984, a plan of activities for implementing the program of action for the 1985–1989 period, in which the compilation and publication of a consolidated volume of national laws designed to combat racism and racial discrimination was suggested.

In order to prepare the compilation, the Secretary-General requested governments to supply the relevant information and received responses from 44 of them. The resulting compilation, in tentative form, was made available to the Assembly in 1988 for consultation. At the same time, an overview of the available texts (UN Doc. A/43/637) was presented to the Assembly. The overview (paras. 13–49) is reproduced below:

The constitutional and legislative texts submitted reflect the concerns and recommendations of the Second World Conference and the General Assembly as outlined above. Each one of the elements for national action dealt with by the Conference and the Assembly found constitutional and legislative expressions in the texts submitted. Most States responding provided information and texts relating to the basic guarantees of equality in the enjoyment of human rights, either taken globally or with regard to specific human rights. They also, in many cases, supplied information on non-discrimination provisions relating to the exercise of specific rights. Information was also provided on the mechanisms established for protecting the enjoyment of human rights and on the sanctions provided for in cases of violation.

A few States submitted the text of legislation dealing specifically with race relations or the promotion of human rights, focusing on the issue of discrimination in many areas and establishing specific procedures in that regard. The following overview seeks to highlight the main points of the texts submitted. It is not exhaustive, and particular States are mentioned by way of example.

A. *Equality and Non-discrimination in the Enjoyment of Human Rights.* It is recognized by the overwhelming majority of States that individuals are entitled to equality of treatment before the law, and most States have passed legislation to this effect. The form and content of such legislation varies from one country to another. Many States do not raise distinctions as regards the class of persons protected by the law, thus ensuring universal equality of treatment. Examples of this would include the constitutions of Brazil—"all are equal before the law"; Canada—"every individual is equal before and under the law"; and El Salvador—"all men are equal before the law". In each of these examples, not only is the class of persons protected an infinite one but it is specifically emphasized that for the purposes of the law in question discrimination on the basis of race is not permitted.

Legislation passed has sometimes raised the distinction of citizenship as regards the class of persons protected. This distinction may be of little practical significance if, as in the case of the Union of Soviet Socialist Republics, another law guarantees non-citizens the rights and freedoms provided by law and specifically mentions that aliens have the right to apply to court to protect their various rights.

Even where it has been officially recognized that individuals are to be treated equally by the law, it has been acknowledged that there might be practical problems in the achievement of this policy. The Constitution of Austria draws attention to this by stating that nationals belonging to a minority should receive the same treatment "in law and in fact".

It is the view of some States that to realize *de facto* equality for all it may be necessary to take affirmative action in support of some groups in society that have already been victims of discrimination. In New Zealand and the United Kingdom of Great Britain and Northern Island, for example, the taking of such action is deemed not to be in breach of the laws against racial discrimination. This position is shared by Canada where, for instance, the law expressly obliges employers to examine situations in which employees might be suffering discrimination and to take steps to eradicate it.

In New Zealand, the State has taken the precaution of legislating against discrimination by subterfuge. Consequently, where a condition is imposed which is not apparently in contravention of a provision but which has a discriminatory effect in a situation that would otherwise be unlawful, then that condition will be deemed to be unlawful unless the person imposing it establishes good reason for its imposition and shows that its imposition is not a subterfuge to avoid complying with that provision.

Many States, such as El Salvador, have recognized the need to ensure that civil rights are enjoyed by all without discrimination. Although it could be argued that the general Declarations of equality provided by most States are enough to ensure this, many of them have gone further in specifically listing at least some of the rights to be enjoyed free of discrimination. For example, some States seek to ensure that all persons are free to marry as they choose. In New Zealand, any condition in restraint of marriage that is based on race will be null and void. The Venezuelan constitution declares that no impediment imposed by another country will be recognized as a bar to an alien wishing to marry in Venezuela. There are some countries, such as Bulgaria, that go further

443

in indicating that any person who takes measures to prevent mixed marriages shall be punished.

The right to own and transfer property is recognized for everyone by the constitutions of, for instance, Portugal and El Salvador. It is recognized in Mauritius that all, regardless of race, have the right to the protection of their property and to be free of deprivation thereof unless they are properly compensated. This sort of protection is also recognized in Tuvalu. In both States, however, the right to property is subject to the rights of others as well as to the national interest.

The right to security of person is one of the utmost importance in ensuring the dignity of human beings and, therefore, one that should be guaranteed by States to all persons, citizens and non-citizens alike. States have legislated on this issue in two principal ways. Some, as illustrated by the constitution of Trinidad and Tobago, have asserted the right of the individual to liberty and the security of the person. Others approach this issue differently, for example, the constitution of the United Arab Emirates seeks to secure the right by declaring that all persons should be free of arbitrary arrest, searches or restriction of liberty. In other States, the constitution also declares that no person should be subjected to torture or degrading treatment. Other examples would include Venezuela, which seeks to ensure this right by allowing asylum for anyone in danger for political reasons, subject to his satisfying the conditions established by law.

Equality and non-discrimination in the exercise of political rights is also important. States often provide that there should be equal and universal suffrage, thus implicitly barring the possibility of racial discrimination. Laws in Austria and Trinidad and Tobago, for example, make this explicit by specifically prohibiting the interference with an individual's rights, *inter alia*, on the ground of race.

Some States have adopted legislation in order to ensure that their political systems are generally free of racial discrimination. In Panama, for instance, the constitution makes it unlawful to form political parties, *inter alia*, on the ground of race. Moreover, the electoral code states that political parties should not discriminate on the ground of race in their admission of members. In Portugal, the constitution indicates that deputies convicted by a court of participating in organizations linked to Fascist idealogy shall forfeit their mandate. The constitution also lists a number of principles governing the conduct of election campaigns, including freedom in canvassing votes, equal treatment and opportunity for all candidates and the impartial treatment of all candidates by the public authorities.

Freedom of association and the right to assembly are provided for all, without distinction of race, by such States as Trinidad and Tobago and Tuvalu. Some States seek to protect the rights of individuals as members of an association. In Panama, a law provides that the beliefs of members of peasant organizations must be respected, regardless, *inter alia*, of race. In the United Kingdom of Great Britain and Northern Ireland, associations may not discriminate in admitting applicants or in the terms on which they will admit them. It is also provided that associations may not discriminate in granting to members access to any benefits of the association, nor may any member be arbitrarily deprived of his membership or made subject to any other detriment simply on the ground of race.

On the other hand, some States take steps to prohibit associations that promote racial discrimination. In Spain, associations formed for the promotion of racial discrimination are viewed as illegal. Similarly, Portugal prohibits Fascist organizations and Panama does not permit associations based on the premise of the superiority of any race. States such as Bulgaria, France and Iran provide for the punishment of individuals who either form or participate in the activities of associations such as these. In France, these types of associations can be dissolved and become null and void.

Freedom of expression is guaranteed to every person in, for example, Cyprus and Nigeria, and certain States explicitly state that it shall be enjoyed without distinction as to race. However, steps are also taken to prohibit the use of freedom of expression to promote racism. In Australia and New Zealand, for example, it is prohibited to publish an advertisement that indicates an intention to perform an act in breach of the laws against racial discrimination. In the United Kingdom of Great Britain and Northern Ireland, no one may advertise an intention to perform an act of racial discrimination, whether such act be unlawful or not. In Portugal, advertisements must not encourage, *inter alia*, racial discrimination. In Mexico, the broadcast of anything racially discriminatory is prohibited, as is the broadcast of anything which might bring ridicule to any person.

Freedom from discrimination in employment is also specifically guaranteed in some texts. In Australia, France, New Zealand and the United Kingdom, one may not refuse to employ or dismiss another on the ground of race. In the United Kingdom, it is stipulated that professional bodies and training courses responsible for conferring the appropriate qualifications may not withhold them on the ground of race, and the laws of Australia, Canada, Finland, New Zealand and the United Kingdom indicate that discrimination as to the conditions of work of employees is prohibited. In Canada, legislation provides that companies should pinpoint and, if necessary, correct by special measures and accommodation of differences, any conditions of disadvantage in employment experienced by racial minority groups.

Access to housing is another area where discrimination is prohibited. In Australia, Canada, New Zealand and the United Kingdom, it is prohibited for individuals to be denied access to property or to be discriminated against regarding the terms on which property is offered simply on the ground of race. These countries also prohibit the ill-treatment of occupants such as by depriving them of benefits they might otherwise have had and arbitrarily evicting them on the ground of race. In Dominica, it is indicated that a landlord may not withhold his licence on the ground of race, nor may an individual be harassed in Canada on the same ground.

Education is another area where discrimination is often specifically prohibited. In Cuba and Panama, all educational establishments are open to all without distinction of race. In Brazil, Colombia, New Zealand and the United Kingdom, it is specifically prohibited to bar the entrance of a student to an educational establishment on the ground of race. As indicated by the laws of Venezuela, the only limitation to access to education should be aptitude. In order to ensure that language is not an impediment to education, students in the Union of Soviet Socialist Republics may choose their language of instruction. In Ecuador, it is stipulated that the indigenous population should be taught in its own language.

Education is an area where the fight against racial discrimination can be carried out. In Portugal, for example, the law states that education shall be used to eradicate all socio-economic prejudices. In Ecuador, the educational system is obliged to impart to children a greater understanding of their culture and society. Colombia shares this position and further stipulates that education should help forge greater links between the various groups in society. In Mexico, education is used to develop a sense of brotherhood in all citizens.

Many States have recognized the right of access to public services or facilities and have legislated in order to ensure that the right is enjoyed by all without discrimination. In Finland, for example, it is provided that anyone who does not serve another in the normal course of his employment, on the ground of racial discrimination, shall be punished. The laws of some other countries differ in two material respects. In Australia, Canada, New Zealand and the United Kingdom, for instance, even when the discrimination impeding an individual's enjoyment of this right is performed outside the normal course of the discriminator's employment, it is generally prohibited. Also, in these same countries, as in countries such as Brazil, Denmark and Norway, the sort of discrimination prohibited is more explicitly stated. They generally prohibit any person from barring another access to, or forcing another to cease the enjoyment of any services, facilities or places generally open to the public solely on the ground of race. Many of those countries also indicate that discrimination in the terms on which such access will be granted is prohibited. In an attempt to facilitate the application of these laws, the laws of New Zealand and the United Kingdom give examples of the sorts of facilities and places to which these laws shall be applicable.

*B. Specific Institutions for the Promotion of Racial Tolerance and Harmony.* Some States have legislated to provide protective measures and institutions so as to facilitate the investigation of problems before they become too acute. Such measures and institutions also provide a mechanism for the mitigation or correction of any situations of discrimination that may arise. Commissions of this nature have been established in Australia, Canada and the United Kingdom of Great Britain and Northern Ireland. They undertake a variety of programmes under the general objective of striving to improve racial relations and promoting equality for all people. They have the task of creating, conducting or supporting research and educational programmes; they monitor the implementation of anti-discriminatory laws and impart their specialized knowledge and advice to other persons interested in the eradication of discrimination. In Australia, the subsidiary Community Relations Council assists the Commission by making recommendations to it as regards various relevant issues, either at request of the Commission or Minister or of its own volition.

Institutions such as the Commissions are also mandated to accept, investigate and try to settle complaints of discrimination, which they often do with the aid of subsidiary conciliatory machinery. These institutions are not merely passive but are entitled to act *suo motu* if they think that the circumstances so warrant.

*C. Recourse Procedures.* Recourse procedures before the courts are available for the protection of the individual's human rights in general, and thus for violations based on racial discrimination (in Venezuela, for example), and they are provided for in some States with specific reference to racial discrimination. In Mauritius, complaints of racial discrimination may be taken to the Supreme Court; in the Federal Republic of Germany, they may be taken to the Federal Constitutional Court. In Nigeria access is provided via the High Courts and in the United Kingdom of Great Britain and Northern Ireland via the county courts, which, for the purposes of handling racial discrimination, are entitled to grant the same sorts of remedies as the High Courts.

Many informal avenues of recourse have also been provided by some States. These are often cheaper and quicker than the formal ones and are therefore essential to an individual already suffering disadvantage. The conciliatory machinery of Australia and New Zealand are examples of such avenues of recourse. Countries such as the Federal Republic of Germany, New Zealand and the United Kingdom also provide access via such specialized bodies as industrial or equal opportunity tribunals. The institution of the Ombudsman in countries such as Austria, Denmark and Portugal provides a further avenue of recourse, while countries such as Portugal and Venezuela preserve the right of the individual to petition anybody in order to protect his rights and freedoms.

A number of specific measures have been undertaken by some States to facilitate access to recourse procedures for all sectors of the population. In Venezuela, the constitution provides that there should be laws ensuring that even those without means will be able to enjoy access. In the United Kingdom an individual contemplating or having actually commenced proceedings may seek assistance from the Commission for Racial Equality, which will grant it only if the circumstances of the case so warrant. As a further aid to complainants in pursuit of a case, the Secretary of State of the United Kingdom is entitled to prescribe forms in which alleged discriminators should be questioned. With the same goal in mind, the Human Rights Commission of Australia and the Conciliator of New Zealand may undertake investigations, either on complaint or *suo moto*, if they feel it appropriate in the circumstances. The Human Rights Commission of Australia is also entitled to convene compulsory conferences in order to fully ascertain the facts of a disputed situation. Within the general intention of facilitating access for complainants, individuals in countries such as Mauritius, Nigeria and Tuvalu do not have to allege that they have been actual victims of discrimination; it is enough that they allege that they are "likely to be". In Australia, it is indicated that where civil proceedings are undertaken to seek a remedy the individual has to prove his case to the reasonable satisfaction of the court only.

*D. Remedies.* Remedies in most countries consist of the possibility of obtaining redress for the violation of one's rights, as well as the possibility of ensuring that steps are taken to terminate ongoing infringements and to prohibit any potential infringements. In Mauritius and Nigeria, the courts are authorized to secure the enjoyment of rights by issuing such writs and making such orders and directions as they consider to be appropriate. Such wide discretion is also provided for in the United Kingdom of Great Britain and Northern Ireland, where complaint of racial discrimination may be pursued in court in the same manner as any claim in tort or for breach of statutory duty.

Some countries specify at least a few of the remedies available to individuals whose rights have been violated. In Hungary, for instance, an individual may apply to court to establish the commission of a wrong or for some other forms of satisfaction, such as a declaration by the wrongdoer. In Australia and Canada, specific performance may be sought in order to ensure that a person responsible for a discriminatory act takes measures to compensate for those actions. A variety of other measures may be applied for, some of which appear to be designed to restore the status quo. In Australia, for example, if the discrimination resulted in the making of a contract, such contract may be annulled or have its terms varied. In Canada, a complainant can ensure that opportunities and privileges one was formerly denied should be made available.

Financial compensation is a remedy that is often provided for. In Hungary, for instance, anyone offended in the enjoyment of his rights may apply to court for damages. Such recourse is most often used to cover material losses such as, in the case of Australia, loss of benefits. In Canada one may claim for lost wages and expenses incurred in obtaining alternative goods and services where such losses were brought about by acts of discrimination.

Other remedies exist which are more suited to the termination of ongoing breaches or prohibiting potential ones. In New Zealand, for example, one may seek that an assurance be given to the conciliator that all discriminatory practices will be discontinued and will not be resumed in the future. In Australia, Canada and Hungary, one may apply for an injunction to prevent future breaches of one's rights. Although similar in object and effect, the latter remedy differs from the former in that it is imposed on the discrimination by a judicial body.

*E. Penalties.* In addition to declaring that individuals are entitled to enjoy certain rights free of discrimination, and providing remedies for those whose rights have been violated, some States have sought to secure the enjoyment of rights by imposing various types of penalties for certain acts of racial discrimination. For instance, in Brazil it is a punishable offence to refuse lodging or goods to another person on account of his race. In France and Norway also, discrimination in the provision of services is punishable. Many States punish individuals not only for acts of racial discrimination, but also for advocating or promoting racial discrimination, for example by acts of incitement, agitation and propaganda aimed at arousing racial hatred. Threats of violence, provocation and defamation with the same intent are also punished. Some States impose punishments even in the absence of intent; in the United Kingdom of Great Britain and Northern Ireland, an individual is punished for his actions if, having regard to all the circumstances, racial hatred was likely to be aroused by such actions. A similar law exists in Hungary. In the Netherlands, acts of incitement are punished if done with reasonable cause to suspect what their effect will be, if actual intent is proven, the punishment is doubled.

A wide variety of penalties are employed by States in their attempts to secure the general enjoyment of rights. In the Netherlands, for instance, if a person is convicted for discrimination in the course of his occupation twice within five years, such person may be barred from continuing the same occupation. Similarly, in Brazil, if it is found that discrimination is practised in allowing access to public service, the person in charge of the selection procedure is stripped of his functions. In Ecuador, where a public body is found to be engaging in acts of discrimination the director is imprisoned and loses his political rights for the duration of the prison term. The conviction of an individual in Turkey for using an association to promote discrimination, even if he is later pardoned, bars that individual from later forming another association. In Poland, if discriminatory views are expressed in a publication, the authorities are allowed to confiscate the instruments and objects employed in its production, even if they are not owned by the perpetrator.

However, the most widespread penalties for discrimination include prison sentences, such as may be imposed in Cyprus and Ecuador, or the payment of fines, as is provided for in countries like Finland and France. In Brazil, Denmark, Iran and New Zealand the imposition of either one of these penalties is provided for, and in countries like Dominica, the Federal Republic of Germany, Pakistan and the United Kingdom, the simultaneous imposition of both penalties for the same offence is allowed. In the Byelorussian Soviet Socialist Republic, for example, a term of either imprisonment or of exile may be imposed, and in Czechoslovakia, some other reformatory measure may be applied instead of imprisonment.

Certain factors are viewed by some States as aggravating the normal offence of discrimination and therefore warranting the imposition of stiffer penalties. The use of violence is viewed in this way by such States as Bulgaria, Czechoslovakia, Ecuador and Hungary. Also, in Bulgaria, any individual who instigates, sets up or leads a mob or association to acts of discrimination is punished more severely than the ordinary members of such a group. In Austria, Cyprus, Pakistan and Poland, the use of publications or some other media to promote discrimination attracts greater punishment than would otherwise be the case. In many countries severe punishment is provided for persons guilty of genocide. In Czechoslovakia, such a crime is punished by seven times the term of imprisonment than is normally imposed for discrimination. In Finland and the Federal Republic of Germany, individuals convicted for genocide may be punished with life imprisonment, and in the Bahamas, Bulgaria, Czechoslovakia and Hungary the death penalty is provided for.

*F. Fight against Apartheid.* Many States, in particular in their reports submitted under the International Convention on the Elimination of All Forms of Racial Discrimination, clearly stated their opposition to apartheid and referred to their legislation in that sense, including that establishing in national law the crime of apartheid and laws or decisions cutting off economic relations with South Africa. India provided the text of its Anti-Apartheid Act, which gives force of law to those provisions from the International Convention for the Suppression and Punishment of the Crime of Apartheid annexed to the Act, and Cuba submitted a text providing penalties for certain acts done for the purpose of instituting or maintaining the domination of one racial group over another. Bulgarian legislation provides penalties for the practice of apartheid and Venezuela reported that the International Convention on the Suppression and Punishment of the Crime of Apartheid had become part of Venezuelan internal law. Very severe penalties are imposed for the crime of apartheid; for example, the death penalty is provided for in Bulgaria and India and long prison sentences in Cuba.

Several States reported severing economic relations with South Africa in the context of their activities against racial discrimination. Denmark provided the text of a Parliamentary Resolution dated 20 May 1984 on tightening the policy of sanctions against South Africa, and of a bill on prohibition of new Danish investments in South Africa and Namibia. Qatar submitted legislation halting petroleum exports to South Africa and severing all economic, trade and commercial relations with that country.

*Conclusions.* The global compilation of legislation against racial discrimination is one element in the Second Decade's overall effort aimed at strengthening the protection against racial discrimination on the national level. Other elements, as mentioned above, include, on the one hand, the preparation of basic reference texts such as the "model legislation", a handbook on recourse procedures and the preparation of a manual of existing national institutions and, on the other hand, steps designed to encourage or facilitate the adoption of those measures, such as training courses for legislative draftsmen, regional workshops on the adoption of legislation, and seminars on community relations Commissions and their functions.

The texts submitted for the global consultation, taken together with the reports of seminars and training courses held on these matters and the information submitted in relation to international instruments in this field, provide a good basis for the preparation of "model texts". It is the Secretary-

General's intention to proceed as rapidly as resources permit with the preparation of the "model texts" and with the organization of the seminars or training courses designed to encourage their adoption.

## EQUALITY IN THE ADMINISTRATION OF JUSTICE.

The principle of equality for all in the administration of justice is set out in article 10 of the Universal Declaration of Human Rights as follows:

*Article 10.* Everyone is entitled in full equality to a fair and public hearing by an independent and impartial tribunal, in the determination of his rights and obligations and of any criminal charge against him.

Since the implementation of all human rights and fundamental freedoms depends upon the proper administration of justice, the principle is of great importance. Its meaning is elaborated further in articles 14 and 15 of the International Covenant on Civil and Political Rights, which respectively set out the elements of a fair trial and prohibit the retroactive application of penal law:

*Article 14.* 1. All persons shall be equal before the courts and tribunals. In the determination of any criminal charge against him, or of his rights and obligations in a suit at law, everyone shall be entitled to a fair and public hearing by a competent, independent and impartial tribunal established by law. The Press and the public may be excluded from all or part of a trial for reasons of morals, public order (*ordre public*) or national security in a democratic society, or when the interest of the private lives of the parties so requires, or to the extent strictly necessary in the opinion of the court in special circumstances where publicity would prejudice the interests of justice; but any judgment rendered in a criminal case or in a suit at law shall be made public except where the interest of juvenile persons otherwise requires or the proceedings concern matrimonial disputes or the guardianship of children.

2. Everyone charged with a criminal offence shall have the right to be presumed innocent until proved guilty according to law.

3. In the determination of any criminal charge against him, everyone shall be entitled to the following minimum guarantees, in full equality:

(a) To be informed promptly and in detail in a language which he understands of the nature and cause of the charge against him;

(b) To have adequate time and facilities for the preparation of his defence and to communicate with counsel of his own choosing;

(c) To be tried without undue delay;

(d) To be tried in his presence, and to defend himself in person or through legal assistance of his own choosing; to be informed, if he does not have legal assistance, of this right; and to have legal assistance, of this right; and to have legal assistance assigned to him, in any case where the interests of justice so require, and without payment by him in any such case if he does not have sufficient means to pay for it;

(e) To examine, or have examined, the witnesses against him and to obtain the attendance and examination of witnesses on his behalf under the same conditions as witnesses against him;

(f) To have the free assistance of an interpreter if he cannot understand or speak the language used in court;

(g) Not to be compelled to testify against himself or to confess guilt.

4. In the case of juvenile persons, the procedure shall be such as will take account of their age and the desirability of promoting their rehabilitation.

5. Everyone convicted of a crime shall have the right to his conviction and sentence being reviewed by a higher tribunal according to law.

6. When a person has by a final decision been convicted of a criminal offence and when subsequently his conviction had been reversed or he had been pardoned on the ground that a new or newly discovered fact shows conclusively that there has been a miscarriage of justice, the person who has suffered punishment as a result of such conviction shall be compensated according to law, unless it is proved that the non-disclosure of the unknown fact in time is wholly or partly attributable to him.

7. No one shall be liable to be tried or punished again for an offence for which he has already been finally convicted or acquitted in accordance with the law and penal procedure of each country.

*Article 15.* 1. No one shall be held guilty of any criminal offence on account of any act or omission which did not constitute a criminal offence, under national or international law, at the time when it was committed. Nor shall a heavier penalty be imposed than the one that was applicable at the time when the criminal offence was committed. If, subsequent to the Commission of the offence, provision is made by law for the imposition of the lighter penalty, the offender shall benefit thereby.

2. Nothing in this article shall prejudice the trial and punishment of any person for any act or omission which, at the time when it was committed, was criminal according to general principles of law recognized by the community of nations.

Article 5 of the International Convention on the Elimination of All Forms of Racial Discrimination states:

In compliance with the fundamental obligations laid down in article 2 of this Convention, States Parties undertake to prohibit and to eliminate racial discrimination in all its forms and to guarantee the right of everyone, without distinction as to race, colour, or national or ethnic origin, to equality before the law, notably in the enjoyment of the following rights:

(a) The right to equal treatment before the tribunals and all other organs administering justice.

Article 16 of the Convention Relating to the Status of Refugees (see **REFUGEES**) provides that:

1. A refugee shall have free access to the courts of law on the territory of all Contracting States.

2. A refugee shall enjoy in the Contracting State in which he has his habitual residence the same treatment as a national in matters pertaining to access to the courts, including legal assistance and exemption from *cautio judicatum solvi.*

3. A refugee shall be accorded in the matters referred to

in paragraph 2 in countries other than that in which he has his habitual residence the treatment granted to a national of the country of his habitual residence.

The Convention Relating to the Status of Stateless Persons (see **STATELESSNESS**) contains a corresponding article 16.

After examining reports submitted by States parties to the International Covenant on Civil and Political Rights in accordance with article 40 of that instrument, the UN Human Rights Committee in 1984 adopted a general comment on article 14 setting out its views on the meaning of certain provisions, as follows (UN Doc. A/39/40, Annex VI, paras. 1–19):

The Committee notes that article 14 of the Covenant is of a complex nature and that different aspects of its provisions will need specific comments. All of these provisions are aimed at ensuring the proper administration of justice, and to this end uphold a series of individual rights such as equality before the courts and tribunals and the right to a fair and public hearing by a competent, independent and impartial tribunal established by law. Not all reports provided details on the legislative or other measures adopted specifically to implement each of the provisions of article 14.

In general, the reports of States parties fail to recognize that article 14 applies not only to procedures for the determination of criminal charges against individuals but also to procedures to determine their rights and obligations in a suit at law. Laws and practices dealing with these matters vary widely from State to State. This diversity makes it all the more necessary for States parties to provide all relevant information and to explain in greater detail how the concepts of "criminal charge" and "rights and obligations in a suit at law" are interpreted in relation to their respective legal systems.

The Committee would find it useful if, in their future reports, States parties could provide more detailed information on the steps taken to ensure that equality before the courts, including equal access to courts, fair and public hearings and competence, impartiality and independence of the judiciary are established by law and guaranteed in practice. In particular, States parties should specify the relevant constitutional and legislative texts which provide for the establishment of the courts and ensure that they are independent, impartial and competent, in particular with regard to the manner in which judges are appointed, the qualifications for appointment, and the duration of their terms of office; the conditions governing promotion, transfer and cessation of their functions and the actual independence of the judiciary from the executive branch and the legislature.

The provisions of article 14 apply to all courts and tribunals within the scope of that article whether ordinary or specialized. The Committee notes the existence, in many countries, of military or special courts which try civilians. This could present serious problems as far as the equitable, impartial and independent administration of justice is concerned. Quite often the reason for the establishment of such courts is to enable exceptional procedures to be applied which do not comply with normal standards of justice. While the Covenant does not prohibit such categories of courts, nevertheless the conditions which it lays down clearly indicate that the trying of civilians by such courts should be very exceptional and take place under conditions which genuinely afford the full guarantees stipulated in article 14. The Committee has noted a serious lack of information in this regard in the reports of some States parties whose judicial institutions include such courts for the trying of civilians. In some countries such military and special courts do not afford the strict guarantees of the proper administration of justice in accordance with the requirements of article 14 which are essential for the effective protection of human rights. If States parties decide in circumstances of a public emergency as contemplated by article 4 to derogate from normal procedures required under article 14, they should ensure that such derogations do not exceed those strictly required by the exigencies of the actual situation, and respect the other conditions in paragraph 1 of article 14.

The second sentence of article 14, paragraph 1, provides that "everyone shall be entitled to a fair and public hearing". Paragraph 3 of the article elaborates on the requirements of a "fair hearing" in regard to the determination of criminal charges. However, the requirements of paragraph 3 are minimum guarantees, the observance of which is not always sufficient to ensure the fairness of a hearing as required by paragraph 1.

The publicity of hearings is an important safeguard in the interest of the individual and of society at large. At the same time article 14, paragraph 1, acknowledges that courts have the power to exclude all or part of the public for reasons spelt out in that paragraph. It should be noted that, apart from such exceptional circumstances, the Committee considers that a hearing must be open to the public in general, including members of the press, and must not, for instance, be limited only to a particular category of persons. It should be noted that, even in cases in which the public is excluded from the trial, the judgment must, with certain strictly defined exceptions, be made public.

The Committee has noted a lack of information regarding article 14, paragraph 2, and, in some cases, has even observed that the presumption of innocence, which is fundamental to the protection of human rights, is expressed in very ambiguous terms or entails conditions which render it ineffective. By reason of the presumption of innocence, the burden of proof of the charge is on the prosecution and the accused has the benefit of doubt. No guilt can be presumed until the charge has been proved beyond reasonable doubt. Further, the presumption of innocence implies a right to be treated in accordance with this principle. It is therefore a duty for all public authorities to refrain from prejudging the outcome of a trial.

Among the minimum guarantees in criminal proceedings prescribed by paragraph 3, the first concerns the right of everyone to be informed in a language which he understands of the charge against him (subparagraph (a)). The Committee notes that State reports often do not explain how this right is respected and ensured. Article 14, subparagraph 3 (a) applies to all cases of criminal charges, including those of persons not in detention. The Committee notes further that the right to be informed of the charge "promptly" requires that information is given in the manner described as soon as the charge is first made by a competent authority. In the opinion of the Committee this right must arise when in the course of an investigation a court or an authority of the prosecution decides to take procedural steps against a person suspected of a crime or publicly names him as such. The specific requirements of subparagraph 3 (a) may be met by stating the charge either orally or in writing, provided that the information indicates both the law and the alleged facts on which it is based.

Subparagraph 3 (b) provides that the accused must have adequate time and facilities for the preparation of his defence and to communicate with counsel of his own choosing. What is "adequate time" depends on the circumstance of each case, but the facilities must include access to documents and other evidence which the accused requires to prepare his case, as well as the opportunity to engage and communicate with counsel. When the accused does not want to defend himself in person or request a person or an association of his choice, he should be able to have recourse to a lawyer. Furthermore, this subparagraph requires counsel to communicate with the accused in conditions giving full respect for the confidentiality of their communications. Lawyers should be able to counsel and to represent their clients in accordance with their established professional standards and judgement without any restrictions, influences, pressures or undue interference from any quarter.

Subparagraph 3 (c) provides that the accused shall be tried without undue delay. This guarantee relates not only to the time by which a trial should commence, but also the time by which it should end and judgement be rendered; all stages must take place "without undue delay". To make this right effective, a procedure must be available in order to ensure that the trial will proceed "without undue delay", both in first instance and on appeal.

Not all reports have dealt with all aspects of the right of defence as defined in subparagraph 3 (d). The Committee has not always received sufficient information concerning the protection of the right of the accused to be present during the determination of any charge against him nor how the legal system assures his right either to defend himself in person or to be assisted by counsel of his own choosing, or what arrangements are made if a person does not have sufficient means to pay for legal assistance. The accused or his lawyer must have the right to act diligently and fearlessly in pursuing all available defences and the right to challenge the conduct of the case if they believe it to be unfair. When exceptionally for justified reasons trials in absentia are held, strict observance of the rights of the defence is all the more necessary.

Subparagraph 3 (e) states that the accused shall be entitled to examine or have examined the witnesses against him and to obtain the attendance and examination of witnesses on his behalf under the same conditions as witnesses against him. This provision is designed to guarantee to the accused the same legal powers of compelling the attendance of witnesses and of examining or cross-examining any witnesses as are available to the prosecution.

Subparagraph 3 (f) provides that if the accused cannot understand or speak the language used in court he is entitled to the assistance of an interpreter free of any charge. This right is independent of the outcome of the proceedings and applies to aliens as well as to nationals. It is of basic importance in cases in which ignorance of the language used by a court or difficulty in understanding may constitute a major obstacle to the right of defence.

Subparagraph 3 (g) provides that the accused may not be compelled to testify against himself or to confess guilt. In considering this safeguard the provisions of article 7 and article 10, paragraph 1, should be borne in mind. In order to compel the accused to confess or to testify against himself frequently methods which violate these provisions are used. The law should require that evidence provided by means of such methods or any other form of compulsion is wholly unacceptable.

In order to safeguard the rights of the accused under par-

agraphs 1 and 3 of article 14, judges should have authority to consider any allegations made of violations of the rights of the accused during any stage of the prosecution.

Article 14, paragraph 4, provides that in the case of juvenile persons, the procedure shall be such as will take account of their age and the desirability of promoting their rehabilitation. Not many reports have furnished sufficient information concerning such relevant matters as the minimum age at which a juvenile may be charged with a criminal offence, the maximum age at which a person is still considered to be a juvenile, the existence of special courts and procedures, the laws governing procedures against juveniles and how all these special arrangements for juveniles take account of "the desirability of promoting their rehabilitation". Juveniles are to enjoy at least the same guarantees and protection as are accorded to adults under article 14.

Article 14, paragraph 5, provides that everyone convicted of a crime shall have the right to his conviction and sentence being reviewed by a higher tribunal according to law. Particular attention is drawn to the other language versions of the word "crime" ("infraction", "delito", "prestuplenie") which show that the guarantee is not confined only to the most serious offences. In this connection, not enough information has been provided concerning the procedures of appeal, in particular the access to and the powers of reviewing tribunals, what requirements must be satisfied to appeal against a judgement and the way in which the procedures before review tribunals take account of the fair and public hearing requirements of paragraph 1 of article 14.

Article 14, paragraph 6, provides for compensation according to law in certain cases of a miscarriage of justice as described therein. It seems from many State reports that this right is often not observed or insufficiently guaranteed by domestic legislation. States should, where necessary, supplement their legislation in this area in order to bring it into line with the provisions of the Covenant.

In considering State reports differing views have often been expressed as to the scope of paragraph 7 of article 14. Some States parties have even felt the need to make reservations in relation to procedures for the resumption of criminal cases. It seems to the Committee that most States parties make a clear distinction between a resumption of a trial justified by exceptional circumstances and a retrial prohibited pursuant to the principal of *ne bis in idem* as contained in paragraph 7. This understanding of the meaning of *ne bis in idem* may encourage States parties to reconsider their reservations to article 14, paragraph 7.

***Study on Equality in the Administration of Justice.*** At its 1963 session, the UN Sub-Commission on Prevention of Discrimination and Protection of Minorities decided (resolution 1 [XV]) to undertake a study of equality in the administration of justice, in accordance with article 10 of the Universal Declaration of Human Rights, and appointed one of its members, Mr. Mohammed A. Abu Rannat (Sudan), as Special Rapporteur for the study. The study was completed and presented to the Sub-Commission in 1969 and later was published under the title *Study of Equality in the Administration of Justice* (UN publication, Sales no. E.71.XIV.3).

The study, deriving as it does from article 10 of the Universal Declaration of Human Rights, deals not with substantive law but with equal entitlement to a fair hearing. It notes that, while many legal systems have recognized the importance of equal justice, not all have stressed the elaboration or formal statement of the necessary guarantees, and some have failed to provide the necessary judicial organization or procedures.

Chapter II of the study explores the implications of a fair hearing with a view to indicating the accepted norms so that departures from those norms may be accurately identified. In this connection, it is recognized that the general elements of a fair hearing, which can be derived from the text of article 10, are elaborated in articles 14 and 15 of the International Covenant on Civil and Political Rights.

In chapter III, the grounds on which discrimination operates in the administration of justice are described; they include race or color, sex, language, religion, political or other opinion, national origin or nationality, property, birth or social origin or position, other status (such as that of minors, ministers of religion and diplomats), and the status of the territory to which an individual belongs.

In chapter IV, the wide variety of measures adopted by various States to combat such discrimination is described, including arrangements designed to encourage the total independence and impartiality of the courts, of judges, or jurors, and of members of the legal profession. A number of specific governmental institutions and procedures found in practice to promote equality in the administration of justice—for instance, by improving the working efficiency of the courts and reducing judicial delay—are also described.

Chapter V sets out the Special Rapporteur's conclusions and recommendations with regard to methods of dealing effectively with discrimination in the administration of justice: first, on the national level by the regulation of matters affecting the administration of justice by means of constitutional or statutory provisions or by rules of court and, second, on the international level by the preparation of a Convention, a Declaration, or both. With a view to facilitating decisions in the matter, the special rapporteur prepared a comprehensive series of draft principles on equality in the administration of justice for consideration by the Sub-Commission and its superior bodies.

The Sub-Commission, after examining the study as a whole, considered and amended the draft principles and forwarded them to the Commission on human rights (resolution 3 [XXIII]). In 1972, the Commission decided to give them high priority at its 1973 session and requested the Secretary-General to obtain the views and comments of the governments of member States on them, and comments on the form in which they should be set forth. At its 1973 session, the Commission was again unable to deal with them, and some members pointed out that there was a lack of consensus among governments as to their disposition.

Accordingly, on recommendation of the Commission, the General Assembly on 14 December 1973 (resolution 3144 [XXVIII]) called upon member States "to give due consideration, in formulating legislation and taking other measures affecting equality in the administration of justice, to the draft principles, which may be regarded as setting forth valuable norms, with a view to arriving at the elaboration of an appropriate international Declaration or instrument."

***Draft Principles on Equality in the Administration of Justice.*** The draft principles, as formulated and adopted by the Sub-Commission on Prevention of Discrimination and Protection of Minorities on the basis of texts proposed by the Special Rapporteur, are as follows:

### 1. General Principles

*Principle 1.* To the fullest extent consistent with the nature of the question, matters connected with the administration of justice shall be regulated by constitutional or statutory provisions or by rules of court, whichever may be appropriate, and not by executive decisions. Written constitutions, where they exist, shall lay down at least the basic general rules affecting the administration of justice.

*Principle 2.* The State shall have the exclusive power and obligation to administer justice to persons within its jurisdiction.

*Principle 3.* National laws concerning the rights to equal access to the courts and to equality before the law in general shall provide specifically that these rights shall be accorded to all, without distinction of any kind, such as race, colour, sex, language, religion, political or other opinion, national or social origin, property, birth or other status.

*Principle 4.* In the allocation of jurisdiction and determination of competence of tribunals of whatever characterization, no such allocation or determination shall be made upon the basis of race, colour, sex, language, religion, political or other opinion national or social origin, property, birth or other status.

*Principle 5.* Being essential requirements for promoting equality in the administration of justice, the independence and impartiality of members of all levels of the judiciary shall be ensured by the laws and practices governing their training, selection, jurisdiction, oath or affirmation, privileges and immunities, tenure of office, transfer, salaries and pensions, the limitations placed on their non-judicial activities, the circumstances disqualifying them from acting in particular cases, the protection against improper influences accorded to them by the criminal law and the sanctions applicable to them in the event of their failing to display independence and impartiality in performing their functions.

*Principle 6.* Being essential requirements for promoting equality in the administration of justice, the independence and impartiality of jurors and assessors, where they function, shall be ensured by the laws and practices affecting their selection and compensation, their oath or affirmation, their immunities, the incompatibility of certain activities with service as juror or assessor, the challenges which may be made to their acting in particular cases, the protection against improper influences accorded to them by the criminal law and the sanctions applicable to them in the event of their failing to display independence and impartiality in performing their functions.

*Principle 7.* Being essential requirements for promoting equality in the administration of justice, the independence of lawyers practising before courts and their impartiality in according their services to potential clients shall be ensured by the laws and practices affecting the relationship between such lawyers and their organizations, on the one hand, and the State, on the other, the incompatibility of certain activities with the profession of the law, the circumstances under which a practising lawyer may not accept a case, the grounds on which a practising lawyer may not refuse his services to a client, the access of the individual to his lawyer and the privacy of communication between the two, the preservation of the secrecy of information received by lawyers during professional dealing with their clients, the immunities of lawyers and the sanctions applicable to them.

*Principle 8.* National laws shall ensure that no one shall be denied equal access to the judiciary and to the legal profession, without distinction based upon race, colour, sex, language, religion, political or other opinion, national or social origin, property, birth or other status.

*Principle 9.* Where the State or any other body subsidizes the training of judges, lawyers and court interpreters, they shall do so without distinction of any kind, such as race, colour, sex, language, religion, political or other opinion, national or social origin, property, birth or other status.

*Principle 10.* Judges, jurors, assessors, accused persons, other parties to judicial proceedings, lawyers, witnesses and interpreters shall be permitted to make an affirmation instead of taking an oath if they object to the religious character of any oath required of them in connexion with their roles in the administration of justice.

*Principle 11.* National laws concerning legal aid for the poor shall develop such aid to the utmost extent consistent with the economic resources of the country concerned. Needy persons shall be entitled to be relieved of all charges and expenses in judicial proceedings and to free aid for their defence.

*Principle 12.* Provisions shall be made through legal aid schemes or otherwise for ensuring adequate legal representation to persons whose political opinions may otherwise be a disadvantage to them in judicial proceedings.

*Principle 13.* Aliens in a country shall have the benefits of legal aid to the same extent as citizens.

*Principle 14.* National laws concerning appeals to higher courts shall include provision for appeals on grounds of the discriminatory application of laws relating to jurisdiction and procedure as well as of substantive law.

*Principle 15.* With a view to eliminating discrimination arising out of the status of the territory to which a person belongs, full application shall be given to the Declaration on the Granting of Independence to Colonial Countries and Peoples, proclaimed by the United Nations General Assembly in resolution 1514 (XV) of 14 December 1960, which proclaims the necessity of bringing to an end colonialism in all its forms.

## 2. Principles Relating to All Courts

*Principle 16.* Everyone, without distinction of any kind, such as race, colour, sex, language, religion, political or other opinion, national or social origin, property, birth or other status, shall be guaranteed the following rights in the examination of any criminal charge against him, whether it relates to a crime falling within ordinary jurisdiction or within military or special jurisdiction, or in the determination of his rights and responsibilities through civil, administrative or other judicial proceedings:

(i) The right to access to tribunals;

(ii) The right to be heard by his lawful judge, that is to say, by the competent tribunal previously established by law or established under pre-existing law and not by a tribunal assigned ad hoc or specially set up to hear his case;

(iii) The right to be heard by an independent and impartial tribunal;

(iv) The right to be assisted and represented by counsel of his own choosing;

(v) The right to a prompt and speedy hearing, subject to his being given adequate time to prepare his case;

(vi) The right, either in person or through counsel, to present his case and to produce and examine witnesses and other evidence, or to have such witnesses or other evidence produced and examined;

(vii) The right to a public hearing, subject to the possibility that the press and the public may be excluded from all or part of a hearing for reasons of morals, public order, or national security in a democratic society, or when the interest of the private lives of the parties so requires, or to the extent strictly necessary in the opinion of the court in special circumstances where publicity would prejudice the interests of justice;

(viii) The right to have the decision in his case based only on the evidence placed before the court and known to all the parties;

(ix) The right to have the decision on his case rendered in public, except where the interest of juveniles otherwise requires or the proceedings concern matrimonial disputes or the guardianship of children;

(x) The right to appeal to a higher court.

*Principle 17.* As regards the administration of justice, married women shall be ensured the right to an independent domicile.

*Principle 18.* The distribution of courts within a country and the movements of itinerant judges shall be determined by the distribution of population, subject to the special needs of persons living in isolated areas.

*Principle 19.* In view of the hardship caused in particular to poor persons by delays in judicial proceedings, measures shall be taken, appropriate to the circumstances prevailing in each country concerned, to reduce the delays facing the courts in reaching and dealing with cases to the minimum consistent with the right of accused or other parties to judicial proceedings adequately to prepare and present their cases.

*Principle 20.* National laws relating to the place of hearing or trial shall provide for the change of place of hearing or trial whenever such change is necessary to ensure a fair hearing or trial.

*Principle 21.* Measures taken for the special protection of minors in judicial proceedings shall not diminish their right to equality in the administration of justice.

*Principle 22.* Whatever the jurisdiction of such religious courts as may exist in a country, civil courts shall offer a forum for the settlement of all justifiable disputes. No person shall be without a court to resort to, due to his not belonging to any of the religions whose courts have exclusive jurisdiction over the matter at issue.

*Principle 23.* Interpretation shall be provided free for all accused persons and other parties to judicial proceedings if they do not have a command of the language of the Court. Analogous arrangements shall be made free for accused persons and other parties to judicial proceedings who are handicapped in speech or hearing.

*Principle 24.* The right to a public hearing may be restricted by laws framed so as to prohibit, prior to the final decision of the court, publicity prejudicial to accused persons or other parties to judicial proceedings.

*Principle 25.* Courts shall be required to give their reasons when rendering judgement.

### 3. Principles Relating to Criminal Courts

*Principle 26.* Everyone against whom a criminal charge is preferred shall be guaranteed, in addition to the above-mentioned rights, the following rights, without distinction of any kind, such as race, colour, sex, language, religion, political or other opinion, national or social origin, property, birth or other status:

(i) The right to be presumed innocent until proved guilty according to law;

(ii) The right to be informed promptly and in detail in a language which he understands of the nature and cause of the charge against him;

(iii) The right to be informed of his right to defend himself either in person or through counsel of his choosing;

(iv) The right to have legal assistance assigned to him in any case, if the interests of justice and of the person involved in the judicial proceedings so require, without payment if he does not have sufficient means to pay for it;

(v) The right to compulsory representation by counsel in proceedings for crimes of a grave nature;

(vi) The right to examine, or have examined, the witnesses and documentary evidence against him and to obtain documentary evidence and the attendance and examination of witnesses on his behalf;

(vii) The right to have the free assistance of an interpreter if he cannot understand or speak the language used in court;

(viii) The right not to be compelled to testify against himself or to confess guilt.

*Principle 27.* Judges shall explain to accused persons their essential procedural rights during trial and their right of appeal.

*Principle 28.* National laws concerning provisional release from custody pending or during trial shall be so framed as to eliminate any requirement of pecuniary guarantees and shall be designed also so as to reduce detention pending or during trial to a minimum.

*Principle 29.* No one shall be compelled to incriminate himself. No accused person or witness shall be subject to physical or psychic pressure, including anything calculated to impair his will or violate his dignity. Evidence obtained in breach of this right shall not be admissible, and the extraction of purported confessions by means of such influences shall be an offence. No one shall be compelled to testify against his spouse, ascendants or descendants.

***EQUALITY OF MEN AND WOMEN.*** Although the principle of equality of men and women has won almost universal acceptance, full equality between men and women is far from being realized in practice.

The Copenhagen World Conference of the United Nations Decade for Women, in 1980, the mid-point of the decade, interpreted equality as meaning not only legal equality and the elimination of *de jure* discrimination but also equality of rights, responsibilities, and opportunities for the participation of women in development, both as beneficiaries and as active agents. Later, the Nairobi Forward-Looking Strategies for the Advancement of Women, adopted by the World Conference to Review and Appraise the Achievements of the United Nations Decade for Women, which met in Nairobi, Kenya, from 15 to 26 July 1985, further clarified the meaning of equality as "both a goal and a means whereby individuals are accorded equal treatment under the law and equal opportunities to enjoy their rights and to develop their potential talents and skills so that they can participate in national political, economic, social and cultural development and can benefit from its results. For women in particular, equality means the realization of rights that have been denied as a result of cultural, institutional, behavioral and attitudinal discrimination. Equality is important for development and peace because national and global inequities perpetuate themselves and increase tensions of all types."

The United Nations is committed by its Charter to the principle of equality of men and women and has explored new ways of promoting and protecting that principle. In the preamble of the charter, the peoples of the United Nations proclaim their determination "to reaffirm faith in fundamental human rights, in the worth and dignity of the human person, in the equal rights of men and women and of nations large and small." One of the purposes of the United Nations, as set out in article 1 of the Charter, is to achieve "international co-operation in solving international problems of an economic, social, cultural or humanitarian character, and in promoting and encouraging respect for human rights and fundamental freedoms for all without distinction." Article 8 provides that "the United Nations shall place no restrictions on the eligibility of men and women to participate in any capacity and under conditions of equality in its principal and subsidiary organs." Articles 13, 55, and 75 call for the realization of human rights and fundamental freedoms "for all without distinction as to race, sex, language or religion." Under article 56, member States have pledged themselves to take joint and separate action, in cooperation with the United Nations, to achieve these aims.

A number of specific problems confronting women in various parts of the world in their efforts to attain full equality with men have been dealt with in Conventions and recommendations adopted and opened for ratification or accession by the United Nations or one of its specialized agencies, such as the Convention for the Suppression of the Traffic in Persons and the Exploitation of the Prostitution of Others, approved by the General Assembly in 1949; the Supplementary Convention on the Abolition of Slavery, the Slave Trade, and Institutions and Practices Similar to Slavery, approved by a conference of plenipotentiaries in 1956; the Convention on the Political Rights of Women, approved by the General Assembly in 1952; the Convention on the Nationality of Married Women, approved by the General Assembly in 1957; the Convention on Consent to Marriage, Minimum Age for Marriage, and Registration of Marriages, approved by the General Assembly in 1962; the ILO Discrimination (Employment and Occupation) Convention, approved by the International Labor Conference in 1958; and the UNESCO Convention against Discrimination in Education, approved by the General Conference of UNESCO in 1958.

The Nairobi Forward-Looking Strategies for the Advancement of Women, proposes a number of concrete measures designed to overcome the many obstacles encountered in efforts to achieve the decade's goals and objectives for the advancement of women. These strategies reaffirm the international concern regarding the status of women and provide a framework for renewed commitment by the international community to the advancement of women and the elimination of gender-based discrimination.

In 1989, recognizing that equality for women is closely linked to their economic independence and noting that various affirmative action policies can accelerate the elimination of discrimination against women, the UN Economic and Social Council urged governments to give high priority to measures and temporary affirmative action programs that will more rapidly bring about equality in women's economic participation, in particular to programs that will ensure the following:

(a) women's access to the labor market and to education and training;

(b) elimination of sex segregation in the labor market and in education;

(c) women's participation in trade unions;

(d) equal pay for equal work;

(e) equal access to economic resources, including credit and membership in cooperatives; and

(f) improved conditions in the informal sector including, where desirable, the application of labor standards and the development or improvement of sex-disaggregated statistics that accurately reflect women's work in the informal economic sector.

The Council called upon the Commission on the Status of Women, in carrying out its review and appraisal of the implementation of the Nairobi Forward-Looking Strategies, to consider measures to accelerate the pace of achieving equality in economic and social participation, including the definition and compilation of benchmark statistical indicators that could be used for national, regional, and international reporting, as well as affirmative action programs.

***SEE ALSO*** *Disability; Minorities' Rights; Race; Racial Discrimination; Sexual Orientation; Slavery; Women's Rights.*

**BIBLIOGRAPHY.** Cook, Rebecca J. "International Human Rights Law Concerning Women: Case Notes and Comments," *Vanderbilt Journal of Transnational Law* 23, No. 4 (1990): 779–818. Scholarly article, in English.

Fredman, Sandra. "European Community Discrimination Law: A Critique," *Industrial Law Journal* 21, no. 2 (June 1992): 119–134. Scholarly article, in English.

Freeman, Marsha A. "Measuring Equality: A Comparative Perspective on Women's Legal Capacity and Constitutional Rights in Five Commonwealth Countries," *Commonwealth Law Bulletin* 16, no. 4 (Oct. 1990): 1418–1443. Scholarly article, in English.

Heinze, Eric. "Equality: Between Hegemony and Subsidiarity," *The ICJ Review* (June 1994): 56–65. Scholarly article, in English.

Hepple, Bob. "Discrimination and Equality of Opportunity—Northern Irish Lessons," *Oxford Journal of Legal Studies* 10, no. 3 (Autumn 1990): 408–421. Scholarly article, in English.

International Labor Organization. *Equality of Opportunity and Treatment for Women Workers.* ILO: Report VIII, 60th session, Geneva, 1975.

————. *ILO Standards and Action for the Elimination of Discrimination and the Promotion of Equality of Opportunity in Employment.* ILO: EGALITE/1991D.

Loenen, Titia. "Rethinking Sex Equality as a Human Right," *Netherlands Quarterly of Human Rights* 12, no. 3 (1994): 253–270. Scholarly article, in English.

Minow, Martha. *Making All the Difference: Inclusion, Exclusion, and American Law.* New York: Cornell University Press, 1990. Monograph, in English.

United Nations. *International Standards of Equality and Religious Freedom.* New York: 1990. UN publication UN/DAW.

————. *Regional Seminar on the Civic Responsibilities and Increased Participation of Asian Women in Public Life.* New York: 1959. UN publication ST/TAO/HR/9.

————. *Report on the Protection of Broad Sectors of the Population Against Social and Material Inequalities, as Well as Other Harmful Effects Which May Arrive from the Use of Scientific and Technological Developments.* UN Doc. A/10/146 (1975).

————. *Study of Equality in the Administration of Justice,* by Mohammed Ahmed Abu Rannat, Special Rapporteur. UN publication, Sales no. E.71.XIV.3.

United Nations Committee for the Elimination of Discrimination against Women. *Development of the Concept of Equality and its Consequences for the Reporting Obligations of States Parties to the Convention on the Elimination of All Forms of Discrimination against Women.* New York: 1990. UN publication no. CS/CEDAW/1990/W.P. I.

————. *International Standards of Equality and Religious Freedom: Implications for the Status of Women.* New York: 1990.

United Nations Educational, Scientific, and Cultural Organization. *World Conference of the United Nations Decade of*

# E

*Women: Equality, Development and Peace.* Copenhagen: 1980. UNESCO 113 EX/22, 113/CR/SS.1 and 112 EX/CR/SS.a. Microfiche 80s1244.

**EQUATORIAL GUINEA.** The Republic of Equatorial Guinea is a country in middle Africa, on the Gulf of Guinea; it includes the mainland area of Rio Muni and several islands in the gulf, among them Bioko (formerly known as Fernando Po), Pagalu (formerly known as Annobon), Corisco, Elobey Grande, and Elobey Chico. It has borders with Cameroon and Gabon. Formerly known as Spanish Guinea, it achieved independence from Spain in 1968, and became a member of the United Nations the same year. Its population is estimated to be 394,000. Ethnic groups include the Fang and the Bubi. Languages commonly used include Spanish (official), Fang, Bubi, and several African vernaculars. Christianity (Roman Catholic, 83%; Protestant, 10%) is the predominant religion; 7% adhere to other faiths or have no religious beliefs. Literacy is estimated at 55%.

The government (1994) took the form of a republic. However, the 1973 constitution was suspended after a coup d'etat of 3 August 1979 resulted in a military regime. The Supreme Military Council has since exercised all power, with its chairman, Lieut. Col. Teodoro Obiang Nguema Mbasogo, as president and head of State. No political parties have been permitted.

At its 1979 session, the UN **COMMISSION ON HUMAN RIGHTS** appointed a special rapporteur to study the situation of human rights in Equatorial Guinea. At its 1980 session, the Commission, after examining the Special Rapporteur's report, noted that the new government has expressed an interest in cooperating with the United Nations in order to ensure the effective enjoyment of human rights in that country. After lengthy negotiations, two jurists were sent to Equatorial Africa by the United Nations in 1986 to provide assistance in the drafting and codification of certain basic legal texts. Their mission was not successful because of difficulties caused by the absence of material conditions required to carry out their work: many of the applicable laws, for example, had not been published because of inadequate printing facilities. The jurists could only recommend a number of measures without which the work could not proceed satisfactorily. The report and recommendation of the jurists were transmitted to the government, and the Commission on Human Rights on 10 March 1987 expressed the hope (resolution 1987/36) that the government would give appropriate consideration to the plan of action proposed by the jurists.

At its 1980 session, the Commission decided (resolution 33 [XXXVI]), in response to the request of the government, to appoint an expert with wide experience of the situation in Equatorial Guinea to assist the government in taking the action necessary for the full restoration of human rights and fundamental freedoms; and requested the Secretary-General to provide the assistance necessary to enable the government to take such action. Mr. Fernando Volio Jiménez (Costa Rica), the expert so appointed, drew up a comprehensive plan of action after studying the situation that existed. The plan was accepted by the government.

On 15 August 1982, a new constitution was drawn up under the supervision of the expert and two consultant jurists designated by him. Since then, however, the situation has improved very little if at all. Two Spanish consultants—Sanz Bayón, a supreme court judge, and Corbi, a lawyer—were designated by the UN Center for Human Rights to assist in the drafting of new civil and criminal codes together with corresponding laws and procedures, but found this to be almost impossible because the country has no official gazette in which to publish laws in the course of preparation or coming into force. Because legislation is promulgated only through radio and television, it is almost impossible for residents, and even the courts, to obtain information on existing legal instruments.

In 1988 Fernando Volio Jiménez fell ill, and Arnaldo Ortiz Lopez (Costa Rica) visited Equatorial Guinea in his place, acting as a consultant. Sanz Bayón and Corbi carried out their mission in November and December 1990. On their recommendation Decree Law No. 7/90 of 16 October 1990 established a Committee on Human Rights to receive complaints and to take steps to investigate possible violations. The Committee is authorized to make appropriate recommendations to the President of the Republic, who in the light of those recommendations will adopt suitable measures to restore respect for the rights violated and repair any damage caused. However, the Committee, if established, has never issued a report of its activities.

In resolution 1993/69 of 10 March 1993, the UN Commission on Human Rights examined a report prepared by Fernando Volio Jiménez which indicated that "there has been no change in the human rights situation in Equatorial Guinea. The political and institutional conditions that seriously hinder both the free exercise and due legal protection of fundamental rights persist;" and which pointed out that "the situation is made worse by the fact that the Government of Equatorial Guinea has shown no sign of the necessary readiness to make sincere changes in its present repressive policy" (E/CN.4/1993/48, paras. 23 and 27).

At its 1993 session the Commission on Human Rights, in resolution 1993/69 of 10 March 1993, recalled that the Plan of Action proposed by the United Nations and accepted by the Government of Equatorial Guinea in 1980 had never been satisfactorily implemented by the Government despite the assistance and the advice provided by the UN Center for Human Rights and took note of the report of the Fernando Volio Jiménez (E/CN.4/1993/48) that the human rights situation in that country had continued to deteriorate seriously. It expressed its serious concern at the persistence of politically motivated violations of human rights, such as arbitrary arrests and the application to political prisoners of torture and other cruel, inhuman and degrading treatment or punishment, and called upon the Government to put an end to the use of military courts for trying ordinary law offences and to permit the establishment of an independent judiciary.

The Commission further called upon the Government "to free all political prisoners and to take, as soon as possible, legislative and administrative measures satisfying the requirements laid down in the International Bill of Human Rights and in other relevant international instruments, and providing for the establishment of freedom, democracy and the rule of law, as well as the promotion and effective protection of the human rights and fundamental freedoms of all citizens of Equatorial Guinea." In addition, it urged the Government "to propose to the International Committee of the Red Cross the conclusion of an agreement for the purpose of enabling the Committee to make periodic visits to prisons and civil and military detention centers, including cells in which persons are held incommunicado."

However, the Commission, at its 1994 session, received continued indications of the persistence of violations of human rights from its new special rapporteur, Mr. Alejandro Artucio (Uruguay). In his first report (E/CN.4/1994/56) the Special Rapporteur presented the following conclusions:

The Special Rapporteur was able to establish that some changes have occurred in the human rights situation in Equatorial Guinea. He is pleased to report the positive aspects of a number of measures adopted by the Government that will help to promote greater respect for human rights. They include the acceptance of the principle of a multi-party political system, the legalization of 14 political parties, the release of political prisoners and the steps recently taken, on 12 October 1993, to grant pardon and amnesty to several persons convicted of political or politically motivated acts. Also deserving of mention are the steps taken by the Ministry of Justice and Worship, at the request of the Special Rapporteur, to improve the food of the inmates in the Malabo prison and to make the system of the so-called "closed" prisons more flexible.

Another positive move was the decision taken in August 1993 by the Kingdom of Morocco to withdraw the soldiers who were serving as the security guards of the President of Equatorial Guinea. This Moroccan contingent of some 400 men had been stationed in the country since 1979 and had been involved in police work on more than one occasion. Their withdrawal had been repeatedly demanded at both the national and the international levels.

The measures by the authorities described above are a step forward, but they are still not enough for anyone to claim that human rights are effectively being respected. The Special Rapporteur concludes that serious and persistent violations of human rights and fundamental freedoms continue to occur in the Republic of Equatorial Guinea.

In the discharge of his mandate, the Special Rapporteur became aware that civilian society is allowed little room in the political, social and economic life of Equatorial Guinea, because the areas are dominated by the State. It is therefore of the utmost importance to promote the development mechanisms to enable civilian society to function within a democratic system and thus ensure that it will effectively have the right to create, the right to move ahead and the right to participation.

In the opinion of the Special Rapporteur, the Government should [adopt] various legislative and administrative measures to ensure that an appropriate climate of trust is established between the Government and the political opposition, so that the major national issues can be discussed. The discussion should also include the parties and groups which refused to take part in the general elections of November 1993 on the grounds that no guarantees were provided for their participation. By the same token, the authorities should give clear instructions to police officers and soldiers should stop considering political opponents as enemies.

There have been no changes in the juridical structure of the State [since] the Commission on Human Rights held its forty-ninth session. Power base continues to be concentrated in the hands of the President of the Republic to the detriment of other branches of government, and this obviously hinders functioning of a democratic system and prevents the establishment of a society governed by the rule of law.

Under the present legal system, the independence and impartiality Judiciary are not guaranteed, nor is respect for the right to a defence in a trial. There are obvious shortcomings and irregularities in the operation of the administration of justice, so that sometimes some persons are placed in a situation in which they have no defence at all. This is compounded by a noticeable lack of rigour in the legal system, on account of overlapping rules, gaps in legislation, the residual application of Spanish legislature dating from before 1968 that has been overtaken by time and historical circumstances, and the non-publication of the laws.

Arrest and arbitrary detention of political opponents are still found in different regions, and are often accompanied by torture and cruel and inhuman treatment. This report describes several cases of persons who died as a result of police action, some presumably as a consequence of the treatment received in prison. In the cases which resulted in death, the Special Rapporteur was not aware that any administrative or judicial investigation having been carried out and still less that those responsible had been punished.

The electoral process was pursued without any regard for the observations and recommendations made by the interagency missions sent by the United Nations. In addition, there were detentions, ill-treatment, prohibitions and intimidation by the Government agents of the political opponents, which finally led eight of the big parties to withdraw and to advocate abstention from the general elections on 21 November 1993. The Governments of the countries which are Equatorial Guinea's major aid donors, as well as other intergovernmental institutions, including the United Nations, decided not to send observers to the elections or to give any financial support, because they thought that "the elections were not genuinely pluralist in nature".

Lastly, the authorities of Equatorial Guinea have not fulfilled the obligations to submit periodic reports to the Committees established under the International Covenant on Human Rights, which makes it difficult to monitor the actual implementation of those instruments. These obligations stem from the fact that the state has ratified or acceded to these human rights instruments. Nor have the authorities seen fit to reply to the request for reports made by the Special Rapporteur on the question of torture and the Chairman of the Working Group on Enforced or Involuntary Disappearances.

In the light of the conclusions reproduced above, the Special Rapporteur recommended that the Commission on Human Rights should urge the Government of Equatorial Africa to meet the following basic conditions:

#### (a) In the field of human rights

(i) Put an end to arrests, arbitrary detentions and persecutions on political grounds;

(ii) Put an end immediately to torture and cruel, inhuman or degrading treatment or punishment;

(iii) Characterize torture and cruel, inhuman or degrading treatment or punishment as specific criminal offences;

(iv) Adopt measures to ensure that the police and security forces will act as professional institutions for the prevention and punishment of crime, under the command of civilian authorities and with functions that are clearly distinguished from those of the armed forces;

(v) Place on trial and impose criminal and administrative penalties on any one guilty of violations of human rights, and grant compensation to the victims of abuses of authority;

(vi) Urgently improve the situation of prisoners and detainees, providing them with adequate food and medical care, a paid work programme, and temporary and early release;

(vii) Grant the free and full exercise of political rights to all citizens without discrimination of any kind on grounds of race, national or ethnic origin, sex, political or other opinion;

(viii) Adopt measures to enable all political parties to exercise their right of participation;

(ix) Ensure full respect for the exercise of the right to freedom of opinion, expression and dissemination of ideas, with no restrictions other than those established by the law in any democratic society;

(x) Adopt measures to guarantee the right of persons residing legally in Equatorial Guinea to travel freely throughout the national territory;

(xi) Guarantee the right of nationals to enter and leave their own country. Abolish the entry and exit visa requirement for nationals of Equatorial Guinea;

(xii) Adopt measures to guarantee and facilitate the return of refugees and political exiles, including the signing of agreements with the office of the United Nations High Commissioner for Refugees (UNHCR) and with the International Organization for Migration (IOM);

(xiii) Eliminate discrimination against women and adopt positive measures designed to improve their effective participation in the educational, occupational, social and political fields;

(xiv) Ratify or accede to all the international human rights instruments to which the Republic of Equatorial Guinea is not yet a party;

#### (b) In the field of legislation

(i) Adopt legislative and administrative measures to guarantee the complete independence and impartiality of the Judiciary and to ensure due legal process, including the right to a defence when on trial;

(ii) Restrict the scope of military jurisdiction to cases involving strictly military offences, committed by military personnel;

(iii) Legislate on the remedies of habeas corpus and amparo;

(iv) Amend the laws governing the activity of political parties, religious activity, the freedoms of Assembly and expression, freedom of the press, trade union rights and the electoral law;

(v) Begin actual work on the codification of civil, trade, labour, criminal and procedural law;

(vi) Revise national legislation to ensure that it is in full conformity with international human rights principles and standards;

(vii) Amend the Fundamental Law in order to establish, *inter alia,* the independent functioning of the Legislature and the Judiciary, to guarantee human rights and fundamental freedoms, in particular the right to life, physical integrity and freedom;

(viii) Publicize all legislation and government decrees by regular and constant publication of the *Boletin Oficial del Estado;*

#### (c) In the political process

(i) Conclude a new National Pact between the Government and all political forces, which will enable a consensus to be reached on lending substance to the transition to democracy, the chief objective being democratic and transparent rules of the game, for the purpose of the forthcoming presidential elections in 1996;

(ii) Establish participation mechanisms to monitor compliance with the new National Pact;

(iii) Ensure the free development of political life throughout the national territory and firmly instil in the security forces and all public officials the principles of equality before the law, the right of all people of Equatorial Guinea to express their opinions freely and to associate with others in advancing them.

To meet the basic conditions stated above and to keep the Commission on Human Rights duly informed, it would be necessary to maintain the contacts already established in the course of two successive visits, between the authorities and the Special Rapporteur, assisted by the Human Rights Consultant.

*Technical Assistance to the Government for the Implementation for the Proposed Measures.* In order to give the necessary impetus and the technical support for the adoption of such measures, the Centre for Human Rights together with the United Nations Development Programme should provide the Government of Equatorial Guinea with the following assistance:

(a) Experts should be sent to cooperate with national specialists in compiling existing legislation, drafting codes and other laws and revising national legislation in order to ensure that it is in conformity with the international human rights principles and standards;

(b) An expert should be sent to train officials in preparing the periodic reports to be submitted to the Committees established under human rights treaties, conventions and covenants. The training should also include the necessary steps for ratification of or accession to international human rights instruments;

(c) Training courses should be held on the independence, impartiality and suitability of the Judiciary, democratic principles and national and international human rights law, for judges, prosecutors and senior government officials;

(d) Training courses should be held on human rights and the treatment of detainees and prisoners, for military and police personnel and prison officers;

(e) Training courses should be held on human rights and fundamental freedoms, for leaders of political parties and for representatives of non-governmental organizations and social sectors;

(f) A seminar should be held with papers submitted by national and international experts, on the rights of women and the position of women in the society of Equatorial Guinea. This seminar should be for government officials and representatives of social sectors.

After examining the Special Rapporteur's report at its 1994 session, the Commission on Human Rights expressed (resolution 1994/89 of 9 March 1994) serious concern at continued reports of the persistence of violations of human rights in Equatorial Guinea and also at the fact that the Government had never satisfactorily implemented any of the major proposals for reform which had been prepared under the auspices of the United Nations. The Commission in particular called upon that Government to implement procedures for the release of all persons detained or condemned for political reasons and to adopt, as soon as possible, legislative and administrative measures satisfying the requirements laid down in the International Bill of Human Rights and in other relevant international instruments, with a view to furthering democracy, the rule of law and the observance of human rights and fundamental freedoms of all inhabitants of Equatorial Guinea.

The Commission also encouraged the Government to facilitate the return of exiles and refugees and to adopt measures permitting the full participation of all citizens in the country's political, social, and cultural affairs; and to continue the dialogue with all elements of the political opposition with a view to reaching a consensus on the democratization of Equatorial Guinea. It urged the Government to invite regional and international human rights bodies to make periodic visits to prisons and to civil and military detention centers, without any exceptions; and requested the UN Secretary-General to provide it with technical assistance in the specific areas suggested by the Special Rapporteur in his report.

At its 1995 session, the Commission noted with satisfaction (resolution 1995/71 of 8 March 1995) that "... in June 1994, the Government of Equatorial Guinea took steps to grant pardon and amnesty to a number of prisoners, as requested by the Special Rapporteur on his visit to Equatorial Guinea on 11 May 1994." However, the Commission reiterated its call upon the government to fulfill all its obligations under various international human rights instruments and urged it to ratify or accede to the Convention Against Torture and Other Cruel, Inhuman, or Degrading Treatment or Punishment and the International Convention on the Elimination of All Forms of Racial Discrimination. The Special Rapporteur's mandate was renewed for another year and he was asked to report to the Commission at its next session.

**BIBLIOGRAPHY.** Amnesty International. *Equatorial Guinea: Political Reform without Human Rights: "What Do Human Rights Have To Do With Democracy?"* London: 1993. NGO report, in English.

————. *Equatorial Guinea: Torture.* London and Paris: 1990. NGO factfinding report, in English and French.

————. *Military Trials and the Use of the Death Penalty in Equatorial Guinea.* London: 1987. NGO briefing paper, in English.

Heinz, Wolfgang S. *Ursachen und Folgen von Menschenrechtsverletzungen in der Dritten Welt* (Causes and Consequences of Human Rights Violations in Third World Countries). Saarbrucken, Germany: Verlag Breitenbach, 1986. Scholarly monograph, in German; bibliography on Equatorial Guinea, pp. 217–218.

Liniger-Goumaz, Max. *Comment on s'empare d'un pays: la Guinée Équatoriale* (How to Seize a Country: Equatorial Guinea). Geneva, Switzerland: Editions du Temps, 1989. Scholarly monograph, in French; bibliography, pp. 80–95.

Radda Barnen, International Commission of Jurists (Swedish Section). *UN Assistance for Human Rights.* Stockholm: 1988. NGO report, in English.

SOS Torture. *Equatorial Guinea: Arrests and Court Martials.* Geneva: 1988. NGO urgent action bulletin, in English and French.

UN Commission on Human Rights. *Advisory Services in the Field of Human Rights: Report on Equatorial Guinea Prepared by the Expert, Mr. Fernando Volio Jiménez, in Accordance with Resolution 1991/80, of the Commission on Human Rights.* Geneva, Switzerland: 1992. IGO document, in English and Spanish. (E/CN.4/1992/51).

————. *Equatorial Guinea: Provision of Expert Assistance in the Field of Human Rights . . .* Prepared by Special Rapporteur Fernando Volio Jiménez. Geneva, Switzerland, 1985. IGO report, in English and Spanish.

**ERITREA.** A country in eastern Africa, Eritrea is located on the west coast of the Red Sea. An Italian colony from 1890 to 1952, when it became a province of **ETHIOPIA,** the country was plagued for many years by civil strife engendered by a series of independence movements. From 1961 to 1964, Eritreans fought

# E

against Ethiopian Emperor Haile Selassie and, after 1974, against the Ethiopian government headed by Mengistu Haile Mariam. From 1981 onwards, the fight for independence was led by the Eritrean People's Liberation Front.

Finally declaring itself an independent State on 24 May 1993, Eritrea was admitted to membership in the United Nations later that year. Its population is estimated to be 3,425,000.

Hot, dry, mountainous, and underdeveloped, Eritrea is sparsely populated and produces only a few exportable products including textiles and hides. Its capital, Asmara, is linked to Ethiopia and the Sudan by sporadic road and air service.

*BIBLIOGRAPHY.* Africa Watch. *Eritrea: Freedom of Expression and Ethnic Discrimination in the Educational System: Past and Future.* New York: Human Rights Watch, 1993. NGO report, in English.

————. *Ethiopia: 200 Days in the Death of Asmara—Starvation as a Weapon and Violations of the Humanitarian Laws of War.* New York: Human Rights Watch, 1990. NGO factfinding report, in English.

Keller, Edmond J. "Drought, War, and the Politics of Famine in Ethiopia and Eritrea," *Journal of Modern African Studies* 30, no. 4 (Dec. 1992): 609–624. Scholarly article, in English.

Kibreab, Gaim. *Refugees and Development in Africa: The Case of Eritrea.* Trenton, NJ, USA: Red Sea Press, 1987. Monograph, in English; bibliography, pp. 293–305.

Moussa, Helene. *Storm and Sanctuary: The Journey of Ethiopian and Eritrean Women Refugees.* Dundas, Canada: Artemis Enterprises, 1993. Monograph, in English; bibliography, pp. 272–284.

Oxfam-Canada. *Eritrean Referendum, April 23–25, 1993: Final Report of the Canadian NGO Observation Delegation to Eritrea.* Ottawa, Canada: 1993. NGO factfinding report, in English.

Pateman, Roy, ed. "Eritrea: An Emerging New Nation in Africa's Troubled Horn?" *Africa Today* 38, no. 2: 5–72. Special issue, in English.

Selassie, Bereket Habte. *Eritrea and the United Nations, and Other Essays.* Trenton, NJ, USA: Red Sea Press, 1989. Scholarly monograph, in English.

**ESTABLISHMENT.** See **FREEDOM OF MOVEMENT AND RESIDENCE.**

**ESTONIA.** The Republic of Estonia is a country in northern Europe bordered by the Gulf of Finland on the north, Latvia on the south, the Baltic Sea on the west, and Russia on the east. Its capital city is Tallinn. It declared its independence from the Soviet Union in 1991 and was admitted to the United Nations in the same year. A period of democratic reform followed. However, in nationwide elections in March 1995, voters expressed their frustration with the hardships induced by rapid economic change and ousted the democratic reformist Fatherland Party in favor of the communist Coalition Party. Estonia, along with the other Baltic states of Latvia and Lithuania, signed an agreement of trade and cooperation with the European Union in June 1995. An historical profile of the country is set out in a report to the UN Secretary-General to the **GENERAL ASSEMBLY** entitled "Situation of Human Rights in Estonia and Latvia" issued on 26 October 1993 (A/48/511) as follows:

Estonia has an ethnic population and language that is non-Slavic. Its closest relatives are in Finland. Throughout its history, Estonia was mostly in the spheres of influence of its neighbours, Czarist Russia, the Swedish crown or the German barons. It enjoyed full independence in the period from 24 February 1918 to 16 June 1940, as a parliamentary democracy. In June 1940, pursuant to the 1939 German-Soviet (Ribbentrop-Molotov) Pact, it was occupied by the Soviet Union; in 1941, invaded by Germany; and in 1944, again occupied and annexed by the Soviet Union. It re-emerged as an independent State in 1991 and was admitted to membership in the United Nations. During Soviet rule, thousands of Estonians were killed and tens of thousands of Estonians were deported to other parts of the Soviet Union. Hundreds of thousands of Soviet citizens were brought into the territory of Estonia, mostly as manpower to run the industrial enterprises established in Estonia, especially in the northeast, which were intended to service the centralized Soviet market. Hundreds of thousands of Russians and other ethnic groups took temporary residence in Estonia as members of the military. Hundreds of thousands of persons of non-ethnic Estonian origin, however, became permanent residents of Estonia. In the referendum on the re-establishment of Estonian independence held on 3 March 1991, the vast majority of the voters, including 40 per cent of the population of non-ethnic Estonian origin, endorsed independence.

Of a total population of 1,562,065 according to the January 1992 estimate based on the 1989 census, some 61.5 per cent are ethnic Estonians, while nearly 600,000 or 38.5 per cent, are not ethnic Estonians, of whom 406,628 were born outside Estonia. The population not of ethnic Estonian origin is composed of some 475,000 ethnic Russians (30.3 per cent), 48,000 Ukrainians (3.1 per cent), 23,000 Belarusians (1.5 per cent), 17,000 Finns (1.1 per cent) and 35,000 others (2.5 per cent). At present there is a negative net migration, reflecting primarily the departure of persons not of Estonian origin.

It is estimated that since 1992 as many as 70,000 ethnic Russians, mostly members of the military and their families, have returned to the Russian Federation. Important considerations include the difficulty of the Russian Federation to finance servicemen and their families with hard currency outside the Russian Federation, and the situation of unemployment in Estonia. Because of these and other considerations, it is estimated that the number of ethnic Russians in Estonia will continue to decline over the next few years.

While rural areas of Estonia remain ethnically Estonian, many of the urban areas show majorities of non-Estonian origin, particularly in cities such as Sillamae, Paldiski and Narva, where the ethnic Estonian population is less than 10 per cent; Residents of non-Estonian origin live throughout the country, with a greater concentration in the north-east, adjacent to the Saint Petersburg Oblast of the Russian Federation. Many residents of Narva have relatives across the Narva River in the town of Ivangorod and in other nearby settlements in the Russian Federation.

***RESTRICTIONS ON CITIZENSHIP.*** A United Nations factfinding mission visited Estonia and had consultations in Moscow in February 1993. The following conclusions and recommendations were set out in the Secretary-General's report to the General Assembly (UN Doc. A/48/511, paras. 87–101):

The Estonian Constitution is compatible with the International Covenant on Civil and Political Rights and the Covenant on Economic, Social and Cultural Rights. The citizenship and language laws examined are also compatible with general principles of international human rights law. Problems have arisen, however, in the implementation of these laws.

The central issue is that of citizenship. At present, a great number of permanent residents in Estonia do not have Estonian citizenship. Although the Law on Citizenship Law is liberal, the language requirement, which is not per se objectionable, at present bars the great majority of the ethnic Russian, ethnic Belarusian and ethnic Ukrainian population from acquiring citizenship. The level of proficiency in Estonian initially required was, in the opinion of the Mission, unreasonably high. At present, subsequent to the adoption, on 10 February 1993, of the Law on Estonian Language Requirements for Applicants for citizenship, it appears that the level of proficiency now required would eventually bring citizenship within reach of most of the Russian-speaking population. This law also allows the President to lower the language requirement for invalids and for persons born prior to 1 January 1930. The Mission would recommend that this law be reviewed so as to waive language requirements completely as a prerequisite for citizenship for persons of 60 years and older and for invalids.

Children born in Estonia after 21 January 1992, the date of the entry into force for Estonia of the International Covenant on Civil and Political Rights, are entitled, by virtue of article 24, paragraph 3, of the Covenant, to acquire Estonian nationality, if they would otherwise be stateless.

Although most currently stateless persons in Estonia could acquire Russian, Belarusian or Ukrainian citizenship, they should not be encouraged to do so if they intend to remain as permanent residents of Estonia. They should be encouraged to learn the Estonian language and to apply for Estonian citizenship. It is in the interest of Estonia to take all necessary measures to facilitate their integration so as to maintain and preserve its traditionally peaceful and tolerant multicultural society.

Immigration quotas should allow sufficient flexibility as not to prevent or delay unduly legitimate family reunification. Estonia is invited to review its law and practice to ensure that there are no waiting lists compelling family members to live apart for years.

Travel documents or alien's passports should be provided to stateless persons so that they can freely travel abroad and return to Estonia, in keeping with the right to freedom of movement enshrined in article 12 of the International Covenant on Civil and Political Rights.

While many residents belonging to the non-Estonian part of the population harbour genuine feelings of anxiety as regards their uncertain status and perceive themselves as victims of a discriminatory policy excluding them from full participation in the life of Estonian society, the Mission did not establish or observe any specific instances of discrimination, as such.

The Mission welcomes the establishment of the Estonian Institute of Human Rights, whose mandate should be expanded to permit examination of complaints of alleged human rights violations in Estonia. It could also render an important service by helping in disseminating information about human rights norms and redress procedures.

The solution of the current conflict demands patience on the part of both communities. The Mission notes that the Language Law dates back to 1989 and independence to 1991. In this short period, complete integration could not have been achieved. The Mission did not learn of any instances of violence; rather, it observed an encouraging level of communication, which is continuing.

Since unemployment has been increasing, particularly in the north-east, where the ethnic Russian minority is predominant, state and local authorities should take the necessary measures to organize retraining programmes so as to expedite the reintegration of the unemployed into the workforce.

There is an overriding economic problem, which is responsible for delaying the implementation of the necessary programmes for the full integration of residents of Estonia who are not ethnic Estonians. Most importantly, there is an insufficient number of Estonian language teachers and limited funds to provide for teaching materials, including video cassettes.

Foreign donors, including the Russian Federation, should be invited to finance the production and distribution of materials for the teaching of the Estonian language, in particular for adult education.

The Estonian Defence Ministry may consider offering its draftees the option to spend part or all of the period of military service as teachers of the Estonian language, especially in those areas of Estonia where the lack of language teachers is most acute.

The United Nations Educational, Scientific and Cultural Organization (UNESCO) should be invited to extend its expertise in the teaching of languages. UNESCO could also be called upon to support inter-ethnic cultural activities of the Association of Ethnic Groups in Estonia and of the Union of societies of Slavic Culture. The Mission is of the opinion that intensified cultural exchange among the ethnic groups in Estonia would contribute significantly to good will and cooperation and would enable the population of non-Estonian origin to be more rapidly integrated into Estonian society.

Persons who believe that their human rights are being violated in Estonia are invited to bring their cases before the competent administrative or judicial bodies in Estonia. Following exhaustion of domestic remedies, they may avail themselves of the review mechanism of the United Nations Human Rights Committee under the procedure established pursuant to the optional Protocol to the International Covenant on Civil and Political Rights.

The United Nations Centre for Human Rights is prepared to offer advisory services and technical assistance to Estonia and to cooperate with the Estonian Institute of Human Rights, particularly with regard to dissemination of human rights information.

After considering the Secretary-General's report and the conclusions and recommendations of the factfinding mission, the General Assembly, taking into account the provisions of the Declaration on the Human Rights of Individuals Who are not Nationals of the

Country in which They Live, noted the existence in Estonia of unresolved issues that involved large groups of population of different ethnic origin and welcomed the cooperation that the Government had extended to the factfinding mission (resolution 48/155 of 20 December 1993).

**BIBLIOGRAPHY.** Commission on Security and Cooperation in Europe. *Human Rights and Democratization in Estonia.* Washington, D.C.: U.S. Government Printing Office, 1993. Government report, in English.

————. *Report on the Supreme Soviet Elections in Estonia.* Washington, D.C.: U.S. Government Printing Office, 1990. Government report, in English.

Helsinki Watch. *Integrating Estonia's Non-Citizen Minority.* New York: Human Rights Watch, 1993. NGO report, in English.

Immigration and Refugee Board Documentation Centre. *Estonia: Ethnic Minorities.* Ottawa, Canada: 1992. Government briefing paper, in English and French; bibliography, pp. 18–24.

Miljan, Toivo. "Ethnic and Linguistic Revival in Estonia," in *Language and the State: The Law and Politics of Identity. Proceedings of the Second National Conference on Constitutional Affairs,* ed. David Schneiderman, pp. 227–242. Cowansville, Quebec, Canada: Éditions Blais for Centre for Constitutional Studies, 1991. Conference paper, in English.

Pekkanen, Raimo, and Hans Danelius. "Human Rights in the Republic of Estonia," *Human Rights Law Journal* 13, no. 5–6 (June 1992): 236–244. Scholarly article, in English.

Tarm, Michael, and Mari-Ann Rikken. *Documents from Estonia: Articles, Speeches, Resolutions, Letters, Editorials, Interviews concerning Recent Developments.* 2 vols. New York: Estonian American National Council, 1989 (vol. 1); 1990 (vol 2). NGO document collection, in English.

Vetik, Raivo. "Ethnic Conflict and Accommodation in Post-Communist Estonia," *Journal of Peace Research* 30, no. 3 (May 1993): 271–280. Scholarly article, in English; bibliography, p. 280.

**ETHIOPIA.** A country in eastern Africa, on the Red Sea, Ethiopia has borders with Djibouti, Kenya, Somalia, and Sudan. It achieved independence from Italy first in 1896 and again in 1941 and became a member of the United Nations in 1945. Its population is estimated to be 51,715,000. Ethnic groups include the Oromo, the Amhara, the Tigre, and the Sidama. Languages commonly used include Amharic (official), Arabic, English, Oromegna, Tegrina, Kunamigna, Sidamigna, Seltegna, Afar, Kefamocha, and Sahogna. Religions practiced include Islam (45%), Coptic Christianity (Ethiopian Orthodox) (40%), and other beliefs or none (15%). Literacy is estimated at 25%.

Once a monarchy under Emperor Haile Selassie, Ethiopia was taken over by its armed forces committee in August 1974 after a period of famine caused by drought had led to riots and mutinies. Haile Selassie's palace and estates were nationalized, and he was deposed, after nearly 58 years as emperor, on 12 September 1974. With Parliament dissolved and the constitution suspended, Lt. Col. Mengistu Haile Mariam was named head of State. A communist regime was proclaimed on 10 September 1984.

Ethiopia's recent large-scale human rights problems stem largely from drought, famine, and disease. Between 1974 and 1978, the country was threatened by Somali guerrillas—a conflict that ended only with the help of military aid supplied by Cuba and the Union of Soviet Socialist Republics. In 1986 and 1987, it was compelled to deal with secessionists from Eritrea.

In 1988, Ethiopia was confronted by two massive problems: assistance to refugees from Somalia and assistance to returnees from Djibouti, Somalia, and Suda. The resulting difficulties were eased only by herculean efforts of the United Nations High Commissioner for Refugees, other intergovernmental and voluntary agencies. The General Assembly commended the Office of the High Commissioner for Refugees and cooperating organizations and agencies for their assistance (resolution 45/161 of 18 December 1990) and appealed to Member States to provide adequate material, financial, and technical assistance for the necessary relief and rehabilitation programs.

Soviet support to the regime of Mengistu Haile Mariam was cut off in 1990; and by 1991, Mengistu abdicated leaving a pro-Western group in control of the country. Former communist leaders, living in exile, were tried in absentia for committing or ordering crimes against humanity, including genocide. The new leadership, headed by Meles Zenawi as President and Chairman of the Council of Representatives, has been introducing democratic reforms. The new government, known as the Transitional Government of Ethiopia (TGE) is dominated by the Ethiopian People's Revolutionary Democratic Front.

Among changes introduced is a Transitional Charter, which guarantees basic human rights. A Constitutional Commission has been empowered to draft a new constitution, and a National Electoral Board has been established to oversee elections. More political parties and other associations are now permitted in Ethiopia than before in its history. On the basis of the Freedom of the Press Proclamation (no. 34/1992) licenses have been issued for independent journals and newspapers.

Former President Mengistu fled to Zimbabwe after his abdication; the new government has attempted to have him extradited to stand trial for abuses under his administration. As of the end of 1994, Mengistu was not returned to Ethiopia. Since 1991, about 1,300 officials and proponents of the former regime have been held in detention, without formal charges having been brought against them. However, in October 1994, 66 senior officials of the former regime were formerly charged with a range of offenses.

**BIBLIOGRAPHY.** Africa Watch. *Ethiopia: Human Rights Crisis as Central Power Crumbles—Killings, Detentions, Forcible Conscription and Obstruction of Relief.* New York: Human Rights Watch, 1991. NGO factfinding report, in English.

———. *Ethiopia: 'Mengistu Has Decided to Burn Us Like Wood'—Bombing of Civilians and Civilian Targets by the Air Force.* New York: Human Rights Watch, 1990. NGO factfinding report, in English.

———. *Evil Days: 30 Years of War and Famine in Ethiopia.* New York: Human Rights Watch, 1991. NGO factfinding report, in English.

Amnesty International. *Ethiopia: "Disappearances."* London: 1987. NGO report, in English.

———. *Ethiopia: End of an Era of Brutal Repression—A New Chance for Human Rights.* London: 1991. NGO factfinding report, in English.

———. *Ethiopia: Political Imprisonment and Torture.* London: 1986. NGO report, in English.

Clay, J. W., and B. K. Holcomb. *Politics and the Ethiopian Famine 1984–1985.* Cambridge, MA, USA: Cultural Survival, 1985. NGO report, in English; bibliography, pp. 247–250.

Clay, J. W., S. Steingraber, and P. Niggli. *The Spoils of Famine: Ethiopian Famine Policy and Peasant Agriculture.* Cambridge, MA, USA: Cultural Survival, 1988. NGO report, in English.

Colchester, M., and V. Luling, eds. *Ethiopia's Bitter Medicine: Settling for Disaster: An Evaluation of the Ethiopian Government's Resettlement Programme.* London: Survival International, 1986. NGO report, in English.

Heinz, Wolfgang S. *Ursachen und Folgen von Menschenrechtsverletzungen in der Dritten Welt* (Causes and Consequences of Human Rights Violations in Third World Countries). Saarbrucken, Germany: Verlag Breitenbach, 1986. Scholarly monograph, in German; bibliography on Ethiopia, pp. 273–275.

Jansson, Kurt, Angela Penrose, and Michael Harris. *The Ethiopian Famine.* London: Zed Press, 1990. Scholarly monograph, in English; bibliography, pp. 213–214.

Kessler, D., and T. Parfitt. *The Falashas: The Jews of Ethiopia.* London: Minority Rights Group, 1985. NGO report, in English.

Kibreab, Gaim. *Refugees and Development in Africa: The Case of Eritrea.* Trenton, NJ, USA: Red Sea Press, 1987. Monograph, in English; bibliography, pp. 293–305.

Korn, David A. *Ethiopia: The United States and the Soviet Union.* Carbondale, IL, USA: Southern Illinois University Press, 1986. Scholarly monograph, in English; bibliography, pp. 190–191.

Lyon, A., M. McColgan, C. Rostoker, and D. Malapel. "Torture and the Violation of Human Rights in Tigray, Ethiopia—Mission Report." *La Lettre de la FIDH* (February 1986). NGO special issue, mission report, in English.

Mersha, Gebru. *The State and Civil Society with Special Reference to Ethiopia.* Dakar, Senegal: Council for the Development of Economic and Social Research in Africa, 1990. Conference paper, in English.

Moussa, Helene. *Storm and Sanctuary: The Journey of Ethiopian and Eritrean Women Refugees.* Dundas, Canada: Artemis Enterprises, 1993. Monograph, in English; bibliography, pp. 272–284.

Ruiz, Hiram A. *Beyond the Headlines: Refugees in the Horn of Africa.* Washington, D.C.: United States Committee for Refugees, 1988. NGO issue paper, in English; selective bibliography, p. 44.

———. "Early Warning Is Not Enough: The Failure to Prevent Starvation in Ethiopia, 1990," *International Journal of Refugee Law* (Sept. 1990): 83–98. Scholarly article, in English.

U.S. House of Representatives, Subcommittee on Africa and Subcommittee on Human Rights and International Organizations. *Human Rights and Food in Ethiopia.* Washington, D.C.: U.S. Government Printing Office, 1985. Government hearings, in English.

U.S. House of Representatives, Subcommittee on Human Rights and International Organizations, Subcommittee on International Economic Policy and Trade, and Subcommittee on Africa. *Human Rights in Ethiopia.* Washington, D.C.: U.S. Government Printing Office, 1988. Government hearings, in English.

Zentrale Dokumentationsstelle der Freien Wohlfahrtspflege fur Fluchtling. *Arbeitsmaterialien fur den Unterricht: Die Weltfluchtlingsproblematik und ihre Auswirkungen in der Bundesrepublik Deutschland* (Study Materials: The World Refugee Problem and its Consequences in the Federal Republic of Germany). Bonn, FRG: 1987. NGO edited collection, in German.

## EUROPEAN ACTION OF THE HANDICAPPED.

Established in 1979, this non-governmental organization promotes the interests of disabled individuals throughout Europe. It supports equal opportunity for the physically challenged.

European Action of the Handicapped. Address: Wurzerstr. 2–4, 53175 Bonn, Germany. Telephone: 228–820930. Fax: 228–820943. Officer: Waldemar Brummendorf.

## EUROPEAN CONVENTION ON HUMAN RIGHTS (1950).

Formally entitled *Convention for the Protection of Human Rights and Fundamental Freedoms,* this is the first international treaty which provides for the collective enforcement of a number of human rights and fundamental freedoms set out in the **UNIVERSAL DECLARATION OF HUMAN RIGHTS.** Prepared under the auspices of the **COUNCIL OF EUROPE** and open for signature and ratification by all members of the Council, it defines the rights and freedoms with which it is concerned and their permissible restrictions and establishes the regional machinery to supervise their implementation: the European Court of Human Rights.

The Court may receive petitions from any person, non-governmental organization or group of individuals claiming to be the victim of a violation by one of the high contracting parties of the rights set forth in the Convention, provided that the high contracting party against which the complaint has been lodged has declared that it recognizes the competence of the Court to receive such petitions. The Court may then deal with the petition with a view to effecting a friendly settlement of the complaint. If a solution is not reached, it must draw up a report and transmit it to the Committee of Ministers of the Council of Europe and to the States concerned.

Under article 46, any of the high contracting parties may at any time declare that it recognizes as compulsory *ipso facto* and without special agreement the jurisdiction of the court. Under article 48, a case may be brought before the court by one of the high contracting Parties concerned. The high contracting parties undertake (article 53) to abide by the decision of the court in any case to which they are parties.

The European Convention on Human Rights has been supplemented by eleven protocols: **PROTOCOL I** (1952), **PROTOCOLS II, III,** and **IV** (1963), **PROTOCOL V** (1966), **PROTOCOL VI** (1983), **PROTOCOL VII** (1984), **PROTOCOL VIII** (1985), **PROTOCOL IX** (1990), **PROTOCOL X** (1992), and **PROTOCOL XI** (1994).

The Convention was concluded by the Committee of Ministers of the Council of Europe, convened in Rome, on 4 November 1950, and entered into force on 3 September 1953. Its text (*European Treaty Series* 5), amended in accordance with the provisions of Protocol III, is as follows:

The governments signatory hereto, being Members of the Council of Europe,

Considering the Universal Declaration of Human Rights proclaimed by the General Assembly of the United Nations on 10 December 1948;

Considering that this Declaration aims at securing the universal and effective recognition and observance of the rights therein declared;

Considering that the aim of the Council of Europe is the achievement of greater unity between its Members and that one of the methods by which that aim is to be pursued is the maintenance and further realisation of human rights and fundamental freedoms;

Reaffirming their profound belief in those fundamental freedoms which are the foundation of justice and peace in the world and are best maintained on the one hand by an effective political democracy and on the other by a common understanding and observance of the human rights upon which they depend;

Being resolved, as the governments of European countries which are like-minded and have a common heritage of political traditions, ideals, freedom and the rule of law, to take the first steps for the collective enforcement of certain of the rights stated in the Universal Declaration;

Have agreed as follows:

*Article 1.* The High Contracting Parties shall secure to everyone within their jurisdiction the rights and freedoms defined in Section I of this Convention.

## Section 1

*Article 2.* 1. Everyone's right to life shall be protected by law. No one shall be deprived of his life intentionally save in the execution of a sentence of a court following his conviction of a crime for which this penalty is provided by law.

2. Deprivation of life shall not be regarded as inflicted in contravention of this article when it results from the use of force which is no more than absolutely necessary:

(a) in defence of any person from unlawful violence;

(b) in order to effect a lawful arrest or to prevent the escape of a person lawfully detained;

(c) in action lawfully taken for the purpose of quelling a riot or insurrection.

*Article 3.* No one shall be subjected to torture or to inhuman or degrading treatment or punishment.

*Article 4.* 1. No one shall be held in slavery or servitude.

2. No one shall be required to perform forced or compulsory labour.

3. For the purpose of this article the term "forced or compulsory labour" shall not include:

(a) any work required to be done in the ordinary course of detention imposed according to the provisions of Article 5 of this Convention or during conditional release from such detention;

(b) any service of a military character or, in case of conscientious objectors in countries where they are recognised, service exacted instead of compulsory military service;

(c) any service exacted in case of an emergency or calamity threatening the life or well-being of the community;

(d) any work or service which forms part of normal civic obligations.

*Article 5.* 1. Everyone has the right to liberty and security of person.

No one shall be deprived of his liberty save in the following cases and in accordance with a procedure prescribed by law:

(a) the lawful detention of a person after conviction by a competent court;

(b) the lawful arrest or detention of a person for non-compliance with the lawful order of a court or in order to secure the fulfilment of any obligation prescribed by law;

(c) the lawful arrest or detention of a person effected for the purpose of bringing him before the competent legal authority on reasonable suspicion of having committed an offence or when it is reasonably considered necessary to prevent his committing an offence or fleeing after having done so;

(d) the detention of a minor by lawful order for the purpose of educational supervision or his lawful detention for the purpose of bringing him before the competent legal authority;

(e) the lawful detention of persons for the prevention of the spreading of infectious diseases, of persons of unsound mind, alcoholics or drug addicts or vagrants;

(f) the lawful arrest or detention of a person to prevent his effecting an unauthorised entry into the country or of a person against whom action is being taken with a view to deportation or extradition.

2. Everyone who is arrested shall be informed promptly, in a language which he understands, of the reasons for his arrest and of any charge against him.

3. Everyone arrested or detained in accordance with the provisions of paragraph 1 *(c)* of this article shall be brought promptly before a judge or other officer authorised by law to exercise judicial power and shall be entitled to trial within a reasonable time or to release pending trial. Release may be conditioned by guarantees to appear for trial.

4. Everyone who is deprived of his liberty by arrest or detention shall be entitled to take proceedings by which the

lawfulness of his detention shall be decided speedily by a court and his release ordered if the detention is not lawful.

5. Everyone who has been the victim of arrest or detention in contravention of the provisions of this article shall have an enforceable right to compensation.

*Article 6.* 1. In the determination of his civil rights and obligations or of any criminal charge against him, everyone is entitled to a fair and public hearing within a reasonable time by an independent and impartial tribunal established by law. Judgment shall be pronounced publicly but the press and public may be excluded from all or part of the trial in the interests of morals, public order or national security in a democratic society, where the interests of juveniles or the protection of the private life of the parties so require, or to the extent strictly necessary in the opinion of the court in special circumstances where publicity would prejudice the interests of justice.

2. Everyone charged with a criminal offence shall be presumed innocent until proved guilty according to law.

3. Everyone charged with a criminal offence has the following minimum rights:

(a) to be informed promptly, in a language which he understands and in detail, of the nature and cause of the accusation against him;

(b) to have adequate time and facilities for the preparation of his defence;

(c) to defend himself in person or through legal assistance of his own choosing or, if he has not sufficient means to pay for legal assistance, to be given it free when the interests of justice so require;

(d) to examine or have examined witnesses against him and to obtain the attendance and examination of witnesses on his behalf under the same conditions as witnesses against him;

(e) to have the free assistance of an interpreter if he cannot understand or speak the language used in court.

*Article 7.* 1. No one shall be held guilty of any criminal offence on account of any act or omission which did not constitute a criminal offence under national or international law at the time when it was committed. Nor shall a heavier penalty be imposed than the one that was applicable at the time the criminal offence was committed.

2. This article shall not prejudice the trial and punishment of any person for any act or omission which, at the time when it was committed, was criminal according to the general principles of law recognised by civilised nations.

*Article 8.* 1. Everyone has the right to respect for his private and family life, his home and his correspondence.

2. There shall be no interference by a public authority with the exercise of this right except such as is in accordance with the law and is necessary in a democratic society in the interests of national security, public safety or the economic well-being of the country, for the prevention of disorder or crime, for the protection of health or morals, or for the protection of the rights and freedoms of others.

*Article 9.* 1. Everyone has the right to freedom of thought, conscience and religion; this right includes freedom to change his religion or belief and freedom, either alone or in community with others and in public or private, to manifest his religion or belief, in worship, teaching, practice and observance.

2. Freedom to manifest one's religion or beliefs shall be subject only to such limitations as are prescribed by law and are necessary in a democratic society in the interests of public safety, for the protection of public order, health or morals, or for the protection of the rights and freedoms of others.

*Article 10.* 1. Everyone has the right to freedom of expression. This right shall include freedom to hold opinions and to receive and impart information and ideas without interference by public authority and regardless of frontiers. This article shall not prevent States from requiring the licensing of broadcasting, television or cinema enterprises.

2. The exercise of these freedoms, since it carries with it duties and responsibilities, may be subject to such formalities, conditions, restrictions or penalties as are prescribed by law and are necessary in a democratic society, in the interests of national security, territorial integrity or public safety, for the prevention of disorder or crime, for the protection of health or morals, for the protection of the reputation or rights of others, for preventing the disclosure of information received in confidence, or for maintaining the authority and impartiality of the judiciary.

*Article 11.* 1. Everyone has the right to freedom of peaceful assembly and to freedom of association with others, including the right to form and to join trade unions for the protection of his interests.

2. No restrictions shall be placed on the exercise of these rights other than such as are prescribed by law and are necessary in a democratic society in the interests of national security or public safety, for the prevention of disorder or crime, for the protection of health or morals or for the protection of the rights and freedoms of others. This article shall not prevent the imposition of lawful restrictions on the exercise of these rights by members of the armed forces, of the police or of the administration of the State.

*Article 12.* Men and women of marriageable age have the right to marry and to found a family, according to the national laws governing the exercise of this right.

*Article 13.* Everyone whose rights and freedoms as set forth in this Convention are violated shall have an effective remedy before a national authority notwithstanding that the violation has been committed by persons acting in an official capacity.

*Article 14.* The enjoyment of the rights and freedoms set forth in this Convention shall be secured without discrimination on any ground such as sex, race, colour, language, religion, political or other opinion, national or social origin, association with a national minority, property, birth or other status.

*Article 15.* 1. In time of war or other public emergency threatening the life of the nation any High Contracting Party may take measures derogating from its obligations under this Convention to the extent strictly required by the exigencies of the situation, provided that such measures are not inconsistent with its other obligations under international law.

2. No derogation from Article 2, except in respect of deaths resulting from lawful acts of war, or from Articles 3, 4 (paragraph 1) and 7 shall be made under this provision.

3. Any High Contracting Party availing itself of this right of derogation shall keep the Secretary General of the Council of Europe fully informed of the measures which it has taken and the reasons therefor. It shall also inform the Secretary General of the Council of Europe when such measures have ceased to operate and the provisions of the Convention are again being fully executed.

*Article 16.* Nothing in Articles 10, 11, and 14 shall be regarded as preventing the High Contracting Parties from imposing restrictions on the political activity of aliens.

*Article 17.* Nothing in this Convention may be interpreted as implying for any State, group or person any right to engage in any activity or perform any act aimed at the destruction of any of the rights and freedoms set forth herein or at their limitation to a greater extent than is provided for in the Convention.

*Article 18.* The restrictions permitted under this Convention to the said rights and freedoms shall not be applied for any purpose other than those for which they have been prescribed.

### Section 2

*Article 19.* To ensure the observance of the engagements undertaken by the High Contracting Parties in the present Convention, there shall be set up:

(a) A European Commission of Human Rights hereinafter referred to as "the Commission";

(b) A European Court of Human Rights, hereinafter referred to as "the Court".

### Section 3

*Article 20.* The Commission shall consist of a number of members equal to that of the High Contracting Parties. No two members of the Commission may be nationals of the same State.

*Article 21.* 1. The members of the Commission shall be elected by the Committee of Ministers by an absolute majority of votes, from a list of names drawn up by the Bureau of the Consultative Assembly; each group of the Representatives of the High Contracting Parties in the Consultative Assembly shall put forward three candidates, of whom two at least shall be its nationals.

2. As far as applicable, the same procedure shall be followed to complete the Commission in the event of other States subsequently becoming Parties to this Convention, and in filling casual vacancies.

*Article 22.* 1. The members of the Commission shall be elected for a period of six years. They may be re-elected. However, of the members elected at the first election, the terms of seven members shall expire at the end of three years.

2. The members whose terms are to expire at the end of the initial period of three years shall be chosen by lot by the Secretary General of the Council of Europe immediately after the first election has been completed.

3. A member of the Commission elected to replace a member whose term of office has not expired shall hold office for the remainder of his predecessor's term.

4. The members of the Commission shall hold office until replaced. After having been replaced, they shall continue to deal with such cases as they already have under consideration.

*Article 23.* The members of the Commission shall sit on the Commission in their individual capacity.

*Article 24.* Any High Contracting Party may refer to the Commission, through the Secretary General of the Council of Europe, any alleged breach of the provisions of the Convention by another High Contracting Party.

*Article 25.* 1. The Commission may receive petitions addressed to the Secretary General of the Council of Europe from any person, non-governmental organisation or group of individuals claiming to be the victim of a violation by one of the High Contracting Parties of the rights set forth in this Convention, provided that the High Contracting Party against which the complaint has been lodged has declared that it recognises the competence of the Commission to receive such petitions. Those of the High Contracting Parties

who have made such a Declaration undertake not to hinder in any way the effective exercise of this right.

2. Such Declarations may be made for a specific period.

3. The Declarations shall be deposited with the Secretary General of the Council of Europe who shall transmit copies thereof to the High Contracting Parties and publish them.

4. The Commission shall only exercise the powers provided for in this article when at least six High Contracting Parties are bound by Declarations made in accordance with the preceding paragraphs.

*Article 26.* The Commission may only deal with the matter after all domestic remedies have been exhausted, according to the generally recognised rules of international law, and within a period of six months from the date on which the final decision was taken.

*Article 27.* 1. The Commission shall not deal with any petition submitted under Article 25 which:

(a) is anonymous, or

(b) is substantially the same as a matter which has already been examined by the Commission or has already been submitted to another procedure of international investigation or settlement and if it contains no relevant new information.

2. The Commission shall consider inadmissible any petition submitted under Article 25 which it considers incompatible with the provisions of the present Convention, manifestly ill-founded, or an abuse of the right of petition.

3. The Commission shall reject any petition referred to it which it considers inadmissible under Article 26.

*Article 28.* In the event of the Commission accepting a petition referred to it:

(a) it shall, with a view to ascertaining the facts, undertake together with the representatives of the parties an examination of the petition and, if need be, an investigation, for the effective conduct of which the States concerned shall furnish all necessary facilities, after an exchange of views with the Commission;

(b) it shall place itself at the disposal of the parties concerned with a view to securing a friendly settlement of the matter on the basis of respect for human rights as defined in this Convention.

*Article 29.* After it has accepted a petition submitted under Article 25, the Commission may nevertheless decide unanimously to reject the petition if, in the course of its examination, it finds that the existence of one of the grounds for non-acceptance provided for in Article 27 has been established.

In such a case, the decision shall be communicated to the Parties.

*Article 30.* If the Commission succeeds in effecting a friendly settlement in accordance with Article 28, it shall draw up a report which shall be sent to the States concerned, to the Committee of Ministers and to the Secretary General of the Council of Europe for publication. This report shall be confined to a brief statement of the facts and of the solution reached.

*Article 31.* 1. If a solution is not reached, the Commission shall draw up a report on the facts and state its opinion as to whether the facts found disclose a breach by the State concerned of its obligations under the Convention. The opinions of all the members of the Commission on this point may be stated in the report.

2. The report shall be transmitted to the Committee of Ministers. It shall also be transmitted to the States concerned, who shall not be at liberty to publish it.

3. In transmitting the report to the Committee of Minis-

ters the Commission may make such proposals as it thinks fit.

*Article 32.* 1. If the question is not referred to the Court in accordance with Article 48 of this Convention within a period of three months from the date of the transmission of the report to the Committee of Ministers, the Committee of Ministers shall decide by a majority of two thirds of the members entitled to sit on the Committee whether there has been a violation of the Convention.

2. In the affirmative case the Committee of Ministers shall prescribe a period during which the High Contracting Party concerned must take the measures required by the decision of the Committee of Ministers.

3. If the High Contracting Party concerned has not taken satisfactory measures within the prescribed period, the Committee of Ministers shall decide by the majority provided for in paragraph 1 above what effect shall be given to its original decision and shall publish the report.

4. The High Contracting Parties undertake to regard as binding on them any decision which the Committee of Ministers may take in application of the preceding paragraphs.

*Article 33.* The Commission shall meet in camera.

*Article 34.* Subject to the provisions of Article 29, the Commission shall take its decisions by a majority of the members present and voting.

*Article 35.* The Commission shall meet as the circumstances require. The meetings shall be convened by the Secretary General of the Council of Europe.

*Article 36.* The Commission shall draw up its own rules of procedure.

*Article 37.* The secretariat of the Commission shall be provided by the Secretary General of the Council of Europe.

## Section 4

*Article 38.* The European Court of Human Rights shall consist of a number of judges equal to that of the Members of the Council of Europe. No two judges may be nationals of the same State.

*Article 39.* 1. The members of the Court shall be elected by the Consultative Assembly by a majority of the votes cast from a list of persons nominated by the Members of the Council of Europe; each Member shall nominate three candidates, of whom two at least shall be its nationals.

2. As far as applicable, the same procedure shall be followed to complete the Court in the event of the admission of new Members of the Council of Europe, and in filling casual vacancies.

3. The candidates shall be of high moral character and must either possess the qualifications required for appointment to high judicial office or be jurisconsults of recognised competence.

*Article 40.* 1. The members of the Court shall be elected for a period of nine years. They may be re-elected. However, of the members elected at the first election the terms of four members shall expire at the end of three years, and the terms of four more members shall expire at the end of six years.

2. The members whose terms are to expire at the end of the initial periods of three and six years shall be chosen by lot by the Secretary General immediately after the first election has been completed.

3. A member of the Court elected to replace a member whose term of office has not expired shall hold office for the remainder of his predecessor's term.

4. The members of the Court shall hold office until re-

placed. After having been replaced, they shall continue to deal with such cases as they already have under consideration.

*Article 41.* The Court shall elect its President and Vice-President for a period of three years. They may be re-elected.

*Article 42.* The members of the Court shall receive for each day of duty a compensation to be determined by the Committee of Ministers.

*Article 43.* For the consideration of each case brought before it the Court shall consist of a Chamber composed of seven judges. There shall sit as an ex officio member of the Chamber the judge who is a national of any State party concerned, or, if there is none, a person of its choice who shall sit in the capacity of judge; the names of the other judges shall be chosen by lot by the President before the opening of the case.

*Article 44.* Only the High Contracting Parties and the Commission shall have the right to bring a case before the Court.

*Article 45.* The jurisdiction of the Court shall extend to all cases concerning the interpretation and application of the present Convention which the High Contracting Parties or the Commission shall refer to it in accordance with Article 48.

*Article 46.* 1. Any of the High Contracting Parties may at any time declare that it recognizes as compulsory ipso facto and without special agreement the jurisdiction of the Court in all matters concerning the interpretation and application of the present Convention.

2. The Declarations referred to above may be made unconditionally or on condition of reciprocity on the part of several or certain other High Contracting Parties or for a specified period.

3. These Declarations shall be deposited with the Secretary General of the Council of Europe who shall transmit copies thereof to the High Contracting Parties.

*Article 47.* The Court may only deal with a case after the Commission has acknowledged the failure of efforts for a friendly settlement and within the period of three months provided for in Article 32.

*Article 48.* The following may bring a case before the Court, provided that the High Contracting Party concerned, if there is only one, or the High Contracting Parties concerned, if there is more than one, are subject to the compulsory jurisdiction of the Court or, failing that, with the consent of the High Contracting Party concerned, if there is only one, or of the High Contracting Parties concerned if there is more than one:

(a) the Commission;

(b) a High Contracting Party whose national is alleged to be a victim;

(c) a High Contracting Party which referred the case to the Commission;

(d) a High Contracting Party against which the complaint has been lodged.

*Article 49.* In the event of dispute as to whether the Court has jurisdiction, the matter shall be settled by the decision of the Court.

*Article 50.* If the Court finds that a decision or a measure taken by a legal authority or any other authority of a High Contracting Party is completely or partially in conflict with the obligations arising from the present Convention, and if the internal law of the said Party allows only partial reparation to be made for the consequences of this decision or measure, the decision of the Court shall, if necessary, afford just satisfaction to the injured party.

*Article 51.* 1. Reasons shall be given for the judgment of the Court.

2. If the judgment does not represent in whole or in part the unanimous opinion of the judges, any judge shall be entitled to deliver a separate opinion.

*Article 52.* The judgment of the Court shall be final.

*Article 53.* The High Contracting Parties undertake to abide by the decision of the Court in any case to which they are Parties.

*Article 54.* The judgment of the Court shall be transmitted to the Committee of Ministers which shall supervise its execution.

*Article 55.* The Court shall draw up its own rules and shall determine its own procedure.

*Article 56.* 1. The first election of the members of the Court shall take place after the Declarations by the High Contracting Parties mentioned in Article 46 have reached a total of eight.

2. No case can be brought before the Court before this election.

**Section 5**

*Article 57.* On receipt of a request from the Secretary General of the Council of Europe any High Contracting Party shall furnish an explanation of the manner in which its internal law ensures the effective implementation of any of the provisions of this Convention.

*Article 58.* The expenses of the Commission and the Court shall be borne by the Council of Europe.

*Article 59.* The members of the Commission and of the Court shall be entitled, during the discharge of their functions, to the privileges and immunities provided for in Article 40 of the Statute of the Council of Europe and in the agreements made thereunder.

*Article 60.* Nothing in this Convention shall be construed as limiting or derogating from any of the human rights and fundamental freedoms which may be ensured under the laws of any High Contracting Party or under any other agreement to which it is a Party.

*Article 61.* Nothing in this Convention shall prejudice the powers conferred on the Committee of Ministers by the Statute of the Council of Europe.

*Article 62.* The High Contracting Parties agree that, except by special agreement, they will not avail themselves of treaties, Conventions or Declarations in force between them for the purpose of submitting, by way of petition, a dispute arising out of the interpretation or application of this Convention to a means of settlement other than those provided for in this Convention.

*Article 63.* 1. Any State may at the time of its ratification or at any time thereafter declare by notification addressed to the Secretary General of the Council of Europe that the present Convention shall extend to all or any of the territories for whose international relations it is responsible.

2. The Convention shall extend to the territory or territories named in the notification as from the thirtieth day after the receipt of this notification by the Secretary General of the Council of Europe.

3. The provisions of this Convention shall be applied in such territories with due regard, however, to local requirements.

4. Any State which has made a Declaration in accordance with paragraph 1 of this article may at any time thereafter declare on behalf of one or more of the territories to which the Declaration relates that it accepts the competence of the Commission to receive petitions from individuals, non-governmental organisations or groups of individuals in accordance with Article 25 of the present Convention.

*Article 64.* 1. Any State may, when signing this Convention or when depositing its instrument of ratification, make a reservation in respect of any particular provision of the Convention to the extent that any law then in force in its territory is not in conformity with the provision. Reservations of a general character shall not be permitted under this article.

2. Any reservation made under this article shall contain a brief statement of the law concerned.

*Article 65.* 1. A High Contracting Party may denounce the present Convention only after the expiry of five years from the date on which it became a Party to it and after six months' notice contained in a notification addressed to the Secretary General of the Council of Europe, who shall inform the other High Contracting Parties.

2. Such a denunciation shall not have the effect of releasing the High Contracting Party concerned from its obligations under this Convention in respect of any act which, being capable of constituting a violation of such obligations, may have been performed by it before the date at which the denunciation became effective.

3. Any High Contracting Party which shall cease to be a Member of the Council of Europe shall cease to be a Party to this Convention under the same conditions.

4. The Conventions may be denounced in accordance with the provisions of the preceding paragraphs in respect of any territory to which it has been declared to extend under the terms of Article 63.

*Article 66.* 1. This Convention shall be open to the signature of the Members of the Council of Europe. It shall be ratified. Ratifications shall be deposited with the Secretary General of the Council of Europe.

2. The present Convention shall come into force after the deposit of ten instruments of ratification.

3. As regards any signatory ratifying subsequently, the Convention shall come into force at the date of the deposit of its instrument of ratification.

4. The Secretary General of the Council of Europe shall notify all the Members of the Council of Europe of the entry into force of the Convention, the names of the High Contracting Parties who have ratified it, and the deposit of all instruments of ratification which may be effected subsequently.

Done at Rome this 4th day of November 1950 in English and French, both texts being equally authentic, in a single copy which shall remain deposited in the archives of the Council of Europe. The Secretary General shall transmit certified copies to each of the Signatories.

**BIBLIOGRAPHY.** 5 Breitenmoser, Stephan, and Dagmar Richter. "Proposal for an Additional Protocol to the European Convention on Human Rights Concerning the Protection of Minorities in the Participating States of the CSCE," *Human Rights Law Journal* 12, no. 6–7 (1991): 262–265. Scholarly article, in English.

Council of Europe. *Yearbook of the European Convention on Human Rights,* vol. 1–present. Dordrecht, the Netherlands: Martinus Nijhoff, 1959–present. IGO annual report, in English and French.

Council of Europe, Parliamentary Assembly. *Report on an Additional Protocol on the Rights of Minorities to the European Convention on Human Rights.* Strasbourg, France: 1993. IGO report, in English and French.

Council of Europe, European Commission of Human Rights. *Stock-Taking on the European Convention on Human Rights: A Periodic Note on the Concrete Results Achieved under the Convention. Supplement 1988.* Strasbourg, France: 1989. IGO document, in English.

Danish Center of Human Rights. *The Implementation in National Law of the European Convention on Human Rights. Proceedings of the Fourth Copenhagen Conference on Human Rights, 28 and 29 October 1988.* Copenhagen, Denmark: 1989. NGO conference proceedings, in English.

Delmas-Marty, Mireille, ed. *The European Convention for the Protection of Human Rights: International Protection Versus National Restrictions.* Dordrecht, the Netherlands: Martinus Nijhoff, 1992. Scholarly collective works, in English.

Foster, Nigel. "The European Court of Justice and the European Convention for the Protection of Human Rights," *Human Rights Law Journal* 8, parts 2–4 (1987): 245–272. Scholarly article, in English.

Kamminga, Menno T. "Is the European Convention on Human Rights Sufficiently Equipped to Cope with Gross and Systematic Violations?" *Netherlands Quarterly of Human Rights* 12, no. 2 (1994): 153–164. Scholarly article, in English.

Mower, A. Glenn, Jr. *Regional Human Rights: A Comparative Study of the West European and Inter-American Systems.* Westport, CT, USA: Greenwood Press, 1991. Scholarly monograph, in English; bibliography, pp. 171–174.

Polakiewicz, Jörg, and Valérie Jacob-Foltzer. "The European Human Rights Convention in Domestic Law: The Impact of the Strasbourg Case-Law in States Where Direct Effect Is Given to the Convention," *Human Rights Law Journal* 12, nos. 3 and 4 (March and April 1991): 65–84 (no. 3); 125–141 (no. 4). Scholarly article, in English.

Theodoropoulos, Christos, ed. *Human Rights in Europe and in Africa: A Comparative Analysis.* Athens, Greece: Hellenic University Press, 1992. Scholarly monograph, in English and Greek.

## EUROPEAN CONVENTION ON HUMAN RIGHTS: PROTOCOL I (1952).

The Protocol adds three rights to those set out in the parent Convention: the right to peaceful enjoyment of one's possessions, the right to education, and the right to participate in elections under conditions ensuring the free expression of the opinion of the people in the choice of the legislature.

The Protocol was concluded by the Committee of Ministers of the **COUNCIL OF EUROPE,** convened at Paris, on 20 March 1952, and entered into force on 18 May 1954. The text (*European Treaty Series* 9) is as follows:

The Governments signatory hereto, being Members of the Council of Europe,

Being resolved to take steps to ensure the collective enforcement of certain rights and freedoms other than those already included in section I of the Convention for the Protection of Human Rights and Fundamental Freedoms signed at Rome on 4 November 1950 (hereinafter referred to as "the Convention"),

Have agreed as follows:

*Article 1.* Every natural or legal person is entitled to the peaceful enjoyment of his possessions. No one shall be deprived of his possessions except in the public interest and subject to the conditions provided for by law and by the general principles of international law.

The preceding provisions shall not, however, in any way impair the right of a State to enforce such laws as it deems necessary to control the use of property in accordance with the general interest or to secure the payment of taxes or other contributions or penalties.

*Article 2.* No person shall be denied the right to education. In the exercise of any functions which it assumes in relation to education and to teaching, the State shall respect the right of parents to ensure such education and teaching in conformity with their own religious and philosophical convictions.

*Article 3.* The High Contracting Parties undertake to hold free elections at reasonable intervals by secret ballot, under conditions which will ensure the free expression of the opinion of the people in the choice of the legislature.

*Article 4.* Any High Contracting Party may at the time of signature or ratification or at any time thereafter communicate to the Secretary-General of the Council of Europe a Declaration stating the extent to which it undertakes that the provisions of the present Protocol shall apply to such of the territories for the international relations of which it is responsible as are named therein.

Any High Contracting Party which has communicated a Declaration in virtue of the preceding paragraph may from time to time communicate a further Declaration modifying the terms of any former Declaration or terminating the application of the provisions of this Protocol in respect of any territory.

A Declaration made in accordance with this article shall be deemed to have been made in accordance with paragraph (1) of article 63 of the Convention.

*Article 5.* As between the High Contracting Parties the provisions of articles 1, 2, 3 and 4 of this Protocol shall be regarded as additional articles to the Convention and all the provisions of the Convention shall apply accordingly.

*Article 6.* This Protocol shall be open for signature by the members of the Council of Europe, who are the signatories of the Convention; it shall be ratified at the same time as or after the ratification of the Convention. It shall enter into force after the deposit of ten instruments of ratification. As regards any signatory ratifying subsequently, the Protocol shall enter into force at the date of the deposit of its instrument of ratification.

The instruments of ratification shall be deposited with the Secretary-General of the Council of Europe, who will notify all members of the names of those who have ratified.

## EUROPEAN CONVENTION ON HUMAN RIGHTS: PROTOCOL II (1963).

The Protocol confers upon the European Court of Human Rights competence to give advisory opinions on legal questions concerning the parent Convention and its Protocols. Such advisory opinions may be requested only by the Committee of Ministers of the **COUNCIL OF EUROPE.** The Protocol was concluded by that Committee, convened at

Strasbourg, on 6 May 1963, and entered into force on 21 September 1970. The text (*European Treaty Series* 44) is as follows:

The member States of the Council of Europe signatory hereto:

Having regard to the provisions of the Convention for the Protection of Human Rights and Fundamental Freedoms signed at Rome on 4 November 1950 (hereinafter referred to as "the Convention") and, in particular, Article 19 instituting, among other bodies, a European Court of Human Rights (hereinafter referred to as "the Court");

Considering that it is expedient to confer upon the Court competence to give advisory opinions subject to certain conditions;

Have agreed as follows:

*Article 1.* 1. The Court may, at the request of the Committee of Ministers, give advisory opinions on legal questions concerning the interpretation of the Convention and the Protocols thereto.

2. Such opinions shall not deal with any question relating to the content or scope of the rights or freedoms defined in Section 1 of the Convention and in the Protocols thereto, or with any other question which the Commission, the Court or the Committee of Ministers might have to consider in consequence of any such proceedings as could be instituted in accordance with the Convention.

3. Decisions of the Committee of Ministers to request an advisory opinion of the Court shall require a two-thirds majority vote of the representatives entitled to sit on the Committee.

*Article 2.* The Court shall decide whether a request for an advisory opinion submitted by the Committee of Ministers is within its consultative competence as defined in Article 1 of this Protocol.

*Article 3.* 1. For the consideration of requests for an advisory opinion, the Court shall sit in plenary session.

2. Reasons shall be given for advisory opinions of the Court.

3. If the advisory opinion does not represent in whole or in part the unanimous opinion of the judges, any judge shall be entitled to deliver a separate opinion.

4. Advisory opinions of the Court shall be communicated to the Committee of Ministers.

*Article 4.* The powers of the Court under Article 55 of the Convention extend to the drawing up of such rules and the determination of such procedure as the Court may think necessary for the purposes of this Protocol.

*Article 5.* 1. This Protocol shall be open to signature by member States of the Council of Europe, signatories to the Convention, who may become Parties to it by:

(a) signature without reservation in respect of ratification or acceptance;

(b) signature with reservation in respect of ratification or acceptance, followed by ratification or acceptance.

Instruments of ratification or acceptance shall be deposited with the Secretary-General of the Council of Europe.

2. This Protocol shall enter into force as soon as all States Parties to the Convention shall have become Parties to the Protocol, in accordance with the provisions of paragraph 1 of this Article.

3. From the date of the entry into force of this Protocol, Articles 1 to 4 shall be considered an integral part of the Convention.

4. The Secretary-General of the Council of Europe shall notify the member States of the Council of:

(a) any signature without reservation in respect of ratification or acceptance;

(b) any signature with reservation in respect of ratification or acceptance;

(c) the deposit of any instrument of ratification or acceptance;

(d) the date of entry into force of this Protocol in accordance with paragraph 2 of this Article.

In witness whereof the undersigned, being duly authorised thereto, have signed this Protocol.

Done at Strasbourg, this 6th day of May 1963, in English and in French, both texts being equally authoritative, in a single copy which shall remain deposited in the archives of the Council of Europe. The Secretary General shall transmit certified copies to each of the signatory States.

## EUROPEAN CONVENTION ON HUMAN RIGHTS: PROTOCOL III (1963).

The Protocol amends the parent Convention, simplifying the procedure of the European Commission on Human Rights by abolishing the system of sub-commissions. The Protocol was concluded by the Committee of Ministers of the **COUNCIL OF EUROPE,** convened at Strasbourg, on 6 May 1963 and entered into force on 21 September 1970. The text (*European Treaty Series* 45) is as follows:

The member States of the Council of Europe, signatories to this Protocol,

Considering that it is advisable to amend certain provisions of the Convention for the Protection of Human Rights and Fundamental Freedoms signed at Rome on 4 November 1950 (hereinafter referred to as "the Convention") concerning the procedure of the European Commission of Human Rights,

Have agreed as follows:

*Article 1.* 1. Article 29 of the Convention is deleted.

2. The following provision shall be inserted in the Convention:

"*Article 29*

"After it has accepted a petition submitted under Article 25, the Commission may nevertheless decide unanimously to reject the petition if, in the course of its examination, it finds that the existence of one of the grounds for non-acceptance provided for in Article 27 has been established.

"In such a case, the decision shall be communicated to the parties."

*Article 2.* In Article 30 of the Convention, the word "Sub-Commission" shall be replaced by the word "Commission".

*Article 3.* 1. At the beginning of Article 34 of the Convention, the following shall be inserted:

"Subject to the provisions of Article 29 . . ."

2. At the end of the same Article, the sentence "the Sub-Commission shall take its decisions by a majority of its members" shall be deleted.

*Article 4.* 1. This Protocol shall be open to signature by the member States of the Council of Europe, who may become Parties to it either by:

(a) signature without reservation in respect of ratification or acceptance, or

(b) signature with reservation in respect of acceptance, followed by ratification or acceptance.

Instruments of ratification or acceptance shall be deposited with the Secretary-General of the Council of Europe.

2. This Protocol shall enter into force as soon as all States Parties to the Convention shall have become Parties to the Protocol, in accordance with the provisions of paragraph 1 of this Article.

3. The Secretary-General of the Council of Europe shall notify the member States of the Council of:

(a) any signature without reservation in respect of ratification or acceptance;

(b) any signature with reservation in respect of ratification or acceptance;

(c) the deposit of any instrument of ratification or acceptance;

(d) the date of entry into force of this Protocol in accordance with paragraph 2 of this Article.

In witness whereof the undersigned, being duly authorised thereto, have signed this Protocol.

Done at Strasbourg, this 6th day of May 1963, in English and in French, both texts being equally authoritative, in a single copy which shall remain deposited in the archives of the Council of Europe. The Secretary General shall transmit certified copies to each of the signatory States.


## EUROPEAN CONVENTION ON HUMAN RIGHTS: PROTOCOL IV (1963).

The Protocol secures certain rights and freedoms other than those included in the parent Convention and in **Protocol I** thereto: the right not to be deprived of one's liberty merely on the ground of inability to fulfill a contractual obligation; the right to liberty of movement and freedom to choose one's residence; the right to leave any country, including his own; and the right not to be expelled from the territory of the State of which one is a national. It also prohibits the collective expulsion of aliens.

The Protocol was concluded by the Committee of Ministers of the **Council of Europe,** convened at Strasbourg, on 16 September 1963, and entered into force on 2 May 1968. The text (*European Treaty Series* 46) is as follows:

The Governments signatory hereto, being Members of the Council of Europe,

Being resolved to take steps to ensure the collective enforcement of certain rights and freedoms other than those already included in Section 1 of the Convention for the Protection of Human Rights and Fundamental Freedoms signed at Rome on 4 November 1950 (hereinafter referred to as "the Convention") and in Articles 1 to 3 of the First Protocol to the Convention, signed at Paris on 20 March 1952,

Have agreed as follows:

*Article 1.* No one shall be deprived of his liberty merely on the ground of inability to fulfil a contractual obligation.

*Article 2.* 1. Everyone lawfully within the territory of a State shall, within that territory, have the right to liberty of movement and freedom to choose his residence.

2. Everyone shall be free to leave any country, including his own.

3. No restrictions shall be placed on the exercise of these rights other than such as are in accordance with law and are necessary in a democratic society in the interests of national security or public safety, for the maintenance of *ordre public,* for the prevention of crime, for the protection of health or morals, or for the protection of the rights and freedoms of others.

4. The rights set forth in paragraph 1 may also be subject, in particular areas, to restrictions imposed in accordance with law and justified by the public interest in a democratic society.

*Article 3.* 1. No one shall be expelled, by means either of an individual or of a collective measure, from the territory of the State of which he is a national.

2. No one shall be deprived of the right to enter the territory of the State of which he is a national.

*Article 4.* Collective expulsion of aliens is prohibited.

*Article 5.* 1. Any High Contracting Party may, at the time of signature or ratification of this Protocol, or at any time thereafter, communicate to the Secretary-General of the Council of Europe a Declaration stating the extent to which it undertakes that the provisions of this Protocol shall apply to such of the territories for the international relations of which it is responsible as are named therein.

2. Any High Contracting Party which has communicated a Declaration in virtue of the preceding paragraph may, from time to time, communicate a further Declaration modifying the terms of any former Declaration or terminating the application of the provisions of this Protocol in respect of any territory.

3. A Declaration made in accordance with this Article shall be deemed to have been made in accordance with paragraph 1 of Article 63 of the Convention.

4. The territory of any State to which this Protocol applies by virtue of ratification or acceptance by that State, and each territory to which this Protocol is applied by virtue of a Declaration by that State under this Article, shall be treated as separate territories for the purpose of the references in Articles 2 and 3 to the territory of a State.

*Article 6.* 1. As between the High Contracting Parties the provisions of Articles 1 to 5 of this Protocol shall be regarded as additional Articles to the Convention, and all the provisions of the Convention shall apply accordingly.

2. Nevertheless, the right of individual recourse recognised by a Declaration made under Article 25 of the Convention, or the acceptance of the compulsory jurisdiction of the Court by a Declaration made under Article 46 of the Convention, shall not be effective in relation to this Protocol unless the High Contracting Party concerned has made a statement recognising such right, or accepting such jurisdiction, in respect of all or any of Articles 1 to 4 of the Protocol.

*Article 7.* 1. This Protocol shall be open for signature by the Members of the Council of Europe who are the signatories of the Convention; it shall be ratified at the same time as or after the ratification of the Convention. It shall enter into force after the deposit of five instruments of ratification. As regards any signatory ratifying subsequently, the Protocol shall enter into force at the date of the deposit of its instrument of ratification.

2. The instruments of ratification shall be deposited with the Secretary-General of the Council of Europe, who will notify all Members of the names of those who have ratified.

In witness whereof the undersigned, being duly authorised thereto, have signed this Protocol.

Done at Strasbourg, this 16th day of September 1963, in English and in French, both texts being equally authoritative, in a single copy which shall remain deposited in the archives of the Council of Europe. The Secretary General shall transmit certified copies to each of the signatory States.

## EUROPEAN CONVENTION ON HUMAN RIGHTS: PROTOCOL V (1966).

The Protocol amends articles 22 and 40 of the parent Convention with a view to ensuring as far as possible a periodic turnover in the membership of the European Commission on Human Rights and the European Court of Human Rights, respectively. The Protocol was concluded by the Committee of Ministers of the COUNCIL OF EUROPE, convened at Strasbourg, on 20 January 1966 and entered into force on 21 December 1971. The text (*European Treaty Series* 55), is as follows:

The Governments signatory hereto, being Members of the Council of Europe,

Considering that certain inconveniences have arisen in the application of the provisions of Articles 22 and 40 of the Convention for the Protection of Human Rights and Fundamental Freedoms signed at Rome on 4th November 1950 (hereinafter referred to as "the Convention") relating to the length of the terms of office of the members of the European Commission of Human Rights (hereinafter referred to as "the Commission") and of the European Court of Human Rights (hereinafter referred to as "the Court");

Considering that it is desirable to ensure as far as possible an election every three years of one half of the members of the Commission and of one third of the members of the Court;

Considering therefore that it is desirable to amend certain provisions of the Convention,

Have agreed as follows:

*Article 1.* In Article 22 of the Convention, the following two paragraphs shall be inserted after paragraph (2):

"(3) In order to ensure that, as far as possible, one half of the membership of the Commission shall be renewed every three years, the Committee of Ministers may decide, before proceeding to any subsequent election, that the term or terms of office of one or more members to be elected shall be for a period other than six years but not more than nine and not less than three years.

"(4) In cases where more than one term of office is involved and the Committee of Ministers applies the preceding paragraph, the allocation of the terms of office shall be effected by the drawing of lots by the Secretary General, immediately after the election."

*Article 2.* In Article 22 of the Convention, the former paragraphs (3) and (4) shall become respectively paragraphs (5) and (6).

*Article 3.* In Article 40 of the Convention, the following two paragraphs shall be inserted after paragraph (2):

"(3) In order to ensure that, as far as possible, one third of the membership of the Court shall be renewed every three years, the Consultative Assembly may decide, before proceeding to any subsequent election, that the term or terms of office of one or more members to be elected shall be for a period other than nine years but not more than twelve and not less than six years.

"(4) In cases where more than one term of office is involved and the Consultative Assembly applies the preceding paragraph, the allocation of the terms of office shall be effected by the drawing of lots by the Secretary General immediately after the election."

*Article 4.* In Article 40 of the Convention, the former paragraphs (3) and (4) shall become respectively paragraphs (5) and (6).

*Article 5.* 1. This Protocol shall be open to signature by Members of the Council of Europe, signatories to the Convention, who may become Parties to it by:

(a) Signature without reservation in respect of ratification or acceptance;

(b) Signature with reservation in respect of ratification or acceptance, followed by ratification or acceptance.

Instruments of ratification or acceptance shall be deposited with the Secretary General of the Council of Europe.

2. This Protocol shall enter into force as soon as all Contracting Parties to the Convention shall have become Parties to the Protocol, in accordance with the provisions of paragraph 1 of this Article.

3. The Secretary General of the Council of Europe shall notify the Members of the Council of:

(a) Any signature without reservation in respect of ratification or acceptance;

(b) Any signature with reservation in respect of ratification or acceptance;

(c) The deposit of any instrument of ratification or acceptance;

(d) The date of entry into force of this Protocol in accordance with paragraph 2 of this Article.

In witness whereof the undersigned, being duly authorised thereto, have signed this Protocol.

Done at Strasbourg, this 20th day of January 1966, in English and in French, both texts being equally authoritative, in a single copy which shall remain deposited in the archives of the Council of Europe. The Secretary General shall transmit certified copies to each of the signatory governments.

## EUROPEAN CONVENTION ON HUMAN RIGHTS: PROTOCOL VI (1983).

In the Protocol, member States of the COUNCIL OF EUROPE agree (article 1) that the death penalty shall be abolished and that no one shall be condemned to such penalty or executed. However, according to article 2, a State may make provision in its law for the death penalty in respect of acts committed in time of war or imminent threat of war, provided that such penalty is applied only in instances laid down in the law and in accordance with its provisions.

The Protocol was concluded by the Committee of Ministers of the Council of Europe, convened in Strasbourg, on 28 April 1983 and entered into force on 1 March 1985. The text (*European Treaty Series* 114) is as follows:

The member States of the Council of Europe, signatory to this Protocol to the Convention for the Protection of Human Rights and Fundamental Freedoms, signed at Rome on 4 November 1950 (hereinafter referred to as "the Convention"),

Considering that the evolution that has occurred in several member States of the Council of Europe expresses a general tendency in favour of abolition of the death penalty;

Have agreed as follows:

*Article 1.* The death penalty shall be abolished. No one shall be condemned to such penalty or executed.

*Article 2.* A State may make provision in its law for the death penalty in respect of acts committed in time of war or of imminent threat of war; such penalty shall be applied only in the instances laid down in the law and in accordance with its provisions. The State shall communicate to the Secretary General of the Council of Europe the relevant provisions of that law.

*Article 3.* No derogation from the provisions of this Protocol shall be made under Article 15 of the Convention.

*Article 4.* No reservation may be made under Article 64 of the Convention in respect of the provisions of this Protocol.

*Article 5.* 1. Any State may at the time of signature or when depositing its instrument of ratification, acceptance or approval, specify the territory or territories to which this Protocol shall apply.

2. Any State may at any later date, by a Declaration addressed to the Secretary General of the Council of Europe, extend the application of this Protocol to any other territory specified in the Declaration. In respect of such territory the Protocol shall enter into force on the first day of the month following the date of receipt of such Declaration by the Secretary General.

3. Any Declaration made under the two preceding paragraphs may, in respect of any territory specified in such Declaration, be withdrawn by a notification addressed to the Secretary General. The withdrawal shall become effective on the first day of the month following the date of receipt of such notification by the Secretary General.

*Article 6.* As between the States Parties the provisions of Articles 1 to 5 of this Protocol shall be regarded as additional articles to the Convention and all the provisions of the Convention shall apply accordingly.

*Article 7.* This Protocol shall be open for signature by the member States of the Council of Europe, signatories to the Convention. It shall be subject to ratification, acceptance or approval. A member State of the Council of Europe may not ratify, accept or approve this Protocol unless it has, simultaneously or previously, ratified the Convention. Instruments of ratification, acceptance or approval shall be deposited with the Secretary General of the Council of Europe.

*Article 8.* 1. This Protocol shall enter into force on the first day of the month following the date on which five member States of the Council of Europe have expressed their consent to be bound by the Protocol in accordance with the provisions of Article 7.

2. In respect of any member State which subsequently expresses its consent to be bound by it, the Protocol shall enter into force on the first day of the month following the date of the deposit of the instrument of ratification, acceptance or approval.

*Article 9.* The Secretary General of the Council of Europe shall notify the member States of the Council of:

(a) any signature;

(b) the deposit of any instrument of ratification, acceptance or approval;

(c) any date of entry into force of this Protocol in accordance with Articles 5 and 8;

(d) any other act, notification or communication relating to this Protocol.

In witness whereof the undersigned, being duly authorised thereto, have signed this Protocol.

Done at Strasbourg, the 28 April 1983, in English and French, both texts being equally authentic, in a single copy which shall be deposited in the archives of the Council of Europe. The Secretary General of the Council of Europe shall transmit certified copies to each member State of the Council of Europe.

## EUROPEAN CONVENTION ON HUMAN RIGHTS: PROTOCOL VII (1984).

The Protocol supplements the provisions of the parent Convention by the addition of six articles recognizing new rights (articles 1 to 6 of the Protocol) with a view to ensuring the collective enforcement of those rights by means of the parent Convention. The Protocol was concluded by the Committee of Ministers of the **COUNCIL OF EUROPE,** convened in Strasbourg, on 22 November 1984 and entered into force on 1 November 1988. The text (*European Treaty Series* 117) is as follows:

The member States of the Council of Europe signatory hereto,

Being resolved to take further steps to ensure the collective enforcement of certain rights and freedoms by means of the Convention for the Protection of Human Rights and Fundamental Freedoms signed at Rome on 4 November 1950 (hereinafter referred to as "the Convention");

Have agreed as follows:

*Article 1.* 1. An alien lawfully resident in the territory of a State shall not be expelled therefrom except in pursuance of a decision reached in accordance with law and shall be allowed:

a. to submit reasons against his expulsion,

b. to have his case reviewed, and

c. to be represented for these purposes before the competent authority or a person or persons designated by that authority.

2. An alien may be expelled before the exercise of his rights under paragraph 1(a), (b) and (c) of this Article, when such expulsion is necessary in the interests of public order or is grounded on reasons of national security.

*Article 2.* 1. Everyone convicted of a criminal offence by a tribunal shall have the right to have conviction or sentence reviewed by a higher tribunal. The exercise of this right, including the grounds on which it may be exercised, shall be governed by law.

2. This right may be subject to exceptions in regard to offences of a minor character, as prescribed by law, or in cases in which the person concerned was tried in the first instance by the highest tribunal or was convicted following an appeal against acquittal.

*Article 3.* When a person has by a final decision been convicted of a criminal offence and when subsequently his conviction has been reversed, or he has been pardoned, on the ground that a new or newly discovered fact shows conclusively that there has been a miscarriage of justice, the person who has suffered punishment as a result of such conviction shall be compensated according to the law or the practice of the State concerned, unless it is proved that the non-disclosure of the unknown fact in time is wholly or partly attributable to him.

*Article 4.* 1. No one shall be liable to be tried or punished again in criminal proceedings under the jurisdiction of the same State for an offence for which he has already been finally acquitted or convicted in accordance with the law and penal procedure of that State.

2. The provisions of the preceding paragraph shall not prevent the re-opening of the case in accordance with the law and penal procedure of the State concerned, if there is evidence of new or newly discovered facts, or if there has been a fundamental defect in the previous proceedings, which could affect the outcome of the case.

3. No derogation from this Article shall be made under Article 15 of the Convention.

*Article 5.* 1. Spouses shall enjoy equality of rights and responsibilities of a private law character between them, and in their relations with their children, as to marriage, during marriage and in the event of its dissolution. This Article shall not prevent States from taking such measures as are necessary in the interests of the children.

*Article 6.* 1. Any State may at the time of signature or when depositing its instrument of ratification, acceptance or approval, specify the territory or territories to which this Protocol shall apply and state the extent to which it undertakes that the provisions of this Protocol shall apply to this or these territories.

2. Any State may at any later date, by a Declaration addressed to the Secretary-General of the Council of Europe, extend the application of this Protocol to any other territory specified in the Declaration. In respect of such territory the Protocol shall enter into force on the first day of the month following the expiration of a period of two months after the date of receipt by the Secretary-General of such Declaration.

3. Any Declaration made under the two preceding paragraphs may, in respect of any territory specified in such Declaration, be withdrawn or modified by a notification addressed to the Secretary-General. The withdrawal or modification shall become effective on the first day of the month following the expiration of a period of two months after the day of receipt of such notification by the Secretary-General.

4. A Declaration made in accordance with this Article shall be deemed to have been made in accordance with paragraph 1 of Article 63 of the Convention.

5. The territory of any State to which this Protocol applies by virtue of ratification, acceptance or approval by that State, and each territory to which this Protocol is applied by virtue of a Declaration by that State under this Article, may be treated as separate territories for the purpose of the reference in Article 1 to the territory of a State.

*Article 7.* 1. As between the State Parties, the provisions of Articles 1 to 6 of this Protocol shall be regarded as additional Articles to the Convention, and all the provisions of the Convention shall apply accordingly.

2. Nevertheless, the right of individual recourse recognised by a Declaration made under Article 25 of the Convention, or the acceptance of the compulsory jurisdiction of the Court by a Declaration made under Article 46 of the Convention, shall not be effective in relation to this Protocol unless the State concerned has made a statement recognising such right, or accepting such jurisdiction in respect of Articles 1 to 5 of this Protocol.

*Article 8.* This Protocol shall be open for signature by member States of the Council of Europe which have signed the Convention. It is subject to ratification, acceptance or approval. A member State of the Council of Europe may not ratify, accept or approve this Protocol without previously or simultaneously ratifying the Convention. Instruments of ratification, acceptance or approval shall be deposited with the Secretary General of the Council of Europe.

*Article 9.* 1. This Protocol shall enter into force on the first day of the month following the expiration of a period of two months after the date on which seven member States of the Council of Europe have expressed their consent to be bound by the Protocol in accordance with the provisions of Article 8.

2. In respect of any member State which subsequently expresses its consent to be bound by it, the Protocol shall enter into force on the first day of the month following the expiration of a period of two months after the date of the deposit of the instrument of ratification, acceptance or approval.

*Article 10.* The Secretary General of the Council of Europe shall notify all the member States of the Council of:

(a) any signature;

(b) the deposit of any instrument of ratification, acceptance or approval;

(c) any date of entry into force of this Protocol in accordance with Articles 6 and 9;

(d) any other act, notification or Declaration relating to this Protocol.

In witness whereof the undersigned, being duly authorised thereto, have signed this Protocol.

Done at Strasbourg, the twenty-two November one thousand nine hundred and eighty four, in English and French, both texts being equally authentic, in a single copy which shall be deposited in the archives of the Council of Europe shall transmit certified copies to each member State of the Council.

## EUROPEAN CONVENTION ON HUMAN RIGHTS: PROTOCOL VIII (1985).

The Protocol amends certain provisions of the parent Convention with a view to expediting the functioning of the European Commission on Human Rights. It also amends certain provisions of the parent Convention which relate to the procedures of the European Court of Human Rights. The Protocol was concluded by the Committee of Ministers of the **COUNCIL OF EUROPE,** convened in Vienna, on 19 March 1985. The text (*European Treaty Series* 118) is as follows:

The member States of the Council of Europe, signatories to this Protocol to the Convention for the Protection of Human Rights and Fundamental Freedoms, signed at Rome on 4 November 1950 (hereinafter referred to as "the Convention"),

Considering that it is desirable to amend certain provisions of the Convention with a view to improving and in particular to expediting the procedure of the European Commission of Human Rights,

Considering that it is also advisable to amend certain provisions of the Convention concerning the procedure of the European Court of Human Rights,

Have agreed as follows:

*Article 1.* The existing text of Article 20 of the Convention shall become paragraph 1 of that Article and shall be supplemented by the following four paragraphs:

"2. The Commission shall sit in plenary session. It may, however, set up Chambers, each composed of at least seven members. The Chambers may examine petitions submitted under Article 25 of this Convention which can be dealt with on the basis of established case law or which raise no serious question affecting the interpretation or application of the Convention. Subject to this restriction and to the provisions of paragraph 5 of this Article, the Chambers shall exercise all the powers conferred on the Commission by the Convention.

The member of the Commission elected in respect of a High Contracting Party against which a petition has been lodged shall have the right to sit on a Chamber to which that petition has been referred.

3. The Commission may set up Committees, each composed of at least three members, with the power, exercisable by a unanimous vote, to declare inadmissible or strike from its list of cases a petition submitted under Article 25, when such a decision can be taken without further examination.

4. A Chamber or Committee may at any time relinquish jurisdiction in favour of the plenary Commission, which may also order the transfer to it of any petition referred to a Chamber or Committee.

5. Only the plenary Commission can exercise the following powers:

(a) the examination of applications submitted under Article 24;

(b) the bringing of a case before the Court in accordance with Article 48a;

(c) the drawing up of rules of procedure in accordance with Article 36."

*Article 2.* Article 21 of the Convention shall be supplemented by the following third paragraph:

"3. The candidates shall be of high moral character and must either possess the qualifications required for appointment to high judicial office or be persons of recognised competence in national or international law."

*Article 3.* Article 23 of the Convention shall be supplemented by the following sentence:

"During their term of office they shall not hold any position which is incompatible with their independence and impartiality as members of the Commission or the demands of this office."

*Article 4.* The text, with modifications, of Article 28 of the Convention shall become paragraph 1 of that Article and the text, with modifications, of Article 30 shall become paragraph 2. The new text of Article 28 shall read as follows:

"*Article 28.* 1. In the event of the Commission accepting a petition referred to it:

(a) it shall, with a view to ascertaining the facts, undertake together with the representatives of the parties an examination of the petition and, if need be, an investigation, for the effective conduct of which the States concerned shall furnish all necessary facilities, after an exchange of views with the Commission;

(b) it shall at the same time place itself at the disposal of the parties concerned with a view to securing a friendly settlement of the matter on the basis of respect for Human Rights as defined in this Convention.

2. If the Commission succeeds in effecting a friendly settlement, it shall draw up a Report which shall be sent to the States concerned, to the Committee of Ministers and to the Secretary General of the Council of Europe for publication. This Report shall be confined to a brief statement of the facts and of the solution reached."

*Article 5.* In the first paragraph of Article 29 of the Convention, the word "unanimously" shall be replaced by the words "by a majority of two-thirds of its members."

*Article 6.* The following provision shall be inserted in the Convention:

"*Article 30.* 1. The Commission may at any stage of the proceedings decide to strike a petition out of its list of cases where the circumstances lead to the conclusion that:

(a) the applicant does not intend to pursue his petition, or

(b) the matter has been resolved, or

(c) for any other reason established by the Commission, it is no longer justified to continue the examination of the petition.

However, the Commission shall continue the examination of a petition if respect for Human Rights as defined in this Convention so requires.

2. If the Commission decides to strike a petition out of its list after having accepted it, it shall draw up a Report which shall contain a statement of the facts and the decision striking out the petition together with the reasons therefor. The Report shall be transmitted to the parties, as well as to the Committee of Ministers for information. The Commission may publish it.

3. The Commission may decide to restore a petition to its list of cases if it considers that the circumstances justify such a course."

*Article 7.* In Article 31 of the Convention, paragraph 1 shall read as follows:

"1. If the examination of a petition has not been completed in accordance with Article 28 (paragraph 2), 29 or 30, the Commission shall draw up a Report on the facts and state its opinion as to whether the facts found disclose a breach by the State concerned of its obligations under the Convention. The individual opinions of members of the Commission on this point may be stated in the Report."

*Article 8.* Article 34 of the Convention shall read as follows:

"Subject to the provisions of Articles 20 (paragraph 3) and 29, the Commission shall take its decisions by a majority of the members present and voting."

*Article 9.* Article 40 of the Convention shall be supplemented by the following seventh paragraph:

"7. The members of the Court shall sit on the Court in their individual capacity. During their term of office they shall not hold any position which is incompatible with their independence and impartiality as members of the Court or the demands of this office."

*Article 10.* Article 41 of the Convention shall read as follows:

"The Court shall elects its President and one or two Vice-Presidents for a period of three years. They may be re-elected."

*Article 11.* In the first sentence of Article 43 of the Convention, the word "seven" shall be replaced by the word "nine".

*Article 12.* 1. This Protocol shall be open for signature by member States of the Council of Europe signatories to the Convention, which may express their consent to be bound by:

(a) signature without reservation as to ratification, acceptance or approval, or

(b) signature subject to ratification, acceptance or approval, followed by ratification, acceptance or approval.

2. Instruments of ratification, acceptance or approval shall be deposited with the Secretary General of the Council of Europe.

*Article 13.* This Protocol shall enter into force on the first day of the month following the expiration of a period of three months after the date on which all Parties to the Convention have expressed their consent to be bound by the Protocol in accordance with the provisions of Article 12.

*Article 14*. The Secretary General of the Council of Europe shall notify the member States of the Council of:

   (a)  any signature;

   (b)  the deposit of any instrument of ratification, acceptance or approval;

   (c)  the date of entry into force of this Protocol in accordance with Article 13;

   (d)  any other act, notification or communication relating to this Protocol.

In witness whereof the undersigned, being duly authorised thereto, have signed this Protocol.

Done at Vienna, this 19th day of March 1985, in English and French, both texts being equally authentic, in a single copy which shall be deposited in the archives of the Council of Europe. The Secretary General of the Council of Europe shall transmit certified copies to each member State of the Council of Europe.

**EUROPEAN COMMISSION ON HUMAN RIGHTS.** The European Commission on Human Rights of the **COUNCIL OF EUROPE** was established in 1955 in accordance with article 19 of the **EUROPEAN CONVENTION ON HUMAN RIGHTS** in order to ensure the observance of the engagements undertaken by States parties to that Convention.

Under article 21 of the Convention, any State party may refer to the Commission, through the Secretary-General of the Council of Europe, any alleged breach of the provisions of the Convention by another State party. Moreover, under article 25, the Commission may receive petitions from any person, non-governmental organization, or group of individuals claiming to be the victim of a violation by one of the States parties of the rights set forth in the Convention, provided that the State against which the complaint is lodged has declared that it recognizes the competence of the Commission to receive such petitions. The Commission's first task is to determine whether or not the petition is admissible under the provisions of the Convention, dismissing those that are anonymous, manifestly unfounded, or abusive of the right of petition and those involving situations in which national remedies have not been exhausted. It must then investigate and ascertain the facts and place itself at the disposal of the parties concerned with a view to securing a friendly settlement of the problem. If such a settlement is achieved, the Commission draws up a report and sends it to the parties concerned, the Committee of Ministers, and the Secretary-General of the Council of Europe for publication. If no settlement is reached, the Commission draws up a detailed report outlining the facts and stating its opinion as to whether or not they disclose a breach of any obligation assumed under the Convention. This report is transmitted to the parties concerned and to the Committee of Ministers together with such proposals as the Commission may consider appropriate. The Commission may also refer the matter to the European Court of Human Rights.

The Commission consists of 21 members, that being the number of States members of the Council of Europe, all of which are parties to the Convention. Members are elected by the Committee of Ministers on the basis of nominations submitted by members of the Consultative Committee of the Council. No two members of the Commission may be nationals of the same State. All serve in their personal capacity for a term of four years. The Commission usually holds five or six sessions per year, totaling about 60 session days, all at the headquarters of the Council of Europe in Strasbourg.

The Commission has no permanent subsidiary bodies but usually establishes a sub-Commission, composed of seven of its members, to assist it in the performances of its factfinding and conciliation functions.

**EUROPEAN COURT OF HUMAN RIGHTS.** The Court of Human Rights of the **COUNCIL OF EUROPE** was established in accordance with article 19 of the **EUROPEAN CONVENTION ON HUMAN RIGHTS** in order to ensure observance of the engagements undertaken by States parties to that Convention, and the Court has jurisdiction in all cases concerning its interpretation and application.

Any State party may, at any time, declare that it recognizes as compulsory *ipso facto* and without special agreement the jurisdiction of the Court in all matters concerning the interpretation and application of the Convention (article 46). The Court may deal with a case only after the European Commission on Human Rights has acknowledged the failure of its efforts for a friendly settlement and within a period of three months from the date of transmission of the Commission's report to the Council of Ministers (article 47). A case may be brought before the Court by (a) the Commission, (b) a party whose national is alleged to be a victim, (c) the party which referred the case to the Commission, or (d) a party against which the complaint has been lodged (article 48). If the Court finds that a decision or measure taken by a legal authority or any other authority of a party is completely or partially in conflict with the obligations arising from the Convention, and if the international law of the said party allows only partial reparation to be made for the consequences of this decision or measure, the decision of the Court shall, if necessary, afford just satisfaction to the injured party (article 50). Judgments of the Court are final, and all parties undertake to abide by them. The judgments are transmitted to the Committee of Ministers of the Council of Europe, which is authorized to supervise their execution.

In accordance with article 38 of the Convention, the Court consists of 21 members, that being the number of members States of the Council of Europe, all of which are parties to the Convention. Members are elected by the Consultative Assembly of the Council of Europe on the basis of nominations submitted by the members of the Council of Europe. Under article 39 (3), candidates "shall be of high moral character and must either possess the qualifications required for appointment to high judicial office or be jurisconsults of recognized competence." They serve for a term of nine years.

The Court schedules its sessions as required. All are held in Strasbourg.

For the consideration of each case brought before it, the Court consists of a chamber composed of seven judges. The judge who is a national of any State party concerned sits as an *ex officio* member of the chamber or, if there is none, a person of its choice sits in the capacity as judge. Names of the other judges are chosen by lot by the president before the opening of a case.

## EUROPEAN CONVENTIONS ON SPECIFIC HUMAN RIGHTS QUESTIONS.

In addition to preparing and providing for the implementation of the **EUROPEAN CONVENTION ON HUMAN RIGHTS** and the European Convention for the Prevention of Torture and Inhuman or Degrading Treatment or Punishment (see **TORTURE**) by concerted international action (by the Commission and Court of Human Rights and the Committee for the Prevention of Torture and Inhuman or Degrading Treatment or Punishment), the **COUNCIL OF EUROPE** has prepared a series of instruments which Contracting States have themselves undertaken to implement through cooperative national action. Among these are the following:

*EUROPEAN CONVENTION ON ESTABLISHMENT, AND PROTOCOL (1955).* The Convention, concluded at Paris on 13 December 1955 by the Committee of Ministers of the Council of Europe, regulates the legal and *de facto* treatment of nationals of the contracting States when they travel to territories under the jurisdiction of other contracting States. It has the effect of placing the nationals of the contracting States in a position more favorable than those of other States in such matters as admission, legal protection, taxation, public service benefits, and private and civil rights. It authorizes the establishment of an international standing committee, composed of one representative of each contracting State, to monitor its practical application or, if necessary, to supplement its provisions.

The Convention is followed by a Protocol providing detailed explanations and qualifications of certain provisions. Both the Convention and the Protocol entered

into force on 23 February 1964. For the texts, see *European Treaty Series* 19.

*EUROPEAN CONVENTION ON EXTRADITION (1957), AND PROTOCOLS.* The Convention, concluded at Paris on 13 December 1957 by the Committee of Ministers of the Council of Europe, aims at establishing uniform rules to govern the decisions of States Parties when dealing with requests from other States for the surrender of persons sought either for prosecution or for the carrying out of a sentence or detention order. The Convention entered into force on 18 April 1960. Its provisions were later supplemented by two protocols. The text can be found in *European Treaty Series* 24.

The European Convention on Extradition: Additional Protocol (1975) entered into force on 20 August 1979. It excludes war crimes and crimes against humanity from the category of political offences, set out in article 3 of the parent Convention, to which extradition does not apply. It also authorizes States parties to refuse extradition if the offender has already been tried for the offence, or offences, in respect of which the request is made. The text of the additional protocol can be found in *European Treaty Series* 53.

The Second Additional Protocol to the European Convention on Extradition was concluded by the Committee of Ministers of the Council of Europe meeting in Strasbourg on 17 March 1978 and entered into force on 5 June 1983. It revises provisions of the parent Convention relating to such matters as fiscal offences, judgements in absentia, and amnesty, with a view to facilitating the application of that Convention. The text of the second additional protocol can be found in *European Treaty Series* 98.

*EUROPEAN SOCIAL CHARTER (1961).* The Charter sets out measures to ensure the enjoyment of a number of economic and social rights without discrimination on grounds such as race, color, sex, religion, political opinion, national extraction, or social origin in States members of the **COUNCIL OF EUROPE.** It is, in effect, a counterpart to the **EUROPEAN CONVENTION ON HUMAN RIGHTS** but does not provide for comparable international machinery of implementation.

Under the Charter, States parties undertake to ensure the effective exercise of the enumerated economic and social rights and to report to the Council on the results of their endeavors. The reports are examined first by a Committee of experts, then by a Sub-Committee of the Governmental Social Committee of the Council, and, finally, by the Council's Consultative Assembly. Eventually, the Committee of Ministers of the Council of Europe, after consultation with the

Consultative Assembly, may make recommendations to the contracting parties.

An appendix, which forms an integral part of the charter (article 388), defines the scope of its provisions in terms of the persons protected.

The Charter was concluded by the States Members of the Council of Europe, convened in Turin, on 18 October 1961, and entered into force on 26 February 1965. For the text, see *European Treaty Series* 35.

**EUROPEAN CODE OF SOCIAL SECURITY, AND PROTOCOL (1964).** The Code, two addenda, and the Protocol, were concluded by the Committee of Ministers of the Council, meeting in Strasbourg, on 16 April 1964, and entered into force on 17 March 1968. These instruments spell out in detail the meaning of the right to social security by specifying benefits to be paid to workers in the event of sickness, unemployment, old age, or incapacity. The Protocol sets, for States accepting its provisions, a standard somewhat higher than does the basic Code. Both instruments improve upon the minimum-standard level embodied in the ILO Social Security (Minimum Standards) Convention of 28 June 1952. In the Code, reference is made to the need for a special instrument to deal with questions relating to social security for foreigners and migrants in European countries; such an instrument, the European Convention on Social Security, was concluded in 1972. For the text of the Code and Protocol, see *European Treaty Series* 48.

**EUROPEAN CONVENTION ON THE ADOPTION OF CHILDREN (1967).** The Convention was adopted at Strasbourg on 24 April 1967 by the Committee of Ministers of the Council of Europe. It entered into force on 26 April 1968. It provides for the establishment of common principles and practices for the adoption of children in all contracting States. These States agree to ensure that their laws are in accordance with the "Essential Provisions" set out in Part II of the instrument, and further agree to put into effect as soon as possible the "Supplementary Provisions" enumerated in Part III. For the text of the Convention, see *European Treaty Series* 58.

**EUROPEAN CONVENTION ON REPATRIATION OF MINORS (1970).** Under this Convention, contracting States under take to cooperate in the repatriation of minors who have been taken abroad against the wishes of their parents or guardians in contravention of the applicable laws. While providing that, in normal circumstances, requests for such cooperation should be considered favorably, the Convention refers to circumstances in which favorable action may reasonably be denied or postponed. The Convention was concluded by the Committee of Ministers of the Council of Europe, convened at the Hague on 28 May 1970. For the text of the Convention, see *European Treaty Series* 71.

**EUROPEAN CONVENTION ON THE TRANSFER OF PROCEEDINGS IN CRIMINAL MATTERS (1972).** The Convention provides that, when a person is suspected of having committed an offense under the law of a Contracting State, that State may request another Contracting State to take proceedings against him in certain cases and under certain conditions. Such cases arise, for example, when the suspected person is a national, or is ordinarily resident in, the requested State, or is imprisoned there. Concluded by the Committee of Ministers of the Council of Europe, convened in Strasbourg on 15 May 1972, the Convention entered into force on 30 March 1978. For the text, see *European Treaty Series* 73.

**EUROPEAN CONVENTION ON SOCIAL SECURITY (1972).** The Convention was concluded by the Committee of Ministers of the Council of Europe meeting in Paris, on 14 December 1972 and entered into force on 1 March 1977. Prepared to meet the need for a special instrument to govern questions relating to social security for foreigners and migrants in European countries, foreseen in article 73 of the European Code of Social Security, the Convention aims at ensuring that all persons resident in the territory of a contracting State—including nationals of other contracting parties, refugees, and stateless persons—enjoy equality of treatment with nationals as regards the benefits available to them under social security schemes. The Convention was accompanied by a detailed Agreement as to its application. For the text of the Convention, see *European Treaty Series* 78.

**EUROPEAN CONVENTION ON THE NON-APPLICABILITY OF STATUTORY LIMITATIONS TO CRIMES AGAINST HUMANITY AND WAR CRIMES (1974).** The Convention follows the general lines of the Convention on the Non-Applicability of Statutory Limitations to War Crimes and Crimes Against Humanity adopted by the UN General Assembly on 26 November 1968. Under the European Convention, States Members of the Council of Europe undertake to adopt any measures necessary to ensure that no statutory limitation shall apply to crimes against humanity or war crimes or to the enforcement of sentences imposed for such offenses insofar as they are punishable under domestic law. The Convention was concluded by the Committee of Ministers of the Council of Europe, convened in Strasbourg, on 25 January 1974. For the text, see *European Treaty Series* 82.

**EUROPEAN CONVENTION ON THE LEGAL STATUS OF CHILDREN BORN OUT OF WEDLOCK (1975).** The Convention aims at reducing the differences between the legal and social status of children born out of wedlock as compared to those of children born of married parents. It was concluded in Strasbourg on 15 October 1975 by the Committee of Ministers of the Council of Europe, and entered into force on 11 August 1978. For the text, see *European Treaty Series* 85.

### EUROPEAN CONVENTION ON THE SUPPRESSION OF TERRORISM (1977).

The Convention binds contracting States to extradite persons who have Committee serious terrorist offenses, such as the taking of hostages, the hijacking of an aircraft, or the use of explosives, even though they seek to justify those actions on political grounds. However, a Contracting State may refuse to extradite a person if it has reasonable grounds to believe that the request for extradition has been made for the purpose of prosecuting or punishing a person on account of his race, religion, nationality or political opinion. The Convention was concluded by the Committee of Ministers of the Council of Europe, convened in Strasbourg on 27 January 1978. For the text, see *European Treaty Series* 90.

### EUROPEAN CONVENTION ON THE LEGAL STATUS OF MIGRANT WORKERS (1977).

Concluded by the Committee of Ministers of the Council of Europe, meeting in Strasbourg on 24 November 1977, the Convention's primary purpose is to regulate the legal status of migrant workers in such a way as to ensure that they are treated no less favorably than workers who are nationals of the receiving State in all aspects of living and working conditions. For the text, see *European Treaty Series* 93.

### EUROPEAN CONVENTION ON RECOGNITION AND ENFORCEMENT OF DECISIONS CONCERNING CUSTODY OF CHILDREN AND ON RESTORATION OF CUSTODY OF CHILDREN (1980).

The Convention establishes procedures whereby a child improperly removed from a contracting State to another contracting State, in breach of an enforcable decision relating to its custody, can be returned to the person having custody. Each contracting State undertakes to appoint a central authority to deal with such matters, to whom any person who has obtained a decision in that State relating to the custody of a child and who wishes to have that decision recognized and enforced in another contracting State may submit an application. The central authorities cooperate in locating the child, in obtaining recognition or enforcement of custody decisions, and in restoring the child to the person having custody. The Convention was adopted by the Committee of Ministers of the Council of Europe, convened in Luxembourg, on 20 May 1980 and entered into force

on 1 September 1983. For the complete text, see *European Treaty Series* 105.

### EUROPEAN CONVENTION FOR THE PROTECTION OF INDIVIDUALS WITH REGARD TO AUTOMATIC PROCESSING OF PERSONAL DATA (1981).

States parties to this Convention undertake to enact legislation and to take other necessary measures to ensure that data contained in automated personal data files are not disclosed to unauthorized persons. The Convention sets out a series of basic principles designed to protect the right of privacy of the individual whose personal data are fed into such files. The principles regulate the procedures by which such data are obtained, preserved, revised, or corrected, and made available to others. In particular, they prohibit the processing of data revealing racial origin, political opinions, religious or other beliefs, or information concerning health or sexual life, unless domestic laws provide adequate safeguards against the disclosure of such information. The Convention was adopted by the Committee of Ministers of the Council of Europe, convened at Strasbourg, on 28 January 1981, and entered into force on 1 October 1985. For the text, see *European Treaty Series* 108.

### EUROPEAN CONVENTION FOR THE PREVENTION OF TORTURE AND INHUMAN OR DEGRADING TREATMENT OR PUNISHMENT (1987).

The Convention was concluded by the Committee of Ministers of the Council of Europe on 26 June 1987 and entered into force on 1 February 1989. The Convention provides for the establishment of the European Committee for the Prevention of Torture and Inhuman or Degrading Treatment or Punishment which shall, "by means of visits, examine the treatment of persons deprived of their liberty with a view to strengthening, if necessary, the protection of such persons from torture and from inhuman or degrading treatment or punishment. Each State party to the Convention undertakes to permit visits, in accordance with the Convention, to any place within its jurisdiction where persons are deprived of their liberty by a public authority. The Committee and the competent national authorities undertake to cooperate with each other in implementing the terms of the Convention." For the text of the Convention, see *European Treaty Series* 126.

**EUROPEAN HUMAN RIGHTS.** Established in 1983, this non-governmental organization works to protect freedom of speech and human rights and seeks to expose human rights violations in Europe. It provides assistance to persons incarcerated for reasons relating to freedom of speech. The organization sponsors seminars and debates and provides children's services. It periodically publishes the newsletter *European Human Rights.*

European Human Rights. Address: Marknadsvagen 289, S-183, 34 Taby, Sweden. Secretary: Ditlieb Felderer

## EUROPEAN HUMAN RIGHTS FOUNDATION.

Established in 1980, this non-governmental organization works to protect civil, political, economic, social, and cultural rights as they are established in international instruments. The Foundation makes grants to individuals and non-governmental organizations involved in the field of human rights.

European Human Rights Foundation. Address: Rue Van Campenhout 13, B-1040, Brussells, Belgium. Telephone: (32-2) 734-94-24. Fax: (32-2) 734-68-32. Director: Peter Ashman.

## EUROPEAN HUMAN RIGHTS PRIZE.

Established in 1980, this honorary prize is awarded to an individual or group whose activities have contributed in an exceptional way to the cause of human rights in accordance with the principles of individual freedom, political liberty, and the rule of law.

The prize is awarded every three years. Nominations are made to the Secretary-General of the **COUNCIL OF EUROPE.** The Consultative Assembly of the Council makes known to the Committee of Ministers its recommendations. Based on that recommendation the Committee of Ministers chooses one or two recipients.

Among past recipients are the **INTERNATIONAL COMMISSION OF JURISTS** (1980); the Medical Section of **AMNESTY INTERNATIONAL** (1983); Argentina's President Raul Alfonsin and Austria's former Justice Minister Christian Broda (1986); and Poland's **LECH WALESA** and the International Helsinki Federation for Human Rights (1989).

*AWARD FOR BEST SHORT TELEVISION DOCUMENTARY ON HUMAN RIGHTS.* Since 1984, the Council of Europe also has recognized documentary filmmakers who have presented human rights issues to the public. The annual winner receives a 10,000 franc award.

For more information on either award, contact: Council of Europe, P.O. Box 431 R6F, 67006 Strasbourg Cedex, France. Telephone: (33) 88-41-20-00. Fax: (33) 88-41-27-81.

## EUROPEAN UNION OF WOMEN.

Established in 1953, in Salzburg, Austria, the EUW promotes cooperation among European women in political and civic organizations through the exchange of ideas on practical issues. It seeks to increase and strengthen the influence of women in the political and civic life of their country and in Europe as a whole. The EUW has consultative status with the UN **ECONOMIC AND SOCIAL COUNCIL** (Roster) and the **COUNCIL OF EUROPE.** It has national sections in 18 countries.

EUW publishes *EUW Information* (five times annually) and *EUW Newsletter* (once a year), both in English, French, and German.

European Union of Women. Address: Kärtnerstr 51, A-1010 Wien, Austria. Telephone: (43-1) 515-21326. Fax: (43-1) 512-2468. Secretary-General: Maria Schnenk.

## EXECUTIONS.

In 1981, the UN **GENERAL ASSEMBLY** expressed its alarm at the occurrence on a large scale of summary or arbitrary executions, including extra-legal executions (resolution 37/182). It joined the **ECONOMIC AND SOCIAL COUNCIL** in condemning such executions, and welcomed the Council's appointment of a Special Rapporteur to examine the question and to report to the **COMMISSION ON HUMAN RIGHTS.**

Three years later, after two comprehensive reports had been prepared by the Special Rapporteur, S. Amos Wako, and the subject had been thoroughly examined by the competent bodies, the Council, strongly condemning and deploring the brutal practice of arbitrary or summary executions in various parts of the world, approved a series of Safeguards Guaranteeing the Protection of the Rights of Those Facing the Death Penalty on the understanding that they should not be invoked to delay or prevent the abolition of **CAPITAL PUNISHMENT.** The Safeguards were later endorsed by the Seventh United Nations Congress on the Prevention of Crime and the Treatment of Offenders, meeting in Milan from 26 August to 6 September 1985 (resolution 14); the Congress invited all States retaining the death penalty to adopt them.

Further information on summary or arbitrary executions has since been presented to each annual session of the Commission on Human Rights, and in April 1992 Bacre Waly Ndiaye was appointed to assume the functions of Special Rapporteur by the Chairman of the Commission on Human Rights pursuant to Commission resolution 1992/72 of 5 March 1992. Ndiaye submitted his first report (E/CN.4/1993/46) to the Commission at its 1993 session, and his second report (E/CN.4/1994/7) to its 1994 session. The conclusions and recommendations set out in the latter report (paras. 671–730) are as follows:

As in the past, at the end of a reporting cycle the Special Rapporteur finds himself compelled to report that extrajudicial, summary or arbitrary executions have not ceased to occur. On the contrary, armed struggles for power and territorial control have continued unabated in many parts of the world, often disguised as ethnic, religious or nationalistic conflicts. The former Yugoslavia, Angola, Liberia, Somalia, Rwanda and Burundi, Azerbaijan and Tajikistan are only a few examples that come to mind, where violations of the right to life, in particular of the civilian population, take place on a massive scale. The Special Rapporteur has also continued to receive increasing numbers of allegations of extrajudicial, summary or arbitrary executions and death threats attributed to government forces or groups cooperating with them or enjoying the acquiescence of the authorities.

The Special Rapporteur responded to these continuing violations of the right to life with a marked increase in the range of his activities. On the basis of the information that has come before him, the Special Rapporteur focused his attention on two main areas of concern: violations of the right to life in the context of capital punishment and impunity enjoyed by perpetrators of violations, which has important implications for almost all other types of extrajudicial, summary or arbitrary executions, particularly for their prevention. In compliance with the requests made to him by the Commission on Human Rights, the Special Rapporteur also paid special attention to a number of other issues. This chapter contains his conclusions and recommendations regarding these questions as well as on a number of procedural points and other matters of concern to the Special Rapporteur.

### Capital Punishment

In its resolution 1993/71, the Commission on Human Rights requested the Special Rapporteur to "continue monitoring the implementation of existing international standards on safeguards and restrictions relating to the imposition of capital punishment, bearing in mind the comments made by the Human Rights Committee in its interpretation of article 6 of the International Covenant on Civil and Political Rights, as well as the Second Optional Protocol thereto".

*The desirability of abolition of the death penalty.* Capital punishment is not yet in itself prohibited under international law. However, in its comments on article 6 of the Covenant, the Human Rights Committee observed that this provision "also refers generally to abolition in terms which strongly suggest that abolition is desirable (paras. 6 [2] and [6]). The Committee concludes that all measures of abolition should be considered as progress in the enjoyment of the right to life . . . ."

The desirability of abolition was also expressed repeatedly by the General Assembly. Moreover, in re-approving article 6, paragraph 6, of the International Covenant on Civil and Political Rights, the Economic and Social Council, in its resolution 1984/50, adopted the Safeguards guaranteeing protection of the rights of those facing the death penalty, on the understanding that they should not be invoked to delay or to prevent the abolition of capital punishment.

Article 6, paragraph 2, of the Covenant provides that "in countries which have not abolished the death penalty, sentence of death may be imposed only for the most serious crimes . . .". The General Assembly has referred to article 6 as forming part of the "minimum standard of legal safeguards" for the protection of the right to life in a number of resolutions concerning summary or arbitrary executions, most recently in paragraph 12 of resolution 45/162 of 18 December 1990. In its comments on article 6 of the Cove-

nant, the Human Rights Committee stated that "the expression most serious crimes, must be read restrictively to mean that the death penalty should be a quite exceptional measure", limited to offences with lethal or "other extremely grave consequences".

The Special Rapporteur has received with concern reports of the extension of the scope of capital punishment to offences previously not punishable by death in a number of countries. In *Bangladesh,* the Curbing of Terrorist Activities Act 1992 reportedly extends the scope of the death penalty to a number of offences under the heading of "terrorism", which had previously been sanctioned with imprisonment. In *China,* the range of capital offences has been broadened since the Chinese Penal Code came into force in 1979. Currently, some 65 criminal offences are punishable by death in China, including crimes such as "speculation", "corruption" or "bribery". Law No. 97 of 1992 significantly enlarged the number of capital offences in *Egypt.* In May 1991, *Pakistan* introduced a mandatory death penalty in cases of blasphemy and it was reported that the Government was planning to extend it to drug-related offences in August 1993. The new *Peruvian* Constitution, approved by referendum on 31 October 1993, widens the scope of capital punishment to cover crimes of terrorism and treason (see E/CN.4/1994/7/ Add.2, paras. 74–78). In *Saudi Arabia,* two *fatwas,* in 1987 and 1988, extended the range of capital offences to a number of drug-related offences and to acts of "sabotage" or "corruption on earth" that "undermine security and endanger lives and public or private property". Previously, such offences were punishable by death only if loss of life was involved. According to reports recently received, a federal crime bill is currently being drafted in the *United States of America* which would extend the death penalty to 47 offences which, at present, are not punishable by death.

Loss of life is irreparable. The Special Rapporteur therefore strongly supports the conclusions of the Human Rights Committee and emphasizes that the abolition of capital punishment is most desirable. The scope of application of the death penalty should never be extended and the Special Rapporteur invites those States which have done so to reconsider.

*Fair trial.* All safeguards and guarantees for due process, both at pre-trial stages and during the actual trial before a court, as provided for by several international instruments such as the Universal Declaration of Human Rights (arts. 10 and 11), the International Covenant on Civil and Political Rights (arts. 9, 14 and 15), the Safeguards guaranteeing protection of all those facing the death penalty as well as Economic and Social Council resolution 1989/65 on their implementation, must be fully respected in all cases, and especially where the life of the defendant is at stake.

In particular, proceedings leading to the imposition of capital punishment must conform to the highest standards of independence, competence, objectivity and impartiality of judges and juries. All defendants in capital cases must benefit from the fullest guarantees for an adequate defence at all stages of the proceedings, including adequate provision for State-funded legal aid by competent defence lawyers. Defendants must be presumed innocent until their guilt has been proven without leaving any room for reasonable doubt, in application of the highest standards for the gathering and assessment of evidence. All mitigating factors must be taken into account. A procedure must be guaranteed in which both factual and legal aspects of the case may be reviewed by a higher tribunal, composed of judges other than those who dealt with the case at the first instance. In addition, the defendants' right to seek pardon or commutation of the death sentence must be ensured.

During the past year, the Special Rapporteur received numerous and alarming reports about legislation and practice leading to the imposition and execution of death sentences where the defendants did not fully benefit from these guarantees and safeguards. Such reports concerned the following countries: *Algeria, Azerbaijan, Bangladesh, China, Comoros, Egypt, Iran (Islamic Republic of), Kuwait, Kyrgyzstan, Malawi, Malaysia, Nigeria, Pakistan, Peru, Saudi Arabia, Sierra Leone, South Africa,* the *Syrian Arab Republic, Tajikistan, Turkmenistan, United States of America, Uzbekistan, Yemen.*

The Special Rapporteur is particularly concerned at reports indicating a tendency towards the establishment of special jurisdictions to speed up proceedings leading to capital punishment in certain cases, particularly in response to acts of violence committed by armed opposition groups. Such special courts often lack independence, for example, because the judges are accountable to the executive, or because they are military officers on active duty within the chain-of-command structure of the army. Time-limits which are sometimes set for the conclusion of the different trial stages before such special jurisdictions gravely affect the defendants' right to an adequate defence. Concerns have also been expressed at limitations on the right to appeal in the context of special jurisdictions. In some cases, the law establishing special courts also provides for an extension of the scope of capital offences. The Special Rapporteur notes that, as a general rule, the standards of due process and respect for the right to life before such jurisdictions are lower than in ordinary criminal proceedings. He wishes to refer, in this context, to the sections of this report on *Algeria, Egypt, Kuwait, Malawi, Nigeria, Pakistan, Peru* and the *Syrian Arab Republic.*

The Special Rapporteur wishes to refer to a recent judgement of the Judicial Committee of the Privy Council of the *United Kingdom of Great Britain and Northern Ireland,* wherein it held that the execution of a death sentence five years after it had been handed down would constitute cruel and inhuman punishment. Consequently, the death sentences of two prisoners in Jamaica who had been awaiting execution for more than five years were commuted to life imprisonment. The Supreme Court of *Zimbabwe* recently reached a similar conclusion. While welcoming the decisions, the Special Rapporteur wishes to express concern that they might encourage Governments to carry out executions of death sentences more speedily. This might, in turn, affect defendants' rights to full appeal procedures, including new hearings if additional evidence is discovered even years later. The Special Rapporteur feels that these judgements should rather be interpreted in the light of the desirability of the abolition of capital punishment: if, as a first step, it is recognized that awaiting execution for five years constitutes in itself cruel and inhuman punishment, the second, towards the rejection of capital punishment as such, may be easier to take.

In summary, judicial errors can no longer be remedied once a death sentence has been carried out. The Special Rapporteur urges the Governments of all States in which the death penalty has not yet been abolished to ensure that proceedings which may lead to the imposition of the death penalty are conducted in accordance with the highest standards of due process and that defendants fully benefit from all safeguards and guarantees set forth in the pertinent international instruments.

The Special Rapporteur calls particularly on the Governments of *Algeria, China, Egypt,* the *Islamic Republic of Iran, Kuwait, Malawi, Malaysia, Nigeria, Pakistan, Peru,* the *Syrian Arab Republic, Tajikistan* and the *United States of America* to revise their legislation governing procedures for trials where the imposition of capital punishment is at stake so as to make them conform to the pertinent international instruments.

*Special restrictions on the application of the death penalty.* Article 6, paragraph 5, of the International Covenant on Civil and Political Rights stipulates that "sentence of death shall not be imposed for crimes committed by persons below eighteen years of age". A number of other international instruments also prohibit the capital punishment of juvenile offenders, in particular the Convention on the Rights of the Child, the United Nations Standard Minimum Rules for the Administration of Juvenile Justice ("The Beijing Rules"), and the Safeguards guaranteeing protection of the rights of those facing the death penalty. The reports received concerning the imposition and execution of death sentences in cases involving minors in *Egypt, Pakistan* and the *United States of America* are most disturbing. The Special Rapporteur is also deeply concerned at legislation allowing for death sentences for minors in *Algeria, China* and *Peru.*

Furthermore, international law prohibits the capital punishment of mentally retarded or insane persons, pregnant women and mothers of young children. In this context, the Special Rapporteur refers to allegations he has received concerning executions of mentally retarded persons in the *United States of America.*

The Special Rapporteur urges the Governments of *Algeria, China, Egypt, Pakistan, Peru* and the *United States* to consider which measures may be more suitable than the death penalty to promote rehabilitation and reinsertion into society of juvenile or mentally retarded offenders.

## Impunity

Governments are obliged under international law to carry out exhaustive and impartial investigations into allegations of violations of the right to life, to identify, bring to justice and punish their perpetrators, to grant compensation to the victims or their families, and to take effective measures to avoid future recurrence of such violations. The first two components of this fourfold obligation constitute in themselves the most effective deterrent for the prevention of human rights violations. Conversely, if perpetrators may be certain that they will not be held responsible, such violations are most likely to continue unabated. The recognition of the duty to compensate victims of human rights violations, and the actual granting of compensation to them, presupposes the recognition by the Government of its obligation to ensure effective protection against human rights abuses on the basis of the respect for the fundamental rights and freedoms of every person.

Economic and Social Council resolution 1989/65 of 24 May 1989 on the Principles on the Effective Prevention and Investigation of Extra-legal, Arbitrary and Summary Executions sets forth in detail the aforementioned obligations. In addition, as regards deaths as a result of excessive use of force, the Basic Principles on the Use of Force and Firearms by Law Enforcement Officials provide that arbitrary or abusive use of force and firearms by law enforcement officials is to be punished as a criminal offence under national law (principle 7). In May 1991, the Crime Prevention and Criminal Justice Branch of the United Nations Centre for Social Development and Humanitarian Affairs published a document of major importance for guaranteeing the right to life. Entitled *Manual on the Effective Prevention and Investigation of*

*Extra-legal, Arbitrary and Summary Executions* (ST/CSDHA/ 12), it lays down procedures for conducting investigations into extra-legal executions or killings.

In practice, however, human rights violations and, in particular, violations of the right to life continue to be perpetrated with impunity in very many countries. The reports and allegations that have come before the Special Rapporteur indicate that grave breaches of the above-mentioned obligation occur at all levels.

In some cases, the basis for impunity may be legislation which exempts perpetrators of human rights abuses from prosecution. The Special Rapporteur received reports about amnesty laws in *El Salvador* and *Mauritania*. He was also informed about provisions granting members of the security forces immunity from prosecution in *Bangladesh* (Bangladesh Penal Code) and *South Africa* (Further Indemnity Act). In this context, the Special Rapporteur wishes to emphasize that "under no circumstances . . . shall blanket immunity from prosecution be granted to any person allegedly involved in extra-legal, summary or arbitrary executions" (principle 19 of the Principles on the Effective Prevention and Investigation of Extra-legal, Summary or Arbitrary Executions). Even if, in exceptional cases, Governments may decide that perpetrators should benefit from measures that would exempt them from or limit the extent of their punishment, their obligation to bring them to justice and hold them formally accountable remains, as does the obligation to carry out prompt, thorough and impartial investigations, grant compensation to the victims or their families and adopt effective preventive measures for the future. The Special Rapporteur appeals to all Governments concerned to revise any legislation as may be in force exempting those involved in violations of the right to life from prosecution.

However, in many countries where the law provides for the prosecution of human rights violators, impunity is the practice. Often, no investigation at all is initiated into cases of alleged violations of the right to life. Authorities do not react to complaints filed by the victims, their families or representatives, or by international organs, including the Special Rapporteur. In this context, it should be recalled that Governments are under obligation to initiate inquiries into allegations ex officio as soon as they are brought to their attention, particularly where the alleged violation of the right to life is imminent and effective measures of protection must be adopted by the authorities. Also, legislation should permit victims or their families or representatives to initiate such proceedings. The Special Rapporteur therefore calls on all Governments to enact legislation enabling the competent authorities to fulfil their obligations under international law irrespective of whether or not the victims are able to provide evidence to identify the authors of human rights abuses against them, and to ensure that these obligations are fully implemented in practice.

In other instances, victims or witnesses are said to be too afraid to complain to the authorities, particularly where they perceive to be under threat from exactly the same authorities that are supposed to protect them. The *Philippine* Human Rights Commission, for example, repeatedly informed the Special Rapporteur that persons were too afraid to testify or file complaints before the authorities. Disturbing reports about death threats against, or even extrajudicial killings of persons who had witnessed human rights violations and, in some cases, testified before investigating organs were received concerning *Brazil, Colombia, Guatemala* and *Peru*. In other cases, the State organs which should carry out the investigations were themselves under threat, as was reported

with regard to public prosecutors in *Peru* or the judiciary in *Chad.* The Special Rapporteur urges all Governments to ensure effective protection for all those who participate, as witnesses, prosecutors, judges, court officials or in any other capacity, in investigations of alleged human rights violations.

There are also countries where there is no independent judiciary that could carry out such investigations, or where the justice system simply does not work in practice. *Cambodia* was reported to the Special Rapporteur as an example in this regard. In *Peru* and *Rwanda,* too, the civilian justice system does not function properly. In such cases, reforms should be carried out to enable the judiciary to fulfil its functions. It should count on an adequate number of judges, court officials and prosecutors and sufficient material. The independence of the judges should be guaranteed by law and fully respected in practice.

In the absence of a functioning civilian justice system, or in cases which warrant particular treatment because of their special nature or gravity, Governments may envisage establishing special commissions of inquiry. They must fulfil the same requirements of independence, impartiality and competence as judges in ordinary courts. The results of their investigations should be made public, and their recommendations should be binding for the authorities. The Special Rapporteur is concerned that the establishment of such commissions is sometimes only announced but not put into practice, as was reported in the case of *Chad,* that recommendations made by such commissions are not or not always followed, such as in *Mexico,* or that such commissions do not fulfil the above-mentioned requirements and are, in reality, tools to evade the obligation to carry out thorough, prompt and impartial investigations into alleged violations of the right to life.

In other cases, investigations are initiated without, however, leading to the punishment of members of the security forces or paramilitary and other groups cooperating with them or acting with their acquiescence. Where perpetrators of such violations are brought to justice and sentenced, these sentences are often not proportionate to the gravity of the offences, as was reported in the case of the Santa Cruz massacre in *East Timor* or the killings of peasants in Accomarca and Santa Barbara in *Peru* (see E/CN.4/1994/7/Add.2, paras. 32 and 53). On other occasions, low-ranking members of security forces have been convicted and sentenced for having carried out human rights violations, while those in positions of command escaped their responsibility for having planned and ordered these violations. The Special Rapporteur calls on all Governments to prosecute all those involved in the planning and carrying out of alleged extrajudicial, summary or arbitrary executions, including those who, although in a position of authority, have not made any attempts to prevent them.

The problem of military jurisdiction over alleged perpetrators of human rights violations has once again been raised in this regard. Sometimes, the fact that the civilian justice system does not function properly is invoked by the authorities to justify trials before military tribunals. Ample information received by the Special Rapporteur indicates that, in practice, this almost always results in impunity for the security forces. The Special Rapporteur therefore once again appeals to all Governments concerned to provide for an independent, impartial and functioning civilian judiciary to deal with all cases of alleged violations of the right to life. The Special Rapporteur also calls on the authorities to ensure that the security forces fully cooperate with the civilian justice system in its efforts to identify and bring to justice those responsible for human rights violations.

The Special Rapporteur considers the implementation of Commission resolutions 1993/33 and 1992/24 to be a matter of high priority. In this regard, he would like to stress the need for expertise in forensic pathology, anthropology and archaeology in order to conduct excavations of mass graves and examine human remains found therein. In this context, efforts to establish a standing team of internationally recognized experts in this field who could provide advice and assistance to national investigating organs should be continued.

The link between the effective investigation of human rights violations of the right to life and the prevention of their recurrence in the future cannot be over-emphasized. Consequently, the Special Rapporteur calls on all Governments to comply fully with their obligation under international law to ensure that thorough, prompt and impartial investigations are carried out into all allegations of the right to life and that all those involved in their planning and execution be identified, brought to justice and punished in accordance with the gravity of the offence, regardless of any rank, office or position they may hold.

### Allegations Received and Acted Upon by the Special Rapporteur

*Death threats.* The Special Rapporteur received allegations concerning death threats or fear for the lives and physical security of more than 380 persons. He continues to view urgent appeals on behalf of those under threat as an essential part of his mandate. In the past year, he has transmitted urgent appeals with the aim of preventing loss of life to the Governments of: *Argentina, Bangladesh, Brazil, Burundi, Chad, Ecuador, El Salvador, India, Indonesia, Iran (Islamic Republic of), Panama, Papua New Guinea, Paraguay, Peru, Philippines, Rwanda, South Africa, Sri Lanka, Togo, Turkey, Venezuela* and *Zaire.* In almost all of these countries, the lives of human rights activists, members of the political opposition, trade unions, community workers, writers and journalists were reported to be at serious risk. The Special Rapporteur is particularly concerned about *Colombia,* where he intervened by sending 26 urgent appeals, and *Guatemala,* where he sent 25 urgent appeals. Furthermore, the Special Rapporteur noted with deep concern reports about the alleged execution, while in custody, of a prisoner in *Azerbaijan,* and the killing of two mothers of disappeared children in *Brazil.* In both cases, he had urged the authorities to ensure their protection. It is also most disturbing that in countries such as *Brazil, Colombia, Guatemala, South Africa* and *Turkey,* patterns of intimidation and threats seem to persist for years.

The Special Rapporteur urges all Governments to adopt effective measures, in accordance with the requirements of each particular case, to ensure full protection of those who are at risk of extrajudicial, summary or arbitrary execution. The Special Rapporteur calls on the authorities to conduct investigations into all instances of death threats or attempts against lives which are brought to their attention, regardless of whether or not any judicial or other procedures have been activated by those under threat.

*Deaths in custody.* The Special Rapporteur received numerous reports concerning deaths in custody in *Azerbaijan, Cambodia* and *Sierra Leone.* Such deaths were alleged to be the result of torture or other cruel, inhuman and degrading treatment in *Bangladesh, Cuba, Ecuador, India, Indonesia, Israel, Mexico, Nepal, Peru, South Africa, Turkey* and *Yugoslavia.*

The Special Rapporteur also received allegations of deaths in custody due to medical neglect or otherwise untenable prison conditions in *Cuba, Morocco* and *Togo.* A particular form of death while in detention was reported, as in former years, in *Myanmar,* where Muslim villagers continue to be forced by the military to serve as porters and die after torture or simply because they are too weak to carry on.

The Special Rapporteur appeals to all Governments to ensure that conditions of detention in their countries conform to the Standard Minimum Rules for the Treatment of Prisoners and other pertinent international instruments. He also urges them to make efforts to ensure full respect of the international norms and principles prohibiting any form of torture or other cruel, inhuman or degrading treatment. Prison guards and other law enforcement personnel should receive training so as to be familiar with these norms as well as the rules and regulations concerning the use of force and firearms to prevent escape or control disturbances. The Special Rapporteur also calls on the competent authorities to prosecute and punish all those who, through action or omission, are found responsible for the death of any person held in custody, in breach of the aforementioned international instruments.

*Death due to abuse of force by law enforcement officials.* The Special Rapporteur received a considerable number of allegations concerning violations of the right to life as a consequence of excessive or arbitrary use of force. Cases in this category were reported in *Brazil, Cameroon, Chad, Chile,* the *Comoros, Egypt, Honduras, Israel* and *Venezuela.* In *Bangladesh, Cameroon, Chad, Chile,* the *Central African Republic, El Salvador, India, Lebanon, Malawi, Nepal, South Africa* and *Zaire,* hundreds of people were reportedly killed by security forces using excessive force against participants in demonstrations and other manifestations. The Special Rapporteur was particularly shocked by reports about deliberate use of firearms against young children by Israeli security forces and Brazilian military police.

The Special Rapporteur calls on all Governments to ensure that the security forces receive thorough training in human rights matters and, in particular, with regard to the restrictions on the use of force and firearms in the discharge of their duties. Such training should include methods of keeping crowds of people under control without resorting to excessive force. Full and independent investigations must be carried out into alleged deaths due to abuse of force, and all law enforcement officials responsible for violations of the right to life must be held accountable.

*Violations of the right to life during armed conflicts.* The Special Rapporteur received increasing numbers of reports concerning deaths as a consequence of armed conflicts, both international and internal, in various parts of the world. Massive violations of the right to life were said to have been committed against combatants who had been captured, or after they had laid down their arms, and particularly civilians. This was reported, for example, in *Angola, Azerbaijan, Cambodia, Chad, Djibouti, Liberia, Papua New Guinea, Sierra Leone, Somalia, Sri Lanka,* the *Sudan, Tajikistan, Turkey* and the conflict areas in the former Yugoslavia. Thousands of people were reportedly killed, either as a direct consequence of the hostilities through deliberate and indiscriminate shelling of residential areas, often with heavy weaponry including aerial bombardments, and deliberate executions—or indirectly, as a result of sieges, blocking off water, food and medical supplies, refusal to evacuate sick or wounded persons. Children, elderly and those in poor health are particularly affected by such measures.

The Special Rapporteur calls on all parties to conflicts, international or internal, to respect the norms and standards of international human rights and humanitarian law which protect the lives of the civilian population and those combatants who are captured or lay down their arms. He also appeals to all those involved in armed conflicts to allow convoys of humanitarian aid to reach their destinations as well as to allow the evacuation of the wounded, elderly persons and children. All those responsible for violations of the right to life in situations of armed conflicts must be held accountable. In this context, the Special Rapporteur particularly wishes to endorse the appeals for respect for the right to life made by the Special Rapporteurs on the situation of human rights in the *Sudan* and, on repeated occasions, by the Special Rapporteur on the human rights situation in the territory of the former Yugoslavia.

In this context, the Special Rapporteur wishes to refer to the role of the United Nations in situations of armed conflict. Increasingly often called upon to exercise peace-keeping tasks, United Nations personnel in many countries are operating under very difficult and often dangerous conditions. A high number of United Nations staff have on many occasions risked, and lost, their lives. However, in the recent past reports have been received indicating that members of United Nations forces were themselves involved in extrajudicial, summary or arbitrary killings in Somalia. The Special Rapporteur is of the view that, as each State is bound under international law to respect these standards, an organ representing States in their collectivity has at least the same degree of responsibility. A human rights component should be an integral part of all peace-keeping and observer missions. As such missions under the auspices of the United Nations multiply, it may be desirable to envisage the institution of an organ within the United Nations, or within each peace-keeping or observer mission, to investigate human rights abuses by members of such missions and hold their authors responsible. Provision should also be made to grant compensation to the victims of such abuses or, in the case of extrajudicial killings, their families with a view to preventing such incidents, all members of peace-keeping and observer missions should receive thorough training in human rights matters as well as in mediation and conflict resolution.

*Violations of the right to life in the context of communal violence.* The Special Rapporteur would once again like to draw the attention of the international community to the problem of communal violence, understood as acts of violence committed by groups of citizens of a country against other groups. In *Burundi, Nigeria, Rwanda* and *Zaire*, where violent confrontations were reported between different ethnic groups, government forces allegedly not only did not intervene to stop the violence but actively supported one side in the conflict, or even began it. In other instances, Governments, for example those of *Bangladesh* and *Sri Lanka*, denied their responsibility for killings, asserting that they occurred in the context of communal violence. Such conflicts, if allowed to continue, may degenerate into genocide. Effective steps should therefore be taken by Governments of countries where acts of communal violence occur to curb such disturbances at an early stage. The Special Rapporteur also strongly appeals to all Governments to refrain from supporting groups, on ethnic or other grounds, either actively or by simply tolerating acts of violence committed by them. On the contrary, efforts should be made towards reconciliation and peaceful coexistence of all parts of the population, regardless of ethnic origin, religion or any other distinction. Mass communication media and campaigns of education

and information promoting mutual respect should be used in this regard. Furthermore, all acts of incitement to hatred or violence must be punished.

*Expulsion of persons to a country where their life is in danger.* The Special Rapporteur received reports about the imminent extradition of one or more persons to countries where their lives might be at risk. All Governments should take due notice of the norms and principles contained in international instruments that refer to this particular question. They should refrain from extraditing a person in circumstances where his or her safety is not fully guaranteed.

*Rights of the victims.* As stated earlier, the recognition of the right of victims or their families to receive adequate compensation is both a recognition of the state's responsibility for the acts of its organs and an expression of respect for the human being. Granting compensation presupposes compliance with the obligation to carry out an investigation into allegations of human rights abuses with a view to identifying and prosecuting their perpetrators. Financial or other compensation provided to the victims or their families before such investigations are initiated or concluded, however, does not exempt Governments from this obligation. The Special Rapporteur notes with concern that, with the exception of *Nepal,* no Government provided him with information about any such compensation provided to victims or their dependants. The Special Rapporteur urges States to make pertinent provisions under national legislation and set up funds for those who have suffered damage as a consequence of extrajudicial, summary or arbitrary execution or attempted execution.

## Issues of Special Interest to the Special Rapporteur

*Freedom of opinion and expression.* More than 700 cases which were brought to the attention of the Special Rapporteur during the past year concerned alleged violations of the right to life involving a breach of the right to freedom of opinion and expression, peaceful assembly and association. Extrajudicial killings as a result of abuse of force against demonstrators and participants in other peaceful manifestations have been referred to earlier. The Special Rapporteur is deeply concerned at the large numbers of reported death threats, assassination attempts and extrajudicial executions of members of legal political opposition parties, trade unions, student movements and community organizations, human rights groups and activists, as well as journalists, writers and persons assisting indigenous people and peasants in *Argentina, Brazil, Cambodia, Chad, Colombia, El Salvador, Equatorial Guinea, Guatemala, Haiti, India, Malawi, Paraguay, Peru,* the *Philippines, Rwanda, South Africa, Turkey* and *Zaire.*

The Special Rapporteur is particularly preoccupied by reports of "hit squads, or death squads" linked to the authorities, which are said to be instruments of violent repression of any political opposition. Such groups, often said to be composed of members of the security forces, allegedly carry out orders to intimidate or eliminate persons perceived as a threat to Governments or certain political parties. Disturbing allegations to this effect were received concerning *Brazil, Colombia, Guatemala, El Salvador, Haiti, Kenya, Peru, South Africa* and *Turkey.* Agents linked to the security forces of the *Islamic Republic of Iran* were said to be responsible for the killing of political opponents in *Italy, Pakistan* and *Turkey.*

The Special Rapporteur calls on all Governments to fully respect the right of all persons to freedom of opinion and expression, peaceful assembly and association, as guaranteed in the pertinent international instruments. He urges the authorities of those countries in which death squads or similar structures are alleged to exist to carry out full investigations with a view to eliminating such groups and identifying and prosecuting their members, as well as all those under whose orders they are found to operate.

*Violations of the right to life of women.* In 168 cases, the victims of reported violations of the right to life were women. As stated earlier, this figure does not necessarily reflect the actual proportion of women among those on whose behalf the Special Rapporteur intervened. This is due to the fact that several cases concerned alleged extrajudicial, summary or arbitrary executions of groups of unidentified civilians, where it was not specified how many women were among those killed. In other cases, the Special Rapporteur could not discern the sex of a person simply by the name and the source did not indicate whether the allegation concerned a man or a woman.

However, women make up a relatively small percentage of purported victims of extrajudicial, summary or arbitrary executions or death threats reported to the Special Rapporteur. Women appear not to be particularly targeted for reasons of their sex. This may partly be explained by the fact that women continue to play a small role in the political and economic life of many countries. The underrepresentation of women in positions of influence, for example in political parties or trade unions, or in professions such as law or journalism, means that they are also less exposed to acts of violence at the hands of Governments that may perceive them as a threat. On the other hand, in areas where women are actively participating in public life, they do not seem to be in a different position from their male counterparts, as may be illustrated by the following cases acted upon by the Special Rapporteur in the past year: *Peruvian* journalist Cecilia Valenzuela, allegedly threatened with death by the security forces; human rights activists Hebe de Bonafini and journalists Magdalena Ruiz Guiñazú, Mónica Cahen d'Anvers and Graciela Guadalupe in *Argentina,* missionary Elsa Rosa Zotti, lawyers Valdenia Brito, Katia Costa Pereira and Cecilia Petrina de Carvalho, as well as mothers of disappeared children pressing for an investigation into their abduction in *Brazil,* human rights activists Nineth de Montenegro, Rosalina Tuyuc, Angela María Contreras Chávez and Rigoberta Menchú in *Guatemala,* lawyers Mirna Perla de Anaya in *El Salvador* and Gloria Estrago in *Paraguay,* as well as Leyla Zana, Member of Parliament in *Turkey.*

*Armed groups that spread terror among the population and drug traffickers.* Violence by armed opposition groups constitutes a serious problem in a number of countries: the situations in *Algeria, Colombia, Egypt, Guatemala,* parts of *India, Myanmar, Peru,* the *Philippines, Sri Lanka* and *Turkey* are well-known examples in this regard. The Special Rapporteur wishes to express his most profound repugnance at the acts of violence committed by these armed opposition groups, which are responsible for grave human and material losses in these countries. He fully understands that the Governments concerned and their security forces face an extremely difficult task in attempting to curb violence by such groups, in particular where they resort to terrorist methods, indiscriminately targeting civilians. However, the Special Rapporteur is concerned at reports according to which operations by the security forces aimed at fighting such armed opposition groups very often result in extrajudicial, summary or arbitrary executions. *Algeria* and *Egypt,* for example, have executed death sentences against persons convicted of terrorism after trials which fall short of the international standards for the pro-

tection of those facing capital punishment. In all other aforementioned countries, security forces allegedly extrajudicially executed civilians whom they perceived to be collaborators or sympathizers of the armed opposition groups. In *Colombia, Guatemala* and *Sri Lanka* it was also reported that residential areas were bombarded by the military. In a number of countries, where drug traffickers are also said to be responsible for killings of members of the security forces and civilians. According to the information received, drug traffickers in *Colombia, Costa Rica* and *Peru* have increased their influence by establishing links with armed opposition groups.

In this context, the Special Rapporteur wishes to emphasize that the right to life is absolute and must not be derogated from, even under the most difficult circumstances. This means that Governments must respect the right to life of all persons, including members of armed groups that demonstrate their total disrespect for the lives of both State representatives and civilians. The Special Rapporteur urges the Governments of all countries where such groups are active to ensure that counter-insurgency operations are conducted in a way so as to minimize the loss of lives. Security forces should receive proper training in this regard, and excessive use of force should be sanctioned.

*Civil defence forces.* In several countries, civilians, particularly in rural and/or remote areas, have formed groups of self-defence in situations where they feel that their lives or property are threatened. While such threats may emanate from common criminality, for example cattle thieves, civil defence forces are frequent in areas where armed opposition groups operate. Often, they are supported or even set up by the security forces and integrated into the Governments' counter-insurgency strategy. This was reported to be the case, for example, with the Bangladesh Rifles and Ansar Guards in *Bangladesh,* the civil self-defence patrols (PAC) in *Guatemala,* the *rondas campesinas* and *comités de defensa civil* in *Peru,* the Citizen's Armed Forces Geographical Units (CAFGUs) in the *Philippines,* or the Kontrgerilla and Village Guards in *Turkey.* The Special Rapporteur received numerous reports about extrajudicial, summary or arbitrary executions committed by members of such groups, either in cooperation with units of the security forces or with their acquiescence. With very few exceptions, they were said to enjoy impunity for their actions. Often, the victims of such killings were said to be peasants suspected of being members or sympathizers of the armed opposition because they refused to join the, ostensibly voluntary, civil defence groups.

The Special Rapporteur appeals to the Governments of all countries where such civil defence structures exist to ensure full respect of human rights by the members of these groups. In particular, they should be trained to act in conformity with the restrictions on the use of force and firearms for law enforcement officials. All arms used by such groups, particularly if provided by the military, should be registered and their use subjected to strict control. All abuses should be punished, and effective measures should be taken to prevent their occurrence. Furthermore, no one should be forced to participate in civil defence groups.

*Right to life and administration of justice.* Respect for human rights within the administration of justice is of relevance to the Special Rapporteur's mandate in the field of capital punishment. In this context, the Special Rapporteur wishes to refer to paragraphs 673 to 687 above, concerning the right of defendants in capital cases to benefit fully from all guarantees of due process. In addition, the Special Rapporteur takes fair trial requirements into account when he evaluates proceedings that lead to the conviction and punishment of perpetrators of violations of the right to life. The Special Rapporteur appeals to all Governments to provide for legislation governing trial procedures in full conformity with the safeguards and guarantees embodied in the pertinent international instruments. He also urges all Governments to ensure that these safeguards and guarantees are fully ensured in practice. Effective protection should be ensured for all those forming part of the justice system. Particular attention should be given to the security of judges, prosecutors and lawyers where they may face threats or even attempts against their lives in the context of terrorist violence or corruption among political leaders.

*Violations of the right to life of minors, particularly "street children".* The Special Rapporteur is deeply concerned at reports about violations of the right to life of minors and, in particular, children and adolescents without homes. Death threats against, and extrajudicial killings of "street children" have been reported in *Brazil, Colombia* and *Guatemala.* Reports of attacks against those who provide this particularly vulnerable group with shelter and education programmes, for example the collaborators of Casa Alianza in *Guatemala* or persons linked with the church in *Brazil,* are also very disturbing. The Special Rapporteur also wishes to express deep concern for violations of the right to life of minors in aimed conflicts.

Children are among those who suffer most from lack of food and medicine as a result of deliberate blocking of humanitarian aid and assistance in conflict areas. They were also said to have died in large numbers as victims of indiscriminate attacks against residential areas. In addition, the Special Rapporteur received numerous reports of incidents in which children, even very young ones, were deliberately shot by members of the security forces, for example in the Occupied Territories or in *Sri Lanka.* As regards the question of capital punishment for minors, see above.

The Special Rapporteur calls on all Governments to ensure full respect for the right to life of children. He urges Governments in countries where children are forced to live in the streets to provide them with food, shelter and education programmes and to effectively protect them from violence in any form. . . .

### Procedural Aspects

As stated earlier, the Special Rapporteur received, and transmitted to 73 Governments, allegations of the right to life concerning more than 3,700 persons. In 217 urgent appeals he urged the competent authorities to ensure effective protection of persons whose lives were feared to be at risk. This constitutes an increase of almost 50 per cent, as compared with the number of urgent appeals sent in 1992. In over 90 letters, the Special Rapporteur asked Governments to fulfil their obligation under international law to investigate human rights violations, bring to justice those responsible and grant compensation to the victims. The Special Rapporteur made an effort to transmit these allegations to the Governments earlier in the year to allow for more time to reply, as announced in his report to the Commission on Human Rights at its forty-ninth session. The Special Rapporteur believes that the initiation of the follow-up procedure, as described in chapter 11 of this report, constitutes an important new element in the working of his mandate. The Special Rapporteur also hopes that his visits to the former Yugoslavia, Rwanda and Peru, as well as his participation in numerous public and private events, may contribute to promoting respect for the right to life and awareness of United Nations human rights procedures and mechanisms.

It has become evident, however, that unless the resources of the Secretariat are increased considerably, it will be impossible to assure the day-to-day work of the mandate. The Special Rapporteur continues to count on two staff members at the Centre for Human Rights, only one of them full-time. The amount of work involved in the assessment of the incoming information, almost daily urgent appeals, thorough follow-up, preparation of missions, etc. would require at least three staff members and one secretary working exclusively on the mandate. The Special Rapporteur hopes that the strengthening of the resources of the Secretariat announced at the World Conference on Human Rights in Vienna in June 1993 will soon be put into practice.

While appreciating the opportunity provided at the World Conference to meet with other special rapporteurs, representatives and members of working groups of the Commission on Human Rights for an exchange of views and a discussion on issues of common interest, and to present a common declaration to the plenary of the Conference, the Special Rapporteur regrets that it was not possible to present these concerns before the drafting committee for the Vienna Declaration and Programme of Action. The scant attention given to the problem of violations of the right to life in that document is disappointing. The Special Rapporteur feels that the scale and gravity of extrajudicial, summary or arbitrary executions in many parts of the world would have justified a special heading in the Programme of Action.

### Prevention

During his visits to the former Yugoslavia, Rwanda and Peru, the Special Rapporteur could clearly recognize the enormous, and irreparable, loss of lives in armed conflicts and other situations of internal violence. By establishing the facts and trying to determine the causes for such violence in these countries, it may be possible to discern ways of reducing the extent of violations of the right to life there and preventing their occurrence in other situations. In this context, it is most important to learn to notice signs of incipient conflict situations that may, if allowed to develop, degenerate into humanitarian and human rights crises with very severe consequences. All internal mechanisms for the peaceful solution of such conflicts at the earliest stage should be strengthened. When a country tries to enact such mechanisms, or where there exists a grave humanitarian or human rights crisis, the international community should make every effort to assist with a view to re-establishing peace and preventing a new crisis. Wherever this entails an international peace-building or peace-keeping operation, human rights should be a central component.

In all situations, whether armed conflict or not, the main question to be addressed with a view to prevention of violations of the right to life is the treatment of their authors: impunity is the key to the perpetuation of human rights violations, including extrajudicial, summary or arbitrary executions. Putting an end to impunity requires a genuine will to recognize and enact the safeguards and guarantees for the protection of the right to life of every person. The Special Rapporteur calls once again on all Governments to comply with their obligation under international law to investigate all instances of alleged violations of the right to life, to prosecute and punish their perpetrators and to grant adequate compensation to the victims or their families. The Special Rapporteur also appeals to the international community to continue and reinforce its efforts to curb the phenomenon of extrajudicial, summary or arbitrary executions by putting into practice the international standards already existing, as well as improving them where shortcomings are identified. Finally, the Special Rapporteur reiterates his readiness to provide his full collaboration and assistance in this cause of common concern.

After examining the Special Rapporteur's report, the UN Commission on Human Rights, convinced "of the need for effective action to combat and to eliminate the abhorrent practice of extrajudicial, summary or arbitrary executions, which represents a flagrant violation of the fundamental right to life," appealed urgently to Governments, United Nations bodies and organs, the specialized agencies and intergovernmental and non-governmental organizations to take effective action to combat and eliminate this phenomenon, and requested the Special Rapporteur to continue to examine situations of extrajudicial, summary or arbitrary executions and to continue to submit his findings, conclusions and recommendations to it on an annual basis (resolution 1994/82 of 9 March 1994). It called upon him "in his next report to continue to pay special attention to extrajudicial, summary or arbitrary executions of children and women and to allegations concerning violations of the right to life in the context of violence against participants in demonstrations and other peaceful public manifestations or against persons belonging to national or ethnic, religious and linguistic minorities." Further, it urged him "to draw to the attention of the High Commissioner for Human Rights such situations of extrajudicial, summary and arbitrary executions as are of particularly serious concern to him or where early action might prevent further deterioration."

Welcoming the Manual on the Effective Prevention and Investigation of Extra-legal, Arbitrary and Summary Executions (UN publication, Sales No. E.91.IV.1), the Commission encouraged Governments, United Nations bodies and organs, the specialized agencies and intergovernmental and non-governmental organizations, as appropriate, to initiate, coordinate or support programs designed to train and educate military forces, law enforcement officers, and government officials, as well as members of the United Nations peacekeeping or observer missions, on humanitarian law issues connected with their work; and appealed to the international community to support endeavors to that end. At its 1995 meeting, the Commission reviewed (resolution 1995/73 of 8 March 1995) the report of the Special Rapporteur, reiterated its concerns, and renewed his mandate for a further three years.

**SEE ALSO** *Capital Punishment; Prisoners.*

**BIBLIOGRAPHY.** United Nations. Annual reports on *Summary or Arbitrary Executions* by S. Amos Wako, Special Rapporteur (E/CN.4/1990/22 and Corr. 1; E/CN.4/1991/36; E/CN.4/1992/30 and Corr. 1); Report on visit to Colombia (E/CN.4/1990/22 and Add. 1); Report on mission to Zaire (E/CN.4/1992/30/Add. 1); Annual reports on *Extrajudicial, Summary or Arbitrary Executions* by Bacre Waly Ndiaye, Special Rapporteur (E/CN.4/1993/46 and E/CN.4/1994/7); Human Rights Fact Sheets on *Enforced or Involuntary Disappearances* (No. 6 [1989]); on *Summary or Arbitrary Executions* (No. 11 [1990]).

## EXECUTIONS: PRINCIPLES ON THE EFFECTIVE PREVENTION AND INVESTIGATION OF EXTRA-LEGAL, ARBITRARY AND SUMMARY EXECUTIONS, UN (1989).

In 1978, and frequently thereafter, the UN General Assembly expressed deep concern at reports from various parts of the world relating to enforced or involuntary disappearances and called upon governments to search for the "disappeared" persons and to investigate disappearances with speed and impartiality. More recently, the General Assembly has on a number of occasions

strongly condemned the large number of summary or arbitrary executions, including extra-legal executions, occurring in some areas.

In 1986, the Economic and Social Council requested the UN COMMITTEE ON CRIME PREVENTION AND CONTROL to examine the question of extra-legal, arbitrary, and summary executions with a view to elaborating principles for the effective prevention and investigation of such practices. On recommendation of the Committee, the Council approved, on 24 May 1989, a series of Principles on the Effective Prevention and Investigation of Extra-legal, Arbitrary or Summary Executions and recommended that they should be taken into account and respected by governments within the framework of their national legislation and practices, and should be brought to the attention of law enforcement and criminal justice officials, military personnel, lawyers, members of the executive and legislative bodies of the government, and the public in general. The Council requested the Committee on Crime Prevention and Control to keep the recommendations under constant review, including the implementation of the Principles, taking into account the various socio-economic, political, and cultural circumstances in which extra-legal, arbitrary, and summary executions occur.

The Principles on the Effective Prevention and Investigation of Extra-legal, Arbitrary and Summary Executions adopted by the UN Economic and Social Council (resolution 1989/65, Annex) are as follows:

*Prevention.* 1. Governments shall prohibit by law all extra-legal, arbitrary and summary executions and shall ensure that any such executions are recognized as offences under their criminal laws, and are punishable by appropriate penalties which take into account the seriousness of such offences. Exceptional circumstances including a state of war or threat of war, internal political instability or any other public emergency may not be invoked as a justification of such executions. Such executions shall not be carried out under any circumstances including, but not limited to, situations of internal armed conflict, excessive or illegal use of force by a public official or other person acting in an official capacity or a person acting at the instigation, or with the consent or acquiescence of such person, and situations in which deaths occur in custody. This prohibition shall prevail over decrees issued by governmental authority.

2. In order to prevent extra-legal, arbitrary and summary executions, Governments shall ensure strict control, including a clear chain of command over all officials responsible for the apprehension, arrest, detention, custody and imprisonment as well as those officials authorized by law to use force and firearms.

3. Governments shall prohibit orders from superior officers or public authorities authorizing or inciting other persons to carry out any such extra-legal, arbitrary or summary executions. All persons shall have the right and duty to defy such orders. Training of law enforcement officials shall emphasize the above provisions.

4. Effective protection through judicial or other means shall be guaranteed to individuals and groups who are in danger of extra-legal, arbitrary or summary executions, including those who receive death threats.

5. No one shall be involuntarily returned or extradited to a country where there are substantial grounds for believing that he or she may become a victim of extra-legal, arbitrary or summary execution in that country.

6. Governments shall ensure that persons deprived of their liberty are held in officially recognized places of custody, and that accurate information on their custody and whereabouts, including transfers, is made promptly available to their relatives and lawyer or other persons of confidence.

7. Qualified inspectors, including medical personnel, or an equivalent independent authority, shall conduct inspections in places of custody on a regular basis, and be empowered to undertake unannounced inspections on their own initiative, with full guarantees of independence in the exercise of this function. The inspectors shall have unrestricted access to all persons in such places of custody, as well as to all their records.

8. Governments shall make every effort to prevent extra-legal, arbitrary and summary executions through measures such as diplomatic intercession, improved access of complainants to intergovernmental and judicial bodies, and public denunciation. Intergovernmental mechanisms shall be used to investigate reports of any such executions and to take effective action against such practices. Governments, including those of countries where extra-legal, arbitrary and summary executions are reasonably suspected to occur, shall cooperate fully in international investigations on the subject.

*Investigation.* 9. There shall be a thorough, prompt and impartial investigation of all suspected cases of extra-legal, arbitrary and summary executions, including cases where complaints by relatives or other reliable reports suggest unnatural death in the above circumstances. Governments shall maintain investigative offices and procedures to undertake such inquiries. The purpose of the investigation shall be to determine the cause, manner and time of death, the person responsible, and any pattern or practice which may have

brought about that death. It shall include an adequate autopsy, collection and analysis of all physical and documentary evidence, and statements from witnesses. The investigation shall distinguish between natural death, accidental death, suicide and homicide.

10. The investigative authority shall have the power to obtain all the information necessary to the inquiry. Those persons conducting the investigation shall have at their disposal all the necessary budgetary and technical resources for effective investigation. They shall also have the authority to oblige officials allegedly involved in any such executions to appear and testify. The same shall apply to any witness. To this end, they shall be entitled to issue summons to witnesses, including the officials allegedly involved, and to demand the production of evidence.

11. In cases in which the established investigative procedures are inadequate because of lack of expertise or impartiality, because of the importance of the matter or because of the apparent existence of a pattern of abuse, and in cases where there are complaints from the family of the victim about these inadequacies or other substantial reasons, Governments shall pursue investigations through an independent commission of inquiry or similar procedure. Members of such a commission shall be chosen for their recognized impartiality, competence and independence as individuals. In particular, they shall be independent of any institution, agency or person that may be the subject of the inquiry. The commission shall have the authority to obtain all information necessary to the inquiry and shall conduct the inquiry as provided for under these Principles.

12. The body of the deceased person shall not be disposed of until an adequate autopsy is conducted by a physician, who shall, if possible, be an expert in forensic pathology. Those conducting the autopsy shall have the right of access to all investigative data, to the place where the body was discovered, and to the place where the death is thought to have occurred. If the body has been buried and it later appears that an investigation is required, the body shall be promptly and competently exhumed for an autopsy. If skeletal remains are discovered, they should be carefully exhumed and studied according to systematic anthropological techniques.

13. The body of the deceased shall be available to those conducting the autopsy for a sufficient amount of time to enable a thorough investigation to be carried out. The autopsy shall, at a minimum, attempt to establish the identity of the deceased and the cause and manner of death. The time and place of death shall also be determined to the extent possible. Detailed colour photographs of the deceased shall be included in the autopsy report in order to document and support the findings of the investigation. The autopsy report must describe any and all injuries to the deceased including any evidence of torture.

14. In order to ensure objective results, those conducting the autopsy must be able to function impartially and independently of any potentially implicated persons or organizations or entities.

15. Complainants, witnesses, those conducting the investigation and their families shall be protected from violence, threats of violence or any other form of intimidation. Those potentially implicated in extra-legal, arbitrary or summary executions shall be removed from any position of control or power, whether direct or indirect, over complainants, witnesses and their families, as well as over those conducting investigations.

16. Families of the deceased and their legal representa-

tives shall be informed of, and have access to, any hearing as well as to all information relevant to the investigation, and shall be entitled to present other evidence. The family of the deceased shall have the right to insist that a medical or other qualified representative be present at the autopsy. When the identity of a deceased person has been determined, a notification of death shall be posted, and the family or relatives of the deceased immediately informed. The body of the deceased shall be returned to them upon completion of the investigation.

17. A written report shall be made within a reasonable period of time on the methods and findings of such investigations. The report shall be made public immediately and shall include the scope of the inquiry, procedures and methods used to evaluate evidence as well as conclusions and recommendations based on findings of fact and on applicable law. The report shall also describe in detail specific events that were found to have occurred, and the evidence upon which such findings were based, and list the names of witnesses who testified, with the exception of those whose identities have been withheld for their own protection. The Government shall, within a reasonable period of time, either reply to the report of the investigation, or indicate the steps to be taken in response to it.

*Legal Proceedings.* 18. Governments shall ensure that persons identified by the investigation as having participated in extra-legal, arbitrary or summary executions in any territory under their jurisdiction are brought to justice.

Governments shall either bring such persons to justice or co-operate to extradite any such persons to other countries wishing to exercise jurisdiction. This principle shall apply irrespective of who and where the perpetrators or the victims are, their nationalities or where the offence was committed.

19. Without prejudice to Principle 3 above, an order from a superior officer or a public authority may not be invoked as a justification for extra-legal, arbitrary or summary executions. Superiors, officers or other public officials may be held responsible for acts committed by officials under their hierarchical authority if they had a reasonable opportunity to prevent such acts. In no circumstances, including a state of war, siege or other public emergency, shall blanket immunity from prosecution be granted to any person allegedly involved in extra-legal, arbitrary or summary executions.

20. The families and dependents of victims of extra-legal, arbitrary or summary executions shall be entitled to fair and adequate compensation within a reasonable period of time.

**EXPRESSION.** See **FREEDOM OF OPINION AND EXPRESSION.**

**EXTRADITION.** The term *extradition* refers to the delivery of a suspected or convicted person by the State in which the person is located to the State in the jurisdiction of which the offense was committed or the person convicted. Each State may have its own extradition treaty with any other state. Below are two international extradition treaties: from the **COUNCIL OF EUROPE** and from the **ORGANIZATION OF AMERICAN STATES.**

*EUROPEAN CONVENTION ON EXTRADITION (1957).* The Convention aims at establishing uniform rules to govern the decisions of States parties when dealing with requests from other States for the surrender of persons sought either for prosecution or for the carrying out of a sentence or detention order. The Convention entered into force on 18 April 1960. Its provisions were later supplemented by a first protocol, adopted in 1975 that excludes war crimes and crimes against humanity from the category of political offences, set out in article 3 of the parent Convention, to which extradition does not apply. It also authorizes States parties to refuse extradition if the offender has already been tried for the offence, or offences, in respect of which the request is made and by a second additional protocol, adopted in 1978, that revises provisions of the parent Convention relating to such matters as fiscal offences, judgements *in absentia,* and amnesty.

The text of the parent convention and its two protocols is as follows:

The governments signatory hereto, being Members of the Council of Europe,

Considering that the aim of the Council of Europe is to achieve a greater unity between its Members;

Considering that this purpose can be attained by the conclusion of agreements and by common action in legal matters;

Considering that the acceptance of uniform rules with regard to extradition is likely to assist this work of unification,

Have agreed as follows:

*Article 1. Obligation to Extradite.* The Contracting Parties undertake to surrender to each other, subject to the provisions and conditions laid down in this Convention, all persons against whom the competent authorities of the requesting Party are proceeding for an offence or who are wanted by the said authorities for the carrying out of a sentence or detention order.

*Article 2. Extraditable Offences.* 1. Extradition shall be granted in respect of offences punishable under the laws of the requesting Party and of the requested Party by deprivation of liberty or under a detention order for a maximum period of at least one year or by a more severe penalty. Where a conviction and prison sentence have occurred or a detention order has been made in the territory of the requesting Party, the punishment awarded must have been for a period of at least four months.

2. If the request for extradition includes several separate offences each of which is punishable under the laws of the requesting Party and the requested Party by deprivation of liberty or under a detention order, but of which some do not fulfil the condition with regard to the amount of punishment which may be awarded, the requested Party shall also have the right to grant extradition for the latter offences.

3. Any Contracting Party whose law does not allow extradition for certain of the offences referred to in paragraph 1 of this article may, in so far as it is concerned, exclude such offences from the application of this Convention.

4. Any Contracting Party which wishes to avail itself of the

right provided for in paragraph 3 of this article shall, at the time of the deposit of its instrument of ratification or accession, transmit to the Secretary General of the Council of Europe either a list of the offences for which extradition is allowed or a list of those for which it is excluded and shall at the same time indicate the legal provisions which allow or exclude extradition. The Secretary General of the Council shall forward these lists to the other Signatories.

5. If extradition is subsequently excluded in respect of other offences by the law of a Contracting Party, that Party shall notify the Secretary General. The Secretary General shall inform the other Signatories. Such notification shall not take effect until three months from the date of its receipt by the Secretary General.

6. Any Party which avails itself of the right provided for in paragraphs 4 or 5 of this article may at any time apply this Convention to offences which have been excluded from it. It shall inform the Secretary General of the Council of such changes, and the Secretary General shall inform the other Signatories.

7. Any Party may apply reciprocity in respect of any offences excluded from the application of the Convention under this article.

*Article 3. Political Offences.* 1. Extradition shall not be granted if the offence in respect of which it is requested is regarded by the requested Party as a political offence or as an offence connected with a political offence.

2. The same rule shall apply if the requested Party has substantial grounds for believing that a request for extradition for an ordinary criminal offence has been made for the purpose of prosecuting or punishing a person on account of his race, religion, nationality or political opinion, or that that person's position may be prejudiced for any of these reasons.

3. The taking or attempted taking of the life of a Head of State or a member of his family shall not be deemed to be a political offence for the purposes of this Convention.

4. This article shall not affect any obligations which the Contracting Parties may have undertaken or may undertake under any other international convention of a multilateral character.

*Article 4. Military Offences.* Extradition for offences under military law which are not offences under ordinary criminal law is excluded from the application of this Convention.

*Article 5. Fiscal Offences.* Extradition shall be granted, in accordance with the provisions of this Convention, for offences in connection with taxes, duties, customs and exchange only if the Contracting Parties have so decided in respect of any such offence or category of offences.

*Article 6. Extradition of Nationals.* 1. (a) A Contracting Party shall have the right to refuse extradition of its nationals.

(b) Each Contracting Party may, by a declaration made at the time of signature or of deposit of its instrument of ratification or accession, define as far as it is concerned the term "nationals" within the meaning of this Convention.

(c) Nationality shall be determined as at the time of the decision concerning extradition. If, however, the person claimed is first recognised as a national of the requested Party during the period between the time of the decision and the time contemplated for the surrender, the requested Party may avail itself of the provision contained in sub-paragraph (a) of this article.

2. If the requested Party does not extradite its national, it shall at the request of the requesting Party submit the case to its competent authorities in order that proceedings may

be taken if they are considered appropriate. For this purpose, the files, information and exhibits relating to the offence shall be transmitted without charge by the means provided for in Article 12, paragraph 1. The requesting Party shall be informed of the result of its request.

*Article 7. Place of Commission.* 1. The requested Party may refuse to extradite a person claimed for an offence which is regarded by its law as having been committed in whole or in part in its territory or in a place treated as its territory.

2. When the offence for which extradition is requested has been committed outside the territory of the requesting Party, extradition may only be refused if the law of the requested Party does not allow prosecution for the same category of offence when committed outside the latter Party's territory or does not allow extradition for the offence concerned.

*Article 8. Pending Proceedings for the Same Offences.* The requested Party may refuse to extradite the person claimed if the competent authorities of such Party are proceeding against him in respect of the offence or offences for which extradition is requested.

*Article 9. Non bis in idem.* Extradition shall not be granted if final judgment has been passed by the competent authorities of the requested Party upon the person claimed in respect of the offence or offences for which extradition is requested. Extradition may be refused if the competent authorities of the requested Party have decided either not to institute or to terminate proceedings in respect of the same offence or offences.

*Article 10. Lapse of Time.* Extradition shall not be granted when the person claimed has, according to the law of either the requesting or the requested Party, become immune by reason of lapse of time from prosecution or punishment.

*Article 11. Capital Punishment.* If the offence for which extradition is requested is punishable by death under the law of the requesting Party, and if in respect of such offence the death-penalty is not provided for by the law of the requested Party or is not normally carried out, extradition may be refused unless the requesting Party gives such assurance as the requested Party considers sufficient that the death-penalty will not be carried out.

*Article 12. The Request and Supporting Documents.* 1. The request shall be in writing and shall be communicated through the diplomatic channel. Other means of communication may be arranged by direct agreement between two or more Parties.

2. The request shall be supported by:

(a) the original or an authenticated copy of the conviction and sentence or detention order immediately enforceable or of the warrant of arrest or other order having the same effect and issued in accordance with the procedure laid down in the law of the requesting Party;

(b) a statement of the offences for which extradition is requested. The time and place of their commission, their legal descriptions and a reference to the relevant legal provisions shall be set out as accurately as possible; and

(c) a copy of the relevant enactments or, where this is not possible, a statement of the relevant law and as accurate a description as possible of the person claimed, together with any other information which will help to establish his identity and nationality.

*Article 13. Supplementary Information.* If the information communicated by the requesting Party is found to be insufficient to allow the requested Party to make a decision in pursuance of this Convention, the latter Party shall request the necessary supplementary information and may fix a time-limit for the receipt thereof.

*Article 14. Rule of Speciality.* 1. A person who has been extradited shall not be proceeded against, sentenced or detained with a view to the carrying out of a sentence or detention order for any offence committed prior to his surrender other than that for which he was extradited, nor shall he be for any other reason restricted in his personal freedom, except in the following cases:

(a) When the Party which surrendered him consents. A request for consent shall be submitted, accompanied by the documents mentioned in Article 12 and a legal record of any statement made by the extradited person in respect of the offence concerned. Consent shall be given when the offence for which it is requested is itself subject to extradition in accordance with the provisions of this Convention;

(b) when that person, having had an opportunity to leave the territory of the Party to which he has been surrendered, has not done so within 45 days of his final discharge, or has returned to that territory after leaving it.

2. The requesting Party may, however, take any measures necessary to remove the person from its territory, or any measures necessary under its law, including proceedings by default, to prevent any legal effects of lapse of time.

3. When the description of the offence charged is altered in the course of proceedings, the extradited person shall only be proceeded against or sentenced in so far as the offence under its new description is shown by its constituent elements to be an offence which would allow extradition.

*Article 15. Re-extradition to a Third State.* Except as provided for in Article 14, paragraph 1 (b), the requesting Party shall not, without the consent of the requested Party, surrender to another Party or to a third State a person surrendered to the requesting Party and sought by the said other Party or third State in respect of offences committed before his surrender. The requested Party may request the production of the documents mentioned in Article 12, paragraph 2.

*Article 16. Provisional Arrest.* 1. In case of urgency the competent authorities of the requesting Party may request the provisional arrest of the person sought. The competent authorities of the requested Party shall decide the matter in accordance with its law.

2. The request for provisional arrest shall state that one of the documents mentioned in Article 12, paragraph 2 (a), exists and that it is intended to send a request for extradition. It shall also state for what offence extradition will be requested and when and where such offence was committed and shall so far as possible give a description of the person sought.

3. A request for provisional arrest shall be sent to the competent authorities of the requested Party either through the diplomatic channel or direct by post or telegraph or through the International Criminal Police Organisation (Interpol) or by any other means affording evidence in writing or accepted by the requested Party. The requesting authority shall be informed without delay of the result of its request.

4. Provisional arrest may be terminated if, within a period of 18 days after arrest, the requested Party has not received the request for extradition and the documents mentioned in Article 12. It shall not, in any event, exceed 40 days from the date of such arrest. The possibility of provisional release at any time is not excluded, but the requested Party shall take any measures which it considers necessary to prevent the escape of the person sought.

5. Release shall not prejudice re-arrest and extradition if a request for extradition is received subsequently.

*Article 17. Conflicting Requests.* If extradition is requested concurrently by more than one State, either for the same offence or for different offences, the requested Party shall make its decision having regard to all the circumstances and especially the relative seriousness and place of commission of the offences, the respective dates of the requests, the nationality of the person claimed and the possibility of subsequent extradition to another State.

*Article 18. Surrender of the Person to be Extradited.* 1. The requested Party shall inform the requesting Party by the means mentioned in Article 12, paragraph 1, of its decision with regard to the extradition.

2. Reasons shall be given for any complete or partial rejection.

3. If the request is agreed to, the requesting Party shall be informed of the place and date of surrender and of the length of time for which the person claimed was detained with a view to surrender.

4. Subject to the provisions of paragraph 5 of this article, if the person claimed has not been taken over on the appointed date, he may be released after the expiry of 15 days and shall in any case be released after the expiry of 30 days. The requested Party may refuse to extradite him for the same offence.

5. If circumstances beyond its control prevent a Party from surrendering or taking over the person to be extradited, it shall notify the other Party. The two Parties shall agree a new date for surrender and the provisions of paragraph 4 of this article shall apply.

*Article 19. Postponed or Conditional Surrender.* 1. The requested Party may, after making its decision on the request for extradition, postpone the surrender of the person claimed in order that he may be proceeded against by that Party or, if he has already been convicted, in order that he may serve his sentence in the territory of that Party for an offence other than that for which extradition is requested.

2. The requested Party may, instead of postponing surrender, temporarily surrender the person claimed to the requesting Party in accordance with conditions to be determined by mutual agreement between the Parties.

*Article 20. Handing over of Property.* 1. The requested Party shall, in so far as its law permits and at the request of the requesting Party, seize and hand over property:

(a) which may be required as evidence or

(b) which has been acquired as a result of the offence and which, at the time of the arrest, is found in the possession of the person claimed or is discovered subsequently.

2. The property mentioned in paragraph 1 of this article shall be handed over even if extradition, having been agreed to, cannot be carried out owing to the death or escape of the person claimed.

3. When the said property is liable to seizure or confiscation in the territory of the requested Party, the latter may, in connection with pending criminal proceedings, temporarily retain it or hand it over on condition that it is returned.

4. Any rights which the requested Party or third parties may have acquired in the said property shall be preserved. Where these rights exist, the property shall be returned without charge to the requested Party as soon as possible after the trial.

*Article 21. Transit.* 1. Transit through the territory of one of the Contracting Parties shall be granted on submission of a request by the means mentioned in Article 12, paragraph 1, provided that the offence concerned is not considered by the Party requested to grant transit as an offence of a political or purely military character having regard to Articles 3 and 4 of this Convention.

2. Transit of a national, within the meaning of Article 6, of a country requested to grant transit may be refused.

3. Subject to the provisions of paragraph 4 of this article, it shall be necessary to produce the documents mentioned in Article 12, paragraph 2.

4. If air transport is used, the following provisions shall apply:

(a) when it is not intended to land, the requesting Party shall notify the Party over whose territory the flight is to be made and shall certify that one of the documents mentioned in Article 12, paragraph 2 (a) exists. In the case of an unscheduled landing, such notification shall have the effect of a request for provisional arrest as provided for in Article 16, and the requesting Party shall submit a formal request for transit;

(b) when it is intended to land, the requesting Party shall submit a formal request for transit.

5. A Party may, however, at the time of signature or of the deposit of its instrument of ratification of, or accession to, this Convention, declare that it will only grant transit of a person on some or all of the conditions on which it grants extradition. In that event, reciprocity may be applied.

6. The transit of the extradited person shall not be carried out through any territory where there is reason to believe that his life or his freedom may be threatened by reason of his race, religion, nationality or political opinion.

*Article 22. Procedure.* Except where this Convention otherwise provides, the procedure with regard to extradition and provisional arrest shall be governed solely by the law of the requested Party.

*Article 23. Language to be Used.* The documents to be produced shall be in the language of the requesting or requested Party. The requested Party may require a translation into one of the official languages of the Council of Europe to be chosen by it.

*Article 24. Expenses.* 1. Expenses incurred in the territory of the requested Party by reason of extradition shall be borne by that Party.

2. Expenses incurred by reason of transit through the territory of a Party requested to grant transit shall be borne by the requesting Party.

3. In the event of extradition from a non-metropolitan territory of the requested Party, the expenses occasioned by travel between that territory and the metropolitan territory of the requesting Party shall be borne by the latter. The same rule shall apply to expenses occasioned by travel between the non-metropolitan territory of the requested Party and its metropolitan territory.

*Article 25. Definition of "Detention Order".* For the purposes of this Convention, the expression "detention order" means any order involving deprivation of liberty which has been made by a criminal court in addition to or instead of a prison sentence.

*Article 26. Reservations.* 1. Any Contracting Party may, when signing this Convention or when depositing its instrument of ratification or accession, make a reservation in respect of any provision or provisions of the Convention.

2. Any Contracting Party which has made a reservation shall withdraw it as soon as circumstances permit. Such withdrawal shall be made by notification to the Secretary General of the Council of Europe.

3. A Contracting Party which has made a reservation in respect of a provision of the Convention may not claim application of the said provision by another Party save in so far as it has itself accepted the provision.

*Article 27. Territorial Application.* 1. This Convention shall apply to the metropolitan territories of the Contracting Parties.

2. In respect of France, it shall also apply to Algeria and to the overseas Departments and, in respect of the United Kingdom of Great Britain and Northern Ireland, to the Channel Islands and to the Isle of Man.

3. The Federal Republic of Germany may extend the application of this Convention to the *Land* of Berlin by notice addressed to the Secretary General of the Council of Europe, who shall notify the other Parties of such declaration.

4. By direct arrangement between two or more Contracting Parties, the application of this Convention may be extended, subject to the conditions laid down in the arrangement, to any territory of such Parties, other than the territories mentioned in paragraphs 1, 2 and 3 of this article, for whose international relations any such Party is responsible.

*Article 28. Relations between this Convention and Bilateral Agreements.* 1. This Convention shall, in respect of those countries to which it applies, supersede the provisions of any bilateral treaties, conventions or agreements governing extradition between any two Contracting Parties.

2. The Contracting Parties may conclude between themselves bilateral or multilateral agreements only in order to supplement the provisions of this Convention or to facilitate the application of the principles contained therein.

3. Where, as between two or more Contracting Parties, extradition takes place on the basis of a uniform law, the Parties shall be free to regulate their mutual relations in respect of extradition exclusively in accordance with such a system notwithstanding the provisions of this Convention. The same principle shall apply as between two or more Contracting Parties each of which has in force a law providing for the execution in its territory of warrants of arrest issued in the territory of the other Party or Parties. Contracting Parties which exclude or may in the future exclude the application of this Convention as between themselves in accordance with this paragraph shall notify the Secretary General of the Council of Europe accordingly. The Secretary General shall inform the other Contracting Parties of any notification received in accordance with this paragraph.

*Article 29. Signature, Ratification and Entry into Force.* 1. This Convention shall be open to signature by the Members of the Council of Europe. It shall be ratified. The instruments of ratification shall be deposited with the Secretary General of the Council.

2. The Convention shall come into force 90 days after the date of deposit of the third instrument of ratification.

3. As regards any signatory ratifying subsequently, the Convention shall come into force 90 days after the date of the deposit of its instrument of ratification.

*Article 30. Accession.* 1. The Committee of Ministers of the Council of Europe may invite any State not a Member of the Council to accede to this Convention, provided that the resolution containing such invitation receives the unanimous agreement of the Members of the Council who have ratified the Convention.

2. Accession shall be by deposit with the Secretary General of the Council of an instrument of accession, which shall take effect 90 days after the date of its deposit.

*Article 31. Denunciation.* Any Contracting Party may denounce this Convention in so far as it is concerned by giving notice to the Secretary General of the Council of Europe.

Denunciation shall take effect six months after the date when the Secretary General of the Council received such notification.

*Article 32. Notifications.* The Secretary General of the Council of Europe shall notify the Members of the Council and the government of any State which has acceded to this Convention of:

(a) the deposit of any instrument of ratification or accession;

(b) the date of entry into force of this Convention;

(c) any declaration made in accordance with the provisions of Article 6, paragraph 1, and of Article 21, paragraph 5;

(d) any reservation made in accordance with Article 26, paragraph 1;

(e) the withdrawal of any reservation in accordance with Article 26, paragraph 2;

(f) any notification of denunciation received in accordance with the provisions of Article 31 and by the date on which such denunciation will take effect.

In witness whereof the undersigned, being duly authorised thereto, have signed this Convention.

Done at Paris, this 13th day of December 1957, in English and French, both texts being equally authentic, in a single copy which shall remain deposited in the archives of the Council of Europe. The Secretary General of the Council of Europe shall transmit certified copies to the signatory governments.

## Additional Protocol

### Chapter I

*Article 1.* For the application of Article 3 of the Convention, political offences shall not be considered to include the following:

(a) the crimes against humanity specified in the Convention on the Prevention and Punishment of the Crime of Genocide adopted on 9 December 1948 by the General Assembly of the United Nations;

(b) the violations specified in Article 50 of the 1949 Geneva Convention for the Amelioration of the Condition of the Wounded and Sick in Armed Forces in the Field, Article 51 of the 1949 Geneva Convention for the Amelioration of the Condition of Wounded, Sick and Shipwrecked Members of Armed Forces at Sea, Article 130 of the 1949 Geneva Convention relative to the Treatment of Prisoners of War and Article 147 of the 1949 Geneva Convention relative to the Protection of Civilian Persons in Time of War;

(c) any comparable violations of the laws of war having effect at the time when this Protocol enters into force and of customs of war existing at that time, which are not already provided for in the above-mentioned provisions of the Geneva Conventions.

### Chapter II

*Article 2.* Article 9 of the Convention shall be supplemented by the following text, the original Article 9 of the Convention becoming paragraph 1 and the under-mentioned provisions becoming paragraphs 2, 3 and 4:

"2. The extradition of a person against whom a final judgment has been rendered in a third State, Contracting Party to the Convention, for the offence or offences in respect of which the claim was made, shall not be granted:

(a) if the aforementioned judgment resulted in his acquittal;

(b) if the term of imprisonment or other measure to which he was sentenced:

(i) has been completely enforced;

(ii) has been wholly, or with respect to the part not enforced, the subject of a pardon or an amnesty;

(c) if the court convicted the offender without imposing a sanction.

3. However, in the cases referred to in paragraph 2, extradition may be granted:

(a) if the offence in respect of which judgment has been rendered was committed against a person, an institution or any thing having public status in the requesting State;

(b) if the person on whom judgment was passed had himself a public status in the requesting State;

(c) if the offence in respect of which judgment was passed was committed completely or partly in the territory of the requesting State or in a place treated as its territory.

4. The provisions of paragraphs 2 and 3 shall not prevent the application of wider domestic provisions relating to the effect of *ne bis in idem* attached to foreign criminal judgments."

### Chapter III

*Article 3.* 1. This Protocol shall be open to signature by the member States of the Council of Europe which have signed the Convention. It shall be subject to ratification, acceptance or approval. Instruments of ratification, acceptance or approval shall be deposited with the Secretary General of the Council of Europe.

2. The Protocol shall enter into force 90 days after the date of the deposit of the third instrument of ratification, acceptance or approval.

3. In respect of a signatory State ratifying, accepting or approving subsequently, the Protocol shall enter into force 90 days after the date of the deposit of its instruments of ratification, acceptance or approval.

4. A member State of the Council of Europe may not ratify, accept or approve this Protocol without having, simultaneously or previously, ratified the Convention.

*Article 4.* 1. Any State which has acceded to the Convention may accede to this Protocol after the Protocol has entered into force.

2. Such accession shall be effected by depositing with the Secretary General of the Council of Europe an instrument of accession which shall take effect 90 days after the date of its deposit.

*Article 5.* 1. Any State may, at the time of signature or when depositing its instrument of ratification, acceptance, approval or accession, specify the territory or territories to which this Protocol shall apply.

2. Any State may, when depositing its instrument of ratification, acceptance, approval or accession or at any later date, by declaration addressed to the Secretary General of the Council of Europe, extend this Protocol to any other territory or territories specified in the declaration and for whose international relations it is responsible or on whose behalf it is authorised to give undertakings.

3. Any declaration made in pursuance of the preceding paragraph may, in respect of any territory mentioned in such declaration, be withdrawn according to the procedure laid down in Article 8 of this Protocol.

*Article 6.* 1. Any State may, at the time of signature or

when depositing its instrument of ratification, acceptance, approval or accession, declare that it does not accept one or the other of Chapters I or II.

2. Any Contracting Party may withdraw a declaration it has made in accordance with the foregoing paragraph by means of a declaration addressed to the Secretary General of the Council of Europe which shall become effective as from the date of its receipt.

3. No reservation may be made to the provisions of this Protocol.

*Article 7.* The European Committee on Crime Problems of the Council of Europe shall be kept informed regarding the application of this Protocol and shall do whatever is needful to facilitate a friendly settlement of any difficulty which may arise out of its execution.

*Article 8.* 1. Any Contracting Party may, in so far as it is concerned, denounce this Protocol by means of a notification addressed to the Secretary General of the Council of Europe.

2. Such denunciation shall take effect six months after the date of receipt by the Secretary General of such notification.

3. Denunciation of the Convention entails automatically denunciation of this Protocol.

*Article 9.* The Secretary General of the Council of Europe shall notify the member States of the Council and any State which has acceded to the Convention of:

(a) any signature;

(b) any deposit of an instrument of ratification, acceptance, approval or accession;

(c) any date of entry into force of this Protocol in accordance with Article 3 thereof;

(d) any declaration received in pursuance of the provisions of Article 5 and any withdrawal of such a declaration;

(e) any declaration made in pursuance of the provisions of Article 6, paragraph 1;

(f) the withdrawal of any declaration carried out in pursuance of the provisions of Article 6, paragraph 2;

(g) any notification received in pursuance of the provisions of Article 8 and the date on which denunciation takes effect.

In witness whereof, the undersigned, being duly authorised thereto, have signed this Protocol.

Done at Strasbourg, this 15th day of October 1975, in English and in French, both texts being equally authoritative, in a single copy which shall remain deposited in the archives of the Council of Europe. The Secretary General of the Council of Europe shall transmit certified copies to each of the signatory and acceding States.

## Second Additional Protocol

### Chapter I

*Article 1.* Paragraph 2 of Article 2 of the Convention shall be supplemented by the following provision:

"This right shall also apply to offences which are subject only to pecuniary sanctions."

### Chapter II

*Article 2.* Article 5 of the Convention shall be replaced by the following provisions:

"*Fiscal Offences*". 1. For offences in connection with taxes, duties, customs and exchange extradition shall take place between the Contracting Parties in accordance with the provisions of the Convention if the offence, under the law of the requested Party, corresponds to an offence of the same nature.

2. Extradition may not be refused on the ground that the law of the requested Party does not impose the same kind of tax or duty or does not contain a tax, duty, customs or exchange regulation of the same kind as the law of the requesting Party."

### Chapter III

*Article 3.* The Convention shall be supplemented by the following provisions;

"*Judgments in absentia*". 1. When a Contracting Party requests from another Contracting Party the extradition of a person for the purpose of carrying out a sentence or detention order imposed by a decision rendered against him in absentia, the requested Party may refuse to extradite for this purpose if, in its opinion, the proceedings leading to the judgment did not satisfy the minimum rights of defence recognised as due to everyone charged with criminal offence. However, extradition shall be granted if the requesting Party gives an assurance considered sufficient to guarantee to the person claimed the right to a retrial which safeguards the rights of defence. This decision will authorise the requesting Party either to enforce the judgment in question if the convicted person does not make an opposition or, if he does, to take proceedings against the person extradited.

2. When the requested Party informs the person whose extradition has been requested of the judgment rendered against him in absentia, the requesting Party shall not regard this communication as a formal notification for the purposes of the criminal procedure in that State."

### Chapter IV

*Article 4.* The Convention shall be supplemented by the following provisions:

"*Amnesty*". Extradition shall not be granted for an offence in respect of which an amnesty has been declared in the requested State and which that State had competence to prosecute under its own criminal law."

### Chapter V

*Article 5.* Paragraph 1 of Article 12 of the Convention shall be replaced by the following provisions:

"The request shall be in writing and shall be addressed by the Ministry of Justice of the requesting Party to the Ministry of Justice of the requested Party; however, use of the diplomatic channel is not excluded. Other means of communication may be arranged by direct agreement between two or more Parties."

### Chapter VI

*Article 6.* 1. This Protocol shall be open to signature by the member States of the Council of Europe which have signed the Convention. It shall be subject to ratification, acceptance or approval. Instruments of ratification, acceptance or approval shall be deposited with the Secretary General of the Council of Europe.

2. The Protocol shall enter into force 90 days after the date of the deposit of the third instrument of ratification, acceptance or approval.

3. In respect of a signatory State ratifying, accepting or approving subsequently, the Protocol shall enter into force 90 days after the date of the deposit of its instrument of ratification, acceptance or approval.

4. A member State of the Council of Europe may not ratify, accept or approve this Protocol without having, simultaneously or previously, ratified the Convention.

*Article 7.* 1. Any State which has acceded to the Convention may accede to this Protocol after the Protocol has entered into force.

2. Such accession shall be effected by depositing with the Secretary General of the Council of Europe an instrument of accession which shall take effect 90 days after the date of its deposit.

*Article 8.* 1. Any State may, at the time of signature or when depositing its instrument of ratification, acceptance, approval or accession, specify the territory or territories to which this Protocol shall apply.

2. Any State may, when depositing its instrument of ratification, acceptance, approval or accession or at any later date, by declaration addressed to the Secretary General of the Council of Europe, extend this Protocol to any other territory or territories specified in the declaration and for whose international relations it is responsible or on whose behalf it is authorised to give undertakings.

3. Any declaration made in pursuance of the preceding paragraph may, in respect of any territory mentioned in such declaration, be withdrawn by means of a notification addressed to the Secretary General of the Council of Europe. Such withdrawal shall take effect six months after the date of receipt by the Secretary General of the Council of Europe of the notification.

*Article 9.* 1. Reservations made by a State to a provision of the Convention shall be applicable also to this Protocol, unless that State otherwise declares at the time of signature or when depositing its instrument of ratification, acceptance, approval or accession.

2. Any State may, at the time of signature or when depositing its instrument of ratification, acceptance, approval or accession, declare that it reserves the right:

(a) not to accept Chapter I;

(b) not to accept Chapter II, or to accept it only in respect of certain offences or certain categories of the offences referred to in Article 2;

(c) not to accept Chapter III, or to accept only paragraph 1 of Article 3;

(d) not to accept Chapter IV;

(e) not to accept Chapter V.

3. Any Contracting Party may withdraw a reservation it has made in accordance with the foregoing paragraph by means of a declaration addressed to the Secretary General of the Council of Europe which shall become effective as from the date of its receipt.

4. A Contracting Party which has applied to this Protocol a reservation made in respect of a provision of the Convention or which has made a reservation in respect of a provision of this Protocol may not claim the application of that provision by another Contracting Party; it may, however, if its reservation is partial or conditional, claim the application of that provision in so far as it has itself accepted it.

5. No other reservation may be made to the provisions of this Protocol.

*Article 10.* The European Committee on Crime Problems of the Council of Europe shall be kept informed regarding the application of this Protocol and shall do whatever is needful to facilitate a friendly settlement of any difficulty which may arise out of its execution.

*Article 11.* 1. Any Contracting Party may, in so far as it is concerned, denounce this Protocol by means of a notification addressed to the Secretary General of the Council of Europe.

2. Such denunciation shall take effect six months after the date of receipt by the Secretary General of such notification.

3. Denunciation of the Convention entails automatically denunciation of this Protocol.

*Article 12.* The Secretary General of the Council of Europe shall notify the member States of the Council and any State which has acceded to the Convention of:

(a) any signature of this Protocol;

(b) any deposit of an instrument of ratification, acceptance, approval or accession;

(c) any date of entry into force of this Protocol in accordance with Articles 6 and 7;

(d) any declaration received in pursuance of the provisions of paragraphs 2 and 3 of Article 8;

(e) any declaration received in pursuance of the provisions of paragraph 1 of Article 9;

(f) any reservation made in pursuance of the provisions of paragraph 2 of Article 9;

(g) the withdrawal of any reservation carried out in pursuance of the provisions of paragraph 3 of Article 9;

(h) any notification received in pursuance of the provisions of Article 11 and the date on which denunciation takes effect.

In witness whereof the undersigned, being duly authorised thereto, have signed this Protocol.

Done at Strasbourg, this 17th day of March 1978, in English and in French, both texts being equally authoritative, in a single copy which shall remain deposited in the archives of the Council of Europe. The Secretary General of the Council of Europe shall transmit certified copies to each of the signatory and acceding States.

**INTER-AMERICAN CONVENTION ON EXTRADITION (1981).** The Convention supplements the Convention on Extradition prepared under the auspices of the Organization of American States and adopted on 26 December 1933 (*League of Nations Treaty Series* 162, p. 45), which systematized the process of extradition for OAS member States. It supplements, clarifies, and simplifies the extradition procedures set out in the earlier convention and, in particular, defines extraditable offenses as those punishable "by a penalty of not less than two years of deprivation of liberty under the laws of both the requesting State and the requested State."

Drafted by the Inter-American Council of Jurists and approved by the Inter-American Juridical Committee, the Convention was adopted by the OAS General Assembly, meeting at Caracas, on 25 February 1981.

The text of the Convention (*OAS Treaty Series* 60) is as follows:

Reaffirming their goal of strengthening international co-operation in legal and criminal law matters, which was the inspiration for the agreements reached in Lima on March 27, 1879, in Montevideo on January 23, 1889, in Mexico City on January 28, 1902, in Washington on February 7, 1923, in Havana on February 20, 1928, in Montevideo on December 26, 1933, in Guatemala City on April 12, 1934, and in Montevideo on March 19, 1940;

Taking into consideration resolutions CVII of the Tenth Inter-American Conference (Caracas, 1954), VII of the Third Meeting of the Inter-American Council of Jurists (Mexico, 1956), IV of the Fourth Meeting of that Council (Santiago, Chile, 1959), and AG/RES.91 (II-O/72), 183 (V-O/75) and 310 (VII-O/77) of the General Assembly of the Organization of American States, as well as the draft Conventions proposed by the Inter-American Juridical Committee in 1954, 1957, 1973, and 1977;

Believing that the close ties and the cooperation that exist in the Americas call for the extension of extradition to ensure that crime does not go unpunished, and to simplify procedures and promote mutual assistance in the field of criminal law on a wider scale than provided for by the treaties in force, with due respect to the human rights embodied in the American Declaration of the Rights and Duties of Man and the Universal Declaration of Human Rights; and

Conscious that the fight against crime at the international level will enhance the fundamental value of justice in criminal law matters,

The Member States of the Organization of American States adopt the following Inter-American Convention on Extradition:

*Article 1. Obligation to Extradite.* The States Parties bind themselves, in accordance with the provisions of this Convention, to surrender to other States Parties that request their extradition persons who are judicially required for prosecution, are being tried, have been convicted or have been sentenced to a penalty involving deprivation of liberty.

*Article 2. Jurisdiction.* 1. For extradition to be granted, the offense that gave rise to the request for extradition must have been committed in the territory of the requesting State.

2. When the offense for which extradition is requested has been committed outside the territory of the requesting State, extradition shall be granted provided the requesting State has jurisdiction to try the offense that gave rise to the request for extradition and to pronounce judgment thereon.

3. The requested State may deny extradition when it is competent, according to its own legislation, to prosecute the person whose extradition is sought for the offense on which the request is based. If it denies extradition for this reason, the requested State shall submit the case to its competent authorities and inform the requesting State of the result.

*Article 3. Extraditable Offenses.* 1. For extradition to be granted, the offense for which the person is sought shall be punishable at the time of its commission, by reason of the acts that constitute it, disregarding extenuating circumstances and the denomination of the offense, by a penalty of not less than two years of deprivation of liberty under the laws of both the requesting State and the requested State. Where the principle of retroactivity of penal law exists, it shall be applied only when it is favorable to the offender.

2. If the extradition is to be carried out between States whose laws establish minimum and maximum penalties, the offense for which extradition is requested shall be punishable, under the laws of the requesting and the requested States, by an average penalty of at least two years of deprivation of liberty. Average penalty is understood to be one-half of the sum of the minimum and maximum terms of each penalty of deprivation of liberty.

3. Where the extradition of an offender is requested for the execution of a sentence involving deprivation of liberty, the duration of the sentence still to be served must be at least six months.

4. In determining whether extradition should be granted to a State having a federal form of government and separate federal and state criminal legislation, the requested State shall take into consideration only the essential elements of the offense and shall disregard elements such as interstate transportation or use of the mails or other facilities of interstate commerce, since the sole purpose of such elements is to establish the jurisdiction of the federal courts of the requesting State.

*Article 4. Grounds for Denying Extradition.* Extradition shall not be granted:

1. When the person sought has completed his punishment or has been granted amnesty, pardon or grace for the offense for which extradition is sought, or when he has been acquitted or the case against him for the same offense has been dismissed with prejudice;

2. When the prosecution or punishment is barred by the statute of limitations according to the laws of the requesting State or the requested State prior to the presentation of the request for extradition;

3. When the person sought has been tried or sentenced or is to be tried before an extraordinary or *ad hoc* tribunal of the requesting State;

4. When, as determined by the requested State, the offense for which the person is sought is a political offense, an offense related thereto, or an ordinary criminal offense prosecuted for political reasons. The requested State may decide that the fact that the victim of the punishable act in question performed political functions does not in itself justify the designation of the offenses as political;

5. When, from the circumstances of the case, it can be inferred that persecution for reasons of race, religion or nationality is involved, or that the position of the person sought may be prejudiced for any of these reasons;

6. With respect to offenses that in the requested State cannot be prosecuted unless a complaint or charge has been made by a party having a legitimate interest.

*Article 5. Specific Offenses.* No provision of this Convention shall preclude extradition regulated by a treaty or Convention in force between the requesting State and the requested State whose purpose is to prevent or repress a specific category of offenses and which imposes on such States an obligation to either prosecute or extradite the person sought.

*Article 6. Right of Asylum.* No provision of this Convention may be intercepted as a limitation on the right of asylum when its exercise is appropriate.

*Article 7. Nationality.* 1. The nationality of the person sought may not be invoked as a ground for denying extradition, except when the law of the requested State otherwise provides.

2. In the case of convicted persons, the States Parties may negotiate the mutual surrender of nationals so that they may serve their sentences in the States of which they are nationals.

*Article 8. Prosecution by the Requested State.* If, when extradition is applicable, a State does not deliver the person sought, the requested State shall, when its laws or other treaties so permit, be obligated to prosecute him for the offense with which he is charged, just as if it had been committed within its territory, and shall inform the requesting State of the judgment handed down.

*Article 9. Penalties Excluded.* The States Parties shall not grant extradition when the offense in question is punishable in the requesting State by the death penalty, by life imprisonment, or by degrading punishment, unless the requested State has previously obtained from the requesting State, through the diplomatic channel, sufficient assurances that none of the above-mentioned penalties will be imposed on the person sought or that, if such penalties are imposed, they will not be enforced.

*Article 10. Transmission of Request.* The request for extradition shall be made by the diplomatic agent of the requesting State, or, if none is present, by its consular officer, or, when appropriate, by the diplomatic agent of a third State to which is entrusted, with the consent of the government of the requested State, the representation and protection of the interests of the requesting State. The request may also be made directly from government to government, in accordance with such procedure as the governments concerned may agree upon.

*Article 11. Supporting Documents.* 1. The request for extradition shall be accompanied by the documents listed below, duly certified in the manner prescribed by the laws of the requesting State:

(a) A certified copy of the warrant for arrest, or other document of like nature, issued by a competent judicial authority, or the *Ministerio Público* as well as a certified copy of evidence that, according to the laws of the requested State, is sufficient for the arrest and commitment for trial of the person sought. The last mentioned requirement shall not apply if the laws of the requesting State and of the requested State do not so provide. If the person has been tried and convicted of the offense by the courts of the requesting State, a certified verbatim copy of the final judgment shall suffice.

(b) The text of the legal provisions that define and penalize the alleged crime, as well as those of the statute of limitations governing prosecution and punishment.

2. The request for extradition shall also be accompanied by the translation into the language of the requested State, if appropriate, of the documents enumerated in the previous paragraph, as well as by any personal data that will permit identification of the person sought, indication of his nationality, and, whenever possible, his location within the territory of the requested State, photographs, fingerprints, or any other satisfactory means of identification.

*Article 12. Supplementary Information and Legal Assistance.* 1. The requested State, when it considers that the documents presented are insufficient, in accordance with the provisions of Article 11 of this Convention, shall so inform the requesting State as soon as possible. The requesting State shall correct any omissions or defects observed within a period of thirty days in the event the person sought is already detained or subject to precautionary measures. If, because of special circumstances, the requesting State is unable to correct the omissions or defects within that term, it may ask the requested State to extend the term by thirty days.

2. The requested State shall provide, at no cost to the requesting State, legal assistance to protect the interests of the requesting State before the competent authorities of the requested State.

*Article 13. Rule of Speciality.* 1. A person extradited under this Convention shall not be detained, tried or punished in the territory of the requesting State for an offense, committed prior to the date of the request for extradition, other than that for which extradition has been granted unless:

(a) That person leaves the territory of the requesting State after extradition and voluntarily returns to it; or

(b) That person does not leave the territory of the requesting State within thirty days after being free to do so; or

(c) The competent authority of the requested State consents to that person's detention, trial or punishment for another offense. In such case, the requested State may require the requesting State to submit the documents mentioned in Article 11 of this Convention.

2. When extradition has been granted, the requesting State shall inform the requested State of the final resolution of the case against the person extradited.

*Article 14. Provisional Detention and Precautionary Measures.* 1. In urgent cases, a State Party may request by the means of communication provided for in Article 10 of this Convention, or any other such means, the detention of the person who is judicially required for prosecution, is being tried, has been convicted, or has been sentenced to a penalty involving deprivation of liberty, and may also request the seizure of the objects related to the offense. The request for provisional detention shall contain a statement of intention to present the formal request for the extradition of the person sought, a statement of the existence of a warrant of arrest or of a judgment of conviction against that person issued by a judicial authority, and a description of the offense. The request for provisional detention shall be the sole responsibility of the requesting State.

2. The requested State shall order provisional detention and, when appropriate, the seizure of objects and shall immediately inform the requesting State of the date on which provisional detention commenced.

3. If the request for extradition, accompanied by the documents referred to in Article 11 of this Convention, is not presented within sixty days of the date on which the provisional detention referred to in paragraph 1 of this article commenced, the person sought shall be set free.

4. After the period of time referred to in the preceding paragraph has expired, the detention of the person sought may not be again requested except upon presentation of the documents required under Article 11 of this Convention.

*Article 15. Requests by more than One State.* When the extradition is requested by more than one State for the same offense, the requested State shall give preference to the request of the State in which the offense was committed. If the requests are for different offenses, preference shall be given to the State seeing the individual for the offense punishable by the most severe penalty, in accordance with the laws of the requested State. If the requests involve different offenses that the requested State considers to be of equal gravity, preference shall be determined by the order in which the requests are received.

*Article 16. Legal Rights and Assistance.* 1. The person sought shall enjoy in the requested State all the legal rights and guarantees granted by the laws of that State.

2. The person sought shall be assisted by legal counsel, and if the official language of the country is other than his own, he shall also be assisted by an interpreter.

*Article 17. Communication of the Extradition Decision.* The requested State shall promptly inform the requesting State of its decision on the request for extradition and the reasons for its approval or denial.

*Article 18. Non bis in idem.* Once the request for extradition of a person has been denied, a request may not be made again for the same offense.

*Article 19. Surrender of the Person Sought and Delivery of Property.* 1. The surrender of the person sought to the agents of the requesting State shall be carried out at a place determined by the requested State. This place shall, if possible, be an airport from which direct international flights depart for the requesting State.

2. If the request for provisional detention or for extradition is accompanied by a request for the seizure of documents, money or other objects that result from the alleged offense or may serve as evidence, such objects shall be collected and deposited under inventory by the requested State for subsequent delivery to the requesting State when the extradition is granted and even though the extradition is impeded by *force majeure,* unless the law of the requested State forbids such delivery. In any event, the rights of the third parties shall not be affected.

*Article 20. Deferral of Surrender.* 1. When the person is being tried or is serving a sentence in the requested State for an offense other than that for which the extradition is requested, his surrender may be deferred until he is entitled to be set free by virtue of acquittal, completed service or commutation of sentence, dismissal, pardon, amnesty or grace. No civil suit that the person sought may have pending against him in the requested State may prevent or defer his surrender.

2. When the surrender of the person sought would, for reasons of health, endanger his life, his surrender may be deferred until it would no longer pose such a danger.

*Article 21. Simplified Extradition.* The requested State may grant extradition without a formal extradition proceeding if:

(a) Its laws do not expressly prohibit it;

(b) The person sought irrevocably consents in writing to the extradition after being advised by a judge or other competent authority of his right to a formal extradition proceeding and the protection afforded by such a proceeding.

*Article 22. Period for Taking Custody of the Person Sought.* If the extradition has been granted, the requesting State shall take custody of the person sought within a period of thirty days from the date on which he was placed at its disposal. If it does not take custody within that period, the person sought shall be set free and may not be subjected to a new extradition procedure for the same offense or offenses. This period, however, may be extended for thirty days if the requesting State is unable, owing to circumstances beyond its control, to take custody of the person sought and escort him out of the territory of the requested State.

*Article 23. Custody.* The agents of the requesting State who are in the territory of another State Party to take custody of a person whose extradition has been granted shall be authorized to have custody of him and escort him to the territory of the requesting State, provided, however, that such agents shall be subject to the jurisdiction of the State in which they are.

*Article 24. Transit.* 1. If prior notification has been given from government to government through diplomatic or consular channels, the States Parties shall permit and cooperate in the transit through their territories of a person whose extradition has been granted under the custody of agents of the requesting State and/or the requested State, as the case may be, upon presentation of a copy of the order granting the extradition.

2. Such prior notification shall not be necessary when air transport is used and no landing is scheduled in the territory of the State Party that will be flown over.

*Article 25. Expenses.* Expenses incurred in the detention, custody, maintenance, and transportation of both the person extradited and of the objects referred to in Article 19 of this Convention shall be borne by the requested State up to the moment of surrender and delivery, and thereafter such expenses shall be borne by the requesting State.

*Article 26. Waiver of Legalization.* When the documents provided for in this Convention are communicated through the diplomatic or consular channel, or direct from government to government, their legalization shall not be required.

*Article 27. Signature.* This Convention shall be open for signature by the member states of the Organization of American States.

*Article 28. Ratification.* This Convention is subject to ratification. The instruments of ratification shall be deposited with the General Secretariat of the Organization of American States.

*Article 29. Accession.* 1. This Convention shall be open to accession by any American State.

2. This Convention shall be open to accession by States having the status of permanent observer to the Organization of American States, following approval of the pertinent request by the General Assembly of the Organization.

*Article 30. Reservations.* Each State may, at the time of signature, approval, ratification, or accession, make reservations to this Convention, provided that each reservation concerns one or more specific provisions and is not incompatible with the object and purpose of the Convention.

*Article 31. Entry into Force.* 1. This Convention shall enter into force on the thirtieth day following the date of deposit of the second instrument of ratification.

2. For each State ratifying or acceding to the Convention after the deposit of the second instrument of ratification, the Convention shall enter into force on the thirtieth day after deposit by such State of its instrument of ratification or accession.

*Article 32. Special Cases of Territorial Application.* 1. If a State Party has two or more territorial units in which different systems of law apply in relation to the matters dealt with in this Convention, it shall, the time of signature, ratification, or accession, declare that this Convention shall extend to all its territorial units or only to one or more of them.

2. Such declaration may be modified by subsequent declarations, which shall expressly indicate the territorial unit or units to which this Convention applies. Such subsequent declarations shall be transmitted to the General Secretariat of the Organization of American States, and shall become effective thirty days after the date of their receipt.

*Article 33. Relations with other Conventions on Extradition*
1. This Convention shall apply to the States Parties that ratify it or accede to it and shall not supersede multilateral or bilateral treaties that are in force or were concluded earlier unless the States Parties concerned otherwise expressly declare or agree, respectively.

2. The State Parties may decide to maintain in force as supplementary instruments treaties entered into earlier.

*Article 34. Duration and Denunciation.* This Convention shall remain in force indefinitely, but any of the States Parties may denounce it. The instrument of denunciation shall be deposited with the General Secretariat of the Organization of American States. After one year from the date of deposit of the instrument of denunciation, the Convention shall no longer be in effect for the denouncing State, but shall remain in effect for the other States Parties.

*SEE ALSO* Prisoners.

**BIBLIOGRAPHY.** Baunach, Phyllis J. "The US-UK Supplementary Extradition Treaty: Justice for Terrorists or Terror for Justice?" *Connecticut Journal of International Law* 2, no. 2 (Spring 1987): 463–498. Scholarly article, in English.

Dinstein, Yoram, and Mala Tabory, eds. "Terrorism as an International Crime," *Israel Yearbook on Human Rights* 19 (1989). Special issue of scholarly articles, in English; bibliography, pp. 405–412.

Gappa, David L. "European Court of Human Rights: Extradition—Inhuman or Degrading Treatment or Punishment, Soering Case, 161 Eur.Ct.H.R. (Ser. A) (1989)," *Georgia Journal of International and Comparative Law* 20, no. 2 (1990): 463–488. Case comment, in English.

Gilbert, Geoff. *Aspects of Extradition Law.* Dordrecht, the Netherlands: Martinus Nijhoff, 1991. Scholarly monograph, in English.

Nicholls, Clive. "The Law and Practice of Extradition: Recent Developments," *Commonwealth Law Bulletin* 17 no. 4 (Oct. 1991): 1450–1457. Discussion paper, in English.

Williams, Sharon A. "Human Rights Safeguards and International Cooperation in Extradition: Striking the Balance," *Criminal Law Forum* 3, no. 2 (Winter 1992): 191–224. Scholarly article, in English.

# F

**FAIR TRIAL.** The UN SUB-COMMISSION ON PREVENTION OF DISCRIMINATION AND PROTECTION OF MINORITIES, at its 1989 session, noted (resolution 1989/27) that, although article 10 of the UNIVERSAL DECLARATION OF HUMAN RIGHTS and article 14 of the INTERNATIONAL COVENANT ON CIVIL AND POLITICAL RIGHTS deal with various aspects of a "fair and public hearing," no comprehensive study had been made of recent developments concerning standards guaranteeing the right to a fair trial. The Sub-Commission also noted that, under the Covenant, the right to a fair trial is considered to be a derogable right which may be suspended in certain circumstances, such as in time of public emergency.

***STUDY ON THE RIGHT TO A FAIR TRIAL.*** The Sub-Commission appointed two of its Members, Mr. Stanislav Chernichenko (USSR) and Mr. William Treat (USA) at its 1990 session (resolution 1990/18 of 30 August 1990) as Special Rapporteurs to prepare a study on "The Right to a Fair Trial: Current Recognition and Measures Necessary for its Strengthening." Over a period of several years the two Special Rapporteurs, working as a team, prepared first a preliminary report (E/CN.4/Sub.2/1991/29), then two progress reports (E/CN.4/Sub.2/1992/24 and Add. 1–3 and E/CN.4/Sub.2/1993/24 and Add. 1–2), and a final report (E/CN.4/Sub.2/1994/24).

The final report, presented to the Sub-Commission at its 1994 session, first summarizes the discussion of the preliminary and progress reports. It then summarizes fundamental sources of international fair trial norms identified since the inception of the study (Chapter II); recognizes other developments related to the study (Chapter III); summarizes interpretations of the right to a fair trial which have been made recently by the HUMAN RIGHTS COMMITTEE, the COMMITTEE ON THE ELIMINATION OF RACIAL DISCRIMINATION, the INTER-AMERICAN COMMISSION AND COURT OF HUMAN RIGHTS, and the European Commission and Court of Human Rights (Chapter IV); identifies the right to a fair trial as a non-derogable right (Chapter V); and discusses the right to a remedy as a non-derogable right (Chapter VI). Chapter VII contains the conclusions and recommendations of the

Special Rapporteurs on strengthening the right to a fair trial and to a remedy. Annex I contains the text of a revised draft third optional protocol to the International Covenant on Civil and Political Rights, aiming at guaranteeing under all circumstances the right to a fair trial and a remedy. Annex II contains a draft body of principles on the right to a fair trial and a remedy. Annex III contains a comprehensive bibliography of relevant material identified since the commencement of the study.

The conclusions and recommendations of the Special Rapporteurs, as set out in Chapter VII (paras. 160–184) of the final report, are as follows:

The Special Rapporteurs have reviewed the treaties and other international instruments protecting the right to a fair trial and a remedy. They have studied the interpretations of the right by the Human Rights Committee, the African Commission on Human and Peoples' Rights, the European Commission and Court of Human Rights, and the Inter-American Commission on and Court of Human Rights. They have also prepared a study of the right to habeas corpus, *amparo,* and similar procedures.

The Special Rapporteurs have gathered materials about national constitutions, laws, rules, and practices relating to the right to a fair trial from more than 65 nations. In this regard, they have very much appreciated the information they have received from Governments, as well as intergovernmental organizations, non-governmental organizations, bar associations, and individuals.

The Special Rapporteurs have found that several of the States studied appear to operate dual systems of trial procedures. Some States deviated from standard procedures in emergency situations which threaten national security or when the offence is political in nature. In some States, jurisdiction is lodged in special or military courts, while in others regular criminal courts try the cases but with remarkable deviation from the State's fair trial norms. While these problems do not exist in many countries, the problems indicate the need for greater international protection for the right to a fair trial and a remedy—particularly during periods of public emergency.

### A. Publication and Dissemination of Study

The Special Rapporteurs view each preparatory, preliminary, and progress report in this study as not only an update of the previous report, but also as a separate chapter in the entire study, each focusing on particular aspects of the right to a fair trial and a remedy. In order to avoid unnecessary repetition of the earlier chapters and to produce a relatively compact document for the Sub-Commission, they have chosen not to assemble all the chapters into their final report which would have been quite lengthy. Instead, the Special Rapporteurs recommend that the entire study be compiled in one document to be published under the United Nations Study Series. In preparation for publication by the United Nations, the Special Rapporteurs will undertake, without financial implications, to compile the full study with all its chapters in light of the comments received from Governments, Sub-Commission members and others, as well as the most recent developments up to the date on which the report is ready for publication. This comprehensive document will provide an invaluable source of fair trial norms and remedies, interpretations of those norms, areas where the right can be strengthened, and recommendations to Governments, non-governmental organizations and individual judges, lawyers and lay people of how to implement and protect the basic human right to a fair trial and a remedy. In order to best appreciate this study, it should be published as one comprehensive document which would be translated and be given broad dissemination. The published report should be particularly useful to the International Law Commission in its efforts to draft a statute for an International Criminal Tribunal and to the International Tribunal for the Prosecution of Persons Responsible for Serious Violations of International Humanitarian Law Committed in the Territory of Former Yugoslavia since 1991. It should also be submitted to the Governments, intergovernmental organizations, non-governmental organizations, bar associations and individuals that provided information for this study. In addition, the United Nations should encourage book reviews about the published study on the right to a fair trial and a remedy, so as to disseminate its contents. (Indeed, all United Nations studies should be the subject of such book reviews.) . . .

### B. Draft Third Optional Protocol

In order to provide greater protection to the right to a fair trial and a remedy during periods of public emergency the Special Rapporteurs recommend the development of a third optional protocol to the International Covenant on Civil and Political Rights, aiming at guaranteeing under all circumstances the right to a fair trial and a remedy. The Special Rapporteurs have prepared a revised draft of such a third optional protocol, which is contained in annex I to this final report. As discussed in paragraph 29 above, there is no need to precede the draft third optional protocol with a declaration. Although it is customary to precede a Convention with a declaration, it is not necessary to precede a protocol with a declaration. None the less, the Special Rapporteurs believe that the Sub-Commission should consider drafting a separate declaration on the right to habeas corpus, *amparo,* and similar procedures. Such a declaration could amplify and further define the international meaning of the right to habeas corpus, *amparo,* and similar procedures. The drafting of that declaration could proceed in the Sub-Commission at the same time that the already drafted third optional protocol on the right to a fair trial and a remedy is being considered by the Commission.

The draft third optional protocol makes non-derogable in periods of public emergency both the right to a fair trial and the right to a remedy. The Special Rapporteurs recommend that the right to a fair trial and the right to a remedy be included within the third optional protocol, because these

two rights are very much related. During the past several years, the Commission on Human Rights and the Sub-Commission have reiterated their view that the right to habeas corpus or similar procedures should be made non-derogable and thus should be applicable even during periods of public emergency. The International Covenant on Civil and Political Rights does not specifically guarantee the right to habeas corpus or *amparo,* because those precise procedures are not available in some countries. None the less, the Covenant in articles 2 (3), 9 (3) and 9 (4) provide the essential remedy for violations of human rights available through habeas corpus, *amparo,* or similar procedures. Accordingly, the Special Rapporteurs recommend that the draft third optional protocol make non-derogable not only the right to a fair trial guaranteed by article 14 of the Civil and Political Covenant, but also articles 2 (3), 9 (3) and 9 (4).

The Special Rapporteurs recommend that this final report, including particularly the third optional protocol in annex I, be sent to all Governments and non-governmental organizations for their comments, so that their comments can be considered by the Commission. The previous draft was sent to Governments and non-governmental organizations in 1993, and the optional protocol was revised in the light of the comments received. It would be useful to send the revised draft for further comments. Also, the draft should be submitted for technical review before the drafting process begins in the Commission on Human Rights.

Pursuant to its decision 1994/107, the Commission expects to consider the Special Rapporteurs' recommendations on the third optional protocol at its fifty-first session in 1995. The Special Rapporteurs recommend that the commission establish an open-ended working group to complete the drafting of the third optional protocol. There exist already, however, a number of open-ended working groups established by the Commission including the working group preparing the draft declaration on the right and responsibility of individuals, groups and organs of society to promote and protect universally recognized human rights and fundamental freedoms (also known as the declaration on human rights defenders), the working group drafting the optional protocol to the Convention against Torture, the two working groups drafting protocols to the Convention on the Rights of the Child, and the inter-sessional working group on the organization of the work of the Commission session. In addition, it is expected that the Commission at its fifty-first session will want to establish a new working group to draft a declaration on indigenous rights. Further, the Commission may be asked to consider draft principles on human rights and a healthy environment. Consequently, there exists a real danger of an administrative overload for both the United Nations and the Governments which need to participate in these groups. The Special Rapporteurs believe that a queuing system should be established by the Commission to alleviate this potential overburden of United Nations and government resources. Accordingly, the Special Rapporteurs recommend that the Commission establish the open-ended working group on the draft third optional protocol at such time as one of the present open-ended working groups has completed its drafting efforts. It is understood that the working group on the third optional protocol will not, therefore, begin drafting until after the Commission's fifty-second session or a year or so later. This delay will provide time for the Commission to solicit more comments on the draft third optional protocol and to obtain a technical review of the present draft.

## C. Draft Body of Principles

The Special Rapporteurs have also sought to derive from international interpretations of the-right to a fair trial and a remedy as well as from national laws and practices those common elements which might serve as the basis for a Body of Principles on the Right to a Fair Trial and a Remedy. Bodies of principles or declarations are valuable when developing new international standards, such as the United Nations Declaration on the Protection of All Persons from Enforced Disappearance, the Basic Principles on the Use of Force and Firearms by Law Enforcement Officials, the Guidelines on the Role of Prosecutors and the Basic Principles on the Role of Lawyers. They may also have some value when attempting to improve an interpretation by a treaty body of ill-defined or inadequately defined rights in a regional instrument, such as the resolution on the right to a fair trial adopted by the African Commission on Human and Peoples Rights. When a body of principles or declaration attempts to summarize a voluminous, well-developed, complex and rapidly changing area of law and standards, such as the right to a fair trial, however, it is questionable whether the formulation of a declaration is advisable for an intergovernmental organization. Such codifications or restatements risk overlooking subtleties and long-established interpretations. Rewording inevitably gives rise to questions whether a different meaning is intended. The draft body of principles contained in annex II simply restates and clarifies existing international fair trial norms and interpretations; it is not expected to serve as the basis for the Sub-Commission, the Commission, or the General Assembly to draft a new norm-setting declaration; and it should in no way weaken present fair trial standards.

Accordingly, the Special Rapporteurs have prepared the draft body of principles on the right to a fair trial and a remedy, which is contained in annex II to this final progress report. The Special Rapporteurs encourage the Sub-Commission to view this draft body of principles as a succinct summary of the materials and interpretations collected in this study.

Since most of the information gathered by the Special Rapporteurs related to criminal trials, the study focuses principally, but not exclusively, on trial procedures in such cases. The Special Rapporteurs have been able to gather sufficient material to provide a basis for drafting a body of principles relating to all aspects of the right to a fair trial and a remedy, including administrative, civil, and criminal proceedings. None the less, the Special Rapporteurs recommend that further study of administrative, civil, and other procedures should be undertaken. The massive volume of the material already collected by the Special Rapporteurs, however, indicates that such additional study should be considered separately by the Sub-Commission at some later time.

## D. Working Group on Arbitrary Detention and Other Mechanisms for Implementation

The Special Rapporteurs are encouraged by the efforts of the Working Group on Arbitrary Detention, which has for two years rendered decisions in regard to communications which had been submitted. The Working Group has considered several communications which stated that a person had been imprisoned without a trial or after a trial failing to comply with international fair trial standards. Accordingly, the Working Group determines whether procedures followed in particular cases violated international norms with respect to the right to a fair trial and could thus be considered to be arbitrary within its mandate. The Special Rapporteurs believe that the Working Group on Arbitrary Detention possesses great potential for implementing the right to a fair trial and a remedy in specific cases.

The Working Group on Arbitrary Detention can determine in an expeditious manner whether individuals have been afforded their right to a fair trial and a remedy in the context of administrative detention or criminal prosecution. The Working Group cannot, however, respond to problems of unfair trials in cases which do not result in detention. None the less, the Working Group can respond more promptly to cases of arbitrary detention and thus can supplement the work of the Human Rights Committee, the Inter-American Commission on and Court of Human Rights, the European Commission and Court of Human Rights, and eventually the African Commission on Human and Peoples' Rights. Those latter institutions may consider all fair trial issues—whether civil, criminal, military, or administrative—but only in regard to Governments that have ratified their authorizing treaties and instruments. In that regard, the Working Group on Arbitrary Detention can respond effectively to violations in all countries of the world. Similarly, by its resolution 1994/41 of 4 March 1994, the Commission on Human Rights established the Special Rapporteur on the independence and impartiality of the judiciary, jurors and assessors and the independence of lawyers, which can respond effectively to certain issues relevant to the right to a fair trial and a remedy.

## E. Other Recommendations for Strengthening the Right to a Fair Trial

Pursuant to the Sub-Commission's resolutions 1992/21 of 27 August 1992 and 1993/26 of 25 August 1993, in which this final report was anticipated, the Special Rapporteurs make the following additional recommendations, aimed at Governments and international organizations, for strengthening the implementation of the right to a fair trial and a remedy.

It should be noted at the outset that the Special Rapporteurs recognize that it is very difficult to identify globally applicable methods for strengthening the right to a fair trial and a remedy. None the less, there exist nine pragmatic steps to strengthen the implementation of the right which could be pursued to assure that it is strengthened. Those steps are discussed more fully in the paragraphs below, but could be summarized as follows:

(a) The Government should assure that its constitution, laws, rules, and other written procedural norms comport with international instruments and prevailing international interpretations guaranteeing the right to a fair trial and a remedy;

(b) The Government should provide or facilitate the training of its judges, lay assessors, other decision makers, court administrators, prosecutors, lawyers, law enforcement officers, prison officials, and other personnel involved in the administration of justice, so as to assure that they are fully qualified to protect the right to a fair trial and a remedy. The training should include the principles of national and international law protecting the right to a fair trial and a remedy;

(c) The Government should assure the independence of the judges, lay assessors, other decision makers, prosecutors, and lawyers, so they can protect the right to a fair trial and remedy and can play their appropriate role in the administration of justice. In particular, Governments should take steps to comply with the Basic Principles on the Independence of the Judiciary, the Guidelines on the Role of Prosecutors, the Basic Principles the Role of Lawyers, and related United Nations standards;

(d) The Government should assure that its legal provisions guaranteeing the right to fair trial and a remedy are applied in practice in criminal, civil, administrative, and other proceedings at all times, including during any states of emergency;

(e) The Government should establish adequate mechanisms for assuring that national and international provisions guaranteeing the right to a fair trial and a remedy are applied in practice. Among the mechanisms which the Government should use to assure the implementation of the right to a fair trial and a remedy are: appeal or similar review in higher courts or tribunals; habeas corpus, *amparo* or similar procedures; ombudsmen and independent oversight mechanisms; national and local human rights institutions; etc.;

(f) The Government should ratify those treaties which contain provisions protecting the right to a fair trial and a remedy, including, for example, the International Covenant on Civil and Political Rights and relevant regional human rights treaties. Similarly, the Government should ratify the first Optional Protocol to the International Covenant on Civil and Political Rights and participate in the relevant optional review mechanisms in the human rights treaties;

(g) The Government should adopt and ratify a third optional protocol to the International Covenant on Civil and Political Rights, aiming at guaranteeing under all circumstances the right to a fair trial and a remedy (annex I);

(h) The Government should cooperate with international mechanisms which have been established to monitor compliance with the right to a fair trial and a remedy, including the Human Rights Committee; the relevant regional human rights bodies; the Working Group on Arbitrary Detention; the Special Rapporteur on the independence and impartiality of the judiciary, jurors and assessors and the independence of lawyers; international trial observers sent by intergovernmental organizations, Governments and non-governmental organizations; etc.;

(i) The Government should consider seeking advisory services and technical assistance from the United Nations, other-intergovernmental organizations and non-governmental organizations to assist with the drafting of national laws and procedures so as to comply with international standards on the right to a fair trial and a remedy; with establishing national and local mechanisms for assuring compliance with national laws and international standards relating to the right to a fair trial and a remedy; and with training of judges, prosecutors, lawyers and other personnel in standards, procedures and practices necessary to protect the right to a fair trial and a remedy.

The most fundamental aspect of guaranteeing and strengthening the right to a fair trial and a remedy on the domestic level is to have adequate written procedures and laws which comport with articles 2 (3), 9 (3), 9 (4) and 14 of the International Covenant on Civil and Political Rights as well as the other instruments and international interpretations of the right to a fair trial and a remedy. Various provisions guaranteeing the right to a fair trial and a remedy may exist in a country's constitution, statutory laws, or other procedural rules. Hence, the first step in guaranteeing and strengthening the right to a fair trial and a remedy would be to review those written rules and procedures to assure that they comport with international standards. For instance, are there established written procedures guaranteeing the right

to a fair trial for criminal proceedings as well as similar laws and procedures applicable to administrative and civil proceedings?

In addition to ensuring adequate laws and procedures to guarantee and strengthen the right to a fair trial and a remedy, there is an equally pressing need for adequate personnel to implement the laws and procedures. Judges, court administrators, prosecutors, lawyers, lay assessors, law enforcement personnel and prison officials need to receive the highest level of training available with a special emphasis on the procedures necessary to protect the right to a fair trial and a remedy not only in the courtroom, but throughout the entire judicial process, be it civil, criminal or administrative. After all, the right to a fair trial means little if the persons responsible for protecting that right are unable or unwilling to understand the mechanisms necessary to implement the right. Ideally, all decision makers should be trained as lawyers but where that is not possible or practicable, they should receive as much training as possible with a special emphasis on fair trial procedures. Once again, the Special Rapporteurs recognize that training needs to be adjusted to conform with the legal traditions of the individual countries. In those countries where training is inadequate or unavailable, technical assistance might be appropriate to ensure at the very least the minimum level of competency of the judiciary and the legal profession.

Another important component necessary to strengthen the concrete implementation of the right to a fair trial and a remedy is to guarantee the independence of the judiciary from undue influence. Governments should take steps to comply with the Basic Principles on the Independence of the Judiciary, the Guidelines on the Role of Prosecutors, and the Basic Principles on the Role of Lawyers. These instruments contain provisions guaranteeing that judges, prosecutors, and lawyers are allowed to perform their essential duties without intimidation, hindrance, harassment, or improper influence. The Special Rapporteurs are especially encouraged by the establishment of the Special Rapporteur on the independence and impartiality of the judiciary, jurors and assessors and the independence of lawyers, who will be able to act effectively in regard to certain aspects of the right to a fair trial and a remedy, that is, particularly in cases relating to the independence of judges and lawyers.

Closely related to adequate laws and procedures designed to protect the right to a fair trial and a remedy and the competence of the individuals responsible for implementation of these laws is the degree to which those laws are implemented. There-needs to be domestic implementation of these laws and procedures at every level of proceedings and in every context where the right to a fair trial and a remedy exists, even during states of emergency. The Special Rapporteurs recommend that the right to a fair trial and a remedy be thoroughly implemented in every context at the domestic level in order to protect more fully and strengthen the right.

After identifying the laws and procedures necessary to protect the right to a fair trial and a remedy, the requisite level of training for those individuals responsible for implementing the right, and the necessary degree of domestic implementation of the right, there still exists the need for mechanisms to monitor the implementation of the right. These mechanisms include adequate appeal procedures or other forms of revision, the availability of remedies such as habeas corpus and other similar procedures and the creation of an ombudsman to receive and respond to complaints regarding deprivation of the right to a fair trial and a remedy.

These mechanisms can safeguard the right and adequately check those individuals responsible for implementing the right to ensure that they are satisfactorily complying with their duties. For those countries unable to develop their own internal safeguards, technical assistance such as country visits might be appropriate to help monitor the basic principles necessary to guarantee the right to a fair trial and a remedy.

The Government should ratify those treaties which contain provisions protecting the right to a fair trial and a remedy, including, for example, the International Covenant on Civil and Political Rights and relevant regional human rights treaties.

Notwithstanding the aforementioned recommendations, the necessary domestic laws and procedures may not exist or may prove to be inadequate to protect the right to a fair trial and a remedy. In those situations, Governments may need technical assistance to draft the appropriate legislation. Model legislation could be drafted to provide the basic laws as procedures necessary for guaranteeing and strengthening the right to a fair trial and a remedy. It should be noted, however, that there are many ways to achieve the basic international standards of this right; none the less, if model legislation is drafted, it may need to be adjusted to accompany the different judicial traditions throughout the world such as the Civil Law, Islamic Law, and Common Law. There exists a pressing need for adequate substantive laws as well, because courts cannot function absent substantive laws. In many countries, substantive laws are lacking with respect to civil and administrative areas.

In addition to implementation of the right to a fair trial and a remedy at the domestic level, the Special Rapporteurs recommend that international monitoring of the right continue through such bodies as the Human Rights Committee, the Working Group on Arbitrary Detention, the Special Rapporteur on the independence and impartiality of the judiciary, jurors and assessors and the independence of lawyers, the European Commission and Court of Human Rights, the Inter-American Commission on and Court of Human Rights, the African Commission on Human and Peoples' Rights and international trial observers sent by intergovernmental organizations, Governments and non-governmental organizations. These mechanisms have already played an invaluable role in identifying and protecting the right to a fair trial and a remedy and their continued involvement is necessary to achieve the optimal level of implementation of the right throughout the world.

### F. Conclusion

In conclusion, the two Special Rapporteurs note that the task they have undertaken covers a vast and complex subject. The right to a fair trial and a remedy has a greater importance today than it had when the Special Rapporteurs began their work. Many Governments are taking a fresh look at how they can develop institutions which will provide enduring protection for human rights. Governments should recognize that judicial and administrative structures necessary to guarantee the right to a fair trial and a remedy are indispensable for the protection of all other human rights. The two Special Rapporteurs wish to express their appreciation for the cooperation and assistance they have received from Governments, the Centre for Human Rights, non-governmental organizations, and from the many others who have assisted with this study. The Special Rapporteurs would like to underscore the spirit of cooperation which has reigned between them throughout their period of collaboration on the study and view this spirit of cooperation as a triumph over the political and ideological competition of the cold war years in which this study was begun as well as a harbinger of continuing cooperation between their respective nations and all other countries.

***DRAFT THIRD OPTIONAL PROTOCOL TO THE INTERNATIONAL CONVENTION ON CIVIL AND POLITICAL RIGHTS.*** The Special Rapporteur's draft of such an optional protocol, aiming at guaranteeing under all circumstances the right to a fair trial and a remedy, is presented in Annex I of the Final Report as follows:

*Article 1.* No derogation from articles 2.3, 9.3, 9.4 or 14 of the International Covenant on Civil and Political Rights may be made under the provisions article 4 of the Covenant.

*Article 2.* No reservation is admissible to the present Protocol.

*Article 3.* The States Parties to the present Protocol shall include in the report they submit to the Human Rights Committee, in accordance with article 40 of the Covenant, information on the measures that they have adopted to give effect to the present Protocol.

*Article 4.* With respect to the States Parties to the Covenant that have made a declaration under article 41, the competence of the Human Rights committee to receive and consider communications when a State Party claims that another State Party is not fulfilling its obligations shall extend to the provisions of the present Protocol, unless the State Party concerned has made a statement to the contrary at the moment of ratification or accession.

*Article 5.* With respect to the States Parties to the first Optional Protocol to the International Covenant on Civil and Political Rights adopted on 16 December 1966, the competence of the Human Rights Committee to receive and consider communications from individuals subject to its jurisdiction shall extend to the provisions of the present Protocol.

*Article 6.* The provisions of the present Protocol shall apply as additional provisions to the Covenant.

*Article 7.* 1. The present Protocol is open for signature by any State that has signed the Covenant.

2. The present Protocol is subject to ratification by any State that has ratified the Covenant or acceded to it. Instruments of ratification shall be deposited with the Secretary-General of the United Nations.

3. The present Protocol shall be open to accession by any State that has ratified the Covenant or acceded to it.

4. Accession shall be effected by the deposit of an instrument of accession with the Secretary-General of the United Nations.

5. The Secretary-General of the United Nations shall inform all States that have signed the present Protocol or acceded to it of the deposit of each instrument of ratification or accession.

*Article 8.* 1. The present Protocol shall enter into force three months after the date of the deposit with the Secretary-General of the United Nations of the tenth instrument of ratification or accession.

2. For each State ratifying the present Protocol or acceding to it after the deposit of the tenth instrument of ratification or accession, the present Protocol shall enter into force three months after the date of the deposit of its own instrument of ratification or accession.

*Article 9.* The provisions of the present Protocol shall extend to all parts of federal States without any limitations or exceptions.

*Article 10.* The Secretary-General of the United Nations shall inform all States referred to in article 48, paragraph 1, of the Covenant of the following:

(a) Statements made under article 4 of the present Protocol;

(b) Signatures, ratifications and accessions under article 7 of the present Protocol;

(c) The date of entry into force of the present Protocol under article 8 thereof.

*Article 11.* 1. The present Protocol, of which the Arabic, Chinese, English, French, Russian and Spanish texts are equally authentic, shall be deposited in the archives of the United Nations.

2. The Secretary-General of the United Nations shall transmit certified copies of the present Protocol to all States referred to in article 48 of the Covenant.

*DRAFT BODY OF PRINCIPLES ON THE RIGHT TO A FAIR TRIAL AND A REMEDY.* In Annex II of the Final Report, the Special Rapporteurs present their draft of a Body of Principles on the Right to a Fair Trial and a Remedy. That draft and brief introductory statement explaining its origins read as follows:

*Introduction.* 1. The Special Rapporteurs have reviewed treaties and other international instruments protecting the right to a fair trial. They have studied interpretations of the right to a fair trial by the Human Rights Committee, the committee on the Elimination of Racial Discrimination, the African Commission on Human and Peoples' Rights, the European Commission and Court of Human Rights, and the Inter-American Commission on and Court of Human Rights. They have also prepared a study of the right to habeas corpus, *amparo,* and similar procedures.

2. In addition, the Special Rapporteurs have gathered materials about national constitutions, laws, rules and practices relating to the right to a fair trial and a remedy from more than 65 countries. In this regard, they have very much appreciated the information they have received from 36 Governments, as well as from intergovernmental organizations, non-governmental organizations, bar associations and individuals.

3. In its resolutions 1992/21 of 27 August 1992 and 1993/26 of 25 August 1993, the Sub-Commission anticipated the preparation by the Special Rapporteurs of this final report, containing recommendations for strengthening the implementation of the right to a fair trial in the light of interpretations of the right by international bodies and contemporary national practices.

4. The Special Rapporteurs have sought to derive from international interpretations of the right to a fair trial and a remedy, as well as from national laws and practices, those common elements which might serve as the basis for a draft body of principles on the right to a fair trial and a remedy. Accordingly, the Special Rapporteurs have prepared a draft Body of Principles on the Right to a Fair Trial and a Remedy, which is contained in this annex II to the present report. In this regard the Special Rapporteurs have sought to ensure that the present fair trial standards in existing international law are not weakened in the process of elaborating and delineating the draft body of principles.

5. In order to provide a relatively succinct summary of the norms identified by the Special Rapporteurs, they submit the following draft body of principles on the right to a fair trial and a remedy:

### Provisions Applicable to All Adjudicative Proceedings

1. In the determination of any criminal charge against a person, or of the person's rights and obligations in a suit at law, everyone shall be entitled to a fair and public hearing by a competent, independent and impartial tribunal established by law. Any judgement rendered in a criminal case or in a suit at law shall be made public, except where the interests of juvenile persons otherwise require or the proceedings concern matrimonial disputes or the guardianship of children.

### Fair Hearing

2. A "fair . . . hearing" requires respect for the principle of equality of arms between parties to the proceedings, whether they be civil, criminal, administrative or military.

3. All persons shall be equal before the courts and tribunals. The right of every individual to a fair trial is recognized without any distinction whatsoever as regards race, colour, sex, language, religion, political or other convictions, national or social origin, means or other circumstance.

4. If a person's rights and obligations may be adversely affected in a suit at law or by particularized actions or inactions taken or proposed by a public authority, the court or the public authority shall give the person adequate notice of the nature and purpose of the proceedings and shall give the person a fair and public hearing by a competent, independent and impartial tribunal established by law.

5. A fair hearing requires that a person entitled to adequate notice of the nature and purpose of proceedings shall have the right to:

(a) Be afforded an adequate opportunity to prepare a case;

(b) Present arguments and evidence, and to meet opposing arguments and evidence, either in writing, orally or by both means;

(c) Consult and be represented by counsel or other qualified persons of his or her choice during all stages of the proceedings;

(d) Consult an interpreter during all stages of the proceedings, if he or she cannot understand or speak the language used in the court or tribunal;

(e) Have his or her rights and obligations affected only by a decision based solely on evidence known to parties to public proceedings;

(f) Have his or her rights and obligations affected only by a decision rendered without undue delay and as to which the parties are provided adequate notice thereof and the reasons therefor; (i) Factors relevant to what constitutes undue delay include: the complexity of the case, the conduct of the parties, the conduct of other relevant participants, whether an individual is detained pending proceedings, and the interest of the persons in the proceeding.

(g) Appeal decisions to a higher administrative authority, a judicial tribunal, or both.

### Public Hearing

6. In order to hold a "public hearing", the court or tribunal shall make information about the time and venue of the

public hearing available, and provide adequate facilities for attendance by interested members of the public.

7. In a public hearing, the court or tribunal may not limit attendance only to a particular category of people and should allow local, national and international observers to attend, so as to verify that justice is done and seen to be done. Representatives of the press and of other media may be present at a public hearing.

8. Exceptions to a public hearing shall be narrowly construed. In regard to each exception, the tribunal shall determine whether the strong public and individual interest in seeing that justice is done would be substantially outweighed by the rationale for the exception which is proposed for closure from public attendance. If some degree of closure is found to be justified as an exception, the tribunal should also consider closing only portions of the proceedings or should consider taking evidence in camera so as to implement to the greatest extent possible the right to a public hearing.

9. The press and the public may be excluded from all or part of a trial for reasons of morals, public order or national security in a democratic society; when the interest of the private lives of the parties so requires; or to the extent strictly necessary in the opinion of the court or tribunal in special circumstances where publicity would prejudice the interests of justice.

10. To define further these exceptions to the right to a public hearing: the public may be excluded from hearings on the grounds of morals, where the testimony will have such a corrupting or intimidating influence on the observers or participants as to outweigh the strong public and individual interest in a public hearing. Moral grounds for excluding the public may be asserted primarily in the trial of cases involving sexual offences. The public may be excluded from hearings on the grounds of a grave threat to public order; such a threat may outweigh the strong public and individual interest in a public hearing for cases of disciplinary proceedings in prisons. The public may be excluded from hearings because of national security concerns when hearings involve state defence secrets in a democratic society. Privacy interests may merit excluding the public from hearings relating to family issues, such as divorce and guardianship, and from juvenile proceedings involving sexual offences, in so far as public proceedings would constitute a clearly unwarranted invasion of personal privacy outweighing the strong public and individual interest in a public hearing.

11. A public hearing shall occur where the merits of the case are being examined—either at the trial or appellate level, but not necessarily at both levels.

12. An individual party may waive his or her right to a public hearing if consent is given freely, if it is given in an unequivocal manner and preferably in writing, and if it does not infringe any important public interest in seeing that justice is done.

## Independent Tribunal

13. Every person has the right to a fair hearing of his or her case by a legally constituted competent independent and impartial court or tribunal.

14. In order to be "independent", a tribunal shall be established by law to have adjudicative functions to determine matters within its competence on the basis of rules of law and in accordance with proceedings conducted in a prescribed manner. A tribunal may be established by legislative, executive, or judicial power.

15. The judiciary shall have jurisdiction over all issues of a judicial nature and shall have exclusive authority to decide whether an issue submitted for decision is within the tribunal's competence as defined by law.

16. A tribunal's jurisdiction may be determined, *inter alia,* by considering where the events involved in the dispute or offence took place, where the property in dispute is located, the place of residence or domicile of the parties, and the consent of the parties.

17. Tribunals that do not use the duly established procedures of the legal process shall not be created to displace the jurisdiction belonging to the ordinary courts or judicial tribunals.

18. There shall not be any inappropriate or unwarranted [interruptions] in the judicial process, nor shall judicial decisions by the courts be subject to revision. This provision is without prejudice to judicial review or to mitigation or commutation by competent authorities of sentences by the judiciary, in accordance with the law.

19. A court shall be independent from the executive branch. The executive branch in a State shall not be able to interfere in a court's proceedings and a court shall not act as an agent for the executive against an individual citizen.

20. The term of office of judges and members of a tribunal, their independence, security, adequate remuneration, conditions of service, pensions and the age of retirement shall be adequately secured by law.

21. Judges or members of a tribunal, whether appointed or elected, shall have guaranteed tenure until a mandatory retirement age or the expiry of their term of office, where such exists.

22. Promotion of judges and members of tribunals, where such a system exists, should be based on objective factors, in particular ability, integrity and experience.

23. It is essential that a judge or member of a tribunal should not be subject to any authority in the performance of his or her duties, aside from duly registered appeals after judgement has been announced.

24. A tribunal shall be independent from the parties in the case.

## Impartial Tribunal

25. A tribunal shall be "impartial"; it shall base its decision only on objective arguments and evidence presented. The judiciary shall decide matters before them without any restrictions, improper influence, inducement pressure, threats or interference, direct or indirect, from any quarter or for any reason.

26. The impartiality of a tribunal may be subject to challenge if the public is entitled to question, on the basis of ascertainable facts, that the fairness of the judge or tribunal was capable of appearing open to doubt. Three relevant factors should be considered in determining impartiality: whether the trial judge's position allows him or her to play a crucial role in the proceedings; whether the judge may have a preformed opinion which would weigh heavily on the decision-making; and whether a judge would have to rule on an action taken in a prior capacity.

27. A tribunal lacks impartiality if, inter alia, a former public prosecutor or counsel sits as a judge on a case in which he or she prosecuted or served as counsel to a party; a trial judge actively participated in the secret, preparatory investigation of a case; or a judge has some other connection with the case which might bias the decision.

28. In the circumstances identified in the paragraphs just above and in other cases where impartiality appears open to doubt, judges and members of a tribunal have the obligation to recuse themselves.

29. A judge may not consult a higher authority before rendering a decision in order to ensure that his or her decision will be upheld.

### Right to a Remedy

30. Everyone has the right to an effective remedy by the competent national tribunals for acts violating the rights granted by the constitution, by law, or by the present Body of Principles, notwithstanding that the acts were committed by persons acting in an official capacity.

31. Any person claiming such a remedy shall have such a right determined by competent judicial, administrative or legislative authorities, or by any other competent authority provided for by the legal system of the State, which may include judicial remedy.

32. Any person claiming such a remedy shall have the right to have the remedy enforced by competent authorities.

### Provisions Applicable to Arrest and Detention

33. Everyone has the right to liberty and security of the person. No one shall be subjected to arbitrary arrest or detention. No one shall be deprived of his or her liberty except on such grounds and in accordance with such procedures as are established by law.

34. A person may be detained only for probable cause or pursuant to a warrant from a competent authority.

35. Anyone who is arrested shall be informed, at the time of arrest, of the reasons for his or her arrest and shall be promptly informed of any charges against him or her.

36. Anyone who is arrested or detained on a criminal charge shall be brought promptly before a judge or other officer authorized by law to exercise judicial power and shall be entitled to trial within a reasonable time or to release. It shall not be the general rule that persons awaiting trial shall be detained in custody, but release may be subject to guarantees to appear for trial, at any other stage of the judicial proceedings, and, should occasion arise, for execution of the judgement.

37. Anyone who is deprived of his or her liberty by arrest or detention shall be entitled to take proceedings before a court, in order that that court may decide without delay on the lawfulness of his or her detention and order release if the detention is not lawful.

(a) Any person arrested or detained has the right to be brought within 24 hours before a judge or authorized judicial officer who shall review the lawfulness of his or her detention and shall order release if the detention is not lawful. The judge or judicial officer shall be authorized by law to exercise judicial power.

(b) Any person arrested or detained shall have prompt access to a lawyer, and in any case not later than 24 hours from the time of arrest or detention. Access to a lawyer includes the attributes of the right to counsel prescribed in the paragraphs below relating to that subject.

38. States shall ensure the right to habeas corpus, *amparo* or similar procedures. The courts shall at all times hear and act upon petitions for habeas corpus, *amparo* or similar procedures. No circumstances whatever may be invoked as a justification for denying the right to habeas corpus, *amparo* or similar procedures.

39. Detention shall be administered by competent authorities established by law and duly identified.

40. Detainees shall be housed in places established by law for that purpose and duly identified.

41. The court with judicial control over the detainee shall be promptly informed that a person has been detained. The court with judicial control over the detainee shall have authority over the officials detaining an individual.

42. The authorities which arrest a person, keep him or her under detention, or investigate the case shall exercise only the powers granted to them under the law, and the exercise of these powers shall be subject to a judicial or other authority.

43. The judiciary shall at all times have authority over executive action resulting in detention.

44. Military courts do not have legal authority over civilians except in narrowly defined circumstances, for example, when the civilian has committed an offence in a military facility.

### Right to Humane Treatment

45. All persons under any form of detention or imprisonment shall be treated in a humane manner and with respect for the inherent dignity of the human person. Persons under any form of detention or imprisonment shall not be subjected to torture or cruel, inhuman or degrading treatment or punishment. In particular, such persons shall not be subjected to the following cruel, inhuman or degrading treatment:

(a) No detainee shall be subjected to incommunicado detention. Communication of the detained or imprisoned person with the outside world shall not be denied for more than a matter of days.

(b) No detainee shall be denied prompt and adequate medical care including necessary medication. No detainee shall be subjected to compulsory medical experimentation.

(c) Accused persons shall be segregated from convicted persons and have the right to separate treatment appropriate to their status as unconvicted persons.

(d) Accused juvenile persons shall be segregated from adults and from juvenile persons whose guilt has been adjudicated. States shall set a minimum age below which a juvenile may not be deprived of his or her liberty.

(e) All detainees have the right to write, send and receive correspondence. Correspondence of detainees with their counsel shall not be delayed, intercepted or censored and shall be in full confidentiality. Other restrictions on correspondence shall not constitute an arbitrary or unlawful interference with the detainee's correspondence.

(f) All detainees have the right to receive visits from counsel, persons assisting counsel, family, friends and others at regular intervals under necessary supervision.

46. All detainees have the right to trial within a reasonable time or release. Pretrial detention is justified only to prevent flight, interference with evidence or the recurrence of crime.

47. Pretrial release may be made subject to guarantees, such as bail, to assure appearance at trial.

### Provisions Applicable to Proceedings Relating to Criminal Charges

*Notice [of accusation].* 48. Any person charged with a criminal offence shall be informed promptly, in detail, and in a language which he or she understands, of the nature and cause of the charge against him or her.

(a) The accused has the right to be informed as soon as a charge is first made by a competent authority. A person suspected of a crime shall be notified as soon as a court or the prosecution decides to take procedural steps against him or her, or publicly names him or her as a suspect.

(b) The purpose of notice is to inform the accused in a manner that would allow him or her to prepare a defence. The notice shall be provided in time to allow the accused a fair opportunity to examine or have examined the witnesses against him or her and to secure the attendance of witnesses on his or her behalf. The notice shall be provided before the accused is required to make any statement.

(c) The purpose of notice is also to enable a person to take immediate steps to secure his or her release; hence, the notice shall include details of the charges or applicable law and the alleged facts on which the charge is based sufficient to indicate the substance of the complaint against the accused. The arresting authorities shall have sufficient evidence to show that the detention falls within the law on which the charge is based.

(d) The accused has the right to translation of the notice of charges into a language which he or she understands. The notice of charges shall actually be communicated to the accused and not only to a representative or agent; notice in a language understood only by the defence counsel is insufficient.

### Right to Counsel

49. The accused has the right to defend him or herself in person or through legal assistance of his or her own choosing. Legal representation is regarded as the best means of legal defence against infringements of human rights and fundamental freedoms.

(a) The accused has the right to be informed, if he or she does not have legal assistance, of the right to defend him or herself through legal assistance of his or her own choosing.

(b) This right applies during all stages of any criminal prosecution, including preliminary investigations in which evidence is taken, periods of administrative detention, trial and appeal proceedings.

(c) The accused has the right to choose his or her own counsel freely. This right begins when the accused is first detained or charged. A court may not assign counsel for the accused if a qualified lawyer of the accused's own choosing is available.

### Right to Free Legal Assistance

50. The accused has a right to have legal assistance assigned to him or her in any case where the interests of justice so require, and without payment by the accused in any such case if he or she does not have sufficient means to pay for it.

(a) The interests of justice in a particular case should be determined by consideration of the seriousness of the offence of which the defendant is accused and the severity of the sentence which he or she risks.

(b) The interests of justice always require counsel for an accused in any capital case. An accused person in a capital case has the right to choose his or her own legal representative at all stages of the case. An accused person in a capital case may contest the choice of his or her court-appointed lawyer. A prisoner sentenced to death shall have the right to appointed counsel for petition for post-conviction judicial relief, executive clemency, commutation of sentence, amnesty or pardon.

(c) An accused person may not be denied counsel on the ground that he or she has or has had the opportunity to defend him or herself, but does not wish to defend him or herself.

51. An accused person has a right to an effective defence. Lawyers appointed by the court shall provide effective defence counsel.

(a) When legal assistance is provided by the court, the lawyer appointed shall be qualified to represent and defend the accused.

(b) A lawyer appointed by the court to represent and defend the accused shall have the necessary training and experience corresponding to the nature and seriousness of the matter.

(c) When legal assistance is provided by the court, the lawyer shall be free to exercise his or her professional judgement in an independent manner, free of influence from the State or the court.

(d) When legal assistance is provided by the court, the lawyer shall actually advocate in favour of the accused. The lawyer representing the accused may exercise professional judgement in choosing the strategy of the defence.

(e) Lawyers appointed to defend the accused shall be sufficiently compensated to provide an incentive to accord the accused adequate and effective representation.

### Right to Adequate Time and
### Facilities for the Preparation of a Defence

52. The accused has the right to communicate with counsel and have adequate time and facilities for the preparation of his or her defence.

(a) The accused has a right to see a lawyer during all stages of any criminal proceedings including any preliminary investigation in which evidence is taken, any period of administrative detention, trial and any appeal.

(b) The accused may not be tried without his or her counsel being notified of the trial date and of the charges in time to allow adequate preparation of a defence.

(c) The accused has a right to adequate time for the preparation of a defence appropriate to the nature of the proceedings and the factual circumstances of the case. Factors which may affect the adequacy of time for preparation of a defence include the complexity of the case, the defendant's access to evidence, the length of time provided by rules of procedure prior to particular proceedings, and prejudice to the defence.

(d) The accused has a right to facilities which assist or may assist the accused in the preparation of his or her defence. The essential elements of the right to adequate facilities are the right to communicate with defence counsel and the right to materials necessary to the preparation of a defence.

(i) All arrested, detained or imprisoned persons shall be provided with adequate opportunities, time and facilities to be visited by and to communicate with a lawyer, without delay, interception or censorship and in full confidentiality.

(ii) The right to confer privately with one's lawyer and exchange confidential information or instructions is a fundamental part of the preparation of a defence. Facilities shall be provided such that communications with counsel shall be made under circumstances in which the confidentiality of the communications is preserved.

(iii) Governments shall recognize and respect that all communications and consultations between lawyers and their clients within their professional relationship are confidential.

(iv) The accused or the accused's defence counsel has a right to all relevant information held by the prosecution that could help the accused exonerate him or herself.

(v) It is the duty of the competent authorities to ensure lawyers access to appropriate information, files and documents in their possession or control in sufficient time to enable lawyers to provide effective legal assistance to their clients. Such access should be provided at the earliest appropriate time.

(vi) The accused has a right to consult legal materials reasonably necessary for the preparation of his or her defence.

(vii) Before judgement or sentence is rendered, the accused and his or her defence counsel shall have the right to know all t evidence which may be used to support the decision. All evidence submitted must be considered by the court.

(viii) Following a trial and before any appellate proceeding, the accused or the defence counsel has a right to access to (or to consult) the evidence which the court considered in making a decision and the court's reasoning in arriving at the judgement.

### The Right to an Interpreter

53. The accused has the right to the free assistance of an interpreter if he or she cannot understand or speak the language used in court.

(a) The right to an interpreter applies when the accused or a defence witness has difficulty understanding or expressing him or herself in the court's language.

(b) The right to an interpreter does not extend to the right to express oneself in the language of one's choice if the accused or the defence witness is sufficiently proficient in the language of the court.

(c) The right to an interpreter applies to both nationals and aliens.

(d) The right to an interpreter applies at all stages of the proceedings, including pretrial proceedings.

(e) The right to an interpreter applies to written as well as oral proceedings. The right extends to translation or interpretation of all documents or statements necessary for the defendant to understand the proceedings or assist in the preparation of a defence.

(f) The interpretation or translation provided shall be adequate to permit the accused to understand the proceedings and for the tribunal to understand the testimony of the accused or defence witnesses.

(g) The right to interpretation or translation cannot be qualified by a requirement that the accused pay for the costs of an interpreter or translator. Even if the accused is convicted, he or she cannot be required to pay for the costs of interpretation or translation.

### The Right to Trial Without Undue Delay

54. Every person charged with a criminal offence has the right to a trial without undue delay.

(a) The right to a trial without undue delay means the right to a trial which produces a final judgement and, if appropriate, a sentence without undue delay.

(b) In assessing whether there has been undue delay, the period review of any conviction or sentence shall be included in the assessment review of any conviction assessment.

(c) The right to a trial without undue delay does not depend upon assertion of that right by the accused. The accused is not required to deem a trial without undue delay in order to preserve his or her right in this regard.

(d) Factors relevant to what constitutes undue delay include the complexity of the case, the conduct of the parties, the conduct of other relevant authorities, whether an accused is detained pending proceedings, and the interest of the person at stake in the proceedings.

### Rights During a Trial

55. In criminal proceedings, the principle of equality of arms imposes procedural equality between the accused and the public prosecutor.

(a) The prosecution and defence shall be allowed equal time to present evidence.

(b) Prosecution and defence witnesses shall be given equal treatment on all procedural matters.

(c) Evidence obtained by illegal means constituting a serious violation of internationally protected human rights shall not be used as evidence against the accused or against any other person in any proceeding.

56. The accused is entitled to a hearing in which an individualized consideration of culpability is afforded. Group trials in which many persons are involved may violate the person's right to a fair hearing.

57. In criminal proceedings, the accused has the right to be tried in his or her presence.

(a) The accused has the right to appear in person before the court.

(b) The accused may not be tried in absentia.

(c) If an accused is tried in absentia, the accused shall have the right to petition for a reopening of the proceedings upon a showing that inadequate notice was given, that the notice was not personally served on the accused, or that his or her failure to appear was for exigent reasons beyond his or her control. If the petition is granted, the accused is entitled to a fresh determination of the merits of the charge.

(d) The accused may voluntarily waive the right to appear at a hearing, but such a waiver shall be established in an unequivocal manner and preferably in writing.

58. The accused has the right not to be compelled to testify against him or herself or to confess guilt.

(a) Any confession or other evidence obtained by any form of coercion or force may not be admitted into evidence or considered as probative of any fact at trial or in sentencing. Any confession or admission obtained during incommunicado detention shall be considered to have been obtained by coercion.

(b) Silence by the accused may not be used as evidence to prove guilt and no adverse consequences may be drawn from the exercise of the right to remain silent.

59. Everyone charged with a criminal offence shall have the right to presumed innocent until proved guilty according to law.

(a) The presumption of innocence places the burden of proof during trial in any criminal case on the prosecution. The criminal charge shall be proved to the intimate conviction of the trier of fact or beyond a reasonable doubt, whichever standard of proof provides the greatest protection for the presumption of innocence under national law.

(b) Public officials shall maintain a presumption of innocence. The provision applies to the judge presiding over the trial and to any other public official who deals with the case in any way. The accused is entitled to the benefit of the doubt during the trial. Public officials, including prosecutors, may inform the public about criminal investigations or charges but shall not express a view as to the guilt of any suspect.

(c) Legal presumptions of fact or law are permissible in a criminal case only if they are rebuttable, allowing a defendant to prove his or her innocence.

(d) In applying the presumption of innocence, a State is not required to reimburse a person who has been found not guilty the cost of his or her defence.

(e) In applying the presumption of innocence, the State may not require a person who has been found not guilty of a criminal offence to pay any portion of the costs of prosecution.

60. The accused has a right to examine, or have examined, witnesses against him or her and to obtain the attendance and examination of witnesses on his or her behalf under the same conditions as witnesses against him or her.

(a) The adversary or contentious nature of a trial is regarded as one effective means of ensuring its fairness.

(b) The accused's right to obtain the attendance and examination of witnesses on his or her behalf may be waived by counsel if such a waiver is properly within the professional judgement of the counsel.

(c) The prosecution shall provide the defence with the names of the witnesses it intends to call at trial within a reasonable time prior to trial which allows the defendant sufficient time to prepare his or her defence.

(d) The accused's right to examine witnesses may be limited to those witnesses whose testimony is relevant and likely to assist in ascertaining the truth.

(e) The accused has the right to be present during the testimony of a witness. This right may be limited only in exceptional circumstances such as when a witness reasonably fears reprisal by the defendant, when the accused engages in a course of conduct seriously disruptive of the proceedings, or when the accused repeatedly fails to appear for trivial reasons and after having been duly notified.

(f) A trial may also be conducted in the absence of an individual accused of any offences against the peace and security of humanity, if that individual is a fugitive from justice or has died before the commencement of such a trial but when the consequences of the offences of which the person stands accused are still extant and the court examination is necessary for the protection of human rights and fundamental freedoms and to prevent perpetration of such offences in the future.

(g) If the defendant is excluded or if the presence of the defendant cannot be ensured, the defendant's counsel shall always have the right to be present to preserve the defendant's right to examine the witness.

(h) If the presence of the defendant or any party cannot be ensured when the sentence or decision is announced, measures shall be taken to ensure that the defendant or any other party is informed as quickly as possible concerning the substance of the verdict or decision and the possibility of appeal against it.

(i) If national law does not permit the accused to examine witnesses during pretrial investigations, the defendant shall have the opportunity to cross-examine the witness at trial.

(j) The use of testimony of anonymous witnesses during a trial is a violation of the defendant's right to examine witnesses against him or her.

### Right to Benefit from a Lighter Sentence or Administrative Sanction

61. No one shall be held guilty of any criminal offence on account of any act or omission which did not constitute a criminal offence, under national or international law, at the time when it was committed. Nor shall a heavier penalty be imposed than the one that was applicable at the time when the criminal offence was committed. If, subsequent to the commission of the offence, provision is made by law for the imposition of a lighter penalty, the offender shall benefit thereby.

62. A lighter penalty created any time before an accused's sentence has been fully served should be applied to any offender serving a sentence under the previous penalty.

63. Administrative tribunals conducting disciplinary proceedings shall not impose a heavier penalty than the one that was applicable at the time when the offending conduct occurred. If, subsequent to the conduct, provision is made by law for the imposition of a lighter penalty, the person disciplined shall benefit thereby.

### Second Trial for Same Offense Prohibited

64. No one shall be liable to be tried or punished again for an offence for which he or she has already been finally convicted or acquitted in accordance with the law and penal procedure of each country.

### Sentencing and Punishment

65. Punishments constituting a deprivation of liberty shall have as an essential aim the reform and social readaptation of the prisoners.

### Appeal

66. Everyone convicted in a criminal proceeding shall have the right to review of his or her sentence by a higher tribunal.

(a) The right to appeal shall provide a genuine and timely review of the case. If exculpatory evidence is discovered after a person is tried and convicted, the right to appeal or some other post-conviction procedure shall permit the possibility of correcting the verdict if the new evidence would have been likely to change the verdict, unless it is proved that the non-disclosure of the unknown fact in time is wholly or partly attributable to the accused.

(b) A court shall stay execution of any sentence while the case is on appeal to a higher tribunal, unless the accused voluntarily accepts the earlier implementation of sentence.

67. Anyone sentenced to death shall have the right to appeal to a court of higher jurisdiction, and steps should be taken to ensure that such appeals become mandatory.

68. When a person has by a final decision been convicted of a criminal offence and when subsequently his or her conviction has been reversed or he or she has been pardoned on the ground that a new or newly discovered fact shows

conclusively that there has been a miscarriage of justice, the person who has suffered punishment as a result of such conviction shall be compensated according to law, unless it is proved that the non-disclosure of the unknown fact in time is wholly or partly attributable to him or her.

69. Every person convicted of a crime has a right to seek pardon, amnesty or commutation of sentence. Clemency, commutation of sentence, amnesty or pardon may be granted in all cases of capital punishment.

### General Clauses

70. There shall be no restriction upon or derogation from any element of the right to a fair trial and a remedy recognized or existing in any State pursuant to law, Conventions, regulations or custom on the pretext that this Body of Principles does not recognize such rights or that it recognizes them to a lesser extent.

71. Nothing in this Body of Principles shall be construed as restricting or derogating from any right defined in the International Covenant on Civil and Political Rights or any other relevant treaty or international instrument.

72. While this Body of Principles is not principally intended to apply to proceedings for juvenile offenders, there are certain protections that relate specifically to juvenile offenders. Juvenile offenders should be entitled to procedures no less protective of their rights than the rights provided in this Body of Principles and other international instruments, including the Convention on the Rights of the Child, General Assembly resolution 44/25 of 20 November 1989; the United Nations Standard Minimum Rules for the Administration of Juvenile Justice, adopted by the General Assembly in resolution 40/33 of 29 November 1985; and the United Nations Rules for the Protection of Juveniles Deprived of their Liberty, adopted by the General Assembly in resolution 45/113 of 14 December 1990.

73. No circumstances whatsoever, whether a threat of war, a state of international or non-international armed conflict, internal political instability or any other public-emergency, may be invoked to justify derogations from the right to a fair trial or a remedy.

### Use of Terms

74. For the purposes of the Body of Principles:

(a) A "criminal charge" is defined by the nature of the offence and the nature and degree of severity of the penalty incurred. An accusation may constitute a criminal charge although the offence is not classified as criminal under national law.

(i) Criminal charges relate to all offences with penalties involving a serious deprivation of liberty. Imprisonment is always a serious deprivation of liberty. Expulsion from one's country by administrative decree is also a serious deprivation of liberty which requires the guarantees of a fair criminal trial.

(ii) Criminal charges do not constitute actions by disciplinary bodies when the penalty imposed is only a reprimand or warning.

(b) The "determination of rights and obligations in a suit at law" is defined by the character of the rights at issue. Civil rights and obligations include all proceedings that are decisive for private rights and obligations, including proceedings before administrative tribunals.

(i) Civil rights and obligations may be deter-
mined in proceedings involving such matters as bankruptcy, commitment to a mental institution, compensation claims against domestic authorities, contractual rights and obligations, drivers' licences, family-related issues, health insurance benefits, labour disputes, land consolidation issues, libel, personal injury claims, professional employment qualifications and rights, property rights, and scope and ownership of patents, as well as other proceedings in which a person has the right to appear and present evidence.

(ii) Proceedings as to civil rights and obligations do not require that both parties to the proceedings be private persons; hence, such proceedings encompass hearings before administrative tribunals where one of the parties is a public authority and the other is a private person.

(c) "Arrest" means the act of apprehending a person for the alleged commission of an offence or by the action of an authority.

(d) "Detained person" means any individual deprived of personal liberty except as a result of conviction for an offence.

(e) "Imprisoned person" means any individual deprived of personal liberty as a result of conviction for an offence.

(f) "Detention" means the condition of detained persons as defined above.

(g) "Imprisonment" means the condition of imprisoned persons as defined above.

***SEE ALSO*** *Habeas Corpus; Judiciary; Prisoners; Procedural Guarantees; Remedy.*

***BIBLIOGRAPHY.*** Faúndez Ledesma, Héctor. "El Derecho a un Juicio Justo: Las Condiciones que Debe Reunir Todo Tribunal" (The Right to a Fair Trial: Conditions for All Tribunals), *Boletín—Comisión Andina de Juristas* 33 (June 1992): 43–55. Scholarly article, in Spanish.

Grogan, John. "When is the 'Expectation' of a Hearing 'Legitimate'?" *South African Journal on Human Rights* 6, no. 1 (1990): 36–47. Scholarly article, in English.

Stavros, Stephanos. "The Right to a Fair Trial in Emergency Situations," *International and Comparative Law Quarterly* 41 (April 1992): 343–365. Scholarly article, in English.

United Nations Sub-Commission on Prevention of Discrimination and Protection of Minorities. *The Right to a Fair Trial: Current Recognition and Measures Necessary for Its Strengthening: Second Report Prepared by Mr. Stanislav Chernichenko and Mr. William Treat in Accordance with Resolution 1990/18 of the Sub-Commission and Resolution 1991/43 of the Commission on Human Rights.* Geneva, Switzerland: 1991. IGO document, in English and French.

**FAMILY LAW.** See **MARRIAGE AND THE FAMILY.**

**FEDERATION OF ASSOCIATIONS OF FORMER INTERNATIONAL CIVIL SERVANTS.** An international non-governmental organization in consultative status (Category II) with the UN **ECONOMIC AND SOCIAL COUNCIL,** the federation consists of fourteen associations, representing 6,000 individuals.

Founded in 1975, in Geneva, to link associations of former employees of organizations within the UN system, the federation protects and represents the common interests of former international civil servants, particularly in matters of pensions and health insurance. The group supports the work of UN organizations and bodies, especially regarding health, aging, and housing problems.

Federation of Associations of Former International Civil Servants. Address: Room C-542-1, Palais des Nations, CH-1211, Geneva 10, Switzerland. Telephone: (41-22) 734-60-11. Fax: (41-22) 731-33-30. Executive Secretary: Angela Butler.

**FIJI.** A country consisting of 332 islands in the southwestern Pacific Ocean, including the islands of Viti Levu, Vanua Levu, and Rotuma, the Republic of Fiji achieved independence from Great Britain in 1970 and became a member of the United Nations the same year. About 110 of the islands are inhabited, the total population being estimated at 754,000. Ethnic groups include Fijians (45%), Indians (50%), and Chinese and others (5%). Religions practiced include Christianity (50%), Hinduism (42%), and Islam (8%).

On 6 October 1987 Lieut. Col. Sitivani Rabuka, having led two earlier military coups, formally declared Fiji a republic and proclaimed the right of the "indigenous Fijian race" to govern themselves with their own advancement and welfare in mind. Elected Prime Minister in 1992 in Fiji's first general election, Rabuka's political power declined notably in November 1993 when dissidents in his Fijian Political Party helped to vote down his 1994 budget proposal, claiming that the rate of spending was too high. In January 1994, these dissidents broke away to form the Fijian Association Party.

Able to control Parliament only by virtue of a coalition with the mixed-race General Voters' Party, which had won four seats, and two independents, Rabuka was sworn in for a second term as Prime Minister on 28 February 1994 by Ratu Sir Kamisese Mara, a former Prime Minister who had been appointed President by the country's Council of Chiefs. At the swearing-in ceremony, Mara called for "reconciliation and healing" in the racially divided country, and Rabuka later suggested the possibility that his party might invite Indians to join with it in a "government of national unity."

**BIBLIOGRAPHY.** Amnesty International. *Fiji: Arrests under a New Internal Security Decree.* London: 1988. NGO report, in English.

———. *Fiji: Restrictions on Fundamental Rights.* London: 1987. NGO report, in English.

Hassall, Graham. "Ethnicity and the State: Constitutional Provisions in Some Pacific Island States," *Ethnic Groups* 9 (1991): 83–105. Scholarly article, in English.

Immigration and Refugee Board Documentation Centre. *Fiji: Cultural Profile—The Indo Fijians: History, Culture, Social Structure.* Ottawa, Canada: 1991. Government briefing paper, in English.

International Commission of Jurists, Australian Section. "The Constitution of Fiji," *The ICJ Review* 45 (Dec. 1990): 33–36. NGO article, in English.

Scott-Murphy, J., D. Dunstan, and N. Khan. *Human Rights in Melanesia: The Report of the Evatt Foundation Delegation.* Sydney, Australia: H.V. Evatt Memorial Foundation, 1988. NGO report, in English.

Tinker, H., N. Duraiswamy, Y. Ghai, and M. Ennals. *Fiji.* London: Minority Rights Group, 1987. NGO report, in English.

**FINLAND.** The Republic of Finland is a country in northern Europe, on the Gulf of Bothnia (part of the Baltic Sea) and the Gulf of Finland. It has borders with Norway, Sweden, and Russia. It achieved independence from Russia in 1917 and became a member of the United Nations in 1955. On 1 January 1995, along with Sweden and Austria, Finland became a member of the European Union. Its population is estimated to be 5,074,000. Ethnic groups include the Sami (about 5,700) and the Romany (Gypsy) populations; the latter numbers between 6,000 and 9,000. Languages commonly used include Finnish and Swedish (both official), Sami, and Romany. Christianity (Lutheran National Church, 90%; Greek Orthodox of Finland, 2%) is the predominant religion; 8% reports no religious affiliation. Literacy is estimated at 99%.

The government (1994) took the form of a republic. The president, selected by a popularly elected 301-member electoral college for a term of six years, is head of State; the premier, representing the party or coalition given the majority in the election, is head of government. Legislation is prepared by the unicameral 200-member Diet, known as the *Eduskunta*, members of which are elected for four-year terms by proportional representation. The chancellor of justice (*Oikeuskansleri*) and the solicitor-general (*Oikeusasiamies*) exercise control over the administration of justice. Political parties include the Social Democratic Party, the National Coalition Party, the Centre Party, the People's Democratic League, the Finnish Rural Party, the Swedish People's Party, and the Christian League.

Following a campaign which highlighted economic issues, particularly Finland's 18% unemployment rate and its public debt of 70% of its GNP, a fiscal conservative, Social Democrat Paavo Lipponen, was elected President in April 1995. He has proposed massive spending cuts in agricultural subsidies and welfare nefits to help revive the country.

***RIGHTS OF ALIENS.*** Human rights problems arise infrequently for Finnish citizens, but the situation of aliens in Finland has been a subject of concern.

As regards aliens, the fundamental rights laid down in chapter II of the Finnish Constitution Act apply as such to Finnish citizens only. However, the **INTERNATIONAL COVENANT ON CIVIL AND POLITICAL RIGHTS,** which Finland has ratified and incorporated into its domestic law, applies to all persons subjected to Finnish jurisdiction. Aliens thus enjoy the same procedural rights as Finnish citizens; however, some restrictions on their political rights still apply. They may not become members of political parties and may not vote in general elections. Aliens from Nordic countries have, however, been accorded the right to vote and to be elected in municipal elections since 1976.

*RIGHTS OF ETHNIC MINORITIES.* Finland's ethnic minorities, the Sami and the Romany, have also encountered problems. As regards the Sami and Romany populations, the Government provided the following information in a report to the UN **COMMITTEE ON THE ELIMINATION OF RACIAL DISCRIMINATION** on 19 January 1988 (UN Doc. CERD/C/159/Add. 1, paras. 5–60):

### The Samis

There are 5,700 Samis in Finland of whom 3,900 live in their native area of Utsjoki, Inari or Enontekiö, or the Vuotso area of the Sodankylä municipality. More than one third of the population of the native Sami areas is Sami (Utsjoki 72 per cent, Inari 30 per cent, Enontekiö 16 per cent).

In Finland a person is considered Sami if he, or at least one of his parents or grandparents spoke Sami as the first language. The language has always been the main criterion in determining whether or not a person is Sami. Problems in the Sami culture are the dominance of the Finnish language and the mainstream culture in Sami language and culture in addition to the weak legal safeguards for the rights in respect of land and waterways which the Samis hold on the basis of tenure since time immemorial.

Researchers do not agree about the ethnic origin of the Samis. The Samis themselves, and current anthropological research, include them in the original peoples of the Arcticum. Parallels to them and to their culture can be found in other circumpolar areas of the globe.

The Sami population in Finland, Sweden and Norway is an autochthonous population and constitutes an ethnic group with its own background, language and traditional means of subsistence. They also are the only ethnic group in Finland indigenous to the present areas of habitation. Their historical existence is traced back by archeologists to the beginning of the post-glacial period. It is suggested that from the oldest archeological findings in Northern Fennoscandia one can see continuity to the times when the Samis *ipso facto* inhabited the area. The theory states that the present-day Samis descend from the population following the retreating edge of the continental glacier from Europe up to Scandinavia. Their contacts with the proto-Sami population of Finland and East Karelia resulted in the beginnings of the Sami culture at the beginning of the first millennium B.C.

### The Romany Population

The first written mention of Gypsies or the Romany people in Finland is from the 1500s. From that date until 1809 the same special laws concerning the Romany governed both the Finnish and Swedish Romanies. The ancestors of today's 6,000–9,000 Romanies in Finland first came to Finland in the middle of the sixteenth century. Their history in Finland, as elsewhere, is one of hostility and contempt. The general attitude towards them was formalized in the laws of the seventeenth, eighteenth and nineteenth centuries, which aimed variously at assimilation, expulsion and control. The effect of these laws was quite minimal on the Romanies, and their enforcement not effective, mainly because the Romanies lived in the most sparsely populated rural provinces until well into this century.

So far as the State is concerned, the improvement of Romany housing conditions has been considered the first priority. In 1975 an Act on Improving the Housing of the Romanies was passed. Under this Act, it is the local municipalities' responsibility to improve the housing of the Romanies within their area. The State gave special finance for this purpose to the municipalities.

The Romany economic structure has suffered hard knocks in the wake of general societal change in Finland. Presently the main income for the Finnish Romanies comes from occasional trading, of which the handwork hold by Romany women forms the largest part, and from various social welfare benefits. It must be pointed out here that in Finland there are some third and fourth generation Romany farmers as well, who have retained their Romany cultural characteristics.

In the last few years a large proportion of Finnish Romanies have moved to Sweden, and according to the estimates by social welfare authorities and Romany organizations about 2,000 Finnish Romanies live more or less permanently in Sweden. The migration has been caused by the better standard of living in Sweden.

The Romanies can be understood to form a common and distinct ethnic group mainly on the basis of their clothing. The clothing of Romany women, especially, differs entirely from Finnish clothing, in terms of materials and styles as well as in terms of colours used.

The Finnish Romanies speak Finnish as their mother tongue these days, and this is also their main language of communication with each other. The majority of the Finnish Romanies can speak Romany to some extent, but its usage can be said to be diminishing and is limited to the expression of ideas or feelings which no Finnish equivalent can convey adequately, or when it is desired that communication is limited to those present who can speak Romany. Attempts to retain and develop the Romany language are hampered by the lack of written material, and also by the resistance from the Romanies in allowing the language to be put within reach of non-Romanies.

In 1967, the Romanies organized themselves into a pressure group as the Finnish Gypsy Association. The Association was instrumental in getting some important laws onto the statute books, such as the Law Prohibiting Discrimination on the Basis of Racial or Ethnic Origin (1970), and a law aimed at improving the Romany housing conditions (1975). Under the latter law, the country's Romanies were to have been adequately housed by 1980, but only a small portion were housed with the aid of this law by the decreed time. The work of the Gypsy Association has at least temporarily ceased, owing to some rather serious disagreements on a number of issues—the main problems centre around whether the Association should be run by a reasonably well-known "elite", or by "ordinary" Romanies.

***BIBLIOGRAPHY.*** Beach, Hugh. *The Saami of Lapland.* London: Minority Rights Group, 1988. NGO report, in English; bibliography, p. 16.

Hannikainen, Lauri. *Cultural, Linguistic and Educational Rights in the Aland Islands.* No. 5. Helsinki, Finland: Finland Advisory Board for International Human Rights Affairs, 1992. Government report, in English; bibliography, pp. 98–102.

Hannikainen, Lauri, Raija Hanski, and Allan Rosas. *Implementing Humanitarian Law Applicable in Armed Conflicts: The Case of Finland.* Dordrecht, the Netherlands: Martinus Nijhoff, 1992. Scholarly monograph, in English; bibliography, pp. 165–173.

International Work Group for Indigenous Affairs. *Self-Determination and Indigenous Peoples: Sami Rights and Northern Perspectives.* Copenhagen: 1987. NGO conference proceedings, in English.

Korsmo, Fae L. "Nordic Security and the Saami Minority: Territorial Rights in Northern Fennoscandia," *Human Rights Quarterly* 10, no. 4 (Nov. 1988): 509–524. Scholarly article, in English.

Myntti, Kristian. *The Protection of Persons Belonging to National Minorities in Finland.* Helsinki, Finland: Finland Advisory Board for International Human Rights Affairs, 1993. Scholarly monograph, in English.

Rosas, Allan, ed. *International Human Rights Norms in Domestic Law: Finnish and Polish Perspectives.* Helsinki, Finland: Lakimiesliiton Kustannus / Finnish Lawyers' Publishing Company, 1990. Conference papers, in English.

## FOOD AND AGRICULTURE ORGANIZATION OF THE UNITED NATIONS (FAO).

By its constitution of 1945, the UN Food and Agriculture Organization was established as an autonomous permanent intergovernmental organization with a basic purpose of contributing towards an expanding world economy and ensuring humanity's freedom from hunger. Article 1 of that constitution mandates the FAO to collect, analyze, interpret, and disseminate information relating to nutrition, food, and agriculture; and to promote and recommend national and international action with respect to (1) conducting scientific, technological, social, and economic research relating to nutrition, food, and agriculture; (2) improving education and administration relating to nutrition, food, and agriculture, and spreading public knowledge of nutritional and agricultural science and practice; (3) conserving natural resources and adopting improved methods of agricultural production; (4) improving the processing, marketing, and distribution of food and agricultural products; (5) adopting national and international policies for the provision of adequate agricultural credit; and (6) adopting international policies with respect to agricultural commodity arrangements. The FAO is also authorized to furnish such technical assistance in its field of competence as governments may request.

As regards human rights, the FAO through its "Freedom from Hunger" campaign, launched in 1960, has distributed hundreds of thousands of tons of food to persons throughout the world who suffered from malnutrition. More recently, it joined the United Nations in establishing the World Food Programme which has carried out a far-reaching and highly successful campaign of development assistance through the supply of food.

A total of 156 States are members of the FAO. Its main organs are the General Conference, the Council, and the Secretariat. All members are represented in the General Conference, which determines policy and approves work programs and budgets. The Council, which supervises the day-to-day activities of the organization, is composed of representatives of 49 member States. The Director-General is appointed by the Council and supervises the work of the Secretariat.

The General Conference meets every two years, for a period of about three weeks, usually at FAO headquarters in Rome. The Council usually holds two annual sessions of approximately ten days each, one in June and one in November, also in Rome.

Under the terms of its agreement with the United Nations, the Food and Agriculture Organization transmits reports to UN organs on its activities and complies to the fullest extent possible with requests from those organs for special reports, studies, or information.

## FOOD AND HUMAN RIGHTS.

The right of everyone to an adequate standard of living for himself and his family, including adequate food, is proclaimed in the UNIVERSAL DECLARATION OF HUMAN RIGHTS as follows:

*Article 25.* 1. Everyone has the right to a standard of living adequate for the health and well-being of himself and of his family, including food, clothing, housing and medical care and necessary social services....

The INTERNATIONAL COVENANT ON ECONOMIC, SOCIAL AND CULTURAL RIGHTS contains the following provision:

*Article 11.* 1. The States Parties to the present Covenant recognize the right of everyone to an adequate standard of living for himself and his family, including adequate food, clothing and housing, and to the continuous improvement of living conditions. The States Parties will take appropriate steps to ensure the realization of this right, recognizing to this effect the essential importance of international co-operation based on free consent.

2. The States Parties to the present Covenant, recognizing the fundamental right of everyone to be free from hunger,

shall take, individually and through international co-operation, the measures, including specific programmes, which are needed:

(a) To improve methods of production, conservation and distribution of food by making full use of technical and scientific knowledge, by disseminating knowledge of the principles of nutrition and by developing or reforming agrarian systems in such a way as to achieve the most efficient development and utilization of natural resources;

(b) Taking into account the problems of both food-importing and food-exporting countries, to ensure an equitable distribution of world food supplies in relation to need.

It may be noted that States parties to the Covenant specifically accept to undertake the measures specified there with a view to ensuring the supply of adequate food to everyone.

The **WORLD HEALTH ORGANIZATION (WHO),** both independently and in association with such other United Nations agencies as **FAO, UNESCO,** and **UNICEF,** has been active in seeking to attain the objectives set out in the provisions cited above together with and on behalf of governments. Nevertheless, despite great improvements in agricultural techniques and extension of knowledge of nutritional physiology and pathology, it is probable that at least one half of the world's population still suffers from undernourishment or malnutrition.

*STUDY ON THE RIGHT TO ADEQUATE FOOD AS A HUMAN RIGHT.* In 1983, the UN **ECONOMIC AND SOCIAL COUNCIL** (decision 1983/140) authorized the **SUB-COMMISSION ON PREVENTION OF DISCRIMINATION AND PROTECTION OF MINORITIES** to entrust one of its members, Mr. Asbjørn Eide (Norway), with the preparation of a study on the right to adequate food as a human right. It instructed the Special Rapporteur to take account of all relevant work being done within the United Nations system and to consult with organs and agencies such as the **WORLD FOOD COUNCIL,** the Food and Agriculture Organization of the United Nations, the United Nations Conference on Trade and Development, and relevant non-governmental organizations in the field. He was further instructed "to give special attention to the normative content of the right to food and its significance in relation to the establishment of the new international economic order."

The Special Rapporteur's report (UN Doc. E/CN.4/Sub.2/1987/23) was presented to the Sub-Commission at its 1987 session. In clarifying the issues involved, he quoted estimates made by competent international organizations indicating that:

—more than one billion people are chronically hungry;

—every year, 13 to 18 million people die as a result of hunger and starvation;

—every 24 hours, 35,000 human beings die as a direct or indirect result of hunger and starvation: 24 every minute, 18 of whom are children under five years of age;

—more people have died from hunger in the last two years than were killed in World War I and World War II together;

—340 million people in developing countries (China excluded) did not have enough income to attain a minimum food energy standard (calories) that would prevent serious health problems and stunted growth in children, while 730 million fell below a standard that would allow an active working life. At the same time, the world output of major food crops reached 1,830 million metric tons. The average amount produced per capita was calculated from this to be, given the world population of 4,605 million, more than 400 kilograms, or well over one kilogram per person per day the world over. Thus, if the total amount of food could have been equally distributed to all inhabitants of the earth, there would be more than enough for all.

The conclusions (paras. 274–284) of the Special Rapporteur—after examining the existing situation, the state of recognition of the right to food in international law, and the situation as regards State obligations, international obligations, and the problems involved in monitoring and supervising activities for ensuring the enjoyment by everyone of the right to food—are as follows:

This study has shown that the right to food is widely recognized in international law, both in general and in more specific terms. In its most general formulation, it is found in the Universal Declaration of Human Rights, to which all members of the international community subscribe, whatever legal consequences they draw from it; in more unequivocal terms it is found also in the international Covenant on Economic, Social and Cultural Rights to which at present 85 States are parties.

In more specific terms, it is found in a great variety of contexts which have been listed above. They attest to a widely accepted view that access to food is an essential right which should be respected and protected under all circumstances.

The corresponding obligations, however, are less developed. In particular, the obligations found in the more general provisions are vague, diverse and found in many different instruments. In view of the urgent need to respond to hunger and malnutrition in the world today, it is necessary to consolidate and further develop existing law through the drafting of an appropriate instrument on the right to food. It might contain declaratory and obligatory parts. As a contribution by a non-governmental organization, the International Law Association has established a working group for this purpose.

At the national level, plans for national food security have obtained increasing attention. Properly approached, with a particular focus on the conditions necessary to promote food security at household and community level according to the principles in the "food security matrix" suggested in this report, such plans could constitute the agenda for the implementation of the right to food nation-wide. Country-specific application could then be made of the otherwise general and vague international obligations. This agenda accommodates a wide range of approaches.

There exists in many States the beginning of national arrangements for the monitoring of the progressive realization of the right to food; such efforts should be encouraged in all States where access to food for some groups presents particular problems, and where special attention therefore must be given to the situation of such groups.

It remains the primary responsibility of States to ensure enjoyment of the right to food by all within their jurisdiction. But States have obligations also to the peoples of other States and to the international community. These can be derived from provisions found within human rights law and from a set of principles of international law, as outlined in chapter V.

For the organized international community to be able to enhance the compliance with internal and external obligations of States, there is also a need for international monitoring and supervision. This should be carried out in order to supplement and strengthen the national efforts and to assist in the elimination of obstacles to the realization of the right to food.

It has been argued above that the functions served by international agencies and organs should be to encourage and promote the national efforts, to assist in overcoming obstacles and difficulties, and to react to gross neglect of these obligations wherever such occurs.

International monitoring may be of help in encouraging and promoting national food security efforts. Through international monitoring it may also become feasible to organize adequate international support and assistance, and to create awareness of situations where actions by other States are detrimental to the progressive realization of the right to food inside a State.

At present, however, such international monitoring and supervision is rather weak, as pointed out in chapter VI. The specialized agencies concerned have not approached the issue of food from the perspective of human rights.

The relevant body within the human rights field is the new Committee on Economic, Social and Cultural Rights, which started its work in March 1987, and which will have substantial difficulties to overcome in its important work. Five of the major difficulties have been outlined in chapter VI: (a) the lack of clarity of obligations, (b) the lack of guidance for State reporting, (c) the limited co-operation from the specialized agencies, (d) the non-involvement of non-governmental organizations and (e) the limited time and capacity of the Committee itself.

On the basis of these conclusions, the Special Rapporteur submitted to the Sub-Commission an extensive series of recommendations, as follows:

*States* should:
Draw up plans for national food security according to the overall framework suggested in this study, focusing on household and community food security and building on a nationwide system of identifying local needs and opportunities for achieving such food security;
Identify in particular within such plans the needs of groups which have the greatest difficulties in achieving food security, and set specific goals to ensure sustainable access to adequate food for those groups.
Ensure popular participation in periodically assessing and

analysing local needs and opportunities, and facilitate inputs by the least privileged groups in society into the action plans that should follow from such assessment and analysis;
Indicate specifically the areas in which international assistance is required and spell out details of the assistance needed;
Ensure that an adequate system for monitoring the right to food is developed and put into action, guided by the principles of food security as suggested in this study (enough and adequate food in terms of nutrition and cultural acceptability, viable patterns of procurement of food, and a sustainable food resource base); such a system may build on and integrate information from different systems (e.g. Timely Warning, Nutritional Surveillance, etc., and national data bases in general), if necessary with appropriate assistance from international agencies;
Provide details of the national food security plans and of progress made and obstacles encountered in the implementation of these plans in their reports for States parties to the Covenant;
Recognize and comply with their obligations in regard to the peoples of other States arising from the right to food and from principles of general international law, as outlined in Chapter VI of this study.
*National non-governmental organizations, universities and research institutions* dealing with development and human rights issues should:
Participate in the elaboration of local needs and opportunities for food security and in the formulation and implementation of food security action plans;
Disseminate information about international human rights standards and stimulate local and national debate on the implementation of the right to food.
*The specialized agencies* should:
Examine their mandates for their relevance and relationship to food as a human right, *inter alia* through establishing as needed interdivisional working groups or task forces for this purpose;
Pay increased attention to the food-related work of the human rights organs and be prepared to co-operate with them in setting up the overall framework for promoting the right to food in given national situations and to develop subsequent action plans;
Develop further, advise on and assist in establishing appropriate systems for monitoring aspects of food security within their domains according to the framework suggested in this study, and consider how relevant information from such systems may be utilized and integrated with that of other systems for the purpose of monitoring the realization of the right to food;
Explore the possibility of developing for such co-operation special mechanisms for inter-agency co-operation in this field under the Administrative Committee on Co-ordination or other existing co-ordinating mechanisms.
*The UN Economic and Social Council* should:
Consider requesting the Committee on Economic, Social and Cultural Rights to designate one or two of its members to pay particular attention to the right to food dimensions of the work of the Committee. These members could, from time to time, draft general comments for consideration by the Committee with a view to developing greater understanding of the normative and practical implications of the right to food;
Consider requesting a Working Group of the Committee on Economic, Social and Cultural Rights to undertake a series of hearings at which experts from relevant international

agencies would make submissions and respond to questions with a view to developing a more sophisticated and mutually rewarding understanding of the best ways by which the international community could promote more effectively implementation of the right to food.

Consider the establishment of relevant intersecretariat and inter-agency co-operative arrangements that would facilitate closer working relations between the Centre for Human Rights and other relevant parts of the Secretariat as well as the specialized agencies, to ensure the best performance of the United Nations in promoting the right to food.

*The UN Committee on Economic, Social and Cultural Rights* should:

Improve its guidelines for States parties' reports so that more meaningful data are generated on the extent to which the right to food is not presently enjoyed and on the obstacles which block its enjoyment;

Encourage States parties to the Covenant to involve community groups and non-governmental organizations in the preparation of reports under the Covenant;

Improve the links with the relevant specialized agencies in order to obtain access to information which could be used to make the supervision process more meaningful;

Take measures to implement articles 22 and 23 of the Covenant by encouraging the provision of technical assistance to States parties which have encountered difficulties in realizing the right to food;

Emphasize to States that the obligation contained in article 2 (1) of the Covenant to "take steps" is of immediate application and does not necessarily depend on the availability of extra resources; the most appropriate step under article 2 (1) being the establishment of a system for the preparation of national food security action plans;

Reorganize the periodicity of the handling of reports in order to obtain shorter intervals; for this purpose, more time might need to be allocated to the Committee;

Indicate also, in its comments on State reports, the required compliance with external obligations of States necessary in order to facilitate a satisfactory realization of the right to food;

Make suggestions for further and improved co-operation between States on a voluntary basis, aimed at better worldwide realization of the right to food.

*International non-governmental organizations* should:

Support the efforts to realize the right to food world-wide, through information, awareness-formation and action as appropriate;

Base their food-related efforts on the right to food rather than on policy statements which are often vague and contentious;

Develop or strengthen their co-operation, on the basis of the right to food, with the relevant parts of the Secretariat and the specialized agencies, the Economic and Social Council, and the Committee on Economic, Social and Cultural Rights.

*The UN Sub-Commission on the Prevention of Discrimination and Protection of Minorities* should:

Seek authorization, through the Commission on Human Rights, from the Economic and Social Council to initiate an effort to consolidate and further develop existing law through the drafting of an appropriate instrument on the right to food. Such an instrument might contain declaratory and obligatory parts, and should give due account also to methods for monitoring and implementation.

In this endeavour, account should be taken of the efforts currently made within the International Law Association to prepare a model draft instrument on the right to food.

*ACTION TAKEN ON THE STUDY.* At its 1987 session, the Sub-Commission, having examined the Special Rapporteur's study, expressed its appreciation and thanks to Mr. Eide and submitted the study, together with the relevant documentation, to the UN COMMISSION ON HUMAN RIGHTS. Having noted a need for further information on the status of the right to food in domestic law, it called upon the Secretary-General to obtain such information from States and from the Food and Agriculture Organization of the United Nations. It decided that it would return to a debate on the normative content of the right to food at a subsequent session, taking into account the information obtained by the Secretary-General as well as the draft model instrument on the right to food then under elaboration by the International Law Association.

The Economic and Social Council, at its first regular session, in 1988, noted (resolution 1988/33) the study with satisfaction, decided that it should be published by the United Nations and given the widest possible circulation, and drew it to the attention of the COMMITTEE ON ECONOMIC, SOCIAL AND CULTURAL RIGHTS, inviting the Committee to submit its observations thereon to the Council. Further, the Council decided to take steps to ensure better coordination between specialized agencies and organs dealing with food-related matters and human rights bodies of the United Nations, if possible through interagency co-operative arrangements.

The Committee on Economic, Social and Cultural Rights devoted two meetings at its third session, held at the United Nations office in Geneva from 6 to 24 February 1989, to a general discussion on article 11 of the International Covenant on Economic, Social and Cultural Rights and in particular to the study on the right to adequate food as a human right prepared by Mr. Eide. On invitation of the Committee, Mr. Eide analyzed the contents of his study and participated in a free exchange of views with members of the Committee.

The essential features of Mr. Eide's analysis are summarized in the 1989 report of the Committee as follows (E/1989/22, chap. IV, sect. B):

(a) that the concept of freedom from want lies at the very heart of economic, social and cultural rights;

(b) that the right to food must be seen in the wider context of civil and political rights and economic, social and cultural rights, all such rights being indivisible and interdependent, and forming part of the overall framework of development, environment and peace;

(c) that the right to food involves not only food production globally and nationally but differential access to food within countries (food entitlements);

(d) that food is a basic need for all human beings and everyone requires access to food which is (i) sufficient, balanced and safe so as to satisfy nutritional requirements, (ii) culturally acceptable and (iii) accessible in a manner that does not destroy one's dignity as a human being;

(e) that the argument as to whether the right to food proclaimed in article 11 of the Covenant was an individual human right or a broadly formulated programme for governmental policies in the economic and social field; or that the rights were not justiciable so as to entitle the individual to have recourse to the Courts for their enforcement—all these arguments were sterile and a pragmatic approach was required for the understanding and realization of the right to food;

(f) that apart from whether human rights, including the right to food, are classified jurisprudentially as constituting legal relations between the individual and the State and the individual as a subject of international law, there were three (3) basic obligations, namely: (i) *the obligation to respect* the freedom of the individual to provide for his well being; (ii) *the obligation to protect* the individual against the action of others and (iii) *the obligation to fulfil* by securing the right to food for those individuals who are marginalized and afflicted by poverty;

(g) that the three basic obligations to *respect, protect* and *fulfil,* arose at both the national and international level; that despite the somewhat vague nature of the language in which the right to food is formulated, the State's obligations clearly emerged from a number of provisions in the Covenant, including articles 2, 11, 22 and 25; and the obligations under international law were founded upon the Charter of the United Nations (especially Article 1, para 3 and Article 55 (a), (b), (c)), the Universal Declaration of Human Rights (especially article 25, para. 1 as well as articles 2, 3, 22, 28, 29), the Covenant on Economic, Social and Cultural Rights (especially article 11, as well as article 2, paras. 1 and 2 and articles 6, 9, 10, and 12) as well as various resolutions and instruments of international organizations;

(h) that the right to food is of particular importance in the context of poverty since poverty was a global problem which permeated both the industrialized and developing countries;

(i) that the right to food was particularly critical in times of famine and disasters (natural and artificial) and posed serious problems in relation to distribution and access to food;

(j) that although it is the primary responsibility of the State to secure the enjoyment of the right to food to all within its jurisdiction, all States had international obligations to ensure humanity's survival by the guarantee of adequate food for all;

(k) that there was a need for a Global Food Security System to complement and strengthen national systems; such a system would recognize the need to guarantee access to food at (i) the household level, (ii) the national level and (iii) the global level; and that it was important to recognize the significance of access to food at the *household level* since "for those who do not have the purchasing power or other entitlements to food, it does not help much that enough food is being produced". At the national level there was the need for States to draw up plans for food security, identify needs and goals, ensure popular participation in the elaboration of these plans, indicate areas of international assistance, recognize its international obligations and establish an adequate system for monitoring the right to food;

(l) that monitoring at the international level was rather weak and there was need for a co-ordinated approach among international agencies in seeing the issue of food from the perspective of human rights. In this regard it was necessary to provide a greater amount of advice and assistance and was desirable to establish an inter-agency consultative mechanism;

(m) that the Committee seek to clarify the obligations of States, provide guidance for State Reporting in respect of their obligations under article 11 of the Covenant and be provided with more time and support for carrying out its monitoring and supervisory responsibility under the Covenant.

In a related statement to the Committee, the representative of the Food and Agriculture Organization of the United Nations (FAO) fully supported the concept of States having

international obligations in guaranteeing the right to food, although he considered that whether that duty was owed to the individual or to the State was an open question. Issues of sovereignty were involved. He was of the view that if the recommendation of FAO regarding World Food Security and the Principles and Plan of Action of the World Conference on Agrarian Reform and Rural Development were more fully implemented, this would go a long way towards the realization of the right to food. But it was first necessary for three elements to be in place, namely (a) the political will (b) the allocation of necessary resources and (c) the full use of the programme and mechanisms of FAO, WFP and IFAD.

The FAO representative submitted that the right to be free from hunger was proclaimed to be a fundamental right in article 11 (2) of the Covenant and this clearly related to the right to life recognized by the Universal Declaration of Human Rights. In this context any discretionary power of States, both developed and developing, in securing the right to food would be limited by the fundamental nature of the right to be free from hunger as an integral part of the right to life.

The observations put forward by various members of the Committee in the course of the exchange of views are summarized in the Committee's report as follows (Ibid., sect. C, paras. 319–326):

The observations made by members of the Committee were varied and far-reaching. Some members noted the lack of clarity in the formulation of the right to food and the obligations of States and pointed out the difficulty of the provisions of article 11 fitting into traditional concepts of rights and obligations. It was not clear in the view of these members whether the individual had an international legal right or merely a moral or social right. Other members considered that the legal foundation of the right to food was established by treaty law under the Covenant and other international instruments and that the obligations of States flowed directly from these provisions; that since the individual was clearly intended to be the beneficiary of those rights, it was within the power of the individual, increasingly recognized as a subject of international law, to demand respect for the obligations of the Covenant.

It was generally agreed that the right to food was much more extensive than the right to stand in line for food and that the individual should have the right to receive food not simply as an act of mercy; that the right to receive food was not simply a question of calories but adequate nutrition; and it had to be culturally acceptable. It was also suggested that all members of the population should receive an adequate income so as to make food affordable by all.

Some members of the Committee considered that every country should take immediate steps to ensure the realization of the right to food; that ultimate realization at the fullest acceptable level may in the circumstances of some countries be achieved progressively but the national and international obligations arising under the Covenant meant that with co-ordinated efforts a meaningful start could be made immediately in all States, whilst it was generally agreed that the primary responsibility for ensuring the right to food rested with the individual. Some members felt that there was a point at which the denial of the human need for food constituted a violation of a human right; that such a right was analogous to a right in public law; that such a right was important to the protection of the disadvantaged and marginalized affected by poverty; that there should be a common law right of action against the State where (a) there was a systematic deprivation of access to food for individuals or the community and (b) the State by its action or inaction had behaved so outrageously as to offend the dignity of the human personality.

It was further contended by some members that the obligations of States at the international level in relation to the right to food supported the thesis that there was an obligation on the part of all States to make food available so as to guarantee the fundamental right of freedom from hunger, that accordingly it could be said that the excess world food resources were the common heritage of mankind's hungry and impoverished and that it would be a denial of justice to refuse access to such resources by the hungry and the starving. This was not to be seen in terms of charity but in terms of human rights. The international obligations of States should be reflected in the reports by states, indicating the extent to which they participate in food aid programmes, multilaterally or bilaterally.

It was the widespread view among members that many of the problems relating to the production and distribution of food, particularly in developing countries dependent upon agriculture, related to the inequitable terms of trade between the primary producers of agricultural products and producers of manufactured products; that the prices received for the primary agricultural products did not keep pace with the prices of manufactured products which producing countries had to import with their limited export earnings from primary agricultural products. It was therefore an important part of the solution of the problem of the right to food that there should be an adjustment in the terms of trade as called for by the new international economic and social order. The role of transnationals would also have to receive attention.

Considerable emphasis was placed by some members on the need to see the right to food not as an isolated phenomenon but as part of the right to life. It was generally agreed that the right to food was necessary for human life and that without adequate food other human rights may be non-existent or meaningless. There was an interdependence and indivisibility between civil and political rights and economic, social and cultural rights.

There was considerable discussion in the Committee as to whether the right to humanitarian assistance transcended sovereignty so as to give the victim the right to require assistance directly rather than through the State. It was recognized that it was important to guarantee the individual's access to food.

Members examined the role of the Committee in making recommendations to States on compliance with the obligations arising under article 11 of the Covenant. The question was asked as to how far the Committee could go in this direction. It was recognized that the position was an evolving one and that by constructive dialogue with States, greater clarity could be achieved as to the extent of the obligation of States and the development of those obligations. Our understanding of human rights evolved with the development and evolution of the human personality and the Committee was a part of this process. Members of the Committee considered that the monitoring and supervisory mechanism was an important part of the Committee's function and that it was necessary to establish, through constructive dialogue, the guidelines for reporting and the bench marks for assessing compliance. It was said that the Committee had a choice between adopting a "positivist" and a "possibilist" approach. In this context it was necessary to continuously improve the co-operation between the Committee and States. It was also necessary to recognize that the Committee constituted an important means of recourse for the fulfilment of the right to food and that the Committee, in co-ordination with other United Nations agencies and non-governmental organizations, would need to intensify its efforts, which in turn would require the provision of adequate time and resources for the Council and the Committee to fulfil their obligations with respect to the Covenant. It was important that the Economic and Social Council bear this is mind in the allocation of resources to the Committee.

There has been little further international consideration of the question of food as a human right, as noted by the General Assembly at its 1992 session. In resolution 47/150 of 18 December of that year, the Assembly expressed its deep concern about the gravity of the world food security situation, in particular the worsening problems of hunger and malnutrition; stressed the urgent need for a more effective and well-coordinated United Nations response to world food and hunger problems; and underscored the increasing importance of intergovernmental policy guidance in this field. In this connection it noted with concern that, despite its efforts, the World Food Council, by its own acknowledgment, had not been able to achieve political leadership and coordination to the extent expected by its founders.

The Assembly went on to affirm "the critical importance of establishing the most effective arrangements for the management and coordination of the United Nations response to world food and hunger problems," and to underline "the need to consider the role of the World Food Council, and how its mandate and functions might best be carried out within the wider context of the overall restructuring of the social and economic activities of the United Nations system." It decided to address these issues in the context of the discussions on restructuring and revitalization of the United Nations in the economic, social, and related fields.

*SEE ALSO* Hunger and Malnutrition; Standard of Living.

**BIBLIOGRAPHY.** Brownlie, Ian. *The Human Right to Food.* London: Commonwealth Secretariat, 1987. IGO study, in English.

Burr, Millard. *Sudan 1990–1992: Food Aid, Famine, and Failure.* Washington, D.C.: U.S. Committee for Refugees, 1993. NGO report, in English.

Clark, John. *For Richer for Poorer: An Oxfam Report on Western Connections with World Hunger.* Oxford, UK: Oxfam, 1986. NGO report and scholarly monograph, in English.

Drèze, Jean, and Amartya Sen. *Hunger and Public Action.* Oxford, UK: Oxford University Press & Clarendon Press, 1989. Scholarly monograph, in English; bibliography, pp. 281–357.

Fenton, T. P., and M. J. Heffon. *Food, Hunger, Agribusiness: A Directory of Resources.* Maryknoll, NY, USA: Orbis Books, 1987. Directory/bibliography, in English.

Independent Commission on International Humanitarian Issues. *Famine: A Man-Made Disaster?* New York: Vintage Books, 1985. NGO report, in English.

Jonassohn, Kurt. *The Tragic Circle of Famine, Genocide and Refugees.* Montreal, Canada: Institute for Genocide and Human Rights Studies, 1992. NGO report, in English.

Jonsson, Urban. *Nutrition and the United Nations Convention on the Rights of the Child.* Florence, Italy: UNICEF, International Child Development Centre, 1993. (Innocenti Occasional Papers, Child Rights Series, 5). Scholarly paper, in English.

Keller, Edmond J. "Drought, War, and the Politics of Famine in Ethiopia and Eritrea," *Journal of Modern African Studies* 30, no. 4 (Dec. 1992): 609–624. Scholarly article, in English.

Lappe, F. M., and J. Collins. *World Hunger: Twelve Myths.* New York: Grove Press for the Institute for Food and Development Policy, 1986. NGO monograph, in English.

Lappe, F. M., R. Schurman, and K. Danaher. *Betraying the National Interest.* New York: Grove Press for the Institute for Food and Development Policy, 1987. NGO monograph, in English.

Low, Martin, et al. "The Right to Food," in *Human Rights in the Twenty-First Century: A Global Challenge,* eds. Kathleen E. Mahoney and Paul Mahoney, pp. 459–477. Dordrecht, the Netherlands: Martinus Nijhoff, 1993. Scholarly article, in English.

Tomasevski, Katarina, ed. *The Right to Food: Guide through Applicable International Law.* Dordrecht, the Netherlands: Martinus Nijhoff, 1987. Compilation of international instruments, in English.

United Nations. *The Right to Adequate Food as a Human Right,* by Asbjørn Eide, Special Rapporteur. Human Rights Study Series No. 1 (1989). United Nations publication, Sales no. E.89.XIV.2.

**FORCED LABOR.** Forced or compulsory labor is a practice which produces effects similar to slavery or develops into conditions analogous to slavery. International problems resulting from forced or compulsory labor were studied by the International Labor Office from 1922 onwards; and, in 1929, the office issued a report (International Labor Conference, 12th session, Geneva, 1929: *Forced Labour: Report and Draft Questionnaire*) surveying the law and practice in this field. The report distinguished between three "purposes for which compulsion is employed": (1) forced labor for general public purposes, such as the requisitioning of labor for public works, compulsory porterage, and compulsory cultivation of the land; (2) forced labor for local public purposes, such as the cleaning of village streets, disposal of refuse, or the construction and maintenance of government buildings and schools; and (3) forced labor for private employers, such as the labor which landowners sometimes may exact by law or custom from the population on their lands or the provision of convict labor to work for private employers.

The report indicated that, over a period of years, there had been a tendency both in law and in practice to eliminate the most brutal and unfair forms of forced labor and that the stage was set for international regulations banning the most reprehensible practices while making them subject to restrictive regulations in order to avoid abuses. This was the purpose of the ILO Forced Labor Convention (ILO Convention No. 29), adopted by the International Labor Conference on 28 June 1930.

***ILO FORCED LABOR CONVENTION (1930).*** The Convention defines "forced or compulsory labor" as "all work or service which is exacted from any person under the menace of any penalty and for which the said person has not offered himself voluntarily." However, article 2 (2) lists a number of forms of forced or compulsory labor which are excluded from the general definition and consequently are not banned or regulated by the Convention, among them:

(a) any work or service exacted in virtue of compulsory military service laws for work of a purely military character;

(b) any work or service which forms part of normal civic obligations of citizens of a fully self-governing country;

(c) any work or service exacted from any person as a consequence of a conviction in a court of law, provided that the said work or service is carried out under the supervision and control of a public authority and that the said person is not hired to or placed at the disposal of private individuals, companies or associations;

(d) any work or services exacted in cases of emergency, that is to say, in the event of war or of a calamity or threatened calamity, such as fire, flood, famine, earthquake, violent epidemic or epizootic diseases, invasion by animal, insect or vegetable pests, and in general any circumstance that would endanger the existence or the well-being of the whole or part of the population;

(e) minor communal services of a kind which, being performed by the members of the community in the direct interest of the said community, can therefore be considered as a normal civic obligations incumbent upon the members of the community, provided that the members of the community or their direct representatives shall have the right to be consulted in regard to the need for such services.

Under article 8, the power to exact forced or compulsory labor is vested in the highest civil authority of the territory concerned, which may, in certain cases, delegate that power to the highest local authorities. Article 9 provides that, before deciding to have recourse to forced or compulsory labor, the competent authority must satisfy itself (a) that the work to be done or the service to be rendered is of important direct interest for the community called upon to do the work or render the service; (b) that the work or service is of present or imminent necessity; (c) that it has been impossible to obtain voluntary labor for carrying out the work or rendering the service by the offer of rates for wages and conditions of work not less favorable than those prevailing in the area concerned for similar work or service; and (d) that the work or service will not lay too heavy a burden upon the present population, having regard to the labor available and its capacity to undertake the work.

Article 11 sets out conditions limiting the persons or types of persons who may be called upon for forced or compulsory labor, and article 12 limits the period for which a person may be taken for such labor to 60 days in any one period of 12 months. Under article 23, the competent authority is required to issue complete and precise regulations governing the use of forced or compulsory labor in order to give effect to the Convention.

The 1930 Forced Labor Convention was applied primarily by the colonial powers with respect to the territories which they administered. In such territories, it considerably strengthened the movement towards full freedom of employment. However, circumstances created by World War II gave rise to a revival of forced or compulsory labor, not only in the dependent territories but in some independent countries as well; and the ILO Committee of Experts on the Application of Conventions and Recommendations found it necessary to draw the attention of governments to the fact that the 1930 Convention applied to independent as well as to dependent countries and territories.

### REPORT OF THE COMMITTEE ON FORCED LABOR (1953).

After the establishment of the United Nations, an item entitled "Survey of Forced Labor and Measures for its Abolition" was placed on the agenda of the ECONOMIC AND SOCIAL COUNCIL at the request of the American Federation of Labor (AFL). Subsequently, in 1951, the United Nations and the International Labor Organization jointly established the temporary Committee on Forced Labor, which re-

ceived and investigated numerous allegations that such labor existed in various parts of the world.

The Committee finished its work in 1953. The report which it submitted to the Economic and Social Council of the United Nations and the Governing Body of the International Labor Office (UN Doc. E/2431, paras. 548–555, 557–561) set out the following general observations:

The Committee's enquiry has revealed the existence in the world of two principal systems of forced labour, the first being employed as a means of political coercion or punishment for holding or expressing political views, the second being employed for important economic purposes.

*A system of forced labour as a means of political coercion* was found by the Committee to be established in certain countries, to be probably in existence in several other countries, and to be possible of establishment in others. Such a system was found to exist in its fullest form and in the form which most endangers human rights where it is expressly directed against people of a particular "class" (or social origin) and even against political "ideas" or "attitudes" in men's minds; where a person may be sentenced to forced labour for the offence of having in some way expressed his ideological opposition to the established political order, or even because he is only suspected of such hostility; when he may be sentenced by procedures which do not afford him full rights of defence, often by a purely administrative order; and when, in addition, the penalty of forced labour to which he is condemned is intended for his political "correction" or "re-education", that is, to alter his political convictions to the satisfaction of the government in power. Such a system is, by its very nature and attributes, a violation of the fundamental rights of the human person as guaranteed by the Charter of the United Nations and proclaimed in the Universal Declaration of Human Rights. Apart from the physical suffering and hardship involved, what makes the system most dangerous to human freedom and dignity is that it trespasses on the inner convictions and ideas of persons to the extent of forcing them to change their opinions, convictions and even mental attitudes to the satisfaction of the State.

The Committee has also found that the systems of forced labour as a means of political coercion are applied with varying degrees of intensity in a number of countries, but it has observed in the trend of the laws and the aims and purposes of legislative enactments and administrative practices a tendency for countries which have less severe systems to approximate them to the more severe described above. The possibility of the extension of this system of forced labour as a means of political coercion to other countries or territories where unsettled conditions may prevail cannot be ignored.

While less seriously jeopardising the fundamental rights of the human person, *systems of forced labour for economic purposes* are no less a violation of the Charter of the United Nations and the Universal Declaration of Human Rights. Although such systems may be found in different parts of the world, their nature and scope are not everywhere the same.

These systems—still found to exist in some countries or territories where a large indigenous population lives side by side with a population of another origin—most often result from a combination of various practices or institutions affecting only the indigenous populations, and involving direct or indirect compulsion to work, such as compulsory labour properly so-called, various coercive methods of recruiting, the infliction of heavy penalties for breaches of contracts of employment, the abusive use of vagrancy legislation, restrictions on freedom of movement, restrictions on the possession and use of land, and other similar measures.

For nearly 25 years the International Labour Organisation has been striving to bring about the abolition of such practices and to improve the situation of indigenous workers. Conventions Nos. 29, 50, 64 and 65, and a number of supplementary Recommendations adopted by this Organisation, have shown the way of advance. The Committee's investigation has revealed that many of the countries concerned have ratified these Conventions and accepted the Recommendations, and in several of these countries or territories progress is commendable inasmuch as many of these practices have either been eliminated or are gradually declining. But progress has not been as rapid elsewhere. . . .

The Committee's enquiry has revealed that, while the forms of forced labour contemplated in the Conventions of the International Labour Organisation were virtually in relation to "indigenous" inhabitants of dependent territories, the systems of forced labour for economic purposes found to exist in some fully self-governing countries (where there is no "indigenous" population) raise new problems and call for action either by the countries concerned or at the international level.

Such systems of forced labour affecting the working population of fully self-governing countries result from various general measures involving compulsion in the recruitment, mobilisation or direction of labour. The Committee finds that these measures, taken in conjunction with other restrictions on the freedom of employment and stringent rules of labour discipline—coupled with severe penalties for any failure to observe them—go beyond the "general obligation to work" embodied in several modern Constitutions, as well as the "normal civic obligations" and "emergency" regulations contemplated in international labour Convention No. 29. They often deprive the individual of the free choice of employment and freedom of movement, and in this and other ways are contrary to the principles of the Universal Declaration of Human Rights.

In view of these findings, the Committee is of the opinion that the problems of compulsory labour, labour recruiting, the length of contracts of employment, penal sanctions for breaches of such contracts and other measures which have been examined in greater detail in regard to individual countries in Section IV, and which the International Labour Organisation has so far considered mainly in connection with indigenous workers, should now be examined also in connection with workers in fully self-governing countries.

The Committee has come to the conclusion that, however attractive the idea of using such methods with a view to promoting the economic progress of a country may seem to be, the result is a system of forced labour which not only subjects a section of the population to conditions of serious hardship and indignity, but which must gradually lower the status and dignity of even the free workers in such countries. The Committee suggests that, wherever necessary, international action be taken, either by framing new Conventions or by amending existing Conventions, so that they may be applicable to the position regarding forced labour conditions found to exist among the workers of fully self-governing countries.

The Committee undertook its work as a fact-finding body; its enquiry has revealed the existence of facts relating to systems of forced labour of so grave a nature that they seriously threaten fundamental human rights and jeopardise the free-

dom and status of workers in contravention of the obligations and provisions of the Charter of the United Nations. The Committee feels, therefore, that these systems of forced labour, in any of their forms, should be abolished, to ensure universal respect for, and observance of, human rights and fundamental freedoms.

***SEE ALSO*** *Debt Bondage; Slavery.*

**BIBLIOGRAPHY.** Center for the Progress of Peoples. "Forced Labour for the 'Bamboo Wall.'" 23 Feb. 1987. NGO urgent action bulletin, in English.

Commission on Security and Cooperation in Europe. *Soviet Forced Labor Practices.* Washington, D.C.: 1986. Government hearings, in English.

Committee against Repression and for Democratic Rights in Iraq. *Facts about Abu Graib, the Notorious Prison in Iraq.* London: 1987. NGO report, in English.

Cronje, Suzanne. *Equatorial Guinea—The Forgotten Dictatorship. Forced Labour and Political Murder in Central Africa.* London: Anti-Slavery Society, 1976. NGO report, in English.

M'Baye, Keba. "Les Realities du Monde Noir et les Droits de l'Homme" (The Realities of the Black World and Human Rights), *Revue des Droits de l'Homme: Droit International et Droit Compare* 2, no. 3 (1969): 382–394. Scholarly article, in English.

Plant, Roger. *Sugar and Modern Slavery: A Tale of Two Countries.* London: Zed Press, 1987. Scholarly monograph, in English.

Sathyaraj, Ranjit. "Human Rights Violations in the Northeast." Bangalore, India: 1987. Unpublished scholarly paper, in English.

United Nations. *Report of the Ad Hoc Committee on Forced Labor,* 1953, issued jointly by the United Nations and the International Labor Office. Supplement No. 13 in the Official Records of the Sixteenth session of the UN Economic and Social Council (E/2431) and No. 36 in the Studies and Reports (New Series) of the International Labor Office.

**FORENSIC SCIENCE AND HUMAN RIGHTS.** The UN **COMMISSION ON HUMAN RIGHTS,** at its 1993 session, received a report submitted by the Secretary-General pursuant to its resolution 1992/24, on human rights and forensic science (E/CN.4/1993/20), in which he noted "the increasing references by experts of the Commission on Human Rights to the need for forensic expertise in the determination of alleged violations brought to their attention and the prevailing difficulties in obtaining such assistance." In the report the Secretary -General referred to the activities of forensic scientists in the conduct of medico-legal investigations, in forensic training, and in the development of international medico-legal standards for investigations, as follows (paras. 7–21):

The bodies of victims of summary executions or disappearances are often buried in shallow, unmarked graves. The remains found in these graves have become invaluable sources of information for forensic scientists in conducting their investigations. Forensic experts exhume these graves, perform initial and second autopsies, observe official inquests into and/or assist in court-ordered investigations of these suspicious deaths.

For the particularly difficult tasks of identifying the remains found in unmarked graves or any other places, the scientists employ multidisciplinary techniques involving medicine, anthropology, archaeology, sociology and law. Their tasks are threefold.

First, they conduct interviews and review documents to ascertain the location of the burial sites and the victims whose remains were probably buried in those sites. Scientists interview the people who live in the locality, sometimes grave-diggers who have been hired to bury the bodies, or civilians who may have heard rumours that a certain area is used as a burial site or who can provide information on other details leading to the identification of the victims. They also review documents, sometimes official records, which indicate where the bodies of certain individuals may have been interred. In some cases the governmental authorities kept detailed records on persons arrested by them. The Special Rapporteur on the situation of human rights in Iraq has reported that such records have been found with regard to a considerable number of persons followed, wanted or detained in northern Iraq, many of whom subsequently disappeared (E/CN.4/1993/45).

Second, they conduct the exhumation in the appropriate scientific manner in order to be able to obtain the optimal amount of information. Because information from both the remains themselves and from the spatial features of the graves is useful, it is crucial that both be preserved and documented carefully. Hence, archaeological techniques much like those used in excavating prehistoric sites are used. The graves are marked so that the exact coordinates of where each item is uncovered can be identified. The soil and dirt are removed in such a manner as to ensure that no piece of evidence, however minute (e.g., teeth, bullets, etc.), will be missed. More important, the remains are exhumed with the care and deliberation that will ensure the least amount of damage and alteration to the surface and placement of the remains. Failure to employ the proper method of exhumation can lead to the destruction of the evidence. For example, according to a report by the Argentine Team of Forensic Anthropology, this occurred in Argentina when bulldozers were run through some graves. As a result, no useful information could be obtained from either the spatial features of the graves or the remains themselves.

Third, they examine the remains to determine the cause and manner of death, and attempt to establish the identity of the victim. Forensic experts analyse the skeletal remains to determine the physical characteristics of the victim, together with the cause, manner, time and place of death with a view to ascertaining the victim's identity. In doing so, they use techniques in pathology, odontology, radiology, etc. For instance, teeth and skeletal x-rays are taken to identify the victim. Also, anthropological studies may be undertaken to determine the skeleton's age at death, sex, race, stature and handedness. The results are then compared to the antemortem characteristics of the deceased. Forensic anthropologists can also distinguish various types of trauma to the bone which help determine the manner and cause of death.

For several years specialized non-governmental organizations have conducted missions to various countries in order to assist in the identification of the remains of victims of disappearances or extrajudicial executions. For example, experts sponsored by the AAAS [American Association for the Advancement of Science] worked in Argentina in 1984, at the request of the governmental Commission on Disap-

peared Persons (CONADEP); in El Salvador in 1988; in Chile in 1989; in Israel in 1989; in Bolivia in 1989; in El Salvador in 1989; again in Argentina in 1990; in Brazil in 1990; in Panama in 1991 and in Mexico in 1991. Similar missions were carried out by experts of the Danish Committee of Concerned Forensic Scientists and Physicians for the Documentation of Human Rights Abuses to Bolivia in 1986 and to El Salvador in 1988 and by the American non-governmental organization Physicians for Human Rights to Kenya in 1987; to Israel from 1988 to 1992 (10 different missions to observe and participate in the autopsies of the bodies of Palestinians who had died in detention or under suspicious circumstances); to Brazil in 1990; to Guatemala from 1990 to 1992 (five different missions for the exhumation and identification of dead bodies found in mass graves); to northern Iraq from 1991 to 1992 (two missions for the exhumation and identification of the dead bodies of Kurds presumed to have been victims of summary executions) and to the territory of the former Yugoslavia in 1992. The Argentine Team of Forensic Anthropology, in addition to its permanent involvement in the exhumation and identification of the remains of victims of disappearance in Argentina, performed, at the request of governmental bodies or non-governmental organizations, the following missions during the period 1975–1983: to the Philippines in 1986; to Bolivia in 1986, 1989 and 1992; to Chile in 1989; to the United States of America in 1989; to Nicaragua in 1990; to Venezuela in 1990; to Guatemala in 1991 and 1992; to Panama in 1992; to Iraq in 1992 and to El Salvador in 1992.

Forensic scientists cite three reasons why they investigate the graves of the victims of extrajudicial killings. First, from a humanitarian perspective, they hope to be able to inform the families of the deceased of the fate of their loved ones. Second, from a legal standpoint, they aim to uncover legally admissible evidence that will result in the conviction of those responsible for any crimes. Third, they hope to deter future violation by creating awareness, through forensic documentation and subsequent litigation, that those responsible will be held accountable for their actions.

The Working Group on Enforced or Involuntary Disappearances and other mechanisms of the Commission on Human Rights have repeatedly stressed that the impunity resulting from inadequate investigations is an important factor contributing to the persistence of human rights violations and to the lack of confidence in the ability or efficiency of national institutions to cope with crimes committed by government forces or groups linked to them. Even when inquests are ordered by Governments, it is not always easy to ascertain the facts surrounding extrajudicial executions. The remains of victims who had previously disappeared are often found long after their executions took place. This complicates the identification of the body due to the natural decomposition of its soft tissue which erases evidence of trauma such as bruises, gunpowder burns or marks from beatings. In addition, eye-witnesses or other people who could provide evidence are frequently reluctant to do so for fear of reprisals. National mechanisms for the investigation of human rights abuses often fail to obtain conclusive evidence because they lack the necessary cooperation of certain authorities, particularly where the death may have been caused by the police, the army or agents related to them.

At present, there are very few forensic scientists trained in the newest techniques currently available in this particular field of activity in comparison with the magnitude of disappearances and summary executions which have occurred over the years and which need to be investigated. Thus, the need for more well-trained and experienced forensic scientists is apparent, particularly in countries where these practices occur on a large scale.

In response to this need, forensic scientists have organized and conducted training workshops on the application of forensic sciences in conducting human rights investigations in different countries. Local physicians and scientists receive instruction in the exhumation and identification of skeletal remains, collection of antemortem data, autopsy procedures, investigation of allegations of torture, and application of international standards for the medico-legal investigation of suspicious deaths.

For a long time, and particularly during the last decade, some non-governmental organizations have been involved in training activities relating to forensic science in different regions of the world. Their courses dealt with modern technology applied to forensic science and with a new multi-disciplinary approach, which requires the participation of professionals from different fields of activity. Examples of this are the training workshops and courses carried out by the AAAS in Argentina in 1985, the Philippines in 1986, Costa Rica in 1989 and Guatemala in 1992; the Argentine Team of Forensic Anthropology in Uruguay in 1988, in Chile in 1989 and 1990, in Bolivia in 1989, Colombia in 1991 and in El Salvador in 1992; and the Danish Committee of Concerned Forensic Scientists and Physicians for the Documentation of Human Rights Abuses in the Philippines and Costa Rica. As a result of such efforts, many more scientists are now able to conduct medico-legal investigations in their home countries. Furthermore, national forensic anthropology teams have even been formed in countries such as Chile, Guatemala and Colombia.

In his report to the Commission on Human Rights (E/CN.4/1992/46) the Special Rapporteur on extrajudicial, summary or arbitrary executions stated that violations of the right to life persist in a variety of forms, ranging from isolated cases, through a more systematic pattern favoured by a "hands-off" policy on the part of the authorities, to killings and death threats as a deliberate state policy which at times touches the limits of war crimes and genocide. While ensuring the rights of the victims of such human rights abuses and their families, the efforts made by the international community to curb the phenomenon of extrajudicial, summary or arbitrary execution in the long term must focus on ways and means of preventing them from taking place. These include a genuine will and effective measures to put into practice the international standards already existing, as well as endeavours to improve them where shortcomings are identified.

In view of the need to develop standards for obtaining evidence when ignored or covered up by the authorities, by official forces or by groups tolerated by them, the international community began formulating a set of principles and medico-legal standards for the investigation and prevention of extra-legal, summary or arbitrary executions. That work, which started in the early 1980s, made considerable advances with the preparation of the Principles on the Effective Prevention and Investigation of Extra-legal, Arbitrary and Summary Executions recommended by the Committee on Crime Prevention and Control at its tenth session in Vienna in 1988. The Principles were adopted by the Economic and Social Council in the annex to its resolution 1989/65 of 24 May 1989 and endorsed by the General Assembly in its resolution 44/162 of 15 December 1989. They are reproduced in the *Manual on the Effective Prevention and Investigation of Extra-legal, Arbitrary and Summary Executions* (ST/CSDHA/12).

The *Manual* contains the general principles establishing a standard of investigation and also sets out procedures for the medico-legal investigations of suspicious deaths, an autopsy protocol, and sample charts and diagrams used in reporting injuries. It likewise describes methods for exhuming and examining skeletal remains and detecting post-mortem signs of torture.

The preparation of the *Manual* was greatly facilitated by the Minnesota Lawyers International Human Rights Committee, which obtained the assistance of an international group of experts in forensic science, lawyers, human rights experts and experts in other disciplines in the drafting of the Principles and in following up their implementation, the contents of which constitute the major part of the *Manual*. The AAAS and the Danish Committee of Concerned Forensic Scientists and Physicians for the Documentation of Human Rights Abuses also had an active participation in the preparation of the *Manual*.

The Secretary-General also reported on consultations held by the Working Group on Enforced or Involuntary Disappearances with organizations in the field of forensic science and human rights with a view to creating a standing team of forensic experts and other relevant disciplines, as follows (paras. 22–27):

In compliance with Commission on Human Rights resolution 1992/24, in which the Working Group on Enforced or Involuntary Disappearances was requested to render active assistance to the Secretary-General in his consultations with a view to creating, under United Nations auspices, a standing team of forensic experts and experts in other relevant disciplines, the Working Group on Enforced or Involuntary Disappearances assisted the Secretary-General in his consultations with appropriate professional organizations in the field of forensic science. As a starting point for such consultations, the Working Group held meetings with the following four professional organizations known for their involvement in missions for the exhumation and identification of corpses of probable victims of human rights violations as well as in training activities in this field: the American Association for the Advancement of Science, the Argentine Team of Forensic Anthropology, Physicians for Human Rights and the Committee of Concerned Forensic Scientists and Physicians of the University Institute of Forensic Medicine, Odense (Denmark).

The Working Group also contacted the following organizations or groups of experts: the Medical Action Group of Manila; the Mahidol University of Bangkok; the Association of Physicians for Humanism in Seoul; the Chilean Forensic Anthropology Group in Santiago; the *Nucleo de Estudos da Violencia* of São Paulo University, Brazil; and the Guatemalan Team of Forensic Anthropology.

Taking into account the suggestions received from those organizations, the Working Group elaborated a preliminary scheme, containing the following elements:

(a) A list of organizations with confirmed experience in human rights and forensic science will be maintained by the Working Group on Enforced or Involuntary Disappearances;

(b) These organizations will designate experts to work on the relevant activities envisaged by different programmes;

(c) Three types of programmes for forensic activities in relation to human rights can be foreseen: (i) programmes requested by Governments; (ii) programmes initiated at the request of special rapporteurs, working groups or other

United Nations organs; (iii) programmes requested by non-governmental organizations. If a programme is requested by a Government, the Working Group will provide it with the names of the organizations listed. In the second case, special rapporteurs, working groups or other United Nations organs will decide, in consultation with the Governments concerned, on the organization that will carry out the forensic activities in connection with their respective mandates. With regard to the third type of programme, non-governmental organizations may inform the Working Group on Enforced or Involuntary Disappearances of their wish to undertake such programme, indicating the experts or organization they wish to work with. At their request, the Working Group may initiate consultations with the Government concerned. Whenever such consultations have already taken place and an agreement has been reached with national, municipal or other local authorities, the Working Group may take note of the agreement and may recommend the relevant programme to be sponsored by the United Nations, provided that it falls under the terms and spirit of resolution 1992/24;

(d) Sponsorship by the United Nations will not imply any financial involvement in the activities of the programme. It will, however, imply that the programme is considered to respond to the terms of resolution 1992/24 and that the experts and the Government concerned will be committed to respect the international human rights standards at all times. The experts will have the legal status of Experts on Mission in accordance with sections 22 and 23 of article VI of the Convention on the Privileges and Immunities of the United Nations of 13 February 1946 and will be requested to perform its duties in accordance with general principles governing the activities of such experts.

During the first stage of the consultations, the Working Group only addressed organizations or groups specialized in medico-legal or anthropological activities related to forensic science and human rights. The Working Group is, however, aware that, in view of the multidisciplinary nature of these activities, experts in other related disciplines and human rights organizations which promote and sometimes fund such activities or which are involved in several different aspects leading to their accomplishment of forensic work should be contacted as well. Among the international non-governmental organizations, mention should be made of the activities performed in this field by Amnesty International, Human Rights Watch and the Minnesota Lawyers Human Rights Committee, which have been actively involved in the documentation and verification of torture, in the establishment of ethical standards for the medical profession and other professions performing forensic activities and in the exhumation and identification of victims of human rights violations. In addition, some organizations of relatives of victims of human rights violations could provide valuable insight into the technical and practical difficulties encountered when undertaking any kind of forensic activities relating to victims of human rights violations.

The Working Group on Enforced or Involuntary Disappearances also included in its report to the Commission on Human Rights information on forensic activities carried out in specific countries in the framework of investigations into cases of disappearances (E/CN.4/1993/25, paras. 50–55, 85, 95, 99–101, 132 and 239).

In the conclusions and recommendations formulated in its report, the Working Group included the following:

"Exhumation and identification of possible victims of human rights violations has proved to be significant in the investigation of cases of disappearances. In compliance with Commission resolution 1992/24, the Working Group has given special attention to the role of forensic experts in this matter. The Working Group will continue to devote its thinking to the topic and expects to receive comments from the Commission on the preliminary scheme which is included in the present report. Consultations will continue during 1993.

"In a number of countries, exhumation and identification of corpses is being carried out by local authorities. In some, the authorities cooperate closely with international forensic teams, an example to be emulated elsewhere. In a few instances, however, forensic teams, whether local or international, have been subjected to reprisals and acts of intimidation. The Working Group expresses its deep concern about this. Any such act is reprehensible as a matter of principle, but in addition the effectiveness of the exercise may be frustrated as a result." (paras. 517–518)

The Secretary-General further reported on the relevant activities of other United Nations bodies, in particular those of the Special Rapporteur on extrajudicial, summary or arbitrary executions and the Commission of Experts established pursuant to Security Council resolution 780 (1992), both in relation to alleged violations in the territory of the former Yugoslavia (paras. 28–30):

In his report to the Commission on Human Rights, the Special Rapporteur on extrajudicial, summary or arbitrary executions made the following specific recommendation:

"The Special Rapporteur would like to refer to the moves towards the institution of a standing team of forensic experts who could assist special rapporteurs in assessing, among other things, the reasons for the decease of a person purported to be a victim of extrajudicial, summary or arbitrary execution. They may also provide invaluable assistance in the examination of mass graves or clandestine cemeteries. This was shown clearly during the second mission to Yugoslavia in October 1992, in which two forensic experts participated. The Special Rapporteur wishes to encourage the international community to create a team of forensic experts, as was envisaged in Commission on Human Rights resolution 1992/24" (E/CN.4/1993/46, para. 698).

In his report on a mission to investigate allegations of mass graves in the territory of the former Yugoslavia, the Special Rapporteur on extrajudicial, summary or arbitrary executions outlined the practical conditions which must prevail before further investigations into those graves are undertaken. He stated that the exploration and excavation of sites as well as the exhumation and examination of bodies require specialists working on a full-time basis for a considerable period of time. Facilities are needed for the examination and conservation of human remains as well as office space, accommodation, transportation, etc. Funds for the remuneration of the experts and to cover all other costs must be made available. Mass graves containing victims of extrajudicial executions must be regarded as the scene of a crime and therefore treated as such. From the very first visit to a grave until the end of the investigation, the site must be protected so as to preserve the evidence. The personal security of the specialists working at the site must be guaranteed. If mass graves are located in areas that are considered as war zones, those guilty of war crimes may still be present, a factor which may generate serious security problems for those involved in the investigations.

Under resolution 780 (1992) of the United Nations Security Council an agreement has recently been signed between the United Nations and Physicians for Human Rights, by which the latter will carry out investigations into a mass grave site located near Vukovar, and into similar mass grave sites as may be agreed upon between the parties with a view to providing the Secretary-General with its conclusions on the evidence of serious breaches of the Geneva Conventions of 1949 and other violations of international humanitarian law committed in the territory of the former Yugoslavia. This agreement, with the necessary changes adapting it to the needs of the different situations in which forensic work will be carried out, might be taken as a basis for future agreements in this field.

The Commission considered and welcomed the Secretary-General's report (resolution 1993/33) and requested him "to consult with Governments, relevant United Nations bodies, professional organizations of forensic experts, the organizations mentioned in his report and other interested institutions with a view to identifying individual experts who might be asked to join forensic teams or to provide advice or assistance to thematic or country mechanisms, advisory services and technical assistance programmes." The Commission also requested the Secretary-General to establish "a list of forensic experts and experts in related fields who could be requested to help international mechanisms in the field of human rights, Governments and the Centre for Human Rights in providing technical and advisory services, advice in regard to the monitoring of human rights violations and training of local teams and/or assistance in the reunification of families of the disappeared." The Secretary-General was further requested to make the aforementioned list available to the Special Rapporteurs and experts of United Nations human rights mechanisms so that they might draw upon the list in carrying out their mandates. Finally, the Secretary-General was requested to report to the Commission at its fiftieth session on progress made in this area and to make such recommendations as he considered appropriate.

The resulting report of the Secretary-General (E/CN.4/1994/24) was welcomed by the Commission at its 1994 session (resolution 1994/31 of 4 March 1994). The Commission invited States to take measures to introduce into their rules and practices the international standards set out in the Principles on the Effective Prevention and Investigation of Extra-legal, Arbitrary and Summary Executions, as well as the model autopsy protocol set forth in the *Manual on the Effective Prevention and Investigation of Extra-legal, Arbitrary and Summary Executions*, and requested the Secretary-General to undertake further consultations with a view to:

(a) Identifying individual experts who might be asked to join forensic teams or to provide advice or assistance to thematic or country mechanisms, advisory services and technical assistance programmes;

(b) Submitting biographical data on the experts, including professional qualifications, current employment, contact address, gender (the nomination of female experts is encouraged) and the kinds of assistance they could provide; and

(c) Seeking their advice as to the elaboration of principles, guidance, procedures, mechanisms and training, in addition to the *Manual on the Effective Prevention and Investigation of Extra-legal, Arbitrary and Summary Executions.*

**SEE ALSO** *Science and Technology.*

**FOUNDATION FOR THE RIGHTS OF THE FAMILY.** Founded in 1981 in Madrid as a private cultural foundation, this non-governmental organization promotes study and research on family issues and values from social, educational, ethical, legal, religious, and political viewpoints. It has consultative status with the UN ECONOMIC AND SOCIAL COUNCIL (Category II) and has members in 23 countries.

Foundation for the Rights of the Family. Address: Zurbano 66-3A, 28010 Madrid, Spain. Secretary-General: Santa Olalia.

**FOUR ARROWS (CUATRO FLECHAS).** Established in 1968 to protect the human rights of indigenous peoples in the Americas, this non-governmental organization promotes intercultural exchange and communication among Indian peoples. It has members in four regional groups in North, South, and Central America. Four Arrows has sponsored projects in educational and agricultural development for Mexican Indian youth and development projects in Guatemala. Among its publications is *Guatemala: The Horror and the Hope.*

Four Arrows. Address: P.O. Box 1332, Ottawa, Ontario, Canada K1P 5R4. Telephone: (613) 234-5887

**FRANCE.** The French Republic is a country in western Europe, on the Atlantic Ocean, the Mediterranean Sea, and the English Channel. It has borders with Belgium, Germany, Italy, Luxembourg, Spain, and Switzerland, and includes the Mediterranean island of Corsica. It became a member of the United Nations in 1945. France became one of seven countries in the European Union to implement the Schengen Agreement in March 1995 whereby border controls between the seven would be eradicated and external controls enhanced. The other countries are Belgium, Germany, Luxembourg, the Netherlands, Portugal, and Spain.

In a period report (document CERD/C/225/Add. 2) to the **COMMITTEE ON THE ELIMINATION OF RACIAL DISCRIMINATION** of the United Nations, dated 28 May 1993, the Government stated that metropolitan France has 57.2 million inhabitants, of whom 3,580,000 are foreigners (6.3 per cent), and 25.1 million working people, of whom 1,624,000 are foreigners (6.5 per cent). The foreign population is numerically stable and composed mainly of: Portuguese: 649,714; Algerians: 614,207; Moroccans: 572,652; Italians: 252,759; Spaniards: 216,047; Tunisians: 206,336; and Turks: 197,712. The population of the overseas departments (Guadeloupe, French Guiana, Martinique, Reunion), the overseas territories (New Caledonia, French Polynesia, Wallis and Futuna Islands) and the territorial communities (Saint Pierre and Miquelon, Mayotte) is 1,896,800.

Ethnic groups in metropolitan France include persons of Celtic, Latin, Teutonic, Slavic, North African, Indochinese, and Basque origins. Languages commonly used are French (official), Arabic, German, and English. Religions practiced include Christianity (Roman Catholic, 90%; Protestant denominations, 5%), Islam (3%), and Judaism (2%). Literacy is estimated at 99%.

The Government (1994) took the form of a republic. The president, elected by popular vote for a term of seven years, is head of State. He appoints the premier, who together with the cabinet is responsible to Parliament. The bi-cameral Parliament includes a 577-member National Assembly and a senate. The president has the right to dissolve the National Assembly or to ask Parliament to reconsider a law. The judicial system includes the Court of Cassation (civil and criminal law), Council of State (administrative law), and Constitutional Council (constitutional law). Political parties include the Socialist Party, the Rally for the Republic, the Union for French Democracy, the National Front, and the Communist Party. François Mitterrand, a socialist, was elected to a second seven-year term as president on 8 May 1988. In May 1995, Jacques Chirac of the neo-Gaulist Rally for the Republic replaced Mitterrand. Chirac's campaign focus was on France's unemployment rate and greater control of the rate of integration within the European Union. Shortly after taking office, President Chirac announced plans to resume underground nuclear weapons testing in the South Pacific.

*TERRITORIES.* The Government of France retained, or undertook, responsibility for the administration of a number of overseas departments and territories after the establishment of the United Nations,

among them, overseas departments in French Guiana, Guadeloupe, Martinique, and Reunion; overseas territories in French Polynesia, New Caledonia and dependencies, Saint Pierre and Miquelon, the southern and Atlantic lands and the Wallis and Futuna Islands; and the island of Mayotte, which for some years has been the subject of a dispute. In 1974, and again in 1976, the largely Christian population of Mayotte voted against joining the Federal Islamic Republic of the **COMOROS** and declared its independence, retaining its close ties to France.

As regards the islands of New Caledonia, which are part of the chain of Melanesian islands spreading east and southeast from Papua New Guinea, Solomon Islands, and Vanuatu to Fiji, the territory was annexed by France on 24 September 1953. The colonization was resisted by the indigenous Melanesian Kanaks, resulting in bloody uprisings in which the Kanak population was decimated. By 1983, when the Kanaks had been reduced to 61,870—42.6% of the total population of 145,368—there was mounting pressure for independence for New Caledonia, which has rich mineral deposits including 40% of the world's known reserves of nickel. After a round-table conference between France and all parties in New Caledonia was held in July 1983, the French government recognized "the territory, including their innate and active right to independence. . . ."

In May 1984, France proposed, under the so-called Lemoine Statute, internal self-government for five years and a referendum in 1989 to choose between maintaining the status quo or independence. The statute, however, enfranchised any French citizen resident in New Caledonia for more than six months and failed to recognize demands of pro-independence parties for electoral reform and an earlier date for the proposed referendum. It was abandoned in 1985 in favor of a new concept—independence in association with France, to be the subject of a referendum in 1987. However, up to the end of 1988, the referendum had not been held.

France has consistently maintained that New Caledonia is an overseas territory of the French republic, not a colonial territory of which France is the administering power; and has claimed that it was the "sole judge of the state of emancipation reached by peoples under its administration." The majority of UN member States held, however, that it was for the United Nations to decide when a territory ceased to be non-self-governing.

On 22 November 1988, the UN **GENERAL ASSEMBLY** noted (resolution 43/34) that a dialogue with the peoples of New Caledonia had been initiated under the auspices of the French authorities on the status of the territory and noted that those authorities were taking positive measures to promote political, economic, and social development in New Caledonia to provide a framework for the peaceful progress of that territory to self-determination. The Assembly urged all the parties involved, in the interest of all the people of New Caledonia, to continue that dialogue and to refrain from acts of violence.

A year later, on 11 December 1989, the Assembly noted (resolution 44/89) "the positive measures being pursued in New Caledonia by the French authorities, in co-operation with all sectors of the population, to promote political, economic and social development in the Territory, in order to provide a framework for its peaceful progress to self-determination." Further, it invited all the parties involved to continue promoting a framework for the peaceful progress of the territory towards an act of self-determination in which all options are open and which would safeguard the rights of all New Caledonians.

Resolutions containing identical terms were adopted in 1990, 1991, 1992, and 1993, most recently Assembly resolution 48/50 of 10 December 1993.

As regards the question of the Comorian island of Mayotte, a dispute between France and the Comoros has persisted since December 1974, when the latter acceded to independence as the result of a referendum in which the peoples of the islands of Anjouan, Grande-Comore, and Moheli voted for self-government, while those of the island of Mayotte voted to retain close ties with France. The government of the Comoros, maintaining that the results of the referendum were to be considered on a global basis and not island-by-island under the terms of an agreement with France, has repeatedly expressed a wish to initiate as soon as possible a frank and serious dialogue with the French Government with a view to accelerating the return of the Comorian island of Mayotte to the Federal Islamic Republic of the Comoros. The position of the Government of the Comoros is supported by the United Nations, the ORGANIZATION OF AFRICAN UNITY, the Movement of Non-Aligned Countries, and the ORGANIZATION OF THE ISLAMIC CONFERENCE. On 18 October 1989, the General Assembly, bearing in mind decisions on the subject taken by the aforementioned international organizations, reaffirmed the sovereignty of the Islamic Federal Republic of the Comoros over the island of Mayotte and invited the government of France to honor the commitments entered into prior to the referendum on the self-determination of the Comoro archipelago of 22 December 1974 concerning respect for the unity and territorial integrity of the Comoros. It urged the Government of France to accelerate the process of negotiations with the Government of the Comoros with a view to ensuring the return of Mayotte to the Comoros.

Resolutions containing identical terms were adopted in 1990, 1991, 1992, and 1993, the most recent being General Assembly resolution 48/56 of 13 December 1993.

*PROBLEMS OF ALIENS.* For some time, the increasing number of aliens in France has been a matter of concern. Between 31 December 1981 and 31 December 1982, for example, the increase amounted to 235,000 persons, including 120,000 illegal aliens whose status was regularized and 30,000 persons who benefited from family unification measures. The largest national groups included Portuguese, Algerians, Moroccans, Italians, Spaniards, Tunisians, and Turks. In addition, there were 129,000 refugees from other countries.

French policy provides for extra French language courses to be provided for children who need them, in order to raise foreign children's knowledge of the language to a minimum level required to integrate them into normal classes. Education also is provided in the language and culture of origin with the aim of facilitating both the integration of foreign students and, if necessary, their return to their country of origin.

In recent years, resentment has mounted in France against an estimated three million Muslim Arab immigrants now living in the country, and the extremist right-wing National Front has called for the eviction of all of France's total of about five million immigrants. In March 1990, after a bomb destroyed a mosque in western France, President Mitterrand denounced racism and added that "what is not acceptable is a crime that has its origin in the rejection of others and that is inspired by instinctive hatred." In 1993, however, the French government enacted laws restricting entry into the country and allowing the government to expel foreigners under certain circumstances.

*RIGHTS OF THE CHILD.* The UN COMMITTEE ON THE RIGHTS OF THE CHILD considered the initial report of France under the Convention on the Rights of the Child (see CHILDREN'S RIGHTS) (UN Doc. CRC/C/3/Add. 15) at meetings held on 11 and 12 April 1994, and on 22 April 1994 adopted the following concluding observations (paras. 4–28):

### Positive Aspects

The Committee is particularly encouraged by the State party's commitment to reflect on and review the measures taken and policy chosen to implement the provisions and principles of the Convention in the light of the changing reality of the situation of children.

The Committee recognizes the importance of the annual meeting held between the public authorities and the non-governmental community on the anniversary of the adoption of the Convention on the Rights of the Child by the General Assembly of the United Nations. The Committee stresses the value of such a meeting in launching a fruitful dialogue between the Government and the "civil society", as well as in ensuring a serious evaluation of the governmental policies adopted for the promotion and protection of the rights of the child.

The Committee also welcomes the decision taken by the Government to submit an annual report to the Parliamentary Assemblies on the implementation of the Convention and on its policies in relation to the situation of children in the world. This procedure will contribute to emphasizing the importance of the principle of the best interests of the child, which is a primary consideration to be taken into account in all actions concerning children, including those undertaken by legislative bodies.

The Committee welcomes the measures taken by the State party to recognize the right of the child to have his or her views heard and taken into account in proceedings affecting the child. Note is taken of the various initiatives to inform children about their rights and to encourage children to express their opinion through special councils established within schools and the local community.

The Committee is further encouraged by the steps taken to train certain professional groups about the rights of the child. It also commends the initiatives undertaken by members of the legal profession to establish a system of legal information and assistance to children in the field of juvenile justice.

The Committee notes the active participation of France in international cooperation activities, including in the area of development assistance.

The Committee also notes the significant contribution being made by the State party to the international campaign addressing the issue of the hazardous impact of anti-personnel land-mines on the civilian population and, in particular, on children.

### Principal Subjects of Concern

The Committee notes with concern the reservation made by the State party to article 30 of the Convention. The Committee wishes to emphasize that the Convention on the Rights of the Child seeks to protect and guarantee the individual rights of children, including the rights of children belonging to minorities.

In view of article 55 of the Constitution, referred to in the core document submitted by the State party to the human rights treaty bodies, which provides that the norms of international human rights instruments are self-executing in France and may be invoked before national courts, the Committee is unclear as to the status of the Convention on the Rights of the Child in the national legal framework, namely in the light of recent decisions adopted by the Court of Cassation in this regard.

The Committee is concerned about the need to take sufficient safeguards against the possible negative social impact of decentralization, for instance in order to avoid the risk of aggravated disparities between the regions, in regard to the standard of living, and to minimize the possible adverse effects on the enjoyment of economic and social rights by children, especially those belonging to the most vulnerable groups.

Regarding the right of the child to know his or her origins, including in cases of a mother requesting that her identity remain secret during the birth and declaration of the birth, adoption and medically-assisted procreation, the Committee is concerned that the legislative measures being taken by the State party might not fully reflect the provisions of the Convention, particularly its general principles.

The Committee is concerned at the situation of unaccompanied children who arrive "unexpectedly in France to obtain refugee status" (as referred to in para. 389 of the State party's report). It is also concerned about the lack of a comprehensive system of protection involving the social and/or judicial authorities which would apply to those children while they are subject to the jurisdiction of the State party, as well as in the process of returning to their country of origin.

The Committee is also concerned that legislation and practice relating to arrest, detention, sentencing and imprisonment within the system of the administration of juvenile justice might not be fully consistent with the provisions and principles of the Convention, and in particular articles 37 and 40.

### Suggestions and Recommendations

The Committee wishes to encourage the State party to consider reviewing its reservation to article 30 of the Convention with a view to withdrawing it.

The Committee also wishes to suggest that the State party envisage the establishment of a permanent mechanism of coordination, evaluation and follow-up for policies taken to implement the Convention on the Rights of the Child.

The Committee wishes to emphasize the importance of close cooperation between the central Government and the local authorities, including on budgetary matters, to minimize disparities which may arise between the regions as to the provision of services. It also emphasizes the value of adopting a comprehensive approach to the implementation of the rights of the child which is both effective and consistent with the provisions and general principles of the Convention, particularly the best interests of the child and non-discrimination which apply irrespective of budgetary resources.

While the Committee notes with satisfaction the measures in place to guarantee minimum social income and to improve access to housing for the most disadvantaged groups, it recommends that the State party in this period of economic recession carefully monitor the enjoyment of the individual rights of children. In this connection, it is suggested that the necessary measures be taken to ensure the full realization of the economic and social rights of children belonging to the poorest and most vulnerable sectors of society, including those living in suburbs, the children of migrant workers and socially marginalized children.

The Committee draws the attention of the State party to the recommendations of United Nations organs and specialized agencies which emphasize the prioritization of social programmes within the framework of development assistance. It would like to suggest that the State party consider these aspects of the promotion of social development within its international cooperation programme.

Within the framework of legal reform and in light of the basic principles of the Convention, particularly its article 2, the Committee suggests that the State party consider reviewing the present law on minimum age for marriage.

The Committee would like to suggest that further consideration be given to ways of encouraging the expression of views by children and those views being given due weight in the decision-making processes affecting their lives, in particular within school and the local community.

The Committee would also like to suggest that further awareness-raising and educational measures be undertaken to prevent child abuse and the physical punishment of children.

In view of the fact that, following the submission of the initial report, important legislation has been adopted, namely in the fields of nationality, entry and residence of foreigners, refugees and asylum-seekers as well as family reunification, the Committee would appreciate receiving, by 1 October 1994, additional written information on those areas and on the way the new legislative measures might affect the enjoyment of the rights of the child as recognized by the Convention, in particular its articles 7, 9, 10 and 22 and taking into due account the general principles of the Convention.

The Committee encourages the State party to consider its legislation in the field of the administration of juvenile justice, in particular with regard to children deprived of their liberty, in order to ensure that deprivation of liberty is used only as a measure of last resort and for the shortest period of time, in the light of the provisions of the Convention, notably its articles 37, 39 and 40, as well as relevant international standards, namely the "Beijing Rules", the "Riyadh Guidelines" and the United Nations Rules for the Protection of Juveniles Deprived of their Liberty.

In the light of the best interests of the child and other provisions of the Convention on the Rights of the Child, as well as those of ILO Convention No. 138 to which France is a party, the Committee believes that the employment of children who have not yet completed their compulsory schooling, as admitted by the legislation in the case of domestic servants and family enterprises, including in the area of agriculture, deserves reconsideration by the State party. It also encourages the State party to review the access by children to activities in the fashion industry in order to ensure that this only takes place on the basis of a case-by-case approach and in the light of the best interests of the child.

In light of the importance the Committee attaches to the monitoring of the implementation of the Convention at the national level, it would appreciate receiving a copy of the annual reports to be submitted by the Government to the Parliamentary Assemblies on the policies adopted to ensure the realization of the rights of the child recognized by the Convention.

**BIBLIOGRAPHY.** Amnesty International. "France (New Caledonia): Statement to the United Nations Special Committee on Decolonization," August 1988. NGO statement, in English.

Association internationale des juristes démocrates. *Les droits de l'homme: universalité, et renouveau 1789–1989* (Human Rights: Universality and Renewal, 1789–1989). Paris: Harmattan, 1990. Collective works, in French.

Duffar, Jean. "L'objection de conscience en droit français" (Conscientious Objection in French Law), *Revue de droit public et de science politique en France et à l'étranger* 107, no. 3 (1991): 657–695. Scholarly article, in French.

France, Commission nationale consultative des droits de l'homme. *1990: La lutte contre le racisme et la xénophobie* (1990: The Fight against Racism and Xenophobia). Paris: Documentation française, 1991. Research report, in French.

France, Conseil d'État. *Statut et protection de l'enfant* (Status and Protection of Children). Paris: Documentation française, 1991. Government research report, in French.

France, Conseil national des populations immigrées. *Égalité des droits: rapport présenté par Mme Danielle Lochak* (Equality of Rights: Report Presented by Ms. Danielle Lochak). Paris: Ministère des Affaires sociales et de l'intégration, 1991. Government report, in French.

*Freedom of Information and Expression in France.* London: Article 19, 1989. NGO report, in English.

Husbands, Christopher T. "The Mainstream Right and the Politics of Immigration in France: Major Developments in the 1980s," *Ethnic and Racial Studies* 14, no. 2 (April 1991): pp. 170–198. Scholarly article, in English; bibliography, pp. 196–198.

Ligue des Droits de l'Homme (League for Human Rights). "Une Declaration sur la Situation en Nouvelle Caledonie" (A Declaration on the Situation in New Caledonia). Paris: 1987. NGO statement, in French.

Miles, Robert, and Jeanne Singer-Kérel, eds. "Migration and Migrants in France," *Ethnic and Racial Studies* 14, no. 3 (July 1991): 265–416. Special issue, in English.

Peuchot, Éric. "Droit de vote et condition de nationalité" (Right to Vote and the Nationality Requirement), *Revue de droit public et de science politique en France et à l'étranger* 107, no. 2 (1991): 481–524. Scholarly article, in French.

Robert, Jacques, ed. *Colloque franco-suédois sur "les nouveaux enjeux des droits de l'homme" (Stockholm, 20–21 avril 1989)* (Franco-Swedish Colloquium on "New Implications for Human Rights" [Stockholm, April 20–21, 1989]), *Revue du droit public* 106, no. 5 (Sept.–Oct. 1990): 1229–1402. Scholarly conference papers, in English.

Ruzie, Davie. "Klaus Barbie and the French Legal Process," *Patterns of Prejudice* 20, no. 3 (July 1986): 27–33. NGO article, in English.

Smith, Eivid, ed. *Les droits de l'homme dans le droit national en France et en Norvège* (Human Rights in the National Law of France and Norway). Aix-en-Provence & Paris, France: Presses universitaires d'Aix-Marseille; Economica, 1990. Scholarly collective papers, in French.

**FRANCE: DECLARATION OF THE RIGHTS OF MAN AND OF THE CITIZEN.** Inspired by the American Declaration of Independence, the Declaration of the Rights of Man and of the Citizen was drafted by the French revolutionary clergyman, pamphleteer, and statesman Emmanuel Joseph (Abbé) Sieyes and decreed by the French National Assembly in morning sessions held on 20, 21, 22, 23, 24, and 26 August 1789. It was signed by Louis XVI on 5 October 1789 and was later embodied as a preamble in the French constitution of 1791.

### Preamble

The representatives of the French people, organized in the National Assembly, considering that ignorance, forgetfulness or contempt of the rights of man are the sole causes of the public miseries and of the corruption of governments, have resolved to set forth in a solemn declaration the natural, inalienable, and sacred rights of man, in order that this declaration, being ever present to all the members of the social body, may unceasingly remind them of their rights and duties; in order that the acts of the legislative power and those of the executive power may be each moment compared with the aim of every political institution and thereby may be more respected; and in order that the demands of the citizens, grounded henceforth upon simple and incontestable principles, may always take the direction of maintaining the constitution and the welfare of all.

In consequence, the National Assembly recognizes and declares in the presence and under the auspices of the Supreme Being, the following rights of man and of the citizen:

I. Men are born and remain free and equal in rights. Social distinctions can be based only upon public utility.

II. The aim of every political association is the preservation of the natural and imprescriptible rights of man. These rights are liberty, property, security and resistance to oppression.

III. The source of all sovereignty is essentially in the nation; no body, no individual can exercise authority that does not proceed from it in plain terms.

IV. Liberty consists in the power to do anything that does not injure others; accordingly, the exercise of the natural rights of each man has for its only limits those that secure to the other members of society the enjoyment of these same rights. These limits can be determined only by law.

V. The law has the right to forbid only such actions as are injurious to society. Nothing can be forbidden that is not interdicted by the law, and no one can be constrained to do that which it does not order.

VI. Law is the expression of the general will. All citizens have the right to take part personally or by their representatives in its formation. It must be the same for all, whether it protects or punishes. All citizens, being equal in its eyes, are equally eligible to all public dignities, places employments, according to their capacities, and without other distinction than that of their virtues and their talents.

VII. No man can be accused, arrested or detained except in the cases determined by the law and according to the forms that it has prescribed. Those who procure, expedite, execute or cause to be executed arbitrary orders ought to be punished; but every citizen summoned or seized in virtue of the law ought to render instant obedience; he makes himself guilty by resistance.

VIII. The law ought to establish only penalties that are strictly and obviously necessary and no one can be punished except in virtue of a law established and promulgated prior to the offence and legally applied.

IX. Every man being presumed innocent until he has been pronounced guilty, if it is thought indispensable to arrest him, all severity that may not be necessary to secure his person ought to be strictly suppressed by law.

X. No one ought to be disturbed on account of his opinions, even religious, provided their manifestation does not derange the public order established by law.

XI. The free communication of ideas and opinions is one of the most precious of the rights of man; every citizen can freely speak, write, and print, subject to responsibility for the abuse of this freedom in the cases determined by law.

XII. The guarantee of the rights of man and of the citizen requires a public force; this force then is instituted for the advantage of all and not for the personal benefit of those to whom it is entrusted.

XIII. For the maintenance of the public force and for the expenses of administration a general tax is indispensable; it ought to be equally apportioned among all the citizens according to their means.

XIV. All the citizens have the right to ascertain, by themselves or by their representatives, the necessity of the public tax, to consent to it freely, to follow the employment of it, and to determine the quota, the assessment, the collection and the duration of it.

XV. Society has the right to call for an account from every public agent of its administration.

XVI. Any society in which the guarantee of the rights is not secured or the separation of powers not determined has no constitution at all.

XVII. Property being a sacred and inviolable right, no one can be deprived of it unless a legal established public necessity evidently demands it, under the condition of a just and prior indemnity.

***BIBLIOGRAPHY.*** Fondation Marangopoulos pour les droits de l'homme. *La déclaration française des droits de l'homme et du citoyen: un rayonnement bicentenaire* (The French Declaration of the Rights of Man and the Citizen: Two Hundred Years of Influence). Athens, Greece: Editions Ant. N. Sakkoulas, 1991. NGO conference report, in English and French.

Fenet, Alain, and Soulier, Gérard, eds. *Les minorités et leurs droits depuis 1789* (Minorities and Their Rights Since 1789). Paris: Éditions L'Harmattan for the Centre de relations internationales et de sciences politiques d'Amiens and Groupement pour les droits des minorités, 1989. Scholarly conference papers, in French.

## FREEDOM AWARD.

Established in 1943, this award is presented at irregular intervals to individuals and organizations that have played an active role in advancing liberty throughout the world. The award is sponsored by Freedom House, a nonpartisan, non-profit human rights organization dedicated to promoting political rights and civil liberties worldwide. Freedom House was established in 1941 by Eleanor Roosevelt and Wendell Wilkie.

Two or three winners are chosen by the Freedom House Board of Trustees. Past winners include Czech President Vaclav Havel and His Holiness the Dalai Lama of Tibet (1991). No award was presented in 1993 or 1994.

For more information, contact: Freedom House, 120 Wall St., New York, NY 10005, USA. Telephone: (212) 514-8040. Fax: (212) 514-8050.

## FREEDOM OF PEACEFUL ASSEMBLY AND ASSOCIATION.

The right of everyone to freedom of peaceful assembly and association is proclaimed in two articles of the **UNIVERSAL DECLARATION OF HUMAN RIGHTS,** as follows:

*Article 20.* 1. Everyone has the right to freedom of peaceful assembly and association.

2. No one may be compelled to belong to an association. . . .

*Article 23.* 4. Everyone has the right to form and join trade unions for the protection of his interests.

Measures to promote and protect the right to freedom of peaceful assembly are set out in both International Covenants on Human Rights. The **INTERNATIONAL COVENANT ON ECONOMIC, SOCIAL AND CULTURAL RIGHTS** provides that:

*Article 8.* 1. The States Parties to the present Covenant undertake to ensure:

(a) The right of everyone to form trade unions and join the trade union of his choice, subject only to the rules of the organization concerned, for the promotion and protection of his economic and social interests. No restrictions may be placed on the exercise of this right other than those prescribed by law and which are necessary in a democratic society in the interests of national security or public order or for the protection of the rights and freedoms of others;

(b) The right of trade unions to establish national federations or confederations and the right of the latter to form or join international trade-union organizations;

(c) The right of trade unions to function freely subject to no limitations other than those prescribed by law and which are necessary in a democratic society in the interests of national security or public order or for the protection of the rights and freedoms of others;

(d) The right to strike, provided that it is exercised in conformity with the laws of the particular country.

2. This article shall not prevent the imposition of lawful restrictions on the exercise of these rights by members of the armed forces or of the police or of the administration of the State.

3. Nothing in this article shall authorize States Parties to the International Labour Organisation Convention of 1948 concerning Freedom of Association and Protection of the Right to Organize to take legislative measures which would prejudice, or apply the law in such a manner as would prejudice, the guarantees provided for in that Convention.

The **INTERNATIONAL COVENANT ON CIVIL AND POLITICAL RIGHTS** provides that:

*Article 21.* The right of peaceful assembly shall be recognized. No restrictions may be placed on the exercise of this right other than those imposed in conformity with the law and which are necessary in a democratic society in the interests of national security or public safety, public order (*ordre public*), the protection of public health or morals or the protection of the rights and freedoms of others.

*Article 22.* 1. Everyone shall have the right to freedom of association with others, including the right to form and join trade unions for the protection of his interests.

2. No restrictions may be placed on the exercise of this right other than those which are prescribed by law and which are necessary in a democratic society in the interests of national security or public safety, public order (*ordre public*), the protection of public health or morals or the protection of the rights and freedoms of others. This article shall not prevent the imposition of lawful restrictions on members of the armed forces and of the police in their exercise of this right.

3. Nothing in this article shall authorize States Parties to the International Labour Organisation Convention of 1948 concerning Freedom of Association and Protection of the Right to Organize to take legislative measures which would prejudice, or to apply the law in such a manner as to prejudice, the guarantees provided for in that Convention.

The International Convention on the Elimination of All Forms of Racial Discrimination (see **RACIAL DISCRIMINATION**) deals with freedom of peaceful assembly and association from a different perspective in articles 4 and 5, as follows:

*Article 4.* States Parties condemn all propaganda and all organizations which are based on ideas or theories of superiority of one race or group of persons of one colour or ethnic origin, or which attempt to justify or promote racial hatred and discrimination in any form, and undertake to adopt immediate and positive measures designed to eradicate all incitement to, or acts of, such discrimination and, to this end, with due regard to the principles embodied in the Universal Declaration of Human Rights and the rights expressly set forth in article 5 of this Convention, *inter alia:*

(a) Shall declare an offence punishable by law all dissemination of ideas based on racial superiority or hatred, incitement to racial discrimination, as well as all acts of violence or incitement to such acts against any race or group of persons of another colour or ethnic origin, and also the provision of any assistance to racist activities, including the financing thereof;

(b) Shall declare illegal and prohibit organizations, and also organized and all other propaganda activities, which promote and incite racial discrimination, and shall recognize participation in such organizations or activities as an offence punishable by law;

(c) Shall not permit public authorities or public institutions, national or local, to promote or incite racial discrimination.

*Article 5.* In compliance with the fundamental obligations laid down in article 2 of this Convention, States Parties undertake to prohibit and to eliminate racial discrimination in all its forms and to guarantee the right of everyone, without distinction as to race, colour, or national or ethnic origin, to equality before the law, notably in the enjoyment of the following rights:

(d) Other civil rights, in particular: . . .

(ix) The right to peaceful assembly and association.

The **AMERICAN CONVENTION ON HUMAN RIGHTS,** open for acceptance by member States of the **ORGANIZATION OF AMERICAN STATES,** deals with the right of freedom of peaceful assembly and association in articles 15 and 16, as follows:

*Article 15.* The right of peaceful assembly, without arms, is recognized. No restrictions may be placed on the exercise of this right other than those imposed in conformity with the law necessary in a democratic society in the interest of national security, public safety or public order, or to protect public health or morals or the rights or freedoms of others.

*Article 16.* 1. Everyone has the right to associate freely for ideological, religious, political, economic, labor, social, cultural, sports, or other purposes.

2. The exercise of this right shall be subject only to such restrictions established by law as may be necessary in a democratic society, in the interest of national security, public safety or public order, or to protect public health or morals or the rights and freedoms of others.

3. The provisions of this article do not bar the imposition of legal restrictions, including even deprivation of the exer-

cise of the right of association, on members of the armed forces and the police.

The **AFRICAN CHARTER ON HUMAN AND PEOPLES' RIGHTS** also deals with the subject in two separate paragraphs, as follows:

*Article 10.* 1. Every individual shall have the right to free association provided that he abides by the law.
2. Subject to the obligation of solidarity provided for in Article 29 no one may be compelled to join an association.
*Article 11.* Every individual shall have the right to assemble freely with others. The exercise of this right shall be subject only to necessary restrictions provided for by law in particular those enacted in the interest of national security, the safety, health, ethics and rights and freedoms of others.

The **EUROPEAN CONVENTION ON HUMAN RIGHTS,** open for acceptance by member States of the **COUNCIL OF EUROPE,** contains the following provision:

*Article 11.* 1. Everyone has the right to freedom of peaceful assembly and to freedom of association with others, including the right to form and to join trade unions for the protection of his interests.
2. No restrictions shall be placed on the exercise of these rights other than such as are prescribed by law and are necessary in a democratic society in the interests of national security or public safety, for the prevention of disorder or crime, for the protection of health or morals or for the protection of the rights and freedoms of others. This article shall not prevent the imposition of lawful restrictions on the exercise of these rights by members of the armed forces, of the police or of the administration of the State.

Article 6 of the Declaration on the Elimination of All Forms of Intolerance and of Discrimination Based on Religion or Belief (see **FREEDOM OF THOUGHT, CONSCIENCE AND RELIGION**) provides that:

In accordance with article 1 of the present Declaration, and subject to the provisions of article 1, paragraph 3, the right to freedom of thought, conscience, religion or belief shall include, *inter alia,* the following freedoms:
(a) to worship or assemble in connection with a religion or belief, and to establish and maintain places for these purposes; ...
(e) to teach a religion in places suitable for these purposes; ...
(h) to observe days of rest and to celebrate holidays and ceremonies in accordance with the precepts of one's religion or belief;
(i) to establish and maintain communications with individuals and communities in matters of religion and belief at the national and international levels.

***INTERNATIONAL STUDIES.*** The Study of Discrimination in the Matter of Religious Rights and Practices, prepared by Mr. Arcot Krishnaswami (India), Special Rapporteur of the UN Sub-Commission on Prevention of Discrimination and Protection of Minorities (United Nations publication, Sales no. 60. XIV.2),

presents the following comments on article 20 of the Universal Declaration of Human Rights:

In view of the generality of the terms of this article, there can be no doubt that it extends to the sphere of religion or belief. However, certain facts relating to the two freedoms here involved—freedom of assembly on the one hand and freedom of association and the right to organize on the other hand—must be pointed out.

History and contemporary practice show a remarkable difference in the attitude of public authorities towards these two freedoms when they are applied in the field of religion or belief, and when they are applied in other fields. In many fields freedom of association and the right to organize have been more readily conceded than freedom of assembly. But in the field of religion, freedom of association and the right to organize have often been, and still are, denied or severely curtailed, whereas freedom of assembly in houses of worship has been recognized first, at least for the dominant religion, and later for a number of recognized—or even all—religions or beliefs. The difference is not accidental; public authorities consider that, in fields other than religion, there is less of a threat to public order and security in the existence of permanent organizations than in the congregation in one place of a large number of people. In the religious field, on the other hand, a meeting held for purposes related purely to matters of religion or belief does not generally present a threat to public order and security, whereas the establishment of a new and permanent organization may be considered dangerous because of the considerable impact which a religion or belief normally has upon its followers. Moreover, freedom of association and the right to organize may have quite a different meaning in the field of religion from that which they have in other fields: such questions as the structure of the religious organization and the management of its religious affairs are often, to a large extent, questions of dogma and therefore not matters of voluntary choice.

Although freedom of assembly for individuals of a particular faith does not raise such complicated issues as freedom of association and the right to organize, conflicts may arise even here between freedom of assembly and considerations of morality, public order, the general welfare, or respect for the rights and freedoms of others.

With regard to articles 4 and 5 of the International Convention on the Elimination of All Forms of Racial Discrimination, the UN **COMMITTEE ON THE ELIMINATION OF RACIAL DISCRIMINATION** has adopted a series of general recommendations. The first, approved at its fifth session, held from 14 to 25 February 1972, was as follows (UN Doc. A/8718, chap. IX A, general recommendation I):

On the basis of the consideration at its fifth session of reports submitted by States Parties under article 9 of the International Convention on the Elimination of All Forms of Racial Discrimination, the Committee found that the legislation of a number of States Parties did not include the provisions envisaged in article 4 (a) and (b) of the Convention, the implementation of which (with due regard to the principles embodied in the Universal Declaration of Human Rights and the rights expressly set forth in article 5 of the

Convention) is obligatory under the Convention for all States Parties.

The Committee accordingly recommends that the States Parties whose legislation was deficient in this respect should consider, in accordance with their national legislative procedures, the question of supplementing their legislation with provisions conforming to the requirements of article 4 (a) and (b) of the Convention.

One year later, the Committee, at its seventh session, held from 16 April to 4 May 1973, reaffirmed the earlier recommendation and requested States parties to the Convention (UN Doc. A/9018, chap. X, decision 3 [VII]):

1. to indicate what specific penal internal legislation designed to implement the provisions of article 4 (a) and (b) has been enacted in their respective countries and to transmit to the Secretary-General in one of the official languages the texts concerned as well as such provisions of general penal law as must be taken into account when applying such specific legislation;

2. where no such specific legislation has been enacted, to inform the Committee of the manner and the extent to which the provisions of the existing penal laws, as applied by the Courts, effectively implement their obligations under article 4 (a) and (b), and to transmit to the Secretary-General in one of the official languages the texts of those provisions. . . .

At its 32nd session, held from 5 to 23 August 1985, the Committee again reaffirmed general recommendation I. Noting that, in a number of States parties, the necessary legislation to implement article 4 of the Convention had not been enacted and that many States parties had not fulfilled all the requirements of article 4 (a) and (b) of the Convention and recalling that, in accordance with the first paragraph of article 4, States parties "undertake to adopt immediate and positive measures designed to eradicate all incitement to, or acts of, such discrimination" with due regard to the principles embodied in the Universal Declaration of Human Rights and the rights expressly set forth in article 5 of the Convention, the Committee recommended (UN Doc. A/40/18, chap. VII B, general recommendation VII): (1) that those States parties whose legislation does not satisfy the provisions of article 4 (a) and (b) of the Convention take the necessary steps with a view to satisfying the mandatory requirements of that article, and (2) that those States parties which had not done so inform the Committee more fully in their periodic reports of the manner and extent to which the provisions of article 4 (a) and (b) are effectively implemented and quote the relevant parts of the texts in their reports. The Committee further requested those States parties which had not done so to endeavor to provide in their periodic reports more information concerning decisions taken by the competent national tribunals and other State institutions

regarding acts of racial discrimination and in particular those offences dealt with in article 4 (a) and (b).

***TRADE UNION RIGHTS.*** The right to form and join trade unions is dealt with in both International Covenants on Human Rights primarily because these rights, although clearly economic and social in nature, constitute an important aspect of the right to freedom of peaceful assembly and association. The International Covenant on Economic, Social and Cultural Rights recognizes (article 8.1 [d]) the right to strike, but only if that right is exercised "in conformity with the laws of the particular country"—an appreciable restriction. No INTERNATIONAL LABOR ORGANIZATION (ILO) convention or recommendation recognizes the right to strike or defines the extent to which it may be exercised.

Within the United Nations system, the lead agency concerned with freedom of association and trade union rights is the ILO, which assumed major responsibilities in this field some five months before the proclamation of the Universal Declaration of Human Rights when its General Conference, on 9 July 1948, adopted the ILO Freedom of Association and Protection of the Right to Organize Convention. This instrument was followed closely by the ILO Right to Organize and Collective Bargaining Convention, 1949; and supplemented later by the ILO Workers' Representatives Convention (1971), the ILO Rural Workers' Organizations Convention (1975), and the ILO Labor Relations (Public Service) Convention (1978).

Under the Freedom of Association and Protection of the Right to Organize Convention, which entered into force on 4 July 1950, States parties guarantee:

(a) that workers and employers, without any distinction whatsoever, shall have the right to establish and, subject only to the rules of the organization concerned, to join organizations of their own choosing without previous authorization;

(b) that workers' and employers' organizations shall have the right to draw up their constitutions and rules, to elect their representatives in full freedom, to organize their administration and activities, and to formulate their programs;

(c) that the public authorities shall refrain from any interferences which would restrict this right or impede the lawful exercise thereof;

(d) that workers' and employers' organizations shall not be liable to be dissolved or suspended by administrative authority; and

(e) that workers' and employers' organizations shall have the right to establish and join federations and confederations, and that any such organization, federation, or confederation shall have the right to affiliate with international organizations of workers and employers.

Under the Right to Organize and Collective Bargaining Convention, which entered into force on 18 July 1951, States parties undertake to provide protection for workers against acts of anti-union discrimination and for workers' and employers' organizations against mutual acts of interference in their establishment, to establish appropriate machinery for this purpose, and to encourage and promote voluntary collective negotiation between employers or employers' organizations and workers' organizations.

Under the Workers' Representatives Convention, which entered into force on 30 June 1973, the term "workers' representatives" is defined as meaning persons recognized as such under national law or practice, whether they be trade union representatives—namely representatives designated or elected by trade unions or by members of such unions—or elected representatives, namely representatives freely elected by the workers of the undertaking whose functions do not include activities recognized as the exclusive prerogative of trade unions in the country concerned. It provides that such representatives shall enjoy effective protection against any act prejudicial to them, including dismissal, based on their status or activities as a workers' representative or on union membership or participation in union activities, insofar as they act in conformity with existing laws or collective agreements or other jointly agreed arrangements. It further provides that they will be afforded such facilities as may be appropriate in order to enable them to carry out their functions promptly and efficiently, as long as the granting of such facilities does not impair the efficient functioning of the undertaking concerned. It further provides that, where there exist in the same undertaking both trade union representatives and elected representatives, appropriate measures shall be taken, wherever necessary, to ensure that the existence of elected representatives is not used to undermine the position of the trade unions concerned or of their representatives.

The standards set out in the instruments mentioned above have been reinforced by a number of recommendations and resolutions adopted by the ILO General Conference concerning various aspects of labor–management relations (negotiation of collective agreements, voluntary conciliation and arbitration, cooperation at the level of the undertaking, consultations between employers and workers, and the right to strike).

**INTERNATIONAL SUPERVISION.** In 1949, the UN Economic and Social Council was informed, by the Director-General of the International Labor Organi-

zation, that the ILO Governing Body had approved the establishment of a factfinding and conciliation commission to provide international supervision of the realization of freedom of association. The Council (resolution 239 [IX]) called upon the UN Secretary-General and the ILO Director-General to work out a procedure for making the services of that commission available to the United Nations with respect to States members of the UN but not of the ILO. With their agreement, the Council formulated, in 1950, a procedure for dealing with allegations concerning infringements of trade union rights; it decided (resolution 277 [X]) that it would forward to the ILO Governing Body, for its consideration for referral to the Factfinding and Conciliation Commission, all such allegations received from governments or trade union or employers' organizations against ILO States members; and invited the ILO to refer to the Council any such allegations against a member of the United Nations which was not a member of ILO.

In 1951, the ILO Governing Body established its own Committee on Freedom of Association to make preliminary examinations of allegations concerning infringements of trade union rights and to advise it on the appropriateness of referring such allegations to the factfinding and conciliation commission.

Since their establishment, the Committee and the Fact-Finding and Conciliation Commission on Freedom of Association have examined complaints of violations of freedom of association without regard as to whether the State concerned has ratified the relevant ILO Conventions; and the Conciliation Commission may even examine complaints against non-member States if the State concerned agrees. The Committee on Freedom of Association has become one of the most active and effective human rights complaints bodies in the international system, and is often called upon to deal with situations of extreme urgency when workers' and employers' organizations or representatives are under fire from their governments. The Committee, and the ILO Director-General on its behalf, often intervenes to secure the release from prison of trade unionists, or permission for them to return from exile. It is also called upon to decide, from time to time, whether a particular kind of action is a proper trade union function.

The Fact-Finding and Conciliation Commission of the ILO has, on the other hand, tended to base its decisions on the results of on-the-spot missions, such as one which it undertook in South Africa in 1992. Its report on that mission was submitted to the UN Economic and Social Council in accordance with the established procedure.

The ILO's supervisory activity in the area of freedom of association is supplemented by intense training and assistance to members of workers' organizations and, to a slightly smaller extent, to those of employers.

Another international body active in the same field is the Ad Hoc Working Group of Experts on Southern Africa of the UN Commission on Human Rights, authorized as early as 1967 and 1968 by the Economic and Social Council (resolutions 1216 [XLII] and 1302 [XLIV] respectively) to deal with allegations concerning violations of human rights in South Africa, which at that time had ceased to be a member of the ILO. On the basis of reports prepared by that Working Group, the Council on 28 May 1988 condemned (resolution 1988/41) the increased repression of the independent black trade union movement by the (then) Government of South Africa, demanded that the persecution of black trade unionists and repression of the independent black trade union movement cease; requested immediate recognition of the right of the entire population of South Africa to exercise freedom of association and to form and join trade unions without impediment or discrimination of any kind; and demanded the immediate unconditional release of all trade unionists imprisoned for exercising their legitimate trade union rights.

On 14 February 1994, shortly before the new government headed by Nelson Mandela was installed in the country, the Commission on Human Rights requested its Ad Hoc Working Group of Experts (resolution 1994/110) "to continue, in cooperation with the Special Committee against Apartheid and other investigatory and monitoring bodies, to examine the situation regarding the violation of human rights in South Africa, including, in particular, reports of torture, ill-treatment and deaths of detainees, infringements of trade union rights, as well as the situation of women and children."

**SEE ALSO** *Civil and Political Rights; Freedom of Opinion and Expression; International Covenant on Civil and Political Rights; Political Rights.*

**BIBLIOGRAPHY.** Daniel, John, Frederieck de Vlaming, Nigel Hartley, Manfred Nowak, eds. *Academic Freedom 2: A Human Rights Report.* Geneva, Switzerland: World University Service, 1993. Scholarly monograph, in English.

International Centre for Trade Union Rights. *Trade Union Rights in the 1990s and Beyond.* Prague, Czechoslovakia: 1991. Report, in English.

International Confederation of Free Trade Unions. *Annual Survey on Violations of Trade Union Rights 1991.* Brussels, Belgium: 1991. Annual report, in English.

International Labor Office. *International Labor Standards: A Workers' Education Manual.* Geneva, Switzerland: 1990. Educational material, in English.

International Labor Organization. *Freedom of Association and Collective Bargaining: General Survey on the Reports relating to the Freedom of Association and Protection of the Right to Organize Convention, 1948 (No. 87) and the Right to Organize and Collective Bargaining Convention, 1949 (No. 98).* ILO report III, Part B. International Labour Conference, 58th session, Geneva, 1973.

————. *Freedom of Association and Collective Bargaining: General Survey by the Committee of Experts on the Application of Conventions and Recommendations.* ILO, report III (Part 4 B). International Labour Conference, 69th session, Geneva, 1983.

————. *Reports of the Governing Body, Committee on Freedom of Association.* First 12 reports published as appendices in the sixth to eighth reports of the ILO to the United Nations (1952–1954). Later reports published in the *ILO Official Bulletin.*

Perry, Michael S. *1990 Survey: Critique of Trade Union Rights in Countries Affiliated with the League of Arab States.* New York: Jewish Labour Committee, 1990. Report, in English.

Rosen, Sumner M. "Protecting Labour Rights in Market Economies," *Human Rights Quarterly* 14, no. 3 (Aug. 1992): 371–382. Scholarly article, in English.

Scoble, H. M., and L. S. Wiseberg. *Freedom of Association for Human Rights Organizations.* Washington, D.C.: Human Rights Internet, 1981. Monograph, in English.

Sedler, Robert A. "The Constitutional Protection of Freedom of Religion, Expression, and Association in Canada and the United States: A Comparative Analysis," *Case Western Reserve Journal of International Law* 20, no. 2 (Summer 1988): 577–621. Scholarly article, in English.

Servais, J. M. "Freedom of Association and the Inviolability of Trade Union Premises and Communications," *International Labour Review* 119, no. 2, (March–April 1980). Scholarly article, in English.

United Nations Advisory Services Program. *International Seminar on Freedom of Association.* ST/TAO/HR/12. New York: 1948.

Wiseberg, Laurie S. *Defending Human Rights Defenders: The Importance of Freedom of Association for Human Rights NGOs.* No. 3 in series *Essays on Human Rights and Democratic Development.* Montreal, Canada: International Centre for Human Rights and Democratic Development, 1993. Scholarly essay, in English and French.

**FREEDOM OF INFORMATION.** A most important element of freedom of expression and opinion is the right to freedom of information. While this right appears to enjoy almost universal acceptance in broad principle, a precise definition of its meaning and scope has eluded the international community for more than 50 years.

The **GENERAL ASSEMBLY** of the United Nations, at the first part of its first session, held in London in 1946, discussed a Philippine proposal to call an International Press Conference to ensure the establishment, operation, and movement of a free press throughout the world. On 9 February 1946, the Assembly instructed the Secretary-General (resolution 59 [I]) to place the question of the organization of such a conference on the agenda of the second part of that session.

In the resolution, the General Assembly declared

that "freedom of information is a fundamental right and is the touchstone of all the freedoms to which the United Nations is consecrated," and resolved "to authorize the holding of a conference of all Members of the United Nations on freedom of information." The **ECONOMIC AND SOCIAL COUNCIL** was instructed to undertake the convocation of such a conference, the purpose of which would be to formulate views concerning the rights, obligations, and practices that should be included in the concept of freedom of information. The Assembly specified that delegations to the conference should include, in each instance, persons actually engaged or experienced in press, radio, motion pictures, and other media for the dissemination of information.

Accordingly, the Council convened (resolution 74 [V]) the United Nations Conference on Freedom of Information, which met in Geneva in March–April 1948. The Conference prepared three draft Conventions—on the gathering and international transmission of news, on the institution of an international right of correction, and on freedom of information, as well as draft articles for inclusion in the **UNIVERSAL DECLARATION OF HUMAN RIGHTS** and the proposed Covenant on Human Rights. In addition, the Conference adopted a series of general principles to be applied in the promotion and protection of freedom of information. These general principles are as follows:

Whereas

Freedom of information is a fundamental right of the people, and is the touchstone of all the freedoms to which the United Nations is dedicated, without which world peace cannot well be preserved; and

Freedom of information carries the right to gather, transmit, and disseminate news anywhere and everywhere without fetters; and

Freedom of information depends for its validity upon the availability to the people of a diversity of sources of news and of opinion; and

Freedom of information further depends upon the willingness of the Press and other agencies of information to employ the privileges derived from the people without abuse, and to accept and comply with the obligation to seek the facts without prejudice and to spread knowledge without malicious intent; and

Freedom of information further depends upon the effective enforcement of recognized responsibilities,

The United Nations Conference on Freedom of Information Resolves, therefore,

1. That everyone shall have the right to freedom of thought and expression: this shall include freedom to hold opinions without interference; and to seek, receive and impart information and ideas by any means and regardless of frontiers;

2. That the right of news personnel to have the widest possible access to the sources of information, to travel unhampered in pursuit thereof, and to transmit copy without unreasonable or discriminatory limitations, should be guaranteed by action on the national and international plane;

3. That the exercise of these rights should be limited only by recognition of and respect for the rights of others, and the protection afforded by law to the freedom, welfare, and security of all;

4. That in order to prevent abuses of freedom of information, Governments in so far as they are able should support measures which will help to improve the quality of information and to make a diversity of news and opinion available to the people;

5. That it is the moral obligation of the Press and other agencies of information to seek the truth and report the facts, thereby contributing to the solution of the world's problems through free interchange of information bearing on them, promoting respect for human rights and fundamental freedoms without discrimination, fostering understanding and co-operation between peoples, and helping maintain international peace and security;

6. That this moral obligation, under the spur of public opinion, can be advanced through organizations and associations of journalists and through individual news personnel;

7. That encouragement should be given to the establishment and to the functioning within the territory of a State of one or more non-official organizations of persons employed in the collection and dissemination of information to the public, and that such organization or organizations should encourage the fulfilment *inter alia* of the following obligations by all individuals or organizations engaged in the collection and dissemination of information;

(a) To report facts without prejudice and in their proper context and to make comment without malicious intent;

(b) To facilitate the solution of the economic, social and humanitarian problems of the world as a whole through the free interchange of information bearing on such problems;

(c) To help promote respect for human rights and fundamental freedoms without discrimination;

(d) To help maintain international peace and security;

(e) To counteract the spreading of intentionally false or distorted reports which promote hatred or prejudice against States, persons or groups of different race, language, religion or philosophical conviction;

8. That observance of the obligations of the Press and other agencies of information, except those of a recognized legal nature, can also be effectively advanced by the people served by these instrumentalists, provided that news and opinion reach them through a diversity of sources and that the people have adequate means of obtaining and promoting a better performance from the Press and other agencies of information.

At the same time, the conference recognized (resolution no. 2) that the attainment of a just and lasting peace depends in great degree upon the free flow of true and honest information to all peoples and upon the spirit of responsibility with which all personnel of the press and other agencies of information seek the truth and report the facts; and that peoples have been misled and their mutual understanding seriously endangered by inaccurate reports, by defective or distorted presentation, and by deliberate or malicious misinterpretation of facts in various parts of the world. It condemned all propaganda either designed or likely to provoke or encourage any threat to the peace, breach of the peace, or act of aggression, and all distortion and falsification of news through whatever channels, private or governmental, since such activities can only promote misunderstanding and mistrust between the peoples of the world and thereby endanger the lasting peace which the United Nations is consecrated to maintain.

The Conference also noted that there are, in some countries, media of information which disseminate racial and national hatred and recommended that the governments of such countries should encourage the widest possible dissemination of free information through a diversity of sources as the best safeguard against the creation of racial and national hatred and prejudice, encourage suitable and effective non-legislative measures against the dissemination of such hatred and prejudice, and encourage dissemination of information promoting friendly relations between races and nations based upon the purposes and principles of the United Nations.

On 13 May 1949, the Assembly approved, but did not open for signature or ratification, the draft Convention on the International Transmission of News and Right of Correction, which consisted of an amalgamation of the provisions of the draft Convention on the Gathering and International Transmission of News and Convention on the Institution of an International Right of Correction. The Assembly, however, decided that the Convention it had approved should not be open for acceptance by member States until the Assembly had taken definite action on the draft Convention on Freedom of Information.

On 16 December 1952, the General Assembly decided to open for signature the substantive provisions of the Convention that it had approved in 1949. Consequently, it adopted and opened for signature the Convention on the International Right of Correction (resolution 630 [VII]). The Convention has been in force since 24 August 1962.

The "definite action" on the draft Convention on Freedom of Information which the General Assembly contemplated in 1949 had not been taken by the Assembly up to the end of 1994. However, a Committee established by the Assembly in 1950 prepared a new version of the draft Convention (Annex I), and on the basis of its work the Assembly's Third Committee approved the preamble and four operative paragraphs (Annex II). These texts are reproduced below. Up to the end of 1994, they had not been approved by the Assembly in plenary session.

In 1960, the Economic and Social Council prepared a draft Declaration on Freedom of Information and transmitted it to the Assembly for consideration. The draft declaration is reproduced below (Annex III). Up to the end of 1994, it had not been considered or approved by the Assembly.

## Annex I

### Preamble

The States Parties to this Convention,

Bearing in mind the Charter of the United Nations and the Universal Declaration of Human Rights,

Considering that freedom of expression, information and opinions are fundamental human rights,

Considering that the free interchange of accurate, objective and comprehensive information and of opinions, both in the national and in the international spheres, is essential to the causes of democracy and peace and for the achievement of political, social, cultural and economic progress,

Considering that freedom of information implies respect for the right of everyone to form an opinion through the fullest possible knowledge of the facts,

Desiring to co-operate fully with one another to guarantee these freedoms and to promote democratic institutions, friendly relations between States and peoples and the peace and welfare of mankind, and

Recognizing that in order to achieve these aims the media of information should be free from pressure or dictation, but that these media, by virtue of their power for influencing public opinion, bear to the peoples of the world a great responsibility, and have the duty to respect the truth and to promote understanding among nations,

Have accepted the following provisions:

*Article 1.* Subject to the provisions of this Convention,

(a) Each Contracting State undertakes to respect and protect the right of every person to have at his disposal diverse sources of information;

(b) Each Contracting State shall secure to its own nationals, and to such of the nationals of every other Contracting State as are lawfully within its territory, freedom to gather, receive and impart without governmental interference, save as provided in article 2, and regardless of frontiers, information and opinions orally, in writing or in print, in the form of art or by duly licensed visual or auditory devices;

(c) No Contracting State shall regulate or control the use or availability of any of the means of communication referred to in the preceding paragraph in any manner discriminating against any of its own nationals or of such of the nationals of any other Contracting State as are lawfully within its territory on political grounds or on the basis of their race, sex, language or religion.

*Article 2.* (a) The exercise of the freedom referred to in article 1 carries with it duties and responsibilities. It may, however, by subject only to such necessary restrictions as are clearly defined by law and applied in accordance with the law in respect of: national security and public order (*ordre public*); systematic dissemination of false reports harmful to friendly relations among nations and of expressions inciting to war or to national, racial or religious hatred; attacks on founders of religions; incitement to violence and crime; public health and morals; the rights, honour and reputation of others; and the fair administration of justice.

(b) The restrictions specified in the preceding paragraph shall not be deemed to justify the imposition by any State of prior censorship on news, comments and political opinions

F

and may not be used as grounds for restricting the right to criticize the Government.

*Article 3.* Nothing in the present Convention may be interpreted as limiting or derogating from any of the rights and freedoms to which the present Convention refers which may be guaranteed under the laws of any Contracting State or any Convention to which it is a party.

*Article 4.* The Contracting States recognize that the right of reply is a corollary of freedom of information and may establish appropriate means for safeguarding that right.

## Annex II

*Article 5.* Each Contracting State shall encourage the establishment and functioning within its territory of one or more non-official organizations of persons employed in the dissemination of information and opinions to the public, so that such persons may thus be encouraged to observe high standards of professional conduct and, in particular, the moral obligations to report facts without prejudice and in their proper context and to make comments without malicious intent, and thereby to:

(a) Facilitate the solution of the economic, social and humanitarian problems of the world as a whole, by the free exchange of information bearing on them;

(b) Help to promote respect for human rights and fundamental freedoms without discrimination;

(c) Help to maintain international peace and security;

(d) Counteract the dissemination of false or distorted reports which offend the national dignity of peoples or promote hatred or prejudice against other States, or against persons or groups of different race, language, religion or philosophical conviction; or

(e) Combat any form of propaganda for war.

*Article 6.* Nothing in the present Convention shall affect the right of any Contracting State to take measures which it deems necessary in order to safeguard its external financial position and balance of payments.

*Article 7.* Nothing in the present Convention shall affect the right of any Contracting State to take measures which it deems necessary in order:

(a) To develop and protect its national news enterprises until such time as they are fully developed;

(b) To prevent restrictive or monopolistic practices or agreements in restraint of the free flow of information and opinions;

(c) To control international broadcasting originating within its territory, provided that such measures may not be used as a means of preventing the entry, movement or residence of nationals of other Contracting States engaged in the gathering and transmission of information and opinions for dissemination to the public.

*Article 8.* Nothing in the present Convention shall prevent a Contracting State from reserving under its legislation to its own nationals the right to edit newspapers or news periodicals produced within its territory, or the right to own or operate telecommunication facilities, including radio broadcasting stations, within its territory.

*Article 9.* (a) Nothing in the present Convention shall limit the discretion of any Contracting State to refuse entry into its territory to any particular person, or to restrict the period of his residence therein.

(b) The present Convention shall not apply to any national of a Contracting State who, while not otherwise admissible into the territory or another Contracting State, is nevertheless admitted conditionally, in accordance with an agreement between that other Contracting State and the United Nations or a specialized agency thereof, or pursuant to a special arrangement made by that other Contracting State in order to facilitate the entry of such national.

*Article 10.* As between the Contracting States which become parties to any general agreement on human rights sponsored by the United Nations and containing provisions relating to the freedom of information, in so far as any provision of the general agreement relates to the same subject matter, the two provisions shall, whenever possible, be treated as complementary so that both provisions shall be applicable and neither shall narrow the effect of the other; but in any case of incompatibility the provisions of the general agreement shall prevail.

*Article 11.* (a) In time of war or other public emergency, a Contracting State may take measures derogating from its obligations under the present Convention to the extent strictly limited by the exigencies of the situation.

(b) Any Contracting State availing itself of this right of derogation shall promptly inform the Secretary-General of the United Nations of the measures which it has thus adopted and of the reasons therefor. It shall also inform him as and when the measures cease to operate.

*Article 12.* Any dispute between any two or more Contracting States concerning the interpretation or application of the present Convention which is not settled by negotiations shall be referred to the International Court of Justice for decision unless the Contracting States agree to another mode of settlement.

*Article 13.* (a) The present Convention shall be open for signature to all States Members of the United Nations, to every State invited to the United Nations Conference on Freedom of Information held at Geneva in 1948, and to every other State which the General Assembly may declare to be eligible.

(b) The present Convention shall be ratified by the States signatory hereto in conformity with their respective constitutional processes. The instruments of ratification shall be deposited with the Secretary-General of the United Nations.

*Article 14.* (a) The present Convention shall be open for accession to the States referred to in paragraph (a) of article 13.

(b) Accession shall be effected by the deposit of an instrument of accession with the Secretary-General of the United Nations.

*Article 15.* (a) The present Convention shall come into force on the thirtieth day following the date of deposit of the sixth instrument of ratification or accession.

(b) For each State ratifying or acceding to the Convention after the deposit of the sixth instrument of ratification or accession, the Convention shall enter into force thirty days after the deposit by such State of its instrument of ratification or accession.

*Article 16.* The provisions of the present Convention shall extend to or be applicable equally to a signatory metropolitan State and to all the territories, be they non-self-governing, trust or colonial territories, which are being administered or governed by such metropolitan State.

*Article 17.* (a) Any Contracting State may denounce the present Convention by notification of denunciation to the Secretary-General of the United Nations.

(b) Denunciation shall take effect six months after the date of receipt by the Secretary-General of the United Nations of the notification of denunciation.

*Article 18.* The Secretary-General of the United Nations

538

shall notify the States referred to in paragraph (a) of article 13 of the following:

(a)  Information received in accordance with article 11;

(b)  Signatures, ratifications and accessions received in accordance with articles 13 and 14;

(c)  The date upon which the present Convention comes into force in accordance with article 15;

(d)  Notifications received in accordance with article 17.

*Article 19.*  (a)  The present Convention, of which the Chinese, English, French, Russian and Spanish texts shall be equally authentic, shall be deposited in the archives of the United Nations.

(b)  The Secretary-General of the United Nations shall transmit a certified copy to each State referred to in paragraph (a) of article 13.

## Annex III
### Draft Declaration on Freedom of Information

#### Preamble

Whereas the development of friendly relations among nations and the promotion of respect for human rights and fundamental freedoms for all are basic purposes of the United Nations,

Whereas the Universal Declaration of Human Rights affirms: "Everyone has the right to freedom of opinion and expression; this right includes freedom to hold opinions without interference and to seek, receive and impart information and ideas through any media and regardless of frontiers",

Whereas freedom of information is essential to the respect for other human rights and fundamental freedoms, since no other liberty is secure if information cannot be freely sought, received and imparted,

Whereas freedom of information is also fundamental to peaceful and friendly relations between peoples and nations, since the erection of barriers to the free flow of information obstructs international understanding and thus impairs prospects for world peace,

Whereas newspapers, periodicals, books, radio, television, films and other media of information play an important role in enabling people to acquire the knowledge of public affairs necessary for the discharge of their responsibilities as citizens, and in shaping the attitudes of peoples and nations to each other, and therefore bear a great responsibility for conveying accurate information,

Now, therefore, the General Assembly,

Desiring to reaffirm the principles which should be upheld and observed and which domestic law and international Conventions and other instruments for the protection of freedom of information should support and endeavour to promote,

Proclaim this Declaration on Freedom of Information in proof of its determination that all peoples should fully enjoy free interchange of information and access to all media of expression:

*Article 1.*  The right to know and the right freely to seek the truth are inalienable and fundamental rights of man. Everyone has the right, individually and collectively, to seek, receive and impart information.

*Article 2.*  All Governments should pursue policies under which the free flow of information, within countries and across frontiers, will be protected. The right to seek and transmit information should be assured in order to enable the public to ascertain facts and appraise events.

*Article 3.*  Media of information should be employed in the service of the people. No Government or public or private body or interests should exercise such control over media for disseminating information as to prevent the existence of a diversity of sources of information or to deprive the individual of free access to such sources. The development of independent national media of information should be encouraged.

*Article 4.*  The exercise of these rights and freedoms entails special responsibilities and duties. Those who disseminate information must strive in good faith to ensure the accuracy of the facts reported and respect the rights and the dignity of nations, and of groups and individuals without distinction as to race, nationality or creed.

*Article 5.*  The rights and freedoms proclaimed above should be universally recognized and respected, and may in no case be exercised contrary to the purposes and principles of the United Nations. They should be subject only to such limitations as are determined by law solely for the purpose of securing due recognition and respect for the rights and freedoms of others and of meeting the just requirements of national security, public order, morality and the general welfare in a democratic society.

---

*DECLARATION OF WINDHOEK ON PROMOTING AN INDEPENDENT AND PLURALISTIC AFRICAN PRESS.*  A seminar on promoting an African Press, sponsored jointly by the United Nations and **UNESCO,** was held in Windhoek, Namibia, from 29 April to 3 May 1991. The Declaration of Windhoek, prepared by its participants, includes the following statements (UN Doc. A/CONF.157/PC/61/Add. 6):

1.  Consistent with article 19 of the Universal Declaration of Human Rights, the establishment, maintenance and fostering of an independent, pluralistic and free press is essential to the development and maintenance of democracy in a nation, and for economic development.

2.  By an independent press, we mean a press independent from governmental, political or economic control or from control of materials and infrastructure essential for the production and dissemination of newspapers, magazines and periodicals.

3.  By a pluralistic press, we mean the end of monopolies of any kind and the existence of the greatest possible number of newspapers, magazines and periodicals reflecting the widest possible range of opinion within the community.

4.  The welcome changes that an increasing number of African States are now undergoing towards multi-party democracies provide the climate in which an independent and pluralistic press can emerge.

5.  The worldwide trend towards democracy and freedom of information and expression is a fundamental contribution to the fulfilment of human aspirations.

6.  In Africa today, despite the positive developments in some countries, in many countries journalists, editors and publishers are victims of repression—they are murdered, arrested, detained and censored, and are restricted by economic and political pressures such as restrictions on newsprint, licensing systems which restrict the opportunity to publish, visa restrictions which prevent the free movement of journalists, restrictions on the exchange of news and information, and limitations on the circulation of newspapers

within countries and across national borders. In some countries, one-party States control the totality of information.

7. Today, at least 17 journalists, editors or publishers are in African prisons, and 48 African journalists were killed in the exercise of their profession between 1969 and 1990.

8. The General Assembly of the United Nations should include in the agenda of its next session an item on the declaration of censorship as a grave violation of human rights falling within the purview of the Commission on Human Rights.

9. African States should be encouraged to provide constitutional guarantees of freedom of the press and freedom of association.

10. To encourage and consolidate the positive changes taking place in Africa, and to counter the negative ones, the international community—specifically, international organizations (governmental as well as non-governmental), development agencies and professional associations—should as a matter of priority direct funding support towards the development and establishment of non-governmental newspapers, magazines and periodicals that reflect the society as a whole and the different points of view within the communities they serve.

11. All funding should aim to encourage pluralism as well as independence. As a consequence, the public media should be funded only where authorities guarantee a constitutional and effective freedom of information and expression and the independence of the press.

12. To assist in the preservation of the freedoms enumerated above, the establishment of truly independent, representative associations, syndicates or trade unions of journalists, and associations of editors and publishers, is a matter of priority in all the countries of Africa where such bodies do not now exist.

13. The national media and labour relations laws of African countries should be drafted in such a way as to ensure that such representative associations can exist and fulfil their important tasks in defence of press freedom.

14. As a sign of good faith, African Governments that have jailed journalists for their professional activities should free them immediately. Journalists who have had to leave their countries should be free to return to resume their professional activities.

15. Cooperation between publishers within Africa, and between publishers of the North and south (for example through the principle of twinning), should be encouraged and supported.

16. As a matter of urgency, the United Nations and UNESCO, and particularly the International Programme for the Development of Communication (IPDC), should initiate detailed research, in cooperation with governmental (especially UNDP) and non-governmental donor agencies, relevant non-governmental organizations and professional associations, into the following specific areas:

(i) identification of economic barriers to the establishment of news media outlets, including restrictive import duties, tariffs and quotas for such things as newsprint, printing equipment, and typesetting and word processing machinery, and taxes on the sale of newspapers, as a prelude to their removal;

(ii) training of journalists and managers and the availability of professional training institutions and courses;

(iii) legal barriers to the recognition and effective operation of trade unions or associations of journalists, editors and publishers;

(iv) a register of available funding from development

and other agencies, the conditions attaching to the release of such funds, and the methods of applying for them;

(v) the state of press freedom, country by country, in Africa.

17. In view of the importance of radio and television in the field of news and information, the United Nations and UNESCO are invited to recommend to the General Assembly and the General Conference the convening of a similar seminar of journalists and managers of radio and television services in Africa, to explore the possibility of applying similar concepts of independence and pluralism to these media.

18. The international community should contribute to the achievement and implementation of the initiatives and projects set out in the annex to this Declaration.

19. This Declaration should be presented by the Secretary-General of the United Nations to the United Nations General Assembly, and by the Director-General of UNESCO to the General Conference of UNESCO.

***DECLARATION OF ALMA ATA.*** A seminar on promoting independent and pluralistic Asian media, sponsored jointly by the United Nations and UNESCO, was held in Alma Ata, Kazakhstan, from 5 to 9 October 1992. The Declaration of Alma Ata, prepared by its participants, includes the following specific project proposals (UN Doc. AICONF. 157/PC/61/Add. 6):

In Asia and the Pacific, including the newly independent Central Asian Republics of the former Soviet Union, which identify with the Asian region, we seek practical application of the principles enshrined in the Declaration of Windhoek, in conjunction with relevant national and international professional organizations and relevant United Nations agencies, in the following specific project proposals and in the following fields:

*I. Legislation*

To give expert advice and legal drafting assistance to replace redundant press laws inherited at independence with laws that create enforceable rights to freedom of expression, freedom of opinion, access to information and freedom of the press; to abolish monopolies and all forms of discrimination in broadcasting and allocation of frequencies, in printing, newspaper and magazine distribution, and in newsprint production and distribution; and to abolish barriers to launching new publications, and discriminatory taxation.

*II. Training*

To promote a programme of national in-country and subregional seminars and/or training courses covering:

(a) professional skills, including extensive training and treatment of development issues;

(b) management, marketing and technical skills for the print and broadcast media;

(c) international principles of freedom of speech, freedom of expression, freedom of information and freedom of the press;

(d) international principles of freedom of association, management/staff relations, collective bargaining skills and the rights and responsibilities of representative associations of journalists, editors, broadcasters and publishers;

(e) principles of journalists' independence and the relationship between the editorial department of a newspaper, the board of directors and the administrative, advertising and commercial departments;

(f) appropriate curricula and training methodology for journalism training institutions (including tutor/lecturer exchange programmes) and special trainer programmes;

(g) access to training programmes and facilities;

(h) codes of conduct relating to advertising in the broadcast media;

(i) the rights of women in the media, and the rights of minority groups within societies.

*III. Free Flow of Information*

As a matter or urgency:

(a) To support the establishment of media resource centres in the Central Asian Republics where journalists and other media personnel can gain access to international news and information, manuals, textbooks and study materials, and where they can utilize desk-top publishing equipment to prepare material for publication;

(b) to assist independent media in the upgrading of production, content and presentation of television news and current affairs programmes through the provision of new technology and the exposure of staff to modern and alternative production techniques and values;

(c) to assist in the establishment of an inter-country news exchange service, in order to increase the flow of international, national and regional news and information to and from neighbouring countries, and to help upgrade technology and develop more extensive communication links.

*IV. Safety of Journalists*

To support the right of journalists to exercise their profession safely and to establish a protection centre (or centres) in the region to link up with the proposed IFEX (International Freedom of Information Exchange) Action Alert Network for Asia, aiming specifically at the safety of journalists and press freedom issues.

*V. Public Service Broadcasting*

To encourage the development of journalistically independent public service broadcasting in place of existing State-controlled broadcasting structures, and to promote the development of community radio.

To upgrade educational broadcasting through support for distance education programmes such as English-language instruction and formal and non-formal education, literacy programmes, and information programmes on AIDS, the environment, children, etc.

*VI. Professional Associations*

To assist Central Asian journalists, editors publishers and broadcasters in establishing truly independent representative associations, syndicates or trade unions of journalists and associations of editors, publishers and broadcasters where such bodies do not yet exist.

*VII. Special Economic Issues*

To identify economic barriers to the creation of new, independent media in Central Asia and in particular to arrange a feasibility study into alternative methods of acquiring and distributing newsprint, alternative facilities for printing and distributing newspapers and magazines and alternative means of obtaining low-interest credit.

The above projects, while identified as specific needs of Central Asian media, have region-wide applications. The participants call on UNESCO and its International Programme for the Development of Communication (IPDC), the United Nations, in particular the United Nations Economic and Social Commission for Asia and the Pacific (ESCAP), the United Nations Development Programme (UNDP), international professional organizations, donor countries, foundations and other interested parties to contribute generously to, and cooperate in, the Implementation of these initiatives.

The participants request that this Declaration be presented by the Secretary-General of the United Nations to the United Nations General Assembly, and by the Director-General of UNESCO to the General Conference of UNESCO.

*SEE ALSO* *Information and Communication Order; Journalists; Media.*

**BIBLIOGRAPHY.** Article 19. *Information, Freedom and Censorship World Report 1991*. London: Library Association Publishing, 1991. NGO report, in English.

————. *Truth From Below: The Emergent Press in Africa*. London: 1991. NGO report, in English.

Collins, Richard. "Broadcasting Policy for a Post Apartheid South Africa," *Critical Arts: A Journal for Cultural Studies* 6, no. 1 (1992): 26–51. Scholarly article, in English.

Committee to Protect Journalists. *Attacks on the Press, 1985: A Worldwide Survey*. New York: 1986–present. NGO annual report, in English.

Corrigall, Jim, Elaine Unterhalter, and Gillian Slovo. *Subverting Apartheid: Education, Information and Culture under Emergency Rule*. London: IDAF Publications, 1990. Monograph, in English.

Dag Hammarskjöld Foundation. "The Right to Inform and Be Informed: Another Development and the Media," *Development Dialogue* 1989 no. 2 (1991). Special issue, in English.

Eek, Hilding. *Report on Developments in the Field of Freedom of Information since 1954*. H. Eek, consultant, 1961 (E/3443). New York: United Nations, 1961.

Fund for Free Expression. *Freedom of Expression and the War: Press and Speech Restrictions in the Gulf and F.B.I. Activity in U.S. Raise First Amendment Issues*. New York: Human Rights Watch, 1991. NGO report, in English.

Hull, Elizabeth. *Taking Liberties: National Barriers to the Free Flow of Ideas*. New York: Praeger, 1990. Scholarly monograph, in English; bibliography, pp. 159–166.

Human Rights Watch. *Off Limits: Censorship and Corruption*. New York: 1991. NGO report, in English.

————. *Threats to Press Freedoms: A Report Prepared for the Free Media Seminar Commission on Security and Cooperation in Europe*. New York: 1993. NGO report, in English.

International Commission for the Study of Communication Problems. *From Freedom of Information to Free Flow of Information; From Free Flow of Information to the Free and Balanced Flow of Information*. (Microfiche 79s1036). Geneva, Switzerland: UNESCO, 1978.

————. *Towards a New International Information Order: The Right to Information in Relation to the New International Economic Order*. (ADS.78/CONF. 401/2). Geneva, Switzerland: UNESCO, 1978.

Linfield, Michael. *Freedom under Fire: U.S. Civil Liberties in Times of War*. Boston, MA, USA: South End Press, 1990. Scholarly monograph, in English; bibliography, pp. 259–268.

Lopez, Salvador P. *Freedom of Information*. S. P. Lopez, Special Rapporteur, Economic and Social Council (E/2426 and Add. 1–5). New York: United Nations, 1953.

Maja-Pearce, Adewale. "The Press in West Africa," *Index on Censorship* 19, no. 6 (June–July 1990): 44–80. NGO article, in English.

Reporters Sans Frontières. *La liberté de la presse dans le monde, rapport 1991–present*. Paris: 1991–present; *Freedom of the Press Throughout the World, 1993–Present*. London: John Libbey, 1993–present. NGO annual report, in French and English.

Shetreet, Shimon, ed. *Free Speech and National Security*. Dordrecht, the Netherlands: Martinus Nijhoff, 1991. Scholarly collective works, in English.

Strozzi, Girolamo. "Liberté de l'information de droit international" (Freedom of Information and International Law), *Revue générale de droit international public* 94, no. 4 (1990): 947–996. Scholarly article, in French.

Sussman, Leonard R. *Power, the Press and the Technology of Freedom: The Coming Age of ISDN*. New York: Freedom House, 1990. NGO monograph, in English.

Suttner, Raymond. "Freedom of Speech," *South African Journal on Human Rights* 6, Part 3 (1990): 372–393. Scholarly article, in English.

United Nations Ad Hoc Committee on Freedom of Information of the Commission on Human Rights. *Freedom of Information 1957*. (E/CN.4/762 and Corr. 1). New York: 1957.

United Nations Advisory Services Program. *Regional Seminars on Freedom of Information (1962 and 1964)*. (ST/TAO/HR13 and 20). New York: 1962, 1964.

United Nations Educational, Scientific, and Cultural Organization. *Activities of UNESCO in the Field of Freedom of Information during the Period March 1949–March 1950*. (E/CN.4/Sub. 1/109). Geneva, Switzerland: 1950.

## FREEDOM OF INFORMATION: EUROPEAN DECLARATION ON FREEDOM OF EXPRESSION AND INFORMATION (1982).

The Declaration draws attention to the fact that freedom of expression and information, as proclaimed in article 19 of the **UNIVERSAL DECLARATION OF HUMAN RIGHTS** and in article 10 of the **EUROPEAN CONVENTION ON HUMAN RIGHTS,** is a basic element of a democratic and pluralist society. It establishes goals for States to aim at with a view to ensuring the full enjoyment of this fundamental freedom and indicates the willingness of European Sates to endeavor to achieve those goals.

The Declaration was adopted by the Committee of Ministers of the **COUNCIL OF EUROPE,** convened at Strasbourg, on 29 April 1982. The text of the Declaration (Council of Europe Press Release C[82] 22) is as follows:

The member States of the Council of Europe,

1. Considering that the principles of genuine democracy, the rule of law and respect for human rights form the basis of their co-operation, and that the freedom of expression and information is a fundamental element of those principles;

2. Considering that this freedom has been proclaimed in national constitutions and international instruments, and in particular in Article 19 of the Universal Declaration of Human Rights and Article 10 of the European Convention on Human Rights;

3. Recalling that through that Convention they have taken steps for the collective enforcement of the freedom of expression and information by entrusting the supervision of its application to the organs provided for by the Convention;

4. Considering that the freedom of expression and information is necessary for the social, economic, cultural and political development of every human being, and constitutes a condition for the harmonious progress of social and cultural groups, nations and the international community;

5. Convinced that the continued development of information and communication technology should serve to further the right, regardless of frontiers, to express, to seek, to receive and to impart information and ideas, whatever their source;

6. Convinced that States have the duty to guard against infringements of the freedom of expression and information and should adopt policies designed to foster as much as possible a variety of media and a plurality of information sources, thereby allowing a plurality of ideas and opinions;

7. Noting that, in addition to the statutory measures referred to in the second paragraph of Article 10 of the European Convention on Human Rights, codes of ethics have been voluntarily established and are applied by professional organisations in the field of the mass media;

8. Aware that a free flow and wide circulation of information of all kinds across frontiers is an important factor for international understanding, for bringing peoples together and for the mutual enrichment of cultures,

I. Reiterate their firm attachment to the principles of freedom of expression and information as a basic element of democratic and pluralist society;

II. Declare that in the field of information and mass media they seek to achieve the following objectives:

(a) protection of the right of everyone, regardless of frontiers, to express himself, to seek and receive information and ideas, whatever their source, as well as to impart them under the conditions set out in Article 10 of the European Convention on Human Rights;

(b) absence of censorship or any arbitrary controls or constraints on participants in the information process, on media content or on the transmission and dissemination of information;

(c) the pursuit of an open information policy in the public sector, including access to information, in order to enhance the individual's understanding of, and his ability to discuss freely political, social, economic and cultural matters;

(d) the existence of a wide variety of independent and autonomous media, permitting the reflection of diversity of ideas and opinions;

(e) the availability and access on reasonable terms to adequate facilities for the domestic and international transmission and dissemination of information and ideas;

(f) the promotion of international co-operation and assistance, through public and private channels, with a view to fostering the free flow of information and improving communication infrastructures and expertise;

III. Resolve to intensify their co-operation in order:

(a) to defend the right of everyone to the exercise of the freedom of expression and information;

(b) to promote, through teaching and education, the effective exercise of the freedom of expression and information;

(c) to promote the free flow of information, thus contributing to international understanding, a better knowledge of convictions and traditions, respect for the diversity of opinions and the mutual enrichment of cultures;

(d) to share their experience and knowledge in the media field;

(e) to ensure that new information and communication techniques and services, where available, are effectively used to broaden the scope of freedom of expression and information.

**FREEDOM OF MOVEMENT AND RESIDENCE.**
The right to freedom of movement and residence is proclaimed in article 13 of the **UNIVERSAL DECLARATION OF HUMAN RIGHTS,** which reads:

*Article 13.* 1. Everyone has the right to freedom of movement and residence within the borders of each State.

2. Everyone has the right to leave any country, including his own, and to return to his country.

Freedom of movement and residence is also the subject of articles 12 and 13 of the **INTERNATIONAL COVENANT ON CIVIL AND POLITICAL RIGHTS,** which read as follows:

*Article 12.* 1. Everyone lawfully within the territory of a State shall, within that territory, have the right to liberty of movement and freedom to choose his residence.

2. Everyone shall be free to leave any country, including his own.

3. The above-mentioned rights shall not be subject to any restrictions except those which are provided by law, are necessary to protect national security, public order (*ordre public*), public health or morals or the rights and freedoms of others, and are consistent with the other rights recognized in the present Covenant.

4. No one shall be arbitrarily deprived of the right to enter his own country.

*Article 13.* An alien lawfully in the territory of a State Party to the present Covenant may be expelled therefrom only in pursuance of a decision reached in accordance with law and shall, except where compelling reasons of national security otherwise require, be allowed to submit the reasons against his expulsion and to have his case reviewed by, and be represented for the purpose before, the competent authority or a person or persons especially designated by the competent authority.

Discrimination denying freedom of movement and residence on the grounds of race, color, or national or ethnic origin is prohibited by article 5 of the International Convention on the Elimination of All Forms of Racial Discrimination (see **RACIAL DISCRIMINATION**), which reads in part as follows:

*Article 5.* In compliance with the fundamental obligations laid down in article 2, States Parties undertake to prohibit and to eliminate racial discrimination in all its forms and to guarantee the right of everyone, without distinction as to race, colour, or national or ethnic origin, to equality before the law, notably in the enjoyment of the following rights: . . .

(d) other civil rights, in particular:

(i) The right to freedom of movement and residence within the border of the State;

(ii) The right to leave any country, including his own, and to return to one's country. . . .

(f) The right of access to any place or service intended for use by the general public, such as transport, hotels, restaurants, cafes, theatres, and parks.

Discrimination denying freedom of movement and residence on the ground of sex is prohibited by article

15 of the Convention on the Elimination of All Forms of Discrimination Against Women, which reads in part as follows:

*Article 15.* 4. States parties shall accord to men and women the same rights with regard to the law relating to the movement of persons and the freedom to choose their residence and domicile.

The **AMERICAN CONVENTION ON HUMAN RIGHTS,** open for acceptance by members of the **ORGANIZATION OF AMERICAN STATES,** provides that:

*Article 22.* 1. Every person lawfully in the territory of a State Party has the right to move about in it, and to reside in it subject to the provisions of the law.

2. Every person has the right to leave any country freely, including his own.

3. The exercise of the foregoing rights may be restricted only pursuant to a law to the extent necessary in a democratic society to prevent crime or to protect national security, public safety, public order, public morals, public health, or the rights or freedoms of others.

4. The exercise of the rights recognized in paragraph 1 may also be restricted by law in designated zones for reasons of public interest.

The **AFRICAN CHARTER ON HUMAN AND PEOPLES' RIGHTS,** open for acceptance by members of the **ORGANIZATION OF AFRICAN UNITY,** contains the following provision:

*Article 12.* 1. Every individual shall have the right to freedom of movement and residence within the borders of a State provided he abides by the law.

2. Every individual shall have the right to leave any country including his own, and to return to his country. This right may only be subject to restrictions, provided for by law for the protection of national security, law and order, public health or morality.

3. Every individual shall have the right, when persecuted, to seek and obtain asylum in other countries in accordance with the laws of those countries and international Conventions.

4. A non-national legally admitted in a territory of a State Party to the present Charter, may only be expelled from it by virtue of a decision taken in accordance with the law.

5. The mass expulsion of non-nationals shall be prohibited. Mass expulsion shall be that which is aimed at national, racial, ethnic or religious groups.

The **EUROPEAN CONVENTION ON HUMAN RIGHTS: PROTOCOL IV** adds the following provisions to the text of the Convention:

*Article 2.* 1. Everyone lawfully within the territory of a State shall, within that territory, have the right to liberty of movement and freedom to choose his residence.

2. Everyone shall be free to leave any country, including his own.

3. No restrictions shall be placed on the exercise of these rights other than such as are in accordance with law and are

necessary in a democratic society in the interests of national security or public safety, for the maintenance of *ordre public,* for the prevention of crime, for the protection of health or morals, or for the protection of the rights and freedoms of others.

4. The rights set forth in paragraph 1 may also be subject, in particular areas, to restrictions imposed in accordance with law and justified by the public interest in a democratic society.

*Article 3.* 1. No one shall be expelled, by means either of an individual or of a collective measure, from the territory of the State of which he is a national.

2. No one shall be deprived of the right to enter the territory of the State of which he is a national.

*Article 4.* Collective expulsion of aliens is prohibited.

The **European Convention on Human Rights: Protocol VI** adds the following provision:

*Article 1.* 1. An alien lawfully resident in the territory of a State shall not be expelled therefrom except in pursuance of a decision reached in accordance with law and shall be allowed:

(a) to Submit reasons against his expulsion,

(b) to have his case reviewed, and

(c) to be represented for these purposes before the competent authority or a person or persons designated by that authority.

2. An alien may be expelled before the exercise of his rights under paragraph 1(a), (b) and (c) of this Article, when such expulsion is necessary in the interests of public order or is grounded on reasons of national security.

**EXPULSION.** After examining reports submitted by States parties on the International Covenant on Civil and Political Rights in accordance with article 40 of that instrument, the UN **Human Rights Committee** adopted, in 1986, general comments on article 13 of that instrument, as follows (UN Doc. A/41/40, Annex VI, paras. 9–10):

Many reports have given insufficient information on matters relevant to article 13. That article is applicable to all procedures aimed at the obligatory departure of an alien, whether described in national law as expulsion or otherwise. If such procedures entail arrest, the safeguards of the Covenant relating to deprivation of liberty (arts. 9 and 10) may also be applicable. If the arrest is for the particular purpose of extradition, other provisions of national and international law may apply. Normally an alien who is expelled must be allowed to leave for any country that agrees to take him. The particular rights of article 13 only protect those aliens who are lawfully in the territory of a State party. This means that national law concerning the requirements for entry and stay must be taken into account in determining the scope of that protection, and that illegal entrants and aliens who have stayed longer than the law or their permits allow, in particular, are not covered by its provisions. However, if the legality of an alien's entry or stay is in dispute, any decision on this point leading to his expulsion or deportation ought to be taken in accordance with article 13. It is for the competent authorities of the State party, in good faith and in the exercise of their powers, to apply and interpret the domestic law, observing, however, such requirements under the Covenant as equality before the law (art. 26).

Article 13 directly regulates only the procedure and not the substantive grounds for expulsion. However, by allowing only those carried out "in pursuance of a decision reached in accordance with law", its purpose is clearly to prevent arbitrary expulsions. On the other hand, it entitles each alien to a decision in his own case and, hence, article 13 would not be satisfied with laws or decisions providing for collective or mass expulsions. This understanding, in the opinion of the Committee, is confirmed by further provisions concerning the right to submit reasons against expulsion and to have the decision reviewed by and to be represented before the competent authority or someone designated by it. An alien must be given full facilities for pursuing his remedy against expulsion so that this right will in all the circumstances of his case be an effective one. The principles of article 13 relating to appeal against expulsion and the entitlement to review by a competent authority may only be departed from when "compelling reasons of national security" so require. Discrimination may not be made between different categories of aliens in the application of article 13.

*STUDY OF DISCRIMINATION IN RESPECT OF THE RIGHT OF EVERYONE TO LEAVE ANY COUNTRY, INCLUDING HIS OWN, AND TO RETURN TO HIS OWN COUNTRY.* In 1960, the UN Sub-Commission on Prevention of Discrimination and Protection of Minorities decided (resolution 5 [XII]) to initiate a study of discrimination in respect of the right of everyone to leave any country, including his own, and to return to his country, as provided in article 13, para. 2, of the Universal Declaration of Human Rights. Mr. Jose D. Ingles (Philippines), a member of the Sub-Commission, was appointed as Special Rapporteur to carry out the study.

The Special Rapporteur completed his study in 1963, and it was published the following year (UN publication, Sales no. 64.XIV.2). It concluded with proposals for action by States and by the international community which included the adoption of a series of principles. Draft principles, formulated by the Special Rapporteur, were set out in annex VI of the study. After examination by the Sub-Commission, the draft was forwarded to the Commission on Human Rights for further consideration and adoption.

However, it was only in 1973 that the study received the attention of the Commission on Human Rights and the **Economic and Social Council.** At that time, the Council took no action other than to request the Commission to deal with the subject further at three-year intervals.

In 1982, the Sub-Commission called upon one of its members, Mr. C. L. C. Mubanga-Chipoya (Zambia), to prepare an analysis of current trends and developments in respect of the right of everyone to leave any country, including his own, and to return to his country. The analysis (UN Doc. E/CN.4/Sub.2/1988/35 and Add. 1 and Corr. 1), Submitted to the Sub-Commission in 1988, included the Special Rapporteur's proposal for a revised set of draft principles, reproduced below.

At the request of the Sub-Commission (resolution 1988/39), the Secretary-General transmitted the revised draft principles to UN member States and to the intergovernmental and non-governmental organizations concerned for their comments. The comments received were presented to the Sub-Commission at its 1989 session (UN Doc. E/CN.4/Sub.2/1989/44).

After considering the draft declaration and comments thereon, the Sub-Commission requested the Secretary-General (resolution 1989/25) to prepare an analytical summary of them. It decided that it would establish, at its 1990 session, an open-ended working group with a view to preparing a revised version of the draft declaration for submission to its parent bodies.

The *Draft Declaration on Freedom and Non-Discrimination in Respect of the Right of Everyone to Leave any Country, including his Own, and to Return to his Country,* prepared by Special Rapporteur Mr. C. L. C. Mubanga-Chipoya, is as follows:

### Preamble

Whereas the peoples of the United Nations in the Charter solemnly reaffirmed their faith in fundamental human rights, in the dignity and worth of the human person, in the equal rights of men and women and of nations large and small, and expressed their determination to promote social progress and better standards of life in larger freedom,

Whereas the Charter declares that it is one of the purposes of the United Nations to promote and encourage universal respect and observance of human rights and fundamental freedoms for all without distinction as to race, sex, language or religion,

Recognizing that respect for human rights and fundamental freedoms is essential for peace, justice and well-being and is necessary to ensure the development of friendly relations and co-operation among all States,

Recalling that the Universal Declaration of Human Rights, the International Covenant on Civil and Political Rights, and the International Convention on the Elimination of All Forms of Racial Discrimination, as well as regional Conventions, recognize the fundamental principle, based on general international law, that everyone has the right to leave any country, including one's own, and to return to one's own country,

Emphasizing that the right of everyone to leave any country and to enter one's own country is indispensable for the full enjoyment of all civil, political, economic, social and culture rights and the free and untrammelled exercise of this right is a sure means of fostering mutual understanding, cooperation and beneficial exchanges among the peoples of the world so that they may practise tolerance and live together in peace as good neighbors,

Recognizing that an individual has duties to himself and to his family as well as to the community in which he lives and in which alone the full and free development of his personality is possible,

Concerned that the denial of this right is the cause of widespread human suffering, a source of international tensions, and an object of international concern,

Whereas this right can only be effectively guaranteed when formally acknowledged in national law consistent with the principles of the Charter of the United Nations, the Universal Declaration of Human Rights and the International Covenant on Civil and Political Rights,

Now therefore the following principles are hereby proclaimed as of universal application to ensure recognition and enjoyment of the right of everyone to leave any country, including his own, and to return to his country, and other related rights, and to prevent discrimination in respect of these rights and urges upon all nations the elaboration, implementation and enforcement of the following principles through effective international machinery and international laws and processes.

### Part I

### General Provisions

*Article 1.* Everyone has the right to leave any country, including one's own, and to enter one's own country, without distinction as to race, colour, sex, language, religion, political or other opinion, national or social origin, property, birth, marriage, age (except for minors not *sui juris* independently of their parents) or other status.

*Article 2.* (a) Every State shall adopt such legislative or other measures as may be necessary to ensure the full and effective enjoyment of the rights set forth in this Declaration.

(b) All laws, administrative regulations or other provisions affecting the enjoyment of these rights shall be published and made easily accessible.

(c) The conditions prescribed by law of administrative regulations for the exercise of this right shall be the same for all nationals of a country.

### Part II

### Right to Leave

*Article 3.* Every State shall recognize, implement and enforce, the right of any person to leave its territory, temporarily or permanently.

*Article 4.* In the implementation of the right to leave every State shall prevent adverse economic consequences through the "brain drain" and shall make bilateral and multilateral arrangements for the benefit of the developing countries concerned.

*Article 5.* No person nor members of his family shall be subjected to any sanction, penalty, official or unofficial reprisals or harassments for seeking to exercise or for exercising the right to leave a country, such as acts which adversely affect, *inter alia,* employment, housing, residence status of social, economic or educational benefits.

(a) No person shall be required to renounce his or her nationality in order to leave a country, nor shall a person be deprived of his nationality for seeking to exercise or for exercising his right to leave a country.

(b) No person shall be denied the right to leave a country on the grounds that that person wished to renounce or has renounced his or her nationality. . . .

*Article 7.* (a) No restriction may be imposed on the right to leave any country including one's own or to enter any country except those which are

(i) Provided by law;

(ii) Necessary to protect national security, "public order" (*ordre public*), public health or morals or the rights and freedoms of others;

(iii) Consistent with internationally recognized human rights and other international legal obligations.

Any such restriction shall be narrowly construed.

(b) Any restriction on the right to leave or enter shall be clear, specific and not subject to arbitrary application.

(c) A restriction shall be considered "necessary" only if it responds to a pressing public and social need, pursues a legitimate aim and is proportionate to that aim.

(d) A restriction based on "national security" may be invoked only in situations where the exercise of the right poses a clear, imminent and serious danger to the State. When this restriction is invoked on the grounds that an individual acquired military secrets, the restriction shall be applicable only for a limited time, appropriate to the specific circumstances, which should not be more than five years after the individual acquired such secrets.

(e) A restriction based on "public order" (*ordre public*) shall be directly related to the specific interest which is sought to be protected. "Public order" (*ordre public*) means the universally accepted fundamental principles, consistent with respect for human rights, on which democratic society is based.

(f) "Public health" may be invoked when there is a serious threat to the health of the population or individual members of the population.

(g) "Public morals" may be invoked when it is essential to the maintenance of respect for fundamental moral values of the community.

(h) A restriction based on "the rights and freedoms of others" shall not imply that relatives (except for parents with respect to minors not *sui juris*), employers or other persons may prevent, by withholding their consent, the departure (entry) of any person seeking to leave (to enter) a country.

*Article 8.* (a) No fees, taxes or other exactions shall be imposed for seeking to exercise or exercising the right to leave a country, with the exception of nominal fees related to travel documents.

(b) No deposit or other security shall be required to ensure the repatriation or return of any national.

(c) Currency or other economic controls shall not be used as a means of preventing any national from leaving his country.

(d) Any national prevented from leaving his country because of non-compliance with obligations towards the State, or towards another person, shall be allowed to make reasonable arrangements for satisfying these obligations.

*Article 9.* (a) Any person leaving a country shall be entitled to take out of that country

(i) His or her personal property, including household effects and property connected with the exercise of that person's profession or skills;

(ii) All other property or the proceeds thereof, subject only to the satisfaction of legal monetary obligations, such as maintenance obligations to family members, and to general controls imposed by law to safeguard the national economy, provided that such controls do not have the effect of denying the exercise of the right.

(b) Property or the proceeds thereof which cannot be taken out of the country shall remain in the possession of the departing owner, who shall be free to dispose of such property or proceeds within the country.

## Part III

### The Right to Learn

*Article 10.* (a) No one shall be deprived of the right to enter [to return to] his own country.

(b) The right of everyone to return to his country shall not be subject to any arbitrary restrictions.

(c) No person shall be deprived of nationality or citizenship in order to enforce exile or to prevent that person from exercising the right to enter his or her country.

(d) No entry visa or fees or taxes may be required to enter one's own country.

*Article 11.* Permanent legal residents who leave their country of residence shall not be denied the right to return to that country except for reasonable cause identical to those applicable under article 7 of this Declaration.

## Part IV

### The Right of a Foreigner to Leave the Country

*Article 12.* (a) Every foreigner has the right to leave the country of his sojourn.

(b) Every foreigner, legally within the territory of a country shall not be accorded lesser rights than a national in the exercise of his right to leave that country.

(c) The right of every foreigner to leave the country of his sojourn shall not be subject to any arbitrary restrictions.

(d) No foreigner shall be prevented from seeking the diplomatic assistance of his own country in order to ensure the enjoyment of his right to leave the country of his sojourn.

## Part V

### Travel Documents and Procedural Safeguards

*Article 13.* (a) Everyone has the right to obtain such travel or other documents as may be necessary to leave any country or to enter one's own country. No one shall be denied such documents and permits.

(b) Such documents shall be issued free of charge or subject only to nominal fees.

*Article 14.* (a) Any national procedures or requirements affecting the exercise of the rights set forth in this Declaration shall be established by law or administrative regulations adopted pursuant to law.

(b) No State shall refuse to issue the documents referred to in article 13 (a) or shall otherwise impede the exercise of the right to leave, on the grounds of the applicant's inability to present authorization to enter another country.

(c) Procedures for the issuance of the documents referred to in article 13 (a) shall be expeditious and shall not be unreasonably lengthy or burdensome.

(d) Everyone filing an application for any document referred to in article 13 (a) shall be entitled to obtain promptly a duly certified receipt for the application filed. Decisions regarding issuance of such documents shall be taken within a reasonable period of time specified by law. The applicant shall be promptly informed in writing of any decision denying, withdrawing, cancelling or postponing issuance of any such document; the specific reasons therefor; the facts upon which the decision is based; and the administrative or other remedies available to appeal the decision.

*Article 15.* The right to appeal to higher administrative or judicial authority shall be provided in all instances in which the right to leave or enter is denied. The appellant shall have a full opportunity to present the grounds for the appeal, to be represented by counsel of his or her choice, and to challenge the validity of any fact upon which a denial or restriction has been founded. The results of any appeal, specifying the reasons for the decision, shall be communicated promptly in writing to the appellant.

*Article 16.* Any person claiming violation of his rights set forth in this Declaration shall have effective recourse to a judicial or other independent tribunal to seek enforcement of those rights.

*Article 17.* (a) No State may impede communication by any person with an international organization outside the State with regard to the rights set forth in this Declaration. No sanction, penalty, reprisal or harassment may be imposed on anyone exercising this right of communication.

(b) No one shall be hindered in or penalized for communicating with or petitioning the United Nations or other intergovernmental or non-governmental organizations complaining of the denial of the rights set forth in this Declaration or seeking their assistance in the exercise of these rights.

(c) No one shall be penalized for or prevented from communicating with foreign consular or diplomatic officials with a view to obtaining travel documents or permits.

(d) A person who claims to be a national of another State shall not be prevented from seeking the assistance of that State in order to ensure his right to leave or return.

**Part VI**

**Final Provisions**

*Article 18.* The enjoyment of the rights set forth in this Declaration shall not be limited because of activities protected under internationally recognized human rights or other international legal obligations.

*Article 19.* Nothing in this Declaration shall be interpreted as implying for any State, group or person any right to engage in any activity or perform any act aimed at destroying any of the rights set forth herein or at limiting them to a greater extent than is provided for in this Declaration.

*Article 20.* The present Declaration shall not be interpreted to limit the enjoyment of any human right protected by international law.

The Sub-Commission was not able, at its 1988 session, to consider the final report of the Special Rapporteur or the preliminary draft Declaration, but decided to take them up at its 1989 session. Meanwhile, it transmitted the text of the draft Declaration to member States, specialized agencies, and other intergovernmental organizations for their comments.

At its 1990 session, the Sub-Commission set up an open-ended working group to complete the revision of the draft Declaration. In 1991, it transmitted the report of the working group (E/CN.4/Sub.2/1991/45) to the Commission on Human Rights and invited the Commission to provide comments and guidance on the issues mentioned therein. The requested comments and guidance had not been made available up to the end of 1994.

**BIBLIOGRAPHY.** Alternative Information Center. *The Right to Family Unity: The Denial of Residency to Spouses of Non-Jewish Citizens of Israel: A Preliminary Report by Israeli-Palestinian Project for Family Reunification.* Jerusalem, Israel: 1992. NGO report, in English.

Amnesty International. *The Imprisonment of Persons Seeking to Leave a Country or to Return to Their Own Country.* London: 1986. NGO report, in English.

Barist, J. O., C. Pell, E. Oshman, and M. E. Hamel. *Who May Leave: A Review of Soviet Practice Restricting Emigration on Grounds of Knowledge of "State Secrets" in Comparison with Standards of International Law and the Policies of Other States.* New York: National Conference on Soviet Jewry and White & Case, 1987. NGO report, in English.

Drinnon, Richard. *Keeper of Concentration Camps: Dillion S. Myer and American Racism.* Berkeley, CA, USA: University of California Press, 1987. Scholarly monograph, in English.

Ecumenical Commission for Displaced Families and Communities. *Primer: Displacement in the Philippines—Nature, Causes, Effects, Extent, Limits, Remedies and Victims' Rights.* Quezon City, Philippines: 1987. NGO manual, in English.

Helsinki Watch. *Destroying Ethnic Identity: The Kurds of Turkey—An Update.* New York: Human Rights Watch, 1988. NGO report, in English.

———. *Ten Years Later: Violation of the Helsinki Accords.* New York: Human Rights Watch, 1985. NGO report, in English.

International Gesellschaft fur Menschenrechte (International Society for Human Rights). *CSCE and Human Rights: Divided Families and the Denial of Freedom of Movement (Documentation).* Frankfurt/Main, FRG: 1987. NGO document collection, in English.

Plender, Richard, ed. *International Migration Law.* 2nd rev. ed. Dordrecht, the Netherlands: Martinus Nijhoff, 1988. Scholarly edited collection, in English.

Research-Action Institute for the Koreans in Japan. *Appeal of Cooperation for Establishment of the Right of Permanent Residents to Return to Their Country of Residence.* Tokyo, Japan: 1990. NGO statement, in English.

United Nations Sub-Commission on Prevention of Discrimination and Protection of Minorities. *Analysis of the Current Trends and Developments Regarding the Right to Leave Any Country, Including One's Own, and to Return to One's Country, and Some Other Rights or Considerations Arising Therefrom,* by C. L. C. Mubanga-Chipoya, Special Rapporteur of the Sub-Commission. New York: 1987 (UN Doc. E/CN.4/Sub.2/1987/10).

———. *Study of Discrimination in Respect of the Right of Everyone to Leave Any Country, Including His Own, and to Return to His Country,* by Jose D. Ingles, Special Rapporteur of the Sub-Commission. New York: n.d. (UN publication, Sales no. E.64.XIV.2).

**FREEDOM OF OPINION AND EXPRESSION.** This right is proclaimed in the **UNIVERSAL DECLARATION OF HUMAN RIGHTS** in the following terms:

*Article 19.* Everyone has the right to freedom of opinion and expression; this right includes freedom to hold opinions without interference and to seek, receive, and impart information and ideas through any media and regardless of frontiers.

Freedom of opinion and expression is dealt with in two articles of the **INTERNATIONAL COVENANT ON CIVIL AND POLITICAL RIGHTS,** as follows:

*Article 19.* 1. Everyone shall have the right to hold opinions without interference.

2. Everyone shall have the right to freedom of expression; this right shall include freedom to seek, receive and impart information and ideas of all kinds, regardless of frontiers, either orally, in writing or in print, in the form of art, or through any other media of his choice.

3. The exercise of the rights provided for in paragraph 2 of this article carries with it special duties and responsibilities. It may therefore be subject to certain restrictions, but these shall only be such as are provided by law and are necessary:

(a) For respect of the rights or reputations of others;

(b) For the protection of national security or of public order (*ordre public*), or of public health or morals.

*Article 20.* 1. Any propaganda for war shall be prohibited by law.

2. Any advocacy of national, racial or religious hatred that constitutes incitement to discrimination, hostility or violence shall be prohibited by law.

The International Convention on the Elimination of All Forms of Racial Discrimination (see **RACIAL DISCRIMINATION**) refers to freedom of opinion and expression in two of its articles, as follows:

*Article 4.* States Parties condemn all propaganda and all organizations which are based on ideas or theories of superiority of one race or group of persons of one colour or ethnic origin, or which attempt to justify or promote racial hatred and discrimination in any form, and undertake to adopt immediate and positive measures designed to eradicate all incitement to, or acts of, such discrimination, and to this end, with due regard to the principles embodied in the Universal Declaration of Human Rights and the rights expressly set forth in article 5 of this Convention, *inter alia*:

(a) Shall declare an offence punishable by law all dissemination of ideas based on racial superiority or hatred, incitement to racial discrimination, as well as acts of violence or incitement to such acts against any race or group of persons of another colour or ethnic origin, and also the provision of any assistance to racist activities, including the financing thereof;

(b) Shall declare illegal and prohibit organizations, and also organized and all other propaganda activities, which promote and incite racial discrimination, and shall recognize participation in such organizations or activities as an offence punishable by law;

(c) Shall not permit public authorities or public institutions, national or local, to promote or incite racial discrimination.

*Article 5.* In compliance with the fundamental obligations laid down in article 2, States Parties undertake to prohibit and to eliminate racial discrimination in all its forms and to guarantee the right of everyone, without distinction as to race, colour, or national or ethnic origin, to equality before the law, notably in the enjoyment of the following rights: . . .

(d) Other civil rights, in particular: . . .

(viii) The right to freedom of opinion and expression.

The **AMERICAN CONVENTION ON HUMAN RIGHTS,** open for acceptance by members of the **ORGANIZATION OF AMERICAN STATES,** provides that:

*Article 13.* 1. Everyone has the right to freedom of thought and expression. This right includes freedom to seek, receive, and impart information and ideas of all kinds, regardless of frontiers, either orally, in writing, in print, in the form of art, or through any other medium of one's choice.

2. The exercise of the right provided for in the foregoing paragraph shall not be subject to prior censorship but shall be subject to subsequent imposition of liability, which shall be expressly established by law to the extent necessary to ensure:

(a) respect for the rights or reputations of others; or

(b) the protection of national security, public order, or public health or morals.

3. The right of expression may not be restricted by indirect methods or means, such as the abuse of government or private controls over newsprint, radio broadcasting frequencies, or equipment used in the dissemination of information, or by any other means tending to impede the communication and circulation of ideas and opinions.

4. Notwithstanding the provisions of paragraph 2 above, public entertainments may be subject by law to prior censorship for the sole purpose of regulating access to them for the moral protection of childhood and adolescence.

5. Any propaganda for war and any advocacy of national, racial, or religious hatred that constitute incitements to lawless violence or to any other similar illegal action against any person or group of persons on any grounds including those of race, color, religion, language, or national origin shall be considered as offenses punishable by law.

The **AFRICAN CHARTER ON HUMAN AND PEOPLES' RIGHTS,** open for acceptance by members of the **ORGANIZATION OF AFRICAN UNITY,** provides that:

*Article 9.* (1) Every individual shall have the right to receive information.

(2) Every individual shall have the right to express and disseminate his opinions within the law.

The **EUROPEAN CONVENTION ON HUMAN RIGHTS,** open for acceptance by members of the **COUNCIL OF EUROPE,** provides that:

*Article 10.* (1) Everyone has the right to freedom of expression. This right shall include freedom to hold opinions and to receive and impart information and ideas without interference by public authority and regardless of frontiers. This Article shall not prevent States from requiring the licensing of broadcasting, television or cinema enterprises.

(2) The exercise of these freedoms, since it carries with it duties and responsibilities, may be subject to such formalities, conditions, restrictions or penalties as are prescribed by law and are necessary in a democratic society, in the interests of national security, territorial integrity or public safety, for the prevention of disorder or crime, for the protection of health or morals, for the protection of the reputation or rights of others, for preventing the disclosure of information received in confidence, or for maintaining the authority and impartiality of the judiciary.

After examining reports submitted by States parties to the International Convention on the Elimination of All Forces of Racial Discrimination in accordance with article 9 of that instrument, the UN **Committee on the Elimination of Racial Discrimination** adopted, in 1972, the following general comments concerning the implementation of article 4:

On the basis of the consideration at its fifth session of reports submitted by States Parties under article 9 of the International Convention on the Elimination of all Forms of Racial Discrimination, the Committee found that the legislation of a number of countries did not include the provisions envisaged under article 4 (a) and (b) of the Convention, the implementation of which (with due regard to the principles embodied in the Universal Declaration of Human Rights and the rights expressly set forth in article 5 of the Convention) is obligatory under the Convention for all States parties.

The Committee accordingly recommends that the States parties whose legislation is deficient in this request should consider, in accordance with their national legislative procedures, the question of supplementing their legislation with provisions conforming to the requirements of article 4 (a) and (b) of the Convention.

After examining reports submitted by States parties to the International Covenant on Civil and Political Rights in accordance with article 40 of that instrument, the UN **Human Rights Committee** adopted, in 1983, the following general comments relating to the implementation of articles 19 and 20:

*Comments on article 19.* 1. Paragraph 1 requires protection of "the right to hold opinions without interference". This is a right to which the Covenant permits no exception or restriction. The Committee would welcome information from States parties concerning paragraph 1.

2. Paragraph 2 requires protection of the right of freedom of expression, which includes not only freedom to "impart information and ideas of all kinds", but also freedom to "seek" and "receive" them "regardless of frontiers" and in whatever medium, "either orally, in writing or in print, in the form of art, or through any other media" of one's choice. Not all States parties have provided information concerning all aspects of the freedom of expression. For instance, little attention has so far been given to the fact that, because of the development of modern mass media, effective measures are necessary to prevent such control of the media as would interfere with the right of everyone to freedom of expression in a way that is not provided for in paragraph 3.

3. Many reports of States parties confine themselves to mentioning that freedom of expression is guaranteed under the Constitution or the law. However, in order to know the precise régime of freedom of expression, in law and in practice, the Committee needs in addition pertinent information about the rules which either define the scope of freedom of expression or which set forth certain restrictions, as well as any other conditions which in practice affect the exercise of this right. It is the interplay between the principle of freedom of expression and such limitations and restrictions which determines the actual scope of the individual's right.

4. Paragraph 3 expressly stresses that the exercise of the right to freedom of expression carries with it special duties and responsibilities and, for this reason, certain restrictions on that right are permitted which may relate either to the interests of other persons or to those of the community as a whole. However, when a State party imposes certain restrictions on the exercise of freedom of expression, these may not put in jeopardy the right itself. Paragraph 3 lays down conditions and it is only subject to these conditions that restrictions may be imposed: the restrictions must be "provided by law"; they may only be imposed for one of the purposes set out in subparagraphs (a) and (b) of paragraph 3; and they must be justified as being "necessary" for that State party for one of those purposes.

*Comments on article 20.* 1. Not all reports submitted by States parties have provided sufficient information as to the implementation of article 20 of the Covenant. In view of the nature of article 20, States parties are obliged to adopt the necessary legislative measures prohibiting the actions referred to therein. However, the reports have shown that in some States such actions are neither prohibited by law nor are appropriate efforts intended or made to prohibit them. Furthermore, many reports failed to give sufficient information concerning the relevant national legislation and practice.

2. Article 20 of the Covenant states that any propaganda for war and any advocacy of national, racial or religious hatred that constitutes incitement to discrimination, hostility or violence shall be prohibited by law. In the opinion of the Committee, these required prohibitions are fully compatible with the right of freedom of expression as contained in article 19, the exercise of which carries with it special duties and responsibilities. The prohibition under paragraph 1 extends to all forms of propaganda threatening or resulting in an act of aggression or breach of the peace contrary to the Charter of the United Nations, while paragraph 2 is directed against any advocacy of national, racial or religious hatred that constitutes incitement to discrimination, hostility or violence, whether such propaganda or advocacy has aims which are internal or external to the State concerned. The provisions of article 20, paragraph 1, do not prohibit advocacy of the sovereign right of self-defence or the right of peoples to self-determination and independence in accordance with the Charter. For article 20 to become fully effective there ought to be a law making it clear that propaganda and advocacy as described therein are contrary to public policy and providing for an appropriate sanction in case of violation. The Committee, therefore, believes that States parties which have not yet done so should take the measures necessary to fulfil the obligations contained in article 20, and should themselves refrain from any such propaganda or advocacy.

**DETENTION OF PERSONS WHO EXERCISE THE RIGHT TO FREEDOM OF OPINION AND EXPRESSION.** At annual sessions held between 1984 and 1988, the UN **Commission on Human Rights** repeatedly expressed its concern (resolutions 1984/26, 1985/17, 1986/46, 1987/32, and 1988/37) at the extensive occurrence in many parts of the world of detention of persons who exercise their right to freedom of opinion and expression as affirmed in the Universal Declaration of Human Rights and the International Covenant on Civil and Political Rights. The Commission appealed

**F**

to all States to ensure respect and support for the rights of all persons who exercise the right to freedom of opinion and expression and, where any persons have been detained solely for exercising that right, to release them immediately.

In resolution 1988/37, the Commission welcomed releases of persons who had been detained for exercising the right to freedom of opinion and expression, encouraged further progress in this regard in all parts of the world, and expressed the view that the effective promotion of the human rights of persons who exercise that right is of fundamental importance to the safeguarding of human dignity. The Commission requested its **SUB-COMMISSION ON PREVENTION OF DISCRIMINATION AND PROTECTION OF MINORITIES** to continue its consideration of the right to freedom of opinion and expression as laid down in the Covenant and to make recommendations to the Commission on further measures which may be required at the national and international levels to safeguard the right.

The Sub-Commission, at its 1988 session, requested one of its members (decision 1988/110), Mr. Danilo Türk (Yugoslavia), to prepare a working paper containing a proposal for carrying out the study aimed at clarifying the conceptual and methodological questions involved.

The Commission on Human Rights at its 1989 session took note (resolution 1989/31) of the Sub-Commission's request to Mr. Türk and decided to review the question of freedom of opinion and expression when Mr. Türk's study had been completed.

In the working paper that Mr. Türk later prepared for the Sub-Commission (UN Doc. E/CN.4/Sub.2/26), he made the following recommendations (paras. 63–65):

Given the nature of the *problematique* dealt with in this paper, I suggest that the Sub-Commission appoint two of its members to work jointly on the study entitled "The right to freedom of opinion and expression: current problems of its realization and measures necessary for its strengthening and promotion".

The priority area within the scope of the study should be the political dimension of the right to freedom of opinion and expression. Within this priority area special attention should be paid to the following problems:

(a) the legal regulation of limitations and restrictions constituting the actual régimes of the right to freedom of expression;

(b) the questions of negative sanctions affecting individuals who express their opinion (particular attention should be paid to the problems relating to detention);

(c) the question of measures (legislative, administrative and others) which are to be taken to promote, safeguard and strengthen the right to freedom of opinion and expression.

At the initial phase of the preparation of the study particular attention should be paid to the methods of collection of information and to other methodological questions.

Approving these recommendations, the Sub-Commission decided (resolution 1989/14) that, subject to approval of its parent bodies, it would entrust preparation of the study to two of its members, Mr. Türk and Mr. Louis Joinet (France).

The Commission, and later the Economic and Social Council, approved the Sub-Commission's request to Mr. Joinet and Mr. Türk to prepare a study on the right to freedom of opinion and expression.

The two Special Rapporteurs submitted their reports and their final conclusions and recommendations to the Sub-Commission at its 1990, 1991, and 1992 sessions (E/CN.4/Sub.2/1990/11, E/CN.4/Sub.2/1991/9, and E/CN.4/Sub.2/1992/9 and Add. 1). The Commission on Human Rights took note of them at its 1993 session (resolution 1993/45), at its 1994 session (resolution 1994/33), and again at its 1995 session (resolution 1995/41). In both resolutions it expressed its concern

(a) at the extensive occurrence of detention of, as well as discrimination, threats and acts of violence and harassment, including persecution and intimidation, directed at persons who exercise the right to freedom of opinion and expression as affirmed in the Universal Declaration of Human Rights and, where applicable, the International Covenant on Civil and Political Rights;

(b) at the extensive occurrence of detention of, as well as discrimination, threats and acts of violence and harassment, including persecution and intimidation, directed at persons who exercise the intrinsically linked rights to freedom of thought, conscience and religion, of peaceful assembly and freedom of association, and the right to take part in the conduct of public affairs as affirmed in the Universal Declaration of Human Rights and, where applicable, the International Covenant on Civil and Political Rights; and

(c) at the extensive occurrence in many parts of the world of detention of, as well as discrimination, threats and acts of violence and harassment, including persecution and intimidation, directed at persons who seek to promote and defend these rights and freedoms.

In both resolutions, also, the Commission appealed to all states "to ensure respect and support for the rights of all persons who exercise the right to freedom of opinion and expression, the rights to freedom of thought, conscience and religion, peaceful assembly and association, and the right to take part in the conduct of public affairs, or who seek to promote and defend these rights and freedoms and where any persons have been detained, subjected to violence or threats of violence and to harassment, including persecution and intimidation, solely for exercising these rights, . . . and to take the appropriate steps to ensure the immediate cessation of these acts and to create the conditions in which these acts may be less liable to occur." It also appealed to all States "to ensure that persons seeking to exercise these rights and freedoms are not discriminated against, particularly in such areas as employment, housing and social services.''

The Commission then requested its Chairman to appoint, for a period of three years, an individual of recognized international standing as its Special Rapporteur on the promotion and protection of the right to freedom of opinion and expression. It requested the Special Rapporteur ''to gather all relevant information, wherever it may occur, of discrimination against, threats or use of violence and harassment, including persecution and intimidation, directed at persons seeking to exercise or to promote the exercise of the right to freedom of opinion and expression.''

**BIBLIOGRAPHY.** Africa Watch (AW). *Academic Freedom and Human Rights Abuses in Africa.* New York: Human Rights Watch, 1991. NGO research report, in English.

Article 19. *The Article 19 Freedom of Expression Manual: International and Comparative Law, Standards and Procedures.* London: 1993. NGO handbook, in English.

———. *Information, Freedom and Censorship World Report 1991.* London: Library Association

Publishing, 1991. NGO report, in English.

———. *Forging War: The Media in Serbia, Croatia and Bosnia-Hercegovina.* London: 1994. NGO report, in English.

Coliver, Sandra, ed. *Striking a Balance: Hate Speech, Freedom of Expression and Non-Discrimination.* London: Article 19, International Centre against Censorship & Human Rights Centre, University of Essex, 1992. Collection of scholarly articles, in English; bibliography, pp. 402–412.

Committee to Protect Journalists. *Attacks on the Press, 1985–present: A Worldwide Survey.* New York: 1986–present. NGO annual report, in English.

d'Almeida Ribeiro, Angelo. *Implementation of the Declaration on the Elimination on All Forms of Intolerance and of Discrimination Based on Religion or Belief.* A. d'Almeido Ribeiro, Special Rapporteur of the Sub-Commission on Prevention of Discrimination and Protection of Minorities (E/CN.4/Sub.2/ 1987/35, 1988/45 and Add. 1, 1989/44, 1990/46, 1991/48, 1992/52, and 1993/62 and Corr. 1 and Add. 1).

Dinstein, Yoram, ed. "International Legal Colloquium on Racial and Religious Hatred and Group Libel," *Israel Yearbook on Human Rights* 22 (1993). Scholarly collection of articles, in English.

Eide, Asbjørn, and C. L. C. Mubanga-Chipoya. *Study of the Question of Conscientious Objection to Military Service.* A. Eide and C. L. C. Mubanga-Chipoya, Special Rapporteurs of the Sub-Commission on Prevention of Discrimination and Protection of Minorities (E/CN.4.Sub.2/1983/30).

Fund for Free Expression. *Freedom of Expression and the War: Press and Speech Restrictions in the Gulf and F.B.I. Activity in U.S. Raise First Amendment Issues.* New York: Human Rights Watch, 1991. NGO report, in English.

Hull, Elizabeth. *Taking Liberties: National Barriers to the Free Flow of Ideas.* New York: Praeger, 1990. Scholarly monograph, in English; bibliography, pp. 159–166.

Human Rights Watch. *Electrifying Speech: New Communications Technologies and Traditional Civil Liberties.* New York: 1992. NGO report, in English.

———. *Free Expression Project.* New York: irregular publication. NGO report (formerly "Fund for Free Expression"), in English.

———. *"Hate Speech" and Freedom of Expression.* New York: 1992. NGO report, in English.

Krishnaswami, A. *Study of Discrimination in the Matter of Religious Rights and Practices.* A. Krishnaswami, Special Rapporteur of the Sub-Commission on Prevention of Discrimination and Protection of Minorities. United Nations publication, Sales no. 60/XIV.2.

MacDonogh, Steve, ed. *The Rushdie Letters: Freedom to Speak, Freedom to Write.* Lincoln, NE, USA: University of Nebraska, 1993. Collection of articles, in English.

Odio-Benito, Elizabeth. *Elimination of All Forms of Intolerance and Discrimination Based on Religion or Belief.* E. Odio-Benito, Special Rapporteur of the Sub-Commission on Prevention of Discrimination and Protection of Minorities. United Nations publication, Sales no. E/89/XIV.3.

Owsley, Brian. "Racist Speech and 'Reasonable People': A Proposal for a Tort Remedy," *Columbia Human Rights Law Review* 24, no. 2 (Summer 1993): 323–367. Scholarly article, in English.

Shetreet, Shimon, ed. *Free Speech and National Security.* Dordrecht, the Netherlands: Martinus Nijhoff, 1991. Scholarly collective works, in English.

United Nations Advisory Services Program. *International Seminar on the Encouragement of Understanding, Tolerance and Respect in Matters Relating to Religion or Belief.* ST/HR/SER. A/ 16.

United Nations Educational, Scientific, and Cultural Organization. *Meeting of Experts on the Place of Human Rights in Cultural and Religious Traditions.* Bangkok: 1979. UNESCO SS.79/CONF. 607/10. Geneva, Switzerland: 1979.

**FREEDOM OF THOUGHT, CONSCIENCE AND RELIGION.** The right is proclaimed in the **UNIVERSAL DECLARATION OF HUMAN RIGHTS** in the following terms:

*Article 18.* Everyone has the right to freedom of thought, conscience and religion; this right includes freedom to change his religion or belief, and freedom, either alone or in community with others and in public or in private, to manifest his religion or belief in teaching, practice, worship and observance.

The **INTERNATIONAL COVENANT ON ECONOMIC, SOCIAL AND CULTURAL RIGHTS** contains the following provisions:

*Article 3.* 1. The States Parties to the present Covenant recognize the right of everyone to education. They agree that education shall be directed to the full development of the human personality and the sense of its dignity, and shall strengthen the respect for human rights and fundamental freedoms. They further agree that education shall enable all persons to participate effectively in a free society, promote understanding, tolerance and friendship among all nations and all racial, ethnic or religious groups, and further the activities of the United Nations for the maintenance of peace. . . .

3. The States Parties to the present Covenant undertake to have respect for the liberty of parents and, when applicable, legal guardians to choose for their children schools, other than those established by the public authorities, which

conform to such minimum educational standards as may be laid down or approved by the State and to ensure the religious and moral education of their children in conformity with their own convictions.

The **INTERNATIONAL COVENANT ON CIVIL AND POLITICAL RIGHTS** deals with this right in the following provisions:

*Article 18.* 1. Everyone shall have the right to freedom of thought, conscience and religion. This right shall include freedom to have or to adopt a religion or belief of his choice, and freedom, either individually or in community with others and in public or private, to manifest his religion or belief in worship, observance, practice and teaching.

2. No one shall be subject to coercion which would impair his freedom to have or to adopt a religion or belief of his choice.

3. Freedom to manifest one's religion or beliefs may be subject only to such limitations as are prescribed by law and are necessary to protect public safety, order, health, or morals or the fundamental rights and freedoms of others.

4. The States Parties to the present Covenant undertake to have respect for the liberty of parents and, when applicable, legal guardians to ensure the religious and moral education of their children in conformity with their own convictions.

Article 4 (2) of the Covenant specifies that no derogation may be made from article 18.

The International Convention on the Elimination of All Forms of Racial Discrimination (see **RACIAL DISCRIMINATION**) contains the following provision:

*Article 5.* In compliance with the fundamental obligations laid down in article 2 of this Convention, States parties undertake to prohibit and to eliminate racial discrimination in all its forms and to guarantee the right of everyone, without distinction as to race, colour, or national or ethnic origin, to equality before the law, notably in the enjoyment of the following rights: . . .

(d) other civil rights, in particular . . .

   (vii) The right to freedom of thought, conscience and religion.

The **AMERICAN CONVENTION ON HUMAN RIGHTS,** open for acceptance by member States of the **ORGANIZATION OF AMERICAN STATES,** provides that:

*Article 12.* 1. Everyone has the right to freedom of conscience and of religion. This right includes freedom to maintain or to change one's religion or beliefs, and freedom to profess or disseminate one's religion or beliefs, either individually or together with others, in public or in private.

2. No one shall be subject to restrictions that might impair his freedom to maintain or to change his religion or beliefs.

3. Freedom to manifest one's religion and beliefs may be subject only to the limitations prescribed by law that are necessary to protect public safety, order, health, or morals, or the rights or freedoms of others.

4. Parents or guardians, as the case may be, have the right to provide for the religious and moral education of their children or wards that is in accord with their own convictions.

The **AFRICAN CHARTER ON HUMAN AND PEOPLES' RIGHTS,** open for acceptance by member States of the **ORGANIZATION OF AFRICAN UNITY,** provides that:

*Article 8.* Freedom of conscience, the profession and free practice of religion shall be guaranteed. No one may, subject to law and order, be submitted to measures restricting the exercise of these freedoms.

The **EUROPEAN CONVENTION ON HUMAN RIGHTS,** open for acceptance by member States of the **COUNCIL OF EUROPE,** provides that:

*Article 9.* 1. Everyone has the right to freedom of thought, conscience and religion; this right includes freedom to change his religion or belief and freedom, either alone or in community with others and in public or private, to manifest his religion or belief, in worship, teaching, practice and observance.

2. Freedom to manifest one's religion or beliefs shall be subject only to such limitations as are prescribed by law and are necessary in a democratic society in the interests of public safety, for the protection of public order, health or morals, or for the protection of the rights and freedoms of others.

*HUMAN RIGHTS COMMITTEE COMMENTS ON ARTICLE 18.* The following General Comment No. 22 (48) on Article 18 of the International Covenant on Civil and Political Rights was adopted by the Human Rights Committee at its 1247th meeting (forty-eighth session) on 20 July 1993:

1. The right to freedom of thought, conscience and religion (which includes the freedom to hold beliefs) in article 18 (1) is far-reaching and profound; it encompasses freedom of thought on all matters, personal conviction and the commitment to religion or belief, whether manifested individually or in community with others. The Committee draws the attention of States parties to the fact that the freedom of thought and the freedom of conscience are protected equally with the freedom of religion and belief. The fundamental character of these freedoms is also reflected in the fact that this provision cannot be derogated from, even in time of public emergency, as stated in article 4 (2) of the Covenant.

2. Article 18 protects theistic, non-theistic and atheistic beliefs, as well as the right not to profess any religion or belief. The terms belief and religion are to be broadly construed. Article 18 is not limited in its application to traditional religions or to religions and beliefs with institutional characteristics or practices analogous to those of traditional religions. The Committee therefore views with concern any tendency to discriminate against any religion or belief for any reasons, including the fact that they are newly established or represent religious minorities that may be the subject of hostility by a predominant religious community.

3. Article 18 distinguishes the freedom of thought, conscience, religion or belief from the freedom to manifest religion or belief. It does not permit any limitations whatsoever on the freedom of thought and conscience or on the free-

dom to have or adopt a religion or belief of one's choice. These freedoms are protected unconditionally, as is the right of everyone to hold opinions without interference in article 19 (1). In accordance with articles 18 (2) and 17, no one can be compelled to reveal his thoughts or adherence to a religion or belief.

4. The freedom to manifest religion or belief may be exercised "either individually or in community with others and in public or private". The freedom to manifest religion or belief in worship, observance, practice and teaching encompasses a broad range of acts. The concept of worship extends to ritual and ceremonial acts giving direct expression to belief, as well as various practices integral to such acts, including the building of places of worship, the use of ritual formulas and objects, the display of symbols, and the observance of holidays and days of rest. The observance and practice of religion or belief may include not only ceremonial acts but also such customs as the observance of dietary regulations, the wearing of distinctive clothing or head coverings, participation in rituals associated with certain stages of life and the use of a particular language customarily spoken by a group. In addition, the practice and teaching of religion or belief includes acts integral to the conduct by religious groups of their basic affairs, such as, *inter alia,* the freedom to choose their religious leaders, priests and teachers, the freedom to establish seminaries or religious schools and the freedom to prepare and distribute religious texts or publications.

5. The Committee observes that the freedom to "have or to adopt" a religion or belief necessarily entails the freedom to choose a religion or belief, including, *inter alia,* the right to replace one's current religion or belief with another or to adopt atheistic views, as well as the right to retain one's religion or belief. Article 18 (2) bars coercion that would impair the right to have or adopt a religion or belief, including the use or threat of physical force or penal sanctions to compel believers or non-believers to adhere to their religious beliefs and congregations, to recant their religion or belief or to convert. Policies or practices having the same intention or effect, such as, for example, those restricting access to education, medical care, employment or the rights guaranteed by article 25 and other provisions of the Covenant are similarly inconsistent with article 18 (2). The same protection is enjoyed by holders of all beliefs of a non-religious nature.

6. The Committee is of the view that article 18 (4) permits public school instruction in subjects such as the general history of religions and ethics if it is given in a neutral and objective way. The liberty of parents or legal guardians to ensure that their children receive a religious and moral education in conformity with their own convictions, set forth in article 18 (4), is related to the guarantees of the freedom to teach a religion or belief stated in article 18 (1). The Committee notes that public education that includes instruction in a particular religion or belief is inconsistent with article 18 (4) unless provision is made for non-discriminatory exemptions or alternatives that would accommodate the wishes of parents and guardians.

7. According to article 20, no manifestation of religions or beliefs may amount to propaganda for war or advocacy of national, racial or religious hatred that constitutes incitement to discrimination, hostility or violence. As stated by the Committee in its general comment No. 11 (19), States parties are under the obligation to enact laws to prohibit such acts.

8. Article 18 (3) permits restrictions on the freedom to manifest religion or belief only if limitations are prescribed by law and are necessary to protect public safety, order, health or morals, or the fundamental rights and freedoms of others. The freedom from coercion to have or to adopt a religion or belief and the liberty of the parents and guardians to ensure religious and moral education cannot be restricted. In interpreting the scope of permissible limitation clauses, States parties should proceed from the need to protect the rights guaranteed under the Covenant, including the right to equality and non-discrimination on all grounds specified in articles 2, 3 and 26. Limitations imposed must be established by law and must not be applied in a manner that would vitiate the rights guaranteed in article 18. The Committee observes that article 18, paragraph 3, is to be strictly interpreted: restrictions are not allowed on grounds not specified there, even if they would be allowed as restrictions to other rights protected in the Covenant, such as national security. Limitations may be applied only for those purposes for which they were prescribed and must be directly related and proportionate to the specific need on which they are predicated. Restrictions may not be imposed for discriminatory purposes or applied in a discriminatory manner. The Committee observes that the concept of morals derives from many social, philosophical and religious traditions; consequently, limitations on the freedom to manifest a religion or belief for the purpose of protecting morals must be based on principles not deriving exclusively from a single tradition. Persons already subject to certain legitimate constraints, such as prisoners, continue to enjoy their rights to manifest their religion or belief to the fullest extent compatible with the specific nature of the constraint. States parties' reports should provide information on the full scope and effects of limitations under article 18 (3), both as a matter of law and of their application in specific circumstances.

9. The fact that a religion is recognized as a State religion or that it is established as official or traditional or that its followers comprise the majority of the population shall not result in any impairment of the enjoyment of any of the rights under the Covenant, including articles 18 and 27, nor in any discrimination against adherents of other religions or non-believers. In particular, certain measures discriminating against the latter, such as measures restricting eligibility for government service to members of the predominant religion or giving economic privileges to them or imposing special restrictions on the practice of other faiths, are not in accordance with the prohibition of discrimination based on religion or belief and the guarantee of equal protection under article 26. The measures contemplated by article 20, paragraph 2, of the Covenant constitute important safeguards against infringements of the rights of religious minorities and of other religious groups to exercise the rights guaranteed by articles 18 and 27, and against acts of violence or persecution directed toward those groups. The Committee wishes to be informed of measures taken by States parties concerned to protect the practices of all religions or beliefs from infringement and to protect their followers from discrimination. Similarly, information as to respect for the rights of religious minorities under article 27 is necessary for the Committee to assess the extent to which the freedom of thought, conscience, religion and belief has been implemented by States parties. States parties concerned should also include in their reports information relating to practices considered by their laws and jurisprudence to be punishable as blasphemous.

10. If a set of beliefs is treated as official ideology in constitutions, statutes, proclamations of the ruling parties, etc.,

or in actual practice, this shall not result in any impairment of the freedoms under article 18 or any other rights recognized under the Covenant nor in any discrimination against persons who do not accept the official ideology or who oppose it.

11. Many individuals have claimed the right to refuse to perform military service (conscientious objection) on the basis that such a right derives from their freedoms under article 18. In response to such claims, a growing number of States have in their laws exempted from compulsory military service citizens who genuinely hold religious or other beliefs that forbid the performance of military service and replaced it with alternative national service. The Covenant does not explicitly refer to a right of conscientious objection, but the Committee believes that such a right can be derived from article 18, inasmuch as the obligation to use lethal force may seriously conflict with the freedom of conscience and the right to manifest one's religion or belief. When this right is recognized by law or practice, there shall be no differentiation among conscientious objectors on the basis of the nature of their particular beliefs; likewise, there shall be no discrimination against conscientious objectors because they have failed to perform military service. The Committee invites States parties to report on the conditions under which persons can be exempted from military service on the basis of their rights under article 18 and on the nature and length of alternative national service.

*SPECIAL RAPPORTEURS' REPORTS.* The UN Sub-Commission on Prevention of Discrimination and Protection of Minorities, at its 1956 session, decided to examine the problem of religious discrimination and intolerance, and appointed one of its members, Mr. Arcot Krishnaswami (India), as its Special Rapporteur. Mr. Krishnaswami's *Study of Discrimination in the Matter of Religious Rights and Practices* was completed in 1959 and published in 1960 (UN publication, Sales no. 60/XIV.2). On the basis of the conclusions and recommendations set out therein, the Sub-Commission prepared and adopted a series of draft principles on freedom and non-discrimination in the matter of religious rights and practices (subsequently annexed to the published study), which the Sub-Commission proposed should serve as the basis for an international instrument on the subject.

It was not until 1981, however, that the General Assembly was able to adopt and proclaim (resolution 36/55) the Declaration on the Elimination of All Forms of Intolerance and of Discrimination Based on Religion or Belief. At its 1982 session, the General Assembly requested (resolution 37/187) the Commission on Human Rights to consider what measures may be necessary to implement the Declaration and to encourage understanding, tolerance, and respect in matters relating to freedom of religion or belief. The Commission called upon the Sub-Commission (resolution 1983/40) to undertake "a comprehensive and thorough study of the current dimensions of the prob-

lems of intolerance and of discrimination on grounds of religion or belief," using the Declaration as its terms of reference. The Sub-Commission subsequently appointed (resolution 1983/31) one of its members, Mrs. Elizabeth Odio-Benito (Costa Rica) as its Special Rapporteur for the study.

The Special Rapporteur's *Study of the Current Dimensions of the Problems of Intolerance and of Discrimination on Grounds of Religion or Belief* (UN Doc. E/CN.4/Sub.2/1987/26) was considered by the Sub-Commission at its 1987 session. In it, the Special Rapporteur concludes that intolerance and discrimination based on religion or belief subsist in the contemporary world and indeed that, in some areas, prejudice and bigotry have given rise to outright hatred, persecution, and repression. She describes, as the root causes of such intolerance and discrimination, such factors as ignorance and lack of understanding of the most basic elements of various religions or beliefs, each of which is unique in certain respects; the constant changes in public religiosity which have occurred and still occur in many parts of the world as a result of the struggle for predominance between the phenomenon of secularization or anti-clericalism and the phenomenon of sacralization or clericalism; developments of history, such as the use of religious intolerance and discrimination by colonial powers in their struggle to subdue and conquer the peoples of developing countries; and social tensions which deny their victims—such as foreign immigrants or migrant workers—the right to live in dignity and to enjoy the fruits of social progress.

The Sub-Commission (resolution 1987/33) welcomed the study's many recommendations, in particular those relating to the need for further study of major aspects of the issue, the need for the elaboration of a binding international instrument, and the need for educational measures to promote tolerance, understanding, and respect in matters relating to religion or belief. It requested its chairman to entrust one of its members with the following tasks: (a) to consider which aspects of this issue should be studied in greater depth by the Sub-Commission; (b) to examine information, recommendations, and other materials which may be Submitted by governments, specialized agencies, non-governmental organizations, academic institutions, and religious bodies; (c) to examine the issues and factors which should be considered before any definitive drafting of a binding international instrument takes place; and (d) to report to the Sub-Commission at its 1989 session. Mr. Theo van Boven (Netherlands) was assigned to this task.

The Sub-Commission further recommended that the Special Rapporteur's study should be published in all official languages of the United Nations and widely disseminated. On 10 March 1986, the UN Commission on Human Rights recalled (resolution 1986/20) that the General Assembly had requested it to consider measures to implement the Declaration on the Elimination of All Forms of Intolerance and of Discrimination Based on Religion or Belief and expressed deep concern about reports of incidents and governmental actions in all parts of the world which were inconsistent with the provisions of that Declaration. Accordingly, it decided to appoint its own Special Rapporteur to examine such incidents and actions and to recommend remedial measures, including the promotion of a dialogue between communities of religion or belief and their governments. Mr. Angelo Vidal d'Almeida Ribero (Portugal) was later designated as Special Rapporteur for the study.

In addition, the Special Rapporteur's annual reports (UN Docs. E/CN.4/1987/35, E/CN.4/1988/45 and Add. 1, E/CN.4/1989/44, E/CN.4/1990/46, E/CN.4/1991/48, E/CN.4/1992/52, and E/CN.4/1993/62 and Corr. 1 and Add. 1) were considered in detail by the Commission at each annual session. However, after Mr. Angelo Vidal D'Almeida resigned as Special Rapporteur, Mr. Abdelfattah Amor (Tunisia) was named to replace him as Special Rapporteur by the chairman of the Commission.

In his report to the 1994 session of the Commission, Mr. Abdelfattah Amor summarized the conclusions and recommendations he had formulated on the basis of the information available to him as follows (E/CN.4/1994/79, paras. 94–114):

The implementation of the Declaration on the Elimination of All Forms of Intolerance and of Discrimination Based on Religion or Belief cannot be dissociated from the general question of respect for all human rights, which cannot be truly promoted in the absence of democracy and development. Any measures for the promotion of human rights should therefore be simultaneous on the one hand with measures to establish, strengthen or protect democracy as the expression of human rights at the political level and, on the other hand, with measures to contain and gradually reduce extreme poverty and encourage the right of individuals and peoples to development as the expression of human rights and solidarity at the economic, social and cultural level. This means, as highlighted by the Vienna Conference, that "Democracy, development and respect for human rights and fundamental freedoms are interdependent and mutually reinforcing" and that "All human rights are universal, indivisible and interdependent and interrelated".

The Special Rapporteur is of the opinion that any dissociation of the elements of the trilogy—just as any selectivity in this area—would tend to have the effect of reducing human rights to a discourse of variable consistency and scope, which could have an unfavourable impact on the mechanisms and procedures for the protection of human rights.

If the protection of human rights constitutes a legitimate concern of the international community, it is because, on principle, it is above individual contingencies and considerations and because its motives as well as its aims are by definition supposed to be and to remain justifiable, since there is a need to ensure that human rights are respected and prevail over any selectivity and over any other aims and objectives. The Special Rapporteur is of the view that it would be desirable to give greater assurance to all the parties concerned by respect for human rights and to assert more forcefully the need to ensure the protection of human rights from anything which is alien to it by steering equally clear of interference, rejection or evasion.

Hatred, intolerance and acts of violence, including those prompted by religious extremism, could serve to create situations that might, in one way or another, threaten or jeopardize international peace and security and adversely affect the right of individuals and peoples to peace. It is the view of the Special Rapporteur that the preservation of the right to peace should encourage greater development of international solidarity, in order to stamp out religious extremism, whatever its source, by attacking both its causes and its effects, without selectivity or ambivalence, and by laying down initially a minimum set of joint rules and principles of conduct and behaviour in regard to religious extremism.

It is in the minds of men that all forms of intolerance and discrimination based on religion or belief take form and it is at this level much more than at others, that action should primarily be taken. Education could be the key instrument for combating discrimination and intolerance. It could contribute decisively to instilling the values that focus on human rights and on the emergence among both individuals and groups, of attitudes and behaviour exhibiting tolerance and non-discrimination and thus participate in disseminating the culture of human rights. The school has a vital place in the educational system. Therefore, special attention should be paid the world over to what school curricula impart about religious freedom or tolerance, particularly at the primary and secondary levels. The Special Rapporteur is deeply convinced that lasting progress with regard to tolerance and non-discrimination in the matter of religion or belief could be achieved first and foremost through the school. He feels that it would be appropriate to conduct a survey on the questions that fall within his mandate in the form in which they could appear in school curricula. Such a survey would make it possible to envisage the formulation, jointly with the specialized international organizations in particular, of an international school strategy to combat all forms of intolerance and discrimination based on religion or belief. This strategy could centre on the elaboration and realization of a minimum joint programme of tolerance and non-discrimination.

For the eighth consecutive year, the Special Rapporteur has examined, under the mandate entrusted to him by the Commission on Human Rights, incidents and governmental measures reported to be inconsistent with the provisions of the Declaration on the Elimination of All Forms of Intolerance and of Discrimination Based on Religion or Belief. This year, even more than in the past, he wishes to express to the Commission and to the States members of the Commission his deep gratitude for their trust in him so far and for the useful dialogue which he has already had with some of them.

In the course of the present reporting period, the Special Rapporteur has received many allegations concerning violations of the rights and freedoms set out in the Declaration and has thus been able to gain a clearer idea of the factors impeding its implementation. The positive dialogue which has been established between him and Governments over the years has enabled him to ask the latter specific questions about particular incidents or cases which involve their countries. He welcomes the spirit of openness, the readiness to

**F**

listen, the sustained interest, as well as the willingness to arrive at practical solutions which he encountered among the Governments approached during this initial phase of his mandate. He also appreciates the remarkable progress made in some countries such as Albania and Bulgaria in relation to various questions falling within his mandate. Lastly, he notes the efforts made by other countries such as the Republic of Moldova and Romania to contain and resolve the difficulties posed by some particular aspects of the religious problems which they face.

The Special Rapporteur wishes especially to thank the non-governmental organizations for the excellent cooperation which they have extended to him and to emphasize the dynamic role which they have played in order to provide him constantly with new information about the facts and problems falling within his mandate. The information communicated to the Special Rapporteur demonstrates the complexity of the concerns felt by the international community about the problems of religious intolerance and discrimination and the genuine efforts being made by many Governments to limit their impact. Once again, the role of the Special Rapporteur is not to make value judgements or level accusations but, rather, to identify factors or even certain of the causes underlying the emergence of phenomena of religious intolerance or discrimination. In this way, he hopes to mobilize the active sectors of international public opinion and to establish a lively dialogue with the Governments and any other parties concerned. With this in mind, the Special Rapporteur intends to use the internationally recognized norms on religious freedom as the basis for his action. These include article 18 of the Universal Declaration of Human Rights and of the International Covenant on Civil and Political Rights as well as all the provisions of the Declaration on the Elimination of All Forms of Intolerance and of Discrimination Based on Religion or Belief.

During the period covered by this report, the Special Rapporteur received complaints from virtually all regions of the world. Various manifestations of religious intolerance have persistently occurred in countries at varying stages of development and with different political and social systems and have not been confined to a particular faith. The majority of the complaints concerned violations of the right to have the religion or belief of one's choice, the right to change one's religion or belief, the right to manifest and practise one's religion in public and in private, the right to celebrate holidays and ceremonies in accordance with the precepts of one's religion or belief and the right not to be subjected to discrimination on these grounds by any State, institution or group of persons.

As the Special Rapporteur has already highlighted in his previous reports, the infringement of the rights mentioned above jeopardizes to a greater or lesser degree the enjoyment of other fundamental rights and freedoms enshrined in both the International Covenant on Civil and Political Rights and the International Covenant on Economic, Social and Cultural Rights, as well as in other human rights instruments. During the present reporting period, the failure to respect certain provisions of the Declaration has had a negative bearing on the right to life, the right to physical integrity and to liberty and security of person, the right to freedom of expression, the right not to be subjected to torture or other cruel, inhuman or degrading treatment or punishment, and the right not to be arbitrarily arrested or detained. The Special Rapporteur notes once again that the rights of persons belonging to religious minorities have been fre-

quently infringed, often seriously, in the countries with an official or clearly predominant majority religion.

Acts of religious intolerance and discrimination have been characterized in many instances by the use or threat of violence. In most cases, they have encompassed the prohibition and repression of external manifestations relating to a particular religion. Confrontations between followers of different faiths have continued as have physical and mental persecution. Many measures of intimidation and even of repression have been applied for belonging to a specific faith or religious group, such as arbitrary detention, heavy prison sentences or life imprisonment, ill-treatment or torture, abduction or even summary or extrajudicial execution. Persons who have converted to another, especially minority, religion, are still severely punished in several countries. The Special Rapporteur notes that there are sometimes veiled economic motives for these measures. In other countries, mandatory religious instruction has been given to persons not belonging to the official religion.

There is also the continuing application of administrative sanctions, against members of certain faiths, such as confiscation of their property, denial of access to education and employment, exclusion from public service and even denial of salaries and pensions. Certain legal safeguards such as the right to a fair trial and the right of legal recourse are no longer respected or applied by several countries. Members of the clergy belonging to various denominations have continued to be subjected to discrimination or even to receive death threats as a result of their work in their respective communities performed alongside their religious functions.

This year again, the Special Rapporteur has received alarming reports of acts of religious intolerance and discrimination being performed by groups of individuals with little or no intervention on the part of the security forces. He is also deeply concerned by allegations that the armed forces or members of the security services actually participated in such activities in a number of cases. The Special Rapporteur has once again noted how difficult it is to curb or eradicate the propagation of extremist or fanatical opinions and overcome the distrust inspired by members and groups of certain denominations or adherents to sects. Although the manifestations of religious discrimination and intolerance are often caused by a variety of historical, economic, social, political or cultural factors, they are frequently also the result of sectarian and dogmatic attitudes. In view of their possible adverse effect on the stability of international relations, the Special Rapporteur is of the opinion that States should remain particularly vigilant in this regard and make determined efforts to combat religious discrimination and intolerance at all levels.

The Special Rapporteur is deeply concerned over the developments in certain countries and in particular in Algeria, where there has been considerable loss of life. Academics, doctors, journalists and clergymen have also been the victims of violence which reflects attitudes and behaviour of intolerance and discrimination based on religion or belief. The Special Rapporteur is also concerned about the mounting tension and antagonism between religious groups or groups claiming to draw inspiration from certain religions in several regions of the world. In his report to the Commission on Human Rights at its forty-eighth session (E/CN.4/1992/52, paras. 47 and 48), the Special Rapporteur mentioned the attack on the sixteenth-century Babri Mosque in Ayodya, India, which was destroyed by Hindu militants at the beginning of December 1992 in clashes which had resulted in more than 1,000 deaths at the time when the report was being finalized. This deplorable incident also gave rise to the demolition of several Hindu temples in retaliation for this act as well as to violent outbursts of religious intolerance both in India and in a number of neighbouring and other countries. The Special Rapporteur is also deeply concerned over the allegations of systematic violations of a wide range of human rights of members of the Muslim community in Myanmar. He feels, furthermore, that greater attention should be paid in the immediate future to the increasing number of problems posed by religious extremism, religious minorities, and sects and other similar or comparable communities.

The Special Rapporteur also notes that the claims to recover their property by several churches in different Eastern European countries such as Romania have not been fully met, although appropriate legislation has been passed to that effect. He considers that the efforts made by the authorities concerned deserve to be supported and encouraged, all the more so as the changes needed are sometimes difficult to carry out and as, in any transition, real obstacles can be encountered which it will take time to eliminate.

The Special Rapporteur is deeply concerned over the critical situation that has developed in the territory of the former Yugoslavia. The policy of demolishing the religious and cultural foundations being pursued there, the destruction of religious and cultural monuments and sites as well as the threats to exterminate the Muslim community are a constant challenge to the entire international community. It is appropriate to point out, once again, that in his latest report to the Commission on Human Rights, the Special Rapporteur responsible for examining the human rights situation in the territory of the former Yugoslavia "reminds the world that the Muslim community in Bosnia and Herzegovina is threatened with extermination" (E/CN.4/1994/47, para. 228).

The Special Rapporteur considers that the establishment of interdenominational dialogue among the main religions is of the utmost importance in combating the injurious effects of the sectarian ideas and intransigence demonstrated by certain extremist groups and enhancing religious tolerance throughout the world. The prerequisite for the establishment of a climate conducive to dialogue and understanding is respect for the rule of law and the proper functioning of democratic institutions. The development of the rights and freedoms established in the 1981 Declaration on the Elimination of All Forms of Intolerance and of Discrimination Based on Religion or Belief can only be achieved if special attention is given to the complex underlying factors which hamper the exercise of these rights, for the sectarian ideas and intransigence and even manifestations of violence to which they can lead, are often linked to socioeconomic or other inequalities. The strengthening of democracy in many countries and the introduction of appropriate adjustments to the legal and constitutional framework will contribute decisively to the creation of a genuine climate of religious tolerance.

The Special Rapporteur wishes to reiterate the recommendations already formulated in his previous reports regarding the urgent need for those States which have not already done so to ratify the relevant international human rights instruments and to avail themselves of the existing machinery for monitoring the implementation of those instruments. States should also examine the possibility of preparing a binding international instrument on the elimination of intolerance and discrimination based on religion or belief, pursuant to the recommendations made by Mr. Theo van Boven, expert of the Sub-Commission on Prevention of Discrimination and Protection of Minorities, in his 1989 study (E/CN.4/Sub.2/1989/32). Such an instrument should not, however, be hastily drafted. Time is still needed to achieve significant progress in respect of religious freedom and to combat intolerance and discrimination based on religion or belief.

The Special Rapporteur hopes that States will remain alert to situations that could lead to violations of any of the rights embodied in the Declaration and take the necessary measures to detect any gaps in their own legislation and make the necessary amendments, and at the same time establish the constitutional and legal safeguards that will ensure the protection of these rights. In the event of incompatibility with the provisions of the Declaration, States should adopt the necessary constitutional and legislative amendments.

States should also make available to persons who are victims of acts of religious intolerance or discrimination the relevant administrative and judicial remedies in order to punish such incidents. States should also give thought to the conciliation mechanisms that should be established in order to settle disputes resulting from acts of religious intolerance. Since impunity encourages the persistence of human rights violations, States should also create national institutions to promote tolerance in matters of religion and belief. For example, the Government of India issued an ordinance, on 28 September 1993, for the establishment of a national human rights Commission, similar Commissions in several States of India as well as the relevant human rights courts.

The Special Rapporteur would like, finally, to highlight the crucial importance of disseminating the principles contained in the Declaration among lawmakers, judges, lawyers and civil servants in order to encourage them to work actively for the elimination of some of the root causes of religious intolerance. He would like to emphasize again the need to promote the ideals of tolerance and understanding in matters of religion and belief through education, the introduction of national and international human rights standards in school and university curricula and the proper training of teaching staff. Furthermore, he wishes to emphasize the important role of press conferences and information seminars in achieving the broadest possible dissemination of the principles set forth in the 1981 Declaration and encouraging understanding and tolerance in matters of religion and belief.

Having considered the Special Rapporteur's report and other relevant documentation at its 1994 session, the Commission on Human Rights, in resolution 1994/18 of 25 February 1994, reaffirmed that freedom of thought, conscience, religion, and belief is a human right derived from the inherent dignity of the human person and guaranteed to all without discrimination; noted with concern the continuing instances of hatred, intolerance, and acts of violence, based on intolerance of religion and belief and upon religious extremism which threaten all human rights and fundamental freedoms; and condemned all such acts, including those motivated by religious extremism in all its forms, as well as practices of discrimination against women.

The Commission urged States to ensure that their constitutional and legal systems provide adequate guarantees of freedom of thought, conscience, religion, and belief, including the provision of effective

# F

remedies where there is intolerance or discrimination based on religion or belief. Recognizing however that legislation alone is not enough to prevent violations of human rights, it urged all States to take appropriate measures to combat hatred, intolerance, and acts of violence, including those motivated by religious extremism, and to encourage understanding, tolerance, and respect in matters relating to freedom of religion or belief.

The Commission encouraged the Special Rapporteur to continue to examine incidents and governmental actions in all parts of the world that are incompatible with the provisions of the Declaration, and to recommend appropriate remedial measures.

SEE ALSO *Religious Discrimination.*

**BIBLIOGRAPHY.** Dinstein, Yoram. "Freedom of Religion and the Protection of Religious Minorities," *Israel Yearbook on Human Rights* 20 (1990): 155–179. Scholarly article, in English.

Goy, Raymond. "La garantie européenne de la liberté de religion: l'article 9 de la Convention de Rome," *Revue du droit public* 107 (1991): 5–59. Scholarly article, in French.

Lerner, Natan. *Group Rights and Discrimination in International Law.* Dordrecht, the Netherlands: Martinus Nijhoff, 1991. Scholarly monograph, in English.

Matscher, Franz, ed. *The Prohibition of Torture and Freedom of Religion and Conscience: Comparative Aspects.* Kehl am Rhein, Austria: N.P. Engel Verlag, 1991. Scholarly monograph, in English and German.

Mayer, Ann Elizabeth. *Islam and Human Rights: Tradition and Politics.* San Francisco, CA, USA: Westview Press, 1991. Scholarly monograph, in English. (Published also by Pinter Press, London, 1991.)

Rahman, Anika. "Religious Rights Versus Women's Rights in India: A Test Case for International Human Rights Law," *Columbia Journal of Transnational Law* 28, no. 2 (1990): 473–498. Scholarly article, in English.

Salzberg, John P. *The Question of a United Nations Convention on Religious Tolerance.* Washington, D.C.: 1990. Report, in English.

Van Boven, Theo. "Advances and Obstacles in Building Understanding and Respect between People of Diverse Religions and Beliefs," *Human Rights Quarterly* 13, no. 4 (1991): 437–449. Scholarly article, in English.

## FREEDOM OF THOUGHT, CONSCIENCE AND RELIGION: DECLARATION ON THE ELIMINATION OF ALL FORMS OF INTOLERANCE AND OF DISCRIMINATION BASED ON RELIGION OR BELIEF, UN (1981).

The Declaration elaborates upon the meaning of the principles of non-discrimination and equality before the law as applied to the right to freedom of thought, conscience, religion, and belief. It aims at promoting understanding, tolerance, and friendship for all religions or beliefs, whether theistic, non-theistic, or atheistic. It was adopted by the UN

GENERAL ASSEMBLY on 25 November 1981 (resolution 36/55). The text is as follows:

The General Assembly,

Considering that one of the basic principles of the Charter of the United Nations is that of the dignity and equality inherent in all human beings, and that all Member States have pledged themselves to take joint and separate action in co-operation with the United Nations to promote and encourage universal respect for and observance of human rights and fundamental freedoms for all, without distinction as to race, sex, language or religion,

Considering that the Universal Declaration of Human Rights and the International Covenants on Human Rights proclaim the principles of non-discrimination and equality before the law and the right to freedom of thought, conscience, religion or belief,

Considering that the disregard and infringement of human rights and fundamental freedoms, in particular of the right to freedom of thought, conscience, religion or whatever belief, have brought, directly or indirectly, wars and great suffering to mankind, especially where they serve as a means of foreign interference in the internal affairs of other States and amount to kindling hatred between peoples and nations,

Considering that religion or belief, for anyone who professes either, is one of the fundamental elements in his conception of life and that freedom of religion or belief should be fully respected and guaranteed,

Considering that it is essential to promote understanding, tolerance and respect in matters relating to freedom of religion or belief and to ensure that the use of religion or belief for ends inconsistent with the Charter, other relevant instruments of the United Nations and the purposes and principles of the present Declaration is inadmissible,

Convinced that freedom of religion or belief should also contribute to the attainment of the goals of world peace, social justice and friendship among peoples and to the elimination of ideologies or practices of colonialism and racial discrimination,

Noting with satisfaction the adoption of several, and the coming into force of some, conventions, under the aegis of the United Nations and of the specialized agencies, for the elimination of various forms of discrimination,

Concerned by manifestations of intolerance and by the existence of discrimination in matters of religion or belief still in evidence in some areas of the world,

Resolved to adopt all necessary measures for the speedy elimination of such intolerance in all its forms and manifestations and to prevent and combat discrimination on the grounds of religion or belief,

Proclaims this Declaration on the Elimination of All Forms of Intolerance and of Discrimination Based on Religion or Belief:

*Article 1.* 1. Everyone shall have the right to freedom of thought, conscience and religion. This right shall include freedom to have a religion or whatever belief of his choice, and freedom, either individually or in community with others and in public or private, to manifest his religion or belief in worship, observance, practice and teaching.

2. No one shall be subject to coercion which would impair his freedom to have a religion or belief of his choice.

3. Freedom to manifest one's religion or belief may be subject only to such limitations as are prescribed by law and

are necessary to protect public safety, order, health or morals or the fundamental rights and freedoms of others.

*Article 2.* 1. No one shall be subject to discrimination by any State, institution, group of persons or person on the grounds of religion or belief.

2. For the purposes of the present Declaration, the expression "intolerance and discrimination based on religion or belief" means any distinction, exclusion, restriction or preference based on religion or belief and having as its purpose or as its effect nullification or impairment of the recognition, enjoyment or exercise of human rights and fundamental freedoms on an equal basis.

*Article 3.* Discrimination between human beings on the grounds of religion or belief constitutes an affront to human dignity and a disavowal of the principles of the Charter of the United Nations, and shall be condemned as a violation of the human rights and fundamental freedoms proclaimed in the Universal Declaration of Human Rights and enunciated in detail in the International Covenants on Human Rights, and as an obstacle to friendly and peaceful relations between nations.

*Article 4.* 1. All States shall take effective measures to prevent and eliminate discrimination on the grounds of religion or belief in the recognition, exercise and enjoyment of human rights and fundamental freedoms in all fields of civil, economic, political, social and cultural life.

2. All States shall make all efforts to enact or rescind legislation where necessary to prohibit any such discrimination, and to take all appropriate measures to combat intolerance on the grounds of religion or belief in this matter.

*Article 5.* 1. The parents or, as the case may be, the legal guardians of the child have the right to organize the life within the family in accordance with their religion or belief and bearing in mind the moral education in which they believe the child should be brought up.

2. Every child shall enjoy the right to have access to education in the matter of religion or belief in accordance with the wishes of his parents or, as the case may be, legal guardians, and shall not be compelled to receive teaching on religion or belief against the wishes of his parents or legal guardians, the best interests of the child being the guiding principle.

3. The child shall be protected from any form of discrimination on the grounds of religion or belief. He shall be brought up in a spirit of understanding, tolerance, friendship among peoples, peace and universal brotherhood, respect for freedom of religion or belief of others, and in full consciousness that his energy and talents should be devoted to the service of his fellow men.

4. In the case of a child who is not under the care either of his parents or of legal guardians, due account shall be taken of their expressed wishes or of any other proof of their wishes in the matter of religion or belief, the best interests of the child being the guiding principle.

5. Practices of a religion or belief in which a child is brought up must not be injurious to his physical or mental health or to his full development, taking into account article 1, paragraph 3, of the present Declaration.

*Article 6.* In accordance with article 1 of the present Declaration, and subject to the provisions of article 1, paragraph 3, the right to freedom of thought, conscience, religion or belief shall include, *inter alia*, the following freedoms:

(a) To worship or assemble in connection with a religion or belief, and to establish and maintain places for these purposes;

(b) To establish and maintain appropriate charitable or humanitarian institutions;

(c) To make, acquire and use to an adequate extent the necessary articles and materials related to the rites or customs of a religion or belief;

(d) To write, issue and disseminate relevant publications in these areas;

(e) To teach a religion or belief in places suitable for these purposes;

(f) To solicit and receive voluntary financial and other contributions from individuals and institutions;

(g) To train, appoint, elect or designate by succession appropriate leaders called for by the requirements and standards of any religion or belief;

(h) To observe days of rest and to celebrate holidays and ceremonies in accordance with the precepts of one's religion or belief;

(i) To establish and maintain communications with individuals and communities in matters of religion or belief at the national and international levels.

*Article 7.* The rights and freedoms set forth in the present Declaration shall be accorded in national legislations in such a manner that everyone shall be able to avail himself of such rights and freedoms in practice.

*Article 8.* Nothing in the present Declaration shall be construed as restricting or derogating from any right defined in the Universal Declaration of Human Rights and the International Covenants on Human Rights.

**FREEDOM-TO-WRITE AWARD.** This annual award, established in 1987, honors two writers who have fought for freedom of expression. Selection is made by the PEN Freedom-to-Write Committee, which campaigns against censorship both in the USA and abroad.

The 1994 awards were presented to two men serving prison sentences for exercising their right to freedom of expression. Edip Polat is a Kurdish writer and biologist who has published five books about Kurdish concerns and advocates Kurdish causes. He is currently serving a sentence for producing "separatist propaganda" in his book *We Made Each Dawn a Newraz,* which describes his experiences in a Turkish military prison. The second recipient was Doan Viet Hoat, a Vietnamese journalist and scholar, who was sentenced in 1993 to 20 years in prison for his role in publishing the newsletter "Freedom Forum," which advocates freedom of speech and release of all political prisoners. As of the end of 1994, both men were still imprisoned.

For more information, contact: PEN American Center, 568 Broadway, New York, NY 10012, USA. Telephone: (212) 334-1660. Fax: (212) 334-2181.

**FRIED, ALFRED HERMANN (1864–1921).** This co-recipient of the 1911 **NOBEL PEACE PRIZE** was cited by the Nobel Committee as "the most industrious literary pacifist of the past 20 years." An Austrian book-seller and publisher by profession, Fried was an ardent believer that international legal and political organizations could end war. To this end, he founded the German and Austrian Peace Societies. He also edited several journals, including *Die Waffen Nieder,* which he co-founded with another Nobel Peace Prize winner, **BERTHA VON SUTTNER**; and *Die Friedenswarte,* the most influential pacifist journal of its time.

In addition to his work with the German and Austrian Peace Societies, Fried also was a member of the **INTERNATIONAL PEACE BUREAU,** the International Conciliation for Central Europe, and the International Union of the Press for Peace.

During World War I, Fried was accused by Austria of treason because of his ardent pacifism; he fled to Switzerland where he worked with prisoners of war.

*BIBLIOGRAPHY.* Gray, Tony. *Champions of Peace.* London: Paddington Press, 1976.

Schlessinger, Bernard S., and June H. Schlessinger, eds. *Who's Who of Nobel Prize Winners.* Phoenix, AZ, USA: Oryx Press, 1991.

## FRIENDS WORLD COMMITTEE FOR CONSULTATION.

An international non-governmental organization in consultative status with the UN **ECONOMIC AND SOCIAL COUNCIL** (Category II), and with **UNESCO, UNICEF,** and UNCTAD, the Committee coordinates the work of Quaker organizations in 80 countries and territories. It maintains regional section offices for Africa, the Americas, Asia-West Pacific, and Europe and the Near East. The Committee also has UN representation in New York and Geneva.

The Committee was established in September 1937 in Swarthmore, Pennsylvania (USA) at a worldwide conference of the Religious Society of Friends, to encourage the spiritual life and solidarity of Quakers everywhere and to promote understanding between Friends and members of other faiths. It works to ensure human rights, disarmament, and resolution of conflicts, with an emphasis on the rights of minority peoples, the welfare of refugees, the promotion of conscientious objection, and education in disarmament and world peace.

FWCC's publications include the *Quaker Information Network* (issued six times a year) and *Friends World News* (issued two times a year). In addition, individual national Peace and Service organizations issue their own publications concerning human rights' issues.

Friends World Committee for Consultation. Address: 4 Byng Place, London WC1E 7JH, UK. Telephone: (44-71) 388-0497. Secretary-General: Thomas F. Taylor.

# G

**GABON.** The Gabonese Republic is a country in western Africa, on the Atlantic Ocean. It has borders with Cameroon, Congo, and Equatorial Guinea. It achieved independence from France in 1960 and became a member of the United Nations the same year. Its population is estimated to be 1,115,000. Ethnic groups include the Fang people, who constitute one-third of its population, and numerous tribal groups. Languages commonly used are French (official) and a variety of Bantu tongues. Christianity (Roman Catholic, 64%; Protestant faiths, 19%) is the predominant religion; Animism and other faiths make up the remaining 17%. Literacy is estimated at 65%.

The government (1994) took the form of a republic. The president, elected by popular vote for a term of seven years, is head of State; the premier, appointed by him, is head of government. Legislation is prepared by the 120-member unicameral National Assembly. The predominant political party is the Gabonese Democratic Party. After anti-government demonstrations, one-party rule ended in elections in 1990. A new constitution was enacted in 1991.

An abundance of natural resources and an influx of foreign investment capital have made Gabon one of the most prosperous countries in western Africa.

*BIBLIOGRAPHY.* Agbabiaka, Tunde. "Gabon: 25 Years After," *West Africa,* 9 September 1985. News article, in English.

"Gabon: Opponents Granted Clemency," *West Africa,* 30 June 1986. News article, in English.

**GAMBIA.** The Republic of the Gambia is a country in western Africa, on the Atlantic Ocean. It is surrounded on three sides by Senegal. It achieved independence from Great Britain in 1965 and became a member of the United Nations the same year. Its population is estimated to be 916,000. Ethnic groups include a number of tribal populations. Languages in common use include English (official) and tribal vernaculars. Religions practiced include Islam (85%), Animism (13%), and Christianity (2%). Literacy is estimated at 20%.

The government (1994) took the form of a republic and member of the Commonwealth. In the Gambia, executive authority is exercised by the president, who is elected by popular vote and serves for a term of five years. Legislation is prepared by the 35-member unicameral House of Representatives; the president selects his vice president and cabinet from among its members. The predominant political party is the People's Progressive Party. In July 1994, the president since elections in 1970, Sir Dawda Jawara, was ousted in a bloodless coup by soldiers who proceeded to suspend the constitution, impose a curfew, and establish a Provisional Council of the Armed Forces. Senior military officers attempted to overthrow this military government in November 1994 and were arrested when they failed.

***RIGHT OF DEROGATION.*** Questions have been raised concerning the provisions of section 26 of the Gambian constitution, which permit derogation from the right to non-discrimination during a period of public emergency. The government has explained to the UN **HUMAN RIGHTS COMMITTEE** that

what article 26 is designed to do is to enable the Government to deal effectively with any threat to the security or the integrity of the nation that may be posed by the actions of any particular religious, tribal or racial group. Such situations have arisen before in several countries. Where there is such a threat from any such group it is obvious that any action taken by the Government to remedy the situation will be directed at that particular group, not out of any desire to discrimination against that group, but in fulfilment of the duty of the State to preserve order, security and the integrity of the nation. Furthermore such action by the State can only be of a temporary nature and is only authorized during a period of public emergency. . . .

***REPORT OF THE UN COMMITTEE ON ECONOMIC, SOCIAL AND CULTURAL RIGHTS.*** Although the Government of the Gambia, a State Party to the International Covenant on Economic, Social and Cultural Rights, had not submitted its report to the Committee on Economic, Social and Cultural Rights as required under articles 16 and 17 of the Covenant, the Committee examined the state of implementation of the Covenant in that country at its tenth session and adopted the following concluding observations at its twenty-third meeting, held on 18 May 1994 (E/C.12/1994/9):

## A. Review of the Implementation of the Covenant

1. At its seventh session, the Committee on Economic, Social and Cultural Rights decided to proceed to a consideration of the state of implementation of the Covenant on Economic, Social and Cultural Rights in a number of States parties which, despite many requests to do so, have not fulfilled their reporting obligations under articles 16 and 17 of the Covenant.

2. The purpose of the reporting system established by the Covenant is for the States parties to report to the competent monitoring body, the Committee on Economic, Social and Cultural Rights, and through it, to the Economic and Social Council, on the measures which they have adopted, the progress made, and the difficulties encountered in achieving the observance of the rights recognized in the Covenant. Non-performance by a State party of its reporting obligations, in addition to constituting a breach of the Covenant, creates a severe obstacle for the fulfilment of the Committee's functions. Nevertheless, the Committee has to perform its supervisory role in such cases, and must do so on the basis of all reliable information available to it.

3. In situations in which a government has not supplied the Committee with any information as to how it evaluates its own compliance with its obligations under the Covenant, the Committee has to base its observations on a variety of materials stemming from both intergovernmental and non-governmental sources, while the former provide mainly statistical information and apply important economic and social indicators, the information gathered from the relevant academic literature, from non-governmental organizations and from the press tends by its very nature, to be more critical of the political, economic and social conditions in the countries concerned. Under normal circumstances, the constructive dialogue between a State party reporting and the Committee will provide an opportunity for the government concerned to voice its own view, and to seek to refute such criticism and convince the Committee of the conformity of its policies with what is required by the Covenant. Non-submission of reports and non-appearance before the Committee deprives a government of this possibility to set the record straight.

## B. The Gambia—Introduction

4. The Gambia has been a party to the International Covenant on Economic, Social and Cultural Rights since 29 March 1979, the date of its entry into force. Since then, it has not submitted a single report. The Committee strongly urges the Government of the Gambia to fulfil its reporting obligations as soon as possible, so that the International Covenant on Economic, Social and Cultural Rights can be given full effect for the benefit of the people of the Gambia. The Committee considers that non-fulfilment of a State party's reporting obligations constitutes a grave impediment to effective and adequate implementation of the Covenant.

## C. Factors and Difficulties Impeding Implementation

5. The Committee takes note of the fact that the fulfilment by the Government of the Gambia of the obligations imposed by the International Covenant on Economic, Social and Cultural Rights cannot be evaluated without taking into consideration the political, economic and social conditions prevailing in the country at the present time. Although the Gambia has consistently held a prominent position in the promotion of human rights in Africa, within the framework of a political system of multiparty democracy, since the proclamation of its independence in 1965, its acknowledged political stability came under threat in the period before the general elections held in April 1992.

6. The Committee notes that the Gambia is one of the least developed countries in Africa and that poverty is widespread, especially in the rural areas where, according to UNDP figures, 200,000 people (25 per cent of the population) live below the poverty line. In terms of the human development index, the Gambia ranked 167th out of 173 in 1993.

7. The Committee notes in particular the socio-economic situation of women, whose disadvantage appears to be rooted in traditional practices and in lack of education, among other things.

8. The Committee also notes the absence until recently of a National Population Policy, the successful implementation of which could be a critical factor in translating optimistic growth projections into the improvement of living standards for all citizens of the Gambia.

9. The committee further notes that, in spite of the widely acclaimed Economic Recovery Programme supported by the World Bank, benefits deriving from economic growth have not been equitably shared by all citizens. The rural population in particular continues to suffer deterioration in living standards.

## D. Positive Aspects

10. The Committee notes that human rights are constitutionally protected in the Gambia and that the Government exerts efforts to promote observance of human rights. In particular, it notes the establishment of the African Centre for Democracy and Human Rights Studies, which aims to promote greater respect for human rights in Africa. The Committee also notes that the Gambia is an active contributor to the work of the Organization of African Unity's Commission on Human and People's Rights.

11. The Committee welcomes the enactment of the Labour Act of 1990, which ensures the freedom to form associations including trade unions, protects the right to organize and bargain collectively, and also sets minimum standards of contracts in the areas of hiring, training, terms of employment, wages and termination of employment.

## E. Principal Subjects of Concern

12. In relation to the rights contained in articles 6 to 9 of the Covenant, the Committee notes with concern that income levels of females generally remain below the government minimum wage scale, particularly those of the female labour force working in contract farming production. The Committee takes particular note that only 20 per cent of the labour force are in effect covered by minimum wage legislation while the remainder is informally employed, chiefly in agriculture.

13. The Committee also notes with concern that, as of January 1994, the Gambia had not ratified any of the International Labour Organisation (ILO) Conventions.

14. With regard to article 10 of the Covenant, the Com-

mittee expresses its profound concern over the situation of those women in the Gambia whose marriages are arranged for them by parents or guardians without their full and free consent as provided for in the Covenant. The Committee notes that polygamy is allowed in the Gambia, and observes that in accordance with articles 2 and 3 of the Covenant, the legal status of women should not be prejudiced.

15. With regard to the right to an adequate standard of living recognized in article 11 of the Covenant, the Committee is concerned about the reported inadequacy of food supply in the country. UNDP figures for 1992 show that 68.8 per cent of urban families did not have enough food and that the diet of 64 per cent of rural families was insufficient to withstand the rainy season. There are indications that chronic malnutrition among children could be as high as 40 per cent. The Committee regrets that it has no information on the right to housing in the Gambia.

16. Regarding the right to health in article 12 of the Covenant, the Committee expresses its deep concern over the extremely high maternal mortality rate of 1,050 per 100,000 live births. UNICEF identifies the main causes to be haemorrhage and infection related to the lack of access to and poor services. The Committee is equally concerned over the alarming UNDP figures of infant mortality and fertility rates of the Gambia, which are among the highest in Africa: 145.1 per 1,000 live births in 1986–87 and a 6.5 fertility rate during the same period. The Committee deplores the practice of female genital mutilation which is still prevalent in the Gambia. Independent experts report that more than half of the female population in the Gambia have undergone this procedure.

17. With regard to the right to education in article 13 of the Covenant, the Committee deeply regrets the absence of compulsory education in the Gambia and draws the attention of the Government to its obligation under the Covenant to ensure that "primary education shall be compulsory and available free for all". The Committee also draws the attention of the Government of the Gambia to the obligation, under article 14 of the Covenant, in cases where free compulsory education has not been assured, to "work out and adopt a detailed plan of Action for the progressive implementation, within a reasonable number of years," of the relevant right. The Committee expresses its concern not only at the high rates of illiteracy but also the gender disparities apparent in the figures. The latest UNICEF data reports that over 75 per cent of adults between the ages of 15 and 54 are functionally illiterate and that 90 per cent of the total are women. The same data source reports how women are disadvantaged educationally, females comprising only one-third of primary-school students and only one-fourth of high school students. The Committee is also concerned that, as a result of the absence of compulsory education legislation and because of the paucity of secondary school opportunities, most children complete their formal education by age 14 and informally enter the work force.

### F. Suggestions and Recommendations

18. The Committee reiterates its request that the Government of the Gambia actively participate in a constructive dialogue with the Committee as to how the obligations arising from the International Covenant on Economic, Social and Cultural Rights can be fulfilled in a more adequate manner. It calls to the Government's attention the fact that the Covenant creates a legal obligation for all States parties to submit periodic reports and that the Gambia has been in breach of this obligation for many years.

19. The Committee recommends that the Government of the Gambia avail itself of the advisory services of the United Nations Centre for Human Rights in order to enable it to submit as soon as possible a comprehensive report on the implementation of the Covenant in conformity with the Revised General Guidelines adopted by the Committee in 1990 (E/C.12/1991/1) and with particular emphasis on the issues raised and concerns expressed in the present concluding observations.

***BIBLIOGRAPHY.*** Hunt, Paul. "Children's Rights in West Africa: The Case of the Gambia's Almudos," *Human Rights Quarterly* 15, no. 3 (Aug. 1993): 499–532. Scholarly article, in English.

U. S. Department of Justice, Immigration and Naturalization Service, Resource Information Center. *Gambia: Human Rights since the July 1994 coup.* Washington, D.C.: 1995. Government briefing paper, in English.

**GARCÍA ROBLES, ALFONSO (1911–).** Co-recipient of the 1982 **NOBEL PEACE PRIZE,** this Mexican diplomat was born in Zamora, Michoacan, and educated at the University of Mexico, the University of Paris, and the Academy of International Law. Immediately after receiving his L.L.D. in 1938, García Robles entered into a diplomatic career.

García Robles' major contribution to world peace was the Treaty of Tlateloco, which banned nuclear weapons from Latin America. The Treaty was signed by 22 countries.

In selecting him for the Prize, the Nobel Committee stated that the award was "not only a reward for almost 20 years of work on disarmament, but also vindication of the virtues of patient and methodical negotiation."

***BIBLIOGRAPHY.*** Schlessinger, Bernard S., and June H. Schlessinger, eds. *Who's Who of Nobel Prize Winners.* Phoenix, AZ, USA: Oryx Press, 1991.

**GENERAL ARAB WOMEN FEDERATION.** Founded in 1944, as the All Arab Women's Federation, this non-governmental organization strives to reinforce the spirit of cooperation and solidarity among Arab women, promote women's equality and their role in the family and in children's education, enhance women's education and knowledge of their rights, and integrate women in society and the development process. The GAWF has consultative status with the UN **ECONOMIC AND SOCIAL COUNCIL** (Category II) and **UNESCO.** It publishes *Arab Women* twice a year and *Nis'al-Arab* periodically.

General Arab Women Federation. Address: Hay-Al-Maghreg, Mahaela 304, Baghdad, Iraq. Telephone:

(964-1) 422-7117. Telex: 213014. Secretary-General: Manal Y. A. Razzak.

**GENERAL ASSEMBLY, UN.** The General Assembly of the United Nations was established in accordance with article 7 of the **UNITED NATIONS CHARTER.** Its principal functions and powers are (1) to discuss any questions or any matters within the scope of the Charter or relating to the powers and functions of any organs provided for in the Charter, and to make recommendations to member States or to the Security Council, or both, on any such questions and matters; (2) to consider the general principles of cooperation in the maintenance of international peace and security, and to make recommendations with regard to such principles; (3) to discuss any questions relating to the maintenance of international peace and security brought before it by any member State, or by the Security Council, or by a non-member State, unless the Security Council is dealing with the question; and (4) to call the attention of the Security Council to situations which are likely to endanger international peace and security. Article 13 of the charter empowers the assembly to initiate studies and make recommendations for the purpose of "promoting international co-operation in the economic, social, cultural, educational and health fields, and assisting in the realization of human rights and fundamental freedoms for all without distinction as to race, sex, language or religion." Under article 14, it may recommend measures for the peaceful adjustment of any situation, regardless of origin, which it deems likely to impair the general welfare or friendly relations among nations. Under article 15, it receives and considers reports from the other UN organs, including the Security Council. Under article 16, it performs certain functions with respect to the international trusteeship system, including the approval of trusteeship agreements for the areas not designated as strategic. Under article 17, it considers and approves the budget of the United Nations and its financial and budgetary arrangements with the specialized agencies.

All members of the United Nations, which is open to every state which accepts the obligations set out in the UN Charter and is judged able and willing to carry out those obligations, are members of the General Assembly. The Assembly admits them to membership on recommendation of the Security Council. In a few cases, States have been suspended or expelled by a decision of the Assembly on recommendation of the Security Council, and in a few cases States have withdrawn from membership.

The General Assembly has three procedural committees: (1) the General Committee, which deals with the organization of its work; (2) the Committee on Conferences, which deals with the scheduling of sessions of subsidiary bodies; and (3) the Credentials Committee, which examines and reports on the credentials of representatives. In addition, it establishes six main committees at each session: the First (Disarmament and Related Matters) Committee, the Second (Economic and Financial) Committee, the Third (Social, Humanitarian and Cultural) Committee, the Fourth (Special Political and Decolonization) Committee, the Fifth (Administrative and Budgetary) Committee, and the Sixth (Legal Matters) Committee. Some matters are considered by the Assembly directly without reference to a main committee.

The role of the main committees is to consider in detail items referred to it by the General Assembly on recommendation of the General Committee, which is composed of the President of the General Assembly, its Vice Presidents, and the Chairmen of its main committees, and to draft resolutions or decisions for adoption by the Assembly in plenary session. Items relating to human rights are normally referred to the Third Committee.

**GENEVA INFORMAL MEETING OF INTERNATIONAL NONGOVERNMENTAL YOUTH ORGANIZATIONS.** Founded in 1980, the GIM serves as a collective communication channel on issues of concern between the United Nations system and the sector of organized youth. The organization also promotes the exchange of views among youth organizations throughout the world on issues affecting young people. It has consultative status with the UN **ECONOMIC AND SOCIAL COUNCIL** (Category II) and the **ILO.** Geneva Informal Meeting of International Nongovernmental Youth Organizations. Address: Youth Unit-CSDHA, P.O. Box 500, A-1400 Wien, Austria.

**GENEVA RED CROSS CONVENTIONS (1949) AND PROTOCOLS (1977).** Concluding several months of grueling negotiations at the Diplomatic Conference convened at Geneva by the Government of Switzerland, the representatives of 154 States on 12 August 1949 approved and opened for signature and acceptance by their governments four major international multilateral treaties, dealing respectively with (I) Amelioration of the Condition of Wounded and Sick an Armed Forces in the Field; (II) Amelioration of the Condition of Wounded, Sick and Shipwrecked Members of Armed Forces at Sea; (III) Treatment of Prisoners of War; and (IV) Protection of Civilian Persons in Time of War. Conventions I and IV were to serve as replacements for equivalent but outdated Geneva Red Cross Conventions adopted in 1929.

Twenty-eight years later, on 8 June 1977, another Diplomatic Conference sponsored by Switzerland completed and opened for acceptance two Protocols to the Geneva Red Cross Conventions: (I) on the Protection of Victims of International Armed Conflicts and (II) on the Protection of Victims of Non-International Armed Conflicts. Non-International conflicts, such as civil wars, had never before been dealt with in an international multilateral treaty.

The key provisions of Geneva Red Cross Conventions which deal with human rights concerns are extracted below. The provisions of Protocols I and II which deal with those are reproduced in full. For the full texts of the four Geneva Conventions, see 75/UNTS/31. For the full texts of the Protocols, see 1977/UNJYB 95.

### GENEVA RED CROSS CONVENTION III, ON TREATMENT OF PRISONERS OF WAR. Key provisions of the Convention include the following:

#### Part II

#### General Protection of Prisoners of War

*Article 12.* Prisoners of war are in the hands of the enemy Power, but not of the individuals or military units who have captured them. Irrespective of the individual responsibilities that may exist, the Detaining Power is responsible for the treatment given them.

Prisoners of war may only be transferred by the Detaining Power to a Power which is a party to the Convention and after the Detaining Power has satisfied itself of the willingness and ability of such transferee Power to apply the Convention. When prisoners of war are transferred under such circumstances, responsibility for the application of the Convention rests on the Power accepting them while they are in its custody.

Nevertheless if that Power fails to carry out the provisions of the Convention in any important respect the Power by whom the prisoners of war were transferred shall, upon being notified by the Protecting Power, take effective measures to correct the situation or shall request the return of the prisoners of war. Such requests must be complied with.

*Article 13.* Prisoners of war must at all times be humanely treated. Any unlawful act or omission by the Detaining Power causing death or seriously endangering the health of a prisoner of war in its custody is prohibited and will be regarded as a serious breach of the present Convention. In particular, no prisoner of war may be subjected to physical mutilation or to medical or scientific experiments of any kind which are not justified by the medical, dental or hospital treatment of the prisoner concerned and carried out in his interest.

Likewise, prisoners of war must at all times be protected, particularly against acts of violence or intimidation and against insults and public curiosity.

Measures of reprisal against prisoners of war are prohibited.

*Article 14.* Prisoners of war are entitled in all circumstances to respect for their persons and their honour.

Women shall be treated with all the regard due to their sex and shall in all cases benefit by treatment as favourable as that granted to men.

Prisoners of war shall retain the full civil capacity which they enjoyed at the time of their capture. The Detaining Power may not restrict the exercise, either within or without its own territory, of the rights such capacity confers except in so far as the captivity requires.

*Article 15.* The Power detaining prisoners of war shall be bound to provide free of charge for their maintenance and for the medical attention required by their state of health.

*Article 16.* Taking into consideration the provisions of the present Convention relating to rank and sex, and subject to any privileged treatment which may be accorded to them by reason of their state of health, age or professional qualifications, all prisoners of war shall be treated alike by the Detaining Power, without any adverse distinction based on race, nationality, religious belief or political opinions, or any other distinction founded on similar criteria.

#### Part III

#### Captivity

#### Section I—Beginning of Captivity

*Article 17.* Every prisoner of war, when questioned on the subject is bound to give only his surname, first names and rank, date of birth, and army, regimental, personal or serial number, or failing this, equivalent information.

If he wilfully infringes this rule he may render himself liable to a restriction of the privileges accorded to his rank or status.

Each Party to a conflict is required to furnish the persons under its jurisdiction who are liable to become prisoners of war, with an identity card showing the owner's surname, first names, rank, army, regimental, personal or serial number or equivalent information, and date of birth. The identity card may, furthermore, bear the signature or the fingerprints, or both, of the owner, and may bear, as well, any other information the Party to the conflict may wish to add concerning persons belonging to its armed forces. As far as possible the card shall measure 6.5 x 10 cm. and shall be issued in duplicate. The identity card shall be shown by the prisoner of war upon demand, but may in no case be taken away from him.

No physical or mental torture, nor any other form of coercion may be inflicted on prisoners of war to secure from them information of any kind whatever. Prisoners of war who refuse to answer may not be threatened, insulted, or exposed to any unpleasant or disadvantageous treatment of any kind.

Prisoners of war who, owing to their physical or mental condition, are unable to state their identity shall be handed over to the medical service. The identity of such prisoners shall be established by all possible means, subject to the provisions of the preceding paragraph.

The questioning of prisoners of war shall be carried out in a language which they understand.

*Article 18.* All effects and articles of personal use, except arms, horses, military equipment and military documents, shall remain in the possession of prisoners of war, likewise their metal helmets and gas masks and like articles issued for personal protection. Effects and articles used for their clothing or feeding shall likewise remain in their possession, even if such effects and articles belong to their regulation military equipment.

At no time should prisoners of war be without identity documents. The Detaining Power shall supply such documents to prisoners of war who possess none.

Badges of rank and nationality, decorations and articles having above all a personal or sentimental value may not be taken from prisoners of war.

Sums of money carried by prisoners of war may not be taken away from them except by order of an officer, and after the amount and particulars of the owner have been recorded in a special register and an itemized receipt has been given, legibly inscribed with the name, rank and unit of the person issuing the said receipt. Sums in the currency of the Detaining Power, or which are changed into such currency at the prisoner's request, shall be placed to the credit of the prisoner's account as provided in Article 64.

The Detaining Power may withdraw articles of value from prisoners of war only for reasons of security; when such articles are withdrawn, the procedure laid down for sums of money impounded shall apply.

Such objects, likewise the sums taken away in any currency other than that of the Detaining Power, and the conversion of which has not been asked for by the owners, shall be kept in the custody of the Detaining Power and shall be returned in their initial shape to prisoners of war at the end of their captivity.

*Article 19.* Prisoners of war shall be evacuated as soon as possible after their capture, to camps situated in an area far enough from the combat zone for them to be out of danger.

Only those prisoners of war who, owing to wounds or sickness, would run greater risks by being evacuated than by remaining where they are, may be temporarily kept back in a danger zone.

Prisoners of war shall not be unnecessarily exposed to danger while awaiting evacuation from a fighting zone.

*Article 20.* The evacuation of prisoners of war shall always be effected humanely and in conditions similar to those for the forces of the Detaining Power in their changes of station.

The Detaining Power shall supply prisoners of war who are being evacuated with sufficient food and potable water, and with the necessary clothing and medical attention. The Detaining Power shall take all suitable precautions to ensure their safety during evacuation, and shall establish as soon as possible a list of the prisoners of war who are evacuated.

If prisoners of war must, during evacuation, pass through transit camps, their stay in such camps shall be as brief as possible.

### Section II—Internment of Prisoners of War

#### Chapter I—General Observations

*Article 21.* The Detaining Power may subject prisoners of war to internment. It may impose on them the obligation of not leaving, beyond certain limits, the camp where they are interned, or if the said camp is fenced in, of not going outside its perimeter. Subject to the provisions of the present Convention relative to penal and disciplinary sanctions, prisoners of war may not be held in close confinement except where necessary to safeguard their health and then only during the continuation of the circumstances which make such confinement necessary.

Prisoners of war may be partially or wholly released on parole or promise, in so far as is allowed by the laws of the Power on which they depend. Such measures shall be taken particularly in cases where this may contribute to the improvement of their state of health. No prisoner of war shall be compelled to accept liberty on parole or promise.

Upon the outbreak of hostilities, each Party to the conflict shall notify the adverse Party of the laws and regulations allowing or forbidding its own nationals to accept liberty on parole or promise. Prisoners of war who are paroled or who have given their promise in conformity with the laws and regulations so notified, are bound on their personal honour scrupulously to fulfil, both towards the Power on which they depend and the Power which has captured them, the engagements of their paroles or promises. In such cases, the Power on which they depend is bound neither to require nor to accept from them any service incompatible with the parole or promise given.

*Article 22.* Prisoners of war may be interned only in premises located on land and affording every guarantee of hygiene and healthfulness. Except in particular cases which are justified by the interest of the prisoners themselves, they shall not be interned in penitentiaries.

Prisoners of war interned in unhealthy areas, or where the climate is injurious for them, shall be removed as soon as possible to a more favourable climate.

The Detaining Power shall assemble prisoners of war in camps or camp compounds according to their nationality, language and customs, provided that such prisoners shall not be separated from prisoners of war belonging to the armed forces with which they were serving at the time of their capture, except with their consent.

*Article 23.* No prisoner of war may at any time be sent to, or detained in areas where he may be exposed to the fire of the combat zone, nor may his presence be used to render certain points or areas immune from military operations.

Prisoners of war shall have shelters against air bombardment and other hazards of war, to the same extent as the local civilian population. With the exception of those engaged in the protection of their quarters against the aforesaid hazards, they may enter such shelters as soon as possible after the giving of the alarm. Any other protective measure taken in favour of the population shall also apply to them.

Detaining Powers shall give the Powers concerned, through the intermediary of the Protecting Powers, all useful information regarding the geographical location of prisoner-of-war camps.

Whenever military considerations permit, prisoner-of-war camps shall be indicated in the daytime by the letters PW or PG, placed so as to be clearly visible from the air. The Powers concerned may, however, agree upon any other system of marking. Only prisoner-of-war camps shall be marked as such.

*Article 24.* Transit or screening camps of a permanent kind shall be fitted out under conditions similar to those described in the present Section, and the prisoners therein shall have the same treatment as in other camps.

#### Chapter II—Quarters, Food and Clothing of Prisoners of War

*Article 25.* Prisoners of war shall be quartered under conditions as favourable as those for the forces of the Detaining Power who are billeted in the same area. The said conditions shall make allowance for the habits and customs of the prisoners and shall in no case be prejudicial to their health.

The foregoing provisions shall apply in particular to the dormitories of prisoners of war as regards both total surface and minimum cubic space, and the general installations, bedding and blankets.

The premises provided for the use of prisoners of war individually or collectively, shall be entirely protected from dampness and adequately heated and lighted, in particular between dusk and lights out. All precautions must be taken against the danger of fire.

In any camps in which women prisoners of war, as well as men, are accommodated, separate dormitories shall be provided for them.

*Article 26.* The basic daily food rations shall be sufficient in quantity, quality and variety to keep prisoners of war in good health and to prevent loss of weight or the development of nutritional deficiencies. Account shall also be taken of the habitual diet of the prisoners.

The Detaining Power shall supply prisoners of war who work with such additional rations as are necessary for the labour on which they are employed.

Sufficient drinking water shall be supplied to prisoners of war. The use of tobacco shall be permitted.

Prisoners of war shall, as far as possible, be associated with the preparation of their meals; they may be employed for that purpose in the kitchens. Furthermore, they shall be given the means of preparing, themselves, the additional food in their possession.

Adequate premises shall be provided for messing.

Collective disciplinary measures affecting food are prohibited.

*Article 27.* Clothing, underwear and footwear shall be supplied to prisoners of war in sufficient quantities by the Detaining Power, which shall make allowance for the climate of the region where the prisoners are detained. Uniforms of enemy armed forces captured by the Detaining Power should, if suitable for the climate, be made available to clothe prisoners of war.

The regular replacement and repair of the above articles shall be assured by the Detaining Power. In addition, prisoners of war who work shall receive appropriate clothing, wherever the nature of the work demands.

*Article 28.* Canteens shall be installed in all camps, where prisoners of war may procure foodstuffs, soap and tobacco and ordinary articles in daily use. The tariff shall never be in excess of local market prices.

The profits made by camp canteens shall be used for the benefit of the prisoners; a special fund shall be created for this purpose. The prisoners' representative shall have the right to collaborate in the management of the canteen and of this fund.

When a camp is closed down, the credit balance of the special fund shall be handed to an international welfare organization, to be employed for the benefit of prisoners of war of the same nationality as those who have contributed to the fund. In case of a general repatriation, such profits shall be kept by the Detaining Power, subject to any agreement to the contrary between the Powers concerned.

**Chapter III—Hygiene and Medical Attention**

*Article 29.* The Detaining Power shall be bound to take all sanitary measures necessary to ensure the cleanliness and healthfulness of camps, and to prevent epidemics.

Prisoners of war shall have for their use, day and night, conveniences which conform to the rules of hygiene and are maintained in a constant state of cleanliness. In any camps in which women prisoners of war are accommodated, separate conveniences shall be provided for them.

Also, apart from the baths and showers with which the

camps shall be furnished, prisoners of war shall be provided with sufficient water and soap for their personal toilet and for washing their personal laundry; the necessary installations, facilities and time shall be granted them for that purpose.

*Article 30.* Every camp shall have an adequate infirmary where prisoners of war may have the attention they require, as well as appropriate diet. Isolation wards shall, if necessary, be set aside for cases of contagious or mental disease.

Prisoners of war suffering from serious disease, or whose condition necessitates special treatment, a surgical operation or hospital care, must be admitted to any military or civil medical unit where such treatment can be given, even if their repatriation is contemplated in the near future. Special facilities shall be afforded for the care to be given to the disabled, in particular to the blind, and for their rehabilitation, pending repatriation.

Prisoners of war shall have the attention, preferably, of medical personnel of the Power on which they depend and, if possible, of their nationality.

Prisoners of war may not be prevented from presenting themselves to the medical authorities for examination. The detaining authorities shall, upon request, issue to every prisoner who has undergone treatment an official certificate indicating the nature of his illness or injury, and the duration and kind of treatment received. A duplicate of this certificate shall be forwarded to the Central Prisoners of War Agency.

The costs of treatment, including those of any apparatus necessary for the maintenance of prisoners of war in good health, particularly dentures and other artificial appliances, and spectacles, shall be borne by the Detaining Power.

*Article 31.* Medical inspections of prisoners of war shall be made at least once a month. They shall include the checking and the recording of the weight of each prisoner of war. Their purpose shall be, in particular, to supervise the general state of health, nutrition and cleanliness of prisoners and to detect contagious diseases, especially tuberculosis, malaria and venereal disease. For this purpose the most efficient methods available shall be employed, e.g. periodic mass miniature radiography for the early detection of tuberculosis.

*Article 32.* Prisoners of war who, though not attached to the medical service of their armed forces, are physicians, surgeons, dentists, nurses or medical orderlies, may be required by the Detaining Power to exercise their medical functions in the interests of prisoners or war dependent on the same Power. In that case they shall continue to be prisoners of war, but shall receive the same treatment as corresponding medical personnel retained by the Detaining Power. They shall be exempted from any other work under Article 49.

**Chapter IV—Medical Personnel and Chaplains Retained to Assist Prisoners of War**

*Article 33.* Members of the medical personnel and chaplains while retained by the Detaining Power with a view to assisting prisoners of war, shall not be considered as prisoners of war. They shall, however, receive as a minimum the benefits and protection of the present Convention, and shall also be granted all facilities necessary to provide for the medical care of, and religious ministration to prisoners of war.

They shall continue to exercise their medical and spiritual functions for the benefit of prisoners of war, preferably those belonging to the armed forces upon which they depend, within the scope of the military laws and regulations of the Detaining Power and under the control of its competent services, in accordance with their professional etiquette. They shall also benefit by the following facilities in the exercise of their medical or spiritual functions:

(a) They shall be authorized to visit periodically prisoners of war situated in working detachments or in hospitals outside the camp. For this purpose, the Detaining Power shall place at their disposal the necessary means of transport.

(b) The senior medical officer in each camp shall be responsible to the camp military authorities for everything connected with the activities of retained medical personnel. For this purpose, Parties to the conflict shall agree at the outbreak of hostilities on the subject of the corresponding ranks of the medical personnel, including that of societies mentioned in Article 26 of the Geneva Convention for the Amelioration of the Condition of the Wounded and Sick in Armed Forces in the Field of August 12, 1949. This senior medical officer, as well as chaplains, shall have the right to deal with the competent authorities of the camp on all questions relating to their duties. Such authorities shall afford them all necessary facilities for correspondence relating to these questions.

(c) Although they shall be subject to the internal discipline of the camp in which they are retained, such personnel may not be compelled to carry out any work other than that concerned with their medical or religious duties.

During hostilities, the Parties to the conflict shall agree concerning the possible relief of retained personnel and shall settle the procedure to be followed.

None of the preceding provisions shall relieve the Detaining Power of its obligations with regard to prisoners of war from the medical or spiritual point of view.

## Chapter V—Religious, Intellectual and Physical Activities

*Article 34.* Prisoners of war shall enjoy complete latitude in the exercise of their religious duties, including attendance at the service of their faith, on condition that they comply with the disciplinary routine prescribed by the military authorities.

Adequate premises shall be provided where religious services may be held.

*Article 35.* Chaplains who fall into the hands of the enemy Power and who remain or are retained with a view to assisting prisoners of war, shall be allowed to minister to them and to exercise freely their ministry amongst prisoners of war of the same religion, in accordance with their religious conscience. They shall be allocated among the various camps and labour detachments containing prisoners of war belonging to the same forces, speaking the same language or practicing the same religion. They shall enjoy the necessary facilities, including the means of transport provided for in Article 33, for visiting the prisoners of war outside their camp. They shall be free to correspond, subject to censorship, on matters concerning their religious duties with the ecclesiastical authorities in the country of detention and with the international religious organizations. Letters and cards which they may send for this purpose shall be in addition to the quota provided for in Article 71.

*Article 36.* Prisoners of war who are ministers of religion, without having officiated as chaplains to their own forces, shall be at liberty, whatever their denomination, to minister freely to the members of their community. For this purpose, they shall receive the same treatment as the chaplains retained by the Detaining Power. They shall not be obliged to do any other work.

*Article 37.* When prisoners of war have not the assistance of a retained chaplain or of a prisoner of war minister of their faith, a minister belonging to the prisoners' or a similar denomination, or in his absence a qualified layman, if such a course is feasible from a confessional point of view, shall be appointed at the request of the prisoners concerned to fill this office. This appointment, subject to the approval of the Detaining Power, shall take place with the agreement of the community of prisoners concerned and, wherever necessary, with the approval of the local religious authorities of the same faith. The person thus appointed shall comply with all regulations established by the Detaining Power in the interests of discipline and military security.

*Article 38.* While respecting the individual preferences of every prisoner, the Detaining Power shall encourage the practice of intellectual, educational and recreational pursuits, sports and games amongst prisoners, and shall take the measures necessary to ensure the exercise thereof by providing them with adequate premises and necessary equipment.

Prisoners shall have opportunities for taking physical exercise including sports and games and for being out of doors. Sufficient open spaces shall be provided for this purpose in all camps.

## Chapter VI—Discipline

*Article 39.* Every prisoner-of-war camp shall be put under the immediate authority of a responsible commissioned officer belonging to the regular armed forces of the Detaining Power. Such officer shall have in his possession a copy of the present Convention; he shall ensure that its provisions are known to the camp staff and the guard and shall be responsible, under the direction of his government, for its application.

Prisoners of war, with the exception of officers, must salute and show to all officers of the Detaining Power the external marks of respect provided for by the regulations applying in their own forces.

Officer prisoners of war are bound to salute only officers of a higher rank of the Detaining Power; they must, however, salute the camp commander regardless of his rank.

*Article 40.* The wearing of badges of rank and nationality, as well as of decorations, shall be permitted.

*Article 41.* In every camp the text of the present Convention and its Annexes and the contents of any special agreement provided for in Article 6, shall be posted, in the prisoners' own language, at places where all may read them. Copies shall be supplied, on request, to the prisoners who cannot have access to the copy which has been posted.

Regulations, orders, notices and publications of every kind relating to the conduct of prisoners of war shall be issued to them in a language which they understand. Such regulations, orders and publications shall be posted in the manner described above and copies shall be handed to the prisoners' representative. Every order and command addressed to prisoners of war individually must likewise be given in a language which they understand.

*Article 42.* The use of weapons against prisoners of war, especially against those who are escaping or attempting to escape, shall constitute an extreme measure, which shall always be preceded by warnings appropriate to the circumstances.

## Chapter VII—Rank of Prisoners of War

*Article 43.* Upon the outbreak of hostilities, the Parties to the conflict shall communicate to one another the titles and ranks of all the persons mentioned in Article 4 of the present Convention, in order to ensure equality of treatment between prisoners of equivalent rank. Titles and ranks which are subsequently created shall form the subject of similar communications.

The Detaining Power shall recognize promotions in rank which have been accorded to prisoners of war and which have been duly notified by the Power on which these prisoners depend.

*Article 44.* Officers and prisoners of equivalent status shall be treated with the regard due to their rank and age.

In order to ensure service in officers' camps, other ranks of the same armed forces who, as far as possible, speak the same language, shall be assigned in sufficient numbers, account being taken of the rank of officers and prisoners of equivalent status. Such orderlies shall not be required to perform any other work.

Supervision of the mess by the officers themselves shall be facilitated in every way.

*Article 45.* Prisoners of war other than officers and prisoners of equivalent status shall be treated with the regard due to their rank and age.

Supervision of the mess by the prisoners themselves shall be facilitated in every way.

## Chapter VIII—Transfer of Prisoners of War after Their Arrival in Camp

*Article 46.* The Detaining Power, when deciding upon the transfer of prisoners of war, shall take into account the interests of the prisoners themselves, more especially so as not to increase the difficulty of their repatriation.

The transfer of prisoners of war shall always be effected humanely and in conditions not less favourable than those under which the forces of the Detaining Power are transferred. Account shall always be taken of the climatic conditions to which the prisoners of war are accustomed and the conditions of transfer shall in no case be prejudicial to their health.

The Detaining Power shall supply prisoners of war during transfer with sufficient food and drinking-water to keep them in good health, likewise with the necessary clothing, shelter and medical attention. The Detaining Power shall take adequate precautions especially in case of transport by sea or by air, to ensure their safety during transfer, and shall draw up a complete list of all transferred prisoners before their departure.

*Article 47.* Sick or wounded prisoners of war shall not be transferred as long as their recovery may be endangered by the journey, unless their safety imperatively demands it.

If the combat zone draws closer to a camp, the prisoners of war in the said camp shall not be transferred unless their transfer can be carried out in adequate conditions of safety, or if they are exposed to greater risks by remaining on the spot than by being transferred.

*Article 48.* In the event of transfer, prisoners of war shall be officially advised of their departure and of their new postal address. Such notifications shall be given in time for them to pack their luggage and inform their next of kin.

They shall be allowed to take with them their personal effects, and the correspondence and parcels which have arrived for them. The weight of such baggage may be limited, if the conditions of transfer so require, to what each prisoner can reasonably carry, which shall in no case be more than twenty-five kilograms per head.

Mail and parcels addressed to their former camp shall be forwarded to them without delay. The camp commander shall take, in agreement with the prisoners' representative, any measures needed to ensure the transport of the prisoners' community property and of the luggage they are unable to take with them in consequence of restrictions imposed by virtue of the second paragraph of this Article.

The costs of transfers shall be borne by the Detaining Power.

## Section III—Labour of Prisoners of War

*Article 49.* The Detaining Power may utilize the labour of prisoners of war who are physically fit, taking into account their age, sex, rank and physical aptitude, and with a view particularly to maintaining them in a good state of physical and mental health.

Non-commissioned officers who are prisoners of war shall only be required to do supervisory work. Those not so required may ask for other suitable work which shall, so far as possible, be found for them.

If officers or persons of equivalent status ask for suitable work, it shall be found for them, so far as possible, but they may in no circumstances be compelled to work.

*Article 50.* Besides work connected with camp administration, installation or maintenance, prisoners of war may be compelled to do only such work as is included in the following classes:

(a) agriculture;

(b) industries connected with the production or the extraction of raw materials, and manufacturing industries, with the exception of metallurgical, machinery and chemical industries; public works and building operations which have no military character or purpose;

(c) transport and handling of stores which are not military in character or purpose;

(d) commercial business, and arts and crafts;

(e) domestic service;

(f) public utility services having no military character or purpose.

Should the above provisions be infringed, prisoners of war shall be allowed to exercise their right of complaint, in conformity with Article 78.

*Article 51.* Prisoners of war must be granted suitable working conditions, especially as regards accommodation, food, clothing and equipment; such conditions shall not be inferior to those enjoyed by nationals of the Detaining Power employed in similar work; account shall also be taken of climatic conditions.

The Detaining Power, in utilizing the labour of prisoners of war, shall ensure that in areas in which prisoners are employed, the national legislation concerning the protection of labour and, more particularly, the regulations for the safety of workers, are duly applied.

Prisoners of war shall receive training and be provided with the means of protection suitable to the work they will have to do and similar to those accorded to the nationals of the Detaining Power. Subject to the provisions of Article 52, prisoners may be submitted to the normal risks run by these civilian workers.

Conditions of labour shall in no case be rendered more arduous by disciplinary measures.

*Article 52.* Unless he be a volunteer, no prisoner of war may be employed on labour which is of an unhealthy or dangerous nature.

No prisoner of war shall be assigned to labour which would be looked upon as humiliating for a member of the Detaining Power's own forces.

The removal of mines or similar devices shall be considered as dangerous labour.

*Article 53.* The duration of the daily labour of prisoners of war, including the time of the journey to and fro, shall not be excessive, and must in no case exceed that permitted for civilian workers in the district, who are nationals of the Detaining Power and employed on the same work.

Prisoners of war must be allowed, in the middle of the day's work, a rest of not less than one hour. This rest will be the same as that to which workers of the Detaining Power are entitled, if the latter is of longer duration. They shall be allowed, in addition, a rest of twenty-four consecutive hours every week, preferably on Sunday or the day of rest in their country of origin. Furthermore, every prisoner who has worked for one year shall be granted a rest of eight consecutive days, during which his working pay shall be paid him.

If methods of labour such as piece work are employed, the length of the working period shall not be rendered excessive thereby.

*Article 54.* The working pay due to prisoners of war shall be fixed in accordance with the provisions of Article 62 of the present Convention.

Prisoners of war who sustain accidents in connection with work, or who contract a disease in the course, or in consequence of their work, shall receive all the care their condition may require. The Detaining Power shall furthermore deliver to such prisoners of war a medical certificate enabling them to submit their claims to the Power on which they depend, and shall send a duplicate to the Central Prisoners of War Agency provided for in Article 123.

*Article 55.* The fitness of prisoners of war for work shall be periodically verified by medical examinations, at least once a month. The examinations shall have particular regard to the nature of the work which prisoners of war are required to do.

If any prisoner of war considers himself incapable of working, he shall be permitted to appear before the medical authorities of his camp. Physicians or surgeons may recommend that the prisoners who are, in their opinion, unfit for work be exempted therefrom.

*Article 56.* The organization and administration of labour detachments shall be similar to those of prisoner-of-war camps.

Every labour detachment shall remain under the control of and administratively part of a prisoner-of-war camp. The military authorities and the commander of the said camp shall be responsible, under the direction of their government, for the observance of the provisions of the present Convention in labour detachments.

The camp commander shall keep an up-to-date record of the labour detachments dependent on his camp, and shall communicate it to the delegates of the Protecting Power, of the International Committee of the Red Cross, or of other agencies giving relief to prisoners of war, who may visit the camp.

*Article 57.* The treatment of prisoners of war who work for private persons, even if the latter are responsible for guarding and protecting them, shall not be inferior to that which is provided for by the present Convention. The Detaining Power, the military authorities and the commander of the camp to which such prisoners belong shall be entirely responsible for the maintenance, care, treatment, and payment of the working pay of such prisoners of war.

Such prisoners of war shall have the right to remain in communication with the prisoners' representatives in the camps on which they depend.

## Section IV—Financial Resources of Prisoners of War

*Article 58.* Upon the outbreak of hostilities, and pending an arrangement on this matter with the Protecting Power, the Detaining Power may determine the maximum amount of money in cash or in any similar form, that prisoners may have in their possession. Any amount in excess, which was properly in their possession and which has been taken or withheld from them, shall be placed to their account, together with any monies deposited by them, and shall not be converted into any other currency without their consent.

If prisoners of war are permitted to purchase services or commodities outside the camp against payment in cash, such payments shall be made by the prisoner himself or the camp administration who will charge them to the accounts of the prisoners concerned. The Detaining Power will establish the necessary rules in this respect.

*Article 59.* Cash which was taken from prisoners of war, in accordance with Article 18, at the time of their capture, and which is in the currency of the Detaining Power, shall be placed to their separate accounts, in accordance with the provisions of Article 64 of the present Section.

The amounts, in the currency of the Detaining Power, due to the conversion of sums in other currencies that are taken from the prisoners of war at the same time, shall also be credited to their separate accounts.

*Article 60.* The Detaining Power shall grant all prisoners of war a monthly advance of pay, the amount of which shall be fixed by conversion, into the currency of the said Power, of the following amounts:

*Category I:* Prisoner ranking below sergeants: eight Swiss francs.

*Category II:* Sergeants and other non-commissioned officers, or prisoners of equivalent rank: twelve Swiss francs.

*Category III:* Warrant officers and commissioned officers below the rank of major or prisoners of equivalent rank: fifty Swiss francs.

*Category IV:* Majors, lieutenant-colonels, colonels or prisoners of equivalent rank: sixty Swiss francs.

*Category V:* General officers or prisoners of war of equivalent rank: seventy-five Swiss francs.

However, the Parties to the conflict concerned may by special agreement modify the amount of advances of pay due to prisoners of the preceding categories.

Furthermore, if the amounts indicated in the first paragraph above would be unduly high compared with the pay of the Detaining Power's armed forces or would, for any reason, seriously embarrass the Detaining Power, then, pending the conclusion of a special agreement with the Power on which the prisoners depend to vary the amounts indicated above, the Detaining Power:

(a) shall continue to credit the accounts of the prisoners with the amounts indicated in the first paragraph above;

(b) may temporarily limit the amount made available from these advances of pay to prisoners of war for their own use, to sums which are reasonable, but which, for Category I, shall never be inferior to the amount that the Detaining Power gives to the members of its own armed forces.

The reasons for any limitations will be given without delay to the Protecting Power.

*Article 61.* The Detaining Power shall accept for distribution as supplementary pay to prisoners of war sums which the Power on which the prisoners depend may forward to them, on condition that the sums to be paid shall be the same for each prisoner of the same category, shall be payable to all prisoners of that category depending on that Power, and shall be placed in their separate accounts, at the earliest opportunity, in accordance with the provisions of Article 64. Such supplementary pay shall not relieve the Detaining Power of any obligation under this Convention.

*Article 62.* Prisoners of war shall be paid a fair working rate of pay by the detaining authorities direct. The rate shall be fixed by the said authorities, but shall at no time be less than one-fourth of one Swiss franc for a full working day. The Detaining Power shall inform prisoners of war, as well as the Power on which they depend, through the intermediary of the Protecting Power, of the rate of daily working pay that it has fixed.

Working pay shall likewise be paid by the detaining authorities to prisoners of war permanently detailed to duties or to a skilled or semi-skilled occupation in connection with the administration, installation or maintenance of camps, and to the prisoners who are required to carry out spiritual or medical duties on behalf of their comrades.

The working pay of the prisoners' representative, of his advisers, if any, and of his assistants, shall be paid out of the fund maintained by canteen profits. The scale of this working pay shall be fixed by the prisoners' representative and approved by the camp commander. If there is no such fund, the detaining authorities shall pay these prisoners a fair working rate of pay.

*Article 63.* Prisoners of war shall be permitted to receive remittances of money addressed to them individually or collectively.

Every prisoner of war shall have at his disposal the credit balance of his account as provided for in the following Article, within the limits fixed by the Detaining Power, which shall make such payments as are requested. Subject to financial or monetary restrictions which the Detaining Power regards as essential, prisoners of war may also have payments made abroad. In this case payments addressed by prisoners of war to dependents shall be given priority.

In any event, and subject to the consent of the Power on which they depend, prisoners may have payments made in their own country, as follows: the Detaining Power shall send to the aforesaid Power through the Protecting Power, a notification giving all the necessary particulars concerning the prisoners of war, the beneficiaries of the payments, and the amount of the sums to be paid, expressed in the Detaining Power's currency. The said notification shall be signed by the prisoners and countersigned by the camp commander. The Detaining Power shall debit the prisoners' account by a corresponding amount; the sums thus debited shall be placed by it to the credit of the Power on which the prisoners depend.

To apply the foregoing provisions, the Detaining Power may usefully consult the Model Regulations in Annex V of the present Convention.

*Article 64.* The Detaining Power shall hold an account for each prisoner of war, showing at least the following:

(1) The amounts due to the prisoner or received by him as advances of pay, as working pay or derived from any other source; the sums in the currency of the Detaining Power which were taken from him; the sums taken from him and converted at his request into the currency of the said Power.

(2) The payments made to the prisoner in cash, or in any other similar form; the payments made on his behalf and at his request; the sums transferred under Article 63, third paragraph.

*Article 65.* Every item entered in the account of a prisoner of war shall be countersigned or initialled by him, or by the prisoners' representative acting on his behalf.

Prisoners of war shall at all times be afforded reasonable facilities for consulting and obtaining copies of their accounts, which may likewise be inspected by the representatives of the Protecting Powers at the time of visits to the camp.

When prisoners of war are transferred from one camp to another, their personal accounts will follow them. In case of transfer from one Detaining Power to another, the monies which are their property and are not in the currency of the Detaining Power will follow them. They shall be given certificates for any other monies standing to the credit of their accounts.

The Parties to the conflict concerned may agree to notify to each other at specific intervals through the Protecting Power, the amount of the accounts of the prisoners of war.

*Article 66.* On the termination of captivity, through the release of a prisoner of war or his repatriation, the Detaining Power shall give him a statement, signed by an authorized officer of that Power, showing the credit balance then due to him. The Detaining Power shall also send through the Protecting Power to the government upon which the prisoner of war depends, lists giving all appropriate particulars of all prisoners of war whose captivity has been terminated by repatriation, release, escape, death or any other means, and showing the amount of their credit balances. Such lists shall be certified on each sheet by an authorized representative of the Detaining Power.

Any of the above provisions of this Article may be varied by mutual agreement between any two Parties to the conflict.

The Power on which the prisoner of war depends shall be responsible for settling with him any credit balance due to him from the Detaining Power on the termination of his captivity.

*Article 67.* Advances of pay, issued to prisoners of war in conformity with Article 60, shall be considered as made on behalf of the Power on which they depend. Such advances of pay, as well as all payments made by the said Power under Article 63, third paragraph, and Article 68, shall form the subject of arrangements between the Powers concerned, at the close of hostilities.

*Article 68.* Any claim by a prisoner of war for compensation in respect of any injury or other disability arising out of work shall be referred to the Power on which he depends, through the Protecting Power. In accordance with Article 54, the Detaining Power will, in all cases, provide the prisoner of war concerned with a statement showing the nature of the injury or disability, the circumstances in which it arose and particulars of medical or hospital treatment given for it. This statement will be signed by a responsible officer of the Detaining Power and the medical particulars certified by a medical officer.

Any claim from a prisoner of war for compensation in respect of personal effects, monies or valuables impounded by the Detaining Power under Article 18 and not forthcoming on his repatriation, or in respect of loss alleged to be due to the fault of the Detaining Power or any of its servants, shall likewise be referred to the Power on which he depends. Nevertheless, any such personal effects required for use by the prisoners of war whilst in captivity shall be replaced at the expense of the Detaining Power. The Detaining Power will, in all cases, provide the prisoner of war with a statement, signed by a responsible officer, showing all available information regarding the reasons why such effects, monies or valuable have not been restored to him. A copy of this statement will be forwarded to the Power on which he depends through the Central Agency for Prisoners of War provided for in Article 123.

### Section V—Relations of Prisoners of War with the Exterior

*Article 69.* Immediately upon prisoners of war falling into its power, the Detaining Power shall inform them and the Powers on which they depend, through the Protecting Power, of the measures taken to carry out the provisions of the present Section. They shall likewise inform the parties concerned of any subsequent modifications of such measures.

*Article 70.* Immediately upon capture, or not more than one week after arrival at a camp, even if it is a transit camp, likewise in case of sickness or transfer to hospital or another camp, every prisoner of war shall be enabled to write direct to his family, on the one hand, and to the Central Prisoners of War Agency provided for in Article 123, on the other hand, a card similar, if possible, to the model annexed to the present Convention, informing his relatives of his capture, address and state of health. The said cards shall be forwarded as rapidly as possible and may not be delayed in any manner.

*Article 71.* Prisoners of war shall be allowed to send and receive letters and cards. If the Detaining Power deems it necessary to limit the number of letters and cards sent by each prisoner of war, the said number shall not be less than two letters and four cards monthly, exclusive of the capture cards provided for in Article 70, and conforming as closely as possible to the models annexed to the present Convention. Further limitations may be imposed only if the Protecting Power is satisfied that it would be in the interests of the prisoners of war concerned to do so owing to difficulties of translation caused by the Detaining Power's inability to find sufficient qualified linguists to carry out the necessary censorship. If limitations must be placed on the correspondence addressed to prisoners of war, they may be ordered only by the Power on which the prisoners depend, possibly at the request of the Detaining Power. Such letters and cards must be conveyed by the most rapid method at the disposal of the Detaining Power; they may not be delayed or retained for disciplinary reasons.

Prisoners of war who have been without news for a long period, or who are unable to receive news from their next of kin or to give them news by the ordinary postal route, as well as those who are at a great distance from their homes, shall be permitted to send telegrams, the fees being charged against the prisoners of war's accounts with the Detaining Power or paid in the currency at their disposal. They shall likewise benefit by this measure in cases of urgency.

As a general rule, the correspondence of prisoners of war shall be written in their native language. The Parties to the conflict may allow correspondence in other languages.

Sacks containing prisoner-of-war mail must be securely sealed and labelled so as clearly to indicate their contents, and must be addressed to offices of destination.

*Article 72.* Prisoners of war shall be allowed to receive by post or by any other means individual parcels or collective shipments containing, in particular, foodstuffs, clothing, medical supplies and articles of a religious, educational or recreational character which may meet their needs, including books, devotional articles, scientific equipment, exami-

nation papers, musical instruments, sports outfits and materials allowing prisoners of war to pursue their studies or their cultural activities.

Such shipments shall in no way free the Detaining Power from the obligations imposed upon it by the virtue of the present Convention.

The only limits which may be placed on these shipments shall be those proposed by the Protecting Power in the interest of the prisoners themselves, or by the International Committee of the Red Cross or any other organization giving assistance to the prisoners, in respect of their own shipments only, on account of exceptional strain on transport or communications.

The conditions for the sending of individual parcels and collective relief shall, if necessary, be the subject of special agreements between the Powers concerned, which may in no case delay the receipt by the prisoners of relief supplies. Books may not be included in parcels of clothing and foodstuffs. Medical supplies shall, as a rule, be sent in collective parcels.

*Article 73.* In the absence of special agreements between the Powers concerned on the conditions for the receipt and distribution of collective relief shipments, the rules and regulations concerning collective shipments, which are annexed to the present Convention, shall be applied.

The special agreements referred to above shall in no case restrict the right of prisoners' representatives to take possession of collective relief shipments intended for prisoners of war, to proceed to their distribution or to dispose of them in the interest of the prisoners.

Nor shall such agreements restrict the right of representatives of the Protecting Power, the International Committee of the Red Cross or any other organization giving assistance to prisoners of war and responsible for the forwarding of collective shipments, to supervise their distribution to the recipients.

*Article 74.* All relief shipments for prisoners of war shall be exempt from import, customs and other dues.

Correspondence, relief shipments and authorized remittances of money addressed to prisoners of war or despatched by them through the post office, either direct or through the Information Bureaux provided for in Article 122 and the Central Prisoners of War Agency provided in Article 123, shall be exempt from any postal dues, both in the countries of origin and destination, and in intermediate countries.

If relief shipments intended for prisoners of war cannot be sent through the post office by reason of weight or for any other cause, the cost of transportation shall be borne by the Detaining Power in all the territories under its control. The other Powers party to the Convention shall bear the cost of transport in their respective territories.

In the absence of special agreements between the Parties concerned, the costs connected with transport of such shipments, other than costs covered by the above exemption, shall be charged to the senders.

The High Contracting Parties shall endeavour to reduce, so far as possible, the rates charged for telegrams sent by prisoners of war, or addressed to them.

*Article 75.* Should military operations prevent the Powers concerned from fulfilling their obligation to assure the transport of the shipments referred to in Articles 70, 71, 72 and 77, the Protecting Powers concerned, the International Committee of the Red Cross or any other organization duly approved by the Parties to the conflict may undertake to ensure the conveyance of such shipments by suitable means (railway wagons, motor vehicles, vessels or aircraft, etc.). For this purpose, the High Contracting Parties shall endeavour to supply them with such transport and to allow its circulation, especially by granting the necessary safe-conducts.

Such transport may also be used to convey:

(a) correspondence, lists and reports exchanged between the Central Information Agency referred to in Article 123 and the National Bureaux referred to in Article 122;

(b) correspondence and reports relating to prisoners of war which the Protecting Powers, the International Committee of the Red Cross or any other body assisting the prisoners, exchange either with their own delegates or with the Parties to the conflict.

These provisions in no way detract from the right of any Party to the conflict to arrange other means of transport, if it should so prefer, nor preclude the granting of safe-conducts, under mutually agreed conditions, to such means of transport.

In the absence of special agreements, the costs occasioned by the use of such means of transport shall be borne proportionally by the Parties to the conflict whose nationals are benefited thereby.

*Article 76.* The censoring of correspondence addressed to prisoners of war or despatched by them shall be done as quickly as possible. Mail shall be censored only by the despatching State and the receiving State, and once only by each.

The examination of consignments intended for prisoners of war shall not be carried out under conditions that will expose the goods contained in them to deterioration; except in the case of written or printed matter, it shall be done in the presence of the addressee, or of a fellow-prisoner duly delegated by him. The delivery to prisoners of individual or collective consignments shall not be delayed under the pretext of difficulties of censorship.

Any prohibition of correspondence ordered by Parties to the conflict, either for military or political reasons, shall be only temporary and its duration shall be as short as possible.

*Article 77.* The Detaining Powers shall provide all facilities for the transmission, through the Protecting Power or the Central Prisoners of War Agency provided for in Article 123, of instruments, papers or documents intended for prisoners of war or despatched by them, especially powers of attorney and wills.

In all cases they shall facilitate the preparation and execution of such documents on behalf of prisoners of war; in particular, they shall allow them to consult a lawyer and shall take what measures are necessary for the authentication of their signatures.

### Section VI—Relations between Prisoners of War and the Authorities

### Chapter I—Complaints of Prisoners of War Respecting the Conditions of Captivity

*Article 78.* Prisoners of war shall have the right to make known to the military authorities in whose power they are, their requests regarding the conditions of captivity to which they are subjected.

They shall also have the unrestricted right to apply to the representatives of the Protecting Powers either through their prisoners' representative or, if they consider it necessary, direct, in order to draw their attention to any points on which they may have complaints to make regarding their conditions of captivity.

These requests and complaints shall not be limited nor considered to be a part of the correspondence quota referred to in Article 71. They must be transmitted immediately. Even if they are recognized to be unfounded, they may not give rise to any punishment.

Prisoners' representatives may send periodic reports on the situation in the camps and the needs of the prisoners of war to the representatives of the Protecting Powers.

### Chapter II—Prisoners of War Representatives

*Article 79.* In all places where there are prisoners of war, except in those where there are officers, the prisoners shall freely elect by secret ballot, every six months, and also in case of vacancies, prisoners' representatives entrusted with representing them before the military authorities, the Protecting Powers, the International Committee of the Red Cross and any other organization which may assist them. These prisoners' representatives shall be eligible for re-election.

In camps for officers and persons of equivalent status or in mixed camps, the senior officer among the prisoners of war shall be recognised as the camp prisoners' representative. In camps for officers, he shall be assisted by one or more advisers chosen by the officers; in mixed camps, his assistant shall be chosen from among the prisoners of war who are not officers and shall be elected by them.

Officer prisoners of war of the same nationality shall be stationed in labour camps for prisoners of war, for the purpose of carrying out the camp administration duties for which the prisoners of war are responsible. These officers may be elected as prisoners' representatives under the first paragraph of this Article. In such a case the assistants to the prisoners' representatives shall be chosen from among those prisoners of war who are not officers.

Every representative elected must be approved by the Detaining Power before he has the right to commence his duties. Where the Detaining Power refuses to approve a prisoner of war elected by his fellow prisoners of war, it must inform the Protecting Power of the reason for such refusal.

In all cases the prisoners' representative must have the same nationality, language and customs as the prisoners of war whom he represents. Thus, prisoners of war distributed in different sections of a camp, according to their nationality, language or customs, shall have for each section their own prisoners' representative, in accordance with the foregoing paragraphs.

*Article 80.* Prisoners' representatives shall further the physical, spiritual and intellectual well-being of prisoners of war.

In particular, where the prisoners decide to organize amongst themselves a system of mutual assistance, this organization will be within the province of the prisoners' representative, in addition to the special duties entrusted to him by other provisions of the present Convention.

Prisoners' representatives shall not be held responsible, simply by reason of their duties, for any offences committed by prisoners of war.

*Article 81.* Prisoners' representatives shall not be required to perform any other work, if the accomplishment of their duties is thereby made more difficult.

Prisoners' representatives may appoint from amongst the prisoners such assistants as they may require. All material facilities shall be granted them, particularly a certain freedom of movement necessary for the accomplishment of their duties (inspections of labour detachments, receipt of supplies, etc.).

Prisoners' representatives shall be permitted to visit premises where prisoners of war are detained, and every prisoner of war shall have the right to consult freely his prisoners' representative.

All facilities shall likewise be accorded to the prisoners' representatives for communication by post and telegraph with the detaining authorities, the Protecting Powers, the International Committee of the Red Cross and their delegates, the Mixed Medical Commission and with the bodies which give assistance to prisoners of war. Prisoners' representatives of labour detachments shall enjoy the same facilities for communication with the prisoners' representatives of the principal camp. Such communications shall not be restricted, nor considered as forming a part of the quota mentioned in Article 71.

Prisoners' representatives who are transferred shall be allowed a reasonable time to acquaint their successors with current affairs.

In case of dismissal, the reasons therefor shall be communicated to the Protecting Power.

### Chapter III—Penal and Disciplinary Sanctions

#### (I) General Provisions

*Article 82.* A prisoner of war shall be subject to the laws, regulations and orders in force in the armed forces of the Detaining Power; the Detaining Power shall be justified in taking judicial or disciplinary measures in respect of any offence committed by a prisoner of war against such laws, regulations or orders. However, no proceedings or punishments contrary to the provisions of this Chapter shall be allowed.

If any law, regulation or order of the Detaining Power shall declare acts committed by a prisoner of war to be punishable, whereas the same acts would not be punishable if committed by a member of the forces of the Detaining Power, such acts shall entail disciplinary punishments only.

*Article 83.* In deciding whether proceedings in respect of an offence alleged to have been committed by a prisoner of war shall be judicial or disciplinary, the Detaining Power shall ensure that the competent authorities exercise the greatest leniency and adopt, wherever possible, disciplinary rather than judicial measures.

*Article 84.* A prisoner of war shall be tried only by a military court, unless the existing laws of the Detaining Power expressly permit the civil courts to try a member of the armed forces of the Detaining Power in respect of the particular offence alleged to have been committed by the prisoner of war.

In no circumstances whatever shall a prisoner of war be tried by a court of any kind which does not offer the essential guarantees of independence and impartiality as generally recognized, and, in particular, the procedure of which does not afford the accused the rights and means of defence provided for in Article 105.

*Article 85.* Prisoners of war prosecuted under the laws of the Detaining Power for acts committed prior to capture shall retain, even if convicted, the benefits of the present Convention.

*Article 86.* No prisoner of war may be punished more than once for the same act or on the same charge.

*Article 87.* Prisoners of war may not be sentenced by the military authorities and courts of the Detaining Power to any penalties except those provided for in respect of members of the armed forces of the said Power who have committed the same acts.

When fixing the penalty, the courts or authorities of the Detaining Power shall take into consideration, to the widest extent possible, the fact that the accused, not being a national of the Detaining Power, is not bound to it by any duty of allegiance, and that he is in its power as the result of circumstances independent of his own will. The said courts or authorities shall be at liberty to reduce the penalty provided for the violation of which the prisoner of war is accused, and shall therefore not be bound to apply the minimum penalty prescribed.

Collective punishment for individual acts, corporal punishments, imprisonment in premises without daylight and, in general, any form of torture or cruelty, are forbidden.

No prisoner of war may be deprived of his rank by the Detaining Power, or prevented from wearing his badges.

*Article 88.* Officers, non-commissioned officers and men who are prisoners of war undergoing a disciplinary or judicial punishment, shall not be subjected to more severe treatment than that applied in respect of the same punishment to members of the armed forces of the Detaining Power of equivalent rank.

A woman prisoner of war shall not be awarded or sentenced to a punishment more severe, or treated whilst undergoing punishment more severely, than a woman member of the armed forces of the Detaining Power dealt with for a similar offence.

In no case may a woman prisoner of war be awarded or sentenced to a punishment more severe, or treated whilst undergoing punishment more severely, than a male member of the armed forces of the Detaining Power dealt with for a similar offence.

Prisoners of war who have served disciplinary or judicial sentences may not be treated differently from other prisoners of war.

#### (II) Disciplinary Sanctions

*Article 89.* The disciplinary punishments applicable to prisoners of war are the following:

(1) a fine which shall not exceed 50 per cent of the advances of pay and working pay which the prisoner of war would otherwise receive under the provisions of Articles 60 and 62 during a period of not more than thirty days.

(2) Discontinuance of privileges granted over and above the treatment provided for by the present Convention.

(3) Fatigue duties not exceeding two hours daily.

(4) Confinement.

The punishment referred to under (3) shall not be applied to officers.

In no case shall disciplinary punishments be inhuman, brutal or dangerous to the health of prisoners of war.

*Article 90.* The duration of any single punishment shall in no case exceed thirty days. Any period of confinement awaiting the hearing of a disciplinary offence or the award of disciplinary punishment shall be deducted from an award pronounced against a prisoner of war.

The maximum of thirty days provided above may not be exceeded, even if the prisoner of war is answerable for several acts at the same time when he is awarded punishment, whether such acts are related or not.

The period between the pronouncing of an award of disciplinary punishment and its execution shall not exceed one month.

When a prisoner of war is awarded a further disciplinary punishment, a period of at least three days shall elapse between the execution of any two of the punishments, if the duration of one of these is ten days or more.

*Article 91.* The escape of a prisoner of war shall be deemed to have succeeded when:

(1) he has joined the armed forces of the Power on which he depends, or those of an allied Power;

(2) he has left the territory under the control of the Detaining Power, or of an ally of the said Power;

(3) he has joined a ship flying the flag of the Power on which he depends, or of an allied Power, in the territorial waters of the Detaining Power, the said ship not being under the control of the last named Power.

Prisoners of war who have made good their escape in the sense of this Article and who are recaptured, shall not be liable to any punishment in respect of their previous escape.

*Article 92.* A prisoner of war who attempts to escape and is recaptured before having made good his escape in the sense of Article 91 shall be liable only to a disciplinary punishment in respect of this act, even if it is a repeated offence.

A prisoner of war who is recaptured shall be handed over without delay to the competent military authority.

Article 88, fourth paragraph, notwithstanding, prisoners of war punished as a result of an unsuccessful escape may be subjected to special surveillance. Such surveillance must not affect the state of their health, must be undergone in a prisoner of war camp, and must not entail the suppression of any of the safeguards granted them by the present Convention.

*Article 93.* Escape or attempt to escape, even if it is a repeated offence, shall not be deemed an aggravating circumstance if the prisoner of war is subjected to trial by judicial proceedings in respect of an offence committed during his escape or attempt to escape.

In conformity with the principle stated in Article 83, offences committed by prisoners of war with the sole intention of facilitating their escape and which do not entail any violence against life or limb, such as offences against public property, theft without intention of self-enrichment, the drawing up or use of false papers, the wearing of civilian clothing, shall occasion disciplinary punishment only.

Prisoners of war who aid or abet an escape or an attempt to escape shall be liable on this count to disciplinary punishment only.

*Article 94.* If an escaped prisoner of war is recaptured, the Power on which he depends shall be notified thereof in the manner defined in Article 122, provided notification of his escape has been made.

*Article 95.* A prisoner of war accused of an offence against discipline shall not be kept in confinement pending the hearing unless a member of the armed forces of the Detaining Power would be so kept if he were accused of a similar offence, or if it is essential in the interests of camp order and discipline.

Any period spent by a prisoner of war in confinement awaiting the disposal of an offence against discipline shall be reduced to an absolute minimum and shall not exceed fourteen days.

The provisions of Articles 97 and 98 of this Chapter shall apply to prisoners of war who are in confinement awaiting the disposal of offences against discipline.

*Article 96.* Acts which constitute offences against discipline shall be investigated immediately.

Without prejudice to the competence of courts and superior military authorities, disciplinary punishment may be ordered only by an officer having disciplinary powers in his capacity as camp commander, or by a responsible officer who replaces him or to whom he has delegated his disciplinary powers.

In no case may such powers be delegated to a prisoner of war or be exercised by a prisoner of war.

Before any disciplinary award is pronounced, the accused shall be given precise information regarding the offences of which he is accused, and given an opportunity of explaining his conduct and of defending himself. He shall be permitted, in particular, to call witnesses and to have recourse, if necessary, to the services of a qualified interpreter. The decision shall be announced to the accused prisoner of war and to the prisoners' representative.

A record of disciplinary punishments shall be maintained by the camp commander and shall be open to inspection by representatives of the Protecting Power.

*Article 97.* Prisoners of war shall not in any case be transferred to penitentiary establishments (prisons, penitentiaries, convict prisons, etc.) to undergo disciplinary punishment therein.

All premises in which disciplinary punishments are undergone shall conform to the sanitary requirements set forth in Article 25. A prisoner of war undergoing punishment shall be enabled to keep himself in a state of cleanliness, in conformity with Article 29.

Officers and persons of equivalent status shall not be lodged in the same quarters as non-commissioned officers or men.

Women prisoners of war undergoing disciplinary punishment shall be confined in separate quarters from male prisoners of war and shall be under the immediate supervision of women.

*Article 98.* A prisoner of war undergoing confinement as a disciplinary punishment, shall continue to enjoy the benefits of the provisions of this Convention except in so far as these are necessarily rendered inapplicable by the mere fact that he is confined. In no case may he be deprived of the benefits of the provisions of Articles 78 and 126.

A prisoner of war awarded disciplinary punishment may not be deprived of the prerogatives attached to his rank.

Prisoners of war awarded disciplinary punishment shall be allowed to exercise and to stay in the open air at least two hours daily.

They shall be allowed, on their request, to be present at the daily medical inspections. They shall receive the attention which their state of health requires and, if necessary, shall be removed to the camp infirmary or to a hospital.

They shall have permission to read and write, likewise to send and receive letters. Parcels and remittances of money, however, may be withheld from them until the completion of the punishment; they shall meanwhile be entrusted to the prisoners' representative, who will hand over to the infirmary the perishable goods contained in such parcels.

**(III) Judicial Proceedings**

*Article 99.* No prisoner of war may be tried or sentenced for an act which is not forbidden by the law of the Detaining Power or by International Law, in force at the time the said act was committed.

No moral or physical coercion may be exerted on a prisoner of war in order to induce him to admit himself guilty of the act of which he is accused.

No prisoner of war may be convicted without having had an opportunity to present his defence and the assistance of a qualified advocate or counsel.

*Article 100.* Prisoners of war and the Protecting Powers shall be informed, as soon as possible, of the offences which are punishable by the death sentence under the laws of the Detaining Power.

Other offences shall not thereafter be made punishable

by the death penalty without the concurrence of the Power upon which the prisoners of war depend.

The death sentence cannot be pronounced on a prisoner of war unless the attention of the court has, in accordance with Article 87, second paragraph, been particularly called to the fact that since the accused is not a national of the Detaining Power, he is not bound to it by any duty of allegiance, and that he is in its power as the result of circumstances independent of his own will.

*Article 101.* If the death penalty is pronounced on a prisoner of war, the sentence shall not be executed before the expiration of a period of at least six months from the date when the Protecting Power receives, at an indicated address, the detailed communication provided for in Article 107.

*Article 102.* A prisoner of war can be validly sentenced only if the sentence has been pronounced by the same courts according to the same procedure as in the case of members of the armed forces of the Detaining Power, and if, furthermore, the provisions of the present Chapter have been observed.

*Article 103.* Judicial investigations relating to a prisoner of war shall be conducted as rapidly as circumstances permit and so that his trial shall take place as soon as possible. A prisoner of war shall not be confined while awaiting trial unless a member of the armed forces of the Detaining Power would be so confined if he were accused of a similar offence, or if it is essential to do so in the interests of national security. In no circumstances shall this confinement exceed three months.

Any period spent by a prisoner of war in confinement awaiting trial shall be deducted from any sentence of imprisonment passed upon him and taken into account in fixing any penalty.

The provisions of Articles 97 and 98 of this Chapter shall apply to a prisoner of war whilst in confinement awaiting trial.

*Article 104.* In any case in which the Detaining Power has decided to institute judicial proceedings against a prisoner of war, it shall notify the Protecting Power as soon as possible and at least three weeks before the opening of the trial. This period of three weeks shall run as from the day on which such notification reaches the Protecting Power at the address previously indicated by the latter to the Detaining Power.

The said notification shall contain the following information:

(1) Surname and first names of the prisoner of war, his rank, his army, regimental, personal or serial number, his date of birth, and his profession or trade, if any.

(2) Place of internment or confinement.

(3) Specification of the charge or charges on which the prisoner of war is to be arraigned, giving the legal provisions applicable.

(4) Designation of the court which will try the case, likewise the date and place fixed for the opening of the trial.

The same communication shall be made by the Detaining Power to the prisoners' representative.

If no evidence is submitted, at the opening of a trial, that the notification referred to above was received by the Protecting Power, by the prisoner of war and by the prisoners' representative concerned, at least three weeks before the opening of the trial, then the latter cannot take place and must be adjourned.

*Article 105.* The prisoner of war shall be entitled to assistance by one of his prisoner comrades, to defence by a qualified advocate or counsel of his own choice, to the calling of witnesses and, if he deems necessary, to the services of a competent interpreter. He shall be advised of these rights by the Detaining Power in due time before the trial.

Failing a choice by the prisoner of war, the Protecting Power shall find him an advocate or counsel, and shall have at least one week at its disposal for the purpose. The Detaining Power shall deliver to the said Power, on request, a list of persons qualified to present the defence. Failing a choice of an advocate or counsel by the prisoner of war or the Protecting Power, the Detaining Power shall appoint a competent advocate or counsel to conduct the defence.

The advocate or counsel conducting the defence on behalf of the prisoner of war shall have at his disposal a period of two weeks at least before the opening of the trial, as well as the necessary facilities to prepare the defence of the accused. He may, in particular, freely visit the accused and interview him in private. He may also confer with any witnesses for the defence, including prisoners of war. He shall have the benefit of these facilities until the term of appeal or petition has expired.

Particulars of the charge or charges on which the prisoner of war is to be arraigned, as well as the documents which are generally communicated to the accused by virtue of the laws in force in the armed forces of the Detaining Power, shall be communicated to the accused prisoner of war in a language which he understands, and in good time before the opening of the trial. The same communication in the same circumstances shall be made to the advocate or counsel conducting the defence on behalf of the prisoner of war.

The representatives of the Protecting Power shall be entitled to attend the trial of the case, unless, exceptionally, this is held *in camera* in the interest of State security. In such a case the Detaining Power shall advise the Protecting Power accordingly.

*Article 106.* Every prisoner of war shall have, in the same manner as the members of the armed forces of the Detaining Power, the right of appeal or petition from any sentence pronounced upon him, with a view to the quashing or revising of the sentence or the reopening of the trial. He shall be fully informed of his right to appeal or petition and of the time limit within which he may do so.

*Article 107.* Any judgment and sentence pronounced upon a prisoner of war shall be immediately reported to the Protecting Power in the form of a summary communication, which shall also indicate whether he has the right of appeal with a view to the quashing of the sentence or the re-opening of the trial. This communication shall likewise be sent to the prisoners' representative concerned. It shall also be sent to the accused prisoner of war in a language he understands, if the sentence was not pronounced in his presence. The Detaining Power shall also immediately communicate to the Protecting Power the decision of the prisoner of war to use or to waive his right of appeal.

Furthermore, if a prisoner of war is finally convicted or if a sentence pronounced against a prisoner of war in the first instance is a death sentence, the Detaining Power shall as soon as possible address to the Protecting Power a detailed communication containing:

(1) the precise wording of the finding and sentence;

(2) a summarized report of any preliminary investigation and of the trial, emphasizing in particular the elements of the prosecution and the defence;

(3) notification, where applicable, of the establishment where the sentence will be served.

The communications provided for in the forgoing sub-paragraphs shall be sent to the Protecting Power at the address previously made known to the Detaining Power.

*Article 108.* Sentences pronounced on prisoners of war after a conviction has become duly enforceable shall be served in the same establishments and under the same conditions as in the case of members of the armed forces of the Detaining Power. These conditions shall in all cases conform to the requirements of health and humanity.

A woman prisoner of war on whom such a sentence has been pronounced shall be confined in separate quarters and shall be under the supervision of women.

In any case, prisoners of war sentenced to a penalty depriving them of their liberty shall retain the benefit of the provisions of Articles 78 and 126 of the present Convention. Furthermore, they shall be entitled to receive and despatch correspondence, to receive at least one relief parcel monthly, to take regular exercise in the open air, to have the medical care required by their state of health, and the spiritual assistance they may desire. Penalties to which they may be subjected shall be in accordance with the provisions of Article 87, third paragraph.

## Part IV

### Termination of Captivity

#### Section I—Direct Repatriation and Accommodation in Neutral Countries

*Article 109.* Subject to the provisions of the third paragraph of this Article, Parties to the conflict are bound to send back to their own country, regardless of number or rank, seriously wounded and seriously sick prisoners of war, after having cared for them until they are fit to travel, in accordance with the first paragraph of the following Article.

Throughout the duration of hostilities, Parties to the conflict shall endeavour, with the co-operation of the neutral Powers concerned, to make arrangements for the accommodation in neutral countries of the sick and wounded prisoners of war referred to in the second paragraph of the following Article. They may, in addition, conclude agreements with a view to the direct repatriation or internment in a neutral country of able-bodied prisoners of war who have undergone a long period of captivity.

No sick or injured prisoner of war who is eligible for repatriation under the first paragraph of this Article, may be repatriated against his will during hostilities.

*Article 110.* The following shall be repatriated direct:

(1) Incurably wounded and sick whose mental or physical fitness seems to have been gravely diminished.

(2) Wounded and sick who, according to medical opinion, are not likely to recover within one year, whose condition requires treatment and whose mental or physical fitness seems to have been gravely diminished.

(3) Wounded and sick who have recovered, but whose mental or physical fitness seems to have gravely and permanently diminished.

The following may be accommodated in a neutral country:

(1) Wounded and sick whose recovery may be expected within one year of the date of the wound or the beginning of the illness, if treatment in a neutral country might increase the prospects of a more certain and speedy recovery.

(2) Prisoners of war whose mental or physical health, according to medical opinion, is seriously threatened by continued captivity, but whose accommodation in a neutral country might remove such a threat.

The conditions which prisoners of war accommodated in a neutral country must fulfil in order to permit their repatriation shall be fixed, as shall likewise their status, by agreement between the Powers concerned. In general, prisoners of war who have been accommodated in a neutral country, and who belong to the following categories, should be repatriated:

(1) Those whose state of health has deteriorated so as to fulfil the conditions laid down for direct repatriation;

(2) Those whose mental or physical powers remain, even after treatment, considerably impaired.

If no special agreements are concluded between the Parties to the conflict concerned, to determine the cases of disablement or sickness entailing direct repatriation or accommodation in a neutral country, such cases shall be settled in accordance with the principles laid down in the Model Agreement concerning direct repatriation and accommodation in neutral countries of wounded and sick prisoners of war and in the Regulations concerning Mixed Medical Commissions annexed to the present Convention.

*Article 111.* The Detaining Power, the Power on which the prisoners of war depend, and a neutral Power agreed upon by these two Powers, shall endeavour to conclude agreements which will enable prisoners of war to be interned in the territory of the said neutral Power until the close of hostilities.

*Article 112.* Upon the outbreak of hostilities, Mixed Medical Commissions shall be appointed to examine sick and wounded prisoners of war, and to make all appropriate decisions regarding them. The appointment, duties and functioning of these Commissions shall be in conformity with the provisions of the Regulations annexed to the present Convention.

However, prisoners of war who, in the opinion of the medical authorities of the Detaining Power, are manifestly seriously injured or seriously sick, may be repatriated without having to be examined by a Mixed Medical Commission.

*Article 113.* Besides those who are designated by the medical authorities of the Detaining Power, wounded or sick prisoners of war belonging to the categories listed below shall be entitled to present themselves for examination by the Mixed Medical Commissions provided for in the forgoing Article:

(1) Wounded and sick proposed by a physician or surgeon who is of the same nationality, or a national of a Party to the conflict allied with the Power on which the said prisoners depend, and who exercises his functions in the camp.

(2) Wounded and sick proposed by their prisoners' representative.

(3) Wounded and sick proposed by the Power on which they depend, or by an organization duly recognized by the said Power and giving assistance to the prisoners.

Prisoners of war who do not belong to one of the three foregoing categories may nevertheless present themselves for examination by Mixed Medical Commissions, but shall be examined only after those belonging to the said categories.

The physician or surgeon of the same nationality as the prisoners who present themselves for examination by the Mixed Medical Commission, likewise the prisoners' representative of the said prisoners, shall have permission to be present at the examination.

*Article 114.* Prisoners of war who meet with accidents shall, unless the injury is self-inflicted, have the benefit of the provisions of this Convention as regards repatriation or accommodation in a neutral country.

*Article 115.* No prisoner of war on whom a disciplinary punishment has been imposed and who is eligible for repatriation or for accommodation in a neutral country, may be kept back on the plea that he has not undergone his punishment.

Prisoners of war detained in connection with a judicial prosecution or conviction and who are designated for repatriation or accommodation in a neutral country, may benefit by such measures before the end of the proceedings or the completion of the punishment, if the Detaining Power consents.

Parties to the conflict shall communicate to each other the names of those who will be detained until the end of the proceedings or the completion of the punishment.

*Article 116.* The costs of repatriating prisoners of war or of transporting them to a neutral country shall be borne, from the frontiers of the Detaining Power, by the Power on which the said prisoners depend.

*Article 117.* No repatriated person may be employed on active military service.

### Section II—Release and Repatriation of Prisoners of War at the Close of Hostilities

*Article 118.* Prisoners of war shall be released and repatriated without delay after the cessation of active hostilities.

In the absence of stipulations to the above effect in any agreement concluded between the Parties to the conflict with a view to the cessation of hostilities, or failing any such agreement, each of the Detaining Powers shall itself establish and execute without delay a plan of repatriation in conformity with the principle laid down in the foregoing paragraph.

In either case, the measures adopted shall be brought to the knowledge of the prisoners of war.

The costs of repatriation of prisoners of war shall in all cases be equitably apportioned between the Detaining Power and the Power on which the prisoners depend. This apportionment shall be carried out on the following basis:

(a) If the two Powers are contiguous, the Power on which the prisoners of war depend shall bear the costs of repatriation from the frontiers of the Detaining Power.

(b) If the two Powers are not contiguous, the Detaining Power shall bear the costs of transport of prisoners of war over its own territory as far as its frontier or its port of embarkation nearest to the territory of the Power on which the prisoners of war depend. The Parties concerned shall agree between themselves as to the equitable apportionment of the remaining costs of the repatriation. The conclusion of this agreement shall in no circumstances justify any delay in the repatriation of the prisoners of war.

*Article 119.* Repatriation shall be effected in conditions similar to those laid down in Articles 46 to 48 inclusive of the present Convention for the transfer of prisoners of war, having regard to the provisions of Article 118 and to those of the following paragraphs.

On repatriation, any articles of value impounded from prisoners of war under Article 18, and any foreign currency which has not been converted into the currency of the Detaining Power, shall be restored to them. Articles of value and foreign currency which, for any reason whatever, are not restored to prisoners of war on repatriation, shall be despatched to the Information Bureau set up under Article 122.

Prisoners of war shall be allowed to take with them their personal effects, and any correspondence and parcels which have arrived for them. The weight of such baggage may be limited, if the conditions of repatriation so require, to what each prisoner can reasonably carry. Each prisoner shall in all cases be authorized to carry at least twenty-five kilograms.

The other personal effects of the repatriated prisoner shall be left in the charge of the Detaining Power which shall have them forwarded to him as soon as it has concluded an agreement to this effect, regulating the conditions of transport and the payment of the costs involved, with the Power on which the prisoner depends.

Prisoners of war against whom criminal proceedings for an indictable offence are pending may be detained until the end of such proceedings, and, if necessary, until the completion of the punishment. The same shall apply to prisoners of war already convicted for an indictable offence.

Parties to the conflict shall communicate to each other the names of any prisoners of war who are detained until the end of proceedings or until punishment has been completed.

By agreement between the Parties to the conflict, commissions shall be established for the purpose of searching for dispersed prisoners of war and of assuring their repatriation with the least possible delay.

### Section III—Death of Prisoners of War

*Article 120.* Wills of prisoners of war shall be drawn up so as to satisfy the conditions of validity required by the legislation of their country of origin, which will take steps to inform the Detaining Power of its requirements in this respect. At the request of the prisoner of war and, in all cases, after death, the will shall be transmitted without delay to the Protecting Power; a certified copy shall be sent to the Central Agency.

Death certificates, in the form annexed to the present Convention, or lists certified by a responsible officer, of all persons who die as prisoners of war shall be forwarded as rapidly as possible to the Prisoner of War Information Bureau established in accordance with Article 122. The death certificates or certified lists shall show particulars of identity as set out in the third paragraph of Article 17, and also the date and place of death, the cause of death, the date and place of burial and all particulars necessary to identify the graves.

The burial or cremation of a prisoner of war shall be preceded by a medical examination of the body with a view to confirming death and enabling a report to be made and, where necessary, establishing identity.

The detaining authorities shall ensure that prisoners of war who have died in captivity are honourably buried, if possible according to the rites of the religion to which they belonged, and that their graves are respected, suitably maintained and marked so as to be found at any time. Wherever possible, deceased prisoners of war who depended on the same Power shall be interred in the same place.

Deceased prisoners of war shall be buried in individual graves unless unavoidable circumstances require the use of collective graves. Bodies may be cremated only for imperative reasons of hygiene, on account of the religion of the deceased or in accordance with his express wish to this effect. In case of cremation, the fact shall be stated and the reasons given in the death certificate of the deceased.

In order that graves may always be found, all particulars of burials and graves shall be recorded with a Graves Registration Service established by the Detaining Power. Lists of graves and particulars of the prisoners of war interred in cemeteries and elsewhere shall be transmitted to the Power on which such prisoners of war depended. Responsibility for the care of these graves and for records of any subsequent moves of the bodies shall rest on the Power controlling the territory, if a party to the present Convention. These provisions shall also apply to the ashes which shall be kept by the Graves Registration Service until proper disposal thereof in accordance with the wishes of the home country.

*Article 121.* Every death or serious injury of a prisoner of war caused or suspected to have been caused by a sentry, another prisoner of war, or any other person, as well as any death the cause of which is unknown, shall be immediately followed by an official enquiry by the Detaining Power.

A communication on this subject shall be sent immediately to the Protecting Power. Statements shall be taken from witnesses, especially from those who are prisoners of war, and a report including such statements shall be forwarded to the Protecting Power.

If the enquiry indicates the guilt of one or more persons, the Detaining Power shall take all measures for the prosecution of the person or persons responsible.

## Part V

## Information Bureaux and Relief Societies for Prisoners of War

*Article 122.* Upon the outbreak of a conflict and in all cases of occupation, each of the Parties to the conflict shall institute an official Information Bureau for prisoners of war who are in its power. Neutral or non-belligerent Powers who may have received within their territory persons belonging to one of the categories referred to in Article 4, shall take the same action with respect to such persons. The Power concerned shall ensure that the Prisoners of War Information Bureau is provided with the necessary accommodation, equipment and staff to ensure its efficient working. It shall be at liberty to employ prisoners of war in such a Bureau under the conditions laid down in the Section of the present Convention dealing with work by prisoners of war.

Within the shortest possible period, each of the Parties to the conflict shall give its Bureau the information referred to in the fourth, fifth and sixth paragraphs of this Article regarding any enemy person belonging to one of the categories referred to in Article 4, who has fallen into its power. Neutral or non-belligerent Powers shall take the same action with regard to persons belonging to such categories whom they have received within their territory.

The Bureau shall immediately forward such information by the most rapid means to the Powers concerned through the intermediary of the Protecting Powers and likewise of the Central Agency provided for in Article 123.

This information shall make it possible quickly to advise the next of kin concerned. Subject to the provisions of Article 17, the information shall include, in so far as available to the Information Bureau, in respect of each prisoner of war, his surname, first names, rank, army, regimental, personal or serial number, place and full date of birth, indication of the Power on which he depends, first name of the father and maiden name of the mother, name and address of the person to be informed and the address to which correspondence for the prisoner may be sent.

The Information Bureau shall receive from the various departments concerned information regarding transfers, releases, repatriations, escapes, admissions to hospital, and deaths, and shall transmit such information in the manner described in the third paragraph above.

Likewise, information regarding the state of health of prisoners of war who are seriously ill or seriously wounded shall be supplied regularly, every week if possible.

The Information Bureau shall also be responsible for replying to all enquiries sent to it concerning prisoners of war, including those who have died in captivity; it will make any enquiries necessary to obtain the information which is asked for if this is not in its possession.

All written communications made by the Bureau shall be authenticated by a signature or a seal.

The Information Bureau shall furthermore be charged with collecting all personal valuables, including sums in currencies other than that of the Detaining Power and documents of importance to the next of kin, left by prisoners of war who have been repatriated or released, or who have escaped or died, and shall forward the said valuables to the Powers concerned. Such articles shall be sent by the Bureau in sealed packets which shall be accompanied by statements giving clear and full particulars of the identity of the person to whom the articles belonged, and by a complete list of the contents of the parcel. Other personal effects of such prisoners of war shall be transmitted under arrangements agreed upon between the Parties to the conflict concerned.

*Article 123.* A Central Prisoners of War Information Agency shall be created in a neutral country. The International Committee of the Red Cross shall, if it deems necessary, propose to the Powers concerned the organization of such an Agency.

The function of the Agency shall be to collect all the information it may obtain through official or private channels respecting prisoners of war, and to transmit it as rapidly as possible to the country of origin of the prisoners of war or to the Power on which they depend. It shall receive from the Parties to the conflict all facilities for effecting such transmissions.

The High Contracting Parties, and in particular those whose nationals benefit by the services of the Central Agency, are requested to give the said Agency the financial aid it may require.

The foregoing provisions shall in no way be interpreted as restricting the humanitarian activities of the International Committee of the Red Cross, or of the relief Societies provided for in Article 125.

*Article 124.* The national Information Bureaux and the Central Information Agency shall enjoy free postage for mail, likewise all the exemptions provided for in Article 74, and further, so far as possible, exemption from telegraphic charges or, at least, greatly reduced rates.

*Article 125.* Subject to the measures which the Detaining Powers may consider essential to ensure their security or to meet any other reasonable need, the representatives of religious organizations, relief societies, or any other organization assisting prisoners of war, shall receive from the said Powers, for themselves and their duly accredited agents, all necessary facilities for visiting the prisoners, distributing relief supplies and material, from any source, intended for religious, educational or recreative purposes, and for assisting them in organizing their leisure time within the camps. Such societies or organizations may be constituted in the territory of the Detaining Power or in any other country, or they may have an international character.

The Detaining Power may limit the number of societies and organizations whose delegates are allowed to carry out their activities in its territory and under its supervision, on condition, however, that such limitation shall not hinder the effective operation of adequate relief to all prisoners of war.

The special position of the International Committee of the Red Cross in this field shall be recognized and respected at all times.

As soon as relief supplies or material intended for the above-mentioned purposes are handed over to prisoners of war, or very shortly afterwards, receipts for each consignment, signed by the prisoners' representative, shall be forwarded to the relief society or organization making the shipment. At the same time, receipts for these consignments shall be supplied by the administrative authorities responsible for guarding the prisoners.

**Part VI**

**Execution of the Convention**

**Section I—General Provisions**

*Article 126.* Representatives or delegates of the Protecting Powers shall have permission to go to all places where prisoners of war may be, particularly to places of internment, imprisonment and labour, and shall have access to all premises occupied by prisoners of war; they shall also be allowed to go to the places of departure, passage and arrival of prisoners who are being transferred. They shall be able to interview the prisoners, and in particular the prisoners' representatives, without witnesses, either personally or through an interpreter.

Representatives and delegates of the Protecting Powers shall have full liberty to select the places they wish to visit. The duration and frequency of these visits shall not be restricted. Visits may not be prohibited except for reasons of imperative military necessity, and then only as an exceptional and temporary measure.

The Detaining Power and the Power on which the said prisoners of war depend may agree, if necessary, that compatriots of these prisoners of war be permitted to participate in the visits.

The delegates of the International Committee of the Red Cross shall enjoy the same prerogatives. The appointment of such delegates shall be submitted to the approval of the Power detaining the prisoners of war to be visited.

*Article 127.* The High Contracting Parties undertake, in time of peace as in time of war, to disseminate the text of the present Convention as widely as possible in their respective countries, and, in particular, to include the study thereof in their programmes of military and, if possible, civil instruction, so that the principles thereof may become known to all their armed forces and to the entire population.

Any military or other authorities, who in time of war assume responsibilities in respect of prisoners of war, must possess the text of the Convention and be specially instructed as to its provisions.

*Article 128.* The High Contracting Parties shall communicate to one another through the Swiss Federal Council and, during hostilities, through the Protecting Powers, the official translations of the present Convention, as well as the laws and regulations which they may adopt to ensure the application thereof.

*Article 129.* The High Contracting Parties undertake to enact any legislation necessary to provide effective penal sanctions for persons committing, or ordering to be committed, any of the grave breaches of the present Convention defined in the following Article.

Each High Contracting Party shall be under the obligation to search for persons alleged to have committed, or to have ordered to be committed, such grave breaches, and shall bring such persons, regardless of their nationality, before its own courts. It may also, if it prefers, and in accordance with the provisions of its own legislation, hand such persons over for trial to another High Contracting Party concerned, provided such High Contracting Party has made out a *prima facie* case.

Each High Contracting Party shall take measures necessary for the suppression of all acts contrary to the provisions of the present Convention other than the grave breaches defined in the following Article.

In all circumstances, the accused persons shall benefit by safeguards of proper trial and defence, which shall not be less favourable than those provided by Article 105 and those following of the present Convention.

*Article 130.* Grave breaches to which the preceding Article relates shall be those involving any of the following acts, if committed against persons or property protected by the Convention: wilful killing, torture or inhuman treatment, including biological experiments, wilfully causing great suffering or serious injury to body or health, compelling a prisoner of war to serve in the forces of the hostile Power, or wilfully depriving a prisoner of war of the rights of fair and regular trial prescribed in this Convention.

*Article 131.* No High Contracting Party shall be allowed to absolve itself or any other High Contracting Party of any liability incurred by itself or by another High Contracting Party in respect of breaches referred to in the preceding Article.

*Article 132.* At the request of a Party to the conflict, an enquiry shall be instituted, in a manner to be decided between the interested Parties, concerning any alleged violation of the Convention.

If agreement has not been reached concerning the procedure for the enquiry, the Parties should agree on the choice of an umpire who will decide upon the procedure to be followed.

Once the violation has been established, the Parties to the conflict shall put an end to it and shall repress it with the least possible delay.

***GENEVA RED CROSS CONVENTION IV, ON PROTECTION OF CIVILIAN PERSONS IN TIME OF WAR.*** The provisions of the Convention are as follows:

The undersigned Plenipotentiaries of the Governments represented at the Diplomatic Conference held at Geneva from April 21 to August 12, 1949, for the purpose of establishing a Convention for the Protection of Civilian Persons in Time of War, have agreed as follows:

**Part I**

**General Provisions**

*Article 1.* The High Contracting Parties undertake to respect and to ensure respect for the present Convention in all circumstances.

*Article 2.* In addition to the provisions which shall be implemented in peacetime, the present Convention shall apply to all cases of declared war or of any other armed conflict which may arise between two or more of the High Contracting Parties, even if the state of war is not recognized by one of them.

The Convention shall also apply to all cases of partial or total occupation of the territory of a High Contracting Party, even if the said occupation meets with no armed resistance.

Although one of the Powers in conflict may not be a party

to the present Convention, the Powers who are parties thereto shall remain bound by it in their mutual relations. They shall furthermore be bound by the Convention in relation to the said Power, if the latter accepts and applies the provisions thereof.

*Article 3.* In the case of armed conflict not of an international character occurring in the territory of one of the High Contracting Parties, each Party to the conflict shall be bound to apply, as a minimum, the following provisions:

(1) Persons taking no active part in the hostilities, including members of armed forces who have laid down their arms and those placed *hors de combat* by sickness, wounds, detention, or any other cause, shall in all circumstances be treated humanely, without any adverse distinction founded on race, colour, religion or faith, sex, birth or wealth, or any other similar criteria.

To this end, the following acts are and shall remain prohibited at any time and in any place whatsoever with respect to the above-mentioned persons:

(a) violence to life and person, in particular murder of all kinds, mutilation, cruel treatment and torture;

(b) taking of hostages;

(c) outrages upon personal dignity, in particular humiliating and degrading treatment;

(d) the passing of sentences and the carrying out of executions without previous judgment pronounced by a regularly constituted court, affording all the judicial guarantees which are recognized as indispensable by civilized peoples.

(2) The wounded and sick shall be collected and cared for.

An impartial humanitarian body, such as the International Committee of the Red Cross, may offer its services to the Parties to the conflict.

The Parties to the conflict should further endeavour to bring into force, by means of special agreements, all or part of the other provisions of the present Convention.

The application of the preceding provisions shall not affect the legal status of the Parties to the conflict.

*Article 4.* Persons protected by the Convention are those who, at a given moment and in any manner whatsoever, find themselves, in case of a conflict or occupation, in the hands of a Party to the conflict or Occupying Power of which they are not nationals.

Nationals of a State which is not bound by the Convention are not protected by it. Nationals of a neutral State who find themselves in the territory of a belligerent State, and nationals of a co-belligerent State, shall not be regarded as protected persons while the State of which they are nationals has normal diplomatic representation in the State in whose hands they are.

The provisions of Part II are, however, wider in application, as defined in Article 13.

Persons protected by the Geneva Convention for the Amelioration of the Condition of the Wounded and Sick in Armed Forces in the Field of August 12, 1949, or by the Geneva Convention for the Amelioration of the Condition of Wounded, Sick and Shipwrecked Members of Armed Forces at Sea of August 12, 1949, or by the Geneva Convention relative to the Treatment of Prisoners of War of August 12, 1949 shall not be considered as protected persons within the meaning of the present Convention.

*Article 5.* Where, in the territory of a Party to the conflict, the latter is satisfied that an individual protected person is definitely suspected of or engaged in activities hostile to the security of the State, such individual person shall not be en-

titled to claim such rights and privileges under the present Convention as would, if exercised in the favour of such individual person, be prejudicial to the security of such State.

Where in occupied territory an individual protected person is detained as a spy or saboteur, or as a person under definite suspicion of activity hostile to the security of the Occupying Power, such person shall, in those cases where absolute military security so requires, be regarded as having forfeited rights of communication under the present Convention.

In each case, such persons shall nevertheless be treated with humanity, and in case of trial, shall not be deprived of the rights of fair and regular trial prescribed by the present Convention. They shall also be granted the full rights and privileges of a protected person under the present Convention at the earliest date consistent with the security of the State or Occupying Power, as the case may be.

*Article 6.* The present Convention shall apply from the outset of any conflict or occupation mentioned in Article 2.

In the territory of Parties to the conflict, the application of the present Convention shall cease on the general close of military operations.

In the case of occupied territory, the application of the present Convention shall cease one year after the general close of military operations; however, the Occupying Power shall be bound, for the duration of the occupation, to the extent that such Power exercises the functions of government in such territory, by the provisions of the following Articles of the present Convention: 1 to 12, 27, 29 to 34, 47, 49, 51, 52, 53, 59, 61 to 77, 143.

Protected persons whose release, repatriation or reestablishment may take place after such dates shall meanwhile continue to benefit by the present Convention.

*Article 7.* In addition to the agreements expressly provided for in Articles 11, 14, 15, 17, 36, 108, 109, 132, 133 and 149, the High Contracting Parties may conclude other special agreements for all matters concerning which they may deem it suitable to make separate provision. No special agreement shall adversely affect the situation of protected persons, as defined by the present Convention, nor restrict the rights which it confers upon them.

Protected persons shall continue to have the benefit of such agreements as long as the Convention is applicable to them, except where express provisions to the contrary are contained in the aforesaid or in subsequent agreements, or where more favourable measures have been taken with regard to them by one or other of the Parties to the conflict.

*Article 8.* Protected persons may in no circumstances renounce in part or in entirety the rights secured to them by the present Convention, and by the special agreements referred to in the foregoing Article, if such there be.

*Article 9.* The present Convention shall be applied with the cooperation and under the scrutiny of the Protecting Powers whose duty it is to safeguard the interests of the Parties to the conflict. For this purpose, the Protecting Powers may appoint, apart from their diplomatic or consular staff, delegates from amongst their own nationals or the nationals of other neutral Powers. The said delegates shall be subject to the approval of the Power with which they are to carry out their duties.

The Parties to the conflict shall facilitate to the greatest extent possible the task of the representatives or delegates of the Protecting Powers.

The representatives or delegates of the Protecting Powers

shall not in any case exceed their mission under the present Convention. They shall, in particular, take account of the imperative necessities of security of the State wherein they carry out their duties.

*Article 10.* The provisions of the present Convention constitute no obstacle to the humanitarian activities which the International Committee of the Red Cross or any other impartial humanitarian organization may, subject to the consent of the Parties to the conflict concerned, undertake for the protection of civilian persons and for their relief.

*Article 11.* The High Contracting Parties may at any time agree to entrust to an organization which offers all guarantees of impartiality and efficacy the duties incumbent on the Protecting Powers by virtue of the present Convention.

When persons protected by the present Convention do not benefit or cease to benefit, no matter for what reason, by the activities of a Protecting Power or of an organization provided for in the first paragraph above, the Detaining Power shall request a neutral State, or such an organization, to undertake the functions performed under the present Convention by a Protecting Power designated by the Parties to a conflict.

If protection cannot be arranged accordingly, the Detaining Power shall request or shall accept, subject to the provisions of this Article, the offer of the services of a humanitarian organization, such as the International Committee of the Red Cross, to assume the humanitarian functions performed by Protecting Powers under the present Convention.

Any neutral Power, or any organization invited by the Power concerned or offering itself for these purposes, shall be required to act with a sense of responsibility towards the Party to the conflict on which persons protected by the present Convention depend, and shall be required to furnish sufficient assurances that it is in a position to undertake the appropriate functions and to discharge them impartially.

No derogation from the preceding provisions shall be made by special agreements between Powers one of which is restricted, even temporarily, in its freedom to negotiate with the other Power or its allies by reason of military events, more particularly where the whole, or a substantial part, of the territory of the said Power is occupied.

Whenever in the present Convention mention is made of a Protecting Power, such mention applies to substitute organizations in the sense of the present Article.

The provisions of this Article shall extend and be adapted to cases of nationals of a neutral State who are in occupied territory or who find themselves in the territory of a belligerent State in which the State of which they are nationals has not normal diplomatic representation.

*Article 12.* In cases where they deem it advisable in the interest of protected persons, particularly in cases of disagreement between the Parties to the conflict as to the application or interpretation of the provisions of the present Convention, the Protecting Powers shall lend their good offices with a view to settling the disagreement.

For this purpose, each of the Protecting Powers may, either at the invitation of one Party or on its own initiative, propose to the Parties to the conflict a meeting of their representatives, and in particular of the authorities responsible for protected persons, possibly on neutral territory suitably chosen. The Parties to the conflict shall be bound to give effect to the proposals made to them for this purpose. The Protecting Powers may, if necessary, propose for approval by the Parties to the conflict, a person belonging to a neutral Power or delegated by the International Committee of the Red Cross, who shall be invited to take part in such a meeting.

**Part II**

**General Protection of Populations Against Certain Consequences of War**

*Article 13.* The provisions of Part II cover the whole of the populations of the countries in conflict, without any adverse distinction based, in particular, on race, nationality, religion or political opinion, and are intended to alleviate the sufferings caused by war.

*Article 14.* In time of peace, the High Contracting Parties and, after the outbreak of hostilities, the Parties thereto, may establish in their own territory and, if the need arises, in occupied areas, hospital and safety zones and localities so organized as to protect from the effects of war, wounded, sick and aged persons, children under fifteen, expectant mothers and mothers of children under seven.

Upon the outbreak and during the course of hostilities, the Parties concerned may conclude agreements on mutual recognition of the zones and localities they have created. They may for this purpose implement the provisions of the Draft Agreement annexed to the present Convention, with such amendments as they may consider necessary.

The Protecting Powers and the International Committee of the Red Cross are invited to lend their good offices in order to facilitate the institution and recognition of these hospital and safety zones and localities.

*Article 15.* Any Party to the conflict may, either direct or through a neutral State or some humanitarian organization, propose to the adverse Party to establish, in the regions where fighting is taking place, neutralized zones intended to shelter from the effects of war the following persons, without distinction:

(a) wounded and sick combatants or non-combatants;

(b) civilian persons who take no part in hostilities, and who, while they reside in the zones, perform no work of a military character.

When the Parties concerned have agreed upon the geographical position, administration, food supply and supervision of the proposed neutralized zone, a written agreement shall be concluded and signed by the representatives of the Parties to the conflict. The agreement shall fix the beginning and the duration of the neutralization of the zone.

*Article 16.* The wounded and sick, as well as the infirm, and expectant mothers, shall be the object of particular protection and respect.

As far as military considerations allow, each Party to the conflict shall facilitate the steps taken to search for the killed and wounded, to assist the shipwrecked and other persons exposed to grave danger, and to protect them against pillage and ill-treatment.

*Article 17.* The Parties to the conflict shall endeavour to conclude local agreements for the removal from besieged or encircled areas, of wounded, sick, infirm, and aged persons, children and maternity cases, and for the passage of ministers of all religions, medical personnel and medical equipment on their way to such areas.

*Article 18.* Civilian hospitals organized to give care to the wounded and sick, the infirm and maternity cases, may in no circumstances be the object of attack, but shall at all times be respected and protected by the Parties to the conflict.

States which are Parties to a conflict shall provide all civilian hospitals with certificates showing that they are civilian hospitals and that the buildings which they occupy are not used for any purpose which would deprive these hospitals of protection in accordance with Article 19.

Civilian hospitals shall be marked by means of the emblem provided for in Article 38 of the Geneva Convention for the Amelioration of the Condition of the Wounded and Sick in Armed Forces in the Field of August 12, 1949, but only if so authorized by the State.

The Parties to the conflict shall, in so far as military considerations permit, take the necessary steps to make the distinctive emblems indicating civilian hospitals clearly visible to the enemy land, air and naval forces in order to obviate the possibility of any hostile action.

In view of the dangers to which hospitals may be exposed by being close to military objectives, it is recommended that such hospitals be situated as far as possible from such objectives.

*Article 19.* The protection to which civilian hospitals are entitled shall not cease unless they are used to commit, outside their humanitarian duties, acts harmful to the enemy. Protection may, however, cease only after due warning has been given, naming, in all appropriate cases, a reasonable time limit, and after such warning has remained unheeded.

The fact that sick or wounded members of the armed forces are nursed in these hospitals, or the presence of small arms and ammunition taken from such combatants and not yet handed to the proper service, shall not be considered to be acts harmful to the enemy.

*Article 20.* Persons regularly and solely engaged in the operation and administration of civilian hospitals, including the personnel engaged in the search for, removal and transporting of and caring for wounded and sick civilians, the infirm and maternity cases, shall be respected and protected.

In occupied territory and in zones of military operations, the above personnel shall be recognizable by means of an identity card certifying their status, bearing the photograph of the holder and embossed with the stamp of the responsible authority, and also by means of a stamped, water-resistant armlet which they shall wear on the left arm while carrying out their duties. This armlet shall be issued by the State and shall bear the emblem provided for in Article 38 of the Geneva Convention for the Amelioration of the Condition of the Wounded and Sick in Armed Forces in the Field of August 12, 1949.

Other personnel who are engaged in the operation and administration of civilian hospitals shall be entitled to respect and protection and to wear the armlet, as provided in and under the conditions prescribed in this Article, while they are employed on such duties. The identity card shall state the duties on which they are employed.

The management of each hospital shall at all times hold at the disposal of the competent national or occupying authorities an up-to-date list of such personnel.

*Article 21.* Convoys of vehicles or hospital trains on land or specially provided vessels on sea, conveying wounded and sick civilians, the infirm and maternity cases, shall be respected and protected in the same manner as the hospitals provided for in Article 18, and shall be marked, with the consent of the State, by the display of the distinctive emblem provided for in Article 38 of the Geneva Convention for the Amelioration of the Condition of the Wounded and Sick in Armed Forces in the Field of August 12, 1949.

*Article 22.* Aircraft exclusively employed for the removal of wounded and sick civilians, the infirm and maternity cases, or for the transport of medical personnel and equipment, shall not be attacked, but shall be respected while flying at heights, times and on routes specifically agreed upon between all the Parties to the conflict concerned.

They may be marked with the distinctive emblem provided for in Article 38 of the Geneva Convention for the Amelioration of the Condition of the Wounded and Sick in Armed Forces in the Field of August 12, 1949.

Unless agreed otherwise, flights over enemy or enemy-occupied territory are prohibited.

Such aircraft shall obey every summons to land. In the event of a landing thus imposed, the aircraft with its occupants may continue its flight after examination, if any.

*Article 23.* Each High Contracting Party shall allow the free passage of all consignments of medical and hospital stores and objects necessary for religious worship intended only for civilians of another High Contracting Party, even if the latter is its adversary. It shall likewise permit the free passage of all consignments of essential foodstuffs, clothing and tonics intended for children under fifteen, expectant mothers and maternity cases.

The obligation of a High Contracting Party to allow the free passage of the consignments indicated in the preceding paragraph is subject to the condition that this Party is satisfied that there are no serious reasons for fearing:

(a) that the consignments may be diverted from their destination,

(b) that the control may not be effective, or

(c) that a definite advantage may accrue to the military efforts or economy of the enemy through the substitution of the above-mentioned consignments for goods which would otherwise be provided or produced by the enemy or through the release of such material, services or facilities as would otherwise be required for the production of such goods.

The Power which allows the passage of the consignments indicated in the first paragraph of this Article may make such permission conditional on the distribution to the persons benefited thereby being made under the local supervision of the Protecting Powers.

Such consignments shall be forwarded as rapidly as possible, and the Power which permits their free passage shall have the right to prescribe the technical arrangements under which such passage is allowed.

*Article 24.* The Parties to the conflict shall take the necessary measures to ensure that children under fifteen, who are orphaned or are separated from their families as a result of the war, are not left to their own resources, and that their maintenance, the exercise of their religion and their education are facilitated in all circumstances. Their education shall, as far as possible, be entrusted to persons of a similar cultural tradition.

The Parties to the conflict shall facilitate the reception of such children in a neutral country for the duration of the conflict with the consent of the Protecting Power, if any, and under due safeguards for the observance of the principles stated in the first paragraph.

They shall, furthermore, endeavour to arrange for all children under twelve to be identified by the wearing of identity discs, or by some other means.

*Article 25.* All persons in the territory of a Party to the conflict, or in a territory occupied by it, shall be enabled to give news of a strictly personal nature to members of their families, wherever they may be, and to receive news from them. This correspondence shall be forwarded speedily and without undue delay.

If, as a result of circumstances, it becomes difficult or impossible to exchange family correspondence by the ordinary post, the Parties to the conflict concerned shall apply to a neutral intermediary, such as the Central Agency provided for in Article 140, and shall decide in consultation with it how to ensure the fulfilment of their obligations under the best possible conditions, in particular with the cooperation of the National Red Cross (Red Crescent, Red Lion and Sun) Societies.

If the Parties to the conflict deem it necessary to restrict family correspondence, such restrictions shall be confined to the compulsory use of standard forms containing twenty-five freely chosen words, and to the limitation of the number of these forms despatched to one each month.

*Article 26.* Each Party to the conflict shall facilitate enquiries made by members of families dispersed owing to the war, with the object of renewing contact with one another and of meeting, if possible. It shall encourage, in particular, the work of organizations engaged on this task provided they are acceptable to it and conform to its security regulations.

## Part III

### Status and Treatment of Protected Persons

#### Section I—Provisions Common to the Territories of the Parties to the Conflict and to Occupied Territories

*Article 27.* Protected persons are entitled, in all circumstances, to respect for their persons, their honour, their family rights, their religious convictions and practices, and their manners and customs. They shall at all times be humanely treated, and shall be protected especially against all acts of violence or threats thereof and against insults and public curiosity.

Women shall be especially protected against any attack on their honour, in particular against rape, enforced prostitution, or any form of indecent assault.

Without prejudice to the provisions relating to their state of health, age and sex, all protected persons shall be treated with the same consideration by the Party to the conflict in whose power they are, without any adverse distinction based, in particular, on race, religion or political opinion.

However, the Parties to the conflict may take such measures of control and security in regard to protected persons as may be necessary as a result of the war.

*Article 28.* The presence of a protected person may not be used to render certain points or areas immune from military operations.

*Article 29.* The Party to the conflict in whose hands protected persons may be, is responsible for the treatment accorded to them by its agents, irrespective of any individual responsibility which may be incurred.

*Article 30.* Protected persons shall have every facility for making application to the Protecting Powers, the International Committee of the Red Cross, the National Red Cross (Red Crescent, Red Lion and Sun) Society of the country where they may be, as well as to any organization that might assist them.

These several organizations shall be granted all facilities for that purpose by the authorities, within the bounds set by military or security considerations.

Apart from the visits of the delegates of the Protecting Powers and of the International Committee of the Red Cross, provided for by Article 143, the Detaining or Occupying Powers shall facilitate as much as possible visits to protected persons by the representatives of other organizations whose object is to give spiritual aid or material relief to such persons.

*Article 31.* No physical or moral coercion shall be exercised against protected persons, in particular to obtain information from them or from third parties.

*Article 32.* The High Contracting Parties specifically agree that each of them is prohibited from taking any measure of such a character as to cause the physical suffering or extermination of protected persons in their hands. This prohibition applies not only to murder, torture, corporal punishment, mutilation and medical or scientific experiments not necessitated by the medical treatment of a protected person, but also to any other measures of brutality whether applied by civilian or military agents.

*Article 33.* No protected person may be punished for an offence he or she has not personally committed. Collective penalties and likewise all measures of intimidation or of terrorism are prohibited.

Pillage is prohibited.

Reprisals against protected persons and their property are prohibited.

*Article 34.* The taking of hostages is prohibited.

#### Section II—Aliens in the Territory of a Party to the Conflict

*Article 35.* All protected persons who may desire to leave the territory at the outset of, or during a conflict, shall be entitled to do so, unless their departure is contrary to the national interests of the State. The applications of such persons to leave shall be decided in accordance with regularly established procedures and the decision shall be taken as rapidly as possible. Those persons permitted to leave may provide themselves with the necessary funds for their journey and take with them a reasonable amount of their effects and articles of personal use.

If any such person is refused permission to leave the territory, he shall be entitled to have such refusal reconsidered as soon as possible by an appropriate court or administrative board designated by the Detaining Power for that purpose.

Upon request, representatives of the Protecting Power shall, unless reasons of security prevent it, or the persons concerned object, be furnished with the reasons for refusal of any request for permission to leave the territory and be given, as expeditiously as possible, the names of all persons who have been denied permission to leave.

*Article 36.* Departures permitted under the foregoing Article shall be carried out in satisfactory conditions as regards safety, hygiene, sanitation and food. All costs in connection therewith, from the point of exit in the territory of the Detaining Power, shall be borne by the country of destination, or, in the case of accommodation in a neutral country, by the Power whose nationals are benefited. The practical details of such movements may, if necessary, be settled by special agreements between the Powers concerned.

The foregoing shall not prejudice such special agreements as may be concluded between Parties to the conflict concerning the exchange and repatriation of their nationals in enemy hands.

*Article 37.* Protected persons who are confined pending proceedings or serving a sentence involving loss of liberty, shall during their confinement be humanely treated.

As soon as they are released, they may ask to leave the territory in conformity with the foregoing Articles.

*Article 38.* With the exception of special measures authorized by the present Convention, in particular by Articles 27 and 41 thereof, the situation of protected persons shall continue to be regulated, in principle, by the provisions concerning aliens in time of peace. In any case, the following rights shall be granted to them:

(1) They shall be enabled to receive the individual or collective relief that may be sent to them.

(2) They shall, if their state of health so requires, receive medical attention and hospital treatment to the same extent as the nationals of the State concerned.

(3) They shall be allowed to practise their religion and to receive spiritual assistance from ministers of their faith.

(4) If they reside in an area particularly exposed to the dangers of war, they shall be authorised to move from that area to the same extent as the nationals of the State concerned.

(5) Children under fifteen years, pregnant women and mothers of children under seven years shall benefit by any preferential treatment to the same extent as the nationals of the State concerned.

*Article 39.* Protected persons who, as a result of the war, have lost their gainful employment, shall be granted the opportunity to find paid employment. That opportunity shall, subject to security considerations and to the provisions of Article 40, be equal to that enjoyed by the nationals of the Power in whose territory they are.

Where a Party to the conflict applies to a protected person methods of control which result in his being unable to support himself, and especially if such a person is prevented for reasons of security from finding paid employment on reasonable conditions, the said Party shall ensure his support and that of his dependents.

Protected persons may in any case receive allowances from their home country, the Protecting Power, or the relief societies referred to in Article 30.

*Article 40.* Protected persons may be compelled to work only to the same extent as nationals of the Party to the conflict in whose territory they are.

If protected persons are of enemy nationality, they may only be compelled to do work which is normally necessary to ensure the feeding, sheltering, clothing, transport and health of human beings and which is not directly related to the conduct of military operations.

In the cases mentioned in the two preceding paragraphs, protected persons compelled to work shall have the benefit of the same working conditions and of the same safeguards as national workers, in particular as regards wages, hours of labour, clothing and equipment, previous training and compensation for occupational accidents and diseases.

If the above provisions are infringed, protected persons shall be allowed to exercise their right of complaint in accordance with Article 30.

*Article 41.* Should the Power in whose hands protected persons may be consider the measures of control mentioned in the present Convention to be inadequate, it may not have recourse to any other measure of control more severe than that of assigned residence or internment, in accordance with the provisions of Articles 42 and 43.

In applying the provisions of Article 39, second paragraph, to the cases of persons required to leave their usual places of residence by virtue of a decision placing them in assigned residence elsewhere, the Detaining Power shall be guided as closely as possible by the standards of welfare set forth in Part III, Section IV of this Convention.

*Article 42.* The internment or placing in assigned residence of protected persons may be ordered only if the security of the Detaining Power makes it absolutely necessary.

If any person, acting through the representatives of the Protecting Power, voluntarily demands internment, and if his situation renders this step necessary, he shall be interned by the Power in whose hands he may be.

*Article 43.* Any protected person who has been interned or placed in assigned residence shall be entitled to have such action reconsidered as soon as possible by an appropriate court or administrative board designated by the Detaining Power for that purpose. If the internment or placing in assigned residence is maintained, the court or administrative board shall periodically, and at least twice yearly, give consideration to his or her case with a view to the favourable amendment of the initial decision, if circumstances permit.

Unless the protected persons concerned object, the Detaining Power shall, as rapidly as possible, give the Protecting Power the names of any protected persons who have been interned or subjected to assigned residence, or who have been released from internment or assigned residence. The decisions of the courts or boards mentioned in the first paragraph of the present Article shall also, subject to the same conditions, be notified as rapidly as possible to the Protecting Power.

*Article 44.* In applying the measures of control mentioned in the present Convention, the Detaining Power shall not treat as enemy aliens exclusively on the basis of their nationality *de jure* of an enemy State, refugees who do not, in fact, enjoy the protection of any government.

*Article 45.* Protected persons shall not be transferred to a Power which is not a party to the Convention.

This provision shall in no way constitute an obstacle to the repatriation of protected persons, or to their return to their country of residence after the cessation of hostilities.

Protected persons may be transferred by the Detaining Power only to a Power which is a party to the present Convention and after the Detaining Power has satisfied itself of the willingness and ability of such transferee Power to apply the present Convention. If protected persons are transferred under such circumstances, responsibility for the application of the present Convention rests on the Power accepting them, while they are in its custody. Nevertheless, if that Power fails to carry out the provisions of the present Convention in any important respect, the Power by which the protected persons were transferred shall, upon being so notified by the Protecting Power, take effective measures to correct the situation or shall request the return of the protected persons. Such request must be complied with.

In no circumstances shall a protected person be transferred to a country where he or she may have reason to fear persecution for his or her political opinions or religious beliefs.

The provisions of this Article do not constitute an obstacle to the extradition, in pursuance of extradition treaties concluded before the outbreak of hostilities, of protected persons accused of offences against ordinary criminal law.

*Article 46.* In so far as they have not been previously withdrawn, restrictive measures taken regarding protected persons shall be cancelled as soon as possible after the close of hostilities.

Restrictive measures affecting their property shall be cancelled, in accordance with the law of the Detaining Power, as soon as possible after the close of hostilities.

## Section III—Occupied Territories

*Article 47.* Protected persons who are in occupied territory shall not be deprived, in any case or in any manner whatsoever, of the benefits of the present Convention by any change introduced, as the result of the occupation of a territory, into the institutions or government of the said territory, nor by any agreement concluded between the authorities of the occupied territories and the Occupying Power, nor by any annexation by the latter of the whole or part of the occupied territory.

*Article 48.* Protected persons who are not nationals of the Power whose territory is occupied, may avail themselves of the right to leave the territory subject to the provisions of Article 35, and decisions thereon shall be taken according to the procedure which the Occupying Power shall establish in accordance with the said Article.

*Article 49.* Individual or mass forcible transfers, as well as deportations of protected persons from occupied territory to the territory of the Occupying Power or to that of any other country, occupied or not, are prohibited, regardless of their motive.

Nevertheless, the Occupying Power may undertake total or partial evacuation of a given area if the security of the population or imperative military reasons so demand. Such evacuations may not involve the displacement of protected persons outside the bounds of the occupied territory except when for material reasons it is impossible to avoid such displacement. Persons thus evacuated shall be transferred back to their homes as soon as hostilities in the area in question have ceased.

The Occupying Power undertaking such transfers or evacuations shall ensure, to the greatest practicable extent, that proper accommodation is provided to receive the protected persons, that the removals are effected in satisfactory conditions of hygiene, health, safety and nutrition, and that members of the same family are not separated.

The Protecting Power shall be informed of any transfers and evacuations as soon as they have taken place.

The Occupying Power shall not detain protected persons in an area particularly exposed to the dangers of war unless the security of the population or imperative military reasons so demand.

The Occupying Power shall not deport or transfer parts of its own civilian population into the territory it occupies.

*Article 50.* The Occupying Power shall, with the cooperation of the national and local authorities, facilitate the proper working of all institutions devoted to the care and education of children.

The Occupying Power shall take all necessary steps to facilitate the identification of children and the registration of their parentage. It may not, in any case, change their personal status, nor enlist them in formations or organizations subordinate to it.

Should the local institutions be inadequate for the purpose, the Occupying Power shall make arrangements for the maintenance and education, if possible by persons of their own nationality, language and religion, of children who are orphaned or separated from their parents as a result of the war and who cannot be adequately cared for by a near relative or friend.

A special section of the Bureau set up in accordance with Article 136 shall be responsible for taking all necessary steps to identify children whose identity is in doubt. Particulars of their parents or other near relative should always be recorded if available.

The Occupying Power shall not hinder the application of any preferential measures in regard to food, medical care and protection against the effects of war, which may have been adopted prior to the occupation in favour of children under fifteen years, expectant mothers, and mothers of children under seven years.

*Article 51.* The Occupying Power may not compel protected persons to serve in its armed or auxiliary forces. No pressure or propaganda which aims at securing voluntary enlistment is permitted.

The Occupying Power may not compel protected persons to work unless they are over eighteen years of age, and then only on work which is necessary either for the needs of the army of occupation, or for the public utility services, or for the feeding, sheltering, clothing, transportation or health of the population of the occupied country. Protected persons may not be compelled to undertake any work which would involve them in the obligation of taking part in military operations. The Occupying Power may not compel protected persons to employ forcible means to ensure the security of the installations where they are performing compulsory labour.

The work shall be carried out only in the occupied territory where the persons whose services have been requisitioned are. Every such person shall, so far as possible, be kept in his usual place of employment. Workers shall be paid a fair wage and the work shall be proportionate to their physical and intellectual capacities. The legislation in force in the occupied country concerning working conditions, and safeguards as regards, in particular, such matters as wages, hours of work, equipment, preliminary training and compensation for occupational accidents and diseases, shall be applicable to the protected persons assigned to the work referred to in this Article.

In no case shall requisition of labour lead to a mobilization of workers in an organization of a military or semi-military character.

*Article 52.* No contract, agreement or regulation shall impair the right of any worker, whether voluntary or not and wherever he may be, to apply to the representatives of the Protecting Power in order to request the said Power's intervention.

All measures aiming at creating unemployment or at restricting the opportunities offered to workers in an occupied territory, in order to induce them to work for the Occupying Power, are prohibited.

*Article 53.* Any destruction by the Occupying Power of real or personal property belonging individually or collectively to private persons, or to the State, or to other public authorities, or to social or cooperative organizations, is prohibited, except where such destruction is rendered absolutely necessary by military operations.

*Article 54.* The Occupying Power may not alter the status of public officials or judges in the occupied territories, or in any way apply sanctions to or take any measures of coercion or discrimination against them, should they abstain from fulfilling their functions for reasons of conscience.

This prohibition does not prejudice the application of the second paragraph of Article 51. It does not affect the right of the Occupying Power to remove public officials from their posts.

*Article 55.* To the fullest extent of the means available to it, the Occupying Power has the duty of ensuring the food and medical supplies of the population; it should, in particular, bring in the necessary foodstuffs, medical stores and other articles if the resources of the occupied territory are inadequate.

The Occupying Power may not requisition foodstuffs, articles or medical supplies available in the occupied territory, except for use by the occupation forces and administration personnel, and then only if the requirements of the civilian population have been taken into account. Subject to the provisions of other international Conventions, the Occupying Power shall make arrangements to ensure that fair value is paid for any requisitioned goods.

The Protecting Power shall, at any time, be at liberty to verify the state of the food and medical supplies in occupied territories, except where temporary restrictions are made necessary by imperative military requirements.

*Article 56.* To the fullest extent of the means available to it, the Occupying Power has the duty of ensuring and maintaining, with the cooperation of national and local authorities, the medical and hospital establishments and services, public health and hygiene in the occupied territory, with particular reference to the adoption and application of the prophylactic and preventive measures necessary to combat the spread of contagious diseases and epidemics. Medical personnel of all categories shall be allowed to carry out their duties.

If new hospitals are set up in occupied territory and if the competent organs of the occupied State are not operating there, the occupying authorities shall, if necessary, grant them the recognition provided for in Article 18. In similar circumstances, the occupying authorities shall also grant recognition to hospital personnel and transport vehicles under the provisions of Articles 20 and 21.

In adopting measures of health and hygiene and in their implementation, the Occupying Power shall take into consideration the moral and ethical susceptibilities of the population of the occupied territory.

*Article 57.* The Occupying Power may requisition civilian hospitals only temporarily and only in cases of urgent necessity for the care of military wounded and sick, and then on condition that suitable arrangements are made in due time for the care and treatment of the patients and for the needs of the civilian population for hospital accommodation.

The material and stores of civilian hospitals cannot be requisitioned so long as they are necessary for the needs of the civilian population.

*Article 58.* The Occupying Power shall permit ministers of religion to give spiritual assistance to the members of their religious communities.

The Occupying Power shall also accept consignments of books and articles required for religious needs and shall facilitate their distribution in occupied territory.

*Article 59.* If the whole or part of the population of an occupied territory is inadequately supplied, the Occupying Power shall agree to relief schemes on behalf of the said population, and shall facilitate them by all the means at its disposal.

Such schemes, which may be undertaken either by States or by impartial humanitarian organizations such as the International Committee of the Red Cross, shall consist, in particular, of the provision of consignments of foodstuffs, medical supplies and clothing.

All Contracting Parties shall permit the free passage of these consignments and shall guarantee their protection.

A Power granting free passage to consignments on their way to territory occupied by an adverse Party to the conflict shall, however, have the right to search the consignments, to regulate their passage according to prescribed times and routes, and to be reasonably satisfied through the Protecting Power that these consignments are to be used for the relief of the needy population and are not to be used for the benefit of the Occupying Power.

*Article 60.* Relief consignments shall in no way relieve the Occupying Power of any of its responsibilities under Articles 55, 56 and 59. The Occupying Power shall in no way whatsoever divert relief consignments from the purpose for which they are intended, except in cases of urgent necessity,

in the interests of the population of the occupied territory and with the consent of the Protecting Power.

*Article 61.* The distribution of the relief consignments referred to in the foregoing Articles shall be carried out with the cooperation and under the supervision of the Protecting Power. This duty may also be delegated, by agreement between the Occupying Power and the Protecting Power, to a neutral Power, to the International Committee of the Red Cross or to any other impartial humanitarian body.

Such consignments shall be exempt in occupied territory from all charges, taxes or customs duties unless these are necessary in the interests of the economy of the territory. The Occupying Power shall facilitate the rapid distribution of these consignments.

All Contracting Parties shall endeavour to permit the transit and transport, free of charge, of such relief consignments on their way to occupied territories.

*Article 62.* Subject to imperative reasons of security, protected persons in occupied territories shall be permitted to receive the individual relief consignments sent to them.

*Article 63.* Subject to temporary and exceptional measures imposed for urgent reasons of security by the Occupying Power:

(a) recognized National Red Cross (Red Crescent, Red Lion and Sun) Societies shall be able to pursue their activities in accordance with Red Cross principles, as defined by the International Red Cross Conferences. Other relief societies shall be permitted to continue their humanitarian activities under similar conditions;

(b) the Occupying Power may not require any changes in the personnel or structure of these societies, which would prejudice the aforesaid activities.

The same principles shall apply to the activities and personnel of special organizations of a non-military character, which already exist or which may be established, for the purpose of ensuring the living conditions of the civilian population by the maintenance of the essential public utility services, by the distribution of relief and by the organization of rescues.

*Article 64.* The penal laws of the occupied territory shall remain in force, with the exception that they may be repealed or suspended by the Occupying Power in cases where they constitute a threat to its security or an obstacle to the application of the present Convention. Subject to the latter consideration and to the necessity for ensuring the effective administration of justice, the tribunals of the occupied territory shall continue to function in respect of all offences covered by the said laws.

The Occupying Power may, however, subject the population of the occupied territory to provisions which are essential to enable the Occupying Power to fulfill its obligations under the present Convention, to maintain the orderly government of the territory, and to ensure the security of the Occupying Power, of the members and property of the occupying forces or administration, and likewise of the establishments and lines of communication used by them.

*Article 65.* The penal provisions enacted by the Occupying Power shall not come into force before they have been published and brought to the knowledge of the inhabitants in their own language. The effect of these penal provisions shall not be retroactive.

*Article 66.* In case of a breach of the penal provisions promulgated by it by virtue of the second paragraph of Article 64, the Occupying Power may hand over the accused to its properly constituted, non-political military courts, on condition that the said courts sit in the occupied country. Courts of appeal shall preferably sit in the occupied country.

*Article 67.* The courts shall apply only those provisions of law which were applicable prior to the offence, and which are in accordance with general principles of law, in particular the principle that the penalty shall be proportionate to the offence. They shall take into consideration the fact that the accused is not a national of the Occupying Power.

*Article 68.* Protected persons who commit an offence which is solely intended to harm the Occupying Power, but which does not constitute an attempt on the life or limb of members of the occupying forces or administration, nor a grave collective danger, nor seriously damage the property of the occupying forces or administration or the installations used by them, shall be liable to internment or simple imprisonment, provided the duration of such internment or imprisonment is proportionate to the offence committed. Furthermore, internment or imprisonment shall, for such offences, be the only measure adopted for depriving protected persons of liberty. The courts provided for under Article 66 of the present Convention may at their discretion convert a sentence of imprisonment to one of internment for the same period.

The penal provisions promulgated by the Occupying Power in accordance with Articles 64 and 65 may impose the death penalty on a protected person only in cases where the person is guilty of espionage, of serious acts of sabotage against the military installations of the Occupying Power or of intentional offences which have caused the death of one or more persons, provided that such offences were punishable by death under the law of the occupied territory in force before the occupation began.

The death penalty may not be pronounced against a protected person unless the attention of the court has been particularly called to the fact that since the accused is not a national of the Occupying Power, he is not bound to it by any duty of allegiance.

In any case, the death penalty may not be pronounced against a protected person who was under eighteen years of age at the time of the offence.

*Article 69.* In all cases, the duration of the period during which a protected person accused of an offence is under arrest awaiting trial or punishment shall be deducted from any period of imprisonment awarded.

*Article 70.* Protected persons shall not be arrested, prosecuted or convicted by the Occupying Power for acts committed or for opinions expressed before the occupation, or during a temporary interruption thereof, with the exception of breaches of the laws and customs of war.

Nationals of the occupying Power who, before the outbreak of hostilities, have sought refuge in the territory of the occupied State, shall not be arrested, prosecuted, convicted or deported from the occupied territory, except for offences committed after the outbreak of hostilities, or for offences under common law committed before the outbreak of hostilities which, according to the law of the occupied State, would have justified extradition in time of peace.

*Article 71.* No sentence shall be pronounced by the competent courts of the Occupying Power except after a regular trial.

Accused persons who are prosecuted by the Occupying Power shall be promptly informed, in writing, in a language which they understand, of the particulars of the charges preferred against them, and shall be brought to trial as rapidly as possible. The Protecting Power shall be informed of all proceedings instituted by the Occupying Power against protected persons in respect of charges involving the death penalty or imprisonment for two years or more; it shall be enabled, at any time, to obtain information regarding the state of such proceedings. Furthermore, the Protecting Power shall be entitled, on request, to be furnished with all particulars of these and of any other proceedings instituted by the Occupying Power against protected persons.

The notification to the Protecting Power, as provided for in the second paragraph above, shall be sent immediately, and shall in any case reach the Protecting Power three weeks before the date of the first hearing. Unless, at the opening of the trial, evidence is submitted that the provisions of this Article are fully complied with, the trial shall not proceed. The notification shall include the following particulars:

(a) description of the accused;

(b) place of residence or detention;

(c) specification of the charge or charges (with mention of the penal provisions under which it is brought);

(d) designation of the court which will hear the case;

(e) place and date of the first hearing.

*Article 72.* Accused persons shall have the right to present evidence necessary to their defence and may in particular, call witnesses. They shall have the right to be assisted by a qualified advocate or counsel of their own choice, who shall be able to visit them freely, and shall enjoy the necessary facilities for preparing the defence.

Failing a choice by the accused, the Protecting Power may provide him with an advocate or counsel. When an accused person has to meet a serious charge and the Protecting Power is not functioning, the Occupying Power, subject to the consent of the accused, shall provide an advocate or counsel.

Accused persons shall, unless they freely waive such assistance, be aided by an interpreter, both during preliminary investigation and during the hearing in court. They shall have the right at any time to object to the interpreter and to ask for his replacement.

*Article 73.* A convicted person shall have the right of appeal provided for by the laws applied by the court. He shall be fully informed of his right to appeal or petition and of the time limit within which he may do so.

The penal procedure provided in the present Section shall apply, as far as it is applicable, to appeals. Where the laws applied by the Court make no provision for appeals, the convicted person shall have the right to petition against the finding and sentence to the competent authority of the Occupying Power.

*Article 74.* Representatives of the Protecting Power shall have the right to attend the trial of any protected person, unless the hearing has, as an exceptional measure, to be held *in camera* in the interests of the security of the Occupying Power, which shall then notify the Protecting Power. A notification in respect of the date and place of trial shall be sent to the Protecting Power.

Any judgment involving a sentence of death, or imprisonment for two years or more, shall be communicated, with the relevant grounds, as rapidly as possible to the Protecting Power. The notification shall contain a reference to the notification made under Article 71, and, in the case of sentences of imprisonment, the name of the place where the sentence is to be served. A record of judgments other than those referred to above shall be kept by the court and shall be open to inspection by representatives of the Protecting Power. Any period allowed for appeal in the case of sentences involving the death penalty, or imprisonment of two years or more, shall not run until notification of judgment has been received by the Protecting Power.

*Article 75.* In no case shall persons condemned to death be deprived of the right of petition for pardon or reprieve.

No death sentence shall be carried out before the expiration of a period of at least six months from the date of receipt by the Protecting Power of the notification of the final judgment confirming such death sentence, or of an order denying pardon or reprieve.

The six months period of suspension of the death sentence herein prescribed may be reduced in individual cases in circumstances of grave emergency involving an organized threat to the security of the Occupying Power or its forces, provided always that the Protecting Power is notified of such reduction and is given reasonable time and opportunity to make representations to the competent occupying authorities in respect of such death sentences.

*Article 76.* Protected persons accused of offences shall be detained in the occupied country, and if convicted they shall serve their sentences therein. They shall, if possible, be separated from other detainees and shall enjoy conditions of food and hygiene which will be sufficient to keep them in good health, and which will be at least equal to those obtaining in prisons in the occupied country.

They shall receive the medical attention required by their state of health.

They shall also have the right to receive any spiritual assistance which they may require.

Women shall be confined in separate quarters and shall be under the direct supervision of women.

Proper regard shall be paid to the special treatment due to minors.

Protected persons who are detained shall have the right to be visited by delegates of the Protecting Power and of the International Committee of the Red Cross, in accordance with the provisions of Article 143.

Such persons shall have the right to receive at least one relief parcel monthly.

*Article 77.* Protected persons who have been accused of offences or convicted by the courts in occupied territory, shall be handed over at the close of occupation, with the relevant records, to the authorities of the liberated territory.

*Article 78.* If the Occupying Power considers it necessary, for imperative reasons of security, to take safety measures concerning protected persons, it may, at the most, subject them to assigned residence or to internment.

Decisions regarding such assigned residence or internment shall be made according to a regular procedure to be prescribed by the Occupying Power in accordance with the provisions of the present Convention. This procedure shall include the right of appeal for the parties concerned. Appeals shall be decided with the least possible delay. In the event of the decision being upheld, it shall be subject to periodical review, if possible every six months, by a competent body set up by the said Power.

Protected persons made subject to assigned residence and thus required to leave their homes shall enjoy the full benefit of Article 39 of the present Convention.

### Section IV—Regulations for the Treatment of Internees

#### Chapter I—General Provisions

*Article 79.* The Parties to the conflict shall not intern protected persons, except in accordance with the provisions of Articles 41, 42, 43, 68 and 78.

*Article 80.* Internees shall retain their full civil capacity and shall exercise such attendant rights as may be compatible with their status.

*Article 81.* Parties to the conflict who intern protected persons shall be bound to provide free of charge for their maintenance, and to grant them also the medical attention required by their state of health.

No deduction from the allowances, salaries or credits due to the internees shall be made for the repayment of these costs.

The Detaining Power shall provide for the support of those dependent on the internees, if such dependents are without adequate means of support or are unable to earn a living.

*Article 82.* The Detaining Power shall, as far as possible, accommodate the internees according to their nationality, language and customs. Internees who are nationals of the same country shall not be separated merely because they have different languages.

Throughout the duration of their internment, members of the same family, and in particular parents and children, shall be lodged together in the same place of internment, except when separation of a temporary nature is necessitated for reasons of employment or health or for the purposes of enforcement of the provisions of Chapter IX of the present Section. Internees may request that their children who are left at liberty without parental care shall be interned with them.

Wherever possible, interned member of the same family shall be housed in the same premises and given separate accommodation from other internees, together with facilities for leading a proper family life.

### Chapter II—Places of Internment

*Article 83.* The Detaining Power shall not set up places of internment in areas particularly exposed to the dangers of war.

The Detaining Power shall give the enemy Powers, through the intermediary of the Protecting Powers, all useful information regarding the geographical location of places of internment.

Whenever military considerations permit, internment camps shall be indicated by the letters IC, placed so as to be clearly visible in the daytime from the air. The Powers concerned may, however, agree upon any other system of marking. No place other than an internment camp shall be marked as such.

*Article 84.* Internees shall be accommodated and administered separately from prisoners of war and from persons deprived of liberty for any other reason.

*Article 85.* The Detaining Power is bound to take all necessary and possible measures to ensure that protected persons shall, from the outset of their internment, be accommodated in buildings or quarters which afford every possible safeguard as regards hygiene and health, and provide efficient protection against the rigours of the climate and the effects of the war. In no case shall permanent places of internment be situated in unhealthy areas, or in districts the climate of which is injurious to the internees. In all cases where the district, in which a protected person is temporarily interned, is in an unhealthy area or has a climate which is harmful to his health, he shall be removed to a more suitable place of internment as rapidly as circumstances permit.

The premises shall be fully protected from dampness, adequately heated and lighted, in particular between dusk and lights out. The sleeping quarters shall be sufficiently spacious and well ventilated, and the internees shall have suitable bedding and sufficient blankets, account being taken of the climate, and the age, sex, and state of health of the internees.

Internees shall have for their use, day and night, sanitary conveniences which conform to the rules of hygiene and are constantly maintained in a state of cleanliness. They shall be provided with sufficient water and soap for their daily personal toilet and for washing their personal laundry; installations and facilities necessary for this purpose shall be granted to them. Showers or baths shall also be available. The necessary time shall be set aside for washing and for cleaning.

Whenever it is necessary, as an exceptional and temporary measure, to accommodate women internees who are not members of a family unit in the same place of internment as men, the provision of separate sleeping quarters and sanitary conveniences for the use of such women internees shall be obligatory.

*Article 86.* The Detaining Power shall place at the disposal of interned persons, of whatever denomination, premises suitable for the holding of their religious services.

*Article 87.* Canteens shall be installed in every place of internment, except where other suitable facilities are available. Their purpose shall be to ensure internees to make purchases, at prices not higher than local market prices, of foodstuffs and articles of everyday use, including soap and tobacco, such as would increase their personal well-being and comfort.

Profits made by canteens shall be credited to a welfare fund to be set up for each place of internment, and administered for the benefit of the internees attached to such place of internment. The Internee Committee provided for in Article 102 shall have the right to check the management of the canteen and of the said fund.

When a place of internment is closed down, the balance of the welfare fund shall be transferred to the welfare fund of a place of internment for internees of the same nationality, or, if such a place does not exist, to a central welfare fund which shall be administered for the benefit of all internees remaining in the custody of the Detaining Power. In case of a general release, the said profits shall be kept by the Detaining Power, subject to any agreement to the contrary between the Powers concerned.

*Article 88.* In all places of internment exposed to air raids and other hazards of war, shelters adequate in number and structure to ensure the necessary protection shall be installed. In case of alarms, the internees shall be free to enter such shelters as quickly as possible, excepting those who remain for the protection of their quarters against the aforesaid hazards. Any protective measures taken in favour of the population shall also apply to them.

All due precautions must be taken in places of internment against the danger of fire.

### Chapter III—Food and Clothing

*Article 89.* Daily food rations for internees shall be sufficient in quantity, quality and variety to keep internees in a good state of health and prevent the development of nutritional deficiencies. Account shall also be taken of the customary diet of the internees.

Internees shall also be given the means by which they can prepare for themselves any additional food in their possession.

Sufficient drinking water shall be supplied to internees. The use of tobacco shall be permitted.

Internees who work shall receive additional rations in proportion to the kind of labour which they perform.

Expectant and nursing mothers, and children under fifteen years of age, shall be given additional food, in proportion to their physiological needs.

*Article 90.* When taken into custody, internees shall be given all facilities to provide themselves with the necessary clothing, footwear and change of underwear, and later on, to procure further supplies if required. Should any internees not have sufficient clothing, account being taken of the climate, and be unable to procure any, it shall be provided free of charge to them by the Detaining Power.

The clothing supplied by the Detaining Power to internees and the outward markings placed on their own clothes shall not be ignominious nor expose them to ridicule.

Workers shall receive suitable working outfits, including protective clothing, whenever the nature of their work so requires.

### Chapter IV—Hygiene and Medical Attention

*Article 91.* Every place of internment shall have an adequate infirmary, under the direction of a qualified doctor, where internees may have the attention they require, as well as an appropriate diet. Isolation wards shall be set aside for cases of contagious or mental diseases.

Maternity cases and internees suffering from serious diseases, or whose condition requires special treatment, a surgical operation or hospital care, must be admitted to any institution where adequate treatment can be given and shall receive care not inferior to that provided for the general population.

Internees shall, for preference, have the attention of medical personnel of their own nationality.

Internees may not be prevented from presenting themselves to the medical authorities for examination. The medical authorities of the Detaining Power shall, upon request, issue to every internee who has undergone treatment an official certificate showing the nature of his illness or injury, and the duration and nature of the treatment given. A duplicate of this certificate shall be forwarded to the Central Agency provided for in Article 140.

Treatment, including the provision of any apparatus necessary for the maintenance of internees in good health, particularly dentures and other artificial appliances and spectacles, shall be free of charge to the internee.

*Article 92.* Medical inspections of internees shall be made at least once a month. Their purpose shall be, in particular, to supervise the general state of health, nutrition and cleanliness of internees, and to detect contagious diseases, especially tuberculosis, malaria, and venereal diseases. Such inspections shall include, in particular, the checking of weight of each internee and, at least once a year, radioscopic examination.

### Chapter V—Religious, Intellectual and Physical Activities

*Article 93.* Internees shall enjoy complete latitude in the exercise of their religious duties, including attendance at the services of their faith, on condition that they comply with the disciplinary routine prescribed by the detaining authorities.

Ministers of religion who are interned shall be allowed to minister freely to the members of their community. For this purpose, the Detaining Power shall ensure their equitable allocation amongst the various places of internment in which there are internees speaking the same language and belonging to the same religion. Should such ministers be too few in number, the Detaining Power shall provide them with the necessary facilities, including means of transport, for moving from one place to another, and they shall be authorized to visit any internees who are in hospital. Ministers of religion shall be at liberty to correspond on matters concerning their ministry with the religious authorities in the country of detention and, as far as possible, with the international religious organizations of their faith. Such correspondence shall not be considered as forming a part of the quota mentioned in Article 107. It shall, however, be subject to the provisions of Article 112.

When internees do not have at their disposal the assistance of ministers of their faith, or should these latter be too few in number, the local religious authorities of the same faith may appoint, in agreement with the Detaining Power, a minister of the internees' faith or, if such a course is feasible from a denominational point of view, a minister of similar religion or a qualified layman. The latter shall enjoy the facilities granted to the ministry he has assumed. Persons so appointed shall comply with all regulations laid down by the Detaining Power in the interests of discipline and security.

*Article 94.* The Detaining Power shall encourage intellectual, educational and recreational pursuits, sports and games amongst internees, whilst leaving them free to take part in them or not. It shall take all practicable measures to ensure the exercise thereof, in particular by providing suitable premises.

All possible facilities shall be granted to internees to continue their studies or to take up new subjects. The education of children and young people shall be ensured; they shall be allowed to attend schools either within the place of internment or outside.

Internees shall be given opportunities for physical exercise, sports and outdoor games. For this purpose, sufficient open spaces shall be set aside in all places of internment. Special playgrounds shall be reserved for children and young people.

*Article 95.* The Detaining Power shall not employ internees as workers, unless they so desire. Employment which, if undertaken under compulsion by a protected person not in internment, would involve a breach of Articles 40 or 51 of the present Convention, and employment on work which is of a degrading or humiliating character are in any case prohibited.

After a working period of six weeks, internees shall be free to give up work at any moment, subject to eight days' notice.

These provisions constitute no obstacle to the right of the Detaining Power to employ interned doctors, dentists and other medical personnel in their professional capacity on behalf of their fellow internees, or to employ internees for administrative and maintenance work in places of internment and to detail such persons for work in the kitchens or for other domestic tasks, or to require such persons to undertake duties connected with the protection of internees against aerial bombardment or other war risks. No internee may, however, be required to perform tasks for which he is, in the opinion of a medical officer, physically unsuited.

The Detaining Power shall take entire responsibility for all working conditions, for medical attention, for the payment of wages, and for ensuring that all employed internees receive compensation for occupational accidents and diseases. The standards prescribed for the said working conditions and for compensation shall be in accordance with the national laws and regulations, and with the existing practice;

they shall in no case be inferior to those obtaining for work of the same nature in the same district. Wages for work done shall be determined on an equitable basis by special agreements between the internees, the Detaining Power, and, if the case arises, employers other than the Detaining Power, due regard being paid to the obligation of the Detaining Power to provide for free maintenance of internees and for the medical attention which their state of health may require. Internees permanently detailed for categories of work mentioned in the third paragraph of this Article, shall be paid fair wages by the Detaining Power. The working conditions and the scale of compensation for occupational accidents and diseases to internees thus detailed, shall not be inferior to those applicable to work of the same nature in the same district.

*Article 96.* All labour detachments shall remain part of and dependent upon a place of internment. The competent authorities of the Detaining Power and the commandant of a place of internment shall be responsible for the observance in a labour detachment of the provisions of the present Convention. The commandant shall keep an up-to-date list of the labour detachments subordinate to him and shall communicate it to the delegates of the Protecting Power, of the International Committee of the Red Cross and of other humanitarian organizations who may visit the places of internment.

## Chapter VI—Personal Property and Financial Resources

*Article 97.* Internees shall be permitted to retain articles of personal use. Monies, cheques, bonds, etc., and valuables in their possession may not be taken from them except in accordance with established procedure. Detailed receipts shall be given therefor.

The amounts shall be paid into the account of every internee as provided for in Article 98. Such amounts may not be converted into any other currency unless legislation in force in the territory in which the owner is interned so requires or the internee gives his consent.

Articles which have above all a personal or sentimental value may not be taken away.

A woman internee shall not be searched except by a woman.

On release or repatriation, internees shall be given all articles, monies or other valuables taken from them during internment and shall receive in currency the balance of any credit to their accounts kept in accordance with Article 98, with the exception of any articles or amounts withheld by the Detaining Power by virtue of its legislation in force. If the property of an internee is so withheld, the owner shall receive a detailed receipt.

Family or identity documents in the possession of internees may not be taken away without a receipt being given. At no time shall internees be left without identity documents. If they have none, they shall be issued with special documents drawn up by the detaining authorities, which will serve as their identity papers until the end of their internment.

Internees may keep on their persons a certain amount of money, in cash or in the shape of purchase coupons, to enable them to make purchases.

*Article 98.* All internees shall receive regular allowances, sufficient to enable them to purchase goods and articles, such as tobacco, toilet requisites, etc. Such allowances may take the form of credits or purchase coupons.

Furthermore, internees may receive allowances from the Power to which they owe allegiance, the Protecting Powers, the organizations which may assist them, or their families, as well as the income on their property in accordance with the law of the Detaining Power. The amount of allowances granted by the Power to which they owe allegiance shall be the same for each category of internees (infirm, sick, pregnant women, etc.), but may not be allocated by that Power or distributed by the Detaining Power on the basis of discriminations between internees which are prohibited by Article 27 of the present Convention.

The Detaining Power shall open a regular account for every internee, to which shall be credited the allowances named in the present Article, the wages earned and the remittances received, together with such sums taken from him as may be available under the legislation in force in the territory in which he is interned. Internees shall be granted all facilities consistent with the legislation in force in such territory to make remittances to their families and to other dependants. They may draw from their accounts the amounts necessary for their personal expenses, within the limits fixed by the Detaining Power. They shall at all times be afforded reasonable facilities for consulting and obtaining copies of their accounts. A statement of accounts shall be furnished to the Protecting Power on request, and shall accompany the internee in case of transfer.

### Chapter VII—Administration and Discipline

*Article 99.* Every place of internment shall be put under the authority of a responsible officer, chosen from the regular military forces or the regular civil administration of the Detaining Power. The officer in charge of the place of internment must have in his possession a copy of the present Convention in the official language, or one of the official languages, of his country and shall be responsible for its application. The staff in control of internees shall be instructed in the provisions of the present Convention and of the administrative measures adopted to ensure its application.

The text of the present Convention and the texts of special agreements concluded under the said Convention shall be posted inside the place of internment, in a language which the internees understand, or shall be in the possession of the Internee Committee.

Regulations, orders, notices and publications of every kind shall be communicated to the internees and posted inside the places of internment, in a language which they understand.

Every order and command addressed to internees individually, must likewise, be given in a language which they understand.

*Article 100.* The disciplinary regime in places of internment shall be consistent with humanitarian principles, and shall in no circumstances include regulations imposing on internees any physical exertion dangerous to their health or involving physical or moral victimization. Identification by tattooing or imprinting signs or markings on the body, is prohibited.

In particular, prolonged standing and roll-calls, punishment drill, military drill and manoeuvres, or the reduction of food rations, are prohibited.

*Article 101.* Internees shall have the right to present to the authorities in whose power they are, any petition with regard to the conditions of internment to which they are subjected.

They shall also have the right to apply without restriction through the Internee Committee or, if they consider it necessary, direct to the representatives of the Protecting Power, in order to indicate to them any points on which they may have complaints to make with regard to the conditions of internment.

Such petitions and complaints shall be transmitted forthwith and without alteration, and even if the latter are recognized to be unfounded, they may not occasion any punishment.

Periodic reports on the situation in places of internment and as to the needs of the internees, may be sent by the Internee Committees to the representatives of the Protecting Powers.

*Article 102.* In every place of internment, the internees shall freely elect by secret ballot every six months, the members of a Committee empowered to represent them before the Detaining and the Protecting Powers, the International Committee of the Red Cross and any other organization which may assist them. The members of the committee shall be eligible for re-election.

Internees so elected shall enter upon their duties after their election has been approved by the detaining authorities. The reasons for any refusals or dismissals shall be communicated to the Protecting Powers concerned.

*Article 103.* The Internee Committees shall further the physical, spiritual and intellectual well-being of the internees.

In case the internees decide, in particular, to organize a system of mutual assistance amongst themselves, this organization would be within the competence of the Committees in addition to the special duties entrusted to them under other provisions of the present Convention.

*Article 104.* Members of Internee Committees shall not be required to perform any other work, if the accomplishment of their duties is rendered more difficult thereby.

Members of Internee Committees may appoint from amongst the internees such assistants as they may require. All material facilities shall be granted to them, particularly a certain freedom of movement necessary for the accomplishment of their duties (visits to labour detachments, receipt of supplies, etc.).

All facilities shall likewise be accorded to members of Internee Committees for communication by post and telegraph with the detaining authorities, the Protecting Powers, the International Committee of the Red Cross and their delegates, and with the organizations which give assistance to internees. Committee members in labour detachments shall enjoy similar facilities for communication with their Internee Committee in the principal place of internment. Such communications shall not be limited, nor considered as forming a part of the quota mentioned in Article 107.

Members of Internee Committees who are transferred shall be allowed a reasonable time to acquaint their successors with current affairs.

### Chapter VIII—Relations with the Exterior

*Article 105.* Immediately upon interning protected persons, the Detaining Powers shall inform them, the Power to which they owe allegiance and their Protecting Power of the measures taken for executing the provisions of the present Chapter. The Detaining Powers shall likewise inform the Parties concerned of any subsequent modifications of such measures.

*Article 106.* As soon as he is interned, or at the latest not more than one week after his arrival in a place of internment, and likewise in cases of sickness or transfer to another place of internment or to a hospital, every internee shall be enabled to send direct to his family, on the one hand, and to the Central Agency provided for by Article 140, on the other, an internment card similar, if possible, to the model annexed to the present Convention, informing his relatives of his detention, address and state of health. The said cards shall be forwarded as rapidly as possible and may not be delayed in any way.

*Article 107.* Internees shall be allowed to send and receive letters and cards. If the Detaining Power deems it necessary to limit the number of letters and cards sent by each internee, the said number shall not be less than two letters and four cards monthly; these shall be drawn up so as to conform as closely as possible to the models annexed to the present Convention. If limitations must be placed on the correspondence addressed to internees, they may be ordered only by the Power to which such internees owe allegiance, possibly at the request of the Detaining Power. Such letters and cards must be conveyed with reasonable despatch; they may not be delayed or retained for disciplinary reasons.

Internees who have been a long time without news, or who find it impossible to receive news from their relatives, or to give them news by the ordinary postal route, as well as those who are at a considerable distance from their homes, shall be allowed to send telegrams, the charges being paid by them in the currency at their disposal. They shall likewise benefit by this provision in cases which are recognized to be urgent.

As a rule, internees' mail shall be written in their own language. The Parties to the conflict may authorize correspondence in other languages.

*Article 108.* Internees shall be allowed to receive, by post or by any other means, individual parcels or collective shipments containing in particular foodstuffs, clothing, medical supplies, as well as books and objects of a devotional, educational or recreational character which may meet their needs. Such shipments shall in no way free the Detaining Power from the obligations imposed upon it by virtue of the present Convention.

Should military necessity require the quantity of such shipments to be limited, due notice thereof shall be given to the Protecting Power and to the International Committee of the Red Cross, or to any other organization giving assistance to the internees and responsible for the forwarding of such shipments.

The conditions for the sending of individual parcels and collective shipments shall, if necessary, be the subject of special agreements between the Powers concerned, which may in no case delay the receipt by the internees of relief supplies. Parcels of clothing and foodstuffs may not include books. Medical relief supplies shall, as a rule, be sent in collective parcels.

*Article 109.* In the absence of special agreements between Parties to the conflict regarding the conditions for the receipt and distribution of collective relief shipments, the regulations concerning collective relief which are annexed to the present Convention shall be applied.

The special agreements provided for above shall in no case restrict the right of Internee Committees to take possession of collective relief shipments intended for internees, to undertake their distribution and to dispose of them in the interests of the recipients.

Nor shall such agreements restrict the right of representatives of the Protecting Powers, the International Committee of the Red Cross, or any other organization giving assistance to internees and responsible for the forwarding of collective shipments, to supervise their distribution to the recipients.

*Article 110.* All relief shipments for internees shall be exempt from import, customs and other dues.

All matter sent by mail, including relief parcels sent by parcel post and remittances of money, addressed from other countries to internees or despatched by them through the post office, either direct or through the Information Bureaux provided for in Article 136 and the Central Information Agency provided for in Article 140, shall be exempt from all postal dues both in the countries of origin and destination and in intermediate countries. To this end, in particular, the exemption provided by the Universal Postal Convention of 1947 and by the agreements of the Universal Postal Union in favour of civilians of enemy nationality detained in camps or civilian prisons, shall be extended to the other interned persons protected by the present Convention. The countries not signatory to the above-mentioned agreements shall be bound to grant freedom from charges in the same circumstances.

The cost of transporting relief shipments which are intended for internees and which, by reason of their weight or any other cause, cannot be sent through the post office, shall be borne by the Detaining Power in all the territories under its control. Other Powers which are Parties to the present Convention shall bear the cost of transport in their respective territories.

Costs connected with the transport of such shipments, which are not covered by the above paragraphs, shall be charged to the senders.

The High Contracting Parties shall endeavour to reduce, so far as possible, the charges for telegrams sent by internees, or addressed to them.

*Article 111.* Should military operations prevent the Powers concerned from fulfilling their obligation to ensure the conveyance of the mail and relief shipments provided for in Articles 106, 107, 108 and 113, the Protecting Powers concerned, the International Committee of the Red Cross or any other organization duly approved by the Parties to the conflict may undertake the conveyance of such shipments by suitable means (rail, motor vehicles, vessels or aircraft, etc.). For this purpose, the High Contracting Parties shall endeavour to supply them with such transport, and to allow its circulation, especially by granting the necessary safe-conducts.

Such transport may also be used to convey:

(a) correspondence, lists and reports exchanged between the Central Information Agency referred to in Article 140 and the National Bureaux referred to in Article 136;

(b) correspondence and reports relating to internees which the Protecting Powers, the International Committee of the Red Cross or any other organization assisting the internees exchange either with their own delegates or with the Parties to the conflict.

These provisions in no way detract from the right of any Party to the conflict to arrange other means of transport if it should so prefer, nor preclude the granting of safe-conducts, under mutually agreed conditions, to such means of transport.

The costs occasioned by the use of such means of transport shall be borne, in proportion to the importance of the shipments, by the Parties to the conflict whose nationals are benefited thereby.

*Article 112.* The censoring of correspondence addressed to internees or despatched by them shall be done as quickly as possible.

The examination of consignments intended for internees

shall not be carried out under conditions that will expose the goods contained in them to deterioration. It shall be done in the presence of the addressee, or of a fellow-internee duly delegated by him. The delivery to internees of individual or collective consignments shall not be delayed under the pretext of difficulties of censorship.

Any prohibition of correspondence ordered by the Parties to the conflict either for military or political reasons, shall be only temporary and its duration shall be as short as possible.

*Article 113.* The Detaining Powers shall provide all reasonable facilities for the transmission, through the Protecting Power or the Central Agency provided for in Article 140, or as otherwise required, of wills, powers of attorney, letters of authority, or any other documents intended for internees or despatched by them.

In all cases the Detaining Powers shall facilitate the execution and authentication in due legal form of such documents on behalf of internees, in particular by allowing them to consult a lawyer.

*Article 114.* The Detaining Power shall afford internees all facilities to enable them to manage their property, provided this is not incompatible with the conditions of internment and the law which is applicable. For this purpose, the said Power may give them permission to leave the place of internment in urgent cases and if circumstances allow.

*Article 115.* In all cases where an internee is a party to proceedings in any court, the Detaining Power shall, if he so requests, cause the court to be informed of his detention and shall, within legal limits, ensure that all necessary steps are taken to prevent him from being in any way prejudiced, by reason of his internment, as regards the preparation and conduct of his case or as regards the execution of any judgment of the court.

*Article 116.* Every internee shall be allowed to receive visitors, especially near relatives, at regular intervals and as frequently as possible.

As far as is possible, internees shall be permitted to visit their homes in urgent cases, particularly in cases of death or serious illness of relatives.

### Chapter IX—Penal and Disciplinary Sanctions

*Article 117.* Subject to the provisions of the present Chapter, the laws in force in the territory in which they are detained will continue to apply to internees who commit offences during internment.

If general laws, regulations or orders declare acts committed by internees to be punishable, whereas the same acts are not punishable when committed by persons who are not internees, such acts shall entail disciplinary punishments only.

No internee may be punished more than once for the same act, or on the same count.

*Article 118.* The courts or authorities shall in passing sentence take as far as possible into account the fact that the defendant is not a national of the Detaining Power. They shall be free to reduce the penalty prescribed for the offence with which the internee is charged and shall not be obliged, to this end, to apply the minimum sentence prescribed.

Imprisonment in premises without daylight and, in general, all forms of cruelty without exception are forbidden.

Internees who have served disciplinary or judicial sentences shall not be treated differently from other internees.

The duration of preventive detention undergone by an internee shall be deducted from any disciplinary or judicial penalty involving confinement to which he may be sentenced.

Internee Committees shall be informed of all judicial proceedings instituted against internees whom they represent, and of their result.

*Article 119.* The disciplinary punishments applicable to internees shall be the following:

(1) A fine which shall not exceed 50 per cent of the wages which the internee would otherwise receive under the provisions of Article 95 during a period of not more than thirty days.

(2) Discontinuance of privileges granted over and above the treatment provided for by the present Convention.

(3) Fatigue duties, not exceeding two hours daily, in connection with the maintenance of the place of internment.

(4) Confinement.

In no case shall disciplinary penalties be inhuman, brutal or dangerous for the health of internees. Account shall be taken of the internee's age, sex and state of health.

The duration of any single punishment shall in no case exceed a maximum of thirty consecutive days, even if the internee is answerable for several breaches of discipline when his case is dealt with, whether such breaches are connected or not.

*Article 120.* Internees who are recaptured after having escaped or when attempting to escape, shall be liable only to disciplinary punishment in respect of this act, even if it is a repeated offence.

Article 118, paragraph 3, notwithstanding, internees punished as a result of escape or attempt to escape, may be subjected to special surveillance, on condition that such surveillance does not affect the state of their health, that it is exercised in a place of internment and that it does not entail the abolition of any of the safeguards granted by the present Convention.

Internees who aid and abet an escape or attempt to escape, shall be liable on this count to disciplinary punishment only.

*Article 121.* Escape, or attempt to escape, even if it is a repeated offence, shall not be deemed an aggravating circumstance in cases where an internee is prosecuted for offences committed during his escape.

The Parties to the conflict shall ensure that the competent authorities exercise leniency in deciding whether punishment inflicted for an offence shall be of a disciplinary or judicial nature, especially in respect of acts committed in connection with an escape, whether successful or not.

*Article 122.* Acts which constitute offences against discipline shall be investigated immediately. This rule shall be applied, in particular, in cases of escape or attempt to escape. Recaptured internees shall be handed over to the competent authorities as soon as possible.

In case of offences against discipline, confinement awaiting trial shall be reduced to an absolute minimum for all internees, and shall not exceed fourteen days. Its duration shall in any case be deducted from any sentence of confinement.

The provisions of Articles 124 and 125 shall apply to internees who are in confinement awaiting trial for offences against discipline.

*Article 123.* Without prejudice to the competence of courts and higher authorities, disciplinary punishment may be ordered only by the commandant of the place of internment, or by a responsible officer or official who replaces him, or to whom he has delegated his disciplinary powers.

Before any disciplinary punishment is awarded, the accused internee shall be given precise information regarding the offences of which he is accused, and given an opportunity of explaining his conduct and of defending himself. He shall be permitted, in particular, to call witnesses and to have recourse, if necessary, to the services of a qualified interpreter. The decision shall be announced in the presence of the accused and of a member of the Internee Committee.

The period elapsing between the time of award of a disciplinary punishment and its execution shall not exceed one month.

When an internee is awarded a further disciplinary punishment, a period of at least three days shall elapse between the execution of any two of the punishments, if the duration of one of these is ten days or more.

A record of disciplinary punishments shall be maintained by the commandant of the place of internment and shall be open to inspection by representatives of the Protecting Power.

*Article 124.* Internees shall not in any case be transferred to penitentiary establishments (prisons, penitentiaries, convict prisons, etc.) to undergo disciplinary punishment therein.

The premises in which disciplinary punishments are undergone shall conform to sanitary requirements; they shall in particular be provided with adequate bedding. Internees undergoing punishment shall be enabled to keep themselves in a state of cleanliness.

Women internees undergoing disciplinary punishment shall be confined in separate quarters from male internees and shall be under the immediate supervision of women.

*Article 125.* Internees awarded disciplinary punishment shall be allowed to exercise and to stay in the open air at least two hours daily.

They shall be allowed, if they so request, to be present at the daily medical inspections. They shall receive the attention which their state of health requires and, if necessary, shall be removed to the infirmary of the place of internment or to a hospital.

They shall have permission to read and write, likewise to send and receive letters. Parcels and remittances of money, however, may be withheld from them until the completion of their punishment; such consignments shall meanwhile be entrusted to the Internee Committee, who will hand over to the infirmary the perishable goods contained in the parcels.

No internee given a disciplinary punishment may be deprived of the benefit of the provisions of Articles 107 and 143 of the present Convention.

*Article 126.* The provisions of Articles 71 to 76 inclusive shall apply, by analogy, to proceedings against internees who are in the national territory of the Detaining Power.

## Chapter X—Transfers of Internees

*Article 127.* The transfer of internees shall always be effected humanely. As a general rule, it shall be carried out by rail or other means of transport, and under conditions at least equal to those obtaining for the forces of the Detaining Power in their changes of station. If, as an exceptional measure, such removals have to be effected on foot, they may not take place unless the internees are in a fit state of health, and may not in any case expose them to excessive fatigue.

The Detaining Power shall supply internees during transfer with drinking water and food sufficient in quantity, quality and variety to maintain them in good health, and also with the necessary clothing, adequate shelter and the necessary medical attention. The Detaining Power shall take all suitable precautions to ensure their safety during transfer, and shall establish before their departure a complete list of all internees transferred.

Sick, wounded or infirm internees and maternity cases shall not be transferred if the journey would be seriously detrimental to them, unless their safety imperatively so demands.

If the combat zone draws close to a place of internment, the internees in the said place shall not be transferred unless their removal can be carried out in adequate conditions of safety, or unless they are exposed to greater risks by remaining on the spot than by being transferred.

When making decisions regarding the transfer of internees, the Detaining Power shall take their interests into account and, in particular, shall not do anything to increase the difficulties of repatriating them or returning them to their own homes.

*Article 128.* In the event of transfer, internees shall be officially advised of their departure and of their new postal address. Such notification shall be given in time for them to pack their luggage and inform their next of kin.

They shall be allowed to take with them their personal effects, and the correspondence and parcels which have arrived for them. The weight of such baggage may be limited if the conditions of transfer so require, but in no case to less than twenty-five kilograms per internee.

Mail and parcels addressed to their former place of internment shall be forwarded to them without delay.

The commandant of the place of internment shall take, in agreement with the Internee Committee, any measures needed to ensure the transport of the internees' community property and of the luggage the internees are unable to take with them in consequence of restrictions imposed by virtue of the second paragraph.

## Chapter XI—Deaths

*Article 129.* The wills of internees shall be received for safekeeping by the responsible authorities; and in the event of the death of an internee his will shall be transmitted without delay to a person whom he has previously designated.

Deaths of internees shall be certified in every case by a doctor, and a death certificate shall be made out, showing the causes of death and the conditions under which it occurred.

An official record of the death, duly registered, shall be drawn up in accordance with the procedure relating thereto in force in the territory where the place of internment is situated, and a duly certified copy of such record shall be transmitted without delay to the Protecting Power as well as to the Central Agency referred to in Article 140.

*Article 130.* The detaining authorities shall ensure that internees who die while interned are honourably buried, if possible according to the rites of the religion to which they belonged, and that their graves are respected, properly maintained, and marked in such a way that they can always be recognized.

Deceased internees shall be buried in individual graves unless unavoidable circumstances require the use of collective graves. Bodies may be cremated only for imperative reasons of hygiene, on account of the religion of the deceased or in accordance with his expressed wish to this effect. In case of cremation, the fact shall be stated and the reasons given in the death certificate of the deceased. The ashes shall be retained for safe-keeping by the detaining authorities and shall be transferred as soon as possible to the next of kin on their request.

As soon as circumstances permit, and not later then the close of hostilities, the Detaining Power shall forward lists of graves of deceased internees to the Powers on whom the deceased internees depended, through the Information Bureaux provided for in Article 136. Such lists shall include all particulars necessary for the identification of the deceased internees, as well as the exact location of their graves.

*Article 131.* Every death or serious injury of an internee, caused or suspected to have been caused by a sentry, another internee or any other person, as well as any death the cause of which is unknown, shall be immediately followed by an official enquiry by the Detaining Power.

A communication on this subject shall be sent immediately to the Protecting Power. The evidence of any witnesses shall be taken, and a report including such evidence shall be prepared and forwarded to the said Protecting Power.

If the enquiry indicates the guilt of one or more persons, the Detaining Power shall take all necessary steps to ensure the prosecution of the person or persons responsible.

**Chapter XII—Release Repatriation and Accommodation in Neutral Countries**

*Article 132.* Each interned person shall be released by the Detaining Power as soon as the reasons which necessitated his internment no longer exist.

The Parties to the conflict shall, moreover, endeavour during the course of hostilities, to conclude agreements for the release, the repatriation, the return to places of residence or the accommodation in a neutral country of certain classes of internees, in particular children, pregnant women and mothers with infants and young children, wounded and sick, and internees who have been detained for a long time.

*Article 133.* Internment shall cease as soon as possible after the close of hostilities.

Internees in the territory of a Party to the conflict against whom penal proceedings are pending for offences not exclusively subject to disciplinary penalties, may be detained until the close of such proceedings and, if circumstances require, until the completion of the penalty. The same shall apply to internees who have been previously sentenced to a punishment depriving them of liberty.

By agreement between the Detaining Power and the Powers concerned, committees may be set up after the close of hostilities, or of the occupation of territories, to search for dispersed internees.

*Article 134.* The High Contracting Parties shall endeavour, upon the close of hostilities or occupation, to ensure the return of all internees to their last place of residence, or to facilitate their repatriation.

*Article 135.* The Detaining Power shall bear the expense of returning released internees to the places where they were residing when interned, or, if it took them into custody while they were in transit or on the high seas, the cost of completing their journey or of their return to their point of departure.

Where a Detaining Power refuses permission to reside in its territory to a released internee who previously had his permanent domicile therein, such Detaining Power shall pay the cost of the said internee's repatriation. If, however, the internee elects to return to his country on his own respon-

sibility or in obedience to the Government of the Power to which he owes allegiance, the Detaining Power need not pay the expenses of his journey beyond the point of his departure from its territory. The Detaining Power need not pay the costs of repatriation of an internee who was interned at his own request.

If internees are transferred in accordance with Article 45, the transferring and receiving Powers shall agree on the portion of the above costs to be borne by each.

The foregoing shall not prejudice such special agreements as may be concluded between Parties to the conflict concerning the exchange and repatriation of their nationals in enemy hands.

**Section V—Information Bureaux and Central Agency**

*Article 136.* Upon the outbreak of a conflict and in all cases of occupation, each of the Parties to the conflict shall establish an official Information Bureau responsible for receiving and transmitting information in respect of the protected persons who are in its power.

Each of the Parties to the conflict shall, within the shortest possible period, give its Bureau information of any measure taken by it concerning any protected persons who are kept in custody for more than two weeks, who are subjected to assigned residence or who are interned. It shall, furthermore, require its various departments concerned with such matters to provide the aforesaid Bureau promptly with information concerning all changes pertaining to these protected persons, as, for example, transfers, releases, repatriations, escapes, admittances to hospitals, births and deaths.

*Article 137.* Each national Bureau shall immediately forward information concerning protected persons by the most rapid means to the Powers of whom the aforesaid persons are nationals, or to Powers in whose territory they resided, through the intermediary of the Protecting Powers and likewise through the Central Agency provided for in Article 140. The Bureaux shall also reply to all enquiries which may be received regarding protected persons.

Information Bureaux shall transmit information concerning a protected person unless its transmission might be detrimental to the person concerned or to his or her relatives. Even in such a case, the information may not be withheld from the Central Agency which, upon being notified of the circumstances, will take the necessary precautions indicated in Article 140.

All communications in writing made by any Bureau shall be authenticated by a signature or a seal.

*Article 138.* The information received by the national Bureau and transmitted by it shall be of such a character as to make it possible to identify the protected person exactly and to advise his next of kin quickly. The information in respect of each person shall include at least his surname, first names, place and date of birth, nationality, last residence and distinguishing characteristics, the first name of the father and the maiden name of the mother, the date, place and nature of the action taken with regard to the individual, the address at which correspondence may be sent to him and the name and address of the person to be informed.

Likewise, information regarding the state of health of internees who are seriously ill or seriously wounded shall be supplied regularly and if possible every week.

*Article 139.* Each national Information Bureau shall, furthermore, be responsible for collecting all personal valuables left by protected persons mentioned in Article 136, in particular those who have been repatriated or released, or who have escaped or died; it shall forward the said valuables to those concerned, either direct, or, if necessary, through the Central Agency. Such articles shall be sent by the Bureau in sealed packets which shall be accompanied by statements giving clear and full identity particulars of the person to whom the articles belonged, and by a complete list of the contents of the parcel. Detailed records shall be maintained of the receipt and despatch of all such valuables.

*Article 140.* A Central Information Agency for protected persons, in particular for internees, shall be created in a neutral country. The International Committee of the Red Cross shall, if it deems necessary, propose to the Powers concerned the organization of such an Agency, which may be the same as that provided for in Article 123 of the Geneva Convention relative to the Treatment of Prisoners of War of August 12, 1949.

The function of the Agency shall be to collect all information of the type set forth in Article 136 which it may obtain through official or private channels and to transmit it as rapidly as possible to the countries of origin or of residence of the persons concerned, except in cases where such transmissions might be detrimental to the persons whom the said information concerns, or to their relatives. It shall receive from the Parties to the conflict all reasonable facilities for effecting such transmissions.

The High Contracting Parties, and in particular those whose nationals benefit by the services of the Central Agency, are requested to give the said Agency the financial aid it may require.

The foregoing provisions shall in no way be interpreted as restricting the humanitarian activities of the International Committee of the Red Cross and of the relief societies described in Article 142.

*Article 141.* The national Information Bureaux and the Central Information Agency shall enjoy free postage for all mail, likewise the exemptions provided for in Article 110, and further, so far as possible, exemption from telegraphic charges or, at least, greatly reduced rates.

## Part IV

### Execution of the Convention

### Section I—General Provisions

*Article 142.* Subject to the measures which the Detaining Powers may consider essential to ensure their security or to meet any other reasonable need, the representatives of religious organizations, relief societies, or any other organizations assisting the protected persons, shall receive from these Powers, for themselves or their duly accredited agents, all facilities for visiting the protected persons, for distributing relief supplies and material from any source, intended for educational, recreational or religious purposes, or for assisting them in organizing their leisure time within the places of internment. Such societies or organizations may be constituted in the territory of the Detaining Power, or in any other country, or they may have an international character.

The Detaining Power may limit the number of societies and organizations whose delegates are allowed to carry out their activities in its territory and under its supervision, on condition, however, that such limitation shall not hinder the supply of effective and adequate relief to all protected persons.

The special position of the International Committee of

the Red Cross in this field shall be recognized and respected at all times.

*Article 143.* Representatives or delegates of the Protecting Powers shall have permission to go to all places where protected persons are, particularly to places of internment, detention and work.

They shall have access to all premises occupied by protected persons and shall be able to interview the latter without witnesses, personally or through an interpreter.

Such visits may not be prohibited except for reasons of imperative military necessity, and then only as an exceptional and temporary measure. Their duration and frequency shall not be restricted.

Such representatives and delegates shall have full liberty to select the places they wish to visit. The Detaining or Occupying Power, the Protecting Power and when occasion arises the Power of origin of the persons to be visited, may agree that compatriots of the internees shall be permitted to participate in the visits.

The delegates of the International Committee of the Red Cross shall also enjoy the above prerogatives. The appointment of such delegates shall be submitted to the approval of the Power governing the territories where they will carry out their duties.

*Article 144.* The High Contracting Parties undertake, in time of peace as in time of war, to disseminate the text of the present Convention as widely as possible in their respective countries, and, in particular, to include the study thereof in their programmes of military and, if possible, civil instruction, so that the principles thereof may become known to the entire population.

Any civilian, military, police or other authorities, who in time of war assume responsibilities in respect of protected persons, must possess the text of the Convention and be specially instructed as to its provisions.

*Article 145.* The High Contracting Parties shall communicate to one another through the Swiss Federal Council and, during hostilities, through the Protecting Powers, the official translations of the present Convention, as well as the laws and regulations which they may adopt to ensure the application thereof.

*Article 146.* The High Contracting Parties undertake to enact any legislation necessary to provide effective penal sanctions for persons committing, or ordering to be committed any of the grave breaches of the present Convention defined in the following Article.

Each High Contracting Party shall be under the obligation to search for persons alleged to have committed, or to have ordered to be committed, such grave breaches, and shall bring such persons, regardless of their nationality, before its own courts. It may also, if it prefers, and in accordance with the provisions of its own legislation, hand such persons over for trial to another High Contracting Party concerned, provided such High Contracting Party has made out a *prima facie* case.

Each High Contracting Party shall take measures necessary for the suppression of all acts contrary to the provisions of the present Convention other than the grave breaches defined in the following Article.

In all circumstances, the accused persons shall benefit by safeguards of proper trial and defence, which shall not be less favourable than those provided by Article 105 and those following of the Geneva Convention relative to the Treatment of Prisoners of War of August 12, 1949.

*Article 147.* Grave breaches to which the preceding Article relates shall be those involving any of the following acts, if committed against persons or property protected by the present Convention: wilful killing, torture or inhuman treatment, including biological experiments, wilfully causing great suffering or serious injury to body or health, unlawful deportation or transfer or unlawful confinement of a protected person, compelling a protected person to serve in the forces of a hostile Power, or wilfully depriving a protected person of the rights of fair and regular trial prescribed in the present Convention, taking of hostages and extensive destruction and appropriation of property, not justified by military necessity and carried out unlawfully and wantonly.

*Article 148.* No High Contracting Party shall be allowed to absolve itself or any other High Contracting Party of any liability incurred by itself or by another High Contracting Party in respect of breaches referred to in the preceding Article.

*Article 149.* At the request of a Party to the conflict, an enquiry shall be instituted, in a manner to be decided between the interested Parties, concerning any alleged violation of the Convention.

If agreement has not been reached concerning the procedure for the enquiry, the Parties should agree on the choice of an umpire who will decide upon the procedure to be followed.

Once the violation has been established, the Parties to the conflict shall put an end to it and shall repress it with the least possible delay.

### Section II—Final Provisions

*Article 150.* The present Convention is established in English and in French. Both texts are equally authentic.

The Swiss Federal Council shall arrange for official translations of the Convention to be made in the Russian and Spanish languages.

*Article 151.* The present Convention, which bears the date of this day, is open to signature until February 12, 1950, in the name of the Powers represented at the Conference which opened at Geneva on April 21, 1949.

*Article 152.* The present Convention shall be ratified as soon as possible and the ratifications shall be deposited at Berne.

A record shall be drawn up of the deposit of each instrument of ratification and certified copies of this record shall be transmitted by the Swiss Federal Council to all the Powers in whose name the Convention has been signed, or whose accession has been notified.

*Article 153.* The present Convention shall come into force six months after not less than two instruments of ratification have been deposited.

Thereafter, it shall come into force for each High Contracting Party six months after the deposit of the instrument of ratification.

*Article 154.* In the relations between the Powers who are bound by The Hague Conventions respecting the Laws and Customs of War on Land, whether that of July 29, 1899, or that of October 18, 1907, and who are parties to the present Convention, this last Convention shall be supplementary to Sections II and III of the Regulations annexed to the above mentioned Conventions of The Hague.

*Article 155.* From the date of its coming into force, it shall be open to any Power in whose name the present Convention has not been signed, to accede to this Convention.

*Article 156.* Accessions shall be notified in writing to the Swiss Federal Council, and shall take effect six months after the date on which they are received.

The Swiss Federal Council shall communicate the accessions to all the Powers in whose name the Convention has been signed, or whose accession has been notified.

*Article 157.* The situations provided for in Articles 2 and 3 shall give immediate effect to ratifications deposited and accessions notified by the Parties to the conflict before or after the beginning of hostilities or occupation. The Swiss Federal Council shall communicate by the quickest method any ratifications or accessions received from Parties to the conflict.

*Article 158.* Each of the High Contracting Parties shall be at liberty to denounce the present Convention.

The denunciation shall be notified in writing to the Swiss Federal Council, which shall transmit it to the Governments of all the High Contracting Parties.

The denunciation shall take effect one year after the notification thereof has been made to the Swiss Federal Council. However, a denunciation of which notification has been made at a time when the denouncing Power is involved in a conflict shall not take effect until peace has been concluded, and until after operations connected with the release, repatriation and re-establishment of the persons protected by the present Convention have been terminated.

The denunciation shall have effect only in respect of the denouncing Power. It shall in no way impair the obligations which the Parties to the conflict shall remain bound to fulfil by virtue of the principles of the law of nations, as they result from the usages established among civilized peoples, from the laws of humanity and the dictates of the public conscience.

*Article 159.* The Swiss Federal Council shall register the present Convention with the Secretariat of the United Nations. The Swiss Federal council shall also inform the Secretariat of the United Nations of all ratifications, accessions and denunciations received by it with respect to the present Convention.

In witness whereof the undersigned, having deposited their respective full powers, have signed the present Convention.

Done at Geneva this twelfth day of August, 1949, in the English and French languages. The original shall be deposited in the Archives of the Swiss Confederation. The Swiss Federal Council shall transmit certified copies thereof to each of the signatory and acceding States.

***PROTOCOL I, ADDITION TO THE 1949 GENEVA RED CROSS CONVENTIONS AND RELATING TO THE PROTECTION OF VICTIMS OF INTERNATIONAL ARMED CONFLICTS.*** The Protocol revises and supplements the Geneva Conventions of 12 August 1949, broadening the scope of their protection of victims of armed conflicts in many respects. In particular, article 1 (4) of the Protocol clarifies the definition of **ARMED CONFLICT,** which appears in article 2 common to each of the four Geneva Conventions so as to include "armed conflicts in which people are fighting against colonial domination and alien occupation and against racist regimes in the exercise of their right of self-determination as enshrined in the Charter of the United Nations and the Declaration on Principles of International Law concerning Friendly Relations and Co-operation among States in accordance with the Charter of the United Nations."

The Protocol also authorizes the establishment (article 90) of an international factfinding commission, consisting of 15 members of high moral standing elected by the high contracting parties, with competence to (1) inquire into any facts alleged to be a grave breach as defined in the conventions and in this Protocol or other serious violation of the conventions or of the Protocol, and (2) facilitate, through its good offices, the restoration of an attitude of respect for the Conventions and the Protocol.

The Protocol was prepared by the Diplomatic Conference on the Reaffirmation and Development of International Humanitarian Law, convened in 1974, 1975, 1976, and 1977 by the Swiss Federal Council with the cooperation of the **INTERNATIONAL COMMITTEE OF THE RED CROSS.** It was adopted by the Conference on 8 June 1977 and entered into force on 7 December 1978. The text (UN Doc. A/32/144, annex I) is as follows:

### Preamble

The High Contracting Parties,

Proclaiming their earnest wish to see peace prevail among peoples,

Recalling that every State has the duty, in conformity with the Charter of the United Nations, to refrain in its international relations from the threat or use of force against the sovereignty, territorial integrity or political independence of any State, or in any other manner inconsistent with the purposes of the United Nations,

Believing it necessary nevertheless to reaffirm and develop the provisions protecting the victims of armed conflicts and to supplement measures intended to reinforce their application,

Expressing their conviction that nothing in this Protocol or in the Geneva Conventions of 12 August 1949 can be construed as legitimizing or authorizing any act of aggression or any other use of force inconsistent with the Charter of the United Nations,

Reaffirming further that the provisions of the Geneva Conventions of 12 August 1949 and of this Protocol must be fully applied in all circumstances to all persons who are protected by those instruments, without any adverse distinction based on the nature or origin of the armed conflict or on the causes espoused by or attributed to the Parties to the conflict,

Have agreed on the following:

### Part I

### General Provisions

*Article 1. General Principles and Scope of Application.* 1. The High Contracting Parties undertake to respect and to ensure respect for this Protocol in all circumstances.

2. In cases not covered by this Protocol or by other international agreements, civilians and combatants remain under the protection and authority of the principles of international law derived from established custom, from the principles of humanity and from dictates of public conscience.

3. This Protocol, which supplements the Geneva Conven-

tions of 12 August 1949 for the protection of war victims, shall apply in the situations referred to in Article 2 common to those Conventions.

4. The situations referred to in the preceding paragraph include armed conflicts in which peoples are fighting against colonial domination and alien occupation and against racist régimes in the exercise of their right of self-determination, as enshrined in the Charter of the United Nations and the Declaration on Principles of International Law concerning Friendly Relations and Co-operation among States in accordance with the Charter of the United Nations.

*Article 2. Definitions.* For the purposes of this Protocol:

(a) "First Convention", "Second Convention", "Third Convention" and "Fourth Convention" mean, respectively, the Geneva Convention for the Amelioration of the Condition of the Wounded and Sick in Armed Forces in the Field of 12 August 1949; the Geneva Convention for the Amelioration of the Condition of Wounded, Sick and Ship-wrecked Members of Armed Forces at Sea of 12 August 1949; the Geneva Convention relative to the Treatment of Prisoners of War of 12 August 1949; the Geneva Convention relative to the Protection of Civilian Persons in Time of War of 12 August 1949; "the Conventions" means the four Geneva Conventions of 12 August 1949 for the protection of war victims;

(b) "Rules of international law applicable in armed conflict" means the rules applicable in armed conflict set forth in international agreements to which the Parties to the conflict are Parties and the generally recognized principles and rules of international law which are applicable to armed conflict;

(c) "Protecting Power" means a neutral or other State not a Party to the conflict which has been designated by a Party to the conflict and accepted by the adverse Party and has agreed to carry out the functions assigned to a Protecting Power under the Conventions and this Protocol;

(d) "Substitute" means an organization acting in place of a Protecting Power in accordance with Article 5.

*Article 3. Beginning and End of Application.* Without prejudice to the provisions which are applicable at all times:

(a) the Conventions and this Protocol shall apply from the beginning of any situation referred to in Article 1 of this Protocol;

(b) the application of the Conventions and of this Protocol shall cease, in the territory of Parties to the conflict, on the general close of military operations and, in the case of occupied territories, on the termination of the occupation, except, in either circumstance, for those persons whose final release, repatriation or re-establishment takes place thereafter. These persons shall continue to benefit from the relevant provisions of the Conventions and of this Protocol until their final release repatriation or re-establishment.

*Article 4. Legal Status of the Parties to the Conflict.* The application of the Conventions and of this Protocol, as well as the conclusion of the agreements provided for therein, shall not affect the legal status of the Parties to the conflict. Neither the occupation of a territory nor the application of the Conventions and this Protocol shall affect the legal status of the territory in question.

*Article 5. Appointment of Protecting Powers and of their Substitute.* 1. It is the duty of the Parties to a conflict from the beginning of that conflict to secure the supervision and implementation of the Conventions and of this Protocol by the application of the system of Protecting Powers, including *inter alia* the designation and acceptance of those Powers, in accordance with the following paragraphs. Protecting Powers shall have the duty of safeguarding the interests of the Parties to the conflict.

2. From the beginning of a situation referred to in Article 1, each Party to the conflict shall without delay designate a Protecting Power for the purpose of applying the Conventions and this Protocol and shall, likewise without delay and for the same purpose, permit the activities of a Protecting Power which has been accepted by it as such after designation by the adverse Party.

3. If a Protecting Power has not been designated or accepted from the beginning of a situation referred to in Article 1, the International Committee of the Red Cross, without prejudice to the right of any other impartial humanitarian organization to do likewise, shall offer its good offices to the Parties to the conflict with a view to the designation without delay of a Protecting Power to which the Parties to the conflict consent. For that purpose it may *inter alia* ask each Party to provide it with a list of at least five States which that Party considers acceptable to act as Protecting Power on its behalf in relation to an adverse Party and ask each adverse Party to provide a list of at least five States which it would accept as the Protecting Power of the first Party; these lists shall be communicated to the Committee within two weeks after the receipt of the request; it shall compare them and seek the agreement of any proposed State named on both lists.

4. If, despite the foregoing, there is no Protecting Power, the Parties to the conflict shall accept without delay an offer which may be made by the International Committee of the Red Cross or by any other organization which offers all guarantees of impartiality and efficacy, after due consultations with the said Parties and taking into account the result of these consultations, to act as a substitute. The functioning of such a substitute is subject to the consent of the Parties to the conflict; every effort shall be made by the Parties to the conflict to facilitate the operations of the substitute in the performance of its tasks under the Conventions and this Protocol.

5. In accordance with Article 4, the designation and acceptance of Protecting Powers for the purpose of applying the Conventions and this Protocol shall not affect the legal status of the Parties to the conflict or of any territory, including occupied territory.

6. The maintenance of diplomatic relations between Parties to the conflict or the entrusting of the protection of a Party's interests and those of its nationals to a third State in accordance with the rules of international law relating to diplomatic relations is no obstacle to the designation of Protecting Powers for the purpose of applying the Conventions and this Protocol.

7. Any subsequent mention in this Protocol of a Protecting Power includes also a substitute.

*Article 6. Qualified Persons.* 1. The High Contracting Parties shall, also in peacetime, endeavour, with the assistance of the national Red Cross (Red Crescent, Red Lion and Sun) Societies, to train qualified personnel to facilitate the application of the Conventions and of this Protocol, and in particular the activities of the Protecting Powers.

2. The recruitment and training of such personnel are within domestic jurisdiction.

3. The International Committee of the Red Cross shall hold at the disposal of the High Contracting Parties the lists of persons so trained which the High Contracting Parties may have established and may have transmitted to it for that purpose.

4. The conditions governing the employment of such personnel outside the national territory shall, in each case, be the subject of special agreements between the Parties concerned.

*Article 7. Meetings.* The depositary of this Protocol shall convene a meeting of the High Contracting Parties, at the request of one or more of the said Parties and upon the approval of the majority of the said Parties, to consider general problems concerning the application of the Conventions and of the Protocol.

### Part II

### Wounded, Sick and Shipwrecked

### Section I—General Protection

*Article 8. Terminology.* For the purposes of this Protocol:

1. "Wounded" and "sick" mean persons, whether military or civilian, who, because of trauma, disease or other physical or mental disorder or disability, are in need of medical assistance or care and who refrain from any act of hostility. These terms also cover maternity cases, new-born babies and other persons who may be in need of immediate medical assistance or care, such as the infirm or expectant mothers, and who refrain from any act of hostility;

2. "Shipwrecked" means persons, whether military or civilian, who are in peril at sea or in other waters as a result of misfortune affecting them or the vessel or aircraft carrying them and who refrain from any act of hostility. These persons, provided that they continue to refrain from any act of hostility, shall continue to be considered shipwrecked during their rescue until they acquire another status under the Conventions or this Protocol;

3. "Medical personnel" means those persons assigned, by a Party to the conflict, exclusively to the medical purposes enumerated under (5) or to the administration of medical units or to the operation or administration of medical transports. Such assignments may be either permanent or temporary. The term includes:

(a) medical personnel of a Party to the conflict, whether military or civilian, including those described in the First and Second Conventions, and those assigned to civil defence organizations;

(b) medical personnel of national Red Cross (Red Crescent, Red Lion and Sun) Societies and other national voluntary aid societies duly recognized and authorized by a Party to the conflict;

(c) medical personnel of medical units or medical transports described in Article 9, paragraph 2.

4. "Religious personnel" means military or civilian persons, such as chaplains, who are exclusively engaged in the work of their ministry and attached:

(a) to the armed forces of a Party to the conflict;

(b) to medical units or medical transports of a Party to the conflict;

(c) to medical units or medical transports described in Article 9, paragraph 2; or

(d) to civil defence organizations of a Party to the conflict. The attachment of religious personnel may be either permanent or temporary, and the relevant provisions mentioned under (11) apply to them;

5. "Medical units" means establishments and other units, whether military or civilian, organized for medical purposes, namely the search for, collection, transportation, diagnosis

or treatment—including first-aid treatment—of the wounded, sick and shipwrecked, or for the prevention of disease. The term includes, for example, hospitals and other similar units, blood transfusion centres, preventive medicine centres and institutes, medical depots and the medical and pharmaceutical stores of such units. Medical units may be fixed or mobile, permanent or temporary;

6. "Medical transportation" means the conveyance by land, water or air of the wounded, sick, shipwrecked, medical personnel, religious personnel, medical equipment or medical supplies protected by the Conventions and by this Protocol;

7. "Medical transports" means any means of transportation, whether military or civilian, permanent or temporary, assigned exclusively to medical transportation and under the control of a competent authority of a Party to the conflict;

8. "Medical vehicles" means any medical transports by land;

9. "Medical ships and craft" means any medical transports by water;

10. "Medical aircraft" means any medical transports by air;

11. "Permanent medical personnel", "permanent medical units" and "permanent medical transports" mean those assigned exclusively to medical purposes for an indeterminate period. "Temporary medical personnel", "temporary medical units" and "temporary medical transports" mean those devoted exclusively to medical purposes for limited periods during the whole of such periods. Unless otherwise specified, the terms "medical personnel", "medical units" and "medical transports" cover both permanent and temporary categories;

12. "Distinctive emblem" means the distinctive emblem of the red cross, red crescent or red lion and sun on a white ground when used for the protection of medical units and transports, or medical and religious personnel, equipment or supplies;

13. "Distinctive signal" means any signal or message specified for the identification exclusively of medical units or transports in Chapter III of Annex I to this Protocol.

*Article 9. Field of Application.* 1. This Part, the provisions of which are intended to ameliorate the condition of the wounded, sick and shipwrecked, shall apply to all those affected by a situation referred to in Article 1, without any adverse distinction founded on race, colour, sex, language, religion or belief, political or other opinion, national or social origin, wealth, birth or other status, or on any other similar criteria.

2. The relevant provisions of Articles 27 and 32 of the First Convention shall apply to permanent medical units and transports (other than hospital ships, to which Article 25 of the Second Convention applies) and their personnel made available to a Party to the conflict for humanitarian purposes:

(a) by a neutral or other State which is not a Party to that conflict;

(b) by a recognized and authorized aid society of such a State;

(c) by an impartial international humanitarian organization.

*Article 10. Protection and Care.* 1. All the wounded, sick and shipwrecked, to whichever Party they belong, shall be respected and protected.

2. In all circumstances they shall be treated humanely and shall receive, to the fullest extent practicable and with the least possible delay, the medical care and attention required by their condition. There shall be no distinction among them founded on any grounds other than medical ones.

*Article 11. Protection of Persons.* 1. The physical or mental health and integrity of persons who are in the power of the adverse Party or who are interned, detained or otherwise deprived of liberty as a result of a situation referred to in Article 1 shall not be endangered by any unjustified act or omission. Accordingly, it is prohibited to subject the persons described in this Article to any medical procedure which is not indicated by the state of health of the person concerned and which is not consistent with generally medical standards which would be applied under similar medical circumstances to persons who are nationals of the Party conducting the procedure and who are in no way deprived of liberty.

2. It is, in particular, prohibited to carry out on such persons, even with their consent:

(a) physical mutilations;

(b) medical or scientific experiments;

(c) removal of tissue or organs for transplantation, except where these acts are justified in conformity with the conditions provided for in paragraph 1.

3. Exceptions to the prohibition in paragraph 2 (c) may be made only in the case of donations of blood for transfusion or of skin for grafting, provided that they are given voluntarily and without any coercion or inducement, and then only for therapeutic purposes, under conditions consistent with generally accepted medical standards and controls designed for the benefit of both the donor and the recipient.

4. Any wilful act or omission which seriously endangers the physical or mental health or integrity of any person who is in the power of a Party other than the one on which he depends and which either violates any of the prohibitions in paragraphs 1 and 2 or fails to comply with the requirements of paragraph 3 shall be a grave breach of this Protocol.

5. The persons described in paragraph 1 have the right to refuse any surgical operation. In case of refusal, medical personnel shall endeavour to obtain a written statement to that effect, signed or acknowledged by the patient.

6. Each Party to the conflict shall keep a medical record for every donation of blood for transfusion or skin for grafting by persons referred to in paragraph 1, if that donation is made under the responsibility of that Party. In addition, each Party to the conflict shall endeavour to keep a record of all medical procedures undertaken with respect to any person who is interned, detained or otherwise deprived of liberty as a result of a situation referred to in Article 1. These records shall be available at all times for inspection by the Protecting Power.

*Article 12. Protection of Medical Units.* 1. Medical units shall be respected and protected at all times and shall not be the object of attack.

2. Paragraph 1 shall apply to civilian medical units, provided that they:

(a) belong to one of the Parties to the conflict;

(b) are recognized and authorized by the competent authority of one of the Parties to the conflict; or

(c) are authorized in conformity with Article 9, paragraph 2, of this Protocol or Article 27 of the First Convention.

3. The Parties to the conflict are invited to notify each other of the location of their fixed medical units. The absence of such notification shall not exempt any of the Parties from the obligation to comply with the provisions of paragraph 1.

4. Under no circumstances shall medical units be used in an attempt to shield military objectives from attack. Whenever possible, the Parties to the conflict shall ensure that medical units are so sited that attacks against military objectives do not imperil their safety.

*Article 13. Discontinuance of Protection of Civilian Medical Units.* 1. The protection to which civilian medical units are entitled shall not cease unless they are used to commit, outside their humanitarian function, acts harmful to the enemy. Protection may, however, cease only after a warning has been given setting, whenever appropriate, a reasonable time-limit, and after such warning has remained unheeded.

2. The following shall not be considered as acts harmful to the enemy:

(a) that the personnel of the unit are equipped with light individual weapons for their own defence or for that of the wounded and sick in their charge;

(b) that the unit is guarded by a picket or by sentries or by an escort;

(c) that small arms and ammunition taken from the wounded and sick, and not yet handed to the proper service, are found in the units;

(d) that members of the armed forces or other combatants are in the unit for medical reasons.

*Article 14. Limitations on Requisition of Civilian Medical Units.* 1. The Occupying Power has the duty to ensure that the medical needs of the civilian population in occupied territory continue to be satisfied.

2. The Occupying Power shall not, therefore, requisition civilian medical units, their equipment, their *matériel* or the services of their personnel, so long as these resources are necessary for the provision of adequate medical services for the civilian population and for the continuing medical care of any wounded and sick already under treatment.

3. Provided that the general rule in paragraph 2 continues to be observed, the Occupying Power may requisition the said resources, subject to the following particular conditions:

(a) that the resources are necessary for the adequate and immediate medical treatment of the wounded and sick members of the armed forces of the Occupying Power or of prisoners of war;

(b) that the requisition continues only while such necessity exists; and

(c) that immediate arrangements are made to ensure that the medical needs of the civilian population, as well as those of any wounded and sick under treatment who are affected by the requisition, continue to be satisfied.

*Article 15. Protection of Civilian Medical and Religious Personnel.* 1. Civilian medical personnel shall be respected and protected.

2. If needed, all available help shall be afforded to civilian medical personnel in an area where civilian medical services are disrupted by reason of combat activity.

3. The Occupying Power shall afford civilian medical personnel in occupied territories every assistance to enable them to perform, to the best of their ability, their humanitarian functions. The Occupying Power may not require that, in the performance of those functions, such personnel shall give priority to the treatment of any person except on medical grounds. They shall not be compelled to carry out tasks which are not compatible with their humanitarian mission.

4. Civilian medical personnel shall have access to any place where their services are essential, subject to such supervisory and safety measures as the relevant Party to the conflict may deem necessary.

5. Civilian religious personnel shall be respected and protected. The provisions of the Conventions and of this Protocol concerning the protection and identification of medical personnel shall apply equally to such persons.

*Article 16. General Protection of Medical Duties.* 1. Under no circumstances shall any person be punished for carrying out medical activities compatible with medical ethics, regardless of the person benefiting therefrom.

2. Persons engaged in medical activities shall not be compelled to perform acts or to carry out work contrary to the rules of medical ethics or to other medical rules designed for the benefit of the wounded and sick or to the provisions of the Conventions or of this Protocol, or to refrain from performing acts or from carrying out work required by those rules and provisions.

3. No person engaged in medical activities shall be compelled to give to anyone belonging either to an adverse Party, or to his own Party except as required by the law of the latter Party, any information concerning the wounded and sick who are, or who have been, under his care, if such information would, in his opinion, prove harmful to the patients concerned or to their families. Regulations for the compulsory notification of communicable diseases shall, however, be respected.

*Article 17. Role of the Civilian Population and of Aid Societies.* 1. The civilian population shall respect the wounded, sick and shipwrecked, even if they belong to the adverse Party, and shall commit no act of violence against them. The civilian population and aid societies, such as national Red Cross (Red Crescent, Red Lion and Sun) Societies, shall be permitted, even on their own initiative, to collect and care for the wounded, sick and shipwrecked, even in invaded or occupied areas. No one shall be harmed, prosecuted, convicted or punished for such humanitarian acts.

2. The Parties to the conflict may appeal to the civilian population and the aid societies referred to in paragraph 1 to collect and care for the wounded, sick and shipwrecked, and to search for the dead and report their location; they shall grant both protection and the necessary facilities to those who respond to this appeal. If the adverse Party gains or regains control of the area, that Party also shall afford the same protection and facilities for so long as they are needed.

*Article 18. Identification.* 1. Each Party to the conflict shall endeavour to ensure that medical and religious personnel and medical units and transports are identifiable.

2. Each Party to the conflict shall also endeavour to adopt and to implement methods and procedures which will make it possible to recognize medical units and transports which use the distinctive emblem and distinctive signals.

3. In occupied territory and in areas where fighting is taking place or is likely to take place, civilian medical personnel and civilian religious personnel should be recognizable by the distinctive emblem and an identity card certifying their status.

4. With the consent of the competent authority, medical units and transports shall be marked by the distinctive emblem. The ships and craft referred to in Article 22 of this Protocol shall be marked in accordance with the provisions of the Second Convention.

5. In addition to the distinctive emblem, a Party to the conflict may, as provided in Chapter III of Annex I to this Protocol, authorize the use of distinctive signals to identify medical units and transports. Exceptionally, in the special cases covered in that Chapter, medical transports may use distinctive signals without displaying the distinctive emblem.

6. The application of the provisions of paragraphs 1 to 5 of this article is governed by Chapters I to III of Annex I to this Protocol. Signals designated in Chapter III of the Annex for the exclusive use of medical units and transports shall not, except as provided therein, be used for any purpose other than to identify the medical units and transports specified in that Chapter.

7. This article does not authorize any wider use of the distinctive emblem in peacetime than is prescribed in Article 4 of the First Convention.

8. The provisions of the Conventions and of this Protocol relating to supervision of the use of the distinctive emblem and to the prevention and repression of any misuse thereof shall be applicable to distinctive signals.

*Article 19. Neutral and Other States not Parties to the Conflict.* Neutral and other States not Parties to the conflict shall apply the relevant provisions of this Protocol to persons protected by this Part who may be received or interned within their territory, and to any dead of the Parties to that conflict whom they may find.

*Article 20. Prohibition of Reprisals.* Reprisals against the persons and objects protected by this Part are prohibited.

### Section II—Medical Transportation

*Article 21. Medical Vehicles.* Medical vehicles shall be respected and protected in the same way as mobile medical units under the Conventions and this Protocol.

*Article 22. Hospital Ships and Coastal Rescue Craft.* 1. The provisions of the Conventions relating to:

(a) vessels described in Articles 22, 24, 25 and 27 of the Second Convention.

(b) their lifeboats and small craft,

(c) their personnel and crews, and

(d) the wounded, sick and shipwrecked on board, shall also apply where these vessels carry civilian wounded, sick and shipwrecked who do not belong to any of the categories mentioned in Article 13 of the Second Convention. Such civilians shall not, however, be subject to surrender to any Party which is not their own, or to capture at sea. If they find themselves in the power of a Party to the conflict other than their own they shall be covered by the Fourth Convention and by this Protocol.

2. The protection provided by the Conventions to vessels described in Article 25 of the Second Convention shall extend to hospital ships made available for humanitarian purposes to a Party to the conflict:

(a) by a neutral or other State which is not a Party to that conflict; or

(b) by an impartial international humanitarian organization, provided that, in either case, the requirements set out in that Article are complied with.

3. Small craft described in Article 27 of the Second Convention shall be protected even if the notification envisaged by that Article has not been made. The Parties to the conflict are, nevertheless, invited to inform each other of any details of such craft which will facilitate their identification and recognition.

*Article 23. Other Medical Ships and Craft.* 1. Medical ships and craft other than those referred to in Article 22 of this Protocol and Article 38 of the Second Convention shall, whether at sea or in other waters, be respected and protected in the same way as mobile medical units under the Conventions and this Protocol. Since this protection can only be effective if they can be identified and recognized as medical ships or craft, such vessels should be marked with the distinctive emblem and as far as possible comply with the second paragraph of Article 43 of the Second Convention.

2. The ships and craft referred to in paragraph 1 shall remain subject to the laws of war. Any warship on the surface able immediately to enforce its command may order them to stop, order them off, or make them take a certain course, and they shall obey every such command. Such ships and craft may not in any other way be diverted from their medical mission so long as they are needed for the wounded, sick and shipwrecked on board.

3. The protection provided in paragraph 1 shall cease only under the conditions set out in Articles 34 and 35 of the Second Convention. A clear refusal to obey a command given in accordance with paragraph 2 shall be an act harmful to the enemy under Article 34 of the Second Convention.

4. A Party to the conflict may notify any adverse Party as far in advance of sailing as possible of the name, description, expected time of sailing, course and estimated speed of the medical ship or craft, particularly in the case of ships of over 2,000 gross tons, and may provide any other information which would facilitate identification and recognition. The adverse Party shall acknowledge receipt of such information.

5. The provisions of Article 37 of the Second Convention shall apply to medical and religious personnel in such ships and craft.

6. The provisions of the Second Convention shall apply to the wounded, sick and shipwrecked belonging to the categories referred to in Article 13 of the Second Convention and in Article 44 of this Protocol who may be on board such medical ships and craft. Wounded, sick and shipwrecked civilians who do not belong to any of the categories mentioned in Article 13 of the Second Convention shall not be subject, at sea, either to surrender to any Party which is not their own, or to removal from such ships or craft; if they find themselves in the power of a Party to the conflict other than their own, they shall be covered by the Fourth Convention and by this Protocol.

*Article 24. Protection of Medical Aircraft.* Medical aircraft shall be respected and protected, subject to the provisions of this Part.

*Article 25. Medical Aircraft in Areas not Controlled by an Adverse Party.* In and over land areas physically controlled by friendly forces, or in and over sea areas not physically controlled by an adverse Party, the respect and protection of medical aircraft of a Party to the conflict is not dependent on any agreement with an adverse Party. For greater safety, however, a Party to the conflict operating its medical aircraft in these areas may notify the adverse Party, as provided in Article 29, in particular when such aircraft are making flights bringing them within range of surface-to-air weapons systems of the adverse Party.

*Article 26. Medical Aircraft in Contact or Similar Zones.* 1. In and over those parts of the contact zone which are physically controlled by friendly forces and in and over those areas the physical control of which is not clearly established, protection for medical aircraft can be fully effective only by prior agreement between the competent military authorities of the Parties to the conflict, as provided for in Article 29. Although, in the absence of such an agreement, medical aircraft operate at their own risk, they shall nevertheless be respected after they have been recognized as such.

2. "Contact zone" means any area on land where the forward elements of opposing forces are in contact with each other, especially where they are exposed to direct fire from the ground.

*Article 27. Medical Aircraft in Areas Controlled by an Adverse Party.* 1. The medical aircraft of a Party to the conflict shall continue to be protected while flying over land or sea areas physically controlled by an adverse Party, provided that prior agreement to such flights has been obtained from the competent authority of that adverse Party.

2. A medical aircraft which flies over an area physically controlled by an adverse Party without, or in deviation from the terms of, an agreement provided for in paragraph 1, either through navigational error or because of an emergency affecting the safety of the flight, shall make every effort to identify itself and to inform the adverse Party of the circumstances. As soon as such medical aircraft has been recognized by the adverse Party, that Party shall make all reasonable efforts to give the order to land or to alight on water, referred to in Article 30, paragraph 1, or to take other measures to safeguard its own interests, and, in either case, to allow the aircraft time for compliance, before resorting to an attack against the aircraft.

*Article 28. Restrictions on Operations of Medical Aircraft.* 1. The Parties to the conflict are prohibited from using their medical aircraft to attempt to acquire any military advantage over an adverse Party. The presence of medical aircraft shall not be used in an attempt to render military objectives immune from attack.

2. Medical aircraft shall not be used to collect or transmit intelligence data and shall not carry any equipment intended for such purposes. They are prohibited from carrying any persons or cargo not included within the definition in Article 8 (6). The carrying on board of the personal effects of the occupants or of equipment intended solely to facilitate navigation, communication or identification shall not be considered as prohibited.

3. Medical aircraft shall not carry any armament except small arms and ammunition taken from the wounded, sick and shipwrecked on board and not yet handed to the proper service, and such light individual weapons as may be necessary to enable the medical personnel on board to defend themselves and the wounded, sick and shipwrecked in their charge,

4. While carrying out the flights referred to in Article 26 and 27, medical aircraft shall not, except by prior agreement with the adverse Party, be used to search for the wounded, sick and shipwrecked.

*Article 29. Notifications and Agreements concerning Medical Aircraft.* 1. Notifications under Article 25, or requests for prior agreement under Articles 26, 27, 28, paragraph 4, or 31 shall state the proposed number of medical aircraft, their flight plans and means of identification, and shall be understood to mean that every flight will be carried out in compliance with Article 28.

2. A Party which receives a notification given under Article 25 shall at once acknowledge receipt of such notification.

3. A Party which receives a request for prior agreement under Articles 26, 27, 28, paragraph 4, or 31 shall, as rapidly as possible, notify the requesting Party:

(a) that the request is agreed to;

(b) that the request is denied; or

(c) of reasonable alternative proposals to the request. It may also propose a prohibition or restriction of other flights in the area during the time involved. If the Party which submitted the request accepts the alternative proposals, it shall notify the other Party of such acceptance.

4. The Parties shall take the necessary measures to ensure that notifications and agreements can be made rapidly.

5. The Parties shall also take the necessary measures to disseminate rapidly the substance of any such notifications and agreements to the military units concerned and shall instruct those units regarding the means of identification that will be used by the medical aircraft in question.

*Article 30. Landing and Inspection of Medical Aircraft.* 1. Medical aircraft flying over areas which are physically controlled by an adverse Party, or over areas the physical control of which is not clearly established, may be ordered to land or to alight on water, as appropriate, to permit inspection in accordance with the following paragraphs. Medical aircraft shall obey any such order.

2. If such an aircraft lands or alights on water, whether ordered to do so or for other reasons, it may be subjected to inspection solely to determine the matters referred to in paragraphs 3 and 4. Any such inspection shall be commenced without delay and shall be conducted expeditiously. The inspecting Party shall not require the wounded and sick to be removed from the aircraft unless their removal is essential for the inspection. That Party shall in any event ensure that the condition of the wounded and sick is not adversely affected by the inspection or by the removal.

3. If the inspection discloses that the aircraft:

(a) is a medical aircraft within the meaning of Article 8 (10),

(b) is not in violation of the conditions prescribed in Article 28, and

(c) has not flown without or in breach of a prior agreement where such agreement is required, the aircraft and those of its occupants who belong to the adverse Party or to a neutral or other State not a Party to the conflict shall be authorized to continue the flight without delay.

4. If the inspection discloses that the aircraft:

(a) is not a medical aircraft within the meaning of Article 8 (10),

(b) is in violation of the conditions prescribed in Article 28, or

(c) has flown without or in breach of a prior agreement where such agreement is required, the aircraft may be seized. Its occupants shall be treated in conformity with the relevant provisions of the Conventions and of this Protocol. Any aircraft seized which had been assigned as a permanent medical aircraft may be used thereafter only as a medical aircraft.

*Article 31. Neutral or Other States not Parties to the Conflict.* 1. Except by prior agreement, medical aircraft shall not fly over or land in the territory of a neutral or other State not a Party to the conflict. However, with such an agreement, they shall be respected throughout their flight and also for the duration of any calls in the territory. Nevertheless they shall obey any summons to land or to alight on water, as appropriate.

2. Should a medical aircraft, in the absence of an agreement or in deviation from the terms of an agreement, fly over the territory of a neutral or other State not a Party to the conflict, either through navigational error or because of an emergency affecting the safety of the flight, it shall make every effort to give notice of the flight and to identify itself. As soon as such medical aircraft is recognized, that State shall make all reasonable efforts to give the order to land or to alight on water referred to in Article 30, paragraph 1, or to take other measures to safeguard its own interests, and, in either case, to allow the aircraft time for compliance, before resorting to an attack against the aircraft.

3. If a medical aircraft, either by agreement or in the cir-

cumstances mentioned in paragraph 2, lands or alights on water in the territory of a neutral or other State not Party to the conflict, whether ordered to do so or for other reasons, the aircraft shall be subject to inspection for the purposes of determining whether it is in fact a medical aircraft. The inspection shall be commenced without delay and shall be conducted expeditiously. The inspecting Party shall not require the wounded and sick of the Party operating the aircraft to be removed from it unless their removal is essential for the inspection. The inspecting Party shall in any event ensure that the condition of the wounded and sick is not adversely affected by the inspection or the removal. If the inspection discloses that the aircraft is in fact a medical aircraft, the aircraft with its occupants, other than those who must be detained in accordance with the rules of international law applicable in armed conflict, shall be allowed to resume its flight, and reasonable facilities shall be given for the continuation of the flight. If the inspection discloses that the aircraft is not a medical aircraft, it shall be seized and the occupants treated in accordance with paragraph 4.

4. The wounded, sick and shipwrecked disembarked, otherwise than temporarily, from a medical aircraft with the consent of the local authorities in the territory of a neutral or other State not a Party to the conflict shall, unless agreed otherwise between that State and the Parties to the conflict, be detained by that State where so required by the rules of international law applicable in armed conflict, in such a manner that they cannot again take part in the hostilities. The cost of hospital treatment and internment shall be borne by the State to which those persons belong.

5. Neutral or other States not Parties to the conflict shall apply any conditions and restrictions on the passage of medical aircraft over, or on the landing of medical aircraft in, their territory equally to all Parties to the conflict.

### Section III—Missing and Dead Persons

*Article 32. General Principle.* In the implementation of this Section, the activities of the High Contracting Parties, of the Parties to the conflict and of the international humanitarian organizations mentioned in the Conventions and in this Protocol shall be prompted mainly by the right of families to know the fate of their relatives.

*Article 33. Missing Persons.* 1. As soon as circumstances permit, and at the latest from the end of active hostilities, each Party to the conflict shall search for the persons who have been reported missing by an adverse Party. Such adverse Party shall transmit all relevant information concerning such persons in order to facilitate such searches.

2. In order to facilitate the gathering of information pursuant to the preceding paragraph, each Party to the conflict shall, with respect to persons who would not receive more favourable consideration under the Conventions and this Protocol:

(a) record the information specified in Article 138 of the Fourth Convention in respect of such persons who have been detained, imprisoned or otherwise held in captivity for more than two weeks as a result of hostilities or occupation, or who have died during any period of detention;

(b) to the fullest extent possible, facilitate and, if need be, carry out the search for and the recording of information concerning such persons if they have died in other circumstances as a result of hostilities or occupation.

3. Information concerning persons reported missing pursuant to paragraph 1 and requests for such information shall be transmitted either directly or through the Protecting Power or the Central Tracing Agency of the International Committee of the Red Cross or national Red Cross (Red Crescent, Red Lion and Sun) Societies. Where the information is not transmitted through the International Committee of the Red Cross and its Central Tracing Agency, each Party to the conflict shall ensure that such information is also supplied to the Central Tracing Agency.

4. The Parties to the conflict shall endeavour to agree on arrangements for teams to search for, identify and recover the dead from battlefield areas, including arrangements, if appropriate, for such teams to be accompanied by personnel of the adverse Party while carrying out these missions in areas controlled by the adverse Party. Personnel of such teams shall be respected and protected while exclusively carrying out these duties.

*Article 34. Remains of Deceased.* 1. The remains of persons who have died for reasons related to occupation or in detention resulting from occupation or hostilities and those of persons not nationals of the country in which they have died as a result of hostilities shall be respected, and the gravesites of all such persons shall be respected, maintained and marked as provided for in Article 130 of the Fourth Convention, where their remains or gravesites would not receive more favourable consideration under the Conventions and this Protocol.

2. As soon as circumstances and the relations between the adverse Parties permit, the High Contracting Parties in whose territories graves and, as the case may be, other locations of the remains of persons who have died as a result of hostilities or during occupation or in detention are situated, shall conclude agreements in order:

(a) to facilitate access to the gravesites by relatives of the deceased and by representatives of official graves registration services and to regulate the practical arrangements for such access;

(b) to protect and maintain such gravesites permanently;

(c) to facilitate the return of the remains of the deceased and of personal effects to the home country upon its request or, unless that country objects, upon the request of the next of kin.

3. In the absence of the agreements provided for in paragraph 2 (b) or (c) and if the home country of such deceased is not willing to arrange at its expense for the maintenance of such gravesites, the High Contracting Party in whose territory the gravesites are situated may offer to facilitate the return of the remains of the deceased to the home country. Where such an offer has not been accepted the High Contracting Party may, after the expiry of five years from the date of the offer and upon due notice to the home country, adopt the arrangements laid down in its own laws relating to cemeteries and graves.

4. A High Contracting Party in whose territory the gravesites referred to in this Article are situated shall be permitted to exhume the remains only:

(a) in accordance with paragraphs 2 (c) and 3, or

(b) where exhumation is a matter of overriding public necessity, including cases of medical and investigative necessity, in which case the High Contracting Party shall at all times respect the remains, and shall give notice to the home country of its intention to exhume the remains together with details of the intended place of reinterment.

**Part III**

**Methods and Means of Warfare / Combatant
and Prisoner-of-War Status**

**Section I—Methods and Means of Warfare**

*Article 35. Basic Rules.* 1. In any armed conflict, the right of the Parties to the conflict to choose methods or means of warfare is not unlimited.

2. It is prohibited to employ weapons, projectiles and material and methods of warfare of a nature to cause superfluous injury or unnecessary suffering.

3. It is prohibited to employ methods or means of warfare which are intended, or may be expected, to cause widespread, long-term and severe damage to the natural environment.

*Article 36. New Weapons.* In the study, development, acquisition or adoption of a new weapon, means or method of warfare, a High Contracting Party is under an obligation to determine whether its employment would, in some or all circumstances, be prohibited by this Protocol or by any other rule of international law applicable to the High Contracting Party.

*Article 37. Prohibition of Perfidy.* 1. It is prohibited to kill, injure or capture an adversary by resort to perfidy. Acts inviting the confidence of an adversary to lead him to believe that he is entitled to, or is obliged to accord, protection under the rules of international law applicable in armed conflict, with intent to betray that confidence, shall constitute perfidy. The following acts are examples of perfidy:

(a) the feigning of an intent to negotiate under a flag of truce or of a surrender;

(b) the feigning of an incapacitation by wounds or sickness;

(c) the feigning of civilian, non-combatant status; and

(d) the feigning of protected status by the use of signs, emblems or uniforms of the United Nations or of neutral or other States not Parties to the Conflict.

2. Ruses of war are not prohibited. Such ruses are acts which are intended to mislead an adversary or to induce him to act recklessly but which infringe no rule of international law applicable in armed conflict and which are not perfidious because they do not invite the confidence of an adversary with respect to protection under that law. The following are examples of such ruses: the use of camouflage, decoys, mock operations and misinformation.

*Article 38. Recognized Emblems.* 1. It is prohibited to make improper use of the distinctive emblem of the red cross, red crescent or red lion and sun or of other emblems, signs or signals provided for by the Conventions or by this Protocol. It is also prohibited to misuse deliberately in an armed conflict other internationally recognized protective emblems, signs or signals, including the flag of truce, and the protective emblem of cultural property.

2. It is prohibited to make use of the distinctive emblem of the United Nations, except as authorized by that Organization.

*Article 39. Emblems of Nationality.* 1. It is prohibited to make use in an armed conflict of the flags or military emblems, insignia or uniforms of neutral or other States not Parties to the conflict.

2. It is prohibited to make use of the flags or military emblems, insignia or uniforms of adverse Parties while engaging in attacks or in order to shield, favour, protect or impede military operations.

3. Nothing in this Article or in Article 37, paragraph 1 (d), shall affect the existing generally recognized rules of international law applicable to espionage or to the use of flags in the conduct of armed conflict at sea.

*Article 40. Quarter.* It is prohibited to order that there shall be no survivors, to threaten an adversary therewith or to conduct hostilities on this basis.

*Article 41. Safeguard of an Enemy Hors de Combat.* 1. A person who is recognized or who, in the circumstances should be recognized to be *hors de combat* shall not be made the object of attack.

2. A person is *hors de combat* if:

(a) he is in the power of an adverse Party;

(b) he clearly expresses an intention to surrender; or

(c) he has been rendered unconscious or is otherwise incapacitated by wounds or sickness, and therefore is incapable of defending himself; provided that in any of these cases he abstains from any hostile act and does not attempt to escape.

3. When persons entitled to protection as prisoners of war have fallen into the power of an adverse Party under unusual conditions of combat which prevent their evacuation as provided for in Part III, Section I, of the Third Convention, they shall be released and all feasible precautions shall be taken to ensure their safety.

*Article 42. Occupants of Aircraft.* 1. No person parachuting from an aircraft in distress shall be made the object of attack during his descent.

2. Upon reaching the ground in territory controlled by an adverse Party, a person who has parachuted from an aircraft in distress shall be given an opportunity to surrender before being made the object of attack, unless it is apparent that he is engaging in a hostile act.

3. Airborne troops are not protected by this Article.

**Section II—Combatant and Prisoner-of-War Status**

*Article 43. Armed Forces.* 1. The armed forces of a Party to a conflict consist of all organized armed forces, groups and units which are under a command responsible to that Party for the conduct of its subordinates, even if that Party is represented by a government or an authority not recognized by an adverse Party. Such armed forces shall be subject to an internal disciplinary system which, *inter alia,* shall enforce compliance with the rules of international law applicable in armed conflict.

2. Members of the armed forces of a Party to a conflict (other than medical personnel and chaplains covered by Article 33 of the Third Convention) are combatants, that is to say, they have the right to participate directly in hostilities.

3. Whenever a Party to a conflict incorporates a paramilitary or armed law enforcement agency into its armed forces it shall so notify the other Parties to the conflict.

*Article 44. Combatants and Prisoners of War.* 1. Any combatant, as defined in Article 43, who falls into the power of an adverse Party shall be a prisoner of war.

2. While all combatants are obliged to comply with the rules of international law applicable in armed conflict, violations of these rules shall not deprive a combatant of his right to be a combatant or, if he falls into the power of an adverse Party, of his right to be a prisoner of war, except as provided in paragraphs 3 and 4.

3. In order to promote the protection of the civilian population from the effects of hostilities, combatants are obliged to distinguish themselves from the civilian population while

they are engaged in an attack or in a military operation preparatory to an attack. Recognizing, however, that there are situations in armed conflicts where, owing to the nature of the hostilities an armed combatant cannot so distinguish himself, he shall retain his status as a combatant, provided that, in such situations, he carries his arms openly:

(a) during each military engagement, and

(b) during such time as he is visible to the adversary while he is engaged in a military deployment preceding the launching of an attack in which he is to participate. Acts which comply with the requirements of this paragraph shall not be considered as perfidious within the meaning of Article 37, paragraph 1 (c).

4. A combatant who falls into the power of an adverse Party while failing to meet the requirements set forth in the second sentence of paragraph 3 shall forfeit his right to be a prisoner of war, but he shall, nevertheless, be given protections equivalent in all respects to those accorded to prisoners of war by the Third Convention and by this Protocol. This protection includes protections equivalent to those accorded to prisoners of war by the Third Convention in the case where such a person is tried and punished for any offences he has committed.

5. Any combatant who falls into the power of an adverse Party while not engaged in an attack or in a military operation preparatory to an attack shall not forfeit his rights to be a combatant and a prisoner of war by virtue of his prior activities.

6. This Article is without prejudice to the right of any person to be a prisoner of war pursuant to Article 4 of the Third Convention.

7. This Article is not intended to change the generally accepted practice of States with respect to the wearing of the uniform by combatants assigned to the regular, uniformed armed units of a Party to the conflict.

8. In addition to the categories of persons mentioned in Article 13 of the First and Second Conventions, all members of the armed forces of a Party to the conflict, as defined in Article 43 of this Protocol, shall be entitled to protection under those Conventions if they are wounded or sick or, in the case of the Second Convention, shipwrecked at sea or in other waters.

*Article 45. Protection of Persons Who Have Taken Part in Hostilities.* 1. A person who takes part in hostilities and falls into the power of an adverse Party shall be presumed to be a prisoner of war, and therefore shall be protected by the Third Convention, if he claims the status of prisoner of war, or if he appears to be entitled to such status, or if the Party on which he depends claims such status on his behalf by notification to the detaining Power or to the Protecting Power. Should any doubt arise as to whether any such person is entitled to the status of prisoner of war, he shall continue to have such status and, therefore, to be protected by the Third Convention and this Protocol until such time as his status has been determined by a competent tribunal.

2. If a person who has fallen into the power of an adverse Party is not held as a prisoner of war and is to be tried by that Party for an offence arising out of the hostilities, he shall have the right to assert his entitlement to prisoner-of-war status before a judicial tribunal and to have that question adjudicated. Whenever possible under the applicable procedure, this adjudication shall occur before the trial for the offence. The representatives of the Protecting Power shall be entitled to attend the proceedings in which that question is adjudicated, unless, exceptionally, the proceedings are held *in camera* in the interest of State security. In such a case

the detaining Power shall advise the Protecting Power accordingly.

3. Any person who has taken part in hostilities, who is not entitled to prisoner-of-war status and who does not benefit from more favourable treatment in accordance with the Fourth Convention shall have the right at all times to the protection of Article 75 of this Protocol. In occupied territory, any such person, unless he is held as a spy, shall also be entitled, notwithstanding Article 5 of the Fourth Convention, to his rights of communication under that Convention.

*Article 46. Spies.* 1. Notwithstanding any other provision of the Conventions or of this Protocol, any member of the armed forces of a Party to the conflict who falls into the power of an adverse Party while engaging in espionage shall not have the right to the status of prisoner of war and may be treated as a spy.

2. A member of the armed forces of a Party to the conflict who, on behalf of that Party and in territory controlled by an adverse Party, gathers or attempts to gather information shall not be considered as engaging in espionage if, while so acting, he is in the uniform of his armed forces.

3. A member of the armed forces of a Party to the conflict who is a resident of territory occupied by an adverse Party and who, on behalf of the Party on which he depends, gathers or attempts to gather information of military value within that territory shall not be considered as engaging in espionage unless he does so through an act of false pretences or deliberately in a clandestine manner. Moreover, such a resident shall not lose his right to the status of prisoner of war and may not be treated as a spy unless he is captured while engaging in espionage.

4. A member of the armed forces of a Party to the conflict who is not a resident of territory occupied by an adverse Party and who has engaged in espionage in that territory shall not lose his right to the status of prisoner of war and may not be treated as a spy unless he is captured before he has rejoined the armed forces to which he belongs.

*Article 47. Mercenaries.* 1. A mercenary shall not have the right to be a combatant or a prisoner of war.

2. A mercenary is any person who:

(a) is specially recruited locally or abroad in order to fight in an armed conflict;

(b) does, in fact, take a direct part in the hostilities;

(c) is motivated to take part in the hostilities essentially by the desire for private gain and, in fact, is promised, by or on behalf of a Party to the conflict, material compensation substantially in excess of that promised or paid to combatants of similar ranks and functions in the armed forces of that Party;

(d) is neither a national of a Party to the conflict nor a resident of territory controlled by a Party to the conflict;

(e) is not a member of the armed forces of a Party to the conflict; and

(f) has not been sent by a State which is not a Party to the conflict on official duty as a member of its armed forces.

## Part IV

### Civilian Population

#### Section I—General Protection against Effects of Hostilities

#### Chapter I—Basic Rule and Field of Application

*Article 48. Basic Rule.* In order to ensure respect for and protection of the civilian population and civilian objects, the Parties to the conflict shall at all times distinguish between the civilian population and combatants and between civilian objects and military objectives and accordingly shall direct their operations only against military objectives.

*Article 49. Definition of Attacks and Scope of Application.* 1. "Attacks" means acts of violence against the adversary, whether in offence or in defence.

2. The provisions of this Protocol with respect to attacks apply to all attacks in whatever territory conducted, including the national territory belonging to a Party to the conflict but under the control of an adverse Party.

3. The provisions of this section apply to any land, air or sea warfare which may affect the civilian population, individual civilians or civilian objects on land. They further apply to all attacks from the sea or from the air against objectives on land but do not otherwise affect the rules of international law applicable in armed conflict at sea or in the air.

4. The provisions of this section are additional to the rules concerning humanitarian protection contained in the Fourth Convention, particularly in part II thereof, and in other international agreements binding upon the High Contracting Parties, as well as to other rules of international law relating to the protection of civilians and civilian objects on land, at sea or in the air against the effects of hostilities.

### Chapter II—Civilians and Civilian Population

*Article 50. Definition of Civilians and Civilian Population.* 1. A civilian is any person who does not belong to one of the categories of persons referred to in Article 4 (A) (1), (2), (3) and (6) of the Third Convention and in Article 43 of this Protocol. In case of doubt whether a person is a civilian, that person shall be considered to be a civilian.

2. The civilian population comprises all persons who are civilians.

3. The presence within the civilian population of individuals who do not come within the definition of civilians does not deprive the population of its civilian character.

*Article 51. Protection of the Civilian Population.* 1. The civilian population and individual civilians shall enjoy general protection against dangers arising from military operations. To give effect to this protection, the following rules, which are additional to other applicable rules of international law, shall be observed in all circumstances.

2. The civilian population as such, as well as individual civilians, shall not be the object of attack. Acts or threats of violence the primary purpose of which is to spread terror among the civilian population are prohibited.

3. Civilians shall enjoy the protection afforded by this section, unless and for such time as they take a direct part in hostilities.

4. Indiscriminate attacks are prohibited. Indiscriminate attacks are:

(a) those which are not directed at a specific military objective;

(b) those which employ a method or means of combat which cannot be directed at a specific military objective; or

(c) those which employ a method or means of combat the effects of which cannot be limited as required by this Protocol; and consequently, in each such case, are of a nature to strike military objectives and civilians or civilian objects without distinction.

5. Among others, the following types of attacks are to be considered as indiscriminate:

(a) an attack by bombardment by any methods or means which treats as a single military objective a number of clearly separated and distinct military objectives located in a city, town, village or other area containing a similar concentration of civilians or civilian objects; and

(b) an attack which may be expected to cause incidental loss of civilian life, injury to civilians, damage to civilian objects, or a combination thereof, which would be excessive in relation to the concrete and direct military advantage anticipated.

6. Attacks against the civilian population or civilians by way of reprisals are prohibited.

7. The presence or movements of the civilian population or individual civilians shall not be used to render certain points or areas immune from military operations, in particular in attempts to shield military objectives from attacks or to shield, favour or impede military operations. The Parties to the conflict shall not direct the movement of the civilian population or individual civilians in order to attempt to shield military objectives from attacks or to shield military operations.

8. Any violation of these prohibitions shall not release the Parties to the conflict from their legal obligations with respect to the civilian population and civilians, including the obligation to take the precautionary measures provided for in Article 57.

### Chapter III—Civilian Objects

*Article 52. General Protection of Civilian Objects.* 1. Civilian objects shall not be the object of attack or of reprisals. Civilian objects are all objects which are not military objectives as defined in paragraph 2.

2. Attacks shall be limited strictly to military objectives. In so far as objects are concerned, military objectives are limited to those objects which by their nature, location, purpose or use make an effective contribution to military action and whose total or partial destruction, capture or neutralization, in the circumstances ruling at the time, offers a definite military advantage.

3. In case of doubt whether an object which is normally dedicated to civilian purposes, such as a place of worship, a house or other dwelling or a school, is being used to make an effective contribution to military action, it shall be presumed not to be so used.

*Article 53. Protection of Cultural Objects and of Places of Worship.* Without prejudice to the provisions of the Hague Convention for the Protection of Cultural Property in the Event of Armed Conflict of 14 May 1954, and of other relevant international instruments, it is prohibited:

(a) to commit any acts of hostility directed against the historic monuments, works of art or places of worship which constitute the cultural or spiritual heritage of peoples;

(b) to use such objects in support of the military effort;

(c) to make such objects the object of reprisals.

*Article 54. Protection of Objects Indispensable to the Survival of the Civilian Population.* 1. Starvation of civilians as a method of warfare is prohibited.

2. It is prohibited to attack, destroy, remove or render useless objects indispensable to the survival of the civilian population, such as food-stuffs, agricultural areas for the production of food-stuffs, crops, livestock, drinking water installations and supplies and irrigation works, for the specific purpose of denying them for their sustenance value to the civilian population or to the adverse Party, whatever the motive, whether in order to starve out civilians, to cause them to move away, or for any other motive.

3. The prohibitions in paragraph 2 shall not apply to such of the objects covered by it as are used by an adverse Party:

(a) as sustenance solely for the members of its armed forces; or

(b) if not as sustenance, then in direct support of military action, provided, however, that in no event shall actions against these objects be taken which may be expected to leave the civilian population with such inadequate food or water as to cause its starvation or force its movement.

4. These objects shall not be made the object of reprisals.

5. In recognition of the vital requirements of any Party to the Conflict in the defence of its national territory against invasion, derogation from the prohibitions contained in paragraph 2 may be made by a Party to the conflict within such territory under its own control where required by imperative military necessity.

*Article 55. Protection of the Natural Environment.* 1. Care shall be taken in warfare to protect the natural environment against widespread, long-term and severe damage. This protection includes a prohibition of the use of methods or means of warfare which are intended or may be expected to cause such damage to the natural environment and thereby to prejudice the health or survival of the population.

2. Attacks against the natural environment by way of reprisals are prohibited.

*Article 56. Protection of Works and Installations containing Dangerous Forces.* 1. Works or installations containing dangerous forces, namely dams, dykes and nuclear electrical generating stations, shall not be made the object of attack, even where these objects are military objectives, if such attack may cause the release of dangerous forces and consequent severe losses among the civilian population. Other military objectives located at or in the vicinity of these works or installations shall not be made the object of attack if such attack may cause the release of dangerous forces from the works or installations and consequent severe losses among the civilian population.

2. The special protection against attack provided by paragraph 1 shall cease:

(a) for a dam or a dyke only if it is used for other than its normal function and in regular, significant and direct support of military operations and if such attack is the only feasible way to terminate such support;

(b) for a nuclear electrical generating station only if it provides electric power in regular, significant and direct support of military operations and if such attack is the only feasible way to terminate such support;

(c) for other military objectives located at or in the vicinity of these works or installations only if they are used in regular, significant and direct support of military operations and if such attack is the only feasible way to terminate such support.

3. In all cases, the civilian population and individual civilians shall remain entitled to all the protection accorded them by international law, including the protection of the precautionary measures provided for in Article 57. If the protection ceases and any of the works, installations or military objectives mentioned in paragraph 1 is attacked, all practical precautions shall be taken to avoid the release of the dangerous forces.

4. It is prohibited to make any of the works, installations or military objectives mentioned in paragraph 1 the object of reprisals.

5. The Parties to the conflict shall endeavour to avoid locating any military objectives in the vicinity of the works or installations mentioned in paragraph 1. Nevertheless, installations erected for the sole purpose of defending the protected works or installations from attack are permissible and shall not themselves be made the object of attack, provided that they are not used in hostilities except for defensive actions necessary to respond to attacks against the protected works or installations and that their armament is limited to weapons capable only of repelling hostile action against the protected works or installations.

6. The High Contracting Parties and the Parties to the conflict are urged to conclude further agreements among themselves to provide additional protection for objects containing dangerous forces.

7. In order to facilitate the identification of the objects protected by this article, the Parties to the conflict may mark them with a special sign consisting of a group of three bright orange circles placed on the same axis, as specified in Article 16 of Annex I to this Protocol. The absence of such marking in no way relieves any Party to the conflict of its obligations under this Article.

### Chapter IV—Precautionary Measures

*Article 57. Precautions in Attack.* 1. In the conduct of military operations, constant care shall be taken to spare the civilian population, civilians and civilian objects.

2. With respect to attacks, the following precautions shall be taken:

(a) those who plan or decide upon an attack shall:

(i) do everything feasible to verify that the objectives to be attacked are neither civilians nor civilian objects and are not subject to special protection but are military objectives within the meaning of paragraph 2 of Article 52 and that it is not prohibited by the provisions of this Protocol to attack them;

(ii) take all feasible precautions in the choice of means and methods of attack with a view to avoiding, and in any event to minimizing, incidental loss of civilian life, injury to civilians and damage to civilian objects;

(iii) refrain from deciding to launch any attack which may be expected to cause incidental loss of civilian life, injury to civilians, damage to civilian objects, or a combination thereof, which would be excessive in relation to the concrete and direct military advantage anticipated;

(b) an attack shall be cancelled or suspended if it becomes apparent that the objective is not a military one or is subject to special protection or that the attack may be expected to cause incidental loss of civilian life, injury to civilians, damage to civilian objects, or a combination thereof, which would be excessive in relation to the concrete and direct military advantage anticipated;

(c) effective advance warning shall be given of attacks which may affect the civilian population, unless circumstances do not permit.

3. When a choice is possible between several military objectives for obtaining a similar military advantage, the objective to be selected shall be that the attack on which may be expected to cause the least danger to civilian lives and to civilian objects.

4. In the conduct of military operations at sea or in the air, each Party to the conflict shall, in conformity with its rights and duties under the rules of international law applicable in armed conflict, take all reasonable precautions to avoid losses of civilian lives and damage to civilian objects.

5. No provision of this article may be construed as authorizing any attacks against the civilian population, civilians or civilian objects.

*Article 58. Precautions Against the Effects of Attacks.* The Parties to the conflict shall, to the maximum extent feasible:

(a) without prejudice to Article 49 of the Fourth Convention, endeavour to remove the civilian population, individual civilians and civilian objects under their control from the vicinity of military objectives;

(b) avoid locating military objectives within or near densely populated areas;

(c) take the other necessary precautions to protect the civilian population, individual civilians and civilian objects under their control against the dangers resulting from military operations.

## Chapter V—Localities and Zones under Special Protection

*Article 59. Non-defended localities.* 1. It is prohibited for the Parties to the conflict to attack, by any means whatsoever, non-defended localities.

2. The appropriate authorities of a Party to the conflict may declare as a non-defended locality any inhabited place near or in a zone where armed forces are in contact which is open for occupation by an adverse Party. Such a locality shall fulfil the following conditions:

(a) all combatants, as well as mobile weapons and mobile military equipment must have been evacuated;

(b) no hostile use shall be made of fixed military installations or establishments;

(c) no acts of hostility shall be committed by the authorities or by the population; and

(d) no activities in support of military operations shall be undertaken.

3. The presence, in this locality, of persons specially protected under the Conventions and this Protocol, and of police forces retained for the sole purpose of maintaining law and order, is not contrary to the conditions laid down in paragraph 2.

4. The declaration made under paragraph 2 shall be addressed to the adverse Party and shall define and describe, as precisely as possible, the limits of the non-defended locality. The Party to the conflict to which the declaration is addressed shall acknowledge its receipt and shall treat the locality as a non-defended locality unless the conditions laid down in paragraph 2 are not in fact fulfilled, in which event it shall immediately so inform the Party making the declaration. Even if the conditions laid down in paragraph 2 are not fulfilled, the locality shall continue to enjoy the protection provided by the other provisions of this Protocol and the other rules of international law applicable in armed conflict.

5. The Parties to the conflict may agree on the establishment of non-defended localities even if such localities do not fulfil the conditions laid down in paragraph 2. The agreement should define and describe, as precisely as possible, the limits of the non-defended locality; if necessary, it may lay down the methods of supervision.

6. The Party which is in control of a locality governed by such an agreement shall mark it, so far as possible, by such signs as may be agreed upon with the other Party, which shall be displayed where they are clearly visible, especially on its perimeter and limits and on highways.

7. A locality loses its status as a non-defended locality when its ceases to fulfil the conditions laid down in paragraph 2 or in the agreement referred to in paragraph 5. In such an eventuality, the locality shall continue to enjoy the protection provided by the other provisions of this Protocol and the other rules of international law applicable in armed conflict.

*Article 60. Demilitarized Zones.* 1. It is prohibited for the Parties to the conflict to extend their military operations to zones on which they have conferred by agreement the status of demilitarized zone, if such extension is contrary to the terms of this agreement.

2. The agreement shall be an express agreement, may be concluded verbally or in writing, either directly or through a Protecting Power or any impartial humanitarian organization, and may consist of reciprocal and concordant declarations. The agreement may be concluded in peacetime, as well as after the outbreak of hostilities, and should define and describe, as precisely as possible, the limits of the demilitarized zone and, if necessary, lay down the methods of supervision.

3. The subject of such an agreement shall normally be any zone which fulfils the following conditions:

(a) all combatants, as well as mobile weapons and mobile military equipment, must have been evacuated;

(b) no hostile use shall be made of fixed military installations or establishments;

(c) no acts of hostility shall be committed by the authorities or by the population; and

(d) any activity linked to the military effort must have ceased.

The Parties to the conflict shall agree upon the interpretation to be given to the condition laid down in subparagraph (d) and upon persons to be admitted to the demilitarized zone other than those mentioned in paragraph 4.

4. The presence, in this zone, of persons specially protected under the Conventions and this Protocol, and of police forces retained for the sole purpose of maintaining law and order, is not contrary to the conditions laid down in paragraph 3.

5. The Party which is in control of such a zone shall mark it, so far as possible, by such signs as may be agreed upon with the other Party, which shall be displayed where they are clearly visible, especially on its perimeter and limits and on highways.

6. If the fighting draws near to a demilitarized zone, and if the Parties to the conflict have so agreed, none of them may use the zone for purposes related to the conduct of military operations or unilaterally revoke its status.

7. If one of the Parties to the conflict commits a material breach of the provisions of paragraphs 3 or 6, the other Party shall be released from its obligations under the agreement conferring upon the zone the status of demilitarized zone. In such an eventuality, the zone loses its status but shall continue to enjoy the protection provided by the other provisions of this Protocol and the other rules of international law applicable in armed conflict.

## Chapter VI—Civil Defence

*Article 61. Definitions and Scope.* For the purpose of this Protocol:

1. "Civil defence" means the performance of some or all of the undermentioned humanitarian tasks intended to protect the civilian population against the dangers, and to help it to recover from the immediate effects, of hostilities or disasters and also to provide the conditions necessary for its survival. These tasks are:

(a) warning;

(b) evacuation;

(c) management of shelters;

(d) management of blackout measures;

(e) rescue;

(f) medical services, including first aid, and religious assistance;

(g) fire-fighting;

(h) detection and marking of danger areas;

(i) decontamination and similar protective measures;

(j) provision of emergency accommodation and supplies;

(k) emergency assistance in the restoration and maintenance of order in distressed areas;

(l) emergency repair of indispensable public utilities;

(m) emergency disposal of the dead;

(n) assistance in the preservation of objects essential for survival;

(o) complementary activities necessary to carry out any of the tasks mentioned above, including, but not limited to, planning and organization;

2. "Civil defence organizations" means those establishments and other units which are organized or authorized by the competent authorities of a Party to the conflict to perform any of the tasks mentioned under 1, and which are assigned and devoted exclusively to such tasks;

3. "Personnel" of civil defence organizations means those persons assigned by a Party to the conflict exclusively to the performance of the tasks mentioned under 1, including personnel assigned by the competent authority of that Party exclusively to the administration of these organizations;

4. "Matériel" of civil defence organizations means equipment, supplies and transports used by these organizations for the performance of the tasks mentioned under 1.

*Article 62. General Protection.* 1. Civilian civil defence organizations and their personnel shall be respected and protected, subject to the provisions of this Protocol, particularly the provisions of this section. They shall be entitled to perform their civil defence tasks except in case of imperative military necessity.

2. The provisions of paragraph 1 shall also apply to civilians who, although not members of civilian civil defence organizations, respond to an appeal from the competent authorities and perform civil defence tasks under their control.

3. Buildings and *matériel* used for civil defence purposes and shelters provided for the civilian population are covered by Article 52. Objects used for civil defence purposes may not be destroyed or diverted from their proper use except by the Party to which they belong.

*Article 63. Civil Defence in Occupied Territories.* 1. In occupied territories, civilian civil defence organizations shall receive from the authorities the facilities necessary for the performance of their tasks. In no circumstances shall their personnel be compelled to perform activities which would interfere with the proper performance of these tasks. The Occupying Power shall not change the structure or personnel of such organizations in any way which might jeopardize the efficient performance of their mission. These organizations shall not be required to give priority to the nationals or interests of that Power.

2. The Occupying Power shall not compel, coerce or induce civilian civil defence organizations to perform their tasks in any manner prejudicial to the interests of the civilian population.

3. The Occupying Power may disarm civil defence personnel for reasons of security.

4. The Occupying Power shall neither divert from their proper use nor requisition buildings or *matériel* belonging to or used by civil defence organizations if such diversion or requisition would be harmful to the civilian population.

5. Provided that the general rule in paragraph 4 continues to be observed, the Occupying Power may requisition or divert these resources, subject to the following particular conditions:

(a) that the buildings or *matériel* are necessary for other needs of the civilian population; and

(b) that the requisition or diversion continues only while such necessity exists.

6. The Occupying Power shall neither divert nor requisition shelters provided for the use of the civilian population or needed by such population.

*Article 64. Civilian Civil Defence Organizations of Neutral or Other States not Parties to the Conflict and International Co-ordinating Organizations.* 1. Articles 62, 63, 65 and 66 shall also apply to the personnel and *matériel* of civilian civil defence organizations of neutral or other States not Parties to the conflict which perform civil defence tasks mentioned in Article 61 in the territory of a Party to the conflict, with the consent and under the control of that Party. Notification of such assistance shall be given as soon as possible to any adverse Party concerned. In no circumstances shall this activity be deemed to be an interference in the conflict. This activity should, however, be performed with due regard to the security interests of the Parties to the conflict concerned.

2. The Parties to the conflict receiving the assistance referred to in paragraph 1 and the High Contracting Parties granting it should facilitate international co-ordination of such civil defence actions when appropriate. In such cases the relevant international organizations are covered by the provisions of this Chapter.

3. In occupied territories, the Occupying Power may only exclude or restrict the activities of civilian civil defence organizations of neutral or other States not Parties to the conflict and of international co-ordinating organizations if it can ensure the adequate performance of civil defence tasks from its own resources or those of the occupied territory.

*Article 65. Cessation of Protection.* 1. The protection to which civilian civil defence organizations, their personnel, buildings, shelters and *matériel* are entitled shall not cease unless they commit or are used to commit, outside their proper tasks, acts harmful to the enemy. Protection may, however, cease only after a warning has been given setting, whenever appropriate, a reasonable time-limit, and after such warning has remained unheeded.

2. The following shall not be considered as acts harmful to the enemy:

(a) that civil defence tasks are carried out under the direction or control of military authorities;

(b) that civilian civil defence personnel co-operate with military personnel in the performance of civil defence tasks, or that some military personnel are attached to civilian civil defence organizations;

(c) that the performance of civil defence tasks may incidentally benefit military victims, particularly those who are *hors de combat*.

3. It shall also not be considered as an act harmful to the enemy that civilian civil defence personnel bear light individual weapons for the purpose of maintaining order or for self-defence. However, in areas where land fighting is taking place or is likely to take place, the Parties to the conflict shall undertake the appropriate measures to limit these weapons to handguns, such as pistols or revolvers, in order to assist in distinguishing between civil defence personnel and combatants. Although civil defence personnel bear other light in-

dividual weapons in such areas, they shall nevertheless be respected and protected as soon as they have been recognized as such.

4. The formation of civilian civil defence organizations along military lines, and compulsory service in them, shall also not deprive them of the protection conferred by this Chapter.

*Article 66. Identification.* 1. Each Party to the conflict shall endeavour to ensure that its civil defence organizations, their personnel, buildings and *matériel* are identifiable while they are exclusively devoted to the performance of civil defence tasks. Shelters provided for the civilian population should be similarly identifiable.

2. Each Party to the conflict shall also endeavour to adopt and implement methods and procedures which will make it possible to recognize civilian shelters as well as civil defence personnel, buildings and *matériel* on which the international distinctive sign of civil defence is displayed.

3. In occupied territories and in areas where fighting is taking place or is likely to take place, civilian civil defence personnel should be recognizable by the international distinctive sign of civil defence and by an identity card certifying their status.

4. The international distinctive sign of civil defence is an equilateral blue triangle on an orange ground when used for the protection of civil defence organizations, their personnel, buildings and *matériel* and for civilian shelters.

5. In addition to the distinctive sign, Parties to the conflict may agree upon the use of distinctive signals for civil defence identification purposes.

6. The application of the provisions of paragraphs 1 to 4 is governed by Chapter V of Annex I to this Protocol.

7. In time of peace, the sign described in paragraph 4 may, with the consent of the competent national authorities, be used for civil defence identification purposes.

8. The High Contracting Parties and the Parties to the conflict shall take the measures necessary to supervise the display of the international distinctive sign of civil defence and to prevent and repress any misuse thereof.

9. The identification of civil defence medical and religious personnel, medical units and medical transports is also governed by Article 18.

*Article 67. Members of the Armed Forces and Military Units Assigned to Civil Defence Organizations.* 1. Members of the armed forces and military units assigned to civil defence organizations shall be respected and protected, provided that:

(a) such personnel and such units are permanently assigned and exclusively devoted to the performance of any of the tasks mentioned in Article 61;

(b) if so assigned, such personnel do not perform any other military duties during the conflict;

(c) such personnel are clearly distinguishable from the other members of the armed forces by prominently displaying the international distinctive sign of civil defence, which shall be as large as appropriate, and such personnel are provided with the identity card referred to in Chapter V of Annex I to this Protocol certifying their status;

(d) such personnel and such units are equipped only with light individual weapons for the purpose of maintaining order or for self-defence. The provisions of Article 65, paragraph 3 shall also apply in this case;

(e) such personnel do not participate directly in hostilities, and do not commit, or are not used to commit, outside their civil defence tasks, acts harmful to the adverse Party.

(f) such personnel and such units perform their civil

defence tasks only within the national territory of their Party. The non-observance of the conditions stated in (e) above by any member of the armed forces who is bound by the conditions prescribed in (a) and (b) above is prohibited.

2. Military personnel serving within civil defence organizations shall, if they fall into the power of an adverse Party, be prisoners of war. In occupied territory they may, but only in the interest of the civilian population of that territory, be employed on civil defence tasks in so far as the need arises, provided however that, if such work is dangerous, they volunteer for such tasks.

3. The buildings and major items of equipment and transports of military units assigned to civil defence organizations shall be clearly marked with the international distinctive sign of civil defence. This distinctive sign shall be as large as appropriate.

4. The matériel and buildings of military units permanently assigned to civil defence organizations and exclusively devoted to the performance of civil defence tasks shall, if they fall into the hands of an adverse Party, remain subject to the laws of war. They may not be diverted from their civil defence tasks, except in case of imperative military necessity, unless previous arrangements have been made for adequate provision for the needs of the civilian population.

### Section II—Relief in Favour of the Civilian Population

*Article 68. Field of Application.* The provisions of this Section apply to the civilian population as defined in this Protocol and are supplementary to Articles 23, 55, 59, 60, 61 and 62 and other relevant provisions of the Fourth Convention.

*Article 69. Basic Needs in Occupied Territories.* 1. In addition to the duties specified in Article 55 of the Fourth Convention concerning food and medical supplies, the Occupying Power shall, to the fullest extent of the means available to it and without any adverse distinction, also ensure the provision of clothing, bedding, means of shelter, other supplies essential to the survival of the civilian population of the occupied territory and objects necessary for religious worship.

2. Relief actions for the benefit of the civilian population of occupied territories are governed by Articles 59, 60, 61, 62, 108, 109, 110 and 111 of the Fourth Convention, and by Article 71 of this Protocol, and shall be implemented without delay.

*Article 70. Relief Actions.* 1. If the civilian population of any territory under the control of a Party to the conflict, other than occupied territory, is not adequately provided with the supplies mentioned in Article 69, relief actions which are humanitarian and impartial in character and conducted without any adverse distinction shall be undertaken, subject to the agreement of the Parties concerned in such relief actions. Offers of such relief shall not be regarded as interference in the armed conflict or as unfriendly acts. In the distribution of relief consignments, priority shall be given to those persons, such as children, expectant mothers, maternity cases and nursing mothers, who, under the Fourth Convention or under this Protocol, are to be accorded privileged treatment or special protection.

2. The Parties to the conflict and each High Contracting Party shall allow and facilitate rapid and unimpeded passage of all relief consignments, equipment and personnel provided in accordance with this Section, even if such assistance is destined for the civilian population of the adverse Party.

3. The Parties to the conflict and each High Contracting Party which allows the passage of relief consignments, equipment and personnel in accordance with paragraph 2:

(a) shall have the right to prescribe the technical arrangements, including search, under which such passage is permitted;

(b) may make such permission conditional on the distribution of this assistance being made under the local supervision of a Protecting Power;

(c) shall, in no way whatsoever, divert relief consignments from the purpose for which they are intended nor delay their forwarding, except in cases of urgent necessity in the interest of the civilian population concerned.

4. The Parties to the conflict shall protect relief consignments and facilitate their rapid distribution.

5. The Parties to the conflict and each High Contracting Party concerned shall encourage and facilitate effective international co-ordination of the relief actions referred to in paragraph 1.

*Article 71. Personnel Participating in Relief Actions.* 1. Where necessary, relief personnel may form part of the assistance provided in any relief action, in particular for the transportation and distribution of relief consignments; the participation of such personnel shall be subject to the approval of the Party in whose territory they will carry out their duties.

2. Such personnel shall be respected and protected.

3. Each Party in receipt of relief consignments shall, to the fullest extent practicable, assist the relief personnel referred to in paragraph 1 in carrying out their relief mission. Only in case of imperative military necessity may the activities of the relief personnel be limited or their movements temporarily restricted.

4. Under no circumstances may relief personnel exceed the terms of their mission under this Protocol. In particular they shall take account of the security requirements of the Party in whose territory they are carrying out their duties. The mission of any of the personnel who do not respect these conditions may be terminated.

### Section III—Treatment of Persons in the Power of a Party to the Conflict

### Chapter I—Field of Application and Protection of Persons and Objects

*Article 72. Field of Application.* The provisions of this Section are additional to the rules concerning humanitarian protection of civilians and civilian objects in the power of a Party to the conflict contained in the Fourth Convention, particularly Parts I and III thereof, as well as to other applicable rules of international law relating to the protection of fundamental human rights during international armed conflict.

*Article 73. Refugees and Stateless Persons.* Persons who, before the beginning of hostilities, were considered as stateless persons or refugees under the relevant international instruments accepted by the Parties concerned or under the national legislation of the State of refuge or State of residence shall be protected persons within the meaning of Parts I and III of the Fourth Convention, in all circumstances and without any adverse distinction.

*Article 74. Reunion of Dispersed Families.* The High Contracting Parties and the Parties to the conflict shall facilitate in every possible way the reunion of families dispersed as a result of armed conflicts and shall encourage in particular the work of the humanitarian organizations engaged in this task in accordance with the provisions of the Conventions and of this Protocol and in conformity with their respective security regulations.

*Article 75. Fundamental Guarantees.* 1. In so far as they are affected by a situation referred to in Article 1 of this Protocol, persons who are in the power of a Party to the conflict and who do not benefit from more favourable treatment under the Conventions or under this Protocol shall be treated humanely in all circumstances and shall enjoy, as a minimum, the protection provided by this Article without any adverse distinction based upon race, colour, sex, language, religion or belief, political or other opinion, national or social origin, wealth, birth or other status, or on any other similar criteria. Each Party shall respect the person, honour, convictions and religious practices of all such persons.

2. The following acts are and shall remain prohibited at any time and in any place whatsoever, whether committed by civilian or by military agents:

(a) violence to the life, health, or physical or mental well-being of persons, in particular:

(i) murder;

(ii) torture of all kinds, whether physical or mental;

(iii) corporal punishment; and

(iv) mutilation;

(b) outrages upon personal dignity, in particular humiliating and degrading treatment, enforced prostitution and any form of indecent assault;

(c) the taking of hostages;

(d) collective punishments; and

(e) threats to commit any of the foregoing acts.

3. Any person arrested, detained or interned for actions related to the armed conflict shall be informed promptly, in a language he understands, of the reasons why these measures have been taken. Except in cases of arrest or detention for penal offences, such persons shall be released with the minimum delay possible and in any event as soon as the circumstances justifying the arrest, detention or internment have ceased to exist.

4. No sentence may be passed and no penalty may be executed on a person found guilty of a penal offence related to the armed conflict except pursuant to a conviction pronounced by an impartial and regularly constituted court respecting the generally recognized principles of regular judicial procedure, which include the following:

(a) the procedure shall provide for an accused to be informed without delay of the particulars of the offence alleged against him and shall afford the accused before and during his trial all necessary rights and means of defence;

(b) no one shall be convicted of an offence except on the basis of individual penal responsibility;

(c) no shall be accused or convicted of a criminal offence on account of any act or omission which did not constitute a criminal offence under the national or international law to which he was subject at the time when it was committed; nor shall a heavier penalty be imposed than that which was applicable at the time when the criminal offence was committed; if, after the commission of the offence, provision is made by law for the imposition of a lighter penalty, the offender shall benefit thereby;

(d) anyone charged with an offence is presumed innocent until proved guilty according to law;

(e) anyone charged with an offence shall have the right to be tried in his presence;

(f) no one shall be compelled to testify against himself or to confess guilt;

(g) anyone charged with an offence shall have the right to examine, or have examined, the witnesses against him and to obtain the attendance and examination of witnesses on his behalf under the same conditions as witnesses against him;

(h) no one shall be prosecuted or punished by the same Party for an offence in respect of which a final judgement acquitting or convicting that person has been previously pronounced under the same law and judicial procedure;

(i) anyone prosecuted for an offence shall have the right to have the judgement pronounced publicly; and

(j) a convicted person shall be advised on conviction of his judicial and other remedies and of the time-limits within which they may be exercised.

5. Women whose liberty has been restricted for reasons related to the armed conflict shall be held in quarters separated from men's quarters. They shall be under the immediate supervision of women. Nevertheless, in cases where families are detained or interned, they shall, whenever possible, be held in the same place and accommodated as family units.

6. Persons who are arrested, detained or interned for reasons related to the armed conflict shall enjoy the protection provided by this Article until their final release, repatriation or re-establishment, even after the end of the armed conflict.

7. In order to avoid any doubt concerning the prosecution and trial of persons accused of war crimes or crimes against humanity, the following principles shall apply:

(a) persons who are accused of such crimes should be submitted for the purpose of prosecution and trial in accordance with the applicable rules of international law; and

(b) any such persons who do not benefit from more favourable treatment under the Conventions of this Protocol shall be accorded the treatment provided by this Article, whether or not the crimes of which they are accused constitute grave breaches of the Conventions or of this Protocol.

8. No provision of this Article may be construed as limiting or infringing any other more favourable provision granting greater protection, under any applicable rules of international law, to persons covered by paragraph 1.

## Chapter II—Measures in Favour of Women and Children

*Article 76. Protection of Women.* 1. Women shall be the object of special request and shall be protected in particular against rape, forced prostitution and any other form of indecent assault.

2. Pregnant women and mothers having dependent infants who are arrested, detained or interned for reasons related to the armed conflict, shall have their cases considered with the utmost priority.

3. To the maximum extent feasible, the Parties to the conflict shall endeavour to avoid the pronouncement of the death penalty on pregnant women or mothers having dependent infants, for an offence related to the armed conflict. The death penalty for such offences shall not be executed on such women.

*Article 77. Protection of Children.* 1. Children shall be the object of special respect and shall be protected against any form of indecent assault. The Parties to the conflict shall provide them with the care and aid they require, whether because of their age or for any other reason.

2. The Parties to the conflict shall take all feasible measures in order that children who have not attained the age of fifteen years do not take a direct part in hostilities and, in particular, they shall refrain from recruiting them into their armed forces. In recruiting among those persons who have attained the age of fifteen years but who have not attained the age of eighteen years the Parties to the conflict shall endeavour to give priority to those who are oldest.

3. If, in exceptional cases, despite the provisions of paragraph 2, children who have not attained the age of fifteen years take a direct part in hostilities and fall into the power of an adverse Party, they shall continue to benefit from the special protection accorded by this Article, whether or not they are prisoners of war.

4. If arrested, detained or interned for reasons related to the armed conflict, children shall be held in quarters separate from the quarters of adults, except where families are accommodated as family units as provided in Article 75, paragraph 5.

5. The death penalty for an offence related to the armed conflict shall not be executed on persons who had not attained the age of eighteen years at the time the offence was committed.

*Article 78. Evacuation of Children.* 1. No Party to the conflict shall arrange for the evacuation of children, other than its own nationals, to a foreign country except for a temporary evacuation where compelling reasons of the health or medical treatment of the children or, except in occupied territory, their safety, so require. Where the parents or legal guardians can be found, their written consent to such evacuation is required. If these persons cannot be found, the written consent to such evacuation of the persons who by law or custom are primarily responsible for the care of the children is required. Any such evacuation shall be supervised by the Protecting Power in agreement with the Parties concerned, namely, the Party arranging for the evacuation, the Party receiving the children and any Parties whose nationals are being evacuated. In each case, all Parties to the conflict shall take all feasible precautions to avoid endangering the evacuation.

2. Whenever an evacuation occurs pursuant to paragraph 1, each child's education, including his religious and moral education as his parents desire, shall be provided while he is away with the greatest possible continuity.

3. With a view to facilitating the return to their families and country of children evacuated pursuant to this Article, the authorities of the Party arranging for the evacuation and, as appropriate, the authorities of the receiving country shall establish for each child a card with photographs, which they shall send to the Central Tracing Agency of the International Committee of the Red Cross. Each card shall bear, whenever possible, and whenever it involves no risk of harm to the child, the following information:

(a) surname(s) of the child;

(b) the child's first name(s);

(c) the child's sex;

(d) the place and date of birth (or, if that date is not known, the approximate age);

(e) the father's full name;

(f) the mother's full name and her maiden name;

(g) the child's next-of-kin;

(h) the child's nationality;

(i) the child's native language, and any other languages he speaks;

(j) the address of the child's family;

(k) any identification number for the child;

(l) the child's state of health;

(m) the child's blood group;

(n) any distinguishing features;

(o) the date on which and the place where the child was found;

(p) the date on which and the place from which the child left the country;

(q) the child's religion, if any;

(r) the child's present address in the receiving country;

(s) should the child die before his return, the date, place and circumstances of death and place of interment.

**Chapter III—Journalists**

*Article 79. Measures of Protection for Journalists.* 1. Journalists engaged in dangerous professional missions in areas of armed conflict shall be considered as civilians within the meaning of Article 50, paragraph 1.

2. They shall be protected as such under the Conventions and this Protocol, provided that they take no action adversely affecting their status as civilians, and without prejudice to the right of war correspondents accredited to the armed forces to the status provided for in Article 4 (A) (4) of the Third Convention.

3. They may obtain an identity card similar to the model in Annex II of this Protocol. This card, which shall be issued by the government of the State of which the journalist is a national or in whose territory he resides or in which the news medium employing him is located, shall attest to his status as a journalist.

**Part V**

**Execution of the Convention and of This Protocol**

**Section I—General Provisions**

*Article 80. Measures for Execution.* 1. The High Contracting Parties and the Parties to the conflict shall without delay take all necessary measures for the execution of their obligations under the Conventions and this Protocol.

2. The High Contracting Parties and the Parties to the conflict shall give orders and instructions to ensure observance of the Conventions and this Protocol, and shall supervise their execution.

*Article 81. Activities of the Red Cross and Other Humanitarian Organizations.* 1. The Parties to the conflict shall grant to the International Committee of the Red Cross all facilities within their power so as to enable it to carry out the humanitarian functions assigned to it by the Conventions and this Protocol in order to ensure protection and assistance to the victims of conflicts; the International Committee of the Red Cross may also carry out any other humanitarian activities in favour of these victims, subject to the consent of the Parties to the conflict concerned.

2. The Parties to the conflict shall grant to their respective Red Cross (Red Crescent, Red Lion and Sun) organizations the facilities necessary for carrying out their humanitarian activities in favour of the victims of the conflict, in accordance with the provisions of the Conventions and this Protocol and the fundamental principles of the Red Cross as formulated by the International Conferences of the Red Cross.

3. The High Contracting Parties and the Parties to the conflict shall facilitate in every possible way the assistance which Red Cross (Red Crescent, Red Lion and Sun) organizations and the League of Red Cross Societies extend to the victims of conflicts in accordance with the provisions of the Conventions and this Protocol and with the fundamental

principles of the Red Cross as formulated by the International Conferences of the Red Cross.

4. The High Contracting Parties and the Parties to the conflict shall, as far as possible, make facilities similar to those mentioned in paragraphs 2 and 3 available to the other humanitarian organizations referred to in the Conventions and this Protocol which are duly authorized by the respective Parties to the conflict and which perform their humanitarian activities in accordance with the provisions of the Conventions and this Protocol.

*Article 82. Legal Advisers in Armed Forces.* The High Contracting Parties at all times, and the Parties to the conflict in time of armed conflict, shall ensure that legal advisers are available, when necessary, to advise military commanders at the appropriate level on the application of the Conventions and this Protocol and on the appropriate instruction to be given to the armed forces on this subject.

*Article 83. Dissemination.* 1. The High Contracting Parties undertake, in time of peace as in time of armed conflict, to disseminate the Conventions and this Protocol as widely as possible in their respective countries and, in particular, to include the study thereof in their programmes of military instruction and to encourage the study thereof by the civilian population, so that those instruments may become known to the armed forces and to the civilian population.

2. Any military or civilian authorities who, in time of armed conflict, assume responsibilities in respect of the application of the Conventions and this Protocol shall be fully acquainted with the text thereof.

*Article 84. Rules of Application.* The High Contracting Parties shall communicate to one another, as soon as possible, through the depositary and, as appropriate, through the Protecting Powers, their official translations of this Protocol, as well as the laws and regulations which they may adopt to ensure its application.

**Section II—Repression of Breaches of the Conventions and of This Protocol**

*Article 85. Repression of Breaches of this Protocol.* 1. The provisions of the Conventions relating to the repression of breaches and grave breaches, supplemented by this Section, shall apply to the repression of breaches and grave breaches of this Protocol.

2. Acts described as grave breaches in the Conventions are grave breaches of this Protocol if committed against persons in the power of an adverse Party protected by Articles 44, 45 and 73 of this Protocol, or against the wounded, sick and shipwrecked of the adverse Party who are protected by this Protocol, or against those medical or religious personnel, medical units or medical transports which are under the control of the adverse Party and are protected by this Protocol.

3. In addition to the grave breaches defined in Article 11, the following acts shall be regarded as grave breaches of this Protocol, when committed wilfully, in violation of the relevant provisions of this Protocol, and causing death or serious injury to body or health:

(a) making the civilian population or individual civilians the object of attack;

(b) launching an indiscriminate attack affecting the civilian population or civilian objects in the knowledge that such attack will cause excessive loss of life, injury to civilians or damage to civilian objects, as defined in Article 57, paragraph 2 (a) (iii);

(c) launching an attack against works or installations containing dangerous forces in the knowledge that such attack will cause excessive loss of life, injury to civilians or damage to civilian objects, as defined in Article 57, paragraph 2 (a) (iii);

(d) making non-defended localities and demilitarized zones the object of attack;

(e) making a person the object of attack in the knowledge that he is *hors de combat;*

(f) the perfidious use, in violation of Article 37, of the distinctive emblem of the red cross, red crescent or red lion and sun or of other protective signs recognized by the Conventions or this Protocol.

4. In addition to the grave breaches defined in the preceding paragraphs and in the Conventions, the following shall be regarded as grave breaches of this Protocol, when committed wilfully and in violation of the Conventions or the Protocol:

(a) the transfer by the occupying Power of parts of its own civilian population into the territory it occupies, or the deportation or transfer of all or parts of the population of the occupied territory within or outside this territory, in violation of Article 49 of the Fourth Convention;

(b) unjustifiable delay in the repatriation of prisoners of war or civilians;

(c) practices of *apartheid* and other inhuman and degrading practices involving outrages upon personal dignity, based on racial discrimination;

(d) making the clearly-recognized historic monuments, works of art or places of worship which constitute the cultural or spiritual heritage of peoples and to which special protection has been given by special arrangement, for example, within the framework of a competent international organization, the object of attack, causing as a result extensive destruction thereof, where there is no evidence of the violation by the adverse Party of Article 53, subparagraph (b), and when such historic monuments, works of art and places of worship are not located in the immediate proximity of military objectives;

(e) depriving a person protected by the Conventions or referred to in paragraph 2 of this Article of the rights of fair and regular trial.

5. Without prejudice to the application of the Conventions and of this Protocol, grave breaches of these instruments shall be regarded as war crimes.

*Article 86. Failure to Act.* 1. The High Contracting Parties and the Parties to the conflict shall repress grave breaches, and take measures necessary to suppress all other breaches, of the Conventions or of this Protocol which result from a failure to act when under a duty to do so.

2. The fact that a breach of the Conventions or of this Protocol was committed by a subordinate does not absolve his superiors from penal disciplinary responsibility, as the case may be, if they knew, or had information which should have enabled them to conclude in the circumstances at the time, that he was committing or was going to commit such a breach and if they did not take all feasible measures within their power to prevent or repress the breach.

*Article 87. Duty of Commanders.* 1. The High Contracting Parties and the Parties to the conflict shall require military commanders, with respect to members of the armed forces under their command and other persons under their control, to prevent and, where necessary, to suppress and to report to competent authorities breaches of the Conventions and of this Protocol.

2. In order to prevent and suppress breaches, High Con-

tracting Parties and Parties to the conflict shall require that, commensurate with their level of responsibility, commanders ensure that members of the armed forces under their command are aware of their obligations under the Conventions and this Protocol.

3. The High Contracting Parties and Parties to the conflict shall require any commander who is aware that subordinates or other persons under his control are going to commit or have committed a breach of the Conventions or of this Protocol, to initiate such steps as are necessary to prevent such violations of the Conventions or this Protocol, and, where appropriate, to initiate disciplinary or penal action against violators thereof.

*Article 88. Mutual Assistance in Criminal Matters.* 1. The High Contracting Parties shall afford one another the greatest measure of assistance in connexion with criminal proceedings brought in respect of grave breaches of the Conventions or of this Protocol.

2. Subject to the rights and obligations established in the Conventions and in Article 85, paragraph 1 of this Protocol, and when circumstances permit, the High Contracting Parties shall co-operate in the matter of extradition. They shall give due consideration to the request of the State in whose territory the alleged offence has occurred.

3. The law of the High Contracting Party requested shall apply in all cases. The provisions of the preceding paragraphs shall not, however, affect the obligations arising from the provisions of any other treaty of a bilateral or multilateral nature which governs or will govern the whole or part of the subject of mutual assistance in criminal matters.

*Article 89. Co-operation.* In situations of serious violations of the Conventions or of this Protocol, the High Contracting Parties undertake to act jointly or individually, in co-operation with the United Nations and in conformity with the United Nations Charter.

*Article 90. International Fact-Finding Commission.* 1. (a) An International Fact-Finding Commission (hereinafter referred to as "the Commission") consisting of 15 members of high moral standing and acknowledged impartiality shall be established;

(b) When not less than 20 High Contracting Parties have agreed to accept the competence of the Commission pursuant to paragraph 2, the depositary shall then, and at intervals of five years thereafter, convene a meeting of representatives of those High Contracting Parties for the purpose of electing the members of the Commission. At the meeting, the representatives shall elect the members of the Commission by secret ballot from a list of persons to which each of those High Contracting Parties may nominate one person;

(c) The members of the Commission shall serve in their personal capacity and shall hold office until the election of new members at the ensuing meeting;

(d) At the election, the High Contracting Parties shall ensure that the persons to be elected to the Commission individually possess the qualifications required and that, in the Commission as a whole, equitable geographical representation is assured;

(e) In the case of a casual vacancy, the Commission itself shall fill the vacancy, having due regard to the provisions of the preceding subparagraphs;

(f) The depositary shall make available to the Commission the necessary administrative facilities for the performance of its functions.

2. (a) The High Contracting Parties may at the time of signing, ratifying or acceding to the Protocol, or at any other

subsequent time, declare that they recognize *ipso facto* and without special agreement, in relation to any other High Contracting Party accepting the same obligation, the competence of the Commission to inquire into allegations by such other Party, as authorized by this Article;

(b) The declaration referred to above shall be deposited with the depositary, which shall transmit copies thereof to the High Contracting Parties;

(c) The Commission shall be competent to:

(i) inquire into any facts alleged to be a grave breach as defined in the Conventions and this Protocol or other serious violation of the Conventions or of this Protocol;

(ii) facilitate, through its good offices, the restoration of an attitude of respect for the Conventions and this Protocol;

(d) In other situations, the Commission shall institute an inquiry at the request of a Party to the conflict only with the consent of the other Party or Parties concerned;

(e) Subject to the foregoing provisions of this paragraph, the provisions of Article 52 of the First Convention, Article 53 of the Second Convention, Article 132 of the Third Convention and Article 149 of the Fourth Convention shall continue to apply to any alleged violation of the Conventions and shall extend to any alleged violation of this Protocol.

3. (a) Unless otherwise agreed by the Parties concerned, all inquiries shall be undertaken by a Chamber consisting of seven members appointed as follows:

(i) five members of the Commission, not nationals of any Party to the conflict, appointed by the President of the Commission on the basis of equitable representation of the geographical areas, after consultation with the Parties to the conflict;

(ii) two *ad hoc* members, not nationals of any Party to the conflict, one to be appointed by each side;

(b) Upon receipt of the request for an inquiry, the President of the Commission shall specify an appropriate time-limit for setting up a Chamber. If any *ad hoc* member has not been appointed within the time-limit, the President shall immediately appoint such additional member or members of the Commission as may be necessary to complete the membership of the Chamber.

4. (a) The Chamber set up under paragraph 3 to undertake an inquiry shall invite the Parties to the conflict to assist it and to present evidence. The Chamber may also seek such other evidence as it deems appropriate and may carry out an investigation of the situation *in loco;*

(b) All evidence shall be fully disclosed to the Parties, which shall have the right to comment on it to the Commission;

(c) Each Party shall have the right to challenge such evidence.

5. (a) The Commission shall submit to the Parties a report on the findings of fact of the Chamber, with such recommendations as it may deem appropriate;

(b) If the Chamber is unable to secure sufficient evidence for factual and impartial findings, the Commission shall state the reasons for that inability;

(c) The Commission shall not report its findings publicly, unless all the Parties to the conflict have requested the Commission to do so.

6. The Commission shall establish its own rules, including rules for the presidency of the Commission and the presidency of the Chamber. Those rules shall ensure that the functions of the President of the Commission are exercised at all times and that, in the case of an inquiry, they are exercised by a person who is not a national of a Party to the conflict.

7. The administrative expenses of the Commission shall be met by contributions from the High Contracting Parties which made declarations under paragraph 2, and by voluntary contributions. The Party or Parties to the conflict requesting an inquiry shall advance the necessary funds for expenses incurred by a Chamber and shall be reimbursed by the Party or Parties against which the allegations are made to the extent of 50 per cent of the costs of the Chamber. Where there are counter-allegations before the Chamber each side shall advance 50 per cent of the necessary funds.

*Article 91. Responsibility.* A Party to the conflict which violates the provisions of the Conventions or of this Protocol shall, if the case demands, be liable to pay compensation. It shall be responsible for all acts committed by persons forming part of its armed forces.

## Part VI

### Final Provisions

*Article 92. Signature.* This Protocol shall be open for signature by the Parties to the Conventions six months after the signing of the Final Act and will remain open for a period of twelve months.

*Article 93. Ratification.* This Protocol shall be ratified as soon as possible. The instruments of ratification shall be deposited with the Swiss Federal Council, depositary of the Conventions.

*Article 94. Accession.* This Protocol shall be open for accession by any Party to the Conventions which has not signed it. The instruments of accession shall be deposited with the depositary.

*Article 95. Entry into Force.* 1. This Protocol shall enter into force six months after two instruments of ratification or accession have been deposited.

2. For each Party to the Conventions thereafter ratifying or acceding to this Protocol, it shall enter into force six months after the deposit by such Party of its instrument of ratification or accession.

*Article 96. Treaty Relations upon Entry into Force of This Protocol.* 1. When the Parties to the Conventions are also Parties to this Protocol, the Conventions shall apply as supplemented by this Protocol.

2. When one of the Parties to the conflict is not bound by this Protocol, the Parties to the Protocol shall remain bound by it in their mutual relations. They shall furthermore be bound by this Protocol in relation to each of the Parties which are not bound by it, if the latter accepts and applies the provisions thereof.

3. The authority representing a people engaged against a High Contracting Party in an armed conflict of the type referred to in Article 1, paragraph 4, may undertake to apply the Conventions and this Protocol in relation to that conflict by means of a unilateral declaration addressed to the depositary. Such declaration shall, upon its receipt by the depositary, have in relation to that conflict the following effects:

(a) the Conventions and this Protocol are brought into force for the said authority as a Party to the conflict with immediate effect;

(b) the said authority assumes the same rights and obligations as those which have been assumed by a High Contracting Party to the Conventions and this Protocol; and

(c) the Conventions and this Protocol are equally binding upon all Parties to the conflict.

*Article 97. Amendment.* 1. Any High Contracting Party may propose amendments to this Protocol. The text of any proposed amendment shall be communicated to the depositary, which shall decide, after consultation with all the High Contracting Parties and the International Committee of the Red Cross, whether a conference should be convened to consider the proposed amendment.

2. The depositary shall invite to that conference all the High Contracting Parties as well as the Parties to the Conventions, whether or not they are signatories of this Protocol.

*Article 98. Revision of Annex I.* 1. Not later than four years after the entry into force of this Protocol and thereafter at intervals of not less than four years, the International Committee of the Red Cross shall consult the High Contracting Parties concerning Annex I to this Protocol and, if it considers it necessary, may propose a meeting of technical experts to review Annex I and to propose such amendments to it as may appear to be desirable. Unless, within six months of the communication of a proposal for such a meeting to the High Contracting Parties, one third of them object, the International Committee of the Red Cross shall convene the meeting, inviting also observers of appropriate international organizations. Such a meeting shall also be convened by the International Committee of the Red Cross at any time at the request of one third of the High Contracting Parties.

2. The depositary shall convene a conference of the High Contracting Parties and the Parties to the Conventions to consider amendments proposed by the meeting of technical experts if, after that meeting, the International Committee of the Red Cross or one third of the High Contracting Parties so request.

3. Amendments to Annex I may be adopted at such a conference by a two-thirds majority of the High Contracting Parties present and voting.

4. The depositary shall communicate any amendment so adopted to the High Contracting Parties and to the Parties to the Conventions. The amendment shall be considered to have been accepted at the end of a period of one year after it has been so communicated, unless within that period a declaration of non-acceptance of the amendment has been communicated to the depositary by not less than one third of the High Contracting Parties.

5. An amendment considered to have been accepted in accordance with paragraph 4 shall enter into force three months after its acceptance for all High Contracting Parties other than those which have made a declaration of non-acceptance in accordance with that paragraph. Any Party making such a declaration may at any time withdraw it and the amendment shall then enter into force for that Party three months thereafter.

6. The depositary shall notify the High Contracting Parties and the Parties to the Conventions of the entry into force of any amendment, of the Parties bound thereby, of the date of its entry into force in relation to each Party, of declarations of non-acceptance made in accordance with paragraph 4, and of withdrawals of such declarations.

*Article 99. Denunciation.* 1. In case a High Contracting Party should denounce this Protocol, the denunciation shall only take effect one year after receipt of the instrument of denunciation. If, however, on the expiry of that year the denouncing Party is engaged in one of the situations referred to in Article I, the denunciation shall not take effect before the end of the armed conflict or occupation and not, in any case, before operations connected with the final release, repatriation or re-establishment of the persons protected by the Convention or this Protocol have been terminated.

2. The denunciation shall be notified in writing to the depositary, which shall transmit it to all the High Contracting Parties.

3. The denunciation shall have effect only in respect of the denouncing Party.

4. Any denunciation under paragraph 1 shall not affect the obligations already incurred, by reason of the armed conflict, under this Protocol by such denouncing Party in respect of any act committed before this denunciation becomes effective.

*Article 100. Notifications.* The depositary shall inform the High Contracting Parties as well as the Parties to the Conventions, whether or not they are signatories of this Protocol, of:

(a) signatures affixed to this Protocol and the deposit of instruments of ratification and accession under Articles 93 and 94;

(b) the date of entry into force of this Protocol under Article 95;

(c) communications and declarations received under Articles 84, 90 and 97;

(d) declarations received under Article 96, paragraph 3, which shall be communicated by the quickest methods; and

(e) denunciations under Article 99.

*Article 101. Registration.* 1. After its entry into force, this Protocol shall be transmitted by the depositary to the Secretariat of the United Nations for registration and publication, in accordance with Article 102 of the Charter of the United Nations.

2. The depositary shall also inform the Secretariat of the United Nations of all ratifications, accessions and denunciations received by it with respect to this Protocol.

*Article 102. Authentic Texts.* The original of this Protocol, of which the Arabic, Chinese, English, French, Russian and Spanish texts are equally authentic, shall be deposited with the depositary, which shall transmit certified true copies thereof to all the Parties to the Conventions.

## Annex 1 to Protocol

### Regulations concerning Identification

### Chapter I—Identity Cards

*Article 1. Identity Card for Permanent Civilian Medical and Religious Personnel.* 1. The identity card for permanent civilian medical and religious personnel referred to in Article 18, paragraph 3, of the Protocol should:

(a) bear the distinctive emblem and be of such size that it can be carried in the pocket;

(b) be as durable as practicable;

(c) be worded in the national or official language (and may in addition be worded in other languages);

(d) mention the name, the date of birth (or, if that date is not available, the age at the time of issue) and the identity number, if any, of the holder;

(e) state in what capacity the holder is entitled to the protection of the Conventions and of the Protocol;

(f) bear the photograph of the holder as well as his signature or his thumbprint, or both;

(g) bear the stamp and signature of the competent authority;

(h) state the date of issue and date of expiry of the card.

2. The identity card shall be uniform throughout the territory of each High Contracting Party and, as far as possible,

of the same type for all Parties to the conflict. The Parties to the conflict may be guided by [a] single-language model. . . . At the outbreak of hostilities, they shall transmit to each other a specimen of the model they are using. The identity card shall be made out, if possible, in duplicate, one copy being kept by the issuing authority, which should maintain control of the cards which it has issued.

3. In no circumstances may permanent civilian medical and religious personnel by deprived of their identity cards. In the event of the loss of a card, they shall be entitled to obtain a duplicate copy.

*Article 2. Identity Card for Temporary Civilian Medical and Religious Personnel.* 1. The identity card for temporary civilian medical and religious personnel should, whenever possible, be similar to that provided for in Article 1 of these Regulations.

2. When circumstances preclude the provision to temporary civilian medical and religious personnel of identity cards similar to those described in Article 1 of these Regulations, the said personnel may be provided with a certificate signed by the competent authority certifying that the person to whom it is issued is assigned to duty as temporary personnel and stating, if possible, the duration of such assignment and his right to wear the distinctive emblem. The certificate should mention the holder's name and date of birth (or if that date is not available, his age at the time when the certificate was issued), his function and identity number, if any. It shall bear his signature or his thumbprint, or both. . . .

**Chapter II—The Distinctive Emblem**

*Article 3. Shape and Nature.* 1. The distinctive emblem (red on a white ground) shall be as large as appropriate under the circumstances [in the] shapes of the cross, the crescent or the lion and sun. . . .

2. At night or when visibility is reduced, the distinctive emblem may be lighted or illuminated; it may also be made of materials rendering it recognizable by technical means of detection.

*Article 4. Use.* 1. The distinctive emblem shall, whenever possible, be displayed on a flat surface or on flags visible from as many directions and from as far away as possible.

2. Subject to the instructions of the competent authority, medical and religious personnel carrying out their duties in the battle area shall, as far as possible, wear headgear and clothing bearing the distinctive emblem.

**Chapter III—Distinctive Signals**

*Article 5. Optional Use.* 1. Subject to the provisions of Article 6 of these Regulations, the signals specified in this Chapter for exclusive use by medical units and transports shall not be used for any other purpose. The use of all signals referred to in this Chapter is optional.

2. Temporary medical aircraft which cannot, either for lack of time or because of their characteristics, be marked with the distinctive emblem, may use the distinctive signals authorized in this Chapter. The best method of effective identification are recognition of medical aircraft is, however, the use of a visual signal, either the distinctive emblem or the light signal specified in Article 6, or both, supplemented by the other signals referred to in Articles 7 and 8 of these Regulations.

*Article 6. Light Signal.* 1. The light signal, consisting of a flashing blue light, is established for the use of medical air-

craft to signal their identity. No other aircraft shall use this signal. The recommended blue colour is obtained by using, as trichromatic co-ordinates:

green boundary—$y = 0.065 + 0.805x$
white boundary—$y = 0.400 - x$
purple boundary—$x = 0.133 + 0.600y$

The recommended flashing rate of the blue light is between 60 and 100 flashes per minute.

2. Medical aircraft should be equipped with such lights as may be necessary to make the light signal visible in as many directions as possible.

3. In the absence of a special agreement between the Parties to the conflict reserving the use of flashing blue lights for the identification of medical vehicles and ships and craft, the use of such signals for other vehicles or ships is not prohibited.

*Article 7. Radio Signal.* 1. The radio signal shall consist of a radiotelephonic or radiotelegraphic message preceded by a distinctive priority signal to be designated and approved by a World Administrative Radio Conference of the International Telecommunication Union. It shall be transmitted three times before the call sign of the medical transport involved. This message shall be transmitted in English at appropriate intervals on a frequency or frequencies specified pursuant to paragraph 3. The use of the priority signal shall be restricted exclusively to medical units and transports.

2. The radio message preceded by the distinctive priority signal mentioned in paragraph 1 shall convey the following data:

    (a) call sign of the medical transport;
    (b) position of the medical transport;
    (c) number and type of medical transports;
    (d) intended route;
    (e) estimated time en route and of departure and arrival, as appropriate;
    (f) any other information such as flight altitude, radio frequencies guarded, languages and secondary surveillance, radar modes and codes.

3. In order to facilitate the communications referred to in paragraphs 1 and 2, as well as the communications referred to in Articles 22, 23, 25, 26, 27, 28, 29, 30 and 31 of the Protocol, the High Contracting Parties, the Parties to a conflict, or one of the Parties to a conflict, acting in agreement or alone, may designate, in accordance with the Table of Frequency Allocations in the Radio Regulations annexed to the International Telecommunication Convention, and publish selected national frequencies to be used by them for such communications. These frequencies shall be notified to the International Telecommunication Union in accordance with procedures to be approved by a World Administrative Radio Conference.

*Article 8. Electronic Identification.* 1. The Secondary Surveillance Radar (SSR) system, as specified in Annex 10 to the Chicago Convention on International Civil Aviation of 7 December 1944, as amended from time to time, may be used to identify and to follow the course of medical aircraft. The SSR mode and code to be reserved for the exclusive use of medical aircraft shall be established by the High Contracting Parties, the Parties to a conflict, or one of the Parties to a conflict, acting in agreement or alone, in accordance with procedures to be recommended by the International Civil Aviation Organization.

2. Parties to a conflict may, by special agreement between them, establish for their use a similar electronic system for the identification of medical vehicles, and medical ships and craft.

## Chapter IV—Communications

*Article 9. Radiocommunications.* The priority signal provided for in Article 7 of these Regulations may precede appropriate radiocommunications by medical units and transports in the application of the procedures carried out under Articles 22, 23, 25, 26, 27, 28, 29, 30 and 31 of the Protocol.

*Article 10. Use of International Codes.* Medical units and transports may also use the codes and signals laid down by the International Telecommunication Union, the International Civil Aviation Organization and the Inter-Governmental Maritime Consultative Organization. These codes and signals shall be used in accordance with the standards, practices and procedures established by these Organizations.

*Article 11. Other Means of Communication.* When two-way radiocommunication is not possible, the signals provided for the International Code of Signals adopted by the Inter-Governmental Maritime Consultative Organization or in the appropriate Annex to the Chicago Convention on International Civil Aviation of 7 December 1944, as amended from time to time, may be used.

*Article 12. Flight Plans.* The agreements and notifications relating to flight plans provided for in Article 29 of the Protocol shall as far as possible be formulated in accordance with procedures laid down by the International Civil Aviation Organization.

*Article 13. Signals and Procedures for the Interception of Medical Aircraft.* If an intercepting aircraft is used to verify the identity of a medical aircraft in flight or to require it to land in accordance with Articles 30 and 31 of the Protocol, the standard visual and radio interception procedures prescribed by Annex 2 to the Chicago Convention on International Civil Aviation of 7 December 1944, as amended from time to time, should be used by the intercepting and the medical aircraft.

## Chapter V—Civil Defence

*Article 14. Identity Card.* 1. The identity card of the civil defence personnel provided for in Article 66, paragraph 3, of the Protocol is governed by the relevant provisions of Article 1 of these Regulations. . . .

3. If civil defence personnel are permitted to carry light individual weapons, an entry to that effect should be made on the card mentioned.

*Article 15. International Distinctive Sign.* 1. The international distinctive sign of civil defence provided for in Article 66, paragraph 4, of the Protocol is an equilateral blue triangle on an orange ground. . . .

2. It is recommended that:

(a) if the blue triangle is on a flag or armlet or tabard, the ground to the triangle be the orange flag, armlet or tabard;

(b) one of the angles of the triangle be pointed vertically upwards;

(c) no angle of the triangle touch the edge of the orange ground.

3. The international distinctive sign shall be as large as appropriate under the circumstances. The distinctive sign shall, whenever possible, be displayed on flat surfaces or on flags visible from as many directions and from as far away as possible. Subject to the instructions of the competent authority, civil defence personnel shall, as far as possible, wear headgear and clothing bearing the international distinctive sign. At night or when visibility is reduced, the sign may be lighted or illuminated; it may also be made of materials rendering it recognizable by technical means of detection.

## Chapter VI—Works and Installations Containing Dangerous Forces

*Article 16. International Special Sign.* 1. The international special sign for works and installations containing dangerous forces, as provided for in Article 56, paragraph 7, of the Protocol, shall be a group of three bright orange circles of equal size, placed on the same axis, the distance between each circle being one radius . . .

2. The sign shall be as large as appropriate under the circumstances. When displayed over an extended surface it may be repeated as often as appropriate under the circumstances. It shall, whenever possible, be displayed on flat surfaces or on flags so as to be visible from as many directions and from as far away as possible.

3. On a flag, the distance between the outer limits of the sign and the adjacent sides of the flag shall be one radius of a circle. The flag shall be rectangular and shall have a white ground.

4. At night or when visibility is reduced, the sign may be lighted or illuminated. It may also be made of materials rendering it recognizable by technical means of detection . . .

### Annex II to Protocol I

### Identity Card for Journalists on Dangerous Professional Missions

[Annex II presents sample figures of identity cards for journalists.]

***PROTOCOL II, RELATING TO THE PROTECTION OF VICTIMS OF NON-INTERNATIONAL ARMED CONFLICTS.*** This Protocol revises and supplements the Geneva Conventions of 12 August 1949, providing protection for the victims of non-international armed conflicts such as civil wars, which had not been mentioned in the 1949 Conventions. The broadened material and personal fields of application are set out in articles 1 and 2.

The Protocol was prepared by the Diplomatic Conference on the Reaffirmation and Development of International Humanitarian Law, convened in 1974, 1975, 1976, and 1977 by the Swiss Federal Council with the cooperation of the International Committee of the Red Cross. It was adopted by the Conference on 8 June 1977 and entered into force on 7 December 1978. The text (UN Doc. A/32/144, annex II) is as follows:

The High Contracting Parties,

Recalling that the humanitarian principles enshrined in Article 3 common to the Geneva Conventions of 12 August 1949, constitute the foundation of respect for the human person in cases of armed conflict not of an international character,

Recalling furthermore that international instruments relating to human rights offer a basic protection to the human person,

Emphasizing the need to ensure a better protection for the victims of those armed conflicts,

Recalling that, in cases not covered by the law in force,

the human person remains under the protection of the principles of humanity and the dictates of the public conscience,

Have agreed on the following:

## Part I

### Scope of This Protocol

*Article 1. Material Field of Application.* 1. This Protocol, which develops and supplements Article 3 common to the Geneva Conventions of 12 August 1949 without modifying its existing conditions of application, shall apply to all armed conflicts which are not covered by Article 1 of the Protocol Additional to the Geneva Conventions of 12 August 1949, and relating to the Protection of Victims of International Armed Conflicts (Protocol I) and which take place in the territory of a High Contracting Party between its armed forces and dissident armed forces or other organized armed groups which, under responsible command, exercise such control over a part of its territory as to enable them to carry out sustained and concerted military operations and to implement this Protocol.

2. This Protocol shall not apply to situations of internal disturbances and tensions, such as riots, isolated and sporadic acts of violence and other acts of a similar nature, as not being armed conflicts.

*Article 2. Personal Field of Application.* 1. This Protocol shall be applied without any adverse distinction founded on race, colour, sex, language, religion or belief, political or other opinion, national or social origin, wealth, birth or other status, or on any other similar criteria (hereinafter referred to as "adverse distinction") to all persons affected by an armed conflict as defined in Article 1.

2. At the end of the armed conflict, all the persons who have been deprived of their liberty or whose liberty has been restricted for reasons related to such conflict, as well as those deprived of their liberty or whose liberty is restricted after the conflict for the same reasons, shall enjoy the protection of Articles 5 and 6 until the end of such deprivation or restriction of liberty.

*Article 3. Non-intervention.* 1. Nothing in this Protocol shall be invoked for the purpose of affecting the sovereignty of a State or the responsibility of the government, by all legitimate means, to maintain or re-establish law and order in the State or to defend the national unity and territorial integrity of the State.

2. Nothing in this Protocol shall be invoked as a justification for intervening, directly or indirectly, for any reason whatever, in the armed conflict or in the internal or external affairs of the High Contracting Party in the territory of which that conflict occurs.

## Part II

### Humane Treatment

*Article 4. Fundamental Guarantees.* 1. All persons who do not take a direct part or who have ceased to take part in hostilities, whether or not their liberty has been restricted, are entitled to respect for their person, honour and convictions and religious practices. They shall in all circumstances by treated humanely, without any adverse distinction. It is prohibited to order that there shall be no survivors.

2. Without prejudice to the generality of the foregoing, the following acts against the persons referred to in paragraph 1 are and shall remain prohibited at any time and in any place whatsoever:

(a) violence to the life, health and physical or mental well-being of persons, in particular murder as well as cruel treatment such as torture, mutilation or any form of corporal punishment;

(b) collective punishments;

(c) taking of hostages;

(d) acts of terrorism;

(e) outrages upon personal dignity, in particular humiliating and degrading treatment, rage, enforced prostitution and any form of indecent assault;

(f) slavery and the slave trade in all their forms;

(g) pillage;

(h) threats to commit any of the foregoing acts.

3. Children shall be provided with the care and aid they require, and in particular:

(a) they shall receive an education, including religious and moral education, in keeping with the wishes of their parents, or in the absence of parents, of those responsible for their care;

(b) all appropriate steps shall be taken to facilitate the reunion of families temporarily separated;

(c) children who have not attained the age of fifteen years shall neither be recruited in the armed forces or groups nor allowed to take part in hostilities;

(d) the special protection provided by this Article to children who have not attained the age of fifteen years shall remain applicable to them if they take a direct part in hostilities despite the provisions of subparagraph (c) and are captured;

(e) measures shall be taken, if necessary, and whenever possible with the consent of their parents or persons who by law or custom are primarily responsible for their care, to remove children temporarily from the area in which hostilities are taking place to a safer area within the country and ensure that they are accompanied by persons responsible for their safety and well-being.

*Article 5. Persons whose Liberty has been Restricted.* 1. In addition to the provisions of Article 4 the following provisions shall be respected as a minimum with regard to persons deprived of their liberty for reasons related to the armed conflict, whether they are interned or detained:

(a) the wounded and the sick shall be treated in accordance with Article 7;

(b) the persons referred to in this paragraph shall, to the same extent as the local civilian population, be provided with food and drinking water and be afforded safeguards as regards health and hygiene and protection against the rigours of the climate and the dangers of the armed conflict;

(c) they shall be allowed to receive individual or collective relief;

(d) they shall be allowed to practise their religion and, if requested and appropriate, to receive spiritual assistance from persons, such as chaplains, performing religious functions;

(e) they shall, if made to work, have the benefit of working conditions and safeguards similar to those enjoyed by the local civilian population.

2. Those who are responsible for the internment or detention of the persons referred to in paragraph 1 shall also, within the limits of their capabilities, respect the following provisions relating to such persons:

(a) except when men and women of a family are accommodated together, women shall be held in quarters separated from those of men and shall be under the immediate supervision of women;

(b) they shall be allowed to send and receive letters and cards, the number of which may be limited by competent authority if it deems necessary;

(c) places of internment and detention shall not be located close to the combat zone. The persons referred to in paragraph 1 shall be evacuated when the places where they are interned or detained become particularly exposed to danger arising out of the armed conflict, if their evacuation can be carried out under adequate conditions of safety;

(d) they shall have the benefit of medical examinations;

(e) their physical or mental health and integrity shall not be endangered by any unjustified act or omission. Accordingly, it is prohibited to subject the persons described in this Article to any medical procedure which is not indicated by the state of health of the person concerned, and which is not consistent with the generally accepted medical standards applied to free persons under similar medical circumstances.

3. Persons who are not covered by paragraph 1 but whose liberty has been restricted in any way whatsoever for reasons related to the armed conflict shall be treated humanely in accordance with Article 4 and with paragraphs 1 (a), (c) and (d), and 2 (b) of this Article.

4. If it is decided to release persons deprived of their liberty, necessary measures to ensure their safety shall be taken by those so deciding.

*Article 6. Penal Prosecutions.* 1. This Article applies to the prosecution and punishment of criminal offences related to the armed conflict.

2. No sentence shall be passed and no penalty shall be executed on a person found guilty of an offence except pursuant to a conviction pronounced by a court offering the essential guarantees of independence and impartiality. In particular:

(a) the procedure shall provide for an accused to be informed without delay of the particulars of the offence alleged against him and shall afford the accused before and during his trial all necessary rights and means of defence;

(b) no one shall be convicted of an offence except on the basis of individual penal responsibility;

(c) no one shall be held guilty of any criminal offence on account of any act or omission which did not constitute a criminal offence, under the law, at the time when it was committed; nor shall a heavier penalty be imposed than that which was applicable at the time when the criminal offence was committed; if, after the commission of the offence, provision is made by law for the imposition of a lighter penalty, the offender shall benefit thereby;

(d) anyone charged with an offence is presumed innocent until proved guilty according to law;

(e) anyone charged with an offence shall have the right to be tried in his presence;

(f) no one shall be compelled to testify against himself or to confess guilt.

3. A convicted person shall be advised on conviction of his judicial and other remedies and of the time-limits within which they may be exercised.

4. The death penalty shall not be pronounced on persons who were under the age of eighteen years at the time of the offence and shall not be carried out on pregnant women or mothers of young children.

5. At the end of hostilities, the authorities in power shall endeavour to grant the broadest possible amnesty to persons who have participated in the armed conflict, or those deprived of their liberty for reasons related to the armed conflict, whether they are interned or detained.

## Part III

### Wounded, Sick and Shipwrecked

*Article 7. Protection and Care.* 1. All the wounded, sick and shipwrecked, whether or not they have taken part in the armed conflict, shall be respected and protected.

2. In all circumstances they shall be treated humanely and shall receive to the fullest extent practicable and with the least possible delay, the medical care and attention required by their condition. There shall be no distinction among them founded on any grounds other than medical ones.

*Article 8. Search.* Whenever circumstances permit and particularly after an engagement, all possible measures shall be taken, without delay, to search for and collect the wounded, sick and shipwrecked, to protect them against pillage and ill-treatment, to ensure their adequate care, and to search for the dead, prevent their being despoiled, and decently dispose of them.

*Article 9. Protection of Medical and Religious Personnel.* 1. Medical and religious personnel shall be respected and protected and shall be granted all available help for the performance of their duties. They shall not be compelled to carry out tasks which are not compatible with their humanitarian mission.

2. In the performance of their duties medical personnel may not be required to give priority to any person except on medical grounds.

*Article 10. General Protection of Medical Duties.* 1. Under no circumstances shall any person be punished for having carried out medical activities compatible with medical ethics, regardless of the person benefiting therefrom.

2. Persons engaged in medical activities shall neither be compelled to perform acts or to carry out work contrary to, nor be compelled to refrain from acts required by, the rules of medical ethics or other rules designed for the benefit of the wounded and sick, or this Protocol.

3. The professional obligations of persons engaged in medical activities regarding information which they may acquire concerning the wounded and sick under their care shall, subject to national law, be respected.

4. Subject to national law, no person engaged in medical activities may be penalized in any way for refusing or failing to give information concerning the wounded and sick who are, or who have been, under his care.

*Article 11. Protection of Medical Units and Transports.* 1. Medical units and transports shall be respected and protected at all times and shall not be the object of attack.

2. The protection to which medical units and transports are entitled shall not cease unless they are used to commit hostile acts, outside their humanitarian function. Protection may, however, cease only after a warning has been given setting, whenever appropriate, a reasonable time-limit, and after such warning has remained unheeded.

*Article 12. The Distinctive Emblem.* Under the direction of the competent authority concerned, the distinctive emblem of the red cross, red crescent or red lion and sun on a white ground shall be displayed by medical and religious personnel and medical units, and on medical transports. It shall be respected in all circumstances. It shall not be used improperly.

**Part IV**

**Civilian Population**

*Article 13. Protection of the Civilian Population.* 1. The civilian population and individual civilians shall enjoy general protection against the dangers arising from military operations. To give effect to this protection, the following rules shall be observed in all circumstances.

2. The civilian population as such, as well as individual civilians, shall not be the object of attack. Acts or threats of violence the primary purpose of which is to spread terror among the civilian population are prohibited.

3. Civilians shall enjoy the protection afforded by this part, unless and for such time as they take a direct part in hostilities.

*Article 14. Protection of Objects Indispensable to the Survival of the Civilian Population.* Starvation of civilians as a method of combat is prohibited. It is therefore prohibited to attack, destroy, remove or render useless, for that purpose, objects indispensable to the survival of the civilian population such as food-stuffs, agricultural areas for the production of food-stuffs, crops, livestock, drinking water installations and supplies and irrigation works.

*Article 15. Protection of Works and Installations containing Dangerous Forces.* Works or installations containing dangerous forces, namely dams, dykes and nuclear electrical generating stations, shall not be made the object of attack, even where these objects are military objectives, if such attack may cause the release of dangerous forces and consequent severe losses among the civilian population.

*Article 16. Protection of Cultural Objects and of Places of Worship.* Without prejudice to the provisions of the Hague Convention for the Protection of Cultural Property in the Event of Armed Conflict of 14 May 1954, it is prohibited to commit any acts of hostility directed against historic monuments, works of art or places of worship which constitute the cultural or spiritual heritage of peoples, and to use them in support of the military effort.

*Article 17. Prohibition of Forced Movement of Civilians.* 1. The displacement of the civilian population shall not be ordered for reasons related to the conflict unless the security of the civilians involved or imperative military reasons so demand. Should such displacements have to be carried out, all possible measures shall be taken in order that the civilian population may be received under satisfactory conditions of shelter, hygiene, health, safety and nutrition.

2. Civilians shall not be compelled to leave their own territory for reasons connected with the conflict.

*Article 18. Relief Societies and Relief Actions.* 1. Relief societies located in the territory of the High Contracting Party, such as Red Cross (Red Crescent, Red Lion and Sun) organizations, may offer their services for the performance of their traditional functions in relation to the victims of the armed conflict. The civilian population may, even on its own initiative, offer to collect and care for the wounded, sick and shipwrecked.

2. If the civilian population is suffering undue hardship owing to a lack of the supplies essential for its survival, such as food-stuffs and medical supplies, relief actions for the civilian population which are of an exclusively humanitarian and impartial nature and which are conducted without any adverse distinction shall be undertaken subject to the consent of the High Contracting Party concerned.

**Part V**

**Final Provisions**

*Article 19. Dissemination.* This Protocol shall be disseminated as widely as possible.

*Article 20. Signature.* This Protocol shall be open for signature by the Parties to the Conventions six months after the signing of the Final Act and will remain open for a period of twelve months.

*Article 21. Ratification.* This Protocol shall be ratified as soon as possible. The instruments of ratification shall be deposited with the Swiss Federal Council, depositary of the Conventions.

*Article 22. Accession.* This Protocol shall be open for accession by any Party to the Conventions which has not signed it. The instruments of accession shall be deposited with the depositary.

*Article 23. Entry into Force.* 1. This Protocol shall enter into force six months after two instruments of ratification and accession have been deposited.

2. For each Party to the Conventions thereafter ratifying or acceding to this Protocol, it shall enter into force six months after the deposit by such Party of its instrument of ratification or accession.

*Article 24. Amendment.* 1. Any High Contracting Party may propose amendments to this Protocol. The text of any proposed amendment shall be communicated to the depositary which shall decide, after consultation with all the High Contracting Parties and the International Committee of the Red Cross, whether a conference should be convened to consider the proposed amendment.

2. The depositary shall invite to that conference all the High Contracting Parties as well as the Parties to the Conventions, whether or not they are signatories of this Protocol.

*Article 25. Denunciation.* 1. In case a High Contracting Party should denounce this Protocol, the denunciation shall only take effect six months after receipt of the instrument of denunciation. If, however, on the expiry of six months, the denouncing Party is engaged in the situation referred to in Article 1, the denunciation shall not take effect before the end of the armed conflict. Persons who have been deprived of liberty, or whose liberty has been restricted, for reasons related to the conflict shall nevertheless continue to benefit from the provisions of this Protocol until their final release.

2. The denunciation shall be notified in writing to the depositary, which shall transmit it to all the High Contracting Parties.

*Article 26. Notifications.* The depositary shall inform the High Contracting Parties as well as the Parties to the Conventions, whether or not they are signatories of this Protocol, of:

(a) signatures affixed to this Protocol and the deposit of instruments of ratification and accession under Articles 21 and 22;

(b) the date of entry into force of this Protocol under Article 23; and

(c) communications and declarations received under Article 24.

*Article 27. Registration.* 1. After its entry into force, this Protocol shall be transmitted by the depositary to the Secretariat of the United Nations for registration and publication, in accordance with Article 102 of the Charter of the United Nations.

2. The depositary shall also inform the Secretariat of the

**G**

United Nations of all ratifications, accessions and denunciations received by it with respect to this Protocol.

*Article 28. Authentic Texts.* The original of this Protocol, of which the Arabic, Chinese, English, French, Russian and Spanish texts are equally authentic shall be deposited with the depositary, which shall transmit true copies thereof to all the Parties to the Conventions.

***SEE ALSO*** *Armed Conflict.*

**BIBLIOGRAPHY.** Aldrich, George H. "Prospects for United States Ratification of Additional Protocol I to the 1949 Geneva Conventions," *American Journal of International Law* 85, no. 1 (Jan. 1991): 1–20. Scholarly article, in English.

Gardam, Judith Gail. *Non-Combatant Immunity as a Norm of International Humanitarian Law.* Dordrecht, the Netherlands: Martinus Nijhoff, 1993. Scholarly monograph, in English; bibliography, pp. 183–193.

Hannikainen, Lauri, Raija Hanski, and Allan Rosas. *Implementing Humanitarian Law Applicable in Armed Conflicts: The Case of Finland.* Dordrecht, the Netherlands: Martinus Nijhoff, 1992. Scholarly monograph, in English; bibliography, pp. 165–173.

Krill, Françoise. "The International Fact-Finding Commission—The Role of the ICRC," *International Review of the Red Cross* no. 281 (March–April 1991): 190–207. Scholarly article, in English and French.

**GENOCIDE.** In the first multilateral human rights treaty adopted and opened for ratification or accession by the UN **GENERAL ASSEMBLY,** the Convention on the Prevention and Punishment of the Crime of Genocide, contracting parties confirm that "genocide" is a crime under international law which they undertake to prevent and punish. Genocide is defined there as meaning

any of the following acts committed with intent to destroy, in whole or in part, a national, ethnical, racial or religious group, as such:
(a) killing members of the group;
(b) causing serious bodily or mental harm to members of the group;
(c) deliberately inflicting on the group conditions of life calculated to bring about its physical destruction in whole or in part;
(d) imposing measures intended to prevent births within the group; and
(e) forcibly transferring children of the group to another group.

In the Convention, States parties placed it beyond doubt that genocide (and conspiracy, incitement, and attempts to commit it and complicity in it), even if perpetrated by a government in its own territory against its own citizens, is not a matter essentially within the domestic jurisdiction of States but a matter of international concern. When genocide occurs, any contracting party can call upon the appropriate United Nations organs to intervene.

Under the Convention, genocide is a crime whether committed in time of peace or in time of war. Persons committing genocide, or conspiring, inciting, or attempting to commit it, are to be punished, whether they are constitutionally responsible rulers, public officials, or private citizens. Persons charged with this crime are to be tried by a competent tribunal of the State in the territory of which the act was committed or by such international penal tribunals as may have jurisdiction with respect to those contracting parties which will have accepted its jurisdiction.

Although the Convention has achieved almost universal acceptance by members of the United Nations, its effectiveness has often been questioned. It is clear that, as long as an international criminal court has not been established, the Convention can have only a limited scope. A trial of persons accused of genocide before the courts of the State on whose territory the act was committed is hardly likely to produce a finding of guilt.

Periodically, reports reach the United Nations of actual or potential situations involving genocide in the contemporary world. The UN **COMMISSION ON HUMAN RIGHTS** has on several occasions been presented with clear evidence that, in some of these situations, entire groups of persons have been liquidated or threatened with liquidation. In one case, the Commission was advised that more than a million persons had died.

In 1992, the General Assembly condemned unreservedly certain policies and practices of "ethnic cleansing" which bear a close resemblance to those of genocide, reaffirmed that "ethnic cleansing" and racial hatred are totally incompatible with universally recognized human rights and fundamental freedoms, and reiterated its conviction that those who commit or order the commission of acts of "ethnic cleansing" are individually responsible and should be brought to justice (resolution 47-80).

Because no international criminal court existed for this purpose, the UN **SECURITY COUNCIL** established on 25 May 1993 (resolution 827 [1993]) the International Tribunal for the Prosecution of Persons Responsible for Serious Violations of International Humanitarian Law Committed in the Territory of the Former Yugoslavia since 1991, and on 11 February 1994 that Tribunal was able to begin its work by adopting its Rules of Procedure and Evidence.

The first comprehensive study of the prevention and punishment of the crime of genocide was completed in 1978 (UN Doc. E/CN.4/Sub.2/416) by Mr. Nicodeme Ruhashyankiko (Rwanda), a Special Rapporteur of the **SUB-COMMISSION ON PREVENTION OF DISCRIMINATION AND PROTECTION OF MINORITIES.** One of the Special Rapporteur's conclusions was that:

A number of allegations of genocide have been made since the adoption of the 1948 Convention. In the absence of a prompt investigation of these allegations by an impartial body, it has not been possible to determine whether they are well-founded. Either they have given rise to sterile controversy or, because of the political circumstances, nothing further has been heard of them. For these reasons, the Special Rapporteur feels that the Commission on Human Rights should consider the setting up of *ad hoc* Committees to inquire into allegations of genocide brought to the knowledge of the Commission by a member State or an international organization and supported by sufficient *prima facie* evidence.

The study concluded with the following recommendation:

... since no international criminal court has yet been established, the question of universal punishment should be considered again if it is decided to prepare new international instruments for the prevention and punishment of genocide, since in practice, even if a Government were to commit serious acts of genocide there would be, as there has always been, some doubt as to the possibility of indicting it, unless it were replaced by a régime that would take the necessary legal action. While recognizing the political implications of the application of the principle of universal punishment for the crime of genocide, the Special Rapporteur remains convinced that the adoption of this principle would help to make the Genocide Convention more effective. Moreover, the adoption of the principle should not automatically entail the obligation to prosecute persons guilty of genocide. It would merely be an option that could be used, particularly in the case of Governments, in the light of all the circumstances and of the advisability of taking appropriate action. Moreover, a new international instrument on genocide, establishing the principle of universal jurisdiction, would offer the choice between extradition and the punishment of the crime by the State on whose territory the guilty person was found.

Continuing concern about the question of genocide led the UN **Economic and Social Council,** in 1983, to request the Sub-Commission (resolution 1983/33) to appoint a new Special Rapporteur to revise and update the study which had been prepared by Mr. Ruhashyankiko. The Sub-Commission designated one of its members, Mr. Benjamin C. G. Whitaker (United Kingdom of Great Britain and Northern Ireland), as Special Rapporteur for this purpose. The revised and updated study (UN Doc. E/CN.4/Sub.2/1985/6) was presented to the Sub-Commission at its 1985 session.

In the study, Mr. Whitaker describes the development of the concept of genocide in the following paragraphs (14–22, 24):

Genocide is the ultimate crime and the gravest violation of human rights it is possible to commit. Consequently, it is difficult to conceive of a heavier responsibility for the international community and the Human Rights bodies of the United Nations than to undertake any effective steps possible to prevent and punish genocide in order to deter its recurrence.

It has rightly been said that those people who do not learn from history, are condemned to repeat it. This belief underpins much of the Human Rights work of the United Nations. In order to prescribe the optimal remedies to prevent future genocide, it can be of positive assistance to diagnose past cases in order to analyse their causation together with such lessons as the international community may learn from the history of these events.

Genocide is a constant threat to peace, and it is essential to exercise the greatest responsibility when discussing a subject so emotive. It is certainly not the intention of this Study in any way to comment on politics or to awaken bitterness or feelings of revenge. The purpose and hope of this Study is exactly the opposite: to deter future violence by strengthening collective international responsibility and remedies. It would undermine this purpose, besides violating historical truth as well as the integrity of United Nations Studies, were anybody guilty of genocide to believe that international concern might be averted or historical records changed because of political or other pressure. If such an attempt were to succeed, that would serve to encourage those in the future who may be contemplating similar crimes. Equally, it is necessary to warn that nothing in these historical events should be used to provide an excuse for further violence or vendettas: this Study is a warning directed against violence. Its object is to deter terrorism or killing of whatever scale, and to encourage understanding and reconciliation. The scrutiny of world opinion and an honest recognition of the truth about painful past events have been the starting-point for a foundation of reconciliation, with, for example, post-war Germany, which will help to make the future more secure for humanity.

Amongst all human rights, the primacy of the right to life is unanimously agreed to be pre-eminent and essential: it is the *sine qua non,* for all other human rights (apart from that to one's posthumous reputation) depend for their potential existence on the preservation of human life. Every right can also only survive as a consequence of the exercise of responsibilities. The right of a person or people not to be killed or avoidably left to die depends upon the reciprocal duty of other people to render protection and help to avert this. The concept of this moral responsibility and interdependence in human society has in recent times received increasing international recognition and affirmation. In cases of famine in other countries, for example, the States parties to the International Covenant on Economic, Social and Cultural Rights in "recognizing the fundamental right of everyone to be free from hunger" have assumed responsibility to take "individually and through international co-operation" the measures required "to ensure an equitable distribution of world food supplies in relation to need". The core of the right not to starve to death is a corollary of the right not to be killed, concerning which the duty of safeguarding life is recognized to extend not just to the individual's or group's own Government but to the international community as well.

More serious problems arise when the body responsible for threatening and causing death is—or is in complicity with—a State itself. The potential victims in such cases need to turn individually and collectively for protection not to, but from, their own Government. Groups subject to extermination have a right to receive something more helpful than tears and condolences from the rest of the world. Action under the Charter of the United Nations is indeed specifically authorized by the Convention on the Prevention and

Punishment of the Crime of Genocide, and might as appropriate be directed for example to the introduction of United Nations trusteeship. States have an obligation, besides not to commit genocide, in addition to prevent and punish violations of the crime by others; and in cases of failure in this respect too, the 1948 Convention recognizes that intervention may be justified to prevent or suppress such acts and to punish those responsible "whether they are constitutionally responsible rulers, public officials or private individuals".

The Convention on Genocide was unanimously adopted by the United Nations General Assembly on 9 December 1948, and therefore preceded—albeit by one day—the Universal Declaration of Human Rights itself. While the word "genocide" is a comparatively recent neologism for an old crime, the Convention's preamble notes that "at all periods of history genocide has inflicted great losses on humanity, and being convinced that, in order to liberate mankind from such an odious scourge, international co-operation is required".

Throughout recorded human history, war has been the predominant cause or pretext for massacres of national, ethnic, racial or religious groups. Wars in ancient and classical eras frequently aimed to exterminate if not enslave other peoples. Religious intolerance could also be a predisposing factor: in religious wars of the Middle Ages as well as in places in the Old Testament, some genocide was sanctioned by Holy Writ. The twentieth century equally has seen examples of "total wars" involving the destruction of civilian populations and which the development of nuclear weapons makes an almost inevitable matrix for future major conflicts. In the nuclear era, indeed the logical conclusion of this may be "omnicide".

Genocide, particularly of indigenous peoples, has also often occurred as a consequence of colonialism, with racism and ethnic prejudice commonly being predisposing factors. In some cases occupying forces maintained their authority by the terror of a perpetual threat of massacre. Examples could occur either at home or overseas: the English for example massacred native populations in Ireland, Scotland and Wales in order to deter resistance and to "clear" land for seizure, and the British also almost wholly exterminated the indigenous people when colonizing Tasmania as late as the start of the nineteenth century. Africa, Australasia and the Americas witnessed numerous other examples. The effect of genocide can be achieved in different ways: today, insensitive economic exploitation can threaten the extinction of some surviving indigenous peoples.

But genocide, far from being only a matter of historical study, is an aberration which also is a modern danger to civilization. No stronger evidence that the problem of genocide has—far from receding—grown in contemporary relevance is required than the fact that the gravest documented example of this crime is among the most recent, and furthermore occurred in the so-called developed world. Successive advances in killing-power underline that the need for international action against genocide is now more urgent than ever. It has been estimated that the Nazi holocaust in Europe slaughtered some 6 million Jews, 5 million Protestants, 3 million Catholics and half a million Gypsies. This was the product not of international warfare, but a calculated State political policy of mass murder that has been termed "a structural and systematic destruction of innocent people by a State bureaucratic apparatus". The Nazi intention to destroy particular human nations, races, religions, sexual groups, classes and political opponents as a premeditated plan was manifested before the Second World War. The war

later offered the Nazi German leaders an opportunity to extend this policy from their own country to the peoples of occupied Poland, parts of the Soviet Union and elsewhere, with an intention of Germanizing their territories. The "final solution" included (as evidenced at the Nuremberg trial) "delayed-action genocide" aimed at destroying groups' biological future through sterilization, castration, abortion, and the forcible transfer of their children. . . .

The Nazi aberration has unfortunately not been the only case of genocide in the twentieth century. Among other examples which can be cited as qualifying are the German massacre of Hereros in 1904, the Ottoman massacre of Armenians in 1915–16, the Ukrainian pogrom of Jews in 1919, the Tutsi massacre of the Ache Indians prior to 1974, the Khmer Rouge massacre in Kampuchea between 1975 and 1978, and the contemporary Iranian killings of Baha'is. . . .

As regards future progress in the prevention and punishment of genocide, the Special Rapporteur presents the following suggestions (paras. 71–72, 74–77):

The fact remains that although the Convention has been in force since 12 January 1951, any ascertainable effect of it is difficult to quantify, whereas all too much evidence continues to accumulate that acts of genocide are still being committed in various parts of the world. Certainly in its present form, the Convention therefore must be judged to be not enough. Further evolution of international measures against genocide are necessary and indeed overdue.

It is important that the historic momentum of the spirit of international unity against genocide displayed by Nuremberg and the Convention should not be allowed to falter or lapse. Failure to make effective international legal provisions is likely to threaten peace, to drive nations to desperate unilateral measures (such as the abduction of Adolf Eichmann in Argentina to bring him to trial in Israel for genocidal acts of 1961), or to open excuses for the deplorable violence of terrorist reprisals. For too many centuries war and violence have been the standard method of avenging grievances, or of creating new ones. Now in the era of atomic weapons, human society depends for its future survival upon establishing in time alternative international legal means to resolve such disputes peacefully. Despite the problems in doing so, the size of the risk permits little further time for any more delay. . . .

Although a historic impetus of international agreement achieved the unprecedented establishment of the Nuremberg and Tokyo Tribunals, these were open to the accusation that they were set up *ad hoc* to enable victors to pass judgement on vanquished. It would be a preferable concept to have instead an impartial but respected international body with permanent authority. None the less the final Count in the Nuremberg Charter broke new ground by charging defendants with "Crimes against Humanity", a term used to cover the persecution of racial and religious groups and the wholesale exploitation of peoples. Doenitz suggested in his memoirs that the acts the Tribunal had examined were a purely German affair: Germans, he said, should have been allowed to "investigate and then bring to justice those who had been responsible for the inhuman enormities that had taken place". But what some of the international lawyers at Nuremberg hoped was that the trial would be the foundation of a new legal order. They wanted international law to be advanced and to govern the future conduct of nations. Robert Jackson reported to President Truman subsequently that the London agreement, prior to Nuremberg, had for the first time made explicit that:

"to persecute, oppress, or do violence to individuals or minorities on political, racial, or religious grounds in connection with such a war; or to exterminate, enslave or deport civilian populations is an international crime and that for the commission of such crimes individuals are responsible."

However once the International Military Tribunal at Nuremberg finished its work, there was no international criminal court. President Truman welcomed Biddle's recommendation that the United Nations be invited to draft a code of international criminal law. It has not yet been drafted. As historians of the Nuremberg cases observe, "it is in the broadest sense a political question whether nations prefer to have some objective body of law and an impartial institution to administer it or whether they prefer to settle disputes and fulfil their ambitions by force".

It has equally been suggested that the influence of historical events also caused the character of the Convention to constitute more of a protest against immediate past crimes than to create an effective instrument for the prevention or repression of genocide. Critics have in fact alleged that the Convention represents at best almost a dead letter, and at worst has been perverted into a weapon of political warfare, instead of being an instrument to liberate, unite and reconcile mankind. What should, and can be done?

One basic difficulty is that although the Convention concentrates on punishment of the crime, this is nearly meaningless at the international level in the absence of an International Penal Tribunal. Hence, it is only the Governments of States in the territories of which the crime was committed, that can institute proceedings for its punishment. However, in the case of "domestic" genocides, these are generally committed by or with the complicity of Governments, with the bizarre consequence that the Governments would be required to prosecute themselves. In actual practice, mass murderers are protected by their own Governments, save in exceptional cases, where these Governments have been overthrown. Thus in Equatorial Guinea, Macias was found guilty of a number of crimes, including genocide, and executed. In Kampuchea, however, Pol Pot is still at large, protected by his own army, and presumably also in some measure, by the continued international recognition of his régime.

There exists support for a Supplementary Convention or Protocols to improve the Convention, though consensus would be hard to achieve amongst all Governments. It is possible, and indeed to be hoped, though improbable, that the existence of the Convention may have deterred more genocide from being committed. But as in attitudes to improving United Nations human rights' effectiveness generally, too often respect for State sovereignty, domestic jurisdiction and territorial integrity can, and does, take precedence over the wider human concern for protection against genocide. In these circumstances, there is a need for some new ideas or for institutions, relatively independent of the deliberations of the delegations of member States, such as an International Penal Court, and a High Commissioner for Human Rights, or else for forms of organized action outside the United Nations by, for example, the international non-governmental organizations. The recent United Nations support for the new Convention on Torture (reproduced as an appendix to this study) may afford fresh grounds for optimism, as well as some useful parallels. It is important to be practical and realistic, but also to work hard and without delay in view of the gravity of the subject.

The Special Rapporteur's proposals call for (1) anticipation of potential genocide through the systematic study of up-to-date information, (2) the setting up of a system to provide an "early warning" of impending genocide, and (3) the establishment of an international body competent to deal with genocide when it occurs. These proposals are elaborated in the following paragraphs (78–87) of the study:

*1. Prevention.* Punishment after the event does not meet the priority problem of preventing great loss of life. Those personalities who are psychologically prepared to commit genocide are not always likely to be deterred by retribution, at least in this world. Perhaps, the Convention's most conspicuous weakness is that it insufficiently formulates preventive measures. Such international short-term and long-term action would need to relate to different stages in the evolution of a genocidal process—anticipation of its happening; early warning of its commencement; and action to be taken at the outset of or during a genocide itself to stop it.

Intelligent anticipation of potential cases could be based on a data bank of continuously updated information, which might enable remedial, deterrent or averting measures to be planned ahead. Reliable information is the essential oxygen for human rights: this could be facilitated by the development of a United Nations satellite communications network. Comparisons could be made with the lessons, both positive and negative, of previous cases. Experienced international conciliators and mediators, from the United Nations and its agencies or other bodies such as the International Committee of the Red Cross, could serve to defuse tension.

H. G. Wells rightly stated that "Human history becomes more and more a race between education and catastrophe". Another highly important area of study is interdisciplinary research (to be co-ordinated perhaps by the United Nations University) into the psychological character and motivation of individuals and groups who commit genocide or racism, or the psychopathic dehumanizing of vulnerable minorities or scapegoats. In all human rights work, it is essential to go beyond condemnation of violations to analysing their causation.

The results of such research could help form one part of a wide educational programme throughout the world against such aberrations, starting at an early age in schools. Without a strong basis of international public support, even the most perfectly redrafted Convention will be of little value. Conventions and good Governments can give a lead, but the mobilization of public awareness and vigilance is essential to guard against any recurrence of genocide and other crimes against humanity and human rights. There has recently occurred an encouraging change from preoccupation with particular genocides to wider concern for effective measures to deal with the general phenomenon itself.

As a further safeguard, public awareness should be developed internationally to reinforce the individual's responsibility, based on the knowledge that it is illegal to obey a superior order or law that violates human rights. Although some Governments may be reluctant to agree, such a concept has been an honoured tradition in many different parts of the world. Gandhi's and Martin Luther King's ideas on civil disobedience to unjust laws were developments of the earlier thinking of people such as Thoreau, who went to prison rather than acquiesce in the forced return of runaway slaves to their owners. (Thoreau in turn based his philosophy on the ideas of Granville Sharp who in the 1770's resigned from the London War Office rather than authorize arms to put down the American revolution; Sharp's ideas in turn helped to inspire Jefferson and others who drafted the Declaration of Independence.) All these people followed their conscience, at personal danger; the safeguarding of human rights in the final resort will always need to depend upon such integrity and courage.

*2. Early Warning.* In cases where evidence appears of an impending genocidal conflict, mounting repression, increasing polarization or the first indications of an unexpected case, an effective early warning system could help save several thousands of lives. This requires an efficient co-ordinating network, maintained in a state of permanent readiness, which could possibly also watch for early indications of mass famine and exoduses of refugees in conjunction with bodies such as the Office of the United Nations Disaster Relief Coordinator and the International Committee of the Red Cross.

On an early warning alert being received, the steps to be taken could include: the investigation of allegations; activating different organs of the United Nations and related organizations, both directly and through national delegations, and making representations to national Governments and to interregional organizations for active involvement; seeking support of the international press in providing information; enlisting the aid of other media to call public attention to the threat, or actuality, of genocidal massacre; asking relevant racial, communal and religious leaders, in appropriate cases, to intercede, and arranging the immediate involvement of suitable mediators and conciliators at the outset. Finally, there are the possibility of sanctions which could be applied with public support, by means of economic boycotts, the refusal to handle goods to or from offending States, and selective exclusion from participation in international activities and events. Representations would also be made to Governments to enlist their support in the application of sanctions.

*3. An International Body to Deal with Genocide.* Cogent support has been expressed for the establishment of a new impartial and respected international body whose special concern would be to deal over-all with genocide. Such a body could perhaps be created under the "competent organs" Article VIII of the Convention. Support for such a body has been expressed, *inter alia,* by the Government of Spain. A constructive possible formulation for such a body has been proposed by a non-governmental organization, the Baha'i International:

"We believe that, at the present time, the most effective means of preventing and controlling genocide is through the establishment by the United Nations of a new international body dealing exclusively with genocide and charged with responsibility for considering allegations of genocide, carrying out investigations in connection with those allegations and taking urgent steps to put a stop to genocide wherever it is known to be taking place. Since secrecy is the greatest ally of any Government that seeks to engage in genocide, and international publicity and condemnation the greatest enemy, it might be expected that the opprobrium that would attach to any Government which was identified as a violator of the Convention by a high-level international body of known competence and impartiality would, on its own, act as a deterrent to that Government, quite apart from any action that the international body itself was able to generate. We accordingly suggest that consideration be given to revising the existing Convention by adding to it appropriate provisions for the creation of a Committee on Genocide whose

existence would derive directly from the Convention and which would concern itself exclusively with the subject-matter contained in its parent Convention.

"We envisaged that this Committee would concern itself primarily with questions of fact rather than with questions of law. It would, we envisage, hold a 'watching brief' on genocide: it would be the body to which any allegations of genocide were automatically referred and it would be responsible for investigating those allegations. In order to enable it to react effectively in cases where there were strong and reliable indications that genocide was, in fact, taking place, the Committee should, we suggest, be empowered to (a) invite the State party concerned to submit its observations with regard to the allegations of genocide; and (b) if it decided that the situation warranted it, designate one or more of its members to make a confidential inquiry and to report to the Committee urgently. In short, we envisage the Committee being given powers in this regard similar to those proposed for the Torture Committee in the Convention against torture and other cruel, inhuman or degrading treatment or punishment.

"We envisage that the Committee on Genocide, in common with other bodies created under the provisions of international human rights instruments (which it would very closely resemble in membership and procedures), would report annually to the General Assembly, but we suggest that the Committee should also be empowered to bring any situations of urgency to the immediate attention of the Secretary-General of the United Nations. We believe that the advantages of establishing a Committee under the provisions of the Convention would be:

"(a) To remove the subject of genocide as far as possible from the political arena;

"(b) To attract a high-calibre 'independent expert' membership;

"(c) To speed the international response to genocidal situations by obviating the necessity for cases of genocide to proceed through the hierarchical mechanisms of the United Nations human rights system;

"(d) To provide the high-profile, international focus for genocide that is currently lacking.

"We are, of course, aware that any proposed revision of the existing Convention must be requested by a State party and must then win the approval of the United Nations General Assembly and we are fully conscious of the difficulties attendant upon obtaining such approval. Nevertheless, we feel that it is appropriate to consider this course of action, bearing in mind the status of genocide as the major 'crime against humanity', the disturbing fact that genocide persists in the contemporary world, and the urgent need for determined international action to combat it. Failing agreement on the creation of a Committee on Genocide under the provisions of the Convention, we would suggest that a Working Group on Genocide be established under the aegis of the Commission on Human Rights."

*4. An International Human Rights Tribunal or Court.* Support has been expressed by, *inter alia,* the Government of El Salvador that:

"Regarding the possibility of setting up an international penal tribunal as proposed in article VI of the Convention on the Prevention and Punishment of the Crime of Genocide, the Government of El Salvador considers that, in view of the international importance of this crime, it would be appropriate to set up an international penal court competent to judge this and similar crimes. However, the binding and enforceable character of the decisions of such a court would require to be formally stated in the international instrument establishing it."

The Government of Morocco also suggests "the establishment of a full-scale international court with a prosecutor's office and an investigating arm". The Government of Chad likewise supports the idea of an international penal tribunal and an international body entrusted with carrying out investigations. It might obviate much argument about which massacres technically are, or are not, genocide, if such a Tribunal or Court dealt with all major crimes against humanity.

Other opinion and replies indicate a preference for instituting universality of jurisdiction, or for both proposals to provide a "fail-safe" or double system of safeguard.

The Special Rapporteur concluded his study by pointing out that "the reforms recommended will, like most things worthwhile in human progress, not be easy. They would, however, be the best living memorial to all the past victims of genocide. To do nothing, by contrast, would be to invite responsibility for helping cause future victims."

The Special Rapporteur's study was considered and debated by the Sub-Commission on Prevention of Discrimination and Protection of Minorities at its 1985 session. The Sub-Commission (resolution 1985/9), noting that divergent views had been expressed about the content and proposals of the study, limited itself to recommending "that the United Nations renew its efforts so as to make ratification by States Members of the Convention on the Prevention and Punishment of the Crime of Genocide universal as soon as possible."

Both the UN General Assembly and the Commission on Human Rights have reviewed the observance of the provisions of the Genocide Convention from time to time, and both have recognized repeatedly that genocide is a crime that violates the norms of international law and runs counter to the spirit and aims of the United Nations. Both have strongly condemned genocide and have reaffirmed the need for international cooperation in order to liberate mankind from such an odious crime. At the same time, they have noted with some satisfaction that more than 100 States have accepted the Genocide Convention and have urged all other States to become parties to it without delay.

**SEE ALSO** *Crimes against the Peace and Security of Mankind; War Crimes.*

**BIBLIOGRAPHY.** Akhavan, Payam. "Lessons from Iraqi Kurdistan: Self-Determination and Humanitarian Intervention against Genocide," *Netherlands Quarterly of Human Rights* 11, no. 1 (1993): 41–62. Scholarly article, in English.

Bassiouni, M. Cherif. *Crimes against Humanity in International Criminal Law.* Dordrecht, the Netherlands: Martinus Nijhoff, 1992. Scholarly monograph, in English.

Bauman, Zygmut. *Modernity and the Holocaust.* Ithaca, NY, USA: Cornell University Press, 1991. Scholarly monograph, in English.

Chalk, Frank, and Kurt Jonassohn. *The History and Sociology of Genocide: Analyses and Case Studies.* New Haven, CT, USA: Yale University Press with the Montreal Institute for Genocide Studies, 1990. Scholarly collection of articles, in English; bibliography, pp. 429–461.

Fein, Helen. "Genocide: A Sociological Perspective," *Current Sociology* 38, no. 1 (Spring 1990): 1–126. Scholarly article, in English; bibliography, pp. 113–126.

Fein, Helen, ed. *Genocide Watch.* New Haven, CT, USA: Yale University Press, 1992. Scholarly monograph, in English.

Mbemba, Jean-Martin. *L'autre mémoire du crime contre l'humanité* (The Other Memory of Crimes Against Humanity). Dakar, Senegal: Présence africaine, 1990. Monograph, in French.

Parsons, William, and Samuel Totten, eds. "Teaching about Genocide," *Social Education* 55, no. 2 (Feb. 1991): 84–133. Special issue, in English.

Ruhashyankiko, Nicodeme. *Study on the Question of the Prevention and Punishment of the Crime of Genocide,* by Special Rapporteur (UN Doc. E/CN.4/Sub.2/416 [1978]). New York: 1978. IGO document, in English.

Sunga, Lyal S. *Individual Responsibility in International Law for Serious Human Rights Violations.* Dordrecht, the Netherlands: Martinus Nijhoff, 1992. Scholarly monograph, in English.

Tennant, C. C., and M. E. Turpel. "A Case Study of Indigenous People: Genocide, Ethnocide and Self-Determination," *Nordic Journal of International Law* 59, no. 4 (1990): 287–319. Scholarly article, in English.

Whitaker, Benjamin. *Revised and Updated Report on the Question of the Prevention and Punishment of the Crime of Genocide,* by Special Rapporteur (UN Doc. E/CN.4/Sub.2/1985/6 and Corr. 1). New York: 1986. IGO document, in English.

**GENOCIDE: CONVENTION ON THE PREVENTION AND PUNISHMENT OF THE CRIME OF GENOCIDE (1948).** At the second part of its first session, on 11 December 1946, the UN **GENERAL ASSEMBLY** affirmed (resolution 96 [I]) that **GENOCIDE** is a crime under international law which the civilized world condemns, and that those guilty of it, whoever they are and for whatever reason they committed it, are punishable. Recognizing the need to organize international cooperation for this purpose, the UN General Assembly called upon the **ECONOMIC AND SOCIAL COUNCIL** to undertake the necessary studies for drawing up a draft convention on the crime of genocide. The Council instructed the Secretary-General to prepare a preliminary draft with the assistance of three experts. On the basis of their work, and with the assistance of its *Ad Hoc* Committee on Genocide, the Council was able to transmit the draft convention to the Assembly in 1948. The Assembly completed the Convention and, on 9 December 1948 (resolution 260 A [III]), adopted it and opened it for signature and ratification or accession. It entered into force on 12 January 1951.

The text of the Convention (United Nations, *Treaty Series* 78, p. 277) is as follows:

The Contracting Parties,

Having considered the declaration made by the General Assembly of the United Nations in its resolution 96 (I) dated 11 December 1946 that genocide is a crime under international law, contrary to the spirit and aims of the United Nations and condemned by the civilized world,

Recognizing that at all periods of history genocide has inflicted great losses on humanity, and

Being convinced that, in order to liberate mankind from such an odious scourge, international co-operation is required,

Hereby agree as hereinafter provided:

*Article 1.* The Contracting Parties confirm that genocide, whether committed in time of peace or in time of war, is a crime under international law which they undertake to prevent and to punish.

*Article 2.* In the present Convention, genocide means any of the following acts committed with intent to destroy, in whole or in part, a national, ethnical, racial or religious group, as such:

(a) Killing members of the group;

(b) Causing serious bodily or mental harm to members of the group;

(c) Deliberately inflicting on the group conditions of life calculated to bring about its physical destruction in whole or in part;

(d) Imposing measures intended to prevent births within the group;

(e) Forcibly transferring children of the group to another group.

*Article 3.* The following acts shall be punishable:

(a) Genocide;

(b) Conspiracy to commit genocide;

(c) Direct and public incitement to commit genocide;

(d) Attempt to commit genocide;

(e) Complicity in genocide.

*Article 4.* Persons committing genocide or any of the other acts enumerated in article 3 shall be punished, whether they are constitutionally responsible rulers, public officials or private individuals.

*Article 5.* The Contracting Parties undertake to enact, in accordance with their respective Constitutions, the necessary legislation to give effect to the provisions of the present Convention and, in particular, to provide effective penalties for persons guilty of genocide or any of the other acts enumerated in article 3.

*Article 6.* Persons charged with genocide or any of the other acts enumerated in article 3 shall be tried by a competent tribunal of the State in the territory of which the act was committed, or by such international penal tribunal as may have jurisdiction with respect to those Contracting Parties which shall have accepted its jurisdiction.

*Article 7.* Genocide and the other acts enumerated in article 3 shall not be considered as political crimes for the purpose of extradition.

The Contracting Parties pledge themselves in such cases to grant extradition in accordance with their laws and treaties in force.

*Article 8.* Any Contracting Party may call upon the competent organs of the United Nations to take such action under the Charter of the United Nations as they consider appropriate for the prevention and suppression of acts of genocide or any of the other acts enumerated in article 3.

*Article 9.* Disputes between the Contracting Parties relating to the interpretation, application or fulfilment of the present Convention, including those relating to the responsibility of a State for genocide or for any of the other acts enumerated in article 3, shall be submitted to the International Court of Justice at the request of any of the parties to the dispute.

*Article 10.* The present Convention, of which the Chinese, English, French, Russian and Spanish texts are equally authentic, shall bear the date of 9 December 1948.

*Article 11.* The present Convention shall be open until 31 December 1949 for signature on behalf of any Member of the United Nations and of any non-member State to which an invitation to sign has been addressed by the General Assembly.

The present Convention shall be ratified, and the instruments of ratification shall be deposited with the Secretary-General of the United Nations.

After 1 January 1950, the present Convention may be acceded to on behalf of any Member of the United Nations and of any non-member State which has received an invitation as aforesaid.

Instruments of accession shall be deposited with the Secretary-General of the United Nations.

*Article 12.* Any Contracting Party may at any time, by notification addressed to the Secretary-General of the United Nations, extend the application of the present Convention to all or any of the territories for the conduct of whose foreign relations that Contracting Party is responsible.

*Article 13.* On the day when the first twenty instruments of ratification or accession have been deposited, the Secretary-General shall draw up a *procès-verbal* and transmit a copy thereof to each Member of the United Nations and to each of the non-member States contemplated in article 11.

The present Convention shall come into force on the ninetieth day following the date of deposit of the twentieth instrument of ratification or accession.

Any ratification or accession effected, subsequent to the latter date shall become effective on the ninetieth day following the deposit of the instrument of ratification or accession.

*Article 14.* The present Convention shall remain in effect for a period of ten years as from the date of its coming into force.

It shall thereafter remain in force for successive periods of five years for such Contracting Parties as have not denounced it at least six months before the expiration of the current period.

Denunciation shall be effected by a written notification addressed to the Secretary-General of the United Nations.

*Article 15.* If, as a result of denunciations, the number of Parties to the present Convention should become less than sixteen, the Convention shall cease to be in force as from the date on which the last of these denunciations shall become effective.

*Article 16.* A request for the revision of the present Convention may be made at any time by any Contracting Party by means of a notification in writing addressed to the Secretary-General.

The General Assembly shall decide upon the steps, if any, to be taken in respect of such request.

*Article 17.* The Secretary-General of the United Nations shall notify all Members of the United Nations and the non-member States contemplated in article 11 of the following:

(a) Signatures, ratifications and accessions received in accordance with article 11;

(b) Notifications received in accordance with article 12;

(c) The date upon which the present Convention comes into force in accordance with article 13;

(d) Denunciations received in accordance with article 14;

(e) The abrogation of the Convention in accordance with article 15;

(f) Notifications received in accordance with article 16.

*Article 18.* The original of the present Convention shall be deposited in the archives of the United Nations.

A certified copy of the Convention shall be transmitted to each Member of the United Nations and to each of the non-member States contemplated in article 11.

*Article 19.* The present Convention shall be registered by the Secretary-General of the United Nations on the date of its coming into force.

**BIBLIOGRAPHY.** Akhavan, Payam. "Enforcement of the Genocide Convention through the Advisory Opinion Jurisdiction of the International Court of Justice," *Human Rights Law Journal* 12, no. 8–9 (Sept. 1991): 285–299. Scholarly article, in English.

LeBlanc, Lawrence J. *The United States and the Genocide Convention.* Durham, NC, USA: Duke University Press, 1991. Scholarly monograph, in English.

Lerner, Natan. *Group Rights and Discrimination in International Law.* Dordrecht, the Netherlands: Martinus Nijhoff, 1991. Scholarly monograph, in English.

Thornberry, Patrick. *International Law and the Rights of Minorities.* Oxford, UK: Oxford University Press, 1991. Scholarly monograph, in English; bibliography, pp. 431–443.

**GEORGE MASON UNIVERSITY, INSTITUTE FOR CONFLICT ANALYSIS AND RESOLUTION.** The Institute for Conflict Analysis and Resolution (ICAR) offers a Ph.D. and an M.S. degree in conflict analysis and resolution. Both degree programs are among the first in this field and are part of the mission of the Institute: to advance the understanding and resolution of significant and persistent human conflicts among individuals, small groups, communities, ethnic groups, and nations.

*MASTER'S PROGRAM.* Begun in 1982, this program prepares students for practice in such processes as negotiation, mediation, third-party facilitation, and analytical problem-solving. In this two-year, full-time curriculum, students apply theory in laboratory/simulation courses and in field internships in agencies in the Washington, D.C., area and abroad.

*DOCTORAL PROGRAM.* Established in 1987, this program prepares students as researchers, theoreticians, and teachers in higher education; and as policy administrators, analysts, and consultants in both the public and private sectors. Doctoral students must show competence in a foreign language.

George Mason University, ICAR. Address: Fairfax, VA 22030-4444, USA. Telephone: (703) 993-1300.

**GEORGIA.** The Republic of Georgia is a country lying south of the Caucasus Mountains, bordered by Russia on the north, Turkey and Armenia on the south, Azerbaijan on the east, and the Black Sea on the west. It declared its independence from Russia in 1991 and became a member of the United Nations the same year. It is a member of the Commonwealth of Independent States.

Georgia's population, estimated to be 6,795,000, is composed of ethnic Georgians (about 70%), Russians (7.5%), Azerbaijanis (4.6%), and others (17.9%). Languages in common use include Georgian and Russian. Religious activities are conducted by the Orthodox Church of Georgia.

The government (1994) took the form of a republic, headed by Eduard Shevardnadze, former foreign minister of the Union of Soviet Socialist Republics, who acts as Chairman of the Parliament. Although this provisional government has endeavored to ensure to all the inhabitants of Georgia the full enjoyment of their human rights and fundamental freedoms, it has not been able to put an end to persistent civil strife in the country, which has persisted in the regions of South Ossetia and Abkhazia. At Georgia's request, the United Nations and other international organizations, including the Conference on Security and Cooperation in Europe, have sent missions to these regions to broker cease-fire arrangements, to supervise the implementation of peace-keeping pacts, and to provide technical assistance designed to promote the trend towards democratization supported by the government. Both the United States of America and Russia have supported these efforts. On 4 April 1994, at negotiations held in Moscow, representatives of Georgia and Abkhazia signed two documents: the "Declaration on Measures for a Political Settlement of the Georgian/Abkhaz Conflict" and the "Quadripartite Agreement on Voluntary Return of Refugees and Displaced Persons."

As early as 10 March 1993 the UN **COMMISSION ON HUMAN RIGHTS** requested the Secretary-General (resolution 1993/85) to assist the Georgian government in such activities as the drafting of legal instruments and constitutional provisions safeguarding human rights, and assistance in conducting national elections. One year later, on 4 March 1994, the Commission was able to note with satisfaction (resolution 1994/59) "the efforts within the United Nations system in organizing missions to Georgia, including Abkhazia, to investigate abuses and human rights violations which are being committed on all sides, and to initiate a country program of the Center for Human Rights for technical assistance to Georgia, to be implemented in 1994."

However, while noting with appreciation "the efforts of the personal representative of the Secretary-General to support a speedy political solution to the conflict in Georgia, including Abkhazia, at the peace talks in Geneva, as well as the positive contribution of the mission of the Conference on Security and Cooperation in Europe to the consolidation of an effective cease-fire in South Ossetia and Abkhazia," the Commission expressed "its serious concern at the persistence of numerous and grave violations of human rights in Georgia, including Abkhazia, such as extrajudicial executions, torture and ill-treatment, including rape, inhuman or degrading treatment of prisoners, looting and burning of houses, and deportations of the civilian population."

The Commission strongly condemned such reprehensible acts and abuses committed by troops or armed groups, urged the Government of Georgia and the authorities in Abkhazia to carry out investigations into all allegations of human rights violations, with a view to identifying and prosecuting those responsible; and appealed to those in control in the territory of Abkhazia "to implement and ensure law and order, to guarantee fully the enjoyment of human rights, and to ensure the right of displaced persons to return to Abkhazia and to recover their property." In April 1994, Georgia and Abkhazia did sign a cease-fire agreement and a plan for the return of refugees.

The Commission, further, encouraged a speedy agreement on the country program discussed between the Center for Human Rights and the Government of Georgia and the provision of technical assistance to the government, including *inter alia* the following components: assistance in creating a national institution for the promotion and protection of human rights, a seminar on minority issues, needs assessment and reform of the system for the administration of justice and the penal code, and training of law enforcement officers, including police, military, and prison officers. The Commission suggested that the program should be coordinated by a human rights officer to be posted in Georgia.

*UN OBSERVER MISSION IN GEORGIA (UNOMIG).* On 24 August 1993, the UN Security Council (resolution 858) established the United Nations Observer Mission in Georgia, comprising up to 88 military observers, plus minimal civilian staff necessary to support the mission, with the mandate to: verify compliance with the cease-fire agreement of 27 July 1993 with special attention to the situation in the city of Sukhumi (where UNOMIG is headquartered); investigate re-

ports of cease-fire violations and attempt to resolve such incidents; and report to the UN Secretary-General on the implementation of its mandate, in particular in regard to cease-fire violations. In September 1993, UNOMIG's mandate was declared invalid because of violations of the cease-fire; but, by resolution 881 (1993), the Security Council approved its continued presence in Georgia until 31 January 1994. This deadline was itself extended and, by 30 April 1994, UNOMIG had a strength of 21 observers.

**BIBLIOGRAPHY.** Benifand, Alexander. "The Russian Policy and the Intensification of Civil Wars in Georgia, Tajikistan and Moldova," *Refuge* 12, no. 7 (Feb. 1993): 12–15. Article, in English.

Gudava, Tengiz, and Eduard Gudava. "Georgia: A Historical Survey of the Georgian National Liberation Movements," *Nationalities Papers* 17, no. 2 (Fall 1989): 228–235. Scholarly article, in English.

Helsinki Watch (HW). *Conflict in Georgia: Human Rights Violations by the Government of Zviad Gamsakhurdia.* New York: Human Rights Watch, 1991. NGO report, in English.

Human Rights Watch. "Georgia," in *Human Rights Watch World Report 1995,* pp. 205–208. New York: 1995. NGO report, in English.

Immigration and Refugee Board Documentation Centre. *CIS, Baltic States and Georgia: Nationality Legislation.* Ottawa, Canada: 1992. Government briefing paper, in English and French; bibliography, pp. 20–23.

———. *CIS, Baltic States and Georgia: Situation of the Jews.* Ottawa, Canada: 1992. Government briefing paper, in English and French; bibliography, pp. 30–35.

**GERMAN ASSOCIATION OF JUDGES (DEUTSCHER RICHTERBUND) HUMAN RIGHTS PRIZE.** See **DEUTSCHER RICHTERBUND (GERMAN ASSOCIATION OF JUDGES) HUMAN RIGHTS PRIZE.**

**GERMANY.** The largest country of central Europe, the Federal Republic of Germany has borders on the north with the North and the Baltic Seas and with Denmark, on the west with the Netherlands, Belgium, Luxembourg, and France, on the south with Switzerland, Austria, and the Czech Republic, and on the east with Poland. Separated into the Federal Republic of Germany (West Germany) and the German Democratic Republic (East Germany) after its unconditional surrender to the Allied Forces in 1945, the two areas were reunited and again became a single State known as Germany in 1990. Bonn is its temporary capital pending restoration of its traditional seat of government, Berlin. Germany is a member of the United Nations and the European Union. Its population is estimated to be 80,590,000. It became one of seven countries in the European Union to implement the Schengen Agreement in March 1995 whereby border controls between the seven would be eradicated and external controls enhanced. The other countries are Belgium, France, Luxembourg, the Netherlands, Portugal, and Spain.

The process of reunification initiated a period of social and economic turbulence, shaking up the governing coalition which had functioned effectively since 1990: the Christian Democratic Alliance headed by Chancellor Helmut Kohl and the liberal Free Democrats, which combined to provide only a 10-seat majority in elections held on 17 October 1994. The causes for the decline from an earlier margin of 134 seats were clear: in the west, voters had tired of financing the absorption and rehabilitation of the former Democratic Republic and of retraining its workers while in the east they had failed to adjust to a market economy, to the loss of security of employment, and to many aspects of the process of democratization.

One bright side of the election picture, however, lay in the fact that the radical right-wing Republican Party—which had created frightening disturbances two years earlier as hundreds of thousands of foreigners had poured into the country seeking automatic political asylum—had registered only 1.9% of the national vote, thus becoming an insignificant splinter party and eliminating what at one time had appeared to be a possible threat to German democracy. As part of the government's crack-down on extreme right groups and anti-semitic violence, the constitutional court in February 1995 placed a ban on a number of parties whose beliefs were too extreme and not truly political.

*SITUATION OF MINORITIES.* On 3 February 1993, the Government of Germany submitted its twelfth periodic report pursuant to article 9 of the International Convention on the Elimination of All Forms of Racial Discrimination (see **RACIAL DISCRIMINATION**) to the UN **COMMITTEE ON THE ELIMINATION OF RACIAL DISCRIMINATION** (UN Doc. CERD/C/226/Add. 7). The report covered the entire territory of the Federal Republic of Germany, including the former German Democratic Republic, and presented extensive new information on measures taken by the government for the protection of minorities and other groups, for the prohibition of racialist organizations, for assistance to foreign workers in the country, for the elimination of racist attacks, and for the education of school children to have respect for human rights.

After detailed consideration of the report at its meetings on 11 August 1993, the Committee adopted the following concluding observations on 18 August 1993 (UN Doc. A/48/18, paras. 443–452):

### Positive Aspects

The Committee welcomed the efforts of the German authorities to fight xenophobia and racial discrimination, in compliance with its obligations under the Convention. In that connection, the Committee welcomed legal and other measures taken by the German authorities to give effect to the provisions of article 4 of the Convention. The Committee noted that the Government had the necessary will to cope with the problem of racial hatred. The Committee also noted with appreciation that in many German cities large popular demonstrations had been held against recent expressions of racist violence and xenophobia.

### Principal Subjects of Concern

The Committee expressed serious concern at the manifestations of xenophobia, anti-semitism, racial discrimination and racial violence that had recently occurred in Germany. In spite of the Government's efforts to counteract and to prevent them, it appeared that those manifestations were increasing and that the German police system had in many instances failed to provide effective protection to victims and potential victims of xenophobia and racial discrimination, as required by the Convention. The Committee particularly held that all those who carried out functions in public and political life should in no way encourage sentiments of racism and xenophobia.

### Suggestions and Recommendations

In view of the serious nature of the manifestations of xenophobia, racism and racial discrimination in Germany, the Committee recommended that practical measures should be strengthened with a view to preventing such manifestations, particularly acts of violence on an ethnic basis, and to punishing those who committed them. Measures should be taken, in that regard, against the organizations and groups involved.

At the same time, taking into account that practices of racial discrimination in such areas as access to employment, housing and other rights referred to in article 5 (f) of the Convention were not always effectively dealt with, the German authorities should give serious consideration to the enactment of a comprehensive anti-discrimination law. Such a law would constitute a clear reaffirmation by the Germany authorities that racial discrimination was absolutely unacceptable, detrimental to human rights and human dignity. Other preventive measures, such as information campaigns, educational programmes and training programmes addressed particularly to law enforcement officials, in accordance with article 7 of the Convention and general recommendation XIII of the Committee, would strengthen the effectiveness of legal provisions.

The Committee was also of the view that the Government should guarantee equal protection to all minority groups living in Germany. In addition, the Government should consider reviewing certain restrictive provisions recently adopted with regard to asylum-seekers, to ensure that they did not result in any discrimination in effect on grounds of ethnic origin.

While commending the Government of Germany for taking measures to prohibit extremist organizations disseminating ideas based on racial superiority or hatred, the Committee was of the view that appropriate measures should also be strictly applied against such organizations and especially against persons and groups who were implicated in racially motivated crimes.

In accordance with its general recommendation XI, the

Committee appealed to the Government of Germany to continue reporting fully upon legislation on foreigners and its implementation.

The Committee further invited Germany, taking into account statements to that effect by the World Conference on Human Rights, to make the declaration under article 14 of the Convention recognizing the competence of the Committee to receive and consider communications from individuals or groups of individuals within its jurisdiction claiming to be victims of a violation of any of the rights set forth in the Convention.

The Committee was of the view that the situation in Germany should be kept under close scrutiny and expected Germany, in its thirteenth periodic report, to inform the Committee on further measures taken in compliance with the Convention and pursuant to recommendations and suggestions put forward in connection with the examination of the eleventh and twelfth reports.

***RECENT RULING ON FREEDOM OF SPEECH.*** **HUMAN RIGHTS WATCH,** a non-governmental organization in consultative status with the UN **ECONOMIC AND SOCIAL COUNCIL,** reported that, in April 1994, the German constitutional court ruled that "individuals who spread the 'Auschwitz Lie'—propaganda that the Holocaust never happened—would not be protected by freedom of speech and could be prohibited from stating their views publicly." One justice stated that "proven untruthful statements do not have the protection of freedom of speech."

***BIBLIOGRAPHY.*** Human Rights Watch. "Germany," in *Human Rights Watch World Report 1995*, pp. 208–210. New York: 1995. NGO report, in English.

Neuman, Gerald L. "Immigration and Judicial Review in the Federal Republic of Germany," *New York University Journal of International Law & Politics* 23, no. 1 (Fall 1990): 35–85. Scholarly article, in English.

Wetzel, Juliane. "The Judicial Treatment of Incitement against Ethnic Groups and of the Denial of National Socialist Mass Murder in the Federal Republic of Germany," in *Under the Shadow of Weimar: Democracy, Law, and Racial Incitement in Six Countries*, eds. Louis Greenspan and Cyril Levitt, pp. 83–106. Westport, CO, USA: Praeger, 1993. Scholarly article, in English.

**GHANA.** The Republic of Ghana is a country in western Africa, on the Gulf of Guinea. It has borders with Burkina Faso, the Ivory Coast, and Togo. It achieved independence from Great Britain in 1957 and became a member of the United Nations the same year. Its population is estimated to be 16,445,000. Under a government directive of 21 March 1972, it is illegal for anyone to collect or disseminate information on the ethnic composition of Ghana's population. Languages commonly used include English (official), Akanand, Twi, Fanti, Ga, Ewe, Dagbani, and other African vernaculars. Religions practiced include Christianity

(65%), Islam (15%), and Animism (20%). Literacy is estimated at 45%.

The government (1994) took the form of a republic and member of the Commonwealth, the Organization of African Unity, and the Non-Aligned Movement. However, on 31 December 1981, the constitution was suspended, and all executive and legislative powers were exercised by the Provisional National Defense Council, composed of six members of the military. The chairman of the Council acted as head of State and government. A National Commission for Democracy was established to formulate a program for a more effective realization of democracy based on Ghanian traditions and experience. The judicial system remains as it was before the imposition of military rule; but public tribunals have been established to try specified offenses such as economic crimes, sedition, corruption, and mismanagement by public officials. These courts operate side-by-side with the regular ones. For many years, there were no political parties; however, a new constitution, approved in April 1992, allows for multi-party politics.

Ghana's President, Flight Lt. Jerry Rawlings, first seized power on 4 June 1979, charging the military government then headed by Lt. Gen. Frederick Akuffo with repression and corruption. Rawlings then stepped aside to permit the election and installation of a civilian government headed by Hilla Limann. Two years later, however, he staged a second coup, again charging repression and corruption. Shortly after he took over as chairman of the Provisional National Defense Council, the Council abrogated Ghana's 1979 constitution and replaced it by "Directive Principles of State Policy" designed to provide the basic framework for the exercise of all powers of government. These principles envisaged that:

(a) a basis of social justice is to be established, particular attention being paid to the deprived sections of the community and to the reconstruction of the society in a revolutionary process directed against the previous structures of injustice and exploitation;

(b) respect for fundamental human rights and for the dignity of the human person are to be cultivated among all sections of the society and established as part of the basis of social justice;

(c) corrupt practices, exploitation in all its forms, as well as abuse of power are to be eradicated;

(d) national integration is to be encouraged and discrimination on grounds of ethnic origin discouraged. A spirit of loyalty to Ghana overriding sectional, ethnic or other loyalties, is to be cultivated among the people of Ghana. . . .

***BIBLIOGRAPHY.*** Africa Watch. *Ghana: Revolutionary Injustice: Abuse of the Legal System under the PNDC Government.* New York: Human Rights Watch, 1992. NGO report, in English.

Amnesty International. *The Death Penalty in Ghana*. London: 1985. NGO report, in English.

————. *Ghana: Political Imprisonment and the Death Penalty*. London: 1991. NGO report, in English.

Graft-Johnson, K. E. de. *Measures Taken in Ghana to Ensure the Effective Exercise of Human Rights for Disadvantaged Social Groups*. Paper presented at International Experts Meeting on Ways and Means to Ensure Effective Exercise of Human Rights by Disadvantaged Groups, Quebec, Canada, 29 November 1985. Conference paper, in English.

Gyimah-Boadi, E. "Notes on Ghana's Current Transition to Constitutional Rule," *Africa Today* 38, no. 4 (1991): 5–17. Article, in English.

Hawley, Edward A., ed. "Ghana: The Process of Political and Economic Change, 1991–1992," *Africa Today* 38, no. 4 (1991): 4–48. Special issue, in English.

Head, Ivan L. "International Standards of Civil Procedure: The Aliens in the Courts of Ghana," *St. Louis University Law Journal* 12, no. 3 (Spring 1986): 392–417. Scholarly article, in English.

Immigration and Refugee Board Documentation Centre. *Ghana: Country Profile*. Ottawa, Canada: 1990. Government briefing paper, in English and French; bibliography, pp. 51–57 (in English); pp. 54–61 (in French).

James, Stanlie. "Some Impressions of the Ghanaian Version of Black Feminism," in *Emerging Human Rights: The African Political Economy Context*, eds. G. W. Shepherd, Jr., and M. O. C. Anikpo, pp. 181–196. New York: Greenwood Press, 1990. Scholarly article, in English.

Opoku-Dapaah, Edward. "Ghana 1981–1991: A Decade of Forced Repression and Migration," *Refuge* 11, no. 3 (March 1992): 8–13. Article, in English.

## GOBAT, CHARLES ALBERT (1843–1914).

Co-winner of the 1902 **NOBEL PEACE PRIZE** along with **ELIE DUCOMMUN**, Charles Gobat was born in Tremelan, Switzerland. He received a doctorate in law from the University of Heidelberg in 1867; he practiced law in Bern and taught law at Bern University from 1882 to 1912 for many years. He was involved in local and national politics from 1882 until his death.

Gobat was an ardent supporter of the Interparliamentary Union and served as the general secretary and director of the Interparliamentary Bureau from 1892. In 1906, he became the director of the **INTERNATIONAL PEACE BUREAU**, itself a Nobel Peace Prize recipient in 1910. As president of the Bern International Peace Bureau and administrative head of the Interparliamentary Union, he simultaneously directed the two largest peace organizations in the world. He died in 1914 while addressing the International Peace Bureau.

An ardent believer in arbitration as the way to achieve a peaceful resolution to conflicts, Gobat called on the United States of America to intervene in the Russo-Japanese War. He recalled this in his Nobel Prize lecture: "At the beginning of the war between Russia and Japan, the president of the United States persisted in offering his good services to the Russians

and Japanese. Neither party chose to condemn the offer as an unfriendly act. . . . President [Theodore] Roosevelt was the first head of state to apply the rules of The Hague Convention concerning the preservation of general peace."

**BIBLIOGRAPHY.** Gray, Tony. *Champions of Peace*. London: Paddington Press, 1976.

Schlessinger, Bernard S., and June H. Schlessinger, eds. *Who's Who of Nobel Prize Winners*. Phoenix, AZ, USA: Oryx Press, 1991.

## GORBACHEV, MIKHAIL SERGEYEVICH (1931– ).

Born in the southern Russian village of Privolnoye, in the Stavropol territory, Mikhail Gorbachev, recipient of the 1990 **NOBEL PEACE PRIZE,** received his law degree from Moscow State University in 1955. While at the university, he joined the Communist party in 1952 and became active in the Young Communist League. After graduation, he applied his law degree to party work where he rose steadily in the ranks.

From 1956 to 1958, Gorbachev was first secretary of the Stavropol city Young Communist League; later he became deputy chief of the propaganda department; next, second secretary, then, first secretary. In 1962, he was promoted to party organizer for the territorial production board of collective and state farms and, in that same year, became chief of the agricultural department for the Stavropol region. Throughout the rest of the 1960s and the 1970s, Gorbachev rose rank-by-rank through the party hierarchy—often being the youngest member of any committee or department to which he was appointed—finally becoming secretary of agriculture in 1978. In October 1980, under the patronage of Yuri Andropov, he attained full membership in the Politburo, the Central Committee's policy-making organ.

When Andropov became general secretary of the Communist party, Gorbachev became his "right-hand" man, implementing many of Andropov's proposed reforms and introducing a measure of decentralization and technological innovation in industry. When Andropov died, despite the succession of Konstantin Chernenko to the position of general secretary, Gorbachev was in position to assume power when his own time came.

That time came in May 1985, hours after Chernenko's death, when Gorbachev was elected general secretary. He immediately initiated economic reforms, "socialist self-government," and limited democratization. Throughout the world, two Russian terms *glasnost* ("openness") and *perestroika* (a radical program of reform and restructuring) became well-known. For the first time since World War II, relations between the

USSR and the West were no longer strained. Gorbachev visited the British Parliament and met with Prime Minister Margaret Thatcher in 1984; and held a summit talk with American President Ronald Reagan in Geneva in 1985, at which Gorbachev took the initiative in discussing a moratorium on nuclear tests. He later visited Washington, D.C., and addressed the American Congress. Indeed, in citing Gorbachev for the Peace Prize, the committee stressed his "decisive contributions [to the] dramatic changes to take place in the relationship between the East and West." In the USSR itself, Gorbachev's reforms allowed greater civil liberties and journalistic and cultural freedom. He also withdrew Soviet troops from their disastrous, decade-long involvement in Afghanistan in 1989.

It has been argued that Gorbachev did not intend to dismantle the centralized planning system of the USSR—merely to make it more efficient. Whatever Gorbachev's intentions truly were, the USSR's member states began to demand more freedom from central control, beginning first with Lithuania's declaration of independence in 1990, and, finally, to break away into independent republics. In August 1991, a coup attempted to overthrow Gorbachev, placing him under house arrest; but the insurgents were defeated, largely through the efforts of Boris Yeltsin, the president of the Russian S.S.R. and a longtime Gorbachev opponent, who defiantly aroused public opinion against the coup. In 1991, with the formal dissolution of the Soviet Union, Gorbachev was forced to resign as general secretary of the Communist party.

**BIBLIOGRAPHY.** *Current Biography.* New York: W.H. Wilson & Co., 1985.

Schlessinger, Bernard S., and June H. Schlessinger, eds. *Who's Who of Nobel Prize Winners.* Phoenix, AZ, USA: Oryx Press, 1991.

Zemtsov, Ilya, and John Farrar. *Gorbachev.* New Brunswick, NJ, USA: Transaction Books, 1989.

**GREECE.** The Hellenic Republic is a country on the Balkan Peninsula in southern Europe, on the Mediterranean between the Aegean and Ionian Seas. It has borders with Albania, Bulgaria, Turkey, and Yugoslavia and includes a number of islands, among them Crete, Rhodes, and numerous islets of the Ionian, Cyclades, and Dodecanese groups. It achieved independence in 1827 and became a member of the United Nations in 1945. Its population is estimated to be 10,075,000. There are a large number of ethnic groups, the Greeks having mingled through many centuries with invaders from the Balkans, Africa, and Asia. Languages commonly used include Greek, French, English, and Turkish. Christianity (Greek Orthodox) is the predominant religion. Literacy is estimated at 95%.

The government (1994) took the form of a republic, established by a referendum of December 1974 which ended the monarchy. The president, elected by popular vote, is head of State. The premier, representing the party or coalition given a majority in an election, is head of government and exercises executive authority; he is responsible directly to Parliament, which is a unicameral body of 300 members. Political parties include the Panhellenic Socialist Movement, the New Democratic Party, the Communist Party, the Democratic Renewal, and the Communist Party of the Interior.

King Constantine II was forced into exile in 1967 by a coup d'etat staged by rightist officers led by Col. George Papadopoulos. The new regime—which came to be known as "the colonels"—suspended Parliament and replaced the 1952 constitution with one that established a "crown parliamentary democracy," under which royal authority was exercised by a regent and Papadopoulos became premier. This became a "presidential parliamentary democracy" in 1973, with Papadopoulos as president. However, efforts by the colonels "to restore democracy" by suspending civil rights and resorting to torture and arbitrary detention backfired when parliamentary elections were postponed indefinitely, and they were forced out by another military coup. General Phaidon Gizikis, who became president, returned the government to civilian control in 1974. The 1952 civilian constitution and its guarantees of civil rights were restored on 1 August 1974, martial law was lifted in October of that year, and the monarchy was abolished by a referendum held on 8 December. On 18 October 1981, the first socialist government in Greek history was elected, and Andreas Papandreou became premier. The socialist victory in parliamentary elections was repeated on 1 June 1985.

Charged with corruption in 1989, Papandreou was stripped of office in 1989, and in April 1990 Constantine Mitsotakis became premier as a result of on electoral victory by the center-right forces. Mr. Mitsotakis's New Democratic Party won the elections with 46.9% of the vote and 150 seats, after failing by a few seats in elections held in June and November 1989. However, after Andreas Papandreou had been acquitted of all charges in 1992, he resumed his role in government, first as leader of the opposition and later once again as premier.

A problem relating to the enjoyment of freedom of religion or belief continues to be of concern to human rights groups as well as to Greeks who are not members of the Eastern Orthodox Church. Article 13 of the constitution guarantees the freedom of "known" religions. This formula, which is primarily historical in origin, has been interpreted in legal decisions as establishing freedom to practice all religions whose beliefs are "known" as opposed to "secret." However, the constitution also qualifies the Eastern Orthodox Church as the "predominant Church" and prohibits proselytism. In the course of 1983 and 1984, more than 160 lawsuits were brought for proselytism, and none of the requests for authorization to open new places of worship was granted. Under a 1939 law still in force, such authorization cannot be given without the prior agreement of the Orthodox Church.

**BIBLIOGRAPHY.** Amnesty International. *Greece: Conscientious Objection.* London: 1988. NGO report, in English.

*Greece: Deliberate Violations of Human Rights.* Neufvilles, Belgium: Human Rights without Frontiers, 1992. Special issue, in English.

Helsinki Watch. *Destroying Ethnic Identity: The Turks of Greece.* New York: Human Rights Watch, 1990. NGO factfinding report, in English.

Marangopoulos Foundation for Human Rights. *La déclaration française des droits de l'homme et du citoyen: un rayonnement bicentenaire* (The French Declaration of the Rights of Man and the Citizen: Two Hundred Years of Influence). Athens, Greece: Editions Ant. N. Sakkoulas, 1991. NGO conference report, in English and French.

Pollis, Adamantia. "The State, the Law and Human Rights in Modern Greece," *Human Rights Quarterly* 9, no. 4 (November 1987): 587–614. Scholarly article, in English.

## GREEK ORTHODOX ARCHDIOCESAN COUNCIL OF NORTH AND SOUTH AMERICA.

The GOAC promotes universal peace and security; works for better welfare, education, and health conditions; encourages the enhancement of the status of women; and condemns racism. It has consultative status with the UN Economic and Social Council (Category I) and has a membership of approximately 3 million people in 13 countries. It publishes the bimonthly *Orthodox Observer* and the monthly *Mission.*

Greek Orthodox Archdiocesan Council of North and South America. Address: Greek Orthodox Archhouse, 8-10 E. 79th Street, New York, NY 10021, USA.

## GRENADA.

The State of Grenada is a country which occupies the southernmost portion of the Windward Islands, in the Caribbean Sea, 120 miles north of South America. Grenada achieved independence from Great Britain in 1974 and became a member of the United Nations in the same year. Its population is estimated to be 97,000. Ethnic groups include Amerindians and Caribs. Languages commonly used include English (official) and a French *patois.* Christianity (Roman Catholic, 64%; Anglican and other Protestant denominations, 25%) is the predominant religion.

The government (1994) took the form of a parliamentary State member of the Commonwealth. Executive power is vested in the governor-general, who represents the crown. He appoints the prime minister, who represents the party or coalition given the majority in a popular election. There is a 15-member parliament and a judiciary organized along British lines. Political parties include the New National Party, the Grenada Unity Labor Party, the New Jewel Movement, the Democratic Labor Party, and the Christian Democratic Labor Party.

Abuses of power by the Prime Minister Sir Eric Gairy led to a Marxist takeover in 1979 and the installation of Maurice Bishop as prime minister. Bishop was killed by radical elements in his New Jewel Movement in 1983, prompting an invasion on 25 October by 1,900 U.S. marines and rangers and small military contingents from Antigua, Barbados, Dominica, Jamaica, St. Lucia, and St. Vincent. Resistance by Cuban military personnel on the island ended after one day when Pearls Airport was re-opened and 1,000 U.S. citizens were evacuated. After subsequent elections, Nicholas Braithwaite emerged as Prime Minister, Minister of Finance, and Minister of National Security.

**BIBLIOGRAPHY.** Ferguson, James. *Grenada: Revolution in Reverse.* London: Latin America Bureau, 1990. NGO report, in English.

Ramshaw, P., and T. Steers. *Intervention on Trial: The New York War Crimes Tribunal on Central America and the Caribbean.* New York: Praeger Publishers and National Lawyers Guild, 1987. Scholarly study, in English.

Sandford, Gregory. *The New Jewel Movement: Grenada's Revolution, 1979–1983.* Washington, D.C.: U.S. Department of State, Foreign Service Institute, 1985. Government monograph, in English.

Thompson, Robert. *Green Gold: Bananas and Dependency in the Eastern Caribbean.* London: Latin American Bureau, 1987. NGO monograph, in English.

## GUATEMALA.

The Republic of Guatemala is a country in Central America. It has borders with Belize, El Salvador, Honduras, and Mexico. Once a Mayan Indian empire, it became a colony of Spain in 1524 and achieved independence from that country in 1821. The republic was established in 1839. It became a member of the United Nations in 1945. Its population is estimated to be 9,705,000. Ethnic groups include Maya (55%), Mestizos (42%), and descendants of Spanish and other European settlers (3%). Languages commonly used include Spanish, English, and Amerindian vernaculars. Christianity (Roman Catholic, 80%; various Protestant denominations, 10%) and Mayan (10%) are the predominant religions. Literacy is estimated at 50%.

The government (1994) took the form of a republic. After the first civilian government of recent years was ousted by the army in 1982, there was a period of political violence which caused more than 200,000 Guatemalans to seek refuge in Mexico and Central American countries. A second military coup occurred in 1983, ending the reign of terror and promising to restore power to an elected civilian president. A Constituent Assembly was elected on 1 July 1984 and proceeded to prepare a new constitution. Elections for president, vice president and members of Congress took place in November and December 1985; and, on 14 January 1986, the new civilian government assumed power. Active political parties included the Christian Democrats, the *Union del Centro Nacional*, and the Social Democratic Party.

*CONCERNS OF THE COMMISSION ON HUMAN RIGHTS.* During the period of transition, the UN **COMMISSION ON HUMAN RIGHTS** continued to receive reports of continuing, serious violations of human rights in Guatemala, including reports of violence against non-combatants, widespread repression, and the killing and massive displacement of rural and indigenous peoples. On 8 March 1983, the Commission appointed one of its members, Viscount Colville of Culross (United Kingdom) as its Special Representative to study and report on the situation (resolution 1983/37). The Special Representative subsequently submitted a number of reports to the commission and to the **GENERAL ASSEMBLY** (UN Docs. A/38/485, E/CN.4/1984/30, A/39/635, E/CN.4/1985/19, A/40/865, E/CN.4/1986/23, and E/CN.4/1987/24). In the final report, the Special Representative summed up his general impressions in the following terms (UN Doc. E/CN.4/1987/24, paras. 7–8):

... In the course of seven visits since the summer of 1983, the Special Representative has been observing the situation as it can only be perceived (however imperfectly) in the country itself. Whatever the past criticisms, which have been many and justified, there is now a democratically elected President and Congress. The President's attitude is that the country should be governed under civilian control, through himself (including his role as Commander-in-Chief of the armed forces), the Minister of Interior and other Ministers. Even the briefest visit to Congress indicates a lively, urgent parliamentary activity. The media seem now to be all persuasive, increasingly well-informed and, so far as the Special Representative is concerned, responsible in their reporting. Trade union protests and placards opposite the National Palace are new. The Special Representative is much indebted to the Army on earlier occasions for their safe-keeping and their transport, with many other kindnesses and facilities; nevertheless the 1986 visit was in civilian hands throughout and the differences were significant.

The Government faces huge political, practical and economic problems. The scale of crime is unacceptable to everyone, within and without the country. The poverty, especially when you see it at first hand, is hard to comprehend. Yet the dignity and friendliness of the people, in city or rural hamlet, cannot fail to impress. The Special Representative has noted the tributes paid, often in publications which are generally critical of the human rights situation in Guatemala, to the quality of the country's present leaders; he has attempted to describe the policies where they are pursuing. The Special Representative ventures to suggest that the efforts they are making to implement the new legal order for the protection of human rights and to guarantee the full enjoyment of fundamental freedoms, even if not yet perfect or complete, should receive the support of the international community....

After considering the report at its 1987 session, the Commission on Human Rights noted (resolution 1987/53) the measures that had been taken by the government to guarantee the protection of human rights and fundamental freedoms, expressed the hope that the appropriate authorities would investigate human rights violations reported to them and would make all possible efforts to clarify the fate of the disappeared persons, expressed its gratitude to Viscount Colville of Culross and terminated his mandate, and requested the Secretary-General to appoint an expert to formulate recommendations for the further restoration of human rights in Guatemala. Accordingly, the Secretary-General appointed Mr. Hector Gros Espiell (Uruguay) as the expert "with a view to assisting the Government of Guatemala, through direct contacts, in taking the necessary action for the further restoration of human rights."

Mr. Gros Espiell, in his first report to the Commission (UN Doc. E/CN.4/1988/42, para. 16) stated that he believed that his mandate was to deal with the possibility offered to the constitutional government of Guatemala of requesting advisory services and other forms of assistance with a view to fostering advances in democracy and strengthening respect for human rights. After considering the report, the Commission noted (resolution 1988/50) that the government of Guatemala was prepared "to guarantee the protection of human rights and fundamental freedoms in that country. However, after the expert submitted his second report (UN Doc. E/CN.4/1989/39) to the Commission at its 1989 session, the Commission expressed (in resolution 1989/74) "its serious concern at the harmful conditions that still exist and that place severe limitations on any genuine process of improving the human rights situation in Guatemala" and urged the government "to intensify its efforts to ensure that all its authorities and security forces fully respect the human rights and fundamental freedoms of all its citizens."

In his report to the 1990 session of the Commission (UN Doc. E/CN.4/1990/45 and Add. 1), Mr. Gros Espiell reviewed the situation of human rights in Guatemala on the basis of his visits to that country in May and October–November 1989 and reported on a technical assistance program on human rights questions carried out in 1988 and 1989 as a result of a request made by Guatemalan authorities to the UN **Center for Human Rights.** The program was financed in its entirety (US$222,000) by the United Nations Voluntary Fund for Advisory Services and Technical Assistance in the Field of Human Rights.

The expert's general conclusions from the study of the human rights situation in Guatemala, as summarized in the report, were as follows (UN Doc. E/CN.4/1990/45, chap. VI, paras. 66–70):

(a) The development and progress in the legal framework for recognizing, guaranteeing and protecting human rights in Guatemala are undeniable;

(b) The Government's political will to ensure respect for these rights is definite. In the view of the Expert, its efforts in this regard cannot be doubted. But it lacked the firm and unrelenting determination to carry out a human rights policy at the proper time and, most important, at present it has no possibility to act with all the constitutional and political authority that is needed to achieve the desired goals;

(c) Virtually nothing has been done either by the Government or by the judiciary to investigate and punish earlier human rights violations;

(d) Major *de facto* harmful conditions still exist and place severe limitations on any genuine process of improving the human rights situation in Guatemala;

(e) A climate of social violence continues to exist. What is more, it has grown and become worse. A human rights culture will have to be developed in which tolerance takes the place of the present contempt for pluralism and opposing views among many sections of the population;

(f) Violations of civil and political rights, especially deaths and disappearances, are still taking place and have increased in number. These are apparently the outcome not of government orders on policy but of factors, of acts committed by power circles and a persistent climate of violence that are still beyond effective government control. The Government has proved powerless and incapable of remedying this situation. Its scope for action has lessened as the violence and violations have increased;

(g) It is necessary to make sure that people are not compelled to join civilian self-defence patrols and do not suffer reprisals for not doing so;

(h) Serious deficiencies remain in the situation regarding respect for economic, social and cultural rights. Society as a whole is still conditioned by injustice and discrimination;

(i) The situation of the indigenous populations continues to be a crucial problem. The habitual discrimination and exploitation of these populations has been a constant source of human rights violations. The Government is aware of this difficult problem and an examination and comprehensive plan of the political, economic, social and cultural aspects of the question is under way (see the conclusions of consultant Willemsen Diaz, especially on the legislation which is being drafted);

(j) If the democratic process grows stronger and takes root and if it is maintained without any institutional breakdowns, the slow process of improvement initiated by the constitutional Government can be expected to continue;

(k) For this to happen, aside from the essential political will and the commitment that the Guatemalan people and their freely elected authorities alone can provide, continued international assistance and support are required;

(l) The dialogue for national reconciliation should be encouraged whole-heartedly and there should be no unjustified exclusions from it. The Government should participate actively, demonstrating total political will in continuing this dialogue;

(m) The technical capability and efficiency of the police should be upgraded in accordance with the conclusions of the report by the consultant, J. Maier;

(n) The operation of the Judiciary should be improved as recommended by the consultant, J. Maier, in his conclusions;

(o) The Procurator for Human Rights should be given greater support to enable him to continue, extend and complete the work he has begun. (In this connection, see the conclusions of the experts from the Parliamentary High Commissioner of Spain);

(p) More emphasis should be placed on training in civics and democracy, in an atmosphere of respect for human rights, for senior officers of the armed forces;

(q) The total subordination in matters of jurisdiction of members of the armed forces to the ordinary system of justice should be studied;

(r) With reference to the problem of refugees (paras. 34–39), since repatriation depends on political, economic, and social conditions and the level of violence, efforts must be continued to encourage, freely the speeding up of the repatriation process which has experienced some vicissitudes.

These conclusions coincide in general with those the Expert put forward in his previous reports to the Commission. Political difficulties, the continuing climate of violence and the influence of the negative factors referred to above have prevented the Government, in its weakened state, from ensuring full safeguards and respect for human rights.

Events have not justified the relative and cautious optimism felt in 1987 and 1988. This is serious, disturbing and unfortunate.

International assistance and co-operation are essential if this process is to continue, through the application of the provisions of the international instruments ratified by Guatemala and through the promotion of human rights in the manner indicated in paragraph 71 (c) and (d).

Only in a pluralistic and representative democracy, with a fully operative Constitution, with free elections and with everyone subject to a single and legitimate civil authority, can the future be contemplated and can there be an improvement in the human rights situation in Guatemala. The present constitutional Government, notwithstanding its shortcomings and omissions should, therefore, be supported, as should future democratic Governments.

The expert's recommendations to the Commission were as follows (chap. VII, paras. 71–72):

(a) It is necessary for the Commission to continue to observe the situation of human rights in whatever way it deems appropriate, bearing in mind the present situation in Guatemala;

(b) Conclusions (l) to (p) should be borne in mind;

(c) It is essential to continue the broad programme of assistance to the Government to help the democratic process, since this institutional framework is a necessary but not the only prerequisite for the future improvement of the situation which is undeniably tied in with the maintenance of democracy;

(d) In keeping with what has already been done, this programme should, *inter alia*, continue to consist of:

(i) Assistance to introduce human rights courses at all levels of education. This should include not only State education but also education in private schools, colleges and universities;

(ii) Assistance for courses and seminars intended for judges and officials of the Judiciary;

(iii) Assistance for courses and seminars for police officials. It must be ensured that human rights are included as a subject in the continuous training of senior police officials;

(iv) Assistance for courses and seminars intended for officers in the armed forces. Human rights must be included at all times as a subject in the courses in the Military College and in the courses for officers on the General Staff. Such courses should not be confined to international humanitarian law but should cover the overall topic of human rights.

Without prejudice to these specific recommendations, the Expert would also like to draw the attention to the value of:

(a) Continuing to provide suitable advice and assistance for the organization and activities of the Office of the Procurator for Human Rights;

(b) Continuing to provide multidisciplinary and sectoral support to help in devising an overall policy on development, assistance and non-discrimination in regard to the indigenous populations;

(c) Supporting and complementing bilateral aid, already negotiated and in the process of being furnished, for technical reform and material improvement of the police force, so that it will become an effective democratic organization protecting and guaranteeing law and order and everyone's rights and freedoms.

The expert ended his report to the Commission with the following concluding remarks (chap. VIII, paras. 74–83):

In the course of monitoring the situation in Guatemala for almost four years, the Expert has ascertained that extensive sections of Guatemalan society have begun to understand the problem of human rights, its conception and the limitations and obligations involved. Previously, it was a problem that did not impinge on the social conscience, one which was alien to a "culture", that had other components. But today, the start of a process of change can be glimpsed. It is a difficult and complex process and cannot be expected to come about automatically or rapidly. However, it is the only one that can bring about a legal situation, in the context of which the present and future democratic governments can work more effectively and efficiently than they have been able to do so far. This beginning of a change in thinking and a new awareness of the need to respect human rights—seen as deriving directly from the dignity of all human beings without any kind of discrimination—is perhaps the most important progress achieved in Guatemala in recent years and gives some ground for optimism about the future. Human rights violations are not confined to the Government or public officials acting in an official capacity. Human rights are also violated by terrorists and the guerrilla—especially in a democratic State, which, because it is pluralistic, guarantees the free expression of opposing political views by legitimate

means—by armed fringe groups which act outside the control of the army or the police, or which are in the pay of private interests, by common criminals and by all who resort to violence in order to settle any kind of conflict or to express hatred, and to indicate the inability to conceive that there can be divergent views in freedom. But the many and varied causes of human rights violations in Guatemala as well as the injustice of placing the blame solely at the door of the Government must be borne in mind. it is equally true and should always be remembered that the Government has a legal, political and moral obligation both nationally and internationally, to guarantee the enjoyment of human rights to all persons under its jurisdiction.

For personal reasons, the Expert is unable to continue the mandate which the Commission had assigned him, and this report is therefore his last. He wishes to thank the Commission for the confidence shown him and the support which he received and to say that the case of Guatemala and the changes which occurred in the human rights situation during the years in which he was required to observe the process at firsthand enabled him to study a complex and difficult situation, which raises serious doubts and questions.

First of all, there is an apparently insurmountable gulf between law and reality, between what should be and what is and between the rule and what is actually done. This is a particularly serious matter in Guatemala and has already been referred to by the Expert in other reports. Until this gulf is bridged, until this breach begins to close, the human rights situation will not improve. The traditional legal approach, the belief that problems can be solved because a rule, full of fine-sounding words exists, but is not applied is one of the worst obstacles to progress on human rights issues. However, one should not think that the law does not play an extremely important role in the overall process of improvement. Legal standards are absolutely essential. Without the law, there can be no progress in human rights but if the law is not applied and no serious attempt is made to enforce it, maintain it and keep it alive and effective it is of little use. The law should be applied and should serve as a means of forcing a change in the situation and it is one's bounden duty to use it and not keep it there as an ethereal, distant, unattainable realization, divorced from reality.

Second, if material, economic, social and cultural conditions do not change, if there is no movement away from a society of exploitation, of immutable privileges and of entrenched injustice towards a society which is supportive, tolerant and fair, human rights cannot become a living reality, available to all, the basis for peace and progress.

Third, without democracy, without free elections, without constitutional Governments, it is not possible to contemplate an improvement in the human rights situation. However, one must recognize that the democratic Governments in Latin America which have succeeded military dictatorships have managed to achieve very little. This is not due only to the economic and social situation but to other real factors of power. These factors, which are outside the government apparatus, but which sometimes infiltrate the Government, the police and the armed forces, have proven to be stronger than even the Government itself, which is unable to dominate them.

The Government itself may respect human rights, but it lacks the ability, power or authority to ensure that they are fully and freely exercised and is unable to punish violations and guarantee peace and order based on freedom. It lives in fear, a prisoner of forces which it cannot control. This is a tragedy, a formidable problem, which has not been solved and with no prospect of an immediate solution. It has a negative and decisive impact on the situation in Guatemala which cannot be understood or tackled if it is not taken into account.

It should be acknowledged, with modesty and relativism, that it will not be possible to achieve any significant improvement in the human rights situation in the short term. A strengthened democratic Government, which is a genuine source of authority, based on the Constitution, public order safeguarded by the law, illegal centres of power brought under control or eliminated outright, a society that believes and trusts in the law, violence eschewed and tolerance embraced, an understanding of the need for pluralism and co-existence for all ideologies in a context of freedom, an acceptance, intellectually and at the practical level of the "human rights culture" are the conditions that must be met in order to improve the human rights situation in what can only be a lengthy and arduous process.

In order to advance in this process, democracy must perforce continue, there must be elections and the Constitution must be maintained. If there is any interruption of this process, the Government would not even be able to do what it has done so far despite its shortcomings, limitations and adverse conditions, but with sincerity and conviction, and there would be a backsliding into a maelstrom of unconfined violence and the horror of widespread and continued human rights violations, perpetrated, fanned and encouraged by governmental authority. This would be unacceptable. The Expert, therefore, believes that the maintenance of constitutional democracy in Guatemala, despite its limitations, shortcomings and weaknesses, is vital in order to envisage the protection of human rights in the future.

The Expert wished to make these comments as this will be his last report to the Commission. He considered that it was his duty to state his views in complete frankness, and without reticence of any kind.

During these years of contacts with the situation in Guatemala he has come to love the country and its people as if they were his own. That is why he is confident that Guatemala is capable of overcoming the anti-democratic violence and of securing respect for human rights, based on a fully effective Constitution and on the far-reaching changes needed in the present economic and social situation.

After examining the expert's final report, the Commission on Human Rights adopted on 7 March 1990 a resolution entitled "Assistance to Guatemala in the Field of Human Rights" (resolution 1990/80), the operative paragraphs of which are as follows (paras. 1–15):

Expresses its gratitude to the Expert for the work done during his term of office and thanks him for his report and recommendations;

Expresses its appreciation also to the Government of Guatemala for its collaboration with the Commission on Human Rights in carrying out its advisory activities, as well as for the facilities and co-operation afforded to the Expert;

Recognizes that, while the Government of Guatemala has upheld its commitment to guaranteeing the protection of fundamental rights and freedoms, it has been unable to implement the decision with sufficient authority, so that the social violence and violations of human rights have continued;

Supports therefore the recommendations contained in the Expert's report (E/CN.4/1990/45) that the programme of assistance and advisory services in the field of human rights should be continued and strengthened;

Urgently appeals to the Government of Guatemala to continue to accord priority to its undertaking under the Esquipulas II Agreements and to promote and participate more actively in the national reconciliation dialogue, as one of the ways of consolidating the democratic process;

Deeply deplores the increase in murders, kidnappings and attacks on and threats against persons involved in political activities as jeopardizing the democratization process;

Expresses its profound concern at the resurgence of the criminal activities of the "death squads", as indicated in the report of the Special Rapporteur to examine questions relevant to torture (E/CN.4/1990/17);

Deplores, in particular, the recent murders of a member of the National Revolutionary Movement Party (MNR) of El Salvador, Secretary for Latin America of the Socialist International, and of a Guatemalan lawyer, on 12 January 1990 in Guatemala, and requests the Government of Guatemala to continue and strengthen the investigation already under way, with a view to identifying and punishing the culprits;

Requests the Government of Guatemala to intensify its efforts to ensure that all its authorities and security forces fully respect the human rights and fundamental freedoms of the Guatemalan people;

Urges the Government of Guatemala to initiate or intensify, as the case may be, investigations aimed at identifying and bringing to justice those responsible for acts of torture, disappearance, murders and extra-legal executions;

Further urges the Government of Guatemala to promote any measures necessary to identify and punish members of "death squads";

Encourages the Government of Guatemala to strengthen policies and programmes relating to the situation of the indigenous populations, taking into account their proposals and aspirations, to enable them to enjoy fully their fundamental rights and freedoms;

Requests the Secretary-General to continue to provide the Government of Guatemala with such advisory services and other forms of assistance in the field of human rights as may be necessary to foster and strengthen the consolidation of the democratic process, and to promote a human rights culture;

Requests the Secretary-General to appoint an independent expert as his representative to examine the human rights situation in Guatemala and continue assistance to the Government in the field of human rights who, within the framework of his mandate, shall prepare a report with appropriate recommendations for submission to the Commission at its forty-seventh session;

Decides to consider this matter at its forty-seventh session under an item of the agency to be determined in the light of the above-mentioned report and of the situation of human rights and fundamental freedoms in Guatemala.

The independent expert appointed to carry out this task, Mr. Christian Tomuschat (Germany), visited Guatemala in 1990 and again in 1991, and informed the Commission on Human Rights about the unstable human rights situation in that country in two reports (UN Docs. E/CN.4/1991/5 and Add. 1). He visited Guatemala again in 1992, and reported on the continuing violation of human rights there (E/CN.4/1992/5). After a fifth visit to the country, he submitted a final report to the Commission in which he set out his overall conclusions and observations in the following terms (E/CN.4/1993/10, paras. 236–281):

As in the two preceding years, the Expert wishes to express his sincere gratitude to the Government of Guatemala for its willingness to cooperate with him. No obstacles or restrictions were placed in his way. He could freely travel to all parts of the country he wanted to visit and talk without any hindrance to persons from all walks of life. The President himself spent a whole day with him, showing him a number of social institutions designed to benefit the least favoured persons of Guatemalan society. On that occasion, the Expert had the opportunity to raise with the President many of the issues dealt with in the present report.

*Guatemalan Society and the Nobel Peace Prize.* One of the most outstanding events of 1992 was the award of the Nobel Peace Prize to Rigoberta Menchú Tum, a fighter for the human rights of indigenous peoples. This recognition of her work by the international community underlines the importance of indigenous peoples in countries where, although forming the majority of the population, as in Guatemala, they have suffered centuries-long discrimination by the authorities. In this connection Rigoberta Menchú stated in the Third Committee of the General Assembly on 17 November 1992 that her role as the new Nobel Laureate ". . . is to be a force for peace and the human rights of indigenous peoples", in the sense that "the internal armed conflict in my country and in other countries of the world has its causes, and it is only by dealing with these structural and historical causes that the conflict itself will be resolved politically".

*Overall Governmental Policies in the Field of Human Rights.* One of the major merits of the policies inaugurated by President Serrano is his unequivocal commitment to the peace process through negotiations with the URNG. The problem remains how a policy of respect for human rights and fundamental freedoms can be made the unmistakable hallmark of governmental policies at all levels. It is still doubtful whether the President has in that regard the unconditional support of the entire governmental machinery. No great strides ahead which would permit the elimination of this situation of structural tension can be expected in the near future.

*Public Insecurity.* The general climate of violence still remains one of the dominant features of Guatemala. Public authorities have not been able to effectively stem the wave of crimes against the life and physical integrity of individuals from almost all social sectors. However, the indigenous communities in the rural areas seem to be the group most affected. In most cases, it is extremely difficult to determine whether an offence should be categorized as being committed by common criminals or whether there has been involvement of the security forces of the State. All observers, among whom the most reliable source is the Human Rights Procurator, agree that many attacks on the life and physical integrity of individuals are in fact to be attributed to these forces, including the civilian self-defence patrols. On the other hand, the number of such crimes at the hands of security agents shows a significant decrease according to the statistics available for the first six months of 1992. However, it should be pointed out that the well-known pattern of extrajudicial executions persists: the targeted victims during 1992 were university professors and students, human rights defenders including union leaders, political leaders and members of the Catholic Church.

The civilian authorities continued their efforts directed towards making the rule of law the effective guiding principle of every state agent. However, the Expert is not aware that the recommendations contained in paragraph 188 of his last report (E/CN.4/1992/5), to the effect that the reliability of every member of the security forces should be checked by one and that, in order to create conditions of transparency, the organigrams of the national police and the armed forces should be made accessible to members of the public, have been heeded. He hereby formally renews this suggestion.

*Machinery for the Prevention and Repression of Crime—the National Police.* The National Police of Guatemala has not yet been able significantly to alter its profile of low effectiveness. The reopening of the Police Academy as well as some improvements of the salary structure may pave the way for a higher degree of professionalization tantamount to an increase in investigative power. Changes at the head of the National Police as well as in the post of the Minister of the Interior demonstrate the enormous difficulties experienced in trying to reorganize the police forces and raise their level of performance. As an emergency measure to counter a wave of violent crime in the capital in the spring of 1992, the task force "Hunapú", made up of elements of the National Police, the Policia Militar Ambulante and the Guardia de Hacienda, was established with the aim of patrolling the streets of Guatemala city. This task force again links the National Police closely with the armed forces. Although its creation, like that of the Sistema de Protección Civil (SIPROCI), may have been justified during a momentary crisis situation which seemed to overwhelm the capacity of the National Police, "Hunapú", together with SIPROCI, should again be dissolved at the earliest time. The existence of such special task forces creates the unfortunate and erroneous impression that even outside zones of armed conflict public order cannot be maintained without the assistance of the armed forces. Accordingly, the recommendation of the Expert to create a specialized unit within the National Police, to be entrusted with the investigation of all cases of enforced disappearance, extrajudicial killings and other political crimes, is now renewed and emphasized.

Efforts to make the National Police a professional instrument for the prevention and repression of crime and a disciplined body of the State which enjoys the confidence of all citizens must be continued and intensified. It should be the aim of the police authorities to attract candidates with a good level of education. Moreover, a strict organizational separation between the armed forces and the National Police should be established. In particular, the different police departments should be headed by civilians instead of military officers. The general intelligence services for matters other than those strictly of a military character should be under the National Police. Therefore, the present competences of the Servicio de Inteligencia Militar (G-2) should be reviewed to meet democratic standards. This approach should also be adopted by the Executive branch in order to replace what is now the Estado Mayor Presidencial by a civilian body composed of advisers to the President of the Republic.

*Machinery for the Prevention and Prosecution of Crime—Prosecutorial Authorities and the Judicial System.* The machinery for the prevention and repression of crime is still largely ineffective. In most cases of offences against the life and physical integrity of human beings, it is impossible to collect sufficient evidence to bring an indictment against any presumed perpetrators. If a person is put on trial, proceedings normally advance slowly and often end with an acquittal for lack of evidence so that the Commission of the crime remains without any sanction. It has again been reported that judges are put under pressure in connection with trials under their jurisdiction. The Public Procurator's office has appealed all of the judgements which to the outsider seemed to be marred by a hardly understandable leniency. In mid-November 1992, the final decision is still outstanding in many cases that are likely to shed a clear light on the ability of the judicial system of Guatemala effectively and objectively to deal with cases having a political background.

The recommendation made by the Expert (E/CN.4/1992/5, para. 190) to adopt the new Code of Criminal Procedure as a matter of urgency was heeded by the National Congress. The new Code will enter into force in September 1993, after a transitional period of one year. The new President of the Supreme Court has elaborated far-reaching plans to monitor the activities of judges, which again correspond to some extent to a recommendation by the Expert. It should be stressed, however, that efforts to prevent abuses of judicial independence must not impair and undermine that independence. While general examination of every single judicial act would simply appear to be excessive, swift action should be possible in instances where there exist clear indications that a judge has made use of the powers of his office in an irregular manner.

The extension of the military jurisdiction is excessive and is a blatant obstacle to the proper conduct of the legal proceedings in which members of the armed forces are accused of serious violations of human rights. In a democratic society the military jurisdiction is reserved exclusively for offences of a military nature committed by servicemen against servicemen. Apart from such cases, jurisdictional competence should rest with the ordinary courts of justice.

As far as the Public Prosecutor's office is concerned, the Expert urges the Government, in particular President Serrano, upon whom the Constitution confers direct responsibility (art. 252), to do everything in its power to ensure the effectiveness of the institution during the absence of its head officer, the Procurador General de la Nación. The National Congress should complete its consideration of the draft law on the Public Prosecutor's office as soon as possible in order to ensure that the new Code of Criminal Procedure may become effective in 1993 as currently planned.

*The Human Rights Procurator.* The Human Rights Procurator and his deputies in 1992 once again confirmed their well-deserved reputation as public officers committed in total independence and impartiality to the cause of human rights. Care will have to be taken that all collaborators, in particular the heads of the subsidiary offices in the Departments, are all inspired by the same spirit of attachment to the rule of law and show a similar firmness in denouncing attacks against the basic rights of individuals.

Taking into account the marginalized situation of the indigenous populations in Guatemala, the Human Rights Procurator should consider the strengthening of his office by the creation of a department dealing specifically with indigenous issues.

The activities of the Human Rights Procurator deserve the full support of the National Congress and the international community.

*Other Institutions for the Promotion and Protection of Human Rights.* The Presidential Coordinating Commission on Executive Policy in the Field of Human Rights (COPREDEH) received the necessary financial and human resources and became fully operational in the course of 1992. It serves, in particular, as a useful documentation centre for the Government with regard to all issues directly concerning human rights.

Within this context, COPREDEH should be the focal point of the Government to coordinate its efforts to comply with the international obligations contracted by Guatemala in the field of human rights. In particular, COPREDEH should *inter alia*: (i) coordinate the preparation of periodic reports under United Nations human rights conventions and, bearing in mind the recommendations of the Commission on Human Rights in its resolution 1992/54 on national institutions, to involve in such preparation the Human Rights Procurator and other interested organizations and make the national reports available to the general public; (ii) coordinate the preparation of replies to the United Nations extraconventional special procedures; (iii) promote the ratification of international human rights instruments such as the two Optional Protocols to the International Covenant on Civil and Political Rights, ILO Convention No. 169 concerning Indigenous and Tribal Peoples in Independent Countries; and to accept the declarations under article 22 of the Convention Against Torture and Other Cruel, Inhuman or Degrading Treatment or Punishment and article 14 of the Convention on the Elimination of All Forms of Racial Discrimination; (iv) review with the National Police and the armed forces all manuals used for training their personnel in order to ascertain whether these manuals take account of the generally accepted United Nations standards; (v) review the Military Code, Second Part (Code of Criminal Procedure) to comply with the requirements of the International Covenant on Civil and Political Rights; (vi) review domestic legislation to comply with the international human rights standards, in particular those of the International Covenant on Civil and Political Rights.

*The Armed Forces.* The Minister of Defence has on many occasions emphasized the unreserved loyalty of the armed forces to the democratically elected Government. Although many sources report strong tensions among top-rank military leaders, the armed forces have manifested that loyalty, in particular by fully and unreservedly participating in the peace negotiations with the URNG. The strategies employed by the armed forces in their fight against the guerrilla units still do not correspond to elementary rules on warfare since indiscriminate bombing and shelling of targets which are not strictly military ones continue.

There are still widespread allegations, based on solid evidence, that some elements of the armed forces are involved in attacks on the life and physical integrity of other citizens. The draft system has slightly improved, but is still marred by irregularities and discrimination to the detriment of the indigenous population.

It must be stressed once again that the armed forces need clear combat rules directing their units not to harm the civilian population in the disputed zones. A profound revision of the strategies employed appears all the more necessary since a large part of the refugees returning from Mexico intend to settle in the Ixcán area. The armed forces should generally follow the rules laid down in Additional Protocol II to the Geneva Conventions of 12 August 1949, as provisionally agreed in the peace negotiations with the URNG.

The draft bill on military and social service which has been elaborated in accordance with a corresponding recommendation of the Expert (E/CN.4/1992/5, para. 204) should be enacted by the National Congress as soon as possible. During the consideration of the bill, every effort should be made to ensure that none of its provisions contains regulatory elements which may turn out to legitimize discriminatory treatment to the detriment of members of indigenous communities.

Control mechanisms permitting the monitoring of compliance by the armed forces with their obligations under the Constitution and the laws of Guatemala are largely lacking. There is no public accountability. Rather, the armed forces still act to a large extent as a closed society. In particular, little preparedness exists to cooperate in investigating serious crimes attributed to members of the military. Thus, in the Estado Mayor Presidencial no disciplinary inquiry was initiated when it emerged that an officer of that unit was charged by the Public Prosecutor's office with being one of the murderers of the sociologist Myrna Mack. The armed forces must radically change their practices in that regard in order to restore military honour and to establish their legitimacy in a democratic society by winning the confidence of all Guatemalans.

*Civilian Self-Defense Patrols.* In most rural areas where civilian self-defence patrols and military Commissioners exist, pressure is being exerted on the local population to join the ranks of the patrols in contravention of article 34 of the Constitution. The patrols and the military Commissioners are responsible for many acts of violence against persons who disagree with their philosophy of unconditional warfare against any kind of "subversion". Additionally, they tend to undermine the authority of the civilian authorities at the local level. The Expert, while maintaining the recommendations contained in paragraph 193 of the previous report (E/CN.4/1992/5), welcomes the provisional agreement reached between the Government and the URNG and emphasizes that this agreement should be considered a first step for the definitive abolition of the patrols.

*The Guerilla Forces.* As in previous years, the Human Rights Procurator attributes a considerable number of violent attacks against civilians to the guerrilla forces. Like the armed forces, the guerrilla units should abide by the rules of warfare contained in Additional Protocol II to the Geneva Conventions of 12 August 1949. The guerrilla forces continued in 1992 their strategy of blowing up bridges and electric power lines. No justification can be found for such destruction, which harms the people of Guatemala. The guerrilla forces should desist forthwith from any activities which are capable of jeopardizing the rights of the large majority of Guatemalans who are not involved in the armed conflict.

*Freedom of Expression.* Although Guatemala continues to enjoy a remarkably high degree of freedom of expression, there exists a fatal tendency in Guatemalan society, including holders of public office, to stigmatize any views containing fundamental criticisms of governmental policies as "subversive", in particular if such criticisms coincide with positions defended by the URNG. As a consequence of this attitude, once again a number of journalists were physically attacked and received death threats.

Everyone must realize that freedom of opinion means first and foremost freedom to criticize. Of course, journalists in particular are required to report objectively and truthfully. But to inform the public about events that have actually happened, to analyse the background of these events and to articulate views as to the lessons to be drawn from the events is the right of everyone and constitutes a professional duty for every journalist. The fight against impunity, if pursued forcefully and with determination, would at the same time strengthen freedom of expression, which is one of the cornerstones of a democratic society.

*Freedom of Association.* The present system for the conferral of juridical personality on groups wishing to establish themselves as associations is unsatisfactory. It allows judgments to be made on political grounds and is flawed by excessive procedural delays in a manner inconsistent with freedom of association as a fundamental right of every citizen.

Human rights organizations, which have become an essential feature of Guatemalan society under the democratic Constitution of 1985, have not yet been fully accepted by the Government as legitimate groups acting as an opposition not only to the Government, but also to the other political forces represented in the National Congress. Assaults and threats against members of these groups have not stopped in 1992. Criminal charges brought against the leader of CERJ (Council of Ethnic Communities Runujel Junam) for alleged smuggling of arms to the guerrilla forces appear highly implausible to the outside observer. The prevailing situation raises all the more concerns since many of the human rights organizations were set up by members of the indigenous communities.

*Freedom of Correspondence and Communication.* According to widespread allegations, the security forces of the State have established a system for the control and opening of mail and the tapping of telephones. There is no law permitting such activities which would, if proved, constitute a serious violation of the fundamental rights of all Guatemalan citizens. The Government should look into the matter and submit a detailed report to the National Congress.

*Economic and Social Rights.* The situation of social and economic rights remains precarious in Guatemala. The deficiencies signalled in last year's report (E/CN.4/1992/5, paras. 153–170, 195) remain largely unchanged. Although Guatemala is still an economically weak country and a tradition of social neglect that has continued for decades cannot be remedied at once, the State of Guatemala has a direct responsibility in a number of areas. Greater efforts should be undertaken in the field of health care. Within a relatively short time-span, every child should be provided with essential basic needs, in particular food, health care, shelter and the opportunity to attend at least primary school. The present policies can be acknowledged as a first step in the right direction. But more drastic shifts in the budget of the nation are needed in order to satisfy all legitimate needs. A greater percentage of public spending should be devoted to the rural areas. The National Congress, in particular, is called upon to promote understanding for a greater degree of national solidarity and to shape its budget policies accordingly.

No real progress can be observed as far as the enforcement of minimum living standards is concerned. Unfortunately, some foreign investors, in particular in the textile industry, exploit the weak economic situation of Guatemala in an unscrupulous manner by threatening to close their factories if public control mechanisms should attempt to penalize them for breaches of the law in force.

*Indigenous Populations.* Through the award of the 1992 Nobel Peace Prize to Rigoberta Menchú, the whole of Guatemalan society has become aware of the unique position of Guatemala in Central America. The Nobel Prize citation itself emphasized that "the recognition of ethnic plurality and cultural diversity are keys to enabling countries such as Guatemala to define their true character as nations. The recognition of indigenous peoples as forming a majority in society is one of the starting points for recognition and respect of such profound values as the conception of the world, language, the forms of social organization, mankind's relationship with nature and, in short, his history". Nearly 70 per cent of the population are members of indigenous communities. In the political life of the nation, however, the indigenous people play only a modest role. In the National Congress, only 10 to 15 per cent of the deputies are of indigenous origin. A sign of a new constructive spirit is that the National Congress is considering the approval of the ratification of the ILO Convention No. 169 concerning Indigenous and Tribal Peoples in Independent Countries.

In the years to come, Guatemala will have to make a considerable effort to integrate the indigenous communities more closely into the life of the nation in the manner in which those communities themselves see fit. Bilingual education in Spanish as well as in the vernacular languages, already begun in some areas, should be intensified. It should also be stressed again that the Government and the society of Guatemala must accept the human rights organizations which, precisely because they articulate specific indigenous concerns, were in the past regarded with a high degree of mistrust. If the provisions of the Constitution (articles 66 to 70), as well as ILO Convention No. 169, are faithfully implemented, the current concerns of the indigenous communities will largely be met.

The Expert renews his recommendation (E/CN.4/1992/5, para. 198), which so far has gone unheeded, that a Ministry for Indigenous Affairs be established. At the same time, he wishes to state his satisfaction that the work on a law implementing the principles enshrined in the Constitution on indigenous communities has again been taken up with the services provided by Mr. A. Willemsen Díaz, a consultant of the United Nations Centre for Human Rights.

*The Democratic Process.* It is gratifying to note that the National Congress and the Government, both entrusted with a mandate by the electorate in 1990, have been able to discharge their constitutional responsibilities without any hindrance. On the other hand, in order to be fully effective, the democratic process requires full participation by all citizens without any discrimination. It is a fact that the indigenous communities are still to a great extent outside that process, hampered by their lack of education in articulating their needs and often unable, because of the deficient means of communication, to understand what is going on in the capital.

The Expert renews the recommendations contained in last year's report (E/CN.4/1992/5, para. 200). He insists, in particular, on the need to get rid of the highly pernicious concept of "subversion" in political struggles of an ideological nature. No one should be stigmatized as a foe of the national community as long as he is prepared to respect the rights of his fellow citizens. The Government is of course fully entitled to defend the positions which it considers best suited to the common interest of the nation. But it must accept that other political groups have a similar right to hold that governmental policies should take a different direction.

*The Negotiating Process between the Government and the URNG.* The negotiating process, although still focused on the first point of the agreed agenda, namely human rights, has made considerable progress in 1992. The two sides disagree only on the nature and the starting date of the verification system concerning the future agreement of human rights.

The armed conflict has already lasted too long. The loss of human lives and the material damages entailed by it are a heavy burden which has poisonous repercussions in all fields of social life. The Expert had hoped that the agenda of the peace negotiations could be disposed of by the end of 1992, an expectation which has not materialized. He urges both sides to complete their work early in 1993. If the negotiations were to drag on beyond 1993, they would definitively lose any momentum and both sides would be harmed equally; any chance that a peace agreement could be con-

cluded before the end of the term of office of President Serrano would be lost. Both sides must be reminded of their responsibilities vis-à-vis the people of Guatemala, which have just one desire, namely to live in peace. It is the people of Guatemala who are the great losers if no compromise solution is reached.

*Refugees and Displaced Persons.* The conclusion of an agreement on the return of the refugees living in Mexico, which took place on 8 October 1992 between the permanent Commissions of refugees and CEAR, the body entrusted in the Government of Guatemala with the relevant responsibilities, can be seen as a first step in a long-term process of normalization, made possible by the existence of a democratically elected Government in Guatemala. The agreement sets forth important guarantees to the benefit of the returnees. In particular, they have received firm assurances that they will not have to serve in the civilian self-defence patrols; that, on account of the heavy burden which building a new existence entails, they are exempted from military service for a duration of three years; and that the Government will assist them in recovering their former possessions or acquiring new land.

A carefully balanced verification mechanism, which includes the Expert, will ensure that the agreement is dutifully complied with. Under the new verification mechanism, the Expert would be assisted in the field by an official of the Centre for Human Rights who, as a delegate of the Expert, would monitor the fulfilment of the conditions stipulated in the agreement and report to the Expert, who would present his reports to the Commission on Human Rights. In this context it is essential that the Commission takes the Appropriate action so that funds are made available for the financing of the Expert's delegate to be posted in Guatemala on a permanent basis during the period of repatriation of the Guatemalan refugees from Mexico.

The Expert appeals to both sides to implement the agreement in good faith in order to make it a model for future arrangements that should emerge from the peace process. The agreement should not be considered a political "victory" by either party. Any such interpretation could have disturbing negative repercussions.

The situation of the "Comunidades de Población en Resistencia" (CPR) in the areas affected by the armed conflict has not significantly improved in 1992. They are still largely cut off from contacts with the rest of the country, although they have been able to establish an office in the capital. The State of Guatemala is required to treat the members of those communities like all other Guatemalan citizens. On the other hand, the CPR must accept that the areas in which they live are an integral part of the territory of Guatemala, not subject to any special status. It is deplorable that they imperilled the health of their children by not permitting a vaccination campaign prepared by the International Committee of the Red Cross to be carried out, simply because the Government insisted that the medical team be accompanied by an employee of the Ministry of Public Health.

The Expert urges both sides to reconsider their positions and to normalize the situation in the relevant areas. It is clear that the armed forces bear a particularly heavy responsibility in this regard. If they continue to treat the CPR with suspicion, equating them with the guerilla forces, the anomalous situation as it exists today cannot be overcome.

*Further Action by the Commission.* The Expert has noted many positive elements in the reports; on the other hand, numerous negative elements cannot be overlooked either. Under these circumstances, he feels that the human rights situation in Guatemala requires essentially a political assessment which can only be made by a political body. Consequently, he confirms his earlier recommendation, suggesting that Guatemala's human rights record should continue to be observed by the Commission on Human Rights, leaving the appropriate method of observation to the discretion of the Commission.

### Final Observations

Progress towards ending the armed conflict has been slow, albeit real and tangible, in 1992. It has been said many times and remains true that human rights can flourish only under conditions of peace. The main obstacle impeding swift progress in the negotiations between the Government and the URNG is mutual distrust. The Government fears that by making too many concessions it could destabilize the country. The URNG, for its part, is haunted by the fear that any pledges made by the Government could reveal themselves very quickly to be mere paper constructions, lacking any real substance. Thus, a deliberate effort at mutual confidence building, which needs no contractual basis, should accompany the negotiating process.

As pointed out elsewhere in this report, the URNG should forthwith desist from attacking and destroying elements of the social infrastructure of the country. It could thus demonstrate that the common interest of the nation is its primary objective. The Government, on its part, should rid itself of the fears and anxieties of a past where the cold war may have posed a real threat of foreign domination through groups inspired by a worldwide ideology alien to Guatemala. In order to prevent any sympathies for "leftist" ideas from taking root, even the mere expression of opinions that did not conform to a canon of conservative orthodoxy was made subject to prosecution and persecution. Under a democratic constitution, which sets forth freedom of expression and political equality of all citizens, such practices must be definitively abandoned. Times have changed. Guatemala finds itself today in a different international context. The simple fact is that views are now being voiced which for decades could not be articulated on the national soil. This is not the price, but the fruit of freedom. Only by permitting everyone to avail himself freely of all the rights that are the normal prerogatives of a citizen in a genuinely democratic country can Guatemala hope to accomplish modernization and raise its level of development in all fields.

Full and unreserved recognition of the equal rights of all citizens is the core element of a process of mutual confidence building. It requires tolerance not only of all actors in the political arena, but of every single citizen. The ugly concept of subversion must be renounced once and for all because it encompasses in a pernicious fashion attacks on the basic political philosophy of a liberal State, namely recourse to violent means, and advocacy of political ideas by canvassing in a peaceful manner strategies alternative to those pursued by the Government. Guatemala must accept the challenge of such alternative blueprints for its society. If the leading elites opt for suppressing the free competition of ideas, they risk imperilling the long-term stability of the country. The Expert trusts that all parties involved—the social organizations, the political parties, the indigenous communities, the National Congress, the Government and the URNG—are aware of the basic truth that Guatemala is the homeland of all of them and that mechanisms for the peaceful vindication and coordination of their rights and interests must be found if the nation as a whole is to live in human dignity.

At its 1994 session, the UN Commission on Human Rights examined the first report of the new independent expert, Ms. Mónica Pinto (E/CN.4/1994/10), together with information concerning the situation in Guatemala appearing in reports of the Special Rapporteur on Enforced or Involuntary Disppearances (E/CN.4/1994/26 and Corr. 1 and Add. 1), the Special Rapporteur on Extrajudicial, Summary or Arbitrary Executions (E/CN.4/1994/7 and Corr. 1–2 and Add. 1–2), and the Working Group on Enforced or Involuntary Disappearances (E/CN.4/1994/26 and Corr. 1 and Add. 1). On the basis of information contained in those reports, the Commission, in resolution 1994/58 of 4 March 1994, "welcomed the mobilization of the people of Guatemala, which has made possible the restoration of the constitutional order and the rule of law following the events of 25 May 1993 and which has led to the appointment as constitutional President of the Republic of Mr. Ramiro de León Carpio, whose work as Human Rights Procurator has been widely recognized by Guatemalan society." It took note in particular of "the legal and institutional reforms introduced by the Government with a view to combatting impunity and guaranteeing the full enjoyment of human rights and fundamental freedoms by everyone in Guatemala."

At the same time the Commission took into account "the fact that the continuation of the internal armed conflict is a factor affecting the human rights situation in Guatemala," and expressed its concern "that there continue to be human rights violations attributed to members of the armed forces and security forces, and to the so-called voluntary civil self-defense committees," and that "situations of impunity continue to exist and that in cases of human rights violations there has been little progress in the investigations and/or the judicial proceedings."

On 29 March 1994, representatives of the Government of Guatemala met in Mexico City with those of the Guatemalan National Revolutionary Union and concluded a UN-sponsored agreement that includes a schedule for putting a stop to the 33-year-old civil war by the end of 1994. Under the agreement a UN human rights verification commission will investigate allegations of human rights abuses in Guatemala with the right to travel freely and to interview any person having information relevant to its probe. Previously, the military had opposed any such investigations on the ground that they might only provide a basis for anti-army propaganda.

The 29 March agreement bars all paramilitary organizations and secret detention centers, ends forced recruitment into the army, and affirms the rights of freedom of movement and of association. It further provides for the demobilization of units of the National Revolutionary Union and their reintegration into Guatemalan society by December 1994, when a "lasting peace agreement" was expected to be signed. However, fighting continued and in April 1994, President de León Carpio authorized the military to oversee the internal security of the country, a short time after the assassination of the President of the Constitutional Court. Negotiations continued on issues such as resettlement of refugees, and UN-sponsored peace talks again took place in early 1995 with the URNG and the government agreeing to offer recognition to indigenous people.

**BIBLIOGRAPHY.** American Association for the Advancement of Science. *Guatemala: Case Reports 1980–1985.* Washington, D.C.: 1986. NGO report, in English.

American Association for the International Commission of Jurists. *Guatemala: A New Beginning.* New York: 1987. NGO report, in English.

Americas Watch. *Guatemala: Rights Abuses Escalate as Elections Near.* New York: Human Rights Watch, 1990. NGO factfinding report, in English.

Amnesty International. *Guatemala: Extrajudicial Executions and Human Rights Violations against Street Children.* London: 1990. NGO factfinding report, in English and French.

————. *Guatemala: The Human Rights Record.* London: 1987. NGO report, in English.

Asociacion Centroamericana de Familiares de Detenidos-Desaparecidos (Central American Association of Families of the Detained and Disappeared). *La Practica de la Desaparicion Forzada de Personas en Guatemala* (The Practice of Forced Disappearance of Persons in Guatemala). San Jose, Costa Rica: 1988. NGO report, in Spanish; bibliography (annotated by key words), pp. 297–304.

Balsells Tojo, Edgar Alfredo. *El Procurador de los Derechos Humanos* (The Human Rights Ombudsman). Guatemala City, Guatemala: Procurador de los derechos humanos, 1990. Government report, in Spanish.

Ciencia y Tecnologia para Guatemala (Science and Technology for Guatemala). *Tortura y Legalidad en Guatemala* (Torture and Legality in Guatemala). Mexico City, Mexico: 1986. NGO monograph, in Spanish.

Clark, Roger, George Lovell, and Katharine Pearson. *Guatemala in the 90's: Civilian Face, Military Reality.* Ottawa, Canada: Central America Monitoring Group, 1991. NGO factfinding report, in English.

Comision de Derechos Humanos de Guatemala (Guatemala Human Rights Commission). *El Niño Guatemalteco en la Coyuntura Actual* (Guatemalan Children in the Current Coyuntura Actual). Mexico City, Mexico: 1986. NGO report, in Spanish.

————. *Regarding the Status of Human Rights for the Indigenous Population of Guatemala.* Geneva: 1985. NGO bulletin, in English.

————. *Report on the Situation of Human Rights in Guatemala.* Mexico City, Mexico: 1991. NGO factfinding report, in Spanish.

Comision para la Defensa de los Derechos Humanos (Commission for the Defense of Human Rights). *Informe sobre la Situacion de los Derechos Humanos en Centro-america, 1986* (Report on the Human Rights Situation in Central America, 1986). San Jose, Costa Rica: 1987. NGO monograph, in English.

Comite Pro-Justicia y Paz de Guatemala (Justice and Peace Committee of Guatemala). *Human Rights in Guatemala.* Mexico City, Mexico: 1987. NGO report, in English.

Fédération Internationale des Droits de l'Homme, Fondation Danielle Mitterand. *Rapport de mission: Guatemala, 4–12 avril 1991* (Mission Report: Guatemala, 4–12 April 1991). Paris: 1991. NGO factfinding report, in French.

Guatemala Human Rights Commission (USA). *Report on the Situation of Human Rights in Guatemala.* Washington, D.C.: 1986. NGO report, in English.

Heinz, Wolfgang S. *Ursachen und Folgen von Menschenrechtsverletzungen in der Dritten Welt* (Causes and Consequences of Human Rights Violations in Third World Countries). Saarbrucken, FRG: Verlag Breitenbach, 1986. Scholarly monograph, in German; bibliography on Guatemala, pp. 529–530.

Hey, Hilde. "Human Rights and Guatemalan Displaced Persons," *Netherlands Quarterly of Human Rights* 10, no. 4 (1992): 461–480. Scholarly article, in English.

Human Rights Watch. "Guatemala," in *Human Rights Watch World Report 1995,* pp. 93–99. New York, 1995. NGO report, in English.

Inter-Church Committee on Human Rights in Latin America. *1986 Annual Report on the Human Rights Situation in Guatemala.* Toronto, Canada: 1987. NGO report, in English.

————. *1987 Annual Report on the Human Rights Situation in Guatemala.* Toronto, Canada: 1987. NGO report, in English.

International Human Rights Law Group and Washington Office on Latin America. *Political Transition and the Rule of Law in Guatemala.* Washington, D.C.: 1988. NGO mission report, in English.

Klothen, Kenneth L. *Children without Childhood: Violations of Children's Rights in Guatemala, 1990.* Swarthmore, PA, USA: Children's Rights International, 1990. NGO factfinding report, in English.

Krueger, C., and K. Enge. *Security and Development Conditions in the Guatemalan Highlands.* Washington, D.C.: Washington Office on Latin America, 1985. NGO mission report, in English; bibliography, p. 68.

Lawyers Committee for Human Rights. *The UN Advisory Services Program in Guatemala.* New York: 1990. NGO report, in English.

Lytton, Timothy. "Exodus and the Struggle for Deliverance: Guatemalan Refugees in Mexico," *International Journal of Refugee Law* (Sept. 1990): 173–180. Scholarly article, in English.

Manz, Beatriz. *Refugees of a Hidden War: The Aftermath of Counterinsurgency in Guatemala.* Albany, NY, USA: State University of New York Press, 1988. Scholarly monograph, in English.

Martin, Julie Carleton, and Jeffrey Svoboda. "Unearthing the Truth: Grassroots Organizing in the Guatemalan Highlands," *Harvard Human Rights Journal* 3 (Spring 1990): 240–245. Scholarly article, in English.

Minnesota Lawyers International Human Rights Committee. *Expectations Denied: Habeas Corpus and the Search for Guatemala's Disappeared.* Minneapolis, MN, USA: 1988. NGO report, in English.

————. *Justice Suspended: The Failure of the Habeas Corpus System in Guatemala.* Minneapolis, MN, USA: 1990. NGO factfinding report, in English.

Organization of American States. *Annual Report of the Inter-American Commission on Human Rights 1986–1987.* Washington, D.C.: 1987. IGO annual report, in English.

Painter, John. *Guatemala: False Hope, False Freedom.* London: Latin America Bureau and Catholic Institute for International Relations, 1987. NGO monograph, in English.

Petersen, Kurt. *The Maquiladora Revolution in Guatemala.* New Haven, CT, USA: Orville H. Schell Jr. Center for International Human Rights, Yale Law School, 1992. Scholarly monograph, in English.

Rouquette, R., A. Garapon, and A. Breton. *Guatemala: Sur la Situation Generale et Notamment Celle des Droits de l'Homme* (Guatemala: The General Situation and Current Status of Human Rights). Paris: Federation Internationale des Droits de l'Homme, 1985. NGO mission report, in French.

Simon, Jean-Marie. *Guatemala: Eternal Spring—Eternal Tyranny.* New York: W. W. Norton, 1987. Monograph, in English.

United Nations Commission on Human Rights. *Report by the Independent Expert, Mr. Christian Tomuschat, on the Situation of Human Rights in Guatemala.* Geneva, Switzerland: 1991. IGO document, in English and French.

————. *Report on the Situation of Human Rights in Guatemala.* Prepared by Special Rapporteur Viscount Colville of Culross. 13 February 1986. IGO document, in English; *Report . . . on the Situation of Human Rights in Guatemala.* Prepared by Special Rapporteur Viscount Colville of Culross, E/CN.4/1987/24. 5 December 1986. IGO document, in English.

Washington Office on Latin America. *Habits of Repression: Military Accountability for Human Rights Abuse Under the Serrano Government in Guatemala, 1991–1992.* Washington, D.C.: 1992. NGO report, in English.

**GUINEA.** The Republic of Guinea is a country in western Africa, on the Atlantic Ocean. It has borders with Guinea-Bissau, the Ivory Coast, Liberia, Mali, Senegal, and Sierra Leone. It achieved independence from France in 1958 and became a member of the United Nations the same year. Its population is estimated to be 7,726,000. Ethnic groups include the Fulani (40%), Malinke (26%), Susu (11%), Kissi (5%), and many others. Languages commonly used include French (official), Malinke, Susu, and Fulani. Religions practiced include Islam (70%), Animism (29%), and Christianity (1%). Literacy is estimated at 30%.

The government (1994) took the form of a republic. However, following a military coup in March 1984, the constitution was suspended. All State power was assumed by the *Comite Militaire de Redressement National,* the chairman of which became president of the republic. He was assisted by a vice president and council of ministers appointed by himself. One of the first acts of the military government was to release all political prisoners, to declare the observance of human rights to be one of its primary objectives, and to reorganize the judiciary to increase its independence.

President Lansana Conté, who promoted himself from colonel to brigadier-general after the 1984 coup, succeeded Sékou Touré, who had made Guinea Africa's first Marxist State and who had ruled with scant regard for human rights for 26 years. Touré died in the United States following surgery.

Guinea became independent by overwhelmingly rejecting the proposal that it should remain voluntarily as part of French West Africa under the Fifth Republic constitution drafted in 1958 by Gen. Charles de Gaulle. Angered by the 95% "no" vote, de Gaulle withdrew more than 4,000 French administrators, doctors, judges, technicians, and teachers from the territory with a view to teaching a lesson to other colonies considering total independence. The departing French civil servants burned their records, files, blueprints, and operating manuals, and left the country in an administrative shambles.

The efforts of Guinea's first president, Ahmed Sékou Touré, to replace French workers with substitutes from eastern-bloc nations was unsuccessful. Although Guinea was the first marxist State in Africa, the Soviet Union and other eastern countries provided little administrative help or guidance. Guinea's capital, Conakry, became the K.G.B. center for West Africa, and its airstrip was used to ferry Cuban soldiers into the area. Once considered the "pearl of West Africa" because of its wealth in gold, diamonds, and bauxite, Guinea saw its mining industries disintegrate from neglect and its people reduced to famine by collectivist farm policies.

President Lansana Conté's first official act was to send a mission to Paris, seeking assistance in rebuilding the nation's railroads, highways, and buildings, in paving its streets, and in restoring its public transportation. Since that time, French has been reintroduced in Guinean primary schools, and French instructors have retrained Guinean soldiers, policemen, journalists, teachers, and members of the medical professions. French entrepreneurs have opened stores, beauty parlors, restaurants, and discotheques.

President Conté's opposition maintains that the French are trampling Guinea's dignity and national independence. The reply of the government is to express the hope that Americans, Germans, and Italians will join the French in aiding Guinea's reconstruction.

The president has promised the people of Guinea a new constitution, including a bill of rights, an independent judiciary, periodic multi-party elections, and a government that functions by majority rule. He has also introduced a program of economic rehabilitation meeting the free-market requirements of the World Bank and has eliminated State-operated collective farms.

***REPORT ON THE INTERNATIONAL COVENANT ON CIVIL AND POLITICAL RIGHTS.*** As a State party to the **INTERNATIONAL COVENANT ON CIVIL AND POLITICAL RIGHTS,** Guinea submitted its second periodic report (CCPR/C/79/Add. 30) to the **HUMAN RIGHTS COMMITTEE** at its forty-seventh session. After considering the report at its 1222nd to 1224th meetings, held on

1 and 2 April 1992, the Committee adopted the following observations (CCPR/C/79/Add. 20):

### Positive Aspects

Since the consideration of the initial report, it should be pointed out that Guinea has adopted a basic law which has the value of a constitution and contains a title concerning fundamental rights and freedoms; the Law was adopted by referendum on 23 December 1990. The military courts and the State Security Court have been discontinued. The delegation announced that Guinea would soon accede to the optional Protocol.

### Factors and Difficulties that Impede Implementation of the Covenant

According to the representative of Guinea, the legacy of the former regime, which was responsible for torturing several thousands of people and for mass disappearances, has left marks and bad habits in the Administration. Instances of violations (irregular arrests and ill-treatment) are not reported because the victims are resigned. The force of tradition and custom is an obstacle to the exercise of the rights of the Covenant concerning, more particularly, customs and the family.

### Main Grounds for Concern

The Committee expressed concern at the general character of the provisions of article 22 of the Basic Law which permit it to limit the rights and freedoms of the individual for reasons relating to public order. It fears that implementation of these provisions might lead Guinea to enact laws instituting restrictions on rights and freedoms that go beyond those permitted by the Covenant. The Committee expressed concern at the establishment under the Basic Law of the Supreme Court of Justice which does not seem to it to comply with the requirements of article 14 of the Covenant. Several cases of ill-treatment and torture have been reported and have remained unpunished. There have been arrests and detentions for reasons of a political nature during the period covered by the report. Peaceful demonstrations have ended in bloodshed owing to excessive use of firearms by the police. The Committee is also concerned regarding the implementation of article 27 of the Covenant.

### Suggestions and Recommendations

The Committee recommended that, during this period of major legislative change, the Government of the Republic of Guinea take account of the provisions of the Covenant with a view to introducing them into its internal legislation. It suggested, in particular, that the Government adopt detailed regulations governing firearms to enable it to respect article 6 of the Covenant and also rules applicable to police custody and detention consistent with article 9 of the Covenant. Investigations should be ordered systematically when a violation is reported. An appropriate penalty should be imposed on the guilty when they are identified. Measures should also be taken to fully implement the guarantees provided for in article 27 of the Covenant.

The Committee emphasized the need to develop programmes of education concerning human rights and specific programmes to be used in training law enforcement officers with the assistance, where necessary, of the Centre for Human Rights.

The Government was invited to promote the development of organizations specializing in the protection and promotion of human rights.

**BIBLIOGRAPHY.** Amnesty International. *A Summary of Amnesty International's Concerns in the Republic of Guinea.* London: 1986. NGO report, in English.

*Freedom of Information and Expression in Guinea.* London: Article 19, 1989. NGO report, in English.

Ligue Francaise pour la Defense des Droits de l'Homme et du Citoyen (French League for the Defense of Human Rights and the Citizen). "Un Communique de la Ligue des Droits de l'Homme sur les Declarations Recentes des Dirigeants Guineens" (Communiqué of the League for the Defense of Human Rights on the Recent Declarations of the Guinean Authorities), 24 July 1985. NGO press release, in French.

Radda Barnen, International Commission of Jurists (Swedish Section). *UN Assistance for Human Rights.* Stockholm: 1988. NGO report, in English.

**GUINEA-BISSAU.** The Republic of Guinea-Bissau is a country in western Africa, on the Atlantic Ocean; its territory includes about 25 islands off the coast. It has borders with Guinea and Senegal. It achieved independence from Portugal in 1974 and became a member of the United Nations the same year. Its population is estimated to be 1,060,000. Ethnic groups include the Balante (27%), Fulani (23%), Malinke (12%), Mandjako (11%), and Pepel (10%). Languages commonly used include Portuguese (official) and Crioulo. Religions practiced include Animism (65%), Islam (30%), and Christianity (5%). Literacy is estimated at 10%.

The government (1994) took the form of a republic. However, the constitution was suspended in 1980 when a military *coup d'etat* deposed the president, and all State power was assumed by the nine-member Council of the Revolution. The president of the Council, Brig. General Joao Bernardo Vieira, is president of the republic and head of State and government; he is assisted by a 15-member Council of Ministers and five State secretaries. The only political party is the African Party for the Independence of Guinea-Bissau and Cape Verde.

**BIBLIOGRAPHY.** Amnesty International. "Guinea Bissau: Death Penalty," 14 July 1986. NGO urgent action bulletin, in English.

**GUYANA.** The Cooperative Republic of Guyana is a country in tropical South America, on the Atlantic Ocean. It has borders with Brazil, Suriname, and Venezuela. Formerly known as British Guiana, it achieved independence from Great Britain in 1966 and became a member of the United Nations the same year. Its population is estimated to be 737,000. Ethnic groups include persons of East Indian (51%), African (30%), and Amerindian (6%) descent. Languages commonly used include English (official), Hindi, and Urdu. Religions practiced include Christianity (Roman Catholic, 18%; Anglican 16%; other Protestant denominations, 18%), Hinduism (34%), and Islam (14%). Literacy is estimated at 86%.

The government (1994) took the form of a republic and member of the Commonwealth. In Guyana, executive power is exercised by the president, Hugh Desmond Hoyte, who is head of State and of government and leader of a 24-member cabinet. Legislation is dealt with by the unicameral National Assembly, composed of 53 members elected by popular vote and 12 elected by local councils, all for five-year terms. Elections are held under a single-list system with proportional representation. Political parties include the People's National Congress, the People's Progressive Party, the United Force, and the Working People's Alliance.

**BIBLIOGRAPHY.** Americas Watch Committee and Parliamentary Human Rights Group. *Political Freedom in Guyana.* New York: 1985. NGO mission report, in English.

Amnesty International. "Death Penalty: Guyana," 1 July 1986. NGO urgent action bulletin, in English.

Colchester, Marcus. "Sacking Guyana," *Multinational Monitor* 12, no. 9 (Sept. 1991): 8–14. NGO article, in English.

Forcese, Craig. *Decolonizing Guyana's Interior: Recommendations on the Reform of Laws Pertaining to the Amerindian Peoples of Guyana.* Georgetown, Guyana: Canadian Lawyers Association for International Human Rights and Amerindian Peoples Association, 1994. NGO report, in English.

Guyana Human Rights Association. *Brief on Police Violence.* Georgetown, Guyana: 1988. NGO report, in English.

———. *Guyana Human Rights Report 1989.* Georgetown, Guyana: 1988. NGO annual report, in English.

Participating Consulting Team. *The Challenge of Democratic Development in Guyana, Participlan, March 1993.* Canada: 1993. NGO report, in English.

# H

**HABEAS CORPUS.** An order of habeas corpus legally requires that a detained person be brought before a judge or court within a specified time for investigation of the legality of his detention.

The **INTERNATIONAL COVENANT ON CIVIL AND POLITICAL RIGHTS** provides in article 9 (4) that: "Anyone who is deprived of his liberty by arrest or detention shall be entitled to take proceedings before a court, in order that the court may decide without delay on the lawfulness of his detention and order his release if the detention is not lawful."

Bearing this provision in mind, the UN **COMMISSION ON HUMAN RIGHTS** invited its **SUB-COMMISSION ON PREVENTION OF DISCRIMINATION AND PROTECTION OF MINORITIES** (resolution 1991/34) to consider the question of the effectiveness of this procedure, commonly known as habeas corpus, and similar remedies during states of emergency, and to formulate its suggestions thereon.

The Sub-Commission, at its 1991 session, considered (1) recommendations prepared by its Working Group on Detention, (2) article 9 of the draft declaration which the Sub-Commission had adopted one year earlier on the protection of all persons from enforced or involuntary disappearances (resolution 1990/33) providing that States shall ensure under all circumstances, including emergencies, to right to an effective judicial remedy, including habeas corpus, as a means of determining the whereabouts or the state of health of persons deprived of their liberty and/or identifying the authority ordering or carrying out the deprivation of liberty; and (3) the draft guidelines for the development of legislation on states of emergency contained in the report of the Special Rapporteur on human rights and states of emergency (E/CN.4/Sub.2/1991/28, annex I), and in particular section 8 thereof, which provides that "No person deprived of his liberty . . . shall be denied . . . the right to challenge the legality of the deprivation before a court of law by habeas corpus or other prompt and effective remedy."

On the basis of these considerations, the Sub-Commission proposed, and the Commission on Human Rights later adopted, resolution 1992/35 of 28 February 1992, in which it called upon "all States that have not yet done so to establish a procedure such as habeas corpus by which anyone who is deprived of his or her liberty by arrest or detention shall be entitled to institute proceedings before a court, in order that the court may decide without delay on the lawfulness of his or her detention and order his or her release if the detention is found to be unlawful"; and also called upon all States "to maintain the right to such a procedure at all times and under all circumstances, including during states of emergency."

**SEE ALSO** *Fair Trial.*

**BIBLIOGRAPHY.** Eguiguren, Francisco P., and Milagros Maraví Sumar. "Análisis de las Principales Tendencias Cuantitativas en la Jurisprudencia de Hábeas Corpus en el Perú (1983–1990)" (Analysis of the Principal Quantitative Tendencies in Habeas Corpus Jurisprudence in Peru), *Boletín—Comisión Andina de Juristas* 28 (March 1991): 9–21. Scholarly article, in Spanish.

International Commission of Jurists, Centre for the Independence of Judges and Lawyers. *Chile: A Time of Reckoning: Human Rights and the Judiciary.* Geneva, Switzerland: 1992. NGO report, in English.

Mandler, John P. "Habeas Corpus and the Protection of Human Rights in Argentina," *The Yale Journal of International Law* 16, no. 1 (Winter 1991): 1–72. Scholarly article, in English.

Minnesota Lawyers International Human Rights Committee. *Justice Suspended: The Failure of the Habeas Corpus System in Guatemala.* Minneapolis, MN, USA: 1990. NGO factfinding report, in English.

United Nations Advisory Services Program. *Regional Seminar on Amparo, Habeas Corpus, and Other Similar Remedies.* New York: 1961. ST/TAO/HR/12.

Villavicencio C., Miguel. "Protección del Derecho a la Integridad Personal en el Perú" (Protection of the Right to Security of the Person in Peru), *Boletín—Comisión Andina de Juristas* 28 (March 1991): 35–54. Scholarly article, in Spanish.

**HABITAT INTERNATIONAL COALITION.** Founded in 1976, in the aftermath of the UN Conference on Human Settlements in Vancouver, Canada, HIC acts as an international pressure group to defend the rights of the homeless, the poor, and the inadequately housed. HIC recognizes the right of everyone to secure a place in which to live in peace and dignity. It actively provides advice, training, and information on the organization, management, and use of techniques in such fields as shelter, building materials, employment, infrastructure, and services. HIC has members in 72 countries and is in consultative status with the UN **ECONOMIC AND SOCIAL COUNCIL** (Roster) and **UNESCO.** HIC publishes the quarterly *HIC News* in English, Spanish, and French.

Habitat International Coalition. Address: Cordobanes 24, San José Insurgentes, 03900 Mexico DF, Mexico. Telephone: (52-5) 651-68-07. Fax: (52-5) 593-51-94. Secretary: Enrique Ortiz.

**HAITI.** The Republic of Haiti is a country which occupies the western third of the island of Hispaniola, in the West Indies. It has a border with the Dominican Republic, which occupies the remainder of the island. It achieved independence from France in 1804 and became a member of the United Nations in 1945. Its population is estimated to be 6,509,000. Ethnic groups include persons of African (90%), French (5%), and mixed (5%) descent. Languages commonly used are French (official) and Creole. Religions practiced include Christianity (Roman Catholic and several Protestant denominations) and a variety of folk beliefs. Literacy is estimated at 20%.

The government (1994) took the form of a republic. However, in recent years it has been governed for the most part by military dictatorships headed, respectively, by Francois "Papa Doc" Duvalier, his son Jean Claude "Baby Doc" Duvalier, General Henri Namphy and General Raoul Cédras.

Jean-Claude Duvalier, the son of former dictator Francois Duvalier, who had seized power and established a regime based on the use of secret police in 1957, was no less ruthless than his father in suppressing any hint of opposition. After succeeding his father "Papa Doc" in 1971, "Baby Doc" ruled over the poorest and most densely populated country in the western hemisphere, until forced to flee the country in 1985 in the face of public protests and the threat of an uprising.

After Baby Doc Duvalier fled the country in February 1986, a military-civilian council headed by Gen. Henri Namphy assumed control; and in, 1987, voters approved a new constitution. In elections of January 1988, Leslie Manigat was named president, but opposition leaders charged widespread fraud. Gen. Namphy seized control in June of that year, naming himself as president, but he was ousted by a coup in September 1988. By mid-1990, five governments had been in power since the exile of Baby Doc Duvalier.

Between 1981 and 1990, the UN **COMMISSION ON HUMAN RIGHTS** examined materials relating to the human rights situation in Haiti within the framework of its confidential "communications" procedure, under which neither the allegations nor the response of the government is made public. These materials showed that the basic civil rights of Haitian citizens, including freedoms of expression, opinion, press, assembly, and association in trade unions, had been arbitrarily suspended or suppressed. Haitians were alleged to be regularly arrested without charge, detained without trial, and denied fair hearings and due process of law. Haitian lawyers were said to be fearful of representing their clients and of being subjected to intimidation in cases of political trial. The courts and the administration of justice were reported to be run by judges, appointed by the "President for Life" (the Duvaliers), who lacked the independence to make judgments against abuses of human rights.

The special security officers or militia, known as the *Tonton Macoutes,* were said to be responsible for large-scale corruption, violence, and harassment, including illegal arrests, detention in unknown places, interrogation under torture, and killings; they also engaged in activities of extortion and raids on public meetings. Human rights activists, political opponents, independent journalists, radio broadcasters, trade union leaders, and priests were reported to have been imprisoned without charge.

On 12 March 1990, Gen. Prosper Avril, leader of the Haitian army and of the unofficial Tonton Macoutes, left Haiti aboard a craft provided by the government of the United States of America. Justice Ertha Pascal-Trouillot, the only woman on Haiti's Supreme Court, was nominated as provisional president after civilian political leaders had rejected Chief Justice of the Supreme Court Gilbert Austin because of his past association with Gen. Avril. Mrs. Pascal-Trouillot announced that her principal task would be to lead the country to early elections.

On 16 December 1990, the Rev. Jean-Bertrand Aristide was elected president of Haiti by a large majority of voters in that country's first free and peaceful election, monitored by representatives of the United Nations, the **ORGANIZATION OF AMERICAN STATES,** and a number of governmental and non-governmental representatives. He was sworn in on 7 February 1991, but his presidency was overthrown by the military establishment on 30 September of that year as the result of a violent coup led by Lieut. General Raoul Cédras.

After Aristide had made a factual presentation of the situation to the UN **SECURITY COUNCIL** on 3 October (S/PV.3011), the UN **GENERAL ASSEMBLY** (resolution 46/7) strongly condemned both the attempted illegal replacement of the constitutional president of Haiti and the use of violence, military coercion, and the violation of human rights in that country, and affirmed as unacceptable "any entity resulting from that illegal situation." It demanded "the immediate restoration of the legitimate Government of President Jean-Bertrand Aristide, together with the full application of the National Constitution and hence the full observance of human rights in Haiti."

During 1992 the situation in Haiti continued to deteriorate, and the General Assembly, in resolution 42/20 of 24 November, expressed its great alarm at "the persistence and worsening of gross violations of human rights, in particular summary and arbitrary executions, involuntary disappearances, reports of torture and rape, arbitrary arrests and detentions, as well as the denial of freedom of expression, of assembly and of association." It was concerned "that the persistence of this situation contributes to a climate of fear of persecution and economic dislocation which could increase the number of Haitians seeking refuge in neighboring Member States, and convinced that a reversal of this situation is needed to prevent its negative repercussions on the region." For these reasons it requested the UN Secretary-General to take the necessary measures in order to assist, in cooperation with the Organization of American States, in the solution of the Haitian crisis.

On 17 June 1993, the UN Security Council imposed a severe arms and oil embargo on Haiti. After a series of negotiations brokered by the UN, Aristide and Cédras signed the Governors Island Agreement (UN Doc. A/47/975) on 3 July, calling for Cédras to resign, Aristide to return to the presidency, and democratic order to be restored in Haiti by 30 October. A further agreement, the New York Pact, was signed on 16 July, and the sanctions were lifted at that time.

However, on 13 October 1993, the sanctions were reimposed by the Security Council after a two-day rampage by Haitian gunmen prevented an American ship, the *Harlan County*, from landing although they were to be deployed as part of the United Nations Mission to Haiti. The action was taken by the Council in the light of a report by the Secretary-General (S/26573) that the military authorities of Haiti, including the metropolitan police of Port-au-Prince, had not complied with the Governors Island Agreement. When the 30 October deadline for Aristide to return to Haiti passed, he remained in the United States of America.

The UN General Assembly, on 6 December 1993, again strongly condemned the attempt to replace unlawfully the constitutional president of Haiti, the employment of violence and military coercion and the violation of human rights in this country, and also condemned "all attempts to delay or prevent the immediate reinstatement of President Jean-Bertrand Aristide as the constitutional President of Haiti." It expressed its profound concern for the fate of the Haitian people and reasserted that the Haitian military authorities were fully responsible for the suffering resulting directly from their disrespect for the Haitian

Constitution and for their public commitments to the Governors Island Agreement.

In May 1994, the Security Council tightened its sanctions on Haiti, banning travel by its military leaders and all commerce except food, medicine, cooking oil and journalistic supplies. President Bill Clinton of the United States of America reversed his policy of returning Haitian "boat people" to their country without a hearing on their claims for refugee status, and commercial air traffic between the United States and Haiti was cut off.

On 7 July 1994, some 2,000 U.S. marines appeared in waters off Haiti to "practice for an invasion." On 31 July the Security Council voted, 12 to 0, with 2 abstentions, to authorize the use of force against Haiti. On 17 September President Clinton sent former U.S. President Jimmy Carter, Chief of Staff General Colin Powell, and Senator Sam Nunn to negotiate with Cédras. An agreement was reached under which Cédras would step down when Parliament had passed an amnesty law exonerating his followers from prosecution for their activities or on 15 October, whichever came first.

On 19 September U.S. forces, as authorized by the Security Council, began to land in Haiti, and were warmly welcomed. On 10 October, Cédras resigned and shortly thereafter left for Panama, which had offered him asylum. And on 15 October Aristide resumed his presidency and began the enormous task of restoring civil and human rights to his ravaged nation.

Haitian refugees in "safe havens" in various countries were forcefully repatriated when they refused to return home. The U.S. military contingent was replaced by 6,000 UN peacekeepers in March 1995 as concerns about security mounted following the assassination of an opposition politician who had planned to stand in the 1995 presidential elections. She was one of several victims of such slayings.

**BIBLIOGRAPHY.** Americas Watch. *Fugitives from Injustice: The Crisis of Internal Displacement in Haiti.* New York: Human Rights Watch, 1994. NGO report, in English.

————. *Rape in Haiti: A Weapon of Terror.* New York: Human Rights Watch, 1994. NGO report, in English.

————. *Terror Prevails in Haiti: Human Rights Violations and Failed Diplomacy.* New York: Human Rights Watch, 1994. NGO report, in English.

Americas Watch and National Coalition for Haitian Refugees. *Silencing a People: The Destruction of Civil Society in Haiti.* New York: Human Rights Watch, 1993. NGO factfinding report, in English.

Americas Watch, National Coalition for Haitian Refugees, and Caribbean Rights. *Haiti: The Aristide Government's Human Rights Record.* New York: Human Rights Watch, 1991. NGO factfinding report, in English.

Americas Watch, National Coalition for Haitian Refugees, and Physicians for Human Rights. *Return to the Darkest Days: Human Rights in Haiti since the Coup.* Boston, MA, USA: 1991. NGO factfinding report, in English.

Amnesty International. *Haiti: Deaths in Detention, Torture and Inhuman Prison Conditions.* London: 1987. NGO report, in English.

Anderson, Leslie, E. J. Kelley, and Zarakivi Kinnunen. *Restavek: Child Domestic Labor in Haiti.* Minneapolis, MN, USA: Minnesota Lawyers International Human Rights Committee, 1990. NGO factfinding report, in English.

Comite Haitiano-Venezolano de Defensa de los Derechos Humanos (Haitian-Venezuela Committee for the Defense of Human Rights). "Mujeres de Haiti" (Haitian Women), *Bambu, Voz de la Libertad* 9 (January–March 1985). NGO special issue, in Spanish.

Human Rights Watch. "Haiti," in *Human Rights Watch World Report 1995,* pp. 99–104. New York: 1995. NGO report, in English.

Latin American Bureau. *Haiti: Family Business.* London: 1985. Monograph, in English; bibliography, pp. 83–84.

Lawyers Committee for Human Rights. *Expulsions of Haitians and Dominico-Haitians from the Dominican Republic.* New York: 1991. NGO factfinding report, in English.

———. *Refugee Refoulement: The Forced Return of Haitians under the U.S.-Haitian Interdiction Agreement.* New York: 1990. NGO factfinding report, in English.

———. *Warning Signs in Haiti: The Multinational Force and Prospects for the Rule of Law.* New York: 1994. NGO report, in English.

Legomsky, Stephen H. "The Haitian Interdiction Programme, Human Rights, and the Role of Judicial Protection," *International Journal of Refugee Law* (Sept. 1990): 180–189. Scholarly article in special issue, in English.

National Coalition for Haitian Refugees and Americas Watch. *In the Army's Hands: Human Rights in Haiti on the Eve of the Elections.* New York: 1990. NGO factfinding report, in English.

O'Neill, W. G., and E. J. Schrage. *Paper Laws, Steel Bayonets: Breakdown of the Rule of Law in Haiti.* New York: Lawyers Committee for Human Rights, 1990. NGO factfinding report, in English.

Organization of American States, Inter-American Commission on Human Rights. *Report on the Situation of Human Rights in Haiti.* Washington, D.C.: 1993. Annual report. IGO report, in English.

Plant, Roger. *Sugar and Modern Slavery: A Tale of Two Countries.* London: Zed Press, 1987. Scholarly monograph, in English.

Trouillot, Michel-Rolph. *Haiti: State against Nation. The Origins and Legacy of Duvalierism.* New York: Monthly Review Press, 1990. Monograph, in English.

**HAMMARSKJÖLD, DAG (1905–1961).** Recipient of the 1961 **NOBEL PEACE PRIZE,** Dag Hammarskjöld is the only person to be awarded the prize posthumously. Born in Jonkoping, Sweden, Hammarskjöld descended from a family of Swedish statesmen, his father Hjalmar having been prime minister, a member of the Hague Tribunal, and chairman of the board of the Nobel Foundation. Hammarskjöld received a B.A. in 1925, an M.A. in 1928, and a law degree in 1930 from Uppsala University; and a Ph.D. in economics from the University of Stockholm in 1934.

After a briefing teaching stint at the University of Stockholm, Hammarskjöld began his career as a public servant, often serving in more than one capacity at a time. At first, he served as secretary of the Bank of Sweden in 1935 and was later to be head of this institution (1941–1948); concurrently, from 1936 to 1945, he served as under-secretary of the Swedish Department of Finance. In 1946, he took on another job, serving as financial adviser to the Swedish Ministry of Foreign Affairs. In 1951, he became deputy foreign minister, in which position he kept Sweden free of a military commitment to NATO. Finally, in 1949, he served as the Swedish delegate to the United Nations, a post he held again from 1951 to 1953. In addition to these posts, he served as Swedish representative to the **COUNCIL OF EUROPE** and to the Organization for European Economic Cooperation during the 1940s.

In 1953, the UN **SECURITY COUNCIL** elected Hammarskjöld Secretary-General of the United Nations, a post he held until his death in 1961 and the position for which he is remembered. During his tenure as Secretary-General, Hammarskjöld redefined the role, becoming an active participant in world affairs, employing negotiation between parties to maintain peace in the world's hotspots. His first success came in 1955 when he secured the release of fifteen American airmen who had been shot down over China. In 1955, he defused the Suez Crisis between Israel and Egypt by setting up demarcation lines and sending in the first UN peacekeeping mission—UNEF I. Sent in November 1956, UNEF I was withdrawn in June 1967; its mission was to secure and supervise the cessation of hostilities first in the Suez Canal sector and the Sinai peninsula and to serve as a buffer between Egyptian and Israeli forces.

In 1958, Hammarskjöld established the United Nations Observation Group in Lebanon (UNOGIL), whose brief mission (June to December 1958) was to ensure that no illegal personnel or arms crossed the border between Lebanon and Syria.

Then, in 1960, civil war threatened the Congo, which had achieved independence from Belgium a few months earlier. In July, Hammarskjöld installed the United Nations Operations in the Congo (ONUC) initially to ensure withdrawal of Belgian forces and to assist the fledgling government in maintaining law. Soon, however, the ONUC was maintaining the territorial integrity and political independence of the new nation and trying to remove all foreign military, paramilitary, and advisory personnel, including mercenaries, not under UN command. As the complicated situation worsened, Hammarskjöld personally visited the Congo to confer with the president of Katanga province, where fighting had recently broken out between UN forces and Katangan troops. On the night of 17–18 September 1961, his plane crashed near the border between the Congo and Rhodesia. He and fifteen others were killed.

**BIBLIOGRAPHY.** *Current Biography.* New York: W.H. Wilson & Company, 1953; Obituary, 1961.

Gray, Tony. *Champions of Peace.* London: Paddington Press, 1976.

Hammarskjöld, Dag. *Servant of Peace.* New York: Harper & Row, 1962.

Schlessinger, Bernard S., and June H. Schlessinger, eds. *Who's Who of Nobel Prize Winners.* Phoenix, AZ, USA: Oryx Press, 1991.

**HANDICAP INTERNATIONAL.** Established in 1982 in Lyon, France, this non-governmental organization works for the rehabilitation of physically disabled persons in third-world countries. HI trains local technicians in appropriate technologies to create small prosthetics (using locally available materials) and physical rehabilitation units. In 1994, specialized technicians, physiotherapists, and medical doctors associated with HI worked in 65 rehabilitation programs in 26 countries and territories.

HI publishes the quarterly *Handicap International* in French.

Handicap International. Address: 14 Ave. Berthelot, F-69361, Lyon, Cedex 107 France. Telephone: (33) 7969-7979. Fax: (33) 7869-7994. President: Jean-Nobel Serseron.

**HANDICAPPED PERSONS' RIGHTS: DECLARATION ON THE RIGHTS OF MENTALLY RETARDED PERSONS, UN (1971).** In adopting this Declaration, the UN GENERAL ASSEMBLY drew international attention to the necessity of assisting mentally retarded persons to develop their abilities in various fields and to promote their integration as far as possible into normal life.

The Declaration was adopted by the General Assembly on 20 December 1971 (resolution 2856 [XXVI]). The text, annexed to the resolution, is as follows:

The General Assembly,

Mindful of the pledge of the States Members of the United Nations under the Charter to take joint and separate action in cooperation with the Organization to promote higher standards of living, full employment and conditions of economic and social progress and development,

Reaffirming faith in human rights and fundamental freedoms and in the principles of peace, of the dignity and worth of the human person and of social justice proclaimed in the Charter,

Recalling the principles of the Universal Declaration of Human Rights, the International Covenants on Human Rights, the Declaration of the Rights of the Child and the standards already set for social progress in the constitutions, conventions, recommendations and resolutions of the International Labour Organisation, the United Nations Educational, Scientific and Cultural Organization, the World Health Organization, the United Nations Children's Fund and other organizations concerned,

Emphasizing that the Declaration on Social Progress and Development has proclaimed the necessity of protecting the rights and assuring the welfare and rehabilitation of the physically and mentally disadvantaged,

Bearing in mind the necessity of assisting mentally retarded persons to develop their abilities in various fields of activities and of promoting their integration as far as possible in normal life,

Aware that certain countries, at their present stage of development, can devote only limited efforts to this end,

Proclaims this Declaration on the Rights of Mentally Retarded Persons and calls for national and international action to ensure that it will be used as a common basis and frame of reference for the protection of these rights:

1. The mentally retarded person has, to the maximum degree of feasibility, the same rights as other human beings.

2. The mentally retarded person has a right to proper medical care and physical therapy and to such education, training, rehabilitation and guidance as will enable him to develop his ability and maximum potential.

3. The mentally retarded person has a right to economic security and to a decent standard of living. He has a right to perform productive work or to engage in any other meaningful occupation to the fullest possible extent of his capabilities.

4. Whenever possible, the mentally retarded person should live with his own family or with foster parents and participate in different forms of community life. The family with which he lives should receive assistance. If care in an institution becomes necessary, it should be provided in surroundings and other circumstances as close as possible to those of normal life.

5. The mentally retarded person has a right to a qualified guardian when this is required to protect his personal well-being and interests.

6. The mentally retarded person has a right to protection from exploitation, abuse and degrading treatment. If prosecuted for any offence, he shall have a right to due process of law with full recognition being given to his degree of mental responsibility.

7. Whenever mentally retarded persons are unable, because of the severity of their handicap, to exercise all their rights in a meaningful way or it should become necessary to restrict or deny some or all of these rights, the procedure used for that restriction or denial of rights must contain proper legal safeguards against every form of abuse. This procedure must be based on an evaluation of the social capability of the mentally retarded person by qualified experts and must be subject to periodic review and to the right of appeal to higher authorities.

**HARVARD LAW SCHOOL HUMAN RIGHTS PROGRAM.** Established in 1984, the Human Rights Program offered by Harvard Law School, Cambridge, MA, USA, supplies impetus and direction to the school's concern for the universal realization of human rights and fundamental freedoms. By making work in the field of human rights a significant part of legal education, the program complements domestic law courses by stressing the international and comparative dimensions of human rights.

The courses, conducted by Harvard Law faculty and visiting lecturers in human rights, explore political and civil rights and topics such as torture and arbitrary detention, race and gender discrimination, conflicts between religious and secular order, freedom of expression and modes of political participation, the organization and protection of labor, the provision of food and health care, and ethnic conflict and self-determination. The program also encourages independent advocacy and policy-oriented research that may be pursued in the academic environment or that may involve field work in the U.S. or abroad, and invites visiting fellows for varying periods.

In addition to regular courses and independent research, HRP offers Harvard law students summer internships to work for two months with public interest groups or international organizations concerned with human rights; some positions are in the United States, but most are in other countries.

In the spring of 1988, the Human Rights Program published the inaugural issue of the *Harvard Human Rights Journal*. This student-edited publication includes articles of general interest written by scholars, student-written notes reviewing human rights aspects of U.S. foreign policy, personal reflections of Harvard interns on their experiences, and reviews of books on human rights.

Human Rights Program, Harvard Law School. Address: Pound Hall 401, Harvard Law School, Cambridge, MA 02138, USA. Telephone: (617) 495-9362. Fax: (617) 495-1110. Administrative Director: Jack Tobin.

## HEALTH AS A HUMAN RIGHT.

The **UNIVERSAL DECLARATION OF HUMAN RIGHTS,** of 10 December 1948, proclaims that:

*Article 25.* Everyone has the right to a standard of living adequate for the health and well-being of himself and of his family, including food, clothing, housing and medical care and necessary social services, and the right to security in the event of unemployment, sickness, disability, widowhood, old age or other lack of livelihood in circumstances beyond his control.

The Declaration of the Rights of the Child (see **CHILDREN'S RIGHTS**), proclaimed on 29 November 1959, states:

*Principle 4.* The child shall enjoy the benefits of social security. He shall be entitled to grow and develop in health; to this end special care and protection shall be provided to him and to his mother, including adequate pre-natal and post-natal care. The child shall have the right to adequate nutrition, housing, recreation and medical services.

The **INTERNATIONAL COVENANT ON ECONOMIC, SOCIAL AND CULTURAL RIGHTS** contains the following provision:

*Article 12.* 1. The States Parties to the present Covenant recognize the right of everyone to the enjoyment of the highest attainable standard of physical and mental health.

2. The steps to be taken by the States Parties to the present Covenant to achieve the full realization of this right shall include those necessary for:

(a) the provision for the reduction of the stillbirth-rate and of infant mortality and for the healthy development of the child;

(b) The improvement of all aspects of environmental and industrial hygiene;

(c) The prevention, treatment, and control of epidemic, endemic, occupational, and other diseases;

(d) The creation of conditions which would assure to all medical service and medical attention in the event of sickness.

The International Convention on the Elimination of All Forms of Racial Discrimination (see **RACIAL DISCRIMINATION**), of 21 December 1965, states:

*Article 5.* In compliance with the fundamental obligations laid down in article 2 of this Convention, States Parties undertake to prohibit and to eliminate racial discrimination in all its forms and to guarantee the right to everyone, without distinction as to race, colour, or national or ethnic origin, to equality before the law, notably in the enjoyment of the following rights: . . .

(e) . . . (iv). The right to public health, medical care, social security and social services.

The Declaration on the Rights of Mentally Retarded Persons, of 20 December 1971, states:

2. The mentally-retarded person has a right to proper medical care and physical therapy and to such education, training, rehabilitation and guidance as will enable him to develop his ability and maximum potential.

The Declaration on the Rights of Disabled Persons, of 9 December 1975, states:

6. Disabled persons have the right to medical, psychological and functional treatment, including prosthetic and orthetic appliances, to medical and social rehabilitation, education, vocational training and rehabilitation, aid, counselling, placement services and other services which will enable them to develop their capabilities and skills to the maximum and will hasten the process of their social integration or reintegration.

The Convention on the Elimination of All Forms of Discrimination against Women, of 18 December 1979, states:

*Article 14.* 2. States Parties shall take all appropriate measures to eliminate discrimination against women in rural areas in order to ensure, on a basis of equality of men and women, that they participate in and benefit from rural development and, in particular, shall ensure to such women the right: . . .

(b) to have access to adequate health care facilities, including information, counseling and services in family planning.

The Body of Principles for the Protection of All Persons Under Any Form of Detention or Imprisonment (see **PRISONERS**), of 9 December 1988, states:

*Principle 22.* No detained or imprisoned person shall, even with his consent, be subjected to any medical or scientific experiment which may be detrimental to his health.

*Principle 24.* A proper medical examination shall be offered to a detained or imprisoned person as promptly as possible after his admission to the place of detention or imprisonment, and thereafter medical care and treatment shall be provided whenever necessary. This care and treatment shall be provided free of charge.

The Convention on the Rights of the Child (see **CHILDREN'S RIGHTS**), of 20 November 1989, includes the following provision:

*Article 24.* 1. States Parties recognize the right of the child to the enjoyment of the highest attainable standard of health and to facilities for the treatment of illness and rehabilitation of health. States Parties shall strive to ensure that no child is deprived of his or her right of access to such health care facilities.

2. States Parties shall pursue full implementation of this right and, in particular, shall take appropriate measures:

(a) To diminish infant and child mortality;

(b) To ensure the provision of necessary medical assistance and health care to all children with emphasis on the development of primary health care;

(c) To combat disease and malnutrition, including within the framework of primary health care, through, inter alia, the application of readily available technology and through the provision of adequate nutritious foods and clean drinking-water, taking into consideration the dangers and risks of environmental pollution;

(d) To ensure appropriate prenatal and postnatal health care for mothers;

(e) To ensure that all segments of society, in particular parents and children, are informed, have access to education and are ]supported in the use of basic knowledge of child health and nutrition, the advantages of breast-feeding, hygiene and environmental sanitation and the prevention of accidents;

(f) To develop preventive health care, guidance for parents and family planning education and services.

3. States Parties shall take all effective and appropriate measures with a view to abolishing traditional practices prejudicial to the health of children.

4. States Parties undertake to promote and encourage international co-operation with a view to achieving progressively the full realization of the right recognized in the present article. In this regard, particular account shall be taken of the needs of developing countries.

The International Convention on the Protection of the Rights of All Migrant Workers and Members of Their Families (see **MIGRANT WORKERS**), of 18 December 1990, states:

*Article 28.* Migrant workers and members of their families shall have the right to receive any medical care that is urgently required for the preservation of their life or the avoidance of irreparable harm to their health on the basis of equality of treatment with nationals of the State concerned. Such emergency medical care shall not be refused them by reason of any irregularity with regard to stay or employment.

The Principles for the Protection of Persons with Mental Illness and the Improvement of Mental Health Care, of 17 December 1991, state:

*Principle I .* (1) All persons have the right to the best available mental health care, which shall be part of the health and social care system.

***DECLARATION OF ALMA-ATA (1978).*** The Declaration was adopted by the International Conference on Primary Health Care, convened at Alma-Ata, Union of Soviet Socialist Republics, from 6 to 12 September 1978, under the joint sponsorship of the **WORLD HEALTH ORGANIZATION** and the **UNITED NATIONS CHILDREN'S FUND**. It was endorsed by the UN **GENERAL ASSEMBLY** on 29 November 1979 (resolution 34/58), in which the Assembly noted with approval the decision which the World Health Assembly had taken (resolution WHA 32.30) stating that the development of the programs of the World Health Organization and the allocation of its resources at the global, regional, and country levels should reflect the commitment of that organization to the priority of the achievement of health for all by the year 2000. The Assembly called upon every competent United Nations body to coordinate with, and support, the efforts of the World Health Organization to achieve that goal. The text of the declaration (UN Doc. E/ICEF/L. 1387, annex, sect. V) is as follows:

The International Conference on Primary Health Care, meeting in Alma-Ata this twelfth day of September in the year nineteen hundred and seventy-eight, expressing the need for urgent action by all governments, all health and development workers, and the world community to protect and promote the health of all the people of the world, hereby makes the following Declaration:

*I.* The Conference strongly reaffirms that health, which is a state of complete physical, mental and social wellbeing, and not merely the absence of disease or infirmity, is a fundamental human right and that the attainment of the highest possible level of health is a most important world-wide social goal whose realization requires the action of many other social and economic sectors in addition to the health sector.

*II.* The existing gross inequality in the health status of the people particularly between developed and developing countries as well as within countries is politically, socially and economically unacceptable and is, therefore, of common concern to all countries.

*III.* Economic and social development, based on a New International Economic Order, is of basic importance to the fullest attainment of health for all and to the reduction of the gap between the health status of the developing and developed countries. The promotion and protection of the health of the people is essential to sustained economic and social development and contributes to a better quality of life and to world peace.

*IV.* The people have the right and duty to participate individually and collectively in the planning and implementation of their health care.

*V.* Governments have a responsibility for the health of their people which can be fulfilled only by the provision of adequate health and social measures. A main social target of governments, international organizations and the whole world community in the coming decades should be the attainment by all peoples of the world by the year 2000 of a level of health that will permit them to lead a socially and economically productive life. Primary health care is the key to attaining this target as part of development in the spirit of social justice.

*VI.* Primary health care is essential health care based on practical, scientifically sound and socially acceptable methods and technology made universally accessible to individuals and families in the community through their full participation and at a cost that the community and country can afford to maintain at every stage of their development in the spirit of self-reliance and self-determination. It forms an integral part both of the country's health system, of which it is the central function and main focus, and of the overall social and economic development of the community. It is the first level of contact of individuals, the family and community with the national health system bringing health care as close as possible to where people live and work, and constitutes the first element of a continuing health care process.

*VII.* Primary health care:

1. reflects and evolves from the economic conditions and socio-cultural and political characteristics of the country and its communities and is based on the application of the relevant results of social, biomedical and health services research and public health experience;

2. addresses the main health problems in the community, providing promotive, preventive, curative and rehabilitative services accordingly;

3. includes at least: education concerning prevailing health problems and the methods of preventing and controlling them; promotion of food supply and proper nutrition; an adequate supply of safe water and basic sanitation; maternal and child health care, including family planning; immunization against the major infectious diseases; prevention and control of locally endemic diseases; appropriate treatment of common diseases and injuries; and provision of essential drugs;

4. involves, in addition to the health sector, all related sectors and aspects of national and community development, in particular agriculture, animal husbandry, food, industry, education, housing, public works, communications and other sectors; and demands the coordinated efforts of all those sectors;

5. requires and promotes maximum community and individual self-reliance and participation in the planning, organization, operation and control of primary health care, making fullest use of local, national and other available resources; and to this end develops through appropriate education the ability of communities to participate;

6. should be sustained by integrated, functional and mutually-supportive referral systems, leading to the progressive improvement of comprehensive health care for all, and giving priority to those most in need;

7. relies, at local and referral levels, on health workers, including physicians, nurses, midwives, auxiliaries and community workers as applicable, as well as traditional practitioners as needed, suitably trained socially and technically to work as a health team and to respond to the expressed health needs of the community.

*VIII.* All governments should formulate national policies, strategies and plans of action to launch and sustain primary health care as part of a comprehensive national health system and in coordination with other sectors. To this end, it will be necessary to exercise political will, to mobilize the country's resources and to use available external resources rationally.

*IX.* All countries should cooperate in a spirit of partnership and service to ensure primary health care for all people since the attainment of health by people in any one country directly concerns and benefits every other country. In this context the joint WHO/UNICEF report on primary health care constitutes a solid basis for the further development and operation of primary health care throughout the world.

*X.* An acceptable level of health for all the people of the world by the year 2000 can be attained through a fuller and better use of the world's resources, a considerable art of which is now spent on armaments and military conflicts. A genuine policy of independence, peace, détente and disarmament could and should release additional resources that could well be devoted to peaceful aims and in particular to the acceleration of social and economic development of which primary health care, as an essential part, should be allotted its proper share.

The International Conference on Primary Health Care calls for urgent and effective national and international action to develop and implement primary health care throughout the world and particularly in developing countries in a spirit of technical cooperation and in keeping with a New International Economic Order. It urges governments, WHO and UNICEF, and other international organizations, as well as multilateral and bilateral agencies, non-governmental organizations, funding agencies, all health workers and the whole world community to support national and international commitment to primary health care and to channel increased technical and financial support to it, particularly in developing countries. The Conference calls on all the aforementioned to collaborate in introducing, developing and maintaining primary health care in accordance with the spirit and content of this Declaration.

*THE WORLD HEALTH ORGANIZATION.* Within the United Nations system, primary responsibility for the preparation and supervision of international measures relating to the right to health lies with the **WORLD HEALTH ORGANIZATION.** Before the World Health Organization was established in 1948, international instruments having a bearing upon the right to health were prepared mainly by the **INTERNATIONAL LABOR ORGANIZATION,** which, as early as 1921, concluded a convention calling for annual health examinations of seamen under the age of 16 and the provision of medical certificates to them; or by regional organizations such as the Pan American Union, which in 1924 promulgated the Pan American Sanitary Code with a view to preventing the international spread of communicable diseases. That code, and many similar regional agreements, was replaced by the comprehensive International Health Regulations adopted in Boston on 25 July 1969 by the World Health Assembly.

From its inception the World Health Organization has devoted all its efforts and available resources to the realization of the basic principle stated in the preamble to its constitution: "The enjoyment of the highest attainable standard of health is one of the fundamental rights of every human being without distinction of race, religion, political belief, economic and social conditions." WHO's definition of health includes "physical, mental and social well being." WHO has declared (UN Doc. A/CONF. 32/8):

Without health, other rights have little meaning. The right to health, however, cannot be exercised by the people unless the conditions which make a healthy life possible are provided and unless health services and health facilities are available. WHO considers that the basic health services essential for the provision of adequate health protection to the community should cover:
  —care of mothers and children including midwifery;
  —nutrition;
  —prevention and control of communicable diseases;
  —sanitation and water supply;
  —health education;
  —occupational health.

These also, in the main, are the fields of WHO's activity and since 1948 have received an increasingly greater share of the Organization's efforts. The study of WHO's current program reveals that they are still among its major concerns. But there have been significant changes of method in approaching these problems, as a result of accumulated experience.

*Care of Mothers and Children, including Midwifery.* Health is a fundamental right of the child and the mother. This means a right to special care and protection and the ability to live and develop in a healthy and normal manner. Without care and education at home and at school, all acquired rights of adults may be limited or unattainable. Increased value is placed on the health and well-being of women and children. Recent years have witnessed a widening in demand for maternal and child health services throughout the world and a new awareness of the importance of health and the fact that children need not suffer and die.

The services needed to protect and promote the health of mothers and children are closely interrelated. They include pre-natal supervision, including treatment of important infections and other diseases,

correction of anemia and malnutrition, natal and post-natal care, the very important education of pregnant women in mothercraft, continuing health supervision, and total medical care of all children from birth through childhood and adolescence.

WHO advocates integration of originally separate maternal and child health services into the basic health services, as it is a suitable arrangement for countries short of staff and funds and as it is an instrument for widening the health coverage given to the child population.

*Nutrition.* It is alarming to record that about two-thirds of the world's population is still suffering from under-nutrition or malnutrition, in spite of a tremendous improvement in techniques and possibilities for increasing the food crops of the earth. The most important and widespread disorders of malnutrition are protein-calorie deficiency diseases, lack of vitamin A, nutritional anemias and endemic goiter. Of these, protein-calorie deficiency disease and hypovitaminosis A principally affect weaning infants and pre-school children, while nutritional anemias, particularly of the iron deficiency type, are widespread among women of child-bearing age.

Experience has shown that improved nutrition lowers infant mortality and the mortality of children under five years of age, in which malnutrition or undernutrition are clearly among the main factors. The devastating interaction of malnutrition and the ordinary infectious diseases of childhood is now well known.

WHO's efforts to relieve malnutrition and to promote good nutrition include the implementation of applied nutrition programs with the assistance of **FAO** and **UNICEF,** and assistance in organizing nutritional rehabilitation centers in areas where malnutrition of young children is prevalent. The Organization also supports research into nutritional diseases and methods for their control, and into protein requirements of children.

*Control of Communicable Diseases.* It is becoming increasingly clear that the improvement of the people's health depends largely on the extent to which the developing countries can rid themselves of communicable diseases, which are responsible for an enormous amount of sickness, disability and loss of working time.

Much has already been accomplished, but very much remains to be done. The experience of recent years has shown that the communicable diseases still continue to be a most important challenge to the health, welfare and happiness of mankind. Cholera, small pox and tuberculosis are still currently and potentially major causes of death and morbidity. Malaria is still far from being eradicated. Governments express general concern at the increased incidence of such diseases as venereal diseases, infectious hepatitis, bilharziasis, etc. It is WHO's task to assist them in their efforts to bring the communicable diseases under control.

It is now generally recognized that eradication of the major communicable diseases can be achieved, provided that the following conditions are fulfilled: strengthening of the basic health services, systematic expansion of health facilities, establishment of priorities and the synchronization of efforts in neighboring countries. Experience in the field has shown that the control of communicable diseases can only be carried out through a comprehensive network of health centers. The WHO-assisted control programs today tend to put more emphasis on the development of rural health services, improvement in sanitation and health education, and integration of specialized programs into the general public health services.

*Sanitation and Water Supply.* The need for clean and abundant water supplies is a primary one for all living creatures. Of almost equal importance to the health of man is the need for efficient and adequate disposal of human and other wastes. Population growth, urbanization and industrialization are causing an increase in the scope and complexity of environmental health problems. Contaminated water and insanitary conditions play a major role in the spread of cholera and other enteric diseases. Water-borne diseases are one of the causes of the high infant mortality in developing countries. These diseases also place a heavy burden on families and communities. It has however long been recognized that health conditions are bound to improve greatly with the introduction of satisfactory sanitation conditions.

These considerations have led WHO to assign major importance to the improvement of environmental hygiene. The Organization's present program aims at strengthening national community water supply and waste disposal programs, development of country projects and training of sanitary engineers and sanitarians.

*Health Education.* The attainment of the highest standard of health is not only the right of every human being, it is also his duty to use his own resources to improve his health and standard of living. Improvement in health conditions depends, to a large extent, upon action by the community and therefore education of the public is an important factor. The main aim of health education is to help people achieve health by their own actions and efforts and to stimulate them to take an active and responsible part in support of various efforts designed to strengthen and promote health services.

WHO's program in health education includes assistance in the planning and organization of the education services in the national health programs, integration of the health education services into the general public health administration, training of health work-

ers in health education, and assistance to health education in schools.

*Occupational Health.* The protection and promotion of the health of people at work is an increasingly important element of every health program. This is particularly the case in developing countries where many classes of skilled labor are in short supply and where there is a direct, and major, relationship between health and productivity.

The scope of occupational health has been defined by the Joint ILO/WHO Committee on Occupational Health as "the promotion and maintenance of the highest degree of physical, mental and social well-being of workers in all occupations; the prevention among workers of departures from health caused by their working conditions, the protection of workers in their employment from risks resulting from factors adverse to health; the placing and maintenance of the worker in an occupational environment adapted to his physiological and psychological equipment and to summarize: the adaptation of work to man and of each man to his job."

Apart from giving advice on specific toxicological matters and supporting certain research, WHO, since 1950, has played a direct part in enabling governments to evaluate what type of occupational health program is needed, to train nationals, to assist in the formulation of control measures, including legislation and in-plant programs, and in the establishment of occupational health institutes. These activities have been carried out mainly with respect to manufacturing industries and agriculture. In all such matters there is close liaison with the International Labour Office.

***HEALTH DEVELOPMENTS AFFECTING THE ENJOYMENT OF HUMAN RIGHTS.*** An analysis of the effect of certain scientific and technological developments in the field of health on the enjoyment of human rights and fundamental freedoms (UN Doc. USA/8055/Add. 1) was presented to the UN General Assembly at its 1970 session by the World Health Organization. The analysis indicated that such developments had both positive and negative consequences, some of the latter tending to give rise to serious infringements of human rights. WHO pointed out that, in considering the effect of such advances, it is important to emphasize the great advantages which have accrued to millions of people by reason of the application of new health techniques rather than to concentrate upon any concomitant disadvantages or on the occasional abuse which may occur.

Among the developments dealt with in the analysis are the following (paras. 34–90):

### Protection of the Human Personality
### and Its Physical and Intellectual Integrity

*(a) Developments in Genetics.* A number of discoveries in biology have prompted writers to probe into the future, even though it is not yet certain whether these innovations are applicable to human beings.

Changes in the hereditary endowment have been achieved in such organisms as viruses and bacteria, where the processes of "transformation" and "transduction" often result in the acquisition of new genetic specificities by the organisms involved. Similar hereditary changes have been obtained also in mammalian cells cultured *in vitro* but, at present, they seem to be unstable.

The possibility of inducing desired changes in the genotype of human cells exists, but it seems quite remote at this stage of development of molecular genetics. The concern of some writers, that gene-manipulation is potentially capable of changing the human species and jeopardizing the integrity of human beings, would seem to be premature, but thought given to future implications would be desirable.

*(b) Tissue or Organ Transplantations.* Many people die as the result of disease or injury of a particular organ or pair of organs, or from burns associated with excessive loss of skin. Others are incapacitated by loss of limbs, eyes, teeth and other structures. In many cases lives would be saved, or the disability alleviated if a diseased or injured organ or tissue could be replaced by a functionally effective substitute. The types of substitute which are available are of two kinds—mechanical substitutes (prostheses) and transplants.

Transplantation of skin, cartilage or bone from one site to another in the same person requires only skill in plastic surgery and since there is no tissue-incompatibility, there is no immunological reaction leading to rejection of the transplant. Transplants from a donor to another recipient may often be successful in special sites—e.g. corneal transplantation. On the other hand, the commonest form of tissue transplant, blood transfusion, requires tissue compatibility between donor and recipient, and this is achieved by red blood cell typing. In more complex tissues, like the skin or in organs such as the kidney, tissue incompatibility leading to rejection of the transplant by the recipient is always a major problem, except in the case of transplants between identical twins.

Although there has recently been some success in minimizing tissue-incompatibility by the use of tissue typing to select appropriate donors, and considerable progress had been made in overcoming graft rejection by the use of immunosuppressive drugs and sera, the best transplants are still those which are provided by blood relatives.

Transplants from cadavers are less successful (unless by chance there is better compatibility than with a blood relative) though they are the only source of unpaired organs such as the heart and liver. Transplants from animal species are so far not feasible because the immunological reaction to tissue of a foreign species is difficult to suppress.

The many problems in human rights arising in organ transplantations are best seen by a study of kidney transplantations of which several thousand have now been carried out in various parts of the world.

Foremost amongst these problems is the question of consent by the donor in case a living donor is used. He is required to undergo a major operation and in addition loses the factor of safety and reserve provided by a second kidney in the event of accident to the remaining kidney.

It is therefore essential that the donor should be fully informed of the risks and that his or her consent to the sacrifice of the kidney should be absolutely voluntary. Since the potential donor of the most suitable kidney is usually a member of the family it is sometimes difficult to avoid the problem of whether moral pressure is being brought to bear on suitable individuals. It is recognized by transplantation surgeons that persuasion must be avoided.

With regard to the ordinary donor, there can be no question of a violation of human rights if care is taken to ensure that the consent is personal, informed, understanding and voluntary. It is doubtful whether a parent or guardian should give consent on behalf of a young dependent, not of legal age. It is now accepted that it is an infringement of human rights to take advantage of prisoners as donors of organs, even if no special privileges are involved.

At the present time most kidney transplantations are made from cadaver donors. The removal of the kidney can be effected if the deceased person has given his consent, or in the absence of his consent, with the authorization of close relatives. In many countries, legal measures have been taken in this respect.

There remains the ethical question of "triage"—the selection of patients to receive "transplants" when transplant material, technical personnel and supporting services are in short supply. This problem does not raise any question of human rights. In the case of the individual patient the selection is usually made by the medical head of the transplantation service, though in some centres it has become the practice to delegate this responsibility to a small committee.

*(c) Heart Transplantations.* Despite their rarity, heart transplantations create their own problems of which the time of death of the donor has caused the most discussion and controversy. Modern methods of resuscitation involving the use of artificial respirators enable cardiac and respiratory functions to be maintained even though the patient has sustained irreversible brain damage resulting in "brain death". Nevertheless the viability of the donor's heart and his artificially continued respiration are facts which conflict with the traditional criteria of death, namely the inability to maintain cardiac and respiratory function.

Fear undoubtedly exists in lay circles that some over-zealous transplantation surgeon may operate before the donor actually dies. To eliminate this problem the decision as to death should be made by two or more physicians not concerned with the performance of the transplantation.

The question of a new definition of death has therefore been extensively discussed at conferences held under the auspices of the CIBA Foundation (London 1966), the Council for International Organization of Medical Sciences (CIOMS, Geneva 1968), and the World Medical Association (Sydney, 1968). As a result new series of criteria have been prepared.

Certain governments are considering legislation establishing new criteria for the definition of death, but legal opinion on the subject still tends to await further medical action. It is felt that the criteria must first be endorsed by the medical associations representative of the profession as being ethically correct as well as pragmatic.

*(d) Radical Medical Techniques in General.* Human lives can be prolonged in certain cases by sophisticated and expensive techniques of which Renal Dialysis or the Artificial Kidney is a typical example. Because of their present cost and heavy demands for trained personnel, these techniques are not available for everyone who can benefit from them.

Renal dialysis is to some extent an alternative to renal

transplantation and is applicable to the same type of patient, namely persons suffering from chronic uraemia.

Apart from the question of who should benefit from the technique, the fundamental questions are those of cost, effort and personnel, and whether it is justifiable to allocate funds for this purpose which, if applied to the development and extension of less sophisticated therapeutic or preventive procedures, could benefit many more people.

There is nothing quite comparable to renal dialysis. The intensive treatment of certain types of cancer, involving multiple operations, irradiation and powerful cytotoxic drugs, is not nearly as expensive. Questions, however, have been raised as to whether the effort and cost of these procedures is justifiable in incurably ill or very elderly patients. But, failure to provide these types of service could be regarded as a denial of human rights. From the medical point of view, long term medical care of the elderly and incurable cases must continue on humanitarian grounds.

The choice of patients to receive special forms of treatment such as renal dialysis may raise difficult ethical problems. Wherever possible appropriate criteria for determining choice should be drawn up by the professional groups most intimately concerned.

## Experiments on Human Subjects

In one sense a great deal of modern therapy is experimental. Standard courses of treatment do not always apply and the physician with a wide range of powerful drugs available will adjust the treatment of his patient in accordance with the development of his illness. But in other circumstances, the human being is often used as a experimental subject. And it is these situations which have caused public concern. In brief, there is a feeling that certain experiments on human subjects are infringements of human rights. Article 7 of the International Covenant on Civil and Political Rights states, *inter alia:* "In particular no one shall be subjected without his consent to medical or scientific experimentation".

In the present context, "experiments on human subjects" will be considered very briefly under the three heads, which however are not intended to cover all the possibilities.

*(a) Experiments on Human Subjects in Physiology, Pathology and Psychology.* There are many examples of the use of human beings to advance knowledge of human physiology, the subjects concerned being often the experimenter himself, medical students, nurses, soldiers, etc. Recorded experiments have involved almost all physiological systems—cardiovascular, respiratory, nervous, muscular and metabolic.

Pathological studies have also been made particularly in the field of the communicable diseases. One heroic example was the ingestion of a culture of cholera vibrio; another was the use of conscientious objectors to military service to demonstrate the ecology of the scabies mite, and to compare methods of treating the infestation.

If any of these experiments has been undertaken without the knowledge and consent of the subjects, it would have constituted a definite violation of their human rights. But in the great majority of cases the subjects were genuine volunteers, many of whom had a personal scientific interest in the experiment. In such circumstances, no question of a violation of human rights or of ethical misconduct could arise.

*(b) Clinical Testing of Drugs.* In recent years, there has been world-wide interest in ensuring the safety of the increasing number of powerful drugs.

The World Health Organization has been especially active

in encouraging and supporting these developments, and the Director-General was requested by the 17th World Health Assembly in 1964 "to undertake with the assistance of the (WHO) Advisory Committee on Medical Research, the formulation of generally accepted principles and requirements for the evaluation of the safety and efficacy of drugs". In compliance with this request, several meetings of leading experts were convened, and their reports have been the basis of much subsequent activity by national governments and the pharmaceutical industry.

For the investigation of drugs, planned scientific studies involving both animals and man are essential. It is not always recognized that it is unethical to introduce into general use a drug that has been inadequately tested. Adherence to ethical and humanitarian principles as well as economic and technical considerations limit the number of subjects and the number and quality of organized studies on man as compared with animals. It is therefore important not to waste human and economic resources. The prerequisites of a schema for effective drug control involves the following:

—pre-clinical testing in animals

—clinical evaluation on human subjects

—a monitoring system to collect and report adverse reactions to drugs in use.

The World Health Organization, through its advisory machinery, has formulated two sets of principles for the pre-clinical testing of drugs and for their clinical evaluation which have obtained a large measure of acceptance. Following upon a resolution of the Twenty-third World Health Assembly in May 1970, it has also accepted financial responsibility for the establishment of a monitoring service at WHO headquarters in Geneva.

With regard to clinical evaluation on human subjects, it is suggested that this should be done on healthy adults, patients suffering from the disease against which the drug is going to be used, and patients suffering from other diseases. Even when this recommendation is strictly followed there still remains the question of formal therapeutic trial to determine the usefulness of the drug and to compare it with existing therapy. In formulating rules for the organization of these trials, the outstanding consideration is to obtain the personal, informed, understanding and voluntary consent of the participants.

In some countries, these trials are operated by the pharmaceutical industry, with varying degrees of governmental surveillance and legal regulation. In others, governmental supervision and control operates primarily and throughout.

*(c) The Use of Chemical Additives in Foods and Potable Fluids.* The use of simple chemical substances such as salt to preserve foods, and of colouring materials (usually of vegetable origin) to improve their appearance is of very long standing. In recent years, many new synthetic chemicals have been developed for use as food additives. They serve to prevent spoilage, to stop food from becoming rancid, to improve the colour, flavour or texture of a food, to render food more amenable to mass production and processing, etc. The increased use of food additives stems from such social and technological changes as urbanization, development of long-distance food transport, and the demand for ready-to-serve foods.

The fact that additives are present in most processed and many semi-processed foods narrows the choice of foods for those who wish to avoid eating all or certain food additives. In this sense the wide-spread use of food additives is an encroachment on one aspect of human rights. However, this consideration must be balanced against the technological value of these additives as well as their contribution towards an abundant supply of wholesome and easy-to-serve food. (The addition of iodine and antimalarial drugs to salt is easily justified on health grounds and, in these cases, there is no infringement of human rights because medicaments-free salt is also available to the public.)

The main reason that some individuals consider the addition of chemicals to foods or drinks as undesirable is that they are not convinced that all these chemicals are absolutely free from health hazards. In fact, certain additives which were in use have since been found to possess potential health hazards.

Realizing this problem, many governments have legal means to control the use of food additives. Furthermore, the World Health Assembly also expressed concern at its Sixth Session in 1953, and subsequently a series of meetings of the Expert Committee on Food Additives were convened by WHO in conjunction with FAO to provide toxicological evaluations of food additives. These evaluations were transmitted to governmental agencies for information. More recently these have been made use of in the elaboration of food standards in the framework of the Joint FAO/WHO Food Standards Programme.

### Deterioration of the Human Environment

Several human rights are prejudiced by the many prevailing manifestations of the deterioration of the environment. They include at least two accepted rights—the right to life, and the right to a standard of life adequate for the health of the individual and his family, which implies the right to enjoy life. Environmental deterioration also derogates from the highest attainable standard of health. The manifestations of deterioration are almost universal wherever human beings settle, live and work, and the causal factors have increased *pari passu* with technological developments.

To the traditional factors of air, soil and water pollution, and urbanization have been added noise, traffic congestion, the accumulation of wastes, soil erosion, oil pollution of the sea, and the waste products of nuclear energy plants. Urbanization and the trend towards urban industrial societies are manifest increasingly in both developed and developing countries. Together with bad housing they create physical, social and psychological problems which have impacts on health and infringe the human rights referred to.

To all these detrimental factors there has been added in recent years the all-pervading pesticides. Certain pesticides which have shown themselves as great benefactors in the control of such vector borne diseases as malaria, and in agriculture, if used improperly or unrestrictedly, are capable of producing detrimental effects on many forms of life—because of their indestructibility and toxicity. Certain governments have been so alarmed by the extent of the invasion of soil, water and sea by some persistent pesticides that they have restricted or forbidden the use of these substances. But universal prohibition of the use of certain insecticides would need to be balanced against the inevitable recrudescence of such diseases as malaria; this is unthinkable unless effective and economic substitute control methods are developed.

Against this recital of the negative developments, attention should be drawn to the technological advances in water supply which have so improved that the provision of water to all people as a health measure is now technically feasible.

Action against the deterioration of the environment postulates a recognition of the modes of pollution, public education as to their importance, legislative control and inten-

sive research. Some countries have already achieved considerable success in the control of smoke pollution, and in the purification of effluent wastes, but much remains to be done.

In its own field, WHO had instituted or is associated with a large number of research projects, which can be summarized as follows:

*Environmental pollution* studies of water, air, soil and radioactive pollution in an effort to prevent pollution from reaching levels which interfere with the health and well-being of individuals.

*Wastes disposal* research and establishment of scientific technical information and wastes management and control.

*Vector biology and control* research and development on ecology, vector surveillance, insecticide resistance, genetics and genetic control, biological control, the development and evaluation of alternative insecticides, rodent control and methods of aircraft disinfection.

*Pesticides* assessment of hazards of pesticides and promotion of their safe use.

In addition, the Twenty-third World Health Assembly in 1970 expressed its growing concern that the consequences of factors in the environment are adversely affecting the condition of human health. It further requested the Director-General to develop and submit to the Twenty-fourth World Health Assembly a long-term programme for environmental health, including, in so far as might be found practicable, a programme for a worldwide system of surveillance and monitoring in close collaboration with national and international efforts. Attention was also directed to the need for the establishment of environmental health criteria, guidelines for preventive measures, and methods of determining priorities and allocating resources based on the health problems and needs in both developing and developed countries.

The organization has also co-operated with other members of the United Nations system, and in particular with FAO and UNESCO, on these problems. It is also participating in the preparations for the United Nations Conference on the Human Environment which is to be held in Stockholm, Sweden, in 1972.

### Human Rights Aspects of the Delivery of Health Services

The right to health and medical care is widely accepted in the basic documents of the United Nations and WHO.

Prevention, treatment and control of disease constitute the *raison d'être* for the provision of health services and medical care. The components of this human right have been frequently identified by WHO in various official documents and can be summarized as follows: general medical services for prevention, treatment and rehabilitation; maternal and child care, including family planning advice and services; control of communicable disease; mental health; occupational health; health education and nutrition.

These services, other than occupation health services, but including certain aspects of environmental control, are commonly provided through what are described as the basic or community health services.

*(a) Methods of Provision and Administration of Health and Medical Services.* The systems of provision and administration of these services vary from country to country, and are entirely matters for the national government to determine. The pattern of provision is to some extent influenced by the financial situation of the country, and the sources from which the cost of providing the services is met. There are three

main patterns. The first is where the government itself organizes and runs the health services and where it is the exclusive source of finance.

The second comprises health and medical care services which are provided to a certain extent by the State and partly under a compulsory insurance scheme.

Under the third arrangement, the cost of medical care is met from individual private funds and/or voluntary private insurance. Sometimes the cost of preventive services is borne by the State.

No question of an infringement of human rights would appear to arise by the imposition of any of these forms of provision, but the range and coverage of the services provided may give rise to certain questions relevant to human rights.

Obviously financial resources can determine the range of the services provided. Some developing countries can give no more than the barely essential services. Certain developed countries may provide a comprehensive range of services, elaborately equipped hospitals, and access to costly methods of treatment. If a government is offering to all its citizens the best possible it can provide within its powers and resources, there can be no question of any deprivation of human rights.

On the other hand, if services are not evenly distributed, and if certain groups appear to benefit more than others without due reason, complaints will undoubtedly arise and may indicate an infringement. It may be reasonable, however, to give certain groups special consideration as, for example, expectant and nursing mothers and young children.

*(b) Cost of Health Services and Medical Care.* There is universal anxiety about the rising cost of health and medical care services as they exist at present, but the future is even more ominous. The development of other expensive techniques comparable to those now available for the intensive care of patients or for renal dialysis, together with further advances in the transplantation of kidneys, livers, hearts and skin (in the treatment of major burns) will all add to the financial burden, and to the manpower requirements.

The question may then arise as to who shall receive the full treatment and who shall be denied. But this question has already arisen in respect of transplantations and renal dialysis (paragraphs 45 and 51) at any rate for individual hospitals. The responsibility for the decision is usually accepted by the head of the services, with or without the assistance of a small committee.

At the national level, the decision *on principle* must be taken by the government, preferably with guidance from representatives of the medical and associated professions.

***EFFECTS OF TRADITIONAL PRACTICES ON WOMEN AND CHILDREN.*** On 24 May 1984, the UN **ECONOMIC AND SOCIAL COUNCIL** requested the Secretary-General (resolution 1984/34) to entrust to a working group composed of experts designated by the **SUB-COMMISSION ON PREVENTION OF DISCRIMINATION AND PROTECTION OF MINORITIES**; the **UNITED NATIONS EDUCATIONAL, SCIENTIFIC AND CULTURAL ORGANIZATION**; and the World Health Organization the task of conducting a comprehensive study on the phenomenon of traditional practices affecting the health of women and children; and requested all in-

terested non-governmental organizations to cooperate in the study.

The Working Group on Traditional Practices Affecting the Health of Women and Children held three sessions at the European office of the United Nations in Geneva, the first in March 1985, the second in September of that year, and the third in January 1986. On the basis of the documentation available to it, the Working Group submitted a report to the **COMMISSION ON HUMAN RIGHTS** (UN Doc. E/CN.4/1986/42) in which it accorded priority consideration to such practices as (a) female circumcision, (b) preferential treatment for male children, and (c) traditional birth practices.

***Female Circumcision.*** The term, as used by the Working Group, refers to the traditional practice which consists in cutting away all, or part, of the external female genital organs. Although in most countries where it is practiced it is an integral part of the "initiation rite," the operation has been shown to involve significant risks of damage to the mental and physical health of girls and women.

The conclusions reached by the Working Group, with regard to this practice (paras. 108–120), are as follows:

*A. Functions.* Female circumcision is a practice that has complex social, ethnic, religious, economic and psychological aspects which vary from one social group to another.

As a social phenomenon, circumcision has an evolutionary aspect which can be understood and evaluated only in the context of the societies in which it is practiced.

In some societies, female circumcision has had and continues to have an initiatory function which varies from one social group to another. Moreover, there is a perceptible evolution of the role and function of female circumcision from the rural environment to the urban environment. Traditional practices have a more symbolic and ritual character, and their social and economic functions are easier to determine. These practices continue to have significant relationships with other aspects of social and cultural life.

The function of social integration is stronger and more instrumental within populations confronted with situations comprising contradictions and conflicts of values.

Generally speaking, attachment to traditions which have lost some of their significance is to a certain extent the consequence of the basic problem which these societies are facing. This function of the social integration of young girls is strengthened by the image which women and the community have of themselves and by the difference between the roles of men and women in society and the forms of discrimination resulting therefrom.

*B. Evolution.* There has been an evolution in the functions inherent in female circumcision and the methods and forms employed. In urban environments, in particular, a change of attitude has been noted in relation to certain variables (education, sex, age). This evolution may even go as far as the simulation of circumcision in the practice of the most benign form. Despite the positive evolution of these practices, it must not be forgotten that this evolution is often felt to be insufficient by certain population groups within which new models of societies have emerged.

*C. Consequences.* Female circumcision has consequences on the mental and physical health of women and children, the gravity of which increases with the degree of mutilation.

The consequences of these practices continue to be significant regardless of forms and procedures, in particular in groups of women or populations confronted with changing life patterns, whether in urban or other areas. The seriousness of the consequences cannot be diminished by evolution extending to the medicalization of the act. Medicalization entailing normalization and institutionalization of these practices would have particularly adverse consequences since it would deprive these acts of any ritual content and, in most cases, would not diminish the effects of mutilation on the physiological functioning of the genital organs of women and young girls.

It is interesting to note that some traditional practices were aimed, in traditional societies, at the closer incorporation of the individual within his social environment in order to enable him to benefit from all the rights of the individual which these societies recognized.

Today, because of the evolution in traditional societies due to various factors, these traditional practices are at variance with new standards defined by various international instruments relating to human rights.

In the light of these principles which today have the force of law, all countries which have ratified the International Covenants on Human Rights and the Convention on the Elimination of All Forms of Discrimination Against Women and which have morally endorsed the principles enunciated in the Universal Declaration of Human Rights and the United Nations Declaration on the Rights of the Child are currently confronted with the incompatibility which exists between these principles and the obligations they assume as States parties to the above-mentioned instruments, and the maintenance of certain traditional practices, especially since these practices have proved prejudicial to the physical and mental health of women and children.

During their consideration of this question, the members of the Working Group have been unable to avoid noting this incompatibility.

In conclusion, the Working Group, wishing to facilitate the work of the members of the Commission on Human Rights, makes the following suggestions relating to the study of this problem.

The working group offers the following suggestions for action:

The legislative efforts to abolish female circumcision by the Government of Egypt should be noted with satisfaction and an appeal should be made to other Governments, which had not yet had the possibility of adopting clear-cut policies and appropriate legislation to abolish female circumcision, to take such action.

These measures should be preceded and followed up by public education.

To ensure the implementation of such legislation there is a need to set up an effective mechanism.

Note could be taken of the important action by African women in efforts to combat practices which are prejudicial to the health and well-being of women and children and which impede the full realization of their fundamental rights.

It would be desirable for Governments to support and reinforce this action: (a) decision-makers and professionals, professional bodies and non-governmental organizations, as well as the mass media, should be alerted with a view to obtaining their co-operation in order to implement attitudes to obtain their co-operation in order to influence attitudes towards the eradication of female circumcision; (b) opinion-builders at grass-root levels, such as village leaders and community health and development workers which should also be alerted.

The Working Group further suggests that Governments should encourage and support by all available means the associations and organizations engaged in the process of eradicating female circumcision.

*Specific Action.* With a view to attaining the goal of health for all by the year 2000, national health policies should include among their priorities strategies aimed at the eradication of female circumcision in their primary health care programmes. The Working Group recommends that the competent public services should describe the adverse effects of female circumcision to birth attendants, nurses, mobile health teams, social workers, rural teachers and community auxiliaries at the beginning of their courses, not forgetting vocational health personnel and any other socio-vocational category concerned.

The Working Group further considers that information should also be given in health centres, pre-natal centres, women's development centres, handicraft centres and governmental-run social institutions.

Appropriate pedagogical material should be prepared for the training of educational, medical and paramedical personnel and even psychologists in order to enable them to tackle this problem adequately within the populations concerned.

Alternative training should be provided for the traditional practitioners whose main source of income derives from female circumcision.

In the area of education, sex education should be given in schools, including information on female circumcision and its eradication. This question should also be included in literacy campaigns. Moreover, the problem of female circumcision should be included in teacher-training programmes and curricula at all levels, and in all the disciplines concerned, not forgetting civic or religious education programmes.

In countries with an Islamic majority or which have a large Muslim population, stress must be laid on the importance accorded to women, on the condemnation of ill-treatment, and on the fact that female circumcision is not mentioned in the Koran and is in no way a religious obligation.

*Education.* In view of the limited amount of study and research on the socio-cultural aspects of the problem, multidisciplinary research programmes should be established and supported, taking account of the complex and multiple aspects of this practice with a view to formulating action programmes.

Effective evaluation mechanisms should be instituted at the national level in order to build on the progress achieved in the area of the eradication of female circumcision.

Meetings should be organized at the international, regional and national levels enabling men and women from the countries concerned to exchange their views and experiences on female circumcision and means of achieving its eradication.

It would be appropriate to congratulate the international organizations on the efforts made and support extended by them and to call upon them to renew and reinforce such support.

The action and support provided so far by the international non-governmental organizations to national efforts for eradicating female circumcision and continuation of such international collaboration on a large scale for the realization of programmes to eliminate female circumcision should be noted with satisfaction.

It should be noted with satisfaction that progress has been made in work against female circumcision through the creation of the Inter-African Committee and its national bodies. Such national and regional efforts should be encouraged and supported.

*Son Preference.* Preference of parents for male children is a tradition in many parts of the world and often manifests itself in neglect, deprivation, or discriminatory treatment of girls to the detriment of their mental and physical health. According to the report of the Working Group, "it refers to a whole range of values and attitudes that are manifested in many different practices whose common feature is preference for the male child with daughter neglect often a concomitant result. It may mean that a female child is disadvantaged since its birth, and may determine the quality and quantity of parental care and extent of investment on the child's development. It may lead to acute discrimination, particularly in settings where resources are scarce. Although neglect is the rule, in extreme cases son preference may lead to selective abortion or female infanticide—but more often it involves neglect."

The areas most affected by the practice, the Working Group found, "seem to be South Asia (Bangladesh, India, Nepal, and Pakistan), the Middle East (Algeria, Egypt, Jordan, Libya, Morocco, Syria, Tunisia, and Turkey), and parts of Africa (Cameroon, Liberia, Madagascar, and Senegal). In Latin America, there is evidence of abnormal sex ratios in mortality in Ecuador, Mexico, Peru, and Uruguay."

The reasons for this practice are set out by the Working Group as follows:

Those who have studied the low value accorded to daughters in several societies argue that: (a) where women's economic productivity is high or where there is a high demand for female labor in agriculture, discrimination against girls is less prevalent, but where women are economically dependent upon men they are put at a disadvantage since they have no control over their own lives; (b) sons are economic assets to their family and bring in an extra pair of hands for work when they marry; (c) parents view sons as having far greater obligations towards them in their old age whereas daughters are lost to the family after marriage; (d) sons are needed to carry on the family lineage; (e) most religious beliefs seem to consider women as inferior and so unfit to perform sacred duties and rituals; and (f) in certain societies, the lack of understanding and the misinterpretation of the female physiology results in the devalorization of the female person.

The main conclusion of the working group with regard to son preference is that "sex favoritism does affect the self-esteem and self-image of the less preferred female children and socializes them to be dependent

upon men." Other conclusions include the following (paras. 173–177):

Son preference is not necessarily a danger for daughters, but when it is often accompanied by neglect and discrimination towards female children it leads to serious health consequences which account for between 500,000 to 1 million deaths among female children.

In particular, such discrimination is reflected in food distribution, in which female children are disadvantaged and thus particularly suffer from malnutrition.

Likewise, an explicit manifestation of neglect towards girls is lack of care, in comparison with boys, in case of illness.

The following conclusions should be highlighted.

—There is an interdependence between the economic system and the family system. Where women's productivity is high or women are much in demand as agricultural workers, there is less discrimination against and undervaluation of women and girls.

—Food distribution on the basis of sex is heightened in times of shortage, whether resulting from seasonal scarcity, famine or chronic poverty. This discrimination on grounds of sex occurs in both poor and less poor families, which would appear to indicate that a better food supply would be a necessary but not a sufficient condition for eliminating food discrimination against female members of the family.

—Underinvestment in the education of girls seriously affects the health of future generations, since maternal education has a decisive influence on child health mortality.

—Excess female mortality in childhood is an indicator of serious external influences against the normal biological advantages with which nature has endowed the female.

—The neglect of daughters because of son preference affects both the health and the status of women directly and through each other.

Higher female than male infant and/or child mortality or even more female than male deaths among infants and children are a sure indicator of the existence of serious discrimination against girls.

The Working Group's recommendations on the question of son preference are as follows (paras. 178–190):

Even where they have taken up the question of son preference, the World Fertility Survey and other demographic studies have unfortunately focused on the influence of that preference on fertility and not on the ensuing consequences for female children.

The same is true of the many studies carried out (a bibliography of which is attached to this report) whose concern was the nutritional status of children rather than nutritional differences on grounds of sex. It is, however, worthy to note that although these studies were not carried out with the principal aim of exploring male and female discrimination, nevertheless they all indicate without any doubt that the problems outlined above exist and are acute in many parts of the world.

Consequently, the first recommendation must be:

(a) To identify the problem of son preference,

(b) An essential prerequisite for action, in the short term, is information that helps to identify whether the problem exists in a given country. Most countries have at least some sources of information that can provide valuable data without having to initiate additional data collection.

There are a number of indicators which can be used as a signalling device to alert those responsible for planning and implementing health and development interventions.

(a) The mortality rates of female infants and children between 1 and 4 years of age is perhaps *the most crucial indicator*. Higher female than male infant and/or child mortality, or even more female than male deaths among infants and children, are a sure indicator of the existence of serious discrimination against girls. Where civic registration is poor or non-existent sex specific mortality data may not exist, although community surveys carried out for other purposes may yield useful data. The absence of a female excess in mortality does not however mean the absence of neglect of female children. It is necessary, therefore, to examine other indicators, such as sex differentials in nutritional status of children.

(b) An analysis by sex of *anthropometric data* collected in child-health clinics, school health records, child growth records maintained by health programmes etc. can reveal significant differences between the nutritional status of boys and girls. Community nutritional and/or health surveys are however more reliable sources of data, since clinic data could reflect an inherent sex-bias in clinic attendance—more malnourished boys than girls may be brought to clinics even if more girls than boys were malnourished in the child population as a whole.

(c) *Analysis by sex of clinic and hospital records and immunization records* would show if there is systematic bias against girls in seeking medical care—preventive or curative. In the case of curative care this would be true if in addition to there being a greater number of boys than girls attending the clinic, the girls who are brought show more advanced symptoms. This implies that there was a greater delay in seeking medical care for girls.

*On-going Monitoring.* It should become common practice for future demographic surveys and censuses to record and analyse infant and child mortality rates and to calculate life expectancies by sex in order to bring about sex differentials. Analysis by sex of community health surveys, hospital and immunization records and nutritional surveys should also become routine; such on-going monitoring will not only alert planners to sex-differential treatment of children, but also serve as a useful device to measure the impact of preventive action.

*Preventive Action.* If an examination on the basis of indicators such as the above shows the existence of widespread and systematic discrimination against female children, corrective measures will need to be planned and implemented without delay.

*Combating Existing Practices.* Although the elimination of undervaluation of daughters implies long-term and protracted action to change entrenched attitudes and values, several short-term measures can be initiated to prevent and compensate for the serious health consequences that result from it.

For example, all countries with excess female and child mortality may gear all health interventions towards the attainment of at least equal female and male infant and child mortality rates and, ultimately, the more normal 5–10 per cent higher male than female mortality rate in infancy and childhood. Feeding and other nutritional intervention programmes and immunization campaigns may need to include targets as to the minimal proportion of female children to be covered.

Another measure that may help improve the access to

medical care of female infants and children is provision of services to all children on a compulsory basis and even free-of-charge.

(a) Health planners and practitioners, women's organizations, development agencies, community workers and all others concerned including legislators should be made aware of the gravity of the problems and encouraged to re-examine the situation in their countries, to document existing practices, and to plan corrective action.

(b) It would be necessary to sensitize the health staff about this discrimination and its effects.

(c) An information campaign should be launched through the mass media and health education programmes set up with a view to changing attitudes as regards discriminatory practices against female children, particularly in nutrition and access to health care.

*Eliminating the Underlying Causes.* Long-term measures to deal with the phenomenon of son preference and its implications would include enactment and implementation of legislation against discrimination on the grounds of sex.

Provision of free and compulsory primary education to all children may not be adequate to ensure girls' access to education, and suitable social support measures may have to be introduced in an attempt to minimize the disadvantages to the family due to the girls' schooling, adequate social security when possible for older people so that a son is no longer a must for security in old age. The social and economic status of women should be enhanced. Parents should be encouraged by incentives to send their girl children to school.

*At the International Level.* The specialized agencies concerned, such as WHO, UNESCO and UNICEF, should provide technical and other assistance to Governments which so request in order to eliminate this practice:

(a) Seminars should be organized under the auspices of the regional economic commissions, in particular to exchange information and experience in this field.

(b) The organs responsible for the implementation of conventions concerning the elimination of discrimination against women and equality of access of girls to education should give special attention to this problem when studying reports submitted by States parties.

Finally, it is worth ending on an optimistic note. Some Asian countries are not indifferent to the enormous problems arising from son preference to the detriment of female children. Although their efforts remain limited, they should be supported in order to encourage more dynamic action.

***Traditional Childbirth Practices.*** In its consideration of traditional childbirth practices, the Working Group points out in its report that not all of them are harmful, and some are either beneficial or at least harmless.

Among the beneficial practices, it lists breastfeeding, especially traditional "on demand" 12-month breastfeeding, which results in protection from infections and better nutrition and prolongs the intervals between births, and other traditional methods of birth spacing.

Among the harmful practices, it describes some of those considered to be the most harmful, including culturally prescribed dietary practices during pregnancy and puerperium, such as restrictions, in various

667

localities, on the eating of meat, eggs, green vegetables, fruit, rice, milk, potatoes, and other nourishing foods; childbirth attended only by traditional birth attendants (TBAs), relatives, or no one at all in dark, secluded, and unsterile hideaways; unhygienic examinations, procedures, and operations; and improper treatment of complications, especially when TBAs delay recourse to trained medical assistance.

The Working Group puts forward the following recommendations for dealing with traditional childbirth practices (paras. 222–229):

*At the National Level.* Since not all traditional childbirth practices are harmful, but on the contrary some are beneficial or at least harmless, it is recommended that each country should examine these practices in its own context, to identify those which are harmful and need to be eliminated, those which are beneficial and should be encouraged, and those which need no action at all.

Believing that in most cases the persistence of harmful traditional practices is largely due to the unavailability of trained assistance in pregnancy and childbirth, it is strongly recommended that Governments recall the commitments universally undertaken at the Alma Ata Conference on Primary Health Care and the subsequent adoption by the World Health Assembly and the United Nations General Assembly of the Strategy for Health for All by the Year 2000, and recall also the recommendations of the International Population Conference in Mexico in 1984 and the World Conference to Review and Appraise the Achievements of the United Nations Decade for Women: Equality, Development and Peace of 1985 about ensuring the availability of trained assistance in pregnancy and childbirth for all women who need it, and that Governments redouble their efforts to achieve this aim by elevating the level of priority which is given to maternity care in national development plans and budget allocations.

Aware that the registration of, training and supervision of Traditional Birth Attendants (TBAs) has been historically one of the means by which most countries who today provide adequate maternity care have achieved this, and aware also that this approach is in tune with both the development philosophy and practical possibilities of most developing countries, it is recommended that determined efforts should be made in the next few years to apply this approach nationwide wherever appropriate, and to provide adequate support to the TBAs in the form of training, supervision and support.

Countries are recommended to carry out campaigns of public education:

(a) Specifically to combat harmful traditional practices and to promote beneficial practices,

(b) To encourage women to use fully such opportunities as do exist for trained help in pregnancy and childbirth.

In public education and in collaboration with Governments in making available adequate maternity care, the non-government organizations of developing countries have a major role to play.

*At the Regional Level.* The Working Group noted with interest the creation of the Inter-African Committee on Traditional Practices Affecting the Health of Women and Children and the setting up so far of 12 national committees with the approval of Governments. An appeal should be made to all Governments concerned to support the Inter-African

Committee which deals with the various practices studied at the Dakar Seminar. It should be also recommended, in appealing to Governments, to give higher priority to national action in this field, it is believed that at this early stage of action small regional meetings between countries might be useful.

*At the International Level.* The Commission on Human Rights should call upon all appropriate regional economic commissions and international agencies, such as WHO, UNICEF, UNESCO, UNFPA, UNDP and the World Bank and the regional development banks again to take cognizance that still today over 50 per cent of women in developing countries have no trained assistance in childbirth, and therefore to give a very high priority to collaboration with and support to countries in improving their provision of maternal health care at primary and secondary levels.

The group also recommends to bilateral aid donors and to international NGOs who wish to assist health development to give particular emphasis to the provision of maternity care in order to resolve the gross discrepancies and inequities which prevail at present in this regard.

***Action Taken on the Report.*** After examining the Working Group's report, the UN **COMMISSION ON HUMAN RIGHTS** requested the Sub-Commission on Prevention of Discrimination and Protection of Minorities (resolution 1988/57) to consider, at its 1988 session, measures to be taken at the national and international levels to eliminate the practices described therein. The Sub-Commission, responding to that request, called upon Mrs. Halima Embarek Warzazi (Morocco), who had acted as Chairman/Rapporteur of the Working Group, to study, on the basis of information to be gathered from governments, specialized agencies, other intergovernmental and non-governmental organizations concerned, recent developments with regard to traditional practices affecting the health of women and children and to bring the results of her study to the attention of the Sub-Commission at its 1989 session.

In the preliminary report presented to the Sub-Commission at its 1989 session (UN Doc. E/CN.4/Sub.2/1989/42 and Add. 1), the Special Rapporteur summarized the information she had gathered from 16 governments, two United Nations organs, one specialized agency, and 12 non-governmental organizations and stated (chap. V) that the consultations had led her to make the following recommendations:

(a) The mandate given by the Sub-Commission should be extended by two years to make it possible to obtain the information needed in order appropriately to strengthen the report requested by the Sub-Commission;

(b) Study visits should be envisaged to selected countries in certain regions where traditional practices affecting women and children are prevalent and whose Governments have not yet sent a reply. The purpose of these visits would be to prepare for the holding of international seminars organized by the Centre for Human Rights; these seminars would study the effect of traditional practices on human rights and ways of eradicating traditional practices that adversely affect families and the community and of encouraging practices that are beneficial. The visits would also have the purpose of demonstrating the importance of holding such international seminars, aimed at government officials and national and international NGOs, and of mobilizing the NGO community at the national and international levels in support of such seminars;

(c) Sources of financing for holding these seminars should be sought in the Centre for Human Rights and other United Nations agencies, particularly UNDP. The Centre for Human Rights should provide Mrs. Halima Embarek Warzazi with all possible support to enable her to fulfill the mandate entrusted to her;

(d) United Nations agencies, regional economic and social commissions of the United Nations and other interested bodies should be asked to provide any information they have collected on traditional practices and on measures taken to eradicate traditional practices affecting the health of women and children;

(e) There should be greater co-operation between the Centre for Human Rights and the Inter-African Committee and national NGOs, and with Governments and international NGOs, including their national branches, in order to ensure implementation of the recommendations contained in the report of the Working Group on Traditional Practices affecting the health of women and children;

(f) The Sub-Commission should recommend to WHO to invite Mrs. Halima Embarek Warzazi to address the Ministers of Health at the next World Health Assembly, at Geneva, on the subject of traditional practices affecting the health of women and children.

At that same session, the Sub-Commission took note (resolution 1989/16) of the Special Rapporteur's report, shared the concern she had expressed about the lack of information on the subject made available to her, and expressed the view that the issue of traditional practices is a matter of serious concern to the international community because of its human rights implications.

The Sub-Commission recommended (resolution 1989/16) that its parent bodies, the Commission on Human Rights and the Economic and Social Council, review the question in 1990 and arrange (a) for the mandate of the Special Rapporteur to be extended for two years to enable her to present a more complete report, (b) for her to undertake field missions if possible in two countries where harmful traditional practices are prevalent, and (c) for international regional seminars to be organized in Africa and Asia to consider the subject of harmful traditional practices.

At its 1991 session, the Sub-Commission studied with interest the Special Rapporteur's final report (E/CN.4/Sub.2/1991/6) as well as the report of the regional seminar held in Burkina Faso from 29 April to 3 May 1991. It recommended that the mandate of the Special Rapporteur be extended for two years so as to enable her to submit to the Sub-Commission a plan of action for the elimination of harmful traditional prac-

tices affecting the health of women and children, and a report on the Asian regional seminar. These recommendations also were approved by the Commission.

In April 1993 Sri Lanka offered to act as host to the Asian seminar, which was subsequently held in that country from 4 to 8 July 1994.

**SEE ALSO** *Standard of Living.*

**BIBLIOGRAPHY.** Abraham, Martin. *The Lessons of Bhopal: A Community Action Resource Manual on Hazardous Technologies.* Penang, Malaysia: International Organization of Consumers Unions, 1985. NGO report, in English.

Agarwal, A., J. Merrifield, and R. Tandon. *No Place to Run: Local Realities and Global Issues of the Bhopal Disaster.* New Market, TN, USA: Highlander Research and Education Center and Society for Participatory Research in Asia, 1985. NGO report, in English.

*Apartheid Medicine: Health and Human Rights in South Africa: A Report to the American Association for the Advancement of Science, American Psychiatric Association, American Public Health Association, Institute of Medicine of the National Academy of Sciences.* Washington, D.C.: AAAS, 1990. NGO factfinding report, in English.

*Bhopal: Industrial Genocide? A Unique Compilation of Documents from Indian Publications.* Hong Kong: Asian Regional Exchange for New Alternatives, 1985. Edited collection, in English.

Breum, M., and A. Hendriks, eds. *AIDS and Human Rights: An International Perspective.* Copenhagen, Denmark: Danish Center of Human Rights, 1988. Edited collection, in English.

Chetley, Andrew. *A Healthy Business?: World Health and the Pharmaceutical Industry.* London, UK: Zed Books, 1990. Monograph, in English.

Claude, R., E. Stover, and J. Lopez. *Health Professionals and Human Rights in the Philippines.* Washington, D.C.: American Association for the Advancement of Science, 1987. NGO report, in English.

Coordinating Committee for Primary Health Care of Thai NGOs. *Proceedings of International Conference on Primary Health Care and People's Movement, Cholburi, Thailand, 23–28 Feb. 1986.* Bangkok, Thailand: 1986. NGO conference proceedings, in English.

Evers, T., P. Molan, and P. Burgess. *The Treatment of Disabled Persons in Social Security and Taxation Law.* Canberra, Australia: Human Rights Commission, 1986. Government monograph, in English.

"Female Circumcision Endangers 75 Million," *Canadian Human Rights Advocate* 2, no. 6 (June 1986): 12–13. NGO bulletin article, in English.

*Health and Human Rights.* Boston, MA, USA: François-Xavier Bagnoud Center for Health and Human Rights, Harvard School of Public Health. Scholarly periodical, in English; began publication in fall 1994.

"Health Protection and Medical Assistance in Disaster Situations," *International Review of the Red Cross* no. 284 (Sept.–Oct. 1991): 435–532; no. 791 (Sept.–Oct. 1991): 459–566 (French). Scholarly article, in English and French.

International Commission of Health Professions. *Health and Human Rights.* Geneva, Switzerland: 1986. NGO document collection, in English, French, and Spanish.

International Confederation of Free Trade Unions. *Occupational Health, Safety and the Environment in Central and*

*Eastern Europe.* Brussels, Belgium: 1990. Issue paper, in English.

Jaising, Indira. *The Bhopal Tragedy: What Really Happened and What It Means for American Workers and Communities at Risk.* New York: Council on International and Public Affairs, 1986. Background report, in English.

Johannes Wier Foundation for Health and Human Rights. *Health and Human Rights in the Philippines.* The Hague, the Netherlands: 1991. NGO report, in English.

Johannes Wier Foundation for Health and Human Rights and Physicians for Human Rights. *South Africa 1991: Apartheid and Health Care in Transition—A Report on Progress, Impediments and Means of Support.* No. 5. Amersfoort, the Netherlands: 1992. NGO report, in English.

Leary, Virginia. "The Right to Health in International Human Rights Law," *Health and Human Rights* 1, no. 1 (Fall 1994): 24–56. Scholarly article, in English.

Mann, Jonathan, et al. "Health and Human Rights," *Health and Human Rights* 1, no. 1 (Fall 1994): 6–23. Scholarly article, in English.

Panos Institute. *AIDS and the Third World.* 2nd ed. London: 1987. NGO report, in English.

Physicians for Human Rights. *Casualties of Conflict: Medical Care and Human Rights in the West Bank and Gaza Strip: Report of a Medical Fact-Finding Mission by Physicians for Human Rights.* Somerville, MA, USA: 1988. NGO mission report, in English.

―――. *El Salvador: Health Care under Siege—Violations of Medical Neutrality during the Civil Conflict.* Somerville, MA, USA: 1990. NGO report, in English.

―――. *Medical Testimony on Victims of Torture: A Physician's Guide to Political Asylum Cases.* Boston, MA, USA: 1991. NGO guidelines, in English.

"The Right to Health," in *Human Rights in the Twenty-First Century: A Global Challenge,* eds. Kathleen E. Mahoney and Paul Mahoney, pp. 447–516. Dordrecht, the Netherlands: Martinus Nijhoff, 1993. Scholarly contributions, in English.

Sabatier, Renee. *Blaming Others: Prejudice, Race and Worldwide AIDS.* London: Panos Institute and the Norwegian Red Cross, 1988. Monograph, in English.

Sheehan, R., and J. Jardine. *Epilepsy and Human Rights.* Canberra, Australia: Human Rights Commission, 1984. Government monograph, in English.

Tomasevski, Katarina. *Prison Health: International Standards and National Practices in Europe.* Helsinki, Finland: Helsinki Institute for Crime Prevention and Control, 1992. Report, in English.

"Women, Ecology and Health: Rebuilding Connections," *Development Dialogue* nos. 1–2 (1992). Special issues, in English.

**HELLMAN/HAMMETT GRANTS.** Established in 1990 with funds from the estates of American writers Lillian Hellman and Dashiell Hammett, the Hellman/Hammett Grants are given annually by **HUMAN RIGHTS WATCH** to writers around the world who are in financial need because of political persecution. In the first five years of the program, more than 160 writers received awards. In 1995, grants were awarded to 48 writers from 23 countries. Not all of the recipients are acknowledged publicly because of possible danger to them and their families; however, some of the 1995 grant recipients are the following:

Fikret Baskaya (Turkey), columnist for a now-banned pro-Kurdish newspaper who was sentenced to 20 months in prison for "disseminating enemy propaganda"; Kenneth Best (Liberia), founder of the first independent newspaper in Liberia, now in exile in the United States; Tsegay Gabre-Medhin (Ethiopia), a poet-playwright whose plays were once banned by Emperor Haile Selassie and the military junta, and now are banned by the current regime; Vasila Inoiatove (Uzbekistan), a poet whose political views have interfered with publication of her work; Hadi Khorsandi (Iran), a poet and journalist under death threats from Islamic militants for writing satirical articles about the revolution; Aicha Lemsine (Algeria), novelist and journalist, called "the most dangerous woman in Algeria" by Islamic militants, now in exile in the United States; Liao Yiwu (China), arrested for making audio tapes criticizing the 1989 Beijing massacre; Fatos Lubonja (Albania), a poet, novelist, and essayist imprisoned for 17 years for "decadent" writings; Bonar Tigor Naipospos (Indonesia), a journalist sentenced to eight and a half years in prison for expressing Marxist views; Nguyen Van Thuan (Vietnam), a journalist imprisoned in 1990 for publishing *Freedom Forum,* an underground newsletter advocating peaceful political reform; Fr. Richardo Rezende (Brazil), a parish priest and author who works with landless rural workers; and Alexandra Sviridova (Russia), journalist and filmmaker, whose investigative reports exposed rights abuses and corruption under the communist regime, now in exile in the United States.

Hellman/Hammett Grants. Address: Human Rights Watch, 485 Fifth Avenue, New York, NY 10017, USA. Telephone: (212) 972-8400. Contact: Marcia Allina.

**HENDERSON, ARTHUR (1863–1935).** The 1934 **NOBEL PEACE PRIZE** went to a man who championed the rights of labor and liberal governmental policies all of his adult life and who fervently worked for peace, even as the world prepared for war. Arthur Henderson was born in Glasgow, Scotland, to working-class parents and received little formal education; yet he had a profound impact on British policies during his lifetime. He was a foundry worker and union activist from 1875 to 1903. From 1903 to his death, he served in public office as a Labor Party leader; indeed, Henderson was instrumental in founding Britain's Labor Party and served as its secretary from 1911 to 1934.

After World War I, as a Labor Party minister in the governments of Lloyd George and Ramsay MacDonald, Henderson worked to ease the tensions between the victorious and the vanquished. In 1918, he called for a conference to be held in Berne, Switzerland, where delegates from combatants in the war would send recommendations on the peace treaty to Versailles. Under MacDonald's leadership, Henderson worked to draft the Geneva protocol for settlement of international disputes by arbitration. As foreign secretary under MacDonald, he reopened diplomatic relations between Britain and the Soviet Union and arranged for France to withdraw her troops from the Rhineland before the date settled in the Treaty of Versailles.

Henderson supported the notion of a world commonwealth as an end to war and national divisions. To this end, he worked in the League of Nations as head of its disarmament effort. It was for his leadership of the Disarmament Conference in 1932–34 that Henderson received the Nobel Prize. Although the Conference began with great hopes, it lost momentum in 1933, when Germany, under Adolph Hitler, withdrew from the conference and continued on its military buildup.

**BIBLIOGRAPHY.** Gray, Tony. *Champions of Peace.* London: Paddington Press, 1976.

Schlessinger, Bernard S., and June H. Schlessinger, eds. *Who's Who of Nobel Prize Winners.* Phoenix, AZ, USA: Oryx Press, 1991.

# HIGH COMMISSIONER FOR HUMAN RIGHTS, UN.

In resolution 48/141 of 20 December 1993, entitled "High Commissioner for the Promotion and Protection of All Human Rights," the UN **GENERAL ASSEMBLY** created the post of High Commissioner for Human Rights and set out the functions and responsibilities of the person appointed to that office. Subsequently the Secretary-General appointed José Ayala Lasso, the Permanent Representative of Ecuador to the United Nations, as the first High Commissioner for Human Rights, for a term of four years beginning on 28 February 1994.

The full text of the High Commissioner's Report to the Fifty-First Session of the Commission on Human Rights is reproduced below (E/CN.4/1995/98):

### Introduction

The General Assembly at its forty-eighth session in resolution 48/141 decided to create the post of High Commissioner for Human Rights. On 14 February 1994 and pursuant to the terms of that resolution, the General Assembly confirmed the Secretary-General's nomination of Mr. José Ayala Lasso as first United Nations High Commissioner for Human Rights. On 5 April 1994 the High Commissioner took up his functions at Geneva.

The establishment of the post of the High Commissioner for Human Rights is a result of the consensus reached at the World Conference on Human Rights on approaching the sensitive issue of human rights from a global perspective and on seeking global solutions to human rights problems. The "spirit of Vienna" resulted in the Declaration and Programme of Action, adopted by the World Conference. The

High Commissioner has reaffirmed his intention to preserve and constantly strengthen this spirit of international cooperation and solidarity so that the important tasks entrusted to him can be dealt with effectively.

The States Members of the United Nations, in creating the post by consensus, endowed the High Commissioner with political authority to express, in the area of human rights, the moral conscience of mankind. In keeping with the mandate, determined and multidimensional activities aimed at better promotion and protection of human rights are carried out in cooperation with Governments, United Nations specialized agencies, regional organizations, national institutions, non-governmental organizations and grass-roots organizations. The High Commissioner has committed himself to carrying out his functions with the sole objective of improving respect for all the human rights of every person in the world.

Since it was established in 1945, the United Nations has elaborated a comprehensive body of international human rights standards and put into place a complex system of international supervision of national respect for those standards which provide the High Commissioner with a solid foundation on which to build up his own specific activities. It was not intended that the High Commissioner would replace or duplicate the existing mechanisms. Rather, the High Commissioner is charged, inter alia, with using the tools of diplomacy to establish a dialogue with Governments in order to secure the greatest possible respect for all human rights and to provide needed assistance. Of course, these new methods are backed up by the ongoing work of the United Nations human rights programme.

The High Commissioner addressed the Economic and Social Council during its substantive session for 1994 (July 1994). Pursuant to the request contained in paragraph 5 of General Assembly resolution 48/141, the High Commissioner submitted a report (A/49/36) to the General Assembly at its forty-ninth session and is submitting the present report to the Commission on Human Rights at its fifty-first session. Since a relatively short time has passed since the submission of the report to the General Assembly, the present report provides an up-date of the High Commissioner's activities and should be read against the background of that report.

Pursuant to the request contained in paragraph 9 of Commission resolution 1994/95, this report contains a section (sect. III) on progress towards the full implementation of the recommendations contained in the Vienna Declaration and Programme of Action. That part has been prepared in the context of the report of the Secretary-General on the follow-up to the World Conference on Human Rights, submitted to the General Assembly at its forty-ninth session (A/49/668).

### Mandate of the High Commissioner

Pursuant to General Assembly resolution 48/141, the High Commissioner for Human Rights is the United Nations official with principal responsibility for United Nations human rights activities, under the direction and authority of the Secretary-General and within the framework of the overall competence, authority and decisions of the General Assembly, the Economic and Social Council and the Commission on Human Rights. Resolution 48/141 provides that the High Commissioner is to carry out his duties in an impartial, objective, non-selective and effective manner within the framework of the Charter of the United Nations, the Universal Declaration of Human Rights and other international instruments of human rights and international law, and that he is to be guided by the recognition that all human rights—civil, cultural, economic, political and social—are universal, indivisible, interdependent and interrelated. The High Commissioner has based his activities on three main principles: international cooperation at all levels; a comprehensive and integrated approach to the promotion and protection of human rights; and the participation of all actors in programmes, plans and projects to promote human rights at the international, national and local levels. These principles are applied in a spirit of dialogue, consensus and solidarity.

In keeping with his mandate and in the context of the Vienna Declaration and Programme of Action, the High Commissioner has oriented his activities towards:

Promoting international cooperation in the field of human rights;

Strengthening implementation of all human rights;

Responding to serious violations of human rights;

Acting to prevent violations of human rights from becoming serious or widespread;

Assisting countries in transition to democracy;

Providing advisory services and technical assistance in the field of human rights;

Coordinating human rights activities within the United Nations system;

Adapting the United Nations human rights machinery to current and future needs;

Promoting the right to development and the enjoyment of cultural, economic and social rights;

Combating racial discrimination; promoting the rights of persons belonging to groups requiring special protection: women, children, minorities and indigenous people;

Combating the most atrocious human rights violations, such as torture and involuntary disappearances;

Promoting human rights education and public information activities;

Implementing the Vienna Declaration and Programme of Action.

## Main Fields of the High Commissioner's Activity

### A. Promoting International Cooperation in the Field of Human Rights, Including the Universal Ratification of Human Rights Instruments

Close cooperation between the High Commissioner and Governments, the United Nations agencies and programmes, other international organizations, national institutions for the promotion and protection of human rights and non-governmental organizations is an important instrument for strengthening national protection of human rights and building support for the United Nations human rights programme in general.

A key element in the High Commissioner's mandate as set out by the General Assembly is the responsibility of engaging in a dialogue with all Governments with a view to securing respect for all human rights. To ensure that his actions are effective, the High Commissioner must have the support and cooperation of Governments. The High Commissioner has invited all Governments to engage in a frank dialogue, without conditions or prejudice. The response to that call has been very encouraging. In pursuit of this dialogue, the High Commissioner has visited Switzerland, as the host country, Austria, Bhutan, Burundi, Cambodia, Colombia, Cuba, Denmark, Estonia, Finland, Germany, Japan, the

Republic of Korea, Latvia, Lithuania, Malawi, Nepal, Norway, Rwanda and Sweden.

In the framework of his missions, the High Commissioner has urged States to ratify the human rights treaties they have not so far ratified and discussed strengthening national implementation of human rights through the preparation of national plans of action, the establishment of national institutions such as human rights commissions or an ombudsman, and the promotion of human rights education. He has stressed the need to promote and protect cultural, economic and social rights, as well as the right to development, and to consider the impact of various policies on those rights, especially with regard to the most vulnerable groups in society. The High Commissioner has raised issues relating to the promotion of the rights of women; the status of minorities and the status of non-citizens; the legal status of refugees and asylum seekers; the protection of the rights of children; and the conformity of national legislation with international standards. He has also paid attention to the need for strengthening international cooperation on human rights, and for support for the United Nations human rights programme.

A permanent dialogue has been maintained with all the United Nations bodies dealing with human rights, including the Commission on Human Rights, the Sub-Commission on Prevention of Discrimination and Protection of Minorities and the various working groups they have established, as well as the treaty monitoring bodies. Cooperation has been developed with intergovernmental and national development agencies, with a view to integrating a human rights dimension into their development programmes.

Strengthening cooperation with all regional organizations dealing with human rights is an important objective. The tripartite meeting of the Council of Europe, the Conference on Security and Cooperation in Europe and Geneva-based United Nations programmes, held on 1 September 1994 and attended by the High Commissioner, dealt inter alia with these issues. Working contacts on various issues have been developed.

The High Commissioner has also initiated a dialogue with States and non-governmental organizations (NGOs) in order to develop or establish regional arrangements in the field of human rights. In the framework of the Third Asia-Pacific Workshop on Human Rights Issues (July 1994, Republic of Korea) he discussed questions related to setting up a regional or subregional human rights arrangement in Asia.

National institutions and non-governmental organizations are natural partners of the High Commissioner. Meetings and consultations with such institutions and organizations have become an important component of his country missions.

The High Commissioner will continue determined action aimed at promoting the universal ratification of human rights instruments, guided by the call of the World Conference for the universal ratification of the Convention on the Rights of the Child by the end of 1995, and of the Convention on Elimination of All Forms of Discrimination against Women by the year 2000. In cooperation with the United Nations Development Programme (UNDP) resident coordinators, the Secretary-General's letter to Governments encouraging ratification of international instruments will be followed up.

The High Commissioner has granted a large number of interviews to television, radio and the press, to enhance coverage of human rights issues, including international cooperation in this field, by the mass media, which have a very important role to play in human rights education and information.

## B. Strengthening the Implementation of all Human Rights

The United Nations human rights programme today increasingly focuses its activities on the implementation of the international human rights standards. The country rapporteurs, thematic special rapporteurs, working groups and the treaty bodies attach great importance to developing methods and means to improve the implementation of human rights. The General Assembly at its forty-ninth session, in resolution 49/178, identified steps to be taken in this respect and reiterated its support for the related efforts and recommendations of the treaty bodies. It also urged States parties to make every effort to meet their reporting obligations and to address, as a matter of priority, at their next scheduled meetings, the issue of States parties consistently not complying with their treaty obligations. In its resolution 49/145, the General Assembly welcomed the innovatory procedures adopted by the Committee on the Elimination of Racial Discrimination for reviewing the implementation of the Convention in States whose reports are overdue. The General Assembly also, in resolution 49/178, recognized the important role of non-governmental organizations in the effective implementation of all human rights.

In keeping with his mandate, the High Commissioner is determined to contribute to a better implementation of human rights worldwide. During his missions to countries and on other occasions, he has stressed that although the adoption of legislation consistent with international standards is of paramount importance, it is still necessary to apply it in practice. Furthermore, the efficient functioning of the international human rights machinery, which assists the implementation of the international human rights standards, depends on the cooperation of the Member States. The High Commissioner, guided by the relevant resolutions of the General Assembly and the Commission on Human Rights, will assist the special procedures and the treaty bodies in their efforts towards better implementation of human rights.

The Commission on Human Rights, at its fiftieth session, observed encouraging trends. A growing number of countries have developed a working relationship with the Commission and its mechanisms. A number of countries have improved their human rights record. The language of the resolutions relating to South Africa reflects the momentous change in that country. The end of apartheid and the beginning of democracy through free elections are the achievements of a human rights process embodied in the presidency of Nelson Mandela. Another example of the worldwide process of transition to democracy and human rights is the return of President Aristide to Haiti, which was strongly demanded by the Commission on Human Rights, inter alia. Resolutions adopted by and the statement of the Commission at its fiftieth session under the agenda item concerning advisory services in the field of human rights have guided the provision of assistance to Albania, Cambodia, El Salvador, Georgia, Guatemala, Romania and Somalia.

The positive developments, however, are accompanied by the concern expressed by the General Assembly and the Commission with regard to (a) obstacles to the enjoyment of all human rights by all, (b) serious human rights violations and (c) difficult human rights situations in a relatively large number of countries. Resolutions of these bodies have drawn the attention of Governments, the United Nations system and the general public and have called for action with regard to extreme poverty and problems related to sustainable development, international debt, impunity, racial discrimination and discrimination against women, ethnic and religious intolerance, mass exoduses and refugee flows, armed conflicts and terrorism, and lack of the rule of law as major obstacles to human rights. The outcome of the intensive work concerning the right to development, as well as the strengthening of the interlinkage between democracy, development and human rights should provide a helpful strategy to meet the needs in this respect. The General Assembly and the Commission and its mechanisms have for many years alerted the international community to widespread crimes of torture and enforced disappearance; arbitrary detention; violence against women, children and vulnerable groups; the problem of internally displaced persons; extrajudicial, summary or arbitrary executions, etc. The Commission has also elaborated measures to combat these violations at the national and international levels which should be applied with the greatest determination. Under the agenda item related to the question of violations of human rights and fundamental freedoms in any part of the world, with particular reference to colonial and other dependent countries and territories, the Commission expressed its concern about the human rights situation in Afghanistan, Angola, Burundi, Cuba, East Timor, Equatorial Guinea, Haiti, the Islamic Republic of Iran, Iraq, Kosovo, Myanmar, the Papua New Guinea island of Bougainville, the territory of the former Yugoslavia: Bosnia and Herzegovina, Croatia, and the Federal Republic of Yugoslavia (Serbia and Montenegro), southern Lebanon, Sudan and Zaire. Under agenda item 4, the Commission considered violations of human rights in the occupied Arab territories, including Palestine, and under agenda items 5 and 6, the situation in South Africa. In addition, various thematic procedures in their reports to the Commission pointed out serious human rights problems in a number of countries and made recommendations in this regard. Under the procedure established in Economic and Social Council resolution 1503 (XLVIII), the Commission had before it for consideration the human rights situations in Armenia, Azerbaijan, Chad, Estonia, Germany, Kuwait, Rwanda, Somalia and Viet Nam. The Commission decided to discontinue consideration of the human rights situation in Estonia, Germany, Kuwait, Somalia and Viet Nam. The High Commissioner in his dialogue with Governments raises issues related to specific situations with a view to securing respect for all human rights.

A particularly difficult situation arises when Governments refuse or limit their cooperation with the Commission or its mechanisms. This is a major obstacle to providing assistance to Governments and to those members of society who need it. The General Assembly at its forty-ninth session, in resolution 49/186, urged again all States to cooperate with the Commission on Human Rights in the promotion and protection of human rights and fundamental freedoms. Unfortunately, resolutions of the Commission give instances of non-compliance with this recommendation. For example, in its resolution 1994/39, the Commission noted with concern that, as the Working Group on Enforced or Involuntary Disappearances had stressed in its report, some Governments had never provided substantive replies concerning enforced disappearances alleged to have occurred in their countries, and deplored the fact that some Governments had not acted on the recommendations of the Working Group concerning them. In the same resolution, the Commission urged the Governments concerned, particularly those which had not yet acted with regard to communications transmitted to them, to intensify their cooperation with the Working Group. (See also General Assembly resolution A/49/l93 on the question of enforced disappearances.) The very fact that the appeal to Governments to cooperate with the special procedures has been repeated by the General Assembly and the Commission in a number of their resolutions proves that cooperation is insufficient. Also, in resolutions adopted at its fiftieth session, the Commission frequently stressed its concern about the lack of or inadequate cooperation with the United Nations machinery, in particular with the Commission's mechanisms. The Commission, in resolution 1994/72, deplored and condemned the continual refusal of the Bosnian Serbs authorities to permit the Special Rapporteur to conduct investigations in territory under their control. In resolution 1994/71, the Commission noted with deep regret the continued failure of the Government of Cuba to cooperate with the Special Rapporteur and its refusal to permit him to visit Cuba in order to fulfil his mandate. The Commission, in its resolution 1994/73, while noting that the Government of the Islamic Republic of Iran had responded to the Special Representative's request for information, also noted that it had not allowed him to pay a fourth visit to the country so that he might obtain direct and first-hand information on the current human rights situation. In its resolution 1994/74, the Commission expressed its regret that the Government of Iraq had not seen fit to respond to the formal request of the Special Rapporteur on the situation of human rights in Iraq to visit Iraq and that, despite the formal cooperation extended to the Special Rapporteur by the Government of Iraq, such cooperation needed to be improved. The Commission, in its resolution 1994/79, noted with displeasure the interference by the Government of the Sudan with the visit to the Sudan of the Special Rapporteur during September 1993. In its resolution 1994/81, the Commission expressed its concern that the Government of Papua New Guinea had not provided information to the Commission on actions it had taken during the previous year. The Commission was also gravely concerned that in southern Lebanon, occupied by Israel, the International Committee of the Red Cross and other humanitarian organizations had been impeded from accomplishing their humanitarian mission (resolution 1994/83) and deplored the fact that the Myanmar authorities had denied the Special Rapporteur on the situation in Myanmar access to the Nobel Prize laureate—Daw Aung San Suu Kyi (resolution 1994/85), who despite the resolution of the Commission is still under house arrest. General Assembly resolutions also refer to the majority of the aforementioned cases. In its resolution 49/196, the General Assembly condemned the continuing refusal of the Federal Republic of Yugoslavia (Serbia and Montenegro) and the Bosnian Serbs authorities to permit the Special Rapporteur to conduct investigations in territories under their control, and in resolution 49/204 considered that the re-establishment of the international presence in Kosovo to monitor and investigate the situation of human rights was of great importance in preventing the situation in Kosovo from deteriorating into a violent conflict. In keeping with his mandate, the High Commissioner assists the Commission, its mechanisms and other relevant parts of the United Nations human rights machinery, as well as Governments, in establishing and developing mutual working contacts with a view to implementing relevant Commission resolutions. Also, while undertaking missions to various countries, the High

Commissioner is paving the way for cooperation between Governments and United Nations organs and bodies. His visits, however, do not replace missions and other activities of other competent mechanisms.

The implementation of human rights requires unimpeded cooperation of individuals and groups with the United Nations and representatives of its human rights bodies. The Commission reiterated in resolution 1994/70 its concern at the continued reports of intimidation and reprisals against private individuals and groups who seek such cooperation. The General Assembly referred, in its resolutions 49/197 and 49/198, to acts of deprivation of freedom of people who contacted or were seeking to communicate with the respective special rapporteurs in Myanmar and in the Sudan. The High Commissioner will pay close attention to this issue in all his contacts with Governments, as well as with NGOs and other parts of civil society. No one should be deprived of his or her freedom because of cooperation with the United Nations and representatives of its bodies.

## C. Activities in the Period November 1994–January 1995

After the submission of his first report to the General Assembly, which contained information on his visits to countries, the High Commissioner undertook missions to Colombia and Cuba at the invitation of the respective Governments. The purpose of these visits was the advancement of the promotion and protection of human rights and the strengthening of ties between the countries concerned and the United Nations human rights programme.

From 15 to 19 November 1994, the High Commissioner visited Cuba. The main purpose of his visit was to establish a dialogue with the Government on all matters concerning the promotion and protection of human rights, including the United Nations human rights programme as a whole; the right to development; the human rights situation in Cuba; and the implementation of the mandate of the High Commissioner for Human Rights. In addition, it was the desire of the High Commissioner to facilitate contacts and cooperation between the mechanisms of the Commission on Human Rights and the Government of Cuba. The mission was primarily action oriented and directed at making measurable progress in the field of human rights. The High Commissioner discussed human rights matters with the President and other high authorities of the country. He also met representatives of civil society, including informal non-governmental organizations. The High Commissioner had the opportunity to become acquainted with the efforts of the Government with regard to the infrastructure for cultural, economic and social rights. The authorities informed him about the obstacles to development which, in the view of the Government, limited the results of its action. The High Commissioner emphasized with all his interlocutors matters relating to the better promotion and protection of human rights, including ratification of international human rights instruments; the need for improvements in national legislation to make it fully consistent with international human rights standards; the importance of establishing national institutions for the promotion and protection of human rights and of ensuring the independence of the judiciary. The High Commissioner also stressed the obligation of all Governments to ensure respect for and observance of all human rights, including civil and political rights, and to cooperate with the United Nations organs, bodies and mechanisms acting in the field of human rights, including the country rapporteur established by the Commission on Human Rights. He expressed his deep concern about the number of persons who were reported to be political prisoners. While making reference to the linkage between democracy, development and human rights, the High Commissioner referred to the pertinent resolutions of the General Assembly and stipulations of the Vienna Declaration and Programme of Action which stressed the role of normal economic and trade relations in creating conditions for sustainable development in all spheres of life, including the area of cultural, economic, and social rights. The High Commissioner offered advisory services and technical assistance to the efforts aimed at the protection of human rights. It was agreed that the dialogue would continue. The representatives of the Government assured the High Commissioner that his opinions and comments would be carefully examined with a view to implementing them.

From 12 to 14 December 1994, the High Commissioner visited Colombia. This mission took place relatively shortly after a new Government had been installed and the President had made a statement announcing a new policy in the field of human rights. The President acknowledged that his country was facing serious human rights problems and announced that all necessary measures would be taken in order to overcome the situation. A positive attitude to close cooperation with the Commission on Human Rights and its thematic mechanisms was also a part of this approach to human rights issues. At the invitation of the Government of Colombia, the Special Rapporteur on extrajudicial, summary and arbitrary executions and the Special Rapporteur on torture visited the country. In his dialogue with the President and other high ranking representatives of the Government, as well with the human rights community, the High Commissioner stressed the need for concerted efforts to improve the human rights infrastructure and prevent human rights violations. Joint efforts were all the more important in the context of the challenges presented by the high rate of crime and other acute social problems. The question of the responsibility of perpetrators of human rights violations was also one of the major topics discussed by the High Commissioner with the authorities. It is worth noting in this respect that the President announced his determination to combat impunity, which will, however, require a number of legislative reforms. Several interlocutors from non-governmental organizations and parliamentary circles expressed the need to establish a United Nations mechanism that could provide assistance on human rights issues. A programme of advisory services and technical assistance will be developed in Colombia by the Centre for Human Rights, especially in connection with legislative reforms and the administration of justice. A follow-up needs assessment mission should be sent to Santa Fe de Bogota very soon. The High Commissioner also met the heads of the various United Nations agency and programme offices in Colombia.

The High Commissioner has undertaken action with regard to the human rights situation in Chechnya. He carried out a number of consultations with Permanent Representatives at Geneva, including the Permanent Representative of the Russian Federation, as well as with United Nations agencies and international organizations, including the Organization for Security and Cooperation in Europe, and non-governmental organizations. During his meeting with the Minister for Foreign Affairs of the Russian Federation in Geneva on 17 January 1995, the High Commissioner reiterated his profound preoccupation at the reports of violations of human rights and humanitarian law in Chechnya, charac-

terized by a large number of civilian victims, and appealed once again for an immediate end to violence and violations of human rights in full respect for the Charter of the United Nations, the Universal Declaration of Human Rights, international human rights instruments and humanitarian law. The High Commissioner offered the cooperation of his office in connection with the promotion of human rights and the provision of technical assistance for the re-establishment of basic human rights infrastructure. He also reiterated his proposal to send as soon as possible a mission to Moscow and Chechnya to meet with all concerned.

### D. Responding to Serious Violations of Human Rights

The General Assembly entrusted the High Commissioner with the responsibility of playing an active role in preventing the continuation of human rights violations throughout the world, as reflected in the Vienna Declaration and Programme of Action. The activities of the High Commissioner in this regard opened a new avenue of United Nations action. His appeals addressing specific problems or cases created a new framework for a continuing dialogue on human rights with all the actors involved.

The High Commissioner responded with a comprehensive action to the tragic human rights situation in Rwanda. He undertook two missions to this country and urged in May 1994 from its capital all the protagonists to put an end to the massive violations of human rights, to conclude a cease-fire without delay and to allow humanitarian aid to be dispatched to all those who needed it. On 24 and 25 May 1994, at the request of the Government of Canada, following a suggestion by the High Commissioner, the Commission on Human Rights held its third special session, to consider the human rights situation in Rwanda. Pursuant to Commission resolution S-3/1, a special rapporteur for Rwanda was appointed and was requested to report to the Commission on the human rights situation in that country and to gather and compile information on possible violations of human rights and acts which might constitute breaches of international humanitarian law and crimes against humanity, including acts of genocide. The High Commissioner presented to the Commission at its third special session a report on his mission to Rwanda and the region (E/CN.4/S-3/3), and made recommendations for specific action to bring the cycle of violence in that country to an end. On 15 September 1994, after his second visit to Rwanda, the High Commissioner presented a detailed preliminary operational plan for the human rights field operation in Rwanda, designed to support the work of the Special Rapporteur and the Commission of Experts established pursuant to Security Council resolution 935 (1994), and to provide advisory services. That plan described the legal and conceptual framework for the High Commissioner's activities in Rwanda and laid out the resource requirements. A revised operational plan was presented during the UNDP round table on Rwanda on 18 and 19 January 1995.

Through his local office, the High Commissioner is conducting a human rights field operation in Rwanda (a) to carry out investigations into violations of human rights and humanitarian law, (b) to monitor the ongoing human rights situation, essentially for the purposes of the mandate of the Special Rapporteur, (c) to cooperate with other international agencies in re-establishing confidence and thus facilitate the return of refugees and displaced persons and the rebuilding of civic society, (d) to implement programmes of technical cooperation in the field of human rights. In the framework of this human rights field operation, more than 100 personnel are employed in Rwanda at present. The High Commissioner participated on 18 and 19 January 1995 in a round table on assistance to Rwanda, organized by UNDP, and on 20 January 1995 in a consolidated appeal on Rwanda organized by the Department of Humanitarian Affairs. Both events took place at Geneva. The case of Rwanda exemplifies the spirit in which the High Commissioner may act in emergency human rights situations.

Since his appointment, the High Commissioner has been in close contact with the Special Rapporteur on the human rights situation in the former Yugoslavia, whose mandate is served by a field operation of the Centre for Human Rights. He has also established contacts with the Special Representative of the Secretary-General for the former Yugoslavia with a view to strengthening and enhancing human rights activities in Bosnia and Herzegovina. In the light of the request of the Government for assistance, following the establishment of the Federation of Bosnia and Herzegovina, and the terms of the December 1994 agreements on cease-fire and cessation of hostilities, the High Commissioner for Human Rights, after consultation with the Secretary-General and his Special Representative, took the initiative of convening a meeting on 3 February 1995 to develop, in close cooperation with other United Nations bodies operating in Bosnia and Herzegovina, a coordinated and more effective response to human rights requirements in the country.

The cooperation of countries is strongly required in securing support needed to carry out activities rapidly and effectively in situations of serious human rights violations and where preventive action is necessary. The following areas are of particular importance: (a) logistical assistance capacity on a standby basis to provide material, communications and other support for emergency or preventive field missions; (b) the establishment and maintenance of an international roster of specialized staff to be available at short notice for human rights field missions (investigation teams, human rights field officers, legal experts, etc.); (c) increased contributions to the Voluntary End for Technical Cooperation in order to cover the financial needs of field missions and advisory services assistance. The response of Governments, international organizations and United Nations agencies and programmes, as well as non-governmental organizations, to the request by the High Commissioner for assistance in the above-mentioned areas has been very encouraging. However, meeting these needs requires continuous cooperation.

### E.  Acting to Prevent Violations of Human Rights From Becoming Serious or Widespread

In accordance with General Assembly resolution 48/141, the High Commissioner has the responsibility to play an active role in removing the current obstacles and in meeting the challenges to full realization of all human rights. The High Commissioner himself has repeatedly stressed that the prevention of human rights violations constitutes an essential part of his action. He avails himself of every possibility of acting at the diplomatic level to obtain rapid and substantive results with individual Governments and in relation to specific matters. Close cooperation between the High Commissioner and the special procedures and treaty bodies and the relevant agencies and programmes can play a most useful role both in providing early warning of future disasters and in mitigating or even avoiding such disasters. Experience has

shown that the provision of advisory services and technical assistance in appropriate cases can be an important element in preventing violations of human rights.

A system-wide policy for preventing serious human rights violations is being devised. It will be based on early-warning arrangements and other forms of interaction between United Nations agencies and relevant departments of the United Nations Secretariat. It will be important in the future to have as early notice as possible of situations in which various elements of the United Nations human rights programme could play a role in preventing the outbreak of serious violations of human rights. In this connection, the High Commissioner has written to the Chairpersons of human rights treaty bodies, to the special rapporteurs and representatives, experts, and working groups established by the Commission on Human Rights, as well as to United Nations agencies and programmes and non-governmental organizations to invite them to call his attention to situations which might need preventive action. At their fifth meeting, from 19 to 23 September 1994, the Chairpersons of the human rights treaty bodies urged those bodies to take all appropriate measures in response to situations of massive violations of human rights, including bringing those violations to the attention of the High Commissioner for Human Rights, as well as of the Secretary-General. The High Commissioner has already taken steps to enhance the Centre's capacity to analyse and review information resulting from the activities of special rapporteurs, working groups of the Commission on Human Rights and the treaty bodies with respect to situations which might need preventive action.

The United Nations human rights presence which has been set up in Burundi in cooperation with the Government provides an example of preventive action taken by the High Commissioner. The crisis in Rwanda could have had negative repercussions in Burundi, which had managed to maintain relative calm after the death of its President on 6 April 1994. The High Commissioner visited Burundi twice to support the action of the Government and others in promoting respect for human rights and thus contributing to a stabilization of the situation. Benefiting from the cooperation and expertise of the Special Representative of the Secretary-General of the United Nations in Burundi, the UNDP Resident Representative and other United Nations field officers, the High Commissioner elaborated proposals concerning a programme of cooperation and technical assistance in the field of human rights for Burundi. Agreement with the Government of Burundi was reached on this programme, which will be part of a comprehensive integrated approach to be carried out in close cooperation with all United Nations agencies and programmes present in Burundi.

An office of the High Commissioner has been established in Bujumbura to implement the above agreement. It has since been agreed with the Government to strengthen the assistance programme in the following areas: (a) training and educational activities (particularly for the judiciary, the police, the gendarmerie and the military); (b) advisory services of experts on human rights (particularly for the military and the judiciary); (c) human rights fellowships; (d) human rights documentation; (e) promotional activities for a human rights culture; (f) support for the Centre for Human Rights of Bujumbura; and (g) assistance to the human rights promotional activities of national human rights NGOs, such as the two human rights leagues. Since his second visit to Burundi, the High Commissioner has stressed the importance that an enhanced human rights presence within the framework of his office would have in ensuring the promotion of human rights and acting as a deterrent with respect to possible future violations. In view of the deteriorating situation in Burundi, the Security Council decided to send a mission there in February 1995. From 15 to 17 February 1995, the Organization of African Unity and UNHCR organized a regional conference in Bujumbura on the issues of refugees and displaced persons. Representatives of the High Commissioner attended a number of meetings organized by NGOs on Burundi, most recently a meeting organized by International Alert in London on 3 February 1995.

The General Assembly, in its resolution 49/204, requested the Secretary-General to seek ways and means, including through consultations with the High Commissioner and relevant regional organizations, to establish an adequate monitoring presence in Kosovo and to report thereon to the General Assembly.

### F. Assisting Countries in Transition to Democracy

A number of countries worldwide are in transition from authoritarian to democratic rule, which opens the avenue to the full protection of human rights in those countries. This crucial process requires encouragement and international cooperation, as stressed by the World Conference on Human Rights in the Vienna Declaration and Programme of Action. The provision of assistance aimed at establishing and strengthening human rights infrastructure, the rule of law and democracy is a momentous responsibility of the United Nations and, in particular, of its human rights programme. To ensure this assistance, emphasis has been placed on two major objectives: (a) the elaboration of national human rights programmes which should be carried out in cooperation with the United Nations and (b) the strengthening of the related United Nations infrastructure. The reaction of Governments to the High Commissioner's initiatives in this respect has been very positive.

The cooperation of the United Nations with the Government of Malawi is an example of assistance to countries in transition. The Centre for Human Rights provided advisory services to Malawi in connection with that country's 1993 referendum on multiparty democracy, the preparations for the multiparty elections of 1994 and the drafting of a new constitution. During his visit to Malawi, the High Commissioner and the Vice-President of the Republic signed a Joint Declaration of Cooperation for the Development of Programmes for the Promotion and Protection of Human Rights in Malawi. The programme will run for two years from 1 January 1995. It covers several areas of priority need, such as constitutional reform, assistance to the judiciary, training of the police and the military, human rights education in primary and secondary schools, support to the civil society, to the Parliament and to structures concerned with the administration of justice, such as jails and detention centres. The office of the High Commissioner for Human Rights in Lilongwe was opened in mid-November 1994 for the purpose of assisting in the implementation of the programme.

### G. Providing Advisory Services and Technical Assistance in the Field of Human Rights

The United Nations programme of advisory services and technical assistance is a crucial instrument for the promotion of human rights. The General Assembly, in resolution 48/141, entrusted the High Commissioner with the responsibility for providing, through the Centre for Human Rights or other appropriate institutions, such services and assistance at the request of the State concerned and, where appropriate, the regional human rights organizations, with a view to supporting actions and programmes in the field of human rights. The strengthening of this United Nations programme was strongly recommended by the World Conference on Human Rights as one of the principal means for achieving the objectives laid down in the Vienna Declaration and Programme of Action. The General Assembly in its resolution 49/178 requested the High Commissioner to report regularly to the Commission on possible technical assistance projects identified by the treaty bodies.

The present objectives of the programme of advisory and technical assistance implemented by the Centre for Human Rights result predominantly from the Vienna Declaration and Programme of Action and are oriented towards: facilitating the process of ratification or accession to international human rights instruments; assisting legislative reforms bringing national laws into line with international human rights standards; assisting States in implementing the recommendations of human rights treaty bodies; the protection of groups rendered vulnerable, such as minorities, indigenous people, women, children, migrant workers, disabled persons, refugees and displaced persons; strengthening the rule of law and democratic institutions, assistance to the judiciary, including training in the administration of justice and police officials as an important element for improving the observance of human rights, as well as of human rights aspects of electoral assistance; assisting States in meeting their reporting obligations under the various human rights treaties. The Centre also assists in the elaboration of national plans of action in the field of human rights, which are supported by the programme of technical assistance. In an increasing number of States, comprehensive country programmes are being carried out in the framework of advisory services and technical assistance.

The coordination of advisory services programmes in the field of human rights is the responsibility of the High Commissioner and the Centre for Human Rights. The latter is a focal point and a clearing house for requests by Member States for technical cooperation in the field of human rights. The High Commissioner developed his vision of a new and enhanced partnership with relevant human rights institutions and NGOs in the implementation of technical assistance programmes. He underlined the availability of the advisory services and technical assistance to the whole human rights constituency, including national institutions, non-governmental organizations, academic institutions and grassroots organizations. Furthermore, non-governmental organizations and academic institutions are expected to contribute to the advisory services and technical assistance programme, if their capacities permit it.

In the context of the transition in Haiti, the General Assembly, in its resolution 49/201, requested the Secretary-General, through the High Commissioner and the Centre for Human Rights, to take appropriate steps for the urgent establishment, in conjunction with the International Civilian Mission to Haiti, of a special programme of assistance to the Government and people of Haiti in their efforts to ensure the observance of human rights. Appropriate preparatory steps, especially with regard to financial and human resources, are being taken.

Multidimensional programmes of advisory services and technical assistance are conducted by the Centre for Human Rights in the Eastern and Central European countries which are in transition from authoritarian to democratic rule. They range from constitutional and legislative assistance; human rights training in the administration of justice, for teachers, police and prison administrators; assistance for parliamentarians, academic institutions and non-governmental organizations, to assistance in human rights aspects of the electoral process.

The High Commissioner discussed advisory services and technical assistance programmes in particular during his visits to Burundi, Bhutan, Cambodia, Colombia, Cuba, Estonia, Latvia, Lithuania, Malawi and Nepal (see the report of the High Commissioner to the General Assembly at its forty-ninth session (A/49/36)).

## H. Coordinating Human Rights Activities Within the United Nations System

United Nations agencies and programmes, other international organizations, national human rights institutions and non-governmental organizations all have important contributions to make to promoting human rights. Cooperation and coordination among those bodies is essential for contributing to the achievement of the purposes of the United Nations in the field of human rights through better management, greater efficiency and cost effectiveness. Pursuant to General Assembly resolution 48/141, the High Commissioner is responsible for system-wide coordination of activities aiming at the promotion and protection of human rights. A permanent dialogue with the United Nations agencies and programmes has been established to maintain systematic exchange of information, experience and expertise; in addition, operational cooperation and coordination are being developed. Working agreements or memoranda of understanding between the High Commissioner and the United Nations agencies have been concluded or are under preparation. They are based on the identification of areas of common interest and joint action in the field of human rights. The High Commissioner took part in the 11-12 April 1994 session of the Administrative Committee on Coordination concerning the coordination of efforts aimed at the full implementation of the Vienna Declaration and Programme of Action.

Coordination of activities was among the central objectives of meetings and contacts the High Commissioner had with the heads of UNICEF, UNDP, UNHCR and UNESCO and other United Nations agencies and programmes and the International Organization for Migration. It should be noted that cooperation with United Nations agencies and programmes has increased substantially in connection with the human rights field operations and provided a solid base for cooperation in other areas as well. Operations in Rwanda, Burundi, Malawi, Bosnia and Herzegovina, Croatia and the former Yugoslav Republic of Macedonia are examples of such cooperation.

Reinforcing coordination and cooperation is closely connected with the rationalization of the United Nations machinery in the field of human rights. In this context, the High Commissioner chaired the first meeting of special rapporteurs, experts and chairpersons of working groups of the Commission on Human Rights, held at Geneva from 30 May to 1 June 1994. The High Commissioner stressed that the work of the special rapporteurs, experts and working groups was an important pillar of the implementation of human rights and that he did not intend to duplicate or substitute himself for those mechanisms. He has overall competence for the promotion and protection of human rights and special rappor-

teurs are entrusted with mandates relating to specific subjects or situations. These mandates require fact-finding, investigation and the assessment of phenomena, situations and cases, and, as far as advisory services experts are concerned, the development of comprehensive programmes of human rights assistance and training. In this framework, the mandate of the High Commissioner is essentially one of facilitation and coordination and of promoting follow-up action to implement recommendations made by special rapporteurs, experts and working groups. The priority areas, where enhanced cooperation and exchange of information with and among special rapporteurs, working groups, and treaty bodies should be ensured, are the following: (a) early warning on emergency human rights situations; (b) field missions by the various special rapporteurs or working groups; (c) follow-up action of the High Commissioner to recommendations made by special rapporteurs and working groups; (d) the work of other implementation mechanisms and the provision of advisory services and technical assistance to Member States.

During the fifth meeting of the Chairpersons of human rights treaty bodies, the High Commissioner underlined the importance of the treaty bodies to the human rights activities of the United Nations, as was recognized by the World Conference, stressed his commitment to supporting the work of those bodies. The regular meetings of the Chairpersons are an important method of improving and coordinating the work of the United Nations human rights machinery.

## I. Adapting the United Nations Human Rights Machinery to Current and Future Needs

The mandate of the High Commissioner includes specific responsibility for rationalization, adaptation, strengthening and streamlining of the United Nations machinery in the field of human rights with a view to improving its efficiency and effectiveness. The World Conference on Human Rights recognized the necessity for a continuing adaptation of the United Nations human rights machinery to current and future needs in the promotion and protection of human rights, as reflected in the Vienna Declaration and Programme of Action, within the framework of balanced and sustainable development. In line with the Vienna Declaration and Programme of Action, measures should be taken urgently to make the human rights machinery: (a) more effective and cost efficient; (b) able to act swiftly and to respond appropriately to human rights situations; (c) stronger, through international cooperation in the field of human rights, based on mutual confidence; and (d) more transparent and understandable to the outside world. The activities of the machinery should be supported by an easy accessible and efficient overall system of information and documentation based on modern technology. Paragraph 9 of General Assembly resolution 49/208, in which the Assembly requested the High Commissioner to submit a report with a detailed plan of the human and financial resource requirements for the implementation of the recommendations of the Vienna Declaration and Programme of Action, requires an integrated approach to the reform of the United Nations human rights machinery.

The High Commissioner bases his activities related to the adaptation of the United Nations machinery to the current and future needs in the field of human rights on the following premises:

(a) The adjustment of a given organ or body to the new needs remains the primary responsibility of this organ or of another organ vested with a special competence to take proper decisions. The High Commissioner thus assists and facilitates human rights organs and bodies in their endeavours;

(b) In cooperation with the relevant organs and bodies, the High Commissioner will analyse the existing United Nations human rights machinery with a view to working out proposals for its overall adaptation to current and anticipated needs and for better coordination of human rights activities;

(c) The High Commissioner in cooperation with these organs and bodies will undertake measures to strengthen the implementation of their recommendations and decisions (for example, cooperation with special procedures and treaty bodies in this regard).

The adaptation of the machinery should be perceived as a multidimensional and continuing process in the framework of which reforms relating to specific organs or procedures are placed against the background of the overall adaptation of the United Nations human rights machinery. New solutions should be introduced gradually, taking into account the need for practical verification and the possibility of change, if necessary. It is of vital importance to start the process of adaptation in practical terms without unnecessary delay.

In accordance with General Assembly resolution 48/141, the High Commissioner for Human Rights has responsibility for the overall supervision of the Centre for Human Rights. The Centre, as the principal unit of the Secretariat dealing with human rights issues, and the High Commissioner for Human Rights represent a unity of action whereby the High Commissioner sets the policy directions and the Centre implements those policies. The High Commissioner for Human Rights and the Centre for Human Rights maintain an office at United Nations Headquarters in New York.

The High Commissioner will assess needs related to the adaptation of the United Nations secretariat structures dealing with human rights, including the Centre for Human Rights. In that regard, the Office for Inspections and Investigations, the predecessor of the Office of Internal Oversight Services, carried out, in June 1994, a review of the programme and administrative practices of the Centre for Human Rights which gave rise to a number of recommendations, concerning inter alia: the translation of the Vienna Declaration and Programme of Action into strategic priorities and objectives; the reappraisal and restructuring of the Centre's programme of work; the reorganization of the Centre's secretariat to respond more adequately to the programme of work and facilitate the implementation of its interrelated objectives and priorities; the strengthening of the Centre's administrative services; and the training in management and administration of the staff of the Centre. The Under-Secretary-General for Internal Oversight Services discussed those recommendations with the High Commissioner and the Centre for Human Rights. The High Commissioner, within the context of his mandate, has decided on the following approach in order to implement the recommendations of the June 1994 review. As a first step, a discussion at the level of the Centre's secretariat will assess the Centre's experience in the implementation of its work programme, identify the gaps and weaknesses in the existing methods, and determine the changes needed to address the issues raised in the June 1994 review. Parallel to that, consideration will be given to basic themes under which the mandates of the Human Rights programme as reflected in the Vienna Declaration, the High Commissioner's mandate and the specific mandates given to the Centre by policy making organs could be organized. Based on the information and ideas so generated, a detailed study will be carried out on how best to adapt the structure of the secretariat to the new priorities of the Vienna Declaration and Programme of Action and to respond to the gaps and weaknesses identified inter alia in the June 1994 review. The recommendations will then be reviewed and implemented. The time-frame for the above exercise is expected to be from mid-March to the end of June 1995. In addition to the above, steps have already been taken to strengthen the administrative services of the Centre and to provide training to staff in administration and management.

## J. Promoting the Right to Development and Cultural, Economic, and Social Rights

The High Commissioner is specifically charged with promoting and protecting the realization of the right to development and enhancing support from relevant bodies of the United Nations system for this purpose. This mandate is placed firmly within the perspective of the World Conference, which clearly announced the interdependent, interrelated and indivisible nature of all human rights, and called for action at the national and international levels to promote and protect those rights.

It is essential to give high priority to promoting cultural, economic, and social rights and the right to development as areas which have not always received adequate attention. The High Commissioner has participated in two sessions of the Working Group on the Right to Development of the Commission on Human Rights and met with the Committee on Economic, Social and Cultural Rights to present his views on these matters. The High Commissioner is also following closely the implementation of the Commission's request for high-level consultations with heads of State or Government, heads of multilateral financial institutions, specialized agencies and intergovernmental and non-governmental organizations on adequate measures to be implemented to find a durable solution to the debt crises of the developing countries.

Protecting cultural, economic, and social rights is particularly important during periods of structural adjustment and during transitions to market economies. Too often basic rights such as those to health, food, shelter and education receive insufficient protection and the victims are often children. This is a matter which government policy makers and parliaments in particular should keep in mind.

In order to provide direction and focus to the implementation of his mandate in this area the High Commissioner is undertaking the formulation of a strategy for the implementation of the right to development and the protection of cultural, economic, and social rights. This will be done in consultation with the organizations, agencies, programmes, bodies and organs involved in the various aspects of the subject and will include: cooperation with the agencies and treaty-based bodies, especially the Committee on Economic, Social and Cultural Rights, and experts of the Sub-Commission in order to identify ways of improving implementation of the right to development and cultural, economic, and social rights; consideration of the application of findings and recommendations made by the Working Group on the Right to Development; concluding the preparation of the procedures to enable communications to be made concerning cultural, economic, and social rights; pilot projects to implement the right to development and cultural, economic, and social rights; promotion of the right to development and cultural, economic and social rights at the national level; and identification of the international action necessary to promote the right to development. Cooperation with international/regional finance and development organizations and with the regional economic commissions will be an important part of the strategy. In its resolution 49/183, the General Assembly expressed its support for the current initiatives of the High Commissioner to consult with all relevant bodies, funds, programmes and specialized agencies of the United Nations system on how they may promote the right to development.

Another important part of the strategy will be the translation of the multidimensional concept of the right to development to the national level. Here, the United Nations advisory services and technical assistance programme in the field of human rights has an important role to play. Criteria can be elaborated which could be applied in needs assessment country missions to identify areas where assistance focusing on cultural, economic, and social rights and the right to development might be suggested. Model projects in this area to provide a basis for decision, a roster of experts, and a manual on promoting the right to development could be developed. Training programmes at the national and local levels addressed to policy makers, parliamentarians and others whose decisions affect human rights could be designed to raise awareness of the interdependent nature of human rights and social and economic development activities. Finally, concrete projects supporting popular participation may be proposed.

The results of the dialogue established within the Administrative Committee on Coordination concerning the development of indicators of progress in human rights and the assessment of the impact of the strategies and policies of the various agencies and programmes on the enjoyment of all human rights will play an important role in promoting the right to development and cultural, economic and social rights. In addition, a senior-level meeting of experts will be convened to evaluate results achieved in the implementation of cultural, economic, and social rights. These measures will be carried out in the context of the Secretary-General's Agenda for Development.

## K. Combating Discrimination and Promoting the Rights of Persons Belonging to Groups Requiring Special Protection: Equal Status and Rights of Women, the Rights of the Child and the Rights of Minorities and Indigenous People

The effective promotion and protection of human rights require concerted efforts to eliminate racial discrimination and racism and to strengthen mutual tolerance between groups and individuals. During his missions to countries, the High Commissioner has raised these matters and suggested steps which might help to eliminate discrimination.

States should consider, if they have not already done so, adopting legislation which declares discrimination illegal. Such legislation must be enforced by the judicial and the executive branches. This is important, not least because law and its enforcement are powerful tools of education. Model legislation against racial discrimination, which has been prepared recently by the United Nations, may also be a useful tool in this connection.

Human rights education and the creation of a climate of tolerance and understanding between different communities should play a significant role in combating discrimination. In this context, the different cultures, which constitute

a common heritage of all, have an important role to play. Cultural multiplicity must be perceived as a means of enriching human values and strengthening human rights standards and not as an opposition to the universality of these rights. Sensitivity training in the early school years and the broader based community action programmes are important tools to achieve this objective.

Consideration should also be given to setting up community relations commissions not only in areas where tensions have actually emerged but also as a general mechanism in all communities. Such commissions could reinforce existing inter-group understanding and identify at an early stage the seeds of future tension so as to act preventively. The participation of vulnerable groups in the elaboration of national and local plans of action is also crucial as a tangible recognition of their dignity and of the principle of equality.

The rise in xenophobia and new forms of racial and ethnic discrimination, including "ethnic cleansing", and in reported attacks on migrant workers, immigrants, asylum seekers and refugees are matters of serious concern. During his missions, the High Commissioner raised this issue. He received assurances that the authorities concerned were determined to take the necessary measures to deal with such manifestations. In this context, the European Union's Declaration on the subject, adopted at the Corfu summit in June 1994, is to be welcomed.

The activities of the International Year of Tolerance proclaimed by the General Assembly for 1995 and the follow-up programme for the Year for which UNESCO is the lead organization must be supported and highlighted. Close cooperation between UNESCO and the High Commissioner/Centre for Human Rights should contribute to the accomplishment of the objectives of the Year. The High Commissioner is cooperating with UNESCO in the drafting of the declaration of principles and programme of action resulting from the Year.

Equal status and human rights of women are of the utmost importance. Impetus is being given to the integration of the human rights of women into the mainstream of the activities and programmes of work of the Centre for Human Rights. In addition, regular briefings and discussions are held with both the staff of the Centre and the human rights bodies, i.e. chairpersons of treaty-based bodies, working groups, thematic and country specific special rapporteurs and experts, with a view to ensuring that a gender perspective and gender neutral language are comprehensively included in their work. The High Commissioner has given priority to these activities and provides guidance to the Centre for Human Rights in that regard.

There must be strong human rights input to the Fourth World Conference on Women. The Conference should encourage universal ratification of the Convention on the Elimination of All Forms of Discrimination against Women and of all human rights treaties. For basic human rights treaties, such as the International Covenant on Civil and Political Rights and the International Covenant on Economic, Social and Cultural Rights, not only contain anti-discrimination provisions but also identify areas of specific gender discrimination which require that State parties enact legal and administrative measures including affirmative action to achieve equality between men and women.

The issue of the equal status and rights of women should be systematically analysed by government and non-governmental organizations. Attention should be paid inter alia to the impact of economic adjustment or transitional policies on the rights of women.

The recommendations of the World Conference outline the directions of national and international efforts for promoting respect for the rights of the child. To implement these recommendations and achieve the objectives of the Plan of Action of the World Summit for Children, the High Commissioner has developed close cooperation with the agencies and programmes of the United Nations system, especially with UNICEF and the Committee on the Rights of the Child. Achievement of the goal of universal ratification of the Convention on the Rights of the Child in 1995 and its effective implementation is being facilitated through technical assistance and supported in the framework of the aforementioned cooperation.

Promoting and protecting the human rights of the child require strengthening the Committee on the Rights of the Child as the key international mechanism monitoring respect for those rights. Taking into account the suggestions and requests of the Committee, the High Commissioner has prepared a plan of action to strengthen substantive support for the Committee's work and provide advisory services and technical assistance when needed to implement the Committee's recommendations. The plan of action was discussed and supported by the Committee on the Rights of the Child at its sessions in October 1994 and in January 1995. It is now under discussion with Governments and will be coordinated with UNICEF and other relevant agencies and institutions. The plan foresees establishing within the Centre for Human Rights an interdisciplinary substantive support team to: assist the Committee on the Rights of the Child in its work of analysing country reports and developing recommendations; assist States in preparing reports; support field visits by the Committee; and support improved implementation of the Committee's recommendations through advisory services and technical cooperation.

The General Assembly in its resolution 49/192 has given to the High Commissioner a particular responsibility to promote the implementation of the principles contained in the Declaration on the Rights of Persons Belonging to National or Ethnic, Religious and Linguistic Minorities and to continue to engage in a dialogue with Governments concerned for that purpose. In his contacts with Governments and the wider human rights community, the High Commissioner is raising the issue of the rights of persons belonging to minorities, with a view to protecting human rights and promoting better understanding. During some of his country visits, for instance to Estonia, Latvia and Lithuania, the High Commissioner has referred to issues relating to minorities as very difficult human problems. The High Commissioner appealed for full respect of the rights of persons belonging to minorities, as expressed in the Declaration, the International Covenant on Civil and Political Rights and other international instruments, including those adopted by the Conference on Security and Cooperation in Europe. In addition, the High Commissioner appealed for government policies which would respond to the legitimate expectations of all people living in the country and enable everyone to feel secure in their rights.

The effective protection of the rights of indigenous people is equally important. The High Commissioner has placed emphasis on the preparation of the plan of activities for the International Decade of the World's Indigenous People and participated in the inauguration ceremony of the Decade in December 1994. He is also encouraging work by the Centre for Human Rights on advisory services projects of direct benefit to indigenous people, as called for by the World Conference, and on the preparation of information for the public on the rights of indigenous people.

## L. Combating the Most Atrocious Human Rights Violations, Such as Torture and Involuntary Disappearances

It is essential to implement effectively the Convention against Torture and Other Cruel, Inhuman or Degrading Treatment or Punishment. On 28 June 1994, at the Copenhagen Centre for the Rehabilitation of Victims of Torture, the High Commissioner made a worldwide appeal for the immediate cessation of all forms of torture, the universal ratification of the Convention, and the full implementation of its provisions.

In cooperation with the Working Group on Enforced or Involuntary Disappearances and the relevant treaty monitoring bodies, as well as NGOs, the High Commissioner has taken steps to study recommendations for the effective implementation of the Declaration on the Protection of All Persons from Enforced Disappearance.

Campaigns for strengthening Member States' assistance to victims of torture and involuntary disappearance, including increased support for the Voluntary Fund for the Victims of Torture, are being carried out. Measures and methods applied in this regard require further examination as to their efficiency. In cooperation with the World Health Organization (WHO) and NGOs, the Centre will take concrete steps to ensure that principles of medical ethics are made familiar to physicians and other relevant professions. The Committee against Torture, the Working Group on Enforced or Involuntary Disappearances and the Special Rapporteur on the question of torture are to be provided with all the necessary support. Interaction between them and the advisory services and technical assistance programme will be strengthened.

## M. Promoting Human Rights Education and Public Information Activities

Human rights education and information aimed at creating a universal culture of human rights is an essential element in a long-term strategy to improve respect for human rights. This was recognized by the World Conference on Human Rights. The High Commissioner attaches special importance to that part of his mandate which gives him responsibility for the coordination of relevant United Nations education and public information programmes in the field of human rights.

Human rights education is vital for the encouragement of harmonious intercommunity relations, for mutual tolerance and understanding and, finally, for peace. All individuals, all groups and all people should be informed of the rights to which they can aspire and the machinery which exists to protect those rights. In educational activities, special attention should be given to those groups that are in a position to exercise an influence on the human rights of others such as primary and secondary school teachers (the "training of trainers"), magistrates, senior government officials and members of the police and the armed forces.

To strengthen interagency cooperation and coordination with regard to human rights education, the High Commissioner brought this issue to the attention of the Administrative Committee on Coordination during its session in 1994. He has also discussed this question with Governments, members of treaty bodies and non-governmental organizations, and stressed the importance of human rights education in the programmes of advisory services and technical cooperation.

As requested by the Commission on Human Rights, the High Commissioner, with the contributions of Member States, the treaty bodies, international organizations, competent non-governmental organizations and other relevant organs prepared a plan of action for a United Nations decade for human rights education. The Plan of Action (A/49/261/Add. 1, annex) was submitted to the General Assembly, which, in resolution 49/184, proclaimed the 10-year period beginning on 1 January 1995 the United Nations Decade for Human Rights Education and welcomed the Plan of Action for the Decade. The High Commissioner participated in the inauguration ceremony of the Decade in December 1994. In resolution 49/184 also, the General Assembly invited the Secretary-General to submit proposals, taking into account the views expressed by Governments, for the implementation of the Plan of Action. The Assembly also requested the High Commissioner for Human Rights to coordinate the implementation of the Plan of Action, and the Centre for Human Rights and the Commission on Human Rights, in cooperation with Member States, human rights treaty bodies, other appropriate bodies and competent nongovernmental organizations, to support efforts of the High Commissioner in this respect. In this connection, infrastructure for the implementation of the Decade should be established at the earliest possible opportunity. Capacity to meet the needs of the Decade will be created within the Centre for Human Rights. The establishment of national committees for the Decade should be strongly encouraged.

A universal culture of human rights depends to a large extent on information being made available to the general public. This is to be accomplished through a revitalized World Public Information Campaign for Human Rights with two major themes: firstly, the need to provide encouragement and support to national efforts by Governments, human rights institutions or non-governmental organizations for activities aimed at disseminating public knowledge of human rights and at providing information as to how anyone can act to protect his or her own rights or the rights of others, and as to the benefits respect for human rights bring to all; secondly, the World Public Information Campaign for Human Rights should also include readily understandable information on what the United Nations does in the field of human rights. The General Assembly called upon the High Commissioner, in resolution 49/187, to coordinate and harmonize human rights information strategies within the United Nations system.

will be continued. By 15 February 1995, a report will be prepared with a detailed plan of the human and financial resource requirements for the implementation of the recommendations of the Vienna Declaration and Programme of Action, as requested by the General Assembly in resolution 49/208. In this context, the High Commissioner is placing primary emphasis on: (a) the strengthening of human rights organs and bodies; (b) follow-up of their recommendations and decisions; (c) coordination of their participation in the implementation of the Vienna Declaration and Programme of Action. In the same resolution, the General Assembly also requested the High Commissioner to include in his annual report to the Assembly a section on the measures taken and the progress achieved in the comprehensive implementation of the Vienna Declaration and Programme of Action.

On 25 June 1994, the High Commissioner invited all Governments and intergovernmental organizations, including regional ones, to inform him annually concerning the implementation of the Vienna Declaration and Programme of Action. The answers are being analysed with a view to continuing cooperation aimed at the realization of the recommendations adopted by the World Conference.

On 12 August 1994, the High Commissioner invited national human rights institutions and NGOs to present annually their views concerning the implementation of the Vienna Declaration and Programme of Action. More than 100 national institutions and non-governmental organizations from all regions shared their experience and opinions with the High Commissioner, providing information on activities undertaken to implement the recommendations of the Vienna Conference and on related needs and expectations. Proposals were also made as to activities that could be undertaken by the United Nations. The responses received are being thoroughly reviewed. A debate on the implementation of the Vienna Declaration and Programme of Action will take place during consultation meetings between the High Commissioner and national institutions and non-governmental organizations, which will be a forum for evaluating existing practice and for outlining future objectives and methods of cooperation. Regional meetings with regional/national grass-roots organizations active in the field of human rights and development will have a similar purpose.

Also on 12 August 1994, the High Commissioner addressed all the United Nations agencies and programmes with a request for information about their contribution to the implementation of the Vienna Declaration and Programme of Action as well as about follow-up action on the conclusions of the ACC meeting. The substantive responses received, which include specific proposals for joint activities, provide a solid basis for enhancing yet further inter-agency cooperation in the field of human rights.

## N. Implementing the Vienna Declaration and Programme of Action

The full implementation of the Vienna Declaration and Programme of Action is a priority of the United Nations. As the United Nations official with principal responsibility for United Nations human rights activities, the High Commissioner provides policy direction and guidance concerning its implementation, including coordination of efforts to that end. Cooperation with United Nations agencies and programmes, human rights bodies, regional organizations, national institutions and NGOs aimed at the full implementation of the Vienna Declaration and Programme of Action

## Progress Towards the Full Implementation of the Recommendations Contained in the Vienna Declaration and Programme of Action

### A. The Outcome of Vienna—a Promise and Challenge to the International Community

The Vienna Declaration and Programme of Action, adopted by the World Conference on Human Rights on 25 June 1993, is a reaffirmation of the solemn commitment of all States to promote and protect all human rights and fundamental freedoms. This document, in essence, charts the course of action of the international community well into the next century.

It is a universal document adopted after all nations of the world had the opportunity to seek and determine their own human rights preoccupations, also in the framework of regional and local human rights institutions. It constitutes the crowning piece of a long process of consultation and joint action in which not only Governments participated, but also United Nations organs and bodies, human rights treaty bodies and regional intergovernmental organizations, as well as organizations representing a wide spectrum of civil society, including national institutions and NGOs.

The Vienna Declaration and Programme of Action provides the United Nations with a framework of principles and a programme of activities, approved by consensus, to achieve the objectives of the Charter of the United Nations in the field of human rights. The World Conference took an integrated and symmetric approach regarding the protection of human rights. It identified major obstacles to the implementation of human rights and shortcomings, especially in the international protection of these rights, and specified concrete measures which should help to overcome the existing difficulties.

The World Conference on Human Rights reaffirmed the universality of all human rights as the birthright of all human beings. It recognized that their promotion and protection is the first responsibility of Governments and, in the framework of the purposes and principles of the United Nations, constitute a legitimate concern of the international community. The Conference stressed the close interrelationship between democracy, development and respect for human rights and reaffirmed the right to development as a human right. It underlined that all human rights, civil, cultural, economic, political and social, are universal, indivisible, interdependent and interrelated and must be treated globally in a fair and equal manner and with the same emphasis.

The General Assembly in its resolution 48/121 of 20 December 1993 endorsed the Vienna Declaration and Programme of Action. In that resolution and in resolution 49/208, the Assembly called upon all States to take further action with a view to the full realization of human rights in the light of the recommendations of the Conference and requested the Secretary-General, the General Assembly, the Commission on Human Rights and other organs and bodies of the United Nations system related to human rights to take further action with a view to the full implementation of all the recommendations of the Conference.

The implementation of the Vienna Declaration and Programme of Action requires more than a number of isolated activities. International cooperation and an organizational framework to that end is strongly needed. An updated plan for the implementation of the Vienna Declaration and Programme of Action, enriched by the input of specialized agencies and United Nations programmes, continuously verified in practice, will guide the United Nations activities.

The World Conference on Human Rights has already had a positive impact on activities in the field of human rights. The international community should continue with determination its efforts to implement fully recommendations which were adopted voluntarily and by consensus by participating Governments. The implementation of the Vienna Declaration and Programme of Action depends primarily on activities at the national level, undertaken by Governments, as well as institutions and organizations representing all parts of civil society. The role of the United Nations is to provide all possible support to these activities in the framework of international cooperation.

**B. Universal Ratification of Human Rights Instruments**

The World Conference called for universal acceptance of international human rights instruments, if possible without reservations. Following this call the Secretary-General addressed letters to all Heads of State urging that their Governments accept those principal human rights treaties to which they were not yet a party. The High Commissioner, in his contacts and dialogue with high-level governmental officials, also encourages universal accession to international human rights treaties. The Chairpersons of the human rights treaty bodies during their fifth meeting welcomed these initiatives. The Chairpersons of the Human Rights Committee and the Committee on the Elimination of Racial Discrimination undertook separate initiatives in which they called upon States of the former Soviet Union to notify their succession to the International Covenant on Civil and Political Rights or the International Convention on the Elimination of All Forms of Racial Discrimination, if they had not yet done so.

Although the number of States parties to the international human rights treaties is increasing, too many countries have still not acceded to the international human rights instruments. By way of example, as of 31 December 1994 the International Covenant on Economic, Social and Cultural Rights had been ratified by 131 countries and International Covenant on Civil and Political Rights by 129 countries. Worldwide action is being carried out to achieve universal ratification of the Convention of the Rights of the Child by the end of 1995 (in close cooperation with UNICEF) and the Convention on the Elimination of Discrimination against Women by the year 2000, which was the subject of a call by the World Conference. As of 31 December 1994, 168 States had ratified the Convention on the Rights of the Child and 138 States had ratified the Convention on the Elimination of Discrimination against Women.

**C. International Cooperation and Coordination of Human Rights Activities; Adaptation and Strengthening of United Nations Machinery for Human Rights**

The Vienna Declaration and Programme of Action stresses the importance of international cooperation in the promotion and protection of human rights and reflects the generally shared view that better coordination of the human rights efforts of the United Nations system is essential to improve their efficiency and effectiveness. The central role in the coordination of human rights activities throughout the United Nations system is played by the High Commissioner. A new avenue was opened by the Administrative Committee on Coordination (ACC) at its meeting on 11 and 12 April 1994, in which the High Commissioner participated. Discussing human rights for the first time, and considering the High Commissioner's recommendations for further action, the Committee stressed the need for a permanent dialogue within the system to promote human rights through a systematic exchange of information, experience and expertise. All agencies committed themselves to the implementation of the Vienna Declaration and Programme of Action and to assess the impact of their strategies and policies on the enjoyment of human rights. The members of ACC declared their support for the action taken by the High Commissioner to fulfil his mandate with regard to the system-wide coordination of human rights activities. ACC will continue the examination of this question. Generally, while the initial steps towards better coordination of activities have already been taken, determined efforts in this direction must continue.

Adaptation of the United Nations machinery for human rights to current and future needs and its strengthening was perceived by the World Conference as a prerequisite for the implementation of the United Nations human rights programme. Both the General Assembly and the Commission on Human Rights have taken steps in this direction. After the establishment of the post of High Commissioner for Human Rights the Working Group of the Third Committee of the General Assembly is continuing its work during the current session of the General Assembly to consider other aspects of the implementation of the recommendations of the Vienna Declaration and Programme of Action. The Commission on Human Rights, in decision 1994/111, established an informal, open-ended working group to discuss problems related to the reform of this organ. The Chairman will report on the outcome of its session to the Commission at its current session.

It is to be borne in mind that the adaptation of the infrastructure of the United Nations human rights programme should be based on interlinkage between: structural reform of the United Nations human rights machinery, a plan of action for the implementation of the Vienna Declaration and Programme of Action, and the provision of adequate human and financial resources. A correlation between these dimensions of the process leading to strengthening of the human rights machinery is indispensable.

The experience gained in Rwanda requires a careful future oriented analysis from the point of view of the need for logistical support and human resources in actions responding to serious human rights violations. Stand-by arrangements are already being concluded in order to enable the High Commissioner to act more promptly in response to such crises in the future.

## D. Racism, Racial Discrimination, Xenophobia and Other Forms of Intolerance

The Third Decade to Combat Racism and Racial Discrimination provides the framework for the international activities with regard to elimination of racism and racial discrimination. The General Assembly at its forty-ninth session, in resolution 49/146, adopted a revised plan for implementation of the Programme of Action for the Third Decade.

The General Assembly at its forty-eighth session, in resolution 48/126, proclaimed 1995 the United Nations Year of Tolerance. At its forty-ninth session, in resolution 49/213, the Assembly recommended that the specialized agencies, regional commissions and other organizations of the United Nations system consider in their respective forums the contribution they could make to the success of the United Nations Year for Tolerance. The Assembly also requested UNESCO to prepare for the conclusion of the Year a declaration of principles and a programme of action as a follow-up to the Year.

Problems related to racism, racial discrimination, xenophobia, "ethnic cleansing" and religious and other forms of intolerance are on the agenda of the Third Committee of the General Assembly, the Commission on Human Rights, the Sub-Commission on Prevention of Discrimination and Protection of Minorities, and the treaty bodies, in particular the Committee on the Elimination of Racial Discrimination. Special procedures have been established to carry out studies and

investigations. The international organs and bodies focus on the analysis of contemporary forms and root causes of these phenomena, with a view of proposing specific methods of combating them. The international norms and rules provide a useful tool for preventing and combating discrimination. However, legislation against racial discrimination alone is not enough to prevent violations of human rights in this area. The international community should focus on the further implementation of the related human rights instruments and declarations, as well as recommendations of the treaty bodies and special procedures. A periodical complex review of measures adopted to give effect to them is required.

## E. Equal Status and Human Rights of Women

The call of the World Conference for worldwide efforts to ensure the equal status and rights of women has met with a positive response throughout the United Nations system. This objective is also one of the keynotes of the preparation of the Fourth World Conference on Women: Action for Equality, Development and Peace, to be held in Beijing in 1995.

United Nations agencies and programmes, human rights organs and treaty bodies, especially the Commission on the Status of Women, the Commission on Human Rights, the Committee on the Elimination of Discrimination against Women have taken numerous initiatives against violations of the human rights of women and to promote and protect these rights. The Fourth World Conference on Women is expected to consider the question of integrating the human rights of women into the mainstream of United Nations system-wide activity. The appointment by the Commission on Human Rights in its resolution 1994/45, of a special rapporteur on violence against women, including its causes and its consequences, strengthens the involvement of the special procedures of the Commission on Human Rights in the area of the protection of the rights of women. Issues, which have attracted the particular attention of the United Nations in this context, are: obstacles to the realization of the human rights of women; the elimination of gender-based violence against women in public and private life and measures, ways and means, at the national, regional and international levels, to eliminate violence against women and its causes, and to remedy its consequences; traditional practices affecting the health of women and girl children; cooperation and coordination between relevant United Nations organs and bodies; reflection of the problems related to the human rights of women in the reporting guidelines and procedures of various human rights treaty bodies.

The Commission on the Status of Women in its resolution 1994/35/2, entitled "Mainstreaming women's human rights", requested the Secretary-General to assess the preparation of a joint workplan on women's human rights for the Centre for Human Rights and the Division for the Advancement of Women on an annual basis. The coordinated efforts should contribute to a greater effectiveness of the promotion and protection of women's rights.

The lack of educational opportunities offered to girls and women have often contributed to reinforcing the traditional female role, denying their full partnership in society. Equal access by women to education and education free from gender stereotypes will be an important part of the United Nations Decade for Human Rights Education.

Within the Centre for Human Rights priority has been given to action aimed at ensuring cooperation and coordination with the Division for the Advancement of Women of the Secretariat and other United Nations bodies related to women. The Centre for Human Rights incorporated issues relating to the human rights of women in all its activities and its publications. Particular account is being taken of the situation of women in the programme of technical assistance in the field of human rights.

### F. Persons Belonging to Vulnerable Groups: Children, Minorities, Indigenous People, Migrant Workers, Disabled Persons

Activities aimed at protection of the rights of the child are developed throughout the United Nations system. Their particular dynamics, if continued, should allow for real progress in the protection of children. A great number of initiatives have been developed by the High Commissioner for Human Rights to implement the recommendations contained in the Vienna Declaration and Programme of Action, which include: (a) the establishment by the Commission on Human Rights, in resolutions 1994/90 and 1994/91 of two open-ended working groups to consider draft optional protocols to the Convention on the Rights of the Child concerning the prevention and eradication of the sale of children, child prostitution and child pornography, and the involvement of children in armed conflicts; (b) steps aimed at a better co-ordination of United Nations efforts, inter alia, the conclusion of a working agreement between UNICEF and the Centre for Human Rights; (c) strengthening the Centre's capacity with regard to children's rights; (d) system-wide co-operation to pursue the achievement of the objectives set up by the Plan of Action of the World Summit for Children; (e) contacts of the Centre with relevant organizations concerned with the protection of children traumatized by war; (f) a study on children affected by armed conflict.

Problems related to national or ethnic, religious and linguistic minorities are widely recognized as one of the major sources of international and internal conflicts involving widespread human rights violations. The international community, including Governments, human rights organs and treaty bodies, as well as non-governmental organizations, are taking a number of initiatives to protect effectively persons belonging to minorities. The Commission on Human Rights, in its resolution 1994/22 and the General Assembly in its resolution 49/192, which place emphasis on promoting and giving effect to the Declaration on the Rights of Persons Belonging to National or Ethnic, Religious and Linguistic Minorities, have provided a strong impetus to the protection of rights of persons belonging to minorities. The examination of peaceful and constructive solutions to situations involving minorities recommended by the Sub-Commission on Prevention of Discrimination and Protection of Minorities in its resolution 1994/4 can lead to relevant conclusions. The General Comment on article 27 of the International Covenant on Civil and Political Rights, adopted by the Human Rights Committee during its fiftieth session (1994) contributed to making more precise the legal obligations with regard to the protection of minorities.

Further progress in the field of the protection of minorities depends on concerted efforts by Governments and international and non-governmental organizations aimed at the creation of an open culture, at dissemination of understanding of the richness which exists in a multicultural and multiethnic society. The protection of persons belonging to minorities, based on mutual tolerance and acceptance, promises new perspectives, free of the disasters familiar to many regions of the world. The Centre for Human Rights, in close cooperation with other departments of the Secretariat, United Nations bodies and organs, is developing activities aimed at facilitating the full participation of persons belonging to national or ethnic, religious and linguistic minorities in all aspects of the political, economic, social, religious and cultural life of their societies and in the economic progress and development of their countries.

The international community reaffirmed in the Vienna Declaration and Programme of Action commitment to the economic, social and cultural well-being of indigenous people and their enjoyment of the fruits of sustainable development. The establishment of a permanent forum for indigenous people within the United Nations, which should be considered by the Commission as a matter of priority, in accordance with General Assembly resolution 48/163, and the eventual adoption of the Declaration on the Rights of Indigenous People will further enhance the system-wide involvement in this area. The Sub-Commission on Prevention of Discrimination and Protection of Minorities has submitted a draft declaration to the fifty-first session of the Commission on Human Rights (E/CN.4/1995/2-E/CN.4/1995/56, resolution 1994/45, annex).

The General Assembly, in resolution 48/163, proclaimed the International Decade of the World's Indigenous People. In its resolution 49/214, the Assembly adopted the short-term programme of activities for 1995 and invited Governments to submit comments with a view to the preparation of a final comprehensive programme of action for the Decade. The Centre has recently published a newsletter containing basic information concerning the Decade of the World's Indigenous People.

The entering into force of the International Convention on the Rights of All Migrant Workers and Members of their Families is crucial for establishing proper protection of this vulnerable group of people. Therefore, in its resolution 1994/17, the Commission on Human Rights called upon all States to accede to this Convention as a matter of priority. The Secretary-General also has addressed Governments on this issue. And the Commission has invited all organizations and agencies of the United Nations system, as well as intergovernmental and non-governmental organizations to disseminate information on promoting understanding of the Convention. The General Assembly, in its resolution 48/110, called for action to be taken by all countries, trade unions, treaty bodies and non-governmental organizations to protect the human rights of women migrant workers, who are doubly vulnerable because of their gender and their status as foreigners.

It is a moral responsibility of society as a whole to ensure that persons with disabilities can enjoy all human rights and fundamental freedoms. However, the question also has economic, organizational, and cultural dimensions and, therefore, the efforts of all actors concerned with human rights and development are necessary to assist disabled persons. The framework for activities dealing with this issue is provided by the World Programme of Action concerning Disabled Persons, the continuing value and validity of which was reaffirmed by the General Assembly in its resolution 48/99. In addition, the Standard Rules on the Equalization of Opportunities for Persons with Disabilities, adopted by the General Assembly in its resolution 48/96, also constitute important guidelines in this respect. They have been brought to the attention of the relevant committees, working groups and special rapporteurs. Publication of these Standard Rules is expected to sensitize public opinion. The Special Rapporteur appointed by the Commission for Social Development has an important role to play in monitoring the implementation of the Standard Rules. The Asian and Pacific Decade of Disabled Persons, 1993-2002, is an encouraging regional initiative.

### G. Torture and Enforced Disappearance

Torture remains one of the most atrocious violations against human dignity and one of the most shameful phenomena. The call of the World Conference for its eradication is not only a political guideline but, first and foremost, a fundamental moral imperative. Human rights organs and treaty bodies have undertaken numerous steps to implement the recommendation contained in the Vienna Declaration and Programme of Action. However, torture and cruel, inhuman or degrading treatment or punishment are still tolerated in many parts of the world. Full support should be given by Governments, the relevant United Nations organs and bodies, international and non-governmental organizations to the specific measures outlined by the Commission on Human Rights in resolution 1994/37, with a view to preventing or combating torture, as well as assisting victims of torture. Also, the Commission's call upon, in the same resolution, all States to become parties to the Convention against Torture and Other Cruel, Inhuman and Degrading Treatment or Punishment should be heeded. The draft optional protocol to the Convention, under discussion in the open-ended working group of the Commission, envisages an important method of preventing torture. The call of the World Conference for its completion should be implemented at the earliest. The General Assembly, in its resolution 49/177, noted with appreciation the activities of the open-ended working group, while expressing its concern at the pace of its progress in elaborating a draft optional protocol.

Involuntary disappearances unfortunately are increasing in various parts of the world, particularly as the consequence of internal conflicts on a large scale. The Commission on Human Rights, in its resolution 1994/39, invited all Governments to take effective steps to prevent and punish the practice of enforced disappearances. In this regard, it recalled that all acts of enforced disappearance are offences punishable by appropriate penalties which take into account their extreme seriousness under criminal law. The Working Group on Enforced or Involuntary Disappearances helps prevent or combat this phenomenon. To that end, Governments concerned should intensify their cooperation with the Group and take action on the recommendations it addresses to them.

### H. The Right to Development, Advisory Services and Technical Assistance

The World Conference set out the vision of supporting democracy, development and human rights through increased international cooperation.

The reaffirmation by consensus that the universal and inalienable right to development, as established in the Declaration on the Right to Development, must be implemented and realized, was one of the major achievements of the World Conference. The Conference gave also priority to the effective implementation of economic, social, and cultural rights. In order to implement the recommendations of the World Conference in this regard, the United Nations human

rights programme is pursuing the following objectives: enhancing cooperation between the Committee on Economic, Social and Cultural Rights and NGOs, as well as relevant United Nations organs and agencies; identifying further social and economic indicators which should facilitate assessing the progressive realization of cultural, economic, and social rights and addressing violations of these rights; establishing a communication procedure with regard to rights laid down in the International Covenant on Economic, Social and Cultural Rights; clarifying the particular content of specific cultural, economic and social rights; formulating comprehensive and effective measures to eliminate obstacles to the implementation and realization of the Declaration on the Right to Development and recommending ways and means towards the realization of the right to development; preparing plans to enable NGOs and grass-roots organizations active in development and human rights to play an increased role in the implementation of the Declaration on the Right to Development; elaborating adequate measures to be implemented in order to find a durable solution to the debt crisis of developing countries. The General Assembly, at its forty-ninth session, in resolution 49/186, reiterated its decision that the approaches to future work within the United Nations system on human rights matters should take into account the content of the Declaration on the Right to Development and the need for the implementation thereof.

The forthcoming World Summit for Social Development will address matters of great importance for human rights, in particular cultural, economic, and social rights and the right to development. The High Commissioner and numerous human rights organs and bodies are contributing to the preparatory work for this conference. In this regard, it has been underlined that social development issues are directly connected to human rights and that maintaining and reinforcing high human rights standards will contribute to the achievement of social development worldwide.

The United Nations Development Programme has an important role to play with regard to the implementation of the right to development and of cultural, economic and social rights. Its activities can significantly contribute to the implementation of the Vienna Declaration and Programme of Action in this respect.

The World Conference put emphasis on developing and building institutions relating to human rights, strengthening a pluralistic civil society and protecting groups which have been rendered vulnerable. The United Nations human rights organs and bodies, in particular the Commission on Human Rights and its Subcommission and mechanisms, the treaty bodies, and the Centre for Human Rights, aim, in particular, at: providing assistance to Governments with regard to the development of national structures which have a direct impact on the overall observance of human rights; strengthening the rule of law and the administration of justice; the promotion of freedom of expression; the human rights aspects of elections and participation of the people in decision-making; drawing up related national plans of action.

The programme of advisory services and technical assistance through its multidimensional character has an essential place in the United Nations human rights activities. The World Conference on Human Rights stressed the need for it to be strengthened and its resources increased. Upon the request of States, assistance should be made available for the implementation of comprehensive plans of action to promote and protect human rights, including strengthening human rights institutions and the institutions of democracy, the legal protection of human rights, training of public officials, and broad-based education and public information activities aimed at promoting respect for human rights.

### I. National Institutions and Non-governmental Organizations

The United Nations counts on the support of NGOs, academic communities, members of Parliaments and other parts of civil society. As part of the human rights infrastructure, these institutions are active partners in the realization of the Vienna Declaration and Programme of Action. Their continuing participation in the promotion and protection of human rights is indispensable for worldwide progress in this respect. The General Assembly welcomed the principles relating to the status of national institutions (resolution 48/134, annex). The Centre for Human Rights offers assistance through training and making available United Nations human rights publications to national institutions and NGOs. It assists States in establishing or strengthening such institutions inter alia through organizing workshops at the regional and subregional levels. The Third International Workshop on National Institutions for the Promotion and Protection of Human Rights, held in April 1995 in Manila at the invitation of the Government of the Philippines, opened new avenues for the activities of national institutions. Recently prepared by the Centre for Human Rights, a manual on national institutions for the promotion and protection of human rights will assist States, as well as all those active in this area, in establishing or strengthening their national institutions. The edition by the Centre for Human Rights of an information newsletter will also enhance communication with the wider human rights community.

Cooperation with academic institutions should be one of the important vehicles in the implementation of the Vienna Declaration and Programme of Action. A number of such institutions have already offered their cooperation in preparing background policy studies in important human rights areas (for example, prevention of human rights violations, the right to development, economic, social and cultural rights, the protection of minorities, information and documentation). Academic institutions are also ready to cooperate actively in the realization of the United Nations Decade for Human Rights Education and the implementation of the Vienna Declaration and Programme of Action.

### J. Education and Dissemination of Information

Following the recommendation of the World Conference, the General Assembly considered the idea of a Decade for Human Rights Education and proclaimed the Decade in its resolution 49/184. The Decade should promote and streamline activities of the international community in the field of human rights education. The Centre for Human Rights, in cooperation with UNESCO and other relevant agencies and bodies, assists Member States to develop specific programmes and strategies for ensuring human rights education for all. In this framework, the development of curricula, pedagogical techniques and teaching materials, such as manuals for primary and secondary schools, is supported. Manuals for public officials and the general public have been published or are under preparation. In organizing educational and promotional activities the Centre cooperates with the national or regional institutes for human rights, such as the African Centre in Banjul, the Arab Institute for Human Rights in Tunis, the Asia-Pacific Hu-

man Rights Center in Osaka, the Instituto de Promocion de Derechos Humanos in Buenos Aries, the Inter-American Institute of Human Rights in San Jose, the International Institute of Human Rights in Strasbourg, the Nordic institutes of human rights in Copenhagen, Lund, Oslo and Turku, the Slovak Human Rights Centre in Bratislava, and others. The revitalized World Public Information Campaign for Human Rights provides the framework for informing people worldwide about the United Nations human rights activities. In the human rights publications programme, preference has been given to publications for use in technical cooperation projects, such as specialized manuals for the training of police, lawyers and judges, election officials and social workers. Emphasis has also been placed on publication of Fact Sheets focusing on priority issues, such as the protection of indigenous populations, the rights of the child, and child exploitation.

The Decade for Human Rights Education and the World Public Information Campaign should enhance efforts aimed at the dissemination of knowledge and information on human rights, which should be available to all people worldwide. This is the very foundation of any efforts aimed at the promotion and protection of human rights, at the international and national levels.

UNESCO attaches great importance to the implementation of the Vienna Declaration and Programme of Action with regard to education in the field of human rights. A number of projects are carried out or planned jointly with the Centre for Human Rights. The forty-fourth session of the International Conference on Education (3–8 October 1994) took note of the Integrated Framework of Action on Education for Peace, Human Rights and Democracy, which takes into account all related action plans and proposes a conceptual framework and a system of concrete activities to be implemented at the national and international levels. UNESCO and the Centre for Human Rights will assist the High Commissioner in the preparation and issuing of a report on the state of human rights education at the local, national, regional and international levels.

### K. Implementation and Monitoring

While stressing that the implementation of human rights is a primary obligation of Governments, the World Conference paid special attention to the international mechanisms and procedures which should assist the international community in its endeavours in this area. It stressed the importance of preserving and strengthening the system of special procedures, rapporteurs, representatives, experts and working groups of the Commission on Human Rights.

The significant role of special procedures established by the Commission on Human Rights and treaty based bodies in human rights implementation was also emphasized at the first meeting of special rapporteurs/representatives/experts and chairmen of working groups on the special procedures (30 May–1 June 1994) and the fifth meeting of persons chairing the human rights treaty bodies (September 1994). They resulted in a number of important conclusions for the work of the human rights implementation machinery. Periodic meetings of the procedures and mechanisms will enable them to harmonize and rationalize their work.

The chairpersons of treaty bodies deplored a growing tendency in the United Nations on the part of bodies concerned with some aspects of human rights to ignore or in some cases to redefine in their activities the standards codified in the international human rights treaties. The intergovernmental organs and treaty bodies should pay close attention to this warning. New perspectives in the implementation of human rights standards have been opened by the endeavours of treaty bodies to develop, within the scope of their respective mandates, procedures aimed at preventing human rights violations. Further efforts in this regard will be encouraged.

It must be underlined that adequate human and material resources within the Centre for Human Rights are required to strengthen the system of special procedures and treaty bodies. They are indispensable to provide special rapporteurs, working groups and treaty bodies with the necessary facilities, including a human rights database, easily accessible also by the rapporteurs and experts during their missions.

The question of impunity has acquired a growing importance. The initiative taken by the Sub-Commission on the Prevention of Discrimination and Protection of Minorities in its resolution 1994/34 to prepare reports on this issue might contribute to clarifying related problems. One report should deal with the impunity of perpetrators of violations of civil and political rights and another with that of perpetrators of violations of cultural, economic, and social rights.

Strengthening the implementation of human rights requires adequate protection of human rights defenders. Therefore, the World Conference called for the speedy completion and adoption of a draft declaration on the rights and responsibilities of individuals, groups and organs of society to promote and protect universally recognized human rights and fundamental freedoms. It is to be hoped that the several years spent by the Working Group discussing the draft will soon bear fruit in the form of the adoption of a declaration by the General Assembly. The High Commissioner addressed the Working Group on 17 January 1995 and called for the speedy preparation of the final version of the draft declaration.

## Conclusions

Today, respect for human rights has become of overriding importance to people all over the world and a central concern in human affairs nationally and internationally. People increasingly judge national authorities and international organizations by how well they respond to the challenge of protecting human rights.

Internationally, this dynamic process coming from all societies has given rise to the Vienna Declaration and Programme of Action, the establishment of the post of United Nations High Commissioner for Human Rights and greatly increased calls upon the United Nations system to respond to serious violations of human rights, prevent their outbreak and to help improve respect for human rights in countries throughout the world. Both the Vienna Declaration and the mandate of the High Commissioner are based on a number of common premises: that respect for human rights is a matter of legitimate concern to the international community; that every person in the world is, on a basis of equality, entitled to enjoy all the human rights enumerated in United Nations standards; that all human rights are interdependent and that economic, social and cultural rights and the right to development deserve particular attention; that democracy, development and human rights are interrelated; that international action to promote human rights must be based on cooperation and undertaken in a balanced, objective and non-selective manner; and that the primary responsibility for protecting human rights rests with Governments.

Nationally, the establishment in many countries of national institutions to protect human rights, wide ranging reviews of legislation and practice from the human rights point of view, the strengthening of democratic institutions, the establishment of numerous human rights non-governmental organizations, open public debates on human rights issues, increased ratification of human rights treaties and the growth of requests for technical cooperation in the field of human rights all witness the importance people attach to human rights.

Today, a truly global sense of human rights solidarity runs across all borders and reaches to all continents. This is reflected in the large media coverage of violations and in the widely held conviction that the international community has a clear responsibility for effective action to bring them to an end. This increased sensitivity to human rights comes at a time when it is impossible to deny the existence of violations of human rights, whether in the poverty and exclusion found in poor and rich societies alike, or in the horrors of the extreme situations of massive violations, many of which are well documented before United Nations organs. Meeting the need for effective action to bring violations to an end is at the core of our human rights challenge. And it is of first importance to the credibility and success of all international activities that this challenge be met successfully.

The Vienna Declaration and Programme of Action, in the 18 months since its adoption, has shown itself to be a dynamic and creative framework for action at all levels to promote and protect human rights. The organs of the United Nations system now place their human rights activities well within the perspective of the Vienna Declaration and have resolved on specific actions to achieve its objectives. Governments have repeatedly stated the relevance of the Declaration to national needs and the importance of cooperating internationally within its framework, especially with the High Commissioner for Human Rights. Nationally and internationally, non-governmental organizations have been inspired by the Declaration and many report adopting new methods and initiating new activities to achieve its objectives.

The creation of the United Nations High Commissioner for Human Rights was the most concrete result of the Vienna Declaration and the High Commissioner has taken that Declaration and its objectives as the foundation of his own activities. International cooperation is at the heart of the High Commissioner's mandate and the High Commissioner has focused significant attention on engaging in a dialogue with all Governments with a view to enhancing respect for human rights. This involves a wide range of activities including action to bring violations to an end and action to prevent the outbreak of serious violations. Prevention has become central to international human rights preoccupations as the international community sees years of development efforts destroyed overnight by outbreaks of serious violations and the generation of refugees, internally displaced persons and mass exoduses. The High Commissioner avails himself of every opportunity to use his diplomacy to obtain results on specific matters with Governments and he also, when circumstances require, uses the many other tools at his disposal, including the provision of human rights technical cooperation, to help prevent violations.

The interlinkage of human rights, democracy and development requires a comprehensive and integrated approach to the promotion and protection of human rights on the part of the High Commissioner. He has adopted this approach both in relation to Governments and in his activities of international coordination, in particular within the United Nations system. In order for international efforts to promote human rights to be effective, they must permeate the activities of all international agencies so that each, within its own mandate, can make its own important contribution to the common objective. This is especially true with regard to the right to development and economic, social and cultural rights.

One of the important objectives of the United Nations in establishing the post of High Commissioner for Human Rights was to ensure more effective coordination of the numerous activities in favour of human rights throughout the system and to increase the efficiency and strengthen the impact of United Nations human rights machinery. The High Commissioner does not seek to replace existing organs, bodies or procedures, but to strengthen them and better coordinate their activities within the framework of the objectives of the Vienna Declaration. Today's new demands on the United Nations system and the heightened expectations of Governments and public opinion require a more operational approach to the international promotion and protection of human rights and the development of new methods of work and new capacities for action.

The High Commissioner for Human Rights has today become a recognized and important part of the United Nations system. The highest policy making bodies have welcomed his initiatives in various fields, have sought to identify ways of cooperating with him and have reacted positively to his suggestions and recommendations. And, in regard to sensitive issues, they have called upon him to make his own contribution to dealing with them.

The success of the activities of the human rights programme and of the High Commissioner in the future will depend upon the support and understanding of the international community and the cooperation received from Governments, international organizations, non-governmental organizations and people throughout the world. This must include adequate human and financial resources for the implementation of the Vienna Declaration and Programme of Action, the activities of the High Commissioner and the Centre for Human Rights. That support will help respond to the hopes and expectations generated by the World Conference on Human Rights and the establishment of the post of High Commissioner for Human Rights and help promote international peace and security and better standards of life in larger freedom as embodied in the Charter of the United Nations.

**HIGH COMMISSIONER FOR REFUGEES, UN.** On 14 December 1950, the UN General Assembly adopted the Statute of the Office of the United Nations High Commissioner for Refugees. The office came into existence, as authorized by the statute, on 1 January 1951, originally for a period of three years. The mandate of the office has since been renewed many times, most recently for a period of five years beginning 1 January 1989 (General Assembly resolution 42/108).

Assistance to refugees was first organized under international auspices in 1921 with the appointment of Dr. **FRIDTJOF NANSEN,** of Norway, as League of Nations High Commissioner for Refugees. During World War II, the United Nations Relief and Rehabilitation Administration (UNRRA) was established in 1943 to assist persons displaced because of the hostil-

ities, many of whom were reluctant or unwilling to be repatriated to their countries of origin. UNRRA was succeeded by the International Refugees Organization (IRO) in 1946; by the time IRO ceased operations in 1952, it had resettled more than a million displaced persons and refugees and had repatriated about 73,000 to their former homelands. On 3 December 1949, the UN General Assembly recognized the continuing responsibility of the United Nations for the international protection of refugees after the termination of IRO and decided to appoint a United Nations High Commissioner for Refugees.

The Statute of the Office of the High Commissioner, adopted by the General Assembly on 14 December 1950 (resolution 428 [V], specifies that the High Commissioner's work shall be of an entirely non-political character; that it shall be humanitarian and social; and that it shall relate, as a rule, to groups and categories of refugees. The High Commissioner's policy directives are given by the General Assembly or the Economic and Social Council. The High Commissioner is mandated to provide for the protection of refugees within the competence of his office by (1) promoting the conclusion and ratification of international conventions for the protection of refugees, supervising their application, and proposing amendments thereto; (2) promoting through special agreements with governments the execution of any measures calculated to improve the situation of refugees and to reduce the number requiring protection; (3) assisting governmental and private efforts to promote voluntary repatriation or assimilation with new national communities; (4) promoting the admission of refugees, not excluding those in the most destitute categories, to the territories of States; (5) endeavoring to obtain permission for refugees to transfer their assets, and especially those necessary for their resettlement; (6) obtaining from governments information concerning the number and conditions of refugees in their territories and the laws and regulations concerning them; (7) keeping in close touch with the governments and intergovernmental organizations concerned; (8) establishing contact in such manner as he may think best with private organizations dealing with refugee questions; and (9) facilitating the coordination of efforts of private organizations concerned with the welfare of refugees.

Refugees in "divided countries" are not a responsibility of the High Commissioner, nor is there a concern with refugees for which another UN body has assumed full responsibility, such as the Arab refugees from Palestine, which fall within the mandate of UNRWA. The High Commissioner's primary concerns are those persons who, owing to well-founded fear of persecution for reasons of race, religion, nationality, or political opinion, are outside their country of origin and cannot, or do not, owing to such fear, avail themselves of the protection of that country.

In addition to providing international protection to refugees within its mandate, the Office of the UN High Commissioner for Refugees provides them with various forms of assistance until they are settled. On 2 February 1952, the General Assembly authorized the High Commissioner to appeal for funds to enable emergency aid to be given to the most needy groups of refugees within his mandate (resolution 538 [VI]); in 1954, this emergency fund was incorporated into a new voluntary UN Refugee Fund.

The High Commissioner is elected by the General Assembly on recommendation of the Secretary-General. The program of the High Commissioner is administered by an executive committee composed of representatives of 43 states which are UN members or members of a specialized agency, elected by the Economic and Social Council on the widest geographical basis from those states with a demonstrated interest in, and devotion to, the solution of the refugee problem. Members of the executive committee serve for the duration of the High Commissioner's mandate.

The executive committee holds one session per year, of about ten days' duration, at the United Nations office in Geneva. It has two subsidiary bodies: the Sub-Committee of the Whole on International Protection and the Sub-Committee on Administrative and Financial Matters; these usually meet in Geneva a few days prior to the opening of the session of the executive committee.

The Office of the League of Nations High Commissioner for Refugees was awarded the Nobel Peace Prize in 1938. The Office of the UN High Commissioner for Refugees has been awarded the Prize twice: in 1954 and again in 1981.

*STATUTE.* The statute, adopted by the UN General Assembly on 14 December 1950 (resolution 428 [V]), authorizes the establishment of the Office of the United Nations High Commissioner for Refugees. The text of the statute, annexed to the resolution, is as follows:

### Chapter I—General Provisions

1. The United Nations High Commissioner for Refugees, acting under the authority of the General Assembly, shall assume the function of providing international protection, under the auspices of the United Nations, to refugees who fall within the scope of the present Statute and of seeking permanent solutions for the problem of refugees by assisting governments and, subject to the approval of the governments concerned, private organizations to facilitate the voluntary repatriation of such refugees, or their assimilation within new national communities.

In the exercise of his functions, more particularly when difficulties arise, and for instance with regard to any controversy concerning the international status of these persons, the High Commissioner shall request the opinion of an advisory committee on refugees if it is created.

2. The work of the High Commissioner shall be of an entirely non-political character; it shall be humanitarian and social and shall relate, as a rule, to groups and categories of refugees.

3. The High Commissioner shall follow policy directives given him by the General Assembly or the Economic and Social Council.

4. The Economic and Social Council may decide, after hearing the views of the High Commissioner on the subject, to establish an advisory committee on refugees, which shall consist of representatives of States Members and States non-members of the United Nations, to be selected by the Council on the basis of their demonstrated interest in and devotion to the solution of the refugee problem.

5. The General Assembly shall review, not later than at its eighth regular session, the arrangements for the Office of the High Commissioner with a view to determining whether the Office should be continued beyond 31 December 1963.

### Chapter II—Functions of the High Commissioner

6. The competence of the High Commissioner shall extend to:

A. (i) Any person who has been considered a refugee under the Arrangements of 12 May 1926 and 30 June 1928 or under the Conventions of 28 October 1933 and 10 February 1938, the Protocol of 14 September 1939 or the Constitution of the International Refugee Organization;

(ii) Any person who, as a result of events occurring before 1 January 1951 and owing to well-founded fear of being persecuted for reasons of race, religion, nationality or political opinion, is outside the country of his nationality and is unable or, owing to such fear or for reasons other than personal convenience, is unwilling to avail himself of the protection of that country; or who, not having a nationality and being outside the country of his former habitual residence, is unable or, owing to such fear or for reasons other than personal convenience, is unwilling to return to it.

Decisions as to eligibility taken by the International Refugee Organization during the period of its activities shall not prevent the status of refugee being accorded to persons who fulfil the conditions of the present paragraph;

The competence of the High Commissioner shall cease to apply to any person defined in section A above if:

(a) He has voluntarily re-availed himself of the protection of the country of his nationality; or

(b) Having lost his nationality, he has voluntarily re-acquired it; or

(c) He has acquired a new nationality, and enjoys the protection of the country of his new nationality; or

(d) He has voluntarily re-established himself in the country which he left or outside which he remained owing to fear of persecution; or

(e) He can no longer, because the circumstances in connexion with which he has been recognized as a refugee have ceased to exist, claim grounds other than those of personal convenience, for continuing to refuse to avail himself of the protection of the country of his nationality. Reasons of a purely economic character may not be invoked; or

(f) Being a person who has no nationality, he can

no longer, because the circumstances in connexion with which he has been recognized as a refugee have ceased to exist and he is able to return to the country of his former habitual residence, claim grounds other than those of personal convenience for continuing to refuse to return to that country;

B. Any other person who is outside the country of his nationality or, if he has no nationality, the country of his former habitual residence, because he has or had well-founded fear of persecution by reason of his race, religion, nationality or political opinion and is unable or, because of such fear, is unwilling to avail himself of the protection of the government of the country of his nationality, or, if he has no nationality, to return to the country of his former habitual residence.

7. Provided that the competence of the High Commissioner as defined in paragraph 6 above shall not extend to a person:

(a) Who is a national of more than one country unless he satisfies the provisions of the preceding paragraph in relation to each of the countries of which he is a national; or

(b) Who is recognized by the competent authorities of the country in which he has taken residence as having the rights and obligations which are attached to the possession of the nationality of that country; or

(c) Who continues to receive from other organs or agencies of the United Nations protection or assistance; or

(d) In respect of whom there are serious reasons for considering that he has committed a crime covered by the provisions of treaties of extradition or a crime mentioned in article VI of the London Charter of the International Military Tribunal or by the provisions of article 14, paragraph 2, of the Universal Declaration of Human Rights.

8. The High Commissioner shall provide for the protection of refugees falling under the competence of his Office by:

(a) Promoting the conclusion and ratification of international conventions for the protection of refugees, supervising their application and proposing amendments thereto;

(b) Promoting through special agreements with governments the execution of any measures calculated to improve the situation of refugees and to reduce the number requiring protection;

(c) Assisting governmental and private efforts to promote voluntary repatriation or assimilation within new national communities;

(d) Promoting the admission of refugees, not excluding those in the most destitute categories, to the territories of States;

(e) Endeavouring to obtain permission for refugees to transfer their assets and especially those necessary for their resettlement;

(f) Obtaining from governments information concerning the number and conditions of refugees in their territories and the laws and regulations concerning them;

(g) Keeping in close touch with the governments and inter-governmental organizations concerned;

(h) Establishing contact in such manner as he may think best with private organizations dealing with refugee questions;

(i) Facilitating the co-ordination of the efforts of private organizations concerned with the welfare of refugees.

9. The High Commissioner shall engage in such additional activities, including repatriation and resettlement, as

the General Assembly may determine, within the limits of the resources placed at his disposal.

10. The High Commissioner shall administer any funds, public or private, which he receives for assistance to refugees, and shall distribute them among the private and, as appropriate, public agencies which he deems best qualified to administer such assistance.

The High Commissioner may reject any offers which he does not consider appropriate or which cannot be utilized.

The High Commissioner shall not appeal to governments for funds or make a general appeal, without the prior approval of the General Assembly.

The High Commissioner shall include in his annual report a statement of his activities in this field.

11. The High Commissioner shall be entitled to present his views before the General Assembly, the Economic and Social Council and their subsidiary bodies.

The High Commissioner shall report annually to the General Assembly through the Economic and Social Council; his report shall be considered as a separate item on the agenda of the General Assembly.

12. The High Commissioner may invite the co-operation of the various specialized agencies.

### Chapter III—Organization and Finances

13. The High Commissioner shall be elected by the General Assembly on the nomination of the Secretary-General. The terms of appointment of the High Commissioner shall be proposed by the Secretary-General and approved by the General Assembly. The High Commissioner shall be elected for a term of three years, from 1 January 1951.

14. The High Commissioner shall appoint, for the same term, a Deputy High Commissioner of a nationality other than his own.

15. (a) Within the limits of the budgetary appropriations provided, the staff of the Office of the High Commissioner shall be appointed by the High Commissioner and shall be responsible to him in the exercise of their functions.

(b) Such staff shall be chosen from persons devoted to the purposes of the Office of the High Commissioner.

(c) Their conditions of employment shall be those provided under the staff regulations adopted by the General Assembly and the rules promulgated thereunder by the Secretary-General.

(d) Provision may also be made to permit the employment of personnel without compensation.

16. The High Commissioner shall consult the governments of the countries of residence of refugees as to the need for appointing representatives therein. In any country recognizing such need, there may be appointed a representative approved by the government of that country. Subject to the foregoing, the same representative may serve in more than one country.

17. The High Commissioner and the Secretary-General shall make appropriate arrangements for liaison and consultation on matters of mutual interest.

18. The Secretary-General shall provide the High Commissioner with all necessary facilities within budgetary limitations.

19. The Office of the High Commissioner shall be located in Geneva, Switzerland.

20. The Office of the High Commissioner shall be financed under the budget of the United Nations. Unless the General Assembly subsequently decides otherwise, no expen-

diture, other than administrative expenditures relating to the functioning of the Office of the High Commissioner, shall be borne on the budget of the United Nations, and all other expenditures relating to the activities of the High Commissioner shall be financed by voluntary contributions.

21. The administration of the Office of the High Commissioner shall be subject to the Financial Regulations of the United Nations and to the financial rules promulgated thereunder by the Secretary-General.

22. Transactions relating to the High Commissioner's funds shall be subject to audit by the United Nations Board of Auditors, provided that the Board may accept audited accounts from the agencies to which funds have been allocated. Administrative arrangements for the custody of such funds and their allocation shall be agreed between the High Commissioner and the Secretary-General in accordance with the Financial Regulations of the United Nations and rules promulgated thereunder by the Secretary-General.

*BIBLIOGRAPHY.* Burgess, Jan. "New UNHCR Guidelines for Protection of Women," *Refugees* 87 (Oct. 1991): 40-41. Article, in English and French.

Cohen, Roberta. *Human Rights and Humanitarian Emergencies: New Roles for UN Human Rights Bodies.* Washington, DC: Center for Policy Analysis and Research on Refugee Issues; Refugee Policy Group, 1992. NGO discussion paper, in English.

Dewey, Arthur E. "UNHCR and the New World Order," *Refugees* 87 (Oct. 1991): 27-29. Article, in English and French.

Goodwin-Gill, Guy S. "New Mandate? What New Mandate?" *Refugees* 88 (Jan. 1992: 38-40. Article, in English and French.

Goodwin-Gill, Guy S., ed. "Human Rights and Refugees in Crisis: An Overview and Introduction," *International Journal of Refugee Law* (Sept. 1990). Special issue, in English.

Gowlland, Vera, and Klaus Samson, eds. *Problems and Prospects of Refugee Law: Papers Presented at the Colloquium Organized by the Graduate Institute of International Studies in Collaboration with the Office of the United Nations High Commissioner for Refugees, Geneva, 23 and 24 May, 1991.* Geneva, Switzerland: Graduate Institute of Internationsl Studies, 1992. Conference paper, in English.

Lawyers Committee for Human Rights. *The UNHCR at 40: Refugee Protection at the Crossroads.* New York: 1991. NGO report, in English.

**HOLY SEE.** The Vatican City State occupies a small territory within the city of Rome, on the right bank of the Tiber River, and is the site of the central administration of the Catholic Church throughout the world. It is sovereign and independent, and the Roman Catholic Pope exercises temporal as well as spiritual authority over it. Its religious functions are carried on by 11 congregations, three tribunals, three secretariats, and a number of councils, commissions, and committees, while its external relations are in the hands of the Papal Secretary of State.

Although not a member of the United Nations, the Holy See has observer status there. Its population is estimated to be 800, of whom about 85% are of Italian origin. Languages in common use include Italian and Latin.

Pope John Paul II—Polish Cardinal Karol Wojtyla—was chosen by the College of Cardinals in 1978 to succeed Pope John Paul I, who died only 34 days after his election. The first non-Italian to be elected Pope in 456 years, John Paul II has since established himself as "the people's Pope" largely by visiting many nations with large Catholic populations.

A Church-State treaty between Italy and the Holy See, which entered into force in 1985, affirmed the independence of the Vatican but ended the status of Catholicism as Italy's State religion and the designation of Rome as a "sacred city." A ban on diplomatic relations with the Vatican adopted by the Congress of the United States of America in 1867 was repealed in 1984.

**HOMOSEXUALITY.** In 1982, the UN **HUMAN RIGHTS COMMITTEE** examined a communication which it had received under article 5, para. 4, of the **INTERNATIONAL COVENANT ON CIVIL AND POLITICAL RIGHTS: OPTIONAL PROTOCOL,** which contained allegations concerning discrimination on the ground of homosexuality. The action taken by the Committee is summarized in its 1982 report to the **GENERAL ASSEMBLY** as follows (UN Doc. A/37/40, annex XIV, paras. 18–24):

The authors of this communication claimed that the authorities of their country, including organs of the State-controlled broadcasting company, had interfered with their right of freedom of expression and information, as laid down in article 19 of the International Covenant on Civil and Political Rights, by imposing sanctions against participants in, or censuring, radio and television programmes dealing with homosexuality. According to the communication, it was extremely difficult, if not impossible, for a journalist to prepare a programme in which homosexuals were portrayed as anything other than sick, disturbed, criminal or wanting to change their sex.

The State party concerned, while rejecting the allegation that it was in breach of article 19 of the Covenant, stressed that the purpose of the prohibition of public encouragement to indecent behaviour between persons of the same sex was to reflect the prevailing moral conceptions in the country as interpreted by parliament and by large groups of the population. It further contended that discussions in the parliament indicated that the word "encouragement" was to be interpreted in a narrow sense. Moreover, the Legislation Committee of the parliament expressly provided that the law should not hinder the presentation of factual information on homosexuality. As to the decision of the broadcasting company concerning the programmes referred to by the authors, the State party contended that it did not involve the application of censorship but was based on "general considerations of programme policy in accordance with the internal rules of the company".

In an additional submission the authors argued that article 19 of the Covenant, when read in connection with article

2, paragraph 1, required the State party to ensure that its broadcasting company "not only deals with the subject of homosexuality in its programmes but also that it affords a reasonable and, in so far as is possible, an impartial coverage of information and ideas on the subject, in accordance with its own programme regulations".

In its examination of the communication, the Committee pointed out that its task was confined to clarifying whether the restrictions applied against the alleged victims, irrespective of the scope of penal prohibitions under the State party's penal law, revealed a breach of any of the rights under the Covenant. In addition, the Committee stressed that it was limited to examining whether an individual had suffered an actual violation of his rights. It could not review in the abstract whether national legislation contravened the Covenant. With regard to the claim of one of the authors, the Committee observed that the sole fact that he took a personal interest in the dissemination of information about homosexuality did not make him a victim in the sense required by the Optional Protocol. The Committee accepted, however, the contention of two of the authors that their rights under article 19, paragraph 2, of the Covenant had been restricted. On the other hand, the Committee observed that article 19, paragraph 3, permitted certain restrictions on the exercise of the rights protected by article 19, paragraph 2, as were provided by law and were necessary for the protection of public order or of public health or morals. Concerning the communication under consideration, the Government of the State party had specifically invoked public morals as justifying the actions complained of.

In formulating its views, the Committee emphasized that public morals differed widely. There was no universally applicable common standard. Consequently, in that respect, a certain margin of discretion had to be accorded to national authorities. The Committee found that it could not question the decision of those authorities that radio and television were not the appropriate forums to discuss issues related to homosexuality, as far as a programme could be judged as encouraging homosexual behaviour. According to article 19, paragraph 3, the exercise of the rights provided for in article 19, paragraph 2, carried with it special duties and responsibilities for those organs. As far as radio and television programmes were concerned, the audience could not be controlled, and, in particular, harmful effects on minors could not be excluded. Accordingly, the Committee was of the view that there had been no violation of the rights of the authors of the communication under article 19, paragraph 2, of the Covenant.

In an individual opinion appended to the Committee's views, one member of the Committee, although he agreed with the conclusion of the Committee, wished to clarify the following points:

"This conclusion prejudges neither the right to be different and live accordingly, protected by article 17 of the Covenant, nor the right to have general freedom of expression in this respect, protected by article 19. Under article 19, paragraph 2, and subject to article 19, paragraph 3, everyone must in principle have the right to impart information and ideas—positive or negative—about homosexuality and discuss any problem relating to it freely, through any media of his choice and on his own responsibility.

"Moreover, in my view the conception and contents of 'public morals' referred to in article 19, paragraph 3, are relative and changing. State-imposed restrictions on freedom of expression must allow for this fact and should not be applied so as to perpetuate prejudice or promote intolerance. It is of special importance to protect freedom of expression as regards minority views, including those that offend, shock or disturb the majority. Therefore, even if . . . laws . . . may reflect prevailing moral conceptions, this is in itself not sufficient to justify it under article 19, paragraph 3. It must also be shown that the application of the restriction is 'necessary'.

"However, as the Committee has noted, this law has not been directly applied to any of the alleged victims. The question remains whether they have been more indirectly affected by it in a way which can be said to interfere with their freedom of expression, and if so, whether the grounds were justifiable.

"It is clear that nobody—and in particular no State—has any duty under the Covenant to promote publicity for information and ideas of all kinds. Access to media operated by others is always and necessarily more limited than the general freedom of expression. It follows that such access may be controlled on grounds which do not have to be justified under article 19, paragraph 3.

"It is true that self-imposed restrictions on publishing, or the internal programme policy of the media, may threaten the spirit of freedom of expression. Nevertheless, it is a matter of common sense that such decisions either entirely escape control by the Committee or must be accepted to a larger extent than externally imposed restrictions such as enforcement of criminal law or official censorship, neither of which took place in the present case. Not even media controlled by the State can under the Covenant be under an obligation to publish all that may be published. It is not possible to apply the criteria of article 19, paragraph 3, to self-imposed restrictions: quite apart from the 'public morals' issue, one cannot require that they shall be only such as are 'provided by law and are necessary' for the particular purpose. Therefore I prefer not to express any opinion on the possible reasons for the decisions complained of in the present case.

"The role of mass media in public debate depends on the relationship between journalists and their superiors who decide what to publish. I agree with the authors of the communication that the freedom of journalists is important, but the issues arising here can only partly be examined under article 19 of the Covenant."

Two other members of the Human Rights Committee associated themselves with the individual opinion expressed above.

**HONDURAS.** The Republic of Honduras is a country in Central America, on the Pacific Ocean and the Caribbean Sea. It has borders with El Salvador, Guatemala, and Nicaragua. It achieved independence from Spain in 1921 and became a member of the United Nations in 1945. Its population is estimated to be 5,164,000. Ethnic groups include Mestizos (mixed European and Amerindian ancestry), 90%; Europeans, 10%; and Amerindians, 10%. Languages commonly used include Spanish and a number of Amerindian vernaculars. Christianity is the predominant religion. Literacy is estimated at 56%.

The government (1994) took the form of a republic. In 1982, Honduras returned to civilian government after 18 years of military rule. The president, elected by popular vote for a term of four years, is head of State and of government. Political parties include the Liberal Party, the National Party, the Innovation and Unity Party, and the Christian Democratic Party.

Up to 1982, Honduras, the least-developed country in Central America, was frequently the victim of internal conflicts and border disputes. American marines quelled serious disorders in 1903 and 1923, and government forces suppressed revolutions in 1931, 1932, and 1937. El Salvador invaded the country in 1969, charging that Honduras had unfairly deported migrant workers of Salvadoran nationality and left only after intervention by the Organization of American States.

Military rule prevailed, except for brief intervals, between 1955 and 1978, when the ruling *junta* organized open elections for members of the Constituent Assembly. After the Assembly had prepared a new constitution and electoral law, general elections were held in 1981, and Roberto Suazo Cordova was inaugurated as president. A new president, Jose Azcona Hoyo, was elected in 1985, and the change of government represented the first peaceful transfer of power from one democratically elected head of State to another in 50 years. In 1993, Carlos Roberto Reina Idiaquez was elected president.

*INTERAGENCY ON HUMAN RIGHTS.* On 16 February 1987, the Government of Honduras forwarded to the Commission on Human Rights a copy of press communique No. 014-87 of 6 February 1987 from the office of the director for information and the press of the secretariat for foreign affairs, which reads as follows (UN Doc. E/CN.4/1987/54):

On 29 January, on the instructions of the President of the Republic, José Azcona H., the Interagency Commission on Human Rights entered into operation, for the purpose of furnishing a proper response to reports which may be made at both the national and the international level concerning violations of human rights.

The Commission is chaired by the Attorney-General, Rubén D. Zepeda. Reports presented at the international level on alleged human rights violations will be accepted by the Secretariat for Foreign Affairs, which will forward them to the Attorney-General, who, in addition to undertaking appropriate investigations, will bring them to the attention of the members of the Commission. On the basis of any reports supplied by the members of the Commission, and the results of the steps taken by the Attorney-General, the Secretariat for Foreign Affairs will communicate with international organizations as appropriate concerning the reported facts. Domestically, any person who considers that his rights have been violated may present a report to the Attorney-General, upon which appropriate action will be taken immediately.

It should be pointed out that Honduras is one of the few countries in Latin America which has voluntarily accepted the mandatory jurisdiction of the Inter-American Court of Human Rights.

The Commission is composed of representatives of the Office of the Attorney-General, the Supreme Court, the armed forces, the National Congress, the Ministry of the Interior and Justice and the Secretariat for Foreign Affairs.

*SUPPORT OF NICARAGUAN CONTRAS.* In recent years, Honduras sheltered units of the U.S. army and of the U.S.-backed opponents of the Sandinista regime in Nicaragua known as the "contras." In March 1988, more than 3,000 American combat troops were rushed to Palmerola Air Base, near Tegucigalpa, following reports that Nicaraguan troops had crossed into Honduras in pursuit of contras and engaged in "military exercises" for a period of ten weeks. In September of that year, when talks between the contras and the Sandinistas broke down after a five-month truce, thousands of contras began moving out of Nicaragua into base camps in Honduras.

In February 1989, five Central American presidents agreed that the contras should be demobilized, and Nicaraguan President Daniel Ortega Saavedra agreed to free elections in 1990. In those elections, the Sandinistas were defeated, and the contras, after some delay, agreed to disband 12,000 troops then in Honduran base camps.

*DECISION OF THE INTER-AMERICAN COURT OF HUMAN RIGHTS.* A series of public hearings was held by the **INTER-AMERICAN COURT OF HUMAN RIGHTS** between 30 September and 7 October 1987, concerning cases involving the forced disappearances of Alfredo Manfredo Velasquez Rodríguez, Saul Godinez, Francisco Fairen, and Yolanda Solis. At the hearings, the Court received evidence submitted by the **INTER-AMERICAN COMMISSION ON HUMAN RIGHTS,** as well as hearing statements by representatives of the Commission and of the Government of Honduras. In a landmark judgment on 29 July 1988, the Court decided unanimously that Honduras had failed, in the case of Velasquez Rodríguez, a young student who had been detained by government authorities and who later disappeared, to ensure the student's right to personal liberty, his right to humane treatment, and his right to life. The Court further decided unanimously that Honduras should pay fair compensation to the victim's next-of-kin. This judgment represents the first time an international court of human rights, in effect, found a government guilty in the disappearance of a citizen.

*BIBLIOGRAPHY.* Americas Watch. *Honduras: Torture and Murder by Government Forces Persist despite End of Hostilities.* New York: Human Rights Watch, 1991. NGO report, in English.

———. *Human Rights in Honduras: Central America's "Sideshow."* New York: Human Rights Watch, 1987. NGO report, in English.

————. *The Sumus in Nicaragua and Honduras: An Endangered People*. New York: Human Rights Watch, 1987. NGO report, in English.

Amnesty International. *Honduras: Civilian Authority and Military Power: Human Rights Violations in the 1980s*. London: 1988. NGO report, in English.

Asociacion Centroamericana de Familiares de Detenidos-Desaparecidos (Central American Association of Families of the Detained-Disappeared). *Honduras Desaparecidos, Juicio y Condena* (Honduras: Disappearances, Trial and Sentence). San Jose, Costa Rica: 1989. NGO report, in Spanish.

Centro de Documentacion de Honduras (Honduras Documentation Center). *Honduras: Realidad Nacional y Crisis Regional* (Honduras: National Reality and Regional Crisis). Tegucigalpa, Honduras: 1986. NGO edited collection/conference proceedings, in Spanish.

————. *La Contra in Honduras* (The Contras in Honduras). Tegucigalpa, Honduras: 1987. NGO report, in Spanish.

————. *La Tortura en Honduras* (Torture in Honduras). Tegucigalpa, Honduras: 1987. NGO report, in Spanish.

Comité para la Defensa de los Derechos Humanos en Honduras (Committee for the Defense of Human Rights in Honduras). *La Situación de los Derechos Humanos en Honduras 1990* (Annual Report on the Situation of Human Rights in Honduras 1990). Tegucigalpa, Honduras: 1990. Annual report, in English and Spanish.

Human Rights Watch. "Honduras," in *Human Rights Watch World Report 1995*, pp. 104–108. New York: 1995. NGO report, in English.

Instituto de Investigaciones Socio-Economicas de Honduras (Honduran Institute for Socio-Economic Research). *Honduras 1989: Intervencionismo y Ascenso de Nueva Derecha* (Honduras 1989: Interventionism and the Rise of the New Right). Mexico City, Mexico: 1990. NGO report, in Spanish.

————. *Honduras: Fuerzas Armadas 1988, Contrainsurgencia Interna y Disuasion Regional* (Honduras: Armed Forces 1988, Internal Counterinsurgency and Regional Dissuasion). Mexico City, Mexico: 1988. NGO report, in Spanish.

Inter-American Court of Human Rights. *Corte Interamericana de Derechos Humanos: Caso Godinez Cruz, Sentencia del 20 de Enero de 1989* (Inter-American Court of Human Rights: Godinez Cruz Case, January 20, 1989, Decision). San Jose, Costa Rica: 1989. IGO document, in Spanish.

Inter-Church Committee on Human Rights in Latin America. *1990 Annual Report on the Human Rights Situation in Honduras*. Toronto, Canada: 1991. Annual report, in English.

Peckenham, N., and A. Street, eds. *Honduras: Portrait of a Captive Nation*. New York: Praeger, 1985. Edited collection, in English.

Rosenberg, M. B., and P. L. Shepherd, eds. *Honduras Confronts Its Future*. Boulder, CO, USA: Lynne Rienner Publishers, 1986. Document collection, in English.

Tillet, Rebecca. *Investigacion sobre el Habeas Corpus en la Corte Suprema de Justicia Honduras, C A, 1980–1985* (Investigation of Habeas Corpus Practice and Procedure in the Honduran Supreme Court, 1980–1985). Tegucigalpa, Honduras: Comite para la Defensa de los Derechos Humanos en Honduras, 1986. NGO report, in Spanish.

**HOSTAGES.** Acts of hostage-taking and abduction have been recognized by the competent international organs as grave violations of human rights, exposing the hostages to privation, hardship, anguish, and danger to life and health. They are contrary to the principles set out in the UNIVERSAL DECLARATION OF HUMAN RIGHTS, which proclaims the right to life, liberty, and security of person; freedom from torture and other degrading treatment; freedom of movement; and protection against arbitrary detention. They are prohibited by the International Convention against the Taking of Hostages, adopted and opened for ratification and accession by the UN GENERAL ASSEMBLY in 1979 (resolution 34/146, annex), which recognizes the taking of hostages as an offense of grave concern to the international community and provides for its punishment by the State having jurisdiction over that offence. Recently such acts were unequivocally condemned in a resolution adopted unanimously by the UN Security Council (resolution 579 [1985]), in which the Council called for the immediate safe release of all hostages and abducted persons, wherever and by whomever they are being held, and affirmed the obligation of all States in whose territory hostages or abducted persons are held urgently to take all appropriate measures to secure their safe release and to prevent the commission of acts of hostage-taking and abduction in the future. In this connection the Council called for the further development of international cooperation among States in devising and adopting effective measures which are in accordance with the rules of international law to facilitate the prevention, prosecution, and punishment of all acts of hostage-taking and abduction as manifestations of international terrorism.

The UN COMMISSION ON HUMAN RIGHTS and the SUB-COMMISSION ON PREVENTION OF DISCRIMINATION AND PROTECTION OF MINORITIES have repeatedly pointed out that the taking of hostages constitutes a grave violation of human rights. At its 1989 session, the Commission, alarmed by the number of cases of hostage-taking throughout the world, expressed its distress at these unacceptable displays of violence towards innocent victims and at the anxiety and suffering of the families concerned; strongly condemned the taking of any person hostage, whoever is responsible and whatever the circumstances, whether or not the hostage is chosen at random and whatever his nationality; censured the actions of all persons responsible for taking hostages, whatever their motives, and demanded that they should immediately release those they are holding; and called upon States to take any measures necessary to prevent and punish the taking of hostages and to put an immediate end to cases of abduction and unlawful restraint on their territory.

Likewise, the Sub-Commission on Prevention of Discrimination and Protection of Minorities, on 1 September 1989, condemned (resolution 1989/26) hostage-taking and the torture and murder which frequently accompany such practices; condemned all who actively participate in or implicitly tolerate such activities by failing to take the appropriate corrective steps; specifically condemned the abduction and murder of United Nations personnel as exemplified by the brutal murder of the Commander of the United Nations Truce Supervision Organization in Lebanon, Lt. Col. William R. Higgins; and expressed its deepest sympathy and grief to the families of United Nations personnel whose members have been abducted and/or murdered.

The Sub-Commission called upon all States to take steps to prevent hostage-taking and bring to trial, in conformity with international standards, any who may participate in such an undertaking; and called upon all governments to become parties to the International Convention Against the Taking of Hostages and to observe faithfully its terms, in particular, the obligation to prosecute or extradite hostage-takers without exception. Further, it urged the Secretary-General to take all possible measures to stop hostage-taking and to seek the release of all hostages being unlawfully detained and to provide the Sub-Commission with a complete list of all United Nations personnel held in captivity with all available information concerning the names and whereabouts of the captors, if known.

More recently, the UN General Assembly, in resolution 46/51 of 9 December 1991, firmly called for the immediate and safe release of all hostages and abducted persons, wherever and by whomever they are being held, and called upon all States "to use their political influence in accordance with the Charter of the United Nations and the principles of international law to secure the safe release of all hostages and abducted persons and to prevent the commission of acts of hostage-taking and abduction."

**SEE ALSO** *Terrorism; Victims' Rights.*

**HOSTAGES: INTERNATIONAL CONVENTION AGAINST THE TAKING OF HOSTAGES (1979).** In 1976, the UN **GENERAL ASSEMBLY** decided (resolution 31/103) to establish an *ad hoc* committee to draft an international convention against the taking of hostages, composed of 35 Member States, and to request it to prepare the draft of such a convention bearing in mind suggestions and proposals received from any State.

In doing so, the Assembly bore in mind that both the **UNIVERSAL DECLARATION OF HUMAN RIGHTS** and the **INTERNATIONAL COVENANT ON CIVIL AND POLITICAL RIGHTS** provide that everyone has the right to life, liberty, and security. It also recalled the prohibitions of the taking of hostages in articles 3 and 34 of the Geneva Convention relative to the Protection of Civilian Persons in Time of War of 12 August 1949, the Convention for the Suppression of Unlawful Acts against the Safety of Civil Aviation, and the Convention on the Prevention and Punishment of Crimes against Internationally Protected Persons, including Diplomatic Agents, as well as the Assembly's own resolution of 25 November 1970 (resolution 2645 [XXV]), condemning aerial hijacking or interference with civil air travel.

The ad hoc committee completed the draft of a convention against the taking of hostages in 1979; and, on 17 December 1979, the Assembly adopted (resolution 34/146) the International Convention against the Taking of Hostages. The text of the convention, annexed to that resolution, is as follows:

The States Parties to this Convention,

Having in mind the purposes and principles of the Charter of the United Nations concerning the maintenance of international peace and security and the promotion of friendly relations and co-operation among States,

Recognizing, in particular, that everyone has the right to life, liberty and security of person, as set out in the Universal Declaration of Human Rights and the International Covenant on Civil and Political Rights,

Reaffirming the principle of equal rights and self-determination of peoples as enshrined in the Charter of the United Nations and the Declaration on Principles of International Law concerning Friendly Relations and Co-operation among States in accordance with the Charter of the United Nations, as well as in other relevant resolutions of the General Assembly,

Considering that the taking of hostages is an offence of grave concern to the international community and that, in accordance with the provisions of this Convention, any person committing an act of hostage taking shall be either prosecuted or extradited,

Being convinced that it is urgently necessary to develop international co-operation between States in devising and adopting effective measures for the prevention, prosecution and punishment of all acts of taking of hostages as manifestations of international terrorism.

Have agreed as follows:

*Article 1.* 1. Any person who seizes or detains and threatens to kill, to injure or to continue to detain another person (hereinafter referred to as the "hostage") in order to compel a third party, namely, a State, an international intergovernmental organization, a natural or juridical person, or a group of persons, to do or abstain from doing any act as an explicit or implicit condition for the release of the hostage commits the offence of taking of hostages ("hostage-taking") within the meaning of this Convention.

2. Any person who:

(a) Attempts to commit an act of hostage-taking, or

(b) Participates as an accomplice of anyone who commits or attempts to commit an act of hostage-taking likewise commits an offence for the purposes of this Convention.

*Article 2.* Each State Party shall make the offences set forth in article 1 punishable by appropriate penalties which take into account the grave nature of those offences.

*Article 3.* 1. The State Party in the territory of which the hostage is held by the offender shall take all measures it considers appropriate to ease the situation of the hostage, in particular, to secure his release and, after his release, to facilitate, when relevant, his departure.

2. If any object which the offender has obtained as a result of the taking of hostages comes into the custody of a State Party, that State Party shall return it as soon as possible to the hostage or the third party referred to in article 1, as the case may be, or to the appropriate authorities thereof.

*Article 4.* States Parties shall co-operate in the prevention of the offences set forth in article 1, particularly by:

(a) Taking all practicable measures to prevent preparations in their respective territories for the commission of those offences within or outside their territories, including measures to prohibit in their territories illegal activities of persons, groups and organizations that encourage, instigate, organize or engage in the perpetration of acts of taking of hostages;

(b) Exchanging information and co-ordinating the taking of administrative and other measures as appropriate to prevent the commission of those offences.

*Article 5.* 1. Each State Party shall take such measures as may be necessary to establish its jurisdiction over any of the offences set forth in article 1 which are committed:

(a) In its territory or on board a ship or aircraft registered in that State;

(b) By any of its nationals or, if that State considers it appropriate, by those stateless persons who have their habitual residence in its territory;

(c) In order to compel that State to do or abstain from doing any act; or

(d) With respect to a hostage who is a national of that State, if that State considers it appropriate.

2. Each State Party shall likewise take such measures as may be necessary to establish its jurisdiction over the offences set forth in article 1 in cases where the alleged offender is present in its territory and it does not extradite him to any of the States mentioned in paragraph 1 of this article.

3. This Convention does not exclude any criminal jurisdiction exercised in accordance with internal law.

*Article 6.* 1. Upon being satisfied that the circumstances so warrant, any State Party in the territory of which the alleged offender is present shall, in accordance with its laws, take him into custody or take other measures to ensure his presence for such time as is necessary to enable any criminal or extradition proceedings to be instituted. That State Party shall immediately make a preliminary inquiry into the facts.

2. The custody or other measures referred to in paragraph 1 of this article shall be notified without delay directly or through the Secretary-General of the United Nations to:

(a) The State where the offence was committed;

(b) The State against which compulsion has been directed or attempted;

(c) The State of which the natural or juridical person against whom compulsion has been directed or attempted is a national;

(d) The State of which the hostage is a national or in the territory of which he has his habitual residence;

(e) The State of which the alleged offender is a national or, if he is a stateless person, in the territory of which he has his habitual residence;

(f) The international intergovernmental organization against which compulsion has been directed or attempted;

(g) All other States concerned.

3. Any person regarding whom the measures referred to in paragraph 1 of this article are being taken shall be entitled:

(a) To communicate without delay with the nearest appropriate representative of the State of which he is a national or which is otherwise entitled to establish such communication or, if he is a stateless person, the State in the territory of which he has his habitual residence;

(b) To be visited by a representative of that State.

4. The rights referred to in paragraph 3 of this article shall be exercised in conformity with the laws and regulations of the State in the territory of which the alleged offender is present, subject to the proviso, however, that the said laws and regulations must enable full effect to be given to the purposes for which the rights accorded under paragraph 3 of this article are intended.

5. The provisions of paragraphs 3 and 4 of this article shall be without prejudice to the right of any State Party having a claim to jurisdiction in accordance with paragraph 1 (b) of article 5 to invite the International Committee of the Red Cross to communicate with and visit the alleged offender.

6. The State which makes the preliminary inquiry contemplated in paragraph 1 of this article shall promptly report its findings to the States or organization referred to in paragraph 2 of this article and indicate whether it intends to exercise jurisdiction.

*Article 7.* The State Party where the alleged offender is prosecuted shall, in accordance with its laws, communicate the final outcome of the proceedings to the Secretary-General of the United Nations, who shall transmit the information to the other States concerned and the international intergovernmental organizations concerned.

*Article 8.* 1. The State Party in the territory of which the alleged offender is found shall, if it does not extradite him, be obliged, without exception whatsoever and whether or not the offence was committed in its territory, to submit the case to its competent authorities for the purpose of prosecution, through proceedings in accordance with the laws of that State. Those authorities shall take their decision in the same manner as in the case of any ordinary offence of a grave nature under the law of that State.

2. Any person regarding whom proceedings are being carried out in connexion with any of the offences set forth in article 1 shall be guaranteed fair treatment at all stages of the proceedings, including enjoyment of all the rights and guarantees provided by the law of the State in the territory of which he is present.

*Article 9.* 1. A request for the extradition of an alleged offender, pursuant to this Convention, shall not be granted if the requested State Party has substantial grounds for believing:

(a) That the request for extradition for an offence set forth in article 1 has been made for the purpose of prosecuting or punishing a person on account of his race, religion, nationality, ethnic origin or political opinion; or

(b) That the person's position may be prejudiced:

(i) For any of the reasons mentioned in subparagraph (a) of this paragraph, or

(ii) For the reason that communication with him by the appropriate authorities of the State entitled to exercise rights of protection cannot be effected.

2. With respect to the offences as defined in this Convention, the provisions of all extradition treaties and arrangements applicable between States Parties are modified as between States Parties to the extent that they are incompatible with this Convention.

*Article 10.* 1. The offences set forth in article 1 shall be deemed to be included as extraditable offences in any extradition treaty existing between States Parties. States Parties undertake to include such offences as extraditable offences in every extradition treaty to be concluded between them.

2. If a State Party which makes extradition conditional on the existence of a treaty receives a request for extradition from another State Party with which it has no extradition treaty, the requested State may at its opinion consider this Convention as the legal basis for extradition in respect of the offences set forth in article 1. Extradition shall be subject to the other conditions provided by the law of the requested State.

3. States Parties which do not make extradition conditional on the existence of a treaty shall recognize the offences set forth in article 1 as extraditable offences between themselves, subject to the conditions provided by the law of the requested State.

4. The offences set fort in article 1 shall be treated, for the purpose of extradition between States Parties, as if they had been committed not only in the place in which they occurred but also in the territories of the States required to establish their jurisdiction in accordance with paragraph 1 of article 5.

*Article 11.* 1. States Parties shall afford one another the greatest measure of assistance in connexion with criminal proceedings brought in respect of the offences set forth in article 1, including the supply of all evidence at their disposal necessary for the proceedings.

2. The provisions of paragraph 1 of this article shall not affect obligations concerning mutual judicial assistance embodied in any other treaty.

*Article 12.* In so far as the Geneva Conventions of 1949 for the protection of war victims or the Protocols Additional to those Conventions are applicable to a particular act of hostage-taking, and in so far as States Parties to this Convention are bound under those conventions to prosecute or hand over the hostage-taker, the present Convention shall not apply to an act of hostage-taking committed in the course of armed conflicts as defined in the Geneva Conventions of 1949 and the Protocols thereto, including armed conflicts, mentioned in article 1, paragraph 4, of Additional Protocol 1 of 1977 in which peoples are fighting against colonial domination and alien occupation and against racist régimes in the exercise of their right of self-determination, as enshrined in the Charter of the United Nations and the Declaration on Principles of International Law concerning Friendly Relations and Co-operation among States in accordance with the Charter of the United Nations.

*Article 13.* This Convention shall not apply where the offence is committed within a single State, the hostage and the alleged offender are nationals of that State and the alleged offender is found in the territory of that State.

*Article 14.* Nothing in this Convention shall be construed as justifying the violation of the territorial integrity or political independence of a State in contravention of the Charter of the United Nations.

*Article 15.* The provisions of this Convention shall not affect the application of the Treaties on Asylum, in force at the date of the adoption of this Convention, as between the States which are parties to those Treaties; but a State Party to this Convention may not invoke those Treaties with respect to another State Party to this Convention which is not a party to those Treaties.

*Article 16.* 1. Any dispute between two or more States Parties concerning the interpretation or application of this Con-

vention which is not settled by negotiation shall, at the request of one of them, be submitted to arbitration. If within six months from the date of the request for arbitration the parties are unable to agree on the organization of the arbitration, any one of those parties may refer the dispute to the International Court of Justice by request in conformity with the Statute of the Court.

2. Each State may at the time of signature or ratification of this Convention or accession thereto declare that it does not consider itself bound by paragraph 1 of this article. The other Sates Parties shall not be bound by paragraph 1 of this article with respect to any State Party which has made such a reservation.

3. Any State Party which has made a reservation in accordance with paragraph 2 of this article may at any time withdraw that reservation by notification to the Secretary-General of the United Nations.

*Article 17.* 1. This Convention is open for signature by all States until 31 December 1980 at United Nations Headquarters in New York.

2. This Convention is subject to ratification. The instruments of ratification shall be deposited with the Secretary-General of the United Nations.

3. This Convention is open for accession by any State. The instruments of accession shall be deposited with the Secretary-General of the United Nations.

*Article 18.* 1. This Convention shall enter into force on the thirtieth day following the date of deposit of the twenty-second instrument of ratification or accession with the Secretary-General of the United Nations.

2. For each State ratifying or acceding to the Convention after the deposit of the twenty-second instrument of ratification or accession, the Convention shall enter into force on the thirtieth day after deposit by such State of its instrument of ratification or accession.

*Article 19.* 1. Any State Party may denounce this Convention by written notification to the Secretary-General of the United Nations.

2. Denunciation shall take effect one year following the date on which notification is received by the Secretary-General of the United Nations.

*Article 20.* The original of this Convention, of which the Arabic, Chinese, English, French, Russian and Spanish texts are equally authentic, shall be deposited with the Secretary-General of the United Nations, who shall send certified copies thereof to all States.

In witness whereof, the undersigned, being duly authorized thereto by their respective Governments, have signed this Convention, opened for signature at New York on 18 December 1979.

**HOUSING AS A HUMAN RIGHT.** The **UNIVERSAL DECLARATION OF HUMAN RIGHTS,** of 10 December 1948, proclaims that:

*Article 25.* (1) Everyone has the right to a standard of living adequate for the health and well-being of himself and his family, including food, clothing, housing and medical care and necessary social services, and the right to security in the event of unemployment, sickness, disability, widowhood, old age or other lack of livelihood in circumstances beyond his control.

The Convention Relating to the Status of Refugees (see **REFUGEES**), of 28 July 1951, states:

*Article 21.* As regards housing, the Contracting States, in so far as the matter is regulated by laws or regulations or is subject to the control of public authorities, shall accord to refugees lawfully staying in their territory treatment as favourable as possible and, in any event, not less favourable than that accorded to aliens generally in the same circumstances.

The Declaration of the Rights of the Child (see **CHILDREN'S RIGHTS**), of 29 November 1959, states:

*Principle 4.* The child shall enjoy the benefits of social security. He shall be entitled to grow and develop in health; to this end special care and protection shall be provided to him and his mother, including adequate pre-natal and post-natal care. The child shall have the right to adequate nutrition, housing, recreation and medical services.

The ILO Recommendation on Worker's Housing (no. 115), of 7 June 1961, states:

*Principle 2.* It should be an objective of the national (housing) policy to promote, within the framework of general housing policy, the construction of housing and related community facilities with a view to ensuring that adequate and decent housing accommodation and a suitable living environment are made available to all workers and their families. A degree of priority should be accorded to those whose needs are most urgent.

The International Convention on the Elimination of all Forms of Racial Discrimination (see **RACIAL DISCRIMINATION**), of 21 December 1965, states:

*Article 5.* In compliance with the fundamental obligations laid down in article 2 of this Convention, States Parties undertake to prohibit and eliminate racial discrimination in all its forms and to guarantee the right of everyone, without distinction as to race, colour, or national or ethnic origin, to equality before the law, notably in the enjoyment of the following rights: . . . (e) Economic, Social and Cultural rights in particular: . . . (iii) The right to housing.

The **INTERNATIONAL COVENANT ON ECONOMIC, SOCIAL AND CULTURAL RIGHTS**, of 16 December 1966, states:

*Article 11.* (1) The States Parties to the present Covenant recognize the right of everyone to an adequate standard of living for himself and his family, including adequate food, clothing and housing, and to the continuous improvement of living conditions. The States Parties will take appropriate steps to ensure the realization of this right, recognizing to this effect the essential importance of international co-operation based on free consent.

The Declaration on Social Progress and Development (see **DEVELOPMENT**), of 11 December 1969, states:

*Part II.* Social progress and development shall aim at the continuous raising of the material and spiritual standards of living of all members of society, with respect for and in compliance with human rights and fundamental freedoms, through the attainment of the following main goals: . . .
10(f). The provision for all, particularly persons in low-income groups and large families, of adequate housing and community services.

The Vancouver Declaration on Human Settlements, of 11 June 1976, adopted by HABITAT, the United Nations Conference on Human Settlements, states:

*Section III.* (8) Adequate shelter and services are a basic human right which places an obligation on governments to ensure their attainment by all people, beginning with direct assistance to the least advantaged through guided programmes of self-help and community action. Governments should endeavour to remove all impediments hindering attainment of these goals. Of special importance is the elimination of social and racial segregation, inter alia, through the creation of better balanced communities, which blend different social groups, occupations, housing and amenities.

The Convention on the Elimination of All Forms of Discrimination Against Women, of 18 December 1979, states:

*Article 14.* (2) States Parties shall take all appropriate measures to eliminate discrimination against women in rural areas in order to ensure, on a basis of equality of men and women, that they participate in and benefit from rural development and, in particular, shall ensure to such women the right: . . . (h) To enjoy adequate living conditions, particularly in relation to housing, sanitation, electricity and water supply, transport and communications.

The Declaration on the Right to Development (see **DEVELOPMENT**), of 4 December 1986, states:

*Article 8.* (1) States should undertake, at the national level, all necessary measures for the realization of the right to development and shall ensure, inter alia, equality of opportunity for all in their access to basic resources, education, health services, food, housing, employment and the fair distribution of income. Effective measures should be undertaken to ensure that women have an active role in the development process. Appropriate economic and social reforms should be carried out with a view to eradicating all social injustices.

The Convention on the Rights of the Child (see **CHILDREN'S RIGHTS**), of 20 November 1989, states:

*Article 27.* (3) States Parties, in accordance with national conditions and within their means, shall take appropriate measures to assist parents and others responsible for the child to implement this right and shall in case of need provide material assistance and support programmes, particularly with regard to nutrition, clothing and housing.

The International Convention on the Protection of the Rights of All Migrant Workers and Members of

Their Families (see **MIGRANT WORKERS**), of 18 December 1990, states:

Article 43 (1) Migrant workers shall enjoy equality of treatment with nationals of the State of employment in relation to: . . .

(d) access to housing, including social housing schemes, and protection against exploitation in respect of rents.

*THE RIGHT TO ADEQUATE HOUSING.* At its sixth (1991) session, the UN **COMMITTEE ON ECONOMIC, SOCIAL AND CULTURAL RIGHTS** adopted its General Comment No. 4, on the right to adequate housing (art. 11 (1) of the International Covenant on Economic, Social and Cultural Rights), as follows:

1. Pursuant to article 11 (1) of the Covenant, States parties "recognize the right of everyone to an adequate standard of living for himself and his family, including adequate food, clothing and housing, and to the continuous improvement of living conditions". The human right to adequate housing, which is thus derived from the right to an adequate standard of living, is of central importance for the enjoyment of all economic, social and cultural rights.

2. The Committee has been able to accumulate a large amount of information pertaining to this right. Since 1979, the Committee and its predecessors have examined 75 reports dealing with the right to adequate housing. The Committee has also devoted a day of general discussion to the issue at each of its third (see E/1989/22, para. 312) and fourth sessions (E/1990/23, paras. 281–285). In addition, the Committee has taken careful note of information generated by the International Year of Shelter for the Homeless (1987) including the Global Strategy for Shelter to the Year 2000 adopted by the General Assembly in its resolution 42/191 of 11 December 1987. The Committee has also reviewed relevant reports and other documentation of the Commission on Human Rights and the Sub-Commission on Prevention of Discrimination and Protection of Minorities.

3. Although a wide variety of international instruments address the different dimensions of the right to adequate housing article 11 (1) of the Covenant is the most comprehensive and perhaps the most important of the relevant provisions.

4. Despite the fact that the international community has frequently reaffirmed the importance of full respect for the right to adequate housing, there remains a disturbingly large gap between the standards set in article 11 (1) of the Covenant and the situation prevailing in many parts of the world. While the problems are often particularly acute in some developing countries which confront major resource and other constraints, the Committee observes that significant problems of homelessness and inadequate housing also exist in some of the most economically developed societies. The United Nations estimates that there are over 100 million persons homeless worldwide and over 1 billion inadequately housed. There is no indication that this number is decreasing. It seems clear that no State party is free of significant problems of one kind or another in relation to the right to housing.

5. In some instances, the reports of States parties examined by the Committee have acknowledged and described difficulties in ensuring the right to adequate housing. For the most part, however, the information provided has been insufficient to enable the Committee to obtain an adequate picture of the situation prevailing in the State concerned. This General Comment thus aims to identify some of the principal issues which the Committee considers to be important in relation to this right.

6. The right to adequate housing applies to everyone. While the reference to "himself and his family" reflects assumptions as to gender roles and economic activity patterns commonly accepted in 1966 when the Covenant was adopted, the phrase cannot be read today as implying any limitations upon the applicability of the right to individuals or to female-headed households or other such groups. Thus, the concept of "family" must be understood in a wide sense. Further, individuals, as well as families, are entitled to adequate housing regardless of age, economic status, group or other affiliation or status and other such factors. In particular, enjoyment of this right must, in accordance with article 2 (2) of the Covenant, not be subject to any form of discrimination.

7. In the Committee's view, the right to housing should not be interpreted in a narrow or restrictive sense which equates it with, for example, the shelter provided by merely having a roof over one's head or views shelter exclusively as a commodity. Rather it should be seen as the right to live somewhere in security, peace and dignity. This is appropriate for at least two reasons. In the first place, the right to housing is integrally linked to other human rights and to the fundamental principles upon which the Covenant is premised. This "the inherent dignity of the human person" from which the rights in the Covenant are said to derive requires that the term "housing" be interpreted so as to take account of a variety of other considerations, most importantly that the right to housing should be ensured to all persons irrespective of income or access to economic resources. Secondly, the reference in article 11 (1) must be read as referring not just to housing but to adequate housing. As both the Commission on Human Settlements and the Global Strategy for Shelter to the Year 2000 have stated: "Adequate shelter means . . . adequate privacy, adequate space, adequate security, adequate lighting and ventilation, adequate basic infrastructure and adequate location with regard to work and basic facilities—all at a reasonable cost".

8. Thus the concept of adequacy is particularly significant in relation to the right to housing since it serves to underline a number of factors which must be taken into account in determining whether particular forms of shelter can be considered to constitute "adequate housing" for the purposes of the Covenant. While adequacy is determined in part by social, economic, cultural, climatic, ecological and other factors, the Committee believes that it is nevertheless possible to identify certain aspects of the right that must be taken into account for this purpose in any particular context. They include the following:

(a) *Legal security of tenure.* Tenure takes a variety of forms, including rental (public and private) accommodation, cooperative housing, lease, owner-occupation, emergency housing and informal settlements, including occupation of land or property. Notwithstanding the type of tenure, all persons should possess a degree of security of tenure which guarantees legal protection against forced eviction, harassment and other threats. States parties should consequently take immediate measures aimed at conferring legal security of tenure upon those persons and households currently lacking such protection, in genuine consultation with affected persons and groups;

(b) *Availability of services, materials, facilities and infrastructure.* An adequate house must contain certain facilities essential for health, security, comfort and nutrition. All beneficiaries of the right to adequate housing should have sustainable access to natural and common resources, safe drinking water, energy for cooking, heating and lighting, sanitation and washing facilities, means of food storage, refuse disposal, site drainage and emergency services;

(c) *Affordability.* Personal or household financial costs associated with housing should be at such a level that the attainment and satisfaction of other basic needs are not threatened or compromised. Steps should be taken by States parties to ensure that the percentage of housing-related costs is, in general, commensurate with income levels. States parties should establish housing subsidies for those unable to obtain affordable housing, as well as forms and levels of housing finance which adequately reflect housing needs. In accordance with the principle of affordability, tenants should be protected by appropriate means against unreasonable rent levels or rent increases. In societies where natural materials constitute the chief sources of building materials for housing, steps should be taken by States parties to ensure the availability of such materials;

(d) *Habitability.* Adequate housing must be habitable, in terms of providing the inhabitants with adequate space and protecting them from cold, damp, heat, rain, wind or other threats to health, structural hazards, and disease vectors. The physical safety of occupants must be guaranteed as well. The Committee encourages States parties to comprehensively apply the *Health Principles of Housing* prepared by WHO which view housing as the environmental factor most frequently associated with conditions for disease in epidemiological analyses; i.e. inadequate and deficient housing and living conditions are invariably associated with higher mortality and morbidity rates;

(e) *Accessibility.* Adequate housing must be accessible to those entitled to it. Disadvantaged groups must be accorded full and sustainable access to adequate housing resources. Thus, such disadvantaged groups as the elderly, children, the physically disabled, the terminally ill, HIV-positive individuals, persons with persistent medical problems, the mentally ill, victims of natural disasters, people living in disaster-prone areas and other groups should be ensured some degree of priority consideration in the housing sphere. Both housing law and policy should take fully into account the special housing needs of these groups. Within many States parties increasing access to land by landless or impoverished segments of the society should constitute a central policy goal. Discernible governmental obligations need to be developed aiming to substantiate the right of all to a secure place to live in peace and dignity, including access to land as an entitlement;

(f) *Location.* Adequate housing must be in a location which allows access to employment options, health-care services, schools, child-care centres and other social facilities. This is true both in large cities and in rural areas where the temporal and financial costs of getting to and from the place of work can place excessive demands upon the budgets of poor households. Similarly, housing should not be built on polluted sites nor in immediate proximity to pollution sources that threaten the right to health of the inhabitants;

(g) *Cultural adequacy.* The way housing is constructed, the building materials used and the policies supporting these must appropriately enable the expression of cultural identity and diversity of housing. Activities geared towards development or modernization in the housing sphere should ensure that the cultural dimensions of housing are not sacrificed, and that, inter alia, modern technological facilities, as appropriate are also ensured.

9. As noted above, the right to adequate housing cannot be viewed in isolation from other human rights contained in the two International Covenants and other applicable international instruments. Reference has already been made in this regard to the concept of human dignity and the principle of non-discrimination. In addition, the full enjoyment of other rights—such as the right to freedom of expression, the right to freedom of association (such as for tenants and other community-based groups), the right to freedom of residence and the right to participate in public decision-making—is indispensable if the right to adequate housing is to be realized and maintained by all groups in society. Similarly, the right not to be subjected to arbitrary or unlawful interference with one's privacy, family, home or correspondence constitutes a very important dimension in defining the right to adequate housing.

10. Regardless of the state of development of any country, there are certain steps which must be taken immediately. As recognized in the Global Strategy for Shelter and in other international analyses, many of the measures required to promote the right to housing would only require the abstention by the Government from certain practices and a commitment to facilitating "self-help" by affected groups. To the extent that any such steps are considered to be beyond the maximum resources available to a State party, it is appropriate that a request be made as soon as possible for international cooperation in accordance with articles 11 (1), 22 and 23 of the Covenant, and that the Committee be informed thereof.

11. States parties must give due priority to those social groups living in unfavourable conditions by giving them particular consideration. Policies and legislation should correspondingly not be designed to benefit already advantaged social groups at the expense of others. The Committee is aware that external factors can affect the right to a continuous improvement of living conditions, and that in many States parties overall living conditions declined during the 1980s. However, as noted by the Committee in its General Comment 2 (1990) (E/1990/23, annex III), despite externally caused problems, the obligations under the Covenant continue to apply and are perhaps even more pertinent during times of economic contraction. It would thus appear to the Committee that a general decline in living and housing conditions, directly attributable to policy and legislative decisions by States parties, and in the absence of accompanying compensatory measures, would be inconsistent with the obligations under the Covenant.

12. While the most appropriate means of achieving the full realization of the right to adequate housing will inevitably vary significantly from one State party to another, the Covenant clearly requires that each State party take whatever steps are necessary for that purpose. This will almost invariably require the adoption of a national housing strategy which, as stated in paragraph 32 of the Global Strategy for Shelter, "defines the objectives for the development of shelter conditions, identifies the resources available to meet these goals and the most cost-effective way of using them and sets out the responsibilities and time-frame for the implementation of the necessary measures". Both for reasons of relevance and effectiveness, as well as in order to ensure respect for other human rights, such a strategy should reflect

extensive genuine consultation with, and participation by, all of those affected, including the homeless, the inadequately housed and their representatives. Furthermore, steps should be taken to ensure coordination between ministries and regional and local authorities in order to reconcile related policies (economics, agriculture, environment, energy, etc.) with the obligations under article 11 of the Covenant.

13. Effective monitoring of the situation with respect to housing is another obligation of immediate effect. For a State party to satisfy under article 11 (1) it must demonstrate, inter alia, that it has taken whatever steps are necessary, either alone or on the basis of international cooperation, to ascertain the full extent of homelessness and housing within its jurisdiction. In this regard, the revised general guidelines regarding the form and contents of reports adopted by the Committee (E/C.12/1991/1) emphasize the need to "provide detailed information about those groups within . . . society that are vulnerable and disadvantaged with regard to housing". They include, in particular, homeless persons and families, those inadequately housed and without ready access to basic amenities, those living in "illegal" settlements, those subject to forced evictions and low-income groups.

14. Measures designed to satisfy a State party's obligations in respect of the right to adequate housing may reflect whatever mix of public and private sector measures considered appropriate. While in some States public financing of housing might most usefully be spent on direct construction of new housing, in most cases, experience has shown the inability of Governments to fully satisfy housing deficits with publicly built housing. The promotion by States parties of "enabling strategies", combined with a full commitment to obligations under the right to adequate housing, should thus be encouraged. In essence, the obligation is to demonstrate that, in aggregate, the measures being taken are sufficient to realize the right for every individual in the shortest possible time in accordance with the maximum of available resources.

15. Many of the measures that will be required will involve resource allocations and policy initiatives of a general kind. Nevertheless, the role of formal legislative and administrative measures should not be underestimated in this context. The Global Strategy for Shelter (paras. 66–67) has drawn attention to the types of measures that might be taken in this regard and to their importance.

16. In some States, the right to adequate housing is constitutionally entrenched. In such cases the Committee is particularly interested in learning of the legal and practical significance of such an approach. Details of specific cases and of other ways in which entrenchment has proved helpful should thus be provided.

17. The Committee views many component elements of the right to adequate housing as being at least consistent with the provision of domestic legal remedies. Depending on the legal system, such areas might include, but are not limited to: (a) legal appeals aimed at preventing planned evictions or demolitions through the issuance of court-ordered injunctions; (b) legal procedures seeking compensation following an illegal eviction; (c) complaints against illegal actions carried out or supported by landlords (whether public or private) in relation to rent levels, dwelling maintenance, and racial or other forms of discrimination; (d) allegations of any form of discrimination in the allocation and availability of access to housing; and (e) complaints against landlords concerning unhealthy or inadequate housing conditions. In some legal systems it would also be appropriate to explore the possibility of facilitating class action suits in situations involving significantly increased levels of homelessness.

18. In this regard, the Committee considers that instances of forced eviction are prima facie incompatible with the requirements of the Covenant and can only be justified in the most exceptional circumstances, and in accordance with the relevant principles of international law.

19. Finally, article 11 (1) concludes with the obligation of States parties to recognize "the essential importance of international cooperation based on free consent". Traditionally, less than 5 per cent of all international assistance has been directed towards housing or human settlements, and often the manner by which such funding is provided does little to address the housing needs of disadvantaged groups. States parties, both recipients and providers, should ensure that a substantial proportion of financing is devoted to creating conditions leading to a higher number of persons being adequately housed. International financial institutions promoting measures of structural adjustment should ensure that such measures do not compromise the enjoyment of the right to adequate housing. States parties should, when contemplating international financial cooperation, seek to indicate areas relevant to the right to adequate housing where external financing would have the most effect. Such requests should take full account of the needs and views of the affected groups.

***REPORTS OF THE SPECIAL RAPPORTEUR ON THE RIGHT TO ADEQUATE HOUSING.*** The UN SUB-COMMISSION ON PREVENTION OF DISCRIMINATION AND PROTECTION OF MINORITIES, at its 1991 session, entrusted Mr. Rajindar Sachar with the task of preparing a working paper on the right to adequate housing (resolution 1991/26). The working paper (E/CN.4/Sub.2/15) was considered by the Sub-Commission at its 1992 session, which expressed its appreciation to the author and encouraged all States to pursue effective policies and legislation aimed at creating conditions designed to ensure the full realization of the right to adequate housing of the entire population, concentrating on those vulnerable groups that are homeless or inadequately housed. It decided to appoint Mr. Rajindar Sachar as Special Rapporteur on promoting the realization of the right to adequate housing, and the Commission on Human Rights endorsed that decision.

The Special Rapporteur's first progress report was submitted to the Sub-Commission at its 1993 session, (E/CN.4/Sub.2/1993/15). Its central focus was to elaborate and clarify States' obligations concerning the human right to adequate housing, as well as other legal dimensions of this fundamental right. The Special Rapporteur also set out a few preliminary conclusions and recommendations, as follows (paras. 159–165):

Although it is too early in his mandate for the Special Rapporteur to put forward a comprehensive list of conclusions and recommendations on promoting the full realization of the right to adequate housing, it is possible to make a series of preliminary remarks. These are designed to begin what will necessarily be a much longer-term process towards ensuring housing rights to all persons, families and communities. The Special Rapporteur would appreciate receiving comments and ideas concerning these preliminary remarks during the consideration of this report.

At the most fundamental level, the preceding analysis exposes a situation wherein much greater attention and coverage has been devoted to all levels of the right to adequate housing than is generally known. These many inspiring developments, however, remain disproportionately rhetorical in nature, when seen against the legal protection which should be accorded to those of the world's citizens whose right to a safe, secure and dignified place to live has yet to be realized.

There continues to be a pressing need for long-term and practical strategies to be elaborated and implemented aimed at ensuring the full realization of housing rights. There is a clear need for permanent and sufficient United Nations mechanisms for monitoring the global status of housing rights and for accurately delineating global housing needs and the costs and measures required for assessing and alleviating the situation. It may be advisable for the United Nations advisory services programme to develop expertise in the area of housing rights.

Along the same lines, procedures, both legal and political in orientation, should be developed which lead to an enhancement of governmental accountability vis-à-vis housing rights. The arguments supporting the utilization of housing as a guiding principle of State policy are deemed compelling by the Special Rapporteur.

These issues and the points raised above suggest that a more in-depth examination as to the utility of considering the eventual adoption of an international convention on housing rights designed to alleviate the on-going and often irreducible problems associated with housing rights is in order in the next report of the Special Rapporteur.

The Special Rapporteur has received a large quantity of information on the topic of this study, the majority of which could not be included in this progress report because of space constraints.

In order, therefore, to grasp fully the true nature of the housing rights struggle, and given the many valiant efforts under way—legal and otherwise—in different countries towards this goal, the Special Rapporteur would consider visits to several countries as an indispensable component of his future work. The Special Rapporteur requests the support of the Sub-Commission towards this end.

The second progress report of the special rapporteur (E/CN.4/Sub.2/1994/20), submitted to the Sub-Commission at its 1994 session, included a preliminary examination of the feasibility of the adoption by the United Nations of an international declaration or convention on the right to adequate housing, as requested by the Sub-Commission, and the draft of such a convention. In addition, it set out the following preliminary recommendations and conclusions (chap. X, para. 118):

The Special Rapporteur is convinced of the present and future need for the United Nations to expand its mechanisms and activities relevant to promoting, protecting and monitoring housing rights. In this chapter preliminary rec-

ommendations are put forward as to the direction which both United Nations system action and government action at the national level might take to begin to tackle the enormous problems that confront dwellers worldwide as they struggle for their housing rights. The Special Rapporteur will attempt in his final report to develop comprehensive and detailed recommendations.

## A. Recommendations for the United Nations System

1. The foremost need, to guarantee continued attention to the global housing rights situation, is for the Commission on Human Rights to consider the appointment of a Special Rapporteur of the Commission on the realization of the right to adequate housing. Such an appointment could lead to the production of annual reports on the global housing rights situation. The Commission might also consider developing, through this mechanism, an early warning system on housing rights infringements and violations. Most importantly, such an appointment would bring necessary attention to one of the grave problems facing millions worldwide seeking a secure place to live, a problem that is either ignored by all relevant actors or is given little attention.

2. As mentioned by the Special Rapporteur in his earlier reports, the phenomenon of forced evictions continues to confront people and communities worldwide. The appointment by the Commission on Human Rights of a Special Rapporteur on Forced Evictions could be one practical way of tackling what remains perhaps the gravest of housing rights violations.

3. For the remainder of his mandate, in order to grasp fully the true nature of the global housing rights struggle, and based upon the valuable insights already gained from private visits, the Special Rapporteur would consider visits to several countries essential for the fulfilment of his mandate. The Special Rapporteur requests the support of the Sub-Commission for this purpose.

4. As mentioned by the Rapporteur in his first progress report, it may be advisable for the United Nations programme of advisory services in the field of human rights to develop expertise in the area of housing rights.

5. It would be of great use were the Committee on Economic, Social and Cultural Rights to consider the feasibility of adopting a general comment on forced evictions and the precise relationship this practice has with the housing rights provisions contained in the Covenant and elsewhere in international law. Such a general comment could facilitate a clear understanding of the essential illegality of the practice of forced evictions and serve to delineate which forms of induced or enforced movement of persons by States and their agents are incompatible with international law. Moreover, such a general comment would be useful in expounding on the legal issues arising from internationally financed development displacement by agencies such as the World Bank.

6. The Special Rapporteur would like to recommend that the preparatory process leading up to the Social Summit in 1995 take fully into account economic, social and cultural rights as they have been developed and are being enforced in the United Nations system. The synthesis developed by the Special Rapporteur on State obligations in his first progress report needs particular attention. The Special Rapporteur would also recommend that the Committee on Economic, Social and Cultural Rights be given the mandate to carry out the follow-up work that will emerge from the Social Summit.

There exists a need to garner State support for housing

rights initiatives within the United Nations system, and more importantly within States. Presently, governmental support for even the notion that housing exists as a core component of human rights is piercingly lacking.

7. The Special Rapporteur would recommend that the second preparatory committee for Habitat II, to be held in Nairobi in mid-1995, take fully into account the ongoing work on the right to housing. This would entail going beyond the recognition of the right to housing as a thematic principle to evolving practical application of the obligations that arise for States from the recognition of the right to housing.

## B. Recommendations for Governments at the National Level

1. At the national level, the Special Rapporteur would recommend to States adopting the following approaches towards the practice of forced evictions: (i) end forced evictions; (ii) repeal legislation impinging on housing rights; (iii) sell, share or swap land, but do not evict; (iv) no evictions without freely accepted relocation; (v) develop land sites for affordable housing within 25 km of city centres; (vi) grant security of tenure to all; (vii) strengthen housing finance programmes for the poor; (viii) expropriate land only as a last resort; (ix) regulate rents (fair rents); (x) prosecute violators of housing rights laws; (xi) if government human rights commissions exist, broaden mandates to include monitoring of and awarding relief from forced evictions and other violations of housing rights; and (xii) long-term planning for future housing needs.

2. To broaden the perspectives necessary to tackle the many dimensions of the housing crisis the Special Rapporteur would recommend that States recognize the housing rights entitlements of the following groups:

Homeless citizens (no permanent residence);
—Pavement dwellers (permanent residence on pavement);
—Slum dwellers (residents of informal settlements, tenements, squatter areas, etc.);
—Public sector tenants (residents of social housing units);
—Private sector tenants (residents of private sector housing units);
—Owner-occupiers (own (or paying mortgage) and residing in own home);
—Victims of eviction, demolition, natural disasters, etc. (temporarily or permanently displaced and dehoused);
—Workers (employees of employers responsible for the provision of housing);
—Families (families of every size or status);
—Women (all women of any status);
—Children (all children of any status);
—Disabled persons (all physically and mentally disabled persons, including persons with chronic health problems);
—Migrant workers (non-nationals employed in third countries);
—Elderly persons (all persons over 60 years);
—Refugees and asylum seekers (all accepted refugees and asylum seekers legally within third countries);
—Low-income groups (all groups living under, at or near to the accepted poverty line in any society);
—Ethnic, national, racial, social or other minority groups (all members of any distinct groups);
—Indigenous and tribal peoples (all members of societies which self-identify as indigenous and tribal peoples);

—Civilians and other victims of war and armed conflict (all non-combatants affected by war, including internally displaced persons);
—Occupied populations (all persons belonging to peoples and States illegally occupied by another State).

**FORCED EVICTIONS.** In resolution 1993/77 of 10 March 1994, the UN Commission on Human Rights reaffirmed that every woman, man and child has the right to a secure place to live in peace and dignity, and expressed its concern that, according to United Nations statistics, in excess of one billion persons throughout the world are homeless or inadequately housed, and that this number is growing. Recognizing that the practice of forced eviction involves the involuntary removal of persons, families and groups from their homes and communities, resulting in increased levels of homelessness and in inadequate housing and living conditions, the Commission was disturbed that forced evictions and homelessness intensify social conflict and inequality and invariably affect the poorest, most socially, economically, environmentally and politically disadvantaged and vulnerable sectors of society.

The Commission affirmed, in the resolution, that the practice of forced eviction constitutes a gross violation of human rights, in particular the right to adequate housing, and urged all Governments to undertake immediate measures, at all levels, aimed at eliminating that practice. In particular it called upon Governments to provide "immediate restitution, compensation, and/or appropriate and sufficient alternative accommodation or land, consistent with their wishes and needs, to persons and communities that have been forcibly evicted, following mutually satisfactory negotiations with the affected persons or groups." The Secretary-General was requested to transmit the resolution to Governments, and to compile an analytical report on the practice of forced evictions, based on an analysis of international law, for consideration by the Commission at its 1994 session.

At that session, the Commission received the Secretary-General's analytical report on forced evictions (E/CN.4/1994/20), but did not consider it in detail. The conclusions and recommendations set out in that report are as follows (paras. 140–185):

### Conclusions

Whether a gross violation of human rights, in particular of the right to adequate housing, or in the context of displacements, resettlements, population transfers or removals, the practice of forced evictions continues to exist throughout the world. However, not only does the practice of forced evictions continue to persist worldwide, but, as stated in Commission resolution 1993/77, it is actually increasing in terms of the number of people affected as well as in the severity of its impact.

While the practice of forced evictions may take various forms and affect individual households, as well as whole communities, there exist certain common characteristics associated with it: the victims of forced evictions are almost always the poorest, socially most disadvantaged sectors of society and a certain degree of violence is involved.

From this analysis it can be observed that in most cases evictions can be prevented and in all cases the adverse consequences can be avoided. In cases where evictions are unavoidable, there exists an obligation on the part of the proponents of evictions to undertake measures to compensate the victims, so as to reduce the adverse consequences to a minimum.

It has further been shown that the practice of forced evictions is increasing globally, despite the attention paid to the phenomenon by international human rights bodies and organs. The fact that the practice of forced evictions constitutes an act which violates the right to adequate housing, and other human rights by implication, leads to the conclusion that there exists a substantial gap between legal norms and practice. The involuntary removal of persons, families and groups from their homes is a current practice in many countries which, in most cases, is contradictory to, if not a blatant infringement of, fundamental, internationally recognized human rights law.

Such circumstances disclose a compelling need to create new legislation and effective mechanisms geared to the prevention of forced evictions at national, regional and international levels, with a view to enforcing the implementation mechanisms of the right to adequate housing.

Furthermore, there exists a clear and inherent relationship between housing rights and evictions; by implication, a wide variety of civil, political, economic, social and cultural rights are also closely linked to the practice. In addition, the fact that international human rights bodies, in particular the Committee on Economic, Social and Cultural Rights, have addressed the question of forced evictions squarely in the context of the human rights implications of the practice has resulted in an increased acceptance that the consequences of the practice are serious and that it is appropriate to apply the norms of international human rights law.

It is without doubt necessary that the issue of forced evictions be considered in greater detail in the future deliberations of all United Nations human rights bodies. Furthermore, in an attempt to rationalize and streamline the work of the Commission on Human Rights and the Sub-Commission on Prevention of Discrimination and Protection of Minorities, it is proposed that the Special Rapporteurs on the right to adequate housing, population transfers, internally displaced persons and the environment study with particular care in their next reports the relationship between their respective mandates and the practice of forced evictions.

### Recommendations

On the basis of the facts and analyses of the present report, the Secretary-General wishes to make the following recommendations to the Commission on Human Rights at its fiftieth session. The first part of the recommendations will address methods for the prevention and elimination of forced evictions, whereas the second part will elaborate methods for the mitigation of the adverse consequences of forced evictions when these cannot be prevented.

### A. Preventive Measures

States parties to the International Covenant on Economic, Social and Cultural Rights have agreed to take appropriate steps to ensure the realization of the rights contained in the Covenant by all appropriate means, including in particular the adoption of legislative measures.

In the case of forced evictions, many national housing acts, laws or statutes already contain clauses expressly prohibiting illegal evictions. The 1977 Protection from Eviction Act of the United Kingdom includes legal protection from "illegal eviction and harassment" and the creation of offences for violations of the Act. The existence of such legal provisions indicates that it would be reasonable for countries lacking such provisions to consider adopting them. In fact, areas of national law in need of revision or repeal may be revealed by the legislative review function of the State reporting procedure.

Eviction impact statements may also contribute to the protection of the potential victims, the reduction of social tension and the mitigation of the inhabitants' hardship, as long as they are viewed only as interim measures and not as substitutes for legislative authority which, if improperly carried out, may even justify an eviction process. Under such a procedure, permission to remove occupants from any given site will not be granted unless such statements, prepared by persons or organs fully independent of the actor requesting the eviction are provided to the competent authorities, and if the statements do not reveal that the target community is inadequately protected.

One of the most urgent measures to be taken by Governments in eliminating the practice of forced evictions is the enforcement of housing rights. This study has argued that economic and developmental considerations are among the main motivations behind forced evictions. The incentives of economic growth and development for society often overshadow the basic need of individuals for a decent and secure place to live. The right to property is in constant conflict with the right to housing. Therefore, enforcing the right to housing implies a step-by-step approach leading only gradually to the full, society-wide enjoyment of the right.

It is, therefore, recommended that the steps to be taken towards the full enjoyment of the right to adequate housing include, inter alia, the undertaking of comprehensive and systematic legislative reviews of all national laws relevant to or affecting the right to housing to ensure their conformity with international standards, to initiate nationwide public information campaigns on the various provisions on the issue of housing, as well as the regular inclusion in State's reports, to the Committee on Economic, Social and Cultural Rights of data relevant to evictions, resettlement and homelessness.

One specific legally based action Governments should undertake to curtail the practice of forced evictions is the universal conferral of security of tenure. Security of tenure, namely the legal right to protection from arbitrary or forced eviction—equally relevant to owners, tenants and squatters—may play a significant role in discouraging the eviction process.

The principle of security of tenure has been repeatedly recognized. In resolution 1993/77 the Commission on Human Rights urged all Governments to "confer legal security of tenure on all persons currently threatened with forced eviction and to adopt all necessary measures giving full protection against forced eviction, based upon effective participation, consultation and negotiation with affected persons or groups".

General Comment No. 4 (1991) on the right to adequate housing, unanimously adopted by the Committee on Economic, Social and Cultural Rights clearly places security of tenure into the category of legal entitlements assumed under the International Covenant on Economic, Social and Cultural Rights. The Committee, in defining the meaning of "adequate housing", expressly stated that:

"Tenure takes a variety of forms, including rental (public and private) accommodation, cooperative housing, lease, owner-occupation, emergency housing and informal settlements, including occupation of land or property. Notwithstanding the type of tenure, all persons should possess a degree of security of tenure which guarantees legal protection against forced eviction, harassment and other threats. States parties should consequently take immediate measures aimed at conferring legal security of tenure upon those persons and households currently lacking such protection, in genuine consultation with affected persons and groups" (para. 8 (a)).

The Sub-Commission on Prevention of Discrimination and Protection of Minorities, in its resolution 1991/12, recommended that the Commission on Human Rights encourage Governments "to undertake policy and legislative measures aimed at curtailing the practice of forced eviction, including the conferral of legal security of tenure to those currently threatened with forced eviction, based upon effective consultation and negotiation with affected persons or groups".

The Commission on Human Settlements, in its resolution 14/6 of 5 May 1993, unanimously urged States to establish appropriate monitoring mechanisms and indicators on the extent of homelessness, inadequate housing conditions and persons without security of tenure, as well as other issues arising from the right to adequate housing.

Read in conjunction with each other and considering all other foundations of housing rights in international law, security of tenure for everyone, notwithstanding the type of housing, has become increasingly entrenched in the legal interpretation of the right to adequate housing.

The United Nations Centre for Human Settlements (Habitat) is strongly against the eradication of urban slums and squatter settlements and against the forced eviction of families in cases of competing land-use interests. Habitat reports that with the adoption of national shelter strategies by most countries, including regularization and upgrading policies, some progress is being made in securing respect for peoples' efforts to house themselves where the State or the private sector is unable to offer acceptable and adequate housing.

In such cases, Governments are often not required to do more than refrain from forced evictions in order to respect the right to adequate housing, as long as a commitment to provide support to the self-help housing efforts of the poor exist—through technical, legal and financial assistance. In this situation, one of the most far-reaching measures is the provision of security of tenure. According to Habitat, legal protection in the form of granting an occupancy permit or title to a piece of land destined for residential use is the single most important step Governments can take in honouring their commitment to the right to adequate housing, and to the eradication of the practice of forced evictions. These steps in turn often trigger an impressive level of investment in self-help housing, especially among the poor in developing countries.

Nevertheless, security of tenure alone, without adequate safeguards for affordability and an acceptable level of habitability, would not fully satisfy the legal requirements inherent in housing rights.

In a situation of conflicting interests between the landowner and persons who have illegally occupied housing or land sites, land-sharing, a proposal advocated by Habitat and COHRE, is a development option which can provide a mutually satisfactory solution to the dispute. This preventive method of avoiding forced evictions has been successfully applied in Hyderabad, India, and Bangkok, Thailand. In many cities in developing countries, the legal system limits the possibilities for immediate removal of the squatters and therefore forces the landlord to pursue complicated and time-consuming legal procedures; land-sharing offers landlords the benefit of immediate repossession and development of the land, a likely increase in land value and the elimination of legal or other fees involved in the act of eviction.

The principle of land-sharing is the development of the site under dispute in such a way that one part of the site is reserved for housing the people who lived there while allowing the owner to develop the other part according to his/her own wishes. Land-sharing can be considered a form of on-site relocation. For the potential victims of forced evictions, this alternative offers security of tenure, the elimination of eviction threats and litigation, incentives to build safer and healthier housing of permanent building materials, as well as an asset for future generations. In addition, public agencies have the advantage of avoiding social unrest, the provision of public services is facilitated and the incentives for pursuing upgrading programmes are greater when occupants possess security of tenure.

The "buy-out" option is a unique alternative to forced evictions and has been carried out with varied, small-scale success in some countries, although the global applicability of this solution might be limited. The "buy-out" option concerns essentially properties, inhabited by squatters which have been occupied for a long period of time but which require renovation.

This option recognizes both the responsibility of public authorities to ensure a habitable housing situation, as well as the rights of dwellers to tenure. Since many occupied dwellings are owned by private persons, the buy-out option involves the purchase by local councils of the dwelling in question, with the subsequent right and duty of the council to renovate the building.

The squatter inhabitants are involved in the process throughout, are offered either financial assistance or alternative housing during the renovation phase, and are permitted to re-inhabit the renovated building following completion of the project. The squatters then become tenants, generally at a reasonable rent, and have both the benefits of returning to their dwelling and a substantially improved and maintained home. This option precludes eviction, protects the rights of the inhabitants and increases habitable living space.

Additional preventive methods could include, inter alia, the following:

(a) The creation of social awareness and participation in the planning and implementation of mitigation, as well as preparedness and preventive, measures to reduce losses resulting from planned evictions;

(b) Contributing to poverty alleviation measures and better living conditions for the poor by protecting private and social assets, promoting private and social medium- and long-term investment and providing employment opportunities and skills;

(c) Strengthening community development to carry out shared responsibilities for the rehabilitation and reconstruction, protection and increase of social and public services and infrastructure—with the people themselves assessing and ordering their needs, planning and carrying out remedies and being responsible for maintenance.

In recognition of the severe human traumas associated with forced evictions, relocation guidelines have been developed, notably by the World Bank and the OECD, as referred to above. Habitat has also taken clearly positive initiatives in this direction, participating in the elaboration of guidelines of good practice which should be promoted at a policy level, guidelines for the management of relocation processes and guidelines for the different planning and implementation steps of relocation procedures.

Such guidelines may assist policy makers of donor countries in deciding against funding a project involving evictions, but will have only limited impact upon Governments in recipient countries which continue the practice. Where outside agencies, such as donors and/or bilateral organizations, are able to exert influence through project guidelines, as in the case of the World Bank, such guidelines may indeed play a positive role. However, it is imperative to develop guidelines which can have an impact on development situations where special leverage is not available or outside agencies are not involved. In this context, the guidelines elaborated by Habitat contain the following elements: avoidance of relocation if at all possible; if relocation is unavoidable, sufficient resources, including the assistance of NGOs and community-based organizations, must be allocated to ensure that the urban poor do not suffer from the process; the parties benefiting from the development causing the relocation should pay the full costs of the relocation process including the socio-economic rehabilitation of relocatees.

Nevertheless, it is vital to understand that such guidelines might also constitute a tacit acceptance of the practice of forced evictions, although this report advocates as its main recommendation that forced evictions must be avoided if at all possible and only carried out if absolutely necessary. Guidelines for relocation are important, however, and, if pursued realistically and faithfully by all the actors involved, can assist in finding alternatives to the eviction process and the consequent violations of the right to adequate housing.

This report argues that evictions often occur in connection with major international events, such as Olympic Games, beauty pageants, official State visits, international conferences, etc., which, on the one hand, have positive implications for the host country such as media attention and higher revenues but, on the other hand, should not be seen as reasonable justifications for the practice of forced evictions.

There thus seems to be an arguable need for the drafting and adoption of guidelines for the planning of international events, which could be initiated by such United Nations bodies as the Commission on Human Rights and the Commission on Human Settlements. Elements to be considered in the drafting of such guidelines include: the discouraging of external donors if evictions are likely to result from the planned event; public hearings conducted prior to the decision to adopt the plan in order to address the likelihood of evictions in connection with the event; persons threatened with forced evictions shall have the right to bring the matter before a court of law and the right to appeal before a higher court; if no alternatives to evictions exist, minimum periods of warning, possibilities of relocation and adequate financial compensation and participation in the process must be guaranteed.

It should also be noted that the Special Rapporteur on the right to adequate housing has been requested by the Sub-Commission to examine the feasibility of an international convention on housing rights which would provide an opportunity for an in-depth debate on the issue of housing rights at the international level.

The role of non-governmental organizations in the prevention and elimination of the practice of forced evictions is one of great importance and should be promoted to the full. Their involvement as intermediaries between policy makers and affected persons for the mutual benefit of all actors involved and especially to defend the interests of the victims must be stressed. Well-informed non-governmental organizations may help to obtain political support and to alert public opinion to deter planned forced evictions, they may coordinate and assist in the resettlement, as their role is often crucial in the relocation process. In addition, people often do not know what their rights and options are in situations of looming forced evictions, and NGOs can give legal and professional assistance.

A practical example of influential work carried out by NGOs in the field of housing rights and forced evictions are the activities of Habitat International Coalition (HIC), a Mexican-based organization, as well as the Netherlands NGO, COHRE which have also contributed substantively to the present report. The latter has published a manual on forced evictions and human rights, which contains the relevant United Nations resolutions on forced eviction in all the official United Nations languages and practical suggestions as to their use at the national level. This example of grass-roots-level activity will doubtless contribute to the elimination of the practice of forced evictions by raising awareness amongst the affected communities.

One aspect of international population movements, or international migration across boundaries, should be the study of its causes and how development affects international migration; with particular reference to forced evictions, the study should address how forced evictions as a "by-product" of development affect the number of "economic migrants" (as opposed to political refugees). UNDP, in its contribution to the present report, noted that "UNDP recognizes that international population movements can affect and be affected by virtually all aspects of the development process", in relation to which a comprehensive strategy entails taking into account both causes and impacts of population movements. Furthermore, UNDP is firmly committed to preventing conditions resulting in forced migrations, such as the elimination of "broad contextual conditions (e.g. the availability of housing".

### B. Compensatory Measures

In this context, resolution 1993/77, states that: "all Governments [should] provide immediate restitution, compensation and/or appropriate and sufficient alternative accommodation or land, consistent with their wishes and needs, to persons and communities that have been forcibly evicted, following mutually satisfactory negotiations with the affected persons or groups".

In addition, the Special Rapporteur of the Sub-Commission on the right to restitution, compensation and rehabilitation for victims of gross violations of human rights and fundamental freedoms, Mr. Theo van Boven, recognizes in his final report that "the issue of forced removals and forced evictions has in recent years reached the international human rights agenda because it is considered a practice that does grave and disastrous harm to the basic civil, political, economic, social and cultural rights of large numbers of people, both individual persons and collectivities". (E/CN.4/Sub.2/1993/8, para. 21).

The Committee on Economic, Social and Cultural Rights, in its General Comment No. 4 (1991), deemed legal procedures seeking compensation following an illegal eviction one of the possible remedies in connection with the right to adequate housing:

"The Committee views many component elements of the right to adequate housing as being at least consistent with the provision of domestic legal remedies. Depending on the legal system, such areas might include, but are not limited to: (a) legal appeals aimed at preventing planned evictions or demolitions through the issuance of court-ordered injunctions; (b) legal procedures seeking compensation following an illegal eviction; (c) complaints against illegal actions carried out or supported by landlords (whether public or private) in relation to rent levels, dwelling maintenance, and racial or other forms of discrimination; (d) allegations of any form of discrimination in the allocation and availability of access to housing; and (e) complaints against landlords concerning unhealthy or inadequate housing conditions". (E/1992/23-E.C.12/1991/4, annex III, para. 17).

Compensation and restitution may take various forms. Cash payments represent the most frequent form of compensation, although experience shows that the money offered is usually insufficient and it its argued that this type of indemnity by itself is an inadequate form of countering the problems involved with forced evictions.

Alternative accommodation at relocation sites is one of the most feasible ways to reduce the adverse effects of evictions. However, overcrowding, long distances from employment opportunities and previous neighbours, lack of basic amenities and a general decline in living conditions are too frequently characteristics of this alternative. At the other extreme, the costs of the alternative housing offered may far exceed the means of the evicted persons. Furthermore, in many cases the victims are offered no compensation whatsoever. Therefore, the situation with regard to the consequences resulting from the practice of forced evictions is clearly unsatisfactory and point to the urgent need to avoid and eliminate the practice in the first instance, rather than trying to "soften the blow" afterwards.

A study published by Habitat suggests the following essential areas of compensation: financial arrangements to cover investments made in the house/land left behind; compensation for the problems caused by being resettled in a place away from the original living environment, such as transport subsidies; compensation for the loss of income due to eviction.

In this connection, the Declaration of Basic Principles of Justice for Victims of Crime and Abuse of Power, adopted by the General Assembly in its resolution 40/34, provides a variety of compensatory principles which could be applied to the victims of forced evictions. These are, inter alia:

(a) Victims are entitled to the mechanisms of justice and to prompt redress;

(b) Victims should be informed of their rights in seeking redress through such mechanisms;

(c) Offenders or third parties responsible for their behaviour should make fair restitution to victims, their families or dependents, including the return of property or payment for the harm or loss suffered, reimbursement of expenses incurred as a result of the victimization, the provision of services and the restoration of rights;

(d) When compensation is not fully available from the offender or other sources, States should endeavour to provide financial compensation;

(e) Victims should receive the necessary material, medical, psychological and social assistance and support.

It is evident that these provisions are applied in very few circumstances, not least because the persons affected by the practice of forced eviction are not always perceived as victims, but by squatting or using services illegally, as violators of the law.

Finally, as a result of the analysis of the practice of forced evictions and the observations contained in this report, the Commission on Human Rights might wish to consider the establishment of a more permanent mechanism, such as a special rapporteur on the practice of forced evictions, with a view to redressing the adverse consequences of forced evictions carried out in the past and preventing forced evictions from happening in the future.

***INTERNATIONAL YEAR OF SHELTER FOR THE HOMELESS (1987).*** In 1980, the UN General Assembly first expressed the view (resolution 35/76) that an international year devoted to the problems of homeless people in urban and rural areas of the developing countries could be an appropriate occasion to focus attention of the international community on those problems. Two years later, the Assembly proclaimed (resolution 37/221) the year 1987 International Year of Shelter for the Homeless.

In so doing, the Assembly expressed its concern that, despite the efforts of governments at the national and local levels and of international organizations, the living conditions of the majority of the people in slums and squatter areas and rural settlements, especially in developing countries, continue to deteriorate in both relative and absolute terms; and its conviction that a special effort to address this fundamental issue will strengthen overall national economic and social development.

At the close of the international year, the Assembly welcomed (resolution 43/180) the success achieved in attaining the objectives of the year and took note with appreciation of the numerous and encouraging reports received from a total of 130 countries as at 31 December 1987, on activities, policies, programs, and projects undertaken by those countries within the context of the year and towards the successful attainment of its objectives. It requested governments to sustain the momentum generated during the program for the year and to continue implementing concrete and innovative activities aimed at improving the shelter and neighborhoods of the poor and the disadvantaged and requested the Secretary-General to keep it informed periodically on the progress achieved.

***SEE ALSO*** Shelter; Standard of Living.

***BIBLIOGRAPHY.*** Agnelli, Susanna. *Street Children: A Growing Urban Tragedy.* London: Independent Commission on International Humanitarian Issues and Weidenfield and Nicolson, 1986. NGO monograph, in English.

Aliran Kesedaran Negara. "Eviction: The Moral Aspects," *Aliran Monthly* 6, no. 9 (Sept.–Oct. 1986): 11–13. NGO article, in English.

Amnesty International. "Slum Dwellers: The Less Privileged Segment of Urban Population: A Case of Bangkok Slum and Squatter Settlements," *Human Rights Forum* 1, no. 4 (Oct.–Dec. 1985): 9–16. NGO magazine article, in English.

Asian Coalition for Housing Rights and Habitat International Coalition for Asia. *Urban Poor Housing Rights in South Korea and Hong Kong.* Bangkok, Thailand: 1991. NGO fact-finding report, in English.

Centre on Housing Rights and Evictions. *Bibliography on Housing Rights and Evictions.* Utrecht, the Netherlands: 1993. Bibliography, in English.

———. *Legal Provisions on Housing Rights: International and National Approaches.* Utrecht, the Netherlands: 1994. NGO monograph, in English.

Committee on the Right to Housing. *Slum and Pavement Dwellers Eviction: The Human Face.* Bombay, India: 1986. NGO pamphlet, in English.

Conroy, J. D. *Shelter for the Homeless: Asian-Pacific Needs and Australian Responses.* Canberra, Australia: Australian Council for Overseas Aid, 1987. NGO report, in English.

Cortese, Michele. "Property Rights and Human Values: A Right of Access to Private Property for Tenant Organizers," *Columbia Human Rights Law Review* 17, no. 2 (Spring -Summer 1986): 257–282. Scholarly article, in English.

Das, P. K., and C. Gonsalves. *The Struggle for Housing: A Peoples' Manifesto.* Bombay, India: Nivara Hakk Suraksha Samit, 1987. NGO report, in English; bibliography: basic statistics on Bombay, plus information on housing, social services, and slum population.

Gomez, Terence. "Struggle for Shelter: The Plight of the Kampung Jaya Squatters," *Aliran Monthly* 7, no. 9 (Sept.–Oct. 1987): 13–15. NGO article, in English.

Gordon, P., and D. A. Newnham. *Different Worlds: Racism and Discrimination in Britain.* 2nd rev. ed. London: The Runnymede Trust, 1986. NGO report, in English.

Habitat International Coalition. *Towards an International Charter of Housing Rights: Habitat International Coalition, Cartagena, Colombia, 1989.* Mexico City, Mexico: 1990. NGO policy statement, in English.

Hebel, Herman von. "The Implementation of the Right to Housing in Article 11 of the U.N. Covenant on Economic, Social and Cultural Rights," *SIM Newsletter* no. 20 (Dec. 1987): 26–41. Scholarly article, in English.

Kozol, Jonathan. *Rachel and Her Children: Homeless Families in America.* New York: Crown Publishers, 1988. Scholarly monograph, in English; bibliography, pp. 249–252.

Lapierre, Dominique. *The City of Joy.* Trans. Kathryn Spink. Garden City, NY, USA: Doubleday & Co., 1985. Novel, originally published in French as *La Cite de la Joie* (Editions Robert Laffont).

Leckie, Scott. "The Legal Struggle for Housing Rights: One NGO's Search for the Elusive," *Beyond Law* 2, no. 4 (July 1992). Article, in English.

———. *Towards an International Convention on Housing Rights: Options at Habitat II.* Washington, D.C.: American Society of International Law, 1994. (Issue Papers on World Conferences, No. 4.). Scholarly paper, in English.

———. "The UN Committee on Economic, Social and Cultural Rights and the Right to Adequate Housing: Towards an Appropriate Approach," *Human Rights Quarterly* 11, no. 4 (Nov. 1989): 522–560. Scholarly article, in English.

Metcalf, G. R. *Fair Housing Comes of Age.* Westport, CT, USA: Greenwood Press, 1988. Scholarly monograph, in English.

People's Union for Democratic Rights. "India: Children Jailed for Want of Homes," *International Children's Rights Monitor* 3, no. 3 (3rd quarter 1986): 16. NGO article, in English.

Pontifical Commission "Justicia et Pax." *What Have You Done to Your Homeless Brother? The Church and the Housing Problem.* Vatican City: 1985. Church statement, in English.

United Nations Department of Public Information. *Building for the Homeless.* New York: 1987. IGO report, in official UN languages.

———. *The Human Right to Adequate Housing.* Fact Sheet no. 21. New York and Geneva, Switzerland: n.d. IGO booklet, in official UN languages.

## HOWARD LEAGUE FOR PENAL REFORM.

This non-governmental organization was founded in 1921 with the aim of advancing constructive penal and social policies through systematic research. The Howard League has 30 affiliates worldwide, with a membership of 1,300 individuals. It has consultative status with the UN **ECONOMIC AND SOCIAL COUNCIL.** The League publishes the quarterly *Howard Journal of Criminal Justice* and the annual *Criminal Justice Magazine.*

Howard League for Penal Reform. Address: 708 Holloway Road, London N193NL, UK. Telephone: (44-1) 71-281-7722. Fax: (44-1) 71-281-5506. Director: Frances Crook.

## HULL, CORDELL (1871–1955).

Cordell Hull rose from humble beginnings to become the United States Secretary of State during World War II and was awarded the 1945 **NOBEL PEACE PRIZE.** Born in Overton County, TN, USA, in a log cabin, Hull received a law degree from Cumberland University (Tennessee) in 1891. Almost immediately, he began a political career, first as a member of the Tennessee House of Representatives (1893–1897), then as a judge (1903), and then as member of the U.S. House of Representatives from the Fourth Tennessee District (1907–1931). In 1931, Hull was elected senator from Tennessee, but left that position two years later when President Franklin D. Roosevelt picked Hull as his secretary of state.

Although an influential American congressman, Hull was to make his mark on the world through the cabinet position he held for twelve years (1933–1945), the longest tenure of any American secretary of state. Always a proponent of co-existence among nations and an opponent of tariffs, Hull used his national position to establish diplomatic and trade relations among the countries of the Americas. The initiator of Roosevelt's "good neighbor policy," Hull negotiated treaties with 21 Latin and South American countries and, through the Trade Agreements of 1934, signed reciprocal trade agreements that lowered tariffs. All of these achievements were to figure in his receiving the Nobel Prize.

During World War II, Hull laid the foundations for the United Nations system to replace the ineffective **LEAGUE OF NATIONS.** Although ill health impeded Hull from being at the forefront of the actual institution of the United Nations (he resigned his cabinet position in 1944 for medical reasons), he served as a senior advisor at the 1945 United Nations Conference in San Francisco. Franklin Roosevelt referred to Hull as "the father of the United Nations," a title to which the Nobel Peace Prize Committee agreed. In its citation of Hull, the Committee recognized his "long and indefatigable work for understanding between nations; for his prominent role in establishing the United Nations; for his efforts in lowering trade barriers to improve international relations; and for implementing Franklin D. Roosevelt's 'good neighbor policy.'"

Although unable to attend the Oslo ceremonies to receive his prize, Hull centered his acceptance speech on the promise of the new organization: "I am firmly convinced that, with all its imperfections, the United Nations organization offers the peace-loving nations of the world, now, a fully workable mechanism which will give them peace, if they want peace. . . . The searing lessons of this latest war and the promise of the United Nations organization will be the cornerstone of a new edifice of enduring peace and the guideposts of a new era of human progress."

**BIBLIOGRAPHY.** Gray, Tony. *Champions of Peace.* London: Paddington Press, 1976.

Hull, Cordell. *The Memoirs of Cordell Hull.* 2 vols. New York: Macmillan, 1948.

Pratt, Julius. *Cordell Hull, 1933–44.* 2 vols. New York: Cooper Square Publishers, 1964.

Schlessinger, Bernard S., and June H. Schlessinger, eds. *Who's Who of Nobel Prize Winners.* Phoenix, AZ, USA: Oryx Press, 1991.

**HUMANITAS HUMAN RIGHTS AWARD.** Established in 1991, this award honors those individuals who preserve human rights and promote nonviolence. The first recipients of the award were Jigme Yugay, Tibetan human rights activist; Jan Urban, Czech activist; and Ron Hampton, American opponent of the death penalty. The prize carries a $10,000 award.

For more information, contact: Humanitas, P.O. Box 818, Menlo Park, CA 94026, USA.

**HUMAN RIGHTS.** The term "human rights" comes somewhat late in the vocabulary of mankind; but, throughout history, philosophy, law, and religion have been concerned with establishing guidelines for the protection of the individual and the peaceful coexistence of the species. One can only speculate as to when it was that human beings first envisaged certain rights and freedoms as belonging to all men and women, equally and irrevocably, simply because they are members of the human family. There were hints of this approach in the 13th-century teaching of Thomas Aquinas and even more so in the 17th- and 18th-century philosophies of such men as John Locke of England and Jean-Jacques Rosseau and Voltaire of France. But it was in the great documents of freedom of the 18th century—the American Declaration of Independence (see **UNITED STATES OF AMERICA**) and the French Declaration of the Rights of Man and of the Citizen (see **FRANCE**)—that such a concept was clearly expounded (even though many of the great 18th-century Western thinkers tended to recognize landowning, Caucasian men as "superior" to all other members of the human family).

When the horrors and brutality of World War I were fully recognized, people throughout the world began equating the way governments treat the people they govern with the way they treat other nations and began seeing peace as a way to safeguard the rights of all peoples. The **LEAGUE OF NATIONS** was the first attempt at an intergovernment worldwide organization that would ensure peaceful resolution of international conflicts, but the failure of the League to stop the aggression of the Axis powers (German, Italy, and Japan) throughout the 1930s dashed hopes for universal peace. Moreover, the League did not concern itself so much with the needs of individuals or groups of people as it did with the needs of nations.

The term "human rights" was first used in the **DECLARATION BY UNITED NATIONS** of 1 January 1942 by the representatives of 26 nations that were fighting against the Axis powers. In this document, the signers spoke of the need "to preserve human rights and justice in our [own] lands as well as in other lands." At the close of World War II, in 1945, representatives of fifty nations meet in San Francisco, CA, USA, to draft the **UNITED NATIONS CHARTER,** to establish for a second time an intergovernmental organization that would preserve peace through cooperation. In addition to affirming peace, the Charter also states that one of the purposes of the United Nations is "to achieve international co-operation . . . in promoting and encouraging respect for human rights and for fundamental freedoms of all without distinction as to race, sex, language or religion." This affirmation appears all the more significant when we understand that, up to that time, neither the notion that every individual has certain human rights and fundamental freedoms that all other individuals and organizations are bound to respect, nor the notion that every citizen has certain political rights and freedoms that must be honored by the government of his country, had ever before won worldwide recognition. The Charter, thus, made the rights and freedoms of every human being, and of every people, matters not only of local and national interest but also of international concern. Never again could any government validly maintain that whatever it chose to do with the individuals or peoples who lived within its jurisdiction was its own private affair or that the world community, no matter how outraged it might be, had no authority to intervene.

The Charter, however, did not answer one key question: what are the rights and freedoms to which every man and woman is entitled? A partial answer to this question was provided by the **UNIVERSAL DECLARATION OF HUMAN RIGHTS** of 10 December 1948, which set out the common understanding of UN members concerning human rights and fundamental freedoms. The Declaration was especially far-reaching because it characterized as genuine human rights a whole series of what had, up to that time, been considered little more than social and cultural aspirations. The so-called **INTERNATIONAL BILL OF HUMAN RIGHTS,** a collective term applied to four major international instruments (the Universal Declaration of Human Rights, the **INTERNATIONAL COVENANT ON ECONOMIC, SOCIAL AND CULTURAL RIGHTS,** and the **INTERNATIONAL COVENANT ON CIVIL AND POLITICAL RIGHTS** and its **OPTIONAL PROTOCOL**) has laid the basis from which other covenants, conventions, and declarations have been constructed. Over the years, the answer to the question of what rights and freedoms compose the field of human rights has been enhanced in individual documents that examine the rights of peoples and groups not seriously considered in the past—groups such as women, children, indigenous peoples, ethnic minorities, the handicapped, colonized peoples, and combatants fighting against abusive regimes, to name a few.

Put most simply, human rights are the universally accepted principles and rules that support morality and that make it possible for each member of the human family to realize his or her full potential and to live life in an atmosphere of freedom, justice, and peace. They include both "traditional" civil and political rights and the more recently recognized economic, social, and cultural rights. The definition is ever-expanding and may include rights still in the process of discovery and formulation, such as the right to an environment that permits a life of health and well-being and the right to development. Intergovernmental organizations such as the United Nations, the **COUNCIL OF EUROPE,** the **ORGANIZATION OF AMERI-** **CAN STATES,** and the **ORGANIZATION OF AFRICAN UNITY**; non-governmental organizations; and individual scholars and thinkers throughout the world continually re-evaluate the concept of human rights. The process of examining the inherent rights and freedoms due each human being is ongoing, perhaps never-ending. Human rights and fundamental freedoms represent the basic moral values of our modern world and are thus truly an expression of the conscience of mankind.

*HUMAN RIGHTS INSTRUMENTS.* International multilateral instruments concerned with human rights—usually designated as "treaties," "conventions," "covenants," or "protocols," are like other international multilateral instruments opened for signature and ratification or acceptance by States in accordance with the provisions of each particular instrument. Signature normally indicates only general approval of an instrument and the willingness of State authorities to consider definitive acceptance. Ratification or accession occurs when the head of State notifies the depository of the instrument—usually the UN Secretary-General, another State, or an intergovernmental organization designated as such in the instrument—that it accepts to be bound to apply the provisions of the instrument in territories under its control.

The question of the acceptance of human rights treaties, conventions, protocols, and other instruments is, therefore, of great importance; and several international bodies have concerned themselves with seeking out, and trying to correct, the most common causes of delay. Although these causes differ from State to State and from instrument to instrument, certain common factors have been identified. These factors were described in a paper (UN Doc. A/CONF.32/ 15) prepared by the **UNITED NATIONS INSTITUTE FOR TRAINING AND RESEARCH** (UNITAR) and presented to the **TEHERAN INTERNATIONAL CONFERENCE ON HUMAN RIGHTS** held in 1968, as follows:

*Lack of Expertise.* The question of ratification of or accession to human rights treaties is far from a simple policy decision to be taken at the level of the foreign minister or head of State. It often involves investigation into the substantive scope of the treaties and the effects of the conventions upon existing law and policy of States. Not infrequently, ratification of treaties necessitates adoption of new legislation, and, consequently, the drafting of legislative bills. In addition, where the language of a State is not one of the official languages of the United Nations, the texts of conventions need to be translated into the official language or languages of the State. All this requires a machinery and personnel having the necessary expertise. In many States, and especially the newly independent States, there seems to be a shortage of administrative and legal expertise to carry out the necessary tasks.

*Constitutional Questions.* In some States, the executive is possessed of the power to ratify a treaty internationally, without the prior consent or approval of parliament; but, as some of the human rights treaties belong to the category of treaties which need to be implemented through national legislation, there is a need for legislative action. Seldom do States ratify or accede to a treaty internationally before the necessary legislation has been adopted. Preparation of new legislation entails time and is, in any case, conditioned by factors such as the business or agenda before the legislature, the items needing priority, and the policy of the government towards the subject-matter of a treaty.

*Federal–State Questions.* In some countries, arguments as to whether or not the balance between federal and state jurisdiction would be altered by acceptance of certain international human rights treaties have delayed or prevented the acceptance of such treaties.

*Parallel Treaties.* In some cases where there are a number of international treaties dealing with a single subject—such as, for example, the traffic in human beings—some States which are parties to the earlier treaties consider them to be adequate for the purpose and accordingly do not accept the newer ones. Similarly, in some cases where regional treaties cover either the same or similar questions as do the international treaties, States are reluctant to accept both.

Since 1979, the UN Sub-Commission on Prevention of Discrimination and Protection of Minorities has given concentrated attention to the task of encouraging all States which have not done so to ratify or accede to international human rights instruments. At its 1979 session, the Sub-Commission decided (resolution 1 B [XXXII]) that it would establish each year a sessional working group to assist it in this task and requested the Secretary-General to call upon the governments concerned to inform the Sub-Commission of the circumstances which have not enabled them to ratify or accede to the instruments in question and to explain any particular difficulties they might face. The working group was authorized to consider what forms of assistance could be provided to governments by the United Nations, with a view to assisting them to adhere to the conventions as soon as possible. However, the activities of the working group did not produce the desired results, and its activities were suspended in 1984. At that time, the Sub-Commission requested its chairman to appoint one of its members to report to it on the basis of information obtained by the Secretary-General. Mr. Marc Bossuyt (Belgium) accordingly was appointed and presented a brief analysis of the information submitted by governments at the Sub-Ccommission's 1985 session (UN Doc. E/CN.4/Sub. 2/1985/27).

At its 1987 session, the sub-commission noted (in resolution 1987/1) that, as of 15 June of that year, only 90 States had accepted the International Covenant on Economic, Social and Cultural Rights; only 86 had accepted the International Covenant on Civil and Political Rights; and only 38 had accepted the optional protocol to the latter covenant, although more than 20 years had elapsed since the adoption of those instruments by the General Assembly; and that a substantial number of States parties to the covenants and related instruments had failed to produce the regular reports required by those instruments.

The Sub-Commission suggested that the General Assembly, recognizing that repeated exhortations had not brought the desired results and that more specific measures were required, should call upon all States which had not ratified the covenants to consider doing so and to call upon all States parties to the covenants and related instruments to file regularly and without delay the reports which they had undertaken to produce for submission to the bodies set up to supervise their implementation. It further suggested that a worldwide campaign should be launched, aimed at the universal acceptance of the international instruments relating to human rights.

The Secretary-General submitted to the Sub-Commission at its 1988 session a summary of new information on the subject he had received since 1985 (UN Doc. E/CN.4/Sub.2/1988/27). The Sub-Commission, while thanking the States that had supplied the information and calling upon the Secretary-General to continue collecting it, requested him further (a) to examine the idea of offering technical assistance, in the form of legal training of local staff or by providing human rights experts to assist in the drafting of appropriate national legislation and regulations, with a view to enabling States to ratify or accede to international human rights instruments; (b) to keep under review the idea of designating regional advisors on international human rights standards, whose function would include advising the States concerned on acceptance and implementation of such instruments; and (c) to continue holding informal discussions concerning prospects for ratification of human rights instruments with government delegations, giving priority to instruments drafted by the Commission on Human Rights such as the International Covenants on Human Rights, the International Convention on the Elimination of All Forms of Racial Discrimination, the International Convention on the Suppression and Punishment of the Crime of *Apartheid,* and the Convention against Torture and Other Cruel, Inhuman or Degrading Treatment or Punishment.

***APPROACH TO FUTURE WORK.*** Each year, the UN **GENERAL ASSEMBLY** and **COMMISSION ON HUMAN RIGHTS** intensively review recent activities within the United Nations system aimed at the promotion and protection of human rights and fundamental freedoms and consider the approach to be taken to future work in this field.

The operative part of General Assembly resolution 47/137, of 18 December 1992, entitled "Alternative approaches and ways and means within the United Nations system for improving the effective enjoyment of human rights and fundamental freedoms," provides an indication of the approach to future work recommended to organs and agencies within the United Nations system. The document

1. Reiterates its request that the Commission on Human Rights should continue its current work on overall analysis with a view to further promoting and strengthening human rights and fundamental freedoms, including the question of the programme and working methods of the Commission, and on the overall analysis of the alternative approaches and ways and means for improving the effective enjoyment of human rights and fundamental freedoms in accordance with the provisions and ideas set forth in General Assembly resolution 32/130;

2. Affirms that a primary aim of international cooperation in the field of human rights is a life of freedom, dignity and peace for all peoples and for every human being, that all human rights and fundamental freedoms are indivisible

and interrelated and that the promotion and protection of one category of rights should never exempt or excuse States from promoting and protecting the others;

3. Reaffirms that equal attention and urgent consideration should be given to the implementation, promotion and protection of civil and political rights and of economic, social and cultural rights;

4. Reiterates once again that the international community should accord, or continue to accord, priority to the search for solutions to mass and flagrant violations of human rights of peoples and individuals affected by situations such as those mentioned in paragraph 1 (e) of General Assembly resolution 32/130, paying due attention also to other situations of violations of human rights;

5. Considers that the issues mentioned in paragraph 4 above should be approached with due attention in the preparatory work for the World Conference on Human Rights so as to evaluate during the Conference the obstacles to achieving progress in the field of human rights;

6. Reaffirms that the right to development is an inalienable human right;

7. Reaffirms also that international peace and security are essential elements for achieving full realization of the right to development;

8. Recognizes that all human rights and fundamental freedoms are indivisible and interdependent;

9. Considers it necessary for all Member States to promote international cooperation on the basis of respect for the independence, sovereignty and territorial integrity of each State, including the right of every people to choose freely its own socio-economic and political system, with a view to solving international economic, social and humanitarian problems;

10. Urges all States to cooperate with the Commission on Human Rights in the promotion and protection of human rights and fundamental freedoms;

11. Reaffirms once again that, in order to facilitate the full enjoyment of all human rights without diminishing personal dignity, it is necessary to promote the rights to education, work, health and proper nourishment through the adoption of measures at the national level, including those that provide for the right of workers to participate in management, as well as the adoption of measures at the international level, entailing a restructuring of existing international economic relations;

12. Decides that the approaches to future work within the United Nations system on human rights matters should take into account the content of the Declaration on the Right to Development and the need for the implementation thereof.

***UNIVERSAL AND REGIONAL HUMAN RIGHTS COMMISSIONS.*** There are four international human rights commissions which operate on a universal or a regional basis: (1) the UN Commission on Human Rights, authorized by article 68 of the United Nations Charter, which is universal in the scope of its operations; (2) the European Commission on Human Rights, which functions on a regional basis within the framework of the Council of Europe; (3) the **INTER-AMERICAN COMMISSION ON HUMAN RIGHTS,** which functions on a regional basis within the framework of the **ORGANIZATION OF AMERICAN STATES**; (4) and the **AFRICAN COMMISSION ON HUMAN AND PEOPLES'**

**RIGHTS,** which functions on a regional basis within the framework of the **ORGANIZATION OF AFRICAN UNITY.**

***NATIONAL HUMAN RIGHTS COMMISSIONS.*** Organs have been established by national or local governments with a view to ensuring that laws and regulations concerning the protection of human rights are effectively applied and to educating the public about the purpose and operation of such legislation. The role and functions of such commissions are described in general terms in the UN Secretary-General's report entitled *National Institutions for the Protection and Promotion of Human Rights* (UN Doc. E/CN.4/1987/37, paras. 59–71), prepared at the request of the General Assembly (resolution 40/123), as follows:

Human rights commissions are concerned primarily with the protection of citizens against discrimination as well as with the protection of civil and other human rights. These commissions and similar public bodies at the national level are generally designed to hear and investigate individual charges of human rights violations or discriminatory acts committed in violation of existing law. Most human rights commissions are collegial bodies, comprised of members who, in most cases, are selected by the Executive. In many cases the commissions enjoy statutory independence, and are responsible for reporting on a regular basis, to the legislative body. In some cases, as in Canada and Japan, the human rights commissions are organized within the Ministry of Justice. Similarly, the Ministry of Foreign Affairs is responsible for the selection of the members of the Norwegian Human Rights Committee, and the same is true in Denmark.

Commission members may be selected from a number of fields, but preference is generally given to person having prior experience in the field of human rights. For instance, in Denmark, the members of the Human Rights Committee include representatives from the Foreign Ministry, other ministries and various nongovernmental organizations concerned with human rights. In some cases, restrictions are place on selection of commission members. For example, in the United States, members of the Civil Rights Commission are selected by the President and must be confirmed by the Senate, with the requirement that not more than half of the Commission's members belong to the same political party. In Japan, the Ministry of Justice selects the members of the Civil Liberties Bureau from among citizens in each locality of the Bureau's eight offices across the country. The citizens chosen as Commissioners include social workers, schoolteachers, attorneys, media personnel and manual workers in agriculture and forestry.

Generally the laws or statutes which create a human rights commission define its jurisdiction, since they codify the range of discriminatory or violative conduct that the Commission is empowered to investigate. For example, the Australian Human Rights Commission (established in 1981) is authorized to hear and investigate complaints of violations of any rights defined in the Racial Discrimination Act and the Human Rights Commission Act. The United States Civil Rights Commission may hear and investigate complaints alleging discrimination on the grounds of race, colour, religion, sex or national origin. An even broader range of rights is protected in Canada, in accordance with the Canadian

Human Rights Act which empowers the Human Rights Commission to investigate allegations of discrimination based on race, national or ethnic origin, colour, religion, age, sex, marital status, conviction for an offence for which a pardon has been issued, and discriminatory employment practices against physically handicapped persons.

The procedures followed by human rights commissions in the investigation and resolution of complaints vary from country to country. It is true however, that in almost all countries the human rights commission does not have the power to make binding decisions itself in resolving a complaint. In most cases, the human rights commission attempts to arrive at settlements between parties. If the settlement or appropriate remedial steps suggested by the commission are not implemented, it frequently has the authority to seize the courts or the Prosecutor's Office for adjudication or prosecution of the matter. The commission may, as in Australia, merely submit the matter to the Attorney-General with a recommendation as to the appropriate legal action.

In cases in which no settlement can be reached, the law often provides the procedures to be followed. In Canada, for example, the Provincial Minister of Justice concerned, may, upon the recommendation of the Human Rights Commission, set up a Board of Inquiry. The Board's membership is entirely independent of the Commission. If the Board decides that a human rights violation has indeed been committed, it may determine the appropriate remedial action to be taken, including the payment of damages. When the Board's recommendation is not implemented, it may be enforced by the courts, or in some Provinces, by the Human Rights Commission itself. In one Canadian Province, in which no Board of Inquiry exists, the Human Rights Commission may, with the plaintiff's consent, seek an injunction from the court, in the event that its recommendation has not been implemented.

In some cases, a human rights commission may hear and investigate complaints, but may not be empowered to act upon them. This is true of the United States Civil Rights Commission. The Commission's function is, primarily, to review the status of compliance with civil rights law and to study the situation concerning respect for human rights. The Commission is empowered, however, to hear complaints and to receive information regarding those complaints. In fulfilling its responsibilities, the United States Civil Rights Commission may issue subpoenas and hold formal hearings.

One of the most important functions of a human rights commission is its power to review systematically existing government policy toward human rights and to suggest improvements. For instance, in addition to its competence to hear, investigate and apply remedies to cases involving human rights violations, the National Commission for the Promotion and Protection of Human Rights in Nicaragua conducts periodic reviews of the legislative and administrative systems and recommends to the Government ways in which these systems might be improved. Similarly, the Standing Advisory Commission on Human Rights for Northern Ireland advises Parliament on the adequacy and effectiveness of existing laws in preventing discrimination based on religious belief and political opinion.

Many human rights commissions engage in monitoring State legislative compliance with existing human rights law. In its review of every newly enacted State law, the Senate Legal Committee of Zimbabwe, for example, seeks to ensure that all new legislation complies with the Declaration of Rights embodied in the Zimbabwean Constitution. The Committee also advises the Government on whether any pro-

visions in the new legislation would be in violation of the Declaration of Rights. Similarly, the Italian Interministerial Committee on Human Rights engages in a systematic review of legislative and administrative measures in an effort to ensure that Italy meets its obligations under international conventions on human rights. Also, in New Zealand, the Human Rights Commission is responsible for advising the Prime Minister on the acceptance by New Zealand of any international instruments on human rights. It may, in addition, give advice on the human rights implications of any policy or legislation proposed by the Government.

Most human rights commissions are also actively engaged in educating the public about their function and purpose, as well as about various important issues in the field of human rights. This has been referred to in previous reports as the "promotional role" of human rights commissions. They generally fulfil this function through seminars, counselling services and meetings, as well as through the distribution of periodic repots, studies and bulletins prepared by the commission or other human rights institutions. In fact recently, the Australian Human Rights Commission published its own handbook on human rights. Frequently, responsibility for educating the public on human rights issues is part of a human rights commission's statutory mandate. For example, part of the mandate of the Japanese Civil Liberties Bureau is to provide educational activities and to encourage community campaigns and non-governmental organization activities, which promote respect for human rights. Even more specifically, the Canadian Human Rights Act requires its Human Rights Commission to provide assistance and advice with respect to special programmes; to institute information programmes to foster public understanding of the Canadian Human Rights Act; to carry out research programmes and undertake studies concerning discrimination, to consider recommendations received concerning human rights and individual freedoms; to take steps and encourage others to ensure that the physically handicapped have access to goods, services, facilities and accommodations that are customarily available to other people; to provide assistance and advice directed at ensuring compliance with the Act; and to maintain close liaison with bodies or authorities in the Provinces that are working against discrimination.

In some cases, commissions are created for the sole purpose of carrying out promotional and educational human rights duties. In fact, in 1984, Suriname reported that it had established a Commission for Information and Guidance regarding Human Rights in Suriname. Such a commission would, ostensibly, be solely devoted to providing promotional services to the community in heightening an awareness of human rights issues. Suriname later expressed its intention to broaden the scope of this Commission beyond its merely promotional duties, and eventually to establish a national institution for the promotion and protection of human rights pursuant to General Assembly resolution 38/123.

What appears to be the most essential ingredient for an effective human rights commission is a strong connection between the law, the commission and the courts. First, the human rights commission requires a broad and clearly codified mandate (as part of the Constitution or of the law) to establish its jurisdiction, and to ensure its statutory independence from the Executive or parliamentary control. An effective human rights commission further requires recourse to the courts or the Prosecutor's Office, to enforce the results and recommendations of its investigations. Without this important connection (between the law, the commission and the court), a human rights commission would be largely impotent. The power to investigate complaints without the power to enforce the recommendations resulting from such investigations, may render a human rights commission powerless, and may ultimately discourage citizens from seeking recourse to such organs. The purpose and role of a human rights commission is highly questionable if a citizen must initiate another action, either in the courts or with another agency, after utilizing the offices of the commission, particularly since many individuals who have suffered some form of discrimination or a violation of their rights may be unwilling to initiate a second action after the first had produced an unenforceable decision and no actual relief.

In order to maintain low administrative costs (by eliminating the need for citizens to take their complaints to more than one agency), to ease the burden on the courts (by settling matters without the high cost of an independent adjudicative investigation), and most of all, to encourage citizens to seek redress for violations of their civil and human rights, human rights commissions must be empowered to enforce compliance with their recommendations, either by seizing the court or the Prosecutor's Office, or through an independent grant of power, enabling the human rights commissions to make binding decisions.

Another very important consideration to bear in mind in the development of a human rights commission is a mechanism for the equitable selection of commission members, as problems may arise if the selection procedure is unfair. Moreover, maintaining close ties with the community, and dispelling the image of human rights commissions as lofty government agencies, can only benefit the standing of human rights commissions as effective institutions for the protection of the human and civil rights of the ordinary citizen.

### NATIONAL AGENCIES AND PARTICULAR GROUPS.

Institutions have been established by national or local governments with a view to protecting and promoting the rights of members of particular groups, such as ethnic and linguistic minorities, indigenous populations, aliens, migrants and immigrants, children and minors, and women. The role and functions of such institutions are described by the UN Secretary-General's report entitled *National Institutions for the Protection and Promotion of Human Rights* (UN Doc. E/CN.4/1987/37, paras. 72–90), prepared at the request of the General Assembly (resolution 40/123), as follows:

In recognition of the fact that particular groups in the community are often subject to an inordinately high incidence of discrimination, many States have established institutions designed to protect and promote the rights of individuals in such groups. Members of the community who are most often recognized by Governments as needed specialized human rights agencies to protect their interests are persons belonging to ethnic and linguistic minorities, aliens, refugees, indigenous populations, women and children, as well as members of religious minority groups. For the most part, these agencies are designed to promote government and social policy which protects the rights of these groups, to investigate instances and patterns of discrimination and against individuals in the group and against the group as a whole, and to provide materials and consultative assistance to members of the group.

Such agencies are generally not empowered to make binding decisions or to initiate legal action. Most often, agencies for the protection of the rights of specific groups are consultative and advisory commissions to the parliament and executive branch of government, and are required to examine the status of human rights violations as regards the group concerned. These agencies are also generally responsible for monitoring the effectiveness of existing statutory and constitutional safeguards aimed at protecting the rights of specific groups in the community, and are additionally empowered to investigate claims of discrimination brought by members of the community against State and local authorities.

Agencies for the protection of minorities have been established in many States over the past several decades to protect the rights of members of ethnic and linguistic minority groups, who are traditionally subject to discrimination. For instance, in Yugoslavia, commissions have been established to address the specific problems faced by minorities and to promote the principle of equality and collective rights. Other organizations of a similar nature are designed primarily to investigate the grievances of minority group members charging State or local authorities with engaging in discriminatory practices. In Pakistan, for example, District Minority Committees have been organized under the chairmanship of Minority Officers to redress, at the local level, the grievances of the minority communities expressed by their representatives.

A broad mandate was contemplated when the Indian Minorities Commission was created in 1978. The functions of the Commission are:

(1) To evaluate the working of the various safeguards provided for in the Constitution and in laws passed by the Union and State Governments for the protection of minorities;

(2) To make recommendations with a view to ensuring the effective implementation and enforcement of all the safeguards and laws;

(3) To undertake a review of the implementation of the policies pursued by the Union and the State Governments with respect to minorities;

(4) To look into specific complaints regarding deprivation of rights and safeguards of minorities;

(5) To conduct studies, research and analysis on the question of avoidance of discrimination against minorities;

(6) To suggest appropriate legal and welfare measures in respect of any minority to be undertaken by the central or State Governments;

(7) To serve as a national clearing-house for information in respect of the conditions of minorities;

(8) To make periodical reports at prescribed intervals to the Government.

Such a body can clearly have a great impact on human rights policy in the country, as well as on the immediate problems facing minorities with regard to discrimination in the community.

In accordance with its Constitution, Singapore has established a Presidential Council for Minority Rights. The Council considers and reports on information received from Parliament or the Government on matters concerning persons belonging to racial and religious minorities. The Council is especially requested to report on any proposed legislation or regulation which may result in discriminatory or unequal treatment of persons in particular communities. For the protection of the rights of linguistic minorities, India has established a Commissioner for Linguistic Minorities. In accordance with article 350A of the Indian Constitution, all States must provide adequate facilities for instruction in the mother tongue at the primary school level of education. The

Indian Commissioner for Linguistic Minorities investigates all matters relating to the safeguards provided for in the Constitution regarding the rights of linguistic minorities. The Commissioner is also required to report directly to the President on these matters. Another example of an organ established for the protection of linguistic minorities is the Austrian system of contact committees for the Slovene-speaking and Croatian-speaking minorities, organized within the Austrian Federal Chancellery. The contact committees meet at regular intervals and are comprised of members of the Federal Government, the provincial government concerned, the political parties represented in parliament and the provincial legislative assemblies concerned. Representatives of the minority groups also serve on these committees. The primary function of the committees is to consider measures for the implementation of the provisions of the State treaty of 1955 regarding minority rights. The committees are also charged with the consideration of all action relating to the peaceful cohabitation of the various ethnic groups and may deal with problems concerning individual members of the various ethnic groups or the groups as a whole.

Concerning ethnic groups more specifically, countries with an ethnically diverse population often create special commissions designed to ensure that the rights of the various ethnic groups in the community will be protected. For instance, in India, the Commissioner for Scheduled Castes and Tribes was empowered to investigate all matters relating to the safeguards provided for the scheduled castes and tribes under the Constitution. The Commissioner was responsible for submitting an annual report to the President, which was subsequently presented to both Houses of Parliament. Because of the magnitude of the problem however, a Commission for Scheduled Castes and Tribes—composed of a Chairman and four members—was organized to address the issues concerned in the protection of the rights of scheduled castes and tribes more effectively.

It has also been suggested that such commissions may be even more needed in ethnically homogeneous countries, in which small ethnic groups are virtually without representation at the State and local level and may be subject to a high incidence of discrimination in the community. Organizations established to protect the rights of such ethnic groups are often additionally charged with promoting respect for the various cultures present in the community. In Finland, for example, the Advisory Board for Gypsy Affairs has developed projects for the teaching of the Gypsy language, culture and history.

*Agencies for the Protection of Indigenous Populations.* Increasingly, the countries concerned have created organs to protect and promote the rights of indigenous populations, which are often subject to discrimination, dispossession of land and other human rights abuses.

In New Zealand for example, the Department of Maori and Island Affairs and the New Zealand Maori Council have been established to address the concerns of the Maori population. The Department of Maori and Island Affairs is responsible for co-ordinating and implementing government policy with respect to Maoris. The New Zealand Maori Council is a consultative body, which expresses its views on all proposed legislation affecting the Maori population. Norway, Finland and Sweden have all created independent commissions to deal with the concerns and problems of their respective Sami (formerly referred to as Lappish) populations. The Finnish Commission for Lappish Affairs is composed of representatives of the Ministries of Justice, Education and Agriculture, and of representatives of various Sami

organizations. The main function of the Commission is to advise the Council of State on proposed measures designed to promote the culture of the Sami. The Commission is also consulted by State and local authorities on all matters concerning the Sami population. The Swedish Commission on Sami Affairs, created in 1970, is designed to examine the various problems confronting the Sami in Swedish society. The Commission is particularly concerned with addressing the needs of those Sami who have left reindeer husbandry and moved away from the breeding areas. Norway has created two organs to deal with Sami issues and concerns. The first, the Norwegian Lapp Council, is comprised of eight members, who are all Sami. The Council is primarily an advisory body, which may make recommendations on matters concerning the economic, social and cultural situation of the Sami. Norway has also established a Select Committee, comprised of government and Sami representatives. The Committee, organized under the Ministry of Church and Education, examines questions relating to the educational development of the Sami.

Another example of an organ created to address the concerns of indigenous populations is the Mexican Instituto Nacional Indigenista (National Institute for Indigenous Affairs), which was established to study issues concerning the indigenous populations, and to report on the implementation of measures taken to improve the situation of Mexico's indigenous populations.

*Agencies for the Protection of Aliens, Migrants and Immigrants.* To address the problems of discrimination against foreign migrants and refugees, many countries have created agencies to protect these individuals against discrimination and other obstacles which may obstruct the full exercise of their rights in the community. The Australian Ethnic Affairs Council, for example, advises the Minister for Immigration and Ethnic Affairs on matters relating to the integrations of migrants into the Australian community, particularly in the area of community services. In addition, the Australian Government has opened two Multi-Cultural Resource Centres established to provide an information and advisory service to meet the special needs of immigrants, and to provide information on the availability of benefits and services at the State and local level. The Centres are designed to provide premises for the centralized distribution of multilingual information material, such as pamphlets on social security benefits and other relevant information.

In Belgium in 1952, the Aliens Advisory Commission was created. This Commission must be consulted by the King in all cases in which an alien can only be removed from the country by an expulsion order. The Belgian Minister of Justice may seek the Commission's opinion before making a decision concerning an alien. If the Commission is not consulted prior to a decision which is the subject of an application for review, the Minister of Justice must obtain the Commission's views before ruling on that application. Similarly, concern with protecting the rights of immigrants resulted in the creation of the Norwegian Foreign Workers' Association, which is aimed at safeguarding the economic, social and cultural interests of Norway's many new immigrant groups. The Association receives substantial financial assistance from the Norwegian Government, and emphasis is placed on an increased commitment to permitting immigrant groups to exercise greater influence on matters which particularly concern them. In Sweden, the Commission on Ethnic Prejudice and Discrimination may propose to the Government, measures concerning the improvement of the situation of aliens. Finally, it was recently reported that, in

716

an effort to address the needs of its growing refugee population, Denmark has created a Directorate for Aliens and a Refugee Board. The Directorate is the authority of first instance for decisions concerning refugee status. Such decisions are appealable to the Refugee Board, which functions procedurally like a court.

*Agencies for the Protection of Children and Minors.* Although in most countries protection of children's rights is primarily the responsibility of parents and legal guardians, mechanisms have been established by States for the protection of children whose parents do not fulfil their recognized duties, or who may be particularly vulnerable to exploitation. One of the primary concerns of such agencies is the exploitation of children in the labour market. Examples of institutions concerned with the prevention of child labour include the Egyptian Supreme Council for the Child, the Indian National Children's Board, the National Council for Children's Affairs in Bangladesh, the Chinese People's National Committee for the Defence of Children, the National Council for the Child in the Dominican Republic, and the United States Federal Inter-Agency Committee for Children and Youth.

In some states, these agencies function as subsidiary organs of the legislative body. For instance, questions concerning the rights of the child are carried out by the Juvenile Welfare Board in Norway, the Commission on Children's Rights in Sweden, and the Child Care Board in Barbados. In India, the National Children's Board, established in accordance with the National Policy for the Children Resolution adopted by the Legislature in 1974, is headed by the Prime Minister. This Children's Board was designed to provide "a focus and a forum to plan and review and properly co-ordinate the multiplicity of services, striving to meet the needs of children."

Many agencies for the protection of children are increasingly concerned with the social protection of homeless and abandoned children. In Poland, for example, the Society of the Friends for Children renders special assistance to children's homes and day-care centres. Also concerned with the social protection of children, the Minors' Association of Mexico provides both moral and material assistance to young persons who have committed offences or who are socially abandoned.

*Agencies for the Protection of Women.* States have increasingly recognized the need for agencies which are equipped to deal with the problem of discrimination against and exploitation of women. Many of these organizations are concerned with the high incidence of discrimination against women in the area of employment. Several of these agencies have already been discussed in the section of the report on equal employment agencies. However, other organs for the protection of women are more broadly designed to promote the rights of women, and to protect women from discrimination, not only in the workplace, but in all areas. One such organization is the Australian National Women's Advisory Council, which was created to give all Australian women a consultative voice at the federal level with a view to protecting the interests of women in the national sphere. This Council advises the Federal Government on issues affecting women through the Minister for Home Affairs. The women who serve on the Council are selected from different parts of the country and are of diverse backgrounds and interests. To eliminate discrimination against women in the federal sphere, and to monitor potential discrimination inherent in proposed federal laws and practices, Australia also has established the Office of Women's Affairs. This Office is additionally responsible for co-ordinating the work of women's affairs

units in other departments. Another example of an agency designed to monitor potential discrimination in the law is the Commission on Women's Rights, created by the Government of Barbados in 1977. This Commission was established to examine all aspects of the law relating to women. The Commission presents reports, containing the results of its ongoing examination, to the Attorney-General, whose Ministry has a Department of Women's Affairs. In India, both the Committee on the Status of Women and the National Committee on Women are designed to promote the rights of women. The Committee on the Status of Women in India is concerned primarily with emphasizing the need to co-ordinate agencies and communication in the implementation of measures to improve the status of women. The National Committee on Women is responsible for an ongoing review of the progress of programmes for women. The National Committee on Women is chaired by the Prime Minister of India, and the position of Vice-Chairman is held by the Minister of Education, Social Welfare and Culture. Other members of the National Committee are generally leading public figures in the field of women's issues.

Agencies created to protect groups in the community from the deleterious effects of discrimination and exploitation would seem to be an essential part of any comprehensive national programme for the protection and promotion of human rights. In all countries, groups characterized by race, ethnicity, national origin, religion or sex, may be, in varying degrees, subject to instances and practices of discrimination. When there is a tradition of bias or long-standing discrimination in a community, such groups are often underrepresented at the State and local official level, and subsequently may have little or no readily accessible means of alerting the proper authorities to redress such acts of discrimination. Moreover, when acts of discrimination are perpetrated by State or local authorities, the recourse available to members of particular groups in the community may be non-existent. Organizations which deal solely with the protection of these groups can offer an accessible and effective recourse to members of the community who traditionally lack responsive administrative machinery at the State and local level.

Finally, the high incidence of refugee and migratory movement, the continued abuse of the land rights of indigenous populations, and the pervasive level of racial and sexual discrimination which exist in countries throughout the world, overwhelmingly heighten the need for special agencies to address the problems and concerns which face particular groups of the community, which often suffer from inordinately high levels of discrimination.

**HUMAN RIGHTS DEFENDERS.** The protection of persons who participate in proceedings before international organs competent to deal with allegations concerning violations of human rights has been a matter of concern for some years. It has been proposed that standardized rules setting out the immunities of such persons, and of their lawyers, witnesses, and experts called upon to assist them, should be adopted. Such rules are already in effect in Europe.

In 1969, the Committee of Ministers of the Council of Europe adopted the European Agreement relating to Persons Participating in Proceedings of the European Commission and Court of Human Rights. The agreement applies to (a) agents of the contracting parties and advisors and advocates assisting them; (b) persons taking part in proceedings instituted before the Commission under article 25 of the Convention, whether in their own names or as representatives of one of the applicants enumerated in article 25; (c) barristers, solicitors, or professors of law, taking part in proceedings in order to assist one of the persons enumerated in (b) above; (d) persons chosen by the delegates of the Commission to assist them in proceedings before the Court; and (e) witnesses, experts, and other persons called upon by the Commission or the Court to take part in proceedings before the Commission or the Court. Article 2 states that these persons "shall have immunity from legal process in respect of oral or written statements made, or documents or other evidence submitted by them before or to the Commission or the Court." Under article 3, the contracting parties undertake to respect the right of these persons to correspond freely with the Commission and the Court; and, under article 4, they undertake not to hinder the free movement and travel, for the purpose of attending and returning from proceedings before the Commission or the Court, the above-mentioned persons whose presence has in advance been authorized by the Commission or the Court.

In 1970, the UN Secretary-General, at the request of the **COMMISSION ON HUMAN RIGHTS,** prepared draft model rules for United Nations bodies dealing with violations of human rights (UN Doc. E/CN.4/1020), in which it was proposed that all United Nations bodies investigating such violations should make the arrangements necessary with the State concerned to ensure that no obstacle prevented representatives or witnesses from attending meetings of the body and assuring any witness or any individual appearing before the body due protection against any acts of violence or intimidation, any threats or reprisals, or any discriminatory measures which might be directed against them because they attend the meetings or give their testimony, and against any legal proceedings which might be instituted against them because of their testimony. However, these proposals were not adopted; and it has since been the practice of UN bodies assigned to make on-the-spot factfinding investigations of human rights violations to work out individual agreements with the governments concerned in which the government assures the group of its assistance in the protection of the persons the group desires to meet.

The **INTERNATIONAL FEDERATION OF HUMAN RIGHTS,** a nongovernmental organization in consultative status, has been studying various aspects of the problem. In a written statement submitted to the UN **SUB-COMMISSION ON PREVENTION OF DISCRIMINATION AND PROTECTION OF MINORITIES** at its 1988 session (UN Doc. E/CN.4/Sub.2/1988/NGO/6), the Federation pointed out that

. . . United Nations human rights agencies have increased the number of organs and procedures for direct access, thus enabling them to deal with individual communications and complaints and, on that basis, to report on the various situations involving violations of human rights. There has thus been steady progress towards a regular system for reporting violations and for monitoring offending States, although no specific measure to protect those individuals who have recourse to those procedures has been adopted. The duty of protecting human rights is becoming a particularly dangerous responsibility for persons who are denied the guarantees of the law. For regimes based on force, the affirmation of the primacy of the law becomes a subversive activity.

Usually the mere fact of alerting, informing or attempting, either through us or directly, to contact United Nations agencies causes those who are helping the victims to become victims in their turn. The various organs of the Commission have been able to verify on a number of occasions that a more selective repression is now directed particularly against human rights activists. The threat overthrowing the future of human rights through the persecution of their champions is very serious and the time and energy devoted to adopting a declaration by the General Assembly is too precious. Such a declaration should not merely confine itself to an abstract reaffirmation of rights but should, if it is to be effective, reaffirm and strengthen the freedom of association and propose universal rules for its exercise. In the interests of effectiveness, it is vital to have a prior knowledge of the status of the law in that regard. The FIDH requests the Sub-Commission to instruct one of its experts:

(a) To conduct a study on the national legislation regulating the protection of human rights advocates; [and]

(b) To prepare model rules for the use of those countries that do not yet provide measures of protection for these persons in their domestic law.

The Inter-American Commission on Human Rights commented on the difficulties faced by human rights activists and their organizations in its annual report for 1985–1986 (OAS Ser. L/V/II.68, Doc. 8 rev. 1, pp. 194–195) as follows:

Limitations or weakness of the judiciary have led human rights organizations, particularly non-governmental ones, to play an active role in the protection of human rights, the denunciation of violations, and the movement to investigate such violations.

In some cases, the activities carried out by these organizations have helped to correct abuses; in other cases, as the Commission has regrettably found in examining the situation of human rights in various states, these organizations or their leaders have been persecuted by government authorities, which has enormously hampered their valuable work.

Several cases of such persecution can be cited. In some instances, human rights organizations have been denied legal status or juridical personality. In others, their offices have been raided and their property confiscated. Moreover, in at least three countries, their leaders have been subjected to threats, smear campaigns, harassment and even detention, in which the flimsiest pretexts have been used to block their functions and activities.

Since many of these methods have regrettably been used more intensively in recent years in some member states, the Commission feels obligated to reiterate to those member states where such organizations are carrying out their important functions under such precarious conditions, their obligation to guarantee the autonomy and freedom of activity of such human rights organizations, as well as the integrity and full freedom of their leaders.

The UN Commission on Human Rights, at its 1988 session, adopted a resolution (resolution 1988/39) in which it expressed its concern that, in many parts of the world, numerous persons are detained for seeking to exercise peacefully their human rights and fundamental freedoms, in particular the rights to freedom of expression, of assembly, and of association, or to promote and defend those rights and freedoms; and that these persons are often exposed to special dangers as regards the protection of their human rights and fundamental freedoms.

The Commission requested all governments to release all persons deprived of their liberty for seeking peacefully to exercise these rights and freedoms or to promote and defend them; and called on all governments, pending such release, to take effective measures to safeguard the human rights and fundamental freedoms of such persons.

The Sub-Commission on Prevention of Discrimination and Protection of Minorities also adopted a resolution in 1988 (resolution 1988/38) in which it expressed its concern at the incidence of detention, torture, disappearances, and extra-legal executions of individuals, in particular those within their own countries who are working to promote and protect universally recognized human rights and fundamental freedoms, including lawyers complying with their professional ethical obligations to defend the legal rights of their clients.

The Sub-Commission called for the release of all persons detained, in violation of the rights to freedom of speech, association, and assembly; for defending the human rights of others; and for publicizing alleged violations of human rights. It further called for effective measures of protection for those working to promote and protect the human rights of others, as well as the rights of complainants, witnesses, and those who are threatened with violations of their own rights, particularly intimidation or threats to life or limb. It decided that, where relevant, studies being carried out by the Sub-Commission should pay particular attention to the rights of persons promoting and protecting the human rights of others and their violation; and urged the Commission on Human Rights to finalize as soon as possible its work on the drafting of a declaration on the right and responsibility of individuals, groups, and organs of society to promote and protect

universally recognized human rights and fundamental freedoms.

Since 1990 the UN Commission on Human Rights had campaigned against intimidation of and reprisals against private individuals and groups seeking to cooperate with the United Nations, and against representatives of UN human rights bodies (resolutions 1990/76, 1991/70, 1992/59 and 1993/64), after receiving and considering reports by the Secretary-General on this question.

Having examined the 1994 report (E/CN.4/1994/52), which indicated clearly that such activities had not declined, the Commission reiterated its concern about them in resolution 1994/70 of 5 March 1994, and in particular urged Governments to refrain from any such acts of intimidation or reprisal against:

(a) Those who seek to cooperate or have cooperated with representatives of United Nations human rights bodies, or who have provided testimony or information to them;
(b) Those who avail or have availed themselves of procedures established under United Nations auspices for the protection of human rights and fundamental freedoms and all those who have provided legal assistance to them for this purpose;
(c) Those who submit or have submitted communications under procedures established by human rights instruments;
(d) Those who are relatives of victims of human rights violations.

The Commission further requested all representatives of United Nations human rights bodies to continue to take urgent steps to help prevent the occurrence of any such intimidation, reprisal, or hampering of access to established procedures, and to report all such incidents—and the action taken against them—to the United Nations bodies concerned.

***HUMAN RIGHTS PROMOTION AND PROTECTION.*** On 11 March 1982, the UN Commission on Human Rights restated (resolution 1982/30) a view which it had adopted on earlier occasions—that individuals, groups, and organs of society have a right and a responsibility to promote and protect the rights recognized in the Universal Declaration of Human Rights, the International Covenants on Human Rights, and all other relevant international instruments, without prejudice to articles 29 and 30 of the Universal Declaration. In this connection, the Commission emphasized that, in the exercise of these rights and freedoms, the individual shall be subject only to such limitations as are determined in the United Nations Charter, the Universal Declaration, and other relevant instruments; and that the imposition of other limitations or the persecution or punishment of anyone exercising, individually or collectively, his universally recognized human rights and fundamental freedoms is at variance with the obligations of States under these instruments to work for the full and effective enjoyment of those rights and freedoms.

The Commission called upon the Secretary-General to prepare, for consideration by the Sub-Commission on Prevention of Discrimination and Protection of Minorities, elements for a draft body of principles on the right and responsibility of individuals, groups, and organs of society to promote and protect human rights and fundamental freedoms; and requested the Sub-Commission to prepare, taking these elements into account, a report containing a draft of such a body of principles.

The Sub-Commission received and noted, at its 1982 session, the Secretary-General's report (UN Doc. E/CN.4/Sub.2/1982/12) setting out elements for a draft body of principles as requested. Recalling that the proposal for such a body of principles had initially been put forward in the study prepared by one of its members, Mrs. Erica-Irene A. Daes (Greece), entitled *Study of the Individual's Duties to the Community and the Limitations on Human Rights and Freedoms under Article 29 of the Universal Declaration of Human Rights—A Contribution to the Freedom of the Individual under Law* (United Nations publication, Sales no. E.82.XIV.1), the Sub-Commission requested Mrs. Daes (resolution 1982/24) to prepare the draft principles. It received her report (UN Doc. E/CN.4/Sub.2/1985/30) at its 1985 session and referred it (resolution 1985/30) and other relevant documentation to the Commission on Human Rights for consideration by an open-ended working group which the Commission had already established for the purpose (decision 1985/112).

The working group met before and during sessions of the Commission held in 1986, 1987, 1988, 1989, 1990, 1991, 1992 and 1993, but was not able to complete the preparation of the proposed declaration. The Commission accordingly decided (resolution 1994/96) to urge the working group to make every effort to complete its task and submit the draft declaration to it at its 1995 session. In doing so it recalled that the World Conference on Human Rights had recommended speedy completion and adoption of the draft declaration, but recognized the importance of taking into account the opinions of all States and interested inter-governmental and non-governmental organizations before finalizing the text.

***HUMAN RIGHTS PUBLICITY.*** The following general comment on article 2 of the International Covenant on Civil and Political Rights was adopted by the UN Human Rights Committee on 28 July 1981:

The Committee notes that article 2 of the Covenant generally leaves it to the States parties concerned to choose their method of implementation in their territories within the framework set out in that article. It recognizes, in particular, that the implementation does not depend solely on constitutional or legislative enactments, which in themselves are often not *per se* sufficient. The Committee considers it necessary to draw the attention of States parties to the fact that the obligation under the Covenant is not confined to the respect of human rights, but that States parties have also undertaken to ensure the enjoyment of these rights to all individuals under their jurisdiction. This aspect calls for specific activities by the States parties to enable individuals to enjoy their rights. This is obvious in a number of articles, but in principle this undertaking relates to all rights set forth in the Covenant.

In this connexion, it is very important that individuals should know what their rights under the Covenant (and the Optional Protocol, as the case may be) are and also that all administrative and judicial authorities should be aware of the obligations which the State party has assumed under the Covenant. To this end, the Covenant should be publicized in all official languages of the State and steps should be taken to familiarize the authorities concerned with its contents as part of their training. It is desirable also to give publicity to the State party's co-operation with the Committee.

***HUMAN RIGHTS TEACHING.*** At its 1971 session, the UN Commission on Human Rights examined a report prepared by the **UNITED NATIONS EDUCATIONAL, SCIENTIFIC AND CULTURAL ORGANIZATION** (UN Doc. E/CN.4/1027) which drew attention to the difficulties encountered by educators in the teaching of human rights in schools and universities, and requested UNESCO (resolution 11 C [XXVII]) "to consider the desirability of envisaging the systematic study and the development of an independent scientific discipline of human rights, taking into account the principal legal systems of the world with a view to facilitating the understanding, comprehension, study and teaching of human rights at the university level, and subsequently at other educational levels. . . ." The UNESCO General Conference later invited the Director-General to carry out a feasibility study on the "creation of an international clearing-house for the teaching of human rights and for exchange of information on the curricula and on existing courses at all levels, as well as on specialized research."

Generally speaking, according to a report of the Director-General transmitted to the UN General Assembly in November 1988 (UN Doc. A/43/96), UNESCO's action with regard to human rights education has developed on the following five lines:

(a) cooperation with institutions specializing in human rights teaching, including universities;

(b) preparation of educational and teaching materials;

(c) development of human rights teaching methods;

720

(d) training at the primary, secondary, and higher levels, including teacher training; and

(e) knowledge of the basic texts on the protection and promotion of human rights, notably the International Bill of Human Rights.

In the report (paras. 7, 12–14), the Director-General pointed out that:

These five lines of approach are interconnected in many ways and cannot be completely dissociated in practice. They should, however, be distinguished according to the main objective sought by a given activity. The experience of co-operating with bodies specializing in human rights teaching, and with universities, shows that as an agency for international intellectual co-operation, UNESCO has a very important role to play in diversifying educational projects and in promoting exchanges of experience, both successful and unsuccessful. . . .

While at the pre-school and primary levels classroom life and relations within the school are vital for human rights teaching, at the level of secondary education equally great importance is given to knowledge of international human rights instruments and the 1974 UNESCO Recommendation on Education for International Understanding, Co-operation and Peace and Education relating to Human Rights and Fundamental Freedoms.

It is obvious that teacher-training institutions have a particularly vital role to play in human rights education. Admittedly in certain cases this education is part of their curricula. However, many examples attest that it is often on the initiative of a few teachers or a school principal that this subject is included in the curriculum of a teacher-training school. In this connection it should be noted that the International Days proclaimed by the United Nations General Assembly (for example, United Nations Day, Human Rights Day or the International Day of Peace) all provide opportunities for a school to launch educational activities concerning human rights.

Generally speaking, while it is recognized that in human rights teaching there is a conceptual aspect of the acquisition of knowledge (definitions, ideas and theories), it is nevertheless a fact that in this field emphasis should be placed on forming the intellectual and moral aptitudes required for observance of human rights. Care should therefore be taken not to overlook the aspect of the transmission of values by teachers. UNESCO has accordingly encouraged exchanges of teachers from different cultures and countries in order to make them aware of the importance of culture in education and to strengthen their vigilance with regard to prejudice, intolerance and racism so that they in turn can communicate their own experience of respect for other peoples. A workshop on teacher training for combating prejudice, intolerance and racism in the field of education was held in Chad in 1985. A practical guide for secondary school teachers, containing suggestions on ways of combating all forms of discrimination, was prepared for publication in 1989. In parallel with these exchanges, UNESCO encourages Member States to revise their textbooks so as to eliminate any references of a discriminatory nature.

The feasibility study authorized by the UNESCO General Conference was entrusted in 1985 to the Netherlands Institute of Human Rights in Utrecht. Its purpose

is to examine the different possibilities for coordinating the dissemination and circulation of human rights information and documentation on the basis of knowledge gained by efforts in this field by other intergovernmental and non-governmental organizations.

UNESCO has organized two major international conferences on the teaching of human rights: the International Congress on the Teaching of Human Rights, held at Vienna in 1978, and the International Congress on Human Rights Teaching, Information and Documentation, held at Malta in 1987. Both were preceded by a number of regional meetings, and both made assessments of the progress achieved in the field. Recommendations of the congresses, and of the regional preparatory meetings, were summed up as follows in the Director-General's report (paras. 62–89):

*Universality of Human Rights.* The universality of the human rights proclaimed by the Universal Declaration of Human Rights and recognized by the International Covenants of 1966 is reiterated. UNESCO's action should be placed within this framework. However, as regards international co-operation, the methodological approach to human rights education and teaching and the priorities given to research, information and documentation may vary from one region to another.

All of UNESCO's programme activities in the field of human rights should continue to draw on the guiding principles affirmed in resolution 34/46 of 23 November 1979, in which the United Nations General Assembly reaffirmed its conviction that all human rights are indivisible and interdependent, and that equal attention should be given to the implementation, promotion and protection of both civil and political, and economic, social and cultural rights.

*Human Rights Education.* Instruction in human rights should be given at all levels and in all forms of education, integrated into the different disciplines and reflected in the curricula.

For such education to be effective, the very atmosphere of social and cultural institutions must reflect respect for human rights; such education should be founded on a basis of reciprocity, solidarity and justice.

Educational action should take into account cultural diversity throughout the world, and be based on the cultural identity, social values, language, socialization and communication systems, etc. specific to each country.

The training of trainers is essential in the field of human rights. A particular effort should be made to encourage innovations and pilot projects in teacher-training colleges.

Teaching methods in human rights education should be active, with the maximum possible recourse to discovery and creative work by pupils or students. Data collection, interviews, exhibitions, etc. promote an in-depth understanding of human rights problems.

At present, there is a dearth of teaching materials in this area. It is therefore necessary to encourage the production and distribution of materials which have been tested and evaluated in practice. Particular attention should be paid to audiovisual aids, a teaching medium that has been little exploited so far.

Human rights education should be the basis of non-formal or mass education programmes, particularly in adult education. Innovative experiments carried out in many regions, particularly in rural areas, deserve support and encouragement. Education should take into account the situation of disadvantaged groups such as refugees, ethnic, linguistic and religious minorities, and so on. It should also be noted that non-formal education is one of the responsibility of, for example, trade unions, professional associations and learned societies.

In the context of lifelong or continuing education, specific teaching should be designed for the professionals most directly concerned with human rights, such as magistrates, lawyers, civil servants, policemen, members of the armed forces, journalists, trade unionists, social workers, health personnel, etc., with due regard for the type of problems with which they have to deal.

Human rights education and teaching should be provided in the language(s) used by those concerned, and be accessible to them in that/those language(s).

*Research in the Social and Human Sciences.* Since the rapid development of human rights education and teaching depends to a great extent on pedagogical research, such research should be encouraged, particularly from a comparative viewpoint and with a view to valuating the results of this education.

The introduction of human rights curricula should be encouraged, not only in law faculties but in faculties of literature, human sciences, social and economic sciences and also in faculties of science, medicine, pharmacy, etc., adopting the approach specific to each discipline.

The establishment of specialized human rights training, research and documentation centres or institutes, and their strengthening in countries where they already exist, should be promoted on multidisciplinary lines.

Interregional and regional research and researcher-training programmes should be encouraged, particularly with a view to co-operation among developing countries, together with exchanges of experience and of teachers and researchers.

Publications should be used to disseminate research findings and to contribute to a knowledge of the institutions specializing in training, research and documentation in the field of human rights.

The relationship between ethics, human rights and recent progress in the biological sciences and technology should be studied more deeply. For example, a study should be made of the links between professional ethics and human rights, especially with a view to training the professionals most directly concerned with human rights.

Human rights research should help to bring out the connection with the highly topical problems facing different societies and the international community as a whole (development, peace, discrimination, intolerance, etc.). Research should also take into account the radical changes at work in society and the emergence of new social movements, new patterns of social organization, etc.

*Human Rights Information and Documentation.* The mass media play a predominant role in disseminating knowledge about human rights to the general public. Experiments and innovations in this field, particularly in information programmes, deserve to be encouraged.

It is possible that insufficient recourse has been had to non-conventional communication media in disseminating knowledge of human rights. Here also greater use should be made of the theatre, painting, the cinema, songs or even educational or social games.

Documentation centres should be established or strengthened in order to support educational work and research. A network of documentation centres should gradually be established with a view to improved dissemination at the international level.

Special attention should be paid to educational documentation, with a view not only to production but also to improved dissemination.

Training should be provided in documentation (collection, processing, storage, circulation) which will take account of the specific nature of the human rights field.

The possibility of preparing a human rights thesaurus should be studied in collaboration with the relevant international and regional organizations.

Whenever possible and wherever the need is most keenly felt, encouragement and support should be given to the creation of a liaison or information newsletters and their circulation to universities, teachers and organizations concerned with human rights in different geographical, linguistic or cultural regions.

*Role of Non-governmental Organizations.* Co-operation with non-governmental organizations at the national, regional and international levels is equally vital. The leading role that they play in the fields of education and training, research, information and documentation deserves to be emphasized.

*Dissemination by Member States of Basic Human Rights Texts.* Resolution 217 (III) D, adopted by the United Nations General Assembly on 10 December 1948, appealed to all Member States to give due publicity to the text of the Universal Declaration of Human Rights and to "cause it to be disseminated, displayed, read and expounded principally in schools and other educational institutions". The dissemination of basic human rights texts is thus a long-standing commitment for all Governments.

It is therefore necessary to seek funds and request the co-operation of Member States in order to ensure the dissemination of basic human rights texts such as the Universal Declaration of Human Rights, the International Covenants of 1966, international conventions and other standards and procedures approved at the international level. It is recognized that Member States will not be in a position to meet their international commitments as long as there is no access to the basic texts in the languages required for the teaching and training activities which are carried out, in either a formal or a non-formal context.

**HUMAN RIGHTS TEACHING PRIZE.** At its 1993 session, the General Assembly, in accordance with its resolution 2217 (XVI) of 19 December 1966 and decisions 47/429 and 48/410A, awarded nine prizes to the following individuals and organizations that had made outstanding contributions to the promotion and protection of human rights: Bassib Ben Ammar (Tunisia); Dr. Erica Daes (Greece); James Grant (USA); International Commission of Jurists; Medical Personnel of the Central Hospital of Sarajevo (Bosnia and Herzegovina); Dr. Sonia Picado Sotela (Costa Rica); Ganesh Man Singh (Nepal); Sudanese Women's Union (Sudan); Father Julio Tumiri Javier (Bolivia).

**HUMAN RIGHTS DAY (DECEMBER 10).** On 10 December 1948, the UN General Assembly adopted and proclaimed (resolution 217 A [III]) the Universal Declaration of Human Rights. Two years later, on 4 December 1950, it invited (resolution 423 [V]) all States and interested organizations to adopt December 10 of each year as "Human Rights Day," to observe this day to celebrate the proclamation of the Declaration, and to exert increasing efforts in this field of human progress. The Assembly expressed the view that the anniversary should be appropriately commemorated in all countries as part of the common effort to bring the principles set out in the Declaration to the attention of all the peoples of the world and expressed its appreciation to those countries that had already begun to observe the anniversary.

Up to the end of 1989, Human Rights Day had been celebrated for 39 years in all parts of the world, with the most extensive celebrations occurring on the 10th anniversary of the Declaration (1958), the 20th (1968), the 30th (1978), and the 40th (1988).

The General Assembly decided on 4 December 1986 (resolution 41/150) to celebrate the 40th anniversary of the Universal Declaration of Human Rights (10 December 1988) and invited member States, specialized agencies, regional intergovernmental organizations, and non-governmental organizations throughout the world to take appropriate measures and to support appropriate activities aimed at encouraging the promotion and universal observance of human rights and fundamental freedoms. On 7 December 1987 (resolution 42/131), it reiterated that decision and resolved further that the 1988 celebration should be used as an occasion to highlight the achievements of the United Nations in its efforts to promote and protect human rights universally, to renew the commitment of the organization in this area and to encourage member States to ensure the promotion and protection of the rights enshrined in the Universal Declaration. The Assembly again held a special commemorative meeting, on 8 December 1988, to observe the anniversary.

A worldwide program of activities for the observance of the 40th anniversary of the Declaration was coordinated by the UN CENTER FOR HUMAN RIGHTS and the Department of Public Information. Activities began on World AIDS Day, 1 December, and ended on Human Rights Day. At UN headquarters in New York, a series of daily seminars was held dealing with various aspects of human rights, such as economic and social rights; human rights aspects of AIDS; human rights writers; the right to education as reflected in the proposed convention on the rights of the child; women and human rights; the role of non-governmental organizations in the work of the United Nations in the field of human rights; and the situation of United Nations staff members whose human rights have been violated. Film screenings and musical, cultural, and social events were also held.

In addition, on Human Rights Day 1988, the UN Secretary-General accepted the Nobel Peace Prize at Oslo on behalf of the United Nations PEACEKEEPING FORCES, and ceremonies were held in Paris at the *Palais de Chaillot,* the site of the adoption of the Universal Declaration of Human Rights by the General Assembly on 10 December 1948.

In a decision adopted on 8 December 1988 (resolution 43/90) the General Assembly reaffirmed the significance of the Universal Declaration of Human Rights as a source of inspiration for national and international efforts to promote and protect human rights and fundamental freedoms. Underlining the importance of the teaching of human rights at all levels, it noted the progress made up to that time in the field of human rights, including standard-setting and codification, but expressed its concern at mass and flagrant violations of human rights, including those stemming from racism and all forms of racial discrimination and *apartheid,* and at all violations of human rights that continue to take place in many parts of the world. Further, it affirmed the responsibility of the United Nations in protecting and promoting human rights and fundamental freedoms and expressed the determination of the United Nations to deal, through appropriate United Nations bodies, with violations of human rights and fundamental freedoms.

Reaffirming the importance of the observance and effective implementation of universally recognized standards in the field of human rights contained in international human rights instruments, the Assembly invited the UN Commission on Human Rights to consider a program of action which would include:

(a) measures to promote the universal ratification of or accession to United Nations instruments in the field of human rights and to strengthen United Nations machinery for the promotion and protection of human rights and fundamental freedoms enshrined in the Declaration;

(b) activities to develop human rights institutions and infrastructures, drawing upon the assistance of the United Nations Program for Advisory Services in the Field of Human Rights, including the Voluntary Fund for Technical Assistance and Advisory Services, and drawing also upon the relevant capabilities of the specialized agencies in this field, and other available multilateral and bilateral assistance;

(c) activities in the area of public information as may be determined by the Commission in considering the world campaign for human rights; and

(d) measures to enhance national and existing regional institutions for the promotion of human rights, through appropriate educational, judicial, legal, and other channels, including direct contact among them.

On 10 December 1993, the forty-fifth anniversary of

the University Declaration of Human Rights, the General Assembly recognized the significance of the Declaration as a source of inspiration for national and international efforts for the promotion and protection of all human rights, and decided to include on the agenda of its 53rd session (1999) an item entitled "Fiftieth Anniversary of the Universal Declaration of Human Rights."

### INTERNATIONAL YEAR FOR HUMAN RIGHTS (1968).

The 20th anniversary of the Universal Declaration of Human Rights, 1968, was designated by the General Assembly as the "International Year for Human Rights" and was marked by the convening of the International Conference on Human Rights. The Assembly decided (resolution 2081 [XX]) on 20 December 1965:

to promote further the principles contained in the Universal Declaration of Human Rights, to develop and guarantee political, civil, economic, social and cultural rights and to end all discrimination and denial of human rights and fundamental freedoms on grounds of race, colour, sex, language or religion, and in particular to permit the elimination of *apartheid*, an International Conference on Human Rights should be convened during 1968 in order to:

(a) Review the progress which has been made in the field of human rights since the adoption of the Universal Declaration of Human Rights;

(b) Evaluate the effectiveness of the methods used by the United Nations in the field of human rights, especially with respect to the elimination of all forms of racial discrimination and the practice of the policy of *apartheid*;

(c) Formulate and prepare a programme of further measures to be taken subsequent to the celebrations of the International Year for Human Rights.

The program approved by the General Assembly (resolution 2081 [XX], annex) gave first priority to the elimination of certain practices constituting some of the grosser forms of the denial of human rights. It then called for further study by United Nations bodies of international measures for the guarantee or protection of human rights and for the establishment of programs designed to promote the full enjoyment by all of human rights and fundamental freedoms. The national programs envisaged by the Assembly called upon governments, *inter alia*, to embark upon a complementary program of education, including both adult and child education, designed to produce new thinking on the part of many people in regard to human rights, this program to aim at mobilizing some of the energies of:

(a) universities, colleges, and other institutions of higher learning, both private and public, within member States;

(b) the teaching staff of primary and secondary schools;

(c) foundations and charitable, scientific, and research institutions; and

(d) media of information and mass communication, including the press, radio, and television.

A further program approved by the General Assembly on 19 December 1966 (resolution 2217 A [XXI], annex), called upon the Secretary-General to do all in his power to publicize the 20th anniversary of the Universal Declaration and the observance of the International Year for Human Rights, recommended a long list of activities to be undertaken during 1968 by governments and interested organizations, and proposed that all the commemorative activities be coordinated by the Secretary-General.

The International Conference on Human Rights, convened at Teheran from 22 April to 13 May 1968, adopted the Proclamation of Teheran, by which it "affirmed its faith in the principles of the Universal Declaration of Human Rights and other international instruments in this field" and urged all peoples and governments to dedicate themselves to those principles and "to redouble their efforts to provide for all human beings a life consonant with freedom and dignity and conducive to physical, mental, social and spiritual welfare." The Conference adopted 29 resolutions on various aspects of human rights.

After reviewing the Final Act of the Conference, the Assembly on 19 December 1968 expressed satisfaction (resolution 2442 [XXIII]) with the Conference's work, endorsed the Proclamation of Teheran, and urged all States and concerned organizations to encourage and assist all media of mass communication in giving widespread publicity to the Proclamation and to the work of the Conference. The Assembly also called upon all States and concerned organizations to take further action with a view to the full realization of human rights in the light of the recommendations of the Conference.

**BIBLIOGRAPHY. A. General.** Agence de Coopération Culturelle et Technique. *Promotion et protection des droits de l'homme dans l'espace francophone: Communications des participants au séminaire international tenu à Bordeaux du 29 juin au 10 juillet 1992* (Human Rights Promotion and Protection in French-Speaking Communities: Speeches delivered by Participants at the International Seminar held in Bordeaux from June 29 to July 10, 1992). Talence, France: 1992. IGO conference report, in French.

Bello, Emmanuel G., and Bola A. San Ajibola, eds. *Essays in Honour or Judge Tasim Olawale Elias, Vol. I: Contemporary International Law and Human Rights.* Dordrecht, the Netherlands, and Boston, MA, USA: Martinus Nijhoff, 1992. Scholarly collection of articles, in English, French, and Spanish.

Bokatola, Isse Omanga. *L'organisation des nations unies et la protection des minorités* (The United Nations Organization and the Protection of Minorities). Brussels, Belgium: Émile Bruylant, 1992. Scholarly monograph, in French; bibliography, pp. 263–274.

Buergenthal, Thomas, Robert Norris, and Dinah Shelton. *Protecting Human Rights in the Americas: Selected Problems*. Kehl, Germany: International Institute of Human Rights and N.P.Engel Publisher, 1990. Scholarly monograph, in English; bibliography, pp. 463–472.

Butler, W. E. *Control over Compliance with International Law*. Dordrecht, the Netherlands: Martinus Nijhoff, 1991. Scholary monograph, in English.

Claude, Richard Pierre, and Burns H. Weston, eds. *Human Rights in the World Community: Issues and Action*. Philadelpia, PA, USA: University of Pennsylvania Press, 1992. Scholarly collection of articles, in English.

Cohen, Roberta. *Human Rights and Humanitarian Emergencies: New Roles for UN Human Rights Bodies*. Washington, D.C.: Center for Policy Analysis and Research on Refugee Issues and Refugee Policy Group, 1992. NGO discussion paper, in English.

Cohn, Cindy A. "The Early Harvest: Domestic Legal Changes Related to the Human Rights Committee and the Covenant on Civil and Political Rights," *Human Rights Quarterly* 13, no. 3 (August 1991): 295–321. Scholarly article, in English.

Commonwealth Secretariat, Human Rights Unit. *Statutory Human Rights Bodies in the Commonwealth: Directory*. London: Commonwealth Secretariat, 1990. IGO directory, in English.

Council of Europe. *Yearbook of the European Convention on Human Rights,* vol. 1–present. Dordrecht, the Netherlands: Martinus Nijhoff, 1959–present. IGO annual report, in English and French.

Donnelly, Jack. *International Human Rights*. Boulder, CO, USA: Westview Press, 1993. Scholarly monograph, in English.

Eide, Asbjorn, and Jan Helgesen, eds. *The Future of Human Rights Protection in a Changing World: Fifty Years Since the Four Freedoms Address: Essays in Honour of Torkel Opsahl*. Oslo, Norway: Norwegian University Press, 1991. Scholarly collection of articles, in English.

Fisler, Lori, and David J. Scheffer, eds. *Law and Force in the New International Order*. Boulder, CO, USA: Westview Press for the American Society of International Law, 1991. Scholarly collection of articles, in English.

Gaer, Felice D. "First Fruits: Reporting by States under the African Charter on Human and Peoples' Rights," *Netherlands Quarterly of Human Rights* 10, no. 1 (1992). Scholarly article, in English.

Gillies, David W. "Evaluating National Human Rights Performance: Priorities for the Developing World," *Bulletin of Peace Proposals* 21, no. 1 (1990): 15–27. Scholarly article, in English.

Hannum, Hurst, ed. *Guide to International Human Rights Practice*. Washington, D.C., and Philadelphia, PA, USA: University of Pennsylvania Press, 1992. Scholarly monograph, in English.

"The Hierarchy of Constitutional Norms and Its Function in Protecting Human Rights: Reports to the 8th Conference of the European Constitutional Courts," *Human Rights Law Journal* 13, no. 3 (March 1992): 81–111. Scholarly article, in English.

Howard, Rhoda E. "Monitoring Human Rights: Problems of Consistency," *Ethics and International Affairs* 4 (1990): 33–51. Scholarly article, in English.

Inter-American Commission on Human Rights. *Annual Report of the Inter-American Commission on Human Rights,* vol. 1–present. Washington, D.C.: Organization of American States, 1971–present. Annual report, in English.

Kamarotos, Alexander S. *A View into NGO Networks in Human Rights Activities: NGO Action with Special Reference to the UN Commission on Human Rights and its Sub-Commission*. Geneva, Switzerland: Graduate Institute of International Studies, 1990. Scholarly monograph, in English.

Kedzia, Zdizislaw, Anna Korula, and Manfred Nowak, eds. "Perspectives of an All-European System of Human Rights Protection: The Role of the Council of Europe, the CSCE, and the European Communities—Proceedings and Recommendations of an International Conference, Poznan, Poland, 8–11 October 1990," *All-European Human Rights Yearbook* 1 (1991). Special issue of scholarly collective works, in English.

Lillich, Richard B. *International Human Rights: Law, Policy and Process*. Boston, MA, USA: Little, Brown, 1991. Educational material, in English.

"Modernizing Customary International Law: The Challenge of Human Rights," *Virginia Journal of International Law* 31 (Winter 1991): 211–247. Scholarly article, in English.

Muller, Joachim W. *The Reform of the United Nations, Vol. I: Report ; Vol. II: Resolutions, Decisions and Documents*. New York and London: Oceana Publications, 1992. Scholarly monograph, in English.

Newman, Frank, and David Weissbrodt. *International Human Rights: Law, Policy, and Process*. Cincinnati, OH, USA: Anderson Publishing, 1990. Educational material, in English; bibliography, pp. 733–762.

Ramcharan, B. G. "The Security Council and Humanitarian Emergencies," *Netherlands Quarterly of Human Rights* 9, no. 1 (1991): 19–35. Scholarly article, in English.

———. "Security Council Patterns for Dealing with Ethnic Conflicts and Minority Problems," in *Broadening The Frontiers of Human Rights: Essays in Honour of Asbjorn Eide*, pp. 27–40. New York: Scandinavian University Press, 1993. Scholarly contribution, in English.

———. "Strategies for the International Protection of Human Rights in the 1990s," *Human Rights Quarterly* 13, no. 2 (May 1991): 155–169. Scholarly article, in English.

Rivlin, Benjamin, and Leon Gordenker, eds. *The Challenging Role of the UN Secretary-General: Making the "Most Impossible Job in the World" Possible*. Westport, CT, USA: Praeger, 1993. Scholarly monograph, in English.

Roht-Arriaza, Naomi. "State Responsibility to Investigate and Prosecute Grave Human Rights Violations in International Law," *California Law Review* 78, no. 2 (March 1990): 449–513. Scholarly article, in English.

Rosas, Allan, Jan Helgesen, and Donna Gomien, eds. *Human Rights in a Changing East-West Perspective*. London: Pinter Publishers, 1991. Scholarly collective works, in English.

Schmidt, Markus G. "Achieving Much With Little: The Work of the United Nations Centre for Human Rights," *Netherlands Quarterly of Human Rights* 8, no. 4 (1990): 371–380. Scholarly article, in English.

Skogly, Sigrun I. "Human Rights Reporting: The 'Nordic' Experience," *Human Rights Quarterly* 12, no. 4 (Nov. 1990): 513–528. Scholarly article, in English.

United Nations, Center for Human Rights. *The International Bill of Human Rights*. Fact sheet, no. 2. New York: n.d. Booklet, in official UN languages.

———. *United Nations Training Course on International Norms and Standards in the Field of Human Rights: Proceedings, Moscow (USSR), 27 November–1 December 1989*. Geneva, Switzerland: 1990. IGO document, in English and French.

United Nations, Center for Human Rights and UN Institute for Training and Research. *Manual on Human Rights Reporting under Six Major International Human Rights Instru-*

*ments.* New York and Geneva, Switzerland: 1991. IGO guidelines, in English; bibliography, pp. 195–202.

United Nations, Secretariat. *Compilation of General Comments and General Recommendations Adopted by Human Rights Treaty Bodies.* New York and Geneva, Switzerland: 1992. IGO document, in English and French.

***B. Universal and Regional Human Rights Commissions.*** African Commission on Human and Peoples' Rights. "Second Activity Report of the African Commission on Human and Peoples' Rights adopted on 14 June 1989" and "Third Activity Report of the African Commission on Human and Peoples' Rights, adopted on 28 April 1990," *Human Rights Law Journal* 11, no. 3–4 (1990): 390–429, 432–440. Report, in English.

Brody, Reed, Penny Parker, and David Weissbrodt. "Major Developments in 1990 at the UN Commission on Human Rights," *Human Rights Quarterly* 12, no. 4 (Nov. 1990): 559–588. Scholarly article, in English.

Craven, Matthew, and Caroline Dommen. "Making Room for Substance: Fifth Session of the Committee on Economic, Social and Cultural Rights," *Netherlands Quarterly of Human Rights* 9, no. 1 (1991): 83–95. Report, in English.

Davidse, Koen M. "The 48th Session of the UN Commission on Human Rights and UN Monitoring of Violations of Civil and Political Rights," *Netherlands Quarterly of Human Rights* 10, no. 3 (1992): 283–302. Article, in English.

Leckie, Scott. "An Overview and Appraisal of the Fifth Session of the UN Committee on Economic, Social and Cultural Rights," *Human Rights Quarterly* 13, no. 4 (Nov. 1991): 545–572. Scholarly article, in English.

Medina, Cecilia. "The Inter-American Commission on Human Rights and the Inter-American Court of Human Rights: Reflections on a Joint Venture," *Human Rights Quarterly* 12, no. 4 (Nov. 1990): 439–464. Scholarly article, in English.

Mower, A. Glenn, Jr. *Regional Human Rights: A Comparative Study of the West European and Inter-American Systems.* Westport, CT, USA: Greenwood Press, 1991. Scholarly monograph, in English; bibliography, pp. 171–174.

Omozurike, U. O. "The African Commission on Human and Peoples' Rights: An Introduction," *Review of the African Commission on Human and Peoples' Rights* 1 (Oct. 1991): 5–15. Scholarly article, in English.

Parker, Penny, and David Weissbrodt. "Major Developments at the UN Commission on Human Rights in 1991," *Human Rights Quarterly* 13, no. 4 (Nov. 1991): 573–613. Scholarly article, in English.

Theodoropoulos, Christos, ed. *Human Right in Europe and in Africa: A Comparative Analysis.* Athens, Greece: Hellenic University Press, 1992. Scholarly monograph, in English and Greek.

Welch, Claude E. "The African Commission on Human and Peoples' Rights: A Five-Year Report and Assessment," *Human Rights Quarterly* 14, no. 1 (Feb. 1992): 43–61. Report, in English.

Zoller, Adrien-Claude. "46th Session of the United Nations Commission on Human Rights (Geneva, 29 January–9 March 1990)," *Netherlands Quarterly of Human Rights* 8, no. 2 (1990): 140–175. Report, in English.

———. "Reform, Independence and Expertise: Analysis of the 42nd Session of the United Nations Sub-Commission," *Human Rights Monitor* no. 10–11 (Nov. 1990): 3–15. Report, in English.

———. "Consolidation of the Sub-Commission: Analytical Report of the 43rd Session of the Sub-Commission," *Human Rights Monitor* no. 14 (Oct. 1991): 3–17. Article, in English.

***C. National and Local Human Rights Commissions.*** Amankwah, H. A., and K. I. Omar. "Buttressing Constitutional Protection of Fundamental Rights in Developing Nations: The Ombudsman Commission of Papua New Guinea—A New Hybrid," *Melanesian Law Journal* 18 (1990): 74–99. Scholarly article, in English.

Baehr, Peter R. "Human Rights: A Common Standard of Achievement?," *Netherlands Quarterly of Human Rights* 9, no. 1 (1991): 5–18. Scholarly article, in English.

Carver, Richard, and Paul Hunt. *National Human Rights Institutions in Africa.* Banjul, Gambia: African Centre for Democracy and Human Rights Studies, 1991. NGO research report, in English.

Comisión Nacional de Derechos Humanos (National Commission on Human Rights [Mexico]). *First Biannual Report: June-December 1990.* Mexico City, Mexico: 1990. Government annual report, in English and Spanish.

Commonwealth Human Rights Initiative. *Put Our World to Rights: Towards a Commonwealth Human Rights Policy. A Report by a Non-Governmental Advisory Group Chaired by the Hon. Flora MacDonald.* London: 1991. NGO report, in English.

Commonwealth Secretariat, Human Rights Unit. *National Human Rights Institutions in the Commonwealth: Directory—Survey and Analysis.* London: 1992. Directory, in English.

Menon, Madhava. "Some Thoughts on the National Commission on Human Rights: A Discussion Note," *Law and Society Trust Forthnightly Review* 3, no. 54 (1 March 1993): 4–8. Article, in English.

***D. Human Rights Defenders.*** Beigbeder, Yves. *The Role and Status of International Humanitarian Volunteers Organizations: The Right and Duty to Humanitarian Assistance.* Dordrecht, the Netherlands: Martinus Nijhoff, 1991. Scholarly monograph, in English; bibliography, pp. 395–400.

Burgers, Jan Herman. "The Road to San Francisco: The Revival of the Human Rights Idea in the Twentieth Century," *Human Rights Quarterly* 14, no. 4 (Nov. 1992): 447–477. Scholarly article, in English.

Harries-Jones, Peter, ed. *Making Knowledge Count: Advocacy and Social Science.* Montreal, Canada and London, UK: McGill-Queen's University Press, 1991. Scholarly conference papers, in English; bibliography.

Human Rights Watch. *The Persecution of Human Rights Monitors: December 1989 to December 1990–A Worldwide Survey.* New York: 1990. Annual report, in English.

Wiseberg, Laurie S. *Defending Human Rights Defenders: The Importance of Freedom of Association for Human Rights NGOs.* Montreal, Canada: International Centre for Human Rights and Democratic Development, 1993. (Essays on Human Rights and Democratic Development 3). Scholarly monograph, in English and French.

———. "Protecting Human Rights Activists and NGOs: What More Can Be Done?" *Human Rights Quarterly* 13, no. 4 (Nov. 1991): 525–544. Scholarly article, in English.

***E. Human Rights Promotion.*** Ekins, Paul. *A New World Order: Grassroots Movements for Global Change.* London and New York: Routledge, 1992. Monograph, in English; bibliography, pp. 224–234.

Feyter, Koen de. "The Red Cross and Raising Human Rights Awareness in Europe," *Netherlands Quarterly of Human Rights* 9, no. 1 (1991): 36–49. Scholarly article, in English.

Gomien, Donna, ed. *Broadening the Frontiers of Human Rights: Essays in Honour of Asbjørn Eide.* New York: Scandinavian University Press, 1993. Scholarly monograph, in English.

Martin, Ian. "Promotion of Human Rights," *Law and Society Trust Fortnightly Review* 3, no. 53 (16 February 1993): 1–9. Conference paper, in English.

**F. Human Rights Teaching.** Barbier, Mireille. *Système de référence pour l'évaluation pédagogique de matériel audiovisuel existant en matière d'éducation aux droits de l'homme: rapport à la Direction des droits de l'homme du Conseil de l'Europe [. . .]* (A System of References for Pedagogical Evaluation of Audio-Visual Material in the Area of Human Rights Education: Report to the Human Rights Directorate of the Council of Europe [. . .]). Geneva, Switzerland: Centre international de formation à l'enseignement des droits de l'homme et de la paix, 1990. NGO report, in French.

Bassiouni, M. Cherif. "The Arab Human Rights Program of the International Institute of Higher Studies in Criminal Sciences, Siracusa, Italy," *Human Rights Quarterly* 12, no. 3 (Aug. 1990): 365–396. Scholarly article, in English.

Burns, Cynthia, Anne Campbell, and Yos Hut Khemacaro. *A Human Rights Teaching Curriculum for Cambodians.* Aranyaprathet, Thailand: UNBRO, 1991. Educational material, in English.

Caloz-Tschopp, Marie Claire, ed. "Droits de l'homme: actualité et enseignement" (Human Rights: New Developments and Education), *Equinoxe—Revue romande de sciences humaines* 4 (Fall 1990): 1–191. Special issue, in French.

Centre international de formation à l'enseignement des droits de l'homme et de la paix (International Centre for Teaching Human Rights and Peace). *Recueil des Documents de la 2e session africaine de formation à l'enseignement des droits de l'homme pour les professeurs des écoles secondaires d'Afrique francophone* (Collection of Documents from the Second African Training Session on Teaching Human Rights for High School Teachers in Francophone Africa). Geneva, Switzerland: 1991. NGO Conference papers, in French.

Claude, Richard Pierre. *Human Rights Education in the Philippines.* Quezon City, Philippines: 1991. Research paper, in English.

Dias, Clarence J., ed. *Initiating Human Rights Education at the Grassroots: Asian Experiences.* Bangkok, Thailand: Asian Cultural Forum on Development, 1991. Educational material, in English.

Magendzo, Abraham, ed. *¿Superando la Racionalidad Instrumental? Ensayos en busca de un nuevo paradigma para la educación y la discusión de los Derechos Humanos* (Transcending Instrumental Rationality? In Search of a New Paradigm for Human Rights Education and Discussion). Santiago, Chile: Programa Interdisciplinario de Investigaciones en Educación, 1991. Scholarly monograph, in Spanish.

Parsons, William, and Samuel Totten, eds. "Teaching about Genocide," *Social Education* 55, no. 2 (Feb. 1991): 84–133. Special issue, in English.

Seck, Moustapha. "A Plea for Human Rights Education in Africa," *Human Rights Law Journal* 11, no. 3–4 (1990): 283–299. Scholarly article, in English.

Starkey, Hugh, ed. *The Challenge of Human Rights Education.* London: Cassell and Council of Europe, 1991. Scholarly collection of articles, in English; references at the end of each article.

*The Teaching of Human Rights.* Geneva, Switzerland: UN Center for Human Rights, 1989. Report of an international seminar held at the United Nations Office at Geneva, Switzerland, from 5 to 9 December 1988 as part of the observance of the 40th anniversary of the proclamation of the Universal Declaration of Human Rights. UN publication HR/PUB/89/3.

Ty, Reynaldo R., ed. *Truth and Freedom: Understanding and Teaching Human Rights.* Manila, Philippines: Task Force Detainees of the Philippines, 1990. Educational material, in English.

**HUMAN RIGHTS ADVOCATES.** An international non-governmental organization in consultative status (Category II) with the UN **ECONOMIC AND SOCIAL COUNCIL,** HRA has submitted briefs to and participated in the work of the UN **COMMISSION ON HUMAN RIGHTS,** its **SUB-COMMISSION ON PREVENTION OF DISCRIMINATION AND PROTECTION OF MINORITIES,** and the **ORGANIZATION OF AMERICAN STATES.** The organization has members in 15 countries.

Founded in 1978, HRA is composed mainly of lawyers and human rights specialists who perform legal services (free of charge) to protect the rights of such persons as migrant workers, the mentally retarded, and the destitute. It also works closely with freedom fighters and liberation movements and provides technical assistance in the preparation of constitutions, bills of rights, and human rights legislation.

HRA publishes *Human Rights Advocates Newsletter* triannually and has published numerous articles on human rights laws and their application.

Human Rights Advocates. Address: 2918 Florence Street, Berkeley, CA 94705, USA. Telephone: (415) 841-2928. Executive Director: Rita Maran.

**HUMAN RIGHTS COMMITTEE, UN.** The Committee was established in accordance with article 28 of the **INTERNATIONAL COVENANT ON CIVIL AND POLITICAL RIGHTS,** adopted by the UN **GENERAL ASSEMBLY** on 16 December 1966 (resolution 2200 A [XXI]). The Covenant entered into force on 23 March 1976. Each State party to the Covenant undertakes to respect and ensure to all individuals within its territory and subject to its jurisdiction the rights recognized therein, to adopt such legislative and other measures as may be necessary to give effect to those rights, to ensure that any person whose rights are violated shall have an effective remedy, to ensure that any person claiming such a remedy shall have his right thereto determined by competent authorities, and to ensure that those authorities enforce such remedies when granted. In addition, each State party undertakes to ensure the equal right of men and women to the enjoyment of all the rights set forth in the Covenant. The responsibilities of the Committee, set out in articles 40 to 45 of the Covenant, are summarized in the following paragraphs.

***CONSIDERATION OF REPORTS OF STATES PARTIES.***
Under article 40, para. 1, States parties to the Covenant undertake to submit to the Secretary-General for consideration by the Committee reports on the measures they have adopted which give effect to the rights recognized therein and on the progress made in the enjoyment of those rights. The Committee is empowered to study the reports and to transmit them, and such general comments as it may consider appropriate, to the States parties and to the Economic and Social Council.

The consideration of reports submitted under article 40 of the Covenant takes place in public meetings and in the presence of representatives of the State party concerned. The purpose of such meetings is to establish a constructive dialogue between the Committee and the State party. The main function of the Committee is to assist State parties in fulfilling their obligations under the Covenant, to make available to them the experience the Committee has acquired in its examination of other reports, and to discuss with them various issues relating to the enjoyment of the rights enshrined in the Covenant. In fulfilling this function, members of the Committee pose questions to the representatives of the State party in order to obtain information or clarification on any factual or legal matter or factor that may affect the implementation of the Covenant. In dealing with periodic reports, the Committee identifies in advance the various matters which might most usefully be discussed with the representatives of the State party.

***GENERAL COMMENTS.*** The practice of preparing general comments on selected articles of the Covenant was initiated by the Committee in 1981, after it had acquired considerable experience in examining State reports. General comments draw attention to certain aspects of the Covenant but do not purport to be restrictive or to attribute any priority among the different aspects in terms of implementation. They are intended to make the Committee's experience available for the benefit of all States parties, so as to promote more effective implementation of the Covenant; to draw their attention to insufficiencies disclosed by a large number of reports; to suggest improvements in the reporting procedure; and to stimulate the activities of States parties and international organizations in the promotion and protection of human rights. General comments are also intended to be of interest to other States, especially those preparing to become parties to the Covenant, and generally to strengthen cooperation among States in the universal promotion and protection of human rights.

***CONCLUDING OBSERVATIONS ON STATES PARTIES' REPORTS.*** Since its forty-fourth session (March/April 1992), the Committee has been adopting comments reflecting the views of the Committee as a whole on each State party report considered during a given session. Such comments are additional to, and do not replace, comments made by individual members at the conclusion of the consideration of a report. A Rapporteur is selected in each case to draft a text, in consultation with the Chairman and other members, for adoption by the Committee in closed meeting. Such comments are dispatched to the State party concerned as soon as practicable, published in a separate document and included in the annual report of the Committee, together with the concluding observations by individual members. Comments drafted during a given session are normally adopted by the Committee on the penultimate day of the session.

The comments of the Committee provide a general evaluation of a State party's report and of the dialogue with the delegation and make note of positive developments that may have occurred during the period under review of factors and difficulties affecting the implementation of the Covenant, and of specific issues of concern relating to the application of the provisions of the Covenant. They also include suggestions and recommendations to the State party concerned.

***THE COMMITTEE'S PROCEDURES IN DEALING WITH EMERGENCY SITUATIONS.*** In 1991 and 1992, in the light of events indicating that the enjoyment of human rights protected under the Covenant had been seriously affected in certain States parties, the Committee has resorted to the practice of requesting the States parties concerned to submit reports on the situation urgently, generally within three months. Such decisions have been taken regarding, in chronological order, Iraq (11 April 1991), the Federal Republic of Yugoslavia (4 November 1991), Peru (10 April 1992), Bosnia and Herzegovina, Croatia and the Federal Republic of Yugoslavia (Serbia and Montenegro) (6 October 1992). In all cases, the States concerned complied with the Committee's request and participated in the consideration of the report. Additionally, the Committee has agreed that, if an exceptional situation arises in the interim between sessions, the Chairman, acting in consultation with the members of the Committee, may direct a request for the submission of a report under article 40, paragraph 1 (b), of the Covenant by the State party concerned. The Committee has also given its support to the Secretary-General's proposal that ways should be explored of empowering human rights bodies to bring massive human rights violations to the attention of the Security Council.

The Committee is also considering, in cases where

it had been unable to obtain required information and as a follow-up to recommendations included in earlier concluding comments, to request the State party concerned to agree to receive a mission, consisting of one or two members of the Committee, with a view to collecting information the Committee needs to carry out its functions under the Covenant. Such a decision would only be taken after the Committee had satisfied itself that no adequate alternative approach was available and that such an approach was warranted by information in the Committee's possession.

At its 47th (March/April 1993) session, the Committee discussed in detail the possibility of modifying its methods of work under article 40 of the Covenant. Various suggestions were made to adapt the Committee's procedures in dealing with emergency situations. The possibility of making known the Committee's views on matters within its competence, as well as its comments on States parties' reports, particularly on reports submitted pursuant to special decisions taken by the Committee, to the appropriate United Nations bodies, including the Security Council, was envisaged. It was also considered that, when it had not been able to ascertain whether its recommendations included in its concluding observations had been acted upon, the Committee might request the State party concerned to accept a mission, consisting of one or two members of the Committee, with a view to learning the responses of the State concerned to the specific proposals for the better enjoyment of human rights. The working group that was to meet prior to the forty-eighth session was requested to study the matter further.

In order to react more efficiently to exceptional situations arising when the Committee was not in session, on 8 April 1993 (1233rd meeting) the Committee amended its rules of procedure to the effect that, in such circumstances, a request for the submission of a report might be made through the Chairperson, acting in consultation with the members of the Committee.

### CONSIDERATION OF COMPLAINTS OF STATES PARTIES AGAINST OTHER STATES PARTIES.

Under article 41, a State party to the Covenant may declare that it recognizes the competence of the Committee to receive and consider communications to the effect that another State party is not fulfilling its obligations under the Covenant. With respect to such complaints, the Committee is authorized (1) to deal with the matter when referred to it by either State after it has ascertained that all domestic remedies have been invoked and exhausted; (2) if the matter is not thus resolved to the satisfaction of the States parties concerned, to appoint an ad hoc conciliation commission which shall make its good offices available to those States with a view to an amicable solution of the matter; (3) to com-

municate the report of the ad hoc commission to the States parties concerned so that they may indicate whether or not they accept its contents; and (4) to report on the matter to the General Assembly.

### CONSIDERATION OF COMMUNICATIONS FROM INDIVIDUALS.

Under articles 1 to 3 of the Optional Protocol to the International Covenant on Civil and Political Rights, and subject to the conditions set out there, the Committee may receive and consider communications from individuals who claim that any of their rights enumerated in the Covenant have been violated and who indicate that they have exhausted all available domestic remedies. With respect to such complaints, the Committee is authorized (1) to consider their admissibility, screening out communications which are anonymous or which it considers to be an abuse of the right of submission or to be incompatible with the provisions of the Covenant; (2) to bring them to the attention of the State party alleged to be violating any provision of the Covenant; (3) to consider them in the light of all written information made available to it by the individual and by the State party concerned; (4) to forward its views to the State party concerned and to the individual; and (5) to report on these activities to the General Assembly through the Economic and Social Council.

Under article 3 of the second optional protocol, aiming at the abolition of the death penalty, States parties to that protocol are to include in the reports they submit to the Human Rights Committee information on the measures they have adopted to give effect to the second optional protocol. Under article 4, which applies with respect to States parties to the Covenant that have made a declaration under article 41, the competence of the Human Rights Committee to receive and consider communications when a State party claims that another State party is not fulfilling its obligations shall extend to the provisions of the protocol, unless the State party concerned has made a statement to the contrary at the moment of ratification or accession.

### METHODS OF WORK.

The Committee normally holds three sessions each year, of from two to three weeks' duration. Most of the sessions are held at the United Nations office in Geneva, but occasionally one is held at the headquarters of the United Nations in New York. The Committee submits an annual report to the General Assembly through the Economic and Social Council, covering its activities under the Covenant and its optional protocol.

The Committee's practice has been to establish two working groups, which meet prior to each of its sessions. The first makes recommendations regarding communications received under the optional protocol; the second makes suggestions concerning the committee's work program and prepares draft texts for consideration by the Committee.

In addition, since 1991 the Committee has designated one of its Members as Special Rapporteur on New Communications in order to expedite the processing of those communications and lighten the burden of the Committee. The terms of reference of the Special Rapporteur, adopted at the 1087th meeting of the Committee on 24 July 1991, are as follows:

(a) To examine all new communications received by the Committee and to take whatever action is necessary pursuant to rule 91 of the Committee's rules of procedure;

(b) To issue rule 86 requests, whether coupled with a request under rule 91 or not;

(c) To inform the Committee at each session on action taken under rules 86 and 91;

(d) To draft recommendations for the Committee's consideration to declare communications inadmissible under articles 1, 2, 3 and 5 of the Optional Protocol. In particular, the Special Rapporteur may recommend inadmissibility *ratione materiae, personae* or *temporis,* notably, but not exclusively, on grounds of an author's lack of standing to submit a communication, insufficient substantiation of allegations, abuse of the right of submission, incompatibility with the provisions of the Covenant, lack of competence by the Committee under the Optional Protocol, non-exhaustion of domestic remedies, preclusion because of a State party's reservation or simultaneous examination under another procedure of international investigation or settlement.

***RULES RELATING TO THE FUNCTIONS OF THE COMMITTEE.*** The Committee adopted provisional rules of procedure at its first and second sessions, and subsequently amended them as necessary. The rules relating to the functions of the Committee, as amended at its third, seventh, thirty-sixth, forty-seventh, forty-ninth and fiftieth sessions, are as follows:

### XV. Reports from States Parties under Article 40 of the Covenant

*Rule 66.* 1. The States parties to the Covenant shall submit reports on the measures they have adopted which give effect to the rights recognized in the Covenant and on the progress made in the enjoyment of those rights. Reports shall indicate the factors and difficulties, if any, affecting the implementation of the Covenant.

2. Requests for submission of a report under article 40, paragraph 1 (b), of the Covenant may be made in accordance with the periodicity decided by the Committee or at any other time the Committee may deem appropriate. In the case of an exceptional situation when the Committee is not in session, a request may be made through the Chairman, acting in consultation with the members of the Committee.

3. Whenever the Committee requests States parties to submit reports under article 40, paragraph 1 (b), of the Covenant, it shall determine the dates by which such reports shall be submitted.

4. The Committee may, through the Secretary-General, inform the States parties of its wishes regarding the form and content of the reports to be submitted under article 40 of the Covenant.

*Rule 67.* 1. The Secretary-General may, after consultation with the Committee, transmit to the specialized agencies concerned copies of such parts of the reports from States members of those agencies as may fall within their field of competence.

2. The Committee may invite the specialized agencies to which the Secretary-General has transmitted parts of the reports to submit comments on those parts within such time-limits as it may specify.

*Rule 68.* The Committee shall, through the Secretary-General, notify the States parties as early as possible of the opening date, duration and place of the session at which their respective reports will be examined. Representatives of the States parties may be present at the meetings of the Committee when their reports are examined. The Committee may also inform a State party from which it decides to seek further information that it may authorize its representative to be present at a specified meeting. Such a representative should be able to answer questions which may be put to him by the Committee and make statements on reports already submitted by his State, and may also submit additional information from his State.

*Rule 69.* 1. At each session the Secretary-General shall notify the Committee of all cases of non-submission of reports or additional information requested under rules 66 and 70 of these rules. In such cases the Committee may transmit to the State party concerned, through the Secretary-General, a reminder concerning the submission of the report or additional information.

2. If, after the reminder referred to in paragraph 1 of this rule, the State party does not submit the report or additional information required under rules 66 and 70 of these rules, the Committee shall so state in the annual report which it submits to the General Assembly of the United Nations through the Economic and Social Council.

*Rule 70.* 1. When considering a report submitted by a State party under article 40 of the Covenant, the Committee shall first satisfy itself that the report provides all the information required under rule 66 of these rules.

2. If a report of a State party to the Covenant, in the opinion of the Committee, does not contain sufficient information, the Committee may request that State to furnish the additional information which is required, indicating by what date the said information should be submitted.

3. On the basis of its examination of the reports and information supplied by a State party, the Committee in accordance with article 40, paragraph 4, of the Covenant, make such comments as it may consider appropriate.

*Rule 71.* 1. The Committee shall, through the Secretary-General, communicate to the States parties for their observations the general comments it has made under article 40, paragraph 4, of the Covenant on the basis of its examination of the reports and information furnished by States parties. The Committee may, where necessary, indicate a time-limit for the receipt of observations from States parties.

2. The Committee may also transmit to the Economic and

Social Council the comments referred to in paragraph 1 of this rule, together with copies of the reports it has received from the States parties to the Covenant and the observations, if any, submitted by them.

## XVI. Procedure for the Consideration of Communications Received under Article 41 of the Covenant

*Rule 72.* 1. A communication under article 41 of the Covenant may be referred to the Committee by either State party concerned by notice given in accordance with paragraph 1 (b) of that article.

2. The notice referred to in paragraph 1 of this rule shall contain or be accompanied by information regarding:

(a) Steps taken to seek adjustment of the matter in accordance with article 41, paragraphs 1 (a) and (b), of the Covenant, including the text of the initial communication and of any subsequent written explanations or statements by the States parties concerned which are pertinent to the matter;

(b) steps taken to exhaust domestic remedies;

(c) Any other procedure of international investigation or settlement resorted to by the States parties concerned.

*Rule 73.* The Secretary-General shall maintain a permanent register of all communications received by the Committee under article 41 of the Covenant.

*Rule 74.* The Secretary-General shall inform the members of the Committee without delay of any notice given under rule 72 of these rules and shall transmit to them as soon as possible copies of the notice and relevant information.

*Rule 75.* The Committee shall examine communications under article 41 of the Covenant at closed meetings.

2. The Committee may, after consultation with the States parties concerned, issue communiques, through the Secretary-General, for the use of the information media and the general public regarding the activities of the Committee at its closed meetings.

*Rule 76.* A communication shall not be considered by the Committee unless:

(a) Both States parties concerned have made declarations under article 41, paragraph 1, of the Covenant which are applicable to the communication;

(b) The time-limit prescribed in article 41, paragraph 1 (b), of the Covenant has expired;

(c) The Committee has ascertained that all available domestic remedies have been invoked and exhausted in the matter in conformity with the generally recognized principles of international law, or that the application of the remedies is unreasonably prolonged.

*Rule 77A.* Subject to the provisions of rule 76 of these rules, the Committee shall proceed to make its good offices available to the States parties concerned with a view to a friendly solution of the matter on the basis of respect for human rights and fundamental freedoms as recognized in the Covenant.

*Rule 77B.* The Committee may, through the Secretary-General, request the States parties concerned or either of them to submit additional information or observations orally or in writing. The Committee shall indicate a time-limit for the submission of such written information or observations.

*Rule 77C.* 1. The States parties concerned shall have the right to be represented when the matter is being considered in the Committee and to make submissions orally and/or in writing.

2. The Committee shall, through the Secretary-General, notify the States parties concerned as early as possible of the

opening date, duration and place of the session at which the matter will be examined.

3. The procedure for making oral and/or written submissions shall be decided by the Committee, after consultation with the States parties concerned.

*Rule 77D.* 1. Within 12 months after the date on which the Committee received the notice referred to in rule 72 of these rules, the Committee shall adopt a report in accordance with article 41, paragraph 1 (h), of the Covenant.

2. The provisions of paragraph 1 of rule 77C of these rules shall not apply to the deliberations of the Committee concerning the adoption of the report.

3. The Committee's report shall be communicated, through the Secretary-General, to the States parties concerned.

*Rule 77E.* If a matter referred to the Committee in accordance with article 41 of the Covenant is not resolved to the satisfaction of the States parties concerned, the Committee may, with their prior consent, proceed to apply the procedure prescribed in article 42 of the Covenant.

## XVII. Procedure for the Consideration of Communications Received under the Optional Protocol

### A. Transmission of Communications to the Committee

*Rule 78.* 1. The Secretary-General shall bring to the attention of the Committee, in accordance with the present rules, communications which are or appear to be submitted for consideration by the Committee under article 1 of the Protocol.

2. The Secretary-General, when necessary, may request clarification from the author of a communication as to his wish to have his communication submitted to the Committee for consideration under the Protocol. In case there is still doubt as to the wish of the author, the Committee shall be seized of the communication.

3. No communication shall be received by the Committee or included in a list under rule 79 if it concerns a State which is not a party to the Protocol.

*Rule 79.* 1. The Secretary-General shall prepare lists of the communications submitted to the Committee in accordance with rule 78 above, with a brief summary of their contents, and shall circulate such lists to the members of the Committee at regular intervals. The Secretary-General shall also maintain a permanent register of all such communications.

2. The full text of any communication brought to the attention of the Committee shall be made available to any member of the Committee upon his request.

*Rule 80.* 1. The Secretary-General may request clarification from the author of a communication concerning the applicability of the Protocol to his communication, in particular regarding:

(a) The name, address, age and occupation of the author and the verification of his identity;

(b) The name of the State party against which the communication is directed;

(c) The object of the communication;

(d) The provision or provisions of the Covenant alleged to have been violated;

(e) The facts of the claim;

(f) Steps taken by the author to exhaust domestic remedies;

(g) The extent to which the same matter is being examined under another procedure of international investigation or settlement.

2. When requesting clarification or information, the Secretary-General shall indicate an appropriate time-limit to the author of the communication with a view to avoiding undue delays in the procedure under the Protocol.

3. The Committee may approve a questionnaire for the purpose of requesting the above-mentioned information from the author of the communication.

4. The request for clarification referred to in paragraph 1 of the present rule shall not preclude the inclusion of the communication in the list provided for in rule 79, paragraph 1, of these rules.

*Rule 81.* For each registered communication the Secretary-General shall as soon as possible prepare and circulate to the members of the Committee a summary of the relevant information obtained.

## B. General Provisions Regarding the Consideration of Communications by the Committee or Its Subsidiary Bodies

*Rule 82.* Meetings of the Committee or its subsidiary bodies during which communications under the Protocol will be examined shall be closed. Meetings during which the Committee may consider general issues such as procedures for the application of the Protocol may be public if the Committee so decides.

*Rule 83.* The Committee may issue communiques, through the Secretary-General, for the use of the information media and the general public regarding the activities of the Committee at its closed meetings.

*Rule 84.* 1. A member shall not take part in the examination of a communication by the Committee:

(a) If he has any personal interest in the case; or

(b) If he has participated in any capacity in the making of any decision on the case covered by the communication.

2. Any question which may arise under paragraph 1 above shall be decided by the Committee.

*Rule 85.* If, for any reason, a member considers that he should not take part or continue to take part in the examination of a communication, he shall inform the Chairman of his withdrawal.

*Rule 86.* The Committee may, prior to forwarding its views on the communication to the State party concerned, inform that State of its views as to whether interim measures may be desirable to avoid irreparable damage to the victim of the alleged violation. In doing so, the Committee shall inform the State party concerned that such expression of its views on interim measures does not imply a determination on the merits of the communication.

### C. Procedure to Determine Admissibility

*Rule 87.* 1. The Committee shall decide as soon as possible and in accordance with the following rules whether the communication is admissible or is inadmissible under the Protocol.

2. A working group established under rule 89, paragraph 1, may also declare a communication admissible when it is composed of five members and all the members so decide.

*Rule 88.* 1. Communications shall be dealt with in the order in which they are received by the Secretariat, unless the Committee or a working group established under rule 89, paragraph 1, decides otherwise.

2. Two or more communications may be dealt with jointly if deemed appropriate by the Committee or a working group established under rule 89, paragraph 1.

*Rule 89.* 1. The Committee may establish one or more working groups of no more than five of its members to make recommendations to the Committee regarding the fulfilment of the conditions of admissibility laid down in articles 1, 2, 3 and 5 (2) of the Protocol.

2. The rules of procedure of the Committee shall apply as far as possible to the meetings of the working group.

3. The Committee may designate special rapporteurs from among its members to assist in the handling of communications.

*Rule 90.* With a view to reaching a decision on the admissibility of a communication, the Committee, or a working group established under rule 89, paragraph 1, shall ascertain:

(a) That the communication is not anonymous and that it emanates from an individual, or individuals, subject to the jurisdiction of a State party to the Protocol;

(b) That the individual claims, in a manner sufficiently substantiated, to be a victim of a violation by that State party of any of the rights set forth in the Covenant. Normally, the communication should be submitted by the individual himself or by his representative; a communication submitted on behalf of an alleged victim may, however, be accepted when it appears that he is unable to submit the communication himself;

(c) That the communication is not an abuse of the right to submit a communication under the Protocol;

(d) That the communication is not incompatible with the provisions of the Covenant;

(e) That the same matter is not being examined under another procedure of international investigation or settlement;

(f) That the individual has exhausted all available domestic remedies.

*Rule 91.* 1. The Committee or a working group established under rule 89, paragraph 1, or a special rapporteur designated under rule 89, paragraph 3, may request the State party concerned or the author of the communication to submit additional written information or observations relevant to the question of the admissibility of the communication. To avoid undue delays, a time-limit for the submission of such information or observations shall be indicated.

2. A communication may not be declared admissible unless the State party concerned has received the text of the communication and has been given an opportunity to furnish information or observations as provided in paragraph 1 of this rule.

3. A request addressed to a State party under paragraph 1 of this rule shall include a statement of the fact that such a request does not imply that any decision has been reached on the question of admissibility.

4. Within fixed time-limits, each party may be afforded an opportunity to comment on submissions made by the other party pursuant to this rule.

*Rule 92.* 1. Where the Committee decides that a communication is inadmissible under the Protocol it shall as soon as possible communicate its decision, through the Secretary-General, to the author of the communication and, where the communication has been transmitted to a State party concerned, to that State party.

2. If the Committee has declared a communication inadmissible under article 5, paragraph 2, of the Protocol, this decision may be reviewed at a later date by the Committee upon a written request by or on behalf of the individual concerned containing information to the effect that the reasons

for inadmissibility referred to in article 5, paragraph 2, no longer apply.

3. Any member of the Committee may request that a summary of his individual opinion shall be appended to the Committee's decision declaring a communication inadmissible under the Protocol.

### D. Procedure for the Consideration of Communications on Merit

*Rule 93.* 1. As soon as possible after the Committee or a working group acting under rule 87, paragraph 2, has taken a decision that a communication is admissible under the Protocol, that decision and the text of the relevant documents shall be submitted, through the Secretary-General, to the State party concerned. The author of the communication shall also be informed, through the Secretary-General, of the decision.

2. Within six months, the State party concerned shall submit to the Committee written explanations or statements clarifying the matter under consideration and the remedy, if any, that may have been taken by that State.

3. Any explanations or statements submitted by a State party pursuant to this rule shall be communicated, through the Secretary-General, to the author of the communication, who may submit any additional written information or observations within fixed time-limits.

4. Upon consideration of the merits, the Committee may review a decision that a communication is admissible in the light of any explanations or statements submitted by the State party pursuant to this rule.

*Rule 94.* 1. If the communication is admissible, the Committee shall consider it in the light of all written information made available to it by the individuals and by the State party concerned and shall formulate its views thereon. For this purpose the Committee may refer the communication to a working group of not more than five of its members or to a special rapporteur to make recommendations to the Committee.

2. The views of the Committee shall be communicated to the individual and to the State party concerned.

3. Any member of the Committee may request that a summary of his individual opinion shall be appended to the views of the Committee.

### E. Rules Concerning Confidentiality

*Rule 95.* 1. All decisions not of a final nature adopted by the Committee in the course of consideration of a communication under the Protocol are confidential. They are transmitted to the parties solely for information or for the purpose of soliciting information, observations or clarifications in respect of (a) questions of admissibility; (b) the merits of the claims; or (c) any remedial action that may have been taken by the State party. No publicity shall be given by the parties to the content of these decisions, which will remain confidential except to the extent that they may be reflected in later decisions of a final nature.

2. Notwithstanding paragraph 1 above, interim measures requested under rule 86 shall not be subject to the rule of confidentiality.

3. Decisions of a final nature are normally made public by the Committee.

(a) Decisions declaring communications inadmissible under the Protocol will normally become public shortly after they have been forwarded to the parties. As a rule, the identity of the authors will be indicated in the text made public, unless the Committee decides otherwise;

(b) The Committee's views on the merits of the claims become public shortly after they have been forwarded to the parties under article 5, paragraph 4, of the Protocol.

4. The text of a decision made public shall carry an indication to that effect.

*Rule 96.* 1. All submissions made by the parties in respect of communications considered under the Protocol shall remain confidential until a final decision has been forwarded to the parties pursuant to rule 95. The parties are under an obligation to observe and respect this rule of confidentiality and shall refrain from giving publicity to any submissions while a communication is under consideration. Thereafter, both parties are free to release their own submissions.

2. If the identity of the author of a communication declared inadmissible has not been disclosed by the Committee, the State party shall refrain from disclosing his identity.

*Rule 97.* All working documents issued for the Committee by the Secretariat, or placed before a working group established pursuant to rule 89, paragraph 1, or placed before a Special Rapporteur designated pursuant to rule 89, paragraph 3, are confidential and remain confidential after consideration of a communication is concluded, unless the Committee decides otherwise. This includes the Secretariat summaries of communications, prepared pursuant to rule 79, paragraph 1, which may be made available to States parties at the time when they are requested, under rule 91, paragraph 1, to submit information or observations relevant to the question of admissibility of a communication.

*Rule 98.* Information furnished by the parties within the framework of follow-up to the Committee's views is not subject to confidentiality, unless the Committee decides otherwise. Decisions of the Committee relating to follow-up activities are equally not subject to confidentiality, unless the Committee decides otherwise.

**BIBLIOGRAPHY.** Cohen, Roberta. *Human Rights and Humanitarian Emergencies: New Roles for UN Human Rights Bodies.* Washington, D.C.: Center for Policy Analysis and Research on Refugee Issues and Refugee Policy Group, 1992. NGO discussion paper, in English.

United Nations Office of Public Information. *Civil and Political Rights: The Human Rights Committee.* Human Rights Fact Sheet No. 15. New York: 1991. IGO booklet, in official UN languages.

**HUMAN RIGHTS DATABASES.** See **DIANA, HUMAN RIGHTS INTERNET** and **HURIDOCS.**

**HUMAN RIGHTS INFORMATION AND DOCUMENTATION SYSTEM.** See **HURIDOCS.**

**HUMAN RIGHTS IN MEDIA AWARD.** Established in 1986, this annual, honorary award is presented in recognition of exceptional contributions to the cause of human freedom through the media. Past recipients include Ted Koppel (1988), Abe Rosenthal (1991), and David Kaplan and Roy Gutman (1992).

For more information, contact: International League of Human Rights, 432 Park Ave., S., Room 1103, New York, NY, 10016, USA. Telephone: (212) 684-1221. Fax: (212) 684-1690.

**HUMAN RIGHTS INTERNET.** A nonprofit, participatory international communications network founded in 1976 to provide a worldwide clearinghouse on matters related to human rights, Human Rights Internet (HRI) is a nonpartisan and independent organization designed to support, in particular, non-governmental organizations. It has consultative status with the UN ECONOMIC AND SOCIAL COUNCIL and with UNICEF and observer status with the African Commission on Human and Peoples' Rights.

HRI's constituency is a broad one, including NGOs, international and national officials, lawyers, journalists, students, and the general public. Its main objectives are (1) to gather and disseminate information relating to the status of human rights in various parts of the world, the work of human rights organizations, and relevant developments in international law; (2) to promote research and teaching in the human rights field; and (3) to stimulate communication and coordination with the human rights community. HRI's activities include the following.

*DOCUMENTATION.* HRI communicates by telephone, fax, mail, and the information highway with more than 5,000 organizations and individuals worldwide. Its international documentation center offers more than 100,000 documents, the largest such storehouse of this specialized information. Staffed by two librarians, HRI's documentation center provides services to international scholars, activists, asylum lawyers, and other researchers.

*DATABASE/SEARCH SERVICE.* To facilitate the exchange of information, HRI maintains several computerized databases, including (1) HRIO, which provides information on the location, mandate, activities, and publications of more than 5,000 human rights organizations throughout the world; (2) HRIP, with over 10,000 bibliographic abstracts of NGO, IGO, and academic literature published since 1985; and (3) FUND, with information on foundations and other sources interested in human rights.

*DOCUMENTATION ON MICROFICHE.* In cooperation with HRI, IDC distributes documents from selected human rights organizations on microfiche, including newsletters, journals, pamphlets, books, manuscripts, reports, press releases, action alerts, and brochures. The collection lists about 300 organizations and contains material going back to 1980.

*PUBLICATIONS.* HRI maintains an extensive publication program. Among its publications are the following: *The Reporter,* a comprehensive review, with abstracts of thousands of publications received by HRI each year; recent editions have focused on specific themes but still include major relevant documents; *The Human Rights Tribune,* a magazine that analyzes human rights situations worldwide; and the *Masterlist,* a directory that is often referred to as the human rights community's phonebook, listing phone, fax, addresses, and e-mail addresses of more than 4,000 human rights organizations throughout the world. In addition, HRI has produced regional directories on Latin America, Africa, Western Europe, Eastern Europe, and North America. Finally, *The Funding Directory* contains information on foundations and other sources that contribute to human rights causes.

HRI also offers internships in human rights documentation and research.

Human Rights Internet. Address: 8 York Street, Suite 202, Ottawa, Ontario K1N 5S6, Canada. Telephone: (613) 789-7407. Fax: (613) 789-7417. E-mail: hri@hri.ca. Executive Director: Laurie Wiseberg.

**HUMAN RIGHTS LAW JOURNAL.** Established in 1980, this quarterly journal is published in association with the International Institute of Human Rights in Strasbourg, France. It provides up-to-date and systematic reporting and commentary on international, constitutional, and supreme court decisions from European countries. It also reproduces the papers of international or regional symposia and documents of IGOs. Annually, it produces a chart indicating the countries that have ratified or acceded to major international human rights instruments.

*Human Rights Law Journal.* Address: N.P. Engel, Gutenbergstr. 29, B.P. 1940, D-7640 Kehl, Germany; or 3608 S. 12th Street, Arlington, VA 22204, USA.

**HUMAN RIGHTS LITERARY AWARD.** Since 1978, the *Prix Litterarie des Droits de l'Homme* (Human Rights Literary Award) has been sponsored by Nouveaux Droits de l'Homme in recognition of a work of literature that has contributed most to the understanding of human rights issues. The work must be published in French (originally or in translation) during the previous year. Recent winners are Daniel Cohen (1994) for *Les gènes de l'espoir,* Jean-Marie Le Clezio (1993) for *Etoile Errante,* Aung San Suu Kyi (1992) for *Se libèrer de la Peur,* and Ismaïl Kadare (1991) for *Le Palais des Rêves.* In 1990 Ahmadou Kourouma received the award for his book *Monne, Outrages de Defis.*

For more information, contact: Nouveaux Droits de l'Homme, 14 Citè Vaneau, 75007 Paris, France. Telephone: (33-1) 47-53-78-78. Fax: (33-1) 45-56-07-06.

**HUMAN RIGHTS QUARTERLY.** The *Human Rights Quarterly* is an interdisciplinary journal that covers human rights matters encompassed by the Universal Declaration of Human Rights. Published by the Johns Hopkins University Press, the oldest university press in the United States, *HRQ* was established in 1983, and has published over 200 articles since its inception. In addition to individual articles, several numbers are symposium issues focused on a specific topic. The *Quarterly* is edited by staff of the **URBAN MORGAN INSTITUTE FOR HUMAN RIGHTS**; fellows of the Institute participate on the editorial staff.

*Human Rights Quarterly.* Address: The Johns Hopkins University Press, Journals Publishing Division, 701 W. 40th Street, Baltimore, MD 21211, USA.

**HUMAN RIGHTS WATCH.** Established in 1978 with the founding of its Helsinki division (formerly called Helsinki Watch), Human Rights Watch is an independent, non-governmental organization supported by contributions from private individuals and foundations. Its divisions currently cover Africa, the Americas, Asia, the Middle East, and the signatories of the Helsinki Accords. These divisions work jointly with five thematic projects: arms; free expression; prisoners' rights; women's rights; and since 1994, a children's rights project.

With a staff including over 45 country specialists, Human Rights Watch annually sends more than 100 investigative missions to gather current, first-hand human rights information. The missions meet with government officials, opposition leaders, local human rights groups, church officials, labor leaders, journalists, college faculty members, lawyers, relief groups, doctors, and others to gather information on human rights practices. Where possible, the mission interviews victims, members of their families, and witnesses to abuses; the group also attends court proceedings and examines court records. In recent missions, HRW has investigated the widespread devastation caused by land mines, police and death squad murders of adolescents in Brazil, discrimination against Gypsies in Hungary, summary executions by Indian security forces in Kashmir, state-sponsored ethnic violence in Kenya, and the limits on freedom of expression in Iran.

Human Rights Watch conducts an extensive publication program with individual country reports from each of its divisions and the Free Expression and Women's Rights Projects. Each January it also issues *The Human Rights Watch World Report*. Its quarterly newsletter is titled *Human Rights Watch*.

Human Rights Watch. Address: 485 Fifth Avenue, New York, NY 10017, USA. Telephone: (212) 972-8400. Fax: (212) 972-0905. Executive Director: Aryeh Neier.

**HUNGARY.** The Republic of Hungary is a country in the Carpathian Basin in central Europe. It has borders with the Czech Republic and Slovakia on the north, Austria on the west, Ukraine and Romania on the east, and Croatia and Yugoslavia on the south. It achieved independence in 1949 and became a Member of the United Nations in 1955. Its population was recorded at 10, 375,000 in 1990 and was estimated (1993) to be 10,305,000. This population includes 200,000 to 220,000 Germans, 100,000 to 110,000 Slovaks, 80,000 to 100,000 Southern Slavs, 20,000 to 25,000 Romanians, and 500,000 to 700,000 Gypsies. The government has set up a National Office for National and Ethnic Minorities, which operates under a minister without portfolio, to ensure that the rights of these groups are observed. The language in common use is Hungarian; however, the Bulgarians, Poles, Greeks, and Gypsies tend to use their own languages, as do members of the linguistic minorities: Southern Slavs (Croatians, Serbs, and Slovenes), Germans, and Romanians and Slovaks.

The government (1994) took the form of a republic. Under the constitution, the supreme body of State power is the 21-member Presidential Council, elected by the National Assembly and headed by the president. Administrative power is exercised by the Council of Ministers, headed by the prime minister. The 352-member unicameral People's Assembly, whose members are elected by popular vote for terms of four years, is the national legislature. The administration of justice is the responsibility of the procurator-general, who is elected by the National Assembly.

Hungary's transition from a single-party State to a multi-party democracy was a gradual one which followed a sharp decline in the membership of the Communist Party and the emergence of numerous informal groups of dissidents which developed into full-fledged opposition parties.

In mid-March 1986, a group of Hungarian citizens attempted to march through Budapest to mark the anniversary of the 1956 uprising which had been crushed by Soviet tanks; the march was broken up by police using truncheons and tear gas. In mid-March 1987, about 3,000 Hungarians attempted such a march again; this time the march was tolerated by the Communist authorities. In mid-March 1988, more than 10,000 people paraded through the center of Budapest after several members of the growing opposition had been arrested for "subversion" in a series of dawn raids; they chanted "Democracy!" and carried banners that demanded "press freedom," "real reforms," and "freedom of assembly." This time the police did not attempt to block the march.

In September 1989, the government, after months of negotiations, reached agreement with leaders of the opposition calling for the enactment of a more democratic electoral law, the creation of a stronger presidency, the legalization of political parties, and the liberalization of the penal code and rules of criminal procedure.

In October, a three-member body of the Communist Party took office and adopted a social democratic program in the hope of attracting aid from the West; at that time, it changed its name to the Socialist Party. In a referendum held on 26 November—the first free national vote in 42 years—voters rejected the party's plan for election of the president in January 1990, when it would still control Parliament. Instead, a timetable was established for multi-party elections to Parliament to be held on 25 March 1990, with the president to be elected by members of the new Parliament at a later date.

Twelve major political parties participated in the parliamentary elections: the Hungarian Socialist Party, the Hungarian Democratic Reform, the Alliance of Free Democrats, the Independent Smallholders' Party, the Federation of Young Democrats, the Social Democratic Party of Hungary, the Christian Democratic People's Party, the Hungarian People's Party, the Hungarian Socialist Workers Party, the Entrepreneurs Party, the Patriotic Election Coalition, and the Agrarian Federation.

Arpad Goncz, a leading writer who had spent six months in jail after receiving a life sentence for the part he played in the 1956 uprising, was selected as head of Parliament and, thus, interim president of Hungary on 2 May 1990, receiving 339 of the 370 votes cast in the first freely elected Parliament convened in that country in four decades. On the same day, by agreement between the center-right Hungarian Democratic Forum and his own liberal opposition party, the Free Democrats, Mr. Goncz was selected to serve as Hungary's president.

However, in elections in 1994, the Socialists won 209 of the 386 seats, in contrast to their 33 seats in 1990, and formed a government. Privatization of state-owned property continued with parliamentary action in 1995.

### HUNGARY AS A COMMUNIST STATE.
A monarchy for more than 1,000 years and part of the Austro–Hungary monarchy from 1867 until its collapse in 1918, Hungary fought in World War II as an ally of Germany but, nevertheless, fell under German occupation. German forces were driven out by Soviet armies early in 1945, but the Soviet troops remained until 1949. In 1947, a new constitution was promulgated proclaiming Hungary a People's Republic.

In 1956, open criticism of the regime by Hungarian writers, students, and intellectuals led to demonstrations and street fighting in Budapest. The trial and sentencing of Jozsef Cardinal Mindszenty, the Roman Catholic pri-

mate of Hungary, aroused further angry demonstrations, and Soviet troops temporarily withdrew from Budapest. Premier Nagy, assenting to popular demand, proclaimed Hungary's neutrality and its withdrawal from the Warsaw Pact and announced the government's intention to hold free, multi-party elections.

Three days after these announcements, Soviet armed forces crushed the national uprising on 3 November 1956. Three decades later, Hungary has developed the reputation of being somewhat freer than most Eastern European States; however, its economic development is reported to have deteriorated slightly.

### HUMAN RIGHTS PROVISIONS.
As regards human rights, Hungary is bound by article 2 of the Peace Treaty with the Allied and Associated Powers at Paris on 10 February 1947, which provides that:

1. Hungary shall take all measures necessary to secure to all persons under Hungarian jurisdiction, without distinction as to race, sex, language or religion, the enjoyment of human rights and of the fundamental freedoms, including freedom of expression, of press and publication, of religious worship, of political opinion and of public meeting.
2. Hungary further undertakes that the laws in force in Hungary shall not, either in their content or in their application, discriminate or entail any discrimination between persons of Hungarian nationality on the ground of their race, sex, language or religion, whether in reference to their persons, prosperity, business, professional or financial interests, status, political or civil rights or any other matter.

### FORM OF GOVERNMENT.
In a report to a United Nations monitoring body issued in 1992, the Government of Hungary supplied the following details concerning its coalition form of government:

*The Government.* On 8 May 1990 the President of the Republic of Hungary requested the President of the largest Parliamentary party, the Hungarian Democratic Forum, to form a new Government, and Parliament elected József Antall Prime Minister on 24 May 1990. A coalition Government was formed with the participation of the Hungarian Democratic Forum, the Christian Democratic People's Party and the Independent Smallholders' Party.

*The Government's consultative bodies.* The Government sets up a cabinet, a government committee, a college and a consultative body, and appoints government commissioners.

Present-day Hungarian regulations and constitutional practice have imbued the concept of a cabinet with a special meaning. What this boils down to is that the Cabinet is a consultative body that prepares government decisions, and presents preliminary views on every question within its competence that requires a government decision or concerns the realization of the Government's political and economic goals. The Government created the Economic Cabinet to consult on strategic issues concerning the economy.

The Government Committee prepares decisions and is a

coordinative and supervisory body that also has the power to take decisions in certain cases. Recently, a Committee on Science Policy and a Council on Science Policy were set up.

The College and the Consultative Body, which assist the work of the Government in preparing decisions, occasionally submit reports on their work to the Government.

The Government Commissioners are empowered to act on behalf of the Government, and periodically report on their activities and what measures they have taken. There is a government commissioner, for instance, for the Budapest-Vienna World Expo, and one for the Danube water barrage.

Developing a new type of public administration is a long-term programme, one the law on State secretaries goes some way to bring about. Similarly, certain conclusions can be drawn from the Law on Local Governments:

(a) The public administration set-up and personnel under the political State secretaries are to become politically neutral. Professionalism will be the determining factor and staff will be engaged under indefinite contracts.

(b) Contrary to earlier solutions, the functions, organization and activities of public administration, and the functions of local Governments will be entirely separate both in theory and practice. In other words, the system of hierarchy that prevailed until now between the two systems will cease to exist.

Certain urgent administrative measures have already been taken: an Office for National and Ethnic Minorities has been set up, for instance. The tasks of this office include preparing the Government's minority policy; shaping minority policy concepts; following up how national and minority rights are observed; and promoting respect for these rights; keeping in constant touch with the Parliamentary Commissioner for Minorities; and promoting exchanges of opinions and information between the Government and minority organizations.

The Office for National and Ethnic Minorities is an independent public administration body operating under the supervision of a minister without portfolio: its president is appointed by the Prime Minister on the recommendation of the minister without portfolio concerned.

The Republic of Hungary has a parliamentary system of Government. Hungarian parliamentarism has certain special features which are worth noting.

*The President of the Republic.* The President of the Republic of Hungary is the country's head of State. He stands for national unity and oversees the democratic operation of the State. Not in all areas which fall under his umbrella can the President of the Republic act independently: to exercise some aspects of his authority, he first needs the counter-signature of the competent minister (concluding international treaties, the appointment and accreditation of ambassadors and envoys, exercising clemency, etc.); other fields of his competence—including the presidential privilege of participation and speaking at parliamentary sessions and at the meetings of the parliamentary committees, and initiating legislation and referenda—do not require counter-signature. One interesting feature of the Constitution is that not only does it ensure the President the right to initiate legislation, but it also gives him a limited veto: before a law is promulgated, he may return it to Parliament once for reconsideration.

If Parliament cannot be convened, the President of the Republic may declare a state of war or a state of emergency. It is up to a body consisting of the Prime Minister, the President of the Constitutional Court and the Speaker of Parliament to decide whether there are sufficient grounds for calling a state of war and/or a state of emergency in the first

place, and whether Parliament is really prevented from going into session.

The President of the Republic is the Commander-in-Chief of the country's armed forces.

If the President of the Republic so requests, Parliament has to be convened. On the other hand, Parliament may only be dissolved if the Government has been defeated at least four times within 12 months, or if Parliament does not elect the Prime Minister proposed by the President of the Republic within 40 days. Parliament elects the President of the Republic for a term of five years; he may be re-elected for a second term.

If the President of the Republic violates the Constitution or any other law, he may be stripped of his office. If he commits a criminal offence, he is liable to be tried and sentenced by the Constitutional Court.

*Specific features of Hungarian parliamentarism.* One of the specific features of Hungarian parliamentarism is that under the Constitution, the Prime Minister is the supreme authority as regards government activity and responsibility.

The Prime Minister is elected by Parliament on the recommendation of the President of the Republic; his election requires a majority vote from MPs. Ministers are appointed and relieved by the President of the Republic on the recommendation of the Prime Minister. The Government is formed when the ministers have been appointed. After the formation of the Government, its members take the oath of office. The Government cannot operate without the confidence of Parliament: its mandate ceases when Parliament withdraws this confidence.

The Constitution lays down that a constructive vote of no confidence is possible against the Government. This means that MPs can raise a motion of no confidence against the Government only if at the same time they make a proposal as to the new Prime Minister. In other words, carrying a no-confidence vote automatically invests the person proposed with the office of Prime Minister.

*No confidence.* The significance of the institution of the constructive no-confidence motion is that in order to oust the Government, it is not enough for the opposition parties to be agreed on this point: they also have to arrive at a consensus on who the new Prime Minister is to be.

A vote of no confidence may be initiated only against the Prime Minister, and cannot be proposed against individual ministers. The other side of the coin is that no confidence against individual ministers counts as no confidence in the Prime Minister.

The Government itself may raise the issue of confidence through the Prime Minister. The Government, again through the Prime Minister, may also recommend that voting on a particular proposal it has submitted should at the same time be cast as a confidence vote.

*The Prime Minister and his cabinet.* The present Constitution has made for a government system that expects almost total political solidarity with the Prime Minister from his ministers. In other words, the governmental system is built on ministers' political solidarity with the Prime Minister. In this way, the relationship between the Prime Minister and the individual ministers could almost be likened to the sort of relationship that has developed between the President of the United States and his secretaries under the Constitution of the United States. As a matter of fact, it is not the scope of authority of the Prime Minister, but that of the Government and the individual ministers, that the Constitution and other legal provisions generally deal with, though the Prime Minister is free to set the political limits on their sphere of authority.

This relationship between the Prime Minister and his ministers as regulated by the Constitution is, however, modified by shifts in the balance of power effective at any one time in Parliament; that is, if the Prime Minister wants to rely on a parliamentary majority, he has to take into consideration the political intentions of the ministers the coalition parties have "delegated".

***MINORITY RIGHTS.*** In the same document, the Government also supplied the following information on minority rights in Hungary:

Principles of the regulatory provisions regarding the national and ethnic minorities are laid down in the Constitution, which states that "the national and ethnic minorities living in the Republic of Hungary are participants in the power of the people and constituent components of the State". Besides this declaration, the Constitution guarantees the collective participation of the minorities in public life, the promotion of their cultures, the wide usage of their languages, their right to have education in their mother tongues as well as their right to use their names in accordance with the rules of their respective languages.

It is also the Constitution that defines the legal status and the tasks of the parliamentary ombudsman (Commissioner for Citizens' Rights). This legal institution makes the redress of grievances possible for the national and ethnic minorities as well.

Beyond these regulatory enactments, the whole of the legal system supports the enforcement of minority rights. The free use of the mother tongue is guaranteed by law. At the same time, criminal acts against national, ethnic, racial or religious groups, as well as racial discrimination, are also prohibited and punishable by law.

The number of lower level statutes regulating everyday life is between 18 and 22. Their subjects range from the rules regarding the protection of historic buildings to the norms defining the tasks of the education system.

The enforcement of the rights of the national and ethnic minorities is promoted by the laws on local government, which have facilitated the entry of representatives of the minorities into local governmental bodies. The assertion of minority rights is one of the compulsory tasks for any local government.

There are several prevailing statutes by which the framework for freely conducted economic activity in accordance with the requirements of a market economy is guaranteed for the minorities, too.

Though the Hungarian legal system is fundamentally protective of the minorities, the processes of legal codification and legislation have not yet come to an end. Work is under way on a codex summarizing the rights of national and ethnic minorities; the international agreements and recommendations on minority rights are to serve as its theoretical basis.

After coming into force, this legal measure will define the minorities individual and collective rights, including the legal institutions of minority local governments, the parliamentary commissioner for minority rights and local minority spokesman. This law will also lay down the rights of the minorities regarding language usage, public education, culture and mass media. The Parliament is expected to debate this bill as early as 1991.

*Minorities in politics and public life.* The dearth of constitutionality in the last four and a half decades has had a cumulative negative impact on the national and ethnic minor-ities. Their traditional communities have been crushed by political reprisals such as resettlement, the removal or exchange of populations, and the confiscation of property on the one hand and by the economic processes which have affected the country as a whole, such as the forced collectivization of agriculture and the accelerated pace of both industrialization and urbanization on the other.

These structural processes have had a negative effect on the minorities' consciousness and on the state of their languages. Indeed, both the assimilation and the eclipse of their languages have speeded up.

Under the conditions of the one-party dictatorship at first and, then, under State paternalism, no effective organizations or representation groups could develop to safeguard the interests of the minorities; the process of their spontaneous self-organization from below could not even get started.

The so-called "democratic associations" of the minorities were functioning without members, their activities being limited to the promotion of cultural traditions. In fact, they were nothing but obedient executives of the Communist party's policy on minorities. Moreover, gypsies were not even considered a minority before the end of the 1980s.

The democratic political institutions coming into existence after the fundamental change in the economic and social system in Hungary, i.e. the freely elected Parliament and Government, have framed new ideas on minority policy which are related to the traditions and norms of Europe. A twofold process has begun: on the one hand, the Hungarian Government declared those principles which would guide its attitude towards the national and ethnic minorities; on the other hand, the minorities themselves are also gradually establishing organizations to safeguard their interests.

The cornerstone of the new Hungarian Government's minority policy is to arrest and, if possible, to reverse the process of assimilation.

***LEGAL FRAMEWORK.*** In the same document, the Government summarized the general legal framework within which human rights are protected in Hungary, as follows:

Besides the judicial authorities, nearly all organs vested with administrative powers have jurisdiction affecting human rights. Thus, for instance, the sanitary and epidemic inspector may impose restrictions on the personal freedom of citizens. The trends of legislation nevertheless indicate that human rights and fundamental freedoms cannot be restricted in the future except by court decision and that judicial review will be available in cases of restriction by other authorities. These trends will be strengthened by the ratification of the European Convention on Human Rights, which is expected to take place in 1992.

Various legal remedies are available to individuals who claim that any of their human rights have been violated depending on the type of procedure or act by which violations of human rights have occurred. Recourse is typical under the criminal law and the civil law on personal rights. In specific cases, remedy can also be sought in administrative proceedings.

Human rights are protected in a comprehensive way by the general (Chapter I) as well as the specific provisions (Chapter XII) of the Constitution. In its general provisions the Constitution, inter alia, states: "The Republic of Hungary recognizes the inviolable and inalienable fundamental human rights; to respect and to protect thereof shall be of a primary duty of the State". Human rights are regulated by legislative enactments, but the essential content of such fundamental rights cannot be restricted even by legislation. "In the Republic of Hungary, the rules respecting fundamental rights and obligations shall be determined by law which, however, shall not limit the substantial contents of any fundamental right."

Suspension of the exercise of these rights is allowed only in exceptional circumstances, but certain rights cannot be suspended even in the presence of such circumstances. Restrictions on the exercise of the fundamental rights to life, human dignity, etc. cannot be justified even by a state of public emergency, siege or peril (Art. 8, paras. 1, 2, 4 of the Constitution). Fundamental human rights are specified by Chapter XII of the Constitution.

Although these rights are covered and protected by the basic law, the need for elaboration of sufficiently detailed procedural rules and guarantees justifies the adoption of separate laws on particular rights, which are regulated in greater detail by several essential laws adopted since 1989, such as:

(a) Act II of 1989 on the Freedom of Association;

(b) Act III of 1989 on the Freedom of Assembly;

(c) Act VII of 1989 on Strike;

(d) Act XXVIII of 1989 on Travel Abroad and Passports;

(e) Act XIX of 1989 on Emigration and Immigration;

(f) Act XXXIII of 1989 on the Functioning and Finances of Political Parties;

(g) Act IV of 1990 on the Freedom of Conscience and Religion and on the Churches;

(h) Act XVII of 1990 on the Parliamentary Representation of National and Linguistic Minorities living in the Republic of Hungary;

(i) Act IV of 1991 on Employment Promotion and Provision for the Unemployed.

Various authorities are intensively working on the preparation of other significant laws such as the law on the press, the radio and television; the law on the protection of personal data and the publicity of data of public interest; the law on the parliamentary ombudsman for civil rights.

The norms of international law become part of Hungarian law indirectly, i.e. to be applicable, they must be promulgated by Hungarian legislation. This transformational procedure regulated by the Hungarian legal system has the following phases:

(a) Under the Constitution, the Republic of Hungary shall accept the generally recognized rules of international law and shall ensure their harmony with the domestic law (Art. 7);

(b) The mechanism for this is determined by a separate law, Act XI of 1987 on Legislation, which provides (in Art. 2 (a)) that the fundamental rights and duties of citizens, the conditions for and the restrictions on their exercise, and the rules for their enforcement must exclusively be subject to legislation. The Act enumerates these rights exemplificatively (restrictions on personal freedom, right to travel abroad and to passport, freedom of association and assembly, rules on marriage and the family, etc.). The relevant regulations are also applicable to international treaties, but the Act deems it important to state in particular that "an international treaty containing a generally binding rule of conduct shall be promulgated by an act of legislation at the level appropriate to the content thereof" (Art. 16). International treaties affecting fundamental human rights are subject to ratification by Parliament and are incorporated into the Hungarian legal system by parliamentary enactments;

(c) Finally, in the third phase, Law-Decree No. 27 of 1982 on Procedures Concerning International Treaties lays down the technical rules for incorporation of international legal norms into Hungarian Law. The relevant act of national legislation may be promulgated concurrently with, or following upon, the entry into force of international legislation.

Settlement of conflicts between an international treaty adopted and the internal law in force is within the jurisdiction of the Constitutional Court. Act XXXI of 1989 on the Constitutional Court establishes two procedures for the settlement of such conflicts: If the legislative provision promulgating an international treaty is in conflict with a rule of internal law equal in hierarchy or subordinate to it, the Constitutional Court shall annul, wholly or partly, the rule of internal law. If an international treaty is in conflict with a rule of internal law superior to it, the Constitutional Court shall invite the organ or law-making body having concluded the international treaty to remove the conflict. The law-making organ may happen to fail in a duty emanating from an international treaty. Decision in such cases also lies with the Constitutional Court, which shall, by setting a time-limit, invite the body in default to comply with its duty in accordance with the international treaty.

It is accordingly necessary that international law regulating human rights should be transformed into internal law to be invoked or to have access to national organs for enforcing it in case of violation.

The relevant legislation in force empowers the Procurator's Office to oversee the implementation of human rights, but the Parliament is considering a bill on the parliamentary ombudsman for civil rights, which will place the protection of human and civil rights on a completely new organizational basis. The parliamentary ombudsmen of national and ethnic minorities will be covered by the Act on Minorities, which is likewise in the process of preparation.

Hungary is a party to most of the international treaties concluded under the auspices of the United Nations and covering specific aspects of human rights. Under previous practice, Hungary—while acceding to the important international conventions regulating specific areas of human rights—did not, in its reservations made to them, undertake to apply the related control mechanisms. After the profound change of its social and political system those reservations have gradually been revoked. Thus Hungary at present recognizes the competence of the Human Rights Committee, the Committee on the Elimination of Racial Discrimination and the Committee against Torture to receive and consider individual communications and is ready to cooperate with the competent treaty bodies. Hungary has also recognized and attaches special importance to the competence of the Committee against Torture under article 20 of the Convention against Torture.

Hungary is a signatory to the European Convention for the Protection of Human Rights and Fundamental Freedoms as much as to its Protocols. The ratification process of this Convention and its Protocols is currently under way.

**BIBLIOGRAPHY.** Bency, Gyorgy. *Censored and Alternative Modes of Cultural Expression in Hungary.* New York: Human Rights Watch, 1985. NGO report, in English.

Budapest "Eotvos Lorand" University Research Group. *Human Rights in Today's Hungary.* Budapest, Hungary: Mezon, 1990. Scholarly edited collection, in English.

Commission on Security and Cooperation in Europe. *Basket I—Implementation of the Final Act of the Conference on Security and Cooperation in Europe: Findings Eleven Years after Helsinki.*

Washington, D.C.: GPO, 1987. Government report, in English.

————. *Report on the Parliamentary Elections in the Republic of Hungary*. Washington, D.C.: U.S. Government Printing Office, 1990. Government report, in English.

Fleischman, Janet. *Violations of the Helsinki Accords: Hungary*. New York: U.S. Helsinki Watch Committee, 1986. NGO report, in English.

Helsinki Watch. *From Below: Independent Peace and Environmental Movements in Eastern Europe and the USSR*. New York: Human Rights Watch, 1987. NGO report, in English.

————. "Hungary," in *Ten Years Later: Violation of the Helsinki Accords*, pp. 55–68. New York: Human Rights Watch, 1985. NGO report, in English.

————. *Struggling for Ethnic Identity: The Gypsies of Hungary*. New York: Human Rights Watch, 1993. NGO report, in English.

Human Rights Watch. "Hungary," in *Human Rights Watch World Report 1995*, pp. 210–212. New York: 1995. NGO report, in English.

Plichtová, Jana, ed. *Minorities in Politics . . . Cultural and Languages Rights: Proceeding from International Symposium on Minorities in Central Europe*. Bratislava, Czechoslovakia: Czechoslovak Committee in the European Cultural Foundation, 1992. Conference report, in English.

Tóth, Judith. "Changing Refugee Policy in Hungary," *Migration World* 20, no. 2 (1992): 10–13. Article, in English.

**HUNGER AND MALNUTRITION.** The **WORLD FOOD COUNCIL,** meeting in Nicosia, Republic of Cyprus, from 23 to 26 May 1988, reviewed recent food and hunger trends in the world, examined the situation of global food-stocks and possible ways for their utilization as a means of development assistance, and addressed ecological issues vital to ensuring the food security of the present and future generations. In its report to the **GENERAL ASSEMBLY,** the Council evaluated the situation at that time as follows (UN Doc. A/43/19, part I):

*Global State of Hunger and Malnutrition.* The untenable trends of growing hunger and malnutrition, to which the Council's Beijing Declaration drew the world's attention, are continuing. Famine again threatens large numbers of people in Africa, and millions of people in Asia and Latin America face extraordinary food shortages, in the wake of natural calamities or civil strife. Food consumption per person, which has been declining in a large number of developing countries throughout this decade, decreased further in all developing regions in 1987–indicating a tragic rise in the number of hungry people. More children are now suffering from malnutrition than a decade ago. According to United Nations estimates, over 14 million children under the age of five die needlessly every year from malnutrition and disease in the developing countries.

The living conditions of the poorest people continue to deteriorate in the difficult national and international economic conditions. Despite some slight improvements in 1987, the developing regions' economies continue to suffer from depressed international commodity prices, protectionism and worsening terms of trade, growing debt-service obligations, and reduced and—in many cases—negative net resource transfer abroad. It was recognized that a more equitable income distribution could contribute to the alleviation of hunger, malnutrition and poverty.

However, our review should also give rise to some hope. Social concern is growing. Many countries are seeking to protect the food security and well-being of their low-income people in the economic difficulties of this decade. International agencies are asked to continue to better respond to the assistance needs of these countries, for which purpose the agencies should have the necessary resources available.

We note with satisfaction that some progress has been made since the Beijing session with regard to disarmament, detente and regional peace efforts. Peace is a prerequisite for sound development, which should have the well-being of all people as its central objective.

The current imbalances that characterize the world economy challenge the entire international community to halt and reverse the trend of growing hunger and malnutrition. We reiterate our Beijing call for fundamental policy changes to improve the human condition. Specifically, we call for a joint effort by all countries and international agencies to improve the food condition and protect the nutritional levels of low-income groups during economic adjustment. We request the WFC secretariat to provide us regularly at future Council sessions with comprehensive analyses on policy options, country experiences and progress in the fight against hunger.

We emphasize that the alleviation of hunger and malnutrition requires that more resources be channelled, nationally and internationally, to the world's poor. Equitable economic development is essential to the alleviation of hunger and poverty and requires greater resource flows to developing countries through improved international trade conditions, feasible approaches to the debt problem and stepped-up development assistance.

*Potential for Hunger Reduction through Food-Surplus-Based Development Assistance.* Growing hunger amidst food surpluses is a cruel fact of our times. As follow-up to the Council's Beijing (thirteenth) session, we have sought to put this problem into perspective by assessing the current and prospective food-stock situation, reviewing the developing countries' food needs and examining possible ways for surplus utilization in support of accelerated food-security focused development in developing countries.

Global cereal stocks increased during most of the 1980s, reaching record levels in 1987. They are expected to decline over the next two years. But in any event, stocks are likely to fluctuate above the levels considered "safe" for global food security and surpluses will persist in the medium term. While some developed countries are trying to draw down their stocks, developing nations are finding it increasingly difficult to feed their people. In many developing countries, food production has not kept pace with population growth, financial constraints have reduced food imports per person, non-emergency food aid has remained stagnant, and food consumption levels have been declining.

Against this background, we examined a proposal by the WFC secretariat for an international hunger initiative based on a combination of concessional food transfers from food-surplus countries, financial assistance from non-food-surplus developed countries and the efforts by developing countries to alleviate hunger and poverty. While the proposal met with widespread interest and drew wide support, it was observed that food "surpluses" and hunger were separate problems. The Council's primary concern is the solution of the problems of hunger.

From this perspective, the secretariat's proposal represented a limited contribution to the much broader efforts required to address hunger problems. Our discussions brought to the fore that past policies and programmes had not succeeded in reducing hunger and malnutrition. Future progress will critically hinge on a better understanding of why efforts of the international community have proved insufficient. At the same time, we emphasize that more studies will not feed hungry people. Rather, immediate and more effective action is required, which draws upon the lessons of the past. In this spirit, we have decided to launch the following:

*Cyprus Initiative against Hunger in the World.* The Cyprus Initiative calls for an urgent review and assessment of the efforts made to date in hunger reduction and for the identification of ways for improving current policies and programmes and of pragmatic, feasible and potentially effective new initiatives towards meeting the Council's fundamental objective: the elimination of hunger and malnutrition. We call on the Council's President to present a full, action-oriented report to the Council at its fifteenth ministerial session in mid-1989. In order to assist the President in this complex task, we have agreed to establish an informal *ad hoc* consultative group along the following lines:

*Composition.* Representatives of States Members of the United Nations convened by the regional Vice-Presidents of WFC, relevant international organizations and the President, thus constituting a small group.

*Mandate.* The group should, in particular:

(a) Review and assess the policies and instruments at present available to combat chronic hunger and malnutrition in developing countries, particularly in low-income food-deficit countries, and identify the reasons and obstacles that may have hindered their greater impact;

(b) Consider concrete and realistic measures that could make existing policies and instruments more effective;

(c) Identify workable initiatives;

(d) Recommend a course of action to combat hunger more effectively.

*Implementation.* The proposals of the group should be examined first in a meeting of the bureau of WFC before the end of 1988. They shall thereafter be presented to the fifteenth ministerial session of the Council.

**ACTION BY THE GENERAL ASSEMBLY.** On 20 December 1988, the UN General Assembly reaffirmed (resolution 43/191) the Universal Declaration on the Eradication of Hunger and Malnutrition and noted with concern that hunger and malnutrition had been increasing since the World Food Conference in 1974, that the number of people suffering from hunger and malnutrition had increased since the 1980s, and that the central objective of the World Food Conference remained largely unfulfilled. It welcomed the conclusions and recommendations of the World Food Council, in particular the Cyprus Initiative against Hunger in the World, and called upon governments and international and non-governmental organizations to assist the Council fully in implementing that objective.

The Assembly stressed, in particular, the need for coordinated international action to tackle the long-term problems of migratory pest control, particularly in Africa, and, expressing gratitude for the support of donors and recognizing the efforts made by the affected coun-

tries in the fight against the grasshopper and locust infection, called upon donors to continue to give high priority to the implementation and continued coordination by the **FAO** of emergency control programs, as well as longer-term measures, against grasshoppers and locusts currently affecting vast areas of Africa, as well as other regions of the developing world, and to remain prepared to provide financial and technical assistance to affected countries at short notice.

The Assembly urged the World Food Council to continue to assess the overall impact of structural adjustment programs in developing countries on the nutritional levels of their populations, especially among children and low-income groups, and to suggest remedial measures in that area, including ways of stimulating the provision of resources to eliminate the suffering of those groups.

At its 47th (1992) session, the General Assembly again expressed its deep concern about the gravity of the world food security situation, in particular the worsening problems of hunger and malnutrition, and affirmed the critical importance of establishing the most effective arrangements for the management and coordination of the United Nations response to those problems (resolution 47/150). It decided to address these issues as a matter of priority.

**UNIVERSAL DECLARATION ON THE ERADICATION OF HUNGER AND MALNUTRITION (1974).** The Declaration was adopted by the World Food Conference, convened at Rome from 5 to 16 November 1974 by the UN General Assembly (resolution 3180 [XXVIII]). It sought to develop ways and means whereby the international community as a whole could act to resolve the world's food problem. The Declaration, charting a course for future work, also served to remind the world that "every man, woman and child had the inalienable right to be free from hunger and malnutrition in order to develop fully and maintain their physical and mental faculties."

The text of the Declaration (*Report of the World Food Conference,* United Nations publication, Sales no. E.75.II.A.3, chap. I), adopted by the Conference on 16 November 1974 and endorsed by the General Assembly on 17 December 1974 (resolution 3348 [XXIX]), is as follows:

The World Food Conference,
Recognizing that:
(a) The grave food crisis that is afflicting the peoples of the developing countries where most of the world's hungry and ill-nourished live and where more than two thirds of the world's population produce about one third of the world's food—an imbalance which threatens to increase in the next 10 years—is not only fraught with grave economic and social implications, but also acutely jeopardizes the most fundamen-

tal principles and values associated with the right to life and human dignity as enshrined in the Universal Declaration of Human Rights;

(b) The elimination of hunger and malnutrition, included as one of the objectives in the United Nations Declaration on Social Progress and Development, and the elimination of the causes that determine this situation are the common objectives of all nations;

(c) The situation of the peoples afflicted by hunger and malnutrition arises from their historical circumstances, especially social inequalities, including in many cases alien and colonial domination, foreign occupation, racial discrimination, *apartheid* and neo-colonialism in all its forms, which continue to be among the greatest obstacles to the full emancipation and progress of the developing countries and all the peoples involved;

(d) This situation has been aggravated in recent years by a series of crises to which the world economy has been subjected, such as the deterioration in the international monetary system, the inflationary increase in import costs, the heavy burdens imposed by external debt on the balance of payments of many developing countries, a rising food demand partly due to demographic pressure, speculation, and a shortage of, and increased costs for, essential agricultural inputs;

(e) These phenomena should be considered within the framework of the on-going negotiations on the Charter of Economic Rights and Duties of States, and the General Assembly of the United Nations should be urged unanimously to agree upon, and to adopt, a Charter that will be an effective instrument for the establishment of new international economic relations based on principles of equity and justice;

(f) All countries, big or small, rich or poor, are equal. All countries have the full right to participate in the decisions on the food problem;

(g) The well-being of the peoples of the world largely depends on the adequate production and distribution of food as well as the establishment of a world food security system which would ensure adequate availability of, and reasonable prices for, food at all times, irrespective of periodic fluctuations and vagaries of weather and free of political and economic pressures, and should thus facilitate, amongst other things, the development process of developing countries;

(h) Peace and justice encompass an economic dimension helping the solution of the world economic problems, the liquidation of under-development, offering a lasting and definitive solution of the food problem for all peoples and guaranteeing to all countries the right to implement freely and effectively their development programmes. To this effect, it is necessary to eliminate threats and resort to force and to promote peaceful co-operation between States to the fullest extent possible, to apply the principles of non-interference in the internal affairs of other States, full equality of rights and respect of national independence and sovereignty, as well as to encourage the peaceful co-operation between all States, irrespective of their political, social and economic systems. The further improvement of international relations will create better conditions for international co-operation in all fields which should make possible large financial and material resources to be used, *inter alia,* for developing agricultural production and substantially improving world food security;

(i) For a lasting solution of the food problem all efforts should be made to eliminate the widening gaps which today separate developed and developing countries and to bring about a new international economic order. It should be possible for all countries to participate actively and effectively in the new international economic relations by the establishment of suitable international systems, where appropriate, capable of producing adequate action in order to establish just and equitable relations in international economic co-operation;

(j) Developing countries reaffirm their belief that the primary responsibility for ensuring their own rapid development rests with themselves. They declare, therefore, their readiness to continue to intensify their individual and collective efforts with a view to expanding their mutual co-operation in the field of agricultural development and food production, including the eradication of hunger and malnutrition;

(k) Since, for various reasons, many developing countries are not yet always able to meet their own food needs, urgent and effective international action should be taken to assist them, free of political pressures,

Consistent with the aims and objectives of the Declaration on the Establishment of a New International Economic Order and the Programme of Action adopted by the General Assembly at its sixth special session,

The Conference consequently solemnly proclaims:

1. Every man, woman and child has the inalienable right to be free from hunger and malnutrition in order to develop fully and maintain their physical and mental faculties. Society today already possesses sufficient resources, organizational ability and technology and hence the competence to achieve this objective. Accordingly, the eradication of hunger is a common objective of all the countries of the international community, especially of the developed countries and others in a position to help.

2. It is a fundamental responsibility of Governments to work together for higher food production and a more equitable and efficient distribution of food between countries and within countries. Governments should initiate immediately a greater concerted attack on chronic malnutrition and deficiency diseases among the vulnerable and lower income groups. In order to ensure adequate nutrition for all, Governments should formulate appropriate food and nutrition policies integrated in over-all socio-economic and agricultural development plans based on adequate knowledge of available as well as potential food resources. The importance of human milk in this connexion should be stressed on nutritional grounds.

3. Food problems must be tackled during the preparation and implementation of national plans and programmes for economic and social development, with emphasis on their humanitarian aspects.

4. It is a responsibility of each State concerned, in accordance with its sovereign judgement and internal legislation, to remove the obstacles to food production and to provide proper incentives to agricultural producers. Of prime importance for the attainment of these objectives are effective measures of socio-economic transformation by agrarian, tax, credit and investment policy reform and the reorganization of rural structures, such as the reform of the conditions of ownership, the encouragement of producer and consumer co-operatives, the mobilization of the full potential of human resources, both male and female, in the developing countries for an integrated rural development and the involvement of small farmers, fishermen and landless workers in attaining the required food production and employment targets. Moreover, it is necessary to recognize the key role of women in agricultural production and rural economy in many countries, and to ensure that appropriate education, extension programmes and financial facilities are made available to women on equal terms with men.

5. Marine and inland water resources are today becoming

more important than ever as a source of food and economic prosperity. Accordingly, action should be taken to promote a rational exploitation of these resources, preferably for direct human consumption, in order to contribute to meeting the food requirements of all peoples.

6. The efforts to increase food production should be complemented by every endeavour to prevent wastage of food in all its forms.

7. To give impetus to food production in developing countries and in particular in the least developed and most seriously affected among them, urgent and effective international action should be taken, by the developed countries and other countries in a position to do so, to provide them with sustained additional technical and financial assistance on favourable terms and in a volume sufficient to their needs on the basis of bilateral and multilateral arrangements. This assistance must be free of conditions inconsistent with the sovereignty of the receiving States.

8. All countries, and primarily the highly industrialized countries, should promote the advancement of food production technology and should make all efforts to promote the transfer, adaptation and dissemination of appropriate food production technology for the benefit of the developing countries and, to that end, they should *inter alia* make all efforts to disseminate the results of their research work to Governments and scientific institutions of developing countries in order to enable them to promote a sustained agricultural development.

9. To assure the proper conservation of natural resources being utilized, or which might be utilized, for food production, all countries must collaborate in order to facilitate the preservation of the environment, including the marine environment.

10. All developed countries and others able to do so should collaborate technically and financially with the developing countries in their efforts to expand land and water resources for agricultural production and to assure a rapid increase in the availability, at fair costs, of agricultural inputs such as fertilizers and other chemicals, high-quality seeds, credit and technology. Co-operation among developing countries, in this connexion, is also important.

11. All States should strive to the utmost to readjust, where appropriate, their agricultural policies to give priority to food production, recognizing, in this connexion the interrelationship between the world food problem and international trade. In the determination of attitudes towards farm support programmes for domestic food production, developed countries should take into account, as far as possible, the interest of the food-exporting developing countries, in order to avoid detrimental effect on their exports. Moreover, all countries should co-operate to devise effective steps to deal with the problem of stabilizing world markets and promoting equitable and remunerative prices, where appropriate through international arrangements, to improve access to markets through reduction or elimination of tariff and non-tariff barriers on the products of interest to the developing countries, to substantially increase the export earnings of these countries, to contribute to the diversification of their exports, and apply to them, in the multilateral trade negotiations, the principles as agreed upon in the Tokyo Declaration, including the concept of non-reciprocity and more favourable treatment.

12. As it is common responsibility of the entire international community to ensure the availability at all times of adequate world supplies of basic food-stuffs by way of appropriate reserves, including emergency reserves, all countries should co-operate in the establishment of an effective system of world food security by:

(a) Participating in and supporting the operation of the Global Information and Early Warning System on Food and Agriculture;

(b) Adhering to the objectives, policies and guidelines of the proposed International Undertaking on World Food Security as endorsed by the World Food Conference;

(c) Earmarking, where possible, stocks or funds for meeting international emergency food requirements as envisaged in the proposed International Undertaking on World Food Security and developing international guidelines to provide for the co-ordination and the utilization of such stocks;

(d) Co-operating in the provision of food aid for meeting emergency and nutritional needs as well as for stimulating rural employment through development projects.

All donor countries should accept and implement the concept of forward planning of food aid and make all efforts to provide commodities and/or financial assistance that will ensure adequate quantities of grains and other food commodities.

Time is short. Urgent and sustained action is vital. The Conference, therefore, calls upon all peoples expressing their will as individuals, and through their Governments and non-governmental organizations, to work together to bring about the end of the age-old scourge of hunger.

The Conference affirms:

The determination of the participating States to make full use of the United Nations system in the implementation of this Declaration and the other decisions adopted by the Conference.

**SEE ALSO** *Food and Human Rights; Standard of Living.*

**BIBLIOGRAPHY.** Africa Watch. *Ethiopia: 200 Days in the Death of Asmara—Starvation as a Weapon and Violations of the Humanitarian Laws of War.* New York: Human Rights Watch, 1990. NGO factfinding report, in English.

Ardanaz, Jose. "Democracias Debiles y Dictaduras Criminales en America Latina: Por Luchar Contra el Hambre y la Represion Hay Millones de Personas Represaliadas" (Weak Democracies and Criminal Dictatorships in Latin America: Thousands Repressed for Their Involvement in the Struggle against Hunger and Oppression), *Madres de Plaza de Mayo 2,* no. 19 (June 1986): 10–11. NGO newspaper article, in English.

Brennan, T. O. *Uprooted Angolana: From Crisis to Catastrophe.* Washington, D.C.: U.S. Committee for Refugees, 1987. NGO report, in English.

Burr, Millard. *Sudan 1990–1992: Food Aid, Famine, and Failure.* Washington, D.C.: U.S. Committee for Refugees, 1993. NGO report, in English.

Clark, John. *For Richer for Poorer: An Oxfam Report on Western Connections with World Hunger.* Oxford, UK: Oxfam, 1986. NGO report/scholarly monograph, in English.

Clay, J. W., S. Steingraber, and P. Niggli. *The Spoils of Famine: Ethiopian Famine Policy and Peasant Agriculture.* Cambridge, MA, USA: Cultural Survival, 1988. NGO report, in English.

Defense for Children International—USA. *Database on the Rights of the Child.* New York: 1987. NGO bibliography, in English.

Drèze, Jean, and Amartya Sen. *Hunger and Public Action.* Oxford, UK: Oxford University Press, 1989. Scholarly monograph, in English.

Ecumenical Committee on the Andes. "Peru: Hunger,

Poverty and Economic Crisis," *Andean Focus* 4, no. 1 (Feb. 1987): 1–4. NGO article, in English.

Edelman, M. W., and J. D. Weill. "Status of Children in the 1980s," *Columbia Human Rights Law Review* 17, no. 2 (Spring–Summer 1986): 139–158. Scholarly article, in English.

Fenton, T. P., and M. J. Heffon. *Food, Hunger, Agribusiness: A Directory of Resources.* Maryknoll, NY, USA: Orbis Books, 1987. Directory/bibliography, in English.

Gesellschaft fur Bedrohte Volker (Association for Endangered Peoples). "Menschenrechtesverletzungen in Athiopien 1974 bis 1985" (Human Rights Violations in Ethiopia 1974 to 1985), *Pogrom* 115 (June 1985): 1–16. NGO magazine article, in German.

———. "Fragwurdige Methoden sur Bekamfpung der Hungersnot: Athiopien—Deportationer und Zwangsarbeitslager" (Questionable Methods of Fighting the Hunger Emergency: Ethiopia Deportation and Forced Labor), *Pogrom* 25/85 (28 May 1985): 1–80. NGO bulletin article, in German.

Hopkins, Raymond F. "Ending Hunger in Africa," *Issue: A Journal of Africanist Opinion* 16, no. 2 (1988): 36–44. Scholarly article, in English.

International Committee of the Red Cross. "The Beirut Delegation Appeals," *ICRC Bulletin* 133 (Feb. 1987): 1. NGO article, in English.

Internationale Gesellschaft fur Menschenrechte (International Society for Human Rights). "Terror, Mord, und Hunger in Uganda" (Terror, Death and Hunger in Uganda), *Menschenrechte* (March–April 1987): NGO article, in German.

Keller, Edmond J. "Drought, War, and the Politics of Famine in Ethiopia and Eritrea," *Journal of Modern African Studies* 30, no. 4 (Dec. 1992): 609–624. Scholarly article, in English.

Kibola, H. S. "Some Conceptual Aspects of Human Rights: The Basis for the Right to Development in Africa." Paper presented at a seminar on "Law and Human Rights in Development," 24–28 May 1982, Gaborone, Botswana. Unpublished paper, in English.

Kutzner, P., and N. Lagoudakis. *Who's Involved with Hunger: An Organization Guide for Education and Advocacy.* 4th ed. Washington, D.C.: World Hunger Education Service, 1985. Directory, in English.

Lappe, F. M., and J. Collins. *World Hunger: Twelve Myths.* New York: Grove Press, for Institute for Food and Development Policy, 1986. NGO monograph, in English.

Middle East Research and Information Project. "Food and the Future of the Middle East," *Middle East Report* 20, no. 5 (Sept.–Oct. 1990): 4–30. NGO article, in English.

Refugee Studies Programme, International Development Centre—Queen Elizabeth House. *Responding to the Nutrition Crisis among Refugees: The Need for New Approaches—Report of the International Symposium, Oxford, 17–20 March 1991.* Oxford, UK: 1991. Conference report, in English.

Ruiz, Hiram A. "Early Warning Is Not Enough: The Failure to Prevent Starvation in Ethiopia, 1990," *International Journal of Refugee Law* (Sept. 1990): 83–98. Scholarly article, in English.

Rupesinghe, Kumar, and Michiko Kuroda, eds. *Early Warning and Conflict Resolution.* London and New York: Macmillan and St. Martin's Press for the International Peace Research Institute, 1992. Scholarly collective papers, in English; bibliography, pp. 232–238.

Vicaria de la Solidaridad, Arzobispado de Santiago (Vicariate of Solidarity, Archbishop of Santiago). "Hambre: Mucho mas de lo que se confiesa" (Much More Hunger than Admitted), *Solidaridad, Compromiso con la Verdad* 214 (14 Dec. 1985): 12–15. NGO newspaper article, in Spanish.

Wallace, Tina. "Refugees and Hunger in Eastern Sudan," *Review of African Political Economy* 33 (Aug. 1985): 64–68. Scholarly article, in English.

**HUNGER PROJECT.** A non-governmental organization founded in 1977, Hunger Project works to end world hunger by the year 2000 and to generate a new global climate or environment to transform this possibility into a reality. The group carries out initiatives and activities that range from mobilizing volunteers in developed countries for education and advocacy to establishing participatory, multi-sectoral approaches to planning and action in developing countries. It presents the annual "Africa Prize for Leadership for the Sustainable End of Hunger." Hunger Project has consultative status with the UN **ECONOMIC AND SOCIAL COUNCIL** (Roster) and sponsors projects in more than 30 countries.

Hunger Project. Address: One Madison Ave., 8A, New York, NY 10010, USA. Telephone: (212) 532-4255. Fax: (212) 532-9785. Executive Director: Joan Holmes.

**HURIDOCS (HUMAN RIGHTS INFORMATION AND DOCUMENTATION SYSTEMS).** A nonprofit, participatory international communications network founded in Strasbourg, France, in 1979, HURIDOCS provides a worldwide clearinghouse for information and documentation relating to human rights. Established by human rights organizations and interested individuals from more than 50 countries, the organization reviews, analyzes, and systematizes the information it receives and makes it available for use in the promotion and protection of human rights. In addition, it conducts conferences and seminars on questions relating to human rights and issues their reports. HURIDOCS is an open network with no formal membership structure; currently, over 1,750 organizations in 130 countries and territories are involved in various ways in the network.

HURIDOCS has an extensive publication program. In addition to its periodical *HURIDOCS News*, HURIDOCS has published *List of Organizations, Serial Numbers, and Acronyms, Standard Formats for the Recording and Exchange of Information on Human Rights* (Bjorn Stormorken, 1985); *BIBSYS: A Database System for Handling Bibliographic Data on Microcomputers* (Stormorken, 1986); *Bibliographic Database Model Using HURIDOCS Standard Formats* (Jeannine Thomas, 1989); *Media and Information Technology for Human Rights: A Select Bibliography* (1992); and *Standard Formats: A Tool in the Documentation of Human Rights Violations* (1992).

HURIDOCS. Address: Advice and Support Unit/Secretariat, Torggate 27, N-0183, Oslo 1, Norway. Telephone: (47-2) 200-247. Fax: (47-2) 110-501. E-mail: GEONET GEO2 HURDOCS. Chairman: Kuman Rupesinghe.

# I

**ICELAND.** The Republic of Iceland is a country that occupies an island in the north Atlantic Ocean, east of Greenland. It achieved independence in 1944 and became a member of the United Nations in 1946. Its population is estimated to be 260,000. Ethnic groups include descendants of the Norse and Celtic settlers. Languages commonly used include Icelandic, Danish, and English. Christianity is the predominant religion; the Evangelical Lutheran Church is the established Church of Iceland. Literacy is estimated at 99.9%.

The government (1994) took the form of a republic. The president, elected by universal suffrage for a term of four years, is head of State. Vigdis Finnbogadottir, elected as the country's first woman president in 1980, was re-elected in 1984, 1988 and 1992. The prime minister, appointed by the president, represents the party or coalition obtaining the majority in a popular election and exercises executive authority with the assistance of the cabinet. The 60-member bicameral elected *Althing* is the National Parliament. The 60 members who are elected select 20 of themselves to constitute the Upper House; the remaining 40 sit in the Lower House. The judiciary is protected by the constitution against interference by other branches of government. Political parties include the Independence Party, the Progressive Party, the Social Democratic Party, the Social Democratic Alliance, and the Women's League.

Iceland's *Althing*, established in 930 A.D., is the oldest parliament in the world. It did not function during the period when Norway, and later Denmark, assumed control over Iceland; but when Denmark granted Iceland a constitution in 1843, it was reestablished as a consultative assembly. When home rule was granted in 1903, the Danish minister for Icelandic affairs was made responsible to the *Althing*.

Iceland was neutral in World War II but cooperated with the Allied powers. Following German occupation from 1940 to 1944, the country was established as an independent republic on 17 June 1944. It became a charter member of the North American Treaty Alliance—the only NATO member without military forces of its own. Under a treaty between Iceland and the United States of America signed in 1951, the United States assumed responsibility for Iceland's defense.

*REPORT ON ECONOMIC, SOCIAL, AND CULTURAL RIGHTS.* The UN **Committee on Economic, Social and Cultural Rights** considered the initial report of Iceland on articles 1 to 15 of the Covenant on Economic, Social and Cultural Rights (E/1990/5/Add. 6 and 14) at its meetings on 25 and 26 November 1993 and, on 8 December 1993, adopted the following concluding observations (E/1994/23, paras. 217–225):

### Positive Aspects

The Committee welcomes the efforts undertaken by the Government of Iceland in order to implement the rights recognized in the Covenant. It notes with satisfaction that the Government of Iceland pays a great deal of attention in its activities to the promotion and protection of economic, social and cultural rights in accordance with the obligations undertaken under article 2 of the Covenant and that the Government has in recent years enacted a series of important laws of direct relevance to these rights.

In that regard, the Committee notes with particular satisfaction that Law No. 28/1991 on Equal Status and Equal Rights of Women and Men secures equal rights of men and women in general, and not only with regard to remuneration, as was the case before the adoption of that law. The Committee also notes with interest the establishment of the Equal Rights Council with the aim of ensuring the proper implementation of the Equal Rights Law and forming the policies to be followed by the authorities in matters concerning gender equality. The Committee also welcomes the establishment of a committee to hear and investigate complaints relating to alleged instances of gender discrimination. The Committee notes with interest, in the context of the measures undertaken to implement provisions of articles 3 and 7 of the covenant, the work being carried out by the Icelandic Wage Investigation Committee and the adoption by the Government in 1988, on the initiative Of the Equal Status Council and the Ministry of Social Affairs, of the equal opportunity programmes to be implemented by ministries and State institutions.

The Committee expresses its appreciation of the range and quality of the services provided to the whole population, including particularly, the elderly, in relation to social security, protection of the family, health care and education.

The Committee appreciates the amendments to the legislation concerning unemployment insurance (Law No. 69/1993), which, in contrast to previous legislation, extends benefits also to non-members of a trade union. It also appreciates information according to which, currently, all workers between the ages of 16 and 71, resident in Iceland, are entitled to unemployment benefits, the only condition being that they have worked in the previous 12 months for a total of no less than 425 hours in insurable employment, and regarding the fact that benefits have been extended to the self-employed.

### Factors and Difficulties Impeding the Application of the Covenant

The Committee is aware of the difficulties encountered by Iceland with regard to the full implementation of the right to strike embodied in article 8 of the Covenant, which the State party attributes to the fact that the economy of Iceland is heavily dependent upon fishing. In the view of the Committee, this circumstance does not relieve the State party of its obligation to take steps to achieve progressively the full realization of the rights recognized in the Covenant, including the right to strike.

### Principal Subjects of Concern

The Committee notes that, in spite of numerous legislative measures undertaken to ensure equality between the sexes, inequality between men and women still exists in practice, especially in relation to the rights recognized in articles 6 and 7 of the Covenant. The Committee encourages the Government to continue its endeavours to eliminate the persisting disparities in remuneration for men and women.

### Suggestions and Recommendations

The Committee recommends that the State party should accord equal treatment to both International Human Rights Covenants in terms of their domestic legal status and that, if measures are taken to incorporate civil and political rights treaty obligations, consideration should be given to similar measures in relation to economic, social and cultural rights.

The Committee emphasizes that further measures should be taken to ensure that the provisions of the Covenant are more widely disseminated, particularly among the legal profession and members of the judiciary.

The Committee urges that the reporting obligations of the State party under articles 16 and 17 of the Covenant be strictly observed and that the second periodic report be submitted within the time-limit to be determined by the Committee.

**ILO.** See **INTERNATIONAL LABOR ORGANIZATION.**

**IMPUNITY.** The term "impunity" refers to a pardon, often a general amnesty, granted to individuals or groups accused of heinous crimes; impunity is sometimes granted by national courts in an effort to make a clean start after a period of major upheaval. In a communication circulated as an official document to the UN **COMMISSION ON HUMAN RIGHTS** in February 1988 (UN Doc. E/CN.4/1988/NGO/51), 18 non-governmental organizations in consultative status with the UN **ECONOMIC AND SOCIAL COUNCIL** expressed their deep concern about indiscriminate amnesty laws which provide what they described as impunity to repressive forces responsible for gross violations of human rights. The communication reads as follows:

We, concerned non-governmental organizations, have noted an alarming trend in many parts of the world: civilian Governments, and in some cases the military themselves, are allowing virtual impunity to repressive forces which have been responsible for crimes of torture, "disappearance", murder—in some cases to the point of genocide—and other human rights violations.

This impunity has been accomplished through various means: amnesty laws granted by Governments, constitutional statutes and decrees, and the simple *de facto* method of failure by Governments to implement existing laws. We call this cluster of methods impunity because it places criminals above the law and leaves crimes unpunished, which in essence reinforces these patterns of behaviour by military, paramilitary and security forces and gives them the freedom to continue these practices, or to threaten to do so.

At the trial of Klaus Barbie, the Nazi criminal, it was clear that the end of the Second World War and the passage of 40 years did not diminish the horror of the atrocities committed nor the necessity for justice to be done. Yet under national security doctrines and counter-insurgency programmes, crimes of great magnitude have also been carried out more recently in many countries, and in others are still being carried out.

In a number of countries in Latin America, Africa and Asia, civilian Governments have in fact absolved or ignored the crimes of armies and individuals, and are still doing so in some cases. This effort is explained as necessary to consolidate democracy or avoid more bloodshed. In other countries where military rule still exists, although there are loudly proclaimed moves towards democracy, military rulers have taken measures to avoid ever being prosecuted for human rights violations. Sometimes, these provisions for impunity have been taken to the level of the national constitutions or "legalized" in national law. Often, in fact, civilian Governments and new "democracies" are subservient to former military rulers precisely because impunity has been granted to them by these Governments.

We state very firmly that the issue is larger than a single nation's constitution or internal law. It is an issue of international human rights law. Since the Nürnberg trials following the Second World War, international law has been clear on the necessity for the military of each country to respect the principles of human rights. The 1984 United Nations Convention against Torture and Other Cruel, Inhuman or Degrading Treatment or Punishment, in upholding the Nürnberg decision concerning the use of torture, stated: "No exceptional circumstances whatsoever, whether a state of war or a threat of war, internal political instability or any other public emergency, may be invoked as a justification of torture." Other international standards uphold absolute respect for human rights, including the International Convention on Civil and Political Rights and the 1968 Convention on the Non-Applicability of Statutory Limitations to War Crimes and Crimes against Humanity. Yet, the kinds of impunity laws being granted to military and repressive forces place them above international law and thus threaten all of civilization.

It has been argued that granting this sort of impunity is a necessary price for establishing democracy. While we welcome the transition to constitutional rule in countries which have suffered serious violations of human rights by armies in power, we see this as only the first step towards real democracy. We believe that laws granting impunity, rather than consolidating democracy, in fact weaken constitutional rule and may open the way for its reversal by a defiant army. These laws prevent justice from being done and allow powerful military forces to continue their domination behind the scenes through a persistent climate of intimidation and terror. Moreover, they perpetuate the bitter divisions that have plagued society. Democracy is more than formal elections or the turning over of government from military forces to civilians. Democracy must mean, among other things, an effective set of laws and a judiciary that can hold accountable criminals and violators of human rights. There can be no real democracy in a society where there is no justice, where murderers and torturers go free, where victims can achieve no legitimate rights for their loved ones and there is no accounting of what happened.

We believe that this issue, due to its magnitude, deserves the attention of the Commission on Human Rights. Some background work has been done by non-governmental organizations, human rights organizations, concerned individuals and this coalition, but we consider it necessary for the United Nations to start addressing this problem. In this sense we suggest the following measures:

1. Approval of a resolution expressing concern for indiscriminate amnesty and laws and measures leading to impunity;

2. Appointment of an *ad hoc* group of experts to study the consequences for human rights of granting impunity laws and decrees to repressive forces, expanding the work of document E/CN.4/Sub.2/1987/16 on the administration of justice and the human rights of detainees, particularly the practice of administrative detention without charge or trial;

3. Request to the Sub-Commission on Prevention of Discrimination and Protection of Minorities to analyze the problem in depth, as it has affected many peoples;

4. Reaffirmation of existing international law covering crimes against humanity, and work towards a convention to prevent impunity for these crimes.

We know that full implementation of the measures here could take a long time, but we feel it is necessary for the United Nations to send a visible signal to all concerned, especially to the peoples who have suffered widespread and gross violations of human rights. Civilian Governments must see that the world cares and supports their efforts to democratize. Victims of past repression must see others join their demand for justice. Military and repressive forces must see that they cannot act with impunity and trample international and national law as well as respect for human rights.

In its Vienna Declaration and Program of Action (para. II.91), the World Conference on Human Rights supported the efforts of the Commission and Sub-Commission to intensify opposition to the impunity of perpetrators of serious violations of human rights.

The UN SUB-COMMISSION ON PREVENTION OF DISCRIMINATION AND PROTECTION OF MINORITIES has established Special Rapporteurs to look into the question of impunity. The progress report of a Special Rapporteurs (E/CN.4/Sub.2/1993/6), submitted to the Sub-Commission at its 1993 session, set out the following conclusions and recommendations (paras. 127–135):

National reconciliation is only possible beyond the stage of forgiving and forgetting. That is why, in the short- or medium-term, we prefer to use the expression "conciliation", which is more respectful of the distress of the victims. There again, the final report should define the possible "hard core" that should be respected in any process of national conciliation. Discussions might focus on the following six guidelines:

I. Action should be guided by the sole objective of civil peace, with a view to guaranteeing the security of the most disadvantaged persons as a matter of priority, since social injustice is more often than not at the origin of the troubles that engender impunity (see the earlier reference to the concept of serious violations of economic and social rights).

II. A decision should be taken to discontinue proceedings against prisoners of opinion and to release them immediately (not to grant them an amnesty, since this would signify acknowledgment of the criminal nature of their actions, when in fact all they have done is to exercise a legitimate right, and the true offender is the perpetrator of the arbitrary detention).

III. Impunity should not be encouraged, which means that the instigators and highly placed persons responsible should be brought to justice and tried.

IV. A commission for the establishment of the truth should be set up in order to preserve the "right to know" of victims and to incorporate the historical dimension of conciliation, which means acquiring awareness and not forgetting.

V. Perpetrators other than those covered by principle III should be tried, or at least purged.

VI. The following measures should be taken in support of victims:

(a) Compensation for injury suffered;

(b) Reinstatement in their employment of persons dismissed for political reasons;

(c) Right of return for exiles and measures for their reintegration.

Only after this lengthy sequence can national reconciliation be envisaged, and then only if the perpetrators of violations, especially those who have not been tried, agree to openly repent, failing which the victims cannot be asked to participate in a process of forgiveness. Without a minimum of repentance, any clemency measure may be interpreted as an endorsement. It may be noted that a display of repentance by all the parties concerned facilitates such a process. The importance of this point is demonstrated, in the case of El Salvador, by the public act of self-criticism made by the FMLN in order to facilitate conciliation within the framework of the National Commission for the Consolidation of Peace (COPAZ). This is particularly true since, under the Peace Agreements, FMLN members responsible for serious violations will not be able to accede to public office. This agreed purging measure deserves to be acknowledged in an equally responsible manner by the State party in order to facilitate the purging of the armed forces.

Without being exhaustive, this report has tried to identify the many facets of organized impunity more clearly, with the aim of facilitating the formulation of a strategy geared to the historical period through which the country is passing; such a strategy must give priority, in turn, to prevention through training and advisory services and to law enforcement as a means not only of inflicting punishment, but also of perpetuating the memory of history as it actually was and not as revisionism always wants to rewrite it.

The campaign against impunity must employ a variety of

means and be organized on a long-term basis, setting itself the following four additional goals:

(a) Trying the perpetrators of serious violations;

(b) Ensuring the victims' right to know and to obtain reparation;

(c) Guarding against forgetting and revisionism, particularly through the keeping of records;

(d) At a given point in time, taking account of aspirations for national reconciliation while respecting certain limits beyond which national reconciliation would be the accomplice of impunity.

To conclude this progress report on impunity, the authors make the following recommendations:

1. The final report should take greater account of the suggestions made by Mr. Theo van Boven in his study concerning the right to restitution, compensation and rehabilitation for victims of gross violations of human rights and fundamental freedoms.

2. The present study may be expected to be followed by a specific report on action to combat impunity for serious violations of economic and social rights.

3. Non-governmental organizations should be given a greater role in the strategy for combating impunity.

4. The scope of due obedience in the light of the theory of mitigating circumstances should be more clearly delimited in order to restrict its effects.

5. A comparative study should be made of the various experiences of the truth-finding commissions in order to assess the feasibility and desirability of establishing some guidelines on the subject.

6. Efforts should be made to find ways and means of overcoming the obstacles posed by the *in absentia* procedure before a possible international court.

7. Guidelines for conserving and regulating access to the files and records of the security and intelligence services should be drawn up.

8. A specific study should be prepared, in conjunction with the Human Rights Committee and the regional commissions and courts, on the scope of the right of every person to a hearing, and particularly on whether or not this right is subject to derogation.

9. A comparative analysis should be made of the various purging policies implemented in recent decades in order to identify possible guidelines regarding grounds that may legitimize such policies and the safeguards to be afforded.

10. Ways and means of eradicating the practice of death squads should be studied.

11. Guidelines for the implementation of national reconciliation policies, including in particular a hard core of principles which may not be violated in any circumstances, should be worked out.

12. A programme of action ensuring the optimum application of the provisions of the Geneva Conventions and Protocols which can be used to combat impunity should be formulated.

The primary beneficiaries of these treaty norms are the victims, followed by States as the entities responsible for their implementation, without of course forgetting the specific assistance that can be provided by the International Committee of the Red Cross (ICRC) pursuant to the provisions common to the four Conventions. Making these norms more effective involves taking certain initiatives, namely:

(a) The launching of an awareness campaign aimed at inducing States parties to incorporate in their criminal legislation the enforcement provisions laid down in the Conventions;

(b) The conduct of a study designed to elucidate the following two points in order to identify more clearly the reasons for this ineffectiveness:

(i) Conclusions to be drawn from the few cases in which the perpetrators of serious crimes have actually been sentenced on the basis of the Geneva Conventions (for example, the United States, where war crimes are also offences under the United States Uniform Code of Military Justice, which the Criminal Investigation Division is responsible for prosecuting. Between 1965 and 1973, 36 cases in which indictments were preferred against army personnel for war crimes were brought before the court martial; 20 of them resulted in convictions);

(ii) Conclusions to be drawn concerning the use, or otherwise, of the universal jurisdiction clause contained in the Conventions;

(c) The development of coordinated action by non-governmental organizations vis-à-vis States parties to ensure that, on a case-by-case basis, States parties give full effect to the aforementioned article 1 common to the four Conventions, by which they undertake not only to respect those instruments but also to ensure respect for them, even if they are not parties to the conflict;

(d) The expansion of the role of victims and the relevant non-governmental organizations in ensuring the application of the Conventions, particularly through a revised interpretation of the concept of a legitimate interest in action which takes better account of the spirit, and indeed the letter, of the Geneva Conventions, so as to enable certain NGOs to bring proceedings before the competent national or, as appropriate, international courts. In that connection, it would be desirable to explore the possibilities of a joint interpretation by National Red Cross Societies, on behalf of the victims, of the statutes of the International Federation of Red Cross and Red Crescent Societies, on the one hand, and of the Conventions, on the other (for example, Convention IV, art. 142, and, in particular, protocol I, art. 81, para. 3);

(e) Promotion of the use of the means afforded by the International Fact-Finding Commission, a body of inquiry provided for by article 90 of protocol I.

We would like to conclude this progress report on a hopeful note. It is possible to combat impunity and render justice without jeopardizing the possibilities for national reconciliation, as demonstrated by the recent decision of the Supreme Court of Bolivia (21 April 1993), which served to restore confidence in the judiciary, one of the cornerstones of any democracy. After a seven-year campaign against impunity, human rights associations and democratic organizations hailed this ruling as the "judgement of the century". Judge Gualberto Davalos, sharing this view, observed that this decision "constitutes an important precedent for the strengthening of democracy and a warning in Bolivia as in other countries of Latin America" to anyone contemplating a coup d'état.

The perpetrators of the most serious violations, who had ousted the constitutional Government of Lydia Gueiler, together with 44 of their accomplices, received the following sentences:

The former dictator Luis García Neza: 30 years' imprisonment without the possibility of a pardon;

The former Minister of the Interior, Luis Arce Gomez, the former chief of the repressive apparatus, Guido Benavidez, the former chief of the National Department of Investigation, Freddy Quiroga, the former chief of the Special Security Service and his deputy Tito Montano: 30 years' imprisonment.

It is fitting that a report on the adverse effects of impunity should conclude with a tribute to those responsible for such a decision, which, far beyond the country's frontiers, does honour to justice in Bolivia, gives renewed hope to all victims and their relatives, and shows that justice can prevail over impunity.

Having examined the Special Rapporteurs' progress report, the Sub-Commission on Prevention of Discrimination and Protection of Minorities welcomed it and shared the opinion of the Special Rapporteurs that they should undertake the final study in two stages: first with respect to civil and political rights and thereafter with respect to economic, social and cultural rights (resolution 1993/37 of 26 August 1993). This decision was later approved by the Commission on Human Rights and the Economic and Social Council.

**SEE ALSO** Amnesty.

**BIBLIOGRAPHY.** Americas Watch. *Chile: The Struggle for Truth and Justice for Past Human Rights Violations.* New York: Human Rights Watch, 1992. NGO report, in English.
―――――. *South Africa: Accounting for the Past: The Lessons for South Africa from Latin America.* New York: Human Rights Watch, 1992. NGO report, in English.
―――――. *Truth and Partial Justice in Argentina: An Update.* New York: Human Rights Watch, 1991. NGO factfinding report, in English.
Artucio, Alejandro. "La Comunidad Internacional Frente a la Impunidad por los Crímenes de la Dictadura: Ley 15.848" (The International Community's Opposition to the Impunity over the Crimes of the Dictatorship. Law 15.848), *Revista de IELSUR* no. 6 (July 1990): 24–32. Article, in Spanish.
Asia Watch and Physicians for Human Rights. *A Pattern of Impunity: The Human Rights Crisis in Kashmir.* New York: Human Rights Watch, 1993. NGO report, in English.
Dokumentation und Informationszentrum Menschenrechte in Lateinamerika/Centro de Documentación e Información sobre Derechos Humanos en América Latina. "Impunidad en América Latina" (Impunity in Latin America), *Memoria: Boletín informativo del DIML* no. 1–2 (1990): 1–84. Special issue, in Spanish.
International Commission of Jurists and the Centre for the Independence of Judges and Lawyers. *Chile: A Time of Reckoning—Human Rights and the Judiciary.* Geneva, Switzerland: 1992. NGO report, in English.
Kokott, Juliane. "No Impunity for Human Rights Violations in the Americas," *Human Rights Law Journal* 14, no. 5–6 (June 1993): 153–159. Scholarly article, in English.

**INDIA.** The Republic of India is a country in southern Asia occupying most of the Indian sub-continent, located between the Arabian Sea and the Bay of Bengal; it also includes three groups of islands: the Andamans (204 islands) and the Nicobars (19 islands) in the Bay of Bengal and the Laccadives (14 islands) in the Arabian Sea. It has borders with Bangladesh, Bhutan, China, Myanmar, Nepal, and Pakistan. It achieved independence from Great Britain in 1947 and became a member of the United Nations in 1945. Its population is estimated by the UN to be 854,897,000. Ethnic groups include Indo–Aryan (72%), Dravidian (25%), and Mongoloid (2%). The population also includes members of "scheduled castes" and "scheduled tribes," for which special provisions are included in the 1950 constitution with the aim of helping them to attain equality in real terms; these provisions, and a wide variety of special programs and measures undertaken by the government, are not considered by the government to violate the principle of equality but rather to benefit all the peoples of India. More than 200 languages are in common use, including Hindi (official) and 14 languages recognized in the constitution: Assamese, Bengali, Gujarati, Kannada, Kannarese, Kashmiri, Malayam, Marathi, Oriya, Punjabi, Sindhi, Tamil, Telegu, and Urdu. Religions practiced include Hinduism (83%), Islam (11%), Christianity (3%), Animism (1%), and others including the Sikh, Jain, Parsi, and Buddhist faiths (2%). Literacy is estimated at 40%.

The government (1994) took the form of a republic and member of the Commonwealth. It is described in the constitution as "a Sovereign, Socialist, Secular, Democratic Republic." The president, elected by popular vote for a term of five years, is head of State. He appoints, and is advised by, the prime minister and cabinet, who represent the party or coalition given a majority in a popular election. Parliament is bicameral, consisting of the Council of States (*Rajya Sabha*) and the House of the People (*Lok Sabha*). Members of the Council of States represent the constituent units of the republic: 22 states and nine union territories. Members of the House of the People are elected by popular vote for terms of five years. Political parties include the Congress Party, the Lok Dal Party, the Congress II Party, the Communist Party and the Communist Party of India.

History has made India the home of people with diverse origin, many of whom came from beyond the country's borders. Hinduism, Buddhism, Jainism and later Sikhism were faiths cradled by India. Christianity, in the coastal regions of Western India, goes back to apostolic times. Islam came to India within the first century of its emergence. India is thus composed of a wonderful mosaic of different religions and cultures. It has a tolerant, eclectic society where people of many different faiths and persuasions have joined together in building the world's largest democracy, a democracy in which universally recognized human rights and fundamental freedoms are guaranteed to all without any discrimination on grounds of creed or community. At the time of the 1981 census the total population of India was 683,997,512. Since 1971 it had shown an increase of 24.78%. The census mentions that more than 1,500 languages are spoken in the country. Of these 15 are specified and recognized in the VIIIth schedule of the Constitution; 90% of the Indian population speaks one of these 15 languages.

In spite of the diversity, India is the largest democracy in the world where elections are held periodically on the basis of universal and equal adult franchise; and article 325 of the constitution provides that no person shall be ineligible for inclusion in the general electoral roll on grounds only of religion, race, caste, sex, or any of them. Indian citizens enjoy the right to participate in public affairs, and all Indians have equal access to employment in the public services. While guaranteeing these rights, the constitution provides for reservations in favor of the scheduled castes and tribes and other disadvantaged classes.

India's traditional lack of any sort of unity—physical, political, social, linguistic, or religious—periodically gives rise to serious human rights problems. Controlled by force during the early years of British colonial rule, which began in 1757, these problems multiplied soon after World War I when the All-India Congress Party, led by Mohandas K. Gandhi, spearheaded nonviolent but effective revolts against British authority. The party's main demand was for a measure of self-government for India, which had sent more than six million troops into the war. The British responded in 1919 by giving India a federal form of government and a measure of self-rule.

In 1942, as Japanese troops approached India's eastern borders, the Congress Party demanded that the British leave India. In an effort to avoid further confrontations, the Indian government arrested Gandhi and other party leaders and announced its determination to transfer power to "responsible Indian hands" by June 1948 even if a constitution recognizing Indian independence had not been completed by that time.

In June 1947, Lord Mountbatten, as viceroy, reached an agreement on independence which called for the partitioning of British India into two dominions: India, with a Hindu majority, and Pakistan, with a Moslem majority. Two provinces, Bengal and the Punjab, which the Moslems had claimed, were to be split between the two new states. The Indian Independence Act was quickly adopted by the British Parliament and received royal assent on 8 July 1947. On 15 August, the Indian empire passed into history.

The resultant flight of large groups of Hindus and Moslems who suddenly found themselves in hostile territory was accompanied by the outright murder of millions of refugees as communal passions exceeded all bounds. The hostility between India and newly established Pakistan was subsequently aggravated by warfare over the princely states of Hyderabad and Kashmir.

***SYSTEM OF CASTES.*** In today's India, the most persistent human rights problem relates to the situation of the "scheduled castes" and "scheduled tribes," designated as such by presidential orders in accordance with articles 341 and 342 of the constitution. According to the 1981 census, the population of scheduled castes was 104,754,623 and that of scheduled tribes was 51,628,638; together they comprise about 24% of the country's population.

In a report submitted to the United Nations on 26 June 1986 (UN Doc. CERD/C/149/Add. 11, paras. 14–22), the government of India stated that:

The Constitution prescribes protection and safeguards for the scheduled castes and scheduled tribes and other weaker sections, either specially or by way of insisting on their general rights as citizens, with the object of promoting their educational and economic interests and of removing the social disabilities. The main safeguards are:

(i) Abolition of "untouchability" and forbidding of its practice in any form (art. 17);

(ii) Promotion of their educational and economic interests and their protection from social injustice and all forms of exploitation (art. 46);

(iii) Throwing open by law of Hindu religious institutions of a public character to all classes and sections of Hindus (art. 25b);

(iv) Removal of any disability, liability, restriction or condition with regard to access to shops, public restaurants, hotels and places of public entertainment or the use of wells, tanks, bathing ghats, roads and places of public resort maintained wholly or partially out of State funds or dedicated to the use of the general public (art. 15(2));

(v) Curtailment by law in the interests of any scheduled tribe, of the general rights of all citizens to move freely, reside and settle in any part of India (art. 19(5));

(vi) Permitting the State to make reservation for the backward classes in public services in case of inadequate representations and requiring the State to consider the claims of the scheduled castes and scheduled tribes in the making of appointments to public services (arts. 16 and 335);

(vii) Reservation of seats in the *Lok Sabha* and the State Legislatures (*vidhan sabhas*) to scheduled castes and tribes (arts. 330, 332 and 334);

(viii) The setting up of tribes advisory councils and separate departments in the states and the appointment of a special officer at the centre to promote their welfare and safeguard their interests (arts. 244 and 338 and 5th Schedule);

(ix) Special provision for the administration and control of scheduled and tribal areas (art. 244 and 5th and 6th Schedules); and

(x) Prohibition of traffic in human beings and forced labour (art. 23).

To enlarge the scope and make the penal provision more stringent, the Untouchability (Offences) Act, 1955 was comprehensively amended by the Untouchability (Offences) Amendment and Miscellaneous Provisions Act, 1976, which came into force from 19 November 1976. With this amendment, the name of the principal Act has been changed to the Protection of Civil Rights Act, 1955. The Act provides penalties for preventing a person, on the ground of untouchability, from enjoying the rights accruing out of abolition of untouchability. Enhanced penalties/punishment have also been provided for subsequent offences.

Under section 8 of the Representation of the People Act, 1951, a person who is convicted of an offence under the Act is disqualified from contesting elections to Parliament and State legislatures for a period of six years commencing from the date of such conviction.

The Protection of Civil Rights Act, 1955, is administered by the state governments also from time to time. Under a provision in the Act, the Government also lays before each House of Parliament an annual report on the working of the provisions of section 15A of the Act.

Under articles 330 and 332 of the Constitution, seats are reserved for scheduled castes and scheduled tribes in the *Lok Sabha* or the Lower House of Parliament and State *vidhan sabhas* or legislatures in proportion to their population. This concession was initially for a period of 10 years from the commencement of the Constitution but has been extended, through amendments up to 25 January 1990. Parliamentary Acts provide for such reservations in the Union territories having legislatures. Following the introduction of *panchayati raj*, safeguards have been provided for proper representation of the members of the scheduled castes and tribes by reserving seats for them in the *gram panchayats* and other local bodies.

Article 335 of the Constitution provides that the claims of the members of the scheduled castes and scheduled tribes shall be taken into consideration, consistent with the maintenance of efficiency of administration, in making appointments to posts and services, in connection with the affairs of the Union or of a state. Article 16(4) permits reservation in favour of citizens of backward classes, who may not be adequately represented in services. In pursuance of these provisions, the Government has made reservations for scheduled castes and scheduled tribes in the services under their control.

A Commission for the scheduled castes and scheduled tribes consisting of a chairman and four members, including the special officer appointed under article 338 of the Constitution known as the Commissioner for Scheduled Castes and Scheduled Tribes, was set up in August 1978. The Commission is to investigate all matters relating to Constitutional safeguards, reservation in public services; to study the implementation of the Protection of Civil Rights Act, 1955, with particular reference to the objective of removal of untouchability and invidious discrimination arising therefrom; and to ascertain the socio-economic and other relevant circumstances responsible for the commission of offences against persons belonging to scheduled castes and tribes with a view to recommending appropriate remedial measures.

A number of voluntary organizations also promote the welfare of the scheduled castes and scheduled tribes. Important organizations of all-India character are: Harijan Sevak Sangh, Delhi; Bharatiya Depressed Classes League, New Delhi; Ishwar Saran Ashram, Allahabad; Indian Red Cross Society, New Delhi; Hind Sweepers Sevak Samaj, New Delhi; Ramakrishnan Mission, Narendrapur, West Bengal; Bharatiya Adimjati Sevak Sangh, New Delhi; Andhra Rashtra Adimjati Sevak Sangh, Nellore, Remakrishna Mission, Cheerapunchi, Ranchi, Puri, Silchar and Shillong; Thakkar Bapa Ashram, Numakhandi, Orissa; Servants of India Society, Pune; and Social Work and Research Centre, Tilonia, Rajasthan.

Government provides grants-in-aid to non-official voluntary organizations working among scheduled castes and scheduled tribes.

**BONDED LABOR.** Since 1978 the Indian government has sponsored a plan for rehabilitation of freed bonded laborers, which provides for matching assistance to the extent of 50% of the total cost subject to a ceiling of 2,000 rupees per bonded laborer. The individual state governments have been asked to treat the plan as a national program for the effective and permanent rehabilitation of identified and freed bonded labor. By 30 September 1983, 158,946 bonded laborers had been identified and freed; of these, 116,917 had been rehabilitated.

Despite the government's efforts to end bonded labor schemes, the practice continues to be a major human rights problem. The **ANTI-SLAVERY SOCIETY FOR THE PROTECTION OF HUMAN RIGHTS,** a non-governmental organization in consultative status, submitted the following information to the UN Working Group on Contemporary Forms of Slavery at the working group's 1988 session (UN Doc. E/CN.4/Sub.2/AC.2/1988/7/Add. 1):

In its report to the Working Group on Slavery last year, the Anti-Slavery Society pointed out that it had several times raised the issue of bonded labour in India in the United Nations. On each occasion, the official response, as relayed by the Indian representative on the Sub-Commission on Prevention of Discrimination and Protection of Minorities, was that the problem was being resolved with all the despatch and vigour that Delhi and the State capitals could command. Therefore there was no cause for concern.

The Anti-Slavery Society maintains there is cause for concern. India is not the only country where debt bondage occurs, but it is home to the largest number of bonded labourers in the world. By extrapolation, and using the 1983 judgement of the Supreme Court of India, those trapped in debt bondage could form 10 per cent of the population: 80 million bonded labourers, the greatest number of contemporary slaves on the face of the earth.

The Anti-Slavery Society has recently finished its own investigation into the malleable nature of contemporary bonded labour, particularly as it affects the landless in and migrating from Bihar.

Bihar has been described as being India's most feudal State. Thousands of Biharis migrate to economically more advanced areas every year, and frequently they are forced to do so by the village money-lender. This may sometimes lead to the debtor being able, eventually, to pay off his debt because the money he earns away from his home and family is significantly more than is available in Bihar. Until the loan is repaid in full, the debtor is in bondage and his family form a living surety for his return or repayment.

North Bihar provides seasonal workers for Punjab's agrarian sector. These come from the scheduled castes. South Bihar annually provides some 10,000 migrant workers drawn from the scheduled tribes. These become agricultural workers bonded to creditor-employers or labour contractors in Punjab itself.

Share-cropping continues to be a means of entrapping borrowers into debt bondage. Land ownership in Bihar is unequal—72 per cent of cultivators own fewer than five acres—and the 1961 Bihar Land Reform Act had the unintended consequence of increasing dependence on large landowners. Tenants were evicted and re-engaged as simple share-croppers.

A poor peasant farmer may become a share-cropper when, during a lean period, he falls further into debt and his land is taken in lieu of unredeemed loans. He then joins the ranks of the landless.

A landless labourer or a poor peasant with insufficient land may be forced through circumstance and the lack of alternative local employment to share-crop for a large landlord or rich peasant. He becomes indebted to his "partner" through taking out loans, in cash or in kind, in order to perform his role as a share-cropper.

The eventual result is an increase in debt bondage.

It is the view of the Anti-Slavery Society that the introduction of new technology in the more economically advanced States, particularly in Punjab and Haryana, has aggravated and not relieved the age-old condition of debt bondage in India. This development, allied with traditional practices and obligations, has resulted in an increase in contemporary slavery.

The Anti-Slavery Society repeats its pleas of previous years made in this Working Group, and urges the Government of India to take all measures not only to free its most vulnerable people from slavery, but to ensure freed bonded labourers receive the full rehabilitation sums due to them under the 1976 Bonded Labour (Abolition) Act.

***CHILDREN WORKERS.*** Of particular concern is the problem of child bonded labor, especially in the carpetmaking industry. Child carpet weavers, usually boys below the age of 15, are reported to suffer from practices similar to slavery. In its 1988 report to the Working Group on Contemporary Forms of Slavery, the Anti-Slavery Society for the Protection of Human Rights furnished the following information:

Professor B.N. Juyal quotes Shridar Mishra, a leading figure in India's carpet-making industry, as saying that the Government is considering proposals "to raise the minimum wages on the pretext of regulating the wages of bonded child workers, which shall prove suicidal to the development of the industry."

This is revealing on two counts: it implies ruthless employment practices and it explicitly admits the existence of bonded child labour.

Carpet-making is an officially designated hazardous industry and, consequently, children are prohibited from working in it by article 24 of the Constitution and by the 1938 Employment of Children Act.

Even under the much-criticized new legislation, the Child Labour (Regulation) Act, 1986, children are prohibited from making carpets except as part of a family labour force and in familial conditions.

The Anti-Slavery Society's latest research into labour conditions in the Mirzapur-Varanasi-Bhadohi carpet belt in the State of Uttar Pradesh reveals that school-age boys are being employed in contravention of the law, and that they are underpaid (if paid at all), ill-treated, badly fed, unhealthy, kept illiterate and innumerate, kidnapped and sold deliberately or naively into bondage.

India today has at least 100,000 juvenile carpet-making slaves. They are slaves as defined by the United Nations 1956 Supplementary Convention on the Abolition of Slavery, the Slave Trade and Institutions and Practices similar to Slavery because:

(a) They suffer gross labour exploitation;
(b) They are below the age of 15;
(c) 15 per cent of them are aged between 6 and 11;
(d) Some of them have been sold into debt bondage.

It is difficult to know the precise number of bonded children. It is certain that in the main they come from the scheduled castes and scheduled tribes of Bihar, and that sometimes they are kidnapped. When this occurs, the parents do not even receive the approximately £25 which is the common advance on the wages their children will supposedly earn.

In addition, the "industry" is composed of some 55,000 looms located in about 15,000 villages scattered over a large area. The loom owners in fact are frequently tied to specific manufacturers who have advanced them the money to buy the loom. Because they are one-man-and-a-couple-of-boys operations, they do not even have to register under either the Factory Act or the Shops and Establishment Act. These unregistered premises account for 95 per cent of the carpet belt's production.

The boys working at the looms are passed off as sons or nephews, and this in spite of about half the child labour force having been brought in from other areas.

What is greatly disturbing is that the Indian authorities not only know about the gross exploitation of the carpet-making boys, are not only aware of the daily and wholesale contravention of legislation, but they may be regarded as being originally responsible for this contemporary form of slavery. In 1975, the Government set up training centres for children who were required to work over six hours a day and so denied schooling. In 1981, the Government claimed to be turning out 30,000 child carpet-makers under the age of 15.

A recital of statistics does not convey the misery of exploited child labour.

The Anti-Slavery Society appreciates the difficulties involved in eradicating exploitative child labour in the carpet industry. It does not advocate emancipation in a void; accordingly, it is proud to announce the founding of Project Mala.

Project Mala aims to raise the standard of life and the future expectations of children working in the carpet industry by offering them benefits which are in fact guaranteed under the Indian Constitution: education, training, health and an adequate diet. Although it is only boys who work at the looms, Project Mala will not discriminate sexually, and girls will be entitled to equal benefit.

It is intended to set up six schools during the next three years. Each school will serve a cluster of villages so that children will be able to walk to and from school each day. One of the schools will, however be a boarding school to cater for those children who have been "imported", by whatever means, from further afield. This boarding school will almost certainly be established in the Palamau region on the Uttar Pradesh-Bihar border, since it is from there that the majority of bonded children come.

The school day will be divided into two: one half will be devoted to basic education along the Gandhian lines and the other half to vocational training of an appropriate kind. For the boys, this vocational training may indeed centre on carpet-weaving but girls will learn other skills which will help them to generate their own incomes and thus relieve them from utter dependency on their menfolk. By education along Gandhian lines is meant a learning process which will be relevant to the children's circumstances and way of life, rather than an externally imposed system to which they would find it difficult to relate.

Great importance will be attached to personal hygiene and, since tuberculosis is endemic in the region, children will be regularly screened so that the disease can be caught in its earliest stages when it is relatively easy to cure. Care for the children's health will be reinforced by the good, well-balanced midday meal which will be provided in all the schools. In the boarding school all meals as well as decent accommodation will be provided.

The conditions in which the weavers work, and this applies to adults as well as to children, are usually very bad. The weaving huts are badly lit, with poor ventilation, and the looms themselves are usually of rudimentary and inefficient design. The Intermediate Technology Group has been asked to advise on improvements to both the looms and the huts. It is hoped that this will result in much better working conditions, as well as a reduction in the quantity of rejected carpets. This improved efficiency will increase significantly the income from each loom as well as providing a better quality of goods.

Children are driven to difficult work by a simple economic necessity. The weavers are usually poor farmers who turn to carpet-making to eke out a penurious living during slack seasons or when harvests are poor. Now that there is an increased demand for carpets, weaving tends to occupy more of a family's time and it is this increased demand which has given rise to abuses such as the sale or kidnapping of children. Essentially, it is sheer poverty, allied to the lack of educational and other facilities, which drives children to work. Without the children's income most families would be hard put to it to survive.

Project Mala takes account of this economic necessity by paying a stipend to each child in school and this stipend will increase annually so that the family will suffer no loss of income; indeed, with girls as well as boys benefiting in this way, a family's income should be significantly greater. It is hoped that this simple economic fact will help overcome the inherent conservatism of the villagers and that they will accept the opportunity for improving their children's chances in life which Project Mala offers.

The scheme is unique in that it brings together for the first time a group of voluntary organizations, the State Government of Uttar Pradesh and representatives of the carpet industry. The scheme also enjoys the blessing of the Union Ministry of Labour in Delhi and is attracting the interest and support of both the British Overseas Development Administration and the European Community in Brussels. The International Labour Organisation is also following the scheme's progress with interest and with its moral support.

A site for the first school has been found near Mirzapur. The buildings already *in situ* are readily adaptable for the purposes of the school, vocational training centre and other facilities. Project Mala should have its first school in operation by the end of the year, and it is hoped that this collaborative effort may serve as a model for similar schemes in other industries and, perhaps, in other countries.

Although India, unlike many third world countries, has succeeded in preserving its constitutional democracy and has improved its national income, its health standards, and its production of food, the improvements have not kept pace with the rapid increase in its population. Observance of the 40th anniversary of India's independence on 15 August 1987 evoked a flood of soul-searching introspection about its future.

One problem is the declining efficiency of the civil service bureaucracy; once so well trained that it was able to assume the responsibilities of government overnight when the British left the country, it has been wracked by disclosures of systematic bribery, illicit kickback payments, and tax evasion. Another is that the separation of church and State, enshrined in the constitution, has been threatened by resurgences of domination by the Hindu majority and by clashes between religious extremists and the government. A third is that little, if any, new leadership has emerged to fight for reform and to compel the nation to pay more attention to the plight of its poor and deprived. A fourth is that the Congress Party, which since the days of Mahatma Gandhi held the confidence and respect of the Indian people, seems to have lost some of its mass support.

***RELIGIOUS CONFLICTS.*** In recent years, one of India's major human rights problems has involved antagonisms between religious groups. In 1984, Prime Minister Indira Ghandi ordered a military invasion of the Golden Temple in Amritsar to rout out military Sikhs who had occupied it, demanding restoration of their civil rights. Four months later, she was assassinated by her Sikh bodyguards. Her son and successor, Rajiv Ghandi, fought a continuous and sometimes successful battle against Sikh terrorists but never won their trust. Prime Minister V. P. Singh, who took office in December 1989, journeyed to Amritsar to pray at the Golden Temple as his first official trip outside New Delhi and set up a non-partisan conference to deal with the Sikh demands for an independent homeland to be known as Khalistan.

Two Sikh men, found guilty of killing Mrs. Ghandi, were later hanged. But although thousands of suspects, including members of the governing Congress Party, were the subject of government inquiries as possible instigators of the mobs that roamed through Sikh areas for four days—killing more than 3,000 men and boys and destroying thousands of homes and businesses—fewer than ten were convicted and many others are said to remain active in the government of the current Prime Minister, P. V. Narasimha Rao.

***KASHMIR.*** In Kashmir Valley, a predominantly Muslim territory largely occupied by India, there have been frequent attacks on Indian officials and installations by militants demanding the withdrawal of Indian troops and the holding of a UN-supervised plebescite. India has persistently refused to permit such a plebescite in its part of the Muslim-majority valley; however Pakistan, which occupies the remainder, strongly favors it, knowing that Kashmir's population feels strongly bound to it by ties of religion.

Islamic militancy has swept through Kashmir Valley on the ground that India has failed to make good its promises of economic development and better links with the outside world. Calling themselves "Allah's Tigers," long-unemployed young men have taken to roaming the streets of Srinagar in groups, halting the sale of alcoholic drinks, and monitoring the dress of women. Their stated aim is restoration of the human rights of the Kashmiri people and ending what they term the Indian "reign of terror."

Since the partition of the Indian sub-continent in 1947, India and Pakistan have twice gone to war over Kashmir without conclusive results. Efforts to mediate the dispute have been dismissed as interference in the "domestic affairs" of India, and from time to time India has suspended the elected Kashmiri government and substituted direct rule from New Delhi.

At the 1994 session of the UN **COMMISSION ON HUMAN RIGHTS**, Pakistan proposed that India should be given an international reprimand for violating the human rights of Kashmiris, and that a UN mission should be sent to investigate the numerous allegations of abuse. However, the proposal was withdrawn on 9 March before it had been put to the vote. And on 10 March India announced that it would not permit a mission organized by Amnesty International to enter Kashmir to investigate such allegations on the ground that organization "has not been fair or balanced or just with regard to India."

**BIBLIOGRAPHY.** Agarwal, A., J. Merrifield, and R. Tandon. *No Place to Run: Local Realities and Global Issues of the Bhopal Disaster.* New Market, TN, USA: Highlander Research and Education Center and Society for Participatory Research in Asia, 1985. NGO report, in English.

Amnesty International. *Human Rights Violations in Punjab: Use and Abuse of the Law.* London: 1991. NGO factfinding report, in English.

———. *India: Allegations of Extrajudicial Killings by the Provincial Armed Constabulary in and around Meerut, 22–23 May 1987.* London: 1987. NGO report, in English.

———. *India: "An Unnatural Fate": Disappearances and Impunity in the Indian States of Jammu, Kashmir, and Punjab.* London: 1993. NGO report, in English.

———. *India: Examination of Second Periodic Report by the Human Rights Committee: Recommendations to Bring Indian Laws and Practices in Line with International Human Rights Standards.* London: 1993. NGO report, in English.

———. *India: Operation Bluebird: A Case Study of Torture and Extrajudicial Executions in Manipur.* London: 1990. NGO factfinding report, in English.

———. *India: Torture, Rape and Deaths in Custody.* London: 1992. NGO factfinding report, in English.

———. *The Need to Review Cases against 324 Sikhs Held for More Than Four Years in Jodhpur Jail, Rajasthan.* London: 1988. NGO issue paper, in English.

Andreassen, B. A., and A. Eide, eds. *Human Rights in Developing Countries 1987/88: A Yearbook on Human Rights in Countries Receiving Nordic Aid.* Copenhagen, Denmark: Christian Michelsen Institute, 1988. NGO report, in English; bibliography, pp. 357–372.

Asia Watch. *Dead Silence: The Legacy of Abuses in Punjab.* New York: Human Rights Watch, 1994. NGO report, in English.

———. *Human Rights in India: Kashmir under Siege.* New York: Human Rights Watch, 1991. NGO factfinding report, in English.

———. *Prison Conditions in India.* New York: Human Rights Watch, 1991. NGO report, in English.

———. *Punjab in Crisis: Human Rights in India.* New York: Human Rights Watch, 1991. NGO factfinding report, in English.

Asia Watch and Physicians for Human Rights. *A Pattern of Impunity: The Human Rights Crisis in Kashmir.* New York: Human Rights Watch, 1993. NGO report, in English.

Bhargava, Ashok. "The Bhopal Incident and Union Carbide: Ramifications of an Industrial Accident," *Bulletin of Concerned Asian Scholars* 18, no. 4 (October–December 1986): 2–19. NGO article, in English.

*Bhopal: Industrial Genocide? A Unique Compilation of Documents from Indian Publications.* Hong Kong: Asian Regional Exchange for New Alternatives, 1985. Edited collection, in English.

Center for the Independence of Judges and Lawyers. *The Independence of the Judiciary in India.* Geneva, Switzerland: International Commission of Jurists, 1990. Conference report, in English.

Chatterjee, Amrita. *India: The Forgotten Children of the Cities.* Florence, Italy: UNICEF International Child Development Centre, 1992. IGO monograph, in English.

Committee for Initiative for Human Rights. *India's Kashmir War.* New Delhi, India: 1990. NGO factfinding report, in English.

Cross, Peter. *Kashmiri Carpet Children: Exploited Village Weavers.* London: Anti-Slavery International, 1991. NGO monograph, in English.

Cultural Survival. "Mountain Peoples," *Cultural Survival Quarterly* 10, no. 3 (1986). Edited collection, in special issue, in English.

de Villiers, Bertus. "Directive Principles of State Policy and Fundamental Rights: The Experience of India," *South African Journal on Human Rights* 8, part 1 (1992): 29–49. Scholarly article, in English.

Donnelly, J., and R. E. Howard, eds. *International Handbook on Human Rights.* Westport, CT, USA: Greenwood Press, 1987. Scholarly edited collection, in English.

Gunewardene, Roshani M. "The Caste System: A Violation of Fundamental Human Rights?" *Human Rights Law Journal* 11, no. 1–2 (1990): 35–55. Scholarly article, in English.

Guttal, G. H. "Human Rights: The Indian Law," *Indian Journal of International Law* 26, no. 1 and 2 (January–June 1986): 53–71. Scholarly article, in English.

"Inde: Pays Riche, Peuple Pauvre," *Bulletin CRIDEV* 53 (November 1985). NGO special issue bulletin, in French.

International Commission of Jurists. *The Independence of Judges and Lawyers in South Asia.* Geneva, Switzerland: 1988. NGO conference report, in English.

———. "India: Situation in the State of Punjab," *The Review* 36 (June 1986): 7–12. NGO article, in English.

International Work Group for Indigenous Affairs. *The*

*Naga Nation and its Struggle against Genocide.* Copenhagen, Denmark: 1986. NGO report, in English.

Joshi, Barbara R., ed. *Untouchable! Voices of the Dalit Liberation Movement.* London: Minority Rights Group, 1986. Edited collection, in English.

Kothari, Smithu. "Ecology vs. Survival: The Struggle for Survival in India," in *The International Context of Rural Poverty in the Third World: Issues for Research and Action by Grassroots Organizations and Legal Activists,* pp. 203–224. Center for Law in Development, 1986. NGO monograph, in English.

Lawyers Committee for Human Rights. *India: The Human Rights Commissions Bill, 1993.* New York: 1993. NGO report, in English.

Liddle, J., and R. Joshi. *Daughters of Independence: Gender, Caste, and Class in India.* London: Zed Books, 1986. Scholarly monograph, in English.

Mendelsohn, Oliver. "Life and Struggles in the Stone Quarries of India: A Case-Study," *Journal of Commonwealth and Comparative Politics* 29, no. 1 (1991). Scholarly article, in English.

Moon, Minakshi, and Pawar, Urmila. "We Made History Too: Women in the Early Untouchable Movement," *South Asia Bulletin* 9, no. 2 (1989): 68–71. Scholarly article, in English.

Omvedt, Gail. "The Anti-Caste Movement and the Discourse of Power," *Race & Class: A Journal for Black and Third World Liberation* 33, no. 2 (October–December 1991): 15–28. Scholarly article, in English.

Physicians for Human Rights and Asia Watch. *The Crackdown in Kashmir: Torture of Detainees and Assaults on the Medical Community.* New York: 1993. NGO report, in English.

"The Politics of Human Rights," *Lokayan Bulletin* 5, no. 4/5 (1987). Collection of scholarly articles in special issue, in English.

Rahman, Anika. "Religious Rights Versus Women's Rights in India: A Test Case for International Human Rights Law," *Columbia Journal of Transnational Law* 28, no. 2 (1990): 473–498. Scholarly article, in English.

Raj, Antony. *Children of a Lesser God.* Madurai, Tamilnadu, India: Dalit Christian Liberation Movement, 1992. NGO report, in English.

Reddy, O. Chinnappa. "Human Rights Movement in India," *Socio-Legal Concern Newsletter* 2, no. 6 (June 1986): 2–10. NGO article, in English.

———. *The Indian Legal System and Human Rights.* Madras, India: Centre for Socio-Legal Research and Documentation Service, 1987. Speech, in English.

"Safeguards to Human Rights under the Indian Constitution," *Socio-Legal Concern Newsletter* 4, no.11 and 12 (November–December 1988): 8–23. NGO article, in English.

Sangari, K., and S. Said. "Sati in Modern India: A Report," *Economic and Political Weekly* (1 August 1981): 1284–1288. Journal article, in English.

Sigler, Jay A., ed. *International Handbook on Race and Race Relations.* Westport, CT, USA: Greenwood Press, 1987. Scholarly edited collection, in English; bibliography, pp. 449–454.

Singh, R., B. Joshi, and S. Singh, eds. *The Turning Point—India's Future Direction?* Syracuse, NY, USA: 1985. Edited collection, in English.

Sinha, Arun. *Against the Few: Struggles of India's Rural Poor.* London: Zed Books, 1991. Monograph, in English.

U.S. Committee for Refugees. *From Isolation to Exile: Refugees from the Chittagong Hill Tracts of Bangladesh.* Washington, D.C.: 1988. NGO report, in English.

Vigil India Movement. "Cultural Rights vs. Human Rights," *Vigil India* 44 (February 1988). NGO bulletin special issue, in English.

Widmalm, Sten. *Dowry Crime and Law Implementation in India.* Uppsala, Sweden: University of Uppsala, Department of Government, 1990. Research report, in English.

**INDIAN COUNCIL OF SOUTH AMERICA.** An international non-governmental organization in consultative status (Roster) with the UN **ECONOMIC AND SOCIAL COUNCIL,** best known by its Spanish title *Consejo Indio de Sudamérica (CISA),* the Council is affiliated with 15 organizations in 10 American countries.

Established in 1980 with the participation of delegations from 10 South American countries, CISA works to promote and secure the human rights of Indians of Latin America, to improve the economies of Indian communities, and to regain territory taken from indigenous peoples. CISA publishes *Pueblo Indio* (in Peruvian and international editions) and *Boletín Informativo CISA* (in Spanish).

Indian Council of South America. Address: Ave. J. de Canterac 373, Apdo Postal 2054, Correo Postal, Lima 100, Peru. Telephone: (51-14) 236-955. Administrator: Adrian Orozco Huaytalla.

**INDIGENOUS PEOPLES.** The **INTERNATIONAL LABOR ORGANIZATION (ILO)** has been concerned with the situation of indigenous and tribal peoples since 1921, and in 1957 adopted its Indigenous and Tribal Populations Convention (no. 107). Thirty-two years later it replaced that instrument by the adoption on 27 June 1989 of the **ILO INDIGENOUS AND TRIBAL PEOPLES CONVENTION** (no. 169). The ILO's pervasive long-term interest in the subject is traced in a document which it prepared and circulated to the Preparatory Committee for the World Conference on Human Rights (UN Doc. A/CONF.157/PC/61/Add. 10), which reads in part as follows:

According to conservative figures, there are about 300 million indigenous and tribal peoples around the world, representing 4.8% of the world population. There are profound differences among them in terms of the ecological environment they inhabit, cultural integrity, economic organisation, social and religious practices, and degree and terms of relationship to national political and economic systems.

Notwithstanding these differences, indigenous and tribal peoples share many common characteristics, and many common problems. These include exploitation and social exclusion, weak representation in national political systems, limited access to basic assets and services, and cultural discrimination. In rural areas, indigenous and tribal peoples have been gradually losing control over their traditional lands thus becoming landless, debt peons, tenants or marginal farmers. In urban areas, they are an uprooted, unskilled, unorganised and unprotected labour force. Indigenous and tribal peoples are often caught up in armed conflicts, where they are the victims of abuses not only by government forces but also by armed opposition groups.

Only in recent years has the wider international community started to become concerned with the social disruption, cultural destruction and physical disappearance of indigenous and tribal peoples. There is an increasing recognition that cultural diversity is not an obstacle to national development, but on the contrary can foster and contribute to it. Closely linked to this point is the increasing awareness that a wealth of accumulated knowledge adapted to local conditions is being lost with the extinction of indigenous societies. This has become a particularly important issue, with many indigenous and tribal peoples living in ecologically threatened areas and being the most vulnerable to environmental resource crisis.

Moreover, the sharp growth in inter-ethnic conflicts worldwide has made apparent the need for a new relationship between the State and indigenous and tribal peoples (and, of course, other minority groups). The conceptual national model based on the imposition of a unique model of development and of artificial cultural homogeneity has failed to guarantee a Pacific and fruitful coexistence.

The ILO's principal goals in this field are to promote the human rights of indigenous and tribal peoples, and to enhance their position within national societies, with respect for their cultural specificity. To attain these goals the ILO has two means of action: specific standards on the subject and a targeted technical cooperation programme. These two instruments are closely linked to one another and are mutually supportive.

ILO standards on the subject provide the guidelines for operational activities, while development assistance contributes to the creation of the environment conducive to the exercise of the rights established by them. Standards can be a very powerful tool of social transformation, but they are not sufficient. Complementary efforts have to be made to empower indigenous and tribal peoples economically, socially and politically.

*CONCERN OF THE UNITED NATIONS.* In 1971 the UN ECONOMIC AND SOCIAL COUNCIL, on recommendation of the SUB-COMMISSION ON PREVENTION OF DISCRIMINATION AND PROTECTION OF MINORITIES, authorized Mr. José Martinez Cobo, a member of the Sub-Commission, to act as its Special Rapporteur in preparing a study of discrimination against indigenous populations (Council resolution 1589 (L)). The study was completed only in 1985. At the request of the Council, Parts I and II were issued as a consolidated document (E/CN.4/Sub.2/1986/7), while Part III, setting out the Special Rapporteur's conclusions was printed (UN publication, Sales no. E.86.XIV.3).

One of the questions considered in detail in Part III is that of the definition of "indigenous populations" from the international point of view. In this connection, the Special Rapporteur points out that "the fundamental assertion must be that indigenous populations must be recognized according to their own perception and conception of themselves in relation to other groups; there must be no attempt to define

them according to the perception of others through the values of foreign societies or of the dominant sections in such societies." On this subject, he continues (paras. 369–382, 402–403):

The right of indigenous peoples themselves to define what and who is indigenous must be recognized.

The correlative of this faculty is, obviously, the faculty of defining or determining what or who is not indigenous.

No State may take, by legislation, regulations or other means, measures that interfere with the power of indigenous nations or groups to determine who are their members.

Artificial, arbitrary or manipulative definitions must, in any event, be rejected.

As regards the circumstance that gave rise to the notion of indigenous populations, it must be said that the special position of indigenous populations within the society of nation-States existing today derives from their historical rights to their lands, as well as from their right to be different and to be considered as different.

Much of their land has been taken away and whatever land is left to them is subject to constant encroachment. Their culture and their social and legal institutions and systems have been constantly under attack at all levels, through the media, the law and the public educational systems. It is only natural, therefore, that there should be resistance to further loss of their land and rejection of the distortion or denial of their history and culture and defensive/offensive reaction to the continual linguistic and cultural aggressions and attacks on their way of life, their social and cultural integrity and their very physical existence. They have a right to continue to exist, to defend their lands, to keep and to transmit their culture, their language, their social and legal institutions and systems and their way of life, which have been illegally and unjustifiably attacked.

It is in the context of these situations and these rights that the question of definition should arise. Social scientists have reached the conclusion that ethnic groups can be characterized only by the distinctions which they themselves perceive between themselves and other groups with which they have to interact. They exist as such ethnic groups as long as they consider themselves different from those other groups. Ethnic groups determine their rules concerning membership, contemplating inclusion or exclusion of individuals whom they may accept or reject as members, or those they will adopt or ostracize, and those who may or may not represent them. On an individual basis, belonging to such groups depends on two main factors: self-identification as members of the group (group consciousness) and recognition by the group that those given individuals belong to it (acceptance by the group). Thus the group may, under its own rules governing membership, and inclusion and exclusion of individuals, accept or reject some persons as its members, while adopting or ostracizing others. It may, further, keep these rules unchanged or modify them as it wishes, without any outside interference.

It is clear that indigenous peoples consider themselves to be different from the other groups that form the society of present-day nation-States in which they now find themselves included. They consider themselves to be the historical successors of the peoples and nations that existed on their territories before the coming of the invaders of these territories, who eventually prevailed over them and imposed on them colonial or other forms of subjugation, and whose historical successors now form the predominant sectors of society. It is also abundantly clear that indigenous peoples consider themselves different from those other peoples and demand the right to be considered different by other sectors of society and by the international community.

Indigenous peoples wish to keep whatever territory has been left to them and to regain land illegally taken from them, so as to have an adequate land base for their existence as different peoples. They also want their culture, language, social and legal institutions, which they consider essential for their own organization and existence, to be respected and recognized in those nation-States. They wish to keep, develop and transmit to future generations their territories, social and legal institutions and systems, their culture and their language.

Indigenous populations may, therefore, be defined as follows for the purposes of international action that may be taken affecting their future existence:

Indigenous communities, peoples and nations are those which, having a historical continuity with pre-invasion and pre-colonial societies that developed on their territories, consider themselves distinct from other sectors of the societies now prevailing in those territories, or parts of them. They form at present nondominant sectors of society and are determined to preserve, develop and transmit to future generations their ancestral territories, and their ethnic identity, as the basis of their continued existence as peoples, in accordance with their own cultural patterns, social institutions and legal systems.

This historical continuity may consist of the continuation, for an extended period reaching into the present, of one or more of the following factors:

(a) Occupation of ancestral lands, or at least of part of them;

(b) Common ancestry with the original occupants of these lands;

(c) Culture in general, or in specific manifestations (such as religion, living under a tribal system, membership of an indigenous community, dress, means of livelihood, life-style, etc.);

(d) Language (whether used as the only language, as mother-tongue, as the habitual means of communication at home or in the family, or as the main, preferred, habitual, general or normal language);

(e) Residence in certain parts of the country, or in certain regions of the world;

(f) Other relevant factors.

On an individual basis, an indigenous person is one who belongs to these indigenous populations through self-identification as indigenous (group consciousness) and is recognized and accepted by these populations as one of its members (acceptance by the group).

This preserves for these communities the sovereign right and power to decide who belongs to them, without external interference. . . .

Diversity is not, in itself, contrary to unity, any more than uniformity itself necessarily produces the desired unity. Indeed, there can be weakness and hostility within artificially produced uniformity, just as there can be strength in diversity co-ordinated within a harmonious, yet many-faceted whole, based on respect for the special nature of each component part.

Pluralism, self-management, self-government, autonomy and self-determination within a policy of ethnic development, as defined in the San José Declaration, appear to be the formula called for by the times in which we are now living and to do justice to the aspirations and desires of indigenous populations, which have for so long been subjected to interference and imposed conditions of all kinds. The Special Rapporteur is convinced that, following these guidelines would not be promoting artificial distinctions or separatist aspirations where such feelings do not exist, but would simply be recognizing the multiform nature of the societies of States with indigenous populations. It is essential not to prevent such groups from fully regaining a historical awareness of their own existence as such and to enable them to control their future according to their own aspirations and traditions. To do otherwise is to prolong the subjugation and oppression of groups and cultures capable of making a significant contribution to mankind, today as in the past. They should be afforded that opportunity like any other people on our planet, if frictions and conflicts caused by lack of understanding and injustice are to be avoided.

The Special Rapporteur then suggests a number of steps which, in his view, should be taken by the governments of countries having indigenous populations with a view to eliminating discrimination against such populations and their individual members, as follows (para. 405):

Governments which have not yet done so should consider establishing institutions, machinery and specialized administrative procedures, since entities with specific and clearly defined mandates are in a better position to accord due attention to solving the difficult and complex problems currently facing indigenous populations in the countries in which they live.

A second question considered in detail in Part II of the study relates to the status of the treaties which govern the relationships between various indigenous populations and the states in which they live. Because of the paramount importance of this question, the Special Rapporteur proposes that a thorough and careful study should be made of the subject in its entirety, including the official force of such treaties; the observance, or lack of observance, of their provisions; and the consequences for the population concerned.

As regards the policy to be adopted in dealing with the problem of discrimination against indigenous populations, the Special Rapporteur offers the following views (paras. 399–401, 406–412):

The Special Rapporteur is fully aware that each country will determine its ethnic, cultural, linguistic and religious policies on the basis of prevailing conditions and other criteria which it deems pertinent. The suggestions put forward in this regard are based on the existing alternatives and the preferences which the needs of indigenous populations and current world thinking appear to demand. While the recommendations do not represent any attempt to dictate policies to any sovereign State, a number of suggestions can nevertheless be made.

States should seek to gear their policies to the wish of indigenous populations to be considered different, as well as to the ethnic identity explicitly defined by such populations. In the view of the Special Rapporteur, this should be done within a context of socio-cultural and political pluralism which affords such populations the necessary degree of autonomy, self-determination and self-management commensurate with the concepts of ethnic development described in chapters IX and XV.

The unity which is a legitimate concern of many States, particularly those which have most recently acceded to independence, can be achieved most fully and profoundly through a genuine diversity which respects differences between existing groups aspiring to a distinct identity within society as a whole. The desired unity will be achieved more fully if it is based on diversity, rather than on an imposed uniformity inconsistent with the genuine feelings of the population. Within that diversity, each group would participate more fully since it would do so on the basis of its own conceptions, values and patterns, rather than attempting to use modes of expression which are foreign to it. . . .

Governments which have divided responsibility for indigenous population affairs among a number of ministries, departments or institutions should consider the advantages of setting up a special body to co-ordinate such efforts. They should also consider the possibility of authorizing that or some other body to co-ordinate and harmonize private programmes with government policy.

Governments with parliamentary systems should endeavour to set up legislative committees and sub-committees specializing in indigenous affairs, with a view to according more careful study and specialized consideration to legislation in this area.

Governments should consider setting up consultative or advisory bodies, either of a general or a specialized nature, and at the national or local level, to make use of the specialized knowledge of non-governmental experts and, in particular, to encourage the participation of authentic representatives of indigenous populations. This would ensure the greater involvement of those populations in the formulation and implementation of official policy and programmes, the revision and amendment of which should be based on their points of view.

The selection and immovability of the staff of departments concerned with indigenous affairs should be governed by the norms generally applicable to civil service or administrative personnel. Special measures should be adopted, however, to secure the services of specially qualified individuals and, in particular, of members of indigenous communities, to occupy such posts, with a number of key and decision-making posts being reserved for them. Pre-service or in-service training programmes on the problems of indigenous populations and possible solutions should also be regarded as essential for the effective preparation and utilization of available staff and resources.

Special efforts should be made to ensure the adequate funding of institutions and administrative programmes concerned with indigenous affairs at all times. Consideration should be given to the possibility of establishing trust funds to provide the necessary stability for certain budgetary provisions and to supplement regular appropriations in specific critical areas. Entities or undertakings which generate their own income should be subjected to annual reviews by joint consultative or advisory bodies (governmental and non-governmental, indigenous and non-indigenous), in order to ensure that the attainment of the proposed income targets does not conflict with general policy, which should constitute a compact and meaningful body of guiding principles serving the interests of indigenous populations, as they themselves conceive such interests.

Governments should consider ways of encouraging non-governmental organizations and, in particular, those established by indigenous populations, through normative measures and the necessary financial assistance, and of promoting the participation of indigenous communities in consultative and advisory bodies and proceedings.

Governments should recognize the pertinence and special competence of indigenous communities and organizations in this area and should increasingly incorporate them into policy-making and policy-implementing bodies and processes and programmes of fundamental importance to indigenous populations. The need for the participation of such communities and organizations in advisory and consultative procedures should be recognized explicitly, and increasing efforts should be made in daily life with regard to indigenous affairs.

As areas requiring special attention if discrimination against indigenous populations is to be eliminated, the Special Rapporteur cites health, housing, education, language, culture, employment, land use and development, political rights, and religious rights and practices.

His basic proposal for dealing with the problem of discrimination against indigenous populations is to begin by formulating specific principles for use as guidelines by governments in their relationships with such populations, on a basis of respect for the ethnic identity of such populations and for the rights and freedoms to which they are entitled:

Such principles must necessarily contain any additional and specific provisions which, following careful study, may be deemed necessary for the fuller recognition and protection of the indispensable rights and freedoms of indigenous populations. . . . When the ideas and measures considered fundamental have been organized into a set of principles, the Sub-Commission may deem it advisable to recommend to its subsidiary organs the need to prepare a declaration of the rights and freedoms of indigenous populations as a possible basis for a convention on that question.

In fact, the Sub-Commission did enlist the assistance of its Working Group on Indigenous Populations in preparing the draft Universal Declaration on Indigenous Rights.

***DRAFT DECLARATION ON THE RIGHTS OF INDIGENOUS PEOPLES.*** In 1985, the Working Group on Indigenous Populations decided to proceed with the preparation of a draft declaration on indigenous rights for eventual proclamation by the General Assembly. Pursuant to this decision it prepared and adopted provisional texts in 1985 and 1987, and in the latter year recommended that its Chairman/Rapporteur, Mrs. Erica-Irene A. Daes, be entrusted with the preparation of a working paper consisting of a full set of preambular paragraphs and principles for insertion in the draft declaration.

The Chairman/Rapporteur's working paper (UN

Doc. E/CN.4/Sub.2/1988/25) was accepted by the working group at its 1988 session and was forwarded to the Sub-Commission as an annex to the working group's report (UN Doc. E/CN.4/Sub.2/1988/24, annex II). The Sub-Commission examined it at its 1988 session, endorsed (resolution 1988/18) the working group's decision to adopt it as the framework for the drafting of a universal declaration on indigenous rights, and requested the Secretary-General to transmit the working group's report to governments, indigenous peoples, and to intergovernmental and non-governmental organizations, for their specific comments and proposals. It recommended that the Chairman/Rapporteur should later be entrusted with preparing a revised text of the draft declaration on the basis of the comments and proposals received and the discussion in the working group.

The working group, at its 1989 session, examined the first revised text of the draft Universal Declaration on the Rights of Indigenous Peoples (E/CN.4/Sub.2/1989/33) and recommended that its Chairman/Rapporteur be entrusted with the task of preparing and presenting in 1990 a further revision based on comments received in writing and those made at sessions of the working group.

At its 1993 session, the working group, having agreed on the text of a draft declaration, submitted it to the Sub-Commission for consideration. After examining the text and expressing its appreciation and satisfaction to the working group for its valuable work, the Sub-Commission decided (a) to postpone until its 1995 session consideration of the draft declaration; (b) to request the Secretary-General to submit the draft declaration to the appropriate services within the Centre for Human Rights for its technical revision; and (c) to request the Secretary-General to transmit the technically revised text of the draft declaration to governments, intergovernmental and non-governmental organizations and to indigenous peoples and organizations no later than 31 March 1994 and to note explicitly that no further amendments to the technically revised text will be accepted during the future proceedings of the working group but that the report of the working group on its 1994 session will contain a summary of general views expressed by the participants on the draft declaration. The Commission on Human Rights later (resolution 1994/29 of 4 March 1994) urged the Sub-Commission to complete its consideration of the draft declaration and to submit it to the Commission at its 1995 session.

The draft declaration, as agreed upon by the members of the Working Group, is as follows (E/CN.4/Sub.2/1994/2/Add. 1):

Affirming that indigenous peoples are equal in dignity and rights to all other peoples, while recognizing the right of all peoples to be different, to consider themselves different, and to be respected as such,

Affirming also that all peoples contribute to the diversity and richness of civilizations and cultures, which constitute the common heritage of humankind,

Affirming further that all doctrines, policies and practices based on or advocating superiority of peoples or individuals on the basis of national origin, racial, religious, ethnic or cultural differences are racist, scientifically false, legally invalid, morally condemnable and socially unjust,

Reaffirming also that indigenous peoples, in the exercise of their rights, should be free from discrimination of any kind,

Concerned that indigenous peoples have been deprived of their human rights and fundamental freedoms, resulting, *inter alia*, in their colonization and dispossession of their lands, territories and resources, thus preventing them from exercising, in particular, their right to development in accordance with their own needs and interests,

Recognizing the urgent need to respect and promote the inherent rights and characteristics of indigenous peoples, especially their rights to their lands, territories and resources, which derive from their political, economic and social structures and from their cultures, spiritual traditions, histories and philosophies,

Welcoming the fact that indigenous peoples are organizing themselves for political, economic, social and cultural enhancement and in order to bring an end to all forms of discrimination and oppression wherever they occur,

Convinced that control by indigenous peoples over developments affecting them and their lands, territories and resources will enable them to maintain and strengthen their institutions, cultures and traditions, and to promote their development in accordance with their aspirations and needs,

Recognizing also that respect for indigenous knowledge, cultures and traditional practices contributes to sustainable and equitable development and proper management of the environment,

Emphasizing the need for demilitarization of the lands and territories of indigenous peoples, which will contribute to peace, economic and social progress and development, understanding and friendly relations among nations and peoples of the world,

Recognizing in particular the right of indigenous families and communities to retain shared responsibility for the upbringing, training, education and well-being of their children,

Recognizing that indigenous peoples have the right freely to determine their relationships with States in a spirit of coexistence, mutual benefit and full respect,

Considering that treaties, agreements and other arrangements between States and indigenous peoples are properly matters of international concern and responsibility,

Acknowledging that the Charter of the United Nations, the International Covenant on Economic, Social and Cultural Rights and the International Covenant on Civil and Political Rights affirm the fundamental importance of the right of self-determination of all peoples, by virtue of which they freely determine their political status and freely pursue their economic, social and cultural development,

Bearing in mind that nothing in this Declaration may be used to deny any peoples their right of self-determination,

Encouraging States to comply with and effectively implement all international instruments, in particular those related to human rights, as they apply to indigenous peoples, in consultation and cooperation with the Peoples concerned,

Emphasizing that the United Nations has an important and continuing role to play in promoting and protecting the rights of indigenous peoples,

Believing that this Declaration is a further important step forward for the recognition, promotion and protection of the rights and freedoms of indigenous peoples and in the development of relevant activities of the United Nations system in this field,

Solemnly proclaims the following United Nations Declaration on the Rights of Indigenous Peoples:

*Article 1.* Indigenous peoples have the right to the full and effective enjoyment of all human rights and fundamental freedoms recognized in the Charter of the United Nations, the Universal Declaration of Human Rights and international human rights law.

*Article 2.* Indigenous individuals and peoples are free and equal to all other individuals and peoples in dignity and rights, and have the right to be free from any kind of adverse discrimination, in particular that based on their indigenous origin or identity.

*Article 3.* Indigenous peoples have the right of self-determination. By virtue of that right they freely determine their political status and freely pursue their economic, social and cultural development.

*Article 4.* Indigenous peoples have the right to maintain and strengthen their distinct political, economic, social and cultural characteristics, as well as their legal systems, while retaining their rights to participate fully, if they so choose, in the political, economic, social and cultural life of the State.

*Article 5.* Every indigenous individual has the right to a nationality.

*Article 6.* Indigenous peoples have the collective right to live in freedom, peace and security as distinct peoples and to full guarantees against genocide or any other act of violence, including the removal of indigenous children from their families and communities under any pretext.

In addition, they have the individual rights to life, physical and mental integrity, liberty and security of person.

*Article 7.* Indigenous peoples have the collective and individual right not to be subjected to ethnocide and cultural genocide, including prevention of and redress for:

(a) Any action which has the aim or effect of depriving them of their integrity as distinct peoples, or of their cultural values or ethnic identities;

(b) Any action which has the aim or effect of dispossessing them of their lands, territories or resources;

(c) Any form of population transfer which has the aim or effect of violating or undermining any of their rights;

(d) Any form of assimilation or integration by other cultures or ways of life imposed on them by legislative, administrative or other measures;

(e) Any form of propaganda directed against them.

*Article 8.* Indigenous peoples have the collective and individual right to maintain and develop their distinct identities and characteristics, including the right to identify themselves as indigenous and to be recognized as such.

*Article 9.* Indigenous peoples and individuals have the right to belong to an indigenous community or nation, in accordance with the traditions and customs of the community or nation concerned. No disadvantage of any kind may arise from the exercise of such a right.

*Article 10.* Indigenous peoples shall not be forcibly removed from their lands or territories. No relocation shall take place without the free and informed consent of the indigenous peoples concerned and after agreement on just and fair compensation and, where possible, with the option of return.

*Article 11.* Indigenous peoples have the right to special protection and security in periods of armed conflict.

States shall observe international standards, in particular the Fourth Geneva Convention of 1949, for the protection of civilian populations in circumstances of emergency and armed conflict, and shall not:

(a) Recruit indigenous individuals against their will into the armed forces and, in particular, for use against other indigenous peoples;

(b) Recruit indigenous children into the armed forces under any circumstances;

(c) Force indigenous individuals to abandon their lands, territories or means of subsistence, or relocate them in special centres for military purposes;

(d) Force indigenous individuals to work for military purposes under any discriminatory conditions.

*Article 12.* Indigenous peoples have the right to practise and revitalize their cultural traditions and customs. This includes the right to maintain, protect and develop the past, present and future manifestations of their cultures, such as archaeological and historical sites, artifacts, designs, ceremonies, technologies and visual and performing arts and literature, as well as the right to the restitution of cultural, intellectual, religious and spiritual property taken without their free and informed consent or in violation of their laws, traditions and customs.

*Article 13.* Indigenous peoples have the right to manifest, practise, develop and teach their spiritual and religious traditions, customs and ceremonies; the right to maintain, protect, and have access in privacy to their religious and cultural sites; the right to the use and control of ceremonial objects; and the right to the repatriation of human remains.

States shall take effective measures, in conjunction with the indigenous peoples concerned, to ensure that indigenous sacred places, including burial sites, be preserved, respected and protected.

*Article 14.* Indigenous peoples have the right to revitalize, use, develop and transmit to future generations their histories, languages, oral traditions, philosophies, writing systems and literatures, and to designate and retain their own names for communities, places and persons.

States shall take effective measures, whenever any right of indigenous peoples may be threatened, to ensure this right is protected and also to ensure that they can understand and be understood in political, legal and administrative proceedings, where necessary through the provision of interpretation or by other appropriate means.

*Article 15.* Indigenous children have the right to all levels and forms of education of the State. All indigenous peoples also have this right and the right to establish and control their educational systems and institutions providing education in their own languages, in a manner appropriate to their cultural methods of teaching and learning.

Indigenous children living outside their communities have the right to be provided access to education in their own culture and language.

States shall take effective measures to provide appropriate resources for these purposes.

*Article 16.* Indigenous peoples have the right to have the dignity and diversity of their cultures, traditions, histories and aspirations appropriately reflected in all forms of education and public information.

States shall take effective measures, in consultation with the indigenous peoples concerned, to eliminate prejudice and discrimination and to promote tolerance, understanding and good relations among indigenous peoples and all segments of society.

*Article 17.* Indigenous peoples have the right to establish their own media in their own languages. They also have the right to equal access to all forms of non-indigenous media.

States shall take effective measures to ensure that State-owned media duly reflect indigenous cultural diversity.

*Article 18.* Indigenous peoples have the right to enjoy fully all rights established under international labour law and national labour legislation.

Indigenous individuals have the right not to be subjected to any discriminatory conditions of labour, employment or salary.

*Article 19.* Indigenous peoples have the right to participate fully, if they so choose, at all levels of decision-making in matters which may affect their rights, lives and destinies through representatives chosen by themselves in accordance with their own procedures, as well as to maintain and develop their own indigenous decision-making institutions.

*Article 20.* Indigenous peoples have the right to participate fully, if they so choose, through procedures determined by them, in devising legislative or administrative measures that may affect them.

States shall obtain the free and informed consent of the peoples concerned before adopting and implementing such measures.

*Article 21.* Indigenous peoples have the right to maintain and develop their political, economic and social systems, to be secure in the enjoyment of their own means of subsistence and development, and to engage freely in all their traditional and other economic activities. Indigenous peoples who have been deprived of their means of subsistence and development are entitled to just and fair compensation.

*Article 22.* Indigenous peoples have the right to special measures for the immediate, effective and continuing improvement of their economic and social conditions, including in the areas of employment, vocational training and retraining, housing, sanitation, health and social security.

Particular attention shall be paid to the rights and special needs of indigenous elders, women, youth, children and disabled persons.

*Article 23.* Indigenous peoples have the right to determine and develop priorities and strategies for exercising their right to development. In particular, indigenous peoples have the right to determine and develop all health, housing and other economic and social programmes affecting them and, as far as possible, to administer such programmes through their own institutions.

*Article 24.* Indigenous peoples have the right to their traditional medicines and health practices, including the right to the protection of vital medicinal plants, animals and minerals.

They also have the right to access, without any discrimination, to all medical institutions, health services and medical care.

*Article 25.* Indigenous peoples have the right to maintain and strengthen their distinctive spiritual and material relationship with the lands, territories, waters and coastal seas and other resources which they have traditionally owned or otherwise occupied or used, and to uphold their responsibilities to future generations in this regard.

*Article 26.* Indigenous peoples have the right to own, develop, control and use the lands and territories, including the total environment of the lands, air, waters, coastal seas, sea-ice, flora and fauna and other resources which they have traditionally owned or otherwise occupied or used. This includes the right to the full recognition of their laws, traditions and customs, land-tenure systems and institutions for the development and management of resources, and the right to effective measures by States to prevent any interference with, alienation of or encroachment upon these rights.

*Article 27.* Indigenous peoples have the right to the restitution of the lands, territories and resources which they have traditionally owned or otherwise occupied or used, and which have been confiscated, occupied, used or damaged without their free and informed consent. Where this is not possible, they have the right to just and fair compensation. Unless otherwise freely agreed upon by the peoples concerned, compensation shall take the form of lands, territories and resources equal in quality, size and legal status.

*Article 28.* Indigenous peoples have the right to the conservation, restoration and protection of the total environment and the productive capacity of their lands, territories and resources, as well as to assistance for this purpose from States and through international cooperation. Military activities shall not take place in the lands and territories of indigenous peoples, unless otherwise freely agreed upon by the peoples concerned.

States shall take effective measures to ensure that no storage or disposal of hazardous materials shall take place in the lands and territories of indigenous peoples.

States shall also take effective measures to ensure, as needed, that programmes for monitoring, maintaining and restoring the health of indigenous peoples, as developed and implemented by the peoples affected by such materials, are duly implemented.

*Article 29.* Indigenous peoples are entitled to the recognition of the full ownership, control and protection of their cultural and intellectual property.

They have the right to special measures to control, develop and protect their sciences, technologies and cultural manifestations, including human and other genetic resources, seeds, medicines, knowledge of the properties of fauna and flora, oral traditions, literatures, designs and visual and performing arts.

*Article 30.* Indigenous peoples have the right to determine and develop priorities and strategies for the development or use of their lands, territories and other resources, including the right to require that States obtain their free and informed consent prior to the approval of any project affecting their lands, territories and other resources, particularly in connection with the development, utilization or exploitation of mineral, water or other resources. Pursuant to agreement with the indigenous peoples concerned, just and fair compensation shall be provided for any such activities and measures taken to mitigate adverse environmental, economic, social, cultural or spiritual impact.

*Article 31.* Indigenous peoples, as a specific form of exercising their right to self-determination, have the right to autonomy or self-government in matters relating to their internal and local affairs, including culture, religion, education, information, media, health, housing, employment, social welfare, economic activities, land and resources management, environment and entry by non-members, as well as ways and means for financing these autonomous functions.

*Article 32.* Indigenous peoples have the collective right to determine their own citizenship in accordance with their customs and traditions. Indigenous citizenship does not impair the right of indigenous individuals to obtain citizenship of the States in which they live.

Indigenous peoples have the right to determine the structures and to select the membership of their institutions in accordance with their own procedures.

*Article 33.* Indigenous peoples have the right to promote, develop and maintain their institutional structures and their distinctive juridical customs, traditions, procedures and practices, in accordance with internationally recognized human rights standards.

*Article 34.* Indigenous peoples have the collective right to determine the responsibilities of individuals to their communities.

*Article 35.* Indigenous peoples, in particular those divided by international borders, have the right to maintain and develop contacts, relations and cooperation, including activities for spiritual, cultural, political, economic and social purposes, with other peoples across borders.

States shall take effective measures to ensure the exercise and implementation of this right.

*Article 36.* Indigenous peoples have the right to the recognition, observance and enforcement of treaties, agreements and other constructive arrangements concluded with States or their successors, according to their original spirit and intent, and to have States honour and respect such treaties, agreements and other constructive arrangements. Conflicts and disputes which cannot otherwise be settled should be submitted to competent international bodies agreed to by all parties concerned.

*Article 37.* States shall take effective and appropriate measures, in consultation with the indigenous peoples concerned, to give full effect to the provisions of this Declaration. The rights recognized herein shall be adopted and included in national legislation in such a manner that indigenous peoples can avail themselves of such rights in practice.

*Article 38.* Indigenous peoples have the right to have access to adequate financial and technical assistance from States and through international cooperation, to pursue freely their political, economic, social, cultural and spiritual development and for the enjoyment of the rights and freedoms recognized in this Declaration.

*Article 39.* Indigenous peoples have the right to have access to and prompt decision through mutually acceptable and fair procedures for the resolution of conflicts and disputes with States, as well as to effective remedies for all infringements of their individual and collective rights. Such a decision shall take into consideration the customs, traditions, rules and legal systems of the indigenous peoples concerned.

*Article 40.* The organs and specialized agencies of the United Nations system and other intergovernmental organizations shall contribute to the full realization of the provisions of this Declaration through the mobilization, *inter alia,* of financial cooperation and technical assistance. Ways and means of ensuring participation of indigenous peoples on issues affecting them shall be established.

*Article 41.* The United Nations shall take the necessary steps to ensure the implementation of this Declaration including the creation of a body at the highest level with special competence in this field and with the direct participation of indigenous peoples. All United Nations bodies shall promote respect for and full application of the provisions of this Declaration.

*Article 42.* The rights recognized herein constitute the minimum standards for the survival, dignity and well-being of the indigenous peoples of the world.

*Article 43.* All the rights and freedoms recognized herein are equally guaranteed to male and female indigenous individuals.

*Article 44.* Nothing in this Declaration may be construed as diminishing or extinguishing existing or future rights indigenous peoples may have or acquire.

*Article 45.* Nothing in this Declaration may be interpreted as implying for any State group or person any right to engage in any activity or to perform any act contrary to the Charter of the United Nations.

***INDIGENOUS PEOPLES AND THE ENVIRONMENT.*** The Rio Declaration on Environment and Development, adopted on 14 June 1992 by the United Nations Conference on Environment and Development, convened at Rio de Janeiro, proclaims (Principle 22) that: "Indigenous people and their communities and other local communities have a vital role to play in environmental management and development because of their knowledge and traditional practices. States should recognize and duly support their identity, culture and interests and enable their effective participation in the achievement of sustainable development."

The Conference developed a comprehensive program to meet these objectives, as set out in Chapter 26 of its report (UN publication, Sales no. E.93.I). Entitled "Recognizing and Strengthening the Role of Indigenous People in their Communities," the chapter reads in part as follows:

### Basis for Action

Indigenous people and their communities have an historical relationship with their lands and are generally descendants of the original inhabitants of such lands. In the context of this chapter the term "lands" is understood to include the environment of the areas which the people concerned traditionally occupy. Indigenous people and their communities represent a significant percentage of the global population. They have developed over many generations a holistic traditional scientific knowledge of their lands, natural resources and environment. Indigenous people and their communities shall enjoy the full measure of human rights and fundamental freedoms without hindrance or discrimination. Their ability to participate fully in sustainable development practices on their lands has tended to be limited as a result of factors of an economic, social and historical nature. In view of the interrelationship between the natural environment and its sustainable development and the cultural, social, economic and physical well-being of indigenous people, national and international efforts to implement environmentally sound and sustainable development should recognize, accommodate, promote and strengthen the role of indigenous people and their communities. . . .

### Objectives

In full partnership with indigenous people and their communities, Governments and, where appropriate, intergovernmental organizations should aim at fulfilling the following objectives:

(a) Establishment of a process to empower indigenous people and their communities through measures that include:

(i) Adoption or strengthening of appropriate policies and/or legal instruments at the national level;

(ii) Recognition that the lands of indigenous people and their communities should be protected from activities that are environmentally unsound or that the indigenous people concerned consider to be socially and culturally inappropriate;

(iii) Recognition of their values, traditional knowledge and resource management practices with a view to promoting environmentally sound and sustainable development;

(iv) Recognition that traditional and direct dependence on renewable resources and ecosystems, including sustainable harvesting, continues to be essential to the cultural, economic and physical well-being of indigenous people and their communities;

(v) Development and strengthening of national dispute-resolution arrangements in relation to settlement of land and resource-management concerns;

(vi) Support for alternative environmentally sound means of production to ensure a range of choices on how to improve their quality of life so that they effectively participate in sustainable development;

(vii) Enhancement of capacity-building for indigenous communities, based on the adaptation and exchange of traditional experience, knowledge and resource-management practices, to ensure their sustainable development;

(b) Establishment, where appropriate, of arrangements to strengthen the active participation of indigenous people and their communities in the national formulation of policies, laws and programmes relating to resource management and other development processes that may affect them, and their initiation of proposals for such policies and programmes;

(c) Involvement of indigenous people and their communities at the national and local levels in resource management and conservation strategies and other relevant programmes established to support and review sustainable development strategies, such as those suggested in other programme areas of Agenda 21.

## Activities

Some indigenous people and their communities may require, in accordance with national legislation, greater control over their lands, self-management of their resources, participation in development decisions affecting them, including, where appropriate, participation in the establishment or management of protected areas. The following are some of the specific measures which Governments could take:

(a) Consider the ratification and application of existing international conventions relevant to indigenous people and their communities (where not yet done) and provide support for the adoption by the General Assembly of a declaration on indigenous rights;

(b) Adopt or strengthen appropriate policies and/or legal instruments that will protect indigenous intellectual and cultural property and the right to preserve customary and administrative systems and practices.

United Nations organizations and other international development and finance organizations and Governments should, drawing on the active participation of indigenous people and their communities, as appropriate, take the following measures, *inter alia,* to incorporate their values, views and knowledge, including the unique contribution of indigenous women, in resource management and other policies and programmes that may affect them:

(a) Appoint a special focal point within each international organization, and organize annual interorganizational coordination meetings in consultation with Governments and indigenous organizations, as appropriate, and develop a procedure within and between operational agencies for assisting Governments in ensuring the coherent and coordinated incorporation of the views of indigenous people in the design and implementation of policies and programmes. Under this procedure, indigenous people and their communities should be informed and consulted and allowed to participate in national decision-making, in particular regarding regional and international cooperative efforts. In addition, these policies and programmes should take fully into account strategies based on local indigenous initiatives;

(b) Provide technical and financial assistance for capacity-building programmes to support the sustainable self-development of indigenous people and their communities;

(c) Strengthen research and education programmes aimed at:

(i) Achieving a better understanding of indigenous people's knowledge and management experience related to the environment, and applying this to contemporary development challenges;

(ii) Increasing the efficiency of indigenous people's resource management systems, for example, by promoting the adaptation and dissemination of suitable technological innovations;

(d) Contribute to the endeavours of indigenous people and their communities in resource management and conservation strategies. . . .

Governments, in full partnership with indigenous people and their communities should, where appropriate:

(a) Develop or strengthen national arrangements to consult with indigenous people and their communities with a view to reflecting their needs and incorporating their values and traditional and other knowledge and practices in national policies and programmes in the field of natural resource management and conservation and other development programmes affecting them;

(b) Cooperate at the regional level, where appropriate, to address common indigenous issues with a view to recognizing and strengthening their participation in sustainable development.

## Means of Implementation

*(a) Financing and cost evaluation.* The Conference secretariat has estimated the average total annual cost (1993–2000) of implementing the activities of this programme to be about $3 million on grant or concessional terms. These are indicative and order-of-magnitude estimates only and have not been reviewed by Governments. Actual costs and financial terms, including any that are non-concessional, will depend upon the specific strategies and programmes Governments decide upon for implementation.

*(b) Legal and administrative frameworks.* Governments should incorporate, in collaboration with the indigenous

I

people affected, the rights and responsibilities of indigenous people and their communities in the legislation of each country, suitable to the country's specific situation. Developing countries may require technical assistance to implement these activities.

*(c) Human resource development.* International development agencies and Governments should commit financial and other resources to education and training for indigenous people and their communities to develop their capacities to achieve their sustainable self-development, and to contribute to and participate in sustainable and equitable development at the national level. Particular attention should be given to strengthening the role of indigenous women.

### INTERNATIONAL DECADE OF THE WORLD'S INDIGENOUS PEOPLE.

The UN **GENERAL ASSEMBLY**, in resolution 48/163 of 21 December 1993, proclaimed the International Decade of the World's Indigenous People, commencing on 10 December 1994, and decided that the goal of the decade should be the strengthening of international cooperation for the solution of problems faced by indigenous people in such areas as human rights, development, education and health. At the same time, the Assembly also decided that, beginning in the first year of the decade, one day of every year shall be observed as the International Day of Indigenous People.

At its 1994 session, the Commission on Human Rights considered a working paper prepared by the Secretariat summarizing the results of a technical meeting on the International Year and the International Decade (E/CN.4/1994/AC.4/TM.4/3), Part I of which related to the activities of the Assistant Secretary-General who had been appointed as Coordinator for the International Decade as requested in the General Assembly resolution, and Parts II to VI of which set out proposals for activities of the United Nations system, for regional activities, national activities, activities to be carried out in indigenous people, non-governmental organizations and other organizations, institutions or groups, and ways and means of financing these activities.

In resolution 1994/26 of 4 March 1994, the Commission welcomed the decision of the General Assembly to proclaim the International Decade of the World's Indigenous People, requested the Coordinator of the Decade to coordinate the international program of activities in full collaboration and consultation with Governments, competent bodies, regional organizations, the International Labor Organization and other specialized agencies, and indigenous and non-governmental bodies; and urged United Nations bodies and specialized agencies to designate focal points for coordination with the Center for Human Rights of activities related to the decade. Further, it requested the Secretary-General to establish a voluntary fund for the decade, and to seek, accept and administer contributions from governments, organizations and individuals.

### INTERNATIONAL YEAR OF THE WORLD'S INDIGENOUS PEOPLE.

The "Study of the Problem of Discrimination against Indigenous Populations," completed in 1986 by Mr. José Martinez Cobo, Special Rapporteur of the Sub-Commission on Prevention of Discrimination and Protection of Minorities, included a proposal that the United Nations should proclaim an international year of the world's indigenous people (E/CN.4/Sub.2/1986/7/Add. 4, para. 633). Two years later, the Commission on Human Rights recommended to its parent bodies that such an observance should be proclaimed when appropriate. The Assembly made such a proclamation in 1990 (resolution 45/164) "with a view to strengthening international cooperation for the solution of problems faced by indigenous communities in such areas as human rights, the environment, development, education, health and so on," and designated 1993 as the International Year of the World's Indigenous People.

Subsequently a program of activities for the year was adopted by the Assembly (resolution 46/128, annex), and the Under-Secretary-General for Human Rights was designated as Coordinator of the Year. After the year came to an end, the Assembly requested the Commission on Human Rights to convene a meeting of participants in its programs and projects to assess what conclusions could be drawn from the activities. The conclusions reached at that meeting, held in Geneva from 20 to 22 July 1994, testified to the success of the observance. As summarized in the report of the meeting, they were as follows (E/CN.4/1994/AC.4/TM.4/2, paras. 242–249):

Although not all objectives were fully achieved within the short space of 12 months, a great deal was accomplished in this time; indigenous peoples everywhere intensified their campaigns for the recognition of their civil, political, cultural, economic and social rights. The success of the Year was due to the endeavours of many people, both indigenous and non-indigenous, all over the world.

The Goodwill Ambassador for the Year and 1992 Nobel Peace Prize winner, Mrs. Rigoberta Menchú Tum, was an inspiration to indigenous peoples, and her efforts contributed significantly to the success of the Year.

Considering the extensive programme of activities that took place all over the world; the efforts of individuals such as the Goodwill Ambassador, the Chairperson-Rapporteur of the Technical Meeting on the Year, Mrs. Ligía Galvis, and the Chairperson of the Working Group on Indigenous Populations, Ms. Erica-Irene A. Daes; the efforts of indigenous peoples both collectively and individually; and the programmes undertaken by the non-governmental sector, the conclusion must be drawn that the Year was a success.

One of the lessons learned from the Year is that communications networks need to be strengthened and a study on how best to spread information amongst indigenous peoples needs to be undertaken. The dissemination of information has to be in indigenous languages, it has to reach peoples on time, and often has to reach very remote areas. Communications strategies need to be practical, workable and accessible. The secretariat considered that one of the major practical limitations was the lack of facilities to develop a comprehensive communications strategy.

Adequate resources, the means to develop a well-planned programme, sufficient time and a substantial communications strategy are essential elements for the preparation of and the successful implementation of international year or decade programmes. Furthermore, it would have been wise to have identified resources, possibly from the Voluntary Fund for the International Year of the World's Indigenous People itself, to have allowed the secretariat to carry out fund-raising and promotional activities. Some travel with a fund-raising goal could have encouraged contributions far in excess of any amount absorbed by the secretariat in travel costs.

Indigenous peoples opened dialogues with many United Nations agencies and some serious deficiencies in the various programmes with respect to indigenous peoples were identified. The organs of the United Nations system need to build upon the lessons learned in the Year.

## PERMANENT FORUM IN THE UNITED NATIONS FOR INDIGENOUS PEOPLE.

The World Conference on Human Rights, in its Vienna Declaration and Program of Action, recommended that consideration should be given to the establishment of a permanent forum for indigenous people in the United Nations system, and the General Assembly later (resolution 48/163 of 21 December 1993) recognized the importance of considering the establishment of such a forum in the framework of the International Decade of the World's Indigenous People. On 4 March 1994 the Commission on Human Rights requested the UN Assistant Secretary-General for Human Rights (resolution 1994/28) "to invite Governments and indigenous organizations to express their views pertaining to the possibility of establishing such a permanent forum and to transmit to the Working Group on Indigenous Populations contributions received together with a technical note addressing institutional issues."

The technical note on the subject, prepared by the UN Secretariat, was presented to the Working Group at its 1994 session (UN Doc. E/CN.4/Sub.2/AC.4/1994/11), and reads in part as follows:

### Purpose of a Permanent Forum

The recommendation to consider the establishment of a permanent forum for indigenous people is linked, *inter alia*, to the decision to proclaim an International Decade of the World's Indigenous People. The World Conference, for example, recommended the establishment of such a forum in the framework of the proposed international decade and the General Assembly made its request to the Commission on Human Rights in its resolution proclaiming the Decade. It may be inferred that the establishment of a permanent forum is, *inter alia*, to promote the goal of the Decade which

as stated by the General Assembly is "the strengthening of international cooperation for the solution of problems faced by indigenous people in areas such as human rights, the environment, development, education and health". The same resolution also invites Governments "to ensure that activities and objectives for the Decade are planned and implemented on the basis of full consultation and collaboration with indigenous people".

Given these two elements, it may be considered useful to consider whether one purpose of the proposed permanent forum could be to contribute to the strengthening of international cooperation in the areas referred to in the General Assembly resolution on the basis of full consultation and collaboration with indigenous people.

In this regard, note may be taken of recent developments in other parts of the United Nations system, in particular concerning recommendations to involve indigenous people in the process of planning and implementation of projects. The United Nations Conference on Environment and Development in chapter 26 of the Programme of Action (Agenda 21) states, *inter alia*, that United Nations organizations and other international and finance organizations should, draw on the active participation of indigenous people and their communities, incorporate their values, views, and knowledge in resource management and other policies and programmes that may affect them. Agenda 21 suggests that an annual interorganizational coordination meeting in consultation with Governments and indigenous organizations take place (A/CONF.151/26, vol. III). The World Bank has adopted Operational Directive 4.20 of September 1991 in which it recognizes the need for "culturally appropriate development based on full consideration of the options preferred by the indigenous people affected by the project".

Note may also be taken of the range of suggestions and comments made by indigenous delegates at the inauguration of the International Year of the World's Indigenous People in New York on 10 December 1992, as well as at the forty-ninth session of the Commission on Human Rights and the World Conference on Human Rights. These included the proposal to establish a Commission on Indigenous Peoples within the United Nations, an advisory body, a permanent seat for indigenous people, an office for indigenous affairs, a High Commissioner for Indigenous Peoples, and a suggestion that observer status be granted to one or more indigenous organization at the General Assembly. Many indigenous organizations spoke generally about making a permanent place for indigenous peoples and enhancing their participation in United Nations forums.

Bearing in mind the points made by indigenous people at United Nations meetings as well as the resolutions referred to above, a number of objectives for the proposed permanent forum may be discerned. A new forum might provide an opportunity for indigenous peoples:

(a) To take part in decision-making in the United Nations system;

(b) To offer advice to the appropriate organs and agencies of the United Nations system on matters of concern to them, particularly in areas such as development, health, environment and culture;

(c) To present information on violations of human rights with a view to receiving attention and action by the relevant bodies and mechanisms, including possibly the monitoring of the implementation of the declaration on the rights of indigenous peoples;

(d) To engage in dialogue with States and to elaborate research and other activities of mutual interest.

It might also be useful to consider whether the proposed permanent forum could play a role in advancing the objectives of the Decade in a direct way. The programme of activities of the Decade will hopefully be approved by the General Assembly at its forty-ninth and fiftieth sessions and the designated coordinating body, the Centre for Human Rights, charged with the execution of the programme within the limited resources available. However, the proposed permanent forum may be in a position to offer advice and guidance to the Coordinator on programme planning or implementation and in identifying priorities for the Voluntary Fund for the International Decade. Furthermore, in the light of the recommendations of the General Assembly to Governments and indigenous peoples to establish national committees for the Decade and to United Nations agencies to appoint focal points on indigenous people, the proposed permanent forum might address its suggestions, recommendations and advice, through the Coordinator, to these newly created institutions.

Finally, it is clearly desirable that the proposed permanent forum be an effective body which offers something new to United Nations activities and contributes to practical and measurable improvements in the well-being of indigenous peoples. It is not in the interest of Governments, indigenous people or the overstretched United Nations Secretariat to establish a forum whose advice and recommendations are ignored and its decisions unrealizable because of lack of resources or of consensus among the key partners.

### The Working Group on Indigenous Populations and Its Relationship with the Proposed Permanent Forum

In order to avoid duplication of work and waste of resources, any proposed new forum within the United Nations should address areas of activity currently undeveloped. For these reasons, it may not be desirable for the proposed permanent forum to take on tasks currently dealt with under the mandate of the Working Group on Indigenous Populations. The two-fold mandate of the Working Group is expressed in Economic and Social Council resolution 1982/34 as:

(a) To review developments pertaining to the promotion and protection of the human rights and fundamental freedoms of indigenous populations, including information requested by the Secretary-General annually from Governments, specialized agencies, regional intergovernmental organizations and non-governmental organizations in consultative status, particularly those of indigenous peoples, to analyse such materials, and to submit its conclusions to the Sub-Commission, bearing in mind the final report of the Special Rapporteur of the Sub-Commission, Mr. José R. Martínez Cobo, entitled "Study of the problem of discrimination against indigenous populations" (E/CN.4/Sub.2/1986/7 and Add. 1–4);

(b) To give special attention to the evolution of standards concerning the rights of indigenous populations, taking account of both the similarities, and the differences in the situations and aspirations of indigenous populations throughout the world.

In addition to the review of developments and the evolution of international standards, the Working Group has over the years considered a number of other issues. These include the question of treaties, agreements and other constructive arrangements between States and indigenous peoples, the Voluntary Fund for Indigenous Populations, recent meetings and seminars, and the International Year of the World's Indigenous People. Since its establishment in 1982, the agenda of the Working Group has evolved and broadened considerably in an effort to cover matters of interest and concern to indigenous peoples. In practice, the Working Group has become the primary forum within the United Nations system for consideration of this question and its advice is increasingly sought by its parent bodies such as the Commission on Human Rights and the General Assembly. It will be necessary to consider carefully the future division of labour between the Working Group and the permanent forum. One possibility might be to let the Working Group take care of all human rights aspects while the permanent forum could deal with other issues such as development, culture, environment and health.

Furthermore, the Working Group on Indigenous Populations has begun its own reflection on its future role. The Chairperson-Rapporteur of the Working Group, Ms. Erica-Irene Daes, submitted a note on the question at the eleventh session of the Group (E/CN.4/Sub.2/AC.4/1993/8) and Mr. Miguel Alfonso Martinez, a member of the Working Group, is due to present further suggestions and comments in a note to its twelfth session (E/CN.4/Sub.2/AC.4/1994/10). The World Conference on Human Rights recommended that the Commission on Human Rights "consider the renewal and updating of the mandate of the Working Group on Indigenous Populations upon completion of the drafting of a declaration on the rights of indigenous people". Neither these initiatives nor the completion of the drafting of the declaration should bring into doubt the status of the Working Group which is authorized by the Economic and Social Council to meet annually for up to five days. It will, therefore, continue to hold meetings on this basis.

### Authority to Which the Permanent Forum Might Report

Consideration will need to be given to where in the United Nations system the proposed permanent forum would be placed. Within the complex organigram of commissions, committees, ad hoc bodies, expert consultative groups, working groups and other entities which make up the United Nations organization, for the purposes of this discussion four levels may be considered: the General Assembly, the Economic and Social Council, its functional Commissions and their subsidiary bodies, of which the Sub-Commission on Prevention of Discrimination and Protection of Minorities is one. Without prejudice to the discussion which will take place at the twelfth session of the Working Group on Indigenous Populations, it may be observed, on the one hand, that the treaty bodies which report to the General Assembly or the Economic and Social Council are established by the International Conventions on Human Rights which are binding legal instruments for those Governments which have ratified them. It may not be thought useful to make comparisons with such bodies since no such binding legal instrument on indigenous rights exists. On the other hand, if consideration is given to a permanent body reporting to a subsidiary body of a functional commission, it may not constitute a significant change from the present arrangement by which the Working Group on Indigenous Populations reports to the Sub-Commission.

For these reasons, attention may perhaps be focused at the levels of the Economic and Social Council and the functional commissions. The subsidiary machinery of the Economic and Social Council includes functional commissions such as the Commission on Human Rights, the regional commissions, and standing committees and expert bodies. The last two groups may be of interest since they include committees whose members are nominated by Governments (Committee on Natural Resources) or by the Secretary-General in consultation with Governments (Committee for Development Planning). Article 68 of the Charter of the United Nations empowers the Economic and Social Council to set up commissions in the economic and social fields for the promotion of human rights.

If consideration is to be given to the proposed permanent forum reporting to one of the functional commissions, it may be thought appropriate to examine the Commission on Human Rights or the newly established Commission on Sustainable Development. The former has under its authority the Sub-Commission on Prevention of Discrimination and Protection of Minorities, a body of 26 independent experts nominated by Governments and elected by the Commission on Human Rights, as well as a number of working groups. The working groups of the Commission have been established to draft new legal instruments or, as in the case of the Working Group on the Right to Development, to consider ways of enhancing implementation of an adopted international standard. It might also be considered possible to create a permanent forum reporting to two functional commissions, as appropriate, so that human rights on the one hand and development and environmental matters on the other are channelled to the appropriate body.

The Working Group in its discussions on this question may wish to consider whether the permanent forum could not act as an advisory body reporting directly to the Secretary-General or another high-level official such as the High Commissioner for Human Rights. It may be noted in this regard that the Secretary-General has recently established a high-level advisory board on sustainable development. However, such an advisory board may not be considered a permanent forum as such as it is directly linked to the post of Secretary-General.

It might be useful at this point to recall that United Nations organizations responsible for major programme areas of interest to indigenous people are themselves subject to their own separate policy-making bodies. The executive boards or governing bodies of such organizations as the United Nations Development Programme, the United Nations Children's Fund, the World Health Organization, the Food and Agriculture Organization or the International Labour Organisation are, in practice, their policy-making organs. Any permanent forum established by the Economic and Social Council would need to recognize its limitations and to explore ways in which its advice might be made available to the appropriate United Nations agencies.

### Mandate

Although no binding legal instrument on indigenous rights has yet been adopted by the United Nations General Assembly, sufficient guidance for drafting the mandate and terms of reference for the proposed forum may exist in the form of General Assembly and Commission on Human Rights resolutions, recommendations of high-level conferences such as the United Nations Conference on Environment and Development and the World Conference on Human Rights, and certain existing declarations and conventions. In addition, the ILO Convention No. 169 on indigenous and tribal peoples may also be useful in determining the areas which might fall under the mandate of the permanent forum.

As was noted earlier, the Working Group on Indigenous Populations is authorized to pay attention to the evolution of standards and the review of developments pertaining to the human rights of indigenous peoples. It might, therefore, not be advisable under the present circumstances to include standard-setting in the mandate. However, the experience of the Working Group over its 12 years of life is that a range of other matters have been raised on which it is not competent to act. Indigenous delegates have made allegations of human rights violations, expressed concerns about rights which are not protected in existing human rights instruments, and made comments and offered substantive opinions on health, development, environment, education, culture, refugee, social, youth and many other issues. It may be understood that the proposed permanent forum would provide an effective channel for these diverse matters.

At the intergovernmental level, a similar expression of interest in the views of indigenous communities has been noted. For example, in a resolution adopted by the World Health Assembly at its 47th session in May 1994, WHO requested its regional offices to work, along with the Governments of the member States concerned, with indigenous people, including by establishing a core advisory group of indigenous representatives with special knowledge of the health needs and resources of their communities.

Given the interest in a permanent forum demonstrated by Governments, the United Nations system and indigenous organizations themselves, it may be considered possible to elaborate, following consultations, an agenda for the proposed forum which accommodates the diverse interests and concerns. The proposed permanent forum might also be empowered to establish working groups of experts on questions of concern such as health or environment, or even regional working groups.

The terms of reference for such a forum, especially if human rights questions are discussed, will also need to be developed through a consultation process. It would not be desirable that the proposed permanent forum consider human rights questions which are dealt with by the treaty bodies or by bodies such as the Commission on Human Rights. Furthermore, in the absence at the present time of a United Nations instrument recognizing the specific rights of indigenous peoples, there would not be a possibility of considering individual cases. However, these qualifications made, indigenous people have expressed their hope that a better means of protecting their human rights will be established. This is particularly important since indigenous people do not have access to the major human rights meetings because most of their non-governmental organizations do not enjoy consultative status with the Economic and Social Council.

### Authority of the Permanent Forum

All United Nations forums have the possibility of taking decisions and making recommendations. It will, therefore, be necessary to consider the kinds of decisions and the nature of the recommendations to be made by the permanent forum, and the means by which these are to be carried out. Equally, it will be necessary to identify the areas in which the forum would not be given authority to act. Mention has been made of the areas which a permanent forum might examine but the question of what matters it will be empowered to decide upon and what kinds of recommendations will be received by its parent body will need to be determined.

With regard to the decisions or recommendations that the

permanent forum could be authorized to take, the following might be considered: its agenda, the creation of expert thematic or regional working groups, the appointment of special rapporteurs, the holding of expert meetings, the elaboration of studies, activities under the programme of activities for the Decade, projects supported by the Voluntary Fund for the Decade, action in the area of indigenous peoples that might be undertaken by the High Commissioner for Human Rights, technical and expert advice to other United Nations specialist agencies. Such a list is not exhaustive nor should these matters fall necessarily within the competence of the proposed forum. It may in the long run be advisable to allow the permanent forum to remain as flexible as possible so that it can establish its competence over time as it is able to demonstrate its expertise, usefulness, and capacity to find agreement between the different partners.

## Membership

The question of membership of the proposed permanent forum may be considered in the light of the functions and responsibilities attributed to it. Thus, if the permanent forum is to be established to provide expert advice to the United Nations system, it might be assumed that it will draw upon the experiences of indigenous and other experts. If the forum is to take decisions or make recommendations which require implementation by the United Nations, it will need the participation and approval of Member States. It may also be asserted that if indigenous people are not a part of the membership of the proposed permanent forum they will probably have little interest or confidence in it. Equally, if States, the constituency that makes up the United Nations, are not members, the forum will not be given any authority to take decisions or offer recommendations. Given this perspective, a range of possibilities may be envisaged which brings together not only representatives of Governments and indigenous organizations but, if deemed useful, could also include other interested parties such as independent experts on human rights (such as those composing the Sub-Commission) or on health, education or environment, or nongovernmental organizations having a long-standing interest in indigenous affairs.

It may be noted that the United Nations has experience of establishing different committees and expert technical bodies to allow them to draw upon the wealth of knowledge that exists in academic institutions, the scientific community, specialist non-governmental organizations, national institutions and other such groups or bodies. The Committee on Crime Prevention and Control, before its name and terms of reference were changed in accordance with ECOSOC resolution 1992/1, was composed of experts possessing the necessary qualifications and professional knowledge; the membership of the human rights treaty bodies is also composed of persons with a high moral character and recognized competence in the field of human rights. It may also be noted that the United Nations technical meetings and expert seminars often bring together experts from all fields in order to broaden the information and expertise available. Representatives of indigenous people have, thus, been invited by the Secretary-General to participate together with Governments in technical meetings on questions of concern. This was the case, for example, for the United Nations Technical Conference on Practical Experience in the Realization of Sustainable and Environmentally Sound Self-development of Indigenous Peoples (E/CN.4/Sub.2/1992/31 and Add. 1). Note

may also be taken of the terms of reference of the Board of Trustees of the Voluntary Fund for Indigenous Populations established in accordance with General Assembly resolution 40/131 of 13 December 1985 which authorizes the Secretary-General to appoint Board members with experience in indigenous matters, at least one of whom should be a representative of a widely recognized organization of indigenous people.

Expert committees are also established in other parts of the United Nations system to provide advice on specific areas of work. FAO and UNESCO, for example, have created advisory groups which include non-governmental organizations. Of interest also are organizations such as ILO whose governing body is composed of Governments, and employers' and employees, organizations, and the International Union for the Conservation of Nature (IUCN) whose membership comprises States, governmental agencies, and national and international non-governmental organizations. The recently established Fund for the Development of the Indigenous Peoples of Latin America and the Caribbean may serve as an example of trying to integrate indigenous people into the decision-making process. Under article 3.2 (ii) of the Agreement establishing the Fund, the General Meeting is composed of government delegates and one indigenous peoples, delegate for each State of the region that is a member of the Indigenous Fund, accredited by his Government following the relevant consultations with the indigenous organizations of the State.

An additional consideration for determining the membership of the proposed permanent forum will be the procedure that is established for appointment or election. In the case of certain meetings or committees, the responsibility for appointing experts is given to the Secretary-General, sometimes but not always following consultations with States. In other cases, States, nominate experts for subsequent election by a United Nations body. This is the case of the Sub-Commission whose members are nominated by States and elected by the Commission on Human Rights. In other cases, States, in accordance with an agreed rotation and equitable geographical distribution, nominate experts without recourse to an electoral process. As is the case for the Latin American and Caribbean Development Fund for Indigenous Peoples, Governments nominate indigenous delegates following consultations with their organizations. It may also be thought desirable to invite indigenous organizations to elect or select representatives.

However, these procedures apart, some consideration may be given to the practices developed in the Working Group on Indigenous Populations. The Chairperson, Ms. Erica-Irene A. Daes, and members of the Working Group have welcomed the participation of indigenous experts and representatives selected by the indigenous organizations themselves. This is also the established practice followed by the Board of Trustees of the Voluntary Fund. Indigenous people have appreciated the open character of their participation in the Working Group. It might be thought useful to examine the working practices of the Working Group to see whether such independent selection of representation by the indigenous organizations themselves cannot also be formalized in a way that allows for a similar procedure for election of the membership of the proposed permanent forum.

## Participation of Indigenous Organizations

Another question of relevance is the procedures that would be established for the proposed permanent forum to allow participation by observer States, the United Nations system, indigenous organizations and non-governmental organizations. Two questions may be raised: firstly, would indigenous representatives from organizations without consultative status with the Economic and Social Council be authorized to provide written information, make oral statements, and fully participate in the meeting; and second, given the extremely restricted economic circumstances of most indigenous organizations, would funds be available to assist indigenous people to travel to the sessions of the permanent forum?

Once again, consideration may be given to the procedures developed during the 12 years of activity of the Working Group on Indigenous Populations. In order to assist the Working Group in its work, written information and oral statements have been accepted from indigenous organizations in an open spirit. This has been of particular value as 11 of the 12 indigenous organizations with consultative status have their headquarters in a developed country and the Working Group considered it important to ensure equitable geographical distribution and participation of indigenous organizations. As regards the problems that may be encountered by indigenous organizations wishing to participate in the proposed permanent forum but lacking resources to do so, it may be desirable to consider how the Voluntary Fund for Indigenous Populations may be used to assist them.

### Secretariat Implications of a Permanent Forum

The establishment of a permanent forum has implications for the secretariat which will also need to be considered. A permanent forum will require additional funds to cover the travel costs and daily subsistence allowances of members, the additional conference services expenses associated with preparation, translation and printing of documentation, interpretation, and other support activities, as well as the staff necessary for servicing and following up on decisions. It will also be necessary to ensure that any future forum hold its sessions at a suitable and practical date taking into account the calendar of human rights meetings.

Finally, it may be appropriate to note the ongoing preparations to enhance staffing for indigenous issues and to establish an indigenous peoples unit within the Centre for Human Rights, in accordance with General Assembly resolution 48/163 and Commission on Human Rights resolution 1994/26. It may be envisaged that the measures being taken by the United Nations Secretariat to increase resources in this area in order to respond to the growing interest and workload, as well as to implement the programme of activities for the Decade, will be further strengthened in the event of a permanent forum being established.

***PROTECTION OF THE HERITAGE OF INDIGENOUS PEOPLES.*** On 29 August 1991 the UN Sub-Commission on Prevention of Discrimination and Protection of Minorities decided (resolution 1991/32) to entrust Mrs. Erica-Irene A. Daes, as Special Rapporteur, with the task of preparing a study of measures which should be taken by the international community to strengthen respect for the cultural property of indigenous peoples. After considering a preliminary report (E/CN.4/Sub.2/1993/28) at its 1993 session, the Sub-Commission endorsed the Special Rapporteur's con-

clusions and recommendations, decided that the title of the study should be "Protection of the Heritage of the Indigenous Peoples," and requested the Special Rapporteur to expand the study with a view to elaborating draft principles and guidelines for the protection of the heritage of the indigenous peoples and to submit a preliminary report, containing such principles and guidelines, to it at its 1994 session.

The preliminary report (E/CN.4/Sub.2/1994/31) included an Annex setting out the Special Rapporteur's proposed principles and guidelines (reproduced below). In explaining the basis for her formulation of these proposals, the Special Rapporteur included in her report the following discussion (paras. 4–10):

In the Rio Declaration on Environment and Development, the United Nations Conference on Environment and Development stressed the "vital role" that indigenous peoples may play in achieving sustainable development "because of their knowledge and traditional practices" (A/CONF.151/26 (vol. I), annex I, principle 22). The Conference also called on Governments and intergovernmental organizations, "in full partnership with indigenous peoples", to take measures to recognize traditional forms of knowledge and enhance capacity-building for indigenous communities based on the adaptation and exchange of traditional knowledge (A/CONF.151/26 (vol. III), para. 26.3). It is the view of the Special Rapporteur that these conclusions and recommendations not only apply to indigenous knowledge which is narrowly biological, botanical or ecological but—in view of the special relationship that exists between indigenous peoples and their territories—to all aspects of indigenous peoples, heritage.

The Special Rapporteur has also been particularly mindful of the principle that "every people has the right and the duty to develop its culture", adopted by the General Conference of UNESCO in article 1 of the UNESCO Declaration of the Principles of International Cultural Co-operation (4 November 1966). The central role of traditional forms of cultural transmission and education has been stressed in the guidelines set out in the annex to the present report in the belief that this will be the most effective means of ensuring that indigenous peoples control the further development of their own heritage, as well as its interpretation and use by others.

In elaborating the principles and guidelines, contained in the annex to this report, the Special Rapporteur has drawn extensively on the Kari-Oca Declaration of the World Conference of Indigenous Peoples on Territory, Environment and Development (Kari-Oca, Brazil, 15–30 May 1992) and the Mataatua Declaration of the First International Conference on Cultural and Intellectual Property Rights of Indigenous Peoples. Their own conception of the nature of their heritage and their own ideas for ensuring the protection of their heritage are central to the "new partnership" with indigenous peoples symbolized by the International Year of the World's Indigenous People in 1993.

The Special Rapporteur wishes to underscore the fact, emphasized by the Mataatua Declaration, that indigenous peoples have repeatedly expressed their willingness to share their useful knowledge with all humanity, provided that their fundamental rights to define and control this knowledge are protected by the international community. Greater protection of the indigenous peoples, control over their own heritage will not, in the opinion of the Special Rapporteur, decrease the sharing of traditional cultural knowledge, arts and sciences with other peoples. On the contrary, indigenous peoples' willingness to share, teach, and interpret their heritage will increase.

In developing the principles and guidelines, the Special Rapporteur found it useful to bear in mind that the heritage of an indigenous people is not merely a collection of objects, stories and ceremonies, but a complete knowledge system with its own concepts of epistemology, philosophy, and scientific and logical validity. The diverse elements of an indigenous people's heritage can only be fully learned or understood by means of the pedagogy traditionally employed by these peoples themselves, including apprenticeship, ceremonies and practice. Simply recording words or images fails to capture the whole context and meaning of songs, rituals, arts or scientific and medical wisdom. This also underscores the central role of indigenous peoples' own languages, through which each people's heritage has traditionally been recorded and transmitted from generation to generation.

The Special Rapporteur also considers it fundamental to recognize and renew the central and indispensable role of land as the classroom in which the heritage of each indigenous people has traditionally been taught. Heritage is learned through a lifetime of personal experience travelling through and conducting ceremonies on the land. Much or all of an indigenous people's traditional territory must therefore remain accessible to and under the control of the people themselves, so that they can continue to teach, develop and renew their knowledge systems fully by their own means of cultural transmission. Indeed, ceremonies and traditional artistic works are regarded as means of renewing human relationships with the land, even as "deeds" to the territory, so that they can never be detached geographically, and used elsewhere, without completely losing their meaning.

This special relationship is not merely with the physical aspects of the land, but is conceived of as a direct and personal kinship with each of the species of animals and plants that co-exist with people in the same territory. Biological, zoological and botanical knowledge is not simply a matter of learning the names, habits and uses of species, but of carefully maintaining and periodically renewing ancient social and ceremonial relationships with each species. An indigenous person does not only harvest medicinal plants, for instance, but visits them, prays with them and, through ceremonies, helps them. For this reason, indigenous peoples do not believe that their knowledge of ecology, the uses of plants and animals, rituals or medicine can ever be alienated completely. Like human family relationships, these forms of knowledge are permanent and collective. They can be shared, however, under the right circumstances, with properly initiated persons.

In conclusion, the Special Rapporteur recommended:

that the Sub-Commission decide to request the Secretary-General to submit the attached principles and guidelines to indigenous peoples' organizations, Governments, specialized agencies and non-governmental organizations concerned for their comments. On the basis of these comments and those of the members of the Sub-Commission, the Spe-

cial Rapporteur should be entrusted with presenting her final report to the Sub-Commission at its 47th session, in 1995, for the Sub-Commission to consider and adopt these principles and guidelines, as a first formal step towards committing the United Nations to the protection of indigenous peoples' heritage. With the support of indigenous peoples, these principles and guidelines may be transmitted to the General Assembly, through the Commission on Human Rights and the Economic and Social Council, for adoption.

These recommendations were later accepted by the Sub-Commission, the Commission, and the Economic and Social Council.

***PRINCIPLES AND GUIDELINES FOR THE PROTECTION OF THE HERITAGE OF INDIGENOUS PEOPLES.*** The proposed principles and guidelines annexed to the report of the Special Rapporteur are as follows:

### Principles

1. The effective protection of indigenous peoples' heritage will be of long-term benefit to all humanity. Cultural diversity contributes to the adaptability and creativity of the human species as a whole.

2. To be effective, the protection of indigenous peoples' heritage should be based broadly on the principle of self-determination, which includes the right and the duty of indigenous peoples to develop their own cultures and knowledge systems.

3. Indigenous peoples should be recognized as the primary guardians and interpreters of their cultures, arts and sciences, whether created in the past or developed by them in the future.

4. International recognition and respect for indigenous peoples' own customs, rules and practices for the transmission of their heritage to future generations, and for the sharing of their heritage with others, is essential to these peoples' enjoyment of human rights and dignity.

5. Indigenous peoples' ownership and custody of their heritage must continue to be collective, permanent and inalienable, as prescribed by the customs, rules and practices of each people.

6. The discovery, use and teaching of indigenous peoples' knowledge, arts and cultures is inextricably connected with the traditional lands and territories of each people. Control over traditional territories and resources is essential to the continued transmission of indigenous peoples' heritage to future generations and its full protection.

7. To protect their heritage indigenous peoples must control their own means of cultural transmission and education. This includes their right to the continued use and, wherever necessary, the restoration of their own languages and orthographies.

8. To protect their heritage indigenous peoples must also exercise control over all research conducted within their territories, or which uses their people as subjects of study.

9. The free and informed consent of the traditional owners should be an essential precondition of any agreements which may be made for the recording, study, use or display of indigenous peoples' heritage.

10. Any agreements which may be made for the recording, study, use or display of indigenous peoples' heritage must be revocable and ensure that the peoples concerned

continue to be the primary beneficiaries of commercial application.

### Guidelines

*Definitions.* 11. The heritage of indigenous peoples is comprised of all objects, sites and knowledge, the nature or use of which has been transmitted from generation to generation, and which is regarded as pertaining to a particular peoples' clan or territory. The heritage of an indigenous people also includes objects, knowledge and literary or artistic works which may be created in the future based upon its heritage.

12. The heritage of indigenous peoples includes all moveable cultural property as defined by the relevant conventions of UNESCO; all kinds of literary and artistic works such as music, dance, song, ceremonies, symbols and designs, narratives and poetry; all kinds of scientific, agricultural, technical and ecological knowledge, including cultigens, medicines and the phenotypes and genotypes of flora and fauna; human remains; immoveable cultural property such as sacred sites, sites of historical significance, and burials; and documentation of indigenous peoples' heritage on film, photographs, videotape or audiotape.

13. Every element of an indigenous peoples' heritage has traditional owners, which may be the whole people, a particular family or clan, an association or society, or individuals who have been specially taught or initiated to be its custodians. The traditional owners of heritage must be determined in accordance with indigenous peoples' own customs, laws and practices.

*Transmission of Heritage.* 14. Indigenous peoples' heritage should ordinarily be learned only by the means customarily employed by its traditional owners for teaching the specific knowledge concerned. Each indigenous people's rules and practices for the transmission of heritage and sharing of its use must be recognized generally in the national legal system.

15. In the event of a dispute over the custody or use of any element of an indigenous people's heritage, judicial and administrative bodies should be guided by the advice of indigenous elders who are recognized by the indigenous communities or peoples concerned as having specific knowledge of traditional laws.

16. Governments, international organizations and private institutions should support the development of educational, research and training centres which are controlled by indigenous communities, and strengthen these communities' capacity to document, protect, teach and apply all aspects of their heritage.

17. Governments, international organizations and private institutions should support the development of regional and global networks for the exchange of information and experience among indigenous peoples in the fields of science, culture, education and the arts. This may include electronic networks where feasible and appropriate.

18. Governments, with international cooperation, should provide the necessary financial resources and institutional support to ensure that every indigenous child has the opportunity to achieve both fluency and literacy in his/her own traditional language.

*Recovery and Restitution of Heritage.* 19. Governments, with the assistance of international organizations, should assist indigenous peoples and communities in recovering control and possession of their moveable cultural property and other heritage.

20. In cooperation with indigenous peoples, UNESCO should establish a programme to mediate the recovery of moveable cultural property from across international borders, at the request of the traditional owners of the property concerned.

21. Human remains and associated funeral objects must be returned to their descendants and territories in a culturally appropriate manner, as determined by the indigenous peoples concerned. Documentation may be retained, displayed or otherwise used only in such form and manner as may be agreed upon with the peoples concerned.

22. Moveable cultural property should be returned wherever possible to its traditional owners, particularly if shown to be of significant cultural, religious or historical value to them. Moveable cultural property should only be retained by universities, museums, private institutions or individuals in accordance with the terms of a recorded agreement with the traditional owners for the sharing of the custody and interpretation of the property.

23. Under no circumstances should objects or any other elements of an indigenous people's heritage be publicly displayed, except in a manner deemed appropriate by the peoples concerned.

24. In the case of objects or other elements of heritage which were removed or recorded in the past, the traditional owners of which can no longer be identified precisely, the traditional owners are presumed to be the entire people associated with the territory from which these objects were removed, or where the recordings were made, or the direct descendants of that people.

*National Programmes and Legislation.* 25. National laws should guarantee that indigenous peoples can obtain prompt, effective and affordable judicial or administrative action to prevent, punish and obtain full restitution and compensation for the acquisition, documentation or use of their heritage without proper authorization of the traditional owners.

26. National laws should deny to any person or corporation the right to obtain patent, copyright, or other legal protection for any element of indigenous peoples' heritage without adequate documentation of the free and informed consent of the traditional owners to an arrangement for the sharing of ownership, control and benefits.

27. National laws should ensure the labelling and correct attribution of indigenous peoples' artistic, literary and cultural works whenever they are offered for public display or sale. Attribution should be in the form of a trademark or an appellation of origin, authorized by the peoples or communities concerned.

28. National laws for the protection of indigenous peoples' heritage should be adopted following consultations with the peoples concerned, in particular the traditional owners and teachers of religious, sacred and spiritual knowledge, and wherever possible, should have the consent of the peoples concerned.

29. National laws should ensure that the use of traditional languages in education, arts and the mass media is respected and, to the extent possible, promoted and strengthened.

30. Governments should provide indigenous communities with financial and institutional support for the control of local education, through community-managed programmes, and with use of traditional pedagogy and languages.

31. Governments should take immediate steps, in cooperation with the indigenous peoples concerned, to identify sacred and ceremonial sites, including burial sites, and protect them from unauthorized entry or use.

*Researchers and Scholarly Institutions.* 32. All researchers and scholarly institutions should take immediate steps to provide indigenous peoples and communities with comprehensive inventories of the cultural property, and documentation of indigenous peoples' heritage, which they may have in their custody.

33. Researchers and scholarly institutions should return all elements of indigenous peoples' heritage to the traditional owners upon demand, or obtain formal agreements with the traditional owners for the shared custody, use and interpretation of their heritage.

34. Researchers and scholarly institutions should decline any offers for the donation or sale of elements of indigenous peoples' heritage, unless they have first contacted the peoples or communities directly concerned and ascertaining the wishes of the traditional owners.

35. Researchers and scholarly institutions must refrain from engaging in any study of previously-undescribed species or cultivated varieties of plants, animals or microbes, or naturally-occurring pharmaceuticals, without first obtaining satisfactory documentation that the specimens were acquired with the consent of the traditional owners, if any.

36. Researchers must not publish information obtained from indigenous peoples or the results of research conducted on flora, fauna, microbes or materials discovered through the assistance of indigenous peoples' without identifying the traditional owners and obtaining their consent to publication.

37. Researchers should agree to an immediate moratorium on the Human Genome Diversity Project. Further research on the specific genotypes of indigenous peoples should be suspended unless and until broadly and publicly supported by indigenous peoples to the satisfaction of United Nations human rights organs.

38. Researchers and scholarly institutions should make every possible effort to increase indigenous peoples' access to all forms of medical, scientific and technical education, and participation in all research activities which may affect them or be of benefit to them.

39. Professional associations of scientists, engineers and scholars, in collaboration with indigenous peoples, should sponsor seminars and disseminate publications to promote ethical conduct in conformity with these guidelines and discipline members who act in contravention.

*Business and Industry.* 40. In dealings with indigenous peoples, business and industry should respect the same guidelines as researchers and scholarly institutions.

41. Business and industry should agree to an immediate moratorium on making contracts with indigenous peoples for the rights to discover, record and use previously-undescribed species or cultivated varieties of plants, animals or microbes, or naturally-occurring pharmaceuticals. No further contracts should be negotiated until indigenous peoples and communities themselves are capable of supervising and collaborating in the research process.

42. Business and industry should refrain from offering incentives to any individuals to claim traditional rights of ownership or leadership within an indigenous community, in violation of their trust within the community and the laws of the indigenous peoples concerned.

43. Business and industry should refrain from employing scientists or scholars to acquire and record traditional knowledge or other heritage of indigenous peoples in violation of these guidelines.

44. Business and industry should contribute financially and otherwise to the development of educational and research institutions controlled by indigenous peoples and communities.

45. All forms of tourism based on indigenous peoples' heritage must be restricted to activities which have the approval of the peoples and communities concerned, and which are conducted under their supervision and control.

*Artists, Writers and Performers.* 46. Artists, writers and performers should refrain from incorporating elements derived from indigenous heritage into their works without the informed consent of the traditional owners.

47. Artists, writers and performers should support the full artistic and cultural development of indigenous peoples and encourage public support for the development and greater recognition of indigenous artists, writers and performers.

48. Artists, writers and performers should contribute, through their individual works and professional organizations, to greater public understanding and respect for the indigenous heritage associated with the country in which they live.

*Public Information and Education.* 49. The mass media in all countries should take effective measures to promote understanding of and respect for indigenous peoples' heritage, in particular through special broadcasts and public-service programmes prepared in collaboration with indigenous peoples.

50. Journalists should respect the privacy of indigenous peoples, in particular concerning traditional religious, cultural and ceremonial activities, and refrain from exploiting or sensationalizing indigenous peoples' heritage.

51. Journalists should actively assist indigenous peoples in exposing any activities, public or private, which destroy or degrade indigenous peoples' heritage.

52. Educators should ensure that school curricula and textbooks teach understanding and respect for indigenous peoples' heritage and history and recognize the contribution of indigenous peoples to the creativity and cultural diversity of the country as a whole.

*International Organizations.* 53. The Secretary-General should publish an annual report, based upon information from all available sources, and in particular information requested from UNESCO, the World Intellectual Property Organization (WIPO) and indigenous communities, on problems and solutions experienced in the protection of indigenous peoples' heritage in all countries.

54. The Secretary-General should also prepare a note, in cooperation with indigenous peoples' organizations, on progress made and problems still to be overcome for the protection of indigenous peoples' heritage, for consideration by the World Summit for Social Development in 1995.

55. In cooperation with indigenous peoples, WIPO should bring these principles and guidelines to the attention of the member States of all of the intellectual and industrial property unions which are under its administration, with a view to promoting the strengthening of national legislation and international conventions in this field.

56. Indigenous peoples and their representative organizations should enjoy direct access to all relevant negotiations administered by WIPO and the World Trade organization, to share their views on measures to improve the protection of their heritage through international law.

57. In collaboration with indigenous peoples, UNESCO should develop a list of sacred and ceremonial sites that require special measures for their protection and conservation, and provide financial and technical assistance to indigenous peoples for these purposes.

58. In collaboration with indigenous peoples, UNESCO

should also establish a trust fund with a mandate to act as a global agent for the recovery of compensation for the unconsented or inappropriate use of indigenous peoples' heritage, and to provide assistance to indigenous peoples to strengthen their institutional capacity to protect their own heritage.

59. United Nations operational agencies, as well as the international financial institutions, and regional and bilateral development assistance programmes, should give priority to providing financial and technical support to indigenous communities for capacity-building and exchanges of experience focused on local control of research and education.

## STUDY ON TREATIES, AGREEMENTS AND OTHER CONSTRUCTIVE ARRANGEMENTS BETWEEN STATES AND INDIGENOUS POPULATIONS.

At its 1992 session, the Sub-Commission on Prevention of Discrimination and Protection of Minorities considered the first progress report on the study of treaties, agreements and other constructive arrangements between States and indigenous populations (E/CN.4/Sub.2/1992/32), prepared by its Special Rapporteur, Mr. Miguel Alfonso Martínez. An earlier preliminary report (E/CN.4/Sub.2/1991/33) had been the subject of debate at the 1991 session of the Working Group on Indigenous Populations, which had requested that a questionaire prepared by the Special Rapporteur should again be distributed to governments, intergovernmental organizations and organizations of indigenous peoples with the request that they make the information sought by the Special Rapporteur available not later than 15 March 1992.

In the 1992 progress report, the Special Rapporteur endeavored (a) to inform the Sub-Commission and its Working Group of his activities, (b) to establish some anthropological and historical premises which appeared of importance to him with respect to several key issues directly related to the central purpose of the study, (c) to further elaborate on some juridical issues that he considered to be of prime importance for the study, and (d) to review and summarize a number of cases that he considered to be useful to illustrate the vast diversity of juridical situations existing in various parts of the world which may be relevant to the study.

Having reviewed the progress report, the Sub-Commission requested the Special Rapporteur to submit a second progress report to the Working Group and to the Sub-Commission at their 1994 sessions.

**SEE ALSO** *Cultural Rights; Minorities' Rights.*

**BIBLIOGRAPHY.** American Friends Service Committee, Latin America and Caribbean Programs. *Struggle over Autonomy: A Report on the Atlantic Coast of Nicaragua.* Philadelphia, PA, USA: 1987. NGO report, in English.

Amnesty International. *Brazil: Cases of Killings and Ill-Treatment of Indigenous People.* London: 1988. NGO report, in English.

————. *Guatemala: The Human Rights Record.* London: 1987. NGO report, in English.

————. *Mexico Human Rights in Rural Areas: Exchange of Documents with the Mexican Government on Human Rights Violations in Oaxaca and Chiapas.* London: 1986. NGO mission report, in English.

Association Henri-Capitant, Section québécoise. *Droit civil et droits autochtones: confrontation ou complémentarité? Recueil des textes présentés à la conférence Henri-Capitant du 12 avril 1991 à la Faculté de droit de l'Université de Montréal* (Civil Law and Indigenous Rights: Papers Presented at Henri-Capitant Conference held on April 12, 1991 at the Faculty of Law, University of Montreal). Outremont, Canada: June 1992. Scholarly conference report, in French.

Barsh, Russell L. "Indigenous Peoples in the 1990s: From Object to Subject of International Law," *Harvard Human Rights Journal* 7 (Spring 1994): 33–86. Scholarly article, in English.

Branford, S., and O. Glock. *The Last Frontier: Fighting over Land in the Amazon.* London: Zed Press, 1985. Scholarly monograph, in English.

Brölmann, Catherine, Rene Lefeber, and Marjoleine Zieck, eds. *Peoples and Minorities in International Law.* Dordrecht, the Netherlands: Martinus Nijhoff, 1993. Scholarly monograph, in English.

Burger, Julian, and Paul Hunt. "Towards the International Protection of Indigenous Peoples' Rights," *Netherlands Quarterly of Human Rights* 12, no. 4 (1994): 405–423. Scholarly article, in English.

Castillo, Eduardo V., and Jorge E. Sanderson E. *Pueblos Indígenas: Normas Constitucionales y Derecho Internacional* (Indigenous Peoples: Constitutional Norms and International Law). Santiago, Chile: Chilean Commission of Human Rights, Human Rights and Indigenous Peoples Program, 1990. Research paper, in Spanish.

Clinton, Robert N. "The Right of Indigenous Peoples as Collective Group Rights," *Arizona Law Review* 32, no. 4 (1990): 739–747. Scholarly article, in English.

Colchester, Marcus. *Pirates, Squatters and Poachers: The Political Ecology of Dispossession of the Native Peoples of Sarawak.* London: Survival International Institute of Social Analysis, 1992. NGO report, in English; bibliography, pp. 82–85.

Comeau, Pauline, and Aldo Santin. *The First Canadians: A Profile of Canada's Native People Today.* Toronto, Canada: James Lorimer, 1990. Monograph, in English.

Comisión Chilena de Derechos Humanos and the Chilean Commission for Human Rights. *Pueblo, Tierra, Desarrollo: Conceptos Fundamentales Para una Nueva Ley Indígena* (People, Earth, Development: Fundamental Concepts for a New Indigenous Law). Santiago, Chile: 1992. NGO report, in Spanish.

Corkill, D., and D. Cubitt. *Ecuador: Fragile Democracy.* London: Latin American Bureau, 1988. NGO report, in English; bibliography: books in English on Ecuador, 1978–1988, p. 113.

Durand, A., and H. Carolos. *Minorias Nacionales y Derechos Humanos: El Caso de los Triquis de Oaxaca, Mexico* (National Minorities and Human Rights: The Case of the Triquis of Oaxaca, Mexico). Chapingo, Mexico: Asociacion Americana de Juristas, 1987. NGO report, in Spanish.

Einfeld, Marcus. *Bicentennial Oration: Human Rights and Constitutional Entrenchment, Statement by . . . President of the Australian Human Rights and Equal Opportunity Commission on the Presentation of the Report of the Commission's Inquiry into the Social and Material Needs of the Residents of Toomelah, Boggabilwindi.*

Sydney, Australia: Australian Human Rights and Equal Opportunity Commission, 1988. Speeches, in English.

Gray, Andrew, comp. *IWGIA Yearbook 1987: Indigenous Peoples and Development.* Copenhagen, Denmark: International Work Group for Indigenous Affairs, 1987. NGO report, in English.

Heinz, W. S. *Indigenous Populations, Ethnic Minorities and Human Rights.* Berlin, FRG: Quorum Verlag, 1988. Scholarly monograph, in English.

Indigenous Work Group for Indigenous Affairs. *Indigenous Women on the Move.* Copenhagen, Denmark: 1990. NGO monograph, in English.

International Work Group for Indigenous Affairs. *The Indigenous World, 1993–94.* Copenhagen, Denmark: 1994. NGO annual report, in English.

Iturralde, Diego A. "Los Pueblos Indígenas y Sus Derechos en América Latina" (The Indigenous Peoples and Their Rights in Latin America), *Revista IIDH* no. 15 (June 1992): 11–28. Scholarly article, in Spanish.

Leonel, Mauro, Betty Mindlin, and Carmen Junqueira. "The Joint Responsibility of the International Community in the Indigenous and Environmental Issues of the Brazilian Amazon," *IWGIA Newsletter* no. 3 (Aug./Sept. 1992): 6–19. Scholarly article, in English; bibliography, p. 19.

Marcus, Alan R. *Out in the Cold: The Legacy of Canada's Inuit Relocation Experiment in the High Arctic.* Document 71. Copenhagen, Denmark: International Work Group for Indigenous Affairs, 1992. NGO monograph, in English; bibliography, pp. 91–102.

McRae, H., G. Nettheim, and L. Beacroft. *Aboriginal Legal Issues: Commentary and Materials.* Melbourne, Australia: Law Book Company, 1991. Educational material, in English; bibliography, pp. xxi–xxxvii.

Mey, Wolfgang. *Wir Wollen Nicht Euch—Wir Wollen Eurer Land* (We Don't Want You—We Want Your Land). Goettingen, FRG: Gesellschaft fur Bedrohte Volker, 1988. NGO report, in German.

Nettheim, Garth. *International Law and Indigenous Political Rights: Yesterday, Today and Tomorrow.* Sydney, Australia: 1991. Conference paper, in English.

Ortiz, R. D. *The Miskito Indians of Nicaragua.* London: Minority Rights Group, 1988. NGO monograph, in English; bibliography, pp. 16–19.

Pearce, Elizabeth A. "Self-Determination for Native Americans: Land Rights and the Utility of Domestic and International Law," *Columbia Human Rights Law Review* 22, no. 2 (Spring 1991): 361–400. Scholarly article, in English.

Ryser, Rudolph C. "The World Bank's Tribal Economic Policy: A Change in International Economic Development Strategies?" *Fourth World Journal* 2, no. 3 (Winter 1990): 185–194. Article, in English.

Shutkin, William Andrew. "International Human Rights Law and the Earth: The Protection of Indigenous Peoples and the Environment," *Virginia Journal of International Law* 31 (Spring 1991): 479–511. Scholarly article, in English.

Sill, Marc A., and Glenn T. Morris. *Indigenous Peoples' Politics: An Introduction.* Denver, CO, USA: Fourth World Center for the Study of Indigenous Law and Politics, University of Colorado at Denver, 1993. Textbook, in English.

Tennant, C. C. "Indigenous Peoples, International Institutions, and the International Legal Literature from 1945–1993," *Human Rights Quarterly* 16, no. 1 (Feb. 1994): 1–57. Scholarly article, in English.

Tennant, C. C., and M. E. Turpel. "A Case Study of Indigenous People: Genocide, Ethnocide and Self-Determination," *Nordic Journal of International Law* 59, no. 4 (1990): 287–319. Scholarly article, in English.

Torres, Raidza. "The Rights of Indigenous Populations: The Emerging International Norm," *The Yale Journal of International Law* 16, no. 1 (Winter 1991): 127–175. Scholarly article, in English.

U.S. Committee for Refugees. *From Isolation to Exile: Refugees from the Chittagong Hill Tracts of Bangladesh.* Washington, D.C.: 1988. NGO report, in English.

United Nations Sub-Commission on Prevention of Discrimination and Protection of Minorities. *Report of the Working Group on Indigenous Populations on Its Ninth Session. Chairperson/Rapporteur: Mrs. Erica-Irene A. Daes.* Geneva, Switzerland: 1991. IGO document, in English and French.

————. *Study on Treaties, Agreements and Other Constructive Arrangements between States and Indigenous Populations. Preliminary Report Submitted by Mr. Miguel Alfonso Martínez, Special Rapporteur.* Geneva, Switzerland: 1991. IGO document, in English and French.

Vries, Gijs de. "Report: Broken Promises: Canada and its Aboriginal Peoples," *Netherlands Quarterly of Human Rights* 10, no. 2 (1992): 166–183. Scholarly article, in English.

## INDIGENOUS PEOPLES: ILO INDIGENOUS AND TRIBAL PEOPLES CONVENTION (1989).

During the drafting of the Indigenous and Tribal Peoples Convention (ILO Convention No. 169), a special appeal was made to governments to consult indigenous and tribal peoples in formulating their views on the proposed instrument. For the first time a space was made for non-governmental organizations representing indigenous and tribal peoples in the written consultations and in the meetings of the Conference to express their views, to submit amendments to the draft during the discussion (indirectly through the workers' representatives), and to address both the Committee and the plenary sittings of the Conference.

Convention No. 169 fixes goals and priorities, and contains standards defining the minimum level below which the conduct of government must not descend. It sets goals toward which governments should work, while laying down guidelines for a participatory approach to decision-making and providing a number of specific protections.

The basic principle of this Convention is respect for the cultures and ways of life of indigenous and tribal peoples, and their right to continued existence and to development, along the lines they themselves wish. The Convention contains provisions to orient the relationship between indigenous and tribal peoples and the State, including protection against discrimination, protection of their cultural and religious heritage and a requirement for impact studies in relation to development projects, whenever appropriate.

Convention No. 169 recognizes that these peoples have the right to self-identification, and accords them the respect of designating them as "peoples." It provides that governments must consult with indigenous and tribal peoples within their countries on development projects and other activities affecting them, and lays down criteria for these consultations. It provides for respect not only for cultural manifestations, but for traditional ways of life and legal systems, within the framework of national and international law. It includes provisions on land rights which require respect for traditional occupation and provide for measures to recognize and protect these rights. These rights include participation in the management and benefits of resource exploitation on indigenous and tribal peoples' lands, and the right to refuse displacement from their lands except in exceptional circumstances and against compensation. The Convention provides for educational and health protection, and recognizes the right of these peoples to assume progressively the management of their educational and health services when they are capable of doing so. It provides special protection for them in labor, where they are often particularly vulnerable. Finally, it recognizes that the situation of indigenous and tribal peoples in different countries, and even within the same country, may vary enormously, and stipulates that the Convention is to be applied in a flexible manner.

The Convention revises the ILO Convention No. 107 of 1957, which had been oriented towards the integration and assimilation of indigenous peoples. Convention No. 169 was adopted by the International Labor Conference (76th session) on 27 June 1989. The text of the Convention is as follows:

The General Conference of the International Labour Organisation,

Having been convened at Geneva by the Governing Body of the International Labour Office, and having met in its 76th Session on 7 June 1989, and

Noting that the international standards contained in the Indigenous and Tribal Populations Convention and Recommendation, 1957, and

Recalling the terms of the Universal Declaration of Human Rights, the International Covenant on Economic, Social and Cultural Rights, the International Covenant on Civil and Political Rights, and the many international instruments on the prevention of discrimination, and

Considering that the developments which have taken place in international law since 1957, as well as developments in the situation of indigenous and tribal peoples in all regions of the world, have made it appropriate to adopt new international standards on the subject with a view to removing the assimilationist orientation of the earlier standards, and

Recognising the aspirations of these peoples to exercise control over their own institutions, ways of life and economic development and to maintain and develop their identities, languages and religions, within the framework of the States in which they live, and

Noting that in many parts of the world these peoples are unable to enjoy their fundamental human rights to the same degree as the rest of the population of the States within which they live, and that their laws, values, customs and perspectives have often been eroded, and

Calling attention to the distinctive contributions of indigenous and tribal peoples to the cultural diversity and social and ecological harmony of humankind and to international co-operation and understanding, and

Noting that the following provisions have been framed with the co-operation of the United Nations, the Food and Agriculture Organisation of the United Nations, the United Nations Educational, Scientific and Cultural Organisation and the World Health Organisation, as well as of the Inter-American Indian Institute, at appropriate levels and in their respective fields, and that it is proposed to continue this co-operation in promoting and securing the application of these provisions, and

Having decided upon the adoption of certain proposals with regard to the partial revision of the Indigenous and Tribal Populations Convention, 1957, (No. 107), which is the fourth item on the agenda of the session, and

Having determined that these proposals shall take the form of an international Convention revising the Indigenous and Tribal Populations Convention, 1957;

Adopts this twenty-seventh day of June of the year one thousand nine hundred and eighty-nine the following Convention, which may be cited as the Indigenous and Tribal Peoples Convention, 1989:

### Part I. General Policy

*Article 1.* 1. This Convention applies to:

(a) tribal peoples in independent countries whose social, cultural and economic conditions distinguish them from other sections of the national community, and whose status is regulated wholly or partially by their own customs or traditions or by special laws or regulations;

(b) peoples in independent countries who are regarded as indigenous on account of their descent from the populations which inhabited the country, or a geographical region to which the country belongs, at the time of conquest or colonisation or the establishment of present state boundaries and who, irrespective of their legal status, retain some or all of their own social, economic, cultural and political institutions.

2. Self-identification as indigenous or tribal shall be regarded as a fundamental criterion for determining the groups to which the provisions of this Convention apply.

3. The use of the term "peoples" in this convention shall not be construed as having any implications as regards the rights which may attach to the term under international law.

*Article 2.* 1. Governments shall have the responsibility for developing, with the participation of the peoples concerned, co-ordinated and systematic action to protect the rights of these peoples and to guarantee respect for their integrity.

2. Such action shall include measures for:

(a) ensuring that members of these peoples benefit on an equal footing from the rights and opportunities which national laws and regulations grant to other members of the population;

(b) promoting the full realisation of the social, economic and cultural rights of these peoples with respect for their social and cultural identity, their customs and traditions and their institutions;

(c) assisting the members of the peoples concerned to

eliminate socio-economic gaps that may exist between indigenous and other members of the national community, in a manner compatible with their aspirations and ways of life.

*Article 3.* 1. Indigenous and tribal peoples shall enjoy the full measure of human rights and fundamental freedoms without hindrance or discrimination. The provisions of the Convention shall be applied without discrimination to male and female members of these peoples.

2. No form of force or coercion shall be used in violation of the human rights and fundamental freedoms of the peoples concerned, including the rights contained in this Convention.

*Article 4.* 1. Special measures shall be adopted as appropriate for safeguarding the persons, institutions, property, labour, cultures and environment of the peoples concerned.

2. Such special measures shall not be contrary to the freely-expressed wishes of the peoples concerned.

3. Enjoyment of the general rights of citizenship, without discrimination, shall not be prejudiced in any way by such special measures.

*Article 5.* In applying the provisions of this Convention:

(a) the social, cultural, religious and spiritual values and practices of these peoples shall be recognised and protected, and due account shall be taken of the nature of the problems which face them both as groups and as individuals;

(b) the integrity of the values, practices and institutions of these peoples shall be respected;

(c) policies aimed at mitigating the difficulties experienced by these peoples in facing new conditions of life and work shall be adopted, with the participation and co-operation of the peoples affected.

*Article 6.* 1. In applying the provisions of this Convention, governments shall:

(a) consult the peoples concerned, through appropriate procedures and in particular through their representative institutions, whenever consideration is being given to legislative or administrative measures which may affect them directly;

(b) establish means by which these peoples can freely participate, to at least the same extent as other sectors of the population, at all levels of decision-making in elective institutions and administrative and other bodies responsible for policies and programmes which concern them;

(c) establish means for the full development of these peoples' own institutions and initiatives, and in appropriate cases provide the resources necessary for this purpose.

2. The consultations carried out in application of this Convention shall be undertaken, in good faith and in a form appropriate to the circumstances, with the objective of achieving agreement or consent to the proposed measures.

*Article 7.* 1. The peoples concerned shall have the right to decide their own priorities for the process of development as it affects their lives, beliefs, institutions and spiritual well-being and the lands they occupy or otherwise use, and to exercise control, to the extent possible, over their own economic, social and cultural development. In addition, they shall participate in the formulation, implementation and evaluation of plans and programmes for national and regional development which may affect them directly.

2. The improvement of the conditions of life and work and level of health and education of the peoples concerned, with their participation and co-operation, shall be a matter of priority in plans for the overall economic development of areas they inhabit. Special projects for development of the areas in question shall also be so designed as to promote such improvement.

3. Governments shall ensure that, whenever appropriate, studies are carried out, in co-operation with the peoples concerned, to assess the social, spiritual, cultural and environmental impact on them of planned development activities. The results of these studies shall be considered as fundamental criteria for the implementation of these activities.

4. Government shall take measures, in co-operation with the peoples concerned, to protect and preserve the environment of the territories they inhabit.

*Article 8.* 1. In applying national laws and regulations to the peoples concerned, due regard shall be had to their customs or customary laws.

2. These peoples shall have the right to retain their own customs and institutions, where these are not incompatible with fundamental rights defined by the national legal system and with internationally recognized human rights. Procedures shall be established, whenever necessary, to resolve conflicts which may arise in the application of this principle.

3. The application of paragraphs 1 and 2 of this Article shall not prevent members of these peoples from exercising the rights granted to all citizens and from assuming the corresponding duties.

*Article 9.* 1. To the extent compatible with the national legal system and internationally recognized human rights, the methods customarily practised by the peoples concerned for dealing with offences committed by their members shall be respected.

2. The customs of these peoples in regard to penal matters shall be taken into consideration by the authorities and courts dealing with such cases.

*Article 10.* 1. In imposing penalties laid down by general law on members of these peoples account shall be taken of their economic, social and cultural characteristics.

2. Preference shall be given to methods of punishment other than confinement in prison.

*Article 11.* The exaction from members of the peoples concerned of compulsory personal services in any form, whether paid or unpaid, shall be prohibited and punishable by law, except in cases prescribed by law for all citizens.

*Article 12.* The peoples concerned shall be safeguarded against the abuse of their rights and shall be able to take legal proceedings, either individually or through their representative bodies, for the effective protection of these rights. Measures shall be taken to ensure that members of these peoples can understand and be understood in legal proceedings, where necessary through the provision of interpretation or by other effective means.

## Part II. Land

*Article 13.* 1. In applying the provisions of this Part of the Convention governments shall respect the special importance for the cultures and spiritual values of the peoples concerned of their relationship with the lands or territories, or both as applicable, which they occupy or otherwise use, and in particular the collective aspects of this relationship.

2. The use of the term "lands" in Articles 15 and 16 shall include the concept of territories, which covers the total environment of the areas which the peoples concerned occupy or otherwise use.

*Article 14.* 1. The rights of ownership and possession of the peoples concerned over the lands which they traditionally occupy shall be recognised. In addition, measures shall be taken in appropriate cases to safeguard the right of the peoples concerned to use lands not exclusively occupied by them, but to which they have traditionally had access for their subsistence and traditional activities. Particular attention shall be paid to the situation of nomadic peoples and shifting cultivators in this respect.

2. Governments shall take steps as necessary to identify the lands which the peoples concerned traditionally occupy, and to guarantee effective protection of their rights of ownership and possession.

3. Adequate procedures shall be established within the national legal system to resolve land claims by the peoples concerned.

*Article 15.* 1. The rights of the peoples concerned to the natural resources pertaining to their lands shall be specially safeguarded. These rights include the right of these peoples to participate in the use, management and conservation of these resources.

2. In cases in which the State retains the ownership of mineral or sub-surface resources or rights to other resources pertaining to lands, governments shall establish or maintain procedures through which they shall consult these peoples, with a view to ascertaining whether and to what degree their interests would be prejudiced, before undertaking or permitting any programmes for the exploration or exploitation of such resources pertaining to their lands. The peoples concerned shall wherever possible participate in the benefits of such activities, and shall receive fair compensation for any damages which they may sustain as a result of such activities.

*Article 16.* 1. Subject to the following paragraphs of this Article, the peoples concerned shall not be removed from the lands which they occupy.

2. Where the relocation of these peoples is considered necessary as an exceptional measure, such relocation shall take place only with their free and informed consent. Where their consent cannot be obtained, such relocation shall take place only following appropriate procedures established by national laws and regulations, including public inquiries where appropriate, which provide the opportunity for effective representation of the peoples concerned.

3. Whenever possible, these peoples shall have the right to return to their traditional lands, as soon as grounds for relocation cease to exist.

4. When such return is not possible, as determined by agreement or, in the absence of such agreement, through appropriate procedures, these peoples shall be provided in all possible cases with lands of quality and legal status at least equal to that of the lands previously occupied by them, suitable to provide for their present needs and future development. Where the peoples concerned express a preference for compensation in money or in kind, they shall be so compensated under appropriate guarantees.

5. Persons thus relocated shall be fully compensated for any resulting loss or injury.

*Article 17.* 1. Procedures established by the peoples concerned for the transmission of land rights among members of these peoples shall be respected.

2. The peoples concerned shall be consulted whenever consideration is being given to their capacity to alienate their lands or otherwise transmit their rights outside their own community.

3. Persons not belonging to these peoples shall be prevented from taking advantage of their customs or of lack of understanding of the laws on the part of their members to secure the ownership, possession or use of land belonging to them.

*Article 18.* Adequate penalties shall be established by law for unauthorised intrusion upon, or use of, the lands of the

peoples concerned, and governments shall take measures to prevent such offences.

*Article 19.* National agrarian programmes shall secure to the peoples concerned treatment equivalent to that accorded to other sectors of the population with regard to:

(a) the provision of more land for these peoples when they have not the area necessary for providing the essentials of a normal existence, or for any possible increase in their numbers;

(b) the provision of the means required to promote the development of the lands which these peoples already possess.

## Part III. Recruitment and Conditions of Employment

*Article 20.* 1. Governments shall, within the framework of national laws and regulations, and in co-operation with the peoples concerned, adopt special measures to ensure the effective protection with regard to recruitment and conditions of employment of workers belonging to these peoples, to the extent that they are not effectively protected by laws applicable to workers in general.

2. Governments shall do everything possible to prevent any discrimination between workers belonging to the peoples concerned and other workers, in particular as regards:

(a) admission to employment, including skilled employment, as well as measures for promotion and advancement;

(b) equal remuneration for work of equal value;

(c) medical and social assistance, occupational safety and health, all social security benefits and any other occupationally related benefits, and housing;

(d) the right of association and freedom for all lawful trade union activities, and the right to conclude collective agreements with employers or employers' organisations.

3. The measures taken shall include measures to ensure:

(a) that workers belonging to the peoples concerned, including seasonal, casual and migrant workers in agricultural and other employment, as well as those employed by labour contractors, enjoy the protection afforded by national law and practice to other such workers in the same sectors, and that they are fully informed of their rights under labour legislation and of the means of redress available to them;

(b) that workers belonging to these peoples are not subjected to working conditions hazardous to their health, in particular through exposure to pesticides or other toxic substances;

(c) that workers belonging to these peoples are not subjected to coercive recruitment systems, including bonded labour and other forms of debt servitude;

(d) that workers belonging to these peoples enjoy equal opportunities and equal treatment in employment for men and women, and protection from sexual harassment.

4. Particular attention shall be paid to the establishment of adequate labour inspection services in areas where workers belonging to the peoples concerned undertake wage employment, in order to ensure compliance with the provisions of this Part of this Convention.

## Part IV. Vocational Training, Handicrafts and Rural Industries

*Article 21.* Members of the peoples concerned shall enjoy opportunities at least equal to those of other citizens in respect of vocational training measures.

*Article 22.* 1. Measures shall be taken to promote the voluntary participation of members of the peoples concerned in vocational training programmes of general application.

2. Whenever existing programmes of vocational training of general application do not meet the special needs of the peoples concerned, governments shall, with the participation of these peoples, ensure the provision of special training programmes and facilities.

3. Any special training programmes shall be based on the economic environment, social and cultural conditions and practical needs of the peoples concerned. Any studies made in this connection shall be carried out in co-operation with these peoples, who shall be consulted on the organisation and operation of such programmes. Where feasible, these peoples shall progressively assume responsibility for the organisation and operation of such special training programmes, if they so decide.

*Article 23.* 1. Handicrafts, rural and community based industries, and subsistence economy and traditional activities of the peoples concerned, such as hunting, fishing, trapping and gathering, shall be recognised as important factors in the maintenance of their cultures and in their economic self-reliance and development. Governments shall, with the participation of these people and whenever appropriate, ensure that these activities are strengthened and promoted.

2. Upon the request of the peoples concerned, appropriate technical and financial assistance shall be provided wherever possible, taking into account the traditional technologies and cultural characteristics of these peoples, as well as the importance of sustainable and equitable development.

### Part V. Social Security and Health

*Article 24.* Social security schemes shall be extended progressively to cover the peoples concerned, and applied without discrimination against them.

*Article 25.* 1. Governments shall ensure that adequate health services are made available to the peoples concerned, or shall provide them with resources to allow them to design and deliver such services under their own responsibility and control, so that they may enjoy the highest attainable standard of physical and mental health.

2. Health services shall, to the extent possible, be community-based. These services shall be planned and administered in co-operation with the peoples concerned and take into account their economic, geographic, social and cultural conditions as well as their traditional preventive care, healing practices and medicines.

3. The health care system shall give preference to the training and employment of local community health workers, and focus on primary health care while maintaining strong links with other levels of health care services.

4. The provision of such health services shall be co-ordinated with other social, economic and cultural measures in the country.

### Part VI. Education and Means of Communication

*Article 26.* Measures shall be taken to ensure that members of the peoples concerned have the opportunity to acquire education at all levels on at least an equal footing with the rest of the national community.

*Article 27.* 1. Education programmes and services for the peoples concerned shall be developed and implemented in co-operation with them to address their special needs, and shall incorporate their histories, their knowledge and technologies, their value systems and their further social, economic and cultural aspirations.

2. The competent authority shall ensure the training of members of these peoples and their involvement in the formulation and implementation of education programmes, with a view to the progressive transfer of responsibility for the conduct of these programmes to these peoples as appropriate.

3. In addition, governments shall recognize the right of these peoples to establish their own educational institutions and facilities, provided that such institutions meet minimum standards established by the competent authority in consultation with these peoples. Appropriate resources shall be provided for this purpose.

*Article 28.* 1. Children belonging to the peoples concerned shall, wherever practicable, be taught to read and write in their own indigenous language or in the language most commonly used by the group to which they belong. When this is not practicable, the competent authorities shall undertake consultations with these peoples with a view to the adoption of measures to achieve this objective.

2. Adequate measures shall be taken to ensure that these peoples have the opportunity to attain fluency in the national language or in one of the official languages of the country.

3. Measures shall be taken to preserve and promote the development and practice of the indigenous languages of the peoples concerned.

*Article 29.* The imparting of general knowledge and skills that will help children belonging to the peoples concerned to participate fully and on an equal footing in their own community and in the national community shall be an aim of education for these peoples.

*Article 30.* 1. Governments shall adopt measures appropriate to the traditions and cultures of the peoples concerned, to make known to them their rights and duties, especially in regard to labour, economic opportunities, education and health matters, social welfare and their rights deriving from this Convention.

2. If necessary, this shall be done by means of written translations and through the use of mass communications in the languages of these peoples.

*Article 31.* Educational measures shall be taken among all sections of the national community, and particularly among those that are in most direct contact with the peoples concerned, with the object of eliminating prejudices that they may harbour in respect of these peoples. To this end, efforts shall be made to ensure that history textbooks and other educational materials provide a fair, accurate and informative portrayal of the societies and cultures of these peoples.

### Part VII. Contacts and Co-operation across Borders

*Article 32.* Governments shall take appropriate measures, including by means of international agreements, to facilitate contacts and co-operation between indigenous and tribal peoples across borders, including activities in the economic, social, cultural, spiritual and environmental fields.

### Part VIII. Administration

*Article 33.* 1. The governmental authority responsible for the matters covered in this Convention shall ensure that agencies or other appropriate mechanisms exist to administer the programmes affecting the peoples concerned, and shall ensure that they have the means necessary for proper fulfilment of the functions assigned to them.

2. These programmes shall include:

(a) the planning, co-ordination, execution and evaluation, in co-operation with the peoples concerned, of the measures provided for in this convention;

(b) the proposing of legislative and other measures to the competent authorities and supervision of the application of the measures taken, in co-operation with the peoples concerned.

### Part IX. General Provisions

*Article 34.* The nature and scope of the measures to be taken to give effect to this Convention shall be determined in a flexible manner, having regard to the conditions characteristic of each country.

*Article 35.* The application of the provisions of this Convention shall not adversely affect rights and benefits of the peoples concerned pursuant to other Conventions and Recommendations, international instruments, treaties, or national laws, awards, custom or agreements.

### Part X. Final Provisions

*Article 36.* This Convention revises the Indigenous and Tribal Populations Convention, 1957.

*Article 37.* The formal ratifications of this Convention shall be communicated to the Director-General of the International Labour Office for registration.

*Article 38.* 1. This Convention shall be binding only upon those Members of the International Labour Organisation whose ratifications have been registered with the Director-General.

2. It shall come into force twelve months after the date on which the ratifications of two Members have been registered with the Director-General.

3. Thereafter, this Convention shall come into force for any Member twelve months after the date on which its ratification has been registered.

*Article 39.* 1. A Member which has ratified this Convention may denounce it after the expiration of ten years from the date on which the Convention first comes into force, by an act communicated to the Director-General of the International Labour Office for registration. Such denunciation shall not take effect until one year after the date on which it is registered.

2. Each Member which has ratified this Convention and which does not, within the year following the expiration of the period of ten years mentioned in the preceding paragraph, exercise the right of denunciation provided for in this Article, will be bound for another period of ten years and, thereafter, may denounce this Convention at the expiration of each period of ten years under the terms provided for in this Article.

*Article 40.* 1. The Director-General of the International Labour Office shall notify all Members of the International Labour Organisation of the registration of all ratifications and denunciations communicated to him by the Members of the Organisation.

2. When notifying the Members of the Organisation of the registration of the second ratification communicated to him, the Director-General shall draw the attention of the Members of the Organisation to the date upon which the Convention will come into force.

*Article 41.* The Director-General of the International Labour Office shall communicate to the Secretary-General of the United Nations for registration in accordance with Article 102 of the Charter of the United Nations full particulars of all ratifications and acts of denunciation registered by him in accordance with the provisions of the preceding Articles.

*Article 42.* At such times as it may consider necessary the Governing Body of the International Labour Office shall present to the General Conference a report on the working of this Convention and shall examine the desirability of placing on the agenda of the Conference the question of its revision in whole or in part.

*Article 43.* 1. Should the Conference adopt a new Convention revising this Convention in whole or in part, then, unless the new Convention otherwise provides—

(a) the ratification by a Member of the new revising Convention shall *ipso jure* involve the immediate denunciation of this Convention, notwithstanding the provisions of Article 39 above, if and when the new revising Convention shall have come into force;

(b) as from the date when the new revising Convention comes into force this Convention shall cease to be open to ratification by the Members.

2. This Convention shall in any case remain in force in its actual form and content for those Members which have ratified it but have not ratified the revising Convention.

*Article 44.* The English and French versions of the text of this Convention are equally authoritative.

**BIBLIOGRAPHY.** Berman, Howard R. "ILO and Indigenous Peoples: Revision of ILO Convention 107," *ICJ Review* no. 41 (Dec. 1988): 48–57. NGO article, in English.

Gray, Andrew. "The ILO Meeting at the UN, Geneva, June 1989: Report on International Labor Organization Revision of Convention 107," *IWGIA Yearbook* (1990): 173–191. Conference report, in English.

Lerner, Natan. "The 1989 ILO Convention on Indigenous Populations: New Standards?," *Israel Yearbook on Human Rights* 20 (1990): 223–241. Scholarly article, in English.

**INDIGENOUS WORLD ASSOCIATION.** An international non-governmental organization in consultative status (Category II) with the UN **ECONOMIC AND SOCIAL COUNCIL,** the IWA is affiliated with six organizations in four countries.

Founded in 1981, the Association promotes the values and programs of the United Nations and the rights of indigenous peoples, refugees, migrant workers, and minorities. It promotes the development of international human rights law and supports the work of the UN Working Group on Indigenous Populations. IWA publishes the *IWA Bulletin*.

Indigenous World Association. Address: 275 Grand View Avenue, San Francisco, CA 94114, USA. Telephone: (415) 647-1966. Director: Roxanne Dunbar Ortiz.

**INDONESIA.** The Republic of Indonesia is a country in southeastern Asia consisting of the Malay Archipelago, a large island group in the Indian Ocean, including the Sunda Islands (including Java and Sunatra), the Lesser Sundas (including Bali), Borneo, the Celebes, and the Moluccas. It has borders with Malaysia and Papua New Guinea. It achieved independence from the Netherlands in 1945 and became a member of the United Nations in 1950. Its population is estimated to be 186,180,000. The complex ethnic structure of the population is the result of several great migrations, many centuries ago, from Asia and the South Pacific. The Chinese are the most numerous of the non-indigenous peoples. The so-called Coast Malays, who inhabit the coastal areas of the major islands, are of mixed stock: Chinese, Arab, East Indian, and Malayan. Languages commonly used include Bahasa Indonesian (official), Javanese, Dutch, and English. Islam is the predominant religion (90%); Christianity, Buddhism, and Hinduism comprise the remaining 10%.

The government (1994) took the form of a republic. The president, elected by the 920-member People's Assembly, serves as head of State and government. The House of Representatives, composed of 464 members of the assembly, is the legislative authority. The house meets at least once a year; the assembly only once every five years. Political parties include the Sekber Golkar Party, the Islamic United Development Party, and the Democratic Party.

Occupied by the Japanese during World War II, the Dutch colony of Indonesia enjoyed virtual self-government until the Japanese surrendered to the Allies on 17 August 1945, at which time President Sukarno proclaimed his country's independence from the Netherlands. British troops fought the Indonesian nationalists until Dutch units arrived; then Dutch and Indonesian forces fought sporadically until leaders of the two countries agreed upon terms of a Dutch-Indonesian union under the Dutch crown. But the union, established in 1949, was abrogated by Indonesia in 1956.

*MALAYSIA.* Indonesia was involved in an international dispute concerning the right of self-determination in 1963–1964, relating to the formation of Malaysia. A United Nations mission determined that the people of Sabah and Sarawak had decided to realize their independence through freely chosen association with the people of the Federation of Malaysia and Singapore, with whom they felt ties of ethnic association, heritage, language, religion, culture, ideals, and objectives. When the Federation of Malaysia was proclaimed on 16 September 1963, Indonesia's representative at the United Nations objected. In January 1965, after Malaysia had been seated as a member of the Security Council, Indonesia withdrew from the United Nations. However, it resumed participation in UN activities in September 1966.

*"DISAPPEARANCE" OF CITIZENS.* During the two decades when President Sukarno was in power in Indonesia, the influence of the Indonesian Communist Party gradually increased, until fear of a takeover led to an attempted *coup d'etat*. The coup, directed against Sukarno, was thwarted by the army under the command of Gen. Suharto and was followed by an intensive campaign against "subversives" in which thousands are said to have "disappeared" or lost their lives.

Gen. Suharto replaced Sukarno as president in 1967, stabilized the country economically, and reorganized its government. However, the "disappearances" continued and, indeed, intensified between 1982 and 1984 under the influence of legislation that made it a crime, subject to the death penalty, to undertake action aimed at undermining or contradicting the ideology of the State.

*EAST TIMOR.* In 1975, after Portugal had withdrawn from its administration of the eastern portion of a Malaysian island known as East Timor, Indonesian troops invaded the area and the Government of Indonesia proclaimed it a province of that country. The move was not recognized by the United Nations, and for some time Indonesia did not participate in the work of that organization.

The question of East Timor has remained on the agenda of the **GENERAL ASSEMBLY,** without solution, since that time, although the people of South Timor have campaigned vigorously for its recognition as an independent nation.

In 1991, Indonesian forces opened fire on a crowd of mourners in Dili, the capital of East Timor, and the UN Secretary-General sent his personal envoy, Mr. S. Amos Wako, to Indonesia and East Timor to seek clarification of the reasons for that tragic incident. After a series of contacts with the parties concerned, the Secretary-General invited the Foreign Ministers of Indonesia and Portugal to hold informal consultations in New York, under his auspices and without preconditions, with the object of arriving at a mutually acceptable format for resuming substantive discussions on the matter. Three rounds of talks were held between December 1992 and September 1993, and the Secretary-General advised the General Assembly that while it had proved difficult to make progress on the core question, he was modestly encouraged by the substance and tone of the discussions.

In November 1994—the third anniversary of the gunning down of the mourners in Dili—hundreds of young people rampaged through the streets of that town, armed with sticks, iron rods and stones, breaking windows and setting cars on fire. At the same time, about 30 demonstrators staged a sit-in at the United States Embassy in Jakarta, to meet visiting American President Bill Clinton to request his help in obtaining the release of the leader of a guerrilla movement imprisoned for fighting for East Timor's independence.

A Special Rapporteur's analysis of the events of 1991 following his visit in 1994 included the following (E/CN.4/1995/61/Add. 1, paras. 41–42, 48, 52, 70–73, 77):

### Conclusions

The Special Rapporteur based the following conclusions on the information given to him during the meetings he held in Jakarta and in East Timor, on documentary evidence brought to his attention before and during his mission and on the various reliable testimonies he gathered. It should be noted once again that during his visit the Special Rapporteur requested, both orally and by a letter dated 11 July 1994, that some important official documents referred to by the Indonesian authorities, mostly reports regarding the Santa Cruz killings, be made available to him. At the time of the completion of the present report, this request had not been satisfied.

The Special Rapporteur believes that, in examining the situation of the right to life in East Timor, other grave human rights violations attributed to the Indonesian armed forces in Indonesia itself (for instance in Aceh and Iryan Jaya), as described in his previous reports to the Commission, should be borne in mind. In particular, the patterns of dealing violently with political dissent and the virtual impunity enjoyed by members of the security forces responsible for human rights violations should be recalled.

### The Government's Responsibility in the Killings

The Special Rapporteur, after careful consideration of the available evidence, including the numerous eye-witness testimonies he gathered, reached in the following conclusions:

(a) A proper crowd control operation could have been set up beforehand to deal with the demonstration, thus avoiding the killings;

(b) The forces that perpetrated the killings on 12 November 1991 were regular members of the armed forces;

(c) The procession that took place in Dili on 12 November 1991 was a peaceful demonstration of political dissent by unarmed civilians; the claims of some officials that the security forces had fired in self-defence and had respected the principles of the necessity and the proportionality of the use of lethal force are unsubstantiated;

(d) There are, therefore, reasons to believe that the actions of the security forces were not a spontaneous reaction to a riotous mob, but rather a planned military operation designed to deal with a public expression of political dissent in a way not in accordance with international human rights standards.

### Analysis of the Investigations

From the information he gathered during meetings with the representative of the East Timor judiciary and law enforce-ment authorities, the Special Rapporteur concluded the following:

(a) The investigation carried out by the police forces was not thorough, as will be shown below;

(b) Given that the police is itself a part of the armed forces and the grave allegations concerning the adverse role of the police in the Santa Cruz killings and subsequent incidents, the conditions for an independent and impartial investigation were not present;

(c) The forensic examination was inadequate. Although a medical examination was carried out by the hospital on the 19 acknowledged corpses, no adequate autopsies were performed. The Chief of Police told the Special Rapporteur that the necessary technological means were not available in East Timor, and that no forensic expert was sent from Jakarta. Likewise, no ballistic examination was conducted to connect the bullets fired with the weapons of the members of the security forces present at the cemetery, even though such an analysis could have been conducted later in the capital;

(d) The criminal investigation was inadequate, failing to clarify either the identity of the perpetrators or the victims, nor even the number of the latter. It did not determine the fate and whereabouts of the missing persons. In fact, it appears that the witnesses interrogated by the police were questioned on their involvement in the organization of the demonstrations rather than on possible unlawful acts carried out by members of the security forces, or the identity of the killed and disappeared.

### Analysis of the Prosecution of the Members of the Security Forces Responsible for the Killings and Disappearances

As regards the prosecution of the perpetrators of the Santa Cruz killings and connected grave human rights violations, the Special Rapporteur reached the following conclusions:

(a) According to the information brought to the attention of the Special Rapporteur, torture, murder and kidnapping are criminal offences under Indonesian law. They are also prohibited by the Military Criminal Code and by a variety of ministerial regulations. Other provisions of the Military Criminal Code are designed to curtail the abuse of authority by members of the security forces and to ensure that commanding officers take responsibility for crimes committed by their subordinates. Thus, the minimum instruments allowing for the prosecution of the perpetrators exist. However, members of the armed forces, including the police, who have committed crimes or have abused their authority can stand trial only before military courts, even in cases where the victims are civilians;

(b) In spite of the recommendations formulated by the Special Rapporteur on the question of torture subsequent to his visit to Indonesia and East Timor in November 1991 (E/CN.4/1992/17/Add. 1, para. 80), victims of human rights violations or their relatives still do not have direct access to the judicial system in cases of abuses perpetrated by members of the security forces. Consequently, such complaints have to be filed with the police, which belongs to the armed forces. In practice, investigations are, therefore, rarely concluded. This can hardly be called an effective remedy. The Special Rapporteur is not aware of any provision entitling a civilian to bring such a complaint before a judicial or other authority if the police have rejected the complaint or refused to carry out an investigation. Even the Prosecutor has no authority to order the police to carry out an investigation. If the police find a complaint filed by a civilian to be well founded, the file is transmitted to the office of the Military Attorney-General, since the suspect would have to stand trial before a military court. This means that no civilian authority is involved in any way in dealing with a complaint filed by a civilian of an alleged encroachment on his fundamental rights. The Special Rapporteur feels that a system which places the task of correcting and suppressing abuses of authority by members of the army in that same institution will not easily inspire confidence. The Special Rapporteur believes that there is no reason why persons belonging to the military should be tried by military courts for offences committed against civilians during the essentially civil task of maintaining law and order.

(c) Despite the fundamental shortcomings of its investigation, NCI reached conclusions that engaged the responsibility of the security forces to a greater extent than was admitted by the police during the Special Rapporteur's visit: "according to information received from the Military Operational Command, the death toll reached 19 . . . but according to the account of other eye-witnesses and sources, the death toll exceeded 19 and their figures varied from 50, 60 to over 100. . . . Although the casualty toll until now was set at 19 dead and 91 wounded, the Commission feels that there are sufficiently strong grounds to conclude that the death casualties totalled about 50 while the wounded exceeded 91". NCI, however, gave no indication as to why the figure of "about 50" had been retained. During his visit, the Special Rapporteur was told by all the officials he met that only 19 persons had died as a result of the 12 November 1991 event. The Chief of the East Timor Police declared that 6 persons had died at the hospital on that same day, in the afternoon, and 13 at the site of the incident. The Special Rapporteur reiterates his view that the dispute over the actual number of the dead and missing should not obscure the need and the obligation to identify the dead and reveal the whereabouts of their remains, to bring the perpetrators to justice and to compensate the families of the victims;

(d) The report of NCI concluded that "action must be taken against all those involved in the 12 November 1991 incident in Dili and suspected of having violated the law, and they must be brought to trial in accordance with the rule of law, Pancasila and the 1945 Constitution". However, this statement does not specify or recommend who should be brought to justice;

(e) The Special Rapporteur feels that the court martial set up as a response to the Santa Cruz killings was an encouraging first step towards the accountability of members of the armed forces for violations of human rights. However, as mentioned above, the Court examined only the cases of 10 low-ranking members of the security forces, who were accused of having acted "without command and beyond acceptable norms". They were charged under article 103, paragraph 1, of the Military Criminal Code for disobeying orders. Only one of them was charged with assault, in violation of article 351 of the code, for cutting off the ears of a demonstrator. That is to say that none of the few military personnel accused was charged with homicide, serious assault, or for having committed enforced disappearances. Likewise, there did not seem to have been any attempts made by the prosecution, for example by using ballistic evidence, to attribute to the accused the shots which caused deaths or wounds. The sentences meted out by the military tribunal ranged from 8 to 18 months, which, considering the seriousness of the human rights violations that were committed on 12 November 1991 and possibly subsequently, seem to the Special Rapporteur to be inappropriately light penalties.

Furthermore, the fate of the missing persons continues to be unknown;

(f) The Honorary Military Council appointed by the President dealt with the cases of six senior officers and found them guilty of misconduct. This procedure was not public and did not involve the participation of the families or of independent observers. Many elements about it therefore remain obscure; for instance, the exact grounds for punishing those officers is not known, and in any event they were never brought to justice;

(g) The Special Rapporteur is of the opinion that the inadequacy of the charges and the inappropriately light sentences imposed by the court martial on the few members of the armed forces accused of having been implicated in the 12 November 1991 incident are in no way a fulfilment of the obligation to punish perpetrators, and thus to provide a deterrent for the recurrence of a similar tragedy in the future. On the contrary, he feels that they illustrate that little importance is given to the respect of the right to life by Indonesian law enforcement officials in East Timor. On the other hand, the 13 civilians involved in peaceful protest during and after 12 November 1991 were sentenced to terms of up to life imprisonment. In paragraph 4 of its resolution 1993/97, the Commission regretted "the disparity in the severity of sentences imposed on those civilians not indicted for violent activities—who should have been released without delay—on the one hand, and to the military involved in the violent incident, on the other". The Special Rapporteur is also of the opinion that there was an unreasonable disparity between the sentences passed upon the perpetrators and upon the victims; the latter were, in fact, those really blamed for the killings. He believes that this disparity is much more illustrative of an implacable determination to suppress political dissent than a genuine commitment to protect the right to life and prevent extrajudicial executions.

## Compensation of the Families and Dependents of the Victims

Principle 20 states: "The families and dependents of victims of extra-legal, summary or arbitrary executions shall be entitled to fair and adequate compensation within a reasonable period of time."

Article 19 of the Declaration states: "The victims of acts of enforced disappearance and their families shall obtain redress and shall have the right to adequate compensation, including the means for as complete a rehabilitation as possible. In the event of the death of the victim as a result of an act of enforced disappearance, their dependants shall also be entitled to compensation."

With respect to the above:

(a) According to the information brought to the attention of the Special Rapporteur, existing procedures for the redress and compensation of victims and relatives are ineffective and cumbersome. Members of the public with a human rights grievance face the daunting prospect of complaining to the armed forces, the very authority they believe to be responsible;

(b) According to the information gathered by the Special Rapporteur, the judiciary are largely shackled by the executive branch and the military, and the legal system suffers widespread corruption. The Special Rapporteur is concerned that there is no real right to defence in Indonesian courts. The few lawyers practicing in East Timor are reportedly not trusted by the population, because they are considered to be linked to the Indonesian authorities;

(c) In the case of the Santa Cruz killings, no compensation has been granted, and no special mechanism has been created for that purpose. The Special Rapporteur believes that the first step towards compensation should be the identification of the dead and disappeared, which, in turn, requires the recognition by the Government of its responsibility.

### Recommendation

The Special Rapporteur believes that the Santa Cruz killings should not be considered as a thing of the past. They must not be forgotten, and there is still time to correct the shortcomings, noted at all levels, in the way in which violations of the right to life have been dealt with by the Indonesian authorities in East Timor: it is not too late to conduct proper investigations, to identify and bring to justice the perpetrators, to determine the fate and whereabouts of the missing persons, to grant compensation to the victims or their relatives, and to prevent the occurrence of further killings.

*OBSERVATIONS OF THE COMMITTEE ON THE RIGHTS OF THE CHILD.* The UN **COMMITTEE ON THE RIGHTS OF THE CHILD** considered the initial report of Indonesia under the Convention on the Rights of the Child (see **CHILDREN'S RIGHTS**) (CRC/C/15/Add. 7) at meetings held on 22 and 23 September 1993. In view of the fact that there was not sufficient time during the session to fully clarify a number of questions relating to the implementation of the Convention, the Committee decided to continue its consideration of the report at a future session and adopted the following preliminary observations:

*Positive aspects.* The Committee notes with satisfaction the importance Indonesia attaches to the Committee's advice and assistance on measures to be taken to improve the implementation of the rights of the child and welcomes the State party's commitment to cooperating with the Committee and other United Nations bodies and agencies with a view to reviewing and developing policies and programmes to enhance the situation of children.

The Committee takes note of the willingness expressed by the State party to review its national legislation in the light of its obligations under the Convention and as reflected in the "Beijing consensus" of August 1992. It also welcomes the State party's commitment to review the reservations it has made to the Convention with a view to considering withdrawing them.

The Committee also notes the steps taken to give higher priority to children's concerns, especially within the context of development strategies.

*Factors and difficulties impeding the implementation of the Convention.* The Committee takes note of the difficulties impeding the rapid implementation of the Convention in the State party, particularly the existence of 360 ethnic groups, the dispersal of the population throughout the Indonesian archipelago, as well as the economic problems still facing the State party in general and sectors of the Indonesian population, in particular.

*Principal subjects of concern.* The Committee is deeply concerned at the extent of the reservations made to the Convention by the State party. The Committee feels that the broad and imprecise nature of these reservations raises serious concern as to their compatibility with the object and purposes of the Convention.

While the Committee takes note of the delegation's statement that the rights of the child as contained in the Convention are not in contradiction with the Constitution, it is concerned that national legislation does not appear to ensure that all children, including non-nationals, are protected by the rights guaranteed in the Convention.

The Committee is also concerned that the rights contained in article 14 of the Convention are not fully protected, in spite of the fact that they are non-derogable.

It is also a concern of the Committee that national legislation with respect to the age at which a child may marry may not be compatible with the non-discrimination provisions of the Convention, as reflected in its article 2.

The Committee expresses its concern at the insufficient efforts undertaken to make the principles and provisions of the Convention widely known to children.

The Committee is also concerned at the lack of participation of non-governmental organizations, particularly of human rights groups in the promotion and protection of the rights of the child as well as at the absence of efforts to provide training about the rights of the child to personnel working directly with children.

The Committee is concerned that insufficient attention is given to the implementation of the general principles of the Convention, particularly its articles 2, 3 and 12. The Committee wishes to emphasize that the implementation of these principles is not to be made dependent on budgetary resources.

The Committee is concerned at the small proportion of the budget devoted to the social sectors, particularly primary health care and primary education. In this connection, the Committee draws the State party's attention to the need to respect the provisions of article 4 of the Convention, which emphasize that economic, social and cultural rights should be implemented to the maximum extent of available resources. The Committee emphasizes that such action is required, regardless of the economic model followed by the State party.

The Committee expresses its concern as regards the implementation of article 14 of the Convention, as it relates to freedom of religion. The Committee deems it important to underline the fact that limiting official recognition to certain religions may give rise to practices of discrimination.

The Committee regrets that the written information requested on special protection measures was not provided and also expresses its concern at the lack of compatibility of the system of administration of juvenile justice with articles 37, 39 and 40 of the Convention and other United Nations standards relating to juvenile justice.

The Committee expresses its concern at the absence of a reply from the Government of Indonesia to its urgent communication of November 1991 relating to excessive use of violence by security forces against demonstrating children in Santa Cruz, Dili. In this regard, the Committee draws the attention of the Government of Indonesia to its request for information about the safeguards established in accordance with the provisions of articles 37 and 40 of the Convention, to ensure that such violations would not occur again. The Committee also requests information on the strategies formulated and facilities provided to rehabilitate the victims of serious human rights violations, in accordance with the provisions of article 39 of the Convention.

The Committee is also concerned at the lack of information provided about the situation of child labour and the situation of children who, to survive, are forced to work or live in the street (often known as "street children").

*Further action.* The Committee encourages the Government of Indonesia to undertake a review of child-related laws so as to ensure their conformity with the provisions of the Convention and, in this regard, draws attention to the activities developed by the Programme of Advisory Services and Technical Assistance of the United Nations Centre for Human Rights. In the foregoing connection, the Committee welcomes the delegation's invitation to members of the Committee to visit the State party. The Committee requests information in writing on the concerns raised during its dialogue with the delegation, as spelled out in paragraphs 7–18 of the present document. The Committee also requests that this written information be forwarded to the secretariat by 31 December 1993 with a view to the Committee formulating its concluding observations on the initial report of Indonesia by September/October 1994.

**BIBLIOGRAPHY.** Amnesty International. *East Timor: State of Fear: Statement before the United Nations Special Committee on Decolonization.* London: 1993. NGO report, in English.

———. *East Timor Violations of Human Rights: Extrajudicial Executions, "Disappearances," Torture and Political Imprisonment.* London: 1985. NGO report, in English.

———. *East Timor: Who is to Blame?: Statement Before the UN Special Committee on Decolonization, July 1994.* London: 1994. NGO report, in English.

———. *Indonesia: The Application of the Death Penalty.* London: 1987. NGO report, in English.

———. *Indonesia: Continuing Human Rights Violations in Irian Jaya.* London: 1991. NGO factfinding report, in English.

———. *Indonesia: "Shock Therapy": Restoring Order in Aceh 1989–1993.* London: 1994. NGO report, in English.

———. *Indonesia/East Timor: A New Order? Human Rights in 1992.* London: 1993. NGO report, in English.

———. *Indonesia and East Timor: Political Prisoners and the "Rule of Law."* London: 1995. NGO report, in English.

———. *Indonesia and East Timor: Power and Impunity—Human Rights under the New Order.* London: 1994. NGO report, in English.

———. *Question of the Violation of Human Rights and Fundamental Freedoms in Any Part of the World, With Particular Reference to Colonial and Other Dependent Countries and Territories: Situation in East Timor/Statement by Amnesty International to the United Nations Special Committee on Decolonization (August 1990).* Geneva, Switzerland: United Nations, 1991. NGO report, in English and French.

Asia Watch. *Human Rights in Indonesia and East Timor.* New York: Human Rights Watch, 1989. NGO factfinding report, in English.

———. *Indonesia: Continuing Human Rights Violations in Aceh.* New York: Human Rights Watch, 1991. NGO report, in English.

———. *Indonesia: Human Rights Abuses in Aceh.* New York: Human Rights Watch, 1990. NGO factfinding report, in English.

———. *Injustice, Persecution, Eviction: A Human Rights Update on Indonesia and East Timor.* New York: Human Rights Watch, 1990. NGO report, in English.

———. *The Limits of Openness: Human Rights in Indonesia and East Timor.* New York: Human Rights Watch, 1994. NGO report, in English.

———. *Prison Conditions in Indonesia.* New York: Human Rights Watch, 1990. NGO factfinding report, in English.

———. *Remembering History in East Timor: The Trial of Xanana Gusmao and a Follow-up to the Dili Massacre.* New York: Human Rights Watch, 1993. NGO report, in English.

Australian Council for Overseas Aid. *East Timor: Keeping the Flame of Freedom Alive.* Canberra, Australia: 1991. NGO factfinding report, in English.

Bizot, Jack. *The Forgotten Cause: East Timor's Right to Self-Determination.* London: Parliamentary Human Rights Group, 1988. NGO report, in English.

Canada-Asia Working Group. "Human Rights in Asia: Submission Prepared for the 44th Session of the United Nations Commission on Human Rights," *Currents* 10, no. 1 (February 1988): 1–55. NGO report, in English.

Catholic Institute for International Relations. *East Timor: A Christian Reflection.* London: 1987. NGO statement, in English and French.

Eldridge, Philip. *Aid, Basic Needs and the Politics of Reform in Indonesia.* Clayton, Australia: Monash University, Centre of Southeast Asian Studies, 1980. Scholarly monograph, in English.

Federation Internationale des Droits de l'Homme (International Federation of Human Rights). *Indonesie: Dossier sur la Situation des Droits de l'Homme* (Indonesia: Dossier on the Human Rights Situation). Paris: 1987. NGO report, in French.

Heinz, Wolfgang S. *Ursachen und Folgen von Menschenrechtsverletzungen in der Dritten Welt* (Causes and Consequences of Human Rights Violations in Third World Countries). Saarbrucken, FRG: Verlag Breitenbach, 1986. Scholarly monograph, in German; bibliography on Indonesia, pp. 400–402.

Hiorth, F. *Timor Past and Present.* Townsville, Australia: James Cook University of North Queensland, Centre for Southeast Asian Studies, 1985. Scholarly monograph, in English.

Human Rights Council of Australia. *Irian Jaya and Human Rights: A Working Group Report.* Canberra, Australia: 1986. NGO report, in English.

"Human Rights in South and Southeast Asia." Papers presented at the State University of New York at Buffalo, NY 25–26 May 1988. Conference proceedings, in English.

Human Rights Watch. "Indonesia and East Timor," in *Human Rights Watch World Report 1995*, pp. 157–163. New York: 1995. NGO report, in English.

Ichiro, Suzuki, et al. "Suharto's Indonesia: Development and Death," *AMPO: Japan-Asia Quarterly Review* 22, no. 1 (1990): 2–39. Articles, in English.

Indonesian Documentation and Information Centre. *Indonesian Workers and their Right to Organise: Developments 1987–88.* Leiden, the Netherlands: 1988. NGO report, in English.

Lawyers Committee for Human Rights. *Broken Laws Broken Bodies.* New York: 1993. NGO factfinding report, in English.

Lev, Daniel S. "Legal Aid in Indonesia." Department of Political Science, University of Washington, Seattle, WA 98195. Unpublished scholarly paper, in English.

Meagher, J. Patrick. *Reflections on the Human Rights Situation in Indonesia.* Jakarta: Institute for Development Studies, 1987. Research paper, in English.

Morgan, S., and E. Colson, eds. *People in Upheaval.* Staten Island, NY, USA: Center for Migration Studies of New York, 1987. NGO document collection, in English.

Nietschmann, Bernard. "Economic Development by Invasion of Indigenous Nations: Cases of Indonesia and Bangladesh," *Cultural Survival Quarterly* 10, no. 2 (1986): 2–12. NGO article, in English.

Otten, Mariel. *Transmigrasi: Myths and Realities—Indonesian Resettlement Policy, 1965–1985.* Copenhagen: International Work Group for Indigenous Affairs, 1986. NGO monograph, in English.

Ramos-Horta, J. *Funu: The Unfinished Saga of East Timor.* Trenton, NJ, USA: Red Sea Press, 1987. Scholarly monograph, in English.

Sasono, Adi. "The Role of NGOs in Promoting Human Rights: Some Notes on Indonesian Experiences," *Human Rights Forum* 1, no. 1 (1985): 15–18. NGO article, in English.

TAPOL, British Campaign for the Defence of Political Prisoners and Human Rights in Indonesia. *Indonesia: Muslims on Trial.* London: 1987. NGO report, in English.

Taswell, Ruth, ed. *Southeast Asian Tribal Groups and Ethnic Minorities.* Cambridge, MA, USA: Cultural Survival, 1987. NGO conference proceedings, in English.

Thoolen, Hans, ed. *Indonesia and the Rule of Law: Twenty Years of "New Order" Government.* London: Frances Pinter Publishers for the International Commission of Jurists and the Netherlands Institute of Human Rights, 1987. Scholarly monograph, in English.

United Nations Economic and Social Council. *Question of the Human Rights of All Persons Subjected to Any Form of Detention or Imprisonment, in Particular Torture and Other Cruel, Inhuman or Degrading Treatment or Punishment: Report of the Special Rapporteur, Mr. P. Kooijmas, Pursuant to Commission on Human Rights Resolution 1991/38–Addendum: Visit by the Special Rapporteur to Indonesia and East Timor.* Geneva, Switzerland: 1992. NGO document, in English.

Witjes, Ben. "The Indonesian Law on Social Organizations." Nijmegen, the Netherlands. Unpublished research paper, in English.

## INFORMATION AND COMMUNICATION ORDER.

On 18 December 1978, the UN GENERAL ASSEMBLY affirmed (resolution 33/115 B) the need to establish a new, more just, and more effective international information and communication order, intended to strengthen peace and international understanding and based on the free circulation and wider and better-balanced dissemination of information. On the same date one year later, the Assembly affirmed (resolution 34/182) its primary role in elaborating, coordinating, and harmonizing policies and activities in this field and requested the Director-General of UNESCO to submit to it a progress report on the establishment of a new world information and communication order.

The UNESCO General Conference, convened in Belgrade in October–November 1980, adopted (resolution 21 C/19) the following considerations upon which a new world information and communication order could be based:

(a) elimination of the imbalances and inequalities which characterize the present situation;

(b) elimination of the negative effects of certain monopolies, public or private, excessive concentrations;

(c) removal of the internal and external obstacles to a free flow and wider and better balanced dissemination of information and ideas;

(d) plurality of sources and channels of information;

(e) freedom of the press and information;

(f) freedom of journalists and all professionals in the communication media, a freedom inseparable from responsibility;

(g) the capacity of developing countries to achieve improvement of their own situations, notably by providing their own equipment, by training their personnel, by improving their infrastructures, and by making their information and communication media suitable to their needs and aspirations;

(h) the sincere will of developed countries to help them attain these objectives;

(i) respect for each people's cultural identity and for the right of each nation to inform the world public about its interests, its aspirations, and its social and cultural values;

(j) respect for the right of all peoples to participate in international exchanges of information on the basis of equality, justice, and mutual benefit; and

(k) respect for the right of public, ethnic, and social groups and of individuals to have access to information sources and to participate actively in the communication process.

UNESCO has continued to conduct studies on the notion of a new world information and communication order; the studies have dealt with different aspects of the right to communicate, such as the democratization of communication, communication and human rights, obstacles to the free flow of information, and the legal implications of an international instrument on the subject.

The UN General Assembly concluded its consideration of proposals relating to a new world information and communication order by urging (resolution 43/60 of 6 December 1988) the full implementation of the following recommendations:

(1) All countries, the United Nations system as a whole and all others concerned should co-operate in the establishment of a new world information and communication order, seen as an evolving and continuous process, and based, *inter alia,* on the free circulation and wider and better balanced dissemination of information guaranteeing diversity of sources of information and free access to information and, in particular, the urgent need to change the dependent status of the developing countries in the field of information and communication, as the principle of sovereign equality among nations extends also to this field, and intended also to strengthen peace and international understanding, enabling all persons to participate effectively in political, economic, social and cultural life and promoting human rights, understanding and friendship among all nations. The ongoing efforts of the United Nations Educational, Scientific and Cultural Organization, which retains the central role in this field, to eliminate gradually the existing imbalances in the field of information and communication and to encourage a free flow and a wider and better balanced dissemination of information in accordance with the relevant resolu-

tions of that organization, adopted by consensus, should be reaffirmed;

(2) Considering the important role that the media worldwide can freely play, particularly under the present situation, it is recommended that:

(a) The mass media should be encouraged to give wider coverage to the efforts of the international community towards global development and, in particular, the efforts of the developing countries to achieve economic, social and cultural progress;

(b) The United Nations system as a whole should co-operate in a concerted manner, through its information services, in promoting a more comprehensive and realistic image of the activities and potential of the United Nations system in all its endeavours, in accordance with the principles and purposes of the Charter of the United Nations and General Assembly resolutions, with particular emphasis on the right to self-determination and the elimination of all forms of racism, aggression, foreign domination and occupation, in order to create a climate of confidence, the strengthening of multilateralism and the promotion of the development activities in the United Nations system;

(c) All countries should be urged to extend assistance to journalists for the free and effective performance of their professional tasks and to ensure respect for their physical integrity;

(3) Considering the existing imbalances in the international distribution of news, particularly that affecting the developing countries, it is recommended that urgent attention should be given to the elimination of existing imbalances by, inter alia, diversifying the sources of information and respecting the interests, aspirations and sociocultural values of all peoples;

(4) The United Nations system as a whole, particularly the United Nations Educational, Scientific and Cultural Organization, and the developed countries should be urged to co-operate in a concerted manner with the developing countries towards strengthening the information and communication infrastructures in the latter countries and promoting their access to advanced communication technology, in accordance with the priorities attached to such areas by the developing countries, with a view to enabling them to develop their own information and communications policies freely and independently and in the light of their social and cultural values, taking into account the principle of freedom of the press and information. In this regard, support should be provided for the continuation and strengthening of practical training programmes for broadcasters and journalists from developing countries;

(5) Note should be taken with appreciation of regional efforts, especially among the developing countries, as well as co-operation between developed and developing countries to develop further the media infrastructure in the developing countries, especially in the areas of training and dissemination of information, with a view to encouraging a free flow and a wider and better balanced dissemination of information;

(6) Article 19 of the Universal Declaration of Human Rights, which provides that everyone has the right to freedom of opinion and expression and that this right includes freedom to hold opinions without interference and to seek, receive and impart information and ideas through any media and regardless of frontiers, and article 29, which stipulates that these rights and freedoms may in no case be exercised contrary to the purposes and principles of the United Nations, should be recalled;

(7) The relevant paragraphs of General Assembly resolution 59 (I) of 14 December 1946, in which the Assembly stated, inter alia, that freedom of information is a fundamental human right, must be reiterated.

Since 1989, the General Assembly has considered questions relating to information and communication primarily on the basis of reports prepared by its Committee on Information and the Secretary-General. In 1993, its decisions on these questions were set out in resolution 48/44 A, entitled "Information in the Service of Humanity," as follows:

The General Assembly,

Taking note of the comprehensive and important report of the Committee on Information (A/48/21),

Also taking note of the report of the Secretary-General on questions relating to information (A/48/407),

Urges that all countries, organizations of the United Nations system as a whole and all others concerned, reaffirming their commitment to the principles of the Charter of the United Nations and to the principles of freedom of the press and freedom of information, as well as to those of the independence, pluralism and diversity of the media, deeply concerned by the disparities existing between developed and developing countries and the consequences of every kind arising from those disparities that affect the capability of the public, private or other media and individuals in developing countries to disseminate information and communicate their views and their cultural and ethical values through endogenous cultural production, as well as to ensure the diversity of sources and their free access to information, recognizing the call in this context for what in the United Nations and at various international forums has been termed "a new world information and communication order, seen as an evolving and continuous process", should:

(a) Cooperate and interact with a view to reducing existing disparities in information flows at all levels by increasing assistance for the development of communication infrastructures and capabilities in developing countries, with due regard for their needs and the priorities attached to such areas by those countries, and in order to enable them and the public, private or other media in developing countries to develop their own information and communication policies freely and independently and increase the participation of media and individuals in the communication process, and to ensure a free flow of information at all levels;

(b) Ensure for journalists the free and effective performance of their professional tasks and condemn resolutely at attacks against them;

(c) Provide support for the continuation and strengthening of practical training programmes for broadcasters and journalists from public, private and other media in developing countries;

(d) Enhance regional efforts and cooperation among developing countries, as well as cooperation between developed and developing countries, to strengthen communication capacities and to improve the media infrastructure and communication technology in the developing countries, especially in the areas of training and dissemination of information;

(e) Aim, in addition to bilateral cooperation, at providing all possible support and assistance to the developing countries and their media, public, private or other, with due regard to their interests and needs in the field of information and to action already adopted within the United Nations system, including:

(i) The development of the human and technical resources that are indispensable for the improvement of information and communication systems in developing countries and support for the continuation and strengthening of practical training programmes, such as those already operating under both public and private auspices throughout the developing world;

(ii) The creation of conditions that will enable developing countries and their media, public, private or other, to have, by using their national and regional resources, the communication technology suited to their national needs, as well as the necessary programme material, especially for radio and television broadcasting;

(iii) Assistance in establishing and promoting telecommunication links at the subregional, regional and interregional levels, especially among developing countries;

(iv) The facilitation, as appropriate, of access by the developing countries to advanced communication technology available on the open market;

(f) Provide full support for the International Programme for the Development of Communication of the United Nations Educational, Scientific and Cultural Organization, which should support both public and private media.

*SEE ALSO* Development; Freedom of Information; Media.

## INSTITUTE FOR THE TEACHING OF HUMAN RIGHTS.
Established in 1978, the Institute organizes educational programs based on UNESCO guidelines for lawyers, judges, and scholars. It also helps in research projects. The seminars and programs are taught in French. The Institute publishes the quarterly *Bulletin Institut Droits de l'Homme* in French.

Institute for the Teaching of Human Rights. Address: 4 sq. la Bruyere, F-75009 Paris, France. Telephone: 428-04-954. President: Louis Pettiti.

## INSTITUTE OF INTERNATIONAL LAW.
Founded in Ghent, Belgium, in 1873, the Institute was the 1904 recipient of the **NOBEL PEACE PRIZE,** the first institution to achieve this status. The Institute promotes the progress of international law by striving to formulate general principles in this area, by cooperating in its gradual and progressive codification, and by adjudicating controversial cases.

The Institute was founded, at first as a private organization, by Dr. Rolin-Jaquemyns, editor of the *Revue de Droit International* (*International Law Review*). The Institute has consultative status with the UN **ECONOMIC AND SOCIAL COUNCIL** (Roster). On the basis of income from the Special James Scott Brown Prize Fund, it awards prizes to authors of the best dissertations devoted to a specific topic of public international

law. The Institute currently has members in 45 countries.

Institute of International Law. Address: 132 rue de Lausanne, CP 36, CH-1211, Geneva 21, Switzerland. Telephone: (41-22) 731-1730. Fax: (41-22) 738-4306. Secretary-General: Christian Domincé.

## INTER-AFRICAN COMMITTEE ON TRADITIONAL PRACTICES AFFECTING THE HEALTH OF WOMEN AND CHILDREN IN AFRICA.
This nongovernmental organization was founded in 1984 to continue the work of the Seminar on Traditional Practices Affecting the Health of Women and Children in Africa, held 6–10 February 1984 in Dakar, Senegal. The IAC organizes educational programs to sensitize the public to the harmful effects of female circumcision, early marriage and pregnancy, nutritional taboos, and other harmful traditional practices. It conducts the Training Information Campaign and the Traditional Birth Attendants program and works with government ministries, medical practitioners, and women's organizations in its effort to inform the public.

IAC has consultative status with the UN **ECONOMIC AND SOCIAL COUNCIL** (Category II) and has participated in sessions of the UN **HUMAN RIGHTS COMMISSION.** It has national committees in 16 African countries.

Inter-African Committee on Traditional Practices affecting the Health of Women and Children in Africa. Address: c/o UNECA/ATCW, P.O. Box 2001, Addis Ababa, Ethiopia. Telephone: (251-1) 51-7200. Fax: (251-1) 51-4682.

## INTER-AMERICAN CHARTER OF SOCIAL GUARANTEES, OAS (1948).
The Charter is a proclamation of principles to protect workers of all kinds, setting out the rights to which they are entitled in the American States. Its purpose is to encourage the raising of standards of living throughout the American continent through economic development linked to cooperation between workers and employers. It was adopted as a resolution by the Ninth International Conference of American States, convened at Bogota, on 2 May 1948, and included in the Final Act of the Conference. The text of the Charter is as follows:

### General Principles

*Article 1.* It is the aim of the present Charter of Social Guarantees to proclaim the fundamental principles that must protect workers of all kinds, and it sets forth the minimum rights they must enjoy in the American States, without prejudice to the fact that the laws of each State may extend such rights or recognize others that are more favourable.

This Charter of Social Guarantees gives equal protection to men and women. It is recognized that the supremacy of these rights and the progressive raising of the standard of living of the community in general depend to a large degree upon the development of economic activities, upon increased productivity, and upon co-operation between workers and employers, expressed in harmonious relations and in mutual respect for and fulfilment of their rights and duties.

*Article 2.* The following principles are considered to be fundamental in the social legislations of the American countries:

(a) Labour is a social function; it enjoys the special protection of the State and must not be considered as a commodity.

(b) Every worker must have the opportunity for a decent existence and the right to fair working conditions.

(c) Intellectual, as well as technical and manual labour, must enjoy the guarantees established in labour laws, with the distinctions arising from the application of the law under the different circumstances.

(d) There should be equal compensation for equal work, regardless of the sex, race, creed or nationality of the worker.

(e) The rights established in favour of workers may not be renounced, and the laws that recognize such rights are binding on and benefit all the inhabitants of the territory, whether nationals or aliens.

*Article 3.* Every worker has the right to engage in his occupation and to devote himself to whatever activity suits him. He is likewise free to change employment.

*Article 4.* Every worker has the right to receive vocational and technical training in order to perfect his skills and knowledge, obtain a greater income from his work, and contribute effectively to the advancement of production. To this end, the State shall organize adult education and the apprenticeship of young people, in such a way as to assure effective training in a given trade or work, at the same time that it provides for their cultural, moral and civic development.

*Article 5.* Workers have the right to share in the equitable distribution of the national well-being, by obtaining the necessary food, clothing, and housing at reasonable prices. To achieve these purposes, the State must sponsor the establishment and operation of popular farms and restaurants and of consumer and credit co-operatives, and should organize institutions to promote and finance such farms and establishments, as well as to supply low-cost, comfortable, hygienic housing for labourers, salaried employees and rural workers.

### Individual Labour Contracts

*Article 6.* The law shall regulate individual labour contracts, for the purpose of guaranteeing the rights of workers.

### Collective Labour Contracts and Agreements

*Article 7.* The law shall recognize and regulate collective labour contracts and agreements. In the enterprises that are governed by these contracts and agreements, the provisions shall apply not only to the workers affiliated with the trade association that signed them, but also to the other workers who are or shall be employed in those enterprises. The law shall establish the procedure for extending collective contracts and agreements to all the activities in respect to which they were made and for widening the geographical sphere of their application.

### Wages

*Article 8.* Every worker has the right to earn a minimum wage, fixed periodically with the participation of the State and of workers and employers, which shall be sufficient to cover his normal home needs, material, moral and cultural, taking into account the characteristics of each type of work, the special conditions of each region and each job, the cost of living, the worker's relative aptitude, and the wage systems prevalent in the enterprises. A minimum occupational wage shall also be set up for those activities in which this matter is not regulated by a collective contract or agreement.

*Article 9.* Workers have the right to an annual bonus, in proportion to the number of days worked during the year.

*Article 10.* Wages and social benefits, in the amount fixed by law, are not subject to attachment, with the exception of payments for support that the worker has been ordered by a court to pay. Wages should be paid in cash in legal tender. The value of wages and social benefits constitutes a privileged claim in the case of the bankruptcy of the employer, or a meeting of his creditors.

*Article 11.* Workers have the right to a fair share in the profits of the enterprises in which they work, in the form and amount and under the conditions that the law provides.

### Work Periods, Rest and Vacations

*Article 12.* The ordinary effective work period should not exceed eight hours a day or forty-eight hours a week. The maximum duration of the work period in agricultural, livestock, or forestry work, shall not exceed nine hours a day or fifty-four hours a week. The daily limits may be extended up to one hour in each case, provided that the work period of one or more days during the week is shorter than the indicated limit, without prejudice to the provisions with respect to a weekly rest period. The period for night work, and that for dangerous or unhealthful work, shall be less than the daytime work period.

The work period limitation shall not apply in cases of *force majeure.*

Overtime work shall not exceed a daily and weekly maximum. In work that is by nature hazardous or unhealthful, the limit of the work period may not be exceeded by means of overtime work.

The laws of each country shall determine both the length of the intervals that are to interrupt the work period when for reasons of health the nature of the task demands it, and the intervals that should come between two work periods.

Workers may not exceed the limit of the work period, whether working for the same or for another employer.

Night and overtime work shall give the right to extra pay.

*Article 13.* Every worker has a right to a weekly paid rest period in the form established by the law of each country.

Workers who do not enjoy the rest period referred to in the foregoing paragraph shall be entitled to special pay for the services rendered on those days and to a compensatory rest period.

*Article 14.* Workers shall also have the right to a paid rest period on the civil and religious holidays established by law, with the exceptions that the law itself may determine, for the same reasons that justify work on the weekly days of rest. Those who do not enjoy the rest period on these days have a right to extra pay.

*Article 15.* Every worker who has to his credit a minimum of service rendered during a given period shall be entitled to paid annual vacations, on work days, the length of such vacations to be in proportion to the number of years of service. Monetary compensation may not be given in lieu of vacations, and the obligation of the worker to take them shall follow from the obligation of the employer to grant them.

### Child Labour

*Article 16.* Persons less than fourteen years of age, and those who, having reached that age, are still subject to the compulsory education laws of the country, may not be employed in any type of work. The authorities responsible for supervising the work of such minors may authorize their employment when it is essential for their own maintenance, or that of their parents or brothers and sisters, provided that the minimum compulsory education requirements are met.

The work period for those under sixteen years of age may not be greater than six hours daily or thirty-six hours weekly in any type of work.

*Article 17.* Night work and work hazardous or injurious to health is forbidden for persons under eighteen years of age; exceptions concerning weekly rest set forth in the laws of the respective countries may not be applied to such workers.

### The Work of Women

*Article 18.* In general, night work is forbidden for women in industrial establishments, whether public or private, and in work that is hazardous or injurious to health, except in cases where only the members of the same family are employed, in cases of *force majeure* that render it necessary, in cases where women perform administrative or responsible duties not normally requiring manual labour, and in other cases expressly provided for by law.

By industrial establishments and by work that is hazardous or injurious to health are understood those so defined by law or by international labour conventions.

Exceptions concerning weekly rest set forth in the laws of the respective countries may not be applied to women.

### Tenure

*Article 19.* The law shall guarantee stability of employment, due consideration being given to the nature of the respective industries and occupations and justifiable causes for dismissal. In case of unjustified discharge, the worker shall have the right to indemnification.

### Apprenticeship Contracts

*Article 20.* Apprenticeship contracts shall be regulated by a law, to assure to the apprentice instruction in his trade or occupation, just treatment, fair pay and the benefits of social security and welfare.

### Work at Home

*Article 21.* Work at home is subject to social legislation. Home workers have the right to an officially determined minimum wage, to compensation for time lost because of the employer's delay in ordering or receiving the work, or for arbitrary or unjustified suspension of the supply of work. Home workers shall be entitled to a legal status similar to that of other workers, due consideration being given to the special nature of their work.

### Domestic Work

*Article 22.* Domestic workers have a right to the protection of the law with respect to wages, work periods, rest periods, vacations, dismissal pay and social benefits in general; the extent and nature of this protection shall be determined with due regard to the conditions and special nature of their work. Those who render services of a domestic nature in industrial, commercial, social and other similar establishments should be considered as manual workers, and granted the rights to which such workers are entitled.

### Work in the Merchant Marine and Aviation

*Article 23.* The law shall regulate the contracts of those serving in the merchant marine and in aviation, in accordance with the special character of their work.

### Public Employees

*Article 24.* Public employees have the right to be protected in their administrative careers by being guaranteed, so long as they perform their duties satisfactorily, permanent employment, the right to promotion, and the benefits of social security. Such employees also have the right to be protected by a special court of administrative-contentious jurisdiction and, in case penalties are imposed, the right to defend themselves in the respective proceedings.

### Intellectual Workers

*Article 25.* Independent intellectual workers and the product of their activity should be the subject of protective legislation.

### The Right of Association

*Article 26.* Workers and employers, without distinction as to sex, race, creed or political ideas, have the right freely to form associations for the protection of their respective interests, by forming trade associations or unions, which in turn may form federations among themselves. These organizations have the right to enjoy juridical personality and to be duly protected in the exercise of their rights. Their suspension or dissolution may not be ordered save by due process of law.

Conditions of substance and of form that must be met for the constitution and functioning of trade and union organizations should not go so far as to restrict freedom of associations.

The organization, functioning and dissolution of federations and confederations shall be subject to the same formalities as those prescribed for unions.

Members of boards of directors of trade unions, in the number established by the respective law and during their term of office, may not be discharged, transferred or given less satisfactory working conditions, without just cause having been previously determined by competent authority.

### The Right to Strike

*Article 27.* Workers have the right to strike. The law shall regulate the conditions and exercise of that right.

## Social Security and Welfare

*Article 28.* It is the duty of the State to provide measures of social security and welfare for the benefit of workers.

*Article 29.* States should promote and provide for recreational and welfare centres that can be freely utilized by workers.

*Article 30.* The State should take adequate measures to ensure healthful, safe and moral conditions at places of work.

*Article 31.* Workers, including agricultural workers; home workers; domestic workers; public servants; apprentices, even when not receiving wages; and independent workers, when it is possible to include them, have the right to a system of compulsory social security designed to realize the following objectives:

(a) To provide for the elimination of hazards that might deprive workers of their wage-earning ability and means of support;

(b) To re-establish as quickly and as completely as possible the wage-earning ability lost or reduced as a result of illness or accident;

(c) To supply means of support in case of the termination or interruption of occupational activity as a result of illness or accident, maternity, temporary or permanent disability, unemployment, old age, or premature death of the head of the family.

Compulsory social security should provide for protection of the members of the worker's family and should establish additional benefits for those of the insured who have large families.

*Article 32.* In countries where a social security system does not yet exist, or in those in which one does exist but does not cover all occupational and social hazards, employers shall be responsible for providing adequate welfare and assistance benefits.

*Article 33.* Every working woman shall be entitled to have leave with pay for a period of not less than six weeks before and six weeks after childbirth, to keep her job, and to receive medical attention for herself and the child and financial assistance during the nursing period.

The law shall make it obligatory for employers to install and maintain nurseries and playrooms for the children of workers.

*Article 34.* Independent workers have a right to the co-operation of the State in joining associations of social protection organized to give them benefits equal to those of wage earners. Persons who practise the liberal professions and are not employed by third parties have a similar right.

## Supervision of Labour Conditions

*Article 35.* Workers have a right to have the State maintain a service of trained inspectors to ensure faithful compliance with legal provisions in regard to labour and social security, assistance and welfare, to study the results of such provisions and to suggest the indicated improvements.

## Labour Courts

*Article 36.* Each State shall have a special system of labour courts and an adequate procedure for the prompt settlement of disputes.

## Conciliation and Arbitration

*Article 37.* It is the duty of the State to promote conciliation and arbitration as means of obtaining peaceful solutions for collective labour disputes.

## Rural Work

*Article 38.* Rural or farm workers have the right to be guaranteed an improvement in their present standard of living, to be furnished proper hygienic conditions and to have effective social assistance organized for them and their families.

The State shall carry on planned and systematic activity directed towards putting agricultural development on a rational basis, organizing and distributing credit, improving rural living conditions, and achieving the progressive economic and social emancipation of the rural population.

The law shall establish the technical and other conditions, consistent with the national interest of each State, under which effect shall be given to the exercise of the right which the State recognizes on behalf of associations of rural workers, and individuals suited to agricultural work who lack land or do not possess it in sufficient quantity, to be granted land and the means necessary to make it productive.

*Article 39.* In countries where the problem of an indigenous population exists, the necessary measures shall be adopted to give protection and assistance to the Indians, safeguarding their life, liberty and property, preventing their extermination, shielding them from oppression and exploitation, protecting them from want and furnishing them an adequate education.

The State shall exercise its guardianship in order to preserve, maintain and develop the patrimony of the Indians or their tribes; and it shall foster the exploitation of the natural, industrial or extractive resources or any other sources of income proceeding from or related to the aforesaid patrimony, in order to ensure in due time the economic emancipation of the indigenous groups.

Institutions or agencies shall be created for the protection of Indians, particularly in order to ensure respect for their lands, to legalize their possession thereof, and to prevent encroachment upon such lands by outsiders.

***SEE ALSO*** *American Convention on Human Rights and Protocols; American Declaration of the Rights and Duties of Man.*

**INTER-AMERICAN COMMISSION ON HUMAN RIGHTS, OAS.** The Inter-American Commission on Human Rights of the **ORGANIZATION OF AMERICAN STATES** was established in 1959 and in 1965 was authorized to examine complaints received from individuals alleging violations of the principles set out in the **AMERICAN DECLARATION OF THE RIGHTS AND DUTIES OF MAN.** Under the **AMERICAN CONVENTION ON HUMAN RIGHTS,** which entered into force on 18 July 1978, the Commission is authorized (a) to develop an awareness of human rights among the people of America; (b) to make recommendations to the governments of the member States for the adoption of progressive measures in favor of human rights; (c) to prepare studies and reports; (d) to request the governments of member States to supply it with information on the measures adopted by them in matters of human rights; (e) to respond, through the General Secretariat of the Organization of American States, to inquiries made by the member States on matters related to human rights and, within the limits of its possibilities, to provide those States with the advisory services they request; (f) to take action on petitions and other communications under the provisions of the convention; and (g) to submit an annual report to the General Assembly of the Organization of American States.

Under article 42 of the Convention, States parties transmit to the Commission copies of the reports that they submit annually to the Executive Committee of the Inter-American Economic and Social Council and the Inter-American Council for Education, Science and Culture. The task of the Commission with regard to such reports is to "watch over the promotion of human rights implicit in the economic, social, educational, scientific and cultural standards set forth in the Charter of the Organization of American States as amended by the Protocol of Buenos Aires."

Under article 45, any State party to the Convention may declare that it recognizes the competence of the Commission to receive and examine communications in which a State party alleges that another State party has committed a violation of a human right set forth in the Convention. The Commission may examine such communications only if they are presented by a State that has made such a declaration and are directed against a State that has also made such a declaration. The Commission first considers the admissibility of such communications (articles 46 and 47). In the case of those found to be admissible, it requests relevant information from the government of the State indicated as being responsible for the alleged violations. On the basis of such information, it may close the case. If not, it first establishes the facts and then seeks to secure a friendly settlement. If such a settlement is reached, it draws up a report to be transmitted to the petitioner and to the States parties to the Convention, as well as to the Secretary-General for publication. If unsuccessful, it draws up a report setting out the facts and stating its conclusions, to be transmitted to the States concerned. If the matter has not been settled or submitted to the **INTER-AMERICAN COURT OF HUMAN RIGHTS** within three months, the Commission may set forth its opinions and conclusions, make pertinent recommendations, and prescribe a period within which the State may be expected to take measures to remedy the situation. If the prescribed period expires without action, the Commis-

sion may decide by majority vote (a) whether the State has taken adequate measures and (b) whether to publish its report on the situation. In addition to such reports, the Commission submits an annual report to the General Assembly of the Organization of American States.

**COMPOSITION.** The Commission consists of seven members, elected by the OAS General Assembly from a list of candidates proposed by the governments of member States; they serve in their personal capacity for a term of four years. The Commission usually holds three sessions per year at its headquarters, the General Secretariat of the Organization of American States, Washington, D.C. Occasionally, it meets elsewhere, or upon invitation conducts on-site observation in a particular country.

**RULES RELATING TO THE FUNCTIONS OF THE COMMISSION.** The regulations of the Commission (OAS Doc. OEA/Ser. L/V/II.65, Doc. 6) set out rules relating to the handling of the petitions and communications regarding States parties to the American Convention on Human Rights, as follows:

### Title II—Procedures

### Chapter I

### General Provisions

*Article 25. Official Languages.* 1. The official languages of the Commission shall be Spanish, French, English and Portuguese. The working languages shall be those decided on by the Commission every two years, in accordance with the languages spoken by its members.

2. A member of the Commission may allow omission of the interpretation of debates and the preparation of documents in his language.

*Article 26. Presentation of Petitions.* 1. Any person or group of persons or nongovernmental entity legally recognized in one or more of the Member States of the Organization may submit petitions to the Commission, in accordance with these Regulations, on one's own behalf or on behalf of third persons, with regard to alleged violations of a human rights recognized, as the case may be, in the American Convention on Human Rights or in the American Declaration of the Rights and Duties of Man.

2. The Commission may also, *motu proprio,* take into consideration any available information that it considers pertinent and which might include the necessary factors to begin processing a case which in its opinion fulfills the requirements for the purpose.

*Article 27. Form.* 1. The petition shall be lodged in writing.

2. The petitioner may appoint, in the petition itself, or in another written petition, an attorney or other person to represent him before the Commission.

*Article 28. Special Missions.* The Commission may designate one or more of its members or staff members of the Secretariat to take specific measures, investigate facts or make the necessary arrangements for the Commission to perform its functions.

*Article 29. Precautionary Measures.* 1. The Commission may, at its own initiative, or at the request of a party, take any action it considers necessary for the discharge of its functions.

2. In urgent cases, when it becomes necessary to avoid irreparable damage to persons, the Commission may request that provisional measures be taken to avoid irreparable damage in cases where the denounced facts are true.

3. If the Commission is not in session, the Chairman, or in his absence, one of the Vice-Chairmen, shall consult with the other members, through the Secretariat, on implementation of the provisions of paragraphs 1 and 2 above. If it is not possible to consult within a reasonable time, the Chairman shall take the decision on behalf of the Commission and shall so inform its members immediately.

4. The request for such measures and their adoption shall not prejudice the final decision.

*Article 30. Initial Processing.* 1. The Secretariat of the Commission shall be responsible for the study and initial processing of petitions lodged before the Commission and that fulfill all the requirements set forth in the Statute and in these Regulations.

2. If a petition or communication does not meet the requirements called for in these Regulations, the Secretariat of the Commission may request the petitioner or his representative to complete it.

3. If the Secretariat has any doubt as to the admissibility of a petition, it shall submit it for consideration to the Commission or to the Chairman during recesses of the Commission.

## Chapter II

### Petitions and Communications Regarding States Parties to the American Convention on Human Rights

*Article 31. Condition for Considering the Petition.* The Commission shall take into account petitions regarding alleged violations by a state party of human rights defined in the American Convention on Human Rights, only when they fulfill the requirements set forth in that Convention, in the Statute and in these Regulations.

*Article 32. Requirements for the Petitions.* Petitions addressed to the Commission shall include:

(a) the name, nationality, profession or occupation, postal address, or domicile and signature of the person or persons making the denunciation; or in cases where the petitioner is a nongovernmental entity, its legal domicile or postal address, and the name and signature of its legal representative or representatives;

(b) an account of the act or situation that is denounced, specifying the place and date of the alleged violations and, if possible, the name of the victims of such violations as well as that of any official that might have been apprised of the act or situation that was denounced;

(c) an indication of the state in question which the petitioner considers responsible, by Commission or omission, for the violation of a human right recognized in the American Convention on Human Rights in the case of States Parties thereto, even if no specific reference is made to the article alleged to have been violated;

(d) information on whether the remedies under domestic law have been exhausted or whether it has been impossible to do so.

*Article 33. Omission of Requirements.* Without prejudice to the provisions of Article 26, if the Commission considers that the petition is inadmissible or incomplete, it shall notify the petitioner, whom it shall ask to complete the requirements omitted in the petition.

*Article 34. Initial Processing.* 1. The Commission, acting initially through its Secretariat, shall receive and process petitions lodged with it in accordance with the standards set forth below:

(a) it shall enter the petition in a register especially prepared for that purpose, and the date on which it was received shall be marked on the petition or communication itself;

(b) it shall acknowledge receipt of the petition to the petitioner, indicating that it will be considered in accordance with the Regulations;

(c) if it accepts, in principle, the admissibility of the petition, it shall request information from the government of the State in question and include the pertinent parts of the petitions.

2. In serious or urgent cases or when it is believed that the life, personal integrity or health of a person is in imminent danger, the Commission shall request the promptest reply from the government, using for this purpose the means it considers most expeditious.

3. The request for information shall not constitute a prejudgment with regard to the decision the Commission may finally adopt on the admissibility of the petition.

4. In transmitting the pertinent parts of a communication to the government of the State in question, the identity of the petitioner shall be withheld, as shall any other information that could identify him, except when the petitioner expressly authorizes in writing the disclosure of his identity.

5. The Commission shall request the affected government to provide the information requested within 90 days after the date on which the request is sent.

6. The government of the State in question may, with justifiable cause, request a 30 day extension, but in no case shall extensions be granted for more than 180 days after the date on which the first communication is sent to the government of the State concerned.

7. The pertinent parts of the reply and the documents provided by the government shall be made known to the petitioner or to his representative, who shall be asked to submit his observations and any available evidence to the contrary within 30 days.

8. On receipt of the information or documents requested, the pertinent parts shall be transmitted to the government, which shall be allowed to submit its final observations within 30 days.

*Article 35. Preliminary Questions.* The Commission shall proceed to examine the case and decide on the following matters:

(a) whether the remedies under domestic law have been exhausted, and it may determine any measures it considers necessary to clarify any remaining doubts;

(b) other questions related to the admissibility of the petition of its manifest inadmissibility based upon the record or submission of the parties;

(c) whether grounds for the petition exist or subsist, and if not, to order the file closed.

*Article 36. Examination by the Commission.* The record shall be submitted by the Secretariat to the Commission for consideration at the first session held after the period referred to in Article 31, paragraph 5, if the government has not provided the information on that occasion, or after the periods indicated in paragraphs 7 and 8 have elapsed if the petitioner has not replied or if the government has not submitted its final observations.

*Article 37. Exhaustion of Domestic Remedies.* 1. For a petition to be admitted by the Commission, the remedies under domestic jurisdiction must have been invoked and exhausted in accordance with the general principles of international law.

2. The provisions of the preceding paragraph shall not be applicable when:

(a) the domestic legislation of the State concerned does not afford due process of law for protection of the right or rights that have allegedly been violated;

(b) the party alleging violation of his rights has been denied access to the remedies under domestic law or has been prevented from exhausting them;

(c) there has been unwarranted delay in rendering a final judgment under the aforementioned remedies.

3. When the petitioner contends that he is unable to prove exhaustion as indicated in this Article, it shall be up to the government against which this petition has been lodged to demonstrate to the Commission that the remedies under domestic law have not previously been exhausted, unless it is clearly evident from the background information contained in the petition.

*Article 38. Deadline for the Presentation of Petitions.* 1. The Commission shall refrain from taking up those petitions that are lodged after the six-month period following the date on which the party whose rights have allegedly been violated has been notified of the final ruling in cases where the remedies under domestic law have been exhausted.

2. In the circumstances set forth in Article 34 (2) of these Regulations, the deadline for presentation of a petition to the Commission shall be within a reasonable period of time, in the Commission's judgment, as from the date on which the alleged violation of rights has occurred, considering the circumstances of each specific case.

*Article 39. Duplication of Procedures.* 1. The Commission shall not consider a petition in cases where the subject of the petition:

(a) is pending settlement in another procedure under an international governmental organization of which the State concerned is a member;

(b) essentially duplicates a petition pending or already examined and settled by the Commission or by another international governmental organization of which the state concerned is a member.

2. The Commission shall not refrain from taking up and examining a petition in cases provided for in paragraph 1 when:

(a) the procedure followed before the other organization or agency is one limited to an examination of the general situation on human rights in the State in question and there has been no decision on the specific facts that are the subject of the petition submitted to the Commission, or is one that will not lead to an effective settlement of the violation denounced;

(b) the petitioner before the Commission or a family member is the alleged victim of the violation denounced and the petitioner before the organizations in reference is a third party of a nongovernmental entity having no mandate from the former.

*Article 40. Separation and Combination of Cases.* 1. Any petition that states different facts that concern more than one person, and that could constitute various violations that are unrelated in time and place shall be separated and processed as separate cases, provided the requirements set forth in Article 32 are met.

2. When two petitions deal with the same facts and persons, they shall be combined and processed in a single file.

*Article 41. Declaration of Inadmissibility.* The Commission shall declare inadmissible any petition when:

(a) any of the requirements set forth in Article 32 of these Regulations has not been met;

(b) when the petition does not state facts that constitute a violation of rights referred to in Article 31 of these Regulations in the case of the States Parties to the American Convention on Human Rights;

(c) the petition is manifestly groundless or inadmissible on the basis of the statement by the petitioner himself or the government.

*Article 42. Presumption.* The facts reported in the petition whose pertinent parts have been transmitted to the government of the State in reference shall be presumed to be true if, during the maximum period set by the Commission under the provision of Article 34 paragraph 5, the government has not provided the pertinent information, as long as other evidence does not lead to a different conclusion.

*Article 43. Hearing.* 1. If the file has not been closed and in order to verify the facts, the Commission may conduct a hearing following a summons to the parties and proceed to examine the matter set forth in the petition.

2. At that hearing, the Commission may request any pertinent information from the representative of the State in question and shall receive, if so requested, oral or written statements presented by the parties concerned.

*Article 44. On-site Investigation.* 1. If necessary and advisable, the Commission shall carry out an on-site investigation, for the effective conduct of which it shall request, and the States concerned shall furnish to it, all necessary facilities.

2. However, in serious and urgent cases, only the presentation of a petition or communication that fulfills all the formal requirements of admissibility shall be necessary in order for the Commission to conduct an on-site investigation with the prior consent of the State in whose territory a violation has allegedly been committed.

3. Once the investigatory stage has been completed, the case shall be brought for consideration before the Commission, which shall prepare its decision in a period of 180 days.

*Article 45. Friendly Settlement.* 1. At the request of any of the parties, or on its own initiative, the Commission shall place itself at the disposal of the parties concerned, at any stage of the examination of a petition, with a view to reaching a friendly settlement of the matter on the basis of respect for the human rights recognized in the American Convention on Human Rights.

2. In order for the Commission to offer itself as an organ of conciliation for a friendly settlement to the matter it shall be necessary for the positions and allegations of the parties to be sufficiently precise; and in the judgment of the Commission, the nature of the matter must be susceptible to the use of the friendly settlement procedure.

3. The Commission shall accept the proposal to act as an organ of conciliation for a friendly settlement presented by one of the parties if the circumstances described in the above paragraph exist and if the other party to the dispute expressly accepts the procedure.

4. The Commission, upon accepting the role of an organ of conciliation for a friendly settlement shall designate a Special Commission or an individual from among its members. The Special Commission or the member so designated shall

inform the Commission within the time period set by the Commission.

5. The Commission shall fix a time for the reception and gathering of evidence, it shall set dates for the holding of hearings, if appropriate, it shall plan an on-site observation, which will be carried out following the receipt of consent of the State to be visited and it shall fix a time for the conclusion of the procedure, which the Commission may extend.

6. If a friendly settlement is reached, the Commission shall prepare a report which shall be transmitted to the parties concerned and referred to the Secretary General of the Organization of American States for publication. This report shall contain a brief statement of the facts and of the solution reached. If any party in the case so requests, it shall be provided with the fullest possible information.

7. In a case where the Commission finds, during the course of processing the matter, that the case, by its very nature, is not susceptible to a friendly settlement; or finds that one of the parties does not consent to the application of this procedure; or does not evidence good will in reaching a friendly settlement based on the respect for human rights, the Commission, at any stage of the procedure shall declare its role as organ of conciliation for a friendly settlement to have terminated.

*Article 46. Preparation of the Report.* 1. If a friendly settlement is not reached, the Commission shall examine the evidence provided by the government in question and the petitioner, evidence taken from witnesses to the facts or that obtained from documents, records, official publications, or through an on-site investigation.

2. After the evidence has been examined, the Commission shall prepare a report stating the facts and conclusions regarding the case submitted to it for its study.

*Article 47. Proposals and Recommendations.* 1. In transmitting the report, the Commission may make such proposals and recommendations as it sees fit.

2. If, within a period of three months from the date of the transmittal of the report of the Commission to the States concerned, the matter has not been settled or submitted by the Commission, or by the State concerned, to the Court and its jurisdiction accepted, the Commission may, by the vote of an absolute majority of its members, set forth its opinion and conclusions concerning the question submitted for its consideration.

3. The Commission may make the pertinent recommendation and prescribe a period within which the government in question must take the measures that are incumbent upon it to remedy the situation examined.

4. If the report does not represent, in its entirety, or, in part, the unanimous opinion of the members of the Commission, any member may add his opinion separately to that report.

5. Any verbal or written statement made by the parties shall also be included in the report.

6. The report shall be transmitted to the parties concerned, who shall not be authorized to publish it.

*Article 48. Publication of the Report.* 1. When the prescribed period has expired, the Commission shall decide by the vote of an absolute majority of its members whether the State has taken suitable measures and whether to publish its report.

2. That report may be published by including it in the Annual Report to be presented by the Commission to the General Assembly of the Organization or in any other way the Commission may consider suitable.

*Article 49. Communications from a Government.* 1. Commun-ications presented by the government of a State Party to the American Convention on Human Rights, which has accepted the competence of the Commission to receive and examine such communications against other States Parties, shall be transmitted to the State Party in question, whether or not it has accepted the competence of the Commission. Even if it has not accepted such competence, the communication shall be transmitted so that the State can exercise its option under the provisions of Article 45 (3) of the Convention to recognize the Commission's competence in the specific case that is the subject of the communication.

2. Once the State in question has accepted the competence of the Commission to take up the communication of the other State Party, the corresponding procedure shall be governed by the provisions of Chapter II insofar as they may be applicable.

*Article 50. Referral of the Case to the Court.* 1. If a State Party to the Convention has accepted the Court's jurisdiction in accordance with Article 62 of the Convention, the Commission may refer the case to the Court, subsequent to transmittal of the report referred to in Article 46 of these Regulations to the government of the State in question.

2. When it is ruled that the case is to be referred to the Court, the Executive Secretary of the Commission shall immediately notify the Court, the petitioner and the government of the State in question.

3. If the State Party has not accepted the Court's jurisdiction, the Commission may call upon that State to make use of the option referred to in Article 62, paragraph 2 of the Convention to recognize the Court's jurisdiction in the specific case that is the subject of the report.

## Chapter III

## Petitions Concerning States that Are Not Parties to the American Convention on Human Rights

*Article 51. Receipt of the Petitions.* The Commission shall receive and examine any petition that contains a denunciation of alleged violations of the human rights set forth in the American Declaration of the Rights and Duties of Man, concerning the Member States of the Organization that are not parties to the American Convention on Human Rights.

*Article 52. Applicable Procedure.* The procedure applicable to petitions concerning Member States of the Organization that are not parties to the American Convention on Human Rights shall be that provided for in the General Provisions included in Chapter I of Title II, in Articles 32 to 43 of these Regulations, and in the articles indicated below.

*Article 53. Final Decision.* 1. In addition to the facts and conclusions, the Commission's final decision shall include any recommendations the Commission deems advisable and a deadline for their implementation.

2. That decision shall be transmitted to the State in question.

3. If the State does not adopt the measures recommended by the Commission within the deadline referred to in paragraphs 1 or 3, the Commission may publish its decision.

4. The decision referred to in the preceding paragraph may be published in the Annual Report to be presented by the Commission to the General Assembly of the Organization or in any other manner the Commission may see fit.

*Article 54. Request for Reconsideration.* 1. When the State in question, prior to the expiration of the 90 day deadline, invokes new facts or legal arguments which have not been previously considered, it may request a reconsideration of the conclusions or recommendations of the Commission's Report. The Commission shall decide to maintain or modify its decision, fixing a new deadline for compliance, where appropriate.

2. The Commission, if it considers it necessary, may request the petitioner to present any observations to the affected State's request for reconsideration.

3. The reconsideration procedure may be utilized only once.

4. The Commission shall consider the request for reconsideration during the first regular session following its presentation.

5. If the State does not adopt the measures recommended by the Commission within the deadline referred to in paragraph 1, the Commission may publish its decision in conformity with Article 48 (2) and 53 (4) of the present Regulations.

### Chapter IV

### On-Site Observations

*Article 55. Designation of the Special Commission.* On-site observations shall be carried out in each case by a Special Commission named for that purpose. The number of members of the Special Commission and the designation of its Chairman shall be determined by the Commission. In cases of great urgency, such decision may be made by the Chairman subject to the approval of the Commission.

*Article 56. Disqualification.* A member of the Commission who is a national of or who resides in the territory of the State in which the on-site observation is to be carried out shall be disqualified from participating therein.

*Article 57. Schedule of Activities.* The Special Commission shall organize its own activities. To that end, it may appoint its own members and, after hearing the Executive Secretary, any staff members of the Secretariat or personnel necessary to carry out any activities related to its mission.

*Article 58. Necessary Facilities.* In extending an invitation for an on-site observation or in giving its consent, the government shall furnish to the Special Commission all necessary facilities for carrying out its mission. In particular, it shall bind itself not to take any reprisals of any kind against any persons or entities cooperating with the Special Commission or providing information or testimony.

*Article 59. Other Applicable Standards.* Without prejudice to the provisions in the preceding article, any on-site observation agreed upon by the Commission shall be carried out in accordance with the following standards:

(a) the Special Commission or any of its members shall be able to interview freely and in private, any persons, groups, entities or institutions, and the government shall grant the pertinent guarantees to all those who provide the Commission with information, testimony or evidence of any kind;

(b) the members of the Special Commission shall be able to travel freely throughout the territory of the country, for which purpose the government shall extend all the corresponding facilities, including the necessary documentation;

(c) the government shall ensure the availability of local means of transportation;

(d) the members of the Special Commission shall have access to the jails and all other detention and interrogation centers and shall be able to interview in private those persons imprisoned or detained;

(e) the government shall provide the Special Commission with any document related to the observance of human rights that it may consider necessary for the presentation of its reports;

(f) the Special Commission shall be able to use any method appropriate for collecting, recording or reproducing the information it considers useful;

(g) the government shall adopt the security measures necessary to protect the Special Commission;

(h) the government shall ensure the availability of appropriate lodging for the members of the Special Commission;

(i) the same guarantees and facilities that are set forth here for the members of the Special Commission shall also be extended to the Secretariat staff;

(j) any expenses incurred by the Special Committee, any of its members and the Secretariat staff shall be borne by the Organization, subject to the pertinent provisions.

**INTER-AMERICAN COURT OF HUMAN RIGHTS, OAS.** The Inter-American Court of Human Rights of the **ORGANIZATION OF AMERICAN STATES** was established in accordance with article 33 of the **AMERICAN CONVENTION ON HUMAN RIGHTS,** which entered into force on 18 July 1978. It is an autonomous judicial institution whose purpose is the application and interpretation of the Convention. As regards application, the Court may adjudicate disputes relating to charges that a State party has violated the Convention. As regards interpretation, it may interpret the Convention and certain other human rights treaties in proceedings in which it is not called upon to adjudicate a specific dispute. Only the States parties and the **INTER-AMERICAN COMMISSION ON HUMAN RIGHTS** have the right to submit a case to the Court (article 61.1 of the Convention); this, however, does not mean that a case arising out of an individual's complaint cannot reach the Court but only that it must be referred to the Court by the Inter-American Commission or by a State party to the Convention.

A State party does not subject itself to the contentious jurisdiction of the Court by ratifying the Convention; it must, in addition, recognize the Court's jurisdiction either by a special declaration or a special agreement (article 63). After hearing a case, the Court must decide whether there has been a breach of the Convention and, if so, what rights the injured party should be accorded. Moreover, the Court may also determine the steps that should be taken to remedy the breach and the amount of damages to which the injured party is entitled (article 63.1). In addition to regular judgments, the Court also has the power to grant temporary injunctions "in cases of extreme gravity and urgency, and when necessary to avoid irreparable damage to persons" (article 63.2). Judgments of the Court are final and not subject to appeal, and all States parties to the Convention have undertaken to comply with such judgments in any case to which they are parties. Enforcement of judgments of the Court is the responsibility of the OAS General Assembly.

As regards the Court's advisory jurisdiction, it is authorized to interpret the provisions of any OAS treaty concerning the protection of human rights in the American States at the request of any OAS member State or of OAS organs such as the Commission on Human Rights and the Commission of Women on matters within their competence (article 64).

**COMPOSITION.** The Court consists of seven judges, "nationals of the member States of the OAS, elected in an individual capacity from among jurists of the highest moral authority and of recognized competence in the field of human rights, who possess the qualifications required for the exercise of the highest judicial functions in conformity with the law of the State of which they are nationals or of the State that proposes them as candidates. . . . No two judges may be nationals of the same State. . . . The judges shall be elected by secret ballot by an absolute majority vote of the States Parties to the Convention in the General Assembly of the Organization, from a panel of candidates proposed by those States. . . ." (articles 52–53). The term of office is six years. The Court has its seat in San Jose, Costa Rica.

The Court submits a report on its work during the previous year to each regular session of the OAS General Assembly. In the report, the Court specifies, in particular, any cases in which a State has not complied with its judgments and makes any pertinent recommendations (article 65).

**RULES RELATING TO THE FUNCTIONS OF THE COURT.** Rules relating to the handling of cases brought before the Court were adopted by the Court at its third regular session, held from 30 July to 9 August 1980, and are set out in the Court's *Rules of Procedure* (OAS Doc. OEA/Ser. 1/V/II.65, Doc. 6, Title II, chaps. I–VI) as follows:

### Title II

### Chapter I

### General Rules

*Article 19. Official Languages.* 1. The official languages of the Court are those of the Organization of American States.

2. The working languages are those of the nationalities of the judges and, whenever required, those of the parties as long as they are the official languages.

3. The working language shall be determined at the beginning of the proceedings in each case.

4. The Court may authorize any party, agent, advocate, adviser, witness, expert, or other person who appears before it to use his own language if he does not have sufficient knowledge of an official language. The Court shall, in that event, make the necessary arrangements for the interpreta-

tion of the statements of such persons into the working language mentioned in the preceding paragraphs.

5. In all cases the authentic text shall be designated accordingly.

*Article 20. Representation of the Parties.* The parties shall be represented by agents who may have the assistance of advocates, advisers, or any other person of their choice.

*Article 21. Representation of the Commission.* The Commission shall be represented by the delegates whom it designates. These delegates may, if they so wish, have the assistance of any person of their choice.

*Article 22. Communications, Notifications and Summonses Addressed to Persons other than the Agents of the Parties or Delegates of the Commission.* 1. If, for any communication, notification or summons addressed to persons other than the agents of the parties or delegates of the Commission, the Court considers it necessary to have the assistance of the government of the State on whose territory such communication, notification or summons is to have effect, the President shall address an appropriate request to that government to obtain the same.

2. The same procedure shall apply when the Court wishes to undertake or arrange for an investigation in the territory of a State for the purpose of establishing the facts or procuring evidence, or when it orders the appearance of a person resident in, or having to cross, that territory.

*Article 23. Interim Measures.* 1. At any stage of the proceeding involving cases of extreme gravity and urgency and when necessary to avoid irreparable damage to persons, the Court may, in matters it has under consideration, adopt whatever provisional measures, based on the provisions of Article 63 (2) of the Convention, it deems appropriate.

2. With respect to matters not yet submitted to it, the Court may act at the request of the Commission.

3. Such request may be presented to the President or any judge of the Court by any means of communication.

4. If the Court is not sitting, the President shall convoke it immediately. Pending the meeting of the Court, the President, in consultation with the Permanent Commission or with the judges, if possible, shall call upon the parties, whenever necessary, to act so as to permit any decision of the Court regarding the request for provisional measures to have its appropriate effect.

5. The Court may at any time determine, *motu proprio* at the request of one of the parties, whether the circumstances of the case require the adoption of provisional measures.

*Article 24. Procedure by Default.* 1. When a party fails to appear in or to continue with a case, the Court shall, *motu proprio,* subject to the provisions of Article 42 of these Rules, take whatever measures are necessary to complete consideration of the case.

2. When a party, having the right to enter a case, does so at a later stage, it shall take the proceedings at that stage.

### Chapter II

### Institution of the Proceedings

*Article 25. Filing of the Application.* 1. A State Party which intends to bring a case before the Court in accordance with the provisions of Article 61 of the Convention shall file with the Secretary an application, in twenty copies, indicating the object of the application, the human rights involved, and the name and address of its agent, including, if pertinent, its objections to the opinion of the Commission. On receipt of the application, the Secretary shall immediately request the report of the Commission.

2. If the Commission intends to bring a case before the Court in accordance with the provisions of Article 61 of the Convention, it shall file with the Secretary, together with its report, in twenty copies, its duly signed application which shall indicate the object of the application, the human rights involved, and the names of its delegates.

*Article 26. Communication of the Application.* 1. On receipt of the application provided for in Article 25 of these Rules, the Secretary shall notify the Commission whenever the application is submitted under Article 25 (1) as well as the States concerned in the case, transmitting copies thereof to them.

2. The Secretary shall inform the other States Parties and the Secretary General of the OAS of the receipt of the application.

3. When giving the notice provided for in paragraph 1, the Secretary shall request the State concerned to designate, within a period of two weeks, an agent who shall have an address for service at the seat of the Court to which all communications concerning the case shall be sent. If the State does not do so, a decision shall be deemed to have been notified twenty-four hours after it was rendered.

*Article 27. Preliminary Objections.* 1. A preliminary objection must be filed, in twenty copies, no later than the expiration of the time fixed for the beginning of the written proceedings with respect to the party making the objection.

2. The preliminary objection shall set out the facts and the law on which the objection is based, the submissions and a list of the documents in support; it shall mention any evidence which the party may wish to produce. Copies of the supporting documents shall be attached.

3. The receipt by the Secretary of a preliminary objection shall not cause the suspension of the proceedings on the merits. The Court, or the President, if the Court is not sitting, shall fix the time-limit within which the other party may present a written statement of its observations and submissions.

4. The Court shall, after having received the replies or comments of every other party and of the delegates of the Commission, give its decision on the objection or join the objection to the merits.

## Chapter III

### Examination of the Cases

*Article 28. Stages of the Proceedings.* The proceedings before the Court shall consist of a written and an oral part.

*Article 29. Fixing of Time-limits.* Before the Court meets, the President shall ascertain the views of the agents of the parties and the delegates of the Commission or, if they have not yet been appointed, the Chairman of the Commission, regarding the procedure to be followed. He shall then direct in what order and within what time-limits memorials, counter-memorials and other documents are to be filed.

*Article 30. Written Proceeding.* 1. The written part of the proceedings in a case shall consist of a Memorial and a Counter-Memorial.

2. The Court may, in special circumstances, authorize additional written submissions consisting of a Reply and a Rejoinder.

3. A Memorial shall contain a statement of the relevant facts, a statement of law, and the submissions.

4. A Counter-Memorial shall contain an admission or denial of the facts stated in the Memorial; any additional facts,

if necessary; observations concerning the statement of law in the Memorial; a statement of law in answer thereto; and the submissions.

5. The Reply and Rejoinder, whenever authorized by the Court, shall not merely repeat the contentions of the parties, but shall be directed to bringing out the issues that still divide them.

6. The Memorials, Counter-Memorials, and accompanying documents shall be deposited with the Secretary in twenty copies. The Secretary shall send copies of this documentation to the agents of the parties and the delegates of the Commission.

*Article 31. Joinder of Cases.* 1. In the event that two cases are presented which have common elements, the Court shall decide whether to join the cases.

2. The Court may at any time direct that the proceedings in two or more cases be joined.

*Article 32. Oral Proceedings.* When the case is ready for hearing, the President shall, after consulting the agents of the parties and the delegates of the Commission, fix the date for the opening of the oral proceedings.

*Article 33. Conduct of the Hearings.* The President shall direct the hearings. He shall prescribe the order in which the agents, the advocates or advisers of the parties, and the delegates of the Commission, as well as any other person appointed by them in accordance with Article 21, shall be called upon to speak.

*Article 34. Inquiry, Expert Opinion and other Measures for Obtaining Information.* 1. The Court may, at the request of a party or the delegates of the Commission, or *motu proprio*, decide to hear as a witness, expert, or in any other capacity, any person whose testimony or statements seem likely to assist it in carrying out its functions.

2. The Court may, in consultation with the parties, entrust any body, office, commission, or authority of its choice with the task of obtaining information, expressing an opinion, or making a report upon any specific point.

3. Any report prepared in accordance with the preceding paragraph shall be sent to the Secretary and shall not be published until so authorized by the Court.

*Article 35. Convocation of Witnesses, Experts and other Persons.* 1. Witnesses, experts, or other persons whom the Court decides to hear, shall be summoned by the Secretary. If they are called by a party, the expenses of their appearance shall be fixed by the President and borne by that party. In other cases, such expenses shall be fixed by the President and borne by the Court.

2. The summons shall indicate:

    (a) the name of the party or parties;

    (b) the object of the inquiry, expert opinion, or any other measure for obtaining information ordered by the Court;

    (c) any provision for the payment of the sum due to the person summoned.

*Article 36. Oath or Solemn Declaration by Witness and Experts.* 1. After the establishment of his identity and before giving evidence, every witness shall take the following oath or make the following solemn declaration: "I swear"—or "I solemnly declare upon my honor and conscience"——"that I will speak the truth, the whole truth and nothing but the truth."

2. After the establishment of his identity and before carrying out his task, every expert shall take the following oath or make the following solemn declaration: "I swear"—"I solemnly declare"—"that I will discharge my duty as an expert honorably and conscientiously."

3. This oath shall be taken or this declaration made before the Court or before any of its judges who have been so delegated by the Court.

*Article 37. Objection to a Witness or Expert; Hearing of a Person for Purpose of Information.* The Court shall decide any dispute arising from an objection to a witness or expert. If the Court considers it necessary, it may nevertheless, hear, for purposes of information, a person who cannot be heard as a witness.

*Article 38. Questions Put During the Hearing.* 1. Any judge may put questions to the agents, advocates, or advisers of the parties, to the witnesses and experts, to the delegates of the Commission, and to any other person appearing before the Court.

2. Subject to the control of the President, who has the power to decide as to the relevance of the questions put, the witnesses, experts, and other persons referred to in Article 34, may be examined by the agents, advocates or advisers of the parties, by the delegates of the Commission, and by any person appointed by them in accordance with Article 21.

*Article 39. Failure to Appear or False Evidence.* 1. When without good reason, a witness or any other person who has been duly summoned, fails to appear or refuses to give evidence, the Secretary shall, on being so required by the President, inform the State to whose jurisdiction such witness or other person is subject. The same provision shall apply when a witness or expert has, in the opinion of the Court, violated the oath or solemn declaration mentioned in Article 36.

2. The State may not try any person on account of their testimony before the Court. The Court may, however, request the States to take the measures provided for in their domestic legislation against those who, in the opinion of the Court, have violated the oath or solemn declaration.

*Article 40. Minutes of Hearings.* 1. Minutes shall be made of each hearing; they shall be signed by the President and the Secretary.

2. These minutes shall include:

(a) the names of the judges present;

(b) the names of the agents, advocates, advisers, and delegates of the Commission present;

(c) the names, description and residence of the witnesses, experts, or other persons heard;

(d) the declaration expressly made for insertion in the minutes on behalf of the parties or the Commission;

(e) a summary record of the questions put by the judges and the responses thereto;

(f) any decision by the Court delivered during the hearing.

3. Copies of the minutes shall be given to the agents of the parties and the delegates of the Commission.

4. The minutes shall be deemed to constitute the certified record.

*Article 41. Transcript of the Hearings.* 1. The Secretary shall ensure that a transcript of the hearings be made.

2. The agents, advocates, and advisers of the parties, the delegates of the Commission and witnesses, experts, and other persons mentioned in Articles 21 and 34, shall receive the transcript of their arguments, statements or evidence, to enable them, subject to the control of the Secretary, to make corrections within the time-limits fixed by the President.

*Article 42. Discontinuance.* 1. When the party which has brought the case before the Court notifies the Secretary of its intention not to proceed with the case and when the other parties agree to such discontinuance, the Court shall, after having obtained the opinion of the Commission, decide whether it is appropriate to approve the discontinuance and, accordingly, to strike the case off its list.

2. When, in a case brought before the Court by the Commission, the Court is informed of a friendly settlement, arrangement or other fact of a kind to provide a solution of the matter, it may, after having obtained the opinion, if necessary, of the delegates of the Commission, strike the case off its list.

3. The Court may, having regard to its responsibilities, decide that it should proceed with the consideration of the case, notwithstanding the notice of discontinuance, friendly settlement, arrangement or other fact referred to in the two preceding paragraphs.

*Article 43. Question of the Application of Article 63 (1) of the Convention.* If proposals or observations on the question of the application of Article 63 (1) of the Convention have not been presented to the Court in the document instituting the proceedings, they may be presented by a party or by the Commission at any stage of the written or oral proceedings.

*Article 44. Decisions.* 1. The judgments, advisory opinions, and the interlocutory decisions that put an end to a case or proceedings, shall be decided by the Court.

2. The other decisions shall be taken by the Court, if it is sitting, or, if not, by the President, pursuant to the instructions of the Court.

## Chapter IV

### Judgments

*Article 45. Contents of the Judgment.* 1. A judgment shall contain:

(a) the names of the judges and the Secretary;

(b) the date on which it was delivered at a hearing in public;

(c) a description of the party or parties;

(d) the names of agents, advocates or advisers of the party or parties;

(e) the names of the delegates of the Commission;

(f) the statement of the proceedings;

(g) the submission of the party or parties and, if any, of the delegates of the Commission;

(h) the facts of the case;

(i) the legal arguments;

(j) the operative provisions of the judgment;

(k) the allocation, if any, of compensation;

(l) the decision, if any, in regard to costs;

(m) the number of judges constituting the majority;

(n) a statement as to which text is authentic.

2. Where the Court finds that there is a breach of the Convention, it shall give in the same judgment a decision on the application of Article 63 (1) of the Convention if that question, after being raised under Article 43 of these Rules, is ready for decision; if the question is not ready for decision, the Court shall decide on the procedure to follow. If, on the other hand, the matter has not been raised under Article 43, the Court shall determine the period within which it may be presented by a party or by the Commission.

3. If the Court is informed that an agreement has been reached between the victim of the violation and the State Party concerned, it shall verify the equitable nature of such agreement.

*Article 46. Delivery and Communication of the Judgment.* 1. When the case is ready for a decision, the Court shall meet in private, take a preliminary vote, name one or more rapporteurs among the judges of the respective majority and minority, and fix the date of the deliberation and final vote.

2. In the final deliberation, the Court shall take a final vote, approve the wording of the judgment, and fix the date of the public hearing at which it shall be communicated to the parties.

3. Until the aforementioned communication, the votes and details thereof, the texts, and the legal arguments shall remain secret.

4. The judgments shall be signed by all of the judges who participated in the voting and the dissents and concurring opinions shall be signed by the judges supporting them. A judgment shall, however, be valid if signed by a majority of the judges.

5. An order of communication and execution, sealed and signed by the President and the Secretary, shall appear at the end of the judgment.

6. The originals of the decisions shall be placed in the archives of the Court. The Secretary shall send certified copies to the party or parties, the Commission, the Chairman of the Permanent Council, the Secretary General, and any other person directly concerned.

7. The Secretary shall transmit the judgment to all the States Parties.

*Article 47. Publication of Judgments, Decision and Other Documents.* 1. The Secretary shall be responsible for the publication of:

(a) judgments and other decisions of the Court;

(b) documents relating to the proceedings, including the report of the Commission, but excluding any particulars relating to the attempt to reach a friendly settlement;

(c) the transcripts of the public hearings;

(d) any other document whose publication the President considers useful.

2. Documents deposited with the Secretary and not published shall be accessible to the public unless otherwise decided by the President, either on his own initiative, at the request of a party, the Commission, or any other person concerned.

*Article 48. Request for an Interpretation of a Judgment.* 1. Requests for an interpretation allowed under the terms of Article 67 of the Convention shall be presented in twenty copies and shall indicate precisely the points in the operative provision of the judgment on which interpretation is requested. It shall be filed with the Secretary.

2. The Secretary shall communicate the request to any other party and, where appropriate, to the Commission, and shall invite them to submit, in twenty copies, any written comments within a period fixed by the President.

3. The nature of the proceedings shall be determined by the Court.

4. A request for interpretation shall not suspend the effect of the judgment.

## Chapter V

### Advisory Opinions

*Article 49. Interpretation of the Convention.* 1. The request for an advisory opinion provided for in Article 64 (1) of the Convention shall be instituted by means of an application that shall state the specific questions on which the opinion of the Court is sought.

2. If an interpretation of the Convention is requested by:

(a) A Member State—the application shall indicate the provisions to be interpreted, the considerations giving rise to the consultation, and the name and address of the agent of the applicant;

(b) An OAS Organ—the application shall indicate the provisions to be interpreted, how the consultation relates to its sphere of competence, the considerations giving rise to the consultation, and the name and address of its delegates.

*Article 50. Interpretation of Other Treaties.* 1. If an interpretation is requested of other treaties concerning the protection of human rights in the American states, as provided for in Article 64 (1) of the Convention, the application shall indicate the name of, and parties to, the treaty, the specific questions on which the opinion of the Court is sought, and the considerations giving rise to the consultation.

2. In the case of an application submitted by one of the OAS organs referred to in Article 64 (1) of the Convention, the provisions of Article 49 (2) (b) of these rules shall apply, *mutatis mutandis.*

*Article 51. Interpretation Relating to Domestic Laws.* 1. The request for an advisory opinion, provided for in Article 64 (2) of the Convention, shall be instituted by means of an application that shall identify:

(a) the domestic laws, the provisions of the Convention and/or international treaties forming the subject of the consultation;

(b) the specific questions on which the opinion of the Court is sought;

(c) the name and address of the applicant's agent.

2. Ten copies of the domestic laws referred to in the preceding paragraph shall accompany the application.

*Article 52.* 1. Upon receipt of the request for an advisory opinion, under Articles 49 and 50 of these Rules, the Secretary shall transmit copies thereof to any State which might be concerned in this matter, as well as to the Secretary General of the OAS for transmission to the organs mentioned in Article 64 (1) of the Convention. He shall likewise inform the aforementioned and the Commission that the Court is prepared to receive within a time-limit fixed by the President their written observations. These observations or other relevant documents shall be filed with the Secretariat in forty copies and shall be transmitted to the Commission, to the States and to the other bodies mentioned in Article 64 (1) of the Convention.

2. At the conclusion of the written proceedings, the Court shall decide upon the format of the oral proceedings, and fix the order of presentation and time-limits for the hearing.

*Article 53.* When the circumstances require, the Court may apply any of the rules governing contentious proceedings to advisory proceedings.

*Article 54.* 1. The hearings and advisory opinions shall be public.

2. When the Court has completed its deliberations and adopted its advisory opinion, it shall be read in public and shall contain:

(a) a statement of the questions submitted to the Court;

(b) the date on which it is delivered;

(c) the names of the judges;

(d) a summary of the proceedings;

(e) a summary of the considerations giving rise to the request;

(f) the conclusions of the Court;

(g) the legal arguments;

(h) a statement indicating which text of the opinion shall be deemed authoritative.

3. A judge may, if he so wishes, attach his individual opinion to the advisory opinion of the Court, whether he dissents from the majority or not, and may record his concurrence or dissent.

*Article 55.* These Rules may be amended or supplemented by the vote of an absolute majority of the titular judges of the Court.

**INTER-AMERICAN INSTITUTE OF HUMAN RIGHTS.** The Institute was founded in 1980 as an autonomous international body. Its purpose is to assume educational, research, and promotional functions in the human rights field that are beyond the mandate of both the **INTER-AMERICAN COURT OF HUMAN RIGHTS** and the **INTER-AMERICAN COMMISSION ON HUMAN RIGHTS,** but which will support these **OAS** bodies and their work. The Institute conducts conferences, colloquia, and seminars for teaching human rights; serves as a clearinghouse on human rights information; develops publication programs; maintains a human rights library; and conducts human rights research.

In the area of teaching, the Institute works with centers and personnel planning education programs for teaching a human rights curriculum in regional educational systems. It has developed and offered such courses as an interdisciplinary course in Costa Rica, a training course for lawyers of the human rights commissions of Central America, and an inter-American seminar on human rights education. In addition, among its current research projects are such programs as a study of the constitutional protection of human rights in Latin America, a preliminary study on incorporating human rights into secondary education, and research into human rights and democratization in South America.

Inter-American Institute of Human Rights. Address: P.O. 10.081, CR 1000 San Jose, Costa Rica. Telephone: (506) 34-04-04. Fax: (506) 34-09-55. President: Thomas Buergenthal.

**INTER-AMERICAN PRESS ASSOCIATION.** An international non-governmental organization in consultative status with the UN **ECONOMIC AND SOCIAL COUNCIL** (Category II), and with **UNESCO,** IAPA has over 1,300 associate life members (newspapers and magazines published six or more times a year) in 34 countries, mostly in Latin and South America. It is a non-profit organization of western hemisphere publications devoted to the promotion and protection of freedom of the press and the people's right to know in the New World.

During its first years, the Association was largely a Latin American body, and few North Americans attended the meetings. But in 1946, a small group of United States editors and publishers established the Inter-American Press Association of the United States as a national chapter of the hemispheric institution.

IAPA's objectives are to foster and protect the interests of the daily and periodical press of the Americas; to promote and maintain the dignity, rights, and responsibilities of journalism; to encourage uniform standards of professional and business conduct; to exchange ideas and information which contribute to the cultural, material, and technical development of the press; and to foster a wider knowledge and greater interchange among the peoples of the Americas. The Association campaigns via protests, press releases, and missions on behalf of journalists whose rights are violated or endangered. It has protested against the closing of newspapers in Nicaragua, Panama, and Paraguay.

In addition to its primary concerns, IAPA supports the Inter-American Press Association Scholarship Fund, which awards 10 scholarships annually; the IAPA Technical Center, which provides members—especially those in Latin America—with technical and modern management information; the Office of Certified Circulation, which gives members a tool for measuring circulation; and the IAPA awards, which are presented annually to newspersons and publications in South and Central America for outstanding community and journalistic work and to North American newspapers for their work on behalf of Inter-American friendship and understanding.

IAPA's publications include the *IAPA News, Noticiero SIP,* and *El Boletín del Centro Técnico.*

Inter-American Press Association. Address: 2911 N.W. 39th Street, Miami, FL 33142, USA. Telephone: (305) 634-2465. Fax: (305) 635-2272. Executive Director: Bill Williamson.

**INTERGOVERNMENTAL COMMITTEE FOR MIGRATION.** A committee consisting of the representatives of 33 governments, established in Brussels in 1951 as an outgrowth of the International Migration Conference, the Intergovernmental Committee for Migration has observer status with a number of intergovernmental organs rendering assistance to refugees and other migrants, including the United Nations **HIGH COMMISSIONER FOR REFUGEES** and the **WORLD HEALTH ORGANIZATION,** and also with many non-governmental organizations active in this field such as the **INTERNATIONAL CATHOLIC MIGRATION COMMISSION** and the **LEAGUE OF THE RED CROSS AND RED CRESCENT SOCIETIES.** Since 1952, ICM has arranged the movement of more than 3.5 million migrants—whether refugees, displaced persons, asylum seekers, or nationals in need of international assistance—to countries of resettlement. Its member governments, and 15 additional governments participating in its work as observers, adhere to the principle of free movement of people. At the request of these governments, ICM provides a wide variety of migration services including recruitment, selection, orientation, counseling, medical examination, provision of medical escorts, reception, placement, immigration assistance, and language training. Its largest emergency operations involved refugees from Hungary in 1956, from Czechoslovakia in 1968, from Uganda in 1972, and from Vietnam from 1975 onwards. It also assisted in the transfer of detainees out of Chile in 1973, out of Bolivia in 1980–1981, and out of El Salvador in 1983.

Among ICM's publications are the quarterly *International Migration* and the *Monthly Dispatch;* it also issues an annual report entitled *Review of Achievements* and numerous pamphlets, booklets, and leaflets.

Intergovernmental Committee for Migration. Address: 17 Route des Morillons, P.O. Box 71, CH-1211, Geneva 19, Switzerland. Telephone: (41-22) 717-9-11. Cable: Promigrant Geneva. Telex: 22-155/22-193. Director-General: James N. Purcell.

**INTERNALLY DISPLACED PERSONS.** The UN **COMMISSION ON HUMAN RIGHTS** received, at its 1992 session, an analytical report by the Secretary-General on the situation of internally displaced persons (E/CN.4/1992/23) indicating that 24 million people, largely women and children, were estimated to be displaced within the borders of their own countries, while the refugee population was estimated at 17 million. The report stated that armed conflict, forced relocation, communal violence, natural and ecological disasters, systematic violations of human rights, as well as traditionally recognized sources of persecution had combined to produce these massive involuntary movements within state borders. Vulnerable and unable to find places of safety, the internally displaced had often suffered persistent violations of basic human rights and their humanitarian needs had not been met.

The crisis of the internally displaced from the perspective of the international community, the report stated, was that they fell within the domestic jurisdiction of their own countries and were therefore not covered by the protection normally accorded those who cross international borders and become refugees. In the absence of clear mandates and an international body with special responsibility for the protection of such displaced persons, the international response to their plight had been ad hoc, limited and unsatisfactory. In 1991 the Secretary-General had appointed an Emergency Relief Coordinator to improve the provi-

sion of relief and assistance to those caught up in humanitarian emergencies, and in the same year the problem had first been drawn to the attention of the Commission. The Commission had requested the Secretary-General (resolution 1991/25) to prepare "an analytical report on internally displaced persons."

The report (E/CN.4/1992/23) concluded that the protection of the human rights of internally displaced persons would require large-scale involvement of United Nations human rights bodies, and suggested that the Commission on Human Rights should create mechanisms by which it could "deal with existing problems in this area with the necessary degree of urgency and in a concrete manner, bringing them to the attention of the international community and trying to generate the cooperation of all interested and concerned Governments."

Taking note of the report, the Commission requested the Secretary-General (resolution 1992/73) "to designate a representative to seek again views and information from all Governments on the human rights issues related to internally displaced persons, including an examination of existing human rights, humanitarian and refugee law and standards and their applicability to the protection of and relief assistance to internally displaced persons." Information on these issues was to be sought also from the specialized agencies, relevant United Nations organs, regional intergovernmental and non-governmental organizations and experts in all regions.

At its 1993 session, the Commission received and considered the resulting study, prepared by the Representative of the Secretary-General, Mr. Francis M. Deng (E/CN.4/1993/35). Its findings and recommendations, as summarized briefly by the author, were as follows (paras. 278–294):

The purpose of the study is to analyse and evaluate international legal instruments and mechanisms with a view to developing a strategy to deal with the problem of internally displaced persons. More specifically, resolution 1992/73 of the Commission on Human Rights mandated the Secretary-General, and therefore his Representative, to study existing laws and mechanisms and make recommendations on ways of strengthening them to be more effective in providing protection for the internally displaced.

The nature of the problem and the challenge it presents to the international community was articulated by the Under-Secretary-General for Human Rights in his letter conveying the appointment and the terms of the mandate to the designated Representative of the Secretary-General. "I am sure . . . you will agree that protecting the human rights of displaced persons is one of the most critical challenges facing the international community today, affecting hundreds of thousands in Africa, Asia, Europe and Latin America", the Under-Secretary-General wrote. "It is a problem which has only recently begun to be addressed, and the study requested by the Commission on Human Rights can be expected to make an important contribution to determining the legal and policy approaches which will be adopted by the United Nations in this regard." These words were later reflected by the Representative of the Secretary-General in his letter requesting information from the sources stipulated in the resolution. From a statistical point of view, the magnitude of the crisis is greater than the figures quoted in the letter would suggest. Estimates now place internally displaced persons worldwide at some 24 million and even that figure may already be outdated by recent developments throughout the world. From this mandate, there are two critical sets of issues involved: those relating to the legal doctrine and those pertaining to the mechanism of implementation.

*Legal Doctrine.* With respect to the law, there is a difference of opinion between two sets of perspectives. One argues that the existing standards sufficiently cover the internally displaced and that the principal problem is lack of implementation. Another maintains that there are gaps that need to be filled in order to make the coverage complete and adequate. Both points of view emanate from the need to strengthen protection for the displaced. The first point of view favours building on what already exists. The second believes that setting new standards would not only fill existing gaps, but also focus international attention and thereby raise the level of public awareness of the problem and the need for remedies.

The study finds that in so far as the principles of the law are concerned, there indeed appears to be fairly adequate protection under human rights and humanitarian law. There are, however, obvious gaps in the existing law with respect to the specific needs of internally displaced persons. Just as added attention and protection are required for certain vulnerable groups, such as minorities, women, children, the disabled or refugees, a specific regime for protecting the internally displaced would serve as a useful focus on their special needs.

Combining the argument that there are gaps in the existing law with the chronic problem of insufficient implementation would tend to favour the development of a legal instrument specifically addressing the problem of internal displacement. Such an instrument could also serve as a means of focusing international attention on the crisis. But preparing such an instrument takes time and can only be conceived in a long-term perspective. Meanwhile, the compelling conditions and urgent needs of the internally displaced call for a speedy remedy.

The study recommends that while it might be useful to begin work on a legal instrument, it will be necessary to move ahead with other means of addressing the problems of internal displacement. What is envisaged in this transitional phase is an initial statement of principles which, though not legally binding, would focus international attention, raise the level of awareness, and stimulate practical measures of alleviating the crisis. It would also help to prepare the ground for a more legally binding document.

Several documents are envisaged in this transitional phase. One would be a compilation of rules and norms now existing in various forms and in a variety of legal instruments. Another would be in the form of a code of conduct comprising guiding principles to govern the treatment of internally displaced persons. The third would be the closest to an authoritative legal document and could take the form of a declaration. These documents need not be prepared in sequence; indeed, it might be advantageous to conduct work on them concurrently.

*Institutional Mechanism.* There is at present no single organization within the United Nations system specifically mandated to assume responsibility for the protection of the internally displaced. Given° the global magnitude of the problem and the urgent need for solutions, it has become imperative for the United Nations to explore ways to better assist and protect these internally displaced. One way would be to explicitly add internally displaced persons to the mandates of UNHCR or DHA, or an equivalent body might be established to cater to the needs of the internally displaced. Pending the resolution of this institutional issue, it would be useful for each of the major organs of the United Nations system whose mandate is relevant to the internally displaced to consider establishing units to focus on the problem. But protection still would need to be addressed by United Nations human rights bodies. An effective mechanism established by the Commission on Human Rights would serve the purpose by utilizing the existing institutional structures and the resources of the United Nations system.

The functions of such a mechanism may be classified into three principal sets of activities. One involves monitoring, gathering information, processing it, reporting to pertinent authorities within the system, and otherwise issuing alert bulletins that could act as an early warning of impending displacement crises and a call for action against occurring violations. The second comprises making contacts with Governments and other pertinent actors to play a more delicate diplomatic function of facilitating dialogue and otherwise seeking ways of ameliorating the suffering of the displaced masses. The third is the invocation of alternative enforcement mechanisms where intercession and dialogue fail to produce constructive results.

There is the question of which of the mechanisms now available to the Commission—Representative of the Secretary-General, Rapporteur or Working Group—would be more suited to the task of utilizing the potential of the United Nations system as a whole. Each of these mechanisms offers particular advantages, but perhaps a pivotal factor in selecting between them may be the need to liaise with other competent United Nations bodies, including the General Assembly and, ultimately, the Security Council, in which the good offices of the Secretary-General may be an added facility. If this suggests the mechanism of Representative of the Secretary-General, the broad rubric under which he or she would operate should allow flexibility to permit the creative use of information received through the parallel processes of monitoring, reporting, alerting and otherwise putting in motion early warning systems in order to reinforce diplomatic initiatives before any more drastic measures may be considered.

*Operational Strategy.* The principles of the legal doctrine and institutional mechanism outlined above can be put into operation through a strategy involving three phases: the monitoring, reporting, and early warning phase; the phase of intercession, dialogue, and mediation; and the last phase consisting of the mobilization of eventual humanitarian collective action.

Phase one will aim at detecting and identifying the problem through various mechanisms for information collection, evaluation, and reporting. This phase should make use of the pertinent United Nations network, including the United Nations early warning system recommended by the ACC which aims at establishing a building process beginning with the creation of an inter-agency consultative mechanism. This United Nations early warning system would especially benefit from the reports of field representatives and other monitors of such operational bodies as UNHCR, UNDP, UNICEF and other intergovernmental and non-governmental bodies, including regional organizations such as OAU and OAS.

The result of collecting, analysing and reporting pertinent data would be to declare the existence of a problem, its magnitude or dimension and the need for some measures to be taken. This should invoke the mechanism envisaged for phase two, although by that time enough would already have been known about the situation to warrant the involvement of the Representative or alternative mechanisms of the Commission. This implies a certain amount of functional overlap between the monitoring, reporting and early warning phase and the role of the proposed Representative, Rapporteur, or Working Group. Through country missions, the Representative or the alternative entities could also detect developments which might lead to massive displacement and bring them to the attention of the international community.

The results of the Representative's discussions with the Government will determine whether or not action is needed. The Representative may become convinced, by the information available and the results of the analyses at phase one or by insights gained during an initial trip to the country concerned, that some sort of humanitarian action is urgently needed. Nevertheless, he/she might choose to continue with the dialogue in the country in question.

If the situation continues to threaten lives, the Representative will need to engage other bodies within the United Nations system and other actors in the effort, if necessary, through the good offices of the Secretary-General himself. In this context, the principles of the legal doctrine and especially the guiding principles envisioned in the code of conduct come into focus as the yardstick for determining the form of action required in the circumstances. As already indicated, the clarification of those principles could be an important aspect of prevention. The expectation that if specified standards are not met, certain consequences will follow, can be an effective deterrent.

What is outlined in this study is a framework for dealing with the grave problem of internal displacement with a focus on the concerns of the Commission on Human Rights. For the international community to develop an adequate response to this global crisis, a great deal more will have to be done with respect to the legal instruments and, in particular, enforcement mechanisms. Equally important is the realization that internal displacement, acute and critical as it is, constitutes an aspect of a larger problem of civil wars and domestic violence which will have to be addressed if a comprehensive and lasting solution is to be found. Consequently, the mechanisms and procedures envisaged for enhancing protection and assistance to the internally displaced will have to be strategically connected and coordinated with other pertinent institutions, mechanisms and procedures for peace-making, peace-keeping and peace-building.

With United Nations bodies pragmatically mobilized and coordinated to provide effective protection and assistance, with monitoring and early warning systems in place for the detection of impending or prevailing crises of displacement, with procedures under way for the consolidation of existing international instruments into a code, a declaration, or a convention, with organizational arrangements made to cater both to protection and assistance and with diplomatic initiatives taken as appropriate to avert, alleviate, or correct humanitarian tragedies or human rights violations, there should develop within the United Nations system and in the international community a more favourable climate for policy-making, an institutional framework and an operational network that should be effective in elevating and promoting the rights of the internally displaced persons to an acceptable standard of human dignity.

Having taken note of the study and of the useful suggestions and recommendations contained therein, the Commission on Human Rights commended the Representative of the Secretary-General and requested the Secretary-General (resolution 1993/95) "to mandate his representative for a period of two years to continue his work aimed at a better understanding of the general problems faced by internally displaced persons and their possible long-term solutions, with a view to identifying, where required, ways and means of improving protection for and assistance to internally displaced persons."

*SEE ALSO* *Refugees.*

## INTERNATIONAL ABOLITIONIST FEDERATION.
An international non-governmental organization in consultative status with the UN ECONOMIC AND SOCIAL COUNCIL (Category II) and with ILO, UNESCO, and the COUNCIL OF EUROPE, IAF has national branches in India, France, Belgium, Switzerland, West Germany, and Great Britain; in addition, it has 40 affiliated organizations in 50 countries and individual members in 39 countries.

The Federation was founded in London in 1875. It engages in scientific study of the problems of prostitution and the traffic in persons, seeking the causes thereof and the means of preventing and eliminating such traffic. It also strives to promote the social rehabilitation of persons engaged in prostitution and victims of traffic in persons. Each year IAF delegates participate in the work of the UN Working Group on Contemporary Forms of Slavery of the UN COMMISSION ON HUMAN RIGHTS. IAF publishes *Revue Abolitionniste.*

International Abolitionist Federation. Address: 7 rue Gautier, CH-1201, Geneva, Switzerland. Telephone: (41-22) 731-33-69. Fax: (41-22) 738-92-68. Executive Secretary: Anne Schutt.

## INTERNATIONAL ACTION FOR THE RIGHTS OF THE CHILD.
Founded in 1986, this non-governmental organization informs and intervenes, without any discrimination, when children suffer or are exploited. The IARC assists children in need—especially street children, jailed children, and worker children—and takes into account their requirements and aspirations. IARC provides food, lodging, and medical and psychological support, searches for families when necessary, and operates a residential aid center (*La Porte*

*Ouverte*). The group has published *Philippines: Les enfants du mépris* (1989) and *Pour les enfants du monde* (1991).

International Action for the Rights of the Child. Address: B.P. 427, F-75870, Paris Cedex 18, France. Fax: (33-1) 42-05-552. General Manager: Jean Dallais.

## INTERNATIONAL ALERT.

Founded in 1985 by development and human rights groups concerned that ethnic and other internal conflicts inhibited development, violated human rights, and could lead to mass killings and genocide, International Alert is a non-governmental organization in consultative status with the UN **ECONOMIC AND SOCIAL COUNCIL** (Category II). The group provides initiative in conflict resolution and attempts to identify the root causes of conflicts that may escalate to mass killings. In these efforts, International Alert conducts seminars and missions in conflict-resolution training and research.

International Alert. Address: 379/381 Brixton Road, London SW9 7DE, UK. Telephone: (44-71) 978-9480. Fax: (44-71) 738-6265. Director: Dr. Kumar Rupesinghe.

## INTERNATIONAL ALLIANCE OF WOMEN.

An international non-governmental organization in consultative status with the UN **ECONOMIC AND SOCIAL COUNCIL** (Category I), and with **ILO, UNESCO,** and the **COUNCIL OF EUROPE,** and also known by its full title, "International Alliance of Women: Equal Rights–Equal Responsibilities," the organization brings together national affiliates in 56 countries.

Founded in 1902 in Washington, D.C., under the name "International Alliance of Women for Suffrage and Citizenship," inspired by Susan B. Anthony and Elizabeth Stanton, the Alliance promotes all reforms necessary to establish a real equality of liberties, status, and opportunities between men and women and urges women to use their rights and influence in public life to ensure respect for the rights of all individuals. The Alliance cooperates with other non-governmental organizations and with the UN specialized agencies on peace, nationality of married women, equal pay and discrimination in employment, discrimination in education, slavery and suppression of traffic in persons, elimination of discrimination against women, better family living, equal access to technology, and violence against women in the family. The group sponsors a triennial congress and annual regional conferences. IAW publishes *International Women's News* (six times a year) in English and French.

International Alliance of Women. Address: One Lycavittou St., 10672, Athens, Greece. Telephone: (30-1) 362-61-11. Fax: (30-1) 362-24-52. President: Prof. Alice Marangopoulos.

## INTERNATIONAL ASSOCIATION AGAINST TORTURE.

Founded as an international non-governmental organization in Milan, Italy, in 1977, the Association has consultative status (Category II) with the UN **ECONOMIC AND SOCIAL COUNCIL** and has national sections in 15 countries.

The International Association against Torture organizes campaigns to denounce torture and those who practice it, to investigate its causes, and to assist its victims. The Association has published numerous monographs and pamphlets, including *Torture, Executions and Disappearances, The Fate of Political Prisoners in Regimes in Latin America* (1983), *Latin America: A Governmental System* (1984), and *Latin America: A Tortured Continent.*

International Association against Torture. Address: P.O. Box 1752, Cathedral Station, New York, NY 10025, USA. Telephone: (212) 927-9050. Fax: (212) 928-2757.

## INTERNATIONAL ASSOCIATION FOR THE DEFENSE OF RELIGIOUS LIBERTY.

An international non-governmental organization in consultative status with the UN **ECONOMIC AND SOCIAL COUNCIL** (Category II) and with **UNESCO** and the **COUNCIL OF EUROPE,** the Association has individual members and national affiliates in 39 countries.

Founded in France in 1946, the International Association crusades against all forms of intolerance and fanaticism and conducts the World Congress on Religious Liberty, jointly with the International Religious Liberty Association. It publishes the biannual *Conscience et liberté* in four languages.

International Association for the Defense of Religious Liberty. Address: Schosshaldenstrasse 17, CH-3006 Berne, Switzerland. Telephone: (41-31) 44-62-62. Fax: (41-31) 44-62-66. Secretary-General: Gianfranco Rossi.

## INTERNATIONAL ASSOCIATION OF DEMOCRATIC LAWYERS.

An international non-governmental organization in consultative status with the UN **ECONOMIC AND SOCIAL COUNCIL** (Category II) and **UNESCO.** At its inception, the IADL brought together lawyers from mainly European countries; however, IADL currently has 165,000 members from 82 countries.

IADL was founded on 24 October 1946 by lawyers who had fought fascism, nazism, and militarism during World War II. The organization promotes cooperation among lawyers for defense of peace, support for the principles of the United Nations Charter, support for international law, and defense of fundamental human and peoples' rights. To achieve these goals, IADL supports political, economic, social, cultural, and institutional independence and actively promotes a democratic international order. The Association also strives for respect for modern international law as a law of peace and coexistence and attempts to safeguard fundamental rights of defense, in particular through guaranteeing the independence of the judiciary and the Bar. In the past 40 years, IADL has sent working groups and special missions to investigate and report on human rights conditions in countries on all continents; has supported liberation movements in Asia, Africa, and Latin America; and has sent legal observers to trials to insure the defense of political prisoners.

Among its special projects is the IADL Study Centre, created in 1975 to reflect on the main legal themes concerning national and international law for reports for the United Nations and its affiliated agencies; to provide education in law for officers of national or international organizations; and to provide legal advice on behalf of countries, especially third world countries, or organizations which seek it.

IADL's primary publication is the *International Review of Contemporary Law,* and it also publishes reports, pamphlets, and brochures on human rights situations in individual countries.

International Association of Democratic Lawyers. Address: 263 Avenue Albert, 1180 Brussels, Belgium. Telephone: (32-2) 345-14-71. Fax: (32-2) 343-35-96. Secretary-General: Amar Bentoumi.

**INTERNATIONAL ASSOCIATION OF EDUCATORS FOR WORLD PEACE.** An international non-governmental organization in consultative status with the UN **ECONOMIC AND SOCIAL COUNCIL** (Category II), and with **UNESCO,** the Association has 20,000 members in 88 countries.

Founded in the United States in 1969, IAEWP fosters international understanding and world peace, using education as a medium, and furthers the realization of the Universal Declaration of Human Rights through the promotion of social progress, broader international communications at the personal level, and the development of peaceful co-existence. The IAEWP supports academic departments at the Institute of International Relations and Intercultural Studies and the Graduate School of World Problems, Huntsville, AL, USA; the *Institut des affaires internationales,* Boissy

Saint Léger, France; and the *Fundación Universidad para la Pax,* Argentina.

The Association organizes quadrennial world congresses and publishes *Peace Education* and *Peace Progress* annually. It also issues the IAWEP *Newsletter* from time to time, as well as occasional case studies, monographs, and progress reports.

International Association of Educators for World Peace. Address: P.O. Box 3282, Mastin Lake Station, Huntsville, AL 35810-0282 (USA). Telephone: (205) 534-5501. Fax: (205) 536-1018. Executive Vice-President: Dr. Charles Mercieca.

**INTERNATIONAL ASSOCIATION OF GERONTOLOGY.** Established in 1950 at the First International Congress of Gerontology, IAG promotes research in the biological, medical, and social fields on the subject of aging and supports the training of qualified professional personnel in this field. With consultative status with the UN **ECONOMIC AND SOCIAL COUNCIL** (Roster), IAG organizes quadrennial world and regional congresses. It has national societies in 51 countries.

Among its information services, IAG has an extensive library and data bank of institutions and human resources on aging. It publishes the *IAG Newsletter* and the annual *IAG Newsletter for Developing Countries* and has issued the books *Aging in the Eighties and Beyond, Aging: The Universal Human Experience,* and *The IAG Chronicle 1950–1986.*

International Association of Gerontology. Address: Av Prol División del Norte 4271-4273, Tlalpan 14350, Mexico DR, Mexico. Telephone: (52-5) 684-3204. Fax: (52-5) 679-5842. President: Samuel Bravo-Williams.

**INTERNATIONAL ASSOCIATION OF PENAL LAW.** An international non-governmental organization in consultative status with the UN **ECONOMIC AND SOCIAL COUNCIL** (Category II), and with **UNESCO** and the **COUNCIL OF EUROPE,** the association has members in 75 countries.

IAPL was founded in Paris in 1924 as the successor to the International Union of Penal Law, which had functioned since 1889. The Association encourages the exchange of ideas and close collaboration between those who are concerned with the study or application of criminal law or with research on crime and its causes, with a view to promoting theoretical and practical development of international penal law and rules of procedure. The Association has conducted studies on the evolution of the methods and means of penal law, on drug traffic and abuse, on indemnification of victims of penal infractions, and on the suppression of hijacking. It is also working on the creation of an International Criminal Tribunal with an International Criminal Court as its judicial organ.

The Association publishes the *Revue international de droit pénal* (twice a year) in English and French.

International Association of Penal Law. Address: DePaul University, College of Law, 25 E. Jackson Blvd., Chicago, IL 60604, USA. President: Prof. M. Cherif Bassiouni.

## INTERNATIONAL BAR ASSOCIATION.

An international non-governmental organization in consultative status with the UN ECONOMIC AND SOCIAL COUNCIL (Category II) and with the COUNCIL OF EUROPE, the Association has over 140 national or local affiliates and over 15,000 individual members in 117 countries and territories.

Founded in New York in 1947 as a federation of national bar associations, IBA works to establish and maintain permanent relations and exchanges between bar associations and law societies throughout the world, to advance the science of jurisprudence by common study of practical legal problems, to promote uniformity and definition in appropriate fields of law, and to promote the administration of justice under law among the peoples of the world. The Bar Association maintains the following special sections: Section on Business Law (26 committees) formed in 1970; Section on General Practice (22 committees) formed in 1974; Section on Energy and Natural Resources (6 committees) formed in 1983. The Bar also has standing committees on Arab region credentials, confidentiality, finance, general professional programs, human rights, and international liaison with legal organizations.

The IBA publishes several journals and newsletters: *International Business Lawyer* (11 times a year), *International Bar Journal* (six times a year), *International Legal Practitioner* (four times a year), and the *Journal of Natural Resources Law* (four times a year). It also publishes the *International Code of Professional Ethics*, conference reports, books, pamphlets, and papers on various phases of the law.

International Bar Association. Address: 2 Harewood Place, Hanover Square, London W1R 9HB, UK. Telephone: (44-71) 629-1206. Fax: (44-71) 409-0456. Executive Director: Madeleine May.

## INTERNATIONAL BILL OF HUMAN RIGHTS.

A collective term applied to four major international instruments in the field of human rights: the UNIVERSAL DECLARATION OF HUMAN RIGHTS, the INTERNATIONAL COVENANT ON ECONOMIC, SOCIAL AND CULTURAL RIGHTS, the INTERNATIONAL COVENANT ON CIVIL AND POLITICAL RIGHTS and its OPTIONAL PROTOCOLS. A fifth instrument, the International Convention on the Elimination of All Forms of Racial Discrimination (see RACIAL DISCRIMINATION), is sometimes recognized as part of the International Bill of Human Rights.

## INTERNATIONAL CATHOLIC CHILD BUREAU.

An international non-governmental organization in consultative status (Category II) with the UN ECONOMIC AND SOCIAL COUNCIL and the COUNCIL OF EUROPE, ICCB is affiliated with 194 organizations in 47 countries.

The Bureau studies and documents children's issues and works in areas of non-material needs of refugee children—religious information, spiritual growth, family issues—and many other child-related projects. ICCB participated in the preparation of the Declaration of the Rights of the Child and the more recent Convention on the Rights of the Child (see CHILDREN'S RIGHTS). The Bureau's current programs include ones on the psychosocial needs of refugee children, hidden disabled children, street children, sexually exploited children, and intercultural training of educators.

ICCB publishes the international review *Children Worldwide* triannually in English and French and the quarterly *Enfants de partout* (in French), as well as brochures, special statements, reports of workshops and symposia, and specialized publications from national members.

International Catholic Child Bureau. Address: 63-65 rue de Lausanne, CH-1202 Geneva, Switzerland. Telephone: (41-22) 731-32-48. Fax: (44-22) 731-77-93. President: Amin Fahim.

## INTERNATIONAL CATHOLIC MIGRATION COMMISSION.

An international non-governmental organization in consultative status with the UN ECONOMIC AND SOCIAL COUNCIL (Category II), and with the COUNCIL OF EUROPE, the ICMC was established by the Holy See in 1951 to deal with problems of refugees, migrants, and displaced persons. ICMC works mainly through 97 national affiliates and liaison offices for the resettlement of refugees and local integration self-help projects. In recent years, the Commission has emphasized the problems of refugees; it also assists other migrants through funds, loans, and subsidies and in counseling, transport, resettlement, and local integration.

ICMC publishes the biannuals *Migration News* and the *Migrations* in French and the quarterly *ICMC Today* in English and French.

International Catholic Migration Commission. Address: 37-39 Rue Vermont CP 96, CH-1211 Geneva 20

CIC Switzerland. Telephone: (41-22) 733-41-50. Fax: (41-22) 734-79-29. Secretary-General: Dr. André Van Chau.

## INTERNATIONAL CATHOLIC UNION OF THE PRESS.

An international non-governmental organization in consultative status with the UN ECONOMIC AND SOCIAL COUNCIL (Category II) and with UNESCO, ICUP consists of four international federations: the International Federation of Associations of Church Press, the International Federation of Catholic Dailies and Periodicals, the International Federation of Catholic Journalists, and the International Federation of Catholic Press Agencies.

Founded in Brussels in 1927 as the "International Bureau of Catholic Journalists," ICUP serves as a link for Catholics who exercise an influence on public opinion through the press and supports high standards of professional conscience in its members. It conducts research on the problems of the press and religious news and promotes the Catholic press in developing countries. It has been instrumental in establishing the International Catholic Association of Teachers and Research Fellows in the Sciences and Techniques of Information; the *Union catholique africaine de la press*; the Union of Catholic Asian News; and the Catholic Media Council.

ICUP publishes the quarterly *UCIP Information* in English, French, and German.

International Catholic Union of the Press. Address: UCIP, 37-39 rue de Vermont, CP 197, CH-1211. Geneva 20, Switzerland. Telephone: (41-22) 734-00-17. Fax: (41-22) 731-1051. Secretary-General: P. Bruno Holtz.

## INTERNATIONAL CENTER FOR THE LEGAL PROTECTION OF HUMAN RIGHTS.

Founded in 1983, "Interights" is a non-governmental organization in consultative status (Category II) with the UN ECONOMIC AND SOCIAL COUNCIL. The group provides legal advice and information free of charge. It occasionally makes direct representation to the European Commission of Human Rights, the UN COMMISSION ON HUMAN RIGHTS, and the INTER-AMERICAN COMMISSION ON HUMAN RIGHTS. It also assists lawyers and other non-governmental organizations in preparing submissions to international and regional tribunals. In addition, Interights provides advice *amicus curiae* in cases raising important problems of interpretation concerning fundamental rights.

International Center for the Legal Protection of Human Rights. Address: 5-15 Cromer St., London WC1H

8LS, UK. Telephone: (44-71) 278-3230. Fax: (44-71) 278-4334. Executive Director: Nuala Mole.

## INTERNATIONAL CENTER OF SOCIOLOGICAL, PENAL AND PENITENTIARY RESEARCH AND STUDIES.

An international non-governmental organization in consultative status with the UN ECONOMIC AND SOCIAL COUNCIL (Category II) and with the COUNCIL OF EUROPE, INTERCENTER brings together scientific committee branches in 12 countries.

Founded in Messina, Italy, in 1977 by a number of leading Italian and international personalities, the center studies various forms of criminality considered to be compromising to democratic society or threatening democratic institutions. INTERCENTER also sponsors international study seminars and round-table discussions, finances research, and conducts courses in higher specialization of police forces. In collaboration with UNESCO, the center also organizes annual human rights sessions. Since 1978, INTERCENTER has published approximately 50 volumes of proceedings of its various courses and seminars. It also publishes the quarterly *Violence in its Penitentiary Implications*.

International Center of Sociological, Penal and Penitentiary Research and Studies. Address: Via Ghibellina, 59, 1-98100 Messina, Italy. Telephone: (39-90) 710-554. Fax: (39-90) 321-1990. Secretary-General: Domenico Cucchiara.

## INTERNATIONAL CHILDREN'S CENTER.

Founded in Paris in 1949, by French ministerial decree following proposals initiated through UNICEF, ICC promotes the physical, mental, and social well-being and health of children and their environment, particularly in developing countries, and encourages the training of specialized staff and the study of problems affecting children. It operates the Communicable Diseases and Immunization Service to research the efficacy of various immunizations used in childhood and conducts international courses, seminars, and research and exchange programs. ICC also maintains a library and documentation center, acting as a data bank for information on problems concerning children, and has produced a CD-ROM containing all references of the BIRD database. ICC publishes *Children in the Tropics* six times a year in English and French.

International Children's Center. Address: Chateau de Longchamp, Carrefour de Longchamp, Bois de Boulogne, F-75016, Paris, France. Telephone: (33-1) 4520-7992. Fax: (33-1) 4525-7367. Director-General: Jean Brouste.

**INTERNATIONAL COMMISSION OF HEALTH PROFESSIONALS FOR HEALTH AND HUMAN RIGHTS.** An international non-governmental organization in consultative status with the UN **ECONOMIC AND SOCIAL COUNCIL** (Category II), ICHP has national affiliates in five countries.

Founded in Geneva in 1985, the Commission works to secure the commitment of health professionals to respect human rights and professional ethics. ICHP investigates general situations and individual cases in which human rights relevant to health questions have been violated and takes action to secure their observance. The Commission publishes *Up to Date,* a biannual newsletter; *ICHP Yearbook,* a collection of articles; and reports on its activities.

International Commission of Health Professionals for Health and Human Rights. Address: 15 Route des Morillons, Grand Saconnex, CH-1218, Geneva, Switzerland. Telephone: (41-22) 98-89-81. Telex: 27-935 ICA CH. Secretary-General: Dr. Robert Bannerman.

**INTERNATIONAL COMMISSION OF JURISTS.** An international non-governmental organization in consultative status with the UN **ECONOMIC AND SOCIAL COUNCIL** (Category II), **UNESCO,** and the **COUNCIL OF EUROPE,** ICJ limits membership by statute to 45 eminent jurists representative of different legal systems, but others may join as associates; at the present time, ICJ has 40 members from 40 countries and 63 affiliated associations in 51 countries.

Founded in 1952, in Geneva, the Commission concentrates upon advancing the principles of justice which constitute the basis of the rule of law, and mobilizing jurists throughout the world to support and defend the rule of law and the legal protection of human rights. ICJ has initiated inquiries and published reports on human rights and political and legal situations in British Guiana, South and South West Africa, Brazil, Uruguay, Chile, Iran, Suriname, and Sri Lanka, among others. It has also established, at its Geneva headquarters, the Centre for the Independence of Judges and Lawyers, to promote the independence of these professions and to organize support by legal organizations for victims of harassment and persecution. For its work, ICJ was awarded in 1980 the first **EUROPEAN HUMAN RIGHTS PRIZE** by the Council of Europe; and, in 1985, it received the Wateler Peace Prize and, in 1989, the Erasmus Prize.

The organization sponsors several publications: the quarterly *ICJ Newsletter* in English; and the biannuals *ICJ Review* and *ICJ Yearbook,* both in English, French, and Spanish.

International Commission of Jurists. Address: P.O. Box 160, Chemin de Joinville, Cointrin, CH-1216 Geneva, Switzerland. Telephone: (41-22) 788-4747. Fax: (41-22) 788-4880. Secretary-General: Adama Dieng.

**INTERNATIONAL COMMITTEE OF THE RED CROSS.** An international non-governmental organization in consultative status (Category II) with the UN **ECONOMIC AND SOCIAL COUNCIL,** ICRC is composed exclusively of Swiss nationals, not exceeding 25 members, selected by choice or election, and making corporate decisions.

The International Committee of the Red Cross is an independent, private institution, neutral in regard to politics, ideology and religion. The Committee was established in Geneva in 1863, based on the humanitarian writings of **HENRI DUNANT,** and is the founder body of the **LEAGUE OF THE RED CROSS AND RED CRESCENT SOCIETIES.** In time of international or national armed conflict, ICRC endeavours to ensure that the victims of such conflict, whether civilian or soldiers, receive protection and humanitarian assistance. ICRC also works for the development of international humanitarian law and for the understanding and dissemination of the Geneva Conventions. For its humanitarian service, ICRC has been awarded the **NOBEL PEACE PRIZE** three times: in 1917, in 1944, and in 1963, when it shared the Prize with the Red Cross Societies League.

Among its numerous activities, ICRC has instituted two humanitarian divisions, the Central Tracing Agency and the International Tracing Service. The Central Tracing Agency, under various names, has been active since 1870 when it was begun by Swiss humanitarians during the Franco-Prussian War to locate prisoners of war and to notify their families of their location. During World War II, as during World War I, ICRC opened an information agency in Geneva to transmit details concerning military personnel in captivity. Currently, the agency's work consists of registering and forwarding any information obtained on prisoners of war, civilian internees, persons released or repatriated, etc., mainly on the basis of lists of names which it receives. It traces civilians and soldiers missing during conflicts and informs their families. It also draws up captivity and death certificates. The agency has a card index of 60 million cards, representing 30 million individual cases.

The second humanitarian agency is the International Tracing Service, whose headquarters is in Arolsen, FRG, today the most important center of information concerning persons deported or displaced during the Second World War, whether in Germany or in countries occupied by German troops. Responsibility for administering the service was entrusted to the ICRC in 1955. The International Tracing Service has a card index of 25 million cards, representing 2 million inquiries received since 1951.

ICRC has an extensive publication program, sponsoring books and pamphlets on its own work, international humanitarian law, and human rights. Among its periodical publications are the *ICRC Annual Report, ICRC* (annually), *International Review of the Red Cross* (bi-monthly), *Dissemination* (quarterly), and the *ICRC Bulletin* (monthly). The *ICRC Annual Report, ICRC,* and *Dissemination* are published in English, French, Spanish, German, and Arabic. The *International Review of the Red Cross* and *ICRC Bulletin* are published in English, French, Spanish, and German.

International Committee of the Red Cross. Address: 19 avenue de la Paix, CH-1202 Geneva, Switzerland. Telephone: (41-22) 734-6001. Fax: (41-22) 733-8280.

## INTERNATIONAL CONFEDERATION OF FREE TRADE UNIONS.

An international non-governmental organization in consultative status with the UN **ECONOMIC AND SOCIAL COUNCIL** (Category I), and with **ILO, UNESCO,** and **FAO,** ICFTU has 164 affiliated organizations, totaling over 113,000,000 in 117 countries.

Its constitution, adopted in December 1949, declares that the Confederation exists to unite workers organized in free and democratic trade unions throughout the world and to afford a means of consultation and collaboration between them to further the right of individuals to achieve social justice and a full and decent life; to work and choose their own employment; to secure their employment and the income deriving from it; to protect their lives and health in the working environment; to protect workers' interests through independent trade unions; and to guarantee democratic means of changing their government. The Confederation also works to raise living standards; to promote international cooperation, peace, and disarmament; to defend fundamental human and trade union rights, and to combat discrimination based on race, color, creed, or sex. These aims are summarized in the motto "Bread, Peace and Freedom."

The ICFTU maintains the International Solidarity Fund, which helps in the development of free trade unions in developing countries by makings grants for national trade union action programs, educational activities, practical advice, and assistance. It has also provided assistance to workers who have been victimized by repressive regimes or hostile governments or employers.

Among its publications, ICFTU publishes the monthly *Free Labour World*. It also publishes annually a survey of violations of trade union rights throughout the world, published in English, French, German, and Spanish editions.

International Confederation of Free Trade Unions. Address: Rue Montagne-aux-Herbes-Potagères, 37-41, B-1000 Brussels, Belgium. Telephone: (32-2) 217-8085. Fax: (32-2) 218-8415. General Secretary: Enzo Friso.

## INTERNATIONAL CONFERENCE ON HUMAN RIGHTS. See TEHERAN INTERNATIONAL CONFERENCE ON HUMAN RIGHTS.

## INTERNATIONAL CONVENTION AGAINST APARTHEID IN SPORTS. See APARTHEID: INTERNATIONAL CONVENTION AGAINST APARTHEID IN SPORTS.

## INTERNATIONAL CONVENTION AGAINST THE RECRUITMENT, USE, FINANCING AND TRAINING OF MERCENARIES. See MERCENARISM: INTERNATIONAL CONVENTION AGAINST THE RECRUITMENT, USE, FINANCING AND TRAINING OF MERCENARIES.

## INTERNATIONAL CONVENTION AGAINST THE TAKING OF HOSTAGES. See HOSTAGES: INTERNATIONAL CONVENTION AGAINST THE TAKING OF HOSTAGES.

## INTERNATIONAL CONVENTION ON THE ELIMINATION OF ALL FORMS OF RACIAL DISCRIMINATION. See RACIAL DISCRIMINATION: INTERNATIONAL CONVENTION ON THE ELIMINATION OF ALL FORMS OF RACIAL DISCRIMINATION.

## INTERNATIONAL CONVENTION ON THE SUPPRESSION AND PUNISHMENT OF THE CRIME OF APARTHEID. See APARTHEID: INTERNATIONAL CONVENTION ON THE SUPPRESSION AND PUNISHMENT OF THE CRIME OF APARTHEID.

## INTERNATIONAL COUNCIL FOR ADULT EDUCATION.

An international non-governmental organization in consultative status with the UN **ECONOMIC AND SOCIAL COUNCIL** (Category II), **UNESCO,** the **FAO,** and the **ILO,** the Council has grown to include member associations in 91 countries and to maintain liaison with national and international groups in those countries. Its activities focus on research, training, advocacy, and the exchange of information. Among its primary concerns are health care, problems relating to the equality of men and women, literacy and peace workers' education.

The Council publishes *ICAE News* and the newsletter *Convergence,* as well as newsletters from its various programs: *Peace Letter, Voices Rising, Participatory Research International Networking Memo, Health and Popular Education, Education and Criminal Justice,* and *Participatory 'Formation'.*

International Council for Adult Education. Address: 720 Bathurst Street, Suite 500, Toronto, Ontario M5S 2R4, Canada. Telephone: (416) 588-1211. Fax: (416) 588-5725. Secretary-General: Ana Maria Quiroz.

## INTERNATIONAL COUNCIL OF ENVIRONMENTAL LAW.

An international non-governmental organization in consultative status (Category II) with the UN ECONOMIC AND SOCIAL COUNCIL, ICEL has members in 68 countries.

Founded in 1969 in New Delhi, the Council promotes the exchange of information on legal, administrative, and policy aspects of environmental conservation and cooperates with organizations active in those fields. It co-sponsors *Environmental Policy and Law* (issued eight times a year) in English and French and publishes the *ICEL Directory* and *ICEL References.*

International Council of Environmental Law. Address: Adenauerallee 214, D-5300 Bonn 1, Germany. Telephone: (49-228) 2692-240. Fax: (49-228) 2692-250.

## INTERNATIONAL COUNCIL OF JEWISH WOMEN.

An international non-governmental organization in consultative status with the UN ECONOMIC AND SOCIAL COUNCIL (Category II), UNESCO, and the COUNCIL OF EUROPE, ICJW, established in 1912, links Jewish women from 41 countries on five continents with a total individual membership of approximately 1.5 million. Among its objectives are cooperation with national and international organizations working for good will and equal rights among all peoples for realization of the principles set out in the Universal Declaration of Human Rights. It participates in the work of intergovernmental human rights bodies including the UN COMMISSION ON HUMAN RIGHTS, the COMMISSION ON THE STATUS OF WOMEN, and the SUB-COMMISSION ON PREVENTION OF DISCRIMINATION AND PROTECTION OF MINORITIES, and encourages its affiliates to take part in the activities of the United Nations.

ICJW publishes the biannual *ICJW Newsletter* in English and Spanish; *Links around the World,* a community service newsletter; occasional bulletins; and Action Alerts.

International Council of Jewish Women. Address: 1110 Finch Ave. W., Suite 518, Downsview, Ontario M3J 2T2, Canada. Telephone: (416) 665-82512. Fax: (416) 665-8702. President: Helen Marr.

## INTERNATIONAL COUNCIL OF VOLUNTARY AGENCIES.

An international non-governmental organization in consultative status with the UN ECONOMIC AND SOCIAL COUNCIL (Category I), the ILO, and the COUNCIL OF EUROPE, the ICVA has members in 35 countries. It is an independent association of non-governmental, nonprofit organizations active in the fields of humanitarian assistance and development cooperation. Established in 1962 to promote the development of voluntary agencies, ICVA today provides a permanent international liaison structure for voluntary agency consultation and cooperation. ICVA does not implement relief or development projects itself but provides services and support to its member agencies to enable them to cooperate and perform more effectively.

The ICVA has established many working groups on humanitarian affairs, among them the Working Group on Institutional Development and the Working Group on Refugees, Displaced Persons, and Migrants. It also maintains sub-groups on Latin America and the Caribbean, the Middle East, and Refugee Children and Adolescents; and a contact group on Southern Africa.

The Council publishes the quarterly *NGO Management* on behalf of the NGO Management Network, and special reports and publications concerning the activities of voluntary agencies. It also publishes the "Sustainable Development Series."

International Council of Voluntary Agencies. Address: Case 216, CH-1211, Geneva 21, Switzerland. Telephone: (41-22) 732-6600. Fax: (41-22) 738-9904. Executive Director: Delmar Blasco.

## INTERNATIONAL COUNCIL OF WOMEN.

An international non-governmental organization in consultative status with the UN ECONOMIC AND SOCIAL COUNCIL (Category I), and with ILO, UNESCO, FAO, and WHO, the International Council brings together 76 national councils of women's voluntary organizations.

Founded in Washington, D.C., in 1888, the Council seeks to promote the welfare of all people, the family, and the individual through recognition of and respect for human rights and the removal of all forms of discrimination. It is particularly active in pursuing equal rights and responsibilities for both sexes in all spheres, in stimulating women to participate in public life, and in integrating them in development and decision-making bodies. It is assisted by international standing committees on such subjects as international relations and peace, laws and the status of women, migration, and women and employment.

In addition to issuing its resolutions and reports at regular intervals, ICW publishes the *ICW Newsletter* three times a year and occasional books including *Women and the UN* and *World Anthology of Poetry by Women.*

International Council of Women. Address: 13 rue Caumartin, F-75009 Paris, France. Telephone: (33-1) 4742-1940. Fax: (33-1) 4266-2623. General-Secretary: Jacqueline Barbet-Massin.

## INTERNATIONAL COUNCIL ON JEWISH SOCIAL AND WELFARE SERVICES.

INTERCO was established in 1961 in London to exchange information concerning the problems of Jewish social and welfare services, including medical care, old age, welfare, child care, rehabilitation, technical assistance, vocational training, agricultural and other resettlement, economic assistance, refugees, migration, and integration. INTERCO has consultative status with the UN **ECONOMIC AND SOCIAL COUNCIL** (Category II), **UNESCO, FAO,** UNHCR, **WHO,** and the **COUNCIL OF EUROPE.**

International Council on Jewish Social and Welfare Services. Address: Drayton House, 30 Gordon Street, London WC1H OAN, UK. Telephone: (44-71) 387-3925. Fax: (44-71) 383-4810. Executive Secretary: Cheryl Mariner.

## INTERNATIONAL COUNCIL ON SOCIAL WELFARE.

An international non-governmental organization in consultative status with the UN **ECONOMIC AND SOCIAL COUNCIL** (Category I), and with **ILO, UNESCO, FAO, WHO,** and the **COUNCIL OF EUROPE,** the Council has national committees in 69 countries.

Founded in Paris in 1928 at the First International Conference of Social Work as the "Permanent Committee of the International Conference of Social Work," ICSW was reorganized in 1946 and again in 1966, and its constitution was amended in 1982. Its main functions are to foster and promote social development on a global basis, to define social needs and stimulate awareness of these needs, to facilitate the dialogue between different groups of society concerned with the promotion of social justice and human well-being, and in general to act as a catalyst, platform, and resource center for the sharing of knowledge, experience, and information on social development. It organizes international and regional seminars, conferences, and workshops and participates in studies and research regarding the development of effective new social policies.

ICSW publishes *International Social Work* quarterly and issues the proceedings of its Biennial Conferences.

International Council on Social Welfare. Address: Kostlergasse 1/29, A-1060, Vienna, Austria. Telephone: (43-1) 587-8164. Fax: (43-1) 587-9951. Secretary-General: Sirpa Utrainen.

## INTERNATIONAL COURT OF JUSTICE.

The Court, which has its headquarters at The Hague, is the principal judicial organ of the United Nations. The statute of the International Court—based on the Statute of the Permanent Court of International Justice instituted by the **LEAGUE OF NATIONS** in 1920 but dissolved in 1946—is an integral part of the **UNITED NATIONS CHARTER.** All States members of the United Nations are *ipso facto* parties to the statute. A State which is not a UN member may become a party to the statute of the Court on conditions to be determined in each case by the UN **GENERAL ASSEMBLY** on recommendation of the Security Council.

In accordance with Article 38 of the statute, the Court's primary function is "to decide in accordance with international law such disputes as are submitted to it." In so doing, the Court applies (1) international conventions, (2) international custom, (3) the general principles of law recognized by civilized nations, and (4) judicial decisions and the teachings of the most highly qualified publicists as subsidiary means for determining the rules of law. The Court may also decide a case *ex aequo et bono*—i.e., in accordance with the principles of equity—if the parties concerned agree. The court may also give an advisory opinion on any legal question at the request of the UN General Assembly, the **SECURITY COUNCIL,** or other UN organs or specialized agencies when authorized by the General Assembly. The Security Council can be called upon to determine measures to be taken to effect a judgment of the Court if the other party fails to perform its obligations under that judgment. The reports of the International Court of Justice are considered by the General Assembly.

*COMPOSITION.* The Court is composed of 15 independent judges of different nationalities "from among persons of high moral character who possess the qualifications required in their respective countries for appointment to the highest judicial offices, or are jurisconsults of recognized competence in international law." Candidates are nominated by national groups of legal experts. From the list of candidates, the General Assembly and the Security Council, voting independently, elect the members of the court, an absolute majority being required. If, after three meetings, concurring majorities have not been achieved in the two organs, a special joint conference is applied. Judges are elected for a term of nine years, the terms of five of the 15 judges expiring at the end of every three years.

**SESSIONS.** The Court remains permanently in session, except during judicial vacations. It has no subsidiary bodies, but from time to time may establish chambers of three or more judges to deal with particular categories of cases (for example, labor cases). The Registry is the administrative organ of the Court, and the registrar directs the work of the staff, of which he is the head.

Since the court met for the first time in The Hague on 1 April 1946, it has dealt with a number of contentious cases relating to human rights matters, among them: *Haya de la Torre* (Colombia v. Peru), 1950–51; *Nottebohm* (Liechtenstein v. Guatemala), 1951–55; *South West Africa* (Ethiopia v. South Africa; Liberia v. South Africa), 1960–61; *Trial of Pakistani Prisoners of War* (Pakistan v. India), 1973; and *U.S. Diplomatic and Consular Staff in Teheran* (United States of America v. Iran), 1979–81. It has also given advisory opinions on legal questions relating to human rights in a number of cases, among them: *Interpretation of Peace Treaties with Bulgaria, Hungary and Romania* (1949–50), *International Status of South West Africa* (1949–50), *Reservations to the Convention on the Prevention and Punishment of the Crime of Genocide* (1950–51), and *Legal Consequences for States of the Continued Presence of South Africa in Namibia (South West Africa) notwithstanding Security Council resolution 276 (1970)* (1970–71).

**BIBLIOGRAPHY.** Akhavan, Payam. "Enforcement of the Genocide Convention through the Advisory Opinion Jurisdiction of the International Court of Justice," *Human Rights Law Journal* 12, no. 8–9 (Sept. 1991): 285–299. Scholarly article, in English.

Fisler, Lori, and David J. Scheffer, eds. *Law and Force in the New International Order.* Boulder, CO, USA: Westview Press, 1991. Collection of scholarly articles, in English.

Van Baarda, Th. A. "Is It Expedient to Let the World Court Clarify, in an Advisory Opinion, the Applicability of the Fourth Geneva Convention in the Occupied Territories?" *Netherlands Quarterly of Human Rights* 10, no. 1 (1992). Scholarly article, in English.

# INTERNATIONAL COVENANT ON CIVIL AND POLITICAL RIGHTS (1966) AND OPTIONAL PROTOCOLS.

The Covenant is the third instrument—after the **UNIVERSAL DECLARATION OF HUMAN RIGHTS** and the **INTERNATIONAL COVENANT ON ECONOMIC, SOCIAL AND CULTURAL RIGHTS**—constituting the **INTERNATIONAL BILL OF HUMAN RIGHTS.** The fourth is the Optional Protocol to the International Covenant on Civil and Political Rights. The fifth is the Second Optional Protocol, which aims at the abolition of the death penalty.

The Covenant defines the civil and political rights which it aims to protect and the permissible limitations on the enjoyment of those rights, authorizes the establishment of a monitoring organ, the **HUMAN RIGHTS COMMITTEE,** to supervise the implementation of its provisions, and provides (article 41) for the handling by the Committee of complaints by one State party that another State party is not fulfilling its obligations under the Covenant, provided that both States have made a declaration recognizing the competence of the Committee to receive and consider such communications.

Under the optional protocol, the Committee may also deal with complaints from individuals claiming to be victims of violations of any of the rights set out in the Covenant provided that the State concerned is a party both to the Covenant and to the optional protocol. Under the Second Optional Protocol, States parties agree that no one within their jurisdiction shall be executed, and that each State Party shall take all necessary measures to abolish the death penalty within its jurisdiction.

The International Covenant on Civil and Political Rights was adopted by the UN **GENERAL ASSEMBLY** on 16 December 1966 (resolution 2200 A [XXI]), and entered into force on 23 March 1976. The Declaration Regarding Article 41 of the International Covenant on Civil and Political Rights entered into force on 28 March 1979. The text of the Covenant, annexed to resolution 2200 A (XXI), is as follows:

### Preamble

The States Parties to the present Covenant,

Considering that, in accordance with the principles proclaimed in the Charter of the United Nations, recognition of the inherent dignity and of the equal and inalienable rights of all members of the human family is the foundation of freedom, justice and peace in the world,

Recognizing that these rights derive from the inherent dignity of the human person,

Recognizing that, in accordance with the Universal Declaration of Human Rights, the ideal of free human beings enjoying civil and political freedom and freedom from fear and want can only be achieved if conditions are created whereby everyone may enjoy his civil and political rights, as well as his economic, social and cultural rights,

Considering the obligation of States under the Charter of the United Nations to promote universal respect for, and observance of, human rights and freedoms,

Realizing that the individual, having duties to other individuals and to the community to which he belongs, is under a responsibility to strive for the promotion and observance of the rights recognized in the present Covenant,

Agree upon the following articles:

## Part I

*Article 1.* 1. All peoples have the right of self-determination. By virtue of that right they freely determine their political status and freely pursue their economic, social and cultural development.

2. All peoples may, for their own ends, freely dispose of their natural wealth and resources without prejudice to any obligations arising out of international economic co-operation, based upon the principle of mutual benefit, and international law. In no case may a people be deprived of its own means of subsistence.

3. The States Parties to the present Covenant, including those having responsibility for the administration of Non-Self-Governing and Trust Territories, shall promote the realization of the right of self-determination, and shall respect that right, in conformity with the provisions of the Charter of the United Nations.

## Part II

*Article 2.* 1. Each State Party to the present Covenant undertakes to respect and to ensure to all individuals within its territory and subject to its jurisdiction the rights recognized in the present Covenant, without distinction of any kind, such as race, colour, sex, language, religion, political or other opinion, national or social origin, property, birth or other status.

2. Where not already provided for by existing legislative or other measures, each State Party to the present Covenant undertakes to take the necessary steps, in accordance with its constitutional processes and with the provisions of the present Covenant, to adopt such legislative or other measures as may be necessary to give effect to the rights recognized in the present Covenant.

3. Each State Party to the present Covenant undertakes:

(a) To ensure that any person whose rights or freedoms as herein recognized are violated shall have an effective remedy, notwithstanding that the violation has been committed by persons acting in an official capacity;

(b) To ensure that any person claiming such a remedy shall have his right thereto determined by competent judicial, administrative or legislative authorities, or by any other competent authority provided for by the legal system of the State, and to develop the possibilities of judicial remedy;

(c) To ensure that the competent authorities shall enforce such remedies when granted.

*Article 3.* The States Parties to the present Covenant undertake to ensure the equal right of men and women to the enjoyment of all civil and political rights set forth in the present Covenant.

*Article 4.* 1. In time of public emergency which threatens the life of the nation and the existence of which is officially proclaimed, the States Parties to the present Covenant may take measures derogating from their obligations under the present Covenant to the extent strictly required by the exigencies of the situation, provided that such measures are not inconsistent with their other obligations under international law and do not involve discrimination solely on the ground of race, colour, sex, language, religion or social origin.

2. No derogation from articles 6, 7, 8 (paragraphs 1 and 2), 11, 15, 16 and 18 may be made under this provision.

3. Any State Party to the present Covenant availing itself of the right of derogation shall immediately inform the other States Parties to the present Covenant, through the intermediary of the Secretary-General of the United Nations, of the provisions from which it has derogated and of the reasons by which it was actuated. A further communication shall be made, through the same intermediary, on the date on which it terminates such derogation.

*Article 5.* 1. Nothing in the present Covenant may be interpreted as implying for any State, group or person any right to engage in any activity or perform any act aimed at the destruction of any of the rights and freedoms recognized herein or at their limitation to a greater extent than is provided for in the present Covenant.

2. There shall be no restriction upon or derogation from any of the fundamental human rights recognized or existing in any State Party to the present Covenant pursuant to law, conventions, regulations or custom on the pretext that the present Covenant does not recognize such rights or that it recognizes them to a lesser extent.

## Part III

*Article 6.* 1. Every human being has the inherent right to life. This right shall be protected by law. No one shall be arbitrarily deprived of his life.

2. In countries which have not abolished the death penalty, sentence of death may be imposed only for the most serious crimes in accordance with the law in force at the time of the commission of the crime and not contrary to the provisions of the present Covenant and to the Convention on the Prevention and Punishment of the Crime of Genocide. This penalty can only be carried out pursuant to a final judgment rendered by a competent court.

3. When deprivation of life constitutes the crime of genocide, it is understood that nothing in this article shall authorize any State Party to the present Covenant to derogate in any way from any obligation assumed under the provisions of the Convention on the Prevention and Punishment of the Crime of Genocide.

4. Anyone sentenced to death shall have the right to seek pardon or commutation of the sentence. Amnesty, pardon or commutation of the sentence of death may be granted in all cases.

5. Sentence of death shall not be imposed for crimes committed by persons below eighteen years of age and shall not be carried out on pregnant women.

6. Nothing in this article shall be invoked to delay or to prevent the abolition of capital punishment by any State Party to the present Covenant.

*Article 7.* No one shall be subjected to torture or to cruel, inhuman or degrading treatment or punishment. In particular, no one shall be subjected without his free consent to medical or scientific experimentation.

*Article 8.* 1. No one shall be held in slavery; slavery and the slave-trade in all their forms shall be prohibited.

2. No one shall be held in servitude.

3. (a) No one shall be required to perform forced or compulsory labour;

(b) Paragraph 3 (a) shall not be held to preclude, in countries where imprisonment with hard labour may be imposed as a punishment for a crime, the performance of hard labour in pursuance of a sentence to such punishment by a competent court;

(c) For the purpose of this paragraph the term "forced or compulsory labour" shall not include:

(i) Any work or service, not referred to in sub-paragraph (b), normally required of a person who is under detention in consequence of a lawful order of a court, or of a person during conditional release from such detention;

(ii) Any service of a military character and, in countries where conscientious objection is recognized, any national service required by law of conscientious objectors;

(iii) Any service exacted in cases of emergency or calamity threatening the life or well-being of the community;

(iv) Any work or service which forms part of normal civil obligations.

*Article 9.* 1. Everyone has the right to liberty and security of person. No one shall be subjected to arbitrary arrest or detention. No one shall be deprived of his liberty except on such grounds and in accordance with such procedure as are established by law.

2. Anyone who is arrested shall be informed, at the time of arrest, of the reasons for his arrest and shall be promptly informed of any charges against him.

3. Anyone arrested or detained on a criminal charge shall be brought promptly before a judge or other officer authorized by law to exercise judicial power and shall be entitled to trial within a reasonable time or to release. It shall not be the general rule that persons awaiting trial shall be detained in custody, but release may be subject to guarantees to appear for trial, at any other stage of the judicial proceedings, and, should occasion arise, for execution of the judgement.

4. Anyone who is deprived of his liberty by arrest or detention shall be entitled to take proceedings before a court, in order that that court may decide without delay on the lawfulness of his detention and order his release if the detention is not lawful.

5. Anyone who has been the victim of unlawful arrest or detention shall have an enforceable right to compensation.

*Article 10.* 1. All persons deprived of their liberty shall be treated with humanity and with respect for the inherent dignity of the human person.

2. (a) Accused persons shall, save in exceptional circumstances, be segregated from convicted persons and shall be subject to separate treatment appropriate to their status as unconvicted persons;

(b) Accused juvenile persons shall be separated from adults and brought as speedily as possible for adjudication.

3. The penitentiary system shall comprise treatment of prisoners the essential aim of which shall be their reformation and social rehabilitation. Juvenile offenders shall be segregated from adults and be accorded treatment appropriate to their age and legal status.

*Article 11.* No one shall be imprisoned merely on the ground of inability to fulfil a contractual obligation.

*Article 12.* 1. Everyone lawfully within the territory of a State shall, within that territory, have the right to liberty of movement and freedom to choose his residence.

2. Everyone shall be free to leave any country, including his own.

3. The above-mentioned rights shall not be subject to any restrictions except those which are provided by law, are necessary to protect national security, public order (*ordre public*), public health or morals or the rights and freedoms of others, and are consistent with the other rights recognized in the present Covenant.

4. No one shall be arbitrarily deprived of the right to enter his own country.

*Article 13.* An alien lawfully in the territory of a State Party to the present Covenant may be expelled therefrom only in pursuance of a decision reached in accordance with law and shall, except where compelling reasons of national security otherwise require, be allowed to submit the reasons against his expulsion and to have his case reviewed by, and be represented for the purpose before, the competent authority or a person or persons especially designated by the competent authority.

*Article 14.* 1. All persons shall be equal before the court and tribunals. In the determination of any criminal charge against him, or of his rights and obligations in a suit at law, everyone shall be entitled to a fair and public hearing by a competent, independent and impartial tribunal established by law. The Press and the public may be excluded from all or part of a trial for reasons of morals, public order (*ordre public*) or national security in a democratic society, or when the interest of the private lives of the parties so requires, or to the extent strictly necessary in the opinion of the court in special circumstances where publicity would prejudice the interests of justice; but any judgement rendered in a criminal case or in a suit at law shall be made public except where the interest of juvenile persons otherwise requires or the proceedings concern matrimonial disputes or the guardianship of children.

2. Everyone charged with a criminal offence shall have the right to be presumed innocent until proved guilty according to law.

3. In the determination of any criminal charge against him, everyone shall be entitled to the following minimum guarantees, in full equality:

(a) To be informed promptly and in detail in a language which he understands of the nature and cause of the charge against him;

(b) To have adequate time and facilities for the preparation of his defence and to communicate with counsel of his own choosing;

(c) To be tried without undue delay;

(d) To be tried in his presence, and to defend himself in person or through legal assistance of his own choosing; to be informed, if he does not have legal assistance, of this right; and to have legal assistance assigned to him, in any case where the interests of justice so require, and without payment by him in any such case if he does not have sufficient means to pay for it;

(e) To examine, or have examined, the witnesses against him and to obtain the attendance and examination of witnesses on his behalf under the same conditions as witnesses against him;

(f) To have the free assistance of an interpreter if he cannot understand or speak the language used in court;

(g) Not to be compelled to testify against himself or to confess guilt.

4. In the case of juvenile persons, the procedure shall be such as will take account of their age and the desirability of promoting their rehabilitation.

5. Everyone convicted of a crime shall have the right to his conviction and sentence being reviewed by a higher tribunal according to law.

6. When a person has by a final decision been convicted of a criminal offence and when subsequently his conviction has been reversed or he has been pardoned on the ground that a new or newly discovered fact shows conclusively that there has been a miscarriage of justice, the person who has suffered punishment as a result of such conviction shall be compensated according to law, unless it is proved that the non-disclosure of the unknown fact in time is wholly or partly attributable to him.

7. No one shall be liable to be tried or punished again

for an offence for which he has already been finally convicted or acquitted in accordance with the law and penal procedure of each country.

*Article 15.* 1. No one shall be held guilty of any criminal offence on account of any act or omission which did not constitute a criminal offence, under national or international law, at the time when it was committed. Nor shall a heavier penalty be imposed than the one that was applicable at the time when the criminal offence was committed. If, subsequent to the commission of the offence, provision is made by law for the imposition of the lighter penalty, the offender shall benefit thereby.

2. Nothing in this article shall prejudice the trial and punishment of any person for any act or omission which, at the time when it was committed, was criminal according to the general principles of law recognized by the community of nations.

*Article 16.* Everyone shall have the right to recognition everywhere as a person before the law.

*Article 17.* 1. No one shall be subjected to arbitrary or unlawful interference with his privacy, family, home or correspondence, nor to unlawful attacks on his honour and reputation.

2. Everyone has the right to the protection of the law against such interference or attacks.

*Article 18.* 1. Everyone shall have the right to freedom of thought, conscience and religion. This right shall include freedom to have or to adopt a religion or belief of his choice, and freedom, either individually or in community with others and in public or private, to manifest his religion or belief in worship, observance, practice and teaching.

2. No one shall be subject to coercion which would impair his freedom to have or to adopt a religion or belief of his choice.

3. Freedom to manifest one's religion or beliefs may be subject only to such limitations as are prescribed by law and are necessary to protect public safety, order, health, or morals or the fundamental rights and freedoms of others.

4. The States Parties to the present Covenant undertake to have respect for the liberty of parents and, when applicable, legal guardians to ensure the religious and moral education of their children in conformity with their own convictions.

*Article 19.* 1. Everyone shall have the right to hold opinions without interference.

2. Everyone shall have the right to freedom of expression; this right shall include freedom to seek, receive and impart information and ideas of all kinds, regardless of frontiers, either orally, in writing or in print, in the form of art, or through any other media of his choice.

3. The exercise of the rights provided for in paragraph 2 of this article carries with it special duties and responsibilities. It may therefore be subject to certain restrictions, but these shall only be such as are provided by law and are necessary:

(a) For respect of the rights or reputations of others;

(b) For the protection of national security or of public order (*ordre public*), or of public health or morals.

*Article 20.* 1. Any propaganda for war shall be prohibited by law.

2. Any advocacy of national, racial or religious hatred that constitutes incitement to discrimination, hostility or violence shall be prohibited by law.

*Article 21.* The right of peaceful assembly shall be recognized. No restrictions may be placed on the exercise of this right other than those imposed in conformity with the law and which are necessary in a democratic society in the interests of national security or public safety, public order (*ordre public*), the protection of public health or morals or the protection of the rights and freedoms of others.

*Article 22.* 1. Everyone shall have the right to freedom of association with others, including the right to form and join trade unions for the protection of his interests.

2. No restrictions may be placed on the exercise of this right other than those which are prescribed by law and which are necessary in a democratic society in the interests of national security or public safety, public order (*ordre public*), the protection of public health or morals or the protection of the rights and freedoms of others. This article shall not prevent the imposition of lawful restrictions on members of the armed forces and of the police in their exercise to this right.

3. Nothing in this article shall authorize States Parties to the International Labour Organisation Convention of 1948 concerning Freedom of Association and Protection of the Right to Organize to take legislative measures which would prejudice, or to apply the law in such a manner as to prejudice the guarantees provided for in that Convention.

*Article 23.* 1. The family is the natural and fundamental group unit of society and is entitled to protection by society and the State.

2. The right of men and women of marriageable age to marry and to found a family shall be recognized.

3. No marriage shall be entered into without the free and full consent of the intending spouses.

4. States Parties to the present Covenant shall take appropriate steps to ensure equality of rights and responsibilities of spouses as to marriage, during marriage and at its dissolution. In the case of dissolution, provision shall be made for the necessary protection of any children.

*Article 24.* 1. Every child shall have, without any discrimination as to race, colour, sex, language, religion, national or social origin, property or birth, the right to such measures of protection as are required by his status as a minor, on the part of his family, society and the State.

2. Every child shall be registered immediately after birth and shall have a name.

3. Every child has the right to acquire a nationality.

*Article 25.* Every citizen shall have the right and the opportunity, without any of the distinctions mentioned in article 2 and without unreasonable restrictions:

(a) To take part in the conduct of public affairs, directly or through freely chosen representatives;

(b) To vote and to be elected at genuine periodic elections which shall be by universal and equal suffrage and shall be held by secret ballot, guaranteeing the free expression of the will of the electors;

(c) To have access, on general terms of equality, to public service in his country.

*Article 26.* All persons are equal before the law and are entitled without any discrimination to the equal protection of the law. In this respect, the law shall prohibit any discrimination and guarantee to all persons equal and effective protection against discrimination on any ground such as race, colour, sex, language, religion, political or other opinion, national or social origin, property, birth or other status.

*Article 27.* In those States in which ethnic, religious or linguistic minorities exist, persons belonging to such minorities shall not be denied the right, in community with the other members of their group, to enjoy their own culture, to profess and practise their own religion, or to use their own language.

**Part IV**

*Article 28.* 1. There shall be established a Human Rights Committee (hereafter referred to in the present Covenant as the Committee). It shall consist of eighteen members and shall carry out the functions hereinafter provided.

2. The Committee shall be composed of nationals of the States Parties to the present Covenant who shall be persons of high moral character and recognized competence in the field of human rights, consideration being given to the usefulness of the participation of some persons having legal experience.

3. The members of the Committee shall be elected and shall serve in their personal capacity.

*Article 29.* 1. The members of the Committee shall be elected by secret ballot from a list of persons possessing the qualifications prescribed in article 28 and nominated for the purpose by the States Parties to the present Covenant.

2. Each State Party to the present Covenant may nominate not more than two persons. These persons shall be nationals of the nominating State.

3. A person shall be eligible for renomination.

*Article 30.* 1. The initial election shall be held no later than six months after the date of the entry into force of the present Covenant.

2. At least four months before the date of each election to the Committee, other than an election to fill a vacancy declared in accordance with article 34, the Secretary-General of the United Nations shall address a written invitation to the States Parties to the present Covenant to submit their nominations for membership of the Committee within three months.

3. The Secretary-General of the United Nations shall prepare a list in alphabetical order of all the persons thus nominated, with an indication of the States Parties which have nominated them, and shall submit it to the States Parties to the present Covenant no later than one month before the date of election.

4. Elections of the members of the Committee shall be held at a meeting of the States Parties to the present Covenant convened by the Secretary-General of the United Nations at the Headquarters of the United Nations. At that meeting, for which two thirds of the States Parties to the present Covenant shall constitute a quorum, the persons elected to the Committee shall be those nominees who obtain the largest number of votes and an absolute majority of the votes of the representatives of States Parties present and voting.

*Article 31.* 1. The Committee may not include more than one national of the same State.

2. In the election of the Committee, consideration shall be given to equitable geographical distribution of membership and to the representation of the different forms of civilization and of the principal legal systems.

*Article 32.* 1. The members of the Committee shall be elected for a term of four years. They shall be eligible for re-election if renominated. However, the terms of nine of the members elected at the first election shall expire at the end of two years; immediately after the first election, the names of these nine members shall be chosen by lot by the Chairman of the meeting referred to in article 30, paragraph 4.

2. Elections at the expiry of office shall be held in accordance with the preceding articles of this part of the present Covenant.

*Article 33.* 1. If, in the unanimous opinion of the other members, a member of the Committee has ceased to carry out his functions for any cause other than absence of a temporary character, the Chairman of the Committee shall notify the Secretary-General of the United Nations, who shall then declare the seat of that member to be vacant.

2. In the event of the death or the resignation of a member of the Committee, the Chairman shall immediately notify the Secretary-General of the United Nations, who shall declare the seat vacant from the date of death or the date on which the resignation takes effect.

*Article 34.* 1. When a vacancy is declared in accordance with article 33 and if the term of office of the member to be replaced does not expire within six months of the declaration of the vacancy, the Secretary-General of the United Nations shall notify each of the States Parties to the present Covenant, which may within two months submit nominations in accordance with article 29 for the purpose of filling the vacancy.

2. The Secretary-General of the United Nations shall prepare a list in alphabetical order of the persons thus nominated and shall submit it to the States Parties to the present Covenant. The election to fill the vacancy shall then take place in accordance with the relevant provisions of this part of the present Covenant.

3. A member of the Committee elected to fill a vacancy declared in accordance with article 33 shall hold office for the remainder of the term of the member who vacated the seat on the Committee under the provisions of that article.

*Article 35.* The members of the Committee shall, with the approval of the General Assembly of the United Nations, receive emoluments from United Nations resources on such terms and conditions as the General Assembly may decide, having regard to the importance of the Committee's responsibilities.

*Article 36.* The Secretary-General of the United Nations shall provide the necessary staff and facilities for the effective performance of the functions of the Committee under the present Covenant.

*Article 37.* 1. The Secretary-General of the United Nations shall convene the initial meeting of the Committee at the Headquarters of the United Nations.

2. After its initial meeting, the Committee shall meet at such times as shall be provided in its rules of procedure.

3. The Committee shall normally meet at the Headquarters of the United Nations or at the United Nations Office at Geneva.

*Article 38.* Every member of the Committee shall, before taking up his duties, make a solemn declaration in open Committee that he will perform his functions impartially and conscientiously.

*Article 39.* 1. The Committee shall elect its officers for a term of two years. They may be re-elected.

2. The Committee shall establish its own rules of procedure, but these rules shall provide, *inter alia,* that:

(a) Twelve members shall constitute a quorum;

(b) Decisions of the Committee shall be made by a majority vote of the members present.

*Article 40.* 1. The States Parties to the present Covenant undertake to submit reports on the measures they have adopted which give effect to the rights recognized herein and on the progress made in the enjoyment of those rights:

(a) Within one year of the entry into force of the present Covenant for the States Parties concerned;

(b) Thereafter whenever the Committee so requests.

2. All reports shall be submitted to the Secretary-General of the United Nations, who shall transmit them to the Committee for consideration. Reports shall indicate the factors

and difficulties, if any, affecting the implementation of the present Covenant.

3. The Secretary-General of the United Nations may, after consultation with the Committee, transmit to the specialized agencies concerned copies of such parts of the reports as may fall within their field of competence.

4. The Committee shall study the reports submitted by the States Parties to the present Covenant. It shall transmit its reports, and such general comments as it may consider appropriate, to the States Parties. The Committee may also transmit to the Economic and Social Council these comments along with the copies of the reports it has received from States Parties to the present Covenant.

5. The States Parties to the present Covenant may submit to the Committee observations on any comments that may be made in accordance with paragraph 4 of this article.

*Article 41.* 1. A State Party to the present Covenant may at any time declare under this article that it recognizes the competence of the Committee to receive and consider communications to the effect that a State Party claims that another State Party is not fulfilling its obligations under the present Covenant. Communications under this article may be received and considered only if submitted by a State Party which has made a declaration recognizing in regard to itself the competence of the Committee. No communication shall be received by the Committee if it concerns a State Party which has not made such a declaration. Communications received under this article shall be dealt with in accordance with the following procedure:

(a) If a State Party to the present Covenant considers that another State Party is not giving effect to the provisions of the present Covenant, it may, by written communication, bring the matter to the attention of that State Party. Within three months after the receipt of the communication the receiving State shall afford the State which sent the communication an explanation, or any other statement in writing clarifying the matter which should include, to the extent possible and pertinent, reference to domestic procedures and remedies taken, pending, or available in the matter.

(b) If the matter is not adjusted to the satisfaction of both States Parties concerned within six months after the receipt by the receiving State of the initial communication, either State shall have the right to refer the matter to the Committee, by notice given to the Committee and to the other State.

(c) The Committee shall deal with a matter referred to it only after it has ascertained that all available domestic remedies have been invoked and exhausted in the matter, in conformity with the generally recognized principles of international law. This shall not be the rule where the application of the remedies is unreasonably prolonged.

(d) The Committee shall hold closed meetings when examining communications under this article.

(e) Subject to the provisions of sub-paragraph (c), the Committee shall make available its good offices to the States Parties concerned with a view to a friendly solution of the matter on the basis of respect for human rights and fundamental freedoms as recognized in the present Covenant.

(f) In any matter referred to it, the Committee may call upon the States Parties concerned, referred to in sub-paragraph (b), to supply any relevant information.

(g) The States Parties concerned, referred to in sub-paragraph (b), shall have the right to be represented when the matter is being considered in the Committee and to make submissions orally and/or in writing.

(h) The Committee shall, within twelve months after the date of receipt of notice under sub-paragraph (b), submit a report:

(i) If a solution within the terms of sub-paragraph (e) is reached, the Committee shall confine its report to a brief statement of the facts and of the solution reached;

(ii) If a solution within the terms of sub-paragraph (e) is not reached, the Committee shall confine its report to a brief statement of the facts; the written submissions and record of the oral submissions made by the State Parties concerned shall be attached to the report. In every matter, the report shall be communicated to the States Parties concerned.

2. The provisions of this article shall come into force when ten States Parties to the present Covenant have made declarations under paragraph 1 of this article. Such declarations shall be deposited by the States Parties with the Secretary-General of the United Nations, who shall transmit copies thereof to the other States Parties. A declaration may be withdrawn at any time by notification to the Secretary-General. Such a withdrawal shall not prejudice the consideration of any matter which is the subject of a communication already transmitted under this article; no further communication by any State Party shall be received after the notification of withdrawal of the declaration has been received by the Secretary-General, unless the State Party concerned has made a new declaration.

*Article 42.* 1. (a) If a matter referred to the Committee in accordance with article 41 is not resolved to the satisfaction of the States Parties concerned, the Committee may, with the prior consent of the States Parties concerned, appoint an *ad hoc* Conciliation Commission (hereinafter referred to as the Commission). The good offices of the Commission shall be made available to the States Parties concerned with a view to an amicable solution of the matter on the basis of respect for the present Covenant;

(b) The Commission shall consist of five persons acceptable to the States Parties concerned. If the States Parties concerned fail to reach agreement within three months on all or part of the composition of the Commission, the members of the Commission concerning whom no agreement has been reached shall be elected by secret ballot by a two-thirds majority vote of the Committee from among its members.

2. The members of the Commission shall serve in their personal capacity. They shall not be nationals of the States Parties concerned, or of a State not party to the present Covenant, or of a State Party which has not made a declaration under article 41.

3. The Commission shall elect its own Chairman and adopt its own rules of procedure.

4. The meetings of the Commission shall normally be held at the Headquarters of the United Nations or at the United Nations Office at Geneva. However, they may be held at such other convenient places as the Commission may determine in consultation with the Secretary-General of the United Nations and the States Parties concerned.

5. The secretariat provided in accordance with article 36 shall also service the commission appointed under this article.

6. The information received and collated by the Committee shall be made available to the Commission and the Commission may call upon the States Parties concerned to supply any other relevant information.

7. When the Commission has fully considered the matter, but in any event not later than twelve months after having been seized of the matter, it shall submit to the Chairman of the Committee a report for communication to the States Parties concerned:

817

(a) If the Commission is unable to complete its consideration of the matter within twelve months, it shall confine its report to a brief statement of the status of its consideration of the matter.

(b) If an amicable solution to the matter on the basis of respect for human rights as recognized in the present Covenant is reached, the Commission shall confine its report to a brief statement of the facts and of the solution reached;

(c) If a solution within the terms of sub-paragraph (b) is not reached, the Commission's report shall embody its findings on all questions of fact relevant to the issues between the States Parties concerned, and its views on the possibilities of an amicable solution of the matter. This report shall also contain the written submissions and a record of the oral submissions made by the States Parties concerned;

(d) If the Commission's report is submitted under subparagraph (c), the States Parties concerned shall, within three months of the receipt of the report, notify the Chairman of the Committee whether or not they accept the contents of the report of the Commission.

8. The provisions of this article are without prejudice to the responsibilities of the Committee under article 41.

9. The States Parties concerned shall share equally all the expenses of the members of the Commission in accordance with estimates to be provided by the Secretary-General of the United Nations.

10. The Secretary-General of the United Nations shall be empowered to pay the expenses of the members of the Commission, if necessary, before reimbursement by the States Parties concerned, in accordance with paragraph 9 of this article.

*Article 43.* The members of the Committee, and of the *ad hoc* conciliation commissions which may be appointed under article 42, shall be entitled to the facilities, privileges and immunities of experts on mission for the United Nations as laid down in the relevant sections of the Convention on the Privileges and Immunities of the United Nations.

*Article 44.* The provisions for the implementation of the present Covenant shall apply without prejudice to the procedures prescribed in the field of human rights by or under the constituent instruments and the conventions of the United Nations and of the specialized agencies and shall not prevent the States Parties to the present Covenant from having recourse to other procedures for settling a dispute in accordance with general or special international agreements in force between them.

*Article 45.* The Committee shall submit to the General Assembly of the United Nations, through the Economic and Social Council, an annual report on its activities.

## Part V

*Article 46.* Nothing in the present Covenant shall be interpreted as impairing the provisions of the Charter of the United Nations and of the constitutions of the specialized agencies which define the respective responsibilities of the various organs of the United Nations and of the specialized agencies in regard to the matters dealt with in the present Covenant.

*Article 47.* Nothing in the present Covenant shall be interpreted as impairing the inherent right of all peoples to enjoy and utilize fully and freely their natural wealth and resources.

## Part VI

*Article 48.* 1. The present Covenant is open for signature by any State Member of the United Nations or member of any of its specialized agencies, by any State Party to the Statute of the International Court of Justice, and by any other State which has been invited by the General Assembly of the United Nations to become a party to the present Covenant.

2. The present Covenant is subject to ratification. Instruments of ratification shall be deposited with the Secretary-General of the United Nations.

3. The present Covenant shall be open to accession by any State referred to in paragraph 1 of this article.

4. Accession shall be effected by the deposit of an instrument of accession with the Secretary-General of the United Nations.

5. The Secretary-General of the United Nations shall inform all States which have signed this Covenant or acceded to it of the deposit of each instrument of ratification or accession.

*Article 49.* 1. The present Covenant shall enter into force three months after the date of the deposit with the Secretary-General of the United Nations of the thirty-fifth instrument of ratification or instrument of accession.

2. For each State ratifying the present Covenant or acceding to it after the deposit of the thirty-fifth instrument of ratification or instrument of accession, the present Covenant shall enter into force three months after the date of the deposit of its own instrument of ratification or instrument of accession.

*Article 50.* The provisions of the present Covenant shall extend to all parts of federal States without any limitations or exceptions.

*Article 51.* 1. Any State Party to the present Covenant may propose an amendment and file it with the Secretary-General of the United Nations. The Secretary-General of the United Nations shall thereupon communicate any proposed amendments to the States Parties to the present Covenant with a request that they notify him whether they favour a conference of States Parties for the purpose of considering and voting upon the proposals. In the event that at least one third of the States Parties favours such a conference, the Secretary-General shall convene the conference under the auspices of the United Nations. Any amendment adopted by a majority of the States Parties present and voting at the conference shall be submitted to the General Assembly of the United Nations for approval.

2. Amendments shall come into force when they have been approved by the General Assembly of the United Nations and accepted by a two-thirds majority of the States Parties to the present Covenant in accordance with their respective constitutional processes.

3. When amendments come into force, they shall be binding on those States Parties which have accepted them, other States Parties still being bound by the provisions of the present Covenant and any earlier amendment which they have accepted.

*Article 52.* Irrespective of the notifications made under article 48, paragraph 5, the Secretary-General of the United Nations shall inform all States referred to in paragraph 1 of the same article of the following particulars:

(a) Signatures, ratifications and accessions under article 48;

(b) The date of the entry into force of the present Covenant under article 49 and the date of the entry into force of any amendments under article 51.

*Article 53.* 1. The present Covenant, of which the Chinese, English, French, Russian and Spanish texts are equally authentic, shall be deposited in the archives of the United Nations.

2. The Secretary-General of the United Nations shall transmit certified copies of the present Covenant to all States referred to in article 48.

## OPTIONAL PROTOCOL TO THE INTERNATIONAL COVENANT ON CIVIL AND POLITICAL RIGHTS (1966).

The Optional Protocol provides for consideration by the UN Human Rights Committee of communications from individuals or groups of individuals who claim to be victims of violations of any of the rights set out in the International Covenant on Civil and Political Rights. However, States parties to the Covenant have the options of accepting, or not accepting, the Optional Protocol; and such communications can only be considered by the Committee if the complaint is directed against a State which has ratified or acceded to the Optional Protocol.

The Optional Protocol was adopted by the UN General Assembly on 16 December 1966 (resolution 2200 A [XXI]) and entered into force on 23 March 1976. The text, annexed to that resolution, is as follows:

The States Parties to the Present Protocol,

Considering that in order further to achieve the purposes of the Covenant on Civil and Political Rights (hereinafter referred to as the Covenant) and the implementation of its provisions it would be appropriate to enable the Human Rights Committee set up in part IV of the Covenant (hereinafter referred to as the Committee) to receive and consider, as provided in the present Protocol, communications from individuals claiming to be victims of violations of any of the rights set forth in the Covenant.

Have agreed as follows:

*Article 1.* A State Party to the Covenant that becomes a party to the present Protocol recognizes the competence of the Committee to receive and consider communications from individuals subject to its jurisdiction who claim to be victims of a violation by that State Party of any of the rights set forth in the Covenant. No communication shall be received by the Committee if it concerns a State Party to the Covenant which is not a party to the present Protocol.

*Article 2.* Subject to the provisions of article 1, individuals who claim that any of their rights enumerated in the Covenant have been violated and who have exhausted all available domestic remedies may submit a written communication to the Committee for consideration.

*Article 3.* The Committee shall consider inadmissible any communication under the present Protocol which is anonymous, or which it considers to be an abuse of the right of submission of such communications or to be incompatible with the provisions of the Covenant.

*Article 4.* 1. Subject to the provisions of article 3, the Committee shall bring any communications submitted to it under the present Protocol to the attention of the State Party to the present Protocol alleged to be violating any provision of the Covenant.

2. Within six months, the receiving State shall submit to the Committee written explanations or statements clarifying the matter and the remedy, if any, that may have been taken by that State.

*Article 5.* 1. The Committee shall consider communications received under the present Protocol in the light of all written information made available to it by the individual and by the State Party concerned.

2. The Committee shall not consider any communication from an individual unless it has ascertained that:

(a) The same matter is not being examined under another procedure of international investigation or settlement;

(b) The individual has exhausted all available domestic remedies. This shall not be the rule where the application of the remedies is unreasonably prolonged.

3. The Committee shall hold closed meetings when examining communications under the present Protocol.

4. The Committee shall forward its views to the State Party concerned and to the individual.

*Article 6.* The Committee shall include in its annual report under article 45 of the Covenant a summary of its activities under the present Protocol.

*Article 7.* Pending the achievement of the objectives of resolution 1514 (XV) adopted by the General Assembly of the United Nations on 14 December 1960 concerning the Declaration on the Granting of Independence to Colonial Countries and Peoples, the provisions of the present Protocol shall in no way limit the right of petition granted to these peoples by the Charter of the United Nations and other international conventions and instruments under the United Nations and its specialized agencies.

*Article 8.* 1. The present Protocol is open for signature by any State which has signed the Covenant.

2. The present Protocol is subject to ratification by any State which has ratified or acceded to the Covenant. Instruments of ratification shall be deposited with the Secretary-General of the United Nations.

3. The present Protocol shall be open to accession by any State which has ratified or acceded to the Covenant.

4. Accession shall be effected by the deposit of an instrument of accession with the Secretary-General of the United Nations.

5. The Secretary-General of the United Nations shall inform all States which have signed the present Protocol or acceded to it of the deposit of each instrument of ratification or accession.

*Article 9.* 1. Subject to the entry into force of the Covenant, the present Protocol shall enter into force three months after the date of the deposit with the Secretary-General of the United Nations of the tenth instrument of ratification or instrument of accession.

2. For each State ratifying the present Protocol or acceding to it after the deposit of the tenth instrument of ratification or instrument of accession, the present Protocol shall enter into force three months after the date of the deposit of its own instrument of ratification or instrument of accession.

*Article 10.* The provisions of the present Protocol shall extend to all parts of federal States without any limitations or exceptions.

*Article 11.* 1. Any State Party to the present Protocol may propose an amendment and file it with the Secretary-General of the United Nations. The Secretary-General shall thereupon communicate any proposed amendments to the States Parties to the present Protocol with a request that they notify him whether they favour a conference of States Parties for the purpose of considering and voting upon the proposal. In the event that at least one third of the States Parties favours such a conference, the Secretary-General shall convene the conference under the auspices of the United Nations. Any amendment adopted by a majority of the States Parties present and voting at the conference shall be submitted to the General Assembly of the United Nations for approval.

2. Amendments shall come into force when they have been approved by the General Assembly of the United Nations and accepted by a two-thirds majority of the States Parties to the present Protocol in accordance with their respective constitutional processes.

3. When amendments come into force, they shall be binding on those States Parties which have accepted them, other States Parties still being bound by the provisions of the present Protocol and any earlier amendment which they have accepted.

*Article 12.* 1. Any State Party may denounce the present Protocol at any time by written notification addressed to the Secretary-General of the United Nations. Denunciation shall take effect three months after the date of receipt of the notification by the Secretary-General.

2. Denunciation shall be without prejudice to the continued application of the provisions of the present Protocol to any communication submitted under article 2 before the effective date of denunciation.

*Article 13.* Irrespective of the notifications made under article 8, paragraph 5, of the present Protocol, the Secretary-General of the United Nations shall inform all States referred to in article 48, paragraph 1, of the Covenant of the following particulars:

(a) Signatures, ratifications and accessions under article 8;

(b) The date of the entry into force of the present Protocol under article 9 and the date of the entry into force of any amendments under article 11;

(c) Denunciations under article 12.

*Article 14.* 1. The present Protocol, of which the Chinese, English, French, Russian and Spanish texts are equally authentic, shall be deposited in the archives of the United Nations.

2. The Secretary-General of the United Nations shall transmit certified copies of the present Protocol to all States referred to in article 48 of the Covenant.

### SECOND OPTIONAL PROTOCOL TO THE INTERNATIONAL COVENANT ON CIVIL AND POLITICAL RIGHTS

*(1989).* The Second Optional Protocol, adopted and opened for signature and ratification or accession by the UN General Assembly on 15 December 1989, provides States that choose to do so the opportunity to join in an international commitment to abolish the death penalty. The purpose of the Second Optional Protocol is to ensure the enjoyment by everyone of the right to life as set out in article 3 of the Universal Declaration of Human Rights and in article 6 of the International Covenant on Civil and Political Rights. The implementation of its provisions is supervised by the Human Rights Committee.

The General Assembly requested the UN Commission on Human Rights to consider the idea of a Second Optional Protocol on 18 December 1982 (resolution 37/192). The Commission asked its **SUB-COMMISSION ON PREVENTION OF DISCRIMINA-**

**TION AND PROTECTION OF MINORITIES** to prepare a draft text, and the Sub-Commission entrusted the task to one of its members, Mr. Marc Bossuyt (Belgium) as its Special Rapporteur.

The Special Rapporteur submitted his report (UN Doc. E/CN.4/Sub.2/1987/20) to the Sub-Commission at its 1987 session. On the basis of the Special Rapporteur's proposals, the Sub-Commission transmitted a draft of the Second Optional Protocol to the Commission in 1988. The Commission forwarded the draft, through the Economic and Social Council, to the General Assembly, which considered it in detail in 1989.

The Second Optional Protocol to the International Covenant on Civil and Political Rights, Aiming at the Abolition of the Death Penalty, was adopted and opened for signature, ratification, and accession by the General Assembly on 15 December 1989 (resolution 44/128); it entered into force on 11 July 1991. The text of the Second Optional Protocol, annexed to that resolution, is as follows:

The States parties to the present Protocol,

Believing that abolition of the death penalty contributes to enhancement of human dignity and progressive development of human rights,

Recalling article 3 of the Universal Declaration of Human Rights adopted on 10 December 1948 and article 6 of the International Covenant on Civil and Political Rights adopted on 16 December 1966,

Noting that article 6 of the International Covenant on Civil and Political Rights refers to abolition of the death penalty in terms that strongly suggest that abolition is desirable,

Convinced that all measures of abolition of the death penalty should be considered as progress in the enjoyment of the right to life,

Desirous to undertake hereby an international commitment to abolish the death penalty,

Have agreed as follows:

*Article 1.* 1. No one within the jurisdiction of a State party to the present Optional Protocol shall be executed.

2. Each State party shall take all necessary measures to abolish the death penalty within its jurisdiction.

*Article 2.* 1. No reservation is admissible to the present Protocol, except for a reservation made at the time of ratification or accession that provides for the application of the death penalty in time of war pursuant to a conviction for a most serious crime of a military nature committed during wartime.

2. The State party making such a reservation shall at the time of ratification or accession communicate to the Secretary-General of the United Nations the relevant provisions of its national legislation applicable during wartime.

3. The State party having made such a reservation shall notify the Secretary-General of the United Nations of any beginning or ending of a state of war applicable to its territory.

*Article 3.* The States parties to the present Protocol shall include in the reports they submit to the Human Rights Committee, in accordance with article 40 of the Covenant, information on the measures that they have adopted to give effect to the present Protocol.

*Article 4.* With respect to the States parties to the Covenant that have made a declaration under article 41, the competence of the Human Rights Committee to receive and consider communications when a State party claims that another State party is not fulfilling its obligations shall extend to the provisions of the present Protocol, unless the State party concerned has made a statement to the contrary at the moment of ratification or accession.

*Article 5.* With respect to the States parties to the (First) Optional Protocol to the International Covenant on Civil and Political Rights adopted on 16 December 1966, the competence of the Human Rights Committee to receive and consider communications from individuals subject to its jurisdiction shall extend to the provisions of the present Protocol, unless the State party concerned has made a statement to the contrary at the moment of ratification or accession.

*Article 6.* 1. The provisions of the present Protocol shall apply as additional provisions to the Covenant.

2. Without prejudice to the possibility of a reservation under article 2 of the present Protocol, the right guaranteed in article 1, paragraph 1, of the present Protocol shall not be subject to any derogation under article 4 of the Covenant.

*Article 7.* 1. The present Protocol is open for signature by any State that has signed the Covenant.

2. The present Protocol is subject to ratification by any State that has ratified the Covenant or acceded to it. Instruments of ratification shall be deposited with the Secretary-General of the United Nations.

3. The present Protocol shall be open to accession by any State that has ratified the Covenant or acceded to it.

4. Accession shall be effected by the deposit of an instrument of accession with the Secretary-General of the United Nations.

5. The Secretary-General of the United Nations shall inform all States that have signed the present Protocol or acceded to it of the deposit of each instrument of ratification or accession.

*Article 8.* 1. The present Protocol shall enter into force three months after the date of the deposit with the Secretary-General of the United Nations of the tenth instrument of ratification or accession.

2. For each State ratifying the present Protocol or acceding to it after the deposit of the tenth instrument of ratification or accession, the present Protocol shall enter into force three months after the date of the deposit of its own instrument of ratification or accession.

*Article 9.* The provisions of the present Protocol shall extend to all parts of federal States without any limitations or exceptions.

*Article 10.* The Secretary-General of the United Nations shall inform all States referred to in article 48, paragraph 1, of the Covenant of the following particulars:

(a) Reservations, communications and notifications under article 2 of the present Protocol;

(b) Statements made under its articles 4 or 5;

(c) Signatures, ratifications and accessions under its article 7;

(d) The date of the entry into force of the present Protocol under its article 8.

*Article 11.* 1. The present Protocol, of which the Arabic, Chinese, English, French, Russian and Spanish texts are equally authentic, shall be deposited in the archives of the United Nations.

2. The Secretary-General of the United Nations shall transmit certified copies of the present Protocol to all States referred to in article 48 of the Covenant.

**GENERAL COMMENTS ADOPTED BY THE HUMAN RIGHTS COMMITTEE.** Under article 40, para. 4. of the International Covenant on Civil and Political Rights, the Human Rights Committee "shall study the reports submitted by the States Parties. . . . It shall transmit its reports, and such general comments as it may consider appropriate, to the States Parties. The Committee may also transmit to the Economic and Social Council these comments along with the copies of the reports it has received from States Parties to the present Covenant." Under para. 5 of that article, "States Parties may submit to the Committee observations on any comments that may be made in accordance with para. 4 of this article."

In the introduction to the document setting out its first general comments (CCPR/C/21/Rev. 1 of 19 May 1989), the Committee explained that

The purpose of these general comments is to make this experience available for the benefit of all States parties in order to promote their further implementation of the Covenant; to draw their attention to insufficiencies disclosed by a large number of reports; to suggest improvements in the reporting procedure and to stimulate the activities of these States and international organizations in the promotion and protection of human rights. These comments should also be of interest to other States, especially those preparing to become parties to the Covenant and thus to strengthen the cooperation of all States in the universal promotion and protection of human rights.

General comments adopted by the Committee, up to the close of its fiftieth (1994) session, are as follows:

*GENERAL COMMENT 1: Reporting Obligation (13th session, 1981).* States parties have undertaken to submit reports in accordance with article 40 of the Covenant within one year of its entry into force for the States parties concerned and, thereafter, whenever the Committee so requests. Until the present time only the first part of this provision, calling for initial reports, has become regularly operative. The Committee notes, as appears from its annual reports, that only a small number of States have submitted their reports on time. Most of them have been submitted with delays ranging from a few months to several years and some States parties are still in default despite repeated reminders and other actions by the Committee. The fact that most States parties have nevertheless, even if somewhat late, engaged in a constructive dialogue with the Committee suggests that the States parties normally ought to be able to fulfil the reporting obligation within the time limit prescribed by article 40 (1) and that it would be in their own interest to do so in the future. In the process of ratifying the Covenant, States should pay immediate attention to their reporting obligation since the proper preparation of a report which covers so many civil and political rights necessarily does require time.

*GENERAL COMMENT 2: Reporting Guidelines (13th session, 1981).* 1. The Committee has noted that some of the reports submitted initially were so brief and general that the Committee found it necessary to elaborate general guidelines regarding the form and content of reports. These guidelines were designed to ensure that reports are presented in a uniform manner and to enable the Committee and States parties to obtain a complete picture of the situation in each State as regards the implementation of the rights referred to in the Covenant. Despite the guidelines, however, some reports are still so brief and general that they do not satisfy the reporting obligations under article 40.

2. Article 2 of the Covenant requires States parties to adopt such legislative or other measures and provide such remedies as may be necessary to implement the Covenant. Article 40 requires States parties to submit to the Committee reports on the measures adopted by them, on the progress made in the enjoyment of the Covenant rights and the factors and difficulties, if any, affecting the implementation of the Covenant. Even reports which were in their form generally in accordance with the guidelines have in substance been incomplete. It has been difficult to understand from some reports whether the Covenant had been implemented as part of national legislation and many of them were clearly incomplete as regards relevant legislation. In some reports the role of national bodies or organs in supervising and in implementing the rights had not been made clear. Further, very few reports have given any account of the factors and difficulties affecting the implementation of the Covenant.

3. The Committee considers that the reporting obligation embraces not only the relevant laws and other norms relating to the obligations under the Covenant but also the practices and decisions of courts and other organs of the State party as well as further relevant facts which are likely to show the degree of the actual implementation and enjoyment of the rights recognized in the Covenant, the progress achieved and factors and difficulties in implementing the obligations under the Covenant.

4. It is the practice of the Committee, in accordance with Rule 68 of its Provisional Rules of Procedure, to examine reports in the presence of representatives of the reporting States. All States whose reports have been examined have cooperated with the Committee in this way but the level, experience and the number of representatives have varied. The Committee wishes to state that, if it is to be able to perform its functions under article 40 as effectively as possible and if the reporting State is to obtain the maximum benefit from the dialogue, it is desirable that the States representatives should have such status and experience (and preferably be in such number) as to respond to questions put, and the comments made, in the Committee over the whole range of matters covered by the Covenant.

*GENERAL COMMENT 3: Article 2: Implementation at the National Level (13th session, 1981).* 1. The Committee notes that article 2 of the Covenant generally leaves it to the States parties concerned to choose their method of implementation in their territories within the framework set out in that article. It recognizes, in particular, that the implementation does not depend solely on constitutional or legislative enactments, which in themselves are often not per se sufficient. The Committee considers it necessary to draw the attention of States parties to the fact that the obligation under the Covenant is not confined to the respect of human rights, but that States parties have also undertaken to ensure the enjoyment of these rights to all individuals under their jurisdiction. This aspect calls for specific activities by the States parties to enable individuals to enjoy their rights. This is obvious in a number of articles (e.g. art. 3 which is dealt with in

General Comment 4 below), but in principle this undertaking relates to all rights set forth in the Covenant.

2. In this connection, it is very important that individuals should know what their rights under the Covenant (and the Optional Protocol, as the case may be) are and also that all administrative and judicial authorities should be aware of the obligations which the State party has assumed under the Covenant. To this end, the Covenant should be publicized in all official languages of the State and steps should be taken to familiarize the authorities concerned with its contents as part of their training. It is desirable also to give publicity to the State party's cooperation with the Committee.

*GENERAL COMMENT 4: Article 3 (13th session 1981).* 1. Article 3 of the Covenant requiring, as it does, States parties to ensure the equal right of men and women to the enjoyment of all civil and political rights provided for in the Covenant, has been insufficiently dealt with in a considerable number of States reports and has raised a number of concerns, two of which may be highlighted.

2. Firstly, article 3, as articles 2 (1) and 26 in so far as those articles primarily deal with the prevention of discrimination on a number of grounds, among which sex is one, requires not only measures of protection but also affirmative action designed to ensure the positive enjoyment of rights. This cannot be done simply by enacting laws. Hence, more information has generally been required regarding the role of women in practice with a view to ascertaining what measures, in addition to purely legislative measures of protection, have been or are being taken to give effect to the precise and positive obligations under article 3 and to ascertain what progress is being made or what factors or difficulties are being met in this regard.

3. Secondly, the positive obligation undertaken by States parties under that article may itself have an inevitable impact on legislation or administrative measures specifically designed to regulate matters other than those dealt with in the Covenant but which may adversely affect rights recognized in the Covenant. One example, among others, is the degree to which immigration laws which distinguish between a male and a female citizen may or may not adversely affect the scope of the right of the woman to marriage to non-citizens or to hold public office.

4. The Committee, therefore, considers that it might assist States parties if special attention were given to a review by specially appointed bodies or institutions of laws or measures which inherently draw a distinction between men and women in so far as those laws or measures adversely affect the rights provided for in the Covenant and, secondly, that States parties should give specific information in their reports about all measures, legislative or otherwise, designed to implement their undertaking under this article.

5. The Committee considers that it might help the States parties in implementing this obligation, if more use could be made of existing means of international cooperation with a view to exchanging experience and organizing assistance in solving the practical problems connected with the insurance of equal rights for men and women.

*GENERAL COMMENT 5: Article 4 (13th session, 1981).* 1. Article 4 of the Covenant has posed a number of problems for the Committee when considering reports from some States parties. When a public emergency which threatens the life of a nation arises and it is officially proclaimed, a State party may derogate from a number of rights to the extent strictly required by the situation. The State party, however, may not derogate from certain specific rights and may not take discriminatory measures on a number of grounds.

The State party is also under an obligation to inform the other States parties immediately, through the Secretary-General, of the derogations it has made including the reasons therefor and the date on which the derogations are terminated.

2. States parties have generally indicated the mechanism provided in their legal systems for the declaration of a state of emergency and the applicable provisions of the law governing derogations. However, in the case of a few States which had apparently derogated from Covenant rights, it was unclear not only whether a state of emergency had been officially declared but also whether rights from which the Covenant allows no derogation had in fact not been derogated from and further whether the other States parties had been informed of the derogations and of the reasons for the derogations.

3. The Committee holds the view that measures taken under article 4 are of an exceptional and temporary nature and may only last as long as the life of the nation concerned is threatened and that, in times of emergency, the protection of human rights becomes all the more important, particularly those rights from which no derogations can be made. The Committee also considers that it is equally important for States parties, in times of public emergency, to inform the other States parties of the nature and extent of the derogations they have made and of the reasons therefor and, further, to fulfil their reporting obligations under article 40 of the Covenant by indicating the nature and extent of each right derogated from together with the relevant documentation.

*GENERAL COMMENT 6: Article 6 (16th session, 1982).* 1. The right to life enunciated in article 6 of the Covenant has been dealt with in all State reports. It is the supreme right from which no derogation is permitted even in time of public emergency which threatens the life of the nation (art. 4). However, the Committee has noted that quite often the information given concerning article 6 was limited to only one or other aspect of this right. It is a right which should not be interpreted narrowly.

2. The Committee observes that war and other acts of mass violence continue to be a scourge of humanity and take the lives of thousands of innocent human beings every year. Under the Charter of the United Nations the threat or use of force by any state against another State, except in exercise of the inherent right of self-defence, is already prohibited. The Committee considers that States have the supreme duty to prevent wars, acts of genocide and other acts of mass violence causing arbitrary loss of life. Every effort they make to avert the danger of war, especially thermonuclear war, and to strengthen international peace and security would constitute the most important condition and guarantee for the safeguarding of the right to life. In this respect, the Committee notes, in particular, a connection between article 6 and article 20, which states that the law shall prohibit any propaganda for war (para. 1) or incitement to violence (para. 2) as therein described.

3. The protection against arbitrary deprivation of life which is explicitly required by the third sentence of article 6 (1) is of paramount importance. The Committee considers that States parties should take measures not only to prevent and punish deprivation of life by criminal acts, but also to prevent arbitrary killing by their own security forces. The deprivation of life by the authorities of the State is a matter of the utmost gravity. Therefore, the law must strictly control and limit the circumstances in which a person may be deprived of his life by such authorities.

4. States parties should also take specific and effective measures to prevent the disappearance of individuals, something which unfortunately has become all too frequent and leads too often to arbitrary deprivation of life. Furthermore, States should establish effective facilities and procedures to investigate thoroughly cases of missing and disappeared persons in circumstances which may involve a violation of the right to life.

5. Moreover, the Committee has noted that the right to life has been too often narrowly interpreted. The expression "inherent right to life" cannot properly be understood in a restrictive manner, and the protection of this right requires that States adopt positive measures. In this connection, the Committee considers that it would be desirable for States parties to take all possible measures to reduce infant mortality and to increase life expectancy, especially in adopting measures to eliminate malnutrition and epidemics.

6. While it follows from article 6 (2) to (6) that States parties are not obliged to abolish the death penalty totally they are obliged to limit its use and, in particular, to abolish it for other than the "most serious crimes". Accordingly, they ought to consider reviewing their criminal laws in this light and, in any event, are obliged to restrict the application of the death penalty to the "most serious crimes". The article also refers generally to abolition in terms which strongly suggest (paras. 2 (2) and (6)) that abolition is desirable. The Committee concludes that all measures of abolition should be considered as progress in the enjoyment of the right to life within the meaning of article 40, and should as such be reported to the Committee. The Committee notes that a number of States have already abolished the death penalty or suspended its application. Nevertheless, States' reports show that progress made towards abolishing or limiting the application of the death penalty is quite inadequate.

7. The Committee is of the opinion that the expression "most serious crimes" must be read restrictively to mean that the death penalty should be a quite exceptional measure. It also follows from the express terms of article 6 that it can only be imposed in accordance with the law in force at the time of the commission of the crime and not contrary to the Covenant. The procedural guarantees therein prescribed must be observed, including the right to a fair hearing by an independent tribunal, the presumption of innocence, the minimum guarantees for the defence, and the right to review by a higher tribunal. These rights are applicable in addition to the particular right to seek pardon or commutation of the sentence.

*GENERAL COMMENT 7: Article 7 (16th session, 1982).* General Comment 7 was replaced by General Comment 20 (Forty-fourth session, 1992).

*GENERAL COMMENT 8: Article 9 (16th session, 1982).* 1. Article 9 which deals with the right to liberty and security of persons has often been somewhat narrowly understood in reports by States parties, and they have therefore given incomplete information. The Committee points out that paragraph 1 is applicable to all deprivations of liberty, whether in criminal cases or in other cases such as, for example, mental illness, vagrancy, drug addiction, educational purposes, immigration control, etc. It is true that some of the provisions of article 9 (part of para. 2 and the whole of para. 3) are only applicable to persons against whom criminal charges are brought. But the rest, and in particular the important guarantee laid down in paragraph 4, i.e. the right to control by a court of the legality of the detention, applies to all persons deprived of their liberty by arrest or detention. Furthermore, States parties have in accordance with article

2 (3) also to ensure that an effective remedy is provided in other cases in which an individual claims to be deprived of his liberty in violation of the Covenant.

2. Paragraph 3 of article 9 requires that in criminal cases any person arrested or detained has to be brought "promptly" before a judge or other officer authorized by law to exercise judicial power. More precise time-limits are fixed by law in most States parties and, in the view of the Committee, delays must not exceed a few days. Many States have given insufficient information about the actual practices in this respect.

3. Another matter is the total length of detention pending trial. In certain categories of criminal cases in some countries this matter has caused some concern within the Committee, and members have questioned whether their practices have been in conformity with the entitlement "to trial within a reasonable time or to release" under paragraph 3. Pre-trial detention should be an exception and as short as possible. The Committee would welcome information concerning mechanisms existing and measures taken with a view to reducing the duration of such detention.

4. Also if so-called preventive detention is used, for reasons of public security, it must be controlled by these same provisions, i.e. it must not be arbitrary, and must be based on grounds and procedures established by law (para. 1), information of the reasons must be given (para. 2) and court control of the detention must be available (para. 4) as well as compensation in the case of a breach (para. 5). And if, in addition, criminal charges are brought in such cases, the full protection of article 9 (2) and (3), as well as article 14, must also be granted.

*GENERAL COMMENT 9: Article 10 (16th session, 1982).* General Comment 9 was replaced by General Comment 21 (Forty-fourth session, 1992).

*GENERAL COMMENT 10: Article 19 (19th session, 1983).* 1. Paragraph 1 requires protection of the "right to hold opinions without interference". This is a right to which the Covenant permits no exception or restriction. The Committee would welcome information from States parties concerning paragraph 1.

2. Paragraph 2 requires protection of the right to freedom of expression, which includes not only freedom to "impart information and ideas of all kinds", but also freedom to "seek" and "receive" them "regardless of frontiers" and in whatever medium, "either orally, in writing or in print, in the form of art, or through any other media of his choice". Not all States parties have provided information concerning all aspects of the freedom of expression. For instance, little attention has so far been given to the fact that, because of the development of modern mass media, effective measures are necessary to prevent such control of the media as would interfere with the right of everyone to freedom of expression in a way that is not provided for in paragraph 3.

3. Many State reports confine themselves to mentioning that freedom of expression is guaranteed under the Constitution or the law. However, in order to know the precise regime of freedom of expression in law and in practice, the Committee needs in addition pertinent information about the rules which either define the scope of freedom of expression or which set forth certain restrictions, as well as any other conditions which in practice affect the exercise of this right. It is the interplay between the principle of freedom of expression and such limitations and restrictions which determines the actual scope of the individual's right.

4. Paragraph 3 expressly stresses that the exercise of the right to freedom of expression carries with it special duties and responsibilities and for this reason certain restrictions on the right are permitted which may relate either to the interests of other persons or to those of the community as a whole. However, when a State party imposes certain restrictions on the exercise of freedom of expression, these may not put in jeopardy the right itself. Paragraph 3 lays down conditions and it is only subject to these conditions that restrictions may be imposed: the restrictions must be "provided by law"; they may only be imposed for one of the purposes set out in subparagraphs (a) and (b) of paragraph 3; and they must be justified as being "necessary" for that State party for one of those purposes.

*GENERAL COMMENT 11: Article 20 (19th session, 1983).* 1. Not all reports submitted by States parties have provided sufficient information as to the implementation of article 20 of the Covenant. In view of the nature of article 20, States parties are obliged to adopt the necessary legislative measures prohibiting the actions referred to therein. However, the reports have shown that in some States such actions are neither prohibited by law nor are appropriate efforts intended or made to prohibit them. Furthermore, many reports failed to give sufficient information concerning the relevant national legislation and practice.

2. Article 20 of the Covenant states that any propaganda for war and any advocacy of national, racial or religious hatred that constitutes incitement to discrimination, hostility or violence shall be prohibited by law. In the opinion of the Committee, these required prohibitions are fully compatible with the right of freedom of expression as contained in article 19, the exercise of which carries with it special duties and responsibilities. The prohibition under paragraph 1 extends to all forms of propaganda threatening or resulting in an act of aggression or breach of the peace contrary to the Charter of the United Nations, while paragraph 2 is directed against any advocacy of national, racial or religious hatred that constitutes incitement to discrimination, hostility or violence, whether such propaganda or advocacy has aims which are internal or external to the State concerned. The provisions of article 20, paragraph 1, do not prohibit advocacy of the sovereign right of self-defence or the right of peoples to self-determination and independence in accordance with the Charter of the United Nations. For article 20 to become fully effective there ought to be a law making it clear that propaganda and advocacy as described therein are contrary to public policy and providing for an appropriate sanction in case of violation. The Committee, therefore, believes that States parties which have not yet done so should take the measures necessary to fulfil the obligations contained in article 20, and should themselves refrain from any such propaganda or advocacy.

*GENERAL COMMENT 12: Article 1 (21st session, 1984).* 1. In accordance with the purposes and principles of the Charter of the United Nations, article 1 of the International Covenant on Civil and Political Rights recognizes that all peoples have the right of self-determination. The right of self-determination is of particular importance because its realization is an essential condition for the effective guarantee and observance of individual human rights and for the promotion and strengthening of those rights. It is for that reason that States set forth the right of self-determination in a provision of positive law in both Covenants and placed this provision as article 1 apart from and before all of the other rights in the two Covenants.

2. Article 1 enshrines an inalienable right of all peoples as described in its paragraphs 1 and 2. By virtue of that right they freely "determine their political status and freely pursue

their economic, social and cultural development''. The article imposes on all States parties corresponding obligations. This right and the corresponding obligations concerning its implementation are interrelated with other provisions of the Covenant and rules of international law.

3. Although the reporting obligations of all States parties include article 1, only some reports give detailed explanations regarding each of its paragraphs. The Committee has noted that many of them completely ignore article 1, provide inadequate information in regard to it or confine themselves to a reference to election laws. The Committee considers it highly desirable that States parties' reports should contain information on each paragraph of article 1.

4. With regard to paragraph 1 of article 1, States parties should describe the constitutional and political processes which in practice allow the exercise of this right.

5. Paragraph 2 affirms a particular aspect of the economic content of the right of self-determination, namely the right of peoples, for their own ends, freely to "dispose of their natural wealth and resources without prejudice to any obligations arising out of international economic cooperation, based upon the principle of mutual benefit, and international law. In no case may a people be deprived of its own means of subsistence". This right entails corresponding duties for all States and the international community. States should indicate any factors or difficulties which prevent the free disposal of their natural wealth and resources contrary to the provisions of this paragraph and to what extent that affects the enjoyment of other rights set forth in the Covenant.

6. Paragraph 3, in the Committee's opinion, is particularly important in that it imposes specific obligations on States parties, not only in relation to their own peoples but *vis-à-vis* all peoples which have not been able to exercise or have been deprived of the possibility of exercising their right to self-determination. The general nature of this paragraph is confirmed by its drafting history. It stipulates that "The States Parties to the present Covenant, including those having responsibility for the administration of Non-Self-Governing and Trust Territories, shall promote the realization of the right of self-determination, and shall respect that right, in conformity with the provisions of the Charter of the United Nations". The obligations exist irrespective of whether a people entitled to self-determination depends on a State party to the Covenant or not. It follows that all States parties to the Covenant should take positive action to facilitate realization of and respect for the right of peoples to self-determination. Such positive action must be consistent with the States' obligations under the Charter of the United Nations and under international law: in particular, States must refrain from interfering in the internal affairs of other States and thereby adversely affecting the exercise of the right to self-determination. The reports should contain information on the performance of these obligations and the measures taken to that end.

7. In connection with article 1 of the Covenant, the Committee refers to other international instruments concerning the right of all peoples to self-determination, in particular the Declaration on Principles of International Law concerning Friendly Relations and Co-operation among States in accordance with the Charter of the United Nations, adopted by the General Assembly on 24 October 1970 (General Assembly resolution 2625 (XXV)).

8. The Committee considers that history has proved that the realization of and respect for the right of self-determination of peoples contributes to the establishment of friendly relations and cooperation between States and to strengthening international peace and understanding.

*GENERAL COMMENT 13: Article 14 (21st session, 1984).* 1. The Committee notes that article 14 of the Covenant is of a complex nature and that different aspects of its provisions will need specific comments. All of these provisions are aimed at ensuring the proper administration of justice, and to this end uphold a series of individual rights such as equality before the courts and tribunals and the right to a fair and public hearing by a competent, independent and impartial tribunal established by law. Not all reports provided details on the legislative or other measures adopted specifically to implement each of the provisions of article 14.

2. In general, the reports of States parties fail to recognize that article 14 applies not only to procedures for the determination of criminal charges against individuals but also to procedures to determine their rights and obligations in a suit at law. Laws and practices dealing with these matters vary widely from State to State. This diversity makes it all the more necessary for States parties to provide all relevant information and to explain in greater detail how the concepts of "criminal charge" and "rights and obligations in a suit at law" are interpreted in relation to their respective legal systems.

3. The Committee would find it useful if, in their future reports, States parties could provide more detailed information on the steps taken to ensure that equality before the courts, including equal access to courts, fair and public hearings and competence, impartiality and independence of the judiciary are established by law and guaranteed in practice. In particular, States parties should specify the relevant constitutional and legislative texts which provide for the establishment of the courts and ensure that they are independent, impartial and competent, in particular with regard to the manner in which judges are appointed, the qualifications for appointment, and the duration of their terms of office; the condition governing promotion, transfer and cessation of their functions and the actual independence of the judiciary from the executive branch and the legislative.

4. The provisions of article 14 apply to all courts and tribunals within the scope of that article whether ordinary or specialized. The Committee notes the existence, in many countries, of military or special courts which try civilians. This could present serious problems as far as the equitable, impartial and independent administration of justice is concerned. Quite often the reason for the establishment of such courts is to enable exceptional procedures to be applied which do not comply with normal standards of justice. While the Covenant does not prohibit such categories of courts, nevertheless the conditions which it lays down clearly indicate that the trying of civilians by such courts should be very exceptional and take place under conditions which genuinely afford the full guarantees stipulated in article 14. The Committee has noted a serious lack of information in this regard in the reports of some States parties whose judicial institutions include such courts for the trying of civilians. In some countries such military and special courts do not afford the strict guarantees of the proper administration of justice in accordance with the requirements of article 14 which are essential for the effective protection of human rights. If States parties decide in circumstances of a public emergency as contemplated by article 4 to derogate from normal procedures required under article 14, they should ensure that such derogations do not exceed those strictly required by the exigencies of the actual situation, and respect the other conditions in paragraph 1 of article 14.

5. The second sentence of article 14, paragraph 1, pro-

vides that "everyone shall be entitled to a fair and public hearing". Paragraph 3 of the article elaborates on the requirements of a "fair hearing" in regard to the determination of criminal charges. However, the requirements of paragraph 3 are minimum guarantees, the observance of which is not always sufficient to ensure the fairness of a hearing as required by paragraph 1.

6. The publicity of hearings is an important safeguard in the interest of the individual and of society at large. At the same time article 14, paragraph 1, acknowledges that courts have the power to exclude all or part of the public for reasons spelt out in that paragraph. It should be noted that, apart from such exceptional circumstances, the Committee considers that a hearing must be open to the public in general, including members of the press, and must not, for instance, be limited only to a particular category of persons. It should be noted that, even in cases in which the public is excluded from the trial, the judgement must, with certain strictly defined exceptions, be made public.

7. The Committee has noted a lack of information regarding article 14, paragraph 2 and, in some cases, has even observed that the presumption of innocence, which is fundamental to the protection of human rights, is expressed in very ambiguous terms or entails conditions which render it ineffective. By reason of the presumption of innocence, the burden of proof of the charge is on the prosecution and the accused has the benefit of doubt. No guilt can be presumed until the charge has been proved beyond reasonable doubt. Further, the presumption of innocence implies a right to be treated in accordance with this principle. It is, therefore, a duty for all public authorities to refrain from prejudging the outcome of a trial.

8. Among the minimum guarantees in criminal proceedings prescribed by paragraph 3, the first concerns the right of everyone to be informed in a language which he understands of the charge against him (subpara. (a)). The Committee notes that State reports often do not explain how this right is respected and ensured. Article 14 (3) (a) applies to all cases of criminal charges, including those of persons not in detention. The Committee notes further that the right to be informed of the charge "promptly" requires that information is given in the manner described as soon as the charge is first made by a competent authority. In the opinion of the Committee this right must arise when in the course of an investigation a court or an authority of the prosecution decides to take procedural steps against a person suspected of a crime or publicly names him as such. The specific requirements of subparagraph 3 (a) may be met by stating the charge either orally or in writing, provided that the information indicates both the law and the alleged facts on which it is based.

9. Subparagraph 3 (b) provides that the accused must have adequate time and facilities for the preparation of his defence and to communicate with counsel of his own choosing. What is "adequate time" depends on the circumstances of each case, but the facilities must include access to documents and other evidence which the accused requires to prepare his case, as well as the opportunity to engage and communicate with counsel. When the accused does not want to defend himself in person or request a person or an association of his choice, he should be able to have recourse to a lawyer. Furthermore, this subparagraph requires counsel to communicate with the accused in conditions giving full respect for the confidentiality of their communications. Lawyers should be able to counsel and to represent their clients in accordance with their established professional standards and judgement without any restrictions, influences, pressures or undue interference from any quarter.

10. Subparagraph 3 (c) provides that the accused shall be tried without undue delay. This guarantee relates not only to the time by which a trial should commence, but also the time by which it should end and judgement be rendered; all stages must take place "without undue delay". To make this right effective, a procedure must be available in order to ensure that the trial will proceed "without undue delay", both in first instance and on appeal.

11. Not all reports have dealt with all aspects of the right of defence as defined in subparagraph 3 (d). The Committee has not always received sufficient information concerning the protection of the right of the accused to be present during the determination of any charge against him nor how the legal system assures his right either to defend himself in person or to be assisted by counsel of his own choosing, or what arrangements are made if a person does not have sufficient means to pay for legal assistance. The accused or his lawyer must have the right to act diligently and fearlessly in pursuing all available defences and the right to challenge the conduct of the case if they believe it to be unfair. When exceptionally for justified reasons trials in absentia are held, strict observance of the rights of the defence is all the more necessary.

12. Subparagraph 3 (e) states that the accused shall be entitled to examine or have examined the witnesses against him and to obtain the attendance and examination of witnesses on his behalf under the same conditions as witnesses against him. This provision is designed to guarantee to the accused the same legal powers of compelling the attendance of witnesses and of examining or cross-examining any witnesses as are available to the prosecution.

13. Subparagraph 3 (f) provides that if the accused cannot understand or speak the language used in court he is entitled to the assistance of an interpreter free of any charge. This right is independent of the outcome of the proceedings and applies to aliens as well as to nationals. It is of basic importance in cases in which ignorance of the language used by a court or difficulty in understanding may constitute a major obstacle to the right of defence.

14. Subparagraph 3 (g) provides that the accused may not be compelled to testify against himself or to confess guilt. In considering this safeguard the provisions of article 7 and article 10, paragraph 1, should be borne in mind. In order to compel the accused to confess or to testify against himself, frequently methods which violate these provisions are used. The law should require that evidence provided by means of such methods or any other form of compulsion is wholly unacceptable.

15. In order to safeguard the rights of the accused under paragraphs 1 and 3 of article 14, judges should have authority to consider any allegations made of violations of the rights of the accused during any stage of the prosecution.

16. Article 14, paragraph 4, provides that in the case of juvenile persons, the procedure shall be such as will take account of their age and the desirability of promoting their rehabilitation. Not many reports have furnished sufficient information concerning such relevant matters as the minimum age at which a juvenile may be charged with a criminal offence, the maximum age at which a person is still considered to be a juvenile, the existence of special courts and procedures, the laws governing procedures against juveniles and how all these special arrangements for juveniles take account of "the desirability of promoting their rehabilita-

tion." Juveniles are to enjoy at least the same guarantees and protection as are accorded to adults under article 14.

17. Article 14, paragraph 5, provides that everyone convicted of a crime shall have the right to his conviction and sentence being reviewed by a higher tribunal according to law. Particular attention is drawn to the other language versions of the word "crime" (*infraction, delito, prestuplenie*) which show that the guarantee is not confined only to the most serious offences. In this connection, not enough information has been provided concerning the procedures of appeal, in particular the access to and the powers of reviewing tribunals, what requirements must be satisfied to appeal against a judgement, and the way in which the procedures before review tribunals take account of the fair and public hearing requirements of paragraph 1 of article 14.

18. Article 14, paragraph 6, provides for compensation according to law in certain cases of a miscarriage of justice as described therein. It seems from many State reports that this right is often not observed or insufficiently guaranteed by domestic legislation. States should, where necessary, supplement their legislation in this area in order to bring it into line with the provisions of the Covenant.

19. In considering State reports differing views have often been expressed as to the scope of paragraph 7 of article 14. Some States parties have even felt the need to make reservations in relation to procedures for the resumption of criminal cases. It seems to the Committee that most States parties make a clear distinction between a resumption of a trial justified by exceptional circumstances and a re-trial prohibited pursuant to the principle of *ne bis in idem* as contained in paragraph 7. This understanding of the meaning of *ne bis in idem* may encourage States parties to reconsider their reservations to article 14, paragraph 7.

*GENERAL COMMENT 14: Article 6 (23rd session, 1984)*. 1. In its general comment 6 [16] adopted at its 378th meeting on 27 July 1982, the Human Rights Committee observed that the right to life enunciated in the first paragraph of article 6 of the International Covenant on Civil and Political Rights is the supreme right from which no derogation is permitted even in time of public emergency. The same right to life is enshrined in article 3 of the Universal Declaration of Human Rights adopted by the General Assembly of the United Nations on 10 December 1948. It is basic to all human rights.

2. In its previous general comment, the Committee also observed that it is the supreme duty of States to prevent wars. War and other acts of mass violence continue to be a scourge of humanity and take the lives of thousands of innocent human beings every year.

3. While remaining deeply concerned by the toll of human life taken by conventional weapons in armed conflicts, the Committee has noted that, during successive sessions of the General Assembly, representatives from all geographical regions have expressed their growing concern at the development and proliferation of increasingly awesome weapons of mass destruction, which not only threaten human life but also absorb resources that could otherwise be used for vital economic and social purposes, particularly for the benefit of developing countries, and thereby for promoting and securing the enjoyment of human rights for all.

4. The Committee associates itself with this concern. It is evident that the designing, testing, manufacture, possession and deployment of nuclear weapons are among the greatest threats to the right to life which confront mankind today. This threat is compounded by the danger that the actual use of such weapons may be brought about, not only in the event of war, but even through human or mechanical error or failure.

5. Furthermore, the very existence and gravity of this threat generates a climate of suspicion and fear between States, which is in itself antagonistic to the promotion of universal respect for and observance of human rights and fundamental freedoms in accordance with the Charter of the United Nations and the International Covenants on Human Rights.

6. The production, testing, possession, deployment and use of nuclear weapons should be prohibited and recognized as crimes against humanity.

7. The Committee accordingly, in the interest of mankind, calls upon all States, whether Parties to the Covenant or not, to take urgent steps, unilaterally and by agreement, to rid the world of this menace.

*GENERAL COMMENT 15: The Position of Aliens under the Covenant (27th session, 1986)*. 1. Reports from States parties have often failed to take into account that each State party must ensure the rights in the Covenant to "all individuals within its territory and subject to its jurisdiction" (art. 2, para. 1). In general, the rights set forth in the Covenant apply to everyone, irrespective of reciprocity, and irrespective of his or her nationality or statelessness.

2. Thus, the general rule is that each one of the rights of the Covenant must be guaranteed without discrimination between citizens and aliens. Aliens receive the benefit of the general requirement of non-discrimination in respect of the rights guaranteed in the Covenant, as provided for in article 2 thereof. This guarantee applies to aliens and citizens alike. Exceptionally, some of the rights recognized in the Covenant are expressly applicable only to citizens (art. 25), while article 13 applies only to aliens. However, the Committee's experience in examining reports shows that in a number of countries other rights that aliens should enjoy under the Covenant are denied to them or are subject to limitations that cannot always be justified under the Covenant.

3. A few constitutions provide for equality of aliens with citizens. Some constitutions adopted more recently carefully distinguish fundamental rights that apply to all and those granted to citizens only, and deal with each in detail. In many States, however, the constitutions are drafted in terms of citizens only when granting relevant rights. Legislation and case law may also play an important part in providing for the rights of aliens. The Committee has been informed that in some States fundamental rights, though not guaranteed to aliens by the Constitution or other legislation, will also be extended to them as required by the Covenant. In certain cases, however, there has clearly been a failure to implement Covenant rights without discrimination in respect of aliens.

4. The Committee considers that in their reports States parties should give attention to the position of aliens, both under their law and in actual practice. The Covenant gives aliens all the protection regarding rights guaranteed therein, and its requirements should be observed by States parties in their legislation and in practice as appropriate. The position of aliens would thus be considerably improved. States parties should ensure that the provisions of the Covenant and the rights under it are made known to aliens within their jurisdiction.

5. The Covenant does not recognize the right of aliens to enter or reside in the territory of a State party. It is in principle a matter for the State to decide who it will admit to its territory. However, in certain circumstances an alien may enjoy the protection of the Covenant even in relation to entry or residence, for example, when considerations of non-

discrimination, prohibition of inhuman treatment and respect for family life arise.

6. Consent for entry may be given subject to conditions relating, for example, to movement, residence and employment. A State may also impose general conditions upon an alien who is in transit. However, once aliens are allowed to enter the territory of a State party they are entitled to the rights set out in the Covenant.

7. Aliens thus have an inherent right to life, protected by law, and may not be arbitrarily deprived of life. They must not be subjected to torture or to cruel, inhuman or degrading treatment or punishment; nor may they be held in slavery or servitude. Aliens have the full right to liberty and security of the person. If lawfully deprived of their liberty, they shall be treated with humanity and with respect for the inherent dignity of their person. Aliens may not be imprisoned for failure to fulfil a contractual obligation. They have the right to liberty of movement and free choice of residence; they shall be free to leave the country. Aliens shall be equal before the courts and tribunals, and shall be entitled to a fair and public hearing by a competent, independent and impartial tribunal established by law in the determination of any criminal charge or of rights and obligations in a suit at law. Aliens shall not be subjected to retrospective penal legislation, and are entitled to recognition before the law. They may not be subjected to arbitrary or unlawful interference with their privacy, family, home or correspondence. They have the right to freedom of thought, conscience and religion, and the right to hold opinions and to express them. Aliens receive the benefit of the right of peaceful assembly and of freedom of association. They may marry when at marriageable age. Their children are entitled to those measures of protection required by their status as minors. In those cases where aliens constitute a minority within the meaning of article 27, they shall not be denied the right, in community with other members of their group, to enjoy their own culture, to profess and practise their own religion and to use their own language. Aliens are entitled to equal protection by the law. There shall be no discrimination between aliens and citizens in the application of these rights. These rights of aliens may be qualified only by such limitations as may be lawfully imposed under the Covenant.

8. Once an alien is lawfully within a territory, his freedom of movement within the territory and his right to leave that territory may only be restricted in accordance with article 12, paragraph 3. Differences in treatment in this regard between aliens and nationals, or between different categories of aliens, need to be justified under article 12, paragraph 3. Since such restrictions must, inter alia, be consistent with the other rights recognized in the Covenant, a State party cannot, by restraining an alien or deporting him to a third country, arbitrarily prevent his return to his own country (art. 12, para. 4).

9. Many reports have given insufficient information on matters relevant to article 13. That article is applicable to all procedures aimed at the obligatory departure of an alien, whether described in national law as expulsion or otherwise. If such procedures entail arrest, the safeguards of the Covenant relating to deprivation of liberty (arts. 9 and 10) may also be applicable. If the arrest is for the particular purpose of extradition, other provisions of national and international law may apply. Normally an alien who is expelled must be allowed to leave for any country that agrees to take him. The particular rights of article 13 only protect those aliens who are lawfully in the territory of a State party. This means that national law concerning the requirements for entry and stay must be taken into account in determining the scope of that protection, and that illegal entrants and aliens who have stayed longer than the law or their permits allow, in particular, are not covered by its provisions. However, if the legality of an alien's entry or stay is in dispute, any decision on this point leading to his expulsion or deportation ought to be taken in accordance with article 13. It is for the competent authorities of the State party, in good faith and in the exercise of their powers, to apply and interpret the domestic law, observing, however, such requirements under the Covenant as equality before the law (art. 26).

10. Article 13 directly regulates only the procedure and not the substantive grounds for expulsion. However, by allowing only those carried out "in pursuance of a decision reached in accordance with law", its purpose is clearly to prevent arbitrary expulsions. On the other hand, it entitles each alien to a decision in his own case and, hence, article 13 would not be satisfied with laws or decisions providing for collective or mass expulsions. This understanding, in the opinion of the Committee, is confirmed by further provisions concerning the right to submit reasons against expulsion and to have the decision reviewed by and to be represented before the competent authority or someone designated by it. An alien must be given full facilities for pursuing his remedy against expulsion so that this right will in all the circumstances of his case be an effective one. The principles of article 13 relating to appeal against expulsion and the entitlement to review by a competent authority may only be departed from when "compelling reasons of national security" so require. Discrimination may not be made between different categories of aliens in the application of article 13.

*GENERAL COMMENT 16: Article 17 (32nd session, 1988).* 1. Article 17 provides for the right of every person to be protected against arbitrary or unlawful interference with his privacy, family, home or correspondence as well as against unlawful attacks on his honour and reputation. In the view of the Committee this right is required to be guaranteed against all such interferences and attacks whether they emanate from State authorities or from natural or legal persons. The obligations imposed by this article require the State to adopt legislative and other measures to give effect to the prohibition against such interferences and attacks as well as to the protection of this right.

2. In this connection, the Committee wishes to point out that in the reports of States parties to the Covenant the necessary attention is not being given to information concerning the manner in which respect for this right is guaranteed by legislative, administrative or judicial authorities, and in general by the competent organs established in the State. In particular, insufficient attention is paid to the fact that article 17 of the Covenant deals with protection against both unlawful and arbitrary interference. That means that it is precisely in State legislation above all that provision must be made for the protection of the right set forth in that article. At present the reports either say nothing about such legislation or provide insufficient information on the subject.

3. The term "unlawful" means that no interference can take place except in cases envisaged by the law. Interference authorized by States can only take place on the basis of law, which itself must comply with the provisions, aims and objectives of the Covenant.

4. The expression "arbitrary interference" is also relevant to the protection of the right provided for in article 17. In the Committee's view the expression "arbitrary interference" can also extend to interference provided for under the law.

The introduction of the concept of arbitrariness is intended to guarantee that even interference provided for by law should be in accordance with the provisions, aims and objectives of the Covenant and should be, in any event, reasonable in the particular circumstances.

5. Regarding the term "family", the objectives of the Covenant require that for purposes of article 17 this term be given a broad interpretation to include all those comprising the family as understood in the society of the State party concerned. The term "home" in English, "manzel" in Arabic, "zhùzhái" in Chinese, "domicile" in French, "zhilische" in Russian and "domicilio" in Spanish, as used in article 17 of the Covenant, is to be understood to indicate the place where a person resides or carries out his usual occupation. In this connection, the Committee invites States to indicate in their reports the meaning given in their society to the terms "family" and "home".

6. The Committee considers that the reports should include information on the authorities and organs set up within the legal system of the State which are competent to authorize interference allowed by the law. It is also indispensable to have information on the authorities which are entitled to exercise control over such interference with strict regard for the law, and to know in what manner and through which organs persons concerned may complain of a violation of the right provided for in article 17 of the Covenant. States should in their reports make clear the extent to which actual practice conforms to the law. State party reports should also contain information on complaints lodged in respect of arbitrary or unlawful interference, and the number of any findings in that regard, as well as the remedies provided in such cases.

7. As all persons live in society, the protection of privacy is necessarily relative. However, the competent public authorities should only be able to call for such information relating to an individual's private life the knowledge of which is essential in the interests of society as understood under the Covenant. Accordingly, the Committee recommends that States should indicate in their reports the laws and regulations that govern authorized interferences with private life.

8. Even with regard to interferences that conform to the Covenant, relevant legislation must specify in detail the precise circumstances in which such interferences may be permitted. A decision to make use of such authorized interference must be made only by the authority designated under the law, and on a case-by-case basis. Compliance with article 17 requires that the integrity and confidentiality of correspondence should be guaranteed de jure and de facto. Correspondence should be delivered to the addressee without interception and without being opened or otherwise read. Surveillance, whether electronic or otherwise, interceptions of telephonic, telegraphic and other forms of communication, wire-tapping and recording of conversations should be prohibited. Searches of a person's home should be restricted to a search for necessary evidence and should not be allowed to amount to harassment. So far as personal and body search is concerned, effective measures should ensure that such searches are carried out in a manner consistent with the dignity of the person who is being searched. Persons being subjected to body search by State officials, or medical personnel acting at the request of the State, should only be examined by persons of the same sex.

9. States parties are under a duty themselves not to engage in interferences inconsistent with article 17 of the Covenant and to provide the legislative framework prohibiting such acts by natural or legal persons.

10. The gathering and holding of personal information on computers, databanks and other devices, whether by public authorities or private individuals or bodies, must be regulated by law. Effective measures have to be taken by States to ensure that information concerning a person's private life does not reach the hands of persons who are not authorized by law to receive, process and use it, and is never used for purposes incompatible with the Covenant. In order to have the most effective protection of his private life, every individual should have the right to ascertain in an intelligible form, whether, and if so, what personal data is stored in automatic data files, and for what purposes. Every individual should also be able to ascertain which public authorities or private individuals or bodies control or may control their files. If such files contain incorrect personal data or have been collected or processed contrary to the provisions of the law, every individual should have the right to request rectification or elimination.

11. Article 17 affords protection to personal honour and reputation and States are under an obligation to provide adequate legislation to that end. Provision must also be made for everyone effectively to be able to protect himself against any unlawful attacks that do occur and to have an effective remedy against those responsible. States parties should indicate in their reports to what extent the honour or reputation of individuals is protected by law and how this protection is achieved according to their legal system.

*GENERAL COMMENT 17: Article 24 (35th session, 1989).* 1. Article 24 of the International Covenant on Civil and Political Rights recognizes the right of every child, without any discrimination, to receive from his family, society and the State the protection required by his status as a minor. Consequently, the implementation of this provision entails the adoption of special measures to protect children, in addition to the measures that States are required to take under article 2 to ensure that everyone enjoys the rights provided for in the Covenant. The reports submitted by States parties often seem to underestimate this obligation and supply inadequate information on the way in which children are afforded enjoyment of their right to a special protection.

2. In this connection, the Committee points out that the rights provided for in article 24 are not the only ones that the Covenant recognizes for children and that, as individuals, children benefit from all of the civil rights enunciated in the Covenant. In enunciating a right, some provisions of the Covenant expressly indicate to States measures to be adopted with a view to affording minors greater protection than adults. Thus, as far as the right to life is concerned, the death penalty cannot be imposed for crimes committed by persons under 18 years of age. Similarly, if lawfully deprived of their liberty, accused juvenile persons shall be separated from adults and are entitled to be brought as speedily as possible for adjudication; in turn, convicted juvenile offenders shall be subject to a penitentiary system that involves segregation from adults and is appropriate to their age and legal status, the aim being to foster reformation and social rehabilitation. In other instances, children are protected by the possibility of the restriction—provided that such restriction is warranted—of a right recognized by the Covenant, such as the right to publicize a judgement in a suit at law or a criminal case, from which an exception may be made when the interest of the minor so requires.

3. In most cases, however, the measures to be adopted are not specified in the Covenant and it is for each State to

determine them in the light of the protection needs of children in its territory and within its jurisdiction. The Committee notes in this regard that such measures, although intended primarily to ensure that children fully enjoy the other rights enunciated in the Covenant, may also be economic, social and cultural. For example, every possible economic and social measure should be taken to reduce infant mortality and to eradicate malnutrition among children and to prevent them from being subjected to acts of violence and cruel and inhuman treatment or from being exploited by means of forced labour or prostitution, or by their use in the illicit trafficking of narcotic drugs, or by any other means. In the cultural field, every possible measure should be taken to foster the development of their personality and to provide them with a level of education that will enable them to enjoy the rights recognized in the Covenant, particularly the right to freedom of opinion and expression. Moreover, the Committee wishes to draw the attention of States parties to the need to include in their reports information on measures adopted to ensure that children do not take a direct part in armed conflicts.

4. The right to special measures of protection belongs to every child because of his status as a minor. Nevertheless, the Covenant does not indicate the age at which he attains his majority. This is to be determined by each State party in the light of the relevant social and cultural conditions. In this respect, States should indicate in their reports the age at which the child attains his majority in civil matters and assumes criminal responsibility. States should also indicate the age at which a child is legally entitled to work and the age at which he is treated as an adult under labour law. States should further indicate the age at which a child is considered adult for the purposes of article 10, paragraphs 2 and 3. However, the Committee notes that the age for the above purposes should not be set unreasonably low and that in any case a State party cannot absolve itself from its obligations under the Covenant regarding persons under the age of 18, notwithstanding that they have reached the age of majority under domestic law.

5. The Covenant requires that children should be protected against discrimination on any grounds such as race, colour, sex, language, religion, national or social origin, property or birth. In this connection, the Committee notes that, whereas non-discrimination in the enjoyment of the rights provided for in the Covenant also stems, in the case of children, from article 2 and their equality before the law from article 26, the non-discrimination clause contained in article 24 relates specifically to the measures of protection referred to in that provision. Reports by States parties should indicate how legislation and practice ensure that measures of protection are aimed at removing all discrimination in every field, including inheritance, particularly as between children who are nationals and children who are aliens or as between legitimate children and children born out of wedlock.

6. Responsibility for guaranteeing children the necessary protection lies with the family, society and the State. Although the Covenant does not indicate how such responsibility is to be apportioned, it is primarily incumbent on the family, which is interpreted broadly to include all persons composing it in the society of the State party concerned, and particularly on the parents, to create conditions to promote the harmonious development of the child's personality and his enjoyment of the rights recognized in the Covenant. However, since it is quite common for the father and mother to be gainfully employed outside the home, reports by States parties should indicate how society, social institutions and the State are discharging their responsibility to assist the family in ensuring the protection of the child. Moreover, in cases where the parents and the family seriously fail in their duties, ill-treat or neglect the child, the State should intervene to restrict parental authority and the child may be separated from his family when circumstances so require. If the marriage is dissolved, steps should be taken, keeping in view the paramount interest of the children, to give them necessary protection and, so far as is possible, to guarantee personal relations with both parents. The Committee considers it useful that reports by states parties should provide information on the special measures of protection adopted to protect children who are abandoned or deprived of their family environment in order to enable them to develop in conditions that most closely resemble those characterizing the family environment.

7. Under article 24, paragraph 2, every child has the right to be registered immediately after birth and to have a name. In the Committee's opinion, this provision should be interpreted as being closely linked to the provision concerning the right to special measures of protection and it is designed to promote recognition of the child's legal personality. Providing for the right to have a name is of special importance in the case of children born out of wedlock. The main purpose of the obligation to register children after birth is to reduce the danger of abduction, sale of or traffic in children, or of other types of treatment that are incompatible with the enjoyment of the rights provided for in the Covenant. Reports by States parties should indicate in detail the measures that ensure the immediate registration of children born in their territory.

8. Special attention should also be paid, in the context of the protection to be granted to children, to the right of every child to acquire a nationality, as provided for in article 24, paragraph 3. While the purpose of this provision is to prevent a child from being afforded less protection by society and the State because he is stateless, it does not necessarily make it an obligation for States to give their nationality to every child born in their territory. However, States are required to adopt every appropriate measure, both internally and in cooperation with other States, to ensure that every child has a nationality when he is born. In this connection, no discrimination with regard to the acquisition of nationality should be admissible under internal law as between legitimate children and children born out of wedlock or of stateless parents or based on the nationality status of one or both of the parents. The measures adopted to ensure that children have a nationality should always be referred to in reports by States parties.

*GENERAL COMMENT 18: Non-discrimination (37th session, 1989).* 1. Non-discrimination, together with equality before the law and equal protection of the law without any discrimination, constitute a basic and general principle relating to the protection of human rights. Thus, article 2, paragraph 1, of the International Covenant on Civil and Political Rights obligates each State party to respect and ensure to all persons within its territory and subject to its jurisdiction the rights recognized in the Covenant without distinction of any kind, such as race, colour, sex, language, religion, political or other opinion, national or social origin, property, birth or other status. Article 26 not only entitles all persons to equality before the law as well as equal protection of the law but also prohibits any discrimination under the law and guarantees to all persons equal and effective protection against discrimination on any ground such as race, colour, sex, language, religion, political or other opinion, national or social origin, property, birth or other status.

2. Indeed, the principle of non-discrimination is so basic that article 3 obligates each State party to ensure the equal right of men and women to the enjoyment of the rights set forth in the Covenant. While article 4, paragraph 1, allows States parties to take measures derogating from certain obligations under the Covenant in time of public emergency, the same article requires, inter alia, that those measures should not involve discrimination solely on the ground of race, colour, sex, language, religion or social origin. Furthermore, article 20, paragraph 2, obligates States parties to prohibit, by law, any advocacy of national, racial or religious hatred which constitutes incitement to discrimination.

3. Because of their basic and general character, the principle of non-discrimination as well as that of equality before the law and equal protection of the law are sometimes expressly referred to in articles relating to particular categories of human rights. Article 14, paragraph 1, provides that all persons shall be equal before the courts and tribunals, and paragraph 3 of the same article provides that, in the determination of any criminal charge against him, everyone shall be entitled, in full equality, to the minimum guarantees enumerated in subparagraphs (a) to (g) of paragraph 3. Similarly, article 25 provides for the equal participation in public life of all citizens, without any of the distinctions mentioned in article 2.

4. It is for the States parties to determine appropriate measures to implement the relevant provisions. However, the Committee is to be informed about the nature of such measures and their conformity with the principles of non-discrimination and equality before the law and equal protection of the law.

5. The Committee wishes to draw the attention of States parties to the fact that the Covenant sometimes expressly requires them to take measures to guarantee the equality of rights of the persons concerned. For example, article 23, paragraph 4, stipulates that States parties shall take appropriate steps to ensure equality of rights as well as responsibilities of spouses as to marriage, during marriage and at its dissolution. Such steps may take the form of legislative, administrative or other measures, but it is a positive duty of States parties to make certain that spouses have equal rights as required by the Covenant. In relation to children, article 24 provides that all children, without any discrimination as to race, colour, sex, language, religion, national or social origin, property or birth, have the right to such measures of protection as are required by their status as minors, on the part of their family, society and the State.

6. The Committee notes that the Covenant neither defines the term "discrimination" nor indicates what constitutes discrimination. However, article 1 of the International Convention on the Elimination of All Forms of Racial Discrimination provides that the term "racial discrimination" shall mean any distinction, exclusion, restriction or preference based on race, colour, descent, or national or ethnic origin which has the purpose or effect of nullifying or impairing the recognition, enjoyment or exercise, on an equal footing, of human rights and fundamental freedoms in the political, economic, social, cultural or any other field of public life. Similarly, article 1 of the Convention on the Elimination of All Forms of Discrimination against Women provides that "discrimination against women" shall mean any distinction, exclusion or restriction made on the basis of sex which has the effect or purpose of impairing or nullifying the recognition, enjoyment or exercise by women, irrespec-

tive of their marital status, on a basis of equality of men and women, of human rights and fundamental freedoms in the political, economic, social, cultural, civil or any other field.

7. While these conventions deal only with cases of discrimination on specific grounds, the Committee believes that the term "discrimination" as used in the Covenant should be understood to imply any distinction, exclusion, restriction or preference which is based on any ground such as race, colour, sex, language, religion, political or other opinion, national or social origin, property, birth or other status, and which has the purpose or effect of nullifying or impairing the recognition, enjoyment or exercise by all persons, on an equal footing, of all rights and freedoms.

8. The enjoyment of rights and freedoms on an equal footing, however, does not mean identical treatment in every instance. In this connection, the provisions of the Covenant are explicit. For example, article 6, paragraph 5, prohibits the death sentence from being imposed on persons below 18 years of age. The same paragraph prohibits that sentence from being carried out on pregnant women. Similarly, article 10, paragraph 3, requires the segregation of juvenile offenders from adults. Furthermore, article 25 guarantees certain political rights, differentiating on grounds of citizenship.

9. Reports of many States parties contain information regarding legislative as well as administrative measures and court decisions which relate to protection against discrimination in law, but they very often lack information which would reveal discrimination in fact. When reporting on articles 2 (1), 3 and 26 of the Covenant, States parties usually cite provisions of their constitution or equal opportunity laws with respect to equality of persons. While such information is of course useful, the Committee wishes to know if there remain any problems of discrimination in fact, which may be practised either by public authorities, by the community, or by private persons or bodies. The Committee wishes to be informed about legal provisions and administrative measures directed at diminishing or eliminating such discrimination.

10. The Committee also wishes to point out that the principle of equality sometimes requires States parties to take affirmative action in order to diminish or eliminate conditions which cause or help to perpetuate discrimination prohibited by the Covenant. For example, in a State where the general conditions of a certain part of the population prevent or impair the enjoyment of human rights, the State should take specific action to correct those conditions. Such action may involve granting for a time to the part of the population concerned certain preferential treatment in specific matters compared with the rest of the population. However, as long as such action is needed to correct discrimination in fact, it is a case of legitimate differentiation under the Covenant.

11. Both article 2, paragraph 1, and article 26 enumerate grounds of discrimination such as race, colour, sex, language, religion, political or other opinion, national or social origin, property, birth or other status. The Committee has observed that in a number of constitutions and laws not all the grounds on which discrimination is prohibited, as cited in article 2, paragraph 1, are enumerated. The Committee would therefore like to receive information from States parties as to the significance of such omissions.

12. While article 2 limits the scope of the rights to be protected against discrimination to those provided for in the Covenant, article 26 does not specify such limitations. That is to say, article 26 provides that all persons are equal before the law and are entitled to equal protection of the law with-

out discrimination, and that the law shall guarantee to all persons equal and effective protection against discrimination on any of the enumerated grounds. In the view of the Committee, article 26 does not merely duplicate the guarantee already provided for in article 2 but provides in itself an autonomous right. It prohibits discrimination in law or in fact in any field regulated and protected by public authorities. Article 26 is therefore concerned with the obligations imposed on States parties in regard to their legislation and the application thereof. Thus, when legislation is adopted by a State party, it must comply with the requirement of article 26 that its content should not be discriminatory. In other words, the application of the principle of non-discrimination contained in article 26 is not limited to those rights which are provided for in the Covenant.

13. Finally, the Committee observes that not every differentiation of treatment will constitute discrimination, if the criteria for such differentiation are reasonable and objective and if the aim is to achieve a purpose which is legitimate under the Covenant.

*GENERAL COMMENT 19: Article 23 (39th session, 1990).* 1. Article 23 of the International Covenant on Civil and Political Rights recognizes that the family is the natural and fundamental group unit of society and is entitled to protection by society and the State. Protection of the family and its members is also guaranteed, directly or indirectly, by other provisions of the Covenant. Thus, article 17 establishes a prohibition on arbitrary or unlawful interference with the family. In addition, article 24 of the Covenant specifically addresses the protection of the rights of the child, as such or as a member of a family. In their reports, States parties often fail to give enough information on how the State and society are discharging their obligation to provide protection to the family and the persons composing it.

2. The Committee notes that the concept of the family may differ in some respects from State to State, and even from region to region within a State, and that it is therefore not possible to give the concept a standard definition. However, the Committee emphasizes that, when a group of persons is regarded as a family under the legislation and practice of a State, it must be given the protection referred to in article 23. Consequently, States parties should report on how the concept and scope of the family is construed or defined in their own society and legal system. Where diverse concepts of the family, "nuclear" and "extended", exist within a State, this should be indicated with an explanation of the degree of protection afforded to each. In view of the existence of various forms of family, such as unmarried couples and their children or single parents and their children, States parties should also indicate whether and to what extent such types of family and their members are recognized and protected by domestic law and practice.

3. Ensuring the protection provided for under article 23 of the Covenant requires that States parties should adopt legislative, administrative or other measures. States parties should provide detailed information concerning the nature of such measures and the means whereby their effective implementation is assured. In fact, since the Covenant also recognizes the right of the family to protection by society, States parties' reports should indicate how the necessary protection is granted to the family by the State and other social institutions, whether and to what extent the State gives financial or other support to the activities of such institutions, and how it ensures that these activities are compatible with the Covenant.

4. Article 23, paragraph 2, of the Covenant reaffirms the right of men and women of marriageable age to marry and to found a family. Paragraph 3 of the same article provides that no marriage shall be entered into without the free and full consent of the intending spouses. States parties' reports should indicate whether there are restrictions or impediments to the exercise of the right to marry based on special factors such as degree of kinship or mental incapacity. The Covenant does not establish a specific marriageable age either for men or for women, but that age should be such as to enable each of the intending spouses to give his or her free and full personal consent in a form and under conditions prescribed by law. In this connection, the Committee wishes to note that such legal provisions must be compatible with the full exercise of the other rights guaranteed by the Covenant; thus, for instance, the right to freedom of thought, conscience and religion implies that the legislation of each State should provide for the possibility of both religious and civil marriages. In the Committee's view, however, for a State to require that a marriage, which is celebrated in accordance with religious rites, be conducted, affirmed or registered also under civil law is not incompatible with the Covenant. States are also requested to include information on this subject in their reports.

5. The right to found a family implies, in principle, the possibility to procreate and live together. When States parties adopt family planning policies, they should be compatible with the provisions of the Covenant and should, in particular, not be discriminatory or compulsory. Similarly, the possibility to live together implies the adoption of appropriate measures, both at the internal level and as the case may be, in cooperation with other States, to ensure the unity or reunification of families, particularly when their members are separated for political, economic or similar reasons.

6. Article 23, paragraph 4, of the Covenant provides that States parties shall take appropriate steps to ensure equality of rights and responsibilities of spouses as to marriage, during marriage and at its dissolution.

With regard to equality as to marriage, the Committee wishes to note in particular that no sex-based discrimination should occur in respect of the acquisition or loss of nationality by reason of marriage. Likewise, the right of each spouse to retain the use of his or her original family name or to participate on an equal basis in the choice of a new family name should be safeguarded.

During marriage, the spouses should have equal rights and responsibilities in the family. This equality extends to all matters arising from their relationship, such as choice of residence, running of the household, education of the children and administration of assets. Such equality continues to be applicable to arrangements regarding legal separation or dissolution of the marriage.

Thus, any discriminatory treatment in regard to the grounds and procedures for separation or divorce, child custody, maintenance or alimony, visiting rights or the loss or recovery of parental authority must be prohibited, bearing in mind the paramount interest of the children in this connection. States parties should, in particular, include information in their reports concerning the provision made for the necessary protection of any children at the dissolution of a marriage or on the separation of the spouses.

*GENERAL COMMENT 20: Article 7 (44th session, 1992).* 1. This general comment replaces general comment 7 (the sixteenth session, 1982) reflecting and further developing it.

2. The aim of the provisions of article 7 of the International Covenant on Civil and Political Rights is to protect

both the dignity and the physical and mental integrity of the individual. It is the duty of the State party to afford everyone protection through legislative and other measures as may be necessary against the acts prohibited by article 7, whether inflicted by people acting in their official capacity, outside their official capacity or in a private capacity. The prohibition in article 7 is complemented by the positive requirements of article 10, paragraph 1, of the Covenant, which stipulates that "All persons deprived of their liberty shall be treated with humanity and with respect for the inherent dignity of the human person".

3. The text of article 7 allows no limitation. The Committee also reaffirms that, even in situations of public emergency such as those referred to in article 4 of the Covenant, no derogation from the provision of article 7 is allowed and its provisions must remain in force. The Committee likewise observes that no justification or extenuating circumstances may be invoked to excuse a violation of article 7 for any reasons, including those based on an order from a superior officer or public authority.

4. The Covenant does not contain any definition of the concepts covered by article 7, nor does the Committee consider it necessary to draw up a list of prohibited acts or to establish sharp distinctions between the different kinds of punishment or treatment; the distinctions depend on the nature, purpose and severity of the treatment applied.

5. The prohibition in article 7 relates not only to acts that cause physical pain but also to acts that cause mental suffering to the victim. In the Committee's view, moreover, the prohibition must extend to corporal punishment, including excessive chastisement ordered as punishment for a crime or as an educative or disciplinary measure. It is appropriate to emphasize in this regard that article 7 protects, in particular, children, pupils and patients in teaching and medical institutions.

6. The Committee notes that prolonged solitary confinement of the detained or imprisoned person may amount to acts prohibited by article 7. As the Committee has stated in its general comment No. 6 (16), article 6 of the Covenant refers generally to abolition of the death penalty in terms that strongly suggest that abolition is desirable. Moreover, when the death penalty is applied by a State party for the most serious crimes, it must not only be strictly limited in accordance with article 6 but it must be carried out in such a way as to cause the least possible physical and mental suffering.

7. Article 7 expressly prohibits medical or scientific experimentation without the free consent of the person concerned. The Committee notes that the reports of States parties generally contain little information on this point. More attention should be given to the need and means to ensure observance of this provision. The Committee also observes that special protection in regard to such experiments is necessary in the case of persons not capable of giving valid consent, and in particular those under any form of detention or imprisonment. Such persons should not be subjected to any medical or scientific experimentation that may be detrimental to their health.

8. The Committee notes that it is not sufficient for the implementation of article 7 to prohibit such treatment or punishment or to make it a crime. States parties should inform the Committee of the legislative, administrative, judicial and other measures they take to prevent and punish acts of torture and cruel, inhuman and degrading treatment in any territory under their jurisdiction.

9. In the view of the Committee, States parties must not expose individuals to the danger of torture or cruel, inhu-man or degrading treatment or punishment upon return to another country by way of their extradition, expulsion or refoulement. States parties should indicate in their reports what measures they have adopted to that end.

10. The Committee should be informed how States parties disseminate, to the population at large, relevant information concerning the ban on torture and the treatment prohibited by article 7. Enforcement personnel, medical personnel, police officers and any other persons involved in the custody or treatment of any individual subjected to any form of arrest, detention or imprisonment must receive appropriate instruction and training. States parties should inform the Committee of the instruction and training given and the way in which the prohibition of article 7 forms an integral part of the operational rules and ethical standards to be followed by such persons.

11. In addition to describing steps to provide the general protection against acts prohibited under article 7 to which anyone is entitled, the State party should provide detailed information on safeguards for the special protection of particularly vulnerable persons. It should be noted that keeping under systematic review interrogation rules, instructions, methods and practices as well as arrangements for the custody and treatment of persons subjected to any form of arrest, detention or imprisonment is an effective means of preventing cases of torture and ill-treatment. To guarantee the effective protection of detained persons, provisions should be made for detainees to be held in places officially recognized as places of detention and for their names and places of detention, as well as for the names of persons responsible for their detention, to be kept in registers readily available and accessible to those concerned, including relatives and friends. To the same effect, the time and place of all interrogations should be recorded, together with the names of all those present and this information should also be available for purposes of judicial or administrative proceedings. Provisions should also be made against incommunicado detention. In that connection, States parties should ensure that any places of detention be free from any equipment liable to be used for inflicting torture or ill-treatment. The protection of the detainee also requires that prompt and regular access be given to doctors and lawyers and, under appropriate supervision when the investigation so requires, to family members.

12. It is important for the discouragement of violations under article 7 that the law must prohibit the use of admissibility in judicial proceedings of statements or confessions obtained through torture or other prohibited treatment.

13. States parties should indicate when presenting their reports the provisions of their criminal law which penalize torture and cruel, inhuman and degrading treatment or punishment, specifying the penalties applicable to such acts, whether committed by public officials or other persons acting on behalf of the State, or by private persons. Those who violate article 7, whether by encouraging, ordering, tolerating or perpetrating prohibited acts, must be held responsible. Consequently, those who have refused to obey orders must not be punished or subjected to any adverse treatment.

14. Article 7 should be read in conjunction with article 2, paragraph 3, of the Covenant. In their reports, States parties should indicate how their legal system effectively guarantees the immediate termination of all the acts prohibited by article 7 as well as appropriate redress. The right to lodge complaints against maltreatment prohibited by article 7 must be recognized in the domestic law. Complaints must be investigated promptly and impartially by competent authorities

so as to make the remedy effective. The reports of States parties should provide specific information on the remedies available to victims of maltreatment and the procedure that complainants must follow, and statistics on the number of complaints and how they have been dealt with.

15. The Committee has noted that some States have granted amnesty in respect of acts of torture. Amnesties are generally incompatible with the duty of states to investigate such acts; to guarantee freedom from such acts within their jurisdiction; and to ensure that they do not occur in the future. States may not deprive individuals of the right to an effective remedy, including compensation and such full rehabilitation as may be possible.

*GENERAL COMMENT 21: Article 10 (Forty-fourth session, 1992)*. 1. This general comment replaces general comment 9 (the sixteenth session, 1982) reflecting and further developing it.

2. Article 10, paragraph 1, of the International Covenant on Civil and Political Rights applies to any one deprived of liberty under the laws and authority of the State who is held in prisons, hospitals—particularly psychiatric hospitals—detention camps or correctional institutions or elsewhere. States parties should ensure that the principle stipulated therein is observed in all institutions and establishments within their jurisdiction where persons are being held.

3. Article 10, paragraph 1, imposes on States parties a positive obligation towards persons who are particularly vulnerable because of their status as persons deprived of liberty, and complements for them the ban on torture or other cruel, inhuman or degrading treatment or punishment contained in article 7 of the Covenant. Thus, not only may persons deprived of their liberty not be subjected to treatment that is contrary to article 7, including medical or scientific experimentation, but neither may they be subjected to any hardship or constraint other than that resulting from the deprivation of liberty; respect for the dignity of such persons must be guaranteed under the same conditions as for that of free persons. Persons deprived of their liberty enjoy all the rights set forth in the Covenant, subject to the restrictions that are unavoidable in a closed environment.

4. Treating all persons deprived of their liberty with humanity and with respect for their dignity is a fundamental and universally applicable rule. Consequently, the application of this rule, as a minimum, cannot be dependent on the material resources available in the State party. This rule must be applied without distinction of any kind, such as race, colour, sex, language, religion, political or other opinion, national or social origin, property, birth or other status.

5. States parties are invited to indicate in their reports to what extent they are applying the relevant United Nations standards applicable to the treatment of prisoners: the Standard Minimum Rules for the Treatment of Prisoners (1957), the Body of Principles for the Protection of All Persons under Any Form of Detention or Imprisonment (1988), the Code of Conduct for Law Enforcement Officials (1978) and the Principles of Medical Ethics relevant to the Role of Health Personnel, particularly Physicians, in the Protection of Prisoners and Detainees against Torture and Other Cruel, Inhuman or Degrading Treatment or Punishment (1982).

6. The Committee recalls the provisions that have a bearing on the national legislative and administrative provisions that have a bearing on the right provided for in article 10, paragraph 1. The Committee also considers that it is necessary for reports to specify what concrete measures have been taken by the competent authorities to monitor the effective application of the rules regarding the treatment of persons deprived of their liberty. States parties should include in their reports information concerning the system for supervising penitentiary establishments, the specific measures to prevent torture and cruel, inhuman or degrading treatment, and how impartial supervision is ensured.

7. Furthermore, the Committee recalls that reports should indicate whether the various applicable provisions form an integral part of the instruction and training of the personnel who have authority over persons deprived of their liberty and whether they are strictly adhered to by such personnel in the discharge of their duties. It would also be appropriate to specify whether arrested or detained persons have access to such information and have effective legal means enabling them to ensure that those rules are respected, to complain if the rules are ignored and to obtain adequate compensation in the event of a violation.

8. The Committee recalls that the principle set forth in article 10, paragraph 1, constitutes the basis for the more specific obligations of States parties in respect of criminal justice, which are set forth in article 10, paragraphs 2 and 3.

9. Article 10, paragraph 2 (a), provides for the segregation, save in exceptional circumstances, of accused persons from convicted ones. Such segregation is required in order to emphasize their status as unconvicted persons who at the same time enjoy the right to be presumed innocent as stated in article 14, paragraph 2. The reports of States parties should indicate how the separation of accused persons from convicted persons is effected and explain how the treatment of accused persons differs from that of convicted persons.

10. As to article 10, paragraph 3, which concerns convicted persons, the Committee wishes to have detailed information on the operation of the penitentiary system of the State party. No penitentiary system should be only retributory; it should essentially seek the reformation and social rehabilitation of the prisoner. States parties are invited to specify whether they have a system to provide assistance after release and to give information as to its success.

11. In a number of cases, the information furnished by the State party contains no specific reference either to legislative or administrative provisions or to practical measures to ensure the re-education of convicted persons. The Committee requests specific information concerning the measures taken to provide teaching, education and re-education, vocational guidance and training and also concerning work programmes for prisoners inside the penitentiary establishment as well as outside.

12. In order to determine whether the principle set forth in article 10, paragraph 3, is being fully respected, the Committee also requests information on the specific measures applied during detention, e.g., how convicted persons are dealt with individually and how they are categorized, the disciplinary system, solitary confinement and high-security detention and the conditions under which contacts are ensured with the outside world (family, lawyer, social and medical services, nongovernmental organizations).

13. Moreover, the Committee notes that in the reports of some States parties no information has been provided concerning the treatment accorded to accused juvenile persons and juvenile offenders. Article 10, paragraph 2 (b), provides that accused juvenile persons shall be separated from adults. The information given in reports shows that some States parties are not paying the necessary attention to the fact that this is a mandatory provision of the Covenant. The text also provides that cases involving juveniles must be considered as speedily as possible. Reports should specify the measures taken by States parties to give effect to that provision. Lastly,

under article 10, paragraph 3, juvenile offenders shall be segregated from adults and be accorded treatment appropriate to their age and legal status in so far as conditions of detention are concerned, such as shorter working hours and contact with relatives, with the aim of furthering their reformation and rehabilitation. Article 10 does not indicate any limits of juvenile age. While this is to be determined by each State party in the light of relevant social, cultural and other conditions, the Committee is of the opinion that article 6, paragraph 5, suggests that all persons under the age of 18 should be treated as juveniles, at least in matters relating to criminal justice. States should give relevant information about the age groups of persons treated as juveniles. In that regard, States parties are invited to indicate whether they are applying the United Nations Standard Minimum Rules for the Administration of Juvenile Justice, known as the Beijing Rules (1987).

*GENERAL COMMENT 22: Article 18 (48th session 1993).* 1. The right to freedom of thought, conscience and religion (which includes the freedom to hold beliefs) in article 18.1 is far-reaching and profound; it encompasses freedom of thought on all matters, personal conviction and the commitment to religion or belief, whether manifested individually or in community with others. The Committee draws the attention of States parties to the fact that the freedom of thought and the freedom of conscience are protected equally with the freedom of religion and belief. The fundamental character of these freedoms is also reflected in the fact that this provision cannot be derogated from, even in time of public emergency, as stated in article 4.2 of the Covenant.

2. Article 18 protects theistic, non-theistic and atheistic beliefs, as well as the right not to profess any religion or belief. The terms "belief" and "religion" are to be broadly construed. Article 18 is not limited in its application to traditional religions or to religions and beliefs with institutional characteristics or practices analogous to those of traditional religions. The Committee therefore views with concern any tendency to discriminate against any religion or belief for any reason, including the fact that they are newly established, or represent religious minorities that may be the subject of hostility on the part of a predominant religious community.

3. Article 18 distinguishes the freedom of thought, conscience, religion or belief from the freedom to manifest religion or belief. It does not permit any limitations whatsoever on the freedom of thought and conscience or on the freedom to have or adopt a religion or belief of one's choice. These freedoms are protected unconditionally, as is the right of everyone to hold opinions without interference in article 19.1. In accordance with articles 18.2 and 17, no one can be compelled to reveal his thoughts or adherence to a religion or belief.

4. The freedom to manifest religion or belief may be exercised "either individually or in community with others and in public or private". The freedom to manifest religion or belief in worship, observance, practice and teaching encompasses a broad range of acts. The concept of worship extends to ritual and ceremonial acts giving direct expression to belief, as well as various practices integral to such acts, including the building of places of worship, the use of ritual formulae and objects, the display of symbols, and the observance of holidays and days of rest. The observance and practice of religion or belief may include not only ceremonial acts but also such customs as the observance of dietary regulations, the wearing of distinctive clothing or head coverings, participation in rituals associated with certain stages

of life, and the use of a particular language customarily spoken by a group. In addition, the practice and teaching of religion or belief includes acts integral to the conduct by religious groups of their basic affairs, such as the freedom to choose their religious leaders, priests and teachers, the freedom to establish seminaries or religious schools and the freedom to prepare and distribute religious texts or publications.

5. The Committee observes that the freedom to "have or to adopt" a religion or belief necessarily entails the freedom to choose a religion or belief, including the right to replace one's current religion or belief with another or to adopt atheistic views, as well as the right to retain one's religion or belief. Article 18.2 bars coercion that would impair the right to have or adopt a religion or belief, including the use of threat of physical force or penal sanctions to compel believers or non-believers to adhere to their religious beliefs and congregations, to recant their religion or belief or to convert. Policies or practices having the same intention or effect, such as, for example, those restricting access to education, medical care, employment or the rights guaranteed by article 25 and other provisions of the Covenant, are similarly inconsistent with article 18.2. The same protection is enjoyed by holders of all beliefs of a non-religious nature.

6. The Committee is of the view that article 18.4 permits public school instruction in subjects such as the general history of religions and ethics if it is given in a neutral and objective way. The liberty of parents or legal guardians to ensure that their children receive a religious and moral education in conformity with their own convictions, set forth in article 18.4, is related to the guarantees of the freedom to teach a religion or belief stated in article 18.1. The Committee notes that public education that includes instruction in a particular religion or belief is inconsistent with article 18.4 unless provision is made for non-discriminatory exemptions or alternatives that would accommodate the wishes of parents and guardians.

7. In accordance with article 20, no manifestation of religion or belief may amount to propaganda for war or advocacy of national, racial or religious hatred that constitutes incitement to discrimination, hostility or violence. As stated by the Committee in its General Comment 11 [19], States parties are under the obligation to enact laws to prohibit such acts.

8. Article 18.3 permits restrictions on the freedom to manifest religion or belief only if limitations are prescribed by law and are necessary to protect public safety, order, health or morals, or the fundamental rights and freedoms of others. The freedom from coercion to have or to adopt a religion or belief and the liberty of parents and guardians to ensure religious and moral education cannot be restricted. In interpreting the scope of permissible limitation clauses, States parties should proceed from the need to protect the rights guaranteed under the Covenant, including the right to equality and non-discrimination on all grounds specified in articles 2, 3 and 26. Limitations imposed must be established by law and must not be applied in a manner that would vitiate the rights guaranteed in article 18. The Committee observes that paragraph 3 of article 18 is to be strictly interpreted: restrictions are not allowed on grounds not specified there, even if they would be allowed as restrictions to other rights protected in the Covenant, such as national security. Limitations may be applied only for those purposes for which they were prescribed and must be directly related and proportionate to the specific need on which they are predicated. Restrictions may not be imposed for discrimi-

natory purposes or applied in a discriminatory manner. The Committee observes that the concept of morals derives from many social, philosophical and religious traditions; consequently, limitations on the freedom to manifest a religion or belief for the purpose of protecting morals must be based on principles not deriving exclusively from a single tradition. Persons already subject to certain legitimate constraints, such as prisoners, continue to enjoy their rights to manifest their religion or belief to the fullest extent compatible with the specific nature of the constraint. States parties' reports should provide information on the full scope and effects of limitations under article 18.3, both as a matter of law and of their application in specific circumstances.

9. The fact that a religion is recognized as a state religion or that it is established as official or traditional or that its followers comprise the majority of the population, shall not result in any impairment of the enjoyment of any of the rights under the Covenant, including articles 18 and 27, nor in any discrimination against adherents to other religions or non-believers. In particular, certain measures discriminating against the latter, such as measures restricting eligibility for government service to members of the predominant religion or giving economic privileges to them or imposing special restrictions on the practice of other faiths, are not in accordance with the prohibition of discrimination based on religion or belief and the guarantee of equal protection under article 26. The measures contemplated by article 20, paragraph 2 of the Covenant constitute important safeguards against infringement of the rights of religious minorities and of other religious groups to exercise the rights guaranteed by articles 18 and 27, and against acts of violence or persecution directed towards those groups. The Committee wishes to be informed of measures taken by States parties concerned to protect the practices of all religions or beliefs from infringement and to protect their followers from discrimination. Similarly, information as to respect for the rights of religious minorities under article 27 is necessary for the Committee to assess the extent to which the right to freedom of thought, conscience, religion and belief has been implemented by States parties. States parties concerned should also include in their reports information relating to practices considered by their laws and jurisprudence to be punishable as blasphemous.

10. If a set of beliefs is treated as official ideology in constitutions, statutes, proclamations of ruling parties, etc., or in actual practice, this shall not result in any impairment of the freedoms under article 18 or any other rights recognized under the Covenant nor in any discrimination against persons who do not accept the official ideology or who oppose it.

11. Many individuals have claimed the right to refuse to perform military service (conscientious objection) on the basis that such right derives from their freedoms under article 18. In response to such claims, a growing number of States have in their laws exempted from compulsory military service citizens who genuinely hold religious or other beliefs that forbid the performance of military service and replaced it with alternative national service. The Covenant does not explicitly refer to a right to conscientious objection, but the Committee believes that such a right can be derived from article 18, inasmuch as the obligation to use lethal force may seriously conflict with the freedom of conscience and the right to manifest one's religion or belief. When this right is recognized by law or practice, there shall be no differentiation among conscientious objectors on the basis of the nature of their particular beliefs; likewise, there shall be no discrimination against conscientious objectors because they

have failed to perform military service. The Committee invites States parties to report on the conditions under which persons can be exempted from military service on the basis of their rights under article 18 and on the nature and length of alternative national service.

*GENERAL COMMENT 23: Article 27 (50th session, 1994).* 1. Article 27 of the Covenant provides that, in those States in which ethnic, religious or linguistic minorities exist, persons belonging to these minorities shall not be denied the right, in community with the other members of their group, to enjoy their own culture, to profess and practise their own religion, or to use their own language. The Committee observes that this article establishes and recognizes a right which is conferred on individuals belonging to minority groups and which is distinct from, and additional to, all the other rights which, as individuals in common with everyone else, they are already entitled to enjoy under the Covenant.

2. In some communications submitted to the Committee under the Optional Protocol, the right protected under article 27 has been confused with the right of peoples to self-determination proclaimed in article 1 of the Covenant. Further, in reports submitted by States parties under article 40 of the Covenant, the obligations placed upon States parties under article 27 have sometimes been confused with their duty under article 2.1 to ensure the enjoyment of the rights guaranteed under the Covenant without discrimination and also with equality before the law and equal protection of the law under article 26.

3.1. The Covenant draws a distinction between the right to self-determination rights protected under article 27. The former is expressed to be a right belonging to peoples and the Covenant. Self-determination is not a right cognizable under the Optional Protocol. Article 27, on the other hand, relates to rights conferred on individuals as such and is included, like the articles relating to other personal rights conferred on individuals, in Part III of the Covenant and is cognizable under the Optional Protocol. See *Official Records of the General Assembly, Thirty-ninth Session, Supplement No. 40* (A/39/40), annex VI, General Comment No. 12 (21) (article 1), also issued in document CCPR/C/21/Rev.1; ibid., *Forty-fifth Session, Supplement No. 40,* (A/45/40), vol. II, annex IX, sect. A, Communication No. 167/1984 (*Bernard Ominayak, Chief of the Lubicon Lake Band v. Canada*), views adopted on 26 March 1990.

3.2. The enjoyment of the rights to which article 27 relates does not prejudice the sovereignty and territorial integrity of a State party. At the same time, one or other aspect of the rights of individuals protected under that article—for example, to enjoy a particular culture—may consist in a way of life which is closely associated with territory and use of its resources. (See ibid., *Forty-third Session, Supplement No. 40* [A/43/40], annex VII, sect. G, Communication No. 197/1985 [*Kitok v. Sweden*], views adopted on 27 July 1988.) This may particularly be true of members of indigenous communities constituting a minority.

4. The Covenant also distinguishes the rights protected under article 27 from the guarantees under articles 2.1 and 26. The entitlement, under article 2.1, to enjoy the rights under the Covenant without discrimination applies to all individuals within the territory or under the jurisdiction of the state whether or not those persons belong to a minority. In addition, there is a distinct right provided under article 26 for equality before the law, equal protection of the law, and non-discrimination in respect of rights granted and obligations imposed by the States. It governs the exercise of all rights, whether protected under the Covenant or not, which

the State party confers by law on individuals within its territory or under its jurisdiction, irrespective of whether they belong to the minorities specified in article 27 or not. (See ibid., *Forty-second Session. Supplement No. 40* [A/42/40], annex VIII, sect. D, Communication No. 182/1984 [*F.H. Zwaan-de Vries v. the Netherlands*], views adopted on 9 April 1987; ibid., sect. C, Communication No. 180/1984 [*L.G. Danning v. the Netherlands*], views adopted on 9 April 1987.) Some States parties who claim that they do not discriminate on grounds of ethnicity, language or religion, wrongly contend, on that basis alone, that they have no minorities.

5.1. The terms used in article 27 indicate that the persons designed to be protected are those who belong to a group and who share in common a culture, a religion and/or a language. Those terms also indicate that the individuals designed to be protected need not be citizens of the State party. In this regard, the obligations deriving from article 2.1 are also relevant, since a State party is required under that article to ensure that the rights protected under the Covenant are available to all individuals within its territory and subject to its jurisdiction, except rights which are expressly made to apply to citizens, for example, political rights under article 25. A State party may not, therefore, restrict the rights under article 27 to its citizens alone.

5.2. Article 27 confers rights on persons belonging to minorities which "exist" in a State party. Given the nature and scope of the rights envisaged under that article, it is not relevant to determine the degree of permanence that the term "exist" connotes. Those rights simply are that individuals belonging to those minorities should not be denied the right, in community with members of their group, to enjoy their own culture, to practise their religion and speak their language. Just as they need not be nationals or citizens, they need not be permanent residents. Thus, migrant workers or even visitors in a State party constituting such minorities are entitled not to be denied the exercise of those rights. As any other individual in the territory of the State party, they would, also for this purpose, have the general rights, for example, to freedom of association, of assembly, and of expression. The existence of an ethnic, religious or linguistic minority in a given State party does not depend upon a decision by that State party but requires to be established by objective criteria.

5.3. The right of individuals belonging to a linguistic minority to use their language among themselves, in private or in public, is distinct from other language rights protected under the Covenant. In particular, it should be distinguished from the general right to freedom of expression protected under article 19. The latter right is available to all persons, irrespective of whether they belong to minorities or not. Further, the right protected under article 27 should be distinguished from the particular right which article 14.3 (f) of the Covenant confers on accused persons to interpretation where they cannot understand or speak the language used in the courts. Article 14.3 (f) does not, in any other circumstances, confer on accused persons the right to use or speak the language of their choice in court proceedings. See ibid., *Forty-fifth Session, Supplement No. 40,* (A/45/40), vol. II, annex X, sect. A, Communication No. 220/1987 (*T.K. v. France*), decision of 8 November 1989; ibid., sect. B, Communication No. 222/1987 (*M.K. v. France*), decision of 8 November 1989.

6.1. Although article 27 is expressed in negative terms, that article, nevertheless, does recognize the existence of a "right" and requires that it shall not be denied. Consequently, a State party is under an obligation to ensure that the existence and the exercise of this right are protected against their denial or violation. Positive measures of protection are, therefore, required not only against the acts of the State party itself, whether through its legislative, judicial or administrative authorities, but also against the acts of other persons within the State party.

6.2. Although the rights protected under article 27 are individual rights, they depend in turn on the ability of the minority group to maintain its culture, language or religion. Accordingly, positive measures by States may also be necessary to protect the identity of a minority and the rights of its members to enjoy and develop their culture and language and to practise their religion, in community with the other members of the group. In this connection, it has to be observed that such positive measures must respect the provisions of articles 2.1 and 26 of the Covenant both as regards the treatment between different minorities and the treatment between the persons belonging to them and the remaining part of the population. However, as long as those measures are aimed at correcting conditions which prevent or impair the enjoyment of the rights guaranteed under article 27, they may constitute a legitimate differentiation under the Covenant, provided that they are based on reasonable and objective criteria.

7. With regard to the exercise of the cultural rights protected under article 27, the Committee observes that culture manifests itself in many forms, including a particular way of life associated with the use of land resources, especially in the case of indigenous peoples. That right may include such traditional activities as fishing or hunting and the right to live in reserves protected by law. (See notes 1 and 2 above, Communication No. 167/1984 [*Bernard Ominavak, Chief of the Lubicon Lake Band v. Canada*], views adopted on 26 March 1990, and Communication No. 197/1985 [*Kitok v. Sweden*], views adopted on 27 July 1988.) The enjoyment of those rights may require positive legal measures of protection and measures to ensure the effective participation of members of minority communities in decisions which affect them.

8. The Committee observes that none of the rights protected under article 27 of the Covenant may be legitimately exercised in a manner or to an extent inconsistent with the other provisions of the Covenant.

9. The Committee concludes that article 27 relates to rights whose protection imposes specific obligations on States parties. The protection of these rights is directed towards ensuring the survival and continued development of the cultural, religious and social identity of the minorities concerned, thus enriching the fabric of society as a whole. Accordingly, the Committee observes that these rights must be protected as such and should not be confused with other personal rights conferred on one and all under the Covenant. States parties, therefore, have an obligation to ensure that the exercise of these rights is fully protected and they should indicate in their reports the measures they have adopted to this end.

***BIBLIOGRAPHY.*** Bok, Marcia. *Civil Rights and the Social Programs of the 1960s: The Social Justice Functions of Social Policy.* Westport, CT, USA: Praeger, 1992. Scholarly monograph, in English; bibliography, pp. 161–172.

Claude, Richard Pierre, and B. H. Weston, eds. *Human Rights in the World Community: Issues and Action.* Philadelphia, PA, USA: University of Pennsylvania Press, 1992. Collection of scholarly articles, in English.

Cohn, Cindy A. "The Early Harvest: Domestic Legal Changes Related to the Human Rights Committee and the Covenant on Civil and Political Rights," *Human Rights Quar-*

*terly* 13, no. 3 (Aug. 1991): 295–321. Scholarly article, in English.

Eide, Asbjorn, and Jan Helgesen, eds. *The Future of Human Rights Protection in a Changing World: Fifty Years Since the Four Freedoms Address—Essays in Honour of Torkel Opsahl.* Oslo, Norway: Norwegian University Press (Universitetsforlaget), 1991. Collection of scholarly articles, in English.

Mahoney, Kathleen E., and Paul Mahoney, eds. *Human Rights in the Twenty-First Century: A Global Challenge.* Dordrecht, the Netherlands: Martinus Nijhoff, 1993. Scholarly monograph, in English.

Nowak, Manfred. *CCPR Commentary: Commentary on the UN Covenant on Civil and Political Rights.* Arlington, VA, USA, and Kehl am Rhein, Germany: N.P. Engel, 1993. Scholarly monograph, in English.

Pathak, R. S., and R. P. Dhokalia, eds. *International Law in Transition: Essays in Memory of Judge Nagendra Singh.* New Delhi, India, and Dordrecht, the Netherlands: Lancer Books and Martinus Nijhoff Publishers, on behalf of the Indian Society of International Law, 1992. Collective scholarly works, in English.

Rosas, Allan. *The Strength of Diversity: Human Rights and Pluralist Democracy.* Dordrecht, the Netherlands: Martinus Nijhoff, 1992. Scholarly monograph, in English.

Sieghart, Paul. *An Introduction to the International Covenants on Human Rights.* Paper prepared for the Commonwealth Secretariat. London: 1988. Article, in English.

**INTERNATIONAL COVENANT ON ECONOMIC, SOCIAL AND CULTURAL RIGHTS (1966).** The Covenant is the second instrument—after the **UNIVERSAL DECLARATION OF HUMAN RIGHTS**—constituting the **INTERNATIONAL BILL OF HUMAN RIGHTS,** the third, fourth, and fifth being the **INTERNATIONAL COVENANT ON CIVIL AND POLITICAL RIGHTS** and the two Optional Protocols to that Covenant, respectively.

The Covenant defines the economic, social, and cultural rights which it aims to protect and the permissible limitations on the enjoyment of those rights and authorizes the United Nations **ECONOMIC AND SOCIAL COUNCIL** to monitor the implementation of its provisions. The Council established the **COMMITTEE ON ECONOMIC, SOCIAL AND CULTURAL RIGHTS** to assist it in this task.

The Covenant was adopted by the UN **GENERAL ASSEMBLY** on 16 December 1966 (resolution 2200 A [XXI]), and entered into force on 3 January 1976. The text, annexed to that resolution, is as follows:

### Preamble

The States Parties to the present Covenant,

Considering that, in accordance with the principles proclaimed in the Charter of the United Nations, recognition of the inherent dignity and of the equal and inalienable rights of all members of the human family is the foundation of freedom, justice and peace in the world,

Recognizing that these rights derive from the inherent dignity of the human person,

Recognizing that, in accordance with the Universal Declaration of Human Rights, the ideal of free human beings enjoying freedom from fear and want can only be achieved if conditions are created whereby everyone may enjoy his economic, social and cultural rights, as well as his civil and political rights,

Considering the obligation of States under the Charter of the United Nations to promote universal respect for, and observance of, human rights and freedoms,

Realizing that the individual, having duties to other individuals and to the community to which he belongs, is under a responsibility to strive for the promotion and observances of the rights recognized in the present Covenant,

Agree upon the following articles:

### Part I

*Article 1.* 1. All peoples have the right of self-determination. By virtue of that right they freely determine their political status and freely pursue their economic, social and cultural development.

2. All peoples may, for their own ends, freely dispose of their natural wealth and resources without prejudice to any obligations arising out of international economic co-operation, based upon the principle of mutual benefit, and international law. In no case may a people be deprived of its own means of subsistence.

3. The States Parties to the present Covenant, including those having responsibility for the administration of Non-Self-Governing and Trust Territories, shall promote the realization of the right of self-determination, and shall respect that right, in conformity with the provisions of the Charter of the United Nations.

### Part II

*Article 2.* 1. Each State Party to the present Covenant undertakes to take steps, individually and through international assistance and co-operation, especially economic and technical, to the maximum of its available resources, with a view to achieving progressively the full realization of the rights recognized in the present Covenant by all appropriate means, including particularly the adoption of legislative measures.

2. The States Parties to the present Covenant undertake to guarantee that the rights enunciated in the present Covenant will be exercised without discrimination of any kind as to race, colour, sex, language, religion, political or other opinion, national or social origin, property, birth or other status.

3. Developing countries, with due regard to human rights and their national economy, may determine to what extent they would guarantee the economic rights recognized in the present Covenant to non-nationals.

*Article 3.* The States Parties to the present Covenant undertake to ensure the equal right of men and women to the enjoyment of all economic, social and cultural rights set forth in the present Covenant.

*Article 4.* The States Parties to the present Covenant recognize that, in the enjoyment of those rights provided by the State in conformity with the present Covenant, the State may subject such rights only to such limitations as are determined by law only in so far as this may be compatible with the nature of these rights and solely for the purpose of promoting the general welfare in a democratic society.

*Article 5.* 1. Nothing in the present Covenant may be interpreted as implying for any State, group or person any right to engage in any activity or to perform any act aimed at the destruction of any of the rights or freedoms recognized herein, or at their limitation to a greater extent than is provided for in the present Covenant.

2. No restriction upon or derogation from any of the fundamental human rights recognized or existing in any country in virtue of law, conventions, regulations or custom shall be admitted on the pretext that the present Covenant does not recognize such rights or that it recognizes them to a lesser extent.

## Part III

*Article 6.* 1. The States Parties to the present Covenant recognize the right to work, which includes the right of everyone to the opportunity to gain his living by work which he freely chooses or accepts, and will take appropriate steps to safeguard this right.

2. The steps to be taken by a State Party to the present Covenant to achieve the full realization of this right shall include technical and vocational guidance and training programmes, policies and techniques to achieve steady economic, social and cultural development and full and productive employment under conditions safeguarding fundamental political and economic freedoms to the individual.

*Article 7.* The States Parties to the present Covenant recognize the right of everyone to the enjoyment of just and favourable conditions of work which ensure, in particular:

(a) Remuneration which provides all workers, as a minimum, with:

(i) Fair wages and equal remuneration for work of equal value without distinction of any kind, in particular women being guaranteed conditions of work not inferior to those enjoyed by men, with equal pay for equal work;

(ii) A decent living for themselves and their families in accordance with the provisions of the present Covenant;

(b) Safe and healthy working conditions;

(c) Equal opportunity for everyone to be promoted in his employment to an appropriate higher level, subject to no considerations other than those of seniority and competence;

(d) Rest, leisure and reasonable limitation of working hours and periodic holidays with pay, as well as remuneration for public holidays.

*Article 8.* 1. The States Parties to the present Covenant undertake to ensure:

(a) The right of everyone to form trade unions and join the trade union of his choice, subject only to the rules of the organization concerned, for the promotion and protection of his economic and social interests. No restrictions may be placed on the exercise of this right other than those prescribed by law and which are necessary in a democratic society in the interests of national security or public order or for the protection of the rights and freedoms of others;

(b) The right of trade unions to establish national federations or confederations and the right of the latter to form or join international trade-union organizations;

(c) The right of trade unions to function freely subject to no limitations other than those prescribed by law and which are necessary in a democratic society in the interests of national security or public order or for the protection of the rights and freedoms of others;

(d) The right to strike, provided that it is exercised in conformity with the laws of the particular country.

2. This article shall not prevent the imposition of lawful restrictions on the exercise of these rights by members of the armed forces or of the police or of the administration of the State.

3. Nothing in this article shall authorize States Parties to the International Labour Organisation Convention of 1948 concerning Freedom of Association and Protection of the Right to Organize to take legislative measures which would prejudice, or apply the law in such a manner as would prejudice, the guarantees provided for in that Convention.

*Article 9.* The States Parties to the present Covenant recognize the right of everyone to social security, including social insurance.

*Article 10.* The States Parties to the present Covenant recognize that:

1. The widest possible protection and assistance should be accorded to the family, which is the natural and fundamental group unit of society, particularly for its establishment and while it is responsible for the care and education of dependent children. Marriage must be entered into with the free consent of the intending spouses.

2. Special protection should be accorded to mothers during a reasonable period before and after childbirth. During such period working mothers should be accorded paid leave or leave with adequate social security benefits.

3. Special measures of protection and assistance should be taken on behalf of all children and young persons without any discrimination for reasons of parentage or other conditions. Children and young persons should be protected from economic and social exploitation. Their employment in work harmful to their morals or health or dangerous to life or likely to hamper their normal development should be punishable by law. States should also set age limits below which the paid employment of child labour should be prohibited and punishable by law.

*Article 11.* 1. The States Parties to the present Covenant recognize the rights of everyone to an adequate standard of living for himself and his family, including adequate food, clothing and housing, and to the continuous improvement of living conditions. The States Parties will take appropriate steps to ensure the realization of this right, recognizing to this effect the essential importance of international co-operation based on free consent.

2. The States Parties to the present Covenant, recognizing the fundamental right of everyone to be free from hunger, shall take, individually and through international co-operation, the measures, including specific programmes, which are needed:

(a) To improve methods of production, conservation and distribution of food by making full use of technical and scientific knowledge, by disseminating knowledge of the principles of nutrition and by developing or reforming agrarian systems in such a way as to achieve the most efficient development and utilization of natural resources;

(b) Taking into account the problems of both food-importing and food-exporting countries, to ensure an equitable distribution of world food supplies in relation to need.

*Article 12.* 1. The States Parties to the present Covenant recognize the right of everyone to the enjoyment of the highest attainable standard of physical and mental health.

2. The steps to be taken by the States Parties to the present Covenant to achieve the full realization of this right shall include those necessary for:

(a) The provision for the reduction of the stillbirthrate and of infant mortality and for the healthy development of the child;

(b) The improvement of all aspects of environmental and industrial hygiene;

(c) The prevention, treatment and control of epidemic, endemic, occupational and other diseases;

(d) The creation of conditions which would assure to all medical service and medical attention in the event of sickness.

*Article 13.* 1. The States Parties to the present Covenant recognize the right of everyone to education. They agree that education shall be directed to the full development of the human personality and the sense of its dignity, and shall strengthen the respect for human rights and fundamental freedoms. They further agree that education shall enable all persons to participate effectively in a free society, promote understanding, tolerance and friendship among all nations and all racial, ethnic or religious groups, and further the activities of the United Nations for the maintenance of peace.

2. The States Parties to the present Covenant recognize that, with a view to achieving the full realization of this right:

(a) Primary education shall be compulsory and available free to all;

(b) Secondary education in its different forms, including technical and vocational secondary education, shall be made generally available and accessible to all by every appropriate means, and in particular by the progressive introduction of free education;

(c) Higher education shall be made equally accessible to all, on the basis of capacity, by every appropriate means, and in particular by the progressive introduction of free education;

(d) Fundamental education shall be encouraged or intensified as far as possible for those persons who have not received or completed the whole period of their primary education;

(e) The development of a system of schools at all levels shall be actively pursued, an adequate fellowship system shall be established, and the material conditions of teaching staff shall be continuously improved.

3. The States Parties to the present Covenant undertake to have respect for the liberty of parents and, when applicable, legal guardians to choose for their children schools, other than those established by the public authorities, which conform to such minimum educational standards as may be laid down or approved by the State and to ensure the religious and moral education of their children in conformity with their own convictions.

4. No part of this article shall be construed so as to interfere with the liberty of individuals and bodies to establish and direct educational institutions, subject always to the observance of the principles set forth in paragraph 1 of this article and to the requirement that the education given in such institutions shall conform to such minimum standards as may be laid down by the State.

*Article 14.* Each State Party to the present Covenant which, at the time of becoming a Party, has not been able to secure in its metropolitan territory or other territories under its jurisdiction compulsory primary education, free of charge, undertakes, within two years, to work out and adopt a detailed plan of action for the progressive implementation, within a reasonable number of years, to be fixed in the plan, of the principle of compulsory education free of charge for all.

*Article 15.* 1. The States Parties to the present Covenant recognize the right of everyone:

(a) To take part in cultural life;

(b) To enjoy the benefits of scientific progress and its applications;

(c) To benefit from the protection of the moral and material interests resulting from any scientific, literary or artistic production of which he is the author.

2. The steps to be taken by the States Parties to the present Covenant to achieve the full realization of this right shall include those necessary for the conservation, the development and the diffusion of science and culture.

3. The States Parties to the present Covenant undertake to respect the freedom indispensable for scientific research and creative activity.

4. The States Parties to the present Covenant recognize the benefits to be derived from the encouragement and development of international contacts and co-operation in the scientific and cultural fields.

**Part IV**

*Article 16.* 1. The States Parties to the present Covenant undertake to submit in conformity with this part of the Covenant reports on the measures which they have adopted and the progress made in achieving the observance of the rights recognized herein.

2. (a) All reports shall be submitted to the Secretary-General of the United Nations, who shall transmit copies to the Economic and Social Council for consideration in accordance with the provisions of the present Covenant;

(b) The Secretary-General of the United Nations shall also transmit to the specialized agencies copies of the reports, or any relevant parts therefrom, from States Parties to the present Covenant which are also members of these specialized agencies in so far as these reports, or parts therefrom, relate to any matters which fall within the responsibilities of the said agencies in accordance with their constitutional instruments.

*Article 17.* 1. The States Parties to the present Covenant shall furnish their reports in stages, in accordance with a programme to be established by the Economic and Social Council within one year of the entry into force of the present Covenant after consultation with the States Parties and the specialized agencies concerned.

2. Reports may indicate factors and difficulties affecting the degree of fulfilment of obligations under the present Covenant.

3. Where relevant information has previously been furnished to the United Nations or to any specialized agency by any State Party to the present Covenant, it will not be necessary to reproduce that information, but a precise reference to the information so furnished will suffice.

*Article 18.* Pursuant to its responsibilities under the Charter of the United Nations in the field of human rights and fundamental freedoms, the Economic and Social Council may make arrangements with the specialized agencies in respect of their reporting to it on the progress made in achieving the observance of the provisions of the present Covenant falling within the scope of their activities. These reports may include particulars of decisions and recommendations on such implementation adopted by their competent organs.

*Article 19.* The Economic and Social Council may transmit to the Commission on Human Rights for study and general recommendation or, as appropriate, for information the reports concerning human rights submitted by States in accordance with articles 16 and 17, and those concerning human rights submitted by the specialized agencies in accordance with article 18.

*Article 20.* The States Parties to the present Covenant and the specialized agencies concerned may submit comments to the Economic and Social Council on any general recommendation under article 19 or reference to such general recommendation in any report of the Commission on Human Rights or any documentation referred to therein.

*Article 21.* The Economic and Social Council may submit from time to time to the General Assembly reports with recommendations of a general nature and a summary of the information received from the States Parties to the present Covenant and the specialized agencies on the measures taken and the progress made in achieving general observance of the rights recognized in the present Covenant.

*Article 22.* The Economic and Social Council may bring to the attention of other organs of the United Nations, their subsidiary organs and specialized agencies concerned with furnishing technical assistance any matters arising out of the reports referred to in this part of the present Covenant which may assist such bodies in deciding, each within its field of competence, on the advisability of international measures likely to contribute to the effective progressive implementation of the present Covenant.

*Article 23.* The States Parties to the present Covenant agree that international action for the achievement of the rights recognized in the present Covenant includes such methods as the conclusion of conventions, the adoption of recommendations, the furnishing of technical assistance and the holding of regional meetings and technical meetings for the purpose of consultation and study organized in conjunction with the Governments concerned.

*Article 24.* Nothing in the present Covenant shall be interpreted as impairing the provisions of the Charter of the United Nations and of the constitutions of the specialized agencies which define the respective responsibilities of the various organs of the United Nations and of the specialized agencies in regard to the matters dealt with in the present Covenant.

*Article 25.* Nothing in the present Covenant shall be interpreted as impairing the inherent right of all peoples to enjoy and utilize fully and freely their natural wealth and resources.

### Part V

*Article 26.* 1. The present Covenant is open for signature by any State Member of the United Nations or member of any of its specialized agencies, by any State Party to the Statute of the International Court of Justice, and by any other State which has been invited by the General Assembly of the United Nations to become a party to the present Covenant.

2. The present Covenant is subject to ratification. Instruments of ratification shall be deposited with the Secretary-General of the United Nations.

3. The present Covenant shall be open to accession by any State referred to in paragraph 1 of this article.

4. Accession shall be effected by the deposit of an instrument of accession with the Secretary-General of the United Nations.

5. The Secretary-General of the United Nations shall inform all States which have signed the present Covenant or acceded to it of the deposit of each instrument of ratification or accession.

*Article 27.* 1. The present Covenant shall enter into force three months after the date of the deposit with the Secretary-General of the United Nations of the thirty-fifth instrument of ratification or instrument of accession.

2. For each State ratifying the present Covenant or acceding to it after the deposit of the thirty-fifth instrument of ratification or instrument of accession, the present Covenant shall enter into force three months after the date of the deposit of its own instrument of ratification or instrument of accession.

*Article 28.* The provisions of the present Covenant shall extend to all parts of federal States without any limitations or exceptions.

*Article 29.* 1. Any State Party to the present Covenant may propose an amendment and file it with the Secretary-General of the United Nations. The Secretary-General shall thereupon communicate any proposed amendments to the States Parties to the present Covenant with a request that they notify him whether they favour a conference of States Parties for the purpose of considering and voting upon the proposals. In the event that at least one third of the States Parties favours such a conference, the Secretary-General shall convene the conference under the auspices of the United Nations. Any amendment adopted by a majority of the States Parties present and voting at the conference shall be submitted to the General Assembly of the United Nations for approval.

2. Amendments shall come into force when they have been approved by the General Assembly of the United Nations and accepted by a two-thirds majority of the States Parties to the present Covenant in accordance with their respective constitutional processes.

3. When amendments come into force they shall be binding on those States Parties which have accepted them, other States Parties still being bound by the provisions of the present Covenant and any earlier amendment which they have accepted.

*Article 30.* Irrespective of the notifications made under article 26, paragraph 5, the Secretary-General of the United Nations shall inform all States referred to in paragraph 1 of the same article of the following particulars:

(a) Signatures, ratifications and accessions under article 26;

(b) The date of the entry into force of the present Covenant under article 27 and the date of the entry into force of any amendments under article 29.

*Article 31.* 1. The present Covenant, of which the Chinese, English, French, Russian and Spanish texts are equally authentic, shall be deposited in the archives of the United Nations.

2. The Secretary-General of the United Nations shall transmit certified copies of the present Covenant to all States referred to in article 26.

**GENERAL COMMENTS BY THE COMMITTEE ON ECONOMIC, SOCIAL AND CULTURAL RIGHTS.** At its 1988 session, the Committee decided, pursuant to an invitation addressed to it by the Economic and Social Council (resolution 1987/5) and endorsed by the General Assembly (resolution 42/102) to begin, as from its 1989 session, the preparation of general comments based on various articles and provisions of the International Covenant on Economic, Social and Cultural Rights with a view to assisting States parties in fulfilling their reporting obligations.

General comments adopted by the Committee, up to the close of its 1994 session, relate to reporting by States parties, international technical assistance measures, the nature of States parties obligations, and the right to adequate housing. The first three of these comments are reproduced below.

*A. Reporting by States Parties.* 1. The reporting obligations which are contained in part IV of the Covenant are designed principally to assist each State party in fulfilling its obligations under the Covenant and, in addition, to provide a basis on which the Council, assisted by the Committee, can discharge its responsibilities for monitoring States parties' compliance with their obligations and for facilitating the realization of economic, social and cultural rights in accordance with the provisions of the Covenant. The Committee considers that it would be incorrect to assume that reporting is essentially only a procedural matter designed solely to satisfy each State party's formal obligation to report to the appropriate international monitoring body. On the contrary, in accordance with the letter and spirit of the Covenant, the processes of preparation and submission of reports by States can, and indeed should, serve to achieve a variety of objectives.

2. A *first objective,* which is of particular relevance to the initial report required to be submitted within two years of the Covenant's entry into force for the State party concerned, is to ensure that a comprehensive review is undertaken with respect to national legislation, administrative rules and procedures, and practices in an effort to ensure the fullest possible conformity with the Covenant. Such a review might, for example, be undertaken in conjunction with each of the relevant national ministries or other authorities responsible for policy-making and implementation in the different fields covered by the Covenant.

3. A *second objective* is to ensure that the State party monitors the actual situation with respect to each of the rights on a regular basis and is thus aware of the extent to which the various rights are, or are not, being enjoyed by all individuals within its territory or under its jurisdiction. From the Committee's experience to date, it is clear that the fulfilment of this objective cannot be achieved only by the preparation of aggregate national statistics or estimates, but also requires that special attention be given to any worse-off regions or areas and to any specific groups or subgroups which appear to be particularly vulnerable or disadvantaged. Thus, the essential first step towards promoting the realization of economic, social and cultural rights is diagnosis and knowledge of the existing situation. The Committee is aware that this process of monitoring and gathering information is a potentially time-consuming and costly one and that international assistance and cooperation, as provided for in article 2, paragraph 1 and articles 22 and 23 of the Covenant, may well be required in order to enable some States parties to fulfil the relevant obligations. If that is the case, and the State party concludes that it does not have the capacity to undertake the monitoring process which is an integral part of any process designed to promote accepted goals of public policy and is indispensable to the effective implementation of the Covenant, it may note this fact in its report to the Committee and indicate the nature and extent of any international assistance that it may need.

4. While monitoring is designed to give a detailed overview of the existing situation, the principal value of such an overview is to provide the basis for the elaboration of clearly stated and carefully targeted policies, including the establishment of priorities which reflect the provisions of the Covenant. Therefore, a *third objective* of the reporting process is to enable the Government to demonstrate that such principled policy-making has in fact been undertaken. While the Covenant makes this obligation explicit only in article 14 in cases where "compulsory primary education, free of charge" has not yet been secured for all, a comparable obligation "to work out and adopt a detailed plan of action for the progressive implementation" of each of the rights contained in the Covenant is clearly implied by the obligation in article 2, paragraph 1 "to take steps . . . by all appropriate means . . .".

5. A *fourth objective* of the reporting process is to facilitate public scrutiny of government policies with respect to economic, social and cultural rights and to encourage the involvement of the various economic, social and cultural sectors of society in the formulation, implementation and review of the relevant policies. In examining reports submitted to it to date, the Committee has welcomed the fact that a number of States parties, reflecting different political and economic systems, have encouraged inputs by such non-governmental groups into the preparation of their reports under the Covenant. Other States have ensured the widespread dissemination of their reports with a view to enabling comments to be made by the public at large. In these ways, the preparation of the report, and its consideration at the national level can come to be of at least as much value as the constructive dialogue conducted at the international level between the Committee and representatives of the reporting State.

6. A *fifth objective* is to provide a basis on which the State party itself, as well as the Committee, can effectively evaluate the extent to which progress has been made towards the realization of the obligations contained in the Covenant. For this purpose, it may be useful for States to identify specific benchmarks or goals against which their performance in a given area can be assessed. Thus, for example, it is generally agreed that it is important to set specific goals with respect to the reduction of infant mortality, the extent of vaccination of children, the intake of calories per person, the number of persons per health-care provider, etc. In many of these areas, global benchmarks are of limited use, whereas national or other more specific benchmarks can provide an extremely valuable indication of progress.

7. In this regard, the Committee wishes to note that the Covenant attaches particular importance to the concept of "progressive realization" of the relevant rights and, for that reason, the Committee urges States parties to include in their periodic reports information which shows the progress over time, with respect to the effective realization of the relevant rights. By the same token, it is clear that qualitative, as well as quantitative, data are required in order for an adequate assessment of the situation to be made.

8. A *sixth objective* is to enable the State party itself to develop a better understanding of the problems and shortcomings encountered in efforts to realize progressively the full range of economic, social and cultural rights. For this reason, it is essential that States parties report in detail on the "factors and difficulties" inhibiting such realization. This process of identification and recognition of the relevant difficulties then provides the framework within which more appropriate policies can be devised.

9. A *seventh objective* is to enable the Committee, and the States parties as a whole, to facilitate the exchange of information among States and to develop a better understanding of the common problems faced by States and a fuller appreciation of the type of measures which might be taken to promote effective realization of each of the rights contained in the Covenant. This part of the process also enables the Committee to identify the most appropriate means by which the international community might assist States, in accordance with articles 22 and 23 of the Covenant. In order to underline the importance which the Committee attaches to this objective, a separate general comment on those articles will be discussed by the Committee at its fourth session.

*B. International Technical Assistance Measures (Art. 22 of the Covenant).* 1. Article 22 of the Covenant establishes a mechanism by which the Economic and Social Council may bring to the attention of relevant United Nations bodies any matters arising out of reports submitted under the Covenant "which may assist such bodies in deciding, each within its field of competence, on the advisability of international measures likely to contribute to the effective progressive implementation of the . . . Covenant". While the primary responsibility under article 22 is vested in the Council, it is clearly appropriate for the Committee on Economic, Social and Cultural Rights to play an active role in advising and assisting the Council in this regard.

2. Recommendations in accordance with article 22 may be made to any "organs of the United Nations, their subsidiary organs and specialized agencies concerned with furnishing technical assistance". The Committee considers that this provision should be interpreted so as to include virtually all United Nations organs and agencies involved in any aspect of international development cooperation. It would therefore be appropriate for recommendations in accordance with article 22 to be addressed, *inter alia,* to the Secretary-General, subsidiary organs of the council such as the Commission on Human Rights, the Commission on Social Development and the Commission on the Status of Women, other bodies such as UNDP, UNICEF and CDP, agencies such as the World Bank and IMF, and any of the other specialized agencies such as ILO, FAO, UNESCO and WHO.

3. Article 22 could lead either to recommendations of a general policy nature or to more narrowly focused recommendations relating to a specific situation. In the former context, the principal role of the Committee would seem to be to encourage greater attention to efforts to promote economic, social and cultural rights within the framework of international development cooperation activities undertaken by, or with the assistance of, the United Nations and its agencies. In this regard the Committee notes that the Commission on Human Rights, in its resolution 1989/13 of 2 March 1989, invited it "to give consideration to means by which the various United Nations agencies working in the field of development could best integrate measures designed to promote full respect for economic, social and cultural rights in their activities".

4. As a preliminary practical matter, the Committee notes that its own endeavours would be assisted, and the relevant agencies would also be better informed, if they were to take a greater interest in the work of the Committee. While recognizing that such an interest can be demonstrated in a variety of ways, the Committee observes that attendance by representatives of the appropriate United Nations bodies at its first four sessions has, with the notable exceptions of ILO, UNESCO and WHO, been very low. Similarly, pertinent materials and written information had been received from only a very limited number of agencies. The Committee considers that a deeper understanding of the relevance of economic, social and cultural rights in the context of international development cooperation activities would be considerably facilitated through greater interaction between the Committee and the appropriate agencies. At the very least, the day of general discussion on a specific issue, which the Committee undertakes at each of its sessions, provides an ideal context in which a potentially productive exchange of views can be undertaken.

5. On the broader issues of the promotion of respect for human rights in the context of development activities, the Committee has so far seen only rather limited evidence of specific efforts by United Nations bodies. It notes with satisfaction in this regard the initiative taken jointly by the Centre for Human Rights and UNDP in writing to United Nations Resident Representatives and other field-based officials, inviting their "suggestions and advice, in particular with respect to possible forms of cooperation in ongoing projects [identified] as having a human rights dimension or in new ones in response to a specific Government's request". The Committee has also been informed of longstanding efforts undertaken by ILO to link its own human rights and other international labour standards to its technical cooperation activities.

6. With respect to such activities, two general principles are important. The first is that the two sets of human rights are indivisible and interdependent. This means that efforts to promote one set of rights should also take full account of the other. United Nations agencies involved in the promotion of economic, social and cultural rights should do their utmost to ensure that their activities are fully consistent with the enjoyment of civil and political rights. In negative terms this means that the international agencies should scrupulously avoid involvement in projects which, for example, involve the use of forced labour in contravention of international standards, or promote or reinforce discrimination against individuals or groups contrary to the provisions of the Covenant, or involve large-scale evictions or displacement of persons without the provision of all appropriate protection and compensation. In positive terms, it means that, wherever possible, the agencies should act as advocates of projects and approaches which contribute not only to economic growth or other broadly defined objectives, but also to enhanced enjoyment of the full range of human rights.

7. The second principle of general relevance is that development cooperation activities do not automatically contribute to the promotion of respect for economic, social and cultural rights. Many activities undertaken in the name of "development" have subsequently been recognized as ill-conceived and even counter-productive in human rights terms. In order to reduce the incidence of such problems, the whole range of issues dealt with in the Covenant should, wherever possible and appropriate, be given specific and careful consideration.

8. Despite the importance of seeking to integrate human rights concerns into development activities, it is true that proposals for such integration can too easily remain at a level of generality. Thus, in an effort to encourage the operationalization of the principle contained in article 22 of the Covenant, the Committee wishes to draw attention to the following specific measures which merit consideration by the relevant bodies:

(a) As a matter of principle, the appropriate United Nations organs and agencies should specifically recognize the intimate relationship which should be established between development activities and efforts to promote respect for human rights in general, and economic, social and cultural rights in particular. The Committee notes in this regard the failure of each of the first three United Nations Development Decade Strategies to recognize that relationship and urges that the fourth such strategy, to be adopted in 1990, should rectify that omission;

(b) Consideration should be given by United Nations agencies to the proposal, made by the Secretary-General in a report of 1979 (E/CN.4/1334, para. 314) that a "human rights impact statement" be required to be prepared in connection with all major development cooperation activities;

(c) The training or briefing given to project and other personnel employed by United Nations agencies should include a component dealing with human rights standards and principles;

(d) Every effort should be made, at each phase of a development project, to ensure that the rights contained in the Covenants are duly taken into account. This would apply, for example, in the initial assessment of the priority needs of a particular country, in the identification of particular projects, in project design, in the implementation of the project, and in its final evaluation.

9. A matter which has been of particular concern to the committee in the examination of the reports of States parties is the adverse impact of the debt burden and of the relevant adjustment measures on the enjoyment of economic, social and cultural rights in many countries. The Committee recognizes that adjustment programmes will often be unavoidable and that these will frequently involve a major element of austerity. Under such circumstances, however, endeavours to protect the most basic economic, social and cultural rights become more, rather than less, urgent. States parties to the Covenant, as well as the relevant United Nations agencies, should thus make a particular effort to ensure that such protection is, to the maximum extent possible, built-in to programmes and policies designed to promote adjustment. Such an approach, which is sometimes referred to as "adjustment with a human face," or as promoting "the human dimension of development" requires that the goal of protecting the rights of the poor and vulnerable should become a basic objective of economic adjustment. Similarly, international measures to deal with the debt crisis should take full account of the need to protect economic, social and cultural rights through, *inter alia,* international cooperation. In many situations, this might point to the need for major debt relief initiatives.

10. Finally, the Committee wishes to draw attention to the important opportunity provided to States parties, in accordance with article 22 of the Covenant, to identify in their reports any particular needs they might have for technical assistance or development cooperation.

*C. The Nature of States Parties Obligations (Art. 2, Para. 1 of the Covenant).* 1. Article 2 is of particular importance to a full understanding of the Covenant and must be seen as having a dynamic relationship with all of the other provisions of the Covenant. It describes the nature of the general legal obligations undertaken by States parties to the Covenant. Those obligations include both what may be termed (following the work of the International Law Commission) obligations of conduct and obligations of result. While great emphasis has sometimes been placed on the difference between the formulations used in this provision and that contained in the equivalent article 2 of the International Covenant on Civil and Political Rights, it is not always recognized that there are also significant similarities. In particular, while the

Covenant provides for progressive realization and acknowledges the constraints due to the limits of available resources, it also imposes various obligations which are of immediate effect. Of these, two are of particular importance in understanding the precise nature of States parties obligations. One of these, which is dealt with in a separate General Comment, and which is to be considered by the Committee at its sixth session, is the "undertaking to guarantee" that relevant rights "will be exercised without discrimination . . . ".

2. The other is the undertaking in article 2 (1) "to take steps", which in itself, is not qualified or limited by other considerations. The full meaning of the phrase can also be gauged by noting some of the different language versions. In English the undertaking is "to take steps", in French it is "to act" ("s'engage à agir") and in Spanish it is "to adopt measures" ("a adoptar medidas"). Thus while the full realization of the relevant rights may be achieved progressively, steps towards that goal must be taken within a reasonably short time after the Covenant's entry into force for the States concerned. Such steps should be deliberate, concrete and targeted as clearly as possible towards meeting the obligations recognized in the Covenant.

3. The means which should be used in order to satisfy the obligation to take steps are stated in article 2 (1) to be "all appropriate means, including particularly the adoption of legislative measures". The Committee recognizes that in many instances legislation is highly desirable and in some cases may even be indispensable. For example, it may be difficult to combat discrimination effectively in the absence of a sound legislative foundation for the necessary measures. In fields such as health, the protection of children and mothers, and education, as well as in respect of the matters dealt with in articles 6 to 9, legislation may also be an indispensable element for many purposes.

4. The Committee notes that States parties have generally been conscientious in detailing at least some of the legislative measures that they have taken in this regard. It wishes to emphasize, however, that the adoption of legislative measures, as specifically foreseen by the Covenant, is by no means exhaustive of the obligations of States parties. Rather, the phrase "by all appropriate means" must be given its full and natural meaning. While each State party must decide for itself which means are the most appropriate under the circumstances with respect to each of the rights, the "appropriateness" of the means chosen will not always be self-evident. It is therefore desirable that States parties' reports should indicate not only the measures that have been taken but also the basis on which they are considered to be the most "appropriate" under the circumstances. However, the ultimate determination as to whether all appropriate measures have been taken remains one for the Committee to make.

5. Among the measures which might be considered appropriate, in addition to legislation, is the provision of judicial remedies with respect to rights which may, in accordance with the national legal system, be considered justiciable. The Committee notes, for example, that the enjoyment of the rights recognized, without discrimination, will often be appropriately promoted, in part, through the provision of judicial or other effective remedies. Indeed, those States parties which are also parties to the International Covenant on Civil and Political Rights are already obligated (by virtue of arts. 2 (paras. 1 and 3), 3 and 26) of that Covenant to ensure that any person whose rights or freedoms (including the right to equality and non-discrimination) recognized in that Covenant are violated, "shall have

an effective remedy" (art. 2 [3] [a]). In addition, there are a number of other provisions in the International Covenant on Economic, Social and Cultural Rights, including articles 3, 7 (a) (i), 8, 10 (3), 13 (2) (a), (3) and (4) and 15 (3) which would seem to be capable of immediate application by judicial and other organs in many national legal systems. Any suggestion that the provisions indicated are inherently non-self-executing would seem to be difficult to sustain.

6. Where specific policies aimed directly at the realization of the rights recognized in the Covenant have been adopted in legislative form, the Committee would wish to be informed, *inter alia,* as to whether such laws create any right of action on behalf of individuals or groups who feel that their rights are not being fully realized. In cases where constitutional recognition has been accorded to specific economic, social and cultural rights, or where the provisions of the Covenant have been incorporated directly into national law, the Committee would wish to receive information as to the extent to which these rights are considered to be justiciable (i.e. able to be invoked before the courts). The Committee would also wish to receive specific information as to any instances in which existing constitutional provisions relating to economic, social and cultural rights have been weakened or significantly changed.

7. Other measures which may also be considered "appropriate" for the purposes of article 2 (1) include, but are not limited to, administrative, financial, educational and social measures.

8. The Committee notes that the undertaking "to take steps . . . by all appropriate means including particularly the adoption of legislative measures" neither requires nor precludes any particular form of government or economic system being used as the vehicle for the steps in question, provided only that it is democratic and that all human rights are thereby respected. Thus, in terms of political and economic systems the Covenant is neutral and its principles cannot accurately be described as being predicated exclusively upon the need for, or the desirability of a socialist or a capitalist system, or a mixed, centrally planned, or laisser-faire economy, or upon any other particular approach. In this regard, the Committee reaffirms that the rights recognized in the Covenant are susceptible of realization within the context of a wide variety of economic and political systems, provided only that the interdependence and indivisibility of the two sets of human rights, as affirmed *inter alia* in the preamble to the Covenant, is recognized and reflected in the system in question. The Committee also notes the relevance in this regard of other human rights and in particular the right to development.

9. The principal obligation of result reflected in article 2 (1) is to take steps "with a view to achieving progressively the full realization of the rights recognized" in the Covenant. The term "progressive realization" is often used to describe the intent of this phrase. The concept of progressive realization constitutes a recognition of the fact that full realization of all economic, social and cultural rights will generally not be able to be achieved in a short period of time. In this sense the obligation differs significantly from that contained in article 2 of the International Covenant on Civil and Political Rights which embodies an immediate obligation to respect and ensure all of the relevant rights. Nevertheless, the fact that realization over time, or in other words progressively, is foreseen under the Covenant should not be misinterpreted as depriving the obligation of all meaningful content. It is on the one hand a necessary flexibility device, reflecting the realities of the real world and the difficulties

involved for any country in ensuring full realization of economic, social and cultural rights. On the other hand, the phrase must be read in the light of the overall objective, indeed the raison d'être, of the Covenant which is to establish clear obligations for States parties in respect of the full realization of the rights in question. It thus imposes an obligation to move as expeditiously and effectively as possible towards that goal. Moreover, any deliberately retrogressive measures in that regard would require the most careful consideration and would need to be fully justified by reference to the totality of the rights provided for in the Covenant and in the context of the full use of the maximum available resources.

10. On the basis of the extensive experience gained by the Committee, as well as by the body that preceded it, over a period of more than a decade of examining States parties' reports the Committee is of the view that a minimum core obligation to ensure the satisfaction of, at the very least, minimum essential levels of each of the rights is incumbent upon every State party. Thus, for example, a State party in which any significant number of individuals is deprived of essential foodstuffs, of essential primary health care, of basic shelter and housing, or of the most basic forms of education is, prima facie, failing to discharge its obligations under the Covenant. If the Covenant were to be read in such a way as not to establish such a minimum core obligation, it would be largely deprived of its raison d'être. By the same token, it must be noted that any assessment as to whether a State has discharged its minimum core obligation must also take account of resource constraints applying within the country concerned. Article 2 (1) obligates each State party to take the necessary steps "to the maximum of its available resources". In order for a State party to be able to attribute its failure to meet at least its minimum core obligations to a lack of available resources it must demonstrate that every effort has been made to use all resources that are at its disposition in an effort to satisfy, as a matter of priority, those minimum obligations.

11. The Committee wishes to emphasize, however, that even where the available resources are demonstrably inadequate, the obligation remains for a State party to strive to ensure the widest possible enjoyment of the relevant rights under the prevailing circumstances. Moreover, the obligations to monitor the extent of the realization, or more especially of the non-realization, of economic, social and cultural rights, and to devise strategies and programmes for their promotion, are not in any way eliminated as a result of resource constraints. The Committee has already dealt with these issues in its General Comment 1 (1989).

12. Similarly, the Committee underlines the fact that even in times of severe resources constraints whether caused by a process of adjustment, of economic recession, or by other factors the vulnerable members of society can and indeed must be protected by the adoption of relatively low-cost targeted programmes. In support of this approach the Committee takes note of the analysis prepared by UNICEF entitled "Adjustment with a human face: protecting the vulnerable and promoting growth," the analysis by UNDP in its *Human Development Report 1990* and the analysis by the World Bank in the *World Development Report 1990.*

13. A final element of article 2 (1), to which attention must be drawn, is that the undertaking given by all States parties is "to take steps, individually and through international assistance and cooperation, especially economic and technical . . .". The Committee notes that the phrase "to the maximum of its available resources" was intended by the

drafters of the Covenant to refer to both the resources existing within a State and those available from the international community through international cooperation and assistance. Moreover, the essential role of such cooperation in facilitating the full realization of the relevant rights is further underlined by the specific provisions contained in articles 11, 15, 22 and 23. With respect to article 22 the Committee has already drawn attention, in General Comment 2 (1990), to some of the opportunities and responsibilities that exist in relation to international cooperation. Article 23 also specifically identifies "the furnishing of technical assistance" as well as other activities, as being among the means of "international action for the achievement of the rights recognized . . .".

14. The Committee wishes to emphasize that in accordance with Articles 55 and 56 of the Charter of the United Nations, with well-established-principles of international law, and with the provisions of the Covenant itself, international cooperation for development and thus for the realization of economic, social and cultural rights is an obligation of all States. It is particularly incumbent upon those States which are in a position to assist others in this regard. The Committee notes in particular the importance of the Declaration on the Right to Development adopted by the General Assembly in its resolution 41/128 of 4 December 1986 and the need for States parties to take full account of all of the principles recognized therein. It emphasizes that, in the absence of an active programme of international assistance and cooperation on the part of all those States that are in a position to undertake one, the full realization of economic, social and cultural rights will remain an unfulfilled aspiration in many countries. In this respect, the Committee also recalls the terms of its General Comment 2 (1990).

***TOWARDS AN OPTIONAL PROTOCOL TO THE INTERNATIONAL COVENANT ON ECONOMIC, SOCIAL AND CULTURAL RIGHTS.*** The preparation of an Optional Protocol to the Covenant was proposed, and the issues involved were explained, in an analytical paper adopted by the Committee on Economic, Social and Cultural Rights at its seventh session, on 11 December 1992. The paper, included as an annex (annex IV) to the Committee's report of that session (UN Doc. E/1993/22), reads in part as follows:

1. At its fifth session the Committee on Economic, Social and Cultural Rights requested its Rapporteur at the time to present it with a discussion note outlining the principal issues that would arise in connection with the drafting of an optional protocol to the International Covenant on Economic, Social and Cultural Rights "which would permit the submission of communications pertaining to some or all of the rights recognized in the Covenant" (E/1991/23, para. 285).

2. Accordingly, a discussion note was presented to the Committee at its sixth session (E/C.12/1991/WP.2). As the Committee's report on that session notes:

"The members of the Committee . . . supported the drafting of an optional protocol since that would enhance the practical implementation of the Covenant as well as the dialogue with States parties and would make it possible to focus the attention of public opinion to a greater extent on economic, social and cultural rights. The Covenant would no longer be considered as a 'poor relation' of the human rights instruments. Members stressed that the doctrine of the interdependence and indivisibility of human rights should form the basis of any work done by the Committee on drawing up such a draft. In the course of that work, without underestimating the difficulties stemming from the nature and the complexity of the rights guaranteed in the Covenant, it would be appropriate to initiate a dialogue or process which would make it possible, on the one hand, to identify the areas that lent themselves to the gradual development of such a recourse procedure and, on the other hand, to avoid any possible overlapping with the procedures existing under other international human rights instruments" (E/1992/23, para. 362).

3. In the context of the same debate within the Committee, a number of issues were identified in relation to which it was considered that further analysis would be desirable. For that reason, the Committee agreed at its sixth session to request that a supplementary working paper, addressing the specific issues raised in the preceding discussions, be drafted for consideration at its seventh session.

4. A further working paper (E/C.12/1992/2) was prepared accordingly and discussed by the Committee at its seventh session. The details of its consideration of that paper are recorded in the summary record (E.C.12/1992/SR. 14). The Committee endorsed the general approach and requested the preparation of a revised and consolidated document which would combine the two discussion papers presented at the Committee's sixth and seventh sessions and which would also take account of the main points made during the debate at the Committee's seventh session.

5. The Committee expressed its strong support for the drafting and adoption of an optional protocol to the International Covenant on Economic, Social and Cultural Rights. In order to facilitate further consideration of this proposal by the appropriate organs and by States parties, the Committee decided that the present analytical paper should be annexed both to the report on its seventh session and to the statement which it adopted to be sent to the World Conference on Human Rights.

6. The Committee also noted that the preparation of an optional protocol was expressly recommended by the Special Rapporteur of the Sub-Commission on Prevention of Discrimination and Protection of Minorities on the realization of economic, social and cultural rights in his final report (E/CN.4/Sub.2/1992/16, para. 211). It therefore expressed the hope that the matter would be discussed further by the relevant United Nations organs and noted that it might decide to pursue the issue again at future sessions.

The Commission on Human Rights, at its 1994 session, recalled (resolution 1994/20) that the World Conference on Human Rights had encouraged it, in cooperation with the Committee on Economic, Social and Cultural Rights, to continue the examination of Optional Protocols to the International Covenant on Economic, Social and Cultural Rights, and took note of the steps taken by that Committee for the drafting of an Optional Protocol granting the right of individuals or groups to submit communications concerning noncompliance with the Covenant. The Commission invited the Committee to report to it on that subject at its 1995 session.

*STUDY OF THE REALIZATION OF ECONOMIC, SOCIAL AND CULTURAL RIGHTS BY THE COMMISSION ON HUMAN RIGHTS.* Since 1975, the UN Commission on Human Rights has studied at each annual session an item which in 1994 was worded: "Question of the realization in all countries of the economic, social and cultural rights contained in the Universal Declaration of Human Rights and in the International Covenant on Economic, Social and Cultural Rights, and study of special problems which the developing countries face in their efforts to achieve these human rights."

Under this item, the Commission has repeatedly affirmed "that all human rights and fundamental freedoms are universal, indivisible, interdependent and interrelated, and that the promotion and protection of one category of rights should never exempt or excuse States from the promotion and protection of the other rights."

In 1994, after reviewing the situation then existing, the Commission pointed out that "the full respect for the rights contained in the International Covenant on Economic, Social and Cultural Rights is inextricably linked with the process of development, the central purpose of which is the realization of the potentialities of the human person in harmony with the effective participation of all members of society in relevant decision-making processes as agents and beneficiaries of development, as well as fair distribution of the benefits of development." It welcomed the work of the Committee on Economic, Social and Cultural Rights, and encouraged States parties to continue to give their full support and cooperation to its activities. In particular it invited Member States "to consider the desirability of drawing up a national action plan identifying steps to improve the situation of human rights, as well as to seek the participation of communities affected by the non-realization of these rights; and to identify specific national benchmarks designed to give effect to the minimum core obligation to ensure the satisfaction of the minimum essential levels of each of the rights."

**SEE ALSO** *Civil and Political Rights: Siracusa Principles.*

**BIBLIOGRAPHY.** Craven, Matthew, and Caroline Dommen. "Making Room for Substance: Fifth Session of the Committee on Economic, Social and Cultural Rights," *Netherlands Quarterly of Human Rights* 9, no. 1 (1991): 83–95. Report, in English.

Sieghart, Paul. *An Introduction to the International Covenants on Human Rights.* Paper prepared for the Commonwealth Secretariat. London: 1988. Article, in English.

**INTERNATIONAL CRIMINAL POLICE ORGANIZATION (INTERPOL).** INTERPOL is an intergovernmental organization composed of affiliates in 158 countries, providing international coordination for the police authorities in its member States and centralized documentation pertaining to international crime. Police authorities in each participating country operate a National Central Bureau which is constantly in touch with INTERPOL's headquarters by means of a private radio network of more than 70 stations. Information concerning criminal activities is thus passed rapidly from one country to another to prevent individuals who commit crimes in one country to escape arrest by moving quickly to another, and to expedite extradition proceedings.

INTERPOL endeavors to ensure the widest possible mutual assistance between police authorities in the spirit of the **UNIVERSAL DECLARATION OF HUMAN RIGHTS** and to establish and develop institutions and procedures which will contribute to the prevention and suppression of crime. The organization's constitution strictly forbids it to intervene in any activities of a political, military, religious, or racial character.

Policy questions arising within INTERPOL are dealt with by its **GENERAL ASSEMBLY,** which meets annually. On the international level, INTERPOL participates on a continuing basis, under a special arrangement, with the UN **ECONOMIC AND SOCIAL COUNCIL** and its subsidiary bodies, including the **SUB-COMMISSION ON PREVENTION OF DISCRIMINATION AND PROTECTION OF MINORITIES.** In particular, it supplies information when available concerning institutions and practices resembling slavery or the slave trade to the Sub-Commission's Working Group on Contemporary Forms of Slavery.

INTERPOL publishes the *International Criminal Police Review* (issued six times per year) in Arabic, English, French, and Spanish; and the *INTERPOL Information Bulletin.* It also conducts seminars and training courses on various aspects of police work.

International Criminal Police Organization. Address: BP 6401, F-69411 Lyon CEDEX 06, France. Telephone: (33) 7244-7000. Fax: (33) 7244-7163. Secretary-General: Raymond E. Kendall.

**INTERNATIONAL EDUCATIONAL DEVELOPMENT.** This non-governmental organization was founded in 1962 and has consultative status (Roster) with the UN **ECONOMIC AND SOCIAL COUNCIL.** The group acts as a catalyst and consultant for cooperative effort in integral human development. It has consultants and informal affiliates in 50 countries.

International Educational Development. Address 8124 W. Third Street, Suite 105, Los Angeles, CA 90048, USA. Telephone: (213) 658-7156. Executive Director: Patricia Krommer.

**INTERNATIONAL FALCON MOVEMENT.** This non-governmental organization was founded in 1947 in Amsterdam, replacing the pre-World War II Socialist Educational International. The group has consultative status (Roster) with the UN **Economic and Social Council, UNICEF,** and the **Council of Europe.** It has full members in 20 countries.

The International Falcon Movement provides opportunities on an international level for discussion and development of principles, strategies, and practice of socialist education. It also represents the interests of working class children and youth in international labor movement forums. The Movement organizes seminars and conferences, camps, and study tours. Its educational projects include research work on new teaching methods, practical work (such as noncompetitive games, new forms of camp activities, and political education), and an institute for training and education.

International Falcon Movement. Address: Rue de Waelhem 71, B-1030, Brussells, Belgium. Telephone: (32-2) 215-7927. Fax: (32-2) 245-0083. Secretary-General: Jacqui Cottyn.

**INTERNATIONAL FEDERATION FOR THE PROTECTION OF THE RIGHTS OF ETHNIC, RELIGIOUS, LINGUISTIC AND OTHER MINORITIES.** Founded in 1984 in Washington, D.C., this non-governmental organization monitors human rights violations and reports to international organizations concerned with this subject. It has consultative status with the UN **Economic and Social Council** (Roster) and publishes a newsletter.

International Federation for the Protection of the Rights of Ethnic, Religious, Linguistic and Other Minorities. Address: 11-25 30th Avenue, Long Island City, NY 11102, USA. Secretary-General: Menalaos Tzelios.

**INTERNATIONAL FEDERATION OF BUSINESS AND PROFESSIONAL WOMEN.** An international non-governmental organization in consultative status with the UN **Economic and Social Council** (Category I) and with **ILO, UNESCO,** and the **Council of Europe.**

Established as an international organization in 1930, the Federation has national federations in 44 countries; associate clubs in 27 countries and territories; and individual associates in 11 countries. Its main function is to encourage women and girls to acquire advanced education and occupational training. It also strives for equal opportunities for all and for improved status for women in all phases of economic, civil, and political life.

To accomplish these goals, the Federation employs concerted action to press governments to ratify such instruments as the Convention on the Elimination of All Forms of Discrimination against Women, makes statements on women's rights to organs within the United Nations system, and issues general statements in support of peace and in condemnation of *apartheid.*

IFBPW publishes two journals, the biannual *Widening Horizons* and the quarterly *Circular.* In addition, it gives wide circulation to the proceedings and the resolutions of its conferences.

International Federation of Business and Professional Women. Address: Cloisters House, 8 Battersea Park Rd., London SW8 4BG, UK. Telephone: (44-71) 622-8528. Fax: (44-71) 622-8528. General Secretary: Marianne Haslegrave.

**INTERNATIONAL FEDERATION OF FREE JOURNALISTS.** Founded in London in 1948, this non-governmental organization defends freedom of the press in all countries. It cooperates in inter-European affairs and maintains contacts with the new states of central and eastern Europe through their diplomatic representatives. The Federation has consultative status (Roster) with the UN **Economic and Social Council.** It publishes the annual *IFFJ Bulletin.*

International Federation of Free Journalists. Address: 4 Overton Road, London N14 4SY, UK. Telephone: (44-71) 360-2991. Secretary-General: Krstyna Asipowicz.

**INTERNATIONAL FEDERATION OF HUMAN RIGHTS.** An international non-governmental organization in consultative status with the UN **Economic and Social Council** (Category II) and with **UNESCO** and the **Council of Europe,** best known by its French title, *Federation internationale des droits de l'homme* (FIDH), the Federation has a membership of national leagues or associations in 50 countries and territories.

Founded in 1922, FIDH is primarily concerned with the application of the **Universal Declaration of Human Rights** and with disseminating in all countries the principles of justice, liberty, and equality laid down in the French declarations of the rights of man of 1789 and 1793. It specializes in sending missions to countries (more than 400 missions to more than 60 countries since 1960) in which human rights violations are reported; these missions of inquiry and observation have in many cases resulted in improvements in the realization of human rights in such countries.

FIDH publishes reports of its investigative missions, the weekly *La lettre de la FIDH,* the *Revue annuelle de la*

*Fédération internationale des droits de l'homme,* and reports of its missions of inquiry.

International Federation of Human Rights. Address: 27 rue Jean-Dolent, F-75014 Paris, France. Telephone: (33-1) 4331-9495. Fax: (33-1) 4336-3543. President: Michèle Gourarier.

## INTERNATIONAL FEDERATION OF NEWSPAPER PUBLISHERS.

A non-governmental organization in consultative status with the UN ECONOMIC AND SOCIAL COUNCIL (Roster), and with UNESCO and the COUNCIL OF EUROPE, also known by its French title, *Fédération internationale des éditeurs de journaux (FIEJ),* the Federation is a union of national organizations of newspaper publishers and directors (full members) and individuals (associate members). It has members in 41 countries.

Founded in Paris in 1948, the Federation promotes the free flow of ideas by word and image and defends freedom of information. It also works to safeguard the ethical and economic interests of the press by studying and supporting all means to promote press activities. It holds an annual congress.

The Federation publishes the quarterly *FIEJ Bulletin* in French and English.

International Federation of Newspaper Publishers. Address: 25 rue d'Astorg, F-75008 Paris, France. Telephone: (33-1) 4742-8500. Fax: (33-1) 4742-4948. General-Director: Timothy Balding.

## INTERNATIONAL FEDERATION OF RURAL ADULT CATHOLIC MOVEMENTS.

An international non-governmental organization in consultative status with the UN ECONOMIC AND SOCIAL COUNCIL (Roster), and with UNESCO, the Federation has affiliated and associated movements in 41 countries and territories.

Founded in 1964 at Fatima, Portugal, the International Federation of Rural Adult Catholic Movements promotes a lifelong human and Christian education of rural adults, thereby contributing to the development of rural populations. The Federation holds a quadrennial general assembly and continental regional sessions between assemblies. It publishes the quarterly *Cahiers du monde rural* in English, French, Portuguese, and Spanish; and *Voix du monde rural* in English, French, Portuguese, and Spanish.

International Federation of Rural Adult Catholic Movements. Address: Rue Africaine 92, B-1050 Brussels, Belgium. Telephone: (32-2) 538-7842. Fax: (32-2) 534-3884. Secretary-General: Joseph Pirson.

## INTERNATIONAL FEDERATION OF SOCIAL WORKERS.

An international non-governmental organization in consultative status with the UN ECONOMIC AND SOCIAL COUNCIL (Category II) and with UNESCO, WHO, OAS, and the COUNCIL OF EUROPE, IFSW has as members national associations of social workers in 53 countries.

A successor to the International Permanent Secretariat of Social Workers which was launched in Paris in 1928, the International Federation of Social Workers was established in 1956 at the Munich International Conference on Social Welfare. Its principal activities are to promote social work as a profession, to represent that profession on the international level, and to organize international symposia and regional seminars for discussion of the problems of social workers. In addition, IFSW has assisted in liberating social workers held as prisoners of conscience in Chile, the Philippines, and South Africa. In 1987, it was awarded the designation as "Peace Messenger" by the UN Secretary-General in connection with the observance of the International Year of Peace.

Among its publications, IFSW issues the quarterly journal *International Social Work,* the triannual *IFSW Newsletter,* the *International Social Workers Code of Ethics,* and *Policy Paper on Human Rights.*

International Federation of Social Workers. Address: 33 rue de l'Athénée, CH-1206 Geneva, Switzerland. Telephone: (41-22) 347-1236. Fax: (41-22) 346-8657. Secretary-General: Andrew Mouravieff-Apostol.

## INTERNATIONAL FEDERATION OF THE ACTION OF CHRISTIANS FOR THE ABOLITION OF TORTURE.

Established in 1987, the IFACAT works to sensitize Christians to the atrocity of torture and to invite all members to act on behalf of tortured prisoners. This non-governmental organization, in consultative with the UN ECONOMIC AND SOCIAL COUNCIL (Roster) and the COUNCIL OF EUROPE, promotes and disseminates legal instruments against torture and organizes seminars and symposia on the subject. It has national sections in 19 countries.

IFACAT publishes the quarterly *IFACAT News* and periodical reports.

International Federation of the Action of Christians for the Abolition of Torture. Address: 252 rue Saint-Jacques, F-75005 Paris, France. Telephone: (33-1) 4329-8852. Fax: (33-1) 4046-0183. President: Guy Aurenche.

## INTERNATIONAL FEDERATION OF THE PERIODICAL PRESS.

An international non-governmental organization in consultative status with the UN

**ECONOMIC AND SOCIAL COUNCIL** (Roster), and with **UNESCO** and the **COUNCIL OF EUROPE,** the Federation has national sections in 31 countries, representing 100 periodical publishing companies.

Founded in 1910 in Brussels, the Federation develops the interests of the periodical press by supporting freedom in the dissemination of the news, protecting its ethical and material interests, and raising its standards. The Federation holds a biennial congress.

International Federation of the Periodical Press. Address: Imperial House, 15-19 Kingsway, London WC2B 6UN, UK. Telephone: (44-71) 379-3822. Fax: (44-71) 379-3866. Managing Director: Per Mortensen.

## INTERNATIONAL FEDERATION OF UNIVERSITY WOMEN.

An international non-governmental organization in consultative status with the UN **ECONOMIC AND SOCIAL COUNCIL** (Category II), and with **UNESCO,** the Federation was founded in 1919 by women graduates who wanted to do all they could to prevent another catastrophe such as World War I. Since its foundation, IFUW has been concerned and active in education, the advancement of women, and the promotion of international understanding, working primarily for the elimination of all forms of discrimination against women. IFUW undertakes studies and compiles reports dealing with the legal, social, economic, and educational status of women. Individual national affiliates (of which there are 50, representing some 200,000 university women internationally) carry out a variety of activities: vocational guidance for school-aged girls, literacy projects, adult education, self-help training for rural women, hostels for working young women and students, child care, and scholarships—among other endeavors.

Every three years, a study and action program is suggested to the national affiliates; themes have included "Beyond the Decade for Women: Planning towards 2000" (1983–1986), "Women, Leadership, and Development" (1986–1989), and "Women's Role in Changing Society" (1989–1992). In addition, the Federation's Hegg-Hoffet Fund provides assistance for university women in need as a result of war, political upheavals, and natural disasters.

IFUW publishes the *IFUW Newsletter* six times a year in English, French, and Spanish; and the *IFUW Information Papers* in English and French.

International Federation of University Women. Address: 37 Quai Wilson, CH-1201 Geneva, Switzerland. Telephone: (41-22) 731-2380. Fax: (41-22) 738-0440. Secretary-General: Dorothy Davies.

## INTERNATIONAL FEDERATION OF WOMEN IN LEGAL CAREERS.

An international non-governmental organization in consultative status with the UN **ECONOMIC AND SOCIAL COUNCIL** (Category II), and with **ILO, UNESCO,** and **FAO,** the Federation's membership includes national associations in 72 countries as well as individual members.

Founded in 1929, the Federation works to establish relations between women of all countries and to promote their access to all careers in the legal profession. IFWLC also studies on an international level the various rules of law, particularly those relating to the family and the individual, with a view to putting forward a law of the individual and of the family equally acceptable in all countries. It sets up mutual aid and legal research projects for women who are students of law, economics, or social or political sciences from developing countries, particularly Africa. It also campaigns to publicize questions such as the prostitution of children, the legal rights of women in rural areas, and the problems of migrant workers and their families. The Federation maintains three commissions: Unification of Family Law; Practical Implementation of International Conventions; and Labour Law. Its Center of Comparative Law and Jurisprudence handles family law.

IFWLC publishes the *IFWLC Bulletin* (quarterly) in English and French. Other publications include the *Dictionaire international des professions juridiques, Some Aspects of Family, Children Whose Parents are in Prison,* and *Information Tour on the Human Rights Situation in Chile, Argentina, Uruguay, Paraguay and Brazil.*

International Federation of Women in Legal Careers. Address: Via R Giovagnoli 6, 1-10052 Rome, Italy. Telephone: (39-6) 5818-107. President: T. A. Brugiateli.

## INTERNATIONAL FEDERATION OF WOMEN LAWYERS.

An international non-governmental organization in consultative status with the UN **ECONOMIC AND SOCIAL COUNCIL** (Category II), and with **ILO** and **UNESCO,** the Federation has affiliated organizations and individual members in 74 countries.

Founded in 1944 in Mexico City during the third Conference of the Inter-American Bar Association, IFWL works to establish friendly international relations on a basis of equality and mutual respect of all peoples, to promote the principles and aims of the United Nations in their legal and social aspects, and to enhance and promote the welfare of women and children. To assist in this work, it has established 21 standing committees, including committees on comparative civil and commercial law, on domestic relations, on immigration, on nationality and naturalization, and on the legal status of women.

IFWL publishes the quarterly *La Abogada Newsletter,* for distribution to its members, and occasionally issues *La*

*Abogada Internacional* in English, French, and Spanish.

International Federation of Women Lawyers. Address: 186 Fifth Avenue, New York, NY 10010, USA. Telephone: (212) 206-1666. President: Mary Eugenia Charles.

## INTERNATIONAL FELLOWSHIP OF RECONCILIATION.

An international non-governmental organization in consultative status with the UN ECONOMIC AND SOCIAL COUNCIL (Category II), and with UNESCO, the Fellowship is an interreligious movement committed to nonviolence as a principle of life for a world community of peace and liberation. Founded in Holland in 1919, IFOR now has over 100,000 members internationally in 24 countries.

The abolition of war has long been an IFOR goal, and the group advocates total disarmament and works for the creation of nuclear-weapon-free zones as steps toward disarmament. IFOR also strives for solidarity among peoples and nonviolent change and works for human rights for all peoples. The fellowship has given special attention to working for the release of "prisoners of peace"—those arrested and imprisoned for their human rights and nonviolence. Through coordinated efforts, including petitions, letter-writing campaigns, and visits with government officials, IFOR has helped to free political prisoners in Argentina, Vietnam, and South Africa. ADOLFO PÉREZ ESQUIVEL, 1980 NOBEL PEACE PRIZE winner, was the focus of such an IFOR campaign that began with his imprisonment in 1977.

Five times annually, IFOR publishes *Reconciliation International.*

International Fellowship of Reconciliation. Address: Spoorstraat 38, NL-1815 BK, Alkmaar, the Netherlands. Telephone: (31-72) 12-30-14. Fax: (31-72) 15-11-02. General Secretary: David Atwood.

## INTERNATIONAL FREEDOM AWARD.

Established in 1992, this annual award honors either a non-governmental organization that is independent of any party or government affiliation or an individual committed to nonviolence for defending or promoting human rights and democratic development. The winner is chosen by a panel of five human rights activists. The first recipient was the Instituto de Defensa Legal of Lima, Peru. Institutions that are chosen receive a $30,000 award, while individuals receive $15,000.

For more information, contact: International Centre for Human Rights and Democratic Development, 63 rue de Bresoles, Montreal, Quebec H2Y IV7, Canada. Telephone: (514) 283-6073. Fax: (514) 283-3792.

## INTERNATIONAL HELSINKI FEDERATION FOR HUMAN RIGHTS.

Established in 1982 in Bellagio, Italy, the IHF promotes compliance with the human rights provisions of the Final Act of the Helsinki Conference on Security and Cooperation in Europe and the follow-up documents by the 35 states that signed the Final Act in 1975. This non-governmental organization has regular contact with the COUNCIL OF EUROPE and has national committees in 20 countries.

International Helsinki Federation for Human Rights. Address: Rummelhardtgasse 2/18, A-1090 Vienna, Austria. Telephone: (43-1) 427-387. Fax: (43-1) 487-444. Secretary-General: Gerald Nagler.

## INTERNATIONAL HUMANIST AND ETHICAL UNION.

An international non-governmental organization in consultative status with the UN ECONOMIC AND SOCIAL COUNCIL (Roster) and with UNESCO and the COUNCIL OF EUROPE, the Union has full member organizations in nine countries and associate organizations in 31 countries.

IHEU endeavors to bring into active association groups and individuals throughout the world interested in promoting ethical and scientific humanism. It stimulates cooperation and the exchange of information between its members in various fields, including human rights and, in 1983, established its own International Humanist *Ombudsman*—since renamed IHEU Commissioner for Human Rights. In addition to investigating and reporting on allegations concerning violations of human rights, the union also deals with infringements of the principle of Church and State and provides legal services to persons in need. The IHEU also has established the Humanistic Institute for Cooperation with Developing Countries.

IHEU issues the quarterly publication *International Humanist*. It also issues the proceedings of its congresses and has published monographs.

International Humanist and Ethical Union. Address: Nieuwegracht 69A, NL-3512 LG Utrecht, the Netherlands. Telephone: (31-30) 32-21-55. Fax: (31-30) 36-71-04. Executive Director: Ernst van Brakel.

## INTERNATIONAL HUMANITARIAN SERVICE AWARD.

Established in 1988 by the American Red Cross, this annual award recognizes an individual or group whose work exemplifies or inspires the humanitarian values of dignity, respect, compassion, protection, and assistance.

In 1994, a group of talented anonymous individuals from Hanover, VA, USA, called "The Knitters Group" received the award. This group is composed of individuals who responded to an emergency call from a teacher in Bucharest, Romania, who had written that her students suffered from the winter cold. The letter found its way to Mrs. Jane Wells, manager of Volunteer and Youth Services for the local Red Cross chapter, who was aware of a knitting group that had been making blankets for patients at a veterans hospital. The group was enlisted to supply sweaters and caps for the children; and, after this project, they went on to knit warm clothing for children in Armenia and Moldavia.

In addition, past recipients include the First Aid Teams of the Lebanese Red Cross (1988); Dr. Neil Boothby, of Save the Children, who worked in Mozambique with children who are war victims (1989); Mrs. Zhang Zhenkun, a nurse with the Red Cross Society of China (1990); Mohammed Al-Hadid, vice president of the National Red Crescent Society of Jordan (1992); and the Somali Red Crescent Society, for providing medical, relief, and humanitarian services to the people of Somalia in the face of internecine conflict, famine, and collapse of the country's infrastructure (1993).

For more information, contact: American Red Cross, 431 18th St., NW, Washington, D.C., 20006, USA. Telephone: (202) 639-3306. Fax: (202) 639-3932.

## INTERNATIONAL HUMAN RIGHTS INTERNSHIP PROGRAM.

The Internship Program promotes international human rights by helping to strengthen human rights organizations through support of professional training opportunities for their staff or volunteers and for individuals committed to human rights work. The program offers grants to organizations to improve their staff; in this regard, the program's priority is the development of human rights organizations in Africa, Asia, the Middle East, Latin America and the Caribbean, East Central Europe, and the former Soviet republics. Grants are also offered to individuals from these same countries who require training in building human rights organizations.

Participants are trained in such areas as factfinding, documentation, reporting, use of international machineries, legal aid, medical work, human rights education, and internal management. A trainee may be placed as a temporary staff member of a host organization, may conduct research into an issue or area by visiting and consulting with two or more human rights institutions in one or more countries, or may attend a training course or seminar.

In addition, since 1992, the Internship Program has undertaken a systematic effort to increase its base of information about non-governmental legal-aid organizations, human rights public-interest law initiatives, and clinical legal education programs in law faculties in various countries. The "Legal Resources Project" helps the Program to design specifically tailored training projects in law-related human rights work and serves as a clearinghouse of information for other organizations.

The Internship Program is administered by the Institute of International Education and receives funding from the Ford Foundation, the Swedish NGO Foundation for Human Rights, the Danish Ministry of Foreign Affairs, the Joyce Mertz-Gilmore Foundation, the John Merck Fund, the Royal Norwegian Ministry of Foreign Affairs, and the General Service Foundation.

International Human Rights Internship Program. Address: Institute of International Education, 1400 K Street, N.W., Suite 650, Washington, D.C., 20005, USA. Fax: (202) 962-8827.

## INTERNATIONAL INDIAN TREATY COUNCIL.

An international non-governmental organization in consultative status (Category II) with the UN ECONOMIC AND SOCIAL COUNCIL, the Council includes representatives from 98 Indian nations in the Americas.

Founded in 1974 in the United States of America, the Council works to inform the international community about treaty rights of Indians of the western hemisphere and about human rights violations and denial of land rights of this indigenous people. The Council maintains the American Indian Treaty Council Information Center in South Dakota (USA). IITC publishes the quarterly *Treaty Council News*.

International Indian Treaty Council. Address: 444 Second Ave., No. 32A, New York, NY 10010-2528, USA. Executive Director: William Means.

## INTERNATIONAL INSTITUTE FOR PEACE.

Founded in 1957 in Vienna, the Institute undertakes scientific research on the problems of peace, disarmament, security, development, international cooperation, and other global problems. It initiates international projects and participates in scientific projects of Austrian and other national and international organizations. The Institute has a membership of individuals and corporate bodies in the East and the West in 44 countries.

The Institute has consultative status (Roster) with the UN ECONOMIC AND SOCIAL COUNCIL and UNESCO. It publishes the quarterly *Peace and the Sciences* in English and German.

International Institute for Peace. Address: Möllwaldplatz 5, A-1040, Vienna, Austria. Telephone: (43-1) 504-4376. Fax: (43-1) 505-3236. Secretary-General: Peter Stania.

**INTERNATIONAL INSTITUTE OF HUMANITARIAN LAW.** An international non-governmental organization in consultative status with the UN Economic and Social Council (Category II) and with UNESCO and the Council of Europe, the Institute was founded in San Remo, Italy, in September 1970, to reaffirm, develop, and disseminate the principles of international humanitarian law, which is primarily concerned with the protection of combatants and civilians and the protection of refugees, in time of war. It organizes courses on the law of armed conflicts and on international refugee law. It is also concerned with protection of the rights of victims of disasters and migrations.

The Institute has established seven academic committees: Human Rights, Humanitarian Law, Military Courses, International Refugee Law, Relief Law, Migrations, and Protection of Cultural Property.

IIHL conducts an extensive publications program and disseminates documentation generated by its program of conferences, symposia, round-tables, and meetings of experts. Its publications include *International Protection of Refugees in Armed Conflicts* (1981), *International Humanitarian Law of Coerced Movements of People across State Boundaries* (1983), *The Status of Refugees in Denmark* (1985), and *El Derecho de los Refugiados y el Articulo 2 de la Convencion Americana sobre Derechos Humanos* (1987).

International Institute of Humanitarian Law. Address: Villa Ormond, Corso Cavallotti 115, I-18038 San Remo, Italy. Telephone: 184-690848. Fax: 184-541-600. Secretary-General: Dr. Ugo Genesio.

**INTERNATIONAL INSTITUTE OF HUMAN RIGHTS.** Founded by Nobel Peace Prize recipient René Cassin, the International Institute of Human Rights organizes annually during the month of July a specialized study session that provides advanced courses on international and comparative law of human rights. The session is directed toward: advanced students in law, political science, humane studies, and social sciences; professors and researchers; members of legal professions; national and international civil servants; and members of non-governmental organizations. The two official languages of the session are French and English; the participants must write, speak, and understand one of the two official languages and be proficient enough in the other to understand the courses and debates (no simultaneous translation is provided).

In addition, during each study session, the International Center for University Human Rights Teaching (CIEDHU) offers university professors and researchers an intensive study program that trains them to develop specialized research and teaching in human rights at their own universities and centers.

Applications for admission to either program must reach the Institute by May 31. Financial aid forms must be submitted by April 30.

International Institute of Human Rights. Address: 1, quai Lezay-Marnésia, 67000 Strasbourg. Telephone: (33-88) 35-05-50. Fax: (33-88) 36-38-55

**INTERNATIONAL INSTITUTE ON AGING.** The Institute, authorized by the UN Economic and Social Council in 1987 (resolution 1987/41), was inaugurated by the UN Secretary-General on 15 April 1988. With headquarters in Valletta, Malta, the Institute is funded from voluntary contributions by governments, non-governmental organizations, and philanthropic institutions and individuals.

The Institute provides training in gerontology to policymakers, planners, program executives, educators, scientists, professionals, and para-professionals. It conducts annually short-term courses in Social Gerontology, Income Security for the Elderly, and Medical Geriatrics; and long-term courses in Gerontology (in conjunction with the University of Malta). It promotes cooperation on various aspects of AGING and analyzes and disseminates information on aging to the developing countries. It operates under the direction of an international board, which formulates principles and guidelines for its activities, approves its work program and budget, and assists in fundraising activities. The UN Secretary-General has appointed the Director-General of the United Nations office at Vienna as chairperson of the board. The Institute publishes the quarterly *Bold.*

International Institute on Aging. Address: 117 St. Paul St., Valletta VLT07, Malta. Telephone: (356) 243-044. Fax: (356) 230-248. Director: Alfred Grech.

**INTERNATIONAL LABOR ORGANIZATION (ILO).** In accordance with the International Labor Organization constitution of 1919, the ILO was established as an autonomous permanent intergovernmental organization mandated to promote world wide programs to achieve (1) full employment and the raising of standards of living; (2) the employment of workers in occupations in which they can have the satisfaction of giving the fullest measure of their skill and attainments and can make their contribution to the common well-being; (3) the provision, as a means to attaining this end, and under adequate guarantees for all concerned, of facilities for training and the transfer of labor, including migration for employment and settlement; (4) policies in regard to wages and earnings, hours and other conditions of work, calculated to insure a just share of the fruits of progress to all, and a minimum living wage to all employed and in need of such protection; (5) the effective recognition of the right of collective bargaining, the cooperation of management and labor in the continuous improvement of productive efficiency, and the collaboration of workers and employers in the preparation and application of social and economic measures; (6) the extension of social security measures to provide a basic income to all in need of such protection and comprehensive medical care; (7) adequate protection for the life and health of workers in all occupations; (8) provision for child welfare and maternity protection; (9) the provision of adequate nutrition, housing, and facilities for recreation and culture; and (10) the assurance of equality of educational and vocational opportunity.

ILO's main organs are the General Conference, composed of representatives of each member State, and the Governing Body composed of 56 members—28 of them representing governments, 14 representing employees, and 14 representing employers. The conference elects members of the Governing Body, sets international labor standards by preparing and adopting conventions and recommendations, and provides a forum for the discussion of questions relating to the treatment of labor. The Governing Body elects the Director-General, establishes administrative policy and work programs, and supervises the activities of the International Labor Office (the ILO Secretariat, headed by the Director-General).

The General Conference meets annually for a period of about three weeks, usually at the United Nations office in Geneva during the month of June. The Governing Body holds three sessions per year, the first in February/March, the second in May/June, and the third in November, all in Geneva.

The Governing Body has two standing committees which deal with human rights matters: the ILO Freedom of Association Committee and the ILO Committee of Experts on the Application of Conventions and Recommendations. The former considers and investigates complaints alleging infringement of trade union rights; the latter supervises the application of a number of international instruments that deal with human rights matters, prepared under the auspices of the ILO. In addition, the Governing Body from time to time establishes tri-partite committees to examine representations made under article 24 of the ILO constitution relating to discrimination in employment; most of these allege nonobservance of the ILO Discrimination (Employment and Occupation) Convention.

***COMMITTEE OF EXPERTS ON THE APPLICATION OF CONVENTIONS AND RECOMMENDATIONS.*** Established by the Governing Body in 1926, the Committee's func-

tion is to determine and to point out, in complete independence, the extent to which each State member of the International Labor Organization applies the provisions of ILO conventions and recommendations and lives up to the obligations undertaken by its acceptance of the constitution of the International Labor Organization. Each convention is a formal legal instrument regulating some aspect of labor administration, social welfare, or human rights and is binding upon all States that have ratified or acceded to it. Recommendations are more informal but apply equally to all member States. More than 250 conventions and recommendations have been adopted since the ILO was established in 1919, and together they constitute the International Labor Code (see Appendix E).

Member States are not bound to ratify a particular convention, even though they may have voted for its adoption. However, under the ILO constitution, they are required as a minimum to bring all conventions adopted by the International Labor Conference to the attention of their legislative authorities. If a convention is ratified, the ratifying State undertakes to report periodically to the ILO on the measures taken for the implementation of its provisions. Similarly, member States are expected to report from time to time on their position with respect to conventions that they have not ratified and recommendations that they have not accepted. It is on these reports that the Committee of Experts bases its conclusions and recommendations to the governing body.

Originally composed of six members, the committee has since been enlarged progressively to 20, four of whom are from Asian countries, three from African countries, three from eastern European countries, five from western European countries, three from South American countries, and two from countries in North and Central America. In establishing the committee, the governing body decided that its members should be selected from among persons of recognized technical competence whose complete impartiality could not be challenged; that they should, in no sense, be considered as representatives of governments; and that, therefore, they must be persons of independent standing, not directly connected with a government service or a trade organization. The experts accordingly are drawn from the judiciary, from academic circles, and from persons with considerable experience in public administration. They are appointed in their personal capacity by the governing body, on the proposal of the Director-General, and serve for a term of three years.

The Committee of Experts schedules its meetings as required; usually it convenes at least once a year at ILO headquarters in Geneva.

### FREEDOM OF ASSOCIATION COMMITTEE OF THE GOVERNING BODY.

The Governing Body's Committee on Freedom of Association was established in 1951 for the preliminary examination of complaints of infringements of trade union rights. Its main function is to consider the appropriateness of referring particular complaints to the ILO Freedom of Association Fact-finding and Conciliation Commission and to make recommendations concerning such action to the governing body.

The Committee has established its own rules and procedures for dealing with such complaints, particularly regarding their receivability and regarding communication with the complainants on the one hand and with the governments concerned on the other. It is composed of nine members of the governing body: three government representatives, three employers' representatives, and three workers' representatives. Members are appointed by the governing body on proposal of the Director-General.

The Committee has no subsidiary bodies; but, in urgent cases, the Director-General may, with the prior consent of the committee and of the government concerned, send a representative to the country named in a complaint with a view to ascertaining relevant facts.

Since its establishment, the Committee has considered many hundreds of allegations concerning infringements of trade union rights. In only a few cases was it necessary to refer such cases to the Fact-Finding and Conciliation Commission.

### FREEDOM OF ASSOCIATION FACT-FINDING AND CONCILIATION COMMISSION.

One year earlier, in 1950, the Governing Body had established the Freedom of Association Fact-finding and Conciliation Commission to secure, by factfinding and conciliation, friendly settlements of complaints alleging infringements of trade union rights submitted by governments or by workers' or employers' organizations. Such complaints must be referred to the Commission either by the Governing Body or by the ECONOMIC AND SOCIAL COUNCIL, the latter of which decided, on 17 February 1950 (resolution 277 [X]):

(a) to accept on behalf of the United Nations the services of the International Labour Organisation and the Fact-finding and Conciliation Commission as established by the International Labour Organisation;

(b) to forward to the Governing Body of the International Labour Office, for its consideration as to referral to the Commission, all allegations regarding infringements of trade union rights received from Governments or trade union or employers' organizations against member States of the International Labour Organisation;

(c) (i) that, before acting on such allegations regarding any Member of the United Nations which is not a member of the International Labour Organisation the Secretary-General, on behalf of the Council, will seek the consent of the Government concerned; (ii) that upon receiving such consent, the Council will transmit to the Fact-finding and Conciliation Commission, through the Governing Body of the International Labour Office, any allegations regarding infringements of trade-union rights by Members of the United Nations which are not members of the International Labour Organisation, received from Governments or trade-union or employers' organizations, which it considers suitable for transmittal; (iii) that if such consent is not forthcoming, the Council will give consideration to such refusal with a view to taking any appropriate alternative action designed to safeguard the rights relating to freedom of information involved in the case.

Reports of the Commission are submitted to the ILO Governing Body. In addition, the ILO Director-General includes in the ILO's annual report to the UN GENERAL ASSEMBLY an account of the work of the Fact-finding and Conciliation Commission.

The Commission is composed of nine independent members appointed by the ILO Governing Body on proposal of the Director-General. They serve for an indeterminate term and meet as required to perform their functions. The Commission sometimes works in panels consisting of not less than three or more than five members.

### INTERNATIONAL LABOR OFFICE.

The staff of the International Labor Organization consists of more than 3,000 international civil servants appointed and directed by the Director-General under regulations approved by the governing body. In accordance with the ILO constitution, the responsibilities of the Director-General and of the staff are exclusively international in character (article 9). Their main functions include the collection and distribution of information on all subjects relating to the international adjustment of conditions of industrial life and labor, particularly the examination of subjects which it is proposed to bring before the International Labor Conference with a view to the conclusion of international conventions and the conduct of such investigations as may be ordered by the conference or by the governing body (article 10).

### ILO PROTECTION OF SPECIFIC GROUPS.

In a statement prepared by the International Labor Organization and circulated to the Preparatory Committee for the World Conference on Human Rights, which met in Geneva from 19 to 30 April 1993, the work of the ILO for the protection of specific groups is summarized (UN Doc. A/CONF.157/PC/61/Add. 10) as follows:

Protection of specific groups, including those most in need of protection, is an essential part of the ILO's work. The ILO naturally carries out this task within its mandate, which does not aim at the overall protection for these groups which is the approach of the United Nations itself (there is one exception, concerning indigenous and tribal peoples; in this instance the ILO acts on behalf of the United Nations system as a whole), but which allows a concentrated effort within the limits of the ILO's competence.

The ILO's mandate concentrates, of course, on the world of work. Yet this is a wider framework than it might seem at first glance. A very large part of the effects of discrimination or of exploitation is expressed through the means of access to or denial of the right to participate in economic activity. Forced labour, discrimination in employment, child labour, and freedom of association are all questions of fundamental human rights, in which various groups require protection in relation to work. The ILO concentrates on their protection within the economic sphere.

*The Groups Protected by the ILO.* The "Declaration of Philadelphia", which is annexed to the ILO Constitution, defines the principal groups which the Organisation is to protect. These include workers and employers exercising freedom of association, women, children and migrant workers. By mandating the ILO also to work for the abolition of discrimination in employment, other groups are brought within its action.

The ILO's principal means of action is the adoption of International Conventions and Recommendations, and the supervision of their implementation by ratifying States. These Conventions and Recommendations often define groups to be specially protected. There are, for example, 11 ILO Conventions intended specifically to protect children from being employed or working; and many others which set such conditions as the hours of work permitted for young workers, require medical examinations before they can be employed, etc. The ILO has also adopted Conventions dealing with the conditions of work of seafarers and fishermen, agricultural workers, older workers and other designated groups in need of special protection, but special attention will be given to a selection of the groups protected by the ILO in the context of the World Conference on Human Rights.

In addition to the activities described below, the ILO has worked for many years for the improvement of the situation of workers affected by apartheid, and workers in the occupied Arab territories. While no information on these extensive activities is included in the present paper, these activities have been reported in detail to the United Nations bodies working in these areas.

This paper will concentrate on the following specific groups:

(a) workers' and employers' organizations protected by the ILO's instruments on freedom of association;

(b) those subject to discrimination in employment and work on the basis of race, colour, sex, religion, political opinion, national extraction or social origin;

(c) women at work;

(d) children and young workers;

(e) migrant workers;

(f) disabled workers; and

(g) indigenous and tribal peoples.

Specific ILO standards, examined below, have been adopted for all of these groups, and other Conventions and Recommendations contain provisions specially applicable to them. When they are implemented through the ILO's highly-developed system for supervision of obligations, supported by its programme of technical assistance, they form the basis for national action in almost all the countries of the world.

An explanation of the ILO's system for the adoption and

supervision of standards is contained in UN Doc. A/CONF.157/PC/6/Add. 3, submitted to the first session of the Preparatory Committee for the World Conference.

## I. Protection of the Right of Freedom of Association

This is of course one of the most basic ILO principles: that workers and employers have the right to organise freely to protect their interests, to join and form organisations of their own choice for the purpose, and to run their own affairs without undue interference from each other or from the government.

Do these organizations require specific protection? Most certainly. Both the organizations and the individuals composing and representing them are subject to attack and discrimination, and are protected by ILO standards. If trade unions have acquired considerable influence in some developed countries, in most of the developing world they remain subject to manipulation and exploitation by governments and by employers. Their leaders are often the subject of arrest and imprisonment, torture and exile. In most countries of the world, trade unions are the only organized force in the country outside the army, explaining why they are often the first to be imprisoned or exiled when there is unrest in the country. The representatives of workers' organizations are often subjected to discrimination and ill-treatment in the workplace. Employers' organizations also can be subject to brutal repression, for instance in countries where private enterprise is held to be ideologically unacceptable, and are in equal need of protection.

The principle of freedom of association is contained in the Declaration of Philadelphia, and is considered to be a fundamental part of the ILO's mandate. Two of the best-known ILO Conventions develop the principles of freedom of association: the Freedom of Association and Protection of the Right to Organise Convention, 1948 (No. 87), and the Right to Organise and Collective Bargaining Convention, 1949 (No. 98). There are also other Conventions on specific aspects of the subject, such as the Rural Workers' Organisations Convention, 1975 (No. 141), and the Workers' Representatives Convention, 1971 (No. 135). Their implementation is examined by the ILO's regular supervisory bodies whenever the country concerned has ratified them.

Convention No. 87 provides for the right of workers and employers, without any distinction whatsoever, to establish and join organizations of their own choosing with a view to furthering and defending their interests. These organizations have the rights to run their affairs, to establish and join federations and confederations which shall enjoy the same rights and guarantees, and to affiliate with international organizations. Convention No. 98 goes on to provide protection for workers when they are exercising the right to organize; lays down the principle of non-interference between workers' and employers' organizations; and promotes voluntary collective bargaining.

It should be noted that in Article 8 of the International Covenant on Economic, Social and Cultural Rights which guarantees the right to freedom of association, paragraph 3 states that "Nothing in this article shall authorize States Parties to the International Labour Organisation Convention concerning Freedom of Association and Protection of the Right to Organise to take legislative measures which would prejudice, or apply the law in such a manner as would prejudice, the guarantees provided for in that Convention."

Compliance with the Conventions on freedom of association is supervised by the ILO Committee of Experts on the Application of Conventions and Recommendations in the same manner as all other ILO instruments. A special procedure applies in this regard, however, which is not available in the ILO to protect other rights. The Committee on Freedom of Association of the ILO Governing Body, and the Fact-Finding and Conciliation Commission on Freedom of Association, were established in the ILO after agreement with the Economic and Social Council of the United Nations in 1950. They examine complaints of violations of freedom of association without regard to whether the State concerned has ratified the relevant ILO Conventions; and the Fact-Finding and Conciliation Commission can even examine complaints against non-Member States if the State concerned agrees. The Committee on Freedom of Association is one of the most active and effective human rights complaints bodies in the international system. It is often called upon to deal with situations of extreme urgency when workers' and employers' organizations or representatives are under fire from their governments. The Committee, and the Director-General on its behalf, often intervenes to secure the release from prison of trade unionists, or permission for them to return from exile. It may be called upon to decide on delicate problems of whether a particular kind of action is a proper trade union function, or whether it goes over into the political arena. The ILO has become a very active participant in the protection of these organizations all over the world.

In a recent case of significant interest, the Fact-Finding and Conciliation Commission of the ILO examined a complaint against South Africa in 1992, and carried out an on-the-spot mission with three independent personalities to examine the situation. It adopted a report in May 1992 which was then submitted to the UN Economic and Social Council in accordance with the established procedure.

The supervisory activity carried out by the ILO under these Conventions, and in accordance with the principles of freedom of association, is supplemented by intense training and assistance for workers' organizations and, to a slightly smaller extent, for employers' organizations. This includes seminars carried out by the technical unit responsible for supervising these principles, the Department of International Labour Standards and Human Rights, and by the Workers' Education service. The principle of freedom of association is integrated into all the ILO activities, and is of course reflected in the structure of the ILO itself.

## II. The Right to Be Free from Discrimination in Employment and Occupation

The annotations to the "Report on Studies and Documentation for the World Conference" states that the study under objective 1 "should focus on equality as the fundamental rule of international human rights law", and states that this should be examined taking into account, inter alia, instruments adopted by the ILO.

Most ILO Conventions apply without distinction to all persons in the workplace, with the exception of those intended to protect special categories of persons (women, children, etc.) The ILO also has the mission to promote equality or opportunity and treatment in respect of employment and occupation more generally.

The Discrimination (Employment and Occupation) Convention, 1958 (No. 111) requires ratifying States to promote equality of opportunity and treatment through a national policy aimed at eliminating all forms of discrimination in respect of employment and occupation. Discrimination is defined as any distinction, exclusion or preference based on race, colour, sex, religion, political opinion, national extraction or social origin. The State concerned may also designate other grounds on which it undertakes to apply the Convention. The Convention covers access to vocational training, access to employment and to particular occupations, and terms and conditions of employment. The Convention also provides that special measures of protection or assistance provided for in other ILO Conventions or Recommendations shall not be deemed to be discrimination; nor shall any distinction, exclusion or preference in respect of a particular job based on the inherent requirements thereof. The Convention has been ratified by 112 countries.

The implementation of the Convention has certainly known some success over the years. Most countries of the world have provisions in their labour legislation which prohibit discrimination in employment, and the majority of them are modeled on Convention No. 111 or take account of it. An increasing number of countries have established machinery to combat discrimination in employment, and significant differences can be discerned in recent years in many of them in the treatment of various minority or other disadvantaged groups.

Nevertheless, in its 1988 General Survey on the application of Convention No. 111, the Committee of Experts on the Application of Conventions and Recommendations noted that equality in employment could not be fully realised in a general context of inequality. Inequality in social status leads inevitably to inequality of treatment, and above all to inequality of opportunity in employment. Achievement of a general climate of equality of opportunity and treatment does not depend solely on law and regulations, but must be based also on education which covers employment but is not limited to it.

There is in fact no country in the world in which the problem of discrimination does not arise. Far from receding, situations of discrimination are multiplying as situations which have their origins in tribal, ethnic or religious differences grow into active conflicts.

## III. The Elimination of Discrimination Against Women

The ILO Constitution contains, in the Declaration of Philadelphia, the affirmation that "all human beings, irrespective of race, creed or sex, have the right to pursue their material well-being and their spiritual development in conditions of freedom and dignity, of economic security and equal opportunity", and that "the attainment of the conditions under which this shall be possible must constitute the central aim of national and international policy".

Although most international labour standards apply without distinction to men and women workers, there are a number of Conventions and Recommendations which refer specifically to women. The ILO's standard-setting work in this area has been based on two central concerns. The first has been to guarantee equality of opportunity and treatment as concerns access to training, employment, promotion, organisation and decision-making, as well as securing equal conditions of remuneration, benefits, social security and welfare services provided in connection with employment. The second has been to protect women workers especially in relation to conditions of work which may entail risks for maternity.

There are three principal ILO Conventions which cover this subject.

1. *The Equal Remuneration Convention, 1951 (No. 100)* provides for equal remuneration for men and women for work of equal value. The Convention is supplemented by the Equal Remuneration Recommendation, 1951 (No. 90). The principle may be applied by means of national laws or regulations, legal machinery for wage determination, collective agreements or a combination of these means, including the objective appraisal of jobs. The Convention has been ratified by 114 countries.

Even beyond their international engagement, a growing number of States have taken legislative measures to ensure the application of the principle of equal remuneration. However, the ILO views with a certain concern the fact that the definitions and criteria used in national legislation to compare the value of jobs are often more limited than those defined in the Convention (and in the International Covenant on Economic, Social and Cultural Rights which later took up this same idea in shorter form in Article 7(a)(i)). Many of them speak of "equal pay for equal work", a much more limited concept. In order to guarantee equal remuneration to men and women for work of equal value, it is important that there exist a mechanism and a procedure which allows a guarantee that the criterion of sex is not taken into consideration when comparing the value of jobs.

Given the many causes of inequality of remuneration between men and women workers, the best results appear to have been obtained in countries in which global action has been taken to correct all aspects of the situation at once. Some countries have established specialised bodies or agencies with sufficiently wide powers to draw up programmes and coordinate measures to promote equality of opportunity and treatment in general, including equality of remuneration.

The ILO Committee of Experts on the Application of Conventions and Recommendations carried out a General Survey of the application of Convention No. 100 in 1986. It noted in that Survey that, whatever the measures put into place to achieve equality of remuneration, it was essential that organisations of employers and workers be fully engaged in achieving the objectives of the Convention in order to ensure as fully and rapidly as possible that discrimination be eliminated on all wage scales as well as in collective agreements. This engagement is particularly important in times of economic hardship when there is a temptation to give priority to other questions.

2. *The Discrimination (Employment and Occupation) Convention, 1958 (No. 111)* (supplemented by Recommendation No. 111 of the same title) is the other major ILO Convention that promotes equality of rights between men and women in the workplace, and is examined in detail above. The ILO has given special attention in recent years to the application of these principles to discrimination on the basis of sex.

3. *The Workers with Family Responsibilities Convention. 1981 (No. 156).* The objective of this instrument is to create effective equality of opportunity and treatment for men and women workers with family responsibilities. It applies to both men and women workers with responsibilities for their dependent children or other members of their immediate families where such responsibilities restrict their possibilities of participating in economic activity.

4. *Protective Measures for Women.* It is important to remember in this connection that a number of ILO Conventions provide protection for women in employment especially in relation to conditions of work which may entail risks for maternity. A large number of ILO Conventions provide for special conditions of work and special protection for women when they would be endangered by exposure to particular substances or situations in the workplace; and others provide for social security protection for women in pregnancy and child-bearing.

5. *Operational Considerations.* Three characteristics of work by women provide the most striking evidence of discrimination in employment on the basis of sex, and are the prime focuses of the ILO's attention.

The first is occupational segregation, which operates by designating certain occupations as more "appropriate" for one sex or the other. Occupational segregation can take place on a horizontal basis, in the form of a reduced list of sectors of activity and types of occupations which include a high proportion of women, as compared to the wider range of activities occupied mainly by men; or in the vertical sense, as evidenced by the "glass ceiling" which prevents women from having access to posts with greater responsibility and decision-making power.

The second characteristic is the gap in remuneration between men and women, based to a large degree on occupational segregation but which also involves discrepancies in remuneration for work of equal value.

The third characteristic lies in the "double work day" which faces women who carry out an economic activity, but who must also assume family and domestic responsibilities almost alone. This involves an unequal workload between the sexes, as well as imposing limitations on the ability of women to compete on equal terms with men in the labour market.

In spite of continuing increases in the rates of participation by women in the labour force during the last twenty years, women continue to encounter greater difficulties than men in access to employment, and they are the group most vulnerable to unemployment. The great majority of women workers are found in jobs involving the least qualifications, lowest remuneration and least security, and worst working conditions. Discriminated against in the formal labour market, women in the developing countries in particular resort more often than men to work in the informal urban sector and to subsistence activities in rural areas.

Discrimination against women in work is largely the result of cultural factors which assign different social roles to men and women in both the public and private spheres. Women are often restricted to family and domestic tasks, reducing the importance of their economic role. This results in women being considered a secondary labour force, whose income is simply a complement to the family unit. In fact, however, the large majority of women want and need to work, and their income-earning capacity is essential for their own survival and that of their families. In addition, women are principally responsible for the economic subsistence of approximately one-third of households in the world.

The ILO's action in this field has taken the form of combating these discriminatory practices, and in assisting member States to adopt policies and measures which guarantee real equality of opportunity for men and women in the context of work. Activities include research, evaluation, meetings, technical cooperation and dissemination of information on the subject, and they have contributed to increasing consciousness of the forms and magnitude of discrimination against women and of its significance in terms of human rights, social justice and lost potential for development. The ILO's practical activities have therefore concentrated on stimulating an increase in the quantity and quality of employment accessible to women, increasing and diversifying their opportunities for training, and improving their working conditions, ability to organise for their own defense and participation in decision-making.

The ILO considers participation by women in working life on an equal footing to be a key element in economic and social development. Women should not simply be allowed to have equal access to the benefits of development, they should also be able to participate actively in its construction. They constitute an underutilised human resource and their economic contribution remains largely invisible and undervalued. The question of gender should always be taken into account in development planning, so that the needs, interests and contributions of both women and men can be taken fully into account on an equal basis.

The ILO's work takes place within the general context of action by the UN system as a whole to improve the situation of women. The Division for the Advancement of Women, located in the United Nations Office in Vienna, acts as the focal point for coordination in the system, and regularly convenes interagency meetings in which common strategies can be agreed upon and contributions can be made to the International Commission on the Status of Women.

### IV. Migrant Workers

The Declaration of Philadelphia mandated the ILO to work for the protection of migrant workers, along with other vulnerable groups among the economically active population. The first of the principal ILO instruments on the subject is the Migration for Employment Convention (Revised), 1947 (No. 97), which requires ratifying States to establish services to assist and protect migrants for employment and their families, and to provide for equality of treatment with its own nationals for migrants lawfully in the country. Ratifying States should conclude agreements with other States from which significant numbers of migrants come, in order to provide further protection. The Migrant Workers (Supplementary Provisions) Convention, 1975 (No. 143) aims at suppressing illegal migration for employment, and provides for additional measures to assure equality of treatment for migrant workers. The Equality of Treatment (Social Security) Convention, 1962 (No. 118) provides for equal treatment of migrant workers in terms of social security, on a reciprocal basis with other countries which have ratified the same Convention.

The United Nations adopted, in 1990, an International Convention on the Protection of the Rights of all Migrant Workers and Members of their Families. The ILO took an active part in the deliberations leading to its adoption and when the Convention comes into force, will also participate in its supervision.

Recent events involving massive expulsions of workers have illustrated the importance of putting into place workable mechanisms for the protection of the workers—and, of course, the protection of the countries from which they have come. The sudden repatriation of large numbers of workers can be disastrous for their countries of origin, which often have highly precarious economic conditions, putting workers and their national economies at terrible risk. Such situations have also pointed up the terrible conditions under which migrant workers must often survive, and their need for protection.

Recent operational activities in this field cover a wide range of activities. Attention has been focused on female domestic workers in recent case studies carried out in several counties in Europe, Latin America and Asia. The ILO's Asian Regional Programme on Labour Migration has provided training in social security protection for migrant workers in that region, and the training of labour attaches has been addressed in a recent seminar which concentrated on migrants' problems in Middle Eastern countries of employment. Another seminar took place in Tunis in December 1992 to familiarize North and West Africa trade unionists with national and international law designed to protect migrant workers.

Another activity launched recently concerns discrimination at the workplace of non-national migrant workers, and national workers of different origin, in countries where discrimination is prohibited by law but subsists in practice. This will measure the effectiveness of redress mechanisms, evaluate training courses given by enterprises and governments, and examine how this training can be improved.

With a view to giving concrete shape to the idea of providing alternatives to international migration, the ILO and the United Nations High Commission for Refugees held a meeting in May 1992 to evaluate case studies they had carried out on international aid as a means to reduce the need for emigration. This research has shown that it is possible to target international development assistance on population groups or regions characterised by a high degree of emigration. As a result of this work, a programme for the Mahgreb countries is under preparation.

The proposals for the Programme and Budget of the ILO for 1994 and 1995 provide for a special Inter-Departmental Project to protect and promote the rights of migrant workers.

### V. Disabled Workers

In accordance with international labour standards, workers enjoy social protection in the event of disability, the principal aim being to ensure that disabled workers have equitable access to employment and income from work. The underlying concept is that disabled workers who are job-ready, after a process of rehabilitation, are not unjustifiably barred from access to jobs and are not denied the opportunity to choose their employment freely. The ILO's Vocational Rehabilitation and Employment (Disabled Persons) Convention, 1983 (No.159), which has been ratified by 43 countries, reaffirms the right of disabled people to equal treatment in training and employment, and calls on governments and on employers' and workers' organizations to ensure that policies are pursued which protect disabled peoples' right to secure, retain and advance in employment.

The need for protective legal provisions to ensure employment equity for disabled workers is a reflection of persistent discrimination experienced by disabled job-seekers and/or disabled employees. Labour market participation rates are significantly lower among disabled people than among the total working population. Jobs held by disabled persons are often precarious jobs, which in times of enterprise restructuring or in a depressed economy are among the first to be abolished. Finally, disabled employees often hold only low-paid jobs and are frequently excluded from career advancement and related upgrading or retraining measures.

The right to choose employment freely and to earn a fair income from work is not applied where the only real opportunity open to disabled people is to work in sheltered conditions, frequently under sub-standard conditions of employment and remuneration. Another form of discrimination is occupational segregation, which means that certain occupations or the manufacturing of certain products are considered specifically appropriate for a certain category of disability, and disabled people are thus compelled to exercise this activity irrespective of their inclinations, desires and abilities.

Discrimination in employment is frequently the result of discrimination in education and vocational training, which makes it difficult for disabled people to compete on the open labour market despite their varied talents and abilities. Also deeply rooted fears, negative attitudes towards disability and false assumptions about disabled peoples' work capacity lead to exclusion and segregation. One of the most forceful grounds for discrimination against disabled persons in employment remains in most countries the fact that society has erected many physical barriers, e.g. in transport, housing and in the workplace, so that disabled people meet obstacles which prevent them from realizing realistic job opportunities. These objective obstacles—and not the disability as such—are often referred to by employers when rejecting job applications by disabled persons.

ILO action to combat discrimination against disabled persons includes advice on policy and anti-discriminatory legal provisions, the development of services which strengthen the capacity of disabled persons to be competitive on the open labour market, advice on adjustments at training and worksites and the introduction of support systems which facilitate the integration of disabled persons in the labour market and the strengthening of grassroots organizations of disabled persons to empower them to become competent self-advocates and to stand up for their rights. It is an essential part of the ILO's efforts to promote a more accomodating environment for the integration of disabled people into employment that the role of employers' and workers' organizations in this field is strengthened.

The ILO also participates actively in the efforts of the United Nations to develop Standard Rules on the Equalisation of Opportunities, and to formulate and implement a long-term strategy for the period after the UN Decade of Disabled Persons, which has as its guiding principle a "Society for All". In this framework it will be the ILO's task to promote the concept that the diversity of society—including its vulnerable groups—is fully reflected in the workforce.

## VI. Indigenous and Tribal Peoples

The ILO has been concerned with the situation of indigenous and tribal peoples since 1921. According to conservative figures there are about 300 million indigenous and tribal peoples around the world, representing 4.8% of the world population. There are profound differences among them in terms of the ecological environment they inhabit, cultural integrity, economic organisation, social and religious practices, and degree and terms of relationship to national political and economic systems.

Notwithstanding these differences, indigenous and tribal peoples share many common characteristics, and many common problems. These include exploitation and social exclusion, weak representation in national political systems, limited access to basic assets and services, and cultural discrimination. In rural areas, indigenous and tribal peoples have been gradually losing control over their traditional lands thus becoming landless, debt peons, tenant or marginal farmers. In urban areas, they are an uprooted, unskilled, unorganised and unprotected labour force. Indigenous and tribal peoples are often caught up in armed conflicts, where they are the victims of abuses not only by government forces but also by armed opposition groups.

Only in recent years has the wider international community started to become concerned with the social disruption, cultural destruction and physical disappearance of indigenous and tribal peoples. There is an increasing recognition that cultural diversity is not an obstacle to national development, but on the contrary can foster and contribute to it. Closely linked to this point is the increasing awareness that a wealth of accumulated knowledge adapted to local conditions is being lost with the extinction of indigenous societies. This has become a particularly important issue, with many indigenous and tribal peoples living in ecologically threatened areas and being the most vulnerable to environmental resource crisis.

Moreover, the sharp growth in inter-ethnic conflicts worldwide has made apparent the need for a new relationship between the State and indigenous and tribal peoples (and, of course, other minority groups). The conceptual national model based on the imposition of a unique model of development and of artificial cultural homogeneity has failed to guarantee a pacific and fruitful coexistence.

The ILO's principal goals in this field are to promote the human rights of indigenous and tribal peoples, and to enhance their position within national societies, with respect for their cultural specificity. To attain these goals the ILO has two means of action: specific standards on the subject and a targeted technical cooperation programme. These two instruments are closely linked to one another and are mutually supportive.

ILO standards on the subject provide the guidelines for operational activities, while development assistance contributes to the creation of the environment conducive to the exercise of the rights established by them. Standards can be a very powerful tool of social transformation, but they are not sufficient. Complementary efforts have to be made to empower indigenous and tribal peoples economically, socially and politically.

### The Legal Dimension of ILO Action

ILO Conventions Nos. 107 and 169 are the only two international legal instruments adopted specifically on the subject by the international community.

The Indigenous and Tribal Populations Convention, 1957 (No. 107), ratified by 27 countries, was the only Convention on the subject for 32 years. Adopted by the ILO with the full cooperation and collaboration of a number of other organizations in the United Nations system, it covers a wide number of issues, ranging from the working and labour conditions, and recruitment of indigenous and tribal peoples, to land rights, health and education.

During the last part of the 1970s and throughout the 1980s some indigenous organisations, and a number of intergovernmental agencies and governments, started expressing disagreement with the philosophy and approach of Convention No. 107, since it was perceived as having an "integrationist" orientation. In June 1989 the International Labour Conference adopted Convention No. 169 on Indigenous and Tribal Peoples, which took a very different approach.

***STANDARD FINAL PROVISIONS OF ILO CONVENTIONS.*** During the first ten sessions of the International Labor Conference, the final provisions of the conventions adopted varied widely. Beginning with the 11th session (1928), however, the Conference framed the final provisions of all conventions in a form that became standardized under six main headings: ratifications, entry into force, denunciations, notification of ratification to members, examination of revision, and authoritative texts. In 1929, the Conference added a seventh standard final provision, relating to the effect of revision of the convention; and, in 1946, an eighth was added, relating to notification of ratification to the Secretary-General of the United Nations. The texts of the provisions are as follows:

*Ratifications.* The formal ratifications of this Convention shall be communicated to the Director-General of the International Labour Office for registration.

*Entry into Force.* 1. This Convention shall be binding only upon those Members of the International Labour Organisation whose ratifications have been registered with the Director-General.

2. It shall come into force twelve months after the date on which the ratifications of two Members have been registered with the Director-General.

3. Thereafter, this Convention shall come into force for any Member twelve months after the date on which its ratification has been registered.

*Denunciation.* 1. A Member which has ratified this Convention may denounce it after the expiration of ten years from the date on which the Convention first comes into force, by an act communicated to the Director-General of the International Labour Office for registration. Such denunciation shall not take effect until one year after the date on which it is registered.

2. Each Member which has ratified this Convention and which does not, within the year following the expiration of the period of ten years mentioned in the preceding paragraph, exercise the right of denunciation provided for in this Article, will be bound for another period of ten years and, thereafter, may denounce this Convention at the expiration of each period of ten years under the terms provided for in this Article.

*Notification of Ratifications to Members.* 1. The Director-General of the International Labour Office shall notify all Members of the International Labour Organisation of the registration of all ratifications and denunciations communicated to him by the Members of the Organisation.

2. When notifying the Members of the Organisation of the registration of the second ratification communicated to him, the Director-General shall draw the attention of the Members of the Organisation to the date upon which the Convention will come into force.

*Communication to the United Nations.* The Director-General of the International Labour Office shall communicate to the Secretary-General of the United Nations for registration in accordance with article 102 of the Charter of the United Nations full particulars of all ratifications and acts of denunciation registered by him in accordance with the provisions of the preceding Articles.

*Note:* This provision does not appear in Conventions Nos. 1–67. However, it is made applicable to these Conventions by Article 1, paragraph 3, of the Final Articles Revision Convention, 1946 (No. 80).

*Examination of Revision.* At such times as it may consider necessary the Governing Body of the International Labour Office shall present to the General Conference a report on the working of this Convention and shall examine the desirability of placing on the agenda of the Conference the question of its revision in whole or in part.

*Note:* In Conventions Nos. 1–98 this provision originally provided for reports by the Governing Body every ten years after entry into force. It was replaced in these Conventions by the present text, under the terms of the Final Articles Revision Convention, 1961 (No. 116).

*Effect of Revising Convention.* 1. Should the Conference adopt a new Convention revising this Convention in whole or in part, then, unless the new Convention otherwise provides—

(a) the ratification by a Member of the new revising Convention, shall *ipso jure* involve the immediate denunciation of this Convention, notwithstanding the provisions of Article 3 above, if and when the new revising Convention shall have come into force;

(b) as from the date when the new revising Convention comes into force this Convention shall cease to be open to ratification by the Members.

2. This Convention shall in any case remain in force in its actual form and content for those Members which have ratified it but have not ratified the revising Convention.

*Note:* This provision does not appear in Conventions Nos. 1–26. Conventions Nos. 27–33 do not contain the words "then, unless the new Convention otherwise provides".

*Authoritative Texts.* The English and French versions of the text of this Convention are equally authoritative.

*Note:* In Conventions Nos. 1–67 this provision reads "The French and English texts of this Convention shall both be authentic."

***BIBLIOGRAPHY.*** International Confederation of Free Trade Unions. *Annual Survey of Violations of Trade Union Rights.* Brussels, Belgium. NGO yearbook, in English.

International Labour Office. *Child Labour: Law and Practice.* Vol. 10, No. 1. Geneva, Switzerland: 1991. IGO topical issue, in English.

————. *International Labour Conventions and Recommendations, 1919–1981.* Geneva, Switzerland: 1982. Document collection, in English.

————. *International Labour Standards and Women Workers.* Geneva, Switzerland: 1993. IGO information kit, in English.

————. *International Labour Standards: A Workers' Education Manual.* Geneva, Switzerland: 1990. Educational material, in English.

————. *World Labour Report.* Geneva, Switzerland: 1985–present. IGO annual report, in English.

Joyce, James A. *World Labour Rights and Their Protection.* London: Croom Helm, 1980. Scholarly study, in English.

Plant, Roger. *Labour Standards and Structural Adjustment.* Geneva, Switzerland: International Labour Office, 1994. Monograph, in English.

## INTERNATIONAL LABOR ORGANIZATION HUMAN RIGHTS CONVENTIONS.

A number of international conventions prepared and implemented by the **INTERNATIONAL LABOR ORGANIZATION** deal with basic human rights issues, such as freedom of association, the prohibition of forced labor, or equality of opportunity and treatment in employment.

Other ILO conventions deal with related issues such as industrial relations, occupational safety and health, and social security, which have important implications for human rights although the protection of those rights is not their primary concern. Such conventions are summarized briefly below and presented in chronological order:

*ILO Forced Labor Convention (1930).* Formally entitled *Convention (No. 29) concerning Forced or Compulsory Labor,* the Convention was prepared first as a temporary transitional agreement aimed at suppressing **FORCED LABOR** or compulsory labor exacted of citizens by their own governments. Its provisions were later broadened and updated in the ILO Abolition of Forced Labor Convention of 1957. The Forced Labor Convention was adopted by the International Labor Conference (14th session) on 28 June 1930, and entered into force on 1 May 1932.

*Freedom of Association and Protection of the Right to Organize Convention* (1948). Formally entitled *Convention (No. 87) concerning Freedom of Association and Protection of the Right to Organize,* the Convention was adopted on 9 July 1948 by the International Labor Conference (31st session) and entered into force on 4 July 1950. It is the first ILO convention on freedom of association applicable to non-agricultural workers and employers. It states specifically:

*Article 2.* Workers and employers, without distinction whatsoever, shall have the right to establish and, subject, only to the rules of the organisation concerned, to join organisations of their own choosing without previous authorisation.

*Article 3.* 1. Workers' and employers' organisations shall have the right to draw up their constitutions and rules, to elect their representatives in full freedom, to organise their administration and activities and to formulate their programmes.

2. The public authorities shall refrain from any interference which would restrict this right or impede the lawful exercise thereof.

*Article 4.* Workers' and employers' organisations shall not be liable to be dissolved or suspended by administrative authority.

*Article 5.* Workers' and employers' organisations shall have the right to establish and join federations and confederations and any such organisation, federation or confederation shall have the right to affiliate with international organisations of workers and employers.

*Article 6.* The provisions of articles 2, 3 and 4 hereof apply to federations and confederations of workers' and employers' organisations.

*Article 7.* The acquisition of legal personality by workers' and employers' organisations, federations and confederations shall not be made subject to conditions of such a character as to restrict the application of the provisions of articles 2, 3 and 4 hereof.

*Article 8.* 1. In exercising the rights provided for in this Convention workers and employers and their respective organisations, like other persons or organised collectivities, shall respect the law of the land.

2. The law of the land shall not be such as to impair, nor shall it be so applied as to impair, the guarantees provided for in this Convention.

*Article 9.* 1. The extent to which the guarantees provided for in this Convention shall apply to the armed forces and the police shall be determined by national laws or regulations.

2. In accordance with the principle set forth in paragraph 8 of article 19 of the Constitution of the International Labour Organisation the ratification of this Convention by any Member shall not be deemed to affect any existing law, award, custom or agreement in virtue of which members of the armed forces or the police enjoy any right guaranteed by this Convention.

*Article 10.* In this Convention the term "organisation" means any organisation of workers or of employers for furthering and defending the interests of workers or of employers.

*Article 11.* Each Member of the International Labour Organisation for which this Convention is in force undertakes to take all necessary and appropriate measures to ensure that workers and employers may exercise freely the right to organise. . . .

*Right to Organize and Collective Bargaining Convention (1949).* Formally entitled *Convention (No. 98) concerning the Application of the Principles of the Right to Organize and to Bargain Collectively, 1949,* the Convention was adopted on 1 July 1949 by the International Labor Conference (32nd session) and entered into force on 18 July 1951. It aims at providing safeguards against acts of anti-union discrimination, as is specified in the first two articles of the Convention:

*Article 1.* 1. Workers shall enjoy adequate protection against acts of anti-union discrimination in respect of their employment.

2. Such protection shall apply more particularly in respect of acts calculated to:

(a) Make the employment of a worker subject to the condition that he shall not join a union or shall relinquish trade union membership;

(b) Cause the dismissal of or otherwise prejudice a worker by reason of union membership or because of participation in union activities outside working hours or, with the consent of the employer, within working hours.

*Article 2.* 1. Workers' and employers' organisations shall enjoy adequate protection against any acts of interference by each other or each other's agents or members in their establishment, functioning or administration.

2. In particular, acts which are designed to promote the establishment of workers' organisations under the domination of employers or employers' organisations, or to support workers' organisations by financial or other means, with the object of placing such organisations under the control of employers or employers' organisations, shall be deemed to constitute acts of interference within the meaning of this article.

*Equal Remuneration Convention (1951).* Formally entitled *Convention (No. 100) concerning Equal Remuneration for Men and Women Workers for Work of Equal Value,* the Convention was adopted on 29 June 1951 by the International Labor Conference (34th session) and entered into force on 23 May 1953. Under the Convention, contracting States agree to enforce the basic principle—embodied in the Preamble to the constitution of the ILO—that men and women shall receive equal remuneration for work of equal value. This principle is to be applied, under the Convention, either by national laws and regulations, by legally established or recognized machinery for wage negotiation, by collective agreements between workers and employers, or by a combination of those methods.

*Abolition of Forced Labor Convention (1957).* Formally entitled *Convention (No. 105) concerning the Abolition of Forced Labor,* this instrument provides for States parties to undertake to suppress, and refrain from using, any form of **FORCED LABOR** or compulsory labor for any of the purposes set out in article 1. The Convention was adopted by the International Labor Conference (40th session) on 25 June 1957 and entered into force on 17 January 1959. It updates and broadens the scope of the groundbreaking ILO Forced Labor Convention of 1936. The 1957 Convention specifically condemns forced labor in the following terms:

(a) as a means of political coercion or education or as a punishment for holding or expressing political views or views ideologically opposed to the established political, social or economic system;
(b) as a method of mobilising and using labour for purposes of economic development;
(c) as a means of labour discipline;
(d) as a punishment for having participated in strikes;
(e) as a means of racial, social, national or religious discrimination.

*Discrimination (Employment and Occupation) Convention (1958).* Formally entitled *Convention (No. 111) concerning Discrimination in Respect of Employment and Occupation, 1958,* the Convention was adopted on 25 June 1958 by the International Labor Conference (42nd session) and entered into force on 15 June 1960. It was the first human rights instrument prepared by the ILO at the request of the United Nations. Between 1952 and 1954, the **SUB-COMMISSION ON PREVENTION OF DISCRIMINATION AND PROTECTION OF MINORITIES** decided to undertake preliminary studies on the question of discrimination in employment. After the UN **ECONOMIC AND SOCIAL COUNCIL** had indicated (resolution 502 H [XVI]) that such a study should be undertaken by the specialized agency concerned, the Sub-Commission was advised that the ILO was willing to prepare the study. At its 1958 session, the Sub-Commission, after examining provisional drafts of a convention and a recommendation on the subject prepared by the ILO, discontinued its

own studies. Later that year, both the draft convention and the draft recommendation were adopted by the International Labor Conference. Although the substantive provisions of both are similar, the Convention is legally binding only upon its contracting States, whereas the recommendation is morally binding upon all States.

In Article 1, the Convention defines the term "discrimination" in the following way:

(a) Any distinction, exclusion or reference made on the basis of race, colour, sex, religion, political opinion, national extraction or social origin, which has the effect of nullifying or impairing equality of opportunity or treatment in employment or occupation;
(b) Such other distinction, exclusion or preference which has the effect of nullifying or impairing equality of opportunity or treatment in employment or occupation as may be determined by the Member concerned after consultation with representative employers; and workers' organisations, where such exist, and with other appropriate bodies.
2. Any distinction, exclusion or preference in respect of a particular job based on the inherent requirements thereof shall not be deemed to be discrimination.

The Convention requires all signatories to enact the following:

(a) To seek the co-operation of employers' and workers' organisations and other appropriate bodies in promoting the acceptance and observance of this policy;
(b) To enact such legislation and to promote such educational programmes as may be calculated to secure the acceptance and observance of the policy;
(c) To repeal any statutory provisions and modify any administrative instructions or practices which are inconsistent with the policy;
(d) To pursue the policy in respect of employment under the direct control of a national authority;
(e) To ensure observance of the policy in the activities of vocational guidance, vocational training and placement services under the direction of a national authority;
(f) To indicate in its annual reports on the application of the Convention the action taken in pursuance of the policy and the results secured by such action.

*Workers' Representatives Convention (1971).* Formally entitled *Convention (No. 135) concerning Protection and Facilities to be Afforded to Workers' Representatives in the Undertaking,* the Convention reinforces two basic conventions relating to trade union rights: the Freedom of Association and Protection of the Right to Organize Convention, 1948, and the Right to Organize and Collective Bargaining Convention, 1949. It aims at ensuring that the representatives of workers are protected against dismissal or other discriminatory acts because of their status or activities and puts responsibility upon employers to provide those representatives with facilities which will enable them to perform their functions promptly and efficiently. The Convention was adopted by the International Labor Conference (56th session) on 23 June 1971 and entered into force on 30 June 1973.

*Rural Workers' Organizations Convention (1975).* Formally entitled *Convention (No. 141) concerning Organizations of Rural Workers and their Role in Economic and Social Development,* the Convention requires States parties to ensure freedom of association to rural workers, defined in article 2 as "any person engaged in agriculture, handicrafts or a related occupation in a rural area, whether as a wage earner" and further as "a self-employed person such as a tenant, sharecropper or small owner-occupier." It was adopted by the International Labor Conference (60th session) on 23 June 1975 and entered into force on 24 November 1977.

*Labor Relations (Public Service) Convention (1978).* Formally entitled *Convention (No. 151) concerning Protection of the Right to Organize and Procedures for Determining Conditions of Employment in the Public Service,* the Convention protects the right of public employees to organize and to be protected against anti-union discrimination. It was adopted by the International Labor Conference (64th session) on 27 June 1978 and entered into force on 25 February 1981.

*Workers with Family Responsibilities Convention (1981).* Formally entitled *Convention (No. 156) concerning Equal Opportunities and Equal Treatment for Men and Women Workers with Family Responsibilities,* the Convention was adopted by the International Labor Conference (67th session) on 23 June 1981 and entered into force on 11 June 1983. It updates the ILO Discrimination (Employment and Occupation) Convention, 1958, taking into account the perceived need for a change in the traditional role of men, as well as in the role of women in society and in the family, as a prerequisite to the achievement of full equality between men and women and their "responsibilities in relation to their dependent children, where such responsibilities restrict their possibilities of preparing for, entering, participating in or advancing in economic activity" (article 1). In addition, this Convention addresses the need of male and female workers to take care of "other members of their immediate family who clearly need their care or support" (article 1).

*Collective Bargaining Convention (1981).* Formally entitled *Convention (No. 154) concerning the Promotion of Collective Bargaining,* the Convention was adopted on 19 June 1981 by the International Labor Conference. It complements and updates provisions of earlier conventions concerning collective bargaining: the Freedom of Association and Protection of the Right to Organize Convention (1948) and the Right to Organize and Collective Bargaining Convention (1949), defining the term "collective bargaining" in article 2 as "negotiations which take place between an employer, a group of employers or one or more employers' organisations, on the one hand, and one or more workers' organisations, on the other, for (a) determining working conditions and terms of employment; and/or (b) regulating relations between employers and workers; and/or (c) regulating relations between employers or their organisations and a workers' organisation or workers' organisations."

The Convention also specifically calls for the promotion of labor organizations.

*Indigenous and Tribal Peoples Convention (1989).* Formally entitled *Convention (No. 169) concerning Indigenous and Tribal Peoples in Independent Countries,* the Convention was adopted by the International Labor Conference, at its 76th session, on 27 June 1989. It revises the ILO Indigenous and Tribal Populations Convention (No. 107) of 1957. Whereas the earlier instrument had been oriented towards the integration and assimilation of indigenous peoples, the revision is based on the assumption that they would continue to exist as distinct elements within national societies. Accordingly, the revised document reaffirms the principle of respect for the cultures and traditions of indigenous peoples everywhere and their right to a voice in consultations and decisions about any measures which might affect them. The full text of the Convention may be found under the entry **INDIGENOUS PEOPLES: ILO INDIGENOUS AND TRIBAL PEOPLES CONVENTION.**

***OTHER ILO CONVENTIONS HAVING A BEARING ON THE ENJOYMENT OF HUMAN RIGHTS.*** A number of international conventions, prepared and implemented by organs of the International Labor Organization, have a bearing upon the recognition and realization of human rights although their main thrust is the stimulation of improvements in employment policy, trade union arrangements, social security standards, etc. Such conventions are summarized briefly below, in the chronological order of their adoption by the International Labor Conference. The complete texts can be found in *International Labor Conventions and Recommendations, 1919–1981.*

*Labor Inspection Convention (1947).* Formally entitled *Convention (No. 81) concerning Labor Inspection in Industry and Commerce,* the Convention was adopted on 11 July 1947 by the International Labor Conference (30th session) and entered into force on 7 April 1950. The ILO had long considered it to be of great importance that every country should have a labor inspection service worthy of the name, it being obvious that labor legislation that did not provide for inspection represented more of a theoretical exercise than a binding obligation. The Convention establishes standards for operational inspection programs.

*Night Work (Women) Convention, Revised (1948).* Formally entitled *Convention (No. 89) concerning Night Work of Women Employed in Industry*, the Convention was adopted by the International Labor Conference (31st session) on 9 July 1948 and entered into force on 27 February 1951. It increases the restrictions on industrial night work employment of women previously established in the Night Work (Women) Convention (1919) and the Night Work (Women) Convention, Revised (1934).

*Protection of Wages Convention (1949).* Formally entitled *Convention (No. 95) concerning the Protection of Wages*, the Convention was adopted on 1 July 1949 by the International Labor Conference (32nd session) and entered into force on 24 September 1952. The Convention provides full and prompt payment of wages to all wage-earners in a manner which provides protection against abuse.

*Migration for Employment Convention, Revised (1949).* Formally entitled *Convention (No. 97) concerning Migration for Employment (Revised 1949)*, the Convention aims at assisting migrant workers in their search for employment and in achieving equality of treatment in respect of their human rights. The Convention was adopted by the International Labor Conference (32nd session) on 1 July 1949 and entered into force on 22 January 1952.

*Maternity Protection Convention, Revised (1952).* Formally entitled *Convention (No. 103) concerning Maternity Protection (Revised 1952)*, the Convention provides that an employed woman, after producing a medical certificate indicating that she is pregnant and stating the presumed date of her confinement, shall be entitled to a period of maternity leave of at least 12 weeks, including a period of compulsory leave after confinement. It applies to women employed in industrial undertakings and in non-industrial and agricultural occupations, including women wage-earners working at home. The Convention was adopted by the International Labor Conference (35th session) on 28 June 1952 and entered into force on 7 September 1955.

*Social Security (Minimum Standards) Convention (1952).* Formally entitled *Convention (No. 102) concerning Minimum Standards of Social Security*, the Convention was adopted by the International Labor Conference (35th session) on 28 June 1952 and entered into force on 27 April 1955. The Convention deals with nine main branches of social security—medical care, sickness benefit, unemployment benefit, old-age benefit, employment injury benefit, family benefit, maternity benefit, invalidity benefit, and survivors' benefit—and establishes minimum standards for such benefits.

*Equality of Treatment (Social Security) Convention (1962).* Formally entitled *Convention (No. 118) concerning Equality of Treatment of Nationals and Non-Nationals in Social Security*, the Convention provides that nation-

als and non-nationals shall be treated equally in all matters of social security. It was adopted by the International Labor Conference (46th session) on 28 June 1962 and entered into force on 25 April 1964.

*Social Policy (Basic Aims and Standards) Convention (1962).* Formally entitled *Convention (No. 117) concerning Basic Aims and Standards of Social Policy, 1962*, the Convention was adopted by the International Labor Conference (46th session) on 23 June 1962, and entered into force on 23 April 1964. Its basic aim is to improve standards of living in such fields as public health, housing, nutrition, education, the welfare of children, the status of women, conditions of employment, the remuneration of wage earners and independent producers, the protection of migrant workers, social security, standards of public services and general production, primarily by steps taken at the appropriate international, regional and national levels.

*Employment Policy Convention (1964).* Formally entitled *Convention (No. 122) concerning Employment Policy*, this instrument was adopted on 9 July 1964 by the International Labor Conference (48th session) and entered into force on 15 July 1966. Recognizing that employment is normally the first concern of every worker, the Convention provides that each contracting State undertake to pursue, as a major goal, an active policy designed to promote full, productive and freely chosen employment.

*Medical Care and Sickness Benefits Convention (1969).* Formally entitled *Convention (No. 130) concerning Medical Care and Sickness Benefits, 1969*, the Convention revises two earlier instruments which had been adopted by the ILO in 1927: the Sickness Insurance (Industry) Convention and the Sickness Insurance (Agriculture) Convention. It provides for the regulation by the contracting States of the scope and character of State medical care (Part I) and of sickness benefits (Part II), with a view to ensuring that such care and benefits are made available to all persons on a basis of equality and without discrimination.

*Holidays with Pay Convention, Revised (1970).* Formally entitled *Convention (No. 132) concerning Annual Holidays with Pay (Revised 1970)*, the Convention provides that all employed persons in a contracting State—seafarers are the only exception specifically mentioned—are entitled to annual paid holidays of not less than three working weeks for one year of service. Public or customary holidays are not counted as part of the minimum annual holiday, and a worker on holiday must be paid at least his normal or average remuneration. The Holidays with Pay Convention was adopted by the International Labor Conference on 24 June 1970 (54th session) and entered into force on 30 June 1973. It revises and updates the earlier Holidays with Pay Convention (No. 52) of 24 June 1936 and the

ILO Holidays with Pay (Agriculture) Convention (No. 101) of 26 June 1952.

*Minimum Wage Fixing Convention (1970)*. Formally entitled *Convention (No. 131) concerning Minimum Wage Fixing, with Special Reference to Developing Countries*, the Convention was adopted by the International Labor Conference (54th session) on 22 June 1970 and entered into force on 29 April 1972. It establishes a system of minimum wages, and the machinery by which they may be adjusted periodically.

*Minimum Age Convention (1973)*. Formally entitled *Convention (No. 138) concerning Minimum Age for Admission for Employment*, the Convention aims at the abolition of child labor and the establishment of a minimum age for employment high enough to ensure the fullest physical and mental development of young persons. It provides that each State party shall specify a minimum age for admission to employment or work within its territory and not permit anyone under that age to work in any occupation and that the minimum age specified shall not be less than the age of completion of compulsory schooling and, in any case, not less than 15 years. It revises all earlier ILO conventions relating to minimum age of employment to conform to its Standard. The Convention was adopted by the International Labor Conference (58th session) on 26 June 1973 and entered into force on 19 June 1976.

*Paid Educational Leave Convention (1974)*. Formally entitled *Convention (No. 140) concerning Paid Educational Leave*, the Convention was adopted on 24 June 1974 by the International Labor Conference (59th session) and entered into force on 26 September 1976. It defines "paid educational leave" as leave granted to workers for educational purposes for a specified period during working hours, with adequate financial entitlements; and provides that States Parties should grant such leave as necessary for (a) training at any level, (b) general, social, and civic education, and (c) trade union education.

*Human Resources Development Convention (1975)*. Formally entitled *Convention (No. 142) concerning Vocational Guidance and Vocational Training in the Development of Human Resources, 1975*, the Convention provides that States parties "shall adopt and develop comprehensive and coordinated policies and programs of vocational guidance and vocational training, closely linked with employment, in particular through public employment services."

*Migrant Workers (Supplementary Provisions) Convention (1975)*. Formally entitled *Convention (No. 143) concerning Migrations in Abusive Conditions and the Promotion of Equality of Opportunity and Treatment of Migrant Workers*, the Convention supplements the earlier Migration for Employment Convention (Revised), and provides that States parties undertake to respect the basic human rights of all migrant workers, take steps to eliminate abusive work conditions, and actively promote equality of opportunity and treatment.

*Collective Bargaining Convention (1981)*. Formally entitled *Convention (No. 154) concerning the Promotion of Collective Bargaining*, the Convention complements and updates the provisions of earlier conventions concerning collective bargaining between employers and employees, including the ILO Freedom of Association and Protection of the Right to Organize Convention (1948) and the ILO Right to Organize and Collective Bargaining Convention (1949). It provides that measures adapted to national conditions shall be taken to promote collective bargaining after prior consultations between organizations of employers and employees, and that provisions for such measures should be incorporated in national laws or regulations.

**INTERNATIONAL LAW.** On 8 May 1981, the UN **ECONOMIC AND SOCIAL COUNCIL** authorized (decision 1981/142) the **SUB-COMMISSION ON PREVENTION OF DISCRIMINATION AND PROTECTION OF MINORITIES** to appoint Mrs. Erica-Irene A. Daes (Greece) as Special Rapporteur to undertake a study on the status of the individual and contemporary international law.

The final report on the study was presented to the Sub-Commission at its 1989 session (UN Doc. E/CN.4/Sub.2/1989/40). Based on the information received, in response to a questionnaire, from 38 States, four specialized agencies, the Office of the United Nations High Commissioner for Refugees, and a number of international agencies and organizations, the Special Rapporteur reviewed developments relating to the subjectivity of the individual in international law with the aim of demonstrating, both from the theoretical and from the practical point of view, that the individual is indeed a bearer of international rights and responsibilities and that he has a restricted procedural capacity directly under international law and should be considered, at least alongside the State, as a subject of contemporary international law.

Her final conclusions were (1) that the individual is the beneficiary of international law and, in certain cases, bears the liabilities and disabilities which it imposes; (2) that the growing and ever-changing needs and the interdependence of communities and the real interest of modern society require, in most cases, the existence of various subjects of international law; and (3) that the individual, at the present time, should at least be considered on a parallel with the State as a subject of international law.

On the basis of these conclusions, the Special Rapporteur proposed that the Sub-Commission consider making the following recommendations to the **COMMISSION ON HUMAN RIGHTS** (chap. X, paras. 567–568):

*A. General Recommendations.* (a) Greater popularization of the international standards of human rights and dissemination of information concerning the promotion, protection and restoration of universally-recognized human rights, especially of measures related to teaching and education for the promotion of, respect for, and the implementation of international human rights.

(b) It is considered necessary to use the mass communication media, such as radio, television, newspapers and magazines to the greatest possible extent for constant campaigning on issues related in particular to the international protection of human rights. In this connection, it is important not only to refer to reports of human rights violations but also to the popularization of international rights standards and to every aspect that might contribute to the exaltation of the individual as the worthiest creature in the universe, over and above all racial, national, social, cultural, ideological or political differences.

(c) In some less developed countries, individuals should, when necessary, be enlightened with regard to their rights and in the manner in which they should be protected and safeguarded mainly at the regional and international level.

(d) The petition system in the Human Rights Committee represents a considerable advance over any other system of implementation existing at the universal level within the framework of the United Nations, but it is still inadequate.

(e) The creation of more effective institutions is considered of great importance. These should be accessible to the individual for the protection of their rights. Thus, it is recommended the establishment and development of international rules and procedures for more effective protection of the individual in international law, for example, on the lines of the individual's right to petition under article 25 of the European Convention on Human Rights.

(f) Developing new mechanisms by which individuals might seek international judicial review of alleged violations of their human rights, once domestic remedies have been exhausted.

(g) Adopting proper enforcement mechanisms capable of ensuring the redress of specific human rights violations. The individual must have some form of ultimate international redress.

(h) The individual should have the right to appeal to procedures provided by international law when his fundamental human rights are being violated.

(i) The individual must be given his place at the centre of international courts and international law; he must have easier access to international courts and tribunals, not only for actions falling within the competence of municipal courts but also for all real and major actions directly related to international law.

(j) The revision of the provisions of the Statute of the International Court of Justice should be considered by States and the United Nations so that even the World Court may offer free access to every individual who may be denied justice in the courts of any municipal jurisdiction.

(k) International treaties, other intergovernmental instruments relating in particular to the protection of the human rights and fundamental freedoms of every individual, should be duly ratified by the States in order to become municipal law and to be applied by the competent authorities as substantive law.

(l) States should recognize that true supranational protection and enforcement of human rights norms is es-sential for the practical enjoyment of human rights by every individual.

(m) Rules of international law, including humanitarian and human rights law, and resolutions of the competent organs and bodies of the United Nations system, related in particular to the international protection of the individual should be fully respected by every State of the international community.

(n) In particular, the disrespect and violation of human rights resolutions by Governments should be strongly condemned by the competent United Nations organs.

(o) The individual should be accorded personality under international law and should have certain rights and responsibilities as a subject of international law.

*B. Specific Recommendations.* (a) A study should be undertaken on the status of the liberation movements and contemporary international law. It should be noted that there are clear signs that recognized liberation movements are in a state of transition, which may well have an important impact on the norms of international law pertaining to them. Taking into account this ongoing evolution, it may be appropriate to delay the implementation of this recommendation until developments provide the United Nations with a clearer and firmer basis for formulating relevant criteria and standards;

(b) A study should be undertaken on the status of the "Indigenous Peoples and Nations" under contemporary international law. The study of the Problem of Discrimination Against Indigenous Populations, prepared by J.R. Martinez Cobo, Special Rapporteur of the Sub-Commission, the reports of the United Nations Working Group on Indigenous Populations, the relevant reports and the work of the ILO, including, in particular, the relevant work on the revision of the Convention No. 107/1957, and the Draft Universal Declaration on the rights of indigenous peoples under elaboration, will, *inter alia*, constitute sources of information and the key-documents for the justification of such a study. In addition to these sources, the report of the United Nations Seminar on the Effects of Racism and Racial Discrimination on the Social and Economic Relations between Indigenous Peoples and States provides a wealth of relevant information, data and reasons, and valuable conclusions and recommendations;

(c) Action should be taken by the competent bodies and organs of the United Nations and efforts should be doubled to revive the appropriate procedures for the consideration of the establishment of an objective international criminal jurisdiction;

(d) The formulation and adoption of certain general principles which could lead to international norms and standards related specifically to the status of the individual in contemporary international law; and,

(e) The present study should be transmitted through the appropriate United Nations channels to the International Law Commission for its information.

The Sub-Commission, which had examined a draft of the report at its 1988 session, received and considered the final version at its 1989 session. On 1 September 1989, it expressed (resolution 1989/46) its appreciation to the Special Rapporteur and recommended that her study, entitled "The Status of the Individual and Contemporary International Law," should be published and widely disseminated by the United Nations.

# I

**INTERNATIONAL LAW COMMISSION.** Established by the Statute of the International Law Commission, adopted by the UN **GENERAL ASSEMBLY** on 21 November 1947 (resolution 174 [II]), the Commission endeavors to promote the progressive development of international law and its codification. The term "progressive development of international law" is defined in article 15 of the statute as meaning the preparation of draft conventions on subjects which have not been heretofore regulated by international law, or in regard to which the law has not yet sufficiently developed in the practice of States. The term "codification of international law" is defined as meaning the more precise formulation and systemization of rules of international law in fields where there already has been extensive State practice, precedent, and doctrine.

*COMPOSITION.* In accordance with the statute, as amended by the General Assembly (resolutions 1103 [XI], 1647 [XVI], and 36/39), the Commission consists of 34 members "who shall be persons of recognized competence in international law." Members are elected by the Assembly from a list of candidates nominated by the governments of member States, prepared by the Secretary-General. Under the terms of the statute, the electors bear in mind that the persons chosen should individually possess the qualifications required and that, in the Commission as a whole, representation of the main forms of civilization and of the principal legal systems of the world should be insured. Under resolution 36/39, members are elected according to the following pattern: eight nationals from African States; seven from Asian States, three from Eastern European States; six from Latin American States; eight from Western European and other States; one from African or Eastern European States, in rotation; and one from Asian or Latin American States, in rotation. The term of office is five years.

*SESSIONS.* Normally, the Commission holds one session, of 12 weeks' duration, each year at the United Nations European office in Geneva. It has occasionally held meetings at other places, including New York City (first session), Paris (sixth session), and Monaco (2nd part of its 17th session). The Commission reports annually to the General Assembly.

The Commission frequently appoints one of its members as Special Rapporteur to prepare a study and report on a topic of its agenda and takes action on the basis of such a study or report. It occasionally makes use of a drafting committee composed so as to achieve a balance between its working languages or sets up small working groups or sub-committees to deal with particular topics.

*HUMAN RIGHTS RECORD.* As regards human rights, the Commission was responsible for drafting several important international instruments, including the Convention on the Nationality of Married Women, the Convention on the Reduction of Statelessness, and the Convention relating to the Status of Stateless Persons (see **STATELESSNESS**).

On 21 November 1947, the UN General Assembly directed the Commission (resolution 177 [II]) to: (a) formulate the principles of international law recognized in the charter of the Nuremberg Tribunal and in the judgment of the tribunal, and (b) prepare a draft code of offenses against the peace and security of mankind, indicating clearly the place to be accorded to the principles mentioned in (a) above.

At its 1950 session, the Commission adopted a formulation of the Principles of International Law Recognized in the Charter of the Nuremberg Tribunal and in the Judgment of the Tribunal, and submitted these principles to the General Assembly. In 1954, it completed and submitted to the General Assembly a draft code of offenses against the peace and security of mankind.

At that time, the General Assembly concluded (resolution 897 [IX]) that the draft code formulated by the Commission raised questions closely related to those of the definition of **AGGRESSION,** which it had entrusted to a special committee. It, therefore, postponed consideration of the draft code until the special committee had completed its work.

On 14 December 1974, the assembly adopted (resolution 3314 [XXIX]) the definition of aggression. Some time later, it invited the International Law Commission to resume its work on elaborating the proposed draft code of offenses against the peace and security of mankind.

Both the proposed "Draft Code of Crimes against the Peace and Security of Mankind" and the related question of a draft statute for an internal criminal court have been under discussion for some time in the International Law Commission, and the General Assembly has invited States to submit to the Secretary-General written comments on the draft articles under consideration. The Assembly, in resolution 48/31 of 9 December 1993, requested the International Law Commission to continue its work on this question as a matter of priority with a view to elaborating a draft statute if possible in 1994.

The Commission publishes *The Yearbook of the International Law Commission.* Another publication, *The*

*Work of the International Law Commission,* is brought up-to-date every seven years.

International Law Commission: Address: Palais des Nations, CH-1211, Geneva 10, Switzerland. Telephone: (41-22) 734-6011. Secretary: Vladmir Kotliar.

## INTERNATIONAL LAW: DECLARATION ON PRINCIPLES OF INTERNATIONAL LAW CONCERNING FRIENDLY RELATIONS AND CO-OPERATION AMONG STATES IN ACCORDANCE WITH THE CHARTER OF THE UNITED NATIONS

**(1970).** In adopting this Declaration, on the occasion of the 25th anniversary of the United Nations, the UN **GENERAL ASSEMBLY** expressed its strong conviction that the new instrument, by promoting the rule of law among nations and universal application of the principles of the **UNITED NATIONS CHARTER,** would strengthen world peace and constitute a landmark in the development of international law and of relations between States.

The Declaration was adopted by the UN General Assembly on 24 October 1970 (resolution 2625 [XXV]). The text, annexed to the resolution, includes the following sections relevant to human rights concerns:

### Preamble

The General Assembly,

Reaffirming in the terms of the Charter of the United Nations that the maintenance of international peace and security and the development of friendly relations and co-operation between nations are among the fundamental purposes of the United Nations,

Recalling that the peoples of the United Nations are determined to practise tolerance and live together in peace with one another as good neighbours,

Bearing in mind the importance of maintaining and strengthening international peace founded upon freedom, equality, justice and respect for fundamental human rights and of developing friendly relations among nations irrespective of their political, economic and social systems or the levels of their development,

Bearing in mind also the paramount importance of the Charter of the United Nations in the promotion of the rule of law among nations,

Considering that the faithful observance of the principles of international law concerning friendly relations and co-operation among States and the fulfilment in good faith of the obligations assumed by States, in accordance with the Charter, is of the greatest importance for the maintenance of international peace and security and for the implementation of the other purposes of the United Nations,

Noting that the great political, economic and social changes and scientific progress which have taken place in the world since the adoption of the Charter give increased importance to these principles and to the need for their more effective application in the conduct of States wherever carried on,

Recalling the established principle that outer space, including the Moon and other celestial bodies, is not subject to national appropriation by claim of sovereignty, by means of use or occupation, or by any other means, and mindful of the fact that consideration is being given in the United Nations to the question of establishing other appropriate provisions similarly inspired,

Convinced that the strict observance by States of the obligation not to intervene in the affairs of any other State is an essential condition to ensure that nations live together in peace with one another, since the practice of any form of intervention not only violates the spirit and letter of the Charter, but also leads to the creation of situations which threaten international peace and security,

Recalling the duty of States to refrain in their international relations from military, political, economic or any other form of coercion aimed against the political independence or territorial integrity of any State,

Considering it essential that all States shall refrain in their international relations from the threat or use of force against the territorial integrity or political independence of any State, or in any other manner inconsistent with the purposes of the United Nations,

Considering it equally essential that all States shall settle their international disputes by peaceful means in accordance with the Charter,

Reaffirming, in accordance with the Charter, the basic importance of sovereign equality and stressing that the purposes of the United Nations can be implemented only if States enjoy sovereign equality and comply fully with the requirements of this principle in their international relations,

Convinced that the subjection of peoples to alien subjugation, domination and exploitation constitutes a major obstacle to the promotion of international peace and security,

Convinced that the principle of equal rights and self-determination of peoples constitutes a significant contribution to contemporary international law, and that its effective application is of paramount importance for the promotion of friendly relations among States, based on respect for the principle of sovereign equality,

Convinced in consequence that any attempt aimed at the partial or total disruption of the national unity and territorial integrity of a State or country or at its political independence is incompatible with the purposes and principles of the Charter,

Considering the provisions of the Charter as a whole and taking into account the role of relevant resolutions adopted by the competent organs of the United Nations relating to the content of the principles,

Considering that the progressive development and codification of the following principles:

(a) The principle that States shall refrain in their international relations from the threat or use of force against the territorial integrity or political independence of any State, or in any other manner inconsistent with the purposes of the United Nations,

(b) The principle that States shall settle their international disputes by peaceful means in such a manner that international peace and security and justice are not endangered,

(c) The duty not to intervene in matters within the domestic jurisdiction of any State, in accordance with the Charter,

(d) The duty of States to co-operate with one another in accordance with the Charter,

(e) The principle of equal rights and self-determination of peoples,

(f) The principle of sovereign equality of States,

(g) The principle that States shall fulfil in good faith the obligations assumed by them in accordance with the Charter, so as to secure their more effective application within the international community, would promote the realization of the purposes of the United Nations,

Having considered the principles of international law relating to friendly relations and co-operation among States,

1. Solemnly proclaims the following principles: . . .

*The Principle Concerning the Duty not to Intervene in Matters Within the Domestic Jurisdiction of any State, in Accordance with the Charter.* No State or group of States has the right to intervene, directly or indirectly, for any reason whatever, in the internal or external affairs of any other State. Consequently, armed intervention and all other forms of interference or attempted threats against the personality of the State or against its political, economic and cultural elements, are in violation of international law.

No State may use or encourage the use of economic, political or any other type of measures to coerce another State in order to obtain from it the subordination of the exercise of its sovereign rights and to secure from it advantages of any kind. Also, no State shall organize, assist, foment, finance, incite or tolerate subversive, terrorist or armed activities directed towards the violent overthrow of the régime of another State, or interfere in civil strife in another State.

The use of force to deprive peoples of their national identity constitutes a violation of their inalienable rights and of the principle of nonintervention.

Every State has an inalienable right to choose its political, economic, social and cultural systems, without interference in any form by another State.

Nothing in the foregoing paragraphs shall be construed as affecting the relevant provisions of the Charter relating to the maintenance of international peace and security.

*The Principle of Equal Rights and Self-Determination of Peoples.* By virtue of the principle of equal rights and self-determination of peoples enshrined in the Charter of the United Nations, all peoples have the right freely to determine, without external interference, their political status and to pursue their economic, social and cultural development, and every State has the duty to respect this right in accordance with the provisions of the Charter.

Every State has the duty to promote, through joint and separate action, realization of the principle of equal rights and self-determination of peoples, in accordance with the provisions of the Charter, and to render assistance to the United Nations in carrying out the responsibilities entrusted to it by the Charter regarding the implementation of the principle, in order:

(a) To promote friendly relations and cooperation among States; and

(b) To bring a speedy end to colonialism, having due regard to the freely expressed will of the peoples concerned; and bearing in mind that subjection of peoples to alien subjugation, domination and exploitation constitutes a violation of the principle, as well as a denial of fundamental human rights, and is contrary to the Charter.

Every State has the duty to promote through joint and separate action universal respect for and observance of human rights and fundamental freedoms in accordance with the Charter.

The establishment of a sovereign and independent State, the free association or integration with an independent State or the emergence into any other political status freely determined by a people constitutes modes of implementing the right of self-determination by that people.

Every State has the duty to refrain from any forcible action which deprives peoples referred to above in the elaboration of the present principle of their right to self-determination and freedom and independence. In their actions against, and resistance to, such forcible action in pursuit of the exercise of their right to self-determination, such peoples are entitled to seek and to receive support in accordance with the purposes and principles of the Charter.

The territory of a colony or other Non-Self-Governing Territory has, under the Charter, a status separate and distinct from the territory of the State administering it; and such separate and distinct status under the Charter shall exist until the people of the colony or Non-Self-Governing Territory have exercised their right of self-determination in accordance with the Charter, and particularly its purposes and principles.

Nothing in the foregoing paragraphs shall be construed as authorizing or encouraging any action which would dismember or impair, totally or in part, the territorial integrity or political unity of sovereign and independent States conducting themselves in compliance with the principle of equal rights and self-determination of peoples as described above and thus possessed of a government representing the whole people belonging to the territory without distinction as to race, creed or colour.

Every State shall refrain from any action aimed at the partial or total disruption of the national unity and territorial integrity of any other State or country. . . .

2. Declares that:

In their interpretation and application the above principles are interrelated and each principle should be construed in the context of the other principles.

Nothing in this Declaration shall be construed as prejudicing in any manner the provisions of the Charter or the rights and duties of Member States under the Charter or the rights of peoples under the Charter, taking into account the elaboration of these rights in this Declaration.

3. Declares further that:

The principles of the Charter which are embodied in this Declaration constitute basic principles of international law, and consequently appeals to all States to be guided by these principles in their international conduct and to develop their mutual relations on the basis of the strict observance of these principles.

**INTERNATIONAL LEAGUE FOR HUMAN RIGHTS.** An international non-governmental organization in consultative status with the UN **ECONOMIC AND SOCIAL COUNCIL** (Category II), and with **ILO, UNESCO, OAS,** and the **COUNCIL OF EUROPE,** the League has 43 affiliates in 28 countries and individual members in 60 countries.

Founded in 1941 in New York City as the "International League for the Rights of Man," the league now seeks to promote realization of the human rights and fundamental freedoms set out in the Universal Declaration of Human Rights and other international human rights instruments. It monitors the application of those instruments, investigates human rights violations, intervenes directly with governments, makes representations before international bodies, conducts research and educational programs, publishes special reports on human rights conditions, assists victims, sends observers to political trials, dispatches special investigative missions to inquire into specific violations and to effect redress, supports and helps establish human rights national groups, and, in general, works to establish international human rights standards. It publishes the monthly *Human Rights Bulletin* and the *ILHR Annual Review*.

**INTERNATIONAL LEAGUE FOR HUMAN RIGHTS AWARD.** Established in 1980, this annual, honorary award recognizes exceptional contributions to the cause of human freedom on an international level. Past recipients include Poland's Solidarity movement (1980); Kim Dae Jung of South Korea and Helen Suzman of South Africa (1983); Andrei Sahkarov of the USSR, Mario Soares of Portugal, and Elie Wiesel of the USA (1985); and Sandro Pertini of Italy and Fang Li Zhi of China (1991).

International League for Human Rights. Address: 432 Park Avenue South, New York, NY 10002, USA. Telephone: (212) 684-1221. Executive Director: Felice Gaer.

**INTERNATIONAL LEAGUE FOR THE RIGHTS AND LIBERATION OF PEOPLES.** An international non-governmental organization in consultative status with the UN **ECONOMIC AND SOCIAL COUNCIL** (Roster), the League has individual members and national branches in 47 countries.

Founded in Rome in 1976, the League works to uphold and promote the principles of the Declaration on the Granting of Independence to Colonial Countries and Peoples. To this end, it organizes conferences, seminars, and symposia and participates in UN seminars and conferences on human rights. It publishes the *Diritti dei popoli* in Italian, six times a year; *Derechos de los pueblos* in Spanish, also six times a year; and *Ligan* in Swedish, twice a year.

International League for the Rights and Liberation of Peoples. Address: Via Bagutta 12, 1-20121 Milan, Italy. Telephone: (39-2) 78-08-11. Secretary-General: Piero Basso.

**INTERNATIONAL LESBIAN AND GAY ASSOCIATION.** A non-governmental organization in consultative status with the UN **ECONOMIC AND SOCIAL COUNCIL** and **WHO,** ILGA was founded in 1978 in Coventry, UK, to work for the liberation of lesbian/gay women and gay men from legal, social, cultural, and economic discrimination. The Association has members in 56 countries.

ILGA maintains the International Gay and Lesbian Archives and the European Discrimination Documentation Center. It also has "information pools" on topics such as asylum, Christian churches, the military, and youth. It conducts the Gay and Lesbian Prisoners Project. ILGA publishes *ILGA Bulletin* five times a year in English; and has published *The Pink Book* (3rd edition 1993).

International Lesbian and Gay Association. Address: Rue Marché-au-Charbon 81, B-1000 Brussels, Belgium. Telephone: (32-2) 502-2471. Fax: (32-2) 502-2471. Secretary-General: Rebecca Sevilla.

**INTERNATIONAL MOVEMENT ATD FOURTH WORLD.** An international non-governmental organization in consultative status with the UN **ECONOMIC AND SOCIAL COUNCIL** (Category I) and with **UNESCO** and the **COUNCIL OF EUROPE,** the Movement has over 12,000 active members in 24 countries.

The Fourth World Movement was founded by Fr. Joseph Wresinski and the poor people of the shantytown Noisy-le-Grand, France, in 1957. The Movement defends human rights by fighting against the cultural and economic insecurity into which the poor are born and works to enable the poorest and most excluded to participate in their communities and to change their destiny; it campaigns on both grassroots and international levels for decent housing, health care, job training, education, and an understanding of the problems of the poor. It sends volunteers into ghettos, barios, and public housing units in 106 countries; and organizes preschools and libraries, as well as offering internships and running training programs. In February 1987, the Economic and Social Council of France adopted the Movement's "Report on Economic and Social Poverty and Insecurity," which includes a detailed plan to combat poverty. The plan is now being implemented in 12 of France's 95 *départements* on an experimental basis.

The Movement publishes the journals *The Fourth World Journal* and *Tapori* (for children). It has also produced the books *Children of our Time, The Fourth World Speaks, Children Lead the Way in Burkina Faso, Blessed are You the Poor,* and *Passport to Bringing Computers to the Most Disadvantaged*.

International Movement ATD Fourth World. Address: 29 rue du Stade, F-77720 Champeaux, France. Telephone: (33-1) 6066-9128. Fax: (33-1) 6069-9717.

**INTERNATIONAL MOVEMENT FOR FRATERNAL UNION AMONG RACES AND PEOPLES.** An international non-governmental organization in consultative status with the UN **ECONOMIC AND SOCIAL COUN-**

CIL (Category II) and with **UNESCO**, the Movement was founded in Paris in 1952 and currently has national branches in 37 countries.

The group promotes mutual understanding and fraternal collaboration among races and peoples in the spirit of the Universal Declaration of Human Rights. Since the majority of its members are women, it accords high priority to questions relating to the status of women and children, especially in situations of oppression and underdevelopment.

The Movement publishes the *Grail Review* in English and the *UFER Bulletin* and *Intercom* in English and French.

International Movement for Fraternal Union among Races and Peoples. Address: UFER, Rue Eugene Smits 74, B-1030 Brussels, Belgium. Secretary-General: Magda Van Malder.

## INTERNATIONAL ORGANIZATION FOR THE DEVELOPMENT OF FREEDOM OF EDUCATION.

Founded in 1985 by 40 statesmen, educators, and parents of school children, this non-governmental organization collaborates with international organizations in their efforts to protect the right to freedom of education and assists in establishing, managing, and financing educational centers. The organization has consultative status with the UN **ECONOMIC AND SOCIAL COUNCIL** (Category II) and **UNESCO** and with the **COUNCIL OF EUROPE.** It publishes the newsletter *Education et Liberté* and periodical reports.

International Organization for the Development of Freedom of Education. Address: 10 rue Richemont, CH-1202 Geneva, Switzerland. Telephone: (41-22) 731-1300. Fax: (41-22) 731-4929. Director-General: Alfred Fernandez.

## INTERNATIONAL ORGANIZATION FOR THE ELIMINATION OF ALL FORMS OF RACIAL DISCRIMINATION.

An international non-governmental organization in consultative status with the UN **ECONOMIC AND SOCIAL COUNCIL** (Category II) and with **UNESCO**, EAFORD unites individual members in 21 countries.

Established in 1976 in Tripoli by an international symposium on Zionism, the organization seeks to advance understanding of international law and world consensus on the question of racism; to further the elimination of all forms of racial discrimination; to conduct, support, and publish scholarly research on racism and racial conflict; and to engage in other activities and projects aimed at the protection of human rights and the elimination of racial discrimination. The group grants fellowship awards to postgraduate students and presents awards for the furtherance of human understanding and for the best book published in Arabic, English, French, Portuguese, or Spanish on the question of racism. EAFORD investigates racism, in particular, as it relates to the Palestine conflict, the situation in South Africa, and the conditions of indigenous peoples everywhere. Among its publications are *Treatment of Palestinians in Israeli-occupied West Bank and Gaza* (1978) and *Witness of War Crimes in Lebanon* (1983).

International Organization for the Elimination of all Forms of Racial Discrimination. Address: 41 Rue de Zurich, CH-1201 Geneva, Switzerland. Telephone: (41-22) 732-5534. Fax: (41-22) 732-5082. Executive Director: Hanan Shafeddin.

## INTERNATIONAL ORGANIZATION OF JOURNALISTS.

An international non-governmental organization in consultative status with the UN **ECONOMIC AND SOCIAL COUNCIL** (Category II) and with **UNESCO**, the Organization has over 250,000 members in 120 countries.

Founded in Copenhagen in 1946, IOJ is the oldest and largest organization of professional journalists. It endeavors, by stimulating the flow of free and true information, to help maintain peace and friendship between nations; to defend freedom of the press and of journalists, in particular; to fight for better material and social conditions for journalists; and to support friendly cooperation among journalists all over the world, especially those engaged in dangerous missions. It organizes conferences, seminars, and training courses to achieve these purposes, conducts mass media research, and establishes data bases.

The Organization has published more than 250 textbooks, handbooks, and pamphlets on journalism. It also produces the monthly journal *Democratic Journalists* and the bimonthly *Newsletter.*

International Organization of Journalists. Address: Parizska 9, 110 01 Prague 1, Czechoslovakia. Telephone: 2328015, 232-83-71, or 232-59-89. Cable: INTORGJOUR PRAGUE. Telex: 122631 JOUR C. General Secretary: Dusan Ulcak.

## INTERNATIONAL PEACE BUREAU.

Founded in 1891 in Rome by the Third World Peace Congress to promote international cooperation and understanding among individuals, movements, and institutions and to develop nonviolent solutions to potential or actual violent conflicts, the International Peace Bureau has consultative status with the UN **ECONOMIC AND SOCIAL COUNCIL** (Roster) and **UNESCO.**

Through a worldwide network of member organizations in 40 countries, this non-governmental organization organizes international peace events, conferences, and seminars; supplies information and other services; and maintains a central address database of peace organizations worldwide.

The International Peace Bureau has an extensive publications program. In addition to the quarterly *IPB News*, the Bureau has published *Children's Campaign for Nuclear Disarmament* (1985), *Women and the Military System* (1988), *From Hiroshima to the Hague* (1992) by Keith Mothersson, and *Tackling the Flow of Arms* (1992) by Ernst Gülcher.

International Peace Bureau. Address: Rue de Zurich 41, CH-1201 Geneva, Switzerland. Telephone: (41-22) 731-6429. Fax: (41-22) 738-9419. Secretary-General: Colin Archer.

**INTERNATIONAL PEN.** Founded in 1921 in London, under the presidency of the author John Galsworthy, International PEN is a world association of writers, editors, and translators in all branches and classes of literature, belles lettres, poetry, drama, fiction, history, biography, science, translation, and philosophy. Unconcerned with national or party politics, the PEN charter affirms that literature should remain the common currency in spite of political or international upheavals and that works of art are the property of humanity at large. PEN works for friendship and intellectual cooperation and freedom of expression in all countries. International PEN maintains autonomous chapters in 82 countries and has consultative status with the UN **ECONOMIC AND SOCIAL COUNCIL** (Roster), **UNESCO,** and the World Intellectual Property Organization. It publishes *PEN International* twice a year in English and French.

International PEN. Address: 9-10 Charterhouse Buildings, Goswell Road, London EC1M 7AT, UK. Telephone: (44-71) 253-4308. Fax: (44-71) 253-5711. International Secretary: Alexandre Blokh.

**INTERNATIONAL PHYSICIANS FOR THE PREVENTION OF NUCLEAR WAR.** When a **NOBEL PEACE PRIZE** is given to an organization, that prize is usually considered a "safe" choice, one around which no argument will arise. Such a choice was the 1985 Peace Prize awarded to a relatively little-known international group of doctors. The Prize Committee cited the organization for performing a "considerable service to mankind by spreading authoritative information and by creating an awareness of the catastrophic consequences of atomic warfare." Unfortunately, while

the group itself was not an issue, controversy arose around one of its leaders.

Established in 1980, this Boston-based group is dedicated to publicizing the medical effects of nuclear war and to urging that money spent on nuclear armaments be used to improve the health and well-being of all peoples. At the time of the award, the group had 135,000 members worldwide, particularly among American physicians and doctors from what was then the USSR. At present, the group has over 200,000 members, with affiliated groups in 76 countries. The IPPNW has consultative status with the UN **ECONOMIC AND SOCIAL COUNCIL** (Roster) and with **WHO.** In addition to the 1985 Nobel Peace Prize, the group received the 1984 UNESCO Education for Peace Award. It publishes the quarterly *Vital Signs*.

When the Nobel Prize was announced in 1985, the co-presidents of the group decided to attend the Oslo ceremonies to accept the award: the American Dr. Bernard Lown of the Harvard School of Public Health and the Russian Dr. Yevgeny Chazov, personal cardiologist to the top members of the Communist Party. It was Dr. Chazov's participation that sparked the ensuing controversy. In 1973, Dr. Chazov was one of 25 Soviet doctors who signed an open letter to Andrei Sakharov, published in *Izvestia*, denouncing the Russian physicist for his criticism of Soviet domestic and foreign policies. Dr. Chazov never repudiated the letter or made any comments on Soviet human rights policy (or the situation of Sakharov, in particular, who, at that time, was under house arrest in Gorky). Because of Dr. Chazov's participation, the American and West German ambassadors were instructed to boycott the award ceremony, and Great Britain officially protested the award.

In their Nobel lectures, the co-presidents stressed the necessity of medical personnel actively interceding in public policy. Dr. Lown stated, "We physicians who shepherd human life from birth to death have a moral imperative to resist . . . the drift toward the brink. The threatened inhabitants on this planet must speak out for those generations yet unborn." Dr. Chazov remarked, "True to the Hippocratic oath, we cannot keep silent knowing what the final epidemic—nuclear war—can bring to humankind. The bell of Hiroshima rings . . . not as a funeral knell but as an alarm."

International Physicians for the Prevention of Nuclear War. Address: 126 Rogers Street, Cambridge, MA 02142, USA. Telephone: (617) 868-5050. Fax: (617) 868-2560. Executive Director: Ralph Fine.

**INTERNATIONAL PLANNED PARENTHOOD FEDERATION.** Founded in 1952 in Bombay, India, to promote the education of all peoples in family planning and responsible parenthood; to preserve and protect good mental and physical health of parents and children; and to stimulate research in all aspects of human fertility and its regulation, Planned Parenthood has grown to 109 national associations, in addition to regional offices for Africa, for East and Southeast Asia, for Oceania, for the Arab world, and for the western hemisphere. This non-governmental organization encourages family-planning services and helps associations offer contraceptives services, set and maintain high clinical standards, and train all levels of personnel. It has consultative status with the UN ECO-NOMIC AND SOCIAL COUNCIL (Category I), **UNESCO, FAO, ILO, UNICEF, WHO,** and the UN Population Fund, and maintains a Geneva representative. It also cooperates with the Organization of American States.

The International Planned Parenthood Federation maintains an extensive publication program, among its offerings: the monthly *Information Package* in English; *IPPF Medical Bulletin* (six times a year) in English, French, and Spanish; the quarterly *People and the Planet* in English; the biannual *Planned Parenthood Challenges;* and *The Family Planning Handbook for Doctors* in English, French, and Spanish. It has also published a trilingual edition of the *IPPF Directory of Hormonal Contraceptives* (1992) and offers a wide range of medical books and educational publications.

International Planned Parenthood Federation. Address: Regent's College, Inner Circle, Regent's Park, London NW1 4NS, UK. Telephone: (44-71) 486-0741. Fax: (44-71) 487-7950. Secretary-General: Halfdan Mahler.

**INTERNATIONAL PRESS INSTITUTE.** An international non-governmental organization in consultative status with the UN ECONOMIC AND SOCIAL COUNCIL (Roster) and with **UNESCO** and the COUNCIL OF EUROPE, IPI has 1,800 members in 75 countries.

Founded in Paris in 1951, the Institute promotes free access to news, free expression of views, and free publication of newspapers. It also promotes understanding among editors, the exchange of accurate and balanced news, and the improvement of journalistic practices. The Institute's Press Center provides information on press freedom and editorial research. IPI also conducts Asian conferences and African training programs, as well as seminars in Africa, the Americas, Asia, and Europe.

The Institute publishes the monthly *IPI Report* in English, as well as studies on the international media.

International Press Institute. Address: Dilke House, Malet Street, London WC1E 7JA, UK. Telephone: (44-71) 636-0703. Fax: (44-71) 580-8349. Director: Peter Galliner.

**INTERNATIONAL PROGRESS ORGANIZATION.** An international non-governmental organization in consultative status with the UN ECONOMIC AND SOCIAL COUNCIL (Roster) and with **UNESCO,** IPO has members in 66 countries. The Organization was founded in 1972 in Innsbruck, Austria, by students from Europe, Asia, and Africa who were concerned about human rights. IPO sponsors international conferences and research seminars on topics such as human rights, international law, and economic development. It encourages cultural exchanges between all nations, attempts to promote tolerance towards all nationalities and cultures, and emphasizes human liberties, social and economic development, and peace.

IPO conducts an extensive publication program, most prominently the series "Studies in International Relations," which includes among its titles *Cultural Self-Comprehension of Nations* (1978), *The Principles of International Law and Human Rights* (1981), *The Principles of Non-Alignment* (1982), and *Democracy in International Relations* (1986). Among its published monographs are *The Concept of Monotheism in Islam and Christianity* (1982), *The Crisis of Representative Democracy* (1986), *Ethical Relativism Versus Human Rights* (1987), *Democracy and Human Rights,* and *The United Nations and the New World Order* (1992).

International Progress Organization. Address: Kohlmarkt 4, A-1010 Vienna, Austria. Telephone: (43-1) 533-2877. Fax: (43-1) 533-296221. President: Hans Köchler.

**INTERNATIONAL PUBLISHERS ASSOCIATION.** Founded in Paris in 1896, this non-governmental organization has consultative status with the UN ECONOMIC AND SOCIAL COUNCIL (Roster), **UNESCO,** and the World Intellectual Property Organization. The group has member organizations in 48 countries.

IPA works to defend freedom of publishers to publish and distribute all works and to overcome illiteracy. The group keeps the flow of books from one country to another free of tariffs and other obstructions. IPA publishes the quarterly *International Publishers Bulletin.*

International Publishers Association. Address: Ave. de Miremont 3, CH-1206 Geneva, Switzerland. Telephone: (41-22) 346-3018. Fax: (41-22) 347-5717. Secretary-General: J. Alexis Koutchoumow.

**INTERNATIONAL RED CROSS.** This organization comprises the INTERNATIONAL COMMITTEE OF THE RED CROSS, the LEAGUE OF THE RED CROSS AND RED

CRESCENT SOCIETIES, and about 145 national Red Cross and Red Crescent Societies. The International Red Cross oversees the realization, in all parts of the Red Cross/Red Crescent movement, of certain basic principles: humanity, impartiality, neutrality, independence, voluntary service, unity, and universality.

The first Red Cross national societies came into being in 1863; in 1864, the emblem of a red cross on a white background—the inverse of the Swiss flag—was created to insure the protection of those wounded in war and those who care for them. The emblem has no religious significance; however, in 1876, during the Russo–Turkish war, the Ottoman Society for Relief to the Wounded replaced the cross with a red crescent. The red crescent has since been adopted by a number of Islamic countries and is recognized and granted equal status with the red cross.

The work of the national societies in time of armed conflict is well known; originally created for service in wartime, to help army medical personnel care for the sick and wounded, the national societies moved off the battlefields to help civilian victims of conflicts. In addition, the societies expanded their efforts to help in peacetime. After World War I, the national societies used their training and experience to attend to the urgent medical and social needs of populations ravaged by that conflict. Since that time, the national societies have played important roles in founding hospitals, training nurses, and conducting education programs in child care and public health; in pioneering ambulances, mountain, and sea rescue services; in providing first-aid training; and in caring for the elderly and the handicapped.

Nearly every society has a youth section and promotes blood transfusion services. Since World War II, the national societies in industrialized countries have further widened their field of activities to address social problems like drug addiction, unemployment, and delinquency. In developing countries, the societies work for improved health and welfare, engaging in projects to combat fatal infantile diseases, give basic health education, and mount intensive vaccination campaigns.

Finally, throughout the 1980s, due to the enormous increase in refugees, especially in third world countries, the national societies have provided relief and social services for this population. In addition to its many other services, the national societies continue one of their oldest peacetime activities: providing relief and emergency services for victims of natural disasters.

International Red Cross. Address: 17 Avenue de la Paix, CH-1202 Geneva, Switzerland. Telephone: 22-346001. Cable: INTERCROIXROUGE. Telex: 22269. Contact: Michel Testuz.

## INTERNATIONAL SERVICE FOR HUMAN RIGHTS.

The International Service for Human Rights is a nongovernmental organization that was created in 1984 to help human rights organizations, witnesses, and victims who wish to address themselves to the international procedures concerning human rights. The Service provides information on human rights sessions in the United Nations, explains how to present complaints and eyewitness reports in accordance with international procedures, and technically and logistically assists those who come to witness before international bodies.

Since 1989, the International Service has developed its activities in the southern continents. In particular, the International Service has developed the "Internship Program for Human Rights Defenders from the South," giving priority to situations in Africa and Asia. The interns work in Geneva and receive training in international procedures during the sessions of the UN COMMISSION ON HUMAN RIGHTS and of the SUB-COMMISSION FOR THE PREVENTION OF DISCRIMINATION AND PROTECTION OF MINORITIES. The interns help at human rights meetings by preparing reports and notes. Their training is of service to their organizations and communities.

The International Service publishes the quarterly *Human Rights Monitor* in English and French.

International Service for Human Rights. Address: 1 rue de Varembé, P.O. Box 16, Ch-1211 Geneva, Switzerland. Telephone: (41-22) 733-51-23. Fax: (41-22) 733-08-26. Director: Adrien-Claude Zoller.

## INTERNATIONAL SOCIAL SERVICE.

An international non-governmental organization in consultative status with the UN ECONOMIC AND SOCIAL COUNCIL (Category II), ISS has national branches in 14 countries.

Founded in 1921 by the World YWCA and originally called the "International Migration Service," ISS assists individuals who, as a consequence of voluntary or forced migration or other social problems of an international character, have to overcome personal or family difficulty. It also studies, from an international viewpoint, the conditions and consequences of migration regarding the individual and family life. The ISS General Secretariat in Geneva handles annually about 500 cases involving individual or family difficulty arising from migration or from residence in a foreign country. The service also works with groups and communities as required and endeavors to procure legal documents, where needed.

ISS publishes annual activity reports and has published *International Naming and Addressing Directory, ISS*

*History,* and *60 Years of International Social Service.*

International Social Service. Address: 32 Quai du Seujet, CH-1201, Geneva, Switzerland. Telephone: 31-74-54 or 31-74-55. Cable: Migranto Geneva. Telex: 28-92-83. Secretary-General: Marcelle L. Brisson.

## INTERNATIONAL SOCIETY FOR HUMAN RIGHTS.

An international non-governmental organization in consultative status with the **COUNCIL OF EUROPE,** ISHR brings together 18 national organizations in 17 countries.

Founded in 1972 in Frankfurt-Main—originally as the "Society for Human Rights"—ISHR works to achieve universal respect for and observance of human rights, to provide support and relief to victims of discrimination, and to support the Universal Declaration of Human Rights and other international human rights instruments. It defends non-violent human rights activists and assists "prisoners of conscience" and their families. It also promotes family reunions within the framework of the final act of the Helsinki Accord.

Among the society's publications are *Menschenrechte, Menschenrechte in Latein Amerika, Menschenrechte in Afrika, DDR Heute, Boletin en America Latina, USSR Aktuell,* and *Human Rights in Brief.*

International Society for Human Rights. Address: Kaiserstrasse 72, Postfach 101132, D-6000 Frankfurt/Main 1, German FR. Telephone: 69-23-69-71. Telex: 4-185-181-IGFM. Fax: (49-69) 23-41-00. Executive Director: Ivan Agrusow.

## INTERNATIONAL STUDIES ASSOCIATION.

An international non-governmental organization in consultative status (Roster) with the UN **ECONOMIC AND SOCIAL COUNCIL,** ISA is associated with 16 organizations in 21 countries. It has more than 2,000 individual members, including scientists, students, officials of governments and international organizations, and officials of transnational corporations.

The Association focuses primarily on issues of academic freedom and the unimpeded transnational flow of persons and ideas. ISA organizes an annual international convention (with approximately 1,200 attendees) and the biennial World Assembly of International Studies Research. In addition to individual papers and studies, ISA regularly publishes the *International Studies Newsletter* (10 times per year), *International Studies Quarterly,* and *IS Notes* (four times per year).

International Studies Association. Address: Byrnes International Center, University of South Carolina, Columbia, SC 29208, USA. Telephone: (803) 777-2933. Telex: 805038. USC INTL CLB. Executive Director: William A. Welsh.

## INTERNATIONAL THEATER INSTITUTE.

Established in 1948 in Prague, Czechoslovakia, under the auspices of **UNESCO,** the International Theater Institute is a non-governmental organization in consultative status with the UN **ECONOMIC AND SOCIAL COUNCIL** and the **COUNCIL OF EUROPE.** The Institute promotes the exchange of knowledge and practices in the area of performing arts and attempts to make the public aware of the ways that artistic creation can influence development, mutual understanding between nations, and peace.

The Institute maintains eight permanent committees: Dramatic Theater Committee, the Dance Committee, the Music Theater Committee, the Playwrights Committee, the Committee for Theater Education, the Publication Committee, the New Theater Committee, and the Committee for Cultural Identity and Development. It also helps to celebrate World Theater Day every March 27 and organizes the biennial festival Theater of Nations. In addition the group operates the University of the Theater of Nations, which offers training courses to young postgraduate professionals from all theater disciplines. ITI publishes the triannual *ITI News.*

International Theater Institute. Address: 1 rue Miollis, F-75732 Paris CEDEX 15, France. Telephone: (33-1) 4568-2650. Fax: (33-1) 4306-8798. Secretary-General: André Louis Perinetti.

## INTERNATIONAL UNION OF LATIN NOTARIES.

Established in 1948 in Buenos Aires, Argentina, to promote the study and standardization of notarial legislation and to establish offices for international notarial exchange, the Union has consultative status (Category II) with the UN **ECONOMIC AND SOCIAL COUNCIL, UNESCO,** the **COUNCIL OF EUROPE,** and the **ORGANIZATION OF AMERICAN STATES.** Its membership consists of notaries in over 50 countries.

The Union represents notariats before international organizations and organizes exchanges and diffusion of information and publications on law, international private law, and comparative legislation. It maintains consultative bureaus in member countries. The Union publishes the quarterly *Revista Internacional del Notariado* in Spanish and French.

International Union of Latin Notaries. Address: Via Locatelli 5, 1-20124 Milan, Italy. Telephone: (39-2) 875-657. Fax: (39-2) 874-734. European Permanent Secretary: Emanuele Ferrari.

**INTERNATIONAL UNION OF LAWYERS.** An international non-governmental organization in consultative status with the UN ECONOMIC AND SOCIAL COUNCIL (Category II) and with the COUNCIL OF EUROPE, best known by its French title, *Union internationale des avocats* (UIA), the organization is affiliated with regional associations and national bar associations (55) in 41 countries.

Founded in 1927 in Belgium, the Union works to establish permanent relations and exchanges between national federations or associations of lawyers and supports their action and work. It promotes joint study of questions concerning legal organization and contributes to the establishment of an international legal order. The Union publishes *Bulletin de l'UIA*.

International Union of Lawyers. Address: 18 Ave. Charles de Gaulle, F-92200 Neuilly, France. Telephone: (33-1) 4738-1311. Fax: (33-1) 4738-6138.

**INTERNATIONAL UNION OF STUDENTS.** An international non-governmental organization in consultative status with the UN ECONOMIC AND SOCIAL COUNCIL (Category II) and with UNESCO, the Union has 109 full organizations in 117 countries.

Founded in 1946 in Prague, Czechoslovakia, the Union works for the right of all young people to enjoy primary, secondary, and higher education, regardless of sex, economic circumstances, social standing, political or religious convictions, color, or race. It organizes and sponsors conferences, seminars, and winter and summer sports and work camps. It also supports student campaigns for peace, student relief and welfare activities, and works against colonialism and racial discrimination. The Union also arranges student exchanges, travel, and cultural events and operates a documentation center.

Among IUS' publications are the monthly *World Student News,* published in English, French, Spanish and German; and the *Democratization of Education, Sports Bulletin,* and the cultural monthly *Students Life Magazine* in English, French, and Spanish.

International Union of Students. Address: 17th November Street, P.O. Box 58, 11001 Prague 01, Czech Republic. Telephone: (42-2) 231-2812. Fax: (42-2) 231-6100.

**INTERNATIONAL UNION OF YOUNG CHRISTIAN DEMOCRATS.** An international non-governmental organization in consultative status with the UN ECONOMIC AND SOCIAL COUNCIL (Category II) and with UNESCO, IUYCD has national affiliates in 42 countries.

Founded in 1959, the Union supports the establishment throughout the world of a social, economic, and political democracy based on Christian democratic ideals. In addition to its quadrennial world congress, it conducts international, regional, and national congresses, seminars, and round-table discussions, focusing on issues related to human rights, social justice, and pluralism in society.

IUYCD publishes the *IUYCD Newsletter* fortnightly in three languages and *Debate* triannually, also in three languages.

International Union of Young Christian Democrats. Address: Rue de La Victoire, B-1060 Brussels, Belgium. Telephone: (32-2) 537-2589. Fax: (32-2) 537-9348. Secretary-General: Marcos Vilasmil.

**INTERNATIONAL WOMEN'S TRIBUNE CENTRE.** Founded in New York in 1976, IWTC is an international non-governmental organization in consultative status with the UN ECONOMIC AND SOCIAL COUNCIL (Roster). IWTC serves as a communication link for 16,000 individuals and groups in 160 countries throughout the world. It is supported by grants from the development agencies of the Governments of Canada, Sweden, the Netherlands, Norway, and Australia, with additional funds coming from church and foundation groups in the United States.

The Centre was established following the International Women's Year Tribune (a non-governmental conference) in Mexico City in 1975. IWTC promotes equal rights and opportunities for women worldwide, in particular supporting the initiatives of third-world women who are working to promote the more equitable and active participation of women within the development process. Through a program of technical assistance and training, information, and networking services, IWTC's work focuses on four areas: organizing women, coordinating communication services, promoting community economic development, and training individuals and groups in appropriate technology.

Among its resources for women, IWTC has an extensive publication program. Its principal organ is *The Tribune: A Women and Development Quarterly* published in English, French, and Spanish since 1976. The Centre also publishes training manuals and resource kits, bibliographies, directories, guides to specialized informational resources, and slide-tape sets.

International Women's Tribune Centre. Address: 777 United Nations Plaza, New York, NY 10017, USA. Telephone: (212) 687-8633. Fax: (212) 661-2704. Director: Anne S. Walker.

**INTERNATIONAL WORK GROUP FOR INDIGENOUS AFFAIRS.** Founded in 1968 in Stuttgart, Germany, to establish the right of indigenous peoples to self-determination, the IWGIA has consultative status with the UN **ECONOMIC AND SOCIAL COUNCIL** (Category II) and with the **ILO**. It has members in 60 countries. The group documents information and performs research to publicize problems of indigenous peoples and provides practical and financial support for congresses that are undertaken by indigenous peoples' own organizations. It also organizes humanitarian projects and emergency action in cases of land rights abuse, human rights violations, or genocide. It publishes the *IWGIA Newsletter* in English and Spanish, the triannual *IWGIA Documents* in English and Spanish, and the *IWGIA Yearbook*.

International Work Group for Indigenous Affairs. Address: Fiolstraede 10, DK-1171, Copenhagen, Denmark. Telephone: (45) 3312-4724. Fax: (45) 3314-7749. Chairman: Rene Fuerst.

## INTERNATIONAL YOUNG CATHOLIC STUDENTS.

An international non-governmental organization in consultative status with the UN **ECONOMIC AND SOCIAL COUNCIL** (Roster) and with **UNESCO** and the **COUNCIL OF EUROPE**, IYCS has affiliated organizations and individual members in 78 countries and territories.

Founded in 1946 in Fribourg, Switzerland, as the *Centre international de documentation et d'information*, International Young Catholic Students supports student movements in all countries. Its regional secretariats organize study sessions. IYCS maintains regional secretariats and committees in Africa, Latin America, North America, Europe, the Middle East, Asia, and the Pacific. The group publishes *IYCS Newsletter* (quarterly) in English, French, and Spanish; *Info-Rapid* (bimonthly); and *SPES: Boletin de Información para los Movimientos de América Latina* (quarterly) in Spanish. The regional secretariats also publish quarterly bulletins.

International Young Catholic Students. Address: 171 rue de Rennes, F-75006 Paris, France. Telephone: (33-1) 4548-1472. Fax: (33-1) 4284-0453. Secretary-General: Jean-François Bickel.

## INTERNATIONAL YOUNG CHRISTIAN WORKERS.

An international non-governmental organization in consultative status with the UN **ECONOMIC AND SOCIAL COUNCIL** (Category II) and with **ILO, UNESCO, FAO,** and the **COUNCIL OF EUROPE**, IYCW brings together national organizations in 50 countries and territories.

Founded in 1945 in Brussels as the "European Young Christian Workers," International Young Christian Workers—through surveys, meetings, and congresses—studies aspects of young workers lives: working conditions, displacements, living conditions, etc.

The group organizes young working people in groups to discuss their problems and means of solving them. IYCW publishes the quarterly *Info* in English, French, and Spanish; the annual *African Info* in English and French; and the annual *Continental Bulletin of America* in French and Spanish.

International Young Christian Workers. Address: Rue Plantin 11, B-1070 Brussels, Belgium. Telephone: (32-2) 521-6983. Fax: (32-2) 521-6944. International President: Glynn Cloete.

## INTERNATIONAL YOUTH AND STUDENT MOVEMENT FOR THE UNITED NATIONS.

An international non-governmental organization in consultative status with the UN **ECONOMIC AND SOCIAL COUNCIL** (Category I) and with **UNESCO,** the Movement has members in 42 countries and territories.

Founded in Rome in 1948 as the "Student Commission of the World Federation of United Nations Associations," the International Youth and Student Movement for the United Nations is now an independent organization. It works with students and young people to promote national liberation; economic, social, and cultural justice; and peace, disarmament, and human rights. It opposes colonialism, neocolonialism, imperialism, and repression in all forms and promotes a wider knowledge of the UN's activities and of its potential. The group organizes seminars, workshops, and study tours; and disseminates information on UN and international affairs.

ISMUN publishes the monthly *ISMUN Newsletter* and *Analysis and Action Reports*. An occasional publication is the *Human Rights Bulletin*.

International Youth and Student Movement for the United Nations. Address: Palais des Nations, Pavillons du Petit-Saconnex, 16 avenue Jean-Tremblay, CH-1211 Geneva 10, Switzerland. Telephone: (41-22) 798-5850, Ext. 498. Fax: (41-22) 733-4838. Secretary-General: Jan Lönn.

## INTER-PARLIAMENTARY UNION.

An international non-governmental organization in consultative status with the UN **ECONOMIC AND SOCIAL COUNCIL** (Category I), the **COUNCIL OF EUROPE**, the **LEAGUE OF ARAB STATES**, the **ORGANIZATION OF AMERICAN STATES**, and the **ORGANIZATION OF AFRICAN UNITY**, IPU is composed of Inter-Parliamentary national groups in 118 countries.

The Union was the first worldwide political organization to promote the concept of peace and international arbitration. Its origins date back to 1889, when the first Inter-Parliamentary Conference for International Arbitration met in Paris. From its inception, IPU has been active in the peace movement and was instrumental in setting up what is now the Permanent Court of Arbitration in the Hague. Over the years, eight **Nobel Peace Prizes**—including recipients for the first three years of the award, **Frederick Passy, Charles Albert Gobat,** and **William Randal Cremer**—were shared by leaders of the IPU.

IPU addresses all international problems suitable for settlement by parliamentary action and promotes improvements in the working methods of parliamentary institutions. Through organizing specialized worldwide or regional meetings, IPU studies problems in the fields of international security, economic development, and social affairs, including problems in European security and cooperation, disarmament, the environment, population, health, employment, drug control, and women's and children's rights. IPU also safeguards the rights of parliamentarians; in a 1987 report of the Special Committee on Violations of the Human Rights of Parliamentarians, the committee stated that, in its ten years of operation, it has investigated nearly 600 individual situations in 47 countries and has examined cases involving violations of freedom of expression, exile, disappearance, murder and execution, and restriction or suspension of civil and political rights.

The Union has five established committees: the Political Questions Committee, the International Security and Disarmament Questions Committee; the Parliamentary, Juridical, and Human Rights Questions Committee; the Economic and Social Questions Committee; and the Education, Science, Culture and Environment Committee. In 1989, the Union established the permanent Ad Hoc Committee on Environment.

IPU publishes the *Inter-Parliamentary Bulletin,* its official organ, issued quarterly in English and French, among others.

Inter-Parliamentary Union. Address: Place du Petit-Saconnex, CP 438, CH-1211, Geneva 19, Switzerland. Telephone: (41-22) 734-4150. Fax: (41-22) 733-3141. Secretary-General: Pierre Comillon.

## INTIFADA (UPRISING) OF THE PALESTINIAN PEOPLE. See PALESTINIAN PEOPLE'S RIGHTS.

## INUIT CIRCUMPOLAR CONFERENCE. Established in 1977 in Barrow, AK, USA, to protect the resources of the Inuit homeland in the Arctic regions and to promote unity among the Inuit in protection of their rights, culture, and environment, this non-governmental organization has consultative status (Category II) with the UN **Economic and Social Council** and the **ILO.** The group has official delegates representing Inuit people from each of its four member countries and territories: Canada, Alaska (USA), Greenland, and Russia.

The ICC maintains the Inuit Regional Conservation Strategy and the Creation of a Comprehensive Artic Policy project. It publishes the *ICC Artic Policy Review.*

Inuit Circumpolar Conference. Address: 3111 C Street, Suite 506, Anchorage, AK 99503, USA. Telephone: (907) 561-7611. Fax: (907) 562-4376. President: Eilene MacLean.

## IRAN. The Islamic Republic of Iran is a country in southern Asia, on the Caspian Sea, the Gulf of Oman, and the Persian Gulf. It has borders with Afghanistan, Armenia, Azerbaijan, Iraq, Pakistan, Turkey, and Turkmenistan. It achieved independence in 1925 from Russia and England, which had divided the country (then known as Persia) into two spheres of influence, when Gen. Reza Pahlavi seized the government and was elected hereditary shah. It became a member of the United Nations in 1945. Its population is estimated to be 60,500,000. Ethnic groups include persons of Turkish, Kurdish, and Syrian descent. Languages commonly used include Farsi (Persian), various Turkic vernaculars, Kurdish, Luri, and Baluchi. Islam (Shi'ite, 96%; Sunni, 3%) is the predominant religion; non-Muslim denominations account for the remainder.

The government (1994) took the form of a republic. Under the constitution, the president, elected for a term of four years, exercises executive authority. He appoints the prime minister and members of the cabinet, subject to the approval of the unicameral National Consultative Assembly, members of which are elected by popular vote for terms of four years. The judicial system is based on Islamic law. However, from 1982 to the end of 1988 all State policy was determined by a religious leader, the Ayatollah Ruhollah Khomeini, who, together with the National Consultative Assembly, aimed to ensure adherence to Islamic principles in every aspect of Iranian life.

In ancient days, the territory now known as Iran lay at the heart of the Persian Empire, one of the greatest empires the world has ever known. In 626 A.D. Arab invaders brought foreign rule, and the new religion of Islam, to the country. Independence was re-established many centuries later when the Safavid dynasty (1499–1733), under its leader Shah Ismael, drove out the Arabs and converted the population to the Shi'ite branch of Islam. Subsequently, Iran experienced periods of prosperity and expansion mixed with periods of conquest and exploitation of its vast natural resources by various European countries, including England, Portugal, and Russia.

Gen. Reza Pahlavi was deposed as Shah in 1941 in favor of his son, Mohammed Reza Pahlavi. Although conditions of life improved notably in Iran during the regime of the new shah, he was widely criticized for his efforts to modernize the country and to improve the status of its women, as well as for misuse of the secret police force known as *Sadak* to suppress opposition. In 1968, Iran acted as host to the International Conference on Human Rights, held to commemorate the 20th anniversary of the UNIVERSAL DECLARATION OF HUMAN RIGHTS.

Massive demonstrations demanding the return to Iran of opposition leader Ayatollah Ruhollah Khomeini from France, where he had lived for some years in exile, led to the imposition of martial law in 1978. When riots and strikes continued despite the appointment of another opposition leader, Shahpur Bakhtiar, as premier, Shah Mohammed Reza Pahlavi handed over power to a regency council and left Iran on 16 January 1979. Khomeini returned to Iran on 1 February and established a new government based on fundamentalist Islamic concepts. The shah died on 17 July 1980 after being admitted to the United States of America for treatment of his terminal cancer.

Since militant "students" invaded the U.S. embassy at Teheran on 4 November 1979 and seized a number of staff members as hostages, the United Nations has been deeply concerned about the human rights situation in Iran. A unanimous appeal by the SECURITY COUNCIL demanding release of the hostages was rejected by the Iranian government, and it was not until Iran's conditions—including release of $8 billion in frozen Iranian assets, return of assets held by the former imperial family, and cancellation of any damage claims against Iran by the U.S.—were met that 52 American hostages were released after 444 days in captivity.

The Security Council, the GENERAL ASSEMBLY, the COMMISSION ON HUMAN RIGHTS, the SUB-COMMISSION ON PREVENTION OF DISCRIMINATION AND PROTECTION OF MINORITIES, and other United Nations bodies have repeatedly, since then, expressed their concern at reports of continuing serious violations of human rights in the Islamic Republic of Iran, and the Commission has appointed a Special Representative to assist it in monitoring the situation.

The Special Representative was first appointed by the Commission at its 1984 session (resolution 1984/54); the Special Representative's mandate later was extended, at each annual Commission session, for a one-year period. The Special Representative is Mr. Reynaldo Galindo Pohl (El Salvador). He prepares, each year, an interim report for consideration by the General Assembly and a final report for consideration by the Commission on Human Rights.

Up to December 1989, all reports of the Special Representative were based on information made available to him by the government of the Islamic Republic of Iran and by other sources, including governmental and non-governmental organizations. However, the situation changed towards the end of that year following the death of the Ayatollah Khomeini, and the UN General Assembly on 15 December (resolution 44/163) welcomed the Iranian Government's invitation to the Special Representative to visit that country (A/C.3/44/9).

Accordingly, Mr. Pohl visited Iran between 20 and 28 January 1990 and met with many representatives of the executive, judicial, and legislative branches of its government. Earlier, between 8 and 19 January 1989, he had heard a number of witnesses in connection with the human rights situation in that country; and, during the period between the announcement of the invitation and the departure of the Special Representative, some 1,500 Iranian emigres or relatives of Iranians living abroad addressed communications to him. Their allegations related to alleged cases of executions, torture, disappearances, and mistreatment of prisoners. Information was also obtained from the Iranian and the international press and from organizations of many types.

The Special Representative's visit was described in detail, and the information placed at his disposal was analyzed, in the report which he presented to the Commission on Human Rights at its 1990 session (UN Doc. E/CN.4/1990/24, chaps. I–IV). Further reports on the situation of human rights in Iran were submitted to the Commission on Human Rights in 1991, 1992, 1993, and 1994 (documents E/CN.4/1991/35, 1992/34, 1993/41, and 1994/50, respectively), and interim reports were made available to the General Assembly in each of those years except 1991 (documents A/45/619, 47/617, and 48/526, respectively).

The conclusions and recommendations set out in the 1994 final report to the Commission are as follows (E/CN.4/1994/50):

*Conclusions.* Comparing recent events with those of previous years, one has the impression that the situation did not change markedly in 1993. The requirements of due process of law have not yet been met, and no plans are known for making good existing legal shortcomings. The same problems occur, and people remain just as unsure of the reactions of officials, especially those responsible for public policy, to events that depart from current guidelines in the view of the authorities concerned.

The official position of the Government of the Islamic Republic of Iran is that this criticism stems from the Special Representative's ignorance of Islamic law. The fact is that international bodies monitoring human rights are required to base themselves on international principles and instruments, and national laws, institutions and practices must change to match international laws, not vice versa. This is a fundamental stumbling-block which constantly gives rise to differences in assessment, and up to now it has not been overcome.

The Special Representative wishes to repeat the general comments made in his report to the General Assembly, and feels there is enough evidence to indicate that the situation of human rights and fundamental freedoms in the Islamic Republic of Iran should remain under international scrutiny.

*Recommendations.* The Special Representative makes the following recommendations to the Commission on Human Rights on action which, from the viewpoint of the international instruments in force, would in his view be appropriate:

(a) To urge the Government of the Islamic Republic of Iran once again to take urgent and effective action to prevent its secret service agents from harassing Iranians living outside the country and their relatives living within it, or mounting attempts on the lives of exiles and refugees, whatever their political leanings; to investigate offences reported, particularly offences in which the authorities of other countries implicate Iranian agents; and to cooperate wholeheartedly with those authorities in investigating and punishing such offences;

(b) To remind the Iranian Government of the need to carry out technical reforms to its penal legislation, and to ensure the due process of law, with special emphasis on the openness of political trials and the presence of a qualified defence lawyer. The Government should also be recommended to recognize full equality of rights between men and women in its civil legislation, and to rely solely on individual beliefs and choice where social traditions and cultural mores are concerned.

(c) As regards the press and freedom of expression, to urge the Government of the Islamic Republic of Iran to deal with the problems caused by groups intimidating the media by attacking media facilities, and to take appropriate legal steps to protect newspapers, magazines and journalists and punish those who instigate and perpetrate outrages, eliminating violence as a means of cowing the spoken and written press;

(d) Since the International Committee of the Red Cross (ICRC) was forced to leave Iran at the Government's request in March 1992, and bearing in mind that there exists a perfectly valid agreement between ICRC and the Government, to urge the Government of the Islamic Republic of Iran to abide by the terms of that agreement;

(e) As regards cooperation by the Government of the Islamic Republic of Iran with the Commission on Human Rights through its Special Representative, it is appropriate to point out that it would be to the advantage of all concerned with human rights as they understand them in Iran were the Government to offer the Special Representative its full cooperation, inter alia by allowing him to pay a fourth visit to the country.

Having examined the report, and noting that the Government of the Islamic Republic of Iran had responded to the Special Representative's request for information concerning allegations of human rights violations in that country but had not allowed him to pay a fourth visit to the country so that he might obtain direct and first-hand information on the human rights situation, adopted, on 9 March 1994, a resolution (1994/73) containing the following operative paragraphs:

The Commission on Human Rights, . . .

1. Takes note with appreciation of the final report of the Special Representative of the Commission and the observations contained therein (E/CN.4/1994/50);

2. Expresses its deep concern at continuing reports of violations of human rights in the Islamic Republic of Iran;

3. Expresses its concern more specifically at the main criticisms of the Special Representative with regard to the human rights situation in the Islamic Republic of Iran, namely, the high number of executions, cases of torture and cruel, inhuman or degrading treatment or punishment, the standard of the administration of justice, the absence of guarantees of due process of law, discriminatory treatment of certain groups of citizens for reason of their religious beliefs, notably the Baha'is, whose existence as a viable religious community in the Islamic Republic of Iran is threatened, as well as the ill-treatment of certain Christians and restrictions on the freedoms of expression, thought, opinion and the press, and that, as noted by the Special Representative, there is continued discrimination against women;

4. Expresses its grave concern at continued use of the death penalty, which the Special Representative had described as excessive;

5. Also expresses its grave concern that there are continuing threats to the life of Mr. Salman Rushdie, whose case is mentioned in the report of the Special Representative, as well as to individuals associated with his work, which have the support of the Government of the Islamic Republic of Iran;

6. Urges the Government of the Islamic Republic of Iran to refrain from activities such as those mentioned in the report of the Special Representative against members of the Iranian opposition living abroad and to cooperate wholeheartedly with the authorities of other countries in investigating and punishing offences reported by them;

7. Regrets that the Government of the Islamic Republic of Iran has still not permitted the Special Representative to visit the country in order to enable him fully to discharge his mandate by according him full cooperation;

8. Urges the Government of the Islamic Republic of Iran to implement existing agreements with international humanitarian organizations;

9. Calls upon the Government of the Islamic Republic of Iran to intensify its efforts to investigate and rectify the human rights issues raised by the Special Representative in his observations, in particular as regards the administration of justice and due process of law;

10. Also calls upon the Government of the Islamic Republic of Iran to comply with international instruments on human rights, in particular the International Covenant on Civil and Political Rights, to which the Islamic Republic of Iran is a party, and to ensure that all individuals within its territory and subject to its jurisdiction, including religious groups, enjoy the rights recognized in these instruments;

11. Endorses the view of the Special Representative that the international monitoring of the human rights situation in the Islamic Republic of Iran should be continued;

12. Decides to extend the mandate of the Special Representative, as contained in Commission resolution 1984/54 of 14 March 1984, for a further year;

13. Calls upon the Government of the Islamic Republic of Iran to cooperate fully with the Special Representative, including allowing him to make another visit to the country;

14. Requests the Special Representative to submit an interim report to the General Assembly at its forty-ninth session on the situation of human rights in the Islamic Republic

of Iran, including the situation of minority groups, such as the Baha'is, and to report to the Commission at its fifty-first session;

15. Requests the Secretary-General to give all necessary assistance to the Special Representative;

16. Decides to continue its consideration of the situation of human rights and fundamental freedoms in the Islamic Republic of Iran, as a matter of priority, at its fifty-first session.

In the course of the preceding year, 1993, other competent United Nations bodies, including the General Assembly, the **COMMITTEE ON ECONOMIC, SOCIAL AND CULTURAL RIGHTS,** the **HUMAN RIGHTS COMMITTEE,** and the Sub-Commission on Prevention of Discrimination and Protection of Minorities, had expressed their views on the human rights situation in the Islamic Republic of Iran, as indicated below.

*REPORT OF THE UN COMMITTEE ON ECONOMIC, SOCIAL AND CULTURAL RIGHTS.* The Committee considered the initial report of the Islamic Republic of Iran (E/1990/5/Add. 9) at meetings held on 18, 19, and 28 May 1993, and on the latter date adopted the following concluding observations (E/C.12/1993/7):

*Positive Aspects.* The committee notes that the rate of unemployment, which had risen to 15 per cent as a result of the war with Iraq has, in the four years since the end of the war, fallen to 10 per cent; that under new labour legislation annual leave has been increased from 12 to 30 days and that the minimum age for employment has been raised from 12 to 15 years; that the Ministry of Labour has established a countrywide network of labour inspectors whose task is to ensure compliance with Labour regulations and who have the authority to shut down part or whole of an enterprise in which safety measures are considered inadequate.

*Factors and Difficulties Impeding the Application of the Covenant.* The Committee notes that the written report submitted by the Government of Iran contains no information on the factors and difficulties affecting the degree of fulfilment of its obligations under the present Covenant as required by article 17 (2) of the Covenant. However, the Committee observes that various articles of the Constitution of Iran subject the enjoyment of universally recognized human rights, including economic, social and cultural rights, to such restrictions as: "provided it is not against Islam" (art. 28); "with due regard to Islamic standards" (art. 20); "in conformity with the Islamic criteria" (art. 20); and "except when it is detrimental to the fundamental principles of Islam" (art. 24). In that connection the Committee considers, in the light of the Covenant provisions and of all the information available to it, that such restrictive clauses negatively affect the application of the Covenant, in particular its articles 2 (2) (non-discrimination), article 3 (equality of rights of men and women), article 6 (right to work), article 12 (right to health), article 13 (right to education) and article 15 (right to take part in cultural life). It is apparent that the authorities in Iran are using the religion as a pretext in order to abuse these rights.

*Principal Subjects of Concern.* The Committee regrets that the documentation made available to it by non-governmental organizations and the report of the Special Rapporteur of the commission on Human Rights, Mr. Reynaldo Galindo Pohl (E/CN.4/1993/41), confirm the broad consensus that there has been practically no progress in ensuring greater respect and protection for rights of the non-Muslim religious communities in the Islamic Republic of Iran in general, and of the economic, social and cultural rights of persons belonging to those minority groups in particular. The Committee draws again the attention to the following concerns expressed at its fifth session in 1990 about the situation of certain minority groups, which have not been satisfactorily answered in the course of the present session:

(a) Violation of the rights of the Baha'i community;

(b) Violation of economic, social and cultural rights in addition to violation of political and civil rights;

(c) Discrimination on religious grounds in the educational system;

(d) Insufficiency of the education offered to the children belonging to the Kurdish minority;

(e) Prohibition of the admission to university of Baha'is;

(f) Restriction of freedom of debate and choice in the university institutions;

(g) The situation of the Kurds and the disparities that exist between the different ethnic and economic groups in the enjoyment of their rights to education, to work, to travel, to housing and to the enjoyment of cultural activities.

The Committee expresses its particular concern with respect to the non-performance by the Government of Iran of its obligation under article 3 of the Covenant, under which the States parties undertake to ensure the equality of men and women to the enjoyment of all economic, social and cultural rights set forth in the Covenant. In that connection the Committee finds that the situations: in which women are not permitted to study engineering, agriculture, mining or metallurgy or to become magistrates; in which they are excluded from a very large number of specific subjects at university level; and in which they need their husbands' permission to work or travel abroad; to be incompatible with the obligations undertaken by the State party under the Covenant. The Committee seeks further clarification as to which women's rights have been "revived" in accordance with article 20 (i) of the constitution.

In relation to the right to take part in cultural life, the Committee would also like to have more precise information on legislation and policies protecting creative freedom. In particular, the committee expresses its grave concern at the negative implications for this right of the issuance of *fatwahs.* During the Committee's examination of the report, several members drew attention in this regard to the case of an author, Mr Salman Rushdie. While appreciating that *fatwahs* are issued by the religious authorities and not by state organizations per se, the question of State responsibility clearly arises in circumstances in which the State does not take whatever measures are available to it to remove clear threats to the rights applicable in Iran in consequence of its ratification of the Covenant. The Committee calls upon the Government of Iran to affirm that it rejects the acceptability, in terms of its international human rights obligations, of the issuance of such *fatwahs.* It also requests the Government to assure the Committee that if such a *fatwah* were to be carried out in Iran, or elsewhere by an Iranian citizen, the Government would ensure the criminal prosecution of the individual(s) concerned.

*Suggestions and Recommendations.* The Committee recommends that the State party should spell out a clear legislative, judicial and administrative basis for giving fullest possible effect to the provisions of the covenant "with a view to achieving progressively the full realization of the rights recognized in the present Covenant by all appropriate means, including particularly the adoption of legislative measures.'' (art. 2 (1) of the Covenant). The Committee invites the Government of Iran to undertake necessary steps, both legislative and practical, in order to ensure that the rights enunciated in the Covenant are able to be exercised without discrimination of any kind as to race, colour, sex, language, religion, political or other opinion, especially in the case of ethnic or religious minorities. The Committee notes that the obligation to ensure equal opportunity for women warrants particular attention, especially in relation to the right to work, family related rights and the right to education.

The Committee further recommends that the second periodic report of Iran should contain information not only on legislative measures adopted, but also on the application of these measures, on the difficulties encountered in the process of their implementation, and on the issues dealt with in the present concluding observations.

### REPORT OF THE UN HUMAN RIGHTS COMMITTEE.
The Committee considered the second periodic report of the Islamic Republic of Iran (CCPR/C/28/Add. 15) at meetings held on 29 and 30 October 1992, 7 April 1993, and 22 and 23 July 1993, and on the latter date adopted the following comments (CCPR/C/79/Add. 25):

*Positive Aspects.* The Committee takes satisfaction in the resumption of its dialogue with the Islamic Republic of Iran after a period of nearly ten years. However, difficulties in the dialogue made it necessary for the Committee to invite the Islamic Republic of Iran to three consecutive sessions and the Committee appreciates the readiness of the State party to do so. It regards the request for the Committee's assistance in the State party's endeavour to bring its domestic law and practice more into line with the provisions of the Covenant as a particularly important feature of the State party representatives concluding remarks.

The Committee notes with interest the establishment of a Human Rights office within the Ministry for Foreign Affairs, the measures under consideration in the Islamic Republic of Iran to improve the status of women and the promise to reconsider the question of corporal punishments. It also notes that efforts have been undertaken to develop an awareness of human rights on the part of senior officials of ministries and administrations, including the promise that the comments of the committee would be brought to their attention. The Committee also appreciates the fact that, at the time of the Gulf war, more than 1.5 million refugees were sheltered by the Islamic Republic of Iran.

*Factors and Difficulties Impeding the Application of the Covenant.* In view of the lack of transparency and predictability in the application of Iranian domestic law, the Committee has found it somewhat difficult to determine the extent to which the latter was compatible with the provisions of the Covenant. It also notes that numerous, explicit or implicit, limitations or restrictions associated with the protection of religious values, as interpreted by Iranian authorities, have also seriously impeded the enjoyment of some human rights protected under the Covenant.

Furthermore, the Committee observes that the emergency measures adopted by the authorities during the war with a neighbouring country, and the parallel destruction of the country's economy, have undoubtedly had negative effects on the enjoyment of the rights and freedoms provided for under the Covenant.

*Principal Subjects of Concern.* The Committee deplores the extremely high number of death sentences that were pronounced and carried out in the Islamic Republic of Iran during the period under review, many of which resulting from trials in which the guarantees of due process of law had not been properly applied. In the light of the provision of article 6 of the Covenant, requiring States parties that have not abolished the death penalty to limit it to the most serious crimes, the Committee considers the imposition of that penalty for crimes of an economic nature, for corruption and for adultery, or for crimes that do not result in loss of life, as being contrary to the Covenant. The Committee also deplores that a number of executions have taken place in public.

The Committee also condemns the fact that a death sentence has been pronounced, without trial, in respect of a foreign writer, Mr. Salman Rushdie, for having produced a literary work and that general appeals have been made or condoned for its execution, even outside the territory of Iran. The fact that the sentence was the result of a *fatwah* issued by a religious authority does not exempt the State party from its obligation to ensure to all individuals the rights provided for under the Covenant, in particular its articles 6, 9, 14 and 19.

In addition, the Committee is concerned about the many cases of extrajudicial executions, disappearances, torture and ill-treatment of persons deprived of their liberty that have been brought to its attention and which are described, *inter alia*, in the last report of the Special Representative of the Commission on Human Rights on the situation of human rights in the Islamic Republic of Iran (E/CN.4/1993/41).

Furthermore, the Committee considers that the application of measures of punishment of extreme severity, such as flogging, lapidation and amputation, is not compatible with the provisions of article 7 of the Covenant. It also has serious questions about requiring repentance from detainees as a condition of their release from custody.

The Committee also deplores the lack of respect for due process of law, particularly before the Revolutionary courts, where trials in camera tend to be the rule and where apparently no real possibility is provided to the accused to prepare a defence. The lack of an independent Bar Association also has an adverse effect on the administration of justice, in the view of the Committee.

The Committee observes that the persistence and extent of discrimination against women is incompatible with the provisions of article 3 of the Covenant and refers, in particular, to the punishment and harassment of women who do not conform with a strict dress code; the need for women to obtain their husband's permission to leave home; their exclusion from the magistracy; discriminatory treatment in respect of the payment of compensation to the families of murder victims, depending on the victim's gender and in respect of the inheritance rights of women; prohibition against the practice of sports in public; and segregation from men in public transportation.

The Committee considers that legal provisions allowing for the possibility of banishing individuals, preventing them from residing in the place of their choice, or compelling them to reside in a given locality, are not compatible with article 12 of the Covenant.

Furthermore, the Committee is concerned at the extent of limitations to the freedom of expression, assembly and association, exemplified by articles 6 and 24 of the Constitution and Article 16 of the Law Pertaining to Activities of Parties, Societies and Political and Professional Associations, noting in this connection that, contrary to the provisions of articles 18 and 19 of the Covenant, members of certain political parties who did not agree with what the authorities believe to be Islamic thinking or who expressed opinions in opposition to official positions have been discriminated against. Self-censorship also seems to be widespread in the media and severe limitations appear to have been placed upon the exercise of freedom of assembly and of association.

Finally, the Committee wishes to express its concern at the extent of the limitations and restrictions on the freedom of religion and belief, noting that conversion from Islam is punishable and that even followers of the three recognized religions are facing serious difficulties in the enjoyment of their rights under article 18 of the Covenant. The Committee is particularly disturbed about the extent of discrimination against followers of nonrecognized religions, notably the Baha'is, whose rights under the Covenant are subject to extremely severe restrictions. In the foregoing connection, the Committee received no satisfactory answer regarding the destruction of places of worship or cemeteries and the systematic persecution, harassment and discrimination of the Baha'is, which is in clear contradiction with the provisions of the Covenant.

*Suggestions and Recommendations.* The Committee recommends that the comments it had made in connection with the consideration of the second periodic report of the Islamic Republic of Iran should be studied by the authorities with a view to adopting necessary legal and practical measures to ensure the effective implementation of all the provisions of the Covenant. The Committee wishes, in particular, to emphasize the following suggestions and recommendations:

The Committee recommends that domestic laws should be revised with a view to curtailing the number of offences currently punishable by the death penalty and to reducing the number of executions. Public executions should be avoided and the accused should, in all cases, be provided with all necessary guarantees, including the right to a fair trial as provided for under article 14 of the Covenant.

Effective measures should be adopted to ensure the strictest observance of articles 7 and 10 of the Covenant. All complaints of extrajudicial executions, disappearances, torture and ill-treatment should be duly investigated, the culprits should be punished and measures should be taken to prevent any recurrence of such acts. Severe forms of punishment incompatible with the Covenant should be removed from law and practice and the conditions of detention of persons deprived of their liberty should be improved. The Committee also recommends that training courses should be organized for members of the police, the armed forces and the security forces as well as for other law enforcement officials, so as to better acquaint them with basic human rights principles and norms.

The Committee recommends that Iranian legislation and practice be brought into line with the provisions of articles 9 and 14 of the Covenant, which provide that all persons should have the right to a fair trial, including the assistance of counsel, the right to be brought promptly before a judge and the right to be tried in public. Urgent consideration should also be given to the abolition of the Revolutionary courts.

The Committee recommends that active measures should be taken to enhance the status of women in the Islamic Republic of Iran in accordance with articles 2, 3 and 23 of the Covenant and to guarantee their equal enjoyment of rights and freedoms.

The Committee recommends that its recently adopted General comment No. 22 (48) be studied by the authorities to bring its legislation and practice into line with the requirements of article 18 of the Covenant. In that regard, the Committee wishes to emphasize that recognition of a religion as a State religion should not result in any impairment of the enjoyment of any of the rights under the Covenant, including articles 18 and 27, nor in any discrimination against adherents of other religions or non-believers, since the right to freedom of religion and belief and the prohibition of discrimination do not depend on the recognition as an official religion or belief. Measures restricting eligibility for government service to members of the predominant religion, or giving economic privileges to such persons, or imposing special restrictions on the practice of other faiths, are incompatible with the prohibition of discrimination based on religion or belief and the guarantee of equal protection under article 26.

The Committee also wishes to invite the Government of the Islamic Republic of Iran to undertake necessary steps to ensure that the rights enunciated in articles 17, 19, 21, 22 and 25 can be exercised without any limitations or restrictions other than those provided for in the Covenant.

### REPORT OF THE UN SUB-COMMISSION ON PREVENTION OF DISCRIMINATION AND PROTECTION OF MINORITIES.

The Sub-Commission, which had called for an end to the situation of human rights in the Islamic Republic of Iran since 1981, adopted a further resolution on the subject at its 1993 session (resolution 1993/14) in which it *inter alia*:

1. Endorses the urgent call of the Special Representative of the Commission on Human Rights to the Government of the Islamic Republic of Iran urging it to comply with the current international norms in the field of human rights;

2. Strongly condemns the continuing flagrant human rights violations of the Islamic Republic of Iran, including:

(a) The use of excessive force and violence to suppress anti-government gatherings and demonstrations;

(b) The continuing execution of political prisoners and the assassination of opponents abroad;

(c) The stoning, torture and degrading treatment of citizens, especially women;

(d) The continued persecution of Baha'is and other religious minorities;

(e) The harassment of Iranian political refugees' relatives inside the Republic of Iran to coerce the refugees to return to the country or on intelligence matters;

3. Rejects any cultural or religious justification of the breach of universal human rights standards;

4. Emphatically urges the Government of the Islamic Republic of Iran to stop its attacks on Iranian dissidents abroad;

5. Reports the continuation of the mandate of Mr. Reynaldo Galindo Pohl, Special Representative of the Commission of Human Rights, and of international monitoring of the human rights situation in the Islamic Republic of Iran.

6. Maintains that the deteriorating conduct of the Islamic Republic of Iran in terms of violations of human rights and fundamental freedoms and the breach of international instruments, the repercussions of which spread beyond its national frontiers, jeopardizes peace and security in other regions;

7. Requests the Special Representative to consider and recommend in his report the strongest measures which could be adopted within the framework of the United Nations to eliminate human rights violations in the Islamic Republic of Iran.

### REPORT OF THE UN GENERAL ASSEMBLY.

The Assembly, at its 1993 session, expressed its deep concern at continuing reports of violations of human rights in the Islamic Republic of Iran, and more specifically at the main criticisms of the Special Representative with regard to that situation, namely, the high number of executions; cases of torture and cruel, inhuman, or degrading treatment or punishment; the standard of the administration of justice; the absence of guarantees of due process of law; discriminatory treatment of certain groups of citizens for reason of their religious beliefs, notably the Baha'is, whose existence as a viable religious community is threatened; and restrictions on the freedom of expression, thought, opinion, and the press; and that, as noted by the Special Representative, there is continued discrimination against women (resolution 48/145 of 20 December 1993). The Assembly also expressed its grave concern "at the continued use of the death penalty, which the Special Representative has described as excessive," and at "continuing threats to the life of a citizen of another State which appear to have the support of the Government . . . as well as to individuals associated with his work."

The Assembly called upon the Government of the Islamic Republic of Iran "to intensify its efforts to investigate and rectify the human rights issues raised by the Special Representative in his considerations and observations, in particular as regards the administration of justice and due process of law," and also "to comply with international instruments on human rights, in particular the International Covenant on Civil and Political Rights, to which the Islamic Republic of Iran is a party, and to ensure that all individuals within its territory and subject to its jurisdiction, including religious groups, enjoy the rights recognized in those instruments."

**BIBLIOGRAPHY.** Amnesty International. *Iran: Persistent Violations of Human Rights.* London: 1988. NGO report, in English.

———. *Iran: Victims of Human Rights Violations.* London: 1993. NGO report, in English.

———. *Iran: Violations of Human Rights 1987–1990.* London: 1990. NGO report, in English.

———. *Religious Intolerance.* London: 1986. NGO report, in English.

———. *Unfair Trials of Political Detainees.* London: 1992. NGO report, in English.

Asia Watch. *Guardians of Thought: Limits on Freedom of Expression in Iran.* New York: Human Rights Watch, 1993. NGO report, in English.

Bakhas, Shaul. *The Reign of the Ayatollahs.* New York: Basic Books, 1984. Scholarly monograph, in English.

Bashiriyeh, Hossein. *The State and Revolution in Iran.* New York: St. Martin's Press, 1984. Scholarly monograph, in English.

Benard, C., and Z. Khalilzad. *"The Government of God": Iran's Islamic Republic.* New York: Columbia University Press, 1984. Scholarly monograph, in English.

Chafiq, Chahla. *La femme et le retour de l'Islam: l'expérience iranienne* (Women and the Return of Islam: The Iranian Experience). Paris: Editions du Félin, 1991. Monograph, in French; bibliography, pp. 145–147.

Dekker, Ige F., and Harry Post, eds. *The Gulf War of 1980–1988: The Iran–Iraq War in International Legal Perspective.* Dordrecht, the Netherlands: Martinus Nijhoff for T.M.C. Asser Institute, 1991. Scholarly monograph, in English.

Elahi, Maryam. "The Rights of the Child under Islamic Law: Prohibition of the Child Soldier," *Columbia Human Rights Law Review* 19, no. 2 (Spring 1988): 259–279. Scholarly article, in English.

Federation Internationale des Droits de l'Homme (International Federation of Human Rights). "Le Martyr du Peuple Kurde" (The Martyrdom of the Kurdish People), *Lettre de la FIDH* 241 (22 March 1988). NGO newsletter, in French.

Femmes sous Lois Musulmanes (Women Living under Muslim Laws). *Dossier No. 1.* Montpellier, France: 1986. NGO document collection, in French and English.

Human Rights Watch. "Iran," in *Human Rights Watch World Report 1995*, pp. 269–275. New York: 1995. NGO report, in English.

International Gesellschaft fur Menschenrechte (International Society for Human Rights). *Menschenrechte in der Islamischen Republik Iran* (Human Rights in the Islamic Republic of Iran). Frankfurt, Germany: 1987. NGO report, in German.

McDowall, David. *The Kurds.* Rev. ed. London: Survival International, 1985. NGO report, in English; bibliography, p. 31.

Meron, Theodor. "Iran's Challenge to the International Law of Human Rights," *Human Rights Internet* 13, no. 1 (Spring 1989). NGO article, in English.

Parliamentary Human Rights Group. *The Abuse of Human Rights in Iran.* London: 1986. NGO report, in English.

Rejali, Darius M. *Torture and Modernity: Self, Society and State in Modern Iran.* Boulder, CO, USA: Westview Press, 1994. Scholarly monograph, in English.

United Nations Commission on Human Rights. *Report of the Human Rights Situation in the Islamic Republic of Iran . . . .* Prepared by Special Rapporteur Reynaldo Galindo Pohl. Geneva, Switzerland: 1987–1994. IGO reports, in English.

United Nations Security Council. *Report of the Mission Dispatched by the Secretary-General on the Situation of Prisoners of War in the Islamic Republic of Iran and Iraq.* 24 August 1988. IGO mission report, in English.

**IRAQ.** The Republic of Iraq is an Arab country in western Asia, once known as Mesopotamia. It has borders with Iran, Jordan, Kuwait, Saudi Arabia, Syria, and Turkey. It achieved independence in 1932, after 12 years as a **LEAGUE OF NATIONS** mandate under British administration, and became a member of the United Nations in 1945. Its population is estimated to be 18,815,000. Arabs and Kurds are the largest ethnic groups; the Kurds are largely concentrated in the northern areas. Numerically, the next largest ethnic group are the Turcomans who, although scattered throughout the country, are concentrated mainly in the area of Kirkuk. Other minorities are the Assyrians, the Chaldeans, and the Armenians, who are concentrated mainly in the governates of Nineva and Dohuk. Languages spoken include Arabic (official), Kurdish, Turcoman, Assyrian, and Armenian. Islam is the predominant religion, 96%; Christians, Sabeans, Yazidis, and Jews make up the remaining 4%. Literacy is estimated at 50%.

The government (1994) took the form of a republic. However, since the revolution of 17 July 1968, the Iraqi government has been directed by the Arab Ba'ath Socialist Party through a Council of Command of the Revolution and a Council of Ministers, both headed by the president who acts as head of State and of government. Legislation is prepared by the National Assembly. The courts are independent of other branches of government and may award damages to any person found to have suffered moral or material harm as a result of violation of his human rights.

*WAR WITH IRAN.* In September 1980, Iraq became involved in a war with neighboring Iran which arose out of a dispute over control of a waterway between the two countries. By the time a UN ceasefire agreement ended the dispute in 1988, countless lives were destroyed. In 1984, Iraq began missile attacks on Iranian oil tankers, prompting Iranian counterattacks and disrupting peaceful trading in the Persian Gulf for three years. In 1987, Kuwait requested that major world powers guarantee safe civilian shipping in the area, which led to the Western powers stationing navy vessels in the Gulf area. In 1988, Iraqi missiles bombed Teheran.

One result of the war was the "disappearance" of large numbers of persons in Iraq between 1980 and 1984. Many of the "disappeared" were Iraqi Shi'ites who were arrested at the outbreak of hostilities and later expelled to Iran. More recent cases, reported to the Working Group on Enforced or Involuntary Disappearances of the COMMISSION ON HUMAN RIGHTS, include 16 women said to have been arrested in reprisal against their husbands. The Working Group's 1990 report to the Commission on Human Rights indicated that it had transmitted a total of 3,045 cases to the Government of Iraq, of which 36 had been clarified by government responses and 17 by non-governmental sources, leaving 2,992 cases outstanding. None of these cases had occurred in the latest year of the survey, 1989.

*USE OF CHEMICAL WEAPONS.* Iraq has also been the subject of international attention since 1984 because of allegations of its use of chemical weapons against Iranian forces and against Kurdish rebels. As early as 1982, the UN GENERAL ASSEMBLY had requested the Secretary-General (resolution 37/98) to investigate, with the assistance of qualified experts, information brought to his attention by any member State concerning activities that may constitute a violation of the Protocol for the Prohibition of the Use of Asphyxiating, Poisonous or Other Gases, and of Bacteriological Methods of Warfare, signed at Geneva on 17 June 1925, or of the relevant rules of customary international law. Accordingly, the Secretary-General dispatched missions to investigate allegations by the Islamic Republic of Iran, and of Iraq, concerning the use of chemical weapons in March 1984, April 1985, February–March 1986, April–May 1987, March–April 1988, and twice in July 1988. The results were summarized by the Secretary-General as follows (UN Doc. E/CN.4/Sub.2/1989/4, paras. 36–38):

In its report of 8 May 1987, the mission stated that, in areas inspected by the mission, chemical weapons had been used against Iranian positions. In addition to military personnel, civilians had also been injured in these attacks. After investigation undertaken in Iran in 1984, 1986 and 1987, in hospitals in Europe in 1985 and in Iraq in 1987, the mission concluded that [UN Doc. S/18852, paras. 18–19]:

"(a) There has been repeated use of chemical weapons against Iranian forces by Iraqi forces, employing aerial bombs and, very probably, rockets. The chemical agents used are mustard gas (yperite) and probably, on some occasions, nerve agents;

"(b) A new dimension is that civilians in Iran also have been injured by chemical weapons;

"(c) Iraqi military personnel have sustained injuries from chemical warfare agents, which are mustard gas (yperite) and a pulmonary irritant, possibly phosgene".

At the request of the Secretary-General, Dr. M. Domingues, a medical specialist, accompanied by Mr. James Holger, a senior official of the United Nations Secretariat, conducted between 8 and 11 April 1988 an investigation into the alleged use of chemical weapons in the Iran-Iraq conflict. He came to the following conclusions [UN Doc. S/19823, para. 16–17]:

"(a) On the basis of the clinical examinations I conducted in the Islamic Republic of Iran, I was able to determine that patients had been affected by chemical weapons. A considerable number of those affected were civilians;

"(b) On the basis of clinical examinations I conducted in Iraq, I was able to determine that the patients—all military personnel—had been affected by chemical weapons."

In its resolutions 612 of 9 May 1988 and 620 of 16 August 1988, the Security Council, having reviewed reports on the investigative missions dispatched to the region by the Secretary-General in April, July and in August, condemned the use of chemical weapons in the conflict between Iran and Iraq. All three missions' reports confirmed the use of chemical weapons in the war (UN Docs. S/19823, S/20060 and Add. 1, S/20063 and Add 1, and S/2 0134).

In September 1988, officials in Turkey charged that Iraq had used chemical weapons in its military campaign against Kurdish rebels within its own borders, causing thousands of Kurds to seek refuge in Turkey.

An investigation by United Nations experts was proposed by Belgium, Great Britain, Japan, the Netherlands, the United States of America, and West Germany. Although Iraq denied that chemical weapons had been used, it refused to cooperate with the proposed investigation on the ground that it would constitute an interference in its internal affairs.

In a report to the UN SECURITY COUNCIL in April 1995, UN weapons inspector Rolf Ekeus stated that Iraq had failed to account for 17 tons of material that can be used to breed bacteria. Ekeus reported that Iraq appears to be pursuing germ warfare capability: "With Iraq's failure to account for the use of . . . items and materials for legitimate purposes, the only conclusion that can be drawn is that there is a high risk that they have been purchased and used for proscribed purpose—acquisition of biological warfare agents." Ekeus heads the UN Special Commission formed after the Persian Gulf war to oversee the destruction of Iraq's nuclear, chemical, and biological weapons, as well as its long-range missiles. The Security Council has mandated the destruction of all such Iraqi weapons as one of its conditions for lifting the economic sanctions imposed on Iraq after its 1990 invasion of Kuwait.

*INVASION OF KUWAIT.* On 2 August 1990, Iraq's armed forces invaded neighboring Kuwait. This action was condemned by the UN Security Council on the following day (resolution 660 [1990]). On 6 August, the Council imposed a mandatory trade embargo against Iraq and occupied Kuwait, calling upon all member States to halt their trade and transportation links with those countries (resolution 661 [1990]). Only twice before had the Council imposed mandatory economic sanctions, as authorized by chap. VII of the UNITED NATIONS CHARTER—against Southern Rhodesia in 1965 and against South Africa in 1977. The sanctions were adopted by a vote of 13 to 0, with Cuba and Yemen abstaining. In addition to the United Nations, the Arab League voted in a tumultuous meeting to condemn Iraq's aggression against its Arab neighbor, by a vote of 13 to 0, with the remaining eight members either abstaining or boycotting the meeting.

The United States of America promptly imposed a trade embargo on Iraq and sent military forces to defend Saudi Arabia at the request of the Saudi Government. Iraq formally annexed Kuwait on 8 August 1990, an act repudiated by the UN Security Council on the following day.

On 18 August 1990, the Security Council demanded the release of foreign hostages—called "guests" by the Iraqi Government. These foreign citizens were trapped in Iraq and occupied Kuwait and reportedly were to be used as "human shields" against military attack; all "guests" were released by Christmas 1990. On 15 August 1990, the Council gave the United States and other countries with warships in the Persian Gulf area the authority to enforce the blockade by halting shipping headed for Iraq or Kuwait.

On 29 November 1990, the Security Council noted that, despite all its efforts, Iraq had refused to implement resolution 660 and subsequent resolutions, and, in resolution 678 (1990), authorized UN member States cooperating with the legitimate Government of Kuwait "to use all necessary means" to uphold and implement its resolutions, unless Iraq were to fully implement them by 15 January 1991.

When Iraq ignored the deadline, the allied coalition began a devastating air attack on military targets in Iraq and occupied Kuwait on 16 January 1991. On 25 February, having achieved air supremacy, the allies undertook a massive ground offensive, which decimated the demoralized Iraqi ground forces. By 27 February, Kuwait had been fully liberated and offensive combat operations were suspended, provided that Iraq would immediately comply with the Security Council's resolutions. As part of the ceasefire agreement, Iraq agreed to destroy all chemical weapons and to allow UN inspectors to inspect all manufacturing sites where such weapons were made. Iraq did not readily comply when inspectors attempted to enter the manufacturing sites in the following months.

On 6 March 1991, the Commission on Human Rights requested its Chairman (resolution 1991/74) to appoint a Special Rapporteur "to make a thorough study of the violations of human rights by the Government of Iraq, and to submit an interim report to the General Assembly at its 1991 session and a final report to the Commission at its 1992 session." Mr. Max van der Stoel was subsequently appointed as Special Rapporteur.

Having examined the interim report (A/46/647, annex), the General Assembly on 17 December 1991 expressed its deep concern (resolution 46/134) about the numerous and detailed allegations of grave human rights violations by the Government of Iraq mentioned by the Special Rapporteur, in particular:

(a) Arbitrary detention, including women, children and the elderly, as well as the systematic practice of torture and other cruel, inhuman or degrading practices, and of enforced or involuntary disappearances as a part of a general structured programme of repression aimed at quelling opposition;

(b) Extrajudicial killings, including political killings and summary or arbitrary executions throughout the country, particularly in the northern Kurdish autonomous region, in southern Shiah centres and in the southern marshes;

(c) Hostage-taking and the use of persons as "human shields", a most grave and blatant violation of Iraq's obligations under international law.

The Assembly called upon the Government of Iraq to abide by its obligations under the International Covenant on Civil and Political Rights and other international human rights instruments, and particularly to respect and ensure these rights to all individuals irrespective of their origin within its territory and subject to its jurisdiction, including Kurds and Shi'ites. It regretted the failure of the Government to provide satisfactory replies to all the allegations of violations of human rights, and urged it to accord its full cooperation to the Special Rapporteur.

The Commission on Human Rights was even more condemnatory of the "massive violations of human rights, of the gravest nature, for which the Government of Iraq is responsible" after examining the Special Rapporteur's report at its forty-eighth session (E/CN.4/1992/31); in resolution 1992/71 of 5 March 1992, it referred to:

(a) Summary and arbitrary executions, orchestrated mass executions and burials, extrajudicial killings, including political killings, in particular in the northern region of Iraq, in southern Shiah centres and in the southern marshes;

(b) Widespread routine practice of systematic torture in its most cruel forms, including the torture of children;

(c) Enforced or involuntary disappearances, routinely practised arbitrary arrest and detention, including of women and children, consistent and routine failure to respect due process and the rule of law;

(d) Hostage-taking and the use of persons as "human shields", a most grave and blatant violation of Iraq's obligations under international law;

(e) Suppression of freedom of thought, expression and association, violations of property rights.

In the same resolution, the Commission further expressed "its special alarm at the repressive policies and practices directed against the Kurds which resulted in the extermination of a part of this population and which continue to have an impact on the lives of the Iraqui people as a whole"; and its deep concern "at the repressive measures taken by the Government of Iraq against the Shiah communities, in particular the suppression of Shiah religious and cultural rights."

***REPORT OF SPECIAL RAPPORTEUR.*** The Special Rapporteur's most comprehensive report on the subject (E/CN.4/1994/58) was presented to the Commission at its 1994 session. In that report he dealt extensively with the legal situation in the country and in its northern Kurdish territory, and with alleged violations of human rights, including those affecting the population as a whole and those affecting ethnic and religious communities. His conclusions and recommendations, as set forth in chapter IV, are as follows:

**Conclusions as to the Facts**

In drawing his conclusions as to the facts of the situation of human rights in Iraq, the Special Rapporteur refers to his previous comments concerning the nature and quality of information before him (E/CN.4/1993/45, paras. 169–179). In doing so, it is worth reiterating that it is the normal practice of a judicial enquiry to establish facts through the combined weight of testimony, documentary evidence and physical evidence. While the Special Rapporteur remains completely aware of the fact that he has not been mandated to conduct a judicial enquiry, he has again endeavoured to employ standards of a judicial nature in order to achieve the highest possible degree of certainty in his conclusions. Consequently, general reports and specific allegations of violations have been again investigated with a discriminating eye on the supporting evidence and attempts to obtain corroborations.

The Special Rapporteur regrets that his efforts to pay a return visit to Iraq have so far failed to obtain a positive response from the Government of Iraq. The Special Rapporteur also regrets that he has still not received replies to many of the questions he put to the Government of Iraq in previous years. Nevertheless, the Special Rapporteur is confident that much of the evidence brought to his attention speaks for itself, especially the laws of Iraq published in the *Official Gazette* and also the 18 metric tons of official Iraqi documents to which he has access. In connection with the evidentiary value of the documents, the Special Rapporteur has noted (and previously commented upon) the Government of Iraq's argument that all the documents are falsifications—including any "future" documents (E/CN.4/1993/45, paras. 163–168). As such, the Special Rapporteur has not felt it necessary to seek the Government of Iraq's views on this evidence, the veracity of which the Special Rapporteur remains convinced (in this connection, see E/CN.4/1993/45, paras. 171–172 and 174).

The Special Rapporteur concludes that extrajudicial, summary or arbitrary executions continue to occur in Iraq and that the legal order permits such violations. In particular, the fact that a large number of minor offenses entail the extremely disproportionate death penalty constitutes a violation of Article 6 (2) of the International Covenant on Civil and Political Rights. In addition, the authority of nonjudicial services to apply the death penalty or to kill persons with impunity constitutes yet more serious violations of the right to life. Indiscriminate use of excessive force of a military character in order to effect police actions also clearly violates the right to life.

Detailed reports of a large number of disappearances continue to reach the Special Rapporteur relating mainly to events of previous years. However, recent reports from southern Iraq indicate that the practice continues. Irrespective of the date and number of disappearances reported to the Special Rapporteur, it is clear that large numbers of individuals have disappeared at the hands of Government forces in Iraq and that their dependents remain seriously affected by their disappearance. The fact that the Government of Iraq has still not established a Commission of Enquiry to facilitate the resolution of these thousands of cases constitutes another violation of human rights. This omission is all the more serious in view of the fact that the Government of Iraq clearly maintains detailed records concerning persons within its jurisdiction and has the capacity to assist those seeking clarifications.

On the subject of torture, the Special Rapporteur sees no

reason to conclude that any steps have been taken by the Government of Iraq to stop practices of torture or other cruel, inhuman or degrading treatment or punishment. In view of the fact that those forces accused of practising torture remain clearly protected from prosecution or any other penalty, the Special Rapporteur concludes that the practice of torture will most probably continue to be reported in the future. Indeed, information before the Special Rapporteur confirms that torture is wide spread in Iraq and results from a system of State-terror directed at subduing the population.

With regard to allegations of arbitrary arrest and detention, the Special Rapporteur does not doubt that such violations take place on a wide scale if for no other reason than an examination of the laws in place which shows that such violations are permitted and may easily occur. At the same time, the absence of an independent judiciary coupled with a host of executive orders criminalizing far too many aspects of normal civilian conduct, prescribing enormously disproportionate penalties and authorizing arrest and detention without judicial review or any other form of judicial authorization leads the Special Rapporteur to conclude that a significant percentage of all arrests and detentions in Iraq are arbitrary as measured by international standards.

On the basis of virtually unanimous reports, testimonies and other information, the Special Rapporteur concludes that there are essentially no freedoms of opinion, expression or association in Iraq. The absolute powers of the State serve to silence opposition and penalize those holding oppositional views or beliefs. No institutions of government or civil society are immune to the impositions of the Baathist ideology of the State. Indeed, the abuses of physical integrity rights have terrorized the population into passive submission to the extent that no oppositional opinions, expressions or associations are apparent in the country. Perhaps most indicative of the severe repression is Revolution Command Council Decree No. 840 of 4 November 1986 which plainly subverts the freedom of expression by prescribing the death penalty for mere insults to the President and other institutions of State and Government.

Turning to the freedoms of movement and residence in Iraq, including the right to leave and re-enter one's own country, the Special Rapporteur concludes that there are clear violations of these freedoms found in Iraqi law and practice. Specifically, severe, unreasonable and sometimes gender-based restrictions are placed on travel abroad. On the matter of internal deportations and forced relocations, the Special Rapporteur concludes that Iraqi laws and Government policies violate the freedoms of movement and residence and, in some cases, constitute discriminatory practices based on ethnic or religious affiliations.

In examining the right to nationality in Iraq, the Special Rapporteur concludes that many Iraqi citizens have been unjustly stripped of their citizenship and expelled from Iraq in violation of international law. Specifically, hundreds of thousands of Iraqis have been stripped of their citizenship and expelled for reasons which are clearly of a political nature based upon real or presumed disloyalty to the Government. To rectify this problem, a comprehensive review of Iraqi citizenship law and Government policies and practices would have to be undertaken.

With respect to the enjoyment of the right to property in Iraq, the Special Rapporteur concludes that the Government of Iraq violates proprietary rights in a variety of ways. In particular, the confiscation of property is a frequent and often disproportionate punishment for minor offenses and is commonly carried out without judicial supervision and in an in-

vidiously discriminatory manner. Property rights are also violated on spurious charges in order to enrich Government officials or provide revenues for the State. Moreover, violations of property rights are used to alter the ethnic composition of communities and to penalize family members for alleged crimes attributed to their relatives.

Among the issues affecting a very large part of the population of Iraq at the present time is the problem of inadequate access to food and health care. The Special Rapporteur concludes that, as long as the Government of Iraq maintains its internal blockades and otherwise discriminates in its distribution of available resources, continues to spend disproportionately on military services to the detriment of resources available for public health, refuses to cooperate fully with international humanitarian organizations in allowing them access to all parts of the country where persons are in need (as required by Security Council resolution 688), refuses to take advantage of the "food for oil" formula available under the terms of Security Council resolutions 706 and 712, and therefore fails to provide those in need, especially the most vulnerable, with adequate food and health care, the Government of Iraq is in violation of its obligations relating to the rights to food and health.

The Special Rapporteur observes that the absence of respect for the rights pertaining to democratic governance seems to be at the root of all other violations of human rights in Iraq insofar as their absence implies a structure of power which is prone to abuse. The Special Rapporteur concludes that genuine and enduring improvements in the situation of human rights in Iraq may not be attained without respect for the rights pertaining to democratic governance. The 1991 Political Parties Act would have been a step in the right direction should it not have suffered from so many inappropriate restrictions and controls.

The Special Rapporteur further observes that the effects of many human rights violations bear disproportionately on women and children. Not only are women and children subject to most of the above mentioned violations, including those of the worst kind, but they also suffer the effects of violations inflicted more directly upon others on whom they are dependent, i.e. their husbands and fathers.

With regard to violations of human rights of specific ethnic and religious communities in Iraq, the Special Rapporteur notes that the driving motivation for most violations is political, i.e. the eradication of opposition. However, in achieving this objective, it is clear that the Government does not hesitate to interfere with the particularities and private domains of ethnic and religious communities. Examination of specific situations viewed in the light of the nature of the Government also reveals chauvinistic and discriminatory prejudices which explain the existence and character of policies directed against certain groups. For example, a pro-Arab chauvinism appears to be at the root of Arabization policies which deny linguistic, cultural and other minority rights to the Assyrian and Turkoman communities.

Without doubt, the ethnic community which has suffered the severest oppression under the Government of Iraq is the Kurdish minority. Notwithstanding the existence of the Law for the Autonomous Region which grants some significant rights to the predominantly Kurdish population, but fails to achieve in practice the political autonomy it suggests (see A/46/647, paras. 47, 55, and 87-88), the Special Rapporteur concludes that the policies directed against the Kurds constitute violations of a variety of human rights. In particular, the policy directed against the Barzani tribe from 1983 to the present which has resulted in the systematic destruction of their homeland together with the disappearance of thousands of their members raises issues of crimes against humanity and violations of the 1948 Genocide Convention. Likewise, and as described in paragraphs 109 to 125 above, the Anfal campaign of 1988 reveals a pattern of gross violations of human rights and clear violations of crimes against humanity which, taken as a whole, may very well constitute another violation of the Genocide Convention.

The continuing crisis facing the Marsh Arab population of southern Iraq causes the Special Rapporteur to conclude that, should no steps be taken to cease the repression, the extent and gravity of the reported violations places the survival of this indigenous population in jeopardy. In particular, the programme to drain the marshes constitutes a massive and soon to be irreparable damage affecting the whole population. There is an urgent need to take steps to reverse the drainage and restore the environment to which the Marsh Arab people are inextricably linked. The indiscriminate military campaign against the population must also be abandoned.

With respect to the Shiah religious community in Iraq, which constitutes over one-half the entire population of the country, the Special Rapporteur concludes that Government policy systematically violates the rights to religious freedom guaranteed by Article 18 of the International Covenant on Civil and Political Rights and constitutes discrimination in violation of Article 2 of the same convention. In general, the Special Rapporteur discerns a policy of repression animated by an anti-Shiah prejudice and aimed at destroying the private and exclusive domain of religious communion which the Government perceives as a real or potential threat to its hold on power. In view of the systematic threats to the Shiah clergy and the continuous assault on the community's religious heritage, there is a clear need to reassure the community that their religious beliefs and practices will be respected and that their historical traditions and institutions will be safeguarded.

### Conclusions as to Causes

### 1. The Structure of Power

*Introduction.* While the Special Rapporteur has reached certain conclusions as to the facts of the situation of human rights in Iraq, he believes that a fuller understanding of the situation permitting the determination of appropriate recommendations requires some analysis of the causes of human rights violations in Iraq. Specifically, in order to understand how a particular violation may come about, what failures of the system are at play and/or which persons may be at fault, the Special Rapporteur offers the following brief review of the structure of power in Iraq on the thesis that most violations of human rights derive from abuses of power which are facilitated in the politico-legal order of the State.

In Iraq, a key feature of the structure of power is the remarkable centralization of power in a very few institutions and persons. These require some description in order to reveal their structural flaws. As in most States, the basis of the order rests upon some articulated constitutional grounds which establish the institutions of government. In the case of Iraq, the institutions are largely defined in the Provisional Constitution of 16 July 1970 (as amended) together with the National Assembly Act No. 55 of 1980. These laws have been published in the *Official Gazette* of Iraq and are open to scrutiny. As mentioned above, the International Commission of Jurists has recently published the results of its study of the

institutions in a report entitled "Iraq and the Rule of Law". The Special Rapporteur offers his own brief analysis herebelow.

According to Article 1 of the 1970 Provisional Constitution, Iraq is a "people's democratic and sovereign Republic, the basic aim of which is to achieve a unified Arab State and establish a socialist system". The Republic is composed of five principal institutions: the Revolution Command Council, the National Assembly, the President of the Republic, the Council of Ministers and the Judiciary. Since the institutions of the National Assembly and the Judiciary have already been described above (and exposed as largely impotent), some detail of the remaining institutions is warranted here.

*The Revolution Command Council.* According to Article 37 (a) of the Provisional Constitution, the Revolution Command Council is the "supreme body of the State which, on 17 July 1968, assumed responsibility for the fulfilment of the general popular will by wresting power from the reactionary, autocratic and corrupt regime and restoring it to the people". It exercises absolute power independently of the people on the pretext that it is "the true representative of the will of the Iraqi people".

The composition of the Revolution Command Council is determined by Article 37 (b) of the Provisional Constitution which literally names the members. It would therefore appear that any change in the composition of the Revolution Command Council requires an amendment to the Constitution. Moreover, since the Chairman of the Revolution Command Council also acts as the President of the Republic, the Head of State can only be removed from office by changing the Constitution by a two-thirds majority decision. The Revolution Command Council elects its new members by a similar majority decision among its members. Neither the Revolution Command Council nor the President of the Republic have any fixed term of office. There is no form of public participation in the election of the members of the Revolution Command Council which means that the Council is not accountable to the people for its decisions or actions. Indeed, the members of the Revolution Command Council enjoy full immunity and no proceedings can be instituted against them without the consent of the Revolution Command Council, the procedures of which are also to be established by the Council itself.

The Iraqi Provisional Constitution gives the Revolution Command Council extensive powers confirming its control over the country's political life. The Provisional Constitution defines the Revolution Command Council as the principal legislative body with the absolute power to promulgate law and decisions in all fields. The Revolution Command Council was the sole legislative body until the elections to the National Assembly in 1980. In theory the Revolution Command Council shares legislative power with the National Assembly. However, if the Revolution Command Council wishes to enact legislation directly, it invokes Article 42 (a) of the Provisional Constitution. This it frequently does. The Revolution Command Council adopts legislation by majority vote in closed meetings and there is no possibility of reviewing the deliberations preceding the enactment of these laws and decisions. Apart from the power to promulgate legislation the Revolution Command Council also may make decisions of a regulatory nature which have the force of law. This procedure is generally used by the Revolution Command Council to criminalize acts for which no provisions are made in the Penal Code, increase the penalty for acts which are already designated as illegal, add new provisions to or amend an existing provision or limit the jurisdiction of courts in ordinary criminal matters. This absolute legislative power enables the Revolution Command Council to control all aspects of political, social and economic life in Iraq and thereby maintain the present order.

Amendments to the Provisional Constitution can, according to Article 66 (b) of the Constitution, only be made by a decision taken by two-thirds of the Revolution Command Council. This means that the Revolution Command Council can amend the Constitution, whenever and however it wants, in closed session, without being obliged to consult any other institutions. Since, in the absence of a Supreme Constitutional Court, there is no control of the constitutionality of legislation enacted by the Revolution Command Council and since the decisions of the Revolution Command Council are not subject to any review procedure, it is possible for the Revolution Command Council to enact legislation contrary to the Provisional Constitution.

Aside from sub-paragraph 42 (a) of the Provisional Constitution, referred to above, two other provisions are also important for the role of the Revolution Command Council. Article 42 (b) enables the Revolution Command Council to "promulgate any decisions needed for the application of the provisions of the legislation in force". However, the Revolution Command Council normally requests the President, who holds the "executive authority", to promulgate the decisions needed for the application of an enactment through a stipulation which appears in the text of the enactment itself. Article 43 (a) of the Constitution gives the Revolution Command Council full authority to supervise defence and security affairs and to promulgate all legislation related to these areas. It is also to be noted that the Revolution Command Council is the only institution with the competence to decide over questions concerning the budgets of the Ministry of Defence and the security services. This obviously gives the Revolution Command Council full control over the armed forces and the security apparatus, which in turn enables it to retain its grip on power.

The Provisional Constitution gives the Revolution Command Council extensive powers over practically every field of government activity. However, the Revolution Command Council does not regard itself as bound by these constitutional provisions. As the "State's supreme body" it is entitled to take any action it deems appropriate. The Revolution Command Council has, e.g., proclaimed numerous amnesties although the Constitution does not contain any provisions on this point. Furthermore, even though the Revolution Command Council has no constitutional power to dissolve the National Assembly, it has this power according to Article 60 of the National Assembly Act. The Revolution Command Council also frequently intervenes in the work of the courts, even though the independence of the judiciary is supposedly guaranteed by the Constitution.

*The President of the Republic.* The President of the Republic is elected by the Revolution Command Council by two-thirds of its members (Article 38 (a) of the Provisional Constitution). Apart from being the Chairman of the Revolution Command Council, the President also acts as Head of State, Commander-in-Chief of the Armed Forces and Secretary-General of the Baath Party. As a member of the Revolution Command Council the President is designated by name in the Provisional Constitution. He has no fixed term of office and can only be dismissed by a two-thirds majority decision of the Revolution Command Council.

The powers of the President are extensive. He is responsible for preserving the country's internal and external security and also controls the armed forces in his capacity as Commander-in-Chief. This enables the President to formulate national defence policies and supervise the work of the security apparatus. The President also promulgates the laws approved by the National Assembly and the legislation and decisions of the Revolution Command Council. It should be noted that the Provisional Constitution does not specify any time-limit by which the President must promulgate legislation. Consequently, the President can obstruct the work of the National Assembly by refusing to accept legislation for lengthy periods of time. The President is the head of the executive authority and is empowered to appoint and dismiss the Prime Minister and Ministers. He supervises the work of the Ministries and other public institutions and can appoint and dismiss judges, civil servants and military personnel.

The President exercises his constitutional powers by issuing decrees (so-called "sovereign acts") which do not require the approval of the competent Ministers and cannot be contested in courts. The President's strong constitutional powers, combined with his dominating position over the ruling Baath Party, the army and the security authorities, have made him the *de facto* ruler of the country. Although the President is accountable to the Revolution Command Council, which has the power to dismiss him, the members of the evolution Command Council can hardly be regarded as more than civil servants following the orders of the Chairman of the Revolution Command Council, i.e. the President of the Republic. This means that the President controls the highest and sole political authority in Iraq and can therefore rule the country as a sovereign.

*The Council of Ministers.* Only two articles of the Provisional Constitution are devoted to the Council of Ministers. According to Article 61 the Council consists of the Deputy Prime Minister and Ministers and is presided over by the President of the Republic. The powers of the Council are regulated by Article 62 of the Provisional Constitution and the Council of Ministers Act of 1991. The Council drafts bills of law which are then submitted to the President for promulgation in accordance with the Provisional Constitution. The Council also drafts and promulgates regulations, with the exception of regulations relating to the Ministry of Defence or the Security authorities which are promulgated by the President without consulting the Council of Ministers. Further, it is the duty of the Council to monitor the application of legislation and the decisions needed for its implementation. The Council of Ministers also has the right to permit the establishment of new political parties, monitor their activities and dissolve them (Political Parties Act of 1991).

The actual power of the Council of Ministers is, however, extremely limited since the President exercises the real executive authority. It should be noted that the Ministers do not countersign decrees promulgated by the President, regardless of their content. The President is also empowered to appoint and dismiss the Ministers, including the Prime Minister, at will. Thus, the Ministers are not accountable to the National Assembly, as is the case in ordinary parliamentary systems, but to the President from whom they receive their orders and directives.

*The Baath Party.* The Revolution Command Council has promulgated a number of enactments and decisions which have consolidated the dominating role of the Baath Party in State affairs and thereby divested the political institutions of much of their independence and credibility. According to the Leading Party Act No. 142 of 1974, all Ministries and Government departments have to adopt the report of the

Eighth Regional Congress of the Baath Party as a guideline for their work. Furthermore, the Revolution Command Council has also made it obligatory for all Government departments to comply with the decisions of the regional leadership of the Baath Party. The Revolution Command Council controls the Baath Party by virtue of Act No. 107 of 1974 which prescribes the death penalty for any member of the Party who deliberately conceals his previous political affiliations or is found to have links to other political groups during his commitment to the Baath Party, and Act No. 145 of 1976 which forbids any member of the Baath Party leaving the Party to join any other political organisation. Under Revolution Command Council Decision No. 437 of 1987, government departments are obliged to impose on any of their employees who are Party members the disciplinary sanctions determined by the leadership of the Baath Party. It is also to be noted that the Baath Party is the only political organisation which is allowed to recruit members from, and operate among, the armed forces and the security services (Political Parties Act of 1991).

*Conclusions.* Upon review of the institutions of the Republic, noting the impotence of the National Assembly, the Council of Ministers and the judiciary, and realizing the enormous powers centralized in the Revolution Command Council and the President of the Republic, it appears obvious that the role of the Provisional Constitution is not to regulate the functions of public institutions nor to safeguard the rights and freedoms of its citizens. Rather, the 1970 Provisional Constitution appears merely to be an instrument through which the Government attempts to legitimize itself and consolidate its total control over the country.

As described above, the politico-legal structure of the State is such that both the legislative and executive powers are held by one single body which is neither accountable to the public nor to any other institution. The Revolution Command Council not only controls the legislation and its implementation, but also has the power to interfere with the administration of justice by obstructing the work of courts or by simply changing their judgements. It can also bypass the official judicial system by establishing special or emergency courts, the judgements of which it may also alter or annul. In the absence of a Supreme Constitutional Court, there is no control over the constitutionality of the activities and decisions of the Revolution Command Council. The independence of the judiciary is therefore only theoretical, which in turn means that there can be no legal safeguards available for the citizens. This analysis confirms the Special Rapporteur's previous characterization of the Iraqi judicial system as a kind of parallel system through which the executive power, i.e. the Revolution Command Council, can bypass the judiciary simply by promulgating the necessary decisions. Therefore, since the authorities can violate the Provisional Constitution without being legally or politically accountable, the Provisional Constitution loses its role as a source of legitimacy and a safeguard for the rights and the freedoms of the citizens.

Another important element of the structure of power in Iraq concerns the relationship between the Revolution Command Council and its Chairman, the President of the Republic. Under the Provisional Constitution, the Revolution Command Council is empowered to appoint and dismiss the President. In fact, however, the President is the head of the armed forces, the security apparatus and the Baath Party. This position enables him to exercise effective control over all branches of government and public life, including the activities of the Revolution Command Council. Thus, the role of the Revolution Command Council is reduced to that of an advisory body to the President, which in turn makes the President the sole *de facto* ruler of the country. The politico-legal structure of the State, therefore, cedes absolute power to the President.

## 2. The Abuse of Power

In having described how the politico-legal organization of the Republic of Iraq constitutes of itself a systematic cause of human rights violations, not only as a matter of individual laws and a general order of laws which by their promulgation constitute violations but also insofar as the organization of the State almost requires violative acts if attributed powers are to be accordingly applied, it seems necessary to underline the fact that the activities of those in positions of power do in fact violate human rights. This may imply some restatement of matters already expounded upon in chapter III above. However, at the risk of some repetition, it is important to show that the persons holding power—the rulers of Iraq—not only can but do abuse their power through constant violations of human rights. Indeed, so routine and abusive are these acts that they have over the years come to constitute an endemic element of government policy intruding entirely into the daily lives of all those within the jurisdiction of the State.

To illustrate the above point, the Special Rapporteur offers the following examples of Revolution Command Council decrees (all of which bear the signature of Saddam Hussein) which have been issued at different times since 16 July 1979, address all aspects of public and private life and affect persons in all parts of the country or beyond. Ranging from petty and personal punishments or favours to the most far-reaching effects upon the lives of millions of persons, the examples offered are hardly isolated or unique acts: the Special Rapporteur could cite many more. In no particular order, they have instructed: the suspension of criminal convictions and terminated judicial processes concerning named individuals (implementation by the competent Ministers); the exemption of a named Imam from mandatory retirement (implementation by the Ministers for Awqaf and Finance); the exemption of a pharmacist from a medical grading requirement (implementation by the Minister of Health); the suspension of a named staff member of the Ministry of Culture and Information (implementation by the Minister of Culture and Information); the award of the highest rank in the Armed Forces to Saddam Hussein (implementation by the competent Ministers); the exemption of a named person from the requirements of a medical grading and appointment of the individual as a physician at the Central Eye Hospital in Baghdad (implementation by the Minister of Health); the exemption of Baath Party offices in the provinces from having to pay water or electricity fees (implementation by the competent Ministers); prohibition of employment in official departments of government, semi-official departments of government or corporations in the public sector to any Iraqi citizen who marries a foreigner (implementation by the competent Ministers); cancelation of an order of dismissal from, and instruction to return to, the College of Education in Baghdad concerning a named individual (implementation by the Minister of Higher Education); the withdrawal of citizenship from, and deportation of, Iraqis of "foreign origin" if they "appear disloyal to the country, the people, and the higher national and social goals of the revolution" (implementation by the Minister of Interior); the payment of large sums of money to Iraqi husbands of Iranian citizens upon divorce and deportation of their wives and remarriage to Iraqi citizens (implementation by the competent Ministers); the immunity from legal process against those assigned to chase military service evaders or deserters, no matter what damage caused or injuries inflicted (implementation by the competent Ministers); the prohibition of conveyancing of movable or immovable property from an Iraqi citizen to a non-Iraqi spouse (implementation by the competent Ministers); the dismissal and retirement of named judges (implementation by the Ministers of Justice and Finance); the award of The Medal of the Revolution, at the First Grade, to "the struggling comrade Saddam Hussein" in acknowledgement of his actual and direct participation in the revolution of 17–30 July 1968 (implementation by the competent Ministers); the suspension of a doctor at the Children's Hospital in Diwaniyah and the withdrawal of his degree (implementation by the Ministers of Health and Finance); the prohibition of the practice of law to two named lawyers; the appointment of Ali Hassan al-Majid as Secretary-General of the Revolution Council for the Organization of the North and granting personal authority over all affairs of civil, military and security agencies including the Executive Council of the Autonomous Region of Kurdistan, all governors and administrative directors under the Ministry of Local Government, the intelligence services of the Ministries of Interior and Defense, and the Popular Army—i.e. a grant of absolute power over millions of people; the doubling and tripling in July 1991 of the salaries of "friends of the President and leader Saddam Hussein" (implementation by the competent Ministers); and, of course, the naming of Saddam Hussein as Chairman of the Revolution Command Council on 16 July 1979.

According to the Provisional Constitution, the 9 named members of the Revolution Command Council clearly hold in their persons the basis of power. However, they are all subject to the power of Saddam Hussein as President of the Republic, Secretary-General of the National Command of the Baath Party (to whom all members of the Government are subordinated) and Commander-in-Chief of the Armed Forces. Because of the absolute and personal power wielded by Saddam Hussein, his close family members have been placed in positions of power with their familial link being more important than any formal status.

Examination and analysis of the order of government in Iraq demonstrates that those in power use their positions in almost every conceivable way in order to eradicate opposition and control all privileges. To defeat opposition and secure the compliance of the population, power is abused as the Government discerns vulnerabilities and exploits them to the fullest. In the process of subjugating the population, power is abused not only vertically, i.e. through direct and immediate oppression upon the population, but by means of horizontal effects whereby social ties are also exploited. For example, family members are routinely held responsible for the alleged "crimes" of their relations, thus instilling a clear interest in every family to check the activities of all family members (see Document No. 19 of Annex I). Other social institutions are also exploited in this way as the Government abuses the traditions and values which imbue tribal and religious communities. For example, tribal and religious leaders are made to swear (on penalty of death and sometimes against their values) the allegiance of themselves and their communities to Saddam Hussein: a breach on the part of any member of the community incurs the responsibility of community leaders and frequently the entire community (see Document No. 20 of Annex I). According to editions of the Iraqi newspapers *Al-Thawra* and *Babil* dated, respectively, 17 February 1993 and 13 December 1993, the obtention of such oaths, which community leaders may feel obliged to make either to save their communities from punishment or to secure some necessary "privilege", continues on a large scale. Further, the fundamental institutions of marriage and motherhood are abused as wives and mothers are held responsible for the alleged "crimes" of their husbands and sons. Moreover, the Special Rapporteur notes that power is further abused and control is further established by, for example, video-taping acts of allegiance (see Document No. 21 of Annex I).

In the process of exploiting the social institutions of Iraqi society, the methods of abuse are extreme. Severe humiliation and degradation range from religious insults, such as the arrangement of a mass marriage celebration on the Shiah holy day of Ashura, to insidious assaults such as requiring members of the Islamic Da'wa Party to carry out the executions of their own Party members (see Document No. 22 of Annex I). Such techniques serve to terrorize the population by highlighting the impotence of resistance. The processes of extreme dehumanization and terror also largely explain the practices of torture, rape and other brutal acts sometimes carried out in the presence of family members.

Some dehumanizing practices appear to surpass any apparent objective. For example, some methods of torture seem only to be explained by cruel and brutal tendencies: one official Iraqi document in the possession of the Special Rapporteur records the fate of a mentally retarded man who, being found in "the demolished village of Shaikh Tawil in the administratively cancelled sub-district of Bibaz", was arrested, killed, decapitated and had his head delivered to the General Directorate of Security (see Document No. 23 of Annex I). Indeed, as so many official Iraqi documents show, those in power accord little or no value to human life. This fact is most evident in the attitude of those in power towards the death penalty. For example, in September 1983, while running a war and an entire modern State, documents show that Saddam Hussein had the time to authorize (and presumably consider and reflect upon) the execution of over 500 persons in the space of just 10 days (see E/CN.4/1993/45, Document 3 of Annex I thereto). Official Iraqi documents further show that, by 15 November 1988 (i.e. after the end of the Iran-Iraq war), Saddam Hussein no longer felt the need to fulfil his constitutional responsibility to review every death sentence as he simply granted the power to the "competent authorities" (see Document No. 17 of Annex I); it may be deduced that Saddam Hussein either did not view the matter as serious enough for his consideration, believed other "competent authorities" to be more appropriate for consideration of such matters, or (perhaps much worse) he could no longer cope with the number of executions at that time. Indeed, the Special Rapporteur understands that the nongovernmental organization Middle East Watch long ago simply stopped keeping track of records of executions found in official Iraqi documents because there are just too many. Clearly, the abuse of power that this implies has been made possible by both the structure of the State and the character of the personalities who dominate it.

The extent of abuse of power obtains perhaps its most disturbing dimension in certain racist views. Aside from the chauvinistic and prejudicial tendencies which have been referred to above, the Special Rapporteur recalls the characterization of the Marsh Arab population as "monkey-faced" (apparently a reference to the dark skin and curly hair of certain Marsh Arabs; see E/CN.4/1992/31, para. 126) and draws attention to Ali Hassan al-Majid's characterization of the Kurdish population as "goats" (apparently a reference to the mountain lifestyle of much of the population who herd goats for their wool, meat and milk). Another disturbing reference found in many official Iraqi documents in the possession of the Special Rapporteur relates to a single Kurdish tribe characterized as "criminal" through simple references to the "Barzanis" and "the scions of treachery" (*salilu al-khiyana*) (apparently references to the descendents of the Barzani tribe formerly headed by Moustapha Barzani who had lead an insurgency against the Government in the early 1970s). Such apparent biological groupings and dehumanization of entire groups may partly explain policies such as those against the "Barzanis" in 1983, the Anfal campaign of 1988 and the present policy in the southern marsh area of the country.

Those in power in Iraq have used the politico-legal structure to bolster an order which permits the secure enjoyment of essentially no human right or freedom. Through the construction of a web of informers including community leaders, friends and family, and the existence of a security apparatus which may intrude into the most private affairs of the individual, it is difficult to speak of the enjoyment of any freedom in Iraq. This order is justified by a revolutionary logic and a militarism which requires severe restrictions of human rights and seems to require an enemy. The continuing effect of such an order is a complex of abusive acts which seem impossible to catalogue or calculate. Insidiously, those in power are able to obtain the compliance of others in carrying out abusive acts under damnation of themselves, their loved ones and their spiritual integrity. In effect, those in power damn the people and then, in the worst way, make the people damn themselves, damn their children, damn their families, damn their neighbours, damn their tribes, damn their religions and damn their futures: the people are stripped of all dignity, shamed and rendered compliant, "guilty" and hopeless. They are pacified.

### Conclusions as to Responsibilities

#### 1. State Responsibility

As a matter of general international law, the State of Iraq must respect all those obligations to which it has freely consented, by virtue of the principle of *pacta sunt servanda*. Consequently, the non-respect of such obligations entails the responsibility of the State for the wrongful act or acts. Since Iraq has freely undertaken a variety of human rights obligations as referred to above in paragraphs 13 and 14, and insofar as the wrongful acts and omissions described in chapter III are imputable to the Government of Iraq acting as agents of the State, it follows that Iraq is responsible in international law for the aforementioned human rights violations. Aside from its responsibility for numerous and most serious violations of, *inter alia,* the instruments forming the International Bill of Human Rights, the Special Rapporteur notes that the information before him also demonstrates State responsibility for serious breaches of the 1925 General Protocol for the Prohibition of the Use in War of Asphyxiating, Poisonous or Other Gases, and of Bacteriological Methods of Warfare and may prove State responsibility for breaches of the 1948 Genocide Convention. Moreover, and as established in his previous reports to the Commission on Human Rights, the Special Rapporteur observes that there are no permissible excuses which the Government of Iraq

may invoke to avoid State responsibility for the situation of human rights in Iraq.

With regard to the special legal obligations which pertain to the State of Iraq pursuant to a host of mandatory Security Council resolutions, the Special Rapporteur further observes that State responsibility is incurred by Iraq's continuing failure to fulfil its special obligations. In relation to human rights obligations, the Special Rapporteur refers to Security Council resolution 688 (1991) together with resolutions 706 (1991) and 712 (1991). More specifically, the Special Rapporteur observes that Iraq continues to be in breach of its special international obligations as long as it: fails to cease its repression of its civilian population; fails to cooperate fully with international humanitarian organizations seeking to relieve the suffering of the people from shortages of essential humanitarian supplies; and fails to take advantage of the "food for oil" arrangement which would enlarge the humanitarian resources available to the population to the amount of at least U.S.$900 million and (as the Secretary General inferred in his 1 February 1994 press conference at United Nations Headquarters (see SG/SM/5216)), perhaps billions of dollars.

#### 2. Individual Responsibility

The Special Rapporteur has previously observed that certain individuals at the highest echelons of government in Iraq carry special and individual responsibility for a large number of violations and that international law would not afford immunities to those responsible (E/CN.4/1993/45, para. 186).

Following further study and analysis, the Special Rapporteur believes that the two persons who hold the most responsibility, of a special and individual nature, for serious human rights violations are Saddam Hussein and Ali Hassan al-Majid. According to the principle of command responsibility, their responsibility is derived from their positions of command, both in terms of their formal positions of State and also their practical positions of command over specific policies, orders and resulting events. To be specific, Saddam Hussein holds the following positions of power: President of the Republic, Chairman of the Revolution Command Council, Secretary-General of the Regional Command of the Baath Party, Secretary-General of the National Command of the Baath Party, and Commander-in-Chief of the Armed Forces; pursuant to Revolution Command Council Decision No. 150 of 9 February 1988, Saddam Hussein oversees the General Directorate of Security and, until May 1991, he was also Prime Minister. Saddam Hussein's cousin Ali Hassan al-Majid is presently the Minister of Defense and also holds, or has held at various significant times, the following positions of power: Director General of the National Secretariat of the Revolution Command Council; Member of the Regional Command of the Baath Party; Member of the National Security Council coordinating the security and intelligence services; Military Governor of Kuwait Governorate; Minister of Interior; Minister of Local Government; and Secretary-General of the Baath Party's Bureau for the Organization of the North.

Notwithstanding the responsibilities held by Saddam Hussein and Ali Hassan al-Majid for acts which constitute crimes against the peace (such as the invasion of Kuwait on 2 August 1990) and crimes of war (such as in relation to events during both the wars with Iran and Kuwait), the Special Rapporteur believes that serious violations of human rights committed against the civilian population of Iraq both in times of war and peace involve crimes against humanity committed under and pursuant to the commands of Saddam Hussein and Ali Hassan al-Majid. Specifically, the use of chemical weapons against numerous communities in northern Iraq and other events that took place pursuant to implementation of order 28/4008 of 20 June 1987, including the Anfal campaign of 1988, constitute crimes against humanity. Other acts, such as those carried out against the "Barzanis" similarly constitute crimes against humanity.

### Recommendations

The Special Rapporteur regrets that he finds it necessary to repeat all of the recommendations made in his report to the Commission on Human Rights in 1993. The Special Rapporteur also finds it necessary to make additional recommendations. The Special Rapporteur recommends:

(a) That the Government of Iraq take immediate steps to bring the capacities and actions permitted of its military and security forces into conformity with the standards of international law, in particular those of the International Covenant on Civil and Political Rights;

(b) That the Government of Iraq abrogate all laws granting impunity to specified forces or persons killing or injuring individuals for any purpose beyond the administration of justice under the rule of law as prescribed by international standards;

(c) That the Government of Iraq immediately establish a national commission on disappearances, take appropriate steps to cooperate closely with the Working Group on Enforced or Involuntary Disappearances to resolve those thousands of cases which have been submitted through this body, and otherwise cooperate fully in the resolution of the cases of disappearances of Kuwaitis and third-country nationals who are said to have disappeared in detention during or subsequent to the Iraqi occupation of Kuwait;

(d) That the Government of Iraq take immediate and unequivocal steps to stop the practices of torture and other cruel, inhuman and degrading treatment or punishment;

(e) That all persons arbitrarily detained be immediately released and that steps be taken to compensate all those who suffered arbitrary arrest, detention or other miscarriages of justice especially under special courts such as the Revolutionary Court;

(f) That the Government of Iraq immediately abrogate all legislation and abolish all policies effecting punishments imposed on persons for the alleged crimes of family members and others of extended relation;

(g) That steps be taken to restore the independence of the judiciary and to subject the executive to the rule of law by means of establishing a constitutional court;

(h) That the Government of Iraq take steps to facilitate the enjoyment of the freedoms of opinion, expression and association, in particular by decriminalizing the expression of oppositional views, relinquishing Government controls over the media and literary and artistic communities, and permitting the formation of independently organized trade unions;

(i) That the Government of Iraq immediately remove all restrictions relating to the entry and exit of citizens to and from the country, including removal of the prohibitous exit tax;

(j) That the Government of Iraq review its citizenship law with a view to safeguarding against the arbitrary or discriminatory withdrawal of citizenship, the repatriation of persons who were previously expelled from Iraq, and with a view to extending full citizenship to the largest number of long term residents who would otherwise be Stateless;

(k) That the Government of Iraq abrogate all discriminatory legislation and cease all discriminatory policies which interfere with the free and equal enjoyment of property, and that those whose property has been arbitrarily or unjustly destroyed or confiscated be appropriately compensated;

(l) That the Government of Iraq end its internal economic embargoes on both the northern and southern regions and take such steps as to cooperate with international humanitarian agencies in the provision of relief to those in need throughout Iraq;

(m) That, especially in view of the extremely serious lack of food and medicine in the country, the Government of Iraq immediately act to take advantage of the "food for oil" formula according to Security Council resolutions 706 and 712 which, as the Secretary-General has recently confirmed, would enable the Government to purchase hundreds of millions, if not billions, of dollars worth of urgently needed foodstuffs and medical supplies;

(n) That the Government of Iraq abrogate all laws discriminating against women and abide by its obligations pursuant to the Convention on the Elimination of Discrimination against Women;

(o) That the Government of Iraq take steps to ensure that no person under the age of 18 be subjected to the death penalty;

(p) That, in the interest of ensuring that the Government of Iraq genuinely reflects the will of the people, steps be taken to render the executive accountable to the citizenry in a clear and meaningful way. Specifically: the institutions of government should benefit from a separation of powers; unreasonable restrictions on the freedoms of opinion, expression and association should be removed along with the legislated "leading role" of the Baath Party; and the repressive restrictions contained in the Political Parties Act should be abolished;

(q) That, in fulfilment of its obligations pursuant to Article 27 of the International Covenant on Civil and Political Rights, the Government of Iraq take steps to ensure the recognition and enjoyment of minority rights on the part of the Assyrian, Kurdish, Marsh Arab, Turkoman and other minorities;

(r) That the Government of Iraq immediately cease its periodic shelling of Kurdish agricultural lands, cooperate in the identification of minefields with a view to facilitating their marking and eventual cleaning, cooperate with international aid agencies in the provision of humanitarian assistance to the northern Kurdish region, and take steps towards the peaceful settlement of the internal dispute;

(s) That, in relation to the southern marsh area and its Marsh Arab population, the Government of Iraq implement the recommendations made by the Special Rapporteur in his interim report to the forty-eighth session of the General Assembly (see A/48/600, para. 82) including, inter alia, the immediate halting and reversal of the draining of the marshes and the cessation of its military activities against the civilian population of the area;

(t) That the Government of Iraq immediately cease its interference in the religious activities of the Shiah community and take such steps as to compensate it for damages and to locate the missing clergy and their families;

(u) That, considering the exceptional gravity of the situation of human rights in Iraq, the Government of Iraq agree to the stationing of human rights monitors throughout the country;

(v) That, irrespective of the Government of Iraq's position with regard to the stationing of human rights monitors within the country, sufficient human and material resources be provided for the sending of human rights monitors to such locations as would facilitate improved information flow and assessment and would help in the independent verification of reports on the situation of human rights in Iraq.

After examining the report, the Commission again condemned what it described as "an all-pervasive order of repression and oppression which is sustained by broad-based discrimination and widespread terror." It demanded that the Government of Iraq (resolution 1994/74) "restore the independence of the judiciary and abrogate all laws granting impunity to specified forces or persons killing or injuring individuals for any purpose beyond the administration of justice under the rule of law as prescribed by international standards." It further demanded that the Iraqi Government:

(a) In fulfilment of its obligation pursuant to article 27 of the International Covenant on Civil and Political Rights, take steps to ensure the recognition and enjoyment of human rights of persons belonging to minorities;

(b) Immediately cease its periodic shelling of agricultural lands belonging to Iraqi Kurds, cooperate in the identification of minefields with a view to facilitating their marking and eventual clearing, cooperate with international aid agencies in the provision of humanitarian assistance to the northern Kurdish region and take steps towards the lifting of the embargo;

(c) In relation to the southern marsh area and its Marsh Arab population implement the recommendations made by the Special Rapporteur in his interim report to the General Assembly at its forty-eighth session (A 48/600, para. 82). . . .

In the same resolution, the Commission also expressed "its special alarm at all internal embargoes which permit essentially no exceptions for humanitarian needs and which prevent the equitable enjoyment of basic foodstuffs and medical supplies, and calls upon Iraq, which has sole responsibility in this regard, to remove them and to take such steps as to cooperate with international humanitarian agencies in the provision of relief to those in need throughout Iraq. . . ."

In addition, the Commission extended the mandate of the Special Rapporteur for another year and requested him to submit further reports to it and to the General Assembly. It requested the Secretary-General, in consultation with the Special Rapporteur, to take the necessary measures in order to send human rights monitors to such locations as would facilitate improved information flows and assessment and would help in the independent verification of reports on the situation in Iraq.

***REPORT BY THE UN COMMITTEE ON ECONOMIC, SOCIAL AND CULTURAL RIGHTS.*** The second periodic report of Iraq, on articles 13–15 of the International Covenant on Economic, Social and Cultural Rights (/ 1990/7/Add. 15), was considered by the Committee on 9 and 10 May 1994. On 19 and 20 May 1994, the Committee adopted the following concluding observations (E/C.12/1994/6):

*Positive Aspects.* The Committee takes note of the State party's policy to provide education at all levels free of charge and to enhance the provision of education in remote areas, through the awarding of additional allowances to teachers serving in those areas.

*Factors and Difficulties Impeding the Implementation of the Covenant.* The Committee is aware that problems caused by long periods of war and their aftermath have hampered the implementation of the Covenant in the State party.

*Principal Subjects of Concern.* The Committee is deeply concerned that the measures being taken by the State party are not sufficient to avoid continued suffering, and even greater deprivation of the economic, social and cultural rights, of the Iraqi people. The Committee is of the opinion that whatever the difficulties caused by the economic embargo, the States parties should none the less do everything possible to promote the realization of the Covenant to the maximum of its available resources.

In addition, the Committee considers that sufficient attention has not been given to the implementation of article 2 of the Covenant, as it relates to non-discrimination, in respect of the policies and measures adopted to promote and protect the economic, social and cultural rights, provided for under articles 13 to 15 of the Covenant, of all persons within the jurisdiction of the State, including, in particular, women and persons belonging to various cultural groups.

The Committee notes the lack of information on the implementation of the provisions of article 13, paragraph 1, specifically in respect to human rights education.

In connection with the implementation of article 13 of the Covenant, the Committee wishes to emphasize the fundamental importance of according equal priority to the education of women, including with regard to the eradication of illiteracy.

The Committee expresses its dissatisfaction at the lack of available statistical and other data which would assist in determining the extent of equality of educational opportunity existing within the country for various sectors of the Iraqi population.

The Committee is seriously concerned at reports it has received of infringements of academic freedom within the State party.

The Committee is alarmed at information brought to its attention concerning the destruction of the cultural heritage of religious communities and minorities.

Equally, the Committee is concerned that clarification remains to be given by the State party as to the compatibility of the steps taken by the Government in its exercise of control over the choice and broadcasting of minority language radio programmes with the implementation of the provisions of the Covenant, including its article 15, paragraph 2.

Moreover, the Committee is concerned at the reports brought to its attention of the adverse impact of recent drainage programmes in areas inhabited by "Marsh Arabs" on the community's ability to conserve its culture and traditional lifestyle and to exercise its right to education.

*Suggestions and Recommendations.* The Committee is of the view that further measures are required to ensure the effective monitoring and implementation of the rights provided for under articles 13 to 15 of the Covenant. In this regard attention is drawn to the contents of General Comment 3 of the Committee and to the obligation of States parties to take the necessary steps to the maximum extent of resources for the implementation of the rights provided for under the Covenant.

The Committee requests the State party to provide full information in the next report on the measures taken to implement article 13, paragraph 1 of the Covenant, in particular in relation to human rights education.

The Committee also recommends that the State party adopt the necessary measures to accord greater priority to the education of women, including the eradication of female illiteracy.

The Committee would appreciate receiving statistical data and other information relating to the admission and graduation of students, particularly of those belonging to religious and ethnic minorities and communities, within different higher educational establishments over the last three years.

The Committee would also appreciate receiving written information regarding the situation of the "Marsh Arabs", the closure of a Shiah college of jurisprudence and other concerns raised during the dialogue with the State party which remained unanswered. In this regard, the State party should refer to the present concluding observations and the summary records of the dialogue with the Committee. Finally, the Committee requests that this information be submitted to it by 30 September 1994.

**BIBLIOGRAPHY.** Akhavan, Payam. "Lessons from Iraqi Kurdistan: Self-Determination and Humanitarian Intervention against Genocide," *Netherlands Quarterly of Human Rights* 11, no. 1 (1993): 41–62. Scholarly article, in English.

Amnesty International. *The Death Penalty in Iraq: Introduction and Background.* London: 1987. NGO background paper, in English.

———. *Executions in Iraq.* London: 1988. NGO briefing paper, in English.

———. *Iraq/Occupied Kuwait: Human Rights Violations since 2 August [1990].* London: 1990. NGO factfinding report, in English and French.

Arab Organization for Human Rights. *Report: Human Rights in the Arab World.* Cairo: 1987. NGO report, in Arabic and English.

Bartram, Roger. "Reflections on Human Rights Issues in Prewar Iraq," *Journal of Palestine Studies* 20, no. 3 (Spring 1991): 87–97. Scholarly article, in English.

Bresheeth, Haim, and Nira Yuval-Davis, eds. *The Gulf War and the New World Order.* London: Zed Books, 1991. Monograph, in English.

Committee against Repression and for Democratic Rights in Iraq. *Saddam's Iraq: Revolution or Reaction?* 2nd ed. London: Zed Books, 1989. NGO edited collection, in English.

Dekker, Ige F., and Harry Post, eds. *The Gulf War of 1980–1988: The Iran-Iraq War in International Legal Perspective.* Dordrecht, the Netherlands: Martinus Nijhoff for T.M.C. Asser Institute, 1991. Scholarly monograph, in English.

Dudley, James. "Human Rights Practices in the Arab States: The Modern Impact of Shari'a Values," *Georgia Journal of International and Comparative Law* 12 (1982): 55–93. Scholarly article, in English.

Federation Internationale des Droits de l'Homme (International Federation of Human Rights). *The Human Rights Situation in Iraq.* Paris: 1986. NGO report, in French.

———. "Le Martyr du Peuple Kurde" (The Martyrdom of the Kurdish People). *Lettre de la FIDH* 241 (22 March 1988). NGO newsletter, in French.

*Freedom of Information and Expression in Iraq: A Commentary by Article 19 on the Report Submitted to the United Nations Committee by the Government of Iraq.* London: Article 19, 1987. NGO report, in English.

Harvard Study Team. *Harvard Study Team Report: Public Health in Iraq after the Gulf War.* Cambridge, MA, USA: 1991. Research report, in English.

Human Rights Watch. "Iraq and Iraqi Kurdistan," in *Human Rights Watch World Report 1995,* pp. 275–281. New York: 1995. NGO report, in English.

———. *Iraq's Crime of Genocide: The Anfal Campaign against the Kurds.* New York: 1994. NGO monograph, in English.

International Commission of Jurists. *Iraq and the Rule of Law.* Geneva, Switzerland: 1994. NGO monograph, in English.

Khalidi, Walid. *The Gulf Crisis: Origins and Consequences.* Washington, D.C.: Institute for Palestine Studies, 1991. Scholarly monograph, in English.

Korn, David. *Human Rights in Iraq.* New York: Human Rights Watch, 1990. NGO report, in English; bibliography, pp. 191–193.

Lawyers Committee for Human Rights. *Asylum under Attack: A Report on the Protection of Iraqi Refugees and Displaced Persons One Year after the Humanitarian Emergency in Iraq.* New York: 1992. NGO factfinding report, in English.

McDowall, David. *The Kurds.* 4th rev. ed. London: Minority Rights Group, 1985. NGO report, in English; bibliography, p. 31.

Middle East Watch. *The Bombing of Iraqi Cities: Middle East Watch Condemns Bombing without Warning or Air Raid Shelter in Baghdad's Al Ameriyya District on February 13.* New York: Human Rights Watch, 1991. NGO factfinding report, in English.

———. *Endless Torment: The 1991 Uprising in Iraq and Its Aftermath.* New York: Human Rights Watch, 1992. NGO report, in English.

———. *Genocide in Iraq: The Anfal Campaign against the Kurds.* New York: Human Rights Watch, 1993. NGO report, in English.

———. *Needless Deaths in the Gulf War: Civilian Casualties during the Air Campaign and Violations of the Laws of War.* New York: Human Rights Watch, 1991. NGO monograph, in English.

Middle East Watch and Physicians for Human Rights. *The Anfal Campaign in Iraqi Kurdistan: The Destruction of Koreme.* New York: Human Rights Watch, 1993. NGO report, in English.

———. *Unquiet Graves: The Search for the Disappeared in Iraqi Kurdistan.* New York: Human Rights Watch, 1992. NGO report, in English.

Physicians for Human Rights. *Winds of Death: Iraq's Use of Poison Gas against its Kurdish Population.* Somerville, MA, USA: 1989. NGO report, in English.

Picard, Elizabeth. *La Question Kurde* (The Kurdish Question). Brussels, Belgium: Éditions Complexe, 1991. Monograph, in French.

Vincent-Daviss, Diana, and Radu Popa. "The International Legal Implications of Iraq's Invasion of Kuwait: A Research Guide," *New York University Journal of International Law and Politics* 23 (1990): 231–321. Bibliography, in English.

# I

**IRELAND.** A country in western Europe, occupying about 84% of the land area of the second largest of the British Isles, situated in the Atlantic Ocean west of Great Britain, from which it is separated by the Irish Sea, the Republic of Ireland has a border with Northern Ireland, which occupies the remainder of the island. It achieved self-rule in 1921 when the Irish Free State was recognized after prolonged anti-British agitation and guerrilla warfare; however, six northern counties chose to remain as part of the United Kingdom. Full independence came with the proclamation of the Republic of Ireland on 18 April 1949, and Ireland became a member of the United Nations in 1955. Its population is estimated to be 3,525,000. Ethnic groups include descendants of Celtic tribes who conquered the island before the Christian era, and of the English invaders who eventually replaced them. Languages commonly used include English and Irish (Gaelic). Christianity (Roman Catholic, 95%; Anglican, 5%) is the predominant religion. Literacy is estimated at 99%.

The government (1994) took the form of a republic. The prime minister (*Taoiseach*), representing the party or coalition given the majority in a popular election, is appointed by the president on nomination by the House of Representatives (*Dáil Eireann*), to which he is responsible. The legislature consists of the president, who signs and promulgates all laws, the 166-member House of Representatives, and the 60-member Senate (*Seanad Eireann*). Members of the House are elected by proportional representation. Members of the Senate are nominated in the following manner: 11 by the prime minister, 6 by the universities, and 43 by vocational panels. Members of both bodies serve for a maximum term of five years. There is an independent judiciary, to which judges are appointed by the president. Political parties include the *Fianna Fáil, Fine Gael*, Labour, Progressive Democrats, Workers' Party, and the Independents.

## UNIFICATION OF IRELAND AND NORTHERN IRELAND.

Efforts to reunite the republic and the six northern provinces—now joined to the United Kingdom—continue sporadically. However, the government in Dublin has outlawed the extremist Irish Republican Army (IRA) and has detained and punished IRA guerrillas operating in territories under its control. The efforts at unification sometimes result in serious violence.

Rioting first broke out on 15 October 1968 as Catholic civil rights workers clashed with police in Londonderry, a small town northwest of Belfast. British troops were dispatched to Northern Ireland in August 1969 after a night of rioting and arson in Belfast. In 1972, after British soldiers had killed 13 members of another

Catholic civil rights march in Londonderry, England assumed direct rule of Northern Ireland.

After a brief year-end ceasefire in 1974, random violence reappeared on both sides: the Irish Republican Army—originally set up to protect Catholic neighborhoods—endeavoring to weaken British resolve by bombing buildings and open areas in London and other British cities, while the Ulster Freedom Fighters and Ulster Volunteers fought back with terrorist tactics which included hit-squads roaming the streets and killing Catholics at random in their homes and public places. At one point Great Britain was compelled to deploy 18,000 troops and 13,000 policemen to maintain a semblance of peace in Northern Ireland.

In 1985 Prime Minister Margaret Thatcher of Britain and Prime Minister Garrett Fitzgerald of Ireland concluded an agreement giving Ireland a voice in Northern Ireland affairs in return for its help in combatting terrorism. However, negotiations on a new arrangement for governing Northern Ireland collapsed in 1992 when the Protestant Unionists withdrew. Towards the end of 1993, however, Britain and Ireland issued the Downing Street Declaration setting out a new "framework for peace." The document mentioned self-determination by the people of Northern Ireland and the possibility of a united Ireland. Although this Declaration was formally rejected by *Sinn Fein*, the political arm of the IRA, a ceasefire was announced on 31 August 1994 by Sinn Fein leader Gerry Adams while on an unannounced visit to the United States of America.

The ceasefire issued on that day by the Irish Republican Army (in Gaelic, the *Oglaigh na h-Eirann*) was as follows:

Recognizing the potential of the current situation and in order to enhance the democratic peace process and underline our definitive commitment to its success, the leadership of Oglaigh na h-Eirann have decided that as of midnight Wednesday, Aug. 31, there will be a complete cessation of military operations. All our units have been instructed accordingly.

At this historic crossroads, the leadership of Oglaigh na h-Eirann salutes and commends our volunteers, other activists, our supporters and the political prisoners who have sustained this struggle, against all odds, for the past 25 years. Your courage, determination and sacrifices have demonstrated that the spirit of freedom and the desire for peace based on a just and lasting settlement cannot be crushed. We remember all those who have died for Irish freedom and we reiterate our commitment to our republican objectives.

Our struggle has seen many gains and advances made by nationalists and for the democratic position. We believe that an opportunity to secure a just and lasting settlement has been created. We are therefore entering into a new situation in a spirit of determination and confidence, determined that the injustices which created this conflict will be removed and confident in the strength and justice of our struggle to achieve this.

We note that the Downing Street Declaration is not a solution, nor was it presented as such by its authors. A solution will only be found as a result of inclusive negotiations. Others, not least the British Government, have a duty to face up to their responsibilities. It is our desire to significantly contribute to the creation of a climate which will encourage this. We urge everyone to approach this new situation with energy, determination and patience.

Concerning freedom of religion, members of the Protestant minority have maintained that laws relating to mixed marriages force the children of such unions into the Catholic faith and that Protestant parents are compelled to pay educational costs considerably higher than those paid by Catholics.

A new ruling coalition in the Dail elected John Bruton from the conservative Fine Gael Party as the new Prime Minister in December 1994.

In February 1995 a plan, drawn up by Prime Ministers Major and Bruton, called for a directly elected, 90-seat Ulster Assembly with legislative responsibility for most issues except security and taxation. This would mark the first "home-rule" for the province since Westminister took direct legislative responsibility in 1974. The plan also called for a "cross-border" group of representatives from the Irish Republic and Northern Ireland who would focus on mutual interests such as the environment, tourism, economic development, and culture.

Within the document the Irish Republic rescinded its constitutional claim to Northern Ireland. Unionists responded with a document of their own, claiming that Britain was conceding union of the north with the Irish Republic. Following a British troop reduction from 30,000 in 1992 to 17,500 in 1995 and an end to day-time patrols in the province, the peace plan proceeded with the first meeting since 1974 between a British government Minister and Sinn Fein.

***BIBLIOGRAPHY.*** Callender, Rosheen, and Frances Meenan. *Equality in Law between Men and Women in the European Community: Ireland.* Dordrecht, the Netherlands: Martinus Nijhoff; Office for Official Publications of the European Communities, 1994. Scholarly monograph, in English.

Fitzgerald, Eithne. "Irish Women Today," *America* 158, no. 10 (12 March 1988): 266–268. NGO article, in English.

Robbins, T., and R. Robertson, eds. *Church-State Relations: Tensions and Transitions.* New Brunswick, NJ, USA: Transaction Books, 1987. Scholarly edited collection, in English.

## ISLAMIC CALL SOCIETY.

**ISLAMIC CALL SOCIETY.** An international non-governmental organization in consultative status with the UN ECONOMIC AND SOCIAL COUNCIL (Roster) and with **UNESCO,** the Society has affiliated organizations and individual members in 36 countries.

Founded in 1972, the group aims to make known the call of Islam in the world by all peaceful means, in particular by diffusing Islamic culture and the Arabic language, promoting peace and international coopera-

tion, classifying Islamic law, compiling and publishing reference works, and creating centers of education.

Islamic Call Society. Address: P.O. Box 2549, Tripoli, Libya. Secretary-General: Mohamed Ahmed Sharif.

## ISRAEL.

**ISRAEL.** The State of Israel is a country in western Asia, on the Mediterranean Sea. It has borders with Egypt, Jordan, Lebanon, and Syria. Formerly Palestine, a LEAGUE OF NATIONS mandate under the administration of Great Britain, the foreign minister of the Provincial Government of Israel informed the UN SECURITY COUNCIL of the "Proclamation of an Independent State of Israel in Palestine" (UN Doc. S/747) on 15 May 1948, one day after the expiration of the mandate. Israel became a member of the United Nations in 1949. Its population is estimated to be 4,593,000. The demographic composition of the population (as of 1983) included Jews (84%), Muslims (13%), Christians (2.3%), and Druze (1.3%). Languages in common use include Hebrew and Arabic (both official), English, and the many national tongues of the immigrant population. Arabic is employed in official publications and as necessary in government offices; it is used by members of the parliament if they so choose, such speeches being simultaneously rendered into Hebrew; and it is used in the publication of ordinances, official notices, and in the press and other media. The *Sharia* (Muslim religious) courts, which have exclusive jurisdiction over members of the Muslim community in matters of personal status (marriage, divorce, inheritance, etc.), conduct their proceedings in Arabic, while, in other courts, translators are appointed to assist those who do not know Hebrew. Literacy is estimated at 94% among Jews and 84% among those of other beliefs.

Among the Jewish population of Israel, there tend to be four main divisions: the non-observant, 45%; the traditional, mostly immigrants from Muslim countries, 35%; the Orthodox, 15%; and the ultra-orthodox Haredim, 5%. Their points of view sometimes conflict, mainly on the question of whether or not Israel should remain a secular State.

While basically secular, Israel has preserved the system of religious communities, or millets, of earlier Turkish and British administrations. Under that system, members of religious communities are governed by the laws of their own religion in matters of personal status, such as marriage, divorce, maintenance, guardianship, etc. For this purpose, the recognized religious communities may establish and administer their own religious courts under rules supervised by the Ministry of Religious Affairs. In addition, recognized communities are governed by religious and cultural councils or boards, which have the capacity to acquire and administer property, to enter into contracts, to raise funds, and to execute deeds. In some cases, they may also have the power to impose upon members of the community contributions and fees for communal purposes.

The government (1994) took the form of a republic, although it does not have a written constitution. The president, elected by the *Knesset* for a term of five years, is head of State. The cabinet, headed by the prime minister, who represents the party or coalition given the majority in a popular election, exercises executive authority. The *Knesset* is composed of 120 members elected for terms of four years under a system of proportional representation. Citizens of Israel vote for national parties rather than for individuals, and any party getting even 1% of the vote wins a seat in parliament. With 17 parties represented in 1990, none could gain a majority without joining with several others.

A special body, independent of the executive, was established in 1971: the Commissioner for Complaints from the Public (or *Ombudsman*). Its function is to examine complaints submitted by anyone who claims to have been injured by an act of a public authority and to seek redress in appropriate cases.

For more than 25 years, the question of the violation of human rights in Arab territories occupied by Israel has been on the agenda of a number of United Nations organs, including the **GENERAL ASSEMBLY,** the Security Council, the UN **COMMISSION ON HUMAN RIGHTS,** the **COMMITTEE ON THE ELIMINATION OF RACIAL DISCRIMINATION,** and the **SUB-COMMISSION ON PREVENTION OF DISCRIMINATION AND PROTECTION OF MINORITIES,** as well as various specialized agencies and intergovernmental bodies (recent conclusions and recommendations of some of these bodies are summarized below).

Peace talks between the leaders of Israel and the **PALESTINE LIBERATION ORGANIZATION (PLO)** resulted in a historic agreement in September 1993. The PLO recognized Israel's right to exist as a State, while Israel recognized the PLO as the representative of the Palestinian people. An agreement for limited Palestinian self-rule in Gaza and in the West Bank, beginning with the city of Jericho, was also signed. One result of these agreements was the awarding of the 1993 **NOBEL PEACE PRIZE** to PLO leader **YASSAR ARAFAT** and to Israeli Prime Minister **YITZHAK RABIN** and Foreign Minister **SHIMON PERES.** Since the initial euphoria, however, the peace talks have stalled, largely due to acts of violence by both sides. The fanatical Islamic group Hamas has conducted bombings and murders of Israeli citizens and soldiers, while Israeli settlers also committed atrocities. The worst violence by an Israeli settler was the mass murder committed at the Ibrahimi mosque in Hebron in February 1994, when Baruch Goldstein entered the shrine during worship and killed 29. The Israeli government initiated a commission to investigate the massacre.

***VIOLATIONS OF HUMAN RIGHTS IN THE OCCUPIED TERRITORIES.*** At its 1993 session the Commission on Human Rights, taking into consideration numerous General Assembly and Security Council resolutions, taking note of reports which the Special Committee to Investigate Israeli Practices Affecting the Human Rights of the Palestinian People and Other Arabs of the Occupied Territories had submitted to the General Assembly since 1968, and noting with great concern "the Israeli refusal to abide by the resolutions of the Security Council, the General Assembly and the Commission on Human Rights," condemned "the policies and practices of Israel, which violate the human rights of the Palestinian people in the Palestinian territory occupied by Israel with military force, including Jerusalem, and, in particular, the opening of fire by the Israeli army and settlers on Palestinian civilians that results in killing and wounding them, as has happened continuously since the eruption of the Palestinian people's intifada against the Israeli military occupation; the imposition of restrictive economic measures; the demolition of houses; the expropriation of houses; the ransacking of property belonging individually or collectively to private persons; collective punishment; arbitrary and administrative detention of thousands of Palestinians; the confiscation of property of Palestinians, including their bank accounts; the expropriation of land; the prevention of travel; the closure of universities and schools; the perpetration of crimes of torture in Israeli prisons and detention centres; and the establishment of Jewish settlements in the occupied Palestinian territory."

The Commission affirmed "the right of the Palestinian people to resist the Israeli occupation by all means, in accordance with the relevent United Nations resolutions, consistent with the purposes and principles of the Charter of the United Nations, as has been expressed by the Palestinian people in their brave *intifada* since December 1987, in legitimate resistance against the Israeli military occupation," and called once more "upon Israel, the occupying Power, to desist from all forms of violation of human rights in the Palestinian and other occupied Arab territories and to respect the bases of international law, the principles of international humanitarian law, and its commitments to the provisions of the Charter and resolutions of the United Nations."

In the resolution the Commission decided to appoint a Special Rapporteur with the following mandate:

(a) to investigate Israel's violations of the principles and bases of international law, international humanitarian law and the Geneva Convention relative to the Protection of Civilian Persons in Time of War, of 12 August 1949, in the Palestinian territories occupied since 1967;

(b) to receive communications, to hear witnesses, and to use such modalities of procedure as he may deem necessary for his mandate; and

(c) to report, with his conclusions and recommendation, to the Commission on Human Rights at its future sessions, until the end of the Israeli occupation of those territories.

At its 1994 session, the Commission received the report on the human rights situation in the Palestinian territories occupied since 1967 submitted by the Special Rapporteur, Mr. René Felber (Un Doc. E/CN.4/1994/14). It welcomed the positive development represented by the Declaration of Principles on Interim Self-Government Arrangements signed by the Government of Israel and the Palestine Liberation Organization on 13 September 1993, but noted that the Special Rapporteur's report referred to information provided to him on confiscation of land by the Israeli authorities before and after the signing of that Declaration. In resolution 1994/1 of 18 February 1994, the Commission reaffirmed "that the installation of Israeli civilians in the occupied territories is illegal and constitutes a violation of the relevant provisions of the Geneva Convention relative to the Protection of Civilian Persons in Time of War," regretted that that Government had not fully complied with the provisions of its earlier resolutions on the subject; and urged it to abstain from installing any settlers in the occupied territories.

In Part A of resolution 1994/3 of 18 February 1994, bearing the same title and based on the same report of the Special Rapporteur, as well as reports which the Special Committee had submitted to the General Assembly since 1968, the Commission on Human rights deeply regretted "the continued violations of human rights in the occupied Palestinian territory since the signing of the Declaration of Principles on Interim Self-Government Arrangements by the Government of Israel and the Palestine Liberation Organization on 13 September 1993," and condemned "the continued violations of the human rights of the Palestinian people in the Palestinian territory occupied by Israel with military force, including Jerusalem, and, in particular, the opening of fire by the Israeli army and settlers on Palestinian civilians that results in killing and wounding them; the imposition of restrictive economic measures; the demolition of houses; the expropriation of houses; collective punishment; arbitrary and administrative detention of thousands of Palestinians without trial; the confiscation of property of Palestinians; the expropriation of land; the prevention of travel; the closure of universities and schools; the perpetration of crimes of torture in Israeli prisons and detention centres; and the establishment of Israeli settlements in the occupied Palestinian territory."

It called once more "upon Israel, the occupying Power, to desist from all forms of violation of human rights in the Palestinian and other occupied Arab territories and to respect the bases of international law, the principles of international humanitarian law, and its commitments to the provisions of the Charter and resolutions of the United Nations." It also called upon Israel "to withdraw from the Palestinian territory, including Jerusalem, and the other occupied Arab territories in accordance with the relevant resolutions of the United Nations and the Commission on Human Rights."

The Secretary-General was requested to bring the resolution to the attention of the Government of Israel, and to report on its implementation by that Government to the Commission at its 1995 session.

In Part B of the same resolution, the Commission on Human Rights reaffirmed "that the Geneva Convention relative to the Protection of Civilian Persons in Time of War, of 12 August 1949, is applicable to the Palestinian and all other Arab territories occupied by Israel since 1967, including Jerusalem, and that Israel's long-standing refusal to apply the Convention to those territories has led to the perpetration by the Israeli authorities of grave violations of human rights against Palestinian citizens," and called upon Israel "to comply with its international commitments, to respect the Convention and to apply it in the occupied Palestinian territory, including Jerusalem." It urged once more all States parties to the Convention to make every effort to ensure the Israeli occupation authorities' respect for and compliance with the provisions of the Convention, and strongly condemned once more "the refusal of Israel to apply the Convention to Palestine and the Arab territories occupied since 1967 and to their inhabitants." In particular it called upon Israel "to allow those who have been deported since 1967 to return to their homeland without delay in implementation of the resolutions of the Security Council, the General Assembly and the Commission on Human Rights."

***HUMAN RIGHTS IN THE OCCUPIED SYRIAN GOLAN.*** In resolution 1994/2 of 18 February 1994, the UN Commission on Human Rights expressed its grave alarm, after considering the report of the Special Committee to Investigate Israeli Practices Affecting the Human Rights of the Palestinian people and other Arabs of the Occupied Territories (A/48/558), over Israel's flagrant and persistent violations of human rights in the Syrian and other Arab territories occupied since 1967, despite the resolutions of the Security Council and the General Assembly which repeatedly called upon Israel to put an end to such occupation. In the resolution, the Commission:

Strongly condemns Israel, the occupying Power, for its refusal to comply with the relevant resolutions of the General Assembly and the Security Council, particularly resolution 497 (1981), in which the Council, *inter alia*, decided that the Israeli decision to impose its laws, jurisdiction and administration on the occupied Syrian Golan was null and void and without international legal effect, and demanded that Israel, the occupying Power, should rescind forthwith its decision;

Condemns the persistence of Israel in changing the physical character, demographic composition, institutional structure and legal status of the occupied Syrian Golan, and emphasizes that the displaced persons of the population of the occupied Syrian Golan must be allowed to return to their homes and to recover their properties;

Determines that all legislative and administrative measures and actions taken or to be taken by Israel, the occupying Power, that purport to alter the character and legal status of the Syrian Golan are null and void, constitute a flagrant violation of international law and of the Geneva Convention relative to the Protection of Civilian Persons in Time of War, of 12 August 1949, and have no legal effect;

Strongly condemns Israel for its attempt to impose forcibly Israeli citizenship and Israeli identity cards on the Syrian citizens in the occupied Syrian Golan and for its practices of annexation, establishment of settlements, confiscation of lands and diversion of water resources and imposing a boycott on their agricultural products; and calls upon Israel to desist from its settlement designs and policies aimed against academic institutions with the goal of serving the objectives of occupation, and to desist from its repressive measures against the population of the occupied Syrian Golan;

Calls once again upon Member States not to recognize any of the legislative or administrative measures and actions referred to in the present resolution;

Requests the Secretary-General to bring the present resolution to the attention of all Governments, the competent United Nations organs, the specialized agencies, regional intergovernmental organizations and international humanitarian organizations and to give it the widest possible publicity, and to report to the Commission on Human Rights at its fifty-first session.

## HUMAN RIGHTS IN SOUTHERN LEBANON.

In resolution 1994/83 of 9 March 1994, the Commission on Human Rights deplored "the repeated Israeli aggression in southern Lebanon, particularly the Israeli attack on the south and west Bekaa in July 1993, which caused a large number of deaths and injuries and the displacement of hundreds of thousands of inhabitants, as well as the destruction of several houses, hospitals, schools and public buildings." It further indicated that it was "gravely concerned by the impeding of the International Committee of the Red Cross and

other humanitarian organizations from accomplishing their humanitarian mission in the occupied area of southern Lebanon, in particular to ascertain reports of ill-treatment of detainees in the detention centers of Khiyam and Marjayoun."

The Commission specifically condemned "the continued Israeli violations of human rights in southern Lebanon, manifested particularly by the arbitrary detention of civilians, the destruction of their houses, the confiscation of their property, their expulsion from the occupied area, the bombardment of villages and civilian areas, and other practices violating human rights," and called upon Israel to put an end to such practices and to implement Security Council resolutions 425 (1978) and 509 (1982) which demand the immediate, total and unconditional withdrawal of Israel from all Lebanese territories and respect for the sovereignty, independence and territorial integrity of Lebanon.

Further, the Commission called upon the Government of Israel, the occupying Power of territories in southern Lebanon and the west Bekaa, "to release immediately all those Lebanese and other prisoners detained in the Israeli prisons and detention centers contrary to all the Geneva Conventions and to other provisions of international law," and also "to facilitate the humanitarian mission of the International Committee of the Red Cross and other humanitarian organizations in that region, and, in particular, to allow these organizations to visit the detention centers of Khiyam and Marjayoun and verify the living conditions of the detainees."

**BIBLIOGRAPHY.** Amnesty International. *Conscientious Objection to Military Service.* London: 1988. NGO report, in English.

————. *Excessive Force: Beatings to Maintain Law and Order.* London: 1988. NGO report, in English.

————. *Israel and the Occupied Territories: Prisoner Cases—September 1987 to February 1988.* London: 1988. NGO report, in English.

Aronson, Geoffrey. *Creating Facts: Israel, Palestinians and the West Bank.* Washington, D.C.: Institute for Palestine Studies, 1987. Scholarly monograph, in English.

————. "Soviet Jewish Emigration, the United States and the Occupied Territories," *Journal of Palestine Studies* 19, no. 4 (Summer 1990): 30–45. Scholarly article, in English.

Association for Civil Rights in Israel. *The Legal and Administrative System.* Jerusalem: 1985. NGO monograph, in English.

Averick, Sara M. *A Human Rights Comparison: Israel Versus the Arab States.* Washington, D.C.: American Israel Public Affairs Committee, 1988. Political report, in English.

Berliner, Marilyn J. "Palestinian Arab Self-Determination and Israeli Settlements on the West Bank: An Analysis of Their Legality Under International Law," *Loyola of Los Angeles International and Comparative Law Journal* 8, no. 3 (1985–1986): 551–552. Scholarly article, in English.

Blanchard, Francis. *Report on the Situation of Workers of the Occupied Arab Territories.* Vol. 2. Geneva: ILO, 1988. IGO report, in English.

Cohen, Esther Rosalind. *Human Rights in the Israeli-Occupied Territories, 1967–1982.* Manchester, England: Manchester University Press, 1985. Scholarly monograph, in English.

Cohen, Roberta. "Israel's Problematic Absorption of Soviet Jews," *International Journal of Refugee Law* 3, no. 1 (Jan. 1991): 60–81. Scholarly article, in English.

Cossali, P., and C. Robson. *Stateless in Gaza.* London: Zed Books, 1986. Documentary, in English.

Dinstein, Yoram, ed. *Israel Yearbook on Human Rights.* Tel Aviv: Alpha Press, 1985–present. Scholarly yearbook, in English.

Donnelly, J., and R. E. Howard, eds. *International Handbook on Human Rights.* Westport, CT, USA: Greenwood Press, 1987. Scholarly edited collection, in English.

Falloon, Virgil. *Excessive Secrecy, Lack of Guidelines: A Report on Military Censorship in the West Bank.* Ramallah, Occupied Territories: Law in the Service of Man/Al-Haq, 1986. NGO report, in English.

Friedman, Hanna, and Hava Halevi, eds. *Moderate Physical Pressure: Interrogation Methods in Israel—Symposium Following the Landau Commission Report 12.7.90.* Jerusalem, Israel: Public Committee against Torture in Israel, 1990. Conference report, in English.

Gordon, Haim, and Rivca Gordon, eds. *Israel/Palestine: The Quest for Dialogue.* New York: Orbis Books, 1991. Monograph, in English.

Halabi, Usama R. "The Legality of Utilizing Administrative Detention in the Israeli Occupied Territories," *Netherlands Quarterly of Human Rights* 9, no. 4 (1991): 398–417. Scholarly article, in English.

Hilterman, Joost R. "L'immigration soviétique et la mainmise sur Jérusalem" (Soviet Immigration and the Control of Jerusalem), *Revue d'études palestiniennes* no. 40 (Summer 1991): 61–76. Article, in French.

Human Rights Watch. "Israeli-Occupied West Bank and the Gaza Strip," in *Human Rights Watch World Report 1995,* pp. 281–290. New York: 1995. NGO report, in English.

Hunt, Paul. *Justice? The Military Court System in the Israeli-Occupied Territories.* Ramallah, Occupied Territories: Law in the Service of Man/Al-Haq and Gaza Centre for Rights and the Law, 1987. NGO report, in English.

Institute for Palestine Studies. *United Nations Resolutions on Palestine and the Arab-Israeli Conflict.* Washington, D.C.: 1988. NGO document collection, in English.

International Standing Committee of Lawyers on the Question of Palestine and Peace in the Middle East and International Association of Democratic Lawyers. *Palestine and Law.* Brussels: 1988. NGO articles/factfinding missions, in English and French (*Palestine et Droit*).

"Israël et l'ONU : 42 ans de non-respect du droit" (Israel and the UN: 42 Years of No Respect for Law), *Revue d'études palestiniennes* no. 38 (Winter 1991): 75–98. Article, in French.

Israeli League for Human and Civil Rights. *Report on the Violations of Human Rights in the Territories during the Uprising, 1988.* Tel Aviv: 1988. NGO report, in English.

Kretzmer, David. *The Legal Status of the Arabs in Israel.* Boulder, CO, USA: Westview Press, 1990. Scholarly monograph, in English.

Law in the Service of Man/Al-Haq. *Punishing a Nation: Human Rights Violations during the Palestinian Uprising, December 1987–December 1988.* Ramallah, Occupied Territories: 1988. NGO report, in English.

Maddrell, Penny. *The Beduin of the Negev.* London: Minority Rights Group, 1990. NGO report, in English.

Middle East Watch. *The Israeli Army and the Intifada: Policies that Contribute to the Killings.* New York: Human Rights Watch, 1990. NGO factfinding report, in English.

———. *A License to Kill: Israeli Undercover Operations against 'Wanted' and Masked Palestinians.* New York: Human Rights Watch, 1993. NGO report, in English.

———. *Prison Conditions in Israel and the Occupied Territories.* New York: Human Rights Watch, 1991. NGO factfinding report, in English.

———. *Torture and Ill-Treatment: Israel's Interrogation of Palestinians from the Occupied Territories.* New York: Human Rights Watch, 1994. NGO report, in English.

Pacheco, Allegra A. "Occupying an Uprising: The Geneva Convention and the Israeli Administrative Detention Policy During the First Year of the Palestinian General Uprising: December 1987–December 1988," *Columbia Human Rights Law Review* 21, no. 2 (Spring 1990): 515–563. Scholarly article, in English.

Physicians for Human Rights. *Casualties of Conflict: Medical Care and Human Rights in the West Bank and Gaza Strip.* Somerville, MA, USA: 1988. NGO mission report, in English.

Playfair, Emma. *Administrative Detention in the Occupied West Bank.* Ramallah, Occupied Territories: Law in the Service of Man/Al-Haq, 1986. NGO study, in English.

———. *Demolition and Sealing of Houses as a Punitive Measure in the Israeli-Occupied West Bank.* Ramallah, Occupied Territories: Law in the Service of Man/Al-Haq, 1987. NGO report, in English.

———, ed. *International Law and the Administration of Occupied Territories.* Oxford, UK: Oxford University Press, 1992. Scholarly monograph, in English; bibliography, pp. 505–522.

Pressberg, Gail. "The Uprising: Causes and Consequences," *Journal of Palestine Studies* 18, no. 3 (Spring 1988): 38–50. Scholarly article, in English.

Quigley, John. *Palestine and Israel: A Challenge to Justice.* Durham, NC, USA: Duke University Press, 1990. Scholarly monograph, in English.

Shalev, Carmel. *The Price of Insurgency: Civil Rights in the Occupied Territories.* Jerusalem: West Bank Database Project, 1988. NGO report, in English.

Shehadeh, Raja. "Occupier's Law and the Uprising," *Journal of Palestine Studies* 18, no. 3 (Spring 1988): 24–37. Scholarly article, in English.

Stendel, Ori. "The Arabs of Israel: Between Hammer and Anvil," *Israel Yearbook on Human Rights,* pp. 287–308. Dordrecht, the Netherlands: Martinus Nijhoff Publishers and the Faculty of Law, Tel Aviv University, 1991. Scholarly article, in English.

United Nations Division for Palestinian Rights. *Seventh United Nations International NGO Meeting on the Question of Palestine. 29–31 August 1990.* Geneva, Switzerland: 1990. IGO conference proceedings, in English.

Vermund, S. H., S. G. Miller, and S. P. Cohen. *Health Status and Services in the West Bank and Gaza Strip—Report of "Cooperation for Development: A Community-Based Health Project,"* New York: Institute for Middle East Peace and Development, 1985. NGO report, in English.

Vitullo, Anita. *Ansar 2: Detention, Humiliation, and Intimidation.* Chicago, IL, USA: Palestine Human Rights Information Center and Human Rights Research and Education Foundation/Database Project, 1987. NGO report, in English.

**ITALY.** The Italian Republic is a country in southern Europe, occupying a peninsula extending into the Mediterranean Sea and several islands including Lampedusa, Linosa, Pantellaria, Sardinia, and Sicily. It has borders with Austria, France, Switzerland, and Slovenia. It achieved independence originally as the Roman Empire, which disintegrated after 1713. Reunited by Giuseppe Garibaldi under Victor Emmanuel II, it was a monarchy until Benito Mussolini seized power as dictator in 1922. After World War II, in which it participated as part of the Rome—Berlin Axis, the resumption of its independence was recognized in the peace treaty of 15 September 1947. Under the peace treaty, Italy renounced all claims in Ethiopia and Greece, ceded the Dodecanese Islands to Greece and five Alpine areas to France, and turned over much of the Istrian Peninsula to Yugoslavia.

Italy became a member of the United Nations in 1955. Its population is estimated to be 56,550,000. Ethnic groups include communities of Albanian, Catalan, Croatian, Germanic, Greek, Gypsy, Sardinian, and Slavic origin; linguistic communities whose mother tongue is French, Franco–Provencal, German, Ladin, Occitan, or Slovene; and foreign workers and refugees, mostly of Mediterranean background. Languages commonly used include Italian and the above-mentioned minority languages. Christianity (Roman Catholic) is the predominant religion. Literacy is estimated at 98%.

The government (1994) took the form of a republic. The constitution, promulgated on 1 January 1948, establishes a bicameral parliament consisting of a 315-member Senate and a 630-member Chamber of Deputies; members are elected for five-year terms. The executive branch consists of a Council of Ministers (cabinet), headed by the president of the council (prime minister). The president of the republic is elected for a term of seven years by parliament sitting jointly with a small number of regional delegates. The resident nominates the prime minister, who chooses the other ministers. The judicial system is based on Roman law, as modified by the Napoleonic Code and subsequent statutes, and there is a Constitutional Court which passes on the constitutionality of laws.

There are many political parties. The Christian Democratic Party is the largest, and Italy's stability is largely due to the fact that it has represented the majority, either alone or in coalition with other parties, since 1945, although Italy has had more than 40 prime ministers during that period. The Italian Communist Party, the second largest, has at times received as much as 34% of the popular vote; in 1983, it won 29.9% of that vote. Other parties include the Italian Socialist Party, the Italian Social Movement, the Italian Republican Party, the Italian Social Democratic Party, the Italian Liberal Party, and the Radical Party.

Bettino Craxi, Italy's first socialist premier, was chosen for that post after the election of June 1983. However, his government suffered an internal crisis after the October 1985 hijacking of the cruise ship *Achille Lauro* and the downing of an Egyptian plane carrying the hijackers and Abu Abbas, a PLO leader believed to have organized the hijacking. The release of Abbas and refusal to turn the hijackers over to U.S. authorities brought Craxi's government to an impasse, and Craxi was forced to resign. He was succeeded in June 1987 by a Christian Democrat, Giovanni Goria, who, in turn, was replaced by Ciriaco De Mita in April 1988. In 1994, when U.S. President Clinton visited Italy as part of a tour commemorating Allied landings in Europe 50 years earlier, Silvio Berlusconi was premier.

He resigned less than seven months later as the rightist coalition was weakened considerably. The widespread investigation into organized crime and official corruption continued despite assassinations of members of the judiciary and others. Numerous government officials and business leaders were implicated, including former Prime Minister Craxi, who was convicted and sentenced for official wrongdoing.

In recent years, Italy has been plagued by frequent outbursts of lawlessness and terrorism, carried out by well-organized bands of kidnappers. In February 1990, the government took steps to reduce the problem by enacting measures lengthening prison terms for cases in which kidnapping victims are ill, very young, or very old, and those in which cruel treatment is involved. At the same time, it called upon parliament to approve a far-reaching policy under which all relatives of a kidnapping victim would immediately have their assets frozen by the State to prevent them from raising money for payment of ransom and would be prohibited from seeking financial help from banks and similar sources. Moreover, an existing ban that makes it illegal for Italian insurance companies to sell anti-kidnapping policies would be extended to foreign companies.

Italy has also experienced an influx of foreigners, attracted by the relative prosperity of the country. The presence among the newcomers of Africans and Gypsies has occasionally been the subject of protests and public demonstrations.

***REPORT OF THE UN HUMAN RIGHTS COMMITTEE.*** The **HUMAN RIGHTS COMMITTEE** considered the third periodic report of Italy on its implementation of the **INTERNATIONAL COVENANT ON CIVIL AND POLITICAL RIGHTS** (CCPR/C/64/Add. 8) at its meeting held on 11 and 12 July 1994, and on 27 July 1994 adopted the following comments (CCPR/C/79/Add. 37):

*Factors and Difficulties Affecting the Implementation of the Covenant.* The Committee notes the emergence in certain parts of the population of Italy of a trend towards racism and intolerance against foreigners, particularly asylum-seekers and migrant workers, and the resurgence of certain elements militating in favour of political movements reminiscent of a past when human rights were seriously violated. The Committee also notes that there are difficulties in implementing the necessary struggle against organized crime and corruption, especially in the highest spheres of power, in a manner that is compatible with the provisions of the Covenant.

*Positive Aspects.* The Committee notes with particular satisfaction the high level of achievement in the respect of human rights in Italy and the strong commitment of the State party to the promotion and protection of human rights at both the national and the international level. In this regard, it welcomes, in particular, the intention of the State party to accede to the Second optional Protocol to the Covenant, aiming at the abolition of the death penalty.

The Committee welcomes the efforts taken by the State party to promote equal opportunities for women, particularly through the work of the commission for Parity and Equality of opportunities for Men and Women, and progress achieved in improving women's participation in public affairs, professions and private economic sector. It also welcomes the adoption, on 26 April 1993, of a law aiming at strengthening the prevention, elimination and punishment of racist acts. The Committee takes note of agreements recently concluded between the State party and certain religious denominations as well as the proposed establishment of a special office on religious freedom. The improvements in the free legal aid scheme and the establishment of an advisory national bioethics committee are also welcomed. Moreover, the Committee appreciates the various measures taken by the State party to protect and promote the rights of persons belonging to linguistic minorities which constitute a positive approach to the full implementation of article 27 of the Covenant.

*Principal Subjects of Concern.* The Committee continues to regret the extent of State party's reservations to the Covenant and that it has yet not envisaged to withdraw some of them.

The Committee regrets that the office of the citizens' advocate has not yet been established at the national level and that similar offices do not exist in all regions of the State party. Furthermore, there appear not to be any guidelines regarding cooperation and coordination between those different offices. These facts combined with distinctions in the powers and functions of the regional and local citizens' advocates, may cause unequal protection for individuals depending on the place where they live.

The Committee is concerned about cases brought to its attention of ill-treatment of persons by police and security forces in public places and police stations. The Committee is also concerned by the increasing number of cases of ill-treatment in prisons. It notes with concern that the Government does not always investigate thoroughly those cases, that torture as such is not punishable in domestic law, and that, consequently, appropriate sanctions are not always imposed on those found guilty.

The Committee is concerned about the duration of preventive detention as provided for under the law which do not appear to be compatible with the requirements of articles 9 and 14 of the Covenant. Delays in judicial proceedings remain worrisome despite attempts at reducing them. The Committee is also concerned at the various problems faced in the administration of prisons and other detention centres, particularly overcrowding.

The Committee is concerned about the excessive concentration of the mass media in a small group of people. Furthermore, it notes that such concentration may affect the enjoyment of the right to freedom of expression and information under article 19 of the Covenant.

The Committee is concerned that the State party's definition of minorities is confined to linguistic minorities within its territory and that, consequently, members of other minorities may not enjoy equal protection of their rights under article 27.

*Suggestions and Recommendations.* The Committee recommends that the State party will review its reservations to the Covenant with a view to withdrawing them.

In view of the fact that criminal legislation does not provide for the death penalty, the Committee wishes to encourage the State party to take the necessary steps to accede to the Second optional Protocol to the Covenant.

The Committee expresses the hope that the Government will undertake the necessary measures to establish a citizens' advocate office at the national level. It also recommends that, at the regional level, where this has not already been done, citizens, advocate offices be established and that functions and powers of regional citizens' advocates be harmonized.

The Committee urges that the State party consider making torture a specific criminal offence. In addition, it suggests that the State party further strengthen measures to protect the rights of detainees; to promptly investigate allegations of ill-treatment and to ensure that appropriate penalties are applied whenever such offences are committed; to prevent the commission of such acts through efforts to ensure the stricter observance of regulations relating to the treatment of detainees and offenders; and to reduce the length of preventive detention, taking into account the principle of presumption of innocence and the complexity of the investigation. The Committee also suggests that more effective and thorough human rights training be provided to law enforcement officials and prison officers.

The Committee recommends that the State party should re-examine the possibility of civil liability of judges in the light of the United Nations Basic Principles on the Independence of the Judiciary.

In order to avoid the inherent risks in the excessive concentration of control of the mass information media in a small group of people, the Committee emphasizes the importance of implementing measures to ensure impartial allocation of resources as well as equitable access to such media, and of adopting anti-trust legislation regulating mass media.

The Committee recommends that the State party continue to strengthen its education and training programmes on multi-culturalism with a view to eliminating racial discrimination, and advancing tolerance and understanding among peoples and races.

Further efforts are required to ensure the equal participation by women in public life and more effective protection of women against all forms of violence.

The Committee would appreciate receiving in the next periodic report information on those matters which due to time constraints remained unanswered, including on the legal measures taken by the State party to allow the implementation of the views of the Committee under the optional Protocol.

*REPORT OF THE UN COMMITTEE ON ECONOMIC, SO-CIAL AND CULTURAL RIGHTS.* The **COMMITTEE ON ECONOMIC, SOCIAL AND CULTURAL RIGHTS** examined the second periodic report of Italy concerning its implementation of the **INTERNATIONAL COVENANT ON ECONOMIC, SOCIAL AND CULTURAL RIGHTS** at meetings held on 3, 4, and 10 December 1992, and on the latter date adopted the following concluding observations (E/1993/22, paras. 187–193):

The Committee welcomed the continuation of its dialogue with Italy on the occasion of the submission of that country's second periodic report on articles 1 to 15. It was gratified by the high level of the delegation selected to present the oral report and to reply to the questions raised by the written report.

The written report dealt very comprehensively with articles 13 to 15 and article 10 (3), but on articles 6 to 9, 10 (1) and 10 (2) it was too sketchy and it did not cover at all the rights contained in article 11, concerning the right of everyone to an adequate standard of living. The oral presentation and the replies to the Committee's questions largely rectified that shortcoming.

The Committee noted that substantial efforts were being made by the Italian Government to reduce unemployment and integrate foreign workers, both from within and outside the European Community. The number of industrial accidents and occupational diseases was falling. Progress was also being made in the employment of women.

However, the policy of privatization and the abolition of the sliding scale system entailed certain risks for the social protection of all the sectors of the population.

In the consideration of the report the Committee devoted particular attention to the right to housing. Although the steady increase in the number of home-owners (currently 62 per cent) was a source of satisfaction, the situation of tenants in the most disadvantaged social categories did not seem to be improving.

The Committee wished to draw the attention of the State party to a number of specific concerns resulting from the dialogue with its representatives. These concerns included the fact that:

(a) The adoption of Act L359/92 in August 1992 seems likely to aggravate the situation of the most economically disadvantaged tenants. The Act partly goes back on Act L392/78 of 1978, which introduced the concept of a "fair rent" (*equo canone*);

(b) It has led to a certain paralysis in the rental market since about 5 million apartments are currently reported to be unoccupied. The scope of exceptions to the fair-rent rule has widened and freedom to set rents is contributing to rental increases;

(c) Given the shortage of low-income housing, which accounts for about 5 per cent of the total housing stock, and since no housing allowance system has been established or is envisaged, the situation of tenants is disturbing. The 10-year low-income housing construction plan, which was partly executed in 1988, has not been amended and remains insufficient;

(d) A further continuing source of concern is the precarious nature of leases, aggravated by the provisions of the Act of August 1992, given the fact that 74 per cent of evictions are based on termination of the lease and, since 1983, one family out of three has been evicted.

The Committee reiterated the importance the Covenant attaches to the right to housing, and recommends that the Italian Government should take all appropriate measures to improve the situation of tenants and to ensure that medium-term solutions are found in order to deal more satisfactorily with housing for the most disadvantaged social categories. It hopes to receive all relevant information on the occasion of Italy's submission of its third periodic report.

Italy has also submitted reports on its application of the International Convention on the Elimination of All Forms of Racial Discrimination to the Committee on the Elimination of Racial Discrimination (see **RACIAL DISCRIMINATION**) (E/CERD/C/104/Add. 2, 156/Add. 1, 182/Add. 12, and 237/Add. 1); and reports on its implementation of articles 21 (controversies between States) and 22 (communications from individuals) of the Convention against Torture and Other Cruel, Inhuman or Degrading Treatment or Punishment (see **TORTURE**) to the **COMMITTEE AGAINST TORTURE** (CAT/C/9/Add. 9).

***BIBLIOGRAPHY.*** Amnesty International. *Amnesty International Concerns in Western Europe: October 1986–March 1987.* London: 1987. NGO report, in English.

————. *Conscientious Objection to Military Service.* London: 1988. NGO report, in English.

Cavallari, Vincenzo. "The Universal Declaration of Human Rights and the Italian System of Penal Protection," *Review of Contemporary Law* 15, no. 2 (1988): 53–56. Scholarly article, in English.

Lorenzo, Ray. *Italy: Too Little Time and Space for Childhood.* Florence, Italy: UNICEF International Child Development Centre, 1991. IGO monograph, in English.

Nascimbene, Bruno. "The Case of Albanians in Italy: Is the Right of Asylum Under Attack?" *International Journal of Refugee Law* 3, no. 4 (Oct. 1991): 714–720. Scholarly article, in English.

Zagrebelsky, Vladimiro. "Measures Taken in Italy to Ensure the Effective Exercise of Human Rights by Migrants and the Unemployed," Paper presented at the International Experts Meeting on Ways and Means to Ensure Effective Exercise of Human Rights by Disadvantaged Groups, Quebec, Canada, 14 November 1985. Unpublished conference paper, in English.

**IVORY COAST.** The *Republique de la Côte d'Ivoire,* which officially changed its name from Ivory Coast in 1985, is a country in western Africa, on the Gulf of Guinea. It has borders with Burkina Faso, Ghana, Guinea, Liberia, and Mali. It achieved independence from France in 1960 and became a member of the United Nations the same year. Its population is estimated to be 12,430,000.

A French trading center and protectorate from 1842, the area was recognized as an autonomous republic in the French Union after World War II. As an independent State, it was once one of the most prosperous and stable tropical African nations. Its population includes more than 60 ethnic groups, among them peoples of many national and racial backgrounds. Languages commonly used are French (official), Diaula, and other African languages. Religions practiced include Animism (45%), Christianity (30%), and Islam (25%). Literacy is estimated at 40%.

The government (1994) took the form of a republic. Its constitution provides for the president, elected by popular vote for a term of five years, to act as head of State and of government. There is a 175-member unicameral National Assembly, also elected by popular vote, and an independent judiciary modeled after the French system of justice. Suffrage is universal for those 21 years of age or over. The Democratic Party of the Ivory Coast is the only political party.

Early in 1990, when world prices for coffee, cocoa, and other products of Africa dipped to their lowest levels in many years, the long-celebrated "economic miracle" of the Ivory Coast slacked off as the country experienced its worst recession since achieving independence.

In mid-February 1990, university students demonstrated in the streets of Abidjan to protest increased school fees, lowered wages, and cuts in scholarships. The government responded by sending police and army units to disperse them with tear gas, stun grenades, and rubber truncheons. But in March a far larger protest march was organized to oppose the government's new austerity program and, incidentally, to complain that money spent by President Felix Houphouët-Boigny—out of his personal funds—to build a Roman Catholic basilica at his birthplace could better

have been spent on health care and housing for the poor. This time the police used stun guns and tear gas to turn the marchers back. As the confrontation escalated, groups of college students threw firebombs at the police and were met with concussion grenades. Demonstrating secondary-school students were sprayed with tear gas by paramilitary troops. And most civil servants in Abijan, including school personnel, went on strike. The protests were aimed, at least in part, at ending single-party rule in the Ivory Coast, where President Houphouët-Boigny, at 84, was Africa's oldest and longest-serving leader.

In April 1990, under growing pressure, the government announced postponement of some of the austerity measures and the creation of a special government panel to review efforts to counter the severe economic downturn.

President Houphouët-Boigny died in 1994.

**BIBLIOGRAPHY.** Amnesty International. *Cote D'Ivoire: Forcible Conscription of Trade Unionists*. London: 1988. NGO report, in English.

————. *Cote d'Ivoire: Freedom of Expression and Association Threatened*. London: 1994. NGO report, in English.

————. *Cote d'Ivoire: Silencing the Opposition—77 Prisoners of Conscience Convicted*. London: 1992. NGO report, in English.

International Commission of Jurists. *Les Services Juridiques en Milieu Rural (Afrique de l'Ouest)* (Legal Services in Rural Areas [West Africa]). Geneva: 1987. NGO report, in French.

Kannyo, Edward. *Human Rights in Africa: Report of a Visit to Nigeria, Ghana, Ivory Coast, Senegal and Upper Volta*. New York: International League for Human Rights, 1981. NGO report, in English.

# J

**JAMAICA.** Jamaica is a country occupying an island of the West Indies, situated in the Caribbean Sea south of Cuba and west of Haiti. It achieved independence from Great Britain in 1962 and became a member of the United Nations the same year. Its population is estimated to be 2,412,000. Ethnic groups include (according to the 1970 census) Negro/Black (90%), White (.7%), Mixed (5.8%), East Indian (1.7%), Chinese (.7%), and others (1.1%). Languages commonly used are English and Creole. Religions practiced include Christianity (Anglican, Baptist, and other Protestant denominations, and Roman Catholic), and Rastafarianism (belief in the spiritual leadership of Emperor Haile Selassie I of Ethiopia). Literacy is estimated at 75%.

The government (1994) took the form of a parliamentary State and member of the Commonwealth. The governor-general, representing the crown, appoints as prime minister the person who, in his view, is best able to command the confidence of a majority of the members of the House of Representatives. The legislature includes, in addition to the 60-member house, elected by popular vote, a 21-member Senate nominated by the governor-general. The judiciary is independent and modeled after the British system of justice. Political parties include the Jamaica Labour Party and the People's National Party. Elections were held on March 30, 1993 in which the People's National Party retained control of the House of Representatives with 52 seats versus the Jamaica Labour Party's 8 seats.

Provisions against discrimination are entrenched in Jamaica's constitution; any proposal to amend or delete such provisions would require a two-thirds' majority in both the House of Representatives and the Senate.

**BIBLIOGRAPHY.** Americas Watch. *Prison Conditions in Jamaica.* New York: Human Rights Watch, 1990. NGO report, in English.

Amnesty International. *Jamaica: The Death Penalty.* London: 1989. NGO report, in English.

————. *Jamaica: Proposal for an Inquiry into Deaths and Ill-Treatment of Prisoners in St. Catherine's District Prison.* London: 1993. NGO report, in English.

Byre, Angela D., and Beverley Y. Byfield, eds. *International Human Rights Law in the Commonwealth Caribbean.* Dordrecht, the Netherlands: Martinus Nijhoff, 1991. Scholarly conference papers, in English.

Chevigny, Paul G. "Police Deadly Force as Social Control: Jamaica, Argentina, and Brazil," *Criminal Law Forum* 1, no. 3 (Spring 1990): 389–425. Scholarly article, in English.

Daly, Denis. *Human Rights Situation in Jamaica and the Prospects for a CARICOM Human Rights Charter.* Georgetown, Guyana: Guyana Human Rights Association, 1986. NGO bulletin, in English.

Donnelly, J., and R. E. Howard, eds. *International Handbook on Human Rights.* Westport, CT, USA: Greenwood Press, 1987. Scholarly edited collection, in English.

Human Rights Watch Children's Rights Project. *Jamaica: Children Improperly Detained in Police Lockups.* New York: Human Rights Watch, 1994. NGO report, in English.

Thompson, Robert. *Green Gold: Bananas and Dependency in the Eastern Caribbean.* London: Latin American Bureau, 1987. NGO monograph, in English.

**JAPAN.** A country which occupies an archipelago off the eastern coast of Asia, between the Pacific Ocean and the Sea of Japan. Its main islands are Hokkaido, Honshu (on which Tokyo and other principal cities are located), Shikoku, and Kyushu. In addition, about 1,000 smaller islands lie in an arc between the ocean and the sea.

Japan resumed its independence under the Japanese Peace Treaty of 1951 and became a member of the United Nations in 1956. Its population is estimated to be 124,710,000. Ethnic groups include Japanese (99.4%), Korean (0.5%), and Chinese (0.1%). Among the Japanese, there are the remnants of a section of the indigenous population traditionally considered as outcastes because of their occupations (killing animals, handling the dead, etc.), and sometimes segregated in special communities (*Tokushu Buraku*). Discrimination against these "Burakumin" has been illegal for many years, but behavior towards them often resembles that directed against India's outcaste groups. In addition, naturalized Korean and Chinese citizens of Japan have often complained about discrimination in housing and employment, leading some foreign-born citizens to adopt Japanese names to prevent such problems.

Japanese is the predominant language, with English and German in frequent use. Religions practiced include Buddhism, Christianity, Confucianism, and

Shintoism. Many Japanese observe both Shinto and Buddhist rituals; and Buddhism has developed special Japanese denominations such as Jodo, Shingon, Nicheren, and Zen. Literacy is estimated at 99%.

The government (1994) took the form of a constitutional monarchy; the institution of emperor exists but no longer is considered to have divine rights. Executive authority is exercised by the Cabinet, nominated by the Diet from among its members, and its chairman, the prime minister. The Diet consists of a 512-member House of Representatives, the members of which are elected for terms of four years; and a 252-member House of Councilors, half of its members being elected every three years for terms of five years. The judicial system is one of civil law, based on Roman Law. Political parties include the Liberal Democratic Party, the Socialist Party, the Clean Government Party, the Communist Party, the Democratic Socialist Party, and the New Liberal Club. The Liberal Democratic Party, which has governed without interruption for 35 years, was returned to power in elections held on 18 February 1990.

After invading Manchuria in 1931 and setting up the state of Manchukuo, Japan resigned from the **LEAGUE OF NATIONS** in 1933. Three years later the "anti-Comintern" pact with Germany was signed. After invading China in 1937, Japan launched its attack on Pearl Harbor in 1941, bringing the United States of America into World War II. After three years and nine months of warfare, in which 3 million Japanese lost their lives, Japan signed an instrument of surrender shortly after the atomic bombings of Hiroshima and Nagasaki. As a result, Japan lost all of its overseas possessions and renounced its claims to Formosa. Manchukuo was dissolved and Manchuria returned to China. The southern Sakhalin and Kuriles Islands were occupied by the Soviet Union.

After the war, Japan was placed under international control of the Allied powers through Supreme Commander General Douglas MacArthur, who ruled Japan through Japanese officials and a freely elected legislature. This arrangement provided for a progressive and orderly transition from strict military control to the eventual restoration of full sovereignty.

Japan's constitution, prepared under American sponsorship, includes a pledge of the people of Japan to uphold human rights and the ideas of democracy and to end the emperor's "divine rights." Accordingly, the emperor now has no powers with respect to the government. The Upper House of the Diet passed a political reform and anti-corruption law on 21 November 1994. Its measures, including the reduction of seats in the Lower House from 511 to 500 and more equitable distribution between rural and urban populations, went into effect in December 1994.

The people of Japan join organs of the State in protecting human rights through a system of voluntary civil liberties commissioners, to whom the Ministry of Justice entrusts the task of keeping a close watch in their own communities to ensure that the human rights of residents are not violated and of taking prompt remedial action if indicated. The commissioners, who include people working in agriculture, industry, forestry, and business, give advice and counsel to citizens on matters relating to their rights and freedoms and organize campaigns to promote respect for those rights.

However, Japan's World War II sexual enslavement program, which forced Korean, Filipino, and other women living in Japan's occupied territories to serve its occupation forces, remains a matter of world-wide concern. In August 1994 Japan announced that it would spend $1 billion on an "atonement program," but offered no compensation to the women victims involved. The **INTERNATIONAL COMMISSION OF JURISTS** and other non-governmental organizations urged in November of that year that direct compensation of at least $40,000 should be paid to each victim.

*REPORT OF THE HUMAN RIGHTS COMMITTEE.* The third periodic report of Japan under the **INTERNATIONAL COVENANT ON CIVIL AND POLITICAL RIGHTS** (CCPR/C/70/Add. 1 and Corr. 1 and 2) was considered by the UN **HUMAN RIGHTS COMMITTEE** at its 1277th to 1280th meetings, held on 27 and 28 October 1993. The Committee adopted the following comments on the report at its 1290th meeting, on 4 November 1993 (paras. 5–19):

### Factors and Difficulties Affecting Implementation

The Committee notes that the Japanese Government sometimes experiences difficulties in taking measures to implement the Covenant due to various social factors, such as the traditional concept of the different roles of the sexes, the unique relationship between individuals and the group they belong to, and the unconscious particularities due to the homogeneity of the population.

### Positive Aspects

The Committee takes note with satisfaction of the serious approach the Japanese Government has taken in dealing with issues relating to civil and political rights, and of its commitment to fulfil its obligations under the Covenant.

The Committee is of the view that the human rights situation in Japan has improved since the consideration of the second periodic report of that State party in 1988, and that there is generally a good regard for human rights in the country.

Furthermore, the Committee notes, with appreciation, that Japan actively assists in the promotion of human rights at the international level. It also notes that there is awareness in the Japanese society of the provisions of the Covenant;

this awareness is confirmed by the interest expressed by many Japanese non-governmental organizations in the Committee's consideration of the third periodic report of Japan.

## Principal Subjects of Concern

The Committee believes that it is not clear that the Covenant would prevail in the case of conflict with domestic legislation and that its terms are not fully subsumed in the Constitution. Furthermore, it is also not clear whether the "public welfare" limitation of articles 12 and 13 of the Constitution would be applied in a particular situation in conformity with the Covenant.

The Committee expresses concern at the continued existence in Japan of certain discriminatory practices against social groups, such as Korean permanent residents, members of the Buraku communities, and persons belonging to the Ainu minority. The requirement that it is a penal offence for alien permanent residents not to carry documentation at all times, while this does not apply to Japanese nationals, is not consistent with the Covenant. Moreover, persons of Korean and Taiwanese origin, who served in the Japanese Army and who no longer possess Japanese nationality, are discriminated against in respect of their pensions.

In addition, the Committee expresses concern at other discriminatory practices that appear to persist in Japan against women, with regard to remuneration in employment, and notes that de facto problems of discrimination more generally continue to exist. The situation regarding mentally ill persons has significantly improved, but problems continue regarding access to employment. The Committee acknowledges the fact that legal measures have been taken by the Japanese authorities to forbid those practices and that there are comprehensive programmes to promote equal opportunity. However, it appears that a certain gap exists in Japan between the adoption of legislation and the actual behaviour of certain sectors of society. The Committee notes that recourse for settlement of claims of discrimination against trade-union activists is very protracted.

The Committee is particularly concerned at the discriminatory legal provisions concerning children born out of wedlock. In particular, provisions and practices regarding the birth registration forms and the family register are contrary to articles 17 and 24 of the Covenant. The discrimination in their right to inherit is not consistent with article 26 of the Covenant.

The Committee is disturbed by the number and nature of crimes punishable by death penalty under the Japanese Penal Code. The Committee recalls that the terms of the Covenant tend towards the abolition of the death penalty, and that those States which have not already abolished the death penalty are bound to apply it only for the most serious crimes. In addition, there are matters of concern relating to conditions of detainees. In particular, the Committee finds that the undue restrictions on visits and correspondence, and the failure of notification of executions to the family are incompatible with the Covenant.

The Committee is concerned that the guarantees contained in articles 9, 10, and 14 are not fully complied with, in that pre-trial detention takes place not only in cases where the conduct of the investigation requires it; the detention is not promptly and effectively brought under judicial control and is left under the control of the police; most of the time interrogation does not take place in the presence of the detainee's counsel, nor rules exist to regulate the length of interrogation; and the substitute prison system (Daiyo Kangoku) is not under the control of an authority separate from the police. In addition, the legal representatives of the defendant do not have access to all relevant material in the police record, in order to enable them to prepare the defence.

The Committee regrets that there appears to be a restrictive approach in certain laws and decisions as to the respect of the right to freedom of expression.

The Committee notes with concern the exclusion of Koreans from the Government's concept of minorities. This is not justified by the Covenant, which does not limit the concept of minority to those who are nationals of the State concerned.

## Suggestions and Recommendations

The Committee recommends that Japan becomes a party to both Optional Protocols to the International Covenant on Civil and Political Rights and to the Convention against Torture and Other Cruel, Inhuman or Degrading Treatment or Punishment.

The Committee also recommends that the Japanese legislation concerning children born out of wedlock be amended and that discriminatory provisions contained therein be removed, to bring it into line with the provisions of articles 2, 24 and 26 of the Covenant. All discriminatory laws and practices still existing in Japan should be abolished in conformity with articles 2, 3 and 26 of the Covenant. The Japanese Government should make efforts to influence the public opinion in this respect.

The Committee further recommends that Japan takes measures towards the abolition of the death penalty and that, in the meantime, that penalty should be limited to the most serious crimes; that the conditions of death row detainees be reconsidered; and that preventive measures of control against any kind of ill-treatment of detainees should be further improved.

With a view to guaranteeing the full application of articles 9, 10 and 14 of the Covenant, the Committee recommends that pre-trial procedures and the operation of the substitute prison system (Daiyo Kangoku) should be made to be compatible with all requirements of the Covenant and, in particular, that all the guarantees relating to the facilities for the preparation of the defence should be observed.

**BIBLIOGRAPHY.** Amnesty International. *Japan: The Death Penalty and the Need for More Safeguards Against Ill-Treatment of Detainees.* London: 1991. NGO factfinding report, in English.

————. *Japan: Human Rights: Open Letter to the Prime Minister.* London: 1993. NGO statement, in English.

————. *Japan: Inadequate Protection for Refugees and Asylum-Seekers.* London: 1993. NGO report, in English.

Buraku Liberation Research Institute. *Discrimination against Buraku Today.* Osaka: 1986. NGO book, in English.

Canada-Asia Working Group. "Human Rights in Asia: Submission Prepared for the 45th Session of the U.N. Commission on Human Rights, Geneva, February 1989," *Currents* 11, no. 1 (February 1989). NGO report, in English.

Donnelly, J., and R. E. Howard, eds. *International Handbook on Human Rights.* Westport, CT, USA: Greenwood Press, 1987. Scholarly edited collection, in English.

Gap Min, Pyong. "A Comparison of the Korean Minorities in China and Japan," *International Migration Review* 26, no. 1

(no. 97) (Spring 1992): 4–21. Scholarly article, in English; bibliography, pp. 20–21.

Good, Martha H. "Freedom of Expression in Comparative Perspective: Japan's Quiet Revolution," *Human Rights Quarterly* 7, no. 3 (August 1985): 429–445. Scholarly article, in English.

Hsiung, James C. *Human Rights in East Asia: A Cultural Perspective.* New York: Pergamon, 1985. Scholarly edited collection, in English.

Human Rights Watch. "Japan," in *Human Rights Watch World Report 1995*, pp. 163–165. New York: 1995. NGO report, in English.

International Commission of Jurists. *Human Rights and Mental Patients in Japan.* Geneva: 1985. NGO report, in English.

Iwasawa, Yuji. *Legal Treatment of Koreans in Japan: The Impact of International Human Rights Law on Japanese Law.* Washington, D.C.: International Human Rights Law Group, 1986. NGO mission report, in English.

Japan Civil Liberties Union. *1993 Report concerning the Present Status of Human Rights in Japan: A Report of JCLU with regard to the Third Periodic Report of the Government of Japan Submitted under the International Covenant on Civil and Political Rights.* Tokyo: 1993. NGO report, in English.

Japan Federation of Bar Associations. *A Report on the Application and Practice in Japan of the International Covenant on Civil and Political Rights.* Tokyo: 1993. NGO report, in English.

Kajimura, Hideki. "Confronting Japanese Racism: Toward a Korean Identity," *AMPO: Japan-Asia Quarterly Review* 20, nos. 1 and 2 (1988): 35–41. NGO article, in English.

Luney, Percy R., Jr., ed. "The Constitution of Japan—The Fifth Decade," *Law and Contemporary Problems* 53, nos. 1 and 2 (Winter–Spring 1990). Special issue of scholarly articles, in English.

Pacific-Asia Resources Center. "Japan's Human Imports," *AMPO: Japan-Asia Quarterly Review* 19, no. 4 (1988): 2–37. NGO articles, in English.

Parker, K., and E. Jaudel. *Police Cell Detention in Japan: The Kaiyo Kangoku System.* Paris: Federation Internationale des Droits de l'Homme and Association of Humanitarian Lawyers, 1989. NGO mission report, in English and French.

Research-Action Institute for the Koreans in Japan. *Japan's Subtle Apartheid: The Korean Minority Now.* Tokyo: 1990. NGO report, in English; bibliography, p. 55.

Sigler, Jay A., ed. *International Handbook on Race and Race Relations.* Westport, CT, USA: Greenwood Press, 1987. Scholarly edited collection, in English; bibliography, pp. 449–454.

Sjoberg, Katarina. "Japan: The Ainu—A Fourth World Population," *IWGIA Newsletter* 48 (December 1986): 42–66. NGO article, in English.

———. " 'Mr. Ainu' in the Japanese Culture," *IWGIA Newsletter* nos. 60–61 (April–Sept. 1990): 79–101. NGO article, in English.

Wessels, D. *Advancing Human Rights: Japan, East Asia, and the World.* Tokyo: Institute of International Relations for Advanced Studies on Peace and Development in Asia, Sophia University, 1986. Scholarly research report, in English.

## JAYCEES INTERNATIONAL.

An international nongovernmental organization in consultative status with the UN **ECONOMIC AND SOCIAL COUNCIL** (Category II) and with **UNESCO** and the **COUNCIL OF EUROPE,** JAYCEES International has members in 80 countries and territories.

Founded in 1944 in Mexico as the "Junior Chamber International," JAYCEES International coordinates the activities of member organizations to develop the individual abilities of young people for the purpose of improving the economic, social, and spiritual well-being of all peoples. JCI encourages an awareness and acceptance of the responsibilities of citizenship, active participation in planning and executing programs for the development of the individual and the community, and furtherance of understanding, good will, and cooperation among all peoples. It adopts major themes in which all members world-wide participate; recent themes have included "Outlook for Children" and "North/South Dialogue."

JCI publishes the quarterly *JCI World* in Chinese, English, French, Japanese, Korean, and Spanish.

JAYCEES International. Address: 400 University Drive, P.O. Box 140577, Coral Gables, FL 33114, USA. Telephone: (305) 446-7608. Cable: JAYCEES. Telex: 441084. Fax: (305) 442-0041. Secretary-General: W. Daniel Lamey.

## JORDAN.

The Hashemite Kingdom of Jordan, formerly known as Transjordan, is an Arab country in western Asia. It has borders with Iraq, Israel, Saudi Arabia, and Syria. A part of the Ottoman Empire from the 16th century until the end of World War I, Jordan became a part of the Palestine mandate of the **LEAGUE OF NATIONS.** Great Britain, which administered the mandate, agreed in 1923 to recognize Jordan's independence under Abdullah, a son of Husein ibn Ali of the Hashemite family. The loyalty of Jordan in World War II led to the termination of the mandate and the proclamation of the kingdom in 1946. Jordan became a member of the United Nations in 1955. Its population is estimated to be 3,632,000, excluding the West Bank. Ethnic groups include Armenians, Circassians, and Kurds. Languages commonly used include Arabic (official), English, and French. Religions practiced include Islam (95%), Christianity (4%), and others (1%). Literacy is estimated at 70%.

The government (1994) took the form of a monarchy, with the king as ruler and head of State. Under the 1952 constitution, executive authority is exercised by the Council of Ministers, of which the prime minister is chairman. The council is responsible to Parliament, which consists of the Chamber of Deputies, the 60 members of which are elected by popular vote for terms of four years, and the Senate, the 30 members of which are appointed by the king. Disputes arising between individuals in matters of personal status, such as divorce, maintenance, and child custody, fall within the jurisdiction of religious courts, which deliver judgments enforceable by the authorities who execute judgment delivered by civil and criminal courts. Following the 1989 parliamentary elections and principles of democratization voted on by the special National Conference in June 1991, 24 political parties were formed. Specific provisions had not yet been passed by the National Assembly.

Jordan acquired control of Jerusalem's Old City and the area on the west bank of the Jordan River in the hostilities of 1948 but lost both to Israel in 1967. For many years, Jordan continued to provide financial and other support to West Bank municipalities, but this policy has been discontinued. Jordan broke diplomatic relations with Egypt in 1979 as a protest against the peace treaty between Egypt and Israel; relations were, however, resumed in 1984. Late in 1994, Jordan and Israel concluded a new peace treaty, called the Washington Declaration, which reopened diplomatic relations and trade between them.

*REPORT OF THE HUMAN RIGHTS COMMITTEE.* The third periodic report of Jordan under the **INTERNATIONAL COVENANT ON CIVIL AND POLITICAL RIGHTS** (CCPR/C/76/Add. 1) was considered by the UN **HUMAN RIGHTS COMMITTEE** at its 1321st to 1324th meetings, held on 5 and 6 July 1994. The Committee adopted the following general comments at its 1354th meeting, held on 27 July 1994 (paras. 3–19).

### Factors and Difficulties Affecting Implementation

The Committee takes note of the difficult economic and social situation faced by Jordan as a result of the Gulf crisis and lack of stability in the region. The presence of a very large number of refugees constitutes another factor which renders the implementation of the Covenant more difficult.

### Positive Aspects

The Committee welcomes the democratic process initiated in 1989, the lifting of the state of emergency, and the abolition of the Martial Law and the 1935 Defence Act, as well as the release of political prisoners, restitution of withdrawn passports, reinstatement of civil servants who had been dismissed for political reasons and the institution of a right to appeal against decisions of the State Security Court to the Supreme Court. The Committee also notes with satisfaction the existence of an appeal procedure to the Supreme Court against administrative decisions, including those concerning civil servants. The efforts to undertake a thorough legal reform have already yielded many accomplishments, in particular with respect to the new Press Act and Political Parties Act. The Committee also appreciates the creation of a Commission for human rights and the establishment of Jordanian sections of the Arab Organization for Human Rights and Amnesty International. These new institutions and the drafting of new bills that may promote human rights, as well as the holding of multiparty elections, clearly illustrate the positive trend towards strengthening democracy and the promotion and protection of human rights in Jordan. Some progress made in recent years in promoting the status of women is also commendable and the notable achievements in the field of life expectancy together with reduction of child mortality rates are positive developments ensuring better respect of the right to life as provided for under article 6 of the Covenant.

### Principal Subjects of Concern

The Committee notes that the Constitution does not contain specific provisions as to the relationship between international conventions and domestic law. Accordingly, there is a need to define the place of the Covenant within the Jordanian legal system to ensure that domestic laws are construed in conformity with the provisions of the Covenant. Furthermore, it notes with concern that the general legal framework is still not in conformity with the provisions of the Covenant. The Committee also regrets that the Constitutional Court has not yet been established.

The Committee is concerned that the State Security Court continues to exercise special jurisdiction and that, in accordance with articles 124 and 125 of the Constitution and under the new Defence Act, ordinary law can be suspended in emergency situations, contrary to the provisions of article 4 of the Covenant which prohibit derogation from some categories of human rights. The lack of clarity with regard to accountability for acts performed under provisions of the Martial Law is also a matter of concern.

The Committee regrets that, although some improvement has been achieved as regards the status of women, the State party has not embarked on all the necessary reforms to combat the factors still impeding equality between men and women. It notes with concern that the Constitution does not guarantee the principle of non-discrimination on the basis of sex, and that there are still gender disparities in law or practice with regard to such issues as status within the family, inheritance rights, the right to leave the country, the acquisition of Jordanian nationality, access to work and participation in the public life.

The Committee is concerned about the excessive number of offences punishable by the death penalty as well as the number of death sentences handed down by the Courts.

The Committee is also concerned that the guarantees contained in articles 7, 9, 10 and 14 of the Covenant are not fully complied with. In particular, it is concerned that torture and ill-treatment of persons deprived of liberty continue to be reported. Cases of administrative detention, denial of access of detainees to legal counsel, long periods of pre-trial detention without charges and incommunicado detention are also matters of great concern. The committee is particularly concerned at conditions of detention in the General Intelligence Department headquarters.

The Committee notes with concern the shortcomings in the observance of the provisions of article 18 of the Covenant, in particular the restrictions affecting the enjoyment by non-recognized or non-registered religious denominations, including the Bahai's, of their right to freedom of religion or belief. Concern is also expressed about the practical limitations to the right to have or adopt a religion or belief of one's choice, which should include the freedom to change religion.

The Committee also expresses concern that in spite of the positive developments resulting from the adoption of the new Press Act, freedom of expression is still restricted by the control exercised by the authorities over the State radio and television and by measures of harassment against some journalists. The Committee is also concerned that a rigid interpretation of the provisions of the new Press Act and Political Parties Act and prosecutions of offences of defamation might affect the effective enjoyment of those rights stipulated under articles 19 and 25 of the Covenant.

## Suggestions and Recommendations

The Committee recommends that the State party continue the legislative review envisaged by the National Charter and use this process to incorporate all substantive provisions of the Covenant into domestic law and ensure that the restrictions imposed under national legislation do not go beyond those permitted under the Covenant.

The Committee hopes that the Government of Jordan will consider becoming a party to the First Optional Protocol to the Covenant.

The Committee further recommends that Jordan envisages measures towards the abolition of the death penalty, including giving consideration to accession to the Second Optional Protocol.

The Committee emphasizes the need for the Government to prevent and eliminate discriminatory attitudes and prejudices towards women and to achieve the effective implementation of article 3 of the Covenant, by adopting promotional measures to overcome the weight of certain traditions and customs.

The Committee recommends that consideration be given to the abolition of the State Security Court; that the detention premises controlled by the Central Intelligence Department be placed under close supervision of the judicial authorities; that necessary measures be taken to make sure that torture, ill-treatment and illegal detention do not occur and that any such cases be investigated in order to bring before the courts those suspected of having committed such acts and to punish them if found guilty. It also recommends that measures of administrative detention and incommunicado detention be restricted to very limited and exceptional cases, and that the guarantees concerning pre-trial detention provided for in article 9, paragraph 3, of the Covenant be implemented.

The Committee emphasizes the need to take further measures to guarantee the freedom of religion and eliminate discrimination on religious grounds, and suggests in this connection that the State party take into account the recommendations contained in the Committee's general comment on article 18 of the Covenant.

The Committee stresses that further measures should be taken to ensure that the provisions of the Covenant be made more widely known. It urges the Government to prepare its fourth periodic report in compliance with the guidelines for the preparation of State party reports, taking into account the general comments adopted by the Committee. The fourth periodic report should contain detailed information on the extent to which each right protected under the Covenant is enjoyed in practice, and refer to specific factors and difficulties that might impede its application. It should also highlight measures taken to follow up on the Committee's suggestions and recommendations.

The Committee recommends that the Jordanian authorities should ensure that the report submitted by the State party and the comments of the Committee be disseminated as widely as possible in order to encourage the involvement of all sectors concerned in the improvement of human rights.

***REPORT ON THE RIGHTS OF THE CHILD.*** The initial report of Jordan (CRC/C/8/Add. 4) under the Convention on the Rights of the Child (see **CHILDREN'S RIGHTS**), was considered by the UN **COMMITTEE ON THE RIGHTS OF THE CHILD** at its 143rd to 145th meetings, held on 13 and 14 April 1994. The Committee adopted the following concluding observations at its 156th meeting, held on 22 April 1994 (paras. 4–29):

### Positive Aspects

The Committee notes with satisfaction the steps taken during the period under review to bring domestic law into line with the Convention, through the enactment of new laws or the adoption of specific programmes aimed at promoting and protecting the rights of the child. It welcomes the fact that a study is currently being undertaken to review national legislation and its compatibility with the provisions and principles of the Convention and that a draft Personal Status Act is also being studied with the same ambition.

The Committee particularly welcomes the notable progress achieved in recent years in such crucial issues as infant mortality and life expectancy, which has demonstrated the authorities' commitment to allocate substantial resources for social expenditures despite stringent economic difficulties.

### Factors and Difficulties Impeding Implementation

The Committee takes note of the economic and social difficulties which have been faced by Jordan in the aftermath of the Gulf crisis and which have, consequently, adversely affected the situation of children.

The presence of a very large number of refugees, particularly of Palestinian origin, constitutes a further difficulty impeding the implementation of the Convention.

The Committee also notes that the survival of certain traditions and customs sometimes constitutes an obstacle to the implementation of the Convention, particularly with regard to the equality of boys and girls.

### Principal Subjects of Concern

The Committee is concerned that the broad nature of the reservations made to articles 14, 20 and 21 of the Convention by the State party may affect the implementation of the rights guaranteed in these articles and may raise questions about the compatibility of the reservations with the object and purpose of the Convention.

The Committee is concerned about the insufficient steps taken in the framework of legal reform to bring existing legislation into full conformity with the Convention, including in the light of the basic principles of the Convention, in order to overcome discrepancies or lacunae in national legislation, particularly in laws relating to marriage age and the administration of juvenile justice.

The Committee is concerned that, although the National Charter guarantees equality between the sexes in Jordan, discriminatory attitudes and prejudices are still vivid within the society, and that there are still disparities in practice, in particular with regard to inheritance rights, the right to leave the country and the acquisition of Jordanian nationality. In this last respect, the Committee is concerned that in the light of Jordanian legislation, cases of statelessness might arise. It is also concerned that, the national legislation with respect to the minimum age for marriage may not be fully compatible with the non-discrimination provisions of the Convention, as reflected in its article 2.

The Committee expresses concern at the uncertainty in the status of children, and the possible ensuing discrimination, resulting from the coexistence of different personal status regulations according to the child's religion. The Committee takes note of the undertaking in this context by the delegation to provide further information in regard to the rights of children of the Baha'i faith.

Another issue relates to groups of refugee children and the concern that they may not be given full protection in view of the fact that the Kingdom of Jordan has not yet ratified relevant international refugee treaties.

The Committee understands that there are under-age children at work in Jordan and that some children in remote areas are even kept from school for such reasons. The Kingdom of Jordan has not acceded to ILO Convention No. 138 and other conventions on the minimum age of employment relating to the protection of children and young persons at work.

The Committee is concerned about the lack of adequate measures taken by the authorities to evaluate and address the problem of domestic violence.

In the field of the administration of juvenile justice, the Committee is concerned about the application of article 92 of the Penal Code, in accordance with which, although no one under 18 years of age may be held criminally responsible, criminal proceedings may be brought against children over 7 years of age. It also deplores the fact that children taken into custody though not convicted of any criminal offence, may nevertheless be kept in detention in the same premises as convicted persons.

### Suggestions and Recommendations

The Committee expresses the hope that the Government will consider the possibility of reviewing its reservations to articles 14, 20 and 21 of the Convention, with a view to the withdrawal of these reservations.

Special efforts should be made to bring the existing legislation fully into line with the principles and provisions of the Convention, including in the context of the preparation of a new Personal Status Act.

The Committee suggests that the Government envisage the establishment of a national mechanism with the purpose of coordinating the implementation of the Convention and the monitoring thereof. Coordination between the various governmental agencies and non-governmental organizations involved in the implementation of the Convention and the monitoring thereof should be strengthened.

Measures should be taken to develop mechanisms for the determination of appropriate indicators and for the collection of statistical data and other information on the status of children as bases for designing programmes to implement the Convention.

The Committee suggests that law enforcement officials, judges, other administration of justice officials and, more generally, members of professions concerned with the implementation of the Convention be provided with adequate training on the basic principles and norms contained in the Convention on the Rights of the Child.

Measures should be taken to prevent and eliminate discriminatory attitudes or prejudice and to ensure effective protection against discrimination, particularly with regard to the girl child and children born out of wedlock, as well as any differentiation resulting from the status of parents.

A study on the extent and nature of domestic violence is recommended. Appropriate follow-up measures should be envisaged, not least in the field of family education and social support.

In line with article 4 of the Jordanian Education Act and article 29 of the Convention, emphasis should be given in school education to the important values of peace, tolerance and respect of human rights. The active participation of children should be encouraged. Similarly, efforts should be undertaken to develop new channels, including membership of associations, through which children may make their views known and have them taken into account.

Steps should be taken to improve school attendance for children living in remote areas, to reduce the school dropout rate and to raise the level of literacy, particularly among females. School curricula should be adjusted to make room for education about the Convention.

In order to ensure that all refugee children or children seeking refugee status enjoy their rights under the Convention, the Committee recommends that the Kingdom of Jordan consider the possibility of ratifying the 1951 Convention relating to the Status of Refugees and its 1967 Protocol.

The Committee recommends that the State party envisage undertaking a comprehensive reform of the system of juvenile justice and that the Convention and other international standards in this field, such as the "Beijing Rules", the "Riyadh Guidelines" and the United Nations Rules for the Protection of Juveniles Deprived of their Liberty, be seen as a guide in this revision. Attention should also be paid to measures for rehabilitation and social reintegration, in line with article 39 of the Convention.

The mechanism already established to monitor the situation of working children should be strengthened in order to assess the implementation of the Convention and to narrow the gap between the law and practice. Furthermore, the Committee encourages the efforts currently under way to prepare for accession to ILO Convention No. 138 and other conventions on the minimum age of employment relating to the protection of children and young persons at work.

The Committee recommends that the report submitted by the State party, the summary records of its consideration and the concluding observations of the Committee be disseminated as widely as possible within the country, particularly to officials and professionals working with children, parliamentarians, non-governmental organizations and the media.

**BIBLIOGRAPHY.** Amnesty International. *Jordan: Human Rights Protection after the State of Emergency*. London: 1990. NGO report, in English.

————. *Jordan: Human Rights Reforms: Achievements and Obstacles*. London: 1994. NGO report, in English.

Arab Organization for Human Rights. *Human Rights in the Arab World*. Cairo, Egypt: 1987. NGO report, in English and Arabic.

Article 19. *Jordan: Democratization without Press Freedom*. London: 1994. NGO report, in English.

Lawyers Committee for Human Rights. *Lawyers and Human Rights: The U.N. Basic Principles on the Role of Lawyers in the Arab World: The Legal Profession in Jordan*. New York: 1992. NGO report, in English.

**JOSEPH PRIZE FOR HUMAN RIGHTS.** Annually, the Anti-Defamation League of **B'NAI B'RITH INTERNATIONAL** awards the Joseph Prize to individuals whose life's work has been the improvement of human relations and the preservation or growth of human rights. The prize is named in honor of the late I. S. and Anna K. Joseph. Recipients are chosen by the ADL Board of Trustees and are awarded a commemorative medal and $10,000.

The 1994 honorees were **F. W. DE KLERK, NOBEL PEACE PRIZE** recipient and former president of South Africa; and John Lewis, U.S. congressman and civil rights leader. Among past recipients are Barbara Jordan, lawyer, educator, and former U.S. congresswomen; Richard von Weizsacker (1989); and George P. Shultz (1988).

For more information, contact: The Anti-Defamation League, 830 UN Plaza, New York, NY 10017, USA. Telephone: (212) 490-2525. Fax: (212) 867-0779.

**JOUHAUX, LÉON (1879–1954).** In 1951, Léon Jouhaux was awarded the **NOBEL PEACE PRIZE** for his lifelong efforts on behalf of the labor movement. Born in Paris, Jouhaux worked in a match factory, alongside his father, from the age of 16; he took part in his first strike action in 1900, protesting against the use of white phosphorous in the manufacture of matches. He was elected to serve as representative of his local chapter to the General Confederation of Labor (*Générale du Travail*) in 1906; from 1909 to 1947, he was the Confederation's secretary-general. Among his achievements as a labor leader was the Martignon Agreement, which gave French workers an eight-hour day, paid vacations, and the right to organize and bargain collectively. He was also instrumental in founding the International Labor Organization and served as the first vice-president of the International Federation of Trade Unions and as vice-president of the Confederation of Free Trade Unions.

During World War II, Jouhaux joined the French Resistance; he was captured and sent to Buchenwald in 1943. After his liberation, in his late sixties, he served as a French delegate to the newly founded United Nations; as president of the European Movement, a forerunner of the **COUNCIL OF EUROPE**; and as president of the French National Economic Council.

Throughout his life, Jouhaux saw the labor movement as allied to the peace movement. In his Nobel lecture, he stressed the connection: "The . . . only valid goal is to extend the well-being of the worker, to give him a more equitable share of the products of collective work, to make Europe a social democracy, and to ensure the peace desired by men of every race. . . . The free trade union movement is called upon to play an essential part in the fight against international crisis and for the advent of true peace. . . . [W]e have been propagating for years. . . the idea that economic disorder and misery are among the determinative causes of war. . . ."

***BIBLIOGRAPHY.*** Gray, Tony. *Champions of Peace.* London: Paddington Press, 1976.

Schlessinger, Bernard S., and June H. Schlessinger, eds. *Who's Who of Nobel Prize Winners.* Phoenix, AZ, USA: Oryx Press, 1991.

**JOURNALISTS.** The safety and protection of journalists was considered by the **SUB-COMMISSION ON PREVENTION OF DISCRIMINATION AND PROTECTION OF MINORITIES** at its 1989 session. The Sub-Commission recalled (resolution 1989/2) that the press and other forms of mass media have served, and continue to serve, as very valuable and indispensable sources of information on gross violations of human rights and that they perform an honorable and useful role under most difficult circumstances, often when their very lives are being constantly threatened.

It expressed its appreciation to the journalists and other mass media personnel who promote human rights and provide valuable information on human rights violations worldwide and called upon them to carry out their mission to expose such violations and to inform the public with maximum neutrality, fairness, and objectivity. It requested one of its members, Mr. Waleed Sadi (Jordan), to prepare a report on the feasibility of a study on ways and means to extend additional protection and assistance to journalists and mass media personnel while they carry out their duties with objectivity and fairness.

The question of the safety and protection of journalists was later drawn to the attention of the UN **COMMISSION ON HUMAN RIGHTS,** at its 1990 session, by the **INTERNATIONAL ORGANIZATION OF JOURNALISTS (IOJ),** which urged the Commission to take immediate action to put an end to what it described as a "grave situation." In its statement to the Commission (E/CN.4/1990/NGO/72), the Organization pointed out that (paras. 2–5):

The journalistic profession has become one of the most dangerous professions in the world. Journalists have been exposed in recent years to increasing risks and dangers. In many instances they have been subjected to harassment, arrest, torture, denial of their rights, and even physical liquidation to prevent them from performing their professional duties. This process of silencing journalists and the media is increasing to an alarming level. Dictatorial regimes and those forces opposed to the responsible flow of information are more and more resorting to violence to prevent journalists from performing their professional duties.

Data at the disposal of the IOJ for the last four years (1986–1989) clearly reflects the gravity of the problem:

(a) *Killed:* in 1986, 19 journalists; in 1987, 25 journalists; in 1988, 38 journalists; in 1989, 60 journalists.

(b) *Kidnapped:* in 1986, 13 journalists; in 1987, 10 journalists; in 1988, 6 journalists; in 1989, 3 journalists.

(c) *Detained:* in 1986, 178 journalists; in 1987, 188 journalists; in 1988, 98 journalists; in 1989, 269 journalists.

**SEE ALSO** *Media.*

**BIBLIOGRAPHY.** Article 19. *Information, Freedom and Censorship World Report 1991.* London: Library Association Publishing, 1991. NGO report, in English.

————. *Truth from Below: The Emergent Press in Africa.* London: 1991. NGO factfinding report, in English.

Committee to Protect Journalists. *Attacks on the Press, 1985–: A Worldwide Survey.* New York: 1986–present. NGO annual report, in English.

Reporters Sans Frontières. *La Liberté de la presse dans le monde, rapport 1991–.* Paris: 1991. *Freedom of the Press throughout the World, 1993–, Report.* London: John Libbey, 1993–present. NGO annual report, in English (since 1993) and French (since 1991).

**JUDICIARY.** Courts—including courts of general jurisdiction, constitutional courts, special courts and tribunals, and administrative courts and tribunals, all having as one of their functions the protection and promotion of human rights—operate within the framework of the judicial system of nearly every country in the world. As described in the UN Secretary-General's report entitled *National Institutions for the Protection and Promotion of Human Rights* (UN Doc. E/CN.4/1987/37, paras. 19–43) prepared at the request of the **GENERAL ASSEMBLY** (resolution 42/123):

The judiciary plays a central role in enforcing and safeguarding human rights at the national level. Courts, and in particular, courts of general jurisdiction, are endowed with great powers through which they may exercise their ability to enforce human rights, including the very basic function of providing a fair, open and impartial hearing for persons accused of crimes and other illegal acts.

The forum of a court room may provide the accused with the opportunity to hear for the first time all of the specified crimes with which he is charged. Clearly, such information is essential in the preparation of an effective defence for the accused. Moreover, it is the court which provides the accused with the opportunity to speak in his own defence, should he choose to do so, and to confront the witnesses who may testify against him. Such provisions are essential to ensure the protection of the rights of the accused, particularly in penal cases where a great advantage is held by the prosecution, which generally has all organs of the State, including the police, at its disposal while prosecuting a case.

Courts of general jurisdiction also provide forums in which individuals can challenge legislative or executive acts, as well as actions by public authorities which may be illegal. Such a recourse is important in that it helps to hold public officials legally accountable for their actions.

In case of deprivation of liberty, one of the most essential requirements for a fair and equitable administration of justice is the existence of effective remedies. Such remedies are generally provided in all legal systems. Particular mention should be made of the procedures of *habeas corpus* and *amparo* (enforcement of constitutional rights)—a procedure found in Latin American countries.

In many countries, the constitution or other laws provide for the special remedies of *habeas corpus* and *amparo* to redress an unlawful violation of fundamental rights. Both *habeas corpus* and *amparo* are procedures primarily designed to provide speedy relief for the individual who has been the victim of wrongful detention or deprivation of liberty, affected for reasons or in a manner not prescribed by law. Such an action may be the result of a civil or criminal matter.

Although countries may apply different rules as regards access to these procedures, the common factor of *habeas corpus* and *amparo* procedures is the speed and simplicity with which these remedies are effected. Generally, a detained person will submit to the competent judge or authority a "petition alleging unlawful custody". The court will then require the responsible official to appear before the court and explain the reasons for detaining the person in custody. The responsible officer must also, at this time, present the detainee to the court. If the judge decides that the person in custody has indeed been unlawfully detained, then the judge must order that the detained person be released immediately.

For example, according to the Constitution of Venezuela, every person who becomes subject to a deprivation or restriction of his or her liberty in violation of constitutional guarantees, has the right to ask the competent judge to issue a writ of *habeas corpus*. The judge shall immediately order the official in whose custody the aggrieved person is held to report within 24 hours, and shall initiate a summary verification. If the judge decides that the legal formalities for deprivation or restriction of liberty were not met, he or she must order the immediate release of the aggrieved or an end to the restriction imposed within 96 hours after the time that request was originally submitted. Moreover, recent decisions of the Venezuelan Supreme Court of Justice have broadened the application of the remedy of *amparo* to the violation of any fundamental right.

Finally, in many countries, actions of *habeas corpus* or *amparo* may be presented directly to the Supreme Court, High Court or Constitutional Court, and no exhaustion of other legal remedies is necessary. This is the case in El Salvador, India and Spain.

### Constitutional Courts

One of the most important ways in which the courts may strengthen the protection of human rights is through judicial examination of the constitutional validity of enacted laws and administrative measures. Courts of this nature have been established in a number of countries. They are solely concerned with determining the constitutionality of enacted laws and are often called constitutional courts. For instance, the Spanish Constitutional Court may declare a law invalid if it contravenes the rights guaranteed under the Constitution. Similarly, in Ecuador, the Constitutional Guarantees Court, created in 1945 and re-established in 1978 after a period of suspension, seeks to ensure respect for the human rights guaranteed by the Constitution. Composed of three judges, the members of the Ecuadorian Constitutional Guarantees Court are elected by the national legislature, the President of the Supreme Court of Justice, the Attorney-General, the President of the Supreme Electoral Court, a representative of the President of the Republic, a representative of the workers, a representative of industrial organizations and two citizens' representatives.

While in many countries separate constitutional courts have been created, a large number of other States have empowered their supreme courts or high courts to determine the constitutionality of laws. In Singapore, for instance, in addition to its authority to hear all disputes and claims, the High Court is also empowered to hear and adjudicate all constitutional disputes. In accordance with section 42 (2) of the Nigerian Constitution, the High Court has special jurisdiction to hear and decide cases of alleged violations of the human rights guaranteed in the Constitution. Similarly, the Canadian Supreme Court at the federal level has ultimate jurisdiction to ensure the conformity of both federal and provincial statutes or administrative measures to the Charter of Rights and Freedoms set out in the Constitution. The United States Supreme Court hears appeals from the decisions of the State courts in cases involving questions of constitutional interpretation, in addition to its authority to adjudicate cases on appeal from federal courts. The Court may declare any executive Act, Congressional Act or State law unconstitutional if such a law denies or abridges the guaranteed civil liberties of the people.

Although the functions of most courts which examine the constitutionality of laws are quite similar, countries vary greatly in granting the right of direct access to such courts. Most countries have strictly limited the access of individuals to such courts. For instance, actions filed with the Spanish Constitutional Court must be filed by either the President, the People's Advocate, 50 deputies, 50 senators, the executive collegiate bodies of the Autonomous Communities, or their legislative assemblies. A judge or a court, either *ex officio* or at the request of a party, may, however, refer a question on the constitutional validity of a law applicable to the case at hand to the Constitutional Court.

Some courts, like the Supreme Court of Papua New Guinea, however, determine questions of constitutional law presented by other courts, organizations or governmental bodies, as well as by individuals. Similarly, the Ecuadorian Constitutional Guarantees Court may receive complaints from individuals or any entity concerning alleged violations of human rights. The Federal Constitutional Court of the Federal Republic of Germany may hear an appeal from any individual who considers that his rights guaranteed in the Basic Law have been violated. In Sri Lanka, every individual has the Constitutional right to apply to the Supreme Court with respect to an alleged infringement or imminent infringement, by executive or administrative action, of a fundamental right recognized by the Constitution. Similarly, the Indian Constitution gives each individual the legal right to challenge before the Supreme Court the measures adopted by the State which affect or threaten to affect his civil and political rights. In some Latin America countries, like El Salvador, Panama and Venezuela, the *acción popular de inconstitucionalidad* permits every citizen, even those not directly affected, to appeal to the Supreme Court to declare any specific law unconstitutional if it violates the rights guaranteed by the constitution. For example, article 112 of the Venezuelan Organic Law of the Supreme Court of Justice states that any person whose rights or interests are affected by a law, regulation, ordinance or other act, created by national deliberative bodies at the State or municipal level or by the national executive power, may demand before the Supreme

Court that such an act be declared void for reasons of unconstitutionality or illegality. In India complainants may appeal to the Supreme Court, even at first instance, to challenge the constitutionality of measures affecting their civil and political rights.

In Canada and the Federal Republic of Germany, complainants are required to exhaust all available State and local remedies before seeking recourse to the Constitutional or Supreme Court for a determination of the constitutionality of a law or action.

## Special Courts and Tribunals

Increasingly, the legal systems in many countries have provided specialized judicial bodies with limited competence, which function apart from courts of general jurisdiction. Such specialized courts are created for a number of reasons. In some instances, they are established to deal with issues of a socially or politically sensitive nature. Moreover, the character of some legal issues and questions may require a certain level of technical knowledge for a fair adjudication of the matter. Clearly, the creation of such courts helps to ease the case-load of the courts of general jurisdiction, which are frequently too overburdened to provide aggrieved parties with a timely decision on their case. Specialized courts are frequently incorporated into the judicial framework in many countries throughout the world to deal with a number of questions. Labour courts and juvenile and children's courts may be mentioned as examples of special courts.

*1. Labour Courts.* During recent years a large number of countries have begun to establish courts, designed to settle, conciliate or arbitrate disputes arising from labour relations between employers, employees and workers' unions. For instance, the constitution of Yugoslavia calls for the establishment of "self-management courts", empowered to conciliate and arbitrate labour disputes. These self-management courts are composed of permanent judges and workers from organized labour, State organs and other self-managed organizations and communities. In Norway, special courts—the *Arbeidsretten*—have been created to adjudicate labour disputes. The decisions of these courts cannot be appealed to ordinary courts or courts of general jurisdiction. Labour courts have also been established in many other countries, including Barbados, the Federal Republic of Germany, India, Kenya, Papua New Guinea and Thailand.

In some countries the organs dealing with the settlement of disputes in the area of labour relations are not always considered fully-fledged judicial bodies. They settle such disputes in quasi-judicial proceedings. For instance, the main competence of the Canadian Labour Relations Board lies in its statutory and regulatory powers. However the Board may hear appeals against safety rulings in cases where imminent danger has been alleged. The Board also rules on complaints by employees that they have been discriminated against or punished for exercising their rights in relation to safety. An important part of the Board's activities is concerned with granting or reviewing certification on the application of trade unions to act as bargaining agents for groups of employees. The Labour Code of some countries—France and Tunisia for example—provides for the establishment of Conseils de Prud'hommes (Councils of Elders), with competence to rule in disputes between workers and employees.

*2. Juvenile and Children's Courts.* The establishment of juvenile and children's courts is based on the principle that children and young persons need special care and different treatment from that accorded to adults under the law. Definitions of the terms "infants", "children", "minors", "young persons", and "juveniles" vary from country to country. Distinctions are also made according to cases. For example, a "minor" in penal matters may not be so considered in civil cases. Juvenile and children's courts usually have broad discretion for the settlement of cases, ranging from the imposition of a sentence, often suspended, upon the accused, to ordering his or her placement in a rehabilitative institution or school, or merely warning or reprimanding the accused.

Children's courts in Australia are entitled to hear all complaints against children concerning summary offences as well as charges against children accused of committing indictable offences other than homicide, or offences punishable by penal servitude for life. In El Salvador, the Juvenile Courts have exclusive competence to try infractions regarded as crimes or offences under ordinary law and attributed to minors of 18 years of age or under, to investigate the situation of minors of 18 years of age or under who are in a state of moral or physical abandon or in danger, and to adopt suitable measures for the care, treatment, placement, supervision and education of minors.

In Tunisia, minors between 13 and 18 years of age charged with a transgression regarded as a crime, or offence, are brought before the children's judge or the Minors' Penal court. The judges in such cases are required to order appropriate measures of protection, assistance, supervision and education. Where the circumstances and the personality of the delinquent appear to warrant this, the Court may deliver a penal sentence against a minor of over 13 years old, in which case the sentence is served in a special establishment.

Some States select individuals to sit on the juvenile court from among professionals in the community who are qualified to bring particular sociological or psychological expertise to the panel, in addition to the legally certified judges who usually sit on the judicial panel in such courts. For instance, in Italy, the Special Juvenile Court, which tries minors of 18 years of age, is composed of a judge of the Court of Appeals and two citizens (a man and a woman) over 30 years of age who are professionals in biology, psychiatry, clinical anthropology or psychology.

Many juvenile and children's courts are concerned with maintaining the privacy of minors in court proceedings. In Barbados for example, the Juvenile Offenders Act provides that juvenile courts may convene in different places and at different times from ordinary courts. The Act also prohibits the publication of information likely to lead to the identification of any juvenile offender. Similarly, in France, the Juvenile Court and the Juvenile Assize Court are always held in private, without a public audience apart from close relatives. Decisions are, however, delivered in open court.

Finally, it is important to note that some States do not try juvenile delinquents before an organized court. In Cyprus, for example, cases involving delinquent minors do not appear before the Court except when a very serious crime has been committed. Instead, in most cases, delinquent minors are supervised by social workers in their own environment.

3. *Other Specialized Courts.* In addition to juvenile courts and labour courts, many countries have reported the existence of a wide range of quasi-judicial organs to settle disputes involving diverse categories of rights. For instance, New Zealand reports the existence of the Maori Land Court, established to adjudicate the land claims of its indigenous population. In the same country, a Deportation Review Tribunal was created in 1978 to examine administrative orders for the expulsion and deportation of foreigners. A special

Social Insurance Court or *Trygderetten*, whose decisions may be brought before the ordinary courts, has been created in Norway.

### Administrative Courts and Tribunals

The protection of human rights may be provided either within a unitary judicial system, or under a dual system of civil courts (competent to hear civil disputes and penal cases) and administrative courts (competent to rule on complaints against administrative acts). Such a dual system is employed in France, where the *Cour de cassation,* at the top of the judicial hierarchy, deals with criminal and civil cases, and the *Conseil d'Etat* is the judicial authority which exercises ultimate control of the administration by giving final rulings on appeal from the Administrative Tribunals *(Tribunaux administratifs).* The *Conseil d'Etat* may declare void administrative acts which are contrary to the law as well as acts by State or local authorities which have exceeded their jurisdiction. Additionally, the *Conseil d'Etat* may declare measures void, if it finds that they have been exercised for purposes other than those intended by the law. The available remedies of the *Conseil d'Etat* are the annulment of challenged acts and the granting of compensation to the victim, which is paid by the administration.

Administrative courts of a similar nature are also found in other countries, notably in Belgium, Greece and Tunisia. For instance, the Tunisian Administrative Tribunal, which was created in 1972, may hear appeals for compensation from the civil courts and appeals for annulment on grounds of misuse of authority lodged against acts of the administration, local public authorities or public administrative bodies.

***STUDY ON JUDICIAL INDEPENDENCE AND IMPARTIALITY.*** In 1980, the UN **ECONOMIC AND SOCIAL COUNCIL** authorized the **SUB-COMMISSION ON PREVENTION OF DISCRIMINATION AND PROTECTION OF MINORITIES** (decision 1980/124) to entrust one of its members, Mr. M. L. Singhvi (India), with the preparation of a report on the independence and impartiality of the judiciary, jurors, and assessors and the independence of lawyers "to the end that there should be no discrimination in the administration of justice and that human rights and fundamental freedoms might be maintained and safeguarded."

The Special Rapporteur's report on the subject (UN Doc. E/CN.4/Sub.2/1985/18 and Add. 1–6) was presented to the Sub-Commission at its 1985 session and included the draft of a Universal Declaration on the Independence of Justice (*Ibid.,* Add. 5/Rev. 1). The Sub-Commission, after reviewing the report, decided (decision 1985/107) (a) to postpone consideration of the report to its 1986 session, (b) to request the Secretary-General to circulate the study to members of the Sub-Commission and to invite those wishing to do so to submit written comments for transmittal to Mr. Singhvi, (c) to request the Secretary-General to circulate the comments received to all members of the Sub-Commission, and (d) to request Mr. Singhvi to take those comments into account when presenting his report at the 1986 session of the Sub-Commission.

At its 1987 session, the Sub-Commission examined the Special Rapporteur's report in detail, expressed (resolution 1987/23) its appreciation and thanks to him, and decided to examine the draft declaration annexed to the report at its 1988 session, on a priority basis as a separate agenda item. It further decided that the draft declaration should meanwhile be transmitted by the Secretary-General to member States and to the UN Centre for Social Development and Humanitarian Affairs for their comments, and called upon the Special Rapporteur to prepare a report on the draft declaration in the light of such comments and the deliberations in the Sub-Commission.

The **COMMISSION ON HUMAN RIGHTS,** in January 1988, approved (resolution 1988/40) these arrangements. It called upon the Sub-Commission to review and finalize the draft declaration with a view to submitting it to the Commission for consideration in 1989.

The Sub-Commission, in August 1988, received a report by the Special Rapporteur (UN Doc. E/CN.4/Sub.2/1988/20 and Add. 1) in which he analyzed the comments he had received, accepted or accommodated most of them, and presented a revised text of the draft declaration. The Sub-Commission amended the title of the draft declaration to read "Draft Declaration on the Independence and Impartiality of the Judiciary, Jurors and Assessors, and the Independence of Lawyers," and decided (resolution 1988/25) to refer the revised draft declaration, and the relevant documentation, to the Commission on Human Rights for further consideration.

*UN SPECIAL RAPPORTEUR ON JUDICIAL INDEPENDENCE AND IMPARTIALITY.* On recommendation of the Sub-Commission on Prevention of Discrimination and Protection of Minorities and the Commission on Human Rights, the Economic and Social Council in 1994 authorized the creation of a monitoring mechanism "to follow up the question of the independence and impartiality of the judiciary, particularly with regard to judges and lawyers, as well as court officials, and the nature of the problems liable to attack this independence and impartiality." The mandate of the Special Rapporteur, as suggested in Commission on Human Rights resolution 1994/41, consists of the following tasks:

(a) To inquire into any substantial allegations transmitted to him or her and to report his or her conclusions thereon;

(b) To identify and record not only attacks on the independence of the judiciary, lawyers and court officials but also progress achieved in protecting and en-

hancing their independence, and make concrete recommendations, including recommendations for the provision of advisory services or technical assistance when they are requested by the State concerned;

(c) To study, for the purpose of making proposals, important and topical questions of principle with a view to protecting and enhancing the independence of the judiciary and lawyers.

**BIBLIOGRAPHY.** Beatty, David M., ed. *Human Rights and Judicial Review: A Comparative Perspective.* Dordrecht, the Netherlands: Martinus Nijhoff, 1994. Collection of scholarly articles, in English. Also in *International Studies in Human Rights* 34.

Benedek, Wolfgang. "The Judiciary and Human Rights in Africa: The Banjul Seminar and the Training Workshop for a Core of Human Rights Advocates of November 1989," *Human Rights Law Journal* 11, no. 1–2 (1990): 247–256. Conference report, in English.

Brody, Reed, ed. *Attacks on Justice: The Harassment and Persecution of Judges and Lawyers, January 1988–June 1989.* Geneva, Switzerland: Centre for the Independence of Judges and Lawyers of the International Commission of Jurists, 1989–present. NGO annual report, in English.

Centre for the Independence of Judges and Lawyers. "The Independence of Judges and Lawyers: A Compilation of International Standards," *CIJL Bulletin* no. 25–26 (April–October 1990). Special issue, in English.

————. *The Independence of the Judiciary in India.* Geneva, Switzerland: International Commission of Jurists, 1990. Conference report, in English.

Cowling, M.G. "Judges and the Protection of Human Rights in South Africa: Articulating the Inarticulate Premise," *South African Journal on Human Rights* 3, pt. 2 (July 1987): 177–201. Scholarly article, in English.

Elias, T. O. "Organisation and Development of the Legal Profession in Africa, in Particular, the Ability of the Bar and Judiciary to Uphold the Rights of Both the Citizen and the State," *African Journal of International Law* 1, no 1 (Summer 1988): 11–30. Scholarly article, in English.

Forsyth, Christopher. "Interpreting a Bill of Rights: The Future Task of a Reformed Judiciary," *South African Journal on Human Rights* 7, no. 1 (1991): 1–23. Scholarly article, in English.

Franck, T. M. *Human Rights in Third World Perspective.* 3 vols. Dobbs Ferry, NY, USA: Oceana Publications, 1982. Compilation of comments and case studies, in English.

Free Legal Assistance Group. *Towards an Independent Competent and Honest Judiciary.* Manila, Philippines: 1986. NGO position paper, in English.

Garcia-Sayan, Diego. *Habeas Corpus y Estados de Emergencia* (Habeas Corpus and States of Emergency). Lima, Peru: Comision Andina de Juristas and the Friedrich Naumann Foundation, 1988. NGO report, in Spanish.

Hunt, Paul. *Justice? The Military Court System in the Israeli-Occupied Territories.* Ramallah, Occupied Territories: Law in the Service of Man (Al-Haq) and Gaza Centre for Rights and Law, 1987. NGO report, in English.

International Commission of Jurists. *The Independence of Judges and Lawyers in South Asia.* Geneva, Switzerland: 1988. NGO conference report, in English.

————. *The Independence of the Judiciary and the Legal Profession in English-Speaking Africa. A Report of Seminars Held in Lusaka from 10–14 Nov. 1986 and in Banjul from 6–10 April*

*1987, Convened Jointly by the Centre for the Independence of Judges and Lawyers, African Bar Association, and International Commission of Jurists.* Geneva, Switzerland: 1988. NGO conference report, in English.

International Commission of Jurists and Centre for the Independence of Judges and Lawyers. *Chile: A Time of Reckoning—Human Rights and the Judiciary.* Geneva, Switzerland: ICJ, 1992. NGO report, in English.

Lawyers Committee for Human Rights. *In Defense of Rights: Attacks on Lawyers and Judges in 1989–.* New York: 1990–present. NGO annual report, in English.

Nwabueze B. O. *Judicialism in Commonwealth Africa: The Role of the Courts in Government.* New York: St. Martin's Press, 1977. Scholarly study, in English.

Thoolen, Hans, ed. *Indonesia and the Rule of Law: Twenty Years of "New Order" Government.* London: Frances Pinter Publishers for the International Commission of Jurists and the Netherlands Institute of Human Rights, 1987. NGO report/scholarly study, in English.

United Nations Sub-Commission on Prevention of Discrimination and Protection of Minorities. *Report on the Independence of the Judiciary and the Protection of Practising Lawyers, Prepared by Mr. Louis Joinet Pursuant to Resolution 1990/23 of the Sub-Commission on Prevention of Discrimination and Protection of Minorities.* Geneva, Switzerland: 1991. IGO document, in English and French.

## JUDICIARY: BASIC PRINCIPLES ON THE INDEPENDENCE OF THE JUDICIARY (1985).

The basic principles set out below are based on draft guidelines concerning the independence of the judiciary elaborated by the **COMMITTEE ON CRIME PREVENTION AND CONTROL,** which the UN **ECONOMIC AND SOCIAL COUNCIL** had submitted to the Seventh United Nations Congress on the Prevention of Crime and the Treatment of Offenders for consideration. Because of the complexity of the subject, in view of the many different judicial systems of the member States, the Congress decided that an abbreviated text of the guidelines, setting out basic principles, would be more appropriate. Such a text was adopted by the Congress in Milan, Italy, on 5 September 1985. It was later endorsed by the UN **GENERAL ASSEMBLY** on 29 November 1985 (resolution 40/32) and on 13 December 1985 (resolution 40/146). The text (UN Doc. A/CONF.121/22, chap. I, sect. D. 2) is as follows:

Whereas in the Charter of the United Nations the peoples of the world affirm, *inter alia,* their determination to establish conditions under which justice can be maintained to achieve international co-operation in promoting and encouraging respect for human rights and fundamental freedoms without any discrimination,

Whereas the Universal Declaration of Human Rights enshrines in particular the principles of equality before the law, of the presumption of innocence and of the right to a fair and public hearing by a competent, independent and impartial tribunal established by law,

Whereas the International Covenants on Economic, Social and Cultural Rights and on Civil and Political Rights both guarantee the exercise of those rights, and in addition, the Covenant on Civil and Political Rights further guarantees the right to be tried without undue delay,

Whereas frequently there still exists a gap between the vision underlying those principles and the actual situation,

Whereas the organization and administration of justice in every country should be inspired by those principles, and efforts should be undertaken to translate them fully into reality,

Whereas rules concerning the exercise of judicial office should aim at enabling judges to act in accordance with those principles,

Whereas judges are charged with the ultimate decision over life, freedom, rights, duties and property of citizens,

Whereas the Sixth United Nations Congress on the Prevention of Crime and the Treatment of Offenders, by its resolution 16, called upon the Committee on Crime Prevention and Control to include among its priorities the elaboration of guidelines relating to the independence of judges and the selection, professional training and status of judges and prosecutors,

Whereas it is, therefore, appropriate that consideration be first given to the role of judges in relation to the system of justice and to the importance of their selection, training and conduct,

The following basic principles, formulated to assist Member States in their task of securing and promoting the independence of the judiciary, should be taken into account and respected by Governments within the framework of their national legislation and practice and be brought to the attention of judges, lawyers, members of the executive and the legislature and the public in general. The principles have been formulated principally with professional judges in mind, but they apply equally, as appropriate, to lay judges, where they exist.

*Independence of the Judiciary.* 1. The independence of the judiciary shall be guaranteed by the State and enshrined in the Constitution or the law of the country. It is the duty of all governmental and other institutions to respect and observe the independence of the judiciary.

2. The judiciary shall decide matters before them impartially, on the basis of facts and in accordance with the law, without any restrictions, improper influences, inducement, pressures, threats or interferences, direct or indirect, from any quarter or for any reason.

3. The judiciary shall have jurisdiction over all issues of a judicial nature and shall have exclusive authority to decide whether an issue submitted for its decision is within its competence as defined by law.

4. There shall not be any inappropriate or unwarranted interference with the judicial process, nor shall judicial decisions by the courts be subject to revision. This principle is without prejudice to judicial review or to mitigation or commutation by competent authorities of sentences imposed by the judiciary, in accordance with the law.

5. Everyone shall have the right to be tried by ordinary courts or tribunals using established legal procedures. Tribunals that do not use the duly established procedures of the legal process shall not be created to displace the jurisdiction belonging to the ordinary courts or judicial tribunals.

6. The principle of the independence of the judiciary entitles and requires the judiciary to ensure that judicial proceedings are conducted fairly and that the rights of the parties are respected.

7. It is the duty of each Member State to provide adequate

resources to enable the judiciary to properly perform its functions.

*Freedom of Expression and Association.* 8. In accordance with the Universal Declaration of Human Rights, members of the judiciary are like other citizens entitled to freedom of expression, belief, association and assembly; provided, however, that in exercising such rights, judges shall always conduct themselves in such a manner as to preserve the dignity of their office and the impartiality and independence of the judiciary.

9. Judges shall be free to form and join association of judges or other organizations to represent their interests, to promote their professional training and to protect their judicial independence.

*Qualifications, Selection and Training.* 10. Persons selected for judicial office shall be individuals of integrity and ability with appropriate training or qualifications in law. Any method of judicial selection shall safeguard against judicial appointments for improper motives. In the selection of judges, there shall be no discrimination against a person on the grounds of race, colour, sex, religion, political or other opinion, national or social origin, property, birth or status, except that a requirement, that a candidate for judicial office must be a national of the country concerned, shall not be considered discriminatory.

*Conditions of Service and Tenure.* 11. The term of office of judges, their independence, security, adequate remuneration, conditions of service, pensions and the age of retirement shall be adequately secured by law.

12. Judges, whether appointed or elected, shall have guaranteed tenure until a mandatory retirement age or the expiry of their term of office, where such exists.

13. Promotion of judges, wherever such a system exists, should be based on objective factors, in particular ability, integrity and experience.

14. The assignment of cases to judges within the court to which they belong is an internal matter of judicial administration.

*Professional Secrecy and Immunity.* 15. The judiciary shall be bound by professional secrecy with regard to their deliberations and to confidential information acquired in the course of their duties other than in public proceedings, and shall not be compelled to testify on such matters.

16. Without prejudice to any disciplinary procedure or to any right of appeal or to compensation from the State, in accordance with national law, judges should enjoy personal immunity from civil suits for monetary damages for improper acts or omissions in the exercise of their judicial functions.

*Discipline, Suspension and Removal.* 17. A charge or complaint made against a judge in his/her judicial and professional capacity shall be processed expeditiously and fairly under an appropriate procedure. The judge shall have the right to a fair hearing. The examination of the matter at its initial stage shall be kept confidential, unless otherwise requested by the judge.

18. Judges shall be subject to suspension or removal only for reasons of incapacity or behaviour that renders them unfit to discharge their duties.

19. All disciplinary, suspension or removal proceedings shall be determined in accordance with established standards of judicial conduct.

20. Decisions in disciplinary, suspension or removal proceedings should be subject to an independent review. This principle may not apply to the decisions of the highest court and those of the legislature in impeachment or similar proceedings.

**PROCEDURES FOR IMPLEMENTATION OF THE BASIC PRINCIPLES (1989).** The Seventh United Nations Congress on the Prevention of Crime and the Treatment of Offenders, when drafting the Basic Principles on the Independence of the Judiciary later endorsed by the UN General Assembly (resolutions 40/32 and 40/146), called upon the Committee on Crime Prevention and Control to consider, as a matter of priority, the implementation of those principles.

On recommendation of that committee, the UN Economic and Social Council adopted, on 24 May 1989, a series of Procedures for the Effective Implementation of the Basic Principles on the Independence of the Judiciary and invited the Eighth United Nations Congress on the Prevention of Crime and the Treatment of Offenders and its preparatory body to accord priority to ways and means of stimulating adherence to those procedures. The procedures adopted by the Council (resolution 1989/60) are as follows:

*Procedure 1.* All States shall adopt and implement in their justice systems the Basic Principles on the Independence of the Judiciary in accordance with their constitutional process and domestic practice.

*Procedure 2.* No judge shall be appointed or elected for purposes, or be required to perform services, that are inconsistent with the Basic Principles. No judge shall accept judicial office on the basis of an appointment or election, or perform services, that are inconsistent with the Basic Principles.

*Procedure 3.* The Basic Principles shall apply to all judges, including, as appropriate, lay judges, where they exist.

*Procedure 4.* States shall ensure that the Basic Principles are widely publicized in at least the main or official language or languages of the respective country. Judges, lawyers, members of the executive, the legislature, and the public in general, shall be informed in the most appropriate manner of the content and the importance of the Basic Principles so that they may promote their application within the framework of the justice system. In particular, States shall make the text of the Basic Principles available to all members of the judiciary.

*Procedure 5.* In implementing principles 8 and 12 of the Basic Principles, States shall pay particular attention to the need for adequate resources for the functioning of the judicial system, including appointing a sufficient number of judges in relation to case-loads, providing the courts with necessary support staff and equipment, and offering judges appropriate personal security, remuneration and emoluments.

*Procedure 6.* States shall promote or encourage seminars and courses at the national and regional levels on the role of the judiciary in society and the necessity for its independence.

*Procedure 7.* In accordance with Economic and Social Council resolution 1986/10, section V, Member States shall inform the Secretary-General every five years, beginning in 1988, of the progress achieved in the implementation of the Basic Principles, including their dissemination, their incorporation into national legislation, the problems faced and difficulties or obstacles encountered in their implementation at the national level and the assistance that might be needed from the international community.

*Procedure 8.* The Secretary-General shall prepare independent quinquennial reports to the Committee on Crime Prevention and Control on progress made with respect to the implementation of the Basic Principles, on the basis of the information received from Governments under procedure 7, as well as other information available within the United Nations system, including information on the technical co-operation and training provided by institutes, experts and regional and interregional advisers. In the preparation of those reports the Secretary-General shall also enlist the co-operation of specialized agencies and the relevant intergovernmental organizations and non-governmental organizations, in particular professional associations of judges and lawyers, in consultative status with the Economic and Social Council, and take into account the information provided by such agencies and organizations.

*Procedure 9.* The Secretary-General shall disseminate the Basic Principles, the present implementing procedures and the periodic reports on their implementation referred to in procedures 7 and 8, in as many languages as possible, and make them available to all States and intergovernmental and non-governmental organizations concerned, in order to ensure the widest circulation of those documents.

*Procedure 10.* The Secretary-General shall ensure the widest possible reference to and use of the text of the Basic Principles and the present implementing procedures by the United Nations in all its relevant programmes and the inclusion of the Basic Principles as soon as possible in the United Nations publication entitled *Human Rights: A Compilation of International Instruments,* in accordance with Economic and Social Council resolution 1986/10, section V.

*Procedure 11.* As part of its technical co-operation programme, the United Nations, in particular the Department of Technical Co-operation for Development and the United Nations Development Programme, shall:

(a) Assist Governments, at their request, in setting up and strengthening independent and effective judicial systems;

(b) Make available to Governments requesting them, the services of experts and regional and interregional advisers on judicial matters to assist in implementing the Basic Principles;

(c) Enhance research concerning effective measures for implementing the Basic Principles, with emphasis on new developments in that area;

(d) Promote national and regional seminars, as well as other meetings at the professional and non-professional levels, on the role of the judiciary in society, the necessity for its independence, and the importance of implementing the Basic Principles to further those goals;

(e) Strengthen substantive support for the United Nations regional and interregional research and training institutes for crime prevention and criminal justice, as well as other entities within the United Nations system concerned with implementing the Basic Principles.

*Procedure 12.* The United Nations regional and interregional research and training institutes for crime prevention and criminal justice as well as other concerned entities within the United Nations system shall assist in the implementation process. They shall pay special attention to ways and means of enhancing the application of the Basic Principles in their research and training programmes, and to providing technical assistance upon the request of Member States. For this purpose, the United Nations institutes, in co-operation with national institutions and intergovernmental and non-governmental organizations concerned, shall develop curricula and training materials based on the Principles and the present implementing procedures, which are

suitable for use in legal education programmes at all levels as well as in specialized courses on human rights and related subjects.

*Procedure 13.* The regional commissions, the specialized agencies and other entities within the United Nations system as well as other concerned intergovernmental organizations shall become actively involved in the implementation process. They shall inform the Secretary-General of the efforts made to disseminate the Basic Principles, the measures taken to give effect to them and any obstacles and shortcomings encountered. The Secretary-General shall also take steps to ensure that non-governmental organizations in consultative status with the Economic and Social Council become actively involved in the implementation process and the related reporting procedures.

*Procedure 14.* The Committee on Crime Prevention and Control shall assist the General Assembly and the Economic and Social Council in following up the present implementing procedures, including periodic reporting under procedures 6 and 7 above. To this end, the Committee shall identify existing obstacles to, or shortcomings in, the implementation of the Basic Principles and the reasons for them. The Committee shall make specific recommendations, as appropriate, to the Assembly and the Council and any other relevant United Nations human rights bodies on further action required for the effective implementation of the Basic Principles.

*Procedure 15.* The Committee on Crime Prevention and Control shall assist the General Assembly, the Economic and Social Council and any other relevant United Nations human rights bodies, as appropriate, with recommendations relating to reports of *ad hoc* inquiry commissions or bodies, with respect to matters pertaining to the application and implementation of the Basic Principles.

**JUSTICE.** See **ADMINISTRATION OF JUSTICE.**

**JUVENILE JUSTICE: STANDARD MINIMUM RULES FOR THE ADMINISTRATION OF JUVENILE JUSTICE, UN (1985).** The United Nations Standard Minimum Rules for the Administration of Juvenile Justice, also known as the "Beijing Rules," were drafted by an Interregional Preparatory Committee held at Beijing, China, from 14 to 18 May 1984, and were recommended for adoption by the Seventh United Nations Congress on the Prevention of Crime and the Treatment of Offenders, held in Milan from 26 August to 6 September 1985. In adopting them on 29 November 1985 (resolution 40/33), the UN **GENERAL ASSEMBLY** recognized that the young, owing to their early stage of human development, require particular care and assistance with regard to physical, mental, and social development and require legal protection in conditions of peace, freedom, dignity, and security.

The Assembly invited member States to adapt their national legislation, policies, and practices, particularly in the training of juvenile justice personnel, to the Beijing Rules, and to report periodically to the UN

**COMMITTEE ON CRIME PREVENTION AND CONTROL** on the results of their efforts to put the rules into effect.

The text of the rules (including the commentaries designed to clarify their meaning), annexed to General Assembly resolution 40/33, is as follows:

### Part One. General Principles

#### 1. Fundamental Perspectives

1.1 Member States shall seek, in conformity with their respective general interests, to further the well-being of the juvenile and her or his family.

1.2 Member States shall endeavour to develop conditions that will ensure for the juvenile a meaningful life in the community, which, during that period in life when she or he is most susceptible to deviant behaviour, will foster a process of personal development and education that is as free from crime and delinquency as possible.

1.3 Sufficient attention shall be given to positive measures that involve the full mobilization of all possible resources, including the family, volunteers and other community groups, as well as schools and other community institutions, for the purpose of promoting the well-being of the juvenile, with a view to reducing the need for intervention under the law, and of effectively, fairly and humanely dealing with the juvenile in conflict with the law.

1.4 Juvenile justice shall be conceived as an integral part of the national development process of each country, within a comprehensive framework of social justice for all juveniles, thus, at the same time, contributing to the protection of the young and the maintenance of a peaceful order in society.

1.5 These Rules shall be implemented in the context of economic, social and cultural conditions prevailing in each Member State.

1.6 Juvenile justice services shall be systematically developed and co-ordinated with a view to improving and sustaining the competence of personnel involved in the services, including their methods, approaches and attitudes.

*Commentary.* These broad fundamental perspectives refer to comprehensive social policy in general and aim at promoting juvenile welfare to the greatest possible extent, which will minimize the necessity of intervention by the juvenile justice system, and in turn, will reduce the harm that may be caused by any intervention. Such care measures for the young, before the onset of delinquency, are basic policy requisites designed to obviate the need for the application of the Rules.

Rules 1.1 to 1.3 point to the important role that a constructive social policy for juveniles will play, *inter alia,* in the prevention of juvenile crime and delinquency. Rule 1.4 defines juvenile justice as an integral part of social justice for juveniles, while rule 1.6 refers to the necessity of constantly improving juvenile justice, without falling behind the development of progressive social policy for juveniles in general and bearing in mind the need for consistent improvement of staff services.

Rule 1.5 seeks to take account of existing conditions in Member States which would cause the manner of implementation of particular rules necessarily to be different from the manner adopted in other States.

#### 2. Scope of the Rules and Definitions Used

2.1 The following Standard Minimum Rules shall be applied to juvenile offenders impartially, without distinction of any kind, for example, as to race, colour, sex, language, religion, political or other opinions, national or social origin, property, birth or other status.

2.2 For purposes of these Rules, the following definitions shall be applied by Member States in a manner which is compatible with their respective legal systems and concepts:

(a) A *juvenile* is a child or young person who, under the respective legal systems, may be dealt with for an offence in a manner which is different from an adult;

(b) An *offence* is any behaviour (act or omission) that is punishable by law under the respective legal systems;

(c) A *juvenile offender* is a child or young person who is alleged to have committed or who has been found to have committed an offence.

2.3 Efforts shall be made to establish, in each national jurisdiction, a set of laws, rules and provisions specifically applicable to juvenile offenders and institutions and bodies entrusted with the functions of the administration of juvenile justice and designed:

(a) To meet the varying needs of juvenile offenders, while protecting their basic rights;

(b) To meet the needs of society;

(c) To implement the following rules thoroughly and fairly.

*Commentary.* The Standard Minimum Rules are deliberately formulated so as to be applicable within different legal systems and, at the same time, to set some minimum standards for the handling of juvenile offenders under any definition of a juvenile and under any system of dealing with juvenile offenders. The Rules are always to be applied impartially and without distinction of any kind.

Rule 2.1 therefore stresses the importance of the Rules always being applied impartially and without distinction of any kind. The rule follows the formulation of principle 2 of the Declaration of the Rights of the Child.

Rule 2.2 defines "juvenile" and "offence" as the components of the notion of the "juvenile offender", who is the main subject of these Standard Minimum Rules (see, however, also rule 3 and 4). It should be noted that age limits will depend on, and are explicitly made dependent on, each respective legal system, thus fully respecting the economic, social, political, cultural and legal systems of Member States. This makes for a wide variety of ages coming under the definition of "juvenile", ranging from 7 years to 18 years or above. Such a variety seems inevitable in view of the different national legal systems and does not diminish the impact of these Standard Minimum Rules.

Rule 2.3 is addressed to the necessity of specific national legislation for the optimal implementation of these Standard Minimum Rules, both legally and practically.

#### 3. Extension of the Rules

3.1 The relevant provisions of the Rules shall be applied not only to juvenile offenders but also to juveniles who may be proceeded against for any specific behaviour that would not be punishable if committed by an adult.

3.2 Efforts shall be made to extend the principles embodied in the Rules to all juveniles who are dealt with in welfare and care proceedings.

3.3 Efforts shall also be made to extend the principles embodied in the Rules to young adult offenders.

*Commentary*. Rule 3 extends the protection afforded by the Standard Minimum Rules for the Administration of Juvenile Justice to cover:

(a) The so-called "status offences" prescribed in various national legal systems where the range of behaviour considered to be an offence is wider for juveniles than it is for adults (for example, truancy, school and family disobedience, public drunkenness, etc.) (rule 3.1);

(b) Juvenile welfare and care proceedings (rule 3.2);

(c) Proceedings dealing with young adult offenders, depending of course on each given age limit (rule 3.3).

The extension of the Rules to cover these three areas seems to be justified. Rule 3.1 provides minimum guarantees in those fields, and rule 3.2 is considered a desirable step in the direction of more fair, equitable and humane justice for all juveniles in conflict with the law.

## 4. Age of Criminal Responsibility

4.1 In those legal systems recognizing the concept of the age of criminal responsibility for juveniles, the beginning of that age shall not be fixed at too low an age level, bearing in mind the facts of emotional, mental and intellectual maturity.

*Commentary*. The minimum age of criminal responsibility differs widely owing to history and culture. The modern approach would be to consider whether a child can live up to the moral and psychological components of criminal responsibility; that is, whether a child, by virtue of her or his individual discernment and understanding, can be held responsible for essentially anti-social behaviour. If the age of criminal responsibility is fixed too low or if there is no lower age limit at all, the notion of responsibility would become meaningless. In general, there is a close relationship between the notion of responsibility for delinquent or criminal behaviour and other social rights and responsibilities (such as marital status, civil majority, etc.).

Efforts should therefore be made to agree on a reasonable lowest age limit that is applicable internationally.

## 5. Aims of Juvenile Justice

5.1 The juvenile justice system shall emphasize the well-being of the juvenile and shall ensure that any reaction to juvenile offenders shall always be in proportion to the circumstances of both the offenders and the offence.

*Commentary*. Rule 5 refers to two of the most important objectives of juvenile justice. The first objective is the promotion of the well-being of the juvenile. This is the main focus of those legal systems in which juvenile offenders are dealt with by family courts or administrative authorities, but the well-being of the juvenile should also be emphasized in legal systems that follow the criminal court model, thus contributing to the avoidance of merely punitive sanctions. (See also rule 14.)

The second objective is "the principle of proportionality". This principle is well-known as an instrument for curbing punitive sanctions, mostly expressed in terms of just desert in relation to the gravity of the offence. The response to young offenders should be based on the consideration not only of the gravity of the offence but also of personal circumstances. The individual circumstances of the offender (for example, social status, family situation, the harm caused by the offence or other factors affecting personal circumstances) should influence the proportionality of the reaction (for example, by having regard to the offender's endeavour

to indemnify the victim or to her or his willingness to turn to a wholesome and useful life).

By the same token, reactions aiming to ensure the welfare of the young offender may go beyond necessity and therefore infringe upon the fundamental rights of the young individual, as has been observed in some juvenile justice systems. Here, too, the proportionality of the reaction to the circumstances of both the offender and the offence, including the victim, should be safeguarded.

In essence, rule 5 calls for no less and no more than a fair reaction in any given case of juvenile delinquency and crime. The issues combined in the rule may help to stimulate development in both regards: new and innovative types of reactions are as desirable as precautions against any undue widening of the net of formal social control over juveniles.

## 6. Scope of Discretion

6.1 In view of the varying special needs of juveniles as well as the variety of measures available, appropriate scope for discretion shall be allowed at all stages of proceedings and at the different levels of juvenile justice administration, including investigation, prosecution, adjudication and the follow-up of dispositions.

6.2 Efforts shall be made, however, to ensure sufficient accountability at all stages and levels in the exercise of any such discretion.

6.3 Those who exercise discretion shall be specially qualified or trained to exercise it judiciously and in accordance with their functions and mandates.

*Commentary*. Rules 6.1, 6.2 and 6.3 combine several important features of effective, fair and humane juvenile justice administration: the need to permit the exercise of discretionary power at all significant levels of processing so that those who make determinations can take the actions deemed to be the most appropriate in each individual case; and the need to provide checks and balances in order to curb any abuses of discretionary power and to safeguard the rights of the young offender. Accountability and professionalism are instruments best apt to curb broad discretion. Thus, professional qualifications and expert training are emphasized here as a valuable means of ensuring the judicious exercise of discretion in matters of juvenile offenders. (See also rules 1.6 and 2.2.) The formulation of specific guidelines on the exercise of discretion and the provision of systems of review, appeal and the like in order to permit scrutiny of decisions and accountability are emphasized in this context. Such mechanisms are not specified here, as they do not easily lend themselves to incorporation into international standard minimum rules, which cannot possibly cover all differences in justice systems.

## 7. Rights of Juveniles

7.1 Basic procedural safeguards such as the presumption of innocence, the right to be notified of the charges, the right to remain silent, the right to counsel, the right to the presence of a parent or guardian, the right to confront and cross-examine witnesses and the right to appeal to a higher authority shall be guaranteed at all stages of proceedings.

*Commentary*. Rule 7.1 emphasizes some important points that represent essential elements for a fair and just trial and that are internationally recognized in existing human rights instruments. (See also rule 14.) The presumption of innocence, for instance, is also to be found in article 11 of the

Universal Declaration of Human Rights and in article 14, paragraph 2, of the International Covenant on Civil and Political Rights.

Rules 14 *seq.* of these Standard Minimum Rules specify issues that are important for proceedings in juvenile cases, in particular, while rule 7.1 affirms the most basic procedural safeguards in a general way.

### 8. Protection of Privacy

8.1 The juvenile's right to privacy shall be respected at all stages in order to avoid harm being caused to her or him by undue publicity or by the process of labelling.

8.2 In principle, no information that may lead to the identification of a juvenile offender shall be published.

*Commentary.* Rule 8 stresses the importance of the protection of the juvenile's right to privacy. Young persons are particularly susceptible to stigmatization. Criminological research into labelling processes has provided evidence of the detrimental effects (of different kinds) resulting from the permanent identification of young persons as "delinquent" or "criminal".

Rule 8 also stresses the importance of protecting the juvenile from the adverse effects that may result from the publication in the mass media of information about the case (for example, the names of young offenders, alleged or convicted). The interest of the individual should be protected and upheld, at least in principle. (The general contents of rule 8 are further specified in rule 21.)

### 9. Saving Clause

9.1 Nothing in these Rules shall be interpreted as precluding the application of the Standard Minimum Rules for the Treatment of Prisoners adopted by the United Nations and other human rights instruments and standards recognized by the international community that relate to the care and protection of the young.

*Commentary.* Rule 9 is meant to avoid any misunderstanding in interpreting and implementing the present Rules in conformity with principles contained in relevant existing or emerging international human rights instruments and standards—such as the Universal Declaration of Human Rights; the International Covenant on Economic, Social and Cultural Rights and the International Covenant on Civil and Political Rights; and the Declaration of the Rights of the Child and the draft convention on the rights of the child. It should be understood that the application of the present Rules is without prejudice to any such international instruments which may contain provisions of wider application. (See also rule 27.)

### Part Two. Investigation and Prosecution

### 10. Initial Contact

10.1 Upon the apprehension of a juvenile, her or his parents or guardian shall be immediately notified of such apprehension, and, where such immediate notification is not possible, the parents or guardian shall be notified within the shortest possible time thereafter.

10.2 A judge or other competent official or body shall, without delay, consider the issue of release.

10.3 Contacts between the law enforcement agencies and a juvenile offender shall be managed in such a way as to respect the legal status of the juvenile, promote the well-being of the juvenile and avoid harm to her or him, with due regard to the circumstances of the case.

*Commentary.* Rule 10.1 is in principle contained in rule 92 of the Standard Minimum Rules for the Treatment of Prisoners.

The question of release (rule 10.2) shall be considered without delay by a judge or other competent official. The latter refers to any person or institution in the broadest sense of the term, including community boards or police authorities having power to release an arrested person. (See also the International Covenant on Civil and Political Rights, article 9, paragraph 3.)

Rule 10.3 deals with some fundamental aspects of the procedures and behaviour on the part of the police and other law enforcement officials in cases of juvenile crime. To "avoid harm" admittedly is flexible wording and covers many features of possible interaction (for example, the use of harsh language, physical violence or exposure to the environment). Involvement in juvenile justice processes in itself can be "harmful" to juveniles; the term "avoid harm" should be broadly interpreted, therefore, as doing the least harm possible to the juvenile in the first instance, as well as any additional or undue harm. This is especially important in the initial contact with law enforcement agencies, which might profoundly influence the juvenile's attitude towards the State and society. Moreover, the success of any further intervention is largely dependent on such initial contacts. Compassion and kind firmness are important in these situations.

### 11. Diversion

11.1 Consideration shall be given, wherever appropriate, to dealing with juvenile offenders without resorting to formal trial by the competent authority, referred to in rule 14.1 below.

11.2 The police, the prosecution or other agencies dealing with juvenile cases shall be empowered to dispose of such cases, at their discretion, without recourse to formal hearings, in accordance with the criteria laid down for that purpose in the respective legal system and also in accordance with the principles contained in these Rules.

11.3 Any diversion involving referral to appropriate community or other services shall require the consent of the juvenile, or her or his parents or guardian, provided that such decision to refer a case shall be subject to review by a competent authority, upon application.

11.4 In order to facilitate the discretionary disposition of juvenile cases, efforts shall be made to provide for community programmes, such as temporary supervision and guidance, restitution, and compensation of victims.

*Commentary.* Diversion, involving removal from criminal justice processing and, frequently, redirection to community support services, is commonly practised on a formal and informal basis in many legal systems. This practice serves to hinder the negative effects of subsequent proceedings in juvenile justice administration (for example, the stigma of conviction and sentence). In many cases, non-intervention would be the best response. Thus, diversion at the outset and without referral to alternative (social) services may be the optimal response. This is especially the case where the offence is of a non-serious nature and where the family, the school or other informal social control institutions have already reacted, or are likely to react, in an appropriate and constructive manner.

As stated in rule 11.2, diversions may be used at any point of decision-making—by the police, the prosecution or other agencies such as the courts, tribunals, boards or Councils. It may be exercised by one authority or several or all authorities, according to the rules and policies of the respective systems and in line with the present Rules. It need not necessarily be limited to petty cases, thus rendering diversion an important instrument.

Rule 11.3 stresses the important requirement of securing the consent of the young offender (or the parent or guardian) to the recommended diversionary measure(s). (Diversion to community service without such consent would contradict the Convention concerning the Abolition of Forced Labour.) However, this consent should not be left unchallengeable, since it might sometimes be given out of sheer desperation on the part of the juvenile. The rule underlines that care should be taken to minimize the potential for coercion and intimidation at all levels in the diversion process. Juveniles should not feel pressured (for example, in order to avoid court appearance) or to be pressured into consenting to diversion programmes. Thus, it is advocated that provision should be made for an objective appraisal of the appropriateness of disposition involving young offenders by a "competent authority upon application". (The "competent authority" may be different from that referred to in rule 14.)

Rule 11.4 recommends the provision of viable alternatives to juvenile justice processing in the form of community-based diversion. Programmes that involve settlement by victim restitution and those that seek to avoid future conflict with the law through temporary supervision and guidance are especially commended. The merits of individual cases would make diversion appropriate, even when more serious offences have been committed (for example, first offense, the act having been committed under peer pressure, etc.).

### 12. Specialization within the Police

12.1 In order to best fulfil their functions, police officers who frequently or exclusively deal with juveniles or who are primarily engaged in the prevention of juvenile crime shall be specially instructed and trained. In large cities, special police units should be established for that purpose.

*Commentary.* Rule 12 draws attention to the need for specialized training for all law enforcement officials who are involved in the administration of juvenile justice. As police are the first point of contact with the juvenile justice system, it is most important that they act in an informed and appropriate manner.

While the relationship between urbanization and crime is clearly complex, an increase in juvenile crime has been associated with the growth of large cities, particularly with rapid and unplanned growth. Specialized police units would therefore be indispensable, not only in the interest of implementing specific principles contained in the present instrument (such as rule 1.6) but more generally for improving the prevention and control of juvenile crime and the handling of juvenile offenders.

### 13. Detention Pending Trial

13.1 Detention pending trial shall be used only as a measure of last resort and for the shortest possible period of time.

13.2 Whenever possible, detention pending trial shall be replaced by alternative measures, such as close supervision, intensive care or placement with a family or in an educational setting or home.

13.3 Juveniles under detention pending trial shall be entitled to all rights and guarantees of the Standard Minimum Rules for the Treatment of Prisoners adopted by the United Nations.

13.4 Juveniles under detention pending trial shall be kept separate from adults and shall be detained in a separate institution or in a separate part of an institution also holding adults.

13.5 While in custody, juveniles shall receive care, protection and all necessary individual assistance—social, educational, vocational, psychological, medical and physical—that they may require in view of their age, sex and personality.

*Commentary.* The danger to juveniles of "criminal contamination" while in detention pending trial must not be underestimated. It is therefore important to stress the need for alternative measures. By doing so, rule 13.1 encourages the devising of new and innovative measures to avoid such detention in the interest of the well-being of the juvenile.

Juveniles under detention pending trial are entitled to all the rights and guarantees of the Standard Minimum Rules for the Treatment of Prisoners as well as the International Covenant on Civil and Political Rights, especially article 9 and article 10, paragraphs 2 *(b)* and 3.

Rule 13.4 does not prevent States from taking other measures against the negative influences of adult offenders which are at least as effective as the measures mentioned in the rule.

Different forms of assistance that may become necessary have been enumerated to draw attention to the broad range of particular needs of young detainees to be addressed (for example, females or males, drug addicts, alcoholics, mentally ill juveniles, young persons suffering from the trauma of arrest for example, etc.).

Varying physical and psychological characteristics of young detainees may warrant classification measures by which some are kept separate while in detention pending trial, thus contributing to the avoidance of victimization and rendering more appropriate assistance.

The Sixth United Nations Congress on the Prevention of Crime and the Treatment of Offenders, in its resolution 4 on juvenile justice standards specified that the Rules, *inter alia,* should reflect the basic principle that pre-trial detention should be used only as a last resort, that no minors should be held in a facility where they are vulnerable to the negative influences of adult detainees and that account should always be taken of the needs particular to their stage of development.

### Part Three. Adjudication and Disposition

### 14. Competent Authority to Adjudicate

14.1 Where the case of a juvenile offender has not been diverted (under rule 11), she or he shall be dealt with by the competent authority (court, tribunal, board, council, etc.) according to the principles of a fair and just trial.

14.2 The proceedings shall be conducive to the best interests of the juvenile and shall be conducted in an atmosphere of understanding, which shall allow the juvenile to participate therein and to express herself or himself freely.

*Commentary.* It is difficult to formulate a definition of the competent body or person that would universally describe an adjudicating authority. "Competent authority" is meant to include those who preside over courts or tribunals (composed of a single judge or of several members), including professional and lay magistrates as well as administrative boards (for example, the Scottish and Scandinavian systems) or other more informal community and conflict resolution agencies of an adjudicatory nature.

The procedure for dealing with juvenile offenders shall in any case follow the minimum standards that are applied almost universally for any criminal defendant under the procedure known as "due process of law". In accordance with due process, a "fair and just trial" included such basic safeguards as the presumption of innocence, the presentation and examination of witnesses, the common legal defences, the right to remain silent, the right to have the last word in a hearing, the right to appeal, etc. (See also rule 7.1)

### 15. Legal Counsel, Parents and Guardians

15.1 Throughout the proceedings the juvenile shall have the right to be represented by a legal advisor or to apply for free legal aid where there is provision for such aid in the country.

15.2 The parents or the guardian shall be entitled to participate in the proceedings and may be required by the competent authority to attend them in the interest of the juvenile. They may, however, be denied participation by the competent authority if there are reasons to assume that such exclusion is necessary in the interest of the juvenile.

*Commentary.* Rule 15.1 uses terminology similar to that found in rule 93 of the Standard Minimum Rules for the Treatment of Prisoners. Whereas legal counsel and free legal aid are needed to assure the juvenile legal assistance, the right of the parents or guardian to participate as stated in rule 15.2 should be viewed as general psychological and emotional assistance to the juvenile—a function extending throughout the procedure.

The competent authority's search for an adequate disposition of the case may profit, in particular, from the co-operation of the legal representatives of the juvenile (or, for that matter, some other personal assistant who the juvenile can and does really trust). Such concern can be thwarted if the presence of parents or guardians at the hearings plays a negative role, for instance, if they display a hostile attitude towards the juvenile; hence, the possibility of their exclusion must be provided for.

### 16. Social Inquiry Reports

16.1 In all cases except those involving minor offences, before the competent authority renders a final disposition prior to sentencing, the background and circumstances in which the juvenile is living or the conditions under which the offence has been committed shall be properly investigated so as to facilitate judicious adjudication of the case by the competent authority.

*Commentary.* Social inquiry reports (social reports or presentence reports) are an indispensable aid in most legal proceedings involving juveniles. The competent authority should be informed of relevant facts about the juvenile, such as social and family background, school career, educational experiences, etc. For this purpose, some jurisdictions use special social services or personnel attached to the court or board. Other personnel, including probation officers, may serve the same function. The rule therefore requires that adequate social services should be available to deliver social inquiry reports of a qualified nature.

### 17. Guiding Principles in Adjudication and Disposition

17.1 The disposition of the competent authority shall be guided by the following principles:

(a) The reaction taken shall always be in proportion not only to the circumstances and the gravity of the offence but also to the circumstances and the needs of the juvenile as well as to the needs of the society;

(b) Restrictions on the personal liberty of the juvenile shall be imposed only after careful consideration and shall be limited to the possible minimum;

(c) Deprivation of personal liberty shall not be imposed unless the juvenile is adjudicated of a serious act involving violence against another person or of persistence in committing other serious offences and unless there is no other appropriate response;

(d) The well-being of the juvenile shall be the guiding factor in the consideration of her or his case.

17.2 Capital punishment shall not be imposed for any crime committed by juveniles.

17.3 Juveniles shall not be subject to corporal punishment.

17.4 The competent authority shall have the power to discontinue the proceedings at any time.

*Commentary.* The main difficulty in formulating guidelines for the adjudication of young persons stems from the fact that there are unresolved conflicts of a philosophical nature, such as the following:

(a) Rehabilitation versus just desert;

(b) Assistance versus repression and punishment;

(c) Reaction according to the singular merits of an individual case versus reaction according to the protection of society in general;

(d) General deterrence versus individual incapacitation.

The conflict between these approaches is more pronounced in juvenile cases than in adult cases. With the variety of causes and reactions characterizing juvenile cases, these alternatives become intricately interwoven.

It is not the function of Standard Minimum Rules for the Administration of Juvenile Justice to prescribe which approach is to be followed but rather to identify one that is most closely in consonance with internationally accepted principles. Therefore, the essential elements as laid down in rule 17.1, in particular in subparagraphs (a) and (c), are mainly to be understood as practical guidelines that should ensure a common starting point; if heeded by the concerned authorities (see also rule 5), they could contribute considerably to ensuring that the fundamental rights of juvenile offenders are protected, especially the fundamental rights of personal development and education.

Rule 17.1 (b) implies that strictly punitive approaches are not appropriate. Whereas in adult cases, and possibly also in cases of severe offences by juveniles, just desert and retributive sanctions might be considered to have some merit, in juvenile cases such considerations should always be outweighed by the interest of safeguarding the well-being and the future of the young person.

In line with resolution 8 of the Sixth United Nations Congress, it encourages the use of alternatives to institutionalization to the maximum extent possible, bearing in mind the need to respond to the specific requirements of the young. Thus, full use should be made of the range of existing alternative sanctions and new alternative sanctions should be developed, bearing the public safety in mind. Probation should be granted to the greatest possible extent via suspended sentences, conditional sentences, board orders and other dispositions.

Rule 17.1 (c) corresponds to one of the guiding principles in resolution 4 of the Sixth Congress which aims at avoiding incarceration in the case of juveniles unless there is no other appropriate response that will protect the public safety.

The provision prohibiting capital punishment in rule 17.2 is in accordance with article 6, paragraph 5, of the International Covenant on Civil and Political Rights.

The provision against corporal punishment is in line with article 7 of the International Covenant on Civil and Political Rights and the Declaration on the Protection of All Persons from Being Subjected to Torture and Other Cruel, Inhuman or Degrading Treatment or Punishment as well as the Convention against Torture and Other Cruel, Inhuman or Degrading Treatment or Punishment and the draft convention on the rights of the child.

The power to discontinue the proceedings at any time (rule 17.4) is a characteristic inherent in the handling of juvenile offenders as opposed to adults. At any time, circumstances may become known to the competent authority which would make a complete cessation of the intervention appear to be the best disposition of the case.

### 18. Various Disposition Measures

18.1 A large variety of disposition measures shall be made available to the competent authority, allowing for flexibility so as to avoid institutionalization to the greatest extent possible. Such measures, some of which may be combined, include:

(a) Care, guidance and supervision orders;

(b) Probation;

(c) Community service orders;

(d) Financial penalties, compensation and restitution;

(e) Intermediate treatment and other treatment orders;

(f) Orders to participate in group counselling and similar activities;

(g) Orders concerning foster care, living communities or other educational settings;

(h) Other relevant orders.

18.2 No juvenile shall be removed from parental supervision, whether partly or entirely, unless the circumstances of her or his case make this necessary.

*Commentary.* Rule 18.1 attempts to enumerate some of the important reactions and sanctions that have been practised and proved successful thus far, in different legal systems. On the whole they represent promising options that deserve replication and further development. The rule does not enumerate staffing requirements because of possible shortages of adequate staff in some regions; in those regions measures requiring less staff may be tried or developed.

The examples given in rule 18.1 have in common, above all, a reliance on and an appeal to the community for the effective implementation of alternative dispositions. Community-based correction is a traditional measure that has taken on many aspects. On that basis, relevant authorities should be encouraged to offer community-based services.

Rule 18.2 points to the importance of the family which, according to article 10, paragraph 1, of the International Covenant on Economic, Social and Cultural Rights, is "the natural and fundamental group unit of society". Within the family, the parents have not only the right but also the responsibility to care for and supervise their children. Rule 18.2, therefore, requires that the separation of children from their parents is a measure of last resort. It may be resorted to only when the facts of the case clearly warrant this grave step (for example, child abuse).

### 19. Least Possible Use of Institutionalization

19.1 The placement of a juvenile in an institution shall always be a disposition of last resort and for the minimum necessary period.

*Commentary.* Progressive criminology advocates the use of non-institutional over institutional treatment. Little or no difference has been found in terms of the success of institutionalization as compared to non-institutionalization. The many adverse influences on an individual that seem unavoidable within any institutional setting evidently cannot be outbalanced by treatment efforts. This is especially the case for juveniles, who are vulnerable to negative influences. Moreover, the negative effects, not only of loss of liberty but also of separation from the usual social environment, are certainly more acute for juveniles than for adults because of their early stage of development.

Rule 19 aims at restricting institutionalization in two regards: in quantity ("last resort") and in time ("minimum necessary period"). Rule 19 reflects one of the basic guiding principles of resolution 4 of the Sixth United Nations Congress: a juvenile offender should not be incarcerated unless there is no other appropriate response. The rule, therefore, makes the appeal that if a juvenile must be institutionalized, the loss of liberty should be restricted to the least possible degree, with special institutional arrangements for confinement and bearing in mind the differences in kinds of offenders, offences and institutions. In fact, priority should be given to "open" over "closed" institutions. Furthermore, any facility should be of a correctional or educational rather than of a prison type.

### 20. Avoidance of Unnecessary Delay

20.1 Each case shall from the outset be handled expeditiously, without any unnecessary delay.

*Commentary.* The speedy conduct of formal procedures in juvenile cases is a paramount concern. Otherwise, whatever good may be achieved by the procedure and the disposition is at risk. As time passes, the juvenile will find it increasingly difficult, if not impossible, to relate the procedure and disposition to the offence, both intellectually and psychologically.

### 21. Records

21.1 Records of juvenile offenders shall be kept strictly confidential and closed to third parties. Access to such records shall be limited to persons directly concerned with the disposition of the case at hand or other duly authorized persons.

21.2 Records of juvenile offenders shall not be used in adult proceedings in subsequent cases involving the same offender.

*Commentary.* The rule attempts to achieve a balance between conflicting interests connected with records or files: those of the police, prosecution and other authorities in improving control versus the interests of the juvenile offender.

(See also rule 8.) "Other duly authorized persons" would generally include, among others, researchers.

## 22. Need for Professionalism and Training

22.1 Professional education, in-service training, refresher courses and other appropriate modes of instruction shall be utilized to establish and maintain the necessary professional competence of all personnel dealing with juvenile cases.

22.2 Juvenile justice personnel shall reflect the diversity of juveniles who come into contact with the juvenile justice system. Efforts shall be made to ensure the fair representation of women and minorities in juvenile justice agencies.

*Commentary.* The authorities competent for disposition may be persons with very different backgrounds (magistrates in the United Kingdom of Great Britain and Northern Ireland and in regions influenced by the common law system; legally trained judges in countries using Roman law and in regions influenced by them; and elsewhere elected or appointed laymen or jurists, members of community-based boards, etc.). For all these authorities, a minimum training in law, sociology, psychology, criminology and behavioural sciences would be required. This is considered as important as the organizational specialization and independence of the competent authority.

For social workers and probation officers, it might not be feasible to require professional specialization as a prerequisite for taking over any function dealing with juvenile offenders. Thus, professional on-the-job instruction would be minimum qualifications.

Professional qualifications are an essential element in ensuring the impartial and effective administration of juvenile justice. Accordingly, it is necessary to improve the recruitment, advancement and professional training of personnel and to provide them with the necessary means to enable them to properly fulfil their functions.

All political, social, sexual, racial, religious, cultural or any other kind of discrimination in the selection, appointment and advancement of juvenile justice personnel should be avoided in order to achieve impartiality in the administration of juvenile justice. This was recommended by the Sixth United Nations Congress. Furthermore, the Sixth Congress called on Member States to ensure the fair and equal treatment for women as criminal justice personnel and recommended that special measures should be taken to recruit, train and facilitate the advancement of female personnel in juvenile justice administration.

## Part Four. Non-institutional Treatment

## 23. Effective Implementation of Disposition

23.1 Appropriate provisions shall be made for the implementation of orders of the competent authority, as referred to in rule 14.1 above, by that authority itself or by some other authority as circumstances may require.

23.2 Such provisions shall include the power to modify the orders as the competent authority may deem necessary from time to time, provided that such modification shall be determined in accordance with the principles contained in these Rules.

*Commentary.* Disposition in juvenile cases, more so than in adult cases, tends to influence the offender's life for a long period of time. Thus, it is important that the competent authority or an independent body (parole board, probation office, youth welfare institutions or others) with qualifications equal to those of the competent authority that originally disposed of the case should monitor the implementation of the disposition. In some countries a *juge d'exécution des peines* has been installed for this purpose.

The composition, powers and functions of the authority must be flexible; they are described in general terms in rule 23 in order to ensure wide acceptability.

## 24. Provision of Needed Assistance

24.1 Efforts shall be made to provide juveniles, at all stages of the proceedings, with necessary assistance such as lodging, education or vocational training, employment or any other assistance, helpful and practical, in order to facilitate the rehabilitative process.

*Commentary.* The promotion of the well-being of the juvenile is of paramount consideration. Thus, rule 24 emphasizes the importance of providing requisite facilities, services and other necessary assistance as may further the best interests of the juvenile throughout the rehabilitative process.

## 25. Mobilization of Volunteers and Other Community Services

25.1 Volunteers, voluntary organizations, local institutions and other community resources shall be called upon to contribute effectively to the rehabilitation of the juvenile in a community setting and, as far as possible, within the family unit.

*Commentary.* This rule reflects the need for a rehabilitative orientation of all work with juvenile offenders. Co-operation with the community is indispensable if the directives of the competent authority are to be carried out effectively. Volunteers and voluntary services, in particular, have proved to be valuable resources but are at present underutilized. In some instances, the co-operation of ex-offenders (including ex-addicts) can be of considerable assistance.

Rule 25 emanates from the principles laid down in rules 1.1 to 1.6 and follows the relevant provisions of the International Covenant on Civil and Political Rights.

## Part Five. Institutional Treatment

## 26. Objectives of Institutional Treatment

26.1 The objective of training and treatment of juveniles placed in institutions is to provide care, protection, education and vocational skills, with a view to assisting them to assume socially constructive and productive roles in society.

26.2 Juveniles in institutions shall receive care, protection and all necessary assistance—social, educational, vocational, psychological, medical and physical—that they may require because of their age, sex and personality and in the interest of their wholesome development.

26.3 Juveniles in institutions shall be kept separate from adults and shall be detained in a separate institution or in a separate part of an institution also holding adults.

26.4 Young female offenders placed in an institution deserve special attention as to their personal needs and problems. They shall by no means receive less care, protection, assistance, treatment and training than young male offenders. Their fair treatment shall be ensured.

26.5 In the interest and well-being of the institutionalized juvenile, the parents or guardians shall have a right of access.

26.6 Inter-ministerial and inter-departmental co-operation shall be fostered for the purpose of providing adequate academic or, as appropriate, vocational training to institutionalized juveniles, with a view to ensuring that they do not leave the institution at an educational disadvantage.

*Commentary.* The objectives of institutional treatment as stipulated in rules 26.1 and 26.2 would be acceptable to any system and culture. However, they have not yet been attained everywhere, and much more has to be done in this respect.

Medical and psychological assistance, in particular, are extremely important for institutionalized drug addicts, violent and mentally ill young persons.

The avoidance of negative influences through adult offenders and the safeguarding of the well-being of juveniles in an institutional setting, as stipulated in rule 26.3, are in line with one of the basic guiding principles of the Rules, as set out by the Sixth Congress in its resolution 4. The rule does not prevent States from taking other measures against the negative influences of adult offenders, which are at least as effective as the measures mentioned in the rule. (See also rule 13.4.)

Rule 26.4 addresses the fact that female offenders normally receive less attention than their male counterparts, as pointed out by the Sixth Congress. In particular, resolution 9 of the Sixth Congress calls for the fair treatment of female offenders at every stage of criminal justice processes and for special attention to their particular problems and needs while in custody. Moreover, this rule should also be considered in the light of the Caracas Declaration of the Sixth Congress, which, *inter alia,* calls for equal treatment in criminal justice administration, and against the background of the Declaration on the Elimination of Discrimination against Women and the Convention on the Elimination of All Forms of Discrimination against Women.

The right of access (rule 26.5) follows from the provisions of rules 7.1, 10.1, 15.2 and 18.2. Inter-ministerial and inter-departmental co-operation (rule 26.6) are of particular importance in the interest of generally enhancing the quality of institutional treatment and training.

## 27. Application of the Standard Minimum Rules for the Treatment of Prisoners Adopted by the United Nations

27.1 The Standard Minimum Rules for the Treatment of Prisoners and related recommendations shall be applicable as far as relevant to the treatment of juvenile offenders in institutions, including those in detention pending adjudication.

27.2 Efforts shall be made to implement the relevant principles laid down in the Standard Minimum Rules for the Treatment of Prisoners to the largest possible extent so as to meet the varying needs of juveniles specific to their age, sex and personality.

*Commentary.* The Standard Minimum Rules for the Treatment of Prisoners were among the first instruments of this kind to be promulgated by the United Nations. It is generally agreed that they have had a world-wide impact. Although there are still countries where implementation is more an aspiration than a fact, those Standard Minimum Rules continue to be an important influence in the humane and equitable administration of correctional institutions.

Some essential protections covering juvenile offenders in institutions are contained in the Standard Minimum Rules for the Treatment of Prisoners (accommodation, architecture, bedding, clothing, complaints and requests, contact with the outside world, food, medical care, religious service, separation of ages, staffing, work, etc.) as are provisions concerning punishment and discipline, and restraint for dangerous offenders. It would not be appropriate to modify those Standard Minimum Rules according to the particular characteristics of institutions for juvenile offenders within the scope of the Standard Minimum Rules for the Administration of Juvenile Justice.

Rule 27 focuses on the necessary requirements for juveniles in institutions (rule 27.1) as well as on the varying needs specific to their age, sex and personality (rule 27.2). Thus, the objectives and content of the rule interrelates to the relevant provisions of the Standard Minimum Rules for the Treatment of Prisoners.

## 28. Frequent and Early Recourse to Conditional Release

28.1 Conditional release from an institution shall be used by the appropriate authority to the greatest possible extent, and shall be granted at the earliest possible time.

28.2 Juveniles released conditionally from an institution shall be assisted and supervised by an appropriate authority and shall receive full support by the community.

*Commentary.* The power to order conditional release may rest with the competent authority, as mentioned in rule 14.1, or with some other authority. In view of this, it is adequate to refer here to the "appropriate" rather than to the "competent" authority.

Circumstances permitting, conditional release shall be preferred to serving a full sentence. Upon evidence of satisfactory progress towards rehabilitation, even offenders who had been deemed dangerous at the time of their institutionalization can be conditionally released whenever feasible. Like probation, such release may be conditional on the satisfactory fulfilment of the requirements specified by the relevant authorities for a period of time established in the decision, for example, relating to "good behaviour" of the offender, attendance in community programmes, residence in half-way houses, etc.

In the case of offenders conditionally released from an institution, assistance and supervision by a probation or other officer (particularly where probation has not yet been adopted) should be provided and community support should be encouraged.

## 29. Semi-Institutional Arrangements

29.1 Efforts shall be made to provide semi-institutional arrangements, such as half-way houses, educational homes, day-time training centres and other such appropriate arrangements that may assist juveniles in their proper reintegration into society.

*Commentary.* The importance of care following a period of institutionalization should not be underestimated. This rule emphasizes the necessity of forming a net of semi-institutional arrangements.

This rule also emphasized the need for a diverse range of facilities and services designed to meet the different needs of young offenders re-entering the community and to provide guidance and structural support as an important step towards successful reintegration into society.

**Part Six. Research, Planning,
Policy Formulation and Evaluation**

**30. Research as a Basis for Planning,
Policy Formulation and Evaluation**

30.1 Efforts shall be made to organize and promote necessary research as a basis for effective planning and policy formulation.

30.2 Efforts shall be made to review and appraise periodically the trends, problems and causes of juvenile delinquency and crime as well as the varying particular needs of juveniles in custody.

30.3 Efforts shall be made to establish a regular evaluative research mechanism built into the systems of juvenile justice administration and to collect and analyse relevant data and information for appropriate assessment and future improvement and reform of the administration.

30.4 The delivery of services in juvenile justice administration shall be systematically planned and implemented as an integral part of national development efforts.

*Commentary.* The utilization of research as a basis for an informed juvenile justice policy is widely acknowledged as an important mechanism for keeping practices abreast of advances in knowledge and the continuing development and improvement of the juvenile justice system. The mutual feedback between research and policy is especially important in juvenile justice. The mutual and often drastic changes in the life-styles of the young and in the forms and dimensions of juvenile crime, the societal and justice responses to juvenile crime and delinquency quickly become outmoded and inadequate.

Rule 30 thus establishes standards for integrating research into the process of policy formulation and application in juvenile justice administration. The rule draws particular attention to the need for regular review and evaluation of existing programmes and measures and for planning within the broader context of overall development objectives.

A constant appraisal of the needs of juveniles, as well as the trends and problems of delinquency, is a prerequisite for improving the methods of formulating appropriate policies and establishing adequate interventions, at both formal and informal levels. In this context, research by independent persons and bodies should be facilitated by responsible agencies, and it may be valuable to obtain and to take into account the views of juveniles themselves, not only those who come into contact with the system.

The process of planning must particularly emphasize a more effective and equitable system for the delivery of necessary services. Towards that end, there should be a comprehensive and regular assessment of the wide-ranging, particular needs and problems of juveniles and an identification of clear-cut priorities. In that connection, there should also be a co-ordination in the use of existing resources, including alternatives and community support that wouldbe suitable in setting up specific procedures designed to implement and monitor established programmes.

The Report of the Secretary-General pursuant to Commission on Human Rights resolution 1993/80 (E/CN.4/1995/100) contained the following:

**Recommendations**

**Standard Setting and Implementation**

*Measures of general application.* We call upon all States which have not yet done so to ratify the Convention on the Rights of the Child and ensure its effective implementation.

We urge States to fully reflect the principles and provisions of the Convention on the Rights of the Child, the United Nations Guidelines for the Prevention of Juvenile Delinquency (the Riyadh Guidelines), the United Nations Standard Minimum Rules for the Administration of Juvenile Justice (the Beijing Rules) and the United Nations Rules for the Protection of Juveniles Deprived of their Liberty in their national legislation and practice, in particular by establishing a child-oriented juvenile justice system, whether criminal, civil or other, which guarantees the rights of children and promotes their sense of dignity and worth, fully respects their age and their right to fully participate in and contribute to society.

We request all States to make the provisions of these instruments widely known to children in child-accessible language, and to adults and professional groups working with and for children.

We recognize the importance of a comprehensive national approach in the area of juvenile justice respecting the interdependence and indivisibility of all of the rights of the child.

We call on States to integrate into the school curricula, particularly at the primary school level, education on the Convention on the Rights of the Child. We further suggest that awareness be raised by other appropriate means, including the provision of information by campaigns on the rights of the child. We request all States to accord priority to the effective training of all those involved in the field of juvenile justice.

We urge States to guarantee those rights and to give the highest priority to the prevention of the violation of the rights of the child, including those arising in the area of juvenile justice. To this end the child should be clearly recognized as an active and responsible participant in society.

We urge States to adopt all necessary measures to ensure the non-derogability of fundamental children's rights and freedoms, including the freedom from discrimination; the right to life; the freedom from torture or other cruel, inhuman or degrading treatment or punishment; the freedom from any form of slavery or exploitation; the freedom of thought, conscience and religion; the right to be recognized as a person before the law; the right to be protected against retroactive penal laws; and the right to full benefit of all legal safeguards in the juvenile system as recognized in all relevant international instruments.

We recommend that States give serious consideration to the establishment of an independent mechanism, such as an ombudsperson, to ensure that the rights and best interests of the child are upheld in the light of existing international standards.

As a measure towards improving quality of life and to ensure greater social justice for all as a protection against exploitation, elimination of poverty must be addressed with a sustained strategy, both in national and international settings. States as well as international organizations such as the World Bank and the International Monetary Fund should reappraise development policies and programmes to integrate child development and protection more concretely into their implementation and to ensure greater equity, income distribution and resource allocation, including land reform and budget restructuring for needy children and their families. "Child impact assessment" indicators and tests should be incorporated into all international, national and local development programmes.

*Specific targets.* We call upon all States to translate into practice, by the year 2000, the Beijing Rules, the Riyadh Guidelines and the United Nations Rules for the Protection of Juveniles Deprived of their Liberty.

We request all States to ensure that the Convention on the Rights of the Child, the Riyadh Guidelines, the Beijing Rules and the United Nations Rules for the Protection of Juveniles Deprived of their Liberty are translated into all national and ethnic languages, and are widely disseminated in respective national territories by the year 2000.

We urge States to ensure that all judges, lawyers, prosecutors, social workers and other professionals concerned with juvenile justice matters receive human rights and juvenile justice training by the year 2000.

We further urge States to incorporate the Convention on the Rights of the Child as well as international juvenile justice instruments as an integral part of all police training at least by the year 2000. Given that children's rights should be guaranteed to every child under the entire jurisdiction of the State, we see particular need for immigration officers to also receive such training by the year 2000.

### Coordination and Technical Cooperation

We urge that the field of juvenile justice be given priority within the United Nations system-wide action, in particular by the Commission on Crime Prevention and Criminal Justice and the Commission on Human Rights, the Committee on the Rights of the Child and UNICEF.

In this regard, we recognize the urgent need for close cooperation between all bodies and mechanisms concerned with this field, including the Committee on the Rights of the Child, the Crime Prevention and Criminal Justice Branch, the Centre for Human Rights and UNICEF. Such cooperation should be strengthened particularly with regard to research, dissemination of information, training, implementation and monitoring of existing standards, as well as in the provision of technical assistance programmes.

The effective implementation of international standards in technical cooperation and advisory services programmes should be ensured by giving particular attention to the following aspects related to protecting and promoting human rights of juveniles in detention, strengthening the rule of law and improving the administration of the juvenile justice system:

(a) Strengthening national capacities and infrastructures;

(b) Training programmes for judges, prosecutors, lawyers, administrators, social workers and other professionals dealing with juvenile justice;

(c) Training programmes for law enforcement officials.

In the elaboration of such programmes, the Centre for Human Rights and the Crime Prevention and Criminal Justice Branch should take into consideration the recommendations of relevant bodies of the United Nations system, in particular those of the Committee on the Rights of the Child, and take them into account in the execution of these programmes as well as in appropriate follow-up activities.

In accordance with his mandate, the High Commissioner for Human Rights, in close cooperation with the Crime Prevention and Criminal Justice Branch, the Committee on the Rights of the Child and UNICEF, should develop strategies in order to ensure effective coordination of the respective technical cooperation programmes in the field of juvenile justice.

Projects under these programmes should be executed on the basis of needs assessments and should include appropri-

ate evaluation and follow-up procedures, preferably by methods of accompanying action research, with the participation of children. Regional institutes, UNICEF and other relevant bodies as well as national institutions and non-governmental organizations should be an integral part of these activities.

We stress the importance of adequate financial and human resources for such programmes. In this context, we underline the need of adequate preparation of the missions of the United Nations Interregional Advisers in crime prevention and criminal justice through needs assessment missions as well as through appropriate follow-up for comprehensive projects.

We recommend that the United Nations crime prevention and criminal justice programme publish and widely distribute a manual on standards of juvenile justice as a matter of priority, in cooperation with the Centre for Human Rights and UNICEF, and that adequate funding be provided for this purpose.

In view of the need to strengthen the monitoring capacity of the United Nations system in the field of juvenile justice, we urge States parties to the Convention on the Rights of the Child to provide in their periodic reports to the Committee comprehensive information on the implementation of the provisions of the Convention and related United Nations standards adopted in this field, in particular the Riyadh Guidelines, the Beijing Rules and the United Nations Rules for the Protection of Juveniles Deprived of their Liberty.

Furthermore, appreciating the establishment of a working group to monitor the application of United Nations norms and standards in crime prevention and criminal justice, we urge the Commission on Crime Prevention and Criminal Justice to introduce juvenile justice standards into the process of information gathering and to request States to submit information to the sixth session of that Commission on the way such United Nations norms and standards are effectively implemented at the national level, the difficulties encountered and the solutions envisaged to remedy the existing shortcomings.

We urge that due attention be paid to a periodic exchange of all of the information gathered between all those United Nations bodies concerned, always maintaining close cooperation with non-governmental organizations and other relevant entities.

### Children and Juveniles Deprived of their Liberty

We call upon the Commission on Crime Prevention and Criminal Justice, the Commission on Human Rights, through its relevant mechanisms, and the Committee on the Rights of the Child to organize joint periodic missions to visit facilities where juveniles are deprived of their liberty or otherwise restricted. In this regard, we invite the Secretary-General to provide the necessary means to effectively organize and carry out such missions, as well as to ensure an appropriate follow-up to them.

We urge States to ensure easy access by relatives, non-governmental organizations and interested individuals to facilities where juveniles are deprived of their liberty or otherwise restricted, in order to maintain a link between the detained juvenile and his or her family and community, to facilitate his or her social reintegration and to allow for monitoring and reporting on the conditions in these facilities. We urge States to allow independent monitoring bodies access to such facilities.

We call upon States, intergovernmental and non-governmental organizations to raise awareness of situations for juveniles deprived of their liberty and, in particular, on the high rate of juveniles on remand and the length of periods for which they are held in custody. In addition, the conditions under which juveniles are deprived of their liberty need to be highlighted with emphasis on, inter alia, overcrowding, lack of programmes for useful activities and exercise, the frequency of physical and sexual assault and the corresponding risk of HIV infection.

In order to ensure greater compliance with international standards concerning the rights of children, States are urged to take, inter alia, the following measures:

(a) Ensuring that legislation concerning the age of criminal responsibility, civil majority and consent does not have the effect of depriving any child of the full enjoyment of the rights recognized by the Convention on the Rights of the Child;

(b) Giving priority to setting up agencies and programmes to provide free legal and other assistance to children, and in particular, to ensure that the right of every child to automatically receive such assistance from the moment of arrest is respected in practice;

(c) Taking appropriate steps to make available throughout the country a broad range of alternative measures in order to ensure compliance with the principle that deprivation of liberty should only be used as a measure of last resort, both before trial and after conviction;

(d) Recognizing that the best interests of the child must be a primary consideration in all decisions and that any deprivation of liberty should be for the shortest appropriate period of time, indeterminate sentences should never be applicable to persons below the age of 18 and children should never be kept in closed institutions under a welfare pretext;

(e) Prohibiting legislation from allowing the application of the death penalty or life imprisonment to persons under the age of 18 at the time of the commission of the offence.

We urge States to adopt all necessary measures to prevent, forbid and eliminate the use of corporal punishment against children. In the light of existing international standards, we reaffirm that States should establish mechanisms to ensure a prompt, thorough and impartial investigation into allegations against public officials of violation of the fundamental rights and freedoms of children and to ensure that the findings of any such investigation are made public without delay and that those found responsible are duly punished.

We call on States to allow access through the judicial system to fair and adequate compensation for all child victims of violations of human rights, including torture and other cruel, inhuman or degrading treatment or punishment, unlawful or arbitrary deprivation of liberty, unjustifiable detention and miscarriage of justice. Necessary legal representation to bring an action within an appropriate court should be provided at State expense.

In all cases of deprivation of the liberty of a child, human rights and legal safeguards recognized by the Convention on the Rights of the Child and other relevant United Nations standards should be fully applied within the legal framework, including those elements relating to immigration. In this regard, special attention should be paid to the situation of unaccompanied minors and others who are internationally displaced. The same principles should be reflected in the revised text of the 1961 Hague Convention on Protection of Minors which is currently under review. In accordance with the principles of deinstitutionalization and decriminalization, we urge States to examine these principles, giving particular attention to children in especially difficult circumstances.

## Instrumental Use of Children and Juveniles by Adults in and for Criminal Activities

We recommend that systematic research into the causes and effects of the phenomenon of the instrumental use of children in and for criminal activities be undertaken, for the purpose of providing policy and decision makers with profound information and guidance which will serve as the basis for the formulation of international and regional strategies and measures to prevent and control such practices. Such research should entail, inter alia, the delineation of topologies of criminal activities in which children are instrumentally used, and the collection, dissemination and exchange of relevant information through electronic networking, including laws, policies, programmes and practices and successful pilot and demonstration projects.

The training of law enforcement and other justice personnel, as well as policy makers, should seek to sensitize these professionals to those situations of social risk which cause children to be manipulated by adults to engage in criminal activities.

The non-governmental sector active in the field of children's rights should receive every encouragement, both at the national and the international level, in their public awareness-raising campaigns and in their efforts to provide direct services or access to communities and social services for exploited children.

The mass media must be invited to engage in public awareness-raising activities to sensitize public opinion to the plight, special circumstances and vulnerability of children used as instruments of crime. At the same time, the mass media should be encouraged not to depict crime and violence as adventure, but to portray it in a responsible, serious manner.

Initiatives such as the provision of telephone hotlines, safe houses and emergency houses should be encouraged and made easily accessible to children.

We recommend that States should give greater attention to the development of educational programmes, to increase the accessibility of children, especially disadvantaged children, to educational facilities, including non-formal and part-time education. States should also establish innovative incentives to decrease school drop-out rates through assistance for families in need, such as the provision of free meals and textbooks and instruction in minority languages.

States should establish and promote adult education programmes to teach parents about the value of education, including education on child rights, and to encourage parental support for their children's education. States should establish and support education programmes for children to promote in them a respect for human rights and the rule of law.

We urge States to establish qualitative and quantitative indicators to monitor the exploitation of children and their instrumental use in and for criminal activities.

Recognizing that a root cause of the instrumental use of children in and for criminal activities is adult criminality, communities should be mobilized to protect children through "community watch" programmes. At the same time, States should pay particular attention to ensuring that such community-based measures conform to the rule of law, and establish safeguards to this effect.

We urge States and national and international organizations to initiate a pro-child-anti-crime network with INTERPOL, national police, immigration and law enforcement agencies, and community groups to guard against the instrumental use of children in and for criminal activities. In order to promote a rapid and effective communication as well as to promote consistent vigilance and relevant action, each entity in this network should have a focal point dealing with the exploitation of children in child prostitution and child pornography.

States and national and international organizations should highlight the responsibility of both the organizer and customer in child exploitation through national and international campaigns. This implies, in particular, a call to incriminate customers of child victims of prostitution and those who make, distribute or possess child pornography.

### Exploitation of Children

With regard to the exploitation of children by adults, we call upon all Governments to ensure, if they have not already done so, that all international norms and standards designed to protect the child against such abuses are thoroughly reflected in regional, national and local legislation and practice. We call upon the judiciary and law enforcement agencies to ensure, as a matter of strengthening the rule of law, that such legislation is consistently applied.

We urge States to enforce their laws relating to exploitation of children, including trafficking in and sexual exploitation of children and exploitation of child labour. In particular, we urge States to apply due diligence to prevent and investigate such acts of exploitation against children and to ensure that appropriate sanctions are applied against the adults who exploit the children, rather than against the children who are victims of such crimes.

We urge States, supported by the United Nations interregional, regional and affiliated institutes, to develop multidisciplinary training, education and information activities for law enforcement and other criminal justice personnel, as well as for those in other relevant professions such as health care and early childhood and primary education, on the sexual exploitation of children including the activities of paedophiles and paedophile networks.

We urge States, in the absence of existing laws, to adopt legislation to punish and redress the wrongs caused to children who are exploited, including making trafficking in children and sexual exploitation of children outside the country by nationals and permanent residents offences.

The United Nations should develop a Code of Conduct on Child Rights for United Nations Peace-keeping Operations to prevent United Nations personnel from becoming involved in child exploitation, and this should become an integral and necessary element of training for all such personnel before embarking on any mission.

We request States to establish legal, administrative and institutional measures to combat sex tourism. We encourage the World Tourism Organization, the Centre for Human Rights, the Crime Prevention and Criminal Justice Branch and UNICEF to cooperate more closely on the establishment of a network which aims at the identification and elimination of all forms of sex tourism. The WTO in particular is encouraged to continue its efforts to combat organized sex tourism by different activities, especially by adopting the draft declaration on organized sex tourism. Its members are urged to respect this declaration, and to assist the WTO in its relevant activities.

States should encourage exchange programmes between law enforcement personnel and other bilateral exchanges to deal with transnational trafficking in children. Such programmes might, for example, also entail the stationing of police personnel of one country in other countries to track nationals of the former where they may be a threat to the children of the latter. Such cooperation may be facilitated by the increased exchange of information, such as lists of known paedophiles and crime-linked data, in conformity with data protection legislation. Close cooperation with regard to transnational activities of these networks needs to be established or fostered between Member States in order to establish an international tracking mechanism.

We urge States to ensure that children who have been sexually exploited or who are at risk of being sexually exploited have access to assistance that meets their needs, including access to the mechanisms of justice such as legal aid, adequate and safe housing, support services, economic assistance, counselling and health and social services to promote their safety, social reintegration and physical and psychological recovery. Special assistance should be given to those children who are suffering from HIV/AIDS and should include measures to protect them against discrimination and other harm. Emphasis should be placed upon family-based and community-based rehabilitation rather than institutionalization.

Where children are trafficked across frontiers, States, national and international organizations should ensure that the true age of the children is ascertained by independent and objective assessment, preferably with the cooperation of the non-governmental sector. This depends, in part, upon effective birth registration of all children in their country of origin. If they are to be returned to the country of origin, their safety must be guaranteed by independent monitoring and follow-up. Pending their return to the country of origin, they should not be treated as illegal migrants by the receiving countries, but should be dealt with humanely as special cases of humanitarian concern. Upon the return of the children, the country of origin should treat them with respect and in accordance with the international human rights principles, backed up by adequate family-based rehabilitation measures.

National laws should explicitly prohibit the exploitation of children for organ transplants, bearing in mind the WHO Guiding Principles on this issue. States and national and international organizations should ensure effective monitoring of organ transplantation, in particular the role of the private sector and clinics, in order to prevent abuses. In this connection, the medical sector and related professional organizations should be mobilized to report on abuses.

States and national and international organizations should ensure public education, including measures aimed at children, on the dangers of child exploitation, in particular child prostitution and other manifestations of the instrumental use of children in and for criminal activities.

A central registry of all missing children should be established in every country, and transfrontier exchanges of information should be fostered to trace and monitor the cases concerned.

States and national and international organizations, including the private business sector, should be encouraged to prepare and adopt a "Business Code on Child Protection" as a basic standard for their conduct towards children in order to counter child abuse, neglect and exploitation. Peer pressure should be exerted on the members of the business community, including transnational corporations, to respect the rights of the child.

States and national and international organizations

should address the fact that legislation should be periodically reviewed to counter the use of new forms of technology for the purposes of child exploitation.

As the sale of children, child prostitution and child pornography are becoming increasingly transnational in character, States should expand extradition arrangements, mutual assistance agreements and other forms of inter-State cooperation to facilitate interchanges.

States and national and international organizations should foster changes to traditions which perpetuate child exploitation, not only through the enactment of legislation but also by educational measures and consciousness-raising.

**BIBLIOGRAPHY.** United Nations Centre for Social Development and Humanitarian Affairs. "Juvenile Justice in International Perspective—Special Double Volume," *International Review of Criminal Policy,* nos. 39–40 (1990). Special issue, in English.

United Nations Sub-Commission on Prevention of Discrimination and Protection of Minorities. *Application of International Standards concerning the Human Rights of Detained Juveniles: Report Prepared by the Special Rapporteur, Mrs. Mary Concepción Bautista, Pursuant to Sub-Commission Resolution 1990/21.* Geneva, Switzerland: 1991. IGO document, in English and French.

# K

## KAMPALA DECLARATION ON HUMAN RIGHTS (1993).

On 6 February 1993, the Asian-African Legal Consultative Committee, meeting for its 32nd session in Kampala, Uganda, adopted the Kampala Declaration of Human Rights. At the request of its Secretary-General, the Declaration was circulated as a document of the Preparatory Committee for the World Conference on Human Rights (A/CONF.157/PC/62/Add. 9).

In the Declaration, the Committee, an intergovernmental organization comprised of 43 Asian and African States, points out that the right to **DEVELOPMENT** is an inalienable right and calls upon all States to co-operate in "the essential task of eradicating poverty as an indispensable requirement for the universal realization of human rights."

The Asian-African Legal Consultative Committee
Having held its 32nd session in Kampala, Uganda, from 1–6 February 1993,
Recalling the provisions of the Charter of the United Nations and the Universal Declaration of Human Rights as well as other international instruments in the field of human rights;
Mindful of General Assembly resolution 45/155 of 18 December 1990, which *inter alia,* called for the convening of the World Conference on Human Rights in 1993,
Mindful also of General Assembly resolution 46/166 and appreciative of the work of the PREPCOM of the World Conference on Human Rights during the preceding sessions,
Bearing in mind the forthcoming final session of the PREPCOM preparing for the World Conference on Human Rights to be held in Vienna in June 1993,
Declares that
1. The Universal Declaration of Human Rights proclaims a common understanding of all the peoples of the world in the field of human rights and gives help, guidance, and inspiration to humanity in the promotion of human rights and fundamental freedoms.
2. Since the adoption of the Universal Declaration of Human Rights, the United Nations has through the adoption of various international instruments, made much progress in defining standards for the promotion, enjoyment, and protection of human rights and fundamental freedoms. It is an obligation of the members of the international community to ensure the observance of these rights and freedoms.
3. The International Covenant on Civil and Political Rights, the International Covenant on Economic, Social and Cultural Rights, the Declaration on the Granting of Independence to Colonial Countries and Peoples, the International Convention on the Elimination of All Forms of Racial Discrimination, Declaration on the Right to Development as well as other conventions, declarations, proclamations, decisions, principles, and resolutions in the field of human rights adopted under the auspices of the United Nations, the specialized agencies and regional intergovernmental organizations, have created new standards and obligations to which all countries should conform.
4. All States that have not yet ratified or acceded to the International Covenant on Civil and Political Rights, the International Covenant on Economic, Social and Cultural Rights, and other international human rights conventions should make every effort to do so.
5. It is the obligation of all members of the international community to ensure that the principles enshrined in the Charter of the United Nations and in other international human rights instruments are enforced. All Governments, organizations, and peoples should promote the universal respect and observance of human rights.
6. Peace and security are a prerequisite for the full realization of all inalienable and indivisible human rights. Efforts should be made to save present and future generations from the scourge of wars and armed conflicts, and to maintain international peace and security in accordance with the Charter of the United Nations.
7. The validity and universality of human rights, whether civil, political, economic, social, or cultural, is indispensable and these rights must be protected, upheld and promoted by all. To this end, all governments have a special duty to ensure that the constitutions and laws of their States that relate to human rights are in compliance with international human rights standards and are observed and respected.
8. The right to development is an inalienable human right. The vital importance of economic and social development to the full enjoyment of human rights should be further recognized and underscored. It is undoubted that the existence of widespread poverty is a main reason resulting in the insufficient enjoyment of human rights by the majority of humanity. Therefore, all states should cooperate in the essential task of eradicating poverty as an indispensable requirement for the universal realization of human rights.
9. Sustainable development and the environment are intrinsically linked and should not be considered in isolation from each other. Sustainable development cannot be merely an abstract concept and should be promoted and strengthened through the process of social and economic development. The human right to a clean and salubrious environment requires to be progressively developed and codified.
10. The principle of the indivisibility and interdependence of human rights has been recognized and must be given effect in policy formulation and implementation. Civil and political rights cannot be disassociated from economic, social, and cultural rights in their conception as well as uni-

versality and the satisfaction of economic, social, and cultural rights are a guarantee for the enjoyment of civil and political rights. None of these rights should be given precedence over the others.

11. The primary responsibility for implementing and giving effect to human rights is at the national level. Consequently, the most effective system or method of promoting and protecting these rights has to take into account the nation's history, culture, traditions, norms, and values. There is no single universally valid prescription model or system. While the international community should be concerned about the observance of these rights, it should not seek to impose or influence the adoption of their criteria and systems on developing countries. It should be sensitive to the unique aspects of each situation and establish impartiality and genuine concern on human rights problems by objective and acceptable factual analysis of events and situations.

12. The promotion and protection of the rights of vulnerable groups such as women, children, refugees, disabled, migrant workers, and minorities should be given special attention and priority.

13. The international community should devise effective action plans and concrete measures to overcome the current obstacles to the full realization of human rights, namely, threats to peace and security, foreign aggression and occupation, colonization, racism, racial discrimination, apartheid, terrorism, xenophobia, ethnic and religious intolerance and human rights abuse thereof, denial of justice, torture, unfair and unjust international economic order, widespread poverty and illiteracy, worsening economic situation of developing countries, and heavy burden of external debts.

14. The rule of law and the administration of justice in every country shall be inspired by the principles enshrined in the Universal Declaration of Human Rights and other international human rights instruments relating to the administration of justice.

15. The international community recognizes the importance of the rule of law, the independence of the judiciary, and the administration of justice in the development process. To this end, governments, regional and international financial institutions, and the donor community are called upon to give necessary financial resources and assistance to enable those entrusted with the administration of justice to carry out their tasks.

16. The international community affirms that training, equipment, and incentives should be provided to those State agencies involved in the administration of justice within the developing countries on the basis of their need and request. To this end, governments, regional, and international financial institutions and the donor community are urged to give the necessary resources.

17. The international community calls upon States to ensure that law enforcement officials shall, in the performance of their duties, respect and protect human dignity and maintain and uphold human rights of all persons in accordance with international standards enshrined in the Universal Declaration of Human Rights and international human rights instruments regarding arrest, prosecution, detention, imprisonment, protection against torture, cruel, inhuman, or degrading treatment or punishment.

18. Cooperation between national, regional, and international organizations in the field of human rights should be encouraged by all peoples of the world.

19. Nongovernmental organizations in the field of human rights have an important role in the promotion of human rights. Their ideals and activities could be mobilized into the process of universal realization of human rights.

20. Public awareness and concerns of human rights should be enhanced. Citizens should have appropriate access to information concerning their rights and the opportunity to participate in the decision-making process. States should encourage and facilitate public awareness and participation.

21. The United Nations system in the field of human rights is urged to use existing mechanisms and resources effectively and efficiently. The improvement of existing institutional mechanisms and the enhancement of their better cooperation and coordination should be undertaken. All members of the international community are called upon to contribute additional financial and other resources for human rights activities.

**KAZAKHSTAN.** The Republic of Kazakhstan, formerly the second largest Republic of the Soviet Union, is bordered by Russia to the north; Turkmenistan, Uzbekistan, and Kirghizia to the south; China to the east; and the Caspian Sea to the west. It declared its independence in 1991–the last of the former Soviet republics to do so—and was admitted to the United Nations in March 1992. It was a founding member of the Commonwealth of Independent States. Its population is estimated to be 17,190,000.

In 1916, a rebellion against Russian rule, which had lasted for over 200 years, was repressed with a loss of 150,000 lives. Civil war then broke out in Kazakhstan following the Bolshevik revolution in 1917, with Bolshevik forces finally overcoming the White Army. In 1920 the region became the Kyrgyz Autonomous Soviet Socialist Republic and in 1925, the Kazakh ASSR. The Kazakhstan ASSR became a full Union Republic of the USSR in 1936.

Deportees from other parts of the USSR to Kazakhstan, particularly during World War II, and the location of a nuclear test site, a space center and large industrial sites, increased the percentage of Russians from 20% in 1926 to 43% in 1959. They now comprise the largest ethnic group (37%) after the Kazakhs (43%). Kazakhs were converted to Islam in the early part of the 19th century and Muslims now comprise 47% of the population, with Russian Orthodox comprising 15%.

After independence, President Nursultan Nazarbayev was the only candidate in elections held on 1 December 1991. The first free multi-party elections were held in 1994, and Nazarbayev was re-elected as president. However, the election results were declared void, parliament was dissolved and Nazarbayev extended his term until the year 2000. A constitution, adopted in January 1993, provides for the equal status of all nationalities, the direct election every five years of both the president and the 177-member Supreme

Kenges (highest legislative body), and the State language of Kazakh. The president appoints the prime minister and most of the cabinet. The country has a civil legal system.

Main political parties include the People's Unity Party (PUP); Communist Party of Kazakhstan, which was suspended in 1991 and re-registered in 1994; the Kazakhstan Peasant's Union; the People's Congress Party of Kazakhstan; Republican Party—Azat; Republican Public Movement—Lad; and the Socialist Party of Kazakhstan.

**BIBLIOGRAPHY.** Helsinki Watch. *Conflict in the Soviet Union: The Untold Story of the Clashes in Kazakhstan.* New York: Human Rights Watch, 1990. NGO report, in English.

Human Rights Watch. "Kazakhstan," in *Human Rights Watch World Report 1995*, pp. 212–213. New York: 1995. NGO report, in English.

U.S. Department of Justice, Immigration and Naturalization Service, Resource Information Center. *Kazakhstan: Political Conditions in the Post-Soviet Era.* Washington, D.C.: 1994. Government briefing paper, in English.

## KELLOGG, FRANK BILLINGS (1865–1937).

Born in Potsdam, NY, USA, the self-educated Frank B. Kellogg received the 1929 **NOBEL PEACE PRIZE**—among numerous other international awards—for concluding the Pact of Paris (also known as the Kellogg-Briand Pact) in 1928, which outlawed war as an instrument of international policy.

An attorney from 1877–1916 (Kellogg read law himself, having no high-school diploma or college degree), Kellogg first gained national attention as one of several lawyers that President Theodore Roosevelt used to break up monopolies; Kellogg handled the prosecution of the Standard Oil Company in 1910–1911. Kellogg entered the political arena as the senator from Minnesota (1917–1923). After serving one year (1924) as the American ambassador to Great Britain, Kellogg was appointed secretary of state under President Calvin Coolidge (1925–1929). He ended his career as a judge on the Permanent Court of International Justice (1930–1935).

As secretary of state, Kellogg developed a reputation as a master arbitrator and had a profound effect on diplomatic relations in the American hemisphere (as was also the case with a later secretary of state and Nobel Prize winner, **CORDELL HULL**). During his tenure, he improved U.S. and Mexican relations, helped to settle a territorial dispute between Chile and Peru, and intervened in a revolution in Nicaragua. In all, Kellogg signed 80 treaties, including conciliation treaties with all Latin and South American countries, except Argentina, and with 15 countries outside the American hemisphere. He also concluded 19 arbitration treaties.

**BIBLIOGRAPHY.** Gray, Tony. *Champions of Peace.* London: Paddington Press, 1976.

Schlessinger, Bernard S., and June H. Schlessinger, eds. *Who's Who of Nobel Prize Winners.* Phoenix, AZ, USA: Oryx Press, 1991.

## KENNEDY (ROBERT F.) HUMAN RIGHTS AWARD.

Established in 1984 by the Robert F. Kennedy Memorial Center for Human Rights, this annual award honors individuals who have combated oppression at great personal risk and who advocate nonviolence.

An International Advisory Committee, comprised of more than 40 human rights advocates, including Archbishop **DESMOND TUTU**, José Alaquett, Carlos Fuentes, and Czeslaw Milosz, presents nominations to a panel of five American judges, who make the final selection. The judges are Rose Styron, chair of the Advisory Council of Amnesty International USA; Robert Bernstein, chair of **HUMAN RIGHTS WATCH**; Patt Derian, former U.S. Asst. Secretary of State for Human Rights; the Honorable A. Leon Higginbotham, Jr., chief judge emeritus of the U.S. Court of Appeals for the Third Circuit; and Burke Marshall, professor at Yale University Law School and former U.S. Asst. Attorney General for Human Rights.

Recent award honorees include Ren Wanding and Wei Jingsheng, imprisoned Chinese dissidents and democracy activists (1994); Bambang Widjojanto, an Indonesian Legal Aid Institute lawyer who defends the rights of the indigenous peoples of Indonesian-controlled Irian Jaya (1993); Chakufwa Chihana, Malawian trade unionist and human rights activist (1992); Avigdor Feldman, director of the Litigation Center for the Association of Civil Rights in Israel, and Raji Sourani, Gaza's foremost human rights lawyer (1991); and Amilcar Mendez Urizar, defender of the rights of Guatemala's indigenous people (1990).

For more information, contact: the R. F. Kennedy Memorial Center for Human Rights, 1206 30th Street, NW, Washington, D.C., 20007, USA. Telephone: (202) 333-1880. Fax: (202) 333-4903. E-mail: rfkmem@igc.apc.org

## KENYA.

The Republic of Kenya is a country in eastern Africa, on the Indian Ocean. It has borders with Ethiopia, Somalia, Sudan, Uganda, and Tanzania. It achieved independence from Great Britain in 1963 and became a member of the United Nations the same year. Its population is estimated to be 26,635,000. Ethnic groups include the Kikuyu (21%), Luhya (14%),

Luo (13%), Kalenjin (11%), Kamba (11%), Kisii (6%), and others (24%). Languages commonly used include Kiswahili (official), Bantu, Kikuyu, Luhya, Luo, and English. Religions practiced include Christianity (Roman Catholic, 28%; Protestant denominations, 28%), Islam (6%), and Animism (38%). Literacy is estimated at 50%.

The government (1990) took the form of a republic and member of the Commonwealth of Nations, of which the British monarch is the symbolic head. Under the 1963 constitution, the president is elected by popular vote in a general election in which suffrage is universal. He is head of State and government and commander-in-chief of the armed forces. Legislative functions are performed by the 171-member unicameral National Assembly, members of which are elected for terms of five years. The judicial system is modeled along British lines; however, Islamic courts exercise limited jurisdiction in matters of personal status where local populations are predominantly of that faith. The Kenyan African National Union is the only political party.

In August 1991, the opposition group the Forum for the Restoration of Democracy (FORD) was founded and immediately outlawed. It survived but split into two groups in 1992: Ford-Asili and Ford-Kenya.

International aid to Kenya was suspended from November 1991 to November 1993, to encourage political and economic reforms. In December 1991, the National Assembly approved constitutional amendments permitting a multi-party political system but in March 1992, the government banned all political rallies and placed restrictions on the press. Although the ban on political rallies was lifted, political strife continued until the first multi-party elections for president and the National Assembly were held on 29 December 1992 during which President Daniel T. Arap Moi was re-elected and sworn in for another five-year term.

Kenya's most serious human rights problem stems from the fact that its population growth rate—about 4.1% per year, estimated to be among the world's highest—is rapidly outstripping its food crop production. Widespread crop failures in 1979 and 1984, and increasing population of the land once available for agriculture, have signaled serious problems in this area and have made large-scale food imports necessary.

*REPORT ON ECONOMIC, SOCIAL, AND CULTURAL RIGHTS.* The UN COMMITTEE ON ECONOMIC, SOCIAL AND CULTURAL RIGHTS considered the state of implementation by Kenya of the rights contained in the INTERNATIONAL COVENANT ON ECONOMIC, SOCIAL AND CULTURAL RIGHTS, at the 4th and 19th meetings of

its eighth session, held on 17 and 27 May 1993, and adopted the following concluding observations on Kenya, which failed to report on its progress in these areas, at its 19th meeting, held on 27 May 1993 (paras. 4–23):

Kenya has been a party to the Covenant since 3 January 1976, the date of its entry into force. Since then, it has not submitted a single report. The Committee strongly urges the Government of Kenya to live up to its reporting obligations as soon as possible so that the Covenant on Economic, Social and Cultural Rights can be given full effect, for the benefit of the people of Kenya. The Committee emphasizes that it considers the non-performance by Kenya of its reporting obligations not only as a violation of the Covenant but also as a grave impediment in the way of an adequate application of the Covenant.

### Factors and Difficulties Impeding the Application of the Covenant

The Committee takes note of the fact that performance by Kenya of the obligations arising from the Covenant on Economic, Social and Cultural Rights cannot be evaluated without taking into consideration the political, economic and social conditions in which the country finds itself at present. Kenya is currently suffering severe political as well as economic turbulence. The transition from the one-party rule exercised by KANU to a truly democratic multi-party system seems to be underway, albeit slowly, and in the face of numerous obstacles set up by those in power. Frictions appear to be severe in all domains of public life, culminating in violent clashes among certain ethnic groups which have cost more than a thousand lives so far. Conditions are aggravated further by the influx of a large number of refugees and displaced persons as well as by the persistent drought in some parts of the country.

The Committee notes that, in the economic field, the international donor community, the World Bank and the International Monetary Fund in particular, are calling for a thorough liberalization of Kenya's economy and finances, a system hitherto marked by pervasive State interventionism. From the viewpoint of the Covenant and its interpretation by the Committee, any reform measures must be accompanied by the adoption of targeted programmes designed to protect specifically the vulnerable groups and members of society. As far as the Committee has been able to ascertain, the Government of Kenya has demonstrated very little awareness or willingness in this regard. A lack of financial resources is cited by way of justification for the comprehensive neglect of such protective measures. The reform process appears to be complicated and slowed down, by mismanagement as well as by a determination to maintain the political status quo.

The Committee further notes that, within the last 12 months, the economic situation of the vast majority of the population of Kenya has deteriorated considerably. Due in part to measures taken by the central bank of Kenya, inflation has increased immensely. This has led to a redistribution of income which made the rich even richer and the poor even poorer than before. Wage rises have been significantly below the rate of inflation.

# K

## Positive Aspects

The Committee notes that Kenya's economy and social welfare system, particularly in the field of education and health care, used to be, and probably still is, more highly developed than that of many other countries in the region.

## Principal Subjects of Concern

The Committee is deeply concerned, however, that the social system will no longer be able to cope with the consequences of the economic and social crisis. If carefully targeted measures are not undertaken, current developments will lead to even greater deprivation of the economic and social rights of the Kenyan people.

More specifically, the Committee notes with concern that the rights recognized by Kenya as a State party to the International Covenant on Economic, Social and Cultural Rights are neither contained in the constitution of Kenya nor in a separate bill of rights; nor do the provisions of the Covenant seem to have been incorporated into the municipal law of Kenya. Neither does there exist any institution or national machinery with responsibility for overseeing the implementation of human rights in the country. According to the information available to the Committee, the High Court does not play an effective role in the enforcement of human rights.

The Committee expresses its concern that no effort has been undertaken by the Government of Kenya to promote awareness of the rights recognized in the Covenant. On the contrary, there are reports according to which the Government has frustrated efforts by non-governmental organizations to spread such awareness.

With regard to the rights contained in articles 6 and 7 of the Covenant the Committee notes with concern that the possibilities of employment creation are extremely limited and, at present, only a small proportion of young persons leaving school can expect to find work. The labour force participation rate is decreasing, as is the level of annual earnings at the minimum wage (in US dollars at the official exchange rate). These minimum wages appear to be far too low to even allow a very modest standard of living. Further the enforcement of minimum wages does not seem to be adequately secured in practice. Generally, wages have not kept pace with the high rise in the rate of inflation.

Concerning the rights contained in article 8 of the Covenant, the Committee is of the view that the domination of the Central Organization of Trade Unions (COTU) by KANU appears to contravene the letter and spirit of the Covenant. The same observation appears to be valid with regard to the regulation of the right to strike in the Trade Disputes Act.

With regard to article 9 of the Covenant, the Committee expresses its concern that married women whose husbands are in taxable employment cannot participate in the scheme of the National Hospital Insurance Fund. The Committee is also concerned by reports of large-scale mismanagement of the National Social Security Fund.

Concerning the rights recognized in article 10 of the Covenant, the Committee expresses its profound concern about the fate of the great number of street (parking) children. The public funds earmarked for destitute children appear to the Committee to be pitifully inadequate. Further, the Committee is distressed about the apparent fact that child prostitution is common in many parts of Kenya and that the Government has thus not ensured children the special protection to which the Covenant entitles them.

As to the right to an adequate standard of living for everyone recognized in article 11 of the Covenant, the Committee reiterates its grave concern that the current economic and fiscal policies of the Government of Kenya are not designed to secure this right for the overwhelming majority of the population. The Committee notes reports that between 1980 and 1989 no less than 44 per cent of the population—in rural areas 55 per cent—lived below the poverty line. The Committee further notes a distressing inequality in income distribution. The Committee is also concerned about the fact that more than 30 per cent of the population of Kenya are reported to suffer from malnutrition. With regard to the right to adequate housing, the Committee notes with great concern that practices of forced evictions without consultation, compensation or adequate resettlement appear to be widespread in Kenya, particularly in Nairobi.

Turning to article 12 of the Covenant on the right to health, the Committee is concerned about the fact that government expenditure on health care appears to be constantly decreasing. It is also concerned that the introduction of fees for treatment in hospitals has its most negative effects on the particularly vulnerable groups and members of Kenyan society.

Regarding the right to education, the Committee expresses its concern about the low school attendance of children in the poorest areas of the country and in nomadic communities. The Committee observes that the obligation of States parties to the Covenant to ensure that "primary education shall be compulsory and available free to all" applies in all situations including those in which local communities are unable to furnish buildings, or individuals are unable to afford any costs associated with attendance at school. The Committee also draws the attention of the Government of Kenya to the obligation, contained in article 14 of the Covenant, and applying in cases where free compulsory education has not assured, to "work out and adopt a detailed plan of action for the progressive implementation, within a reasonable number of years" of the relevant right. The Committee also regrets the significant gender disparities and regional differences with regard to access to education, the significant difference in quality between the government secondary schools and the Harambee or community schools, as well as the difficulties encountered through the introduction of the new 8-4-4 system of education.

With regard to the rights recognized in article 15 of the Covenant, the Committee expresses its deep concern about the fact that, according to information available to it, academic freedom in Kenya is still seriously curtailed through intimidation and a variety of measures such as the need for academics to obtain official research and travel clearance. The Committee also regrets the frequent interventions by the government in cultural life through, for example, the banning of plays and the prohibition of certain books and periodicals.

The Committee expresses its concern that the policies of the Kenyan government to ensure the protection of the economic, social and cultural rights of women and to discourage violence against, and sexual abuse of, women do not appear to be adequate.

The Committee expresses its concern about the marginalization of ethnic minorities in Kenya, particularly of the nomadic pastoralists and the ethnic Somalis in the North Eastern Province.

### Suggestions and Recommendations

The Committee reiterates its request that the Government of Kenya actively participate in a constructive dialogue with the Committee as to how the obligations arising from the International Covenant on Economic, Social and Cultural Rights can be fulfilled in a more adequate manner. It calls to the Government's attention the fact that the Covenant creates a legal obligation for all States parties to submit periodic reports and that Kenya has been in breach of this obligation for many years.

The Committee recommends that the Government of Kenya avail itself of the advisory services of the United Nations Centre for Human Rights in order to enable it to submit as soon as possible a comprehensive report on the implementation of the Covenant in conformity with the Revised General Guidelines adopted by the Committee in 1990 (E/C.12/1991/1) and with particular emphasis on the issues raised and concerns expressed in the present concluding observations.

**BIBLIOGRAPHY.** Africa Watch. *Kenya: Screening of Ethnic Somalis—The Cruel Consequences of Kenya's Passbook System.* New York: Human Rights Watch, 1990. NGO factfinding report, in English.

————. *Political Crackdown Intensifies.* New York: Human Rights Watch, 1990. NGO report, in English.

Africa Watch and Women's Rights Project. *Seeking Refuge, Finding Terror: The Widespread Rape of Somali Women Refugees in North Eastern Kenya.* New York: Human Rights Watch, 1993. NGO factfinding report, in English.

Amnesty International. *Kenya: Silencing Opposition to One-Party Rule.* London: 1990. NGO factfinding report, in English and French.

Andreassen, B. A., and A. Eide, eds. "Kenya," in *Human Rights in Developing Countries 1987/88: A Yearbook on Human Rights in Countries Receiving Nordic Aid,* pp. 40–69. Copenhagen: Akademisk Forlag, 1988. NGO report, in English; bibliography, pp. 358–360.

Committee to Protect Journalists. *Press Conditions in Kenya.* New York: 1991. NGO briefing paper, in English.

Days, D. S., III, et al. *Justice Enjoined: The State of the Judiciary in Kenya.* New York: Robert F. Kennedy Memorial Center for Human Rights, 1992. NGO report, in English.

Goldfarb, Alan. "A Kenyan Wife's Right to Bury Her Husband: Applying the Convention on the Elimination of All Forms of Discrimination Against Women," *ILSA Journal of International Law* 14 (1990): 1–21. Scholarly article, in English.

"The Historic Debate: Law, Democracy and Multiparty Politics in Kenya," *Nairobi Law Monthly* 23 (April–May 1990). Special issue, in English.

Human Rights Watch. "Kenya," in *Human Rights Watch World Report 1995,* pp. 21–25. New York: 1995. NGO report, in English.

————. *Kenya: Multipartyism Betrayed in Kenya—Continuing Rural Violence and Restrictions on Freedom of Speech and Assembly.* New York: 1994. NGO report, in English.

International Centre for Human Rights and Democratic Development and Westminster Foundation for Democracy. *A Long Road to Uhuru: Human Rights and Political Participation in Kenya.* Montreal, Canada: 1993. NGO report, in English.

International Human Rights Law Group. *Facing the Pluralist Challenge: Human Rights and Democratization in Kenya's December 1992 Multi-Party Elections.* Washington, D.C.: 1992. NGO report, in English.

Kibwana, Kivutha, ed. *Law and the Administration of Justice in Kenya.* Nairobi, Kenya: International Commission of Jurists, Kenya Section, 1992. Scholarly collection of articles, in English.

Kirschner, R. H., and K. Hannibal. *Kenya: Medicolegal Aspects of the Inquests into the Death of Peter Njenga Karanja.* New York: American Association for the Advancement of Science, Committee on Scientific Freedom and Responsibility, and Physicians for Human Rights, 1988. NGO report, in English.

Kuria, Gibson Kamau. "The Rule of Law in Kenya and the Status of Human Rights," *The Yale Journal of International Law* 16, no. 1 (Winter 1991): 217–233. Scholarly article, in English.

Mazrui, Ali A. "Human Rights in Kenya," *African Journal of International Law* 1, no. 1 (Summer 1988): 92–98. Scholarly article, in English.

McLean, S., and S. E. Graham, eds. *Female Circumcision, Excision and Infibulation: The Facts and Proposals for Change.* 2nd rev. ed. London: Minority Rights Group, 1985. NGO report, in English; bibliography.

Munyakho, Dorothy. *Kenya: Child Newcomers in the Urban Jungle.* Florence, Italy: UNICEF International Child Development Centre, 1992. IGO monograph, in English.

Ross, Stanley D. "The Rule of Law and Lawyers in Kenya," *Journal of Modern African Studies* 30, no. 3 (1992): 421–442. Scholarly article, in English.

"The Surest Foundation of Nationhood, a Constitution: Essays in Salute of the Republic of Kenya," *Nairobi Law Monthly* 20 (Dec. 1989–Jan. 1990): 7–39. Special issue, in English.

Wamwere, Koigi wa. *Conscience on Trial.* Trenton, NJ, USA: Africa World Press, 1988. NGO report, in English.

### KING BAUDOUIN INTERNATIONAL DEVELOPMENT PRIZE.

Established in 1979, this biennial prize rewards individuals or organizations that have made a substantial contribution toward the development of third world countries or toward cooperation and good relations among industrialized and developing countries and their peoples.

Nominations can be made by a number of organizations, among them: members of the Belgian Government or related agencies; foreign academies; academic staff of Belgian and foreign university-level institutions; governing bodies of the United Nations and associated regional or specialized agencies; governing bodies of regional and world organizations whose objectives correspond to those of the prize; and former laureates. A selection committee reviews all nominations and makes recommendations to the Board, which then chooses the winner.

For more information, contact: King Baudouin Foundation, rue Brederode 21, B-1000 Brussels, Belgium.

### KING, MARTIN LUTHER, JR. (1929–1968).

In 1964, at the age of 35, Martin Luther King, Jr., became the youngest person ever to be awarded a **NOBEL**

# K

**PEACE PRIZE.** The American civil rights leader was cited by the Peace Prize Committee for his adherence to nonviolence while attempting to bring racial integration to the United States of America.

Born in Atlanta, GA, King was educated at Morehouse College (GA), Crozer Theological Seminary (PA), and Boston University, from which he received both an M.A. and a Ph.D. He served his spiritual community as a Baptist minister from 1947–1968, but he served the national community during the last twelve years of his life to an even greater extent by fighting for racial equality for American blacks and people of color. Toward the end of his life, King also became an outspoken opponent of the Vietnam War.

National prominence for the young minister, overseeing a congregation at the Dexter Avenue Baptist Church in Montgomery, AL, seemed far away in December 1955 when Mrs. Rosa Parks, a black housewife and seamstress, was too tired to take a seat in the back of a public bus, as segregation laws in the southern United States decreed. Mrs. Parks was arrested, setting off nonviolent demonstrations in that city. Dr. King and the Rev. Ralph Abernathy, another influential black minister, called for a black boycott of city buses, a strike that lasted for 382 days. During that year-long struggle, King was imprisoned many times, and his home was firebombed. Thurgood Marshall, at that time the chief attorney for the National Association for the Advancement of Colored People (NAACP) and later the first black justice appointed to the U.S. Supreme Court, took the case against segregation through the U.S. court systems, until finally the Supreme Court ruled that bus segregation anywhere in the United States was unconstitutional.

In 1957, King helped formed the Southern Christian Leadership Conference (SCLC), to fight for black dignity through civil disobedience and other nonviolent means. SCLC concentrated its activities at first on voter registration and on ending discrimination on transportation facilities. Later, the full brunt of segregation laws—including the so-called Jim Crow laws—were tested as the SCLC and the NAACP tried to draw the federal government into the fray. Among the many marches that King headed were the 1963 march in Birmingham, AL, during which King was arrested and composed his famous "Letter from Birmingham Jail," and the 1963 March on Washington, in which over 250,000 people demonstrated in support of the pending civil rights legislation. It was at the Washington demonstration that King delivered his famous "I have a dream" speech. In 1963, King was chosen as *Time* magazine's "Man of the Year." As a result of King's efforts and the efforts of myriad other civil rights fighters, the 1964 Civil Rights Bill was passed by the U.S. Congress.

In accepting the Nobel Peace Prize in Oslo, King explained that the black civil rights movement "does not seek to liberate Negroes at the expense of the humiliation and enslavement of the whites. It seeks no victory over anyone. It seeks to liberate American society and to share in the self-liberation of all the people. . . . It seeks to secure moral ends through moral means."

Throughout the next four years, King continued to wage civil disobedience campaigns on behalf of civil rights and also joined the growing number of Americans who were publicly decrying American involvement in the Vietnam War. Even though he was the moral center of the civil rights movement, toward the end of his life, King's ministerial voice was often shouted down by more radical civil rights fighters in the black community who thought that the pace of change was too slow and who advocated violence as a method of forcing change. And in the mid- and late-1960s, black communities in the North erupted in violence in cities such as Detroit and New York.

On 4 April 1968, King was shot dead by a sniper's bullet in Memphis, TN, where he had gone to lend support to a strike of garbage collectors. As news of his death spread, several cities erupted in riots, including parts of Washington, D.C. From the time of his death, many supporters lobbied for a memorial day in King's honor, usually citing January 18, his birthdate. After years of debate, formal citations by many cities and states, and informal acquiescence by businesses, the U.S. Congress declared the third Monday in January as a national holiday in honor of Martin Luther King, Jr.

**BIBLIOGRAPHY.** *Current Biography Yearbook.* New York: W.H. Wilson & Company, 1965.
Gray, Tony. *Champions of Peace.* London: Paddington Press, 1976.
King, M. L., Jr. *Stride toward Freedom.* New York: Harper and Row, 1958.
———. *The Trumpet of Conscience.* New York: Harper and Row, 1968.
———. *Why We Can't Wait.* New York: Harper and Row, 1964.
Schlessinger, Bernard S., and June H. Schlessinger, eds. *Who's Who of Nobel Prize Winners.* Phoenix, AZ, USA: Oryx Press, 1991.

**KISSINGER, HENRY ALFRED (1923–).** Born in the Bavarian city of Fürth, Henry Kissinger arrived in the United States of America in 1938, and it was as secretary of state of this country that he was to achieve international recognition as a diplomat and to become a joint recipient of the 1973 **NOBEL PEACE PRIZE.**

Kissinger received his undergraduate and graduate degrees from Harvard University, where he taught from 1954 to 1969. During those years, Kissinger also wrote a number of books, among them *Nuclear Weapons and Foreign Affairs* (1957), a work that argued for a flexible response in the use of such weapons and which earned him the Woodrow Wilson Prize. This work also brought Kissinger to the attention of a number of American presidents, including Eisenhower, Kennedy, and Johnson. In addition, during his Harvard teaching days, he also served for 18 months as study director on a research project supported by the Council on Foreign Relations; for two years as director of the Rockefeller Brothers Fund; for two years as associate director of Harvard University's Center for International Affairs; and for ten years as director of Harvard's Defense Studies Program. Concurrently, Kissinger consulted for the Eisenhower administration on the Operations Coordinating Board from 1955 to 1956 and on the Weapons Systems Evaluation Group of the Joint Chiefs of Staff from 1955 to 1960; for the Kennedy administration on the National Security Council (1961–1962), in the Arms Control and Disarmament Agency (1961–1967); and for the Johnson administration in the State Department from 1965 to 1969. During this last period, he also acted as President Johnson's emissary in secret meetings with Vietnamese diplomats, which led to the opening of peace talks in 1968.

Kissinger came to the forefront, however, during the administration of Richard Nixon. As chief foreign policy adviser to Nixon, he began the Strategic Arms Limitation Talks (SALT), developed a policy of detente with the USSR, and began negotiations with the People's Republic of China that eventually led to the United States' recognition of that country. In 1973, Nixon appointed Kissinger secretary of state, a position he was to hold until 1977. During those years, Kissinger also engineered a ceasefire between Egypt and Israel, reestablished American relations with Egypt, and helped to produce an accord between Israel and Syria.

Despite his remarkable scholarly and diplomatic accomplishments, Kissinger's citation by the Nobel Peace Prize Committee for "negotiating an end to the Vietnam War" did not meet with universal approbation. Considered the architect of the Nixon administration's policy of Vietnamization—a gradual withdrawal of American troops and advisors that was to allow more active participation by South Vietnamese troops and which was to later have a disastrous result for the South—Kissinger was also considered a proponent of the continuing bombing of North Vietnam during the two-year peace negotiations. His co-winner, **LE DUC THO,** refused to accept his own Nobel Peace Prize on the grounds that his country was still under

attack. Amid the storm of protest over the joint award, two Peace Prize Committee members resigned.

In addition to the Nobel Peace Prize, Kissinger has received many international citations, including *Time* magazine's Man of the Year (1972), the Jefferson Award (1973), the Wateler Peace Prize (1974), and the President's Medal of Freedom (1977). In 1995, he received an honorary knighthood from Britain's Queen Elizabeth.

***BIBLIOGRAPHY.*** *Current Biography Yearbook.* New York: W.H. Wilson & Company, 1972.

Gray, Tony. *Champions of Peace.* London: Paddington Press, 1976.

Hersh, Seymour. *The Price of Power: Kissinger in the White House.* New York: Summit Books, 1983.

Kissinger, Henry A. *White House Years.* New York: Harper, 1977.

Schlessinger, Bernard S., and June H. Schlessinger, eds. *Who's Who of Nobel Prize Winners.* Phoenix, AZ, USA: Oryx Press, 1991.

## KORCZAK (JANUSZ) LITERARY AWARDS.

Established in 1981 by the Anti-Defamation League's Braun Center for Holocaust Studies and the Embassy of the Republic of Poland, this award was named in honor of Dr. Janusz Korczak, a Polish-Jewish physician, educator, author, and orphan-home administrator who kept 200 children alive in a Warsaw ghetto during the Holocaust. The award is made every two years to two authors (and two honorable mentions) for books for and about children that reflect Dr. Korczak's humanitarianism. The book may be fiction or nonfiction but must have been published in English during the two years previous to the award. The recipients receive $1,000 and a commemorative plaque.

Past award winners include: Malka Drucker for *Eliezer Ben-Yehuda: The Father of Modern Hebrew* and Fr. Bruce Ritter for *Covenant House* (1988); Irene Awret for *Days of Honey* and Alice Miller for *Thou Shalt Not Be Aware* (1986); and Susan Cooper for *Seaward* and Eleanor Craig for *If We Could Hear the Grass Grow* (1984).

For more information, contact: ADL, 823 UN Plaza, New York, NY 10017, USA. Telephone: (212) 490-2525. Fax: (212) 867-0779.

## KOREA, NORTH.

The Democratic People's Republic of Korea is a country in east Asia occupying the part of a peninsula jutting into the Sea of Japan and the Yellow Sea that lies above the 38th parallel Military Demarcation Line, which is its border with South Korea. It also has a border with China. It achieved independence in 1948 and has observer status at the

United Nations, although it is not a member. Its population is estimated to be 22,450,000. Ethnic groups are not in evidence because the Korean people are of a homogeneous nature, sharing one language and one culture. There is, however, a small Chinese minority. Religion has been officially discouraged since 1945, but small groups of Buddhists and Christians continue to practice their faith. Literacy is estimated at 99%.

The government (1994) took the form of a Socialist Republic. The Korean Workers' (Communist) Party exercises power through its control of the organs of government. The general secretary of the party is president, chairman of the Central People's Committee, and head of State. The Supreme People's Assembly, composed of 615 deputies elected by popular vote for four-year terms of office, is the chief organ of government but meets rarely and only for short periods. The judicial system is headed by the Supreme Court. There are also military courts, which are subordinate to the Supreme People's Assembly.

The independence of Korea as a whole was recognized in the treaty that ended the Sino–Japanese War of 1894–1895; but, in 1910, Japan annexed the country. At the conclusion of World War II, the Potsdam Conference designated the 38th parallel as the line dividing occupation by Russian troops in the north and American troops in the south. The Democratic People's Republic was founded in May 1948 in the northern zone, with Pyongyang as its capital.

*THE KOREAN WAR.* On 25 June 1950, North Korean military forces attacked the Republic of Korea all along the 38th parallel, and the UN Security Council called for immediate cessation of hostilities. Two days later, the Council, noting that North Korea had neither ceased hostilities nor withdrawn its forces, recommended that all UN member States furnish such assistance to the Republic of Korea as might be necessary to restore international peace and security in the area. On the same day, the United States ordered its naval and sea forces to provide cover and support to the South Korean troops; and, three days later, it set up a naval blockade of the Korean coast. By 8 July, General Douglas MacArthur had been designated commanding general of a command which unified troops provided by 16 member States, and the United Nations embarked upon its first armed conflict to halt aggression.

By the first week of August 1950, the combined UN forces had been trapped in a 4,000-square-mile beachhead in southeast Korea. After standing off North Korean attacks until 15 September, they launched a major amphibious attack at Inchon, behind the communist lines and, by 30 September, were again in complete control of South Korea. Moving northward,

they were attacked by military units of the People's Republic of China and were eventually forced to retreat below the 38th parallel.

Truce negotiations between the opposing military commanders began in July 1951, but hostilities did not cease until after the signing of an armistice agreement on 27 July 1953, at Panmunjom. The armistice remains in effect after a conference of participants in the hostilities, convened in Geneva in 1954, failed to reach an agreed solution.

In the absence of a peace treaty, North Korea maintains that the two Koreas should become autonomous, equal governments in a Confederal Republic of Koryo (Korea's name for several years in the 10th century). In such a unified republic, North and South Korea would each maintain its own economic and political systems. South Korea, rejecting such an arrangement as unworkable, has for some time sought without success to arrange a summit meeting at which the two sides can discuss and resolve the issues that continue to divide the country.

In 1983, 17 persons, including four South Korean cabinet ministers, were killed by a bombing in Rangoon; two North Korean army officers who confessed to setting the bomb were later sentenced to death by Burmese authorities. In 1988, a woman who claimed to be a North Korean agent confessed that she had planted the bomb that had destroyed Korean Airlines flight 858 on 29 November 1987 over the Andaman Sea, off the coast of Myanmar (Burma), with 115 persons aboard. The bombing, she said, had been intended to frighten those who planned to participate in the Olympic games in Seoul in 1984.

On 20 February 1988, the U.S. State Department placed North Korea on its list of States supporting terrorism after concluding that "the evidence of North Korean culpability is compelling."

In July 1990, North and South Korea signed a historic agreement to meet in the fall of that year to discuss the easing of political and military confrontations. Since that time, the talks have stalled. Although once opposed to separate membership for the two Koreas in the United Nations, North Korea announced that it would seek UN membership in 1991. Then, in March 1993, the North became the first nation to withdraw formally from the Nuclear Nonproliferation Treaty, the international pact designed to limit the spread of nuclear weapons, setting the stage for a year-long confrontation with Western powers; however, with the threat of UN economic sanctions and the personal intercession in June 1994 of former U.S. President Jimmy Carter, North Korea suspended its withdrawal.

Because North Korea functions as a closed society dominated since 1948 by the Korean Workers' (Communist) Party and its leader, Kim Il Sung, little information is available concerning the enjoyment of human rights and fundamental freedoms by its citizens. For many years, Kim Il Sung was the object of a personality cult unequaled in the modern world. On his death in 1994, his son, Kim Jong Il, succeeded him as president.

**BIBLIOGRAPHY.** Asia Watch. *1987 Annual Report.* New York: Human Rights Watch, 1987. NGO annual report, in English.

Canada-Asia Working Group. "Report of the Canadian Council of Churches Delegation to the Democratic Republic of Korea, 4–13 November 1988," *Currents* 10, no. 4 (December 1988). NGO mission report, in English; bibliography.

Choi Sung Chul. "Human Rights in North Korea: Related Laws and Systems," *East Asian Review* 6, no. 4 (Winter 1994): 88–107. Article, in English.

Kim, Hakjoon. "North Korea after Kim Il-Song and the Future of North-South Korean Relations," *Security Dialogue* 26, no. 1 (March 1995): 73–91. Scholarly article, in English.

Shaw, William, ed. *Human Rights in Korea: Historical and Policy Perspectives.* Cambridge, MA, USA: East Asian Legal Studies Program of the Harvard Law School, 1991. Scholarly collection of essays, in English.

**KOREA, SOUTH.** The Republic of Korea is a country in east Asia occupying the part of a peninsula jutting into the Sea of Japan and the Yellow Sea that lies below the 38th parallel military demarcation line, which is its border with North Korea. It achieved independence in 1948 and has observer status at the United Nations, although it is not a member. Its population is estimated to be 43,660,000. Ethnic groups are not reported. There is, however, a small Chinese minority. Religions practiced by those who profess a religious belief include Buddhism (37%), Christianity (Protestant denominations, 26%; Roman Catholic, 5%), Animism (2%), and Confucianism (1.8%). Literacy is estimated at 93%.

The government (1994) took the form of a republic. Under the 1980 constitution, the president is elected by an electoral college chosen by popular vote for a term of seven years and serves as head of State. He appoints, and leads, a Council of Ministers. The prime minister, representing the party or coalition given the majority in the parliamentary election, is head of government. The unicameral legislature, the National Assembly, consists of 276 members, of which 184 are elected by popular vote and 92 appointed under a system of proportional representation. Political parties include the Democratic Justice Party, the New Korea Democratic Party, and the Korean National Party.

Throughout much of its history, Korea has been invaded, influenced, and fought over by its neighbors. It became a vassal of China in the early 17th century and was so isolated from foreign contact that it became known as the "Hermit Kingdom." All non-Chinese influences were excluded until Japan annexed Korea in 1910 and initiated a colonial era characterized by almost total control from Tokyo and ruthless efforts to replace the Korean language and culture by that of Japan. This period ended only after Japan's defeat in World War II.

The United States and the Soviet Union agreed at Yalta that the Japanese forces would surrender to the United States south of the 38th parallel and to the Soviet Union north of that line. This temporary arrangement was formalized in 1948 by the establishment of the Korean Republic in the south, with its capital at Seoul, and the People's Republic of Korea in the north, with its capital at Pyongyang. An election held in the south under United Nations supervision resulted in the choice of Syngman Rhee as president of the Republic. An election held in the north under Soviet supervision resulted in the choice of Kim Il Sung, a former Soviet Army major, as president of the People's Republic. On 12 December 1948, the United Nations declared the Republic of Korea to be the only lawful government in Korea.

After the United Nations command withdrew in 1949, North Korean forces invaded South Korea in 1950. The United Nations, thereupon, organized its first collective action to restore the peace by setting up the United Nations Command, to which 16 nations contributed troops and assistance. This international effort was led by the United States, which contributed the largest contingent.

As United Nations forces advanced northward, they were met by Korean forces and "volunteers" from the Chinese Army and forced to withdraw. The battle line finally stabilized north of Seoul, near the 38th parallel. Hostilities continued until 1953, when an armistice agreement was signed at Panmunjom. The armistice called for an international conference to solve the problem of Korea's division, but the conference—held at Geneva in April 1954—ended inconclusively.

Syngman Rhee served as president of the Republic until forced to step down in 1960 by demonstrations of university students against irregularities in the presidential election of that year. There followed a series of shifts between civilian and military rule, the most successful regime being that of Maj. Gen. Park Chung Hee, who was elected president in 1963 and re-elected in 1967, 1971, and 1978—a period marked by rapid industrialization, economic growth, and modernization. However, Park was assassinated in October 1979; and, after a brief power struggle, Maj. Gen. Chun Doo Hwan took over as president.

Chun's opponents demonstrated vigorously through the spring of 1980, and, in mid-May, the government declared martial law, banned all demonstrations, and arrested many political leaders and dissidents. This led to a confrontation in Kwangju City, which left 170 dead according to official estimates. A new constitution, adopted in October 1980, limited the chief executive to a single seven-year term. A new electoral college in 1981 elected President Chun to such a term, and he vowed to step down in 1988.

***PROTESTS FOR DEMOCRACY.*** In 1986 and 1987, students, intellectuals, and clergy, fearing that a way might be found to re-elect Chun, joined in organizing demonstrations demanding an open, free election in which opposition candidates could participate without fear of reprisal. Some of the demonstrations were marked by considerable violence. They subsided only after fair elections practices were guaranteed. On 25 February 1988, Chun's hand-picked successor, Rho Tae Woo, assumed the presidency after the first genuine presidential election since 1971. Although given only 36.6% of the popular vote, he had emerged victorious because a badly splintered opposition divided its support. In 1990, the nations's three largest political parties merged; the result was that some 100,000 students demonstrated, charging that the merger was undemocratic. In 1991, weeks of anti-government demonstrations led to the resignation of then-Prime Minister Ro Ja Bong. Kim Young Sam, elected in December 1992, became the first non-military aligned president since 1960. He vowed to punish corruption and announced an amnesty for nearly 42,000 people.

In 1992 and 1993, Prime Ministers of Japan offered apologies for Japan's actions during colonial rule of Korea, including the World War II sexual enslavement program affecting approximately 100,000 Korean women.

***BIBLIOGRAPHY.*** Amnesty International. *South Korea: Amnesty International's Concerns.* London: 1992. NGO report, in English.

————. *South Korea: Prisoners Held for National Security Offences.* London: 1991. NGO report, in English.

————. *South Korea: Summary of Amnesty International's Concerns.* London: 1994. NGO report, in English.

————. *South Korea: The Test of Practice: The National Security Law and Human Rights.* London: 1993. NGO report, in English.

————. *South Korea: Unfair Trial and Torture: Long-Term Political Prisoners.* London: 1993. NGO report, in English.

Asia Watch. *Assessing Reform in South Korea.* Washington, D.C.: 1988. NGO mission report, in English.

————. *Retreat from Reform: Labor Rights & Freedom of Expression in South Korea.* New York: Human Rights Watch, 1990. NGO factfinding report, in English.

————. *A Stern, Steady Crackdown: Legal Process and Human Rights in South Korea.* New York: 1987. NGO report, in English.

Asian Coalition for Housing Rights–Habitat International Coalition for Asia. *Urban Poor Housing Rights in South Korea & Hong Kong.* Bangkok, Thailand: 1991. NGO factfinding report, in English.

Canada-Asia Working Group. "Human Rights in Asia, Submission Prepared for the 45th Session of the United Nations Commission on Human Rights, Geneva, February 1989," *Currents* 11, no. 1 (February 1989). NGO report, in English.

————. "Human Rights in Asia, Submission to the 43d Session of the United Nations Commission on Human Rights," *Currents* (1987). NGO report, in English.

Greenberg, M., et al. *Broken Promises, Unfulfilled Dreams: Human Rights and Democracy in South Korea.* New York: Robert F. Kennedy Memorial Center for Human Rights, 1992. NGO report, in English.

Hsiung, James C. *Human Rights in East Asia: A Cultural Perspective.* New York: Pergamon, 1985. Scholarly edited collection, in English.

International Labor Movement Institute. *How the Mass Media are Controlled in South Korea—Pre-Censorship by "Instructions to the Press."* Tokyo, Japan: 1986. NGO report, in English.

International League for Human Rights. *Human Rights in the Republic of Korea: Trade Unions and Workers Rights.* New York: 1987. NGO report, in English.

Oxman, S. A., O. Triffterer, and F. B. Cruz. *South Korea: Human Rights in the Emerging Politics—Report on an ICJ Mission from 25 March to 12 April 1987.* Geneva: International Commission of Jurists, 1987. NGO mission report, in English.

Palley, Marian Lief. "Women's Status in South Korea: Tradition and Change," *Asian Survey* 30, no. 12 (Dec. 1990): 1136–1153. Article, in English.

Physicians for Human Rights. *The Use of Tear Gas in the Republic of Korea: A Report by Health Professionals.* Somerville, MA, USA: 1987. NGO mission report, in English.

Shaw, William, ed. *Human Rights in Korea: Historical and Policy Perspectives.* Cambridge, MA, USA: East Asian Legal Studies Program of the Harvard Law School, 1991. Scholarly collection of essays, in English.

Wessels, D. *Advancing Human Rights: Japan, East Asia, and the World.* Tokyo: Institute of International Relations for Advanced Studies on Peace and Development in Asia, Sophia University, 1986. Scholarly research report, in English.

West, J. M., and E. J. Baker. "The 1987 Constitutional Reform in South Korea: Electoral Process and Judicial Independence," *Harvard Human Rights Yearbook* 1 (1988): 135–177. Scholarly article, in English.

World Council of Church. *Behind the Mask: Human Rights in Asia and Latin America, an Inter-Regional Encounter.* Geneva: 1988. NGO report, in English.

Youm, Kyu Ho. "Current Development: South Korea: Press Laws in Transition," *Columbia Human Rights Law Review* 22, no. 2 (Spring 1991): 401–435. Scholarly article, in English.

**KUWAIT.** The State of Kuwait is an Arab country situated in western Asia, on the Persian Gulf. It has borders with Iraq and Saudi Arabia. It achieved independence in 1961 and became a member of the United Nations in 1963. Its population is estimated to be 2,388,000. Ethnic groups include Arabs (84%), Iranians and other Southeast Asians (16%). Non-Kuwaitis constitute about 75% of the total workforce and draw comparatively high pay. Languages commonly used include Arabic (official) and English. Religions practiced include Islam, the official State religion, (92%), Christianity (6%), and others (2%). Literacy is estimated at 71%.

The Kuwaiti government took the form of a monarchy. The amir is ruler and head of State. Upon his death, he is succeeded by the crown prince, who, up to then, had served as prime minister. A new crown prince is then selected, subject to approval by the National Assembly, by members of the Sabah family, which had controlled succession in the State since 1751. The crown prince is chosen from among the direct descendants of Mubarak the Great.

The National Assembly is a 50-member unicameral body elected by vote of the adult males who live in Kuwait prior to 1920, or their male descendants. Women, police officers, and members of the military are not eligible to vote. The Assembly prepares legislative decrees promulgated by the amir. The judicial system, which is independent, is strongly influenced by Islamic legal concepts. There is a constitutional court which interprets constitutional texts, issues rulings in disputes and hears appeals, and the Administrative Division of the General Court which considers disputes arising between individuals and administrative authorities. There are no political parties. Many Kuwaitis have begun to call for democratization of their country, denouncing one-party rule and demanding the return of Parliament, which was abolished by the ruling amir in 1986. They also have called for the lifting of press censorship and for the recognition and protection by the government of all human rights and fundamental freedoms.

*INVASION BY IRAQ.* On 2 August 1990, Kuwait was invaded by the armed forces of its neighbor Iraq and was promptly claimed by Iraq as its province. The Iraqi occupation lasted for more than six months and caused enormous human suffering to the Kuwaiti population, to the non-Kuwaiti workforce, and to other foreigners in that country. During the occupation, civilians remaining in Kuwait were compelled to live under perilous conditions while attacks upon the country's infrastructure undermined their enjoyment of economic, social, cultural, civil, and political rights. Noting that the treatment of prisoners of war and detained civilians in occupied Kuwait failed to conform to international principles, the UN **GENERAL ASSEMBLY** on 18 December 1990 (resolution 45/170) condemned the Iraqi authorities and forces "for their serious violations of human rights against the Kuwaiti people and third-State nationals, and for acts of torture, arrests, summary executions, disappearances and abductions in violation of all relevant international standards of human rights and international law."

An allied coalition—headed by the United States of America and including armed forces of Great Britain, France, Saudi Arabia, Egypt, Syria, and many others—undertook a war to liberate Kuwait on 16 January 1991, acting on the authority of the UN Security Council to enforce 12 resolutions which the Council had adopted following Iraq's act of aggression. The alliance forces prevailed, and the Iraqi occupation collapsed on 27 February 1991. Kuwait's independence was thus restored.

It was reported on 3 February 1994 that the government had ratified "with reservations" the 1979 Convention on the Elimination of All Forms of Discrimination against Women (see **WOMEN'S RIGHTS**). The reservations centered on voting rights and child custody.

*REPORT ON ELIMINATION OF RACIAL DISCRIMINATION.* One of the wealthiest nations on earth because of its oil revenues, Kuwait has experienced a continuing human rights problem in the treatment of non-Kuwaiti workers who are employed in the country. The UN **COMMITTEE ON THE ELIMINATION OF RACIAL DISCRIMINATION** examined the tenth, eleventh and twelfth periodic reports of Kuwait, submitted in a single document (CERD/C/226/Add. 5) under the International Convention on the Elimination of all Forms of Racial Discrimination, and adopted the following concluding observations at its 1008th meeting, held on 17 August 1993 (A/48/18):

### Positive Aspects

The Committee noted with interest the important developments taking place in the National Assembly, where issues concerning the status of Bedoons and criteria determining the granting of Kuwaiti nationality were being debated. The Committee also noted the willingness of the Government to continue to provide further information on the implementation of the Convention.

### Factors and Difficulties Impeding the Application of the Convention

The Committee recognized that, as a consequence of the invasion and occupation of Kuwait by Iraq, the State party had been subjected to serious difficulties that had temporarily affected the full implementation of the provisions of the Convention.

### Principal Subjects of Concern

The Committee was particularly concerned about expulsions and other discriminatory measures against especially vulnerable groups of foreigners, including Palestinians, stateless Arabs, Bedoons, Iraqis and nationals of countries that did not participate in the coalition, and the treatment of foreign domestic servants. The Committee was concerned that no specific measures had been envisaged to eliminate discrimination with respect to descent, national or ethnic origin. In that connection the Committee referred to official discrimination made between two categories of Kuwaiti citizens: those who possessed longstanding Kuwaiti nationality and those who had acquired Kuwaiti nationality in more recent times. Furthermore, the Committee expressed its concern about the lack of penal legislation to implement the provisions of article 4 of the Convention.

The Committee was particularly concerned about discriminatory measures leading to the exodus of foreigners in the period following the liberation of Kuwait.

The Committee regretted the absence of concrete information in the report of the State party on the implementation of the provisions of articles 2 to 7 of the Convention in practice. The Committee noted, in particular, that no information was provided in the report on the situation of non-Kuwaitis residing in Kuwait, although they were thought to constitute the majority of the population.

### Suggestions and Recommendations

The Committee recommended that the comments and concerns it had expressed with regard to the consideration of the tenth, eleventh and twelfth periodic reports of Kuwait should be taken into account by the State party.

The State party should take steps to guarantee the enjoyment by individuals belonging to vulnerable groups of foreigners, including foreign domestic servants, of the rights enshrined in the Convention without any discrimination; to eliminate discrimination deriving from the dual system of citizenship; to revise the Penal Code in order to introduce specific legislation to implement the provisions of article 4 of the convention in accordance with General Recommendations VIII and XV of the Committee; to guarantee the right of recourse in courts to victims of discrimination; and to implement the provisions of article 7 of the Convention, in particular through adequate training in human rights norms of law enforcement personnel in the light of general recommendation XIII of the Committee.

The State party should include, in its thirteenth report, due in January 1994, concrete information about the demographic composition of the population, including the foreign population, and details about the economic, social and political status of non-Kuwaiti residents. That report would enable the Committee to continue its examination of the situation in Kuwait which warranted close monitoring.

**BIBLIOGRAPHY.** Amnesty International. *Iraq-Occupied Kuwait: Human Rights Violations Since 2 August.* London: 1990. NGO factfinding report, in English and French.
————. *Kuwait: Three Years of Unfair Trials.* London: 1994. NGO report, in English.
Arab Organization for Human Rights. *Human Rights in the Arab World.* Cairo, Egypt: 1987. NGO report, in English and Arabic.
Birks, J. S., and C. A. Sinclair. *Nature and Process of Labor Importing: The African in the Gulf States, Kuwait, Bahrain, Qatar, and the United Arab Emirates.* Geneva: ILO, 1978. IGO report, in English.
Bresheeth, Haim, and Nira Yuval-Davis, eds. *The Gulf War and the New World Order.* London: Zed Books, 1991. Monograph, in English.
Centre d'Etudes et de Recherches sur l'Orient Chretien (Middle East Christian Research Center). "Kuwait: The Rights of Women," *Plus* 1, no. 1 (1985): 4–5. NGO article, in English.
Ghabra, Shafeeq. "Democratization in a Middle Eastern State: Kuwait, 1993," *Middle East Policy* 3, no. 1 (1994): 102–119. Article, in English.
Human Rights Watch. "Kuwait," in *Human Rights Watch World Report 1995,* pp. 290–295. New York: 1995. NGO report, in English.
Ismael, Jacqueline S. "The Conditions of Egyptian Labor in the Gulf: A Profile of Kuwait," *Arab Studies Quarterly* 8, no. 4 (Fall 1986): 390–403. Scholarly journal article, in English; bibliography, p. 403.
Lawyers Committee for Human Rights. *Kuwait: Building the Rule of Law: Human Rights in Kuwait after Occupation.* New York: 1992. NGO factfinding report, in English.
————. *Kuwait: Recent Human Rights Developments.* New York: 1990. NGO report, in English.
————. *Laying the Foundations: Human Rights in Kuwait—Obstacles and Opportunities.* New York: 1993. NGO factfinding report, in English.
————. *The Treatment of Alleged Collaborators and Other Security Detainees in Kuwait.* New York: 1991. NGO report, in English.
Middle East Watch. *Kuwait: Deteriorating Human Rights Conditions Since the Early Occupation.* New York: Human Rights Watch, 1990. NGO report, in English.
————. *Nowhere to Go: The Tragedy of the Remaining Palestinian Families in Kuwait.* New York: Human Rights Watch, 1991. NGO report, in English.
Shah, Nasra M., Sulayman S. Al-Qudsi, and Makhdoom A. Shah. "Asian Women Workers in Kuwait," *International Migration Review* 25, no. 3 (no. 95) (Fall 1991): 464–486. Scholarly article, in English; bibliography, pp. 485–486.
United Nations Commission on Human Rights. *Report on the Situation of Human Rights in Kuwait under Iraqi Occupation, Prepared by Mr. Walter Kälin, Special Rapporteur of the Commission on Human Rights, in Accordance with Commission Resolution 1991/67.* Geneva, Switzerland: 1992. (E/CN.4/1992/26). IGO document, in English and French.
United States Senate, Committee on the Judiciary, Subcommittee on Immigration and Refugee Affairs. *Aftermath of War: The Persian Gulf Refugee Crisis: Staff Report.* Washington, D.C.: 1991. Government briefing paper, in English.
Vincent-Daviss, Diana, and Radu Popa. "The International Legal Implications of Iraq's Invasion of Kuwait: A Research Guide," *New York University Journal of International Law and Politics* 23 (1990): 231–321. Bibliography, in English.

**KYRGYZSTAN.** The Republic of Kyrgyzstan, formerly the Kirghiz Socialist Republic of the U.S.S.R., is a landlocked country bordering on Kazakhstan to the north, Uzbekistan to the west, Tadjzhikistan to the south and China to the east. It achieved independence in 1991 and became a member of the United Nations the following year. It was one of the founding nations of the Commonwealth of Independent States.

The peoples of Kyrgyzstan, estimated at a total of 4,613,000, include the majority Kirghiz and minorities of Uzbeks, Ukrainians, Tartars, and Russians. Although Kyrgyz is the state language, Russian is accorded equal status. Islam is the major religion.

At one time Kyrgyzia, as it was known, was technically under Chinese rule although it maintained much of its autonomy. In 1876 it was incorporated into the

Russian empire and came under Soviet authority in 1919 following the 1917 Bolshevik revolution and the civil war that ensued. In 1936 the Kyrgyz Soviet Socialist Republic became a full union republic of the USSR. Its capital became known as Frunze in 1926 until it was restored to its former name of Bishkek in 1991.

Askar Akayev from the Kyrgyz Academy of Sciences was elected to the presidency in 1990 and survived a coup attempt in 1991 and a referendum of confidence in January 1994. However, he resigned in September 1994 pending election of a new president.

A new constitution was approved in May 1993, guaranteeing basic human rights. It includes provision for a directly elected 105-seat legislative body known as the *Zhorgorku Kenesh* after elections were held in 1995 and every five years thereafter. The 350-seat Supreme Soviet elected in 1990 was to continue until that time. The president, directly elected every five years, is to be head of State and to appoint the prime minister.

***BIBLIOGRAPHY.*** Pryde, Ian. "Kyrgyzstan: The Trials of Independence," *Journal of Democracy* 5, no. 1 (Jan. 1994): 109–120. Scholarly article, in English.

# L

**LA FONTAINE, HENRI MARIE (1854–1943).** Born in Paris, Henri Marie de La Fontaine was awarded the 1913 **NOBEL PEACE PRIZE** for establishing and furthering international cooperation. He served as the president of the **INTERNATIONAL PEACE BUREAU** from 1907 until 1943 and was a member of the **INTER-PARLIAMENTARY UNION.**

On receiving a doctorate of law from the University of Brussels in 1877, La Fontaine worked as an attorney from that year until 1893. From 1894 to 1940, he was a professor of law at the University of Brussels, during which time he concomitantly served as a Belgian senator.

A pacifist and socialist, La Fontaine ardently believed in world unification through education and promulgated the ideas of a world school, a world library, an international auxiliary language, a central monetary office, and an international parliament. A prolific writer, his best-known work is *The Great Solution* (1916), in which he outlines a *magnissima charta* that would create a "United States of the World."

**BIBLIOGRAPHY.** Gray, Tony. *Champions of Peace.* London: Paddington Press, 1976.

Schlessinger, Bernard S., and June H. Schlessinger, eds. *Who's Who of Nobel Prize Winners.* Phoenix, AZ, USA: Oryx Press, 1991.

**LANGE, CHRISTIAN LOUIS (1869–1938).** A writer and political activist, Christian Louis Lange was co-winner of the 1921 **NOBEL PEACE PRIZE.** Born in Stavanger, Norway, Lange represented Norway in the **LEAGUE OF NATIONS** from its inception until his death and was largely responsible for Norway's entry into the League.

Lange also was an active member of the Nobel organization from its inception. In 1900, he served as first secretary of the Nobel Peace Prize Committee. An advocate of peaceful resolution to conflict, Lange served as secretary-general of the **INTER-PARLIAMENTARY UNION** from 1909 and later served as the first secretary-general of the Inter-Parliamentary Bureau. Throughout his life, he supported free speech, free trade, universal suffrage, and labor rights. He also supported the theory of internationalism, which he described in his Nobel lecture as "a *social* and a *political* theory, a definite conception of how society should be organized, especially a conception as to how nations should settle their mutual relations . . . , the belief in the unity of mankind."

**BIBLIOGRAPHY.** Gray, Tony. *Champions of Peace.* London: Paddington Press, 1976.

Schlessinger, Bernard S., and June H. Schlessinger, eds. *Who's Who of Nobel Prize Winners.* Phoenix, AZ, USA: Oryx Press, 1991.

**LAOS.** The Lao People's Democratic Republic is a country in southeastern Asia, located on the Indochinese Peninsula. It has borders with Cambodia, China, Myanmar, Thailand, and Vietnam. It achieved independence within the French Union in 1950, achieved full sovereignty under the Paris Agreements of 29 December 1954, and became a member of the United Nations in 1955. Its population is estimated to be 4,507,000.

The census of 1982 indicated the presence of 68 ethnic groups falling into three major groupings: the Lao Loum, who are plain dwellers and make up approximately 50% of the population; the Lao Sung, who are mountain dwellers and make up approximately 33%; and the Lao Theung, who live on the high plateaus and account for the remainder. Languages commonly used include Lao (official), Lao Sung, French, and English. Each ethnic group is free to preserve its own culture, language, and traditions; however, the only official language is Lao, which must be learned by all national ethnic groups. Religions practiced include Buddhism (Therevada), Animism, and various tribal beliefs. Literacy is estimated at 45%.

The government (1994) took the form of a socialist republic. The president is head of State. Executive authority is exercised by the premier, who leads the only political party, the Lao People's Revolutionary Party (*Pathet Lao*).

A small number of American servicemen, missing since the war in Indochina, are alleged to be held by Pathet Lao elements. In 1985, the government cooperated in an effort to locate them, but the search produced few results.

The 50,000 Vietnamese troops once stationed in Laos have been withdrawn, and the country has developed good relations with its neighbors: Cambodia, China, Myanmar, and Vietnam. For many years dependent upon support from the Soviet Union and other eastern European countries for development assistance, Laos has recently sought improved relations with Great Britain, Japan, and the United States. However, although it has made no move towards discarding its rigid one-party system, it has in some cases welcomed foreign investments and encouraged private farming.

**BIBLIOGRAPHY.** Amnesty International. *Lao People's Democratic Republic: The Draft Constitution and Human Rights.* London: 1990. NGO factfinding report, in English.

———. *Laos: Freedom of Expression Still Denied—Multi-Party Advocates and Political Prisoners Sentenced after Unfair Trials.* London: 1993. NGO report, in English.

———. *Laos: Recent Information on "Re-education" in Attapeu Province.* London: 1988. NGO report, in English.

Cultural Survival. "Militarization and Indigenous Peoples: Part I—The Americas and the Pacific," *Cultural Survival Quarterly* 11, no. 3 (1987). NGO special issue, in English.

Francophone Inter-Associative Information and Documentation Centre on the Right to Asylum and Refugees. "Laos," in *Documentation-Réfugiés.* No. 127. Paris: 1990. NGO briefing paper, in French.

Ireson, Carol J. "Changes in Field, Forest, and Family: Rural Women's Work and Status in Post-Revolutionary Laos," *Bulletin of Concerned Asian Scholars* 24, no. 4 (Oct. 1992): 3–18. Research paper, in English.

Morgan, S. M., and E. Colson, eds. *People in Upheaval.* Staten Island, NY, USA: Center for Migration Studies of New York, 1987. NGO document collection, in English.

Rabé, Paul. *Voluntary Repatriation: The Case of Hmong in Ban Vinai.* Scholarly paper no. 2. Bangkok, Thailand: Indochinese Refugee Information Center, Institute of Asian Studies, Chulalongkorn University, 1990. Scholarly paper, in English and Thai.

Stuart-Fox, Martin. "Laos at Crossroads," in *Indochina Issues.* No. 92. Washington, D.C.: Indochina Project, 1991. Factfinding report, in English.

Women's Commission for Refugee Women and Children. *Repatriation and Reintegration: Can Hmong Refugees Begin to Look Homeward?* New York: 1991. NGO report, in English.

## LATIN AMERICAN FEDERATION OF ASSOCIATIONS OF FAMILIES OF THE DISAPPEARED AND DETAINED.

An international non-governmental organization—best known by its Spanish title, *Federación Latinoamericana de Asociaciones Familiares de Detenidos–Desaparecidos* (FEDEFAM)—in consultative status (Category II) with the UN **ECONOMIC AND SOCIAL COUNCIL,** FEDEFAM was founded in 1981 in San José, Costa Rica. The Federation works to secure the release of all people who have forcibly disappeared in Latin Amer-

ica, seeks to locate children who were kidnaped or born in jails, and strives for their reunification with their legitimate families. FEDEFAM also provides social and medical assistance to families and victims after their release. In 1982, FEDEFAM proposed to the United Nations the adoption of a Convention against the Enforced Disappearance of Persons.

The Federation publishes the bi-monthly bulletin *Hasta Encontrarlos* and the annual magazine *FEDEFAM.*

Latin American Federation of Associations of Families of the Disappeared and Detained. Address: P.O. 2444, Carmelitas 1010-A, Caracas, Venezuela. Telephone: (58-2) 564-27-46. Fax: (58-2) 561-11-74. Executive Secretary: Maria del Carmen Pariente.

**LATVIA.** The Republic of Latvia, located in central Europe and bordered by the Baltic Sea on the west, Russia on the east, Lithuania and Belarus on the south, and Estonia on the north, has a population estimated at 2,737,000, comprised of 52% Latvians and 34% Russians. Its main religions are Lutheran, Catholicism, and Russian Orthodox.

The government took the form of a republic (1994). Ruled by Russia from the eighteenth century, it first achieved independence in 1920, but 20 years later was incorporated into the Union of Soviet Socialist Republics by the German-Russian nonaggression treaty. It was 54 years before the last Russian troops left the country on 31 August 1994.

In the late 1980s, Latvians began their struggle for independence, taking advantage of the sympathetic attitude of the Soviet Communist party head Mikhail Gorbachev and his policy of *perestroika.* The effort culminated successfully on 21 August 1991, when Latvia was able to declare its independence. It was admitted to membership in the United Nations in September of the following year.

The country's 1922 constitution, which had been annulled by the events of 1940, was restored in 1993, providing for the direct election of the 100-seat *Saema* (parliament) for a three-year term by secret ballot of the parliament. The president appoints the prime minister, who appoints the cabinet. In July 1993, elections were held and Latvian Way won the most seats (32%), followed by the Latvian National Independence Movement, Harmony for Latvia-Revival of the Economy, and the Latvian Farmers' Union. In mid-July 1994, Prime Minister Valdis Birkaus resigned from that office but continued to serve contingent upon the designation of a new prime minister. In August 1994 parliament voted to remove a quota system from an earlier citizenship law which would have limited citizenship to 2,000 non-Latvians each year.

# L

*RIGHT OF CITIZENSHIP.* In 1991, Latvia passed the Renewal of Citizenship bill, which restored citizenship to those who held Latvian citizenship (and their descendants) prior to the USSR's takeover in 1940. In effect, this rendered as stateless persons approximately 700,000 Russian citizens who had emigrated to Latvia during the years of Soviet control. In August 1994, Latvian President Guntis Ulmanis signed Latvia's Citizenship Law; according to the new law, naturalization began on 1 January 1996, starting with those who were born in Latvia. The naturalization process will proceed in eight steps, culminating on 1 January 2003, when the final group of non-citizens born outside of Latvia are eligible for naturalization.

*BIBLIOGRAPHY.* Commission on Security and Cooperation in Europe. *Elections in the Baltic States and Soviet Republics: A Compendium of Reports on Parliamentary Elections held in 1990.* Washington, D.C.: 1990. Government report, in English.

————. *Renewal and Challenge: The Baltic States 1988–1989.* Washington, D.C.: 1990. Government report, in English.

————. *Report on the Supreme Soviet Elections in Latvia.* Washington, D.C.: 1990. Government report, in English.

De Meyer, Jan, and Christos Rozakis. "Human Rights in the Republic of Latvia," *Human Rights Law Journal* 13, no. 5–6 (June 1992): 244–249. Scholarly article, in English.

Grigorievs, Alexei. "The Controversy over Citizenship in Latvia," *Uncaptive Minds* 4, no. 4 (18) (Winter 1991–92): 57–60. Scholarly article, in English.

Human Rights Watch. "Latvia," in *Human Rights World Report 1995*, pp. 214–216. New York: 1995. NGO report, in English.

Immigration and Refugee Board Documentation Centre. *CIS, Baltic States and Georgia: Nationality Legislation.* Ottawa, Canada: 1992. Government briefing paper, in English and French; bibliography, pp. 20–23.

## LAW ASSOCIATION FOR ASIA AND THE PACIFIC.

Founded in 1966 in Canberra, Australia, LAWASIA promotes the administration of justice and the maintenance of international law; advances legal education; and spreads knowledge of the laws of member countries. This non-governmental organization has consultative status with the UN ECONOMIC AND SOCIAL COUNCIL (Category II), UNESCO, and the World Intellectual Property Organization.

The Association publishes the *LAWASIA Human Rights Newsletter* six times a year, the annual *LAWASIA Directory* and *LAWASIA Journal,* and the biennial *LAWASIA Human Rights Bulletin.*

Law Association for Asia and the Pacific. Address: Law Society House, 33 Barrack Street, Perth 6000, Australia. Telephone: (61-9) 221-2303. Fax: (61-9) 221-5914.

## LAW ENFORCEMENT: BASIC PRINCIPLES FOR THE USE OF FORCE AND FIREARMS BY LAW ENFORCEMENT OFFICIALS (1990).

The Basic Principles were prepared by the Eighth United Nations Congress on Prevention of Crime and Treatment of Offenders, held at Havana, Cuba, from 27 August to 7 September 1990. In the Basic Principles, as in the Code of Conduct for Law Enforcement Officials, the term "law enforcement officials" includes all officers of the law, whether appointed or elected, who exercise police powers, especially the powers of arrest or detention. In countries where police powers are exercised by military authorities, whether uniformed or not, or by State security forces, the definition of law enforcement officials shall be regarded as including officers of such services.

### General Provisions

1. Governments and law enforcement agencies shall adopt and implement rules and regulations on the use of force and firearms against persons by law enforcement officials. In developing such rules and regulations, Governments and law enforcement agencies shall keep the ethical issues associated with the use of force and firearms constantly under review.

2. Governments and law enforcement agencies should develop a range of means as broad as possible and equip law enforcement officials with various types of weapons and ammunition that would allow for a differentiated use of force and firearms. These should include the development of nonlethal incapacitating weapons for use in appropriate situations, with a view to increasingly restraining the application of means capable of causing death or injury to persons. For the same purpose, it should also be possible for law enforcement officials to be equipped with self-defensive equipment such as shields, helmets, bullet-proof vests and bullet-proof means of transportation, in order to decrease the need to use weapons of any kind.

3. The development and deployment of nonlethal incapacitating weapons should be carefully evaluated in order to minimize the risk of endangering uninvolved persons, and the use of such weapons should be carefully controlled.

4. Law enforcement officials, in carrying out their duty, shall, as far as possible, apply nonviolent means before resorting to the use of force and firearms. They may use force and firearms only if other means remain ineffective or without any promise of achieving the intended result.

5. Whenever the lawful use of force and firearms is unavoidable, law enforcement officials shall:

(a) Exercise restraint in such use and act in proportion to the seriousness of the offence and the legitimate objective to be achieved;

(b) Minimize damage and injury, and respect and preserve human life;

(c) Ensure that assistance and medical aid are rendered to any injured or affected persons at the earliest possible moment;

(d) Ensure that relatives or close friends of the injured or affected person are notified at the earliest possible moment.

6. Where injury or death is caused by the use of force and firearms by law enforcement officials, they shall report the

incident promptly to their superiors, in accordance with principle 22.

7. Governments shall ensure that arbitrary or abusive use of force and firearms by law enforcement officials is punished as a criminal offence under their law.

8. Exceptional circumstances such as internal political instability or any other public emergency may not be invoked to justify any departure from these basic principles.

### Special Provisions

9. Law enforcement officials shall not use firearms against persons except in self-defence or defence of others against the imminent threat of death or serious injury, to prevent the perpetration of a particularly serious crime involving grave threat to life, to arrest a person presenting such a danger and resisting their authority, or to prevent his or her escape, and only when less extreme means are insufficient to achieve these objectives. In any event, intentional lethal use of firearms may only be made when strictly unavoidable in order to protect life.

10. In the circumstances provided for under principle 9, law enforcement officials shall identify themselves as such and give a clear warning of their intent to use firearms, with sufficient time for the warning to be observed, unless to do so would unduly place the law enforcement officials at risk or would create a risk of death or serious harm to other persons, or would be clearly inappropriate or pointless in the circumstances of the incident.

11. Rules and regulations on the use of firearms by law enforcement officials should include guidelines that:

(a) Specify the circumstances under which law enforcement officials are authorized to carry firearms and prescribe the types of firearms and ammunition permitted;

(b) Ensure that firearms are used only in appropriate circumstances and in a manner likely to decrease the risk of unnecessary harm;

(c) Prohibit the use of those firearms and ammunition that cause unwarranted injury or present an unwarranted risk;

(d) Regulate the control, storage, and issuing of firearms, including procedures for ensuring that law enforcement officials are accountable for the firearms and ammunition issued to them;

(e) Provide for warnings to be given, if appropriate, when firearms are to be discharged;

(f) Provide for a system of reporting whenever law enforcement officials use firearms in the performance of their duty.

### Policing Unlawful Assemblies

12. As everyone is allowed to participate in lawful and peaceful assemblies, in accordance with the principles embodied in the Universal Declaration of Human Rights and the International Covenant on Civil and Political Rights, Governments and law enforcement agencies and officials shall recognize that force and firearms may be used only in accordance with principles 13 and 14.

13. In the dispersal of assemblies that are unlawful but nonviolent, law enforcement officials shall avoid the use of force or, where that is not practicable, shall restrict such force to the minimum extent necessary.

14. In the dispersal of violent assemblies, law enforcement officials may use firearms only when less dangerous means are not practicable and only to the minimum extent necessary. Law enforcement officials shall not use firearms in such cases, except under the conditions stipulated in principle 9.

### Policing Persons in Custody or Detention

15. Law enforcement officials, in their relations with persons in custody or detention, shall not use force, except when strictly necessary for the maintenance of security and order within the institution, or when personal safety is threatened.

16. Law enforcement officials, in their relations with persons in custody or detention, shall not use firearms, except in self-defence or in the defence of others against the immediate threat of death or serious injury, or when strictly necessary to prevent the escape of a person in custody or detention presenting the danger referred to in principle 9.

17. The preceding principles are without prejudice to the rights, duties, and responsibilities of prison officials, as set out in the Standard Minimum Rules for the Treatment of Prisoners, particularly rules 33, 34, and 54.

### Qualifications, Training, and Counseling

18. Governments and law enforcement agencies shall ensure that all law enforcement officials are selected by proper screening procedures, have appropriate moral, psychological, and physical qualities for the effective exercise of their functions, and receive continuous and thorough professional training. Their continued fitness to perform these functions should be subject to periodic review.

19. Governments and law enforcement agencies shall ensure that all law enforcement officials are provided with training and are tested in accordance with appropriate proficiency standards in the use of force. Those law enforcement officials who are required to carry firearms should be authorized to do so only upon completion of special training in their use.

20. In the training of law enforcement officials, Governments and law enforcement agencies shall give special attention to issues of police ethics and human rights, especially in the investigative process, to alternatives to the use of force and firearms, including the peaceful settlement of conflicts, the understanding of crowd behaviors, and the methods of persuasion, negotiation, and mediation, as well as to technical means, with a view to limiting the use of force and firearms. Law enforcement agencies should review their training programmes and operational procedures in the light of particular incidents.

21. Governments and law enforcement agencies shall make stress counseling available to law enforcement officials who are involved in situations where force and firearms are used.

### Reporting and Review Procedures

22. Governments and law enforcement agencies shall establish effective reporting and review procedures for all incidents referred to in principles 6 and 11 (f). For incidents reported pursuant to these principles, Governments and law enforcement agencies shall ensure that an effective review process is available and that independent administrative or prosecutorial authorities are in a position to exercise jurisdiction in appropriate circumstances. In cases of death and

serious injury or other grave consequences, a detailed report shall be sent promptly to the competent authorities responsible for administrative review and judicial control.

23. Persons affected by the use of force and firearms or their legal representatives shall have access to an independent process, including a judicial process. In the event of the death of such persons, this provision shall apply to their dependents accordingly.

24. Governments and law enforcement agencies shall ensure that superior officers are held responsible if they know, or should have known that law enforcement officials under their command are resorting, or have resorted, to the unlawful use of force and firearms, and they did not take all measures in their power to prevent, suppress, or report such use.

25. Governments and law enforcement agencies shall ensure that no criminal or disciplinary sanction is imposed on law enforcement officials who, in compliance with the Code of Conduct for Law Enforcement Officials and these basis principles, refuse to carry out an order to use force and firearms, or who report such use by other officials.

26. Obedience to superior orders shall be no defence if law enforcement officials knew that an order to use force and firearms resulting in the death or serious injury of a person was manifestly unlawful and had a reasonable opportunity to refuse to follow it. In any case, responsibility also rests on the superiors who gave the unlawful orders.

**LAW ENFORCEMENT: CODE OF CONDUCT FOR LAW ENFORCEMENT OFFICIALS (1979).** This code sets out a series of principles aimed at ensuring the humane performance of law enforcement functions and at protecting the human rights of the men and women who must deal with them. Recognizing that the nature of the functions performed, and the manner in which they may be exercised, can at times produce serious negative effects upon the quality of life citizens enjoy, the code admonishes all law enforcement officials to perform their tasks diligently and with dignity, in full respect for and compliance with the principles of human rights.

The Code of Conduct was adopted by the UN **GENERAL ASSEMBLY** on 17 December 1979 (resolution 34/169). It contains, in addition to eight articles, a series of commentaries which provide information to facilitate the use of the code within the framework of national legislation or practice. The text of the code and commentaries is as follows:

The General Assembly,

Considering that the purposes proclaimed in the Charter of the United Nations include the achievement of international co-operation in promoting and encouraging respect for human rights and for fundamental freedoms for all without distinction as to race, sex, language or religion,

Recalling, in particular, the Universal Declaration of Human Rights and the International Covenants on Human Rights,

Recalling also the Declaration on the Protection of All Persons from Being Subjected to Torture and Other Cruel, Inhuman or Degrading Treatment or Punishment, adopted by the General Assembly in its resolution 3452 (XXX) of 9 December 1975,

Mindful that the nature of the functions of law enforcement in the defence of public order and the manner in which these functions are exercised have a direct impact on the quality of life of individuals as well as of society as a whole,

Conscious of the important task which law enforcement officials are performing diligently and with dignity, in compliance with the principles of human rights,

Aware, nevertheless, of the potential for abuse which the exercise of such duties entails,

Recognizing that the establishment of a code of conduct for law enforcement officials is only one of several important measures for providing the citizenry served by law enforcement officials with protection of all their rights and interests,

Aware that there are additional important principles and prerequisites for the humane performance of law enforcement functions, namely:

(a) That, like all agencies of the criminal justice system, every law enforcement agency should be representative of and responsive and accountable to the community as a whole,

(b) That the effective maintenance of ethical standards among law enforcement officials depends on the existence of a well-conceived, popularly accepted and humane system of laws,

(c) That every law enforcement official is part of the criminal justice system, the aim of which is to prevent and control crime, and that the conduct of every functionary within the system has an impact on the entire system,

(d) That every law enforcement agency, in fulfilment of the first premise of every profession, should be held to the duty of disciplining itself in complete conformity with the principles and standards herein provided and that the actions of law enforcement officials should be responsive to public scrutiny, whether exercised by a review board, a ministry, a procuracy, the judiciary, an ombudsman, a citizens' committee or any combination thereof, or any other reviewing agency,

(e) That standards as such lack practical value unless their content and meaning, through education and training and through monitoring, become part of the creed of every law enforcement official,

Adopts the Code of Conduct for Law Enforcement Officials set forth in the annex to the present resolution and decides to transmit it to Governments with the recommendation that favourable consideration should be given to its use within the framework of national legislation or practice as a body of principles for observance by law enforcement officials.

*Article 1.* Law enforcement officials shall at all times fulfil the duty imposed upon them by law, by serving the community and by protecting all persons against illegal acts, consistent with the high degree of responsibility required by their profession.

*Commentary.* (a) The term "law enforcement officials" includes all officers of the law, whether appointed or elected, who exercise police powers, especially the powers of arrest or detention.

(b) In countries where police powers are exercised by military authorities, whether uniformed or not, or by state security forces, the definition of law enforcement officials shall be regarded as including officers of such services.

(c) Service to the community is intended to include particularly the rendition of services of assistance to those members of the community who by reason of personal, economic, social or other emergencies are in need of immediate aid.

(d) This provision is intended to cover not only all violent, predatory and harmful acts, but extends to the full range of prohibitions under penal statutes. It extends to conduct by persons not capable of incurring criminal liability.

*Article 2.* In the performance of their duty, law enforcement officials shall respect and protect human dignity and maintain and uphold the human rights of all persons.

*Commentary.* (a) The human rights in question are identified and protected by national and international law.

Among the relevant international instruments are the Universal Declaration of Human Rights, the International Covenant on Civil and Political Rights, the Declaration on the Protection of All Persons from Being Subjected to Torture and Other Cruel, Inhuman or Degrading Treatment or Punishment, the United Nations Declaration on the Elimination of All Forms of Racial Discrimination, the International Convention on the Elimination of all Forms of Racial Discrimination, the International Convention on the Suppression and Punishment of the Crime of *Apartheid,* the Convention on the Prevention and Punishment of the Crime of Genocide, the Standard Minimum Rules for the Treatment of Prisoners and the Vienna Convention on Consular Relations.

(b) National commentaries to this provision should indicate regional or national provisions identifying and protecting these rights.

*Article 3.* Law enforcement officials may use force only when strictly necessary and to the extent required for the performance of their duty.

*Commentary.* (a) This provision emphasizes that the use of force by law enforcement officials should be exceptional; while it implies that law enforcement officials may be authorized to use force as is reasonably necessary under the circumstances for the prevention of crime or in effecting or assisting in the lawful arrest of offenders or suspected offenders, no force going beyond that may be used.

(b) National law ordinarily restricts the use of force by law enforcement officials in accordance with a principle of proportionality. It is to be understood that such national principles of proportionality are to be respected in the interpretation of this provision. In no case should this provision be interpreted to authorize the use of force which is disproportionate to the legitimate objective to be achieved.

(c) The use of firearms is considered an extreme measure. Every effort should be made to exclude the use of firearms, especially against children. In general, firearms should not be used except when a suspected offender offers armed resistance or otherwise jeopardizes the lives of others and less extreme measures are not sufficient to restrain or apprehend the suspected offender. In every instance in which a firearm is discharged, a report should be made promptly to the competent authorities.

*Article 4.* Matters of a confidential nature in the possession of law enforcement officials shall be kept confidential, unless the performance of duty, or the needs of justice, strictly require otherwise.

*Commentary.* By the nature of their duties, law enforcement officials obtain information which may relate to private lives or be potentially harmful to the interests, and especially the reputation, of others. Great care should be exercised in safeguarding and using such information, which should be disclosed only in the performance of duty or to serve the needs of justice. Any disclosure of such information for other purposes is wholly improper.

*Article 5.* No law enforcement official may inflict, instigate or tolerate any act of torture or other cruel, inhuman or degrading treatment or punishment, nor may any law enforcement official invoke superior orders or exceptional circumstances such as a state of war or a threat of war, a threat to national security, internal political instability or any other public emergency as a justification of torture or other cruel, inhuman or degrading treatment or punishment.

*Commentary.* (a) This prohibition derives from the Declaration on the Protection of All Persons from Being Subjected to Torture and Other Cruel, Inhuman or Degrading Treatment or Punishment, adopted by the General Assembly, according to which:

Such an act is "an offence to human dignity and shall be condemned as a denial of the purposes of the Charter of the United Nations and as a violation of the human rights and fundamental freedoms proclaimed in the Universal Declaration of Human Rights" and other international human rights instruments.

(b) The Declaration defines torture as follows:

". . . torture means any act by which severe pain or suffering, whether physical or mental, is intentionally inflicted by or at the instigation of a public official on a person for such purposes as obtaining from him or a third person information or confession, punishing him for an act he has committed or is suspected of having committed, or intimidating him or other persons. It does not include pain or suffering arising only from, inherent in or incidental to, lawful sanctions to the extent consistent with the Standard Minimum Rules for the Treatment of Prisoners."

(c) The term "cruel, inhuman or degrading treatment or punishment" has not been defined by the General Assembly, but should be interpreted so as to extend the widest possible protection against abuses, whether physical or mental.

*Article 6.* Law enforcement officials shall ensure the full protection of the health of persons in their custody and, in particular, take immediate action to secure medical attention whenever required.

*Commentary.* (a) "Medical attention", which refers to services rendered by any medical personnel, including certified medical practitioners and paramedics, shall be secured when needed or requested.

(b) While the medical personnel are likely to be attached to the law enforcement operation, law enforcement officials must take into account the judgement of such personnel when they recommend providing the person in custody with appropriate treatment through, or in consultation with, medical personnel from outside the law enforcement operation.

(c) It is understood that law enforcement officials shall also secure medical attention for victims of violations of law or of accidents occurring in the course of violations of law.

*Article 7.* Law enforcement officials shall not commit any act of corruption. They shall also rigorously oppose and combat all such acts.

*Commentary.* (a) Any act of corruption, in the same way as any other abuse of authority, is incompatible with the profession of law enforcement officials. The law must be enforced fully with respect to any law enforcement official who commits an act of corruption, as Governments cannot expect to enforce the law among their citizens if they cannot, or will not, enforce the law against their own agents and within their own agencies.

(b) While the definition of corruption must be subject to national law, it should be understood to encompass the commission or omission of an act in the performance of or in connexion with one's duties, in response to gifts, promises or incentives demanded or accepted, or the wrongful receipt of these once the act has been committed or omitted.

(c) The expression "act of corruption" referred to above should be understood to encompass attempted corruption.

*Article 8.* Law enforcement officials shall respect the law and the present Code. They shall also, to the best of their capability, prevent and rigorously oppose any violations of them.

Law enforcement officials who have reason to believe that a violation of this Code has occurred or is about to occur shall report the matter to their superior authorities and, where necessary, to other appropriate authorities or organs vested with reviewing or remedial power.

*Commentary.* (a) This Code shall be observed whenever it has been incorporated into national legislation or practice. If legislation or practice contains stricter provisions than those of the present Code, those stricter provisions shall be observed.

(b) The article seeks to preserve the balance between the need for internal discipline of the agency on which public safety is largely dependent, on the one hand, and the need for dealing with violations of basic human rights, on the other. Law enforcement officials shall report violations within the chain of command and take other lawful action outside the chain of command only when no other remedies are available or effective. It is understood that law enforcement officials shall not suffer administrative or other penalties because they have reported that a violation of this Code has occurred or is about to occur.

(c) The terms "appropriate authorities or organs vested with reviewing or remedial power" refer to any authority or organ existing under national law, whether internal to the law enforcement agency, or independent thereof, with statutory, customary or other power to review grievances and complaints arising out of violations within the purview of this Code.

(d) In some countries, the mass media may be regarded as performing complaint review functions similar to those described in commentary (c). Law enforcement officials may, therefore, be justified if, as a last resort and in accordance with the laws and customs of their own countries and with the provisions of article 4 of the present Code, they bring violations to the attention of public opinion through the mass media.

(e) Law enforcement officials who comply with the provisions of this Code deserve the respect, the full support and the co-operation of the community and of the law enforcement agency in which they serve, as well as of the law enforcement profession.

***GUIDELINES FOR IMPLEMENTATION OF CODE OF CONDUCT (1989).*** With a view to promoting the implementation of the provisions of the Code of Conduct for Law Enforcement Officials, which the UN General Assembly had adopted in 17 December 1979 (resolution 34/169), the ECONOMIC AND SOCIAL COUNCIL on 24 May 1989 approved (resolution 1989/ 61) a series of Guidelines for the Effective Implementation of the Code of Conduct for Law Enforcement

Officials which had been prepared at its request by the COMMITTEE ON CRIME PREVENTION AND CONTROL. The Council at the same time invited the Eighth United Nations Congress on the Prevention of Crime and the Treatment of Offenders to explore ways and means of stimulating adherence to the guidelines.

The guidelines endorsed by the Council (resolution 1989/61, annex) are as follows:

### I. Application of the Code

*A. General Principles.* 1. The principles embodied in the Code shall be reflected in national legislation and practice.

2. In order to achieve the aims and objectives set out in article 1 of the Code and its Commentaries, the definition of "law enforcement officials" shall be given the widest possible interpretation.

3. The Code shall be made applicable to all law enforcement officials, regardless of their jurisdiction.

4. Governments shall adopt the necessary measures to instruct, in basic training and all subsequent training and refresher courses, law enforcement officials that is connected with the Code as well as other basic texts on the issue of human rights.

*B. Specific Issues.* 1. Selection, education and training. The selection, education and training of law enforcement officials shall be given prime importance. Governments shall also promote education and training through a fruitful exchange of ideas at the regional and interregional levels.

2. Salary and working conditions. All law enforcement officials shall be adequately remunerated and shall be provided with appropriate working conditions.

3. Discipline and supervision. Effective mechanisms shall be established to ensure the internal discipline and external control as well as the supervision of law enforcement officials.

4. Complaints by members of the public. Particular provisions shall be made, within the mechanisms mentioned under paragraph 3 above, for the receipt and processing of complaints against law enforcement officials made by members of the public, and the existence of these provisions shall be made known to the public.

### II. Implementation of the Code

*A. At the National Level.* 1. The Code shall be made available to all law enforcement officials and competent authorities in their own language.

2. Governments shall disseminate the Code and all domestic laws giving effect to it so as to ensure that the principles and rights contained therein become known to the public in general.

3. In considering measures to promote the application of the Code, Governments shall organize symposia on the role and functions of law enforcement officials in the protection of human rights and the prevention of crime.

*B. At the International Level.* 1. Governments shall inform the Secretary-General at appropriate intervals of at least five years on the extent of the implementation of the Code.

2. The Secretary-General shall prepare periodic reports on progress made with respect to the implementation of the Code, drawing also on observations and on the co-operation of specialized agencies and relevant intergovernmental or-

ganizations and non-governmental organizations in consultative status with the Economic and Social Council.

3. As part of the reports mentioned above, Governments shall provide to the Secretary-General copies of abstracts of laws, regulations and administrative measures concerning the application of the Code, any other relevant information on its implementation, as well as information on possible difficulties in its application.

4. The Secretary-General shall submit the above-mentioned reports to the Committee on Crime Prevention and Control for consideration and further action, as appropriate.

5. The Secretary-General shall make available the Code and the present guidelines to all States and intergovernmental and non-governmental organizations concerned, in all official languages of the United Nations.

6. The United Nations, as part of its advisory services and technical co-operation and development programmes, shall:

(a) Make available to Governments requesting them the services of experts and regional and interregional advisers to assist in implementing the provisions of the Code;

(b) Promote national and regional training seminars and other meetings on the Code and on the role and functions of law enforcement officials in the protection of human rights and the prevention of crime.

7. The United Nations regional institutes shall be encouraged to organize seminars and training courses on the Code and to carry out research on the extent to which the Code is implemented in the countries of the region as well as the difficulties encountered.

**BIBLIOGRAPHY.** An-Na'im, A. A., ed. "Police, Security Forces and Human Rights in the Third World," *Third World Legal Studies, 1990* [1990]. Special issue, in English.

Bishop, Jeanne E. "The Right to be Arrested: British Government Summary Executions," *New York Law School Journal of International and Comparative Law* 11, no. 1 & 2 (1990): 207–228. Scholarly article, in English.

Chevigny, Paul G. "Police Deadly Force as Social Control: Jamaica, Argentina, and Brazil," *Criminal Law Forum* 1, no. 3 (Spring 1990): 389–425. Scholarly article, in English.

Fernandez, Lovell. *Police Abuses of Non-Political Criminal Suspects: A Survey of Practices in the Cape Peninsula Area.* Cape Town, South Africa: Institute of Criminology, University of Cape Town, 1991. Scholarly monograph, in English.

Hillyard, Paddy. *Suspect Community: People's Experience of the Prevention of Terrorism Acts in Britain.* Boulder, CO, USA: Westview Press, 1993. Scholarly monograph, in English.

Institute of Criminology, University of Cape Town; Legal Education Action Project; and Criminal Justice Resource Centre. *Kitskonstabels in Crisis: A Closer Look at Black on Black Policing.* Cape Town, South Africa: Institute of Criminology, 1990. Scholarly report, in English.

Jagwanth, Saras. "Policing of the Conflict in the Greater Pietermaritzburg Area: A Perception Study," *South African Journal on Human Rights* 8, Part 4 (1992): 536–555. Scholarly article, in English.

## LAWYERS: BASIC PRINCIPLES ON THE ROLE OF LAWYERS.

The Basic Principles were adopted by the Eighth United Nations Congress on the Prevention of Crime and the Treatment of Offenders, held in Havana, Cuba, from 27 August to 7 September 1990. The text (UN publication, Sales no. E.91.IV.2, p. 118) is as follows:

Whereas in the Charter of the United Nations the peoples of the world affirm, inter alia, their determination to establish conditions under which justice can be maintained, and proclaim as one of their purposes the achievement of international cooperation in promoting and encouraging respect for human rights and fundamental freedoms without distinction as to race, sex, language, or religion,

Whereas the Universal Declaration of Human Rights enshrines the principles of equality before the law, the presumption of innocence, the right to a fair and public hearing by an independent and impartial tribunal, and all the guarantees necessary for the defence of everyone charged with a penal offence,

Whereas the International Covenant on Civil and Political Rights proclaims, in addition, the right to be tried without undue delay and the right to a fair and public hearing by a competent, independent, and impartial tribunal established by law,

Whereas the International Covenant on Economic, Social and Cultural Rights recalls the obligation of States under the charter to promote universal respect for, and observance of, human rights and freedoms,

Whereas the body of Principles for the Protection of All Persons under Any Form of Detention or Imprisonment provides that a detained person shall be entitled to have the assistance of, and to communicate and consult with, legal counsel,

Whereas the Standard Minimum Rules for the Treatment of Prisoners recommends, in particular, that legal assistance and confidential communication with counsel should be ensured to untried prisoners,

Whereas the Safeguards guaranteeing protection of those facing the death penalty reaffirm the right of everyone suspected or charged with a crime for which capital punishment may be imposed to adequate legal assistance at all stages of the proceedings, in accordance with article 14 of the International Covenant on Civil and Political Rights,

Whereas the Declaration of Basic Principles of Justice for Victims of Crime and Abuse of Power recommends measures to be taken at the international and national levels to improve access to justice and fair treatment, restitution, compensation and assistance for victims of crime,

Whereas adequate protection of the human rights and fundamental freedoms to which all persons are entitled, be they economic, social and cultural, or civil and political, requires that all persons have effective access to legal services provided by an independent legal profession,

Whereas professional associations of lawyers have a vital role to play in upholding professional standards and ethics, protecting their members from persecution and improper restrictions and infringements, providing legal services to all in need of them, and cooperating with governmental and other institutions in furthering the ends of justice and public interest,

The Basic Principles on the role of Lawyers, set forth below, which have been formulated to assist Member States in their task of promoting and ensuring the proper role of lawyers, should be respected and taken into account by Governments within the framework of their national legislation and practice and should be brought to the attention of lawyers as well as other persons, such as judges, prosecutors, members of the executive and the legislature, and the public in general. These principles shall also apply, as appropriate, to persons who exercise the functions of lawyers without having the formal status of lawyers.

## Access to Lawyers and Legal Services

1. All persons are entitled to call upon the assistance of a lawyer of their choice to protect and establish their rights and to defend them in all stages of criminal proceedings.

2. Governments shall ensure that efficient procedures and responsive mechanisms for effective and equal access to lawyers are provided for all persons within their territory and subject to their jurisdiction, without distinction of any kind, such as discrimination based on race, color, ethnic origin, sex, language, religion, political or other opinion, national or social origin, property, birth, economic or other status.

3. Governments shall ensure the provision of sufficient funding and other resources for legal services to the poor and, as necessary, to other disadvantaged persons. Professional associations of lawyers shall cooperate in the organization and provision of services, facilities, and other resources.

4. Governments and professional associations of lawyers shall promote programmes to inform the public about their rights and duties under the law and the important role of lawyers in protecting their fundamental freedoms. Special attention should be given to assisting the poor and other disadvantaged persons so as to enable them to assert their rights and, where necessary, call upon the assistance of lawyers.

## Special Safeguards in Criminal Justice Matters

5. Governments shall ensure that all persons are immediately informed by the competent authority of their right to be assisted by a lawyer of their own choice upon arrest or detention or when charged with a criminal offence.

6. Any such persons who do not have a lawyer shall, in all cases in which the interests of justice so require, be entitled to have a lawyer of experience and competence commensurate with the nature of the offence assigned to them in order to provide effective legal assistance, without payment by them if they lack sufficient means to pay for such services.

7. Governments shall further ensure that all persons arrested or detained, with or without criminal charge, shall have prompt access to a lawyer, and in any case not later than 48 hours from the time of arrest or detention.

8. All arrested, detained or imprisoned persons shall be provided with adequate opportunities, time and facilities to be visited by and to communicate and consult with a lawyer, without delay, interception or censorship and in full confidentiality. Such consultations may be within sight, but not with the hearing, of law enforcement officials.

## Qualifications and Training

9. Governments, professional associations of lawyers and educational institutions shall ensure that lawyers have appropriate education and training and be made aware of the ideals and ethical duties of the lawyer and of human rights and fundamental freedoms recognized by national and international law.

10. Governments, professional associations of lawyers and educational institutions shall ensure that there is no discrimination against a person with respect to entry into or continued practice within the legal profession on the grounds of race, colour, sex, ethnic origin, religion, political or other opinion, national or social origin, property, birth, economic or other status, except that a requirement, that a layer must be a national of the country concerned, shall not be considered discriminatory.

11. In countries where there exist groups, communities, or regions whose needs for legal services are not met, particularly where such groups have distinct cultures, traditions or languages or have been the victims of past discrimination, Governments, professional associations of lawyers and educational institutions should take special measures to provide opportunities for candidates from these groups to enter the legal profession and should ensure that they receive training appropriate to the needs of their group.

## Duties and Responsibilities

12. Lawyers shall at all times maintain the honor and dignity of their profession as essential agents of the administration of justice.

13. The duties of lawyers towards their clients shall include:

(a) Advising clients as to their legal rights and obligations, and as to the working of the legal system insofar as it is relevant to the legal rights and obligations of the clients;

(b) Assisting clients in every appropriate way, and taking legal action to protect their interests;

(c) Assisting clients before courts, tribunals, or administrative authorities, where appropriate.

14. Lawyers, in protecting the rights of their clients and in promoting the cause of justice, shall seek to uphold human rights and fundamental freedoms recognized by national and international law and shall at all times act freely and diligently in accordance with the law and recognized standards and ethics of the legal profession.

15. Lawyers shall always loyally respect the interests of their clients.

## Guarantees for the Functioning of Lawyers

16. Governments shall ensure that lawyers (a) are able to perform all of their professional functions without intimidation, hindrance, harassment or improper interference; (b) are able to travel and to consult with their clients freely both within their own country and abroad; and (c) shall not suffer, or be threatened with, prosecution or administrative, economic or other sanctions for any action taken in accordance with recognized professional duties, standards, and ethics.

17. Where the security of lawyers is threatened as a result of discharging their functions, they shall be adequately safeguarded by the authorities.

18. Lawyers shall not be identified with their clients or their clients' causes as a result of discharging their functions.

19. No court or administrative authority before whom the right to counsel is recognized shall refuse to recognize the right of a lawyer to appear before it for his or her client unless that lawyer has been disqualified in accordance with national law and practice and in conformity with these principles.

20. Lawyers shall enjoy civil and penal immunity for relevant statements made in good faith in written or oral pleadings or in their professional appearances before a court, tribunal, or other legal or administrative authority.

21. It is the duty of the competent authorities to ensure lawyers access to appropriate information, files, and documents in their possession or control in sufficient time to enable lawyers to provide effective legal assistance to their cli-

ents. Such access should be provided at the earliest appropriate time.

22. Governments shall recognize and respect that all communications and consultations between lawyers and their clients within their professional relationship are confidential.

### Freedom of Expression and Association

23. Lawyers like other citizens are entitled to freedom of expression, belief, association, and assembly. In particular, they shall have the right to take part in public discussion of matters concerning the law, the administration of justice, and the promotion and protection of human rights and to join or form local, national, or international organizations and attend their meetings, without suffering professional restrictions by reason of their lawful action or their membership in a lawful organization. In exercising these rights, lawyers shall always conduct themselves in accordance with the law and the recognized standards and ethics of the legal profession.

### Professional Associations of Lawyers

24. Lawyers shall be entitled to form and join self-governing professional associations to represent their interests, promote their continuing education and training, and protect their professional integrity. The executive body of the professional associations shall be elected by its members and shall exercise its function without external interference.

25. Professional associations of lawyers shall cooperate with Governments to ensure that everyone has effective and equal access to legal services and that lawyers are able, without improper interference, to counsel and assist their clients in accordance with the law and recognized professional standards and ethics.

### Disciplinary Proceedings

26. Codes of professional conduct for lawyers shall be established by the legal profession through its appropriate organs, or by legislation, in accordance with national law and custom and recognized international standards and norms.

27. Charges or complaints made against lawyers in their professional capacity shall be processed expeditiously and fairly under appropriate procedures. Lawyers shall have the right to a fair hearing, including the right to be assisted by a lawyer of their choice.

28. Disciplinary proceedings against lawyers shall be brought before an impartial disciplinary committee established by the legal profession, before an independent statutory authority, or before a court, and shall be subject to an independent judicial review.

29. All disciplinary proceedings shall be determined in accordance with the code of professional conduct and other recognized standards and ethics of the legal profession and in the light of these principles.

*BIBLIOGRAPHY.* Brody, Reed, ed. *Attacks on Justice: The Harassment and Persecution of Judges and Lawyers January 1988–June 1989.* Geneva, Switzerland: Centre for the Independence of Judges and Lawyers of the International Commission of Jurists, 1989. NGO annual report, in English.

Centre for the Independence of Judges and Lawyers. "The Independence of Judges and Lawyers: A Compilation of International Standards," *CIJL Bulletin* no. 25–26 (April–October 1990). Special issue, in English.

Human Rights in China (HRIC). *Going through the Motions: The Role of Defense Counsel in the Trials of the 1989 Protesters.* New York: 1993. Monograph, in English and Chinese.

Lawyers Committee for Human Rights (LCHR). *In Defense of Rights: Attacks on Lawyers and Judges in 1989.* New York: 1990. NGO annual report, in English.

Murungi, Kiraitu. *A Working Paper on the Role of the Lawyer with Specific Reference to the Implementation of Human Rights.* Ontario, Canada: African Human Rights Research Association, 1990. Scholarly article, in English.

Ross, Stanley D. "The Rule of Law and Lawyers in Kenya," *Journal of Modern African Studies* 30, no. 3 (Sept. 1992): 421–442. Scholarly article, in English.

## LAWYERS: GUIDELINES ON THE ROLE OF PROSECUTORS.

The Guidelines were prepared and adopted by the Eighth United Nations Congress on the Prevention of Crime and the Treatment of Offenders, convened at Havana, Cuba, from 27 August to 7 September 1990, as follows:

Whereas in the Charter of the United Nations the peoples of the world affirm, *inter alia,* their determination to establish conditions under which justice can be maintained, and proclaim as one of their purposes the achievement of international cooperation in promoting and encouraging respect for human rights and fundamental freedoms without distinction as to race, sex, language or religion,

Whereas the Universal Declaration of Human Rights enshrines the principles of equality before the law, the presumption of innocence and the right to a fair and public hearing by an independent and impartial tribunal,

Whereas frequently there still exists a gap between the vision underlying those principles and the actual situation,

Whereas the organization and administration of justice in every country should be inspired by those principles, and efforts undertaken to translate them fully into reality,

Whereas prosecutors play a crucial role in the administration of justice, and rules concerning the performance of their important responsibilities should promote their respect for and compliance with the above-mentioned principles, thus contributing to fair and equitable criminal justice and the effective protection of citizens against crime,

Whereas it is essential to ensure that prosecutors possess the professional qualifications required for the accomplishment of their functions, through improved methods of recruitment and legal and professional training, and through the provision of all necessary means for the proper performance of their role in combating criminality, particularly in its new forms and dimensions,

Whereas the General Assembly, by its resolution 34/169 of 17 December 1979, adopted the Code of Conduct for Law Enforcement Officials, on the recommendation of the Fifth United Nations Congress on the Prevention of Crime and the Treatment of Offenders,

Whereas in resolution 16 of the Sixth United Nations Congress on the Prevention of Crime and the Treatment of Offenders, the Committee on Crime Prevention and Control was called upon to include among its priorities the elaboration of guidelines relating to the independence of judges and the selection, professional training and status of judges and prosecutors,

Whereas the Seventh United Nations Congress on the Prevention of Crime and the Treatment of Offenders adopted the Basic Principles on the Independence of the Judiciary, subsequently endorsed by the General Assembly in its resolutions 40/32 of 29 November 1985 and 40/146 of 13 December 1985,

Whereas the Declaration of Basic Principles of Justice for Victims of Crime and Abuse of Power, recommends measures to be taken at the international and national levels to improve access to justice and fair treatment, restitution, compensation and assistance for victims of crime,

Whereas, in resolution 7 of the Seventh Congress, the Committee was called upon to consider the need for guidelines relating, *inter alia*, to the selection, professional training and status of prosecutors, their expected tasks and conduct, means to enhance their contribution to the smooth functioning of the criminal justice system and their cooperation with the police, the scope of their discretionary powers, and their role in criminal proceedings, and to report thereon to future United Nations congresses,

The Guidelines set forth below, which have been formulated to assist Member States in their tasks of securing and promoting the effectiveness, impartiality and fairness of prosecutors in criminal proceedings, should be respected and taken into account by Governments within the framework of their national legislation and practice, and should be brought to the attention of prosecutors, as well as other persons, such as judges, lawyers, members of the executive and the legislature and the public in general. The present Guidelines have been formulated principally with public prosecutors in mind, but they apply equally, as appropriate, to prosecutors appointed on an ad hoc basis.

## Qualifications, Selection and Training

1. Persons selected as prosecutors shall be individuals of integrity and ability, with appropriate training and qualifications.

2. States shall ensure that:

(a) Selection criteria for prosecutors embody safeguards against appointments based on partiality or prejudice, excluding any discrimination against a person on the grounds of race, colour, sex, language, religion, political or other opinion, national, social or ethnic origin, property, birth, economic or other status, except that it shall not be considered discriminatory to require a candidate for prosecutorial office to be a national of the country concerned;

(b) Prosecutors have appropriate education and training and should be made aware of the ideals and ethical duties of their office, of the constitutional and statutory protections for the rights of the suspect and the victim, and of human rights and fundamental freedoms recognized by national and international law.

## Status and Conditions of Service

3. Prosecutors, as essential agents of the administration of justice, shall at all times maintain the honour and dignity of their profession.

4. States shall ensure that prosecutors are able to perform their professional functions without intimidation, hindrance, harassment, improper interference or unjustified exposure to civil, penal or other liability.

5. Prosecutors and their families shall be physically protected by the authorities when their personal safety is threatened as a result of the discharge of prosecutorial functions.

6. Reasonable conditions of service of prosecutors, adequate remuneration and, where applicable, tenure, pension and age of retirement shall be set out by law or published rules or regulations.

7. Promotion of prosecutors, wherever such a system exists, shall be based on objective factors, in particular professional qualifications, ability, integrity and experience, and decided upon in accordance with fair and impartial procedures.

## Freedom of Expression and Association

8. Prosecutors like other citizens are entitled to freedom of expression, belief, association and assembly. In particular, they shall have the right to take part in public discussion of matters concerning the law, the administration of justice and the promotion and protection of human rights and to join or form local, national or international organizations and attend their meetings, without suffering professional disadvantage by reason of their lawful action or their membership in a lawful organization. In exercising these rights, prosecutors shall always conduct themselves in accordance with the law and the recognized standards and ethics of their profession.

9. Prosecutors shall be free to form and join professional associations or other organizations to represent their interests, to promote their professional training and to protect their status.

## Role in Criminal Proceedings

10. The office of prosecutors shall be strictly separated from judicial functions.

11. Prosecutors shall perform an active role in criminal proceedings, including institution of prosecution and, where authorized by law or consistent with local practice, in the investigation of crime, supervision over the legality of these investigations, supervision of the execution of court decisions and the exercise of other functions as representatives of the public interest.

12. Prosecutors shall, in accordance with the law, perform their duties fairly, consistently and expeditiously, and respect and protect human dignity and uphold human rights, thus contributing to ensuring due process and the smooth functioning of the criminal justice system.

13. In the performance of their duties, prosecutors shall:

(a) Carry out their functions impartially and avoid all political, social, religious, racial, cultural, sexual or any other kind of discrimination;

(b) Protect the public interest, act with objectivity, take proper account of the position of the suspect and the victim, and pay attention to all relevant circumstances, irrespective of whether they are to the advantage or disadvantage of the suspect;

(c) Keep matters in their possession confidential, unless the performance of duty or the needs of justice require otherwise;

(d) Consider the views and concerns of victims when their personal interests are affected and ensure that victims are informed of their rights in accordance with the Declaration of Basic Principles of Justice for Victims of Crime and Abuse of Power.

14. Prosecutors shall not initiate or continue prosecution, or shall make every effort to stay proceedings, when an impartial investigation shows the charge to be unfounded.

15. Prosecutors shall give due attention to the prosecu-

tion of crimes committed by public officials, particularly corruption, abuse of power, grave violations of human rights and other crimes recognized by international law and, where authorized by law or consistent with local practice, the investigation of such offences.

16. When prosecutors come into possession of evidence against suspects that they know or believe on reasonable grounds was obtained through recourse to unlawful methods, which constitute a grave violation of the suspect's human rights, especially involving torture or cruel, inhuman or degrading treatment or punishment, or other abuses of human rights, they shall refuse to use such evidence against anyone other than those who used such methods, or inform the Court accordingly, and shall take all necessary steps to ensure that those responsible for using such methods are brought to justice.

### Discretionary Functions

17. In countries where prosecutors are vested with discretionary functions, the law or published rules or regulations shall provide guidelines to enhance fairness and consistency of approach in taking decisions in the prosecution process, including institution or waiver of prosecution.

### Alternatives to Prosecution

18. In accordance with national law, prosecutors shall give due consideration to waiving prosecution, discontinuing proceedings conditionally or unconditionally, or diverting criminal cases from the formal justice system, with full respect for the rights of suspect(s) and the victim(s). For this purpose, States should fully explore the possibility of adopting diversion schemes not only to alleviate excessive court loads, but also to avoid the stigmatization of pre-trial detention, indictment and conviction, as well as the possible adverse effects of imprisonment.

19. In countries where prosecutors are vested with discretionary functions as to the decision whether or not to prosecute a juvenile, special considerations shall be given to the nature and gravity of the offence, protection of society and the personality and background of the juvenile. In making that decision, prosecutors shall particularly consider available alternatives to prosecution under the relevant juvenile justice laws and procedures. Prosecutors shall use their best efforts to take prosecutory action against juveniles only to the extent strictly necessary.

### Relations with Other Government Agencies or Institutions

20. In order to ensure the fairness and effectiveness of prosecution, prosecutors shall strive to cooperate with the police, the courts, the legal profession, public defenders and other government agencies or institutions.

### Disciplinary Proceedings

21. Disciplinary offences of prosecutors shall be based on law or lawful regulations. Complaints against prosecutors which allege that they acted in a manner clearly out of the range of professional standards shall be processed expeditiously and fairly under appropriate procedures. Prosecutors shall have the right to a fair hearing. The decision shall be subject to independent review.

22. Disciplinary proceedings against prosecutors shall

guarantee an objective evaluation and decision. They shall be determined in accordance with the law, the code of professional conduct and other established standards and ethics and in the light of the present Guidelines.

### Observance of the Guidelines

23. Prosecutors shall respect the present Guidelines. They shall also, to the best of their capability, prevent and actively oppose any violations thereof.

24. Prosecutors who have reason to believe that a violation of the present Guidelines has occurred or is about to occur shall report the matter to their superior authorities and, where necessary, to other appropriate authorities or organs vested with reviewing or remedial power.

**LEAGUE OF ARAB STATES.** An intergovernmental organization composed of the governments of 21 countries of the Arab world, established in Cairo in 1945 at the Arab General Congress when the Pact of the League of Arab States was signed by its seven original members. Its headquarters were transferred to Tunis in 1979. Its member states are Algeria, Bahrain, Djibouti, Egypt, Iraq, Jordan, Kuwait, Lebanon, Libya, Mauritania, Morocco, Oman, Palestine, Qatar, Saudi Arabia, Somalia, Sudan, Syria, Tunisia, the United Arab Emirates, and Yemen. It maintains a permanent mission to the United Nations and has offices and information centers in Argentina, Austria, Belgium, Brazil, Canada, Ethiopia, France, Germany, Greece, India, Italy, Japan, Kenya, Senegal, Spain, the United Kingdom, and the United States.

The League has NGO relations with the **INTERNATIONAL COMMITTEE OF THE RED CROSS**; the International Red Cross and Red Crescent Movement; and the **INTERNATIONAL RED CROSS** and Red Crescent Societies. In addition, the League has special agreements regarding IGO status with the **FAO**, the **ILO**, and the **WHO**, among others.

The functions of the Arab League—as it is popularly known—are to strengthen ties between its member States, to coordinate their political planning, and to safeguard their independence and sovereignty. The League is concerned with a wide variety of matters, including questions of economics and finance, transportation, communications, cultural and social affairs; questions of health; and questions related to nationality, passports, visas, and interstate travel. It supports African development and anticolonial movements and occasionally plays a role in the settlement of regional disputes and in the reinforcement of collective security. Concerning Arab-Israeli relations, the Arab League has formulated a common strategy toward the recognition of a Palestinian homeland and a common economic policy toward the State of Israel.

A large number of specialized bodies have been established under the auspices of the Arab League, including the Arab Human Rights Committee and the Organization of Arab Petroleum Exporting Countries (OAPEC). It has also sponsored occasional Arab summit conferences.

Among its publications are the monthlies *Sh'oun Arabiyya* (Arab Perspectives) and the *Journal of Arab Affairs*, both published in Arabic; and the monthly *LAS Information Bulletin*, published in Arabic and English.

League of Arab States. Address: Box 503, 1080 Tunis, Tunisia. Telephone: (216-1) 890-100. Fax: (216-1) 701-801. Secretary-General: Dr. Esmat Abdel-Meguid.

**LEAGUE OF NATIONS.** Founded at the close of World War I as "a society of nations" for the purpose of maintaining the peace, the League of Nations was the predecessor of the United Nations. The covenant of the League—incorporated in the Treaty of Versailles on 28 June 1919–makes no reference to the rights or freedoms of individuals; indeed, a mild proposal by Japan to include a call for racial equality was hastily set aside on the insistence of Australia.

*THE MANDATES SYSTEM.* The covenant broke new ground in establishing the first international "mandates" system to protect those residents of former German colonies who were considered not yet capable of self-government. Provisions in peace treaties with Austria, Hungary, Bulgaria, and Turkey and in special treaties with Poland, Czechoslovakia, Romania, Yugoslavia, and Greece placed the protection of racial, religious, and linguistic minorities in those States—particularly the minorities created by changes in national boundary lines—under the protection of the League. Moreover, the League was directly involved in activities connected with the abolition of slavery and suppression of the slave trade, and with a wide variety of questions relating to the plight of refugees and of stateless persons.

Under the mandates system, former German colonies were assigned to more economically and industrially advanced States, who were expected to administer them not on their own behalf but as trustees of the League of Nations. Togoland and the Cameroons were divided between France and Great Britain; German East Africa was split between Great Britain and Belgium; and South West Africa was assigned to South Africa. The thinking behind the system was that, in the case of peoples "not yet able to stand by themselves under the strenuous conditions of the modern world," the mandatory States should apply the principle that the well-being and development of such peoples is a sacred trust of civilization.

In accordance with the peace treaties and the special treaties concerning minorities, the governments concerned agreed to ensure full and complete protection of life and liberty to all the inhabitants of the mandated territories, without distinction as to birth, nationality, language, race, or religion. All were guaranteed the free exercise, in public and in private, of any creed, religion, or belief the practice of which would not be inconsistent with public order or public morals. All were further guaranteed the free use of any language in private business and in private schools and the right to instruction in public primary schools in their own language, if they constituted a sizeable proportion of the population. In a few cases, particular privileges, such as the right of Jews to observe their sabbath as a holiday, were ensured. The protection of the rights set out in the treaties was placed in the hands of the League of Nations, and the specific guarantees could not be modified except with consent of a majority of the Council of the League.

The States thus charged with guaranteeing the rights of members of minorities vigorously opposed the treaty provisions and maintained that they had been unfairly compelled to do something which no other State had done, or would do, voluntarily. They looked upon the League's "minorities system" as an infringement upon their sovereignty and feared that it would inflame the separatist tendencies of the minorities concerned and otherwise stir up trouble. But the victorious "Great Powers" insisted that their demands were in the interest of peace in Europe and compelled acceptance of the guarantees.

Thus, while, to a certain extent, the League of Nations was concerned with the rights of individuals as well as the rights of States, this concern was never very broad or well-developed. Its efforts to protect the rights of individuals applied mainly to persons who formed part of an underprivileged group—a people, a class, or a minority—and it was only rarely concerned with the situation of other human beings.

There were, however, two notable exceptions. The first was that the League established, in 1921, the Office of the **HIGH COMMISSIONER FOR REFUGEES.** This office—which arranged repatriation or asylum, where possible, for persons who had left their native land either because they had been expelled or had fled to escape persecution, and which issued international ("Nansen") passports to enable them to move about and find new homes—considerably eased the plight of many such persons. The second was that, under the auspices of the League, the International Slavery Convention was signed at Geneva on 25 September 1926. This important treaty placed responsibility upon the League for the progressive abolition of slavery and suppression of the slave trade and established international machinery for this purpose within the framework of the League.

The United States was never a member of the League; but, at the height of its influence, in the 1920s, the League of Nations had 53 members. When Germany and Japan had resigned from the League in 1933, followed by Italy in 1936, the League, as a power for peace, collapsed. By 1939, as war raged in Europe, it was virtually an afterthought. The League was formally dissolved in 1946, transferring most of its powers to the United Nations.

**LEAGUE OF THE RED CROSS AND RED CRESCENT SOCIETIES.** A non-governmental organization in consultative status with the UN **ECONOMIC AND SOCIAL COUNCIL** (Category I), and with **UNESCO, WHO,** and **FAO,** the League and the **INTERNATIONAL COMMITTEE OF THE RED CROSS** form the International Red Cross and Red Crescent Movement, which includes 145 national Red Cross and Red Crescent Societies with a total membership of more than 230 individuals.

The League, acting as a permanent coordination and liaison body, encourages and assists all forms of humanitarian action on the part of its national affiliates designed to prevent or to alleviate human suffering. In recognition of its efforts, it received the **NOBEL PEACE PRIZE** in 1963, sharing that honor with the International Committee of the Red Cross.

Although the **INTERNATIONAL RED CROSS** was founded in 1863 by the first recipient of the Nobel Peace Prize, **HENRI DUNANT,** the League itself, as a coordinating body, was not instituted until 1919, after the end of World War I, when national societies turned their attention to helping famine victims and the homeless, especially in eastern Europe. Few countries had health ministries at the time, and there were no international bodies capable of organizing large-scale relief operations. Henry P. Davison, of the American Red Cross, convened an international medical conference in 1919 at which he proposed "to federate the Red Cross Societies of the different countries into an organization comparable to that of the League of Nations, in view of a permanent worldwide crusade to improve health, prevent sickness and alleviate suffering." Davison's proposal gained immediate support, and LORCS was established in Paris. Since 1939, its headquarters have been in Geneva.

The League performs a number of duties for the national societies. It contributes to the development of new national societies by providing advisers, equipment, and subsidies. It also acts as an international-level coordinator for emergency operations being carried out by a national society during a natural disaster.

Based on information and requests it receives from the afflicted area, it appeals to other member societies for assistance; forwards donations, foods, or other supplies not available in the stricken area; and, if needed, sends experts—in particular, medical teams—to help in relief operations. In countries often at risk from natural disasters, the League helps the national societies to minimize the toll on human life by developing disaster-preparedness plans, for example, the construction of shelters and the institution of warning systems. The League has also established an international network of warehouses to enable relief supplies to be sent to disaster zones with a minimum of delay.

In addition to its work with national societies, the League also assists refugees outside of conflict areas, a responsibility it often undertakes at the request of the Office of the UN **HIGH COMMISSIONER FOR REFUGEES.** In the area of health protection, the League has developed a variety of national society activities in the fields of community health care, health education, blood transfusion services, and large-scale vaccination campaigns. Finally, to support the many national societies that have responsibility for blood services, the League actively encourages the dissemination of the "Code of Ethics for Blood Donation and Transfusion," established in 1980 by the International Blood Transfusion Society.

The League of the Red Cross and Red Crescent Societies. Address: Chemin des Crêts 17, Petit-Saconnex, CP 372, CH–1211 Geneva 19, Switzerland. Telephone: (41-22) 34-55-80.

**LEBANON.** The Republic of Lebanon is an Arab country in western Asia, on the Mediterranean Sea. It has borders with Israel and Syria. It achieved independence from France in 1943 and became a member of the United Nations in 1945. Its population is estimated by the UN to be 3,098,000. Ethnic groups include Arabs (93%) and Armenians (7%). Languages commonly used include Arabic (official), French, and English. Religions practiced include Christianity (Greek Orthodox, Catholic, Maronite, and various Protestant denominations), Islam (Sunni and Shi'a), and Druze. Literacy is estimated at 75%.

The government (1994) took the form of a republic. Under the constitution, the president is elected by Parliament for a six-year term and serves as head of State. He appoints the Council of Ministers, headed by the premier; the Council is responsible to Parliament. Members of Parliament are elected by universal suffrage by numbers proportionate to the division of religious groups within the population. The judicial system includes religious as well as secular courts. Political parties organized along religious and ethnic considerations are numerous but ineffective because of the absence of parliamentary elections after 1972.

***RELIGIOUS CONFLICT.*** Religion has been a key factor in Lebanese history for many centuries. Together with Syria, Lebanon came under Roman domination and was included in the Byzantine Empire until part of it fell to the Arabs in the 7th century. Long before that, the Maronites, affiliated with the Roman Catholic Church, had established themselves, with the result that Lebanon became predominantly Christian, while Syria became predominantly Muslim. Adherents of the Druze sect, a group deriving from Islam but differing greatly from it, also settled in Lebanon and adjacent portions of Syria, and dissention between the Maronites and Druze led to frequent disturbances. The crusaders were active in Lebanon, and the Christians assisted them. After that time, until World War I, Lebanon was part of the Ottoman Empire.

Massacres of Maronites by Druzes took place in 1841 and 1860, and gave rise to pressure for the protection of Lebanese Christians by European governments. As a result, some local autonomy was granted to Lebanon. When the empire was broken up after the war, Lebanon and Syria were combined in the Levant States Mandate of the **LEAGUE OF NATIONS** and placed under French administration. Lebanon remained in French hands until, after being seized from the Vichy regime by the Free French in 1941, it achieved full independence in 1943.

Lebanon was able to achieve political unity at that time under an agreement between its religious factions known as the National Covenant of 1943, which provided that the president would be a Maronite Christian; the prime minister, a Sunni Muslim; and the president of the National Assembly, a Shi'a Muslim. Article 95 of its constitution provides that religious communities are to be equitably represented in public employment and in the composition of the cabinet.

However, as years passed, it became increasingly clear that Muslims had begun to outnumber Christians. The government did not take an official census, but Muslim leaders in 1977 put the ratio at 55% Muslim and 45% Christian and demanded greater representation in the government.

Full-scale internal conflict broke out in 1975 over difficulties stemming from the large number of Palestinian refugees in the country and the presence of Palestinian commandos. Late in 1976, the Arab Deterrent Force, composed largely of Syrian troops, moved in and separated the combatants.

***UN PEACEKEEPING MISSIONS.*** The first UN peacekeeping mission to Lebanon, the United Nations Observation Group in Lebanon (UNOGIL), was estab-

lished from June to December 1958 to ensure that no illegal infiltration of personnel or supply of arms crossed the Lebanese borders during the Lebanese-Syrian conflict.

Invasion of Lebanon by Israel in 1978 provoked the UN **SECURITY COUNCIL** to create a second peacekeeping force, the UN Interim Force in Lebanon (UNIFIL), with the mandate of confirming the withdrawal of Israel forces from southern Lebanon. A second invasion by Israel, in 1982, resulted in dispersal of **PALESTINE LIBERATION ORGANIZATION** units to other Arab countries. However, the assassination of Lebanon's President-Elect Bashir Gemayel on 14 September 1982 and the massacre by Lebanese Christian troops of hundreds of Palestinian refugees in the Sabra and Shatila camps in Beirut a few days later stepped up the conflict. A multinational peacekeeping force composed of American, British, French, and Italian elements was established in 1983 but withdrew in 1984 after 241 American marines and 58 French soldiers died as a result of separate but related suicide bombings. The mandate for UNIFIL continues to date; the force has headquarters in Naqoura, Lebanon.

On 6 March 1994 the UN **COMMISSION ON HUMAN RIGHTS** expressed (resolution 1984/83) its grave concern about "the persisting practices of the Israeli occupation forces in southern Lebanon, which constitute a violation of the principles of international law regarding the protection of human rights, in particular the Universal Declaration of Human Rights, as well as a grave violation of the relevant provisions of international humanitarian law as contained in the Geneva Convention relative to the Protection of Civilian Persons in Time of War, of 12 August 1949, and the Hague Convention IV of 1907."

In the resolution, the Commission:

1. Condemns the continued Israeli violations of human rights in southern Lebanon, manifested particularly by the arbitrary detention of civilians, the destruction of their houses, the confiscation of their property, their expulsion from the occupied area, the bombardment of villages and civilian areas; and other practices violating human rights;

2. Calls upon Israel to put an end immediately to such practices and to implement the above-mentioned resolutions of the Security Council which demand the immediate, total and unconditional withdrawal of Israel from all Lebanese territories and respect for the sovereignty, independence and territorial integrity of Lebanon;

3. Also calls upon the Government of Israel, the occupying Power of territories in southern Lebanon and the west Bekaa, to comply with the Geneva Conventions of 1949, specifically the Geneva Convention relative to the Protection of Civilian Persons in Time of War;

4. Further calls upon the Government of Israel, the occupying Power of territories in southern Lebanon and the west Bekaa, to release immediately all those Lebanese and other prisoners detained in the Israeli prisons and detention

centres contrary to all the Geneva Conventions and to other provisions of international law;

5. Calls upon the Government of Israel, the occupying Power of territories in southern Lebanon and the west Bekaa, to facilitate the humanitarian mission of the International Committee of the Red Cross and other humanitarian organizations in that region and, in particular, to allow these organizations to visit the detention centres of Khiyam and Marjayoun and verify the living conditions of the detainees.

In addition to Israeli occupation, Syria has provoked conflict in Lebanon; Syria has historically considered Lebanon as part of its territory. A treaty signed in May 1991 between Lebanon and Syria recognized Lebanon as a separate and independent state for the first time since the two countries gained independence in 1943.

Although the country's civil war ended in October 1990 with the Ta'if Accord, which increased the political power of the Muslims, and although most of the militant groups were disarmed, large areas of Lebanon remained under occupation by Israel. Legislative elections held in 1992 resulted in 128 deputies evenly divided between Christians and Muslims. In March 1994 all political programs and newscasts not controlled by the Government were banned. In addition, arrests against government opponents intensified, especially the arrests of suspected supporters of the banned Lebanese Forces and the ousted Gen. Michel Aoun. The non-governmental organization **HUMAN RIGHTS WATCH** reported that, in 1994, "the government increased its reliance on military courts to try civilians accused of offenses considered harmful to national security, often in proceedings falling far short of internationally recognized standards for fair trials."

**BIBLIOGRAPHY.** Arab Organization for Human Rights. *Human Rights in the Arab World.* Cairo: 1987. NGO report, in English and Arabic.

Donnelly, J., and R. E. Howard, eds. *International Handbook on Human Rights.* Westport, CT, USA: Greenwood Press, 1987. Scholarly edited collection, in English.

Human Rights Watch. "Lebanon," in *Human Rights Watch World Report 1995,* pp. 295–299. New York: 1995. NGO report, in English.

Institute for Women's Studies in the Arab World. "Women and the Law in Lebanon," *Al-Raida* 9, no. 49 (May 1990): 3–7. Article, in English.

International Federation of Human Rights Leagues. *Liban: Missions d'enquêtes: situation des droits de l'homme, 1er au 10 mars 1994; situation des réfugiés palestiniens, 3 au 9 juin 1994* (Lebanon: Factfinding Missions: Human Rights Situation, 1–10 March 1994; Palestinian Refugees Situation, 3–9 June 1994). Paris: 1994. NGO factfinding report, in French.

Lassen, Nina, and Jacob Gammelgaard. *Report on the Danish Refugee Council's Mission to Cyprus and Lebanon.* Copenhagen, Denmark: Danish Refugee Council, 1991. NGO factfinding report, in English.

MacDowall, David. *Lebanon: A Conflict of Minorities.* London: Minority Rights Group, 1986. NGO report, in English.

Middle East Research and Information Project. "Leba-non's War: Any End in Sight?," *Middle East Report* no. 162 (Jan.–Feb.) 1990. Special issue, in English.

## LE DUC THO (1911–1991).

Born in northern Vietnam in the village of Dich Le, Le Duc Tho was the first Asian and the first Communist to be cited for the **NOBEL PEACE PRIZE** and the only winner to refuse it. When he was cited in 1973, along with **HENRY KISSINGER,** for "negotiating an end to the war in Vietnam," Le declined the honor because there was no "peace" in his country, citing violations to the peace accords by the South Vietnamese and the United States of America.

Le founded the Communist Party in Indochina in 1930. His life was dedicated to wars of liberation, especially to the independence of Vietnam (then called Indochina) from the French. In 1941, Le helped Ho Chi Minh found the Vietminh, a Communist-led nationalist movement. For his efforts against French rule, he was imprisoned for ten years. When World War II began, the French again imprisoned Le but released him, according to one version of the story, in 1944.

Throughout the long years of warfare to end French rule (1945–1954), Le rose steadily through the ranks of the Communist Party. With the end of the Indochina War, Vietnam was divided in two, and Le returned to his northern homeland. In 1955, he became a member of the politburo of the Lao Dong (Workers) Party and also served as the major Hanoi advisor to the National Liberation Front forces fighting to overthrow the government in South Vietnam. In 1968, when the Vietnam War was at its peak, Le met for the first time with Henry Kissinger to discuss ceasefire arrangements. The talks dragged on for five years, until, in January 1973, Le and Kissinger announced an accord that was based on major concessions by both sides. However, the pact and the ceasefire did not bring about an end to the hostilities, resulting not only in Le's refusal of the Nobel Peace Prize but criticism from many quarters that the Peace Prize had been awarded to two men who were actually waging war.

In 1975, Le engineered Hanoi's final plans for a victorious offensive against the South Vietnamese regime. He resigned his position on the politburo in 1986.

**BIBLIOGRAPHY.** *Current Biography Yearbook.* New York: W.H. Wilson & Company, 1975.

Gray, Tony. *Champions of Peace.* London: Paddington Press, 1976.

Schlessinger, Bernard S., and June H. Schlessinger, eds. *Who's Who of Nobel Prize Winners.* Phoenix, AZ, USA: Oryx Press, 1991.

# L

**LEGISLATIVE BODIES AND HUMAN RIGHTS.**
Legislative organs are institutions, established within
the framework of the government of nearly every
country, which enact the laws and regulations which
promote and protect human rights and fundamental
freedoms. Their role and functions in this respect are
described in a report by the UN Secretary-General entitled *National Institutions for the Protection and Promotion
of Human Rights* (UN Doc. E/CN.4/1987/37, paras. 7–
15) submitted to the UN COMMISSION ON HUMAN
RIGHTS at the request of the GENERAL ASSEMBLY (resolution 40/123):

In most countries the basic foundation for the protection
of the human rights of individuals at the national level is
established in the Constitution and developed by legislative
organs. It is indeed the role of these organs to enact laws
and regulations with a view to implementing the principles
formulated in the Constitution. Countries which do not
function under a written constitution, generally rely on the
parliament or on the equivalent legislative organ to ensure
the protection of human rights.

The essential function of parliament is, of course, its
power to abrogate old laws and make new ones. Because of
the importance of careful drafting of legislation, many parliaments have created select committees, whose primary
function is to scrutinize and draft all proposed legislation.

To strengthen further the role of parliament in the protection of human and civil rights, many countries have instituted organs functioning within the parliament, to heighten
parliament's awareness of corruption in the government,
and increase the parliament's ability to respond to allegations brought by constituents whose rights may have been
violated by illegal or unconstitutional acts, or by public authorities. These legislative organs fall into four basic categories: committees which seek to protect citizens from infringement of rights by the Executive; committees designed
to draft and scrutinize legislation; committees which may receive petitions from citizens asking for a parliamentary investigation into a matter of public or private interest; and
inquiry or investigatory committees.

Committees which are created to protect the rights of citizens from infringement by the Executive, may be either
standing committees or *ad hoc* committees. Standing committees are permanent parliamentary committees which conduct ongoing investigations throughout the year on a particular agenda of issues. *Ad hoc* committees are created to
respond to a particular situation or allegation requiring an
investigation, which involves the public interest. Both standing and *ad hoc* committees may investigate allegations and
report their findings to the entire parliament, urging that
appropriate action be taken. The purpose of these committees is to exercise control over the Executive, with a view to
restraining it from acting in an arbitrary or oppressive manner, to influence the policies of the government and to act
as a liaison between the government and the general public.

The power of parliament to check the powers and activities of the executive branch can also be exercised through
its authority to initiate investigations of executive offices. . . .

Increasingly, legislative bodies in many countries have created standing and *ad hoc* commissions of inquiry or investigation. These commissions are designed primarily to inquire
into matters of public interest which may involve arbitrary

action or violations of law. Both Houses of Congress in the
United States frequently set up standing or *ad hoc* committees to investigate a wide range of matters of public interest.
In 1974, one such committee, the United States Senate Select Committee, conducted hearings which led to the resignation of the President of the United States. Committees of
this nature are generally comprised only of members of the
legislative organ concerned, who have lawyers and independent investigators at their disposal. While such committees
do not have punitive powers or judicial authority, they may
examine witnesses under oath and take testimony.

Many countries throughout the world recognize the right
of individual citizens to petition the parliament or other legislative bodies for the redress of grievances. In the United
Kingdom, for example, the Committee of Petitions, appointed
by the House of Commons, may receive petitions from citizens
with the aim of redressing grievances. Similarly, in India, in
1952, the Lower House created a Committee on Petitions to
inquire into general grievances against the Government.

To redress the grievances of citizens who believe that incorrect information, omissions or unauthorized data about
themselves has been recorded in the State computer system,
New Zealand passed the Wanganui Computer Act in 1976,
which provides for the appointment of a Wanganui Computer Centre Privacy Commissioner as an officer of Parliament. Not a civil servant, and answerable only to Parliament,
the Privacy Commissioner may, if he/she deems it justified
after the completion of an investigation, direct the department concerned to make such deletions or alterations as may
be deemed necessary by the commission. The departments
in question are required to comply with the Commissioner's
directions.

The Spanish Standing Commission on Petitions, which
functions within the Congress of Deputies (the lower house
of the Cortes), is required to consider each individual or
collective petition received by Congress. The Commission
may refer any of these petitions to the President of the
Chamber, the Commission of Congress most suited to respond to the matter in question, the Senate, the Government, the Courts, or the Office of the Government Attorney.
Finally, the Presidiums of the Supreme Soviets in the USSR
have the power to receive and consider petitions from citizens.

***SEE ALSO*** *Constitutional Councils.*

**LESOTHO.** The Kingdom of Lesotho is a country in
southern Africa, surrounded by the territory of South
Africa except for a border with the Republic of Transkei, a South African national State. Formerly known
as the Basutoland Protectorate, Lesotho achieved independence from Great Britain in 1966 and became
a member of the United Nations the same year. Its
population is estimated to be 1,873,000. Ethnic groups
include Sothos (99%), Europeans (0.6%), and Asians
(0.4%). Languages commonly used include English
and Sesotho (both official). Christianity (Roman Catholic, 44%; Lesotho Evangelical, 30%; Anglican, 12%;
and other Protestant denominations, 14%) is the predominant religion. Literacy is estimated at 65%.

The government (1994) took the form of a constitutional monarchy under military control. The king, recognized as head of State and ruler, does not participate in political activities. Executive functions are performed by the prime minister and his cabinet.

On 1 January 1986, South Africa blockaded Lesotho which it claimed had given sanctuary to military units organizing an attempt to overthrow the South African government. A severe economic crisis resulted; and, on 20 January, the government headed by Chief Jonathan was ousted by a military coup. Five days later, the blockade was lifted after the military government agreed to expel the rebel units.

Political parties in Lesotho include the Basotho National Party, the Basutoland Congress, the Marema-tlou Freedom Party, and the United Democratic Party. A new constitution was promulgated in 1993 and elections which were to take the country from military to democratic rule were held in March 1993. In August 1994 King Lestie III dissolved the Cabinet of the first democratic leader, Ntsu Mokhehle, and installed a provisional government. However, in September 1994 the king signed an accord with Mokhehle, agreeing to abdicate and return the throne to his previously deposed father, King Moshoeshoe II.

**BIBLIOGRAPHY.** Amoah, P. K. A. "The Independence of the Judiciary in Botswana, Lesotho and Swaziland," *CIJL Bulletin* 19–20 (April–October 1987): 16–32. NGO article, in English.

Cooper, Dave. "Unions in Botswana: Comparisons with Lesotho," *South African Labour Bulletin* 10, no. 8 (July–August 1985): 103–114. Journal article, in English.

Maope, K. A. *Human Rights in Botswana, Lesotho and Swaziland: A Survey of the BOLESWA Countries.* Roma, Lesotho: Institute of Southern African Studies, 1986. NGO report, in English.

Neff, Stephen C. "Human Rights in Africa: Thoughts on the African Charter on Human and Peoples' Rights in the Light of Case Law from Botswana, Lesotho, and Swaziland," *International and Comparative Law Quarterly* 33 (1984): 331–347. Scholarly article, in English.

———. *Human Rights in Botswana, Lesotho and Swaziland: Implications of Adherence to International Human Rights Treaties.* Roma, Lesotho: Institute of Southern African Studies, 1986. Scholarly study, in English.

Okullu, H., A. Wako, and N. Koshy. *Report of the AAC-WCC Delegation to Lesotho.* Geneva: AAC-WCC, 1985. NGO report, in English.

**LETELIER-MOFFITT MEMORIAL HUMAN RIGHTS AWARD.** Established in 1977, this annual, honorary Award commemorates Orlando Letelier and Ronni Karpen Moffitt, staff members of the Institute for Policy Studies (IPS), who were killed in Washington, D.C., on 21 September 1976 by a car bomb, planted on orders of the Chilean military government. The Award recognizes two persons or organizations

(one from the United States and one from Latin America or the Caribbean) who work for human rights.

The 1994 recipients were Harry Belafonte, American entertainer, for calling public attention to abuses in South Africa, Rwanda, and Central America; the Coalition for Justice in the Maquiladoras for publicizing the deplorable working conditions of poor people in factories along the U.S.-Mexican border; and the Confederation of Indigenous Nationalities of Ecuador for its fight to protect the land rights and cultures of indigenous peoples throughout Latin America.

Other recent recipients include: Bishop Samuel Ruiz Garcia and Fray Bartolome of the Casas Human Rights Center in Chiapas, Mexico, and Marian Kramer and the National Welfare Rights Organization (1993); Evans Paul, former mayor of Port-au-Prince, Haiti, and Samuel Buffone and Michael Tigar, lawyers who won the suit against the Chilean government for the murders of Letelier and Moffitt (1992); La Mujer Obrera, for protecting the rights of Latina women working in the garment industry in El Paso, TX, and Jorge Gomes Lizarazo, founder of the Regional Committee for the Defense of Human Rights in the Magdalena Medio region of Colombia (1991); and the National Human Rights Coordinating Committee of Peru and Richard Trumka, president of the United Mine Workers of America (1990).

For more information, contact: IPS, 1601 Connecticut Ave., NW, Washington, D.C., 20009. Telephone: (202) 234-9382. Fax: (202) 387-7915.

**LIBERAL INTERNATIONAL.** Founded in 1947 in Oxford, UK, Liberal International is a non-governmental organization that promotes the growth of a free society based on personal liberty, personal responsibility, and social justice. It has members in 29 countries and maintains consultative status with the UN ECONOMIC AND SOCIAL COUNCIL (Category II) and UNESCO, and also with the COUNCIL OF EUROPE. Liberal International annually awards the Prize for Freedom.

Liberal International publishes the quarterly *Liberal Times*; the monthly *London Aerogramme*; and pamphlets, reports, and proceedings of specialized conferences.

Liberal International. Address: One Whitehall Place, London SW1A 2HE, UK. Telephone: (44-71) 839-5905. Fax: (44-71) 925-2685. Secretary-General: Julius Maaten.

**LIBERATION.** An international non-governmental organization in consultative status (Roster) with the

UN ECONOMIC AND SOCIAL COUNCIL. Founded in London in 1954 as the Movement of Colonial Freedom, Liberation promotes the rights of peoples to full independence, including self-determination and freedom from external political, economic, and military domination. Liberation also supports economic aid and technical assistance, free of external regulations, to underdeveloped nations and territories. The group publishes the magazine *Liberation* six times a year.

Liberation. Address: 490 Kingsland Road, London E8 4AE, UK. Telephone: (44-1) 254-6223. Secretary-General: Tony Gilbert.

**LIBERIA.** The Republic of Liberia is a country in western Africa, on the Atlantic Ocean. It has borders with Guinea, the Ivory Coast, and Sierra Leone. Founded in 1822 by the American Colonization Society as a place where freed American slaves could resettle, it achieved independence as the Free and Independent Republic of Liberia in 1847 and became a member of the United Nations in 1945.

Liberia's population is estimated to be 2,869,000. Ethnic groups include indigenous tribes (among them the Kpelle, Bassa, Gio, Kru, Grebo, Mano, Krahn, Gola, Gbandi, Loma, Kissi, Vai, Mandingo, and Belle communities) (95%), and descendants of freed American slaves (5%). Languages commonly used include English (official) and a number of African vernaculars. Religions practiced include Islam (20%), Christianity (15%), and Animism and other traditional beliefs (65%). Literacy is estimated at 24%.

The government (1994) took the form of a republic. However, since 1980 it had been under military rule, directed by the 17-member People's Redemption Council. In 1984, the Council was replaced by an appointed National Assembly. There is a civilian court system and a military tribunal; the latter was established to deal with persons charged with crimes against the security of the State.

Government, employment, and social activity remain in the hands of the descendants of American slaves, although they constitute only about 5% of the total population. Only rarely are members of the indigenous populations permitted to exercise their civil rights. Efforts to raise the educational level of those populations have not been notably successful.

Once a progressive, well-ordered country, Liberia in recent years has been the scene of serious outbreaks of violence which have caused many citizens to move to Guinea or to the Ivory Coast. These outbreaks have been centered mainly in Nimba County, in the northeast, and have involved guerillas opposed to Liberia's former president, General Samuel K. Doe, who himself seized power in a 1980 coup.

Government troops sent to Nimba County attacked civilian as well as military targets and Liberian civilians as well as invaders. An estimated 500 civilians lost their lives, and at least 70,000 fled to the Ivory Coast. The government's failure to control its troops gave rise to fear of prolonged civil strife.

In the summer of 1990, fighting between the government and insurgent forces graduated to a full-scale civil war, with the rebels gaining ground and approaching the capital city of Monrovia. Civilians fled to neighboring countries, and atrocities were reported against both sides. On 9 September 1990, President Doe was captured by rebel forces—and reportedly 60 other persons were killed—when he left the headquarters of the five-nation West African peacekeeping forces, which had been sent into Liberia. Prince Johnson, leader of one of the rebel factions, declared himself president of the country until elections could be held. After his capture, Doe was tortured and killed.

Since civil war had begun in December 1989, an estimated 150,000 Liberians had been killed by the end of 1994, and more than half the population had been displaced to refugee camps in Burkina Faso and Guinea. Indeed, more civilians than combatants have been killed. Another disturbing feature of the Liberian civil war is the use of child soldiers. **UNICEF** estimates that approximately 10% of the soldiers are under the age of 15.

In December 1994, the three leaders of the rebel movements signed a peace accord to take over from the interim civilian council appointed in March 1994. Charles Taylor, General Hezekiah Bowen, and Alhaji Kromah called for elections to be held on 10 October 1995.

**BIBLIOGRAPHY.** Africa Watch. *Liberia: Flight from Terror: Testimony of Abuses in Nimba County.* New York: Human Rights Watch, 1990. NGO report, in English.

————. *Liberia: A Human Rights Disaster—Violations of the Laws of War by All Parties to the Conflict.* New York: Human Rights Watch, 1990. NGO factfinding report, in English.

————. *Liberia: Waging War to Keep the Peace: The ECOMOG Intervention and Human Rights.* New York: Human Rights Watch, 1993. NGO factfinding report, in English.

Amnesty International. *Liberia: No Chance for a Lasting Peace without Effective Human Rights Guarantees.* London: 1993. NGO report, in English.

Fund for Free Expression. *Best Friends: Violations of Human Rights in Liberia, America's Closest Ally in Africa.* New York: 1986. NGO mission report, in English.

Geepu-Nah Tiepoh, Moses. "The Liberian Civil War: The Future of Liberian Refugees," *Refuge* 11, no. 3 (March 1992): 14–17. Article, in English.

Hayden, Thomas. *Report on Liberia: Human Rights Issues.* Washington, D.C.: Society of African Missions, 1985. NGO report, in English.

Human Rights Watch. "Liberia," in *Human Rights World Report 1995* pp. 25–30. New York: 1995. NGO report, in English.

Human Rights Watch Children's Rights Project. *Easy Prey: Child Soldiers in Liberia.* New York: 1994. NGO report, in English.

International Commission of Jurists. "Liberia," *ICJ Review* 36 (June 1986): 13–16. NGO article, in English.

Lawyers Committee for Human Rights. *First Steps: Rebuilding the Justice System in Liberia.* New York: 1991. NGO report, in English.

———. *Liberia: A Promise Betrayed, a Report on Human Rights.* New York: 1986. NGO report, in English.

Liebenow, J. Gus. *Liberia: The Quest for Democracy.* Bloomington, IN, USA: Indiana University Press, 1987. Scholarly monograph, in English.

Schneebaum, S. M., L. Garber, and J. Whalen. *Recent Developments in Liberia: The Need for Congressional Response.* Washington, D.C.: International Human Rights Law Group, 1986. NGO comment, in English.

Schneebaum, S. M., and J. Whalen. *Human Rights in Liberia: A Preliminary Report Based on Two Trial Observer Missions (February–March and May 1986).* Washington, D.C.: International Human Rights Law Group, 1986. NGO mission report, in English.

Swiss, Shana. *Liberia: Anguish in a Divided Land.* Physicians for Human Rights, 1992. NGO report, in English.

U.S. House of Representatives, Subcommittee on Human Rights and International Organizations and Subcommittee on Africa. *Liberia: Recent Developments and United States Foreign Policy,* 99th Cong., 2nd sess. Washington, D.C.: U.S. Government Printing Office, 1986. Government hearings, in English.

## LIBERTY.

The right of everyone to liberty is proclaimed in the **UNIVERSAL DECLARATION OF HUMAN RIGHTS** in the following terms:

*Article 3.* Everyone has the right to life, liberty and security of person.

The right to liberty is elaborated in two articles of the **INTERNATIONAL COVENANT ON CIVIL AND POLITICAL RIGHTS** as follows:

*Article 9.* 1. Everyone has the right to liberty and security of person. No one shall be subjected to arbitrary arrest or detention. No one shall be deprived of his liberty except on such grounds and in accordance with such procedures as are established by law.

2. Anyone who is arrested shall be informed, at the time of arrest, of the reasons for his arrest and shall be promptly informed of any charges against him.

3. Anyone arrested or detained on a criminal charge shall be brought promptly before a judge or other officer authorized by law to exercise judicial power and shall be entitled to trial within a reasonable time or to release. It shall not be the general rule that persons awaiting trial shall be detained in custody, but release may be subject to guarantees to appear for trial, at any other stage of the judicial proceedings, and, should occasion arise, for execution of the judgment.

4. Anyone who is deprived of his liberty by arrest or detention shall be entitled to take proceedings before a court, in order that that court may decide without delay on the lawfulness of his detention and order his release if the detention is not lawful.

5. Anyone who has been the victim of unlawful arrest or detention shall have an enforceable right to compensation.

*Article 10.* 1. All persons deprived of their liberty shall be treated with humanity and with respect for the inherent dignity of the human person.

2. (a) Accused persons shall, save in exceptional circumstances, be segregated from convicted persons and shall be subject to separate treatment appropriate to their status as unconvicted persons;

(b) Accused juvenile persons shall be separated from adults and brought as speedily as possible for adjudication.

3. The penitentiary system shall comprise treatment of prisoners the essential aim of which shall be their reformation and social rehabilitation. Juvenile offenders shall be segregated from adults and be accorded treatment appropriate to their age and legal status.

The **AMERICAN CONVENTION ON HUMAN RIGHTS,** open for acceptance by member States of the **ORGANIZATION OF AMERICAN STATES,** deals with the right to personal liberty in the following article:

*Article 7.* 1. Every person has the right to personal liberty and security.

2. No one shall be deprived of his physical liberty except for the reasons and under the conditions established beforehand by the constitution of the State Party concerned or by a law established pursuant thereto.

3. No one shall be subject to arbitrary arrest or imprisonment.

4. Anyone who is detained shall be informed of the reasons for his detention and shall be promptly notified of the charge or charges against him.

5. Any person detained shall be brought promptly before a judge or other officer authorized by law to exercise judicial power and shall be entitled to trial within a reasonable time or to be released without prejudice to the continuation of the proceedings. His release may be subject to guarantees to assure his appearance for trial.

6. Anyone who is deprived of his liberty shall be entitled to recourse to a competent court, in order that the court may decide without delay on the lawfulness of his arrest or detention and order his release if the arrest or detention is unlawful. In State Parties whose laws provide that anyone who believes himself to be threatened with deprivation of his liberty is entitled to recourse to a competent court in order that it may decide on the lawfulness of such threat, this remedy may not be restricted or abolished. The interested party or another person in his behalf is entitled to seek these remedies.

7. No one shall be detained for debt. This principle shall not limit the orders of a competent judicial authority issued for nonfulfillment of duties of support.

The **AFRICAN CHARTER ON HUMAN AND PEOPLES' RIGHTS,** open for acceptance by member States of the **ORGANIZATION OF AFRICAN UNITY,** contains the following provision:

*Article 6.* Every individual shall have the right to liberty and to the security of his person. No one may be deprived of his freedom except for reasons and conditions previously laid down by law. In particular, no one may be arbitrarily arrested or detained.

The **European Convention on Human Rights,** open for acceptance by member States of the **Council of Europe,** provides that:

*Article 5.* 1. Everyone has the right to liberty and security of person. No one shall be deprived of his liberty save in the following cases and in accordance with a procedure prescribed by law;

(a) the lawful detention of a person after conviction by a competent court;

(b) the lawful arrest or detention of a person for non-compliance with the lawful order of a court or in order to secure the fulfillment of any obligation prescribed by law;

(c) the lawful arrest or detention of a person effected for the purpose of bringing him before the competent legal authority on reasonable suspicion of having committed an offence or when it is reasonably considered necessary to prevent his committing an offence or fleeing after having done so;

(d) the detention of a minor by lawful order for the purpose of educational supervision or his lawful detention for the purpose of bringing him before the competent legal authority;

(e) the lawful detention of persons for the prevention of the spreading of infectious diseases, of persons of unsound mind, alcoholics or drug addicts or vagrants;

(f) the lawful arrest or detention of a person to prevent his effecting an unauthorised entry into the country or of a person against whom action is being taken with a view to deportation or extradition.

2. Everyone who is arrested shall be informed promptly, in a language which he understands, of the reasons for his arrest and of any charge against him.

3. Everyone arrested or detained in accordance with the provisions of paragraph 1(*c*) of this Article shall be brought promptly before a judge or other officer authorised by law to exercise judicial power and shall be entitled to trial within a reasonable time or to release pending trial. Release may be conditioned by guarantees to appear for trial.

4. Everyone who is deprived of his liberty by arrest or detention shall be entitled to take proceedings by which the lawfulness of his detention shall be decided speedily by a court and his release ordered if the detention is not lawful.

5. Everyone who has been the victim of arrest or detention in contravention of the provisions of this Article shall have an enforceable right to compensation.

The **European Convention on Human Rights, Protocol IV,** adds the following provision:

*Article 1.* No one shall be deprived of his liberty merely on the ground of inability to fulfil a contractual obligation.

After examining reports submitted by States parties to the International Covenant on Civil and Political Rights in accordance with article 40 of that instrument, the UN **Human Rights Committee** adopted, in 1982, general comments on articles 9 and 10 of that instrument, as follows (UN Doc. A/37/40, annex V):

*Article 9,* which deals with the right to liberty and security of persons, has often been somewhat narrowly understood in reports by States parties, and they have therefore given incomplete information. The Committee points out that par-

agraph 1 is applicable to all deprivations of liberty, whether in criminal cases or in other cases such as, for example, mental illness, vagrancy, drug addiction, educational purposes, immigration control, etc. It is true that some of the provisions of article 9 (part of paragraph 2 and the whole of paragraph 3) are only applicable to persons against whom criminal charges are brought. But the rest, and in particular the important guarantees laid down in paragraph 4, i.e. the right to control by a court of the legality of the detention, applies to all persons deprived of their liberty by arrest or detention. Furthermore, States parties have in accordance with article 2 (3) also to ensure that an effective remedy is provided in other cases in which an individual claims to be deprived of his liberty in violation of the Covenant.

Paragraph 3 of article 9 requires that in criminal cases any person arrested or detained has to be brought "promptly" before a judge or other officer authorized by law to exercise judicial power. More precise time limits are fixed by law in most States parties and, in the view of the Committee, delays must not exceed a few days. Many States have given insufficient information about the actual practices in this respect.

Another matter is the total length of detention pending trial. In certain categories of criminal cases in some countries this matter has caused some concern within the Committee, and members have questioned whether their practices have been in conformity with the entitlement "to trial within a reasonable time or to release" under paragraph 3. Pre-trial detention should be an exception and as short as possible. The Committee would welcome information concerning mechanisms existing and measures taken with a view to reducing the duration of such detention.

Also if so-called preventive detention is used, for reasons of public security, it must be controlled by these same provisions, i.e., it must not be arbitrary, and must be based on grounds and procedures established by law (paragraph 1), information available (paragraph 4) as well as compensation in the case of a breach (paragraph 5). And if, in addition, criminal charges are brought in such cases, the full protection of article 9 (2) and (3), as well as article 14, must also be granted.

*Article 10,* paragraph 1, of the Covenant provides that all persons deprived of their liberty shall be treated with humanity and with respect for the inherent dignity of the human person. However, by no means all the reports submitted by State parties have contained information on the way in which this paragraph of the article is being implemented. The Committee is of the opinion that it would be desirable for the reports of States parties to contain specific information on the legal measures designed to protect that right. The Committee also considers that reports should indicate the concrete measures being taken by the competent State organs to monitor the mandatory implementation of national legislation concerning the humane treatment and respect for the human dignity of all persons deprived of their liberty that paragraph 1 requires.

The Committee notes in particular that paragraph 1 of this article is generally applicable to persons deprived of their liberty, whereas paragraph 2 deals with accused as distinct from convicted persons, and paragraph 3 with convicted persons only. This structure quite often is not reflected in the reports, which mainly have related to accused and convicted persons. The wording of paragraph 1, its context—especially its proximity to article 9, paragraph 1, which also deals with all deprivations of liberty—and its purpose support a broad application of the principle expressed in that provision. Moreover, the Committee recalls that this article supplements article 7 as regards the treatment of all persons deprived of their liberty.

The humane treatment and the respect for the dignity of all persons deprived of their liberty is a basic standard of universal application which cannot depend entirely on material resources. While the Committee is aware that in other respects the modalities and conditions of detention may vary with the available resources, they must always be applied without discrimination, as required by article 2 (1).

Ultimate responsibility for the observance of this principle rests with the State as regards all institutions where persons are lawfully held against their will, not only in prisons but also, for example, hospitals, detention camps or correctional institutions.

Subparagraph 2 (a) of the article provides that, save in exceptional circumstances, accused persons shall be segregated from convicted persons and shall receive separate treatment appropriate to their status as unconvicted persons. Some reports have failed to pay proper attention to this direct requirement of the Covenant and, as a result, to provide adequate information on the way in which the treatment of accused persons differs from that of convicted persons. Such information should be included in future reports.

Subparagraph 2 (b) of the article calls, *inter alia,* for accused juvenile persons to be separated from adults. The information in reports shows that a number of States are not taking sufficient account of the fact that this is an unconditional requirement of the Covenant. It is the Committee's opinion that, as is clear from the text of the Covenant, deviation from States parties' obligations under subparagraph 2 (b) cannot be justified by any consideration whatsoever.

In a number of cases, the information appearing in reports with respect to paragraph 3 of the article has contained no concrete mention either of legislative or of administrative measures or of practical steps to promote the reformation and social rehabilitation of prisoners, by, for example, education, vocational training and useful work. Allowing visits, in particular by family members, is normally also such a measure which is required for reasons of humanity. There are also similar lacunae in the reports of certain States with respect to information concerning juvenile offenders, who must be segregated from adults and given treatment appropriate to their age and legal status.

The Committee further notes that the principles of humane treatment and respect for human dignity set out in paragraph 1 are the basis for the more specific and limited obligations of States in the field of criminal justice set out in paragraphs 2 and 3 of article 10. The segregation of accused persons from convicted ones is required in order to emphasize their status as unconvicted persons who are at the same time protected by the presumption of innocence stated in article 14, paragraph 2. The aim of these provisions is to protect the groups mentioned, and the requirements contained therein should be seen in that light. Thus, for example, the segregation and treatment of juvenile offenders should be provided for in such a way that it promotes their reformation and social rehabilitation.

**LIBERTY INTERNATIONAL.** Founded in 1981, this non-governmental organization has consultative status with the UN **ECONOMIC AND SOCIAL COUNCIL** (Category II). It works to promote understanding throughout the world of the UN Declaration of Human Rights,

to carry out research in the field of human rights, and to monitor and publicize human rights violations. Liberty International has members in 29 countries.

LI publishes *Liberty International Newsletter* six times a year and the quarterly *International Human Rights Monitor,* both in English.

Liberty International. Address: Bar Association Building, Suite 1, Mymensingh, Bangladesh. Telephone: (880-2) 4527. President: A. Mutaleb.

**LIBYA.** The Socialist People's Libyan Arab Jamahiriya is a country in northern Africa, on the Mediterranean Sea. It has borders with Algeria, Chad, Egypt, Niger, Sudan, and Tunisia. It achieved independence from Italy in 1951 and became a member of the United Nations in 1955. Its population is estimated to be 4,552,000. Ethnic groups include Arabs, Berbers, Arab–Berbers, Touaregs, and Tebous. Languages commonly used include Arabic and Italian. Religions practiced include Islam (Sunni) (97%) and others (3%). Literacy is estimated at 55%.

The government (1994) took the form of a *jamahiriya,* or "mass State," composed of multi-layered popular assemblies (People's Congresses) and executive institutions (People's Committees), guided by the General People's Congress. Under military rule since 1969, the Revolutionary Council that establishes all State policy has been re-named the General Secretariat of the General People's Congress. The sole political party is the Arab Socialist Union Organization.

Ruled successively in antiquity by the Phoenicians, the Greeks, the Romans, the Vandals, and the Byzantines, Libya was conquered by the Arabs in the 7th century and by the Ottoman Turks in the 16th century. Italy invaded and seized it in 1911 and held it as a colony until forced to relinquish all claims under the terms of the 1947 peace treaty with the Allies. The treaty provided that Libya's final disposition was to be determined by France, the United Kingdom, the United States of America, and the Soviet Union by 15 September 1948. When those powers failed to reach agreement, they referred the problem to the General Assembly of the United Nations, which decided that Libya should become independent not later than 1 January 1952. A UN commissioner was appointed to assist the Libyans in drawing up a constitution and establishing an independent government.

On 2 December 1950, the Libyan National Assembly declared that Libya should be a federal State with King Idris I, the Emir of Cyrenaica—who had led Libyan resistance to Italian occupation between the two world wars—as head of State. When Libya declared its independence on 24 December 1951, it was the first country to achieve independence through the United

Nations. In 1955, 1958, and 1960, the GENERAL ASSEMBLY adopted resolutions recognizing the special responsibility of the United Nations for the future of the country and providing it with technical and economic assistance. However, the discovery of significant oil reserves in 1959 changed Libya overnight from a poor country to a wealthy one measured in terms of per capita resources and made further outside assistance unnecessary.

The Kingdom of Libya was ruled by King Idris until 1 September 1969, when the government was overthrown in a *coup d'etat* led by the military. The Revolutionary Command Council, which seized power, abolished the monarchy, pledged itself to improve and to encourage domestic policies, and promised an equitable distribution of wealth. By 1970, it had succeeded in closing down British military installations at Tobruk and El Adem and American facilities at Wheelus Air Force Base near Tripoli.

Under Col. Mu'ammar al-Qadhafi, the revolutionary leader who emerged as chairman of the Revolutionary Command Council and *de facto* head of State, the Libyan Government in 1977 convened a General People's Congress, which proclaimed the establishment of "people's power," changed the name of the country to Socialist People's Libyan Arab Jamahiriya, and assumed authority as a legislative body and as an intermediary between the masses and the leadership. Libyan embassies abroad were re-named "People's Bureaus" and their extended staffs sought to win new recruits to revolutionary philosophy and to take direct action to control Libyan nationals abroad.

*LIBYAN AND AMERICAN RELATIONS.* In 1981, the United States Government closed the Libyan Embassy in Washington and accused Libya of supporting international terrorism. Later in that same year, American and Libyan warplanes fought in the airspace above the Gulf of Sidra, which Libya claimed to be within its territory but which the United States held to be an international waterway. Two Libyan Soviet-built SU-22s were shot down by missiles launched by American F-14s. The U.S. Air Force claimed that its planes had merely returned fire in self-defense, but Libya charged that the incident had been carefully planned and provoked.

In March 1986, U.S. and Libyan naval units skirmished in the Gulf of Sidra and two Libyan patrol boats were sunk. In April of that year—after an American serviceman had been killed in a terrorist attack on a West German discotheque—the United States launched an air raid aimed at Tripoli, Benghazi, and nearby "terrorist-related" targets. American President Ronald Reagan announced that he had ordered the air strikes in retaliation for the bombing of the discotheque and to deter future Libyan-directed terrorist attacks and warned of further military action unless Libya ended its alleged support of anti-American terrorism.

The bombing attack, which threatened the lives of Col. Mu'ammar al-Qadhafi and his family (an 18-month-old daughter was killed), was later condemned by the ORGANIZATION OF AFRICAN UNITY and the Organization of the Islamic Conference. The UN General Assembly, in resolution 41/38 of 20 November 1986, also condemned the action, which in its view constituted a serious threat to peace and security in the Mediterranean region. The Assembly called upon the government of the United States to refrain from the threat or use of force in the settlement of disputes with Libya and to resort to peaceful means in accordance with the UNITED NATIONS CHARTER. It further called upon all States to refrain from extending any assistance or facilities for perpetrating acts of aggression against Libya, and affirmed Libya's right to receive appropriate compensation for the material and human losses which had been inflicted upon it.

*TERRORISM.* Libya has been branded by the U.S. State Department as a proponent of State-sponsored terrorism. In December 1985, Libya's Press Bureau praised as "heroic" terrorist attacks by Arab gunmen—said to be linked to the Abu Nidal terrorist group then believed to be based in Libya—who hurled grenades at check-in counters of El Al, Israel's national airline, in airports at Rome and Vienna, killing 18 persons and wounding 111.

In a matter some consider a result of the American retaliatory bombings in 1986, U.S. State Department reports showed a distinct drop in the number of international acts of terrorism in 1987. In the same year, Libyan armed forces suffered a humiliating defeat when Chadian forces captured a strategic airstrip at Wadi Doum, bringing the Libyan offensive against Chad to a halt. In September 1989, Libya and Chad signed a peace treaty to end 16 years of hostility.

In January 1989, intelligence experts in the United States of America reached the conclusion that West German companies had assisted Libya in designing and constructing a plant for the production of chemical weapons and in helping it to develop a capacity for refueling its French-made fighter planes. These reports surfaced again early in March 1990, when Libya was reported to have produced 30 tons of mustard gas and an unknown quantity of Sarin, a nerve gas, in the Rabta plant. Libyan officials maintain that the plant produces only pharmaceuticals.

In April 1992, the United Nations imposed limited sanctions for Libya's failure to extradite two intelligence agents linked to the 1988 bombing of Pan

American Flight 103 over Lockerbie, Scotland, and four others linked to an airplane bombing over Niger.

**BIBLIOGRAPHY.** African-American Institute. "The Press and Africa," *Africa Report* 32, no. 2 (March–April 1987). NGO special issue, in English.

Amnesty International. *Libya: Summary of Amnesty International's Prisoner Concerns in the Great Socialist People's Libyan Arab Jamahiriya.* London: 1987. NGO report, in English.

————. *Summary of Amnesty International's Concerns in Libya.* London: 1991. NGO factfinding report, in English.

Arab Organization for Human Rights. "Libya: Assassination of Opponents Continue," *AOHR Newsletter* 12–13 (December 1987): 1. NGO article, in English.

Centre d'Etudes et de Recherches sur l'Orient Chretien (Middle East Christian Research Center). "Libya: Mass Expulsion of Foreign Workers," *Plus* 1, no. 1 (1985): 14, 22–23, 26. NGO article, in English.

**LIECHTENSTEIN.** The Principality of Liechtenstein is a country in the Alps of western Europe. It has borders with Austria and Switzerland. An independent State since it withdrew from the German Confederation in 1866, it maintains a customs and monetary union with Switzerland, which also administers its postal services. Its population is estimated to be 30,000, and includes persons of Alemannic (south German) descent (95%) and of Italian descent (5%). Languages in common use are German (official) and various Alemannic dialects. Christianity (Roman Catholic, 85%; Protestant, 8%) is the predominant religion. Literacy is estimated at 100%.

Liechtenstein is not a member of the United Nations. Its government (1990) took the form of a monarchy, headed since 1938 by Prince Franz Josef II but ruled in fact since 1984 by his son, Prince Hans Adam, after his father had given up the responsibilities but not his title to the throne.

Under its 1921 constitution, the premier acts as head of government. There is a 15-member legislature, the *Landtag,* elected by direct male suffrage. Women were granted the right to vote only in a referendum held on 1 July 1984. The main political parties are the Homeland Union and the Progressive Citizens Party.

The principality abolished its army in 1868 and has since remained neutral. Because of its low tax rates, it has attracted many international corporations and about one-third of its population consists of workers from other countries.

**LITHUANIA.** The Republic of Lithuania came into being in March 1990, when the country announced its independence from the USSR. It has borders with Latvia on the north; Belarus on the east; and Poland, Russia, and the Baltic Sea on the west. Ethnic groups include native Lithuanians (80%), Russians (9%), and Polish (7%). Catholicism is the major religion. Its population is estimated to be 3,804,000.

For most of the 20th century, Lithuania has been an occupied country, beginning with German occupation during World War I. Shortly thereafter, the newly founded Union of Soviet Socialist Republics annexed Lithuania, but the Soviets were overthrown in 1919. From 1919 to 1926, Lithuania was a democratic republic, but a coup replaced the democratically elected government. An agreement between the USSR and Germany in 1939 assigned Lithuania over to the Soviet Union, which formally annexed the territory in 1940.

On 11 March 1990, Lithuania declared its independence from the USSR. The Soviets retaliated by massing their troops at the borders and by cutting off oil and gas supplies. In August 1991, after a year of hostilities and an abortive Soviet coup, the Western nations formally recognized Lithuania's independence, as did the USSR one month later. In that year, it was admitted as a Member State of the United Nations. In 1992 elections, former communists won an absolute majority in the legislature. The 1992 Constitution provides for direct elections to the 141-seat Parliament and for presidential elections every five years. It also prohibits discrimination based on race, gender, nationality, religion, language, origin and opinion. The country has a civil law system.

**BIBLIOGRAPHY.** Bernhardt, Rudolf, and Henry Schermers. "Lithuanian Law and International Human Rights Standards," *Human Rights Law Journal* 13, no. 5–6 (June 1992): 249–256. Scholarly article, in English.

Commission on Security and Cooperation in Europe. "Elections in the Baltic States and Soviet Republics: A Compendium of Reports on Parliamentary Elections held in 1990." Washington, D.C.: U.S. Government Printing Office, 1990. Government report, in English.

————. *Renewal and Challenge: The Baltic States 1988–1989.* Washington, D.C.: U.S. Government Printing Office, 1990. Government report, in English.

"Lithuanians Declare Independence, March 11, 1990," *Lituanus* 36, no. 2 (Summer 1990). Special issue, in English.

Urban, William. "Ethnic Tensions in the Baltic," *Lituanus* 39, no. 1 (Spring 1993): 67–76. Article, in English.

**LOWENSTEIN (ALLARD K.) INTERNATIONAL HUMAN RIGHTS LAW PROJECT AND CLINIC, YALE UNIVERSITY LAW SCHOOL.** Established by Yale University Law School and named after the human rights advocate and Yale Law School graduate, the Law Project and the Law Clinic are complementary undertakings designed to provide information and practical experience to Yale law students.

**THE LOWENSTEIN INTERNATIONAL HUMAN RIGHTS LAW PROJECT.** Established in 1981 by Yale law students, the Project sponsors term-time student research for international human rights organizations; brings human rights speakers to the law school; and sponsors an annual symposium on human rights issues. Recently, the Project has drafted a model bill of rights and other constitutional documents for the Palestinian National Committee; done research for and offered technical support to the Constitutional Commission of Eritrea; sponsored a workshop for American legal-aid attorneys on strategies for incorporating international human rights norms into domestic litigation; and argued at the United Nations on behalf of Burmese refugees and the protection of human rights in Burma (Myanmar).

**THE LOWENSTEIN INTERNATIONAL HUMAN RIGHTS LAW CLINIC.** Introduced into the Yale Law School curriculum in 1991, the Clinic provides an opportunity for law students, under the supervision of law-school faculty and prominent human rights lawyers, to initiate and prosecute lawsuits under domestic and international law against human rights violators in U.S. courts and other fora. The Clinic has won over $100 million in judgments against human rights violators around the world. Some of these cases include *Cuban American Bar Association v. Christopher* (rights of Cuban refugees being detained by the United States at U.S. military bases at Guantanamo Bay, Cuba, and in Panama); *Haitian Centers Council v. Sale* (two cases involving the rights of Haitian refugees detained by the United States at Guantanamo Bay, and challenging the U.S. policy of interdicting fleeing Haitians on the high seas and summarily returning them to Haiti); and *Todd v. Panjiatan* (a case against an Indonesian general for a massacre in East Timor).

**LUND UNIVERSITY, RAOUL WALLENBERG INSTITUTE OF HUMAN RIGHTS AND HUMANITARIAN LAW.** See **WALLENBERG (RAOUL) INSTITUTE OF HUMAN RIGHTS AND HUMANITARIAN LAW.**

**LUTHERAN WORLD FEDERATION.** An international non-governmental organization in consultative status (Category II) with the UN **ECONOMIC AND SOCIAL COUNCIL**, LWF has 108 member churches and 15 recognized congregations in 87 countries.

Founded in 1947 in Lund, Sweden, as the successor to the Lutheran World Convention, the Federation acts as a free association of Lutheran churches and serves as their agent in such matters as they may assign to it.

LWF cultivates unity of the Lutheran faith and fosters Lutheran interest, concern for, and participation in ecumenical movements. LWF also assists mission and church programs globally, aids in welfare work, develops communications, and sponsors scholarships and exchange programs for leadership training.

Among LWF's publications are *Lutheran World Information* and the *Lutheran Directory*.

Lutheran World Federation. Address: 150 route de Ferney, P.O. Box 66, CH-1211, Geneva 20, Switzerland. Telephone: (41-22) 791-61-11. Fax: (41-22) 798-86-16. Secretary-General: Rev. Gunnar Johan Stalsett.

**LUTHULI, ALBERT JOHN (1898–1967).** A Zulu chieftain and president of the **AFRICAN NATIONAL CONGRESS OF SOUTH AFRICA** from 1952 until the South African Government banned the ANC in 1960, Albert Luthuli received the 1960 **NOBEL PEACE PRIZE** for his efforts to lead nonviolent resistance against the apartheid regime of his homeland. He was the first African to receive the award.

A deeply religious man, Luthuli was held in internal exile in his own country for most of his life. His career began as a teacher in South Africa from 1921 to 1936. In 1935, he was chosen as chief of the Zulu Nation, a position he held until 1952 when the South African government "deposed" him. In 1944, he became a member of the ANC, which, at that time, had adopted a campaign of passive resistance to the apartheid system, favoring work stoppages. Because of his participation in and support of this campaign, the South African banned Luthuli for the first time in 1952 from all public gatherings; that first ban lasted for two years. In 1954, he was again confined, this time to an area within a 25-mile radius of his home for two years. In 1956, he was charged with treason and held in police custody until December 1957. In 1959, he was banished again to his farm under the government's Suppression of Communism Act and the Riotous Assemblies Act. He was also arrested in connection with demonstrations against the Sharpeville massacre. Even after receiving the Nobel Peace Prize, Luthuli was from time to time confined under government orders to an area within a 25-mile radius of his home.

Luthuli was granted a ten-day passport to travel to Oslo, Norway, to receive the Nobel Peace Prize. In his Nobel lecture, he foresaw a time of freedom for all Africans struggling against colonialism: "In a strife-torn world, tottering on the brink of complete destruction by man-made nuclear weapons, a free and independent Africa is in the making, in answer to the injunction and challenge of history: 'Arise and shine, for thy light is come.'"

**BIBLIOGRAPHY.** *Current Biography Yearbook.* New York: W.H. Wilson & Company, 1962.

Gray, Tony. *Champions of Peace.* London: Paddington Press, 1976.

Schlessinger, Bernard S., and June H. Schlessinger, eds. *Who's Who of Nobel Prize Winners.* Phoenix, AZ, USA: Oryx Press, 1991.

**LUXEMBOURG.** The Grand Duchy of Luxembourg is a country in western Europe. It has borders with Belgium, the Federal Republic of Germany, and France. It achieved independence from the Netherlands in 1839 and became a member of the United Nations in 1945. Its population is estimated to be 392,000. Ethnic groups include Germans and Celts. Aliens constitute over 25% of the population, including Portuguese, Italians, French, Germans, and Belgians. Languages commonly used include Luxembourgish, French, German, and English. Christianity (Roman Catholic) is the predominant religion. Literacy is estimated at 100%.

The government (1994) took the form of a monarchy. The Grand Duke is ruler and head of State. The prime minister, representing the party or coalition given a majority in the Chamber of Deputies, exercises executive authority as head of government. Parliament consists of a 59-member Chamber of Deputies, members of which are elected by popular vote for terms of five years. There is also a Council of State. Political parties include the Christian Social Party, the Socialist Labor Party, the Democratic Party, the Communist Party, and the Green Alternative Party.

Originally one of the largest fiefs of the Holy Roman Empire, Luxembourg passed from Spanish to Austrian to French rule before the Congress of Vienna in 1815 made it a Grand Duchy loosely united to the Netherlands. It joined Belgium in revolting against the Netherlands; and, although Belgium on gaining independence in 1839 took over most of the territory of the Grand Duchy, the remainder declared its independence and joined the German Confederation. At the London Conference of 1857, the Grand Duchy was declared a neutral territory. That neutrality was violated twice by Germany, once in 1914 and again in 1940; the country finally was liberated by Allied troops in 1944. In 1948, its permanent neutrality was abolished by revision of the constitution.

*STATUS OF ALIENS.* As of 31 December 1984, the total population of Luxembourg was 365,900, of which 96,700 (slightly more than 26%) were aliens. The largest groups of aliens was the Portuguese (29,300), followed by Italians (22,300), French (11,900), Germans (8,900), and Belgians (7,900). There were also 813 stateless persons and 98 persons of undetermined nationality. The government, feeling that these alien residents have made a substantial contribution to the development of the country and that their presence will also in the future constitute an essential element in the efficient functioning of its economy, undertakes to combat any form of xenophobia and considers that the solution of problems requires a voluntarist integration policy which respects cultural identities.

As regards measures to promote understanding between the people of Luxembourg and its immigrants and alien residents, the government has established consultative services and has reorganized its system of education.

# M

**MACBRIDE, SEAN (1904–1988).** The first Irishman to win the **NOBEL PEACE PRIZE** (in 1974), Sean Mac-Bride was a revolutionary for freedom and justice throughout his life, a trait he may have inherited from his parents: John MacBride, who was executed by the British for his part in the Easter Sunday Uprising of 1916, and Maud Gonne MacBride, who was regularly arrested by British authorities for her work for Irish independence.

MacBride joined the Irish Republican Army (IRA) in 1917 at the age of 13 and spent many years "underground" fighting for a free and united Ireland. He worked with Eamon De Valera, and both opposed the Anglo-Irish Treaty of 1921, which established the Irish Free State and which partitioned Ireland into two sections and allowed dominion status at home but with Crown control abroad. In opposition to this treaty, the IRA ignited a civil war, during which time MacBride was arrested several times. In 1936, he became commander-in-chief of the IRA, but resigned when the group decided to work for German forces in World War II; despite this break, he served as legal counsel for members of the IRA arrested and condemned to death by the De Valera government. The IRA was outlawed by the Government of Ireland in 1939.

After World War II, MacBride founded the *Clann na Poblachta,* or Republican Party, to work for the establishment of an Irish Republic (*Eire*) and an end to the partition of the northern counties. His party forced the forming of a coalition government in 1948, in which MacBride served as Minister for External Affairs. In 1949, largely through his efforts, the Republic of Ireland was established.

Through the 1950s, MacBride worked on European economic recovery and also was instrumental in securing acceptance of the **EUROPEAN CONVENTION ON HUMAN RIGHTS.** In 1961, he was elected president of the International Board of **AMNESTY INTERNATIONAL,** and served as secretary-general of the **INTERNATIONAL COMMISSION OF JURISTS** from 1963 to 1970. He also worked within the United Nations system for many years and was active in the nuclear disarmament movement.

In addition to the Nobel Peace Prize of 1974, Mac-Bride also was awarded the former Soviet Union's Lenin Peace Prize (1977), the International Institute of Human Rights Medal (1978), and the UNESCO Silver Medal (1980).

**BIBLIOGRAPHY.** *Current Biography Yearbook.* New York: W.H. Wilson & Company, 1949.

Gray, Tony. *Champions of Peace.* London: Paddington Press, 1976.

Schlessinger, Bernard S., and June H. Schlessinger, eds. *Who's Who of Nobel Prize Winners.* Phoenix, AZ, USA: Oryx Press, 1991.

**MACEDONIA.** Macedonia is a landlocked country of southeastern Europe, which borders Albania to the west, Serbia to the north, Bulgaria to the east and Greece to the south. Its population is estimated to be 2,179,000.

In the Balkan wars of 1912–1913, the territory was divided among Greece, Serbia, and Bulgaria. The Serbian portion became one of the six constituent republics of Yugoslavia in 1946; but in 1991 Macedonia voted for independence, which was recognized only by Bulgaria. Greece and other countries objected to the new country's use of the name Macedonia; this problem has not been resolved. The republic was admitted to the United Nations under the temporary name of "the Former Yugoslav Republic of Macedonia" and has since been recognized by more than 60 countries, including the United States, Russia, and individual members of the European Union.

In 1989, the Macedonian communist regime amended the constitution to allow for a multi-party system, and the first multi-party elections were held in November and December 1990. The Internal Macedonian Revolutionary Organization -Democratic Party for Macedonian National Unity (IMRO)-DPMNU) won 37 of the 120 seats in the unicameral parliament, the *Sobranje.* The League of Communists of Macedonia-Party for Democratic Reform (LCM-PDR) won 31 and the two Albanian parties won a total of 25. By 1991, a coalition government was formed and a motion adopted formally declaring Macedonia a sovereign territory.

A constitution was approved by the *Sobranje* in November 1991. It guarantees basic human rights, free expression of nationality freedom of religion and conscience. It also provides for a Council for Inter-Nationality Relations to be formed by the legislature.

The first presidential and parliamentary elections since independence in 1991 were held in October 1994. The incumbent President Kiro Gligorov was re-elected for a five-year term with 78% of the vote and the new government was the three-party coalition, Alliance for Macedonia. Approximately 1800 candidates had challenged 120 parliamentary seats. The elections attracted 540 international observers including monitors from the European Union and the Conference on Security and Cooperation in Europe.

Following the Bulgarian occupation during World War II, Marshall Tito took advantage of growing anti-Bulgarian sentiment and fostered Macedonian culture, language, and identity throughout the next several decades. However, another ethnic threat to Macedonian majority rule (approximately 65% of the population) in the region was the 20%-40% Albanian population that increasingly called for greater autonomy, culminating in a demand for a Yugoslav Albanian republic in 1968. An unofficial and unrecognized referendum of ethnic Albanians in January 1992 nearly unanimously supported a separate republic.

### UNITED NATIONS PROTECTION FORCE (UNPROFOR).
The Former Yugoslav Republic of Macedonia is part of the mandate of UNPROFOR. On 11 November 1992, the president of Macedonia requested that the United Nations deploy an observer force in his territory because of his concern about the possible impact of fighting elsewhere in the former Yugoslavia. Such deployment met with the Security Council's approval; and, from 28 November to 3 December 1992, the Secretary-General sent to Macedonia a group of military, police, and civilian personnel to asses the situation and to prepare a report concerning deployment of UNPROFOR in that republic.

On 9 December, the Secretary-General recommended to the Security Council that it expand the mandate and strength of UNPROFOR to establish a UN presence on Macedonia's borders with Albania and the Federal Republic of Yugoslavia (Serbia and Montenegro). The forces's mandate is essentially preventive, to monitor and report any developments in the border areas which could undermine confidence and stability in Macedonia. A battalion of up to 700, 35 military observers, 26 civilian police monitors, 10 civil affairs staff, and 46 administrative staff and local interpreters comprised the first contingent, with headquarters in Skopje. On 18 June 1993, the Security Council authorized an additional 300 troops in the area (resolution 842 [1993]).

BIBLIOGRAPHY. Helsinki Watch. *Human Rights in the Former Yugoslav Republic of Macedonia*. New York: Human Rights Watch, 1994. NGO report, in English.

**MADAGASCAR.** The Republic of Madagascar is a country in eastern Africa occupying one of the largest islands in the world, situated in the Indian Ocean off the Mozambique Channel. It achieved independence from France in 1960 and became a member of the United Nations the same year. Its population is estimated to be 12,800,000. Ethnic groups include Malagasy tribes, Comorans, and persons of Chinese, French, Indian, Malaysian, and Polynesian origin. Languages commonly spoken include Malagasy (official) and French. Religions practiced include Christianity (40%), Islam (5%), and Animism (55%). Article 39 of the constitution provides that "freedom of conscience and religion shall be guaranteed by the neutrality of the State with respect of all beliefs." Literacy is estimated at 53%.

The government (1994) took the form of a republic. In August 1992, following violent clashes in several cities, a new constitution was approved by 72% of the vote in a referendum. The primary conflict was over the question of whether to form a unitary or federal State. The new constitution provides for a unitary State; a 138-member National Assembly to be elected for four-year terms by universal suffrage; a Senate which will have two-thirds of its members elected by an electoral college and one-third appointed by the president; and executive power resting with the prime minister who is appointed by the National Assembly.

Legislation enabling newspapers to be established without government approval and guaranteeing freedom of the press and speech was passed by the National People's Assembly in December 1990.

In presidential elections in February 1993, Albert Zafy defeated the president of the previous 17 years, Didier Ratsiraka, by gaining 67% of the vote in the second round of voting. Elections for the 138 seats in the National Assembly in June 1993 involved 121 political organizations and resulted in Francisque Ravony being appointed prime minister.

### REPORT OF THE UN COMMITTEE ON THE RIGHTS OF THE CHILD.
The initial report of Madagascar (CRC/C/8/Add. 5) under the Convention on the Rights of the Child was considered by the Committee on the Rights of the Child at its 163rd to 165th meetings, held on 29 and 30 September 1994. The Committee adopted the following concluding observations on the report at its 183rd meeting, held on 14 October 1994 (CRC/C/15/Add. 26, paras. 4–23):

*Positive Aspects.* The Committee welcomes the establishment of the Intersectoral Follow-up Committee which drafted the initial report and which is envisaged as a permanent coordinating body to ensure an effective follow-up in close evaluation and monitoring of the situation of children in Madagascar, as well as an appropriate follow-up in close collaboration with NGOs. The Committee expresses its satisfaction that representatives of international organizations are included in the follow-up committee, which may facilitate better coordination in the area of international cooperation and development assistance aimed at improving the situation of children in Madagascar.

*Factors and Difficulties Impeding the Implementation of the Convention.* The Committee notes the difficulties facing the Government of the Republic of Madagascar in a period of political transition.

The Committee also notes that natural disasters and severe economic problems have had a negative impact on the situation of children. The Committee recognizes that certain traditional values in the rural areas have not favoured the rapid implementation of the Convention.

*Principal Subjects of Concern.* The Committee is concerned that the fundamental legal and administrative reforms needed to apply the Convention have still not been fully undertaken in Madagascar. As a result, many of the laws affecting children date from the period immediately following independence and would need to be brought into full conformity with the principles and provisions of the Convention.

The Committee notes with concern the persistence of disparities in the enjoyment of the rights recognized by the Convention between the different regions of the country, to the detriment in particular of girls, rural children and children living in situations of extreme poverty. The Committee is also concerned that lasting prejudices and traditional beliefs affect certain groups of children, including disabled children and children born on a certain day of the week (considered to bring bad luck), preventing them from fully enjoying the rights recognized by the Convention.

The Committee is concerned that the national legislation establishes a different minimum age for marriage between boys and girls and that it authorizes the marriages of girls as young as 14 years of age who have obtained parental consent from the father or the mother. Such situations may raise the question of compatibility with the principles of non-discrimination and the best interests of the child, in particular as these children will be considered as adults and therefore no longer eligible for the protection afforded by the Convention. Furthermore, the Committee is concerned about the legal status of children born out of wedlock, particularly of incestuous unions.

The Committee is concerned at the difficulties to ensure birth registration of children. Such a situation implies the non-recognition of these children as persons before the law, which will affect the level of enjoyment of their fundamental rights and freedoms. In addition, such children are not included in relevant statistical and other information on children and their situation, therefore, cannot be properly monitored.

The Committee is concerned about the problems associated with ill-treatment, abuse and violence directed towards children in school and in the family, which is reinforced by social custom. In this connection, the Committee notes with concern that child abuse has not yet been clearly addressed, that adequate legal remedies for abused children do not exist and that there are inadequate safeguards against reprisals against children who report abuse.

With respect to basic health and welfare, the Committee notes with concern that in Madagascar, children have increasingly had difficulty in obtaining access to adequate primary health care and that many continue to suffer from lack of medicine and safe drinking water. In particular, the Committee is concerned over the alarming trend that child immunization is on the decrease.

With respect to education, the Committee notes with concern that there has been little progress in implementing the relevant articles of the Convention and that, in particular, the number of hours during which schools are open have been restricted, that teacher training has been inadequate and that a high proportion of pupils drop out before finishing primary school. Moreover, the Committee is concerned at the difficulties arising from the changes introduced in the education system as far as the language of instruction is concerned.

With regard to child exploitation, the Committee is concerned that child labour continues to be a serious problem in Madagascar, particularly in the rural areas and in the informal sector. In this connection, the Committee notes with alarm that there is no effective inspection in rural areas to combat this problem nor is there labour legislation covering domestic workers.

With respect to sexual exploitation of the child, the Committee is concerned that insufficient measures have been taken to prevent and combat the incitement to child pornography as well as prostitution involving children living and/or working on the streets, particularly children who are victimized by tourists.

With regard to the administration of juvenile justice, the Committee is concerned that the existing legislation does not reflect the spirit or the provisions of the Convention. In particular, the Committee is concerned that children may be subject to situations of deprivation of liberty, namely lengthy pre-trial detention, and that they might not benefit from the safeguards recognized in the Convention, in the light of articles 37 and 40. The Committee is also concerned by the serious conditions in the correctional facilities which, as recognized by the delegation, may adversely affect the fulfilment of the State party's obligations under the Convention and other international human rights standards.

*Suggestions and Recommendations.* The Committee recommends that the Government develop information and awareness campaigns on the principles and provisions of the Convention on the Rights of the Child, whenever appropriate in close cooperation with community and religious leaders, in order to create a wider awareness and contribute to the eradication of prevailing prejudices and cultural traditions which may be detrimental to the enjoyment of the rights of the child. It further suggests that special attention be paid to the training of professional groups, working with and for children, on the rights of the child.

The Committee recommends that the Government undertake a comprehensive review of national legislation, with a view to ensuring its full compatibility with the principles and provisions of the Convention. New legislation should be adopted in those areas where the protection of children is not yet adequately addressed, such as in the fields of child abuse and national and intercountry adoption or the administration of juvenile justice. To this end, the Committee suggests that the mandate of the Intersectoral Follow-up Committee be broadened accordingly.

The Committee emphasizes the importance of establishing an effective and permanent system of monitoring the implementation of the Convention and newly adopted legislation relating to children, and recognizes that the Intersectoral Follow-up Committee could be envisaged as the focal point for that purpose. The Committee also suggests that such a monitoring mechanism may strengthen its cooperation with NGOs and relevant professional groups, as well as religious and community leaders.

The Committee also recommends that serious consideration be given to the allocation of available resources, including those deriving from international development aid, in order that they be used, to the maximum extent possible, for the effective implementation of the economic, social and cultural rights of children, in particular those belonging to the most vulnerable groups.

With respect to child exploitation, the Committee recommends that efforts to prevent and combat child labour, in particular in the informal sector, be greatly intensified, and that the Government consider ratifying the ILO Minimum Age Convention, 1973 (No. 138). In this regard, the Committee further recommends that the State party consider seeking assistance from ILO, in particular with a view to reinforcing its capacity to monitor the Convention on the Rights of the Child.

With respect to the administration of juvenile justice, the Committee recommends that the necessary facilities be provided to implement fully the provisions of the Convention. The Committee further recommends that the law reform to be undertaken in this field adequately reflect the provisions of the Convention as well as other relevant international standards, such as "The Beijing Rules", the Riyadh Guidelines and the United Nations Rules for the Protection of Juveniles Deprived of their Liberty. In this regard, it is suggested that serious attention be paid to the best interests and the dignity of the child, and the consideration of deprivation of liberty as a measure of last resort and for the minimum period possible. The Committee underlines the importance of technical assistance programmes in this area and encourages the State party to consider requesting such assistance from the Centre for Human Rights as well as from the Crime Prevention and Criminal Justice Branch of the United Nations.

The Committee recommends that in the light of article 44, paragraph 6, of the Convention, the report submitted by the Government be made widely available to the public at large and that the publication of the report be considered, along with the relevant summary records and the concluding observations adopted thereon by the Committee.

**BIBLIOGRAPHY.** Action des Chretiens pour l'Abolition de la Torture (Christian Action for the Abolition of Torture). "Madagascar: des Faits et des Rumeurs" (Madagascar: The Facts and the Rumors), *Courrier de l'ACAT* 70–71 (December 1986): 2–5. NGO article, in French.

**MALAWI.** The Republic of Malawi is a country in eastern Africa, totally surrounded by Mozambique, Tanzania, and Zambia, and bordered on the east by Lake Malawi. Formerly known as Nyasaland, it achieved independence from Great Britain in 1964 and became a member of the United Nations the same year. Its population is estimated to be 9,691,000. Ethnic groups include the Chewa, Nyanja, Tumbuka, Yao, Lomwe, Sena, Tonga, and Ngoni communities and persons of European and Asian descent. Languages commonly used are English and Chichewa (both official). Religions practiced include Christianity (Protestant and Roman Catholic denominations) (60%), Islam (20%), and Animism (20%). Literacy is estimated at 25%.

The government (1994) took the form of a democracy and member of the Commonwealth of Nations. For a time, under the constitution of 1966, President Hastings Kamuzu Banda had been designated "President for Life," and there was only a single political party. However, following amendments approved by referendum in June 1993, a new constitution was promulgated in May 1994. It provided for a president to be elected by universal suffrage for a five-year term; a 177-seat National Assembly to be elected by universal suffrage for a five-year term; and the appointment of a Constitutional Committee and a Human Rights Commission.

The United Nations sponsored a meeting on the transition to democracy in July 1993. By mid-1993, five political parties had registered. In November 1993, the National Assembly repealed laws providing for the life presidency and detention without trial and reduced the voting age from 21 to 18.

In elections in May 1994, President Bakili Muluzi defeated Hastings Kamuzu Banda who had been president since 1966. The United Democratic Front, of which Muluzi was the leader, won 84 seats in the National Assembly, while the longstanding Malawi Congress Party won 55. The new President repealed a ban on the Tumuka language, ordered the release of all political prisoners, and closed three prisons which he alleged had been used for torture in the previous regime.

**REFUGEES FROM MOZAMBIQUE.** In recent years, refugees from neighboring Mozambique have swarmed into Malawi—more than 600,000 in 1988 alone—and continued to do so for the next five years at a rate of about 1,200 a month. They were fleeing the civil war between the government of Mozambique and the Mozambique National Resistance and have totally disrupted normal life in the host country. Malawi has been hospitable to them, despite food shortages and infestations of insects, and has endeavored to follow the dictum of former President Banda: "We are all brothers." By April 1990, one out of every ten persons in Malawi came from Mozambique; in many locations, refugees vastly outnumbered citizens. Food production and water resources in the affected areas were insufficient to satisfy the needs of the Malawi population and the displaced persons; the ecological environment has been severely damaged by woodcutting on, and expanding cultivation to, fragile hillsides; and health, education, and community services have been severely strained. A United Nations interagency mission sent to Malawi to determine the type and magnitude of the assistance required concluded that the Malawi economy would not be able to cope with the expanding emergency conditions without major support from the international community and substantial development investment.

By mid-1992, the number of refugees from Mozambique reached one million; however, the UN High Commissioner for Refugees reported that, in 1993 and 1994, many Mozambicans were returning to their homeland.

**BIBLIOGRAPHY.** Africa Watch. *Where Silence Rules: The Suppression of Dissent in Malawi.* New York: Human Rights Watch, 1990. NGO factfinding report, in English.

Amnesty International. *Malawi: Amnesty International's Recommendations for Permanent Protection of Basic Human Rights Following the Pro-Democracy Vote.* London: 1993. NGO report, in English.

————. *Malawi: International Commitments—National Realities.* London: 1990. NGO report, in English and French.

————. *Malawi: March–July 1992: Mass Arrests of Suspended Government Opponents.* London: 1992. NGO report, in English.

————. *Malawi: A New Future for Human Rights.* London: 1994. NGO report, in English.

————. *Malawi: Preserving the One-Party State—Human Rights Violations and the Referendum.* London: 1993. NGO report, in English.

————. *Malawi: Prison Conditions, Cruel Punishment and Detention Without Trial.* London: 1992. NGO report, in English.

Article 19. *Freedom of Expression in Malawi: The Elections and the Need for Media Reform.* London: 1994. NGO report, in English.

————. *Freedom of Expression Needed in Malawi: More Changes Needed.* London: 1994. NGO report, in English.

————. *Malawi's Elections: Media Monitoring, Freedom of Expression and Intimidation.* London: 1994. NGO report, in English.

Lawyers Committee for Human Rights. *Malawi: Ignoring Calls for Change.* New York: 1992. NGO report, in English.

Scottish Faculty of Advocates, Law Society of England and Wales, General Council of the Bar to Malawi. *Human Rights in Malawi.* s.l.: 1992. NGO factfinding report, in English.

Tolfree, David. *Refugee Children in Malawi: A Study of the Implementation of the UNHCR Guidelines on Refugee Children.* Geneva, Switzerland: International Save the Children Alliance, 1992. NGO report, in English.

**MALAYSIA.** A country in southeastern Asia, occupying the southern portion of the Malay Peninsula and including the territories of Sabah and Sarawak, located on the island of Borneo. West Malaysia, in the mainland, has borders with Singapore and Thailand. East Malaysia, on Borneo, has borders with Borneo and Brunei. The Federation of Malaysia achieved independence from Great Britain in 1957 and became a member of the United Nations the same year. Malaysia's population is estimated to be 18,630,000. Ethnic groups include persons of Malay and indigenous origins (59%), Chinese (32%), and Indian (9%). Languages commonly used include Malay (official), Chinese and Chinese dialects, Tamil, and English. Religions practiced include Islam (official), Buddhism, Christianity, Confucianism, Hinduism, and Taoism. Literacy is estimated at 80% in peninsular Malaysia, 60% in Sabah and Sarawak.

The government (1994) took the form of a federal constitutional monarchy and member of the Commonwealth. The "Paramount Ruler," elected every five years by the hereditary rulers of the States from among themselves, is head of State. He is advised by the prime minister and cabinet. The prime minister, representing the party or coalition given a majority of seats in the House of Representatives, exercises executive authority as head of government. There is a bicameral parliament including the 68-member Senate—partly elected by the legislative assemblies of the various states and partly appointed by the paramount ruler to represent minority and special interests—and the 180-member House of Representatives, members of which are elected by popular vote for terms of five years. The judiciary is organized along British lines. Political parties include the National Front, which is a broad coalition of 11 parties; the Democratic Action Party; the Islamic Party; and the Independents.

A new Paramount Ruler, Tuanku Ja'afar ibni Al-Marhum Tuanku Abdul Rahman, was elected by the nine-member Conference of Rulers in April 1994 for a five-year term. Constitutional amendments had been enacted in March 1993 reducing the Sultan's legal immunity.

**WAR OF LIBERATION.** The Communist Party of Malaysia ended one of the world's longest insurgencies on 2 December 1989 by signing separate agreements with the government of Malaysia and the Internal Security Operations Command of Thailand, pledging to lay down its arms and return to civilian life. The communist "war of liberation" had started in 1948, when Malaya was a British colony. About 1,200 guerillas were involved. The Malaysian government undertook to allow the disbanded units to participate in political activities within the framework of the country's constitution and laws, while the communists agreed to respect the laws of Malaysia and Thailand and to take part in social and economic development.

**PROBLEMS OF MINORITIES.** Tensions occur frequently in Malaysia as a result of feelings within the Malay community that the Chinese and Indian minorities, which together outnumber the Malays and control a large share of the nation's wealth, will assume control of the country in spite of a constitutional provision that the head of State must always be a Malay of the Islamic faith—a provision that, in fact, means that the prime minister is selected by about 1,500 members of the United Malays National Organization.

In April 1990, the UN High Commissioner for Refugees drew attention to the fact that Malaysia was again refusing permission to land, to ethnic Chinese refugees from Vietnam—"boat people"—in violation of an agreement which it had made in June 1989 at a conference in Geneva convened at Malaysia's request. Under the agreement, Malaysia and other "first asylum countries" were to provide temporary shelter for all new arrivals until they could be screened to determine who among them were real refugees with a "well-founded fear of persecution" and who were "economical migrants." Resettlement countries would then take those judged to be refugees, while the economic migrants would be repatriated.

At an April 1992 meeting on the environment in developing countries, the Kuala Lumpur Declaration was signed, calling for a cessation of international criticism of the environmental record of developing nations, greater environmental effort by industrialized countries and rejection of the linkage between developmental aid and human rights. Malaysia's Prime Minister Mahathir delivered the statement to the 1992 UN Conference on the Environment and Development in Brazil.

During 1993 and 1994, relations improved with both the Philippines and Indonesia as discussions on title to disputed territories were held.

***BIBLIOGRAPHY.*** Amnesty International. *Malaysia: "Operation Lallang": Detention without Trial under the Internal Security Act.* London: 1988. NGO report, in English.

————. *Southeast Asia: Human Rights Violations in Brunei, Indonesia, Malaysia, Philippines, Singapore and Thailand.* London: 1987. NGO report, in English.

Boniface, Dorne. *The Human Cost of Sarawak's Timber Revenue.* Kensington, Australia: Law Association for Asia and the Pacific, 1990. NGO report, in English.

Colchester, Marcus. *Pirates, Squatters and Poachers: The Political Ecology of Dispossession of the Native Peoples of Sarawak.* London: Survival International; Institute of Social Analysis, 1992. NGO report, in English; bibliography, pp. 82–85.

Consumers' Association of Penang. *Rape in Malaysia: The Victims and the Rapists—The Myths and the Realities.* Penang, Malaysia: 1988. NGO study, in English.

Dass, Arokia, and Niala Maharaj. *Not Beyond Repair: Reflections of a Malaysian Trade Unionist.* Kowloon, Hong Kong: Asia Monitor Resource Center, 1991. NGO monograph, in English.

Election Watch. *Report on the Eighth Malaysian General Elections Held on 20th and 21st October 1990.* Kuala Lumpur, Malaysia: Aliran Kesedaran Negara, 1990. NGO factfinding report, in English.

Fédération Internationale des Droits de l'Homme. *Mission to Sarawak: Logging, Environment and Human Rights in Sarawak.* Paris: 1991. NGO factfinding report, in English.

Kirby, Justice. "Malaysia—the Judiciary and the Rule of Law," *ICJ Review* 41 (December 1988): 40–43. NGO article, in English.

Ong Puay Liu. "Ethnic Quotas in Malaysia: Affirmative Action or Indigenous Right?" *Asian Profile* 18, no. 4 (August 1990): 325–334. Article, in English.

Regional Council on Human Rights in Asia. *The Law and Practice of Preventive Detention in the ASEAN Region.* Manila, Philippines: 1988. NGO report, in English.

Sigler, Jay A., ed. *International Handbook on Race and Race Relations.* Westport, CT, USA: Greenwood Press, 1987. Scholarly edited collection, in English; bibliography, pp. 449–454.

Taswell, Ruth, ed. *Southeast Asian Tribal Groups and Ethnic Minorities.* Cambridge, MA, USA: Cultural Survival, 1987. NGO conference proceedings, in English.

**MALDIVES.** The Republic of Maldives is a country in southern Asia, occupying about 1,250 atolls in the Pacific Ocean, southwest of Sri Lanka. Formerly a protectorate known as the Maldive Islands, Maldives achieved independence from Great Britain in 1965 and became a member of the United Nations the same year. Its population is estimated to be 235,000. Ethnic groups include Sinhalese, South Indians, and Arabs. The language in common use is Divehi. Islam (Sunni) is the predominant religion.

The government (1994) took the form of a republic and member of the Commonwealth. There are no political parties. President Maumoon Abdul Gayoom, who has held the office of president since 1978, was re-elected to another five-year term of office in 1993 by 93% of the vote.

***INSURGENCY BY TAMIL SEPARATISTS.*** On 3 November 1988, a mercenary force from Sri Lanka tried to overthrow the government of Maldives. The mercenaries were later identified as "members of Tamil secessionist terrorist groups." The Government of Maldives prepared the following statement for the 1989 session of the UN **COMMISSION ON HUMAN RIGHTS** (UN Doc. E/CN.4/1989/80, paras. 2–13):

A heavily armed foreign mercenary/terrorist force landed at Malé, the capital of Maldives, in two small Sri Lankan fishing trawlers at 4 a.m. on 3 November 1988 and proceeded to attack the National Security Headquarters, situated a few hundred yards from the water front, the President's residence and some key government installations. Two Maldivians, Abdulla Luthfy, a businessman living in Sri Lanka, and Sager Nasir, a former seaman, also took part in the hostile operations.

The attackers who, as subsequent investigations have revealed, belonged to a militant Tamil group from Sri Lanka, the People's Liberation Organization of Tamil Elam (PLOT), were armed with assault rifles, machine-guns, mortars, RPG-7 rockets, grenades and explosives. Their main objective was to seize the National Security Service (NSS) Headquarters, and to capture the President and a number of Cabinet Ministers in a bid to overthrow the legitimate Government of President Maumoon Abdul Gayoom, undermine the constitutional order of the State and turn it into a Tamil terrorist base from which they could launch subversive operations in Sri Lanka.

The attackers failed to achieve their objectives owing to the stiff resistance put up by the NSS and the Presidential guards with the result that they were not able to enter the NSS Headquarters or the residence of the President. However, the fighting lasted 18 hours and left eight National Security Servicemen and four civilians dead and 36 wounded. At least three of the attackers were killed, and many more injured.

The armed aggressors also surrounded the main power house and the central telecommunications building in Malé. Although they forced the engineers to cut off the power supply to the entire city, the terrorists were not skilled enough to sever the international telephone links. They also violated the sanctity of the Islamic Centre and Grand Mosque while the early morning prayers were being conducted and took a number of worshippers hostage, including the elderly imam of the Mosque.

Considering the fact that the safety of a large number of civilians as well as the sovereignty and territorial integrity of the nation were at stake, President Gayoom appealed to the Indian Government for military assistance to stop the aggression. This crucial step was taken by the President in the light of his concern over the possibility of reinforcements reaching the invading force, which would inevitably have led to more fierce fighting, resulting in heavy loss of life and destruction of key government buildings, private homes and other infrastructure.

Their failure to capture the President and the courage with which the NSS fought the terrorists, together with the impending arrival of the Indian troops, caused panic among the mercenaries. In their hurry to escape, they captured a Maldivian cargo ship *Progress Light* and resorted to hostage-taking. A total of 28 persons, including the Minister of Transport and Shipping, his wife, and a Member of Parliament who is a senior official at the Ministry of Trade and Industries, were taken as hostages on board the *Progress Light*. One of the fishing craft in which the mercenary group had arrived left Malé before noon, while the other had escaped at about 9 p.m.

On 4 November 1988, at the request of the Maldives Government, Indian navy and air-force planes tracked down the *Progress Light* which was travelling towards Colombo. Two warships of the Indian navy were also directed to intercept the hijacked vessel in an effort to rescue the hostages and apprehend the terrorists. On being ordered to stop and hand over the hostages, the terrorists refused and continued their course towards Colombo.

Negotiations between the Maldivian officials on board the Indian frigates and the mercenaries/terrorists at sea, which continued for two days, were of no avail. Finally, and with the explicit approval of the Maldives Government, the Indian frigates on 6 November 1988 used force to stop the commandeered vessel, rescue the hostages and capture the fleeing terrorists. The terrorists had killed two of the hostages in cold blood, including the imam of the Islamic Centre. After the rescue operation was over, five more hostages were found dead.

A total of 68 mercenaries, along with the two Maldivian collaborators, Abdulla Luthfy and Sagar Nasir, were apprehended and placed in custody in the Maldives. The investi-

gation of the incident and examination of the evidence is currently being carried out in accordance with the laws of the Republic of Maldives and thereafter the trial of the terrorists will begin.

The Government of Maldives is convinced that the 3 November episode was not merely an attempted *coup d'état*, but that it was a foreign mercenary/terrorist aggression aimed at subverting the sovereignty, territorial integrity and political independence of the Republic of Maldives and converting it into a terrorist base which would endanger the security and stability of the South Asian region as a whole. The Government of Maldives has already conveyed the facts of the 3 November aggression to the Secretary-General of the United Nations and has also addressed the issue in other international forums.

The Republic of Maldives condemns in the strongest terms any mercenary or terrorist activities which threaten the sovereignty, political independence and territorial integrity of any State, or create instability in any region. Terrorism and mercenarism have been growing in recent times in different parts of the world. The Republic of Maldives had repeatedly emphasized the urgent need to tackle this menace in the global context and take strong, effective and concerted action, in various international forums.

The Government of Maldives has also addressed the question of mercenaries before the Commonwealth forum and more particularly, has discussed the subject in the regional forum of the South Asian Association for Regional Co-operation (SAARC). The SAARC Regional Convention on Suppression of Terrorism which came into force in August 1988, provides a framework for the countries of the region to co-operate in combatting the menace of terrorism.

***BIBLIOGRAPHY.*** Amnesty International. *SARAN 04/93—Republic of Maldives: Prisoners of Conscience and Unfair Trial Concerns 1990–1993*. London: 1993. NGO report, in English.

**MALI.** The Republic of Mali is a landlocked country in western Africa. It has borders with Algeria, Burkina Faso, Guinea, the Ivory Coast, Mauritania, Niger, and Senegal. Formerly known as French Sudan and from June until August 1960 as the Sudanese Republic, Mali achieved independence from France in 1960 and became a member of the United Nations the same year. Its population is estimated to be 8,754,000. Ethnic groups include two main racial branches (white and black, each living in a particular area of the national territory); however, the people are cosmopolitan, and racially mixed in the urban centers. Languages commonly used include French (official), Bambara, and numerous languages of the various ethnic groups. Religions practiced include Islam (90%), Animism (9%), and Christianity (1%). The members of the white racial group are almost 99% Muslim. Literacy is estimated at 10%.

A report presented to the UN **COMMITTEE ON THE ELIMINATION OF RACIAL DISCRIMINATION** in April 1985 (UN Doc. CERD/C/105/Add. 7, paras. 5–7) provides the following details about the ethnic situation in that country:

Mali occupies a culturally advantageous position, in that it is at the crossroads of the Arab–Berber and black–African worlds. This fact explains the existence of two major racial groups:

(1) the white racial group which comprises the Tuaregs, the Peul, the Arabs and the Moors, and

(2) the black racial group which comprises a large number of ethnic groups including Bambara, Malinke, Solinke, Dogon, Sonrghai, Senufo, Minianka, Bozo, Somono, and Kakoro.

The black racial group is by far the largest; apart from some 600,000 Peul, 200,000 Tuareg, and 60,000 Moors, the rest of the population of 7 million is made up of black ethnic groups. But it cannot be said that there is cultural homogeneity; each of these ethnic groups claims its own culture. Of all the ethnic groups, however, the Bambara group is the largest in number, with more than 2 million people, and the Bambara language is by far the most widely spoken, especially when the neighboring languages (Malinke, Dioula, and Kassomke), which are closely related to Bambara, are taken into account.

The Malian population, therefore, is quite diversified; this diversity occurs over a territory whose frontiers are not very favorable to any kind of homogeneity, since they are the result of successive divisions by the former colonizers designed to form simple administrative units with no regard whatsoever for historical, ethnic or cultural factors; in most cases, frontiers were, quite literally, drawn with a ruler. Mali has virtually no natural frontiers with the seven countries surrounding it. . . .

The government (1994) took the form of a republic. Formerly known as the French Sudan and later (with Senegal) as the Sudanese Republic, it first achieved independent status in 1960 under President Kieta, who was overthrown in 1968 by a military coup led by Colonel Moussa Traiore. Mali returned to civilian control in 1979, with Traiore as its elected president. He was re-elected in 1985, but was overthrown in 1991 following violent demonstrations. He was charged with murder and "economic crimes."

A draft constitution was prepared by 1800 delegates to a National Conference in mid-1991 and approved nearly unanimously by referendum in January 1992. It provided for a secular, multiparty state; a president (who appoints a prime minister) and a 129-seat National Assembly, each to be elected by universal suffrage for five-year terms; separation of powers, including an independent judiciary and a Constitutional Court; free press and association and other individual rights.

By the time of elections to the National Assembly in March 1992, 48 political organizations had registered and ADEMA (Alliance for Democracy in Mali) won 76 of the 129 seats. Voter participation was estimated at 20%. President Alpha Oumar Konare was inaugurated

in June 1992. The Constitutional Court was established in March 1994.

**BIBLIOGRAPHY.** International Commission of Jurists. *Les Services Juridiques en Milieu Rural (Afrique de l'Ouest)* (Legal Services in Rural Areas [West Africa]). Geneva: 1987. NGO report, in French.

International Work Group for Indigenous Affairs. "West Africa: Documentation on the Tuareg—Massacres on Tuaregs in Mali and Niger," *IWGIA Newsletter,* no. 62 (1990): 129–160. NGO articles, in English.

Women's International Network. "Female Circumcision: Genital and Sexual Mutilation," *WIN News* 14, no. 3 (Summer 1988): 24–27; 14, no. 4 (Autumn 1988): 21–26; 15, no. 1 (Winter 1989): 28–29. NGO edited collection, in English.

**MALTA.** The Republic of Malta is a country in southern Europe, occupying the islands of Malta, Gozo, and Comingo in the Mediterranean Sea, 60 miles south of Sicily. It achieved independence from Great Britain in 1964 and became a member of the United Nations the same year. Its total population is estimated to be 360,000. Ethnic groups include Arabs, Italians, and British. Languages commonly used include Maltese and English (both official) and Italian, French, German, and Arabic. Christianity (Roman Catholic) is the predominant religion. Literacy is estimated at 90%.

The government took the form (1994) of a republic and member of the Commonwealth of Nations, of which the British monarch is the symbolic head. The 1964 constitution is based on the **UNIVERSAL DECLARATION OF HUMAN RIGHTS.** Under that constitution, the president is head of State and the prime minister head of government. The prime minister, representing the party or coalition given the majority in a popular election, exercises executive authority with the assistance of his cabinet; he is directly responsible to the House of Representatives, members of which are elected by popular vote. Legislation is prepared by the House of Representatives. The judiciary, modeled after the British system, includes the Constitutional Court. Political parties include the Malta Labor Party and the Nationalist Party.

Students of many countries, races, beliefs, and backgrounds are welcome to study in Malta; in recent years, foreign students attended various primary, secondary, and trade schools, the university, the Libyan–Arab School, and medical and nursing school; they came from the United States, Canada, the United Kingdom, South Africa, Namibia, Ghana, Nigeria, Tanzania, Swaziland, Libya, Pakistan, India, Egypt, Jordan, and several eastern European countries.

Since Malta ratified the **EUROPEAN CONVENTION ON HUMAN RIGHTS** in 1987, individuals may take complaints concerning violations of human rights to the European Commission on Human Rights after exhausting domestic remedies, in accordance with article 25 of that convention.

Formal application was made for full membership in the European Community (now European Union) in July 1990. In legislative elections in February 1992, the Nationalist Party won a majority of the 69 seats in the House of Representatives. President Ugo Mifsud Bonnici was elected to a five-year term by the House in April 1994.

*REPORT OF THE UN HUMAN RIGHTS COMMITTEE.* The initial report of Malta (CCPR/C/68/Add. 4) was considered by the **HUMAN RIGHTS COMMITTEE** at its 1283rd and 1287th meetings, held on 1 and 3 November 1993. The following comments were adopted (paras. 119–131):

*Factors and Difficulties affecting the Application of the Covenant.* The Committee notes that there are no indications in the report or in the oral submission on the factors or difficulties which may impede the effective implementation of the Covenant's provisions.

*Positive Aspects.* The Committee notes the efforts undertaken by the Government of Malta in order to guarantee effectively the protection of civil and political rights. Chapter IV of the national Constitution provides an appropriate basis for the effective protection of most of the human rights contained in the Covenant.

The recent adoption by Parliament of a number of legal measures, such as the Local Council Act, the proposed review of the Civil Code in order better to ensure the equality of children born out of wedlock and to promote the equality of sexes and the proposed revision of the Investigation of Injustices Act, the forthcoming consideration by Parliament of a draft Data Protection Act and Information Practices Act, indicate the commitment of the Government of Malta to bring its national legislation into line with the Covenant.

The Committee notes with satisfaction that, in 1990, Malta acceded to the first Optional Protocol at the same time as it acceded to the Covenant.

*Principal Subjects of Concern.* The Committee is concerned at the fact that the Covenant, unlike the European Convention for the Protection of Human Rights and Fundamental Freedoms, has not yet been incorporated into the national legal order. The Committee also expresses concern over the status of the Covenant within the legal system of Malta and the lack of clarity concerning the resolution of eventual conflicts between the Covenant and domestic legislation.

In this connection, the Committee recalls that, in accordance with article 2, paragraph 2, of the Covenant, each State party to the Covenant undertakes to take the necessary steps to adopt such legislative or other measures as may be necessary to give effect to the rights recognized in the Covenant.

The Committee also expresses concern over the apparent preference accorded, in the domestic law as well as in legal doctrine and jurisprudence, to the European Convention for the Protection of Human Rights and Fundamental Freedoms as against the International Covenant on Civil and Political Rights. In that regard, the attention of the State party is drawn to the fact that the latter guarantees a number of human rights not protected under the former and that permissible restrictions are less broad-based.

The Committee notes that the reservations entered by Malta upon ratification of the Covenant with respect to a number of provisions have an adverse effect on the effective implementation of the Covenant. No convincing reasons have been offered for the reservations to articles 13 and 14, paragraph 6. Additionally, given the actual situation of human rights protection in Malta, some reservations may now have become obsolete.

The Committee further notes that certain requirements of the Covenant, such as those referred to in article 9, paragraphs 3 and 26, are not fully met. In that connection, the attention of the State party is drawn to the pertinent General Comments adopted by the Committee as well as to the Committee's jurisprudence under the Optional Protocol.

*Suggestions and Recommendations.* The Committee recommends that the State party take appropriate measures to incorporate the substantive provisions of the Covenant into domestic law and ensure that the restrictions imposed under domestic law do not go beyond those permissible under the Covenant.

The Committee also recommends that the Government review, with a view to withdrawing, the reservations made upon ratification of the Covenant, particularly those concerning articles 13 and 14 of the Covenant.

The Committee expresses the hope that the Government of Malta will consider ratifying the Second Optional Protocol to the Covenant aiming at the abolition of the death penalty.

The Committee emphasizes that further measures should be taken to ensure that the provisions of the Covenant be made more widely known, particularly among the legal profession, members of the judiciary and administrative authorities. The general public should also be adequately informed of the provisions of the Covenant and those contained in the Optional Protocol.

*BIBLIOGRAPHY.* Amnesty International. *Amnesty International Concerns in Western Europe—October 1986–March 1987.* London: 1987. NGO report, in English.

―――――. *Amnesty International Concerns in Western Europe—March 1986–September 1986.* London: 1986. NGO report, in English.

International Helsinki Federation for Human Rights. *Human Rights in Malta.* Vienna: 1985. NGO mission report, in English.

**MANDELA, NELSON ROLIHLAHLA (1918–).** Nelson Mandela may be the most famous political prisoner of our time. Imprisoned by the *apartheid* Government of South Africa for 27 years—ostensibly for treason, actually for his struggle against the racist regime of his homeland—Mandela is today the president of South Africa. In 1993, he was co-recipient of the **NOBEL PEACE PRIZE,** an honor he shared with **F. W. DE KLERK,** who helped to dismantle the policy of *apartheid.* Mandela is also the president of the once-outlawed **AFRICAN NATIONAL CONGRESS OF SOUTH AFRICA** (ANC) and the second ANC president to receive a Nobel Peace Prize (**ALBERT LUTHULI** was the first).

Born in 1918 in the Transkei territory of the Eastern Cape, Mandela was a prince of the Xhosa-speaking

Tembu tribe, although he renounced his hereditary right to succeed his father as chief. He received a law degree from the University of South Africa in 1942, and, in 1952, he and Oliver Tambo opened the first black law practice in South Africa, in the city of Johannesburg. In 1944, Mandela joined the African National Congress, South Africa's oldest liberation movement. In 1944, Mandela, along with Tambo and Walter Sisulu established the Congress Youth League, a wing of the ANC which eventually dominated the organization. Throughout the 1940s and early 1950s, the Youth League conducted work stoppages, fullscale labor strikes, and civil disobedience, including the 1952 Defiance against Unjust Laws Campaign, which resulted in approximately 8,000 arrests and the banning of Mandela from political life.

The ban against Mandela was lifted in 1955. Under his leadership of the Youth League, the ANC moved toward the left, embracing Marxist policies and eventually abandoning the policy of peaceful resistance. On 6 December 1956, Mandela and others were charged with advocating revolution under the Suppression of Communism Act. The treason trial lasted until March 1961, when all the defendants were acquitted due to lack of evidence. In 1960, Mandela was authorized to create an "army" that would undertake "organized violence." The group, *Umkhonto we Sizwe* (The Spear of the Nation) or MK, as it was commonly called, undertook a policy of sabotage. As Mandela explains in his autobiography, *Long Walk to Freedom,* "Our strategy was to make selective forays against military installations, power plants, telephone lines, and transportation links: targets that would not only hamper the military effectiveness of the state, but frighten national Party supporters, scare away foreign capital, and weaken the economy. This we hoped would bring the government to the bargaining table." Because of his activities, after his acquittal, Mandela was forced to work "underground," often disguising himself to escape detection; in 1962, while posing as a chauffeur, he was apprehended by the South African security police in Natal and was sentenced to prison for five years for inciting strikes and traveling without valid documents. While he was in detention, the government raided ANC headquarters in Rivonia, a Johannesburg suburb, and found documents that advocated, according to the government, high treason and conspiracy to overthrow the government. Mandela was eventually sentenced to life in prison.

Most of his prison years were spent in the maximum security prison on Robben Island; during those years, international campaigns for his release were undertaken. While Mandela was imprisoned, Oliver Tambo was the nominal head of the ANC, but Mandela was the spirit behind the movement, as the government

well understood. In 1982, Mandela was unexpectedly transferred to Pollsmoor Prison, another maximum security installation, but one where he was able to get news of the outside world. In 1985, while recovering from surgery, he received an unexpected visitor: Kobie Coetsee, the South African minister of justice. Through numerous visits with Coetsee, Mandela realized that the government was willing to negotiate in an effort to ease the international tension and to resolve the national situation that worsened with each day, eventually resulting in states of emergency in 1986, 1987, and 1988.

Mandela secretly met with Coetsee and others in the government over the next three years, eventually meeting with President F. W. de Klerk in 1989. As a basis for negotiations, Mandela had written in 1989 to then-President P. W. Botha what he considered as a basis for negotiations:

Two political issues will have to be addressed; firstly, the demand for majority rule in a unitary state, secondly, the concern of white South Africa over this demand, as well as the insistence of whites on structural guarantees that majority rule will not mean domination of the white minority by blacks. The most crucial tasks which will face the government and the ANC will be to reconcile these two positions.

In de Klerk, who had already released from prison, without a "ban," seven of Mandela's Rivonia colleagues, including Walter Sisulu, Mandela saw a man with whom he could "do business." Mandela and de Klerk first met in December 1989. On 2 February 1990, de Klerk announced the lifting of the bans on the ANC, the Pan-African Congress, the South African Communist Party, and other illegal political organizations; the freeing of all political prisoners incarcerated for nonviolent activities; the suspension of capital punishment; and the lifting of the State of Emergency. On 11 February 1990, Nelson Mandela walked out of prison and raised his fist in the "Afrika" salute.

On Tuesday, April 26, 1994, roughly 100,000 black South Africans lined up to vote in the first all-nation vote. Some stayed in lines for seven or eight hours, just so they could cast their first ballot in an election. On Wednesday, April 27, a new South Africa was born with a new flag, a new constitution, and the first full day of voting. By Friday, April 29, after three days of intense voting, the 9,700 polling stations closed. All the ballots were packed in boxes and transferred to the counting stations. Monday, May 2, saw the ANC leading with 63.6% of the vote, although the tallies were still incomplete. By Saturday, May 7, the first real step in the transfer of power to black South Africans occurred with the meeting of the nine provincial legislatures. By Monday, May 9, the new South African Parliament met and unanimously elected Nelson Mandela as the first black president of the Republic of South Africa.

In his autobiography, Mandela sums up his legacy:

I was not born with a hunger to be free. I was born free—free in every way that I could know. . . . But then I slowly saw that not only was I not free, but my brothers and sisters were not free. I saw that it was not just my freedom that was curtailed, but the freedom of everyone who looked like I did. That is when I joined the African National Congress, and that is when the hunger for my own freedom became the greater hunger for the freedom of my people. It was this desire for the freedom of my people to live their lives with dignity and self-respect that animated my life, that transformed a frightened young man into a bold one, that drove a law-abiding attorney to become a criminal, that turned a family-loving husband into a man without a home, that forced a life-loving man to live like a monk. . . . Freedom is indivisible. . . . It was during those long and lonely years that my hunger for the freedom of my own people became a hunger for the freedom of all people, white and black.

**BIBLIOGRAPHY.** *Current Biography Yearbook.* New York: W. H. Wilson, 1984.

Mandela, Nelson. *Long Walk to Freedom.* Boston, MA, USA: Little, Brown and Company, 1994.

## MARRIAGE AND THE FAMILY.

The right to marry and to found a family is proclaimed in the **UNIVERSAL DECLARATION OF HUMAN RIGHTS** in the following terms:

*Article 16.* 1. Men and women of full age, without any limitation due to race, nationality or religion, have the right to marry and to found a family. They are entitled to equal rights as to marriage, during marriage and at its dissolution.

2. Marriage shall be entered into only with the free and full consent of the intending spouses.

3. The family is the natural and fundamental group unit of society and is entitled to protection by society and the State.

The **INTERNATIONAL COVENANT ON ECONOMIC, SOCIAL AND CULTURAL RIGHTS** provides for special measures to be taken to protect the family, mothers, and children, as follows:

*Article 10.* The States Parties to the present Covenant recognize that:

1. The widest possible protection and assistance should be accorded to the family, which is the natural and fundamental group unit of society, particularly for its establishment and while it is responsible for the care and education of dependent children. Marriage must be entered into with the free consent of the intending spouses.

2. Special protection should be accorded to mothers during a reasonable period before and after childbirth. During such period working mothers should be accorded paid leave or leave with adequate social security benefits.

3. Special measures of protection and assistance should be taken on behalf of all children and young persons without any discrimination for reasons of parentage or other conditions. Children and young persons should be protected from economic and social exploitation. Their employment in work harmful to their morals or health or dangerous to life or likely to hamper their normal development should be punishable by law. States should also set age limits below which the paid employment of child labour should be prohibited and punishable by law.

The **INTERNATIONAL COVENANT ON CIVIL AND POLITICAL RIGHTS** also calls for special measures to be taken to protect the family, mothers, and children, as follows:

*Article 23.* 1. The family is the natural and fundamental group unit of society and is entitled to protection by society and the State.

2. The right of men and women of marriageable age to marry and to found a family shall be recognized.

3. No marriage shall be entered into without the free and full consent of the intending spouses.

4. State Parties to the present Covenant shall take appropriate steps to ensure equality of rights and responsibilities of spouse as to marriage, during marriage and at its dissolution. In the case of dissolution, provision shall be made for the necessary protection of any children.

*Article 24.* 1. Every child shall have, without any discrimination as to race, colour, sex, language, religion, national or social origin, property or birth, the right to such measures of protection as are required by his status as a minor, on the part of his family, society and the State.

2. Every child shall be registered immediately after birth and shall have a name.

3. Every child has the right to acquire a nationality.

The International Convention on the Elimination of All Forms of Racial Discrimination (see **RACIAL DISCRIMINATION**) contains the following provision:

*Article 5.* In compliance with the fundamental obligations laid down in article 2 of this Convention, States parties undertake to prohibit and to eliminate racial discrimination in all its forms and to guarantee the right of everyone, without distinction as to race, colour, or national or ethnic origin, to equality before the law, notably in the enjoyment of the following rights: . . .

(d) Other civil rights, in particular: . . .

(iv) The right to marriage and choice of spouse.

The Convention on the Elimination of All Forms of Discrimination against Women contains extensive provisions concerning marriage and the family, as follows:

*Article 4.* 2. Adoption by States parties of special measures, including those measures contained in the present Convention, aimed at protecting maternity, shall not be considered discriminatory. . . .

*Article 12.* 1. States parties shall take all appropriate measures to eliminate discrimination against women in the field of health care in order to ensure, on a basis of equality of men and women, access to health care services, including those related to family planning.

2. Notwithstanding the provisions of paragraph 1 of this

article, States parties shall assure to women appropriate services in connection with pregnancy, confinement and the post-natal period, granting free services where necessary, as well as adequate nutrition during pregnancy and lactation. . . .

*Article 16.* 1. States parties shall take all appropriate measures to eliminate discrimination against women in all matters relating to marriage and family relations and in particular shall ensure, on a basis of equality of men and women:

(a) The same right to enter into marriage;

(b) The same right freely to choose a spouse and to enter into marriage only with their free and full consent;

(c) The same rights and responsibilities during marriage and at its dissolution;

(d) The same rights and responsibilities as parents, irrespective of their marital status, in matters relating to their children; in all cases the interests of the children shall be paramount;

(e) The same rights to decide freely and responsibly on the number and spacing of their children and to have access to the information, education and means to enable them to exercise these rights;

(f) The same rights and responsibilities with regard to guardianship, wardship, trusteeship and adoption of children, or similar institutions where these concepts exist in national legislation; in all cases the interests of the children shall be paramount;

(g) The same personal rights as husband and wife, including the right to choose a family name, a profession and an occupation;

(h) The same rights for both spouses in respect of ownership, acquisition, management, administration, enjoyment and disposition of property, whether free of charge or for a valuable consideration.

2. The betrothal and the marriage of a child shall have no legal effect, and all necessary action, including legislation, shall be taken to specify a minimum age for marriage and to make the registration of marriages in an official registry compulsory.

The **European Convention on Human Rights, Protocol VII,** adds the following provision to the text of the Convention:

*Article 5.* Spouses shall enjoy equality of rights and responsibilities of a private law character between them, and in their relations with their children, as to marriage, during marriage and in the event of its dissolution. This Article shall not prevent States from taking such measures as are necessary in the interests of the children.

*CONSENT TO MARRIAGE, MINIMUM AGE FOR MARRIAGE, AND REGISTRATION OF MARRIAGES.* At the suggestion of the conference of plenipotentiaries convened in 1956 to prepare the Supplementary Convention on the Abolition of Slavery, the Slave Trade and Institutions and Practices Similar to Slavery, the UN **Commission on the Status of Women** initiated a study of the question of marriage with the objective of drawing attention to the desirability of free consent of both parties to a marriage and of the establishment of a minimum age for marriage.

The Commission decided that it would prepare

both an international convention and a recommendation on this subject and was able to complete preliminary drafts of both at its 1960 and 1961 sessions.

The Convention on Consent to Marriage, Minimum Age for Marriage and Registration of Marriages was completed, adopted, and opened for signature and ratification by the UN General Assembly in 1962 (resolution 1763 [XVII]). The recommendation on the same subject was adopted and proclaimed by the Assembly three years later (resolution 2018 [XX]).

The Convention sets out three measures aimed at ensuring that no marriage shall be legally entered into without the full and free consent of both parties. The first (article 1) is that consent must be expressed by the two intending spouses in person after due publicity and in the presence of an authority competent to solemnize the marriage. The second (article 2) is that each State party must specify by law a minimum age for marriage. The third (article 3) is that all marriages must be registered in an appropriate official register by the competent authority.

The Convention provides for a limited exception from the general rule requiring the presence of both parties at the solemnization of the marriage. One of the parties may be absent if the competent authority is satisfied that the circumstances are exceptional and that the party has, before a competent authority and in such a manner as may be prescribed by law, expressed and not withdrawn consent.

The Convention also permits an exception from the general rule that no marriage shall be legally entered into by a person under the age specified by the law of the State. This exception applies when the competent authority has, in the interests of the intending spouses and for serious reasons, granted a dispensation as to age.

The Recommendation, intended to apply generally to all States not parties to the Convention, deals with the same problems. However, whereas the Convention does not specify a minimum age for marriage, the Recommendation expressly provides that the minimum age to be specified in State legislation shall not be less than 15 years.

*INTERNATIONAL YEAR OF THE FAMILY.* At its 1987 session, the UN **General Assembly** invited all States (resolution 42/134) to make known their views concerning possible proclamation of an international year of the family and to offer their comments and proposals thereon to the Secretary-General before 30 April 1988. In doing so, it was guided by the relevant provisions of the Universal Declaration of Human Rights; the International Covenant on Economic, Social and Cultural Rights; and the Declaration on Social Progress and Development, as well as the Guiding

Principles for Developmental Social Welfare Policies and Programmes in the Near Future, which it had endorsed (resolution 42/125) and which calls for social welfare policies to give greater attention to the family.

Taking note of the positive responses reflected in the report submitted by the Secretary-General in 1988 (UN Doc. A/43/570), the General Assembly on 8 December 1988 requested him (resolution 43/135) to submit to its 1989 session a report containing a proposed date and a comprehensive outline of a possible program for an International Year of the Family. Member States, specialized agencies, and interested intergovernmental and non-governmental organizations were, at the same time, invited to submit proposals on their participation in such an international year.

**SEE ALSO** Domestic Violence; Persons Born Out of Wedlock.

**BIBLIOGRAPHY.** Alternative Information Center. *The Right to Family Unity: The Denial of Residency to Spouses of Non-Jewish Citizens of Israel: A Preliminary Report by Israeli-Palestinian Project for Family Reunification*. Jerusalem, Israel: June 1992. NGO report, in English.

Armstrong, Alice, ed. *Women and Law in Southern Africa*. Harare, Zimbabwe: Zimbabwe Publishing House, 1987. Scholarly edited collection, in English.

Bayefsky, A.F., and M. Eberts, eds. *Equality Rights and the Canadian Charter of Rights and Freedoms*. Toronto, Canada: Carswell, 1985. Edited collection, in English.

Centre d'Etudes et de Recherches sur l'Orient Chretien (Middle East Christian Research Center). "Kuwait: The Rights of Women," *Plus* 1, no. 1 (1985): 4–5. NGO magazine article, in English.

Comite Democratique des Femmes d'Iran (Democratic Committee of Iranian Women). "La Situation des Femmes Iraniennes" (The Situation of Iranian Women). Paris: Ligue des Droits de l'Homme, 1986. NGO letter, in English.

Cook, Rebecca. "Human Rights and Development: Are Women Still Separate and Unequal?" *Proceedings of the 1986 Conference of the Canadian Council on International Law on "International Law and Development,"* pp. 315–347. Ottawa, Ontario: Canadian Council on International Law, 1987. Scholarly article, in English.

European Commission of Human Rights. *Stock-taking on the European Convention on Human Rights: A Periodic Note on the Concrete Results Achieved under the Convention, Supplement 1987*. Strasbourg, France: Publications and Documents Divisions, Council of Europe, 1988. IGO report, in English.

Femmes sous Lois Musulmanes (Women Living under Muslim Laws). *Dossier No. 1*. Montpellier, France: 1986. NGO document collection, in English.

———. *Dossier No. 2*. Montpellier, France: 1986. NGO document collection, in English.

Fraser, Arvonne. "For Women, the Whole World Is Still the 'Developing World,'" *Human Rights Internet* (Spring 1989). Commentary, in English.

Ivan-Smith, E., N. Tandom, and J. Connors. *Women in Sub-Saharan Africa*. London: Minority Rights Group, 1988. NGO report, in English.

Kearney, R. N., and B. D. Miller. "The Spiral of Suicide and Social Change in Sri Lanka," *Marga* 8, no. 3 (1986): 1–29. Journal article, in English.

Rahman, Anika. "Religious Rights Versus Women's Rights in India: A Test Case for International Human Rights Law," *Columbia Journal of Transnational Law* 28, no. 2 (1990): 473–498. Scholarly article, in English.

"U.N. International Convention on the Protection of the Rights of All Migrant Workers and Members of Their Families," *International Migration Review* 25, no. 4 (no. 96) (Winter 1991): 685–872. Special issue, in English.

Widmalm, Sten. *Dowry Crime and Law Implementation in India*. Uppsala, Sweden: University of Uppsala, Department of Government, 1990. Research report, in English.

**MARSHALL, GEORGE CATLETT (1880–1959).** Riots broke out around the world when Gen. George Marshall, the chief of staff of the United States Army throughout World War II and a man intimately connected with atomic research and the dropping of the atomic bomb on Hiroshima, was cited as the 1953 **NOBEL PEACE PRIZE** recipient. Marshall himself remarked, "The cost of war in human lives is constantly spread before me, written neatly in many ledgers whose columns are gravestones. I am deeply moved to find some means or method of avoiding another calamity of war." And, as he concluded in his Nobel acceptance speech, the way to avoid war was to "present democracy as a force holding within itself the seeds of unlimited progress by the human race." Marshall attempted to do this through the "Marshall Plan," the popular name for the "European Recovery Program," an American plan for economic recovery of the war-ravaged countries of Europe.

Marshall was an army careerist, graduating from the Virginia Military Institute and from the Infantry-Cavalry School at Fort Leavenworth in 1907 and from the Army Staff College in 1908. He was among the soldiers in the first division of American troops to France in 1917 and later served as chief of operations of the division and aide to General Jack Pershing. Between the wars, he also served in China and could speak fluent Chinese; in 1945–46, he represented President Harry Truman as a special envoy to war-torn China.

In addition to his wartime accomplishments, Marshall also served as secretary of defense for one year during the Korean War under President Truman, during which time he instituted a conscription system for the U.S. Army. In addition to the Nobel Peace Prize, Marshall was honored by governments around the world: he received the Gold Medal, Distinguished Service Cross, and the Victory Medal from the United States; the Grand Croix, Legion of Honor, from France; the Order of the Crown, from Italy; and a knighthood in the Order of the Bath from Great Britain. He also was the recipient of the Freedom House Award (1947) and the Four Freedoms Foundation Award (1952).

*BIBLIOGRAPHY.* Ferrell, Robert H. *George C. Marshall.* New York: Cooper Square Publishers, 1966.

Gray, Tony. *Champions of Peace.* London: Paddington Press, 1976.

Schlessinger, Bernard S., and June H. Schlessinger, eds. *Who's Who of Nobel Prize Winners.* Phoenix, AZ, USA: Oryx Press, 1991.

**MARSHALL ISLANDS.** The Republic of the Marshall Islands lies in the Pacific Ocean, two-thirds of the way between Hawaii and Papua New Guinea, about 2,000 miles south-west of Hawaii and about 1,300 miles south-east of Guam. It comprises two chains of islands, the Ratak and Ralik, and 30 atolls, including Bikini, Eniwetak, and Wajalein, the first two being the site of nuclear testing during the 1940s and 1950s. Its population is estimated to be 51,000. The predominant religion is Christianity. English is widely spoken.

Since the 19th century, when they were discovered by Spanish seamen, portions of the Marshall Islands have been occupied by Spain, Germany, and Japan. The two latter countries administered the islands under a **LEAGUE OF NATIONS** mandate from 1920 until 1944. In 1947, the UN placed the islands, as well as the Caroline Islands and the Northern Mariana Islands (except Guam), under the trusteeship of the United States. There were growing demands for autonomy for the islands from 1965. A constitution was drafted for the Marshall Islands which took effect in May 1979. In October 1982, the United States signed the Compact of Free Association, under which the United States would maintain its military bases on the islands for 15 years. It took effect in 1983. The republic became a member of the UN in 1991 after the UN **SECURITY COUNCIL** had voted in 1990 to formally end the trusteeship agreement.

The government (1994) took the form of a republic. The 1979 constitution provides for the popular election of a unicameral legislature, the 33-seat Nitijela, which in turn elects the president. Amata Kabula was elected as president in 1980. Elections in Nitijela took place in November 1991.

Compensation for victims of U.S. nuclear testing was agreed to in the Compact of Free Association of 1983 but levels of radioactivity on some islands continued to be considered too high for habitation and calls came for release of classified information regarding the extent of testing. Cancer remains a large threat. An average seven children are born to Marshalltese women, and, according to a May 1991 **UNICEF** report, two-thirds of the children were malnourished.

**MATSUNAGA MEDAL OF PEACE.** Established in 1993, the Medal is presented to those who have contributed in extraordinary ways to peace among the nations and peoples of the world, with special attention to peacemaking and conflict management. This $25,000 award is given annually to one or two winners. In 1993, the medal was awarded to former U.S. Presidents Jimmy Carter and Ronald Reagan.

For more information, contact: U.S. Institute of Peace, 1550 M Street, NW, Suite 700, Washington, D.C., 20005, USA. Telephone: (202) 457-1700. Fax: (202) 429-6063.

**MAURITANIA.** The Islamic Republic of Mauritania is a country in western Africa, on the Atlantic Ocean. It has borders with Algeria, Senegal, and Western Sahara. It achieved independence from France in 1960 and became a member of the United Nations in 1961. Its population is estimated to be 2,092,000. Ethnic groups include Moors, Arabs, Berbers, and a black minority (Peuls, Soninkes, and Wolofs). Languages commonly used include Hassaniya Arabic (national) and French (official), Toucouleur, Fula, Sarakole, and Wolof. Islam is the predominant religion. Literacy is estimated at 17%.

The government (1994) took the form of a republic; however, the constitution of 1961 was abolished by decree in 1978 after a military *coup d'etat*, and the army chief of staff assumed the presidency after a *coup d'etat* of 12 December 1984. The president is also head of the Military Committee for National Salvation, which has assumed all legislative functions. The courts, under the Ministry of Justice and Islamic Affairs, follow the *Sharia* (Islamic law).

A national referendum on a new constitution was held in June 1991. Official reports stated that 85% of eligible voters had participated and 98% voted to approve the constitution, while opponents suggested that only 8% of those eligible had cast their vote. In July 1991, the constitution was adopted and legislation enacted to allow for political parties. By late 1993, 18 political parties had been accorded official status.

The constitution provided for a multiparty system; a President elected by universal suffrage for a six-year term; a National Assembly and a Senate; and Arabic as the official language (although French was still used frequently).

In 1992, a Supreme Islamic Council and Constitutional Council were established and elections were held. In January, President Col. Maawiya Ould Sid'Ahmed Taya, who had been in office since 1984, was elected with 63% of the vote and, in March, the Democratic and Social Republican Party (linked to President Taya) won 67 of the 79 seats in the National Assembly. Six opposition parties had withdrawn from the race in protest and amidst allegations of unfair electoral policies and practices. When the 56 members of the Senate were elected by municipal leaders in April 1992, only one party other than the DSRP fielded candidates, and they were unsuccessful. The 17 seats not won by the DSRP were held by independents.

The National Assembly enacted legislation in 1993 which pardoned people who had been engaged in armed conflict during the three years prior to the inauguration of the President. Relations with Senegal and Mali were strained, however, by the effect of policies restricting the rights of their nationals inside Mauritania.

***THE QUESTION OF SLAVERY.*** In 1984, a mission to study the situation prevailing in Mauritania as regards slavery and the slave trade visited the country at the request of the UN **Sub-Commission on Prevention of Discrimination and Protection of Minorities,** the **Commission on Human Rights,** and the **Economic and Social Council** and on invitation of the government of the country. The mission reported to the Sub-Commission at its 1984 session, at which time the observer for Mauritania indicated that his government was determined to eradicate slavery but faced major economic and social problems in implementing this policy. In 1985, the Commission on Human Rights received further information and called upon international and regional organizations to consider what assistance they could give to Mauritania as a contribution towards the eradication of slavery, and authorized the Sub-Commission to continue to monitor the situation.

In a final report on the mission, prepared by an expert of the Sub-Commission, the Government of Mauritania is quoted as follows (UN Doc. E/CN.4/Sub.2/1987/27, para. 18):

The Ministry first wishes to recall that "the abolition of slavery," provided for in Ordinance No. 81-234 of 9 November 1981 reflected in practice the desire of the Mauritanian authorities to eradicate "consequences" which persisted essentially in attitudes and mentalities.

This desire has resulted in the establishment of a body of legal texts and accompanying measures in various areas (rural development, land tenure, justice, education, information, etc.) whose objective, rather than to abolish practices which by then no longer existed, was to promote a general policy designated to correct social inequalities and to raise the living standard of all citizens.

This desire has also been given effect through the sincere and comprehensive exploration of all possible ways to attain the stated objective.

Thus the government of Mauritania took the initiative, in August 1981, of inviting the Sub-Commission to send a mission to carry out an on-the-spot inquiry into the reality of what has been termed "the question of slavery" in Mauritania, whereas in fact, as the expert's report testifies, what are involved are only "consequences", neither more nor less. . . .

The Sub-Commission, in resolution 1987/30 of 4 September 1987, encouraged that government to implement those measures and policies fully in order to eliminate the consequences of slavery and to intensify further its efforts in adopting measures guaranteeing effective emancipation for former slaves.

The *New York Times,* on 20 July 1989, reported that "nearly 40,000 blacks have been forced out of Mauritania since early May in what relief workers and Senegalese officials say are racially motivated expulsions. The flow of refugees began after a minor border dispute between Senegalese farmers and Mauritanian herders erupted into riots. About 100,000 Mauritanian nationals in Senegal and 85,000 Senegalese in Mauritania were repatriated at that time, most of them in an international airlift. Since then, a growing stream of black Mauritanians, many with Mauritanian passports and other national identity papers, have been forced by Government officials across the Senegal River from Mauritania into Senegal." According to the dispatch, the expulsions were directed against black Mauritanians suspected of being Senegalese nationals. About one-third of Mauritania's people are black, while others are of Arab and Berber origin; most Senegalese are black.

**BIBLIOGRAPHY.** Africa Watch. *Mauritania: More than 200 Black Political Detainees Executed or Tortured to Death.* New York: Human Rights Watch, 1991. NGO report, in English.
———. *Mauritania—Slavery: Alive and Well, 10 Years After it Was Last Abolished.* New York: Human Rights Watch, 1990. NGO factfinding report, in English.
Amnesty International. *Mauritania: Human Rights Violations in the Senegal River Valley.* London: 1990. NGO factfinding report, in English and French.
De la Brosse, Véronique. "Le développement rural: un processus non-démocratique dans un 'no-man's land' légal: une étude de cas en Mauritanie" (Rural Development: A Non-Democratic Process in a Legal 'No-Man's Land': A Study of the Case of Mauritania), *International Journal of Refugee Law* 3, no. 4 (October 1991): 721–730. Scholarly article, in French; bibliography, p. 730.
Federation Internationale des Droits de l'Homme (International Federation of Human Rights). "Mauritanie: La Mort de Tene Youssouf Gueye" (Mauritania: The Death of Tene Youssouf Gueye), *Lettre de la FIDH* 269 (3 October 1988): 3. NGO article, in French.
———. "Mauritanie: Rapport sur l'Affaire des Baa'thistes" (Report on the Baa'th Affair), *Lettre de la FIDH* 270 (10 October 1988): 2–5. NGO article, in French.
———. *Rapport de Mission: Mauritanie Avril–Decembre 1987* (Mission Report: Mauritania, April–December 1987). Paris: 1987. NGO mission report, in French.
Human Rights Watch/Africa. *Mauritania's Campaign of Terror: State-Sponsored Repression of Black Africans.* New York: 1994. NGO factfinding report, in English.
Lawless, R., and L. Monahan, eds. *War and Refugees: The Western Sahara Conflict.* London: Refugee Studies Programme, Queen Elizabeth House, 1987. Scholarly edited collection, in English.

Ommar, Rakika, and Janet Fleischman. "Mauritania: Arab vs. African," *Africa Report* 36, no. 4 (July–August 1991): 34–38. Article, in English.

## MAURITIUS.

Mauritius is a country in eastern Africa, occupying an island in the Indian Ocean, east of Madagascar. It achieved independence from Great Britain in 1968 and became a member of the United Nations the same year. Its population is estimated by the UN to be 1,096,000. Ethnic groups include Indo–Mauritians (68%), Creoles (27%), Sino–Mauritians (3%), and Franco–Mauritians (2%). The Indo–Mauritian majority includes descendents of laborers brought from India to work in the sugar plantations after the abolition of slavery in 1934. Languages commonly used include English (official), French, Creole, Hindi, Urdu, Hakka, and Bojpoori. More than 140 religious denominations have followers in the country; the predominant religions are Hinduism and Islam. Under its constitution, Mauritius is a secular State and maintains a system whereby major religious organizations are subsidized by the government. Literacy is estimated at 79%.

The government (1994) took the form of a republic and member of the Commonwealth. Constitutional amendments passed by the Legislative Assembly (now the National Assembly) in 1991, effective March 1992, provided for a president to be elected by a simple majority of the National Assembly; a prime minister and Council of Ministers appointed by the president and responsible to the National Assembly; and the 62-seat National Assembly elected for a five-year term by universal suffrage. The attorney-general sits in the Assembly as well as a possible additional eight members. President Cassam Uteem was elected in June 1992.

***BIBLIOGRAPHY.*** Ecumenical Coalition on Third World Tourism. *Third World People and Tourism: Approaches to a Dialogue.* Bangkok, Thailand: 1986. NGO conference proceedings, in English.

Mukonoweshuro, Eliphas G. "Containing Political Instability in a Poly-Ethnic Society: The Case of Mauritius," *Ethnic & Racial Studies* 14, no. 2 (April 1991): 199–224. Scholarly article, in English.

## MÉDECINS SANS FRONTIÈRES (DOCTORS WITHOUT BORDERS).

This non-governmental organization was incorporated officially in Paris in 1971, but the first steps for its founding were taken in 1968 during the Biafra crisis and in 1970 during the solidarity appeal following the floods in Pakistan in 1970. Médecins sans Frontières (MSF) runs emergency medical missions in countries at war; and provides shelter, communications, water procesing, and food and power supply in cases of disaster. It carries out curative and preventive medicine missions in refugee camps, and longer-term operations in many countries where health facilities have collapsed.

MSF has established two centers for surveillance and applied research in epidemiology and public health and for training of MSF staff and volunteers: the Epicentre in France and AEDES in Belgium. With members in seven countries, about 1,000 volunteers leave for 60 countries each year.

MSF volunteers dedicate six months to two years of service. The teams often are the first to arrive on the scene. Among the countries that MSF is helping in the 1990s are Afghanistan, Azerbaijan, Bosnia-Herzegovina, Rwanda, and Sudan. Although this NGO treats all people in need, of special importance in these conflicts are the children.

Médecins sans Frontières. Address: Boulevard Leopold II 209, B-1080, Brussels, Belgium. Telephone: (32-2) 426-5562. Fax: (32-2) 426-7535.

## MEDIA.

The United Nations Conference on Freedom of Information, held at the European office of the United Nations, Geneva, from 23 March to 21 April 1948, recommended (resolution no. 9) that arrangements should be made for accredited news personnel of all countries to have free access to countries where United Nations meetings are held and to all sources of information connected with such meetings, except in cases where meetings are private.

On the recommendation of the Conference and the Economic and Social Council, the General Assembly adopted a resolution on the subject on 21 October 1949 (resolution 314 [IV]), as follows:

The General Assembly,

Considering that the United Nations, in accordance with the aims and purposes of its Charter, should be prepared to grant all the necessary facilities for enabling media of information to function with full freedom and responsibility in following the course of its work and that of conferences called by it and by its specialized agencies,

Urges all States Members of the United Nations to grant news personnel of all countries who have been accredited to the United Nations or specialized agencies, as the case may be, free access:

(a) To countries where meetings of the United Nations or specialized agencies or any conferences convened by them take place, for the purpose of covering such meetings, in accordance with the terms and conditions of agreements made by the United Nations or its specialized agencies with the Governments of such countries, or, in the absence of such an agreement, on terms and conditions similar to those contained in agreements made by the United Nations or its specialized agencies with other Member States; and

(b) To all public information sources and services of the United Nations and the specialized agencies and to all meetings and conferences of the United Nations or of the specialized agencies which are open to the Press, equally and without discrimination.

*SEE ALSO* *Freedom of Information; Information and Communication Order; Journalists.*

**MEDIA: DECLARATION OF GUIDING PRINCIPLES ON THE USE OF SATELLITE BROADCASTING FOR THE FREE FLOW OF INFORMATION, THE SPREAD OF EDUCATION AND GREATER CULTURAL EXCHANGE, UNESCO (1972).** The UN General Assembly noted on 16 December 1970 (resolution 2733 [XXV]) that the potential benefits of satellite broadcasting have particular significance with regard to better understanding among peoples, the expansion of the flow of information, the wider dissemination of knowledge in the world, and the promotion of cultural exchanges; and invited UNESCO to continue to promote the use of satellite broadcasting for these purposes.

This declaration was one of UNESCO's first efforts in this field. Adopted by the UNESCO General Conference (17th session), held in Paris, on 15 November 1972, the Declaration deals mainly with the questions raised by the development of communications satellites capable of broadcasting to the population of countries other than that of the country of the transmission's origin. Taking into account the principle of **FREEDOM OF INFORMATION**, it emphasizes the necessity for States to reach or promote prior agreements regulating such direct satellite broadcasting.

The text of the Declaration (*UNESCO's Standard-Setting Instruments,* No. IV.C.2) is as follows:

The General Conference of the United Nations Educational, Scientific and Cultural Organization meeting in Paris at its seventeenth session, in 1972,

Recognizing that the development of communication satellites capable of broadcasting programmes for community or individual reception establishes a new dimension in international communication,

Recalling that under its Constitution the purpose of Unesco is to contribute to peace and security by promoting collaboration among the nations through education, science and culture, and that, to realize this purpose, the Organization will collaborate in the work of advancing the mutual knowledge and understanding of peoples through all means of mass communication and to that end recommend such international agreements as may be necessary to promote the free flow of ideas by word and image,

Recalling that the Charter of the United Nations specifies, among the purposes and principles of the United Nations, the development of friendly relations among nations based on respect for the principle of equal rights, the non-interference in matters within the domestic jurisdiction of any State, the achievement of international co-operation and the respect for human rights and fundamental freedoms,

Bearing in mind that the Universal Declaration of Human Rights proclaims that everyone has the right to seek, receive and impart information and ideas through any media and regardless of frontiers, that everyone has the right to education and that everyone has the right freely to participate in the cultural life of the community, as well as the right to the protection of the moral and material interests resulting from any scientific, literary or artistic production of which he is the author,

Recalling the Declaration of Legal Principles Governing the Activities of States in the Exploration of Use of Outer Space (resolution 1962 [XV*AF. I*III]of 13 December 1963), and the Treaty on Principles Governing the Activities of States in the Exploration and Use of Outer Space, including the Moon and Other Celestial Bodies, of 1967, (hereinafter referred to as the Outer Space Treaty),

Taking account of United National General Assembly resolution 110(II) of 3 November 1947, condemning propaganda designed or likely to provoke or encourage any threat to the peace, breach of the peace or act of aggression, which resolution as stated in the preamble to the Outer Space Treaty is applicable to outer space; and the United Nations General Assembly resolution 1721 D (XV*AF. II*) of 20 December 1961 declaring that communication by means of satellites should be available as soon as practicable on a global and non-discriminatory basis,

Bearing in mind the Declaration of the Principles of International Cultural Co-operation adopted by the General Conference of Unesco, at its fourteenth session,

Considering that radio frequencies are a limited natural resource belonging to all nations, that their use is regulated by the International Telecommunications Convention and its Radio Regulations and that the assignment of adequate frequencies is essential to the use of satellite broadcasting for education, science, culture and information,

Noting the United Nations General Assembly resolution 2733 (XXV) of 16 December 1970 recommending that Member States, regional and international organizations, including broadcasting associations, should promote and encourage international co-operation at regional and other levels in order to allow all participating parties to share in the establishment and operation of regional satellite broadcasting services,

Noting further that the same resolution invites Unesco to continue to promote the use of satellite broadcasting for the advancement of education and training, science and culture, and in consultation with appropriate intergovernmental and non-governmental organizations and broadcasting associations, to direct its efforts towards thesolution of problems falling within its mandate,

Proclaims on the 15th day of November 1972, this Declaration of Guiding Principles on the Use of Satellite Broadcasting for the Free Flow of Information, the Spread of Education and Greater Cultural Exchange:

*Article 1.* The use of Outer Space being governed by international law, the development of satellite broadcasting shall be guided by the principles and rules of international law, in particular the Charter of the United Nations and the Outer Space Treaty.

*Article 2.* 1. Satellite broadcasting shall respect the sovereignty and equality of all States.

2. Satellite broadcasting shall be essentially apolitical and shall be conducted with due regard for the rights of individual persons and non-governmental entities as recognized by States and international law.

*Article 3.* 1. The benefits of satellite broadcasting should be available to all countries without discrimination and regardless of their degree of development.

2. The use of satellites for broadcasting should be based on international co-operation, world-wide and regional, intergovernmental and professional.

*Article 4.* 1. Satellite broadcasting provides a new means of disseminating knowledge and promoting better understanding among peoples.

2. The fulfilment of these potentialities requires that account be taken of the needs and rights of audiences, as well as the objectives of peace, friendship and co-operation between peoples, and of economic, social and cultural progress.

*Article 5.* 1. The objective of satellite broadcasting for the free flow of information is to ensure the widest possible dissemination, among the peoples of the world, of news of all countries, developed and developing alike.

2. Satellite broadcasting, making possible instantaneous world-wide dissemination of news, requires that every effort be made to ensure the factual accuracy of the information reaching the public. News broadcasts shall identify the body which assumes responsibility for the news programme as a whole, attributing where appropriate particular news items to their source.

*Article 6.* 1. The objectives of satellite broadcasting for the spread of education are to accelerate the expansion of education, extend educational opportunities, improve the content of school curricula, further the training of educators, assist in the struggle against illiteracy, and help ensure life-long education.

2. Each country has the right to decide on the content of the educational programmes broadcast by satellite to its people and, in cases where such programmes are produced in co-operation with other countries, to take part in their planning and production, on a free and equal footing.

*Article 7.* 1. The objective of satellite broadcasting for the promotion of cultural exchange is to foster greater contact and mutual understanding between peoples by permitting audiences to enjoy, on an unprecedented scale, programmes on each other's social and cultural life including artistic performances and sporting and other events.

2. Cultural programmes, while promoting the enrichment of all cultures, should respect the distinctive character, the value and the dignity of each, and the right of all countries and peoples to preserve their cultures as part of the common heritage of mankind.

*Article 8.* Broadcasters and their national, regional and international associations should be encouraged to cooperate in the production and exchange of programmes and in all other aspects of satellite broadcasting including the training of technical and programme personnel.

*Article 9.* 1. In order to further the objectives set out in the preceding articles, it is necessary that States, taking into account the principle of freedom of information, reach or promote prior agreements concerning direct satellite broadcasting to the population of countries other than the country of origin of the transmission.

2. With respect to commercial advertising, its transmission shall be subject to specific agreement between the originating and receiving countries.

*Article 10.* In the preparation of programmes for direct broadcasting to other countries, account shall be taken of differences in the national laws of the countries of reception.

*Article 11.* The principles of this Declaration shall be applied with due regard for human rights and fundamental freedoms.

**MEDIA: EUROPEAN CONVENTION ON TRANSFRONTIER TELEVISION (1989).** The Convention, concluded at Strasbourg on 5 May 1989 by member States of the **COUNCIL OF EUROPE** and the other States party to the European Cultural Convention (i.e., the Holy See and Yugoslavia), will enter into force "on the first day of the month following the expiration of a period of three months after the date on which seven States, of which at least five are Member States of the Council of Europe, have expressed their consent" to be bound by it.

The Convention reflects the conviction, expressed in article 10 of the **EUROPEAN CONVENTION ON HUMAN RIGHTS,** that freedom of expression and information constitutes one of the essential principles of a democratic society and one of the basic conditions for progress and for the development of every human being.

The text is as follows:

### Preamble

The member States of the Council of Europe and the other States party to the European Cultural Convention, signatory hereto,

Considering that the aim of the Council of Europe is to achieve a greater unity between its members, for the purpose of safeguarding and realising the ideals and principles which are their common heritage;

Considering that the dignity and equal worth of every human being constitute fundamental elements of those principles;

Considering that the freedom of expression and information, as embodied in Article 10 of the Convention for the Protection of Human Rights and Fundamental Freedoms, constitutes one of the essential principles of a democratic society and one of the basic conditions for its progress and for the development of every human being;

Reaffirming their commitment to the principles of the free flow of information and ideas and the independence of broadcasters, which constitute an indispensable basis for their broadcasting policy;

Affirming the importance of broadcasting for the development of culture and the free formation of opinions in conditions safeguarding pluralism and equality of opportunity among all democratic groups and political parties;

Convinced that the continued development of information and communication technology should serve to further the right, regardless of frontiers, to express, to seek, to receive and to impart information and ideas whatever their source;

Being desirous to present an increasing range of choice of programme services for the public, thereby enhancing Europe's heritage and developing its audiovisual creation, and being determined to achieve this cultural objective through efforts to increase the production and circulation of high-quality programmes, thereby responding to the public's expectations in the political, educational and cultural fields;

Recognising the need to consolidate the common broad framework of regulation;

Bearing in mind Resolution No. 2 and the Declaration of

the 1st European Ministerial Conference on Mass Media Policy;

Being desirous to develop the principles embodied in the existing Council of Europe Recommendations on principles on television advertising, on equality between women and men in the media, on the use of satellite capacity for television and sound radio, and on the promotion of audiovisual production in Europe,

Have agreed as follows:

## Chapter I—General Provisions

*Article 1. Object and Purpose.* This Convention is concerned with programme services embodied in transmissions. The purpose is to facilitate, among the Parties, the transfrontier transmission and the retransmission of television programme services.

*Article 2. Terms Employed.* For the purposes of this Convention:

(a) "Transmission" means the initial emission by terrestrial transmitter, by cable, or by satellite of whatever nature, in encoded or unencoded form, of television programme services for reception by the general public. It does not include communication services operating on individual demand;

(b) "Retransmission" signifies the fact of receiving and simultaneously transmitting, irrespective of the technical means employed, complete and unchanged television programme services, or important parts of such services, transmitted by broadcasters for reception by the general public;

(c) "Broadcaster" means the natural or legal person who composes television programme services for reception by the general public and transmits them or has them transmitted, complete and unchanged, by a third party;

(d) "Programme service" means all the items within a single service provided by a given broadcaster within the meaning of the preceding paragraph;

(e) "European audiovisual works" means creative works, the production or co-production of which is controlled by European natural or legal persons;

(f) "Advertisement" means any public announcement intended to promote the sale, purchase or rental of a product or service, to advance a cause or idea or to bring about some other effect desired by the advertiser, for which transmission time has been given to the advertiser for remuneration or similar consideration;

(g) "Sponsorship" means the participation of a natural or legal person, who is not engaged in broadcasting activities or in the production of audiovisual works, in the direct or indirect financing of a programme with a view to promoting the name, trademark or image of that person.

*Article 3. Field of Application.* This Convention shall apply to any programme service transmitted or retransmitted by entities or by technical means within the jurisdiction of a Party, whether by cable, terrestrial transmitter or satellite, and which can be received, directly or indirectly, in one or more other Parties.

*Article 4. Freedom of Reception and Retransmission.* The Parties shall ensure freedom of expression and information in accordance with Article 10 of the Convention for the Protection of Human Rights and Fundamental Freedoms and they shall guarantee freedom of reception and shall not restrict the retransmission on their territories of programme services which comply with the terms of this Convention.

*Article 5. Duties of the Transmitting Parties.* 1. Each transmitting Party shall ensure, by appropriate means and through its competent organs, that all programme services transmitted by entities or by technical means within its jurisdiction, within the meaning of Article 3, comply with the terms of this Convention.

2. For the purposes of this Convention, the transmitting Party shall be:

(a) in the case of terrestrial transmissions, the Party in which the initial emission is effected;

(b) in the case of satellite transmissions:

(i) the Party in which the satellite up-link is situated;

(ii) the Party which grants the use of the frequency or a satellite capacity when the up-link is situated in a State which is not a Party to this Convention;

(iii) the Party in which the broadcaster has its seat when responsibility under the sub-paragraphs i and ii is not established.

3. When programme services transmitted from States which are not Parties to this Convention are retransmitted by entities or by technical means within the jurisdiction of a Party, within the meaning of Article 3, that Party, acting as transmitting Party, shall ensure, by appropriate means and through its competent organs, compliance with the terms of this Convention.

*Article 6. Provision of Information.* 1. The responsibilities of the broadcaster shall be clearly and adequately specified in the authorisation issued by, or contract concluded with, the competent authority of each Party, or by any other legal measure.

2. Information about the broadcaster shall be made available, upon request, by the competent authority of the transmitting Party. Such information shall include, as a minimum, the name or denomination, seat and status of the broadcaster, the name of the legal representative, the composition of the capital, the nature, purpose and mode of financing of the programme service the broadcaster is providing or intends providing.

## Chapter II—Programming Matters

*Article 7. Responsibilities of the Broadcaster.* 1. All items of programme services, as concerns their presentation and content, shall respect the dignity of the human being and the fundamental rights of others.

In particular, they shall not:

(a) be indecent and in particular contain pornography;

(b) give undue prominence to violence or be likely to incite to racial hatred.

2. All items of programme services which are likely to impair the physical, mental or moral development of children and adolescents shall not be scheduled when, because of the time of transmission and reception, they are likely to watch them.

3. The broadcaster shall ensure that news fairly presents facts and events and encourages the free formation of opinions.

*Article 8. Right of Reply.* 1. Each transmitting Party shall ensure that every natural or legal person, regardless of nationality or place of residence, shall have the opportunity to exercise a right of reply or to seek other comparable legal or administrative remedies relating to programmes transmitted or retransmitted by entities or by technical means within its jurisdiction, within the meaning of Article 3. In particular, it shall ensure that timing and other arrangements for the exercise of the right of reply are such that this right can be effectively exercised. The effective exercise of this right or other comparable legal or administrative remedies shall be ensured both as regards the timing and the modalities.

2. For this purpose, the name of the broadcaster responsible for the programme service shall be identified therein at regular intervals by appropriate means.

*Article 9. Access of the Public to Major Events.* Each Party shall examine the legal measures to avoid the right of the public to information being undermined due to the exercise by a broadcaster of exclusive rights for the transmission or retransmission, within the meaning of Article 3, of an event of high public interest and which has the effect of depriving a large part of the public in one or more other Parties of the opportunity to follow that event on television.

*Article 10. Cultural Objectives.* 1. Each transmitting Party shall ensure, where practicable and by appropriate means, that broadcasters reserve for European works a majority proportion of their transmission time, excluding the time appointed to news, sports events, games, advertising and teletext services. This proportion, having regard to the broadcaster's informational, educational, cultural and entertainment responsibilities to its viewing public, should be achieved progressively, on the basis of suitable criteria.

2. In case of disagreement between a receiving Party and a transmitting Party on the application of the preceding paragraph, recourse may be had, at the request of one of the Parties, to the Standing Committee with a view to its formulating an advisory opinion on the subject. Such a disagreement shall not be submitted to the arbitration procedure provided for in Article 26.

3. The Parties undertake to look together for the most appropriate instruments and procedures to support, without discrimination between broadcasters, the activity and development of European production, particularly in countries with a low audiovisual production capacity or restricted language area.

4. The Parties, in the spirit of co-operation and mutual assistance which underlies this Convention, shall endeavour to avoid that programme services transmitted or retransmitted by entities or by technical means within their jurisdiction, within the meaning of Article 3, endanger the pluralism of the press and the development of the cinema industries. No cinematographic work shall accordingly be transmitted in such services, unless otherwise agreed between its rights holders and the broadcaster, until two years have elapsed since the work was first shown in cinemas; in the case of cinematographic works co-produced by the broadcaster, this period shall be one year.

### Chapter III—Advertising

*Article 11. General Standards.* 1. All advertisements shall be fair and honest.

2. Advertisements shall not be misleading and shall not prejudice the interests of consumers.

3. Advertisements addressed to or using children shall avoid anything likely to harm their interests and shall have regard to their special susceptibilities.

4. The advertiser shall not exercise any editorial influence over the content of programmes.

*Article 12. Duration.* 1. The amount of advertising shall

not exceed 15% of the daily transmission time. However, this percentage may be increased to 20% to include forms of advertisements such as direct offers to the public for the sale, purchase or rental of products or for the provision of services, provided the amount of spot advertising does not exceed 15%.

2. The amount of spot advertising within a given one-hour period shall not exceed 20%.

3. Forms of advertisements such as direct offers to the public for the sale, purchase or rental of products or for the provision of services shall not exceed one hour per day.

*Article 13. Form and Presentation.* 1. Advertisements shall be clearly distinguishable as such and recognisably separate from the other items of the programme service by optical or acoustic means. In principle, they shall be transmitted in blocks.

2. Subliminal advertisements shall not be allowed.

3. Surreptitious advertisements shall not be allowed, in particular the presentation of products or services in programmes when it serves advertising purposes.

4. Advertisements shall not feature, visually or orally, persons regularly presenting news and current affairs programmes.

*Article 14. Insertion of Advertisements.* 1. Advertisements shall be inserted between programmes. Provided the conditions contained in paragraphs 2 to 5 of this Article are fulfilled, advertisements may also be inserted during programmes in such a way that the integrity and value of the programme and the rights of the rights holders are not prejudiced.

2. In programmes consisting of autonomous parts, or in sports programmes and similarly structured events and performances comprising intervals, advertisements shall only be inserted between the parts or in the intervals.

3. The transmission of audiovisual works such as feature films and films made for television (excluding series, serials, light entertainment programmes and documentaries), provided their duration is more than forty-five minutes, may be interrupted once for each complete period of forty-five minutes. A further interruption is allowed if their duration is at least twenty minutes longer than two or more complete periods of forty-five minutes.

4. Where programmes, other than those covered by paragraph 2, are interrupted by advertisements, a period of at least twenty minutes should elapse between each successive advertising break within the programme.

5. Advertisements shall not be inserted in any broadcast of a religious service. News and current affairs programmes, documentaries, religious programmes, and children's programmes, when they are less than thirty minutes of duration, shall not be interrupted by advertisements. If they last for thirty minutes or longer, the provisions of the previous paragraphs shall apply.

*Article 15. Advertising of Particular Products.* 1. Advertisements for tobacco products shall not be allowed.

2. Advertisements for alcoholic beverages of all varieties shall comply with the following rules:

(a) they shall not be addressed particularly to minors and no one associated with the consumption of alcoholic beverages in advertisements should seem to be a minor;

(b) they shall not link the consumption of alcohol to physical performance or driving;

(c) they shall not claim that alcohol has therapeutic qualities or that it is a stimulant, a sedative or a means of resolving personal problems;

(d) they shall not encourage immoderate consumption of alcohol or present abstinence or moderation in a negative light;

(e) they shall not place undue emphasis on the alcoholic content of beverages.

3. Advertisements for medicines and medical treatment which are only available on medical prescription in the transmitting Party shall not be allowed.

4. Advertisements for all other medicines and medical treatment shall be clearly distinguishable as such, honest, truthful and subject to verification and shall comply with the requirement of protection of the individual from harm.

*Article 16. Advertising Directed Specifically at a Single Party.* 1. In order to avoid distortions in competition and endangering the television system of a Party, advertisements which are specifically and with some frequency directed to audiences in a single Party other than the transmitting Party shall not circumvent the television advertising rules in that particular Party.

2. The provisions of the preceding paragraph shall not apply where:

(a) the rules concerned establish a discrimination between advertisements transmitted by entities or by technical means within the jurisdiction of that Party and advertisements transmitted by entities or by technical means within the jurisdiction of another Party, or

(b) the Parties concerned have concluded bilateral or multilateral agreements in this area.

### Chapter IV—Sponsorship

*Article 17. General Standards.* 1. When a programme or series of programmes is sponsored in whole or in part, it shall clearly be identified as such by appropriate credits at the beginning and/or end of the programme.

2. The content and scheduling of sponsored programmes may in no circumstances be influenced by the sponsor in such a way as to affect the responsibility and editorial independence of the broadcaster in respect of programmes.

3. Sponsored programmes shall not encourage the sale, purchase or rental of the products or services of the sponsor or a third party, in particular by making special promotional references to those products or services in such programmes.

*Article 18. Prohibited Sponsorship.* 1. Programmes may not be sponsored by natural or legal persons whose principal activity is the manufacture or sale of products, or the provision of services, the advertising of which is prohibited by virtue of Article 15.

2. Sponsorship of news and current affairs programmes shall not be allowed.

### Chapter V—Mutual Assistance

*Article 19. Co-operation between the Parties.* 1. The Parties undertake to render each other mutual assistance in order to implement this Convention.

2. For that purpose:

(a) each Contracting State shall designate one or more authorities, the name and address of each of which it shall communicate to the Secretary General of the Council of Europe at the time of deposit of its instrument of ratification, acceptance, approval or accession;

(b) each Contracting State which has designated more than one authority shall specify in its communication under sub-paragraph a the competence of each authority.

3. An authority designated by a Party shall:

(a) furnish the information foreseen under Article 6, paragraph 2, of this Convention;

(b) furnish information at the request of an authority designated by another Party on the domestic law and practices in the fields covered by this Convention;

(c) co-operate with the authorities designated by the other Parties whenever useful, and notably where this would enhance the effectiveness of measures taken in implementation of this Convention;

(d) consider any difficulty arising from the application of this Convention which is brought to its attention by an authority designated by another Party.

### Chapter VI—Standing Committee

*Article 20. Standing Committee.* 1. For the purposes of this Convention, a Standing Committee shall be set up.

2. Each Party may be represented on the Standing Committee by one or more delegates. Each delegation shall have one vote. Within the areas of its competence, the European Economic Community shall exercise its right to vote with a number of votes equal to the number of its member States which are Parties to this Convention; the European Economic Community shall not exercise its right to vote in cases where the member States concerned exercise theirs, and conversely.

3. Any State referred to in Article 29, paragraph 1, which is not a Party to this Convention may be represented on the Standing Committee by an observer.

4. The Standing Committee may seek the advice of experts in order to discharge its functions. It may, on its own initiative or at the request of the body concerned, invite any international or national, governmental or non-governmental body technically qualified in the fields covered by this Convention to be represented by an observer at one or part of one of its meetings. The decision to invite such experts or bodies shall be taken by a majority of three-quarters of the members of the Standing Committee.

5. The Standing Committee shall be convened by the Secretary General of the Council of Europe. Its first meeting shall be held within six months of the date of entry into force of the Convention. It shall subsequently meet whenever one-third of the Parties or the Committee of Ministers of the Council of Europe so requests, or on the initiative of the Secretary General of the Council of Europe in accordance with the provisions of Article 23, paragraph 2, or at the request of one or more Parties in accordance with the provisions of Articles 21, sub-paragraph c, and 25, paragraph 2.

6. A majority of the Parties shall constitute a quorum for holding a meeting of the Standing Committee.

7. Subject to the provisions of paragraph 4 and Article 23, paragraph 3, the decisions of the Standing Committee shall be taken by a majority of three-quarters of the members present.

8. Subject to the provisions of this Convention, the Standing Committee shall draw up its own Rules of Procedure.

*Article 21. Functions of the Standing Committee.* The Standing Committee shall be responsible for following the application of this Convention. It may:

(a) make recommendations to the Parties concerning the application of the Convention;

(b) suggest any necessary modifications of the Convention and examine those proposed in accordance with the provisions of Article 23;

(c) examine, at the request of one or more Parties, questions concerning the interpretation of the Convention;

(d) use its best endeavours to secure a friendly settlement of any difficulty referred to it in accordance with the provision of Article 25;

(e) make recommendations to the Committee of Ministers concerning States other than those referred to in Article 29, paragraph 1, to be invited to accede to this Convention.

*Article 22. Reports of the Standing Committee.* After each meeting, the Standing Committee shall forward to the Parties and the Committee of Ministers of the Council of Europe a report on its discussions and any decisions taken.

### Chapter VII—Amendments

*Article 23. Amendments.* 1. Any Party may propose amendments to this Convention.

2. Any proposal for amendment shall be notified to the Secretary General of the Council of Europe who shall communicate it to the member States of the Council of Europe, to the other States party to the European Cultural Convention, to the European Economic Community and to any non-member State which has acceded to, or has been invited to accede to this Convention in accordance with the provisions of Article 30. The Secretary General of the Council of Europe shall convene a meeting of the Standing Committee at the earliest two months following the communication of the proposal.

3. The Standing Committee shall examine any amendment proposed and shall submit the text adopted by a majority of three-quarters of the members of the Standing Committee to the Committee of Ministers for approval. After its approval, the text shall be forwarded to the Parties for acceptance.

4. Any amendment shall enter into force on the thirtieth day after all the Parties have informed the Secretary General of their acceptance thereof.

### Chapter VIII—Alleged Violations of this Convention

*Article 24. Alleged Violations of this Convention.* 1. When a Party finds a violation of this Convention, it shall communicate to the transmitting Party the alleged violation and the two Parties shall endeavour to overcome the difficulty on the basis of the provisions of Articles 19, 25 and 26.

2. If the alleged violation is of a manifest, serious and grave nature which raises important public issues and concerns Article 7, paragraphs 1 or 2, 12, 13, paragraph 1, first sentence, 14 or 15, paragraphs 1 or 3, and if it persists within two weeks following the communication, the receiving Party may suspend provisionally the retransmission of the incriminated programme service.

3. In all other cases of alleged violation, with the exception of those provided for in paragraph 4, the receiving Party may suspend provisionally the retransmission of the incriminated programme service eight months following the communication, if the alleged violation persists.

4. The provisional suspension of retransmission shall not be allowed in the case of alleged violations of Article 7, paragraph 3, 8, 9 or 10.

### Chapter IX—Settlement of Disputes

*Article 25. Conciliation.* 1. In case of difficulty arising from the application of this Convention, the parties concerned shall endeavour to achieve a friendly settlement.

2. Unless one of the parties concerned objects, the Standing Committee may examine the question, by placing itself at the disposal of the parties concerned in order to reach a satisfactory solution as rapidly as possible and, where appropriate, to formulate an advisory opinion on the subject.

3. Each party concerned undertakes to accord the Standing Committee without delay all information and facilities necessary for the discharge of its functions under the preceding paragraph.

*Article 26. Arbitration.* 1. If the parties concerned cannot settle the dispute in accordance with the provisions of Article 25, they may, by common agreement, submit it to arbitration, the procedure of which is provided for in the appendix to this Convention. In the absence of such an agreement within six months following the first request to open the procedure of conciliation, the dispute may be submitted to arbitration at the request of one of the parties.

2. Any Party may, at any time, declare that it recognizes as compulsory ipso facto and without special agreement in respect of any other Party accepting the same obligation the application of the arbitration procedure provided for in the appendix to this Convention.

### Chapter X—Other International Agreements and the Internal Law of the Parties

*Article 27. Other International Agreements or Arrangements.* 1. In their mutual relations, Parties which are members of the European Economic Community shall apply Community rules and shall not therefore apply the rules arising from this Convention except in so far as there is no Community rule governing the particular subject concerned.

2. Nothing in this Convention shall prevent the Parties from concluding international agreements completing or developing its provisions or extending their field of application.

3. In the case of bilateral agreements, this Convention shall not alter the rights and obligations of Parties which arise from such agreements and which do not affect the enjoyment of other Parties of their rights or the performance of their obligations under this Convention.

*Article 28. Relations between the Convention and the Internal Law of the Parties.* Nothing in this Convention shall prevent the Parties from applying stricter or more detailed rules than those provided for in this Convention to programme services transmitted by entities or by technical means within their jurisdiction, within the meaning of Article 3.

### Chapter XI—Final Provisions

*Article 29. Signature and Entry into Force.* 1. This Convention shall be open for signature by the member States of the Council of Europe and the other States party to the European Cultural Convention, and by the European Economic Community. It is subject to ratification, acceptance or approval. Instruments of ratification, acceptance or approval shall be deposited with the Secretary General of the Council of Europe.

2. This Convention shall enter into force on the first day of the month following the expiration of a period of three months after the date on which seven States, of which at least five member States of the Council of Europe, have expressed their consent to be bound by the Convention in accordance with the provisions of the preceding paragraph.

3. A State may, at the time of signature or at any later date prior to the entry into force of this Convention in respect of

that State, declare that it shall apply the Convention provisionally.

4. In respect of any State referred to in paragraph 1, or the European Economic Community, which subsequently express their consent to be bound by it, this Convention shall enter into force on the first day of the month following the expiration of a period of three months after the date of deposit of the instrument of ratification, acceptance or approval.

*Article 30. Accession by Non-member States.* 1. After the entry into force of this Convention, the Committee of Ministers of the Council of Europe, after consulting the Contracting States may invite any other State to accede to this Convention by a decision taken by the majority provided for in Article 20.d of the Statute of the Council of Europe and by the unanimous vote of the representatives of the Contracting States entitled to sit on the Committee.

2. In respect of any acceding State, this Convention shall enter into force on the first day of the month following the expiration of a period of three months after the date of deposit of the instrument of accession with the Secretary General of the Council of Europe.

*Article 31. Territorial Application.* 1. Any State may, at the time of signature or when depositing its instrument of ratification, acceptance, approval or accession, specify the territory or territories to which this Convention shall apply.

2. Any State may, at any later date, by a declaration addressed to the Secretary General of the Council of Europe, extend the application of this Convention to any other territory specified in the declaration. In respect of such territory, the Convention shall enter into force on the first day of the month following the expiration of a period of three months after the date of receipt of such declaration by the Secretary General.

3. Any declaration made under the two preceding paragraphs may, in respect of any territory specified in such declaration, be withdrawn by a notification addressed to the Secretary General. The withdrawal shall become effective on the first day of the month following the expiration of a period of six months after the date of receipt of such notification by the Secretary General.

*Article 32. Reservations.* 1. At the time of signature or when depositing its instrument of ratification, acceptance, approval or accession:

(a) any State may declare that it reserves the right to restrict the retransmission on its territory, solely to the extent that it does not comply with its domestic legislation, of programme services containing advertisements for alcoholic beverages according to the rules provided for in Article 15, paragraph 2, of this Convention;

(b) the United Kingdom may declare that it reserves the right not to fulfil the obligation, set out in Article 15, paragraph 1, to prohibit advertisements for tobacco products, in respect of advertisements for cigars and pipe tobacco broadcast by the Independent Broadcasting Authority by terrestrial means on its territory.

No other reservation may be made.

2. A reservation made in accordance with the preceding paragraph may not be the subject of an objection.

3. Any Contracting State which has made a reservation under paragraph 1 may wholly or partly withdraw it by means of a notification addressed to the Secretary General of the Council of Europe. The withdrawal shall take effect on the date of receipt of such notification by the Secretary General.

4. A Party which has made a reservation in respect of a provision of this Convention may not claim the application of that provision by any other Party; it may, however, if its reservation is partial or conditional, claim the application of that provision in so far as it has itself accepted it.

*Article 33. Denunciation.* 1. Any Party may, at any time, denounce this Convention by means of a notification addressed to the Secretary General of the Council of Europe.

2. Such denunciation shall become effective on the first day of the month following the expiration of a period of six months after the date of receipt of the notification by the Secretary General.

*Article 34. Notifications.* The Secretary General of the Council of Europe shall notify the member States of the Council, the other States party to the European Cultural Convention, the European Economic Community and any State which has acceded to, or has been invited to accede to this Convention of:

(a) any signature;

(b) the deposit of any instrument of ratification, acceptance, approval or accession;

(c) any date of entry into force of this Convention in accordance with the provisions of Articles 29, 30 and 31;

(d) any report established in accordance with the provisions of Article 22;

(e) any other act, declaration, notification or communication relating to this Convention.

In witness whereof the undersigned, being duly authorised thereto, have signed this Convention.

Done at . . . . . . . . . . ., the . . . . . . . . . . ., in English and French, both texts being equally authentic, in a single copy which shall be deposited in the archives of the Council of Europe. The Secretary General of the Council of Europe shall transmit certified copies to each member State of the Council of Europe, to the other States party to the European Cultural Convention, to the European Economic Community and to any State invited to accede to this Convention.

### Appendix

*Arbitration.* 1. A request for arbitration shall be notified to the Secretary General of the Council of Europe. It shall include the name of the other party to the dispute and the subject matter of the dispute. The Secretary General shall communicate the information so received to all the Parties to this Convention.

2. In the event of a dispute between two Parties one of which is a member State of the European Economic Community, the latter itself being a Party, the request for arbitration shall be addressed both to the member State and to the Community, which jointly shall notify the Secretary General, within one month of receipt of the request, whether the member State or the Community, or the member State and the Community jointly, shall be party to the dispute. In the absence of such notification within the said time-limit, the member State and the Community shall be considered as being one and the same party to the dispute for the purposes of the application of the provisions governing the constitution and procedure of the arbitration tribunal. The same shall apply when the member State and the Community jointly present themselves as party to the dispute. In cases envisaged by this paragraph, the time-limit of one month foreseen in the first sentence of paragraph 4 hereafter shall be extended to two months.

3. The arbitration tribunal shall consist of three members: each of the parties to the dispute shall appoint one arbitrator; the two arbitrators so appointed shall designate by common agreement the third arbitrator who shall be the

chairman of the tribunal. The latter shall not be a national of either of the parties to the dispute, nor have his usual place of residence in the territory of either of those parties, nor be employed by either of them, nor have dealt with the case in another capacity.

4. If one of the parties has not appointed an arbitrator within one month following the communication of the request by the Secretary General of the Council of Europe, he shall be appointed at the request of the other party by the President of the European Court of Human Rights within a further one-month period. If the President of the Court is unable to act or is a national of one of the parties to the dispute, the appointment shall be made by the Vice-President of the Court or by the most senior judge to the Court who is available and is not a national of one of the parties to the dispute. The same procedure shall be observed if, within a period of one month following the appointment of the second arbitrator, the Chairman of the arbitration tribunal is not designated.

5. The provisions of paragraphs 3 and 4 shall apply, as the case may be, in order to fill any vacancy.

6. Two or more parties which determine by agreement that they are in the same interest shall appoint an arbitrator jointly.

7. The parties to the dispute and the Standing Committee shall provide the arbitration tribunal with all facilities necessary for the effective conduct of the proceedings.

8. The arbitration tribunal shall draw up its own Rules of Procedure. Its decisions shall be taken by majority vote of its members. Its award shall be final and binding.

9. The award of the arbitration tribunal shall be notified to the Secretary General of the Council of Europe who shall communicate it to all the Parties to this Convention.

10. Each party to the dispute shall bear the expenses of the arbitrator appointed by it; these parties shall share equally the expenses of the other arbitrator, as well as other costs entailed by the arbitration.

*SEE ALSO* Journalists.

**BIBLIOGRAPHY.** African-American Institute. "Media: The Press in a Democratic South Africa," *Africa Report* 37, no. 5 (Sept.–Oct. 1992): 61–64. Conference report, in English.

Article 19. *Press Law and Practice: A Comparative Study of Press Freedom in European and Other Democracies.* London: Article 19 for the UNESCO, 1993. NGO monograph, in English.

—————. *Truth from Below: The Emergent Press in Africa.* London: 1991. NGO factfinding report, in English.

Collins, Richard. "Broadcasting Policy for a Post Apartheid South Africa," *Critical Arts: A Journal for Cultural Studies* 6, no. 1 (1992): 26–51. Scholarly article, in English.

Engelbrekt, Kjell. "The Media Adjust to their New Environment," *Report on Eastern Europe* 2, no. 23 (7 June 1991): 6–10. Article, in English.

Louw, Raymond, et al. *Medias in a New South Africa.* Mowbray, South Africa: Institute for a Democratic Alternative for South Africa, 1990. Conference papers, in English.

Reporters Sans Frontières. *La liberté de la presse dans le monde.* Paris: 1991–present. *Freedom of the Press throughout the World.* London: John Libbey, 1993–present. NGO annual report, in English and French.

Trapans, Jan Arveds, comp. "Recent Developments in the Media," *Report on Eastern Europe* 1 no. 9 (1 March 1991): 33–39. Article, in English.

**MEDIA: EUROPEAN DECLARATION ON MASS COMMUNICATION MEDIA AND HUMAN RIGHTS (1970).** The Declaration defines the meaning of the right to freedom of expression when applied to mass communication media and sets out principles to be observed by those media. It calls for freedom of the press to seek, receive, impart, publish, and distribute information and ideas; for independence of the press from control by the State; and for no direct or indirect censorship of the media. At the same time, it indicates ways and means by which the press and other mass media may discharge their functions with a sense of responsibility and ways and means to protect the individual against interference with his right to privacy.

The Declaration was adopted (resolution 428 [1970]) by the Constituent Assembly of the **COUNCIL OF EUROPE,** convened at Strasbourg, on 23 January 1970. The text is as follows:

### A. Status and Independence of the Press and the Other Mass Media

1. The press and the other mass media, though generally not public institutions, perform an essential function for the general public. In order to enable them to discharge that function in the public interest, the following principles should be observed.

2. The right to freedom of expression shall apply to mass communication media.

3. This right shall include freedom to seek, receive, impart, publish and distribute information and ideas. There shall be a corresponding duty for the public authorities to make available information on matters of public interest within reasonable limits and a duty for mass communication media to give complete and general information on public affairs.

4. The independence of the press and other mass media from control by the state should be established by law. Any infringement of this independence should be justifiable by courts and not by executive authorities.

5. There shall be no direct or indirect censorship of the press, or of the contents of radio and television programmes, or of news or information conveyed by other media such as news reels shown in cinemas. Restrictions may be imposed within the limits authorized by Article 10 of the European Convention on Human Rights. There shall be no control by the state of the contents of radio and television programmes, except on the grounds set out in paragraph 2 of that Article.

6. The internal organisation of mass media should guarantee the freedom of expression of the responsible editors. Their editorial independence should be preserved.

7. The independence of mass media should be protected against the dangers of monopolies. The effects of concentration in the press, and possible measures of economic assistance require further consideration.

8. Neither individual enterprises, nor financial groups should have the right to institute a monopoly in the fields of press, radio or television, nor should government-controlled monopoly be permitted. Individuals, social groups, regional or local authorities should have—as far as they comply with the established licensing provisions—the right to engage in these activities.

9. Special measures are necessary to ensure the freedom of foreign correspondents, including the staff of international press agencies, in order to permit the public to receive accurate information from abroad. These measures should cover the status, duties and privileges of foreign correspondents and should include protection from arbitrary expulsion. They impose a corresponding duty of accurate reporting.

### B. Measures to Secure Responsibility of the Press and Other Mass Media

It is the duty of the press and other mass media to discharge their functions with a sense of responsibility towards the community and towards the individual citizens. For this purpose, it is desirable to institute (where not already done):

(a) Professional training for journalists under the responsibility of editors and journalists;

(b) A professional code of ethics for journalists; this should cover *inter alia* such matters as accurate and well balanced reporting, rectification of inaccurate information, clear distinction between reported information and comments, avoidance of calumny, respect for privacy, respect for the right to a fair trial as guaranteed by Article 6 of the European Convention on Human Rights;

(c) Press councils empowered to investigate and even to censure instances of unprofessional conduct with a view to the exercising of self-control by the press itself.

### C. Measures to Protect the Individual Against Interference with his Right to Privacy

1. There is an area in which the exercise of the right of freedom of information and freedom of expression may conflict with the right to privacy protected by Article 8 of the Convention on Human Rights. The exercise of the former right must not be allowed to destroy the existence of the latter.

2. The right to privacy consists essentially in the right to live one's own life with a minimum of interference. It concerns private, family and home life, physical and moral integrity, honour and reputation, avoidance of being placed in a false light, non-relevation of irrelevant and embarrassing facts, unauthorized publication of private photographs, protection against misuse of private communications, protection from disclosure of information given or received by the individual confidentially. Those who, by their own actions, have encouraged indiscreet revelations about which they complain later on, cannot avail themselves of the right to privacy.

3. A particular problem arises as regards the privacy of persons in public life. The phrase "where public life begins, private life ends" is inadequate to cover this situation. The private lives of public figures are entitled to protection, save where they may have an impact upon public events. The fact that an individual figures in the news does not deprive him of a right to a private life.

4. Another particular problem arises from attempts to obtain information by modern technical devices (wire-tapping, hidden microphones, the use of computers, etc.), which infringe the right to privacy. Further consideration of this problem is required.

5. Where regional, national or international computer-data banks are instituted the individual must not become completely exposed and transparent by the accumulation of information referring even to his private life. Data banks should be restricted to the necessary minimum of information required for the purposes of taxation, pension schemes, social security schemes and similar matters.

6. In order to counter these dangers, national law should provide a right of action enforceable at law against persons responsible for such infringements of the right to privacy.

7. The right to privacy afforded by Article 8 of the Convention on Human rights should not only protect an individual against interference by public authorities, but also against interference by private persons or institutions, including the mass media. National legislations should comprise provisions guaranteeing this protection.

**MEDIA: UNESCO DECLARATION ON FUNDAMENTAL PRINCIPLES CONCERNING THE CONTRIBUTION OF THE MASS MEDIA TO STRENGTHENING PEACE AND INTERNATIONAL UNDERSTANDING, TO THE PROMOTION OF HUMAN RIGHTS AND TO COUNTERING RACISM, APARTHEID AND INCITEMENT TO WAR (1978).** The Declaration was adopted and proclaimed by the **UNESCO** General Conference (20th session), meeting in Paris, on 22 November 1978.

The importance of efforts to implement the principles set out in the Declaration was emphasized by the UN **GENERAL ASSEMBLY** on 10 December 1982 (resolution 37/94), which called upon all member States and organizations within the United Nations system to make those principles better known through every means at their disposal.

The text of the Declaration (*UNESCO's Standard-Setting Instruments,* No. IV.C.3) is as follows:

The General Conference,

Recalling that by virtue of its Constitution the purpose of Unesco is to "contribute to peace and security by promoting collaboration among the nations through education, science and culture in order to further universal respect for justice, for the rule of law and for the human rights and fundamental freedoms" (Art. I, 1), and that to realize this purpose the Organization will strive "to promote the free flow of ideas by work and image" (Art. I, 2),

Further recalling that under the Constitution the Member States of Unesco, "believing in full and equal opportunities for education for all, in the unrestricted pursuit of objective truth, and in the free exchange of ideas and knowledge, are agreed and determined to develop and to increase the means of communication between their peoples and to employ these means for the purposes of mutual understanding and a truer and more perfect knowledge of each other's lives" (sixth preambular paragraph),

Recalling the purposes and principles of the United Nations, as specified in its Charter,

Recalling the Universal Declaration of Human Rights, adopted by the General Assembly of the United Nations in 1948 and particularly Article 19 thereof, which provides that "everyone has the right to freedom of opinion and expression; this right includes freedom to hold opinions without interference and to seek, receive and impart information and ideas through any media and regardless of frontiers"; and the International Covenant on Civil and Political Rights, adopted by the General Assembly of the United Nations in 1966, Article 19 of which proclaims the same principles and Article 20 of which condemns incitement to war, the advocacy of national, racial or religious hatred and any form of discrimination, hostility or violence,

Recalling Article 4 of the International Convention on the Elimination of all Forms of Racial Discrimination, adopted by the General Assembly of the United Nations in 1965, and the International Convention on the Suppression and Punishment of the Crime of Apartheid, adopted by the General Assembly of the United Nations in 1973, whereby the States acceding to these Conventions undertook to adopt immediate and positive measures designed to eradicate all incitement to, or acts of, racial discrimination, and agreed to prevent any encouragement of the crime of apartheid and similar segregationist policies or their manifestations,

Recalling the Declaration on the Promotion among Youth of the Ideals of Peace, Mutual Respect and Understanding between Peoples, adopted by the General Assembly of the United Nations in 1965,

Recalling the declarations and resolutions adopted by the various organs of the United Nations concerning the establishment of a new international economic order and the role Unesco is called upon to play in this respect,

Recalling the Declaration of the Principles of International Cultural Co-operation, adopted by the General Conference of Unesco in 1966,

Recalling Resolution 59(I) of the General Assembly of the United Nations, adopted in 1946 and declaring:

"Freedom of information is a fundamental human right and is the touchstone of all the freedoms to which the United Nations is consecrated; . . .

"Freedom of information requires as an indispensable element the willingness and capacity to employ its privileges without abuse. It requires as a basic discipline the moral obligation to seek the facts without prejudice and to spread knowledge without malicious intent;"

Recalling Resolution 110(II) of the General Assembly of the United Nations, adopted in 1947, condemning all forms of propaganda which are designed or likely to provoke or encourage any threat to the peace, breach of the peace, or act of aggression,

Recalling Resolution 127(II), also adopted by the General Assembly in 1947, which invites Member States to take measures, within the limits of constitutional procedures, to combat the diffusion of false or distorted reports likely to injure friendly relations between States, as well as the other resolutions of the General Assembly concerning the mass media and their contribution to strengthening peace, trust and friendly relations among States,

Recalling Resolution 9.12 adopted by the General Conference of Unesco in 1968, reiterating Unesco's objective to help to eradicate colonialism and racism, and Resolution 12.1 adopted by the General Conference in 1976, which proclaims that colonialism, neo-colonialism and racism in all its forms and manifestations are incompatible with the fundamental aims of Unesco,

Recalling Resolution 4.301 adopted in 1970 by the General Conference of Unesco on the contribution of the information media to furthering international understanding and co-operation in the interests of peace and human welfare, and to countering propaganda on behalf of war, racialism, apartheid and hatred among nations, and *aware of*

the fundamental contribution that mass media can make to the realizations of these objectives,

Recalling the Declaration on Race and Racial Prejudice adopted by the General Conference of Unesco at its twentieth session,

Conscious of the complexity of the problems of information in modern society, of the diversity of solutions which have been offered to them, as evidenced in particular by the consideration given to them within Unesco, and of the legitimate desire of all parties concerned that their aspirations, points of view and cultural identity be taken into due consideration,

Conscious of the aspirations of the developing countries for the establishment of a new, more just and more effective world information and communication order,

Proclaims on this twenty-eighth day of November 1978 this Declaration on Fundamental Principles concerning the Contribution of the Mass Media to Strengthening Peace and International Understanding, to the Promotion of Human Rights and to Countering Racialism, Apartheid, and Incitement to War.

*Article 1.* The strengthening of peace and international understanding, the promotion of human rights and the countering of racialism, apartheid and incitement to war demand a free flow and a wider and better balanced dissemination of information. To this end, the mass media have a leading contribution to make. This contribution will be more effective to the extent that the information reflects the different aspects of the subject dealt with.

*Article 2.* 1. The exercise of freedom of opinion, expression and information, recognized as an integral part of human rights and fundamental freedoms, is a vital factor in the strengthening of peace and international understanding.

2. Access by the public to information should be guaranteed by the diversity of the sources and means of information available to it, thus enabling each individual to check the accuracy of facts and to appraise events objectively. To this end, journalists must have freedom to report and the fullest possible facilities of access to information. Similarly, it is important that the mass media be responsive to concerns of peoples and individuals, thus promoting the participation of the public in the elaboration of information.

3. With a view to the strengthening of peace and international understanding, to promoting human rights and to countering racialism, apartheid and incitement to war, the mass media throughout the world, by reason of their role, contribute to promoting human rights, in particular by giving expression to oppressed peoples who struggle against colonialism, neo-colonialism, foreign occupation and all forms of racial discrimination and oppression and who are unable to make their voices heard within their own territories.

4. If the mass media are to be in a position to promote the principles of the Declaration in their activities, it is essential that the journalists and other agents of the mass media, in their own country or abroad, be assured of protection guaranteeing them the best conditions for the exercise of their profession.

*Article 3.* 1. The mass media have an important contribution to make to the strengthening of peace and international understanding and in countering racialism, apartheid and incitement to war.

2. In countering aggressive war, racialism, apartheid and other violations of human rights which are *inter alia* spawned by prejudice and ignorance, the mass media, by disseminating information on the aims, aspirations, cultures and needs of all peoples, contribute to eliminate ignorance and mis-

understanding between peoples, to make nationals of a country sensitive to the needs and desires of others, to ensure the respect of the rights and dignity of all nations, all peoples and all individuals without distinction of race, sex, language, religion or nationality and to draw attention to the great evils which afflict humanity, such as poverty, malnutrition and diseases, thereby promoting the formulation by States of the policies best able to promote the reduction of international tension and the peaceful and equitable settlement of international disputes.

*Article 4.* The mass media have an essential part to play in the education of young peoples in a spirit of peace, justice, freedom, mutual respect and understanding, in order to promote human rights, equality of rights as between all human beings and all nations, and economic and social progress. Equally, they have an important role to play in making known the views and aspirations of the younger generation.

*Article 5.* In order to respect freedom of opinion, expression and information and in order that information may reflect all points of view, it is important that the points of view presented by those who consider that the information published or disseminated about them has seriously prejudiced their effort to strengthen peace and international understanding, to promote human rights or to counter racialism, apartheid and incitement to war be disseminated.

*Article 6.* For the establishment of a new equilibrium and greater reciprocity in the flow of information, which will be conducive to the institution of a just and lasting peace and to the economic and political independence of the developing countries, it is necessary to correct the inequalities in the flow of information to and from the developing countries, and between those countries. To this end, it is essential that their mass media should have conditions and resources enabling them to gain strength and expand, and to co-operate both among themselves and with the mass media in developed countries.

*Article 7.* By disseminating more widely all of the information concerning the universally accepted objectives and principles which are the bases of the resolutions adopted by the different organs of the United Nations, the mass media contribute effectively to the strengthening of peace and international understanding, to the promotion of human rights, and to the establishment of a more just and equitable international economic order.

*Article 8.* Professional organizations, and people who participate in the professional training of journalists and other agents of the mass media and who assist them in performing their functions in a responsible manner should attach special importance to the principles of this Declaration when drawing up and ensuring application of their codes of ethics.

*Article 9.* In the spirit of this Declaration, it is for the international community to contribute to the creation of the conditions for a free flow and wider and more balanced dissemination of information, and of the conditions for the protection, in the exercise of their functions, of journalists and other agents of the mass media. Unesco is well placed to make a valuable contribution in this respect.

*Article 10.* 1. With due respect for constitutional provisions designed to guarantee freedom of information and for the applicable international instruments and agreements, it is indispensable to create and maintain throughout the world the conditions which make it possible for the organizations and persons professionally involved in the dissemination of information to achieve the objectives of this Declaration.

2. It is important that a free flow and wider and better balanced dissemination of information be encouraged.

3. To this end, it is necessary that States facilitate the procurement by the mass media in the developing countries of adequate conditions and resources enabling them to gain strength and expand, and that they support co-operation by the latter both among themselves and with the mass media in developed countries.

4. Similarly, on a basis of equality of rights, mutual advantage and respect for the diversity of the cultures which go to make up the common heritage of mankind, it is essential that bilateral and multilateral exchanges of information among all States, and in particular between those which have different economic and social systems, be encouraged and developed.

*Article 11.* For this declaration to be fully effective it is necessary, with due respect for the legislative and administrative provisions and the other obligations of Member States, to guarantee the existence of favourable conditions for the operation of the mass media, in conformity with the provisions of the Universal Declaration of Human Rights and with the corresponding principles proclaimed in the International Covenant on Civil and Political Rights adopted by the General Assembly of the United Nations in 1966.

## MEDICAL WOMEN'S INTERNATIONAL ASSOCIATION.
An international non-governmental organization in consultative status with the UN **ECONOMIC AND SOCIAL COUNCIL** (Category II), and with **WHO** and **UNICEF**, MWIA is affiliated with national associations and has members in 43 countries.

Founded in 1919 in New York, the Association brings together women in medical fields to study health problems in particular as these relate to women. MWIA promotes international communication among women in medical areas. It also publishes scientific proceedings and reports of its biennial congresses.

Medical Women's International Association. Address: Herbert-Lewin-Strasse 5, Lindenthal, D-5000 Köln 41, Germany. Telephone: (49-221) 400-4558. Secretary-General: Dr. Carolyn Motzel.

## MEIKLEJOHN CIVIL LIBERTIES INSTITUTE.
Founded in 1965, the Meiklejohn Institute helps people use peace law and history in the United States to enforce the right to peace, education, jobs, and justice. It works to combine U.S. and international law and emphasizes connections between civil/political rights and economic/social/cultural rights. The Institute participates in research, education, organizing, networking, and litigation. It also publishes coursebooks, modules, anthologies, and practice materials for litigation.

In addition, the Institute maintains a practitioners' law library and archival collection. It has a unique collection of jury trials and other significant cases not reported in traditional law service.

The Institute offers internships and work-study opportunities to high school, college, law school, and library school students.

Among its regular publications are the *MCLI Newsletter,* published twice a year, and the *Human Rights Organizations and Periodicals Directory* (7th ed., 1993), which contains over 1,000 entries on groups and publications in the United States dedicated to improving human rights. The Institute also publishes the biennial *Human Rights & Peace Law Docket* and *Peace Law Packets.*

Meiklejohn Civil Liberties Institute. Address: P.O. Box 673, Berkeley, CA 94701, USA. Telephone: (510) 848-0599. Fax: (510) 848-6008.

**MENCHÚ, RIGOBERTA (1959–).** This Guatemalan human rights activist is an indigenous Mayan who has gone from obscurity to become an internationally acclaimed spokesperson for the rights of indigenous peoples. In 1992, Menchú was awarded the **Nobel Peace Prize**; her name was entered into nomination by two former Peace Prize recipients, **Adolfo Pérez Esquivel** of Argentina and Bishop **Desmond Tutu** of South Africa. On announcing the award, the Prize Committee cited Menchú as "a uniquely potent symbol of a just struggle." Menchú might have remained a freedom-fighter unknown outside of her native Guatemala had she not told her life story to anthropologist Elisabeth Burgos-Debray, who recorded and edited it, producing Menchú's autobiography *I, Rigoberta Menchú,* which propelled Menchú into the international spotlight.

Menchú is a member of the Quiché tribe, one of 22 groups of Mayan Indians who constitute approximately 80% of Guatemala's population. Born in the village of Chimel, she and her eight brothers and sisters worked alongside their parents as farmers, subsisting on beans and corn. During her childhood, she saw two brothers die, one from inhaling pesticides in the fields and one from starvation. Another brother was burned to death by military authorities for subversion.

The formative influence on Menchú's life was her father Vicente, a community leader who opposed the takeover of indigenous lands by the government and the wealthy. After years of unsuccessfully seeking legal redress of his grievances, Vicente became an underground leader of indigenous forces and was publicly branded as a "Communist." He founded the Committee of Peasant Unity to teach the peasants about the struggle for land rights. In January 1980 Vicente Menchú and other activists overran the radio stations of El Quiché to broadcast news of human rights abuse.

Then, on 31 January 1980, the group occupied the Spanish Embassy in Guatemala City. Guatemalan soldiers lobbed hand-grenades into the building, killing all inside, including Vicente. Three months later, Rigoberta's mother Juana was kidnapped by government forces and left on the side of a road to die.

Rigoberta took on her father's mantle, organizing labor strikes. In February 1980, 8,000 peasants went on strike on the sugar and cotton plantations on the southern coast of Guatemala. In the next year, Menchú founded the 31 January Popular Front, in her father's memory. Because of her anti-government activities, Menchú was forced into hiding, later fleeing to Mexico. From Mexico, where she remains in self-imposed exile, Menchú help to found, in 1987, the National Committee for Reconciliation, which advocates a negotiated settlement between the Guatemalan Government and rebel forces in Guatemala's 13-year-long civil war.

On receiving the Nobel Peace Prize, Menchú stated, "I consider this prize not as an award to me personally, but rather as one of the greatest conquests in the struggle for peace, for human rights, and for the rights of indigenous people, who, along all the 500 years, have been the victims of genocide, repression, and discrimination." With the monetary award for the Prize, Menchú established the Vicente Menchú Foundation, headquartered in Mexico City, Mexico, to work for the human rights and education of indigenous peoples.

In 1993, Menchú served as the UN Goodwill Ambassador for the International Year of the World's Indigenous People. At the opening ceremony for the International Year on 10 December 1993, before the UN **General Assembly,** Menchú summed up her credo:

We believe in the wisdom of our elders and sages, from whom we have inherited strength and learned the art of speech. This has enabled us to reaffirm the validity of our thousand-year history and the justice of our struggles. In turn, this has provided the terrain in which, as indigenous peoples, we have in recent decades broken new ground. The result of this will be the honorable and peaceful renewal of contact between our cultures and the societies in which we live.

**BIBLIOGRAPHY.** *Current Biography Yearbook.* New York: W.H. Wilson & Company, 1993.

Menchú, Rigoberta. *I, Rigoberta Menchú: An Indian Woman in Guatemala,* ed. Elisabeth Burgos-Debray, trans. Anne Wright. London: Verso Editions, 1984.

**MENTAL HEALTH.** The question of establishing mental health as a human right and protecting the human rights of persons considered to be mentally ill has been a matter of concern to international organs and agencies for many years, with the **WORLD HEALTH ORGANIZATION** (WHO) assuming the leading role. The nature and extent of the problem is outlined by WHO in a memorandum presented to the 1970 session of the UN **GENERAL ASSEMBLY** (UN Doc. A/8055/Add. 1, paras. 91–97), as follows:

Mental health is no less a human right than physical health and reasonable social comfort and security. Treatment methods in psychiatry are classified as psychological, biological and social. Biological methods of treatment differ little from those in other branches of medicine, and include the use of drugs, biological products, electricity and surgery. Psychiatric illness may affect the patient's intelligence, judgement, insight and responsibility and if a patient is lacking in one or more of these faculties, his behaviour may be impaired to the extent that he is not aware of what he is doing or that he is a danger to himself or others or is behaving in a way that is an affront to others. Therefore, it may, on occasion, be reasonable to apply treatment for his own good without his consent, since he may be unable to understand the situation and give his consent. Provided that reasonable and acceptable medical care is applied with good judgement and that established ethical practice is followed, there is no question of infringement of human rights. Human rights would be infringed only if treatment were applied to someone who did not require that particular type of treatment or who is not mentally ill and to whom treatment is applied without his understanding and consent.

As a result of the major progress in the treatment of mentally disordered and mentally retarded persons which has occurred during the past three decades, it is now possible for many individuals with mental illness to be treated while living in the community and/or be transferred from institutional care, to the open life of the community and to be usefully employed, to the benefit both of themselves and of the community. If they are refused the right to work because of mental illness their resocialization is slow and their human rights are infringed. In general it is now possible to envisage the necessary after care as one of the functions of the basic health services.

Traditionally mental institutions have always attracted a sometimes undeserved reputation for the infringement of human rights. In consequence systems for external supervision of the work of these institutions, and for appeals against unwarranted detention, have been established and should continue to work satisfactorily and prevent infringement of human rights in this context. Doubts however have been expressed about the human rights aspects of psychotherapy, chemotherapy and psychosurgery.

The misuse of these most helpful methods of treatment is a breach of medical ethics and might constitute a violation of human rights. But such misuse would be no different from delicts in other branches of medicine and surgery.

Mentally retarded individuals constitute a special group which governments must always be concerned to protect whether they are in institutions or living with their families or guardians. Mentally retarded children and adults accommodated in institutions were undoubtedly used in the past for therapeutic trials and the like, and in some cases, e.g. vaccine trials, were exposed to physical risk. The tendency to use these groups for such purposes has happily diminished and where they are so used, the appropriate authorities usually ensure that the investigators follow strict codes of conduct and practice, in order to prevent any infringement of human rights.

In 1980, the UN **SUB-COMMISSION ON PREVENTION OF DISCRIMINATION AND PROTECTION OF MINORITIES** entrusted one of its members, Mrs. Erica-Irene A. Daes (Greece), with the task of elaborating guidelines and principles for the protection of mentally ill persons (resolution 11 [XXXIII]). It received and considered her report on the subject (UN Doc. E/CN.4/Sub.2/1983/17 and Add. 1) at its 1983 session.

On 16 December 1983, the General Assembly, having noted with satisfaction the progress made by the Sub-Commission, called upon it to expedite its consideration of the problems of the mentally ill and to prepare a draft body of principles and guidelines for their protection for its consideration. The Sub-Commission set up a sessional Working Group on the Question of Persons Detained on the Ground of Mental Ill-Health or Suffering from Mental Disorder.

At its 1988 session, the Sub-Commission, after considering the report of the working group at that session containing a draft body of principles and guarantees, adopted (resolution 1988/28) the working group's text and submitted it to the UN **COMMISSION ON HUMAN RIGHTS** for consideration.

The Commission, however, found that because the working group had made only limited progress, the Sub-Commission was still far from concluding its consideration of the draft body of principles and guarantees. It reiterated (resolution 1988/62) the urgent need for such principles and guarantees to prevent the misuse of psychiatry and to safeguard the rights of all individuals, and requested the Sub-Commission (a) to attach much greater emphasis at its 1989 session to the working group and its drafting assignments, (b) to complete the work on the draft body of guidelines, principles, and guarantees as a matter of urgency at that session, and (c) to take into account the memorandum presented to the Commission by the World Health Organization (UN Doc. E/CN.4/1988/66; see below) and to submit it to the working group for consideration.

Later in 1988, the General Assembly took note (resolution 43/109) of the Sub-Commission's action in adopting the draft body of principles and guarantees prepared by its working group and invited the Commission on Human Rights to consider the subject further at its 1989 session. In doing so, the Assembly expressed deep concern at the repeated evidence of the misuse of psychiatry to detain persons on non-medical grounds and reaffirmed its conviction that detention of persons in mental institutions on account of their political views or on other non-medical grounds is a violation of their human rights.

*VIEWS OF THE WORLD HEALTH ORGANIZATION.* In February 1988, the World Health Organization submitted to the UN Commission on Human Rights a written statement on the question of persons detained on the grounds of mental ill-health or suffering from mental disorders (UN Doc. E/CN.4/1988/66), in which it expressed its continued interest in this matter and offered to cooperate in its further development. The statement, in part, was as follows:

. . . WHO has considerable experience in this field, having worked on a number of projects designed to enhance the care of the mentally ill. It has also carried out studies on legislation related to the care of the mentally ill, most recently in 1976 carrying out an empirical study across 35 jurisdictions, examining the legal statutes relating to mental health. The results of this research, as well as an analysis of the handling of the mentally ill across a number of cultures and economic conditions is reported on in the WHO publication *The Law and Mental Health: Harmonizing Objectives* (W.J. Curran and T. Harding, [Geneva: WHO, 1978]). This document still provides a most valuable source of information and guidance on this topic. Over the last two years WHO has obtained advice on the protection of the rights of the mentally ill from members of its expert advisory panel in a number of developed and developing countries, and from a range of non-governmental organizations representing a variety of professional and academic concerns. WHO has convened a number of informal consultations with non-governmental organizations in order to try and obtain a consensus of opinion from a number of perspectives on this subject (March 1987, May 1987, August 1987 and February 1988 in WHO headquarters, Geneva). WHO has also convened a consultation of lawyers and psychiatrists (June 1987, The Hague) in order to formulate a plan of action whereby the organization could assist the United Nations in further developing these principles, guidelines and guarantees.

As a result of these consultations, several points have come to the fore.

1. *Protection against Neglect as well as Protection against Abuse.* Although the report of the Special Rapporteur and the guidelines provided in annex 2 of the report cover many aspects concerning the protection of the civil rights of the mentally ill, it would be desirable to expand the treatment of economic and social rights so as to cover, in particular, the protection of the mentally ill against neglect. WHO recognizes the need for the protection of the mentally ill from potential abuse, and for ensuring that a label of mental illness is not used as an excuse for limiting the rights of people inappropriately. Equally important, however, are the needs of the mentally ill for care and treatment aimed at integrating them within the community. Experiences in some countries have demonstrated that blocking the access of people with mental illness to treatment can result in more deplorable conditions for the mentally ill person and for his or her family and community than if he or she were confined in a mental health facility. The disturbed mental processes of some of those with mental illness make them especially liable to neglect and unable to take advantage of health and social services even when they are provided for their care. It is to be hoped that any international declaration concerning the mentally ill would provide guidance for the treatment, care and protection of the mentally ill against neglect, in addition to the protection that should be provided against abuse and loss of civil rights.

2. *The Desirability of Treating Mental Illness in the Same Way as Other Illnesses.* Most patients with mental illness do not have to be hospitalized and, of those hospitalized, most are admitted at their own request. Only a minority are kept at health care facilities. The laws and regulations governing the treatment of mental patients at their own request and with their own consent should be no different from those governing the treatment of a person with any other illness. To do otherwise is a form of unjustified discrimination against those with mental illness. Similarly the laws and regulations governing the administration of hospitals or parts of hospitals for the mentally ill in voluntary treatment, should be no different from the laws and regulations governing any other hospital.

Nevertheless, a minority of mental patients do have to be kept at health care facilities. This may be because their mental processes are so disturbed that they are incompetent, from a medical point of view, to make their own decisions and run their own lives or it may be because they pose a threat to themselves or others. Under these circumstances it is necessary to have laws and regulations which regulate the conditions under which they may be kept in health care facilities for treatment. Because such patients cannot leave such facilities, the standard of care may need greater regulation than where patients have the option of leaving or refusing treatment. In addition, in situations where patients can be compelled to receive treatment, means have to be available to ensure that such compulsion is in conformity with the relevant laws and regulations.

Recent trends have shown the intention to promote the incorporation of laws and regulations governing the compulsory treatment of the mentally ill into other legislation and regulations governing the compulsory treatment and retention in health care facilities of patients with any illness requiring such a course of action (e.g., quarantine laws governing those with infectious illnesses, treatment for any illness of minors or others not considered competent to make their own decisions). In this case, it is argued, discrimination against those with mental illness, as opposed to those with physical illness, will be diminished. Nevertheless, the particular problems related to mental illness will need to be dealt with, separately, in special legislations and regulations. Guiding principles for this would therefore be of considerable value.

3. *The Problem of Encompassing the Needs of Very Divergent Groups Around the World.* In the context of a declaration of the kind envisaged, there is a particular problem related to the divergent legal, cultural and economic situations of the States Members of the United Nations. The report states outright in its introductory comments that not all of the guidelines are appropriate for all Member States at their present level of development. It is hoped that solutions can be found with a view to developing a set of ideals that are attainable by the maximum number of Member States. This might require some sacrifice of specificity in the guidelines so that the cost of fulfilling their requirements and the administrative infrastructure needed might be within the means of both developed and developing nations.

4. *The Need for Prior Agreement on a Set of Principles for Protecting the Mentally Ill.* Experience dictates that the greater the detail and specificity that any body of recommendations provides, the greater the difficulty in implementing the measures on an international basis. Consideration could therefore be given to dividing annex 2 of the report into two parts.

The first part would be an extract from the draft declaration of universal principles for the treatment, care and protection of the mentally ill, and the second part would provide more specific guidelines for implementing the principles. The set of principles, which would be clearly separated from the guidelines, would provide the conceptual framework necessary for a universal set of goals. The subsequent guidelines would be more dependent on the means and cultural traditions of the Member States. Guidelines would thus be more like a set of suggestions (for example, as is provided by the WHO *List of Essential Drugs* which provides suggestions to Member States) that could be followed in order to adhere to the principles. This would be one way of enabling an international instrument to provide both the breadth and depth that the report envisages. It is appreciated that the task is difficult. A first step could be to ensure that there is complete agreement on the part of all concerned on a set of principles for the care, treatment and protection of the mentally ill. A list of issues which would have to be addressed in the formulation of such principles is as follows:

4.1 The promotion of humanitarian values in the treatment of the mentally ill;

4.2 The protection of the legal rights of the mentally ill including protection against:

(a) Confinement for political, racial or other reasons not directly related to mental illness;

(b) Confinement for reasons of family conflict;

(c) Confinement based on economic interests or gain;

(d) Confinement on the ostensible grounds of mental illness, when the individual does not meet acceptable diagnostic criteria;

(e) Abuses;

4.3 The need to be able to provide treatment and care to the mentally ill under circumstances in which the patient's own judgement is impaired;

4.4 The need for a provision by which those detained or being treated compulsorily can appeal against this decision;

4.5 The protection of the mentally ill against neglect and inadequate treatment. The provision of treatment, care, support and other resources where necessary for patients to be able to live within the community;

4.6 The need for specific guidelines that will be adapted to different cultural contexts with due attention to basic values and the limitations in financial and health resources of the societies in which they will be used;

4.7 The need to take into account differences in legal traditions around the world;

4.8 Facilitation of help for those voluntarily seeking treatment, in order that they can do so in a dignified manner, with easy access, which allows them to maintain their autonomy and self-determination;

4.9 Encouragement of the development of treatment options which may be less intrusive on the individual and the provision of appropriate resources for this;

4.10 Clear conceptualization of the important distinctions which may influence an individual's legal rights between:

(a) voluntary and involuntary admission; (b) competency and incompetency to make decisions; and (c) informed consent to treatment and the right to refuse treatment;

4.11 Protection of the patient's rights to privacy and confidentiality with regard to information about his or her treatment;

4.12 Provision for a patient's access to his or her own treatment information or, where this is not possible, access to such information by an advocate on behalf of the patient;

4.13 Provision of appropriate and universal guidelines for situations where it is unclear whether a person should be handled by the mental health or criminal system;

4.14 Precise and consistent definition of fundamental terms, such as (a) mental illness, (b) patient, (c) mental health care facility, (d) dangerousness to self and others, (e) mental health care provider;

4.15 Provision of special procedures concerning treatments which may be hazardous, irreversible or especially intrusive;

4.16 Protection of mental patients if they are to be involved in medical and psychosocial research.

WHO is at present considering issues of this kind within the framework of its own activities, and would be prepared to contribute further to the debate in the working group of the Subcommission on Prevention of Discrimination and Protection of Minorities or as the case may be in the Commission on Human Rights itself, in accordance with the procedural decisions that the Commission may wish to take in this respect.

***DRAFT BODY OF PRINCIPLES AND GUARANTEES FOR THE PROTECTION OF MENTALLY-ILL PERSONS AND FOR THE IMPROVEMENT OF MENTAL HEALTH CARE.*** Individuals in all parts of the world diagnosed as "mentally ill" require special measures of protection because they lack the capacity to provide for their own needs, to request aid, to testify, or to educate public opinion about their situation.

In 1977, the UN Commission on Human Rights requested its Sub-Commission on Prevention of Discrimination and Protection of Minorities (resolution 10 A [XXXIII]) to study, with a view to formulating guidelines, if possible, the question of the protection of those detained on the ground of mental ill-health against treatment that may adversely affect the human personality and its physical and intellectual integrity. In 1979, the General Assembly urged (resolution 33/53) that the study be given priority. In 1980, the Sub-Commission entrusted preparation of the study to one of its members, Mrs. Erica-Irene A. Daes (Greece), as Special Rapporteur. The study (UN Doc. E/CN.4/Sub.2/1983/17) was completed and submitted to the Sub-Commission at its 1983 session. It contained (annex II) a series of draft principles formulated by the Special Rapporteur.

With the approval of its parent bodies, the Sub-Commission in 1985 established a sessional working group to consider the Special Rapporteur's draft principles. The working group completed its task during the Sub-Commission's 1988 session, and the Sub-Commission adopted them (resolution 1988/28) and forwarded them to the Commission on Human Rights for further consideration.

Taking note of this development, the General Assembly called upon the Commission to consider the subject at its 1990 session with a view to submitting the draft principles and guarantees to the Assembly the same year (resolution 44/134). In doing so, it expressed the belief that all mentally ill persons should be treated with humanity and respect for the inherent dignity of the human person and reaffirmed its conviction that the misuse of psychiatry to detain persons in mental institutions on account of their political views or on other non-medical grounds, as reflected in the Special Rapporteur's report, is a violation of their human rights.

The Commission on Human Rights decided, on 6 March 1989, to establish an open-ended working group of the Commission to examine, revise, and simplify as necessary the draft body of principles prepared by the Sub-Commission and requested the working group to meet for a period of two weeks prior to the Commission's 1990 session. This development was endorsed by the ECONOMIC AND SOCIAL COUNCIL (resolution 1989/76) and by the General Assembly (resolution 44/134).

The Working Group on the Draft Body of Principles and Guarantees for the Protection of Mentally-Ill Persons and for the Improvement of Mental Health Care accordingly met at the United Nations office in Geneva from 8 to 19 January 1990. After putting aside for later consideration the question of the title of the draft as a whole, and also the definitions of terms contained in article 2 of the Sub-Commission's draft, the working group proceeded to revise and simplify that text, taking into account comments and suggestions from governments and intergovernmental and non-governmental organizations.

The articles thus adopted by the working group at its 1990 session are as follows:

### Title [To be Discussed]

*Article 1.* These Principles and Guarantees shall be applied without discrimination of any kind such as disability, race, colour, sex, language, religion, political or other opinion, national or social origin, social status, age, property or birth.

*Article 2.* [To be discussed.]

*Article 3.* 1. All persons have the right to the best available mental health care, which shall be part of the health and social care system.

2. All persons with a mental illness or who are being treated as such persons shall be treated with humanity and respect for the inherent dignity of the human person.

3. All persons with a mental illness or who are being treated as such persons have the right to protection from exploitation, physical or other abuse and degrading treatment.

4. There shall be no discrimination on the grounds of mental illness. Special measures taken for the sole purpose of protecting the rights, or securing the advancement, of persons with mental illness shall not be deemed to be discrimination. Discrimination does not include any distinction, exclusion or preference undertaken in accordance with the procedures in these Principles and necessary to protect the human rights of a person with a mental illness or of other individuals. [Discrimination" means any distinction, exclusion or preference that has the effect of nullifying or impairing equal enjoyment of rights.]

5. Every person with a mental illness shall have the right to exercise all civil, political, economic, social and cultural rights as recognized in the Universal Declaration of Human Rights, International Covenant on Economic, Social and Cultural Rights, International Covenant on Civil and Political Rights and the Declaration on the Rights of Disabled Persons, subject within the limits prescribed by those instruments to the provisions of domestic law relating to incapacity which include those providing for the judicial review of any relevant decision.

6. Where a court or other competent tribunal finds that a person with mental illness is unable to manage his or her own affairs, measures shall be taken, so far as is necessary and appropriate to that person's condition, to ensure the protection of his or her interests.

*Article 4.* 1. A patient in a mental health facility shall be informed as soon as possible after admission in a form and a language which the patient understands of all his or her rights in accordance with these Principles and Guarantees and under domestic law, which information shall include an explanation of these rights and how to exercise them.

2. If and for so long as a patient is unable to understand such information, the rights of the patient shall be communicated to the person or persons best able to represent the patient's interests and willing to do so.

3. A patient who has the necessary capacity has the right to nominate a person who should be informed on his or her behalf.

*Article 5.* 1. Every patient in a mental health facility shall, in particular, have the right to full respect for his or her:

(a) privacy;

(b) freedom of communication which includes freedom to communicate with other persons in the facility; freedom to send and receive uncensored private communications; freedom to receive, in private, visits from a legal or other representative and, at all reasonable times, from other visitors; and freedom of access to postal and telephone services and to newspapers, radio and television;

(c) freedom of religion or belief.

2. The environment and living conditions in mental health facilities shall be as close as possible to those of the normal life of persons of similar age and in particular shall include:

(a) facilities for recreational and leisure activities;

(b) facilities for education;

(c) facilities to purchase or receive items for daily living, recreation and communication;

(d) facilities, and encouragement to use such facilities, for his or her engagement in active occupation suited to his or her social and cultural background and for training designed to promote rehabilitation and reintegration in the community.

3. In no circumstances shall a patient be subject to forced labour.

4. The labour of a patient in a mental health facility shall not be exploited. Every such patient shall have the right to receive the same remuneration for any work which he or she does as would, according to domestic law or custom, be paid for such work to a non-patient. Every such patient shall in any event have the right to receive a fair share of any remuneration which is paid to the mental health facility for his or her work.

*Article 5 (bis)*. The right of a [patient] to confidentiality of information concerning him or her shall be respected.

*Article 6*. 1. A determination that a person has a mental illness shall be in accordance with internationally accepted medical standards.

2. A determination of mental illness shall never be made on the basis of political, economic or social status, or membership in a cultural, racial or religious group, or any other reason not directly relevant to mental health status.

3. Family or professional conflict, or non-conformity with moral, social, cultural or political values or religious beliefs prevailing in a person's community, shall never be a determining factor in diagnosing mental illness.

4. A background of past treatment or hospitalization as a patient shall not of itself justify any present or future determination of mental illness.

5. No person or authority should classify a person as having, or otherwise indicate that a person has, a mental illness except for purposes directly relating to mental illness or the consequences of mental illness.

*Article 6(a)*. No person shall be compelled to undergo mental examination with a view to determining whether or not he or she has a mental illness except in accordance with a procedure authorized by domestic law.

*Article 7*. 1. Every patient shall have the right to be treated and cared for, as far as possible, in the community in which he or she lives.

2. Where treatment takes place in a mental health facility, a patient shall have the right, whenever possible, to be treated near his or her home or the home of his or her relatives or friends and shall have the right to return to the community as soon as possible.

3. Every patient shall have the right to treatment suited to his or her cultural background.

*Article 8*. 1. Every patient shall have the right to receive such health and social care as is appropriate to his or her health needs, and is entitled to care and treatment in accordance with:

(a) the same standards as other ill persons; and

(b) the internationally accepted standards of the mental health professions, including the Principles of Medical Ethics adopted by the United Nations General Assembly.

2. Every patient shall be protected from harm, including unjustified medication, abuse by other patients or staff or other acts causing mental distress or physical discomfort.

*Article 9*. 1. A mental health facility shall have access to the same resources as any other health establishment, and in particular:

(a) qualified medical and other appropriate professional staff in sufficient numbers and adequate space to provide the patient with a programme of appropriate and active therapy and privacy;

(b) diagnostic and therapeutic equipment for the patient;

(c) appropriate professional care; and

(d) adequate, regular and comprehensive treatment, including supplies of medication.

2. Every mental health facility shall be inspected by the competent authorities with sufficient frequency to ensure that the conditions, treatment, and care of patients comply with these [Principles].

*Article 10*. 1. Every patient shall have the right to be treated in the least restrictive environment and with the least restrictive or intrusive treatment appropriate to the patient's health needs and the need to protect the physical safety of others.

2. The treatment and care of every patient shall be based on an individually prescribed plan, discussed with the patient, reviewed regularly, revised as necessary and provided by qualified professional staff.

3. Psychiatric knowledge and skills shall never be abused.

4. The treatment of every patient shall be directed towards preserving and enhancing personal autonomy.

*Article 11*. 1. Medication shall meet the best health needs of the patient and shall be given to a patient only for therapeutic or diagnostic purposes and shall never be administered as a punishment, or for the convenience of others. Subject to the provisions of Article 12 of these Principles, mental health practitioners shall only administer medication of known or demonstrated efficacy.

2. All medication shall be prescribed by a medical practitioner or by another trained person authorized by law and shall be recorded in the patient's records.

*Article 12*. 1. No treatment shall be given to a patient without his or her informed consent, except as provided for in paragraphs 6, 7 and 8.

2. Informed consent is consent obtained freely without threats or improper inducements after appropriate disclosure to the patient of adequate and understandable information in a form and language understood by the patient of:

(a) the diagnostic assessment;

(b) the purpose, method, likely duration and expected benefit of the proposed treatment;

(c) alternative modes of treatment, including those less intrusive; and

(d) possible pain or discomfort, risks and side effects of the proposed treatment.

3. A patient may request the presence of a person or persons of the patient's choosing during the procedure for granting consent.

4. Patients have the right to refuse or stop treatment except as provided for in paragraphs, 6, 7 and 8. The consequences of refusing or stopping treatment must be explained to the patient.

5. A patient shall never be invited or induced to waive the right to informed consent. If the patient should seek to do so, it shall be explained to the patient that the treatment cannot be given without informed consent.

6. Except as provided in paragraph 7 or in paragraphs 12, 13, and 14, a proposed plan of treatment may be given to a patient without a patient's informed consent if the following conditions are satisfied:

(a) the patient is, at the relevant time, held as an involuntary patient; and

(b) a competent and independent authority, established or prescribed by domestic law and having in its possession all relevant information, including the information specified in paragraph 2, is satisfied that, at the relevant time, the patient lacks the capacity to give or withhold informed consent to the proposed plan of treatment; and

(c) the competent authority is satisfied that the proposed plan of treatment is in the best interests of the patient's health needs.

7. Paragraph 6 does not apply to a patient who is a minor or to any other patient with a legal representative empowered by law to consent to treatment for the patient; but except as provided in paragraphs 12, 13 and 14, treatment may be given to such a patient without his or her informed consent if the legal representative, having been given the information described in paragraph 2, consents on the patient's behalf.

8. Except as provided in paragraphs 12, 13 and 14, treatment may also be given to any patient without the patient's informed consent if a qualified medical practitioner or another trained person authorized by law determines that it is urgently necessary in order to prevent immediate or imminent harm to the patient or to other persons. Such treatment shall not be prolonged beyond the period which is strictly necessary for this purpose.

9. Where any treatment is authorized without the patient's informed consent, every effort shall nevertheless be made to inform the patient about the nature of the treatment and any possible alternatives, and to involve the patient as far as practicable in the development of the treatment plan.

10. [All treatment shall be immediately recorded in the patient's medical records, with an indication of whether involuntary or voluntary.]

11. Physical restraint or involuntary seclusion of a patient shall not be employed except in accordance with the officially approved procedures of the mental health facility and only when it is the only means available to prevent immediate or imminent harm to the patient or others. It shall not be prolonged beyond the period which is strictly necessary for this purpose. All instances of physical restraint or involuntary seclusion, the reasons for them, and their nature and extent shall be recorded in the patient's medical record. A patient who is restrained or secluded shall be kept under humane conditions and be under the care and close and regular supervision of qualified members of the staff. The parents of minors or any legal representative shall be given prompt notice of any physical restraint or involuntary seclusion of the patient.

12. Sterilization shall never be carried out as a treatment for mental illness. Notwithstanding the provisions of paragraphs 6, 7 and 8, sterilization can be carried out on a person with a mental illness only where it is considered that it would best serve the health needs of the patient and where the patient gives informed consent, except that where the patient is unable to give informed consent, sterilization should be authorized only after independent external review.

13. Notwithstanding the provisions of paragraphs 6, 7 and 8, psychosurgery and castration can never be carried out on a patient who is an involuntary patient in a mental health facility and can be carried out on any other patient only where the patient has given informed consent and an independent external body has satisfied itself that there is genuine informed consent and that the treatment best serves the health needs of the patient.

14. Clinical trials and experimental treatment shall never be carried out on any patient without informed consent, except that a patient who is unable to give informed consent may be admitted to a clinical trial or given experimental treatment only with the approval of a competent, independent review body specifically constituted for this purpose.

*Article 13.* 1. Where a patient needs treatment in a mental health facility, every effort shall be made to avoid involuntary admission.

2. Access to a mental health facility shall be administered in the same way as access to any other facility for any other illness.

3. Every patient not admitted involuntarily shall have the right to leave the mental health facility at any time unless the criteria for his or her retention as an involuntary patient, as set forth in Article 15, apply, and he or she shall be informed of that right.

*Article 14.* [Deleted, as it becomes paragraph 3 of Article 13.]

*Article 15.* 1. A person shall—

(a) be admitted involuntarily to a mental health facility as a patient; or

(b) having already been admitted voluntarily as a patient, be retained as an involuntary patient in the mental health facility, if and only if a qualified clinician authorized by law for that purpose determines [in accordance with Article 6] that that person has a mental illness and considers:

(i) that, because of that mental illness, there is a serious likelihood of immediate or imminent harm to that person or to other persons; or

(ii) that, in the case of a person whose mental illness is severe and whose judgment is impaired, failure to admit or retain that person is likely to lead to a serious deterioration in his or her condition or will prevent the giving of treatment which can only be given by admission to a mental health facility in accordance with the principle of the least restrictive alternative. In the case referred to in sub-paragraph (ii), a second such clinician should be consulted if possible and, if such consultation takes place, the involuntary admission or retention may not take place unless the second clinician concurs.

2. Involuntary admission or retention shall initially be for a short period specified by domestic law for observation and preliminary treatment pending review of the patient's admission or retention by a judicial or other independent and impartial review body established by domestic law (hereinafter referred to as "the review body") and in accordance with procedures laid down in domestic law. The fact of the admission or retention and the grounds for it shall be communicated without delay to the review body, to the patient's representative (if any) and, unless the patient objects, to the patient's family.

*Draft General Limitation Clause.* The exercise of the rights set forth in these Principles and Guarantees may be subject only to such limitations as are prescribed by law and are necessary to protect the health or safety of the person concerned or of others or otherwise to protect public safety, order, health or morals or the fundamental rights and freedoms of others.

**BIBLIOGRAPHY.** Australian Human Rights and Equal Opportunity Commission. *Human Rights and Mental Illness: Report of the National Inquiry into the Human Rights of People with Mental Illness.* Canberra, Australia: Australian Government Publishing Service, 1993. Government report, in English.

Bayefsky, A.F., and M. Eberts, eds. *Equality Rights and the Canadian Charter of Rights and Freedoms.* Toronto, Canada: Carswell, 1985. Edited collection, in English.

Carney, T., and P. Singer. *Ethical and Legal Issues in Guardianship Options for Intellectually Disadvantaged People.* Canberra, Australia: Human Rights Commission, 1986. Government research paper, in English.

Chalidze, Lisa. "A Comparison of Norms—Rights of the Mentally Ill and Allegedly Mentally Ill," *New York Law School Human Rights Annual* 1 (1983): 75–97. Scholarly article, in English.

Delaney, Sophie. "Autonomy Denied: International Human Rights and the Mental Health Act 1986 (Vic.)," *Melbourne University Law Review* 18, no. 3 (June 1992): 565–583. Scholarly article, in English.

Heginbotham, Chris. *The Rights of Mentally Ill People.* London: Minority Rights Group, 1987. NGO report, in English.

Herr, Stanley S. *Issues in Human Rights: A Guide for Parents, Professionals, Policymakers and All Those who Are Concerned about the Rights of the Mentally Retarded and Developmentally Disabled People.* New York: 1984. Guidebook, in English.

International Commission of Jurists. *Human Rights and Mental Patients in Japan.* Geneva, Switzerland: 1985. NGO mission report, in English.

Sieghart, Paul, ed. *Human Rights in the United Kingdom.* London: Human Rights Network, 1988. NGO monograph, in English; footnotes to articles contain substantial bibliographic references.

Silver, Hedy M. "Voluntary Admission to New York Hospitals: The Rights of the Mentally Ill Homeless," *Columbia Human Rights Law Review* 19, no. 2 (Spring 1988): 333–367. Scholarly article, in English.

United Nations Commission on Human Rights. *Report of the Working Group on the Principles for the Protection of Persons with Mental Illness and for the Improvement of Mental Health Care. Chairman/Rapporteur: Mr. Henry Steel.* Geneva, Switzerland: 1991. IGO document, in English and French.

**MERCENARISM.** In 1986, the UN ECONOMIC AND SOCIAL COUNCIL (resolution 1986/43) expressed its deep concern at the loss of life, substantial damage to property and the long-term negative effects on the economy of southern Africa countries resulting from mercenary aggression, and condemned the increased recruitment, financing, training, assembly, transit, and use of mercenaries, as well as other forms of support to mercenaries, including so-called humanitarian aid, for the purpose of destabilizing and overthrowing the governments of southern African States and fighting against the national liberation movements of people struggling for the exercise of their right to self-determination. The Council denounced any State that persists in the recruitment, or permits or tolerates the recruitment, of mercenaries and provides facilities to them; and called upon States to exercise the utmost vigilance against the menace posed by the activities of mercenaries and to ensure, by both administrative and legislative measures, that their territory and other territories under their control, as well as their nationals, are not used for the recruitment, assembly, financing, training, and transit of mercenaries, or the planning of such activities designed to destabilize or overthrow the government of any State and to fight the national liberation movements struggling against racism, apartheid, colonial domination, and foreign intervention or occupation for their independence, territorial integrity, and national unity.

The Council urged the UN COMMISSION ON HUMAN RIGHTS to appoint a Special Rapporteur on the subject, and its action was later endorsed by the GENERAL ASSEMBLY (resolution 41/102). The Commission decided on 9 January 1987 (resolution 1987/16) to appoint such a Rapporteur "to examine the question of the use of mercenaries as a means of violating human

rights and of impeding the exercise of the right of peoples to self-determination." Mr. Enrique Bernales Ballesteros (Peru) was subsequently designated as Special Rapporteur.

In his first report to the Commission (UN Doc. E/CN./1988/14), the Special Rapporteur outlined the current state of international law on the subject of mercenarism as reflected in the Geneva Convention Relative to the Protection of Civilian Persons in the Time of War, its Protocol I, the OAU Convention for the Elimination of Mercenarism in Africa, and the International Convention against the Recruitment, Use, Financing and Training of Mercenaries, then under preparation in the UN General Assembly and since adopted.

The Commission, at its 1988 session, took note (resolution 1988/7) of the report with appreciation and continued the Special Rapporteur's mandate for one year, requesting him (a) to develop further the position that mercenary acts and mercenarism in general are a means of violating human rights and thwarting the self-determination of peoples, (b) to strengthen his cooperation and coordination with the various bodies concerned with mercenarism within the United Nations system, and (c) to study credible and reliable reports of mercenary activity in African and other developing countries in order to determine the scope and implications of such activities and the possible responsibility of third parties by means, *inter alia*, of on-site visits where appropriate.

The Commission also called upon the Special Rapporteur to submit to it, in 1989, a report on the question of the use of mercenaries as a means of impeding the exercise of the right of peoples to self-determination, together with his conclusions and recommendations; and to submit a preliminary report on the subject to the General Assembly at its 1988 session.

In its resolution, the Commission expressed its concern at the loss of life, the substantial damage to property, and the long-term negative effects of the economy of African, Central American, and other developing countries resulting from mercenary aggressions, and strongly condemned the racist regime of South Africa for its increasing use of groups of armed mercenaries against national liberation movements and for the destabilization of the governments of southern African States. It condemned the increased recruitment, financing, training, assembly, transit, and use of mercenaries, as well as other forms of support to mercenaries for the purpose of destabilizing and overthrowing the governments of Africa and Central America and of other developing States and fighting against the national liberation movements of peoples struggling for the exercise of their right to self-determination. It branded as inadmissible the use of channels of humanitarian and other assistance to finance, train and arm mercenaries, and denounced any State that persists in the recruitment, or permits or tolerates the recruitment, of mercenaries and provides facilities to them for launching armed aggression against other States. Finally, the Commission called upon all States to exercise the utmost vigilance against the menace posed by the activities of mercenaries and to ensure, by both administrative and legislative measures, that the territory of those States and other territories under their control, as well as their nationals, are not used in any manner in the use or encouragement of mercenarism.

### REPORTS OF THE SPECIAL RAPPORTEUR ON MERCENARISM.
The Special Rapporteur has since submitted reports annually to the Commission on Human Rights and the General Assembly, providing up-to-date information on the situation of mercenarism in various parts of the world and offering his recommendations for putting an end to this scourge.

In his report to the 1990 session of the Commission on Human Rights, he presented the following conclusions (UN Doc. E/CN.4/1990/11, chap. X, paras. 157–170):

It is to be concluded from the information, reports and observations received by the Special Rapporteur during 1989 from Member States, recognized national liberation movements, international organizations and non-governmental organizations that mercenary activities have been clearly condemned and repudiated. Such activities have tended to decrease in the armed conflicts in which they were mentioned and which have been or are being settled, thereby highlighting the tendency to make use of mercenaries in low-intensity conflicts. Thus it may be noted that, as the use of mercenaries declines or ceases, there may also be a fall in the number of reports of mercenary activities connected with such conflicts.

Notwithstanding the above conclusion, it can be observed from the reports received that, regrettably, the world offers a supply of individuals who, because of their military experience, for ideological reasons, or for reasons of adventurism, lifestyle or financial motivation, are prepared to hire out their services for unlawful mercenary activities. Such individuals, in turn, are usually involved with organizations which recruit, train and employ them, at the request of third parties, in activities which violate international law, State sovereignty, the exercise of the right of peoples to self-determination, the stability of constitutional governments and human rights. In this way, it may be concluded that the notion of a mercenary has changed as far as the traditional characteristics are concerned and has become a kind of independent criminal occupation. This is so because of the readiness to participate in unlawful acts and acts which may objectively be characterized as mercenary or terrorist acts, by virtue of both the individual perpetrating them and the damage caused in the territory and among the population affected, causing serious prejudice to territorial sovereignty and human life, even when the context in which they occur is not necessarily that of an international armed conflict.

The use of mercenaries is something that particularly affects small States, notably archipelagic States, especially when their geographical position places them close to areas of acute conflict, or when they are of strategic importance to third parties involved in activities relating to the political, military or economic control of the entire area which has been or is intended to be placed under their influence. These small States, many of them recently established, are extremely vulnerable to expansionist policies, invasion from outside, or to internal conspiracies to destabilize the government that make[s] use of mercenaries. Proven mercenary activity in the cases of Benin, Seychelles, Maldives and the Comoros in recent years demonstrates that there are small States exposed to dangerous situations in which mercenaries are used to jeopardize their sovereignty, their right to self-determination, their constitutional stability and the human rights of their peoples.

As regards mercenary activities in southern Africa, the Special Rapporteur would point out that the process of détente and peace embarked upon by Angola and South Africa, and the current process leading to independence in Namibia, have led to a marked reduction in mercenary activity in that part of southern Africa. In fact the Special Rapporteur has received no new reports of operations of that kind. However, he cannot but mention that, until the internal military conflict in Angola is settled and effective national reconciliation achieved, Angola will remain exposed to the risk of mercenary activities on the part of such groups or individuals employed by UNITA. It is well known that the UNITA rebel guerrilla group receives military assistance and funds from outside which, as indicated in the third report (E/CN.4/1989/14, paras. 179–180), are used in part to hire mercenaries. The Special Rapporteur has also received information from Botswana about mercenary attacks; consequently, the mercenary presence cannot be said to have totally disappeared from southern Africa.

The invasion of Maldives by mercenary groups on 3 November 1988 was thwarted, and the mercenaries of Tamil origin were tried under Maldivian law. The Special Rapporteur has kept in touch with the Maldivian authorities, which have pointed to the vulnerability of Maldivian territory and the risk of invasion, terrorist attacks and other forms of violence while an atmosphere of tension reigns in the Indian Ocean region and could spread to threaten Maldives too. The Maldivian authorities have not ruled out the possibility that mercenaries might be used again in an attack on the sovereignty of the State, and have invited the Special Rapporteur to examine the situation in Maldives on the spot.

On December 4, 1989 the General Assembly adopted the International Convention aginst the Recruitment, Use, Financing and Training of Mercenaries. The text of the Convention was prepared by an *ad hoc* committee set up under resolution 35/48 of 4 December 1980. The complex work of discussion and preparation culminated in a convergence of views which broadens, deepens and refines the scope of the definition of a mercenary, the elements and situations which combine to characterize mercenary activity and the qualifications of both the mercenary acts, and any actions which deliberately advance them, as indictable offences. In this sense, the Convention fills a gap, constitutes an important instrument to enable member States to adapt their national legislation on this subject, and also confirms the legal scope of the many United Nations declarations and resolutions condemning mercenary activities.

It is to be concluded from the text, the preamble and the body of the Convention that the extent and the variety of forms of mercenary practices are recognized. Noteworthy in this regard is the preamble to the Convention, which acknowledges the links between the drug traffic and mercenary activities in its reference to "new unlawful international activities linking drug traffickers and mercenaries in the perpetration of violent actions which undermine the constitutional order of the States" (preamble, fifth paragraph). In this regard, as well as through the broad definition in article 1, the Convention brings matters up to date in a way which should contribute to proper observance of the purposes and principles set out in the Charter of the United Nations, without prejudice to the fact that matters which are not regulated will continue to be governed by the rules and principles of international law. After the Convention has been in force for a reasonable period of time, it would be desirable to analyse and review a number of objections raised to the text, for example the requirement that mercenaries must be foreigners, or the amount of payment made.

Lastly, it can be seen from the text that the Convention contains no provision establishing machinery to minitor implementation. However, such monitoring will be a task for the domestic courts of the States parties. Bearing in mind that the Convention refers to the basic rights of peoples, such as political freedoms, human rights, State sovereignty and self-determination, which may be affected by mercenary activities, the Special Rapporteur concludes that part of the international machinery for monitoring this instrument may fall within the competence of the Commission on Human Rights. If this is the case, reports of mercenary activities of various kinds, such as those which have been reaching the Special Rapporteur, might better be studied within flexible Commission machinery under the mandate of the Special Rapporteur, without prejudice to actions falling within the scope of the competent domestic forums. In this way the Commission could contribute to effective implementation of this Convention.

In reply to letters sent by the Special Rapporteur, nongovernmental organizations and the Government of Colombia itself referred to the serious cases of violence which are systematicallly disrupting public order and affecting individuals and public and private property in that country. Preliminary information indicates that such acts of violence involve groups with a political motivation and also paramilitary gangs in the pay of organized drug traffickers. According to this preliminary information, evidence and facts of public record highlight a criminal association between Colombian drug traffickers and mercenaries recruited for them, who have participated in the formation and training of paramilitary gangs. These mercenaries, reported to be of Israeli and British nationality, are said to have prepared and taken part in large-scale attacks and criminal acts designed to subject the Colombian government to pressure on the part of these illegal groups and secure advantages for the drug traffickers. It may thus be concluded that this unlawful association between drug traffickers and mercenaries affects the sovereignty and constitutional stability of the Government of Colombia and the people, creating a situation presenting serious risks for Colombia and the international community itself.

Various press reports have taken up the generally accepted fact of the mercenary invasion of Comoros on 26 November 1989 in a *coup d'etat* which led to the overthrow and assassination of President Ahmed Abdallah Abderemane. The invasion was carried out by Bob Denard and a group of about 30 French and Belgian mercenaries. The mercenaries stayed in the Comoros until 15 December 1989,

and then left for Johannesburg on a South African cargo plane. The departure of the mercenaries was essentially due to French action in support of the sovereignty and legitimate authorities of the Comoros. This event highlighted the vulnerability of the Comoros and, once again, the active presence of mercenaries in Africa. The Special Rapporteur considered it pertinent to draw the attention of the Commission on Human Rights to this serious occurrence, as well as the withdrawal of the mercenaries to South African territory, and would point out the need for a thorough investigation, for which reason he has made appropriate requests for full and detailed information on this regrettable event.

As to the Central American conflict and the role played in it by the United States of America, the Special Rapporteur has continued to examine the extensive information and documentation obtained when he visited the United States. Although open to further analysis, all the material examined so far indicates that, under the Administration of President Reagan and in the context of policy decisions designed to provide assistance to the Nicaraguan resistance and—as the administration saw it—prevent the Sandinista Government from helping the FMLN guerrillas in El Salvador, covert actions and operations did indeed take place and they went beyond the legal authority granted by Congress for aid and funds for the Nicaraguan resistance (or contras). Some of these covert operations, carried out to raise funds for the contras or to perform acts of sabotage against Nicaragua, involved the creation of all-purpose networks and the recruitment and active participation of some foreign mercenaries. This participation by foreigners, on terms corresponding to mercenarism, has been noted in the Iran-*Contra* Affair report prepared by the Committees of the United States Congress, as well as in reports drawn up by experts and investigators working in United States non-governmental organizations dealing with human rights matters. However, it may also be concluded from the information which has been gathered that these illegal acts were carried out by officials acting without authorization from the highest government authorities or from Congress. The United States Government neither recognizes nor acknowledges any connection with mercenary activities, and has stated that any such activities as may have taken place are the sole responsibility of the private organizations which made use of them.

On the basis of the documentation studied, it may also be concluded that the United States public is greatly aware of the Central American issue, opposes anything that might involve the United States in a military conflict and is against anything that might affect the principles and values of United States democracy. It is also important to note that the Bush administration has stated its readiness to contribute to peace in the region, on the understanding that the most appropriate tool for such purpose is the implementation of the Esquipulas II Agreement as a comprehensive and indivisible set of obligations for all the parties. This stance underlies the bipartisan agreement and the Congress's policy of not granting the Nicaraguan resistance funds for military purposes.

The effort made by Central American leaders to promote political negotiation, détente and peace, despite differences of view between some of them, is a matter of record. In this context, the Esquipulas II, Alajuela, Costa del Sol and Tela agreements, and recently those adopted in San Isidro de Coronado, demonstrate a determination on the part of the Governments of Central America to seek and implement effective solutions to achieve peace in Central America. There is no doubt that demobilization of the Nicaraguan resistance, voluntary repatriation of its members to Nicaragua or third countries, resumption of dialogue and holding democratic elections, which are now under way, can constitute genuine measures to accelerate the process of restoring peace and democracy throughout the Central American region.

As a contribution to international co-operation in the relaxation of tension, the United Nations has set up observer machinery and an International Support and Verification Commission (CIAV) to study issues relating to demobilization, such as the acceptance of returned weapons and ammunition and repatriation as well as assistance to persons deciding to return to Nicaragua or resettle in third countries. On the basis of the Tela and San Isidro de Coronado agreements, and the positions in this regard taken up by the Governments of Honduras and Nicaragua, it may be concluded that such United Nations machinery is the most appropriate means of guaranteeing the implementation of the various arrangements for bringing about reconciliation and peace. Consequently, the stronger this machinery and the guarantees for its operation and the greater resources and funds for its activities, the more rapidly and effectively will it be possible to achieve the desired result of peace in Central America.

On the basis of the information he had received and analyzed, and on the conclusions he had drawn, the Special Rapporteur submitted the following recommendations for consideration by the Commission (chap. XI, paras. 172–186):

Bearing in mind that, despite the rejection and condemnation of mercenary activities by the United Nations, they are still being carried out; it is desirable for such a stand to be maintained and strengthened by provisions on concrete measures and actions to help eliminate mercenary activities of all kinds. To this end it will be necessary to take into account the methods used in recent conflict situations in which one of the parties has made use of mercenaries to subject the other to military action and inflict material damage, or to destabilize a sovereign State internally.

Condemnation and punishment of mercenary activities should apply both to the mercenary agents directly involved in such activities and to those who make use of them, as well as to the bodies or individuals recruiting and training them at the request of third parties for participation in actions in violation of international rules, State sovereignty, the excercise of the right of peoples to self-determination, the stability of constitutional Governments and human rights. In addition, to ensure that this recommendation is effectively applied, it should be borne in mind that there are a variety of ways of making use of mercenaries and that mercenaries now form a kind of independent criminal occupation by virtue of their readiness to take part, on agreed terms, in unlawful acts, as well as acts which may objectively be characterized as mercenary acts, by virtue of both the individual perpetrating them and the damage caused to the population and the territory affected.

The use of mercenaries has been particularly intense against small States, especially archipelagic States, when their geographical position places them close to areas of acute conflict, or when they are of strategic importance to the interests of third parties involved in activities relating to the political, military or economic control of the area which has

been or is intended to be placed under their influence. In this context, and bearing in mind attacks by mercenary gangs against Benin, Seychelles, Maldives and the Comoros, it is desirable for the Commission to look into the vunerability of small States and strenghten the principles of self-determination and the unrestricted realization of the human rights of their peoples, by warning against attempts at expansionist policies, invasions from outside or destabilizing internal conspiracies involving the use of mercenaries, thereby violating the sovereignty, self-determination, domestic constitutional order and human rights of nations.

In view of the variety and scope of the uses to which mercenaries may be put, all States should be urged to exercise maximum vigilance and apply legislative and administrative measures to prevent and punish the use of their territory and other territories under their control, as well as their nationals, for the recruitment, concentration, funding, training and transit of mercenaries, as well as their use in activities designed to destabilize or overthrow the Government of any State or combat national liberation movements fighting against racism, *apartheid*, colonial domination and foreign intervention and occupation and for their independence, territorial integrity and national unity.

As to the principles underlying United Nations action, it would be desirable to point out the incompatibility with international rules of any external assistance which can be objectively demonstrated as for use in intervening in the internal affairs of other States and for attacks against the exercise of the rights of peoples to self-determination. The recommendation on incompatibility should include any diversion of programmes of humanitarian or other assistance to cover up actual situations in which mercenaries are financed, trained or used.

In view of the fact that on 4 December 1989 the General Assembly adopted the International Convention against the Recruitment, Use, Financing and Training of Mercenaries, it is desirable for the Commission to express its satisfaction at the successful finalization of the work of the *Ad hoc* Committee and the adoption of the Convention and declare at the same time that this constitutes a meaningful step forward and an important instrument for Member States to adapt their national legislation in this area, and also express the hope that the Convention will be signed by the greatest possible number of States in the shortest possible time, so as to ensure prompt entry into force.

In view of the text of the Convention itself and the fact that there are few States in which domestic legislation specifically classes mercenary activities as unlawful and provides for the prohibition of such activities and the prosecution and punishment of those responsible, States should once again be urged to establish in their domestic legislation that mercenary activities are an offence and stipulate the appropriate penalties.

It is of relevance to point out that the Convention contains no provisions establishing machinery to monitor implementation. Given the legal precedents and the subject-matter of the Convention, it is desirable for the Commission to bear in mind that it can itself form part of the monitoring machinery, in all matters relating to the unrestricted applicability and the protection of human rights. In this context, reports of mercenary activities in violation of the right to self-determination and the human rights of peoples received by the Special Rapporteur might better be studied under the mandate of the Special Rapporteur—without prejudice to any legal action initiated in competent national courts.

In connection with the peace process in the southern African region, and in the light of the peace agreements signed by Angola and South Africa, as well as the current independence process in Namibia, it is recommended that these initiatives should be supported, together with the relaxation of tension discernible in the region, for their successful culmination may consolidate independence in Namibia and lasting peace in Angola. Mercenary practices arose in the context of the existing violence and conflicts in the region, and hence it is to be hoped that halting them will contribute to the disappearance of mercenary activities once and for all. For this same reason, this recommendation should include a reference to internal military conflict in Angola, expressing support for a national reconciliation process which will lead to the disappearance of the UNITA guerrilla movement, together with its use of mercenaries, and seeking peace among Angolans, and their contribution to, and political participation in, the development of their country.

Bearing in mind the fact that, according to a number of reports, mercenary activities have not ceased in Africa, and indeed the recent occupation of the Comoros by a mercenary force highlights the existence of groups intended to affect the sovereignty, self-determination and stability of the Governments of certain States, it is recommended that the Commission should clearly condemn this situation, express full support for the sovereign rights of States and peoples in the region and demand an explanation from the Government of South Africa about its alleged connection with mercenary activities, or in any event, the protection of persons taking part in them.

With regard to the invasion of Maldives by mercenary groups on 3 November 1988, the prosecution and punishment of the mercenaries found guilty of the invasion, and the concern expressed by the Government of Maldives in drawing attention to the vunerability of its territory and the risk of exposure to invasion, attacks, and other forms of violence affecting its sovereignty, self-determination and political stability and the human rights of its people, it is desirable for the Commission to condemn the mercenary agression to which Maldives was subjected and express support for the country's sovereign rights. At the same time, the Commission might reiterate its call on the Governments concerned to continue co-operating with the Special Rapporteur in this regard.

In the light of the reports and evidence which highlight criminal links between organized groups of Colombian drug traffickers and foreign mercenaries recruited to work for them and participate in the formation and training of paramilitary groups and in acts of extreme violence that have disrupted public order and affected individuals and public and private property in Colombia, it is desirable for the Commission to condemn this serious unlawful association, and at the same time assure the Government of Colombia of its readiness to co-operate within the Commission's field of competence in eliminating this association that affects the sovereignty and constitutional stability of Colombia.

The Commission should vigorously condemn the occupation of the Comoros by a mercenary force on 26 November 1989, express support for the sovereign rights of the people of the Comoros, and welcome the French initiative which helped to bring the mercenary occupation of the country to an end and re-establish the sovereignty and constitutional authority of the Comorian Government. At the same time, this recommendation should include the need for an exhaustive investigation of the causes of, and responsibility for, this mercenary act, as well as the legal situation of the mercenaries who have been publicly accused of perpetrating it.

As regards the Central American conflict, particularly the armed actions in Nicaragua which have caused objective harm to its sovereignty, population, territory and economy, and bearing in mind that, in this context, there has been external interference to help one of the parties to the conflict, and mercenaries have been recruited and used through the use of outside funds raised by covert operations that ignored and exceeded the legal authorizations by the United States Congress and the authorities for aid to the Nicaraguan resistance, it is desirable to reaffirm the right of Nicaragua and the other countries in the Central American region to noninterference in their internal affairs, self-determination and full sovereignty, while condemning the mercenary activities of foreigners recruited as mercenaries and the practices and operations that made those activities possible.

Finally, noting the process of détente which has begun in the Central American region by express and agreed decision of the five presidents; that the Esquipulas II, Alajuela, Costa del Sol, Tela and San Isidro de Coronado agreements set out solutions, machinery and procedures for the settlement of all aspects of the conflict in a manner that is satisfactory to all parties; that, in addition to the United States of America, through the bipartisan agreement, has indicated its readiness to co-operate in seeking a peaceful political solution for Central America on the basis of the comprehensive application to the Esquipulas II agreements as an indivisible whole; and that machinery for observation (ONUCA) and verification (the International Support and Verification Commission) has been established under the United Nations to contribute to democratization, détente and demobilization in the region—the Special Rapporteur considers it desirable for the Commission to express explicit support for this comprehensive peaceful political negotiation process, support the initiatives set out in the San Isidro de Coronado agreement designed to speed up the process of comprehensive application of the peace agreements, and invite all Member States to express their support for and co-operation in the negotiations and political settlement under way and in the demobilization of the Nicaraguan resistance forces and their voluntary repatriation to their own or a third country, as well as undertaking to respect the sovereignty and self-determination of the peoples of Central America and their contribution to all actions that strengthen democracy and development in the region as a whole.

The mandate of the Special Rapporteur has continued. In later reports, he updates the Commission on Human Rights concerning continued mercenarism on the African continent and in Latin America; since the breakup of the Soviet Union, the Special Rapporteur has included remarks on the Balkan conflicts. In one of his latest reports to the Commission on Human Rights, he sets out conclusions (paras. 114–133) and recommendations (paras. 134–140) (E/CN.4/1994/23):

### Conclusions

The United Nations considers mercenary activities unlawful and criminal, as mercenaries have been used to commit acts contrary to international law, thereby creating situations that impede self-determination and endanger the sovereignty, constitutional stability and human rights of the peoples who become victims of this criminal activity. In this context, international instruments have been adopted which condemn and punish the recruitment, training, financing and use of mercenaries. At the same time, a growing number of States have included mercenarism as a punishable offence in their national legislation.

The condemnation of mercenarism is a universally accepted fact even in those states which have not yet categorized it as a crime. At this point, the debate tends to focus on the scope and content of this punishable act, but not on its criminal nature. Moreover, without prejudice to the further development of international legal instruments and of the provisions of national law, member States have sufficient capacity to formulate policies on the prevention, prosecution and punishment of mercenary activities, to prevent their territory from being used for the training or transit of mercenaries, and to prevent their financial and economic systems from facilitating operations which finance such activities.

The assumption that mercenary activities are on the decline owing to the adoption of legal provisions for their prosecution and punishment and the fact that the decolonization process in Africa is over bears no relation to contemporary reality. In recent years, and particularly since 1992, a greater number of criminal actions by mercenaries, both in Africa and on other continents, have been referred to the Special Rapporteur, thus confirming a growing trend towards recourse to the use of mercenaries for various unlawful activities that affect the self-determination of peoples and human rights. These unlawful actions also demonstrate that the growth can be attributed to the outbreak of new armed conflicts in the post-cold-war era with the establishment of new States. The fact is that the current international transition is being marred not only by border problems between recently established States, but also by a climate of acute ethnic, religious and nationalist intolerance which, in more than one case, has degenerated into armed conflict. Some of these conflicts have been aggravated by the involvement of foreign mercenaries.

In the analysis of mercenary activities, responsibility does not end with the commission of the criminal act or with the identification and isolation of the agent. The mercenary has been determined to be merely the last link in a chain, in which his recruitment and his subsequent commission of the criminal act are but the execution of an act which has been conceived, planned, organized, financed and supervised by others, whether they are private groups, political opposition organizations, groups which advocate national, ethnic or religious intolerance, clandestine organizations, or Governments which, through covert operations, decide on illegal action against a state or against the life, liberty, physical integrity and safety of persons, and involve mercenaries in that action. Accordingly, responsibility extends to all those who take part in the criminal act, which, in its final phase, is executed by the mercenary agent. This therefore leads to the conclusion that vigilance, control and express prohibition provided for by Member States in their domestic legislation are very important in order to prevent organizations which generate mercenary activities from operating in their territory and, where necessary, to counter any intelligence machinery that, through covert operations, permits the involvement of government agents who recruit mercenaries or do so through third organizations, by prescribing harsh punishment for such unlawful contractual relationships.

In addition to the general observations made above, it can be said that mercenaries are most frequently recruited to commit acts of sabotage against a third country, to carry out selective assassinations of eminent persons, and to participate in armed conflicts. It therefore follows that a mercenary is a criminal who, without prejudice to the punishment applicable to those who recruited and paid him, must be severely punished, in keeping with the categorization of the common crime he has committed, where national law does not envisage the crime of mercenarism as such. In any case, the person's mercenary role should be considered as an aggravating factor.

Based on the information gathered on mercenaries participating in the most recent domestic or international armed conflicts, all Member States should be concerned that the increase in the supply of mercenaries might be influenced by the existence of career military personnel whose personal situation has deteriorated as a result of the reduction in strength or dissolution of the regular armed forces to which they belonged and who have consequently joined the ranks of the unpaid. There would thus appear to be persons with experience or military training who see in any armed conflict an opportunity to become involved in exchange for pay and are shown tolerance when they commit cruel acts or engage in looting, which brings them additional financial gain.

In the light of these new forms of mercenary activity, the Special Rapporteur concludes that there are cases in which legal formulas, or more specifically, standard legal procedures are resorted to in order to conceal a mercenary. He may thus appear to have the legal status of a national of the country where he becomes involved in an armed conflict, or where he will fulfil his criminal assignment, thereby avoiding categorization as a "mercenary". Although this approach legally masks an individual's real mercenary role, the origin of the contractual relationship, the payment he receives, the type of services agreed on, the simultaneous use of other nationalities and passports, etc., must be seen as indications of the true nationality of persons where there are strong grounds for suspecting that they are mercenaries. In this respect, problems arise in relation to persons who legally have dual or multiple nationality and whose acts are deliberately designed to bring criminal harm to one of the countries of which they are a national, on instructions from the other country of which they are a national, from a third State, or from groups organized to perpetrate acts of aggression.

Although mercenaries are most commonly hired to participate in armed conflicts, the fact that they are also hired to commit acts of provocation, aimed at fomenting an armed conflict or the destabilization of a lawful constitutional Government, should not be overlooked. Moreover, as the mercenary is a criminal agent, it is not unusual for him to be connected with arms or drug-trafficking rings and terrorist groups, which are a threat to a country's laws and security. Nor is it unusual for these illegal groups to exchange identities; a terrorist group might also be said to be composed of mercenaries when it moves to the territory of another State in order to provide protection to drug traffickers in exchange for payment, engage in sabotage and other unlawful acts, or take part in a domestic armed conflict.

The sum total of these acts defines the scope and magnitude of mercenary activity as one of the crimes that most seriously harm the self-determination of peoples, constitutional stability, peace and human rights. This therefore highlights the importance of the General Assembly resolution adopted in December 1993 which recommends convening a group of experts, specialists and interested persons who could contribute to the further development of the concepts, categories, studies and proposed solutions contained in the reports which the Special Rapporteur on the question of the use of mercenaries has submitted to both the Commission on Human Rights and the General Assembly itself.

The information gathered confirms that during 1993 Africa was still the continent which suffered most from mercenary aggression. In this connection it should be recalled that the concept of a mercenary, as construed today, took as its point of departure the presence of professionals of war, most of them white, who were active in bloody armed conflicts in various regions of Africa in order to prevent the exercise of the right to self-determination, independence and the formation of sovereign African States, and to form territorial enclaves subordinate to former colonial Powers or to install Governments subordinate to them or to colonialist ventures. In so far as some of these conflicts have been settled, mercenary activities can be said to have subsided. But they have not disappeared completely. Angola, Benin, Botswana, the Comoros, Lesotho, Liberia, Mozambique, Namibia, Zaire, Zambia and Zimbabwe, inter alia, are countries with recent experience of mercenary activity; and in certain cases, outside the region of southern Africa, mercenary attacks have occurred as a result of the policy of apartheid which originated in South Africa but has ramifications and has sparked criminal activities all over Africa and even outside it.

The situation in Angola steadily deteriorated and became more serious in 1993 with the failure of the peace agreements signed on 31 May 1991 and the resumption of hostilities by UNITA against the Government of Angola. The information obtained indicates that the impact of this war on the Angolan people is even worse than it had been up until 1991. Their living conditions have deteriorated to such an extent that starvation is widespread, the number of deaths is estimated at over 1,000 a day and at approximately 500,000 in 1993 as a result of armed conflicts, acts of sabotage, food shortages, infection and the lack of medicines and prompt medical attention in hospitals. United Nations efforts to reduce the suffering of the Angolan people and to end the conflict have not been successful thus far. Hence the importance of Security Council resolution 864 (1993), unanimously adopted on 15 September 1993 pursuant to Chapter VII of the Charter of the United Nations, declaring an embargo on the supply of arms, related matériel and petroleum to UNITA forces. This embargo took effect on 26 September and is expected to put an end to the purchase of weapons, sophisticated military training abroad and the presence of military technicians and strategists, all of which have served to intensify the war and have, at the same time, made it difficult to end it through negotiation. None the less, it should be noted that in early December 1993 UNITA announced its willingness to negotiate a truce and reopen a dialogue with the Government.

On the basis of all the information gathered, the Special Rapporteur concluded, with regard to the aggravation of this armed conflict, that the presence of foreign mercenaries who have participated in training operations, and in combat has been a key factor in the duration and nature of the conflict. Reports from government sources indicate that most of the mercenaries are of South African and Zairian origin. The reports also mention the recruitment of former members of the South African 31st and 32nd battalions as security guards for Angolan oil refineries and installations, who, however, allegedly fought in Huambo alongside UNITA forces. Their recruitment is attributed to a South African company, Executive Outcome. Moreover, UNITA control of Angola's eastern provinces allegedly facilitated the entry into Angola of mercenaries from Zaire to fight alongside rebel forces. In addition, the head of the South African Defence Forces, General Georg Meiring, confirmed on 11 September 1993 that members of the special élite forces and former members of the South African intelligence services were receiving offers of recruitment to fight in Angola as mercenaries. They were being offered one-year contracts and monthly pay of US$10,000. Although from all indications, UNITA is responsible for the use of mercenaries, the Special Rapporteur notes that recent international press reports name the Angolan Government as well in connection with the acceptance of mercenaries of South African origin to act as military instructors in the army, and some of them have taken part in military operations against UNITA. The Special Rapporteur has contacted the Angolan Government in order to transmit this information to it and seek its views.

In relation to the mercenary activities generated in South Africa within the context of the policy of apartheid, whose backdrop has been both South Africa, other countries of the region and even countries outside Africa, the information contained in the report demonstrates that such mercenary activities have substantially abated with the progressive dismantling of apartheid. The most recent development has been the adoption of a provisional constitution that repeals the laws of apartheid and steers South Africa towards a pluralistic democracy free from racial, political, social and cultural discrimination. This development cannot, however, obscure or minimize the existence of extremely violent groups totally opposed to the dismantling of apartheid. Among the various acts of provocation by such groups was the assassination on 10 April 1993 of Chris Hani, a member of the ANC National Executive, at the hands of a Polish mercenary called Janusz Walus. In view of this situation, which has persisted since December 1993, we maintain that while substantial progress has been achieved in the democratization of South Africa, the process is being resisted by groups that advocate an escalation of violence and are prepared to resort to crime and terrorist activities and actions, hiring known mercenaries for this purpose.

The report contains a brief account of the problems caused by political violence in Zaire (paras. 55–60). All the information gathered points to the participation of foreign mercenaries in acts of violence which are endangering the lives of the Zairian people. These mercenaries have participated in the formation and training of a Civil Guard brigade known as the Special Intervention Force (FIS); mercenaries of Egyptian, Israeli and South African origin have also allegedly acted as instructors in the Special Presidential Division and in some élite army units.

For the second consecutive year, the Special Rapporteur is focusing attention on the armed conflicts taking place in the territory of the former Yugoslavia as part of his substantive mandate. He has again received reports—some from the States affected by the conflict—of the presence of foreign mercenaries involved in that conflict. Details of these reports are contained in paragraphs 61–71 of the report and the correspondence, which sets forth the serious charges levelled in connection with the presence of mercenaries, is contained in the files of the Special Procedures Unit of the Centre for Human Rights. It follows from a study of these facts that the presence of foreigners in this conflict is admitted by all parties, although whether some or all of them are mercenaries is in dispute. The Special Rapporteur has requested replies to these charges and reported on the steps taken to the Special Rapporteur appointed by the Commission to investigate the human rights situation in the territory of the former Yugoslavia.

Although the armed conflict is continuing, the various rounds of political negotiations between the parties are keeping alive hopes of reaching an agreement that will end a war which has been marked by extreme violence and cruelty. However, even assuming that the urgently needed peace agreement is reached, the crimes that have been committed are so serious that the Special Rapporteur believes that their investigation should not be halted. Where mercenaries are known to have participated in such crimes, this should be considered an aggravating factor in the imposition of penalties.

Following the breakup of the former Union of Soviet Socialist Republics, the republics which previously formed part of that State have become sovereign and independent States, with the majority of them making up the Commonwealth of Independent States (CIS). Disputes of various sorts have arisen in a number of those countries, some relating to border issues, others to internal relations between territories and republics and their autonomy with respect to the new State. But the disputes which have degenerated into armed conflict are mainly those which involve some ethnic element and strong nationalist or religious feeling, acting as catalysts in the choice between greater autonomy, territorial redistribution involving a move from one State to another or a change in the nature of the political regime. In every case where the deadlock has turned into armed conflict, there has been participation by mercenaries, according to the information analysed by the Special Rapporteur.

Paragraphs 72–103 of the report provide information on the armed conflicts taking place in Armenia and Azerbaijan (Nagorny-Karabakh), Georgia, the Republic of Moldova and Tajikistan, including official correspondence sent to the Special Rapporteur reporting the presence of foreign mercenaries who have been recruited to participate actively in military operations. With the exception of Armenia and Azerbaijan, these conflicts have abated. When the conflict between Georgia and Abkhazia was at its height, foreign mercenaries were involved, according to the claim made by President Shevardnadze himself, speaking before the Georgian Parliament in Tbilisi on 16 March 1993. Similarly, in the case of the Republic of Moldova, the communication dated 23 August 1993 sent to the Special Rapporteur by the Deputy Minister for Foreign Affairs of Moldova is confirmed by the report on the participation of Russian and Cossack citizens as mercenaries in the armed conflict which broke out in the area of the Moldovan Dniester; this report even gives an account of nine persons from the Russian Federation who were arrested for participating in the conflict. The incidents described would appear to demonstrate that a number of foreigners have indeed participated in the armed-conflicts which took place in some of the States formerly making up the Soviet Union. The investigation being conducted by the Special Rapporteur is not closed and it is expected that, with the cooperation of the authorities of each State and international sources, and through the work of NGOs, he will be able to provide the Commission with a more detailed report on this sensitive question.

With regard to the current status of the International Convention against the Recruitment, Use, Financing and Training of Mercenaries, the Special Rapporteur notes that to date only seven States have completed the process for becoming parties to the convention (Barbados, Cyprus, Maldives, Seychelles, Suriname, Togo and Ukraine), and that a further 13 States have signed it. This situation has prompted the conclusion that there is a delay in the process by which Member States express consent to be bound by the Convention through ratification or accession, for until 22 States have ratified or acceded to it, the Convention cannot enter into force.

In accordance with resolution 1993/48 of the Commission on Human Rights, the Special Rapporteur has focused on the adverse consequences for the enjoyment of human rights of acts of violence committed by armed groups that spread terror among the population and by drug traffickers. From the reports and communications on file in the Centre for Human Rights and the supporting documentation, it has been learned that in the course of 1993 populations of various countries have been seriously harmed by the illegal and criminal action of armed groups which, regardless of their ideological motive, have not hesitated to engage in utterly reprehensible conduct, such as massive violation of human rights, attacks on public safety, and acts designed to disrupt the constitutional order and destabilize constitutional governments. These terrorist practices, perpetrated in order to create a general climate of intimidation and terror, have been committed by armed groups on political pretexts, by drug-trafficking rings or by mercenaries. In more than one case, they have joined forces and exchanged favours, forming criminal associations that seriously endanger human life, the safety and integrity of individuals, and the human rights of whole populations.

### Recommendations

The Special Rapporteur, in view of the reports he has received during 1993, confirming that mercenary activities have not subsided and are giving rise to situations that violate the human rights and impede the self-determination of peoples, and taking into account the United Nations declarations and resolutions condemning such activities as serious crimes which give all States cause for profound concern, recommends to the Commission on Human Rights that, taking into account the fact that these acts are being repeated and the precedents deriving from the position taken on this issue, it should reaffirm its condemnation of mercenary activities of any type or form and at any level, and of States or third parties involved in them. He further stresses the need to strengthen the principles of the sovereignty, equality and independence of States, the self-determination of peoples, full respect for human rights and the stability of constitutionally established and lawfully functioning Governments, and full enjoyment of human rights.

Bearing in mind that recourse to mercenaries is aimed at doing harm, whose victim may be a person singled out for his ideas, belief, race or political position, an institution within society, political figures or eminent persons holding public office, or a State, and that mercenary action takes place chiefly, but not exclusively, in the context of armed conflict, as mercenary operations have also been staged where there was no armed conflict, it is recommended that the Commission should stress that the use of mercenaries in itself and their use for unlawful activities are to be condemned, both in cases where such activities are carried out by one or all parties to an armed conflict and in cases where there is no armed conflict, and mercenaries are resorted to for purposes of impeding the self-determination of a people, damaging a country's installations, destabilizing the constitutional Government of a State or endangering the life and safety of persons.

Bearing in mind the nature and forms of mercenary activities, and that they generally make the mercenary an instrument, since his recruitment and his subsequent commission of the criminal act are but the execution of an operation which has been conceived, planned, organized, financed and supervised by others, the Special Rapporteur recommends that the resolution condemning mercenary activities also stress the need for vigilance and explicit prohibition in the domestic legislation of member States in order to prevent organizations linked to mercenaries from operating in their territory, to prohibit public authorities from resorting to mercenarism and to counter any intelligence machinery which through covert operations uses mercenaries or does so through third organizations. The scope of this recommendation should include the prohibition of the transit of mercenaries through national territory and, of course, punishment of nationals or foreign residents who engage in mercenary activities.

Given the complex techniques employed to conceal and alter the identity of mercenaries, the oversupply of career military personnel who are tempted to become mercenaries and the use of legal devices and standard legal procedures to disguise the mercenary's legal status and nationality, or cases of simultaneous dual or multiple nationality, it is recommended that the Commission should consider the views of the General Assembly contained in its recent resolution on the subject adopted in December 1993, under the section calling for a meeting of a group of experts, specialists and interested persons, so that, together with the Special Rapporteur and taking into account the categories of analysis used by him, significant headway may be made in refining and determining the scope of the concepts relating to the question of mercenaries and in proposing solutions aimed at significantly controlling the problem.

Africa is still the continent most affected by mercenary activities, which persist in certain conflicts in the region and continue to pose a latent threat to other African countries. It is therefore recommended that the Commission should reaffirm its strong condemnation of the presence of mercenaries and of those States and third parties which promote mercenary activities in Africa, and its unqualified support for the self-determination and development of the African peoples, and the full enjoyment of their human rights. It should also express its support for the measures taken, in accordance with international and domestic law, in the case of countries affected by the presence of mercenaries.

In monitoring cases of armed conflict in African countries where mercenaries were involved, it has been determined that they redeploy when cease-fire and peace agreements are concluded; however, the main units which are usually made up of mercenaries from other continents or from South Africa, do not leave Africa but rather move on to other African countries, from which they maintain their ties with organizations that traffic in conflict situations and with paramilitary groups, all of which helps them to become mercenaries again in the country where they have taken refuge or in other countries where a situation of violence exists. It is therefore recommended that the Commission should suggest that, in addition to the prohibition of mercenary activities and the applicable penalties, measures be agreed upon to expel from African countries all persons of foreign nationality who have served as mercenaries in armed conflicts or in support of apartheid, whether or not they have served sentences. Nationals who have participated in mercenary activities should also be liable to provisions in the respective legal system of each country which establish penalties of the greatest severity for recidivism.

Taking into account the escalation of the armed conflict in Angola in 1993, it is recommended that the Commission on Human Rights should draw attention to the grave prejudice that the prolongation of the conflict represents for the Angolan people and for the respect and enjoyment of their human rights. At the same time, it should stress the need to put an end to the conflict, within the framework of the peace agreements and initiatives contained in the relevant United Nations and OAU resolutions. The recommendation should also mention the need for strong condemnation of the presence of mercenaries who have become involved in the armed conflict in Angolan territory or from neighbouring countries.

On the basis of the positive developments in the political situation in South Africa, where the adoption of a new provisional constitution, a transition government leading to democracy and general, pluralistic elections in April 1994 are effectively dismantling apartheid, but also taking into account the resistance of white-minority groups who will resort to armed violence in order to prevent the abolition of the racist system and, in that context, to the use of mercenaries, active, vigilant support is recommended for all measures to eliminate apartheid and introduce democracy in South Africa, to report and at the same time condemn acts of violence that are encouraged to prevent or delay this process, and to hold the racist minority groups responsible for using mercenaries and committing acts of violence in order to obstruct the democratization process in South Africa.

Concerning Zaire, where the use of mercenaries has been yet another sign of a deteriorating political situation, it is recommended that that practice be condemned and that a warning be issued to the Zairian Government and to all parties to the conflict that they must cease attacks on the civilian population and refrain from the use of mercenaries, and that they will be punished, expelled from Zaire and banned from re-entering the country if evidence of their participation in criminal acts is uncovered.

Bearing in mind that armed conflicts continued in the territory of the former Federal Republic of Yugoslavia during 1993, and that there is also evidence of the presence of mercenaries who participated in grave human rights violations, it is recommended that the Commission should include in all the resolutions it adopts in this connection the condemnation of the recruitment and use of mercenaries by any of the parties to the conflict and, at the same time, that the evidence gathered on the participation of mercenaries in criminal acts be used to initiate the processes of investigation and judicial punishment for the commission of such criminal acts.

Concerning the armed conflicts which have broken out in some of the States members of the former Union of Soviet Socialist Republics, it is recommended that, in addition to the national and international initiatives for peace and friendship in this vast region, the Commission should expressly condemn the use of mercenaries by any of the parties to the armed conflicts which are still continuing and in those which are over or partially over. The recommendation should also contain an appeal to all States of the region to strengthen their criminal legislation by expressly prescribing punishment for mercenary activities and to impose penalties on anyone who has been acting as a mercenary either individually or by forming an irregular group.

With regard to the International Convention against the Recruitment, Use, Financing and Training of Mercenaries, the Special Rapporteur recommends that it should be suggested to those States which have not yet ratified it or signalled their intention to accede to it that they consider the advisability of speeding up this process, which would contribute to more effective action by the international community against mercenary activities.

Lastly, and taking into account the previous resolutions of the Commission on Human Rights which have focused on the adverse consequences for the enjoyment of human rights of violence committed by armed groups that spread terror among the population and by drug traffickers it is recommended that the language condemning such activities be reaffirmed and strengthened, and that the Commission also draw attention to the need for more effective action in domestic and international efforts to combat these groups, which violate human rights. The Special Rapporteur recommends that the Commission should further consider the advisability of appointing a working group for the systematic evaluation of reports and communications on acts of violence committed by these armed groups, which spread terror among the population, and by drug traffickers, with adverse effects for the enjoyment of human rights. This working group could also be composed of the Commission's current Special Rapporteurs who are fulfilling thematic mandates.

**BIBLIOGRAPHY.** Obbo, G. Okoth. "Mercenaries and Humanitarian Law, with Particular Reference to Protocol 1 Addition to the Geneva Conventions of 1949," *Indian Journal of International Law* 28, no. 1 (Jan.–March 1988): 33–57. Scholarly article, in English.

## MERCENARISM: INTERNATIONAL CONVENTION AGAINST THE RECRUITMENT, USE, FINANCING AND TRAINING OF MERCENARIES

**(1989).** The Convention, adopted and opened for signature, ratification, and accession by the UN **GENERAL ASSEMBLY** on 4 December 1989, reflects repeated earlier denunciations of the practice of using mercenaries against developing countries and national liberation movements, denunciations which appeared in resolutions of the General Assembly, the **SECURITY COUNCIL,** the **COMMISSION ON HUMAN RIGHTS,** and other bodies. These organs had affirmed, on many occasions, that the practice of using mercenaries in such circumstances constitutes a criminal act and that the mercenaries themselves are criminals and had called upon governments to enact legislation declaring the recruitment, financing, and training of mercenaries in their territory, or even their transit through it, to be punishable offences.

In 1980, the General Assembly, recognizing that the activities of mercenaries are contrary to the fundamental principles of international law and seriously impede the progress of people struggling for self-determination and against foreign domination, established (resolution 35/48) the *Ad Hoc* Committee on the Drafting of an International Convention against the Recruitment, Use, Financing and Training of Mer-

cenaries, composed of 35 member States, and called upon it to elaborate such a Convention at the earliest possible date.

Nine years later, during the 1989 session of the General Assembly, a working group that met during that session succeeded in putting into final form the draft convention which the *Ad Hoc* Committee had substantially completed. The Assembly thereupon adopted, without a recorded vote, the International Convention against the Recruitment, Use, Financing and Training of Mercenaries (resolution 44/34, annex) as follows:

The States Parties to the present Convention,

Reaffirming the purposes and principles enshrined in the Charter of the United Nations and in the Declaration on the Principles of International Law concerning Friendly Relations and Co-operation among States in accordance with the Charter of the United Nations.

Being aware of the recruitment, use, financing and training of mercenaries for activities which violate principles of international law such as those of sovereign equality, political independence, territorial integrity of States and self-determination of peoples,

Affirming that the recruitment, use, financing and training of mercenaries should be considered as offences of grave concern to all States and that any person committing any of these offences should either be prosecuted or extradited,

Convinced of the necessity to develop and enhance international co-operation among States for the prevention, prosecution and punishment of such offences,

Expressing concern at new unlawful international activities linking drug traffickers and mercenaries in the perpetration of violent actions which undermine the constitutional order of States,

Also convinced that the adoption of a convention against the recruitment, use, financing and training of mercenaries would contribute to the eradication of these nefarious activities and thereby to the observance of the purposes and principles enshrined in the Charter of the United Nations,

Cognizant that matters not regulated by such a convention continue to be governed by the rules and principles of international law,

Have agreed as follows:

*Article 1.* For the purposes of the present Convention,

1. A mercenary is any person who:

(a) Is specially recruited locally or abroad in order to fight in an armed conflict;

(b) Is motivated to take part in the hostilities essentially by the desire for private gain and, in fact, is promised, by or on behalf of a party to the conflict, material compensation substantially in excess of that promised or paid to combatants of similar rank and functions in the armed forces of that party;

(c) Is neither a national of a party to the conflict nor a resident of territory controlled by a party to the conflict;

(d) Is not a member of the armed forces of a party to the conflict; and

(e) Has not been sent by a State which is not a party to the conflict on official duty as a member of its armed forces.

2. A mercenary is also any person who, in any other situation:

(a) Is specially recruited locally or abroad for the purpose of participating in a concerted act of violence aimed at:

(i) Overthrowing a Government or otherwise undermining the constitutional order of a State; or

(ii) Undermining the territorial integrity of a State;

(b) Is motivated to take part therein essentially by the desire for significant private gain and is prompted by the promise or payment of material compensation;

(c) Is neither a national nor a resident of the State against which such an act is directed;

(d) Has not been sent by a State on official duty; and

(e) Is not a member of the armed forces of the State on whose territory the act is undertaken.

*Article 2.* Any person who recruits, uses, finances or trains mercenaries, as defined in article 1 of the present Convention, commits an offence for the purposes of the Convention.

*Article 3.* 1. A mercenary, as defined in article 1 of the present Convention, who participates directly in hostilities or in a concerted act of violence, as the case may be, commits an offence for the purposes of the Convention.

2. Nothing in this article limits the scope of application of article 4 of the present Convention.

*Article 4.* An offence is committed by any person who:

(a) Attempts to commit one of the offences set forth in the present Convention;

(b) Is the accomplice of a person who commits or attempts to commit any of the offences set forth in the present Convention.

*Article 5.* 1. States Parties shall not recruit, use, finance or train mercenaries and shall prohibit such activities in accordance with the provisions of the present Convention.

2. States Parties shall not recruit, use, finance or train mercenaries for the purpose of opposing the legitimate exercise of the inalienable right of peoples to self-determination, as recognized by international law, and shall take, in conformity with international law, the appropriate measures to prevent the recruitment, use, financing or training of mercenaries for that purpose.

3. They shall make the offences set forth in the present Convention punishable by appropriate penalties which take into account the grave nature of those offences.

*Article 6.* States Parties shall co-operate in the prevention of the offences set forth in the present Convention, particularly by:

(a) Taking all practicable measure to prevent preparations in their respective territories for the commission of those offences within or outside their territories, including the prohibition of illegal activities of persons, groups and organizations that encourage, instigate, organize or engage in the perpetration of such offences;

(b) Co-ordinating the taking of administrative and other measures as appropriate to prevent the commission of those offences.

*Article 7.* States Parties shall co-operate in taking the necessary measures for the implementation of the present Convention.

*Article 8.* Any State Party having reason to believe that one of the offences set forth in the present Convention has been, is being or will be committed shall, in accordance with its national law, communicate the relevant information, as soon as it comes to its knowledge, directly or through the Secretary-General of the United Nations, to the States Parties affected.

*Article 9.* 1. Each State Party shall take such measures as may be necessary to establish its jurisdiction over any of the offences set forth in the present Convention which are committed:

(a) In its territory or on board a ship or aircraft registered in that State;

(b) By any of its nationals or, if that State considers it appropriate, by those stateless persons who have their habitual residence in that territory.

2. Each State Party shall likewise take such measures as may be necessary to establish its jurisdiction over the offences set forth in articles 2, 3 and 4 of the present Convention in cases where the alleged offender is present in its territory and it does not extradite him to any of the States mentioned in paragraph 1 of this article.

3. The present Convention does not exclude any criminal jurisdiction exercised in accordance with national law.

*Article 10.* 1. Upon being satisfied that the circumstances so warrant, any State Party in whose territory the alleged offender is present shall, in accordance with its laws, take him into custody or take such other measures to ensure his presence for such time as is necessary to enable any criminal or extradition proceedings to be instituted. The State Party shall immediately make a preliminary inquiry into the facts.

2. When a State Party, pursuant to this article, has taken a person into custody or has taken such other measures referred to in paragraph 1 of this article, it shall notify without delay either directly or through the Secretary-General of the United Nations:

(a) The State Party where the offence was committed;

(b) The State Party against which the offence has been directed or attempted;

(c) The State Party of which the natural or juridical person against whom the offence has been directed or attempted is a national;

(d) The State Party of which the alleged offender is a national or, if he is a stateless person, in whose territory he has his habitual residence;

(e) Any other interested State Party which it considers it appropriate to notify.

3. Any person regarding whom the measures referred to in paragraph 1 of this article are being taken shall be entitled:

(a) To communicate without delay with the nearest appropriate representative of the State of which he is a national or which is otherwise entitled to protect his rights or, if he is a stateless person, the State in whose territory he has his habitual residence;

(b) To be visited by a representative of that State.

4. The provisions of paragraph 3 of this article shall be without prejudice to the right of any State Party having a claim to jurisdiction in accordance with article 9, paragraph 1 (*b*), to invite the International Committee of the Red Cross to communicate with and visit the alleged offender.

5. The State which makes the preliminary inquiry contemplated in paragraph 1 of this article shall promptly report its findings to the States referred to in paragraph 2 of this article and indicate whether it intends to exercise jurisdiction.

*Article 11.* Any person regarding whom proceedings are being carried out in connection with any of the offences set forth in the present Convention shall be guaranteed at all stages of the proceedings fair treatment and all the rights and guarantees provided for in the law of the State in question. Applicable norms of international law should be taken into account.

*Article 12.* The State Party in whose territory the alleged offender is found shall, if it does not extradite him, be obliged, without exception whatsoever and whether or not the offence was committed in its territory, to submit the case to its competent authorities for the purpose of prosecution, through proceedings in accordance with the laws of that State. Those authorities shall take their decision in the same manner as in the case of any other offence of a grave nature under the law of that State.

*Article 13.* 1. State Parties shall afford one another the greatest measure of assistance in connection with criminal proceedings brought in respect of the offences set forth in the present Convention, including the supply of all evidence at their disposal necessary for the proceedings. The law of the State whose assistance is requested shall apply in all cases.

2. The provisions of paragraph 1 of this article shall not affect obligations concerning mutual judicial assistance embodied in any other treaty.

*Article 14.* The State Party where the alleged offender is prosecuted shall in accordance with its laws communicate the final outcome of the proceeding to the Secretary-General of the United Nations, who shall transmit the information to the other States concerned.

*Article 15.* 1. The offences set forth in articles 2, 3 and 4 of the present Convention shall be deemed to be included as extraditable offences in any extradition treaty existing between States Parties. States Parties undertake to include such offences as extraditable offences in every extradition treaty to be concluded between them.

2. If a State Party which makes extradition conditional on the existence of a treaty receives a request for extradition from another State Party with which it has no extradition treaty, it may at its option consider the present Convention as the legal basis for extradition in respect of those offences. Extradition shall be subject to the other conditions provided by the law of the requested State.

3. States Parties which do not make extradition conditional on the existence of a treaty shall recognize those offences as extraditable offences between themselves, subject to the conditions provided by the law of the requested State.

4. The offences shall be treated, for the purpose of extradition between States Parties, as if they had been committed not only in the place in which they occurred but also in the territories of the States required to establish their jurisdiction in accordance with article 9 of the present Convention.

*Article 16.* The present Convention shall be applied without prejudice to:

(a) The rules relating to the international responsibility of States;

(b) The law of armed conflict and international humanitarian law, including the provisions relating to the status of combatant or of prisoner of war.

*Article 17.* 1. Any dispute between two or more States Parties concerning the interpretation or application of the present Convention which is not settled by negotiation shall, at the request of one of them, be submitted to arbitration. If, within six months from the date of the request for arbitration, the parties are unable to agree on the organization of the arbitration, any one of those parties may refer the dispute to the International Court of Justice by a request in conformity with the Statute of the Court.

2. Each State may, at the time of signature or ratification of the present Convention or accession thereto, declare that it does not consider itself bound by paragraph 1 of this article. The other States Parties shall not be bound by paragraph 1 of this article with respect to any State Party which has made such a reservation.

3. Any State Party which has made a reservation in accor-

dance with paragraph 2 of this article may at any time withdraw that reservation by notification to the Secretary-General of the United Nations.

*Article 18.* 1. The present Convention shall be open for signature by all States until 31 December 1990 at United Nations Headquarters in New York.

2. The present Convention shall be subject to ratification. The instruments of ratification shall be deposited with the Secretary-General of the United Nations.

3. The present Convention shall remain open for accession by any State. The instruments of accession shall be deposited with the Secretary-General of the United Nations.

*Article 19.* 1. The present Convention shall enter into force on the thirtieth day following the date of deposit of the twenty-second instrument of ratification or accession with the Secretary-General of the United Nations.

2. For each State ratifying or acceding to the Convention after the deposit of the twenty-second instrument of ratification or accession, the Convention shall enter into force on the thirtieth day after deposit by such State of its instrument of ratification or accession.

*Article 20.* 1. Any State Party may denounce the present Convention by written notification to the Secretary-General of the United Nations.

2. Denunciation shall take effect one year after the date on which the notification is received by the Secretary-General of the United Nations.

*Article 21.* The original of the present Convention, of which the Arabic, Chinese, English, French, Russian and Spanish texts are equally authentic, shall be deposited with the Secretary-General of the United Nations, who shall send certified copies thereof to all States.

In witness whereof the undersigned, being duly authorized thereto by their respective Governments, have signed the present Convention, opened for signature at New York on 4 December 1989.

**MEXICO.** The United Mexican States constitute a country in the southern part of North America, between the Pacific Ocean and the Gulf of Mexico. Mexico has borders with Belize, Guatemala, and the United States of America. It achieved independence from Spain in 1821 and became a member of the United Nations in 1945. Its population is estimated to be 86,170,000. More than 56 ethnic groups live in the 23 States of the republic, including the following: Huasteco, Huichol, Maya, Mazahva, Mazateco, Mixteco, Nahuatl, Otomi, Tarahumara, Tarasco, Totonaco, Tzeltal, Tzotzil, and Zapoteco; members of these groups together constitute about 8.5% of the country's total population. Languages commonly used include Spanish and a wide variety of indigenous vernaculars. Christianity (Roman Catholic, 97%; Protestant denominations, 3%) is predominant among those who profess a religious belief. Literacy is estimated at 74%.

The government (1994) took the form of a republic, composed of 31 federated States and a federal district. Each State has its own governor, legislature, and judiciary; the mayor of the federal district is appointed by the president. National executive power is exercised by the president, elected by popular vote for a term of 6 years and ineligible to succeed himself; he appoints a cabinet to assist him in this function. National legislative matters are dealt with by a bicameral Congress consisting of a 64-member Senate, members of which are elected for terms of 6 years, and a 400-member Chamber of Deputies, members of which are elected for 3-year terms. The national judiciary includes federal and local systems, and a Supreme Court. Major political parties include the Institutional Revolutionary Party (PRI), the *Partido Acción Nacional,* and the Unified Socialist Party.

Hernan Cortés undertook the conquest of Mexico for Spain in 1519; and, from that time until 1810, Spanish colonists exploited the country's natural resources while endeavoring to convert to Christianity descendants of the ancient Maya, Aztec, and Zapotec civilizations. By the time Mexico took advantage of Napoleon's subjugation of Spain to revolt and achieve independence in 1821, the country's population had developed into three main groups: the white Spaniards, the Amerindians, and the Mestizos (mixed). Although loosely bound together by adherence to the Roman Catholic faith, there was antagonism between these groups: the Spanish-born and Mexican-born white elements vied for economic and political power, while the Amerindians and Mestizos fought a losing battle against sinking into poverty and even peonage.

Liberal reforms instituted by the constitution of 1857, including secularization of Church property, restrictions on the military, and some land distribution improved the lot of the most severely disadvantaged groups but outraged conservatives who, with the help of Napoleon III, established Maximilian as Emperor in 1864. However, the empire lasted only three years; and the regime of Porfirio Diaz, which followed, was one of outstanding national development, unfortunately sometimes at the expense of the underprivileged classes who lost lands, homes, and jobs in the process.

In the 20th century, after a series of revolts and revolutions, Lazaro Cardenas was installed as president in 1934 and initiated a series of measures to improve the lot of the underprivileged, including the indigenous populations. However, Mexico's financial crises of 1983 and 1984, which had worldwide repercussions when the government was unable to make payments on its foreign debt, produced high unemployment and continues to upset the economic balance of the country and its people.

Every presidential election since 1929 has been won by a candidate nominated by the PRI, although voters have frequently expressed displeasure over 60 years of one-party rule. In 1988, Carlos Salinas de Gortari, son of a former president, was elected for a 6-year term with the support of that party and of a coalition of smaller organizations known as the National Democratic Front. He took office on 1 December 1988 as Mexico struggled to end its worst economic decline in 50 years, committing himself to reform and modernization of the troubled economy and the somewhat discredited political system. However, by the end of Salinas' presidency, his administration was mired in controversy and charges of corruption, including possible involvement in political assassinations.

Political assassinations plagued Mexico in 1994. Within six months of each other, the presidential candidate of the 65-year ruling PRI, Luis Donaldo Colosio Murrieta, and the second-ranking official of the party, Francisco Ruiz Massieu, were assassinated. Massieu's brother, the Deputy Attorney General, issued a 98-page report alleging a PRI conspiracy and cover-up in the death of his brother.

The new PRI candidate, Ernesto Zedillo Ponce de Leon, won the 6-year presidency in August 1994 with 50.18% of the vote. PRI candidates also won 277 of the 300 directly contested seats in the Chamber of Deputies, continuing the 65-year domination of the party.

Amid continuing allegations of official abuse of human rights, the establishment of the National Commission for Human Rights was announced in June 1990. Despite several electoral reforms passed by the government, allegations by the opposition of fraud and corruption and unfairness continued. Economic, educational, agrarian and religious reforms were also passed.

***INDIGENOUS POPULATIONS.*** As regards human rights problems, the most vulnerable groups in Mexico are the indigenous and peasant populations in the states of Oaxaca and Chiapas. Members of these groups are frequently subjected to ill-treatment by the police and security forces; and many cases of abduction, disappearance, and torture have not been resolved by those forces. The government body responsible for the welfare of the indigenous peoples is the National Indigenous Institute. Its objectives include strengthening the capacity of those peoples to defend their individual and social status; and its programs for the promotion of cultural heritage help them to exercise their right to enjoy their own cultural life, to profess and practice their own religions or beliefs, and to use their own language. The Department of Public Information, through its Indigenous Education Office, offers a bilingual-bicultural primary education program in which nearly 500,000 students take part.

***CHIAPAS.*** In the south-eastern state of Chiapas, a predominantly indigenous group called Ejercito Zapatista de Liberacion Nacional (EZLN) declared war against the government. In the Declaration of the Lacandona Jungle it demanded social and economic reforms to aid the poor. The Declaration was timed to coincide with the implementation on 1 January 1994 of the North American Free Trade Agreement (NAFTA). After a brief bombardment by the government in January, it announced a unilateral cease-fire. Fighting continued through 1994.

The Mexican army reportedly conducted extrajudicial executions and torture in an attempt to quell the Chiapas rebellion. The force occupied four towns in the Los Altos region on New Year's Day 1994, calling NAFTA "a death certificate for the Indian peoples of Mexico" and calling for the resignation of President Carlos Salinas de Gortari. After two weeks of heavy fighting and the death of 200 people, President Salinas declared a unilateral ceasefire, but talks between the government and the EZLN broke off in June 1994 and had not resumed by the end of the year.

When the PRI governor-elect of Chiapas was sworn into office in December 1994, opponents also swore in the opposition Democratic Revolutionary Party candidate. He vowed to establish a parallel government near the rain forest stronghold of the EZLN. President Zedillo announced reforms of law enforcement and the judicial system in December 1994 and requested the resignation of the entire Supreme Court, to be replaced by justices with a limited 15-year term.

### REPORT OF THE UN HUMAN RIGHTS COMMITTEE.

The Human Rights Committee considered the third periodic report of Mexico (CCPR/C/76/Add. 2, paras. 169–179) from its 1302nd to 1305th, meetings, held on 28 and 29 March 1994 (see CCPR/C/SR. 1302–1305), and adopted the following comments:

*Factors and Difficulties affecting the Application of the Covenant.*
Socio-economic difficulties and extremely widespread poverty have led to the growing marginalization of a vast portion of the population, in particular street children and members of indigenous groups, who, as a result, are denied the protection of the basic rights guaranteed by the Covenant. Moreover, rural populations are isolated because of the remoteness of agrarian zones from decision-making centres and judicial organs, which impedes the realization of human rights throughout the territory of Mexico.

*Positive Aspects.* The Committee welcomes with satisfaction the establishment of the National Human Rights Commission responsible for conducting investigations and making recommendations to the Government. The Committee notes the establishment of similar commissions within each of the States of the Union at the local level. These new institutions and the development of human rights legislation, which, in particular, prescribes punishment for torture and provides for compensation of victims, reflect progress towards the promotion and protection of human rights in Mexico. The extension of the right to vote to persons who had hitherto been deprived of that right and access to the public service by citizens who are not Mexican nationals by birth are positive developments in ensuring respect for article 25 of the Covenant. Allowing non-governmental organizations the opportunity to visit any part of the country, in particular the sensitive areas, demonstrates the Government's willingness to cooperate with organizations for the defence of human rights.

*Principal Subjects of Concern.* The Committee strongly deplores the events that occurred recently in Chiapas which resulted in many violations of the rights guaranteed by the Covenant, in particular, in articles 6, 7 and 9 thereof. The Committee notes that, since a state of emergency was not declared in Chiapas in early 1994, the authorities have restricted the rights provided for in the Covenant, particularly in articles 9 and 12, without respecting the guarantees provided for therein.

The Committee is disturbed by the large number of complaints concerning acts of torture or arbitrary detention when prosecution and sentencing of the guilty parties occurs very infrequently and falls far short of the recommendations of the National Human Rights Commission of Mexico, which has condemned these acts. Similarly, enforced or involuntary disappearances and extrajudicial executions are not systematically followed by investigations in which the perpetrators are identified, brought to justice and punished and the victims compensated. Lastly, the conditions in prison and other detention centres and the slowness of judicial procedures continue to be a major cause for concern.

As *amparo* proceedings have proved to be ineffective, immediate release of a person who has been irregularly detained is not fully guaranteed in accordance with article 9 of the Covenant.

The Committee deplores the gross violation of both the right to life and the right to freedom of expression constituted by the frequent-murder of journalists, which has reached alarming proportions.

The Committee is further concerned by the conditions in which the rights provided for in articles 21 and 22 of the Covenant are exercised, as evidenced by the severe repression of peaceful demonstrations by striking workers.

The Committee has doubts and concerns about the electoral system and practices and the climate of violence in which the most important elections have taken place. It notes that this situation precludes the full guarantee of free choice by all voters and the participation of all citizens in the conduct of public affairs, in particular through freely chosen representatives, in accordance with article 25 of the Covenant.

Lastly, the Committee has expressed concern about the situation of indigenous populations. Article 27 of the Constitution concerning agrarian reform is often implemented to the detriment of persons belonging to such groups. The delay in resolving problems relating to the distribution of land has weakened the confidence of these populations in both local and federal authorities. Moreover, these persons are subject to special laws, particularly in Chiapas, which could create a situation of discrimination within the meaning of article 26 of the Covenant.

*Suggestions and Recommendations.* The Committee recommends that the State party should provide the National Human Rights Commission with the authority necessary for its effective functioning, in complete independence from the political and administrative authorities, and should allow it to refer cases to the competent judicial authorities where it finds that rights guaranteed by the Covenant have been violated.

The Committee strongly recommends that all cases of extrajudicial execution, torture and arbitrary detention be investigated in order to bring those suspected of having committed such acts before the courts, that those found guilty be punished and that the victims be compensated. Law enforcement officials should be properly trained so that ensuring respect for the basic rights of the persons placed under their control becomes an integral part of their task.

***REPORT OF THE COMMITTEE ON ECONOMIC, SOCIAL AND CULTURAL AFFAIRS.*** The Committee on Economic, Social and Cultural Affairs considered the second periodic report of Mexico on articles 1–15 of that Covenant (E/1900/6/Add. 4, paras. 228–238) at its 33rd to 35th meetings held on 29 and 30 November 1993. At its 49th meeting, held on 10 December 1993, it adopted the following concluding observations:

*Positive Aspects.* The Committee welcomes the efforts made by the State party to carry out a number of programmes and reforms designed to solve the serious economic, social or cultural problems being encountered by the country. It notes the many activities being carried out by the Mexican Human Rights Commission.

The Committee notes the adoption of the National Development Plan 1989–1994 (NDP) which aims, *inter alia,* at facilitating progress in the solution of the country's unemployment problem, as well as the Solidarity Programme (PRONASOL), the objective of which is to enhance the opportunities of the socially deprived for earning a livelihood. The Committee also welcomes the statement of the Government that efforts are being made, with the assistance of the Agricultural Attorney's Office, to help agricultural workers to organize.

*Factors and Difficulties Impeding the Implementation of the Covenant.* The Committee notes that the Government should continue to tackle the economic and social difficulties ingrained in the country and characterized by considerable foreign indebtedness, the inadequacy of budgetary resources earmarked for essential social services and the unequal distribution of national wealth. These difficulties severely affect the most vulnerable segments of society, and in particular children, persons living below the poverty threshold and those belonging to minority groups, such as the many indigenous peoples; they are relevant to the departure of many Mexican migrant workers abroad.

*Principal Subjects of Concern.* The Committee finds it disturbing that a particularly large number of persons live in extreme poverty. In this connection it notes with concern the decline in the purchasing power of the minimum wage during recent years, it being no longer adequate to enable people to live above the poverty line.

Another source of concern is the situation of many children, namely abandoned children, street children or children in extremely difficult circumstances, who are unable to enjoy the economic, social and cultural rights set out in the Covenant and who are particularly vulnerable to criminality, drug addiction and sexual exploitation. A very big percentage of children (34 per cent), concentrated in particular in areas with a large Indian population, appear to have left school without even having been able to complete their primary education and are therefore in a situation that is extremely conducive to various forms of exploitation.

The Committee notes with concern the economic, social and cultural situation of many indigenous groups who suffer from the difficult conditions brought about by the economic situation and by the imbalance of wealth in the country. It notes the difficulties being experienced by these groups in preserving their culture and in teaching their language. It notes that, although the Government publishes and distributes textbooks in 25 languages free of charge, overall government programmes devoted to these groups nevertheless remain inadequate.

The Committee is concerned about the fact that a large segment of the population of Mexico has to endure inadequate living and housing conditions, without access to basic services such as sanitation and potable water.

The Committee is also concerned about the prevalence of forced evictions in both urban and rural areas of Mexico. Of particular concern to the Committee is the large number of people already evicted or threatened with eviction owing to the lack of adequate protection.

*Suggestions and Recommendations.* The Committee recommends that efforts should be made to curb the decline in the purchasing power of the minimum wage and to redeploy certain budgetary resources to benefit the most vulnerable segments of society, and particularly children and persons living below the poverty line. Resources should be made available for indigenous groups to enable them to preserve their language, culture and traditional way of life, and at the same time to promote the economic, social and cultural rights provided for in the Covenant. The Committee recommends in particular that the State party should take energetic steps to mitigate any negative impact that the North American Free Trade Agreement (NAFTA) might have on the enjoyment of the rights set out in the Covenant.

The Committee recommends that the Mexican Human Rights Commission should, in the future, devote greater attention to economic, social and cultural rights.

The Committee recommends that steps should be taken urgently to overcome the grave housing crisis in the country. It further recommends the speedy adoption of policies and measures designed to ensure adequate civic services, security of tenure and the availability of resources to facilitate access low-income communities to affordable housing. The Committee also recommends the increased construction of rental housing, as well as the adoption of other measures to enable Mexico to comply fully with its obligations under article 11 of the Covenant, as dealt with in General Comment No. 4 of the Committee.

***BIBLIOGRAPHY.*** Academia Mexicana de Derechos Humanos (Mexican Academy of Human Rights). *Informe de Actividades de la Academia Mexicana de Derechos Humanos, A.C. Junio 1986–Junio 1987* (Report on the Activities of the Mexican Academy of Human Rights June 1986–June 1987). Mexico City: 1987. NGO report, in Spanish.

Alvarez Icaza, Jose. *Donde y Como se Reprimio la Prensa en Mexico: 1984–1986* (Repression of the Mexican Press: 1984–1986). Mexico City: 1987. Scholarly study, in Spanish.

Americas Watch. *Human Rights in Mexico: A Policy of Impunity.* New York: Human Rights Watch, 1990. NGO report, in English.

———. *Mexico: The New Year's Rebellion: Violations of Human Rights and Humanitarian Law during the Armed Revolt in Chiapas.* New York: Human Rights Watch, 1994. NGO report, in English.

————. *Prison Conditions in Mexico.* New York: Human Rights Watch, 1991. NGO factfinding report, in English.

————. *Unceasing Abuses: Human Rights in Mexico One Year after the Introduction of Reform.* New York: Human Rights Watch, 1991. NGO report, in English.

Amnesty International. *Mexico: Exchange of Communications on Reported Violations of Human Rights in Huitzilan de Serdan, Puebla.* London: 1987. NGO report, in English.

————. *Mexico: Exchange of Correspondence with the Mexican Government on Human Rights Violations in the States of Oaxaca and Chiapas.* London: 1987. NGO report, in English.

————. *Mexico Human Rights in Rural Areas: Exchange of Documents with the Mexican Government on Human Rights Violations in Oaxaca and Chiapas.* London: 1986. NGO mission report, in English.

————. *Mexico: Human Rights Violations against Ch'ol and Tzeltal Indian Activists.* London: 1992. NGO report, in English.

————. "Mexico: Peasant and Indian Victims of Abuses," *Amnesty International Newsletter* 16, no. 8 (June 1986): 8. NGO article, in English.

————. *Mexico: The Persistence of Torture and Impunity.* London: 1993. NGO report, in English.

"Behind Bars: Repression and Protest in Chiapas," *The Other Side of Mexico* 4 (January–March 1988): 4, 6, 8. News article, in English.

Comisión Mexicana de Defensa y Promoción de Derechos Humanos (Mexican Commission for the Defense and Promotion of Human Rights). *Informe sobre Violaciones a los Derechos Humanos en México: Julio 1988–Febrero 1990* (Report on Human Rights Violations in Mexico: July 1988–February 1990). Mexico City, Mexico: 1990. NGO report, in Spanish.

Committee to Protect Journalists. "Drugs and Corruption Deadly Beat for Mexican Press," *CPJ Update* 27 (Jan.–Feb. 1987): 1, 5. NGO article, in English.

Cultural Survival. "Mountain Peoples," *Cultural Survival Quarterly* 10, no. 3 (1986). NGO special issue, in English.

Durand Aleantara, Carlos Humberto. *Minorias Nacionales y Derechos Humanos: El Caso de los Triques de Oaxaca, Mexico* (National Minorities and Human Rights: The Case of the Triquis of Oaxaca, Mexico). Chapingo, Mexico: Asociacion Americana de Juristas, 1987. NGO report, in Spanish.

Federation Internationale des Droits de l'Homme (International Federation of Human Rights). *Mexique: Situation des Droits de l'Homme* (Mexico: Human Rights Situation). Paris: 1985. NGO report, in French.

————. *Rapport sur la Situation des Refugies du Guatemala au Mexique* (Report on the Status of Guatemalan Refugees in Mexico). Paris: 1985. NGO mission report, in French.

Ferris, Elizabeth G. *The Central American Refugees.* New York: Praeger, 1987. Scholarly study, in English.

Huerta Lara, Ma. del Rosario. *Los Movimientos de Derechos Humanos de los Pueblos Indios en Mexico* (Human Rights Movements of the Indian Peoples of Mexico). s.l.: Grupo de Apoyo a Pueblos Indios (Indian Peoples' Support Group), 1992. Scholarly article, in Spanish.

Human Rights Watch. "Mexico," in *Human Rights Watch World Report 1995*, pp. 109–114. New York: 1995. NGO report, in English.

————. *Mexico at the Crossroads: Political Rights and the 1994 Presidential and Congressional Elections.* New York: 1994. NGO factfinding report, in English.

Instituto Nacional Indigenista (National Indigenous Institute) and Centro de Investigación Social Aplicada y Atención Psicologica A.C. (Centre for Applied Social Research and Psychological Work). *Una Aproximación a la Violación de los Derechos Humanos de los Indigenas de Mexico* (An Approximation of the Violation of the Human Rights of Indigenous Peoples in Mexico). Mexico City: 1992. Scholarly monograph, in Spanish.

Inter-Church Committee on Human Rights in Latin America. *A "Democracy" Unmasked: Systematic Human Rights Violations in Mexico.* Toronto, Canada: 1994. NGO report, in English.

Lytton, Timothy. "Exodus and the Struggle for Deliverance: Guatemalan Refugees in Mexico," *International Journal of Refugee Law* (Sept. 1990): 173–180. Scholarly article, in English.

Mexico, Comisión Nacional de Derechos Humanos (National Commission on Human Rights). *First Biannual Report: June–December 1990.* Mexico City: 1990. Government annual report, in English.

Minnesota Advocates for Human Rights. *Conquest Continued: Disregard for Human and Indigenous Rights in the Mexican State of Chiapas.* Minneapolis, MN, USA: 1992. NGO report, in English.

Physicians for Human Rights (PHR); Human Rights Watch. *Mexico: Waiting for Justice in Chiapas.* Boston, MA, USA: 1994. NGO factfinding report, in English.

Reding, Andrew. "Mexico at a Crossroads," *World Policy Journal* 5, no. 4 (Fall 1988): 615–650. Scholarly article, in English.

Stavenhagen, Rodolfo. "Mexico y los Derechos Humanos" (Mexico and Human Rights), *Justicia y Paz* 5, no. 1 (Nov. 1988): 15–21. NGO article, in Spanish.

UN High Commission for Refugees. "Asylum in Mexico: A Proud Tradition," *Refugees* 34 (October 1986): 19–31. IGO magazine article, in English.

U.S. Committee for Refugees. *Running the Gauntlet: The Central American Journey through Mexico.* Washington, D.C.: American Council for Nationalities Service, 1991. NGO report, in English; bibliography, pp. 23–24.

Washington Office on Latin America and Academia Mexicana de Derechos Humanos. *The 1994 Mexican Election: A Question of Credibility.* Washington, D.C.: 1994. NGO report, in English.

Wollny, Hans. "Asylum Policy in Mexico: A Survey," *Journal of Refugee Studies* 4, no. 3 (1991): 219–236. Scholarly article, in English.

**MICRONESIA.** The Federated States of Micronesia lie in the northern Pacific Ocean, about three-quarters of the way between Hawaii and Indonesia. They include four major island groups and 607 islands and one comprised of the states of Yap, Pohnpei, Chuuk, and Kosrae. The predominant religion is Christianity. The population is estimated to be 117,000.

Micronesia has been explored since the 16th century by Spain, Germany, and Japan. In 1947, the UN placed it, as well as the Marshall Islands, under the trusteeship of the United States. There were growing demands for autonomy for the islands from 1965.

Its constitution of 1979 provides for a federal 14-member Congress, with four members elected at-large by each of the four states for four-year terms. The remaining ten seats, carrying two-year terms, are distributed proportionately to the state populations.

The president and vice-president are elected by the Congress from among the four senators-at-large.

In November 1986, the United States of America signed the Compact of Free Association, under which the United States would maintain its responsibility for the defense of the Federated States of Micronesia therein recognized as a sovereign state. Micronesia became a member of the United Nations in 1991 after the UN SECURITY COUNCIL voted in 1990 to end the trusteeship agreement.

**MIDDLE EAST WATCH.** See **HUMAN RIGHTS WATCH.**

**MIGRANT WORKERS.** In 1972, the UN ECONOMIC AND SOCIAL COUNCIL noted with alarm and indignation (resolution 1706 [LIII]) newspaper reports of incidents which involved the illegal transportation of African workers to European countries by criminal elements, and the exploitation of those workers in conditions akin to slavery or forced labor. The council condemned all such clandestine trafficking and exploitation, appealed to the governments concerned to put an end to such practices, and called upon the UN COMMISSION ON HUMAN RIGHTS to study the problem and to prepare recommendations for further action.

Later the same year, the GENERAL ASSEMBLY also expressed concern (resolution 2920 [XXVII]) about the *de facto* discrimination against foreign workers in Europe and elsewhere and urged governments to step up their efforts to eliminate such discrimination. In particular, it recommended that governments which had not done so should ratify the ILO Migration for Employment Convention (revised 1949).

In 1973, the Economic and Social Council (resolution 1789 [LIV]) requested the UN COMMISSION ON THE STATUS OF WOMEN and the SUB-COMMISSION ON PREVENTION OF DISCRIMINATION AND PROTECTION OF MINORITIES to study the question in depth and to recommend further measures to protect the human rights of foreign workers. The Sub-Commission responded by appointing one of its members, Ms. Halima Warzazi (Morocco) as Special Rapporteur to prepare a comprehensive study of the subject. Ms. Warzazi's study, entitled *Exploitation of Labor through Illicit and Clandestine Trafficking* (UN publication, Sales no. E.86.XIV.1), was considered by the Sub-Commission at its 1986 session. The Sub-Commission noted it with appreciation and forwarded it to the Commission on Human Rights.

Meanwhile, the General Assembly had examined the question further under the agenda item "Measures to Improve the Situation and Ensure the Human Rights and Dignity of All Migrant Workers." On 16 December 1977, it adopted a resolution (resolution 32/120) calling upon all States, "taking into account the provisions of the relevant instruments adopted by the International Labor Organization and of the International Convention on the Elimination of all Forms of Racial Discrimination, to take measures to prevent and put to an end all discrimination against migrant workers and to ensure the implementation of such measures."

In particular, the Assembly invited all States:

(a) to extend to migrant workers having regular status in their territories treatment equal to that enjoyed by their own nationals with regard to the enjoyment of fundamental human rights, with particular reference to equality of opportunity and of treatment in respect of employment and occupation, social security, trade union and cultural rights and individual and collective freedoms;

(b) to promote and facilitate by all the means in their power the implementation of the relevant international instruments and the adoption of bilateral agreements designed, *inter alia*, to eliminate the illicit traffic in alien workers; and

(c) to take all necessary and appropriate measures to ensure that the fundamental human rights and acquired social rights of all migrant workers, irrespective of their immigration status, are fully respected under their national legislation.

In 1980, the General Assembly established (resolution 34/172) the Working Group on the Drafting of an International Convention on the Protection of the Rights of All Migrant Workers and their Families, open to all States, to elaborate such an international convention. The working group held sessions during and between annual sessions of the General Assembly. The text of the convention can be found in the entry entitled **MIGRANT WORKERS: INTERNATIONAL CONVENTION ON THE PROTECTION OF THE RIGHTS OF ALL MIGRANT WORKERS AND MEMBERS OF THEIR FAMILIES.**

*SEE ALSO* Work.

**BIBLIOGRAPHY.** Americas Watch, National Coalition for Haitian Refugees, and Caribbean Rights. *Half Measures: Reform, Forced Labour and the Dominican Sugar Industry.* New York: Human Rights Watch, 1991. NGO factfinding report, in English.

————. *Harvesting Oppression: Forced Haitian Labor in the Dominican Sugar Industry.* New York: Human Rights Watch, 1990. NGO factfinding report, in English.

Bilsborrow, Richard E., and Hania Zlotnik. "Preliminary Report of the United Nations Expert Group Meeting on the Feminization of Internal Migration," *International Migration Review* 26, no. 1 (no. 97) (Spring 1992): 138–161. IGO conference report, in English.

Birks, J. S., and C. A. Sinclair. *Nature and Process of Labor*

*Importing: The African in the Gulf States, Kuwait, Bahrain, Qatar, and the United Arab Emirates.* Geneva, Switzerland: International Labour Office, 1978. IGO study, in English.

Catholic Institute for International Relations. *The Labour Trade: Filipino Migrant Workers around the World.* London: 1987. NGO report, in English.

Comite Europeen pour la Defense des Refugies et Immigres (European Committee for the Defense of Refugees and Immigrants). *Land and Liberty: The Struggle of Agricultural Workers of Andalusia.* Forcalquier, France: 1985. NGO report, in English.

Commission on Security and Cooperation in Europe. *Implementation of the Helsinki Accords: CSCE Human Dimension Seminar on Migrant Workers, Report, Briefing, and Documentation, Warsaw, Poland, March 21–25, 1994.* Washington, D.C.: 1994. Government conference report, in English.

Downing, T. E., and G. Kushner, eds. *Human Rights and Anthropology.* Cambridge, MA, USA: Cultural Survival, 1988. Edited collection/bibliography, in English.

Fawcett, J. T., and B. V. Carino, eds. *Pacific Bridges: The New Migration from Asia and the Pacific Islands.* Staten Island, NY, USA: Center for Migration Studies of New York, 1987. NGO document collection, in English.

Goldman, Chris. *Human Rights and the Migratory Labour System.* Roma, Lesotho: Institute of Southern African Studies, 1987. Scholarly study, in English.

International Labour Office. *Migrant Workers Affected by the Gulf Crisis.* Geneva, Switzerland: 1990. IGO report, in English.

*International Migration Review* 20, no. 4 (Winter 1986). Special issue with scholarly articles on "Temporary Worker Programs: Mechanism, Conditions, Consequences," in English.

Isis International. *Rural Women in Latin America.* Rome: 1987. NGO monograph, in English.

Keyter, Carl, comp., ed. *Report of Proceedings of the Second Consultation on Migration and Development.* Organized by the Agency for Industrial Mission and the Transformation Resource Centre, held at the National University of Lesotho, Roma, 1–5 June 1986. Maseru, Lesotho: Transformation of Resource Centre, 1986. Conference proceedings, in English.

Komai, Hiroshi. "Are Foreign Trainees in Japan Disguised Cheap Laborers?" *Migration World* 20, no. 1 (1992): 13–17. Article, in English.

Lawyers Committee for Human Rights. *Expulsions of Haitians and Dominico-Haitians from the Dominican Republic.* New York: 1991. NGO factfinding report, in English.

Lurie, Peter. "AIDS and Labour Policy," *South African Labour Bulletin* 12, no. 8 (Oct. 1987): 80–88. NGO article, in English; bibliography, pp. 86–88.

Miles, Robert, and Jeanne Singer-Kérel, eds. "Migration and Migrants in France," *Ethnic and Racial Studies* 14, no. 3. (July 1991): 265–416. Special issue, in English.

Plender, Richard, ed. *International Migration Law.* Rev. 2nd ed. Dordrecht, the Netherlands: Martinus Nijhoff, 1988. Scholarly edited collection, in English.

Rugege, S. *Legal Aspects of Labor Migration from Lesotho to the Southern African Mines.* Geneva, Switzerland: International Labor Office, 1979. IGO study, in English.

Shah, Nasra M., Sulayman S. Al-Qudsi, and Makhdoom A. Shah. "Asian Women Workers in Kuwait," *International Migration Review* 25, no. 3 (no. 95) (Fall 1991): 464–486. Scholarly article, in English; bibliography, pp. 485–486.

Torrealba, R., and F. Urrea, eds. *Migraciones Internacionales en las Americas* (International Migrations in the Americas). Caracas, Venezuela: Centro de Estudios de Pastoral y Asis-

tencia Migratoria, 1987. NGO document collection/conference proceedings, in Spanish.

Transformation Resource Centre. *Report of a Conference on Successful Small Rural Development Projects.* Conference held at Marakabei, Lesotho, 17–20 Nov. 1988. Marakabei, Lesotho: 1988. NGO conference proceedings, in English.

U.S. Congress, House of Representatives Committee on Foreign Affairs. *The Plight of the Haitian Sugarcane Cutters in the Dominican Republic: Hearing before the Subcommittees on Human Rights and International Organizations, and on Western Hemisphere Affairs, June 11, 1991.* Washington, D.C.: 1991. Government report, in English.

White, P., and C. Kesteloot, eds. "Les communautés étrangères en Europe" (Foreign Communities in Europe), *Espace, populations, sociétés* no. 2 (1990). Special issue, in English and French.

Whiteside, A., and C. Patel. *Black Migrant Workers' Rights in South Africa.* Geneva, Switzerland: International Labour Office, 1986. IGO manual, in English.

## MIGRANT WORKERS: EUROPEAN CONVENTION ON THE LEGAL STATUS OF MIGRANT WORKERS, COUNCIL OF EUROPE (1977).

Concluded by the Committee of Ministers of the **COUNCIL OF EUROPE,** meeting in Strasbourg, on 24 November 1977, the Convention entered into force on 1 May 1983. Its primary purpose is to regulate the legal status of migrant workers in such a way as to ensure that they are treated no less favorably than workers who are nationals of the receiving State in all aspects of living and working conditions. The text of the Convention (*European Treaty Series* 93) is as follows:

The member States of the Council of Europe, signatory hereto,

Considering that the aim of the Council of Europe is to achieve a greater unity between its Members for the purpose of safeguarding and realising the ideals and principles which are their common heritage and facilitating their economic and social progress while respecting human rights and fundamental freedoms;

Considering that the legal status of migrant workers who are nationals of Council of Europe member States should be regulated so as to ensure that as far as possible they are treated no less favourably than workers who are nationals of the receiving State in all aspects of living and working conditions;

Being resolved to facilitate the social advancement of migrant workers and members of their families;

Affirming that the rights and privileges which they grant to each other's nationals are conceded by virtue of the close association uniting the member States of the Council of Europe by means of its Statute,

Have agreed as follows:

### Chapter I

*Article 1. Definition.* 1. For the purpose of this Convention, the term "migrant worker" shall mean a national of a Contracting Party who has been authorised by another Contracting Party to reside in its territory in order to take up paid employment.

2. This Convention shall not apply to:

(a) frontier workers;

(b) artists, other entertainers and sportsmen engaged for a short period and members of a liberal profession;

(c) seamen;

(d) persons undergoing training;

(e) seasonal workers; seasonal migrant workers are those who, being nationals of a Contracting Party, are employed on the territory of another Contracting Party in an activity dependent on the rhythm of the seasons, on the basis of a contract for a specified period or for specified employment;

(f) workers, who are nationals of a Contracting Party, carrying out specific work in the territory of another Contracting Party on behalf of an undertaking having its registered office outside the territory of that Contracting Party.

### Chapter II

*Article 2. Forms of Recruitment.* 1. The recruitment of prospective migrant workers may be carried out either by named or by unnamed request and in the latter case shall be effected through the intermediary of the official authority in the State of origin if such an authority exists and, where appropriate, through the intermediary of the official authority of the receiving State.

2. The administrative costs of recruitment, introduction and placing, when these operations are carried out by an official authority, shall not be borne by the prospective migrant worker.

*Article 3. Medical Examination and Vocational Test.* 1. Recruitment of prospective migrant workers may be preceded by a medical examination and a vocational test.

2. The medical examination and the vocational test are intended to establish whether the prospective migrant worker is physically and mentally fit and technically qualified for the job offered to him and to make certain that his state of health does not endanger public health.

3. Arrangements for the reimbursement of expenses connected with medical examination and vocational test shall be laid down when appropriate by bilateral agreements, so as to ensure that such expenses do not fall upon the prospective migrant worker.

4. A migrant worker to whom an individual offer of employment is made shall not be required, otherwise than on grounds of fraud, to undergo a vocational test except at the employer's request.

*Article 4. Right of Exit—Right to Admission—Administrative Formalities.* 1. Each Contracting Party shall guarantee the following rights to migrant workers:

(a) the right to leave the territory of the Contracting Party of which they are nationals;

(b) the right to admission to the territory of a Contracting Party in order to take up paid employment after being authorised to do so and obtaining the necessary papers.

2. These rights shall be subject to such limitations as are prescribed by legislation and are necessary for the protection of national security, public order, public health or morals.

3. The papers required of the migrant worker for emigration and immigration shall be issued as expeditiously as possible free of charge or on payment of an amount not exceeding their administrative cost.

*Article 5. Formalities and Procedure relating to the Work Contract.* Every migrant worker accepted for employment shall be provided prior to departure for the receiving State with a contract of employment or a definite offer of employment, either of which may be drawn up in one or more of the languages in use in the State of origin and in one or more of the languages in use in the receiving State. The use of at least one language of the State of origin and one language of the receiving State shall be compulsory in the case of recruitment by an official authority or an officially recognised employment bureau.

*Article 6. Information.* 1. The Contracting Parties shall exchange and provide for prospective migrants appropriate information on their residence, conditions of and opportunities for family reunion, the nature of the job, the possibility of a new work contract being concluded after the first has lapsed, the qualifications required, working and living conditions (including the cost of living), remuneration, social security, housing, food, the transfer of savings, travel, and on deductions made from wages in respect of contributions for social protection and social security, taxes and other charges. Information may also be provided on the cultural and religious conditions in the receiving State.

2. In the case of recruitment through an official authority of the receiving State, such information shall be provided, before his departure, in a language which the prospective migrant worker can understand, to enable him to take a decision in full knowledge of the facts. The translation, where necessary, of such information into a language that the prospective migrant worker can understand shall be provided as a general rule by the State of origin.

3. Each Contracting Party undertakes to adopt the appropriate steps to prevent misleading propaganda relating to emigration and immigration.

*Article 7. Travel.* 1. Each Contracting Party undertakes to ensure, in the case of official collective recruitment, that the cost of travel to the receiving State shall never be borne by the migrant worker. The arrangements for payment shall be determined under bilateral agreements, which may also extend these measures to families and to workers recruited individually.

2. In the case of migrant workers and their families in transit through the territory of one Contracting Party en route to the receiving State, or on their return journey to the State of origin, all steps shall be taken by the competent authorities of the transit State to expedite their journey and prevent administrative delays and difficulties.

3. Each Contracting Party shall exempt from import duties and taxes at the time of entry into the receiving State and of the final return of the State of origin and in transit:

(a) the personal effects and movable property of migrant workers and members of their family belonging to their household;

(b) a reasonable quantity of hand-tools and portable equipment necessary for the occupation to be engaged in.

The exemptions referred to above shall be granted in accordance with the laws or regulations in force in the States concerned.

### Chapter III

*Article 8. Work Permit.* 1. Each Contracting Party which allows a migrant worker to enter its territory to take up paid employment shall issue or renew a work permit for him (unless he is exempt from this requirement), subject to the conditions laid down in its legislation.

2. However, a work permit issued for the first time may not as a rule bind the worker to the same employer or the same locality for a period longer than one year.

3. In case of renewal of the migrant worker's work permit, this should as a general rule be for a period of at least one year, insofar as the current state and development of the employment situation permits.

*Article 9. Residence Permit.* 1. Where required by national legislation, each Contracting Party shall issue residence permits to migrant workers who have been authorised to take up paid employment on their territory under conditions laid down in this Convention.

2. The residence permit shall in accordance with the provisions of national legislation be issued and, if necessary, renewed for a period as a general rule at least as long as that of the work permit. When the work permit is valid indefinitely, the residence permit shall as a general rule be issued and, if necessary, renewed for a period of at least one year. It shall be issued and renewed free of charge or for a sum covering administrative costs only.

3. The provisions of this Article shall also apply to members of the migrant worker's family who are authorised to join him in accordance with Article 12 of this Convention.

4. If a migrant worker is no longer in employment, either because he is temporarily incapable of work as a result of illness or accident or because he is involuntarily unemployed, this being duly confirmed by the competent authorities, he shall be allowed for the purpose of the application of Article 25 of this Convention to remain on the territory of the receiving State for a period which should not be less than five months.

Nevertheless, no Contracting Party shall be bound, in the case provided for in the above sub-paragraph, to allow a migrant worker to remain for a period exceeding the period of payment of the unemployment allowance.

5. The residence permit, issued in accordance with the provisions of paragraphs 1 to 3 of this Article, may be withdrawn:

(a) for reasons of national security, public policy or morals;

(b) if the holder refuses, after having been duly informed of the consequences of such refusal, to comply with the measures prescribed for him by an official medical authority with a view to the protection of public health;

(c) if a condition essential to its issue or validity is not fulfilled.

Each Contracting Party nevertheless undertakes to grant to migrant workers whose residence permits have been withdrawn, an effective right to appeal, in accordance with the procedure for which provision is made in its legislation, to a judicial or administrative authority.

*Article 10. Reception.* 1. After arrival in the receiving State, migrant workers and members of their families shall be given all appropriate information and advice as well as all necessary assistance for their settlement and adaptation.

2. For this purpose, migrant workers and members of their families shall be entitled to help and assistance from the social services of the receiving State or from bodies working in the public interest in the receiving State and to help from the consular authorities of their State of origin. Moreover, migrant workers shall be entitled, on the same basis as national workers, to help and assistance from the employment services. However, each Contracting Party shall endeavour to ensure that special social services are available, whenever the situation so demands, to facilitate or co-ordinate the reception of migrant workers and their families.

3. Each Contracting Party undertakes to ensure that migrant workers and members of their families can worship freely, in accordance with their faith; each Contracting Party shall facilitate such worship, within the limit of available means.

*Article 11. Recovery of Sums due in respect of Maintenance.* 1. The status of migrant workers must not interfere with the recovery of sums due in respect of maintenance to persons in the State of origin to whom they have maintenance obligations arising from a family relationship, parentage, marriage or affinity, including a maintenance obligation in respect of a child who is not legitimate.

2. Each Contracting Party shall take the steps necessary to ensure the recovery of sums due in respect of such maintenance, making use as far as possible of the form adopted by the Committee of Ministers of the Council of Europe.

3. As far as possible, each Contracting Party shall take steps to appoint a single national or regional authority to receive and despatch applications for sums due in respect of maintenance provided for in paragraph 1 above.

4. This Article shall not affect existing or future bilateral or multilateral agreements.

*Article 12. Family Reunion.* 1. The spouse of a migrant worker who is lawfully employed in the territory of a Contracting Party and the unmarried children thereof, as long as they are considered to be minors by the relevant law of the receiving State, who are dependent on the migrant worker, are authorised on conditions analogous to those which this Convention applies to the admission of migrant workers and according to the admission procedure prescribed by such law or by international agreements to join the migrant worker in the territory of a Contracting Party, provided that the latter has available for the family housing considered as normal for national workers in the region where the migrant worker is employed. Each Contracting Party may make the giving of authorisation conditional upon a waiting period which shall not exceed twelve months.

2. Any State may, at any time, by declaration addressed to the Secretary General of the Council of Europe, which shall take effect one month after the date of its receipt, make the family reunion referred to in paragraph 1 above further conditional upon the migrant worker having steady resources sufficient to meet the needs of his family.

3. Any State may, at any time, by declaration addressed to the Secretary General of the Council of Europe, which shall take effect one month after the date of its receipt, derogate temporarily from the obligation to give the authorisation provided for in paragraph 1 above, for one or more parts of its territory which it shall designate in its declaration, on the condition that these measures do not conflict with obligations under other international instruments. The declaration shall state the special reasons justifying the derogation with regard to receiving capacity.

Any State availing itself of this possibility of derogation shall keep the Secretary General of the Council of Europe fully informed of the measures which it has taken and shall ensure that these measures are published as soon as possible. It shall also inform the Secretary General of the Council of Europe when such measures cease to operate and the provisions of the Convention are again being fully executed.

The derogation shall not, as a general rule, affect requests for family reunion submitted to the competent authorities, before the declaration is addressed to the Secretary General, by migrant workers already established in the part of the territory concerned.

*Article 13. Housing.* 1. Each Contracting Party shall accord to migrant workers, with regard to access to housing and rents, treatment not less favourable than that accorded to its own nationals, insofar as this matter is covered by domestic laws and regulations.

2. Each Contracting Party shall ensure that the competent national authorities carry out inspections in appropriate cases in collaboration with the respective consular authorities, acting within their competence, to ensure that standards of fitness of accommodations are kept up for migrant workers as for its own nationals.

3. Each Contracting Party undertakes to protect migrant workers against exploitation in respect of rents, in accordance with its laws and regulations on the matter.

4. Each Contracting Party shall ensure, by the means available to the competent national authorities, that the housing of the migrant worker shall be suitable.

*Article 14. Pretraining—Schooling—Linguistic Training—Vocational Training and Retraining.* 1. Migrant workers and members of their families officially admitted to the territory of a Contracting Party shall be entitled, on the same basis and under the same conditions as national workers, to general education and vocational training and retraining and shall be granted access to higher education according to the general regulations governing admission to respective institutions in the receiving State.

2. To promote access to general and vocational schools and to vocational training centres, the receiving State shall facilitate the teaching of its language or, if there are several, one of its languages to migrant workers and members of their families.

3. For the purpose of the application of paragraphs 1 and 2 above, the granting of scholarships shall be left to the discretion of each Contracting Party which shall make efforts to grant the children of migrant workers living with their families in the receiving State—in accordance with the provisions of Article 12 of this Convention—the same facilities in this respect as the receiving State's nationals.

4. The workers' previous attainments, as well as diplomas and vocational qualifications acquired in the State of origin, shall be recognised by each Contracting Party in accordance with arrangements laid down in bilateral and multilateral agreements.

5. The Contracting Parties concerned, acting in close cooperation, shall endeavour to ensure that the vocational training and retraining schemes, within the meaning of this Article, cater as far as possible for the needs of migrant workers with a view to their return to their State of origin.

*Article 15. Teaching of the Migrant Worker's Mother Tongue.* The Contracting Parties concerned shall take action by common accord to arrange, so far as practicable, for the migrant worker's children, special courses for the teaching of the migrant worker's mother tongue, to facilitate, inter alia, their return to their State of origin.

*Article 16. Conditions of Work.* 1. In the matter of conditions of work, migrant workers authorised to take up employment shall enjoy treatment not less favourable than that which applies to national workers by virtue of legislative or administrative provisions, collective labour agreements or custom.

2. It shall not be possible to derogate by individual contract from the principle of equal treatment referred to in the foregoing paragraph.

*Article 17. Transfer of Savings.* 1. Each Contracting Party shall permit, according to the arrangements laid down by its legislation, the transfer of all or such parts of the earnings and savings of migrant workers as the latter may wish to transfer.

This provision shall apply also to the transfer of sums due by migrant workers in respect of maintenance. The transfer of sums due by migrant workers in respect of maintenance shall on no account be hindered or prevented.

2. Each Contracting Party shall permit, under bilateral agreements or by any other means, the transfer of such sums as remain due to migrant workers when they leave the territory of the receiving State.

*Article 18. Social Security.* 1. Each Contracting Party undertakes to grant within its territory, to migrant workers and members of their families, equality of treatment with its own nationals, in the matter of social security, subject to conditions required by national legislation and by bilateral and multilateral agreements already concluded or to be concluded between the Contracting Parties concerned.

2. The Contracting Parties shall moreover endeavour to secure to migrant workers and members of their families the conservation of rights in course of acquisition and acquired rights, as well as provision of benefits abroad, through bilateral and multilateral agreements.

*Article 19. Social and Medical Assistance.* Each Contracting Party undertakes to grant within its territory, to migrant workers and members of their families who are lawfully present in its territory, social and medical assistance on the same basis as nationals in accordance with the obligations it has assumed by virtue of other international agreements and in particular of the European Convention on Social and Medical Assistance of 1953.

*Article 20. Industrial Accidents and Occupational Diseases—Industrial Hygiene.* 1. With regard to the prevention of industrial accidents and occupational diseases and to industrial hygiene, migrant workers shall enjoy the same rights and protection as national workers, in application of the laws of a Contracting Party and collective agreements and having regard to their particular situation.

2. A migrant worker who is victim of an industrial accident or who has contracted an occupational disease in the territory of the receiving State shall benefit from occupational rehabilitation on the same basis as national workers.

*Article 21. Inspection of Working Conditions.* Each Contracting Party shall inspect or provide for inspection of the conditions of work of migrant workers in the same manner as for national workers. Such inspection shall be carried out by the competent bodies or institutions of the receiving State and by any other authority authorised by the receiving State.

*Article 22. Death.* Each Contracting Party shall take care, within the framework of its laws and, if need be, within the framework of bilateral agreements, that steps are taken to provide all help and assistance necessary for the transport to the State of origin of the bodies of migrant workers deceased as the result of an industrial accident.

*Article 23. Taxation on Earnings.* 1. In the matter of earnings and without prejudice to the provisions on double taxation contained in agreements already concluded or which may in future be concluded between Contracting Parties, migrant workers shall not be liable, in the territory of a Contracting Party, to duties, charges, taxes or contributions of any description whatsoever either higher or more burdensome than those imposed on nationals in similar circumstances. In particular, they shall be entitled to deductions or exemptions from taxes or charges and to all allowances, including allowances for dependants.

2. The Contracting Parties shall decide between themselves, by bilateral or multilateral agreements on double taxation, what measures might be taken to avoid double taxation on the earnings of migrant workers.

*Article 24. Expiry of Contract and Discharge.* 1. On the expiry of a work contract concluded for a specified period at the end of the period agreed on and in the case of anticipated cancellation of such a contract or cancellation of a work contract for an unspecified period, migrant workers shall be accorded treatment not less favourable than that accorded to national workers under the provisions of national legislation or collective labour agreements.

2. In the event of individual or collective dismissal, migrant workers shall receive the treatment applicable to national workers under national legislation or collective labour agreements, particularly as regards the form and period of notice, the compensation provided for in legislation or agreements or such as may be due in cases of unwarranted cancellation of their work contracts.

*Article 25. Re-employment.* 1. If a migrant worker loses his job for reasons beyond his control, such as redundancy or prolonged illness, the competent authority of the receiving State shall facilitate his re-employment in accordance with the laws and regulations of that State.

2. To this end the receiving State shall promote the measures necessary to ensure, as far as possible, the vocational retraining and occupational rehabilitation of the migrant worker in question, provided that he intends to continue in employment in the State concerned afterwards.

*Article 26. Right of Access to the Courts and Administrative Authorities in the Receiving State.* 1. Each Contracting Party shall secure to migrant workers treatment not less favourable than that of its own nationals in respect of legal proceedings. Migrant workers shall be entitled, under the same conditions as nationals, to full legal and judicial protection of their persons and property and of their rights and interests; in particular, they shall have, in the same manner as nationals, the right of access to the competent courts and administrative authorities, in accordance with the law of the receiving State, and the right to obtain the assistance of any person of their choice who is qualified by the law of that State, for instance in disputes with employers, members of their families or third parties. The rules of private international law of the receiving State shall not be affected by this Article.

2. Each Contracting Party shall provide migrant workers with legal assistance on the same conditions as for their own nationals and, in the case of civil or criminal proceedings, the possibility of obtaining the assistance of an interpreter where they cannot understand or speak the language used in court.

*Article 27. Use of Employment Services.* Each Contracting Party recognises the right of migrant workers and of the members of their families officially admitted to its territory to make use of employment services under the same conditions as national workers subject to the legal provisions and regulations and administrative practice, including conditions of access, in force in that State.

*Article 28. Exercise of the Right to Organise.* Each Contracting Party shall allow to migrant workers the right to organise for the protection of their economic and social interests on the conditions provided for by national legislation for its own nationals.

*Article 29. Participation in the Affairs of the Undertaking.* Each Contracting Party shall facilitate as far as possible the participation of migrant workers in the affairs of the undertaking on the same conditions as national workers.

## Chapter IV

*Article 30. Return Home.* 1. Each Contracting Party shall, as far as possible, take appropriate measures to assist migrant workers and their families on the occasion of their final return to their State of origin, and in particular the steps referred to in paragraphs 2 and 3 of Article 7 of this Convention. The provision of financial assistance shall be left to the discretion of each Contracting Party.

2. To enable migrant workers to know, before they set out on their return journey, the conditions on which they will be able to resettle in their State of origin, this State shall communicate to the receiving State, which shall keep available for those who request it, information regarding in particular:

(a) possibilities and conditions of employment in the State of origin;

(b) financial aid granted for economic reintegration;

(c) the maintenance of social security rights acquired abroad;

(d) steps to be taken to facilitate the finding of accommodation;

(e) equivalence accorded to occupational qualifications obtained abroad and any tests to be passed to secure their official recognition;

(f) equivalence accorded to educational qualifications, so that migrant workers' children can be admitted to schools without down-grading.

## Chapter V

*Article 31. Conservation of Acquired Rights.* No provision of this Convention may be interpreted as justifying less favourable treatment than that enjoyed by migrant workers under the national legislation of the receiving State or under bilateral and multilateral agreements to which that State is a Contracting Party.

*Article 32. Relations between this Convention and the Laws of the Contracting Parties or International Agreements.* The provisions of this Convention shall not prejudice the provisions of the laws of the Contracting Parties or of any bilateral or multilateral treaties, conventions, agreements or arrangements, as well as the steps taken to implement them, which are already in force, or may come into force, and under which more favourable treatment has been, or would be, accorded to the persons protected by the Convention.

*Article 33. Application of the Convention.* 1. A Consultative Committee shall be set up within a year of the entry into force of this Convention.

2. Each Contracting Party shall appoint a representative to the Consultative Committee. Any other member State of the Council of Europe may be represented by an observer with the right to speak.

3. The Consultative Committee shall examine any proposals submitted to it by one of the Contracting Parties with a view to facilitating or improving the application of the Convention, as well as any proposal to amend it.

4. The opinions and recommendations of the Consultative Committee shall be adopted by a majority of the members of the Committee; however, proposals to amend the Convention shall be adopted unanimously by the members of the Committee.

5. The opinions, recommendations and proposals of the Consultative Committee referred to above shall be addressed

to the Committee of Ministers of the Council of Europe, which shall decide on the action to be taken.

6. The Consultative Committee shall be convened by the Secretary General of the Council of Europe and shall meet, as a general rule, at least once every two years and, in addition, whenever at least two Contracting Parties or the Committee of Ministers so requests. The committee shall also meet at the request of one Contracting Party whenever the provisions of paragraph 3 of Article 12 are applied.

7. The Consultative Committee shall draw up periodically, for the attention of the Committee of Ministers, a report containing information regarding the laws and regulations in force in the territory of the Contracting Parties in respect of matters provided for in this Convention.

### Chapter VI

*Article 34. Signature, Ratification and Entry into Force.* 1. This Convention shall be open to signature by the member States of the Council of Europe. It shall be subject to ratification, acceptance or approval. Instruments of ratification, acceptance or approval shall be deposited with the Secretary General of the Council of Europe.

2. This Convention shall enter into force on the first day of the third month following the date of the deposit of the fifth instrument of ratification, acceptance or approval.

3. In respect of a signatory State ratifying, approving or accepting subsequently, the Convention shall enter into force on the first day of the third month following the date of the deposit of its instrument of ratification, acceptance or approval.

*Article 35. Territorial Scope.* 1. Any State may, at the time of signature or when depositing its instrument of ratification, acceptance or approval or at any later date, by declaration addressed to the Secretary General of the Council of Europe, extend the application of this Convention to all or any of the territories for whose international relations it is responsible or on whose behalf it is authorised to give undertakings.

2. Any declaration made in pursuance of the preceding paragraph may, in respect of any territory mentioned in such declaration, be withdrawn. Such withdrawal shall take effect six months after receipt by the Secretary General of the Council of Europe of the declaration of withdrawal.

*Article 36. Reservations.* 1. Any State may, at the time of signature or when depositing its instrument of ratification, acceptance or approval, make one or more reservations which may relate to no more than nine articles of Chapters II to IV inclusive, other than Articles 4, 8, 9, 12, 16, 17, 20, 25, 26.

2. Any State may, at any time, wholly or partly withdraw a reservation it has made in accordance with the foregoing paragraph by means of a declaration addressed to the Secretary General of the Council of Europe, which shall become effective as from the date of its receipt.

*Article 37. Denunciation of the Convention.* 1. Each Contracting Party may denounce this Convention by notification addressed to the Secretary General of the Council of Europe, which shall take effect six months after the date of its receipt.

2. No denunciation may be made within five years of the date of the entry into force of the Convention in respect of the Contracting Party concerned.

3. Each Contracting Party which ceases to be a Member of the Council of Europe shall cease to be a Party to this Convention six months after the date on which it loses its quality as a Member of the Council of Europe.

*Article 38. Notifications.* The Secretary General of the Council of Europe shall notify the member States of the Council of:

(a) any signature;

(b) the deposit of any instrument of ratification, acceptance or approval;

(c) any notification received in respect of paragraphs 2 and 3 of Article 12;

(d) any date of entry into force of this Convention in accordance with Article 34 thereof;

(e) any declaration received in pursuance of the provisions of Article 35;

(f) any reservation made in pursuance of the provisions of paragraph 1 of Article 36;

(g) withdrawal of any reservation carried out in pursuance of the provisions of paragraph 2 of Article 36;

(h) any notification received in pursuance of the provisions of Article 37 and the date on which denunciation takes place.

In witness whereof, the undersigned, being duly authorised thereto, have signed this Convention.

Done at Strasbourg, this 24th day of November 1977, in English and in French, both texts being equally authoritative, in a single copy which shall remain deposited in the archives of the Council of Europe. The Secretary General of the Council of Europe shall transmit certified copies to each of the signatory States.

## MIGRANT WORKERS: ILO MIGRANT WORKERS (SUPPLEMENTARY PROVISIONS) CONVENTION (1975).

Formally entitled Convention (No. 143) concerning Migrations in Abusive Conditions and the Promotion of Equality of Opportunity and Treatment of Migrant Workers, the Convention supplements the earlier ILO Migration for Employment Convention and provides that the States parties undertake to respect the basic human rights of all migrant workers, take steps to eliminate abusive work conditions, and actively promote equality of opportunity and treatment.

The Convention was adopted by the International Labour Conference (60th session) on 24 June 1975 and entered into force on 9 December 1978. The text of the Convention (*International Labour Conventions and Recommendations, 1919–1981,* p. 821), with the exception of the ILO standard final provisions (articles 17–24), is as follows:

The General Conference of the International Labour Organisation,

Having been convened at Geneva by the Governing Body of the International Labour Office, and having met in its Sixtieth Session on 4 June 1975, and

Considering that the Preamble of the Constitution of the International Labour Organisation assigns to it the task of protecting "the interests of workers when employed in countries other than their own", and

Considering that the Declaration of Philadelphia reaffirms, among the principles on which the Organisation is based, that "labour is not a commodity", and that "poverty anywhere constitutes a danger to prosperity everywhere", and recognises the solemn obligation of the ILO to further programmes which will achieve in particular full employment through "the transfer of labour, including for employment . . . ",

Considering the ILO World Employment Programme and the Employment Policy Convention and Recommendation, 1964, and emphasising the need to avoid the excessive and uncontrolled or unassisted increase of migratory movements because of their negative social and human consequences, and

Considering that in order to overcome underdevelopment and structural and chronic unemployment, the governments of many countries increasingly stress the desirability of encouraging the transfer of capital and technology rather than the transfer of workers in accordance with the needs and requests of these countries in the reciprocal interest of the countries of origin and the countries of employment, and

Considering the right of everyone to leave any country, including his own, and to enter his own country, as set forth in the Universal Declaration of Human Rights and the International Covenant on Civil and Political Rights, and

Recalling the provisions contained in the Migration for Employment Convention and Recommendation (Revised), 1949, in the Protection of Migrant Workers (Underdeveloped Countries) Recommendation, 1955, in the Employment Policy Convention and Recommendation, 1964, in the Employment Service Convention and Recommendation, 1948, and in the Fee-Charging Employment Agencies Convention (Revised), 1949, which deal with such matters as the regulation of the recruitment, introduction and placing of migrant workers, the provision of accurate information relating to migration, the minimum conditions to be enjoyed by migrants in transit and on arrival, the adoption of an active employment policy and international collaboration in these matters, and

Considering that the migration of workers due to conditions in labour markets should take place under the responsibility of official agencies for employment or in accordance with the relevant bilateral or multilateral agreements, in particular those permitting free circulation of workers, and

Considering that evidence of the existence of illicit and clandestine trafficking in labour calls for further standards specifically aimed at eliminating these abuses, and

Recalling the provisions of the Migration for Employment Convention (Revised), 1949, which require ratifying Members to apply to immigrants lawfully within their territory treatment not less favourable than that which they apply to their nationals in respect of a variety of matters which it enumerates, in so far as these are regulated by laws or regulations or subject to the control of administrative authorities, and

Recalling that the definition of the term "discrimination" in the Discrimination (Employment and Occupation) Convention, 1958, does not mandatorily include distinctions on the basis of nationality, and

Considering that further standards, covering also social security, are desirable in order to promote equality of opportunity and treatment of migrant workers and, with regard to matters regulated by laws or regulations or subject to the control of administrative authorities, ensure treatment at least equal to that of nationals, and

Noting that, for the full success of action regarding the very varied problems of migrant workers, it is essential that there be close co-operation with the United Nations and other specialised agencies, and

Noting that, in the framing of the following standards, account has been taken of the work of the United Nations and of other specialised agencies and that, with a view to avoiding duplication and to ensuring appropriate co-ordination, there will be continuing co-operation in promoting and securing the application of the standards, and

Having decided upon the adoption of certain proposals with regard to migrant workers, which is the fifth item on the agenda of the session, and

Having determined that these proposals shall take the form of an international Convention supplementing the Migration for Employment Convention (Revised), 1949, and the Discrimination (Employment and Occupation) Convention, 1958, adopts this twenty-fourth day of June of the year one thousand nine hundred and seventy-five the following Convention, which may be cited as the Migrant Workers (Supplementary Provisions) Convention, 1975:

### Part I. Migrations in Abusive Conditions

*Article 1.* Each Member for which this Convention is in force undertakes to respect the basic human rights of all migrant workers.

*Article 2.* 1. Each Member for which this Convention is in force shall systemically seek to determine whether there are illegally employed migrant workers on its territory and whether there depart from, pass through or arrive in its territory any movements of migrants for employment in which the migrants are subjected during their journey, on arrival or during their period of residence and employment to conditions contravening relevant international multilateral or bilateral instruments or agreements, or national laws or regulations.

2. The representative organisations of employers and workers shall be fully consulted and enabled to furnish any information in their possession on this subject.

*Article 3.* Each Member shall adopt all necessary and appropriate measures, both within its jurisdiction and in collaboration with other Members—

(a) to suppress clandestine movements of migrants for employment and illegal employment of migrants, and

(b) against the organisers of illicit or clandestine movements of migrants for employment departing from, passing through or arriving in its territory, and against those who employ workers who have immigrated in illegal conditions, in order to prevent and to eliminate the abuses referred to in Article 2 of this Convention.

*Article 4.* In particular, Members shall take such measures as are necessary, at the national and the international level, for systematic contact and exchange of information on the subject with other States, in consultation with representative organisations of employers and workers.

*Article 5.* One of the purposes of the measures taken under Articles 3 and 4 of this Convention shall be that the authors of manpower trafficking can be prosecuted whatever the country from which they exercise their activities.

*Article 6.* 1. Provision shall be made under national laws or regulations for the effective detection of the illegal employment of migrant workers and for the definition and the application of administrative, civil and penal sanctions, which include imprisonment in their range, in respect of the illegal employment of migrant workers, in respect of the organisation of movements of migrants for employment defined as involving the abuses referred to in Article 2 of this Convention, and in respect of knowing assistance to such movements, whether for profit or otherwise.

2. Where an employer is prosecuted by virtue of the provision made in pursuance of this Article, he shall have the right to furnish proof of his good faith.

*Article 7.* The representative organisations of employers and workers shall be consulted in regard to the laws and regulations and other measures provided for in this Convention and designed to prevent and eliminate the abuses referred to above, and the possibility of their taking initiatives for this purpose shall be recognised.

*Article 8.* 1. On condition that he has resided legally in the territory for the purpose of employment, the migrant workers shall not be regarded as in an illegal or irregular situation by the mere fact of the loss of his employment, which shall not in itself imply the withdrawal of his authorisation of residence or, as the case may be, work permit.

2. Accordingly, he shall enjoy equality of treatment with nationals in respect in particular of guarantees of security of employment, the provision of alternative employment, relief work and retraining.

*Article 9.* 1. Without prejudice to measures designed to control movements of migrants for employment by ensuring that migrant workers enter national territory and are admitted to employment in conformity with the relevant laws and regulations, the migrant worker shall, in cases in which these laws and regulations have not been respected and in which his position cannot be regularised, enjoy equality of treatment for himself and his family in respect of rights arising out of past employment as regards remuneration, social security and other benefits.

2. In case of dispute about the rights referred to in the preceding paragraph, the worker shall have the possibility of presenting his case to a competent body, either himself or through a representative.

3. In case of expulsion of the worker or his family, the cost shall not be borne by them.

4. Nothing in this Convention shall prevent Members from giving persons who are illegally residing or working within the country the right to stay and to take up legal employment.

### Part II. Equality of Opportunity and Treatment

*Article 10.* Each Member for which the Convention is in force undertakes to declare and pursue a national policy designed to promote and to guarantee, by methods appropriate to national conditions and practice, equality of opportunity and treatment in respect of employment and occupation, of social security, of trade union and cultural rights and of individual and collective freedoms for persons who as migrant workers or as members of their families are lawfully within its territory.

*Article 11.* 1. For the purpose of this Part of this Convention, the term "migrant worker" means a person who migrates or who has migrated from one country to another with a view to being employed otherwise than on his own account and includes any person regularly admitted as a migrant worker.

2. This Part of this Convention does not apply to—

(a) frontier workers;

(b) artistes and members of the liberal professions who have entered the country on a short-term basis;

(c) seamen;

(d) persons coming specifically for purposes of training or education;

(e) employees of organisations or undertakings operating within the territory of a country who have been admitted temporarily to that country at the request of their employer to undertake specific duties or assignments, for a limited and defined period of time, and who are required to leave that country on the completion of their duties or assignments.

*Article 12.* Each Member shall, by methods appropriate to national conditions and practice—

(a) seek the co-operation of employers' and workers' organisations and other appropriate bodies in promoting the acceptance and observance of the policy provided for in Article 10 of this Convention;

(b) enact such legislation and promote such educational programmes as may be calculated to secure the acceptance and observance of the policy;

(c) take measures, encourage educational programmes and develop other activities aimed at acquainting migrant workers as fully as possible with the policy, with their rights and obligations and with activities designed to give effective assistance to migrant workers in the exercise of their rights and for their protection;

(d) repeal any statutory provisions and modify any administrative instructions or practices which are inconsistent with the policy;

(e) in consultation with representative organisations of employers and workers, formulate and apply a social policy appropriate to national conditions and practice which enables migrant workers and their families to share in advantages enjoyed by its nationals while taking account, without adversely affecting the principle of equality of opportunity and treatment, of such special needs as they may have until they are adapted to the society of the country of employment;

(f) take all steps to assist and encourage the efforts of migrant workers and their families to preserve their national and ethnic identity and their cultural ties with their country of origin, including the possibility for children to be given some knowledge of their mother tongue;

(g) guarantee equality of treatment, with regard to working conditions, for all migrant workers who perform the same activity whatever might be the particular conditions of their employment.

*Article 13.* 1. A Member may take all necessary measures which fall within its competence and collaborate with other Members to facilitate the reunification of the families of all migrant workers legally residing in its territory.

2. The members of the family of the migrant worker to which this Article applies are the spouse and dependent children, father and mother.

*Article 14.* A Member may—

(a) make the free choice of employment, while assuring migrant workers the right to geographical mobility, subject to the conditions that the migrant worker has resided lawfully in its territory for the purpose of employment for a prescribed period not exceeding two years or, if its laws or regulations provide for contracts for a fixed term of less than two years, that the worker has completed his first work contract;

(b) after appropriate consultation with the representative organisations of employers and workers, make regulations concerning recognition of occupational qualifications acquired outside its territory, including certificates and diplomas;

(c) restrict access to limited categories of employment or functions where this is necessary in the interests of the State.

## Part III. Final Provisions

*Article 15.* This Convention does not prevent Members from concluding multilateral or bilateral agreements with a view to resolving problems arising from its application.

*Article 16.* 1. Any Member which ratifies this Convention may, by a declaration appended to its ratification, exclude either Part I or Part II from its acceptance of the Convention.

2. Any Member which has made such a declaration may at any time cancel that declaration by a subsequent declaration.

3. Every Member for which a declaration made under paragraph 1 of this Article is in force shall indicate in its reports upon the application of this Convention the position of its law and practice in regard to the provisions of the Part excluded from its acceptance, the extent to which effect has been given, or is proposed to be given, to the said provision and the reasons for which it has not yet included them in its acceptance of the Convention. . . .

**MIGRANT WORKERS: INTERNATIONAL CONVENTION ON THE PROTECTION OF THE RIGHTS OF ALL MIGRANT WORKERS AND MEMBERS OF THEIR FAMILIES (1990).** The situation of migrant workers, and of members of their families, has been a subject of international concern since 1939, when the first ILO Migration for Employment Convention (No. 66) was adopted. Updated in 1949 as the ILO Migration for Employment Convention, Revised (No. 97), this basic instrument was supplemented in 1975 by the ILO Migrant Workers (Supplementary Provisions) Convention (No. 143). Provisions relating to migrant workers may also be found in the ILO Forced Labor Convention of 1930 (No. 29) and the ILO Abolition of Forced Labor Convention of 1957 (No. 105).

Taking into account the principles and standards set out in these ILO instruments, and those set out in the basic human rights instruments of the United Nations, the UN GENERAL ASSEMBLY decided at its thirty-fourth session (resolution 34/172 of 17 December 1979) that in spite of the existence of an already-established body of principles and standards there was a need for further efforts to improve the situation and to ensure the human rights of migrants. It established a working group open to all member States to prepare an international instrument to meet this need. The working group submitted its final report (A/C.3/45/1) to the Assembly in 1990. The Assembly adopted the draft convention contained therein without a recorded vote and opened it for signature, ratification and accession on 18 December 1990. The text of the Convention, annexed to resolution 45/158, is as follows:

## Part I: Scope and Definitions

*Article 1.* 1. The present Convention is applicable, except as otherwise provided hereafter, to all migrant workers and members of their families without distinction of any kind such as sex, race, colour, language, religion or conviction, political or other opinion, national, ethnic or social origin, nationality, age, economic position, property, marital status, birth or other status.

2. The present Convention shall apply during the entire migration process of migrant workers and members of their families, which comprises preparation for migration, departure, transit and the entire period of stay and remunerated activity in the State of employment as well as return to the State of origin or the State of habitual residence.

*Article 2.* For the purposes of the present Convention:

1. The term "migrant worker" refers to a person who is to be engaged, is engaged or has been engaged in a remunerated activity in a State of which he or she is not a national.

2. (a) The term "frontier worker" refers to a migrant worker who retains his or her habitual residence in a neighbouring State to which he or she normally returns every day or at least once a week;

(b) The term "seasonal worker" refers to a migrant worker whose work by its character is dependent on seasonal conditions and is performed only during part of the year;

(c) The term "seafarer", which includes a fisherman, refers to a migrant worker employed on board a vessel registered in a State of which he or she is not a national;

(d) The term "worker on an offshore installation" refers to a migrant worker employed on an offshore installation that is under the jurisdiction of a State of which he or she is not a national;

(e) The term "itinerant worker" refers to a migrant worker who, having his or her habitual residence in one State, has to travel to another State or States for short periods, owing to the nature of his or her occupation;

(f) The term "project-tied worker" refers to a migrant worker admitted to a State of employment for a defined period to work solely on a specific project being carried out in that State by his or her employer;

(g) The term "specified-employment worker" refers to a migrant worker:

(i) Who has been sent by his or her employer for a restricted and defined period of time to a State of employment to undertake a specific assignment or duty; or

(ii) Who engages for a restricted and defined period of time in work that requires professional, commercial, technical or other highly specialized skill; or

(iii) Who, upon the request of his or her employer in the State of employment, engages for a restricted and defined period of time in work whose nature is transitory or brief, and who is required to depart from the State of employment either at the expiration of his or her authorized period of stay, or earlier if he or she no longer undertakes that specific assignment or duty or engages in that work;

(h) The term "self-employed worker" refers to a migrant worker who is engaged in a remunerated activity otherwise than under a contract of employment and who earns his or her living through this activity normally working alone or together with members of his or her family, and to any other migrant worker recognized as self-employed by applicable legislation of the State of employment or bilateral or multilateral agreements.

*Article 3.* The present Convention shall not apply to:

(a) Persons sent or employed by international organizations and agencies or persons sent or employed by a State outside its territory to perform official functions, whose admission and status are regulated by general international law or by specific international agreements or conventions;

(b) Persons sent or employed by a State or on its behalf outside its territory who participate in development programmes and other co-operation programmes, whose admission and status are regulated by agreement with the State of employment and who, in accordance with that agreement, are not considered migrant workers;

(c) Persons taking up residence in a State different from their State of origin as investors;

(d) Refugees and stateless persons, unless such application is provided for in the relevant national legislation of, or international instruments in force for, the State Party concerned;

(e) Students and trainees;

(f) Seafarers and workers on an offshore installation who have not been admitted to take up residence and engage in a remunerated activity in the State of employment.

*Article 4.* For the purposes of the present Convention the term "members of the family" refers to migrant workers or having with them a relationship that, according to applicable law, produces effects equivalent to marriage, as well as their dependent children and other dependent persons who are recognized as members of the family by applicable legislation or applicable bilateral or multilateral agreements between the States concerned.

*Article 5.* For the purposes of the present Convention, migrant workers and members of their families:

(a) Are considered as documented or in a regular situation if they are authorized to enter, to stay and to engage in a remunerated activity in the State of employment pursuant to the law of that State and to international agreements to which that State is a party;

(b) Are considered as non-documented or in an irregular situation if they do not comply with the conditions provided for in subparagraph (a) of the present article.

*Article 6.* For the purposes of the present Convention:

(a) The term "State of origin" means the State of which the person concerned is a national;

(b) The term "State of employment" means a State where the migrant worker is to be engaged, is engaged or has been engaged in a remunerated activity, as the case may be;

(c) The term "State of transit" means any State through which the person concerned passes on any journey to the State of employment or from the State of employment to the State of origin or the State of habitual residence.

### Part II: Non-discrimination with Respect to Rights

*Article 7.* States Parties undertake, in accordance with the international instruments concerning human rights, to respect and to ensure to all migrant workers and members of their families within their territory or subject to their jurisdiction the rights provided for in the present Convention without distinction of any kind such as to sex, race, colour, language, religion or conviction, political or other opinion, national, ethnic or social origin, nationality, age, economic position, property, marital status, birth or other status.

### Part III: Human Rights of All Migrant Workers and Members of Their Families

*Article 8.* 1. Migrant workers and members of their families shall be free to leave any State, including their State of ori-

gin. This right shall not be subject to any restrictions except those that are provided by law, are necessary to protect national security, public order (ordre public), public health or morals or the rights and freedoms of others and are consistent with the other rights recognized in the present part of the Convention.

2. Migrant workers and members of their families shall have the right at any time to enter and remain in their State of origin.

*Article 9.* The right to life of migrant workers and members of their families shall be protected by law.

*Article 10.* No migrant worker or member of his or her family shall be subjected to torture or to cruel, inhuman or degrading treatment or punishment.

*Article 11.* 1. No migrant worker or member of his or her family shall be held in slavery or servitude.

2. No migrant worker or member of his or her family shall be required to perform forced or compulsory labour.

3. Paragraph 2 of the present article shall not be held to preclude, in States where imprisonment with hard labour may be imposed as a punishment for a crime, the performance of hard labour in pursuance of a sentence to such punishment by a competent court.

4. For the purpose of the present article the term "forced or compulsory labour" shall not include:

(a) Any work or service not referred to in paragraph 3 of the present article normally required of a person who is under detention in consequence of a lawful order of a court or of a person during conditional release from such detention;

(b) Any service exacted in cases of emergency or calamity threatening the life or well-being of the community;

(c) Any work or service that forms part of normal civil obligations so far as it is imposed also on citizens of the State concerned.

*Article 12.* 1. Migrant workers and members of their families shall have the right to freedom of thought, conscience and religion. This right shall include freedom to have or to adopt a religion or belief of their choice and freedom either individually or in community with others and in public or private to manifest their religion or belief in worship, observance, practice and teaching.

2. Migrant workers and members of their families shall not be subject to coercion that would impair their freedom to have or to adopt a religion or belief of their choice.

3. Freedom to manifest one's religion or belief may be subject only to such limitations as are prescribed by law and are necessary to protect public safety, order, health or morals or the fundamental rights and freedoms of others.

4. States Parties to the present Convention undertake to have respect for the liberty of parents, at least one of whom is a migrant worker, and, when applicable, legal guardians to ensure the religious and moral education of their children in conformity with their own convictions.

*Article 13.* 1. Migrant workers and members of their families shall have the right to hold opinions without interference.

2. Migrant workers and members of their families shall have the right to freedom of expression; this right shall include freedom to seek, receive and impart information and ideas of all kinds, regardless of frontiers, either orally, in writing or in print, in the form of art or through any other media of their choice.

3. The exercise of the right provided for in paragraph 2 of the present article carries with it special duties and responsibilities. It may therefore be subject to certain restric-

tions, but these shall only be such as are provided by law and are necessary:

(a) For respect of the rights or reputation of others;

(b) For the protection of the national security of the States concerned or of public order (ordre public) or of public health or morals;

(c) For the purpose of preventing any propaganda for war;

(d) For the purpose of preventing any advocacy of national, racial or religious hatred that constitutes incitement to discrimination, hostility or violence.

*Article 14.* No migrant worker or member of his or her family shall be subjected to arbitrary or unlawful interference with his or her privacy, family, home, correspondence or other communications, or to unlawful attacks on his or her honour and reputation. Each migrant worker and member of his or her family shall have the right to the protection of the law against such interference or attacks.

*Article 15.* No migrant worker or member of his or her family shall be arbitrarily deprived of property, whether owned individually or in association with others. Where, under the legislation in force in the State of employment, the assets of a migrant worker or a member of his or her family are expropriated in whole or in part, the person concerned shall have the right to fair and adequate compensation.

*Article 16.* 1. Migrant workers and members of their families shall have the right to liberty and security of person.

2. Migrant workers and members of their families shall be entitled to effective protection by the State against violence, physical injury, threats and intimidation, whether by public officials or by private individuals, groups or institutions.

3. Any verification by law enforcement officials of the identity of migrant workers or members of their families shall be carried out in accordance with procedure established by law.

4. Migrant workers and members of their families shall not be subjected individually or collectively to arbitrary arrest or detention; they shall not be deprived of their liberty except on such grounds and in accordance with such procedures as are established by law.

5. Migrant workers and members of their families who are arrested shall be informed at the time of arrest as far as possible in a language they understand of the reasons for their arrest and they shall be promptly informed in a language they understand of any charges against them.

6. Migrant workers and members of their families who are arrested or detained on a criminal charge shall be brought promptly before a judge or other officer authorized by law to exercise judicial power and shall be entitled to trial within a reasonable time or to release. It shall not be the general rule that while awaiting trial they shall be detained in custody, but release may be subject to guarantees to appear for trial, at any other stage of the judicial proceedings and, should the occasion arise, for the execution of the judgement.

7. When a migrant worker or a member of his or her family is arrested or committed to prison or custody pending trial or is detained in any other manner:

(a) The consular or diplomatic authorities of his or her State of origin or of a State representing the interests of that State shall, if he or she so requests, be informed without delay of his or her arrest or detention and of the reasons therefor;

(b) The person concerned shall have the right to communicate with the said authorities. Any communication by the person concerned to the said authorities shall be for-

warded without delay, and he or she shall also have the right to receive communications sent by the said authorities without delay;

(c) The person concerned shall be informed without delay of this right and of rights deriving from relevant treaties, if any, applicable between the States concerned, to correspond and to meet with representatives of the said authorities and to make arrangements with them for his or her legal representation.

8. Migrant workers and members of their families who are deprived of their liberty by arrest or detention shall be entitled to take proceedings before a court, in order that that court may decide without delay on the lawfulness of their detention and order their release if the detention is not lawful. When they attend such proceedings, they shall have the assistance, if necessary without cost to them, of an interpreter, if they cannot understand or speak the language used.

9. Migrant workers and members of their families who have been victims of unlawful arrest or detention shall have an enforceable right to compensation.

*Article 17.* 1. Migrant workers and members of their families who are deprived of their liberty shall be treated with humanity and with respect for the inherent dignity of the human person and for their cultural identity.

2. Accused migrant workers and members of their families shall, save in exceptional circumstances, be separated from convicted persons and shall be subject to separate treatment appropriate to their status as unconvicted persons. Accused juvenile persons shall be separated from adults and brought as speedily as possible for adjudication.

3. Any migrant worker or member of his or her family who is detained in a State of transit or in a State of employment for violation of provisions relating to migration shall be held, in so far as practicable, separately from convicted persons or persons detained pending trial.

4. During any period of imprisonment in pursuance of a sentence imposed by a court of law, the essential aim of the treatment of a migrant worker or a member of his or her family shall be his or her reformation and social rehabilitation. Juvenile offenders shall be separated from adults and be accorded treatment appropriate to their age and legal status.

5. During detention or imprisonment, migrant workers and members of their families shall enjoy the same rights as nationals to visits by members of their families.

6. Whenever a migrant worker is deprived of his or her liberty, the competent authorities of the State concerned shall pay attention to the problems that may be posed for members of his or her family, in particular for spouses and minor children.

7. Migrant workers and members of their families who are subjected to any form of detention or imprisonment in accordance with the law in force in the State of employment or in the State of transit shall enjoy the same rights as nationals of those States who are in the same situation.

8. If a migrant worker or a member of his or her family is detained for the purpose of verifying any infraction of provisions related to migration, he or she shall not bear any costs arising therefrom.

*Article 18.* 1. Migrant workers and members of their families shall have the right to equality with nationals of the State concerned before the courts and tribunals. In the determination of any criminal charge against them or of their rights and obligations in a suit of law, they shall be entitled to a fair and public hearing by a competent, independent and impartial tribunal established by law.

2. Migrant workers and members of their families who are charged with a criminal offence shall have the right to be presumed innocent until proven guilty according to law.

3. In the determination of any criminal charge against them, migrant workers and members of their families shall be entitled to the following minimum guarantees:

(a) To be informed promptly and in detail in a language they understand of the nature and cause of the charge against them;

(b) To have adequate time and facilities for the preparation of their defence and to communicate with counsel of their own choosing;

(c) To be tried without undue delay;

(d) To be tried in their presence and to defend themselves in person or through legal assistance of their own choosing; to be informed, if they do not have legal assistance, of this right; and to have legal assistance assigned to them, in any case where the interests of justice so require and without payment by them in any such case if they do not have sufficient means to pay;

(e) To examine or have examined the witnesses against them and to obtain the attendance and examination of witnesses on their behalf under the same conditions as witnesses against them;

(f) To have the free assistance of an interpreter if they cannot understand or speak the language used in court;

(g) Not to be compelled to testify against themselves or to confess guilt.

4. In the case of juvenile persons, the procedure shall be such as will take account of their age and the desirability of promoting their rehabilitation.

5. Migrant workers and members of their families convicted of a crime shall have the right to their conviction and sentence being reviewed by a higher tribunal according to law.

6. When a migrant worker or a member of his or her family has, by a final decision, been convicted of a criminal offence and when subsequently his or her conviction has been reversed or he or she has been pardoned on the ground that a new or newly discovered fact shows conclusively that there has been a miscarriage of justice, the person who has suffered punishment as a result of such conviction shall be compensated according to law, unless it is proved that the non-disclosure of the unknown fact in time is wholly or partly attributable to that person.

7. No migrant worker or member of his or her family shall be liable to be tried or punished again for an offence for which he or she has already been finally convicted or acquitted in accordance with the law and penal procedure of the State concerned.

*Article 19.* 1. No migrant worker or member of his or her family shall be held guilty of any criminal offence on account of any act or omission that did not constitute a criminal offence under national or international law at the time when the criminal offence was committed, nor shall a heavier penalty be imposed than the one that was applicable at the time when it was committed. If, subsequent to the commission of the offence, provision is made by law for the imposition of a lighter penalty, he or she shall benefit thereby.

2. Humanitarian considerations related to the status of a migrant worker, in particular with respect to his or her right of residence or work, should be taken into account in imposing a sentence for a criminal offence committed by a migrant worker or a member of his or her family.

*Article 20.* 1. No migrant worker or member of his or her family shall be imprisoned merely on the ground of failure to fulfil a contractual obligation.

2. No migrant worker or member of his or her family shall be deprived of his or her authorization of residence or work permit or expelled merely on the ground of failure to fulfil an obligation arising out of a work contract unless fulfilment of that obligation constitutes a condition for such authorization or permit.

*Article 21.* It shall be unlawful for anyone, other than a public official duly authorized by law, to confiscate, destroy or attempt to destroy identity documents, documents authorizing entry to or stay, residence or establishment in the national territory or work permits. No authorized confiscation of such documents shall take place without delivery of a detailed receipt. In no case shall it be permitted to destroy the passport or equivalent document of a migrant worker or a member of his or her family.

*Article 22.* 1. Migrant workers and members of their families shall not be subject to measures of collective expulsion. Each case of expulsion shall be examined and decided individually.

2. Migrant workers and members of their families may be expelled from the territory of a State Party only in pursuance of a decision taken by the competent authority in accordance with law.

3. The decision shall be communicated to them in a language they understand. Upon their request where not otherwise mandatory, the decision shall be communicated to them in writing and, save in exceptional circumstances on account of national security, the reasons for the decision likewise stated. The persons concerned shall be informed of these rights before or at the latest at the time the decision is rendered.

4. Except where a final decision is pronounced by a judicial authority, the person concerned shall have the right to submit the reason he or she should not be expelled and to have his or her case reviewed by the competent authority, unless compelling reasons of national security require otherwise. Pending such review, the person concerned shall have the right to seek a stay of the decision of expulsion.

5. If a decision of expulsion that has already been executed is subsequently annulled, the person concerned shall have the right to seek compensation according to law and the earlier decision shall not be used to prevent him or her from re-entering the State concerned.

6. In case of expulsion, the person concerned shall have a reasonable opportunity before or after departure to settle any claims for wages and other entitlements due to him or her and any pending liabilities.

7. Without prejudice to the execution of a decision of expulsion, a migrant worker or a member of his or her family who is subject to such a decision may seek entry into a State other than his or her State of origin.

8. In case of expulsion of a migrant worker or a member of his or her family the costs of expulsion shall not be borne by him or her. The person concerned may be required to pay his or her own travel costs.

9. Expulsion from the State of employment shall not in itself prejudice any rights of a migrant worker or a member of his or her family acquired in accordance with the law of that State, including the right to receive wages and other entitlements due to him or her.

*Article 23.* Migrant workers and members of their families shall have the right to have recourse to the protection and assistance of the consular or diplomatic authorities of their

State of origin or of a State representing the interests of that State whenever the rights recognized in the present Convention are impaired. In particular, in case of expulsion, the person concerned shall be informed of this right without delay and the authorities of the expelling State shall facilitate the exercise of such right.

*Article 24.* Every migrant worker and every member of his or her family shall have the right to recognition everywhere as a person before the law.

*Article 25.* 1. Migrant workers shall enjoy treatment not less favourable than that which applies to nationals of the State of employment in respect of remuneration and:

(a) Other conditions of work, that is to say, overtime, hours of work, weekly rest, holidays with pay, safety, health, termination of the employment relationship and any other conditions of work which, according to national law and practice, are covered by these terms;

(b) Other terms of employment, that is to say, minimum age of employment, restriction on home work and any other matters which, according to national law and practice, are considered a term of employment.

2. It shall not be lawful to derogate in private contracts of employment from the principle of equality of treatment referred to in paragraph 1 of the present article.

3. States Parties shall take all appropriate measures to ensure that migrant workers are not deprived of any rights derived from this principle by reason of any irregularity in their stay or employment. In particular, employers shall not be relieved of any legal or contractual obligations, nor shall their obligations be limited in any manner by reason of such irregularity.

*Article 26.* 1. States Parties recognize the right of migrant workers and members of their families:

(a) To take part in meetings and activities of trade unions and of any other associations established in accordance with law, with a view to protecting their economic, social, cultural and other interests, subject only to the rules of the organization concerned;

(b) To join freely any trade union and any such association as aforesaid, subject only to the rules of the organization concerned;

(c) To seek the aid and assistance of any trade union and of any such association as aforesaid.

2. No restrictions may be placed on the exercise of these rights other than those that are prescribed by law and which are necessary in a democratic society in the interests of national security, public order (ordre public) or the protection of the rights and freedoms of others.

*Article 27.* 1. With respect to social security, migrant workers and members of their families shall enjoy in the State of employment the same treatment granted to nationals in so far as they fulfil the requirements provided for by the applicable legislation of that State and the applicable bilateral and multilateral treaties. The competent authorities of the State of origin and the State of employment can at any time establish the necessary arrangements to determine the modalities of application of this norm.

2. Where the applicable legislation does not allow migrant workers and members of their families a benefit, the States concerned shall examine the possibility of reimbursing interested persons the amount of contributions made by them with respect to that benefit on the basis of the treatment granted to nationals who are in similar circumstances.

*Article 28.* Migrant workers and members of their families shall have the right to receive any medical care that is urgently required for the preservation of their life or the avoidance of irreparable harm to their health on the basis of equality of treatment with nationals of the State concerned. Such emergency medical care shall not be refused them by reason of any irregularity with regard to stay or employment.

*Article 29.* Each child of a migrant worker shall have the right to a name, to registration of birth and to a nationality.

*Article 30.* Each child of a migrant worker shall have the basic right of access to education on the basis of equality of treatment with nationals of the State concerned. Access to public pre-school educational institutions or schools shall not be refused or limited by reason of the irregular situation with respect to stay or employment of either parent or by reason of the irregularity of the child's stay in the State of employment.

*Article 31.* 1. States Parties shall ensure respect for the cultural identity of migrant workers and members of their families and shall not prevent them from maintaining their cultural links with their State of origin.

2. States Parties may take appropriate measures to assist and encourage efforts in this respect.

*Article 32.* Upon the termination of their stay in the State of employment, migrant workers and members of their families shall have the right to transfer their earnings and savings and, in accordance with the applicable legislation of the States concerned, their personal effects and belongings.

*Article 33.* 1. Migrant workers and members of their families shall have the right to be informed by the State of origin, the State of employment or the State of transit as the case may be concerning:

(a) Their rights arising out of the present Convention;

(b) The conditions of their admission, their rights and obligations under the law and practice of the State concerned and such other matters as will enable them to comply with administrative or other formalities in that State.

2. States Parties shall take all measures they deem appropriate to disseminate the said information or to ensure that it is provided by employers, trade unions or other appropriate bodies or institutions. As appropriate, they shall co-operate with other States concerned.

3. Such adequate information shall be provided upon request to migrant workers and members of their families, free of charge, and, as far as possible, in a language they are able to understand.

*Article 34.* Nothing in the present part of the Convention shall have the effect of relieving migrant workers and the members of their families from either the obligation to comply with the laws and regulations of any State of transit and the State of employment or the obligation to respect the cultural identity of the inhabitants of such States.

*Article 35.* Nothing in the present part of the Convention shall be interpreted as implying the regularization of the situation of migrant workers or members of their families who are non-documented or in an irregular situation or any right to such regularization of their situation, nor shall it prejudice the measures intended to ensure sound and equitable conditions for international migration as provided in part VI of the present Convention.

## Part IV: Other Rights of Migrant Workers and Members of Their Families Who Are Documented or in a Regular Situation

*Article 36.* Migrant workers and members of their families who are documented or in a regular situation in the State of employment shall enjoy the rights set forth in the present part of the Convention in addition to those set forth in part III.

*Article 37.* Before their departure, or at the latest at the time of their admission to the State of employment, migrant workers and members of their families shall have the right to be fully informed by the State of origin or the State of employment, as appropriate, of all conditions applicable to their admission and particularly those concerning their stay and the remunerated activities in which they may engage as well as of the requirements they must satisfy in the State of employment and the authority to which they must address themselves for any modification of those conditions.

*Article 38.* 1. States of employment shall make every effort to authorize migrant workers and members of their families to be temporarily absent without effect upon their authorization to stay or to work, as the case may be. In doing so, States of employment shall take into account the special needs and obligations of migrant workers and members of their families, in particular in their States of origin.

2. Migrant workers and members of their families shall have the right to be fully informed of the terms on which such temporary absences are authorized.

*Article 39.* 1. Migrant workers and members of their families shall have the right to liberty of movement in the territory of the State of employment and freedom to choose their residence there.

2. Migrant rights mentioned in paragraph 1 of the present article shall not be subject to any restrictions except those that are provided by law, are necessary to protect national security, public order (ordre public), public health or morals, or the rights and freedoms of others and are consistent with the other rights recognized in the present Convention.

*Article 40.* 1. Migrant workers and members of their families shall have the right to form associations and trade unions in the State of employment for the promotion and protection of their economic, social, cultural and other interests.

2. No restrictions may be placed on the exercise of this right other than those that are prescribed by law and are necessary in a democratic society in the interests of national security, public order (ordre public) or the protection of the rights and freedoms of others.

*Article 41.* 1. Migrant workers and members of their families shall have the right to participate in public affairs of their State of origin and to vote and to be elected at elections of that State, in accordance with its legislation.

2. The States concerned shall, as appropriate and in accordance with their legislation, facilitate the exercise of these rights.

*Article 42.* 1. States Parties shall consider the establishment of procedures or institutions through which account may be taken, both in States of origin and in States of employment, of special needs, aspirations and obligations of migrant workers and members of their families and shall envisage, as appropriate, the possibility for migrant workers and members of their families to have their freely chosen representatives in those institutions.

2. States of employment shall facilitate, in accordance with their national legislation, the consultation or participation of migrant workers and members of their families in decisions concerning the life and administration of local communities.

3. Migrant workers may enjoy political rights in the State of employment if that State, in the exercise of its sovereignty, grants them such rights.

*Article 43.* 1. Migrant workers shall enjoy equality of treatment with nationals of the State of employment in relation to:

(a) Access to educational institutions and services subject to the admission requirements and other regulations of the institutions and services concerned;

(b) Access to vocational guidance and placement services;

(c) Access to vocational training and retraining facilities and institutions;

(d) Access to housing, including social housing schemes, and protection against exploitation in respect of rents;

(e) Access to social and health services, provided that the requirements for participation in the respective schemes are met;

(f) Access to co-operatives and self-managed enterprises, which shall not imply a change of their migration status and shall be subject to the rules and regulations of the bodies concerned;

(g) Access to and participation in cultural life.

2. States Parties shall promote conditions to ensure effective equality of treatment to enable migrant workers to enjoy the rights mentioned in paragraph 1 of the present article whenever the terms of their stay, as authorized by the State of employment, meet the appropriate requirements.

3. States of employment shall not prevent an employer of migrant workers from establishing housing or social or cultural facilities for them. Subject to article 70 of the present Convention, a State of employment may make the establishment of such facilities subject to the requirements generally applied in that State concerning their installation.

*Article 44.* 1. States Parties, recognizing that the family is the natural and fundamental group unit of society and is entitled to protection by society and the State, shall take appropriate measures to ensure the protection of the unity of the families of migrant workers.

2. States Parties shall take measures that they deem appropriate and that fall within their competence to facilitate the reunification of migrant workers with their spouses or persons who have with the migrant worker a relationship that, according to applicable law, produces effects equivalent to marriage, as well as with their minor dependent unmarried children.

3. States of employment, on humanitarian grounds, shall favourably consider granting equal treatment, as set forth in paragraph 2 of the present article, to other family members of migrant workers.

*Article 45.* 1. Members of the families of migrant workers shall, in the State of employment, enjoy equality of treatment with nationals of that State in relation to:

(a) Access to educational institutions and services, subject to the admission requirements and other regulations of the institutions and services concerned;

(b) Access to vocational guidance and training institutions and services, provided that requirements for participation are met;

(c) Access to social and health services, provided that requirements for participation in the respective schemes are met;

(d) Access to and participation in cultural life.

2. States of employment shall pursue a policy, where appropriate in collaboration with the States of origin, aimed at facilitating the integration of children of migrant workers in the local school system, particularly in respect of teaching them the local language.

3. States of employment shall endeavour to facilitate for

the children of migrant workers the teaching of their mother tongue and culture and, in this regard, States of origin shall collaborate whenever appropriate.

4. States of employment may provide special schemes of education in the mother tongue of children of migrant workers, if necessary in collaboration with the States of origin.

*Article 46.* Migrant workers and members of their families shall, subject to the applicable legislation of the States concerned, as well as relevant international agreements and the obligations of the States concerned arising out of their participation in customs unions, enjoy exemption from import and export duties and taxes in respect of their personal and household effects as well as the equipment necessary to engage in the remunerated activity for which they were admitted to the State of employment:

(a) Upon departure from the State of origin or State of habitual residence;

(b) Upon initial admission to the State of employment;

(c) Upon final departure from the State of employment;

(d) Upon final return to the State of origin or State of habitual residence.

*Article 47.* 1. Migrant workers shall have the right to transfer their earnings and savings, in particular those funds necessary for the support of their families, from the State of employment to their State of origin or any other State. Such transfers shall be made in conformity with procedures established by applicable legislation of the State concerned and in conformity with applicable international agreements.

2. States concerned shall take appropriate measures to facilitate such transfers.

*Article 48.* 1. Without prejudice to applicable double taxation agreements, migrant workers and members of their families shall, in the matter of earnings in the State of employment:

(a) Not be liable to taxes, duties or charges of any description higher or more onerous than those imposed on nationals in similar circumstances;

(b) Be entitled to deductions or exemptions from taxes of any description and to any tax allowances applicable to nationals in similar circumstances, including tax allowances for dependent members of their families.

2. States Parties shall endeavour to adopt appropriate measures to avoid double taxation of the earnings and savings of migrant workers and members of their families.

*Article 49.* 1. Where separate authorizations to reside and to engage in employment are required by national legislation, the States of employment shall issue to migrant workers authorization of residence for at least the same period of time as their authorization to engage in remunerated activity.

2. Migrant workers who in the State of employment are allowed freely to choose their remunerated activity shall neither be regarded as in an irregular situation nor shall they lose their authorization of residence by the mere fact of the termination of their remunerated activity prior to the expiration of their work permits or similar authorizations.

3. In order to allow migrant workers referred to in paragraph 2 of the present article sufficient time to find alternative remunerated activities, the authorization of residence shall not be withdrawn at least for a period corresponding to that during which they may be entitled to unemployment benefits.

*Article 50.* 1. In the case of death of a migrant worker or dissolution of marriage, the State of employment shall favourably consider granting family members of that migrant worker residing in that State on the basis of family reunion an authorization to stay; the State of employment shall take into account the length of time they have already resided in that State.

2. Members of the family to whom such authorization is not granted shall be allowed before departure a reasonable period of time in order to enable them to settle their affairs in the State of employment.

3. The provisions of paragraphs 1 and 2 of the present article may not be interpreted as adversely affecting any right to stay and work otherwise granted to such family members by the legislation of the State of employment or by bilateral and multilateral treaties applicable to that State.

*Article 51.* Migrant workers who in the State of employment are not permitted freely to choose their remunerated activity shall neither be regarded as in an irregular situation nor shall they lose their authorization of residence by the mere fact of the termination of their remunerated activity prior to the expiration of their work permit, except where the authorization of residence is expressly dependent upon the specific remunerated activity for which they were admitted. Such migrant workers shall have the right to seek alternative employment, participation in public work schemes and retraining during the remaining period of their authorization to work, subject to such conditions and limitations as are specified in the authorization to work.

*Article 52.* 1. Migrant workers in the State of employment shall have the right freely to choose their remunerated activity, subject to the following restrictions or conditions.

2. For any migrant worker a State of employment may:

(a) Restrict access to limited categories of employment, functions, services or activities where this is necessary in the interests of this State and provided for by national legislation;

(b) Restrict free choice of remunerated activity in accordance with its legislation concerning recognition of occupational qualifications acquired outside its territory. However, States Parties concerned shall endeavour to provide for recognition of such qualifications.

3. For migrant workers whose permission to work is limited in time, a State of employment may also:

(a) Make the right freely to choose their remunerated activities subject to the condition that the migrant worker has resided lawfully in its territory for the purpose of remunerated activity for a period of time prescribed in its national legislation that should not exceed two years;

(b) Limit access by a migrant worker to remunerated activities in pursuance of a policy of granting priority to its nationals or to persons who are assimilated to them for these purposes by virtue of legislation or bilateral or multilateral agreements. Any such limitation shall cease to apply to a migrant worker who has resided lawfully in its territory for the purpose of remunerated activity for a period of time prescribed in its national legislation that should not exceed five years.

4. States of employment shall prescribe the conditions under which a migrant worker who has been admitted to take up employment may be authorized to engage in work on his or her own account. Account shall be taken of the period during which the worker has already been lawfully in the State of employment.

*Article 53.* 1. Members of a migrant worker's family who have themselves an authorization of residence or admission that is without limit of time or is automatically renewable shall be permitted freely to choose their remunerated activity under the same conditions as are applicable to the said migrant worker in accordance with article 52 of the present Convention.

2. With respect to members of a migrant worker's family who are not permitted freely to choose their remunerated activity, States Parties shall consider favourably granting them priority in obtaining permission to engage in a remunerated activity over other workers who seek admission to the State of employment, subject to applicable bilateral and multilateral agreements.

*Article 54.* 1. Without prejudice to the terms of their authorization of residence or their permission to work and the rights provided for in articles 25 and 27 of the present Convention, migrant workers shall enjoy equality of treatment with nationals of the State of employment in respect of:

(a) Protection against dismissal;

(b) Unemployment benefits;

(c) Access to public work schemes intended to combat unemployment;

(d) Access to alternative employment in the event of loss of work or termination of other remunerated activity, subject to article 52 of the present Convention.

2. If a migrant worker claims that the terms of his or her work contract have been violated by his or her employer, he or she shall have the right to address his or her case to the competent authorities of the State of employment, on terms provided for in article 18, paragraph 1, of the present Convention.

*Article 55.* Migrant workers who have been granted permission engage in a remunerated activity, subject to the conditions attached to such permission, shall be entitled to equality of treatment with nationals of the State of employment in the exercise of that remunerated activity.

*Article 56.* 1. Migrant workers and members of their families referred to in the present part of the Convention may not be expelled from a State of employment, except for reasons defined in the national legislation of that State, and subject to the safeguards established in part III.

2. Expulsion shall not be resorted to for the purpose of depriving a migrant worker or a member of his or her family of the rights arising out of the authorization of residence and the work permit.

3. In considering whether to expel a migrant worker or a member of his or her family, account should be taken of humanitarian considerations and of the length of time that the person concerned has already resided in the State of employment.

## Part V: Provisions Applicable to Particular Categories of Migrant Workers and Members of Their Families

*Article 57.* The particular categories of migrant workers and members of their families specified in the present part of the Convention who are documented or in a regular situation shall enjoy the rights set forth in part III and, except as modified below, the rights set forth in part IV.

*Article 58.* 1. Frontier workers, as defined in article 2, paragraph 2 (a), of the present Convention, shall be entitled to the rights provided for in part IV that can be applied to them by reason of their presence and work in the territory of the State of employment, taking into account that they do not have their habitual residence in that State.

2. States of employment shall consider favourably granting frontier workers the right freely to choose their remunerated activity after a specified period of time. The granting of that right shall not affect their status as frontier workers.

*Article 59.* 1. Seasonal workers, as defined in article 2, paragraph 2 (b), of the present Convention, shall be entitled to the rights provided for in part IV that can be applied to them by reason of their presence and work in the territory of the State of employment and that are compatible with their status in that State as seasonal workers, taking into account the fact that they are present in that State for only part of the year.

2. The State of employment shall, subject to paragraph 1 of the present article, consider granting seasonal workers who have been employed in its territory for a significant period of time the possibility of taking up other remunerated activities and giving them priority over other workers who seek admission to that State, subject to applicable bilateral and multilateral agreements.

*Article 60.* Itinerant workers, as defined in article 2, paragraph 2 (e), of the present Convention, shall be entitled to the rights provided for in part IV that can be granted to them by reason of their presence and work in the territory of the State of employment and that are compatible with their status as itinerant workers in that State.

*Article 61.* 1. Project-tied workers, as defined in article 2, paragraph 2 (a), of the present Convention, and members of their families shall be entitled to the rights provided for in part IV except the provisions of article 43, paragraphs 1 (b) and (c), article 43, paragraph 1 (d), as it pertains to social housing schemes, article 45, paragraph 1 (b), and articles 52 to 55.

2. If a project-tied worker claims that the terms of his or her work contract have been violated by his or her employer, he or she shall have the right to address his or her case to the competent authorities of the State which has jurisdiction over that employer, on terms provided for in article 18, paragraph 1, of the present Convention.

3. Subject to bilateral or multilateral agreements in force for them, the States Parties concerned shall endeavour to enable project-tied workers to remain adequately protected by the social security systems of their States of origin or habitual residence during their engagement in the project. States Parties concerned shall take appropriate measures with the aim of avoiding any denial of rights or duplication of payments in this respect.

4. Without prejudice to the provisions of article 47 of the present Convention and to relevant bilateral or multilateral agreements, States Parties concerned shall permit payment of the earnings of project-tied workers in their State of origin or habitual residence.

*Article 62.* 1. Specified-employment workers as defined in article 2, paragraph 2 (g), of the present Convention, shall be entitled to the rights provided for in part IV, except the provisions of article 43, paragraphs 1 (b) and (c), article 43, paragraph 1 (d), as it pertains to social housing schemes,. article 52, and article 54, paragraph 1 (d).

2. Members of the families of specified-employment workers shall be entitled to the rights relating to family members of migrant workers provided for in part IV of the present Convention, except the provisions of article 53.

*Article 63.* 1. Self-employed workers, as defined in article 2, paragraph 2 (h), of the present Convention, shall be entitled to the rights provided for in part IV with the exception of those rights which are exclusively applicable to workers having a contract of employment.

2. Without prejudice to articles 52 and 79 of the present Convention, the termination of the economic activity of the self-employed workers shall not in itself imply the withdrawal of the authorization for them or for the members of their

families to stay or to engage in a remunerated activity in the State of employment except where the authorization of residence is expressly dependent upon the specific remunerated activity for which they were admitted.

### Part VI: Promotion of Sound, Equitable, Humane and Lawful Conditions in Connection with International Migration of Workers and Members of Their Families

*Article 64.* 1. Without prejudice to article 79 of the present Convention, the States Parties concerned shall as appropriate consult and co-operate with a view to promoting sound, equitable and humane conditions in connection with international migration of workers and members of their families.

2. In this respect, due regard shall be paid not only to labour needs and resources, but also to the social, economic, cultural and other needs of migrant workers and members of their families involved, as well as to the consequences of such migration for the communities concerned.

*Article 65.* 1. States Parties shall maintain appropriate services to deal with questions concerning international migration of workers and members of their families. Their functions shall include, inter alia:

(a) The formulation and implementation of policies regarding such migration;

(b) An exchange of information, consultation and co-operation with the competent authorities of other States Parties involved in such migration;

(c) The provision of appropriate information, particularly to employers, workers and their organizations on policies, laws and regulations relating to migration and employment, on agreements concluded with other States concerning migration and on other relevant matters;

(d) The provision of information and appropriate assistance to migrant workers and members of their families regarding requisite authorizations and formalities and arrangements for departure, travel, arrival, stay, remunerated activities, exit and return, as well as on conditions of work and life in the State of employment and on customs, currency, tax and other relevant laws and regulations.

2. States Parties shall facilitate as appropriate the provision of adequate consular and other services that are necessary to meet the social, cultural and other needs of migrant workers and members of their families.

*Article 66.* 1. Subject to paragraph 2 of the present article, the right to undertake operations with a view to the recruitment of workers for employment in another State shall be restricted to:

(a) Public services or bodies of the State in which such operations take place;

(b) Public services or bodies of the State of employment on the basis of agreement between the States concerned;

(c) A body established by virtue of a bilateral or multilateral agreement.

2. Subject to any authorization, approval and supervision by the public authorities of the States Parties concerned as may be established pursuant to the legislation and practice of those States, agencies, prospective employers or persons acting on their behalf may also be permitted to undertake the said operations.

*Article 67.* 1. States Parties concerned shall co-operate as appropriate in the adoption of measures regarding the orderly return of migrant workers and members of their families to the State of origin when they decide to return or their authorization of residence or employment expires or when they are in the State of employment in an irregular situation.

2. Concerning migrant workers and members of their families in a regular situation, States Parties concerned shall co-operate as appropriate, on terms agreed upon by those States, with a view to promoting adequate economic conditions for their resettlement and to facilitating their durable social and cultural reintegration in the State of origin.

*Article 68.* 1. States Parties, including States of transit, shall collaborate with a view to preventing and eliminating illegal or clandestine movements and employment of migrant workers in an irregular situation. The measures to be taken to this end within the jurisdiction of each State concerned shall include:

(a) Appropriate measures against the dissemination of misleading information relating to emigration and immigration;

(b) Measures to detect and eradicate illegal or clandestine movements of migrant workers and members of their families and to impose effective sanctions on persons, groups or entities which organize, operate or assist in organizing or operating such movements;

(c) Measures to impose effective sanctions on persons, groups or entities which use violence, threats or intimidation against migrant workers or members of their families in an irregular situation.

2. States of employment shall take all adequate and effective measures to eliminate employment in their territory of migrant workers in an irregular situation, including, whenever appropriate, sanctions on employers of such workers. The rights of migrant workers vis-à-vis their employer arising from employment shall not be impaired by these measures.

*Article 69.* 1. States Parties shall, when there are migrant workers and members of their families within their territory in an irregular situation, take appropriate measures to ensure that such a situation does not persist.

2. Whenever States Parties concerned consider the possibility of regularizing the situation of such persons in accordance with applicable national legislation and bilateral or multilateral agreements, appropriate account shall be taken of the circumstances of their entry, the duration of their stay in the States of employment and other relevant considerations, in particular those relating to their family situation.

*Article 70.* States Parties shall take measures not less favourable than those applied to nationals to ensure that working and living conditions of migrant workers and members of their families in a regular situation are in keeping with the standards of fitness, safety, health and principles of human dignity.

*Article 71.* 1. States Parties shall facilitate, whenever necessary, the repatriation to the State of origin of the bodies of deceased migrant workers or members of their families.

2. As regards compensation matters relating to the death of a migrant worker or a member of his or her family, States Parties shall, as appropriate, provide assistance to the persons concerned with a view to the prompt settlement of such matters. Settlement of these matters shall be carried out on the basis of applicable national law in accordance with the provisions of the present Convention and any relevant bilateral or multilateral agreements.

### Part VII: Application of the Convention

*Article 72.* 1. (a) For the purpose of reviewing the application of the present Convention, there shall be established a

Committee on the Protection of the Rights of All Migrant Workers and Members of Their Families (hereinafter referred to as "the Committee");

(b) The Committee shall consist, at the time of entry into force of the present Convention, often and, after the entry into force of the Convention for the forty-first State Party, of fourteen experts of high moral standing, impartiality and recognized competence in the field covered by the Convention.

2. (a) Members of the Committee shall be elected by secret ballot by the States Parties from a list of persons nominated by the States Parties, due consideration being given to equitable geographical distribution, including both States of origin and States of employment, and to the representation of the principal legal system. Each State Party may nominate one person from among its own nationals;

(b) Members shall be elected and shall serve in their personal capacity.

3. The initial election shall be held no later than six months after the date of the entry into force of the present Convention and subsequent elections every second year. At least four months before the date of each election, the Secretary-General of the United Nations shall address a letter to all States Parties inviting them to submit their nominations within two months. The Secretary-General shall prepare a list in alphabetical order of all persons thus nominated, indicating the States Parties that have nominated them, and shall submit it to the States Parties not later than one month before the date of the corresponding election, together with the curricula vitae of the persons thus nominated.

4. Elections of members of the Committee shall be held at a meeting of States Parties convened by the Secretary-General at United Nations Headquarters. At that meeting, for which two thirds of the States Parties shall constitute a quorum, the persons elected to the Committee shall be those nominees who obtain the largest number of votes and an absolute majority of the votes of the States Parties present and voting.

5. (a) The members of the Committee shall serve for a term of four years. However, the terms of five of the members elected in the first election shall expire at the end of two years; immediately after the first election, the names of these five members shall be chosen by lot by the Chairman of the meeting of States Parties;

(b) The election of the four additional members of the Committee shall be held in accordance with the provisions of paragraphs 2, 3 and 4 of the present article, following the entry into force of the Convention for the forty-first State Party. The term of two of the additional members elected on this occasion shall expire at the end of two years; the names of these members shall be chosen by lot by the Chairman of the meeting of States Parties;

(c) The members of the Committee shall be eligible for re-election if renominated.

6. If a member of the Committee dies or resigns or declares that for any other cause he or she can no longer perform the duties of the Committee, the State Party that nominated the expert shall appoint another expert from among its own nationals for the remaining part of the term. The new appointment is subject to the approval of the Committee.

7. The Secretary-General of the United Nations shall provide the necessary staff and facilities for the effective performance of the functions of the Committee.

8. The members of the Committee shall receive emolu-

ments from United Nations resources on such terms and conditions as the General Assembly may decide.

9. The members of the Committee shall be entitled to the facilities, privileges and immunities of experts on mission for the United Nations as laid down in the relevant sections of the Convention on the Privileges and Immunities of the United Nations.

*Article 73.* 1. States Parties undertake to submit to the Secretary-General of the United Nations for consideration by the Committee a report on the legislative, judicial, administrative and other measures they have taken to give effect to the provisions of the present Convention:

(a) Within one year after the entry into force of the Convention for the State Party concerned;

(b) Thereafter every five years and whenever the Committee so requests.

2. Reports prepared under the present article shall also indicate factors and difficulties, if any, affecting the implementation of the Convention and shall include information on the characteristics of migration flows in which the State Party concerned is involved.

3. The Committee shall decide any further guidelines applicable to the content of the reports.

4. States Parties shall make their reports widely available to the public in their own countries.

*Article 74.* 1. The Committee shall examine the reports submitted by each State Party and shall transmit such comments as it may consider appropriate to the State Party concerned. This State Party may submit to the Committee observations on any comment made by the Committee in accordance with the present article. The Committee may request supplementary information from States Parties when considering these reports.

2. The Secretary-General of the United Nations shall, in due time before the opening of each regular session of the Committee, transmit to the Director-General of the International Labour Office copies of the reports submitted by States Parties concerned and information relevant to the consideration of these reports, in order to enable the Office to assist the Committee with the expertise the Office may provide regarding those matters dealt with by the present Convention that fall within the sphere of competence of the International Labour Organisation. The Committee shall consider in its deliberations such comments and materials as the Office may provide.

3. The Secretary-General of the United Nations may also, after consultation with the Committee, transmit to other specialized agencies as well as to intergovernmental organizations, copies of such parts of these reports as may fall within their competence.

4. The Committee may invite the specialized agencies and organs of the United Nations, as well as intergovernmental organizations and other concerned bodies to submit, for consideration by the Committee, written information on such matters dealt with in the present Convention as fall within the scope of their activities.

5. The International Labour Office shall be invited by the Committee to appoint representatives to participate, in a consultative capacity, in the meetings of the Committee.

6. The Committee may invite representatives of other specialized agencies and organs of the United Nations, as well as of intergovernmental organizations, to be present and to be heard in its meetings whenever matters falling within their field of competence are considered.

7. The Committee shall present an annual report to the General Assembly of the United Nations on the implemen-

tation of the present Convention, containing its own considerations and recommendations, based, in particular, on the examination of the reports and any observations presented by States Parties.

8. The Secretary-General of the United Nations shall transmit the annual reports of the Committee to the States Parties to the present Convention, the Economic and Social Council, the Commission on Human Rights of the United Nations, the Director-General of the International Labour Office and other relevant organizations.

*Article 75.* 1. The Committee shall adopt its own rules of procedure.

2. The Committee shall elect its officers for a term of two years.

3. The Committee shall normally meet annually.

4. The meetings of the Committee shall normally be held at United Nations Headquarters.

*Article 76.* 1. A State Party to the present Convention may at any time declare under this article that it recognizes the competence of the Committee to receive and consider communications to the effect that a State Party claims that another State Party is not fulfilling its obligations under the present Convention. Communications under this article may be received and considered only if submitted by a State Party that has made a declaration recognizing in regard to itself the competence of the Committee. No communication shall be received by the Committee if it concerns a State Party which has not made such a declaration. Communications received under this article shall be dealt with in accordance with the following procedure:

(a) If a State Party to the present Convention considers that another State Party is not fulfilling its obligations under the present Convention, it may, by written communication, bring the matter to the attention of that State Party. The State Party may also inform the Committee of the matter. Within three months after the receipt of the communication the receiving State shall afford the State that sent the communication an explanation, or any other statement in writing clarifying the matter which should include, to the extent possible and pertinent, reference to domestic procedures and remedies taken, pending or available in the matter;

(b) If the matter is not adjusted to the satisfaction of both States Parties concerned within six months after the receipt by the receiving State of the initial communication, either State shall have the right to refer the matter to the Committee, by notice given to the Committee and to the other State;

(c) The Committee shall deal with a matter referred to it only after it has ascertained that all available domestic remedies have been invoked and exhausted in the matter, in conformity with the generally recognized principles of international law. This shall not be the rule where, in the view of the Committee, the application of the remedies is unreasonably prolonged;

(d) Subject to the provisions of subparagraph (c) of the present paragraph, the Committee shall make available its good offices to the States Parties concerned with a view to a friendly solution of the matter on the basis of the respect for the obligations set forth in the present Convention;

(e) The Committee shall hold closed meetings when examining communications under the present article;

(f) In any matter referred to it in accordance with subparagraph (b) of the present paragraph, the Committee may call upon the States Parties concerned, referred to in subparagraph (b), to supply any relevant information;

(g) The States Parties concerned, referred to in subparagraph (b) of the present paragraph, shall have the right to be represented when the matter is being considered by the Committee and to make submissions orally and/or in writing;

(h) The Committee shall, within twelve months after the date of receipt of notice under subparagraph (b) of the present paragraph, submit a report, as follows:

(i) If a solution within the terms of subparagraph (d) of the present paragraph is reached, the Committee shall confine its report to a brief statement of the facts and of the solution reached;

(ii) If a solution within the terms of subparagraph (d) is not reached, the Committee shall, in its report, set forth the relevant facts concerning the issue between the States Parties concerned. The written submissions and record of the oral submissions made by the States Parties concerned shall be attached to the report. The Committee may also communicate only to the States Parties concerned any views that it may consider relevant to the issue between them.

In every matter, the report shall be communicated to the States Parties concerned.

2. The provisions of the present article shall come into force when ten States Parties to the present Convention have made a declaration under Paragraph 1 of the present article. Such declarations shall be deposited by the States Parties with the Secretary-General of the United Nations, who shall transmit copies thereof to the other States Parties. A declaration may be withdrawn at any time by notification to the Secretary-General. Such a withdrawal shall not prejudice the consideration of any matter that is the subject of a communication already transmitted under the present article; no further communication by any State Party shall be received under the present article after the notification of withdrawal of the declaration has been received by the Secretary-General, unless the State Party concerned has made a new declaration.

*Article 77.* 1. A State Party to the present Convention may at any time declare under the present article that it recognizes the competence of the Committee to receive and consider communications from or on behalf of individuals subject to its jurisdiction who claim that their individual rights as established by the present Convention have been violated by that State Party. No communication shall be received by the Committee if it concerns a State Party that has not made such a declaration.

2. The Committee shall consider inadmissible any communication under the present article which is anonymous or which it considers to be an abuse of the right of submission of such communications or to be incompatible with the provisions of the present Convention.

3. The Committee shall not consider any communication from an individual under the present article unless it has ascertained that:

(a) The same matter has not been, and is not being, examined under another procedure of international investigation or settlement;

(b) The individual has exhausted all available domestic remedies; this shall not be the rule where, in the view of the Committee, the application of the remedies is unreasonably prolonged or is unlikely to bring effective relief to that individual.

4. Subject to the provisions of paragraph 2 of the present article, the Committee shall bring any communications submitted to it under this article to the attention of the State Party to the present Convention that has made a declaration

under paragraph 1 and is alleged to be violating any provisions of the Convention. Within six months, the receiving State shall submit to the Committee written explanations or statements clarifying the matter and the remedy, if any, that may have been taken by that State.

5. The Committee shall consider communications received under the present article in the light of all information made available to it by or on behalf of the individual and by the State Party concerned.

6. The Committee shall hold closed meetings when examining communications under the present article.

7. The Committee shall forward its views to the State Party concerned and to the individual.

8. The provisions of the present article shall come into force when ten States Parties to the present Convention have made declarations under paragraph 1 of the present article. Such declarations shall be deposited by the States Parties with the Secretary-General of the United Nations, who shall transmit copies thereof to the other States Parties. A declaration may be withdrawn at any time by notification to the Secretary-General. Such a withdrawal shall not prejudice the consideration of any matter that is the subject of a communication already transmitted under the present article; no further communication by or on behalf of an individual shall be received under the present article after the notification of withdrawal of the declaration has been received by the Secretary-General, unless the State Party has made a new declaration.

*Article 78.* The provisions of article 76 of the present Convention shall be applied without prejudice to any procedures for settling disputes or complaints in the field covered by the present Convention laid down in the constituent instruments of, or in conventions adopted by, the United Nations and the specialized agencies and shall not prevent the States Parties from having recourse to any procedures for settling a dispute in accordance with international agreements in force between them.

### Part VIII: General Provisions

*Article 79.* Nothing in the present Convention shall affect the right of each State Party to establish the criteria governing admission of migrant workers and members of their families. Concerning other matters related to their legal situation and treatment as migrant workers and members of their families, States Parties shall be subject to the limitations set forth in the present Convention.

*Article 80.* Nothing in the present Convention shall be interpreted as impairing the provisions of the Charter of the United Nations and of the constitutions of the specialized agencies which define the respective responsibilities of the various organs of the United Nations and of the specialized agencies in regard to the matters dealt with in the present Convention.

*Article 81.* 1. Nothing in the present Convention shall affect more favourable rights or freedoms granted to migrant workers and members of their families by virtue of:

(a) The law or practice of a State Party; or

(b) Any bilateral or multilateral treaty in force for the State Party concerned.

2. Nothing in the present Convention may be interpreted as implying for any State, group or person any right to engage in any activity or perform any act that would impair any of the rights and freedoms as set forth in the present Convention.

*Article 82.* The rights of migrant workers and members of their families provided for in the present Convention may not be renounced. It shall not be permissible to exert any form of pressure upon migrant workers and members of their families with a view to their relinquishing or foregoing any of the said rights. It shall not be possible to derogate by contract from rights recognized in the present Convention. States Parties shall take appropriate measures to ensure that these principles are respected.

*Article 83.* Each State Party to the present Convention undertakes:

(a) To ensure that any person whose rights or freedoms as herein recognized are violated shall have an effective remedy, notwithstanding that the violation has been committed by persons acting in an official capacity;

(b) To ensure that any persons seeking such a remedy shall have his or her claim reviewed and decided by competent judicial, administrative or legislative authorities, or by any other competent authority provided for by the legal system of the State, and to develop the possibilities of judicial remedy;

(c) To ensure that the competent authorities shall enforce such remedies when granted.

*Article 84.* Each State Party undertakes to adopt the legislative and other measures that are necessary to implement the provisions of the present Convention.

### Part IX: Final Provisions

*Article 85.* The Secretary-General of the United Nations is designated as the depositary of the present Convention.

*Article 86.* 1. The present Convention shall be open for signature by all States. It is subject to ratification.

2. The present Convention shall be open to accession by any State.

3. Instruments of ratification or accession shall be deposited with the Secretary-General of the United Nations.

*Article 87.* 1. The present Convention shall enter into force on the first day of the months after the date of the deposit of the twentieth instrument of ratification or accession.

2. For each State ratifying or acceding to the present Convention after its entry into force, the Convention shall enter into force on the first day of the month following a period of three months after the date of the deposit of its own instrument of ratification or accession.

*Article 88.* A State ratifying or acceding to the present Convention may not exclude the application of any part of it, or, without prejudice to article 3, exclude from its application.

*Article 89.* 1. Any State Party may denounce the present Convention, not earlier than five years after the Convention has entered into force for the State concerned, by means of a notification in writing addressed to the Secretary-General of the United Nations.

2. Such denunciation shall become effective on the first day of the month following the expiration of a period of twelve months after the date of the receipt of the notification by the Secretary-General of the United Nations.

3. Such a denunciation shall not have the effect of releasing the State Party from its obligations under the present Convention in regard to any act or omission which occurs prior to the date at which the denunciation becomes effective, nor shall denunciation prejudice in any way the continued consideration of any matter which is already under con-

sideration by the Committee prior to the date at which the denunciation becomes effective.

4. Following the date at which the denunciation of a State Party becomes effective, the Committee shall not commence consideration of any new matter regarding that State.

*Article 90.* 1. After five years from the entry into force of the Convention a request for the revision of the Convention may be made at any time by any State Party by means of a notification in writing addressed to the Secretary-General of the United Nations. The Secretary-General shall thereupon communicate any proposed amendments to the States Parties with a request that they notify him whether the favour a conference of States Parties for the purpose of considering and voting upon the proposals. In the event that within four months from the date of such communication at least one third of the States Parties favours such a conference, the Secretary-General shall convene the conference under the auspices of the United Nations. Any amendment adopted by a majority of the States Parties present and voting shall be submitted to the General Assembly for approval.

2. Amendments shall come into force when they have been approved by the General Assembly of the United Nations and accepted by a two-thirds majority of the States Parties in accordance with their respective constitutional processes.

3. When amendments come into force, they shall be binding on those States Parties that have accepted them, other States Parties still being bound by the provisions of the present Convention and any earlier amendment that they have accepted.

*Article 91.* 1. The Secretary-General of the United Nations shall receive and circulate to all States the text of reservations made by States at the time of signature, ratification or accession.

2. A reservation incompatible with the object and purpose of the present Convention shall not be permitted.

3. Reservations may be withdrawn at any time by notification to this effect addressed to the Secretary-General of the United Nations. who shall then inform all States thereof. Such notification shall take effect on the date on which it is received.

*Article 92.* 1. Any dispute between two or more States Parties concerning the interpretation or application of the present Convention that is not settled by negotiation shall, at the request of one of them, be submitted to arbitration. If within six months from the date of the request for arbitration the Parties are unable to agree on the organization of the arbitration, any one of those Parties may refer the dispute to the International Court of Justice by request in conformity with the Statute of the Court.

2. Each State Party may at the time of signature or ratification of the present Convention or accession thereto declare that it does not consider itself bound by paragraph 1 of the present article. The other States Parties shall not be bound by that paragraph with respect to any State Party that has made such a declaration.

3. Any State Party that has made a declaration in accordance with paragraph 2 of the present article may at any time withdraw that declaration by notification to the Secretary-General of the United Nations.

*Article 93.* 1. The present Convention, of which the Arabic, Chinese, English, French, Russian and Spanish texts are equally authentic, shall be deposited with the Secretary-General of the United Nations.

2. The Secretary-General of the United Nations shall transmit certified copies of the present Convention to all States.

In witness whereof the undersigned plenipotentiaries, being duly authorized thereto by their respective Governments, have signed the present Convention.

**BIBLIOGRAPHY.** Hune, Shirley, and Jan Niessen. "Ratifying the UN Migrant Workers Convention: Current Difficulties and Prospects," *Netherlands Quarterly of Human Rights* 12, no. 4 (1994): 393–404. Scholarly article, in English.

Quaker Office at the United Nations. *Drafting an International Convention on the Protection of the Rights of All Migrant Workers and Their Families.* New York: 1987. NGO conference report, in English.

"U.N. International Convention on the Protection of the Rights of All Migrant Workers and Members of Their Families," *International Migration Review* 25, no. 4 (no. 96) (Winter 1991): 685–872. Special issue, in English.

**MINE CLEARANCE.** The United Nations' recognition of the importance of the activity of clearing land mines is reflected in the following draft resolution (A/49/L8/Rev. 1 and Rev. 1/Add. 1) of 23 December 1994:

The General Assembly, recalling its resolution 48/7 on assistance in mine clearance, adopted without a vote on 19 October 1993, affirming its deep concern at the tremendous humanitarian problem caused by the presence of mines and other unexploded devices that have serious and lasting social and economic consequences for the populations of mine-infested countries and constitute an obstacle to the return of refugees and other displaced persons, to humanitarian aid operations, to reconstruction and economic development as well as to the restoration of normal social conditions.

Stressing its grave alarm at the ever-increasing presence of mines and other unexploded devices as a result of armed conflicts,

Deeply concerned that the number of mines being laid each year exponentially outweighs the number of such mines that can be cleared during that time, and convinced of the necessity and urgency of an increase in mine-clearance efforts by the international community,

Recognizing the importance of recording, where appropriate, the location of mines,

Reiterating its dismay at the high number of victims of mines, especially among civilian populations, and taking note in this context of Commission on Human Rights resolution 1994/94 of 9 March 1994 on the effects of armed conflicts on children's lives,

Bearing in mind the serious threat that mines and other unexploded devices pose to the safety, the health, and the lives of personnel participating in humanitarian, peace-keeping and rehabilitation programmes,

Recalling, in this regard, its resolution 48/79 of 16 December 1983 on the Convention on Prohibitions or Restrictions on the Use of Certain Conventional Weapons Which May Be Deemed to Be Excessively Injurious or to Have Indiscriminate Effects and the convening by the Secretary-General of a conference to review and amend the above-mentioned Convention, taking particular note, in this regard, of the work of the Group of Governmental Experts at present engaged in preparing the review of that Convention and especially the Protocol on Prohibition or Restrictions on the Use of Mines, Booby Traps, and Other Devices (Protocol II) as a matter of priority,

Recalling also its resolution 48/75 K of 16 December 1993, calling for a moratorium on the export of anti-personnel land-mines,

Bearing in mind that significant progress needs to be achieved in these fields,

Recognizing that, in addition to the primary role of States, the United Nations has an important role in the field of assistance in mine clearance,

Welcoming, in this regard, the efforts made by the United Nations to foster the establishment of national mine-clearance capacities in countries where mines constitute a serious threat to the safety, health, and lives of the local population,

Noting with satisfaction the inclusion in the mandates of several peace-keeping operations of provisions relating to mine-clearance work carried out under the direction of the Department of Peace-keeping Operations of the Secretariat, in the context of such operations,

Commending the activities already undertaken by the United Nations system, donor and recipient Governments, the International Committee of the Red Cross and non-governmental organizations in addressing solutions of problems relating to the presence of mines and other unexploded devices,

Commending in particular the activities already undertaken by the Secretary-General, especially the establishment of the Department of Humanitarian Affairs as a focal point within the United Nations for coordinating de-mining and related issues,

Express its appreciation to the Secretary-General for his comprehensive report on assistance in mine clearance, and takes note with interest of the proposals contained therein as well as of the contributions by Member States and bodies that have observer status with the General Assembly in the addendum to the report;

Welcomes the establishment by the Secretary-General of a voluntary trust fund to finance, in particular, information and training programmes relating to mine clearance and to facilitate the launching of mine-clearance operations;

Appeals to Member States as well as to intergovernmental and non-governmental organizations and foundations to contribute to the voluntary trust fund;

Invites all relevant multilateral and national programmes and bodies to include, in coordination with the United Nations, activities related to mine clearance in their humanitarian, social, and economic activities;

Emphasizes again, in this connection, the importance of coordination by the United Nations of activities related to mine clearance, including those by regional organizations, and in particular activities relating to information and training;

Commends the Secretary-General for his efforts to make use of available resources to strengthen the coordination role of the United Nations, and encourages him to continue those efforts with a view to improving the effectiveness of assistance in mine clearance by the United Nations;

Takes note, in this regard, of the creation, in the context of the current reorganization of the Department of Humanitarian Affairs of the Secretariat, of a Mine Clearance and Policy Unit, which, with the support of other Secretariat units, especially the technical expertise provided by the Department of Peace-keeping Operations, is responsible for carrying out the Department's functions as a focal point;

Urges Member States, regional organizations, governmental and non-governmental organizations and foundations to continue to extend full assistance and cooperation to the Secretary-General and, in particular, to provide him with all information and data as well as other pertinent resources which could be useful in strengthening the coordination role of the United Nations in the fields of mine-awareness, training, surveying, mine detection and clearance, scientific research for mine-detection and clearance technology and information on and distribution of medical equipment and supplies;

Calls upon all States, especially those that have the capacity to do so, to provide the necessary information and technical and material assistance, as appropriate, and to remove or otherwise render ineffective minefields, mines and booby-traps in accordance with international law;

Calls upon Member States and governmental and non-governmental organizations that have the ability to do so to promote scientific research aimed at the rapid advancement of mine detection and clearance technology;

Requests the Secretary-General to consider the convening, as early as possible, of an international meeting on mine clearance, to include a meeting of experts and a meeting of potential donors, in order to promote the work of the United Nations and international cooperation in this field;

Requests the Secretary-General to submit to the General Assembly before its fiftieth session a report covering the activities of the United Nations on assistance in mine-clearance activities during the past year and especially the operation of the voluntary trust fund;

Decides to include in the provisional agenda of its fiftieth session the item entitled "Assistance in mine clearance".

**MINNESOTA ADVOCATES INTERNATIONAL HUMAN RIGHTS AWARD.** Established in 1985, this annual award is presented to individuals or organizations that promote free expression.

In 1994, the award was presented to James P. Grant, executive director of **UNICEF** since 1980, who was instrumental in bringing together world leaders for the World Summit for Children, which resulted in the Convention on the Rights of the Child (see **CHILDREN'S RIGHTS**); and *Movimento Nacional de Meninos e Meninas de Rua* (National Street Children's Movement), a Brazilian non-governmental organization whose mission is to defend and promote the rights of marginalized street children through direct advocacy, lobbying, and education; and who work directly with approximately 30,000 children to improve their daily living conditions.

In 1993, the award was shared by Dr. Shana Swiss, director of the Women's Program at Physicians for Human Rights in Boston, MA (USA); and Jadranka Cigelj, an attorney with the Croatian Information Center, who works throughout the free territories of Croatia and Bosnia-Herzegovina to gather testimony from victims of the Serbian armed forces.

In addition, past recipients are Socorro Diokno, director of the Free Legal Assistance Group of the Philippines (1989); Dith Pran, Pan Marann, Sova Niev, and Sos Duong in memory of the victims of genocide in Cambodia (1990); Yuri Afanas'ev, Russian historian (1991); and Fernando E. Solanas, Argentine film director; the Haitian Underground Press; and Laura Waterman Wittstock, president of MIGIZI Communications (1992).

For more information, contact: Minnesota Advocates for Human Rights, 400 Second Ave. South, Suite 1050, Minneapolis, MN 55401, USA. Telephone: (612) 341-3302. Fax: (612) 341-2971.

**MINNESOTA HUMAN RIGHTS CENTER.** See **UNIVERSITY OF MINNESOTA, HUMAN RIGHTS CENTER.**

**MINORITIES' RIGHTS.** Protection of the rights of "minorities" has been a highly controversial question for the international community for many decades. The **LEAGUE OF NATIONS** devoted much time and attention to this question between the two world wars and served as a protective agency for a number of ethnic, linguistic, and national groups living in various countries, particularly in central Europe. But this machinery ceased to exist when the circumstances which had led to its creation ended with the close of World War II, and the emphasis of the United Nations has since been upon protecting the enjoyment of all human rights by every individual rather than upon protecting special rights of any particular groups.

When the UN **GENERAL ASSEMBLY** adopted and proclaimed the **UNIVERSAL DECLARATION OF HUMAN RIGHTS** in 1948, it decided that it would not include a specific provision on the question of minorities. At the same time, it stated (resolution 217 C [III]) "that the United Nations cannot remain indifferent to the fate of minorities" and added that "it is difficult to adopt a uniform solution of this complex and delicate question, which has special aspects in each State in which it arises."

In 1953, the **ECONOMIC AND SOCIAL COUNCIL** recommended (resolution 502 F [XVI]) that "in the preparation of any international treaties, decisions of international organs, or other acts which establish new States, or new boundary lines between States, special attention should be paid to the protection of any minority which may be created thereby."

Several general international instruments, and at least one of regional application, touch upon the question of special protective measures for ethnic, religious, or linguistic groups. The UN Convention on the Prevention and Punishment of the Crime of Genocide (see **GENOCIDE**), for example, defines genocide as any of a number of acts "committed with intent to destroy, in whole or in part, a national, ethnical, racial or religious group, as such," and the contracting parties

"confirm that genocide, whether committed in time of peace or in time of war, is a crime under international law which they undertake to prevent and punish." The ILO Indigenous and Tribal Peoples Convention (see **INDIGENOUS PEOPLES**) places upon governments (article 2) "the primary responsibility for developing co-ordinated and systematic action for the protection of the populations concerned and their progressive integration into the life of their respective countries," and provides (article 3) that "so long as the social, economic and cultural conditions of the populations concerned prevent them from enjoying the benefits of the general laws of the country to which they belong, special measures should be adopted for the protection of the institutions, persons property and labor of these populations." In the UNESCO Convention against Discrimination in Education (see **EDUCATION**), the States parties agree (article 5 [c]) that "it is essential to recognize the right of members of national minorities to carry on their own educational activities, including the maintenance of schools and, depending on the educational policy of each State, the use or the teaching of their own language," and set out the circumstances in which this right may be exercised. The **EUROPEAN CONVENTION ON HUMAN RIGHTS** contains a provision (article 14) in which "association with a national minority" is listed among a series of grounds upon which discrimination is prohibited. And the **INTERNATIONAL COVENANT ON CIVIL AND POLITICAL RIGHTS,** adopted by the UN General Assembly in 1966, includes an article on the rights of persons belonging to minorities which reads:

*Article 27.* In those States in which ethnic, religious or linguistic minorities exist, persons belonging to such minorities shall not be denied the right, in community with other members of their group, to enjoy their own culture, to profess and practice their own religion, or to use their own language.

Among the decisions of principal organs of the United Nations which have dealt with the question of special protective measures for ethnic, religious, or linguistic groups are three resolutions of the General Assembly: (1) on the future government of Palestine (resolution 181 [II]), (2) on the question of the disposal of the former Italian colonies (resolution 289 [IV]), and (3) on the question of Eritrea (resolution 390 [V]). In addition, the Statute of the City of Jerusalem, approved by the UN **TRUSTEESHIP COUNCIL** on 4 April 1950, provides special protective measures for ethnic, religious, or linguistic groups in articles dealing with human rights and fundamental freedoms (article 9), the legislative council (article 21), the judicial system (article 28), official and working languages (article 31), the educational system and cultural and benevolent institutions (article 32), and broadcasting and television (article 33).

From the texts of the instruments and decisions mentioned above, it may be inferred that the term "minority" is applied internationally to two distinct categories of persons: (a) minorities whose members desire equality with dominant groups in the sole sense of non-discrimination, and (b) those whose members desire equality with dominant groups in the sense of non-discrimination and the recognition of certain special rights and the rendering of certain positive services. The kind of "minority rights" that they feel they are entitled to claim if their equality within the State is to be real includes one or more of the following:

(a) provision of adequate primary and secondary education for the minority in its own language and its cultural traditions;

(b) provision for maintenance of the culture of the minority through the establishment and operation of schools, libraries, museums, media of information, and other cultural and educational institutions;

(c) provision of adequate facilities to the minority for the use of its language, either orally or in writing, in the legislature, before the courts, and in administration, and the granting of the right to use that language in private intercourse;

(d) provision for respect of the family law and personal status of the minority and their religious practices and interests; and

(e) provision of a certain degree of autonomy.

The rendering of such services may be effected either out of public funds or at the expense of the minority.

***STUDY OF THE RIGHTS OF MINORITIES.*** At its 1967 session, the UN **Sub-Commission on Prevention of Discrimination and Protection of Minorities** decided (resolution 9 [XX]) to initiate a study of the implementation of the principles set out in article 27 of the International Covenant on Civil and Political Rights, "with special reference to analyzing the concept of the minority taking into account the ethnic, religious and linguistic factors and considering the position of ethnic, religious or linguistic groups in multinational societies." The study was entrusted by the Sub-Commission to one of its members, Mr. Francesco Capotorti (Italy). Completed in 1977, the study (UN Doc. E/CN.4/Sub.2/384 and Add. 1–7) was examined by the Sub-Commission at its session held in August of that year. The Sub-Commission expressed its appreciation (resolution 5 [XXX]) to the Special Rapporteur, endorsed his conclusions and recommendations, and requested him to present the report to the UN **Commission on Human Rights** at its 1978 session. It recommended that the Commission consider the pos-

sibility of drafting a declaration on the rights of minorities within the framework of the principles set out in article 27 of the International Covenant on Civil and Political Rights.

In the study, the Special Rapporteur presented a tentative definition of the term "minority," drawn up with the application of article 27 in mind, suggesting that the term may be taken to mean

a group numerically inferior to the rest of the population of a State, in a non-dominant position, whose members—being nationals of the State—possess ethnic, religious or linguistic characteristics differing from those of the rest of the population and show, if only implicitly, a sense of solidarity, directed towards preserving their culture, traditions, religion or language.

The Special Rapporteur also made a number of recommendations for dealing with the problems of minorities, including (a) full use of the procedures of implementation contained in the International Covenant on Civil and Political Rights with regard to article 27 thereof; (b) provision of adequate procedures at the national level to deal effectively with violations of the rights granted to members of minority groups under article 27; and (c) preparation of a draft declaration on the rights of members of minority groups within the framework of the principles set forth in article 27. The Special Rapporteur also expressed his belief that bilateral agreements dealing with minority rights concluded between States where minorities lived and States from which such minorities originated (especially between neighboring countries) would be extremely useful, provided that cooperation with regard to the rights of members of minority groups was based on mutual respect for the principles of the sovereignty and territorial integrity of the States concerned and non-interference in their internal affairs.

The Sub-Commission (resolution 5 [XXX]) recommended that the Commission consider the drafting of a declaration on the rights of members of minorities, as had been suggested by the Special Rapporteur. The Commission established an open-ended working group for this purpose at its 1978 session and referred to it the draft of a declaration proposed by Yugoslavia (UN Doc. E/CN.4/L.1367/Rev. 1).

The Sub-Commission, which had been following the slow progress of the Commission in this endeavor, took up the question of the protection of minorities again at its 1988 session and expressed the view that there was a need to explore more practical approaches to the subject in line, *inter alia,* with the conclusions of its Special Rapporteur on the subject, Mr. Capotorti. Accordingly, it invited (resolution 1988/36) one of its members, Ms. Claire Palley (United Kingdom) to prepare a working paper on possible ways and means to facilitate the peaceful and constructive resolution of situations involving racial, national, religious, and linguistic minorities. In the working paper which she presented to the Sub-Commission at its 1989 session (E/CN.4/Sub.2/1989/43), Ms. Palley made the following proposal (sect. 5, paras. 23–25):

In its resolution on the "fate of minorities", the General Assembly observed 40 years ago that it is "difficult to adopt a uniform solution to this complex and delicate question, which has special aspects in each State in which it arises". This remains valid, and cautions against any attempt to construct solutions from general theories or a small sample of national experiences. At the same time, it would appear preferable to adopt a thematic approach to the study of situations involving minorities, because this affords a more global perspective and balance than methods which respond to particular cases.

It is also clear that a study of minorities must initially focus on the analysis of examples of successful national action, so that it is possible to determine what kinds of United Nations action, if any, can strengthen the minorities is still an ongoing concern. Since national situations are so varied and complex, the ultimate goal of the exercise must be to contribute to the formation of effective national institutions, based on comparative experience and some useful models, rather than to develop a catalogue of specific prescriptive measures.

To begin this work, the Sub-Commission may wish to consider the appointment of a special rapporteur to prepare a survey of relevant national experience based on information available from all sources with a view to:

(a) identifying positive examples of achieving or surpassing the requirements of article 27, which can serve as models;

(b) identifying situations in which the programme of advisory services could be used effectively to strengthen or restore unity by supporting relevant national institutions for minorities.

Ms. Palley further suggested that in carrying out the mandate, the Special Rapporteur might be guided by the following principles (sect. 6, para. 26):

(a) the paramount importance of non-discrimination, as well as the full participation of all individuals and groups, as contained in the two International Covenants of Human Rights and in the Declaration on the Right to Development;

(b) the necessity of promoting the rights and development of minorities in a manner that is consistent with the unity and stability of States, in light of the Declaration of Principles on Friendly Relations and Co-operation Among States;

(c) the dangers posed by ethnic conflict for regional as well as national security;

(d) the importance of both negative (non-discrimination) and positive (special assistance or status) measures for the effective protection of minorities;

(e) the role of the development process in removing economic and social obstacles to co-operation and mutual respect among all groups in national society;

(f) the necessity of ensuring that measures adopted to protect minorities also respect the human rights of majorities.

Finally, Ms. Palley suggested that, as a first step in developing a useful analysis, the Special Rapporteur circulate a questionnaire to governments and to interested non-governmental organizations, soliciting information of a specific and practical nature. He would then be in a position to present an analytical report for discussion at the Sub-Commission's 1991 session. She included in the working paper, as an annex, the following proposed questionnaire on national experience in the protection of minorities:

The extent to which minorities:

(1) are recognized in States' legal/political institutions;

(2) enjoy educational or cultural institutions specifically designed to meet their needs, or different forms of autonomy;

(3) have continued to use and to be educated in their own languages, and how practical difficulties in this, if any, have been overcome;

(4) have been able to achieve improvements in their social and economic conditions, relative to national society as a whole;

(5) benefit from positive measures or affirmative action, and the experience gained from the use of such measures;

(6) maintain contacts with other members of their group across State borders, and any difficulties experienced with this;

(7) enjoy direct representation in national legislative bodies and participated in elections, holding public office, and public service generally;

(8) participate in the planning, implementation and benefits of development activities, and by what institutional means;

(9) have benefited from agrarian reform or resettlement programmes, and any difficulties encountered.

***SEXUAL MINORITIES.*** In a resolution adopted on 26 May 1983, entitled "Suppression of the traffic in persons and of the exploitation of the prostitution of others," the UN Economic and Social Council requested the **CENTER FOR HUMAN RIGHTS** in Geneva, Switzerland, to prepare, in liaison with the United Nations agencies and organs concerned and with the competent non-governmental organizations, two complementary studies: one on the sale of children and the other on the legal and social problems of sexual minorities, including male prostitution, and to submit those studies as soon as possible to the Sub-Commission on Prevention of Discrimination and Protection of Minorities.

The study entitled "The Legal and Social Problems of Sexual Minorities," (UN Doc. E/CN.4/Sub.2/1988/31), prepared by Mr. Jean Fernand-Laurent at the invitation of the Secretary-General, was transmitted to the Sub-Commission at its 1988 session. It endeavored to answer two questions in particular: (a) Are sexual minorities subjected to *de facto* or *de jure* discrimination, and, (b) if so, is such discrimination justified on any valid grounds? The study deals, in the words of the author, "not with occasional and individual breaches of collective moral standards, but, rather, only with groups of persons who are, implicitly or explicitly, protesting against the established order, who refuse to play the role assigned to them as men or women and who, when possible, set up groups to demand the satisfaction of their particular needs and to help one another. This definition covers male and female homosexuals (lesbians), who set themselves apart by having a relationship with a partner of the same sex, and transsexuals, who refuse the legal sex assigned to them. They will henceforth be referred to as sexual minorities." It attempts to answer the question whether the Universal Declaration of Human Rights is compatible with legislation, regulations, and practices relating to sexual minorities, and to show whether discrimination which might have occurred is justified by valid reasons, such as the protection of the minorities themselves against economic exploitation, concern for public health, and the protection of children.

The study recalls that, in 1982, the UN **HUMAN RIGHTS COMMITTEE** adopted views under article 5 (4) of the International Covenant on Civil and Political Rights: Optional Protocol, with reference to a communication submitted by five Finnish journalists represented by the Organization for Sexual Equality of Finland. The authors of the communication contended that Finnish authorities, including organs of the State-controlled Finnish Broadcasting Company, had interfered with their right of freedom of expression and information, as laid down in article 19 of the Covenant, by imposing sanctions against participants in, or censuring, radio and television programs dealing with homosexuality. At the heart of the dispute was paragraph 9 of chapter 20 of the Finnish Penal Code, which reads:

If someone publicly engages in an act violating sexual morality, thereby giving offense, he shall be sentenced for publicly violating sexual morality to imprisonment for at most six months or to a fine.

Anyone who publicly encourages indecent behavior between persons of the same sex shall be sentenced for encouragement to indecent behavior between members of the same sex as decreed in sub-section 1.

The Finnish Government, while admitting that paragraph 9 of chapter 20 of the Penal Code constitutes a certain restriction on freedom of expression, referred to article 19 (3) of the Covenant, which states that the exercise of the rights provided for in article 19 (2) may be subject to certain restrictions, in so far as these are provided by law and are necessary for the protection of public order, or of public health or morals.

The Committee, after considering the merits of the communication, found (UN Doc. A/37/40, annex XIV)

that it cannot question the decision of the responsible organs of the Finnish Broadcasting Corporation that radio and TV are not the appropriate forums to discuss issues related to homosexuality, as far as a program could be judged as encouraging homosexual behavior. According to article 19 (3), the exercise of the rights provided for in article 19 (2) carries with it special duties and responsibilities for these organs. As far as radio and TV programs are concerned, the audience cannot be controlled. In particular, harmful effects on minors cannot be excluded. Accordingly, the Human Rights Committee is of the view that there has been no violation of the rights of the authors of the communication under article 19 (2) of the Covenant.

The study also recalls that between 1976 and 1981 the European Commission on Human Rights and the European Court of Human Rights considered a petition brought by a British subject against his government, complaining of the existence in Northern Ireland of laws which had the effect of establishing as offenses certain homosexual acts between consenting adults. The Court's judgment, dated 22 October 1981, led to an order by the British Government decriminalizing homosexual acts committed in private by two consenting adults aged 21 or more in Northern Ireland, thus bringing Northern Irish law on this issue into line with the law in force for the rest of the United Kingdom.

After examining in some detail the numerous problems, including those of prejudice and discrimination, encountered by male and female homosexuals, transsexuals, and male prostitutes, the study concludes with the following comments and proposals (paras. 95–106):

In considering three sexual minorities (homosexuals, lesbians and transsexuals), we have approached the depths of human nature and have come upon the most disturbing mysteries on which scholars have been unable to shed any light. These facts are very humbling and keep us from making any hard and fast judgements.

Our research brought us up against one of the basic structures of every society—the distinction between the sexes. It took us into the area of sexual activity which, together with power and money, forms one of the focal points of all private and social morality, and of all ethical thinking. However, the governing rules of morality, which have been widely challenged over the last 30 years in Western societies, no longer apply for young people, or even for some members of their parents' generation. They are no longer an insurmountable obstacle to the realization of any desires. Admittedly, this questioning attitude and trend towards permissiveness have thus far affected only the industrialized market-economy countries, but neither the socialist countries nor the third world can consider themselves safe from such changes. Moreover, in so far as the law is determined to a large extent by social mores, some impact has begun to be seen in the Western countries, in both legislation and court decisions. Moral permissiveness, encouraged by the media, advertising and cultural industries and only tenuously reined in by the courts, may thus be approaching the point where a continuing deterioration would provoke a backlash in the form of a sudden return to traditional moral values and traditional sanctions, and thus the remarginalization of sexual minorities. The Commission for Social Development, in an effort to ensure the physical and mental equilibrium of the child, is already considering proposing to the Economic and Social Council a major United Nations effort on behalf of the family. It is perhaps for the Commission on Human Rights, without questioning the usefulness of such an initiative, to consider which rights of the human person are at stake in the situation experienced by individuals who, because of sexual proclivity, find themselves excluded from a society in which the family constitutes the basic unit.

In individual cases, we have seen a great deal of suffering engendered more often than not by the feeling of being confined in a ghetto. The members of sexual minorities, who are the victims rather than the instigators of this confinement, are asking not that we should pity them, but that we should respect their difference and that our behaviour should be based on fellowship. We must make every effort to eliminate the causes of their suffering and afford them the possibility of escaping from the ghetto and fitting into society.

It would be worthwhile drawing up a general strategy taking account, in particular, of the fact that many of the situations studied are encouraged, if not determined, by the attitude of society. It is likely that societies have emphasized the distinction between the sexes more than necessary to ensure a happy and fruitful family life, and has established excessively hard and fast male and female prototypes. It is more than likely that the assertion of a purported male supremacy has had a deeply disturbing effect on many women and that there would be fewer lesbians if men were able to be more affectionate, more attentive and more tactful. Also, the virility model presented to men, seeming unattainable to many of them, has caused them to drift towards alternative forms of sexual activity. There would be less impotence and homosexuality if men did not feel called on by the social model to achieve with their female partners an exceptionally high level of sexual performance. In short, a considerable effort would have to be made for the long term, through improved education and a thorough review of the conduct of the media, to eliminate the artificiality of the contrast between the sexes and promote more equality and reciprocity between them. This would bring closer that future time hoped for by Ranier Maria Rilke, when "love would no longer be a relationship between man and woman but a relationship between one human being with another. Being more human, it will be infinitely sensitive and considerate, good and clear in all things which it initiates and resolves. It will be that love for which we work so hard—two solitudes protecting one another, complementing one another, limiting one another and yielding to one another."

*In view of the foregoing observations, the Sub-Committee on Prevention of Discrimination and Protection of Minorities may wish to propose that the Commission on Human Rights should recommend to Member States the adoption of a set of coherent measures, first and foremost in the areas of education and communication, the preventive strategy suggested in the following two paragraphs.* [Italics found in study.]

The first preventive action will consist of a policy in support of the family unit and the educational capacity of the parents. At the same time, in formal education, and particularly as part of the moral education and civics training which should begin at nursery school, it would be as well to institute, instead of or in conjunction with simple sex education, education in respect for life, respect for feelings and for the body and mutual respect between the sexes, which would also provide an early preparation for parental responsibilities. These goals are already provided for in a number of ongoing UNESCO programmes (studies of the image presented of men and women in textbooks, research into the influence of the media on the image of women) encouraged by the Economic and Social Council (resolution 1983/30, para. 11).

With regard to the media (cinema, radio and television, the press, cartoon strips, video cassettes, telephone, telematics, etc.) and advertising in the press, on the screen and on hoardings, it would be worth establishing multidisciplinary advisory commissions on which both parents and teachers were represented, as is already the case with regard to the cinema in a number of countries. These commissions would encourage the media to adopt a deontology of respect for women and children and would formulate guidelines which could be approved by Governments, with a view to protecting children against the spread of pornography which could upset the psychological equilibrium of the most insecure individuals and turn them into sex maniacs.

In addition, in the area of positive law, we have noted that changes in moral values have resulted in the non-application of a number of existing laws, so that the public is no longer quite sure what is permitted and what is not; we have also noted that existing laws vary considerably from one country to another and even within countries with federal systems. There should therefore be greater coherence between the law and judicial practice and greater harmony between the laws of various countries. As for the guiding principles, these should of course be, first and foremost, freedom, equality and nondiscrimination as embodied in the Universal Declaration of Human Rights (articles 2 and 7) and in the Covenants, together with the principle of respect for privacy (article 12 of the Universal Declaration) and of the "special safeguards" needed by the child (International Declaration of the Rights of the Child, adopted by the United Nations General Assembly on 20 November 1959).

*In the interests of non-discrimination and respect for privacy, the Sub-Commission on Prevention of Discrimination and Protection of Minorities may wish to propose to the Commission on Human Rights that it should recommend that Member States which have not already done so should take the legislative or regulatory measures described below as the second phase of an overall policy.* [Italics found in study.]

(a) As in the case of racism, any violence or discrimination practised against an individual because of sexual proclivity to be made punishable by law. Norwegian law already provides for this.

(b) All sexual practices to be tolerated between consenting adults, provided that they are practised in private and do not offend public decency.

(c) A genuine transsexual who has obtained a change of sex by medical means to be entitled to a change of civil status to conform to the new identity. This is already provided for by law in the Federal Republic of Germany and Sweden, among others.

(d) Sexual minorities to be authorized to form associations provided their activities do not contravene the law on associations or other laws.

However, as the guardian of the welfare of the community, the State has the right, and perhaps also the duty, to take, in respect of sexual minorities, precautions similar to those which it takes, without being reproached for it, with regard to any activity likely to present a danger to the natural environment, the human environment or the person engaging in the activity himself (as in the case of fishing, hunting, operation of powered equipment, possession and carrying of weapons, selling of alcoholic beverages and drugs, gambling, etc). In this respect, common sense coincides with the underlying ethics of the Universal Declaration of Human Rights in that, in order to make freedom and equality as accessible as possible to all, individuals and the State itself are called on, in a spirit of brotherhood, to protect the weakest and most vulnerable. This leads to the conclusion that, in addition to protecting sexual minorities . . . against any kind of persecution, the State can and must protect society against the potential dangers which such practices represent for "morality, public order and the general welfare" (article 29, 2, of the Universal Declaration). Furthermore, in the event of a conflict between the respective rights of men, women and children, the guiding principle should be to provide greater protection for the most vulnerable person—in many cases women, and in all cases the child.

*As part of their social defence responsibility, Governments and parliaments which feel unable to remain neutral with regard to such burning ethical and social issues could contemplate adopting (as the third element of an overall policy) the following legislation or regulations.* [Italics found in study.]

(a) *With regard to transsexuality,* protect:

The transsexual himself by imposing a period of reflection, requiring him to attend consultations before deciding to undergo an irreversible operation, and even establishing a minimum age for such operations;

The medical profession against the temptation of deriving profit from requests for unnecessary treatment, by making the administering of hormones and sex change operations subject to certain rules;

The spouse against the distortion, by a transsexual spouse, of the meaning and purpose of marriage by according the right to present any objections before an irreversible operation and affording him the possibility of a divorce on the basis of the decision taken.

(b) *With regard to homosexuality,* protect the health of the population and of homosexuals themselves by taking the precautions recommended by the World Health Organization, in so far as the male homosexual community is known . . . to be one of the groups exposed to a number of contagious diseases.

With regard to homosexuals in positions of authority over children (teachers, etc.), a frequently raised question . . . a choice must be made between the wish to avoid exposing children to the influence of a deviant model and the wish to eliminate any possible discrimination against a minority. Although no specific answer will be suggested here, attention is again drawn to the principle, recognized in the International Declaration of the Rights of the Child, of the special safeguards to be afforded to children by virtue of their vulnerability.

(c) *With regard to propaganda for any abnormal sexual practice,* to protect the mental and moral well-being of the population, and in particular of young people, by regulating freedom of expression to the extent authorized by article 19,

paragraph 3, of the International Covenant on Civil and Political Rights, by imposing on propaganda for such practices "certain restrictions, but these shall only be such as are provided by law and are necessary: (a) for respect of the rights or reputations of others; (b) for the protection of national security or of public order (ordre publique) or of public health or morals". This power of the State was recognized by the Human Rights Committee when considering a complaint against Finland.

(d) *With regard to paedophilia,* since minors are unable to protect themselves against adults, prohibit and severely punish any sexual relations between minors and adults (active paedophilia), even if the minor declares himself to be consenting. In view of the opportunities afforded to paedophiles by international tourism, standardize the age of sexual majority (age of consent) in all countries and for both girls and boys. This recommendation has already been made by the Council of Europe Parliamentary Assembly.

(e) *Concerning male prostitution,* proceed as recommended for female prostitution in Economic and Social Council resolution 1983/30, and, in particular, protect:

Young people by prohibiting, among other things, active soliciting in public places and the access of minors to certain establishments;

Prostitutes themselves against exploitation, by punishing procuring and collectively or bilaterally combating international traffic by *inter alia,* prohibiting the residence of foreign prostitutes.

The foregoing three groups of suggestions . . . obviously call for numerous consultations and lengthy consideration in order to weigh the advantages and disadvantages of legislating on moral values which are in a state of transition, in the knowledge that the criminalization of an act generally forces it underground, whereas its decriminalization (as in the case of abortion) leads to its proliferation. Another question is whether the measures . . . designed to protect young people do not run the risk—which it is hoped to avoid—of placing the individuals concerned under surveillance, making their marginalization official and even, as those concerned fear, encouraging a witch hunt. Consequently, the question of the advisability of a measure which would clearly be legitimate under the Universal Declaration of Human Rights and the Covenants, must be considered in the cultural and political context of each State.

The Sub-Commission was not able to consider the study at its 1987 session because, although completed, it had not been issued as a Sub-Commission document. The Sub-Commission requested (resolution 1987/31) that it be made available in document form and submitted at the 1988 session. At that session, the study (UN Doc. E/CN.4/Sub.2/1988/31) was examined in connection with item 14 A of the agenda, "Question of slavery and the slave trade in all their practices and manifestations, including the slavery-like practices of *apartheid* and colonialism."

***ENCLAVED GROUPS.*** At its 36th meeting, the UN Subcommission on Prevention of Discrimination and Protection of Minorities requested Mr. Asbjørn Eide to prepare a working paper on the concept of and issues relating to enclaved groups (Subcommission decision 1994/113). Following is the text of Eide's paper (E/CN.4/sub.2/1995/34, 21 July 1995).

### Introduction

At its 36th meeting, on 26 August 1994, the Subcommission by decision 1994/113, decided without a vote, to request Mr. Asbjørn Eide to prepare, without financial implications, a working paper on the concept and issues relating to "enclaved groups" and to present this paper to the Subcommission at its forty-seventh session. The following note constitutes the implementation of that request.

The notion of "enclaved groups" has not yet been formally defined under international law. It will here be treated on the basis of human rights law, including that of minority protection, but will be seen within the wider perspective of territorial integrity and political independence of States.

### First Distinction: Enclaved Groups Should Be Distinguished from International Enclaves

International enclaves are known under international law. Such enclaves are isolated parts of a foreign State's territory, entirely surrounded by the territory of another State (the surrounding State) so that it has no surface communication with the territory of the State to which it belongs (the mother or main State) other than through the territory of the surrounding State. While being an enclave from the perspective of the surrounding State, the same territory is an exclave from the point of view of the mother State.

In feudal time, thousands of enclaves existed in Europe. From the point of view of the surrounding State, an international enclave is foreign territory subject to the sovereignty of the mother State. One example is Llivia, a Spanish exclave in southern France which was not occupied by the German occupation force in France during the Second World War, since it belonged to a foreign, neutral State.

Under international law, the main State is entitled to establish its legal order throughout its enclave. International enclaves do not as such pose any particular problem to human rights.

### Second Distinction: Enclaved Groups Versus Autonomies

The concept of enclaved groups should be distinguished from majority populations in legally recognized autonomous territories within independent States.

Numerous autonomous areas can be found within sovereign States. Some of them are entirely within the territory of the sovereign State; others have borders with other States or border on international waters. One example of a territory entirely surrounded by territory of the sovereign State concerned is Nagorny Karabakh, under USSR law an autonomy within Azerbaijan. Upon dissolution of the USSR the 15 Union republics were recognized with the borders they had prior to independence, and Nagorny Karabakh was—and is—consequently a territory with a special status within Azerbaijan. Its future status at this point is subject to controversy, the majority of the population being American who have sought to make Nagorny Karabakh an independent State.

Numerous other autonomies existed within the Union republics of the USSR and continue at present as more or less autonomous entities within the independent States which previously were Union republics. They are not international enclaves, since they form part of the sovereign territory of the country in which they are located. The majority inhabitants can normally not be considered as enclaved groups, since they enjoy a degree of self-government within that territory; under special circumstances they might nevertheless suffer the same problems as those in enclaved groups properly speaking.

Those who constitute a minority within the autonomous area, on the other hand, sometimes experience the conditions of enclaved groups, as further defined below.

### Deported Peoples

Some particularly severe cases of enclaved groups existed in the Soviet Union from the time of the Second World War. Reference is made here as to the fate of the deported nationalities—the Kalmyks, the Crimean Tatars, the Volga Germans, the Meshkhetian Turks, the Koreans, the Greeks and the Kurds. Some 3.5 million were deported, and in the areas to which they were deported they lived a life which can only be described as enclaved groups, with very strict restrictions on their conditions of life, including even stricter restriction on their movement than those which applied to the ordinary Soviet citizen of the time. Many of them were condemned to a near cultural death. Their institutions destroyed, books (including those by Marx and Lenin) burned, typographies broken, each reverted to being a non-literate society. During the Gorbachev period, the tragic fate of these people became officially recognized and their right to return started to be implemented.

### Two Different Contexts of Enclaved Groups

It is submitted that enclaved groups in a reasonably restricted sense of the word can be found in two types of situations: (i) in times when ethnic conflict has resulted in a de facto division of territory within sovereign States along ethnic or religious lines, and where the Government does not hold control over part of its territory; (ii) in sovereign States where the Government has control over the whole of its territory finds itself subjected to particular restrictions.

### Enclaved Groups Under Unrecognized *de facto* Authorities

When a division of a territory on ethnic or religious grounds has temporarily been brought about, groups within the separated territory sometimes experience particularly serious hardship.

Under international law and on the basis of existing international recognition, the territory of both Bosnia and Hersegovina and Cyprus are clearly demarcated. The former comprises the whole territory formed by the republic of the same name in the federation of former Yugoslavia; Cyprus comprises the whole of the island of the same name. In both cases, however, there is at present a de facto division of the territory on an ethnic basis, and serious problems have arisen for non-dominant ethnic groups living in parts of the territory under control by the de facto authority. The qualification "enclaved" is justified because the territory has been split from the rest of the country concerned and the groups concerned are subject to particular hardships.

### The Most Serious Contemporary Situation Is Within Bosnia and Herzegovina

The de facto division of that country was initially brought about by intervention by the Yugoslav Army and has subsequently been maintained by the Bosnian Serbs. It has caused extreme violations of enclaved groups. The reports by Mr. Tadeusz Mazowiecki, the Special Rapporteur on the human rights situation in the territory of the former Yugoslavia of the Commission on Human Rights, as well as publications by numerous other institutions document at length the terrible fate of the Muslims and others living as enclaved groups within territories held by the Bosnian Serbs. Among those who have documented these violations are Amnesty International, Human Rights Watch/Helsinki and others.

The Humanitarian Law Centre in Belgrade, which since 1992 has been documenting, analyzing and monitoring human rights violations by all groups in former Yugoslavia, have, *inter alia,* documented the process of ethnic cleansing carried out by Bosnian Serbs against Bosnian Muslims and Bosnian Croats in many areas, such as Banja Luka.

Mr. Mazowiecki has in a recent report (E/CN.4/1996/3, 21 April 1995) provided detailed information about the terrifying events taking place in this region. While the mass murders and rapes of 1992–1993 have now abated, certain towns in the area still suffer sustained campaigns of violence directed principally against the Muslim inhabitants and also against Bosnian Croats. In smaller outlying towns and villages, gangs appear to be operating with impunity. Mr. Mazowiecki reports that on the streets the non-Serb population, especially Muslims, report feeling highly vulnerable. Testimonies that people have remained hidden in their homes for weeks and months at a time are commonplace. Non-Serbs are subject to random beatings and routine humiliations. In addition, men may be summarily detained at any time and held for service in forced labour brigades.

There are, however, according to Mr. Mazowiecki, encouraging reports that significant numbers of the local Serb population refuse to take part in the discriminating practices against the non-Serb population. Those Serbs, however, are also living under constant pressure from extremist nationalistic groups. Mr. Mazowiecki further reports that the Serbian de facto authorities make use on a large scale of civilians for unpaid forced labour. Recruits are almost invariably members of the Muslim, Croat and Roma population.

The forced labour obligation and the virulence of the ongoing campaign of violence have resulted in practically all non-Serbs fervently wishing to leave the Banja Luka area at present. This illustrates one significant point about the practice of establishing "enclaved groups": the underlying purpose, or effect, is to bring the non-wanted ethnic or religious group to leave the territory. At worst, it takes the form of outright physical killing, but more often it consists of creating conditions under which continued residence in the area becomes so unpleasant that at least the young part of the population leaves. In this way, establishing "enclaved group" conditions serves as a process of ethnic cleansing.

### The North of Cyprus: the Karpas Region

A second situation, less severe but very problematic for those who live there, exists in the north of Cyprus, which is under the control of the de facto Turkish Cypriot authorities and with the presence of some 30,000 members of the armed forces of the republic of Turkey. In the Karpas Peninsula the settlement was until 1974 almost entirely Greek Cypriot. Following the military conflict in 1974, the peninsula was entirely separated from the Greek Cypriot remainder of Cyprus, and the peninsula fell under Turkish Cypriot control. Reports indicate that the Greek Cypriot population groups

have been subjected to harassment and difficulties during the 21 years which have passed since the Turkish military intervention, and that the number of Greek Cypriots in the area has declined from 20,000 in 1974 to 10,000 in 1975, some 4,000 in 1976 and a gradual decline until, at the end of 1994, there remained some 520 Greek Cypriots in the Karpas region (s/1994/1407, para. 22).

### Turkish-Cypriot Enclaves from 1964 to 1974

The phenomenon of enclaves in Cyprus did not start in 1974, but has emerged as a consequence of a long, drawn-out confrontation between the two communities since the 1950's, due to competing views on the political future of the island. The initial desire by many Greek Cypriots for enosis, unification with Greece, was seen as a serious threat by the Turkish Cypriots. During the period of intermittent guerilla warfare prior to independence, the Turkish Cypriots, who had previously lived interspersed with the Greek Cypriots all over the island, started to retreat into enclaves, due to fear and pressure. The process continued after independence in 1960. Following the armed confrontations in December 1963, the formation of Turkish Cypriot enclaves intensified. The enclaves were for a time subjected to economic blockade which was continued until 1968 and significantly undermined the economic development of the Turkish Cypriot group and contributed to the widening gap in income and livelihood between Greek Cypriots and the Turkish Cypriots. It was further aggravated by the activities of General Grivas, an extreme nationalist, who sought to destabilize President Makarios and pushed for more violent action to achieve enosis.

### Enclaved Within Sovereign States With Control over the Territory

Enclaved groups can sometimes also be found in established sovereign States not subject to a de facto separation when a group lives compactly together in a part of the country, enjoying autonomy and surrounded by a majority population which is different from it in ethnic or religious terms, and whose members are subject to restrictions on their enjoyment of their human rights, their possibilities for economic and cultural activities, and on their right to freedom of movement, including their freedom to return to their place of residence after temporary departures. The group can be held to be enclaved if it appears probable that the restrictions are such as to block them from normal possibilities for economic and cultural self-realization.

Dr. Sadik Ahmet, living in Komotini, Greece, asserts that there is a large enclaved group of ethnic Turks (some 40,000) in the mountainous area of western Thrace between the Nestos and Evros rivers, encompassing parts of Xanthi, Rodopi and Evros prefectorates. He further asserts that there exists a military-restricted zone, initially established because of the civil war half a century ago but which still remains although the justification for its existence has disappeared. He claims that only ethnic Turks live in this area, that all roads leading to the area are blocked by military checkpoints, and that everyone wanting to visit the area needs special short-duration permits.

There are restrictions on the freedom of movement and restrictions on farming, forestry and manufacturing, and basic facilities are very rudimentary or non-existent. He further alleges that there are serious difficulties for the ethnic Turks to be allowed to cross the border to Bulgaria, when they wish to have "contacts across frontiers with citizens of other States to whom they are related by national or ethnic, religious or linguistic ties" as provided for by the Declaration on the Rights of Persons Belonging to National or Ethnic, Religious and Linguistic Minorities, article 2, paragraph 5.

### Towards a Working Definition

Based on these examples—and others could be added—we could now provide a working definition of enclaved groups:

Enclaved are groups of persons belonging to a national or ethnic, religious or linguistic group who have traditionally lived in the area; who differ from the general population now surrounding them; who are subject to special hardships due to restrictions imposed on them which are more severe than restrictions affecting members of the majority or dominant groups in the area concerned, or who experience fear of attack and maltreatment from members of the majority or dominant group, without being able to rely on effective and impartial protection by the local police and other agents of law.

An indicator of the existence of an enclaved group is when the restrictions have the purpose or effect of impairing their possibility to sustain and reproduce their culture within the territory in which they live.

Another indicator is when there are special restrictions on their movement to and from the area in they live. To attach the notion "enclave" to a minority group is appropriate only when their freedom of movement, including the right to return, is restricted. Mention is again made of article 2, paragraph 5, of the Declaration on the Rights of Persons Belonging to National or Ethnic, Religious and Linguistic Minorities, the whole text of which states:

"Persons belonging to minorities have the right to establish and maintain, without any discrimination, free and peaceful contacts with other members of their group and with persons belonging to other minorities, as well as contacts across frontiers with citizens of other States to whom they are related by national or ethnic, religious or linguistic ties."

Yet another indicator is when the group does not enjoy the same level of effective and impartial protection by the police and other agencies of law and order in the region where they live as do members of the majority or dominant groups in the area.

In my report "Possible ways and means of facilitating the peaceful and constructive resolution problems involving minorities", (E/CN.4/Sub.2/1993/34 and Add. 1–4, 11 August 1993), I noted in addendum 4, recommendation 1:

"The State should be the common home for all parts of its resident population under conditions of equality, with separate group identities being preserved for those who want it under conditions making it possible to develop those identities. Neither majorities nor minorities should be entitled to assert their identity in ways which deny the possibility for others to do the same, or which lead to discrimination against others in equitable sharing of the economic wealth and social benefits of the nation as a whole. Priority in minority protection should be given to members of groups which are truly vulnerable, subject to discrimination and marginalization by the majority."

The enclavement of groups reflects a pathological stage in the evolution of a multicultural society, where hegemonical ethnicity, sometimes reinforced by religion, and surrounded by security threats from various directions, temporarily blocks a mature development of democratic cooperation between all groups and the formation of a civil society cutting across all groups. Contemporary human rights are based on the equality of all human beings living within the territory of any State, without discrimination based, *inter alia*, on race, colour, religion, ethnic or national origin.

**BIBLIOGRAPHY.** Amnesty International. *Protecting Human Rights: International Procedures and How to Use Them.* London: 1987. NGO manual, in English.

Bokatola, Isse Omanga. *L'Organisation des Nations Unies et la Protection des Minorités* (The United Nations Organization and the Protection of Minorities). Brussels, Belgium: Émile Bruylant, 1992. Scholarly monograph, in French; bibliography, pp. 263–274.

Breitenmoser, Stephan, and Dagmar Richter. "Proposal for an Additional Protocol to the European Convention on Human Rights concerning the Protection of Minorities in the Participating States of the CSCE," *Human Rights Law Journal* 12, no. 6–7 (July 1991): 262–265. Scholarly article, in English.

Brölmann, Catherine, René Lefeber, and Marjoleine Zieck, eds. *Peoples and Minorities in International Law.* Dordrecht, the Netherlands: Martinus Nijhoff, 1993. Scholarly monograph, in English.

Burger, Julian. *Report from the Frontier: The State of the World's Indigenous Peoples.* Cambridge, MA, USA, and London: Cultural Survival and Zed Books, 1987. Scholarly study, in English.

Capotorti, Francesco. *Study on the Rights of Persons Belonging to Ethnic, Religious and Linguistic Minorities.* New York: United Nations Centre for Human Rights, 1991. IGO document, in English.

Chaliand, Gerard, ed. *Minority Peoples in the Age of Nation-States.* London: Minority Rights Group, 1989. Scholarly report, in English; originally published in French.

Cholewinski, Ryszard. "The Racial Discrimination Convention and the Protection of Cultural and Linguistic Ethnic Minorities," *Revue de droit international de sciences diplomatiques et politiques* no. 3 (Sept. 1991):157–226. Scholarly article, in English; bibliography, pp. 192–226.

Cultural Survival. *Cultural Survival Quarterly.* NGO quarterly journal, in English.

———. *Cultural Survival Reports.* Cambridge, MA, USA. NGO series of major reports and books on indigenous peoples, in English.

Cuthbertson, Ian M., and Jane Leibowitz, eds. *Minorities: The New Europe's Old Issue.* Institute for East West Studies, 1994. Collection of scholarly articles, in English.

Davies, Peter, ed. *Human Rights.* London: Minority Rights Group, 1988. Collection of essays, in English.

Dinstein, Yoram. "Freedom of Religion and the Protection of Religious Minorities," *Israel Yearbook on Human Rights* 20 (1990): 155–179. Scholarly article, in English.

Dinstein, Yoram, ed. "Specific Problems of Minorities/General Problems of Rights of Minorities," *Israel Yearbook on Human Rights* 21 (1991). Collection of scholarly articles, in English.

Downing, T. E., and G. Kushner, eds. *Human Rights and Anthropology.* Cambridge, MA, USA: Cultural Survival, 1988. Scholarly study, in English.

Garber, Larry. *Guidelines for International Election Observing.* Washington, D.C.: International Human Rights Law Group, 1984. Manual, in English.

Gesellschaft fur bedrohte Volker (Society for Endangered

Peoples). *Pogrom.* Göttingen, FRG. Journal and book-length reports issued as special issues ("Reihe Pogrom"), in German.

————. *Vierte Welt Aktuell.* Göttingen, FRG. Posters and urgent action bulletins, in German.

Gromacki, Joseph P. "The Protection of Language Rights in International Human Rights Law: A Proposed Draft Declaration of Linguistic Rights," *Virginia Journal of International Law* 32, no. 2 (Winter 1992): 515–579. Scholarly article, in English.

Groupement pour les Droits des Minorities (Minority Rights Group—France). *Les Minorities dans les Balkans* (Minorities in the Balkans). Paris: 1987. NGO report, in French.

Hailbronner, Kay. "The Legal Status of Population Groups in a Multinational State Under Public International Law," *Israel Yearbook on Human Rights* 20 (1990): 127–157. Scholarly article, in English.

Hannum, Hurst, ed. *Documents on Autonomy and Minority Rights.* Dordrecht, the Netherlands: Martinus Nijhoff, 1993. Scholarly monograph, in English.

————. *Guide to International Human Rights Practice.* Philadelphia, PA, USA: University of Pennsylvania Press, 1984. Scholarly study, in English.

Heinz, Wolfgang S. *Indigenous Populations, Ethnic Minorities and Human Rights.* Berlin, FRG: Quorum Verlag, 1988. Scholarly study, in English.

Heraclides, Alexis. "Secessionist Minorities and External Involvement," *International Organization* 44, no. 3 (Summer 1990): 341–378. Scholarly article, in English.

Indian Law Resource Center. *Indian Rights—Human Rights: Handbook for Indians on International Human Rights Complaints Procedures.* Washington, D.C.: 1984. NGO manual, in English.

International Work Group for Indigenous Affairs. *IWGIA Documents.* Copenhagen, Denmark. NGO series of special reports, in English.

————. *IWGIA Newsletter.* Copenhagen, Denmark. NGO irregularly issued report, in English.

————. *IWGIA Yearbook.* Copenhagen, Denmark. NGO annual report, in English.

————. *Native Power: The Quest for Autonomy and Nationhood of Indigenous Peoples.* Copenhagen, Denmark: Universitetsforlaget, 1985. NGO study, in English.

Jacoub, Joseph. "Genèse et évolution du concept de minorité: à la recherche d'une définition" (Genesis and Evolution of the Concept of Minority: Research Over a Definition), *Revue de l'Institut des Droits de l'Homme* no. 9 (1992): 6–21. Scholarly article, in French.

Joshi, Barbara, ed. *Untouchable! Voices of the Dalit Liberation Movement.* London: Minority Rights Group, 1986. NGO report, in English.

Kubota, Yo, ed. *Peoples for Human Rights: IMADR Yearbook 1988* 1, no. 1 (1989). Special issue on international efforts to eliminate discrimination, in English.

Kutukdjian, Georges B., and Antonio Papisca, ed. *Rights of Peoples.* Padova, Italy: Center for Training and Research on Human Rights and the Rights of Peoples, University of Padua, 1991. Collection of scholarly articles, in English and French.

Lerner, Natan. *Group Rights and Discrimination in International Law.* Dordrecht, the Netherlands: Martinus Nijhoff, 1991. Scholarly monograph, in English.

Minority Rights Group. *MRG Reports.* NGO series of reports on status of ethnic, religious, or racial minorities in countries throughout the world, in English; up to 1990, 80 reports have been published.

Moody, Roger, ed. *The Indigenous Voice: Visions and Realities.* 2 vols. Copenhagen, Denmark, and London: International Work Group for Indigenous Affairs and Zed Books, 1988. Scholarly study, in English.

Packer, John, and Kristian Myntti, eds. *The Protection of Ethnic and Linguistic Minorities in Europe.* Turku/Abo, Finland: Abo Akademi Institute for Human Rights, 1993. Scholarly monograph, in English.

Phillips, Alan, and Allan Rosas, eds. *The UN Minority Rights Declaration.* London: Abo Akademi Institute for Human Rights; Minority Rights Group International, 1993. Scholarly monograph/conference report, in English.

Ramaga, Philip Vuciri. "The Bases of Minority Identity," *Human Rights Quarterly* 14, no. 3 (Aug. 1992): 409–428. Scholarly article, in English.

————. "The Group Concept in Minority Protection," *Human Rights Quarterly* 15, no. 3 (Aug. 1993): 575–588. Scholarly article, in English.

————. "Relativity of the Minority Concept," *Human Rights Quarterly* 14, no. 1 (Feb. 1992): 104–119. Scholarly article, in English.

Ramcharan, B. G. "Security Council Patterns for Dealing with Ethnic Conflicts and Minority Problems," in *Broadening the Frontiers of Human Rights: Essays in Honour of Asbjorn Eide,* pp. 27–40. New York: Scandinavian University Press, 1993. Scholarly article, in English.

Rodley, Nigel S. "Conceptual Problems in the Protection of Minorities: International Legal Developments," *Human Rights Quarterly* 17, no. 1 (Feb. 1995): 48–71. Scholarly article, in English.

Roth, Stephen J. "Toward a Minority Convention: Its Need and Content," *Israel Yearbook on Human Rights* 20 (1990): 93–126. Scholarly article, in English.

Shaw, Malcolm N. "The Definition of Minorities in International Law," *Israel Yearbook on Human Rights* 20 (1990): 13–43. Scholarly article, in English.

Shepherd, Jr., George W., and David Penna, eds. *Racism and the Underclass: State Policy and Discrimination against Minorities.* Westport, CT, USA: Greenwood Press, 1991. Collection of scholarly works, in English; bibliography, pp. 167–172.

Sieghart, Paul, ed. *Human Rights in the UK.* London: Minority Rights Group, 1988. Collection of essays, in English.

Sigler, J. A., ed. *International Handbook on Race and Race Relations.* Westport, CT, USA: Greenwood Press, 1987. Collection, in English.

————. *Minority Rights: A Comparative Analysis.* Westport, CT, USA: Greenwood Press, 1983. Scholarly study, in English.

Staples, Lee. *Roots to Power: A Manual for Grassroots Organizing.* New York: Praeger, 1984. Manual, in English.

Stormorken, Bjorn, *HURIDOCS Standard Formats for Recording and Exchange of Information on Human Rights.* Kluwer Academic, 1985. Manual, in English.

Survival International. *Survival International News.* London and New York. NGO quarterly, in English.

Tabory, Mala. "Minority Rights in the CSCE Context," *Israel Yearbook on Human Rights* 20 (1990): 197–221. Scholarly article, in English.

Thornberry, Patrick. *International Law and the Rights of Minorities.* Oxford, UK: Oxford University Press, 1991. Scholarly monograph, in English; bibliography, pp. 431–443.

————. *Minorities and Human Rights Law.* London: Minority Rights Group, 1987. NGO report, in English.

Van Dyke, Vernon. *Human Rights, Ethnicity, and Discrimi-*

*nation*. Westport, CT, USA: Greenwood Press, 1985. Scholarly study, in English.

Whitaker, Ben, ed. *Minorities: A Question of Human Rights?* London: Minority Rights Group, 1984. Collection of essays, in English.

Yacoub, Joseph. *Les Assyro-Chaldeens: Un Peuple Oublie de l'Histoire* (The Assyro-Chaldeens: A People Outside of History). London: Minority Rights Group, 1987, in French.

## MINORITIES' RIGHTS: DECLARATION ON THE RIGHTS OF PERSONS BELONGING TO NATIONAL OR ETHNIC, RELIGIOUS AND LINGUISTIC MINORITIES, UN (1992).

At its 1978 session the UN **COMMISSION ON HUMAN RIGHTS** set up a working group, open to all members of the Commission, to consider drafting a declaration on the rights of members of special minorities, within the framework of the principles contained in article 27 of the **INTERNATIONAL COVENANT ON CIVIL AND POLITICAL RIGHTS.** A draft declaration on the rights of persons belonging to national, ethnic, religious, and linguistic minorities was submitted by Yugoslavia (UN Doc. E/CN.4/L.1367/Rev. 1) and used by the working group as a basis for discussion.

In 1981, a revised and consolidated text was prepared by the working groups Chairman/Rapporteur, and this text served as the basis of the completed text below. Adopted by the **GENERAL ASSEMBLY,** without a vote, on 18 December 1992 (resolution 47/135), the text of the Declaration is as follows:

The General Assembly,

Reaffirming that one of the basic aims of the United Nations, as proclaimed in its Charter, is to promote and encourage respect for human rights and for fundamental freedoms for all, without distinction as to race, sex, language or religion,

Reaffirming faith in fundamental human rights, in the dignity and worth of the human person, in the equal rights of men and women and of nations large and small,

Desiring to promote the realization of the principles contained in the Charter of the United Nations, the Universal Declaration of Human Rights, the Convention on the Prevention and Punishment of the Crime of Genocide, the International Convention on the Elimination of All Forms of Racial Discrimination, the International Covenant on Civil and Political Rights, the International Covenant on Economic, Social and Cultural Rights, the Declaration on the Elimination of All Forms of Intolerance and of Discrimination Based on Religion or Belief, and the convention on the Rights of the Child, as well as other relevant international instruments that have been adopted at the universal or regional level and those concluded between individual States Members of the United Nations,

Inspired by the provisions of article 27 of the International Covenant on Civil and Political Rights concerning the rights of persons belonging to ethnic, religious or linguistic minorities,

Considering that the promotion and protection of the rights of persons belonging to national or ethnic, religious and linguistic minorities contribute to the political and social stability of States in which they live,

Emphasizing that the constant promotion and realization of the rights of persons belonging to national or ethnic, religious and linguistic minorities, as an integral part of the development of society as a whole and within a democratic framework based on the rule of law, would contribute to the strengthening of friendship and cooperation among peoples and States,

Considering that the United Nations has an important role to play regarding the protection of minorities,

Bearing in mind the work done so far within the United Nations system, in particular the Commission on Human Rights, the Subcommission on Prevention of Discrimination and Protection of Minorities and the bodies established pursuant to the International Covenants on Human Rights and other relevant international human rights instruments on promoting and protecting the rights of persons belonging to national or ethnic, religious and linguistic minorities,

Taking into account the important work which is carried out by intergovernmental and non-governmental organizations in protecting minorities and in promoting and protecting the rights of persons belonging to national or ethnic, religious and linguistic minorities,

Recognizing the need to ensure even more effective implementation of international instruments with regard to the rights of persons belonging to national or ethnic, religious and linguistic minorities,

Proclaims this Declaration on the Rights of Persons Belonging to National or Ethnic, Religious and Linguistic Minorities:

*Article 1.* 1. States shall protect the existence and the national or ethnic, cultural, religious and linguistic identity of minorities within their respective territories, and shall encourage conditions for the promotion of that identity.

2. States shall adopt appropriate legislative and other measures to achieve those ends.

*Article 2.* 1. Persons belonging to national or ethnic, religious and linguistic minorities (hereinafter referred to as persons belonging to minorities) have the right to enjoy their own culture, to profess and practise their own religion, and to use their own language, in private and in public, freely and without interference or any form of discrimination.

2. Persons belonging to minorities have the right to participate effectively in cultural, religious, social, economic and public life.

3. Persons belonging to minorities have the right to participate effectively in decisions on the national and, where appropriate, regional level concerning the minority to which they belong or the regions in which they live, in a manner not incompatible with national legislation.

4. Persons belonging to minorities have the right to establish and maintain their own associations.

5. Persons belonging to minorities have the right to establish and maintain, without any discrimination, free and peaceful contacts with other members of their group and with persons belonging to other minorities, as well as contacts across frontiers with citizens of other States to whom they are related by national or ethnic, religious or linguistic ties.

*Article 3.* 1. Persons belonging to minorities may exercise their rights, including those set forth in this Declaration, individually as well as in community with other members of their group, without any discrimination.

2. No disadvantage shall result for any person belonging

to a minority as the consequence of the exercise or non-exercise of the rights set forth in this Declaration.

*Article 4.* 1. States shall take measures where required to ensure that persons belonging to minorities may exercise fully and effectively all their human rights and fundamental freedoms without any discrimination and in full equality before the law.

2. States shall take measures to create favourable conditions to enable persons belonging to minorities to express their characteristics and to develop their culture, language, religion, traditions and customs, except where specific practices are in violation of national law and contrary to international standards.

3. States should take appropriate measures so that, wherever possible, persons belonging to minorities have adequate opportunities to learn their mother tongue or to have instruction in their mother tongue.

4. States should, where appropriate, take measures in the field of education, in order to encourage knowledge of the history, traditions, language and culture of the minorities existing within their territory. Persons belonging to minorities should have adequate opportunities to gain knowledge of the society as a whole.

5. States should consider appropriate measures so that persons belonging to minorities may participate fully in the economic progress and development in their country.

*Article 5.* 1. National policies and programmes shall be planned and implemented with due regard to the legitimate interests of persons belonging to minorities.

2. Programmes of cooperation and assistance among States should be planned and implemented with due regard for the legitimate interests of persons belonging to minorities.

*Article 6.* States should cooperate on questions relating to persons belonging to minorities, including exchange of information and experiences, in order to promote mutual understanding and confidence.

*Article 7.* States should cooperate in order to promote respect for the rights set forth in this Declaration.

*Article 8.* 1. Nothing in this Declaration shall prevent the fulfillment of international obligations of States in relation to persons belonging to minorities. In particular, States shall fulfill in good faith the obligations and comittments they have assumed under international treaties and agreements to which they are parties.

2. The exercise of the rights set forth in this Declaration shall not prejudice the enjoyment by all persons of universally recognized human rights and fundamental freedoms.

3. Measures taken by States to ensure the effective enjoyment of the rights set forth in this Declaration shall not *prima facie* be considered contrary to the principle of equality contained in the Universal Declaration of Human Rights.

4. Nothing in this Declaration may be construed as permitting any activity contrary to the purposes and principles of the United Nations, including sovereign equality, territorial integrity and political independence of States.

*Article 9.* The specialized agencies and other organizations of the United Nations system shall contribute to the full realization of the rights and principles set forth in this Declaration, within their respective fields of competence.

**MINORITY RIGHTS GROUP.** An international non-governmental organization in consultative status

(Roster) with the UN **ECONOMIC AND SOCIAL COUNCIL,** MRG is affiliated with 16 organizations in 16 countries.

The Minority Rights Group was established in 1970 following the Biafra conflict in Nigeria. MRG is a global, impartial, and independent specialized research and information unit that has three principal aims: (1) to secure justice for groups suffering discrimination, by investigating their situation and publicizing the facts to educate and alert public opinion throughout the world; (2) to help prevent, through publicity about violations of human rights, such problems from developing into destructive conflicts; and (3) to foster, by its research findings, international understanding of factors which create prejudiced treatment and group tensions. To implement its goals, MRG monitors developments worldwide in minority situations, prepares impartial reports on these subjects, and disseminates the reports to several hundred newspapers and television and radio stations throughout the world, as well as making them available to universities, libraries, schools, and interested individuals. The group also organizes meetings and lectures and commissions multidisciplinary research into the causes of human rights problems and their possible solution. In 1982, in recognition of its work, MRG was awarded the United Nations Association Media Peace Prize.

MRG has an extensive publication program. Its primary publication is the newsletter *Outsider.* Since its inception, MRG has published 77 reports and updates on minority situations, including *Japan's Minorities, Roma: Europe's Gypsies, The Amerindians of South America, Western Europe's Migrant Workers, The Social Psychology of Minorities,* and *The Falashas: the Jews of Ethiopia;* as of 1994, MRG has approximately 80 publications available. On average, MRG produces five new reports and ten updated reports annually.

Minority Rights Group. Address: 379 Brixton Road, London SW9 7DE, UK. Telephone: (44-1) 930-6659. Director: Alan Phillips.

**MOLDOVA.** The Republic of Moldova, located in eastern Europe, is a small land-locked country bordering Ukraine on the north, east, and south and Romania on the west. It declared its independence from the former Soviet Union in August 1991 and was admitted to the UN in 1992. Moldova was an original signatory to the Alma-Ata Declaration of December 1991 establishing the Commonwealth of Independent States and became a full, official member in 1994. Its population is estimated to be 4,474,000, comprising 65% Moldovan/ethnic Romanians, 14% ethnic Ukrainians, and 13% ethnic Russians. An estimated

99% profess the Eastern Orthodox religion and the literacy rate is 100%.

The current republic comprises the eastern half of what was a larger region of Moldovia. The Russian and Ottoman empires divided the region into two parts in 1812. Following the collapse of the Russian Empire in 1918, the territory, known then as Bessarabia, became independant for a brief time but voted to become a provence of the Kingdom of Romania which it did in 1920. However, the Soviet Union annexed the territory in 1940 and it eventually became the Moldovan Soviet Socialist Republic. Following a brief period of reunification with Romania from 1941 to 1944, the Soviet re-annexed it and controlled it through the Communist Party of Moldova until 1991.

Soviet policy denied commonalities of language, history, and culture with Romania and discouraged affiliation by closing the border and resettling Moldovans in Siberia and elsewhere. At the same time, it enforced stronger ties with the other Soviet republics of Ukraine and Russia by encouraging immigration from these areas.

With Soviet President Gorbachev's new era of *glasnost* (openness) during the second half of the 1980s, ethnic Moldovans pressed reforms aimed at diminishing the influence of the Soviet Union. Romanian was made the official language in September 1989, the constitutional power of the Communist Party was revoked in May 1990, and the name of the country was changed to omit the qualifying title of "Soviet Socialist" republic in May 1991. After declaring independence following the unsuccessful coup against Soviet President Gorbachev in August 1991, the Moldovan Parliament banned the Communist Party and demanded the withdrawal of Soviet troops.

Amidst confusion over the question of whether to unite with Romania, Moldova was faced with separatist movements within its own boundaries. In September 1990, the mostly Slav popluation in the eastern part of the country known as Trans Dniester called for secession from Moldova. Following armed conflict and an exodus of an estimated 50,000 people to Ukraine, Moldova and Russia signed a peace agreement in 1992, giving "special status" to Trans Dniester. Another separatist region in the south west, Gagauzia, also demanded statehood but eventually seemed to accept its role, albeit with greater autonomy, within Moldova. No country has recognized the independence of either region.

A new constitution was drafted in 1993 and 1994, providing for direct election of the president and a 104-member unicameral legislature by universal suffrage . The incumbent president, Mircea Snegur, had run unopposed and was elected with 98% of the vote in December 1991. In February 1994 legislative elections, 56 of the 104 seats were won by the Agrarian-Democratic Party, made up largely of the former communist leadership. The pro-Russian Socialist Party gained 28 seats and the two smaller parties favoring union with Romania, the Peasants' Party of Moldova/ Congress of Intelligentsia and Christian Democratic Popular Front Alliance, won 20 seats between them. The elections were boycotted by Trans Dniester but its residents were able to cross into Moldova to vote.

**BIBLIOGRAPHY.** Amnesty International. *Moldova: The Trial of the "Tiraspol Six"*. London: 1993. NGO report, in English.

Benifand, Alexander. "The Russian Policy and the Intensification of Civil Wars in Georgia, Tajikistan and Moldova," *Refuge* 12, no. 7 (Feb. 1993): 12–15. Article, in English.

Ganea, Alexandru. "Testing Times—State Terrorism Two Years on—This Year's August Coup: Interview with Mircea Druc, Former Moldovan Prime Minister," *East European Reporter* 5, no. 4 (July–Aug. 1992): 40–44. Article, in English.

Helsinki Watch. *Human Rights in Moldova: The Turbulent Dniester.* New York: 1993. NGO report, in English.

Immigration and Refugee Board Documentation Centre. *Moldova: Chronology of Events, June 1940–February 1993*. Ottawa, Canada: 1993. Government briefing paper, in English and French.

**MONACO.** The Principality of Monaco is a country in western Europe, on the Mediterranean Sea, almost totally surrounded by France. After 800 years of independence, Monaco was annexed to France in 1793. It was under the protection of Sardinia from 1815 to 1861, when it returned to French guardianship as an independent nation. It became a member of the United Nations in 1993. In elections to the 18-seat National Council in January 1993, two lists of candidates won 17 seats and an independent won one seat. The *Union Nationale et Democratique* (UND) has dominated the previous six elections since 1963.

Monaco's population is estimated to be 31,000. Ethnic and national groups include Monegasque (16%), French (47%), and Italian (16%). Languages in common use include French (official), Italian, and Monegasque. Christianity (Roman Catholic, 95%) is the predominant religion. Literacy is estimated at 99%.

The government (1994) took the form of a monarchy. Under the constitution of 1962, the ruler, Prince Rainier III, is head of State. He is assisted by an 18-member National Council, members of which are elected by popular vote for terms of five years. Executive authority is vested in the Minister of State, who is the head of government. The judicial system includes the Court of First Instance, the Court of Appeal, the Court of High Appeal, the Criminal Court, and the Supreme Court. The only political party is the National and Democratic Union.

# M

**MONETA, ERNESTO TEODORO (1833–1918).** An Italian journalist who shared the 1907 **NOBEL PEACE PRIZE** with **LOUIS RENAULT,** Ernesto Moneta was a soldier and freedom-fighter who turned "militant pacifist" and "nationalistic internationalist." Moneta fought in the war against Austria for Italian independence in a corps of mountain troops organized by Giuseppe Garibaldi.

After the war, Moneta became an editor of the Milan newspaper *Il Secolo,* the most influential newspaper of its day. In 1887, he founded in Milan the International Society for Peace, which favored disarmament and the establishment of an intergovernmental organization that would settle international disputes by arbitration. He also founded the pacifist periodical *La Vita Internazionale* and participated on the Commission of the **INTERNATIONAL PEACE BUREAU** in 1895 and in the 1906 International Peace Conference.

Despite his love of peace, Moneta was a realist who supported Italy's entry into World War I. In his Nobel acceptance speech, he gave his advice: "Keep your powder dry and always be ready to defend yourself; this is for Italy, as well as for others, a hard necessity at the present time."

**BIBLIOGRAPHY.** Gray, Tony. *Champions of Peace.* London: Paddington Press, 1976.

Schlessinger, Bernard S., and June H. Schlessinger, eds. *Who's Who of Nobel Prize Winners.* Phoenix, AZ, USA: Oryx Press, 1991.

**MONGOLIA.** Formerly known as Outer Mongolia, the Mongolian People's Republic is a country in east Asia. Its population is estimated to be 2,336,000.

In 1990, the legislature passed amendments to the constitution as well as electoral laws which allowed for the official registration of political parties. The fourth constitution was approved in January 1992, providing for a unicameral legislature, the 76-seat Great *Hural* elected for a four-year term by universal suffrage; a president elected for a four-year term; and a nine-seat Constitutional Court appointed by the legislature, the president, and the Supreme Court. It also changed the name of the country to Mongolia from the Mongolian People's Republic. Forced labor is permitted as punishment under the constitution and travel at home and abroad may be restricted for security reasons.

In June 1992 elections, the Mongolian People's Revolutionary Party won 71 of the 76 seats. There were 293 candidates. A presidential law was passed in March 1993 and in elections in June of that year the incumbent head of state, Punsalmaagiyn Ochirbat, won with 58% of the vote.

In January 1993 and April 1994, respectively, Mongolia signed Treaties of Friendship and Cooperation with Russia and China. By September 1992, all Russian troops had left Mongolia.

**BIBLIOGRAPHY.** Amnesty International. *Mongolia: Continuing Legislative Reform.* London: 1992. NGO report, in English.

International Human Rights Law Group. *Mongolia in Midstream: A Final Report on the 1990 Mongolian Elections.* Washington, D.C.: 1990. NGO factfinding report, in English.

**MOROCCO.** The Kingdom of Morocco is a country in northern Africa, on the Atlantic Ocean. It has borders with Algeria and Mauritania. It achieved independence from France in 1956 and became a member of the United Nations the same year. Its population is estimated to be 27,005,000. Moroccans are largely of Arab–Berber descent, but the national census provides no breakdown as to race, language, or ethnic group. Languages commonly used include Arabic (official), French, Spanish, and several Berber vernaculars. Islam is the religion of the State; Jewish and Christian communities practice their religion in accordance with Moroccan law, which vests them with legal personality and enables them to own immovable property. Literacy is estimated at 28%.

The government (1994) took the form of a monarchy, with the king as ruler and head of State. Executive authority as head of government is exercised by the prime minister, who represents the party of coalition given the majority of elected seats in the 306-member Chamber of Deputies (of the 306 members, 204 are elected by popular vote, while the remainder is chosen by local councils and groups). Political parties include the Constitutional Union Party, the National Democratic Party, the Popular Movement, and *Isviglol.*

Throughout most of its history, Morocco has been invaded and occupied by colonial forces. Once an outpost of the Roman Empire, it was seized by the Vandals after the Roman collapse. Later the Arabs invaded and brought Islam to the country, all but wiping out Christianity. Jewish colonies in Morocco, however, retained their religion, prospered, and increased in size.

***INDEPENDENCE FROM FRANCE.*** Morocco first became an independent State in 788. But, after a period of unrest, its coastline was seized by Spain and Portugal soon after they had dispelled the Moors (people from Morocco) from the Iberian Peninsula. The Spanish remained in the country through the 20th century. In the 20th century, France seized some of its territory, and the Germans threatened to take it away by force. They agreed, instead, to recognize Morocco as a

French protectorate in exchange for the cession of French territory in Equatorial Africa. French Morocco remained loyal to the Vichy government even after the fall of France in 1940, at which time both France and Germany rushed to reorganize its economy in order to feed their people. Spanish Morocco, however, was partly occupied by Mauritania and eventually the Spanish, who had promised the territory self-determination, withdrew.

The question of Moroccan independence was raised in the UN **GENERAL ASSEMBLY** in 1951, when six Arab States complained of violations by France of the principles of the **UNITED NATIONS CHARTER** and of the **UNIVERSAL DECLARATION OF HUMAN RIGHTS** and asked the assembly to look into the matter. When the assembly postponed consideration of the matter, the question of Morocco was raised again at the next session of the assembly by 13 States which charged that stringent French rule had compromised the sovereignty of the country and that the national movement in Morocco was being oppressed. In a resolution adopted on 19 December 1952, the Assembly expressed its confidence that France would "endeavor to further fundamental liberties of the people of Morocco" and that the parties would "continue negotiations toward developing the free political institutions of the people of Morocco."

In 1953, 15 Asian and African countries requested an urgent meeting of the UN **SECURITY COUNCIL** to investigate the danger to international peace and security arising out of the intervention of France in Morocco and the overthrow of its legitimate sovereign, Sultan Mohammed V. The issue was not included in the Council's agenda, France maintaining that the United Nations had no right to intervene since the question was one of domestic jurisdiction. The issue was later discussed at three sessions of the General Assembly.

On 2 March 1956, a joint declaration on the status of Morocco was signed by France and Morocco by which France recognized the independence of Morocco. A revised Constitution was approved by national referendum in September 1992. Legislation would take effect within one month of passage regardless of whether it had received royal assent; basic human rights were to be guaranteed; and a constitutional council and an economic and social council were to be established.

Elections to the 222 directly elected seats in the Chamber of Representatives took place in June 1993, with the Union Socialiste des Forces Populairs (USFP) winning 48 seats. Elections in 13 constituencies were thereafter annulled by the Constitutional Council for electoral malpractice and by-elections were held in

April 1994. An additional 111 were elected by an electoral college of local officials in September 1994.

*WESTERN SAHARA.* In 1975, many thousands of Moroccans marched into Spanish Sahara in support of their government's claim that the northern part of the area was legally a part of Morocco. The Moroccan Government subsequently annexed the northern two-thirds of Spanish Morocco, and Mauritania annexed the southern one-third. Spain withdrew, giving up its earlier demand for self-determination for the peoples of the sparsely populated area which is rich in phosphates.

The Polisario Front, a guerrilla movement, declared Spanish Sahara to be independent and launched attacks against the two annexing States. Morocco, with military and economic assistance from the United States of America, retained its hold on the northern portion of the territory, but Mauritania withdrew from the southern portion in 1979 after signing a treaty with the Polisario Front. Morocco then completed its annexation of the entire Spanish Sahara. In the face of protests by the leaders of neighboring African countries, Morocco in 1981 agreed to an internationally supervised referendum to determine the fate of the area.

Since 1986, the chairman of the **ORGANIZATION OF AFRICAN UNITY** and the UN Secretary-General have joined in offering their good offices with a view to promoting a just and lasting solution of the question of Western Sahara. On 30 August 1988, their proposals concerning the referendum were agreed in principle by the Kingdom of Morocco and the *Frente Popular.* However, the conditions necessary for holding the referendum—without any administrative or military constraints, and organized and supervised by the United Nations in cooperation with the OAU—had not been met up to 11 December 1989, when the General Assembly appealed (resolution 44/88) to both parties to display the cooperation and the political goodwill necessary to achieve an acceptable solution.

*UNITED NATIONS MISSION FOR THE REFERENDUM IN WESTERN SAHARA (MINURSO).* In 1985, the UN Secretary-General, in cooperation with the Chairman of the Assembly of Heads of State and Government of the Organization of African Unity, initiated a joint mission of good offices in search for a solution to the question of Western Sahara. On 11 August 1988, the Secretary-General presented, in separate meetings, to the Government of Morocco and the Polisario Front a document referred to as "the settlement proposal." The document called for a ceasefire and the holding of a referendum, without military or administrative constraints, to enable the people of Western Sahara to choose between independence or integration with Morocco.

On 29 April 1993, the UN Security Council (resolution 690 [1991]) established MINURSO and budgeted the mission for 20 weeks. The mission, however, is still in effect. A referendum was rescheduled for mid-1994; but, among other problems, voter registration and eligibility lists were in question.

### REPORT OF THE UN HUMAN RIGHTS COMMITTEE.

After reviewing the third periodic report of Morocco under article 40 of the International Covenant on Civil and Political Rights (CCPR/C/76/Add. 3 and 4), the Human Rights Committee adopted, on 2 November 1994, the following comments (CCPR/C/79/Add. 44, paras. 4–24):

*Factors and Difficulties Affecting the Implementation of the Covenant.* The Committee recognizes that the State party has embarked on a wide-ranging process of amending its domestic legislation to bring it into line with the Covenant. The process has not yet been completed and steps remain to be taken to harmonize the Constitution with the Covenant and develop democratic institutions and human rights machinery for better implementation of the Covenant. The remnants of certain traditions and customs constitute an obstacle to the effective implementation of the Covenant, particularly with regard to equality between men and women.

*Positive Aspects.* The Committee recognizes that the attitude of the Government has recently changed towards a greater openness in its handling of human rights issues, including its reporting obligations under the Covenant. In the latter regard, some frank oral answers given during the consideration of the report to questions raised by members regarding issues such as disappearances, the existence of the Tazmamart detention centre, the whereabouts of persons previously detained therein, as well as the fate of the Oufkir family were appreciated.

The Committee welcomes the numerous measures taken during the period under review to improve democracy and institute a legal environment more favourable to the promotion and protection of human rights. The Committee notes with satisfaction the promulgation in 1992 of an amended Constitution and the amnesty of a number of political prisoners. Compensation is being payed to certain persons illegally detained. The Committee was also glad to learn of the commutation of death sentences to life imprisonment sentences, the establishment of the Constitutional Council and the Economic and Social Council, the holding on 27 September 1993 of parliamentary elections, as well as the holding of a national symposium on problems affecting the news, information and communication services to recommend modifications in the legislation to, *inter alia*, bring it into line with international human rights standards, which constitute steps to consolidate the rule of law. Some progress has been made in the promotion of the status of women and women have been elected to Parliament for the first time. It takes note of the expanded role of the Advisory Council on Human Rights and the efforts made to promote public awareness of the rights guaranteed under the Covenant. The Committee also welcomes the information that measures have been taken to teach the Covenant and other international human rights instruments to members of the judiciary and the police. The freedom now given to nongovernmental organizations to be active in the country is also a matter of appreciation.

*Main Subjects of Concern.* The Committee notes that the Constitution does not contain specific provisions as to the relationship between international treaties and domestic law. Accordingly, there is a need to better define the place of the Covenant within the Moroccan legal system to ensure that domestic law is applied in conformity with the provisions of the Covenant.

The Committee is concerned about Morocco's role with regard to the persistent problems faced regarding self-determination in Western Sahara.

The Committee regrets that, although some improvement has been achieved as regards the status of women, the State party has not yet embarked on all the necessary reforms to combat the difficulties still impeding equality between men and women. The Constitution provides for equality only in the area of political rights, and the situation of women in both public and private law continues to be *de jure* or *de facto* the object of discrimination as regards the right to leave the country, freedom of commercial activities, personal status, marriage, divorce, inheritance rights, transmission of nationality, education, access to work and participation in the conduct of public affairs.

The Committee is concerned that the categories of crimes punishable by the death penalty include crimes in respect of which, by reference to article 6 of the Covenant, the death penalty should not be imposed.

Despite the amnesty of political prisoners and the destruction of certain unregistered places of detention, the Committee continues to deplore that a large number of cases of summary and arbitrary executions, enforced or involuntary disappearances, torture and arbitrary or unlawful detention committed by members of the police or the army, including cases concerning persons previously detained in Tazmamart, have not yet been investigated. Furthermore, the perpetrators of such acts were neither brought to justice nor punished. The Committee cannot accept that the names of those charged with these offences were not made public. The Committee deplores that measures of clemency adopted during the period under review were generally not extended to Western Sahara.

The Committee is concerned that guarantees contained in articles 9, 10 and 14 of the Covenant are not complied with. Despite some efforts to build new prisons, the Committee remains concerned about conditions of detention, particularly overcrowding of prisons, which frequently lead to malnutrition, diseases and deaths of detainees. Concern is also expressed over the long period of detention without charge under article 154 of the Code of Criminal Procedure which appears to be incompatible with article 9 of the Covenant. The Committee is also concerned about the obstacles to the independence and impartiality of the judiciary.

The Committee is concerned about the full implementation of the right to freedom of movement, including in particular the restrictions still imposed on members of the Oufkir family.

The Committee notes with regret the shortcomings in the observance of article 18 of the Covenant, in particular the restrictions affecting the Bahais' right to profess and practice their belief and limitations on inter-religious marriage. Concern is also expressed at the impediment placed upon the freedom to change one's religion.

The Committee expresses concern about the extent of the

limitations to the freedom of expression, assembly and association under the Dahir of 1973 and especially limitations on the right to criticise the Government. Governmental control of the media as well as the imprisonment of some journalists for having expressed criticisms give rise to serious concern.

The Committee is concerned that the electoral system, under which two thirds of members of the House of Representatives are elected by direct universal suffrage and one third by an electoral college, may raise issues as to the requirements, under article 25 (b) of the Covenant, that elections be held by "universal and equal suffrage". The wide scope of executive power in the hands of the King has implications for the effective independence of the judiciary and the democratic processes of Parliament.

*Suggestions and Recommendations.* The Committee recommends that the State party consolidate the process of constitutional revision in order to ensure that all the requirements of the Covenant are reflected in the Constitution, thereby bringing the Constitution into true compliance with the Covenant and to ensure that the limitations imposed on the exercise of rights and freedoms under national legislation do not go beyond those permitted under the Covenant.

The Committee expresses the wish that the Government of Morocco gives serious consideration to becoming a party to the first Optional Protocol.

The Committee further recommends that Morocco studies measures to limit the categories of crimes punishable by death penalty to the most serious offences, with a view to its eventual abolition.

The Committee emphasizes the need for the Government to prevent and eliminate discriminatory attitudes and prejudices towards women and to revise domestic legislation with a view to bring it in conformity with articles 2, 3 and 23 of the Covenant, taking into account the recommendations contained in the Committee's general comments Nos. 4, 18 and 19. It recalls in that regard that, although several reservations have been made by Morocco in acceding to the Convention on the Elimination of All Forms of Discrimination against Women, Morocco remains bound to the fullest extent by the provisions of articles 2, 3, 23 and 26 of the Covenant.

The Committee recommends that the Moroccan authorities ensure that summary and arbitrary executions, enforced or involuntary disappearances, torture, ill-treatment and illegal or secret detention do not occur and that any such cases be investigated in order to bring before the courts those suspected of having committed or participated in such crimes, to punish them if found guilty, and to provide compensation to victims. The Committee expresses the wish that any measures of clemency be granted on a non-discriminatory basis in conformity with articles 2 and 26 of the Covenant. It also recommends that measures of administrative detention and incommunicado detention be restricted to very limited and exceptional cases, and that the guarantees concerning pre-trial detention provided for in article 9, paragraph 3, of the Covenant be fully implemented. Further measures should also be taken to improve detention conditions and, particularly, to ensure that the United Nations Standard Minimum Rules for the Treatment of Prisoners are complied with and the relevant regulations and directives known and accessible to prisoners. Proposed measures to strengthen the presumption of innocence should be implemented as soon as possible.

The Committee emphasizes the need to take further measures to guarantee the freedom of religion and to eliminate discrimination on religious grounds. It suggests in this connection that the State party takes into account the recommendations contained in the general comment on article 18 of the Covenant.

The Committee recommends that restrictions imposed to the rights to freedom of expression, assembly and association under the Dahir of 1973 be modified and brought into line with those permitted under the Covenant to ensure their application in conformity with the Covenant on a non-arbitrary basis.

The Committee recommends that the authorities ensure that the third periodic report of Morocco and the comments of the Committee be disseminated as widely as possible in order to encourage the involvement of all sectors concerned on the improvement of human rights.

**BIBLIOGRAPHY.** Amnesty International. *Morocco: Breaking the Wall of Silence: the "Disappeared" in Morocco [includes correction].* London: 1993. NGO report, in English.

—————. *"Disappearances" of People of Western Saharan Origin.* London: 1990. NGO factfinding report, in English and French.

—————. *Morocco: Human Rights Violations in Garde a Vue Detention.* London: 1990. NGO report, in English.

—————. *Morocco: A Pattern of Political Imprisonment, 'Disappearances' and Torture.* London: 1991. NGO factfinding report, in English and French.

—————. *Morocco: The Pattern of Political Imprisonment Must End.* London: 1994. NGO report, in English.

—————. *Morocco: Students and Academics as Victims of Human Rights Violations.* London: 1991. NGO factfinding report, in English and French.

—————. *Torture in Morocco.* New York: 1986. NGO report, in English.

Anti-Slavery Society. *Child Labour in Morocco's Carpet Industry.* London: 1978. NGO report, in English.

Arab Organization for Human Rights. *Human Rights in the Arab World.* Cairo: 1987. NGO report, in English or Arabic.

Bendourou, Omar. "The Exercise of Political Freedoms in Morocco," *ICJ Review* 40 (June 1988): 31–41. NGO article, in English.

Benlakhel, Nadia. "Dossier Maroc: une presse sous haute surveillance" (The Morocco File: The Press under High Surveillance), *Lettre de Reporters Sans Frontières* no. 20 (Dec. 1990): 13–15. NGO article, in French.

Chaoui, Abdelkader. "Blindfold Justice," *Index on Censorship* 18, no. 1 (Jan. 1989): 20–22. NGO article, in English.

Fédération Internationale des Droits de l'Homme. *Rapport de Mission: mission d'observation dans les zones libérées de la République sahraouie démocratique* (Report of an Observer Mission in the Liberated Areas of the Saharawi Democratic Republic). Paris: 1990. NGO factfinding report, in French.

Lawless, R., and L. Monahan, eds. *War and Refugees: The Western Sahara Conflict.* London: Refugee Studies Programme, Queen Elizabeth House, 1987. Scholarly edited collection, in English.

Lederman, N., and A. Weber. *Rapport de Mission: Maroc, Proces de Casablanca, Affaire de Baha'is* (Mission Report: Morocco, Trial of Baha'is in Casablanca). Paris: Fédération International des Droits de l'Homme, 1984. NGO mission report, in French.

Minkowski, A., and C. Rostoker. *Rapport de Mission: La Situation des Grevistes de la Faim de Marrakech (28 Julliet–1 Aout)* (Mission Report: The Situation of the Hunger Strikers of Marrakech [July 28–August 1]). Paris: Fédération Interna-

# M

tionale des Droits de l'Homme, 1985. NGO mission report, in French.

Perregaux, Christiane. *Femmes sahraouies, femmes du désert* (Saharan Women, Women of the Desert). Paris: Harmattan, 1990. Scholarly monograph, in French.

Sivan, Emmanuel. "The Kabyls: An Oppressed Minority in North Africa," in *Case Studies on Human Rights and Fundamental Freedoms: A World Survey*, vol. 1, ed. W. A. Veenhoven, pp. 261–279. The Hague: Martinus Nijhoff, 1975. Edited collection, in English.

Smith, Theresa K. "Human Rights and the Western Sahara War," *Association of Concerned Africa Scholars Bulletin* 23 (Spring 1988): 10–17. Scholarly article, in English.

Weber, Alain. "Morocco: L'Affaire des Baha'is du Maroc devant la Cour Supreme de Rabat" (Morocco: The Trial of Baha'is before the Supreme Court of Rabat) *Lettre de la FIDH* 225 (1 Dec. 1987): 3–4. NGO article, in French.

**MOTHER TERESA.** See **TERESA, MOTHER.**

**MOTT, JOHN RALEIGH (1865–1955).** Chosen as co-winner of the 1946 **NOBEL PEACE PRIZE** (along with **EMILY GREENE BALCH**), John Raleigh Mott represents a Nobel laureate whose life work was devoted to young people and to "Christian ideals of peace and tolerance among nations," as cited by the Prize Committee.

Mott was born in Livingston Manor, NY (USA), and studied philosophy and history at Cornell University, where he first became interested in spreading Christianity among students. He represented his college's Young Men's Christian Association (YMCA) at the first international, interdemoninational conference in 1886 (he also served as president of the Cornell chapter of the YMCA). Upon graduation, he became national secretary of the American and Canadian Intercollegiate YMCA. He served as presiding officer at the World Missionary Conference in 1910; organized the World's Student Christian Federation, and helped set up Christian student movements throughout Europe, Asia, and the Middle East. During the two world wars, Mott worked with his organizations to relieve the conditions of soldiers and prisoners of war. After World War II, at the age of 80, Mott held a world conference in Geneva, Switzerland to bring together the organizations that had been disrupted by the war. In addition to his tireless activity on behalf of the YMCA, Mott also wrote 16 books on evangelism and the organization's world mission.

***BIBLIOGRAPHY.*** Gray, Tony. *Champions of Peace.* London: Paddington Press, 1976.

Schlessinger, Bernard S., and June H. Schlessinger, eds. *Who's Who of Nobel Prize Winners.* Phoenix, AZ, USA: Oryx Press, 1991.

**MOVEMENT AND RESIDENCE.** See **FREEDOM OF MOVEMENT AND RESIDENCE.**

**MOZAMBIQUE.** The Republic of Mozambique is a country in eastern Africa, on the Indian Ocean. It has borders with Malawi, South Africa, Swaziland, Tanzania, Zambia, and Zimbabwe. It achieved independence from Portugal in 1975 and became a member of the United Nations the same year. Its population is estimated to be 15,795,000. Ethnic groups include many indigenous tribal groups and persons of European, Euro–African, and Indian descent. Languages commonly used are Portuguese (official) and a number of Bantu vernaculars. Religions practiced include Animism (48%), Christianity (17%), and Islam (17%). Literacy is estimated at 15%.

The government (1994) took the form of a republic. President Joaquim Alberto Chissano, as head of State and government, exercises executive authority with the assistance of a cabinet which he appoints. Legislation is prepared by the People's Assembly. The judiciary is modelled on the Portuguese system of civil law. The only political party is the National Front for the Liberation of Mozambique (FRELIMO), which was led through the 10-year war for independence by Mr. Chissano. The first multiparty elections in Mozambique's history, monitored by the United Nations, were held over three days in October 1994, with FRELIMO winning 129 of the 250 parliamentary seats and RENAMO (Mozambique National Resistance) winning 112. President Chissano was elected with 53% of the votes while Renamo's leader won 34% of the votes.

A Portuguese colony for 470 years, Mozambique won its guerrilla war for independence after its national liberation movement, FRELIMO, overwhelmed 40,000 troops sent from Portugal and forced a ceasefire in 1974, an event which promised independence. However, the new Marxist government spent the following 14 years in fighting anti-government guerrillas backed by South Africa and in trying to feed its people suffering from a prolonged drought.

Mozambique's economic problems were intensified by the immigration of nearly all the country's white farmers, civil servants, and professionals, many of whom had been subjected to brutality by the insurgents, by increasing indebtedness, by the continuing war against guerrilla forces, and by widespread and persistent shortages of food.

A new constitution went into effect in November 1990, guaranteeing a multi-party system and an electoral reform law followed in February 1991. The constitution provided for direct election of the president for a five-year term and between 200 and 250 deputies to the Assembly of the Republic. It also guaranteed individual freedoms of expression, assembly, association, religion, and the right to a legal defense. It provided broad protection of equality under the law and prohibited the death penalty.

Throughout this troubled period, mass starvation and emigration of refugees to neighboring countries of South Africa, Malawi, Swaziland, and Zambia brought attention from the UN. It was estimated that 4.3 million Mozambicans were threatened by starvation in 1990 and the 1.7 million refugees had left the country by 1993. Voluntary reparation and aid programs were established and some refugees began to return home.

### UNITED NATIONS OPERATION IN MOZAMBIQUE (ONUMOZ).

On 4 October 1992, after 14 years of civil war, President Chissano and Afonso Dhlakam, president of RENAMO, signed a General Peace Agreement, which called for UN participation in monitoring the implementation of the Agreement and in providing technical assistance to the general election. Presidential and legislative elections were to take place within one year, but continued conflict delayed the elections until October 1994. The Agreement went into force on 15 October 1992.

ONUMOZ's mandate includes political, military, electoral, and humanitarian elements:

***Political Aspects of ONUMOZ.*** The Office of the Special Representative provides overall direction of the UN activities and is responsible for political guidance of the peace process, including facilitating the implementation of the General Peace Agreement, in particular by chairing the Supervisory and Monitoring Commission and its subsidiary joint commissions.

***Military Aspects of ONUMOZ.*** ONUMOZ monitors and verifies the ceasefire, the separation and concentration of forces of the two parties, their demobilization and the collection, storage, and destruction of weapons; monitors and verifies the complete withdrawal of foreign forces and provides security in four transport corridors; monitors and verifies the disbanding of private and irregular armed groups; authorizes security arrangements for infrastructure and provides security for UN and other international activities in support of the peace process.

***Electoral Aspects of ONUMOZ.*** ONUMOZ's electoral division monitored and verified all aspects and stages of the elections held in October 1994.

***Humanitarian Aspects of ONUMOZ.*** The 1992 peace accord set out two objectives for international humanitarian assistance to Mozambique: to serve as an instrument of reconciliation and to assist the return of people displaced by war and hunger, whether they had taken refuge in neighboring countries or in provincial and district centers within Mozambique. ONUMOZ's humanitarian component—ONOHAC—was established in Maputo, with suboffices at the regional and provincial levels. Headed by the Humanitarian Coordinator for Emergency Relief Operations, ONOHAC makes available food and other relief for distribution by a technical unit of ONUMOZ.

### REPORT OF THE UN COMMITTEE ON THE ELIMINATION OF RACIAL DISCRIMINATION.

At its 980th and 983rd meetings, held on 17 and 18 March 1993, the **COMMITTEE ON THE ELIMINATION OF RACIAL DISCRIMINATION** reviewed the implementation of the International Convention on the Elimination of All Forms of Racial Discrimination (see **RACIAL DISCRIMINATION**) by Mozambique, and noted that no report had been received since 1984. In concluding the review, the Committee expressed regret that Mozambique had not submitted a report in 1984 and had not been able to respond to the invitation to participate in the meeting and to furnish the relevant information with regard to the application of the Convention. The Committee drew the attention of the State party to the possibility of requesting technical assistance from the **CENTER FOR HUMAN RIGHTS** in the preparation of its report. The Committee hoped to receive a new report shortly. At the same time, the Committee expressed its deep concern at the serious human rights violations in Mozambique and its awareness of the current difficulties there, which it hoped might soon be overcome.

**BIBLIOGRAPHY.** Africa Watch. *Conspicuous Destruction: War, Famine and the Reform Process in Mozambique.* New York: Human Rights Watch, 1992. NGO factfinding report, in English.

———. *Mozambique: New Constitution Protects Basic Rights But Political Prisoners Still Suffer Unfair Trials.* New York: Human Rights Watch, 1991. NGO factfinding report, in English.

Amnesty International. *Mozambique: Monitoring Human Rights: The Task of UN Police Observers.* London: 1994. NGO report, in English.

Andreassen, B. A., and A. Eide, eds. "Mozambique," in *Human Rights in Developing Countries 1987/88: A Yearbook on Human Rights in Countries Receiving Nordic Aid,* pp. 70—89. Copenhagen: Atademiskforlag, 1988. NGO report, in English; bibliography, pp. 350–361.

Berman, Nina. "Project Launched in Mozambique to Aid Children 'Instrumentalized' by War," *Action for Children 3,* no. 4 (1988): 1, 8. NGO article, in English.

Dodge, Cole P., and Magne Raundalen. *Reaching Children in War: Sudan, Uganda and Mozambique.* Bergen, Norway, and Uppsala, Sweden: Nordiska Afrikainstitutet/Scandinavian Institute of African Studies, 1991. Collective works, in English.

Gersony, Robert. *Summary of Mozambican Refugee Accounts of Principally Conflict-Related Experience in Mozambique.* Washington, D.C.: U.S. Department of State, 1988. Government report, in English.

Human Rights Watch. "Mozambique," in *Human Rights*

*Watch World Report 1995*, pp. 30–34. New York: 1995. NGO report, in English.

Magaia, Lina. *Dumba Nengue: Run for your Life*. Trans. from Portuguese by Michael Wolfers. Trenton, NJ, USA: Africa World Press, 1988. Report, in English.

Marshall, Judith. "'What has Ruined our Lives Is the War': Voices from Nampula," *Southern Africa Report* 4, no. 2 (Oct. 1988): 15–18. NGO article, in English.

"Mozambican Refugees: Waiting for Peace to Return," *Refugees* no. 78 (Sept. 1990): 19–34. IGO article, in English and French.

Norwegian Human Rights Project, Christian Michelsen Institute. *Human Rights in Developing Countries 1986*. Oslo: Universitetsforlaget, 1986. Government annual report, in English; bibliography, classified by country.

Southern African Research and Documentation Centre. *Mozambique: The Victims of Apartheid*. Harare, Zimbabwe: 1987. NGO report, in English.

U.S. Committee for Refugees. *Children of Mozambique: The Cost of Survival*. Washington, D.C.: American Council for Nationalities Service, 1991. NGO report, in English.

———. *No Place Like Home: Mozambican Refugees Begin Africa's Largest Repatriation*. Washington, D.C.: American Council for Nationalities Service, 1993. NGO report, in English.

———. *Refugees from Mozambique: Shattered Land, Fragile Asylum*. Washington, D.C.: 1986. NGO report, in English.

———. *World Refugee Survey—1987 Review*. Washington, D.C.: 1988. NGO special issue, in English; bibliography, pp. 81–84.

**MUSLIM WORLD LEAGUE.** An international nongovernmental organization in consultative status with the UN **ECONOMIC AND SOCIAL COUNCIL** (Category I), and with **UNESCO.** Founded in 1962, the League explains and publicizes Islamic culture, teachings, and ideology. It seeks to further Islamic unity and coordinate Muslim policies and to strengthen the struggle of the Muslim people for the restoration of their religious rights. It has branch offices in 26 countries.

MWL has sponsored translations of the Qur'an and other religious books into many languages, has established Islamic centers in a number of countries, and is active in the field of mosque-building around the world. It operates refugee-related assistance programs in Pakistan, Somalia, and Sudan; and orphanages in Bangladesh, India, Uganda, and Afghanistan. The League offers scholarships to Islamic schools and sponsors 725 male and female students in Saudi Arabia and elsewhere.

MWL's publications include *Akhbar Al-Alam Al-Islami* (weekly) in Arabic; *Majalla Rabitah Al-Alam Al-Islami* (monthly) in Arabic; and *The Journal* (monthly) in English.

Muslim World League. Address: P.O. Box 538, Ummul Joud, Makkah, Saudi Arabia. Telephone: (966-2) 544-6700. Fax: (966-2) 543-6202. Secretary-General: Raja Mohummed Zafar-ul-Haq.

**MYANMAR.** The Union of Myanmar, formerly known as Burma, is a country in southeastern Asia, on the Bay of Bengal, occupying the northwest portion of the Indochinese Peninsula. It has borders with Bangladesh, China, India, Laos, and Thailand. It achieved independence from Great Britain in 1948 and became a member of the United Nations the same year. Its population is estimated to be 43,070,000. Ethnic groups include the Burmese (70%), Shan (9%), Karen (7%), Rakhine (4%), Chinese (5%), and Indian (2%). Languages commonly used include Burmese and English. Hinayana Buddhism is the religion of 85% of the population; the remaining 15% practice Christianity, Islam, or Animism. Literacy is estimated at 78%.

The government (1994) took the form of a republic. Up to 1988, the Burma Socialist Program Party held a monopoly on power which lasted for 26 years and was dedicated to the creation of a socialist welfare State. However, on 10 September 1988, that party was forced by widespread antigovernment rioting to end that monopoly and to call for multiparty elections. Later that month, the demonstrations for democracy were crushed by military gunfire, said to have killed more than 3,000 persons and to have forced thousands of students to flee the country. At the time of the uprising, a temporary government, the State Law and Order Restoration Council (SLORC), consisting of members of the military, was established and continues in force.

On 8 March 1989, the UN **COMMISSION ON HUMAN RIGHTS** adopted a decision entitled "Situation in Burma" (decision 1989/112) in which it expressed concern at the reports and allegations of violations of human rights in Myanmar in 1988 and also at the obstacles to be overcome in the way of the implementation of the democratic aspirations of the people. The Commission decided (a) to encourage the government authorities to take all measures necessary to assure fundamental freedoms, including freedom of expression, freedom of assembly, and freedom of association, with a view to enhancing the prospects for democracy; (b) to note that the Myanmar authorities have been responding to the requests by rapporteurs on specific subjects; (c) to welcome the undertaking by the government authorities to organize free and fair multiparty democratic elections; (d) to urge the Myanmar authorities to implement their undertaking as early as possible with a view to assuring the human rights and fundamental freedoms of the people of Myanmar; and (e) to invite the Myanmar delegation to continue to provide the commission with the necessary information on this question.

The name of Burma was changed to Myanmar on 18 June 1989, and the Secretary-General requested the permanent representative of Myanmar to the United Nations office at Geneva to submit any information the government might wish to provide in accordance with Commission decision 1989/112. In a *note verbale* dated 29 January 1990, the permanent representative made the following statement, which was circulated to the Commission on Human Rights at its 1990 session (UN Doc. E/CN.4/1990/69, para. 3):

(a) It is certainly the intention of the Government of the Union of Myanmar to continue to co-operate with the Commission on Human Rights by providing it with the information requested in paragraph (e) of the Commission's aforementioned decision.

(b) The independent five-member Multi-party Democracy General Elections Commission has, as of the date of this note, completed about 70% of the works preparatory to the holding of the general elections which are scheduled to be held on 27 May 1990.

(c) According to the 14-month timetable drawn up by the Multi-party Democracy General Elections Commission, January and February 1990 will be the most fateful months when political parties contesting elections are required to nominate candidates and subsequently start off a fully-fledged public political campaign for canvassing of votes with full democratic rights subject only to the maintenance of public order and morality.

(d) The Elections Commission has also announced dates for the nomination, scrutinization and withdrawal of nominations of candidates. The period for the nomination of Pyithu Hluttaw (Parliament) candidates for various constituencies was from 28 December 1989 to 3 January 1990. The period for the scrutinization of the nominations of candidates was from 5 to 9 January 1990. The last date for withdrawal of the nominations of candidates was 22 January 1990.

(e) It is encouraging to note that the initial announcements made by the political parties indicate the following position:

—117 political parties will be contesting the elections
—6 of them (namely National League for Democracy (NLD), National Unity Party (NUP), Democracy Party, Union Nationals Democracy Party (UNDP), Coalition League for Democratic Multi-party Unity and League for Democracy and Peace (LDP), will contest in more than 300 constituencies (there are altogether 492 constituencies))
—4 will contest between 101 and 200 constituencies
—4 will contest between 51 and 100 constituencies
—31 will contest between 11 and 50 constituencies
—72 will contest between 3 and 10 constituencies.

(f) As of 9 January 1990, a total of 2,392 Pyithu Hluttaw candidates (83 independents and 2,309 from 100 political parties) have put up nomination papers, indicating broad participation in the forthcoming general elections by the whole spectrum of political parties and organizations. It is worth noting that none of the candidates had withdrawn his or her candidatures on or before the closing date for such withdrawal—22 January 1990.

(g) The Government of the Union of Myanmar will arrange to have a delegation to participate in the work of the Commission in the capacity of an observer as in previous years and report to the Commission at an appropriate time and in an appropriate manner during its forth-sixth session in keeping with the provisions of decision 1989/112.

(h) In the meanwhile, as part of the process to keep the Commission informed of the matter, the Permanent Mission of the Union of Myanmar in Geneva will be keeping in close touch with all State members of the Commission on Human Rights.

In the country's first multi-party general elections in 30 years, held as scheduled on 27 May 1990, the opposition National League for Democracy won a stunning upset victory, winning two-thirds of the popular vote and a majority of the 485 National Assembly seats. The National Unity Party, backed by the military regime, received one-third of the popular vote but won only a few Assembly seats. In all, 93 political parties took part in the election.

The first demand of the National League for Democracy was that the military regime release 400 of its members held under house arrest or other forms of detention, including its leader, Daw Aung San Suu Kyi, the daughter of the country's founder, U Aung San, and the recipient of the 1991 **NOBEL PEACE PRIZE**. It then faced the problem of establishing the modalities and a timetable for transition to civilian rule.

When the SLORC was formed after the military coup in 1988, all state organs were disbanded, including the judiciary. Demonstrations were banned and a dusk-to-dawn curfew, which was not lifted until 1992, was imposed nationwide. In addition, several human rights-monitoring organizations, **HUMAN RIGHTS WATCH** among them, have accused the SLORC of employing forced labor, especially on infrastructure projects; arbitrary detention; and torture.

In July 1990, following its low support in the May elections, the SLORC issued Order 1/90, which all political parties were forced to endorse in November, stating that the SLORC would continue as *de facto* government until the drafting of a new constitution. The official announcement that the SLORC would not transfer power to the recently elected Assembly came in April 1991. The SLORC banned some political parties and retroactively amended the 1989 electoral reform law to make it easier to disqualify candidates. Aung San Suu Kyi, still under house arrest since July 1989, was awarded the Nobel Peace Prize in October 1991 for organizing a peaceful campaign for the restoration of democracy in Myanmar.

From 1992 to 1993, the SLORC released 1,700 political prisoners, and a delegation, including a U.S. Congressman, a *New York Times* reporter, and a UN official, was allowed to visit Aung San Suu Kyi in detention in February 1994. Immediately thereafter, however, the SLORC stated that her detention would continue. In September 1994, she met with military ruler Gen. Than Shwe, still stating that she would not negotiate on the issue of her permanent voluntary exile from her country. The meeting coincided with the opening of the UN **GENERAL ASSEMBLY.** In June 1995, the military authorities freed Suu Kyi from house arrest, after six years.

The 1994 UN General Assembly report from a Special Rapporteur which it had authorized to visit Myanmar at the invitation of its government—indicating that he had visited the country but had been denied access to Daw Aung San Suu Kyi (E/CN.4/1994/57)—was deplored by the Commission on Human Rights, which again urged the Government of Myanmar "to take, in conformity with the assurances given at various times, all necessary measures to establish a democratic State in full accordance with the will of the people as expressed in the democratic elections held in 1990" (resolution 1994/85 of 9 March 1994).

**BIBLIOGRAPHY.** Amnesty International. *Burma: Extrajudicial Execution, Torture and Political Imprisonment of Members of the Shan and other Ethnic Minorities.* London: 1988. NGO report, in English.
————. *Burma: Extrajudicial Execution and Torture of Members of Ethnic Minorities.* London: 1988. NGO report, in English.
————. *Burma: The 18 September 1988 Military Takeover and its Aftermath.* London: 1988. NGO report, in English.
————. *Myanmar: The Climate of Fear Continues, Members of Ethnic Minorities and Political Prisoners Still Targeted.* London: 1993. NGO report, in English.
————. *Myanmar: Human Rights Developments, July to December 1993.* London: 1994. NGO report, in English.
————. *Myanmar: 'No Law at All': Human Rights Violations under Military Rule.* London: 1992. NGO report, in English.
Amnesty International—USA. *Myanmar: 'In the National Interest'—Prisoners of Conscience, Torture, Summary Trials under Martial Law.* New York: 1990. NGO factfinding report, in English.
————. *Myanmar: Prisoners of Conscience, Torture, Extrajudicial Executions.* New York: 1990. NGO briefing paper, in English.
————. *State of Fear: Censorship in Burma (Myanmar).* London: 1991. NGO report, in English.
Article 19. *Paradise Lost?: The Suppression of Environmental Rights and Freedom of Expression in Burma.* London: 1994. NGO report, in English.
Asia Watch (AW). *Human Rights in Burma (Myanmar).* New York: Human Rights Watch, May 1990. NGO factfinding report, in English.
Fredholm, Michael. *Burma: Ethnicity and Insurgency.* Westport, CT, USA: Praeger, 1993. Scholarly monograph, in English.
Gesellschaft fur Bedrohte Volker (Association for Endangered Peoples). *Pogrom: Zeitschrift fur Bedrohte Volker* (Pogrom: Journal for Endangered Peoples) 137 (December 1987). NGO article collection, in German.
Human Rights Watch. "Burma (Myanmar)," in *Human Rights Watch World Report 1995,* pp. 132–137. New York: 1995. NGO report, in English.
International Human Rights Law Group. *Post-Election Myanmar: A Popular Mandate Withheld.* Washington, D.C.: 1990. NGO factfinding report, in English.
————. *Report on the Myanmar Election: Election Date: May 27, 1990.* Washington, D.C.: 1990. NGO factfinding report, in English.
International Work Group for Indigenous Affairs. *The Naga Nation and its Struggle against Genocide.* Copenhagen: 1986. NGO report, in English.
Lawyers Committee for Human Rights. *Burma: The International Response to Continuing Human Rights Violations.* New York: 1992. NGO report, in English.
————. *Summary Injustice: Military Tribunals in Burma (Myanmar).* New York: 1991. NGO factfinding report, in English.
Lintner, Bertil. *Outrage: Burma's Struggle for Democracy.* London, UK, and Bangkok, Thailand: White Lotus, 1990. Monograph, in English.
Smith, Martin. *Burma: Insurgency and the Politics of Ethnicity.* London, UK, and Atlantic Highlands, NJ, USA: Zed Books, 1991. Monograph, in English.
Smith, Martin, and Annie Allsebrook. *Ethnic Groups in Burma: Development, Democracy and Human Rights.* London: Anti-Slavery International, 1994. Monograph, in English; bibliography, p. 137.
Steinbok, Maria. "Burma 1988," *Human Rights Newsletter* (Dec. 1988): 1–28. NGO report, in English.
Taswell, Ruth, ed. *Southeast Asian Tribal Groups and Ethnic Minorities.* Cambridge, MA, USA: Cultural Survival, 1987. NGO conference proceedings, in English.
Taylor, Robert H. "Burma's Ambiguous Breakthrough," *Journal of Democracy* (Fall 1990): 62–72. Scholarly article, in English.
U.S. Committee for Refugees. *The War is Growing Worse and Worse: Refugees and Displaced Persons on the Thai-Burmese Border.* Washington, D.C.: American Council for Nationalities Service, 1990. NGO issue paper, in English; bibliography, pp. 23–24.
Walker, J. "Boy Soldiers in a Grown-Up's War," *Child Workers in Asia* 3, no. 1 (Jan.–March 1987): 1–2. NGO article, in English.

**MYRDAL, ALVA (1902–1986).** This Swedish economist was co-recipient of the 1982 **NOBEL PEACE PRIZE** (with **ALFONSO GARCÍA ROBLES**). Born Alva Reimer in Uppsala, Sweden, she attended Stockholm University, graduating with a B.A. in 1924 and marrying Gunnar Myrdal in the same year; in 1934, she received an M.A. from Uppsala University.

Myrdal and her husband pursued studies on social and economic problems and gained worldwide attention in 1934 with the publication of their study "Crisis in the Population Problem." This work, appearing in Danish and Norwegian editions in the same year, had a direct impact on the social policies of the Scandinavian countries during the 1930s. The thesis of the work was that governments had a responsibility to care for children regardless of the parents' economic means. In 1935, Myrdal served as an expert to the Swedish Government Committee on Social Housing and also served as an advisor to the Royal Population Commission, writing its report entitled "Day Care of Children." In 1936, she founded the Training College for Nursery and Kindergarten Teachers, remaining the college's director until 1948. In addition, during the 1930s and 1940s, Myrdal worked on other educational committees and was prominent in the Scandanavian women's movement. After World War II, she was editor of *Via Suecia,* a multilingual weekly published to help refugees, and was active in governmental and civic organizations dedicated to relief efforts.

In 1949, Myrdal was appointed principal director of the UN Department of Social Affairs, making her the highest-ranking woman in the UN Secretariat. In this capacity, she coordinated UN projects such as commissions on social activities, human rights, freedom of information, status of women, and population. In 1951, she was named director of UNESCO. On leaving the United Nations, Myrdal served as Sweden's chief multinational disarmament negotiator from 1961 to 1973.

In addition to the Nobel Peace Prize, Myrdal was awarded the Wateler Prize, of the Hague Academy of International Peace (1973), the Albert Einstein Peace Prize (1980), and the People's Peace Prize of Norway (1981), among other international honors.

**BIBLIOGRAPHY.** *Current Biography Yearbook.* New York: W.H. Wilson & Company, 1950.

Schlessinger, Bernard S., and June H. Schlessinger, eds. *Who's Who of Nobel Prize Winners.* Phoenix, AZ, USA: Oryx Press, 1991.

# N

**NAMIBIA.** Once a German colony and later the Territory of South West Africa mandated by the **LEAGUE OF NATIONS** to South Africa, Namibia has been the subject of intense international contention since 1946. When it achieved independence on 21 March 1990—the last African colony to do so—it became the 160th State member of the United Nations, the 52nd State member of the **ORGANIZATION OF AFRICAN UNITY,** and the 50th State member of the Commonwealth.

The country, which is rich in natural resources, has borders with Angola, Botswana, South Africa, and Zambia. Its total population is estimated to be 1,902,000, of which 82,000 are white; 52,000, colored (mixed); and the remainder, a wide variety of ethnic groups, including 641,000 Ovambo, 120,000 Kavango, 97,000 Damara, 97,000 Herero, 62,000 Nama, 48,000 Caprivian, 37,000 Bushmen, 32,000 Baster, and 8,000 Tswana. Languages in common use include Afrikaans, English, German, and numerous regional vernaculars. Christianity is the predominant religion, although Animism and other indigenous beliefs are widely practiced. Literacy is estimated at 90% for white Africans, 30% for non-whites.

Recent international developments with reference to Namibia were summarized by the Ad Hoc Working Group of Experts on Southern Africa in its report to the 1990 session of the UN **COMMISSION ON HUMAN RIGHTS** as follows (UN Doc. E/CN.4/1990/7, paras. 230–249):

After World War I, the League of Nations assigned Namibia, which was known as German South West Africa, to South Africa as a mandated territory. However, because of grave abuses and violations of contractual obligations by South Africa, the United Nations General Assembly revoked the mandate in 1966. The International Court of Justice adjudicated several times that South Africa has been in illegal occupation of Namibia ever since.

In 1976, the Security Council unanimously adopted resolution 385, which required withdrawal of South Africa and transfer of power to the United Nations. It was proposed that elections would then be held under the aegis of the United Nations, to select delegates to draft a constitution for an independent Namibia.

On 10 April 1978, the United States, United Kingdom, France, West Germany and Canada submitted the main "proposals for a settlement of the Namibian situation" (see S/12636). The aforementioned countries became known as the Contact Group. On 29 August and 28 September 1978, the Secretary-General issued two subsidiary documents (S/12827 and S/12869, respectively) for the purpose of implementing the proposals of the Contact Group and by way of an explanation of the proposals. On the basis of the foregoing the Security Council adopted resolution 435 on 29 September 1978 which, *inter alia,* provides for the establishment of the United Nations Transition Assistance Group (UNTAG), which includes both a civilian and a military component, functioning under the authority of the Security Council resolution 435 (1978) and assisting the Special Representative of the Secretary-General for Namibia in his task of monitoring and supervising the free and fair election of a Constituent Assembly. It may be mentioned that not only the elections but also all aspects of the preceding and subsequent political process must be free and fair.

It may be noted that many units now operating under the effective control of, or in co-operation with, the South African Defence Force (SADF) did not exist when Security Council resolution 435 (1978) was adopted. The South West African Territorial Force (SWATF) and the Counter-insurgency Unit (COIN), popularly known as "Koevoet" ("crowbar"), are examples of such units.

In December 1988, as a result of negotiations held by the parties concerned, the independence agreement for Namibia was concluded (see Annex). It included the following provisions:

(1) Release of political prisoners
(2) Return of political exiles
(3) Repatriation of refugees
(4) Abolition of all discriminatory laws.

On 16 February 1989, the Security Council adopted resolution 632 (1989) by which it decided to implement its resolution 435 (1978) of 29 September 1978 in its original and definitive form to ensure conditions in Namibia which would allow the Namibian people to participate freely and without intimidation in the electoral process under the supervision and control of the United Nations leading to early independence of the territory.

The implementation of the settlement plan began in April 1989, entrusting UNTAG with the task of monitoring the territory's transition to independence.

As in previous years, the Working Group analysed the situation of human rights in Namibia on the basis of the testimonies and other relevant material received from various sources. In addition, taking into account the specificity of the current situation prevailing in Namibia, the Working Group relied extensively on the information contained in the report of the Secretary-General of the United Nations submitted to the Security Council in accordance with paragraph 9 of Council resolution 640 (1989) of 29 August 1989 (see S/20883 and S/20883/Add.1).

As stated in the report of the Secretary-General, under paragraphs 7 (b) and 7 (c) of the United Nations settlement plan, all Namibian political prisoners were required to be set free. It was stated in the report of the United Nations Mission on Detainees that, on 24 May 1989, UNTAG military observers stationed in Angola had been enabled to interview about 201 former detainees who had been released by SWAPO. On 4 July 1989, 153 ex-detainees, including 18 children, were repatriated to Namibia from Angola, followed by two further groups of 63 and 16 on 29 July 1989 and 8 August 1989, respectively.

On 20 July 1989, 25 Namibian political prisoners were released from the central prison in Windhoek by the South African authorities. It was alleged that both SWAPO and the South African authorities were still holding detainees. In reply to these allegations, the Administrator-General for Namibia, on behalf of the South African Government, replied that the persons on the lists submitted to him had either been released or were unknown to the South African authorities.

SWAPO stated that it no longer held any detainees, and invited the international community to conduct an investigation.

The Mission on Detainees, established by the Special Representative of the Secretary-General in pursuance of paragraphs 7 (c) and 7 (d) of the settlement proposal for Namibia visited Angola and Zambia from 2 to 21 September 1989. Its main purpose was to ascertain whether any Namibians were still being detained by SWAPO, at locations already identified or elsewhere in Angola and Zambia, and if so, to ensure that appropriate arrangements for their release and voluntary repatriation were promptly made in order to enable them to participate in the electoral process. Prior to the departure of the Mission, a consolidated list was prepared of the names of persons allegedly detained. It included about 1,100 names of persons reported to have died or to have been released and/or repatriated, and was intended to form a comprehensive reference source.

From 2 to 12 September 1989, the Mission visited a total of 22 locations in Angola, after which, from 14 to 20 September 1989 it visited a total of 8 locations in Zambia. The Mission visited virtually all of the sites where persons had been reported to be held in the two countries. On the basis of its findings, the Mission unanimously concluded that there were no detainees, in any of the alleged detention centres and other places which it visited, and the majority of persons allegedly detained or missing had been repatriated or otherwise accounted for.

The report of the Secretary-General stated that, on 6 June 1989, an amnesty was granted to all Namibian exiles. This permitted the beginning of the repatriation operation which had been entrusted to the United Nations High Commissioner for Refugees (UNHCR).

UNHCR established three air and three land entry points as well as five reception centres in central and northern Namibia, to receive, register and materially assist the returnees. By 29 September 1989, it was reported that 41,748 Namibians from 46 countries had returned home, and all but 579 had resettled in their former communities.

The planned return of Namibian refugees scheduled for mid-May was threatened with delay because of a dispute over abolishing all discriminatory laws, as required by Security Council resolution 435 (1978). The key obstacle reportedly was Proclamation AG.8, a law that makes provision for racially segregated administrations under the territory's two-tier governmental system. South Africa's Administrator-General, Mr. Louis Pienaar, insisted that by merely dissolving the political compound, the administrations themselves can continue to function within the terms of resolution 435 (1978). In the opinion of the Working Group, the delay in the return of refugees could have affected their participation in the electoral process.

The registration of voters began on 3 September 1989 and ended on 23 September 1989. Almost 700,000 voters were registered, with only 593 applications being rejected, in each case with the concurrence of the UNTAG supervisor.

According to information received by the Working Group, the Administrator-General for Namibia issued instructions that schools in Namibia were to remain closed from 30 October to 10 November 1989, to accommodate preparations for the elections.

On 9 February 1990, the Constituent Assembly of Namibia, meeting in Windhoek, approved by consensus the "Constitution for an Independent Namibia." The constitution, which entered into force on the day Namibia achieved its independence, 21 March 1990, contains provisions (articles 1–29, 32–46, 49–50, 63–70, 74–75, 78–84, 89–102, and 131–132) specifically relating to human rights and fundamental freedoms (UN Doc. S/20967/Add. 2, pp. 10–63).

Namibia was eventually given sole control over Walvis Bay and its islands in March 1994, the area having remained under South African control after independence in 1990 and under shared control from August 1992.

During elections for the 13 Regional Councils in November and December 1992, SWAPO won control of 9 of the Councils. Two members from each of the Councils comprised the National Council, the advisory second parliamentary chamber, which was inaugurated in early 1993.

President Sam Nujoma, elected in 1990 by the Constituent Assembly (later the National Assembly), announced in February 1994 that he would seek re-election in 1995.

**BIBLIOGRAPHY.** Africa Watch. *Accountability in Namibia: Human Rights and the Transition to Democracy.* New York: Human Rights Watch, 1992. NGO report, in English.

Amnesty International. *Namibia: The Human Rights Situation at Independence.* London: 1990. NGO factfinding report, in English.

————. *Namibia: Torture and Ill-Treatment of Prisoners.* London: 1987. NGO report, in English.

————. *Statement by Amnesty International to the Ad Hoc Working Group of Experts on Southern Africa.* Geneva, Switzerland: 1985. NGO testimony, in English.

Boggio, Alice. "La Namibie ou le Rapt d'un Vaste Pays" (Namibia or the Rape of a Vast Country), *Courrier de l'ACAT* 85 (May 1988): 2–4. NGO article, in French.

Centre for the Independence of Judges and Lawyers. "Namibia: Economic Harassment Threatens Independence of Lawyers," *CIJL Bulletin* 15 (April 1985): 3–5. NGO article, in English.

Clearly, Sean. "The Utility of Bills of Rights in Culturally Heterogeneous Societies: A Preliminary Examination of the Namibia Model," *South Africa International* 16, no. 4 (April 1986): 175–190. Scholarly article, in English.

Cosslett, Christopher E. "International 'Illegality' and Anomalous Natural Resources Development: The Case of Namibia, 1966–1986," *Lesotho Law Journal* 3, no. 1 (1987): 223–258. Scholarly article, in English.

Forrest, Joseph B. "Namibia: The First Postapartheid Democracy," *Journal of Democracy* 5, no. 3 (July 1994): 88–100. Scholarly article, in English.

Fraenkel, P., P. Murray, and K. Stearman. *The Namibians.* 3rd ed. London: Minority Rights Group, 1985. NGO study, in English; selective bibliography, p. 31.

Kahanovitz, Colin. "The Namibian Bill of Rights: Implications for the Promotion of Procedural and Substantive Justice in Criminal Cases," *Criminal Law Forum* 2, no. 3 (Spring 1991): 569–594. Scholarly article, in English.

Katjavivi, Peter H. *A History of Resistance in Namibia.* Paris: UNESCO, 1988. Scholarly monograph, in English.

Kelso, B. J. "Namibia: A Legacy of Inequity," *Africa Report* 37, no. 6 (Nov.–Dec. 1992): 35–37. Article, in English.

Landis, Elizabeth S. "Namibia: A Transatlantic View," *South African Journal on Human Rights* 3 (Nov. 1987): 347–366. Scholarly article, in English.

Lawyers' Committee for Civil Rights under Law. *South Africa 1987: Choking Internal Resistance.* Washington, D.C.: 1988. NGO annual report, in English.

McDougall, Gay J. "International Law, Human Rights, and Namibian Independence," *Human Rights Quarterly* 8, no. 3 (Aug. 1986): 443–470. Scholarly article, in English.

———. *Statement Read to U.N. Fourth Committee Hearings on Namibia.* Washington, D.C.: Lawyers' Committee for Civil Rights under Law, 1986. NGO speech, in English.

National Society for Human Rights. *Annual Human Rights Report, 1993.* Windhoek, Namibia: 1993. NGO annual report, in English.

Schoombee, Hannes. "An Important Human Rights Decision in Namibia: Katofa v. Administrator-General for SWA 1985 (4) SA 211 (SWA)," *South African Journal on Human Rights* 2, no. 1 (March 1986): 74–79. Scholarly article, in English.

Steytler, Nico. "The Judicialization of Namibian Politics," *South African Journal on Human Rights* 9, no. 4 (1993): 477–499. Scholarly article, in English.

Toronto Committee for the Liberation of Southern Africa. "Namibia: The Next Phase," *Southern Africa Report* 5, no. 4 (Feb. 1990). NGO articles, in English.

Totemeyer, Gerhard. *The Prospects for Democracy and Development in an Independent Namibia.* Mowbray, South Africa: Institute for a Democratic Alternative for South Africa, 1990. Scholarly conference paper, in English.

TransAfrica Forum. "Namibia: Occupation, Apartheid and Quest for Freedom," *TransAfrica Issue Brief* 5, no. 3 (June–July 1986): 1–16. NGO article, in English; selective bibliography.

**NANSEN, FRIDTJOF (1861–1930).** This remarkable man, a Norwegian by birth but a true internationalist, was awarded the 1922 **NOBEL PEACE PRIZE** for "his work in the repatriation of prisoners of war, his work for the Russian refugees, his work in aiding the millions in Russia struggling against famine and . . . his work for the refugees in Asia Minor and Thrace." Nansen was the first High Commissioner for Refugees for the **LEAGUE OF NATIONS,** a post he held from 1921 to 1930.

Undoubtedly, Nansen is the only Nobel Prize winner who was a professional explorer. Among his earliest expeditions was the crossing of the Greenland ice cap in 1888. His most famous adventure was his attempt to cross the North Pole in a ship that would ride on ice floes and drift safely with the current. In 1893, Nansen and 12 associates sailed *The Fram,* a ship Nansen designed, into the Arctic Ocean, where *The Fram* performed as Nansen had predicted. However, the ship by-passed the North Pole, so Nansen and F. H. Johansen attempted to cross the Pole by sledding over ice flows and kayaking. Nansen and Johansen spent the winter of 1894 on Franz Josef Land, living in a hut of walrus hides, eating polar bear and walrus meat, and using blubber as fuel. The two explorers returned to Norway in 1896, where they were reunited with the crew of *The Fram.* Nansen published a two-volume account of his travels, *Farthest North,* in 1897. A zoologist by degree, Nansen was also an oceanographer and responsible for the establishment of the International Council for the Exploration of the Sea.

As famous in scientific circles as his explorations had made him, Nansen's lasting contributions came in his humanitarian efforts. A strong believer in an international organization that could arbitrate settlement of political and military conflicts, Nansen was given the responsibility by the League of Nations in 1920 for repatriating German and Austro-Hungarian prisoners-of-war from Russia. Although the Soviet government did not recognize the League of Nations, it was willing to negotiate personally with this internationally respected diplomat. In 1921, Nansen again intervened in Russia, this time to relieve a famine; in this instance, Nansen personally shifted world opinion, which was largely opposed to providing aid to the Russian people because of their government's ideological stance. A year later, Nansen arranged for the exchange of over one million Greeks living in Asia Minor for about 500,000 Turks living in Greece. Nansen also initiated the "Nansen passport," an identification card for displaced persons, which allowed the bearer to resettle in a new country.

**BIBLIOGRAPHY.** Gray, Tony. *Champions of Peace.* London: Paddington Press, 1976.

Schlessinger, Bernard S., and June H. Schlessinger, eds. *Who's Who of Nobel Prize Winners.* Phoenix, AZ, USA: Oryx Press, 1991.

**NANSEN INTERNATIONAL OFFICE FOR REFUGEES, LEAGUE OF NATIONS.** Established in 1931, after the death of **FRIDTJOF NANSEN,** this organization was awarded the 1938 **NOBEL PEACE PRIZE.** After Nansen's death in 1930, the League Secretariat took over responsibility for the protection of refugees' rights but designated the Nansen International Office to oversee the material well-being of refugees. The Office operated in the face of seemingly insurmountable problems in the 1930s: a worldwide financial depression eroded available funds; the outbreak of conflicts throughout Europe, particularly in Spain, Italy, and Germany produced more refugees in "peacetime" than had been produced in World War I; and the reputation of and respect for the League itself were fast eroding. Indeed, when the Nazi government in Germany expelled Jews in 1933, the problem escalated to such a level that the League established a new commission devoted solely to the Jewish problem. Despite these and other problems, the Nansen International Office still managed some successes: the resettlement of Saar refugees in Paraguay, and Armenians in Syria, Lebanon, and Erivan.

**BIBLIOGRAPHY.** Gray, Tony. *Champions of Peace.* London: Paddington Press, 1976.

**NANSEN MEDAL.** Awarded by the Office of the UN High Commissioner for Refugees (UNHCR), this annual, honorary medal recognizes those who focus their work on the plight and rights of refugees. Awarded 32 times since its inception in 1954, the award commemorates the first High Commissioner for Refugees under the League of Nations, the Norwegian diplomat and explorer **FRIDTJOF NANSEN.** The Nansen Committee is composed of members designated by the Norwegian Government, the Swiss Government, the Council of Europe, the International Council of Voluntary Agencies, and UNHCR.

In 1992, German President Richard von Weizsacker received the Medal for his struggle against **XENOPHOBIA.** The 1993 recipient was **MÉDECINS SANS FRONTIÈRES (DOCTORS WITHOUT BORDERS).** This non-governmental organization, established in France in 1971, has been among the first to arrive on the scene of refugee crises around the world, often risking their lives to provide emergency medical assistance. Seven MSF staff have been killed in the line of duty. In awarding the Medal to MSF, the Nansen Committee also recognized the crucial role played by non-governmental agencies in assisting refugees and advocating their rights.

There was no award winner in 1994.

For more information, contact: UNHCR, Palais des Nations, CH-1211 Geneva 10, Switzerland. Telephone: (41-22) 734-6011. Fax: (41-22) 739-8682.

**NATIONALITY.** The right to a nationality is proclaimed in the **UNIVERSAL DECLARATION OF HUMAN RIGHTS** in the following terms:

*Article 15.* 1. Everyone has the right to a nationality.
2. No one shall be arbitrarily deprived of his nationality nor denied the right to change his nationality.

The **INTERNATIONAL COVENANT ON CIVIL AND POLITICAL RIGHTS** contains the following provision:

*Article 24.* 3. Every child has the right to acquire a nationality.

The International Convention on the Elimination of All Forms of Racial Discrimination (see **RACIAL DISCRIMINATION**) provides that:

*Article 5.* In compliance with the fundamental obligation laid down in article 2 of this Convention, States parties undertake to prohibit and to eliminate racial discrimination in all its forms and to guarantee the right of everyone, without distinction as to race, colour, or national or ethnic origin, to equality before the law, notably in the enjoyment of the following rights: . . .
(d) Other civil rights, in particular: . . .
(iii) The right to nationality.

The Convention on the Elimination of All Forms of Discrimination against Women provides that:

*Article 9.* 1. States parties shall grant women equal rights with men to acquire, change or retain their nationality. They shall ensure in particular that neither marriage to an alien nor change of nationality by the husband during marriage shall automatically change the nationality of the wife, render her stateless or force upon her the nationality of her husband.
2. States parties shall grant women equal rights with men with respect to the nationality of their children.

The **AMERICAN CONVENTION ON HUMAN RIGHTS,** open for acceptance by member States of the **ORGANIZATION OF AMERICAN STATES,** provides that:

*Article 20.* 1. Every person has the right to a nationality.
2. Every person has a right to the nationality of the State in whose territory he was born if he does not have the right to any other nationality.
3. No one shall be arbitrarily deprived of his nationality or of the right to change it.

*CONFLICTS OF NATIONALITY LAWS.* Nationality is a term which refers to a legal bond reflecting a genuine connection between an individual and a particular State by which the individual gives his allegiance to that State and it, in turn, protects and assists him when he is outside the territory under its jurisdiction.

Normally, nationality coincides with citizenship, but some States restrict their citizenship to those who enjoy full political rights. Each State determines who are its nationals by operation of its laws, and the question of whether a particular individual is a national of a particular State can only be determined by that State itself by reference to those laws.

Most individuals acquire nationality automatically by the fact of birth in a particular State. Later, they may acquire another nationality by marriage, naturalization, or otherwise, sometimes retaining and sometimes losing their original nationality in the process. Or they may lose their original nationality (by expulsion, persecution, or failure to comply with legal requirements) without acquiring a new one, and thus become stateless.

International nationality problems arise most frequently out of conflicts between the nationality laws of various States which give rise either to multiple nationality or to statelessness. From the international point of view, it is essential that everyone should have a nationality—preferably not more than one at a time.

One of the most persistent problems in this field is that relating to the nationality of married women. The Hague Convention on Certain Questions Relating to the Conflict of Nationality Laws, of 12 April 1930, was the earliest multilateral instrument prepared to deal with this problem; it endeavored primarily to reconcile various national legislations so as to eliminate cases of conflicts of nationality laws leading to statelessness. Later, the two Montevideo conventions of 26 December 1933, on the nationality of married women, proclaimed for the first time the principle of equality of the sexes as regards nationality. Article 1 of the first of these conventions provided that "there shall be no distinction based on sex as regards nationality" in the legislation or practice of states parties. Articles 5 and 6 of the second convention provided that "neither matrimony nor its dissolution will affect the nationality of the husband or wife," and that "naturalization or loss of nationality by the husband will not affect any members of his family."

On the basis of a survey of existing national legislation prepared by the UN Secretary-General, the COMMISSION ON THE STATUS OF WOMEN identified the urgent need for a new multilateral convention on the nationality of married women which would ensure such women equality with men in the exercise of the right to a nationality and prevent them from becoming stateless, or otherwise suffering hardships, as a consequence of conflicts in nationality laws. The Commission prepared the draft of such an instrument; and, on 29 January 1957, the Convention on the Nationality of Married Women was completed and adopted by the UN GENERAL ASSEMBLY (resolution 1040 [XI]). The Convention was opened for signature and ratification on 20 February of the same year.

**STATELESSNESS.** There are two categories of stateless persons: *de jure* and *de facto*. Stateless persons *de jure* are persons who are not nationals of any State, either because at birth or subsequently they were not given any nationality or because during their lifetime they lost their own nationality and did not acquire a new one. Stateless persons *de facto* are persons who, having left the country of which they were nationals, no longer enjoy the protection and assistance of their national authorities, either because these authorities refuse to grant them protection and assistance or because they themselves renounce the protection and assistance of the countries of which they were nationals. A stateless person, in short, is one who is unable or unwilling to avail himself of the protection of the government of his country of nationality or former nationality.

**SEE ALSO** *Statelessness.*

**BIBLIOGRAPHY.** Amnesty International. *The Imprisonment of Persons Seeking to Leave a Country or to Return to Their Own Country.* London: 1986. NGO report, in English.

Blackburn, Robert, ed. *Rights of Citizenship.* London: Mansell, 1993. Scholarly monograph, in English.

Chan, Johannes M.M. "The Right to a Nationality as a Human Right: The Current Trend towards Recognition," *Human Rights Law Journal* 12, no. 1–2 (Feb. 1991): 1–14. Scholarly article, in English.

Max Planck Institute for Comparative Public and International Law. *Encyclopedia of Public International Law, Vol. 8: Human Rights and the Individual in International Law—International Economic Relations.* New York: North-Holland, 1985. Encyclopedia, in English.

Plender, Richard, ed. *International Migration Law.* Rev. 2nd ed. Dordrecht, the Netherlands: Martinus Nijhoff, 1988. Scholarly edited collection, in English.

Tarzi, Shah M. "The Nation-State, Victim Groups and Refugees," *Ethnic and Racial Studies* 14, no. 4 (Oct. 1991): 441–452. Scholarly article, in English.

**NAURU.** The Republic of Nauru is a country in Micronesia occupying an island in the Pacific Ocean about 2,500 miles southwest of Honolulu. It achieved independence in 1968 and, although a UN trust territory from 1947 to 1948, is not a member of the United Nations. Its population is estimated to be 10,000. Ethnic groups include Nauruan (58%), other Pacific Island peoples (26%), Chinese (8%), and European (8%). Languages commonly used include Nauruan (official) and English. Christianity (Christian-Nauruan Congregational Church, Nauru Independence Church, and Roman Catholic Church) is the predominant religion. Literacy is estimated at 99%.

The government (1994) took the form of a republic. Under the 1968 constitution, the unicameral 18-member Parliament, members of which are elected by popular vote for terms of three years, elects the president from its membership. The president is head of State and government and exercises executive power with the assistance of a five-member cabinet. President Bernard Dowiyogo was re-elected by Parliament in December 1993. The judicial system includes the Family Court, the District Court, and the Supreme Court. There is no political party.

Annexed by Germany in 1888, Nauru was a **LEAGUE OF NATIONS** mandate under joint Australian, New Zealand, and British administration after World War I and a United Nations trust territory under the same administration after World War II.

**NEPAL.** The Kingdom of Nepal is a landlocked country in southern Asia. It has borders with India and the Tibetan autonomous region of China. It achieved independence from Great Britain in 1923 and became a member of the United Nations in 1955. Its population is estimated to be 20,325,000. Ethnic groups include Bhotias, Brahmans, Chetris, Gurungs, Limbus, Magars, Newars, Rais, Sherpas, and Tamangs. Languages commonly used include Nepali (official), Newari, Bhotia, and a variety of local languages. Religions practiced include Hinduism (90%), Buddhism (5%), and Islam (5%). Literacy is estimated at 20%.

Up to 1980, the government took the form of a monarchy, with the king, as ruler and head of State, appointing the prime minister, who exercised executive authority as head of government, a national *Panchayat* (parliament), and a judiciary headed by the Supreme Court. Political parties were banned.

In May 1990, the king replaced the *Panchayat* system with the Council of Ministers, empowered to enact and repeal legislation to make the transition to a multiparty democracy. The death penalty was abolished and freedom of press and association were restored in July. A nine-member Constitutional Recommendation Commission was also established and a new Constitution was drafted and approved by both the Council of Ministers and the king by November 1990.

After initially refusing to approve the diminution of his sovereign powers, the king inserted into the constitution the compromise provision for a Council of State. The 15-member standing committee of this Council would comprise the prime minister and other key ministers, the chief justice and eight members appointed by the king. The constitution states that Nepal is a democratic constitutional monarchy; that Hindu is the dominant religion and Nepali the official language. It also guarantees many and varied individual freedoms and an independent judiciary. The executive power is vested in the king and the Council of

Ministers, comprising the prime minister and the cabinet, who come from within parliament. The bicameral legislature comprises the 205-seat House of Representatives, directly elected for five-year terms, and the 60-seat Senate appointed by the House and the king for six-year terms.

In preparation for the May 1991 general election, 205 constituencies were outlined and 44 political parties registered. To be registered as a political party, 5% of its candidates standing for election must be women. The Nepali Congress Party (NCP) won a majority with 110 of the 205 House seats and Girija Prasad Koirala became prime minister. Communist parties took a total of 82 seats.

Disputes and general strikes persisted, however, with opposition parties protesting alleged government corruption. The rehabilitation and reputation of the former *Panchayat* regime was bolstered by inclusion of former members in the 121-member Council of State in 1993.

When his social and economic programs were defeated in parliament, Prime Minister Koirala resigned in July 1994 and new elections were held in November. The Communist Party of Nepal (United Marxist Leninist) or UML, obtained the largest bloc of seats with 88 of the 205 but was required to form a coalition. UML Chairman Mannohan Adhikary became the first communist prime minister. However, a member of the NCP became Speaker of the House.

***RELATIONS WITH NEIGHBORING COUNTRIES.*** Relations with both India and China were strengthened with official visits by leaders of both these countries. A proposed 1991 visit by the **DALAI LAMA** of Tibet was canceled after China protested and in 1993, Prime Minister Koirala made the first visit by a Nepali premier to Tibet since the 1950s. In eastern Nepal, ethnic Nepalese refugees fleeing ethnic unrest in Bhutan numbered more than 100,000 by October 1993. Despite continued talks by a "high-level joint committee," the situation remained unresolved with Bhutan denying Nepal's contention that all refugees be repatriated to Bhutan.

***REPORT BY THE UN HUMAN RIGHTS COMMITTEE.*** The initial report of Nepal (CCPR/C/74/Add. 2) under the **INTERNATIONAL COVENANT ON CIVIL AND POLITICAL RIGHTS** was examined by the UN **HUMAN RIGHTS COMMITTEE** at its 1359th and 1363rd meetings, held on 17 and 19 October 1994. The Committee adopted the following comments at its 1382nd meeting, held on 2 November 1994 (CCPR/C/19/Add. 42):

*Factors and difficulties affecting the implementation of the Covenant.* The Committee recognizes that Nepal is emerging from a long period of isolation, and that the remnants of authoritarian rule have not yet been overcome. Steps remain to be taken in engaging, consolidating and developing democratic institutions for better implementation of the Covenant. Economic depression, extreme poverty and widespread illiteracy constitute obstacles to the effective implementation of the Covenant.

*Positive aspects.* The Committee welcomes the efforts undertaken by the State party to establish democratic institutions and multipartism as well as its declared commitment to the rule of law and the independence of the judiciary. It takes note, in particular, of the adoption of a new Constitution which provides the basis for a parliamentary system of government based on multi-party democracy as well as for an independent Supreme Court. The right of citizens to petition the Supreme Court to challenge laws which violate human rights and the use of this right is particularly welcomed. The Committee also notes with satisfaction that Nepal has recently acceded to a number of international human rights instruments, including the first Optional Protocol to the Covenant.

**BIBLIOGRAPHY.** Amnesty International. *Nepal: Human Rights Safeguards.* London: 1994. NGO report, in English.

————. *Nepal: A Pattern of Human Rights Violations.* London: 1987. NGO report, in English.

————. *Religious Intolerance.* London: 1986. NGO report, in English.

————. *Nepal: A Summary of Human Rights Concerns.* London: 1992. NGO report, in English.

"Child Labor in Nepal: The Facts behind the Himalayas," *Child Workers in Asia* 1, no. 1 (July–Sept. 1985): 3–5. NGO bulletin article, in English.

Child Workers in Nepal Concerned Center. *Lost Childhood: Survey Research on Street Children of Kathmandu.* Kathmandu, Nepal: 1990. NGO factfinding report, in English.

Forum for Protection of Human Rights. *Dawn of Democracy, People's Power in Nepal: Photo Documentary of the Movement for Restoration of Democracy from February to April 1990.* Kathmandu, Nepal: 1990. NGO photo album, in English and Nepalese.

Informal Sector Service Centre (INSEC). *Human Rights Yearbook: Nepal 1992.* Kathmandu, Nepal: 1993. NGO report, in English.

————. *Nepal and Its Electoral System: An Introduction.* Kathmandu, Nepal: 1991. NGO research report, in English.

International Commission of Jurists. *The Independence of Judges and Lawyers in South Asia.* Geneva: 1988. NGO conference report, in English.

Yami, Hsila. "Nepal: Women and the Democracy Movement," *Manushi* no. 60 (Sept.–Oct. 1990): 29–32. Article, in English.

**NETHERLANDS.** The Kingdom of the Netherlands consists of three countries: the Netherlands, the Netherlands Antilles, and the Island of Aruba—all linked under a legal framework laid down in the charter of the Kingdom of the Netherlands proclaimed on 15 December 1954. The Netherlands is a country in western Europe, on the North Sea, and has borders with Belgium and the Federal Republic of Germany. Its independence was first achieved in 1581 under the Union of Utrecht and was most recently restored after its second period of occupation by Germans in 1945. It became a member of the United Nations the same year. Its population is estimated to be 15,190,000.

The Netherlands Antilles consist of five islands: Curacao, Bonaire, St. Maarten, St. Eustatius, and Saba, with a total population of 176,500. Aruba, formerly a part of the Antilles, has a population of 61,900; it is in the process of exercising its rights to self-determination, to be realized in 1996. Ethnic groups in the Netherlands include migrants from Suriname, the Moluccan Islands, the Netherlands Antilles, and various Mediterranean countries; and non-nationals from Africa, Asia, Europe, the Americas, Oceania, and Hong Kong. Religions practiced include Christianity (Roman Catholic, Dutch Reformed, and other denominations), 55%; Islam, 5%; Judaism, 2%; and other or unaffiliated, 38%. The language commonly used is Dutch (official). Literacy is estimated at 99%. The Antillean community consists of a number of different races and cultural groups; they live together in harmony and without racial discrimination. The normal language of instruction is Dutch. On Curacao, Aruba, and Bonaire, the mother tongue Papiamente is used in some classes in addition to Dutch. On Saba, St. Eustatius, and St. Maarten, the mother tongue English is used as well as Dutch.

Following legislative elections in May 1994, each of the major parties, typically, failed to secure a majority. Wim Kok, leader of the Labour Party-PvdA, led a three-party coalition to become prime minister in August 1994.

One of the first western countries to do so, the Netherlands passed legislation outlining the procedure for euthanasia of an incurably ill patient who repeatedly requests the procedure.

Following 35,500 applications for political asylum in the Netherlands in 1993, legislation came into effect in 1994 restricting the possible bases for granting refugee status.

**BIBLIOGRAPHY.** Advies Commissie Mensenrechten (Dutch Human Rights and Foreign Policy Advisory Committee). *Development Cooperation and Human Rights.* The Hague, the Netherlands: 1987. Government commission report, in English.

Baehr, Peter R., and Monique C. Castermans-Holleman. "The Promotion of Human Rights: The Netherlands at the UN," in *The Netherlands and the United Nations: Selected Issues*, pp. 23–34. The Hague, the Netherlands: T.M.C. Asser Institute, 1990. Scholarly article, in English.

Breum, M., and A. Hendriks, eds. *AIDS and Human Rights: An International Perspective.* Copenhagen: Danish Center of Human Rights, 1988. Edited collection, in English.

Grunfeld, Fred. *Human Rights: The International Protection and Promotion of Human Rights and its Significance for British and Netherlands' Domestic Law.* Course offered at the Faculty of Law, University of Limburg, Netherlands, 1987–1988. Syllabus/university course outline, in English.

Heringa, Aalt Willem. "Recent Dutch Cases Invalidating Discriminatory Social Security Laws," *Netherlands Quarterly of Human Rights* 6, no. 1 (1988): 19–26. NGO article, in English.

Human Rights Watch. "Nepal," in *Human Rights Watch World Report 1995*, pp. 165–167. New York: 1995. NGO report, in English.

Pettman, Ralph. *Incitement to Racial Hatred: The International Experience.* Canberra, Australia: Human Rights Commission, 1982. Government monograph, in English.

Shadid, W. A. "The Integration of Muslim Minorities in The Netherlands," *International Migration Review* 25, no. 2 (Summer 1991): 355–374. Scholarly article, in English; bibliography, pp. 371–374.

Sigler, Jay A., ed. *International Handbook on Race and Race Relations.* Westport, CT, USA: Greenwood Press, 1987. Scholarly edited collection, in English; bibliography, pp. 449–454.

Simpson Snowden, Lynne. "The Impact of Asylum Policy in The Netherlands, France, and Germany," *Migration World* 19, no. 3 (1991): 14–18. Article, in English.

## NETHERLANDS QUARTERLY OF HUMAN RIGHTS.

Published between 1982 and 1987 as the *SIM Newsletter,* this journal focuses on symposium themes such as social rights, women's rights, and the international protection of human rights.

*Netherlands Quarterly of Human Rights.* Address: Netherlands Institute of Human Rights, Janskerkhof 16, 3512 BW Utrecht, the Netherlands.

## NEW INTERNATIONAL ECONOMIC ORDER.

In 1980, the UN ECONOMIC AND SOCIAL COUNCIL (decision 1980/126) authorized the SUB-COMMISSION ON PREVENTION OF DISCRIMINATION AND PROTECTION OF MINORITIES to appoint one of its members, Mr. Raul Ferrero (Peru), as its Special Rapporteur to prepare a study on the new international economic order and the promotion of human rights, taking into account the conclusions of the seminar scheduled to be held later in 1980 within the framework of the program of UN advisory services in the field of human rights on "The Effects of the Existing Unjust International Economic Order on the Economies of the Developing Countries and the Obstacle that This Represents for the Implementation of Human Rights and Fundamental Freedoms, particularly the Right to Enjoy Adequate Standards of Living as Proclaimed in Article 25 of the Universal Declaration of Human Rights."

One conclusion of the seminar, which was widely supported although no consensus was reached, was that the present unjust international order placed obstacles in the way of exercise of the right to DEVELOPMENT by developing countries. These obstacles were identified as (UN Doc. ST/HR/SER A/8, chap. V):

(i) ideological obstacles, reflected in the priority given to the arms race rather than to development;

(ii) institutional obstacles, reflected in the observance of comprehensive negotiating frameworks and the glaring inadequacy of existing institutions;

(iii) legal obstacles in the form of obsolete concepts and principles of international law based on colonial approaches to international trade and contractual undertakings, the lack of control on transnational enterprises, unfavourable structure of the patent system and the refusal to accept the concept of "permanent sovereignty";

(iv) international trade and related obstacles, characterized by unequal exchange of goods and services, inadequate institutional arrangement for commodity trade, tariff and non-tariff barriers and emphasis on unfair concepts such as reciprocity among developed and developing countries;

(v) obstacles to access to finance due to anachronistic objectives and spirit prevailing in international financial institutions, and an unjust approach to the external debt problems of developing countries;

(vi) inadequate mechanisms to promote transfer of technology for a balance growth in scientific and technological development in both developing and developed countries.

The seminar also drew a comparison between the present international economic order and the economic orders of the European countries at the end of the 19th century, as follows:

At that time, national economies in their liberal setting had come to the point where the system-promoted interests of the haves, the entrepreneurs, became incompatible with the system-neglected interests of the have-nots, the working masses. On the brink of violent revolution the ruling classes were forced to allow restriction of liberal enterprise by the enactment of special legislation, which provided for a gradually expanding minimum of social security and economic welfare for the hitherto exploited. In other words, to meet the demands of the less privileged the three basic principles of liberalism underwent the following changes: the principle of freedom was restricted by the introduction of the principle of protection; the principle of legal equality was in part replaced by that of material equality; and the principle of reciprocity was conditioned by the fact that the working class was endowed with rights which restricted the operational freedom of the entrepreneurs. Today, one can observe the tendency towards a similar development on the international scene.

The Sub-Commission received the Special Rapporteur's study, entitled *The New International Economic Order and the Promotion of Human Rights,* in 1983 (issued in 1985 as United Nations publication, Sales no. E.85.XIV.6). In the study, after examining the relevant documentation, the Special Rapporteur presented the following conclusions (chap. XIII A, paras. 250–294):

In discussing the present situation regarding world economic relations, it is not entirely appropriate to speak of an international economic order, for it is not so much an "order" as a world-wide interaction of economic forces and powers resulting from historical causes that need to be understood.

The present economic order began to be imposed at a time when the vast majority of developing countries were still dependent territories and consequently unable to take part in its establishment; it was therefore inevitably inequitable and contrary to their interests. It is well known that international economic and monetary relations are based on three liberal principles, namely, freedom, equality and reciprocity. These principles could well suffice to bring prosperity for all, but in a world of equals, not in a world of unequals. In a world of "potentates" on one side and the "poor" on the other, it is not right to expect the poor to accept principles which profit the powerful alone and harm the weak; in such conditions, the relationship tends to give rise to exploitation, legal equality to produce material inequality, and reciprocal concessions to widen still further the already immense gap between the rich and the poor countries.

The present order is a serious obstacle to the realization of the human rights and fundamental freedoms proclaimed in the Universal Declaration of Human Rights, more particularly in article 25, which declares that everyone has the right to a standard of living adequate for the health and well-being of himself and of his family. However, the fact that an unjust international economic order exists cannot be used to justify failure to secure the realization or observance of human rights. In any event, there are two needs that have to be met side by side. One is the need to change the present international economic order into a more equitable order, and the other is the need to promote and protect human rights and fundamental freedoms in each and every country; they are interrelated needs, but neither of them is a prerequisite for the realization of the other.

A process of decolonization has given birth to innumerable independent States since the Second World War. Unfortunately, such political independence has not generally been followed by economic, social or cultural independence, which are equally important.

As Janez Stanovnik has pointed out, the demand for the new international economic order is of a political nature. The underprivileged peoples who are championing the new order have neither the military nor the economic power to match the dominant forces in the present world. Their strength lies rather in inevitable historical evolution and is therefore essentially on the political plane.

It must be recognized that it was at the Fourth Conference of Heads of State or Government of Non-Aligned Countries, held at Algiers from 5 to 9 September 1973, that the first ideas concerning a new international economic order were formulated. Conceptually, this new order represents the economic aspect of the policy of non-alignment, that is to say, the application of its general principles to the economic sphere. The above-mentioned Conference adopted an Economic Declaration and an Action Programme for Economic Co-operation, confirming that the new objective of the movement would be to seek to establish "a new type of international economic relations" and a new and just international division of labour. Both instruments benefited from the fact that all the non-aligned countries are also members of the Group of 77 and participate in the work of UNCTAD so that they have vast experience in such matters. Another important source of valuable ideas and concepts was the International Development Strategy for the Second United Nations Development Decade, adopted in 1970.

The existing system not only nullifies all efforts to narrow the gap between developing and developed countries, but, still worse, magnifies that difference by depriving the former of their rightful say in decisions on international economic and commercial questions of vital interest to them. The gap between the levels of living of developed and developing countries continues to widen—from roughly 10:1 in the 1950s to 14:1 at the end of the 1970s.

The industrialized countries are trying to solve their unemployment and inflation problems at the expense of the poor countries. To attain the price stability that suits them, they are holding down the prices of primary commodities from the developing world. As a result of this drop in commodity prices compared with those of industrial products, developing countries, which are mainly exporters of primary products, are forced to export a growing volume of raw materials each year in order to acquire the industrial products needed for their development. This phenomenon has been dubbed the "external strangulation of development."

The Brandt Commission has made the dramatic point that in some low-income countries studies have shown as many as 40 per cent of pre-school children exhibiting clinical signs of malnutrition. No one can state the exact numbers in the world who suffer from hunger and malnutrition, but all estimates indicate that they amount to hundreds of millions: millions of persons who will die from lack of food or have their physical development impaired. It is an intolerable situation. The food problem is extremely serious, but what is even worse is that it is continuing to grow more acute, to the extent that one third of mankind is now suffering from hunger.

To resolve the urgent food problem, the developing countries must put an end to the neglect into which agriculture has fallen; in the late 1950s and during the whole of the 1960s, their concern for industrial development led them to disregard the extremely important complementary role which rural development should play. This led to an abandonment of the countryside, the consequences of which we are suffering today.

World Bank projections indicate only modest growth for the developing countries' exports in the next 10 years. But it will be simply impossible to maintain this growth if the protectionist barriers erected by the developed nations are maintained or continue to grow as they have done recently. The fact is that this trend towards protectionism and restrictive trade practices is gathering momentum in all the industrialized nations.

It is essential to establish an international trade organization—as was proposed when the World Bank and IMF were set up—which would carry out the functions both of GATT and of UNCTAD, assuming responsibility for sponsoring agreements, *inter alia,* on such vital issues as the commercial practices of transnational corporations, international investment, problems of double taxation, the transfer of technology and so on, and in its turn act as a forum (as does UNCTAD) for dialogue, debate and negotiations in trade matters.

Insufficient attention is paid to developing countries' interests when establishing monetary and financial policies at the world level. The World Bank and IMF, which came into being as a result of the agreements adopted at the United Nations Monetary and Financial Conference held at Bretton Woods, New Hampshire, in 1944, were two corner-stones of the monetary system established after the Second World War, but they began to display serious limitations in the 1970s, and today these have developed into grave defects and failure to adapt to the needs of developing countries.

At present, the developing countries hold 38.5 per cent of the votes in the World Bank, in comparison with 42.5 per cent for the main industrialized countries and 19 per cent for the other industrialized countries. The fact that the participation of the developing countries is so limited has led to a proposal that votes should be divided equally between developed countries and developing countries. Similar pressure is being exerted in IMF, where the developing countries hold only 28 percent of the votes.

It is essential to change the prevailing view that IMF is a "lender of last resort" and place greater emphasis on the advisability, as indicated by IMF itself, of encouraging countries to seek its assistance when a need first arises and not when the situation has already become critical.

The conditions imposed today by certain international organizations, such as IMF, when granting balance-of-payments assistance, oblige developing countries to impose specified domestic policies which have extremely dangerous consequences, such as growing rates of inflation and unemployment.

One way to iron out the blatant inequalities between developing and developed countries would be to implement the International Development Strategy for the Third United Nations Development Decade, which reiterates the objective proclaimed by the General Assembly, in paragraph 43 of its resolution 2626 (XXV) of 24 October 1970, that the developed countries should provide developing countries with a minimum net amount of 0.7 per cent of their GNP each year in the form of official development assistance.

At the Seventh Conference of Heads of State or Government of Non-Aligned Countries, held in New Delhi in 1983, was pointed out that, despite the growing need on the part of developing countries for assistance on favourable terms, such assistance was in fact decreasing. The net expenditure of all members of DAC on official development assistance in fact amounted to only 0.35 per cent of their GNP in 1981, as compared with 0.51 per cent in 1960. After two decades, the figure attained is barely half the target figure set by the Untied Nations, namely, 0.7 per cent of the GNP of the developed countries.

Efforts in the field of science and technology are directed mainly at improving living standards in the developed countries, and when science and technology can be applied to the problems of the poor countries, the cost is sometimes virtually prohibitive. In addition, technology is rarely developed with the aim of meeting the needs of the developing countries, so that any technology transfer to those countries is mostly inadequate or, what is worse, obsolete.

The gap between the developed and the developing countries in the area of technology is much greater than the corresponding economic gap. While the developing countries have on average a per capita income 15 times lower than that of the developed countries, the application of modern scientific and technological knowledge in the developing countries is some 50 times less than in the developed countries. This explains the frequent references to the "technological gap".

As pointed out in the report of the Director-General for Development and International Economic Co-operation, transnational corporations have acquired considerable market power *vis-à-vis* the Governments and enterprises of developing countries. This has been due in part to their command over resources of various kinds—finance, management, marketing networks and skills, technology and "know-how" generally, in part to their ability to combine and deploy such resources across the world, and in part to the fact that transnational corporations, particularly those enjoying monopolistic positions, have generally integrated their subsidiaries and affiliates into the company as a whole, rather than into the economy of the host countries. Transnational corpo-

rations have been able to take advantage of their strong bargaining positions in a variety of ways—on occasion by interfering in the political affairs of the host country—and the relationships between transnational corporations and host countries have often involved patterns of growth and industrialization which have led to the inequitable distribution of the earnings from investment and associated activities and have limited the ability of developing countries to achieve self-reliant development.

The role of disarmament should also be emphasized. Let us imagine for a moment what it would mean if the huge resources devoted to military ends were used for civilian purposes. How much could be achieved and how many development programmes could be launched? It is moreover essential to bear in mind how difficult it is for the developing countries, in view of the world's armaments-oriented structure, to pursue their own paths towards progress if at the same time they are confronted with threats of intervention and intimidation from outside. As the report of the Secretary-General on the international dimensions of the right to development concluded, disarmament is crucial to realization of the right to development, as it is to realization of the right to peace, the achievement of a new international economic order and the promotion of respect for all human rights.

It is highly alarming that world expenditures on arms in a single year are, on the one hand, equal to the income of half the world's population in the same year and, on the other hand, of a similar order to the total external debt of the developing countries.

The most serious world recession since 1930 is the worst moment for the international financial institutions to impose more stringent conditions on borrowers and cut back their operations with them. It is counter-productive for IMF and the World Bank to have taken such an attitude at precisely the time when the developing countries have to face high oil prices, low prices for their primary goods and high interest rates on existing debts, all this within the context of a general recession on world markets. Countries that are heavily in debt to the developed countries are precisely their best customers, and any serious reduction in lending will have repercussions in the developed countries in the form of reduced demand and fewer imports in the developing countries.

Although the external debt of some countries may be so great as to appear unmanageable, it must not be forgotten that if the international banking system suddenly stops lending, the developing countries will not be able to pay their existing debts either.

No analysis of the crisis centring round the growing indebtedness of the developing countries can disregard the profound consequences which this crisis may have, above all for the most indebted countries. These countries cannot be expected to confine themselves simply to paying their debts conscientiously, neglecting their internal problems or leaving aside their most important concern, namely, their own development. If these countries are subjected to constraint and pressure, the resulting social problems can come as no surprise.

The current situation with regard to the external debt of the developing countries is extremely serious, and it has now reached the point where whole countries are on the verge of collapse. Unless realistic and urgent measures are taken, the entire international financial system may also collapse. However, the problem has not yet been tackled, except through short-term measures which do not provide any genuine medium-term or long-term solution, and the danger of a widespread cessation of payments therefore remains.

The extremely high level of indebtedness of the developing countries makes it necessary to think in terms of global and realistic solutions. It might be useful to consider the advantages of a system whereby the developed countries would buy from private banks the loans granted to countries with payment difficulties. The loans would of course be bought at a rate lower than the nominal value, which would mean that the private banks would lose a certain amount but would recover a considerable part of the total loan. The acquiring Governments would then negotiate a long-term refinancing scheme with the debtor countries, reducing the annual payments to appropriate or bearable levels based on capacity to pay. The debt might perhaps be converted into negotiable instruments guaranteed in some way by the national treasuries or equivalent institutions in the developed countries.

The effect of this colossal indebtedness on human rights is now being seen. Third world countries are making considerable cuts in their development programmes, Governments have had virtually to halt all public works projects, and unemployment and underemployment are increasing uncontrollably.

All this is giving rise to a bad social atmosphere which affects the poorest classes and helps generate a dangerous climate of political insecurity. In the last two years, the construction of schools, hospitals and houses and the improvement of social security services, for example, have become almost a luxury for the developing countries.

It is extremely important to stress the indivisible and interdependent nature of all human rights, without giving priority to any category in particular. The main difficulty is not to settle on the priority but to establish a flexible relationship between civil and political rights and economic, social and cultural rights and take each country's level of socio-economic development fully into account; to do so, it must be appreciated that the implementation of economic, social and cultural rights depends largely on each State's level of development, while the implementation of civil and political rights depends exclusively on the political will of Governments.

The concept of human rights has evolved gradually. After the traditional classification into civil and political rights, or what could be termed "first generation" rights, came economic, social and cultural rights, which may be placed in the second generation, and only in recent times has the need been maintained to recognize the existence of the "rights of solidarity"—which include the right to development, to a healthy environment, to peace and to the common heritage of mankind, and other rights that make up what could be called the third generation in this evolution. These rights, however, have scarcely taken shape and to implement them will require a major effort along a difficult road ahead.

These three categories, or generations, of human rights are to some extent equivalent to the three fundamental principles of the French Revolution of 1789: liberty, equality and fraternity. The human rights which were first recognized, namely civil and political rights, are those based on the "freedom" of the person. Economic, social and cultural rights, which arise in the second stage, may be said to be based on the "equality" of human beings. The rights of solidarity, which represent a third stage, still in process of maturing, are those based on "fraternity" between men and between peoples.

Those who live in absolute poverty cannot even satisfy the minimum needs of a decent life: enough food, a minimum of clothing, living space, drinking water, satisfactory sanitary installations, elementary hygiene, basic schooling for children, etc. The hundreds of millions of people who live in these conditions are permanently denied most of the fundamental and inalienable human rights proclaimed in the Universal Declaration of Human Rights.

Justice and the search for greater equality should be the guiding principles for international action aimed at eliminating the growing disparities between some countries and others. It must be remembered that the very objective of a new international economic order does not relate solely to economic issues as such. Its aim is not only the reassessment of things and their more equitable distribution, but also the development of all men and of all aspects of man, in a global cultural process which embodies values and encompasses the national context, social relations, education and well-being, with the idea of also providing a basis for the development of the international community itself.

The existing unjust international economic order is a genuine obstacle to realization of the human rights and fundamental freedoms proclaimed in the Universal Declaration of Human Rights, in particular in article 25, which states that everyone has the right to a standard of living adequate for the health and well-being of himself and of his family. More than 30 years after the adoption of the Universal Declaration of Human Rights, 850 million people, that is, approximately 40 per cent of the inhabitants of the developing countries, are still living in dire poverty.

It must therefore be emphasized that the central or basic element in its establishment must be man, whose essential dignity must be defined and protected; it must accordingly be understood that the ultimate goal of the new order is respect for human rights and fundamental freedoms.

Interdependence does not mean uniformity. Genuine development does not consist in grafting life-styles from developed countries onto developing countries. It must be understood that interdependence presupposes relations between countries that are different. International co-operation should be aimed at remedying the lack or scarcity of economic resources, and the recipient States are under an obligation to participate in such co-operation. It is implicit in the right to development that States should agree to assist one another when external factors obstruct the effective implementation of human rights.

One method whereby human rights can be truly and effectively safeguarded internally is through fair participation in which the people can express their own will in a free and responsible manner, thus enabling all the members of the community to fulfil themselves and exercise conscious freedom of choice. Workers and their organizations should participate not only in the management of public, economic, social and cultural affairs as part of the democratization of the State, but also in the decision-making processes of economic, labour and social planning, in the determination of social development goals and in the creation of conditions for achieving those goals.

The principle of participation in developing countries with indigenous populations implies the equal recognition of those peoples' right to participate fully in the economic, political and social life of the States of which they form a part, as well as their right to maintain their traditions, customs, languages and other special characteristics, which are expressed in the right to be different. Alienation as an instrument of national and international policy leads to loss of identity for those against whom it is applied.

Any form of economic aggression, as committed by some

developed States against developing States, is similarly unacceptable and must therefore be categorically rejected; such forms of aggression include the use of threats, commercial sanctions or any other form of blockade and measures of coercion or blackmail to the extent that they involve means of political pressure aimed at influencing sovereign decisions.

The new order must take into consideration two important sets of principles contained in the Charter of Economic Rights and Duties of States: (i) the sovereignty, territorial integrity and political independence of States, the sovereign equality of all States, the principles of non-aggression, non-intervention and peaceful coexistence, equal rights and self-determination of peoples and the peaceful settlement of disputes; (ii) the right of the developing countries and of the people of territories under colonial and racial domination or foreign occupation to achieve their liberation and to regain effective control over their natural resources and economic activities.

The concept of "development" should not be interpreted solely in terms of economic and material well-being but in much broader terms covering the physical, moral, intellectual and cultural growth of human beings.

Development is a concept which ought to focus on the human element, on people, who must be both its agents and its beneficiaries, and it should be based on the individual definition which each society forms of it, founded on its own values and objectives.

It is essential today to incorporate the standards applicable to human rights and the corresponding goals into development plans. This is what is known as the "integrated approach to development". If the new international economic order is to produce a substantial improvement in the extent to which the impoverished and oppressed peoples of the world enjoy human rights, it is important for that goal to be fully incorporated in development strategies, national as well as international.

On the basis of these conclusions and the supporting documentation, the Special Rapporteur formulated the following recommendations (chap. XIII B paras. 295–310):

It must be recognized that not much has been achieved through the existing international systems and machinery, and it is therefore essential for the international organizations to adopt a realistic approach to the requirements of the world today, starting with the United Nations, which must be given greater drive by its Member States. In other words, instead of the international organizations being bypassed in the establishment of a new order, as some prefer or seem to prefer, they must be used as tools for correcting the current unjust international relations which allow a few countries to become steadily richer while the vast majority of countries grow poorer and poorer. Today, a stronger and more vigorous United Nations system is needed, and one that is used more effectively.

The new international economic order must be established through action by States in the context of their relations with other States, so as to change existing links, which favour only a small minority of States. This must be the main and immediate task of global negotiations in the framework of the United Nations, which is the organization called upon to direct this task—the more so today, now that a representative of the third world has been elected to the highest office in the Organization.

The global nature of the structural crisis in international economic relations calls for global solutions also. The trend towards bilateralism may have harmful consequences. A new multilateralism is therefore needed, founded on co-ordinated policies in which all groups of countries would take part on an international basis.

Since the establishment of a new international economic order will require a concerted effort on the part of all States, it is essential that the States of Eastern Europe should play a more active and constructive role than has been the case to date. As Leon Zurawicki recently stated ("The NIEO: an Eastern European point of view," *Development and Socio-Economic Progress* (Cairo), 21, (1983/1): 94.), the Eastern European countries should not only specify their own revised doctrine concerning the new international economic order and the related problems but should also indicate a forum where these ideas could be discussed.

It is certainly somewhat discouraging that at the summit meetings of the major developed countries held at Versailles in June 1982 and at Williamsburg in May 1983, those countries failed to grasp fully the immense significance of the demands of the developing countries; the same thing happened at the sixth session of the United Nations Conference on Trade and Development, held in Belgrade in June 1983. This attitude must change, for otherwise the former countries will themselves be largely responsible for the extremely serious consequences which this lack of understanding may have on a world careering towards an unprecedented crisis. Are we not perhaps already on the threshold of a world catastrophe which will have a profound impact on the basic human rights?

On the basis of a survey of the major United Nation instruments relating to the establishment of the new international economic order, it is apparent that the importance of the link between respect for human rights and the establishment of an equitable international order has long been recognized—most notably perhaps in the Charter of the United Nations and in article 28 of the Universal Declaration of Human Rights. In many respects these instruments demonstrate that the programme for the new international economic order is conceptually founded upon the human rights notion of self-determination. It should also be acknowledged, however, that while these instruments contain many references to human rights-related objectives, they tend only very occasionally to use the exact term "human rights". Moreover, references to the relationship between human rights and the new international economic order have tended to go only in one direction—that is to say, while frequent reference is made to the contribution which the new international economic order could make to the realization of human rights, mention is rarely made of the converse position.

Another important issue which has frequently arisen in international forums, although usually not discussed explicitly, is whether the reaffirmation of the objectives of the new international economic order in essentially human rights-related contexts, and vice versa, serves primarily to assure integration of the two objectives, or rather to distract attention from whichever may be treated as the issue of major immediate concern. While such concern may sometimes be justified, it is nevertheless important to ensure that human rights concerns are related to the overall structural framework in which they arise and that they are acknowledged within the mainstream of international negotiations.

The establishment of a linkage or *quid pro quo* between

respect for human rights and promotion of the new international economic order has on occasion been proposed by some scholars. The relevant United Nations instruments on the new international economic order, however, have not endorsed such an approach, although there would appear to be general support for the proposition that progress on both fronts should be sought simultaneously.

The major objective of the present study has been to demonstrate the fundamental links that exist between the achievement of full respect for human rights and the establishment of an equitable international economic order. These links are manifold and complex and it has not been possible either to examine every relevant issue or to go into great detail with respect to some of the more important issues.

The present study has been designed to lay the basic groundwork for the future examination of other specific issues. In this regard it has already borne fruit in the form of the study on the right to adequate food as a human right which the Sub-Commission on Prevention of Discrimination and Protection of Minorities proposed at its thirty-fifth session. Moreover in the course of the stimulating debates that have taken place in the Sub-Commission in recent years, a number of other topics have been proposed for more detailed consideration. Some of them certainly merit separate studies, which could be undertaken in the future by the Sub-Commission.

One of the broad conclusions that emerges very clearly from the present study is that recent progress towards the adoption of specific elements of the package of demands formulated within the framework of the new international economic order has been painfully slow and in some respects non-existent. The very meagre results achieved at the sixth session of the United Nations Conference on Trade and Development have only served to highlight the critical impasse that has been reached. It is therefore imperative that the global negotiations on international economic co-operation for development, the launching of which continues to be stalled, should not be approached by all States concerned with a renewed sense both of commitment and of overriding urgency. The continued deferral of the global negotiations can only have an adverse impact on the prospects for the full realization of human rights, particularly in developing countries.

With respect to more specific issues, one of the most prominent recommendations that emerges from the present study concerns the impact on human rights of the policies and practices of the major international financial institutions, most notably the World Bank and IMF. The study has made clear the seriousness of the current world debt crisis and has emphasized the need to ensure the continuing, and indeed increased, availability of financial resources to facilitate the development efforts of all developing countries and particularly the least developed.

By the same token, it is clear that the assistance provided by the international financial institutions must be of such a nature that its impact on the enjoyment of human rights is positive. The precise implications of this requirement need, however, to be examined in greater detail. Thus, for example, the question of "conditionality" of assistance has been raised in the present study but its deeper ramifications have not been examined. Similarly, the relevance of political concerns in the decision-making of the international financial institutions needs to be examined frankly, as does the issue of equitable global participation in the management of the relevant institutions. If a new Bretton Woods-type conference is to be convened, as has been proposed, an examina-tion of these and other human rights-related issues should be undertaken in advance.

Another issue which would appear to warrant future consideration by the Sub-Commission is the status of the goal, established and accepted well over a decade ago, that developed countries should provide developing countries with a minimum net amount of 0.7 per cent of the GNP each year in the form of official development assistance. At present the amount provided is less than half of that target, and it is clear that the ability of developing countries to ensure the full enjoyment of human rights of their entire populations has suffered accordingly. Many proposals have been made for the creation of mechanisms designed to ensure a regular, guaranteed transfer of resources to developing countries to support their development efforts. Very little progress has been made, however, with respect to an examination of the obligations and entitlements of States to official development assistance under present international law.

The importance of regional endeavours to promote economic co-operation, including, in particular, economic co-operation among developing countries, has also been noted in the present study. One potential means by which human rights concerns might perhaps be more fully taken into account in regional economic decision-making would be the appointment, perhaps within the framework of the United Nations regional commissions, of regional advisers on human rights, as proposed by the Assistant Secretary-General, Centre for Human Rights, Mr. Herndl, in his opening statement to the thirty-ninth session of the Commission on Human Rights, on 31 January 1983.

In concluding the present study, it must be emphasized that the basic challenge, which is to ensure that the establishment of the new international economic order and the promotion of respect for human rights go hand in hand, is never going to be resolved simply by focusing on one particular issue, such as development assistance, commodity prices or the role of transnational corporations. The challenge is in fact a far more pervasive one and requires constant vigilance to see that economic relations, at the international as much as at the national level, are approached in such a way as to ensure that the concepts of the dignity of every individual and of human solidarity are the guiding principles. In the establishment of a new international economic order, full respect for human rights must be seen both as an end in itself and as an essential means.

After examining the study, the Sub-Commission (resolution 1983/35) transmitted it to the UN **COMMISSION ON HUMAN RIGHTS,** drawing attention to the conclusions and recommendations reproduced above. On recommendation of the Sub-Commission, endorsed by the Commission on Human Rights, the Economic and Social Council (decision 1984/133) decided that the study should be published and given the widest possible distribution in all the official languages of the United Nations.

Two years later, the Sub-Commission decided (resolution 1985/34) that it would consider certain items on its agenda—among them the item entitled "The New International Economic Order and the Promotion of Human Rights"—on a biennial basis starting at its 1986 session. However, the Sub-Commission did not meet in 1986 due to the financial situation of the United Nations. The subject was considered again only at the 1989 session, when the Sub-Commission decided (resolution 1989/1) that thenceforth it would consider the item on an annual basis.

*SEE ALSO* *Development; Economic, Social and Cultural Rights.*

**NEW YORK LAW SCHOOL JOURNAL OF HUMAN RIGHTS.** Established in 1983 as an annual in two parts, this publication contains interdisciplinary information for legal practitioners in new areas of human rights law.

*New York Law School Journal of Human Rights.* Address: New York Law School, 57 Worth Street, New York, NY 10013-2960, USA.

**NEW ZEALAND.** A country in Oceania, southeast of Australia, the dominion of New Zealand occupies two principal islands—North Island and South Island—as well as Stewart Island and the Chatham Islands. In addition, it administers Niue and the Cook Islands, which have achieved self-governing status; Tokelau; and the Antarctic region known as the Ross Dependency. It achieved independence from Great Britain as a self-governing dominion in 1907 and became a member of the United Nations in 1945. Its population is estimated to be 3,477,000. Ethnic groups include Europeans (86.8%), Maoris (8.9%), and communities such as the Cook Island Maori, Niuean, Tokelauan, Samoan, Tongan, Chinese, and Indian. Languages commonly used include English and Maori (both official). Christianity is the predominant religion (Roman Catholic, 15%; Anglican, 29%; Presbyterian, 18%; and others 38%). Literacy is estimated at 99%.

The Bill of Rights Act 1990 was passed to protect fundamental freedoms. The Act does not empower a court to hold legislation invalid because it may be inconsistent with the Bill of Rights Act. The principle of Parliamentary sovereignty, under which no law is supreme, remains intact.

Following the victory of the conservative National Party in the general election of 1990, new political coalitions and parties were formed to challenge the main parties. In December 1991, minor parties formed the Alliance, a coalition of the New Labour Party, the New Zealand Democratic Party, the Green Party of Aotearoa-New Zealand, and Mana Motuhake. New Zealand First was formed in July 1993 by Winston Peters who had been dismissed in October 1991 as Minister of Maori Affairs for criticizing the new National Party government for its proposals to reduce public spending on welfare, education, medical services, and old age pensions.

Both were successful in either winning a contested seat or limiting the National Party's majority in subsequent by-elections. However, the National Party was returned to power in the general election of November 1993. The Alliance and New Zealand First won two seats each in the enlarged 99-seat parliament.

Electoral reform was also approved at that time by 54% of the voters and a mixed member system of proportional representation, similar to that of Germany, was scheduled to take effect at the time of the 1996 general election.

In further disputes between the Maoris and the government, the Waitangi Tribunal recommended in August 1992 that one of the smallest tribes, the Ngai Tahu, be given ownership of most of the fisheries of South Island. A Maori consortium was later given NZ$150m by the government to buy a 50% share of the largest inshore fishing company in the country.

***THE INDIGENOUS MAORI.*** In recent years the New Zealand Government has placed a new emphasis on encouraging Maori economic development, educational advancement, and the greater use of the Maori language. There has also been a positive policy of appointing Maoris to positions where they can make the Maori point of view heard. In addition, a significant debate was engendered in the country on human rights questions as a result of the government's preparation and publication of a white paper which included a draft bill of rights for the country. The draft bill would guarantee those fundamental rights and freedoms embodied in the **INTERNATIONAL COVENANT ON CIVIL AND POLITICAL RIGHTS.** The government has also considered the desirability of altering the structure and functions of the New Zealand Human Rights Commission and the Race Relations Office, with the possibility of merging the two bodies. The Commission has recommended the appointment of an extra commissioner with special responsibility for Maori affairs, thus enabling the Commission to take a more active educational role in assisting all New Zealanders in understanding the issues stemming from the New Zealand-Maori Treaty of Waitangi.

On the subject of the treaty and its implications, the government of New Zealand supplied the following information in a report presented to the UN **HUMAN RIGHTS COMMITTEE** on 2 August 1988 (UN Doc. CCPR/C/37/Add. 8, paras. 143–152):

The Treaty of Waitangi was signed in 1840 between representative Maori chiefs of different tribes and the British Crown. In recent years, a positive and dynamic view of the Treaty has emerged whereby it is seen as a living social contract and the corner-stone of a positive bicultural relationship between Maori people and other New Zealanders. Accordingly, the Treaty has been given an enhanced status which has in turn led, amongst other things, to a greater awareness of Maori cultural values.

Government policy introduced in 1986 states that "all future legislation referred to Cabinet at the policy approval stage should draw attention to any implications for recognition of the principles of the Treaty of Waitangi".

The Treaty of Waitangi Tribunal (referred to in New Zealand's reply of 10 November 1983) was established in 1975 to hear grievances and make recommendations about alleged breaches of the Treaty by the Crown. In 1985, its jurisdiction was extended and now Maoris may submit claims arising from the prejudicial consequences of any legislation, policy or action of the Crown since 1840.

In 1987, the Treaty of Waitangi was the subject of one of the most important cases heard before the New Zealand Courts (*New Zealand Maori Council v. Attorney-General* [1987] 1 NZLR 641: a copy of the Court of Appeal's decision is attached as annex Y). The Maori Council had sought to restrain the Crown from transferring certain assets to State-owned enterprises alleging that that would be in breach of a legislative provision which required the Crown not to act inconsistently with the principles of the Treaty. The Court upheld the Maori Council's case declaring that the Crown assets could not be transferred before there was a system in place to ensure that the transfer was consistent with the Treaty's principles. The Court of Appeal Judges placed emphasis on the Treaty as a partnership requiring "the upmost good faith" and calling for the partners to act reasonably towards each other. The interests at issue in the case have since been settled by agreement between the parties and given legislative form in the Treaty of Waitangi (State Enterprises) Act 1988.

These developments all reflect a new awareness of the importance of the Treaty. At the heart of these changes lies a cultural and political resurgence in the Maori community. The governmental machinery for administering Maoridom's needs is undergoing dramatic change. The Department of Maori Affairs leads this change and has itself been the subject of a thorough review. The "Devolution" Programme *(Tukua Te Rangatiratanga)* has as its objective the giving back of *Rangatiratanga* (autonomy) to Maori people. The first step in this process is the transfer of many of the current functions of the Department of Maori Affairs to *Iwi* (or tribal) Authorities.

Other government departments are taking up Maori suggestions in order to introduce a greater cultural awareness and Maori perspective into their fields of responsibility. The *Maatu Whanqai* (and see para. 53 above) programme, jointly funded by the Departments of Justice, Social Welfare and Maori Affairs, has as its aim to prevent the flow of Maori people into penal institutions and to take them out of those institutions and into the care of *Whanau-iwi* (family and tribe). The Department of Justice has recently published a paper entitled "The Maori and the Criminal Justice System: A New Perspective—*He Whaipaanga Hou*". The paper is the first stage of a project to develop a Maori conceptual framework for research into Maori crime. This will be followed by consultation within the Maori community to ascertain further Maori views on the justice system.

Of great importance in the cultural field is the passage of the Maori Language Act 1987, referred to in paragraph 75 above. The Act declares *Te Reo Maori* (the Maori language) to be an official language of New Zealand and establishes the Maori Language Commission. The functions of the Commission include the initiation, development, co-ordination and implementation of policies and procedures to promote the Maori language as an official language of New Zealand. The Commission is to consider and report on any matter relating to the Maori language referred to it by the Minister of Maori Affairs and to promote the Maori language as an ordinary means of communication. The Commission is also vested with the authority to issue certificates of competency in the Maori language. The certificates of competency will be in either interpretation, translation or interpretation and translation of the Maori language. An endorsement may be made on the certificate of competency that the holder is competent to translate and/or interpret in legal proceedings if the Commission is satisfied that the person meets certain criteria. As already noted, the Act gives to persons involved in legal proceedings the right to speak Maori in such proceedings.

Maori as a spoken language is also being given a new boost through the *Kohanga Reo* (language nests) programme. These are family groups where Maori language, values and customs are naturally acquired by pre-school children from their *Kaumatua* (elders). Its purpose is to create a Maori language and cultural environment where Maori pre-schoolers can became fluent in Maori and be culturally competent.

A Maori Radio Board has recently been established with responsibility for setting up an Auckland based national Maori radio network; the network is being funded through the Department of Maori Affairs. Some Maori communities, who feel that a national organization is inappropriate, have proceeded independently to establish local Maori radio stations.

An interdepartmental committee is co-ordinating a review of Maori involvement in the news media, including broadcasting. Its objectives are to report on the current situation and suggest strategies to increase Maori influences in this sphere.

**TERRITORIES.** The Government of New Zealand administers the Cook Islands and Niue, both of which have achieved self-governing status; the Ross Dependency, an Antarctic region placed under its administration in 1923; and Tokelau, an island of the Gilbert–Ellice group, placed under its administration in 1925.

As regards Tokelau, the UN **GENERAL ASSEMBLY** on 22 November 1988 reaffirmed (resolution 43/35) the inalienable right of its people to self-determination and independence and urged the New Zealand Government to continue to respect the wishes of those people in carrying out the territory's political and economic development, in order to preserve their social, cultural, and traditional heritage. At the same time, it urged the administering power, other member States, and organizations of the United Nations system to continue to extend to Tokelau the maximum assistance possible for the rehabilitation and reconstruction of the islands in order to overcome the losses incurred in natural disasters in 1987.

**REPORT TO THE UN COMMITTEE ON ECONOMIC, SOCIAL AND CULTURAL RIGHTS.** The **COMMITTEE ON ECONOMIC, SOCIAL AND CULTURAL RIGHTS** considered the initial report of New Zealand, Tokelau, and Niue on articles 1–15 of the International Covenant on Economic, Social and Cultural Rights (E/1990/5/ Add. 5, 11, and 12) at its 24th, 25th, and 26th meetings on 21 and 23 November 1993 and adopted the following concluding observations at its 40th meeting, on 3 December 1993 (paras. 184–200):

*Positive aspects.* The Committee welcomes the adoption of the Human Rights Act 1993, consolidating and amending the Race Relations Act 1971 and the Human Rights Commission Act 1977, to provide better protection of human rights in New Zealand in accordance with United Nations Covenants and Conventions on Human Rights.

The Committee appreciates the renewal of the mandate of the Human Rights Commission, and the enlargement of the scope of the Human Rights Act 1993. The Committee takes special note in this regard of the innovative recognition of age as a ground covered by the Act.

The Committee notes with satisfaction the enactment of the Health and Safety in Employment Act 1993, as well as the renewed efforts strictly to implement the Equal Pay Act 1972 particularly as it affects women.

The Committee takes note of the State party's programme to realign the system of education in the primary, secondary and tertiary levels aimed at increasing the participation rate of youth, especially in vocational education and in industry skills training.

The Committee takes note with satisfaction of the repeal of the Labour Relations Act of 1987 which appeared to have been in conflict with article 8 of the Covenant. It also notes its appreciation of the fact that the age up to which education is compulsory has been raised to 16.

In relation to Maori and Pacific Islands people, the Committee notes the measures being taken by the State party to improve employment opportunities for Maori and Pacific Islands people, and to facilitate their full participation at all levels of the educational system.

*Factors and difficulties impeding the implementation of the Covenant.* The Committee notes with regret that the balance-of-payments situation and budgetary constraints have led the New Zealand Government to adopt restrictive economic and social policies, thereby affecting the realization of economic, social and cultural rights, particularly of the most vulnerable groups of society.

*Principal subjects of concern.* The Committee, while regarding the adoption of a Bill of Rights as a positive development, expresses its concern that no reference is made to economic, social and cultural rights in the text of the Bill. The Committee notes that the Bill of Rights is in the form of an ordinary statute, and can therefore be overridden by other legislation at any time.

The Committee expresses its concern that recent extensive reforms in the social security and labour relations system may negatively affect the enjoyment of economic, social and cultural rights. In particular, the Committee notes that reforms introduced by the Employment Contracts Act of 1991 raise questions of compatibility in relation to the rights recognized in articles 7 and 8 of the Covenant.

The Committee notes with concern that, despite relevant efforts by the Government, the Maori and Pacific Islands people continue to figure disproportionately in relation to unemployment, low salary levels, and poor educational and technical qualifications.

The Committee notes with regret that, according to the statement of the representative of New Zealand, the State party does not keep statistical information as to the extent of malnutrition, hunger and homelessness in New Zealand, which various welfare groups have claimed to be significant.

*Suggestions and recommendations.* The Committee strongly recommends the reinforcement of the work of the Human Rights Commission in relation to economic, social and cultural rights. The Commission should also ensure the translation of the Covenant into all the principal languages spoken in the country, its widespread dissemination, and the reflection of its content in community education activities.

The Committee encourages the Government of New Zealand to increase its efforts towards ensuring equity for Maori and Pacific Islands people, especially in their access to education, training and employment.

The Committee urges the State party carefully to monitor the effects of unemployment and of the reduction in welfare services with respect to the realization of economic, social and cultural rights of the most vulnerable sectors of society and to take the necessary measures in order to diminish such negative effects.

The Committee recommends that consideration be given to a careful review by the State party of the impact of the Employment Contracts Act 1991 and related legislation on the provisions set forth in articles 6, 7 and 9 of the Covenant and to the elimination of any conflicts identified by such a review.

The Committee expresses its hope that the State party will consider the possibility of ratifying ILO Conventions Nos. 87 (Freedom of Association and Protection of the Rights to Organize, 1948) and 98 (Right to Collective Bargaining, 1949).

The Committee urges the State to collect and publish the statistics on the topics referred to in paragraph 192 above and to provide that information to the Committee in its next periodic report. The Committee also requests, in that context, the provision of statistics of the school drop-out rates broken down by race.

The Committee expresses its hope that the State party will consider the possibility of withdrawing its reservations to the Covenant.

**BIBLIOGRAPHY.** Adzoxornu, Isaacus Komla. "Access to the Personal Grievance Procedures in New Zealand: The Human Rights Dimension," *University of Tasmania Law Review* 10 (1990): 40–58. Scholarly article, in English.

Auckland Ethnic Council. *Multi-Ethnic New Zealand: A Commitment for the Future—Ethnic Groups and the Treaty of Waitangi.* Auckland, New Zealand: 1990. Conference report, in English.

Brownlie, Ian. *Treaties and Indigenous Peoples: The Robb Lectures 1991.* Oxford, UK: Clarendon Press, 1992. Scholarly lectures, in English.

Buchanan, Anne. "150 Years of White Domination in New Zealand," *Race and Class* 31, no. 4 (April–June 1990): 73–80. Scholarly note, in English.

Center for Women Policy Studies. "Responses to Wife Abuse in Four Western Countries," *Response* 8, no. 2 (Spring 1985): 15–18. NGO article, in English.

Fitzgerald, Paul. "Section 7 of the New Zealand Bill of Rights Act 1990: A Very Practical Power or a Well-Intentioned Nonsense," *Victoria University of Wellington Law Review* 22, no. 2 (June 1992): 135–158. Scholarly article, in English.

Hucker, Bruce. "Immigration Bill Still Discriminates," *Accent* 1, no. 7 (December 1986): 24–25. News article, in English.

International Work Group for Indigenous Affairs. "Aoteraoa (New Zealand): The Struggle for Self-Determination," *IWGIA Newsletter* 50 (July 1987): 15–24. NGO article, in English.

"Justice and Waitangi," *Accent* 2, no.2 (March 1987): 6–22. News article, in English.

Sigler, Jay A., ed. *International Handbook on Race and Race Relations.* Westport, CT, USA: Greenwood Press, 1987. Scholarly edited collection, in English; bibliography, pp. 449–454.

Stover, Sue. "Stumbling towards Aotearoa: Race Relations in New Zealand," *National Outlook* 8, no. 5 (June 1986): 11–13. Magazine article, in English.

Tarnopolsky, Walter S. "Race Relations Commissions in Canada, Australia, New Zealand, the United Kingdom and the United States," *Human Rights Law Journal* 6, parts 2–4 (1985): 145–178. Scholarly article, in English.

United Nations Commission on Human Rights. *Implementation of the Declaration on the Elimination of All Forms of Intolerance and of Discrimination Based on Religion or Belief.* Prepared by Special Rapporteur Angelo Vidal d'Almeida Ribero, E/CN.4/1987/35. 1986. IGO document, in English.

**NICARAGUA.** The Republic of Nicaragua is a country in Central America, located between the Pacific Ocean and the Caribbean Sea. It achieved independence from Spain in 1838 and became a member of the United Nations in 1945. Its population is estimated to be 3,932,000. Ethnic groups include descendants of settlers from Spain (19%), and from Jamaica and other Caribbean islands (9%), as well as Amerindians (5%) and Mestizos (mixed Spanish and Amerindian) (67%). Christianity (Roman Catholic, 98%; Protestant denominations, 2%) is the predominant religion. Spanish is the language in common use. Literacy is estimated at 87%.

The government (1994) took the form of a republic. Under a new constitution, which came into effect on 9 January 1987, guarantees are made of freedom of religion, freedom of expression and access to uncensored news, the rights to work and to health, to hold private property, to strike, and to hold meetings and lawful demonstrations. However, most of these liberties may be suspended by the president "in case of war or when national security, economic conditions or national catastrophe require it."

A Spanish colony from 1522 to 1838, Nicaragua was occupied by small contingents of American armed forces between 1912 and 1933 partly because of sporadic outbreaks of civil disorder and partly because the United States held an option to build a canal through the country and to establish naval bases there.

Guerrillas under Gen. Cesar Augusto Sandino fought the U.S. troops from 1927 until the Americans withdrew in 1933. In 1934, Sandino was assassinated and Gen. Anastasio Somoza Garcia established a military dictatorship in the country. When Somoza was himself assassinated in 1956, he was succeeded by his son Luis. Another son, Maj. General Anastasio Somoza Debayle, became president in 1967.

***THE SOMOZA REGIME.*** On 25 August 1978, a coalition of political parties and trade unions launched a national work stoppage, seeking the resignation of President Anastasio Somoza. The government responded with massive arrests. On 8 September, the Sandinista Liberation Front—named after Gen. Sandino—called for a general uprising; and, on 12 September, the government imposed martial law. Major confrontations between the national guard and the Sandinistas took place in the larger cities, and the government again responded with widespread and often indiscriminate waves of arrests and killings. By the beginning of October, the uprising was largely crushed, and the Sandinistas and their followers fled from the cities.

Between 3 and 12 October 1978, the **INTER-AMERICAN COMMISSION ON HUMAN RIGHTS** carried out an on-site observation in Nicaragua. In its report, the Commission concluded that "the Government of Nicaragua is responsible for serious attempts against the right to life, in violation of international humanitarian norms, in repressing, in an excessive and disproportionate manner, the insurrections that occurred last September in the major cities of the country." The report also stated that "many persons were executed in a summary and collective fashion for the mere reason of living in neighborhoods or districts where there had been activity by the *Frente Sandinista de Liberacion Nacional*; and young people and defenceless children were killed."

By November 1978, 27,000 Nicaraguans had fled to Honduras, while about 30,000 had taken refuge in Costa Rica. An **AMNESTY INTERNATIONAL** research mission collected data on about 600 individual cases of political imprisonment in Nicaragua and documentation indicating that many of the prisoners detained by the national guard had been summarily executed, often after torture, rape, or mutilation. The mission also confirmed reports of widespread summary executions of entire families, wounded persons, health workers, and refugees. On 20 November, Amnesty International released a list of 519 Nicaraguan citizens known to be detained by the government.

On 7 December 1978, martial law was lifted. A few days later the UN **GENERAL ASSEMBLY,** in resolution 33/76 of 15 December 1978, censured the repression of the civilian population of Nicaragua and urged the Nicaraguan authorities to ensure respect for the human rights of the citizens of Nicaragua in accordance with their international commitments and the **UNITED NATIONS CHARTER.**

However, the pattern of arbitrary arrests, torture, and summary executions continued unabated in 1979.

The UN COMMISSION ON HUMAN RIGHTS, in resolution 14 (XXXV) of 13 March 1979, condemned these violations, expressed concern that the Government of Nicaragua had taken no steps to respect the human rights of the population, and demanded that the government put an end to the grave situation which existed and restore respect for human rights and fundamental freedoms.

On 23 June 1979, a meeting of foreign ministers of the ORGANIZATION OF AMERICAN STATES adopted a resolution demanding the immediate and definite replacement of President Somoza. On 17 July, Somoza resigned and left the country.

*THE SANDINISTAS AND "CONTRAS."* When the Sandinistas assumed political power two days later, they promised to maintain a non-aligned foreign policy and a multi-party political system. In 1981, however, the United States charged that Nicaragua had aligned itself with Cuba and the Soviet Union in supplying aid to rebels in El Salvador—a charge the Sandinistas denied. Later that year, Nicaraguan counter-revolutionaries, known as "contras," began a guerrilla war to overthrow the Sandinistas.

Daniel Ortega Saavedra, a Sandinista coordinator, won 63% of the vote in elections held on 4 November 1984 and was inaugurated as president on 10 January 1985. Nevertheless, the contras, with the backing of the United States, continued their attacks, sometimes from bases in neighboring Honduras. In October 1985, civil liberties were suspended in Nicaragua; and, in 1986, the sole opposition newspaper, *La Prensa,* was forced to cease publication.

On 6 April 1984, Nicaragua accused the United States of America of mining its ports and called upon the INTERNATIONAL COURT OF JUSTICE to halt these activities. The Court, on 10 May, ruled that all actions designed to blockade or to mine Nicaragua's ports should halt immediately.

In 1985, the U.S. Congress rejected a request by President Ronald Reagan for military aid to the contras; however, it authorized funds to be used for humanitarian assistance to members of that guerrilla group. In June 1986, the U.S. Congress for the first time approved overt assistance—military as well as non-military—to the contras.

The revelation that the proceeds of a secret arms sale to Iran by the U.S. Government had been diverted to assist the contras—an act specifically prohibited by law—provoked a major scandal in the United States, popularly known as the "Iran-Contra Affair." A congressional committee studied the affair; its findings have been published as *Report of the Congressional Committee Investigating the Iran-Contra Affair, With Supplemental, Minority, and Additional Views* (Washington: 1987).

Criminal indictments against some of the perpetrators of the plot were brought by a special prosecutor.

In 1987, leaders of neutral Central American countries signed the Contadora Peace Plan, sponsored by the president of Costa Rica, OSCAR ARIAS SÁNCHEZ, that called for an end to outside support of the parties to the conflict and for negotiations between them. The U.S. Congress later prohibited further military aid to the contras. A ceasefire, arranged after the first direct meetings between the Sandinistas and the contras, went into effect on 1 April 1988. But further talks between the two sides broke down; and, in September, thousands of contra guerrillas moved out of Nicaragua and settled in base camps in the neighboring Honduras. In February 1989, the five Central American presidents who had signed the Contadora Peace Plan agreed that the contras should be demobilized; and President Ortega, concurring, undertook to hold free elections in Nicaragua in 1990.

A national election, held on 25 February 1990, resulted in a landslide victory for Mrs. Violeta Barrios de Chamorro, widow of the newspaper editor, Pedro Joaquin Chamorro Cardenal, whose assassination in 1978 had touched off the uprising that became the Sandinista revolution. Mrs. Chamorro, not a member of any political party, was the candidate of the National Opposition Union, an alliance of 14 political parties and groups ranging from conservatives to radicals and supported by Nicaragua's indigenous Miskito Indian population. Her election was monitored by nearly 2,000 official observers, including 239 from the United Nations, 435 from the Organization of American States, and 39 from the Carter Center and Council of Free-Elected Heads of State, led by former American President Jimmy Carter. She was inaugurated as president on 25 April 1990.

Despite the demobilization of the contras in June 1990 and the tentative end of a civil war which had lasted for 11 years, fighting continued by re-armed contras and Sandinistas. Certain constitutional provisions were suspended in May 1993 in five northern regions as a result of such fighting. In February 1994, a new cease-fire was signed with the assistance of the Organization of American States.

Labor strikes and legislative disputes continued as well. The Sandinista National Liberation Front (FSLN) withdrew its deputies from the National Assembly in 1991 following proposed legislation to revoke previously enacted provisions on land redistribution. When Chamorro vetoed portions of the legislation, she was accused of giving in to pressures from the Sandinistas.

After the legislature convened in September 1992 and an attempt was made by the leadership to recruit substitute deputies to make up for the loss of the

UNO's majority, Chamorro ordered the army to occupy the National Assembly that December and appointed a provisional legislative administration.

When, in January 1993, cabinet posts were given to the FSLN and the *Grupo de Centro* (GC), former UNO deputies who had remained allied with the government, and UNO found itself excluded, the UNO declared itself in open opposition to Chamorro's government by changing its name to Alianza Politica Opositoro (APO). A boycott of the legislature by the APO continued until January 1994.

### THE INDIGENOUS MISKITO INDIANS.

Nicaragua's Miskito Indians, an indigenous population living on the country's isolated east coast, were also engaged in guerrilla warfare against the Government of Nicaragua over a period of about six years. For a time, the Miskitos received financial assistance from the U.S. Government but were cut off after refusing to unite with the contras.

The Indians charged multiple violations of their rights by the Sandinista regime. The government acknowledged, in 1987, that it had mistreated them and invited them to return to their homelands from Honduras, where many had taken refuge.

In October 1987, the commander of 400 of the Indian guerrillas, Uriel Vanagas, signed an agreement with the government under which his men would retain their weapons and serve as police or militia units to defend Indian villages.

### REPORT TO THE UN COMMITTEE ON ECONOMIC, SOCIAL AND CULTURAL RIGHTS.

The Committee on Economic, Social and Cultural Rights considered the initial report of Nicaragua, on articles 10–12 of the Covenant of Economic, Social and Cultural Rights (E/1986/3/Add. 15 and Add. 16) at its 27th and 28th meetings, held on 24 and 25 November 1993, and approved the following observations at its 46th meetings, held on 8 December 1993 (E/C.12/1993/14) (paras. 3–14):

*Positive Aspects.* The Committee appreciates the frankness of the Government of Nicaragua and its willingness to discuss the problems impeding its social development. The Committee takes note of the statement of the Government in relation to the effort being made in institutional terms to combat poverty through a specific action plan (1990) and to improve the overall standard of living through the Ministry of Social Welfare, established in 1993.

The Committee welcomes the proposed establishment of the Office of Human Rights Ombudsman to inquire into human rights violations and to monitor the implementation of international human rights instruments ratified by Nicaragua.

*Factors and Difficulties Impeding the Implementation of the Covenant.* The Committee is aware that the physical and economic destruction of the country as a result of a lengthy war and great natural disasters, the effects of which have been compounded by the ensuing economic adjustment programme, has limited the realization of the rights recognized in the Covenant.

*Principal Subjects of Concern.* To the extent that structural adjustment measures and the privatization of State property have had negative consequences for the enjoyment of the economic, social and cultural rights of the Nicaraguan people, and more specifically for the standard of living of the most vulnerable sectors, the Committee expresses its serious concern. It is particularly concerned at the fact that official figures reveal an alarming deterioration in the standard of living and that 70 per cent of Nicaraguans live below the poverty threshold and that 40 per cent suffer from protein deficiency. This reflects the tragedy of a child population which, in the words of the report itself, constitutes "a genuine national emergency".

The Committee is also concerned at the lack of consistency and effectiveness of the programmes to regularize land ownership and to deal adequately with the problems of housing. In particular, the lack of respect for ownership of low-income dwellings under laws 85 and 86 and the slow pace of procedures established by the Land Use Management Office (OOT) create legal uncertainty for the occupants of the dwellings in question.

The information received by the Committee concerning expulsions by the police of several hundred families (particularly in the Extension La Primavera and El Boer communities in Managua) without any proposed relocation is very disturbing. Expulsions appear to be quite common and the Committee has not received any replies to specific questions asked about particular examples.

*Suggestions and Recommendations.* The Committee requests the Government of Nicaragua to provide precise information on the incidents involving the expulsion of persons who invaded land and to inform it, before May 1994, of the measures it has adopted to deal, in accordance with the undertakings of the Covenant, with the problems of the irregular settlements. In this regard, the Committee considers that instances of forced eviction are prima facie incompatible with the requirements of the Covenant and can only be justified in the most exceptional circumstances and in accordance with relevant principles of international law.

The Committee requests that it should be provided with written replies to the concerns raised during its dialogue with the State party which, due to time constraints, remained unanswered. In particular, the Committee wishes to receive clarification as regards the situation of the removal and threatened eviction of squatters from different settlement communities.

The Committee suggests that the State party ensure the effective implementation of laws 85 and 86 of 1990 with a view to guaranteeing security of tenure and property title. The Committee recommends that the State party develop and implement urgently a comprehensive housing policy consistent with the State party's obligations under international instruments.

In accordance with the revised general guidelines regarding the form and contents of reports to be submitted by States parties, the Committee requests the State party to provide detailed statistical information on the distribution of income and wealth among groups living in rural and urban areas of the country, desegregated by linguistic and ethnic characteristics as listed in paragraph 5 of the report (E/1986/3/Add. 16). Similar statistical information is also required on the mortality rates, birth rates, life expectancy and the rates of school attendance up to the university level.

The Committee reiterates the view expressed in its general comment No. 2 that it is precisely in times of acute economic and social problems that respect for the obligations arising under the Covenant assumes its greatest importance.

The Committee wishes to bring to the attention of the State party the need to ensure that structural adjustment programmes are so formulated and implemented as to provide adequate safety nets for the vulnerable sectors of society in order to avoid a deterioration of the enjoyment of the economic, social and cultural rights for which the Covenant provides protection.

**BIBLIOGRAPHY.** Americas Watch. *Fitful Peace: Human Rights and Reconciliation in Nicaragua Under the Chamorro Government.* New York: Human Rights Watch, 1991. NGO report, in English.

————. *Human Rights in Nicaragua 1986.* New York: 1987. NGO report, in English.

————. *Human Rights in Nicaragua: August 1987 to August 1988.* New York: 1988. NGO report, in English.

————. *Land Mines in El Salvador and Nicaragua: The Civilian Victims.* New York: 1986. NGO report, in English.

————. *The New Year's Day Killings of the Nuns in Nicaragua: A Report on an Investigation.* New York: Human Rights Watch, January 1990. NGO report, in English.

————. *Separating Facts from Fiction: The Work of the Tripartite Commission in Nicaragua.* New York: Human Rights Watch, 1994. NGO report, in English.

————. *The Sumus in Nicaragua and Honduras: An Endangered People.* New York: 1987. NGO report, in English.

Andreassen, B. A., and A. Eide, eds. "Nicaragua," in *Human Rights in Developing Countries 1987/88: A Yearbook on Human Rights in Countries Receiving Nordic Aid.* Copenhagen: Christian Michelsen Institute, 1988. NGO report, in English; bibliography, pp. 357–372, classified by country.

Asociacion Nicaraguense Pro-Derechos Humanos (Nicaraguan Association for Human Rights). *Violation of Human Rights by the Government of Nicaragua.* San José, Costa Rica: 1987. NGO report, in English.

Bourgois, Philippe. "Nicaragua: The Miskitu Conflict on the Atlantic Coast," *IWGIA Newsletter* 49 (April 1987): 69–89. NGO article/conference paper, in English; bibliography, pp. 88–89.

Carter Center of Emory University. *Observing Nicaragua's Elections, 1989–1990: Report of the Council of Freely-Elected Heads of Government.* Atlanta, GA, USA: 1990. Election observer report, in English; bibliography, pp. 119–121.

Catholic Institute for International Relations. *Right to Survive: Human Rights in Nicaragua.* London: 1987. NGO study, in English.

Comision Nacional de Promocion y Proteccion de los Derechos Humanos (National Commission for the Promotion and Protection of Human Rights). *Derechos Humanos en Nicaragua* (Human Rights in Nicaragua). Managua, Nicaragua: 1987. Government report, in Spanish and English.

————. *Discussion and Analysis of the Americas Watch Report, "Human Rights in Nicaragua, 1985–86."* Managua, Nicaragua: 1986. Government report, in English.

Davies, Maureen. "Report on the Current Status of the Miskito Nation of Nicaragua," *International Journal of Refugee Law* 3, no. 4 (Oct. 1991): 709–713. Scholarly article, in English.

Diskin, M., T. Bossert, S. Nahmad, and S. Varese. *Peace and Autonomy on the Atlantic Coast of Nicaragua.* Pittsburgh, PA, USA: Latin American Studies Association, 1986. Scholarly study, in English.

Donnelly, J., and R. E. Howard. *International Handbook on Human Rights.* Westport, CT, USA: Greenwood Press, 1987. Scholarly edited collection, in English.

Gallo, Jeanne. *Responding to the Rights of the Poor: Nicaragua, the Church and the U.S.* Boston, MA, USA: Gritare, 1985. Monograph, in English.

Instituto Historico Centroamericano (Central American Historical Institute). "International Election Observers: Nicaragua under a Microscope," *Envio* 9, no. 103 (Feb. 1990): 20–31. NGO article, in English.

Instituto Interamericano de Derechos Humanos, Centro de Asesoria y Promoción Electoral (Inter-American Institute of Human Rights, Centre for Electoral Assistance and Promotion). *Elecciones Generales—Nicaragua, 25 de Febrero de 1990: Informe de la Misión de Observación* (General Elections—Nicaragua, February 25, 1990: Report of the Observer Mission. San José, Costa Rica: 1990. NGO factfinding report, in Spanish.

Inter-Church Committee on Human Rights in Latin America. *1990 Annual Report on the Human Rights Situation in Nicaragua.* Toronto, Canada: 1991. NGO report, in English.

International League for Human Rights. *Report on Human Rights Defenders in Nicaragua.* New York: 1986. NGO report, in English.

Medina Quiroga, Cecilia. *The Battle of Human Rights: Gross, Systematic Violations and the Inter-American System.* Dordrecht, the Netherlands: Martinus Nijhoff, 1988. Scholarly monograph, in English.

Membreño, Marcos. "Ethnic Communities of the Pacific and North-Central Nicaragua: Denied Existence; Obstinate Persistence," *Envío* 11, no. 136 (Nov. 1992): 21–30. Article, in Spanish.

Morgan, Martha I. "Founding Mothers: Women's Voices and Stories in the 1987 Nicaraguan Constitution," *Boston University Law Review* 70, no. 1 (Jan. 1990): 1–107. Scholarly article, in English.

National Lawyers Guild. *Freedom of Expression in Nicaragua.* New York: 1986. NGO mission report, in English.

North American Congress on Latin America. "Nicaragua: Haunted By the Past," *NACLA Report on the Americas* 24, no. 1 (June 1990): 9–39. NGO article, in English.

Organization of American States. *Inter-American Yearbook on Human Rights 1986.* Dordrecht, the Netherlands: Martinus Nijhoff, 1988. IGO annual report, in Spanish and English.

Payne, Douglas W. *The Democratic Mask.* New York: Freedom House, 1985. Monograph, in English.

Walker, Thomas W., ed. *Nicaragua: The First Five Years.* New York: Praeger, 1985. Edited collection, in English.

Washington Office on Latin America. *Nicaragua: Reconciliation Awaiting Recovery—Politics, the Economy and U.S. Aid under the Chamorro Government.* Washington, D.C.: 1991. NGO report, in English.

**NIGER.** The Republic of Niger is a country in western Africa. It has borders with Algeria, Benin, Burkina Faso, Chad, Libya, Mali, and Nigeria. It achieved independence from France in 1960 and became a member of the United Nations the same year. Its population is estimated to be 8,198,000. Ethnic groups include the Hausa (54%), Jerma (23%), Fulani (10%), Beriberi–Manga (9%), and Tuareg (3%). Languages in common use include French (official), Hausa, Jerma, Peul, Tamashek, Kanuri, Arabic, Toubou, and Gourmanche. Religions practiced include Islam (90%), Animism (9%), and Christianity (1%). Literacy is estimated at 6%.

The government (1994) took the form of a republic. Its constitution was, however, suspended and civilian government displaced by a military regime which assumed power in April 1974. It is administered by the Supreme Military Council of 12 officers led by the president, who is head of State.

The Supreme Military Council was replaced in May 1989 by the Superior Council of National Orientation. Elections were held in December 1989 and the sole presidential candidate, Brig. Saibou, and the single list of 93 pre-approved candidates to the new national assembly won with 99% of the votes to create the Second Republic.

Student and labor protests followed and in 1991, some government offices were demilitarized and the constitution amended to allow for the registration of political parties. Complaints persisted that opposition parties were being denied access to the media.

The National Conference was convened in July 1991 with 1200 delegates from 24 political parties, professional groups, and government. Declaring itself sovereign, it suspended the constitution, dissolved the legislature, and took responsibility for supervising the head of State whom it voted to retain in his then-mostly ceremonial position.

Due to suspension of relations with external creditors and IMF and World Bank programs, payment of salaries of civil servants and military personnel fell into arrears, which caused unrest, including troops taking control of the state broadcasting offices in February and March 1992. When Taiwan promised credit worth US$50m in June 1992, the government resumed diplomatic relations with that country and suspended relations with the People's Republic of China.

A new constitution was eventually endorsed by 90% of the vote in a referendum in December 1992 and promulgated in January 1993. Elections to the new National Assembly took place in February 1993. The MNSD won 29 of the 83 seats but a coalition of other parties created a majority by forming the 50-member Alliance of the Forces of Change (AFC). Its major party was the Democratic and Social Convention Rahama (CDS-Rahama).

Although the MNSD presidential candidate, Col. Mamadou, won in the first round of voting, he was defeated in the second round by Mahamane Ousmane, leader of the CDS-Rahama, who was inaugurated as president of the Third Republic in April 1993.

After the prime minister resigned in September 1994 and was re-appointed two weeks later, the president called for elections in early 1995 since the prime minister could not win a parliamentary majority.

Labor and education unrest continued into 1994, frequently as a result of the inability of the government to pay salary and student grant arrears. Bans on protests and strikes were imposed and fines imposed on newspapers. Leaders of political parties, including Mamadou, were arrested and detained after demonstrations in April 1994 and parliamentary immunity of the participating parties was revoked.

***TUAREG REBELLION.*** Tuareg nomads from Northern Niger who had migrated to Libya, Algeria, and Mali during the early 1980s to escape drought, began returning to Niger in the late 1980s. Despite a meeting in September 1990 between Niger, Algeria, Libya, and Mali to organize the return of refugees, and the discussion of the Tuareg situation during the National Conference in 1991, the Tuareg rebellion in northern Niger flared. The *Front de liberation de l'Air* at l'Azaouad (FLAA), recognized by the government in 1992, called for a federal state in which ethnic groups would have some autonomy. A 1988 census reported that there were about 700,000 Tuaregs in Niger. A Minister of State for National Reconciliation was appointed in January 1993 and several peace agreements were reached but unrest continued into 1994.

***BIBLIOGRAPHY.*** Hosken, Fran. "Women, Health and Development in East and West Africa: A Personal View," *WIN News* 9, no. 2 (April 1983): 1–12. NGO report, in English.

Ibrahim, Jibrin. "Political Exclusion, Democratization and Dynamics of Ethnicity in Niger," *Africa Today* 41, no. 3 (1994): 15–39. Scholarly article, in English.

International Commission of Jurists. *Les Services Juridiques en Milieu Rural (Afrique de l'Ouest)* (Legal Services in Rural Areas [West Africa]). Geneva, Switzerland: 1987. NGO report, in French.

"West Africa: Documentation on the Tuareg—Massacres of Tuaregs in Mali and Niger," *IWGIA Newsletter* no. 62 (Dec. 1990): 129–160. NGO article, in English.

**NIGERIA.** The Federal Republic of Nigeria is a country in western Africa, on the Gulf of Guinea. It has borders with Benin, Cameroon, Chad, and Niger. It achieved independence from Great Britain in 1960 and became a member of the United Nations the same year. Its population is estimated to be 91,700,000. Ethnic groups include the Hausa, the Fulani, and the Kanuri, who are most numerous in the north, and the Yoruba and Ibo, who predominate in the south. Languages commonly used include English (official), Igbo, Efik, Hausa, and Yoruba. Religions practiced include Islam (48%), Christianity (Roman Catholic,

17%; Protestant denominations, 17%), Animism, and other faiths (18%). Literacy is estimated at 42%.

Since 1970, Nigeria has struggled to recover from its disastrous civil war which began in 1966 and which involved intensive conflict between the predominantly Muslim Hausas and the predominantly Christian Ibos. The war led to the secession of the Republic of Biafra in 1967 but ended with its surrender to federal authorities the following year. Nigeria is now believed to have a Muslim majority, but no census has been taken for more than 20 years, partly out of fear of inflaming religious passions by indicating the current population ratios.

*MILITARY RULE.* Gen. Sani Abacha took power in November 1993 and suspended all organs of government including the Senate and House of Representatives, the two-party political system, and the judiciary. This followed years of promises that the government would be transferred to civilian rule and preparation for that transfer.

The ban on political parties was lifted and a new constitution promulgated in May 1989. However, when 35 political parties formed, 13 met the requirements for registration and six were recommended to the Armed Forces Ruling Council (AFRC), President Ibrahim Babangida dissolved all parties. The AFRC then created two political parties, the Social Democratic Party (SDP) and the National Republican Convention (NRC).

Throughout 1990, limited moves were made to demilitarize the government, with civilian deputy governors appointed in each of the states. Local elections took place in December 1990, with 20% of the electorate participating. The NRC was most successful in the north and the SDP in the south. In September 1991, the number of states was increased to 30. Violence continued, however, with repeated clashes between Muslims and Christians and various ethnic groups. In late 1991 and early 1992, thousands were reported killed in ethnic violence in the eastern state of Taruba.

Also in 1991, the federal capital was moved from Lagos to Abuja and a new 20-member Council of Ministers formed. President Babangida repeatedly announced the delay of legislative elections and the transfer to civilian rule. An alliance of human rights organizations formed a new political party, the Campaign for Democracy.

Elections finally took place in July 1992 and the SDP won a majority in both the House of Representatives (314 of 593 seats) and the Senate (52 of 91 seats). The NRC won 275 and 37 seats in the respective chambers. Although the National Assembly was belatedly inaugurated in December, President Babangida further

postponed the presidential election and prohibited the 23 prospective presidential candidates from taking part in political activity during the transition to civilian rule.

In January 1993, the Transitional Council was formed and the Council of Ministers and the AFRC dissolved. The National Electoral Commission (NEC) was empowered throughout this period to decide the suitability of candidates for public office and to delay elections if necessary. A new pro-Babangida group, the Association for a Better Nigeria, which believed in the continuation of military rule, obtained an injunction against holding the election in June. The NEC stated that the injunction was unconstitutional.

The presidential election finally took place in June 1993, with 30% of the electorate participating. The SDP candidate, Muslim businessman Chief Moshood Kastumawo Olawale Abiola, won a majority in 19 of the 30 states. The High Court, however, ruled that the injunction should have been obeyed and that the election results were invalid. Abiola continued to assert his presidency, and the United States and United Kingdom announced military sanctions against Nigeria. Industrial unrest continued with widespread strikes and protests against the government and rising prices, particularly that of petrol. An oil workers' strike involving a reported 100,000 workers lasted from July to September 1994.

President Babangida announced in July 1993 that an Interim National Government (ING) would be established, but he resigned in August 1993 and was replaced by a 32-member Federal Executive Council led by Head of State Chief Ernest Adegunie Shonekan, previously chairman of the Transitional Council. Shonekan was soon replaced in November by Gen. Sani Abacha, who dissolved all organs of state, reinstated military governors of the states, banned political activity, and established a Provisional Ruling Council.

In November 1993 Abacha restored the 1979 constitution, and it was announced that the National Constitutional Conference was to be formed to decide the future of democratic government in Nigeria. However, a new pro-democracy organization was formed to challenge the authority of such a conference and to demand that Abacha resign. The National Democratic Coalition (NADECO) comprised former politicians, retired military officers, and human rights activists. The first round of elections to the conference in May 1994 were boycotted by Moshood Abiola and his supporters, but the conference convened in June. In October 1993, the conference called for democratic government by 1 January 1995 and recommended that the presidency alternate between north and south.

Gen. Abacha issued eight new decrees in September 1994, including one granting government "absolute power." He also closed three opposition newspapers and two magazines. The attorney general was dismissed after saying that the decrees would "sweep away our liberties." He also dismissed four civilian members of the Provisional Ruling Council, raised the number from 11 to 25, and installed 17 new appointees. Abiola, who had announced the formation of an alternative government, to take effect on the first anniversary of his election, was arrested and jailed in June 1994. He rejected the offer of bail and obtained a court ruling in October that his imprisonment was illegal and that the government should pay $45,454 in damages. An appellate court issued a release order in November but no release of the critically ill Abiola had been reported by December 1994. In addition to Abiola, many well-known opposition political figures and human rights activists have been arrested and remain jailed, including Anthony Enahoro, the NADECO vice-chairman; and Ken Saro-Wiwa, leader of the Ogoni ethnic group. Passports have also been seized, including that of 1986 Nobel laureate Wole Soyinka. Soyinka, however, escaped from Nigeria when he was warned of imminent arrest. From a safe haven in Paris, Soyinka told the Associated Press (May 1995), "It's very strange for those of us who thought Nigeria was the great black hope of Africa. Nigeria is going backwards, retreating into the Dark Ages."

**DECISION ON DEPORTATION.** The problem of female circumcision on the African continent was brought to international attention when a Nigerian woman living in the United States argued before U.S. federal courts that deportation to her homeland would endanger her two American-born daughters. The woman, who had undergone female circumcision as a child, argued that her daughters would be forced to undergo the rite if they accompanied her to Nigeria. In March 1995, a U.S. federal immigration judge denied the deportation of the woman, who was divorced from an American citizen, stating that the children were American-born citizens and had the right to the protection of their mother.

**BIBLIOGRAPHY.** Africa-American Institute. "The Press and Africa," *Africa Report* 32, no. 2 (March–April 1987). NGO special issue, in English.

Africa Watch. *Nigeria: Contradicting Itself—An Undemocratic Transition Seeks to Bring Democracy Nearer.* New York: Human Rights Watch, 1992. NGO report, in English.

————. *Nigeria: "The Dawn of a New Dark Age": Human Rights Abuse Rampant as Nigerian Military Declares Absolute Power.* New York: Human Rights Watch, 1994. NGO report, in English.

————. *Nigeria: Military Injustice—Major General Zamani Lekwot and Others Face Government-Sanctioned Lynching.* New York: Human Rights Watch, 1993. NGO report, in English.

Agbaje, Adigun. "Freedom of the Press and Party Politics in Nigeria: Precepts, Retrospect and Prospects," *African Affairs* 89, no. 355 (April 1990): 205–226. Scholarly article, in English.

Aguda, T. *The Challenge of the Nigerian Nation: An Examination of its Legal Development, 1969–1985.* Lagos, Nigeria: Nigerian Institute of Advanced Legal Studies, 1985. Scholarly monograph, in English.

Alubo, S. O. "Human Rights and Militarism in Nigeria," in *Emerging Human Rights: The African Political Economy Context,* eds. G. W. Shepherd, Jr., and Mark O. C. Anikpo, pp. 197–207. New York: Greenwood Press, 1990. Scholarly article, in English.

Amnesty International. *The Use of the Death Penalty in Nigeria.* London: 1985. NGO report, in English.

Chhangani, R. C. "Recent Development in the Extradition Law of Nigeria," *Indian Journal of International Law* 26, nos. 2–3 (July–Dec. 1986): 483–500. Scholarly article, in English.

Civil Liberties Organisation. *Annual Report on Human Rights in Nigeria, 1993.* Lagos, Nigeria: 1994. NGO annual report, in English.

————. *Executive Lawlessness in the Babangida Regime.* Lagos, Nigeria: 1991. NGO factfinding report, in English.

————. *Prison Study No. 1: A Preliminary Survey of Conditions of Inmates in the Prisons.* Lagos, Nigeria: 1988. NGO report, in English.

————. *The Status of Refugee Rights in Nigeria.* Lagos, Nigeria: 1992. NGO report, in English.

Constitutional Rights Project. *The Bail Process and Human Rights in Nigeria.* Lagos, Nigeria: 1992. NGO monograph, in English.

————. *The Crisis of Press Freedom in Nigeria.* Lagos, Nigeria: 1993. NGO monograph, in English.

————. *Human Rights Practices in the Nigerian Police.* Lagos, Nigeria: 1993. NGO report, in English.

————. "The Militarization of Justice in Nigeria," *Constitutional Rights Journal* 1, no. 1 (Dec. 1990): 1–35. Special issue, in English.

————. *Nigeria: The Limits of Justice.* Lagos, Nigeria: 1993. NGO report, in English.

Femmes sous Lois Musulmanes (Women Living under Muslim Laws). *Dossier No. 1.* Montpellier, France: 1986. NGO document collection, in English.

Hayward, Fred M., ed. *Elections in Independent Africa.* Boulder, CO, USA: Westview Press, 1987. Scholarly study, in English.

Howard, Rhoda. "Human Rights and Democratization in Nigeria: Comparisons with Indonesia," *Netherlands Quarterly of Human Rights* 10, no. 4 (1992): 414–446. Scholarly article, in English.

Human Rights Watch. "Nigeria," in *Human Rights Watch World Report 1995,* pp. 34–39. New York: 1995. NGO report, in English.

Isamah, Austin. "Organized Labour Under the Military Regimes in Nigeria," *Africa Development/Afrique et Développement* 15, no. 2 (1990): 81–94. Scholarly article, in English.

Lawyers Committee for Human Rights. *The Nigerian Police: A Culture of Impunity.* Washington, D.C.: 1992. NGO report, in English.

Legal Research and Resource Development Centre. *Proceedings of the 1990 Human Rights Day Symposium: Human Rights for Development in Nigeria—Strategies for the 90s.* Lagos, Nigeria: 1991. Conference report, in English.

McLean S., and S. E. Graham, eds. *Female Circumcision, Excision and Infibulation: The Facts and Proposals for Change.* 2nd rev. ed. London: Minority Rights Group, 1985. NGO report, in English.

"Nigeria: 25 Years, Part I," *West Africa* (30 Sept. 1985): 2019–2048; "Nigeria: 25 Years, Part II," *West Africa* (7 October 1985): 2089–2114. News article, in English.

Nwala, Uzodinma. *Academic Freedom in Africa: The Nigerian Experience*. Dakar, Senegal: Council for the Development of Economic and Social Research in Africa, 1990. Conference paper, in English.

Osaghae, Eghosa E. "Ethnic Minorities and Federalism in Nigeria," *African Affairs* no. 90 (1991): 237–258. Scholarly article, in English.

Saro-Wiwa, Ken. *Genocide in Nigeria: The Ogoni Tragedy*. Lagos, Nigeria: Saros International, 1992. Scholarly monograph, in English.

Women's International Network. "Female Circumcision:Genital and Sexual Mutilation," *WIN News* 14, no. 3 (Summer 1988): 24–27; 14 no. 4 (Autumn 1988): 21–26; 15, no. 1 (Winter 1989): 28–29. NGO edited collection, in English.

**NOBEL PEACE PRIZE.** The Nobel Peace Prize is the oldest, most renowned, and most highly regarded of all human rights prizes. The Prize has been awarded annually, every October, since 1901.

In his 1895 will, Alfred Nobel, the inventor of dynamite, instructed the Norwegian parliament, the *Storting*, to appoint a committee to award an annual peace prize to an individual or organization that has contributed significantly to the promotion of peace (Nobel, a Swede, also stipulated in his will that scientific and literary prizes should be awarded by Swedish institutions). Once appointed, the five-member Nobel Peace Prize Committee is a completely independent body, responsible for thorough investigations and deliberations before an award is announced.

To be valid, nominations must be submitted by February 1 of the year for which the Prize is awarded. The award ceremony takes place on December 10, the anniversary of Nobel's death, with ceremonies for the Peace Prize held in Oslo, Norway (physics, chemistry, medicine, literature, and economics awards are presented on the same date in Stockholm, Sweden). The Peace Prize winner receives 15% of the previous year's yield of the Nobel Fund. The right to nominate candidates for the Peace Prize is restricted to the following:

(a) present and past members of the Nobel Committee or the *Storting*;

(b) members of the different countries' national assemblies and governments and also members of the **INTER-PARLIAMENTARY UNION**;

(c) members of the **INTERNATIONAL COURT OF JUSTICE** and the International Court of Arbitration;

(d) executive members of the Permanent **INTERNATIONAL PEACE BUREAU**;

(e) members of the Institut de Droit International;

(f) present university professors of law, political science, history, and philosophy;

(g) past recipients of the Nobel Peace Prize.

As of 1994, the Nobel Peace Prize has been awarded only 74 times, with no award being given on 19 occasions. These interruptions were mainly due to the two world wars, but also occurred during peaceful times when the Peace Prize Committee was unable to reach a decision.

The following is a list of Nobel Peace Prize recipients. Brief biographies of these individuals and information on these organizations also are included in this volume:

1901—Henri Dunant (Switzerland) and Frederick Passy (France)

1902—Elie Ducommun and Albert Gobat (Switzerland)

1903—Sir William R. Cremer (England)

1904—Institut de Droit International (Belgium)

1905—Bertha von Suttner (Austria)

1906—Theodore Roosevelt (USA)

1907—Ernesto T. Moneta (Italy) and Louis Renault (France)

1908—Klas P. Arnoldson (Sweden) and Frederik Bajer (Denmark)

1909—Auguste M. F. Beernaert (Belgium) and Baron Paul H. B. B. d'Estournelles de Constant de Rebecque (France)

1910—Bureau International Permanent de la Paix (Switzerland)

1911—Tobias M. C. Asser (Holland) and Alfred H. Fried (Austria)

1912—Elihu Root (USA)

1913—Henri La Fontaine (Belgium)

1914—No award

1915—No award

1916—No award

1917—International Red Cross

1918—No award

1919—Woodrow Wilson (USA)

1920—Léon Bourgeois (France)

1921—Karl H. Branting (Sweden) and Christian L. Lange (Norway)

1922—Fridtjof Nansen (Norway)

1923—No award

1924—No award

1925—Sir Austen Chamberlain (England) and Charles G. Dawes (USA)

1926—Aristide Briand (France) and Gustav Stresemann (Germany)

1927—Ferdinand Buisson (France) and Ludwig Quidde (Germany)

1928—No award

1929—Frank B. Kellogg (USA)

1930—Lars O. J. Söderblom (Sweden)

1931—Jane Addams and Nicholas M. Butler (USA)

1932—No award

1933—Sir Norman Angell (England)

1934—Arthur Henderson (England)

1935—Karl von Ossietzky (Germany)

1936—Carlos de S. Lamas (Argentina)

1937—Lord Cecil of Chelwood (England)

1938—Office International Nansen pour les Réfugiés (Switzerland)

1939—No award

1940—No award

1941—No award

1942—No award

1943—No award

1944—International Red Cross

1945—Cordell Hull (USA)

1946—Emily G. Balch and John R. Mott (USA)

1947—American Friends Service Committee (USA) and British Society of Friends' Service Council (England)

1948—No award

1949—Lord John Boyd Orr (Scotland)

1950—Ralph J. Bunche (USA)

1951—Léon Jouhaux (France)

1952—Albert Schweitzer (French Equatorial Africa)

1953—George C. Marshall (USA)

1954—Office of the UN High Commissioner for Refugees

1955—No award

1956—No award

1957—Lester B. Pearson (Canada)

1958—Rev. Dominique Georges Henri Pire (Belgium)

1959—Philip John Noel-Baker (England)

1960—Albert John Luthuli (South Africa)

1961—Dag Hammarskjöld (Sweden)

1962—Linus Pauling (USA)

1963—International Committee of the Red Cross and League of the Red Cross and Red Crescent Societies (Switzerland)

1964—Rev. Dr. Martin Luther King, Jr. (USA)

1965—UNICEF

1966—No award

1967—No award

1968—René Cassin (France)

1969—International Labor Organization

1970—Norman E. Borlaug (USA)

1971—Willy Brandt (West Germany)

1972—No award

1973—Henry A. Kissinger (USA) and Le Duc Tho (North Vietnam)

1974—Eisaku Sato (Japan) and Sean MacBride (Ireland)

1975—Andrei D. Sakharov (USSR)

1976—Mairead Corrigan and Betty Williams (Northern Ireland)

1977—Amnesty International

1978—Menachem Begin (Israel) and Anwar Sadat (Egypt)

1979—Mother Teresa of Calcutta (India)

1980—Adolfo Pérez Esquivel (Argentina)

1981—Office of the UN High Commissioner for Refugees

1982—Alva Myrdal (Sweden) and Alfonso García Robles (Mexico)

1983—Lech Walesa (Poland)

1984—Bishop Desmond Tutu (South Africa)

1985—International Physicians for the Prevention of Nuclear War

1986—Elie Wiesel (USA)

1987—Oscar Arias Sánchez (Costa Rica)

1988—UN Peacekeeping Forces

1989—Dalai Lama (Tibet)

1990—Mikhail S. Gorbachev (USSR)

1991—Daw Aung San Suu Kyi (Myanmar)

1992—Rigoberta Menchú (Guatemala)

1993—F. W. de Klerk and Nelson Mandela (South Africa)

1994—Yitzhak Rabin (Israel), Shimon Peres (Israel), and Yassar Arafat (PLO)

**NOEL-BAKER, PHILIP (1889–1982).** Born in London, Philip Noel-Baker was a British leader of the Labour Party and international diplomat who was awarded the 1959 NOBEL PEACE PRIZE for a lifetime of service.

Educated at Cambridge, and with a background in Quakerism, Noel-Baker's first service to humanity came during World War I, when he organized the Friends' Ambulance Unit on the Western Front and later the British Ambulance Unit for Italy. After the war, Noel-Baker worked in the LEAGUE OF NATIONS, most notably as an assistant to FRIDTJOF NANSEN and ARTHUR HENDERSON, themselves Nobel laureates. Also during this period and throughout the 1930s and 1940s, Noel-Baker served in the British House of Commons; in 1946, he became chairman of the Labour Party. After World War II, he served as British minister of state (1945–46), secretary of state for air (1946–47), secretary of state for commonwealth relations (1947–50), and minister of fuel and power (1950–51). Both in the League of Nations and in the United Nations, Noel-Baker supported arms control and aid to refugees.

Noel-Baker was also a noted writer, especially on the topic of disarmament. In 1926, he published *The League of Nations at Work* and *Disarmament*. In 1959, he published *The Arms Race: A Program for World Disarmament*, which won the Albert Schweitzer book prize in 1961. In 1977, he was created a life peer of the British monarchy.

**BIBLIOGRAPHY.** Gray, Tony. *Champions of Peace.* London: Paddington Press, 1976.

Schlessinger, Bernard S., and June H. Schlessinger, eds. *Who's Who of Nobel Prize Winners.* Phoenix, AZ, USA: Oryx Press, 1991.

## NON-GOVERNMENTAL ORGANIZATIONS (NGO).

All international governmental organizations (IGOs) recognize the competence of non-governmental organizations (NGOs), have special procedures and requirements for the official recognition of NGOs, and rely on the fieldwork of accredited NGOs to supplement the work of the IGO bodies. In the United Nations system, the **ECONOMIC AND SOCIAL COUNCIL,** as authorized by article 71 of the **UNITED NATIONS CHARTER,** has made arrangements for consultation with non-governmental organizations concerned with matters falling within its competence (Council resolution 1296 [XLIV]). This resolution provides for certain principles to be applied in the establishment of consultative relations, among them:

1. The organization shall be concerned with matters falling within the competence of the Economic and Social Council with respect to international economic, social, cultural, educational, health, scientific, technological, and related matters and to questions of human rights;

2. The aims and purposes of the organization shall be in conformity with the spirit, purposes, and principles of the Charter of the United Nations;

3. The organization shall undertake to support the work of the United Nations and to promote knowledge of its principles and activities, in accordance with its own aims and purposes and the nature and scope of its competence and activities;

4. The organization shall be of representative character and of recognized international standing;

5. The organization shall be international in its structure;

6. The basic resources of the international organization shall be derived in main part from the contributions of the national affiliates or other components or from individual members.

This final stipulation is to ensure that no NGO is government-supported or dependent in any way on financing from a governmental source that may seek to influence the NGO.

In addition, NGOs also supply information concerning allegations of violations of human rights to bodies authorized to supervise the application of various international instruments in the field. Under these arrangements the UN **COMMITTEE ON NON-GOVERNMENTAL ORGANIZATIONS** divides such organizations into three groups:

*Category I,* which is made up of NGOs having a basic interest in most of the Council's activities;

*Category II,* which is made up of those having a special competence but are concerned with only a few of the Council's activities; and

The *Roster,* which contains the names of NGOs that can make occasional and useful contributions to the Council's work.

All the organizations in "consultative status" may send observers to public meetings of the Council and its subsidiary bodies. They can submit written statements for circulation and present their views orally. As regards human rights, more than 100 NGOs regularly attend and participate in meetings of the UN **COMMISSION ON HUMAN RIGHTS,** the **SUB-COMMISSION ON PREVENTION OF DISCRIMINATION AND PROTECTION OF MINORITIES,** and the **COMMISSION ON THE STATUS OF WOMEN.** The Economic and Social Council, on 26 May 1987, invited all such organizations to submit to it written statements that might contribute to full and universal recognition and realization of the rights set out in the **INTERNATIONAL COVENANT ON ECONOMIC, SOCIAL AND CULTURAL RIGHTS** and requested the Secretary-General to make those statements available to the Committee on Economic, Social and Cultural Rights.

**NOBEL LAUREATES.** One of the greatest measures of the contributions of NGOs to world peace and stability can be seen in the number of non-governmental organizations that have received the **NOBEL PEACE PRIZE.** Since its inception in 1901, the Nobel Peace Prize has been awarded eight times to non-governmental organizations.

In 1904, the Institut de Droit International (**INSTITUTE OF INTERNATIONAL LAW**) of Belgium was the first non-governmental organization to be recognized with a Peace Prize. A short time later, in 1910, the Bureau International Permanent de la Paix (**INTERNATIONAL PEACE BUREAU**) was awarded the Prize; the Bureau had been established in Berne, Switzerland, in 1891, to "coordinate the activities of the peace societies and promote the concept of peaceful settlement of international disputes." The **INTERNATIONAL RED CROSS** has been awarded the Peace Prize twice, in 1917 and 1944 in the midst of the two world wars; and its subsidiaries, the **INTERNATIONAL COMMITTEE OF THE RED CROSS** and **LEAGUE OF THE RED CROSS AND RED CRESCENT SOCIETIES,** were recognized in 1963. In 1947, the **AMERICAN FRIENDS SERVICE COMMITTEE** and British Society of Friends' Service Council shared the Prize. More recently, the Nobel Committee has recognized **AMNESTY INTERNATIONAL** (1977) and the **INTERNATIONAL PHYSICIANS FOR THE PREVENTION OF NUCLEAR WAR** (1985).

**SEE ALSO** *Committee on Non-Governmental Organizations, UN.*

**BIBLIOGRAPHY.** Beigbeder, Yves. *The Role and Status of International Humanitarian Volunteer Organizations: The Right*

and Duty to Humanitarian Assistance. Dordrecht, the Netherlands: Martinus Nijhoff, 1991. Scholarly monograph, in English; bibliography, pp. 395–400.

Blaser, Arthur W. "How to Advance Human Rights without Really Trying: An Analysis of Nongovernmental Tribunals," *Human Rights Quarterly* 14, no. 3 (Aug. 1992): 339–370. Scholarly article, in English.

Bratton, Michael. "Beyond the State: Civil Society and Associational Life in Africa," *Transnational Associations/Associations Transnationales* 43, no. 3 (May–June 1991): 130–140. Scholarly article, in English; bibliography, p. 130.

Claude, Richard Pierre, and Burns H. Weston, eds. *Human Rights in the World Community: Issues and Action.* Philadelphia, PA, USA: University of Pennsylvania Press, 1992. Scholarly collection of articles, in English.

Covington, Sally. *Urban Popular Movements in Mexico: Grassroots Action for Change.* New York: Bildner Centre for Western Hemisphere Studies, Graduate School and University Centre of the City University of New York, 1990. Scholarly research paper, in English.

Crystall, Jill. "The Human Rights Movement in the Arab World," *American-Arab Affairs* no. 36 (Spring 1991): 14–16. Scholarly article, in English.

Feyter, Koen de. "The Red Cross and Raising Human Rights Awareness in Europe," *Netherlands Quarterly of Human Rights* 9, no. 1 (1991): 36–49. Scholarly article, in English.

Forsythe, David P. "Human Rights and the International Committee of the Red Cross," *Human Rights Quarterly* 12, no. 2 (May 1990): 265–289. Scholarly article, in English.

Frülhing E., Hugo. *El Movimiento de Derechos Humanos y la Transición Democrática en Chile y Argentina* (The Human Rights Movement and the Democratic Transition in Chile and Argentina). Santiago, Chile: Human Rights Program, University Academy of Christian Humanism, 1990. Scholarly paper, in Spanish.

Gross, Bertram. "Towards a Human Rights Century," *Human Rights Quarterly* 13, no. 3 (Aug. 1991): 387–395. Scholarly article, in English.

Juviler, Peter. "Human Rights Associations for a Human Rights Community: A Proposal," *Human Rights Quarterly* 13, no. 3 (Aug. 1991): 396–402. Scholarly article, in English.

Kararotos, Alexander S. *A View into NGO Networks in Human Rights Activities: NGO Action with Special Reference to the UN Commission on Human Rights and Its Sub-Commission.* Paper prepared for the 31st Annual Convention of the International Studies Association, Washington, D.C., 10–14 April 1990. Geneva, Switzerland: Graduate Institute of International Studies, 1990. Scholarly conference paper, in English.

McKinstry Micou, A., and B. Lindsnaes, eds. *The Role of Voluntary Organizations in Emerging Democracies: Experiences and Strategies in Eastern and Central Europe and in South Africa.* Copenhagen, Denmark: Danish Centre for Human Rights; Institute of International Education, 1993. Conference report, in English.

Nederlands Juristen Comité voor de Mensenrechten (Dutch section of the International Commission of Jurists). *The Role of Non-Governmental Organizations in the Promotion and Protection of Human Rights.* Leiden, the Netherlands: 1991. Conference papers, in English.

Orellana, Patricio, and Elizabeth Quay Hutchinson. *El Movimiento de Derechos Humanos en Chile, 1973–1990* (The Human Rights Movement in Chile, 1973–1990). Santiago, Chile: Centro de Estudios Políticos Latinoamericanos Simón Bolívar, 1991. Scholarly monograph, in Spanish; bibliography, pp. 195–198.

Posner, Michael H., and Candy Whittome. "The Status of Human Rights NGOs," *Columbia Human Rights Law Review* 25, no. 2 (Spring 1994): 269–290. Scholarly article, in English.

Ramcharan, B. G. "Strategies for the International Protection of Human Rights in the 1990s," *Human Rights Quarterly* 13, no. 2 (May 1991): 155–169. Scholarly article, in English.

Sikkink, Kathryn. "Human Rights, Principled Issue-Networks, and Sovereignty in Latin America," *International Organization* 47, no. 3 (Summer 1993): 411–441. Scholarly article, in English.

Steiner, Henry J. *Diverse Partners: Non-Governmental Organizations in the Human Rights Movement.* Cambridge, MA, USA: Harvard Law School Human Rights Program and Human Rights Internet, 1991. Conference report, in English.

Thome, Joseph R. "People Versus the Authoritarians: Grass Root Organizations and Chile's Transition to Democracy," *Más Allá del Derecho/Beyond Law: Stories of Law and Social Change from Latin America and Around the World* 1, no. 2 (July 1991): 85–109. Scholarly article, in English; bibliography, pp. 107–109.

Van Boven, Theo. "The Role of Non-Governmental Organizations in International Human Rights Standard-Setting: A Prerequisite of Democracy," *California Western International Law Journal* 20, no. 2 (1989–1990): 207–225. Scholarly article, in English.

Wiseberg, Laurie S. "Protecting Human Rights Activists and NGOs: What More Can Be Done?" *Human Rights Quarterly* 13, no. 4 (Nov. 1991): 525–544. Scholarly article, in English.

**NORWAY.** The Kingdom of Norway is a country in northern Europe, on the Norwegian Sea. It has borders with Finland and Sweden. It achieved independence as a kingdom, in personal union with Sweden, in 1814 and became a member of the United Nations in 1945. Its population is estimated to be 4,308,000. Ethnic groups include descendants of Germanic peoples (Alpine, Baltic, and Nordic), Gypsies, and Sami (Lapplanders), who are concentrated in Arctic areas where they fish and tend herds of reindeer. Languages commonly used are Norwegian (official) and Lappish. The predominant religion is Christianity, and the Evangelical Lutheran denomination is recognized as the State Church. Literacy is estimated at 100%.

The government (1994) took the form of a monarchy. Under the 1814 constitution, the king is sovereign and head of State. The Norwegian Law of Succession was amended in May 1990 to change the succession preference for males and to allow men and women the equal right to inherit the throne.

The prime minister, representing the party or coalition given the majority in the *Storting* (parliament), exercises executive authority as head of government. The *Storting* comprises 157 members elected by popular vote under a system of proportional representation; its member vote as a single body on political and financial questions but divide themselves into two bodies (*Lagting* and *Odelsting*) when considering legislation. The judiciary includes the Supreme Court. Political parties include the Labor Party, the Conservative Party, the Christian Democratic Party, the Center Party, the Socialist Left Party, and the Party of Progress.

In January 1994 Norway became a member of the newly created European Economic Area with fellow members of the EFTA (European Free Trade Association) and members of the European Union. However, following formal application for membership to the European Union, which would have taken effect January 1, 1995, Norwegians defeated the measure by 52.2% of the vote in a nationwide referendum in November 1994. Voter turn-out was a record 88%, with most of the opposition to the union coming from the rural areas where half the population of Norway lives. With the admission of Sweden and Finland in January 1995, Norway now remains the only Scandinavian country not a member of the EU.

### THE INDIGENOUS SAMI.
Although the Sami population is scattered over Norway, it is concentrated in inner Finnmark and is largely engaged in the breeding and care of reindeer. In a report to the UN **COMMITTEE ON THE ELIMINATION OF RACIAL DISCRIMINATION,** the Norwegian Government reported the following (UN Doc. CERD/C/107/Add. 4, paras. 23–24):

According to the Act relating to the Primary School, children in Sami regions are to be taught Sami as their mother tongue if their parents so demand. During the last two years of the primary school. Sami-speaking pupils can choose Sami as one of their two language forms. Attempts are also being made to promote recruitment of Sami-speaking teachers to Sami regions, for instance by offering courses at the college of education in Alta specially designed for Sami students.

The Council for Sami Education, and at the Nordic level, the Nordic Sami Institute, which is a permanent institution financed out of the Nordic cultural budget, have each contributed significantly to increasing Sami awareness of their own cultural identity.

### REPORT TO THE UN HUMAN RIGHTS COMMITTEE.
The Human Rights Committee considered the third report of Norway under the **INTERNATIONAL COVENANT ON CIVIL AND POLITICAL RIGHTS** (CCPR/C/70/Add. 2) at its 1270th to 1272nd meetings, held on 21 and 22 October and adopted the following comments at its 1282nd meeting, held on 29 October 1993 (paras. 87–97):

*Factors and difficulties affecting the implementation of the Covenant.* The Committee notes the emergence in certain parts of the population of Norway of a trend towards intolerance against foreigners, particularly asylum-seekers and migrant workers. With this exception, the Committee notes that there are no important difficulties affecting the implementation of the Covenant in Norway.

*Positive aspects.* The Committee takes note, with particular appreciation, of the level of achievement in the respect of human rights in Norway. Among the positive developments that have been realized since the consideration of the second periodic report in 1988, the Committee notes, *inter alia,* the ratification of the Second Optional Protocol to the Covenant on the abolition of the death penalty and the efforts undertaken with regard to the promotion of greater public awareness of the provisions of the Covenant and the Optional Protocols, particularly in the area of human rights education in schools and universities and through the organization of training courses for members of the police and other law enforcement officials. While noting that it is still not possible to appeal against the reversal by the Court of Appeal of an acquittal by a lower jurisdiction, the Committee also appreciates the efforts made towards the withdrawal of Norway's reservation in connection with article 14, paragraph 5, of the Covenant.

The Committee notes with satisfaction that independent investigative bodies have been set up to inquire into complaints of offences by members of the police and that their reports have been followed up by a number of prosecutions. It further commends the devolution of responsibility to the Sami Assembly *(Sametinqet)* with regard to matters affecting the life and culture of members of the Sami community and notes with satisfaction that the Sami language may be used in contacts with public bodies and before the courts.

With respect to equality and non-discrimination, developments relating to the granting to foreigners of the right to vote in local elections and to hold local office, as well as legislative steps relating to the registration of partnership of the same sex, are welcomed by the Committee. The continuing improvements in the legal and de facto equality of women and the strengthened measures against domestic violence and sexual abuse of children were also noted with satisfaction.

*Principal subjects of concern.* Despite efforts undertaken with regard to the status of the Covenant within domestic law, the Committee regrets that the opportunity has not been taken to fully incorporate the provisions of the Covenant into the Constitution, or otherwise to confer on it a higher status than ordinary legislation. The Committee also notes that certain obsolete laws still exist in Norway, in particular with regard to penal sanctions against defamation.

The Committee expresses its concern over the vagueness of the criterion of "compelling social considerations", under which a foreign national's right to choose his or her place of residence may be restricted, and its conformity with article 12 of the Covenant.

The Committee emphasizes that article 2 of the Constitution, which provides that individuals professing the Evangelical-Lutheran religion are bound to bring up their children in the same faith is in clear contradiction to article 18 of the Covenant.

The Committee notes that the authorities have included multicultural issues education, but is concerned that they have approached these issues only by reference to articles 2 and 26 of the Covenant. This gives a narrow interpretation of article 27 of the Covenant relating to the rights of persons belonging to minorities. The Committee has observed, in this regard, that the rights conferred under article 27 of the Covenant on individuals who are members of a minority avail all such individuals on a State party's territory and must not as enjoined by article 2, paragraph 1, of the Covenant, be restricted to nationals.

*Suggestions and recommendations.* The Committee recommends that further measures be adopted to repeal outdated provisions in the Constitution or in laws relating to the freedom of conscience and religion or the freedom of expression and bring them into line with the provisions of the Covenant.

The Committee recommends that a careful study of the recently enacted amendment to the Criminal Procedure Act be undertaken with regard to the scope of article 14, paragraph 5, of the Covenant, with a view to withdrawing the reservation made in that connection.

The Committee recommends that the laudable efforts already made in connection with the promotion of greater public awareness of the provisions of the Covenant and the Optional Protocols be further pursued.

*BIBLIOGRAPHY.* Beach, Hugh. *The Saami of Lapland.* London: Minority Rights Group, 1988. NGO report, in English.

Breum, M., and A. Hendriks, eds. *AIDS and Human Rights: An International Perspective.* Copenhagen, Denmark: Danish Center of Human Rights, 1988. Edited collection, in English.

Brostad, J., J. Dahl, A. Gray, et al., eds. *Native Power: The Quest for Autonomy and Nationhood of Indigenous Peoples.* Oslo, Norway: International Work Group for Indigenous Affairs and Universitetsforlaget, 1985. Scholarly edited collection, in English.

Flekkoy, Malfrid Grude. *Working for the Rights of Children: The Experience of the Norwegian Ombudsman for Children.* Florence, Italy: United Nations Children's Fund, International Child Development Centre, 1990. Basic information, in English.

Gibney, Mark. *A Critique of Norway's Refugee/Asylum Policy and Proposals for Change.* Oslo, Norway: Norwegian Institute of Human Rights, 1990. NGO report, in English.

International Work Group for Indigenous Affairs. *Self-Determination and Indigenous Peoples: Sami Rights and Northern Perspectives.* Copenhagen, Denmark: 1987. NGO conference proceedings, in English.

Isis International. "Legal Battle in Norway over Sex-tours to Thailand," *Women in Action* no. 88/2 (June 1988). NGO article, in English.

Korsmo, Fae L. "Nordic Security and the Saami Minority: Territorial Rights in Northern Fennoscandia," *Human Rights Quarterly* 10, no. 4 (Nov. 1988): 509–524. Scholarly article, in English.

Whitaker, Alan. "Radiation in Lappland," *Anti-Slavery Newsletter* 2, no. 7 (1986): 1. NGO article, in English.

**NUCLEAR WEAPONS.** For many years, the UN **GENERAL ASSEMBLY,** alarmed by the threat to the survival of mankind and the life-sustaining system posed by nuclear weapons and by their use, and conscious of an increased danger of nuclear war as a result of the intensification of the nuclear arms race and the serious deterioration of the international situation, has called upon all States to participate actively in efforts to bring about conditions in international relations among States in which a code of peaceful conduct of nations in international affairs could be agreed upon and that would preclude the use or threat of use of nuclear weapons. In this connection, it has repeatedly af-

firmed that the use of nuclear weapons would be a violation of the **UNITED NATIONS CHARTER** and a crime against humanity.

On 15 December 1989, the Assembly noted with regret (resolution 44/117 C) that the Conference on Disarmament had not been able during that year to undertake negotiations with a view to achieving agreement on an international convention prohibiting the use or threat of use of nuclear weapons under any circumstances and repeated the request it had made on several earlier occasions, calling upon the Conference to commence negotiations as a matter of priority, taking as a basis the draft Convention on the Prohibition of the Use of Nuclear Weapons annexed to the resolution and reproduced below:

The States Parties to this Convention,

Alarmed by the threat to the very survival of mankind posed by the existence of nuclear weapons,

Convinced that any use of nuclear weapons constitutes a violation of the Charter of the United Nations and a crime against humanity,

Convinced that this Convention would be a step towards the complete elimination of nuclear weapons leading to general and complete disarmament under strict and effective international control,

Determined to continue negotiations for the achievement of this goal,

Have agreed as follows:

*Article 1.* The States Parties to this Convention solemnly undertake not to use or threaten to use nuclear weapons under any circumstances.

*Article 2.* This Convention shall be of unlimited duration.

*Article 3.* 1. This Convention shall be open to all States for signature. Any State that does not sign the Convention before its entry into force in accordance with paragraph 3 of this article may accede to it at any time.

2. This Convention shall be subject to ratification by signatory States. Instruments of ratification or accession shall be deposited with the Secretary-General of the United Nations.

3. This Convention shall enter into force on the deposit of instruments of ratification by twenty-five Governments, including the Governments of the five nuclear-weapon States, in accordance with paragraph 2 of this article.

4. For States whose instruments of ratification or accession are deposited after the entry into force of this Convention, it shall enter into force on the date of the deposit of their instruments of ratification or accession.

5. The depository shall promptly inform all signatory and acceding States of the date of each signature, the date of deposit of each instrument of ratification or accession and the date of the entry into force of this Convention, as well as of the receipt of other notices.

6. This Convention shall be registered by the depository in accordance with Article 102 of the Charter of the United Nations.

*Article 4.* This Convention, of which the Arabic, Chinese, English, French, Russian and Spanish texts are equally authentic, shall be deposited with the Secretary-General of the United Nations, who shall send duly certified copies thereof to the Government of the signatory and acceding States.

In witness whereof, the undersigned, being duly authorized thereto by their respective Governments, have signed this Convention, opened for signature at _____ on the _____ day of _____ one thousand nine hundred and _____.

***NUCLEAR ARMS TREATIES.*** The following is an overview of international treaties concerning nuclear arms and testing:

(1) Nuclear Test Ban Treaty (1963) was signed in Moscow by the United States, the former USSR, and Great Britain. It prohibited testing of nuclear weapons in space, above ground, and under water.

(2) Outer Space Treaty (1967) banned the introduction of nuclear weapons into space.

(3) Nuclear Nonproliferation Treaty (1968) was signed by the United States, the former USSR, and Great Britain. It limited the spread of military nuclear technology by agreeing not to assist non-nuclear countries in getting or making nuclear weapons.

(4) Strategic Arms Limitation Treaty (SALT I) (1972) was signed in Moscow by the United States and the former USSR. The treaty limited antiballistic missiles to two sites of 100 antiballistic missile launchers in each country (amended in 1974 to one site in each country). It also imposed a five-year freeze on testing and deployment of intercontinental ballistic missiles and submarine-launched ballistic missiles. In 1977, the two superpowers agreed to continue to abide by SALT I, despite its expiration date.

(5) Protocol on Antiballistic Missile Systems (1974) limited underground testing of nuclear weapons and was signed in Moscow by the United States and the former USSR.

(6) SALT II (1979) was signed in Vienna, Austria, by the United States and the former USSR. It limited offensive nuclear weapons, permitting each side to 2,400 missile launchers and heavy bombers until 1 January 1985.

(7) Intermediate-Range Nuclear Forces (INF) Treaty (1987) was signed in Washington, D.C., by USSR President Mikhail Gorbachev and U.S. President Ronald Reagan. This treaty eliminated all medium- and short-range nuclear missiles.

(8) Strategic Arms Reduction Treaty (START I) (1991) was signed by USSR President Gorbachev and U.S. President George Bush to reduce strategic offensive arms by approximately 30% in three phases over seven years. START I was the first treaty to mandate reductions by the superpowers. With the breakup of the former Soviet Union, four newly independent States—Russia, Ukraine, Kazakhstan, and Belarus—had nuclear weapons on their territory. The latter three agreed in principle in 1992 to transfer their nuclear weapons to Russia and ratify START I.

(9) START II (1993) was signed in Moscow by U.S. President Bush and Russian President Boris Yeltsin. This treaty calls for reduction of long-range nuclear arsenals to approximately one-third of their then-current levels within a decade and would eliminate entirely land-based multiple-warhead missiles. However, START II will not take effect until START I has been fully ratified.

*SEE ALSO* Chemical Weapons; Conventional Weapons.

**BIBLIOGRAPHY.** Christian Conference of Asia. *Nuclear Free Nation.* Kowloon, Hong Kong: 1988. NGO report, in English.

Clark, R., and S. R. Roof. *Micronesia: The Problem of Palau.* Rev. ed. London: Minority Rights Group, 1987. NGO report, in English.

Donn, Gari, ed. *Missiles, Reactors, and Civil Liberties: Against the Nuclear State.* Glasgow, Scotland: Scottish Council for Civil Liberties, 1981. NGO edited collection, in English.

Gesellschaft fur bedrohte Volker (Association for Endangered Peoples). "Solange radioaktive Flusse fliessen: Uranium Abbau in den Black Hills" (As Long as Radioactive Rivers Flow: Uranium Processing in the Black Hills). *Pogrom* 135 (Aug. 1987): 20–28. NGO article, in German.

International League for Human Rights. *Report of the International Observer Mission: Palau Referendum, Dec. 1986.* New York: 1987. NGO mission report, in English.

Kuper, Leo. *The Prevention of Genocide.* New Haven, CT, USA: Yale University Press, 1985. Scholarly monograph, in English; bibliography, pp. 255–278.

"Militarization and Indigenous Peoples: Part I—The Americas and the Pacific," *Cultural Survival Quarterly* 11, no. 3 (1987). NGO special issue, in English.

Third World Network. *Belauans Struggle to Stay Nuclear Free and to Protect Their Sovereignty.* Penang, Malaysia: 1988. NGO report, in English.

*What is Hiroshima, Mommy? Vision of a Thousand Cranes: A Guide to the 20 Best Films, Videotapes, and Slide Shows for Hiroshima and Nagasaki Days.* New York: Alternative Media Information Center, n.d. Audiovisuals directory, in English.

Whitaker, Alan. "Radiation in Lappland," *Anti-Slavery Newsletter* 2, no. 7 (1986): 1. NGO article, in English.

## NUCLEAR WEAPONS: DECLARATION ON THE PREVENTION OF NUCLEAR CATASTROPHE, UN (1981).

The Declaration, outlawing the use of nuclear weapons and the waging of nuclear war, was adopted by the UN **GENERAL ASSEMBLY** on 9 December 1981 (resolution 36/100). The text of the Declaration is as follows:

The General Assembly,

Bearing in mind that the foremost task of the United Nations, born in the flames of the Second World War, has been, is and will be to save present and succeeding generations from the scourge of war,

Recognizing that all the horrors of past wars and all other calamities that have befallen people would pale in comparison with what is inherent in the use of nuclear weapons capable of destroying civilization on earth,

Reaffirming that the universally accepted objective is to eliminate completely the possibility of the use of nuclear weapons through the cessation of their production, followed by the destruction of their stockpiles, and that, to this end, priority in disarmament negotiations should be given to nuclear disarmament,

Convinced that, as the first step in this direction, the use of nuclear weapons and the waging of nuclear war should be outlawed,

Solemnly proclaims, on behalf of the States Members of the United Nations:

1. States and statesmen that resort first to the use of nuclear weapons will be committing the gravest crime against humanity.

2. There will never be any justification or pardon for statesmen who take the decision to be the first to use nuclear weapons.

3. Any doctrines allowing the first use of nuclear weapons and any actions pushing the world towards a catastrophe are incompatible with human moral standards and the lofty ideals of the United Nations.

4. It is the supreme duty and direct obligation of the leaders of nuclear-weapon States to act in such a way as to eliminate the risk of the outbreak of a nuclear conflict. The nuclear-arms race must be stopped and reversed by joint efforts, through negotiations conducted in good faith and on the basis of equality, having as their ultimate goal the complete elimination of nuclear weapons.

5. Nuclear energy should be used exclusively for peaceful purposes and only for the benefit of mankind.

# O

---

**OAS.** See **ORGANIZATION OF AMERICAN STATES.**

**OAU.** See **ORGANIZATION OF AFRICAN UNITY.**

**OFFICE OF THE HIGH COMMISSIONER FOR HUMAN RIGHTS, UN.** See **HIGH COMMISSIONER FOR HUMAN RIGHTS, UN.**

**OFFICE OF THE HIGH COMMISSIONER FOR REFUGEES, UN.** See **HIGH COMMISSIONER FOR REFUGEES, UN.**

**OMAN.** The Sultanate of Oman is an Arab country in western Africa, located on the southeastern tip of the Arabian peninsula, fronting on the Arabian Sea and the Gulf of Oman. It attained independence from Turkey in 1741 and became a member of the United Nations in 1971. Its population is estimated to be 1,617,000. Ethnic groups include small communities of Arab, Baluchi, Indian, and Zanzibari origins. Languages commonly used include Arabic (official), English, Baluchi, and several Indian dialects. Islam (Ibadhi, 75%; Sunni and Shi'ite, 10%) is the predominant religion; Hinduism is the religion of immigrants from India and their descendants. Literacy is estimated at 20%.

The government (1994) took the form of a monarchy. The sultan is head of State and of government. He is assisted by the Council of Ministers, the Consultative Council, six specialized councils, and a number of personal advisors. There is no legislature. The courts, for the most part, apply traditional Islamic law. There are no political parties. It was announced in June 1994 that for the first time women from the district of the capital of Muscat would be allowed to hold seats in the Consultative Council.

*BIBLIOGRAPHY.* Arab Organization for Human Rights. *Report: Human Rights in the Arab World.* Cairo, Egypt. Annual NGO report, in Arabic or English.

————. "Sultanate of Oman: Torture and Ill-Treatment," *AOHR Newsletter* 11 (Aug. 1987): 4. NGO article, in English.

**OMBUDSMAN.** An ombudsman is a unique institution established in various forms in a number of countries to protect individuals against unjust acts on the part of government officials or agencies. The role and functions of ombudsmen are described in the Secretary-General's report entitled *National Institutions for the Protection and Promotion of Human Rights* (UN Doc. E/CN.4/1987/37), prepared at the request of the **GENERAL ASSEMBLY** (resolution 40/123, paras. 99–111), as follows:

It would be difficult to classify the ombudsman as a legislative, judicial or administrative organ. It is indeed an institution of a *sui generis* nature, having a multi-faceted character. The ombudsman is an independent mediator—and in some instances, a collegiate body—whose primary role is to protect the rights of the individual who believes he is the victim of unjust acts on the part of the public administration. Generally appointed to office by the legislative body, the ombudsman in many instances functions in a supervisory capacity on behalf of parliament, acting on complaints received from aggrieved persons against government officials or agencies. The ombudsman is often perceived as a Scandinavian institution, since it had its beginnings in early nineteenth century *Sweden*, and is firmly established in *Denmark, Norway* and *Finland.* In the past several decades, however, the ombudsman or the office of the mediator has been established in a number of countries outside Scandinavia. *Australia, Austria, Barbados, Canada, France, Ghana, Guyana, India, Jamaica, Japan, Mauritius, New Zealand, Portugal, Spain, Trinidad and Tobago,* the *United Kingdom* and certain areas in the *United States* have all utilized the ombudsman system in one form or another. Moreover, several African countries (*Nigeria,* the *Sudan, Tanzania* and *Zambia*) have established collegiate bodies or commissions, which function with the authority and jurisdiction of the ombudsman.

Essentially, the ombudsman in all countries follows similar procedures in the performance of his duties. He receives complaints from aggrieved parties, and subsequently initiates an investigation if the claim has merit and falls within his jurisdiction. The ombudsman is generally granted access to documents of all authorities within his jurisdiction, which are pertinent to the investigation. He then usually issues a statement of recommendation based on his investigation, which is given to both the complainant and the office or authority against whom the complaint has been lodged. If the recommendation is not acted upon, the ombudsman may then submit his recommendation to parliament. In the Scandinavian countries, the ombudsman may also call both parties to the case to a hearing if necessary, and he is empowered to examine witnesses under oath. In Sweden, the

Ombudsman's investigation generally results in a letter to both parties, stating his opinion on the conduct of the official, and stating his interpretation of the law in question. He may recommend that damages be paid to the injured party by the official, or out of public funds. In rare cases involving major faults, the Swedish Ombudsman may order prosecution before the courts. In minor cases, when the investigation reveals faults, delay or neglect, the Ombudsman may issue a reminder to the official concerned that his handling of the case was faulty or improper. Additionally, in almost all countries, the ombudsman submits an annual report to parliament or the corresponding legislative body. Each country may require its ombudsman to include specific information or recommendations in his report. For instance, the Swedish Ombudsman's annual report may include an opinion on inadequacies in legislation, as well as his views on the meaning of existing laws and statutes and how they should be interpreted and applied. He may also suggest new legislation. Similarly, the French Ombudsman, *le Médiateur*, may suggest in his reports amendments to the laws and regulations. The Austrian *Volksanwaltschaft* may make recommendations to the highest executive authorities in addition to his annual activity report, which is submitted to the *Nationalrat*.

Although he submits annual reports to parliament, the ombudsman is essentially an independent office. The office of ombudsman is frequently provided for in a constitution or by an act of the legislature. As such, the ombudsman is accountable to the legislature, and in most cases, the legislative body will conduct an annual review of the ombudsman's office. Despite annual review by parliament or the Executive, the ombudsman nevertheless enjoys relative independence. For example, the Swedish Ombudsman cannot be removed from office unless a Parliamentary Committee issues a petition for his removal. In the United Kingdom, the Parliamentary Commissioner (Ombudsman) is subject to review by a Select Committee of the House of Commons, but he can only be removed by an address from both Houses of Parliament.

Ombudsmen may sometimes be accountable to the Executive. For example, while the Nigerian Public Complaints Commission and the Sudanese People's Assembly for Administrative Control are accountable to Parliament, the Tanzanian Permanent Commission of Inquiry and the Zambian Commission for Investigations are directly responsible to the head of State.

In most cases, the ombudsman initiates an investigation based on a complaint received at his offices. He may, however, initiate an investigation without such a complaint. For instance, in Sweden, the Ombudsman frequently may begin an investigation on the basis of a newspaper report about illegalities and maladministration. France also provides for investigations by the *Médiateur* without receipt of a complaint, by giving members of parliament the right to request that the *Médiateur* investigate a matter of concern to parliament. Some countries limit recourse to the ombudsman to those complainants who have actually been injured by the challenged act or authority. This is a requirement in Guyana and in Trinidad and Tobago. Recourse to the Austrian *Volksanwaltschaft*, however, is granted to non-citizens and citizens who are "concerned by alleged abuses in the administration of the *Bund*." Spain merely requires that the complainant assert a legitimate interest in the complaint.

Several countries (Austria, Jamaica, New Zealand and the United Kingdom) require that the complainant first exhaust all alternative legal remedies before approaching the ombudsman. While there is generally no statute of limitations on the time within which the complainant must lodge his or her grievance with the ombudsman, there is often a requirement that the complaint to an ombudsman be made within one year of notification of the decision complained of. None the less, some ombudsmen have discretion to consider older grievances.

Access to the ombudsman by an individual complainant varies from country to country. In many countries (Denmark, Finland, New Zealand, Norway, Sweden, the United Republic of Tanzania and Zambia for example) individuals may lodge their complaints directly with the ombudsman's office. Israel additionally provides that the ombudsman may receive sealed complaints in writing from prisoners. However, in France, the Sudan and the United Kingdom, complaints must be submitted to a member of parliament, who forwards to the ombudsman those complaints which fall within his jurisdiction. For example, the French *Médiateur* receives individual complaints first addressed to Deputies or Senators who transfer them to the *Médiateur*. In practice, members of parliament generally forward all complaints received to the ombudsman. Complainants whose cases fall outside the ombudsman's jurisdiction may then receive a communication from the ombudsman's office, explaining why he is unable to act on the complaint.

Complaints made to the ombudsman are generally confidential, and the identity of the complainant will not be disclosed without his consent. In most countries, the identity of the complainant and that of the official against whom the complaint has been lodged are not revealed in the ombudsman's annual report. In Sweden however, upon the completion of a case, the Ombudsman's file is, in most cases, open to inspection by the press.

The jurisdiction of the ombudsman's authority generally reaches all offices of public administration. Nevertheless, the scope of the ombudsman's jurisdiction varies from country to country. For example, Finland and Denmark vest power over Ministers in the Ombudsman. Austria, Australia, New Zealand and Sweden do not permit their ombudsmen to investigate complaints against Ministers. The Tanzanian Permanent Commission has jurisdiction over central and local government, and practically all statutory bodies, as well as over the party and party affiliates. The Commission does not, however, have jurisdiction over residential decisions, or matters of government or public policy. In Nigeria, complaints to the Public Complaints Commission may be made against government departments, functionaries, employers and employees, individuals in the public and private sectors, State governments and local authorities. The Sudan People's Assembly Committee may investigate any complaint charging that an administration decision is the result of: (a) nepotism, corruption or bias, (b) failure to observe sound administrative bases, (c) negligence in carrying out duty, (d) misuse of discretion, (e) incompetence, (f) loss of documents and papers, (g) tardiness and delay, (h) unjust segregation or (i) any similar matter. The Parliamentary Commissioner of the United Kingdom is empowered to investigate maladministration in most departments and authorities dealing with the public. Maladministration is defined as including: incompetence, delay, neglect and bias, but *not* policy. Policy questions fall within the jurisdiction of Parliament. The Commissioner does not have the power to investigate the merits of discretionary decisions. Nor does his jurisdiction extend to the national health service, local government or the police, since other organs exist which are empowered to investigate complaints against these institutions. The Ombudsman of New Zealand has jurisdiction over acts or omissions of the departments of State, a small number of statutory administrative tribunals and local organizations. He has no control over any matter in which there is a right of appeal or review on the merits of the case to any court, no direct control over a Minister, and may not alter a decision he believes is wrong. In Finland, Sweden and the United Republic of Tanzania, the ombudsman is allowed to investigate complaints against the judiciary. Other countries, such as Austria, Denmark and Norway, have left judges entirely outside the ombudsman's jurisdiction because of a strong concern for maintaining the independence of the courts.

In the countries in which the ombudsman has supervisory power over Ministers, the authorities in question are required to support the ombudsman in the exercise of his investigation, including providing all requested documents and testimony. Despite this requirement however, in some instances, Ministers may refuse to give information to the ombudsman if, in the Minister's judgement, the exposure of such information would be prejudicial to national security or defence. In order to prevent abuse of this exception by Ministers, the United Kingdom introduced a provision in its Parliamentary Commissioner Act which grants the Ombudsman access to all information relevant to his investigation, but which gives the Minister the power to prohibit him from disclosing in his report, any information which, in the Minister's judgement, would be "prejudicial to the safety of the State or otherwise contrary to the public interest."

Responsibility for heightening public awareness of the duties and functions of the office seems to rest with the ombudsman's office itself. Radio messages, pamphlets and television documentaries on the history and role of the ombudsman are all methods which may be used to inform the public about the ombudsman's office as an important resource. For example, the Tanzanian and Zambian ombudsman commissions hold public meetings in villages in rural areas to explain the work done by their commission, and to increase their accessibility to individuals residing in outlying areas, who may have grievances against public officials. After these public meetings, the commissions' representatives hold private sessions in which aggrieved parties may report their complaints. These complaints are subsequently investigated and, if necessary, additional visits are made to the villages for follow-up contacts. In its first year, members of the Tanzanian commission visited 14 regions, 53 districts and addressed over 64,000 persons.

The ombudsman is a potentially effective human rights organ, which can be adapted to various political and social systems. A large number of countries have successfully incorporated the ombudsman into their administrative systems. Naturally, the ombudsman's office may only be as effective as its authority and jurisdiction permits. While countries may differ on the breadth of jurisdiction to be bestowed upon that office, it is clear, for instance, that the right to view documents and to question authorities under the parameters of that jurisdiction, appears to be essential for a thorough and accurate investigation. In addition, the effectiveness of the ombudsman's office is largely dependent on the ability of a potential complainant to utilize the services provided by the ombudsman. Therefore, it is important that individuals are not encumbered by confusing petition processes, when attempting to present their grievances to the ombudsman's office. While it is true that most ombudsmen may initiate investigations on their own, independent of a private complaint, the primary function of the office is to provide a recourse to the individual who has been the victim of injustice resulting from governmental or administrative action. As such, all efforts must be made to ensure that the ombudsman's office is easily accessible to all members of the public.

*THE DANISH OMBUDSMAN.* The Danish Ombudsman Act No. 203 of 11 June 1954, as amended, is a typical national statute setting out the functions and powers of an ombudsman and establishing the procedures to be followed by such an official in supervising government administration. The text of the act is as follows:

1. (a) After every general election and when a vacancy occurs the Folketing shall elect an Ombudsman to supervise, on its behalf, civil and military central government administration and local government administration. The jurisdiction of the Ombudsman shall not extend to the functions of judge, chief administrative officers of the courts of justice, the head of the Probate Division of the Copenhagen City Court, clerks of the Supreme Court, and assistant judges.

(b) Upon a general election, the Ombudsman shall continue in office until the new Folketing has elected an Ombudsman as provided in subsection (a) above, and, if he is not re-elected, until the new Ombudsman has taken office. The term of office of the outgoing Ombudsman shall not, except with the consent of the Folketing, exceed six months from the date of the general election.

(c) In the event of the death of the Ombudsman, the Ombudsman Committee of the Folketing shall determine who shall carry out the functions of Ombudsman until the Folketing has elected a new Ombudsman.

(d) Should the Ombudsman cease to enjoy the confidence of the Folketing, it may dismiss him.

2. The Ombudsman, who may not be a member of the Folketing shall be a law graduate.

3. The Folketing shall lay down general rules governing the activities of the Ombudsman. Subject to these rules, the Ombudsman shall be independent of the Folketing in the discharge of his functions.

4. (a) The jurisdiction of the Ombudsman shall extend to ministers, civil servants and all other persons in government service except as provided in section 1, subsection (a).

(b) Persons in local government service shall likewise fall within the jurisdiction of the Ombudsman in so far as regards matters in which recourse to a central government authority is provided for. The activities of local government councils acting as a body shall not fall within the jurisdiction of the Ombudsman except as provided in section 6, subsection (e).

(c) In the exercise of his powers the Ombudsman shall take account of the special conditions under which local governments function.

5. The Ombudsman shall keep himself informed as to whether the persons referred to in section 4 make themselves guilty of errors or neglect in the performance of their duties.

6. (a) Any person may lodge a complaint with the Ombudsman against any of the persons referred to in section 4. Any person deprived of his personal liberty shall be entitled to address written communications to the Ombudsman in sealed envelopes.

(b) A complainant shall state his name and lodge his complaint within twelve months after the commission of the act complained of.

1105

(c) Complaints against decisions which may be set aside by a superior administrative authority cannot be lodged with the Ombudsman until the superior authority has taken a decision in the matter. In that event the time-limit referred to in subsection (b) of this section shall be reckoned from the date of that authority's decision.

(d) The Ombudsman shall determine whether a complaint offers sufficient grounds for investigation.

(e) The Ombudsman may take up a matter for investigation on his own initiative. In that event the restrictions referred to in section 4, subsection (b) shall not apply where violation of essential legal interests is postulated.

7. (a) The persons referred to in section 4 shall be under obligation to furnish the Ombudsman with such information and to produce such documents and records as he may demand *ex officio*.

(b) Demands for information made by the Ombudsman in pursuance of subsection (1) of this section shall be subject to restrictions corresponding to those laid down in section 169, subsections (1) and (3), section 170, subsection (1), the principal rule of section 170, subsection (4), and section 749 of the Administration of Justice Act.

(c) If the Ombudsman wants to take action on a complaint against any of the persons referred to in section 4, the complaint shall, except where absolutely incompatible with the investigation of the matter, be notified to the person complained of at the earliest opportunity. If the person complained of is a civil servant he may always demand that the matter be dealt with under the provisions of section 17, cf. section 18, of the Civil Servants (Salaries and Pensions) Act. If he is a local government official he may, if the by-laws of the local government concerned provide for disciplinary action, demand that the matter be dealt with under the provisions of such by-laws.

(d) The Ombudsman may subpoena persons to give evidence in court on any matter of importance to his investigations. Such procedure shall be subject to the rules governing examination of witnesses for purposes of investigation, cf. Part 74 of the Administration of Justice Act. The hearings shall not be held in open court. The person complained of shall be entitled to attend such examinations of witnesses and to bring a counsel. The rules in force at any given time with respect to payment of the costs of counsel, etc. in cases of disciplinary prosecution of civil servants shall apply by analogy.

8. The Ombudsman shall observe secrecy in any matter coming to his knowledge in the performance of his duty, provided that secrecy is necessary *ipso facto*. The obligation of the Ombudsman to observe secrecy shall not lapse on his retirement.

9. (a) The Ombudsman may direct the Public Prosecutor to institute a preliminary investigation or bring a charge before a court of justice for misconduct in public service or office, subject to the provisions of sections 16 and 60 of the Constitution of 5 June 1953 (The Court of the Realm).

(b) The Ombudsman may direct the appropriate central government administrative authority to institute disciplinary proceedings. Where the by-laws of a local government provide for disciplinary proceedings, he may direct the appropriate local government authority to institute such proceedings.

(c) The Ombudsman may always state his own views of a case to the person complained of.

10. (a) Should the Ombudsman learn of major mistakes or derelictions on the part of any of the persons referred to in section 4, he shall report the matter to the folketing and the responsible minister. In the case of mistakes or derelictions on the part of any of the persons referred to in section 4, subsection (2), he shall report the matter also to the local government concerned.

*INTERNATIONAL OMBUDSMAN INSTITUTE.* The first international conference of ombudsmen, held in Edmonton, Canada, in 1976, resulted in the establishment of the International Ombudsman Institute (IOI), with headquarters at the Law Center for the University of Alberta, Edmonton, in 1978.

IOI promotes the concept of ombudsmanship by conducting research into problems confronting ombudsmen and organizing conferences and seminars on the subject. It publishes the IOI *Newsletter* every two months and also issues the *IOI Directory of Ombudsmen and Other Complaint-Handlers* and the *IOI Bibliography*. In addition, it issues annually the *Ombudsman Journal, Ombudsman and Other Complaint-Handling Systems Survey, Ombudsman Office Profiles*, and *Court Cases of Interest to the Institution of Ombudsman*.

Membership of the Institute consists of ombudsman offices having a legislative status in 40 countries and academies in 20 countries and territories.

**OPEN DOOR INTERNATIONAL.** Open Door International for the Economic Emancipation of the Woman Worker was founded in Berlin, Germany, in 1929 to secure the rights of women to be free to work and be protected as a worker on the same terms as men. The group has consultative status (Roster) with the UN **ECONOMIC AND SOCIAL COUNCIL** and publishes the newsletter *Circular Letter* four to six times a year.

Open Door International. Address: Rue Americaine 16, B-1050, Brussels, Belgium. Telephone: (32-2) 537-6761. Honorable Secretary: Adele Hauwel.

**OPINION AND EXPRESSION.** See **FREEDOM OF OPINION AND EXPRESSION.**

**ORGANIZATION FOR CHILD AND YOUTH WELFARE OF THE WORLD.** Founded in 1963 as an international agency, this non-governmental organization has consultative status with the UN **ECONOMIC AND SOCIAL COUNCIL** (Category II) and **UNICEF.** The Organization promotes the rights, education, and well-being of children by establishing conditions, programs, and practices from prenatal through adolescent periods. The group runs formal, vocational/technical schools, and recreational programs, particularly in rural areas. The Organization has established the Training Institute for Child and Youth Welfare in Bombay, India. The group has members in 55 countries.

Organization for Child and Youth Welfare. Address: Gulistan, 12th Road, Khar, Bombay 400 052, India. Telephone: (91-22) 543-661.

## ORGANIZATION OF AFRICAN UNITY (OAU).
An intergovernmental organization within the United Nations system composed of the governments of 50 African States, including the island States of Comoros and Madagascar.

The Organization endeavors to promote the unity and solidarity of African States: to coordinate and intensify their cooperation and their efforts to achieve a better life for the peoples of Africa; to defend their sovereignty, territorial integrity, and independence; to eradicate all forms of colonialism from Africa; to promote international cooperation, having due regard for the UNITED NATIONS CHARTER and the UNIVERSAL DECLARATION OF HUMAN RIGHTS; and to coordinate and harmonize members' political, diplomatic, economic, educational, cultural, health, welfare, scientific, technical, and defense policies.

The OAU's organizational structure includes the Assembly of Heads of State and Government, the supreme organ, which meets once a year to perform the functions set out in articles 8 to 11 of the ORGANIZATION OF AFRICAN UNITY CHARTER; the Council of Ministers, which meets two times during the year to perform the functions set out in articles 12 through 15 of the Charter; and the OAU General Secretariat, headed by a Secretary-General and assistant secretaries-general for West, Central, North, East, and Southern Africa (articles 16 through 18 of the Charter).

The OAU Coordinating Committee for the Liberation of Africa organizes, supports, and channels financial, military, and logistic support to recognized African liberation movements including the AFRICAN NATIONAL CONGRESS OF SOUTH AFRICA and the South West African People's Organization. Through the efforts of the committee, the United Nations was persuaded to recognize the legitimacy of those movements and to grant them status as observers.

Organization of African Unity. Address: P.O. Box 3243, Addis Ababa, Ethiopia. Telephone: 47480. Cable: OAU ADDIS ABABA. Secretary-General: Peter Onu.

**SEE ALSO** *African Charter on Human and Peoples' Rights; African Commission on Human and Peoples' Rights.*

**BIBLIOGRAPHY.** Naldi, Gino J., ed. *Documents of the Organization of African Unity.* London: Mansell, 1992. Monograph, in English.

## ORGANIZATION OF AFRICAN UNITY CHARTER
(1963). The Charter of the OAU, open to acceptance by any independent sovereign African State, including Madagascar and the islands surrounding Africa, was adopted by the heads of African States and governments, convened at Addis Ababa, on 25 May 1963. It entered into force on 13 September 1963.

The Charter is supplemented by the OAU Protocol of the Commission of Mediation, Conciliation and Arbitration (see below), signed at Cairo on 21 July 1964 by the heads of African States and governments.

The text of the Charter (United Nations, *Treaty Series,* vol. 479, p. 39) is as follows:

We, the Heads of African States and Governments assembled in the City of Addis Ababa, Ethiopia;

Convinced that it is the inalienable right of all people to control their own destiny;

Conscious of the fact that freedom, equality, justice and dignity are essential objectives for the achievement of the legitimate aspirations of the African peoples;

Conscious of our responsibility to harness the natural and human resources of our continent for the total advancement of our peoples in spheres of human endeavour;

Inspired by a common determination to promote understanding among our peoples and co-operation among our States in response to the aspirations of our peoples for brotherhood and solidarity, in a larger unity transcending ethnic and national differences;

Convinced that, in order to translate this determination into a dynamic force in the cause of human progress, conditions for peace and security must be established and maintained;

Determined to safeguard and consolidate the hard-won independence as well as the sovereignty and territorial integrity of our States, and to fight against neo-colonialism in all its forms;

Dedicated to the general progress of Africa;

Persuaded that the Charter of the United Nations and the Universal Declaration of Human Rights, to the principles of which we reaffirm our adherence, provide a solid foundation for peaceful and positive co-operation among states;

Desirous that all African States should henceforth unite so that the welfare and well-being of their peoples can be assured;

Resolved to reinforce the links between our states by establishing and strengthening common institutions;

Have agreed to the present Charter.

### Establishment

*Article 1.* 1. The High Contracting Parties do by the present Charter establish an Organization to be known as the *Organization of African Unity.*

2. The Organization shall include the Continental African States, Madagascar and other Islands surrounding Africa.

### Purposes

*Article 2.* 1. The Organization shall have the following purposes:

(a) to promote the unity and solidarity of the African States;

(b) to coordinate and intensify their co-operation and efforts to achieve a better life for the peoples of Africa;

(c) to defend their sovereignty, their territorial integrity and independence;

(d) to eradicate all forms of colonialism from Africa; and

(e) to promote international co-operation, having due regard to the Charter of the United Nations and the Universal Declaration of Human Rights.

2. To these ends, the Member States shall coordinate and harmonise their general policies, especially in the following fields:

(a) political and diplomatic co-operation;

(b) economic co-operation, including transport and communications;

(c) educational and cultural co-operation;

(d) health, sanitation, and nutritional co-operation;

(e) scientific and technical co-operation; and

(f) co-operation for defence and security.

## Principles

*Article 3.* The Member States, in pursuit of the purposes stated in Article 2, solemnly affirm and declare their adherence to the following principles:

1. the sovereign equality of all Member States;

2. non-interference in the internal affairs of States;

3. respect for the sovereignty and territorial integrity of each State and for its inalienable right to independent existence;

4. peaceful settlement of disputes by negotiation, mediation, conciliation or arbitration;

5. unreserved condemnation, in all its forms, of political assassination as well as of subversive activities on the part of neighbouring States or any other State;

6. absolute dedication to the total emancipation of the African territories which are still dependent;

7. affirmation of a policy of non-alignment with regard to all blocs.

## Membership

*Article 4.* Each independent sovereign African State shall be entitled to become a Member of the Organization.

## Rights and Duties of Member States

*Article 5.* All Member States shall enjoy equal rights and have equal duties.

*Article 6.* The Member States pledge themselves to observe scrupulously the principles enumerated in Article 3 of the present Charter.

## Institutions

*Article 7.* The Organization shall accomplish its purposes through the following principal institutions:

1. the Assembly of Heads of State and Government;

2. the Council of Ministers;

3. the General Secretariat;

4. the Commission of Mediation, Conciliation and Arbitration.

## The Assembly of Heads of State and Government

*Article 8.* The Assembly of Heads of State and Government shall be the supreme organ of the Organization. It shall, subject to the provisions of this Charter, discuss matters of common concern to Africa with a view to co-ordinating and harmonizing the general policy of the Organization. It may in addition review the structure, functions and acts of all the organs and any specialized agencies which may be created in accordance with the present Charter.

*Article 9.* The Assembly shall be composed of the Heads of State and Government or their duly accredited representatives and it shall meet at least once a year. At the request of any Member State and on approval by a two-thirds majority of the Member States, the Assembly shall meet in extraordinary session.

*Article 10.* 1. Each Member State shall have one vote.

2. All resolutions shall be determined by a two-thirds majority of the Members of the Organization.

3. Questions of procedure shall require a simple majority. Whether or not a question is one of procedure shall be determined by a simple majority of all Member States of the Organization.

4. Two-thirds of the total membership of the Organization shall form a quorum at any meeting of the Assembly.

*Article 11.* The Assembly shall have the power to determine its own rules of procedure.

## The Council of Ministers

*Article 12.* 1. The Council of Ministers shall consist of Foreign Ministers or such other Ministers as are designated by the Governments of Member States.

2. The Council of Ministers shall meet at least twice a year. When requested by any Member State and approved by two-thirds of all Member States, it shall meet in extraordinary session.

*Article 13.* 1. The Council of Ministers shall be responsible to the Assembly of Heads of State and Government. It shall be entrusted with the responsibility of preparing conferences of the Assembly.

2. It shall take cognisance of any matter referred to it by the Assembly. It shall be entrusted with the implementation of the decision of the Assembly, of Heads of State and Government. It shall coordinate inter-African cooperation in accordance with the instructions of the Assembly and in conformity with Article 2 (2) of the present Charter.

*Article 14.* 1. Each Member State shall have one vote.

2. All resolutions shall be determined by a simple majority of the members of the Council of Ministers.

3. Two thirds of the total membership of the Council of Ministers shall form a quorum for any meeting of the Council.

*Article 15.* The Council shall have the power to determine its own rules of procedure.

## General Secretariat

*Article 16.* There shall be an Administrative Secretary-General of the Organization, who shall be appointed by the Assembly of Heads of State and Government. The Administrative Secretary-General shall direct the affairs of the Secretariat.

*Article 17.* There shall be one or more Assistant Secretaries-General of the Organization who shall be appointed by the Assembly of Heads of State and Government.

*Article 18.* The functions and conditions of services of the Secretary-General, of the Assistant Secretaries-General and other employees of the Secretariat shall be governed by the provisions of this Charter and the regulations approved by the Assembly of Heads of State and Government.

1. In the performance of their duties the Administrative Secretary-General and the staff shall not seek or receive instructions from any government or from any other authority external to the Organization. They shall refrain from any action which might reflect on their position as international officials responsible only to the Organization.

2. Each member of the Organization undertakes to respect the exclusive character of the responsibility of the Administrative Secretary-General and the Staff and not to seek to influence them in the discharge of their responsibilities.

## Commission of Mediation, Conciliation and Arbitration

*Article 19.* Member States pledge to settle all disputes among themselves by peaceful means and, to this end decide to establish a Commission of Mediation, Conciliation and Arbitration, the composition of which and conditions of service shall be defined by a separate Protocol to be approved by the Assembly of Heads of State and Government. Said Protocol shall be regarded as forming an integral part of the present Charter.

## Specialized Commissions

*Article 20.* The Assembly shall establish such Specialized Commissions as it may deem necessary, including the following:

1. Economic and Social Commission;
2. Educational and Cultural Commission;
3. Health, Sanitation and Nutrition Commission;
4. Defence Commission;
5. Scientific, Technical and Research Commission.

*Article 21.* Each Specialized Commission referred to in Article 20 shall be composed of the Ministers concerned or other Ministers or Plenipotentiaries designated by the Governments of the Member States.

*Article 22.* The functions of the Specialized Commissions shall be carried out in accordance with the provisions of the present Charter and of the regulations approved by the Council of Ministers.

## The Budget

*Article 23.* The budget of the Organization prepared by the Administrative Secretary-General shall be approved by the Council of Ministers. The budget shall be provided by contributions from Member States in accordance with the scale of assessment of the United Nations; provided, however, that no Member State shall be assessed an amount exceeding twenty percent of the yearly regular budget of the Organization. The Member States agree to pay their respective contributions regularly.

## Signature and Ratification of Charter

*Article 24.* 1. This Charter shall be open for signature to all independent sovereign African States and shall be ratified by the signatory States in accordance with their respective constitutional processes.

2. The original instrument, done, if possible in African languages, in English and French, all texts being equally authentic, shall be deposited with the Government of Ethiopia which shall transmit certified copies thereof to all independent sovereign African States.

3. Instruments of ratification shall be deposited with the Government of Ethiopia, which shall notify all signatories of each such deposit.

## Entry into Force

*Article 25.* This Charter shall enter into force immediately upon receipt by the Government of Ethiopia of the instruments of ratification from two thirds of the signatory States.

## Registration of the Charter

*Article 26.* This Charter shall, after due ratification, be registered with the Secretariat of the United Nations through the Government of Ethiopia in conformity with Article 102 of the Charter of the United Nations.

## Interpretation of the Charter

*Article 27.* Any question which may arise concerning the interpretation of this Charter shall be decided by a vote of two thirds of the Assembly of Heads of State and Government of the Organization.

## Adhesion and Accession

*Article 28.* 1. Any independent sovereign African State may at any time notify the Administrative Secretary-General of its intention to adhere or accede to this Charter.

2. The Administrative Secretary-General shall, on receipt of such notification, communicate a copy of it to all the Member States. Admission shall be decided by a simple majority of the Member States. The decision of each Member State shall be transmitted to the Administrative Secretary-General, who shall, upon receipt of the required number of votes, communicate the decision to the State concerned.

## Miscellaneous

*Article 29.* The working languages of the Organization and all its institutions shall be, if possible African languages, English and French.

*Article 30.* The Administrative Secretary-General may accept on behalf of the Organization gifts, bequests and other donations made to the Organization, provided that this is approved by the Council of Ministers.

*Article 31.* The Council of Ministers shall decide on the privileges and immunities to be accorded to the personnel of the Secretariat in the respective territories of the Member States.

## Cessation of Membership

*Article 32.* Any State which desires to renounce its membership shall forward a written notification to the Administrative Secretary-General. At the end of one year from the date of such notification, if not withdrawn, the Charter shall cease to apply with respect to the renouncing State, which shall thereby cease to belong to the Organization.

## Amendment of the Charter

*Article 33*. This Charter may be amended or revised if any Member State makes a written request to the Administrative Secretary-General to that effect; provided, however, that the proposed amendment is not submitted to the Assembly for consideration until all the Member States have been duly notified of it and a period of one year has elapsed. Such an amendment shall not be effective unless approved by at least two thirds of all the Member States.

***PROTOCOL OF THE COMMISSION OF MEDIATION, CONCILIATION AND ARBITRATION (1964)***. The Protocol, approved by the Assembly of Heads of State and Government, convened at Cairo, on 21 July 1964, is considered to be an integral part of the OAU Charter. The text of the Protocol (*International Legal Materials* 3, p. 1116) is as follows:

*Article 1*. The Commission of Mediation, Conciliation and Arbitration established by Article XIX of the Charter of the Organization of African Unity shall be governed by the provisions of the present Protocol.

*Article 2*. 1. The Commission shall consist of twenty-one members elected by the Assembly of Heads of State and Government.

2. No two Members shall be nationals of the same State.

3. The Members of the Commission shall be persons with recognized professional qualifications.

4. Each Member State of the Organization of African Unity shall be entitled to nominate two candidates.

5. The Administrative Secretary-General shall prepare a list of the candidates nominated by Member States and shall submit it to the Assembly of Heads of State and Government.

*Article 3*. 1. Members of the Commission shall be elected for a term of five years and shall be eligible for re-election.

2. Members of the Commission whose terms of office have expired shall remain in office until the election of a new Commission.

3. Notwithstanding the expiry of their terms of office, Members shall complete any proceedings in which they are already engaged.

*Article 4*. Members of the Commission shall not be removed from office except by decision of the Assembly of Heads of State and Government, by a two-thirds majority of the total membership, on the grounds of inability to perform the functions of their office or of proved misconduct.

*Article 5*. 1. Whenever a vacancy occurs in the Commission, it shall be filled in conformity with the provisions of Article 2.

2. A Member of the Commission elected to fill a vacancy shall hold office for the unexpired term of the Member he has replaced.

*Article 6*. 1. A President and two Vice-Presidents shall be elected by the Assembly of Heads of State and Government from among the Members of the Commission who shall each hold office for five years. The President and the two Vice-Presidents shall not be eligible for re-election as such officers.

2. The President and the two Vice-Presidents shall be full-time members of the Commission, while the remaining eighteen shall be part-time Members.

*Article 7*. The President and the two Vice-Presidents shall constitute the Bureau of the Commission and shall have the responsibility of consulting with the parties as regards the appropriate mode of settling the dispute in accordance with this Protocol.

*Article 8*. The salaries and allowances of the Members of the Bureau and the remuneration of the other Members of the Commission shall be determined in accordance with the provisions of the Charter of the Organization of African Unity.

*Article 9*. 1. The Commission shall appoint a Registrar and may provide for such other officers as may be deemed necessary.

2. The terms and conditions of service of the Registrar and other administrative officers of the Commission shall be governed by the Commission's Staff Regulations.

*Article 10*. The Administrative expenses of the Commission shall be borne by the Organization of African Unity. All other expenses incurred in connection with the proceedings before the Commission shall be met in accordance with the Rules of Procedure of the Commission.

*Article 11*. The Seat of the Commission shall be at Addis Ababa, Ethiopia.

### General Provisions

*Article 12*. The Commission shall have jurisdiction over disputes between States only.

*Article 13*. 1. A dispute may be referred to the Commission jointly by the parties concerned, by a party to the dispute, by the Council of Ministers or by the Assembly of Heads of State and Government.

2. Where a dispute has been referred to the Commission as provided in paragraph 1, and one or more of the parties have refused to submit to the jurisdiction of the Commission, the Bureau shall refer the matter to the Council of Ministers for consideration.

*Article 14*. The consent of any party to a dispute to submit to the jurisdiction of the Commission may be evidenced by:

(a) a prior written undertaking by such party that there shall be recourse to Mediation, Conciliation or Arbitration;

(b) reference of a dispute by such party to the Commission; or

(c) submission by such party to the jurisdiction in respect of a dispute referred to the Commission by another State, by the Council of Ministers, or by the Assembly of Heads of State and Government.

*Article 15*. Member States shall refrain from any act or omission that is likely to aggravate a situation which has been referred to the Commission.

*Article 16*. Subject to the provisions of this Protocol and any special agreement between the parties, the Commission shall be entitled to adopt such working methods as it deems to be necessary and expedient and shall establish appropriate rules of procedure.

*Article 17*. The Members of the Commission, when engaged in the business of the Commission, shall enjoy diplomatic privileges and immunities as provided for in the Convention on Privileges and Immunities of the Organization of African Unity.

*Article 18*. Where, in the course of Mediation, Conciliation or Arbitration, it is deemed necessary to conduct an investigation or inquiry for the purpose of elucidating facts or circumstances relating to a matter in dispute, the parties concerned and all other Member States shall extend to those engaged in any such proceedings the fullest co-operation in the conduct of such investigation or inquiry.

*Article 19.* In case of a dispute between Member States, the parties may agree to resort to any one of these modes of settlement: Mediation, Conciliation and Arbitration.

## Mediation

*Article 20.* When a dispute between Member States is referred to the Commission for Mediation, the President shall, with the consent of the parties, appoint one or more members of the Commission to mediate the dispute.

*Article 21.* 1. The role of the mediator shall be confined to reconciling the views and claims of the parties.

2. The mediator shall make written proposals to the parties as expeditiously as possible.

3. If the means of reconciliation proposed by the mediator are accepted, they shall become the basis of a protocol of arrangement between the parties.

## Conciliation

*Article 22.* 1. A request for the settlement of a dispute by conciliation may be submitted to the Commission by means of a petition addressed to the President by one or more of the parties to the dispute.

2. If the request is made by only one of the parties, that party shall indicate that prior written notice has been given to the other party.

3. The petition shall include a summary explanation of the grounds of the dispute.

*Article 23.* 1. Upon receipt of the petition, the President shall, in agreement with the parties, establish a Board of Conciliators, of whom three shall be appointed by the President from among the Members of the Commission, and one each by the parties.

2. The Chairman of the Board shall be a person designated by the President from among the three Members of the Commission.

3. In nominating persons to serve as Members of the Board, the parties to the dispute shall designate persons in such a way that no two Members of it shall be nationals of the same State.

*Article 24.* 1. It shall be the duty of the Board of Conciliators to clarify the issues in dispute and to endeavour to bring about an agreement between the parties upon mutually acceptable terms.

2. The Board shall consider all questions submitted to it and may undertake any inquiry or hear any person capable of giving relevant information concerning the dispute.

3. In the absence of disagreement between the parties, the Board shall determine its own procedure.

*Article 25.* The parties shall be represented by agents, whose duty shall be to act as intermediaries between them and the Board. They may moreover be assisted by counsel and experts and may request that all persons whose evidence appears to the Board to be relevant shall be heard.

*Article 26.* 1. At the close of the proceedings, the Board shall draw up a report stating either:

(a) that the parties have come to an agreement and, if the need arises, the terms of the agreement and any recommendations for settlement made by the Board; or

(b) that it has been impossible to effect a settlement.

2. The Report of the Board of Conciliators shall be communicated to the parties and to the President of the Commission without delay and may be published only with the consent of the parties.

## Arbitration

*Article 27.* 1. Where it is agreed that arbitration should be resorted to, the Arbitral Tribunal shall be established in the following manner:

(a) each party shall designate one arbitrator from among the Members of the Commission having legal qualifications;

(b) the two arbitrators thus designated shall, by common agreement, designate from among the Members of the Commission a third person who shall act as Chairman of the Tribunal;

(c) where the two arbitrators fail to agree, within one month of their appointment, in the choice of the person to be Chairman of the Tribunal, the Bureau shall designate the Chairman.

2. The President may, with the agreement of the parties, appoint to the Arbitral Tribunal two additional Members who need not be Members of the Commission but who shall have the same powers as the other Members of the Tribunal.

3. The arbitrators shall not be nationals of the parties, or have their domicile in the territories of the parties, or be employed in their service, or have served as mediators or conciliators in the same dispute. They shall all be of different nationalities.

*Article 28.* Recourse to arbitration shall be regarded as submission in good faith to the award of the Arbitral Tribunal.

*Article 29.* 1. The parties shall, in each case, conclude a *compromis* which shall specify:

(a) the undertaking of the parties to go to arbitration, and to accept as legally binding, the decision of the Tribunal;

(b) the subject matter of the controversy; and

(c) the seat of the Tribunal.

2. The *compromis* may specify the law to be applied by the Tribunal and the power, if the parties so agree, to adjudicate *ex aequo et bono,* the time-limit within which the award of the arbitrators shall be given, and the appointment of agents and counsel to take part in the proceedings before the Tribunal.

*Article 30.* In the absence of any provision in the *compromis* regarding the applicable law, the Arbitral Tribunal shall decide the dispute according to treaties concluded between the parties, International Law, the Charter of the Organization of African Unity, the Charter of the United Nations and, if the parties agree, *ex aequo et bono.*

*Article 31.* 1. Hearings shall be held in *camera* unless the arbitrators decide otherwise.

2. The record of the proceedings signed by the arbitrators and the Registrar shall alone be authoritative.

3. The arbitral award shall be in writing and shall, in respect of every point decided, state the reasons on which it is based.

## Final Provisions

*Article 32.* The present Protocol shall, after approval by the Assembly of Heads of State and Government, be an integral part of the Charter of the Organization of African Unity.

*Article 33.* This Protocol may be amended or revised in accordance with the provisions of Article 33 of the Charter of the Organization of African Unity.

In faith whereof, We the Heads of African State and Government, have signed this Protocol.

**SEE ALSO** *African Charter on Human and Peoples' Rights.*

# O

**ORGANIZATION OF AMERICAN STATES (OAS).**
A regional intergovernmental organization composed of 32 countries of North, South, and Central America: Antigua and Barbuda, Argentina, Bahamas, Barbados, Bolivia, Brazil, Chile, Colombia, Costa Rica, Cuba, Dominica, Dominican Republic, Ecuador, El Salvador, Grenada, Guatemala, Haiti, Honduras, Jamaica, Mexico, Nicaragua, Panama, Paraguay, Peru, St. Christopher and Nevis, St. Lucia, St. Vincent–Grenadines, Suriname, Trinidad and Tobago, the United States of America, Uruguay, and Venezuela. However, the Government of Cuba has been excluded from participation in the Inter-American System since 1962.

The OAS developed out of the International Union of American Republics, established on 14 April 1890 by the First International Conference of American States, convened in Washington, D.C. The name of the organization was first changed, in 1910, to Union of American Republics, then changed again to Organization of American States on 30 April 1948 when the Ninth International Conference of American States adopted the **ORGANIZATION OF AMERICAN STATES CHARTER.** The 1948 Conference also adopted the **AMERICAN DECLARATION OF THE RIGHTS AND DUTIES OF MAN.**

In 1959, the **INTER-AMERICAN COMMISSION ON HUMAN RIGHTS** was authorized by the Fifth Meeting of Consultation of Ministers of Foreign Affairs, convened in Santiago, Chile. The Commission's statute, approved by the Council, provided that the Commission would function as an autonomous entity of OAS and that the human rights referred to in the statute were those set forth in the American Declaration of the Rights and Duties of Man.

The 1981 Inter-American Conference of American States adopted and opened for signature and ratification or accession the **AMERICAN CONVENTION ON HUMAN RIGHTS,** also known as the Pact of San Jose. When this Convention entered into force in 1978, authority was provided for the establishment of the **INTER-AMERICAN COURT OF HUMAN RIGHTS.**

In 1985, the OAS General Assembly, at a special session in Cartagena, Colombia, approved the Protocol of Amendment to the Charter of the Organization of American States, also known as the Protocol of Cartagena de Indias. The Protocol entered into force in November 1988 upon ratification by two-thirds of the present OAS membership.

In its annual report for 1985–1986 (OAS Doc. OEA/ Ser. L/V/II.68, Doc. 8, Rev. 1), the Inter-American Commission on Human Rights submitted to the OAS General Assembly, as the Assembly had requested in resolution 778 (XV-O/85), a draft additional protocol, incorporating economic, social, and cultural rights into the Convention. The additional protocol was approved unanimously by the OAS General Assembly on 17 November 1988.

*PURPOSE AND FUNCTIONS.* Under the OAS Charter, as amended by the Protocol of Cartagena de Indias, the essential purposes of the organization are (article 2):

(a) To strengthen the peace and security of the continent;

(b) To promote and consolidate representative democracy, with due respect for the principle of nonintervention;

(c) To prevent possible causes of difficulties and to ensure the pacific settlement of disputes that may arise among the Member States;

(d) To provide for common action on the part of those States in the event of aggression;

(e) To seek the solution of political, juridical, and economic problems that may arise among them;

(f) To promote, by cooperative action, their economic, social and cultural development, and

(g) To achieve an effective limitation of conventional weapons that will make it possible to devote the largest amount of resources to the economic and social development of the Member States.

Under the Charter, as amended, the following principles are reaffirmed (article 3):

(a) International law is the standard of conduct of States in their reciprocal relations;

(b) International order consists essentially of respect for the personality, sovereignty, and independence of States, and the faithful fulfillment of obligations derived from treaties and other sources of international law;

(c) Good faith shall govern the relations between States;

(d) The solidarity of the American States and the high aims which are sought through it require the political organization of those States on the basis of the effective exercise of representative democracy;

(e) Every State has the right to choose, without external interference, its political, economic, and social system and to organize itself in the way best suited to it, and has the duty to abstain from intervening in the affairs of another State. Subject to the foregoing, the American States shall cooperate fully among themselves, independently of the nature of their political, economic, and social systems;

(f) The American States condemn war of aggression: victory does not give rights;

(g) An act of aggression against one American State is an act of aggression against all the other American States;

(h) Controversies of an international character arising between two or more American States shall be settled by peaceful procedures;

(i) Social justice and social security are bases of lasting peace;

(j) Economic cooperation is essential to the common welfare and prosperity of the peoples of the continent;

(k) The American States proclaim the fundamental rights of the individual without distinction as to race, nationality, creed, or sex;

(l) The spiritual unity of the continent is based on respect for the cultural values of the American countries and requires their close cooperation for the high purposes of civilization;

(m) The education of peoples should be directed toward justice, freedom and peace.

The functions and procedures of the major organs of the Organization of American States are set out in the Charter, as amended, as follows:

(a) OAS General Assembly (chapter 9);

(b) OAS Meeting of Consultation of Ministers of Foreign Affairs (chapter 10);

(c) OAS Permanent Council (chapter 12);

(d) Inter-American Economic and Social Council (chapter 13);

(e) Inter-American Council for Education, Science and Culture (chapter 14);

(f) Inter-American Juridical Committee (chapter 15);

(g) Inter-American Commission on Human Rights (chapter 16);

(h) OAS General Secretariat (chapter 17); and

(i) Inter-American Specialized Organizations (chapter 19).

**OAS GENERAL ASSEMBLY.** The General Assembly is the supreme organ of the Organization of American States. Its functions, powers, and organizational arrangements are set out in chapter 9 of the Organization of American States Charter.

The General Assembly's basic task is to determine and monitor the general action and policy of the Organization, exercising its powers in accordance with the Charter and other Inter-American treaties. All member States of the OAS are entitled to be represented in the Assembly, which normally convenes once a year.

**OAS MEETING OF CONSULTATION OF MINISTERS OF FOREIGN AFFAIRS.** Composed of ministers of foreign affairs of all member States of the OAS, the group meets at the request of any member State to consider problems of an urgent nature and of common interest. It considers any threat to the peace and security of the American hemisphere in accordance with the Inter-American Treaty of Reciprocal Assistance, signed in Rio de Janeiro in 1947. Its organization and terms of reference are set out in the Organization of American States Charter, chapter 10.

**OAS PERMANENT COUNCIL.** The Permanent Council is the organ of the Organization of American States which assists member States in the peaceful settlement of their disputes. Its functions, powers, and organizational arrangements are set out in chapter 12 of the Organization of American States Charter. It is composed of one representative of each member State, especially appointed by the respective government, with the rank of ambassador.

**OAS SPECIALIZED CONFERENCES.** Arrangements for the convening of intergovernmental meetings to deal with technical matters or to develop specific aspects of inter-American cooperation are set out in chapter 18 of the Organization of American States Charter.

**OAS SPECIALIZED ORGANIZATIONS.** Six organizations which have specific functions with respect to technical matters of common interest to the American States are recognized by the Organization of American States as specialized organizations. They are: The Inter-American Children's Institute, the Inter-American Commission of Women, the Inter-American Indian Institute, the Inter-American Institute for Co-operation on Agriculture, the Pan American Health Organization, and the Pan American Institute of Geography and History. Rules governing relations between the OAS and these specialized organizations are set out in chapter 19 of the Organization of American States Charter.

Organization of American States. Address: 17th and Constitution Ave., NW, Washington, D.C., 20006, USA. Telephone: (202) 789-3000. Cable: OASWSHDC. Telex: 64128-24838. Secretary-General: Joao Clemente Baena Soares.

**SEE ALSO** *American Convention on Human Rights; American Declaration of the Rights and Duties of Man; Inter-American Charter of Social Guarantees; Inter-American Commission on Human Rights; Inter-American Court of Human Rights.*

**BIBLIOGRAPHY.** Buergenthal, Thomas, Robert Norris, and Dinah Shelton. *Protecting Human Rights in the Americas: Selected Problems.* Kehl, Germany: International Institute of Human Rights and N.P. Engel [D], 1990. Scholarly monograph, in English; bibliography, pp. 463–472.

Inter-American Commission on Human Rights and Inter-American Court of Human Rights. *Inter-American Yearbook on Human Rights, 1960–1970.* Boston, MA, USA: Martinus Nijhoff, 1972–present. IGO annual report, in English and Spanish.

Kokott, Juliane. "No Impunity for Human Rights Violations in the Americas," *Human Rights Law Journal* 14, no. 5–6 (June 1993): 153–159. Scholarly article, in English.

LeBlanc, Larry. "The Economic, Social and Cultural Rights Protocol to the American Convention and Its Background," *Netherlands Quarterly of Human Rights* 10, no. 2 (1992): 130–154. Scholarly article, in English.

Medina, Cecilia. "The Inter-American Commission on Human Rights and the Inter-American Court of Human Rights: Reflections on a Joint Venture," *Human Rights Quarterly* 12, no. 4 (Nov. 1990): 439–464. Scholarly article, in English.

Mower, Jr., A. Glenn. *Regional Human Rights: A Comparative Study of the West European and Inter-American Systems.* Westport,

CT, USA: Greenwood Press, 1991. Scholarly monograph, in English; bibliography, pp. 171–174.

## ORGANIZATION OF AMERICAN STATES CHARTER (1948).

The Charter was opened for signature on 30 April 1948 at the Ninth International Conference of American States and entered into force on 13 December 1951. It was amended first by the protocol known as the Protocol of Buenos Aires, signed on 27 February 1967 at the Third Special Inter-American Conference, which entered into force on 27 February 1970, and later by the protocol known as the Protocol of Cartagena de Indias, which entered into force on 16 November 1988.

The integrated text of the Charter, as amended by the protocols, is as follows (*OAS Treaty Series* 1–D):

In the name of their peoples, the States represented at the Ninth International Conference of American States,

Convinced that the historic mission of America is to offer to man a land of liberty and a favorable environment for the development of his personality and the realization of his just aspirations;

Conscious that that mission has already inspired numerous agreements, whose essential value lies in the desire of the American peoples to live together in peace and, through their mutual understanding and respect for the sovereignty of each one, to provide for the betterment of all, in independence, in equality and under law;

Convinced that representative democracy is an indispensable condition for the stability, peace and development of the region;

Confident that the true significance of American solidarity and good neighborliness can only mean the consolidation on this continent, within the framework of democratic institutions, of a system of individual liberty and social justice based on respect for the essential rights of man;

Persuaded that their welfare and their contribution to the progress and the civilization of the world will increasingly require intensive continental cooperation;

Resolved to persevere in the noble undertaking that humanity has conferred upon the United Nations, whose principles and purposes they solemnly reaffirm;

Convinced that juridical organization is a necessary condition for security and peace founded on moral order and on justice; and

In accordance with Resolution IX of the Inter-American Conference on Problems of War and Peace, held in Mexico City,

Have agreed upon the following

### Part One

### Chapter 1: Nature and Purposes

*Article 1.* The American States establish by this Charter the international organization that they have developed to achieve an order of peace and justice, to promote their solidarity, to strengthen their collaboration, and to defend their sovereignty, their territorial integrity, and their independence. Within the United Nations, the Organization of American States is a regional agency.

The Organization of American States has no powers other than those expressly conferred upon it by this Charter, none of whose provisions authorizes it to intervene in matters that are within the internal jurisdiction of the Member States.

*Article 2.* The Organization of American States, in order to put into practice the principles on which it is founded and to fulfill its regional obligations under the Charter of the United Nations, proclaims the following essential purposes:

(a) To strengthen the peace and security of the continent;

(b) To promote and consolidate representative democracy, with due respect for the principle of nonintervention;

(c) To prevent possible causes of difficulties and to ensure the pacific settlement of disputes that may arise among the Member States;

(d) To provide for common action on the part of those States in the event of aggression;

(e) To seek the solution of political, juridical, and economic problems that may arise among them;

(f) To promote, by cooperative action, their economic, social, and cultural development; and

(g) To achieve an effective limitation of conventional weapons that will make it possible to devote the largest amount of resources to the economic and social development of the Member States.

### Chapter 2: Principles

*Article 3.* The American states reaffirm the following principles:

(a) International law is the standard of conduct of States in their reciprocal relations;

(b) International order consists essentially of respect for the personality, sovereignty, and independence of States, and the faithful fulfillment of obligations derived from treaties and other sources of international law;

(c) Good faith shall govern the relations between States;

(d) The solidarity of the American States and the high aims which are sought through it require the political organization of those States on the basis of the effective exercise of representative democracy;

(e) Every State has the right to choose, without external interference, its political, economic, and social system and to organize itself in the way best suited to it, and has the duty to abstain from intervening in the affairs of another State. Subject to the foregoing, the American States shall cooperate fully among themselves, independently of the nature of their political, economic, and social systems;

(f) The American States condemn war of aggression: victory does not give rights;

(g) An act of aggression against one American State is an act of aggression against all the other American States;

(h) Controversies of an international character arising between two or more American States shall be settled by peaceful procedures;

(i) Social justice and social security are bases of lasting peace;

(j) Economic cooperation is essential to the common welfare and prosperity of the peoples of the continent;

(k) The American States proclaim the fundamental rights of the individual without distinction as to race, nationality, creed, or sex;

(l) The spiritual unity of the continent is based on respect for the cultural values of the American countries and requires their close cooperation for the high purposes of civilization;

(m) The education of peoples should be directed toward justice, freedom, and peace.

### Chapter 3: Members

*Article 4.* All American States that ratify the present Charter are Members of the Organization.

*Article 5.* Any new political entity that arises from the union of several Member States and that, as such, ratifies the present Charter, shall become a Member of the Organization. The entry of the new political entity into the Organization shall result in the loss of membership of each one of the States which constitute it.

*Article 6.* Any other independent American State that desires to become a Member of the Organization should so indicate by means of a note addressed to the Secretary General, in which it declares that it is willing to sign and ratify the Charter of the Organization and to accept all the obligations inherent in membership, especially those relating to collective security expressly set forth in Articles 27 and 28 of the Charter.

*Article 7.* The General Assembly, upon the recommendation of the Permanent Council of the Organization, shall determine whether it is appropriate that the Secretary General be authorized to permit the applicant State to sign the Charter and to accept the deposit of the corresponding instrument of ratification. Both the recommendation of the Permanent Council and the decision of the General Assembly shall require the affirmative vote of two thirds of the Member States.

*Article 8.* Membership in the Organization shall be confined to independent States of the Hemisphere that were members of the United Nations as of December 10, 1985, and the nonautonomous territories mentioned in document OEA/Ser. P, AG/doc.1939/85, of November 5, 1985, when they become independent.

### Chapter 4: Fundamental Rights and Duties of States

*Article 9.* States are juridically equal, enjoy equal rights and equal capacity to exercise these rights, and have equal duties. The rights of each State depend not upon its power to ensure the exercise thereof, but upon the mere fact of its existence as a person under international law.

*Article 10.* Every American State has the duty to respect the rights enjoyed by every other State in accordance with international law.

*Article 11.* The fundamental rights of States may not be impaired in any manner whatsoever.

*Article 12.* The political existence of the State is independent of recognition by other States. Even before being recognized, the State has the right to defend its integrity and independence, to provide for its preservation and prosperity, and consequently to organize itself as it sees fit, to legislate concerning its interests, to administer its services, and to determine the jurisdiction and competence of its courts. The exercise of these rights is limited only by the exercise of the rights of other States in accordance with international law.

*Article 13.* Recognition implies that the State granting it accepts the personality of the new State, with all the rights and duties that international law prescribes for the two States.

*Article 14.* The right of each State to protect itself and to live its own life does not authorize it to commit unjust acts against another State.

*Article 15.* The jurisdiction of States within the limits of their national territory is exercised equally over all the inhabitants, whether nationals or aliens.

*Article 16.* Each State has the right to develop its cultural, political, and economic life freely and naturally. In this free development, the State shall respect the rights of the individual and the principles of universal morality.

*Article 17.* Respect for and the faithful observance of treaties constitute standards for the development of peaceful relations among States. International treaties and agreements should be public.

*Article 18.* No State or group of States has the right to intervene, directly or indirectly, for any reason whatever, in the internal or external affairs of any other State. The foregoing principle prohibits not only armed force but also any other form of interference or attempted threat against the personality of the State or against its political, economic, and cultural elements.

*Article 19.* No State may use or encourage the use of coercive measures of an economic or political character in order to force the sovereign will of another State and obtain from it advantages of any kind.

*Article 20.* The territory of a State is inviolable; it may not be the object, even temporarily, of military occupation or of other measures of force taken by another State, directly or indirectly, on any grounds whatever. No territorial acquisitions or special advantages obtained either by force or by other means of coercion shall be recognized.

*Article 21.* The American States bind themselves in their international relations not to have recourse to the use of force, except in the case of self-defense in accordance with existing treaties or in fulfillment thereof.

*Article 22.* Measures adopted for the maintenance of peace and security in accordance with existing treaties do not constitute a violation of the principles set forth in Articles 18 and 20.

### Chapter 5: Pacific Settlement of Disputes

*Article 23.* International disputes between Member States shall be submitted to the peaceful procedures set forth in this Charter.

This provision shall not be interpreted as an impairment of the rights and obligations of the Member States under Articles 34 and 35 of the Charter of the United Nations.

*Article 24.* The following are peaceful procedures: direct negotiation, good offices, mediation, investigation and conciliation, judicial settlement, arbitration, and those which the parties to the dispute may especially agree upon at any time.

*Article 25.* In the event that a dispute arises between two or more American States which, in the opinion of one of them, cannot be settled through the usual diplomatic channels, the parties shall agree on some other peaceful procedure that will enable them to reach a solution.

*Article 26.* A special treaty will establish adequate means for the settlement of disputes and will determine pertinent procedures for such peaceful means such that no dispute between American States may remain without definitive settlement within a reasonable period of time.

## Chapter 6: Collective Security

*Article 27.* Every act of aggression by a State against the territorial integrity or the inviolability of the territory or against the sovereignty or political independence of an American State shall be considered an act of aggression against the other American States.

*Article 28.* If the inviolability or the integrity of the territory or the sovereignty or political independence of any American State should be affected by an armed attack or by an act of aggression that is not an armed attack, or by an extracontinental conflict, or by a conflict between two or more American States, or by any other fact or situation that might endanger the peace of America, the American States, in furtherance of the principles of continental solidarity or collective self-defense, shall apply the measures and procedures established in the special treaties on the subject.

## Chapter 7: Integral Development

*Article 29.* The Member States, inspired by the principles of inter-American solidarity and cooperation, pledge themselves to a united effort to ensure international social justice in their relations and integral development for their peoples, as conditions essential to peace and security. Integral development encompasses the economic, social, educational, cultural, scientific, and technological fields through which the goals that each country sets for accomplishing it should be achieved.

*Article 30.* Inter-American cooperation for integral development is the common and joint responsibility of the Member States, within the framework of the democratic principles and the institutions of the inter-American system. It should include the economic, social, educational, cultural, scientific, and technological fields, support the achievement of national objectives of the Member States, and respect the priorities established by each country in its development plans, without political ties or conditions.

*Article 31.* Inter-American cooperation for integral development should be continuous and preferably channeled through multilateral organizations, without prejudice to bilateral cooperation between Member States.

The Member States shall contribute to inter-American cooperation for integral development in accordance with their resources and capabilities and in conformity with their laws.

*Article 32.* Development is a primary responsibility of each country and should constitute an integral and continuous process for the establishment of a more just economic and social order that will make possible and contribute to the fulfillment of the individual.

*Article 33.* The Member States agree that equality of opportunity, equitable distribution of wealth and income, and the full participation of their peoples in decisions relating to their own development are, among others, basic objectives of integral development. To achieve them, they likewise agree to devote their utmost efforts to accomplishing the following basic goals:

(a) Substantial and self-sustained increase of per capita national product;

(b) Equitable distribution of national income;

(c) Adequate and equitable systems of taxation;

(d) Modernization of rural life and reforms leading to equitable and efficient land-tenure systems, increased agricultural productivity, expanded use of land, diversification of production and improved processing and marketing systems for agricultural products; and the strengthening and expansion of the means to attain these ends;

(e) Accelerated and diversified industrialization, especially of capital and intermediate goods;

(f) Stability of domestic price levels, compatible with sustained economic development and the attainment of social justice;

(g) Fair wages, employment opportunities, and acceptable working conditions for all;

(h) Rapid eradication of illiteracy and expansion of educational opportunities for all;

(i) Protection of man's potential through the extension and application of modern medical science;

(j) Proper nutrition, especially through the acceleration of national efforts to increase the production and availability of food;

(k) Adequate housing for all sectors of the population;

(l) Urban conditions that offer the opportunity for a healthful, productive, and full life;

(m) Promotion of private initiative and investment in harmony with action in the public sector; and

(n) Expansion and diversification of exports.

*Article 34.* The Member States should refrain from practicing policies and adopting actions or measures that have serious adverse effects on the development of other Member States.

*Article 35.* Transnational enterprises and foreign private investment shall be subject to the legislation of the host countries and to the jurisdiction of their competent courts and to the international treaties and agreements to which said counties are parties, and should conform to the development policies of the recipient countries.

*Article 36.* The Member States agree to join together in seeking a solution to urgent or critical problems that may arise whenever the economic development or stability of any Member State is seriously affected by conditions that cannot be remedied through the efforts of that State.

*Article 37.* The Member States shall extend among themselves the benefits of science and technology by encouraging the exchange and utilization of scientific and technical knowledge in accordance with existing treaties and national laws.

*Article 38.* The Member States, recognizing the close interdependence between foreign trade and economic and social development, should make individual and united efforts to bring about the following:

(a) Favorable conditions of access to world markets for the products of the developing countries of the region, particularly through the reduction or elimination, by importing countries, of tariff and nontariff barriers that affect the exports of the Member States of the Organization, except when such barriers are applied in order to diversify the economic structure, to speed up the development of the less-developed Member States, and intensify their process of economic integration, or when they are related to national security or to the needs of economic balance;

(b) Continuity in their economic and social development by means of:

(i) Improved conditions for trade in basic commodities through international agreements, where appropriate; orderly marketing procedures that avoid the disruption of markets, and other measures designed to promote the expansion of markets and to obtain dependable incomes for producers, adequate and dependable supplies for consumers, and stable prices that are both remunerative to producers and fair to consumers;

(ii) Improved international financial cooperation and the adoption of other means for lessening the adverse impact of sharp fluctuations in export earnings experienced by the countries exporting basic commodities;

(iii) Diversification of exports and expansion of export opportunities for manufactured and semimanufactured products from the developing countries; and

(iv) Conditions conducive to increasing the real export earnings of the Member States, particularly the developing countries of the region, and to increasing their participation in international trade.

*Article 39.* The Member States reaffirm the principle that when the more developed countries grant concessions in international trade-agreements that lower or eliminate tariffs or other barriers to foreign trade so that they benefit the less-developed countries, they should not expect reciprocal concessions from those countries that are incompatible with their economic development, financial, and trade needs.

*Article 40.* The Member States, in order to accelerate their economic development, regional integration, and the expansion and improvement of the conditions of their commerce, shall promote improvement and coordination of transportation and communication in the developing countries and among the Member States.

*Article 41.* The Member States recognize that integration of the developing countries of the Hemisphere is one of the objectives of the inter-American system and, therefore, shall orient their efforts and take the necessary measures to accelerate the integration process, with a view to establishing a Latin American common market in the shortest possible time.

*Article 42.* In order to strengthen and accelerate integration in all its aspects, the Member States agree to give adequate priority to the preparation and carrying out of multinational projects and to their financing, as well as to encourage economic and financial institutions of the inter-American system to continue giving their broadest support to regional integration institutions and programs.

*Article 43.* The Member States agree that technical and financial cooperation that seeks to promote regional economic integration should be based on the principle of harmonious, balanced, and efficient development, with particular attention to the relatively less-developed countries, so that it may be a decisive factor that will enable them to promote, with their own efforts, the improved development of their infrastructure programs, new lines of production, and export diversification.

*Article 44.* The Member States, convinced that man can only achieve the full realization of his aspirations within a just social order, along with economic development and true peace, agree to dedicate every effort to the application of the following principles and mechanisms:

(a) All human beings, without distinction as to race, sex, nationality, creed, or social condition, have a right to material well-being and to their spiritual development, under circumstances of liberty, dignity, equality of opportunity, and economic security;

(b) Work is a right and a social duty, it gives dignity to the one who performs it, and it should be performed under conditions, including a system of fair wages, that ensure life, health, and a decent standard of living for the worker and his family, both during his working years and in his old age, or when any circumstance deprives him of the possibility of working;

(c) Employers and workers, both rural and urban, have the right to associate themselves freely for the defense and promotion of their interests, including the right to collective bargaining and the workers' right to strike, and recognition of the juridical personality of associations and the protection of their freedom and independence, all in accordance with applicable laws;

(d) Fair and efficient systems and procedures for consultation and collaboration among the sectors of production, with due regard for safeguarding the interests of the entire society;

(e) The operation of systems of public administration, banking and credit, enterprise, and distribution and sales, in such a way, in harmony with the private sector, as to meet the requirements and interests of the community;

(f) The incorporation and increasing participation of the marginal sectors of the population, in both rural and urban areas, in the economic, social, civic, cultural, and political life of the nation, in order to achieve the full integration of the national community, acceleration of the process of social mobility, and the consolidation of the democratic system. The encouragement of all efforts of popular promotion and cooperation that have as their purpose the development and progress of the community;

(g) Recognition of the importance of the contribution of organizations such as labor unions, cooperatives, and cultural, professional, business, neighborhood, and community associations to the life of the society and to the development process;

(h) Development of an efficient social security policy; and

(i) Adequate provision for all persons to have due legal aid in order to secure their rights.

*Article 45.* The Member States recognize that, in order to facilitate the process of Latin American regional integration, it is necessary to harmonize the social legislation of the developing countries, especially in the labor and social security fields, so that the rights of the workers shall be equally protected, and they agree to make the greatest efforts possible to achieve this goal.

*Article 46.* The Member States will give primary importance within their development plans to the encouragement of education, science, technology, and culture, oriented toward the overall improvement of the individual, and as a foundation for democracy, social justice, and progress.

*Article 47.* The Member States will cooperate with one another to meet their educational needs, to promote scientific research, and to encourage technological progress for their integral development. They will consider themselves individually and jointly bound to preserve and enrich the cultural heritage of the American peoples.

*Article 48.* The Member States will exert the greatest efforts, in accordance with their constitutional processes, to ensure the effective exercise of the right to education, on the following bases:

(a) Elementary education, compulsory for children of school age, shall also be offered to all others who can benefit from it. When provided by the State it shall be without charge;

(b) Middle-level education shall be extended progressively to as much of the population as possible, with a view to social improvement. It shall be diversified in such a way that it meets the development needs of each country without prejudice to providing a general education; and

(c) Higher education shall be available to all, provided that, in order to maintain its high level, the corresponding regulatory or academic standards are met.

*Article 49.* The Member States will give special attention

to the eradication of illiteracy, will strengthen adult and vocational education systems, and will ensure that the benefits of culture will be available to the entire population. They will promote the use of all information media to fulfill these aims.

*Article 50.* The Member States will develop science and technology through educational, research, and technological development activities and information and dissemination programs. They will stimulate activities in the field of technology for the purpose of adapting it to the needs of their integral development. They will organize their cooperation in these fields efficiently and will substantially increase exchange of knowledge, in accordance with national objectives and laws and with treaties in force.

*Article 51.* The Member States, with due respect for the individuality of each of them, agree to promote cultural exchange as an effective means of consolidating inter-American understanding; and they recognize that regional integration programs should be strengthened by close ties in the fields of education, science, and culture.

## Part Two

### Chapter 8: The Organs

*Article 52.* The Organization of American States accomplishes its purposes by means of:

    (a) The General Assembly;

    (b) The Meeting of Consultation of Ministers of Foreign Affairs;

    (c) The Councils;

    (d) The Inter-American Juridical Committee;

    (e) The Inter-American Commission on Human Rights;

    (f) The General Secretariat;

    (g) The Specialized Conferences; and

    (h) The Specialized Organizations.

There may be established, in addition to those provided for in the Charter and in accordance with the provisions thereof, such subsidiary organs, agencies, and other entities as are considered necessary.

### Chapter 9: The General Assembly

*Article 53.* The General Assembly is the supreme organ of the Organization of American States. It has as its principal powers, in addition to such others as are assigned to it by the Charter, the following:

    (a) To decide the general action and policy of the Organization, determine the structure and functions of its organs, and consider any matter relating to friendly relations among the American States;

    (b) To establish measures for coordinating the activities of the organs, agencies, and entities of the Organization among themselves, and such activities with those of the other institutions of the inter-American system;

    (c) To strengthen and coordinate cooperation with the United Nations and its specialized agencies;

    (d) To promote collaboration, especially in the economic, social, and cultural fields, with other international organizations whose purposes are similar to those of the Organization of American States;

    (e) To approve the program-budget of the Organization and determine the quotas of the Member States;

    (f) To consider the reports of the Meeting of Consultation of Ministers of Foreign Affairs and the observations and recommendations presented by the Permanent Council with regard to the reports that should be presented by the other organs and entities, in accordance with the provisions of paragraph f of Article 90, as well as the reports of any organ which may be required by the General Assembly itself;

    (g) To adopt general standards to govern the operations of the General Secretariat; and

    (h) To adopt its own rules of procedure and, by a two-thirds vote, its agenda.

The General Assembly shall exercise its powers in accordance with the provisions of the Charter and of other inter-American treaties.

*Article 54.* The General Assembly shall establish the bases for fixing the quota that each Government is to contribute to the maintenance of the Organization, taking into account the ability to pay of the respective countries and their determination to contribute in an equitable manner. Decisions on budgetary matters require the approval of two thirds of the Member States.

*Article 55.* All member States have the right to be represented in the General Assembly. Each State has the right to one vote.

*Article 56.* The General Assembly shall convene annually during the period determined by the rules of procedure and at a place selected in accordance with the principle of rotation. At each regular session the date and place of the next regular session shall be determined, in accordance with the rules of procedure.

If for any reason the General Assembly cannot be held at the place chosen, it shall meet at the General Secretariat, unless one of the Member States should make a timely offer of a site in its territory, in which case the Permanent Council of the Organization may agree that the General Assembly will meet in that place.

*Article 57.* In special circumstances and with the approval of two thirds of the Member States, the Permanent Council shall convoke a special session of the General Assembly.

*Article 58.* Decisions of the General Assembly shall be adopted by the affirmative vote of an absolute majority of the Member States, except in those cases that require a two-thirds vote as provided in the Charter or as may be provided by the General Assembly in its rules of procedure.

*Article 59.* There shall be a Preparatory Committee of the General Assembly, composed of representatives of all the Member States, which shall:

    (a) Prepare the draft agenda of each session of the General Assembly;

    (b) Review the proposed program-budget and the draft resolution on quotas, and present to the General Assembly a report thereon containing the recommendations it considers appropriate; and

    (c) Carry out such other functions as the General Assembly may assign to it.

The draft agenda and the report shall, in due course, be transmitted to the Governments of the Member States.

### Chapter 10: The Meeting of Consultation of Ministers of Foreign Affairs

*Article 60.* The Meeting of Consultation of Ministers of Foreign Affairs shall be held in order to consider problems of an urgent nature and of common interest to the American States, and to serve as the Organ of Consultation.

*Article 61.* Any Member State may request that a Meeting of Consultation be called. The request shall be addressed to the Permanent Council of the Organization, which shall decide by an absolute majority whether a meeting should be held.

*Article 62.* The agenda and regulations of the Meeting of Consultation shall be prepared by the Permanent Council of the Organization and submitted to the Member States for consideration.

*Article 63.* If, for exceptional reasons, a Minister of Foreign Affairs is unable to attend the meeting, he shall be represented by a special delegate.

*Article 64.* In case of an armed attack on the territory of an American State or within the region of security delimited by the treaty in force, the Chairman of the Permanent Council shall without delay call a meeting of the Council to decide on the convocation of the Meeting of Consultation, without prejudice to the provisions of the Inter-American Treaty of Reciprocal Assistance with regard to the States Parties to that instrument.

*Article 65.* An Advisory Defense Committee shall be established to advise the Organ of Consultation on problems of military cooperation that may arise in connection with the application of existing special treaties on collective security.

*Article 66.* The Advisory Defense Committee shall be composed of the highest military authorities of the American States participating in the Meeting of Consultation. Under exceptional circumstances the Governments may appoint substitutes. Each State shall be entitled to one vote.

*Article 67.* The Advisory Defense Committee shall be convoked under the same conditions as the Organ of Consultation, when the latter deals with matters relating to defense against aggression.

*Article 68.* The Committee shall also meet when the General Assembly or the Meeting of Consultation or the Governments, by a two-thirds majority of the Member States, assign to it technical studies or reports on specific subjects.

## Chapter 11: The Councils of the Organization Common Provisions

*Article 69.* The Permanent Council of the Organization, the Inter-American Economic and Social Council, and the Inter-American Council for Education, Science, and Culture are directly responsible to the General Assembly and each has the authority granted to it in the Charter and other inter-American instruments, as well as the functions assigned to it by the General Assembly and the Meeting of Consultation of Ministers of Foreign Affairs.

*Article 70.* All Member States have the right to be represented on each of the Councils. Each State has the right to one vote.

*Article 71.* The Councils may, within the limits of the Charter and other inter-American instruments, make recommendations on matters within their authority.

*Article 72.* The Councils, on matters within their respective competence, may present to the General Assembly studies and proposals, drafts of international instruments, and proposals on the holding of specialized conferences, on the creation, modification, or elimination of specialized organizations and other inter-American agencies, as well as on the coordination of their activities. The Councils may also present studies, proposals, and drafts of international instruments to the Specialized Conferences.

*Article 73.* Each Council may, in urgent cases, convoke Specialized Conferences on matters within its competence,

after consulting with the Member States and without having to resort to the procedure provided for in Article 127.

*Article 74.* The Councils, to the extent of their ability, and with the cooperation of the General Secretariat, shall render to the Governments such specialized services as the latter may request.

*Article 75.* Each Council has the authority to require the other Councils, as well as the subsidiary organs and agencies responsible to them, to provide it with information and advisory services on matters within their respective spheres of competence. The Councils may also request the same services from the other agencies of the inter-American system.

*Article 76.* With the prior approval of the General Assembly, the Councils may establish the subsidiary organs and the agencies that they consider advisable for the better performance of their duties. When the General Assembly is not in session, the aforesaid organs or agencies may be established provisionally by the corresponding Council. In constituting the membership of these bodies, the Councils, insofar as possible, shall follow the criteria of rotation and equitable geographic representation.

*Article 77.* The Councils may hold meetings in any Member State, when they find it advisable and with the prior consent of the Government concerned.

*Article 78.* Each Council shall prepare its own statutes and submit them to the General Assembly for approval. It shall approve its own rules of procedure and those of its subsidiary organs, agencies, and committees.

## Chapter 12: The Permanent Council of the Organization

*Article 79.* The Permanent Council of the Organization is composed of ne representative of each Member State, especially appointed by the respective Government, with the rank of ambassador. Each Government may accredit an acting representative, as well as such alternates and advisers as it considers necessary.

*Article 80.* The office of Chairman of the Permanent Council shall be held by each of the representatives, in turn, following the alphabetic order in Spanish of the names of their respective countries. The office of Vice Chairman shall be filled in the same way, following reverse alphabetic order.

The Chairman and the Vice Chairman shall hold office for a term of not more than six months, which shall be determined by the statutes.

*Article 81.* Within the limits of the Charter and of inter-American treaties and agreements, the Permanent Council takes cognizance of any matter referred to it by the General Assembly or the Meeting of Consultation of Ministers of Foreign Affairs.

*Article 82.* The Permanent Council shall serve provisionally as the Organ of Consultation in conformity with the provisions of the special treaty on the subject.

*Article 83.* The Permanent Council shall keep vigilance over the maintenance of friendly relations among the Member States, and for that purpose shall effectively assist them in the peaceful settlement of their disputes, in accordance with the following provisions.

*Article 84.* In accordance with the provisions of this Charter, any party to a dispute in which none of the peaceful procedures provided for in the Charter is under way may resort to the Permanent Council to obtain its good offices. The Council, following the provisions of the preceding article, shall assist the parties and recommend the procedures it considers suitable for peaceful settlement of the dispute.

*Article 85.* In the exercise of its functions and with the

consent of the parties to the dispute, the Permanent Council may establish ad hoc committees.

The ad hoc committees shall have the membership and the mandate that the Permanent Council agrees upon in each individual case, with the consent of the parties to the dispute.

*Article 86.* The Permanent Council may also, by such means as it deems advisable, investigate the facts in the dispute, and may do so in the territory of any of the parties, with the consent of the Government concerned.

*Article 87.* If the procedure for peaceful settlement of disputes recommended by the Permanent Council or suggested by the pertinent ad hoc committee under the terms of its mandate is not accepted by one of the parties, or one of the parties declares that the procedure has not settled the dispute, the Permanent Council shall so inform the General Assembly, without prejudice to its taking steps to secure agreement between the parties or to restore relations between them.

*Article 88.* The Permanent Council, in the exercise of these functions, shall take its decisions by an affirmative vote of two thirds of its members, excluding the parties to the dispute, except for such decisions as the rules of procedure provide shall be adopted by a simple majority.

*Article 89.* In performing their functions with respect to the peaceful settlement of disputes, the Permanent Council and the respective ad hoc committee shall observe the provisions of the Charter and the principles and standards of international law, as well as take into account the existence of treaties in force between the parties.

*Article 90.* The Permanent Council shall also:

(a) Carry out those decisions of the General Assembly or of the Meeting of Consultation of Ministers of Foreign Affairs the implementation of which has not been assigned to any other body;

(b) Watch over the observance of the standards governing the operation of the General Secretariat and, when the General Assembly is not in session, adopt provisions of a regulatory nature that enable the General Secretariat to carry out its administrative functions;

(c) Act as the Preparatory Committee of the General Assembly, in accordance with the terms of Article 59 of the Charter, unless the General Assembly should decide otherwise;

(d) Prepare, at the request of the Member States and with the cooperation of the appropriate organs of the Organization, draft agreements to promote and facilitate cooperation between the Organization of American States and the United Nations or between the Organization and other American agencies of recognized international standing. These draft agreements shall be submitted to the General Assembly for approval;

(e) Submit recommendations to the General Assembly with regard to the functioning of the Organization and the coordination of its subsidiary organs, agencies, and committees;

(f) Consider the reports of the other Councils, of the Inter-American Juridical Committee, of the Inter-American Commission on Human Rights, of the General Secretariat, of specialized agencies and conferences, and of other bodies and agencies, and present to the General Assembly any observations and recommendations it deems necessary; and

(g) Perform the other functions assigned to it in the Charter.

*Article 91.* The Permanent Council and the General Secretariat shall have the same seat.

## Chapter 13: The Inter-American Economic and Social Council

*Article 92.* The Inter-American Economic and Social Council is composed of one principal representative, of the highest rank, of each Member State, especially appointed by the respective Government.

*Article 93.* The purpose of the Inter-American Economic and Social Council is to promote cooperation among the American countries in order to attain accelerated economic and social development, in accordance with the standards set forth in Chapter VII.

*Article 94.* To achieve its purpose the Inter-American Economic and Social Council shall:

(a) Recommend programs and courses of action and periodically study and evaluate the efforts undertaken by the Member States;

(b) Promote and coordinate all economic and social activities of the Organization;

(c) Coordinate its activities with those of the other Councils of the Organization;

(d) Establish cooperative relations with the corresponding organs of the United Nations and with other national and international agencies, especially with regard to coordination of inter-American technical assistance programs; and

(e) Promote the solution of the cases contemplated in Article 36 of the Charter, establishing the appropriate procedure.

*Article 95.* The Inter-American Economic and Social Council shall hold at least one meeting each year at the ministerial level. It shall also meet when convoked by the General Assembly, the Meeting of Consultation of Ministers of Foreign Affairs, at its own initiative, or for the cases contemplated in Article 36 of the Charter.

*Article 96.* The Inter-American Economic and Social Council shall have a Permanent Executive Committee, composed of a Chairman and no less than seven other members, elected by the Council for terms to be established in the statutes of the Council. Each member shall have the right to one vote. The principles of equitable geographic representation and of rotation shall be taken into account, insofar as possible, in the election of members. The Permanent Executive Committee represents all of the Member States of the Organization.

*Article 97.* The Permanent Executive Committee shall perform the tasks assigned to it by the Inter-American Economic and Social Council, in accordance with the general standards established by the Council.

## Chapter 14: The Inter-American Council for Education, Science, and Culture

*Article 98.* The Inter-American Council for Education, Science, and Culture is composed of one principal representative, of the highest rank, of each Member State, especially appointed by the respective Government.

*Article 99.* The purpose of the Inter-American Council for Education, Science, and Culture is to promote friendly relations and mutual understanding between the peoples of the Americas through educational, scientific, and cultural cooperation and exchange between Member States, in order to raise the cultural level of the peoples, reaffirm their dignity as individuals, prepare them fully for the tasks of progress, and strengthen the devotion to peace, democracy, and social justice that has characterized their evolution.

*Article 100.* To accomplish its purpose the Inter-American Council for Education, Science, and Culture shall:

(a) Promote and coordinate the educational, scientific, and cultural activities of the Organization;

(b) Adopt or recommend pertinent measures to give effect to the standards contained in Chapter VII of the Charter;

(c) Support individual or collective efforts of the Member States to improve and extend education at all levels, giving special attention to efforts directed toward community development;

(d) Recommend and encourage the adoption of special educational programs directed toward integrating all sectors of the population into their respective national cultures;

(e) Stimulate and support scientific and technological education and research, especially when these relate to national development plans;

(f) Foster the exchange of professors, research workers, technicians, and students, as well as of study materials; and encourage the conclusion of bilateral or multilateral agreements on the progressive coordination of curricula at all educational levels and on the validity and equivalence of certificates and degrees;

(g) Promote the education of the American peoples with a view to harmonious international relations and a better understanding of the historical and cultural origins of the Americas, in order to stress and preserve their common values and destiny;

(h) Systematically encourage intellectual and artistic creativity, the exchange of cultural works and folklore, as well as the interrelationships of the different cultural regions of the Americas;

(i) Foster cooperation and technical assistance for protecting, preserving, and increasing the cultural heritage of the Hemisphere;

(j) Coordinate its activities with those of the other Councils. In harmony with the Inter-American Economic and Social Council, encourage the interrelationship of programs for promoting education, science, and culture with national development and regional integration programs;

(k) Establish cooperative relations with the corresponding organs of the United Nations and with other national and international bodies;

(l) Strengthen the civic conscience of the American peoples, as one of the bases for the effective exercise of democracy and for the observance of the rights and duties of man;

(m) Recommend appropriate procedures for intensifying integration of the developing countries of the Hemisphere by means of efforts and programs in the fields of education, science, and culture; and

(n) Study and evaluate periodically the efforts made by the Member States in the fields of education, science, and culture.

*Article 101.* The Inter-American Council for Education, Science, and Culture shall hold at least one meeting each year at the ministerial level. It shall also meet when convoked by the General Assembly, by the Meeting of Consultation of Ministers of Foreign Affairs, or at its own initiative.

*Article 102.* The Inter-American Council for Education, Science, and Culture shall have a Permanent Executive Committee, composed of a Chairman and no less than seven other members, elected by the Council for terms to be established in the statutes of the Council. Each member shall have the right to one vote. The principles of equitable geographic representation and of rotation shall be taken into account, insofar as possible, in the election of members. The Permanent Executive Committee represents all of the Member States of the Organization.

*Article 103.* The Permanent Executive Committee shall perform the tasks assigned to it by the Inter-American Council for Education, Science, and Culture, in accordance with the general standards established by the Council.

**Chapter 15: The Inter-American Juridical Committee**

*Article 104.* The purpose of the Inter-American Juridical Committee is to serve the Organization as an advisory body on juridical matters; to promote the progressive development and the codification of international law; and to study juridical problems related to the integration of the developing countries of the Hemisphere and, insofar as may appear desirable, the possibility of attaining uniformity in their legislation.

*Article 105.* The Inter-American Juridical Committee shall undertake the studies and preparatory work assigned to it by the General Assembly, the Meeting of Consultation of Ministers of Foreign Affairs, or the Councils of the Organization. It may also, on its own initiative, undertake such studies and preparatory work as it considers advisable, and suggest the holding of specialized juridical conferences.

*Article 106.* The Inter-American Juridical Committee shall be composed of eleven jurists, nationals of Member States, elected by the General Assembly for a period of four years from panels of three candidates presented by Member States. In the election, a system shall be used that takes into account partial replacement of membership and, insofar as possible, equitable geographic representation. No two members of the Committee may be nationals of the same State.

Vacancies that occur for reasons other than normal expiration of the terms of office of the members of the Committee shall be filled by the Permanent Council of the Organization in accordance with the criteria set forth in the preceding paragraph.

*Article 107.* The Inter-American Juridical Committee represents all of the Member States of the Organization, and has the broadest possible technical autonomy.

*Article 108.* The Inter-American Juridical Committee shall establish cooperative relations with universities, institutes, and other teaching centers, as well as with national and international committees and entities devoted to study, research, teaching, or dissemination of information on juridical matters of international interest.

*Article 109.* The Inter-American Juridical Committee shall draft its statutes, which shall be submitted to the General Assembly for approval.

The Committee shall adopt its own rules of procedure.

*Article 110.* The seat of the Inter-American Juridical Committee shall be the city of Rio de Janeiro, but in special cases the Committee may meet at any other place that may be designated, after consultation with the Member State concerned.

**Chapter 16: The Inter-American
Commission on Human Rights**

*Article 111.* There shall be an Inter-American Commission on Human Rights, whose principal function shall be to promote the observance and protection of human rights and to serve as a consultative organ of the Organization in these matters.

An inter-American convention on human rights shall determine the structure, competence, and procedure of this Commission, as well as those of other organs responsible for these matters.

## Chapter 17: The General Secretariat

*Article 112.* The General Secretariat is the central and permanent organ of the Organization of American States. It shall perform the functions assigned to it in the Charter, in other inter-American treaties and agreements, and by the General Assembly, and shall carry out the duties entrusted to it by the General Assembly, the Meeting of Consultation of Ministers of Foreign Affairs, or the Councils.

*Article 113.* The Secretary General of the Organization shall be elected by the General Assembly for a five-year term and may not be reelected more than once or succeeded by a person of the same nationality. In the event that the office of Secretary General becomes vacant, the Assistant Secretary General shall assume his duties until the General Assembly shall elect a new Secretary General for a full term.

*Article 114.* The Secretary General shall direct the General Secretariat, be the legal representative thereof, and, notwithstanding the provisions of Article 90.b, be responsible to the General Assembly for the proper fulfillment of the obligations and functions of the General Secretariat.

*Article 115.* The Secretary General, or his representative, may participate with voice but without vote in all meetings of the Organization.

The Secretary General may bring to the attention of the General Assembly or the Permanent Council any matter which in his opinion might threaten the peace and security of the Hemisphere or the development of the Member States.

The authority to which the preceding paragraph refers shall be exercised in accordance with the present Charter.

*Article 116.* The General Secretariat shall promote economic, social, juridical, educational, scientific, and cultural relations among all the Member States of the Organization, in keeping with the actions and policies decided upon by the General Assembly and with the pertinent decisions of the Councils.

*Article 117.* The General Secretariat shall also perform the following functions:

(a) Transmit *ex officio* to the Member States notice of the convocation of the General Assembly, the Meeting of Consultation of Ministers of Foreign Affairs, the Inter-American Economic and Social Council, the Inter-American Council for Education, Science, and Culture, and the Specialized Conferences;

(b) Advise the other organs, when appropriate, in the preparation of agenda and rules of procedure;

(c) Prepare the proposed program-budget of the Organization on the basis of programs adopted by the Councils, agencies, and entities whose expenses should be included in the program-budget and, after consultation with the Councils or their permanent committees, submit it to the Preparatory Committee of the General Assembly and then to the Assembly itself;

(d) Provide, on a permanent basis, adequate secretariat services for the General Assembly and the other organs, and carry out their directives and assignments. To the extent of its ability, provide services for the other meetings of the Organization;

(e) Serve as custodian of the documents and archives of the Inter-American Conferences, the General Assembly, the Meetings of Consultation of Ministers of Foreign Affairs, the Councils, and the Specialized Conferences;

(f) Serve as depository of inter-American treaties and agreements, as well as of the instruments of ratification thereof;

(g) Submit to the General Assembly at each regular session an annual report on the activities of the Organization and its financial condition; and

(h) Establish relations of cooperation, in accordance with decisions reached by the General Assembly or the Councils, with the Specialized Organizations as well as other national and international organizations.

*Article 118.* The Secretary General shall:

(a) Establish such offices of the General Secretariat as are necessary to accomplish its purposes; and

(b) Determine the number of officers and employees of the General Secretariat, appoint them, regulate their powers and duties, and fix their remuneration.

The Secretary General shall exercise this authority in accordance with such general standards and budgetary provisions as may be established by the General Assembly.

*Article 119.* The Assistant Secretary General shall be elected by the General Assembly for a five-year term and may not be reelected more than once or succeeded by a person of the same nationality. In the event that the office of Assistant Secretary General becomes vacant, the Permanent Council shall elect a substitute to hold that office until the General Assembly shall elect a new Assistant Secretary General for a full term.

*Article 120.* The Assistant Secretary General shall be the Secretary of the Permanent Council. He shall serve as advisory officer to the Secretary General and shall act as his delegate in all matters that the Secretary General may entrust to him. During the temporary absence or disability of the Secretary General, the Assistant Secretary General shall perform his functions.

The Secretary General and the Assistant Secretary General shall be of different nationalities.

*Article 121.* The General Assembly, by a two-thirds vote of the Member States, may remove the Secretary General or the Assistant Secretary General, or both, whenever the proper functioning of the Organization so demands.

*Article 122.* The Secretary General shall appoint, with the approval of the respective Council, the Executive Secretary for Economic and Social Affairs and the Executive Secretary for Education, Science, and Culture, who shall also be the secretaries of the respective Councils.

*Article 123.* In the performance of their duties, the Secretary General and the personnel of the Secretariat shall not seek or receive instructions from any Government or from any authority outside the Organization, and shall refrain from any action that may be incompatible with their position as international officers responsible only to the Organization.

*Article 124.* The Member States pledge themselves to respect the exclusively international character of the responsibilities of the Secretary General and the personnel of the General Secretariat, and not to seek to influence them in the discharge of their duties.

*Article 125.* In selecting the personnel of the General Secretariat, first consideration shall be given to efficiency, competence, and integrity; but at the same time, in the recruitment of personnel of all ranks, importance shall be given to the necessity of obtaining as wide a geographic representation as possible.

*Article 126.* The seat of the General Secretariat is the city of Washington, D.C.

### Chapter 18: The Specialized Conferences

*Article 127.* The Specialized Conferences are intergovernmental meetings to deal with special technical matters or to develop specific aspects of inter-American cooperation. They shall be held when either the General Assembly or the Meeting of Consultation of Ministers of Foreign Affairs so decides, on its own initiative or at the request of one of the Councils or Specialized Organizations.

*Article 128.* The agenda and rules of procedure of the Specialized Conferences shall be prepared by the Councils or Specialized Organizations concerned and shall be submitted to the Governments of the Member States for consideration.

### Chapter 19: The Specialized Organizations

*Article 129.* For the purposes of the present Charter, Inter-American Specialized Organizations are the intergovernmental organizations established by multilateral agreements and having specific functions with respect to technical matters of common interest to the American States.

*Article 130.* The General Secretariat shall maintain a register of the organizations that fulfill the conditions set forth in the foregoing Article, as determined by the General Assembly after a report from the Council concerned.

*Article 131.* The Specialized Organizations shall enjoy the fullest technical autonomy, but they shall take into account the recommendations of the General Assembly and of the Councils, in accordance with the provisions of the Charter.

*Article 132.* The Specialized Organizations shall transmit to the General Assembly annual reports on the progress of their work and on their annual budgets and expenses.

*Article 133.* Relations that should exist between the Specialized Organizations and the Organization shall be defined by means of agreements concluded between each organization and the Secretary General, with the authorization of the General Assembly.

*Article 134.* The Specialized Organizations shall establish cooperative relations with world agencies of the same character in order to coordinate their activities. In concluding agreements with international agencies of a worldwide character, the Inter-American Specialized Organizations shall preserve their identity and their status as integral parts of the Organization of American States, even when they perform regional functions of international agencies.

*Article 135.* In determining the location of the Specialized Organizations consideration shall be given to the interest of all of the Member States and to the desirability of selecting the seats of these organizations on the basis of a geographic representation as equitable as possible.

### Part Three

### Chapter 20: The United Nations

*Article 136.* None of the provisions of this Charter shall be construed as impairing the rights and obligations of the Member States under the Charter of the United Nations.

### Chapter 21: Miscellaneous Provisions

*Article 137.* Attendance at meetings of the permanent organs of the Organization of American States or at the conferences and meetings provided for in the Charter, or held under the auspices of the Organization, shall be in accordance with the multilateral character of the aforesaid organs, conferences, and meetings and shall not depend on the bilateral relations between the Government of any Member State and the Government of the host country.

*Article 138.* The Organization of American States shall enjoy in the territory of each Member such legal capacity, privileges, and immunities as are necessary for the exercise of its functions and the accomplishment of its purposes.

*Article 139.* The representatives of the Member States on the organs of the Organization, the personnel of their delegations, as well as the Secretary General and the Assistant Secretary General shall enjoy the privileges and immunities corresponding to their positions and necessary for the independent performance of their duties.

*Article 140.* The juridical status of the Specialized Organizations and the privileges and immunities that should be granted to them and to their personnel, as well as to the officials of the General Secretariat, shall be determined in a multilateral agreement. The foregoing shall not preclude, when it is considered necessary, the concluding of bilateral agreements.

*Article 141.* Correspondence of the Organization of American States, including printed matter and parcels, bearing the frank thereof, shall be carried free of charge in the mails of the Member States.

*Article 142.* The Organization of American States does not allow any restriction based on race, creed, or sex, with respect to eligibility to participate in the activities of the Organization and to hold positions therein.

*Article 143.* Within the provisions of this Charter, the competent organs shall endeavor to obtain greater collaboration from countries not members of the Organization in the area of cooperation for development.

### Chapter 22: Ratification and Entry Into Force

*Article 144.* The present Charter shall remain open for signature by the American States and shall be ratified in accordance with their respective constitutional procedures. The original instrument, the Spanish, English, Portuguese, and French texts of which are equally authentic, shall be deposited with the General Secretariat, which shall transmit certified copies thereof to the Governments for purposes of ratification. The instruments of ratification shall be deposited with the General Secretariat, which shall notify the signatory States of such deposit.

*Article 145.* The present Charter shall enter into force among the ratifying States when two thirds of the signatory States have deposited their ratifications. It shall enter into force with respect to the remaining States in the order in which they deposit their ratifications.

*Article 146.* The present Charter shall be registered with the Secretariat of the United Nations through the General Secretariat.

*Article 147.* Amendments to the present Charter may be adopted only at a General Assembly convened for that purpose. Amendments shall enter into force in accordance with the terms and the procedure set forth in Article 145.

*Article 148.* The present Charter shall remain in force indefinitely, but may be denounced by any Member State upon written notification to the General Secretariat, which shall communicate to all the others each notice of denunciation received. After two years from the date on which the General

Secretariat receives a notice of denunciation, the present Charter shall cease to be in force with respect to the denouncing State, which shall cease to belong to the Organization after it has fulfilled the obligations arising from the present Charter.

### Chapter 23: Transitory Provisions

*Article 149.* The Inter-American Committee on the Alliance for Progress shall act as the permanent executive committee of the Inter-American Economic and Social Council as long as the Alliance is in operation.

*Article 150.* Until the inter-American convention on human rights, referred to in Chapter XVI, enters into force, the present Inter-American Commission on Human Rights shall keep vigilance over the observance of human rights.

*Article 151.* The Permanent Council shall not make any recommendation nor shall the General Assembly take any decision with respect to a request for admission on the part of a political entity whose territory became subject, in whole or in part, prior to December 18, 1964, the date set by the First Special Inter-American Conference, to litigation or claim between an extracontinental country and one or more Member States of the Organization, until the dispute has been ended by some peaceful procedure. This article shall remain in effect until December 10, 1990.

## ORGANIZATION OF THE ISLAMIC CONFERENCE (OIC).

Established in 1971 in Jeddah, Saudi Arabia, the OIC promotes Islamic solidarity among member states, consolidating cooperation among them in economic, social, cultural, scientific, and other fields of activity. It also coordinates efforts for safeguarding Islamic holy places and supports the struggle of the Palestinian people and Muslim peoples everywhere.

OIC members comprise the following 47 countries: Afghanistan, Algeria, Azerbaijan, Bahrain, Bangladesh, Benin, Brunei Darussalam, Burkina Faso, Cameroon, Chad, Comoros, Djibouti, Egypt, Gabon, Gambia, Guinea, Guinea-Bissau, Indonesia, Iran, Iraq, Jordan, Kuwait, Lebanon, Libya, Malaysia, Maldives, Mali, Mauritania, Morocco, Niger, Nigeria, Oman, Pakistan, Palestine, Qatar, Saudi Arabia, Senegal, Sierra Leone, Somalia, Sudan, Syria, Tunisia, Turkey, Turkmenistan, Uganda, United Arab Emirates, and Yemen.

Among its activities the OIC has investigated the "Palestine Question," the conflict in Afghanistan, the Iran-Iraq conflict, and the problems of Muslim minorities. Concerning human rights, the OIC feels that Islam provides a particular code of human rights. In 1978, the group decided to draw up a "Charter of Islamic Human Rights" in the form of a comprehensive document; experts and scholars from several member States have worked on the preparation of such a document.

Organization of the Islamic Conference. Address: 6 Km Makkah Al-Mukarramah Road, P.O. Box 178, Jeddah, Saudi Arabia. Telephone: (966-2) 680-0800. Fax: (966-2) 687-6568. Secretary-General: Hamid Algabid.

## ORGANIZATION ON SECURITY AND COOPERATION IN EUROPE (OSCE).

Established on July 3, 1973, the Conference on Security and Cooperation in Europe (CSCE) was made a permanent intergovernmental organization on November 21, 1990, under the **CHARTER OF PARIS FOR A NEW EUROPE**, at a Summit meeting in Paris. Commencing January 1, 1995, the CSCE was renamed the Organization on Security and Cooperation in Europe.

Among the OSCE organs are the Meeting of Heads of State or Government, the Ministerial Council of the CSCE, the Senior Council, the Permanent Council, and the Secretariat (based in Prague); the Conflict Prevention Centre (Vienna); the Office for Democratic Institutions and Human Rights; the Forum for Security Cooperation (also known as the Vienna Forum); and the High Commissioner for National Minorities.

The OSCE conducts Summit meetings that set priorities and provide orientation at the highest political level. Brief, operational review conferences oversee the entire range of activities within the organization and propose measures to strengthen it. Special evaluation meetings are organized by the Office for Democratic Institutions and Human Rights (for the human dimension), by the Conflict Prevention Centre (for security measures), and by the Senior Council (for economic measures). The Senior Council, acting on behalf of the Ministerial Council, is responsible for the overview, coordination, and management of all activities under the Helsinki Document, and plays a central role in early warning, crisis management, and peacekeeping operations. Overall responsibility for executive action resides with the Chairman-in-Office, appointed annually to a one-year term.

*HELSINKI ACCORD.* Before becoming a permanent intergovernmental organization, the CSCE held a series of high-level conferences, the first of which commenced at Helsinki in July 1973, continued at Geneva from September 1973 to July 1975, and concluded at Helsinki on August 1, 1975, at which time the Final Act, popularly known as the Helsinki Accord, was adopted. The Final Act contains a number of references to the promotion and protection of human rights and fundamental freedoms in those portions of Part I that set out the "Declaration on Principles Guiding Relations between Participating States" and those sections—informally referred to as "Basket III"—which are contained under the heading "Co-operation in Humanitarian and Other Fields." The Helsinki Accord had a profound effect on the interest in human rights and the growing movement toward democracy within the former Soviet Union.

Of the ten guiding principles of the Helsinki Accord, Principles VI–IX have particular relevance to issues of human rights:

### (a) Declaration on Principles Guiding Relations Between Participating States

The participating States,

Reaffirming their commitment to peace, security and justice and the continuing development of friendly relations and co-operation;

Recognizing that this commitment, which reflects the interest and aspirations of peoples, constitutes for each participating State a present and future responsibility, heightened by experience of the past;

Reaffirming, in conformity with their membership in the United Nations and in accordance with the purposes and principles of the United Nations, their full and active support for the United Nations and for the enhancement of its role and effectiveness in strengthening international peace, security and justice, and in promoting the solution of international problems, as well as the development of friendly relations and co-operation among States;

Expressing their common adherence to the principles which are set forth below and are in conformity with the Charter of the United Nations, as well as their common will to act, in the application of these principles, in conformity with the purposes and principles of the Charter of the United Nations;

Declare their determination to respect and put into practice,each of them in its relations with all other participating States, irrespective of their political, economic or social systems as well as of their size, geographical location or level of economic development, the following principles, which are all of primary significance, guiding their mutual relations:

*I. Sovereign Equality, Respect for the Rights Inherent in Sovereignty . . .*

*II. Refraining from the Threat or Use of Force . . .*

*III. Inviolability of Frontiers . . .*

*IV. Territorial Integrity of States . . .*

*V. Peaceful Settlement of Disputes . . .*

*VI. Non-intervention in Internal Affairs.* The participating States will refrain from any intervention, direct or indirect, individual or collective, in the internal or external affairs falling within the domestic jurisdiction of another participating State, regardless of their mutual relations.

They will accordingly refrain from any form of armed intervention or threat of such intervention against another participating State.

They will likewise in all circumstances refrain from any other act of military, or of political, economic or other coercion designed to subordinate to their own interest the exercise by another participating State of the rights inherent in its sovereignty and thus to secure advantage of any kind.

Accordingly, they will, *inter alia,* refrain from direct or indirect assistance to terrorist activities, or to subversive or other activities directed towards the violent overthrow of the regime of another participating State.

*VII. Respect for Human Rights and Fundamental Freedoms, including the Freedom of Thought, Conscience, Religion or Belief.* The participating States will respect human rights and funda-mental freedoms, including the freedom of thought, conscience, religion or belief, for all without distinction as to race, sex, language or religion.

They will promote and encourage the effective exercise of civil, political, economic, social, cultural and other rights and freedoms all of which derive from the inherent dignity of the human person and are essential for his free and full development.

Within this framework the participating States will recognize and respect the freedom of the individual to profess and practise, alone or in community with others, religion or belief acting in accordance with the dictates of his own conscience.

The participating States on whose territory national minorities exist will respect the right of persons belonging to such minorities to equality before the law, will afford them the full opportunity for the actual enjoyment of human rights and fundamental freedoms and will, in this manner, protect their legitimate interests in this sphere.

The participating States recognize the universal significance of human rights and fundamental freedoms, respect for which is an essential factor for the peace, justice and well-being necessary to ensure the development of friendly relations and cooperation among themselves as among all States.

They will constantly respect these rights and freedoms in their mutual relations and will endeavour jointly and separately, including in co-operation with the United Nations, to promote universal and effective respect for them.

They confirm the right of the individual to know and act upon his rights and duties in this field.

In the field of human rights and fundamental freedoms, the participating States will act in conformity with the purposes and principles of the Charter of the United Nations and with the Universal Declaration of Human Rights. They will also fulfill their obligations as set forth in the international declarations and agreements in this field, including, *inter alia,* the International Covenants on Human Rights, by which they may be bound.

*VIII. Equal Rights and Self-Determination of Peoples.* The participating States will respect the equal rights of peoples and their right to self-determination, acting at all times in conformity with the purposes and principles of the Charter of the United Nations and with the relevant norms of international law, including those relating to territorial integrity of States.

By virtue of the principle of equal rights and self-determination of peoples, all peoples always have the right, in full freedom, to determine, when and as they wish, their internal and external political status, without external interference, and to pursue as they wish their political, economic, social and cultural development.

The participating States reaffirm the universal significance of respect for an effective exercise of equal rights and self-determination of peoples for the development of friendly relations among themselves or among all States; they also recall the importance of the elimination of any form of violation of this principle.

*IX. Co-operation among States.* The participating States will develop their co-operation with one another and with all States in all fields in accordance with the purposes and principles of the Charter of the United Nations. In developing their co-operation the participating States will place special emphasis on the fields as set forth within the framework of the Conference on Security and Co-operation in Europe, with each of them making its contribution in conditions of full equality.

They will endeavour, in developing their co-operation as equals, to promote mutual understanding and confidence, friendly and good-neighbourly relations among themselves, international peace, security and justice. They will equally endeavour, in developing their co-operation, to improve the well-being of peoples and contribute to the fulfilment of their aspirations through, inter alia, the benefits resulting from increased mutual knowledge and from progress and achievement in the economic, scientific, technological, social, cultural and humanitarian fields. They will take steps to promote conditions favourable to making these benefits available to all; they will take into account the interest of all in the narrowing of differences in the levels of economic development, and in particular the interest of developing countries throughout the world.

They confirm that governments, institutions, organizations and persons have a relevant and positive role to play in contributing toward the achievement of these aims of their co-operation.

They will strive, in increasing their co-operation as set forth above, to develop closer relations among themselves on an improved and more enduring basis for the benefit of peoples.

X. *Fulfilment in Good Faith of Obligations under International Law* . . .

After the adoption of the Helsinki Accord, the countries of the OSCE convened conferences in Belgrade (1977), Madrid (1980–1983), Stockholm (1984–1986), Vienna (1986–1989), Sofia and Paris (1989–1990), and Vienna and Copenhagen (1990). Since its establishment as a permanent organization, the OSCE has conducted conferences in Berlin, Geneva, and Moscow (1991); Prague and Helsinki (1992); and Budapest (1994).

As of March 1996, 53 countries were members of the OSCE: Albania, Armenia, Austria, Azerbaijan, Belarus, Belgium, Bosnia and Herzegovina, Bulgaria, Canada, Croatia, Cyprus, Czech Republic, Denmark, Estonia, Finland, France, Georgia, Germany, Greece, Holy See, Hungary, Iceland, Ireland, Italy, Kazakhstan, Kyrgyzstan, Latvia, Liechtenstein, Lithuania, Luxembourg, Malta, Macedonia, Moldova, Monaco, Netherlands, Norway, Poland, Portugal, Romania, Russia, San Marino, Slovakia, Slovenia, Spain, Sweden, Switzerland, Tajikistan, Turkey, Turkmenistan, Ukraine, United Kingdom, United States of America, and Uzbekistan.

Conference on Security and Cooperation in Europe. Address: Thunovská 12–Malá Strana, 110-00 Prague 1, Czech Republic. Telephone: (42-2) 311-9793. Fax: (42-2) 311-6215.

## OSSIETZKY, KARL VON (1889–1938).

Many **NOBEL PEACE PRIZE** recipients have been imprisoned for their political views; but Karl von Ossietzky, the 1935 Peace Prize winner, is the only recipient to have died in a prison, specifically, in a concentration camp. Rec-

ognized for his "valiant contribution to the cause of peace," Ossietzky, a career liberal journalist, was announced as the Prize winner when he was already imprisoned in the Esterwegen-Papenburg concentration camp. The award was viewed as a direct insult to the German Government and Hitler declared that no German citizen might accept a Nobel Peace Prize after the announcement of the award was made.

Born in Hamburg, Germany, Ossietzky became a pacifist after serving in the German military during 1916 and a leader in the German Peace Society. As a liberal journalist, he was viewed with suspicion by the various German administrations. In 1926, Ossietzky became editor of *Die Weltbühne* (The World Stage), which had undertaken a crusade to uncover Germany's secret rearmament policy. His association with the paper led to his first imprisonment in 1927 for a conviction of libel. In 1931, he was sentenced to 18 months in Spandau prison for betraying German military secrets in his paper, but was released in a general amnesty. Then, in 1933, he was arrested by the secret police. He died of tuberculosis.

**BIBLIOGRAPHY.** Gray, Tony. *Champions of Peace.* London: Paddington Press, 1976.

Schlessinger, Bernard S., and June H. Schlessinger, eds. *Who's Who of Nobel Prize Winners.* Phoenix, AZ, USA: Oryx Press, 1991.

**OXFAM.** Founded in 1942 in Oxford, UK, as the Oxford Committee for Famine Relief and renamed "OXFAM" in 1965, this non-governmental organization works to relieve poverty, distress, and suffering in any part of the world. It has consultative status (Category II) with the UN **ECONOMIC AND SOCIAL COUNCIL** and has official relations with **WHO.** OXFAM's fundraising and educational activities regarding worldwide poverty are linked to overseas aid programs. In 1991, the group contributed approximately $55 million (British) to some 2,300 projects in 70 countries. The group runs OXFAM Trading Markets, which handles goods produced by small community groups in developing countries, returning profits to producer groups in the form of dividends of grants. OXFAM Wastesaver operates a British textile and aluminum waste-processing plant. In addition, the group maintains 50 field offices and operates more than 2,900 relief and development projects. OXFAM has members in 38 countries and territories and publishes the quarterly *OXFAM News* and the triannual *Development in Practice.*

OXFAM. Address: 274 Banbury Road, Oxford OX2 7DZ, UK. Telephone: (44-865) 311-311. Fax: (44-865) 312-380. Director: David Bryer.

**OXFORD UNIVERSITY, REFUGEE STUDIES PROGRAM.** Founded in 1982, the Refugee Studies Program (RSP) of Oxford University is devoted to the multidisciplinary investigation of forced migration. The RSP conducts basic and policy-oriented research involving academics, policymakers, professionals, international agency personnel, and refugees. The Program also sponsors a wide range of publications, lectures, seminars, symposia, and workshops. In addition to its academic offerings, the RSP has a large documentation center of materials on forced migration.

Refugee Studies Program. Address: Oxford University, Queen Elizabeth House, 21 St. Giles, Oxford OX1 3LA, UK. Telephone: (44-08-65) 270-722. Fax: (44-08-65) 270-721.

# P

**PAKISTAN.** The Islamic Republic of Pakistan is a country in southern Asia occupying the northwestern portion of the Indian subcontinent, on the Arabian Sea. It has borders with Afghanistan, India, and Iran. It achieved independence from Great Britain in 1947 and became a member of the United Nations the same year. Its population is estimated to be 123,490,000. Ethnic groups include Baluchi, Pathan, Punjabi, Sindhi, and Urdu-speaking Indian elements; precise data on ethnic origin are not collected by the government. Languages commonly used include Urdu (official), Baluchi, English, Punjabi, Pushto, and Sindhi. Islam is the predominant religion, accounting for about 97% of those who profess a religious belief; Christianity and Hinduism account for the remaining 3%. Literacy is estimated at 26%.

The military dictatorship of President Mohammed Zia ul-Haq, who came to power in a coup in 1977 when he deposed Prime Minister Zulfikar Ali Bhutto, ended in 1988 when Zia died in an unexplained airplane crash. In free national elections held in November 1988, the Pakistan People's Party (PPP) won 92 of 215 contested seats in the lower house of Parliament, and its leader, Benazir Bhutto, daughter of the former prime minister, formed a government. The government of Prime Minister Benazir Bhutto initially had strong support from the voters of Pakistan.

Pursuant to constitutional authority, the president declared a state of emergency in August 1990, dismissed Prime Minister Bhutto and the cabinet, and dissolved the National Assembly. Benazir Bhutto and some of her cabinet were indicted on charges of corruption and Bhutto's husband was charged with extortion and kidnaping.

Following general elections held in October 1990 in which the Islamic Democratic Alliance (IDA) won the most seats in the National Assembly, four shy of an absolute majority, Mohammed Nawaz Sharif became the new prime minister. The IDA also won majorities in by-elections and elections to the Senate in early 1991. Over criticism by Bhutto and others, the National Assembly took steps in 1991 to incorporate Islamic principles in the legal, educational, economic, and judicial systems.

In April 1993 the president once again dissolved the National Assembly and dismissed the prime minister and the cabinet. However, in May the Supreme Court ordered the National Assembly, the prime minister, and the cabinet reinstated immediately, ruling that the order had been unconstitutional. Although the order was followed, President Khan was forced to resign in July 1993 after failing in his attempt to assert federal power over the autonomous province of Punjab and threatening to enforce this authority through military force.

A neutral administration ruled until elections in October 1993 when Benazir Bhutto was elected to head a coalition government of her PPP and smaller parties. The PPP candidate for president, Sardar Farooq Ahmad Khan Leghari, was also elected.

Created in 1947 out of areas of British India that were predominantly Muslim in population, Pakistan has endeavored to ensure that the rights of its minorities are protected and that minority members do not face any problems which are peculiar to their belonging to a minority community. A Ministry of Minorities' Affairs has been established to deal with (a) safeguarding the rights of minorities, (b) promotion of the welfare of minorities, (c) protection of minorities against discrimination, (d) international agreements and commitments in respect of minorities and their implementation, and (e) all other matters relating to minorities.

***RIGHTS OF RACIAL AND RELIGIOUS MINORITIES.*** The Government of Pakistan stated, in a report presented to the **COMMITTEE ON THE ELIMINATION OF RACIAL DISCRIMINATION** in 1986 (UN Doc. CERD/ C/149/Add. 12), that it is "committed to protecting and promoting the cultural identity of minorities" in accordance with the constitution, which provides that "any section of citizens having a distinct language, script or culture shall have the right to preserve and promote the same and subject to law establish institutions for that purpose."

As regards people living in the tribal areas (federally administered tribal areas consisting of seven agencies and four frontier regions and having a population of 2,175,000), their participation in the national decision-making process is ensured through constitutional provisions and administrative instructions; their representation is eight seats in the National Assembly and an equal number of seats in the Senate. In addition, a special quota is reserved in central superior and other services for tribal people to facilitate their entry into the service of Pakistan and provincial services.

With reference to one religious community in Pakistan, the **SUB-COMMISSION ON PREVENTION OF DISCRIMINATION AND PROTECTION OF MINORITIES,** in resolution 1985/21 of 29 August 1985, expressed grave concern over Government Ordinance No. XX of 1984, which appeared to single out the Ahmadis for differential treatment. The ordinance, promulgated "to amend the law to prohibit the Quadiani group and Ahmadis from indulging in anti-Islamic activities," was said by the Sub-Commission to violate "the right to liberty and security of persons, the right to freedom from arbitrary arrest or detention, the right to freedom of thought, expression, conscience and religion, the right of religious minorities to profess and practice their own religion, and the right to an effective legal remedy." The Sub-Commission further expressed concern that persons charged with and arrested for violations of the ordinance had reportedly been subjected to various punishments and confiscation of personal property and that the affected groups as a whole had been subjected to discrimination in employment and education and to the defacement of their religious property. The Sub-Commission requested the **COMMISSION ON HUMAN RIGHTS** to call on the Government of Pakistan to repeal Ordinance XX and to restore the human rights and fundamental freedoms of all persons within its jurisdiction and alerted the Commission to the situation in Pakistan which, in its view, was one with great potential to cause a mass exodus, especially of members of the Ahmadi community.

The Commission took no action on the Sub-Commission's request at any open meeting of its 1986 session, and the Sub-Commission did not meet in August of that year, as scheduled, because of financial constraints. Towards the close of the Commission's 1987 session, on 6 March 1987, **ANTI-SLAVERY INTERNATIONAL FOR THE PROTECTION OF HUMAN RIGHTS,** a non-governmental organization in consultative status, circulated a communication to the Commission entitled "Violations of Basic Human Rights of Ahmadi Muslims in Pakistan" (UN Doc. E/CN.4/1987/NGO/67), which reads as follows:

Since the promulgation of Ordinance XX of 26 April 1984 by the then military Government of Pakistan, fundamental human rights of members of the Ahmadiyya Muslim Community in Pakistan have been violated persistently. The following few facts may be noted by all whose concern is the protection of human rights all over the world:

(1) Ordinance XX forbids in clear, unequivocal terms members of the Ahmadiyya Muslim Community in Pakistan to profess, practise and propagate their beliefs, a fact which cannot be denied by any "interpretation" of the said Ordinance;

(2) President Zia of Pakistan declared in a message to an anti-Ahmadiyya conference held in London on 5 August 1985, his measures to "exterminate the cancer of Ahmadiyyat". This, too, is a documented fact;

(3) The Sub-Commission on Prevention of Discrimination and Protection of Minorities in its findings came to the conclusion that the Government of Pakistan was guilty of grossly violating human rights of Ahmadi Muslims. (See resolution 1985/21 of 29 August 1985);

(4) Both the Universal Declaration of Human Rights and the Constitution of Pakistan (art. 20) guarantee the right of religious freedom, whereas Ordinance XX contravenes these provisions;

(5) The issue of a passport is refused to a Muslim in Pakistan if he does not declare in writing that the Founder of the Ahmadiyya Movement in Islam was a liar and an impostor.

Martial law was in force until 30 December 1985. Our organization was told that the lifting of martial law would allow things to improve and normal conditions would return. Yet, in the case of Ahmadi Muslims things have even worsened and their persecution continues unabated, with greater backing by the authorities. Some more facts in this connection may also be noted:

(i) The provisions of Ordinance XX, which was challenged by the Sub-Commission as a grave violation of basic human rights, have been incorporated in the Constitution of the country, thus perpetuating the "legalized" persecution of Ahmadi Muslims;

(ii) Although martial law was lifted on 30 December 1985, sentences of death against two Ahmadi Muslims were announced in February 1986 as having been passed by a special military court (Sahiwal case);

(iii) Two weeks after the above sentences, two more death sentences by a military court were announced in the Sukkur case against Ahmadi Muslims;

(iv) On 11 May 1986, two Ahmadis were brutally murdered in Sukkur;

(v) On 9 May 1986, the Ahmadiyya mosque in Quetta was attacked by a mob under the very eyes of local authorities; 85 Ahmadis were taken into custody, and the mosque was sealed by police;

(vi) On 9 June 1986, an Ahmadi lady was shot dead in Mardan for having visited the Ahmadiyya mosque to offer her prayers;

(vii) That mosque was later (on 17 August 1986) razed to the ground with police and other government officials as onlookers;

(viii) On 9 July 1986, an ex-Amir of Hyderabad was stabbed to death;

(ix) On 9 September 1986, an Ahmadi Muslim of Peshawar was sentenced to seven years gaol and a fine of PRs 10,000 for wearing the insignia bearing his article of faith;

(x) For the same "crime", two more Ahmadi Muslims were sentenced on 17 September 1986 in Mardan to five years gaol and a fine of PRs 25,000 each;

(xi) On 9 September 1986, an Ahmadi of Rabwah was shot dead in Darra Adam Khel;

(xii) In early February 1987, two Ahmadi Muslims of Lyallpur (Faisalabad) were taken to gaol in handcuffs for having displayed the words "Is God not sufficient for His servant?" and "O Living One, the Sustainer". The logic behind these arrests being that such professions of faith by Ahmadi Muslims "injured the religious feelings" of others;

(xiii) The latest news which reached our organization in March 1987 is that yet another Ahmadi Muslim has been murdered in cold blood in the District of Jhelum.

It becomes quite obvious from these incidents that the persecution of Ahmadis in Pakistan has been stepped up since martial law was lifted. The Government is getting itself involved more and more in the campaign of "exterminating" the "cancer" of Ahmadiyyat. These incidents show beyond doubt that the findings of the Sub-Commission were right and its fears well-based.

The Anti-Slavery Society for the Protection of Human Rights urges the Commission on Human Rights to pay greater attention to the simple enough request made by the Sub-Commission in its resolution 1985/21 of 29 August 1985.

*UN PEACEKEEPING MISSIONS.* Relations between Pakistan and India have been tenuous since the birth of both nations, in particular over the state of Jammu and Kashmir. Under the plan of partition provided by the Indian Independence Act of 1947, Kashmir was free to accede to either new nation. When it chose to join with India in 1947, fighting broke out on a massive scale. In 1949, the United Nations Military Observer Group in India and Pakistan (UNMOGIP) was established to patrol a ceasefire line established between the two countries by the Karachi Agreement of 1949. The UNMOGIP has remained in effect since that time, with a current strength of 39 observers. The group has overseen renewed hostilities in 1965 and 1971. At the present time, India no longer recognizes UNMOGIP's mandate because of a change in the demarcation line after the 1971 fighting; Pakistan, however, still recognizes the mandate. Relations between Pakistan and India were severely strained once again in the 1990s over the continuing border skirmishes in Kashmir and allegations by India that Pakistan was involved in bombings in Bombay in March 1993 which killed more than 300 people. The Pakistani consulate in Bombay was closed in March 1994.

A second UN peacekeeping mission was established in recent years, this time to handle strained relations between Pakistan and Afghanistan due to the flow of Afghani refugees into Pakistan. The United Nations Good Offices Mission in Afghanistan and Pakistan (UNGOMAP) lasted from May 1988 until March 1990. Its mandate was to help ensure the implementation of the Agreements on the Settlement of the Situation relating to Afghanistan and to investigate and report possible violations.

**BIBLIOGRAPHY.** Amnesty International. *Children: The Youngest Victims.* London: 1987. NGO report, in English.

―――. *Pakistan: Arrests of Political Opponents in Sindh Province, August 1990–early 1992.* London: 1992. NGO report, in English.

―――. *Pakistan: The Death Penalty.* London: 1988. NGO report, in English.

―――. *Pakistan: Political Prisoners Convicted in Unfair Trials during the Martial Law Period.* London: 1987. NGO statement, in English.

―――. *Pakistan: Reports of Torture and Death in Police Custody.* London: 1991. NGO report, in English.

―――. *Pakistan: Torture, Deaths in Custody and Extrajudicial Executions.* London: 1993. NGO report, in English.

―――. *Pakistan: Violations of Human Rights of Ahmadis.* London: 1991. NGO report, in English.

―――. *Pakistan: The Pattern Persists: Torture, Deaths in Custody, Extrajudicial Executions and "Disappearances" Under the PPP Government.* London: 1995. NGO report, in English.

Andreassen, B. A., and A. Eide, eds. "Pakistan," in *Human Rights in Developing Countries 1987/88: A Yearbook on Human Rights in Countries Receiving Nordic Aid.* Copenhagen: Christian Michelsen Institute, 1988. NGO report, in English; bibliography, pp. 357–372, classified by country.

Asia Watch. *Double Jeopardy: Police Abuse of Women in Pakistan.* New York: Human Rights Watch, 1992. NGO report, in English.

―――. *Persecuted Minorities and Writers in Pakistan.* New York: Human Rights Watch, 1993. NGO report, in English.

Association Amitie Franco-Afghane (Franco-Afghan Friendship Association). "Les Refugies Afghans" (The Afghan Refugees), *Les Nouvelles d'Afghanistan* no. 35–36 (Dec. 1987). NGO special issue, in French.

Carleton University, Research Resource Division for Refugees. *Pakistan: The Mohajirs.* Ottawa, Canada: 1992. Government briefing paper, in English and French.

Centre for the Independence of Judges and Lawyers. *The Independence of Judges and Lawyers in Pakistan: Report of a Seminar 9–10 November 1989 held at Lahore, Pakistan.* Lahore, Pakistan: International Commission of Jurists, 1990. NGO conference report.

Femmes sous Lois Musulmanes (Women Living under Muslim Laws). *Dossier No. 2.* Montpellier, France: 1986. NGO document collection, in English.

Human Rights Commission of Pakistan. *Baluchistan Special Laws.* Lahore, Pakistan: 1990. NGO research report, in English.

―――. *Bonded Labour in Brick Kiln Industry of Pakistan.* Lahore, Pakistan: 1988. NGO mission report, in English.

―――. *One-Day Seminar on the United Nations Convention on the Elimination of All Forms of Discrimination against Women, October 30, 1987.* Lahore, Pakistan: 1988. NGO conference report, in English.

―――. *Sindh Inquiry: Summer 1990.* Lahore, Pakistan: 1990. NGO factfinding report, in English.

Idara-e-Aman-o-Insaf (Christian Conference of Asia). *Pakistan: Struggle for Human Rights.* Kowloon, Hong Kong: 1986. NGO edited collection, in English.

Immigration and Refugee Board Documentation Centre. *Cultural Profile: the Ahmadiyya.* Ottawa, Canada: 1991. Government briefing paper, in English and French.

―――. *The Mohajirs of Pakistan: Issue Paper.* Ottawa, Canada: 1990. Government briefing paper, in English and French.

―――. *Pakistan: Treatment of Ahmadis Who Return.* Ottawa, Canada: 1992. Government briefing paper, in English and French.

*Information, Freedom and Censorship: The ARTICLE 19 World Report 1988.* London: ARTICLE 19, 1988. NGO report, in English; bibliography on suggested further reading, pp. 324—326.

International Catholic Child Bureau. *Children and Drug Abuse*. Geneva:1988. NGO manual, in English.

International Commission of Jurists. *The Independence of Judges and Lawyers in South Asia*. Geneva: 1988. NGO conference report, in English.

International Federation of Human Rights. *Rapport de mission: Pakistan du 20 au 27 mai 1990* (Mission Report: Pakistan, 20–27 May 1990). Paris: 1990. NGO factfinding report, in French.

————. *Rapport de mission: Pakistan. Élections à l'Assemblée Nationale et aux assemblées des quatre provinces du Pakistan les 24 et 27 octobre 1990* (Mission Report: Pakistan. Elections to the National Assembly and Four Provincial Assemblies, 24–27 October 1990). Paris: 1990. NGO factfinding report, in French.

Jahangir, Asma, and Hina Jilani. *The Hudood Ordinances: A Divine Sanction?* Lahore, Pakistan: Rhotas Books, 1990. Monograph, in English.

Lawyers Committee for Human Rights. *Zia's Law: Human Rights under Military Rule in Pakistan*. New York: 1985. NGO mission report, in English.

National Democratic Institute for International Affairs. *The October 1990 Elections in Pakistan*. Washington, D.C.: 1991. NGO monograph, in English.

Refugee Studies Programme. *The Crisis of Migration from Afghanistan: Domestic and Foreign Implications*. Oxford, UK: 1987. Conference proceedings, in English.

Shafi, M. *Labour Policy Dimensions*. Karachi, Pakistan: Bureau of Labour Publications, 1990. Monograph, in English.

Wirsing, Robert. *The Baluchis and Pathans*, rev. ed. London: Minority Rights, 1987. NGO report, in English.

**PALACH (JAN) PRIZE.** The Jan Palach Prize is awarded to individuals or organizations that have made a major contribution to the development of democratic institutions. It is sponsored by the International Committee for Support of Charter 77 in Czechoslovakia (France) and awards 50,000 (FF) to the honoree.

For more information, contact: Comite international pour l'appui a la charte de 77, 5 rue de Medicis, 75006 Paris, France. Telephone: (33-1) 326-5223.

**PALAU.** The Republic of Palau, formerly a U.S.-administered UN Trust Territory, lies in the Pacific Ocean, about 4,500 miles southwest of Hawaii and about 750 miles south of Guam. It comprises, with the Federated States of Micronesia, the Caroline Islands. Its population is officially estimated to be 16,000. The predominant religion is Christianity, and English and Palauan are the official languages. The republic became a member of the United Nations in 1995.

In 1947, the UN placed the Marshall Islands, the Caroline Islands, and the Northern Mariana Islands (except Guam) under the trusteeship of the United States. There were growing demands for autonomy for the islands from 1965. A constitution was drafted for Palau which took effect in January 1981, and in Oc-

tober 1982 the U.S. signed the Compact of Free Association, under which the United States would maintain responsibility for defense. After Palauans failed to ratify the pact by the requisite 75% in seven referenda, the required percentage was changed to 50% and it passed in 1993. In 1993 Kuniwo Nakamura became Palau's president.

The government (1994) took the form of a republic. The 1981 constitution provides for the popular election of a bicameral legislature, the 16-seat House of Delegates, and the 14-seat Senate, and the president and vice-president. High-level corruption and political assassination have plagued Palau. The leader of the Council of Chiefs has demanded compensation from the United States for physical damage during World War II and mismanagement of the trusteeship.

**PALESTINE LIBERATION ORGANIZATION (PLO).** This organization represents the Palestinian people and participates in the work of the UN **GENERAL ASSEMBLY** and other United Nations organs as an observer.

The Assembly granted observer status to the PLO on 22 November 1974 (resolution 3237 [XXIX]), and to the **SOUTH WEST AFRICA PEOPLE'S ORGANIZATION** (SWAPO) on 20 December 1976 (resolution 31/152). Later, on 9 December 1988, it decided (resolution 43/160) that both organizations were entitled to have their communications relating to the sessions and the work of the Assembly issued and circulated directly, and without intermediary, as official Assembly documents; and that both were also entitled to have their communications relating to the sessions and work of all international conferences issued and circulated directly, and without intermediary, as official documents of such conferences. These steps were taken with a view to facilitating the work of the two organizations.

At the 1989 General Assembly session a number of States submitted and supported the adoption of a draft resolution aimed at recognition of the PLO as the government of an independent Palestinian State. The proposal was vigorously opposed by the United States of America, the Union of Soviet Socialist Republics, and a number of developing countries. The sponsors of the draft resolution, however, did not press it to a vote.

Following Middle East peace talks which began in Madrid, Spain, in October 1991, PLO Chairman Yasir Arafat and then-Israeli Prime Minister Yitzhak Rabin signed the Declaration of Principles, or the Oslo accord, in September 1993, mapping out the general plan toward Palestinian autonomy. The Cairo accord in May 1994 provided the details necessary for executing the plan, including initial Israeli military withdrawal from the West Bank and the Gaza Strip and the transfer of administrative powers to the Palestinian National Authority headed by PLO Chairman Yasir Arafat. In July 1994 Arafat returned to Gaza City from a 27-year exile. Chairman Arafat and Prime Minister Rabin were awarded the 1994 Nobel Prize for Peace.

The second phase of the agreement was signed two years after the Declaration of Principles, in September 1995, paving the way for elections to the Palestinian council and the PNA executive in January 1996. The city of Hebron, like the rest of the West Bank, was split into three zones, under Israeli, Palestinian, and joint control, respectively. In the agreement, Israel recognized Hebron as Palestinian and the West Bank and Gaza Strip as a single territory. The Arab League welcomed the agreement and, following the assassination of Prime Minister Rabin by an Israeli extremist in November 1995, support for the accord by Israelis increased.

Approximately 75% of the one million registered voters cast ballots in the January 1996 elections although militant Islamic groups Islamic Jihad and Hamas boycotted them. Arafat defeated his only opponent for President with 88% of the votes. The Council's 88 seats—44 for the West Bank, 37 for the Gaza Strip, and seven for Jerusalem—were contested by approximately 700 candidates, 500 of whom were independents. International election observers, including former U.S. President Jimmy Carter and some 350 European Union observers declined to designate the elections "free and fair" because of Israeli military and police roadblocks and security checks, understood as attempts to deter people from voting. Suicide bombings and other acts of violence continued after the elections.

**PALESTINIAN PEOPLE'S RIGHTS.** In its first report, submitted to the UN **GENERAL ASSEMBLY** in 1976 (UN Doc. A/31/35), the **COMMITTEE ON THE EXERCISE OF THE INALIENABLE RIGHTS OF THE PALESTINIAN PEOPLE** made a number of recommendations designed to enable the Palestinian people to attain and exercise their human rights in Palestine. These recommendations were first endorsed by the General Assembly on 24 November 1976 (resolution 31/20) as a basis for the solution of the question of Palestine. The recommendations are reproduced below.

In each of its subsequent annual reports to the Assembly, the Committee reaffirmed the original recommendations and called for their implementation. On each occasion, they were endorsed overwhelmingly by the Assembly, which has repeatedly renewed and, as necessary, expanded the Committee's man-

date. However, despite the increasing urgency of the appeals by the Committee, the recommendations have not been acted on by the **SECURITY COUNCIL.**

*RECOMMENDATIONS OF THE UN COMMITTEE ON THE EXERCISE OF THE INALIENABLE RIGHTS OF THE PALESTINIAN PEOPLE.* The recommendations of the Committee, endorsed by the UN General Assembly at its 1976 session, are as follows (UN Doc. A/31/35, paras. 59—72):

### I. Basic Considerations and Guidelines

The question of Palestine is at the heart of the Middle East problem, and consequently, the Committee stresses its belief that no solution in the Middle East can be envisaged which does not fully take into account the legitimate aspirations of the Palestinian people.

The legitimate and inalienable rights of the Palestinian people to return to their homes and property and to achieve self-determination, national independence and sovereignty are endorsed by the Committee in the conviction that the full implementation of these rights will contribute decisively to a comprehensive and final settlement of the Middle East crisis.

The participation of the Palestine Liberation Organization, the representative of the Palestinian people, on an equal footing with other parties, on the basis of General Assembly resolutions 3236 (XXIX) and 3375 (XXX) is indispensable in all efforts, deliberations and conferences on the Middle East which are held under the auspices of the United Nations.

The Committee recalls the fundamental principle of the inadmissibility of the acquisition of territory by force and stresses the consequent obligation for complete and speedy evacuation of any territory so occupied.

The Committee considers that it is the duty and responsibility of all concerned to enable the Palestinians to exercise their inalienable rights.

The Committee recommends an expanded and more influential role by the United Nations and its organs in promoting a just solution to the question of Palestine and in the implementation of such a solution. The Security Council, in particular, should take appropriate action to facilitate the exercise by the Palestinians of their right to return to their homes, lands and property. The Committee, furthermore, urges the Security Council to promote action towards a just solution, taking into account all the powers conferred on it by the Charter of the United Nations.

It is with this perspective in view and on the basis of the numerous resolutions of the United Nations, after due consideration of all the facts, proposals and suggestions advanced in the course of its deliberations, that the Committee submits its recommendations on the modalities for the implementation of the exercise of the inalienable rights of the Palestinian people.

### II. The Right of Return

The natural and inalienable right of Palestinians to return to their homes is recognized by resolution 194 (III), which the General Assembly has reaffirmed almost every year since its adoption. This right was also unanimously recognized by the Security Council in its resolution 237 (1967); the time for the urgent implementation of these resolutions is long overdue.

Without prejudice to the right of all Palestinians to return to their homes, lands and property, the Committee considers that the programme of implementation of the exercise of this right may be carried out in two phases:

*Phase One.* The first phase involves the return to their homes of the Palestinians displaced as a result of the war of June 1967. The Committee recommends that:

(i) The Security Council should request the immediate implementation of its resolution 237 (1967) and that such implementation should not be related to any other condition;

(ii) The resources of the International Committee of the Red Cross (ICRC) and/or of the United Nations Relief and Works Agency for Palestine Refugees in the Near East, suitably financed and mandated, may be employed to assist in the solution of any logistical problems involved in the resettlement of those returning to their homes. These agencies could also assist, in co-operation with the host countries and the Palestine Liberation Organization, in the identification of the displaced Palestinians.

*Phase Two.* The second phase deals with the return to their homes of the Palestinians displaced between 1948 and 1967. The Committee recommends that:

(i) While the first phase is being implemented, the United Nations in co-operation with the States directly involved, and the Palestine Liberation Organization as the interim representative of the Palestinian entity, should proceed to make the necessary arrangements to enable Palestinians displaced between 1948 and 1967 to exercise their right to return to their homes and property, in accordance with the relevant United Nations resolutions, particularly General Assembly resolution 194 (III);

(ii) Palestinians not choosing to return to their homes should be paid just and equitable compensation as provided for in resolution 194 (III).

### III. The Right to Self-Determination, National Independence and Sovereignty

The Palestinian people has the inherent right to self-determination, national independence and sovereignty in Palestine. The Committee considers that the evacuation of the territories occupied by force and in violation of the principles of the Charter and relevant resolutions of the United Nations is a *conditio sine qua non* for the exercise by the Palestinian people of its inalienable rights in Palestine. The Committee considers furthermore, that upon the return of the Palestinians to their homes and property and with the establishment of an independent Palestinian entity, the Palestinian people will be able to exercise its rights to self-determination and to decide its form of government without external interference.

The Committee also feels that the United Nations has an historical duty and responsibility to render all assistance necessary to promote the economic development and prosperity of the Palestinian entity.

To these ends, the Committee recommends that:

(a) A timetable should be established by the Security Council for the complete withdrawal by Israeli occupation forces from those areas occupied in 1967; such withdrawal should be completed no later than 1 June 1977;

(b) The Security Council may need to provide temporary peace-keeping forces in order to facilitate the process of withdrawal;

(c) Israel should be requested by the Security Council to desist from the establishment of new settlements and to withdraw during this period from settlements established since 1967 in the occupied territories. Arab property and all essential services in these areas should be maintained intact;

(d) Israel should also be requested to abide scrupulously by the provisions of the Geneva Convention relative to the Protection of Civilian Persons in Time of War, of 12 August 1949 and to declare, pending its speedy withdrawal from these territories, its recognition of the applicability of that Convention;

(e) The evacuated territories, with all property and services intact, should be taken over by the United Nations, which with the co-operation of the League of Arab States, will subsequently hand over these evacuated areas to the Palestine Liberation Organization as the representative of the Palestinian people;

(f) The United Nations should, if necessary, assist in establishing communications between Gaza and the West Bank;

(g) As soon as the independent Palestinian entity has been established, the United Nations, in co-operation with the States directly involved and the Palestinian entity, should, taking into account General Assembly resolution 3375 (XXX), make further arrangements for the full implementation of the inalienable rights of the Palestinian people, the resolution of outstanding problems and the establishment of a just and lasting peace in the region, in accordance with all relevant United Nations resolutions;

(h) The United Nations should provide the economic and technical assistance necessary for the consolidation of the Palestinian entity.

***INTIFADA (UPRISING).*** Beginning on 9 December 1987, the Palestinian people residing in the territories occupied by Israel staged an uprising *(intifada)* against the occupation, one which received significant attention and sympathy from world public opinion. However, the uprising caused the human rights situation in the territories to deteriorate dramatically. The resulting situation was described by the chairman of the UN Special Committee to Investigate Israeli Practices Affecting the Human Rights of the Population of the Occupied Territories, in his letter transmitting the 1988 report of the Special Committee (UN Doc. A/43/694) to the UN Secretary-General, as follows:

The accumulation of frustrations suffered by the civilian population over the years as a result of the persistent policy of annexation and colonization pursued by the Government of Israel in the territories occupied in June 1967, and the humiliation and suffering brought about by that policy, were bound to provoke a violent reaction on the part of the oppressed civilians. The restrictions imposed in the framework of the "iron fist policy" since 1985 and the increasing determination of the young generation of Palestinians to oppose the arbitrary rules set by the occupants had prepared the ground for such a confrontation. Thus, the explosion of violence sparked off by an incident in the Gaza Strip in December 1987 quickly spread to the entire occupied territo-

# P

ries, giving rise to what has since been called the uprising against the occupation.

The uprising has been marked by a heavy toll of casualties among the Palestinian population. Hundreds of civilians have been killed by security forces, settlers, or under various other circumstances. The death toll has included casualties caused by shooting, beating, gas inhalation or electrocution. While several thousands of civilians have been physically injured, the entire Palestinian population has suffered as a result of the implementation by the Israeli authorities of the policy of "force, power and blows".

The day-to-day life in the occupied territories since the start of the uprising has been characterized by constant unrest and violent clashes, sparing almost no single village or locality; the now familiar pattern of disturbances usually includes demonstrations, stone-throwing, commercial strikes on the one hand, and the use of tear gas, clubs, rubber and live bullets, the imposition of curfews and various economic sanctions by the occupation authorities on the other. Acts of aggression committed by Israel settlers against Palestinians have contributed to a further deterioration in the climate of tension and terror prevailing in the occupied territories. Information and evidence collected by the Special Committee reveal other serious infringements of fundamental rights and freedoms, including the arbitrary deportation of Palestinians from the occupied territories; the illegal demolition of houses used as a form of collective punishment; the severe limitations on the freedom of expression, tending in particular to limit or prevent an adequate media coverage of events related to the uprising; the general closure of all educational institutions for several months, resulting in the loss of an academic year for students and serious delays in the schooling of Palestinian children.

The new situation in the occupied territories has endangered a considerable amount of administrative and other forms of detentions. Several thousand Palestinians, including minors, have been or continue to be detained in various prisons and detention centres, sometimes even inside Israel itself. Many of these cases illustrate the fact that legal guarantees such as the right to fair trial are often denied to Palestinians. Furthermore, this unprecedented increase in the prison population has also aggravated the already critical conditions of detention and the plight of the detainees.

The Special Committee has endeavoured, within the constraints and self-restrictions imposed by the financial situation of the United Nations, to provide in its report a faithful and accurate picture of the human rights situation prevailing in the occupied territories. The tragic developments that have cast their shadow over the civilian population clearly illustrate the responsibility of the international community, which so far has unfortunately not been able to adopt effective measures to improve the human rights situation of the Palestinians under occupation. It is the sincere hope of the Special Committee that the present report may serve as a means of assessing the gravity of the plight of the civilian population in the occupied territories and the urgent need to improve its conditions. . . .

That the *intifada* was a serious and long-lived struggle for the human rights of the Palestinian people is apparent from the fact that the UN General Assembly made reference to it, condemning the policies and practices which had provoked so widespread an uprising, in resolutions adopted annually from 1988 to

1993 (resolutions 43/21, 44/2, 45/69, 46/76, 47/70, and 48/41). In 1994, however, with the establishment of the Palestinian Authority, the *intifada* diminished.

*UN SPECIAL COMMITTEE TO INVESTIGATE ISRAELI PRACTICES AFFECTING THE HUMAN RIGHTS OF THE PALESTINIAN PEOPLE AND OTHER ARABS OF THE OCCUPIED TERRITORIES.* The UN General Assembly decided, on 19 December 1968 (resolution 2433 [XXIII]) to establish the Special Committee to Investigate Israeli Practices affecting the Population of the Occupied Territories. Twenty-one years later, on 8 December 1989, the assembly changed the name of the committee (resolution 44/48 A) to the Special Committee to Investigate Israeli Practices affecting the Human Rights of the Palestinian People and Other Arabs of the Occupied Territories.

The Special Committee is composed of the following members, serving in office for indeterminate terms: Mr. Daya Perera, permanent representative of Sri Lanka to the United Nations, chairman; Mr. Alioune Sene, ambassador of Senegal in Bern and permanent representative of Senegal to the United Nations office at Geneva; and Mr. Dragan Jovanic, Yugoslavia.

In its 1989 report to the General Assembly (UN Doc. A/44/599), the Special Committee indicated (chap. III, para. 25) that in interpreting its mandate it had determined that

(a) The territories to be considered as occupied territories referred to the areas under Israeli occupation, namely, the occupied Syrian Arab Golan, the West Bank (including East Jerusalem), the Gaza Strip and the Sinai Peninsula. Following the implementation of the Egyptian-Israeli Agreement on Disengagement Forces of 18 January 1974 and the Agreement on Disengagement between Israeli and Syrian Forces of 31 May 1974, the demarcation of the areas under occupation was altered as indicated in the maps attached to those agreements. The areas of Egyptian territory under Israeli military occupation were further modified in accordance with the Treaty of Peace between the Arab Republic of Egypt and the State of Israel, which was signed on 26 March 1979 and which came into force on 25 April 1979. On 25 April 1982, the Egyptian territory remaining under Israeli military occupation was restituted to the Government of Egypt in accordance with the provisions of the aforementioned agreement. Thus, for the purposes of the present report, the territories to be considered as occupied territories are those remaining under Israeli occupation, namely, the occupied Syrian Arab Golan, the West Bank, including East Jerusalem, and the Gaza Strip;

(b) The persons covered by General Assembly resolution 2443 (XXIII) and therefore the subject of the investigation of the Special Committee were the civilian population residing in the areas occupied as a result of the hostilities of June 1967 and those persons normally resident in the areas that were under occupation but who had left those areas because of the hostilities. However, the Committee noted that resolution 2443 (XXIII) referred to the "population" without any qualification as to any segment of the inhabitants of the occupied territories;

(c) The "human rights" of the population of the occupied territories consisted of two elements, namely, those rights which the Security Council referred to as "essential and inalienable human rights" in its resolution 237 (1967) of 14 June 1967 and, secondly, those rights which found their basis in the protection afforded by international law in particular circumstances such as military occupation and, in the case of prisoners of war, capture. In accordance with General Assembly resolution 3005 (XXVII), the Special Committee was also required to investigate allegations concerning the exploitation and the looting of the resources of the occupied territories, the pillaging of the archaeological and cultural heritage of the occupied territories, and interference in the freedom of worship in the Holy Places of the occupied territories;

(d) The "policies" and "practices" affecting human rights that came within the scope of investigation by the Special Committee referred, in the case of "policies," to any course of action consciously adopted and pursued by the Government of Israel as part of its declared or undeclared intent; while "practices" referred to those actions which, irrespective of whether or not they were in implementation of a policy, reflected a pattern of behaviour on the part of the Israeli authorities towards the civilian population in the occupied areas.

In preparing its report, the Special Committee relied on the following sources: (a) the testimony of persons with first-hand knowledge of the situation of the population of the occupied territories; (b) reports in the Israeli press of pronouncements by responsible persons in the government of Israel; and (c) reports appearing in other news media, including the Arab language press published in the occupied territories in Israel and the international press. The committee also received written statements from the governments of Jordan and the Syrian Arab Republic and from the observer for Palestine. It undertook a series of hearings in Damascus, Amman, and Cairo during its meetings from 22 May to 7 June 1989, at which it heard the testimony of persons having a first-hand knowledge of the human rights situation existing in the occupied territories. It also took note of information reaching it through a variety of sources, such as individuals, organizations, and governments.

In its report, the Special Committee summarized the information which it had examined under the following main headings: (a) general situation; (b) administration of justice, including the right to a fair trial; (c) treatment of civilians; (d) treatment of detainees; (e) annexation and settlements, and (f) information concerning the occupied Syrian Arab Golan. The Committee then summarized its conclusions as follows (UN Doc. A/44/599, chap. V):

During the period relevant to this report, the Government of Israel continued to withhold its co-operation from the Special Committee. However, the Special Committee bene-

fited from the co-operation of the Governments of Egypt, Jordan and the Syrian Arab Republic, and of various Palestinian representatives. The Special Committee, having been precluded from visiting the occupied territories, conducted a series of meetings at Geneva, Damascus, Amman and Cairo in May and June of this year. At Damascus, Amman and Cairo, it heard the evidence of persons who had first-hand knowledge and personal experience of the human rights situation in the occupied territories. In addition, the Special Committee followed the situation in the occupied territories on a day-to-day basis through reports appearing in the Israeli and Palestinian press. The Special Committee examined a number of valuable communications and reports from Governments, organizations and individuals concerning the occupied territories that reached it during the period under review.

The conclusions contained in the present report are formulated on the basis of the information reflected in the periodic report (A/44/352, sect. II) and in section IV of the present report. It must be borne in mind, however, in this connection, that the volume of information received and examined by the Special Committee did not permit its total reflection in these reports; the Special Committee has endeavoured within the constraints imposed by the financial situation of the United Nations to include in the reports, as faithfully as possible, samples of the information it has received in order to illustrate the total reality of the situation of human rights in the occupied territories during the period covered by both reports.

On the basis of information and evidence put before it, the Special Committee reaches the general conclusion that the situation in the occupied territories has been marked by a dangerous level of violence and repression, which has constantly escalated since the start of the uprising of the Palestinian population against occupation in December 1987.

Information and evidence put before the Special Committee illustrate the fact that Israel has continued, during the period under consideration, to pursue its policy of annexation towards the occupied territories. This policy has led to various measures such as establishing settlements, expropriating property, transferring Israeli citizens to the occupied territories and encouraging or compelling, by various means, Palestinians to leave their homeland. The Special Committee emphasizes once again that such an attitude is in violation of the obligations of Israel as a State party to the fourth Geneva Convention relative to the Treatment of Civilians in Time of War. . . .

The report of the Special Committee also contains information on the tension prevailing in the occupied Syrian Arab Golan, illustrated by widespread demonstrations, violently dispersed by the police and border police forces.

In the opinion of the Special Committee, the overall picture drawn from the evidence and information examined by it during the period under consideration, i.e. 26 August 1988 to 25 August 1989, reveals a very alarming situation and a further deterioration in the level of enjoyment of basic human rights and fundamental freedoms by the civilian population. The provisions of the fourth Geneva Convention, which remains the main international instrument in humanitarian law that applies to the occupied territories, continue to be disregarded and violated. In view of the gravity of such developments, the Special Committee once again stresses that urgent measures must be taken in order to ensure an effective protection of the basic rights and freedoms of the civilians in the occupied territories. Such protection can only be ensured, in the long run, through the negotiation of a comprehensive, just and lasting settlement of the Arab-Israeli conflict acceptable to all concerned. In the mean time, the Special Committee wishes to reiterate the following measures which it already suggested in its twentieth report last year and which could, in the view of the Special Committee, contribute to the restoration of the basic human rights of the civilians in the occupied territories:

(a) The full application, by Israel, of the relevant provisions of the fourth Geneva Convention, which remains the main international instrument in humanitarian law that applies to the occupied territories, and whose applicability to those territories has repeatedly been reaffirmed by the Security Council, the General Assembly and other relevant organs of the United Nations;

(b) The full co-operation of the Israeli authorities with the International Committee of the Red Cross (ICRC) in order to facilitate efforts to protect detained persons, in particular by ensuring full access of ICRC representatives to such persons;

(c) The full support, by Member States, of the activities of the ICRC in the occupied territories, and positive response by Member States to eventual appeals for additional assistance including funds to finance the extra activities required by the unprecedented increase in the number of detained persons;

(d) The full support, by Member States, of UNRWA activities in the occupied territories in order to enable UNRWA to improve the general assistance provided to the refugee population.

Having considered the report of the Special Committee and other relevant documentation, the General Assembly commended (resolution 44/48A) the special committee for its efforts in performing the tasks which had been assigned to it and for its impartiality. It deplored the continued refusal by Israel to allow the special committee access to the occupied Palestine territory, including Jerusalem, and other Arab territories occupied by Israel since 1967, and demanded that Israel allow the committee access to those territories. It reaffirmed the fact that occupation itself constitutes a grave violation of the human rights of the Palestinian people in all occupied Palestinian territory.

The Assembly strongly condemned the following Israeli policies and practices:

(a) annexation of parts of the occupied Palestinian territory, including Jerusalem;

(b) imposition of Israeli laws, jurisdiction and administration on the Syrian Arab Golan, which has resulted in the effective annexation of that territory;

(c) illegal imposition and levy of taxes and dues;

(d) establishment of new Israeli settlements and expansion of the existing settlements on private and public Palestinian and other Arab lands, and transfer of an alien population thereto;

(e) eviction, deportation, expulsion, displacement and transfer of Palestinians and other Arabs of those occupied territories and denial of their right to return;

(f) confiscation and expropriation of private and public Palestinian and other Arab property in those occupied territories and all other transactions for the acquisition of land by the Israeli authorities, institutions or nationals;

(g) excavation and transformation of the landscape and the historical, cultural and religious sites, especially at Jerusalem;

(h) pillaging of archaeological and cultural property;

(i) destruction and demolition of Palestinian and other Arab houses;

(j) collective punishment, mass arrests, administrative detention and ill-treatment of Palestinians and other Arabs;

(k) torture of Palestinians and other Arabs;

(l) interference with religious freedoms and practices, as well as family rights and customs;

(m) interference with the system of education and with the social and economic and health development of the Palestinians and other Arabs in those occupied territories;

(n) interference with the freedom of movement of individuals within the occupied Palestinian territory, including Jerusalem, and other Arab territories occupied by Israel since 1967;

(o) illegal exploitation of the natural wealth, resources and labour of those occupied territories.

The General Assembly also condemned, in particular, the following Israeli policies and practices:

(a) implementation of an "iron-fist" policy against the Palestinian people in the occupied Palestinian territory;

(b) escalation of Israeli brutality since the beginning of the uprising *(intifada)* on 9 December 1987;

(c) ill-treatment and torture of children and minors under detention and/or imprisonment;

(d) closure of headquarters and offices of trade unions and social organizations and harassment, including expulsion of their leaders, as well as attacks on hospitals and their personnel;

(e) interference with the freedom of the press, including ownership, detention or expulsion of journalists, closure and suspension of newspapers and magazines, as well as denial of access to international media;

(f) killing and wounding of defenceless demonstrators;

(g) breaking of bones and limbs of thousands of civilians;

(h) house and/or town arrests;

(i) use of toxic gas, which has resulted, *inter alia*, in the killing of many Palestinians.

***THE PALESTINIAN AUTHORITY.*** After 28 years of Israeli occupation in the Gaza Strip and greater Jericho area on the West Bank, Palestinians in these areas, some 800,000 inhabitants, were granted limited self-rule in May 1994 under the first stage of the so-called Oslo Accords. **YASSAR ARAFAT,** head of the PLO, became leader of the Palestinian Authority, which assumed control of these areas.

In September 1995, the second stage of autonomy was agreed to by the Palestinian Authority and Israel. In a 460-page agreement, the parties agreed that the Israeli army would withdraw completely from six major West Bank towns (Jenin, Nablus, Qalqilya, Ramallah, Bethlehem, and Hebron), by March 1996, and would turn over civil and police control to the Palestinians. Israeli troops would also pull back from 450 smaller towns and villages, but would retain the right to move freely in those areas. Israel would keep full control over most of the area's uninhabited territory, as well as military sites and Jewish settlements. Within three weeks of the Israeli troop withdrawal in the spring of 1996, Palestinians will hold internationally monitored elections, in which an 82-member Palestinian Council will be chosen from the West Bank, Gaza, and East Jerusalem. In addition to these major articles, the Israelis agreed to free all Palestinian women prisoners and any men prisoners who are either sick or had completed two-thirds of their sentence; others will be freed on the eve of the elections. The Palestinians agreed to revoke within two years articles of the Palestinian Covenant calling for the destruction of Israel. Jews will be guaranteed freedom of access to sacred sites within the territory, such as Rachel's tomb in Bethlehem and Joseph's tomb in Nablus; the tomb of Abraham, sacred to both Jews and Muslims, will remain with separate times of worships for the two religious groups, under the watch of Israeli forces.

After the Palestinian Authority had been in power for one year, the NGO **HUMAN RIGHTS WATCH** issued a study that was highly critical of the exercise of human rights in the area, stressing the efforts of the security forces to control terrorism. It has been reported that suspects have been tried late at night without legal representation and that freedom of the press has been curtailed. In addition, the people under the Palestinian Authority have complained about the overwhelming governmental bureauracy and its inability to provide day-to-day services such as education, housing, and sewage. However, under the second stage of the Oslo Accords, the Israelis pledged to increase the Palestinians' share of West Bank water.

***SEE ALSO*** *Committee on the Exercise of the Inalienable Rights of the Palestinian People, UN; Division for Palestinian Rights, UN.*

**BIBLIOGRAPHY.** Amnesty International. *Israel and the Occupied Territories: The Military Justice System in the Occupied Territories: Detention, Interrogation and Trial Procedures.* London: 1991. NGO report, in English.

Baker, Ahmad M. "Psychological Response of Palestinian Children to Environmental Stress Associated with Military Occupation," *Journal of Refugee Studies* 4, no. 3 (1991): 237–247. Research article, in English.

Bennis, Phyllis. *From Stone to Statehood: The Palestinian Uprising.* New York and London: Olive Branch Press and Zed Books, 1990. Monograph, in English.

Bevis, Linda. *The Applicability of Human Rights Law to Occupied Territories: The Case of the Occupied Palestinian Territories.* Ramallah, West Bank: Al-Haq, 1994. NGO monograph, in English.

B'Tselem (Israeli Information Center for Human Rights in the Occupied Territories). *Closure of Schools and Other Setbacks to the Education System in the Occupied Territories.* Jerusalem: 1990. NGO factfinding report, in English.

————. *Collective Punishment in the West Bank and the Gaza Strip.* Jerusalem: 1990. NGO factfinding report, in English.

————. *Human Rights in the Occupied Territories during the War in the Persian Gulf.* Jerusalem: 1991. NGO factfinding report, in English.

————. *Violations of Human Rights in the Occupied Territories 1990/1991.* Jerusalem: 1991. NGO factfinding report, in English.

————. *Deportation of Palestinians from the Occupied Territories and the Mass Deportation of December 1992.* Jerusalem: 1993. NGO factfinding report, in English.

Graff, James A., and Mohamed Abdolell. *Palestinian Children and Israeli State Violence.* Toronto, Canada: Near East Cultural and Educational Foundation of Canada and University of Toronto Press, 1991. Monograph, in English.

Hiltermann, Joost R. "The Women's Movement during the Uprising," *Journal of Palestine Studies* 20, no. 3 (Spring 1991): 48–57. Scholarly article, in English.

Human Rights Watch. *The Gaza Strip and Jericho: Human Rights under Palestinian Partial Self-Rule.* New York: 1995. NGO report, in English.

————. *The Israeli Army and the Intifada: Policies that Contribute to the Killings.* New York: 1990. NGO factfinding report, in English.

————. *A License to Kill: Israeli Undercover Operations Against 'Wanted' and Masked Palestinians.* New York: 1993. NGO report, in English.

————. *Prison Conditions in Israel and the Occupied Territories.* New York: 1991. NGO factfinding report, in English.

————. *Torture and Ill-Treatment: Israel's Interrogation of Palestinians from the Occupied Territories.* New York: 1994. NGO report, in English.

Nixon, Anne Elizabeth, Jennifer Bing-Canar, and John Bing-Canar. *The Status of Palestinian Children during the Uprising in the Occupied Territories.* 3 vols. Stockholm, Sweden: Rädda Barnen (Swedish Save the Children), 1990. NGO factfinding report, in English.

Pacheco, Allegra A. "Occupying an Uprising: The Geneva Convention and the Israeli Administrative Detention Policy during the First Year of the Palestinian General Uprising: December 1987–December 1988," *Columbia Human Rights Law Review* 21, no. 2 (Spring 1990): 515–563. Scholarly article, in English.

Peretz, Don. *Intifada: The Palestinian Uprising.* Boulder, CO, USA: Westview Press, 1990. Scholarly monograph, in English.

Playfair, Emma, ed. *International Law and the Administration of Occupied Territories.* Oxford, UK: Oxford University Press, 1992. Scholarly monograph, in English; bibliography, pp. 505–522.

Quigley, John. *Palestine and Israel: A Challenge to Justice.* Durham, NC, USA: Duke University Press, 1990. Scholarly monograph, in English.

Rigby, Andrew. *Living the Intifada.* London and Atlantic Highlands, NJ, USA: Zed Books, 1991. Monograph, in English.

Sabbagh, Suha, and Ghada Talhami, eds. *Images and Reality: Palestinian Women under Occupation and in the Diaspora.* Washington, D.C.: Institute for Arab Women's Studies, 1990. Collected works, in English.

Salam, Nawaf A. "Between Repatriation and Resettlement: Palestinian Refugees in Lebanon," *Journal of Palestine Studies* 24, no. 1 (Autumn 1994): 18–27. Scholarly article, in English.

Shahak, Israel. "Israeli Land Seizure in the Occupied Territories," *Middle East Policy* 1 (July 1992): 96–106. Article, in English.

United Nations, Division for Palestinian Rights. *Seventh United Nations International NGO Meeting on the Question of Palestine. 29–31 August 1990.* Geneva, Switzerland: 1990. IGO conference proceedings, in English.

Zureik, Elia. "Palestinian Refugees and Peace," *Journal of Palestine Studies* 24, no. 1 (Autumn 1994): 5–17. Scholarly article, in English.

**PANAMA.** The Republic of Panama is a country in Central America, between the Pacific Ocean and the Caribbean Sea. It has borders with Colombia and Costa Rica. It achieved independence from Colombia in 1903 and became a member of the United Nations in 1945. Its population is estimated to be 2,555,000. Ethnic groups include descendants of white and black workers employed in the building of the Panama Canal (15%), American Indians (6%), and Mestizos (mixed) (79%). Languages in common use include Spanish (official) and English. Christianity (Roman Catholic, 93%; Protestant denominations, 6%) is the predominant religion. Literacy is estimated at 90%.

The government (1994) took the form of a republic. Under the 1972 constitution, as revised, the president and vice president are elected by popular vote for six-year terms. The president is head of State and government. Legislation is dealt with by a Legislative Council, also elected by popular vote. Overall policy matters are considered by the National Assembly of Community Representatives, composed of representatives of municipal districts chosen on a community rather than a party basis. Political parties include the Democratic Revolutionary Party, the Authentic Panamenista Party, the Liberal Party, the Christian Democratic Party, the Popular Action Party, the Nationalist Republican Liberal Movement, the Popular Nationalist Party, the Labor Party, the People's Party, and the Republican Party.

*INDIGENOUS POPULATIONS.* As regards Panama's indigenous populations, the government stated, in a report presented to the **COMMITTEE ON THE ELIMINATION OF RACIAL DISCRIMINATION** on 17 April 1986 (UN Doc. CERD/C/149, Add. 4, paras. 58–62) that:

Article 120 of the Constitution provides that the State shall give special attention to rural and indigenous communities with a view to promoting their economic, social and political participation in national life. This provision is supplemented by article 123 containing protective measures with respect to land tenure, as follows:

"The State shall guarantee to indigenous communities the reservation of the necessary lands and the collective ownership thereof, to ensure their economic and social welfare. The law shall regulate the procedures to be followed for this purpose and the boundaries within which private appropriation of land is prohibited".

There are three well-known indigenous groups in Panama: the Cunas, Guaymíes and the Emberás; however there are smaller, less well-known groups such as the Teribes and the Bocotás. The Cuna group inhabits the Atlantic coast of the isthmus and occupies the territory of the San Blas *Comarca*; the Guaymíes live in areas of Veraguas, Chiriquí and Bocas del Toro Provinces; the Emberá group, formerly known as the Chocoes, occupies what is now the Emberá *Comarca* in Darién Province; and the other two groups live in small areas of Bocas del Toro Province.

With the participation of these indigenous groups, the National Government has in recent years prepared various draft legislative texts, one of which became Act No. 22, of 8 November 1983, establishing the Emberá *Comarca*. Some of the other drafts are not yet entirely completed and are therefore subject to technical amendment as appropriate. These drafts include one intended to update the special arrangements for the San Blass *Comarca* established by Act No. 16 of 19 February 1953.

Broadly speaking, the above-mentioned drafts and the Embará *Comarca* Act deal with the following aspects: delimitation of the *Comarca* and political division, private property rights, government and administration, administration of justice, economy, natural resources, archeological sites and objects, and education.

A draft legislative text establishing the Cuna reservation of Madugundí de Alto Bayano was also drawn up and was approved by the Cuna leaders on 8 October 1985. The boundaries of the reservation were approved on 11 September 1985. To ensure that these agreements are effective and to control the entry of strangers into the area, the boundaries of the reservation are being marked by boundary stones and wire fences.

*DISCRIMINATION AGAINST PANAMANIAN EMPLOYEES OF THE PANAMA CANAL COMMISSION.* In the same report, the Government of Panama describes "discrimination on the ground of nationality" allegedly practiced against citizens of Panama who are employees of the Panama Canal Commission and who reside in the Canal Zone. The government states that (*Ibid.,* paras. 4–9):

Article XIII, paragraph 3, of the Agreed Minute on the Implementation of article III of the Panama Canal Treaty of 1977 stipulates that, five years after the entry into force of the Treaty, the employees of the Canal Commission who are citizens of the United States and their dependants shall not be authorized to use the military postal services or commissaries, i.e., these privileges end on 30 September 1983. Despite the foregoing, the United States Congress, through Public Law 96–70, adopted on 27 September 1979, section 1206, unilaterally and in contradiction with the Panama Canal Treaty, established a cost-of-living allowance (COLA) not only for United States citizens, but also for personnel recruited from outside the Republic of Panama, whatever their nationality, who were to lose the above-mentioned privileges on 30 September 1984.

By means of this legislation, the United States laid the legal foundation for granting economic benefits to those persons, discriminating on the ground of nationality by failing to establish similar provisions for the Panamanians residing in the Canal Zone Area who, on 1 October 1979, lost their right of eligibility and access to benefits such as housing, fuel, commissary, electricity, water, telephone, and so on. This is an overt downgrading of the terms and conditions of employment of the Panamanian personnel, and constitutes a violation of the provisions of article X, paragraph 2 (b) of the Treaty, which categorically prohibits this type of downgrading.

At the meeting of the Board of Directors of the Panama Canal Commission on 11 and 12 July 1984, the Administrator of the Canal Commission, basing himself on section 1206 of the aforementioned Public Law 96/70 submitted a recommendation, for which he obtained the approval of the United States members of the Board, for granting the following privileges, to be paid out of the Commission budget, to United States employees who lost the use of certain military facilities on 1 October 1984:

(a) Free housing and electricity;

(b) Full use of the diplomatic bag, including the dispatch and receipt of parcels;

(c) Annual travel to the United States of America;

(d) Payment of a transport differential for employees assigned to the Atlantic sector of the Canal Zone Area; and

(e) Two yearly return journeys for dependent students studying outside the Republic of Panama.

The Republic of Panama has opposed this decision, since the Panama Canal Treaty of 1977 does not contain any provision stipulating that the income of the Canal should be used to pay subsidies to United States citizens and their dependents in the employ of the Panama Canal Commission who, on 30 September 1984, lost the above-mentioned privileges, much less to the category of employees referred to in section 1206 of Public Law 96/70.

This is nothing other than an indirect subsidy, the effect of which is to perpetuate the privileges of the United States employees of the Commission, and is a flagrant act of discrimination against the employees of Panamanian nationality.

The Republic of Panama, through its members on the Board of Directors of the Canal Commission, opposed the allocation of the allowances and privileges by the Board since these are not provided for by article X, paragraph 6, of the Treaty, and represent open discrimination against Panamanian employees performing identical work. In addition, these benefits entail substantial additional costs which decrease the profits from the operation of the canal and thus directly reduce the proportion of economic benefits accruing to Panama. In this way, Panama is unjustly and illegally obliged, through a cut in its legitimate revenues, to subsidize the costs of a measure adopted against its judgement and constituting discrimination in remuneration against its own citizens.

A ten-day suspension of certain constitutional guarantees of human rights in June 1987 was explained by the government, in a report presented to the UN **Human Rights Committee** on 8 November 1988 (UN Doc. CCPR/C/42/Add. 7, paras. 30–37), as follows:

The constitutional guarantees were suspended on account of continuous disturbances of public order on Tuesday, 9 and Wednesday, 10 June 1987 in the cities of Panamá and Colón. On 10 June, since these disturbances were the outcome of constant incitement to violence by individuals and political groups of neo-fascist orientation, obviously bent on overthrowing the Government and assuming power

through violence, the Government acting under article 51 of the Constitution, proclaimed a state of emergency and the temporary suspension of the individual guarantees contained in articles 21, 22, 23, 26, 27, 29, 37, 38 and 44 of the Constitution.

In view of the disorder caused by certain opposition groups for patently subversive purposes, the President of the Republic called a meeting of his Cabinet, at which it was decided to exercise the constitutional power provided for in article 51, authorizing the suspension of guarantees "in the event of an internal disturbance threatening peace and public order". The Cabinet Council accordingly enacted Decree No. 56 of 10 June 1987, the preamble to which stated that "the political forces of the opposition, which have made incessant efforts to prolong the disturbances that occurred during the last electoral contest, have embarked on activities designed to extend the subversion to the rest of the country".

In fact, the opposition groups organizing the disturbances had decided to call a general strike to overthrow the constituted authorities and set up a Provisional Government Junta. There were outbreaks of violence in some parts of the capital which affected normal living, involving serious disruption of traffic and clashes with anti-riot squads of the Defence Forces, deployed to protect the life and personal integrity of members of society and private property. There were several instances of looting of commercial establishments in Colón. The disturbances resulted in casualties and damage to property which compelled the authorities to call out the forces of law and order.

The basic guarantees suspended were:

(a) The guarantee of not being deprived of liberty except by virtue of a written order of the competent authorities, issued in accordance with the legal formalities and for a reason previously defined by law (article 21);

(b) The guarantee of not being detained without being informed of the grounds for detention (article 22);

(c) The presumption of innocence (article 22);

(d) The remedy of *habeas corpus* (article 23);

(e) Freedom of movement (article 27);

(f) The inviolability of correspondence and of private telephone communications (article 29);

(g) Freedom to express ideas in the form of the written word or by any other means, without prior censorship (article 37);

(h) The right of assembly (article 38);

(i) The guarantee of private property acquired in accordance with the law (article 44);

The other guarantees remained in force, including those relating to inviolability of the home, equality before the law, the absence of extradition for political offences, religious liberty and the absence of the death penalty and the penalty of confiscation of property. It should also be noted that, although the right of freedom of movement was suspended, the authorities did not order curfews within the national territory or the use of military check-points on public highways.

Ten days later, since the cause for the state of emergency persisted, the Executive, again acting under article 51 of the Constitution, decided to maintain the state of emergency throughout the national territory by Decree No. 57 of 19 June 1987. The Cabinet Council further requested the President of the Republic to call on the Legislative Assembly to take cognizance of the measures adopted.

The Legislative Assembly, also exercising its constitutional and legal powers and having regard to the action taken by the Cabinet Council and the circumstances necessitating the proclamation of a state of emergency and the suspension of the above-mentioned constitutional provisions, decided, through Decree No. 57 of 19 June 1987, fully to endorse the decisions taken by the Cabinet Council.

When the causes responsible for the above-mentioned measures had ceased to exist, the Legislative Assembly, through resolution No. 22 of 29 June 1987, decided to lift the state of emergency and restore the validity of the articles of the Constitution of the Republic of Panama that had been suspended.

*AMERICAN INTERVENTION IN PANAMA.* In February 1988, General Antonio Noriega, commander of Panama's armed forces, was indicted by grand juries in Miami and Tampa, Florida (USA), on drug-trafficking charges. Panamanian President Eric Arturo Delvalle dismissed Noriega, but Delvalle himself was later dismissed by the Panamanian National Assembly.

An election to replace the president was held in May 1989, but international observers, led by former U.S. President Jimmy Carter, found much of the voting to be fraudulent. The government nullified the election before its results had been announced.

On 15 December 1989, the legislature declared Panama in a "state of war" with the United States of America, and appointed General Noriega to prepare a response. On the following day, a U.S. marine lieutenant was killed by Panamanian soldiers who claimed that he had fired shots at Noriega's military headquarters.

On 20 December, American troops were sent to Panama with a view to seizing Noriega, protecting American lives, preserving the integrity of the Panama Canal, and restoring democracy. After seeking refuge at the Vatican embassy, Noriega turned himself over to American authorities and was transferred to Miami, where he was arraigned. In a letter to U.S. President George Bush, he asserted that he was a prisoner of war. His defense lawyers maintained, without success, that he should be tried only in a neutral country by an international court.

On 29 December, the UN GENERAL ASSEMBLY (resolution 44/240) reaffirmed the sovereign and inalienable right of Panama to determine freely its social, economic, and political system and to develop its international relations without any form of foreign intervention, interference, subversion, coercion, or threat; and recalled that, in accordance with article 2, paragraph 4, of the UNITED NATIONS CHARTER, all member States shall refrain in their international relations from the threat or use of force against the territorial integrity or political independence of any State, or in any other manner inconsistent with the purposes of the United Nations. It also reaffirmed the need to restore conditions which will guarantee the full exercise of the human rights and fundamental freedoms of the Panamanian people, and expressed its concern at the serious consequences the armed in-

tervention by the United States of America in Panama might have for peace and security in the Central American region.

The Assembly deplored the intervention in Panama by the armed forces of the United States of America, "which constitutes a flagrant violation of international law and of the independence, sovereignty and territorial integrity of States"; demanded the immediate cessation of the intervention and the withdrawal from Panama of the armed invasion forces of the United States; and demanded also full respect for and strict observance of the letter and spirit of the Torrijos–Carter Treaties.

The UN COMMISSION ON HUMAN RIGHTS adopted a similar resolution on the situation in Panama (resolution 1990/10) on 20 February 1990.

President Endara was inaugurated just before the invasion and survived a series of coup attempts in the early 1990s. In legislative elections for nine seats in the Assembly in January 1991, his newly formed party failed to secure one seat and in March proceedings were undertaken to impeach him.

A Mutual Legal Assistance Treaty was approved in mid-1991, allowing the United States access to Panamanian financial information, amidst evidence suggesting that narcotics activity was at or near the levels of the 1980s.

Constitutional reforms introduced in December 1991, including abolition of the armed forces and establishment of the post of OMBUDSMAN, were rejected by 64% of voters in a referendum in November 1992. In October 1993 Endara established Panama's membership in the Central American Parliament and committed it to increased economic integration through the Central American Common Market.

Despite several reorganizations of his cabinet, Endara lost the election to Ernesto Perez Balladares in May 1994. Members of Balladares' party obtained 34 of the 72 Assembly seats. He was installed as president in September 1994.

**BIBLIOGRAPHY.** Americas Watch. *Human Rights in Panama.* New York: Human Rights Watch, 1988. NGO mission report, in English.

———. *Human Rights in Post-Invasion Panama: Justice Delayed Is Justice Denied.* New York: Human Rights Watch, 1991. NGO factfinding report, in English.

———. *The Laws of War and the Conduct of the Panama Invasion.* New York: Human Rights Watch, 1990. NGO factfinding report, in English.

Amnesty International. *Panama: Assault on Human Rights.* London: 1988. NGO report, in English.

Centro de Asesoria y Promocion Electoral, Instituto Interamericano de Derechos Humanos, Instituto de Investigaciones Juridicas, Universidad Nacional Autonoma de Mexico (Center for Electoral Counseling and Promotion, Inter-American Institute for Human Rights, and the Institute of

Legal Research, National Autonomous University of Mexico). *Legislacion Electoral Comparada: Colombia, Mexico, Panama, Venezuela y Centroamerica* (Electoral Legislation Compared: Colombia, Mexico, Panama, Venezuela, and Central America). San José, Costa Rica: 1986. Research paper, in Spanish.

Centro de Capacitacion Social y Comision Nacional de Derechos Humanos en Panama (Center for Social Training and National Human Rights Commission of Panama). *Informe sobre los Derechos Humanos en Panama a la X Asamblea de CODEHUCA* (Report on the Human Rights Situation in Panama Presented to the Tenth CODEHUCA Assembly). Panama City, Panama: 1988. NGO report, in Spanish.

Centro de Investigacion de los Derechos Humanos y Socorro Juridico de Panama (Human Rights Research Center and Legal Aid of Panama). Issues annual report. Panama: 1987. NGO report, in Spanish.

————. *La Ley 20 y Los Derechos Humanos* (Law 20 and Human Rights). Panama City, Panama: 1987. NGO report, in Spanish.

Comision de Derechos Humanos de la Provincia de Chirique (Human Rights Commission of Chiriqui Province). *Informe sobre Violaciones de los Derechos Humanos en la Provincia de Chiriqui, Rep. de Panama* (Report on Human Rights Violations in Chiriqui Province, Republic of Panama). Panama: 1987. NGO report, in Spanish.

Comisión para la Defensa de los Derechos Humanos en Centroamerica (Commission for the Defense of Human Rights in Central America). *Exhumations in Panama: Breaking the Silence.* San José, Costa Rica: 1990. NGO factfinding report, in English.

Eisenmann, Roberto. "The Struggle Against Noriega," *Journal of Democracy* 1, no. 1 (Winter 1990): 41–46. Scholarly article, in English.

Latin American Documentation. *The Church and Native Peoples.* Lima, Peru: 1986. NGO document collection, in English.

Lusane, Clarence. "Aftermath of the U.S. Invasion: Racism and Resistance in Panama," *Covert Action Information Bulletin* no. 36 (Spring 1991): 60–65. Article, in English.

Physicians for Human Rights. *Operation "Just Cause": The Human Cost of Military Action in Panama.* Boston, MA, USA: 1991. NGO factfinding report, in English.

————. *Panama 1987: Health Consequences of Police and Military Actions.* Somerville, MA, USA: 1988. NGO mission report, in English.

Weeks, John, and Phil Gunson. *Panama: Made in the USA.* London: Latin America Bureau, 1991. Monograph, in English; bibliography, pp. 127–128.

**PAN EUROPEAN UNION.** Founded in 1923, this non-governmental organization works for European political unity through the establishment of a Federation of European states, a nonpartisan political and economic union based on principles of liberty and self-determination. The Union periodically presents the Coudenhove-Halergi Award for human rights. It has members in 26 national groups. Its publications include *International Paneuropia Jugend* (issued six times a year) and the quarterly *Paneuropia* in German, Czechoslovakian, French, and Slovak.

Pan European Union. Address: Karstrasse 57 III, D-8000 Munich, Germany. Telephone: (49-89) 55-74-75. Fax: (49-89) 59-47-68. President: Dr. Otto von Habsburg.

**PANOS INSTITUTE.** Founded in 1986, this non-governmental organization works with the media and other NGOs, especially in Latin America and the Caribbean, to raise public understanding of development that will not destroy the environment. The Institute distributes "Down to Earth," a radio tape and scripted series on sustainable development; and "Panos Pictures," a specialist photo-library on development and the environment. It also conducts regional partnership programs to provide information to third-world journalists and other NGOs. The group publishes the bimonthly *Panoscope* and maintains regional offices in London, Washington, D.C., and Paris.

Panos Institute. Address: 1717 Massachusetts Ave., NW, Suite 301, Washington, D.C., 20036, USA Telephone: (202) 483-0044. Fax: (202) 483-3059. Executive Director: Mencer D. Edwards.

**PAN PACIFIC AND SOUTH-EAST ASIA WOMEN'S ASSOCIATION.** An international non-governmental organization in consultative status with the UN **ECO-NOMIC AND SOCIAL COUNCIL** (Category II), **UNESCO,** and **UNICEF,** the Association has members in 20 countries.

The Pan Pacific and South-East Asia Women's Association was founded in 1928 in Honolulu, Hawaii, at the second Conference of Pan Pacific Women, and was originally called the Pan Pacific Women's Association. It works to promote peace by fostering understanding and friendship among women of the Pacific and Southeast Asian areas and to encourage study and improvement of social conditions. One of the PPSEA-WA's principal activities is to provide finances and volunteers for projects in a number of countries to aid women in participating in rural and small business development.

The Association publishes *PPSEAWA Bulletin.*

Pan Pacific and South-East Asia Women's Association. Address: 2234 New Petchburi Road, Bangkok 10310, Thailand. Telephone: (66-2) 314-4316. President: Thanpuying Sumalee Chartikavanij.

**PAPUA NEW GUINEA.** Papua New Guinea is a country in Melanesia, occupying the eastern half of the island of New Guinea in the Pacific Ocean, north of Australia. It has a border with the Indonesian province of Irian Jaya, which occupies the western half of the island. It achieved independence from Australia in 1975 and became a member of the United Nations the same year. Its population is estimated to be 3,737,000. Ethnic groups include Melanesians, Europeans, Asians, Chinese, Indians, and Africans. Languages commonly used include English, Melanesian Pidgin, Moto, and more than 700 local dialects. Christianity is the predominant religion (Protestant denominations, 65%; Roman Catholic, 33%); Animism is the faith of the remaining 2%. Literacy is estimated at 32%.

The government (1994) took the form of a parliamentary state and member of the Commonwealth, of which the British sovereign is the symbolic head. The governor-general represents the crown and appoints as prime minister the head of the party or coalition given the majority in a popular election. The prime minister exercises executive authority as head of government and is assisted by an appointed cabinet. Legislative matters are dealt with by the unicameral 109-member Parliament, elected by popular vote. The judiciary includes the Supreme Court and the National Court. Political parties include the Pangu Party, the People's Progress Party, the United Party, the People's Democratic Movement, the National Party, the Melanesian Alliance, and the League for National Advancement.

**MULTI-RACIAL RELATIONS.** In a report presented to the UN COMMITTEE ON THE ELIMINATION OF RACIAL DISCRIMINATION on 16 August 1983, the Government of Papua New Guinea stated (UN Doc. CERD/C/101/Add. 4, paras. 3–5 and 7–13) that:

Prior to Independence and self-government, during the early years of the then administration of Papua New Guinea, a degree of racial discrimination existed within Papua New Guinea. With the advent of self-government, and later independence, discrimination on the ground of race virtually disappeared.

There now exists a non-discriminatory multiracial society in Papua New Guinea. The Government is fully conscious of the need to maintain a high degree of harmony amongst the various ethnic groups represented in Papua New Guinea. The Government believes that such harmony can best be maintained by:

(a) the process of education, both formal and nonformal;

(b) the daily interaction of the various ethnic groups in the fields of employment and social and cultural affairs; and

(c) the provision of legal sanctions which punish conduct contrary to that advocated by the International Convention.

The Government is vigilant in ensuring the racial discrimination does not arise. However, it believes that all persons living in Papua New Guinea, whether nationals or non-nationals, are fundamentally opposed to racial discrimination and that this attitude is demonstrated in their daily interaction. . . .

The Constitution provides that citizens of Papua New Guinea have the same rights, privileges, obligations and duties irrespective of race, tribe, place of origin, political opinion, colour, creed, religion or sex (section 55). Section 55 is enforceable under S.57 on application by the person af-

fected or any other person with an interest in the maintenance of the rule of law. In addition, the Supreme and National Courts of Papua New Guinea (which are the two superior Courts) may take enforcement action on their own initiative.

The Constitution also establishes a body called the "Ombudsman Commission" which, *inter alia,* has jurisdiction to investigate complaints of discrimination by governmental bodies.

The Constitution also recognizes and provides for the enjoyment or exercise of basic human rights and fundamental freedoms in the political, social, cultural and economic life of the people. It guarantees the following for all persons: (a) right to life; (b) freedom from inhuman treatment; (c) protection of the law; (d) liberty of the person; (e) freedom from forced labour; (f) freedom from arbitrary search and entry; (g) freedom from conscience, thought, and religion; (h) freedom of expression; (i) freedom of assembly and association; (j) freedom of employment; and (k) right to privacy.

Citizens have special additional rights granted by the Constitution which are: (a) the right to vote and stand for public office; (b) the right to freedom of information; (c) the right to freedom of movement; (d) protection from unjust deprivation of property; and (e) the right to acquire freehold land.

[In addition,] the Discriminatory Practices Act prohibits discriminatory practices by any person based on reasons of colour, race, ethnic, tribal or national origin. It provides for offences relating to the performance of discriminatory practices and incitement to racial hatred punishable by fines and terms of imprisonment.

**CRIME.** The National Parliament passed measures in 1991 and 1993 to combat the serious crime problem. The death penalty was introduced, the foreheads of convicted criminals were to be tattooed, and movement was restricted within the country. Criticism of the extreme measures mounted, and in September 1993 Prime Minister Paias Wingti resigned and immediately reclaimed his seat in Parliament so that, under the 1991 constitutional amendment, a motion of no confidence could not be introduced for 18 months. Amidst demonstrations and calls for Wingti's resignation, the National Court rejected a constitutional challenge to the re-election.

**BOUGAINVILLE.** The people of the island of Bougainville, part of Papua New Guinea, became increasingly demanding in their relations with the government, beginning with compensation claims in 1988 for land mined since 1972 by the Australian company of Bougainville Copper Ltd. The Bougainville Revolutionary Army (BRA) later demanded secession from Papua New Guinea and announced its independence in May 1990 in response to an economic blockade. Although the effect of the declaration was deferred and talks were ongoing, fighting continued. In August 1994, the new prime minister, Sir Julius Chan, who had been prime minister from 1980 to 1982, came to power with the aim of ending the six-year civil war in Bougainville.

Thousands of refugees continued to cross into Papua New Guinea's Western Province from the Indonesian province of Irian Jaya. Border disputes precluded the two sides from coming to an agreement that would resolve the issue of the refugees.

**BIBLIOGRAPHY.** Amankwah, H. A., and K. I. Omar. "Buttressing Constitutional Protection of Fundamental Rights in Developing Nations: The Ombudsman Commission of Papua New Guinea—A New Hybrid," *Melanesian Law Journal* 18 (1990): 74–99. Scholarly article, in English.

Amnesty International. *Papua New Guinea: Human Rights Violations on Bougainville, 1989–1990*. London: 1990. NGO report, in English.

———. *Papua New Guinea: "Under the Barrel of a Gun"—Bougainville 1991 to 1993*. London: 1993. NGO report, in English.

Committee Against Repression in the Pacific and Asia. "Harassment of Papuan Refugees Continues," *Asia Pacific Solidarity* 20 (June 1985): 14–16. NGO article, in English.

Gillespie, Rosemarie. *Inside Bougainville: Behind Papua New Guinea's Curtain*. Melbourne, Australia: Asian Development Foundation, 1992. NGO report, in English.

Human Rights Council of Australia. *Irian Jaya and Human Rights: A Working Group Report*. Canberra, Australia: 1986. NGO report, in English.

International Commission of Jurists, Australian Section. *Refuji: Report of the 1986 Mission to Papua New Guinea*. Sydney, Australia: 1986. NGO mission report, in English.

Laracy, Hugh. "Bougainville Secessionism," *Journal de la Société des Océanistes* no. 92–93 (1991): 53–59. Article, in English.

Renner, Daniela. *People in Between. A Case Study on the Kumil Timber Project. Madang Province, Papua New Guinea*. Copenhagen, Denmark: International Work Group for Indigenous Affairs, 1990. NGO report, in English.

Scott-Murphy, J., D. Dunstan, and N. Khan. *Human Rights in Melanesia: The Report of the Evatt Foundation Delegation*. Sydney, Australia: H.V. Evatt Memorial Foundation, 1988. NGO report, in English.

**PARAGUAY.** The Republic of Paraguay is a landlocked country in tropical South America. It has borders with Argentina, Bolivia, and Brazil. It achieved independence from Spain in 1811 and became a member of the United Nations in 1945. Its population is estimated to be 5,003,000. Ethnic groups include whites (3%), Amerindians (2%), and Mestizos (95%). Languages commonly used include Spanish and Guarani. Christianity is the predominant religion; the Roman Catholic Church is the established church and numbers among its adherents 95% of those who profess a religious belief, while Protestant denominations account for the remaining 5%. Literacy is estimated at 81%.

The government (1994) took the form of a republic. The president is elected by popular vote for a term of five years; he is head of State and government and appoints his own cabinet. The legislature consists of a 45-member Senate and 80-member Chamber of Deputies, all members being elected by popular vote for terms of five years. Two-thirds of the seats in each chamber are allocated to the majority party, and the remaining one-third are shared among the minority parties in proportion to the votes cast. There is also a Council of State, composed of representatives of the government, the armed forces, and other bodies; when Parliament is in recess, the president can govern by decree through that Council.

***ADMINISTRATION OF GEN. STROESSNER.*** Paraguay had a single president, Gen. Alfredo Stroessner, from 1954, when he seized power in a military coup, to 1989, when he lost it in the same way. He ruled as a dictator under a state of siege until 1965, but then was elected to eight successive terms as president; in the eighth, on 14 February 1988, he received 88.6% of the popular vote.

Under Stroessner's rule, Paraguay prospered but became notorious for its suppression of dissent, its mistreatment of its indigenous peoples, and the role it played as a hideout for international criminals, refusing to extradite them to countries where they were wanted for trial for serious offences, including war crimes and crimes against humanity. Stroessner's regime ended suddenly on 3 February 1989, when a military coup led by Gen. Andres Rodriguez forced him to resign as president and commander-in-chief of the armed forces. Gen. Rodriguez took over those functions immediately, and, on 5 February, Stroessner was flown into exile in Brazil.

Under Stroessner, the government's policies toward the Ache Indians of Paraguay's east coast—said to have reduced many of them to involuntary servitude—and its persistent detention of political prisoners were the subjects of much regional and international criticism.

The **INTER-AMERICAN COMMISSION ON HUMAN RIGHTS,** in its annual report issued on 26 September 1986 (OAS Doc. OEA/Ser.L/ . . .), reviewed the status of human rights in Paraguay under Gen. Stroessner and reported the following conclusions:

As regards the massive and most serious violations of the right to life and humane treatment, which were frequent in Paraguay in earlier decades, it is to be pointed out that during the period covered by this report there were no cases of disappearances; the incidence of torture committed by the police authorities has diminished, as well as assassinations for political reasons, although at least one major exception occurred during this period that must be mentioned here. . . .

Constant violations still occur in Paraguay of important rights recognized by the American Declaration of the Rights and Duties of Man. These violations affect, in particular, the right to a fair trial and due process; personal liberty and safety; recognition of legal capacity and other political rights and civil liberties, such as freedom to organize, freedom of association, residence and movement, and freedom of thought and expression.

The Commission once again regrets the continuous and indiscriminate application of the emergency laws contained in Laws Nos. 294 of 1955 and 209 of 1970 on "Defense of Democracy" and "Defence of Public Order and Individual Liberty", as well as the permanent state of siege established in Article 79 of the Constitution, which without fail has been extended, without interruption, every three months.

The absence of a truly autonomous judiciary has been evidenced by a paralysis of the investigations and the failure to bring to trial senior officials and authorities who may be involved in crimes. This happened, for example, with important government authorities who were presumed to have participated in the theft of several hundred million dollars in foreign exchange from the Central Bank, which was reported at the end of 1985. Initially, the courts had sentenced more than a dozen individuals supposedly implicated in the fraud to jail, but all are currently free.

*Habeas corpus,* a right that is guaranteed under Article 78 of the National Constitution, does not function in practice and is not an available remedy: the Supreme Court has continued to abdicate its functions by disqualifying itself from hearing writs of *habeas corpus* filed during the state of siege.

In the area of political and civil rights, the Government continues to regard the opposition parties that make up the "National Accord" as being "illegal" or "irregular". They are not allowed to participate in elections, nor were they permitted to organize ever since the time they were founded in 1970. The Government has also flatly rejected the planned National Dialogue that the Episcopal Conference of the Paraguayan Catholic Church encouraged in early 1986 in an attempt to gain the participation of all political and social sectors in a common, unified effort to facilitate a political transition by peaceful change towards full democracy.

In that context of lack of conditions for the exercise of democracy, the ruling Colorado Party again won municipal elections in October 1985 by an 88% majority of all votes cast in the country. At the same time, notable members of the militant wing of the Colorado Party floated President Stroessner's candidacy for an eighth presidential term in 1988–1993.

. . . . There has been a new wave of mass arrests and attacks on opposition leaders, and a move by the Government and para-police forces to contain and repress demonstrations by the political opposition and the popular demands and protests of the various segments of the population seeking greater democracy in the country. . . .

It should be noted that in most of the cases described here, the detentions lasted for a few hours or days, after which the persons arrested were freed or brought before the appropriate court authorities.

The persons filing the complaints stated that the police and para-police authorities acted with unjustified violence when they broke up the group of the demonstrators, firing their weapons practically over the heads of the marchers and beating them with knuckle-dusters and the butts of their rifles. They also used water cannons and extraordinarily potent, asphyxiating tear-gas.

Freedom of thought, freedom of expression and freedom to publish have continued under severe restrictions, in an atmosphere of an increased number of arrests, threats and intimidation of journalists, newspaper publishers and editors, and managers of radio stations and news agencies.

*NEW CONSTITUTION.* Proposals for a new constitution were approved by the National Congress in 1991 and, despite legislation pushed through Congress by President Rodriguez granting the military greater autonomy and authority, the constitution was promulgated in June 1992. The legislation regarding the military had been ignored. The death penalty was abolished, public employees (except military and police) were granted the right to form trade unions and to strike, and military officers on active duty were prohibited from direct participation in politics. Other guaranteed freedoms included the right to free political association and religion and the rights of the indigenous peoples to protect their ethnic identity.

Presidential and legislative elections were held in May 1993 and Juan Carlos Wasmosy was elected president with 40% of the vote. His party, the Partido Colorado, however, failed to gain a majority in either chamber.

As prices continued to rise, unrest grew, particularly among the rural poor, and in March 1994 an estimated 10,000 marched to the capital. The first general strike in 35 years was called in May and a demand was made for a 40% wage increase.

*REPORT OF THE UN COMMITTEE ON THE RIGHTS OF THE CHILD.* The **COMMITTEE ON THE RIGHTS OF THE CHILD** began its consideration of the report of Paraguay (CRC/C/3/Add. 17) at its 167th and 168th meetings, held on 4 and 5 October 1994, and adopted the following preliminary observations (CRC/C/15/Add. 27, paras. 3–16) at its 183rd meeting, held on 14 October 1994:

*Positive aspects.* The Committee takes note that different mechanisms have been established within the State party to deal with questions relating to the situation of children. The intention of the State party to adopt a new Juvenile Code for improving the protection and promotion of the rights of the child is also noted. Additionally, the Committee wishes to draw attention to the provision incorporated within the Constitution that not less than 20 per cent of the national budget be devoted to education. It also notes that efforts are being undertaken by the State party to provide bilingual programmes within the primary education system.

*Factors and difficulties impeding the implementation of the Convention.* The Committee notes that Paraguay is going through a period of transition to democracy, having only recently emerged from a dictatorship form of governance. The Committee recognizes that the legacy of certain attitudes and traditions from this period hamper the effective implementation of the rights of the child.

*Principal subjects of concern.* The Committee is concerned that sufficient attention does not seem to have been paid to the development of a coordinating institution to monitor the implementation of the rights of the child in Paraguay. The

Committee is equally concerned about the extent to which the bodies established to consider the situation of children are provided with the requisite support and resources in order to permit them to fulfil their designated functions. In addition, the Committee remains unclear as to the extent to which the process of reviewing the implementation of the rights of the child in the State party was designed to encourage and facilitate popular participation and public scrutiny of government policies.

The Committee is of the view that adequate measures have not yet been taken to make the principles and provisions of the Convention known to adults and children alike. Similarly, it is noted that professionals and personnel working with or for children, including military personnel, law enforcement officials, judges, health workers and teachers, lack sufficient training about the Convention on the Rights of the Child and other relevant international standards relating to the rights of the child.

The Committee wishes to express its general concern that the State party does not appear to have fully taken into account the provisions of the Convention, including its general principles, as reflected in its articles 2, 3, 6 and 12, in the legislative and other measures relevant to children in Paraguay. In this connection, the Committee notes that the low marriageable age for girls, presently standing at 12, and the fact that this age is lower for girls than boys are incompatible with the provisions of the Convention, including those of its article 2. In addition, the Committee is of the opinion that other legislation in force in Paraguay relating to the definition of the child with regard to the performance of military service and to the non-validity of children's statements in cases of alleged sexual abuse also raises concern as to its compatibility with the spirit and purpose of the Convention, especially in ensuring that the best interests of the child shall be a primary consideration in all actions concerning children.

The Committee is generally concerned that Paraguayan society is not sufficiently sensitive to the needs and situation of the girl child. It also notes the persistence of discrimination against children belonging to minority and indigenous groups contrary to the provisions of article 2 of the Convention.

Moreover, within the framework of the application of article 4 of the Convention, relating to the allocation of resources to the maximum extent possible, the Committee is concerned about the insufficient portion of the national and local-level budgets allocated to social and human needs, especially with regard to responding to the situation of the most vulnerable groups of children. In this connection, the Committee wishes to emphasize the importance of the provisions of article 3 of the Convention, relating to the best interests of the child, in guiding deliberations and decisions on policy, including with regard to the allocation of human and economic resources for the implementation of the rights guaranteed under the Convention. The Committee also wishes to underline its concern about the adequacy of statistical and other data collection systems existing within the State party to assist in the formulation and design of strategies to implement the rights of the child.

The Committee is concerned that insufficient measures have been taken to implement the provisions of articles 7 and 8 of the Convention, particularly with regard to ensuring birth registration and that children are provided with the necessary registration certificates and other documents which accurately protect and preserve the elements of their identity. It is noted that the absence of appropriate measures for registration may seriously affect the level of the child's enjoyment of other fundamental rights and freedoms.

The Committee expresses its grave concern over the information brought to its attention of alleged trafficking in inter-country adoptions in violation of the provisions and principles of the Convention. It is further concerned about the absence of a normative framework in the field of inter-country adoptions, namely in the light of articles 3, 12 and 21 of the Convention.

The Committee notes that the social inequalities existing in the country, including through the unequal distribution of income and land, have contributed to the considerable problems facing children in Paraguay. The Committee is further concerned that the difficulties being faced by children living in rural and in disadvantaged urban areas may lead to their parents or guardians placing them in the service of wealthier families which frequently leads to the ill-treatment and abuse of these children.

The Committee is very much alarmed at reports it has received of the ill-treatment of children in detention centres. In view of the seriousness of such alleged violations, the Committee is concerned about the insufficient training provided to law enforcement officials and personnel of detention centres on the provisions and principles of the Convention and other relevant international instruments such as "The Beijing Rules", the Riyadh Guidelines and the United Nations Rules for the Protection of Juveniles Deprived of their Liberty.

The Committee is concerned that, in spite of the fact that the educational system is undergoing a considerable process of reform, the problems of a low rate of access to and retention in school, as well as a high level of school drop-out, remain.

*Further action.* The Committee notes that, during the initial dialogue with the State party, matters relating to basic health and special protection measures were not addressed. The Committee recommends that the additional report requested of the State party cover these issues. In addition, the Committee wishes to be informed of the progress achieved with regard to the establishment of a national coordinating mechanism to monitor the rights of the child and of the participation of various bodies involved in promoting and protecting children's rights, including non-governmental organizations, in such monitoring activities. The Committee would also wish to be informed of the measures taken to ensure that the provisions of the Convention, particularly its articles 3, 12 and 21, are fully taken into consideration, including in the determination and application of legislation and procedures pertaining to the matter of adoption. In this connection, the Committee wishes to encourage the Government of Paraguay to consider ratifying the Hague Convention on Protection of Children and Cooperation in respect of Intercountry Adoption of 1993 and concluding bilateral agreements with the countries of prospective adoptive parents.

The Committee notes the statement contained in paragraph 160 of the State party report which indicates the importance the Government of Paraguay attaches to the Committee's advice on measures to be taken to improve the implementation of the rights of the child, and welcomes the State party's commitment to cooperating with the Committee and other United Nations bodies and agencies with a view to promoting and protecting the rights of the child. In this connection, the Committee takes further note of the technical cooperation currently provided to the Government of Paraguay through a joint programme supported by the Centre for Human Rights and the United Nations Development Programme. The Committee recommends that the concerns raised by the Committee with regard to the

# P

realization of the rights of the child should be incorporated within the activities organized under this joint programme.

**BIBLIOGRAPHY.** Alegre Ortiz, Heriberto. *La Sociedad Cautiva* (The Captive Society). Asunción, Paraguay: Comisión de Defensa de los Derechos Humanos del Paraguay (Paraguayan Commission for the Defense of Human Rights), 1987. NGO monograph, in Spanish.

Americas Watch. *Paraguay: An Encouraging Victory in the Search for Truth and Justice.* New York: Human Rights Watch, 1992. NGO report, in English.

————. *Paraguay: Latin America's Oldest Dictatorship under Pressure.* New York: 1986. NGO mission report, in English.

————. *Paraguay: New Outbursts of Violence in Land Disputes.* New York: Human Rights Watch, 1991. NGO factfinding report, in English and Spanish.

————. *Paraguay: Repression in the Countryside.* New York: 1988. NGO report, in English.

Amnesty International. *Human Rights Violations in Paraguay.* London: 1985. NGO report, in English.

————. *Paraguay: Investigations into Past Human Rights Violations.* London: 1990. NGO factfinding report, in English.

Asociación Interamericana de Servicios Legales (Interamerican Association of Legal Services). *Primer Encuentro Nacional de Servicios Legales Populares del Paraguay, Ciudad del Este, Noviembre de 1989* (First National Meeting of Popular Legal Services of Paraguay—Ciudad del Este, November 1989). Bogotá, Colombia: 1990. Conference report, in Spanish.

Barboza, Ramiro. *El Ocaso de la Tiranía: 1986–1989* (The Decline of Tyranny: 1986–1989). Asunción, Paraguay: Comisión de Defensa de los Derechos Humanos del Paraguay, 1990. Monograph, in Spanish.

Bouvier, V. M. *Decline of the Dictator: Paraguay at a Crossroads.* Washington, D.C.: Washington Office on Latin America, 1988. NGO report, in English.

Comité de Iglesias para Ayudas de Emergencia (Committee of Churches for Emergency Aid). "Sesión Paraguaya del Tribunal Permanente de los Pueblos" (Paraguayan Session of the Permanent Tribunal of the People), *Notas Trimestrales* no. 15 (Spring 1990): 21–25. Article, in Spanish.

Davis, Shelton H. *Land Rights and Indigenous Peoples: The Role of the Inter-American Commission on Human Rights.* Cambridge, MA, USA: Cultural Survival, 1988. NGO report, in English.

Instituto Interamericano de Derechos Humanos, Centro de Asesoría y Promoción Electoral (Inter-American Institute of Human Rights, Centre for Electoral Counseling and Promotion). *Paraguay: Hacia la Consolidación Democrática* (Paraguay: Towards Stronger Democracy). San José, Costa Rica: 1990. NGO monograph, in English.

Inter-American Commission on Human Rights. *Report of the Situation of Human Rights in Paraguay.* Washington, D.C.: Annual report. IGO report, in English.

Inter-Church Committee on Human Rights in Latin America. *ICCHRLA Annual Report: General Concerns and Brief Country Reports.* Toronto, Canada. NGO report, in English.

Organization of American States. *Inter-American Yearbook on Human Rights.* Dordrecht, the Netherlands: Martinus Nijhoff. IGO annual report, in Spanish.

Washington Office on Latin America. *Paraguay: A Transition in Search of Democracy.* Washington, D.C.: 1990. NGO report, in English.

**PARLIAMENTARY ASSOCIATION FOR EURO-ARAB COOPERATION.** An international non-governmental organization in consultative status (Roster) with the UN **Economic and Social Council,** PAEAC has members in 19 countries; individual members come from the European community national parliaments and the European Parliament of the **Council of Europe.**

Founded in 1974 in Paris, the Association supports a European-Arab dialogue for cooperation between the European and Arab worlds; particular emphasis is laid on the Palestinian question. PAEAC expresses the Arab point of view through the Parliamentary Assembly of the Council of Europe and supports recognition of the **PLO** and the establishment of a Palestinian State in Palestine. The Association publishes the quarterly *PAEAC Information Bulletin* and the triannual *Euro-Arab Political Fact Sheets.*

Parliamentary Association for Euro-Arab Cooperation. Address: Rue de la Tourelle 21, B-1040 Brussels, Belgium. Telephone: (32-2) 231-1300. Fax: (32-2) 231-0646. Secretary-General: Jean-Michel Dumont.

**PASSY, FREDERICK (1822–1912).** A co-winner of the 1901 **Nobel Peace Prize,** the first ever awarded, Frederick Passy was a renowned pacifist who had founded two of the most influential organizations dedicated to peace in the 19th century—the International Peace League and the **Inter-Parliamentary Union.** He was cited by the Nobel Committee as "the apostle of peace."

Born in Paris, Passy was a lawyer and economist. Early in his career, he was a devotee of free trade, believing that economic advancement would deter war. He also was a strong advocate of labor rights and an opponent of colonialism. In 1867, he founded the International Peace League *(Le Ligue Internationale et Permanente de la Paix),* which was later renamed the French Society of the Friends of Peace. He was instrumental in bringing to fruition the Inter-Parliamentary Union, a society that brought together members of parliaments of all countries to discuss international issues and seek ways to arbitrate disputes between nations.

**BIBLIOGRAPHY.** Gray, Tony. *Champions of Peace.* London: Paddington Press, 1976.

Schlessinger, Bernard S., and June H. Schlessinger, eds. *Who's Who of Nobel Prize Winners.* Phoenix, AZ, USA: Oryx Press, 1991.

**PAULING, LINUS (1901–1994).** This American scientist is the only man in the history of the Nobel Prizes to have won undivided awards in two categories: in

1954, he received the Nobel Prize for chemistry; and in 1962, the **Nobel Peace Prize.**

Born in Portland, OR (USA), Pauling spent his early years working on such projects as the relationship between molecular abnormality and heredity and the chemical basis of mental retardation; and his later years, on the effect of vitamin C on preventing the common cold. His Nobel Prize in chemistry was awarded for "studies of the nature of the chemical bond," work he had undertaken early in his career, culminating in his widely read and influential 1939 monograph *The Nature of the Chemical Bond and the Structure of Molecules and Crystals*, in which he applied quantum mechanics to chemistry.

Related to his scientific work was his crusade for nuclear disarmament, which often took the form of bringing together scientists to testify to the dangers of nuclear testing. His first such effort came in 1946 when he formed the Emergency Committee of Atomic Scientists. In the following decade, he was to concentrate on the problems of the hydrogen bomb, issuing in 1955 the Mainau Declaration, signed by 52 Nobel laureates, for which act he came under suspicion as a Communist sympathizer by the U.S. Congressional Sub-Committee on Un-American Activities and had his passport revoked on several occasions. In 1957, when Pauling began to concentrate his efforts on the effects of nuclear fallout due to testing on human health and heredity, he issued the "Pauling Appeal," signed by 10,000 international scientists, urging the cessation of all nuclear testing. Because of his unceasing work in this area, Pauling is often credited as the force behind the 1963 Nuclear Test Ban Treaty signed by the United States, the USSR, and Great Britain.

Pauling taught at several American universities, his longest tenure being at the California Institute of Technology (1927–1963). After retirement from teaching, he founded the Linus Pauling Institute of Science and Medicine, an independent, nonprofit research and educational institution devoted to "orthomolecular medicine," which makes the optimum use of vitamins, minerals, and other dietary supplements in the treatment of illness.

***BIBLIOGRAPHY.*** Gray, Tony. *Champions of Peace.* London: Paddington Press, 1976.

Hager, Thomas. *Force of Nature: The Life of Linus Pauling.* New York: Simon and Schuster, 1995.

Schlessinger, Bernard S., and June H. Schlessinger, eds. *Who's Who of Nobel Prize Winners.* Phoenix, AZ, USA: Oryx Press, 1991.

**PAX CHRISTI, INTERNATIONAL CATHOLIC PEACE MOVEMENT.** An international non-governmental organization in consultative status with the UN **Economic and Social Council** (Category II), **UNESCO,** and the **Council of Europe,** Pax Christi has national sections in 19 countries.

Founded in 1945, Pax Christi works for universal peace, to help build a world which is genuinely more humane for all people everywhere—a world founded on respect for the life, conscience, and rights of each human being—and to promote the freedom and political and social responsibilities of individuals and communities.

Pax Christi has created international meeting centers, open to all but particularly to young people; it organizes an annual peace march, *"Route international de la paix,"* always in a different country, where participants walk and pray together; and it works with other interested organizations on matters of disarmament, development, and human rights. It has also organized "East-West-South Projects," which hold programs on topics such as security and disarmament, human rights, and peace education.

Pax Christi publishes the bi-monthly *International Pax Christi Bulletin* in English and French.

Pax Christi. Address: Rue du vieux Marché aux Grains 21, B-1000 Brussels, Belgium. Telephone: (32-2) 502-55-50. Fax: (32-2) 502-46-26. International Secretary: Etienne de Jonghe.

**PAX ROMANA–INTERNATIONAL CATHOLIC MOVEMENT FOR INTELLECTUAL AND CULTURAL AFFAIRS (ICMICA).** An international nongovernmental organization in consultative status with the UN **Economic and Social Council** (Category II), **UNESCO,** and the **Council of Europe,** ICMICA has members in 66 countries.

Founded in 1947, when "Pax Romana" was split into two autonomous divisions—ICMICA and **Pax Romana–International Movement of Catholic Students (IMCS)**—ICMICA works to unite Catholic university graduates to search for solutions to problems posed by modern life and to place their intellectual and moral resources at the service of peace. ICMICA has four professional secretariats: lawyers; engineers, agronomists, and industry officials; scientific affairs; and secondary teachers.

ICMICA publishes the quarterly *Pax Romana–ICMICA News* in English, French, and Spanish.

Pax Romana–International Catholic Movement for Intellectual and Cultural Affairs. Address: 37-39 rue de Vermont, P.O. Box 85, CH-1211 Geneva 20-CIC, Switzerland. Telephone: (41-22) 733-6740. Fax: (41-22) 733-6449. Secretary-General: Victor P. Karunan.

**PAX ROMANA–INTERNATIONAL MOVEMENT OF CATHOLIC STUDENTS (IMCS).** Founded in 1921 in Fribourg, Switzerland, this branch of the NGO Pax Romana changed its focus in 1947 from a purely student movement to a world union of Catholic university students and intellectual leaders. The IMCS is concerned with questions of liberation and the involvement of Christian students. The group works for liberation and development in social, economic, and cultural fields; mobilizes the support of churches for world justice; studies ways of adapting the university to the present needs of man and society; and supports the general trend towards greater flexibility and pluralism within the Catholic Church. It maintains consultative status with the UN Economic and Social Council (Category II) and UNESCO. IMCS has national federations in 72 countries, with regional secretariats for Africa, Asia, Europe, and Latin America.

It publishes the *IMCS Newsletter 'Habari'* and, in conjunction with Pax Romana–ICMICA, the quarterly *Convergence*.

Pax Romana–IMCS. Address: 171 rue de Rennes, F-75006 Paris, France. Telephone: (33-1) 4544-7075.

## PEACE AND HUMAN RIGHTS.

It has long been asserted that human rights and peace are codependent: only in an atmosphere of peace and friendly relations can human rights be fully appreciated and enjoyed; and only when human rights are achieved for all people can peace exist. The UNITED NATIONS CHARTER brings the questions of peace and human rights together in its preamble:

We the people of the United Nations determined
to save succeeding generations from the scourge of war, which twice in our lifetime has brought untold sorrow to mankind, and
to reaffirm faith in fundamental human rights, in the dignity and worth of the human person, in the equal rights of men and women and of nations large and small, and . . .
to practice tolerance and live together in peace with one another as good neighbours, and
to unite our strength to maintain international peace and security, and . . .
to employ international machinery for the promotion of the economic and social advancement of all peoples, have resolved to combine our efforts to accomplish these aims.

Article 1 of the Charter further asserts the following:

The purposes of the United Nations are:
1. To maintain international peace and security, and to that end: to take effective collective measures for the prevention and removal of threats to the peace, and for the suppression of acts of aggression or other breaches of the peace, and to bring about by peaceful means, and in conformity with the principles of justice and international law, adjustment or settlement of international disputes or situations which might lead to a breach of the peace;
2. To develop friendly relations among nations based on

respect for the principle of equal rights and self-determination of peoples, and to take other appropriate measures to strengthen universal peace;
3. To achieve international co-operation in solving international problems of an economic, social, cultural, or humanitarian character, and in promoting and encouraging respect for human rights and for fundamental freedoms for all without distinction as to race, sex, language, or religion; and
4. To be a centre for harmonizing the actions of nations in the attainment of these common ends.

## DECLARATION ON THE ESSENTIALS OF PEACE.

In 1949, the United Nations adopted the Declaration concerning Essentials of Peace after a lengthy and heated debate in the GENERAL ASSEMBLY over two proposals: one, by the Union of Soviet Socialist Republics, that the five permanent members of the SECURITY COUNCIL conclude among themselves a "Pact for Strengthening the Peace"; and the second, by the United Kingdom and the United States of America, that the United Nations lay down the basic principles necessary to achieve an enduring peace. The Soviet proposal was criticized as an attempt to create a body superseding the Security Council, while that of the United Kingdom and United States was said to be "wholly unrealistic, inadequate, and composed of phrases culled from the UN Charter." The UK/USA proposal was adopted by 53 votes to 5.

The Declaration, adopted by the UN General Assembly on 1 December 1949 (resolution 290 [IV]), states the following:

The General Assembly
1. Declares that the Charter of the United Nations, the most solemn pact of peace in history, lays down basic principles necessary for an enduring peace; that disregard of these principles is primarily responsible for the continuance of international tension; and that it is urgently necessary for all Members to act in accordance with these principles in the spirit of co-operation on which the United Nations was founded;
Calls upon every nation
2. To refrain from threatening or using force contrary to the Charter;
3. To refrain from any threats or acts, direct or indirect, aimed at impairing the freedom, independence or integrity of any State, or at fomenting civil strife and subverting the will of the people in any State;
4. To carry out in good faith its international agreements;
5. To afford all United Nations bodies full co-operation and free access in the performance of the tasks assigned to them under the Charter;
6. To promote, in recognition of the paramount importance of preserving the dignity and worth of the human person, full freedom for the peaceful expression of political opposition, full opportunity for the exercise of religious freedom and full respect for all the other fundamental rights expressed in the Universal Declaration of Human Rights;
7. To promote nationally and through international co-

operation, efforts to achieve and sustain higher standards of living for all peoples;

8. To remove the barriers which deny to peoples the free exchange of information and ideas essential to international understanding and peace;

Calls upon every Member

9. To participate fully in all the work of the United Nations:

Calls upon the five permanent members of the Security Council

10. To broaden progressively their co-operation and to exercise restraint in the use of the veto in order to make the Security Council a more effective instrument for maintaining peace;

Calls upon every nation

11. To settle international disputes by peaceful means and to co-operate in supporting United Nations efforts to resolve outstanding problems;

12. To co-operate to attain the effective international regulation of conventional armaments; and

13. To agree to the exercise of national sovereignty jointly with other nations to the extent necessary to attain international control of atomic energy which would make effective the prohibition of atomic weapons and assure the use of atomic energy for peaceful purposes only.

**DECLARATION ON THE PREPARATION OF SOCIETIES FOR LIFE IN PEACE.** In 1978, the UN General Assembly reaffirmed the right of individuals, States, and all mankind to peace and pointed out that every State must accept certain duties and responsibilities as its contribution to ensuring the enjoyment of that right.

The Declaration was adopted by the General Assembly on 15 December 1978 (resolution 33/73). The text, annexed to that resolution, is as follows:

The General Assembly

### I

Solemnly invites all States to guide themselves in their activities by the recognition of the supreme importance and necessity of establishing, maintaining and strengthening a just and durable peace for present and future generations and, in particular, to observe the following principles:

1. Every nation and every human being, regardless of race, conscience, language or sex, has the inherent right to life in peace. Respect for that right, as well as for the other human rights, is in the common interest of all mankind and an indispensable condition of advancement of all nations, large and small, in all fields.

2. A war of aggression, its planning, preparation or initiation are crimes against peace and are prohibited by international law.

3. In accordance with the purposes and principles of the United Nations, States have the duty to refrain from propaganda for wars of aggression.

4. Every State, acting in the spirit of friendship and good-neighbourly relations, has the duty to promote all-round, mutually advantageous and equitable political, economic, social and cultural co-operation with other States, notwithstanding their socio-economic systems, with a view to securing their common existence and cooperation in peace, in

conditions of mutual understanding of and respect for the identity and diversity of all peoples, and the duty to take up actions conducive to the furtherance of the ideals of peace, humanism and freedom.

5. Every State has the duty to respect the right of all peoples to self-determination, independence, equality, sovereignty, the territorial integrity of States and the inviolability of their frontiers, including the right to determine the road of their development, without interference or intervention in their internal affairs.

6. A basic instrument of the maintenance of peace is the elimination of the threat inherent in the arms race, as well as efforts towards general and complete disarmament, under effective international control, including partial measures with that end in view, in accordance with the principles agreed upon within the United Nations and relevant international agreements.

7. Every State has the duty to discourage all manifestations and practices of colonialism, as well as racism, racial discrimination and *apartheid,* as contrary to the right of peoples to self-determination and to other human rights and fundamental freedoms.

8. Every State has the duty to discourage advocacy of hatred and prejudice against other peoples as contrary to the principles of peaceful coexistence and friendly co-operation.

### II

Calls upon all States, in order to implement the above principles:

(a) To act perseveringly and consistently, with due regard for the constitutional rights and the role of the family, the institutions and the organizations concerned:

(i) To ensure that their policies relevant to the implementation of the present Declaration, including educational processes and teaching methods as well as media information activities, incorporate contents compatible with the task of the preparation for life in peace of entire societies and, in particular, the young generations;

(ii) Therefore, to discourage and eliminate incitement to racial hatred, national or other discrimination, injustice or advocacy of violence and war;

(b) To develop various forms of bilateral and multilateral cooperation, also in international, governmental and nongovernmental organizations, with a view to enhancing preparation of societies to live in peace and, in particular, exchanging experiences on projects pursued with that end in view;

### III

1. Recommends that the governmental and nongovernmental organizations concerned should initiate appropriate action towards the implementation of the present Declaration;

2. States that a full implementation of the principles enshrined in the present Declaration calls for concerted action on the part of Governments, the United Nations and the specialized agencies, in particular the United Nations Educational, Scientific and Cultural Organization, as well as other interested international and national organizations, both governmental and nongovernmental;

3. Requests the Secretary-General to follow the progress made in the implementation of the present Declaration and to submit periodic reports thereon to the General Assembly, the first such report to be submitted not later than at its thirty-sixth session.

**DECLARATION ON THE RIGHT OF PEOPLES TO PEACE.** In this Declaration, the UN General Assembly points out that recognition and enjoyment of the right of peoples to peace is essential to full implementation of the human rights and fundamental freedoms proclaimed by the United Nations. The Declaration was adopted by the Assembly on 12 November 1984 (resolution 39/11). The text, annexed to that resolution, is as follows:

The General Assembly,

Reaffirming that the principal aim of the United Nations is the maintenance of international peace and security,

Bearing in mind the fundamental principles of international law set forth in the Charter of the United Nations,

Expressing the will and the aspirations of all peoples to eradicate war from the life of mankind and, above all, to avert a world-wide nuclear catastrophe,

Convinced that life without war serves as the primary international prerequisite for the material well-being, development and progress of countries, and for the full implementation of the rights and fundamental human freedoms proclaimed by the United Nations,

Aware that in the nuclear age the establishment of a lasting peace on Earth represents the primary condition for the preservation of human civilization and the survival of mankind,

Recognizing that the maintenance of a peaceful life for peoples is the sacred duty of each State,

1. Solemnly proclaims that the peoples of our planet have a sacred right to peace;

2. Solemnly declares that the preservation of the right of peoples to peace and the promotion of its implementation constitute a fundamental obligation of each State;

3. Emphasizes that ensuring the exercise of the right of peoples to peace demands that the policies of States be directed towards the elimination of the threat of war, particularly nuclear war, the renunciation of the use of force in international relations and the settlement of international disputes by peaceful means on the basis of the Charter of the United Nations;

4. Appeals to all States and international organizations to do their utmost to assist in implementing the right of peoples to peace through the adoption of appropriate measures at both the national and the international level.

**INTERNATIONAL YEAR OF PEACE (1985).** In 1982, the UN General Assembly declared (resolution 37/16) 1986 to be the International Year of Peace as a commemoration of the 40th anniversary of the United Nations. The Proclamation of the International Year of Peace, approved by the General Assembly on 24 October 1985 (resolution 40/3), links the promotion and achievement of the ideals of peace to the promotion and protection of human rights—both being fundamental purposes of the United Nations Charter. The text of the Proclamation, annexed to resolution 40/3, is as follows:

Whereas, the General Assembly has decided unanimously to proclaim solemnly the International Year of Peace on 24 October 1985, the fortieth anniversary of the United Nations,

Whereas the fortieth anniversary of the United Nations provides a unique opportunity to reaffirm the support for and commitment to the purposes and principles of the Charter of the United Nations,

Whereas peace constitutes a universal ideal and the promotion of peace is the primary purpose of the United Nations,

Whereas the promotion of international peace and security requires continuing and positive action by States and peoples aimed at the prevention of war, removal of various threats to peace—including the nuclear threat—respect for the principle of non-use of force, the resolution of conflicts and peaceful settlement of disputes, confidence-building measures, disarmament, maintenance of outer space for peaceful uses, development, the promotion and exercise of human rights and fundamental freedoms, decolonization in accordance with the principle of self-determination, elimination of racial discrimination and *apartheid,* the enhancement of the quality of life, satisfaction of human needs and protection of the environment,

Whereas peoples must live together in peace and practise tolerance, and it has been recognized that education, information, science and culture can contribute to that end,

Whereas the International Year of Peace provides a timely impetus for initiating renewed thought and action for the promotion of peace,

Whereas the International Year of Peace offers an opportunity to Governments, intergovernmental, non-governmental organizations and others to express in practical terms the common aspiration of all peoples for peace,

Whereas the International Year of Peace is not only a celebration or commemoration, but an opportunity to reflect and act creatively and systematically in fulfilling the purposes of the United Nations,

Now, therefore,

The General Assembly

Solemnly proclaims 1986 to be the International Year of Peace and calls upon all peoples to join with the United Nations in resolute efforts to safeguard peace and the future of humanity.

The UN **SUB-COMMISSION ON PREVENTION OF DISCRIMINATION AND PROTECTION OF MINORITIES** continued at its 1989 session its periodic consideration of the question of the interrelationship between human rights and international peace as it had been requested to do by the **COMMISSION ON HUMAN RIGHTS** in 1982 (resolution 1982/7).

The Sub-Commission based its work on a study prepared in 1988 by the Secretary-General (UN Doc. E/CN.4/Sub.2/1988/2), which reviewed the efforts of UN bodies and other organizations to focus attention on this question, pointed out that a number of international instruments made reference to the interrelationship between the realization of human rights and peace, and drew attention to a special category of violations of human rights—termed "gross and flagrant violations"—that presented the most serious threat to peace.

After examining the report, the Sub-Commission

agreed (resolution 1989/47) that the strengthening of international peace and security, as well as the reduction of expenditures for arms, are important conditions for economic and social development and for the materialization of all human rights and that, conversely, the effective realization of human rights in all parts of the world would contribute to the achievement of international peace and security.

As a basis for its further study of the question, the Sub-Commission invited one of its members, Mr. Murlidhar Bhandare (India), to prepare a working paper on the problem of the interrelationship between international peace and the effective materialization of all human rights for consideration at future sessions.

Mr. Bhandare's working paper (E/CN.4/Sub.2/1991/32 and Corr. 1) was submitted to the Sub-Commission at its 1991 session, but was examined only at the 1992 session. At that time the Sub-Commission, after studying the paper with care and discussing it at length, requested Mr. Bhandare to supplement it and to present a further document on the subject to the Sub-Commission in 1994.

**BIBLIOGRAPHY.** Forsythe, David P. *Human Rights and Peace: International and National Dimensions.* Lincoln, NE, USA: University of Nebraska Press, 1993. Scholarly monograph, in English.

Lavielle, Jean-Marc. "Les rapports entre les droits de l'homme, le développement et la paix" (Relationship between Human Rights, Development and Peace), *Revue trimestrielle des droits de l'homme* 1, no. 3 (July 1990): 211–229. Scholarly article, in French.

Nanda, Ved P., ed. "Nuclear Weapons and the Right to Survival, Peace and Development: An Introduction," *Denver Journal of International Law and Policy* 19, no. 1 (Fall 1990): 1–112. Scholarly articles, in English.

Przetacznik, Frank. "The Basic Collective Human Right to Self-Determination of Peoples and Nations as a Prerequisite for Peace," *New York Law School Journal of Human Rights* 8, no. 1 (Fall 1990): 49–109. Scholarly article, in English.

## PEACEKEEPING FORCES, UN.

UN Peacekeeping Forces received the 1988 **NOBEL PEACE PRIZE** for "demanding and hazardous service in the cause of peace." In accepting the Prize, then-Secretary-General Javier Pérez de Cuéllar stated, "Peacekeeping operations symbolize the world community's will to peace and represent the impartial, practical expression of that will. . . . To remain calm in the face of provocation, to maintain composure when under attack, the UN troops—officers and soldiers alike—must show a special kind of courage, one that is more difficult to come by than the ordinary kind."

Peacekeeping was pioneered and developed by the United Nations as one of the means for maintaining international peace and security. Interposed between hostile States—and sometimes between hostile communities within a State, as in the Bosnian conflict—international military personnel under UN command have contributed to creating the conditions necessary for peaceful settlement of disputes. From 1948 through 1995, approximately one million soldiers and civilians have served under the UN flag in 33 peacekeeping operations. Approximately 1,000 have died while monitoring ceasefires, patrolling demilitarized areas, manning buffer zones, and defusing conflicts.

Peacekeeping as a concept and duty of the United Nations is not specifically described in the **UNITED NATIONS CHARTER,** because it goes beyond the purely diplomatic means for the peaceful settlement of disputes described in chapter 6 of the Charter but falls short of the military or other enforcement provisions of chapter 7. Indeed, former UN Secretary-General **DAG HAMMARSKJÖLD,** who was largely responsible for the use of peacekeeping forces, suggested that peacekeeping might be added to the Charter as "chapter six-and-a-half." Because it is not specifically mandated, the functions of peacekeeping forces has evolved from its first employment to the present day. Prior to the ending of the so-called "cold war" around 1988, peacekeeping forces were largely military in composition and in function, entrusted to maintain calm on the front lines while giving warring factions a chance to negotiate a settlement. Since 1988, the "second generation" of peacekeeping forces have responded to new facets of international conflict: rescuing weak institutions or "failed States," collapsing economies, natural disasters, and internal conflicts such as ethnic and tribal warfare. In 1992, UN Secretary-General Boutros Boutros-Ghali issued *An Agenda for Peace,* in which he introduced proposals for more effective UN operations, such as the increased use of confidence-building and factfinding measures and the preventive deployment of a UN presence or establishment of demilitarized zones in potential conflict areas. In January 1995, the Secretary-General again called for changes in peacekeeping operations, in which he asked the **SECURITY COUNCIL** to be clearer in its mandates so that peacekeeping operations are not confused with enforcement. He also argued for strengthening a system of unified command so that troops in a multinational operation would take orders from one commander on the ground and for stockpiling more supplies in regional centers closer to areas of conflict.

The following is a chronological list of UN peacekeeping operations:

| | |
|---|---|
| 1948 to date | UN Truce Supervision Organization (UNTSO) |
| 1949 to date | UN Military Observer Group in India and Pakistan (UNMOGIP) |

| | |
|---|---|
| 1956 to 1967 | First UN Emergency Force (UNEF I) |
| 1958 to 1958 | UN Observation Group in Lebanon (UNOGIL) |
| 1960 to 1964 | UN Operation in the Congo (ONUC) |
| 1962 to 1963 | UN Security Force in West New Guinea (West Irian) (UNSF) |
| 1963 to 1964 | UN Yemen Observation Mission (UNYOM) |
| 1964 to date | UN Peacekeeping Force in Cyprus (UNFICYP) |
| 1965 to 1966 | Mission of the Representative of the Secretary-General in the Dominican Republic |
| 1965 to 1966 | UN India-Pakistan Observation Mission (UNIPOM) |
| 1973 to 1979 | Second UN Emergency Force (UNEF II) |
| 1974 to date | UN Disengagement Observer Force (UNDOF) |
| 1978 to date | United Nations Interim Force in Lebanon (UNIFIL) |
| 1988 to 1990 | UN Good Offices Mission in Afghanistan and Pakistan (UNGOMAP) |
| 1988 to 1991 | UN Iran-Iraq Military Observer Group (UNIIMOG) |
| 1989 to 1991 | UN Angola Verification Mission I (UNAVEM I) |
| 1989 to 1990 | UN Transition Assistance Group in Namibia (UNTAG) |
| 1989 to 1992 | UN Observer Group in Central America (ONUCA) |
| 1991 to date | UN Iraq-Kuwait Observation Mission (UNIKOM) |
| 1991 to date | UN Angola Verification Mission II (UNAVEM II) |
| 1991 to date | UN Observer Mission in El Salvador (ONUSAL) |
| 1991 to date | UN Mission for the Referendum in Western Sahara (MINURSO) |
| 1991 to 1992 | UN Advance Mission in Cambodia (UNTAC) |
| 1992 to 1993 | UN Operation in Somalia I (UNOSOM I) |
| 1992 to date | UN Operation in Mozambique (UNUMOZ) |
| 1993 to date | UN Operation in Somalia II (UNOSOM II) |
| 1993 to date | UN Observer Mission Uganda-Rwanda (UNOMUR) |
| 1993 to date | UN Observer Mission in Georgia (UNOMIG) |
| 1993 to date | UN Observer Mission in Liberia (UNOMIL) |
| 1993 to date | UN Mission to Haiti (UNMIH) |
| 1993 to date | UN Mission in Rwanda (UNAMIR) |
| 1994 to date | UN Aouzou Strip Observer Group (Chad and Libya) (UNASOG) |
| 1994 to date | UN Protection Force in the Former Yugoslavia (UNPROFOR) |

**BIBLIOGRAPHY.** United Nations, Department of Public Information. *United Nations Peace-Keeping.* New York: 1993. Doc. no. DPI/1399-93527. IGO booklet, in English.

————. *Information Notes: United Nations Peace-Keeping (Update: May 1994).* New York: 1994. Doc. no. DPI/1306/Rev. 3. IGO report, in English.

**PEARSON, LESTER B. (1897–1972).** The recipient of the 1957 NOBEL PEACE PRIZE, this Canadian Liberal Party leader and diplomat was recognized for a life dedicated to peace and specifically for his efforts in the Suez Crisis of 1956. As head of the UN Canadian delegation, Pearson was largely responsible for the formation of the first UN emergency peacekeeping force.

Born in Toronto, Canada, Pearson was educated at the University of Toronto and Oxford University, with degrees in history. He began his diplomatic career in 1924 when he became first secretary in the Canadian Department of External Affairs; in this position, he attended many international conferences on peace and disarmament. In later years, he served as the High Commissioner for Canada in the British cabinet, was assistant under-secretary of state for external affairs, and Canadian ambassador to the United States. As ambassador, he headed the Canadian delegation to the San Francisco Conference in 1947, which established the United Nations. He also headed the Canadian delegation to NATO from its inception until 1957, as well as heading the Canadian delegation to the United Nations from 1946 to 1956.

In 1956, President Nasser of Egypt nationalized the Suez Canal, bringing the military forces of Israel, Great Britain, and France. Pearson recommended a neutral international UN peacekeeping force. This action became the measure against which all future peacekeeping missions would be measured. Pearson's Nobel lecture, entitled "The Four Faces of Peace," dealt with prosperity, power, policy, and the needs of the people. After years of international diplomatic service, Pearson served nationally as Canadian prime minister from 1963 to 1968.

**BIBLIOGRAPHY.** *Current Biography Yearbook 1963.* New York: W. H. Wilson.

Gray, Tony. *Champions of Peace.* London: Paddington Press, 1976.

Pearson, Lester. *Democracy in World Politics.* Princeton, NJ, USA: Princeton University Press, 1957.

————. *Diplomacy in the Nuclear Age.* Cambridge, MA, USA: Harvard University Press, 1959.

———. *Peace in the Family of Man.* New York: Oxford University Press, 1969.

Schlessinger, Bernard S., and June H. Schlessinger, eds. *Who's Who of Nobel Prize Winners.* Phoenix, AZ, USA: Oryx Press, 1991.

## PENNSYLVANIA STUDIES IN HUMAN RIGHTS, UNIVERSITY OF PENNSYLVANIA.

A series of works devoted to the study of human rights, this publishing program is a recent venture, begun in the 1990s. It is anticipated that five books a year will be published in the series. Bert B. Lockwood is the series editor. Among recent publications are *Human Rights in the World Community*, eds. Richard P. Claude and Burns H. Weston; *Educating for Human Dignity* by Betty Reardon; *Inter-State Accountability for Violations of Human Rights* by Menno T. Kamminga; *Human Rights in Crisis*, by Joan M. Fitzpatrick; and *Human Rights of Women*, ed. Rebecca J. Cook.

Pennsylvania Studies in Human Rights. Address: University of Pennsylvania Press, Blockley Hall, 418 Service Drive, Philadelphia, PA 19104, USA. Telephone: (215) 898-6262. Fax: (215) 898-0404.

## PERES, SHIMON (1923–).

This Israeli statesman and Labor Party leader received the 1994 **NOBEL PEACE PRIZE**, along with **YASSAR ARAFAT** and **YITZHAK RABIN**, for forging a peace settlement in the Middle East between Israel and the Palestinians, an achievement that he detailed in a recent book *Battling for Peace: A Memoir* (1995).

Born in Poland, Peres immigrated to Palestine with his family in 1931. There he became involved in Zionist activities, joining such organizations as *Hano'ar Ha'oved* (Working Youth) and the *Haganah*, the underground Jewish self-defense organization. In the *Haganah* he met David Ben-Gurion, later Israel's first prime minister, who appointed him as the head of the defense ministry's naval department during Israel's war of independence. From his background in the underground defense forces, Peres had become an expert in weapons procurement; and, after the war ended, he continued to secure weapons for his country's defense.

In 1952, Peres was appointed director-general of Israel's ministry of defense, where, in his seven-year tenure, he supervised Israel's government-owned weapons industry, negotiating an alliance with France to supply weapons and parts, a relationship that proved crucial in Israel's ability to capture the Sinai Peninsula from Egypt in 1956. In the 1960s, Peres forged a partnership with West Germany for weapons, which were important to Israel in the Six-Day War. Later, Peres negotiated a strong weapons-supply policy with the United States. Through the next twenty years, in various governmental positions, Peres stressed the importance of a strong defense.

Peres served in the Knesset from 1959 to 1969. In 1969, then-Prime Minister Golda Meir appointed him to her cabinet. His political fortunes rose and fell with those of the Labor Party, falling dramatically after Israel's defeat in the 1973 Yom Kippur War and rising in the 1980s when he formed a coalition government and served as prime minister from 1984 to 1986.

Despite his reputation as a hardliner, Peres supported the Camp David Peace Accords signed by Israel's **MENACHEM BEGIN** and Egypt's **ANWAR SADAT** in 1978 and worked for improved relations with Israel's Arab neighbors and the Palestinians. As prime minister, he visited Morocco at the invitation of King Hassan II, making him the first Israeli prime minister to visit an Arab country other than Egypt; and he met with Egypt's President Hosni Mubarak. He also coordinated Israel's withdrawal from Lebanon. When he turned over the reins of government to Rabin in 1986, he served as vice-premier and foreign minister. In the 1988 elections, Rabin and Peres' Labor Party platform promised to resolve the Palestinian *intifada* by trading land for peace. Though Labor was unsuccessful in winning this election, another coalition government was formed, with Peres serving as vice-premier and finance minister.

During the 1990s Israeli public opinion changed in favor of a settlement. Peres undertook secret meetings with **PLO** officials. The result was the Oslo Agreement of 1993, which initiated an interim self-government for Palestinians. On accepting the Nobel Peace Prize, Peres said, "There was a time when war was fought for lack of choice; today it is peace that is the 'no choice' for all of us."

**BIBLIOGRAPHY.** *Current Biography* (March 1995): 37–41.

Peres, Shimon. *Battling for Peace: A Memoir.* New York: Random House, 1995.

———. *The New Middle East.* New York: Random House, 1993.

## PÉREZ ESQUIVEL, ADOLFO (1931–).

The recipient of the 1980 **NOBEL PEACE PRIZE**, this Argentine human rights activist was cited by the Nobel Committee as a spokesman "of a revival of respect of human rights . . . , having shone a light through the darkness" of Argentina's military rule.

A deeply religious man, Pérez Esquivel is a Roman Catholic lay leader in his native country, who espouses the doctrines of a socially active theology. In 1973, he founded the **SERVICE FOR PEACE AND JUSTICE IN**

**LATIN AMERICA** *(Servicio Paz y Justicia en América Latina)*, a church-based network that works for social justice based on Gandhian principles of nonviolence and human rights. On behalf of the organization, Pérez Esquivel traveled throughout Central and South America to forge links between like-minded organizations and to work for the rights of the oppressed, such as the land rights of Ecuadoran Indians and the rights of the Agrarian League of Paraguay. After the 1976 coup in Argentina, which installed a military government, the organization concentrated on the human rights of the *desaparecidos,* those who "disappeared" in a political crackdown and were jailed and often executed without trial.

During this time, Pérez Esquivel founded the Ecumenical Movement for Human Rights and served as president of the Permanent Assembly for Human Rights. For his public pronouncements against the Argentine Government, he was imprisoned as a subversive and severely tortured. He was named as a "prisoner of conscience" by **AMNESTY INTERNATIONAL,** and the administration of American President Jimmy Carter interceded on his behalf. Bowing to international pressure, the Argentine Government released him in 1978 but kept him under house arrest for another nine months. When the Nobel Committee announced the Prize in 1980, the Argentine Government stated that Pérez Esquivel had "contributed to the cause of those who promote terrorism in the nation." Ironically, in 1977, the Argentine Government had passed a law that provided a lifetime stipend equal to the salary of a Supreme Court justice to any Argentine who won a Nobel Prize; in 1981, the government reluctantly began Pérez Esquivel's stipend.

**BIBLIOGRAPHY.** *Current Biography Yearbook 1981.* New York: W. H. Wilson.

Pérez Esquivel, Adolfo. *Christ in a Poncho.* New York: Orbis Books, 1973.

Schlessinger, Bernard S., and June H. Schlessinger, eds. *Who's Who of Nobel Prize Winners.* Phoenix, AZ, USA: Oryx Press, 1991.

## PERMANENT COURT OF ARBITRATION.

The Court, also known as the Hague Tribunal, was established in 1899 in accordance with the International Convention for the Pacific Settlement of International Disputes, concluded at the Hague on 29 July 1899. Under the Convention, several means for the peaceful settlement of disputes between States are recognized, including the use of mediation, of good offices, and of international commissions of inquiry and arbitration. The Permanent Court of Arbitration formally came into being with the adoption of a revised version of the Convention on 18 October 1907 in the course of the Second International Peace Conference at the Hague.

Each State party to the Convention appoints to the Court up to four jurists versed in international law. A case is initiated when two or more States agree to submit their dispute to arbitration. The disputants may either select arbitrators from the panel of jurists to hear their case or have two arbitrators choose an umpire before whom the hearing will be held. Tribunals normally sit at the Hague.

After World War I, the Permanent Court of Arbitration lost much of its influence first to the World Court and, after 1945, to the **INTERNATIONAL COURT OF JUSTICE.**

## PERSONS BORN OUT OF WEDLOCK.

Discrimination against persons born out of wedlock was the subject of a study completed in 1967 by Judge Vieno Voitto Saario (Finland), a Special Rapporteur appointed by the UN **SUB-COMMISSION ON PREVENTION OF DISCRIMINATION AND PROTECTION OF MINORITIES.**

Based on data assembled from 71 countries, the study concluded that persons born out of wedlock are frequently the victims of discrimination because they cannot establish a legal relationship with their mother, their father, or both, and thus are left without any family status or even without a birth record or a name. It revealed a general trend toward greater flexibility in the methods used for establishing filiation, despite serious restrictions applied in a number of countries.

*MATERNAL FILIATION.* Regarding maternal filiation, the study concluded (chapter 5) that:

In a large number of countries, the very fact that a woman has given birth to a child results in *de jure* recognition of the maternal relationship. This rule appears to be most beneficial to persons born out of wedlock who can thus, as a consequence of birth, automatically enjoy status as regards their mother.

A variety of methods of acknowledgement, including tacit acknowledgement resulting from the fact that the mother has openly and constantly treated her child as her own, can be discerned in those systems of law requiring express acknowledgement by the mother. The same purpose is fulfilled where the acknowledgement is effected by the mere mention of the mother's name in the birth record if she does not oppose it, or, as is the case in at least one country, where the director of the public institution where the birth took place has the authority to record officially the declaration of acknowledgement made by the mother. Where the mother is incapacitated or dead, and therefore cannot herself acknowledge the child, the maternal grandparents are, in some instances, permitted to acknowledge him.

In a number of countries where the law requires express acknowledgement by the mother, such acknowledgement may occur at any time during the life of the person born out of wedlock, sometimes before the birth, once conception has taken place, or even after his death. However, some special conditions are to be met when acknowledgement occurs after the birth has been registered. In any case, where a system of express acknowledgement is maintained, the procedure should be made as simple and informal as possible.

Analysis of the available data reveals that while the laws of most countries provide for the judicial establishment of the maternal filiation of a person born out of wedlock, in some countries the law does not provide for its establishment as such, the question being solved for each particular case if and when filiation is challenged. In a few instances, the judicial establishment of maternal filiation is not provided for at all. It goes without saying that the right to establish maternal filiation judicially should be embodied in the law of all countries.

As regards the evidence admissible in the proof of maternal filiation, there may sometimes be differences in the admissibility of evidence in cases of births in wedlock and births out of wedlock. It seems of primary importance that every type of evidence to the effect of establishing the respective identities of the mother and the child, as well as the fact of birth, should be admitted in both situations. As is the case in various countries, any party having a legitimate interest should have the right to establish maternal filiation judicially.

**PATERNAL FILIATION.** Regarding paternal filiation when the parents are married to each other, the study concluded that:

Analysis of the available data reveals that the rule *"pater is est quem nuptiae demonstrant"* is incorporated in the legislation of all countries surveyed. This principle is interpreted, in one group of countries, to mean that the husband is presumed to be the father of the children conceived by his wife during the subsistence of the marriage, while in some other countries the presumption is extended to children either conceived or born during the existence of the marriage. According to this wider interpretation, children conceived before the marriage but born during it, children conceived and born during the marriage, and children conceived during the marriage but born after its dissolution are all presumed to be the offspring of the husband and wife. It is evident that this wider interpretation of the rule is preferable, because it establishes paternal filiation within marriage with all its consequences, in all situations mentioned above.

The legislation of most countries provides for a predetermined period of gestation which usually varies from a minimum of 180 days to a maximum of 302 days. A certain flexibility in this regard would certainly seem to be in accordance with present-day medical knowledge. When no specific period of gestation is provided for, reliance on expert medical evidence should be the rule.

In nearly all countries the law recognizes the right of the husband to disavow paternity, mostly through court proceedings, whether as a principal cause of action or in connexion with other proceedings whereby the enforcement of the legal right depends on the legitimacy of the person concerned. Sometimes, however, children conceived before the celebration of the marriage may be disavowed by a mere declaration of non-paternity made in the appropriate manner. Except for the latter case the presumption of paternity is usually destroyed only upon evidence of circumstances establishing that sexual relations did not take place during the

period of conception and that paternity of the husband is impossible. Such a trend should be encouraged and the grounds admitted should be always very serious and strictly limited.

The right to disavow or to challenge paternity is usually granted to the husband, sometimes also to the person concerned as well as to their respective heirs. In a few instances, such right is enjoyed by the wife and by any person having a legitimate interest. In some countries the competent public authority may *ex officio* initiate proceedings and this is usually the case when the interest of the child or of his descendants so requires. Generally, the action has to be exercised within short time-limits. It is evident that the opportunities of initiating proceedings to disavow or challenge paternity should be as limited as possible, in order not to upset the prevailing family situation.

It should be recalled here that the disavowal or challenge of paternity, when it is admitted in connexion with other proceedings where the issue is relevant, can be made usually at any time and by any person whose interest is affected.

As regards paternal filiation when the parents are not married to each other, the study concluded that:

The legislation of most countries provides for the establishment of the paternal filiation of a person born out of wedlock whether it entails a status that is a set of rights and duties, equal or inferior to that of a person born in wedlock or hardly any status at all, but only very limited rights. In some countries the law does not recognize any relationship between a person born out of wedlock and his father. No doubt the child has a fundamental right to have a father and to enjoy status in relation to him. It is, therefor, essential that the paternal filiation of a person born out of wedlock be recognized in law and that provisions to this effect be accordingly made.

The legislation of a great number of countries requires that the acknowledgement of the father be made according to strictly determined forms. The law of various other countries provides for a wide range of forms including, among others, tacit acknowledgement, operation of the presumption of paternity under specific circumstances, the recording of the acknowledgement by the director of the institution where the birth took place. Undoubtedly, this last approach secures paternal filiation in the largest number of cases of birth out of wedlock.

The information gathered for this study reveals that sometimes the approval of the mother is necessary in order for the acknowledgement made by the father to be effective. This requirement constitutes an infringement upon the right of the child to have his paternal filiation established. Because this right should not be denied, the approval of the mother should never constitute a prerequisite to the acknowledgement by the father.

The legislation of a few countries allows the paternal grandfather to acknowledge the child when the natural father is incapacitated or dead. This right should be extended to either paternal grandparent.

In many countries, the judicial establishment of paternal filiation is possible only in a limited number of cases, and in a few instances it is not provided for by law. This is a serious obstacle to securing paternal filiation and status. In order to improve the situation in this regard, the judicial establishment of paternity should be allowed whenever the court is satisfied that sexual relations took place during the time of conception which resulted in the birth. The possibility of establishing paternal relationship should not be denied in case of misconduct of the mother or relations with another man during the legal period of conception, as seems to be the situation in a few countries. If the court is satisfied that the man alleged to be the father is the natural father of the child, paternal filiation should be established.

Paternal filiation is established through court proceedings. However, mention has been made of a simpler form of establishment consisting in a summons to a man to declare before a judge that he believes he is the natural father. In case of default, acknowledgement is considered made. Such procedure permits establishment of paternal filiation in a quick, easy and inexpensive way.

The right to initiate proceedings for the establishment of paternal filiation should be granted to all persons who have a legal interest in doing so, including the competent guardianship or other authorities. As is sometimes the case, these authorities should play an active role in determining paternity by making the necessary investigations and encouraging voluntary acknowledgements of paternity whenever the father of a child born out of wedlock has been identified. In this connexion, the duty to disclose the identity of the father to the competent authorities should be imposed upon all persons having such knowledge as well as direct knowledge of the pregnancy or birth. Such disclosure should be subject to the rules of professional secrecy.

In various countries prohibitions and restrictions exist either as to the acknowledgement or as to the judicial establishment, or both, of the paternal filiation of persons born as a result of adulterous, incestuous or sacrilegious relations. In others, all persons born out of wedlock whether their parents were free or not to marry each other at the time of conception or birth, are entitled to have their paternal filiation established. This last trend should be followed and in so far as possible all existing prohibitions and restrictions should be eliminated so that these categories of persons born out of wedlock may not be denied the right to have a legally recognized paternal filiation.

*CONCLUSIONS OF SPECIAL RAPPORTEUR.* On the basis of his analysis of the information available to him, the Special Rapporteur concluded that:

. . . it appears that the institution of adoption might indeed by considered an effective means to upgrade the status of a person born out of wedlock. It has gained wide acceptance in the major juridical systems of the world and has become an integral part of the family law of almost all of the jurisdictions studied. Also, the fundamental principles under which it is developing are generally agreed upon. These two points indicate that further progress could be achieved which would serve to make the institution still more useful, and transform it into an instrument which would help alleviate the discriminatory practices which persist against persons born out of wedlock.

Additional legislative measures appear to be required because of the numerous provisions which limit the effects of adoption or which may prevent the person born out of wedlock from being adopted, or when he is adopted, from being fully integrated into the adopter's family. Measures of this type are already in force in a few countries, but their general extension could be proposed as they would not conflict with the basic objectives of the laws of any of the countries studies. Such measures, moreover, would not affect the nature of the laws in force; they would only enlarge their scope and the extent of rights already granted.

Some adoption laws restrict the right to adopt in the case of persons who are not of the same religion as that of the child to be adopted. The primary consideration of the competent authorities should be the interest of the child; consequently, they should take the most liberal view, one that would make it possible for the child to be adopted whether or not he belongs to the same race or ethnic or religious group as the adoptive parents.

In the analysis of legal requirements for a valid adoption, it was observed that a number of countries prohibit adoption if the adopter already has children of his own. While the existence of previous children is indeed worthy of factual consideration before an adoption takes place, it does not seem necessary that it should lead to a legal prohibition of adoption. Some latitude could be given to the judge or the competent public authority to at least decide on the merits of each individual case. Better still, this decision should be left to the individual persons concerned.

A similar remark could be made regarding the prohibition of adoption when the prospective adopter is the father or mother of the person to be adopted. Such adoption should not, in principle, be prohibited in any case where the law permits the establishment of filiation. Furthermore, it could even be envisaged that adoption should be authorized in cases where the law prohibits the establishment of filiation.

As has been observed, only the type of adoption called "adoption with full effects" of blood relationship leads to an equalization of rights between the person adopted and the person born to the adopter in lawful wedlock. But the analysis above reveals also that this type of adoption is practised mainly in countries where the law disregards the fact of birth out of wedlock. In countries which differentiate between the two categories of persons, and where therefore the status of persons born out of wedlock is generally inferior to that of persons born in wedlock, the most common type of adoption found is "regular adoption" which grants rights subject to limitations and usually restricts the effects of adoption to a relationship between the adopted and the adoptee. Efforts leading to a more liberal attitude should be encouraged, as the possibility for integration of the person adopted into the adopter's family is absent where it is most needed. In particular, the question of recognition of family relationship should be re-examined in order that "regular adoption" may place the adopted person, with all the consequences that such a step implies, on an equal footing with the person born to the adopter in lawful wedlock.

Finally, when the adoptee is a minor, he should be allowed to acquire, *ipso facto*, the nationality of the adopter in order to facilitate the process of integration.

*DRAFT PRINCIPLES ON THE RIGHTS OF PERSONS BORN OUT OF WEDLOCK.* After examining the conclusions and recommendations set out in the study, the Sub-Commission on Prevention of Discrimination and Protection of Minorities adopted (in 1967) a series of draft principles on equality and nondiscrimination in respect of persons born out of wedlock. These draft principles were as follows:

### Part I

1. Every person born out of wedlock shall be entitled to legal recognition of his maternal and paternal filiation in so far

as compatible with the principle of the protection of the family.

2. The fact of birth of a child shall by itself establish maternal filiation to the woman who gives birth to the child.

3. The establishment of paternal filiation shall be provided for by law through a variety of means, including acknowledgement, recognition of legal presumptions and judicial decision. Judicial proceedings to establish paternal filiation shall not be subject to any time-limits.

4. The husband shall be presumed to be the father of any child born to his wife whether he is conceived or born during the marriage. This presumption may be overcome only by a judicial decision based upon evidence that the husband is not the father. Proceedings to that end shall be initiated within a limited period of time.

5. Any child born of parents who intermarry after the birth of that child shall be considered to be born of that marriage.

6. Every person born in wedlock, or considered to be born in wedlock as a result of the subsequent marriage of his parents, shall retain his status notwithstanding the invalidity or annulment of the marriage.

### Part II

7. Every person, once his filiation has been established, shall have the same legal status as a person born in wedlock.

8. Every person born out of wedlock whose filiation is established in relation to both parents shall have the right to bear a surname determined as in the case of a person born in wedlock. If his filiation is established in relation only to his mother, he shall be entitled to bear her surname, modified, if necessary, in such a manner as not to reveal the fact of birth out of wedlock.

9. The rights and obligations pertaining to parental authority shall be the same, whether the child is born in wedlock or out of wedlock. Unless otherwise decided by the court in the best interest of the child born out of wedlock, parental authority shall be exercised according to the same rules as for a child born in wedlock if his filiation is established in relation to both parents, or by his mother alone if his paternal filiation is not established.

10. The domicile of any child born out of wedlock whose filiation is established in relation to both parents shall be determined according to the same rules as for children born in wedlock.

If the filiation is established in relation to the mother alone, appropriate rules shall ensure in any case that the child has a domicile.

11. Every person born out of wedlock shall, once his filiation has been established, have the same maintenance rights as persons born in wedlock. Birth out of wedlock shall not affect the order of priority of claimants.

12. Every person born out of wedlock shall, once his filiation has been established, have the same inheritance rights as persons born in wedlock. Legal limitations or restrictions on the freedom of a testator to dispose of his property shall afford equal protection to persons entitled to inheritance, whether they are born in wedlock or out of wedlock.

13. The nationality or citizenship of a person born out of wedlock shall be determined by the same rules as those applicable to persons born in wedlock.

Special protection against statelessness shall be provided for persons born out of wedlock. In particular, when only the maternal filiation of a person born out of wedlock is established, its effects shall be the same as in the case of paternal filiation.

14. Political, social, economic and cultural rights shall be enjoyed equally by all persons, whether they are born in wedlock or out of wedlock, without prejudice as regards social welfare services, to the special care which shall be provided to children born out of wedlock and their mothers, by the State or society, when necessary.

### Part III

15. Information in birth and other registers containing personal data which might disclose the fact of birth out of wedlock shall be available only to persons or authorities having a legitimate interest with respect to filiation.

In referring to persons born out of wedlock, any designation which might carry a derogatory connotation shall be avoided.

16. The adoption of a child born out of wedlock shall be subject to the same rules and provisions and shall have the same consequences as the adoption of children born in wedlock.

Restrictions on the right to adopt shall be limited to such requirements as are necessary to establish a parent-child relationship and to assure the best interest of the adoptee. In particular, no restrictions based solely on a difference of race, colour or national origin shall be permitted.

Adoption procedure should be carried out under the supervision of the State and/or a competent social welfare agency to ensure full protection of the child and his well-being.

The study and the draft general principles were reviewed by the UN **COMMISSION ON THE STATUS OF WOMEN** at its 1967 session in connection with that Commission's consideration of questions relating to the status of the unmarried mother. On the initiative of the Commission, the **ECONOMIC AND SOCIAL COUNCIL** adopted resolution 1514 (XLVIII) of 28 May 1970, in which it urged States to take adequate measures of social assistance in favor of the unmarried mother and the child born out of wedlock and invited them to study the problems posed by the integration of the unmarried mother and her child in all spheres of society.

Later, again on the initiative of the Commission on the Status of Women, the Economic and Social Council adopted resolution 1679 (LII) of 2 June 1972, in which it recommended that governments take all possible measures to eliminate any prevailing legal and social discrimination against the family consisting of an unmarried mother and her child and to offer such families all necessary advice and assistance, seeking to obtain a greater comprehension by society of their situation and with a view to eliminating the harm caused by lack of understanding and to securing them an acceptance on an equal footing with other members of society. The Council recommended the following general principles for achieving that end:

(a) Maternal filiation shall be recognized in law, in all cases, automatically as a consequence of the fact of birth;

(b) Whatever the legal system applying in the case of married parents, the unmarried mother, whether paternal filiation is established or not, shall enjoy in all cases, as a parent, the fullest set of rights and duties provided for by law, in particular:

(i) If maternal filiation only is established, the surname of the mother should be transmitted to her child, if possible, in such a manner as not to reveal the fact of birth out of wedlock;

(ii) If maternal filiation only is established, the nationality of the unmarried mother shall be transmitted to her child as a consequence of the fact of birth; if both maternal and paternal filiations are established, the nationality of the child shall be governed by the same rules as those which apply in the case of birth in wedlock;

(iii) The unmarried mother should be vested in law with full parental authority over her child, in all cases, as an automatic consequence of the fact of birth; a family consisting of an unmarried mother and her child should not be subjected to any special control or supervision by the authorities different from that given to other families;

(iv) Maintenance rights and obligations as between the unmarried mother and her child should be the same as between a sole parent and a child born in wedlock; when both paternal and maternal filiations are established, the maintenance obligations of the parents to the child should be the same as if the child was born in wedlock; all appropriate assistance should be offered by the competent authority to the mother to help her (a) to establish paternal filiation and (b) to obtain an agreement by the father or a decision by the competent authority or court for the support of the child by his father; if the father does not fulfil his maintenance obligations, or if it is not possible to establish paternity, benefit should be available from appropriate public sources for the support of the mother and her child according to their needs;

(v) There should be no discrimination against the offspring of unmarried mothers in all matters of inheritance;

(vi) The unmarried mother should enjoy all the measures of social assistance and social security devised for mothers in general and for single parents in particular;

(vii) There should be no discrimination against the unmarried mother in matters of employment, education and training as well as in access to child care facilities.

The Council also recommended, in the same resolution, that member States should consider the development of programs designed to increase awareness of the existing double standard in allocating social responsibility for births out of wedlock, so as to bring about a balance in these social attitudes toward members of both sexes in the responsibility for such births.

**SEE ALSO** *Marriage and the Family.*

**PERU.** The Republic of Peru is a country in tropical South America, on the Pacific Ocean. It has borders with Bolivia, Brazil, Chile, Colombia, and Ecuador. It achieved independence from Spain in 1821 and became a member of the United Nations in 1945. Its population is estimated to be 22,995,000. There is no up-to-date statistical information on the ethnic composition of the population because it is unlawful to indicate such information on any official document. However, it is estimated that 45% of the people are of Indian origin, 37% of Mestizo (mixed) origin, 15% of European origin, and the remainder of African or Asian origin. Languages commonly used include Spanish (official), Quechua, and Aymara. Christianity (Roman Catholic) is the predominant religion; the Roman Catholic faith is protected by the State, and only Roman Catholic religious instruction is permitted in the schools. Literacy is estimated at 72%.

The government (1994) took the form of a republic. Under the 1980 constitution, the president and members of the legislature are elected, by separate ballots, for terms of five years, voting being compulsory for all citizens over the age of 18. The president, as head of State, exercises executive power with the assistance of a premier and the Council of Ministers. The legislature consists of a 120-seat congress. Political parties include the American Popular Revolutionary Alliance, the Democratic Convergence Party, the Popular Action Party, and the United Left (comprising six Marxist parties).

In a report presented to the UN Group of Three of the **COMMISSION ON HUMAN RIGHTS** on 20 December 1985, the Government of Peru provided the following information concerning human rights in that country (UN Doc. E/CN.4/1986/29/Add. 1, paras. 1–3):

Article 80 of the Constitution establishes, among other duties of the State, that of guaranteeing the full exercise of human rights. A special role in fulfilling this mandate is played by the judiciary; by the Office of the Government Attorney, which ensures the independence of judicial bodies and acts as the defender of the people before the administration; and by the National Elections Board, the Court of Constitutional Guarantees and the Commission on Human Rights of the Chamber of Deputies.

In order better to guarantee the full exercise of human rights, the legislative bodies have enacted a set of laws relating, for example, to suffrage for illiterate persons, measures to speed up the judicial process, the establishment of the Reprieve Assessment Commission, the Organizational Law on the Office of the Government Attorney the law re-establishing the Ministry of Justice and the Organizational Law on the Court of Constitutional Guarantees. In addition to these provisions, there is a new *amparo* and *habeas corpus* act; these laws are all designed to guarantee the full exercise of human rights. Parliament is also studying a number of bills and draft codes which must be brought into line with the new mandates of the Constitution currently in force in Peru.

Peru is a zealous defender of human rights and the legislative bodies are currently faced with the challenge either of giving the country new provisions to improve the implementation of the relevant provisions of the Constitution or of adapting already existing ones.

*"DISAPPEARANCES" OF PERSONS*. The UN Working Group on Enforced or Involuntary Disappearances has twice sent missions to Peru to study the situation as regards enforced or involuntary disappearances there, first in 1985 in response to an invitation extended by the government of then-President Fernando Belaunde Terry and again in 1986 in response to an invitation extended by the government by his replacement, President Alan Garcia Perez.

The reports of the two visits (UN Docs. E/CN.4/1986/18/Add. 1 and E/CN.4/1987/15/Add. 1) together provide a picture of the evolving situation regarding enforced and involuntary disappearances which plagued Peru at that time and of the measures taken by the two governments to deal with the problem. The Working Group's concluding observations, prepared after the second visit, were as follows (UN Doc. E/CN.4/1987/15/Add. 1, paras. 42–52):

The Working Group is grateful to the Peruvian Government for providing an opportunity to review the progress made in combating the phenomenon of disappearances in Peru, following its first visit in June of 1985.

As already stated in last year's report, in assessing the situation of missing persons in Peru, the Working Group has to pay due regard to the overall context of violence in which disappearances have been reported to it. For, in both intellectual and practical terms, it is not feasible to divorce the issue of disappearances completely from related violations of human rights or from the socio-political processes that have engendered them. If it did so, the Group would not be exercising its mandate properly in the manner consistently supported over the years by the Commission on Human Rights.

Being faced with a terrorist movement such as Sendero Luminoso amidst a variety of urgent economic and social problems is not an enviable position for any government to be in. Terrorist violence rages unabated, without the least respect for life, limb or property. Worse still, although for a long time it was confined to some provinces of Ayacucho and neighbouring departments, insurgence has now spread to the Departments of Cerro de Pasco (north of Ayacucho) and of Cuzco and Puno (to the south) and the capital itself has become affected. In consequence, the area covered by the state of emergency has been extended.

Clearly, in its contacts with the Working Group, the previous Government was loath to admit that disappearances had indeed occurred in significant numbers and avoided apportioning responsibility for any excesses to the armed forces or the police. It was heartening, therefore, to note that the new President declared upon taking office that his administration would not fight "barbarism with barbarism". Indeed, that promise as well as concrete action bear witness to a firm resolve to call a halt to disappearances and other violations of human rights by government forces. Civil participation has been sought in finding long-term solutions for internal strife and in promoting the cause of human rights. Establishing the National Council for Human Rights is but one example. The present Government has also resolutely opened its doors to international scrutiny of Peru's human rights record. It has taken a much more co-operative attitude towards the Group, swiftly responding to cases transmitted to it and making immediate efforts to clarify them.

In parliament, interest for human rights seems to have increased markedly and this has led to the introduction of legislation designed to remedy lacunae in Peruvian human rights law.

One of the major concerns expressed in the previous report concerned the wide latitude granted by the central Government to the armed forces and the police to fight Sendero Luminoso and restore public order in the manner they saw fit. At the time it was argued that such latitude would almost inevitably lead sooner or later to disappearances and concomitant violations of human rights. It would seem that the present administration has made great strides towards regaining control over the counter-insurgency strategy followed by the armed forces. Consequently, the incidence of disappearances has decreased considerably, particularly since the end of 1985. This is clear from the graph in the annex.

However, disappearances still continue to occur in Peru on an appreciable scale, and other forms of violence at the hands of government forces appear to have increased, particularly since the middle of 1986. The Working Group has transmitted to the Government some 160 cases that occurred in the emergency zone between August 1985 and November 1986. About half of these cases have subsequently been clarified: detention was acknowledged or subjects were turned over to the police by the armed forces or released. While this shows a welcome increase in the measure of responsiveness of the armed forces, it is also indicative of the practice of short-term disappearances as a method of counter-insurgency in breach of Peruvian law.

In last year's report attention was drawn to what was described as some sort of institutional paralysis pertaining to the protection of human rights in the emergency zone. Little progress can be reported in that regard. In the majority of cases prosecutors are still obstructed in their efforts to follow up on denunciations of disappearances. The Judiciary seems ill at ease with *habeas corpus* proceedings, which in any case meet with lack of co-operation from the respondents. Almost without exception civilian courts refer cases involving military and police personnel to military courts, despite the fact that the Code of Military Justice does not cover homicide, maltreatment and the like. The broad powers concentrated in the hands of the military in the emergency zone further diminish the role which civil institutions might otherwise play in applying the rule of law.

Establishing a Human Rights Office under the auspices of the Attorney-General has admirably expedited the processing of cases of missing persons. Yet that fact in itself has not substantially enhanced the measure of protection extended to citizens at large. Undoubtedly, adequate access to registers of arrests maintained by the armed forces would have not only a curative but also a preventive effect. At any rate, the armed forces must be prevailed upon to co-operate more closely in the emergency zone with prosecutors and judicial authorities. Moreover, the latter are in dire need of material and human resources, as was pointed out in last year's report.

The situation of the victims among the indigenous population in the affected areas remains dismal. Humanitarian aid from national and international sources is an increasingly vital necessity. A long-term development strategy, designed to eliminate the poverty and neglect which are among the root causes of the Ayacuchan drama, is slowly getting under way, even though efforts have been set back by terrorist onslaughts.

Violence cannot be countered with violence alone. Only

when the structural factors that contributed to the spiral of terror and counter-terror are properly dealt with, can there be any hope of preventing a recurrence of the excesses of the past. The Peruvian Government seems keenly aware of that fact. Its task remains a formidable one.

In 1985, although the country was engulfed in an acute economic, social, and financial crisis, an elected president was able to transfer power to a constitutionally elected successor for the first time since 1945.

Following the election in June 1990 of President Alberto Fujimori, tough economic reform measures were instituted. Extreme price inflation brought political upheaval as well as protests and violence. The president was granted emergency legislative powers for 150 days in November 1991, and he used them to privatize industries and eliminate some state monopolies. He also issued dozens of decrees aimed at increasing powers of the security forces to combat narcotics trafficking and guerrilla activity. Relations between the president and the Peruvian Congress worsened as a result of severe disagreements over how to achieve economic reforms.

In April 1992 President Fujimori suspended the 1979 constitution, dissolving the legislature and vesting legislative power with himself and the Council of Ministers. Opposition political leaders were placed under house arrest, the parliament was cordoned off by the military, 13 of the 25 Supreme Court judges were dismissed as well as 134 other judges, and the radio stations were ordered to broadcast only military information. The **ORGANIZATION OF AMERICAN STATES** condemned the actions and all humanitarian aid was halted, except aid from the United States. President Fujimori reinstated the constitution, with reservations, the next month and announced the elections for a body which would draft a new constitution.

The 80 members of the Democratic Constituent Congress (CCD) were elected in November 1992 and parties supportive of the president secured 44 seats. The 1979 constitution was formally reinstated in January 1993 and a new constitution drafted. The new constitution was approved by 52% of the voters in a referendum in October 1993. The CCD stated that the constitution was aimed at fighting economic problems and reducing terrorism. The death penalty was introduced for convicted terrorists. Other provisions allowed for the re-election of the president for a successive five-year term and the creation of a 120-seat unicameral *Congreso* to replace the bicameral legislature.

Presidential and legislative elections were held in April 1995. President Fujimori won a decisive victory over former UN Secretary-General Javier Pérez de Cuéllar and five other candidates, being re-elected to a second five-year term with 64% of the vote. Pérez de Cuéllar and the other candidates complained to the OAS election monitors that supporters of Fujimori had launched a scheme to mark 3,000 ballots prior to the election. Although 15 were arrested for involvement in the scheme, investigators found it to be an isolated incident with little bearing on the outcome of the election. Fujimori's Change 90/New Majority coalition won a majority in the 120-seat congress. In election-related violence, 11 people were killed by guerrillas in an Andean village.

*THE SHINING PATH.* The Peruvian Government has been engaged since the 1980s with controlling a terrorist group named *Sendero Luminoso* (the Shining Path). Political violence and guerrilla activity continued and even intensified throughout the early 1990s. Political violence in 1989 had claimed 3,198 lives, according to the Peruvian Senate's Human Rights Commission. In July 1993, the leader of *Sendero Luminoso* was convicted and sentenced to life imprisonment for treason. However, violence on both sides continued; and in December 1993 criminal charges were brought against 11 army officers for the kidnaping and murder of a professor and students suspected of being supporters of *Sendero Luminoso,* the so-called *La Cantuta* Case. Their cases were transferred to military court, under federal Decree Law 26291, which changed the procedure for determining civilian or military jurisdiction, bringing widespread domestic and international condemnation, and nine of the officers received prison sentences ranging between 1 and 20 years.

**BIBLIOGRAPHY.** Americas Watch. *Human Rights in Peru: One Year after Fujimori's Coup.* New York: Human Rights Watch, 1993. NGO factfinding report, in English.

————. *In Desperate Straits: Human Rights in Peru after a Decade of Democracy and Insurgency.* New York: Human Rights Watch, 1990. NGO factfinding report, in English.

Amnesty International. *Peru: Amnesty International's Concerns about Torture and Ill-Treatment.* London: 1994. NGO report, in English.

————. *States of Emergency: Torture and Violations of the Right to Life under States of Emergency.* London: 1988. NGO report, in English.

Andean Commission of Jurists. *Del Golpe de Estado a la Nueva Constitución* (From the Coup to the New Constitution). Lima, Peru: 1993. NGO scholarly monograph (*Lecturas sobre Temas Constitucionales,* 9), in Spanish.

————. *La Constitución de 1993: Análisis y Comentarios* (The 1993 Constitution: Analysis and Commentaries). Lima, Peru: 1994. NGO scholarly collection (*Lecturas sobre Temas Constitucionales,* 10), in Spanish.

Bequele, A., and J. Boyden, eds. *Combating Child Labour.* Geneva, Switzerland: International Labor Organization, 1988. IGO monograph, in English.

Burneo Labrin, Jose. *Derechos de la Persona ante el Juez, la Policia y en la Carcel* (Rights of the Individual before the Judge, the Police, and while in Prison). Lima, Peru: Comision Episcopal de Accion Social, 1985. Research paper, in Spanish.

Centro de Estudios y Promoción del Desarrollo (Center for the Study and Promotion of Development). "Violencia contra la Mujer: El Sonido del Silencio" (Violence against Women: The Sound of Silence), *Quehacer* 64 (May–June 1990): 80–111. NGO report, in Spanish.

Chipoco, C. C., and P. T. De Valdez. *Derechos Humanos: El Pasado no Fue Diferente* (Human Rights: The Past Was No Different). Lima, Peru: Instituto de Defensa Legal, 1986. NGO report, in Spanish.

Cornell, Angelaj, and Kenneth Roberts. "Democracy, Counterinsurgency, and Human Rights: The Case of Peru," *Human Rights Quarterly* 12, no. 4 (Nov. 1990): 529–553. Scholarly article, in English.

Cultural Survival. "Mountain People," *Cultural Survival Quarterly* 10, no. 3 (1986). NGO edited collection, in English.

Cuya, Esteban. *Perú: Cronología Política, 1992* (Peru: Political Chronology, 1992). Nurnberg, Germany: Dokumentations und informationszentrum Menschenrechte in Lateinamerika, 1993. NGO chronology, in Spanish.

Eguiguren P., Francisco. *Los Retos de Una Democracia Insuficiente: Diez Años de Regimen Constitucional en el Perú 1980–1990* (The Dangers of an Insufficient Democracy: Ten Years of Constitutional Regime in Peru 1980–1990). Lima, Peru: Andean Commission of Jurists and Fundación Friedrich Naumann, 1990. Scholarly monograph, in Spanish; bibliography, pp. 271–276.

Eguiguren P., Francisco, and Milagros Maraví Sumars. "Análisis de las Principales Tendencias Cuantitativas en la Jurisprudencia de Hábeas Corpus en el Perú (1983–1990)" (Analysis of the Principal Quantitative Tendencies in Habeas Corpus Jurisprudence in Peru [1983–1990]), *Boletín—Comisión Andina de Juristas* 28 (March 1991): 9–21. Scholarly article, in Spanish.

Escuela de Derechos Humanos. *La Protection Legal de los Derechos Humanos en el Peru* (The Legal Protection of Human Rights in Peru). Lima, Peru: 1986. Scholarly document collection, in English.

Farnsworth, Elizabeth. "Peru: A Nation in Crisis," *World Policy Journal* 5, no. 4 (Fall 1988): 725–746. Scholarly article, in English.

Garcia-Sayan, Diego. *Habeas Corpus y Estados de Emergencia* (Habeas Corpus and States of Emergency). Lima, Peru: Comision Andina de Juristas and the Friedrich Naumann Foundation, 1988. NGO report, in Spanish.

Gray, Andrew. *And After the Gold Rush . . . ? Human Rights and Self-Development among the Amarakaeri of Southeastern Peru.* Copenhagen, Denmark: International Work Group for Indigenous Affairs, 1985. NGO conference report, in English.

Gray, Andrew, and Soren Hvalkof. "Indigenous Land Titling in the Peruvian Amazon," in *IWGIA Yearbook 1989*, pp. 230–243. Copenhagen, Denmark: International Work Group for Indigenous Affairs, 1990. Article, in English.

Human Rights Watch. "Peru," in *Human Rights Watch World Report 1995*, pp. 114–119. New York: 1995. NGO report, in English.

Instituto de Defensa Legal (Institute for Legal Defense). *En la Espiral de la Violencia* (In the Spiral of Violence). Lima, Peru: 1990. NGO annual report, in Spanish.

———. *Los Sucesos de los Penales: Nueva Abdicacion de la Autoridad Democratica. Un Enfoque Juridico* (A New Abdication of Democratic Authority in Peru: A Legal Analysis . . . Recent Events in the Prisons). Lima, Peru: 1986. NGO report, in Spanish.

Interamerican Institute of Human Rights, Centre for Electoral Counseling and Promotion. *Perú: Elecciones Políticas 8 de Abril y 10 de Junio 1990: Informe de la Misión de Observación* (Peru: Political Elections, April 8 and June 10, 1990: Report of the Observer Mission). San José, Costa Rica: 1990. NGO factfinding report, in Spanish.

Inter-Church Committee on Human Rights in Latin America. *Annual Report on the Human Rights Situation in Peru.* Toronto, Canada. NGO annual report, in English.

Isis International. *Rural Women in Latin America.* Rome: 1987. NGO monograph, in English.

Latin American Documentation. *The Church and Native Peoples.* Lima, Peru: 1986. NGO document collection, in English.

North American Congress on Latin America. "Fatal Attraction: Peru's Shining Path," *Report on the Americas* 24, no. 4 (Dec. 1990–Jan. 1991): 9–39. Article, in English.

Organization of American States (OAS). *Report on the Situation of Human Rights in Peru.* Washington, D.C.: 1993. IGO report, in English.

Pedraglio, Santiago. *Armas Para la Paz: Seguridad Democrática Integral* (Arms for Peace: Integral Democratic Security). Lima, Peru: Instituto de Defensa Legal, 1990. NGO monograph, in Spanish; bibliography, pp. 193–198.

Tarazona-Sevillano, Gabriella, and J. B. Reuter. *Sendero Luminoso and the Threat of Narcoterrorism.* Washington, D.C.: Praeger Publishers with the Center for Strategic and International Studies, 1990. Monograph, in English.

United States Committee for Refugees. *The Decade of Chaqwa: Peru's Internal Refugees.* Washington, D.C.: American Council for Nationalities Service, 1991. NGO report, in English.

Villavicencio, Miguel. "Protección del Derecho a la Integridad Personal en el Perú" (Protection of the Right to Security of the Person in Peru), *Boletín—Comisión Andina de Juristas* 28 (March 1991): 35–54. Scholarly article, in Spanish.

Washington Office on Latin America. *After the Autogolpe: Human Rights in Peru and the U.S. Response.* Washington, D.C.: 1994. NGO report, in English.

Women's Rights Project. *Untold Terror: Violence against Women in Peru's Armed Conflict.* New York: Human Rights Watch, 1992. NGO factfinding report, in English.

World Council of Churches. *Peru and Human Rights: Report of an International Ecumenical Delegation to Peru.* Geneva, Switzerland: 1990. NGO factfinding report, in English.

**PHILIPPINES.** The Republic of the Philippines is a country occupying an archipelago of more than 7,000 islands in the Pacific Ocean, off the southeastern coast of Asia, of which the largest are Luzon, Mindanao, Samar, Negros, Palawan, Panay, and Mindoro. It achieved independence from the United States of America in 1946 and became a member of the United Nations in 1945. Its population is estimated to be 65,500,000. Ethnic groups include Malaysians, Chinese, and persons of mixed blood. Languages commonly used include Filipino (the national language, based on Tagalog, a Malaysian dialect), English (the language of the government and of higher education), and more than 75 languages of the Malayo–Polynesian family. Christianity (Roman Catholic, 85%; Aglipayan, 4%; and Protestant denominations, 3%) is the predominant religion; Islam is the religion of about 4%, and Animism and related beliefs the faith of the remaining 4%. Members of the Islamic religion are concentrated on Mindanao and other southern islands of the Sulu Archipelago. Literacy is estimated at 88%.

The government (1994) took the form of a republic. President Corazon Aquino, who took office on 25 February 1986, suspended parliament and set up a provisional government pending preparation of a new constitution. Political parties include the Philippine Democratic Party, the United Nationalist Democratic Organization, the New Society Movement, and the *Partido Nacionalista Philipina.*

Although a Spanish expedition led by Portuguese explorer Ferdinand Magellan first visited the Philippines in 1521, Spanish conquest of the islands—named Las Felipinas after King Philip II—began in earnest only 40 years later, when an expedition arrived and quickly established dominance over thousands of small independent communities which had never had central rule. The Filipino population at that time consisted of local chiefs, freemen who did not pay tribute to the chiefs, freedmen or liberated slaves who were heavily in debt to the chiefs, and slaves who were the chiefs' personal property. Spanish missionaries—Augustinians, Franciscans, Jesuits, and Dominicans—soon won most of that population either to the Roman Catholic Church or to the Philippine Independent (Aglipayan) Church, an offshoot of Catholicism, with the exception of the Moros who were concentrated on Mindanao and the Sulu Peninsula and who retained their Islamic faith.

***RELATIONS WITH THE UNITED STATES.*** After British defeat of the Spanish Armada in 1588, Spanish influence declined in the Philippines, but the religious orders took over some government functions and amassed great wealth and property. Opposition to these activities of the clergy led to the formation of a liberation movement which accepted American aid during the Spanish–American war. After the victory of Adm. Dewey in Manila Bay in 1898, an insurrection broke out. Although it was successful, the treaty that ended the war transferred the Philippines to the United States instead of granting it independence. This led to a revolt against the United States; and, after the islands were subdued, the question of independence for the Philippines remained a political issue for many years. Finally, under the Tydings–McDuffie Independence Act of 1934, the islands began a ten-year transition period of controlled autonomy as the Commonwealth of the Philippines, with complete independence scheduled for 4 July 1946.

However, on 7 December 1941, the Japanese attacked the Philippines without warning and destroyed most of the U.S. aircraft stationed there after wrecking the Cavite Naval Base. After Manila was bombed and occupied on 2 January 1942 after being declared an open city, American and Filipino forces, commanded by Gen. Douglas MacArthur, were compelled to withdraw to the Bataan Peninsula. MacArthur was ordered to go to Australia, but the 36,000-man garrison he left on Bataan was forced to surrender and its survivors were subjected by the Japanese to a brutal "death march" in which thousands perished, and those who survived were eventually crowded into concentration camps where they were subjected to cruel and inhuman treatment.

American troops liberated the Philippines and freed thousands of prisoners in mid-1945, and by September of that year all military rule ended. On 4 July 1946, President Truman proclaimed the independence of the Philippines.

The United States played a major role in rebuilding the government and the economy of the islands, and, until 1972, the country enjoyed democratic rule under its 1935 constitution.

***THE MARCOS REGIME.*** In 1972, President Ferdinand Marcos declared martial law, blaming his action on increasing lawlessness, urban terrorism, and threats of open rebellion by the New People's Army, alleged to be a military wing of the Philippine Communist Party. During the eight-year period of martial law, Marcos ruled largely by decree and progressively restricted democratic institutions and civil liberties. Although a new constitution came into effect in 1973, the Marcos government acted until 1981 under its transitory provisions.

Mounting popular dissatisfaction with the regime and with the deteriorating national economy was further aroused by the assassination, in 1983, of the leader of the opposition, Benigno Aquino, upon his return from exile in the United States. In December 1985, Marcos called for an unscheduled presidential election to be held in February 1986. Although his party won the official election tally, impartial observers, including a delegation of U.S. congressmen, supported the claim of the opposition that it had actually received a large majority of the votes cast. A civilian-military uprising forced Marcos to flee the country, and Corazon Aquino, widow of Benigno Aquino and leader of the opposition party, was declared winner of the election. As president, Mrs. Aquino was given extensive powers under a provisional constitution.

***NEW CONSTITUTION.*** A new constitution, containing a Bill of Rights (article 3), was ratified by the people of the Philippines on 2 February 1987. Its policies and provisions are implemented mainly through the Revised Penal Code, the Civil Code, the Administrative Code, and various executive orders, proclamations, and directives, as well as by laws adopted by the congress.

Under article 13 of the constitution, a national Commission on Human Rights was created with a mandate to investigate, on its own or on a complaint from any party, all forms of human rights violations involving civil and political rights. These rights can be protected and enforced through the regular judicial system or through administrative bodies such as the Civil Service Commission and the National Police Commission.

***REPORT OF THE COMMISSION ON HUMAN RIGHTS OF THE PHILIPPINES.*** On 6 May 1988, the Commission on Human Rights of the Philippines issued a "Statement on Human Rights" and "Guidelines on Visitation and the Conduct of Investigation, Arrest, Detention and Related Operations" (both reproduced below) to which the secretary of National Defense, the chief of staff of the armed forces, and the director-general of the Integrated National Police have conformed.

In a report submitted to the UN **HUMAN RIGHTS COMMITTEE** on 26 August 1988, the Government of the Philippines provided the following information (UN Doc. CCPR/C/50/Add. 1, paras. 10–11):

The Philippines is currently facing a serious insurgency problem and certain extraordinary measures have been taken by the government authorities to cope with the problem. One of these is Executive Order No. 272 issued on 25 July 1987 increasing the period within which, under article 125 of the Revised Penal Code of the Philippines, a person who is detained on legal grounds is to be delivered to the proper judicial authorities: within 12 hours for crimes or offences punishable by light penalties, 18 hours for crimes or offences punishable by correctional penalties, and 36 hours for crimes or offences punishable by afflictive or capital penalties. The previous period of detention allowed was 6, 9 and 18 hours, respectively. Also, the amount of the bail bond for persons accused of bailable offences has been increased by 10 times in certain cases, such as subversion, sedition, rebellion, illegal possession of firearms, car stealing, drug trafficking and other serious offences.

As already stated in paragraph 10, the current serious insurgency problem has given rise to reported violations of human rights allegedly committed by elements of the military and paramilitary civilian groups as well as by elements of rebel and secessionist groups. Reports of such violations are being investigated by the Commission on Human Rights and, where investigations show that violations have indeed occurred, the perpetrators are recommended for immediate prosecution under existing Philippine laws.

The "Statement on Human Rights" issued by the Commission on Human Rights of the Philippines, reads as follows (UN Doc. CCPR/C/50/Add. 1, annex III):

The Commission on Human Rights reiterates its position that the human rights of every person must be observed and respected at all times. This statement encompasses the human rights most affected in the current insurgency situation.

Human Rights are the supreme and inherent rights to life, to dignity and to self-development. It is the essence of these rights that makes man human.

The policy of our constitutional government on Human Rights is embodied in Section 11, Article II of the Constitution, which states:

"The State values the dignity of every human person and guarantees full respect for human rights."

The Constitution guarantees these rights to every human person and has mandated the Commission on Human Rights as an independent constitutional body to investigate, on its own or on complaint by any party, all forms of human rights violations involving civil and political rights (Par. 1, Sec. 18, Article XIII).

The Bill of Rights enshrined in our Constitution (Article III) specifies the rights guaranteed to every person, without distinction as to race, sex, color, religion, or political persuasion. Among these are the right to life, to equal protection under our laws, to freedom from unreasonable searches and seizures, the right to assemble peacefully for redress of grievances and the right to due process, to be heard and to be assisted by legal counsel.

A person may not be detained unlawfully. During his detention, the following are prohibited:

1. The use of torture, force, violence, threat or any means that vitiate his free will;

2. The use of secret detention places, solitary, incommunicado and other similar forms of detention;

3. The employment of physical, psychological, or degrading punishment, or the use of inhuman facilities.

Every Filipino, regardless of whether he is a member of the military force or the police organization, a civilian, or an insurgent, and even a foreigner residing in or visiting the country, is guaranteed these rights.

Corollary to these rights, however, is the primary obligation of every Filipino citizen to protect and defend the Constitution, to respect the rights of others, to uphold the authority of the State, and to observe its laws.

Our government's commitment to human rights is founded in the Filipino's inherent respect for the dignity of man and his human rights enunciated not only in its state policies but also in its commitment to the principles embodied in, among others, the Universal Declaration of Human Rights adopted by the General Assembly of the United Nations on 10 December 1948, the Declaration of the Rights of the Child, the International Covenant on Civil and Political Rights, the International Covenant of Economic, Social and Cultural Rights, and to Protocol II relating to Protection of Victims of Non-International Armed Conflicts adopted on 12 August 1949 by the Geneva Convention.

We enjoin every Filipino citizen, most especially those in the government service whose functions directly involve the protection of the security of the state and its people, to observe and protect these human rights, and enforce laws, substantive and procedural, that uphold them.

The "Guidelines on Visitation and the Conduct of Investigation, Arrest, Detention and Related Operations," adopted by the Commission on Human Rights of the Philippines, are as follows (UN Doc. CCPR/C/50/Add. 1, annex IV):

1. Section 18, Article XIII of the 1987 Constitution specifically grants the Commission on Human Rights certain powers and functions, among which are the following:

(i) Investigate, on its own or on complaint by any party, all forms of human rights violations involving civil and political rights;

(ii) Protect the rights of Filipinos in the Philippines and overseas;

(iii) Exercise visitorial powers over jails, prisons, detention facilities; and

(iv) Request the assistance of any department, bureau, office or agency in the performance of its functions.

2. The armed Forces of the Philippines, the National Police and other law enforcement agencies have the obligation to protect the human rights of citizens and ensure the security of the state and its people. In the performance of these duties, utmost observance and respect for human rights is required.

3. Accordingly, the following guidelines on visitation and the conduct of investigation, arrest, detention and related operations are hereby promulgated for the strict and immediate implementation of all law enforcement agencies:

3.1 The Heads of the various law enforcement agencies shall be responsible for promulgating the rules and regulations to be disseminated to all members of their units or agencies to ensure observance of the rights guaranteed in the Constitution, especially those enumerated in the Commission on Human Rights statement promulgated May 6, 1988, which are incorporated herein by reference.

3.2 Commanders and elements of all units under their command shall extend maximum cooperation and courtesy to members of the Commission on Human Rights and/or their authorized representatives in the exercise of their constitutional authority and functions.

3.3 Recognizing the crucial role of complainants and witnesses in human rights cases, commanders and elements of all units under their command are responsible for their safety and security from potentially adverse or hostile actions.

3.4 Immediate members of the family, extended members of the family, legal counsel and spiritual advisers shall have free access to detained persons, subject to the provisions of applicable laws, rules and regulations.

3.5 An official report on any arrest, detention, investigation or similar operations shall be submitted to the Commission on Human Rights at the Integrated Bar of the Philippines Building, Dona Julia Vargas Avenue, Pasig, Metro Manila or to any of its twelve (12) regional offices, on a quarterly basis concerning the conduct of the foregoing operations and the names and status of all persons arrested or detained by virtue thereof unless a special report is required by the Commission or any of its regional offices.

3.6 In effecting arrests, conducting investigations and during detention, the use of unnecessary force must always be avoided. The resolution of the National Police Commission prescribing policies on arrests and investigations and enjoining strict adherence to Rule 113 of the Rules of Court must be followed, not only by the National Police, but also by other law enforcement agencies.

Presidential, legislative and local elections took place in May 1992. General Fidel Ramos, who had been Chief of Staff of the Armed Forces and Secretary of National Defense in President Aquino's administration, was elected with 24% of the votes. The progovernment LDP won 89 of the 200 seats in the House of Representatives and 16 of the 24 Senate seats.

A National Unification Commission was established by President Ramos in August 1992, aimed at solving the 20-year-old armed struggle between the Muslim separatists, the communist insurgents, and right-wing former members of the armed forces which had claimed an estimated 50,000 lives. A 35-year-old law banning the Communist Party of the Philippines (CPP) was also repealed. In early 1994 a ceasefire, as well as a general amnesty for rebels and members of security forces charged with counterinsurgency offenses, was announced.

The Presidential Anti-Crime Commission, formed in July 1992, found that the Philippine National Police (PNP) had been kidnaping wealthy Chinese Filipinos for ransom. Hundreds of police officers were dismissed in April 1993 following a complete investigation into the PNP. The death penalty was also reinstated.

**BIBLIOGRAPHY.** Amnesty International. *Philippines: "Disappearances" in the Context of Counter-Insurgency.* London: 1991. NGO factfinding report, in English.

————. *Philippines: Human Rights Violations and the Labour Movement.* London: 1991. NGO report, in English.

————. *Philippines: The Killing Goes On.* London: 1992. NGO report, in English.

————. *The Philippines: A Summary of Amnesty International's Concerns.* London: 1990. NGO report, in English.

Asia Watch. *Bad Blood: Militia Abuse in Mindanao, The Philippines.* New York: Human Rights Watch, 1992. NGO factfinding report, in English.

————. *Disappearances in the Philippines.* New York: Human Rights Watch, 1990. NGO report, in English.

————. *The Philippines: Violations of the Laws of War by Both Sides.* New York: Human Rights Watch, 1990. NGO factfinding report, in English.

Asian Human Rights Commission. *Report of the Asian Human Rights Commission Study Mission to the Philippines.* Hong Kong: 1988. NGO report, in English.

Bello, Walden. *U.S.-Sponsored Low-Intensity Conflict in the Philippines.* San Francisco: Institute for Food and Development Policy, 1987. NGO report, in English.

Black, Maggie. *Philippines: Children of the Runaway Cities.* Florence, Italy: UNICEF International Child Development Centre, 1991. IGO monograph, in English.

Canlas, M., M. Miranda, and J. Putzel. *Land Poverty and Politics in the Philippines.* London: Catholic Institute for International Relations, 1988. NGO conference paper, in English.

Catholic Institute for International Relations. *The Labour Trade: Filipino Migrant Workers around the World.* London: 1987. NGO report, in English.

Claude, R., E. Stover, and J. Lopez. *Health Professionals and Human Rights in the Philippines.* Washington, D.C.: American Association for the Advancement of Science and Clearinghouse on Science and Human Rights, 1987. NGO report, in English.

Delacruz, E., A. Jordan, and J. Emmanuel. *Death Squads in the Philippines.* San Francisco: Alliance for Philippine Concerns, 1987. NGO report, in English.

Donnelly, J., and R. E. Howard. *International Handbook on Human Rights*. Westport, CT, USA: Greenwood Press, 1987. Scholarly edited collection, in English.

Duhaylungsod, Levita, and David Hyndman. "Where All That Glitters Is Not Gold: Crossroads of Mining Exploitation in the T'boli Homeland," *Bulletin of Concerned Asian Scholars* 24, no. 3 (Summer 1992): 3–15. Scholarly article, in English.

Eagle, Julian. *A Smouldering Land: Lessons from the Philippines*. London: Catholic Institute for International Relations and Christian Aid, 1987. NGO report, in English.

Ecumenical Commission for Displaced Families and Communities. *Primer: Displacement in the Philippines—Nature, Causes, Effects, Extent, Limits, Remedies and Victims' Rights*. Quezon City, Philippines: 1987. NGO manual, in English.

Fay, Chip. *Counter-Insurgency and Tribal Peoples in the Philippines*. Washington, D.C.: Survival International USA, 1987. NGO report, in English.

Geiger, Danilo. "Conservation and All that Jazz: Lumad Defend Mount Apo National Park Against Government Onslaught," *IWGIA Newsletter* 4 (Fall 1992): 28–37. NGO article, in English.

General Assembly Binding Women for Reforms, Integrity, Equality, Leadership and Action. *Let's Work Together for the Protection of Human Rights of Filipino Women: A Documentation Report on the Human Rights Situation of Filipino Women*. Quezon City, Philippines: 1988. NGO report, in English.

Heinz, Wolfgang S. *Ursachen und Folgen von Menschenrechtsverletzungen in der Dritten Welt* (Causes and Consequences of Human Rights Violations in Third World Countries). Saarbrucken, Germany: Verlag Breitenbach, 1986. Scholarly monograph, in German; bibliography on the Philippines, pp. 447–449.

Hilderbrand, Dale. *To Pay is to Die: The Philippine Foreign Debt Crisis*. Davao City, Philippines: Philippine International Forum, 1991. Monograph, in English.

International Commission of Jurists. *The Failed Promise: Human Rights in the Philippines Since the Revolution of 1986*. Geneva, Switzerland: 1991. NGO report, in English.

Johannes Wier Foundation for Health and Human Rights. *Health and Human Rights in the Philippines*. The Hague, the Netherlands: 1991. NGO monograph, in English.

Kowalewski, David. "Vigilante Counterinsurgency and Human Rights in the Philippines," *Human Rights Quarterly* 12, no. 2 (May 1990) 246–264. Scholarly article, in English.

Lawyers Committee for Human Rights. *Impunity: Prosecutions of Human Rights Violations in the Philippines*. New York: 1991. NGO factfinding report, in English.

———. *Out of Control: Militia Abuses in the Philippines*. New York: 1990. NGO factfinding report, in English.

———. *Vigilantes in the Philippines: A Threat to Democratic Rule*. New York: 1988. NGO factfinding report, in English.

Lawyers Committee for Human Rights and Asia Watch. *Lawyers under Fire: Attacks on Human Rights Attorneys in the Philippines*. New York: 1988. NGO report, in English.

Leary, V., A. A. Ellis, and K. Madlener. *The Philippines: Human Rights after Martial Law*. Geneva: International Commission of Jurists, 1984. NGO mission report, in English.

Minority Rights Group. *The Lumad and Moro of Mindanao*. London: 1993. NGO factfinding report, in English; bibliography, p. 32.

Monzon, Vivian. *Filipino Children in Situations of Armed Conflicts*. Kensington, NSW, Australia: Law Association for Asia and the Pacific, 1990. NGO research report, in English.

National Federation of Sugar Workers—Food and General Trades. *Documentation Report: Trade Union Repression and Human Rights Violations*. Bacolod City, Philippines: 1988. NGO report in English.

O'Brien, Thomas. *Crises and Instability: The Philippines Enters the Nineties*. Davao City, Philippines: Philippine International Forum, 1990. Monograph, in English.

Pablo, L., J. Sayo, E. Mondez, C. Garcia, and N. Garde. *Primer on Militarization*. Quezon City, Philippines: Ecumenical Movement for Justice and Peace, 1988. NGO issue paper, in English.

Philippine Human Rights Information Center. *A Let-Down in Peace, No Let-Up in War: A Human Rights Report on the First Year of the Ramos Government (July 1, 1992—June 30, 1993)*. Manila, Philippines: Philippine Alliance of Human Rights Advocates, 1993. NGO report, in English.

———. *"Philippines 2000" Human Rights*. Manila, Philippines: 1994. NGO policy study paper, in English.

Philippine Senate Commission on Justice and Human Rights. *Report on Vigilante Groups*. Quezon City, Philippines: 1988. Government report, in English.

Presidential Committee on Human Rights. *Annual Report*. Manila, Philippines. Government commission annual report, in English.

Protestant Association for World Mission. *The Pain Will Go On until Justice Is Done: What Can We Do to Enforce Human Rights in the Philippines?* Manila, Philippines: 1986. NGO edited collection, in English.

Starner, F. L. *The Rising Sun and Tangled Roots: A Philippine Profile*. Hong Kong: Christian Conference on Asia, 1986. NGO report, in English.

Task Force Detainees of the Philippines. *Torment and Struggle after Marcos: A Report on Human Rights Trends in the Philippines under Aquino, March 1986—June 1992*. Quezon City, Philippines: 1993. NGO report, in English.

Taswell, Ruth, ed. *Southeast Asian Tribal Groups and Ethnic Minorities*. Cambridge, MA, USA: Cultural Survival, 1987. NGO conference proceedings, in English.

**PIOOM AWARD.** Since 1991, the PIOOM Foundation (Interdisciplinary Projects for the Study of Root Causes of Human Rights Violations), a nonpartisan, Dutch-based organization, has presented an award every two years in the amount of 2,000 (HFL) for the best study on the basic cause for human rights violations. In 1993, a Junior PIOOM Award was instituted for candidates younger than 25 years old; this award is in the amount of 1,000 (HFL).

The texts, whether published or unpublished, must deal with one or both of the following questions: (1) What factors enable gross human rights violations to occur and what factors inhibit them? (2) What is an optimal strategy for (inter)governmental and non-governmental human rights organizations and agencies to counter contemporary human rights violations and to prevent future violations? The texts may be in the form of an article, book, or thesis, but must have been written or published during the previous two years. They must also have been written in, or translated into, Dutch, English, French, or German.

The first recipient of the PIOOM Award was Dr. Helen Fein for her article "Genocide: A Sociological Perspective" (*Current Sociology* 38, no. 1 [Spring 1990]). At the time of the award, Dr. Fein was associated with the Human Rights Project at the Harvard Law School.

In 1993, the second PIOOM Award was presented to Dr. Robert Melson, associate professor of Political Science at Purdue University in Indiana (USA) and both chair and acting director of the Jewish Studies Program at the same university. Dr. Melson's award-winning book *Revolutions and Genocide: On the Origins of the Armenian Genocide and the Holocaust* deals with Armenians in the Ottoman Empire and Jews in Imperial Germany who survived as ethnic and religious minorities until they suffered mass destruction when the old regimes were engulfed by revolution. The central question of the work is whether there is a connection between revolution and genocide in these two instances and in general.

No Junior PIOOM Award had been awarded as of the end of 1994.

For more information, contact: the PIOOM Foundation, c/o LISWO, Leiden University, Wassenaarseweg 52, 2333 AK Leiden, the Netherlands. Telephone: (31-71) 27-38-61. Fax: (31-71) 27-37-88.

**PIRE, REV. DOMINIQUE HENRI (1910–1969).** Born George Pire in Dinant, Belgium, this Dominican priest was awarded the 1958 **NOBEL PEACE PRIZE** for his work with displaced persons, in particular the elderly and sick. Aid to Displaced Persons (*L'Aide aux Personnes Deplacées)*, an organization Fr. Pire founded in 1949, currently operates seven European "villages," at Aachen, Germany; Bregenz, Austria; Augsburg, Germany; Berchem-Sainte Agathe, Belgium (the Fridtjof Nansen village); Spiesen, Germany (the Albert Schweitzer village); Wuppertal, Germany (the Anne Frank village); and Euskirchen, Germany.

Although the establishment of the villages was the specific impetus for the Prize, Fr. Pire had worked with those in need almost from the beginning of his life as a priest. Ordained in 1934, he began a brief teaching career in moral philosophy and sociology at the Huy (Belgium) monastery. He administered to the spiritual needs of impoverished farm workers and soon began to alleviate the physical needs of their children, by establishing in 1938 the Mutual Family Aid Service (*Service d'Entr'aide Familiale)* and Open Air Camps of Huy (*Stations de Plein Air de Huy)* for area youth. When the Nazis overran Belgium, Fr. Pire served as chaplain for the resistance movement and organized an "underground railroad" for downed Allied airmen.

After World War II, Fr. Pire established Aid to Displaced Persons in an effort to help those refugees and displaced persons who were neglected by other agencies. He began with the idea of a sponsorship program, through which refugee families living in camps were put in touch with families willing to send them necessities, even money. The establishment of the villages came when Fr. Pire realized that the families needed an independent and secure existence, where they would share communal tasks and responsibilities. In addition to the seven villages, Fr. Pire founded four homes for the aged.

**BIBLIOGRAPHY.** *Current Biography Yearbook 1959.* New York: W. H. Wilson.
Gray, Tony. *Champions of Peace.* London: Paddington Press, 1976.
Schlessinger, Bernard S., and June H. Schlessinger, eds. *Who's Who of Nobel Prize Winners.* Phoenix, AZ, USA: Oryx Press, 1991.

**PLANETARY CITIZENS.** This non-governmental organization works to alert people to the interdependence of all countries and peoples and to shift their activities to a global perspective and the good of the planet. It has consultative status (Roster) with the UN **ECONOMIC AND SOCIAL COUNCIL** and **UNESCO.** It currently has members in 58 countries.

Founded in 1972, following the Conference on Human Survival (1970), Planetary Citizens presents annually the "Planetary Citizens of the Year Award" at the United Nations in New York to the person who best represents the organization's aims. It periodically publishes *Planet Earth.*

Planetary Citizens. Address: P.O. Box 1509, Shasta, CA 96067, USA.

**POLAND.** The Polish People's Republic is a country in eastern Europe, on the Baltic Sea. It has borders with Czechoslovakia, the former German Democratic Republic, and the former Union of Soviet Socialist Republics. Occupied by Germany during World War II, Poland's boundaries were redefined in 1945 by the establishment of a *de facto* western frontier along the Oder and Neisse Rivers under an agreement reached in Berlin by U.S. President Harry S. Truman, British Prime Minister Clement Attlee, and U.S.S.R. Premier Joseph Stalin, and by a treaty with the Union of Soviet Socialist Republics delimiting the Polish-U.S.S.R. frontier. Poland became a member of the United Nations the same year. Its population is estimated to be 38,330,000. It includes small national minorities of Byelorussians and Ukrainians. Although religious activity is not officially encouraged, 90% of the Polish people are said to maintain religious beliefs; among them, Christianity is predominant (Roman Catholic, 93%; Eastern Orthodox, 5%; Protestant denominations, 1%), while Islam is professed by .5% of the population and Judaism by .5%. State–Church relationships are regulated by laws, including those adopted by Parliament on 17 May 1989 giving the Roman Catholic Church legal status, the right to buy and sell property, and to operate businesses, and authorizing the government to return Church property it had seized in the 1950s. Literacy is estimated at 98%.

The government (1994) took the form of a republic. Under the 1989 "round table" agreements between the State authorities, the union Solidarity *(Solidarno s c),* and other groups concerned, open elections were held on 4 June 1989 for the first time in 40 years to fill 161 open seats in the 460-member *Sejm,* or lower house of parliament, and 100 seats in the newly created Senate. Candidates sponsored by Solidarity won 160 *Sejm* seats and 92 Senate seats. Thus reconstructed, the National Assembly, on 19 July 1989, elected Gen. Wojciech Jaruzelski, who had been general secretary of the United Workers' (Communist) Party and head of State since 1981, as Poland's president. Tadeusz Mazowiecki, a Solidarity official, was elected as Poland's first postwar non-Communist prime minister and took office on 29 July 1989. In elections held in December 1990, Solidarity leader **LECH WALESA** replaced Gen. Jaruzelski as president.

Poland's fate was controlled for many centuries by its neighbors—Austria, Germany, and Russia—and, for more than a century beginning in 1795, it totally disappeared from the map after those powers had partitioned it among themselves.

World War I gave Poland an opportunity to recover its independence, and the armistice of 11 November 1918 led to its reconstitution as an independent State. The Treaty of Versailles gave it access to the Baltic Sea and made Danzig a free city but left it with the problem of reconciling the conflicting interests of numerous linguistic and ethnic minorities, including Germans, Ukrainians, Byelorussians, Lithuanians, and Jews. The Polish Jews, protected in the Middle Ages by the kings, had later suffered intolerance and discrimination in their own country.

***POLAND UNDER THE NAZIS.*** In 1939, Adolph Hitler, brushing aside a ten-year nonaggression pact Germany had signed with Poland in 1934, abruptly demanded the return of Danzig to Germany. Poland refused, and, on 1 September 1939, Nazi troops invaded Poland from the west, precipitating World War II. Soviet troops moved in from the east on 17 September, and a German/Russian agreement partitioned Poland between the two countries. However, after the German attack on the Soviet Union in June 1941, all of Poland was occupied by Germany.

During the war years, Nazi occupation authorities proceeded methodically to exterminate large seg-

ments of the Polish population by massacres, starvation, and mass incineration in concentration camps. Of more than 3 million Polish Jews, all but 100,000 were put to death; nevertheless, Jewish men and women participated in an effective underground resistance movement that culminated in the Warsaw uprising of 1944.

***POLAND AS A COMMUNIST COUNTRY.*** The last German troops were expelled from Poland in 1945 by Russian forces that had entered the country and set up a provisional government at Lublin. When elections were held in 1947, the Polish Committee for National Liberation, with Russian recognition and support, proclaimed itself the Provisional Government of Poland. A new constitution was adopted in 1952, under which Poland became the Polish People's Republic. Poland joined the Warsaw Pact the same year.

In 1980, persistent economic decline led to strikes and rioting in Poland. The largest of the strikes was one organized by a joint committee of workers in the Gdansk (formerly Danzig), Gydnia, and Sopot shipyards, led by Lech Walesa, demanding the right to strike and to form independent unions, abolition of censorship, access to the media of information, and release of political prisoners. It ended with the signing of the "Gdansk Agreements" by Walesa and government officials, recognizing the right of workers to form independent unions and to go on strike.

Shortly thereafter, the leadership of Poland changed, with Edward Heirek stepping down as first secretary of the Communist Party and being replaced by Stanislaw Kania.

On 17 September 1980, a number of trade unions joined in a national confederation, Solidarity, and applied for legal status, which was granted after some hesitation on 29 October. Early in 1981, Solidarity launched a drive for a five-day week for workers in many enterprises. A crisis was narrowly averted when Defense Minister General Wojciech Jaruzelski assumed the added responsibility of prime minister and arranged a moratorium. Jaruzelski became first secretary of the Communist Party after Kania resigned that post on 18 October.

On 13 December 1981, the Council of State imposed martial law throughout Poland, suspended most political and civil liberties, and established a 20-member Military Council of National Salvation to maintain law and order. The union Solidarity was banned, and its leaders were detained along with many political prisoners.

On 8 October 1982, the *Sejm* adopted a law dissolving all registered trade unions, including Solidarity, and establishing a new union system permitting the establishment of trade unions in workplaces but requiring that they pledge support for the Communist Party and the constitution before being accorded recognition. Martial law was suspended in December 1982 and lifted completely in July 1983, and all internees were released. Although Lech Walesa and other Solidarity leaders were freed as internees, 11 of them—not including Walesa—were immediately arrested and charged with political offenses. This "Group of Eleven" was freed only in July 1984.

In November 1983, Lech Walesa was awarded the **NOBEL PEACE PRIZE.** His wife traveled to Oslo to accept it on his behalf. In October 1984 the kidnaping and murder of Father Jerzy Popieluszko, a supporter of Solidarity, shocked and angered the Polish people; the subsequent trial and conviction of four officers of the Polish Security Police was an unprecedented event in the nation.

Earlier, on 10 March 1982, the **COMMISSION ON HUMAN RIGHTS** of the United Nations had expressed deep concern about reports of widespread violations of human rights in Poland and had requested the Secretary-General, or a person designated by him, to make a thorough study of the human rights situation in that country. The Secretary-General followed the situation closely and, on 21 December 1982, designated Under-Secretary-General Hugo Gobbi to continue the task on his behalf.

In 1983, the Commission received Mr. Gobbi's report, indicating that the Polish authorities had not co-operated either with him or with the Secretary-General. The Commission deplored their attitude in the matter and reaffirmed the right of the Polish people to pursue their political, social, and cultural development free from outside interference. It called upon the Polish authorities to terminate the restrictive measures they had imposed on the exercise of human rights and to review the severe prison sentences which had been imposed in the context of the state of martial law.

In September 1983, Mr. Gobbi forwarded a detailed request for information to the Government of Poland. That government did not reply. Under-Secretary-General Patricio Ruedas, who succeeded Mr. Gobbi as the Secretary-General's representative, reported to the Commission at its February 1984 session, presenting information which had reached the Secretary-General and Mr. Gobbi from a wide variety of sources, including personal contacts between the Secretary-General and Polish authorities during a visit to Poland.

In the report, Under-Secretary-General Patricio Ruedas presented the following conclusions (UN Doc. E/CN.4/1984/26, paras. 38–41):

A difficult economic and social situation has existed, and continues to exist, since 1981 in Poland, taxing to the utmost the resources and the stamina of the Polish people and of the Polish Government. Poland is in the process of change. Martial law, imposed in December 1981, lasted formally for 19 months. During that period, numerous arrests were made, including those for political reasons. Furthermore, some Polish citizens died as a result of clashes between demonstrators and the police: at least two, in 1981; at least one in 1982 and at least two in 1983. That the figures are under dispute is not so important as that deaths actually occurred, for one single case is one too much. This is also the view of the Polish authorities, as reported to the Secretary-General.

The suspension and, thereafter, the lifting of martial law, as well as the enactment and implementation of the clemency measures and, subsequently, the amnesty law, have produced conditions favourable to a reconciliation between different sectors of Polish society. The figures . . . are significant in this regard—particularly if comparison is made between the figure of about 1,500 persons detained for political reasons as of 4 January 1983 (E/CN.4/1983/18, para. 35) and that of 281 detainees—most of them on a temporary basis—as of 18 February 1984. These are certainly encouraging developments, to be seen as such by any independent observer.

Some questions can nevertheless be entertained regarding some of the recent (1983) legislation, be it ever temporary. Thus, for example, the amendment to the Polish penal code . . . seems to perpetuate a similar provision which existed in Article 46 (1) of the now defunct martial law. Also the "Special Legal Regulations in the Period of Overcoming the Socio-Economic Crisis", . . . while temporary in nature, provide for extensive powers to the authorities in several domains, including education. As regards the possible exercise of these powers, the writer of this report is impressed by the spirit of moderation evidenced by all members of the Polish Government who met with him, and is authorized by the Secretary-General to say that he, too, noted favourably that spirit. This has permitted the Secretary-General to state that what he heard in Poland was "very encouraging on all fronts".

In the operative paragraph 4 of its resolution 1983/30, the Commission on Human Rights called upon the Polish authorities "to realize fully and without further delay their stated intention to terminate the restrictive measures imposed on the exercise of human rights and fundamental freedoms, particularly in relation to a review of the severe prison sentences imposed in the context of the state of martial law, the lifting of restrictions on the free flow of information, and the repeal of the new restrictions imposed on the Polish people". In the light of the information contained in this report, it seems clear that in at least one very important aspect—the review of prison sentences—effect has been given to the resolution through enactment and implementation of the clemency measures and the amnesty law.

The reports of Under-Secretaries-General Gobbi and Ruedas made it clear that the Government of Poland had seemingly solved one of its major problems by adopting a new law on trade unions which provided for a complete new trade union structure in the country and abolished all existing trade unions without exception. However, this raised the question whether such action was permissible under the terms of relevant international instruments such as the ILO Freedom of Association and Protection of the Right to Organize Convention (1948) and the ILO Right to

Organize and Collective Bargaining Convention (1949), especially when taken in a period of emergency affecting trade union affairs. Analysis of the new law by the International Labor Office raised doubts as to its compatibility with those conventions, and there was a general consensus that the matter could be settled satisfactorily only by utilizing the complaints procedure established in accordance with the 1948 Convention. Thereafter, the Commission on Human Rights took no further action relating to the situation in Poland.

After a long period of ever-increasing labor unrest over wages and living conditions, government authorities organized a series of "round table negotiations" for discussion of issues relating to the trade union movement and the broadening of civil liberties. On 9 March 1989, these talks between the regime and the opposition, which included Solidarity, resulted in the adoption of a program of major political reform.

The program called for the creation of an upper house of parliament which would be democratically elected and which would supplement the work of the 460-member *Sejm*; the two houses together would constitute the National Assembly. All the senators would be chosen by the people in free elections. The 161 open seats in the *Sejm* would likewise be filled by free elections, open to opposition candidates and independents. The president would then be elected by the National Assembly as a whole and would have strong executive powers, including the ability to dissolve the National Assembly. In addition, three dissident organizations were to be legalized: Solidarity, Rural Solidarity, and the Independent Students Association.

Although the round table agreements were not totally satisfactory to either side, they were signed on 5 April 1989 as—in the words of Solidarity's chief negotiator—"one step in a process through which democracy may be rebuilt in an evolutionary manner, not upsetting the political balance or stability."

When General Jaruzelski was inaugurated as president, Solidarity turned down offers to participate in a coalition government and did not permit its members to serve in the cabinet in either their official or individual capacities. It, however, organized a "shadow cabinet" in the National Assembly to prepare for the time when it would be called upon to assume power, as occurred in 1989.

*POLAND AS A DEMOCRACY.* The first free elections in Poland in 50 years were held at the local level in May 1990 and Solidarity won 41% of the seats. Lech Walesa then won election to the presidency with 74% of the votes in second-round voting in December 1990 when President Jaruzelski resigned before the end of his six-year term. In legislative elections in October 1991 none of the 29 successful parties obtained a majority. The Democratic Union (UD), a party formed by the merger of the Solidarity faction formed in opposition to Walesa and two other parties, won the largest number of seats in both the *Sejm* and the Senate.

Labor and political unrest over the government's stringent economic policies continued. Large-scale strikes took place throughout 1992, including those called by Solidarity. When the *Sejm* passed by one vote a motion of "no-confidence" in Prime Minister Hanna Suchocka in May 1993, Walesa refused to accept her resignation, dissolved the chamber, and scheduled new elections for September 1993. That month legislation was passed requiring parties to obtain 5% of the total votes (8% for political alliances) before taking a seat in parliament.

Votes cast for such parties receiving less than 5% constituted 35% of the total votes in the September elections. Participation was 52% of those eligible to vote and parties of the left dominated the results, primarily the Democratic Left Alliance (SLD), which won 37 seats in the Senate, and the Polish Peasant Party (PSL), which won 34 seats. Both groups advocated the abolition of the Senate. This Communist-linked bloc won 303 of the 460 seats in the *Sejm*.

Poland signed several agreements with international organizations in the 1990s, becoming a member of the **Council of Europe** in November 1991, a member of NATO's "partnership for peace" program in 1994, and an associate partner in the Western European Union, also in 1994. An association agreement with the European Union was signed in 1991, and possible membership in the EU by the year 2000 was discussed again in November 1994.

*DISCRIMINATION AGAINST JEWS.* Aside from its political and economic problems, Poland has been plagued from time to time by manifestations of intolerance and discrimination directed against Jews. Once numbering more than 3 million, the bulk of the Jewish population of the country died of starvation or perished in the Nazi death camps on Polish soil during World War II. Only about 250,000 remained in 1967 and 1968, when an official anti-Semitic campaign reflecting a power struggle in the Communist Party caused 9,000 Jewish workers to lose their jobs and drove more than 20,000 to leave the country after being stripped of their citizenship and provided with one-way travel documents. The campaign, supported by Wladyslaw Gomulka, then head of the Polish Communist Party, took the form of party and factory meetings all over Poland denouncing "Zionists" and proclaiming war against liberals and intellectuals, many of whom were Jews. These actions were condemned as "infamous and an embarrassment to Poland" by the

Polish Communist Party weekly *Polityka* some 20 years later, on 18 February 1988.

### REPORT OF THE UN COMMITTEE ON THE ELIMINATION OF ALL FORMS OF RACIAL DISCRIMINATION.

The report of Poland under the International Convention on the Elimination of All Forms of Racial Discrimination (see **RACIAL DISCRIMINATION**) was considered by the **COMMITTEE ON THE ELIMINATION OF RACIAL DISCRIMINATION** (CERD/C/226/Add. 2) at its 981st, 982nd, and 983rd meetings, held on 17 and 18 March 1993 (CERD/C/SR. 981–983). The Committee adopted the following observations on the report (E/CN.4/Sub.2/1993/25, paras. 178–198):

The tenth, eleventh and twelfth periodic reports of Poland, submitted in one document (CERD/C/226/Add.2), were considered by the Committee at its 981st, 982nd and 983rd meetings, held on 17 and 18 March 1993 (CERD/C/SR.981–983).

The report was introduced by the representative of the reporting State, who explained that since the report had been drafted in 1992 there had been no notable developments concerning the situation of racial discrimination in Poland. There were no laws in Poland regarding the legal status of persons that made any distinction on the grounds of race or ethnic origin. The Constitutional Court had ruled on several occasions that the principle of equality before the law constituted the very foundation of the State and was to be strictly respected by all State organs. Poland had a comprehensive system of institutional guarantees for the rule of law based on the independence of the judiciary. Justice was administered not only through the courts, but also through the Commissioner for Human Rights/Ombudsman, who was empowered to act not only in cases involving breaches of the law, but also in cases of violations of accepted principles of community life. Cases of discrimination in Poland were few and were usually related to nationality.

With respect to the application of the international human rights treaties ratified by Poland, the representative informed the Committee that, in accordance with the decision of the Supreme Court in June 1992, such treaties would henceforth become directly applicable and binding provided that they were self-executing. Unfortunately, the International Convention on the Elimination of All Forms of Racial Discrimination, which had been ratified before the constitutional amendment of April 1989, could not yet be considered as directly incorporated in Polish law. However, that situation was expected to change with the adoption of the new Constitution, which would put all human rights treaties ratified by Poland on an equal footing and make them part of the internal legal order irrespective of the date of ratification.

Members of the Committee welcomed the recent trend towards greater democracy in Poland. The ratification by Poland of the European Convention on the Protection of Human Rights and Fundamental Freedoms and its acceptance of the jurisdiction of the European Court on Human Rights, as well as of the procedure whereby individual petitions could be made to the European Commission on Human Rights, were evidence that it had consolidated its status as a democratic State based on the rule of law.

Members of the Committee noted that the report under consideration was somewhat brief and not fully in accordance with the Committee's revised general guidelines. Those guidelines should be taken into account when the next periodic report was prepared. Members wished to have more detailed information on the legal situation in Poland with regard to the implementation of the Convention. They observed that the Government should consider submitting a "core document" containing general information on the situation in the country that could be used by all human rights treaty bodies and which would make the task of reporting easier. Members also wished to have more precise demographic data showing the ethnic and racial situation in Poland. In particular, further information was requested on attitudes and behaviour towards Jews and Gypsies in Poland and on the problem of racial discrimination against immigrants and refugees.

With respect to article 2 of the Convention, members of the Committee indicated that the Polish authorities should take into account the provisions of article 2.1 in connection with any policy which the National and Ethnic Minorities Commission might adopt. The authorities should formulate a more comprehensive policy towards minorities, put it into written form and bring it to the attention of the persons it was intended to protect and those who were required to implement it. Furthermore, a governmental body should be specifically designated as responsible for its coordination. The Committee would welcome further information on all those points in the next report of Poland. Members requested more information with respect to the implementation of article 2.1(d).

With respect to article 4 of the Convention, members of the Committee stated that the report should have been more informative about the Polish National Party, which sought to promote negative attitudes towards Jews. They asked whether the Polish Constitution allowed the establishment of political parties and organizations on racial, ethnic or religious grounds.

With regard to article 5 of the Convention, members of the Committee noted that the information provided in connection with that article related only to legislation and not to the actual situation in the country. Members wished to have more information on the groups organized by the Socio-Cultural Society, which had secured for the German minority a strong representation in local government; on limitations on the right to own property; on the cultural education provided and training in the languages of minority groups; on the national education system and the extent to which it reflected the interests the different ethnic groups.

Referring to article 6 of the Convention, members of the Committee indicated that insufficient detail had been given with respect to the implementation of that article. Further information was requested on the functions of the Ombudsman and of the National and Ethnic Minority Commission. More information was also requested with respect to recent changes in the organization of the judiciary.

Concerning article 14 of the Convention, members of the Committee asked whether Poland planned to make a declaration recognizing the competence of the Committee to receive and consider communications from individuals or groups of individuals claiming to be victims of a violation of any right set forth in the Convention.

Replying to the questions, the representative of the State party stated that, with regard to the demographic composition of Poland, the Minister of Culture had estimated that the population included 300,000 Ukrainians, between 200,000 and 250,000 Belarusians, between 200,000 and

500,000 Germans, between 20,000 and 25,000 Lithuanians, 15,000 Jews, 15,000 Greeks and Macedonians, 3,000 Russians, Tartars, Karaites, Ormians and Czechs, and between 10,000 and 15,000 Gypsies. Ethnic minorities thus totalled some 1.1 million out of a total population of 40 million. Apart from some isolated instances, there was no negative attitude or discrimination towards foreigners in the country.

With regard to article 1 of the Convention, he stated that, although that provision had not been literally incorporated in domestic legislation, there was no doubt that it had influenced the understanding in Poland of what constituted racial discrimination.

Concerning article 2 of the Convention, he gave further information on the status of the Convention in the Polish legal order and indicated that the Convention played an important role in Polish jurisprudence. There were, for example, frequent references to the International Covenants, which similarly had not yet been transformed into domestic law, in the jurisprudence of the Constitutional Court, the Administrative Court and in the activities of the Ombudsman.

With regard to article 4 of the Convention, he explained that, following decades of Communist rule, Poland was still in the initial stage of establishing a multiparty system. The general approach adopted was to limit State interference in that process as much as possible. At present, there were more than 180 political parties active in Poland, most of which were very small with no political influence. That was the case for the National Party under the leadership of Mr. Tejkowski. Because of his statements and other activities, criminal proceedings against Mr. Tejkowski had been initiated, but they had not yet been completed. In that connection, the statute on political parties of 1990 made it possible for the Constitutional Court to declare a political party inconsistent with the Constitution. Legislation on associations provided similar restrictions with regard to organizations other than political parties.

Concerning article 5 of the Convention and the participation of minorities in representative organs, the local administration in Poland was based on the principle of self-government. Representatives of minorities were members of local parliaments, as well as of the national Parliament. In order to facilitate the access of minorities to the legislature, the electoral law of 1991 had established lower criteria for the registration and election of candidates representing minorities. With regard to educational opportunities for minorities, there were no restrictions as to teaching in minority languages. Availability of such instruction depended on the need and on material resources. Since 1 September 1992, German had been taught as a basic language in 7 schools and as an additional language in 170 schools in areas inhabited by the German minority. Ukrainian was taught in 3 primary schools and in 3 general secondary schools, while Belarusian was taught in 48 primary schools and in 2 general secondary schools.

With respect to article 6 of the Convention, the representative stated that the Sejm Committee for National and Ethnic Minorities had been established immediately after the political changes of 1989. It was a standing parliamentary committee that dealt with all matters relevant to the protection of minorities. In particular, the Committee discussed the question of a draft statute on that question.

In regard to article 14 of the Convention, he stated that, in general, Poland recognized the right of individuals to avail themselves of international complaints procedures in instances where they felt that their rights had been violated. It was only for technical reasons that Poland had not yet made the declaration under article 14 recognizing the competence of the Committee in that regard.

In conclusion, he stated that the observations and recommendations made by the members of the Committee would be very useful to the Polish authorities.

The Committee recommended that the Government of Poland, in drafting its next periodic report, should make use of the possibility created by the revised guidelines on reporting to submit a core document covering the general legal, political and economic situation in Poland. It expressed the hope that the next periodic report would provide all the information requested during the Committee's consideration of the tenth, eleventh and twelfth periodic reports.

The Committee reiterated its request for further demographic data in accordance with general recommendation IV and for full information on the situation of ethnic groups.

The Committee considered the form in which the Convention had been incorporated in Polish law and noted that a different system had been provided for under the new Constitution. It recommended to the Government that it should consider giving the Convention the same status in domestic law as other international human rights instruments.

**BIBLIOGRAPHY.** Bartoszewski, W. T. *Polish-Jewish Relations: A Current Debate among Polish Catholics.* London: Institute of Jewish Affairs, 1987. NGO report, in English.

Commission on Security and Cooperation in Europe. *Basket I—Implementation of the Final Act of the Conference on Security and Cooperation in Europe: Findings Eleven Years after Helsinki.* Washington, D.C.: U.S. Government Printing Office, 1987. Government report, in English.

Donnelly, J., and R. E. Howard, eds. *International Handbook on Human Rights.* Westport, CT, USA: Greenwood Press, 1987. Scholarly edited collection, in English.

*Freedom of Information and Expression in Poland: A Commentary by ARTICLE 19 on the Report Submitted to the United Nations' Human Rights Committee by the Government of the Polish People's Republic.* London: ARTICLE 19, 1987. NGO report, in English.

Goodwyn, Lawrence. *Breaking the Barrier: The Rise of Solidarity in Poland.* New York: Oxford University Press, 1991. Scholarly monograph, in English.

Helsinki Committee in Poland. *Human Rights in Poland.* Warsaw, Poland: International Helsinki Federation for Human Rights, 1990. NGO report, in English.

Helsinki Watch. *Prison Conditions in Poland: An Update.* New York: Human Rights Watch, 1991. NGO factfinding report, in English.

Information Centre for Polish Affairs. "The Helsinki Committee in Poland: Violations of Basic Freedoms in the Polish People's Republic from 1 November 1986 to 30 April 1987," *Uncensored Poland News Bulletin* 13 (June 1987). NGO report, in English.

International League for Human Rights. *Human Rights in Poland: Comments on the Second Periodic Report of the Government of Poland to the Human Rights Committee under the International Covenant on Civil and Political Rights.* New York: 1987. NGO report, in English.

Kedzia, Zdzislaw. "Interpretation and Protection of the Constitutional Rights and Freedoms in Poland," *SIM Newsletter: Netherlands Quarterly of Human Rights* 6, no. 1 (1988): 38–53. Scholarly article, in English.

Korba, Irena. "Five Years Underground: The Opposition and the Church in Poland since Martial Law," *Religion in Communist Lands* 15, no. 2 (Summer 1987): 167–181. NGO article, in English.

Moody, J., and R. Boyes. *The Priest and the Policeman: The Courageous Life and Cruel Murder of Father Jerzy Popieluszko.* New York: Summit Books, 1987. Scholarly monograph, in English.

Polish Helsinki Committee. *Human Rights Violations in Poland 1983–1986.* London: Information for Polish Affairs, 1986. NGO report, in English.

Robbins, T., and R. Robertson, eds. *Church-State Relations: Tensions and Transitions.* New Brunswick, NJ, USA: Transaction Books, 1987. Scholarly edited collection, in English.

Rosas, Allan, ed. *International Human Rights Norms in Domestic Law: Finnish and Polish Perspectives.* Helsinki, Finland: Lakimiesliiton Kustannus (Finnish Lawyers' Publishing Company), 1990. Conference papers, in English.

Roth, Kenneth. *Repression Disguised as Law: Human Rights in Poland.* New York: Lawyers Committee for Human Rights, 1987. NGO report, in English.

Stainsby, R. A. "Asylum-Seekers in Poland: Catalyst for a New Refugee and Asylum Policy in Europe," *International Journal of Refugee Law* 2, no. 4 (1990): 636–641. Scholarly article, in English.

U.S. Helsinki Watch Committee. *From Below: Independent Peace and Environmental Movements in Eastern Europe and the USSR.* New York: 1987. NGO report, in English.

———. *Reinventing Civil Society: Poland's Quiet Revolution, 1981–1986.* New York: 1986. NGO report, in English.

**POLITICAL RIGHTS.** The right of everyone to take part in the government of his or her country is proclaimed in the UNIVERSAL DECLARATION OF HUMAN RIGHTS in the following terms:

*Article 2.* (1) Everyone has the right to take part in the government of his country, directly or through freely chosen representatives.

(2) Everyone has the right of equal access to public service in his country.

(3) The will of the people shall be the basis of the authority of government; this will shall be expressed in periodic and genuine elections which shall be by universal and equal suffrage and shall be held by secret vote or by equivalent free voting procedures.

The INTERNATIONAL COVENANT ON CIVIL AND POLITICAL RIGHTS deals with the subject in article 25, which reads:

*Article 25.* (1) Every citizen shall have the right and the opportunity, without any of the distinctions mentioned in article 2 and without unreasonable restrictions:

(a) To take part in the conduct of public affairs, directly or through freely chosen representatives;

(b) To vote and to be elected at genuine periodic elections which shall be by universal and equal suffrage and shall be held by secret ballot, guaranteeing the free expression of the will of the electors;

(c) To have access, on general terms of equality, to public service in his country.

Article 5 of the International Convention on the Elimination of All Forms of Racial Discrimination (see RACIAL DISCRIMINATION) provides that:

*Article 5.* In compliance with the fundamental obligations laid down in article 2 of this Convention, States parties undertake to prohibit and to eliminate racial discrimination in all its forms and to guarantee the right of everyone, without distinction as to race, colour, or national or ethnic origin, to equality before the law, notably in the enjoyment of the following rights: . . .

(c) Political rights, in particular the rights to participate in elections, to vote and to stand for election—on the basis of universal and equal suffrage, to take part in the Government as well as in the conduct of public affairs at any level and to have equal access to public service. . . .

Discrimination against women in respect of the right of everyone to take part in the government of his or her country is dealt with in the Convention on the Elimination of All Forms of Discrimination against Women (see WOMEN'S RIGHTS) as follows:

*Article 7.* States Parties take all appropriate measures to eliminate discrimination against women in the political and public life of the country and, in particular, shall ensure to women, on equal terms with men, the right:

(a) To vote in all elections and public referenda and to be eligible for election to all publicly elected bodies;

(b) To participate in the formulation of government policy and the implementation thereof and to hold public office and perform all public functions at all levels of government;

(c) To participate in non-governmental organizations and associations concerned with the public and political life of the country.

*Article 8.* States Parties shall take all appropriate measures to ensure to women, on equal terms with men and without any discrimination, the opportunity to represent their Governments at the international level and to participate in the work of international organizations.

The AMERICAN CONVENTION ON HUMAN RIGHTS, open for acceptance by members of the ORGANIZATION OF AMERICAN STATES, contains the following provision:

*Article 23.* (1) Every citizen shall enjoy the following rights and opportunities:

(a) to take part in the conduct of public affairs, directly or through freely chosen representatives;

(b) to vote and to be elected in genuine periodic elections, which shall be by universal and equal suffrage and by secret ballot that guarantees the free expression of the will of the voters; and

(c) to have access, under general conditions of equality, to the public service of his country.

(2) The law may regulate the exercise of the rights and opportunities referred to in the preceding paragraph only on the basis of age, nationality, residence, language, education, civil and mental capacity, or sentencing by a competent court in criminal proceedings.

The AFRICAN CHARTER ON HUMAN AND PEOPLES' RIGHTS, open for acceptance by member States of the ORGANIZATION OF AFRICAN UNITY, states that:

*Article 13.* 1. Every citizen shall have the right to participate freely in the government of his country, either directly or through freely chosen representatives in accordance with the provisions of the law.

2. Every citizen shall have the right of equal access to the public service of his country.

3. Every individual shall have the right of access to public property and services in strict equality of all persons before the law.

## STUDIES ON DISCRIMINATION IN THE POLITICAL SPHERE.

The UN SUB-COMMISSION ON PREVENTION OF DISCRIMINATION AND PROTECTION OF MINORITIES first considered the preparation of a study of discrimination in the matter of political rights in 1952. It decided to proceed with such a study at its 1956 session and appointed Mr. Hernan Santa Cruz (Chile) as its Special Rapporteur for the study.

The Sub-Commission considered the Special Rapporteur's final report at its 1962 session. On the basis of drafts presented in that report, it formulated a series of "General Principles on Freedom and Non-Discrimination in the Matter of Political Rights," reproduced below. The report, to which the general principles were annexed, was published by the United Nations in 1963 (UN publication, Sales no. 63.XIV.2).

The Sub-Commission transmitted the report and general principles to the COMMISSION ON HUMAN RIGHTS for further consideration. The Commission did not elaborate them into a separate international instrument, as had been proposed, but took them into account when it prepared drafts, which later were adopted by the GENERAL ASSEMBLY as the Declaration on the Elimination of All Forms of Racial Discrimination (1963) and the International Convention on the Elimination of All Forms of Racial Discrimination.

The UN General Assembly, at its 1988 session, recalled the provisions of those instruments relating to political rights and stressed (resolution 43/157) its conviction that periodic and genuine elections are a necessary and indispensable element of sustained efforts to protect the rights and interests of the governed, and that, as a matter of practical experience, the right of everyone to take part in the government of his or her country is a crucial factor in the effective enjoyment by all of a wide range of other human rights and fundamental freedoms, including political, economic, social, and cultural rights. The Assembly declared, further, "that determining the will of the people requires an electoral process which accommodates distinct alternatives, and that this process should provide an equal opportunity for all citizens to become candidates and put forward their political views, individually and in co-operation with others."

The Assembly also reaffirmed its oft-stated view that APARTHEID should be abolished, that the systematic denial or abridgement of the right to vote on grounds of race or color is a gross violation of human rights and an affront to the conscience and dignity of mankind, and that the right to participate in a political system based on common and equal citizenship and universal franchise is essential for the exercise of the principle of periodic and genuine elections.

The Assembly called upon the Commission on Human Rights to consider appropriate ways and means of enhancing the effectiveness of the principle of periodic and genuine elections, in the context of full respect for the sovereignty of member States, and to report to it on this question in 1989.

The text of the Sub-Commission's "General Principles on Freedom and Non-discrimination in the Matter of Political Rights" appears below:

### General Principles on Freedom and Non-Discrimination in the Matter of Political Rights

#### Preamble

Whereas the peoples of the world in the Charter of the United Nations have proclaimed their determination to reaffirm faith in fundamental human rights, in the dignity and worth of the human person, in the equal rights of men and women and of nations large and small, and to promote social progress and better standards of life in larger freedom,

Whereas the Charter sets forth, as one of the purposes of the United Nations, the promotion and encouragement of respect for human rights and fundamental freedoms for all without distinction as to race, sex, language or religion,

Whereas the Universal Declaration of Human Rights, further elaborating the principle of non-discrimination, proclaims that everyone is entitled to all the rights and freedoms set forth therein without distinction of any kind, including political opinion, and provides that no distinction shall be made on the basis of the political, jurisdictional or international status of the country or territory to which a person belongs,

Whereas, since the interests of the many are often disregarded when political power is in the hands of the few, the right of everyone to take part in the government of his country is the condition indispensable for the effective enjoyment by all of other human rights, including economic, social and cultural rights.

Whereas the exercise of political rights is directly linked to the existence of freedom of opinion and expression and freedom of peaceful assembly and association,

Whereas these rights can only be effectively guaranteed in a world in which the principles of the Charter, especially the principle of self-determination, and the principles enshrined in the declaration on the granting of independence to colonial territories and peoples, contained in General Assembly resolution 1514 (XV) of 14 December 1960, shall have full application.

Now therefore the following general principles are proclaimed to ensure recognition of the right of everyone to take part in the government of his country and of other related political rights, and to prevent discrimination in the enjoyment of these rights:

1. *The Right of All Peoples to Self-determination.* All peoples have the right to self-determination; by virtue of that right

they freely determine their political status and freely pursue their economic, social and cultural development.

2. *Political Rights of Nationals.* (a) Every national of a country is entitled within that country to full and equal political rights without distinction of any kind, such as race, colour, sex, language, religion, political or other opinion, national or social origin, property, birth or other status.

(b) No one shall be denied nationality, or deprived of nationality, as a means of denying him or depriving him of political rights.

(c) The age, length of residence and other conditions prescribed by law for the exercise of any particular political right shall be the same for all nationals of a country or inhabitants of a political unit, as the case may be.

3. *Freedom of Opinion and Association.* Freedom of opinion and expression and freedom of peaceful assembly and association are essential to the enjoyment of political rights. These freedoms, and the access to the facilities and means for their exercise, shall be ensured to all persons at all times.

4. *Universality of Suffrage.* Every national is entitled to vote in any national election, referendum or plebiscite held in his country, and in any such public consultation held in the political or administrative unit thereof in which he resides. The right to vote shall not be dependent upon literacy or any other educational qualifications.

5. *Equality of Suffrage.* (a) Every national is entitled to vote in any election, or other public consultation for which he is eligible, on equal terms, and each vote shall have the same weight.

(b) When voting is conducted on the basis of electoral districts, the said districts shall be established on an equitable basis such as would make the results most accurately and completely reflect the will of all the voters.

(c) For any election or public consultation held by direct vote there shall be one general election roll, and every eligible national shall be included in that roll.

6. *Secrecy of the Vote.* (a) Every voter shall be able to vote in such a manner as not to involve disclosure of how he has voted or intends to vote.

(b) No voter shall be compelled to state, in any legal proceeding or otherwise, how he voted, or intends to vote, and no one shall attempt to obtain from any voter, directly or otherwise, information as to how he has voted or intends to vote.

7. *Periodicity of Elections.* Elections to all elective public offices shall be held at reasonable intervals, in order to ensure that the will of the people shall at all times be the basis of the authority of government.

8. *Genuine Character of Elections and Other Public Consultations.* (a) Every voter shall be free to vote for the candidate or list of candidates he prefers in any election to public office, and shall not be compelled to vote for any specified candidate or list of candidates.

(b) Every voter shall be free to vote for or against any proposal submitted to a plebiscite, referendum, or other public consultation.

(c) The conduct of elections and other public consultations, including the preparation and periodic revision of the electoral roll, shall be supervised by authorities whose independence and impartiality are ensured and whose decisions are subject to appeal to the judicial authorities or other independent and impartial bodies.

(d) Full freedom shall be ensured for the peaceful expression of political opposition, and also for the organization and free functioning of political parties and the right to present candidates for election.

9. *Access to Elective Public Office.* (a) Every national shall be eligible on equal terms for election to any elective public office in his country or in any political or administrative unit thereof in which he resides.

(b) The extent to which this principle shall be applied to those whose election might result in a conflict between their duties or personal interests and the interests of the community as a whole, shall be determined by law.

10. *Access to Non-elective Public Office.* (a) Every national shall be eligible on equal terms to hold any non-elective public office in his country or in any political or administrative unit thereof in which he resides.

(b) The extent to which this principle shall be applied to those whose appointment or assignment to a non-elective public office might result in a conflict between their duties or personal interests and the interests of the community as a whole, shall be determined by law.

(c) All appointments to the career civil service of a country shall be made on an objective and impartial basis.

11. *Measures Which Shall not Be Considered Discriminatory.* The following measures prescribed by law or regulation shall not be considered discriminatory:

(a) Reasonable requirements for the exercise of the right to vote or the right of access to elective public office;

(b) Reasonable qualifications for appointment to public office which stem from the nature of the duties of the office;

(c) Measures establishing a reasonable period which must elapse before naturalized persons may exercise their political rights, provided that they are combined with a liberal naturalization policy.

(d) Special measures taken to ensure:

(i) The adequate representation of an element of the population of a country whose members are in fact prevented by political, economic, religious, social, historical, or cultural conditions from enjoying equality with the rest of the population in the matter of political rights;

(ii) The balanced representation of the different elements of the population of a country; provided that such measures are continued only so long as there is need for them, and only to the extent that they are necessary.

12. *Limitations.* The rights and freedoms proclaimed above shall in no case be exercised contrary to the purposes and principles of the United Nations. They shall be subject only to such limitations as are determined by law solely for the purpose of securing due recognition and respect for the rights and freedoms of others and of meeting the just requirements of public order (*ordre public*), morality and the general welfare in a democratic society. Any limitation which may be imposed shall be consistent with the purposes and principles of the United Nations.

13. *Constitutional Guarantee.* The rights and freedoms proclaimed above shall in no case be subject to repeal or alteration by ordinary legislative procedure.

14. *Recourse to Independent Tribunals.* Any denial or violation of these rights and freedoms shall entitle the aggrieved person or persons to recourse to independent and impartial tribunals.

15. *Application of Principles.* These principles shall apply to all independent countries and to countries which are under alien domination.

***ELECTORAL PROCESS AS A POLITICAL RIGHT.*** On 15 December 1989, the UN General Assembly adopted a resolution (resolution 44/147) entitled "Respect for the Principles of National Sovereignty and Non-Interference in the Internal Affairs of States in their Electoral Processes" in which it reconfirmed the principle set out in the **UNITED NATIONS CHARTER** (article 2, para. 7) that nothing contained in the Charter shall authorize the United Nations to intervene in matters which are essentially within the domestic jurisdiction of any State or shall require the members to submit such matters to settlement under the Charter. The Assembly recognized that the principles of national sovereignty and non-interference in the internal affairs of any State, as set out in the Charter and in other international instruments, including the Declaration on the Granting of Independence to Colonial Countries and Peoples (1960) and The Declaration of Principles of International Law concerning Friendly Relations and Co-operation among States in Accordance with the Charter of the United Nations (1970), should be respected in the holding of elections. It also recognized that there is no single political system or single model for electoral processes equally suited to all nations and their peoples and that political systems and electoral processes are subject to historical, political, cultural, and religious factors.

The Assembly accordingly reiterated that, by virtue of the principle of equal rights and **SELF-DETERMINATION** of people enshrined in the UN Charter, all peoples have the right freely to determine, without external interference, their political status and to pursue their economic, social, and cultural development, and that every State has the duty to respect that right in accordance with the provisions of the Charter. It affirmed that it is the sole concern of peoples to determine methods and to establish institutions regarding the electoral process, as well as the means for its implementation according to constitutional and national legislation. And it also affirmed that any extraneous activities that attempt, directly or indirectly, to interfere in the free development of national electoral processes, in particular in the developing countries, or that tend to sway the results of such processes, violate the spirit and the letter of the principles established in the Charter and in the Declaration of Principles of International Law.

The Assembly urged all States to respect the principle of non-interference in the internal affairs of States and the sovereign rights of peoples to determine their political, economic, and social system; and strongly appealed to all States to abstain from financing or providing, directly or indirectly, any other form of overt or covert support for political parties or groups and from taking actions to undermine the electoral processes in any country. It condemned any act of armed **AGGRESSION** or threat or use of force against

peoples, elected governments, or their legitimate leaders.

Finally, the Assembly called upon the Commission on Human Rights, at its 1990 session, to give priority to the review of the fundamental factors that negatively affect the observance of the principle of national sovereignty and non-interference in the internal affairs of States in their electoral processes and to report on that review to the Assembly's 1990 session.

***PERIODIC AND GENUINE ELECTIONS.*** The UN General Assembly has twice dealt in almost identical terms (resolutions 43/157 of 8 December 1988 and 44/146 of 15 December 1989) with the question of enhancing the effectiveness of the principle of periodic and genuine elections, reaffirming the relevant provisions of the Universal Declaration of Human Rights (article 21) and of the International Covenant on Civil and Political Rights (article 25). Similar views were expressed by the Commission on Human Rights at its 1989 session (resolution 1989/51).

In resolution 44/146, as in the earlier resolution 43/157, the Assembly recalls that all States enjoy sovereign equality and that each State has the right freely to choose and develop its political, social, economic, and cultural systems; and recognizes that there is no single political system or electoral method equally suited to all nations and their people. It further states (paras. 1–7) that it:

Underscores the significance of the Universal Declaration of Human Rights and the International Covenant on Civil and Political Rights, which establish that the authority to govern shall be based on the will of the people, as expressed in periodic and genuine elections;
Stresses its conviction that periodic and genuine elections are a necessary and indispensable element of sustained efforts to protect the rights and interests of the governed and that, as a matter of practical experience, the right of everyone to take part in the government of his or her country is a crucial factor in the effective enjoyment by all of a wide range of other human rights and fundamental freedoms, embracing political, economic, social and cultural rights;
Declares that determining the will of the people requires an electoral process that provides an equal opportunity for all citizens to become candidates and put forward their political views, individually and in co-operation with others within constitutional and national legislation;
Recognizes that the efforts of the international community to enhance the effectiveness of the principle of periodic and genuine elections should not call into question each State's sovereign right freely to choose and develop its political, social, economic and cultural systems, whether or not they conform to the preference of other States;
Underscores the duty of each member of the international community to respect the decisions taken by other States in freely choosing and developing their electoral institutions;
Reaffirms that *apartheid* must be abolished, that the systematic denial or abridgement of the right to vote on the

grounds of race or color is a gross violation of human rights and an affront to the conscience and dignity of mankind, and that the right to participate in a political system based on common and equal citizenship and universal franchise is essential for the exercise of the principle of periodic and genuine elections;

Rejects the tricameral parliament established under the system of *apartheid* as an abhorrent expression of a fundamentally oppressive and flagrantly inhuman political system.

The Assembly called upon the Commission on Human Rights, at its 1990 session, to continue its consideration of appropriate ways and means of enhancing the effectiveness of the principle of periodic and genuine elections, in the context of full respect for the sovereignty of member States, and to submit a report on that subject for consideration by the Assembly in 1990.

The Commission, in resolution 1989/51 of 7 March 1989, recommended to the Assembly the adoption of the "Framework for Future Efforts" in this field, reproduced below. The ECONOMIC AND SOCIAL COUNCIL forwarded the recommendation to the Assembly on 24 May 1989 (decision 1989/145):

*I. The Will of the People Expressed through Periodic and Genuine Elections as the Basis for the Authority of Government*
A. Universal and equal suffrage.
B. The right to take part in the government of one's country, directly or through freely chosen representatives.
C. The right to equal access to public service in one's country.
D. The need for a secret vote or equivalent free voting procedures, guaranteeing the free expression of the will of the electors.
E. The importance of the right to freedom of peaceful assembly.
F. The importance of the right to freedom of association.
G. The importance of the right to freedom of opinion and expression, including the freedom to seek, receive and impart information and ideas of all kinds, either orally, in writing or in print, in the form of art, or through any other media.
H. The right of citizens of a State to change their governmental system through appropriate constitutional means.
*II. The Activities of Candidates for Public Office*
A. Equal opportunity for all citizens to become candidates.
B. The right of candidates to put forward their political views, individually and in co-operation with others.
*III. Operational Aspects: National Institutions.* National institutions should ensure universal and equal suffrage, as well as impartial administration. There is particular need for independent supervision, appropriate voter registration, reliable balloting procedures and methods for preventing electoral fraud and resolving disputes.
*IV. Co-operative Activities of the International Community.* The host country may wish to invite observers or seek advisory services. Either or both may be available from regional organizations or from the United Nations system.

***POPULAR PARTICIPATION AS A POLITICAL RIGHT.***
The UN General Assembly, Economic and Social Council, and the Commission on Human Rights have repeatedly, since 1979, reaffirmed that popular participation in all sectors of public life, including the participation of workers in management and workers' self-management where they exist, constitutes an important factor in socioeconomic development and in the full realization of all human rights and the dignity of the human person.

In 1975 the Council defined (resolution 1929 [LVIII]) popular participation as connoting the voluntary and democratic involvement of people in:
(a) contributing to the development effort;
(b) sharing equitably in the benefits derived therefrom; and
(c) decisionmaking in respect of setting goals, formulating policies, and planning and implementing economic and social development programs.

The Council noted in particular that, to be effective, popular participation should be consciously promoted by governments, with full recognition of civil, political, economic, and cultural rights and through innovative measures, including structural changes and institutional reform and development, as well as through the encouragement of all forms of education, particularly compulsory primary education, designed to involve actively all segments of society. It recommended that governments:

(a) Adopt popular participation as a basic policy measure in national development strategy;
(b) Encourage the widest possible active participation of all individuals and national non-governmental organizations, such as trade unions and youth and women's organizations, in the development process in setting goals, formulating policies and implementing plans;
(c) Include popular participation as an integral element in local, regional and national development plans and programmes in ways that will ensure maximum citizen participation consistent with the requirements of economic growth, social equity and administrative efficiency;
(d) Adopt measures, including structural changes and institutional arrangements, that will facilitate the contribution of the people to the development effort, their equitable sharing in the benefits derived therefrom and their involvement in making decisions on those matters which directly affect their economic advancement and social progress;
(e) Encourage the study, documentation and dissemination, for the information and benefit of other Member States, of innovative measures adopted by them for promoting popular participation in development and for monitoring and assessing their effectiveness; and
(f) Encourage organized training programmes to impart to government officials and local leaders knowledge and skills in promoting and sustaining effective participation by the people in national, regional and local development plans and programmes.

In 1983, the Council (resolution 1983/21) requested the Secretary-General "to undertake a comprehensive analytical study on the right to popular participation in its various forms as an important factor in the full realization of all human rights." The resulting study (UN Doc. E/CN.4/1985/10 and Add. 1 and 2) was received and noted by the Commission on Human Rights (resolution 1985/44) and later by the General Assembly (resolution 40/99). Both the Commission and the Assembly invited the Secretary-General to obtain the comments of governments, the concerned specialized agencies and organs of the United Nations system, and the relevant non-governmental organizations of the study; and the Assembly requested the Commission to continue to consider the question and to inform the Assembly, at its regular 1989 session, of the results of that consideration.

At that session, the Commission received the Secretary-General's study of the laws and practices regarding popular participation (UN Doc. E/CN.4/1989/12) and his report reproducing the comments received on the earlier study of popular participation in its various forms as an important factor in development and in the full realization of all human rights (UN Doc. E/CN.4/1989/11). While taking note of these reports, the Commission again invited comments on the earlier one (resolution 1989/14) and requested the Secretary-General to submit a further report on the subject for consideration at its 1990 session. The General Assembly, confirming the Commission's decision, invited the Commission to consider the question further at its 1991, 1992, and 1993 sessions, and to inform the Assembly in 1993 of the results.

At its 1990 session, the Commission received the Secretary-General's report on the substantive replies received up to that time (UN Doc. E/CN.4/1990/8).

**SEE ALSO** *Civil and Political Rights; Elections; International Covenant on Civil and Political Rights; Women's Rights: Inter-American Convention on the Granting of Political Rights to Women.*

**BIBLIOGRAPHY.** Blackburn, Robert, ed. *Rights of Citizenship.* London: Mansell, 1993. Scholarly monograph, in English.

Bratton, Michael. "Beyond the State: Civil Society and Associational Life in Africa," *Transnational Associations* 43, no. 3 (May–June 1991): 130–140. Scholarly article, in English; bibliography, p. 130.

Council of Europe. *Democracy and Human Rights: Proceedings of the Colloquy Organised by the Government of Greece and the Council of Europe in Co-Operation with the Centre of International and European Economic Law of Thessaloniki, 24–26 September 1987.* Strasbourg, France, and Arlington, VA, USA: N.P. Engel Publisher, 1990. Conference report, in English and French.

Covington, Sally. *Urban Popular Movements in Mexico: Grassroots Action for Change.* New York: Bildner Centre for Western Hemisphere Studies, Graduate School and University Centre of the City University of New York, 1990. Scholarly research paper, in English.

Fox, Gregory H. "The Right to Political Participation in International Law," *Yale Journal of International Law* 17, no. 2 (Summer 1992): 539–608. Scholarly article, in English.

Hart, Roger A. *Children's Participation: From Tokenism to Citizenship.* Florence, Italy: UNICEF International Child Development Centre, 1992. IGO monograph, in English.

Instituto Interamericano de Derechos Humanos, Centro de Asesoría y Promoción Electoral (Inter-American Institute of Human Rights, Advisory and Electoral Promotion Centre). *Transición Democrática en América Latina: Reflexiones Sobre el Debate Actual* (Democratic Transition in Latin America: Some Reflections on the Current Debate). San José, Costa Rica: 1990. Scholarly collective works, in Spanish.

Landell-Mills, Pierre. "Governance, Cultural Change and Empowerment," *Journal of Modern African Studies* 30, no. 4 (Dec. 1992): 543–567. Scholarly article, in English.

Liniger-Goumaz, Max. *La Démocrature: dictature camouflée, démocratie truquée* (Democratorship: Camoflaged Dictatorship, Truncated Democracy). Paris: Harmattan, 1992. Scholarly monograph, in French.

Mahoney, Kathleen E., and Paul Mahoney, eds. *Human Rights in the Twenty-First Century: A Global Challenge.* Dordrecht, the Netherlands: Martinus Nijhoff, 1993. Scholarly monograph, in English.

Molutsi, Patrick P., and John D. Holm. "Developing Democracy When Civil Society is Weak: The Case of Botswana," *African Affairs* 89, no. 356 (July 1990): 323–340. Scholarly article, in English.

Peuchot, Éric. "Droit de vote et condition de nationalité" (Right to Vote and the Nationality Requirement), *Revue de droit public et de science politique en France et à l'étranger* 107, no. 2 (1991): 481–524. Scholarly article, in French.

Rau, Zbigniew, ed. *The Reemergence of Civil Society in Eastern Europe and the Soviet Union.* Boulder, CO, USA: Westview Press, 1991. Scholarly monograph, in English.

Rosas, Allan. *The Strength of Diversity: Human Rights and Pluralist Democracy.* Dordrecht, the Netherlands: Martinus Nijhoff, 1992. Scholarly monograph, in English.

Rosas, Allan, Jan Helgesen, and Donna Gomien, eds. *Human Rights in a Changing East-West Perspective.* London: Pinter Publishers, 1991. Scholarly collective works, in English.

Rosati, Alexander D. "One Person, One Vote: Is It Time for a New Constitutional Principle?" *New York Law School Journal of Human Rights* 8, part 2 (Spring 1991): 523–555. Scholarly article, in English.

Sachs, Wolfgang, ed. *The Development Dictionary: A Guide to Knowledge as Power.* London and Atlantic Highlands, NJ, USA: Zed Books, 1992. Monograph, in English.

Sandbrook, Richard, and Mohamed Halfani, eds. *Empowering People: Building Community, Civil Associations, and Legality in Africa.* Toronto, Canada: Centre for Urban and Community Studies, University of Toronto, 1993. Conference report, in English.

Schmitz, Gerald J., and David Gillies, eds. *The Challenge of Democratic Development: Sustaining Democratization in Developing Countries.* Ottawa, Canada: North-South Institute, 1992. Scholarly monograph, in English and French.

Shelton, Dinah. "Representative Democracy and Human Rights in the Western Hemisphere," *Human Rights Law Journal* 12, no. 10 (Oct. 1991): 353–359. Scholarly article, in English.

Thome, Joseph R. "People Versus the Authoritarians: Grass Root Organizations and Chile's Transition to Democracy," *Más Allá del Derecho* 1, no. 2 (July 1991): 85–109. Scholarly article, in English; bibliography, pp. 107–109.

United Nations Commission on Human Rights. *Popular Participation in Its Various Forms as an Important Factor in Development and in the Full Realization of All Human Rights: Report of the Secretary General.* Geneva, Switzerland: 1991. IGO document, in English and French.

**PORTUGAL.** The Portuguese Republic is a country occupying the western part of the Iberian Peninsula, on the Atlantic Ocean; it includes also the Atlantic archipelagos of the Azores and Madeira. It has a border with Spain. Portugal achieved independence from Spain during the 12th century and became a member of the United Nations in 1955. Its population is estimated to be 10,660,000. Ethnic groups include persons of Mediterranean origin and a small African minority. The language in common use is Portuguese. Christianity (Roman Catholic, 97%; Protestant denominations, 3%) is the predominant religion. Literacy is estimated at 80%.

The government (1994) took the form of a republic. Under the 1982 constitution, the president is directly elected for a term of five years; he may serve for a maximum of two consecutive terms. As head of State, he appoints the premier, representing the party or coalition given the majority in a popular election. On advice of the prime minister, he also appoints other members of the Council of Ministers and the secretaries and under-secretaries of State, who are outside the Council. Legislation is handled by the 230-member Assembly of the Republic, elected for four-year terms by universal adult suffrage under a system of proportional representation. Political parties include the Social Democratic Party, the Democratic Renewal Party, the United People Alliance, and the Centre Social Democrats. As autonomous regions, the Azores and Madeira have their own governments and legislatures.

Portuguese explorers such as Vasco da Gama, Bartholomeu Dias, and Pedro Alvares Cabral helped to found the widespread Portuguese empire which included territories in Africa, South America, and the Far East. Today Portugal's only overseas territory is Macao, consisting of a peninsula and two small islands on the South China coast, not far from Hong Kong.

In 1926, a prominent university professor and economist, Dr. Antonio Salazar, was brought into the Government of Portugal as an expert to solve serious fiscal problems. In 1928, he was appointed finance minister; and, by 1932, he had become prime minister. He ruled Portugal as an authoritarian "corporate" State for 36 years, keeping it neutral during World War II but leasing air and naval bases to the Allies after 1943. His successor, Marcello Caetano, continued the tradition after Salazar died in 1970.

On 25 April 1974, leftist army officers launched a revolution and established the Junta of National Salvation, which called for negotiation with the independence movements in Angola, Portuguese Guinea, and Mozambique; the end of the "corporate" police state; and the introduction of social and economic reforms which would benefit the lower classes.

Once in power, the junta granted independence to Portuguese Guinea, which became the Republic of Guinea-Bissau on 10 September 1974. Following an attempted rightist coup on 11 March 1975, the junta was dissolved, and the Portuguese Communist Party assumed control of the government. The Supreme Revolutionary Council was formed and remained in control until 25 April 1976, when a new constitution was promulgated providing for a government committed to socialist principles. Meanwhile, Mozambique achieved independence on 25 June 1975 and Angola on 11 November 1975.

General Antonio Ramhalo Eanes was elected to a four-year term as president in 1976 with the support of three major parties and chose Mario Alberto Soares to serve as prime minister. Soares' minority socialist government fell in December 1977, but he was elected to the presidency in 1986.

A new constitution, replacing the one promulgated in 1976, was adopted on 12 August 1982. Under it, Portugal is a sovereign, unitary republic and all citizens possess fundamental rights and duties before the law. In a report presented to the UN **COMMITTEE ON THE ELIMINATION OF RACIAL DISCRIMINATION** on 14 November 1986, the government presented the following information relating to that constitution (UN Doc. CERD/C/126/Add. 3, paras. 11–16):

The Portuguese Constitution repeatedly reflects the concern to ensure that human rights are protected and it consistently upholds the principle of full equality before the law and of non-discrimination.

Not unexpectedly, therefore, the fundamental principles of the Constitution include the following:

"The Portuguese Republic is a democratic State subject to the rule of law, founded on the sovereignty of the people, respect for and the safeguard of fundamental rights and freedoms . . ." (art. 2);

"In its international relations Portugal shall abide by the principles . . . of respect for human rights . . ." (art. 7, para. 1);

"The fundamental tasks of the State shall be . . .

(b) To guarantee fundamental rights and freedoms and respect for the principles of a democratic State subject to the rule of law . . ." (art. 9).

13. Also, the section on fundamental rights and duties stipulates that:

"All citizens shall enjoy the rights and shall be subject to the duties laid down in the Constitution . . ." (art. 12, para. 1).

Article 13, for its part, provides:

"1. All citizens shall have the same dignity at the social level and shall be equal before the law.

"2. No one may be privileged, favoured, disadvantaged, deprived of any right or exempt of any duty by virtue of ancestry, sex, race, language, place of origin, religion, political or ideological convictions, education, financial situation or social status."

This principle of equality likewise applies to foreigners and stateless persons, since article 15 of the Constitution stipulates:

"1. Aliens and stateless persons temporarily or permanently resident in Portugal shall enjoy the same rights and be subject to the same duties as Portuguese citizens.

"2. The preceding paragraph shall not apply to political rights, the performance of public duties that are not primarily technical, and rights and duties confined to Portuguese citizens under the Constitution and by law."

The terms of the constitution and the law are interpreted and applied in accordance with the Universal Declaration of Human Rights (art. 16) and therefore prohibit any provisions to the contrary, particularly as regards racial discrimination. The validity of the laws and acts of the State is dependent on whether they are in conformity with the Constitution (art. 3, para. 3) and any person who violates these fundamental principles will be subject to the legal régime prescribed for the protection of fundamental rights, which provides for appeal to the courts, responsibility of offenders, etc. . . .

President Soares was re-elected in January 1991 with 70% of the vote, and in October 1991 the Social Democratic Party (PSD) won an absolute majority, obtaining 136 seats in elections to the 230-seat Assembly of the Republic (reduced from 250 seats). That Assembly passed controversial legislation restricting the rights of refugees to asylum in Portugal and lowering the minimum age of employment to 14 years of age.

**BIBLIOGRAPHY.** Amnesty International. *Portugal: Torture and Ill-Treatment: Summary of Amnesty International's Concerns.* London: October 1993. NGO report, in English.

Williams, Suzanne. *Child Workers in Portugal: A Report on Child Labour in Portugal for Anti-Slavery International.* London: Anti-Slavery International, 1992. NGO report, in English.

**POVERTY.** The UN **Economic and Social Council,** at its first regular 1988 session, expressed its concern that a significant percentage of the world's population lives in conditions of extreme poverty and is forced to live increasingly at the margins of society and noted that insufficient attention had been paid to this phenomenon, which tends to elude international and intergovernmental action and current statistical methods.

Taking into account the provision of the Declaration on Social Progress and Development (see **DEVELOPMENT**) to the effect that social progress and development are the common concerns of the international community, which shall supplement, by concerted international action, national efforts to raise the living standards of peoples, the Council urged the UN Commission for Social Development to suggest, on the basis of an assessment of its studies, strategies that will help put an end to the marginalization of people living in extreme poverty, irrespective of the economic and social system to which they belong, and to submit its views to the Council in 1991.

The General Assembly, on 20 December 1988, joined the Council (resolution 43/195) in expressing its concern about the situation and emphasized the need for new and imaginative approaches to eradicating poverty in developing countries as an integral part of the promotion of growth and development. It urged the international community to achieve, as a priority, a supportive international economic environment for growth and development that will reinforce the efforts of developing countries to revitalize their development process and eradicate poverty; and requested the UN regional Commissions to study options, including new approaches oriented toward the revitalization of developing countries, in order to enable them to address effectively the eradication of poverty.

In the resolution, the **General Assembly** requested the Secretary-General to prepare a report analyzing the impact of the economic crisis in developing countries on the intensity of poverty and recommending effective international policy measures for dealing with this problem.

***REPORT ON THE ERADICATION OF POVERTY.*** The Secretary-General's report on International Co-operation for the Eradication of Poverty (UN Doc. A/44/467) was presented to the General Assembly at its 1989 session. Its analysis of the extent and intensity of poverty in the developing countries was as follows (paras. 2–4):

Constituting close to half of the population of the developing countries as a whole (not including China), the poor during past decades did not share equally in economic progress. During the 1980s, they absorbed much of the brunt of the economic and other crises that beset most developing countries.

Although a heterogeneous group in terms of their economic interests, the poor have one thing in common: their extremely low incomes. Taking as a comparative cut-off line a level of annual income based on detailed studies of extreme poverty in Kenya, which amounts to $US 300 per capita in constant 1980 dollars, two broad trends are revealed. . . . On the one hand, estimates of the share of the total population living in poverty during the 1970s and 1980s show that a significant improvement has occurred. On the other hand, the number of people living in poverty increased substantially during this period because the population itself grew rapidly. The same overall trends are discernible . . . with respect to absolute poverty levels, that is to say, the income levels established by regions below which a minimum nutritionally adequate diet plus essential non-food requirements is not deemed affordable. Poverty being a normative concept, the absolute levels below which the conditions of life are viewed as intolerable vary by region in broad accordance with the general level of development of each region. For instance, the absolute poverty threshold in Latin America is at a higher cut-off income level than in Africa.

A closer look at the data . . . shows a worsening incidence of poverty, both numerically and as a share of the total population, in both Africa and Latin America during the 1980s. In Latin America, moreover, the magnitude of poverty shifted from the rural to the urban areas, reflecting the effects of continued high rates of rural emigration and the impact of the fall in urban incomes in most countries of the region. In Africa, the relatively rapid growth of rural poverty has been due primarily to high population growth rates, continuing low levels of agricultural productivity, and the destitution created in the early 1980s by the worst drought in 15 years. As for the Asian region, what most stands out is that, while the share of the population in poverty improved steadily during the past two decades, the extent and depth of poverty remained staggering. In general, moreover, it can be seen that the share of the population in the 1980s earning less than $US 300 per annum has been considerably higher in Asia and Africa than in Latin America.

As regards the capacity of the poor to cope with the situation in which they found themselves in the 1980s, the Secretary-General reported that (paras. 25–30):

Income and consumption findings are necessary for gauging and analysing the incidence and changes in poverty, but are not sufficient in explaining the full scope of the changes in circumstances experienced by the extremely poor during the present decade. Bearing in mind the risks of generalizing when faced with a wide diversity of conditions and needs, it appears that in various ways the most salient dimension of poverty during the present decade has been the increased vulnerability of the poor.

The coping mechanisms of the poor were put to a severe test during much of the decade. Those mechanisms consisted as ever of continued attempts at diversifying risks and opportunities, with an eye to the future as well as the present; in particular, this has usually meant making use of the ability and willingness of different household members to do different things in different places. Household strategies have typically consisted of keeping some family members on the farm or in nearby off-farm activities, having others migrate to cities or even abroad for work and educating the brightest children as an investment for the future. Such strategies have resulted in a high degree of inter-sectoral labour mobility, with the dry season usually the main time of the year available for such diversification.

As already noted, such anti-destitution strategies were severely tested in the 1980s. In much of Africa, in particular, rural-based livelihoods were reduced or wiped out by drought, environmental degradation and civil conflicts. Many of the rural poor lost, mortgaged or sold in distress most or all of their assets in order to survive until famine relief arrived. Others ended up in refugee camps or withdrew into subsistence farming.

The viability of the migration option also declined. With opportunities for work in cities and abroad substantially reduced, rural school leavers were deployed on family farms and many displaced urban workers returned to live with their families in the rural areas. In some cases, returned migrants who used to work abroad, had to be accommodated, as when Ghana's nationals returned from Nigeria.

What has most stood out has been the tenacity and long view adopted by the poor in attempting to preserve their assets and self-respect in the face of extreme adversity. They, for example, typically went hungry rather than lose the basis of their livelihood. Sacrificing the future to salvage the present was resorted to only as a last resort. Despite their attempts to avoid destitution, however, millions of poor people were subjected to the horrors of famine and malnutrition, war-related violence, the loss or forced sale of all productive assets and holdings and refugee uprooting.

Traditional values of wider family obligation and support systems have played a crucial role, especially in African societies, in enabling the poor and vulnerable to survive the wrenching adjustments of the present decade. Mutual support arrangements and networks, however, came under stress as family and kinship groups became less able to help one another, and especially to help their poorest members. Modernizing trends also weakened traditional support and mutual obligation systems. The privatization of natural resources, such as grazing lands and water resources, and the increasing commercialization of economic activities further marginalized weaker social groups and members who more than ever have had to buy things which they formerly were accustomed to receiving in the form of traditional claims. Such trends, while historically inevitable, have had the effect of further augmenting the vulnerability of the poorest of the poor.

On the basis of this study, the Secretary-General drew the following conclusions (paras. 80–82):

The economic crisis of the 1980s has had a generally adverse impact on poverty in Africa and brought to a halt the amelioration in the conditions of the poor achieved in Latin America during previous years. As a result, poverty has once again become a major issue of concern for many developing countries and the international community.

International co-operation is essential if progress is to be made towards achieving the goal of eradicating poverty on an urgent, lasting and comprehensive basis. Co-operation on international trade and debt matters would help restore the conditions necessary for renewed economic growth in countries undergoing adjustment. Such growth would expand investment and employment opportunities, support increased social expenditures, and thus raise the incomes and living standards of a majority of the poor. Equally, international co-operation in the form of increased official development assistance could play an important role as seed capital in launching poverty-oriented programmes before the effects of economic growth are felt, and as a contribution to special programmes targeted on those pockets of hard-core poverty that lie beyond the spread effects of growth. For their part, it would help if developing country Governments would restructure the composition of their social expenditure to improve the scope and depth of poverty programmes, as well as reform or remove those laws and regulations that make it hard for the poor to start or expand a small shop or enterprise, put a roof over their heads, or help themselves through organized participation.

A variety of approaches—ranging from short-run welfare measures to long-term human capital formation, and from small-scale, targeted activities to macroeconomic policies—may contribute to poverty eradication in important ways. As examined in the present report, the formulation and implementation of policies that have the aim of increasing the earnings capacity of the poor and making them less vulnerable to future crises remain a major and urgent challenge to policy makers and multilateral agencies.

After examining the report at its 1989 session, the General Assembly on 22 December 1989 (resolution 44/212) expressed its deep concern that more than one billion people throughout the world, mostly in developing countries, are still living in abject poverty and misery, with hunger, malnutrition, disease, illiteracy, and premature death as an integral part of their lives, and called upon the international community to strengthen its work, on a priority basis, toward action-oriented programs for the eradication of poverty in support of developing countries' own efforts.

The Assembly requested the Secretary-General to coordinate such activities and to submit to its 1990 session a progress report and to its 1991 session a comprehensive report containing, *inter alia*: (a) an analysis of the diversified impact of adverse international economic conditions on the intensification of poverty in developing countries, (b) a summary of the experience of developing countries in their efforts to combat poverty, (c) specific recommendations for effective policy measures for urgently and permanently eradicating poverty, and (d) an account of the implementation of resolution 44/212.

The **Commission on Human Rights** also examined the question, "Human Rights and Extreme Poverty," at its 1990 session and expressed (resolution 1990/15) concern that, despite the progress achieved by the international community in ensuring the effective enjoyment of the rights of the person, poverty continues to spread throughout the world, seriously affecting the most vulnerable and disadvantaged individuals, families, and groups in all countries, thus hindering them in the exercise of their human rights and fundamental freedoms.

The Commission drew the attention of all United Nations bodies to the contradiction between the existence of situations of extreme poverty and exclusion from society, and the ability to enjoy human rights fully. It urged the **Committee on Economic, Social and Cultural Rights** to give the necessary attention, in its work, to the question of extreme poverty and exclusion from society, and called upon the **Sub-Commission on Prevention of Discrimination and Protection of Minorities** to examine that question in greater depth and to carry out a specific study of the question.

*POVERTY AND HUMAN RIGHTS.* In resolution 47/134 of 18 December 1992, the General Assembly re-

affirmed that extreme poverty and exclusion from society constitute a violation of human dignity and stressed the need for a complete and in-depth study of extreme poverty, based on the experience and the thoughts of the poorest.

Two years later the Assembly, taking note of the preliminary report on the subject prepared by the Special Rapporteur (E/CN.4/Sub.2/1993/16), invited him to give special attention to the following aspects in preparing his reports: (a) the effects of extreme poverty on the enjoyment and exercise of all human rights and fundamental freedoms of those affected by it; (b) efforts by the poorest themselves to exercise their rights and participate fully in the development of the society in which they live; (c) conditions in which the poorest can convey their experiences and ideas and become partners in the enjoyment of human rights; and (d) means of promoting a better understanding of the experiences and ideas of the poorest and those committed to working alongside them (resolution 1994/12).

*SEE ALSO Standard of Living.*

**BIBLIOGRAPHY.** Bok, Marcia. *Civil Rights and the Social Programs of the 1960s: The Social Justice Functions of Social Policy.* Westport, CT, USA, and London: Praeger, 1992. Scholarly monograph, in English; bibliography, pp. 161–172.

Fanelli, Vincent. *The Human Face of Poverty: A Chronicle of Urban America.* New York: Bootstrap Press for NEW/Fourth World Movement, 1990. Monograph, in English.

Pettiti, Louis. "Pauvreté et Convention Européenne des Droits de l'Homme" (Poverty and the European Convention on Human Rights), *Droit Social* 1 (Jan. 1991): 84–88. Case comment, in French.

Sinha, Arun. *Against the Few: Struggles of India's Rural Poor.* London: Zed Books, 1991. Monograph, in English.

United Nations Commission on Human Rights. *Report on the Seminar on Extreme Poverty and the Denial of Human Rights.* Geneva, Switzerland: 1994. IGO document, in English.

United Nations Sub-Commission on Prevention of Discrimination and Protection of Minorities. *The Realization of Economic, Social and Cultural Rights. Final Report Submitted by Mr. Danilo Türk, Special Rapporteur.* Geneva, Switzerland: 1992. IGO document, in English and French.

**PRISONERS.** On 14 December 1990, the UN **General Assembly** adopted, without a vote, a series of basic principles for the treatment of prisoners (resolution 45/111), in which it articulated the principles underlying the Standard Minimum Rules for the Treatment of Prisoners, which had been adopted by the First UN Congress on Prevention of Crime and the Treatment of Offenders in 1955. The text of the statement is as follows:

1. All prisoners shall be treated with the respect due to their inherent dignity and value as human beings.
2. There shall be no discrimination on the grounds of

race, color, sex, language, religion, political or other opinion, national or social origin, property, birth or other status.

3. It is, however, desirable to respect the religious beliefs and cultural precepts of the group to which prisoners belong, whenever local conditions so require.

4. The responsibility of prisons for the custody of prisoners and for the protection of society against crime shall be discharged in keeping with a State's other social objectives and its fundamental responsibilities for promoting the well-being and development of all members of society.

5. Except for those limitations that are demonstrably necessitated by the fact of incarceration, all prisoners shall retain the human rights and fundamental freedoms set out in the Universal Declaration of Human Rights, and where the State concerned is a party, the International Covenant on Economic, Social and Cultural Rights; the International Covenant on Civil and Political Rights and its optional protocol; and such other rights as are set out in other United Nations covenants.

6. All prisoners shall have the right to take part in cultural activities and education aimed at the full development of the human personality.

7. Efforts addressed to the abolition of solitary confinement as a punishment, or to the restriction of its use, should be undertaken and encouraged.

8. Conditions shall be created enabling prisoners to undertake meaningful remunerated employment which shall facilitate their reintegration into the country's labor market and permit them to contribute to their families' financial support and to their own.

9. Prisoners shall have access to the health services available in the country without discrimination on the grounds of their legal situation.

10. With the participation and help of the community and social institutions, and with due regard to the interests of victims, favorable conditions shall be created for the reintegration of the ex-prisoner into society under the best possible conditions.

11. The above principles shall be applied impartially.

**TRANSFER AND TREATMENT OF FOREIGN PRISONERS.** The Seventh United Nations Congress on the Prevention of Crime and the Treatment of Offenders, held in Milan from 26 August to 6 September 1985, recognized the difficulties confronting foreigners detained in prison establishments abroad owing to such factors as differences in language, culture, customs, and religion and expressed the view that the social resettlement of offenders could best be achieved by giving foreign prisoners the opportunity to serve their sentence within their country of nationality or residence.

The Congress accordingly prepared and adopted (1) the Model Agreement on the Transfer of Foreign Prisoners, and (2) a series of recommendations on the treatment of foreign prisoners (UN publication, Sales no. E.86.IV.2, chap. D [1] and [2]), both of which are reproduced below.

The Congress invited member States to take the Model Agreement and the recommendations into account in dealing with questions relating to foreign

prisoners. The General Assembly endorsed its decisions on 29 November 1985 (resolution 40/32).

Desirous of further developing mutual co-operation in the field of criminal justice,

Believing that such co-operation should further the ends of justice and the social resettlement of sentenced persons,

Considering that those objectives require that foreigners who are deprived of their liberty as the result of a criminal offence should be given the opportunity to serve their sentences within their own society,

Convinced that this aim can best be achieved by transferring foreign prisoners to their own countries,

Bearing in mind that the full respect for human rights, as laid down in universally recognized principles, should be ensured,

Have agreed on the following:

### I. General Principles

1. The social resettlement of offenders should be promoted by facilitating the return of persons convicted of crime abroad to their country of nationality or of residence to serve their sentence at the earliest possible stage. In accordance with the above, States should afford each other the widest measure of co-operation.

2. A transfer of prisoners should be effected on the basis of mutual respect for national sovereignty and jurisdiction.

3. A transfer of prisoners should be effected in cases where the offence giving rise to conviction is punishable by deprivation of liberty by the judicial authorities of both the sending (sentencing) State and the State to which the transfer is to be effected (administering State) according to their national laws.

4. A transfer may be requested by either the sentencing or the administering State. The prisoner, as well as close relatives, may express to either State their interest in the transfer. To that end, the contracting State shall inform the prisoner of their competent authorities.

5. A transfer shall be dependent on the agreement of both the sentencing and the administering State, and should also be based on the consent of the prisoner.

6. The prisoner shall be fully informed of the possibility and of the legal consequences of a transfer, in particular whether or not he might be prosecuted because of other offences committed before his transfer.

7. The administering State should be given the opportunity to verify the free consent of the prisoner.

8. Any regulation concerning the transfer of prisoners shall be applicable to sentences of imprisonment as well as to sentences imposing measures involving deprivation of liberty because of the commission of a criminal act.

9. In cases of the person's incapability of freely determining his will, his legal representative shall be competent to consent to the transfer.

### II. Other Requirements

10. A transfer shall be made only on the basis of a final and definitive sentence having executive force.

11. At the time of the request for a transfer, the prisoner shall, as a general rule, still have to serve at least six months of the sentence; a transfer should, however, be granted also in cases of indeterminate sentences.

12. The decision whether to transfer a prisoner shall be taken without any delay.

13. The person transferred for the enforcement of a sentence passed in the sentencing State may not be tried again in the administering State for the same act upon which the sentence to be executed is based.

### III. Procedural Regulations

14. The competent authorities of the administering State shall: (a) continue the enforcement of the sentence immediately or through a court or administrative order; or (b) convert the sentence, thereby substituting for the sanction imposed in the sentencing State a sanction prescribed by the law of the administering State for a corresponding offence.

15. In the case of continued enforcement, the administering State shall be bound by the legal nature and duration of the sentence as determined by the sentencing State. If, however, this sentence is by its nature or duration incompatible with the law of the administering State, this State may adapt the sanction to the punishment or measure prescribed by its own law for a corresponding offence.

16. In the case of conversion of sentence, the administering State shall be entitled to adapt the sanction as to its nature or duration according to its national law, taking into due consideration the sentence passed in the sentencing State. A sanction involving deprivation of liberty shall, however, not be converted to a pecuniary sanction.

17. The administering State shall be bound by the findings as to the facts in so far as they appear from the judgement imposed in the sentencing State. Thus the sentencing State has the sole competence for a review of the sentence.

18. The period of deprivation of liberty already served by the sentenced person in either State shall be fully deducted from the final sentence.

19. A transfer shall in no case lead to an aggravation of the situation of the prisoner.

20. Any costs incurred because of a transfer and related to transportation should be borne by the administering State, unless otherwise decided by both the sentencing and administering States.

### IV. Enforcement and Pardon

21. The enforcement of the sentence shall be governed by the law of the administering State.

22. Both the sentencing and the administering State shall be competent to grant pardon and amnesty.

### V. Final Clauses

23. This agreement shall be applicable to the enforcement of sentences imposed either before or after its entry into force.

24. This agreement is subject to ratification. The instruments of ratification shall be deposited as soon as possible.

25. This agreement shall enter into force on the thirtieth day after the day on which the instruments of ratification are exchanged.

26. Either Contracting Party may denounce this agreement in writing. Denunciation shall take effect six months following the date on which the notification is received.

### Recommendations on the Treatment of Foreign Prisoners

1. The allocation of a foreign prisoner to a prison establishment should not be effected on the grounds of his nationality alone.

2. Foreign prisoners should have the same access as national prisoners to education, work and vocational training.

3. Foreign prisoners should in principle be eligible for measures alternative to imprisonment, as well as for prison leave and other authorized exits from prison according to the same principles as nationals.

4. Foreign prisoners should be informed promptly after reception into a prison, in a language which they understand and generally in writing, of the main features of the prison régime, including relevant rules and regulations.

5. The religious precepts and customs of foreign prisoners should be respected.

6. Foreign prisoners should be informed without delay of their right to request contacts with their consular authorities, as well as of any other relevant information regarding their status. If a foreign prisoner wishes to receive assistance from a diplomatic or consular authority, the latter should be contacted promptly.

7. Foreign prisoners should be given proper assistance, in a language they can understand, when dealing with medical or programme staff and in such matters as complaints, special accommodation, special diets and religious representation and counselling.

8. Contacts of foreign prisoners with families and community agencies should be facilitated, by providing all necessary opportunities for visits and correspondence, with the consent of the prisoner. Humanitarian international organizations, such as the International Committee of the Red Cross, should be given the opportunity to assist foreign prisoners.

9. The conclusion of bilateral and multilateral agreements on supervision of and assistance to offenders given suspended sentences or granted parole could further contribute to the solution of the problems faced by foreign offenders.

***SEE ALSO*** *Arbitrary Arrest, Detention or Exile; Capital Punishment; Disappearances; Extradition.*

***BIBLIOGRAPHY.*** Adorno, Sergio. "Sistema penitenciario no Brasil" (Brazilian Penitentiary System), *Revista Direitos Humanos GAJOP* 6, no. 9 (Jan. 1991): 23–32. NGO article, in Portuguese.

Africa Watch and The Prison Project. *Prison Conditions in South Africa.* New York: Human Rights Watch, 1994. NGO report, in English.

African Centre for Democracy and Human Rights Studies and Penal Reform International. *Prison Conditions in Africa: Report of a Seminar, 2 to 4 April 1993, Banjul, Gambia.* Banjul, Gambia: 1994. NGO conference report, in English.

American Friends Service Committee, Criminal Justice Program. *The Lessons of Marion: The Failure of a Maximum Security Prison—A History and Analysis, with Voices of Prisoners.* Philadelphia, PA, USA: 1985. NGO report, in English.

Americas Watch. *Prison Conditions in Mexico.* New York: Human Rights Watch, 1991. NGO report, in English.

Amnesty International. *Amnesty International Annual Report, 1974/1975–Present. London. NGO annual report, in English.

Asia Watch. *Prison Conditions in India.* New York: Human Rights Watch, 1991. NGO report, in English.

———. *Prison Conditions in Indonesia.* New York: Human Rights Watch, 1990. NGO report, in English.

B'Tselem—Israeli Information Center for Human Rights in the Occupied Territories. *Violence Against Minors in Police Detention.* Jerusalem, Israel: B'Tselem, 1990. NGO report, in English.

Burneo Labrin, Jose. *Derechos de la Persona ante el Juez, la Policia y en la Carcel* (Rights of the Individual before the Judge, the Police, and while in Prison). Lima, Peru: Comision Episcopal de Accion Social, 1985. Research paper, in Spanish.

Committee against Repression and for Democratic Rights in Iraq. *The Great Massacre: First Hand Account of the Great Massacre of Abu-Ghraib Prisoners by an Official of the Iraqi Abu-Ghraib Prison.* London: 1985. NGO report, in English.

Defence for Children International. *Children in Prison in Turkey.* Geneva, Switzerland: 1988. NGO report, in English.

Díaz Serra, Juan Carlos. "Los Derechos Humanos en el Sistema Penitenciario" (Human Rights in the Penitentiary System), *Revista de IELSUR* 7 (Dec. 1990): 11–20. Scholarly article, in Spanish.

Gonsalves, C., M. Desai, and J. Cox. *Leading Cases on Prisoners' Rights.* Bombay, India: Legal Resource Centre, Youth for Unity and Voluntary Action, 1989. NGO study, in English.

Helsinki Watch. *Prison Conditions in Poland: An Update.* New York: Human Rights Watch, 1991. NGO factfinding report, in English.

Human Rights Watch Prison Project. *The Human Rights Watch Global Report on Prisons.* New York: Human Rights Watch, 1993. NGO report, in English; bibliography, pp. 299–303.

Jaradat, Mohammad, Tikva Honig-Parnassa, and Ingrid Gassner-Jaradat, eds. *Hebron Prison—A View from Inside.* Jerusalem: Alternative Information Center, 1992. NGO report, in English.

Kaufman, Edy. "Prisoners of Conscience: The Shaping of a New Human Rights Concept," *Human Rights Quarterly* 13, no. 3 (Aug. 1991): 339–367. Scholarly article, in English.

Middle East Watch. *Prison Conditions in Israel and the Occupied Territories.* New York: Human Rights Watch, 1991. NGO factfinding report, in English.

Minnesota Lawyers International Human Rights Committee and Physicians for Human Rights. *Hidden from View: Human Rights Conditions in the Krome Detention Center.* Minneapolis, MN, and Somerville, MA, USA: 1991. NGO factfinding report, in English.

Neveloff Dubler, Nancy, Catherine M. Bergmann, and Marvin E. Frankel. "Management of HIV Infection in New York State Prisons," *Columbia Human Rights Law Review* 21, no. 2 (Spring 1990): 363–400. Report, in English.

Observatoire International des Prisons (International Prison Watch). *Rapport 1993: les conditions de détention des prisonniers ordinaires* (Report 1993: Prison Conditions). Lyon, France: 1993. NGO report, in French.

Parts, Mark. "The Eighth Amendment and the Requirement of Active Measures to Prevent the Spread of AIDS in Prisons," *Columbia Human Rights Law Review* 22, no. 2 (Spring 1991): 217–249. Scholarly article, in English.

Rodley, Nigel S. *The Treatment of Prisoners under International Law.* Oxford, UK: Oxford University Press, 1987. Scholarly monograph, in English.

Stern, Vivien. *Deprived of their Liberty.* Belleville, Barbados: Caribbean Rights, 1990. NGO research report, in English.

Tomasevski, Katarina. *Prison Health: International Standards and National Practices in Europe.* Helsinki, Finland: Helsinki Institute for Crime Prevention and Control, 1992. Report, in English.

United Nations Sub-Commission on Prevention of Discrimination and Protection of Minorities. *Application of International Standards concerning the Human Rights of Detained Juveniles: Report Prepared by the Special Rapporteur, Mrs. Mary Concepción Bautista, Pursuant to Sub-Commission Resolution 1990/21.* Geneva, Switzerland: 1991. IGO document, in English and French.

## PRISONERS: BODY OF PRINCIPLES FOR THE PROTECTION OF ALL PERSONS UNDER ANY FORM OF DETENTION OR IMPRISONMENT (1988).

The Body of Principles was drafted by the UN **SUB-COMMISSION ON PREVENTION OF DISCRIMINATION AND PROTECTION OF MINORITIES** and by open-ended working groups established by the Third (Social, Humanitarian and Cultural) Committee and the Sixth (Legal) Committee of the UN **GENERAL ASSEMBLY,** and was approved by the assembly on 9 December 1988 (resolution 43/173).

The text of the Body of Principles, annexed to resolution 43/173, is as follows:

*Scope of the Body of Principles.* These Principles apply for the protection of all persons under any form of detention or imprisonment.

*Use of Terms.* For the purposes of the Body of Principles:

(a) "Arrest" means the act of apprehending a person for the alleged commission of an offence or by the action of an authority;

(b) "Detained person" means any person deprived of personal liberty except as a result of conviction for an offence.

(c) "Imprisoned person" means any person deprived of personal liberty as a result of conviction for an offence;

(d) "Detention" means the condition of detained persons as defined above;

(e) "Imprisonment" means the condition of imprisoned persons as defined above;

(f) The words "a judicial or other authority" mean a judicial or other authority under the law whose status and tenure should afford the strongest possible guarantees of competence, impartiality and independence.

*Principle 1.* All persons under any form of detention or imprisonment shall be treated in a humane manner and with respect for the inherent dignity of the human person.

*Principle 2.* Arrest, detention or imprisonment shall only be carried out strictly in accordance with the provisions of the law and by competent officials or persons authorized for that purpose.

*Principle 3.* There shall be no restriction upon or derogation from any of the human rights of persons under any form of detention or imprisonment recognized or existing in any State pursuant to law, conventions, regulations or custom on the pretext that this Body of Principles does not recognize such rights or that it recognizes them to a lesser extent.

*Principle 4.* Any form of detention or imprisonment and all measures affecting the human rights of a person under any form of detention or imprisonment shall be offered by, or be subject to the effective control of, a judicial or other authority.

*Principle 5.* 1. These principals shall be applied to all persons within the territory of any given State, without distinction of any kind, such as race, colour, sex, language, religion or religious belief, political or other opinion, national ethnic or social origin, property, birth or other status.

2. Measures applied under the law and designed solely to protect the rights and special status of women, especially pregnant women and nursing mothers, children and juveniles, aged, sick or handicapped persons shall not be deemed to be discriminatory. The need for, and the application of, such measures shall always be subject to review by a judicial or other authority.

*Principle 6.* No person under any form of detention or imprisonment shall be subjected to torture or to cruel, inhuman or degrading treatment or punishment. (The term "cruel, inhuman or degrading treatment or punishment" should be interpreted so as to extend the widest possible protection against abuses, whether physical or mental, including the holding of a detained or imprisoned person in conditions which deprive him, temporarily or permanently, of the use of any of his natural senses, such as sight or hearing, or of his awareness of place and the passing of time.) No circumstance whatever may be invoked as a justification for torture or other cruel, inhuman or degrading treatment or punishment.

*Principle 7.* 1. States should prohibit by law any act contrary to the rights and duties contained in these Principles, make any such act subject to appropriate sanctions and conduct impartial investigations upon complaints.

2. Officials who have reason to believe that a violation of this Body of Principles has occurred or is about to occur shall report the matter to their superior authorities and, where necessary, to other appropriate authorities or organs vested with reviewing or remedial powers.

3. Any other person who has ground to believe that a violation of the Body of Principles has occurred or is about to occur shall have the right to report the matter to the superiors of the officials involved as well as to other appropriate authorities or organs vested with reviewing or remedial powers.

*Principle 8.* Persons in detention shall be subject to treatment appropriate to their unconvicted status. Accordingly, they shall, whenever possible, be kept separate from imprisoned persons.

*Principle 9.* The authorities which arrest a person, keep him under detentions or investigate the case shall exercise only the powers granted to them under the law and the exercise of these powers shall be subject to recourse to a judicial or other authority.

*Principle 10.* Anyone who is arrested shall be informed at the time of his arrest of the reason for his arrest and shall be promptly informed of any charges against him.

*Principle 11.* 1. A person shall not be kept in detention without being given an effective opportunity to be heard promptly by a judicial or other authority. A detained person shall have the right to defend himself or to be assisted by counsel as prescribed by law.

2. A detained person and his counsel, if any, shall receive prompt and full communication of any order of detention, together with the reasons therefor.

3. A judicial or other authority shall be empowered to review as appropriate the continuance of detention.

*Principle 12.* 1. There shall be duly recorded:

(a) The reasons for the arrest;

(b) The time of the arrest and the taking of the arrested person to a place of custody as well as that of his first appearance before a judicial or other authority;

(c) The identity of the law enforcement officials concerned;

(d) Precise information concerning the place of custody.

2. Such records shall be communicated to the detained person, or his counsel, if any, in the form prescribed by law.

*Principle 13.* Any person shall, at the moment of arrest and at the commencement of detention or imprisonment, or promptly thereafter, be provided by the authority responsible for his arrest, detention or imprisonment, respectively, with information on and an explanation of his rights and how to avail himself of such rights.

*Principle 14.* A person who does not adequately understand or speak the language used by the authorities responsible for his arrest, detention or imprisonment is entitled to receive promptly in a language which he understands the information referred to in principle 10, principle 11, paragraph 2, principle 12, paragraph 1, and principle 13 and to have the assistance, free of charge, if necessary, of an interpreter in connection with legal proceedings subsequent to his arrest.

*Principle 15.* Notwithstanding the exceptions contained in principle 16, paragraph 4, and principle 18, paragraph 3, communication of the detained or imprisoned person with the outside world, and in particular his family or counsel, shall not be denied for more than a matter of days.

*Principle 16.* 1. Promptly after arrest and after each transfer from one place of detention or imprisonment to another, a detained or imprisoned person shall be entitled to notify or to require the competent authority to notify members of his family or other appropriate persons of his choice of his arrest, detention or imprisonment or of the transfer and of the place where he is kept in custody.

2. If a detained or imprisoned person is a foreigner, he shall also be promptly informed of his right to communicate by appropriate means with a consular post or the diplomatic mission of the State of which he is a national or which is otherwise entitled to receive such communication in accordance with international law or with the representative of the competent international organization, if he is a refugee or is otherwise under the protection of an intergovernmental organization.

3. If a detained or imprisoned person is a juvenile or is incapable of understanding his entitlement, the competent authority shall on its own initiative undertake the notification referred to in this principle. Special attention shall be given to notifying parents or guardians.

4. Any notification referred to in this principle shall be made or permitted to be made without delay. The competent authority may however delay a notification for a reasonable period where exceptional needs of the investigation so require.

*Principle 17.* 1. A detained person shall be entitled to have the assistance of a legal counsel. He shall be informed of his right by the competent authority promptly after arrest and shall be provided with reasonable facilities for exercising it.

2. If a detained person does not have a legal counsel of his own choice, he shall be entitled to have a legal counsel

assigned to him by a judicial or other authority in all cases where the interests of justice so require and without payment by him if he does not have sufficient means to pay.

*Principle 18.* 1. A detained or imprisoned person shall be entitled to communicate and consult with his legal counsel.

2. A detained or imprisoned person shall be allowed adequate time and facilities for consultations with his legal counsel.

3. The right of a detained or imprisoned person to be visited by and to consult and communicate, without delay or censorship and in full confidentiality, with his legal counsel may not be suspended or restricted save in exceptional circumstances, to be specified by law or lawful regulations, when it is considered indispensable by a judicial or other authority in order to maintain security and good order.

4. Interviews between a detained or imprisoned person and his legal counsel may be within sight, but not within the hearing, of a law enforcement official.

5. Communications between a detained or imprisoned person and his legal counsel mentioned in this principle shall be inadmissible as evidence against the detained or imprisoned person unless they are connected with a continuing or contemplated crime.

*Principle 19.* A detained or imprisoned person shall have the right to be visited by and to correspond with, in particular, members of his family and shall be given adequate opportunity to communicate with the outside world, subject to reasonable conditions and restrictions as specified by law or lawful regulations.

*Principle 20.* If a detained or imprisoned person so requests, he shall if possible be kept in a place of detention or imprisonment reasonably near his usual place of residence.

*Principle 21.* 1. It shall be prohibited to take undue advantage of the situation of a detained or imprisoned person for the purpose of compelling him to confess, to incriminate himself otherwise or to testify against any other person.

2. No detained person while being interrogated shall be subject to violence, threats or methods of interrogation which impair his capacity of decision or his judgment.

*Principle 22.* No detained or imprisoned person shall, even with his consent, be subjected to any medical or scientific experimentation which may be detrimental to his health.

*Principle 23.* 1. The duration of any interrogation of a detained or imprisoned person and of the intervals between interrogations as well as the identity of the officials who conducted the interrogation and other persons present shall be recorded and certified in such form as may be prescribed by law.

2. A detained or imprisoned person, or his counsel when provided by law, shall have access to the information described above.

*Principle 24.* A proper medical examination shall be offered to a detained or imprisoned person as promptly as possible after his admission to the place of detention or imprisonment, and thereafter medical care and treatment shall be provided whenever necessary. This care and treatment shall be provided free of charge.

*Principle 25.* A detained or imprisoned person or his counsel shall, subject only to reasonable conditions to ensure security and good order in the place of detention or imprisonment, have the right to request or petition a judicial or other authority for a second medical examination or opinion.

*Principle 26.* The fact that a detained or imprisoned person underwent a medical examination, the name of the physician and the results of such an examination shall be duly recorded. Access to such records shall be ensured. Modalities therefor shall be in accordance with relevant rules of domestic law.

*Principle 27.* Non-compliance with these Principles in obtaining evidence shall be taken into account in determining the admissibility of such evidence against a detained or imprisoned person.

*Principle 28.* A detained or imprisoned person shall have the right to obtain within the limits of available resources, if from public source, reasonable quantities of educational, cultural and informational material, subject to reasonable conditions to ensure security and good order in the place of detention or imprisonment.

*Principle 29.* 1. In order to supervise the strict observance of relevant laws and regulations, places of detention shall be visited regularly by qualified and experienced persons appointed by, and responsible to, a competent authority distinct from the authority directly in charge of the administration of the place of detention or imprisonment.

2. A detained or imprisoned person shall have the right to communicate freely and in full confidentiality with the persons who visit the places of detention or imprisonment in accordance with paragraph 1, subject to reasonable conditions to ensure security and good order in such places.

*Principle 30.* 1. The types of conduct of the detained or imprisoned person that constitute disciplinary offences during detention or imprisonment, the description and duration of disciplinary punishment that may be inflicted and the authorities competent to impose such punishment shall be specified by law or lawful regulations and duly published.

2. A detained or imprisoned person shall have the right to be heard before disciplinary action is taken. He shall have the right to bring such action to higher authorities for review.

*Principle 31.* The appropriate authorities shall endeavour to ensure, according to domestic law, assistance when needed to dependent and, in particular, minor members of the families of detained or imprisoned persons and shall devote a particular measure of care to the appropriate custody of children left without supervision.

*Principle 32.* 1. A detained person or his counsel shall be entitled at any time to take proceedings according to domestic law before a judicial or other authority to challenge the lawfulness of his detention in order to obtain his release without delay, if it is unlawful.

2. The proceedings referred to in paragraph 1 shall be simple and expeditious and at no cost for detained persons without adequate means. The detaining authority shall produce without reasonable delay the detained person before the reviewing authority.

*Principle 33.* 1. A detained or imprisoned person or his counsel shall have the right to make a request or complaint regarding his treatment, in particular in case of torture or other cruel, inhuman or degrading treatment, to the authorities responsible for the administration of the place of detention and to higher authorities and, when necessary, to appropriate authorities vested with reviewing or remedial powers.

2. In those cases where neither the detained or imprisoned person nor his counsel has the possibility to exercise his rights under paragraph 1, a member of the family of the detained or imprisoned person or any other person who has knowledge of the case may exercise such rights.

3. Confidentiality concerning the request or complaint shall be maintained if so requested by the complainant.

4. Every request or complaint shall be promptly dealt with

and replied to without undue delay. If the request or complaint is rejected or, in case of inordinate delay, the complainant shall be entitled to bring it before a judicial or other authority. Neither the detained or imprisoned person nor any complaint under paragraph 1 shall suffer prejudice for making a request or complaint.

*Principle 34.* Whenever the death or disappearance of a detained or imprisoned person occurs during his detention or imprisonment, an inquiry into the cause of death or disappearance shall be held by a judicial or other authority, either on its own motion or at the instance of a member of the family of such a person or any person who has knowledge of the case. When circumstances so warrant, such an inquiry shall be held on the same procedural basis whenever the death or disappearance occurs shortly after the termination of the detention or imprisonment. The findings of such inquiry or a report thereon shall be made available upon request, unless doing so would jeopardize an ongoing criminal investigation.

*Principle 35.* 1. Damage incurred because of acts or omissions by a public official contrary to the rights contained in these Principles shall be compensated according to the applicable rules on liability provided by domestic law.

2. Information required to be recorded under these Principles shall be available in accordance with procedures provided by domestic law for use in claiming compensation under this principle.

*Principle 36.* 1. A detained person suspected of or charged with a criminal offence shall be presumed innocent and shall be treated as such until proved guilty according to law in a public trial at which he has had all the guarantees necessary for his defence.

2. The arrest or detention of such a person pending investigation and trial shall be carried out only for the purposes of the administration of justice on grounds and under conditions and procedures specified by law. The imposition of restrictions upon such a person which are not strictly required for the purpose of the detention or to prevent hindrance to the process of investigation or the administration of justice, or for the maintenance of security and good order in the place of detention shall be forbidden.

*Principle 37.* A person detained on a criminal charge shall be brought before a judicial or other authority provided by law promptly after his arrest. Such authority shall decide without delay upon the lawfulness and necessity of detention. No person shall be kept under detention pending investigation or trial except upon the written order of such an authority. A detained person shall, when brought before such an authority, have the right to make a statement on the treatment received by him while in custody.

*Principle 38.* A person detained on a criminal charge shall be entitled to trial within a reasonable time or to release pending trial.

*Principle 39.* Except in special cases provided for by law, a person detained on a criminal charge shall be entitled, unless a judicial or other authority decides otherwise in the interest of the administration of justice, to release pending trial subject to the conditions that may be imposed in accordance with the law. Such authority shall keep the necessity of detention under review.

*General Clause.* Nothing in the present Body of Principles shall be construed as restricting or derogating from any right defined in the International Covenant on Civil and Political Rights.

## PRISONERS: STANDARD MINIMUM RULES FOR THE TREATMENT OF PRISONERS (1957).

The purpose of the Standard Minimum Rules is not to describe in detail how a model system of penal institutions functions but rather to set out what are generally accepted as good principles and practices to be followed in the treatment of prisoners and the management of penal institutions.

The Standard Minimum Rules were adopted by the First United Nations Congress on the Prevention of Crime and the Treatment of Offenders in 1955 and annexed to the report of that Congress (UN publication, Sales no. 1956.IV.4, annex I.A). They were approved and recommended to States by the UN **ECONOMIC AND SOCIAL COUNCIL** on 31 July 1957. In 1977, the Council decided that a new section E (rule 95) should be added to the rules (resolution 2076 [LXII]). The text, thus amended, is as follows:

### Preliminary Observations

1. The following rules are not intended to describe in detail a model system of penal institutions. They seek only, on the basis of the general consensus of contemporary thought and the essential elements of the most adequate systems of today, to set out what is generally accepted as being good principle and practice in the treatment of prisoners and the management of institutions.

2. In view of the great variety of legal, social, economic and geographical conditions of the world, it is evident that not all of the rules are capable of application in all places and at all times. They should, however, serve to stimulate a constant endeavour to overcome practical difficulties in the way of their application, in the knowledge that they represent, as a whole, the minimum conditions which are accepted as suitable by the United Nations.

3. On the other hand, the rules cover a field in which thought is constantly developing. They are not intended to preclude experiment and practices, provided these are in harmony with the principles and seek to further the purposes which derive from the text of the rules as a whole. It will always be justifiable for the central prison administration to authorize departures from the rules in this spirit.

4. (1) Part I of the rules covers the general management of institutions, and is applicable to all categories of prisoners, criminal or civil, untried or convicted, including prisoners subject to "security measures" or corrective measures ordered by the judge.

(2) Part II contains rules applicable only to the special categories dealt with in each section. Nevertheless, the rules under section A, applicable to prisoners under sentence, shall be equally applicable to categories of prisoners dealt with in sections B, C and D, provided they do not conflict with the rules governing those categories and are for their benefit.

5. (1) The rules do not seek to regulate the management of institutions set aside for young persons such as Borstal institutions or correctional schools, but in general part I would be equally applicable in such institutions.

(2) The category of young prisoners should include at least all young persons who come within the jurisdiction of

juvenile courts. As a rule, such young persons should not be sentenced to imprisonment.

## Part I—Rules of General Application

*Basic Principle.* 6. (1) The following rules shall be applied impartially. There shall be no discrimination on grounds of race, colour, sex, language, religion, political or other opinion, national or social origin, property, birth or other status.

(2) On the other hand, it is necessary to respect the religious beliefs and moral precepts of the group to which a prisoner belongs.

*Register.* 7. (1) In every place where persons are imprisoned there shall be kept a bound registration book with numbered pages in which shall be entered in respect of each prisoner received:

(a) Information concerning his identity;

(b) The reasons for his commitment and the authority therefor;

(c) The day and hour of his admission and release.

(2) No person shall be received in an institution without a valid commitment order of which the details shall have been previously entered in the register.

*Separation of Categories.* 8. The different categories of prisoners shall be kept in separate institutions or parts of institutions taking account of their sex, age, criminal record, the legal reason for their detention and the necessities of their treatment. Thus,

(a) Men and women shall so far as possible be detained in separate institutions; in an institution which receives both men and women the whole of the premises allocated to women shall be entirely separate;

(b) Untried prisoners shall be kept separate from convicted prisoners;

(c) Persons imprisoned for debt and other civil prisoners shall be kept separate from persons imprisoned by reason of a criminal offence;

(d) Young prisoners shall be kept separate from adults.

*Accommodation.* 9. (1) Where sleeping accommodation is in individual cells or rooms, each prisoner shall occupy by night a cell or room by himself. If for special reasons, such as temporary overcrowding, it becomes necessary for the central prison administration to make an exception to this rule, it is not desirable to have two prisoners in a cell or room.

(2) Where dormitories are used, they shall be occupied by prisoners carefully selected as being suitable to associate with one another in those conditions. There shall be regular supervision by night, in keeping with the nature of the institution.

10. All accommodation provided for the use of prisoners and in particular all sleeping accommodation shall meet all requirements of health, due regard being paid to climatic conditions and particularly to cubic content of air, minimum floor space, lighting, heating and ventilation.

11. In all places where prisoners are required to live or work,

(a) The windows shall be large enough to enable the prisoners to read or work by natural light, and shall be so constructed that they can allow the entrance of fresh air whether or not there is artificial ventilation;

(b) Artificial light shall be provided sufficient for the prisoners to read or work without injury to eyesight.

12. The sanitary installations shall be adequate to enable every prisoner to comply with the needs of nature when necessary and in a clean and decent manner.

13. Adequate bathing and shower installations shall be provided so that every prisoner may be enabled and required to have a bath or shower, at a temperature suitable to the climate, as frequently as necessary for general hygiene according to season and geographical region, but at least once a week in a temperate climate.

14. All parts of an institution regularly used by prisoners shall be properly maintained and kept scrupulously clean at all times.

*Personal Hygiene.* 15. Prisoners shall be required to keep their persons clean, and to this end they shall be provided with water and with such toilet articles as are necessary for health and cleanliness.

16. In order that prisoners may maintain a good appearance compatible with their self-respect, facilities shall be provided for the proper care of the hair and beard, and men shall be enabled to shave regularly.

*Clothing and Bedding.* 17. (1) Every prisoner who is not allowed to wear his own clothing shall be provided with an outfit of clothing suitable for the climate and adequate to keep him in good health. Such clothing shall in no manner be degrading or humiliating.

(2) All clothing shall be clean and kept in proper condition. Underclothing shall be changed and washed as often as necessary for the maintenance of hygiene.

(3) In exceptional circumstances, whenever a prisoner is removed outside the institution for an authorized purpose, he shall be allowed to wear his own clothing or other inconspicuous clothing.

18. If prisoners are allowed to wear their own clothing, arrangements shall be made on their admission to the institution to ensure that it shall be clean and fit for use.

19. Every prisoner shall, in accordance with local or national standards, be provided with a separate bed, and with separate and sufficient bedding which shall be clean when issued, kept in good order and changed often enough to ensure its cleanliness.

*Food.* 20. (1) Every prisoner shall be provided by the administration at the usual hours with food of nutritional value adequate for health and strength, of wholesome quality and well prepared and served.

(2) Drinking water shall be available to every prisoner whenever he needs it.

*Exercise and Sport.* 21. (1) Every prisoner who is not employed in outdoor work shall have at least one hour of suitable exercise in the open air daily if the weather permits.

(2) Young prisoners, and others of suitable age and physique, shall receive physical and recreational training during the period of exercise. To this end space, installations and equipment should be provided.

*Medical Services.* 22. (1) At every institution there shall be available the services of at least one qualified medical officer who should have some knowledge of psychiatry. The medical services should be organized in close relationship to the general health administration of the community or nation. They shall include a psychiatric service for the diagnosis and, in proper cases, the treatment of states of mental abnormality.

(2) Sick prisoners who require specialist treatment shall be transferred to specialized institutions or to civil hospitals. Where hospital facilities are provided in an institution, their equipment, furnishing and pharmaceutical supplies shall be proper for the medical care and treatment of sick

prisoners, and there shall be a staff of suitably trained officers.

(3) The services of a qualified dental officer shall be available to every prisoner.

23. (1) In women's institutions there shall be special accommodation for all necessary pre-natal and post-natal care and treatment. Arrangements shall be made wherever practicable for children to be born in a hospital outside the institution. If a child is born in prison, this fact shall not be mentioned in the birth certificate.

(2) Where nursing infants are allowed to remain in the institution with their mothers, provision shall be made for a nursery staffed by qualified persons, where the infants shall be placed when they are not in the care of their mothers.

24. The medical officer shall see and examine every prisoner as soon as possible after his admission and thereafter as necessary, with a view particularly to the discovery of physical or mental illness and the taking of all necessary measures; the segregation of prisoners suspected of infectious or contagious conditions; the noting of physical or mental defects which might hamper rehabilitation, and the determination of the physical capacity of every prisoner for work.

25. (1) The medical officer shall have the care of the physical and mental health of the prisoners and should daily see all sick prisoners, all who complain of illness, and any prisoner to whom his attention is specially directed.

(2) The medical officer shall report to the director whenever he considers that a prisoner's physical or mental health has been or will be injuriously affected by continued imprisonment or by any condition of imprisonment.

26. (1) The medical officer shall regularly inspect and advise the director upon:

(a) The quantity, quality, preparation and service of food;

(b) The hygiene and cleanliness of the institution and the prisoners;

(c) The sanitation, heating, lighting and ventilation of the institution;

(d) The suitability and cleanliness of the prisoner's clothing and bedding;

(e) The observance of the rules concerning physical education and sports, in cases where there is no technical personnel in charge of these activities.

(2) The director shall take into consideration the reports and advice that the medical officer submits according to rules 25 (2) and 26 and, in case he concurs with the recommendations made, shall take immediate steps to give effect to those recommendations; if they are not within his competence or if he does not concur with them, he shall immediately submit his own report and the advice of the medical officer to higher authority.

*Discipline and Punishment.* 27. Discipline and order shall be maintained with firmness, but with no more restriction than is necessary for safe custody and well-ordered community life.

28. (1) No prisoner shall be employed, in the service of the institution, in any disciplinary capacity.

(2) This rule shall not, however, impede the proper functioning of systems based on self-government, under which specified social, educational or sports activities or responsibilities are entrusted, under supervision, to prisoners who are formed into groups for the purposes of treatment.

29. The following shall always be determined by the law or by the regulation of the competent administrative authority:

(a) Conduct constituting a disciplinary offence;

(b) The types and duration of punishment which may be inflicted;

(c) The authority competent to impose such punishment.

30. (1) No prisoner shall be punished except in accordance with the terms of such law or regulation, and never twice for the same offence.

(2) No prisoner shall be punished unless he has been informed of the offence alleged against him and given a proper opportunity of presenting his defence. The competent authority shall conduct a thorough examination of the case.

(3) Where necessary and practicable the prisoner shall be allowed to make his defence through an interpreter.

31. Corporal punishment, punishment by placing in a dark cell, and all cruel, inhuman or degrading punishments shall be completely prohibited as punishments for disciplinary offences.

32. (1) Punishment by close confinement or reduction of diet shall never be inflicted unless the medical officer has examined the prisoner and certified in writing that he is fit to sustain it.

(2) The same shall apply to any other punishment that may be prejudicial to the physical or mental health of a prisoner. In no case may such punishment be contrary to or depart from the principle stated in rule 31.

(3) The medical officer shall visit daily prisoners undergoing such punishments and shall advise the director if he considers the termination or alteration of the punishment necessary on grounds of physical or mental health.

*Instruments of Restraint.* 33. Instruments of restraint, such as handcuffs, chains, irons and strait-jackets, shall never be applied as a punishment. Furthermore, chains or irons shall not be used as restraints. Other instruments of restraint shall not be used except in the following circumstances:

(a) As a precaution against escape during a transfer, provided that they shall be removed when the prisoner appears before a judicial or administrative authority;

(b) On medical grounds by direction of the medical officer;

(c) By order of the director, if other methods of control fail, in order to prevent a prisoner from injuring himself or others or from damaging property; in such instances the director shall at once consult the medical officer and report to the higher administrative authority.

34. The patterns and manner of use of instruments of restraint shall be decided by the central prison administration. Such instruments must not be applied for any longer time than is strictly necessary.

*Information to and Complaints by Prisoners.* 35. (1) Every prisoner on admission shall be provided with written information about the regulations governing the treatment of prisoners of his category, the disciplinary requirements of the institution, the authorized methods of seeking information and making complaints, and all such other matters as are necessary to enable him to understand both his rights and his obligations and to adapt himself to the life of the institution.

(2) If a prisoner is illiterate, the aforesaid information shall be conveyed to him orally.

36. (1) Every prisoner shall have the opportunity each week day of making requests or complaints to the director of the institution or the officer authorized to represent him.

(2) It shall be possible to make requests or complaints to the inspector of prisons during his inspection. The

prisoner shall have the opportunity to talk to the inspector or to any other inspecting officer without the director or other members of the staff being present.

(3) Every prisoner shall be allowed to make a request or complaint, without censorship as to substance but in proper form, to the central prison administration, the judicial authority or other proper authorities through approved channels.

(4) Unless it is evidently frivolous or groundless, every request or complaint shall be promptly dealt with and replied to without undue delay.

*Contact with the Outside World.* 37. Prisoners shall be allowed under necessary supervision to communicate with their family and reputable friends at regular intervals, both by correspondence and by receiving visits.

38. (1) Prisoners who are foreign nationals shall be allowed reasonable facilities to communicate with the diplomatic and consular representatives of the State to which they belong.

(2) Prisoners who are nationals of States without diplomatic or consular representation in the country and refugees or stateless persons shall be allowed similar facilities to communicate with the diplomatic representative of the State which takes charge of their interests or any national or international authority whose task it is to protect such persons.

39. Prisoners shall be kept informed regularly of the more important items of news by the reading of newspapers, periodicals or special institutional publications, by hearing wireless transmissions, by lectures or by any similar means as authorized or controlled by the administration.

*Books.* 40. Every institution shall have a library for the use of all categories of prisoners, adequately stocked with both recreational and instructional books, and prisoners shall be encouraged to make full use of it.

*Religion.* 41. (1) If the institution contains a sufficient number of prisoners of the same religion, a qualified representative of that religion shall be appointed or approved. If the number of prisoners justifies it and conditions permit, the arrangement should be on a full-time basis.

(2) A qualified representative appointed or approved under paragraph (1) shall be allowed to hold regular services and to pay pastoral visits in private to prisoners of his religion at proper times.

(3) Access to a qualified representative of any religion shall not be refused to any prisoner. On the other hand, if any prisoner should object to a visit of any religious representative, his attitude shall be fully respected.

42. So far as practicable, every prisoner shall be allowed to satisfy the needs of his religious life by attending the services provided in the institution and having in his possession the books of religious observance and instruction of his denomination.

*Retention of Prisoners' Property.* 43. (1) All money, valuables, clothing and other effects belonging to a prisoner which under the regulations of the institution he is not allowed to retain shall on his admission to the institution be placed in safe custody. An inventory thereof shall be signed by the prisoner. Steps shall be taken to keep them in good condition.

(2) On the release of the prisoner all such articles and money shall be returned to him except in so far as he has been authorized to spend money or send any such property out of the institution, or it has been found necessary on hygienic grounds to destroy any article of clothing. The prisoner shall sign a receipt for the articles and money returned to him.

(3) Any money or effects received for a prisoner from outside shall be treated in the same way.

(4) If a prisoner brings in any drugs or medicine, the medical officer shall decide what use shall be made of them.

*Notification of Death, Illness, Transfer, etc.* 44. (1) Upon the death or serious illness of, or serious injury to a prisoner, or his removal to an institution for the treatment of mental affections, the director shall at once inform the spouse, if the prisoner is married, or the nearest relative and shall in any event inform any other person previously designated by the prisoner.

(2) A prisoner shall be informed at once of the death or serious illness of any near relative. In case of the critical illness of a near relative, the prisoner should be authorized, whenever circumstances allow, to go to his beside either under escort or alone.

(3) Every prisoner shall have the right to inform at once his family of his imprisonment or his transfer to another institution.

*Removal of Prisoners.* 45. (1) When prisoners are being removed to or from an institution, they shall be exposed to public view as little as possible, and proper safeguards shall be adopted to protect them from insult, curiosity and publicity in any form.

(2) The transport of prisoners in conveyances with inadequate ventilation or light, or in any way which would subject them to unnecessary physical hardship, shall be prohibited.

(3) The transport of prisoners shall be carried out at the expense of the administration and equal conditions shall obtain for all of them.

46. (1) The prison administration, shall provide for the careful selection of every grade of the personnel, since it is on their integrity, humanity, professional capacity and personal suitability for the work that the proper administration of the institutions depends.

(2) The prison administration shall constantly seek to awaken and maintain in the minds both of the personnel and of the public the conviction that this work is a social service of great importance, and to this end all appropriate means of informing the public should be used.

(3) To secure the foregoing ends, personnel shall be appointed on a full-time basis as professional prison officers and have civil service status with security of tenure subject only to good conduct, efficiency and physical fitness. Salaries shall be adequate to attract and retain suitable men and women; employment benefits and conditions of service shall be favourable in view of the exacting nature of the work.

47. (1) The personnel shall possess an adequate standard of education and intelligence.

(2) Before entering on duty, the personnel shall be given a course of training in their general and specific duties and be required to pass theoretical and practical tests.

(3) After entering on duty and during their career, the personnel shall maintain and improve their knowledge and professional capacity by attending courses of in-service training to be organized at suitable intervals.

48. All members of the personnel shall at all times so conduct themselves and perform their duties as to influence the prisoners for good by their example and to command their respect.

49. (1) So far as possible, the personnel shall include a sufficient number of specialists such as psychiatrists, psychologists, social workers, teachers and trade instructors.

(2) The services of social workers, teachers and trade

instructors shall be secured on a permanent basis, without thereby excluding part-time or voluntary workers.

50. (1) The director of an institution should be adequately qualified for his task by character, administrative ability, suitable training and experience.

(2) He shall devote his entire time to his official duties and shall not be appointed on a part-time basis.

(3) He shall reside on the premises of the institution or in its immediate vicinity.

(4) When two or more institutions are under the authority of one director, he shall visit each of them at frequent intervals. A responsible resident official shall be in charge of each of these institutions.

51. (1) The director, his deputy, and the majority of the other personnel of the institution shall be able to speak the language of the greatest number of prisoners, or a language understood by the greatest number of them.

(2) Whenever necessary, the services of an interpreter shall be used.

52. (1) In institutions which are large enough to require the services of one or more full-time medical officers, at least one them shall reside on the premises of the institution or in its immediate vicinity.

(2) In other institutions the medical officer shall visit daily and shall reside near enough to be able to attend without delay in cases of urgency.

53. (1) In an institution for both men and women, the part of the institution set aside for women shall be under the authority of a responsible woman officer who shall have the custody of the keys of all that part of the institution.

(2) No male member of the staff shall enter the part of the institution set aside for women unless accompanied by a woman officer.

(3) Women prisoners shall be attended and supervised only by women officers. This does not, however, preclude male members of the staff, particularly doctors and teachers, from carrying out their professional duties in institutions or parts of institutions set aside for women.

54. (1) Officers of the institutions shall not, in their relations with the prisoners, use force except in self-defence or in cases of attempted escape, or active or passive physical resistance to an order based on law or regulations. Officers who have recourse to force must use no more than is strictly necessary and must report the incident immediately to the director of the institution.

(2) Prison officers shall be given special physical training to enable them to restrain aggressive prisoners.

(3) Except in special circumstances, staff performing duties which bring them into direct contact with prisoners should not be armed. Furthermore, staff should in no circumstances be provided with arms unless they have been trained in their use.

*Inspection.* 55. There shall be a regular inspection of penal institutions and services by qualified and experienced inspectors appointed by a competent authority. Their task shall be in particular to ensure that these institutions are administered in accordance with existing laws and regulations and with a view to bringing about the objectives of penal and correctional services.

### Part II—Rules Applicable to Special Categories

### A. Prisoners Under Sentence

*Guiding Principles.* 56. The guiding principles hereafter are intended to show the spirit in which penal institutions should be administered and the purposes at which they should aim, in accordance with the declaration made under Preliminary Observation 1 of the present text.

57. Imprisonment and other measures which result in cutting off an offender from the outside world are afflictive by the very fact of taking from the person the right of self-determination by depriving him of his liberty. Therefore the prison system shall not, except as incidental to justifiable segregation or the maintenance of discipline, aggravate the suffering inherent in such a situation.

58. The purpose and justification of a sentence of imprisonment or a similar measure deprivative of liberty is ultimately to protect society against crime. This end can only be achieved if the period of imprisonment is used to ensure, so far as possible, that upon his return to society the offender is not only willing but able to lead a law-abiding and self-supporting life.

59. To this end, the institution should utilize all the remedial, educational, moral, spiritual and other forces and forms of assistance which are appropriate and available, and should seek to apply them according to the individual treatment needs of the prisoners.

60. (1) The régime of the institution should seek to minimize any differences between prison life and life at liberty which tend to lessen the responsibility of the prisoners or the respect due to their dignity as human beings.

(2) Before the completion of the sentence, it is desirable that the necessary steps be taken to ensure for the prisoner a gradual return to life in society. This aim may be achieved, depending on the case, by a pre-release régime organized in the same institution or in another appropriate institution, or by release on trial under some kind of supervision which must not be entrusted to the police but should be combined with effective social aid.

61. The treatment of prisoners should emphasize not their exclusion from the community, but their continuing part in it. Community agencies should, therefore, be enlisted wherever possible to assist the staff of the institution in the task of social rehabilitation of the prisoners. There should be in connexion with every institution social workers charged with the duty of maintaining and improving all desirable relations of a prisoner with his family and with valuable social agencies. Steps should be taken to safeguard, to the maximum extent compatible with the law and the sentence, the rights relating to civil interest, social security rights and other social benefits of prisoners.

62. The medical services of the institution shall seek to detect and shall treat any physical or mental illnesses or defects which may hamper a prisoner's rehabilitation. All necessary medical, surgical and psychiatric services shall be provided to that end.

63. (1) The fulfillment of these principles requires individualization of treatment and for this purpose a flexible system of classifying prisoners in groups; it is therefore desirable that such groups should be distributed in separate institutions suitable for the treatment of each group.

(2) These institutions need not provide the same degree of security for every group. It is desirable to provide varying degrees of security according to the needs of different groups. Open institutions, by the very fact that they provide no physical security against escape but rely on the self-discipline of the inmates, provide the conditions most favourable to rehabilitation for carefully selected prisoners.

(3) It is desirable that the number of prisoners in closed institutions should not be so large that the individualization of treatment is hindered. In some countries it is

considered that the population of such institutions should not exceed five hundred. In open institutions the population should be as small as possible.

(4) On the other hand, it is undesirable to maintain prisons which are so small that proper facilities cannot be provided.

64. The duty of society does not end with a prisoner's release. There should, therefore, be governmental or private agencies capable of lending the released prisoner efficient after-care directed towards the lessening of prejudice against him and towards his social rehabilitation.

*Treatment.* 65. The treatment of persons sentenced to imprisonment or a similar measure shall have as its purpose, so far as the length of the sentence permits, to establish in them the will to lead law-abiding and self-supporting lives after their release and to fit them to do so. The treatment shall be such as will encourage their self-respect and develop their sense of responsibility.

66. (1) To these ends, all appropriate means shall be used, including religious care in the countries where this is possible, education, vocational guidance and training, social casework, employment counselling, physical development and strengthening of moral character, in accordance with the individual needs of each prisoner, taking account of his social and criminal history, his physical and mental capacities and aptitudes, his personal temperament, the length of his sentence and his prospects after release.

(2) For every prisoner with a sentence of suitable length, the director shall receive, as soon as possible after his admission, full reports on all the matters referred to in the foregoing paragraph. Such reports shall always include a report by a medical officer, wherever possible qualified in psychiatry, on the physical and mental condition of the prisoner.

(3) The reports and other relevant documents shall be placed in an individual file. This file shall be kept up to date and classified in such a way that it can be consulted by the responsible personnel whenever the need arises.

*Classification and Individualization.* 67. The purpose of classification shall be:

(a) To separate from others those prisoners who, by reason of their criminal records or bad characters, are likely to exercise a bad influence;

(b) To divide the prisoners into classes in order to facilitate their treatment with a view to their social rehabilitation.

68. So far as possible separate institutions or separate sections of an institution shall be used for the treatment of the different classes of prisoners.

69. As soon as possible after admission and after a study of the personality of each prisoner with a sentence of suitable length, a programme of treatment shall be prepared for him in the light of the knowledge obtained about his individual needs, his capacities and dispositions.

*Privileges.* 70. Systems of privileges appropriate for the different classes of prisoners and the different methods of treatment shall be established at every institution, in order to encourage good conduct, develop a sense of responsibility and secure the interest and co-operation of the prisoners in their treatment.

*Work.* 71. (1) Prison labour must not be of an afflictive nature.

(2) All prisoners under sentence shall be required to work, subject to their physical and mental fitness as determined by the medical officer.

(3) Sufficient work of a useful nature shall be provided to keep prisoners actively employed for a normal working day.

(4) So far as possible the work provided shall be such as will maintain or increase the prisoners' ability to earn an honest living after release.

(5) Vocational training in useful trades shall be provided for prisoners able to profit thereby and especially for young prisoners.

(6) Within the limits compatible with proper vocational selection and with the requirements of institutional administration and discipline, the prisoners shall be able to choose the type of work they wish to perform.

72. (1) The organization and methods of work in the institutions shall resemble as closely as possible those of similar work outside institutions, so as to prepare prisoners for the conditions of normal occupational life.

(2) The interests of the prisoners and of their vocational training, however, must not be subordinated to the purpose of making a financial profit from an industry in the institution.

73. (1) Preferably institutional industries and farms should be operated directly by the administration and not by private contractors.

(2) Where prisoners are employed in work not controlled by the administration, they shall always be under the supervision of the institution's personnel. Unless the work is for other departments of the government the full normal wages for such work shall be paid to the administration by the persons to whom the labour is supplied, account being taken of the output of the prisoners.

74. (1) The precautions laid down to protect the safety and health of free workmen shall be equally observed in institutions.

(2) Provision shall be made to indemnify prisoners against industrial injury, including occupational disease, on terms not less favourable than those extended by law to free workmen.

75. (1) The maximum daily and weekly working hours of the prisoners shall be fixed by law or by administrative regulation, taking into account local rules of custom in regard to the employment of free workmen.

(2) The hours so fixed shall leave one rest day a week and sufficient time for education and other activities required as part of the treatment and rehabilitation of the prisoners.

76. (1) There shall be a system of equitable remuneration of the work of prisoners.

(2) Under the system prisoners shall be allowed to spend at least a part of their earnings on approved articles for their own use and to send a part of their earnings to their family.

(3) The system should also provide that a part of the earnings should be set aside by the administration so as to constitute a savings fund to be handed over to the prisoner on his release.

*Education and Recreation.* 77. (1) Provision shall be made for the further education of all prisoners capable of profiting thereby, including religious instruction in the countries where this is possible. The education of illiterates and young prisoners shall be compulsory and special attention shall be paid to it by the administration.

(2) So far as practicable, the education of prisoners shall be integrated with the educational system of the country so that after their release they may continue their education without difficulty.

78. Recreational and cultural activities shall be provided

in all institutions for the benefit of the mental and physical health of prisoners.

*Social Relations and After-care.* 79. Special attention shall be paid to the maintenance and improvement of such relations between a prisoner and his family as are desirable in the best interests of both.

80. From the beginning of a prisoner's sentence consideration shall be given to his future after release and he shall be encouraged and assisted to maintain or establish such relations with persons or agencies outside the institution as may promote the best interests of his family and his own social rehabilitation.

81. (1) Services and agencies, governmental or otherwise, which assist released prisoners to re-establish themselves in society shall ensure, so far as is possible and necessary, that released prisoners be provided with appropriate documents and identification papers, have suitable homes and work to go to, are suitably and adequately clothed having regard to the climate and season, and have sufficient means to reach their destination and maintain themselves in the period immediately following their release.

(2) The approved representatives of such agencies shall have all necessary access to the institution and to prisoners and shall be taken into consultation as to the future of a prisoner from the beginning of his sentence.

(3) It is desirable that the activities of such agencies shall be centralized or co-ordinated as far as possible in order to secure the best use of their efforts.

### B. Insane and Mentally Abnormal Prisoners

82. (1) Persons who are found to be insane shall not be detained in prisons and arrangements shall be made to remove them to mental institutions as soon as possible.

(2) Prisoners who suffer from other mental diseases or abnormalities shall be observed and treated in specialized institutions under medical management.

(3) During their stay in a prison, such prisoners shall be placed under the special supervision of a medical officer.

(4) The medical or psychiatric service of the penal institutions shall provide for the psychiatric treatment of all other prisoners who are in need of such treatment.

83. It is desirable that steps should be taken, by arrangement with the appropriate agencies, to ensure if necessary the continuation of psychiatric treatment after release and the provision of social-psychiatric after-care.

### C. Prisoners Under Arrest or Awaiting Trial

84. (1) Persons arrested or imprisoned by reason of a criminal charge against them, who are detained either in police custody or in prison custody (jail) but have not yet been tried and sentenced, will be referred to as "untried prisoners" hereinafter in these rules.

(2) Unconvicted prisoners are presumed to be innocent and shall be treated as such.

(3) Without prejudice to legal rules for the protection of individual liberty or prescribing the procedure to be observed in respect of untried prisoners, these prisoners shall benefit by a special régime which is described in the following rules in its essential requirements only.

85. (1) Untried prisoners shall be kept separate from convicted prisoners.

(2) Young untried prisoners shall be kept separate from adults and shall in principle be detained in separate institutions.

86. Untried prisoners shall sleep singly in separate rooms, with the reservation of different local custom in respect of the climate.

87. Within the limits compatible with the good order of the institution, untried prisoners may, if they so desire, have their food procured at their own expence from the outside, either through the administration or through their family or friends. Otherwise, the administration shall provide their food.

88. (1) An untried prisoner shall be allowed to wear his own clothing if it is clean and suitable.

(2) If he wears prison dress, it shall be different from that supplied to convicted prisoners.

89. An untried prisoner shall always be offered opportunity to work, but shall not be required to work. If he chooses to work, he shall be paid for it.

90. An untried prisoner shall be allowed to procure at his own expense or at the expense of a third party such books, newspapers, writing materials and other means of occupation as are compatible with the interests of the administration of justice and the security and good order of the institution.

91. An untried prisoner shall be allowed to be visited and treated by his own doctor or dentist if there is reasonable ground for his application and he is able to pay any expenses incurred.

92. An untried prisoner shall be allowed to inform immediately his family of his detention and shall be given all reasonable facilities for communicating with his family and friends, and for receiving visits from them, subject only to such restrictions and supervision as are necessary in the interests of the administration of justice and of the security and good order of the institution.

93. For the purposes of his defence, an untried prisoner shall be allowed to apply for free legal aid where such aid is available, and to receive visits from his legal adviser with a view to his defence and to prepare and hand to him confidential instructions. For these purposes, he shall if he so desires be supplied with writing material. Interviews between the prisoner and his legal adviser may be within sight but not within the hearing of a police or institution official.

### D. Civil Prisoners

94. In countries where the law permits imprisonment for debt, or by order of a court under any other non-criminal process, persons so imprisoned shall not be subjected to any greater restriction or severity than is necessary to ensure safe custody and good order. Their treatment shall be not less favourable than that of untried prisoners, with the reservation, however, that they may possibly be required to work.

### E. Persons Arrested or Detained Without Charge

95. Without prejudice to the provisions of article 9 of the International Covenant on Civil and Political Rights, persons arrested or imprisoned without charge shall be accorded the same protection as that accorded under part I and part II, section C. Relevant provisions of part II, section A, shall likewise be applicable where their application may be conducive to the benefit of this special group of persons in custody, provided that no measures shall be taken implying that re-

education or rehabilitation is in any way appropriate to persons not convicted of any criminal offence.

**PRIVACY.** The right of everyone to privacy is set out in the **Universal Declaration of Human Rights** in the following terms:

*Article 12.* No one shall be subjected to arbitrary interference with his privacy, family, home or correspondence, nor to attacks upon his honour and reputation. Everyone has the right to the protection of the law against such interference or attacks.

The **International Covenant on Civil and Political Rights** contains the following provision on the subject:

*Article 17.* 1. No one shall be subjected to arbitrary or unlawful interference with his privacy, family, home or correspondence.
2. Everyone has the right to the protection of the law against such interference or attacks.

The **American Convention on Human Rights,** open for acceptance by member States of the **Organization of American States,** deals with the right to privacy in the following provision:

*Article 11.* 1. Everyone has the right to have his honor respected and his dignity recognized.
2. No one may be the object of arbitrary or abusive interference with his private life, his family, his home, or his correspondence, or of unlawful attacks on his honor or reputation.
3. Everyone has the right to the protection of the law against such interference or attacks.

The **European Convention on Human Rights,** open for acceptance by member States of the **Council of Europe,** contains the following provision:

*Article 8.* 1. Everyone has the right to respect for his private and family life, his home and his correspondence.
2. There shall be no interference by a public authority with the exercise of this right except such as in accordance with the law and is necessary in a democratic society in the interests of national security, public safety or the economic well-being of the country, for the prevention of disorder or crime, for the protection of health or morals, or for the protection of the rights and freedoms of others.

*COMMENT OF THE UN HUMAN RIGHTS COMMITTEE.*
After examining reports submitted by States parties to the International Covenant on Civil and Political Rights in accordance with article 40 of that instrument, the UN **Human Rights Committee** adopted, in 1988, a general comment setting out its views on the meaning of the right to privacy as formulated in article 17 of the Covenant, as follows (UN Doc. A/43/40, annex VI):

1. Article 17 provides for the right of every person to be protected against arbitrary or unlawful interference with his privacy, family, home or correspondence, as well as against unlawful attacks on his honour and reputation. In the view of the Committee, this right is required to be guaranteed against all such interferences and attacks whether they emanate from State authorities or from natural or legal persons. The obligations imposed by this article require the State to adopt legislative and other measures to give effect to the prohibition against such interferences and attacks as well as to the protection of this right.

2. In this connection, the Committee wishes to point out that, in the reports of States parties to the Covenant, the necessary attention is not being given to information concerning the manner in which respect for this right is guaranteed by legislative, administrative or judicial authorities and in general by the competent organs established in the State. In particular, insufficient attention is paid to the fact that article 17 of the Covenant deals with protection against both unlawful and arbitrary interference. That means that it is precisely in State legislation above all that provision must be made for the protection of the right set forth in that article. At present, the reports either say nothing about such legislation or provide insufficient information on the subject.

3. The term "unlawful" means that no interference can take place except in cases envisaged by the law. Interference authorized by States can only take place on the basis of law, which itself must comply with the provisions, aims and objectives of the Covenant.

4. The expression "arbitrary interference" is also relevant to the protection of the right provided for in article 17. In the Committee's view, the expression "arbitrary interference" can also extend to interference provided for under the law. The introduction of the concept of arbitrariness is intended to guarantee that even interference provided for by law should be in accordance with the provisions, aims and objectives of the Covenant and should be, in any event, reasonable in the particular circumstances.

5. Regarding the term "family", the objectives of the Covenant require that, for the purposes of article 17, this term be given a broad interpretation to include all those comprising the family as understood in the society of the State party concerned. The term "home" in English, *"manzel"* in Arabic, *"zhùzhái"* in Chinese, *"domicile"* in French, *"zhilishche"* in Russian and *"domicilio"* in Spanish, as used in article 17 of the Covenant, is to be understood to indicate the place where a person resides or carries out his usual occupation. In this connection, the Committee invites States to indicate in their reports the meaning given in their society to the term "family" and "home".

6. The Committee considers that the reports should include information on the authorities and organs set up within the legal system of the State which are competent to authorize interference allowed by the law. It is also indispensable to have information on the authorities which are entitled to exercise control over such interference with strict regard for the law, and to know in what manner and through which organs persons concerned may complain of a violation of the right provided for in article 17 of the Covenant. In their reports, States should make clear the extent to which actual practice conforms to the law. State party reports

should also contain information on complaints lodged in respect of arbitrary or unlawful interference, and the number of any findings in that regard, as well as the remedies provided in such cases.

7. As all persons live in society, the protection of privacy is necessarily relative. However, the competent public authorities should only be able to call for such information relating to an individual's private life, the knowledge of which is essential in the interests of society as understood under the Covenant. Accordingly, the Committee recommends that States should indicate in their reports the laws and regulations that govern authorized interferences with private life.

8. Even with regard to interferences that conform to the Covenant, relevant legislation must specify in detail the precise circumstances in which such interferences may be permitted. A decision to make use of such authorized interference must be made only by the authority designated under the law, and on a case-by-case basis. Compliance with article 17 requires that the integrity and confidentiality of correspondence should be guaranteed *de jure* and *de facto*. Correspondence should be delivered to the addressee without interception and without being opened or otherwise read. Surveillance, whether electronic or otherwise, interceptions of telephonic, telegraphic and other forms of communication, wire-tapping and recording of conversations should be prohibited. Searches of a person's home should be restricted to a search for necessary evidence and should not be allowed to amount to harassment. So far as personal and body searches are concerned, effective measures should ensure that such searches are carried out in a manner consistent with the dignity of the person who is being searched. Persons being subjected to a body search by State officials, or medical personnel acting at the request of the State, should only be examined by persons of the same sex.

9. States parties are under a duty themselves not to engage in interferences inconsistent with article 17 of the Covenant and to provide the legislative framework prohibiting such acts by natural or legal persons.

10. The gathering and holding of personal information on computers, data banks and other devices, whether by public authorities or private individuals or bodies, must be regulated by law. Effective measures have to be taken by States to ensure that information concerning a person's private life does not reach the hands of persons who are not authorized by law to receive, process and use it, and is never used for purposes incompatible with the Covenant. In order to have the most effective protection of his private life, every individual should have the right to ascertain, in an intelligible form, whether, and if so, what personal data is stored in automatic data files and for what purposes. Every individual should also be able to ascertain which public authorities or private individuals or bodies control or may control their files. If such files contain incorrect personal data or have been collected or processed contrary to the provisions of the law, every individual should have the right to request rectification or elimination.

11. Article 17 affords protection to personal honour and reputation and States are under an obligation to provide adequate legislation to that end. Provision must also be made for everyone effectively to be able to protect himself against any unlawful attacks that do occur and to have an effective remedy against those responsible. States parties should indicate in their reports to what extent the honour or reputation of individuals is protected by law and how this protection is achieved according to their legal system.

***COMPUTERIZED PERSONAL DATA FILES.*** The Proclamation of Teheran, adopted by the International Conference on Human Rights on 13 May 1968, contains the following paragraph 18:

While recent scientific discoveries and technological advances have opened vast prospects for economic, social and cultural progress, such developments may nevertheless endanger the rights and freedoms of individuals and will require continuing attention.

On 19 December 1968, the General Assembly invited the Secretary-General to undertake (resolution 2450 [XXIII]) a study of the problems in connection with human rights arising from developments in science and technology, including one on the uses of electronics which might affect the rights of the person and the limits which should be placed on such uses in a democratic society.

That study, the first part of which is concerned with "computerized personal data systems," was presented to the UN **COMMISSION ON HUMAN RIGHTS** at its 1974 session (UN Doc. E/CN.4/1142 and Corr. 1, and Add. 1 and 2).

The General Assembly, at its 1975 session, adopted the Declaration on the Use of Scientific and Technological Progress in the Interests of Peace and for the Benefit of Mankind (see **SCIENCE AND TECHNOLOGY**), in which it proclaimed that:

All States shall take appropriate measures to prevent the use of scientific and technological developments, particularly by the State organs, to limit or interfere with the enjoyment of the human rights and fundamental freedoms of the individual as enshrined in the Universal Declaration of Human Rights, the International Covenants on Human Rights and other relevant international instruments.

In 1977, when the Commission on Human Rights was able to consider the Sub-Commission's study, it called upon the Sub-Commission (resolution 10 B [XXXIII]) to examine this and other studies in the light of the provisions of the Declaration and to submit its recommendations for further action.

The Sub-Commission, at its 1980 session, noted (resolution 12 [XXXIII]) that one of the consequences of the use of computers was the increasingly frequent recourse to computerized personal files; that the concentration of personal particulars in such files entailed grave risks of interference with the privacy of individuals and the exercise of their freedoms; and that, apart from States, international, intergovernmental, and regional organizations were keeping an increasing number of computerized personal files. It requested its chairman to designate one of its members to undertake a study of guidelines to be adopted in this area.

Mrs. Nicole Questiaux (France) was designated for

this task on the understanding that it would be carried out by her alternate, Mr. Louis Joinet. Mr. Joinet, who in the meantime replaced Mrs. Questiaux as a member of the Sub-Commission, submitted an interim report in 1981 and the final report (UN Doc. E/CN.4/Sub.2/1983/18) in 1983 (reproduced below).

In the report, Mr. Joinet noted that, as early as 1966, the Nordic Council, a regional organization comprising the Scandinavian countries, had set up a special committee to promote the harmonization of legislation on data processing and freedoms in member States, and that, with time, this committee had become an effective organ for cooperation among the national bodies responsible for the supervision of data files. Further, he noted that the **COUNCIL OF EUROPE** and the Organization for Economic Co-operation and Development (OECD) had proposed for adoption by their member States—in the form of resolutions, recommendations, and even a convention—minimum rules, commonly known as the "hard core," which governments should take into account in the rules they were drafting. In particular, the Council of Europe's Council of Ministers adopted, on 28 January 1981, the European Convention for the Protection of Individuals with Regard to Automatic Processing of Personal Data and the OECD Council of Ministers adopted, on 23 September 1980, a recommendation concerning guidelines on the protection of privacy and transborder flows of personal data.

On the basis of these precedents and other materials available to him, Mr. Joinet concluded his study with two main proposals, the first relating to the promotion of human rights in domestic law (paras. 136–148) and the second relating to the files of international organizations and agencies (paras. 149–152), as follows:

*A. The Promotion of Human Rights in Domestic Law.* In order, firstly, to encourage States to promote protective regulations in their domestic legislation, and secondly, to avoid excessive discrepancies between one legislation and another, guidelines should be proposed for adoption by the competent United Nations bodies, possibly in the form of a recommendation, which might be along the following lines:

States should take steps to give effect to the following basic principles in their domestic legislation:

*Principle of Fairness:* information about persons should not be collected or processed in unfair or unlawful ways.

*Principle of Accuracy:* persons responsible for data files should be obliged to check the accuracy of the data recorded and to ensure that they are kept up to date.

*Principle of Purpose Specification:* the main purpose which a file is to serve should be known before it is established in order to make it possible subsequently to check whether: (a) the personal data collected and recorded are relevant to the purpose to be served; (b) the personal data are not used for purposes other than those for which the file was intended;

and (c) the period for which the personal data are kept does not exceed that which would enable the objective for which they were recorded to be achieved.

*Principle of Openness:* measures should be taken to ensure that any person may be in a position to know of the existence of a personal data file.

*Principle of Individual Access:* any person, irrespective of nationality or place of residence, should have the right: (1) to know whether information concerning him is being processed; (2) if the need arises, to have such information communicated to him in an intelligible form, without excessive delay or expense; (3) to have appropriate rectification or erasures made in the case of erroneous, unlawful or inaccurate entries.

*Principle of Security:* appropriate measures should be taken to ensure the essential security of data files and of access to restricted information.

Departures from the application of one or other of these principles might be admitted in regulations concerning security files (police, defence, courts, intelligence), medical records, scientific and statistical data, and press files, provided that the limits of the exceptions were specified and they were embodied in laws or special regulations promulgated in accordance with the juridical system of each State.

Information on racial origin, sexual proclivities, political opinions, religious or philosophical convictions, or trade-union membership should not be recorded. Departures from these prohibitions should not be authorized except by law and should be subject to more rigorous safeguards.

A supervisory body should be established with adequate guarantees of impartiality both for the purpose of advising the persons affected by these new legislative measures and in order to ensure that the above principles are complied with.

The above principles and rules should, at the very least, be applied to public or private computerized files containing data relating to natural persons.

Particular provision might be made to extend the application of these provisions to manual data systems.

*B. The Files of International Organizations and Agencies.* The international organizations and agencies using computerized personnel files should be recommended to take appropriate protective measures unless they accept local jurisdiction where such exists.

The internal statutes and rules of international organizations and agencies should make provision, as concerns their own files, for the application of the aforementioned principles of fairness, accuracy, purpose specification, openness, individual access and security.

A supervisory authority, either of a collegiate or "ombudsman" type, set up under a procedure offering adequate guarantees of impartiality, should be appointed within each organization or agency.

Its task would be to advise those responsible for the operation of data files and to ensure effective enforcement of internal regulations.

Mr. Joinet recommended that the Sub-Commission prepare a resolution embodying in some appropriate way the twofold proposal above, for submission to the Commission on Human Rights. At the same time, he suggested that, as an immediate step, as far as United Nations computerized files are concerned, one member of the Sub-Commission should be appointed to study draft internal regulations with the assistance of the Secretariat.

***GUIDELINES CONCERNING COMPUTERIZED PERSONAL DATA FILES.*** In the *Study of the Relevant Guidelines in the Field of Computerized Personnel Files* (UN Doc. E/CN.4/Sub.2/1983/18) prepared for the **SUB-COMMISSION ON PREVENTION OF DISCRIMINATION AND PROTECTION OF MINORITIES** by its Special Rapporteur, Mr. Louis Joinet (France), the author elaborated a series of provisional draft guidelines on the use of such files with a view to encouraging States to adopt the regulations necessary to ensure the right to privacy.

At the request of the Sub-Commission, the Secretary-General transmitted the provisional draft guidelines to member States and interested international organizations with a request that they submit their comments. The guidelines were revised in the light of the comments received and presented to the Sub-Commission at its 1988 session (UN Doc. E/CN.4/ Sub.2/1988/22).

On 1 September 1988, the Sub-Commission, expressing its satisfaction with the revised draft guidelines, forwarded them through the Commission on Human Rights and the Economic and Social Council to the General Assembly with a recommendation for their adoption (resolution 1988/29). The Assembly, after examining them, invited the Special Rapporteur (resolution 44/132) to submit to the Commission, at its 1990 session, a revised version taking into account the comments and suggestions submitted by eight governments. The Special Rapporteur accordingly submitted a revised text of the "Guidelines concerning Computerized Personal Data Files", reproduced below, to the Commission at its 1990 session (UN Doc. E/CN.4/1990/72):

The procedures for implementing regulations concerning computerized personal data files are left to the initiative of each State subject to the following orientations:

### Principles concerning the Minimum Guarantees that Should Be Provided in National Legislations

1. *Principle of Lawfulness and Fairness.* Information about persons should not be collected or processed in unfair or unlawful ways, nor should it be used for ends contrary to the purposes and principles of the Charter of the United Nations.

2. *Principle of Accuracy.* Persons responsible for the compilation of files or those responsible for keeping them have an obligation to conduct regular checks on the accuracy and relevance of the data recorded and to ensure that they are kept as complete as possible in order to avoid errors of omission and that they are kept up to date regularly or when the information contained in a file is used, as long as they are being processed.

3. *Principle of the Purpose-Specification.* The purpose which a file is to serve and its utilization in terms of that purpose should be specified, legitimate and, when it is established, receive a certain amount of publicity or be brought to the attention of the person concerned, in order to make it possible subsequently to ensure that:

(a) All the personal data collected and recorded remain relevant and adequate to the purposes so specified;

(b) None of the said personal data is used or disclosed, except with the consent of the person concerned, for purposes incompatible with those specified;

(c) The period for which the personal data are kept does not exceed that which would enable the achievement of the purpose so specified.

4. *Principle of Interested-Person Access.* Everyone who offers proof of identity has the right to know whether information concerning him is being processed and to obtain it in an intelligible form, without undue delay or expense, and to have appropriate rectifications or erasures made in the case of unlawful, unnecessary or inaccurate entries and, when it is being communicated, to be informed of the addresses. Provision should be made for a remedy, if need be with the supervisory authority specified in principle 8 below. The cost of any rectification shall be borne by the person responsible for the file. It is desirable that the provisions of this principle should apply to everyone, irrespective of nationality or place of residence.

5. *Principle of Non-Discrimination.* Subject to cases of exceptions restrictively envisaged under principle 6, data likely to give rise to unlawful or arbitrary discrimination, including information on racial or ethnic origin, colour, sex life, political opinions, religious, philosophical or other beliefs as well as membership of an association or trade union, should not be compiled.

6. *Power to Make Exceptions.* Departures from principles 1 to 4 may be authorized only if they are necessary to protect national security, public order, public health or morality, as well as, *inter alia,* the rights and freedoms of others, especially persons being persecuted (humanitarian clause) provided that such departures are expressly specified in a law or equivalent regulation promulgated in accordance with the internal legal system which expressly states their limits and sets forth appropriate safeguards.

Exceptions to principle 5 relating to the prohibition of discrimination, in addition to being subject to the same safeguards as those prescribed for exceptions to principles 1 and 4, may be authorized only within the limits prescribed by the International Bill of Human Rights and the other relevant instruments in the field of protection of human rights and the prevention of discrimination.

7. *Principle of Security.* Appropriate measures should be taken to protect the files against both natural dangers, such as accidental loss or destruction and human dangers, such an unauthorized access, fraudulent misuse of data or contamination by computer viruses.

8. *Supervision and Sanctions.* The law of every country shall designate the authority which, in accordance with its domestic legal system, is to be responsible for supervising observance of the principles set forth above. This authority shall offer guarantees of impartiality, independence *vis-à-vis* persons or agencies responsible for processing and establishing data, and technical competence. In the event of violation of the provisions of the national law implementing the aforementioned principles, criminal or other penalties should be

envisaged together with the appropriate individual remedies.

9. *Transborder Data Flows.* When the legislation of two or more countries concerned by a transborder data flow offers comparable safeguards for the protection of privacy, information should be able to circulate as freely as inside each of the territories concerned. If there are no reciprocal safeguards, limitations on such circulation may not be imposed unduly and only in so far as the protection of privacy demands.

10. *Field of Application.* The present principles should be made applicable, in the first instance, to all public and private computerized files as well as, by means of optional extension and subject to appropriate adjustments, to manual files. Special provision, also optional, might be made to extend all or part of the principles to files on legal persons particularly when they contain some information on individuals.

### Application of the Guidelines to Personal Data Files Kept by Governmental International Organizations

The present guidelines should apply to personal data files kept by governmental international organizations, subject to any adjustments required to take account of any differences that might exist between files for internal purposes such as those that concern personnel management and files for external purposes concerning third parties having relations with the organization.

Each organization should designate the authority statutorily competent to supervise the observance of these guidelines.

Humanitarian clause: a derogation from these principles may be specifically provided for when the purpose of the file is the protection of human rights and fundamental freedoms of the individual concerned or humanitarian assistance.

A similar derogation should be provided in national legislation for governmental international organizations whose headquarters agreement does not preclude the implementation of the said national legislation as well as for non-governmental international organizations to which this law is applicable.

On the recommendation of the UN Commission on Human Rights (resolution 1990/42) and the Economic and Social Council (resolution 1990/38), the General Assembly adopted the Guidelines without a vote on 14 December 1990 (resolution 45/95) and requested governments to take them into account in their legislative and administration regulations.

*SEE ALSO Science and Technology.*

**BIBLIOGRAPHY.** Campbell, D., and J. Fisher, eds. *Data Transmission and Privacy.* Dordrecht, the Netherlands: Martinus Nijhoff, 1994. Scholarly monograph, in English.
McAllister, Debra M. "Refugees and Public Access to Immigration Hearings: A Clash of Constitutional Values," *International Journal of Refugee Law* 2, no. 4 (Oct. 1990): 562–586. Scholarly article, in English.
Michael, James. *Privacy and Human Rights: An International and Comparative Study, with Special Reference to Developments in Information Technology.* London: Dartmouth Publishing, 1994. Scholarly monograph, in English.

Rigaux, Francois. *La Protection de la vie privée et des autres biens de la personnalité* (The Protection of Privacy and Other Rights of the Individual). Brussels, Belgium: Emile Bruylant, 1990. Scholarly monograph, in French; bibliography, pp. 773–783.

## PRIVACY: CONVENTION FOR THE PROTECTION OF INDIVIDUALS WITH REGARD TO AUTOMATIC PROCESSING OF PERSONAL DATA, COUNCIL OF EUROPE (1981).

States parties to this Convention undertake to enact legislation and to take other necessary measures to ensure that data contained in automated personal data files are not disclosed to unauthorized persons. The Convention sets out a series of basic principles designed to protect the right of privacy of the individual whose personal data are fed into such files. The principles regulate the procedures by which such data are obtained, preserved, revised, or corrected, and made available to others. In particular, they prohibit the processing of data revealing racial origin, political opinions, religious or other beliefs, or information concerning health or sexual life, unless domestic laws provide adequate safeguards against the disclosure of such information.

The Convention was adopted by the Committee of Ministers of the **COUNCIL OF EUROPE,** convened in Strasbourg on 28 January 1981, and entered into force on 1 October 1985. The text (*European Treaty Series* 108) is as follows:

### Preamble

The member States of the Council of Europe, signatory hereto,

Considering that the aim of the Council of Europe is to achieve greater unity between its members, based in particular on respect for the rule of law, as well as human rights and fundamental freedoms;

Considering that it is desirable to extend the safeguards for everyone's rights and fundamental freedoms, and in particular the right to the respect for privacy, taking account of the increasing flow across frontiers of personal data undergoing automatic processing;

Reaffirming at the same time their commitment to freedom or information regardless of frontiers;

Recognising that it is necessary to reconcile the fundamental values of the respect for privacy and the free flow of information between peoples,

Have agreed as follows:

### Chapter I—General Provisions

*Article 1. Object and Purpose.* The purpose of this Convention is to secure in the territory of each Party for every individual, whatever his nationality or residence, respect for his rights and fundamental freedoms, and in particular his right to privacy, with regard to automatic processing of personal data relating to him ("data protection").

*Article 2. Definitions.* For the purposes of this Convention:

(a) "personal data" means any information relating to an identified or identifiable individual ("data subject");

(b) "automated data file" means any set of data undergoing automatic processing;

(c) "automatic processing" includes the following operations if carried out in whole or in part by automated means: storage of data, carrying out of logical and/or arithmetical operations on those data, their alteration, erasure, retrieval or dissemination;

(d) "controller of the file" means the natural or legal person, public authority, agency or any other body who is competent according to the national law to decide what should be the purpose of the automated data file, which categories of personal data should be stored and which operations should be applied to them.

*Article 3. Scope.* 1. The Parties undertake to apply this Convention to automated personal data files and automatic processing of personal data in the public and private sectors.

2. Any State may, at the time of signature or when depositing its instrument of ratification, acceptance, approval or accession, or at any later time, give notice by a declaration addressed to the Secretary General of the Council of Europe:

(a) that it will not apply this Convention to certain categories of automated personal data files, a list of which will be deposited. In this list it shall not include, however, categories of automated data files subject under its domestic law to data protection provisions. Consequently, it shall amend this list by a new declaration whenever additional categories of automated personal data files are subjected to data protection provisions under its domestic law;

(b) that it will also apply this Convention to information relating to groups of persons, associations, foundations, companies, corporations and any other bodies consisting directly or indirectly of individuals, whether or not such bodies possess legal personality;

(c) that it will also apply this Convention to personal data files which are not processed automatically.

3. Any State which has extended the scope of this Convention by any of the declarations provided for in sub-paragraph 2 (b) or (c) above may give notice in the said declaration that such extensions shall apply only to certain categories of personal data files, a list of which will be deposited.

4. Any Party which has excluded certain categories of automated personal data files by a declaration provided for in sub-paragraph 2 (a) above may not claim the application of this Convention to such categories by a Party which has not excluded them.

5. Likewise, a Party which has not made one or other of the extensions provided for in sub-paragraphs 2 (b) and (c) above may not claim the application of this Convention on these points with respect to a Party which has made such extensions.

6. The declarations provided for in paragraph 2 above shall take effect from the moment of the entry into force of the Convention with regard to the State which has made them if they have been made at the time of signature or deposit of its instrument of ratification, acceptance, approval or accession, or three months after their receipt by the Secretary General of the Council of Europe if they have been made at any later time. These declarations may be withdrawn, in whole or in part, by a notification addressed to the Secretary General of the Council of Europe. Such withdrawals shall take effect three months after the date of receipt of such notification.

## Chapter II—Basic Principles for Data Protection

*Article 4. Duties of the Parties.* 1. Each Party shall take the necessary measures in its domestic law to give effect to the basic principles for data protection set out in this chapter.

2. These measures shall be taken at the latest at the time of entry into force of this Convention in respect of that Party.

*Article 5. Quality of Data.* Personal data undergoing automatic processing shall be:

(a) obtained and processed fairly and lawfully;

(b) stored for specified and legitimate purposes and not used in a way incompatible with those purposes;

(c) adequate, relevant and not excessive in relation to the purposes for which they are stored;

(d) accurate and, where necessary, kept up to date;

(e) preserved in a form which permits identification of the data subjects for no longer than is required for the purpose for which those data are stored.

*Article 6. Special Categories of Data.* Personal data revealing racial origin, political opinions or religious or other beliefs, as well as personal data concerning health or sexual life, may not be processed automatically unless domestic law provides appropriate safeguards. The same shall apply to personal data relating to criminal convictions.

*Article 7. Data Security.* Appropriate security measures shall be taken for the protection of personal data stored in automated data files against accidental or unauthorised destruction or accidental loss as well as against unauthorised access, alteration or dissemination.

*Article 8. Additional Safeguards for the Data Subject.* Any person shall be enabled:

(a) to establish the existence of an automated personal data file, its main purposes, as well as the identity and habitual residence or principal place of business of the controller of the file;

(b) to obtain at reasonable intervals and without excessive delay or expense confirmation of whether personal data relating to him are stored in the automated data file as well as communication to him of such data in an intelligible form;

(c) to obtain, as the case may be, rectification or erasure of such data if these have been processed contrary to the provisions of domestic law giving effect to the basic principles set out in Articles 5 and 6 of this Convention;

(d) to have a remedy if a request for confirmation or, as the case may be, communication, rectification or erasure as referred to in paragraphs (b) and (c) of this Article is not complied with.

*Article 9. Exceptions and Restrictions.* 1. No exception to the provisions of Articles 5, 6 and 8 of this convention shall be allowed except within the limits defined in this Article.

2. Derogation from the provisions of Articles 5, 6 and 8 of this Convention shall be allowed when such derogation is provided for by the law of the Party and constitutes a necessary measure in a democratic society in the interests of:

(a) protecting State security, public safety, the monetary interests of the State or the suppression of criminal offences;

(b) protecting the data subject or the rights and freedoms of others.

3. Restrictions on the exercise of the rights specified in Article 8, paragraphs (b), (c) and (d), may be provided by law with respects to automated personal data files used for statistics or for scientific research purposes when there is obviously no risk of an infringement of the privacy of the data subjects.

*Article 10. Sanctions and Remedies.* Each Party undertakes to establish appropriate sanctions and remedies for violations of provisions of domestic law giving effect to the basic principles for data protection set out in this chapter.

*Article 11. Extended Protection.* None of the provisions of this chapter shall be interpreted as limiting or otherwise affecting the possibility for a Party to grant data subjects a wider measure of protection than that stipulated in this convention.

## Chapter III—Transborder Data Flows

*Article 12. Transborder Flows of Personal Data and Domestic Law.* 1. The following provisions shall apply to the transfer across national borders, by whatever medium, or personal data undergoing automatic processing or collected with a view to their being automatically processed.

2. A Party shall not, for the sole purpose of the protection of privacy, prohibit or subject to special authorisation transborder flows of personal data going to the territory of another Party.

3. Nevertheless, each Party shall be entitled to derogate from the provisions of paragraph 2:

(a) insofar as its legislation includes specific regulations for certain categories of personal data or of automated personal data files, because of the nature of those data or those files, except where the regulations of the other Party provide an equivalent protection;

(b) when the transfer is made from its territory to the territory of a non-Contracting State through the intermediary of the territory of another Party, in order to avoid such transfers resulting in circumvention of the legislation of the Party referred to at the beginning of this paragraph.

## Chapter IV—Mutual Assistance

*Article 13. Co-operation Between Parties.* 1. The Parties agree to render each other mutual assistance in order to implement this Convention.

2. For that purpose:

(a) each Party shall designate one or more authorities, the name and address of each of which it shall communicate to the Secretary General of the Council of Europe;

(b) each Party which has designated more than one authority shall specify in its communication referred to in the previous sub-paragraph the competence of each authority.

3. An authority designated by a Party shall at the request of an authority designated by another Party:

(a) furnish information on its law and administrative practice in the field of data protection;

(b) take, in conformity with its domestic law and for the sole purpose of protection of privacy, all appropriate measures for furnishing factual information relating to specific automatic processing carried out in its territory, with the exception however of the personal data being processed.

*Article 14. Assistance to Data Subjects Resident Abroad.* 1. Each Party shall assist any person resident abroad to exercise the rights conferred by its domestic law giving effect to the principles set out in Article 8 of this Convention.

2. When such a person resides in the territory of another Party he shall be given the option of submitting his request through the intermediary of the authority designated by that Party.

3. The request for assistance shall contain all the necessary particulars, relating *inter alia* to:

(a) the name, address and any other relevant particulars identifying the person making the request;

(b) the automated personal data file to which the request pertains, or its controller;

(c) the purpose of the request.

*Article 15. Safeguards Concerning Assistance Rendered by Designated Authorities.* 1. An authority designated by a Party which has received information from an authority designated by another Party either accompanying a request for assistance or in reply to its own request for assistance shall not use that information for purposes other than those specified in the request for assistance.

2. Each Party shall see to it that the persons belonging to or acting on behalf of the designated authority shall be bound by appropriate obligations of secrecy or confidentiality with regard to that information.

3. In no case may a designated authority be allowed to make under Article 14, paragraph 2, a request for assistance on behalf of a data subject resident abroad, of its own accord and without the express consent of the person concerned.

*Article 16. Refusal of Requests for Assistance.* A designated authority to which a request for assistance is addressed under Articles 13 or 14 of this Convention may not refuse to comply with it unless:

(a) the request is not compatible with the powers in the field of data protection of the authorities responsible for replying;

(b) the request does not comply with the provisions of this Convention;

(c) compliance with the request would be incompatible with the sovereignty, security or public policy (*ordre public*) of the Party by which it was designated, or with the rights and fundamental freedoms of persons under the jurisdiction of that Party.

*Article 17. Costs and Procedures of Assistance.* 1. Mutual assistance which the Parties render each other under Article 13 and assistance they render to data subjects abroad under Article 14 shall not give rise to the payment of any costs or fees other than those incurred for experts and interpreters. The latter costs or fees shall be borne by the Party which has designated the authority making the request for assistance.

2. The data subject may not be charged costs or fees in connection with the steps taken on his behalf in the territory of another Party other than those lawfully payable by residents of that Party.

3. Other details concerning the assistance relating in particular to the forms and procedures and the languages to be used, shall be established directly between the Parties concerned.

## Chapter V—Consultative Committee

*Article 18. Composition of the Committee.* 1. A Consultative Committee shall be set up after the entry into force of this Convention.

2. Each Party shall appoint a representative to the committee and a deputy representative. Any member State of the Council of Europe which is not a Party to the Convention shall have the right to be represented on the committee by an observer.

3. The Consultative Committee may, by unanimous decision, invite any non-member State of the Council of Europe which is not a Party to the Convention to be represented by an observer at a given meeting.

*Article 19. Functions of the Committee.* The Consultative Committee:

(a) may make proposals with a view to facilitating or improving the application of the Convention;

(b) may make proposals for amendment of this Convention in accordance with Article 21;

(c) shall formulate its opinion on any proposal for amendment of this Convention which is referred to it in accordance with Article 21, paragraph 3;

(d) may, at the request of a Party, express an opinion on any question concerning the application of this Convention.

*Article 20. Procedure.* 1. The Consultative Committee shall be convened by the Secretary General of the Council of Europe. Its first meeting shall be held within twelve months of the entry into force of this Convention. It shall subsequently meet at least once every two years and in any case when one-third of the representatives of the Parties request its convocation.

2. A majority of representatives of the Parties shall constitute a quorum for a meeting of the Consultative Committee.

3. After each of its meetings, the Consultative Committee shall submit to the Committee of Ministers of the Council of Europe a report on its work and on the functioning of the Convention.

4. Subject to the provisions of this Convention, the Consultative Committee shall draw up its own Rules of Procedure.

## Chapter VI—Amendments

*Article 21. Amendments.* 1. Amendments to this Convention may be proposed by a Party, the Committee of Ministers of the Council of Europe or the Consultative Committee.

2. Any proposal for amendment shall be communicated by the Secretary General of the Council of Europe to the member States of the Council of Europe and to every non-member State which has acceded to or has been invited to accede to this Convention in accordance with the provisions of Article 23.

3. Moreover, any amendment proposed by a Party or the Committee of Ministers shall be communicated to the Consultative Committee, which shall submit to the Committee of Ministers its opinion on that proposed amendment.

4. The Committee of Ministers shall consider the proposed amendment and any opinion submitted by the Consultative Committee and may approve the amendment.

5. The text of any amendment approved by the Committee of Ministers in accordance with paragraph 4 of this Article shall be forwarded to the Parties for acceptance.

6. Any amendment approved in accordance with paragraph 4 of this Article shall come into force on the thirtieth day after all Parties have informed the Secretary-General of their acceptance thereof.

## Chapter VII—Final Clauses

*Article 22. Entry into Force.* 1. This Convention shall be open for signature by the member States of the Council of Europe. It is subject to ratification, acceptance or approval. Instruments of ratification, acceptance or approval shall be deposited with the Secretary General of the Council of Europe.

2. This Convention shall enter into force on the first day of the month following the expiration of a period of three months after the date on which five member States of the Council of Europe have expressed their consent to be bound by the Convention in accordance with the provisions of the preceding paragraph.

3. In respect of any member State which subsequently expresses its consent to be bound by it, the Convention shall enter into force on the first day of the month following the expiration of a period of three months after the date of the deposit of the instrument of ratification, acceptance or approval.

*Article 23. Accession by Non-member States.* 1. After the entry into force of this Convention, the Committee of Ministers of the Council of Europe may invite any State not a member of the Council of Europe to accede to this Convention by a decision taken by the majority provided for in Article 20 (d) of the Statute of the Council of Europe and by the unanimous vote of the representatives of the Contracting States entitled to sit on the Committee.

2. In respect of any acceding State, the Convention shall enter into force on the first day of the month following the expiration of a period of three months after the date of deposit of the instrument of accession with the Secretary General of the Council of Europe.

*Article 24. Territorial Clause.* 1. Any State may at the time of signature or when depositing its instrument of ratification, acceptance, approval or accession, specify the territory or territories to which this Convention shall apply.

2. Any State may at any later date, by a declaration addressed to the Secretary General of the Council of Europe, extend the application of this Convention to any other territory specified in the declaration. In respect of such territory the Convention shall enter into force on the first day of the month following the expiration of a period of three months after the date of receipt of such declaration by the Secretary-General.

3. Any declaration made under the two preceding paragraphs may, in respect of any territory specified in such declaration, be withdrawn by a notification addressed to the Secretary General. The withdrawal shall become effective on the first day of the month following the expiration of a period of six months after the date of receipt of such notification by the Secretary General.

*Article 25. Reservations.* No reservation may be made in respect of the provisions of this Convention.

*Article 26. Denunciation.* 1. Any Party may at any time denounce this Convention by means of a notification addressed to the Secretary General of the Council of Europe.

2. Such denunciation shall become effective on the first day of the month following the expiration of a period of six months after the date of receipt of the notification by the Secretary General.

*Article 27. Notifications.* The Secretary General of the Council of Europe shall notify the member States of the Council and any State which has acceded to this Convention of:

(a) any signature;

(b) the deposit of any instrument of ratification, acceptance, approval or accession;

(c) any date of entry into force of this Convention in accordance with Articles 22, 23 and 24;

(d) any other act, notification or communication relating to this Convention.

In witness whereof the undersigned, being duly authorised thereto, have signed this Convention.

Done at Strasbourg, the 28th day of January 1981, in English and in French, both texts being equally authoritative, in a single copy which shall remain deposited in the archives of the Council of Europe. The Secretary General of the Council of Europe shall transmit certified copies to each member State of the Council of Europe and to any State invited to accede to this Convention.

## PROCEDURAL ASPECTS OF INTERNATIONAL LAW INSTITUTE. An international organization in consultative status (Roster) with the UN ECONOMIC AND SOCIAL COUNCIL, PAIL was founded in 1965, initially to study international procedures for the protection of human rights. It conducts research on various procedural aspects of international law and disseminates its findings through publications, seminars, and conferences. In 1978, PAIL established the International Human Rights Law Group, which has functioned as a separate organization since 1983.

Among the publications in the PAIL series are the following: John Carey, *UN Protection of Civil and Political Rights* (1970); Frank G. Dawson and Ivan L. Head, *International Law, National Tribunals, and the Rights of Aliens* (1970); Richard B. Lillich, *Humanitarian Intervention and the United Nations* (1973); David Harris, *The European Social Charter* (1984); Hurst Hannum, ed., *Guide to International Human Rights Practice* (1984); Hurst Hannum and Richard B. Lillich, *Materials on International Human Rights and U.S. Constitutional Law* (1985); and Hurst Hannum, *The Right to Leave and Return in International Law and Practice* (1987).

Procedural Aspects of International Law Institute. Address: 910 17th Street, N.W., Washington, D.C., 20006, USA. Telephone: (202) 659-3228. Executive Director: L. Hurst Hannum.

## PROCEDURAL GUARANTEES. Procedural guarantees are provisions which prescribe the manner in which rights may be exercised or enforced and which provide safeguards to ensure justly administered remedies in the case of violation of those rights. Certain principles relating to procedural guarantees are set out in articles 6, 10, and 11 of the UNIVERSAL DECLARATION OF HUMAN RIGHTS, as follows:

*Article 6.* Everyone has the right to recognition everywhere as a person before the law. . . .

*Article 10.* Everyone is entitled in full equality to a fair and public hearing by an independent and impartial tribunal, in the determination of his rights and obligations and of any criminal charge against him.

*Article 11.* (1) Everyone charged with a penal offense has the right to be presumed innocent until proved guilty according to law in a public trial at which he has had all the guarantees necessary for his defence.

(2) No one shall be held guilty of any penal offence on account of any act or omission which did not constitute a penal offence, under national or international law, at the time when it was committed. Nor shall a heavier penalty be imposed than the one that was applicable at the time the penal offence was committed.

The subject of procedural guarantees is dealt with extensively in the INTERNATIONAL COVENANT ON CIVIL AND POLITICAL RIGHTS, in articles 14 to 16, as follows:

*Article 14.* 1. All persons shall be equal before the courts and tribunals. In the determination of any criminal charge against him, or of his rights and obligations in a suit at law, everyone shall be entitled to a fair and public hearing by a competent, independent and impartial tribunal established by law. The Press and the public may be excluded from all or part of a trial for reasons of morals, public order (*ordre public*) or national security in a democratic society, or when the interest of the private lives of the parties so requires, or to the extent strictly necessary in the opinion of the court in special circumstances where publicity would prejudice the interests of justice; but any judgement rendered in a criminal case or in a suit at law shall be made public except where the interest of juvenile persons otherwise requires or the proceedings concern matrimonial disputes of the guardianship of children.

2. Everyone charged with a criminal offence shall have the right to be presumed innocent until proved guilty according to law.

3. In the determination of any criminal charge against him, everyone shall be entitled to the following minimum guarantees, in full equality:

(a) To be informed promptly and in detail in a language which he understands of the nature and cause of the charge against him;

(b) To have adequate time and facilities for the preparation of his defence and to communicate with counsel of his own choosing;

(c) To be tried without undue delay;

(d) To be tried in his presence, and to defend himself in person or through legal assistance of his own choosing; to be informed, if he does not have legal assistance, of this right; and to have legal assistance assigned to him, in any case where the interests of justice so require, and without payment by him in any such case if he does not have sufficient means to pay for it;

(e) To examine, or have examined, the witnesses against him and to obtain the attendance and examination of witnesses on his behalf under the same condition as witnesses against him;

(f) To have the free assistance of an interpreter if he cannot understand or speak the language used in court;

(g) Not to be compelled to testify against himself or to confess guilt.

4. In the case of juvenile persons, the procedure shall be such as will take account of their age and the desirability of promoting their rehabilitation.

5. Everyone convicted of a crime shall have the right to his conviction and sentence being reviewed by a higher tribunal according to law.

6. When a person has by a final decision been convicted of a criminal offence and when subsequently his conviction has been reversed or he has been pardoned on the ground that a new or newly discovered fact shows conclusively that there has been a miscarriage of justice, the person who has suffered punishment as a result of such conviction shall be compensated according to law, unless it is proved that the non-disclosure of the unknown fact in time is wholly or partly attributable to him.

7. No one shall be liable to be tried or punished again

for an offence for which he has already been finally convicted or acquitted in accordance with the law and penal procedure of each country.

*Article 15.* 1. No one shall be held guilty of any criminal offence on account of any act or omission which did not constitute a criminal offence, under national or international law, at the time when it was committed. Nor shall a heavier penalty be imposed than the one that was applicable at the time when the criminal offence was committed. If, subsequent to the Commission of the offence, provision is made by law for the imposition of the lighter penalty, the offender shall benefit thereby.

2. Nothing in this article shall prejudice the trial and punishment of any person for any act or omission which, at the time when it was committed, was criminal according to the general principles of law recognized by the community of nations.

*Article 16.* Everyone shall have the right to recognition everywhere as a person before the law.

The International Convention on the Elimination of All Forms of Racial Discrimination (see **RACIAL DISCRIMINATION**) deals with procedural guarantees briefly, as follows:

*Article 5.* In compliance with the fundamental obligations laid down in article 2 of this Convention, States parties undertake to prohibit and to eliminate racial discrimination in all its forms and to guarantee the right of everyone, without distinction as to race, colour, or national or ethnic origin, to equality before the law, notably in the enjoyment of the following rights: (a) the right to equal treatment before the tribunals and all other organs administering justice.

The Convention on the Elimination of All Forms of Discrimination against Women contains the following provisions:

*Article 15.* (2) States Parties shall accord to women, in civil matters, a legal capacity identical to that of men and the same opportunities to exercise that capacity. In particular, they shall give women equal rights to conclude contracts and to administer property and shall treat them equally in all stages of procedure in courts and tribunals.

(3) States parties agree that all contracts and all other private instruments of any kind with a legal effect which is directed at restricting the legal capacity of women shall be deemed null and void.

The subject of procedural guarantees is dealt with in the Convention Against Torture and Other Cruel, Inhuman or Degrading Treatment or Punishment (see **TORTURE**), as follows:

*Article 12.* Each State party shall ensure that its competent authorities proceed to a prompt and impartial investigation, wherever there is reasonable ground to believe that an act of torture has been committed in any territory under its jurisdiction.

*Article 13.* Each State party shall ensure that any individual who alleges he has been subjected to torture in any territory under its jurisdiction has the right to complain to, and to have his case promptly and impartially examined by, its com-

petent authorities. Steps shall be taken to ensure that the complainant and witnesses are protected against all ill-treatment or intimidation as a consequence of his complaint or any evidence given.

*Article 14.* (1) Each State party shall ensure in its legal system that the victim of an act of violence obtains redress and has an enforceable right to fair and adequate compensation, including the means for as full rehabilitation as possible. In the event of the death of the victim as a result of an act of torture, his dependents shall be entitled to compensation.

(2) Nothing in this article shall affect any right of the victim or other persons to compensation which may exist under national law.

*Article 15.* Each State party shall ensure that any statement which is established to have been made as a result of torture shall not be invoked as evidence in any proceedings, except against a person accused of torture as evidence that the statement was made.

The **AMERICAN CONVENTION ON HUMAN RIGHTS,** open for acceptance by member States of the **ORGANIZATION OF AMERICAN STATES,** provides that:

*Article 3.* Every person has the right to recognition as a person before the law. . . .

*Article 8.* 1. Every person has the right to a hearing, with due guarantees and within a reasonable time, by a competent, independent, and impartial tribunal, previously established by law, in the substantiation of any accusation of a criminal nature made against him or for the determination of his rights and obligations of a civil, labor, fiscal, or any other nature.

2. Every person accused of a criminal offense has the right to be presumed innocent so long as his guilt has not been proven according to law. During the proceedings, every person is entitled, with full equality, to the following minimum guarantees:

(a) the right of the accused to be assisted without charge by a translator or interpreter, if he does not understand or does not speak the language of the tribunal or court;

(b) prior notification in detail to the accused of the charges against him;

(c) adequate time and means for the preparation of his defense;

(d) the right of the accused to defend himself personally or to be assisted by legal counsel of his own choosing, and to communicate freely and privately with his counsel;

(e) the inalienable right to be assisted by counsel provided by the state, paid or not as the domestic law provides, if the accused does not defend himself personally or engage his own counsel within the time period established by law;

(f) the right of the defense to examine witnesses present in the court and to obtain the appearance, as witnesses, of experts or other persons who may throw light on the facts;

(g) the right not to be compelled to be a witness against himself or to plead guilty; and

(h) the right to appeal the judgment to a higher court.

3. A confession of guilt by the accused shall be valid only if it is made without coercion of any kind.

4. An accused person acquitted by a nonappealable judgment shall not be subjected to a new trial for the same cause.

5. Criminal proceedings shall be public, except insofar as may be necessary to protect the interests of justice.

The **African Charter on Human and Peoples' Rights,** open for acceptance by member States of the **Organization of African Unity,** contains the following provisions:

*Article 5.* Every individual shall have the right to the respect of the dignity inherent in a human being and to the recognition of his legal status. . . .

*Article 7.* 1. Every individual shall have the right to have his cause heard. This comprises:

(a) The right to an appeal to competent national organs against acts violating his fundamental rights as recognized and guaranteed by conventions, laws, regulations and customs in force;

(b) the right to be presumed innocent until proved guilty by a competent court or tribunal;

(c) the right to defence, including the right to be defended by counsel of his choice;

(d) the right to be tried within a reasonable time by an impartial court or tribunal.

2. No one may be condemned for an act or omission which did not constitute a legally punishable offence at the time it was committed. No penalty may be inflicted for an offence for which no provision was made at the time it was committed. Punishment is personal and can be imposed only on the offender.

The **European Convention on Human Rights,** open for acceptance by member States of the **Council of Europe,** provides that:

*Article 6.* 1. In the determination of his civil rights and obligations or of any criminal charge against him, everyone is entitled to a fair and public hearing within a reasonable time by an independent and impartial tribunal established by law. Judgment shall be pronounced publicly but the press and public may be excluded from all or part of the trial in the interest of morals, public order or national security in a democratic society, where the interests of juveniles or the protection of the private life of the parties so require, or to the extent strictly necessary in the opinion of the court in special circumstances where publicity would prejudice the interests of justice.

2. Everyone charged with a criminal offence shall be presumed innocent until proved guilty according to law.

3. Everyone charged with a criminal offence has the following minimum rights:

(a) to be informed promptly, in a language which he understands and in detail, of the nature and cause of the accusation against him;

(b) to have adequate time and facilities for the preparation of his defence;

(c) to defend himself in person or through legal assistance of his own choosing or, if he has not sufficient means to pay for legal assistance, to be given it free when the interests of justice so require;

(d) to examine or have examined witnesses against him and to obtain the attendance and examination of witnesses on his behalf under the same conditions as witnesses against him;

(e) to have the free assistance of an interpreter if he cannot understand or speak the language used in court.

*Article 7.* 1. No one shall be held guilty of any criminal offence on account of any act or omission which did not constitute a criminal offence under national or international law at the time when it was committed. Nor shall a heavier penalty be imposed than the one that was applicable at the time the criminal offence was committed.

2. This Article shall not prejudice the trial and punishment of any person for any act or omission which, at the time when it was committed, was criminal according to the general principles of law recognized by civilised nations.

The **European Convention on Human Rights: Protocol VII** adds the following provisions to the text of the Convention:

*Article 2.* 1. Everyone convicted of a criminal offence by a tribunal shall have the right to have conviction or sentence reviewed by a higher tribunal. The exercise of this right, including the grounds on which it may be exercised, shall be governed by law.

2. This right may be subject to exceptions in regard to offences of a minor character, as prescribed by law, or in cases in which the person concerned was tried in the first instance by the highest tribunal or was convicted following an appeal against acquittal.

*Article 3.* When a person has by a final decision been convicted of a criminal offence and when subsequently his conviction has been reversed, or he has been pardoned, on the ground that a new or newly discovered fact shows conclusively that there has been a miscarriage of justice, the persons who have suffered punishment as a result of such conviction shall be compensated according to the law or the practice of the State concerned, unless it is proved that the non-disclosure of the unknown fact in time is wholly or partly attributable to him.

*Article 4.* 1. No one shall be liable to be tried or punished again in criminal proceedings under the jurisdiction of the same State for an offence for which he has already been finally acquitted or convicted in accordance with the law and penal procedure of that State.

2. The provisions of the preceding paragraph shall not prevent the reopening of the case in accordance with the law and penal procedure of the State concerned, if there is evidence of new or newly discovered facts, or if there has been a fundamental defect in the previous proceedings, which could affect the outcome of the case.

3. No derogation from this Article shall be made under Article 15 of the Convention.

***COMMENT OF THE UN HUMAN RIGHTS COMMITTEE.*** After examining reports submitted by States parties to the International Covenant on Civil and Political Rights in accordance with its article 40, the UN **Human Rights Committee** adopted in 1984 a general comment on article 14 of that Covenant in which it set out the Committee's views on the use of procedural guarantees to ensure the proper administration of justice in the following terms (UN Doc. A/39/40, annex VI):

1. The Committee notes that article 14 of the Covenant is of a complex nature and that different aspects of its provisions will need specific comments. All of these provisions are aimed at ensuring the proper administration of justice,

and to this end uphold a series of individual rights such as equality before the courts and tribunals and the right to a fair and public hearing by a competent, independent and impartial tribunal established by law. Not all reports provided details on the legislative or other measures adopted specifically to implement each of the provisions of article 14.

2. In general, the reports of States parties fail to recognize that article 14 applies not only to procedures for the determination of criminal charges against individuals but also to procedures to determine their rights and obligations in a suit at law. Laws and practices dealing with these matters vary widely from State to State. This diversity makes it all the more necessary for States parties to provide all relevant information and to explain in greater detail how the concepts of "criminal charge" and "rights and obligations in a suit at law" are intercepted in relation to their respective legal systems.

3. The Committee would find it useful if, in their future reports, States parties could provide more detailed information on the steps taken to ensure that equality before the courts, including equal access to courts, fair and public hearings and competence, impartiality and independence of the judiciary are established by law and guaranteed in practice. In particular, States parties should specify the relevant constitutional and legislative texts which provide for the establishment of the courts and ensure that they are independent, impartial and competent, in particular with regard to the manner in which judges are appointed, the qualifications for appointment, and the duration of their terms of office; the conditions governing promotion, transfer and cessation of their functions and the actual independence of the judiciary from the executive branch and the legislature.

4. The provisions of article 14 apply to all courts and tribunals within the scope of that article whether ordinary or specialized. The Committee notes the existence, in many countries, of military or special courts which try civilians. This could present serious problems as far as the equitable, impartial and independent administration of justice is concerned. Quite often the reason for the establishment of such courts is to enable exceptional procedures to be applied which do not comply with normal standards of justice. While the Covenant does not prohibit such categories of courts, nevertheless the conditions which it lays down clearly indicate that the trying of civilians by such courts should be very exceptional and take place under conditions which genuinely afford the full guarantees stipulated in article 14. The Committee has noted a serious lack of information in this regard in the reports of some States parties whose judicial institutions include such courts for the trying of civilians. In some countries such military and special courts do not afford the strict guarantees of the proper administration of justice in accordance with the requirements of article 14 which are essential for the effective protection of human rights. If States parties decide in circumstances of a public emergency as contemplated by article 4 to derogate from normal procedures required under article 14, they should ensure that such derogations do not exceed those strictly required by the exigencies of the actual situation, and respect the other conditions in paragraph 1 of article 14.

5. The second sentence of article 14, paragraph 1, provides that "everyone shall be entitled to a fair and public hearing". Paragraph 3 of the article elaborates on the requirements of a "fair hearing" in regard to the determination of criminal charges. However, the requirements of paragraph 3 are minimum guarantees, the observance of which is not always sufficient to ensure the fairness of a hearing as required by paragraph 1.

6. The publicity of hearings is an important safeguard in the interest of the individual and of society at large. At the same time article 14, paragraph 1, acknowledges that courts have the power to exclude all or part of the public for reasons spelt out in that paragraph. It should be noted that, apart from such exceptional circumstances, the Committee considers that a hearing must be open to the public in general, including members of the press, and must not, for instance, be limited only to a particular category of persons. It should be noted that, even in cases in which the public is excluded from the trial, the judgement must, with certain strictly defined exceptions, be made public.

7. The Committee has noted a lack of information regarding article 14, paragraph 2, and, in some cases, has even observed that the presumption of innocence, which is fundamental to the protection of human rights, is expressed in very ambiguous terms or entails conditions which render it ineffective. By reason of the presumption of innocence, the burden of proof of the charge is on the prosecution and the accused has the benefit of doubt. No guilt can be presumed until the charge has been proved beyond reasonable doubt. Further, the presumption of innocence implies a right to be treated in accordance with this principle. It is therefore a duty for all public authorities to refrain from prejudging the outcome of a trial.

8. Among the minimum guarantees in criminal proceedings prescribed by paragraph 3, the first concerns the right of everyone to be informed in a language which he understands of the charge against him (subparagraph (a)). The Committee notes that State reports often do not explain how this right is respected and ensured. Article 14, subparagraph 3 (a) applies to all cases of criminal charges, including those of persons not in detention. The Committee notes further that the right to be informed of the charge "promptly" requires that information is given in the manner described as soon as the charge is first made by a competent authority. In the opinion of the Committee this right must arise when in the course of an investigation a court or an authority of the prosecution decides to take procedural steps against a person suspected of a crime or publicly names him as such. The specific requirements of subparagraph 3 (a) may be met by stating the charge either orally or in writing, provided that the information indicates both the law and the alleged facts on which it is based.

9. Subparagraph 3 (b) provides that the accused must have adequate time and facilities for the preparation of his defence and to communicate with counsel of his own choosing. What is "adequate time" depends on the circumstances of each case, but the facilities must include access to documents and other evidence which the accused requires to prepare his case, as well as the opportunity to engage and communicate with counsel. When the accused does not want to defend himself in person or request a person or an association of his choice, he should be able to have recourse to a lawyer. Furthermore, this subparagraph requires counsel to communicate with the accused in conditions giving full respect for the confidentiality of their communications. Lawyers should be able to counsel and to represent their clients in accordance with their established professional standards and judgement without any restrictions, influences, pressures or undue interference from any quarter.

10. Subparagraph 3 (c) provides that the accused shall be tried without undue delay. This guarantee relates not only to the time by which a trial should commence, but also the time by which it should end and judgement be rendered; all stages must take place "without undue delay". To make this

right effective, a procedure must be available in order to ensure that the trial will proceed "without undue delay", both in first instance and on appeal.

11. Not all reports have dealt with all aspects of the right of defence as defined in subparagraph 3 (d). The Committee has not always received sufficient information concerning the protection of the right of the accused to be present during the determination of any charge against him nor how the legal system assures his right either to defend himself in person or to be assisted by counsel of his own choosing, or what arrangements are made if a person does not have sufficient means to pay for legal assistance. The accused or his lawyer must have the right to act diligently and fearlessly in pursuing all available defences and the right to challenge the conduct of the case if they believe it to be unfair. When exceptionally for justified reasons trials *in absentia* are held, strict observance of the rights of the defence is all the more necessary.

12. Subparagraph 3 (e) states that the accused shall be entitled to examine or have examined the witnesses against him and to obtain the attendance and examination of witnesses on his behalf under the same conditions as witnesses against him. This provision is designed to guarantee to the accused the same legal powers of compelling the attendance of witnesses and of examining or cross-examining any witnesses as are available to the prosecution.

13. Subparagraph 3 (f) provides that if the accused cannot understand or speak the language used in court he is entitled to the assistance of an interpreter free of any charge. This right is independent of the outcome of the proceedings and applies to aliens as well as to nationals. It is of basic importance in cases in which ignorance of the language used by a court or difficulty in understanding may constitute a major obstacle to the right of defence.

14. Subparagraph 3 (g) provides that the accused may not be compelled to testify against himself or to confess guilt. In considering this safeguard the provisions of article 7 and article 10, paragraph 1, should be borne in mind. In order to compel the accused to confess or to testify against himself frequently methods which violate these provisions are used. The law should require that evidence provided by means of such methods or any other form of compulsion is wholly unacceptable.

15. In order to safeguard the rights of the accused under paragraphs 1 and 3 of article 14, judges should have authority to consider any allegations made of violations of the rights of the accused during any stage of the prosecution.

16. Article 14, paragraph 4, provides that in the case of juvenile persons, the procedure shall be such as will take account of their age and the desirability of promoting their rehabilitation. Not many reports have furnished sufficient information concerning such relevant matters as the minimum age at which a juvenile may be charged with a criminal offence, the maximum age at which a person is still considered to be a juvenile, the existence of special courts and procedures, the laws governing procedures against juveniles and how all these special arrangements for juveniles take account of "the desirability of promoting their rehabilitation". Juveniles are to enjoy at least the same guarantees and protection as are accorded to adults under article 14.

17. Article 14, paragraph 5, provides that everyone convicted of a crime shall have the right to his conviction and sentence being reviewed by a higher tribunal according to law. Particular attention is drawn to the other language versions of the word "crime" (*"infraction"*, *"delito"*, *"prestuplenie"*) which show that the guarantee is not confined only to the most serious offences. In this connection, not enough information has been provided concerning the procedures of appeal, in particular the access to and the powers of reviewing tribunals, what requirements must be satisfied to appeal against a judgement and the way in which the procedures before review tribunals take account of the fair and public hearing requirements of paragraph 1 of article 14.

18. Article 14, paragraph 6, provides for compensation according to law in certain cases of a miscarriage of justice as described therein. It seems from many State reports that this right is often not observed or insufficiently guaranteed by domestic legislation. States should, where necessary, supplement their legislation in this area in order to bring it into line with the provisions of the Covenant.

19. In considering State reports differing views have often been expressed as to the scope of paragraph 7 of article 14. Some States parties have even felt the need to make reservations in relation to procedures for the resumption of criminal cases. It seems to the Committee that most States parties make a clear distinction between a resumption of a trial justified by exceptional circumstances and a retrial prohibited pursuant to the principle of *ne bis in idem* as contained in paragraph 7. This understanding of the meaning of *ne bis in idem* may encourage States parties to reconsider their reservations to article 14, paragraph 7.

***SEE ALSO*** *Civil and Political Rights; Fair Trial; International Covenant on Civil and Political Rights; Remedy.*

**PROPERTY AND HUMAN RIGHTS.** The right of everyone to own property is proclaimed in the UNIVERSAL DECLARATION OF HUMAN RIGHTS in the following terms:

*Article 17.* (1) Everyone has the right to own property alone as well as in association with others.
(2) No one shall be arbitrarily deprived of his property.

The prohibition of discrimination in respect of the right is set out in article 5 of the International Convention on the Elimination of All Forms of Racial Discrimination (see **RACIAL DISCRIMINATION**), which provides that:

*Article 5.* In compliance with the fundamental obligations laid down in article 2 of this Convention, States Parties undertake to prohibit and to eliminate racial discrimination in all its forms and to guarantee the right of everyone, without distinction as to race, colour, or national or ethnic origin, to equality before the law, notably in the enjoyment of the following rights: . . .
(d) Other civil rights, in particular: . . .
(v) The right to own property alone as well as in association with others;
(vi) The right to inherit. . . .

The Convention on the Elimination of Discrimination against Women contains the following provisions:

*Article 13.* States Parties shall take all appropriate measures to eliminate discrimination against women in other areas of economic and social life in order to ensure, on a basis of equality of men and women, the same rights, in particular:

(a) The right to family benefits;

(b) The right to bank loans, mortgages and other forms of financial credit;

(c) The right to participate in recreational activities, sports and all aspects of cultural life. . . .

*Article 15.* (2) States parties shall accord to women, in civil matters, a legal capacity identical to that of men and the same opportunities to exercise that capacity. In particular, they shall give women equal rights to conclude contracts and to administer property and shall treat them equally in all stages of procedure in courts and tribunals.

The **AMERICAN CONVENTION ON HUMAN RIGHTS,** open for acceptance by member States of the **ORGANIZATION OF AMERICAN STATES,** provides that:

*Article 21.* 1. Everyone has the right to the use and enjoyment of his property. The law may subordinate such use and enjoyment to the interest of society.

2. No one shall be deprived of his property except upon payment of just compensation, for reasons of public utility or social interest, and in the cases and according to the forms established by law.

3. Usury and any form of exploitation of man by man shall be prohibited by law.

The **AFRICAN CHARTER ON HUMAN AND PEOPLES' RIGHTS** open for acceptance by member States of the **ORGANIZATION OF AFRICAN UNITY,** provides that:

*Article 14.* The right to property shall be guaranteed. It may only be encroached upon in the interest of public need or in the general interest of the community and in accordance with the provisions of appropriate laws.

The right of property, set out in general terms in article 17 of the Universal Declaration of Human Rights, is not mentioned in either of the International Covenants on Human Rights, the drafters of the Covenants having been unable to reach agreement on the appropriate formulation of the right, its legitimate limitations, or the restrictions which should properly be placed upon action by the State. However, this right is dealt with, as shown above, in several other international conventions; and both the Declaration on Social Progress and Development and the Declaration on the Right to Development (see **DEVELOPMENT**) assign a role to property in the implementation of human rights and fundamental freedoms.

In recent years, the right of property has been examined mainly in the UN **GENERAL ASSEMBLY** and the **COMMISSION ON HUMAN RIGHTS.**

In 1986, the UN General Assembly expressed (resolution 41/132) the conviction that the full enjoyment by everyone of the right to own property, alone as well as in association with others, is of particular significance in fostering widespread enjoyment of other ba-

sic human rights and contributes to securing the goals of economic and social development enshrined in the **UNITED NATIONS CHARTER.** The resolution called upon the Secretary-General to prepare a report, taking into account the views of member States, specialized agencies, and other competent bodies of the United Nations system, on (a) the relationship between the full enjoyment by individuals of human rights and fundamental freedoms, in particular the right of everyone to own property alone as well as in association with others, as set forth in article 17 of the Universal Declaration of Human Rights, and the economic and social development of member States; and (b) the role of the same right in ensuring the full and free participation of individuals in the economic and social systems of States. The Assembly requested the Secretary-General to report his findings to it through the **ECONOMIC AND SOCIAL COUNCIL.**

In 1987, the General Assembly recognized (resolution 42/115) that there exist in member States many forms of legal property ownership, including private, communal, and state forms, each of which should contribute to ensuring the effective development and utilization of human resources through the establishment of sound bases for political, economic, and social justice; and called upon States to ensure that their national legislation with regard to all forms of property shall preclude any impairment of the enjoyment of human rights and fundamental freedoms, without prejudice to their right freely to choose and develop their political, social, economic, and cultural system.

Also in 1987, the Commission on Human Rights dealt with the right to own property in two resolutions. In the first (resolution 1987/17), it urged States to provide, where they have not done so, adequate constitutional and legal provisions to protect the right of everyone to own property alone as well as in association with others and the right not to be deprived arbitrarily of one's property. In the second (resolution 1987/18), it reaffirmed the statement in article 6 of the Declaration on Social Progress and Development, that social progress and development require the establishment, in conformity with human rights and fundamental freedoms, and with the principles of justice and the social function of property, of forms of ownership of land and of the means of production which preclude any kind of exploitation of man, ensure equal rights to property for all, and create conditions leading to genuine equality among people.

The Commission on Human Rights, at its 1988 session, appealed (resolution 1988/18) to member States, specialized agencies, and other competent bodies of the United Nations systems to respond as constructively and factually as possible to the invitation of the General Assembly to communicate their views on the subject to the Secretary-General. In a resolution on the impact of property upon the enjoyment of human rights and fundamental freedoms (resolution 1988/19), it called upon States to ensure that their national legislation with regard to all forms of property precludes any impairment and reiterated the views which had been expressed by the Assembly on this subject in Assembly resolution 42/115. And in another resolution, on the recovery of nations' assets illegally removed by violators of human rights (resolution 1988/20), it joined with the **SUB-COMMISSION ON PREVENTION OF DISCRIMINATION AND PROTECTION OF MINORITIES** in requesting all States concerned to cooperate in the speedy recovery of the assets belonging to the peoples of the Philippines and Haiti illegally removed by the Marcos and Duvalier families, respectively.

In a note presented to the Economic and Social Council and the General Assembly in 1988 (UN Doc. E/1988/24), the Secretary-General informed those bodies of the progress made in preparing his report and pointed out that each of the above-mentioned resolutions had brought forward important issues to be considered, among them the following (paras. 9–11):

The principal focus of Assembly resolution 41/132 and 42/115 and Commission resolutions 1987/17 and 1988/18 [is] on the legal protection of the right to property as a human right and its relationship to the economic and social development of the individual, within his socio-economic system. In those resolutions, the Assembly and the Commission on Human Rights emphasized the right not to be deprived of one's property arbitrarily (art. 17 of the Universal Declaration of Human Rights), that the right to property should be subject only to such limitations as are determined by law solely for the purpose of securing due recognition and respect for the rights and freedoms of others and of meeting the just requirements of morality, public order and the global welfare in a democratic society (art. 29 of the Universal Declaration of Human Rights), that no State, group or person should be engaged in any activity or perform any act aimed at the destruction of, *inter alia,* the right to property (art. 30 of the Universal Declaration of Human Rights) and that States should establish national legislation to protect the rights of everyone to own property alone as well as in association with others. They also stressed the role of individual initiative as a valuable resource in promoting economic and social development.

In Assembly resolution 42/115 and Commission resolutions 1987/18 and 1988/19, other elements were brought forward relating to the links between the right to own property and the right to self-determination, the right to sovereignty over all natural wealth and resources and the establishment of a new international economic order. Referring to article 6 of the Declaration on Social Progress and Development, the Assembly and the Commission reaffirmed that social progress and development require the establishment, in conformity with human rights and fundamental freedoms and with the principles of justice and the social function of property, of forms of ownership of land and of the means of production which preclude any kind of human exploitation,

ensure equal rights to property for all and create conditions leading to genuine equality among people.

The Assembly and the Commission in those resolutions also emphasized the role of the public sector in promoting the economic development of developing countries, expressed their conviction that social justice is a prerequisite for lasting peace and that man can achieve complete fulfilment of his aspirations only within a just social order and called upon States to ensure that their national legislation with regard to all forms of property precludes any impairment of the enjoyment of human rights and fundamental freedoms, without prejudice to their right freely to choose and develop their political, social, economic and cultural systems. Finally, those resolutions dealt with the specific issues of transnational corporations and urged them to ensure that their activities do not adversely affect the process of implementing the human rights in developing countries.

As regards the materials made available for use in the preparation of his report, the Secretary-General stated that (paras. 12–16):

The communications which have so far been received reflect the broad approach to the issue taken by the Assembly and the Commission by describing the different forms of property which exist in countries and their role in promoting economic and social progress.

Governments in their replies generally refer to constitutional provisions or national legislation regulating the protection of the right to property. Some governmental replies describe the role that the different forms of property play in their countries in promoting the socio-economic development process and in creating conditions in which the individuality of every member of the society can flourish.

Other communications received from competent bodies of the United Nations system and non-governmental organizations, emphasize the need to utilize all human resources for the social and economic development and to guarantee equal opportunity for all to participate in these processes. Referring to the various forms of property, it is stated that property rights may be conceived as one of the means for enlarging people's participation in, and the acceleration of, their social and economic development, particularly in developing countries. It is said that the right of everyone to own property has to be seen in the context of general social conditions of the individual. If such a concept is to be established, it should particularly refer to the needs of underdeveloped regions and of special and disadvantaged social groups.

Various replies refer to the relationship between the right of everybody to own property and other political, economic and social rights. Mention is made in this context to the right to freedom of association, freedom from discrimination, freedom of labour, the right to equivalent pay for the work done or service rendered and other rights. Certain replies stressed that holding of property should not increase social discrimination or injustice, prevent or impeded social integration or full participation in the economic or social policy-making processes, increase unemployment and neglect social responsibility. In this regard, attention is drawn to discriminatory factors which may exist to restrict the social integration and advancement of women, the poor, the aged or the young in many parts of the world.

A number of replies argue that the principal issue was to find and guarantee effective ways and means of enabling socially and economically disadvantaged people to have access to different forms of legal property ownership, including private, communal or State forms. It is said that in the development of these ways and means, national distribution and redistribution policies, as well as land and other social and economic reforms had to be taken into account. It is also emphasized that respect for the right of everybody to own property includes the elimination of all forms of discrimination against specific social groups.

Late in 1988, the General Assembly considered (resolution 43/123) two aspects of the right of property. First, it repeated the earlier call of the Commission on Human Rights requesting States to provide adequate constitutional and legal provisions to protect the right to own property alone as well as in association with others and the right not to be deprived arbitrarily of one's property. Second, it requested the Secretary-General to seek the views of member States, specialized agencies, and other competent bodies of the United Nations system on the means whereby and the degree to which the right to own property contributes to the development of individual liberty and initiative, which serve to foster, strengthen, and enhance the exercise of other human rights and fundamental freedoms. It suggested that member States, specialized agencies, and other competent bodies of the United Nations system may wish to address, in particular, the right to own the following types of property: (a) personal property, including the residence of one's self and family; and (b) economically productive property, including property associated with agriculture, commerce, and industry.

**SEE ALSO** *Housing as a Human Right; Shelter; Standard of Living.*

**BIBLIOGRAPHY.** Budlender, Geoff, et al. "Debating the Land Issue," *South African Journal on Human Rights* 6, no. 2 (1990): 155–227. Scholarly article, in English.

Centre for Applied Legal Studies, University of the Witwatersrand. "Land and Property Rights," *South African Journal on Human Rights* 8, no. 3 (1992): 295–450. Special issue, in English.

Magnusson, Roger S. "The Recognition of Proprietary Rights in Human Tissue in Common Law Jurisdictions," *Melbourne University Law Review* 18, no. 3 (June 1992): 601–629. Scholarly article, in English.

Rigaux, Francois. *La Protection de la vie privée et des autres biens de la personnalité* (The Protection of Privacy and Other Rights of the Individual). Brussels, Belgium: Emile Bruylant, 1990. Scholarly monograph, in French; bibliography, pp. 773–783.

**PUBLIC EMERGENCY.** Article 4 of the **INTERNATIONAL COVENANT ON CIVIL AND POLITICAL RIGHTS** reads as follows:

1. In time of public emergency which threatens the life of the nation and the existence of which is officially proclaimed, the States Parties to the present Covenant may take measures derogating from their obligations under the present Covenant to the extent strictly required by the exigencies of the situation, provided that such measures are not inconsistent with their other obligations under international law and do not involve discrimination solely on the ground of race, colour, sex, language, religion or social origin.

2. No derogation from articles 6, 7, 8 (paragraphs 1 and 2), 11, 15, 16 and 18 may be made under this provision.

3. Any State party to the present Covenant availing itself of the right of derogation shall immediately inform the other States Parties to the present Covenant, through the intermediary of the Secretary-General of the United Nations, of the provisions from which it has derogated and of the reasons by which it was actuated. A further communication shall be made, through the same intermediary, on the date on which it terminates the derogation.

A study of the protection of human rights in time of public emergency appears as Part Three of the more comprehensive study entitled *The Individual's Duties to the Community and the Limitations on Human Rights and Freedoms Under Article 29 of the Universal Declaration of Human Rights*, prepared by Mrs. Erica-Irene A. Daes (Greece), Special Rapporteur for the **SUB-COMMISSION ON PREVENTION OF DISCRIMINATION AND PROTECTION OF MINORITIES,** published in 1983 (UN publication, Sales no. E.82.XIV.1). In the study, the Special Rapporteur reviews the legislative history of the preparation of article 4 of the International Covenant on Civil and Political Rights and sets out the requirements for the existence of a public emergency. Her conclusions and recommendations on this subject are as follows (paras. 171–195):

From the foregoing analysis of article 4 of the International Covenant of Civil and Political Rights, the examination of relevant provisions of other international instruments on human rights, the study of the replies of Governments and certain national constitutions and the review of certain cases dealt with by international organs of implementation, the following conclusions may be drawn.

The only kind of emergency envisaged in article 4 is a "public emergency" and according to paragraph 1, such an emergency can occur only when "the life of the nation" is threatened and only when its existence has been "officially proclaimed" by the State party concerned. The concept "public emergency" is of recent date. It was introduced to eliminate, where possible, from legal instruments the "state of war" which has not existed in international law since the Second World War. It also replaces the traditional term "state of siege".

This formulation was chosen in order to provide for a qualification of the kind of public emergency in which a State would be entitled to make derogations from the rights protected by the Covenant which would not be open to abuse.

The present wording requires that the public emergency should be of such a magnitude as to threaten the life of a nation as a whole.

Article 4 rightly does not include war as a form of public emergency, because the United Nations was established with the object of preventing war.

"Public emergency" is a restrictive term which does not cover, for example, natural disasters, which very often, justify a State party in derogating from some, at least, of the rights recognized in the Covenant.

The provision of article 4, paragraph 1, of the Covenant to the effect that the existence of a public emergency should be "officially proclaimed" by the State party concerned is essential in order to prevent States from derogating arbitrarily from their obligations where such action is not warranted by events.

In most countries a public emergency can be declared only under conditions defined by law, and that guarantee would be lost if a requirement of public proclamation were not provided for.

The provisions of article 4 should in no way imply that constitutional and legal limits imposed upon the powers of Governments during a public emergency can be derogated from or that the executive power is not responsible for taking measures which might conflict with national guarantees.

The measures which a State party may take in derogation of its obligations under the Covenant after a public emergency has been proclaimed are subject to three conditions which are specified in paragraph 1 of the article: (*a*) they must be "to the extent strictly required by the exigencies of the situation"; (*b*) they must not be "inconsistent with [the State party's] other obligations under international law"; and (*c*) they must "not involve discrimination solely on the ground of race, colour, sex, language, religion or social origin".

In particular, the measures which may be taken in derogation of the obligations of a State party under the Covenant should not be inconsistent with the purposes and principles of the Charter of the United Nations, the Universal Declaration of Human Rights and other international instruments on human rights.

Paragraph 2 of article 4 of the Covenant enumerates the provisions of the Covenant from which no derogations may be made.

No derogation may be made, even in time of public emergency, from the provisions of the following articles: article 6 (right to life); article 7 (freedom from torture and cruel, inhuman or degrading treatment or punishment and from medical or scientific experimentation); article 8 (freedom from slavery, servitude and forced labour); article 11 (right not to be imprisoned for inability to fulfil a contractual obligation); article 15 (prohibition of retroactive application of criminal law); article 16 (recognition as a person before the law); and article 18 (freedom of thought, conscience and religion).

When a State party avails itself of the right of derogation in time of public emergency, it is required, by paragraph 3 of article 4 of the Covenant, to comply with three steps concerning notifications of its actions. It must in each case "immediately inform" the other States parties, through the intermediary of the Secretary-General: (*a*) of the provisions of the Covenant from which it has derogated; (*b*) of the reasons by which it was actuated; and (*c*) of the date on which it terminates such derogation.

The proclamation of a public emergency and consequential derogation from the provisions of the Covenant is a matter of the gravest concern and the States parties have the right to be notified of such action.

The derogating State should also furnish the reasons by which it was actuated, although this might not include every detail of each particular measure taken. Notification should also be furnished of the date on which the derogation was terminated.

Certain of the international instruments on human rights contain express provisions spelling out that States may interfere with nationally and internationally guaranteed human rights in time of public emergency.

It is often precisely through action of this kind that the rights and freedoms of the individual are violated. States of public emergency and their effects need to be scrutinized by the organs charged with the implementation of the relevant international bill of human rights.

The implementation provisions of the Covenant should apply to article 4 of the Covenant.

The onus of proof as to the existence of a public emergency and to the necessity of the measure should rest on the respondent Government.

Immeasurable criteria such as the margin of appreciation, the onus and standard of proof and the elements of good faith and reasonableness merely constitute useful tools at the disposal of those exercising functions of a judicial or quasi-judicial nature.

States of exception should not always be equated with violations of human rights.

Even in a state of public emergency the fundamental principle of the rule of law should prevail.

In connection with the protection of human rights in a state of public emergency, and in the light and spirit of the conclusions set forth in section A above, the Special Rapporteur proposes that the Sub-Commission on Prevention of Discrimination and Protection of Minorities should consider making the following recommendations to the Commission on Human Rights:

(1) The Commission should recommend to the Economic and Social Council that it authorize the Sub-Commission to elaborate a declaratory resolution containing common principles, guidelines and standards relating to the protection of human rights in time of public emergency.

(2) The Commission should recommend to the Economic and Social Council that it authorize the Sub-Commission to study all other aspects related to the question of the protection of human rights in time of public emergency, including such aspects as whether public emergency is an issue falling within the domestic jurisdiction of a State and the interrelationship of economic and social development and the state of emergency.

**SEE ALSO** *State of Emergency.*

**PUGWASH CONFERENCES ON SCIENCE AND WORLD AFFAIRS.** This non-governmental organization shared the 1995 **NOBEL PEACE PRIZE** with **JOSEPH ROTBLAT,** one of its founders. Cited by the Peace Prize Committee for its efforts "to diminish the part played by nuclear arms in international policies and in the longer run to eliminate such arms," the Pugwash Conferences have stressed the ethical and moral responsibility of scientists for their inventions.

Founded in 1957 by Bertrand Russell, Albert Einstein, and Joseph Rotblat, the group emerged from the first conference held in Pugwash, Nova Scotia,

Canada, which was itself a result of the "Russell-Einstein Manifesto," which declared that nuclear weapons threaten the continued existence of mankind. The group conducts select conferences of scientists for private exchanges on arms control. It has served as a forum for technical and political issues and as a "back channel" for policymakers. Among topics addressed by the conferences have been such complex problems as antiballistic missile systems, test-ban monitoring, and the spread of chemical and biological weapons. The 1995 Prize is the third given specifically to scientists working for nuclear disarmament, the others being to **LINUS PAULING** in 1962 and to the NGO **INTERNATIONAL PHYSICIANS FOR THE PREVENTION OF NUCLEAR WAR** in 1985.

The organization has consultative status (Category II) with the UN **ECONOMIC AND SOCIAL COUNCIL** and has national Pugwash groups in 65 countries. It publishes the quarterly *Pugwash Newsletter* and the series *Annals of Pugwash*.

Pugwash Conferences on Science and World Affairs. Address: 63A Great Russel Street, Flat A, London WC1B 3BJ, UK. Telephone: (44-7) 405-6661. Fax: (44-7) 831-6551. President: Joseph Rotblat.

# Q

**QATAR.** The State of Qatar is an Arab country in western Asia, occupying the Qatar Peninsula that extends into the Persian Gulf from the Arabian Peninsula. It has boundaries with Saudi Arabia and the United Arab Emirates. It achieved independence from Great Britain in 1971 and became a member of the United Nations the same year. Its population is estimated to be 492,000 and includes members of foreign communities needed for the country's socioeconomic development plans. These foreign communities consist of Asians from Iraq, India, Pakistan, Afghanistan, Iran, Thailand, Korea, the Philippines, Japan, and China; Arab and non-Arab nationals from African countries; and Europeans from Great Britain, France, Germany, Italy, Greece, and other countries. The language commonly used is Arabic. Islam is the predominant religion, and all nationals of Qatar are Muslims. Literacy is estimated at 40%.

The government (1994) took the form of a monarchy. The amir, as ruler, is assisted by the 30-member Advisory Council. There is no legislative body as such; all decrees are issued by the amir. There are five courts of justice which proclaim judgements in the name of the amir; only Arab lawyers are permitted to practice before them. There are no political parties.

***RESTRICTIONS ON THE PRACTICE OF LAW.*** In regard to the restrictions placed upon the practice of law, the government provided the following information to the UN **Committee on the Elimination of Racial Discrimination** in a report presented to that body on 11 October 1983 (UN Doc. CERD/C/104/Add. 1, paras. 39–44):

The practice of law and legal consultancy in Qatar are regulated by Act No. 20 of 1980, article 1 of which restricts the exercise of this profession to jurists listed in the permanent or provisional rolls of lawyers. Under articles 2 and 3, inclusion in the permanent and provisional rolls is restricted to Qataris and non-Qatari Arabs, respectively. However, under article 15, lawyers who are not registered in Qatar may be appointed by litigants to plead before the Qatari courts in particular cases, subject to the following conditions:

The lawyer thus appointed must be an Arab national licensed to practise law in his country. He must work in cooperation with a lawyer entered either in the permanent or in the provisional roll in Qatar. Special permission must be obtained from the Minister of Justice. Such treatment must be granted on a reciprocal basis.

This does not constitute discrimination in favour of Arab lawyers. The purpose of this regulation is to further the interests of litigants, since, in addition to familiarity with Arabic, which is the official language of the country, such lawyers are also acquainted with Arab practices, customs and traditions. Moreover, there is considerable similarity between the laws in force in the various Arab countries and it is therefore fairly easy for this category of lawyers to obtain a sound grasp of the laws applicable in the State of Qatar. This type of regulation is applied in a large number of other countries, particularly those whose circumstances are similar to our own.

In a petition presented by 50 prominent Qataris in January 1992, pleas were made for legal, economic, and educational reforms. There was also a call for a consultative assembly which had legislative power.

***REPORT TO THE UN COMMITTEE ON THE ELIMINATION OF RACIAL DISCRIMINATION.*** The eighth periodic report of Quatar (CERD/C/207/Add. 1) under the International Convention on the Elimination of All Forms of Racial Discrimination (see **Racial Discrimination**) was examined by the UN Committee on the Elimination of Racial Discrimination at its 964th and 983rd meetings, held on 5 March 1993, which adopted the following observations (CERD/C/SR. 964 and 983, paras. 87–99):

The report was introduced by the representative of the State party, who underlined that article 9 of the provisional Constitution of Qatar established the equality of all individuals and prohibited the promulgation of laws permitting discrimination on the basis of origin, sex or religion. In addition, article 5 of the provisional Constitution declared the adherence of Qatar to the principles contained in the Charter of the United Nations, which included condemnation of racial discrimination. Discrimination was also prohibited under Islamic law (Shariah), which was the principal source for the legislation of Qatar. Both the International Convention on the Elimination of All Forms of Racial Discrimination and the International Convention on the Suppression and Punishment of the Crime of Apartheid formed part of the domestic law of Qatar and could be invoked before the courts. Courts in Qatar could award compensation to victims of discrimination by invoking article 4 of the Civil Code. However, since acts of racial discrimination were unknown in Qatar, there had not been a need to adopt specific legislation in that regard.

While welcoming the assurances given by the representative that the Convention had been incorporated in domestic law, members of the Committee pointed out that the Convention obligated States parties to undertake legislative, judicial, administrative and other measures to give effect to its provisions. Additionally, legislation expressly prohibiting racial discrimination and racist propaganda would have a useful preventive effect.

Members of the Committee requested further information on the demographic composition of the population and, in particular, statistical indicators on the health, life expectancy and access to housing and education of foreign workers.

With respect to article 2 of the Convention, members of the Committee wished to know whether article 9 of the Constitution, which guaranteed the equality of all individuals in regard to their rights and obligations, also applied to non-citizens; whether non-Arabs were able to acquire Qatar nationality; whether foreign workers were discriminated against; whether the Government intended to adopt legislation prohibiting discrimination against foreign workers; and whether integrationist, multiracial organizations would not be of benefit in Qatar.

In regard to article 5 of the Convention, members asked whether free choice of employment was guaranteed to foreigners; whether foreign workers had access to all professions and trades; whether the Government envisaged measures to eliminate differences between citizens and foreign workers concerning access to all trades; whether non-citizens were eligible to receive social security benefits; and whether freedom to leave the country and return was guaranteed to non-citizens. Noting that the legislation restricting non-Arab lawyers from pleading a case before the courts was discriminatory, members asked for further information on the relevant regulations. With respect to freedom of religion, members asked what facilities were available to non-Muslims for the practice of their religion.

With respect to article 6 of the Convention, members wished to have further information on specific legislation providing for compensation to victims of discrimination, and on the procedures used to decide whether compensation was to be awarded and in what amount, and wished to know what amounts had been awarded in the past as compensation. They also asked what were the respective competences of civil and religious courts in cases concerning racial discrimination; whether the religious courts based their decisions on the Koran, the *sunnah* or on jurisprudence; and what guidelines existed governing access of victims of discrimination to the civil and religious courts. Members also requested further information relating to the role of the Labour Court in protecting persons against discrimination.

Responding to the questions and comments of the members of the Committee, the representative of the State party said that Palestinians had been residing in Qatar for over 40 years and that a number of them had acquired citizenship. During the Gulf war, no Palestinians had been expelled from the country. The Palestinian community enjoyed all rights guaranteed under the law.

Foreign workers signed contracts with their employers for one or two year duration. Medical care was provided free of charge to foreigners and access to medical care was guaranteed to all. Additionally, the right to education was guaranteed to all under the law. The Asiatic and European communities in Qatar had begun to create their own schools under the control of the Ministry of Education and instruction was available in various languages. Freedom of religion was also guaranteed. Anyone could practice the religion of his or her choice, although there were no Christian churches or suddhist temples in Qatar because those religions were celebrated in the homes of their adherents.

The representative stated that the Government envisaged some revision of its laws so that they might conform to modern legislation. Those revisions, if adopted, would accompany the next report Qatar submitted to the Committee. Other questions raised by members of the Committee would also be answered in that report.

The Committee welcomed the Government's willingness in principle to introduce new legislation to bring its existing laws into conformity with the Convention. It repeated its offer of assistance from the advisory services programme of the Centre for Human Rights.

The Committee drew the attention of the Government to General Recommendations I and II and reiterated its request for further demographic data in accordance with general recommendation IV.

While appreciating that there might be little evidence of racial discrimination in Qatar, the Committee emphasized the preventive value of legislative measures.

The Committee noted the view of the Government that the Shariah courts and the civil courts together offered sufficient remedies for any charges of racial discrimination that might be brought. The Committee was concerned about the criteria by which a Shariah court would determine an appropriate punishment and queried the necessity of separate proceedings in the civil court for the victim to obtain compensation in accordance with article 6 of the Convention.

**BIBLIOGRAPHY.** Arab Organization for Human Rights. *Report: Human Rights int he Arab World.* Cairo, Egypt: annual report. NGO report, in Arabic and English.

Birks, J. S., and C. A. Sinclair. *Nature and Process of Laobr Importing: The African in the Gulf States, Kuwait, Bahrain, Qatar, and the United Arab Emirates.* Geneva, Switzerland: ILO, 1978. IGO study, in English.

**QUAID-I-AZAM INTERNATIONAL HUMAN RIGHTS PRIZE.** This annual Prize recognizes outstanding contributions to the promotion and protection of human rights. The Prize is open to individuals only and carries a 500,000 rupee award.

For more information, contact: Quaid-I-Azam Academy, 297 M.A. Jinnah Road, Karachi 5, Pakistan.

**QUIDDE, LUDWIG (1858–1941).** This German historian was awarded the 1927 NOBEL PEACE PRIZE, along with FERDINAND EDOUARD BUISSON, primarily as a symbol of German pacifism at a time when German militarism was again on the rise. Quidde, the founder of the German Peace Society and its president from 1914 to 1929, opposed German militarism during both world wars and was exiled twice for his pacifism.

Independently wealthy, Quidde worked as a historian and editor, founding the *German Review of Histor-*

*ical Sciences* in 1889 and later editing the publication of medieval German Reichstag documents, a post he held until he was removed in 1933 with the ascension of Adolph Hitler to power. His first trouble with the German Government came with his publication of *Caligula: Eine Studie Über Romischen Caesarenwahnsinor* (Leipzig, Germany: Wilhelm Friedrich, 1894), which was ostensibly a historical account of the reign of the Roman emperor Caligula but was widely regarded as an attack on the policies of Kaiser Wilhelm II.

Quidde was active in the international peace movement, and his pacifism carried over into his national politics. He helped to reorganize the German People's Party and served in the Weimar National Assembly.

***BIBLIOGRAPHY.*** Gray, Tony. *Champions of Peace.* London: Paddington Press, 1976.

Schlessinger, Bernard S., and June H. Schlessinger, eds. *Who's Who of Nobel Prize Winners.* Phoenix, AZ, USA: Oryx Press, 1991.

**QUINNIPIAC COLLEGE, THE ALBERT SCHWEITZER INSTITUTE FOR THE HUMANITIES.** See SCHWEITZER INSTITUTE FOR THE HUMANITIES.

# R

**RABIN, YITZHAK (1922–1995).** Yitzhak Rabin, the first prime minister of Israel to be born in the homeland and the first Israeli prime minister to be assassinated by an Israeli citizen, shared the 1994 **NOBEL PEACE PRIZE** with two former opponents: **YASSAR ARAFAT,** the leader of the **PALESTINE LIBERATION ORGANIZATION** (PLO), and **SHIMON PERES,** Rabin's longtime rival within the Israeli Labor Party. In citing the three men for the Prize, the first time a Peace Prize has been shared by more than two people, the Prize Committee stated, "by concluding the Oslo Accords and subsequently following them up, [they] made substantial contributions to a historic process through which peace and cooperation can replace war and hate." On 4 November 1995, after attending a rally in support of the peace process with Peres, Rabin was assassinated by an angry East Bank settler who believed that Rabin had betrayed his country in making peace with the Palestinians.

Yitzhak Rabin was born in Jerusalem in what was then Palestine, to Russian immigrants. He studied agriculture at the Kadoorie Agricultural High School and was accepted at the University of California to study hydraulic engineering. But World War II intervened; he joined the Hagana, the Jewish underground, and was assigned to the Palmach, the secret commando force designed to prevent the Nazis from overruning the Middle East. After the War, Rabin, still with the Palmach, fought against the British who openly opposed the immigration of Holocaust survivors to Palestine; in the summer of 1945, he led a raid at the Atlit detention camp where the British held immigrants, freeing 200 Jewish refugees. He was arrested for his part in the raid and imprisoned for five months.

During the Israeli War of Independence in 1948, Rabin commanded the Palmach's Harel Brigade. When the State of Israel was established, he continued in the armed forces, becoming commander-in-chief of the Northern Front, on the Israel-Syria border, in 1956. In 1964, he was promoted to chief-of-staff of Israel's military forces; in this position, he waged a campaign against the PLO and was often accused of being a warmonger. During the Six-Day War of 1967, Rabin engineered the takeover of the Sinai peninsula, the western bank of the Jordan River, the Gaza Strip, and the Golan Heights, thus tripling the territory of Israel and becoming an Israeli war hero. He was appointed ambassador to the United States in 1968 and was instrumental in negotiating economic and military aid from the Americans. He returned to Israel in 1973, was elected to the Knesset, and took over the leadership of the Labor Party.

Rabin first served as prime minister from 1973 to 1976, resigning in favor of new elections. He withdrew from the elections, however, and lost the leadership of the Labor Party to Peres. He served in the Knesset from 1976 to 1984, when he was appointed defense minister in the coalition government of Shimon Peres and Yitzhak Shamir. In this post, which he was to hold until 1990, Rabin withdrew Israeli forces from Lebanon and dealt unsuccessfully with the Palestinian uprising (*intifada*). It was apparently at this time that he began to devise a political solution to the Palestinian problem. He expressed a willingness to negotiate with the PLO if it would agree to certain conditions, especially a recognition of Israel's right to exist. Because of this courageous stance, Rabin was elected prime minister in the 1992 national elections. Rabin and Peres, Rabin's vice-premier, undertook secret negotiations with the PLO, resulting in the Oslo Accord, which established preliminary Palestinian self-rule. The historic peace agreement was signed in Washington, D.C., on 13 September 1993.

On accepting the Nobel Peace Prize, Rabin said, "The prize is for the whole nation . . . for the bereaved families and the disabled, for the hundreds and thousands who have fought Israel's wars."

**BIBLIOGRAPHY.** *Current Biography,* (Jan. 1995): 42–46. New York: W. H. Wilson, 1995.

Fedarko, Kevin. "Man of Israel," *Time* (13 Nov. 1995): 69–71.

**RACE.** Four statements on the concept of race were prepared by groups of experts on the subject, brought together by the **UNITED NATIONS EDUCATIONAL, SCIENTIFIC AND CULTURAL ORGANIZATION** in 1950, 1951, 1964, and 1967, as part of its program to make known the scientific facts about race and to combat racial prejudice. The findings of the four statements were taken into account in the preparation of the UNESCO Declaration on Race and Racial Prejudice, adopted by the UNESCO General Conference in 1978.

The texts of the four statements are reproduced below. The names and qualifications of the experts responsible for the preparation of each of the statements appear at the end of each. Statement II, entitled "Statement on the Nature of Race and Race Differences," is preceded by an explanation of the reasons for convening the second meeting of experts.

### I. Statement on Race, Prepared at Paris, July 1950

1. Scientists have reached general agreement in recognizing that mankind is one: that all men belong to the same species, *homo sapiens*. It is further generally agreed among scientists that all men are probably derived from the same common stock; and that such differences as exist between different groups of mankind are due to the operation of evolutionary factors of differentiation such as isolation, the drift and random fixation of the material particles which control heredity (the genes), changes in the structure of these particles, hybridization, and natural selection. In these ways groups have arisen of varying stability and degree of differentiation which have been classified in different ways for different purposes.

2. From the biological standpoint, the species *homo sapiens* is made up of a number of populations, each one of which differs from the others in the frequency of one or more genes. Such genes, responsible for the hereditary differences between men, are always few when compared to the whole genetic constitution of man and to the vast number of genes common to all human beings regardless of the population to which they belong. This means that the likenesses among men are far greater than their differences.

3. A race, from the biological standpoint, may therefore be defined as one of the group of populations constituting the species *homo sapiens*. These populations are capable of interbreeding with one another but, by virtue of the isolating barriers which in the past kept them more or less separated, exhibit certain physical differences as a result of their somewhat different biological histories. These represent variations, as it were, on a common theme.

4. In short, the term "race" designates a group or population characterized by some concentrations, relative as to frequency and distribution, of hereditary particles (genes) or physical characters, which appear, fluctuate, and often disappear in the course of time by reason of geographic and/or cultural isolation. The varying manifestations of these traits in different populations are perceived in different ways by each group. What is perceived is largely preconceived, so that each group arbitrarily tends to misinterpret the variability which occurs as a fundamental difference which separates that group from all others.

5. These are the scientific facts. Unfortunately, however, when most people use the term "race" they do not do so in the sense above defined. To most people, a race is any group of people whom they choose to describe as a race. Thus, many national, religious, geographic, linguistic or cultural groups have, in such loose usage, been called "race", when obviously Americans are not a race, nor are Englishmen, nor Frenchmen, nor any other national group. Catholics, Prot-

estants, Moslems, and Jews are not races, nor are groups who speak English or any other language thereby definable as a race; people who live in Iceland or England or India are not races; nor are people who are culturally Turkish or Chinese or the like thereby describable as races.

6. National, religious, geographic, linguistic and cultural groups do not necessarily coincide with racial groups: and the cultural traits of such groups have no demonstrated genetic connexion with racial traits. Because serious errors of this kind are habitually committed when the term "race" is used in popular parlance, it would be better when speaking of human races to drop the term "race" altogether and speak of ethnic groups.

7. Now what has the scientist to say about the groups of mankind which may be recognized at the present time? Human races can be and have been differently classified by different anthropologists, but at the present time most anthropologists agree on classifying the greater part of the present-day mankind into three major divisions as follows: (a) the Mongoloid division; (b) the Negroid division; and (c) the Caucasoid division. The biological processes which the classifier has here embalmed, as it were, are dynamic, not static. These divisions were not the same in the past as they are at present, and there is every reason to believe that they will change in the future.

8. Many sub-groups or ethnic groups within these divisions have been described. There is no general agreement upon their number, and in any event most ethnic groups have not yet been either studied or described by the physical anthropologists.

9. Whatever classification the anthropologist makes of man, he never includes mental characteristics as part of those classifications. It is now generally recognized that intelligence tests do not in themselves enable us to differentiate safely between what is due to innate capacity and what is the result of environmental influences, training and education. Wherever it has been possible to make allowances for differences in environmental opportunities, the tests have shown essential similarity in mental characters among all human groups. In short, given similar degrees of cultural opportunity to realize their potentialities, the average achievement of the members of each ethnic group is about the same. The scientific investigations of recent years fully support the dictum of Confucius (551–478 b.c.): "Men's natures are alike; it is their habits that carry them far apart."

10. The scientific material available to us at present does not justify the conclusion that inherited genetic differences are a major factor in producing the differences between the cultures and cultural achievements of different peoples or groups. It does indicate, however, that the history of the cultural experience which each group has undergone is the major factor in explaining such differences. The one trait which above all others has been at a premium in the evolution of men's mental characters has been educability, plasticity. This is a trait which all human beings possess. It is indeed, a species character of *homo sapiens*.

11. So far as temperament is concerned, there is no definite evidence that there exist inborn differences between human groups. There is evidence that whatever group differences of the kind there might be are greatly overridden by the individual differences, and by the differences springing from environmental factors.

12. As for personality and character, these may be considered raceless. In every human group a rich variety of personality and character types will be found, and there is no

reason for believing that any human group is richer than any other in these respects.

13. With respect to race mixture, the evidence points unequivocally to the fact that this has been going on from the earliest times. Indeed, one of the chief processes of race formation and race extinction or absorption is by means of hybridization between races or ethnic groups. Furthermore, no convincing evidence has been adduced that race mixture of itself produces biologically bad effects. Statements that human hybrids frequently show undesirable traits, both physically and mentally, physical disharmonies and mental degeneracies, are not supported by the facts. There is, therefore, no biological justification for prohibiting intermarriage between persons of different ethnic groups.

14. The biological fact of race and the myth of ''race'' should be distinguished. For all practical social purposes ''race'' is not so much a biological phenomenon as a social myth. The myth of ''race'' has created an enormous amount of human and social damage. In recent years it has taken a heavy toll in human lives and caused untold suffering. It still prevents the normal development of millions of human beings and deprives civilization of the effective co-operation of productive minds. The biological differences between ethnic groups should be disregarded from the standpoint of social acceptance and social action. The unity of mankind from both the biological and social viewpoints is the main thing. To recognize this and to act accordingly is the first requirement of modern man. It is but to recognize what a great biologist wrote in 1875: ''As man advances in civilization, and small tribes are united into larger communities, the simplest reason would tell each individual that he ought to extend his social instincts and sympathies to all the members of the same nation, though personally unknown to him. This point being once reached, there is only an artificial barrier to prevent his sympathies extending to the men of all nations and races.'' These are the words of Charles Darwin in *The Descent of Man* (2nd ed., 1875, p. 187–188). And, indeed, the whole of human history shows that a co-operative spirit is not only natural to men, but more deeply rooted than any self-seeking tendencies. If this were not so we should not see the growth of integration and organization of his communities which the centuries and the millenniums plainly exhibit.

15. We now have to consider the bearing of these statements on the problem of human equality. It must be asserted with the utmost emphasis that equality as an ethical principle in no way depends upon the assertion that human beings are in fact equal in endowment. Obviously individuals in all ethnic groups vary greatly among themselves in endowment. Nevertheless, the characteristics in which human groups differ from one another are often exaggerated and used as a basis for questioning the validity of equality in the ethical sense. For this purpose we have thought it worth while to set out in a formal manner what is at present scientifically established concerning individual and group differences.

(a) In matters of race, the only characteristics which anthropologists can effectively use as a basis or classifications are physical and physiological.

(b) According to present knowledge there is no proof that the groups of mankind differ in their innate mental characteristics, whether in respect of intelligence or temperament. The scientific evidence indicates that the range of mental capacities in all ethnic groups is much the same.

(c) Historical and sociological studies support the view that genetic differences are not of importance in determining the social and cultural differences between different groups of *homo sapiens*, and that the social and cultural

changes in different groups have, in the main, been independent of changes in inborn constitution. Vast social changes have occurred which were not in any way connected with changes in racial type.

(d) There is no evidence that race mixture as such produces bad results from the biological point of view. The social results of race mixture whether for good or ill are to be traced to social factors.

(e) All normal human beings are capable of learning to share in a common life, to understand the nature of mutual service and reciprocity, and to respect social obligations and contracts. Such biological differences as exist between members of different ethnic groups have no relevance to problems of social and political organization, moral life and communication between human beings.

Lastly, biological studies lend support to the ethic of universal brotherhood; for man is born with drives toward co-operation, and unless these drives are satisfied, men and nations alike fall ill. Man is born a social being who can reach his fullest development only through interaction with his fellows. The denial at any point of this social bond between men and man brings with it disintegration. In this sense, every man is his brother's keeper. For every man is a piece of the continent, a part of the main, because he is involved in mankind.

Original statement drafted at Unesco House, Paris, by the following experts: Professor Ernest Beaglehole (New Zealand); Professor Juan Comas (Mexico); Professor L. A. Costa Pinto (Brazil); Professor Franklin Frazier (United States of America); Professor Morris Ginsberg (United Kingdom); Dr. Humayun Kabir (India); Professor Claude Levi-Strauss (France); Professor Ashley Montagu (United States of America) (rapporteur). Text revised by Professor Ashley Montagu, after criticism submitted by Professors Hadley Cantril, E. G. Conklin, Gunnar Dahlberg, Theodosius Dobzhansky, L. C. Dunn, Donald Hager, Julian S. Huxley, Otto Klineberg, Wilbert Moore, H. J. Muller, Gunnar Myrdal, Joseph Needham, Curt Stern.

## II. Statement on the Nature of Race and Race Differences, Prepared at Paris, June 1951

*[Explanation:]* Race is a question of interest to many different kinds of people, not only to the public at large, but to sociologists, anthropologists and biologists, especially those dealing with problems of genetics. At the first discussion on the problem of race, it was chiefly sociologists who gave their opinions and framed the "Statement on Race". That statement had a good effect, but it did not carry the authority of just those groups within whose special province fall the biological problems of race, namely the physical anthropologists and geneticists. Secondly, the first statement did not, in all its details, carry conviction of these groups and, because of this, it was not supported by many authorities in these two fields.

In general, the chief conclusions of the first statement were sustained, but with differences in emphasis and with some important deletions.

There was no delay or hesitation or lack of unanimity in reaching the primary conclusion that there were no scientific grounds whatever for the racialist position regarding purity of race and the hierarchy of inferior and superior races to which this leads.

We agreed that all races were mixed and that intraracial variability in most biological characters was as great as, if not greater than, interracial variability.

We agreed that races had reached their present states by the operation of evolutionary factors by which different proportions of similar hereditary elements (genes) had become characteristic of different, partially separated groups. The source of these elements seemed to all of us to be the variability which arises by random mutation, and the isolating factors bringing about racial differentiation by preventing intermingling of groups with different mutations, chiefly geographical for the main groups such as African, European and Asiatic.

Man, we recognized, is distinguished as much by his culture as by his biology, and it was clear to all of us that many of the factors leading to the formation of minor races of men have been cultural. Anything that tends to prevent free exchange of genes amongst groups is a potential race-making factor and these partial barriers may be religious, social and linguistic, as well as geographical.

We were careful to avoid dogmatic definitions of race, since, as a product of evolutionary factors, it is a dynamic rather than a static concept. We were equally careful to avoid saying that, because races were all variable and many of them graded into each other, therefore races did not exist. The physical anthropologists and the man in the street both know that races exist; the former, from the scientifically recognizable and measurable congeries of traits which he uses in classifying the varieties of man; the latter from the immediate evidence of his senses when he sees an African, a European, an Asiatic and an American Indian together.

We had no difficulty in agreeing that no evidence of differences in innate mental ability between different racial groups has been adduced, but that here too intraracial variability is at least as great as interracial variability. We agreed that psychological traits could not be used in classifying races, nor could they serve as parts of racial descriptions.

We were fortunate in having as members of our conference several scientists who had made special studies of the results of intermarriage between members of different races. This meant that our conclusion that race mixture in general did not lead to disadvantageous results was based on actual experience as well as upon study of the literature. Many of our members thought it quite likely that hydridization of different races could lead to biologically advantageous results, although there was insufficient evidence to support any conclusion.

Since race, as a word, has become coloured by its misuse in connexion with national, linguistic and religious differences, and by its deliberate abuse by racialists, we tried to find a new word to express the same meaning of a biologically differentiated group. On this we did not succeed, but agreed to reserve race as the word to be used for anthropological classification of groups showing definite combinations of physical (including physiological) traits in characteristic proportions.

We also tried hard, but again we failed, to reach some general statement about the inborn nature of man with respect to his behaviour toward his fellows. It is obvious that members of a group show co-operative or associative behaviour towards each other, while members of different groups may show aggressive behaviour towards each other and both of these attitudes may occur within the same individual. We recognized that the understanding of the psychological origin of race prejudice was an important problem which called for further study.

Nevertheless, having regard to the limitations of our present knowledge, all of us believed that the biological differences found amongst human racial groups can in no case justify the views of racial inequality which have been based on ignorance and prejudice, and that all of the differences which we know can well be disregarded for all ethical human purposes.

1. Scientists are generally agreed that all men living today belong to a single species, *homo sapiens*, and are derived from a common stock, even though there is some dispute as to when and how different human groups diverged from this common stock.

The concept of race is unanimously regarded by anthropologists as a classificatory device providing a zoological frame within which the various groups of mankind may be arranged and by means of which studies of evolutionary processes can be facilitated. In its anthropological sense, the word "race" should be reserved for groups of mankind possessing well-developed and primarily heritable physical differences from other groups. Many populations can be so classified but, because of the complexity of human history, there are also many populations which cannot easily be fitted into a racial classification.

2. Some of the physical differences between human groups are due to differences in hereditary constitution and some to differences in the environments in which they have been brought up. In most cases, both influences have been at work. The science of genetics suggests that the hereditary differences among populations of a single species are the results of the action of two sets of processes. On the one hand, the genetic composition of isolated populations is constantly but gradually being altered by natural selection and by occasional changes (mutations) in the material particles (genes) which control heredity. Populations are also affected by fortuitous changes in gene frequency and by marriage customs. On the other hand, crossing is constantly breaking down the differentiations so set up. The new mixed populations, in so far as they, in turn, become isolated, are subject to the same processes, and these may lead to further changes. Existing races are merely the result, considered at a particular moment in time, of the total effect of such processes on the human species. The hereditary characters to be used in the classification of human groups, the limits of their variation within these groups, and thus the extent of the classificatory sub-divisions adopted may legitimately differ according to the scientific purpose in view.

3. National, religious, geographical, linguistic and cultural groups do not necessarily coincide with racial groups; and the cultural traits of such groups have no demonstrated connexion with racial traits. Americans are not a race, nor are Frenchmen, nor Germans; nor *ipso facto* is any other national group. Moslems and Jews are no more races than are Roman Catholics and Protestants; nor are people who live in Iceland or Britain or India, or who speak English or any other language, or who are culturally Turkish or Chinese and the like, thereby describable as races. The use of the term "race" in speaking of such groups may be a serious error, but it is one which is habitually committed.

4. Human races can be, and have been, classified in different ways by different anthropologists. Most of them agree in classifying the greater part of existing mankind into at least three large units, which may be called major groups (in French *grand-races*, in German *Hauptrassen*). Such a classification does not depend on any single physical character, nor does for example, skin colour by itself necessarily distinguish one major group from another. Furthermore, so far as it has been possible to analyse them, the differences in physical structure which distinguish one major group from another give no support to popular notions of any general "superi-

ority" or "inferiority" which are sometimes implied in referring to these groups.

Broadly speaking, individuals belonging to different major groups of mankind are distinguishable by virtue of their physical character, but individual members, or small groups belonging to different races within the same major group are usually not so distinguishable. Even the major groups grade into each other, and the physical traits by which they and the races within them are characterized overlap considerably. With respect to most, if not all, measurable characters, the differences among individuals belonging to the same race are greater than the differences that occur between the observed averages for two or more races within the same major group.

5. Most anthropologists do not include mental characteristics in their classification of human races. Studies within a single race have shown that both innate capacity and environmental opportunity determine the results of tests of intelligence and temperament, though their relative importance is disputed.

When intelligence tests, even non-verbal, are made on a group of non-literate people, their scores are usually lower than those of more civilized people. It has been recorded that different groups of the same race occupying similarly high levels of civilization may yield considerable differences in intelligence tests. When, however, the two groups have been brought up from childhood in similar environments, the differences are usually very slight. Moreover, there is good evidence that, given similar opportunities, the average performance (that is to say, the performance of the individual who is representative because he is surpassed by as many as he surpasses), and the variation round it, do not differ appreciably from one race to another.

Even those psychologists who claim to have found the greatest differences in intelligence between groups of different racial origin and have contended that they are hereditary, always report that some members of the group of inferior performance surpass not merely the lowest ranking member of the superior group but also the average of its members. In any case, it has never been possible to separate members of two groups on the basis of mental capacity, as they can often be separated on a basis of religion, skin colour, hair form or language. It is possible, though not proved, that some types of innate capacity for intellectual and emotional responses are commoner in one human group than in another, but it is certain that, within a single group, innate capacities vary as much as, if not more than, they do between different groups.

The study of the heredity of psychological characteristics is beset with difficulties. We know that certain mental diseases and defects are transmitted from one generation to the next, but we are less familiar with the part played by heredity in the mental life of normal individuals. The normal individual, irrespective of race, is essentially educable. It follows that his intellectual and moral life is largely conditioned by his training and by his physical and social environment.

It often happens that a national group may appear to be characterized by particular psychological attributes. The superficial view would be that this is due to race. Scientifically, however, we realize that any common psychological attribute is more likely to be due to a common historical and social background, and that such attributes may obscure the fact that, within different populations consisting of many human types, one will find approximately the same range of temperament and intelligence.

6. The scientific material available to us at present does not justify the conclusion that inherited genetic differences are a major factor in producing the differences between the cultures and cultural achievements of different peoples or groups. It does indicate, on the contrary, that a major factor in explaining such differences is the cultural experience which each group has undergone.

7. There is no evidence for the existence of so-called "pure" races. Skeletal remains provide the basis of our limited knowledge about earlier races. In regard to race mixture, the evidence points to the fact that human hybridization has been going on for an indefinite but considerable time. Indeed, one of the processes of race formation and race extinction or absorption is by means of hybridization between races. As there is no reliable evidence that disadvantageous effects are produced thereby, no biological justification exists for prohibiting intermarriage between persons of different races.

8. We now have to consider the bearing of these statements on the problem of human equality. We wish to emphasize that equality of opportunity and equality in law in no way depend, as ethical principles, upon the assertion that human beings are in fact equal in endowment.

9. We have thought it worth while to set out in a formal manner what is at present scientifically established concerning individual and group differences:

(a) In matters of race, the only characteristics which anthropologists have so far been able to use effectively as a basis for classification are physical (anatomical and physiological).

(b) Available scientific knowledge provides no basis for believing that the groups of mankind differ in their innate capacity for intellectual and emotional development.

(c) Some biological differences between human beings within a single race may be as great as, or greater than, the same biological differences between races.

(d) Vast social changes have occurred that have not been connected in any way with changes in racial type. Historical and sociological studies thus support the view that genetic differences are of little significance in determining the social and cultural differences between different groups of men.

(e) There is no evidence that race mixture produces disadvantageous results from a biological point of view. The social results of race mixture, whether for good or ill, can generally be traced to social factors.

Text drafted at Unesco House, Paris, on 8 June 1951, by: Professor R. A. M. Borgman, Royal Tropical Institute, Amsterdam; Professor Gunnar Dahlberg, Director, State Institute for Human Genetics and Race Biology, University of Uppsala; Professor L. C. Dunn, Department of Zoology, Columbia University, New York; Professor J. B. S. Haldane, Head, Department of Biometry, University College, London; Professor M. F. Ashley Montagu, Chairman, Department of Anthropology, Rutgers University, New Brunswick, N.J.; Dr. A. E. Mourant, Director, Blood Group Reference Laboratory, Lister Institute, London; Professor Hans Nachtscheim, Director, Institut für Genetik, Freie Universität, Berlin; Dr. Eugène Schreider, Directeur adjoint du Laboratoire d'Anthropologie Physique de l'Ecole des Hautes Etudes, Paris; Professor Harry L. Shapiro, Chairman, Department of Anthropology, American Museum of Natural History, New York; Dr. J. C. Trevor, Faculty of Archaeology and Anthropology, University of Cambridge; Dr. Henri V. Vallois, Professeur au Museum d'Histoire Naturelle, Directeur du Musée de l'Homme, Paris; Professor S. Zuckerman, Head, Department of Anatomy, Medical School, University of Birmingham; Professor Th. Dobzhansky, Department of Zoology, Columbia University, New York; Dr. Julian Huxley contributed to the final wording.

### III. Proposals on the Biological Aspects of Race, Prepared at Moscow, 18 August 1964

The undersigned, assembled by Unesco in order to give their views on the biological aspects of the race question and in particular to formulate the biological part for a statement foreseen for 1966 and intended to bring up to date and to complete the declaration on the nature of race and racial differences signed in 1951, have unanimously agreed on the following:

1. All men living today belong to a single species, *homo sapiens,* and are derived from a common stock. There are differences of opinion regarding how and when different human groups diverged from this common stock.

2. Biological differences between human beings are due to differences in hereditary constitution and to the influence of the environment on this genetic potential. In most cases, those differences are due to the interaction of these two sets of factors.

3. There is great genetic diversity within all human populations. Pure races—in the sense of genetically homogeneous populations—do not exist in the human species.

4. There are obvious physical differences between populations living in different geographical areas of the world, in their average appearance. Many of these differences have a genetic component.

Most often the latter consist in differences in the frequency of the same hereditary characters.

5. Different classifications of mankind into major stocks, and of those into more restricted categories (races, which are groups of populations, or single populations) have been proposed on the basis of hereditary physical traits. Nearly all classifications recognize at least three major stocks.

Since the pattern of geographic variation of the characteristics used in racial classification is a complex one, and since this pattern does not present any major discontinuity, these classifications, whatever they are, cannot claim to classify mankind into clearcut categories; moreover, on account of the complexities of human history, it is difficult to determine the place of certain groups within these racial classifications, in particular that of certain intermediate populations.

Many anthropologists, while stressing the importance of human variation, believe that the scientific interest of these classifications is limited, and even that they carry the risk of inviting abusive generalizations.

Differences between individuals within a race or within a population are often greater than the average differences between races or populations.

Some of the variable distinctive traits which are generally chosen as criteria to characterize a race are either independently inherited or show only varying degrees of association between them within each population. Therefore, the combination of these traits in most individuals does not correspond to the typological racial characterization.

6. In man as well as in animals, the genetic composition of each population is subject to the modifying influence of diverse factors: natural selection, tending towards adaptation to the environment, fortuitous mutations which lead to modifications of the molecules of deoxyribonucleic acid which determine heredity, or random modifications in the frequency of qualitative hereditary characters, to an extent dependent on the patterns of mating and the size of populations.

Certain physical characters have a universal biological value for the survival of the human species, irrespective of the environment. The differences on which racial classifications are based do not affect these characters, and therefore, it is not possible from the biological point of view to speak in any way whatsoever of a general inferiority or superiority of this or that race.

7. Human evolution presents attributes of capital importance which are specific to the species.

The human species which is now spread over the whole world, has a past rich in migrations, in territorial expansions and contractions.

As a consequence, general adaptability to the most diverse environments is in man more pronounced than his adaptation to specific environments.

For long millenniums progress made by man, in any field, seems to have been increasingly, if not exclusively, based on culture and the transmission of cultural achievements and not on the transmission of genetic endowment. This implies a modification in the role of natural selection in man today.

On account of the mobility of human populations and of social factors, mating between members of different human groups which tend to mitigate the differentiations acquired, has played a much more important role in human history than in that of animals. The history of any human population or of any human race, is rich in instances of hybridization and those tend to become more and more numerous.

For man, the obstacles to interbreeding are geographical as well as social and cultural.

8. At all times, the hereditary characteristics of the human populations are in dynamic equilibrium as a result of this interbreeding and of the differentiation mechanisms which were mentioned before. As entities defined by sets of distinctive traits, human races are at any time in a process of emergence and dissolution.

Human races in general present a far less clearcut characterization than many animal races and they cannot be compared at all to races of domestic animals, these being the result of heightened selection for special purposes.

9. It has never been proved that interbreeding has biological disadvantages for mankind as a whole.

On the contrary, it contributes to the maintenance of biological ties between human groups and thus to the unity of the species in its diversity.

The biological consequences of a marriage depend only on the individual genetic make-up of the couple and not on their race.

Therefore, no biological justification exists for prohibiting intermarriage between persons of different races, or for advising against it on racial grounds.

10. Man since his origin has at his disposal ever more efficient cultural means of nongenetic adaptation.

11. Those cultural factors which break social and geographic barriers, enlarge the size of the breeding populations and so act upon their genetic structure by diminishing the random fluctuations (genetic drift).

12. As a rule, the major stocks extend over vast territories encompassing many diverse populations which differ in language, economy, culture, etc.

There is no national, religious, geographic, linguistic or cultural group which constitutes a race *ipso facto*; the concept of race is purely biological.

However, human beings who speak the same language and share the same culture have a tendency to intermarry, and often there is as a result a certain degree of coincidence between physical traits on the one hand, and linguistic and cultural traits on the other. But there is no known causal nexus between these and therefore it is not justifiable to attribute cultural characteristics to the influence of the genetic inheritance.

13. Most racial classifications of mankind do not include mental traits or attributes as a taxonomic criterion.

Heredity may have an influence in the variability shown by individuals within a given population in their responses to the psychological tests currently applied.

However, no difference has ever been detected convincingly in the hereditary endowments of human groups in regard to what is measured by these tests. On the other hand, ample evidence attests to the influence of physical, cultural and social environment on differences in response to these tests.

The study of this question is hampered by the very great difficulty of determining what part heredity plays in the average differences observed in so-called tests of overall intelligence between populations of different cultures.

The genetic capacity for intellectual development, like certain major anatomical traits peculiar to the species, is one of the biological traits essential for its survival in any natural or social environment.

The peoples of the world today appear to possess equal biological potentialities for attaining any civilizational level. Differences in the achievements of different peoples must be attributed solely to their cultural history.

Certain psychological traits are at times attributed to particular peoples. Whether or not such assertions are valid, we do not find any basis for ascribing such traits to hereditary factors, until proof to the contrary is given.

Neither in the field of hereditary potentialities concerning the overall intelligence and the capacity for cultural development, nor in that of physical traits, is there any justification for the concept of "inferior" and "superior" races.

The biological data given above stand in open contradiction to the tenets of racism. Racist theories can in no way pretend to have any scientific foundation and the anthropologists should endeavour to prevent the results of their researches from being used in such a biased way that they would serve non-scientific ends.

[Statement prepared by the following experts:] Professor Nigel Barnicot, Department of Anthropology, University College, London; Professor Jean Benoist, Director, Department of Anthropology, University of Montreal, Montreal; Professor Tadeusz Bielicki, Institute of Anthropology, Polish Academy of Sciences, Wroclaw; Dr. A. E. Boyo, Head, Federal Malaria Research Institute, Department of Pathology and Haematology, Lagos University Medical School, Lagos; Professor V. V. Bunak, Institute of Ethnography, Moscow; Professor Carleton S. Coon, Curator, The University Museum, University of Pennsylvania, Philadelphia, Pa. (United States); Professor G. F. Debetz, Institute of Ethnography, Moscow; Mrs. Adelaide G. de Diaz Ungria, Curator, Museum of Natural Sciences, Caracas; Professor Santiago Genoves, Institute of Historical Research, Faculty of Sciences, University of Mexico, Mexico; Professor Robert Gessain, Director, Centre of Anthropological Research, Musée de l'Homme, Paris; Professor Jean Hiernaux, (Scientific Director of the meeting), Laboratory of Anthropology, Faculty of Sciences, University of Paris, Institute of Sociology, Free University of Brussels; Dr. Yaya Kane, Director, Senegal National Centre of Blood Transfusion, Dakar; Professor Ramakhrishna Mukherjee, Head, Sociological Research Unit, Indian Statistical Institute, Calcutta; Professor Bernard Rensch, Zoological Institute, Westfälische Wilhelms-Universität, Münster (Federal

Republic of Germany); Professor Y. Y. Roguinski, Institute of Ethnography, Moscow; Professor Francisco M. Salzano, Institute of Natural Sciences, Pôrto Alegre, Rio Grande do Sul (Brazil); Professor Alf Sommerfelt, Rector, Oslo University, Oslo; Professor James N. Spuhler, Department of Anthropology, University of Michigan, Ann Arbor, Mich. (United States); Professor Hisashi Suzuki, Department of Anthropology, Faculty of Science, University of Tokyo, Tokyo; Professor J. A. Valsik, Department of Anthropology and Genetics, J. A. Komensky University, Bratislava (Czechoslovakia); Dr. Joseph S. Weiner, London School of Hygiene and Tropical Medicine, University of London, London; Professor V. P. Yakimov, Moscow State University, Institute of Anthropology, Moscow.

### IV. Statement on Race and Racial Prejudice, Prepared at Paris, September 1967

1. "All men are born free and equal both in dignity and in rights." This universally proclaimed democratic principle stands in jeopardy wherever political, economic, social and cultural inequalities affect human group relations. A particularly striking obstacle to the recognition of equal dignity for all is racism. Racism continues to haunt the world. As a major social phenomenon it requires the attention of all students of the sciences of man.

2. Racism stultifies the development of those who suffer from it, perverts those who apply it, divides nations within themselves, aggravates international conflict and threatens world peace.

3. Conference of experts meeting in Paris in September 1967, agreed that racist doctrines lack any scientific basis whatsoever. It reaffirmed the propositions adopted by the international meeting held in Moscow in 1964 which was called to re-examine the biological aspects of the statements on race and racial differences issued in 1950 and 1951. In particular, it draws attention to the following points:

(a) All men living today belong to the same species and descend from the same stock.

(b) The division of the human species into "races" is partly conventional and partly arbitrary and does not imply any hierarchy whatsoever. Many anthropologists stress the importance of human variation, but believe that 'racial' divisions have limited scientific interest and may even carry the risk of inviting abusive generalization.

(c) Current biological knowledge does not permit us to impute cultural achievements to differences in genetic potential. Differences in the achievements of different peoples should be attributed solely to their cultural history. The peoples of the world today appear to possess equal biological potentialities for attaining any level of civilization. Racism grossly falsifies the knowledge of human biology.

4. The human problems arising from so-called "race" relations are social in origin rather than biological. A basic problem is racism, namely, antisocial beliefs and acts which are based on the fallacy that discriminatory intergroup relations are justifiable on biological grounds.

5. Groups commonly evaluate their characteristics in comparison with others. Racism falsely claims that there is a scientific basis for arranging groups hierarchically in terms of psychological and cultural characteristics that are immutable and innate. In this way it seeks to make existing differences appear inviolable as a means of permanently maintaining current relations between groups.

6. Faced with the exposure of the falsity of its biological

doctrines, racism finds ever new stratagems for justifying the inequality of groups. It points to the fact that groups do not intermarry, a fact which follows, in part, from the divisions created by racism. It uses this fact to argue the thesis that this absence of intermarriage derives from differences of a biological order. Whenever it fails in its attempts to prove that the source of group differences lies in the biological field, it falls back upon justifications in terms of divine purpose, cultural differences, disparity of educational standards or some other doctrine which would serve to mask its continued racist beliefs. Thus, many of the problems which racism presents in the world today do not arise merely from its open manifestations, but from the activities of those who discriminate on racial grounds but are unwilling to acknowledge it.

7. Racism has historical roots. It has not been a universal phenomenon. Many contemporary societies and cultures show little trace of it. It was not evident for long periods in world history. Many forms of racism have arisen out of the conditions of conquest, out of the justification of Negro slavery and its aftermath of racial inequality in the West, and out of the colonial relationship. Among other examples is that of anti-semitism, which has played a particular role in history, with Jews being the chosen scapegoat to take the blame for problems and crises met by many societies.

8. The anti-colonial revolution of the twentieth century has opened up new possibilities for eliminating the scourge of racism. In some formerly dependent countries, people formerly classified as inferior have for the first time obtained full political rights. Moreover, the participation of formerly dependent nations in international organizations on terms of equality has done much to undermine racism.

9. There are, however, some instances in certain societies in which groups, victims of racialistic practices, have themselves applied doctrines with racist implications in their struggle for freedom. Such an attitude is a secondary phenomenon, a reaction stemming from men's search for an identity which prior racist theory and racialistic practices denied them. None the less, the new forms of racist ideology, resulting from this prior exploitation, have no justification in biology. They are a product of a political struggle and have no scientific foundation.

10. In order to undermine racism it is not sufficient that biologists should expose its fallacies. It is also necessary that psychologists and sociologists should demonstrate its causes. The social structure is always an important factor. However, within the same social structure, there may be great individual variation in racialistic behaviour, associated with the personality of the individuals and their personal circumstances.

11. The committee of experts agreed on the following conclusions about the social causes of race prejudice:

(a) Social and economic causes of racial prejudice are particularly observed in settler societies wherein are found conditions of great disparity of power and property, in certain urban areas where there have emerged ghettoes in which individuals are deprived of equal access to employment, housing, political participation, education, and the administration of justice, and in many societies where social and economic tasks which are deemed to be contrary to the ethics or beneath the dignity of its members are assigned to a group of different origins who are derided, blamed, and punished for taking on these tasks.

(b) Individuals with certain personality troubles may be particularly inclined to adopt and manifest racial prejudices. Small groups, associations, and social movements of a certain kind sometimes preserve and transmit racial prejudices. The foundations of the prejudices lie, however, in the economic and social system of a society.

(c) Racism tends to be cumulative. Discrimination deprives a group of equal treatment and presents that group as a problem. The group then tends to be blamed for its own condition, leading to further elaboration of racist theory.

12. The major techniques for coping with racism involve changing those social situations which give rise to prejudice, preventing the prejudiced from acting in accordance with their beliefs, and combating the false beliefs themselves.

13. It is recognized that the basically important changes in the social structure that may lead to the elimination of racial prejudice may require decisions of a political nature. It is also recognized, however, that certain agencies of enlightenment, such as education and other means of social and economic advancement, mass media, and law can be immediately and effectively mobilized for the elimination of racial prejudice.

14. The school and other instruments for social and economic progress can be one of the most effective agents for the achievement of broadened understanding and the fulfilment of the potentialities of man. They can equally much be used for the perpetuation of discrimination and inequality. It is therefore essential that the resources for education and for social and economic action of all nations be employed in two ways:

(a) The schools should ensure that their curricula contain scientific understandings about race and human unity, and that invidious distinctions about peoples are not made in texts and classrooms.

(b) (i) Because the skills to be gained in formal and vocational education become increasingly important with the processes of technological development, the resources of the schools and other resources should be fully available to all parts of the population with neither restriction nor discrimination;

(ii) Furthermore, in cases where, for historical reasons, certain groups have a lower average education and economic standing, it is the responsibility of the society to take corrective measures. These measures should ensure, so far as possible, that the limitations of poor environments are not passed on to the children.

In view of the importance of teachers in any educational programme, special attention should be given to their training. Teachers should be made conscious of the degree to which they reflect the prejudices which may be current in their society. They should be encouraged to avoid these prejudices.

15. Governmental units and other organizations concerned should give special attention to improving the housing situations and work opportunities available to victims of racism. This will not only counteract the effects of racism, but in itself can be a positive way of modifying racist attitudes and behaviour.

16. The media of mass communication are increasingly important in promoting knowledge and understanding, but their exact potentiality is not fully known. Continuing research into the social utilization of the media is needed in order to assess their influence in relation to formation of attitudes and behavioural patterns in the field of race prejudice and race discrimination. Because the mass media reach vast numbers of people at different educational and social levels, their role in encouraging or combating race prejudice can be crucial. Those who work in these media should maintain a positive approach to the promotion of understanding between groups and populations. Represen-

tation of peoples in stereotypes and holding them up to ridicule should be avoided. Attachment to news reports of racial designations which are not germane to the accounts should also be avoided.

17. Law is among the most important means of ensuring equality between individuals and one of the most effective means of fighting racism.

The Universal Declaration of Human Rights of 10 December 1948 and the related international agreements and conventions which have taken effect subsequently can contribute effectively, on both the national and international level, to the fight against any injustice of racist origin.

National legislation is a means of effectively outlawing racist propaganda and acts based upon racial discrimination. Moreover, the policy expressed in such legislation must bind not only the courts and judges charged with its enforcement, but also all agencies of government of whatever level or whatever character.

It is not claimed that legislation can immediately eliminate prejudice. Nevertheless, by being a means of protecting the victims of acts based upon prejudice, and by setting a moral example backed by the dignity of the courts, it can, in the long run, even change attitudes.

18. Ethnic groups which represent the object of some form of discrimination are sometimes accepted and tolerated by dominating groups at the cost of their having to abandon completely their cultural identity. It should be stressed that the effort of these ethnic groups to preserve their cultural values should be encouraged. They will thus be better able to contribute to the enrichment of the total culture of humanity.

19. Racial prejudice and discrimination in the world today arise from historical and social phenomena and falsely claim the sanction of science. It is, therefore, the responsibility of all biological and social scientists, philosophers, and others working in related disciplines, to ensure that the results of their research are not misused by those who wish to propagate racial prejudice and encourage discrimination.

This statement was prepared by a committee of experts on race and racial prejudice which met at Unesco House, Paris, from 18 to 26 September 1967. The following experts took part in the committee's work: Professor Muddathir Abdel Rahim, University of Khartoum (Sudan); Professor Georges Balandier, Université de Paris (France); Professor Celio de Oliveira Borja, University of Guanabara (Brazil); Professor Lloyd Braithwaite, University of the West Indies (Jamaica); Professor Leonard Broom, University of Texas (United States); Professor G. F. Debetz, Institute of Ethnography, Moscow (U.S.S.R.); Professor J. Djordjevic, University of Belgrade (Yugoslavia); Dean Clarence Clyde Ferguson, Howard University (United States); Dr. Dharam P. Ghai, University College (Kenya); Professor Louis Guttman, Hebrew University (Israel); Professor Jean Hiernaux, Université Libre de Bruxelles (Belgium); Professor A. Kloskowska, University of Lodz (Poland); Judge Kéba M'Baye, President of the Supreme Court (Senegal); Professor John Rex, University of Durham (United Kingdom); Professor Mariano R. Solveira, University of Havana (Cuba); Professor Hisashi Suzuki, University of Tokyo (Japan); Dr. Romila Thapar, University of Delhi (India); Professor C. H. Waddington, University of Edinburgh (United Kingdom).

## RACE: DECLARATION ON RACE AND RACIAL PREJUDICE, UNESCO (1978).

In 1948, the UN Economic and Social Council advised UNESCO (resolution 116 B [VI]) of the interest of the United Nations in effective educational programs to prevent racial discrimination and suggested collaboration between the UN and UNESCO in the formulation of such programs. In response, the Director-General of UNESCO was authorized by its General Conference to sponsor research on the scientific facts of race.

Four statements on race were prepared by groups of experts convened by UNESCO in 1950, 1951, 1964, and 1967. Each group concluded that doctrines of racism lack any scientific basis whatsoever.

In 1972, the UNESCO General Conference called for the preparation of a Declaration on Race and Racial Prejudice which would take into account the findings of the four groups of experts and would present a set of universal principles. The draft of such a Declaration was prepared by a group of eminent specialists convened by the Director-General in 1977, and the Declaration was adopted by the General Conference (20th session) on 27 November 1978. The text of the Declaration (*UNESCO's Standard-Setting Instruments*, No. III.C.1) is as follows:

The General Conference of the United Nations Educational, Scientific and Cultural Organization, meeting in Paris at its twentieth session, on 27 November 1978 adopted unanimously and by acclamation the following Declaration:

### Preamble

The General Conference of the United Nations Educational, Scientific and Cultural Organization, meeting at Paris at its twentieth session, from 24 October to 28 November 1978,

Whereas it is stated in the Preamble to the Constitution of Unesco, adopted on 16 November 1945, that "the great and terrible war which has now ended was a war made possible by the denial of the democratic principles of the dignity, equality and mutual respect of men, and by the propagation, in their place, through ignorance and prejudice, of the doctrine of the inequality of men and races", and whereas, according to Article I of the said Constitution, the purpose of Unesco "is to contribute to peace and security by promoting collaboration among the nations through education, science and culture in order to further universal respect for justice, for the rule of law and for the human rights and fundamental freedoms . . . which are affirmed for the peoples of the world, without distinction of race, sex, language or religion, by the Charter of the United Nations",

Recognizing that, more than three decades after the founding of Unesco, these principles are just as significant as they were when they were embodied in its Constitution,

Mindful of the process of decolonization and other historical changes which have led most of the peoples formerly under foreign rule to recover their sovereignty, making the international community a universal and diversified whole and creating new opportunities of eradicating the scourge of racism and of putting an end to its odious manifestations in all aspects of social and political life, both nationally and internationally,

Convinced that the essential unity of the human race and

consequently the fundamental equality of all human beings and all peoples, recognized in the loftiest expressions of philosophy, morality and religion, reflect an ideal towards which ethics and science are converging today,

Convinced that all peoples and all human groups, whatever their composition or ethnic origin, contribute according to their own genius to the progress of the civilizations and cultures which, in their plurality and as a result of their interpenetration, constitute the common heritage of mankind,

Confirming its attachment to the principles proclaimed in the United Nations Charter and the Universal Declaration of Human Rights and its determination to promote the implementation of the International Covenants on Human Rights as well as the Declaration on the Establishment of a New International Economic Order,

Determined also to promote the implementation of the United Nations Declaration and the International Convention on the Elimination of all Forms of Racial Discrimination,

Noting the International Convention on the Prevention and Punishment of the Crime of Genocide, the International Convention on the Suppression and Punishment of the Crime of Apartheid and the Convention on the Non-Applicability of Statutory Limitations to War Crimes and Crimes against Humanity,

Recalling also the international instruments already adopted by Unesco, including in particular the Convention and Recommendation against Discrimination in Education, the Recommendation concerning the Status of Teachers, the Declaration of the Principles of International Cultural Co-operation, the Recommendation concerning Education for International Understanding, Co-operation and Peace and Education relating to Human Rights and Fundamental Freedoms, the Recommendation on the Status of Scientific Researchers, and the Recommendation on participation by the people at large in cultural life and their contribution to it,

Bearing in mind the four statements on the race question adopted by experts convened by Unesco,

Reaffirming its desire to play a vigorous and constructive part in the implementation of the programme of the Decade for Action to Combat Racism and Racial Discrimination, as defined by the General Assembly of the United Nations at its twenty-eighth session,

Noting with the gravest concern that racism, racial discrimination, colonialism and apartheid continue to afflict the world in ever-changing forms, as a result both of the continuation of legislative provisions and government and administrative practices contrary to the principles of human rights and also of the continued existence of political and social structures, and of relationships and attitudes, characterized by injustice and contempt for human beings and leading to the exclusion, humiliation and exploitation, or to be forced assimilation, of the members of disadvantaged groups,

Expressing its indignation at these offences against human dignity, *deploring* the obstacles they place in the way of mutual understanding between peoples and *alarmed* at the danger of their seriously disturbing international peace and security,

Adopts and solemnly proclaims this Declaration on Race and Racial Prejudice:

*Article 1.* 1. All human beings belong to a single species and are descended from a common stock. They are born equal in dignity and rights and all form an integral part of humanity.

2. All individuals and groups have the right to be different, to consider themselves as different and to be regarded as such. However, the diversity of life styles and the right to be different may not, in any circumstances, serve as a pretext for racial prejudice; they may not justify either in law or in fact any discriminatory practice whatsoever, nor provide a ground for the policy of apartheid, which is the extreme form of racism.

3. Identity of origin in no way affects the fact that human beings can and may live differently, nor does it preclude the existence of differences based on cultural, environmental and historical diversity nor the right to maintain cultural identity.

4. All peoples of the world possess equal faculties for attaining the highest level in intellectual, technical, social, economic, cultural and political development.

5. The differences between the achievements of the different peoples are entirely attributable to geographical, historical, political, economic, social and cultural factors. Such differences can in no case serve as a pretext for any rank-ordered classification of nations or peoples.

*Article 2.* 1. Any theory which involves the claim that racial or ethnic groups are inherently superior or inferior, thus implying that some would be entitled to dominate or eliminate others, presumed to be inferior, or which bases value judgements on racial differentiation, has no scientific foundation and is contrary to the moral and ethical principles of humanity.

2. Racism includes racist ideologies, prejudiced attitudes, discriminatory behaviour, structural arrangements and institutionalized practices resulting in racial inequality as well as the fallacious notion that discriminatory relations between groups are morally and scientifically justifiable; it is reflected in discriminatory provisions in legislation or regulations and discriminatory practices as well as in anti-social beliefs and acts; it hinders the development of its victims, perverts those who practise it, divides nations internally, impedes international co-operation and gives rise to political tensions between peoples; it is contrary to the fundamental principles of international law and, consequently, seriously disturbs international peace and security.

3. Racial prejudice, historically linked with inequalities in power, reinforced by economic and social differences between individuals and groups, and still seeking today to justify such inequalities, is totally without justification.

*Article 3.* Any distinction, exclusion, restriction or preference based on race, colour, ethnic or national origin or religious intolerance motivated by racist considerations, which destroys or compromises the sovereign equality of States and the right of peoples to self-determination, or which limits in an arbitrary or discriminatory manner the right of every human being and group to full development is incompatible with the requirements of an international order which is just and guarantees respect for human rights; the right to full development implies equal access to the means of personal and collective advancement and fulfilment in a climate of respect for the values of civilizations and cultures, both national and world-wide.

*Article 4.* 1. Any restriction on the complete self-fulfillment of human beings and free communication between them which is based on racial or ethnic considerations is contrary to the principle of equality in dignity and rights; it cannot be admitted.

2. One of the most serious violations of this principle is represented by apartheid, which, like genocide, is a crime against humanity, and gravely disturbs international peace and security.

3. Other policies and practices of racial segregation and

discrimination constitute crimes against the conscience and dignity of mankind and may lead to political tensions and gravely endanger international peace and security.

*Article 5.* 1. Culture, as a product of all human beings and a common heritage of mankind, and education in its broadest sense, offer men and women increasingly effective means of adaptation, enabling them not only to affirm that they are born equal in dignity and rights, but also to recognize that they should respect the right of all groups to their own cultural identity and the development of their distinctive cultural life within the national and international context, it being understood that it rests with each group to decide in complete freedom on the maintenance and, if appropriate, the adaptation or enrichment of the values which it regards as essential to its identity.

2. States, in accordance with their constitutional principles and procedures, as well as all other competent authorities and the entire teaching profession, have a responsibility to see that the educational resources of all countries are used to combat racism, more especially by ensuring that curricula and textbooks include scientific and ethical considerations concerning human unity and diversity and that no invidious distinctions are made with regard to any people; by training teachers to achieve these ends; by making the resources of the educational system available to all groups of the population without racial restriction or discrimination; and by taking appropriate steps to remedy the handicaps from which certain racial or ethnic groups suffer with regard to their level of education and standard of living and in particular to prevent such handicaps from being passed on to children.

3. The mass media and those who control or serve them, as well as all organized groups within national communities, are urged—with due regard to the principles embodied in the Universal Declaration of Human Rights, particularly the principle of freedom of expression—to promote understanding, tolerance and friendship among individuals and groups and to contribute to the eradication of racism, racial discrimination and racial prejudice, in particular by refraining from presenting a stereotyped, partial, unilateral or tendentious picture of individuals and of various human groups. Communication between racial and ethnic groups must be a reciprocal process, enabling them to express themselves and to be fully heard without let or hindrance. The mass media should therefore be freely receptive to ideas of individuals and groups which facilitate such communication.

*Article 6.* 1. The State has prime responsibility for ensuring human rights and fundamental freedoms on an entirely equal footing in dignity and rights for all individuals and all groups.

2. So far as its competence extends and in accordance with its constitutional principles and procedures, the State should take all appropriate steps, *inter alia* by legislation, particularly in the spheres of education, culture and communication, to prevent, prohibit and eradicate racism, racist propaganda, racial segregation and apartheid and to encourage the dissemination of knowledge and the findings of appropriate research in natural and social sciences on the causes and prevention of racial prejudice and racist attitudes, with due regard to the principles embodied in the Universal Declaration of Human Rights and in the International Covenant on Civil and Political Rights.

3. Since laws proscribing racial discrimination are not in themselves sufficient, it is also incumbent on States to supplement them by administrative machinery for the systematic investigation of instances of racial discrimination, by a comprehensive framework of legal remedies against acts of racial discrimination, by broadly based education and research programmes designed to combat racial prejudice and racial discrimination and by programmes of positive political, social, educational and cultural measures calculated to promote genuine mutual respect among groups. Where circumstances warrant, special programmes should be undertaken to promote the advancement of disadvantaged groups and, in the case of nationals, to ensure their effective participation in the decision-making processes of the community.

*Article 7.* In addition to political, economic and social measures, law is one of the principal means of ensuring equality in dignity and rights among individuals, and of curbing any propaganda, any form of organization or any practice which is based on ideas or theories referring to the alleged superiority of racial or ethnic groups or which seeks to justify or encourage racial hatred and discrimination in any form. States should adopt such legislation as is appropriate to this end and see that it is given effect and applied by all their services, with due regard to the principles embodied in the Universal Declaration of Human Rights. Such legislation should form part of a political, economic and social framework conducive to its implementation. Individuals and other legal entities, both public and private, must conform with such legislation and use all appropriate means to help the population as a whole to understand and apply it.

*Article 8.* 1. Individuals, being entitled to an economic, social, cultural and legal order, on the national and international planes, such as to allow them to exercise all their capabilities on a basis of entire equality of rights and opportunities, have corresponding duties towards their fellows, towards the society in which they live and towards the international community. They are accordingly under an obligation to promote harmony among the peoples, to combat racism and racial prejudice and to assist by every means available to them in eradicating racial discrimination in all its forms.

2. In the field of racial prejudice and racist attitudes and practices, specialists in natural and social sciences and cultural studies, as well as scientific organizations and associations, are called upon to undertake objective research on a wide interdisciplinary basis; all States should encourage them to this end.

3. It is, in particular, incumbent upon such specialists to ensure, by all means available to them, that their research findings are not misinterpreted, and also that they assist the public in understanding such findings.

*Article 9.* 1. The principle of the equality in dignity and rights of all human beings and all peoples, irrespective of race, colour and origin, is a generally accepted and recognized principle of international law. Consequently any form of racial discrimination practised by a State constitutes a violation of international law giving rise to its international responsibility.

2. Special measures must be taken to ensure equality in dignity and rights for individuals and groups wherever necessary, while ensuring that they are not such as to appear racially discriminatory. In this respect, particular attention should be paid to racial or ethnic groups which are socially or economically disadvantaged, so as to afford them, on a completely equal footing and without discrimination or restriction, the protection of the laws and regulations and the advantages of the social measures in force, in particular in regard to housing, employment and health; to respect the authenticity of their culture and values; and to facilitate their social and occupational advancement, especially through education.

3. Population groups of foreign origin, particularly migrant workers and their families who contribute to the development of the host country, should benefit from appropriate measures designed to afford them security and respect for their dignity and cultural values and to facilitate their adaptation to the host environment and their professional advancement with a view to their subsequent reintegration in their country of origin and their contribution to its development; steps should be taken to make it possible for their children to be taught their mother tongue.

4. Existing disequilibria in international economic relations contribute to the exacerbation of racism and racial prejudice; all States should consequently endeavour to contribute to the restructuring of the international economy on a more equitable basis.

*Article 10.* International organizations, whether universal or regional, governmental or non-governmental, are called upon to co-operate and assist, so far as their respective fields of competence and means allow, in the full and complete implementation of the principles set out in this Declaration, thus contributing to the legitimate struggle of all men, born equal in dignity and rights, against the tyranny and oppression of racism, racial segregation, apartheid and genocide, so that all the peoples of the world may be forever delivered from these scourges.

### Resolution for Implementation of the Declaration

The General Conference, at its twentieth session, Considering that Unesco, by reason of the responsibilities devolving upon it under its Constitution in the fields of education, science, culture and communication, is required to call the attention of States and peoples to the problems related to all aspects of the question of race and racial prejudice,

Having regard to the Unesco Declaration of Race and Racial Prejudice adopted this twenty-seventh day of November 1978,

1. Urges Member States:

(a) to consider the possibility of ratifying, if they have not yet done so, the international instruments designed to aid in countering and eliminating racial discrimination, and in particular the International Convention on the elimination of all Forms of Racial Discrimination, the International Convention on the Suppression and Punishment of the Crime of Apartheid and the Unesco Convention against Discrimination in Education;

(b) to take appropriate measures, including the passing of laws, guided by the provisions of Articles 4 and 6 of the International Convention on the Elimination of All Forms of Racial Discrimination, with a view to preventing and punishing acts of racial discrimination and ensuring that fair and adequate reparation is made to the victims of racial discrimination;

(c) to communicate to the Director-General all necessary information concerning the steps they have taken to give effect to the principles set forth in the Declaration.

2. Invites the Director-General:

(a) to prepare a comprehensive report on the world situation in the fields covered by the Declaration, on the basis of the information supplied by Member States and of any other information supported by trustworthy evidence which he may have gathered by such methods as he may think fit, and to enlist for this purpose, if he deems it advisable, the help of one or more independent experts of recognized competence in these fields;

(b) to take due account, when preparing his report, which should be accompanied by any observations he may deem appropriate, of the work of the various international bodies set up to give effect to the legal instruments concerning the struggle against racialism and racial discrimination, or contributing to that struggle through their activities in the general field of human rights;

(c) to present his report to the General Conference and to submit to it for decision, on the basis of the said report and of the discussion it will then have held, with due priority, on the problems of race and racial prejudice, any general comments and any recommendations deemed necessary to promote the implementation of the Declaration;

(d) to ensure the widest possible dissemination of the text of the Declaration and, to that end, to publish and arrange for the distribution of the text not only in the official languages but also in as many languages as is possible with the resources available to him;

(e) to communicate the Declaration to the Secretary-General of the United Nations with a request that he place before the United Nations General Assembly appropriate proposals for strengthening the methods of peaceful settlement of disputes concerning the elimination of racial discrimination.

**RACIAL DISCRIMINATION.** Racial discrimination is a practice characterized as "the very negation of the principle of **EQUALITY,** and therefore an affront to human dignity," in the *Study of Racial Discrimination* prepared in 1976 (UN publication, Sales no. E.76.XIV.2) by Mr. Hernan Santa Cruz (Chile), Special Rapporteur of the **SUB-COMMISSION ON PREVENTION OF DISCRIMINATION AND PROTECTION OF MINORITIES.** As Mr. Santa Cruz explains (paras. 68–69):

The principle of equality does not, as one might assume, exclude all possible differentiations between individuals. In particular, it is not concerned with differentiations based upon such individual qualities as mental or physical capacity, talent or innate ability; nor is it concerned with differentiations based upon the individual's capacities, merits, or behaviour in so far as these are within his control. It is rather concerned with differentiations based on factors over which he has no control, such as his race, his colour, his descent, and his national or ethnic origin.

The principle of equality, in short, recognizes that those elements of body and spirit in which all human beings are essentially alike far outweigh and transcend those purely accidental differentiations over which the individual has no control. The principle flows from a basic ethical concept, that of human dignity, which implies, in its simplest terms, that every human being is an end in himself, not a mere means to an end.

It is for these reasons that Mr. Santa Cruz considers racial discrimination "the very negation of the principle of equality" and adds that "it is a negation, also, of the social nature of man, who can reach his fullest development only through interaction with his fellows."

The Special Rapporteur selects, as the most carefully prepared and widely accepted definition of the term "racial discrimination," the one which appears in article 1 of the International Convention on the Elimination of All Forms of Racial Discrimination and which reads as follows:

In this Convention, the term "racial discrimination" shall mean any distinction, exclusion, restriction of preference based on race, colour, descent, or national or ethnic origin which has the purpose or effect of nullifying or impairing the recognition, enjoyment or exercise, on an equal footing, of human rights and fundamental freedoms in the political, economic, social, cultural or any other field of public life....

Special measures taken for the sole purpose of securing adequate advancement of certain racial or ethnic groups or individuals requiring such protection as may be necessary in order to ensure to such groups or individuals equal enjoyment or exercise of human rights and fundamental freedoms shall not be deemed racial discrimination, provided, however, that such measures do not, as a consequence, lead to the maintenance of separate rights for different racial groups and that they shall not be continued after the objectives for which they were taken have been achieved.

This definition, he explains, while intended to serve only for the purpose of the Convention, serves to clarify the meaning of "racial discrimination" in a number of ways:

It specifies the grounds upon which such discrimination may be based: race, colour, descent, and national or ethnic origin. It indicates the kind of acts which lead to discrimination; distinctions, exclusions, restrictions and preferences. It stipulates that discriminatory acts include not only those having the effect of discriminating, but also those having this intent or purpose. It brands as discriminatory those acts which wholly nullify, as well as those which only partially impair, the recognition, enjoyment or exercise of human rights and fundamental freedoms. It spells out not only what discrimination is, but also what it is not, and provides for the measures necessary to secure the advancement of backward racial or ethnic groups or individuals in order to ensure to them the equal enjoyment or exercise of human rights and fundamental freedoms.

One strong cause of racial prejudice and discrimination, according to the Special Rapporteur, is racism, or "the superiority complex," consisting of a set of popular beliefs which includes the following elements: (1) that the differences between groups are due to hereditary biology and nothing can change them; (2) that habits, attitudes, beliefs, behavior, and all the things we learn are determined for us before we are born; (3) that all differences between the non-dominant group and the dominant group are thought to be examples of inferiority on the part of members of the non-dominant group; and (4) that, if there should be biological crossing of the groups, the children will be more degenerate than either of the parent groups. These racist beliefs, he adds, have been so widespread

that, although authoritatively and consistently proved erroneous, they still continue to be an important cause of prejudice.

***REPORT OF THE SPECIAL RAPPORTEUR.*** In a later report (1994) on the subject of racial discrimination, xenophobia, and intolerance a new Special Rapporteur, Mr. Abdelfattah Amor, presented conclusions and recommendations (E/CN.4/1994/66, paras. 50–52), as follows:

In addition to the activities which the Special Rapporteur has outlined in the section dealing with methods of work, he suggests that scientific research should be done on the nature and scope of the problems covered by his mandate, particularly through such projects as:

An interdisciplinary seminar on the problems of the theoretical aspects and specific manifestations of contemporary forms of racial discrimination, together with a study of measures already taken or to be taken;

Workshops (one per continent) during the first two years of his mandate; and

A conference for the purpose of consolidation during the third year of his mandate. These scientific encounters will be organized in close collaboration with the specialized agencies concerned with human rights, the NGOs and experts working in the field.

The Special Rapporteur is convinced of the importance of education and its far-reaching consequences and suggests that measures should be studied to prevent actions and behaviour giving rise to discrimination—prevention being better than cure—and that a system of human rights teaching should be established in all States in close cooperation with specialized agencies such as UNESCO and with Governments. There would be a study of how to make this system mandatory and effective. Could cultural and social racism not be gradually checked by theoretical teaching as well as practical methods (plays and cultural events) which would enable a country's different ethnic or cultural groups to get to know, learn, understand and appreciate each other's culture, and thus facilitate cultural intermingling? Today, in the "finite world" or the "planetary village" we inhabit, ethnic, religious and cultural minorities could, thanks to the large-scale impact of the media, achieve a better mutual understanding in cultural terms and accept each other to a greater extent. Greater tolerance would thus grow progressively between peoples, migrants, immigrant workers and their families and aboriginal or indigenous peoples. In short, the Special Rapporteur attaches great importance to the prevention of manifestations of racism in any form whatsoever by governmental, legislative, administrative, economic and social and above all educational measures.

Lastly, the Special Rapporteur would suggest that some thought might be given, at the conclusion of the Third Decade to Combat Racism and Racial Discrimination to erecting a memorial in honour of the victims of racial discrimination. It could be set up on the Place des Nations within the grounds of the United Nations at Geneva to promote an awareness of the evils of racial discrimination and to draw attention to the continuing and sustained activities of the United Nations against all forms of racism and on behalf of human rights. If this idea were to find favour, the activity would be financed by voluntary contributions. Our world does not lack men of goodwill, humanists or benefactors.

**DECADES TO COMBAT RACISM AND RACIAL DISCRIMINATION.** In 1972, the UN **GENERAL ASSEMBLY** launched the Decade to Combat Racism and Racial Discrimination (resolution 3057 [XXVIII]); this first decade commenced on 10 December 1973, the 25th anniversary of the adoption of the **UNIVERSAL DECLARATION OF HUMAN RIGHTS.** The decade was designed as a period for intensified national, regional, and international action aimed at achieving the total and unconditional elimination of racism and racial discrimination in all its forms.

In 1983, at the end of the decade, the General Assembly, convinced of the need to take continuing and reinforced measures for the elimination of racism, proclaimed a Second Decade to Combat Racism and Racial Discrimination (resolution 38/14), to begin on 10 December 1983. Midway through this second decade, the UN Sub-Commission on Prevention of Discrimination and Protection of Minorities appointed Mr. Asbjørn Eide (Norway) as its Special Rapporteur to prepare a comprehensive analysis of the achievements made and obstacles encountered during the decades. Mr. Eide presented his final report, titled *Study on the Achievements Made and Obstacles Encountered during the Decades to Combat Racism and Racial Discrimination* (UN Doc. E/CN.4/Sub.2/1989/8 and Add. 1), to the Sub-Commission at its 1989 session.

A Third Decade to Combat Racism and Racial Discrimination was proclaimed by the General Assembly, commencing on 10 December 1993 (resolution 49/146). It adopted the "Programme of Action for the Third Decade" as follows:

### Introduction

1. The goals and objectives of the Third Decade to Combat Racism and Racial Discrimination are those adopted by the General Assembly for the first Decade and contained in paragraph 8 of the annex to its resolution 3057 (XXVIII) of 2 November 1973:

"The ultimate goals of the Decade are to promote human rights and fundamental freedoms for all, without distinction of any kind on grounds of race, colour, descent or national or ethnic origin, especially by eradicating racial prejudice, racism and racial discrimination; to arrest any expansion of racist policies, to eliminate the persistence of racist policies and to counteract the emergence of alliances based on mutual espousal of racism and racial discrimination; to resist any policy and practices which lead to the strengthening of the racist regimes and contribute to the sustainment of racism and racial discrimination; to identify, isolate and dispel the fallacious and mythical beliefs, policies and practices that contribute to racism and racial discrimination; and to put an end to racist regimes."

2. In drawing up suggested elements for the Programme of Action for the Third Decade, account has been taken of the fact that current global economic conditions have caused many Member States to call for budgetary restraint, which in turn requires a conservative approach to the number and type of programmes of action that may be considered at this time. The Secretary-General also took into account the relevant suggestions made by the Committee on the Elimination of Racial Discrimination at its forty-first session. The elements presented below have been suggested as those which are essential, should resources be made available to implement them.

### Measures to Remedy the Legacy of Cultural, Economic and Social Disparities Left by Apartheid

3. The successful peaceful transition of South Africa to a democratic and non-racial society with human rights safeguarded by an entrenched Charter of Fundamental Rights has nevertheless left cultural, economic and social inequalities reflecting historical deprivation. Corrective action by human rights bodies will make a constructive contribution.

### Action at the International Level

4. During the discussion at the substantive session of 1992 of the Economic and Social Council concerning the Second Decade to Combat Racism and Racial Discrimination, many delegations expressed their concern with regard to new expressions of racism, racial discrimination, intolerance and xenophobia in various parts of the world. In particular, these affect minorities, ethnic groups, migrant workers, indigenous populations, nomads, immigrants and refugees.

5. The biggest contribution to the elimination of racial discrimination will be that which results from the actions of States within their own territories. International action undertaken as part of any programme for the Third Decade should therefore be directed so as to assist States to act effectively. The International Convention on the Elimination of All Forms of Racial Discrimination has established standards for States, and every opportunity should be seized to ensure that these are universally accepted and applied.

6. The General Assembly should consider more effective action to ensure that all States parties to the International Convention on the Elimination of All Forms of Racial Discrimination fulfil their reporting and financial obligations. National action against racism and racial discrimination should be monitored and improved by requesting an expert member of the Committee on the Elimination of Racial Discrimination to prepare a report on obstacles encountered with respect to the effective implementation of the Convention by States parties and suggestions for remedial measures.

7. The General Assembly requests the Secretary-General to organize regional workshops and seminars. A team from the Committee should be invited to monitor these meetings. The following themes are suggested for the seminars:

(a) Seminar to assess the experience gained in the implementation of the International Convention on the Elimination of All Forms of Racial Discrimination. The seminar would also assess the efficiency of national legislation and recourse procedures available to victims of racism;

(b) Seminar on the eradication of incitement to racial hatred and discrimination, including the prohibition of propaganda activities and of organizations involved in them;

(c) Seminar on the right to equal treatment before tribunals and other judicial institutions, including the provision of reparation for damages suffered as a result of discrimination;

(d) Seminar on the transmission of racial inequality from one generation to another, with special reference to the children of migrant workers and the appearance of new forms of segregation;

(e) Seminar on immigration and racism;

(f) Seminar on international cooperation in the elimination of racial discrimination, including cooperation between States, the contribution of non-governmental organizations, national and regional institutions, United Nations bodies and petitions to treaty-monitoring bodies;

(g) Seminar on the enactment of national legislation to combat racism and racial discrimination affecting ethnic groups, migrant workers and refugees in all parts of the world;

(h) Seminar on flows of refugees resulting from ethnic conflicts or political restructuring of multi-ethnic societies in socio-economic transition and their link with racism in the host country;

(i) Training course on national legislation prohibiting racial discrimination for nationals from countries with and without such legislation;

(j) Regional seminars on nationalism, ethno-nationalism and human rights could also provide an opportunity for broadening knowledge of the causes of today's ethnic conflicts, particularly of the so-called policy of "ethnic cleansing", in order to provide solutions;

(k) Seminar for educational and training experts, including non-governmental organizations, in cooperation with the United Nations Educational, Scientific and Cultural Organization and other appropriate organizations, aimed at the development of educational materials and training courses for teachers and other opinion leaders on eliminating prejudice and fostering tolerance.

8. The General Assembly requests the Department of Public Information of the Secretariat to undertake specific activities that could be carried out by Governments and relevant national non-governmental organizations to commemorate the International Day for the Elimination of Racial Discrimination on 21 March each year. Support should be sought from artists, as well as religious leaders, trade unions, enterprises and political parties, to sensitize the population on the evils of racism and racial discrimination.

9. The Department of Public Information should also publish its posters for the Third Decade and informative brochures on the activities planned for the Decade. Documentary films and reports, as well as radio broadcasts on the damaging effects of racism and racial discrimination, should, moreover, be considered.

10. In cooperation with the United Nations Educational, Scientific and Cultural Organization and the Department of Public Information, the General Assembly supports the organization of a seminar on the role of mass media in combating or disseminating racist ideas.

11. In cooperation with the International Labour Organization, the possibility of organizing a seminar on the role of trade unions in combating racism and racial discrimination in employment should be explored.

12. The General Assembly invites the United Nations Educational Scientific and Cultural Organization to expedite the preparation of teaching materials and teaching aids to promote teaching, training and educational activities against racism and racial discrimination, with particular emphasis on activities at the primary and secondary levels of education.

13. The General Assembly calls upon Member States to make special efforts:

(a) To promote the aim of non-discrimination in all educational programmes and policies;

(b) To give special attention to the civic education of teachers. It is essential that teachers be aware of the principles and essential content of the legal texts relevant to racism and racial discrimination and of how to deal with the problem of relations between children belonging to different communities;

(c) To teach contemporary history at an early age, presenting children with an accurate picture of the crimes committed by fascist and other totalitarian regimes, and more particularly of the crimes of apartheid and genocide;

(d) To ensure that curricula and textbooks reflect anti-racist principles and promote intercultural education.

### Action at the National and Regional Levels

14. The following questions are addressed in the context of action to be undertaken at the national and regional levels: Have there been any successful national models to eliminate racism and racial prejudices that could be recommended to States, for example, for educating children, or principles of equality to tackle racism against migrant workers, ethnic minorities or indigenous peoples? What kind of affirmative action programmes are there at the national or regional level to redress discrimination against specific groups?

15. The General Assembly recommends that States that have not yet done so adopt, ratify and implement legislation prohibiting racism and racial discrimination, such as the International Convention on the Elimination of All Forms of Racial Discrimination and the International Convention on the Protection of the Rights of All Migrant Workers and Members of Their Families.

16. The General Assembly recommends that Member States review their national programmes to combat racial discrimination and its effects in order to identify and to seize opportunities to close gaps between different groups, and especially to undertake housing educational and employment programmes that have proved to be successful in combating racial discrimination and xenophobia.

17. The General Assembly recommends that Member States encourage the participation of journalists and human rights advocates from minority groups and communities in the mass media. Radio and television programmes should increase the number of broadcasts produced by and in cooperation with racial and cultural minority groups. Multicultural activities of the media should also be encouraged where they can contribute to the suppression of racism and xenophobia.

18. The General Assembly recommends that regional organizations cooperate closely with United Nations efforts to combat racism and racial discrimination. Regional organizations dealing with human rights issues could mobilize public opinion in their regions against the evils of racism and racial prejudices directed towards disadvantaged racial and ethnic groups. These institutions could serve an important function in assisting Governments to enact national legislation against racial discrimination and promote adoption and application of international conventions. Regional human rights commissions should be called upon to publicize widely basic texts on existing human rights instruments.

## Basic Research and Studies

19. The long-term viability of the United Nations programme against racism and racial discrimination will depend in part on continuing research into the causes of racism and into the new manifestations of racism and racial discrimination. The General Assembly may wish to examine the importance of preparing studies on racism. The following are some aspects to be studied:

(a) Application of article 2 of the International Convention on the Elimination of All Forms of Racial Discrimination. Such a study might assist States to learn from one another the national measures taken to implement the Convention;

(b) Economic factors contributing to the perpetuation of racism and racial discrimination;

(c) Integration or preservation of cultural identity in a multiracial or multi-ethnic society;

(d) Political rights, including the participation of various processes and their representation in government service;

(e) Civil rights, including migration, nationality and freedom of opinion and association;

(f) Educational measures to combat racial prejudice and discrimination and to propagate the principles of the United Nations;

(g) Socio-economic costs of racism and racial discrimination;

(h) Global integration and the question of racism and the nation State;

(i) National mechanisms against racism and racial discrimination in the fields of immigration, employment, salary, housing, education and ownership of property.

## Coordination and Reporting

20. It may be relevant to recall that, in its resolution 38/14 of 22 November 1983, in which it proclaimed the Second Decade to Combat Racism and Racial Discrimination, the General Assembly charged the Economic and Social Council with coordinating the implementation of the programme and evaluating the activities. The Assembly decides that the following steps should be taken to strengthen the United Nations input into the Third Decade to Combat Racism and Racial Discrimination:

(a) The General Assembly entrusts the Economic and Social Council and the Commission on Human Rights, in cooperation with the Secretary-General, with the responsibility for coordinating the programmes and evaluating the activities undertaken in connection with the Third Decade;

(b) The Secretary-General is invited to provide specific information on activities against racism, to be contained in one annual report, which should be comprehensive in nature and allow a general overview of all mandated activities. This will facilitate coordination and evaluation;

(c) An open-ended working group of the Commission on Human Rights, or other appropriate arrangement under the Commission, may be established to review Decade-related information on the basis of the annual report referred to above, as well as relevant studies and reports of seminars, to assist the Commission in formulating appropriate recommendations to the Economic and Social Council on particular activities, allocation of priorities and so on.

21. Furthermore, an inter-agency meeting should be organized immediately after the proclamation of the Third Decade, with a view to planning working meetings and other activities.

## Regular System-wide Consultations

22. Annual consultations between the United Nations, specialized agencies and non-governmental organizations should take place to review and plan Decade-related activities. In this framework, the Centre for Human Rights should organize inter-agency meetings to consider and discuss further measures to strengthen the coordination and cooperation of programmes related to the issues of combating racism and racial discrimination.

23. The Centre for Human Rights should also strengthen the relationship with non-governmental organizations fighting against racism and racial discrimination by holding consultations and briefings with the non-governmental organizations. Such meetings could help them to initiate, develop and present proposals regarding the struggle against racism and racial discrimination.

24. The Secretary-General should include the activities to be carried out during the Decade, as well as the related resource requirements, in the proposed programme budgets, which will be submitted biennially, during the Decade, starting with the proposed programme budget for the biennium 1994–1995.

*NATIONAL AND LOCAL RECOURSES.* At its 1980 session, the UN Sub-Commission on Prevention of Discrimination and Protection of Minorities requested the Secretary-General (resolution 4 C [XXXIII]) to prepare a report setting out measures which the Sub-Commission might recommend to governments with a view to enhancing and strengthening national and local recourse procedures available to victims of racial discrimination.

In the report, the Secretary-General enumerated (UN Doc. E/CN.4/Sub.2/1982/9) the forms of national and local recourse procedures available, evaluated their impact and effectiveness, and indicated which had been found to be most effective. Excerpts from the report (paras. 3–39) are reproduced below.

### Forms of Recourse Procedures Available

Although the principle of equality of all in the enjoyment of rights and freedoms is now generally accepted by the international community, the proclaimed human rights and fundamental freedoms, in order to be meaningful, must be sanctioned by effective recourse procedures easily available to victims of racial discrimination.

The establishment of such procedures implies the determination and precise definition of the acts which constitute punishable offences. It is essential to examine carefully the various and subtle forms that racial discrimination can take, in order to determine the most opportune forms of procedure to deal with it.

Bearing in mind the multifaceted aspects of the problem of racial discrimination, a wide range of measures have been envisaged by Governments with a view to providing relevant safeguards against the various forms of discrimination.

*A. Legislative Procedures.* The constitutional and other legislative provisions of many countries include recognition of the principle of non-discrimination and legal means to combat all forms of racial discrimination. These provisions bear upon various fields such as labour, family, economic, social and cultural life. Many countries have adopted legislation which declares illegal racist propaganda and racist organizations. Moreover, international instruments adopted in the field of racial discrimination have usually had an important impact on national legislations, either by having an immediate effect at the national level or by leading to the adoption of special laws in order to comply with the relevant provisions of such instruments.

*B. Judicial Procedures.* Protection against discrimination can be provided through penal codes and procedures. Victims of racial discrimination can also find a remedy in procedures before the civil courts. In some cases, public prosecutors can play an important role in acting against discrimination by making an investigation *ex officio* if reasonable grounds exist for believing that an offence has been committed, even if no complaint has been lodged by a victim of racial discrimination. The public prosecutor is also, as a rule, under the obligation to institute criminal proceedings *ex officio* if he feels that an offence has been committed. Should the public prosecutor decide not to institute such proceedings, the victims are, according to the law, entitled to institute criminal proceedings on their own.

*C. Administrative Procedures.* Special procedures have been introduced by some countries for implementation by the administrative authorities with a view to ensuring equality of treatment and access to public places and services.

Among such procedures, mention may be made of the role of institutions such as the ombudsman or similar officials.

The ombudsman is a public official whose function is to represent the individual in cases where the rights of the individual under the law may have been infringed upon or abused by the State or another public authority.

In some countries, the ombudsman has authority to check and investigate inappropriate performance by public officials, including discriminatory acts. He also devotes special attention to the problems of immigrants and helps them to become familiar with the legal system and legal remedies available to them.

Similar institutions exist in other countries: for instance, in some cases the "Chancellor of Justice" of the Government performs functions concerning the investigation of claims of racial discrimination similar to those of an ombudsman, while in other cases the Procurator is entrusted with safeguarding legality. In some developing countries, similar institutions have been established, with some modifications to take account of their respective needs and experience. The Office Lokpal (Protector of the Law) of India, set up to inquire into allegations of misconduct against public men, can be cited as an example of this type of institution.

*D. Other Forms of Procedure.* Among various other forms of recourse procedure reference may be made to the roles played by the following institutions:

(i) National and local commissions on human rights, it has been said, have an important role in the fight against discriminatory action. They can bring about rapid action, particularly in urgent cases such as those relating to housing, employment and similar situations. They can also play a conciliatory role or make necessary arrangements for legal aid;

(ii) Trade unions can initiate action to curtail discriminatory practices, such as discriminatory contracts or conditions of work. Union management grievance procedures sometimes deal with complaints of racial discrimination;

(iii) In addition to legalistic procedures, some countries have encouraged conciliation and informal procedures for the settlement of cases involving violations of human rights; these procedures have usually proved to be useful;

(iv) In some countries political parties can serve as a means of focusing attention on violations of human rights, and provide an effective means of attacking racial practices;

(v) In other countries, the church has played a valuable role as a powerful means of providing assistance to victims of racial discrimination;

(vi) Finally, an important role can be played in supplementing national recourse procedures, by means provided under the pertinent international legal instruments dealing with racial discrimination. In this regard, great importance is attached to the recognition of the individual right to petition as an effective means of recourse.

## Impact and Effectiveness of Existing Recourse Procedures

Reference has been made above to various forms of recourse procedures available to victims of racial discrimination. However, the mere establishment of such procedures cannot suffice to ensure their effectiveness. A number of criteria have to be taken into account in order to determine the real impact of the recourse procedures in practice.

*A. Accessibility of Recourse Procedures.* The first problem which arises in connection with existing recourse procedures is to ensure that they are universally available to all persons and groups, without any distinction between citizens and non-citizens.

However, access to recourse procedures, even when universally available, might prove quite difficult in practice to those portions of the population which, owing to ignorance or insufficient information on existing rights and ways to exercise them, usually are the most vulnerable to acts of racial discrimination. Psychological obstacles also sometimes prevent victims of racial discrimination from using recourse procedures. In order to ensure better access to these procedures, in some countries specific information about available recourse procedures is channelled through regional bureaux for legal assistance established by trade unions, or through "law shops", which offer free legal advice and facilitate access to the courts for disadvantaged groups through reducing psychological and financial barriers.

*B. Flexible Rules for Initiation of Complaints.* In many cases the complexity of the rules relating to the initiation of complaints constitutes an obstacle. In a number of countries it has been noted that very few complaints dealing with racial discrimination are submitted to the courts or other competent institutions. This often stems from lack of information and knowledge about how to initiate a complaint, or from frustration with the complexity of rules relating to the initiation of complaints.

*C. Flexible Evidentiary Criteria and Standards of Proof.* Evidence to prove discrimination can be very difficult to obtain, as some of the discriminatory acts can take a subtle form and be unamenable to physical proof.

Questions of possible discrimination cannot be investigated like ordinary legal problems for which the question is basically one of deciding whether an illegal act has been committed or not. Thus, investigating bodies have to be flexible regarding the sort of evidence they can regard as admissible evidence, and both direct and/or indirect or circumstantial evidence have to be taken into account.

The same principle applies to standard of proof, for which flexibility is also required. In cases where the objective of the investigation is to obtain redress for an individual the standard of proof should be much less than that required by many investigating bodies. On the other hand, stricter standards of proof should be observed if the investigation extends to the trial of someone on criminal charges.

*D. Effectiveness and Speed of Action.* There is a need for prompt and speedy resolution of the cases brought before the competent organs or bodies in order to avoid any kind of denial of justice. In some countries, internal legislation provide for time limits, not only for the action of the administration in response to a complaint but also in matters of control of the constitutionality of laws.

Flexible recourse procedures can play an important role in eliminating undue delay and problems of backlog.

*E. Ability to Grant Legal and Other Assistance.* The granting of legal aid to victims of racial discrimination to bring actions before the courts can contribute in improving the effectiveness of recourse procedures.

In many countries free legal aid is fully or partially available to persons requiring it. In some cases, the State has complete carriage of a case from beginning to end. Other forms of assistance include the provision, at State expense, of the services of an interpreter. In some countries private attorneys are mandated by the State, at its expense, to provide legal assistance to those requiring it. The wide dissemination of legal literature and information constitutes another form of legal assistance improving the effectiveness of recourse procedures.

### Recommended Procedures and Activities

The importance attached, within the United Nations system, to the struggle against racism and racial discrimination, has led, among other things, to the organization under the Programme of the Decade for the Action to Combat Racism and Racial Discrimination, of a number of seminars. Some of these seminars dealt more specifically with recourse procedures available to victims of racial discrimination.

Among the conclusions of these various seminars, many can be retained as concrete and extremely useful suggestions regarding measures that Governments might wish to adopt with a view to enhance and strengthen recourse procedures available to victims of racial discrimination at national and local levels.

### Establishment of Recourse Procedures

Effective recourse procedures, it has been argued, should be instituted as a means of guaranteeing victims of racial discrimination the application of legal provisions relating to the substance of the law. Therefore, common standards should be established in combating racial discrimination and securing the principle of equality. Thus, all States should ratify international instruments adopted under the auspices of the United Nations and dealing with racial discrimination, such as the International Convention on the Elimination of All Forms of Racial Discrimination, the International Covenant on Civil and Political Rights, and the International Covenant on Economic, Social and Cultural Rights.

### Variety of Approaches

Different approaches, it has been emphasized, should be envisaged in the form and content of recourse procedures, bearing in mind the various root causes and manifestations of racial discrimination, and the differing realities in each country. The forms and efficiency of recourse procedures depend, among other things, on the type of violation dealt with and the socio-economic conditions prevailing in each given society. Particular attention should be given to the specific problems and realities of each situation. Therefore, in order to identify the most effective means of dealing with problems raised by racial discrimination, efforts should be made to detect and study the various causes and manifestations of racial discrimination.

### Conditions of Effectiveness of Recourse Procedures

A number of conditions, it has been stressed, should be filled by recourse procedures in order to render them effective. These procedures should be adequate, efficient and easy to initiate, and cover areas of civil as well as general law and administrative disputes. To this end, it has been said that all countries should ensure that the conditions of access to recourse procedures are as broad as possible, and that these procedures are made available to all persons without any distinction between citizens and non-citizens or exclusion of any specific group. Furthermore, the rules for initiation of complaints should be simple and flexible. Complaints of racial discrimination should be dealt with expeditiously. It has been further argued that different standards of proofs should be promoted, such as the balance of probability or preponderance of the evidence. Another proposal strongly recommended is that victims of racial discrimination should be afforded appropriate financial and legal assistance necessary for the investigation and execution of their complaints.

### Compensation of Victims

With regard to the question of compensation of victims it has been recommended that, in addition to repressive action, States should ensure that measures are taken with a view to providing fair and tangible compensation to victims of acts of racial discrimination, as provided for in article 6 of the International Convention on the Elimination of All Forms of Racial Discrimination. Compensation should be provided for material and moral damages, and cover general as well as special damages. Even in cases where the awarding of moral damages is already provided for in the legislation, specific national legislation on the matter of compensation of victims of acts of racial discrimination would reduce ambiguities.

### Appeal Procedures

With respect to appeal procedures, it has been said that the streamlining of appeals procedures would help strengthen the recourse procedures available to victims of racial discrimination, who frequently depend on a fair and effective appeals system in their pursuit of redress.

### Information Activities

In the field of information, it has been suggested that all countries should by all appropriate means publicize effective recourse procedures. Without an appropriate dissemination of information on their availability, such procedures would be meaningless. Among the various measures which could be taken as regards information activities in this field, the following can be cited:

(i) Publishing popular literature about efforts undertaken to combat racial discrimination and for the realization of civil, political, economic, social and cultural rights;

(ii) Dissemination of information through offices of ombudsmen and similar institutions;

(iii) Giving publicity to the operation of the recourse procedures available;

(iv) Dissemination of information for victims or potential victims of racial discrimination;

(v) Radio and television programmes designed to combat racism;

(vi) Articles and publications on recourse procedures available against racial discrimination;

(vii) Dissemination of legal information through special activities to be carried out by central and local administrative bodies and lawyers associations.

### Educational Measures

Educational measures have been mentioned as an important factor in strengthening the recourse procedures.

Governments should introduce, or where it already exists, strengthen and promote teaching relating to human rights in general and to problems connected with racial discrimination in particular. Among particular educational measures which could be used are suitable training of teachers; grants to schools towards the cost of employing extra teachers where needed; extra staff employed at schools with concentration of children of foreign workers; subsidies granted for bicultural education. Pupils from the primary level upwards should be made aware of racial problems and the dangers of racism. Students should be in a position to know that domestic as well as international remedies are available to them if their rights are infringed. Another educational measure which could help strengthen recourse procedures would be the dissemination of human rights documents, including those concerned with racial discrimination, among minority groups, in their respective languages.

### Institutions of Independent Mediators

It has been emphasized that States should be encouraged to adopt the system of ombudsmen or independent mediators. The role of such mediators could differ from country to country, depending on differences of economic and social systems and the varying problems with which countries are faced at different stages of development. The ombudsman system assumes an independent supervisory role over courts as well as administrative bodies in order to leave no gap in protective mechanisms for individual rights. This system represents an additional guarantee for the protection of human rights. The independent mediator should be entitled to make inspections of governmental and administrative bodies in order to suggest improvements in their administrative procedures. This jurisdiction should be as wide as possible, and should operate at all levels of government.

### National and Local Human Rights Institutions

As regards institutions in the field of human rights, it has been recommended that human rights committees and similar national and local institutions for the protection and promotion of human rights be established and enabled to function adequately. Such institutions should be empowered to investigate infringements of human rights and act in a conciliatory capacity. To this end, they should be protected from government persecution or repression.

Among the various tasks national and local institutions for human rights should be entitled to perform in connection with the protection of victims of racial discrimination, reference may be made to the following:

(i) National and local institutions should assist in the provision of free legal aid to the needy;

(ii) They should be authorized, within the framework of their constitution and competence, to investigate complaints alleging that citizens are being deprived of their basic rights;

(iii) They should be authorized, within the framework of their constitution and competence, to apply concrete remedies to individual cases of human rights violations;

(iv) They should, while discharging their functions of fact finding, conciliation or redress, be empowered, in the conduct of their inquiry, with due process of law, into any matter affecting human rights at the national level, to summon witnesses and have access to relevant evidence.

### Protection of Minority Groups

It has also been agreed that States should adopt specific measures to enhance and strengthen recourse procedures available to minority groups particularly vulnerable to acts of racial discrimination, such as indigenous populations or migrant workers.

With regard to indigenous populations, the distinctiveness of the problems of discrimination in each region require innovative approaches in devising recourse procedures. Alongside national and local human rights bodies, such as human rights commissions or race relations commissions, every Government whose population includes indigenous peoples might establish a national ombudsman on the human rights of indigenous peoples, whose task would be to promote and protect the human rights of indigenous peoples. Members of indigenous peoples who are victims of racial discrimination should be afforded appropriate financial and other assistance necessary for the investigation of their complaints.

The ombudsman institution could also play a constructive role in dealing with problems of racial discrimination against migrant workers, who generally are not familiar with the legal system and legal remedies available to them. States should also eliminate, through legislative, judicial and administrative measures, discriminatory practices against migrant workers.

*PREVENTION OF RACIAL DISCRIMINATION.* The COMMITTEE ON THE ELIMINATION OF RACIAL DISCRIMINATION has from time to time considered ways and means of preventing, or combating, attitudes and prejudices based on race, color, or national or ethnic origin, which often give rise to overt acts of racial discrimination. In 1977, the committee decided to draw to the attention of States parties to the International Convention on the Elimination of All Forms of Racial Discrimination the importance of the provisions of article 7 thereof and to invite them to furnish detailed information on the measures which they had adopted in order to give effect to those provisions. It also considered the need to provide the States parties with some guidance on the manner in which the provisions could most effectively be applied and on the role that UNESCO might be willing to play in assisting the Committee and the States parties.

In the course of formulating an appropriate recommendation, the committee heard the representative of UNESCO, who stated that the development of the teaching of human rights could constitute an excellent means of implementing article 7. He analyzed a number of UNESCO activities in human rights teaching, e.g., the preparation of instructional material, teacher training, and the teaching of human rights in the framework of disciplines other than law; and added that UNESCO was organizing an international conference on the teaching of human rights at the university level which would take place in Vienna in September 1978. He also drew the attention of the committee to UNESCO's preparation of a UNESCO Declaration on Race and Racial Prejudice, which aimed at illuminating the biological, sociological, cultural, economic, and political aspects, as well as the juridical, of the race question, thereby going well beyond the legal effects of condemning racism and racial discrimination. The Declaration would, therefore, constitute an extension and a deepening of the Convention and might, because of its multidisciplinary approach, also become a useful element in the Committee's interpretation of the Convention and a synthetic document for the implementation of article 7.

On 13 April 1977, the Committee adopted a recommendation on the subject and authorized its chairman to transmit it to UNESCO with a request for that body's cooperation. The recommendation was also transmitted by the UN Secretary-General to States parties to the Convention for any comments they might wish to make. The recommendations were as follows (UN Doc. A/32/18, chap. VIII, decision 3 [XV], general recommendation V):

The Committee on the Elimination of Racial Discrimination,

Bearing in mind the provisions of articles 7 and 9 of the International Convention on the Elimination of All Forms of Racial Discrimination,

Convinced that combating prejudices which lead to racial discrimination, promoting understanding, tolerance and friendship among racial and ethnic groups, and propagating the principles and purposes of the Charter of the United Nations and of the human rights declarations and other relevant instruments adopted by the General Assembly of the United Nations, are important and effective means of eliminating racial discrimination,

Considering that the obligations under article 7 of the Convention, which are binding on all States parties, must be fulfilled by them, including States which declare that racial discrimination is not practised on the territories under their jurisdiction, and that therefore all States parties are required

to include information on their implementation of the provisions of that article in the reports they submit in accordance with article 9, paragraph 1, of the Convention,

Noting with regret that few States parties have included, in the reports they have submitted in accordance with article 9 of the Convention, information on the measures which they have adopted and which give effect to the provisions of article 7 of the Convention, and that that information has often been general and perfunctory,

Recalling that, in accordance with article 9, paragraph 1, of the Convention, the Committee may request further information from the States parties,

1. Requests every State party which has not already done so to include—in the next report it will submit in accordance with article 9 of the Convention, or in a special report before its next periodic report becomes due—adequate information on the measures which it has adopted and which give effect to the provisions of article 7 of the Convention;

2. Invites the attention of States parties to the fact that, in accordance with article 7 of the Convention, the information to which the preceding paragraph refers should include information on the "immediate and effective measures" which they have adopted, "in the fields of teaching, education, culture and information", with a view to:

(a) "Combating prejudices which lead to racial discrimination";

(b) "Promoting understanding, tolerance and friendship among nations and racial or ethnical groups";

(c) "Propagating the purposes and principles of the Charter of the United Nations, the Universal Declaration of Human Rights, the United Nations Declaration on the Elimination of All Forms of Racial Discrimination" as well as the International Convention on the Elimination of All Forms of Racial Discrimination.

The Committee on the Elimination of Racial Discrimination has since given special attention to the implementation of article 7 by the national bodies concerned; has included in each annual report to the General Assembly a section indicating to what extent the States parties appear to be conforming to the rules laid out in that article; and has highlighted each positive achievement reported to it. However, in 1982, the Committee found it necessary to prepare additional guidelines for the implementation of article 7 (UN Doc. A/37/18, chap. IX, decision 2 [XXV]), as follows:

1. The reports should provide as much information as possible on each of the main subjects mentioned in article 7 under the following separate headings: (1) Education and teaching, (2) Culture, (3) Information.

2. Within these broad parameters, the information provided should reflect the measures taken by the States parties:

(a) To combat prejudices which lead to racial discrimination,

(b) To promote understanding, tolerance and friendship among nations and racial and ethnic groups.

### I. Education and Teaching

3. This part should describe legislative and administrative measures, including some general information on the educational system, taken in the field of education and teaching to combat racial prejudices which lead to racial discrimination.

4. It should indicate whether any steps have been taken to include in school curricula and in the training of teachers and other professionals, programmes and subjects to help promote human rights issues which would lead to better understanding, tolerance and friendship among nations and racial or ethnic groups.

5. It should also provide information on whether the purposes and principles of the instruments mentioned in the Committee's general guidelines (CERD/C/70, art. 7, letter C) are included in education and teaching.

### II. Culture

6. Information should be provided in this part of the report on the role of institutions or associations working to develop national culture and traditions, to combat racial prejudices and to promote intra-national and intra-cultural understanding, tolerance and friendship among nations and racial or ethnic groups.

7. Information should also be included on the work of solidarity committees or United Nations Associations to combat racism and racial discrimination and the observance by States parties of Human Rights Days or campaigns against racism and *apartheid*.

### III. Information

8. This part should provide information:

(a) On the role of State media in the dissemination of information to combat racial prejudices which lead to racial discrimination and to inculcate better understanding of the purposes and principles of the above-mentioned instruments;

(b) On the role of the mass information media, i.e. the press, radio and television, in the publicizing of human rights and disseminating information on the purposes and principles of the above-mentioned human rights instruments.

In 1983, the *Study on the Implementation of Article 7 of the International Convention on the Elimination of All Forms of Racial Discrimination* (UN Doc. A/CONF. 119/11) was prepared by a Special Rapporteur, Mr. Georges Tenekides, a former member of the Committee. The Committee endorsed the study as its contribution to the Second World Conference to Combat Racism and Racial Discrimination.

The study indicated clearly that a number of States parties to the Convention had not adequately fulfilled their obligations under article 7. The most frequently advanced explanation was the absence of racial discrimination in territories under their control. Another was that the existence of anti-discriminatory provisions in the national constitution made it unnecessary to adopt additional legislative, administrative, or other measures. Still another was that certain matters, particularly in the field of information, were outside the authority of the national authorities. The Committee did not consider such explanations to be valid or acceptable, maintaining, for example, that the simple assertion that racism does not exist in a particular country in no way absolves the State from its obligation

to take appropriate measures under article 7, since it is never known what the future might hold in terms, for example, of a re-emergence of racism as a result of new social conditions such as a sudden influx of foreign migrant workers.

After considering the Committee's report, the General Assembly on 3 December 1982 (resolution 37/44) appealed to all States parties to the International Convention on the Elimination of All Forms of Racial Discrimination to fulfill their obligations under the Convention and to submit their reports within the appropriate time.

The significance of the provisions of article 7, and their important human, social, and international implications, are aptly summarized in the conclusions set out by the Special Rapporteur in the above-mentioned study, which are as follows (UN Doc. A/CONF. 119/11, paras. 105–109):

The guidelines contained in article 7 of the Convention are universal in scope since good relations between individuals, States or various ethnic groups will, in the final analysis, depend on the implementation of these and other measures. In any event, article 7 is unique in that, generally speaking, no provision exists, either in the various internal codes regulating social relations or in international treaties, which contains measures designed to prevent the infringement of the provisions of such instruments. To mention only two basic examples, the Charter of the United Nations and the Covenants on human rights do not provide for any measure in the fields of teaching, education, culture or information to encourage governments or individuals to devote greater attention to the fundamental objectives of those instruments, such as the ideals of peaceful co-operation, respect for the sovereign equality of States and respect for the dignity of the human person. The reason for this is that, in the area of racial prejudice, more than for any other social affliction subject to legal, political or economic sanctions, preventive action is called for to shape mental attitudes through teaching, education, culture and the information media.

It is essential that the concrete measures described above should become a reality. States are trusted to implement them. However, since the State is an abstract entity, the responsibility for ensuring the implementation of the relevant measures devolves upon its organs. The insistent and effective implementation of the principles of non-discrimination, understanding, tolerance and friendship among nations or racial or ethnic groups depends on the cultural background and the sense of the universal within an egalitarian perspective, primarily of teachers, but also, to a certain extent, of legislators, members of the administrative and the executive in general and judges, and on the initiatives of the potential victims.

But it is, for CERD, too, to exercise vigilance and to remind States at every opportunity—particularly during consideration of their periodic reports—of their duties under article 7. A similar responsibility devolves upon the United Nations General Assembly, which, when considering CERD's annual report, has the duty—making use of its moral prestige and vast dissemination facilities—to call upon States who have failed to do so to fulfil their obligations. Similar responsibilities are also incumbent on men of culture and writers. In South Africa, Afrikaner writers such as André Brink and Nadine Gordimer have, through their writings, worked effectively for racial equality and against *apartheid*.

Article 7 carries the seeds of part of the philosophy underlying the fundamental provisions of the Charter of the United Nations. For, today, humanity must be seen as oscillating between interdependence dictated by economic and political circumstances and the reality of cultural pluralism, where more and more is heard of multicultural societies. Never before has man gone so far to promote the one-world ideology, and, at the same time, to ensure the acceptance of the individual by the international community on his own terms.

Thus, the right to be different is being claimed on all sides. Positive law in the sphere of human rights proclaims equality with a view to eliminating discrimination, but not to impose a standardization which could prove oppressive, or even, in some cases, repressive. The system for the safeguarding of human rights combines or pairs unity with diversity and interdependence with freedom, and sees the equal dignity of all within the context of the individuality of each.

Every ethnic group and every State, regardless of the politico-social system to which it belongs, has the right to culture in general and to its own culture. If the duty to promote understanding, tolerance and friendship among nations or racial or ethnic groups is added to this, it will be seen that the result prescribed by article 7, namely fruitful dialogue between men of goodwill, accompanied by the unparallelled fertility of a dialogue of cultures, can be achieved only at the expense of an authentic dialogue encompassing all mankind. Healthy dialogue, with the conditions which it presupposes (good faith of the parties involved, dedication to the values advocated by the United Nations), is a means, a mechanism for piercing the veil which separates individuals and peoples. It provides access to understanding and rapprochement with others and saves us from isolation, which is the cause of many forms of anguish or disillusionment at the individual or social level. To withdraw selfishly into oneself, to seek only gain, or to be indifferent or contemptuous towards individuals in general is to render the civic spirit unattainable and the sense of international solidarity inconceivable. By promoting intolerance and enmity this egotistical attitude threatens individuals and society alike. If man wishes to achieve a full understanding of the time in which he lives and to overcome the crises which beset him on all sides, he will reject the unilateral in favour of the universal. The adoption of the universal perspective and the acceptance of flows from other continents which can fertilize any civilization, indisputably contribute to man's vital potential, to his ability to invent and create. At which point, man, in achieving fulfilment, will find infinite joy, and that euphoria will improve him. The achievement of understanding, tolerance and friendship among nations and racial and ethnic groups, is a process which takes place at both the logical and temporal levels. The resulting rapprochement between human beings will contribute effectively to the development of the spirit of international solidarity, to the safeguarding of the security of States and to the strengthening of *peace within justice*, which is the ultimate aim of the United Nations.

**RACIST PROPAGANDA AND ORGANIZATIONS.** Article 4 of the International Convention on the Elimination of All Forms of Racial Discrimination reads as follows:

States parties condemn all propaganda and all organizations which are based on ideas or theories of superiority of one race or group of persons of one colour or ethnic origin, or which attempt to justify or promote racial hatred and discrimination in any form, and undertake to adopt immediate and positive measures designed to eradicate all incitement to, or acts of, such discrimination and, to this end, with due regard to the principles embodied in the Universal Declaration of Human Rights and expressly set forth in article 5 of this Convention, *inter alia*:

(a) Shall declare an offence punishable by law all dissemination of ideas based on racial superiority or hatred, incitement to racial discrimination, as well as all acts of violence or incitement to such acts against any race or group of persons of another colour or ethnic origin, and also the provision of any assistance to racist activities, including the financing thereof;

(b) Shall declare illegal and prohibit organizations, and also organized and all other propaganda activities, which promote and incite racial discrimination, and shall recognize participation in such organization or activities as an offence punishable by law;

(c) Shall not permit public authorities or public institutions, national or local, to promote or incite racial discrimination.

In examining the reports submitted by States parties to the Convention, the UN **COMMITTEE ON THE ELIMINATION OF RACIAL DISCRIMINATION** has consistently maintained that article 4 requires them to enact legislation imposing specific penalties for all acts of a discriminatory nature, as provided in sub-paragraphs (a) and (b), and that no State could be said to have effectively implemented the convention until it had done so. It has not accepted the position of some States parties that article 4 should be interpreted as requiring such States to adopt further legislative measures only insofar as racist propaganda and organizations actually exist in their countries and territories and has maintained that the adoption of specific and appropriate legislation is required for deterrent purposes even in countries free of racism, since no one can foresee what the future holds in store.

Nor has the Committee accepted the view of some States parties that article 4 cannot be read in isolation from the rest of the Convention and should be interpreted as requiring States to adopt further legislative measures only insofar as such measures were consistent with the fundamental right of freedom of opinion and expression, to which reference is made in article 5 of the Convention.

*The Study on the Implementation of Article 4 of the International Convention on the Elimination of All Forms of Racial Discrimination*, prepared by a member of the Committee on the Elimination of Racial Discrimination, Mr. Jose D. Ingles (Philippines), and approved by the committee (UN Doc. A/CONF. 119/10, later issued as UN publication, Sales no. E.85.XIV.2), was presented to the Second World Conference to Combat

Racism and Racial Discrimination, convened at the European office of the United Nations, Geneva, from 1 to 12 August 1983. In the study, Mr. Ingles included the following background information (paras. 2–11):

Article 4 has been aptly described as the "key article" of the Convention. It was the consensus in the General Assembly that the article, as finally adopted, afforded a compromise between those who wished the enactment of positive legislation to penalize not only "incitement to discrimination" but also the "dissemination of ideas based on racial superiority or hatred", and those who did not wish to see freedom of speech or assembly impaired. For example, the representative of the United Kingdom would not accept punishment for the bare expression of an idea or mere incitement to racial discrimination, unless there was incitement to violence. Indeed, the original draft of article 4 *(a)* submitted by the Sub-Commission on Prevention of Discrimination and Protection of Minorities, as subsequently adopted by the Commission on Human Rights, provided for the punishment by law of "all incitement to racial discrimination resulting in or likely to cause acts of violence".

The compromise text proposed by Nigeria (A/ C.3/ L.1250) broadened the scope of article 4 *(a)* by providing for the punishment by law of "all dissemination of ideas based on superiority or hatred, incitement to racial discrimination, as well as acts of violence or incitement to such acts against any race or group of persons. . . ."

That text also included in the introductory paragraph of article 4 the clause "with due regard to the principles embodied in the Universal Declaration of Human Rights and the rights expressly set forth in article 5 of the Convention". This was interpreted by the advocates of free speech and assembly as "not imposing on a State party the obligation to take any action impairing the right to freedom of speech and freedom of association". However, article 29, paragraph 2, of the Universal Declaration of Human Rights allows the limitation of everyone's rights and freedoms "as are determined by law solely for the purpose of securing due recognition and respect for the rights and freedoms of others and of meeting the just requirements of morality, public order and the general welfare in a democratic society". It is clear that a balance must be struck between article 4 *(a)* of the Convention and the right of free speech, and between article 4 *(b)* and the right of free association.

When the Convention entered into force on 4 January 1969, many of the States parties had not yet enacted legislation to implement that particular article. The situation did not change substantially when the number of States parties increased to 118, from the original 28 in 1969. There were a few States parties that had enacted the necessary legislation prior to ratification or accession to the Convention, and still fewer States whose existing legislation may be said to comply substantially with the provisions of article 4.

A few were of the erroneous opinion that, having become parties to the Convention, they had done all that was required of them as States parties. It was contended that, the Convention having become part of domestic law by incorporation with or without transformation, no further measures were necessary to give effect to the Convention.

Others cited the provisions of their respective constitutions prohibiting racial discrimination or racial propaganda, but did not provide legislative texts to carry out the constitutional injunction. In the absence of legislative provisions, a few stated that racial discrimination or incitement thereto, as well as racist organizations and propaganda, would be unconstitutional.

Some stated in their reports that, since racial discrimination did not exist or was unknown in their respective countries, it was not necessary or might even be counter-productive to prohibit it, much less to take measures to eradicate incitement to, or acts of, such discrimination.

The problem of implementation arose in view of the guidelines adopted by the Committee at its first session, on 28 January 1970 (CERD/C/R.12), to assist the States parties in preparing the reports they were required to submit under article 9, paragraph 1, of the Convention. It was asked, *inter alia*, what administrative, legislative, judicial or other measures they had taken to comply with the provisions of article 4 of the Convention.

On 24 February 1972, the Committee adopted general recommendation I, as follows:

"On the basis of the consideration at its fifth session of reports submitted by States parties under article 9 of the International Convention on the Elimination of All Forms of Racial Discrimination, the Committee found that the legislation of a number of States parties did not include the provisions envisaged in article 4 *(a)* and *(b)* of the Convention, the implementation of which (with due regard to the principles embodied in the Universal Declaration of Human Rights and the rights expressly set forth in article 5 of the Convention) is obligatory under the Convention for all States parties.

"The Committee accordingly recommends that the States parties whose legislation was deficient in this respect should consider, in accordance with their national legislative procedures, the question of supplementing their legislation with provisions conforming to the requirements of article 4 *(a)* and *(b)* of the Convention."

The revised general guidelines concerning the form and contents of reports by States parties under article 9, paragraph 1, of the Convention, adopted by the Committee on 9 April 1980 (CERD/C/70), required *inter alia*:

A. Information on the legislative, judicial, administrative or other measures which give effect to the provisions of article 4 of the Convention, in particular measures taken to give effect to the undertaking to adopt immediate and positive measures designed to eradicate all incitement to, or acts of, racial discrimination [with due regard to the principles embodied in the Universal Declaration of Human Rights and the rights expressly set forth in article 5 of the Convention]; in particular:

(1) To declare an offence punishable by law all dissemination of ideas based on racial superiority and hatred, incitement to racial discrimination, as well as all acts of violence or incitement to such acts against any race or group of persons of another colour or ethnic origin, and also the provision of any assistance to racist activities, including the financing thereof;

(2) To declare illegal and prohibit organizations, and also organized and all other propaganda activities, which promote and incite racial discrimination, and to recognize participation in such organizations or activities as an offence punishable by law;

(3) Not to permit public authorities or public institutions, national or local, to promote or incite racial discrimination.

B. Information on appropriate measures taken to give effect to general recommendation I, of 24 February 1972, by which the Committee recommended that the States parties whose legislation was deficient in respect of the implementation of article 4 should consider, in accordance with their national legislative procedures, the question of supplementing their legislation with provisions conforming to the requirements of article 4 *(a)* and *(b)* of the Convention;

C. Information in response to decision 3 (VII) adopted by the Committee on 4 May 1973, by which the Committee requested the States parties:

(1) To indicate what specific penal internal legislation designed to implement the provisions of article 4 *(a)* and *(b)* has been enacted in their respective countries and to transmit to the Secretary-General in one of the official languages the texts concerned, as well as such provisions of general penal law as must be taken into account when applying such specific legislation;

(2) Where no such specific legislation has been enacted, to inform the Committee of the manner and the extent to which the provisions of the existing penal laws, as applied by the courts, effectively implement their obligations under article 4 *(a)* and *(b)*, and to transmit to the Secretary-General in one of the official languages the texts of those provisions.

Mr. Ingles' conclusions and recommendations, set out in chapter IV of the study (paras. 210–246), are as follows:

The practice of States parties in the implementation of the Convention, particularly of article 4, has not been uniform.

Some States point out that their existing legislation prior to the entry into force of the Convention already satisfies the requirements of article 4. In rare instances the claim seems to be justified.

Others have enacted legislation to conform to the Convention before ratification or accession to the Convention. In some cases such legislation is adequate to meet the requirements of article 4.

Many have amended their existing legislation after accession to, or ratification of, the Convention. Some amendments comply fully with article 4.

A few have adopted entirely new legislation to fulfil the conditions laid down in article 4.

Some are still considering the enactment of the necessary legislation, sometimes through special commissions set up for the purpose.

Unlike other articles of the Convention, article 4 is not self-executing. Despite the incorporation or transformation of the Convention as part of domestic law, article 4 can be implemented only if legislation is enacted to do what the article ordains.

The other articles of the Convention vest States parties with ample discretion to adopt such measures as they may deem appropriate to achieve the objectives of the Convention. The introductory paragraph of article 4 follows this general trend in the undertaking of States parties "to adopt immediate and positive measures designed to eradicate all incitement to, or acts of, such discrimination".

However, paragraphs *(a)* and *(b)* of article 4 are not discretionary, but mandatory. These paragraphs are clear-cut and unambiguous. They provide that States parties "shall declare an offence punishable by law" certain acts enumerated in paragraph *(a)* and "shall declare illegal and prohibit organizations, and also organized and all other propaganda activities which promote and incite racial discrimination" as well as "recognize participation in such organization or activities as an offence punishable by law", as required by paragraph *(b)*.

While article 4 (see the introductory paragraph) is generally directed at the eradication of racial discrimination or incitement to such discrimination, paragraphs *(a)* and *(b)* are directed mainly against incitement, or promotion and incitement, to racial discrimination.

It is evident that many States parties have not yet fulfilled all the requirements of article 4 *(a)* and *(b)* of the Convention. This is due in the first instance to the claims of some States parties that there is no racial discrimination in their respective jurisdictions.

However, States parties are bound to enact implementing legislation in accordance with article 4 *(a)* and *(b)* even if they allege that racial discrimination is unknown or that there are no racist organizations in their respective jurisdictions. Article 4 aims at prevention rather than cure; the penalty of the law is supported to deter racism or racial discrimination as well as activities aimed at their promotion or incitement. Of course other measures are recommended by the Convention, particularly in article 7, through teaching, information, education and acculturation, to combat prejudices which lead to racial discrimination and to promote understanding, tolerance and friendship among nations and racial or ethnic groups. But it is also recognized that penal legislation is educative as well as punitive.

Certain States parties have sought to retain the discretion to determine whether and when it is necessary to enact legislation in accordance with the mandatory provisions of article 4. It has been said that this kind of reservation is incompatible with the object and purpose of the Convention and cannot be permitted under article 20, paragraph 2, of the Convention.

It is true that the second sentence of article 20, paragraph 2, provides that "a reservation shall be considered incompatible or inhibitive if at least two thirds of the States parties to this Convention object to it". But this is certainly only one of the modes of determining whether or not a reservation is incompatible with the Convention, withal an extraordinary one. Article 22 of the Convention gives the International Court of Justice the ultimate function of resolving disputes with respect to the interpretation or application of the Convention.

In the absence of a definitive judicial ruling on the admissibility of the reservation in question, the State party concerned might be asked to withdraw its reservation.

Indeed, the Committee has made such a recommendation to one State party.

Another factor hindering the full application of article 4 of the Convention is the interpretation that implementation of that article might impair or jeopardize freedom of opinion and expression and of peaceful assembly and association. This is the extreme position. Midway lies the proposition that a "balance" has to be struck between article 4 *(a)* and freedom of speech, and between article 4 *(b)* and freedom of association. The weight of opinion inclines to the view that the rights of free speech and of free association are not absolute, but subject to limitations.

Liberty is not licence. As the former Secretary-General of the United Nations, Dag Hammarskjöld, aptly said: "There is not now and never has been any such thing as unlimited liberty.... Each man's freedom is limited by that of his neighbours.... The very existence of a society ... imposes certain limitations of the freedom of action of all its members, no matter how loose or disorderly the society or communities may be. Limitations ... on the liberty of individuals are thus inevitable."

Article 29, paragraph 2, of the Universal Declaration of

Human Rights is explicit that the exercise of the rights and freedoms guaranteed therein shall be subject only to such limitations as may be determined by law solely for the purpose of securing due recognition and respect for the rights and freedoms of others, and of meeting the just requirements of morality, public order and the general welfare of a democratic society.

While article 30 of the Universal Declaration provides that nothing in the Declaration may be interpreted as implying for any State, group or person any right to engage in any activity or to perform any act aimed at the destruction of any of the rights and freedoms set forth therein, this does not preclude or prohibit reasonable limitations as are expressly set forth in article 29, paragraph 2, which do not have the purpose or effect of destroying those rights and freedoms. Moreover, article 29, paragraph 3, of the Universal Declaration provides that those rights and freedoms may in no case be exercised contrary to the purposes and principles of the United Nations, as set forth in Articles 1 and 2 of the Charter of the United Nations.

Article 19, paragraph 3, of the International Covenant on Civil and Political Rights expressly authorizes restrictions on the exercise of the right to freedom of expression such as are provided by law and are necessary, *(a)* for respect of the rights or reputation of others, or *(b)* for the protection of national security or of public order or of public health or morals.

Article 21 of the International Covenant on Civil and Political Rights also authorizes such restrictions on the right of peaceful assembly as are in conformity with law and are necessary in a democratic society in the interests of national security or public safety, public order, the protection of public health or morals or the protection of the rights and freedoms of others.

Even in societies most zealous of safeguarding the right of free speech, there are laws against defamation and sedition. Laws against incitement to racial discrimination or hatred are certainly no less necessary to protect public order or the rights of others. The majority of the Committee is convinced that the same applies without distinction to the dissemination of ideas based on racial superiority.

Moreover, racial discrimination is a crime under international law and its eradication is a treaty obligation of the States parties to the Convention. More than that, the eradication of racial discrimination has become a peremptory norm of international law *(jus cogens)*.

Many States parties have incorporated in their Constitutions the principle of equality in the enjoyment of human rights guaranteed therein. Others have provided in their Constitutions the principle of nondiscrimination, particularly on grounds of race or colour. Some of these countries contend as a consequence that any act of discrimination or violation of the principle of equality would be unconstitutional. The victim of an unconstitutional act may apply to the competent court for redress. Some countries, however, also provide for the extraordinary remedy of *amparo* as a constitutional right.

The remedy of *amparo* is generally available in case a public official or authority commits the unconstitutional act of discrimination or of violation of the principle of equality. In the event of an affirmative finding by the appropriate tribunal, the public official or authority concerned is ordered to desist from continuing the commission of the offence. If the public official or authority persists, then the official or officials concerned are summarily dismissed from office. It is possible that the remedy of *amparo* is also available to the

victim of incitement to racial discrimination in case the offender is a public official. But it is clear that, in the absence of legislation, no remedy is available to the victim of racial discrimination, or incitement thereto, if the offender is a private person.

The legislation of some States parties subject the "dissemination of ideas based on racial superiority or hatred" or "incitement to racial discrimination" to certain conditions, for example that the dissemination or incitement must be intentional, or must have certain objectives such as "to stir up hatred", or that they be "threatening, abusive or insulting", or accompanied by "mocking, slander, insult, threat or other means". Obviously, these conditions are restrictive and ignore the fact that article 4 *(a)* of the Convention declares punishable the mere act of dissemination or incitement, without any conditions.

Most penal codes penalize acts of violence or incitement to such acts directed against any individual or group of individuals. These should satisfy one of the requirements of article 4 *(a)*, although it would be within the spirit, if not the letter, of that article to enact legislation specifically referring to violence or incitement thereto directed against "any race or group of persons of another colour or ethnic origin", perhaps making it an aggravating circumstance.

General penal legislation making accomplices or accessories to crime also punishable would cover "the provision of any assistance to racist activities, including the financing thereof", if such racist activities are made a crime in the first place.

Some States parties have Constitutions which guarantee the right of peaceful assembly and association and also provide that associations may be established only for a lawful purpose. The establishment of an organization or association which promotes or incites to racial discrimination would thus be unconstitutional because it was not established for a lawful purpose. The remedy in such a case varies from denial of permit or registration to dissolution, in the event that the organization or association has already been registered or granted a permit. In any case, legislation would still be necessary to penalize those who form or create such an organization or association, or those who participate in its illegal activities, that is, in the promotion of and incitement to racial discrimination.

There is also legislation in most countries against the establishment of associations or organizations with an illegal purpose. In the absence of such legislation, some countries contend that existing legislation, penalizing the promotion of or incitement to discrimination, has the effect of discouraging the establishment of organizations dedicated to such purposes. The Committee takes the view that further legislation is necessary to declare illegal and prohibit such organizations.

Some States prohibit organizations vested with an unlawful purpose. Legislation is directed either to the prohibition of their registration or their dissolution thereafter, or both. In common law countries, the term "unlawful" is distinguished from "illegal" in the sense that an unlawful act may not always give rise to penal sanctions. Unlawful acts usually result in civil liability, as in the case of torts. It follows that the imposition of civil liability falls short of the requirement in article 4 to declare certain acts or activities "as an offence punishable by law".

Article 4 *(b)* requires States parties not only to "declare illegal and prohibit organizations, and also organized and all other propaganda activities, which promote and incite racial discrimination", but also to "recognize participation in such organizations or activities as an offence punishable by law".

It is obvious that this provision of the Convention or any similar provision in the Constitution of a State party requires implementing legislation. *A fortiori*, this applies also to article 4 *(a)*. The Constitution of a State, like the Convention, can only decree that certain acts should be punishable by law. Rarely does a Constitution itself provide the penalty, as in the case of high treason, for example.

It is clear that constitutional provisions alone, without implementing legislation, would not satisfy the mandatory requirements of article 4 of the Convention for States parties to declare an offence punishable by law the acts enumerated in paragraphs *(a)* and *(b)*.

It will be seen that many States parties require time in order to be able to comply with their obligations under the Convention. It is realized that adoption of legislation is a slow process. Nowhere is this observation more apt than with reference to article 4.

It is not enough that the executive should recommend to the legislature or to parliament the enactment of legislation to implement article 4. The experience of at least four States parties shows that the executive should follow up its recommendation. The legislature, no less than the executive, is bound to take action.

However, it should be stated that States parties should complete the process of adjusting their legislation in accordance with article 4 within a reasonable time. A certain amount of political will is necessary to give impetus to the legislative process. It is an accepted principle that treaties should be observed in good faith by contracting parties.

**SEE ALSO** *Committee on the Elimination of Racial Discrimination, UN; Xenophobia.*

**BIBLIOGRAPHY.** Banton, Michael. "International Action Against Racial Discrimination," *Ethnic and Racial Studies* 14, no. 4 (Oct. 1991): 545–556. Scholarly article, in English.

Barber, Benjamin R. "Global Multiculturalism and the American Experiment," *World Policy Journal* 10, no. 1 (Spring 1993): 47–55. Scholarly article, in English.

Bernard-Maugiron, Nathalie. "20 Years After: 38th Session of the Committee on the Elimination of Racial Discrimination," *Netherlands Quarterly of Human Rights* 8, no. 4 (1990): 395–402. Scholarly article, in English.

Bovenkerk, Frank, Robert Miles, and Gilles Verbunt. "Comparative Studies of Migration and Exclusion on the Grounds of 'Race' and Ethnic Background in Western Europe: A Critical Appraisal," *International Migration Review* 25, no. 2 (Summer 1991): 375–391. Scholarly article, in English; bibliography, pp. 389–391.

Buchanan, Anne. "150 Years of White Domination in New Zealand," *Race and Class* 31, no. 4 (April–June 1990): 73–80. Scholarly note, in English.

Castles, Stephen. "The Australian Model of Immigration and Multiculturalism: Is It Applicable to Europe?" *International Migration Review* 26, no. 2 (Summer 1992): 549–567. Scholarly article, in English; bibliography, pp. 565–567.

————. "Strategies for Improving Community Relations," *Migration Action* 13, no. 1 (April 1991): 18–22. NGO article, in English; bibliography, p. 22.

Cholewinski, Ryszard. "The Racial Discrimination Convention and the Protection of Cultural and Linguistic Ethnic Minorities," *Revue de droit international, de sciences diplomatiques et politiques* no. 3 (Sept. 1991): 157–226. Scholarly article, in English; bibliography, pp. 192–226.

Crowley, John. "Le Rôle de la Commission for Racial Equality dans la représentation politique des minorités ethniques britanniques" (The Role of the Commission for Racial Equality in the Political Representation of British Ethnic Minorities), *Revue européenne des migrations internationales* 6, no. 3 (1990): 45–61. Scholarly article, in French.

Dinstein, Yoram, ed. "International Legal Colloquium on Racial and Religious Hatred and Group Libel," *Israel Yearbook on Human Rights* 22 (1993). Collection of scholarly articles, in English.

Fife, Brian L. *Desegregation in American Schools: Comparative Intervention Strategies.* Westport, CT, USA: Praeger, 1992. Scholarly monograph, in English; bibliography, pp. 181–203.

Frederikse, Julie. *The Unbreakable Thread: Non-Racialism in South Africa.* Bloomington, IN, USA: Indiana University Press & Zed Books, 1990. Scholarly monograph, in English.

Fullinwider, Robert. "Multicultural Education," *Report from the Institute for Philosophy & Public Policy* 11, no. 3 (Summer 1991). Article, in English.

Greenspan, Louis, and Cyril Levitt, eds. *Under the Shadow of Weimar: Democracy, Law, and Racial Incitement in Six Countries.* Westport, CT, USA: Praeger, 1993. Scholarly monograph, in English; bibliography, pp. 213–221.

Legal Education Action Project. *Back to the Laager: The Rise of White Right Wing Violence in South Africa.* Cape Town, South Africa: Institute of Criminology, University of Cape Town, 1991. NGO monograph, in English.

Lerner, Natan. *Group Rights and Discrimination in International Law.* Dordrecht, the Netherlands: Martinus Nijhoff, 1991. Scholarly monograph, in English.

*L'intolérance et le droit de l'autre* (Intolerance and the Rights of Others). No. 20. Geneva, Switzerland: Labor et Fides, 1992. Scholarly monograph, in French.

"Racial Divisions, Skills Divisions," *South African Labour Bulletin* 17, no. 2 (March–April 1993): 23–55. Collection of articles, in English.

Schifter, Richard. "Address Delivered before the International Conference on Ethnic Conflict Resolution under Rule of Law: 'To Hate All the People Your Relatives Hate'," *Human Rights Law Journal* 12, no. 8–9 (Sept. 1991): 327–330. Speech, in English.

Shepherd, Jr., George W., and David Penna, eds. *Racism and the Underclass: State Policy and Discrimination against Minorities.* Westport, CT, USA: Greenwood Press, 1991. Collection of scholarly works, in English; bibliography, pp. 167–172.

Tarzi, Shah M. "The Nation-State, Victim Groups and Refugees," *Ethnic and Racial Studies* 14, no. 4 (Oct. 1991): 441–452. Scholarly article, in English.

Thornberry, Patrick. *International Law and the Rights of Minorities.* Oxford, UK: Oxford University Press, 1991. Scholarly monograph, in English; bibliography, pp. 431–443.

Truluck, Anne. *No Blood on Our Hands: Political Violence in the Natal Midlands; 1987 to mid-1992, and the Role of the State, "White" Political Parties and Business.* Pietermaritzburg, South Africa: Black Sash, Natal Midlands Region, 1992. Scholarly monograph, in English.

van Boven, Theo. "Combating Racial Discrimination in the World and in Europe," *Netherlands Quarterly of Human Rights* 11, no. 2 (1993): 163–172. Scholarly article, in English.

Wyzan, Michael L., ed. *The Political Economy of Ethnic Discrimination and Affirmative Action: A Comparative Perspective.* New York: Praeger, 1990. Collection of scholarly articles, in English; bibliography, pp. 217–231.

## RACIAL DISCRIMINATION: INTERNATIONAL CONVENTION ON THE ELIMINATION OF ALL FORMS OF RACIAL DISCRIMINATION (1965).

The Convention was the first human rights instrument adopted by the United Nations to embody international measures of implementation: it authorized establishment of the COMMITTEE ON THE ELIMINATION OF RACIAL DISCRIMINATION, composed of experts serving in their personal capacities, to consider reports from States parties on the legislative, judicial, administrative, or other measures adopted by them and which give effect to the provisions of the Convention, to make suggestions and general recommendations based on its examination of those reports and information received from States parties, and to assist in settling disputes among States parties concerning the application of the Convention.

It also provides (article 14) for the Committee to receive and consider communications from individuals or groups of individuals within the jurisdiction of a State party claiming to be the victims of a violation of any of the rights set forth in the Convention, provided that that State has made a declaration recognizing the competence of the Committee to do so.

The International Convention on the Elimination of All Forms of Racial Discrimination was adopted by the UN GENERAL ASSEMBLY on 21 December 1965 (resolution 2106 [XX]), and entered into force on 2 January 1969. The Declaration regarding article 14 of the Convention entered into force on 3 December 1982. The text of the Convention, annexed to resolution 2106 (XX), is as follows:

The States Parties to this Convention,

Considering that the Charter of the United Nations is based on the principles of the dignity and equality inherent in all human beings, and that all Member States have pledged themselves to take joint and separate action, in cooperation with the Organization, for the achievement of one of the purposes of the United Nations which is to promote and encourage universal respect for and observance of human rights and fundamental freedoms for all, without distinction as to race, sex, language or religion,

Considering that the Universal Declaration of Human Rights proclaims that all human beings are born free and equal in dignity and rights and that everyone is entitled to all the rights and freedoms set out therein, without distinction of any kind, in particular as to race, colour or national origin,

Considering that all human beings are equal before the law and are entitled to equal protection of the law against any discrimination and against any incitement to discrimination,

Considering that the United Nations has condemned colonialism and all practices of segregation and discrimination associated therewith, in whatever form and wherever they exist, and that the Declaration on the Granting of Independence to Colonial Countries and Peoples of 14 December 1960 (General Assembly resolution 1514 (XV)) has affirmed

and solemnly proclaimed the necessity of bringing them to a speedy and unconditional end,

Considering that the United Nations Declaration on the Elimination of All Forms of Racial Discrimination of 20 November 1963 (General Assembly resolution 1904 [XVIII]) solemnly affirms the necessity of speedily eliminating racial discrimination throughout the world in all its forms and manifestations and of securing understanding of and respect for the dignity of the human person,

Convinced that any doctrine of superiority based on racial differentiation is scientifically false, morally condemnable, socially unjust and dangerous, and that there is no justification for racial discrimination, in theory or in practice, anywhere,

Reaffirming that discrimination between human beings on the grounds of race, colour or ethnic origin is an obstacle to friendly and peaceful relations among nations and is capable of disturbing peace and security among peoples and the harmony of persons living side by side even within one and the same State,

Convinced that the existence of racial barriers is repugnant to the ideals of any human society,

Alarmed by manifestations of racial discrimination still in evidence in some areas of the world and by governmental policies based on racial superiority or hatred, such as policies of *apartheid,* segregation or separation,

Resolved to adopt all necessary measures for speedily eliminating racial discrimination in all its forms and manifestations, and to prevent and combat racist doctrines and practices in order to promote understanding between races and to build an international community free from all forms of racial segregation and racial discrimination,

Bearing in mind the Convention concerning Discrimination in respect of Employment and Occupation adopted by the International Labour Organisation in 1958, and the Convention against Discrimination in Education adopted by the United Nations Educational, Scientific and Cultural Organization in 1960,

Desiring to implement the principles embodied in the United Nations Declaration on the Elimination of All Forms of Racial Discrimination and to secure the earliest adoption of practical measures to that end,

Have agreed as follows:

### Part I

*Article 1.* 1. In this Convention, the term "racial discrimination" shall mean any distinction, exclusion, restriction or preference based on race, colour, descent, or national or ethnic origin which has the purpose or effect of nullifying or impairing the recognition, enjoyment or exercise, on an equal footing, of human rights and fundamental freedoms in the political, economic, social, cultural or any other field of public life.

2. This Convention shall not apply to distinctions, exclusions, restrictions or preferences made by a State Party to this Convention between citizens and non-citizens.

3. Nothing in this Convention may be interpreted as affecting in any way the legal provisions of States Parties concerning nationality, citizenship or naturalization, provided that such provisions do not discriminate against any particular nationality.

4. Special measures taken for the sole purpose of securing adequate advancement of certain racial or ethnic groups or individuals requiring such protection as may be necessary in

order to ensure such groups or individuals equal enjoyment or exercise of human rights and fundamental freedoms shall not be deemed racial discrimination, provided, however, that such measures do not, as a consequence, lead to the maintenance of separate rights for different racial groups and that they shall not be continued after the objectives for which they were taken have been achieved.

*Article 2.* 1. States Parties condemn racial discrimination and undertake to pursue by all appropriate means and without delay a policy of eliminating racial discrimination in all its forms and promoting understanding among all races, and, to this end:

(a) Each State Party undertakes to engage in no act or practice of racial discrimination against persons, groups of persons or institutions and to ensure that all public authorities and public institutions, national and local, shall act in conformity with this obligation;

(b) Each State Party undertakes not to sponsor, defend or support racial discrimination by any persons or organizations;

(c) Each State Party shall take effective measures to review governmental, national and local policies, and to amend, rescind or nullify any laws and regulations which have the effect of creating or perpetuating racial discrimination wherever it exists;

(d) Each State Party shall prohibit and bring to an end, by all appropriate means, including legislation as required by circumstances, racial discrimination by any persons, group or organization;

(e) Each State Party undertakes to encourage, where appropriate, integrationist multiracial organizations and movements and other means of eliminating barriers between races, and to discourage anything which tends to strengthen racial division.

2. States Parties shall, when the circumstances so warrant, take, in the social, economic, cultural and other fields, special and concrete measures to ensure the adequate development and protection of certain racial groups or individuals belonging to them, for the purpose of guaranteeing them the full and equal enjoyment of human rights and fundamental freedoms. These measures shall in no case entail as a consequence the maintenance of unequal or separate rights for different racial groups after the objectives for which they were taken have been achieved.

*Article 3.* States Parties particularly condemn racial segregation and *apartheid* and undertake to prevent, prohibit and eradicate all practices of this nature in territories under their jurisdiction.

*Article 4.* States Parties condemn all propaganda and all organizations which are based on ideas or theories of superiority of one race or group of persons of one colour or ethnic origin, or which attempt to justify or promote racial hatred and discrimination in any form, and undertake to adopt immediate and positive measures designed to eradicate all incitement to, or acts of, such discrimination and, to this end, with due regard to the principles embodied in the Universal Declaration of Human Rights and the rights expressly set forth in article 5 of this Convention, *inter alia:*

(a) Shall declare an offence punishable by law all dissemination of ideas based on racial superiority or hatred, incitement to racial discrimination, as well as all acts of violence or incitement to such acts against any race or group of persons of another colour or ethnic origin, and also the provision of any assistance to racist activities, including the financing thereof;

(b) Shall declare illegal and prohibit organizations,

and also organized and all other propaganda activities, which promote and incite racial discrimination, and shall recognize participation in such organizations or activities as an offence punishable by law;

(c) Shall not permit public authorities or public institutions, national or local, to promote or incite racial discrimination.

*Article 5.* In compliance with the fundamental obligations laid down in article 2 of this Convention, States Parties undertake to prohibit and to eliminate racial discrimination in all its forms and to guarantee the right of everyone, without distinction as to race, colour, or national or ethnic origin, to equality before the law, notably in the enjoyment of the following rights:

(a) The right to equal treatment before the tribunals and all other organs administering justice;

(b) The right to security of person and protection by the State against violence or bodily harm, whether inflicted by government officials or by any individual group or institution;

(c) Political rights, in particular the rights to participate in elections—to vote and to stand for election—on the basis of universal and equal suffrage, to take part in the Government as well as in the conduct of public affairs at any level and to have equal access to public service;

(d) Other civil rights, in particular:

(i) The right to freedom of movement and residence within the border of the State;

(ii) The right to leave any country, including one's own, and to return to one's country;

(iii) The right to nationality;

(iv) The right to marriage and choice of spouse;

(v) The right to own property alone as well as in association with others;

(vi) The right to inherit;

(vii) The right to freedom of thought, conscience and religion;

(viii) The right to freedom of opinion and expression;

(ix) The right to freedom of peaceful assembly and association;

(e) Economic, social and cultural rights, in particular:

(i) The rights to work, to free choice of employment, to just and favourable conditions of work, to protection against unemployment, to equal pay for equal work, to just and favourable remuneration;

(ii) The right to form and join trade unions;

(iii) The right to housing;

(iv) The right to public health, medical care, social security and social services;

(v) The right to education and training;

(vi) The right to equal participation in cultural activities;

(f) The right of access to any place or service intended for use by the general public, such as transport, hotels, restaurants, cafés, theatres and parks.

*Article 6.* States Parties shall assure to everyone within their jurisdiction effective protection and remedies, through the competent national tribunals and other State institutions, against any acts of racial discrimination which violate his human rights and fundamental freedoms contrary to this Convention, as well as the right to seek from such tribunals just and adequate reparation or satisfaction for any damage suffered as a result of such discrimination.

*Article 7.* States Parties undertake to adopt immediate and effective measures, particularly in the fields of teaching, education, culture and information, with a view to combating prejudices which lead to racial discrimination and to promoting understanding, tolerance and friendship among nations and racial or ethnical groups, as well as to propagating the purposes and principles of the Charter of the United Nations, the Universal Declaration of Human Rights, the United Nations Declaration on the Elimination of All Forms of Racial Discrimination, and this Convention.

### Part II

*Article 8.* 1. There shall be established a Committee on the Elimination of Racial Discrimination (hereinafter referred to as the Committee) consisting of eighteen experts of high moral standing and acknowledged impartiality elected by States Parties from among their nationals, who shall serve in their personal capacity, consideration being given to equitable geographical distribution and to the representation of the different forms of civilization as well as of the principal legal systems.

2. The members of the Committee shall be elected by secret ballot from a list of persons nominated by the States Parties. Each State Party may nominate one person from among its own nationals.

3. The initial election shall be held six months after the date of the entry into force of this Convention. At least three months before the date of each election the Secretary-General of the United Nations shall address a letter to the States Parties inviting them to submit their nominations within two months. The Secretary-General shall prepare a list in alphabetical order of all persons thus nominated, indicating the States Parties which have nominated them, and shall submit it to the States Parties.

4. Elections of the members of the Committee shall be held at a meeting of States Parties convened by the Secretary-General at United Nations Headquarters. At that meeting, for which two thirds of the States Parties shall constitute a quorum, the persons elected to the Committee shall be those nominees who obtain the largest number of votes and an absolute majority of the votes of the representatives of States Parties present and voting.

5. (a) The members of the Committee shall be elected for a term of four years. However, the terms of nine of the members elected at the first election shall expire at the end of two years; immediately after the first election the names of these nine members shall be chosen by lot by the Chairman of the Committee.

(b) For the filling of casual vacancies, the State Party whose expert has ceased to function as a member of the Committee shall appoint another expert from among its nationals, subject to the approval of the Committee.

6. States Parties shall be responsible for the expenses of the members of the Committee while they are in performance of Committee duties.

*Article 9.* 1. States Parties undertake to submit to the Secretary-General of the United Nations, for consideration by the Committee, a report on the legislative, judicial, administrative or other measures which they have adopted and which give effect to the provisions of this Convention: (a) within one year after the entry into force of the Convention for the State concerned; and (b) thereafter every two years and whenever the Committee so requests. The Committee may request further information from the States Parties.

2. The Committee shall report annually, through the Secretary-General, to the General Assembly of the United

Nations on its activities and may make suggestions and general recommendations based on the examination of the reports and information received from the States Parties. Such suggestions and general recommendations shall be reported to the General Assembly together with comments, if any, from States Parties.

*Article 10.* 1. The Committee shall adopt its own rules of procedure.

2. The Committee shall elect its officers for a term of two years.

3. The secretariat of the Committee shall be provided by the Secretary-General of the United Nations.

4. The meetings of the Committee shall normally be held at United Nations Headquarters.

*Article 11.* 1. If a State Party considers that another State Party is not giving effect to the provisions of this Convention, it may bring the matter to the attention of the Committee. The Committee shall then transmit the communication to the State Party concerned. Within three months, the receiving State shall submit to the Committee written explanations or statements clarifying the matter and the remedy, if any, that may have been taken by that State.

2. If the matter is not adjusted to the satisfaction of both parties, either by bilateral negotiations or by any other procedure open to them, within six months after the receipt by the receiving State of the initial communication, either State shall have the right to refer the matter again to the Committee by notifying the Committee and also the other State.

3. The Committee shall deal with a matter referred to it in accordance with paragraph 2 of this article after it has ascertained that all available domestic remedies have been invoked and exhausted in the case, in conformity with the generally recognized principles of international law. This shall not be the rule where the application of the remedies is unreasonably prolonged.

4. In any matter referred to it, the Committee may call upon the States Parties concerned to supply any other relevant information.

5. When any matter arising out of this article is being considered by the Committee, the States Parties concerned shall be entitled to send a representative to take part in the proceedings to the Committee, without voting rights, while the matter is under consideration.

*Article 12.* 1. (a) After the Committee has obtained and collated all the information it deems necessary, the Chairman shall appoint an *ad hoc* Conciliation Commission (hereinafter referred to as the Commission) comprising five persons who may or may not be members of the Committee. The members of the Commission shall be appointed with the unanimous consent of the parties to the dispute, and its good offices shall be made available to the States concerned with a view to an amicable solution of the matter on the basis of respect for this Convention.

(b) If the States parties to the dispute fail to reach agreement within three months on all or part of the composition of the Commission, the members of the Commission not agreed upon by the States parties to the dispute shall be elected by secret ballot by a two-thirds majority vote of the Committee from among its own members.

2. The members of the Commission shall serve in their personal capacity. They shall not be nationals of the States parties to the dispute or of a State not Party to this Convention.

3. The Commission shall elect its own Chairman and adopt its own rules of procedure.

4. The meetings of the Commission shall normally be held at United Nations Headquarters or at any other convenient place as determined by the Commission.

5. The secretariat provided in accordance with article 10, paragraph 3, of this Convention shall also service the Commission whenever a dispute among States Parties brings the Commission into being.

6. The States parties to the dispute shall share equally all the expenses of the members of the Commission in accordance with estimates to be provided by the Secretary-General of the United Nations.

7. The Secretary-General shall be empowered to pay the expenses of the members of the Commission, if necessary, before reimbursement by the States parties to the dispute in accordance with paragraph 6 of this article.

8. The information obtained and collated by the Committee shall be made available to the Commission, and the Commission may call upon the States concerned to supply any other relevant information.

*Article 13.* 1. When the Commission has fully considered the matter, it shall prepare and submit to the Chairman of the Committee a report embodying its findings on all questions of fact relevant to the issue between the parties and containing such recommendations as it may think proper for the amicable solution of the dispute.

2. The Chairman of the Committee shall communicate the report of the Commission to each of the States parties to the dispute. These States shall, within three months, inform the Chairman of the Committee whether or not they accept the recommendations contained in the report of the Commission.

3. After the period provided for in paragraph 2 of this article, the Chairman of the Committee shall communicate the report of the Commission and the declarations of the States Parties concerned to the other States Parties to this Convention.

*Article 14.* 1. A State Party may at any time declare that it recognizes the competence of the Committee to receive and consider communications from individuals or groups of individuals within its jurisdiction claiming to be victims of a violation by that State Party of any of the rights set forth in this Convention. No communication shall be received by the Committee if it concerns a State Party which has not made such a declaration.

2. Any State Party which makes a declaration as provided for in paragraph 1 of this article may establish or indicate a body within its national legal order which shall be competent to receive and consider petitions from individuals and groups of individuals within its jurisdiction who claim to be victims of a violation of any of the rights set forth in this Convention and who have exhausted other available local remedies.

3. A declaration made in accordance with paragraph 1 of this article and the name of any body established or indicated in accordance with paragraph 2 of this article shall be deposited by the State Party concerned with the Secretary-General of the United Nations, who shall transmit copies thereof to the other States Parties. A declaration may be withdrawn at any time by notification to the Secretary-General but such a withdrawal shall not affect communications pending before the Committee.

4. A register of petitions shall be kept by the body established or indicated in accordance with paragraph 2 of this article, and certified copies of the register shall be filed annually through appropriate channels with the Secretary-General on the understanding that the contents shall not be publicly disclosed.

5. In the event of failure to obtain satisfaction from the body established or indicated in accordance with paragraph 2 of this article, the petitioner shall have the right to communicate the matter to the Committee within six months.

6. (a) The Committee shall confidentially bring any communication referred to it to the attention of the State Party alleged to be violating any provision of this Convention, but the identity of the individual or groups of individuals concerned shall not be revealed without his or their express consent. The Committee shall not receive anonymous communications.

(b) Within three months, the receiving State shall submit to the Committee written explanations or statements clarifying the matter and the remedy, if any, that may have been taken by that State.

7. (a) The Committee shall consider communications in the light of all information made available to it by the State Party concerned and by the petitioner. The Committee shall not consider any communication from a petitioner unless it has ascertained that the petitioner has exhausted all available domestic remedies. However, this shall not be the rule where the application of the remedies is unreasonably prolonged.

(b) The Committee shall forward its suggestions and recommendations, if any, to the State Party concerned and to the petitioner.

8. The Committee shall include in its annual report a summary of such communications and, where appropriate, a summary of the explanations and statements of the States Parties concerned and of its own suggestions and recommendations.

9. The Committee shall be competent to exercise the functions provided for in this article only when at least ten States Parties to this Convention are bound by declarations in accordance with paragraph 1 of this article.

*Article 15.* 1. Pending the achievement of the objectives of the Declaration on the Granting of Independence to Colonial Countries and Peoples, contained in General Assembly resolutions 1514 (XV) of 14 December 1960, the provisions of this Convention shall in no way limit the right of petition granted to these peoples by other international instruments or by the United Nations and its specialized agencies.

2. (a) The Committee established under article 8, paragraph 1, of this Convention shall receive copies of the petitions from, and submit expressions of opinion and recommendations on these petitions to, the bodies of the United Nations which deal with matters directly related to the principles and objectives of this Convention in their consideration of petitions from the inhabitants of Trust and Non-Self-Governing Territories and all other territories to which General Assembly resolution 1514 (XV) applies, relating to matters covered by this Convention which are before these bodies.

(b) The Committee shall receive from the competent bodies of the United Nations copies of the reports concerning the legislative, judicial, administrative or other measures directly related to the principles and objectives of this Convention applied by the administering Powers within the Territories mentioned in subparagraph (a) of this paragraph, and shall express opinions and make recommendations to these bodies.

3. The Committee shall include in its report to the General Assembly a summary of the petitions and reports it has received from United Nations bodies, and the expressions

of opinion and recommendation of the Committee relating to the said petitions and reports.

4. The Committee shall request from the Secretary-General of the United Nations all information relevant to the objectives of this Convention and available to him regarding the Territories mentioned in paragraph 2 (a) of this article.

*Article 16.* The provisions of this Convention concerning the settlement of disputes or complaints shall be applied without prejudice to other procedures for settling disputes or complaints in the field of discrimination laid down in the constituent instruments of, or in conventions adopted by, the United Nations and its specialized agencies, and shall not prevent the States Parties from having recourse to other procedures for settling a dispute in accordance with general or special international agreements in force between them.

## Part III

*Article 17.* 1. This Convention is open for signature by any State Member of the United Nations or member of any of its specialized agencies, by any State Party to the Statute of the International Court of Justice, and by any other State which has been invited by the General Assembly of the United Nations to become a Party to this Convention.

2. This Convention is subject to ratification. Instruments of ratification shall be deposited with the Secretary-General of the United Nations.

*Article 18.* 1. This Convention shall be open to accession by any State referred to in article 17, paragraph 1, of the Convention.

2. Accession shall be effected by the deposit of an instrument of accession with the Secretary-General of the United Nations.

*Article 19.* 1. This Convention shall enter into force on the thirtieth day after the date of the deposit with the Secretary-General of the United Nations of the twenty-seventh instrument of ratification or instrument of accession.

2. For each State ratifying this Convention or acceding to it after the deposit of the twenty-seventh instrument of ratification or instrument of accession, the Convention shall enter into force on the thirtieth day after the date of the deposit of its own instrument of ratification or instrument of accession.

*Article 20.* 1. The Secretary-General of the United Nations shall receive and circulate to all States which are or may become Parties to this Convention reservations made by States at the time of ratification or accession. Any State which objects to the reservation shall, within a period of ninety days from the date of the said communication, notify the Secretary-General that it does not accept it.

2. A reservation incompatible with the object and purpose of this Convention shall not be permitted, nor shall a reservation the effect of which would inhibit the operation of any of the bodies established by this Convention be allowed. A reservation shall be considered incompatible or inhibitive if at least two thirds of the States Parties to this Convention object to it.

3. Reservations may be withdrawn at any time by notification to this effect addressed to the Secretary-General. Such notification shall take effect on the date on which it is received.

*Article 21.* A State Party may denounce this Convention by written notification to the Secretary-General of the United Nations. Denunciation shall take effect one year after the date of receipt of the notification by the Secretary-General.

*Article 22.* Any dispute between two or more States Parties with respect to the interpretation or application of this Convention, which is not settled by negotiation or by the procedures expressly provided for in this Convention, shall, at the request of any of the parties to the dispute, be referred to the International Court of Justice for decision, unless the disputants agree to another mode of settlement.

*Article 23.* 1. A request for the revision of this Convention may be made at any time by any State Party by means of a notification in writing addressed to the Secretary-General of the United Nations.

2. The General Assembly of the United Nations shall decide upon the steps, if any, to be taken in respect of such a request.

*Article 24.* The Secretary-General of the United Nations shall inform all States referred to in article 17, paragraph 1, of this Convention of the following particulars:

(a) Signatures, ratifications and accessions under articles 17 and 18;

(b) The date of entry into force of this Convention under article 19;

(c) Communications and declarations received under articles 14, 20 and 23;

(d) Denunciations under article 21.

*Article 25.* 1. This Convention, of which the Chinese, English, French, Russian and Spanish texts are equally authentic, shall be deposited in the archives of the United Nations.

2. The Secretary-General of the United Nations shall transmit copies of this Convention to all States belonging to any of the categories mentioned in article 17, para. 1, of the Convention.

**GENERAL RECOMMENDATIONS ADOPTED BY THE COMMITTEE.** The Committee on the Elimination of Racial Discrimination is entitled, under article 9, para. 2, of the International Convention, to make suggestions and general recommendations based on its examination of the reports and information received from the States parties. Such suggestions and general recommendations are reported to the General Assembly together with comments, if any, from States Parties. The Committee had adopted, up to the end of 1994, 18 general recommendations, as follows:

*General Recommendation I (Fifth session, 1972) (document A/8718).* On the basis of the consideration at its fifth session of reports submitted by States parties under article 9 of the International Convention on the Elimination of All Forms of Racial Discrimination, the Committee found that the legislation of a number of States parties did not include the provisions envisaged in article 4 (a) and (b) of the Convention, the implementation of which (with due regard to the principles embodied in the Universal Declaration of Human Rights and the rights expressly set forth in article 5 of the Convention) is obligatory under the Convention for all State parties.

The Committee accordingly recommends that the States parties whose legislation was deficient in this respect should consider, in accordance with their national legislative procedures, the question of supplementing their legislation with provisions conforming to the requirements of article 4 (a) and (b) of the Convention.

*General Recommendation II (Fifth session, 1972) (document A/*

*8718).* The Committee has considered some reports from States parties which expressed or implied the belief that the information mentioned in the Committee's communication of 28 January 1970 (CERD/C/R.12), need not be supplied by States parties on whose territories racial discrimination does not exist.

However, inasmuch as, in accordance with article 9, paragraph 1, of the International Convention on the Elimination of All Forms of Racial Discrimination, all States parties undertake to submit reports on the measures that they have adopted and that give effect to the provisions of the Convention and, since all the categories of information listed in the Committee's communication of 28 January 1970 refer to obligations undertaken by the States parties under the Convention, that communication is addressed to all States parties without distinction, whether or not racial discrimination exists in their respective territories. The Committee welcomes the inclusion in the reports from all States parties, which have not done so, of the necessary information in conformity with all the headings set out in the aforementioned communication of the Committee.

*General Recommendation III (Sixth session, 1973) (document 8718).* The Committee has considered some reports from States parties containing information about measures taken to implement resolutions of United Nations organs concerning relations with the racist regimes in southern Africa.

The Committee notes that, in the tenth paragraph of the preamble to the International Convention on the Elimination of All Forms of Racial Discrimination, States parties have "resolved", *inter alia,* "to build an international community free from all forms of racial segregation and racial discrimination".

It notes also that, in article 3 of the Convention, "States parties particularly condemn racial segregation and apartheid".

Furthermore, the Committee notes that, in resolution 2784 (XXVI), section III, the General Assembly, immediately after taking note with appreciation of the Committee's second annual report and endorsing certain opinions and recommendations, submitted by it, proceeded to call upon "all the trading partners of South Africa to abstain from any action that constitutes an encouragement to the continued violation of the principles and objectives of the International Convention on the Elimination of All Forms of Racial Discrimination by South Africa and the illegal regime in Southern Rhodesia".

The Committee expresses the view that measures adopted on the national level to give effect to the provisions of the Convention are interrelated with measures taken on the international level to encourage respect everywhere for the principles of the Convention.

The Committee welcomes the inclusion in the reports submitted under article 9, paragraph 1, of the Convention, by any State Party which chooses to do so, of information regarding the status of its diplomatic, economic and other relations with the racist regimes in southern Africa.

*General Recommendation IV (Eighth session, 1973) (document 9018).*

The Committee on the Elimination of Racial Discrimination,

Having considered reports submitted by States parties under article 9 of the International Convention on the Elimination of All Forms of Racial Discrimination at its seventh and eighth sessions,

Bearing in mind the need for the reports sent by States parties to the Committee to be as informative as possible,

Invites States parties to endeavour to include in their reports under article 9 relevant information on the demographic composition of the population referred to in the revisions of article 1 of the Convention.

*General Recommendation V (Fifteenth session, 1977) (document A/32/18).*

The Committee on the Elimination of Racial Discrimination,

Bearing in mind the provisions of articles 7 and 9 of the International Convention on the Elimination of All Forms of Racial Discrimination,

Convinced that combating prejudices which lead to racial discrimination, promoting understanding, tolerance and friendship among racial and ethnic groups, and propagating the principles and purposes of the Charter of the United Nations and of the human rights declarations and other relevant instruments adopted by the General Assembly of the United Nations, are important and effective means of eliminating racial discrimination,

Considering that the obligations under article 7 of the Convention, which are binding on all States parties, must be fulfilled by them, including States which declare that racial discrimination is not practised on the territories under their jurisdiction, and that therefore all States parties are required to include information on their implementation of the provisions of that article in the reports they submit in accordance with article 9, paragraph 1, of the Convention,

Noting with regret that few States parties have included, in the reports they have submitted in accordance with article 9 of the Convention, information on the measures which they have adopted and which give effect to the provisions of article 7 of the Convention, and that that information has often been general and perfunctory,

Recalling that, in accordance with article 9, paragraph 1, of the Convention, the Committee may request further information from the States parties,

1. Requests every State party which has not already done so to include—in the next report it will submit in accordance with article 9 of the Convention, or in a special report before its next periodic report becomes due—adequate information on the measures which it has adopted and which give effect to the provisions of article 7 of the Convention;

2. Invites the attention of States parties to the fact that, in accordance with article 7 of the Convention, the information to which the preceding paragraph refers should include information on the "immediate and effective measures" which they have adopted, "in the fields of teaching, education, culture and information", with a view to:

(a) "Combating prejudices which lead to racial discrimination";

(b) "Promoting understanding, tolerance and friendship among nations and racial or ethnical groups";

(c) Propagating the purposes and principles of the Charter of the United Nations, the Universal Declaration of Human Rights, the United Nations Declaration on the Elimination of All Forms of Racial Discrimination, as well as the International Convention on the Elimination of All Forms of Racial Discrimination.

*General Recommendation VI (Twenty-fifth session, 1982) (document A/37/18).*

The Committee on the Elimination of Racial Discrimination,

Recognizing the fact that an impressive number of States has ratified, or acceded to, the International Convention on the Elimination of All Forms of Racial Discrimination,

Bearing in mind, however, that ratification alone does not

enable the control system set up by the Convention to function effectively,

Recalling that article 9 of the Convention obliges States parties to submit initial and periodic reports on the measures that give effect to the provisions of the Convention,

Stating that at present no less than 89 reports are overdue from 62 States, that 42 of those reports are overdue from 15 States, each with two or more outstanding reports, and that four initial reports which were due between 1973 and 1978 have not been received,

Noting with regret that neither reminders sent through the Secretary-General to States parties nor the inclusion of the relevant information in the annual reports to the General Assembly has had the desired effect, in all cases,

Invites the General Assembly:

(a) to take note of the situation;

(b) to use its authority in order to ensure that the Committee could more effectively fulfil its obligations under the Convention.

*General Recommendation VII relating to the implementation of article 4 of the Convention (Thirty-second session, 1985) (document A/40/18).*

The Committee on the Elimination of Racial Discrimination,

Having considered periodic reports of States parties for a period of 16 years, and in over 100 cases sixth, seventh and eighth periodic reports of States parties,

Recalling and reaffirming its General Recommendation I of 24 February 1972 and its decision 3 (VII) of 4 May 1973,

Noting with satisfaction that in a number of reports States parties have provided information on specific cases dealing with the implementation of article 4 of the Convention with regard to acts of racial discrimination,

Noting, however, that in a number of States parties the necessary legislation to implement article 4 of the Convention has not been enacted, and that many States parties have not yet fulfilled all the requirements of article 4 (a) and (b) of the Convention,

Further recalling that, in accordance with the first paragraph of article 4, States parties "undertake to adopt immediate and positive measures designed to eradicate all incitement to, or acts of, such discrimination", with due regard to the principles embodied in the Universal Declaration of Human Rights and the rights expressly set forth in article 5 of the Convention,

Bearing in mind the preventive aspects of article 4 to deter racism and racial discrimination as well as activities aimed at their promotion or incitement,

1. Recommends that those States parties whose legislation does not satisfy the provisions of article 4 (a) and (b) of the Convention take the necessary steps with a view to satisfying the mandatory requirements of that article;

2. Requests that those States parties which have not yet done so inform the Committee more fully in their periodic reports of the manner and extent to which the provisions of article 4 (a) and (b) are effectively implemented and quote the relevant parts of the texts in their reports;

3. Further requests those States parties which have not yet done so to endeavour to provide in their periodic reports more information concerning decisions taken by the competent national tribunals and other State institutions regarding acts of racial discrimination and in particular those offences dealt with in article 4 (a) and (b).

*General Recommendation VIII concerning the interpretation and application of article 1, paragraphs 1 and 4, of the Convention (Thirty-eighth session, 1990) (document A/45/18).*

The Committee on the Elimination of Racial Discrimination,

Having considered reports from States parties concerning information about the ways in which individuals are identified as being members of a particular racial or ethnic groups or groups,

Is of the opinion that such identification shall, if no justification exists to the contrary, be based upon self-identification by the individual concerned.

*General Recommendation IX concerning the application of article 8, paragraph 1, of the Convention (Thirty-eighth session, 1990) (document A/45/18).*

The Committee on the Elimination of Racial Discrimination,

Considering that respect for the independence of the experts is essential to secure full observance of human rights and fundamental freedoms,

Recalling article 8, paragraph 1, of the International Convention on the Elimination of All Forms of Racial Discrimination,

Alarmed by the tendency of the representatives of States, organizations and groups to put pressure upon experts, especially those serving as country rapporteurs,

Strongly recommends that they respect unreservedly the status of its members as independent experts of acknowledged impartiality serving in their personal capacity.

*General Recommendation X concerning technical assistance (Thirty-ninth session, 1991) (document A/46/18).*

The Committee on the Elimination of Racial Discrimination,

Taking note of the recommendation of the third meeting of persons chairing the human rights treaty bodies, as endorsed by the General Assembly at its forty-fifth session, to the effect that a series of seminars or workshops should be organized at the national level for the purpose of training those involved in the preparation of State party reports,

Concerned over the continued failure of certain States parties to the International Convention on the Elimination of All Forms of Racial Discrimination to meet their reporting obligations under the Convention,

Believing that training courses and workshops organized on the national level might prove of immeasurable assistance to officials responsible for the preparation of such State party reports,

1. Requests the Secretary-General to organize, in consultation with the States parties concerned, appropriate national training courses and workshops for their reporting officials as soon as practicable;

2. Recommends that the services of the staff of the Centre for Human Rights as well as of the experts of the Committee on the Elimination of Racial Discrimination should be utilized, as appropriate, in the conduct of such training courses and workshops.

*General Recommendation XI on non-citizens (Forty-second session, 1993).*

1. Article 1, paragraph 1, of the Interational Convention on the Elimination of All Forms of Racial Discrimination defines racial discrimination. Article 1, paragraph 2, excepts from this definition actions by a State party which differentiate between citizens and non-citizens. Article 1, paragraph 3, qualifies Article 1, paragraph 2, by declaring that, among non-citizens, States parties may not discriminate against any particular nationality.

2. The Committee has noted that Article 1, paragraph 2, has on occasion been interpreted as absolving States parties from any obligation to report on matters relating to legisla-

tion on foreigners. The Committee therefore affirms that States parties are under an obligation to report fully upon legislation on foreigners and its implementation.

3. The Committee further affirms that Article 1, paragraph 2, must not be interpreted to detract in any way from the rights and freedoms recognized and enunciated in other instruments, especially the Universal Declaration of Human Rights, the International Covenant on Economic, Social and Cultural Rights and the International Covenant on Civil and Political Rights.

*General Recommendation XII on successor States (Forty-second session, 1993) (document A/45/18).*

The Committee on the Elimination of Racial Discrimination,

Emphasizing the importance of universal participation of States in the International Convention on the Elimination of All Forms of Racial Discrimination,

Taking into account the emergence of successor States as a result of the dissolution of States,

1. Encourages successor States that have not yet done so to confirm to the Secretary-General, as depositary of the International Convention on the Elimination of All Forms of Racial Discrimination, that they continue to be bound by obligations under that Convention, if predecessor States were parties to it;

2. Invites successor States that have not yet done so to accede to the International Convention on the Elimination of All Forms of Racial Discrimination if predecessor States were not parties to it;

3. Invites successor States to consider the importance of making the declaration under article 14, paragraph 1, of the International Convention on the Elimination of All Forms of Racial Discrimination, recognizing the competence of the Committee on the Elimination of Racial Discrimination to receive and consider individual communications.

*General Recommendation XIII on the training of law enforcement officials in the protection of human rights (Forty-second session, 1993) (document A/48/18).*

1. In accordance with article 2, paragraph 1, of the International Convention on the Elimination of All Forms of Racial Discrimination, States parties have undertaken that all public authorities and public institutions, national and local, will not engage in any practice of racial discrimination; further, States parties have undertaken to guarantee the rights listed in article 5 of the Convention to everyone without distinction as to race, colour or national or ethnic origin.

2. The fulfilment of these obligations very much depends upon national law enforcement officials who exercise police powers, especially the powers of detention or arrest, and upon whether they are properly informed about the obligations their State has entered into under the Convention. Law enforcement officials should receive intensive training to ensure that in the performance of their duties they respect as well as protect human dignity and maintain and uphold the human rights of all persons without distinction as to race, colour or national or ethnic origin.

3. In the implementation of article 7 of the Convention, the Committee calls upon States parties to review and improve the training of law enforcement officials so that the standards of the Convention as well as the Code of Conduct for Law Enforcement Officials (1979) are fully implemented. They should also include respective information thereupon in their periodic reports.

*General Recommendation XIV on article 1, paragraph 1, of the Convention (Forty-second session, 1993) (document A/48/18).*

1. Non-discrimination, together with equality before the law and equal protection of the law without any discrimination, constitutes a basic principle in the protection of human rights. The Committee wishes to draw the attention of States parties to certain features of the definition of racial discrimination in article 1, paragraph 1, of the International Convention on the Elimination of All Forms of Racial Discrimination. It is of the opinion that the words "based on" do not bear any meaning different from "on the grounds of," in preambular paragraph 7. A distinction is contrary to the Convention if it has either the purpose or the effect of impairing particular rights and freedoms. This is confirmed by the obligation placed upon States parties by article 2, paragraph 1 (c), to nullify any law or practice which has the effect of creating or perpetuating racial discrimination.

2. The Committee observes that a differentiation of treatment will not constitute discrimination if the criteria for such differentiation, judged against the objectives and purposes of the Convention, are legitimate or fall within the scope of article 1, paragraph 4, of the Convention. In considering the criteria that may have been employed, the Committee will acknowledge that particular actions may have varied purposes. In seeking to determine whether an action has an effect contrary to the Convention, it will look to see whether that action has an unjustifiable disparate impact upon a group distinguished by race, colour, descent, or national or ethnic origin.

3. Article 1, paragraph 1, of the Convention also refers to the political, economic, social and cultural fields; the related rights and freedoms are set up in article 5.

*General Recommendation XV on article 4 of the Convention (Forty-second session, 1993) (document A/48/18).*

1. When the International Convention on the Elimination of All Forms of Racial Discrimination was being adopted, article 4 was regarded as central to the struggle against racial discrimination. At that time, there was a widespread fear of the revival of authoritarian ideologies. The proscription of the dissemination of ideas of racial superiority, and of organized activity likely to incite persons to racial violence, was properly regarded as crucial. Since that time, the Committee has received evidence of organized violence based on ethnic origin and the political exploitation of ethnic differences. As a result, implementation of article 4 is now of increased importance.

2. The Committee recalls its General Recommendation VII in which it explained that the provisions of article 4 are of a mandatory character. To satisfy these obligations, States parties have not only to enact appropriate legislation but also to ensure that it is effectively enforced. Because threats and acts of racial violence easily lead to other such acts and generate an atmosphere of hostility, only immediate intervention can meet the obligations of effective response.

3. Article 4 (a) requires States parties to penalize four categories of misconduct: (i) dissemination of ideas based upon racial superiority or hatred; (ii) incitement to racial hatred; (iii) acts of violence against any race or group of persons of another colour or ethnic origin; and (iv) incitement to such acts.

4. In the opinion of the Committee, the prohibition of the dissemination of all ideas based upon racial superiority or hatred is compatible with the right to freedom of opinion and expression. This right is embodied in article 19 of the Universal Declaration of Human Rights and is recalled in article 5 (d) (viii) of the International Convention on the Elimination of All Forms of Racial Discrimination. Its relevance to article 4 is noted in the article itself. The citizen's exercise of this right carries special duties and responsibili-

ties, specified in article 29, paragraph 2, of the Universal Declaration, among which the obligation not to disseminate racist ideas is of particular importance. The Committee wishes, furthermore, to draw to the attention of States parties article 20 of the International Covenant on Civil and Political Rights, according to which any advocacy of national, racial or religious hatred that constitutes incitement to discrimination, hostility or violence shall be prohibited by law.

5. Article 4 (a) also penalizes the financing of racist activities, which the Committee takes to include all the activities mentioned in paragraph 3 above, that is to say, activities deriving from ethnic as well as racial differences. The Committee calls upon States parties to investigate whether their national law and its implementation meet this requirement.

6. Some States have maintained that in their legal order it is inappropriate to declare illegal an organization before its members have promoted or incited racial discrimination. The Committee is of the opinion that article 4 (b) places a greater burden upon such States to be vigilant in proceeding against such organizations at the earliest moment. These organizations, as well as organized and other propaganda activities, have to be declared illegal and prohibited. Participation in these organizations is, of itself, to be punished.

7. Article 4 (c) of the Convention outlines the obligations of public authorities. Public authorities at all administrative levels, including municipalities, are bound by this paragraph. The Committee holds that States parties must ensure that they observe these obligations and report on this.

*General Recommendation XVI concerning the application of article 9 of the Convention (Forty-second session, 1993) (document A/48/18).*

1. Under article 9 of the International Convention on the Elimination of All Forms of Racial Discrimination, States parties have undertaken to submit, through the Secretary-General of the United Nations, for consideration by the Committee, reports on measures taken by them to give effect to the provisions of the Convention.

2. With respect to this obligation of the States parties, the Committee has noted that, on some occasions, reports have made references to situations existing in other States.

3. For this reason, the Committee wishes to remind States parties of the provisions of article 9 of the Convention concerning the content of their reports, while bearing in mind article 11, which is the only procedural means available to States for drawing to the attention of the Committee situations in which they consider that some other State is not giving effect to the revisions of the Convention.

*General Recommendation XVII on the establishment of national institutions to facilitate the implementation of the Convention (Forty-second session, 1993) (document A/48/18).*

The Committee on the Elimination of Racial Discrimination,

Considering the practice of States parties concerning the implementation of the International Convention on the Elimination of All Forms of Racial Discrimination,

Convinced of the necessity to encourage further the establishment of national institutions to facilitate the implementation of the Convention,

Emphasizing the need to strengthen further the implementation of the Convention,

1. Recommends that States parties establish national commissions or other appropriate bodies, taking into account, mutatis mutandis, the principles relating to the status of national institutions annexed to Commission on Human Rights resolution 1992/54 of 3 March 1992, to serve, inter alia, the following purposes:

(a) To promote respect for the enjoyment of human rights without any discrimination, as expressly set out in article 5 of the International Convention on the Elimination of All Forms of Racial Discrimination;

(b) To review government policy towards protection against racial discrimination;

(c) To monitor legislative compliance with the provisions of the Convention;

(d) To educate the public about the obligations of States parties under the Convention;

(e) To assist the Government in the preparation of reports submitted to the Committee on the Elimination of Racial Discrimination;

2. Also recommends that, where such commissions have been established, they should be associated with the preparation of reports and possibly included in government delegations in order to intensify the dialogue between the Committee and the State party concerned.

*General Recommendation XVIII on the establishment of an international tribunal to prosecute crimes against humanity (Forty-fourth session 1994) (document A/49/18).*

The Committee on the Elimination of Racial Discrimination,

Alarmed at the increasing number of racially and ethnically motivated massacres and atrocities occurring in different regions of the world,

Convinced that the impunity of the perpetrators is a major factor contributing to the occurrence and recurrence of these crimes,

Convinced of the need to establish, as quickly as possible, an international tribunal with general jurisdiction to prosecute genocide, crimes against humanity and grave breaches of the Geneva Conventions of 1949 and the Additional Protocols of 1977 thereto,

Taking into account the work already done on this question by the International Law Commission and the encouragement given in this regard by the General Assembly in its resolution 48/31 of 9 December 1993,

Also taking into account Security Council resolution 872 (1993) of 25 May 1993 establishing an international tribunal for the purpose of prosecuting persons responsible for serious violations of international humanitarian law committed in the territory of the former Yugoslavia,

1. Considers that an international tribunal with general jurisdiction should be established urgently to prosecute genocide, crimes against humanity, including murder, extermination, enslavement, deportation, imprisonment, torture, rape persecutions on political, racial and religious grounds and other inhumane acts directed against any civilian population, and grave breaches of the Geneva Conventions of 1949 and the Additional Protocols of 1977 thereto;

2. Urges the Secretary-General to bring the present recommendation to the attention of the competent organs and bodies of the United Nations, including the Security Council;

3. Requests the High Commissioner for Human Rights to ensure that all relevant information pertaining to the crimes referred to in paragraph 1 is systematically collected by the Centre for Human Rights so that it can be readily available to the international tribunal as soon as it is established.

**RATIFICATIONS AND ACCESSIONS.** As of 31 December 1994, the following 141 UN member states had ratified the International Convention on the Elimination of All Forms of Racial Discrimination:

Afghanistan, Albania, Algeria, Antigua and Barbuda, Argentina, Armenia, Australia, Austria

Bahamas, Bahrain, Bangladesh, Barbados, Belarus, Benin, Bolivia, Bosnia Herzegovina, Brazil, Bulgaria, Burundi

Cambodia, Cameroon, Canada, Cape Verde, the Central African Republic, Chad, Chile, China, Colombia, Congo, Costa Rica, Cote d'Ivoire (Ivory Coast), Croatia, Cuba, Cyprus, Czech Republic

Denmark, Dominican Republic

Ecuador, Egypt, El Salvador, Estonia, Ethiopia

Fiji, Finland, France

Gabon, Gambia, Germany, Ghana, Greece, Guatemala, Guinea, Guyana

Haiti, Holy See, Hungary

Iceland, India, Iran, Iraq, Israel, Italy

Jamaica, Jordan

Kuwait

Laos, Latvia, Lebanon, Lesotho, Liberia, Libya, Luxembourg

Macedonia, Madagascar, Maldives, Mali, Malta, Mauritania, Mauritius, Mexico, Moldova, Mongolia, Morocco, Mozambique

Namibia, Nepal, the Netherlands, New Zealand, Nicaragua, Niger, Nigeria, Norway

Oman

Pakistan, Panama, Papua New Guinea, Peru, Philippines, Poland, Portugal

Qatar

Republic of Korea, Romania, Russian Federation, Rwanda

Saint Lucia, Saint Vincent and Grenadines, Senegal, Seychelles, Sierra Leone, Slovakia, Slovenia, Solomon Islands, Somalia, Spain, Sri Lanka, Sudan, Suriname, Swaziland, Sweden, Switzerland, Syria

Tanzania, Togo, Tonga, Trinidad and Tobago, Tunisia, Turkmenistan

Uganda, Ukraine, United Arab Emirates, United Kingdom, United States of America, Uruguay

Venezuela, Vietnam

Yemen, Yugoslavia (Serbia and Montenegro)

Zaire, Zambia, Zimbabwe.

*SIGNATURE.* As of 31 December 1994, the following six UN member States had signed the International Convention on the Elimination of All Forms of Racial Discrimination but had not yet ratified the document: Benin, Bhutan, Grenada, Ireland, South Africa, Turkey.

**REEBOK HUMAN RIGHTS AWARD.** Sponsored by Reebok International, the award was established in 1988 to honor individuals 30 years of age or younger who have made significant contributions to human rights, often against great odds. The candidates cannot advocate violence or belong to an organization that advocates violence and must be working on an issue that directly relates to the UN **UNIVERSAL DECLARATION OF HUMAN RIGHTS.** Four awards are presented annually; a human rights organization designated by each awardee receives $25,000. This is the only corporate-sponsored human rights award; the recipients are chosen by the Reebok Human Rights Board of Advisors, which includes former U.S. President Jimmy Carter; Peter Gabriel, musician; and Rafer Johnson, Olympic decathlete.

The 1994 recipients were Rose-Anne Auguste, 30, of Haiti, who founded the Women's Health Clinic in a downtrodden neighborhood of Port-au-Prince to provide health care to the poor; Adauto Belarmino Alves, 29, of Brazil, a respected activist in the gay rights and AIDS education movements; Dilli Bahadur Chaudhary, 25, of Nepal, who, through his grassroots organization BASE and his own personal efforts, has fought for the legal rights of the native Tharu people and against the practice of bonded labor; and Samuel Kofi Woods, 30, of Liberia, director of the Justice and Peace Commission, which monitors and investigates human rights violations. The 1994 "Youth-in-Action" Award was presented to Iqbal Masih, 12, of Pakistan, who was sold into bondage at the age of 4 but who escaped in 1992 and is currently enrolled in a school for freed bonded children, run by the Bonded Labour Liberation Front.

In 1993, the recipients were Rev. Carl Washington (USA), Marie-France Botte (Belgium), Hisham Mubarak (Egypt), and Sia Kashinawa (Brazil). In 1992, the recipients were Stacey Kabat (USA), Fernando de Araujo (East Timor), Martin O'Brien (Northern Ireland), and Floribert Chebeya Bahizire (Zaire). Recipients for 1991 were Abubacar Sultan (Mozambique), Maria Mirtala Lopez (El Salvador), Sauveur Pierre (USA), and Carlos Toledo (Guatemala).

For more information, contact: Reebok International, 100 Technology Center Drive, Stoughton, MA 02072, USA.

**REFUGEES.** An international term defined in the Statute of the Office of the United Nations **HIGH COMMISSIONER FOR REFUGEES** (Section 6 B) as "any . . . person who is outside the country of his nationality or, if he has no nationality, the country of his former habitual residence, because he has or had well-founded fear of persecution by reason of his race, religion, nationality or political opinion and is unable or, because of such fear, is unwilling to avail himself of the protection of the government of the country of his nationality, or, if he has no nationality, to return to the country of his former habitual residence."

The **Universal Declaration of Human Rights** proclaims that:

*Article 13.* 2. Everyone has the right to leave any country, including his own, and to return to his country.

*Article 14.* 1. Everyone has the right to seek and enjoy in other countries asylum from persecution.

2. This right may not be invoked in the case of prosecutions genuinely arising from non-political crimes or from acts contrary to the purposes and principles of the United Nations.

The Declaration on Territorial Asylum recognizes "that the grant of asylum by a State to persons entitled to invoke article 14 of the Universal Declaration of Human Rights is a peaceful and humanitarian act and that, as such, it cannot be regarded as unfriendly by any other State." It recommends that States should base themselves, in their practices relating to territorial asylum, on the following principles:

*Article 1.* 1. Asylum granted by a State, in the exercise of its sovereignty, to persons entitled to invoke article 14 of the Universal Declaration of Human Rights, including persons struggling against colonialism, shall be respected by all other States.

2. The right to seek and to enjoy asylum may not be invoked by any person with respect to whom there are serious reasons for considering that he has committed a crime against peace, a war crime or a crime against humanity, as defined in the international instruments drawn up to make provision in respect of such crimes.

3. It shall rest with the State granting asylum to evaluate the grounds for the grant of asylum.

*Article 2.* 1. The situation of persons referred to in article 1, paragraph 1, is, without prejudice to the sovereignty of States and the purposes and principles of the United Nations, of concern to the international community.

2. Where a State finds difficulty in granting or continuing to grant asylum, States individually or jointly or through the United Nations shall consider, in a spirit of international solidarity, appropriate measures to lighten the burden on that State.

*Article 3.* 1. No person referred to in article 1, paragraph 1, shall be subjected to measures such as rejection at the frontier or, if he has already entered the territory in which he seeks asylum, expulsion or compulsory return to any State where he may be subjected to persecution.

2. Exception may be made to the foregoing principle only for overriding reasons of national security or in order to safeguard the population, as in the case of a mass influx of persons.

3. Should a State decide in any case that exception to the principle stated in paragraph 1 of this article would be justified, it shall consider the possibility of granting to the person concerned, under such conditions as it may deem appropriate, an opportunity, whether by way of provisional asylum or otherwise, of going to another State.

*Article 4.* States granting asylum shall not permit persons who have received asylum to engage in activities contrary to the purposes and principles of the United Nations.

At the regional level, the main instrument defining standards for the treatment of refugees is the African Convention Governing the Specific Aspects of Refugee Problems in Africa.

Various aspects of the situation of refugees are dealt with in the Convention Relating to the Status of Refugees and its protocol, which define the term "refugee" and define the juridical status and the rights of persons falling within this category.

***THE ROLE OF THE UN HIGH COMMISSIONER FOR REFUGEES.*** Under the Statute of the Office of the United Nations **High Commissioner for Refugees,** such an office is established, and the High Commissioner is authorized to provide international protection to refugees and to seek permanent solutions for their problems. The High Commissioner follows policy directives given him by the UN **General Assembly** and is assisted in his work by the Executive Committee of the High Commissioner's Program.

In his report to the 1988 session of the General Assembly, the High Commissioner summed up the work of his office during the latter half of 1987 and the early months of 1988 as follows (UN Doc. A/43/12, chap. I, paras. 9–15):

Developments in the field of international protection of refugees, during the reporting period, have once again demonstrated the magnitude and complexity of the refugee problem. Concentrations and flows of refugees can be found in all parts of the world. While the circumstances leading to these refugee flows are varied and intricate, their common feature is that the persons concerned have been compelled to leave their respective countries of origin in order to find security and protection elsewhere and they are all in need of, and entitled to, international protection.

It is the responsibility of UNHCR to provide this protection to refugees to compensate for their lack or the denial of national protection. This task can, however, only be achieved through effective co-operation of States and relevant intergovernmental and non-governmental organizations.

The largest concentrations of refugees are currently located in the Asian and Middle Eastern regions. Some of the refugee situations in those regions are also among the most protracted; more than one has now lasted for well over a decade. This is the case, for example, in South-East Asia where several refugee flows have lasted for over 13 years. The period under review saw the onset of further restrictive tendencies in the region with States seeking, at times with appalling results, to stem the flow of asylum-seekers. If further deaths and suffering of refugees are to be avoided, a concerted effort must be undertaken involving the international community at large in support of the first asylum countries in the region. Elsewhere in the Asian region, positive developments occurred that may lead to the cessation of the hostilities that had originally provoked one of the largest refugee flows in recent times. It is hoped that, with the co-operation of all the parties involved, circumstances may now be created that may allow for the voluntary return of the refugees.

To the already substantial portion of the refugee population that is found on the African continent, the period under review witnessed an increase of well over half a million refugees. Even though, in many instances, the reception of the refugees entailed great sacrifices for the receiving countries, they continued, in the main, their policy of hospitality. At the same time, close to 150,000 refugees returned voluntarily to their respective countries of origin. By and large the voluntary repatriats were able to return in conditions of safety and dignity. Experience shows, however, that if larger numbers are to be afforded an opportunity to avail themselves of voluntary repatriation, countries concerned must redress the causes that originally led to the refugee flow. A particular concern in the region was the vulnerable situation in which many of the refugees find themselves because of the fact that they are located within, or in the vicinity of, conflict areas. In several instances, refugees were subjected to military and armed attacks.

In the American hemisphere, the situation of refugees from Central American countries continued to be the main source of concern to the Office. As in other parts of the world, the refugee phenomenon is but part of a larger political, social and economic situation that rendered the task of providing international protection extremely difficult. Even so, encouraging developments took place during the reporting period as the countries in the region sought to find peaceful and humanitarian solutions to the refugee problem. More than 10,000 refugees returned to their countries of origin voluntarily. Nevertheless, considerable problems remain, in particular with regard to the physical safety of the refugees and the need to gain respect by all parties concerned for the strictly humanitarian and civilian character of the refugees' status.

As far as Europe is concerned, the High Commissioner continued a series of consultations with countries in the region with a view to reaching humane solutions to the problems of refugees and asylum-seekers. The primary preoccupation of the Governments concerned continued to be the arrival of non-European asylum-seekers into Western Europe. This situation was compounded by xenophobic attitudes adopted by segments of the population, and the countries concerned responded with a variety of legal and administrative measures aimed at containing the situation. Such measures ranged from continuing to apply an unduly restrictive interpretation of the refugee definition contained in the United Nations Convention of 1951 relating to the Status of Refugees to the rejection of asylum-seekers at the border on the sole ground that they had been present in another country where they could have sought asylum. In seeking humane solutions to the problems of those who, as a result of persecution or out of fear for their safety, seek asylum in European countries, UNHCR also reinforced its co-operation with the European Community as well as with the network of non-governmental organizations established by the European Consultation on Refugees and Exiles.

Although States have generally continued their efforts to ensure that refugees and asylum-seekers are protected, serious problems emerged, sometimes with extremely serious consequences for the refugees and asylum-seekers concerned. Thus, grave problems remain in the areas of admission and asylum, expulsion and detention and the physical protection of refugees. Increased efforts by the international community and UNHCR in these and related areas of the international protection of refugees are needed to ensure that all refugees, irrespective of their race, country or region of origin, ethnic origin, membership of a particular social group or political opinion are treated in accordance with accepted international standards.

In his report, the High Commissioner further sums up the existing situation as regards recognition and enjoyment of the principles of international protection and refugee rights as follows (*Ibid.*, chap. I. B, paras. 16–35):

### 1. Admission and Asylum

For refugees to enjoy basic protection, it is essential that they be admitted into the territory of a State and granted at least temporary asylum. The main international refugee instruments, however, contain no provisions dealing directly with admission and asylum. The closest they come to addressing the issue is in their *non-refoulement* provisions that protect a refugee from forceful return to a country where he or she may face persecution, as well as in articles that hold that refugees should not be penalized for having entered the territory of a State in an illegal manner if they come directly from their country of origin.

The Universal Declaration of Human Rights embodies the principle that everyone has the right to seek and enjoy in other countries asylum from persecution. A similar provision is contained in the 1967 United Nations Declaration on Territorial Asylum, contained in General Assembly resolution 2312 (XXII) of 14 December 1967. Asylum remains, however, an attribute of State sovereignty and the right to be granted, as opposed to seeking asylum, has not been translated into a binding international legal norm.

Given the absence of firm legal obligations to grant asylum, it is encouraging to note that many States continue liberal asylum policies. Whether persons flee their countries for fear of persecution in the sense of article 1 of the United Nations Convention of 1951 relating to the Status of Refugees, or as a result of armed conflict, foreign aggression or occupation, gross violations of human rights or internal upheavals, there is widespread recognition that they should be admitted and granted at least temporary asylum. Thus, the majority of today's asylum-seekers continue to be admitted into the territory of States and granted, *de jure* or *de facto,* some form of asylum. It should be noted that the majority of these countries—particularly those accommodating large-scale influxes—are among the world's poorest.

If the overall situation with respect to admission and asylum remains on the whole positive, some worrying trends need to be highlighted. One of these involves asylum-seekers who sought asylum in countries far away from their own. Sometimes they travelled uninterruptedly from their country, travelling through some other States to a third country. In other instances, they travelled from a country where they might appear already to have found protection, in order to seek asylum or a durable solution in another State, without first obtaining the consent of the authorities of that State. In many instances, the concerned asylum-seekers, in addition, travelled on forged documents and/or destroyed their documents en route with a view to misleading the authorities and frustrating their efforts to return the asylum-seekers to an intermediate country.

Partly as a result of these movements, a growing number of States introduced, or further reinforced, measures aimed at restricting the entry of asylum-seekers. These included: visa restrictions for growing numbers of nationalities, penalties on airlines carrying insufficiently documented asylum-seekers, penalties on persons assisting in organizing the illegal entry of asylum-seekers into the territories of States, screening procedures at national borders, restrictions in assistance and the right to work, and systematic and prolonged detention of asylum-seekers.

At the same time, some States also continued to resort to much stricter interpretations of the notion of a refugee, as defined in the United Nations Convention of 1951 relating to the Status of Refugees and its 1967 Protocol. Some of these States, furthermore, required that asylum-seekers meet unduly high or unrealistic standards of proof. The combined effect of such measures was that large numbers of persons were frustrated in their efforts to seek asylum from persecution and, even when fulfilling refugee criteria in the sense of the United Nations Convention of 1951 relating to the Status of Refugees, were denied the protection stipulated in that Convention.

An equally worrying trend consisted in the practice of some States to refuse admission to asylum-seekers on the grounds that they could, or should, have sought it elsewhere. In some instances, this led to the creation of "orbit" situations, some of which eventually resulted in *refoulement*. In one particular case involving asylum-seekers travelling by small boats, a comparable practice adopted by one country was reported to have resulted in the deaths of more than 100 persons.

A fundamental tenet of the international system for providing protection to refugees is that the granting of asylum is a peaceful and non-hostile act. Nevertheless, in one instance, as a result of the pressure exerted on neighbouring countries by one particular State, refugees from that country could not, for reasons of national security, be granted asylum in those former countries. Other States in the region offered asylum, however, and several hundred asylum-seekers were relocated to these States during the reporting period.

## 2. Non-refoulement and Other Rights

The most fundamental of protection principles and the first of refugee rights is that of *non-refoulement*, which provides that no person shall be subjected to measures such as rejection at the border, or, if already in the territory of a country of refuge, expulsion or compulsory return to any country where he or she may have reason to fear persecution or danger to life, liberty or freedom because of reasons pertinent to refugee status. Apart from being embodied in a large number of international treaties and declarations, this principle is today considered as part of general international law.

As in previous years, most States continued to adhere to the principle of *non-refoulement*. Nevertheless, the reporting period also saw several noteworthy exceptions. Thus, some countries continued their practice of pushing back asylum-seekers. Other States occasionally resorted to the *refoulement* of larger groups of asylum-seekers and even some recognized refugees. The total number of refugees and asylum-seekers who were subject to *refoulement* during the reporting period exceeded several thousand. This constitutes an extremely worrisome and noteworthy deterioration in recent years.

Another basic principle of refugee protection embodied in article 32 of the 1951 United Nations Convention prohibits States from expelling refugees who are lawfully in their territory except on grounds of national security or public order. During the reporting period, expulsions in disregard of article 32 were limited in number but nevertheless affected several groups of refugees. In one instance, many of the expelled refugees were allowed to return to the asylum country concerned after seeking judicial remedy.

Unjustified detention of refugees and asylum-seekers is contrary to basic principles of refugee protection. It will be recalled that, in 1986, the Executive Committee of the Programme of the High Commissioner, at its thirty-seventh session, adopted a conclusion on this matter. Through this conclusion, the members of the Executive Committee confirmed that detention of refugees and asylum-seekers should only be resorted to if necessary and only on grounds prescribed by law for certain purposes. Those purposes were defined as being to verify identity; to determine the elements on which the claim to refugee status was based; to deal with cases where refugees and asylum-seekers have destroyed their travel and/or identity documents or have used false documents; and to protect national security or public order.

Even so, many hundreds of refugees and asylum-seekers were detained during the reporting period for no other reason than illegal entry or for having overstayed the validity of their entry visa. Such detentions were in violation of article 31 of the United Nations Convention of 1951 relating to the Status of Refugees and disregarded the fact that their illegal entry or presence was due entirely to the need to find asylum. In several instances, detention measures were enforced as a means of discouraging further arrivals and/or were part of a deliberate government policy to deny asylum to persons coming from certain countries or regions. In some instances, the conditions of detention gave rise to particular concern as they did not meet internationally-recognized minimum standards of detention. Also worrisome were the facts that many refugees and asylum-seekers had to spend considerable periods in detention, sometimes exceeding one year, with no possibility of judicial or administrative review of the detention measure, and that detention measures were applied equally to refugee children.

Economic and social rights of refugees are important, not only so as to facilitate their integration, but also to preserve their dignity and self-respect; these latter reasons applying equally to asylum-seekers and those who have only received temporary asylum. The most fundamental of these rights—the right to gainful occupation—is reflected in both the United Nations Convention of 1951 relating to the Status of Refugees and in other international instruments, such as the Universal Declaration of Human Rights and the International Covenant on Economic, Social and Cultural Rights (General Assembly resolution 2200 A [XXI], annex).

The enjoyment by refugees of economic and social rights are, however, fraught with limitations. In some situations, this is due to the absence of specific programmes aimed at assisting refugees to find work, obtain training and other facilities, all of which may be required in countries with high rates of unemployment. In some countries, the sheer number of refugees makes the enjoyment of these rights meaningless as no employment is to be found. The difficulty of finding work may be further increased by the absence of appropriate mechanisms whereby refugee status can be recognized, thereby putting the refugees on a par with ordinary aliens or illegal immigrants. As regards asylum-seekers whose status had not been determined, their situation was even more difficult, particularly in countries which introduced or strengthened already existing restrictions on their right to work.

Limitations also existed on the refugees' right to education. Many countries do not have enough educational institutions to meet the needs of their own citizens let alone those of refugees and asylum-seekers. Special assistance programmes went a long way to meet the basic education needs of refugees living in settlements and camps, whereas the needs of refugees living in urban centres were largely unmet.

At its thirty-eighth session, the Executive Committee of the Programme of the High Commissioner considered the issue of Convention travel documents. Although the great majority of States parties to the United Nations Convention of 1951 relating to the Status of Refugees follow the provisions of article 28 of that Convention on the issuance of such documents, certain problems remained. These related in particular to the issuance and renewal of Convention travel documents, their geographic or temporal validity, their recognition for visa and admission purposes and the transfer of responsibility for their issue. In its conclusion on travel documents for refugees, the Executive Committee, *inter alia*, urged States parties to the United Nations Convention of 1951 relating to the Status of Refugees and/or its 1967 Protocol to take appropriate legislative or administrative measures to implement effectively the provisions of these instruments concerning the issue of Convention travel documents.

Many States continued to issue identity documents to refugees during the reporting period, sometimes with UNHCR assistance. In most instances, these documents attested not only to the holders' identity but also to their refugee status, thereby enabling them to benefit from the various rights of refugees.

### 3. Family Reunification

During the period under review, UNHCR noted that certain Governments introduced measures to facilitate family reunification, such as the lifting of restrictions which limited the rights to family reunification to those refugees who had sufficient means to support their family members; or in accepting family members belonging to the extended family, namely, siblings, parents, grandparents, etc. Progress was further achieved in connection with documentation requirements, whereby some States have been more flexible in cases where refugees were unable to provide documentary evidence in support of claimed family relationships. Positive results were also achieved with respect to reuniting refugees with family members who had remained in their country of origin.

Despite the progress made in some areas, obstacles still remained in many countries. These included the length of the administrative procedures prevailing mainly in countries with heavy backlogs in the processing of asylum requests; the lack of resources to support dependent family members; difficulties in securing employment and adequate housing; the inability of some refugees to prove family relationships; and the requirement to obtain exit permits from countries of origin for the purpose of family reunification abroad. As regards the lack of documentation, the Office was particularly concerned that some countries did not hesitate to contact the authorities of the refugee's country of origin to seek verification of documentation.

After considering the report, the General Assembly, on 8 December 1988 (resolution 43/117), recognizing that the enhancement of basic economic and social rights is essential to the achievement of self-sufficiency and family security for refugees, as well as to the process of re-establishing the dignity of the human person and realizing durable solutions to refugee problems, commended those states that, despite severe eco-

nomic and development problems of their own, continue to admit large numbers of refugees and displaced persons and emphasized the need to share the burden of those states to the maximum extent possible through international assistance.

Stressing the need for the international community to continue to provide adequate resettlement opportunities for those refugees for whom no other durable solution may be in sight, in particular for refugees who have already spent an inordinately long time in camps, the Assembly urged all States to support the high commissioner in his efforts to achieve durable solutions to the problem of refugees and displaced persons, primarily through voluntary repatriation or return, including assistance as appropriate to returnees or, wherever appropriate, through integration into countries of asylum or through resettlement in third countries. It also expressed deep appreciation for the valuable material and humanitarian response of receiving countries and urged the international community, in accordance with the principle of international solidarity and burden-sharing, to assist those countries to enable them to cope with the additional burden that the care for refugees and asylum-seekers represents.

*THE PROBLEMS OF REFUGEE CHILDREN.* The particular problems experienced by children who are refugees, which often exposes them to practices having effects similar to those of slavery, have for some time been a matter of special concern to the Office of the United Nations High Commissioner for Refugees. A standing Working Group on Refugee Children at Risk was established in that office early in 1987 to monitor those problems and to suggest ways of ameliorating or remedying them.

In October 1987, the High Commissioner presented a paper to his executive committee (UN Doc. EC/SCP/46) enumerating the problems and the possible solutions. After examining the subject, the executive committee adopted a series of conclusions on refugee children, in which it:

(a) Expressed appreciation to the High Commissioner for his Report on Refugee Children (EC/SCP/46) and noted with serious concern the violations of their human rights in different areas of the world and their special needs and vulnerability within the broader refugee population;

(b) Recognized that refugee children constitute approximately one half of the world's refugee population and that the situation in which they live often gives rise to special protection and assistance problems as well as to problems in the area of durable solutions;

(c) Reiterated the widely-recognized principle that children must be among the first to receive protection and assistance;

(d) Stressed that all action taken on behalf of refugee

children must be guided by the principle of the best interests of the child as well as by the principle of family unity;

(e) Condemned the exposure of refugee children to physical violence and other violations of their basic rights, including through sexual abuse, trade in children, acts or piracy, military or armed attacks, forced recruitment, political exploitation or arbitrary detention, and called for national and international action to prevent such violations and assist the victims;

(f) Urged States to take appropriate measures to register the births of refugee children born in countries of asylum;

(g) Expressed its concern over the increasing number of cases of statelessness among refugee children;

(h) Recommended that children who are accompanied by their parents should be treated as refugees if either of the parents is determined to be a refugee;

(i) Underlined the special situation of unaccompanied children and children separated from their parents, who are in the care of other families, including their needs as regards determination of their status, provision for their physical and emotional support and efforts to trace parents or relatives; and in this connection, recalled the relevant paragraphs of Conclusion No. 24 (XXXII) on Family Reunification;

(j) Called upon the High Commissioner to ensure that individual assessments are conducted and adequate social histories prepared for unaccompanied children and children separated from their parents, who are in the care of other families, to facilitate provision for their immediate needs, the analysis of the long-term as well as immediate viability of existing foster arrangements, and the planning and implementation of appropriate durable solutions;

(k) Noted that while the best durable solution for an un-accompanied refugee child will depend on the particular circumstances of the case, the possibility of voluntary repatriation should at all times be kept under review, keeping in mind the best interests of the child and the possible difficulties of determining the voluntary character of repatriation;

(l) Stressed the need for internationally and nationally supported programmes geared to preventive action, special assistance and rehabilitation for disabled refugee children and encouraged States to participate in the "Twenty or More" Plan providing for the resettlement of disabled refugee children;

(m) Noted with serious concern the detrimental effects that extended stays in camps have on the development of refugee children and called for international action to mitigate such effects and provide durable sessions as soon as possible;

(n) Recognized the importance of meeting the special psychological, religious, cultural and recreational needs of refugee children in order to ensure their emotional stability and development;

(o) Reaffirmed the fundamental right of refugee children to education and called upon all States, individually and collectively, to intensify their efforts, in co-operation with the High Commissioner, to ensure that all refugee children benefit from primary education of a satisfactory quality, that respects their cultural identity and is oriented towards an understanding of the country of asylum;

(p) Recognized the need of refugee children to pursue further levels of education and recommended that the High Commissioner consider the provision of post-primary education within the general programme of assistance;

(q) Called upon all States, in co-operation with UNHCR and concerned agencies, to develop and/or support pro-grammes to address nutritional and health risks faced by refugee children, including programmes to ensure an adequate, well-balanced and safe diet, general immunization and primary health care;

(r) Recommended regular and timely assessment and review of the needs of refugee children, either on an individual basis or through sample surveys, prepared in co-operation with the country of asylum, taking into account all relevant factors such as age, sex, personality, family, religion, social and cultural background and the situation of the local population, and benefiting from the active involvement of the refugee community itself;

(s) Reaffirmed the need to promote continuing and expanded co-operation between UNHCR and other concerned agencies and bodies active in the fields of assistance to refugee children and protection, including through the development of legal and social standards;

(t) Noted the importance of further study of the needs of refugee children by UNHCR, other intergovernmental and non-governmental agencies and national authorities, with a view to identification of additional support programmes and reorientation as necessary of existing ones;

(u) Called upon the High Commissioner to develop further, in consultation with concerned organizations, guidelines to promote co-operation between UNHCR and these organizations to improve the international protection, physical security, well-being and normal psycho-social development of refugee children;

(v) Called upon the High Commissioner to maintain the UNHCR Working Group on Refugee Children at Risk as his focal point on refugee children, to strengthen the Working Group and to inform the members of the Executive Committee, on a regular basis, of its work.

In particular, the High Commissioner has also addressed the problems of women and female children. As indicated in the report of the High Commissioner for Refugees to the 1988 session of the UN General Assembly, covering the period from mid-1987 to mid-1988 (UN Doc. A/43/12, chap. 1, D, paras. 41–44):

In recent years, UNHCR has paid particular attention to the protection needs of refugee women and children. It will be recalled that, in 1985, the Executive Committee of the Programme of the High Commissioner adopted a conclusion on the protection of refugee women in recognition of the fact that refugee women and girls in certain situations are more vulnerable than the refugee population at large. Since then, the Office has worked with States and non-governmental organizations to sensitize them to the particular protection needs of refugee women and girls. Specific measures have also been adopted in a number of refugee situations, as for example, within the framework of the Anti-Piracy Programme referred to above.

Nevertheless, refugee women and girls continue to suffer physical violence, sexual abuse and discrimination. During the reporting period, refugee women were beaten, raped and subjected to other forms of sexual abuse, such as exploitation for the purpose of prostitution. In some instances, such abuse was inflicted on women under the threat of being denied recognition of their refugee status. In other instances, it seemed, at least in part, to be linked to the absence of adequate assistance programmes geared to the specific needs of the female refugee population. The tensions resulting from living in closed camps during protracted periods of time also increased the level of violence of which women were primarily the victims.

The situation of refugee children was subjected to special scrutiny by the Office during the period under review, and was discussed by the Executive Committee of the Programme of the High Commissioner at its thirty-eighth session. In many instances, refugee children are exposed to physical violence, exploitation, forced recruitment and detention. At times they also face particular problems with respect to their registration, determination of their refugee status and their nationality.

In its conclusion on the subject, the Executive Committee recognized that refugee children have special needs within the broader refugee population, and stressed that all action taken on their behalf must be guided by the principle of the best interests of the child, as well as the principle of family unity. It called for national and international action to prevent violations of the basic rights of children and to assist victims. States were also urged to ensure that the births of refugee children born in countries of asylum were registered. Finally, the Executive Committee addressed the situation of particularly vulnerable groups of refugee children, including unaccompanied minors.

After examining the report, the General Assembly on 8 December 1988 (resolution 43/117) commended the High Commissioner for the work undertaken by his office to identify and meet the special needs of refugee children and invited him to pursue his efforts on their behalf, drawing on the valuable contributions of non-governmental organizations in this area. The Assembly also urged States to extend their full cooperation to the High Commissioner in his efforts to ensure that the special needs of refugee women in the fields of protection, assistance, and durable solutions are met.

*THE PROBLEM OF MASSIVE EXODUSES.* At its 1980 session, the attention of the UN COMMISSION ON HUMAN RIGHTS was drawn to movements of large masses of refugees and displaced persons, in various parts of the world, and the immense burden which such massive movements of population—which were frequently the results of violations of human rights—placed on the first host countries. The Commission requested the Secretary-General (resolution 30/XXXVI), in cases where any large-scale exoduses became a matter of international concern, to make concrete recommendations for ameliorating them. Later that year, the General Assembly also expressed deep concern (resolution 35/196) at the large-scale exoduses and displacements and called upon the Commission to recommend solutions for the problems they caused.

In 1981, the Commission invited its chairman (resolution 29 [XXXVII]) to appoint an individual of recognized international standing as Special Rapporteur to study the question of human rights and mass exo-

duses. Sadruddin Aga Khan, former UN High Commissioner for Refugees, was entrusted with this task.

In his *Study on Human Rights and Massive Exoduses* (UN Doc. E/CN.4/1503), presented to the Commission at its 1982 session, the Special Rapporteur pointed out (paras. 1–5) that:

The phenomenon of mass movements of people is not new. From earliest times men have been fleeing one another's intolerance or migrating in search of land and livelihood. For the last several years, however, the number and magnitude of flows of refugees and displaced persons have been such as to cause increasing concern within the international community. By the beginning of the 1980s, numbers exceeded ten million, with the exodus from certain countries reaching haemorrhage proportions. At the same time, increasingly large migratory movements within countries and regions have begun to pose economic and social problems not hitherto experienced on quite the same scale.

In the last 35 years, with the emergence from colonialism of about a hundred new States, often after a considerable struggle and with an inheritance of artificial national boundaries, fragile national unity, underdeveloped economies, too few cadres and boundless logistical problems, the world has seen an unprecedented proliferation of tensions and conflicts. New ideologies misunderstood by and unacceptable to portions of the population, blatant racial discrimination, civil wars, the terror tactics of more than one dictator, foreign invasion or acute economic hardship have caused millions to decide that any life outside their own country must be more bearable than the present one.

The recent mass flights of people to neighbouring countries not only represent wholescale human deprivation and misery, but have come to place upon their hosts and upon the international community as a whole burdens which it is proving increasingly difficult to bear. The three solutions which until recently enabled most refugee situations to be resolved, namely voluntary repatriation, local settlement and resettlement in third countries, can no longer suggest an answer in every case. While circumstances in the home country remain substantially the same and as long as there is no dialogue between the governments most directly concerned, there is no hope of paving the way to a voluntary return. Where the refugees are numbered in hundreds of thousands—or even millions—and land and other resources are scarce, programmes of local integration are practically unthinkable. As for resettlement in third countries, the Indo-Chinese diaspora brought home to over twenty countries which had offered special quotas at the height of the crisis in South East Asia in mid-1979 the difficulty of integrating refugees from an entirely different ethnic and cultural background. Few have found it possible to renew their generous offers of places at anything like the same level—if at all.

Meanwhile, in some underdeveloped areas the presence of millions of uprooted people, sometimes accompanied by as many head of livestock, is playing havoc with the struggling economies of the host countries and posing a dire ecological threat which should not go unchecked. As for economic migrants, world-wide economic recession has meant that they are no longer in demand on the same scale as before. Yet millions still strive to reach more affluent countries in the hope of finding work and a better life.

As a result of all these factors, many governments have reached the conclusion that serious attention must be paid to analysing the forces which get people on the move, with a view particularly to considering whether means can be found to avert new large-scale refugee situations. At the same time, the need has been felt to study the phenomenon of mass exodus in the context of human rights. Hence the initiative of the United Nations Commission on Human Rights contained in its Resolution 29 (XXXVII) to appoint a Special Rapporteur.

Data presented in the study indicate, in the words of the Special Rapporteur, that "all mass exodus which took place during the decade under review (1971–1981) poured forth from regions where the prevailing situation prevented individual citizens from exercising their political rights. It should be noted, however, that this constraint is not, in itself, the essential cause for large movements of population. Indeed, some countries seem to have succeeded in compensating the absence of democracy by ensuring that their peoples have access to material well being. This, coupled with restrictions on freedom of movement, appears to have stemmed the flow of what is still limited one-way traffic from some countries."

A second major cause of mass exodus is described as "conflict between the desire of certain nationalities absorbed within nation-states to retain at least part of their cultural heritage (including their own language), and the policy of the central authorities to phase out (or stamp out) the distinct linguistic and cultural patterns of a homogenous national population. Such conflict between centralization and regionalism has sometimes been violent enough to lead to an exodus of quite considerable proportions."

The Special Rapporteur's conclusions, based on his analysis of mass exodus situations which had developed during the decade under review in 22 countries, in many of which he had personally played a role in his former capacity as UN High Commissioner for Refugees, were as follows (paras. 114–129):

To summarize very briefly the foregoing, the overview of the past decade amply demonstrates that the consequences of mass exodus situations may be measured in terms not only of human suffering but also of threats to national or regional peace and stability.

People leave for a variety of reasons, and usually as a combination of factors rather than a single one. The social contract has failed temporarily or permanently. Modernization and progress have made casualties of people who held certain customs and traditions too dear. In the chaos of war and post-war reconstruction, populations may have been repeatedly uprooted, and thereby conditioned for a further uprooting—from their country—when the going is hard. Colonialism left a heritage of artificial boundaries and structurally imbalanced economies. The repressive tactics of white minority régimes have made many victims. Most provisions of the Declaration of Human Rights have been violated.

These "push factors" must be viewed against a series of economic realities in developing countries, such as high population growth, global food insecurity and a hunger-induced rise in death rates, inflation, unemployment, the flight of skilled manpower and ecological deterioration—which taken in combination may bring large sectors of the population of the world's poorest countries to the threshold of economic distress. Deficiencies in infrastructure, the high cost of equipping modern armed forces, loss or reduction in both trade and aid and the calamitous impact of oil price rises have in the last ten years further handicapped young nations lacking any tradition of statehood. One result has frequently been the attempt to create national cohesion along somewhat authoritarian single-party lines, a fact which helps explain what may be termed the "integrative revolution" facing many developing nations following their accession to independence. Hence the difficulty in creating conditions in which normal human rights could be enjoyed, and hence a high incidence of mass exodus in the countries classified as some of the poorest in the world.

The other side of the coin is a series of "pull factors" which include an increasingly free flow of information from North to South on economic opportunity, and a belief widely shared by beleaguered potential refugees/migrants that their problems will be better understood by the authorities of countries which uphold human rights. The existence of liberalized immigration regulations or refugee quotas must exert some degree of magnetism, particularly in the case of skilled manpower seeking upward mobility, as may the institutionalization of aid close to a troubled country's border.

As a consequence of all these factors, mass movements have become more commonplace, and the principle of the law of asylum has been eroded. It would seem to be time to update refugee, nationality and labour law, and to reexamine asylum practice. Furthermore, to ensure greater clarity in mass influx situations as to numbers of people to be assisted, a mechanism seems to be called for to carry out refugee population census in an impartial manner.

Since mass exodus frequently takes place from economically-disadvantaged countries, and since those governments which generally provide the means to mount humanitarian assistance programmes are very often those which are giving development aid, there appears to be a strong case for a more integrated approach to the planning of aid. Various ways in which this might be tackled are suggested in the preceding chapter. At the same time, when mass exodus does occur, it is important to see the problem in the broad perspective of the position of both "refugee-producing" and "refugee-receiving" countries. A simultaneity of approach should help in identifying the long-term solution, and with regard to the administration of humanitarian assistance, will ensure that this in itself does not constitute a "pull factor" by there being any imbalance in the overall picture. Moreover, standardization of multilateral aid criteria will help to iron out other "wrinkles" in the international community's approach to these most important questions.

It is suggested that the basic concept of an appropriate United Nations presence can be extended to humanitarian emergencies, as distinct from peace-keeping operations in the accepted sense.

It has been found in studying mass exodus that all these situations conform to a certain pattern common to which is the involvement, at an earlier or later stage, of a miscellany of concerned parties, particularly in relation to the provision of essential relief and the production of a considerable volume of informed comment after the event. Yet all the characteristics of this pattern of upheaval and exodus taken together point to certain lacunae which it will be well to attempt to fill if there is to be a lessening of human suffering and of related frictions between States. Three observations are called for here.

Firstly, there is an obvious lack of contact in man-made exodus situations between the authorities of the country of origin and those of the country (or countries) of asylum. It would appear that those who leave are "written off" by their government, more often than not being labelled as traitors, criminals, undesirables, subversives or, at best, misguided elements, while the receiving government is left to handle matters. To be sure, when political circumstances change and negotiated settlements can be initiated, bilateral talks are a prelude to any mass repatriation. Governments seldom get together whilst the exodus is underway, however, and indeed they may not even be enjoying normal diplomatic relations at the time which would permit them to do so.

As a result, the receiving countries with the help of international agencies mount relief and resettlement operations which may develop and grow in a vacuum without any relation to, or detailed knowledge of, the origins or causes of the problem or its likely resolution. Relief agencies, whether they be intergovernmental or non-governmental, continue to refrain from going far into the background to mass movements on the grounds that they have a humanitarian mandate to fulfil and cannot concern themselves with controversial matters, usually of a political nature.

Thus the need for meaningful dialogue with those principally responsible on how to contain the problem remains unmet. Even if the countries or origin should offer a version of the causes which trigger movement which some might qualify as slanted, their responsibility towards their own nationals needs to be upheld—particularly if there is a danger of economic and social disruption in the receiving country and the undermining of peaceful relations between States which share a common border.

Secondly, because funds for humanitarian emergencies are finite, one has to think in both "lateral" and "vertical" terms about the co-ordination of humanitarian assistance. By "lateral" is meant the range of emergencies for which assistance is supplied, extending through man-made disasters to economic difficulties in individual countries. By "vertical" we refer to the co-ordination of humanitarian assistance through the successive phases of relief, rehabilitation, reconstruction and longer-term development. Just as the international community had reached a perception of the need for approaches to development co-operation to be integrated, so, increasingly, it is recognized that contributions must be used in the most cost-effective way possible.

Already it has been seen that in the not infrequent cases where the origins of an exodus are compounded by famine, the apportioning of aid and timely distribution within the country of origin may contribute to circumscribing the flow. At the same time, the presence of international relief officials may help to create a measure of hope and confidence. An improvement in the psychological climate is indeed a key factor in stemming the departure of groups who tend to influence each other until the movement snowballs beyond control. Conversely, in some situations the availability of international assistance very close to the border but exclusively within the receiving country may help precipitate the flow. It seems to be time to take a broader view and fill the existing lacunae.

Thirdly, appropriate organs of the United Nations called upon to deal with causes and, by inference, with prevention tend to be compartmentalized and ponderous, or may be hamstrung by political constraints. At the same time, agencies, subsidiary organs, intergovernmental and non-governmental bodies assisting displaced populations which are victims of man-made or natural disasters have little or no contact with those bodies whose responsibility it is to address the causes. In this, as in other domains, effective co-ordination remains a chronic problem despite the existence of studies and committees dealing with streamlining and restructuring.

As we have recalled in four case studies and an overview of exodus situations of the past decade, large-scale humanitarian emergencies have consistently been met by *ad hoc* measures and the designation of "focal points" or "lead agencies", as well as the appointment of a co-ordinator or special representative of the Secretary-General whose responsibility did not specifically extend to a liaison function, in the case of mass exodus, between the "refugee-producing" country ("cause") and the "refugee-receiving" countries and/or corresponding humanitarian operations ("effect").

The international community is increasingly concerned with causes behind mass exodus and measures to avert new flows of refugees. The General Assembly, at its last session, dealt *inter alia* with this question in Resolution 36/148. This resolution calls for the Group of Experts to take into account the Study submitted by the Special Rapporteur. It is hoped that the two undertakings will be complementary, bearing in mind the distinct history and terms of reference of each initiative. In a wider context, attention should be drawn also to the General Assembly Resolution 36/136 on the proposal for the promotion of a New International Humanitarian Order.

On the basis of these conclusions, the Special Rapporteur discusses ''what might be feasible in terms of prognosis and prescription, prevention and cure,'' in the following terms (paras. 131—140):

In order to give birth to an "early-warning system", it would be necessary to gather, on an ongoing basis, impartial information from proven sources such as governments, the United Nations presence in the countries concerned (whether the UNDP Resident Representative, Specialized Agencies, UNIC or other) and further informed parties in order to gain an understanding of the background and all the facets of a situation, including the ethnic, economic, political and social aspects. Of necessity, there would be visits to the field. After assessing all available data, an appreciation to include a number of possible scenarios for the future development of the situation would be given to the Secretary-General of the United Nations and to the competent intergovernmental organs.

A "trigger mechanism" would be provided by the Secretary-General deciding, after due study of the material and using his executive authority, what action would be required on the part of the United Nations. The Secretary-General might call for further study of the situation, including discussion with the government or governments most closely concerned and/or with the appropriate regional body (Arab League, Council of Europe, Organization of African Unity, Organization of American States) to try to determine how regional containment of the problem cold be achieved, to save it becoming internationalized (that is to say requiring involvement of large-scale United Nations operations).

In the next stage, the executive entrusted with the task would bring the situation to the attention of those who deal with causes (as distinct from effects) to try to encourage, as appropriate, preventive action before the start of a mass movement. In the case of a political question, he would propose to the Secretary-General that the latter take the initiative appearing most indicated, whether it be consulting interested States or drawing the attention of the Security Council, in a suitable manner, to the problem. In the case of human rights issues, the responsible officer would relay the situation to the Commission on Human Rights which could make an investigation and ensure follow up.

It is suggested that after this, there should be liaison on an informal basis with the humanitarian agencies for purposes of consultation. They would thus be alerted and enabled to act swiftly if an exodus did indeed occur, which could be the case even if action were being taken at the source to remove or dissipate the cause(s) of such exodus.

The executive entrusted with responsibility in the situation would keep abreast of the relevant work of the General Assembly, the Security Council, the Commission on Human Rights or other competent body tackling "causes", as the case might be, while at the same time ensuring that humanitarian needs were being covered. He would be responsible for seeing that the question were kept under review by the relevant bodies. Simultaneously, he would be in a position to advise on the best way to apportion aid as between areas affected by the crisis in order to reduce to the maximum extent possible the stress/distress involved. Where necessary, an agency or agencies not so far working on the problem whose expertise were seen to be needed would be invited to participate.

Follow-up work could include monitoring of developments in order to report them to the Secretary-General and informal reporting to governments on the progress of the international effort. In the longer term, work could be carried out on seeking to promote regional reflexes to crisis situations, for example through encouraging the creation and/or development of regional human rights mechanisms, in co-operation with the Commission on Human Rights, and through promoting an active interest in the New International Humanitarian Order.

Measures to be undertaken should be speedy. Their success would be largely dependent on an informed appreciation of each complex situation and its respective origins, based on ongoing research and analysis. Only an impartial monitoring of situations could lead to a more balanced assessment of circumstances lying at the root of potential exodus and contribute thereby to a more adapted response from humanitarian agencies.

Few events go unnoticed in the world today, and the media has been remarkably effective in bringing violations of human rights to the attention of the public. Yet these and other "push factors" are rarely cause for sufficiently active concern until refugees are on the move. Those who could not leave may pay an even higher price for the apparent indifference of their fellow men.

Such an approach as has been outlined is no panacea. It may not always circumscribe exodus but could lead in certain cases to containing or diminishing movement.

The fact that an undertaking is difficult does not mean that it should not be attempted, Governments will inevitably expect that something should be done on this account if there is to be any confidence that the necessary level of humanitarian response to need and distress will be attained.

The Special Rapporteur's recommendations, at the conclusion of the study, are as follows:

It is recommended that consideration be given to the following:

(1) An updating of refugee, nationality and labour law and fresh consideration of asylum practice in the context of the promotion of a New International Humanitarian Order;

(2) A reappraisal of developing countries' economic needs in relation to possible causes of exodus;

(3) Standardization of international aid criteria;

(4) Simultaneity in approach to the country of origin and country of asylum to gain a comprehensive view of the overall situation and thus be able to plan better;

(5) A "bi-multi" aid approach: multilateral aid should take into account bilateral aid, to prevent duplication and ensure an integrated approach;

(6) The introduction of an effective census mechanism to work independently of relief agencies in order to determine in an impartial and professional way the numbers of border-crossers requiring assistance in mass influx situations;

(7) The introduction of an early-warning system based on impartial information gathering and data collection concerning potential mass exodus situations, leading to expeditious reporting to the Secretary-General of the United Nations and competent intergovernmental organs for the purpose of timely action, if required;

(8) The appointment of a Special Representative for Humanitarian Questions whose task, defined briefly in the preceding section, would basically be (a) to forewarn; (b) to monitor; (c) to de-politicize humanitarian situations; (d) to carry out those functions which humanitarian agencies cannot assume because of institutional/mandatory constraints; (e) to serve as an intermediary of goodwill between the concerned parties;

(9) The identification from among groups experienced in humanitarian questions of men and women willing and able to be called upon to form a corps of "humanitarian observers" which, in case of need, could monitor situations and contribute through their presence to a deescalation of tensions. A prerequisite for this role would be the concurrence of the governments concerned. The corps would facilitate the work of the Special Representative for Humanitarian Questions.

The report of the Special Rapporteur was examined in detail by the Group of Governmental Experts on International Cooperation to Avert New Flows of Refugees, which, in turn, presented a comprehensive report on the subject (UN Doc. A/41/324) to the General Assembly in 1986. After endorsing the conclusions and recommendations contained in the report of the group of experts and calling upon member States to respect them, the Assembly—as had been recommended by the group—urged the main organs of the United Nations to make fuller use of their respective competences under the **UN CHARTER** as a means of preventing new massive flows of refugees.

At its 1988 session, the Commission on Human Rights welcomed (resolution 1988/70) the steps taken up to that time by the Secretary-General to establish an early warning system, as well as steps taken by other United Nations bodies to examine the problem of massive outflows of refugees and displaced persons in all its aspects, including its root causes; and invited all governments and concerned international organizations to intensify their cooperation and assistance in world-wide efforts to address these serious problems.

The General Assembly, on 8 December 1988, recognized (resolution 43/154) the fact that human rights violations are one of the multiple and complex factors causing mass exoduses of refugees and displaced persons, as indicated in the study of the Special Rapporteur and in the report of the Group of Governmental Experts on International Cooperation to Avert New Flows of Refugees. Concerned about the increasingly heavy burden being imposed by these sudden mass exoduses and displacements of population upon developing countries with limited resources of their own and upon the international community as a whole, the Assembly requested all governments to ensure the effective implementation of the relevant international instruments, in particular in the field of human rights, as this would contribute to averting new massive flows of refugees and displaced persons.

Since the time of the UN report on massive exoduses, the world witnessed the second greatest mass exodus in recorded history in 1994, when Rwandans fled a genocidal civil war in their country, overflowing into neighboring Zaire. It was estimated that, on one day alone during the mass exodus, over 200,000 people fled their country.

***SECURITY OF REFUGEES.*** As pointed out in the report of the UN High Commissioner for Refugees to the 1988 session of the UN General Assembly, covering the period from mid-1987 to mid-1988 (UN Doc. A/43/12, chap. I, C, paras. 36–40):

The minimum content of the international protection of refugees consists in the enjoyment of fundamental human rights necessary for survival in safety and dignity. This implies, as the *non-refoulement* principle recognizes, protection from loss of life, injury and other bodily harm as well as from any other action that might endanger, or threaten to endanger, the safety and dignity of refugees. As a fundamental element of this protection, the right of refugees to security is fully recognized in international law.

During the reporting period, the security of refugees continued to be at issue, including during flight, in countries of refuge or in connection with their voluntary return to their country of origin. The most flagrant example of the violation of the right to security remained, as in previous years, military and armed attacks on refugee camps and settlements as well as on refugees living in urban centres. Many of these attacks occurred in Africa, the Middle East and in Asia, with resulting loss of life. In one country alone, some 33 attacks were launched on 21 out of 26 settlements that were located in an area suffering from civil strife and armed uprisings. As a result, some 25 refugees lost their lives, 100 were injured, over 150 were raped and between 300 and 400 were abducted.

At its thirty-eighth session, the Executive Committee, for the sixth consecutive year, considered the problem of military and armed attacks on refugee camps and settlements. The Executive Committee adopted a conclusion on this subject which, *inter alia,* condemned all violations of the rights and safety of refugees and asylum-seekers and, in particular, military and armed attacks on refugee camps and settlements; urged States to abstain from these violations, which are against the principles of international law and cannot, therefore, be justified; called upon States and competent international organizations to provide all necessary assistance to relieve the plight of the victims of such attacks; and urged States to take every possible measure to prevent the occurrence of attacks, including measures to ensure that the civilian and humanitarian character of refugee camps and settlements is maintained.

In some refugee situations, the security of refugees is jeopardized through their forced recruitment into armed groups, guerilla bands or regular armies. Such practices continued during the reporting period and affected considerable numbers of young male refugees. Coercing refugees to take part, as active combatants in an armed struggle, amounts to a clear threat to their survival and integrity, is incompatible with their status as refugees and undermines their access to international protection. Furthermore, these violations are contrary to the concept that refugees are civilians, as well as the tenet, reconfirmed by the Executive Committee in its conclusions on military and armed attacks on refugee camps and settlements, that such camps and settlements have a strictly civilian and humanitarian character and that it is essential that States of refuge do all within their capacity to ensure that this character is maintained.

Further examples of violations of the security of refugees were found in the waters of South-East Asia where pirates continued, during the reporting period, to attack asylum-seekers travelling in boats. Efforts to curb such attacks were maintained under the Anti-Piracy Programme previously established by the Royal Thai Government, in co-operation with UNHCR and funded by several donor countries. Similarly, the Rescue at Sea Resettlement Offers (RASRO) scheme and the Disembarkation Resettlement Offers (DISERO) scheme benefited large numbers of asylum-seekers in distress at sea. Elsewhere, national authorities and UNHCR increased their vigilance along flight routes to ensure that refugees in search of protection were not killed, injured, raped or abducted. Even so, during the period under review, several reports reached the Office of violations of refugees' right to security.

After examining the report, the General Assembly on 8 December 1988 (resolution 43/117) noted with particular concern the continued violation, in certain situations, of the principle of *non-refoulement,* stressed the need to strengthen measures to protect refugees against such action and appealed to all states to abide by their international obligations, taking fully into account their legitimate security concerns.

The Assembly condemned all violations of the rights and safety of refugees and asylum-seekers, in particular those perpetrated by military or armed attacks against refugee camps and settlements and other forms of violence; endorsed again the conclusions on military and armed attacks adopted by the Executive Committee of the Programme of the High Commissioner; and renewed its call to all states to observe these principles.

***REFUGEES: INTERNALLY DISPLACED PERSONS.*** Although not included in the traditional definition of "refugee," the internally displaced person shares many of the same hardships and deprivation of rights. These were acknowledged and summarized in a 1994 report by the Representative of the UN Secretary-General on internally displaced persons (E/CN.4/1994/44, paras. 61–63, and E/CN.4/1994/44/Add. 1, paras. 132–175):

It is important to note that the mandate of the Representative calls for a complex, comprehensive and challenging programme of activities, which will require commensurate human and financial resources. From a human resource point of view, only one staff member at the Centre for Human Rights, appointed and reappointed on short-term contracts, has been working on the mandate. While her performance has been outstanding, the needs of the mandate by far surpass what she can humanly do to meet the demands of the mandate. In this connection, it should be acknowledged that the Government of Norway has generously offered to contribute the service of an expert, although the formalities of recruitment have delayed the appointment. In order for the Representative to continue implementing his programme of activities in a meaningful and productive manner, support for his mandate will have to be provided at a much more substantial level and on a more stable basis.

In his report to the General Assembly, the Representative of the Secretary-General made the point that it would be tragically ironic if the international community were to become complacent in addressing the crisis of internal displacement because of the existence of his mandate. Despite the Commission's concern, as demonstrated in the establishment of the mandate, and although the need for effective action is indisputable, the normative principles and the enforcement mechanisms for international action are clearly inadequate and ineffective.

If the international community is to rise to the challenge, then the mandate of the Representative of the Secretary-General must be seen as a catalyst and leverage for the adoption of more effective measures. It is in this connection that the proposed study leading to the development of a comprehensive strategy of international protection for internally displaced persons deserves support. It should, however, not be seen as a new initiative, for all it aims to do is to provide a more credible means of pursuing the objective of the mandate, in particular by facilitating the search for effective ways to address the crisis of internal displacement in a comprehensive, effective and durable manner.

The following are the conclusions reached by the Representative of the Secretary-General on internally displaced persons after his visit to Sri Lanka in November 1993. As they refer to numerous general issues related with the mandate, they have been included in the present document.

### Conclusions and Recommendations

### Observations on Issues

*Definition of "internally displaced persons".* In his comprehensive study submitted to the Commission at its forty-ninth session, the Representative identified a number of tensions with regard to the definition of "internally displaced persons". The working definition suggested in that study was the one used in the analytical report of the Secretary-General, namely, that "internally displaced parsons" are "persons who have been forced to flee their homes suddenly or unexpectedly in large numbers, as a result of armed conflict, internal strife, systematic violations of human rights or natural or man-made disasters; and who are within the territory of their own country" (E/CN.4/1992/23, para.17). It has been argued by some sources that the definition should not be interpreted in such a way as to exclude small numbers or even individuals who are internally displaced. Another concern was that it would be undesirable to distinguish between civilian populations displaced by armed conflict and those who have not been displaced, but whose needs are similar.

While it is often true that the category to which a person is assigned has consequences for the type of relief assistance to which he or she is entitled, in Sri Lanka the Representative did not identify any major gaps in terms of the provision of relief assistance due to the lack of a general and agreed-upon definition of the term "internally displaced". The need for and type of such assistance is much more evident in the case of the camps. Those who are displaced but who are being accommodated with friends or relatives or have managed on their own presumably are harder to delineate as a group for assistance purposes. In terms of entitlements, therefore, it is important that if different groups need different types of assistance, they be defined in practical terms suitable for the specific circumstances in the country. This does not undermine the need of a general definition of the term "internally displaced"; it simply requires that any such definition retain a margin of flexibility to accommodate to the particular conditions in the country.

Generally, therefore, the situation in Sri Lanka confirms that it is very hard to reach a satisfactory and accurate definition. At the same time it exemplifies the fact that a large proportion of the internally displaced can be easily identified by virtue of the fact that they are housed in special camps and that they have special needs for assistance and protection different from the ones for the rest of the population. Another point to bear in mind is that most of these people have been uprooted because of the conflict, and that while many fled the violent incidents of 1983 or 1990, others may have left their homes less "suddenly" but for equally compelling reasons (e.g. military operations in a area, mines, etc.).

*Protection of human rights.* From the point of view of protection of human rights, the Representative was able to establish that at least in Sri Lanka the displaced are more vulnerable than the rest of the population in certain ways: they may be forcibly resettled; more readily subjected to round-ups, arbitrary detentions or arrests; deprived of their dry rations or more frequently unable to get jobs. Those not displaced have been identified as being more self-sufficient and more resilient to the destructive impacts of the conflict.

The issue of resettlement to the original areas of residence in Sri Lanka has highlighted at least one problem which affects only those displaced: the extent to which the authorities of a country are allowed to compel an internally displaced person to return to an area where his/her life, personal security or freedom will be threatened for reasons similar to the ones that compelled his or her displacement in the first place. It is impossible to provide a full legal analysis in the context of this report. Arguably, however, the principle of non-refoulement, which is the foundation of refugee law, could be applied by analogy in the case of internal displacement. The freedom of movement as well as various other instruments prohibiting population transfers support and strengthen this assumption. Obviously, fundamental human rights such as the right to life, physical integrity and personal security, which are guaranteed, for instance, in the International Covenant of Civil and Political Rights, run counter to practices that place them in serious and actual danger.

Irrespective of the precise legal basis, physical coercion or the threat thereof or the use of food as a tool or any other similar means to compel internally displaced to return to an area where they would not be secure is unacceptable. Clarifying the precise legal principles can only sharpen this conclusion and provide a means of empowerment to the potential victims.

The need to clarify a quasi-non-refoulement principle for situations of internal displacement in a case like Sri Lanka will inevitably require formulating a definition of the term "internally displaced person". From a factual point of view, this person will frequently have fled because of a well-founded fear of being targeted and victimized in the course of an armed conflict or systematic violations of human rights. Violence in Sri Lanka offers just one more example of the fact that both the armed conflict and the violations of human rights occur in the context of ethnic, racial, religious, political or social cleavages. Even if it is argued that Government is not at all responsible for these cleavages and the resulting violence, sending the displaced back to a dangerous situation amounts effectively to the same type of targeting and victimization. In such a situation it can be argued that the internally displaced person can no longer count on the protection of his/her own country as promised by the authorities.

Human rights law on its own is never sufficient for the effective protection of human rights. The lack of an effective judicial system almost precludes the implementation of these rights. The Representative was told in Sri Lanka that no legal problems have arisen from the situation of internal displacement at the judicial level. This contrasts sharply with the complaints voiced by the internally displaced themselves. It can only be explained by the general observation that the poorest and dispossessed layers of a society rarely have effective access to the judicial system. Given the number of internally displaced persons in Sri Lanka, the problems identified may be, for the bar associations and the NGOs, issues worth seizing and challenging in the courts.

*The involvement of the international community.* There are three conceivable levels on which mechanisms to monitor the provision of assistance and protection to the internally displaced can be envisaged: the country level, the regional level, and the international level. For different situations different types of activities at these levels are required as illustrated by such cases as Somalia, Liberia or Sri Lanka.

In a country like Sri Lanka it appears appropriate to any that there is no need for a massive mobilization at the international or the regional levels either to provide large amounts of relief assistance or to intervene in order to protect the internally displaced. In Sri Lanka the humanitarian presence of the United Nations agencies and the international NGOs and the significant leverage of the donors afford de facto a significant amount of protection. While their operations may be conducted on an ad hoc basis, this is not necessarily negative: it only exemplifies that dealing with problems in the field often requires ad hoc solutions, and that these solutions are frequently concrete evidence of the will to address the problems in a creative and effective manner.

Many have argued that these ad hoc solutions should remain marginalized and "fluid" and that any attempt to either place them in existing structures or try to create new structures to fit them in will only destroy them. These arguments refer both to the ad hoc nature of the involvement of the United Nations agencies and the de facto nature of the protection they afford to the internally displaced. Therefore, according to these arguments, emphasizing the need for some monitoring presence in the camps, not only for humanitarian but also for human rights purposes, on a regular basis and making representations to the Government on behalf of the displaced would not work. Also, many believe that institutionalizing a post of United Nations officer for internally displaced persons and placing him or her either under UNHCR or UNDP auspices would not be an idea agreeable to the Government or to these agencies.

Despite the rationale of these attitudes, the Representative has found that both the operations of UNHCR and of UNDP vis-à-vis the internally displaced in Sri Lanka have beneficial effects on that population and should be studied and analysed more carefully.

The need to ensure some monitoring presence at the regional level has been stressed by many sources. While contacts with regional organizations, such as the Conference on Security and Cooperation in Europe or of its High Commissioner for National Minorities, the Organization of American States or the Organization of African Unity, need to be established, the Representative hopes to suggest additional means of collection of information on the regional level.

At the international level the Representative is convinced that there is a need for an effective mechanism to have a regular dialogue with the Governments concerned in order to study and analyse the problem in the respective countries and attempt jointly to find solutions. The Representative currently has the possibility to undertake only very few substantive missions a year, with no resources for follow-up visits. This curtails greatly his ability to alert the international community to each and every situation of internal displacement that occurs in the world or take himself any steps to even register them. He is, therefore, committed to submitting as soon as feasible concrete suggestions and proposals as to this issue. Given the complexities, however, as well as the sheer magnitude of the problems involved, any such suggestions can only be modest attempts to deal with some aspects of the problems rather than with the generic problems themselves.

*Addressing the root causes.* The conclusion of the Representative on the situation in Sri Lanka is that unless a political solution to the conflict is found, there can be little hope either of ending the conflict or of solving the problem of internal displacement. The United Nations, or more generally the international community, does not have a mandate to intercede with the Government on this issue, although the Government welcomes their presence and assistance. The Representative does not perceive himself as, nor does he have the mandate of a peace negotiator. However, if he limited his analysis only to the interim situation of the displaced in Sri Lanka, without regard to their long-term prospects of returning home, he would be taking an obvious step with only short-term and limited prospects. He is convinced that it is time that the parties to the conflict should balance carefully their considerations for continuing the war and for jeopardizing the welfare of the people of Sri Lanka. He also believes that the international community should exhibit an interest not only in providing financial assistance but also in ensuring that such assistance advances the cause of peace, security and stability in the country.

## Specific Proposals

*The nature and scope of assistance.* As long as internal displacement persists, assistance to the affected population, food rations being the absolute minimum, will continue to be urgently needed. Other services, such as the quality of shelter and sanitation, also need improvement, especially as displacement appears destined for long duration in the absence of peace. Alternative forms of assistance may also need to be devised for other vulnerable groups. Where the need exists, any discriminatory practices in the provision of assistance or other benefits should be avoided.

On the other hand, the constraints on the resources available to the Government will naturally limit the scope and level of possible assistance. This is one of the reasons why income-generation projects and the provision of employment opportunities should be placed high on the Government's agenda.

The current level of the provision of education is laudable and needs to be maintained. Where facilities are inadequate, efforts are needed to address these inadequacies to keep a uniform level on this area of commendable accomplishment.

*With regard to the security situation.* Efforts to identify missing or disappeared persons and inform their families need to be intensified, especially as aspects of family security may depend on the status of these missing members.

Militant groups should be discouraged from presence in the welfare centres since that tends to provoke adverse relations with the authorities and threatens the security of the civilian population.

Cordon and search operations in or around welfare centres also need to be avoided as far as possible, unless serious security exigencies dictate otherwise. Likewise, military presence and operation in or near the welfare centres and resettlement sites need to be kept to an absolute minimum.

*The issue of resettlement.* Sincere efforts should be made to comply with the Government's resettlement guidelines which should be made more widely known to the local authorities, the NGOs and the displaced.

Any type of coercion, including the threat of cutting dry rations to induce return, should be avoided. Conditions in the camps should not be allowed to become so perilous or dehumanizing that the displaced prefer the fear of being persecuted or victimized to remaining in the camps.

Accurate information regarding the conditions of security and welfare in the area of original residence should be provided to these to be resettled. The relevant committees already in operation should be supported to enhance their efforts in this regard. The development of procedural safeguards for the voluntary nature of the resettlement needs to be considered. For instance, those to be resettled may be required to sign a form declaring their wish to resettle. Such a form would be similar to the one that UNHCR uses for its voluntary repatriation programmes.

Efforts should be made to avoid giving those to be resettled misleading information regarding the benefits they are to expect from the resettlement. Such expectations can only lead to disappointment and increase the already existing tensions.

To allow time and flexibility in addressing the complex issues involved, resettlement should not be carried out with a rigid time schedule. The issue of resettlement is currently connected to the projected referendum and the local elections. It is therefore seen as having become politicized and too rigorously programmed. To the extent that the refer-endum and the local elections are predicted on the resettlement programme, the Government may have to consider postponing them to allow for a smoother, more acceptable process of resettlement.

*The search for durable solutions.* As the settlement projects of populations in the east at this stage appear to be particularly controversial, careful reconsideration of those projects may be necessary. Such reconsiderations also require that members of the communities who originate from that area be given special attention in the settlement process.

Priority needs to be given to developing alternative long-term solutions for those communities that will not be able to return to their original areas of residence in the foreseeable future.

Efforts to come to a negotiated peace agreement need to be vigorously pursued. If the war continues, the prospects of maintaining peace and security even in those areas that are now relatively peaceful may be seriously jeopardized. As increased freedom of information and expression of opinion would facilitate the spread of peace initiatives, publicize the plight of the displaced and give a clear picture of the magnitude of the war and its consequences, initiatives and efforts in that direction should be encouraged and supported.

*The legal framework.* The Government has been urged to sign Protocol II Additional to the Geneva Conventions and also to consider signing the other human rights instruments to which it is not yet a party.

There is also an urgent need to address legally any outstanding discriminatory practices on the basis of ethnicity, religion and language and to reverse any public tendencies that may operate to the disadvantage of the minorities.

*The role of the United Nations agencies.* The presence of UNHCR, especially in the Open Relief Centres, has had significant beneficial effects and needs to be maintained. It guarantees not only better living conditions, but also protection. The ORCs play an important role in assisting the people to remain near their homes and return to them whenever it is safe to do so.

Given their evident beneficial effects, the operations of UNHCR and UNDP in Sri Lanka should be analysed and built upon. They should be financially supported and their authority to continue these operations should be clarified.

The United Nations agencies, in conjunction with the NGOs, should be encouraged to continue their efforts to share information and coordinate their activities.

*The role of the non-governmental community.* Lawyers' associations need to be actively involved in the protection of the fundamental rights of the internally displaced.

The NGO community should make efforts to become more operational in areas where the NGO presence is currently limited. The NGOs should be encouraged to operate without undue interference from the State or other combatant parties.

The LITE should also be called upon to abide by the principles of humanitarian law, cease any further expulsions of Muslims or other ethnic communities and to permit the free exit of Tamils from the areas it controls.

*The role of the donor community.* International efforts towards a negotiated solution need to be stepped up considerably. Such efforts need to be directed towards both the Government and the LITE.

The donor community is encouraged to channel funds for humanitarian assistance and rehabilitation to NGOs and other international agencies. Such assistance should also be given to the Government, in some instances earmarked for the benefit of the tragic victims of internal displacement.

Given the humanitarian tragedy of the conflict raging in Sri Lanka, a strong case can be made for monitoring the manner in which financial or other assistance is used. Donors should scrutinize continuously the progress made in the human rights field and in the efforts to reach a peaceful resolution of the conflict. Foreign assistance should help promote sustainable development, protection of the environment and, above all, peace and security for the country.

**Concluding Comment**

As a concluding comment, several points need to be highlighted about the Representative's experience with Sri Lanka as a case study. First, both in the magnitude of the crisis and the cooperation of the Government with the Representative and the international community, Sri Lanka is indeed a model to be emulated. Second, the Representative has tried to build on this positive model in an attempt to meet the Commission's and the General Assembly's emphasis on country visits and dialogue with Governments on behalf of the internally displaced. Third, and in conformity with the Representative's commensurate emphasis on country profiles, this report has tried to achieve the necessary level of depth of description and analysis which he aspires to follow with respect to other country missions and reports. Fourth, that within the framework of mutual cooperation with Governments which Sri Lanka typifies, the report has been rather thorough and candid in exposing the problems to be addressed, the objective being to facilitate a cooperative resolution to the issues involved. Fifth and finally, the width and depth of the coverage of this and other country profiles aim at producing documents that can be helpful to organizations and individuals concerned and actually or potentially involved in the search for solutions to the problems of internal displacement. It is, therefore, hoped that it is a document that combines the necessary level of scholarly depth, intellectual integrity, sound policy and practical utility.

*VOLUNTARY REPATRIATION.* As indicated in the report of the UN High Commissioner for Refugees to the 1988 session of the UN General Assembly, covering the period from mid-1987 to mid-1988 (UN Doc. A/43/12, chap. 1, E), at least 150,000 refugees returned voluntarily to their countries of origin during that period, the vast majority on the African continent. Significant numbers of refugees, however, also returned to several Central American countries. Voluntary repatriation movements elsewhere were almost negligible. According to the report (paras. 46–48):

A considerable proportion of the refugees concerned returned spontaneously. In one situation, their decision to return was no doubt influenced by the seriously deteriorating security situation in the part of the country of asylum where they had previously found refuge. Elsewhere, the return took place in an organized fashion in which transportation and immediate assistance needs were met both during the return and during the initial period back in the country of origin.

Although by and large the voluntary returns took place in safety and dignity, there were some exceptions. At least one refugee lost his life as a result of violence and many others were subjected to harassment upon return. Yet other refugees faced considerable problems in the reintegration process and several returning refugees were subjected to detention measures. Part of these problems resulted from the fact that returning refugees were denied proper documentation by their countries of origin, thereby denying them effective national protection.

Voluntary repatriation, whenever feasible, is the preferred solution to any refugee situation. It achieves the basic goal of international protection, namely, the re-establishment of refugees in a community, in this case, their own. It is, however, also one of the most delicate solutions to implement. It is, therefore, of the utmost importance that the Office be able to count on the full support and co-operation of the countries concerned, including receiving the requisite material and human resources. If voluntary repatriation is to become a viable solution for more significant numbers of refugees, it is essential that States attend to the root causes of refugee movements. Only by removing the conditions that led to the original flight can larger numbers of refugees return voluntarily to their respective countries of origin in safety and dignity. This task, which is largely political, must be pursued more vigorously by States.

After considering the report, the General Assembly on 8 December 1988 (resolution 43/117) recognized that voluntary repatriation or return remains the most desirable solution to the problems facing refugees and displaced persons, welcomed the fact that in various parts of the world it had been possible for significant numbers of them to return voluntarily to their countries of origin, and urged all States to support the High Commissioner's efforts to solve the basic problems of refugees and displaced persons primarily through voluntary repatriation or return. A program of voluntary repatriation was initiated under United Nations auspices in 1995, in which Rwandan refugees were encouraged to return home from Zaire. Due to the uncertain conditions in their homeland, many of the Rwandan refugees refused to leave their camps and return to their native land.

***SEE ALSO*** *Internally Displaced Persons; Statelessness.*

**BIBLIOGRAPHY.** Ahearn, Frederick L., and Jean L. Athey, eds. *Refugee Children: Theory, Research, and Services.* London and Baltimore, MD, USA: Johns Hopkins University Press, 1991. Scholarly collective works, in English.

Aiboni, S. A. *Protection of Refugees in Africa.* Uppsala, Sweden: Scandinavian Institute of African Studies and Svenska Institutet for Internationell Ratt, 1978. Scholarly study, in English; bibliography, pp. 151–155.

Aleinidoff, T. Alexander. "The Meaning of 'Persecution' in United States Asylum Law," *International Journal of Refugee Law* 3, no. 1 (Jan. 1991): 5–29. Scholarly article, in English.

All Africa Conference of Churches. *The Refugee Problem: A Time Bomb in Africa—A Report of the Seminar on Awareness Building for Church Leaders held from 12th–16th November, 1990, Blantyre, Malawi.* Nairobi, Kenya: 1992. Conference report, in English and French.

Allen, Tim, and Hubert Morsink. *When Refugees Go Home.* London: James Currey, 1994. Scholarly monograph, in English.

American Association for the Advancement of Science.

*Scientists in Exile: Issues and Perspectives on the Refugee Experience.* Washington, D.C.: 1988. NGO report, in English.

American Council for Nationalities Service. *Refugee Reports.* Washington, D.C. NGO journal, in English.

Anthony, Constance G. "Africa's Refugee Crisis: State Building in Historical Perspective," *International Migration Review* 25, no. 3 (no. 95) (Fall 1991): 574–591. Scholarly article, in English; bibliography, pp. 588–591.

Baker, Ron, ed. *The Psychosocial Problems of Refugees.* London: British Refugee Council and European Consultation on Refugees and Exiles, 1983. Scholarly edited collection, in English.

Beyer, Gregg A. "Human Rights Monitoring and the Failure of Early Warning: A Practitioner's View," *International Journal of Refugee Law* 2, no. 1 (1990): 56–82. Scholarly article, in English.

Brennan, T. O. *Uprooted Angolans: From Crisis to Catastrophe.* Washington, D.C.: U.S. Committee for Refugees, 1987. NGO report, in English.

British Refugee Council. *Uprooted: The Displaced of Central America.* London: 1986. NGO report, in English.

Burgess, Jan. "New UNHCR Guidelines for Protection of Women," *Refugees* no. 87 (Oct. 1991): 40–41. Article, in English and French.

Canadian Council for International Cooperation and the Refugee Policy Group. *Conference report: Internally Displaced Persons in Africa, Ottawa, Canada, February 14–16, 1992.* Washington, D.C.: 1992. Conference report, in English.

Center for Documentation on Refugees and Save the Children Alliance. *A Selected and Annotated Bibliography on Refugee Children.* Geneva, Switzerland: 1988. In English.

Center for Migration Studies. *Migration World.* New York. NGO journal devoted to problems of refugees, in English; prior to 1986, *Migration Today.*

Centre Europe Tiers-Monde (Europe-Third World Centre) and Association pour les Troisièmes Assises sur le Droit d'Asile (Association for the Organization of the Third Meeting on the Right to Asylum). *1992: Europe et droit d'asile* (1992: Europe and the Right of Asylum). Geneva, Switzerland: 1991. Conference report, in French.

Central America Resource Center. *Sourcebook on Central American Refugee Policy: A Bibliography with Subject and Country Index.* Austin, TX, USA: Lyndon B. Johnson School of Public Affairs, University of Texas at Austin, 1985. In English and Spanish.

Cohen, Roberta. *Human Rights Protection for Internally Displaced Persons.* Washington, D.C.: Refugee Policy Group, 1991. Scholarly monograph, in English.

———. *Introducing Refugee Issues into the United Nations Human Rights Agenda.* Washington, D.C.: Refugee Policy Group, 1990. NGO issue paper, in English.

Consultation européenne sur les réfugiés et les exilés (European Consultation on Refugees and Exile). *Asile en Europe: guide à l'intention des associations de protection des réfugiés* (Asylum in Europe: A Guide to the Organizations for the Protection of Refugees). Paris: 1990. NGO guidelines, in French.

Druke, Luise. *Preventive Action for Refugee Producing Situations.* Frankfurt, Germany: Peter Lang, 1990. Thesis, in English; bibliography, pp. 249–271.

Egan, Suzanne J. *Civil War Refugees and the Issue of 'Singling Out' in a State of Civil Unrest.* North York, Canada: Refugee Law Research Unit, Osgoode Hall Law School, York University, 1991. Research paper, in English.

Einarsen, Terje. "The European Convention on Human Rights and the Notion of an Implied Right to *de facto* Asylum," *International Journal of Refugee Law* 2, no. 3 (July 1990): 361–389. Scholarly article, in English.

European Consultation on Refugees and Exiles. *Asylum in Europe: A Handbook for Agencies Assisting Refugees,* 3rd ed. The Hague, the Netherlands: 1983. In English.

Fagen, P. W., and S. Aguayo. *Central Americans in Mexico and the United States: Unilateral, Bilateral, and Regional Perspectives.* Washington, D.C.: Center for Immigration Policy and Refugee Assistance, 1988. NGO study, in English.

Ferris, E. G. *The Central American Refugees.* New York: Praeger Publishers, 1987. Scholarly report, in English.

Forbes Martin, Susan. *Refugee Women.* London: Zed Books, 1992. Monograph, in English; bibliography, pp. 130–133.

Gilbert, Geoff. "Root Causes and International Law: Refugee Flows in the 1990's," *Netherlands Quarterly of Human Rights* 11 (1993): 413–436. Scholarly article, in English.

Goodwin-Gill, Guy S., ed. "Human Rights and Refugees in Crisis: An Overview and Introduction," *International Journal of Refugee Law* (Sept. 1990). Special issue, in English.

Gordenker, Leon. *Refugees in International Politics.* New York: Columbia University Press, 1987. Scholarly report, in English; bibliography, pp. 215–220.

Gorman, Robert F. *Coping with Africa's Refugee Burden: A Time for Solutions.* Dordrecht, the Netherlands: Martinus Nijhoff, 1987. Scholarly monograph, in English.

Gowlland, Vera, and Klaus Samson, eds. *Problems and Prospects of Refugee Law: Papers Presented at the Colloquium Organized by the Graduate Institute of International Studies in Collaboration with the Office of the United Nations High Commissioner for Refugees, Geneva, 23 and 24 May, 1991.* Geneva, Switzerland: Graduate Institute of International Studies, 1992. Conference paper, in English.

Grahl-Madsen, Atle. *Territorial Asylum.* Stockholm, Sweden: Almqvist and Wiksell International, in collaboration with Oceana Publications, 1980. Scholarly monograph, in English.

Gros Espiell, Hector, Sonia Picado, and Leo Valladares Lanza. "Principles and Criteria for the Protection of and Assistance to Central American Refugees, Returnees and Displaced Persons in Latin America," *International Journal of Refugee Law* 2, no. 1 (1990): 83–117. Scholarly article, in English.

Harrell-Bond, B. E. *Imposing Aid: Emergency Assistance to Refugees.* Oxford, UK: Oxford University Press, 1986. Scholarly monograph, in English; bibliography, pp. 428–435.

Hathaway, James C. *The Law of Refugee Status.* Toronto, Canada: Butterworths, 1991. Scholarly monograph, in English; bibliography, pp. 235–242.

Helton, Arthur C. "The Comprehensive Plan of Action for Indo-Chinese Refugees: An Experiment in Refugee Protection and Control," *New York Law School Journal of Human Rights* 8, no. 1 (Fall 1990): 111–148. Scholarly article, in English.

Hull, Elizabeth. *Without Justice for All: The Constitutional Rights of Aliens.* Westport, CT, USA: Greenwood Press, 1985. Scholarly monograph, in English.

Institut Africaine pour le Developpement Economique (African Institute for Economic Development). *Les Refugies en Afrique: Bibliographie Commentee* (Refugees in Africa: Annotated Bibliography). Abidjan, Ivory Coast: 1986. In French.

International Refugee Integration Resource Centre. *International Bibliography of Refugee Literature.* Geneva, Switzerland: 1985. In English.

Jacobson, J. L. *Environmental Refugees: A Yardstick of Habitability.* Washington, D.C.: Worldwatch Institute, 1988. NGO monograph, in English.

Joly, Danièle, Clive Nettleton, and Hugh Poulton. *Refugees: Asylum in Europe?* Boulder, CO, USA: Westview Press, 1993. Scholarly monograph, in English; bibliography, pp. 157–160.

Jonassohn, Kurt. *The Tragic Circle of Famine, Genocide and Refugees.* Montreal, Canada: Montreal Institute for Genocide and Human Rights Studies, 1992. NGO report, in English; bibliography, pp. 20–26.

Kibread, Gaim. *African Refugees: Reflections on the African Refugee Problem.* Trenton, NJ, USA: Africa World Press, 1985. Monograph, in English.

Kronenberger, Jane. "Refugee Women: Establishing a prima facie Case Under the Refugee Convention," *ILSA Journal of International Law* 15 (1992): 61–84. Scholarly article, in English.

Lam, Lawrence. "Repatriation: A Solution to the Vietnamese "Boat People" Problem in Hong Kong?" *Refuge* 11, no. 1 (Oct. 1991): 1–4. Article, in English.

Lawless, R., and L. Monahan, eds. *War and Refugees: The Western Sahara Conflict.* London: Refugee Studies Programme, Queen Elizabeth House, 1987. Scholarly edited collection, in English.

Lawyers Committee for Human Rights. *The UNHCR at 40: Refugee Protection at the Crossroads.* New York: 1991. NGO report, in English.

Loescher, G., and A. D. Loescher. *The Global Refugee Crisis: A Reference Handbook.* Santa Barbara, CA, USA: ABC-CLIO, 1994. Handbook, in English; bibliography, pp. 189–235.

Martin, D. A., ed. *The New Asylum Seekers: Refugee Law in the 1980s.* Dordrecht, the Netherlands: Martinus Nijhoff, 1988. Scholarly edited collection, in English.

Morgan, S. M., and E. Colson, eds. *People in Upheaval.* Staten Island, NY, USA: Center for Migration Studies of New York, 1987. NGO document collection, in English.

Nanda, V. P. "The African Refugee Dilemma: A Challenge for International Law and Policy," *Africa Today* 32, nos. 1 and 2 (1st and 2d quarters 1985): 61–75. Conference proceedings in scholarly journal, in English.

———, ed. *Refugee Law and Policy: International and U.S. Responses.* Westport, CT, USA: Greenwood Press, 1989. Scholarly edited collection, in English.

Netherlands Institute of Human Rights and the Dutch Refugee Council. *Refugees in the World: The European Community's Response.* Utrecht, the Netherlands: 1990. NGO conference proceedings, in English.

New Francophone Summary of Information on Refugees and Asylum. *Documentation Refugies.* NGO documentation, in French.

Ohaegbulom, F. U. "Human Rights and the Refugee Situation in Africa," in *Human Rights and Third World Development,* eds. G. W. Shephard, Jr., and V. Nanda, pp. 197–230. Westport, CT, USA: Greenwood Press, 1985. Chapter in scholarly collection, in English.

Ortiz Miranda, Carlos. "Toward a Broader Definition of Refugee: 20th Century Development Trends," *California Western International Law Journal* 20, no. 2 (1989–1990): 315–327. Scholarly article, in English.

Oxford University. *International Journal of Refugee Law.* Oxford, UK: Oxford University Press. Quarterly scholarly journal, in English.

———. *Journal of Refugee Studies.* Oxford, UK: Oxford University Press. Scholarly document collection, in English.

Panjabi, Ranee K. L. "The Global Refugee Crisis: A Search for Solutions," *California Western International Law Journal* 21, no. 2 (1990–1991): 247–263. Scholarly article, in English.

Plender, Richard, ed. *Basic Documents on International Migration Law.* Dordrecht, the Netherlands: Martinus Nijhoff, 1988. Scholarly document collection, in English.

———. *International Migration Law,* rev. 2nd ed. Dordrecht, the Netherlands: Martinus Nijhoff, 1988. Scholarly edited collection, in English.

Rabé, Paul. *Voluntary Repatriation: The Case of Hmong in Ban Vinai.* No. 2. Bangkok, Thailand: Indochinese Refugee Information Center, Institute of Asian Studies, Chulalongkorn University, 1990. Scholarly paper, in English and Thai.

Refugee Studies Programme, Queen Elizabeth House. *The Directory of Current Research on Refugees and Other Forced Migrants,* 2nd ed. Oxford, UK: 1988. In English.

———. *Implementation of the OAU/UN Conventions and Domestic Legislation concerning the Rights and Obligations of Refugees in Africa, 14–28 September 1986: Final Report.* Oxford, UK: 1988. NGO conference proceedings, in English.

———. "Refugee Children," *RPN—Refugee Participation Network* no. 12 (March 1992): 3–20. Special issue, in English.

Robinson, Court. "Buying Time: Refugee Repatriation from Thailand," *World Refugee Survey—1992* (1992): 18–24. Article, in English.

Rogge, J. R. *Too Many, Too Long: Sudan's Twenty-Year Refugee Dilemma.* Totowa, NJ, USA: Rowman and Allanheld, 1985. Scholarly monograph, in English; bibliography, pp. 185–190.

Ruiz, H. A. *Beyond the Headlines: Refugees in the Horn of Africa.* Washington, D.C.: U.S. Committee for Refugees, 1988. NGO issue paper, in English; selected bibliography.

Stein, Barry N., and Fred C. Cuny. "Repatriation Under Conflict," *World Refugee Survey—1991* (1991): 15–21. Article, in English.

Tomasi, Lydio F., ed. *In Defense of the Alien,* vol. 5, *Refugees and Asylum.* New York: Center for Migration Studies, 1983. Conference proceedings, in English.

———. *In Defense of the Alien,* vol. 6, *Immigration and Refugee Policy.* New York: Center for Migration Studies, 1984. Conference proceedings, in English.

United Nations High Commissioner for Refugees. "Conclusions on International Protection Adopted by the Executive Committee of the High Commissioner's Programmes at its 40th Session (1989)," *International Journal of Refugee Law* 2, no. 1 (1990): 143–157. IGO conference proceedings, in English.

United Nations High Commissioner for Refugees, Refugee Documentation Center. *Refugee Abstracts.* Geneva, Switzerland. Quarterly journal, in English; some abstracts may be in French, German, or Spanish.

United Nations High Commissioner for Refugees and Refugee Policy Group. *A Selected and Annotated Bibliography on Refugee Women.* Geneva, Switzerland: 1985. In English.

U.S. Committee for Refugees. *World Refugee Survey, 1980– .* Washington, D.C.: American Council for Nationalities Service, 1980–. NGO annual report and bibliography, in English.

Wierzbicki, Bogdan. "Cooperation in the Refugee Problem in Europe: A New Perspective," *International Journal of Refugee Law* 2, no. 1 (1990): 118–123. Scholarly article, in English.

Williams, C. L. *An Annotated Bibliography on Refugee Mental Health.* Minneapolis, MN, USA: Refugee Assistance Program, Mental Health-Technical Assistance Center, University of Minnesota, 1987. In English.

Winter, Roger P. *Ending Exile: Promoting Successful Reintegration of African Refugees and Displaced People.* Washington, D.C.: U.S. Committee for Refugees, 1990. NGO issue paper, in English.

Women's Commission for Refugee Women and Children. *Going Home: The Prospect of Repatriation for Refugee Women and Children.* Washington, D.C.: 1992. Conference papers, in English.

——. *Repatriation and Reintegration: Can Hmong Refugees Begin to Look Homeward?* New York: 1991. NGO report, in English.

Yundt, Keith W. *Latin American States and Political Refugees.* New York: Praeger Publishers, 1989. Scholarly monograph, in English.

Zimmerman, D., N. Avrin, and O. D. Cava, comps. *A Directory of International Migration Study Centers, Research Programs and Library Resources.* Staten Island, NY, USA: Center for Migration Studies of New York, 1987. In English.

# REFUGEES: CONVENTION RELATING TO THE STATUS OF REFUGEES (1951).

The Convention was adopted on 28 July 1951 by the United Nations Conference of Plenipotentiaries on the Status of Refugees and Stateless Persons, convened at the European office of the United Nations in Geneva in accordance with a decision taken by the UN **GENERAL ASSEMBLY** (resolution 429 [V]) on 14 December 1950. It entered into force on 22 April 1954. The Convention is the most far-reaching instrument relating to the protection of refugees adopted by the international community and has had the effect of encouraging governments to safeguard the basic human rights of refugees by instituting increasingly generous and liberal policies of asylum. The text of the Convention (United Nations, *Treaty Series*, vol. 189, p. 150) is as follows:

## Preamble

The High Contracting Parties,

Considering that the Charter of the United Nations and the Universal Declaration of Human Rights approved on 10 December 1948 by the General Assembly have affirmed the principle that human beings shall enjoy fundamental rights and freedoms without discrimination,

Considering that the United Nations has, on various occasions, manifested its profound concern for refugees and endeavoured to assure refugees the widest possible exercise of these fundamental rights and freedoms,

Considering that it is desirable to revise and consolidate previous international agreements relating to the status of refugees and to extend the scope of and the protection accorded by such instruments by means of a new agreement,

Considering that the grant of asylum may place unduly heavy burdens on certain countries, and that a satisfactory solution of a problem of which the United Nations has recognized the international scope and nature cannot therefore be achieved without international co-operation,

Expressing the wish that all States, recognizing the social and humanitarian nature of the problem of refugees, will do everything within their power to prevent this problem from becoming a cause of tension between States,

Noting that the United Nations High Commissioner for Refugees is charged with the task of supervising international conventions providing for the protection of refugees, and recognizing that the effective co-ordination of measures taken to deal with this problem will depend upon the co-operation of States with the High Commissioner,

Have agreed as follows:

## Chapter I: General Provisions

*Article 1. Definition of the Term "Refugee".* A. For the purposes of the present Convention, the term "refugee" shall apply to any person who:

(1) Has been considered a refugee under the Arrangements of 12 May 1926 and 30 June 1928 or under the Conventions of 28 October 1933 and 10 February 1938, the Protocol of 14 September 1939 or the Constitution of the International Refugee Organization;

Decisions of non-eligibility taken by the International Refugee Organization during the period of its activities shall not prevent the status of refugee being accorded to persons who fulfil the conditions of paragraph 2 of this section;

(2) As a result of events occurring before 1 January 1951 and owing to well-founded fear of being persecuted for reasons of race, religion, nationality, membership of a particular social group or political opinion, is outside the country of his nationality and is unable, or owing to such fear, is unwilling to avail himself of the protection of that country; or who, not having a nationality and being outside the country of his former habitual residence as a result of such events, is unable or, owing to such fear, is unwilling to return to it.

In the case of a person who has more than one nationality, the term "the country of his nationality" shall mean each of the countries of which he is a national, and a person shall not be deemed to be lacking the protection of the country of his nationality if, without any valid reason based on well-founded fear, he has not availed himself of the protection of one of the countries of which he is a national.

B. (1) For the purposes of this Convention, the words "events occurring before 1 January 1951" in article 1, section A, shall be understood to mean either (*a*) "events occurring in Europe before 1 January 1951"; or (*b*) "events occurring in Europe or elsewhere before 1 January 1951;" and each Contracting State shall make a declaration at the time of signature, ratification or accession, specifying which of these meanings it applies for the purpose of its obligations under this Convention.

(2) Any Contracting State which has adopted alternative (*a*) may at any time extend its obligations by adopting alternative (*b*) by means of a notification addressed to the Secretary-General of the United Nations.

C. This Convention shall cease to apply to any person falling under the terms of section A if:

(1) He has voluntarily re-availed himself of the protection of the country of his nationality; or

(2) Having lost his nationality, he has voluntarily reacquired it; or

(3) He has acquired a new nationality, and enjoys the protection of the country of his new nationality; or

(4) He has voluntarily re-established himself in the country which he left or outside which he remained owing to fear of persecution; or

(5) He can no longer, because the circumstances in connexion with which he has been recognized as a refugee have ceased to exist, continue to refuse to avail himself of the protection of the country of his nationality;

Provided that this paragraph shall not apply to a refugee falling under section A (1) of this article who is able to invoke compelling reasons arising out of previous persecution for refusing to avail himself of the protection of the country of nationality;

(6) Being a person who has no nationality he is, because the circumstances in connexion with which he has been recognized as a refugee have ceased to exist, able to return to the country of his former habitual residence;

Provided that this paragraph shall not apply to a refugee falling under section A (1) of this article who is able to invoke compelling reasons arising out of previous persecution for refusing to return to the country of his former habitual residence.

*D.* This Convention shall not apply to persons who are at present receiving from organs or agencies of the United Nations other than the United Nations High Commissioner for Refugees protection or assistance.

When such protection or assistance has ceased for any reason, without the position of such persons being definitively settled in accordance with the relevant resolutions adopted by the General Assembly of the United Nations, these persons shall *ipso facto* be entitled to the benefits of this Convention.

*E.* This Convention shall not apply to a person who is recognized by the competent authorities of the country in which he has taken residence as having the rights and obligations which are attached to the possession of the nationality of that country.

*F.* The provisions of this Convention shall not apply to any person with respect to whom there are serious reasons for considering that:

(*a*) He has committed a crime against peace, a war crime, or a crime against humanity, as defined in the international instruments drawn up to make provision in respect of such crimes;

(*b*) He has committed a serious non-political crime outside the country of refuge prior to his admission to that country as a refugee;

(*c*) He has been guilty of acts contrary to the purposes and principles of the United Nations.

*Article 2. General Obligations.* Every refugee has duties to the country in which he finds himself, which require in particular that he conform to its laws and regulations as well as to measures taken for the maintenance of public order.

*Article 3. Non-discrimination.* The Contracting States shall apply the provisions of this Convention to refugees without discrimination as to race, religion or country of origin.

*Article 4. Religion.* The Contracting States shall accord to refugees within their territories treatment at least as favourable as that accorded to their nationals with respect to freedom to practice their religion and freedom as regards the religious education of their children.

*Article 5. Rights Granted Apart From This Convention.* Nothing in this Convention shall be deemed to impair any rights and benefits granted by a Contracting State to refugees apart from this Convention.

*Article 6. The Term "In the Same Circumstances."* For the purpose of this Convention, the term "in the same circumstances" implies that any requirements (including requirements as to length and conditions of sojourn or residence) which the particular individual would have to fulfil for the enjoyment of the right in question, if he were not a refugee, must be fulfilled by him, with the exception of requirements which by their nature a refugee is incapable of fulfilling.

*Article 7. Exemption From Reciprocity.* 1. Except where this Convention contains more favourable provisions, a Contracting State shall accord to refugees the same treatment as is accorded to aliens generally.

2. After a period of three years' residence, all refugees shall enjoy exemption from legislative reciprocity in the territory of the Contracting States.

3. Each Contracting State shall continue to accord to refugees the rights and benefits to which they were already entitled, in the absence of reciprocity, at the date of entry into force of this Convention for that State.

4. The Contracting States shall consider favourably the possibility of according to refugees, in the absence of reciprocity, rights and benefits beyond those to which they are entitled according to paragraphs 2 and 3, and to extending exemption from reciprocity to refugees who do not fulfil the conditions provided for in paragraphs 2 and 3.

5. The provisions of paragraphs 2 and 3 apply both to the rights and benefits referred to in articles 13, 18, 19, 21 and 22 of this Convention and to rights and benefits for which this Convention does not provide.

*Article 8. Exemption From Exceptional Measures.* With regard to exceptional measures which may be taken against the person, property or interests of nationals of a foreign State, the Contracting States shall not apply such measures to a refugee who is formally a national of the said State solely on account of such nationality. Contracting States which, under their legislation, are prevented from applying the general principle expressed in this article, shall, in appropriate cases, grant exemptions in favour of such refugees.

*Article 9. Provisional Measures.* Nothing in this Convention shall prevent a Contracting State, in time of war or other grave and exceptional circumstances, from taking provisionally measures which it considers to be essential to the national security in the case of a particular person, pending a determination by the Contracting State that that person is in fact a refugee and that the continuance of such measures is necessary in his case in the interests of national security.

*Article 10. Continuity of Residence.* 1. Where a refugee has been forcibly displaced during the Second World War and removed to the territory of a Contracting State, and is resident there, the period of such enforced sojourn shall be considered to have been lawful residence within that territory.

2. Where a refugee has been forcibly displaced during the Second World War from the territory of a Contracting State and has, prior to the date of entry into force of this Convention, returned there for the purpose of taking up residence, the period of residence before and after such enforced displacement shall be regarded as one uninterrupted period for any purposes for which uninterrupted residence is required.

*Article 11. Refugee Seamen.* In the case of refugees regularly serving as crew members on board a ship flying the flag of a Contracting State, that State shall give sympathetic consideration to their establishment on its territory and the issue of travel documents to them or their temporary admission to its territory particularly with a view to facilitating their establishment in another country.

## Chapter II: Juridical Status

*Article 12. Personal Status.* 1. The personal status of a refugee shall be governed by the law of the country of his domicile or, if he has no domicile, by the law of the country of his residence.

2. Rights previously acquired by a refugee and dependent on personal status, more particularly rights attaching to marriage, shall be respected by a Contracting State, subject to

compliance, if this be necessary, with the formalities required by the law of that State, provided that the right in question is one which would have been recognized by the law of that State had he not become a refugee.

*Article 13. Movable and Immovable Property.* The Contracting States shall accord to a refugee treatment as favourable as possible and, in any event, not less favourable than that accorded to aliens generally in the same circumstances, as regards the acquisition of movable and immovable property and other rights pertaining thereto, and to leases and other contracts relating to movable and immovable property.

*Article 14. Artistic Rights and Industrial Property.* In respect of the protection of industrial property, such as inventions, designs or models, trade marks, trade names, and of rights in literary, artistic and scientific works, a refugee shall be accorded in the country in which he has his habitual residence the same protection as is accorded to nationals of that country. In the territory of any other Contracting State, he shall be accorded the same protection as is accorded in that territory to nationals of the country in which he has his habitual residence.

*Article 15. Right of Association.* As regards non-political and non-profit-making associations and trade unions the Contracting States shall accord to refugees lawfully staying in their territory the most favourable treatment accorded to nationals of a foreign country, in the same circumstances.

*Article 16. Access to Courts.* 1. A refugee shall have free access to the courts of law on the territory of all Contracting States.

2. A refugee shall enjoy in the Contracting State in which he has his habitual residence the same treatment as a national in matters pertaining to access to the courts, including legal assistance and exemption from *cautio judicatum solvi.*

3. A refugee shall be accorded in the matters referred to in paragraph 2 in countries other than that in which he has his habitual residence the treatment granted to a national of the country of his habitual residence.

## Chapter III: Gainful Employment

*Article 17. Wage-earning Employment.* 1. The Contracting States shall accord to refugees lawfully staying in their territory the most favourable treatment accorded to nationals of a foreign country in the same circumstances, as regards the right to engage in wage-earning employment.

2. In any case, restrictive measures imposed on aliens or the employment of aliens for the protection of the national labour market shall not be applied to a refugee who was already exempt from them at the date of entry into force of this Convention for the Contracting State concerned, or who fulfils one of the following conditions:

(*a*) He has completed three years' residence in the country;

(*b*) He has a spouse possessing the nationality of the country of residence. A refugee may not invoke the benefit of this provision if he has abandoned his spouse;

(*c*) He has one or more children possessing the nationality of the country of residence.

3. The Contracting States shall give sympathetic consideration to assimilating the rights of all refugees with regard to wage-earning employment to those of nationals, and in particular of those refugees who have entered their territory pursuant to programmes of labour recruitment or under immigration schemes.

*Article 18. Self-employment.* The Contracting States shall accord to a refugee lawfully in their territory treatment as favourable as possible and, in any event, not less favourable than that accorded to aliens generally in the same circumstances, as regards the right to engage on his own account in agriculture, industry, handicrafts and commerce and to establish commercial and industrial companies.

*Article 19. Liberal Professions.* 1. Each Contracting State shall accord to refugees lawfully staying in their territory who hold diplomas recognized by the competent authorities of that State, and who are desirous of practising a liberal profession, treatment as favourable as possible and, in any event, not less favourable than that accorded to aliens generally in the same circumstances.

2. The Contracting States shall use their best endeavours consistently with their laws and constitutions to secure the settlement of such refugees in the territories, other than the metropolitan territory, for whose international relations they are responsible.

## Chapter IV: Welfare

*Article 20. Rationing.* Where a rationing system exists, which applies to the population at large and regulates the general distribution of products in short supply, refugees shall be accorded the same treatment as nationals.

*Article 21. Housing.* As regards housing, the Contracting States, in so far as the matter is regulated by laws or regulations or is subject to the control of public authorities, shall accord to refugees lawfully staying in their territory treatment as favourable as possible and, in any event, not less favourable than that accorded to aliens generally in the same circumstances.

*Article 22. Public Education.* 1. The Contracting States shall accord to refugees the same treatment as is accorded to nationals with respect to elementary education.

2. The Contracting States shall accord to refugees treatment as favourable as possible, and, in any event, not less favourable than that accorded to aliens generally in the same circumstances, with respect to education other than elementary education and, in particular, as regards access to studies, the recognition of foreign school certificates, diplomas and degrees, the remission of fees and charges and the award of scholarships.

*Article 23. Public Relief.* The Contracting States shall accord to refugees lawfully staying in their territory the same treatment with respect to public relief and assistance as is accorded to their nationals.

*Article 24. Labour Legislation and Social Security.* 1. The Contracting States shall accord to refugees lawfully staying in their territory the same treatment as is accorded to nationals in respect of the following matters:

(*a*) In so far as such matters are governed by laws or regulations or are subject to the control of administrative authorities: remuneration, including family allowances where these form part of remuneration, hours of work, overtime arrangements, holidays with pay, restrictions on home work, minimum age of employment, apprenticeship and training, women's work and the work of young persons, and the enjoyment of the benefits of collective bargaining;

(*b*) Social security (legal provisions in respect of employment injury, occupational diseases, maternity, sickness, disability, old age, death, unemployment, family responsibilities and any other contingency which, according to national laws or regulations, is covered by a social security scheme), subject to the following limitations:

(i) There may be appropriate arrangements for the maintenance of acquired rights and rights in course of acquisition;

(ii) National laws or regulations of the country of residence may prescribe special arrangements concerning benefits or portions of benefits which are payable wholly out of public funds, and concerning allowances paid to persons who do not fulfil the contribution conditions prescribed for the award of a normal pension.

2. The right to compensation for the death of a refugee resulting from employment injury or from occupational disease shall not be affected by the fact that the residence of the beneficiary is outside the territory of the Contracting State.

3. The Contracting States shall extend to refugees the benefits of agreements concluded between them, or which may be concluded between them in the future, concerning the maintenance of acquired rights and rights in the process of acquisition in regard to social security, subject only to the conditions which apply to nationals of the States signatory to the agreements in question.

4. The Contracting States will give sympathetic consideration to extending to refugees so far as possible the benefits of similar agreements which may at any time be in force between such Contracting States and non-contracting States.

### Chapter V: Administrative Measures

*Article 25. Administrative Assistance.* 1. When the exercise of a right by a refugee would normally require the assistance of authorities of a foreign country to whom he cannot have recourse, the Contracting States in whose territory he is residing shall arrange that such assistance be afforded to him by their own authorities or by an international authority.

2. The authority or authorities mentioned in paragraph 1 shall deliver or cause to be delivered under their supervision to refugees such documents or certifications as would normally be delivered to aliens by or through their national authorities.

3. Documents or certifications so delivered shall stand in the stead of the official instruments delivered to aliens by or through their national authorities, and shall be given credence in the absence of proof to the contrary.

4. Subject to such exceptional treatment as may be granted to indigent persons, fees may be charged for the services mentioned herein, but such fees shall be moderate and commensurate with those charged to nationals for similar services.

5. The provisions of this article shall be without prejudice to articles 27 and 28.

*Article 26. Freedom of Movement.* Each Contracting State shall accord to refugees lawfully in its territory the right to choose their place of residence and to move freely within its territory subject to any regulations applicable to aliens generally in the same circumstances.

*Article 27. Identity Papers.* The Contracting States shall issue identity papers to any refugee in their territory who does not possess a valid travel document.

*Article 28. Travel Documents.* 1. The Contracting States shall issue to refugees lawfully staying in their territory travel documents for the purpose of travel outside their territory, unless compelling reasons of national security or public order otherwise require, and the provisions of the Schedule to this Convention shall apply with respect to such documents. The Contracting States may issue such a travel document to any other refugee in their territory; they shall in particular give sympathetic consideration to the issue of such a travel document to refugees in their territory who are unable to obtain a travel document from the country of their lawful residence.

2. Travel documents issued to refugees under previous international agreements by parties thereto shall be recognized and treated by the Contracting States in the same way as if they had been issued pursuant to this article.

*Article 29. Fiscal Charges.* 1. The Contracting States shall not impose upon refugees duties, charges or taxes, of any description whatsoever, other or higher than those which are or may be levied on their nationals in similar situations.

2. Nothing in the above paragraph shall prevent the application to refugees of the laws and regulations concerning charges in respect of the issue to aliens of administrative documents including identity papers.

*Article 30. Transfer of Assets.* 1. A Contracting State shall, in conformity with its laws and regulations, permit refugees to transfer assets which they have brought into its territory, to another country where they have been admitted for the purposes of resettlement.

2. A Contracting State shall give sympathetic consideration to the application of refugees for permission to transfer assets wherever they may be and which are necessary for their resettlement in another country to which they have been admitted.

*Article 31. Refugees Unlawfully in the Country of Refuge.* 1. The Contracting States shall not impose penalties, on account of their illegal entry or presence, on refugees who, coming directly from a territory where their life or freedom was threatened in the sense of article 1, enter or are present in their territory without authorization, provided they present themselves without delay to the authorities and show good cause for their illegal entry or presence.

2. The Contracting States shall not apply to the movements of such refugees restrictions other than those which are necessary and such restrictions shall only be applied until their status in the country is regularized or they obtain admission into another country. The Contracting States shall allow such refugees a reasonable period and all the necessary facilities to obtain admission into another country.

*Article 32. Expulsion.* 1. The Contracting States shall not expel a refugee lawfully in their territory save on grounds of national security or public order.

2. The expulsion of such a refugee shall be only in pursuance of a decision reached in accordance with due process of law. Except where compelling reasons of national security otherwise require, the refugee shall be allowed to submit evidence to clear himself, and to appeal to and be represented for the purpose before competent authority or a person or persons specially designated by the competent authority.

3. The Contracting States shall allow such a refugee a reasonable period within which to seek legal admission into another country. The Contracting States reserve the right to apply during that period such internal measures as they may deem necessary.

*Article 33. Prohibition of Expulsion or Return ("Refoulement").* 1. No Contracting State shall expel or return ("refouler") a refugee in any manner whatsoever to the frontiers of territories where his life or freedom would be threatened on account of his race, religion, nationality, membership of a particular social group or political opinion.

2. The benefit of the present provision may not, however, be claimed by a refugee whom there are reasonable grounds

for regarding as a danger to the security of the country in which he is, or who, having been convicted by a final judgment of a particularly serious crime, constitutes a danger to the community of that country.

*Article 34. Naturalization.* The Contracting States shall as far as possible facilitate the assimilation and naturalization of refugees. They shall in particular make every effort to expedite naturalization proceedings and to reduce as far as possible the charges and costs of such proceedings.

### Chapter VI: Executory and Transitory Provisions

*Article 35. Cooperation of the National Authorities With the United Nations.* 1. The Contracting States undertake to co-operate with the Office of the United Nations High Commissioner for Refugees, or any other agency of the United Nations which may succeed it, in the exercise of its functions, and shall in particular facilitate its duty of supervising the application of the provisions of this Convention.

2. In order to enable the Office of the High Commissioner, or any other agency of the United Nations which may succeed it, to make reports to the competent organs of the United Nations, the Contracting States undertake to provide them in the appropriate form with information and statistical data requested concerning:

(*a*) The condition of refugees,

(*b*) The implementation of this Convention, and

(*c*) Laws, regulations and decrees which are, or may hereafter be, in force relating to refugees.

*Article 36. Information on National Legislation.* The Contracting States shall communicate to the Secretary-General of the United Nations the laws and regulations which they may adopt to ensure the application of this Convention.

*Article 37. Relation to Previous Conventions.* Without prejudice to article 28, paragraph 2, of this Convention, this Convention replaces, as between parties to it, the Arrangements of 5 July 1922, 31 May 1924, 12 May 1926, 30 June 1928 and 30 July 1935, the Conventions of 28 October 1933 and 10 February 1938, the Protocol of 14 September 1939 and the Agreement of 15 October 1946.

### Chapter VII: Final Clauses

*Article 38. Settlement of Disputes.* Any dispute between parties to this Convention relating to its interpretation or application, which cannot be settled by other means, shall be referred to the International Court of Justice at the request of any one of the parties to the dispute.

*Article 39. Signature, Ratification and Accession.* 1. This Convention shall be opened for signature at Geneva on 28 July 1951 and shall thereafter be deposited with the Secretary-General of the United Nations. It shall be open for signature at the European Office of the United Nations from 28 July to 31 August 1951 and shall be re-opened for signature at the Headquarters of the United Nations from 17 September 1951 to 31 December 1952.

2. This Convention shall be open for signature on behalf of all States Members of the United Nations, and also on behalf of any other State invited to attend the Conference of Plenipotentiaries on the Status of Refugees and Stateless Persons or to which an invitation to sign will have been addressed by the General Assembly. It shall be ratified and the instruments of ratification shall be deposited with the Secretary-General of the United Nations.

3. This Convention shall be open from 28 July 1951 for accession by the States referred to in paragraph 2 of this article. Accession shall be effected by the deposit of an instrument of accession with the Secretary-General of the United Nations.

*Article 40. Territorial Application Clause.* 1. Any State may, at the time of signature, ratification or accession, declare that this Convention shall extend to all or any of the territories for the international relations of which it is responsible. Such a declaration shall take effect when the Convention enters into force for the State concerned.

2. At any time thereafter any such extension shall be made by notification addressed to the Secretary-General of the United Nations and shall take effect as from the ninetieth day after the day of receipt by the Secretary-General of the United Nations of this notification, or as from the date of entry into force of the Convention for the State concerned, whichever is the later.

3. With respect to those territories to which this Convention is not extended at the time of signature, ratification or accession, each State concerned shall consider the possibility of taking the necessary steps in order to extend the application of this Convention to such territories, subject, where necessary for constitutional reasons, to the consent of the Governments of such territories.

*Article 41. Federal Clause.* In the case of a Federal or non-unitary State, the following provisions shall apply:

(*a*) With respect to those articles of this Convention that come within the legislative jurisdiction of the federal legislative authority, the obligations of the Federal Government shall to this extent be the same as those of Parties which are not Federal States;

(*b*) With respect to those articles of this Convention that come within the legislative jurisdiction of constituent states, provinces or cantons which are not, under the constitutional system of the Federation, bound to take legislative action, the Federal Government shall bring such articles with a favourable recommendation to the notice of the appropriate authorities of states, provinces or cantons at the earliest possible moment;

(*c*) A Federal State Party to this Convention shall, at the request of any other Contracting State transmitted through the Secretary-General of the United Nations, supply a statement of the law and practice of the Federation and its constituent units in regard to any particular provision of the Convention showing the extent to which effect has been given to that provision by legislative or other action.

*Article 42. Reservations.* 1. At the time of signature, ratification or accession, any State may make reservations to articles of the Convention other than to articles 1, 3, 4, 16 (1), 33, 36–46 inclusive.

2. Any State making a reservation in accordance with paragraph 1 of this article may at any time withdraw the reservation by a communication to that effect addressed to the Secretary-General of the United Nations.

*Article 43. Entry Into Force.* 1. This Convention shall come into force on the ninetieth day following the day of deposit of the sixth instrument of ratification or accession.

2. For each State ratifying or acceding to the Convention after the deposit of the sixth instrument of ratification or accession, the Convention shall enter into force on the ninetieth day following the date of deposit by such State of its instrument of ratification or accession.

*Article 44. Denunciation.* 1. Any Contracting State may denounce this Convention at any time by a notification addressed to the Secretary-General of the United Nations.

2. Such denunciation shall take effect for the Contracting

State concerned one year from the date upon which it is received by the Secretary-General of the United Nations.

3. Any State which has made a declaration or notification under article 40 may, at any time thereafter, by a notification to the Secretary-General of the United Nations, declare that the Convention shall cease to extend to such territory one year after the date of receipt of the notification by the Secretary-General.

*Article 45. Revision.* 1. Any Contracting State may request revision of this Convention at any time by a notification addressed to the Secretary-General of the United Nations.

2. The General Assembly of the United Nations shall recommend the steps, if any, to be taken in respect of such request.

*Article 46. Notifications by the Secretary-General of the United Nations.* The Secretary-General of the United Nations shall inform all Members of the United Nations and non-member States referred to in article 39:

(*a*) Of declarations and notifications in accordance with section B of article 1;

(*b*) Of signatures, ratifications and accessions in accordance with article 39;

(*c*) Of declarations and notifications in accordance with article 40;

(*d*) Of reservations and withdrawals in accordance with article 42;

(*e*) Of the date on which this Convention will come into force in accordance with article 43;

(*f*) Of denunciations and notifications in accordance with article 44;

(*g*) Of requests for revision in accordance with article 45.

In faith whereof the undersigned, duly authorized, have signed this Convention on behalf of their respective Governments.

Done at Geneva, this twenty-eighth day of July, one thousand nine hundred and fifty-one, in a single copy, of which the English and French texts are equally authentic and which shall remain deposited in the archives of the United Nations, and certified true copies of which shall be delivered to all Members of the United Nations and to the non-member States referred to in article 39.

**RATIFICATION AND ACCESSION TO MAIN CONVENTION.** As of 31 December 1994, the following UN member States had ratified or acceded to the Convention relating to the Status of Refugees:

Albania, Algeria, Angola, Argentina, Armenia, Australia, Austria, Azerbaijan

Bahamas, Belgium, Belize, Benin, Bolivia, Bosnia Herzegovina, Botswana, Brazil, Bulgaria, Burkina Faso, Burundi

Cambodia, Cameroon, Canada, Central African Republic, Chad, Chile, China, Colombia, Congo, Costa Rica, Cote d'Ivoire (Ivory Coast), Croatia, Cyprus, Czech Republic

Denmark, Djibouti, Dominica, Dominican Republic

Ecuador, Egypt, El Salvador, Equatorial Guinea, Ethiopia

Fiji, Finland, France

Gabon, Gambia, Germany, Ghana, Greece, Guatemala, Guinea, Guinea-Bissau,

Haiti, Holy See, Honduras, Hungary

Iceland, Iran, Ireland, Israel, Italy

Jamaica, Japan

Kenya

Lesotho, Liberia, Liechtenstein, Luxembourg

Malawi, Mali, Malta, Mauritania, Monaco, Morocco, Mozambique

Netherlands, New Zealand, Nicaragua, Niger, Nigeria, Norway

Panama, Papua New Guinea, Paraguay, Peru, Philippines, Poland, Portugal

Republic of Korea (South Korea), Russian Federation, Rwanda

Saint Vincent and Grenadines, Samoa, Sao Tome and Principe, Senegal, Seychelles, Sierra Leone, Slovakia, Slovenia, Somalia, Spain, Sudan, Suriname, Sweden

Tanzania, Tunisia, Turkey, Tuvalu

Uganda, United Kingdom, Uruguay

Yemen, Yugoslavia

Zaire, Zambia, Zimbabwe

***PROTOCOL TO THE CONVENTION RELATING TO THE STATUS OF REFUGEES (1967).*** The purpose of the Protocol is to remove the date contained in the "definition of refugees" (article 1) in the parent Convention and thereby to make the Convention applicable to refugee situations occurring after 1 January 1951. The Protocol, recommended by the Executive Committee of the Program of the UN **HIGH COMMISSIONER FOR REFUGEES,** was approved by the UN **ECONOMIC AND SOCIAL COUNCIL** on 18 November 1966 (resolution 1186 [XLI]) and adopted by the UN General Assembly on 16 December 1966 (resolution 2198 [XXI]). It was opened for signature and ratification or accession on 31 January 1967 and entered into force on 4 October 1967. The text (United Nations, *Treaty Series,* vol. 606, p. 267) is as follows:

The States Parties to the present Protocol,

Considering that the Convention relating to the Status of Refugees done at Geneva on 28 July 1951 (hereinafter referred to as the Convention) covers only those persons who have become refugees as a result of events occurring before 1 January 1951,

Considering that new refugee situations have arisen since the Convention was adopted and that the refugees concerned may therefore not fall within the scope of the Convention.

Considering that it is desirable that equal status should be enjoyed by all refugees covered by the definition in the Convention irrespective of the dateline 1 January 1951,

Have agreed as follows:

*Article 1. General Provision.* 1. The States Parties to the present Protocol undertake to apply articles 2 to 34 inclusive of the Convention to refugees as hereinafter defined.

2. For the purpose of the present Protocol, the term "refugee" shall, except as regards the application of paragraph 3 of this article, mean any person within the definition of

article 1 of the Convention as if the words "As a result of events occurring before 1 January 1951 and . . ." and the words ". . . As a result of such events," in article 1 A (2) were omitted.

3. The present Protocol shall be applied by the States Parties hereto without any geographic limitation, save that existing declarations made by States already Parties to the Convention in accordance with article 1 B (1) (*a*) of the Convention, shall, unless extended under article 1 B (2) thereof, apply also under the present Protocol.

*Article 2. Co-operation of the National Authorities With the United Nations.* 1. The States Parties to the present Protocol undertake to co-operate with the Office of the United Nations High Commissioner for Refugees, or any other agency of the United Nations which may succeed it, in the exercise of its functions, and shall in particular facilitate its duty of supervising the application of the provisions of the present Protocol.

2. In order to enable the Office of the High Commissioner, or any other agency of the United Nations which may succeed it, to make reports to the competent organs of the United Nations, the States Parties to the present Protocol undertake to provide them with the information and statistical data requested, in the appropriate form, concerning:

(*a*) The condition of refugees;

(*b*) The implementation of the present Protocol;

(*c*) Laws, regulations and decrees which are, or may hereafter be, in force relating to refugees.

*Article 3. Information on National Legislation.* The States Parties to the present Protocol shall communicate to the Secretary-General of the United Nations the laws and regulations which they may adopt to ensure the application of the present Protocol.

*Article 4. Settlement of Disputes.* Any dispute between States Parties to the present Protocol which relates to its interpretation or application and which cannot be settled by other means shall be referred to the International Court of Justice at the request of any one of the parties to the dispute.

*Article 5. Accession.* The present Protocol shall be open for accession on behalf of all States Parties to the Convention and of any other State Member of the United Nations or member of any of the specialized agencies or to which an invitation to accede may have been addressed by the General Assembly of the United Nations. Accession shall be effected by the deposit of an instrument of accession with the Secretary-General of the United Nations.

*Article 6. Federal Clause.* In the case of a Federal or non-unitary State, the following provisions shall apply:

(*a*) With respect to those articles of the Convention to be applied in accordance with article 1, paragraph 1, of the present Protocol that come within the legislative jurisdiction of the federal legislative authority, the obligations of the Federal Government shall to this extent be the same as those of States Parties which are not Federal States;

(*b*) With respect to those articles of the Convention to be applied in accordance with article 1, paragraph 1, of the present Protocol that come within the legislative jurisdiction of constituent states, provinces or cantons which are not, under the constitutional system of the Federation, bound to take legislative action, the Federal Government shall bring such articles with a favourable recommendation to the notice of the appropriate authorities of states, provinces or cantons at the earliest possible moment;

(*c*) A Federal State Party to the present Protocol shall, at the request of any other State Party hereto transmitted through the Secretary-General of the United Nations, supply

a statement of the law and practice of the Federation and its constituent units in regard to any particular provision of the Convention to be applied in accordance with article 1, paragraph 1, of the present Protocol, showing the extent to which effect has been given to that provision by legislative or other action.

*Article 7. Reservations and Declarations.* 1. At the time of accession, any State may make reservations in respect of article 4 of the present Protocol and in respect of the application in accordance with article 1 of the present Protocol of any provisions of the Convention other than those contained in articles 1, 3, 4, 16 (1) and 33 thereof, provided that in the case of a State Party to the Convention reservations made under this article shall not extend to refugees in respect of whom the Convention applies.

2. Reservations made by States Parties to the Convention in accordance with article 42 thereof shall, unless withdrawn, be applicable in relation to their obligations under the present Protocol.

3. Any State making a reservation in accordance with paragraph 1 of this article may at any time withdraw such reservation by a communication to that effect addressed to the Secretary-General of the United Nations.

4. Declarations made under article 40, paragraphs 1 and 2, of the Convention by a State Party thereto which accedes to the present Protocol, shall be deemed to apply in respect of the present Protocol, unless upon accession a notification to the contrary is addressed by the State Party concerned to the Secretary-General of the United Nations. The provisions of article 40, paragraphs 2 and 3, and of article 44, paragraph 3, of the Convention shall be deemed to apply *mutatis mutandis* to the present Protocol.

*Article 8. Entry Into Force.* 1. The present Protocol shall come into force on the day of deposit of the sixth instrument of accession.

2. For each State acceding to the Protocol after the deposit of the sixth instrument of accession, the Protocol shall come into force on the date of deposit by such State of its instrument of accession.

*Article 9. Denunciation.* 1. Any State Party hereto may denounce this Protocol at any time by a notification addressed to the Secretary-General of the United Nations.

2. Such denunciation shall take effect for the State Party concerned one year from the date on which it is received by the Secretary-General of the United Nations.

*Article 10. Notifications by the Secretary-General of the United Nations.* The Secretary-General of the United Nations shall inform the States referred to in article 5 above of the date of entry into force, accessions, reservations and withdrawals of reservations to and denunciations of the present Protocol, and of declarations and notifications relating hereto.

*Article 11. Deposit in the Archives of the Secretariat of the United Nations.* A copy of the present Protocol, of which the Chinese, English, French, Russian and Spanish texts are equally authentic, signed by the President of the General Assembly and by the Secretary-General of the United Nations, shall be deposited in the archives of the Secretariat of the United Nations. The Secretary-General will transmit certified copies thereof to all States Members of the United Nations and to the other States referred to in article 5 above.

**RATIFICATIONS AND ACCESSIONS.** The following 120 UN member States had ratified or acceded to the Protocol to the Convention relating to the Status of Refugees as of 31 December 1995:

Albania, Algeria, Angola, Argentina, Armenia, Australia, Austria, Azerbaijan

Bahamas, Belgium, Belize, Benin, Bolivia, Bosnia Herzegovina, Botswana, Brazil, Bulgaria, Burkina Faso, Burundi

Cambodia, Cameroon, Canada, Cape Verde, Central African Republic, Chad, Chile, China, Colombia, Congo, Costa Rica, Cote d'Ivoire (Ivory Coast), Croatia, Cyprus, Czech Republic

Denmark, Dominica, Dominican Republic

Ecuador, Egypt, Ethiopia

Fiji, Finland, France

Gabon, Gambia, Germany, Ghana, Greece, Guatemala, Guinea, Guinea-Bissau

Haiti, Holy See, Honduras, Hungary

Iceland, Iran, Ireland, Israel, Italy

Jamaica, Japan

Kenya

Lesotho, Liberia, Liechtenstein, Luxembourg

Malawi, Mali, Malta, Mauritania, Morocco

Netherlands, New Zealand, Nicaragua, Niger, Nigeria, Norway

Panama, Papua New Guinea, Paraguay, Peru, Philippines, Poland, Portugal

Republic of Korea (South Korea), Romania, Russian Federation, Rwanda

Samoa, Sao Tome and Principe, Senegal, Seychelles, Sierra Leone, Slovakia, Slovenia, Somalia, Spain, Sudan, Suriname, Swaziland, Sweden

Tanzania, Tunisia, Turkey, Tuvalu

Uganda, United Kingdom, United States of America, Uruguay

Venezuela

Yemen, Yugoslavia

Zaire, Zambia, Zimbabwe

**BIBLIOGRAPHY.** "The 1991 Geneva Colloquium on 'The 1951 Convention Relating to the Status of Refugees: Principles, Problems and Potential,' Geneva 22–24 July 1991," *International Journal of Refugee Law* 3, no. 3 (July 1991): 1–673. Conference report, in English; bibliography, pp. 633–663.

Arboleda, Eduardo, and Ian Hoy. "The Convention Refugee Definition in the West: Disharmony of Interpretation and Application," *International Journal of Refugee Law* 5, no. 1 (1993): 66–90. Scholarly article, in English.

Blay, Samuel K. N., and B. Martin Tsamenyi. "Reservations and Declarations under the 1951 Convention and the 1967 Protocol Relating to the Status of Refugees," *International Journal of Refugee Law* 2, no. 4 (Oct. 1990): 527–561. Scholarly article, in English.

Donahue, Claire, and Patricia Hyndman. *International Law and Refugees in South East Asia.* Kensington, Australia: Law Association for Asia and the Pacific, 1990. NGO report, in English.

Hathaway, James C. *The Law of Refugee Status.* Toronto, Canada: Butterworths, 1991. Scholarly monograph, in English; bibliography, pp. 235–242.

**REFUGEES INTERNATIONAL.** Founded in 1979, this non-governmental organization seeks alternative means of handling refugee migration and permanent resettlement. It provides advocacy, information, public education, and community support for refugees and displaced persons throughout the world. The group has 3,000 members worldwide and publishes the monthly *RI Action Alert* and the quarterly *RI Newsletter.*

Refugees International. Address: 21 Dupont Circle NW, Washington, D.C., 20036, USA. Telephone: (202) 828-1001. Fax: (202) 547-3796. Executive Director: Lionel A. Rosenblatt.

**REGIONAL COUNCIL ON HUMAN RIGHTS IN ASIA.** An international non-governmental organization in consultative status (Roster) with the UN **ECONOMIC AND SOCIAL COUNCIL**, the Council's members are civil rights leaders in five Asian and Pacific countries.

Founded in Manila in 1982, the first General Assembly of the Council adopted, in 1983, the Declaration of the Basic Duties of ASEAN Peoples and Governments, a "regional Declaration of Human Rights" that reflects the culture, values, and aspirations of the people of the ASEAN region. The Council—which consists of civil rights leaders from Indonesia, Malaysia, the Philippines, Singapore, and Thailand—promotes respect for individual and collective civil, political, social, economic, and cultural human rights; receives complaints and petitions; assists in redressing violations of these rights; and encourages governments of the region to ratify or concur in the International Covenants on Human Rights. Since 1984, the Council has campaigned for the release of political prisoners in the region.

Regional Council on Human Rights in Asia. Address: 204 Carbrera II Bldg., 64 Timog Ave., Quezon City, the Philippines. Secretary-General: Socorro Diokno.

**RELIGION.** See **FREEDOM OF THOUGHT, CONSCIENCE AND RELIGION.**

**RELIGIOUS DISCRIMINATION.** At its 1986 session, the UN **COMMISSION ON HUMAN RIGHTS** decided (resolution 1986/20) to appoint a Special Rapporteur to examine incidents and governmental actions which are inconsistent with the provisions of the Declaration on the Elimination of All Forms of Intolerance and of Discrimination Based on Religion and designated Mr.

Angelo Vidal d'Almeida Ribero as its Special Rapporteur.

The Special Rapporteur's reports to the 1987 and 1988 sessions of the Commission (UN Docs. E/CN.4/1987/35 and E/CN.4/1988/45 and Add. 1, respectively) presented an analysis, based on the information available to him, of the principal factors which hamper the implementation of the Declaration. After examining them, the Commission (resolutions 1987/15 and 1988/55) urged States to provide, where they had not already done so, adequate constitutional and legal guarantees of freedom of thought, conscience, religion and belief, including the provision of effective remedies where there is intolerance or discrimination based on religion or belief; and urged them also to take all appropriate measures to combat intolerance and to encourage understanding, tolerance, and respect in matters relating to freedom of religion or belief; and, in this context, to examine, where necessary, the supervision and training of their civil servants, educators, and other public officials to ensure that, in the course of their official duties, they respect different religions and beliefs and do not discriminate against persons professing other religions or beliefs.

In his report to the 1990 session of the Commission, the Special Rapporteur presented the following analysis of the information which he had collected (UN Doc. E/CN.4/1990/46, paras. 102—108):

Since his appointment, the Special Rapporteur has been able to gather a considerable amount of information regarding the factors hampering the implementation of the Declaration, the infringements of the rights defined in the Declaration and the various situations in which religious intolerance and discrimination can lead to the violation of other human rights. The Special Rapporteur has pointed out that the most important factors hampering the implementation of the Declaration are: the existence of legal provisions that run counter to the spirit and letter of the Declaration; practices by governmental authorities contradicting not only the principles embodied in international instruments but even provisions enshrined in domestic law which prohibit discrimination on religious grounds; the persistence of political, economic and cultural factors which result from complex historical processes and which are at the basis of current expressions of religious intolerance.

A large number of incidents brought to the attention of the Special Rapporteur, which involved clashes between members of various religious communities, appear to have resulted from the sectarian and intransigent attitude of the followers of a particular religion or belief. In addition to conflicts between entire religious communities, there are situations in which the activities of extremist or fanatical factions are the main cause of discriminatory practices or of violent outbursts of a religious nature. In fact, the intransigence of extremist elements and their demand for a literal interpretation, without consideration of the context of certain religious precepts, is at the root of many of the current manifestations of religious conflicts in the world.

The last few years have seen the emergence of such sectarian and intransigent attitudes regarding religious matters. This regrettable phenomenon has not only affected the freedoms and rights of minority communities in the countries where they have occurred, but has also become a destabilizing factor in the international system and a source of tension and conflict between States. As is usually the case with the different expressions of religious intolerance, these attitudes have led to attempts at curtailing a wide variety of human rights. For example, the condemnation to death of an author of a book which expresses views considered to be offensive by followers of a world religion and the death threats addressed to his publishers have been a matter of serious concern for the Special Rapporteur, not least because such attitudes violate basic principles of international law. The Special Rapporteur implores those responsible for the above-mentioned death threats not to carry them out, as this would constitute a flagrant violation of universally accepted human rights standards.

As in previous years, this year's alleged infringement of the rights defined in the Declaration affect a whole range of rights and freedoms, such as the right to have, to manifest and to practise the religion or belief of one's choice (Declaration, arts. 1 and 6); the freedom from discriminatory treatment on the grounds of religion or belief (Declaration, arts. 2–4); and the right to bring up children in accordance with the religion or belief chosen by their parents (Declaration, art. 5). As regards, for example, the right to have, to manifest and to practise the religion or belief of one's choice, allegations have been received in relation to restrictions on the right to manifest one's religion in public; sanctions for belonging to a specific denomination; the destruction, enforced closure, evacuation or arbitrary occupation of places of worship or assembly for a religion or belief; prohibition of the opening of new places of worship or assembly, or repair of existing premises; restriction of certain activities of a cultural nature relating to a religion or belief; seizure or confiscation of religious property or articles of worship; prohibition on importing, possessing, exhibiting or distributing certain articles of worship; prohibition on publishing, importing or distributing publications relating to a religion or belief; restriction or prohibition of religious publications, sermons or addresses; use for secular purposes of places considered to be sacred for certain religions or beliefs; profanation of burial places; restrictions on the right to set up seminaries to train clergy and on the possibilities for seminarists to receive adequate instruction; and restrictions on the right to appoint sufficient numbers of clergy. Regarding discrimination on the grounds of religion and belief, the allegations received refer to discriminatory measures in relation to access to education, employment, health services, and food rations, as well as to the permanent exclusion of certain groups or movements from public service, the refusal to give injured parties their legal compensation and the denial of the right to obtain a passport on the grounds of religion or belief. Where the education of children in accordance with the religion or belief of their parents is concerned, the allegations received by the Special Rapporteur indicate the continued existence of restrictions on the enjoyment of this freedom.

As has already been noted, and as it becomes clear from careful analysis of the allegations transmitted to Governments by the Special Rapporteur in the present and previous reports, the infringements of the rights and freedoms embodied in the Declaration usually result in the infringement of other human rights, such as the right to life, physical integrity, liberty and security of the person; freedom of movement; and freedom of opinion and expression. Indeed, many persons are still detained, either in prisons, labour camps or psychiatric hospitals, for reasons of religion or belief, while many more are silenced, persecuted or expelled from their countries on the same grounds. Persons held for religious reasons have in some cases allegedly been subjected to ill-treatment and to corporal punishment. Believers and members of the clergy of many denominations or persons holding certain beliefs continue, in a number of regions of the world, to be subjected to death threats, intimidation, physical assault, enforced re-education or enforced indoctrination. Most important, this year there has been an increase in alleged violations of the right to life in connection with the enjoyment of the rights and freedoms of religion and belief. In some cases, these violations affect individuals or groups and result from clashes with governmental forces; in others, they affect individuals or groups and result from communal clashes. In some cases, law enforcement authorities appear to have intervened in time to reduce the damage; in others it seems that they have not taken any measures; in yet others, they appear to have actively encouraged clashes.

The Special Rapporteur wishes to acknowledge the progress made by certain countries in introducing changes in their constitutional and legal systems in order to bring them into line with prevailing international standards in the field of religious rights and freedoms. He also wishes to express his satisfaction with improvements in the policies of certain Governments regarding matters of religion and conscience. The growing co-operation of Governments in the fulfilment of his mandate is also an encouraging development. However, infringements of the rights defined in the Declaration on the Elimination of All Forms of Intolerance and of Discrimination Based on Religion or Belief seem to persist in most regions of the world, as illustrated in the allegations transmitted to Governments by the Special Rapporteur in the course of this year. They concern all the provisions of the Declaration.

Despite the above-mentioned negative trends, the Special Rapporteur wishes once more to express his satisfaction with the positive impact of the policy of openness and transparency in the sphere of religious freedom and manifestations of worship in Eastern Europe. The Special Rapporteur has particularly noted significant improvement in the relations between the Orthodox Church and the Government of the Union of Soviet Socialist Republics. Among the encouraging signs worth mentioning is the election of His Holiness the Patriarch of Moscow and all Russia and two church dignitaries as deputies to the Supreme Soviet, as well as the opening of more than 1,700 new Orthodox parishes; the opening of a new seminary at Zhiovitzy in the Minsk region which adds to the four existing ones in Smolensk, Minsk, Kishinev and Stavropol; the opening of the competition for the design of a Memorial Cathedral to commemorate the 1,000th anniversary of Christianity in Russia; and the publication by the Moscow Patriarchate of a weekly paper entitled "The Church Messenger". Furthermore, the dialogue initiated at the highest level with the Roman Catholic Church during the recent official visit by the President of the Soviet Union, Mr. Gorbachev, to the Holy See is yet another positive manifestation of this new policy.

***CONCLUSIONS AND RECOMMENDATIONS.*** On the basis of the above analysis, the Special Rapporteur sub-

mitted to the Commission the following conclusions and recommendations (*Ibid.,* paras. 109–123):

During the past year, the Special Rapporteur has continued to receive allegations of infringements of the rights and freedoms set out in the Declaration occurring in most regions of the world, especially the right to have the religion or belief of one's choice and freedom from discrimination on grounds of religion or belief. The Special Rapporteur is concerned with the persistence of alarming infringements of other human rights arising out of attacks on freedom of thought, conscience, religion or belief. Noteworthy among them is the growing number of extra-judicial killings that have allegedly taken place in the context of clashes between religious groups or between such groups and security forces. Resorting to violence or the threat of its use in dealing with problems or antagonisms of a religious nature is also a disturbing development which, if unchecked, might endanger international peace. Despite the growing number of allegations concerning infringements of the principles embodied in the Declaration, the Special Rapporteur also wishes to note that the information collected also attests to a definite interest in overcoming the existing restrictions on the enjoyment of the rights and freedoms of thought, conscience, religion or belief. Significant progress achieved in Eastern Europe is particularly encouraging, and the increasing co-operation of almost all States in connection with the mandate of the Special Rapporteur is also praiseworthy.

The Special Rapporteur would like to emphasize that he is aware of the difficulties involved in distinguishing between religions, sects and religious associations. In his view, aspects having to do with the antiquity of a religion, its revealed character and the existence of a scripture, while important, are not sufficient to make a distinction. Even belief in the existence of a Supreme Being, a particular ritual or a set of ethical and social rules are not exclusive to religions but can also be found in political ideologies. So far, a satisfactory and acceptable distinction has not been arrived at. Given the rapid proliferation of religious associations, the lack of a genuine distinction between religions, sects and religious associations sometimes poses serious problems. Experience has shown that many newer sects and religious associations seem to engage in activities which are not always of a legal nature. The Special Rapporteur believes that, in the absence of an international convention which would be more explicit in this regard, the Declaration is the best instrument at the disposal of the international community allowing a distinction to be made between the legal and illegal practices of sects and religious associations. Indeed, the Declaration protects not only religious but also theistic, non-theistic and atheistic beliefs and stipulates in article 1, paragraph 3, that freedom to manifest one's religion or belief is subject only to such limitations as are prescribed by law and are necessary to protect public safety, order, health or morals, or the fundamental rights and freedoms of others.

Regarding communications informing of legal action taken against certain members of sects or religious associations, the Special Rapporteur believes it would be appropriate to await the final decisions of the courts, although he wishes to add that such legal proceedings should be concluded within a reasonable time. Long procedural delays can be harmful to the parties to a dispute and detrimental to the image of a State. Moreover, to allow a trial to drag on for years is a denial of justice sometimes more serious than the allegations that led to the legal action. In any event, the Special Rapporteur is of the opinion that the possible sentencing of one or more individuals in a criminal trial does not mean a condemnation of the religion or belief that they consider themselves to serve. All religions have already experienced similar situations without being themselves affected.

The Special Rapporteur also wishes to express his concern about the difficulties created by certain States in regard to the religious practices of foreigners who hold religious beliefs different from those held by the majority of the nationals of those States. In many cases, such difficulties consist not only in the prohibition of the building of either churches or chapels, but even in the prohibition of private worship. In some cases, such restrictions are imposed by Governments which have been authorized to build places of worship in the countries of origin of those whom they prevent from practising their faith in public. Not long ago, Pope John Paul II said in reference to this situation: "Allow me to confide in you. It is not difficult to understand the astonishment and frustration felt by Christians, say in Europe, who readily welcome believers of other religions and allow them to practise their faith, when they are refused similar rights in countries where such believers are a majority and their religion is the State religion." The Special Rapporteur believes that what is lacking here is the respect for the principle of reciprocity, widely accepted in international law and the day-to-day practice of international relations. Respect for this principle in the context described above, would certainly contribute to enhancing religious tolerance on a world-wide scale.

The Special Rapporteur would like to draw attention to another limitation in the existing international instruments with regard to freedom of thought, conscience, religion or belief. A broadly based school of legal thought maintains that the individual should be free not only to choose among different theistic creeds and to practise the one of his choice freely, but also to have the right to view life from a non-theistic perspective without facing disadvantages *vis-à-vis* believers. The Special Rapporteur thinks that, in the same way as believers must enjoy their right to practise their religion unhindered, non-believers (freethinkers, agnostics and atheists) should not be discriminated against. The rights of non-believers should be properly guaranteed in a new international instrument.

In the analysis of the information received, the Special Rapporteur has established that the most important obstacles to the implementation of the Declaration are, *inter alia*: the existence of provisions in national laws which run counter to the spirit and letter of the Declaration; governmental practices which often conflict with both national laws and international instruments on the matter; persistent economic, political and cultural factors; the influence of complex historical processes on current manifestations of religious intolerance, such as distrust and clashes between members of various religious communities which generate sectarian and intransigent attitudes; extremist and fanatical opinions originating from a literal interpretation of certain religious precepts which result in violent outbursts; extrajudicial killings, death threats, intimidation, enforced re-education, confinement to psychiatric or labour camps; profanation of places of worship and burial grounds, destruction, closing, evacuation or occupation of such places of worship; seizure or confiscation of articles of worship and property; hindering or prohibition of religious publications and their dissemination, their censorship as well as that of sermons, etc. These regrettable phenomena adversely affect not only the rights and freedoms of religious communities but also those of minorities and represent a destabilizing factor in international relations and a source of tensions and conflict between States. The violation or non-respect of religious rights often results in the infringement of other human rights, such as the right to life, physical integrity, liberty and security of the person, freedom of movement and freedom of opinion and expression.

The Special Rapporteur also wishes to underline that progress has been made in this area as well. An example is the introduction of appropriate changes in constitutions and legal systems made by certain countries to bring them into greater accord with international instruments; improved policies of certain Governments regarding matters of religion and conscience; the positive impact of the policy of openness and transparency in Eastern Europe, especially the new dialogue between the Government of the Soviet Union and the Orthodox and Roman Catholic Churches.

Since his appointment, the Special Rapporteur has been collecting information transmitted to him by the Governments, non-governmental organizations and other religious and lay sources, regarding constitutional and legal guarantees of freedom of thought, conscience, religion and belief, measures taken by States to combat intolerance, and incidents and governmental actions which might be inconsistent with the provisions of the Declaration. The information thus gathered has constantly been examined by the Special Rapporteur, since it contains important elements to be taken into account by any future drafters of a new international instrument. The Special Rapporteur, should the Commission decide to renew his mandate, intends to include in his next report a brief analysis of the material collected over the years since his first appointment.

Although the international system already has a number of mandatory norms in the area of freedom of religion or belief, the persistence of the problem of intolerance and discrimination in this field calls for the preparation of an international instrument dealing specifically with the elimination of this phenomenon. The Special Rapporteur is of the opinion that the adoption of such an instrument could give a broader and more profound dimension to international protection against manifestations of intolerance based on religion or belief. Furthermore, the mandatory nature of the provisions of such an instrument could impose on States parties a number of requirements, such as the submission of reports on the application of its provisions, which might encourage greater respect for religious rights and freedoms by such States.

For the purpose of elaborating such an international instrument, the international community might usefully draw upon the principles laid down in the 1981 Declaration, as well as on the practical experience acquired in recent years by the Commission on Human Rights in this regard. The Special Rapporteur would like to insist on the advantage of establishing, within the Commission on Human Rights or its Sub-Commission on Prevention of Discrimination and Protection of Minorities, an open-ended working group to consider the possibility of preparing a new binding international instrument. In his view, such a group should be able to count on the broad participation of States, non-governmental organizations and religious denominations. While such an international instrument is being prepared, the Commission on Human Rights should endeavour to maintain its vigilance and continue to apply the procedure it has introduced with a view to monitoring and, if possible, reducing incidents and measures inconsistent with the provisions of the 1981 Declaration.

In this connection, the Special Rapporteur has noted with

interest the report (E/CN.4/Sub.2/1989/32) prepared by Mr. Theo van Boven, expert of the Sub-Commission on Prevention of Discrimination and Protection of Minorities, pursuant to Commission resolution 1988/55. In relation to the new binding international instrument itself, Mr. van Boven stresses that it should build on the standard already elaborated by the international community; take into account the complexity of the issues involved and, in particular, the need for broad international acceptance on the part of States which would have to undertake legal obligations.

The Special Rapporteur wishes once more to urge States which have not already ratified the relevant international instruments to do so, making provision, in accordance with the norms laid down by those instruments, for the necessary constitutional and legal guarantees for freedom of thought, conscience, religion and belief, including effective remedies in the event of intolerance or discrimination based on religion or belief.

Advantage should be taken of the advisory services made available by the United Nations in the field of human rights, as follows:

(a) Provision of expert advisory services to countries which express the desire to have them for the drafting of new legislative provisions or the adaptation of existing legislation in conformity with the principles set out in the 1981 Declaration; for the establishment of a machinery for the promotion and protection of human rights, particularly in respect of freedom of religion and belief, such as national commissions, the institution of an ombudsman or of reconciliation commissions; or for the inclusion in school curricula of teaching of the ideals of tolerance, understanding and mutual respect among all religious groups;

(b) Organization of regional, subregional and national training courses aimed at greater familiarization with existing principles, norms and remedies in the sphere of freedom of religion and belief. These training courses would be particularly intended for persons occupying key posts in their respective countries, such as legislators, judges, lawyers, law-enforcement officials, members of the administration and educators;

(c) Organization of international, regional and national workshops for representatives of non-governmental organizations in the sphere of human rights, and for representatives of specific religions and ideologies, on the theme of promotion of tolerance and understanding as regards religion and belief and encouragement of inter-denominational dialogue;

(d) Organization, with the collaboration of UNESCO, of media briefings aimed at a broader dissemination of the principles contained in the Declaration so as to prevent the spreading of stereotypes which might lead to lack of comprehension and tolerance.

The Special Rapporteur wishes to insist that non-governmental organizations in general, and groups representing specific religions or ideologies in particular, can and should play an active role in assuring respect for and promoting tolerance and freedom of religion and belief by initiating an inter-denominational dialogue at the national and international levels, in the form of meetings, conferences and seminars whose topics would be aimed at emphasizing the similarities among various religions and beliefs rather than their differences.

Finally, victims of intolerance and discrimination based on religion or belief should have effective remedies available to them. In this connection, the Special Rapporteur is of the opinion that it would be desirable for information on the norms laid down by the 1981 Declaration to be given widespread dissemination among persons responsible for protecting the right to freedom of religion or belief, particularly lawmakers, judges, lawyers and civil servants.

Following the resignation of Mr. d'Almeida Ribero during the forty-ninth session of the Commission, the Chairman appointed Mr. Abdelfattah Amor (Tunisia) as Special Rapporteur. At its fiftieth session the Commission, in resolution 1994/18, encouraged the Special Rapporteur to continue to examine incidents and governmental actions in all parts of the world that are incompatible with the provisions of the Declaration and to recommend appropriate remedial measures. The Commission also requested the Secretary-General to provide all necessary assistance and resources to the Special Rapporteur to enable him to carry out his mandate and to report to the Commission at its fifty-first session. In the same resolution, the Commission requested the Secretary-General to report to it at its fifty-first session on measures taken to implement resolution 1994/18.

**SEE ALSO** *Freedom of Thought, Conscience and Religion.*

**BIBLIOGRAPHY.** Dinstein, Yoram. "Freedom of Religion and the Protection of Religious Minorities," *Israel Yearbook on Human Rights* 20 (1990): 155–179. Scholarly article, in English.

Goy, Raymond. "La garantie européenne de la liberté de religion: l'article 9 de la Convention de Rome," *Revue du droit public* 107 (1991): 5–59. Scholarly article, in French.

Lerner, Natan. *Group Rights and Discrimination in International Law.* Dordrecht, the Netherlands: Martinus Nijhoff, 1991. Scholarly monograph, in English.

Matscher, Franz, ed. *The Prohibition of Torture and Freedom of Religion and Conscience: Comparative Aspects.* Kehl am Rhein, Austria: N.P. Engel Verlag, 1991. Scholarly monograph, in English and German.

Mayer, Ann Elizabeth. *Islam and Human Rights: Tradition and Politics.* San Francisco, CA, USA, and London: Westview Press; Pinter Publishers, 1991. Scholarly monograph, in English.

Rahman, Anika. "Religious Rights Versus Women's Rights in India: A Test Case for International Human Rights Law," *Columbia Journal of Transnational Law* 28, no. 2 (1990): 473–498. Scholarly article, in English.

Salzberg, John P. *The Question of a United Nations Convention on Religious Tolerance.* Washington, D.C.: s.n., 1990. Report, in English.

Van Boven, Theo. "Advances and Obstacles in Building Understanding and Respect between People of Diverse Religions and Beliefs," *Human Rights Quarterly* 13, no. 4 (1991): 437–449. Scholarly article, in English.

**REMEDY.** An individual may enforce his right, prevent it from being violated, or seek redress or compensation in case of its violation through the right of remedy. The right to an effective remedy is proclaimed in article 8 of the **Universal Declaration of Human Rights,** which reads:

*Article 8.* Everyone has the right to an effective remedy by the competent national tribunals for acts violating the fundamental rights granted him by the constitution or by law.

A corresponding provision is to be found in article 2 (3) of the **International Covenant on Civil and Political Rights,** which reads:

*Article 2.* (3) Each State Party to the present Covenant undertakes:
(a) To ensure that any person whose rights or freedoms as herein recognized are violated shall have an effective remedy, notwithstanding that the violation has been committed by persons acting in an official capacity;
(b) To ensure that any person claiming such a remedy shall have his right thereto determined by competent judicial, administrative or legislative authorities, or by any other competent authority provided for by the legal system of the State, and to develop the possibilities of judicial remedy;
(c) To ensure that the competent authorities shall enforce such remedies when granted.

A provision on the subject also appears in article 6 of the International Convention on the Elimination of All Forms of Racial Discrimination (see **Racial Discrimination**), as follows:

*Article 6.* States Parties shall assure to everyone within their jurisdiction effective protection and remedies, through the competent national tribunals and other State institutions, against any acts of racial discrimination which violate his human rights and fundamental freedoms contrary to this Convention, as well as the right to seek from such tribunals just and adequate reparation or satisfaction for any damage suffered as a result of such discrimination.

Articles 13 and 14 of the Convention against Torture and Other Cruel, Inhuman or Degrading Treatment or Punishment (see **Torture**) provides for the right to an adequate remedy in the case of victims of torture in the following articles:

*Article 13.* Each State Party shall ensure that any individual who alleges he has been subjected to torture in any territory under its jurisdiction has the right to complain to, and to have his case promptly and impartially examined by, its competent authorities. Steps shall be taken to ensure that the complainant and witnesses are protected against all ill-treatment or intimidation as a consequence of his complaint or any evidence given.
*Article 14.* 1. Each State Party shall ensure in its legal system that the victim of an act of torture obtains redress and has an enforceable right to fair and adequate compensation, including the means for as full rehabilitation as possible. In the event of the death of the victim as a result of an act of torture, his dependants shall be entitled to compensation.
2. Nothing in this article shall affect any right of the victim or other persons to compensation which may exist under national law.

The **American Convention on Human Rights,** open for acceptance by member States of the **Organization of American States,** provides that:

*Article 10.* Every person has the right to be compensated in accordance with the law in the event he has been sentenced by a final judgement through a miscarriage of justice.

The **European Convention on Human Rights,** open for acceptance by members of the **Council of Europe,** provides that:

*Article 13.* Everyone whose rights and freedoms as set forth in this Convention are violated shall have an effective remedy before a national authority notwithstanding that the violation has been committed by persons acting in an official capacity.

***GENERAL COMMENT BY THE UN HUMAN RIGHTS COMMITTEE.*** After examining reports submitted by states parties to the International Covenant on Civil and Political Rights in accordance with article 40 of that instrument, the **Human Rights Committee** adopted, in 1981, a general comment relating to article 2 of the Covenant in the following terms (UN Doc. A/36/40, annex VII, paras. 1–2):

The Committee notes that article 2 of the Covenant generally leaves it to the States parties concerned to choose their method of implementation in their territories within the framework set out in that article. It recognizes, in particular, that the implementation does not depend solely on constitutional or legislative enactments, which in themselves are often not *per se* sufficient. The Committee considers it necessary to draw the attention of States parties to the fact that the obligation under the Covenant is not confined to the respect of human rights, but that States parties have also undertaken to ensure the enjoyment of these rights to all individuals under their jurisdiction. This aspect calls for specific activities by the States parties to enable individuals to enjoy their rights. This is obvious in a number of articles (e.g. article 3 which is dealt with in general comment 4/13 below), but in principle this undertaking relates to all rights set forth in the Covenant.
In this connexion, it is very important that individuals should know what their rights under the Covenant (and the Optional Protocol, as the case may be) are and also that all administrative and judicial authorities should be aware of the obligations which the State party has assumed under the Covenant. To this end, the Covenant should be publicized in all official languages of the State and steps should be taken to familiarize the authorities concerned with its contents as part of their training. It is desirable also to give publicity to the State party's co-operation with the Committee.

***SEE ALSO*** *Civil and Political Rights; Fair Trial; International Covenant on Civil and Political Rights; Procedural Guarantees.*

***BIBLIOGRAPHY.*** Adzoxornu, Isaacus Komla. "Access to the Personal Grievance Procedures in New Zealand: The Human Rights Dimension," *University of Tasmania Law Review* 10 (1990): 40–58. Scholarly article, in English.

Alston, P., and M. Rodriguez-Bustelo. *Taking Stock of the United Nations Human Rights Procedures: Report of a January 1988 Workshop at Lake Mohonk, NY.* Medford, MA, USA: Fletcher School of Law and Diplomacy, Tufts University, 1988. Conference report, in English.

Amnesty International. *The Human Rights Committee.* Three parts. London: 1986. NGO report, in English; bibliographies in parts 1 and 2 list official documents, books, pamphlets, and articles on the Human Rights Committee (part 1) and resources (part 2).

──────. *The Human Rights Committee—Protecting Human Rights: International Procedures and How to Use Them.* London: 1987. NGO background paper, in English, French, and Spanish; bibliography.

Cancado Trindade, A. A. "O Esgotamento dos Recursos Internos e a Evolucao da Nocao de 'Vitima' no Direito Internacional dos Direitos Humanos" (The Exhaustion of Internal Resources and the Notion of "Victim" in International Human Rights Law), *Revista IIDH* 3 (Jan.–June 1986): 5–78. NGO scholarly article, in Portuguese.

Committee on the Administration of Justice. *Cause for Complaint: The System for Dealing with Complaints against the Police in Northern Ireland.* Belfast, GB: 1990. NGO report, in English.

Commonwealth Human Rights Initiative. *Put Our World to Rights: Towards a Commonwealth Human Rights Policy. A Report by a Non-Governmental Advisory Group Chaired by the Hon. Flora MacDonald.* London: 1991. NGO report, in English.

Crowley, John. *Le Rôle de la Commission for Racial Equality dans la représentation politique desminorités ethniques britanniques* (The Role of the Commission for Racial Equality in the Political Representation of British Ethnic Minorities), *Revue européenne des migrations internationales* 6, no. 3 (1990): 45–61. Scholarly article, in French.

Gibney, Mark. "Suing for Death, Suffering, and Peace," *Human Rights Quarterly* 12, no. 3 (Aug. 1990): 415–425. Scholarly article, in English.

──────, ed. *World Justice? U.S. Courts and International Human Rights.* Boulder, CO, USA: Westview Press, 1991. Scholarly collective works, in English.

Hottelier, Michel. *La requête abusive au sens de l'article 27, de la Convention européenne des droits de l'homme* (An Abuse of the Right of Petition in the Sense of Article 27, paragraph 2 of the European Convention on Human Rights), *Revue trimestrielle des droits de l'homme* 2, no. 7 (July 1991): 301–318. Scholarly article, in French.

Lester, Anthony. "Preparing and Presenting a Human Rights Brief," *Commonwealth Law Bulletin* 17, no. 3 (July 1991): 1055–1071. Conference paper, in English.

Polakiewicz, Jörg, and Valerie Jacob-Foltzer. "The European Human Rights Convention in Domestic Law: The Impact of the Strasbourg Case-Law in States Where Direct Effect Is Given to the Convention," *Human Rights Law Journal* 12, nos. 3 and 4. (March and April 1991): 65–84, 125–141. Scholarly article, in English.

Roht-Arriaza, Naomi. "State Responsibility to Investigate and Prosecute Grave Human Rights Violations in International Law," *California Law Review* 78, no. 2 (March 1990): 449–513. Scholarly article, in English.

Smith, Nicolas. "Affirmative Action: Its Origin and Point," *South African Journal on Human Rights* 8, no. 2 (1992): 234–248. Scholarly article, in English.

Zayas, Alfred de. "Les procédures de communications individuelles devant le Comité des Droits de l'Homme des Nations Unies" (Petitioning the United Nations Human Rights Committee), *Revue trimestrielle des droits de l'homme* 1, no. 4 (Oct. 1990): 339–351. Article, in French.

## RENAULT, LOUIS (1843–1918).

A co-winner of the 1907 **NOBEL PEACE PRIZE,** along with **ERNESTO TEODORO MONETA,** Louis Renault was an expert on international law and a major figure at the second Hague Peace Conference of 1907.

Born in Autun, France, Renault taught international law at the University of Paris from 1881 to 1890, in which year he was appointed legal consultant to the French Foreign Office. From 1890 onwards, Renault was France's leading representative at international conferences on subjects as various as air travel and the abolition of white slavery. He was awarded the rank of minister plenipotentiary and envoy extraordinary in 1903. In 1914 he became president of the Academy of International Law.

***BIBLIOGRAPHY.*** Gray, Tony. *Champions of Peace.* London: Paddington Press, 1976.

Schlessinger, Bernard S., and June H. Schlessinger, eds. *Who's Who of Nobel Prize Winners.* Phoenix, AZ, USA: Oryx Press, 1991.

## REPORTERS SANS FRONTIÈRES (REPORTERS WITHOUT BORDERS).

This non-governmental organization was founded in 1985 in Montpellier, France, to ensure that news of human rights violations and human tragedies of whatever nature are revealed to the world. The group has consultative status with the UN **ECONOMIC AND SOCIAL COUNCIL** and participates in the International Freedom of Expression Exchange.

*Reporters sans Frontières* established the *Fondation de France* Prize in 1992, which is awarded to a journalist who demonstrates the principle of freedom of expression. The first recipient was Zlatko Kisdarevic, editor of *Oslobodjenje*, a chronicle of the Sarajevo siege.

Reporters sans frontières. Address: 1 place du Nombre d'Or "Antigone," F-34000 Montpelier, France. Telephone: (33-1) 6779-8182. President: Robert Menard.

## REVISTA IIDH.

Published bi-annually, *Revista IIDH* is a Spanish publication containing scholarly articles on international and regional human rights, a review of the work of the Inter-American Commission and Court of Human Rights, and comments on important legislation and human rights developments.

*Revista IIDH.* Inter-American Institute of Human Rights, P.O. 10.081, San Jose, Costa Rica.

**REVUE UNIVERSELLE DES DROITS DE L'HOMME.** This monthly is a French version of the **HUMAN RIGHTS LAW JOURNAL**, although it often contains original articles. The *Revue* provides timely and systematic reporting and commentary on international, constitutional, and supreme court decisions from Europe. It also reproduces the papers of important international or regional symposia, and documents of intergovernmental organizations.

*Revue Universelle des Droits de l'Homme.* Address: N.P. Engel, 44, rue Bantain, F-67000 Strasbourg, France.

**RIGHT LIVELIHOOD AWARD.** Sometimes called the "alternative Nobel Prize," the Right Livelihood Award was introduced in 1980 by Jakob von Uexkul, writer and former member of the European Parliament, to honor and support work that pioneers solutions to: war and the arms race, poverty and unemployment, resource depletion and environmental degradation, human repression and social injustice, inappropriate technologies and unethical scientific practices, and cultural and spiritual decline. Since its inception, the Award has been presented to 58 people and projects from some 60 different countries. Presented annually in the Swedish Parliament in Stockholm on the day before the Nobel Prize presentations, the Right Livelihood Award honors two to five recipients who share US$250,000 to use in their specific projects, and one honoree receives a nonmonetary award.

In 1994, the nonmonetary award was presented to Astrid Lindgren, Swedish writer, for her work on behalf of children's rights and animal abuse. The monetary award was shared by Ken Saro-Wiwa and the Movement for the Survival of the Ogoni People (Nigeria) for their fight against the pollution of the Ogoni environment from government oil extraction; Indian doctor H. Sudarshan and his organization Vivekananda Girijana Karyana Kendra, for working for the social, cultural, and economic progress of the tribal Soliga people in the Biligiri Rangana Hills of Karnataka State; and the Trinidadian organization SERVOL (Service Volunteered for All) for its work with preschool and adolescent children and their parents.

In 1993, the recipients were: Arna Mer-Khamis/ Care and Learning (Israel) for their defense and education of Palestinian children; The Organisation of Rural Associations for Progress of Zimbabwe; Vandana Shiva (India); and Mary and Carrie Dann of the Western Shoshone Nation (North America) for their fights for the land rights of indigenous peoples.

For more information, contact: Right Livelihood Awards, P.O. Box 15072, S-10465 Stockholm, Sweden. Telephone: (46-8) 702-0340. Fax: (46-8) 702-0338.

**RIGHT TO DEVELOPMENT.** See **DEVELOPMENT.**

**RIGHT TO LEAVE ANY COUNTRY, INCLUDING ONE'S OWN, AND TO RETURN TO ONE'S OWN COUNTRY.** See **FREEDOM OF MOVEMENT AND RESIDENCE.**

**RIGHT TO LIFE.** A human right proclaimed in the **UNIVERSAL DECLARATION OF HUMAN RIGHTS** as follows:

*Article 3.* Everyone has the right to life, liberty and the security of person.

The meaning and scope of the right to life is clarified in the **INTERNATIONAL COVENANT ON CIVIL AND POLITICAL RIGHTS** in the following provision:

*Article 6.* (1) Every human being has the inherent right to life. This right shall be protected by law. No one shall be arbitrarily deprived of his life.

(2) In countries which have not abolished the death penalty, sentence of death may be imposed only for the most serious crimes in accordance with the law in force at the time of the Commission of the crime and not contrary to the provisions of the present Covenant and to the Convention on the Prevention and Punishment of the Crime of Genocide. This penalty can only be carried out pursuant to a final judgement rendered by a competent court.

(3) When deprivation of life constitutes the crime of genocide, it is understood that nothing in this article shall authorize any State Party to the present Covenant to derogate in any way from any obligation assumed under the provisions of the Convention on the Prevention and Punishment of the Crime of Genocide.

(4) Anyone sentenced to death shall have the right to seek pardon or commutation of the sentence. Amnesty, pardon or commutation of the sentence of death may be granted in all cases.

(5) Sentence of death shall not be imposed for crimes committed by persons below eighteen years of age and shall not be carried out on pregnant women.

(6) Nothing in this article shall be invoked to delay or to prevent the abolition of capital punishment by any State Party to the present Covenant.

The **AMERICAN CONVENTION ON HUMAN RIGHTS,** open for acceptance by member States of the **ORGANIZATION OF AMERICAN STATES,** provides that:

*Article 4.* (1) Every person has the right to have his life respected. This right shall be protected by law and, in general, from the moment of conception. No one shall be arbitrarily deprived of his life.

(2) In countries that have not abolished the death penalty, it may be imposed only for the most serious crimes and pursuant to a final judgment rendered by a competent court and in accordance with a law establishing such punishment, enacted prior to the commission of the crime. The applica-

tion of such punishment shall not be extended to crimes to which it does not presently apply.

(3) The death penalty shall not be reestablished in states that have abolished it.

(4) In no case shall capital punishment be inflicted for political offenses or related common crimes.

(5) Capital punishment shall not be imposed upon persons who, at the time the crime was committed, were under 18 years of age or over 70 years of age; nor shall it be applied to pregnant women.

(6) Every person condemned to death shall have the right to apply for amnesty, pardon, or commutation of sentence, which may be granted in all cases. Capital punishment shall not be imposed while such a petition is pending decision by the competent authority.

The **AFRICAN CHARTER ON HUMAN AND PEOPLES' RIGHTS,** open for acceptance by member States of the **ORGANIZATION OF AFRICAN UNITY,** provides that:

*Article 4. Human beings are inviolable.* Every human being shall be entitled to respect for his life and the integrity of his person. No one may be arbitrarily deprived of this right.

The **EUROPEAN CONVENTION ON HUMAN RIGHTS,** open for acceptance by members of the **COUNCIL OF EUROPE,** provides that:

*Article 2.* (1) Everyone's right to life shall be protected by law. No one shall be deprived of his life intentionally save in the execution of a sentence of a court following his conviction of a crime for which this penalty is provided by law.

(2) Deprivation of life shall not be regarded as inflicted in contravention of this Article when it results from the use of force which is no more than absolutely necessary:

(a) in defense of any person from unlawful violence;

(b) in order to effect a lawful arrest or to prevent the escape of a person lawfully detained;

(c) in action lawfully taken for the purpose of quelling a riot or insurrection.

The **EUROPEAN CONVENTION ON HUMAN RIGHTS, PROTOCOL VI,** contains the following provisions:

*Article 1.* The death penalty shall be abolished. No one shall be condemned to such penalty or executed.

*Article 2.* A State may make provision in its law for the death penalty in respect of acts committed in time of war or of imminent threat of war; such penalty shall be applied only in the instances laid down in the law and in accordance with its provisions. The State shall communicate to the Secretary-General of the Council of Europe the relevant provisions of the law.

In addition, the Convention on the Prevention and Punishment of the Crime of Genocide (see **GENOCIDE**) and the International Convention on the Suppression and Punishment of the Crime of Apartheid (see **APARTHEID**) both define as crimes the killing of members of certain racial or other groups with a view to bringing about the physical destruction of such a group in whole or in part.

*FIRST GENERAL COMMENT BY THE UN HUMAN RIGHTS COMMITTEE.* After examining reports submitted by States parties to the International Covenant of Civil and Political Rights in accordance with article 40 of that instrument, the **HUMAN RIGHTS COMMITTEE** adopted two general comments on article 6 which, although formulated primarily to guide States in the preparation of future reports, incidentally serve to throw light on the meaning and scope which the Committee attributes to certain provisions of the covenant. The first such comment, adopted in 1982, reads:

The right to life enunciated in article 6 of the Covenant has been dealt with in all State reports. It is the supreme right from which no derogations is permitted even in time of public emergency which threatens the life of the nation (article 4). However, the Committee has noted that quite often the information given concerning article 6 has been limited to only one or other aspect of this right. It is a right which should not be interpreted narrowly.

The Committee observes that war and other acts of mass violence continue to be a scourge of humanity and take the lives of thousands of innocent human beings every year. Under the Charter of the United Nations the threat or use of force by any State against another State, except in exercise of the inherent right of self-defence, is already prohibited. The Committee considers that States have the supreme duty to prevent wars, acts of genocide and other acts of mass violence causing arbitrary loss of life. Every effort they make to avert the danger of war, especially thermo-nuclear war, and to strengthen international peace and security would constitute the most important condition and guarantee for the safeguarding of the right to life. In this respect, the Committee notes, in particular, a connexion between article 6 and article 20, which states that the law shall prohibit any propaganda for war (paragraph 1) or incitement to violence (paragraph 2) as therein described.

The protection against arbitrary deprivation of life which is explicitly required by the third sentence of article 6 (1) is of paramount importance. The Committee considers that States parties should take measures not only to prevent and punish deprivation of life by criminal acts, but also to prevent arbitrary killing by their own security forces. The deprivation of life by the authorities of the State is a matter of the utmost gravity. Therefore, the law must strictly control and limit the circumstances in which a person may be deprived of his life by such authorities.

States parties should also take specific and effective measures to prevent the disappearance of individuals, something which unfortunately has become all too frequent and leads too often to arbitrary deprivation of life. Furthermore, States should establish effective facilities and procedures to investigate thoroughly cases of missing and disappeared persons in circumstances which may involve a violation of the right to life.

Moreover, the Committee has noted that the right to life has been too often narrowly interpreted. The expression "inherent right to life" cannot properly be understood in a restrictive manner, and the protection of this right requires that States adopt positive measures. In this connexion, the Committee considers that it would be desirable for States parties to take all possible measures to reduce infant mortality and to increase life expectancy, especially in adopting measures to eliminate malnutrition and epidemics.

While it follows from article 6 (2) to (6) that States parties are not obliged to abolish the death penalty totally, they are obliged to limit its use and, in particular, to abolish it for other than the "most serious crimes". Accordingly, they ought to consider reviewing their criminal laws in this light and, in any event, are obliged to restrict the application of the death penalty to the "most serious crimes". The article also refers generally to abolition in terms which strongly suggest (paras. 2 (2) and (6)) that abolition is desirable. The Committee concludes that all measures of abolition should be considered as progress in the enjoyment of the right to life within the meaning of article 40, and should as such be reported to the Committee. The Committee notes that a number of States have already abolished the death penalty or suspended its application. Nevertheless, States' reports show that progress made towards abolishing or limiting the application of the death penalty is quite inadequate.

The Committee is of the opinion that the expression "most serious crimes" must be read restrictively to mean that the death penalty should be a quite exceptional measure. It also follows from the express terms of article 6 that it can only be imposed in accordance with the law in force at the time of the commission of the crime and not contrary to the Covenant. The procedural guarantees therein prescribed must be observed, including the right to a fair hearing by an independent tribunal, the presumption of innocence, the minimum guarantees for the defence, and the right to review by a higher tribunal. These rights are applicable in addition to the particular right to seek pardon or commutation of the sentence.

### SECOND GENERAL COMMENT BY THE UN HUMAN RIGHTS COMMITTEE.

The second comment, adopted in 1985, reads:

In its general comment 6 (16), adopted at its 378th meeting on 27 July 1982, the Human Rights Committee observes that the right to life enunciated in the first paragraph of article 6 of the International Covenant on Civil and Political Rights is the supreme right from which no derogation is permitted even in time of public emergency. The same right to life is enshrined in article 3 of the Universal Declaration of Human Rights adopted by the General Assembly of the United Nations on 10 December 1948. It is basic to all human rights.

In its previous general comment, the Committee also observes that it is the supreme duty of States to prevent wars. War and other acts of mass violence continue to be a scourge of humanity and take the lives of thousands of innocent human beings every year.

While remaining deeply concerned by the toll of human life taken by conventional weapons in armed conflicts, the Committee has noted that, during successive sessions of the General Assembly, representatives from all geographical regions have expressed their growing concern at the development and proliferation of increasingly awesome weapons of mass destruction, which not only threaten human life but also absorb resources that could otherwise be used for vital economic and social purposes, particularly for the benefit of developing countries, and thereby for promoting and securing the enjoyment of human rights for all.

The Committee associates itself with this concern. It is evident that the designing, testing, manufacture, possession and deployment of nuclear weapons are among the greatest threats to the right to life which confront mankind today. This threat is compounded by the danger that the actual use of such weapons may be brought about, not only in the event of war, but even through human or mechanical error or failure.

Furthermore, the very existence and gravity of this threat generate a climate of suspicion and fear between States, which is in itself antagonistic to the promotion of universal respect for and observance of human rights and fundamental freedoms in accordance with the Charter of the United Nations and the International Covenants on Human Rights.

The production, testing, possession, deployment and use of nuclear weapons should be prohibited and recognized as crimes against humanity.

The Committee accordingly, in the interest of mankind, calls upon all States, whether parties to the Covenant or not, to take urgent steps, unilaterally and by agreement, to rid the world of this menace.

At its 1987 session, the UN **GENERAL ASSEMBLY** adopted a comprehensive resolution (resolution 42/99) on the right to life, based on its conviction that all rights and freedoms, as well as all the material goods and spiritual wealth that both man and nations possess, have a common foundation—the right to life, freedom, peace, and aspiration for happiness.

In the resolution, the Assembly reaffirmed that all peoples and all individuals have an inherent right to life and that the safeguarding of this cardinal right is an essential condition for the enjoyment of the entire range of economic, social, and cultural, as well as civil and political, rights. It stressed the urgent need for the international community to make every effort to strengthen peace, remove the growing threat of war, particularly nuclear war, halt the arms race, and achieve general and complete disarmament under effective international control and prevent violations of the principles of the of the **UNITED NATIONS CHARTER** regarding the sovereignty and territorial integrity of States and the self-determination of peoples, thus contributing to ensuring the right to life. It stressed further the foremost importance of the implementation of practical measures of disarmament to bring to an end the waste of valuable resources and to streamline them to fight economic backwardness and poverty and to accelerate social and economic progress, particularly for the benefit of developing countries.

The Assembly called upon all States, appropriate United Nations organs, specialized agencies, and intergovernmental and non-governmental organizations concerned to take the necessary measures to ensure that the results of scientific and technological progress, the material and intellectual potential of mankind, are used to solve global problems exclusively in the interests of international peace, for the benefit of mankind, and for promoting and encouraging universal respect for human rights and fundamental freedoms.

It also called upon all States that had not done so

to take effective measures with a view to prohibiting, in accordance with the International Covenant on Civil and Political Rights, any propaganda for war, in particular the formulation, propounding, and dissemination of and propaganda for doctrines and concepts aimed at unleashing nuclear war.

The **COMMISSION ON HUMAN RIGHTS** echoed these views at its 1988 session (resolution 1988/60), and expressed profound concern that international peace and security continue to be threatened by the arms race in all its aspects, particularly the nuclear arms race, as well as by violations of the principles of the United Nations Charter regarding the sovereignty and territorial integrity of States and the **SELF-DETERMINATION** of peoples. It recognized that peoples want to live in a better and more equitable world based on recognition of the priority of the values common to all mankind; that the widening availability of technology and scientific and technical advances, bringing new possibilities for peaceful and productive enterprise, open new perspectives for the progress of civilization and provide increasing opportunities to better the conditions of life of peoples and nations, but at the same time present new dangers if used for the creation of new types of deadly weapons, which are already able to transform an armed conflict from human tragedy to human annihilation; and that it is only the creative genius of man that makes progress and the development of civilization possible in a peaceful environment and that human life must be recognized as supreme.

Convinced of the need to intensify efforts to foster the spirit of mutual respect, understanding, and confidence and to combat attempts to incite enmity, hatred, and intolerance and to impose "enemy-image" stereotypes, it emphasized the importance of overcoming prejudices based on intolerance, hatred, and stereotypes of this kind.

The Commission, finally, requested the Secretary-General, in the light of the comments and views of member States, to submit a report on the implementation of its resolution to the Commission at its 1990 session.

On 8 December 1988, the General Assembly (resolution 43/111) reaffirmed that all people have an inherent right to life, recalled the historic responsibility of the governments of all countries of the world to preserve civilization and to ensure that everyone enjoys that right, and called upon all States to do their utmost to assist in implementing the right through the adoption of appropriate measures at both the national and the international levels.

Similarly, on 15 December 1989, the Assembly called upon those governments (resolution 44/133) to do their utmost to assist in implementing the right to life through the adoption of appropriate measures, at the national and international levels, to ensure that the results of scientific and technological progress and the material and intellectual potential of mankind are used for the benefit of mankind and for promoting and encouraging respect for human rights and fundamental freedoms.

*SEE ALSO* *Abortion; Environment; Standard of Living.*

**ROMANIA.** The Socialist Republic of Romania is a country in eastern Europe, on the Black Sea. It has borders with Bulgaria, Hungary, the Union of Soviet Socialist Republics, and Yugoslavia. Its population is estimated to be 23,200,000. It proclaimed its independence from Turkey in 1877, and its status as an independent State was confirmed by the Treaty of Berlin in 1878. It became a kingdom in 1881 and a constitutional monarchy in 1886.

After the election of a communist-dominated government in 1946, King Michael abdicated, and the country became the People's Republic of Romania. As such, it joined the Warsaw Treaty Organization and the United Nations in 1955. Under a new constitution, its name was changed to the Socialist Republic of Romania in 1965.

Nicolae Ceausescu, who succeeded Gheorghe Gheorghiu-Dej as communist party chief in 1965, presided over a government which harshly suppressed dissidents, mistreated the large Hungarian ethnic minority, and totally disregarded consumer needs. Drastic cuts in the use of energy and in the production of the necessities of life, initiated in 1981 with a view to eliminating a foreign debt of more than $11 billion by the end of the decade, reduced living standards to an unbearable level. By 1987, factory workers marched in protest through the streets of several Romanian cities.

*REPORT TO THE UN COMMISSION ON HUMAN RIGHTS.* The human rights situation in Romania was first examined by the UN **COMMISSION ON HUMAN RIGHTS** at its 1989 session on the basis of alarming information received from a number of reliable sources. On 9 March 1989, the Commission expressed its concern (resolution 1989/75) about serious violations of human rights having occurred in the country and authorized its chairman to appoint a Special Rapporteur to look into the situation and prepare a report.

Appointed as the Special Rapporteur, Mr. Joseph Voyame (Switzerland) completed a report (UN Doc. E/CN.4/1990/28) on 18 December 1989 for presentation to the 1990 session of the Commission, scheduled to be convened on 29 January 1990. However, he later found it necessary to prepare an addendum to the report (UN Doc. E/CN.4/1990/28/Rev. 1) in order to take into account the revolutionary events which occurred in Romania between 19 December and 18 February 1989. He submitted the addendum to the Commission on 22 February 1990.

In the basic report, the Special Rapporteur presented the following general information about Romania (paras. 27–36):

Romania has a surface area of 237,500 square kilometres and a population of about 23 million. Nearly half the population (11.8 million persons) live in urban areas. Until the latest administrative reform of 17 April 1989, the country was divided into 40 departments, plus the municipality of Bucharest, 237 towns and 2,705 communes comprising 13,123 villages (which do not have their own administrative structure).

In historical terms, the union, in January 1859, of Moldavia and Walachia laid the foundations for the modern Romanian State. Romania's independence was proclaimed in 1877 and recognized by the Congress of Berlin in 1878. Following the First World War and the dismantling of the Austro-Hungarian Empire, under the 1920 Treaty of Trianon, Romania acquired Transylvania, Bessarabia and Bukovina. During the Second World War, northern Transylvania was attached to Hungary. Northern Bukovina and Bessarabia were ceded to the Soviet Union and southern Dobruja to Bulgaria. The Peace Treaty signed in Paris on 10 February 1947 re-established the 1920 border between Hungary and Romania and Romanian sovereignty over all of Transylvania.

A pro-Soviet Government headed by Petru Groza was installed in March 1945. After the 1946 elections, most government posts were given to the communists. In December 1947, following the abdication of the King, Parliament announced the establishment of a People's Republic (renamed the Socialist Republic of Romania in 1965). The first Constitution of the Republic was adopted in 1948.

According to the 1965 Constitution (republished in 1987), Romania is a unitary State and a socialist republic, where "the Romanian Communist Party is the leading political force of all of society" (art. 3).

The supreme organ of State power is the Grand National Assembly, the sole legislative organ, which usually meets twice a year. Under the electoral law, the Democracy and Socialist Unity Front, (which is composed of all the country's political and social forces and all grass-roots and civic organizations) organizes elections under the leadership of the Communist Party and "nominates deputies to the Grand National Assembly and the people's councils" (art. 3).

The Council of State, the supreme organ of State power which functions on a permanent basis, is subordinate to, and elected by, the Grand National Assembly. The Council is presided over by the President of the Republic. The President of the Republic, Nicolae Ceausescu, was elected in March 1974 and re-elected in 1975, 1980 and 1985 and has been President of the Council of State since December 1967. He has also been General Secretary of the Romanian Communist Party since March 1965 and President of the Democracy and Socialist Unity Front. In addition, he is President of the National Workers' Council, the National Agricultural Council, the Supreme Economic and Social Development Council, to which the State Planning Committee was recently added, and the Defence Council.

The functions of the Council of State are, *inter alia*: to draft legislation (although it is unable to amend the Constitution); to appoint and dismiss the Prime Minister and the Council of Ministers if the Grand National Assembly is not in session; and to interpret the laws in force. The people's councils, which are local organs of State power, are responsible for local government. They ensure "the economic, social, cultural and civic development of the administrative-territorial units where they have been elected, the defence of socialist property, the protection of the rights of citizens, socialist legality and the maintenance of public order" (Constitution, art. 86). The Council of Ministers is an administrative organ which monitors implementation of the decisions of the Grand National Assembly.

Under the Constitution, justice is administered by the Supreme Court, the district courts, the magistrates' courts and the military courts (art. 101). The Supreme Court is elected by the Grand National Assembly. The Procurator-General, who is responsible for the work of the Procurator's Office, is also elected by the Grand National Assembly. The Procurator's Office "monitors the work of the criminal prosecution and sentencing bodies" and ensures respect for legality and the defence of the socialist régime (art. 112). The people's judges and assessors and the chief prosecutors of the departments and the municipality of Bucharest are elected by the people's councils. The Grand National Assembly and, between sessions, the Council of State are empowered to grant amnesty. In the past few years, amnesties have regularly been granted by decree (17 since 1965), notably in 1981, 1984, 1986, 1987 and 1988. Under the amnesty decree published on 27 January 1988, all persons sentenced to 10 years' imprisonment or less were amnestied. Sentences of more than 10 years were reduced by half, and death sentences were commuted to 20 years' imprisonment.

Until the Second World War, there were some 60 religious sects in Romania. Under Decree No. 177/1948 of 1948, sects wishing to organize their activities have to be recognized by decree of the Council of State on the recommendation of the Department of Worship. At present, 14 religious sects carry out their activities on the basis of statutes adopted by agreement with the State. The Orthodox Church has between 16 and 18 million members. The second largest Church is the Roman Catholic Church, with some 1.3 million members, of whom most (about 700,000) are of Hungarian ethnic origin and about 100,000 of German origin. Of the Protestant churches, the largest is the Reformed Church, which is composed primarily of Hungarians. Mention may also be made of the Lutheran Church, composed mainly of Germans, and the Baptist Church. The Jewish community had about 400,000 members after the Second World War, but most of them have emigrated and only about 20,000 are now left. The Churches which are not legally recognized include the Greek (Uniate) Catholic Church, which was officially disbanded by governmental decree on 1 December 1948 and is reported to have more than 1.5 million members, the Army of the Lord, with about 400,000 members, the Jehovah's Witnesses, and the Nazarene Church.

***CONCLUSIONS AND RECOMMENDATIONS.*** The Special Rapporteur's conclusions and recommendations, as set out in the basic report, were as follows (chap. V, paras. 211–235):

The Special Rapporteur has endeavoured to carry out his mandate as fully and objectively as possible. To this end, he has tried to secure the co-operation of the Romanian authorities and to conduct investigations in Romania itself. To his great regret, he met with a refusal; the Romanian Government deems null and void Commission on Human Rights resolution 1989/75, in which the Commission decided to appoint a special rapporteur to examine the human rights situation in Romania. None the less, the Special Rapporteur has studied the Romanian constitutional, legislative and regulatory provisions as fully as possible, to the extent that they relate to his mandate. In addition, he has made every effort to take the position of the Romanian authorities into account on the basis of the reports which they have sent to various United Nations bodies or specialized agencies.

In order to compile the information necessary for the fulfilment of his mandate, he interviewed a large number of persons who had come to Geneva to provide him with information. In addition, he went to Hungary, specifically in the vicinity of the Romanian-Hungarian frontier. There he was able to interview some 60 recent emigrants from Romania who belonged to various ethnic groups and came from all sectors of Romanian society.

Lastly, he consulted a very large number of documents relating to the human rights situation in Romania.

The information thus gathered does not, of course, enable the Special Rapporteur to draw absolutely certain conclusions, such as might derive from a thorough inquiry in Romania itself. Nevertheless, this information is sufficiently precise and consistent for reasonably reliable observations to be made. In this regard, the Special Rapporteur emphasizes that he has not taken account of isolated allegations; each of the points noted is based on several sources of mutually corroborative information. As to the numerous cases listed in annex 1, they are essentially intended to illustrate observations based on more general information. Lastly, the Special Rapporteur has taken into consideration only relatively recent information and has not in principle, dealt with the period before 1980, even though many violations prior to that date were brought to his attention.

In these circumstances, the Special Rapporteur finds that the Commission on Human Rights has justifiably concerned itself with the situation in Romania. This country is indeed a party to most of the international conventions formulated within the United Nations system which universally protect human rights; it submits the reports called for under these instruments and takes part in discussions on them. It is also a party to the Final Act of the Helsinki Conference on Security and Co-operation in Europe, and to the Concluding Document of the Vienna Meeting relating to the Follow-up to the Helsinki Agreements. It should nevertheless be noted that, in practice, these international instruments are frequently ignored or are only partially implemented in Romania. In these conclusions, the Special Rapporteur will not recapitulate everything stated in the earlier parts of this report. He will simply point out what, in his view, constitute the major violations of the various instruments which protect human rights and by which Romania is bound.

With regard to the right to life, the Special Rapporteur was informed of various cases of deaths or disappearances, either following ill-treatment during interrogations or detention periods, or in the course of attempts to leave the country without authorization. He was unable to elucidate these cases.

As to the right to physical and moral integrity, the reports received are numerous and consistent enough to prompt the conclusion that this right is frequently violated: brutal treatment of persons arrested during attempts to cross the frontier illegally; intimidation, psychological humiliation and maltreatment, including torture, of detainees in order to obtain confessions; poor conditions of detention.

Respect for privacy is frequently violated through arbitrary interference, such as searches and seizures, wire-tapping, confiscation or monitoring of correspondence, restriction of personal or telephone contacts, and gynaecological examinations to prevent interruptions of pregnancy.

With regard to the administration of justice, the Romanian Constitution and laws provide guarantees which are in conformity with international standards. But these guarantees are restricted by decrees, ministerial orders and directives, some of which are not published. Thus, searches and arrests are often carried out without a judicial warrant, detainees are sometimes held incommunicado for several months, and prisoners are frequently deprived of their right to know the charges against them, to communicate with their relatives and to be assisted by a lawyer of their choosing. Furthermore, trials are often held *in camera,* and restricted residence is imposed, even though this measure is not provided for under Romanian law.

Freedom of movement is subject to many restrictions. For instance, young people who have completed their education are required to accept the job assigned to them for several years, often far from their families. The right to leave the country is restricted and is frequently applied in an arbitrary fashion; would-be emigrants are often subjected to harassment, sometimes lose their jobs, or are demoted or even imprisoned; persons who attempt to cross the frontier illegally risk prosecution, and it is not unusual for the families of those who have emigrated without authorization to suffer reprisals. It is interesting to note that, despite these dangers, more than 20,000 persons emigrated clandestinely between mid-1987 and October 1989. Lastly, many families are split because their members who have stayed in Romania are not allowed to leave the country.

Freedom of thought, conscience, religion and belief is restricted. Fourteen Churches are recognized; others, such as the Romanian Greek (Uniate) Catholic Church are illegal. The recognized Churches are subject to supervision by the Department of Worship. Faculties of theology can accept students only according to very limited quotas, and even these are being reduced. Religious literature is insufficient; the importation of Bibles, in particular, is subject to severe restrictions. Church members are not allowed to take up certain professions, such as teaching. Some of them have even been subjected to harassment or other penalties.

The broad and sometimes arbitrary interpretation of certain constitutional and legislative provisions leads to serious restrictions on freedom of opinion and expression. Criticism of governmental policy is not permitted. Many persons have for this reason been subjected to various repressive measures, such as police surveillance and summonses, searches, restricted residence, a ban on receiving visitors, disconnection of telephone service, monitoring of correspondence, and even ill-treatment, loss of employment and imprisonment. In addition, writers, journalists and poets have been deprived of the right to publish their works. Contacts with foreign visitors are strictly monitored, as is the possession of typewriters and photocopying machines. Persons who lose their jobs for political reasons are sometimes later prosecuted and convicted of "parasitism".

Freedom of assembly and association is similarly restricted. The general and vague wording of certain constitutional and legislative provisions has made it possible to prohibit any exercise of this freedom which is not in line with governmental policy. In particular, various penalties, including imprisonment, may be imposed on persons who attempt to exercise their right to take part in public affairs by joining a disbanded party, attempting to form a new party or organizing groups of students and young workers who are critical of governmental policy.

The right to work is subject to many infringements. The linking of remuneration to the total output of an enterprise often entails major wage cuts for workers in enterprises which are unable to achieve norms owing to shortages of electricity, raw materials or adequate tools. Working extra hours is common. It should also be noted that workers are assigned to jobs in areas far from their homes and, for various reasons, some are subject to discrimination in the choice of occupation or job and in opportunities for promotion. Trade union rights are also severely restricted. In particular, workers cannot form trade union organizations of their choice and strikes have been harshly suppressed.

The right to an adequate standard of living is relative and depends, of course, on the country's economic situation. It must be admitted, however, that it is not sufficiently guaranteed in Romania. A large segment of the population has great difficulty in obtaining adequate food, especially for young children. In winter, inadequate heating makes life difficult in homes and work places. The rural systematization policy and the abandonment or demolition of individual houses which it entails seem to have aggravated housing conditions, despite the efforts of the authorities to build new homes. Lastly, medical care is often inadequate. Post-natal mortality is high, and elderly persons generally receive only limited medical care.

Cultural rights are under attack in various ways. The cultural heritage is threatened by demolitions in the cities, which have already resulted in the disappearance of many monuments of artistic or historic interest. Similarly, the rural systemization plan is endangering the rich Romanian popular culture, which has been preserved and developed in the villages in particular. Literary and artistic freedom can be exercised only within narrow limits. As stated earlier, authors who criticize the Government's policy are frequently barred from publication or penalized in other ways. The theatres are subject to control by the authorities and very few foreign publications are imported.

The rights of members of minorities are particularly hard hit. In this regard, the Special Rapporteur would point out that, in order to ensure the survival and development of minorities, it is not sufficient to make them subject to the same rules as those applicable to the population as a whole. They must be given special treatment, appropriate to their identity and needs. Nothing of the sort can be seen in Romania. In the first place, it is obvious that minorities, more than the majority, suffer most of the human rights violations referred to above. Thus, the posting of young people to work places far from their families in the long run results in a dispersal of the ethnic minorities and a mixing of populations which places their survival in jeopardy. Likewise, being cut off from home affects them more than the majority, because they need contacts with the outside populations with whom they share language and culture.

In addition, there is a definite trend towards the Romanization of ethnic minorities. Thus, the use of Hungarian and German is disappearing from the civil administration, the courts and enterprises, and from the names of towns and villages and road signs.

This trend is also apparent in education. With a few exceptions, higher education courses are now in Romanian only. In primary, secondary and vocational education, the number of schools and classes in which Hungarian is the language of instruction has declined markedly in favour of Romanian. Restrictions on access to higher education and arbitrary postings, have even led to a shortage of teachers of Hungarian in Transylvania. Moreover, it is not uncommon for ethnic Hungarian or German parents to opt for their children to be educated in Romanian from the beginning, in the expectation that they will thus have better prospects.

At the cultural level, there has been a decrease in creativity and activities in the minority languages. This phenomenon is particularly apparent in the theatre, and on television and radio. While publications in Hungarian are still relatively numerous, they are concentrated in a single publishing house, and the importation of publications from Hungary has been stopped.

The situation of the churches in which a majority of members are ethnic Hungarians or Germans is particularly precarious. The number of theology students, for example, is specially limited and available religious literature is inadequate. Moreover, severe restrictions limit relations with sister Churches in Hungary and other countries. And it seems that, in some Churches, senior members who have been placed in office with official backing themselves help to persecute members of the clergy and congregations who express views critical of governmental policy.

In general, the minorities complain of living in a hostile climate, which is aggravated by the media and school-books.

These are the main points which the Special Rapporteur wishes to highlight. However, it is apparent from a review of the documents forwarded by the Romanian authorities that they deny that human rights are violated in their country or maintain that they limit such violations to isolated cases.

The Special Rapporteur wishes to state that he fully appreciates what has been achieved in Romania during the past few years or decades: the repayment of the external debt, major industrialization, 10 years of compulsory education for all, a figure which is expected to be raised to 12 in 1990. However, he is of the view that these achievements do not justify the infringements of human rights to which he has drawn attention.

In conclusion, the Special Rapporteur proposes to the Commission on Human Rights that it should make the following recommendations to the Romanian authorities:

(a) They should bring all laws, decrees, regulations and directives into line with the international instruments for the protection of human rights to which Romania is a party, and should make them public if they have not already done so;

(b) They should ensure that these international instruments are strictly implemented in practice;

(c) In so doing, they should pay special attention to the situations noted in this report.

*"A SPECIAL VIEW OF THE ROMANIAN CASE."* At its 1989 session, the UN SUB-COMMISSION ON PREVENTION OF DISCRIMINATION AND PROTECTION OF MINORITIES examined and took note of the report entitled *Human Rights and Youth* (UN Doc. E/CN.4/Sub.2/1989/41 and Add. 1), prepared at its request by its Special Rapporteur, Mr. Dumitru Mazilu (Romania).

In the addendum to the report, Mr. Mazilu presents "A Special View of the Romanian Case," in which he describes with revulsion the situation confronting young people in Romania and other countries like it where dictatorial regimes have destroyed traditional values, negated human rights and fundamental freedoms, and courted economic disaster while maintaining that they are democratic.

Once a member of the Romanian State Security Council, a representative of his country at many international conferences, and a propagandist for the Ceausescu regime, Mr. Mazilu wrote from first-hand experience and obvious conviction. However, he was not authorized by the competent Romanian authorities to travel to Geneva in 1987 or 1988 to present his report to the Sub-Commission, and the report itself was issued by the United Nations only after the International Court of Justice had been requested by the UN ECONOMIC AND SOCIAL COUNCIL for an advisory opinion.

On 22 December 1989, a group calling itself the Council of National Salvation announced that it had overthrown the Ceausescu regime and would form a provisional government. Mr. Dumitru Mazilu was first deputy chairman of the Council and chairman of its Constitutional, Legal and Human Rights Working Committee. The chairman of the Council, Ion Iliescu, later was elected president of Romania.

Unwilling to examine Mr. Mazilu's report in detail in his absence, the Sub-Commission on 1 September 1989 called upon him (resolution 1989/45) to update it and decided to consider it at its August 1990 session. The text is as follows:

### I. Unprecedented Aggression Against the Rights and Freedoms of the Younger Generation. Grave Dangers to the Moral Health of Young People

Niccolò Machiavelli came to the conclusion that politics was immoral, that rules behaved cynically and that "the end justified the means"—he was referring to the need to establish a unitary national State in Italy under the aegis of absolute monarchy. Many theorists since his day have exposed the use of political methods and means that conflict with ethical requirements. Jean-Jacques Rousseau disapproves the use of such methods and means, while Montesquieu argues that Government needs to be based on certain laws which, "in the broadest sense, are the necessary relationships that derive from the nature of affairs".

The passage of time has brought to the fore, with ever-increasing insistence, the moral prerequisites for any Government, making it plain that falsehood, hypocrisy and imposture deeply undermine the foundations of any society, endangering the moral health of the younger generations. While anyone is shocked by the falsification of the truth, by the onslaught of falsehood, shuddering when he finds that hypocrisy has become the habitual formula of Government in some countries such as Romania, and that attempts to unmask imposters are put down with a violence and brutality hard to describe, the young generations are simply traumatized by the injustices and wrongs they find proliferating

around them. More than once the desperate cries of the youngest among us have profoundly shaken us and brought us back to the earth of some of the crudest realities, reminding us of the nightmare world we have been thrown into by odious tyrants to whom the most elementary human feelings are unknown and whose "morality" consists in crushing the individual, destroying his personality and keeping him in slavery.

How can it be, the young Romanians ask us, that in our century, in which civilization has attained unimagined heights, whole peoples should be terrorized in the world's plain sight, while criminal tyrants, instead of being removed and punished as they should be, are glorified by a cult of disgusting vulgarity?

How can it be, they wonder, that the greatest imposters should install themselves at the head of nations and become their absolute spokesmen?

How is it possible to endure such humiliation, such violence and such feudal despotism?

What contempt for man, what effrontery and what barbarity have been shown by tyrants who, labelling millions of people as enemies of the people, traitors to the country or foreign agents, have sent them to their deaths with a mere signature, ordering them to be basely executed in death camps!

How has civil society been able for so many decades to allow a few tyrants to expropriate all the property of its members, to reduce their homes to rubble, to destroy their way of life, to crush their personality?

What kind of civil society is this, in which a person's life no longer counts, the individual being transformed into a beast of burden useful only to put into practice the tyrants' plans of aggrandisement, so as to assure their immortality?

How has it been possible to reach the point at which a person is denied the right to food and to heating for his home in severe winters, while children and old people are robbed even of the right to survive?

Not even in a nightmare world does it seem possible to hear that—as is happening in Romania—newly born babies are denied registration for the first three to four weeks, while old people are refused aid in case of need if they have reached the age of 60, and while medicine is out of the question altogether. "Irresponsibility, indifference, recklessness; what is it all about?" civilized society asks itself, and wonders.

There is no doubt that torturing millions of people means bringing together in one place all the filth and all the vileness of the most aberrant and odious dictators known to history.

Only in our own day, after several decades of infinite sufferings, have the younger generations' questions, their desperate cries, begun to receive frank answers. Obviously it is very late but, anyway, better late than never.

The young people's reprobation and bitterness pour out in waves: "How has it been, and how is it still, possible in some countries that evil should reach unimaginable dimensions and the reaction of civil society be paralysed or quasi-paralysed?"

The younger generations vehemently condemn these odious deeds, but at the same time demand guarantees that they will never be repeated.

Gradually madness is giving way to reason. The peoples have begun to expose and condemn the crimes of Stalin and the other tyrants, unmasking the brutal violation of the elementary rights of hundreds of millions of people.

But if the truth comes to light only after the tyrants' death, it means that the societies which have had the misfortune to fall into the hands of despots are condemned to bear unimagined torments until they pass from the scene.

However, the younger generations and contemporary civil society will not accept this any more. Millions upon millions of young people in Romania demand that an end should be put to the repressive barbarity, oppression, humiliation and slavery and that respect for the human being should be guaranteed in a truly civilized society.

The veil of falsehood and hypocrisy has fallen. Anyone who tries to hide behind it nowadays is building vain hopes that he will not be unmasked.

**A. The Attempt to Mislead Millions of People by Empty Promises and to Conceal from Them the Truth Concerning the Economic Disaster into which They Have Been Plunged by a Despotic Government is not Merely a Profoundly Immoral Act but an Unspeakable Crime.** 1. *The High-handedness of Dictators Means the Failure of a Whole National Economy.* For modern society, in which science and technology have reached such high levels, it is unimaginable that one individual, having reached the summit of the social hierarchy—as is happening in Romania—should dictate the installation of large economic units, fix their parameters of operation and draw up their programmes of activity without a single specialized study or a single economic calculation. Any rational person understands that this is an act of madness.

Then how are we to explain the incredible fact that the best specialists in the field concerned have not given their opinion, while ministers, heads of economic departments, their deputies and other managerial staff comply with insane directives, setting economic objectives and building on them, even ahead of time, while aware that they will be a failure, that they will go bankrupt, before they have managed to carry out their production programmes?

If it were a matter of an isolated case, we would doubtless try to find some attenuating circumstances. But when it is a matter of dozens, of hundreds of similar cases, one shudders!

Only by economic diktat has it been possible in Romania to spend billions of dollars buying obsolete factories abroad and to install them in the national territory without a single prospect of marketing their products. The only objective attained has been to save foreign firms from bankruptcy and to increase the foreign debt of the countries concerned by several billion dollars.

Only by economic diktat has it been possible to establish giant petrochemical plants in Romania without having assured raw materials and without any of the necessary commodity markets. In this way, millions of people have been deprived of the strictly necessary fuel for public and private transport.

Only by economic diktat has it been possible to establish mammoth iron and steel plants in this country at a time when the civilized countries have been closing down their large works owing to the inefficiency of this sector. The only "objective" attained has been to increase the dependence of the people in question on sources of raw materials and energy in other countries, even on other continents, and to maintain bankrupt sectors that have no chance of recovery. The population concerned have been deprived of the necessary light and heat for their homes.

The economic diktat in Romania has led to the establishment of industrial sectors at random, in the absence of assured sources of raw materials and energy and of outlets for their products, not to speak of skilled manpower for the peak areas of modern technology.

Folly enthroned, with just enough "gumption" to order, to demand the doing of what is objectively impossible, has cost and is costing the peoples concerned billions of dollars to maintain bankrupt economies. Every month ministers of finance are forced to squeeze money out of dry stone in order to prolong the agony of economic colossi maintained with the means of subsistence snatched from the mouths of millions of people, merely in order that the "genius" of the tyrants who dictated their installation should not be called into question.

But the price is too high. The truth has come to light. The economic disaster is experienced by everybody.

An economy built on the high-handedness of dictators, on incompetence and defiance of the most elementary requirements of modern science and technology, is turning into an unbearable burden for the peoples concerned.

Neither concealment of the real figures nor their systematic falsification can cover up the disaster in Romania any longer.

Then why do not the economic summits demand that the race to catastrophe should be brought to an end immediately?

Romanian youth is horrified by the indolence and lack of dignity of the ruling hierarchy.

The ruling hierarchy, however, is terrorized by the repressive measures of the dictatorial clan. Everyone is afraid to act, especially when that means not only losing one's job but also losing one's freedom and life. Everyone is waiting for the natural dénouement—the disappearance of the tyrants—and hoping for a new order of affairs thereafter. A sad and barbarous option!

Why should we accept falsehood and hypocrisy? Who gains from them? Not even the dictators. No one believes any longer in the claim that they are ignorant of the sad reality.

At first people were surprised that those around the tyrants paved their way with invented achievements, but when they found that even they required them to embellish the reality and conceal the disaster, they grasped the unbelievable dimensions of the enthroned falsehood.

Cowards lie to you and you lie in your turn to others. What vileness! What human squalor!

2. *Two Worlds: the Palaces of the Despots, and Concentration Camps for Millions of People.* While heaping the most savage curses on the leaders who preceded them, accusing them of having ground down and exploited their own peoples, the new masters install themselves in their castles after having invested billions to rebuild them in an incredible profusion of luxury and wealth.

To the existing palaces, ultramodern new ones are added, as is happening in Romania: palaces at a level of luxury unknown even to the most extravagant monarchs. Sumptuous villas and pleasure grounds scattered all over the national territory; fabulous sums in accounts at the biggest international banks; all the countries' forests as hunting grounds, with the game prepared and lured within range of the tyrants' guns; special aircraft that bring in gowns and luxurious furs from famous fashion houses in exchange for exorbitant sums; culinary preparations of the most sophisticated kind, flown in in special containers. . . . And when you think that the dictators do not even have a salary that can be increased or reduced according to need!

This is the world in which the dictatorial cliques take their ease, while millions of people live in some sort of "matchboxes", grouped together in a kind of concentration camp, with wages that do not afford them even the most wretched level of subsistence. In Romania they chase about desperately in search of a morsel of bread with which to feed their children. Unhappily, however, they often return home empty-handed.

No one claims that those invested with certain responsibilities should not benefit from living conditions that allow them to devote their full time to the proper conduct of public affairs, but the concentration of so much display and luxury at one extreme and of squalor and indigence at the other builds up the hatred and indignation of the oppressed against the flagrant injustices sanctioned with the most shameless effrontery by the dictators.

And when you think that the new rulers in Romania sneaked into power with slogans of condemnation directed at the wrongs and injustices committed by previous societies!

Today, with the most alluring promises concerning right, truth and justice, the Romanian people have seen themselves reduced to the cruellest poverty by rulers whose only "merit" consists in lying with even greater shamelessness and subjecting human beings to tortures that even the most ferocious tyrants never imagined.

3. *The Megalomania of Dictators Means the Proliferation of People's Sufferings.* After having assumed discretionary powers for life, the dictators want to remain in history, enduring even after death. The Pharaohs organized the building of the pyramids. The *Roi Soleil* sponsored the erection of Versailles.

The reigning princes of smaller countries have raised churches, cathedrals and other places of worship. Whenever they emerged victorious in the struggle against foreign invaders, they built a holy place in which to raise a hymn of thanksgiving to Almighty God.

The despots of today wish to distinguish themselves, not by erecting holy places, but by destroying them, as is happening in Romania today.

Gigantic structures, of a quality and taste that are dubious to say the least, take the place of old and durable civilizations. They set tens of thousands of men to changing watercourses and building all kinds of canals for which there is not a single practical use, save only to secure their immortality.

And as the despots' desire to endure for centuries grows stronger, their megalomania takes on insane dimensions. And while the tyrants, for the sake of history, raise megalomaniac edifices in immortal memory of themselves, the national economies of their countries are destroyed and the sufferings of millions upon millions of people attain paroxysmal levels.

Even the most faithful disciples of the dictators sense the disaster, glimpse the catastrophe. Natural questions are put with ever-increasing insistence: "Until when?" "How far is it possible to go?"

Until the youngest scion of Romania wants to know why the truth, the bare and unvarnished truth, is not told about the economic depression. Why people lack the necessary shred of dignity to throw their guilt, all their guilt, in the dictators' faces.

"Through your folly and diktat you have overturned the peoples' traditional values!"

"Through your folly and diktat you have destroyed the national economy!"

"Through a megalomaniac and despotic vision you have brought us to the brink of bankruptcy!"

"Through your Government, you have shown the greatest contempt and the deepest disdain for the human being!"

"You must answer to the peoples for your criminal deeds!"

But for falsehood and hypocrisy to be eliminated once and for all from the activity of any Government, that Government must be built on consistently democratic foundations, so that dictatorship and dictators will no longer find a place.

## II. The Younger Generation Has Been Swept Clean of Any Faith in a Political Régime Which, While Practising the Most Odious Dictatorship, Has the Audacity to Maintain That It Is Profoundly Democratic

Since the most ancient times, the world's great thinkers have spoken out in favour of stable social orders based on democracy. Heracleitus holds that the progress of society can be assured if men will learn to promote, to heed and to respect the best among them. Marcus Tullius Cicero points out that democracy ensures freedom and equality, the State being conceived as *res populi* or *res publica*. Thomas Jefferson has demonstrated that the foundation of democracy and progress is liberty, while Nicolae Bălcescu has shown that a true democracy is "the rule of the people by the people". In his view a democratic republic is one in which "the people will be sovereign, that is to say their own master", and will obey only "officials of their own choosing". These officials—says the great thinker—must act and work only in the name and interest of the people, being always prepared "to give back the office that has been entrusted to them, when the time for which they received it has come to an end". The same thinker points out that "the first condition for the moral development of a State, for its political existence, is freedom of the people and equal rights".

In our own day Raymond Aron, Sartre, André Malraux, Allain Touraine, Marian Irish, James Prothro, René Cassin and virtually all the great thinkers of the world regard freedom and equality as the indispensable foundations of democracy.

**A. Discretionary Dissociation.** Democracy has always aimed to participate both in the preparation of decisions and guidelines for economic and social development and in their execution, their practical application. Even the very supporters of forms of Government based on dictatorship recognize, at least theoretically, that participation must be assured, in certain forms, for both components of the leadership. The dissociation of these fundamental components, through the right of decision being monopolized by a few individuals or even by a single individual—as is happening in Romania—is a discretionary act that demonstrates the abandonment of any appearance of democracy and the installation of despotic forms of Government.

1. *The Dictation of Decisions. Unlimited Power Takes Maniacal Forms.* There can be no doubt that the process of decision-making constitutes the most sensitive aspect of Government. For this very reason, precise rules have been framed and laid down concerning the drafting, definition and adoption of decisions with a view to satisfying the requirements of objectivity and timeliness and, more particularly, the requirements of economic and social progress within one or other country. The broader, freer and more genuine the participation in the drafting and preparation of political, economic, social or cultural decisions, the steadier, more useful and more efficient those decisions will be. At the opposite extreme, the more closely restricted and more incompetent the participation in such preparation, the more arbitrary it will prove, regularly conflicting with the most elementary requirements of progress and development.

Notwithstanding these major desiderata, the decision-making process has nevertheless attained in some countries—in Romania for example—such a degree of concentration that nearly all the problems of development are in practice decided by one person or at most two. From economic development plans for the longer or shorter term to the way wheat, barley or maize is to be sown or harvested or some strictly necessary accessories are to be imported, to the approval of a few dollars with which to send a specialist abroad, everything is decided by a single person, who has accumulated powers that are unimaginable save in the most absolute of feudal monarchies. One or two persons lead the sole party that exists, hold all executive power, and subordinate the legislative and judicial powers.

The effects are disastrous, especially in the long term, since in particular, as we have seen, arbitrary decisions on economic problems of major concern have set veritable catastrophes in train and many years of toil and efforts will be needed to set matters right.

2. *The Slavery of Execution.* In the few despotic régimes that still survive, to the great shame of our century, execution of the tyrants' decisions is a field in which no right is reserved any longer, but instead a binding obligation to participate that rests on all members of the society concerned, from elementary schoolchildren to the old and the sick.

When it comes to putting their discretionary decisions into practice, the dictators fix the time, schedule and apply penalties, suspend the payment of wages, dismiss and appoint, send for trial and convict thousands, tens of thousands of people. In the field of execution they are generous, desiring and inviting a very wide, a unanimous participation.

And in order to mark, once again, the "rightness" of the despots' decisions, people are further required to enthuse when they carry out those decisions, to raise hymns of praise and devotion to the "enlightened chiefs, titans among the titans of the world", as the Romanians are required to do. And if they do not do so, they risk their job, with the scrap of remuneration that comes with it; the persecution of whole families; labelling as enemies of the people; conviction, and even death.

Participation only in the execution of the decisions, through discretionary dissociation from participation in their adoption, has become a form of slavery that dishonours the societies which have fallen into the hands of the despots, dishonours the continents on which tyrannical régimes still exist that stand out like so many dark blots on the whole of contemporary civilization.

People, and especially young ones who have greater working capacity, are transformed into a species of robots, being forced to put into effect decisions which have been proved to be not only useless but manifestly harmful.

And when the régimes that practise such forms of dictatorship still have the audacity to maintain that they are profoundly democratic, they show how deep the gulf has become between the rulers and the ruled.

More and more young Romanians are demanding that an end should be put to the barbarity and that there should be a return to civilized ways of governing. They cite more and more frequently the example of the countries where democracy and freedom have triumphed and where officials who do not work in the people's interest are immediately dismissed, while political, economic and social decisions are subject to the direct approval of the people, not through formal and mendacious referenda but through real ones. In these popular consultations, the will of every person counts. He feels that the decisions adopted take this point of view into account.

The younger generations are demanding more and more insistently that their life should no longer be darkened by odious dictatorships and that Government based on democracy and freedom should prevail in all the countries of the world.

**B. Unprecedented Aggression against Man, Pulverization of Freedom and Annihilation of the Personality.** Freedom endures, more than ever, not only in philosophical studies but in political, legal and sociological studies also. Famous poets and writers have dedicated masterpieces to it, while the most talented painters and sculptors have immortalized it in symbolic form.

Freedom, however, is not an abstract idea or merely a subject of theoretical speculation but a major component of people's everyday life. In many countries it has become a shining reality, in others it is recognized but not respected, and in a few countries it continues to be brutally violated.

Developments in several countries over the past few years have led to the release of the adult generations from many sufferings and have filled the hearts of the younger generations with new hopes. The torch of freedom has begun to flicker again even where the chances were thought to be least. Its overwhelming importance in the life of people and of society has started to be rediscovered. Opinions of value concerning it have been taken off the forbidden list, and dogmas are more and more being abandoned and even repudiated.

Many have remembered that Aristotle regards freedom as a major premise of human progress, while Plato regards it as an expression of culture and civilization. Adam Smith appreciates that free initiative lies at the foundation of the modern development of society, while David Ricardo shows that, without freedom, society would mark time, being exposed to phenomena of stagnation with all the adverse consequences that flow from it.

Marx and Engels have shown that freedom is a rational necessity, and on this basis Stalin decreed that anyone who did not understand the requirements of the revolution was not free.

Stalin placed his own interpretations upon the revolution and advanced the thesis that "he who is not with the revolution is against it!" Gradually the diktat made its way in all political, economic, social and military affairs.

In a number of countries, including Romania, the components and manifestations of freedom, one by one, have been negated, stripped of all content, pulverized.

Free initiative has been outlawed and condemned, and its advocates exiled or executed.

The small peasant farm has been wiped out, and those who tried to resist have vanished without trace.

Great personalities have been reduced to silence. The only voice that can be heard is that of the leader. He thinks for everybody. He thinks best and most boldly. All must listen and submit, and those who did not do so have disappeared into the death camps. Millions of crimes, millions of deaths, more millions of sufferings for which there is no cure. . . .

In order to survive, you have only one course: to renounce freedom, dignity and personality and to live in falsehood and hypocrisy.

Pol Pot in Kampuchea went further. In three years he murdered more than a million people. All those who had in some way succeeded in life, all individuals who had accumulated a certain baggage of knowledge, all intellectuals, were executed without mercy and thrown into common graves.

1. *Violence and Barbarous Aggression by Bulldozers against Human Beings.* In our own day, we have met with even more enterprising despots, who have decided to continue the "revolution" with the aid of bulldozers. Thus in Romania small villas, pretty cottages, traditional rural dwellings—the expression of an entire civilization—have been condemned to

disappear because they are regarded as "a breeding-ground of bourgeois liberalism" that still perpetuates "forms of private property". The bulldozers have gone into action! Hundreds of thousands, millions of people have begun to be expropriated overnight. The home erected with such pains and labour or handed down from generation to generation is razed from the face of the earth at the rulers' behest.

Those who have the strength to survive this barbarous vandalism are thrown into some sort of prefabricated concrete boxes in which the last individual liberties are pulverized in a collectivism characteristic of concentration camps. People are obliged to prepare their food in common kitchens, to wash in common bathrooms, to use common lavatories.

Many Romanians have put an end to their lives, unable to bear any longer the barbarous aggression of the bulldozers, the inhuman way of life provided by tyrants. The survivors remain marked for ever.

The young people shudder to find that such horrors can be perpetrated in our century. Everyone's personality is destroyed.

The sufferings are infinite. The tears of mothers are shed in torrents, and old people's hearts are broken.

The civilized world refuses to understand how such violent aggression against man can be borne.

An X-ray, however succinct, of the societies concerned enables us to reveal the concerted and offensive character of the oppression practised by tyrants who have made contempt for man and his needs into their preferred instrument of government.

2. *Hunger, Cold and Fear in the Service of the Subjugation of Man.* The starving of human beings was one method used even in ancient times by the more powerful armies against cities which did not surrender.

In Romania today the acute shortage of strictly necessary foodstuffs, such as milk for children and daily bread, is of such concern to many large human communities that all other problems, however complex and serious they may be, are relegated to the background.

It is even worse when people are deprived of the heating that is so necessary in the cold seasons. Even if the tyrants advise their subjects to put another coat on, there is no way of tricking the cold. Thousands upon thousands of children and old people are carried off without mercy by the bitter cold. And the struggle for survival keeps more and more individuals away from political and social disturbances.

Many Romanians are saying straight out: "First let my kids escape from this pitiless winter!" or "Help my mother and father to survive!", and then: "I'm not going to bother about other problems any more."

A person who is struggling all-out to feed his children, or to save them from dying of the cold to which they have been exposed by the insane measures of the dictators, no longer has the strength to concentrate on ways of improving the Government, much less on the far more complex and far more risky enterprise of changing it.

If we add to hunger and cold the fear generated by merciless systems of repression such as that of Romania, we shall have a fairly complete picture of the inhuman means of government used by tyrants who are increasingly distinguished by their violent offensive against inherent human rights and freedoms.

As the dictators' failures grow more resounding and the discontent of the population spreads, the machinery of oppression comes into more intensive use. No means is too costly for the dictatorial cliques when it comes to hunting down and annihilating those who dare to oppose the insane course of events. Their correspondence is violated, their telephone conversations are intercepted, contacts with foreigners are forbidden them or strictly monitored, and individual trips abroad are virtually impossible.

A dense fabric of collaborationists is being woven around the inhabitants of the country. Distrust of friends, colleagues and even relatives grows day by day. The oppressors maintain that he who does not love the leader does not love the country, and anyone who dare fail to show his devotion to him or who makes any observation about him is put on the blacklist, hunted down, arrested, tortured and condemned. His life is in jeopardy.

Many young Romanians, learning from the terrible experience of their elders in the matter of barbarous repression, prefer to survive, without renouncing the struggle. They engage is a stealthy battle which they wage with resolution and perseverance, sabotaging the despots' plans of grandeur and splendour, exposing the horrors committed and defusing whenever possible the acts of aggression directed against man, human rights and human freedoms.

The struggle is hard and is waged with unequal forces and resources. The pressure against the human being in Romania grow steadily greater, and the dangers that combine to weaken civil society grow ever more numerous.

3. *The Destruction of Human Values Is Sweeping Away Some Shining Ideals of the Younger Generation.* As the imposture becomes more harmful and the tyrants lose more and more of the ground from under their feet, the repression of potential rivals assumes increasingly offensive and violent forms. In Romania, for example, any leader who comes to public notice, any chief with a fair amount of personality who enjoys the respect of those around him and, especially, those who have gained greater popularity through their personal qualities, capacity for work and civilized behaviour in dealings with people, are immediately discredited, removed from the important public offices they hold, and thrown into the remotest recesses of the economic and social machinery, so that nothing more is heard of them.

Even to mention the name of one of those who have been removed is considered a grave affront to the dictatorial cliques and is reprimanded with the greatest severity. And if there is still anyone in the ruling hierarchy bold enough to pay them a last tribute on the occasion of their death, the gesture is classified even more seriously as entering into compacts with "the class enemy", and the courageous one incurs risks that are difficult to imagine.

In Romania one single leader, one single name is cultivated continuously, insistently, exasperatingly—that of the dictator. Around him are kept or drawn only biddable men, passionate admirers of the "bold thinking" and "innovating activity" of the "titan among titans", of the "hero among heroes", of the "great chief".

If any one of them ventures to open his mouth and say something that is not to the liking of the dictator and his clan, he risks never having his voice heard again, and if someone is inspired to raise his head, he loses it before he begins to be noticed.

Understanding the tragedy of the situation, many of the dictator's collaborators develop a split personality: in public they say what pleases the tyrants and sometimes, in private, with many precautions and great prudence, what they truly think. What a chasm, what a horrifying abyss!

Not only the political field, however, but all other fields fall under the pitiless axe of tyranny. Gradually, but with diabolical persistence and perseverance, all persons of value in science and culture and from all sectors of human creativity are compromised, dishonoured, removed and destroyed.

Some of them, humiliated and discouraged, take the road of exile, trying to do, and sometimes succeeding in doing, there what has been denied them in their homeland. Others give up, no longer having the strength to withstand the onslaught of imposture and of a pitiless oppression.

There nevertheless remain a fair number of valiant people whom only unwavering belief in the rightness of their cause and determination to serve their own nation to the end have impelled to continue creative work and scientific activity, enduring with boundless stoicism the pressures devised by tyrants against them. Devotion to science and creativity and sincere love of country give them the strength to endure anonymity. They do not speak of their research even if it is of national or universal value; they do not mention their creations even if they are exceptional.

A deep silence settles over everything that is bright, bold, advanced. From time to time there is talk of collectives of creative workers, in a barbarous endeavour to dissolve individual merit in a formula of amorphous, standardizing collectivism.

And when you think that all this is only in order to accredit tyrants and members of their clan as the greatest "creators", the most valuable persons of science and culture, who should enjoy "the widest possible international recognition"! Scientific diplomas and certificates are collected from everywhere, by dint of the most persistent intervention and at vast expense.

In this way, as the years of oppression and violence pass, the dictators acquire, alongside the "status" of "political titans", that of "men of science", of "culture". They are the greatest, the most powerful and, at the same time, "the most learned"!

Young Romanians are horrified by so much human baseness, especially when they observe with stupefaction that, even after they have cornered countless certificates and diplomas, the tyrants have not even learned their own language properly. A feeling of fury and indignation takes hold of the young people of Romania when they break through into the basement of the sham dictatorial edifice.

The most intimate and most cherished ideals of the younger generation are swept away when they are deprived of the opportunity to glimpse on the horizon the great lights of science, culture and human creativity; when the examples of their predecessors are denied them; when in literature, in art, in the most widely different branches of science and technology, the leading figures disappear.

The example of prominent personalities has always exerted a powerful force of attraction upon the younger generations. Many young people have become the disciples of scholars, great creative artists, research workers who have devoted their lives to the knowledge and progress of the world. Prominent personalities have always represented shining ideals for the youngest members of the human community. Respect for values stimulates values.

In Romania, contempt for prominent personalities levels, standardizes, blocks material and spiritual progress in all segments of society.

All nations have secured their place in history, not through despotic acts of coercion and oppression by tyrants, but through the contribution made to the advancement of science, culture and human civilization by the great personalities to whom they have given birth. The denial and destruction of real values, the discrediting and ruin of promi-

nent personalities, have grave repercussions on the evolution of human civilization.

Millions upon millions of young people understanding the profound sense of these perennial truths, are boldly raising the banners of struggle and hope, reminding the human community that, the more aggressive, barbarous and reckless the offensive against freedom grows, the closer will come the moment of its rebirth.

**C. Discriminatory Policies and Practices Continue to Do Violence to the Human Being, to Trample His Fundamental Rights and Freedoms.** The old saw "Divide and rule" has not disappeared from the theory and practice of the dictators of our times. We observe with sorrow that there are still rulers who have made *apartheid,* segregation and racial discrimination into a State policy, continuing to spread racial "superiority" and hatred and to pursue a policy of discrimination in all spheres of political, economic, social and cultural life. Measures of forced assimilation are applied to national minorities by the denial of traditions and customs, by attempts to destroy an entire past of history and civilization. Neither the cries of millions of the oppressed nor the strenuous protests of the international community cause dictators to cease their oppression. Acts of persecution and discrimination take ever harsher forms; intolerance makes life impossible.

To the young scions of contemporary society, discriminatory policies and practices, restrictions or preferences based on race, colour or national or ethnic origin are the anachronisms of feudal despots which have been perpetuated by brutal interference with the progressive course of history in this century of human civilization.

The United Nations has given priority attention to the elimination of acts of discrimination and of discriminatory policies and practices, describing them as instruments for the degradation and humiliation of the human being. The General Assembly of the world body has demanded the immediate elimination of discrimination inviting the Administering Powers to repeal discriminatory provisions and to lift discriminatory measures. The United Nations has issued normative instruments condemning discriminatory measures; it has established specialized organs for the elimination of racial discrimination; it has organized long-term programmes of action; it has prepared studies and surveys; it has drawn up very useful recommendations to Member States. The approach to these problems has drawn the attention of the international community to the importance and urgency of solving them.

But despite these measures *apartheid* is maintained, segregation and racial discrimination continue stubbornly to be practised.

Tens of thousands of young people who rise against these anachronistic practices, long condemned by history, fall victim to savage oppression, but they do not give up the struggle.

The disastrous national economic policy of certain dictators has led to the mass exodus of ethnic minorities, for the rulers have made a source of revenue out of the sums collected for each emigrant, as is happening in Romania. A shameful trade, a tragic trade!

Many ethnic groups remind us that "there is nothing more precious than freedom!" "If we cannot attain it any other way, we are ready to give everything we have gained in life in order to see our sons and daughters free!" Trading in people's freedom nevertheless remains a deeply immoral act, precisely because it is so inhuman.

The past years have refocused attention on the complex problem of inter-ethnic relations. Hopes of freedom have been reborn for many ethnic communities in different parts of the world. Millions of people are demanding safeguards for their cultural and religious traditions and recognition of their natural, elementary right to use their language officially and to keep up their customs.

It has been confirmed once again that ethnic problems cannot be solved by discriminatory measures, by oppression, by cultural and social genocide, by displacing millions upon millions of people, by deporting them or by sending them to concentration camps.

A lasting solution to all ethnic questions can be found only through consistent application of the principles of freedom and non-discrimination, principles proven by life and confirmed by social practice.

Young people are deeply attached to these noble principles and express the conviction that only on the basis of those principles will the ethnic communities to which they belong develop and thrive steadily, securing and guaranteeing respect for man and the dignity of the human being.

### III. Manipulation of Relations with Other Countries

The younger generation has begun to decode many of the mechanisms of operation of the monolithic societies ruled over by tyrannical, despotic régimes. One of the most critical has proved to be the manipulation of relations with other countries. This mechanism comprises a co-ordinated system in which every link is tested and retested, conversations are controlled, the places to be visited are carefully chosen, the goods offered to foreigners are selected, and so on.

The concern to embellish reality, and hence to falsify truth, which is present in all other fields of action of tyrannical political régimes, becomes positively obsessive in relations with foreigners, as is happening in Romania for example.

The dictators, knowing themselves to blame for political repression, for their economic failures and for cultural stagnation in their respective countries, take quite exceptional measures to block the circulation of real information, trying to sell foreigners "truths" made up of whole cloth.

In Romania, for example, this is done by establishing a special body of people for contact with foreigners. They escort them continuously, are present at foreigners' conversations with authorized persons, provide them with facts prepared in advance and take them to visit specially laid-out sectors or areas. Foreigners are accorded a hospitality that is out of the common. They are put up in special guest-houses or luxury hotels. They are treated to sumptuous meals washed down with choice wines of which the citizens of the countries concerned do not partake even in their wildest dreams. And in the case of important visiting figures, in view of the difficulty of winning their good opinion, special recreation facilities are made available.

The cynicism of certain tyrants has reached the point where they personally place articles of advertisement, and large sums from the budgets of the countries concerned are squandered on their publication.

Romanian youth is revolted by this profoundly immoral form of manipulation of foreigners. The "truths" which are served up to them represent gross falsehoods, a deliberate attempt to mislead. Any means is good enough when it comes to preventing discovery of the discontent and sufferings of the people oppressed by tyrants. But as a rule the lie is exposed and the truth comes to light.

Instead of being wasted on falsifying the truth, such efforts should have been concentrated on giving people the pleas-

ures they deserve, the freedoms that belong to them, a dignified and happy life. There is not a single young person who thinks otherwise.

But then there would be nothing hidden, nothing falsified.

### IV. Non-interference in Domestic Affairs Is not a Tool for Covering Up the Crimes of Tyrants against Man

The principle of non-interference in domestic affairs (non-intervention) was conceived as an instrument for protecting and guaranteeing the sovereign equality of States and the right of peoples to self-determination and to international peace and security. It is unanimously acknowledged that interference or intervention in domestic affairs means an attempt to stifle the aspirations of peoples to free development. Several cases are known in which a great Power, finding that the constitutional Government of a country which is under its influence has attempted to give greater freedom to the people in question, has intervened brutally, stifling in blood the aspirations of millions of people to free development. And to keep up appearances, they have set up puppet Governments which have labelled the constitutional representatives of the countries concerned as "enemies of the people" and have asked foreign Powers to intervene. As a result, it has been only a matter of time before the strivings for freedom of the peoples in question were crushed under the tracks of the foreign tanks invited to intervene.

But whereas in this case we are concerned with intervention of a violent brutality in the domestic affairs of other countries, how can the expression "interference in domestic affairs" be applied to a notification concerning the violation by certain rulers of international undertakings to respect human rights?

To plead non-interference in domestic affairs, as the Romanian rulers are doing, in cases of brutal and systematic violation of the Universal Declaration of Human Rights, the International Covenants on Human Rights and other commitments assumed concerning respect for the inherent rights and freedoms of the human being, including countries' own constitutions, is not only an illegal act but also a profoundly immoral one.

An attempt to cover up acts of violent oppression of the fundamental rights and freedoms of millions upon millions of people by torturing them individually and destroying their personalities, while maintaining that this should be a matter within the domestic competence of the rulers, forms part of the arsenal that the tyrants bring into play in order to give themselves a free hand in committing crimes of varying degrees of gravity in the countries in which they have cornered power. Disregarding any standard of justice or morality, they behave like the most odious of feudal despots, regarding the country in which they exercise their dictatorship as their own estate and the people as their own slaves.

They ostentatiously reject any critical observation concerning the abuses and crimes they commit, admonishing everybody that they are interfering in their domestic affairs and reminding everyone that "at home they do as they see fit!"

They are not interested in what is right and what is wrong, what is legal and what is illegal, much less in what is moral and what is immoral. Their cynicism reaches the point of declaring that "they do everything for the people's good", whereas those who venture to make critical observations "are unacquainted with reality".

It is plain for anyone to see that concern for the respect

of the fundamental rights and freedoms of the human being constitutes a national and international duty of the first order, since man represents the supreme value and since all activities within the frontiers of nations, as well as those within the framework of international co-operation, should be subordinated to his well-being and happiness. The Charter of the United Nations specifies among its purposes and principles priority for international co-operation in promoting and encouraging respect for human rights and for fundamental freedoms for all. At the same time the Charter lays on Member States the obligation to fulfil in good faith the obligations assumed by them.

In the light of these fundamental principles, who can be allowed any longer to maintain that an action to put an end to crimes directed against man would be an interference in domestic affairs?

Who nowadays can have the impudence to assert that, by reminding certain rulers that they are disregarding their own international undertakings in keeping hundreds of thousands of people in terror and slavery we are violating their "right" to apply the world regulations as they choose?

If we add to this the assessments of some great theorists of international law, we shall understand even better the inconsistency of pleading non-interference in domestic affairs when it is a matter of violence being done to such generally recognized values as the freedom and dignity of man. Great thinkers like Oppenheim, Lauterpacht, J. Fawcett, I. Brownlie and others have convincingly demonstrated that concern to assure and guarantee human rights cannot be described as interference in domestic affairs, considering that these values enjoy universal protection. This legal and doctrinal point of view is considered natural in all the civilized countries of the world.

The only people who dispute it are the despots, the tyrants, who are still to be found here and there, evoking periods of the saddest memory from human history.

They, the tyrants who still exist to the shame of the blue planet, reject any critical observation. They, the despots who remind us of barbarism, want to manipulate their subjects without international rules, without criticism, without comments from outside. They, the tyrants, despots and dictators, have no need of outside arbitration. They are the arbiters of their own deeds. And they always note with satisfaction and nonchalance that it.

### CHRONOLOGY OF DOWNFALL OF CEAUSESCU GOVERNMENT.

In the addendum to the report, the Special Rapporteur first presented a chronology of events which had occurred since the completion of the basic report and which had materially altered the situation in Romania. The chronology, based primarily on news items in the international press, was as follows (UN Doc. E/CN.4/1990/28/Add. 1, paras. 9—28):

*16/17 December 1989.* Riots against the Ceausescu Government broke out in Timisoara and were violently put down by the forces of law and order, more particularly the Securitate (State police). The forces of law and order fired into the crowd, killing and wounding many people; the exact number still has not been accurately determined.

*21 December 1989.* A large demonstration was arranged by the Government in Bucharest to support President Ceausescu. However, the demonstration turned against the régime and so triggered the revolution. As a result of attempts to put down the movement, a large number of people were killed and wounded in the capital.

*22 December 1989.* A group of former dissidents and members of the military, proclaiming that they formed the National Salvation Front, announced on television that they had taken control; violent fighting still continued between the army, which had joined the revolution, and members of the Securitate. The Presidential Palace was taken over by the crowd and the President and his wife fled from the capital.

*23 December 1989.* The National Salvation Front announced the release of all political prisoners and the arrest of President Ceausescu and his wife, Elena. Fighting was still going on between the army and the Securitate.

*24 December 1989.* The fighting continued and Mr. Ion Iliescu, the Front's spokesman, proclaimed that the revolution was victorious. He also announced that the presidential couple would be tried by a military court.

*25 December 1989.* The National Salvation Front announced that Nicolae and Elena Ceausescu had been sentenced to death and executed for the following reasons: the genocide of more than 60,000 people in the course of their reign; infiltration by the State by organizing armed action against the people and the authorities; theft and destruction of public property (by demolishing certain buildings and razing towns and villages); misappropriation of the national economy; attempted escape to recover more than 1,000 million dollars in foreign banks.

*26 December 1989.* Mr. Ion Iliescu was appointed Chairman of the Council of the National Salvation Front.

*27 December 1989.* At its first plenary meeting, the Council of the National Salvation Front adopted a number of urgent measures to establish emergency courts to try "terrorists", repeal certain laws of the previous régime, and make arrangements for the distribution of food products.

*28 December 1989.* Mr. Ion Iliescu, Chairman of the Council of the National Salvation Front, described the new organization of power in Romania. The Council, consisting of 36 members, was intended to head the country until elections were held in April 1990. The Council proceeded to appoint members of the government and adopt measures to do away with some earlier legislation and to reorganize the system of government. The Council had an 11-member Executive Bureau headed by Mr. Ion Iliescu.

*29 December 1989.* The Government announced that the new name for the Romanian State was "Romania".

*31 December 1989.* The Chairman of the Council of the National Salvation Front announced the abolition of the death penalty, the introduction of a five-day working week from March onwards and the start of a programme to redistribute collectivized land to the peasants. It was also announced that the Securitate had been dissolved and that its former chief, Iulian Vlad, had been arrested.

*12 January 1990.* At a demonstration by several thousand people in Bucharest, the Chairman of the Front announced that a referendum would be held on 20 January 1990 on restoring the death penalty for "terrorists" and on outlawing the Romanian Communist Party.

*17 January 1990.* The Council of the National Salvation Front repealed the two decrees of 12 January 1990 mentioned above.

*23 January 1990.* The Council of the National Salvation Front announced that free elections were to be held on 20 May 1990 and that the Front, as such, would be a candidate.

*27 January 1990.* The trial began in the Bucharest Military Court of four leaders of the previous régime: Emil Bobu, former number three; Ion Dinca, former Deputy Prime Minister; Manea Manescu, former Deputy Chairman of the Council of State; and Tudor Postelnicu, former Minister of the Interior. On 2 February 1990 they were given life sentences.

*28/29 January 1990.* A demonstration was called in Bucharest by the traditional political parties to protest against the Front's decision to take part in the elections, and a counter-demonstration also took place.

*3 February 1990.* A Provisional Council of National Unity was established to replace the Council of the National Salvation Front. It consists of 241 members, half of the seats being reserved for the political parties (three members each) and the other half for various leading non-governmental figures who played a role in the revolution, as well as for representatives of national minorities.

*9 February 1990.* The Provisional Council of National Unity held its first meeting.

*13 February 1990.* The Provisional Council of National Unity elected Mr. Ion Iliescu Chairman by consensus. The Council decided on a 21-member Executive Bureau. Sixteen standing commissions were set up: Commission on Reconstruction, Economic Development and Foreign Trade; Commission on Agriculture; Commission on Youth; Commission on Foreign Policy; Commission on Science and Technology; Commission on Education; Commission on Culture; Commission on the Environment and Ecological Balance; Commission on National Minorities; Commission on Local Administration; Commission on Organization; National Commission to Consider and Settle Claims and Complaints by Victims of the Dictatorship; Commission on Health; Commission on the Constitution and Human Rights; Commission on Labour and Social Protection; and Commission on Abuses under the Previous Régime.

*18 February 1990.* In a demonstration the government headquarters were stormed and Mr. Gelu Voican-Voiculescu, Deputy Prime Minister of the Provisional Government, was manhandled by demonstrators. In the evening the army took back the government headquarters, after clashes leaving 3 soldiers dead and 20 injured.

While these extraordinary events were taking place, the Special Rapporteur requested the new Romanian authorities to cooperate with him in discharging the mandate given him by the **COMMISSION ON HUMAN RIGHTS,** including the possibility of a one-week visit to Romania to examine the situation on the spot. The request was granted, and the visit took place from 12 to 16 February 1990.

While in Romania, the Special Rapporteur was also able to talk to the leaders of a number of political parties and factions, to representatives of non-governmental organizations concerned with human rights issues, with former dissidents and political prisoners, and with members of the Hungarian and other minorities.

**SECOND REPORT TO THE UN COMMISSION ON HUMAN RIGHTS.** In the addendum to his report to the Commission on Human Rights, the Special Rapporteur summarized and analyzed the information he had received or compiled (chap. II) and presented his con-

clusions and recommendations (chap. III). The conclusions and recommendations are as follows (UN Doc. E/CN.4/1990/28/Add. 1, paras. 65–69):

The Special Rapporteur is pleased to note that respect for human rights has improved considerably in Romania since the revolution of December 1989. The authorities with whom he met were, moreover, unanimous in expressing their firm determination to guarantee both a return to genuine democracy and the full restoration of human rights in all their aspects. They have already taken a number of legislative and regulatory measures for this purpose, together with restructuring measures.

However, although the texts are generally satisfactory, human rights have not actually been re-established; quite frequently, their exercise encounters *de facto* obstacles.

The Special Rapporteur was unable to shed light on the specific cases brought to his attention. He was, however, able to see that there is still an atmosphere of suspicion, if not fear, in Romania and that it will definitely take time to rebuild confidence. Moreover, the idea of the existence of human rights is still not very widespread among the population and measures will have to be taken to make them better known.

The Special Rapporteur particularly wishes to stress that a number of persons who are prominent in political life are still being subjected to threats, including death threats; many are still wary of the Securitate; real freedom to establish and disseminate newspapers and magazines is not yet fully guaranteed; and the problem of ethnic minorities will still require careful consideration and appropriate measures. The Special Rapporteur is obviously not unaware that, in the space of two months, it is impossible to reform institutions, amend legislation and, above all, change ways of thinking in order to re-establish respect for human rights, which have been disregarded for decades. That is a long-term process. For that reason, however, the process calls for constant vigilance on the part of the authorities and citizens.

The Special Rapporteur therefore recommends that the Commission on Human Rights should:

(a) Take note of the considerable improvement in respect for human rights that has taken place in Romania;

(b) Recommend that the Romanian authorities should:

(i) Continue their action to ensure that human rights in all their aspects are respected in their country, both *de jure* and *de facto;*

(ii) Pay particular attention to the points raised in this report by the Special Rapporteur;

(iii) Consider the possibility of using the Voluntary Fund for Advisory Services set up by the Centre for Human Rights in order to establish national institutions for the promotion and protection of human rights and to strengthen existing institutions.

After examining the reports of the Special Rapporteur, the Commission on Human Rights on 6 March 1990 (resolution 1990/50) took note of the considerable improvement in respect for human rights that has taken place in Romania.

The Commission recommended that the Romanian authorities continue their action to ensure that human rights in all their aspects are respected in their country, both *de jure* and *de facto,* and pay particular attention to the points raised in the Special Rapporteur's latter report (UN Doc. E/CN.4/1990/28/Add. 1). It also recommended that the Romanian authorities consider the possibility of using the United Nations Voluntary Fund for Advisory Services as suggested by the Special Rapporteur. Taking note with appreciation of the readiness of the Government of Romania to cooperate with the Commission and its Special Rapporteur, the Commission decided to continue its consideration of the human rights situation in Romania at its 1991 session.

*ROMANIA AS A DEMOCRACY.* On 20 May 1990, Romanian voters went to the polls to participate in the first free national elections in half a century and chose Ion Iliescu as their president. The Iliescu candidacy was opposed, on the one hand, by two long-established political groups, the Peasants Party and the National Liberal Party, and, on the other hand, by a number of new groups, including the Hungarian Democratic Union and the Ecologists Party. Only the Democratic Union, representing the Hungarian minority of more than two million living mostly in Transylvania, made a better-than-expected showing, polling more than 6% of the vote for seats in Parliament.

A new constitution was approved by referendum in December 1991. Based on the French Constitution, it provided for direct election every four years of 143 members of the Senate, 341 members of the Chamber of Deputies and a president who in turn appoints a prime minister.

President Iliescu was reelected with 62% of the vote in a second round of voting in October 1992. However, following the implementation of reforms such as privatization and price increases, large-scale demonstrations and general strikes continued through 1994, including strikes by miners and steel and railway workers.

Ethnic violence continued as well with an increase in violence against Gypsies, forcing many to emigrate to Germany. An agreement was reached in July 1993 on the rights of the substantial Hungarian minority in Transylvania. Training of Hungarian-speaking school teachers and use of bilingual street signs in areas with at least 30% Hungarian populations were both guaranteed by the pact.

Romania entered into an associate agreement with the European Union in February 1993, joined the Western European Union in October 1993 and agreed in December to work toward full EU membership by the year 2000. In May 1994 it became a member of the COUNCIL OF EUROPE, which undertook an investigation of civil liberties in 1994 in Romania.

*REPORT OF THE UN COMMITTEE ON HUMAN RIGHTS.* The COMMITTEE ON HUMAN RIGHTS considered the second periodic report of Romania on articles 13–15 of the International Covenant on Civil and Political Rights (E/1990/7/Add. 14) at its 5th, 7th, and 13th meetings on 4, 5, and 10 May and, at its 25th and 26th meetings tn 19 May 1994, adopted the following concluding observations (paras. 84–100):

*Positive aspects.* The Committee notes with appreciation that the content of the written report and of its oral presentation differ considerably, for the better, from the consideration of Romania's report on articles 10 to 12 in 1988. The new approach of the Government of Romania to international cooperation in the field of human rights, as manifested during the present session, opens new avenues for effective cooperation between the Committee and the State party within the framework of the International Covenant on Economic, Social and Cultural Rights.

The Committee welcomes the efforts made by the State party to carry out a number of programmes and reforms designed to solve the serious economic, social and cultural problems being encountered by the country in its transition to a market economy and to a pluralist democratic political system based on the rule of law and respect for human rights.

The Committee appreciates the willingness and the readiness of the government to cooperate with various regional and global intergovernmental and non-governmental institutions in the field of human rights. In this context, it takes particular note of the cooperation between the Government of Romania and the United Nations Centre for Human Rights under the Country Programme for the period 1992-1994.

The Committee notes that all forms of public education are free in Romania and the particular attention paid by the Government, in a difficult economic context, to the provision of adequate educational facilities for the most disadvantaged groups of children, including the setting up of special schools for children with disabilities.

The Committee takes note of the recognition of the principle of university autonomy, provided for and guaranteed in accordance with article 32, paragraph 6 of the Constitution.

*Factors and difficulties impeding the implementation of the Covenant.* The Committee notes that the structural adjustment programme, now being implemented in Romania, may have adverse consequences for the implementation of economic, social and cultural rights in general and of the rights enshrined in articles 13 and 15 of the Covenant, in particular.

It notes that great practical difficulties exist in the teaching field, especially in terms of a shortage of qualified staff and a lack of adequate premises. Classes are usually overcrowded in spite of a shift system used (with as many as three shifts a day in the same school). Educational materials and necessary technical facilities are also in short supply. In addition, the Committee notes difficulties flowing from the need to develop comprehensive new curricula.

*Principal subjects of concern.* The Committee notes with concern that the whole system of education in Romania is functioning on the basis of governmental decrees and that since the Revolution of 1989 no specific laws have been adopted in this respect.

The Committee is concerned about the absence of a law on minorities in a country such as Romania, given the existence of large gypsy, Hungarian, German and other minority groups.

The Committee is particularly concerned about the realization of the right to education and of the right to take part in cultural life by one of the largest minorities in Romania, namely the gypsy minority. That group, according to the information at the Committee's disposal, continues to suffer many forms of unofficial discrimination which the Government is often unable to prevent or is unwilling to redress. Gypsies continue to face discrimination in workplaces and schools and greater efforts should be made to accommodate the specific cultural and other needs of those groups in relation to these matters. The Committee is concerned that, since the Revolution of 1989, no appreciable improvement has occurred in their situation, and that direct and indirect discrimination appears to continue, especially at the local level.

The Committee is also concerned about the silence in the report with respect to the difficulties encountered by the State party in implementing rights contained in articles 13 to 15 and about the lack of information on the enjoyment of the right to education and the right to take part in cultural life by the gypsy minority.

The Committee wishes to draw the State party's attention to the absence of any reference in the core document to economic, social and cultural rights and to any efforts made for their implementation.

*Suggestions and recommendations.* The Committee recommends that the State party should take vigorous steps to ensure that the right to education and to take part in cultural life is guaranteed to the members of the gypsy minority in full accordance with the provisions of articles 2 (2), 13 and 15 of the Covenant. The Government should: adopt an active non-discrimination policy with respect to this minority; encourage their participation in cultural life; and assure proper participation in educational activities by children belonging to that group.

The Committee also recommends that particular attention should be paid by the Government to the problem of street and abandoned children, and that further efforts should be made to facilitate their access to all forms of primary and secondary education.

The Committee recommends that the Romanian Human Rights Institute, established at the beginning of 1991 in order to foster a better awareness on the part of Romanian public bodies, non-governmental organizations and private citizens of human rights problems, should, in the future, devote greater attention to economic, social and cultural rights.

The Committee, having noted that a joint human rights programme has been implemented in Romania by the United Nations Centre for Human Rights since 1992, encourages the Government of Romania to continue its cooperation with the United Nations and recommends that this programme should be continued in the future. The Committee also recommends that an economic, social and cultural rights component, which is now practically non-existent, should be adequately reflected in that programme.

**BIBLIOGRAPHY.** Fédération Internationale des Droits de l'Homme (International Federation of Human Rights), in *Roumanie: Situation de la Communauté Rom (Tzigane), 1990–91* (Romania: The Situation of the Roma Community [Gypsies], 1990–91). No. 150. Paris: 1992. NGO report, in French.

Funnemark, Bjorn Cato. *SOS Transylvania: A Report on the Suppression of the Hungarian Minority in Romania.* Vienna, Austria: International Helsinki Federation for Human Rights, 1988. NGO report, in English; bibliography, pp. 59–60.

Helsinki Watch. *Destroying Ethnic Identity: The Persecution of Gypsies in Romania.* New York: Human Rights Watch, 1991. NGO factfinding report, in English.

————. *News from Romania: Violent Events of June 13–15.* New York: Human Rights Watch, 1990. NGO factfinding report, in English.

————. *Restrictions on Freedom of the Press in Romania.* New York: 1994. NGO report, in English.

————. *Romania's Orphans: A Legacy of Repression.* New York: Human Rights Watch, 1990. NGO factfinding report, in English.

————. *Romania: Aftermath to the June Violence in Bucharest.* New York: Human Rights Watch, 1991. NGO factfinding report, in English.

————. *Since the Revolution: Human Rights in Romania.* New York: Human Right Watch, 1991. NGO factfinding report, in English.

————. *Struggling for Ethnic Identity: Ethnic Hungarians in Post-Ceausescu Romania.* New York: Human Rights Watch, 1993. NGO report, in English.

Human Rights Watch. "Romania," in *Human Rights Watch World Report 1995,* pp. 216–218. New York: 1995. NGO report, in English.

Index on Censorship. *Romania's Battered Press.* London: 1990. NGO factfinding report, in English.

International Confederation of Free Trade Unions. *Violations by the Government of the Socialist Republic of Romania of the Rights to Freedom of Association and Collective Bargaining.* Brussels, Belgium: 1989. NGO report, in English.

International Federation for the Protection of the Rights of Ethnic, Religious, Linguistic and Other Minorities. *The State of Religious and Human Rights in Albania and Romania.* New York: 1988. NGO report, in English.

Reporters sans frontières. *Roumanie: qui a menti?* (Romania: Who Was Lying?). Montpellier, France: 1990. Conference report, in French.

Shafir, Michael. "Anti-Semitism without Jews in Romania," *Report on Eastern Europe* 2, no. 26 (June 1991): 20–32. Article, in English.

Solso, Christine K. *Ioan Ruta: A Cast Study of Human Rights in Romania.* Minneapolis, MN, USA: Minnesota Lawyers International Human Rights Committee, 1988. NGO report, in English.

United Nations Commission on Human Rights. *Report on the Situation of Human Rights in Romania.* Geneva, Switzerland: 1991. IGO document, in English and French.

**ROOSEVELT (FRANKLIN) FOUR FREEDOMS MEDALS.** Established in 1982, these honorary medals are awarded to individuals or organizations that have been committed to the principles of freedom of speech, freedom of worship, freedom from want, and freedom from fear—the basic democratic principles that President Franklin Delano Roosevelt proclaimed in his historic speech to the U.S. Congress on 6 January 1941. Five medals are awarded annually, one for each freedom and one for overall achievement (the Four Freedoms Medal).

In 1994, His Holiness the **DALAI LAMA** was presented the Four Freedoms award for his efforts to advance human rights in the world and his nonviolent resistance to oppression, particularly in Tibet. Marion Gräfin Dönhoff, journalist and publisher of the Hamburg, Germany, weekly *Die Zeit* received the Freedom of Speech Award for contributing to German democracy. Gerhard M. Riegner, honorary vice-president of the World Jewish Congress, was awarded the Freedom of Worship Medal for his defense of the rights of Jews in particular and human rights in general. Sadako Ogata, UN HIGH COMMISSIONER FOR REFUGEES, received the Freedom from Want honor for her international leadership in alerting the world to its humanitarian responsibilities. And Zdravko Grebo, director of the Soros Foundation Open Society Fund, was honored with the Freedom from Fear Award for his commitment to a multiethnic Bosnian society based on peace, justice, and tolerance.

The 1993 Medal winners were Cyrus R. Vance, diplomat (Four Freedoms Award); Arthur Miller, playwright (Freedom of Speech Award); Rev. Theodore M. Hesburgh, C.S.C., president of Notre Dame University (Freedom of Worship Award); Eunice and Sargent Shriver (Freedom from Want Award); and George W. Ball, diplomat (Freedom from Fear Award).

In 1992, the recipients were Javier Perez de Cuellar (Freedom Medal), Mstislave Rostropovich (Freedom of Speech), Terry Waite (Freedom of Worship), Jan Tinbergen (Freedom from Want), and the Right Hon. Lord Carrington (Freedom from Fear).

For more information, contact: Roosevelt Institute, 511 Albany Post Road, Hyde Park, NY 12538, USA. Telephone: (914) 229-5321. Fax: (914) 229-9046.

**ROOSEVELT, THEODORE (1858–1919).** The 26th president of the United States of America was awarded the 1906 NOBEL PEACE PRIZE for his work in bringing about a peace treaty between Russia and Japan. Celebrated as a great war veteran, the leader of the "Rough Riders" and hero of the Battle of San Juan Hill, Roosevelt was a controversial choice for the Prize because he had not previously been associated with the cause of peace.

A man of valor and integrity, Roosevelt was known throughout his political career as an opponent of corruption and a defender of imperialism. He believed that "civilized powers" could best maintain peace in the world and that a balance of power among strong nations was a guarantor of peace. A staunch Republican, he served early in his political career as Police Commissioner of New York City and a leader of the New York State legislature. He was appointed Assistant Secretary of the Navy from 1897 to 1898, resigning this post at the outbreak of the Spanish-American War to form the First United States Voluntary Cavalry ("the Rough Riders"). Returning to the United States as a

war hero, he was elected Governor of New York State and was picked by Republican presidential candidate William McKinley as his running mate. The McKinley-Roosevelt ticket was victorious in the elections of 1900; when McKinley was assassinated months later, Roosevelt assumed the presidency. He was re-elected in 1904. His presidency was marked on the domestic front by improved conditions for workers and immigrants (although Japanese immigration was restricted under a "Gentlemen's Agreement" negotiated by Secretary of State ELIHU ROOT) and by strong anti-trust legislation.

His foreign policy, however, was strongly imperialist. Among other fronts, Roosevelt was interested in establishing American power in the Pacific. In this vein, he secured Hawaii, Samoa, Guam, and Midway as American territories. At this time, Russia was advancing its interests in China, a move bitterly opposed by Japan. Roosevelt worked to conciliate relations between Russian and Japan largely because he felt that, by restricting Russian power in the Far East, he could maintain a balance of power and further American interests. In 1905, he finalized a treaty, signed in Portsmouth, New Hampshire, between the two powers and averted a war in the Far East. He used the Nobel Peace Prize money to establish an industrial peace committee in Washington, D.C., "to strive for better and more equitable relations among my countrymen who are engaged, whether as capitalists or as wage workers, in industrial and agricultural pursuits."

**BIBLIOGRAPHY.** Gray, Tony. *Champions of Peace.* London: Paddington Press, 1976.

Schlessinger, Bernard S., and June H. Schlessinger, eds. *Who's Who of Nobel Prize Winners.* Phoenix, AZ, USA: Oryx Press, 1991.

**ROOT, ELIHU (1845–1937).** This American Secretary of War and Secretary of State received the 1912 NOBEL PEACE PRIZE for his support of international arbitration. In his career in the American presidential cabinet, Root negotiated 23 treaties of arbitration between the United States and Latin American and European countries, as well as with Japan.

Born in Clinton, New York, Elihu Root received his degrees from Hamilton College and New York University Law School. A close friend of THEODORE ROOSEVELT and, like Roosevelt, a reform-minded Republican, Root was appointed Secretary of War under the short-lived presidency of William McKinley. In this post, Root dealt with a revolt in the Philippines by writing a constitution for territorial administration and also founded the Army War College and created a general staff. In 1905, Roosevelt appointed Root as Sec-

# R

retary of State. In this cabinet position, Root worked to improve relations between North and South America, establishing the Pan-American Bureau in 1908. Because of hostility toward Japanese immigrants in California, he negotiated a "Gentlemen's Agreement" between the United States and Japan restricting Japanese immigration but improving conditions for Japanese immigrants already living in the United States. In later years, he served on the **PERMANENT COURT OF ARBITRATION,** was president of the Carnegie Peace Foundation, supported the **LEAGUE OF NATIONS,** and helped to frame the statute for the Permanent Court of International Justice.

*BIBLIOGRAPHY.* Gray, Tony. *Champions of Peace.* London: Paddington Press, 1976.

Schlessinger, Bernard S., and June H. Schlessinger, eds. *Who's Who of Nobel Prize Winners.* Phoenix, AZ, USA: Oryx Press, 1991.

**ROTBLAT, JOSEPH (1909–).** A scientist who worked to develop the first atomic bomb but who then fought against nuclear weapons for over 40 years, Joseph Rotblat shared the 1995 **NOBEL PEACE PRIZE** with the organization he helped to found, the **PUGWASH CONFERENCES ON SCIENCE AND WORLD AFFAIRS.** The Nobel Committee praised Rotblat for "bringing together scientists and decision makers to collaborate across political divides on constructive proposals for reducing the nuclear threat."

The Polish-born Rotblat was working on a one-year atom-bomb project at Liverpool University in 1944 when he was asked to join "The Manhattan Project" at Los Alamos. At the time, Rotblat and other scientists believed that the Nazis were working on developing their own A-bomb and that the only way to halt Nazi aggression was to develop such a weapon for the Allies, as a form of nuclear deterrence. However, he soon learned that the Nazis had abandoned their weapons plan and that the United States was going ahead with the bomb's development. He left the Project immediately and returned to England, switching from nuclear physics to nuclear medicine; he was horrified when he heard of the bombing of Hiroshima and Nagasaki.

In 1955, Rotblat joined Albert Einstein, Bertrand Russell, and six other scientists in signing the "Russell-Einstein Manifesto," which declared that nuclear weapons threaten the continued existence of humanity. The Manifesto led to the first Pugwash Conference, held in Pugwash, Nova Scotia, Canada, which has been an international force since its inception in lobbying governments for disarmament.

*BIBLIOGRAPHY.* Lemonick, Michael D. "The Prince of Pugwash," *Time* (23 Oct. 1995): 84.

**ROTHKO CHAPEL AWARDS.** Founded by philanthropist and human rights activist Mrs. Dominique de Menil, who cofounded the Carter-Menil Awards, the Rothko Chapel of Houston, TX (USA), has established two human rights awards:

*THE ROTHKO CHAPEL AWARDS FOR COMMITMENT TO TRUTH AND FREEDOM.* Established in 1981, these awards are presented every five years to exceptional people who distinguish themselves by their courage and integrity. Each honoree receives $10,000.

In 1991, the recipients were CONAVIGUA, the National Coordinating Group of Guatemalan Widows; Maria Mirtala Lopez Mejia and CRIPDES, the Christian Committee for the Displaced in El Salvador; Ramon Custodio Lopez and CODEH, the Committee for Human Rights in Honduras; Ramiro de Leon Carpio, human rights prosecutor; and Cesar Alvarez Guadamuz, adjunct prosecutor, shared with Sebastian Perebal Suy of GAM, Mutual Support Group, all of Guatemala; Juan Guillermo Cano Isaza and Ignacio Gomes of *El Espectador* of Colombia.

*ROTHKO CHAPEL OSCAR ROMERO AWARD.* This Award commemorates Oscar Arnulfo Romero, archbishop of San Salvador, who was murdered on 24 March 1980, because he opposed the forces of violence and oppression in his country. The Award is presented biennially to a cleric who works in the cause of human rights. The 1992 recipient was Monsenor Rodolfo Quezada Toruna of Guatemala.

For more information, contact: the Rothko Chapel, 1409 Sul Ross, Houston, TX 77066, USA. Telephone: (713) 524-9839. Fax: (713) 524-7461.

**RUSSIAN FEDERATION.** The Russian Federation, formerly the largest republic of the Soviet Union, occupying more than three quarters of its land mass, is bordered by Azerbaijan, Belarus, China, Estonia, Finland, Georgia, North Korea, Latvia, Lithuania, Mongolia, Norway, Poland, and Ukraine. It declared its independence from the Soviet Union in 1991 and, as the perceived successor to the Soviet Union in international affairs, it was granted the Soviet Union's permanent seat on the United Nations Security Council. It comprises 89 federal territorial units, including 21 autonomous republics. Its population is estimated to be 149,608,953, comprising 82% Russian, 4% Tatar, 3% Ukrainian, as well as many other ethnic groups.

The primary religion is Russian Orthodox; Islam is also practiced.

***THE UNION OF SOVIET SOCIALIST REPUBLICS.*** Formerly the Russian Empire, it was declared a republic after the successful insurrection of the Bolsheviks. The new government, elected by the second all-Russian Congress of Soviets, was headed by V. I. Lenin (a pseudonym for Vladimir Illyich Ulyanov). The constitution of the Russian Soviet Socialist Republic was adopted by the fifth congress on 10 July 1918.

Other Soviet republics, including those set up in the Ukraine, Byelorussia, and Transcaucasia, established treaty relations with the Russian Soviet Federal Socialist Republic and, in 1922, joined it in a Union. The Transcaucasian Republic later split to form the Armenian Soviet Socialist Republic, and Azerbaijan Soviet Socialist Republic, and the Georgian Soviet Socialist Republic, each of which remained within the Union of Soviet Socialist Republics.

Before, during, and after World War II, the Soviet Union acquired additional territories. In August 1940, three independent Balkan countries—Lithuania, Latvia, and Estonia—were annexed and incorporated in the union. A part of East Prussia was transferred to the Union in 1946 in accordance with the Potsdam Declaration of the Governments of the United Kingdom, Soviet Union, and the United States of America. A province which had been ceded to Finland earlier was returned to the union in 1947 by the treaty of peace between the two countries. And the southern portion of the Sakhalin and the Kurile Islands were transferred from Japan to the union after the defeat of Japan, by agreement with the victorious powers.

Russian was the official language of the USSR. However, other major language groups included the Baltic, the Finnish, Turki, Mongol, and Romance. Most citizens of the USSR were said to adhere to atheistic or nonreligious beliefs. Under the former constitution, the Church was separated from the State and the school from the Church. The teaching of religious dogma was prohibited, and all public education was of a secular nature. Parents or legal guardians could, however, give their children a religious upbringing in accordance with their own beliefs.

Under the USSR, the Russian Soviet Federal Socialist Republic was the leading and largest political unit; it occupied more than three-quarters of the Union's territory. Sixteen of the twenty autonomous republics lay within the boundaries of the Russian Soviet Federal Socialist Republic: two in Georgia and one each in Azerbaijan and Uzbekistan.

Agricultural collectivization, the policies of Premier Joseph Stalin, and World War II were particularly difficult for the people of Russia where large numbers lost their lives. Reform measures were introduced by Premier Nikita Khrushchev who succeeded Stalin in 1953, but Khrushchev was replaced by Leonid Brezhnev in 1964. A detente with the West in the 1970s was again followed by the chilling of the Cold War in the 1980s, particularly as a result of the Soviet invasion of Afghanistan in 1979. But by 1985, there was a new, reform-minded General Secretary of the Communist Party, **MIKHAIL GORBACHEV.** In 1988, addressing the UN **GENERAL ASSEMBLY** in New York City, he indicated that the entire system of power and administration in his country had been undergoing a profound democratic reform under the process of *perestroika.* This restructuring, combined with a policy of *glasnost,* or openness, led to increased demands for political freedom and autonomy for the republics.

***POST-COMMUNIST RUSSIA.*** The Russian Supreme Soviet, elected in March 1990, elected Boris Yeltsin as chairman and declared sovereignty in June 1990. The Russian Communist Party was also established at that time. Other institutions such as trade unions, cultural organizations and a broadcasting network began to develop on a national level. Many such institutions had not been established independently of Soviet authority, unlike all of the other republics of the Soviet Union.

In the first free presidential elections in June 1991, Yeltsin was elected with 57% of the vote. The day before the signing of the treaty granting autonomy to the republics of the Soviet Union in August, communist officials attempted to take control of the government. The attempted coup lasted three days and brought about the disintegration of many Soviet institutions. Yeltsin's power, already strong after his resistance to the coup, increased when the 5th Russian Congress of People's Deputies granted him, as prime minister as well as president, special powers of executive law-making authority for one year.

Russia was a founding member of the Commonwealth of Independent States which was established by the Alma-Ata Declaration signed by 14 former Soviet republics in December 1991. The members announced the dissolution of the USSR and Soviet President Gorbachev resigned that month. The name of the country was changed to the Russian Federation.

Stringent economic reforms were instituted, including the removal of price controls and privatization of industry. Widespread opposition to the fast pace of economic reform was evidenced by demonstrations by groups as divergent as the neo-communists and the Civic Union. Yeltsin tried to ban opposition groups and although the Constitutional Court ruled that state property under the control of the Soviet Communist Party could be seized, it declared invalid the ban on local communist parties and the National Salvation Front, an alliance of extreme nationalist and communist groups.

Yeltsin also encountered opposition in the Congress of People's Deputies where his choice of Prime Minister was rejected in December 1992 for being too radical in his suggested pace of economic reform. After the Constitutional Court ruled unconstitutional his decision to rule by decree until the April 1993 constitutional referendum, the Congress drafted four questions for inclusion in the referendum intended to demonstrate a lack of support for Yeltsin. Confidence in Yeltsin (57%) and his social and economic reforms (54%) were unexpectedly high. Following Yeltsin's disempowering of Vice-President Rutskoy, the rejection of a draft constitution by the Congress in mid-1993 and Yeltsin's suspension of both the Congress and the Supreme Soviet, the Supreme Soviet declared Rutskoy president. The Congress approved the measure and also voted to impeach Yeltsin.

The conflict between Yeltsin and his opponents came to a head in late September and early October 1993. Demonstrations on the streets by opposing sides and fighting between deputies (and their armed supporters) inside the parliament building (the White House) and troops outside, left 170 dead over the three-day period. A state of emergency was in effect in Moscow for two weeks. After the deputies surrendered, Yeltsin consolidated his power and rejected early presidential elections in favor of fulfilling his mandate through June 1996.

A new draft constitution, with increased presidential power and decreased legislative power, was approved by 58% of those voting in a December 1993 referendum. This version did not grant authority of secession to the republics within the Federation. The constitution, which went into effect in December, guarantees basic human rights, including freedom of movement, expression, and conscience and the provision of health care, housing, education, and legal assistance. It protects the right to form trade unions and prohibits censorship. Although Russian was declared the official language, people are guaranteed the right to use their native language. The president, directly elected for a maximum of two four-year terms, appoints the prime minister with the approval of the 450-member State Duma (lower house of the Federal Assembly). The president has limited authority to declare a state of emergency and impose martial law. The Federation Council (upper house) comprises 178 members, two from each of the 89 constituent members (regions and republics) of the Russian Federation. Both houses are directly elected for four-year terms.

Elections to the Federal Assembly, monitored by 1,000 international observers, were held in conjunc-

tion with the constitutional referendum in December. The extreme right-wing and nationalist Liberal Democratic Party, led by Vladimir Zhironovsky, won the largest number of seats (64) in the State Duma and the largest share of the vote (23%). The three major pro-communist parties obtained 104 seats between them. The Federation Council comprised mainly nonparty regional officials but was reported to be slightly more pro-Yeltsin than not.

***CHECHNYA.*** The republic of Chechnya boycotted the elections. This oil-rich republic of 1.2 million Muslims declared independence from Russia in November 1991 in a long tradition of fighting and striving for independence. In 1944 Stalin exiled nearly all the population of the Chechen-Ingush Autonomous District (as it was then known) to Kazakhstan, in order to prevent them from collaborating with the Germans in exchange for assistance with gaining independence.

Fighting between pro-Russian rebels and forces loyal to Dzhokar Dudayev broke out in Chechnya in September 1991. Then, in an election that Russia declared illegal, Dudayev, a former Soviet air force general, was elected president in October 1991. Russian President Yeltsin sent troops into the republic in November 1991 but, under pressure from parliament, withdrew them within two days. Several warlords battled Dudayev for power from that date; but, following an invasion of at least 20,000 Russian troops in mid-December 1994, Dudayev and his cause for secession enjoyed widespread popular support. Although the Russian Parliament reiterated that Chechnya was a part of the Russian Federation, it passed a resolution criticizing Yeltsin for the use of force.

When Russia launched another full-scale attack at the end of December on the capital of Grozny, whose population had fallen from 400,000 to 100,000, domestic and international condemnation followed. In its March 1995 report, the UN **COMMISSION ON HUMAN RIGHTS** criticized the use of excessive force in Chechnya. However, strife continued as 250 Chechen separatist rebels took control of a hospital and 2,000 hostages in the town of Budyonnovsk in June. After hostages were killed, Russian troops stormed the hospital and further deaths occurred, approximately 150 over two days. The Russian Government negotiated a settlement and safe passage for the rebels back to Chechnya but the demand of the rebels for a cease-fire in Chechnya was unresolved by mid 1995.

***CRIME IN RUSSIA.*** Crime and violence, particularly organized crime, spread dramatically in Russia in the early 1990s. The government signed a pact with the U.S. Federal Bureau of Investigation (FBI) in May

1994 by which the FBI would open an office in Moscow aimed at sharing expertise and trying to stem the tide of drugs leaving Asia for Western Europe. An anti-crime decree was also issued in June 1994 which provided the government with authority to hold mafia suspects for 30 days without charge and to allow police to search without a warrant, with high crime areas coming under "special control."

Russia contributed to the UN peacekeeping mission in Bosnia and Herzegovina and joined NATO's partnership for peace program in June 1994.

***REPORT ON PRISON CONDITIONS.*** At the request of the UN **HUMAN RIGHTS COMMITTEE,** a Special Rapporteur visited the Russian Federation and issued the following conclusions and recommendations (E/CN.4/1995/34/Add.1, paras. 62–86):

The Special Rapporteur would first of all recall that his visit was undertaken at the initiative of the Government of the Russian Federation. He generally encountered a frank acknowledgement of problems, particularly relating to atrocious conditions in pre-trial detention institutions, and a hope that a fresh view from a United Nations perspective of problems that elicit constant concern amongst the Russian authorities, media and public could identify means of overcoming the problems.

The Special Rapporteur found the officials he met to be generally open and anxious to find means of improving the situation. In particular, those with responsibility for places of detention, especially the grossly overcrowded remand institutions, asserted their view that they were called upon to manage a situation that was not of their making and that the conditions added substantially to the demoralization of a staff already demoralized by low pay, low status, understaffing, insufficient material resources, unpleasant working conditions and inadequate training. Many of the officials in management positions had visited penal establishments abroad and aspired to high standards of professionalism. The reality which they were required to manage was an affront to their professionalism.

Despite this commitment, the constituency concerned with the rights of those deprived of their liberty, whether or not actually convicted of any crime, is limited. In the light of this, the Special Rapporteur was impressed by the concern expressed by all his interlocutors at the problem of the treatment of detained persons. Not only was this the case in respect of non-governmental organizations, the media and government officials, it was also true of members of the State Duma whom he met. Some of these had profound political differences, but all agreed on the need to avoid practices, notably the conditions in institutions of detention or remand, that would fall foul of the international legal prohibition of torture or cruel, inhuman or degrading treatment or punishment.

On the other hand, the Special Rapporteur encountered various degrees of despair that substantially increased material and financial resources would be allocated to resolve the problems. This was a question of political priority and it was hard to secure resources commensurate with the magnitude of the problem. How far solutions indeed depend on the allocation of resources will be addressed below. At this point, the Special Rapporteur merely notes that neither con-siderations of principle nor the scarcity of resources can justify the continuance for a moment longer of the most urgent problem, namely, the conditions of detention in some of the remand centres caused by what is inadequately captured by the anodyne word "overcrowding". The Russian Federation is responsible under its own and international law to put an end to widespread conditions that its own officials describe as "inhuman".

The Special Rapporteur is in possession of numerous allegations of beatings perpetrated by police when first detaining suspects or by police or investigation officials when they have them in temporary detention centres (IVS). Alleged cases of beatings on first detention before delivery to IVS or police lock-up may also occur in the way of individual police using their coercive powers for personal ends. It should be particularly difficult for beatings to take place once a suspect is delivered to an IVS, since there is a careful procedure for logging in new detainees. However, there is an initial period where a person may be held, formally for no more than three hours, for screening, identification checks and verification of any earlier police record. During this period the suspect is not logged in. The logging in only occurs after the investigator has produced a form confirming the details the screening is designed to elicit. During this period, there is no record of the detainee's presence and the Special Rapporteur has been given documents confirming to a detainee's lawyer that a particular suspect was held for over 24 hours in temporary detention. The police had denied the suspect's presence to the lawyer. The same could presumably happen in a police lock-up where there is no IVS. Accordingly, the period of temporary detention could provide an opportunity for abuses to occur.

It was not alleged that beatings or other exactions were routine in this phase. On the other hand, there was official acknowledgement that underpaid, overstretched and insufficiently trained police officers might individually be tempted to resort to illegal practices. Also, there remain traces within the police establishment of a reluctance to abandon the authoritarian style of the previous Soviet period. The Special Rapporteur believes that abuses do occur during this period, albeit not systematically.

Preliminary detention in an IVS can, on the recommendation of investigators, be authorized by a prosecutor beyond the normal maximum of 3 days for up to 10 days. Since the Presidential Decree that period can be extended for a further 20 days in respect of those suspected of involvement in organized crime or banditry. Even though access by a lawyer remains applicable, this leads to a condition of vulnerability in an atmosphere characterized by seeming arbitrary deployment of State power in conditions of discomfort. Despite the controls referred to above that would tend to inhibit abuses after a detainee has been logged in, the Special Rapporteur cannot discount allegations that some investigators have at times used coercive physical methods in IVS interview rooms to secure the "cooperation" of a suspect. At the same time, as long as a suspect may be threatened with transfer to a remand prison ("sizo" or investigatory isolator) and conditions in some isolators remain as described above, investigators' main weapon of coercion could well be the very threat of such transfer.

The continuum of arbitrariness reaches its apotheosis in some of the isolators. In the St. Petersburg remand centre of Lebedeva, the Special Rapporteur found no problems falling within his mandate and indeed found conditions to be reasonably humane, as far as a brief visit to limited parts of the institution could reveal. On the other hand, despite the fact that some of the overflow from Kresty isolator in St. Petersburg had been placed in Lebedeva, Kresty remained with an inmate population double its capacity. This meant that cells designed in czarist times for one prisoner and now considered as appropriate to accommodate six prisoners, in fact usually accommodate 12 prisoners who have to sleep in two shifts. The atmosphere and conditions in Kresty are oppressive and degrading. On their own they would justify the emergency measures that will be recommended below.

However, the conditions of detention in Moscow's Butyrskaya and Matrosskaya Tishina No. 1 remand centres, especially in the so-called general cells of these two centres, contrived to be even more disgusting. They are believed not to be unique in the territory of the Russian Federation.

The Special Rapporteur would need the poetic skills of a Dante or the artistic skills of a Bosch adequately to describe the infernal conditions he found in these cells. The senses of smell, touch, taste and sight are repulsively assailed. The conditions are cruel, inhuman and degrading; they are torturous. To the extent that suspects are confined there to facilitate the investigation by breaking their wills with a view to eliciting confessions and information, they can properly be described as being subjected to torture.

The Special Rapporteur is aware of the difficulties faced by the authorities. These include legal rigidities tending to put a premium on detention rather than encouraging release on bail or recognizance or other forms of conditional release. This is so even in respect of first-time non-violent suspected offenders. To the extent that overcrowding would be alleviated by building new institutions or improving existing ones, this is very resource-intensive and takes time. Already some significant initiatives have been taken in this direction, both by the central Government and by the cities of Moscow and St. Petersburg. In the spring of 1994, a central government programme to build new remand centres aimed at housing 80,000 inmates within five years was announced. If this target can be met, and if the population of pre-trial detainees does not increase commensurately, then this could substantially alleviate the situation. It is an ambitious programme and steps will need to be taken to avoid the risk of the new institutions encouraging yet further resort to the already over used practice of pre-trial detention. In any event, these initiatives do not promise an early enough end to a problem in which, across the territory of the Russian Federation, there is an excess of population over capacity in the isolators of 71,000.

The prohibition of torture or cruel, inhuman or degrading treatment is absolute under international law. Indeed, according to article 3 of the Declaration on the Protection of All Persons from Being Subjected to Torture and Other Cruel, Inhuman or Degrading Treatment or Punishment (General Assembly resolution 3452 (XXX) of 9 December 1975, annex), even "exceptional circumstances such as a state of war or a threat of war, internal political instability or any other public emergency may not be invoked as a justification of torture or other cruel, inhuman or degrading treatment or punishment" (art. 3). It follows inexorably that the Government of the Russian Federation is obliged to put an immediate end to this situation. No State has the right to subject persons to these conditions, regardless of constraints on resources, rigidities in its legal system or the time required to develop new facilities. Below, the Special Rapporteur makes recommendations both for an immediate, temporary solution as well as for measures that could address the problem in the longer term.

The position of convicted prisoners who have exhausted their appeals is substantially different. Most such prisoners serve their sentences in various types of correctional labour "colony" or colony settlement. Perhaps the best evidence of their, at least relative, humaneness is the fact that prisoners in the isolators, who expected to be convicted, were anxious to be transported to colonies. The Special Rapporteur is not in a position to pronounce authoritatively on conditions in the colonies. Certainly in Kolpino colony for juveniles he found a concerned director and staff at pains to run a humane regime with a view to preparing their charges for a law-abiding life in the outside world. However, he was also surprised to find among the inmates juveniles of 15 or 16 who were sentenced for petty offences such as bicycle stealing or more complex, but equally non-violent, offences such as computer fraud. Deprivation of liberty for juveniles offending for the first time in a non-violent manner seemed grossly inappropriate and disproportionate.

Even in the strict regime camp of Fornosova, the Special Rapporteur appreciated the relatively open nature of the facilities. The main problem for this, as for other labour colonies, is that there are now substantially fewer opportunities for productive labour activity (and consequent remuneration) because of the general economic dislocation in the country.

A small portion of convicts (apparently 1 per cent only) may serve their sentences in prisons. The Special Rapporteur met some of them in Matrosskava Tishina No. 1. They seemed to welcome the regime which provided work inside and outside the institution.

*Recommendations for Immediate Action.* The Special Rapporteur believes that only by adopting at once the following recommendation can the Government of the Russian Federation begin to discharge the responsibility of the Russian State to those within its jurisdiction under its own law and under international law to prevent torture or cruel, inhuman or degrading treatment or punishment. He, therefore, appeals to the Government of the Russian Federation to remove from confinement in centres of detention on remand (isolators) all 71,000 detained in excess of the officially proclaimed capacity of existing institutions.

This recommendation should be put into effect by Presidential Decree if necessary. It could probably be achieved by ordering the release pending trial of all non-violent first-time offenders, any remaining overcrowding could be eliminated by opening up, on a temporary basis, indoor stadiums or other comparable public places, and transferring the excess population to such places.

*General Recommendations.* Much greater use should be made of existing provisions in the law for release of suspects on bail or on recognizance (signature), especially as regards suspected first-time non-violent offenders. Instructions or guidelines to this effect should be given by the Minister of the Interior to investigators from his Ministry; by the Procurator General to State, regional and local procuratorial investigators and supervisory prosecutors, and by the Minister of Justice and the Supreme Court of the Russian Federation to all judges handling criminal cases.

To the extent that the law has been so framed or interpreted as to restrict provisions for release on bail or recognizance to prevent the release of first-time, non-violent suspected offenders as a normal measure, the relevant federal and republican laws should be amended to secure this objective.

The draft Code of Criminal Procedure, giving effect to article 22 of the Constitution which places all deprivations of freedom under judicial authority, should be speedily adopted by the State Duma.

To the extent that more extensive use of release on bail or recognizance will not eliminate the overcrowding problem, there should be a crash programme to build new remand centres with sufficient accommodation for the anticipated population.

Existing institutions should be refurbished so that all institutions meet basic standards of humanity and respect for human dignity.

Provision should be made for sufficient food of palatable quality to be available to those whom the State deprives of the means to fend for themselves.

Medical facilities and medicines should be sufficient to meet the needs of inmates, even after the present situation (in which the State effectively subjects inmates to disease by placing them in health-damaging conditions) has been remedied.

The United Nations Programme of Advisory Services and Technical Assistance in respect of the Russian Federation should be intensified in the following areas:

(a) Training of law enforcement, prosecutorial, judicial and penitentiary officials in international standards in the administration of justice (pre-trial, trial and post-trial phases), in cooperation, as necessary, with other organizations, such as the International Committee of the Red Cross and academic institutions;

(b) The mobilizing of material and technical resources existing in Member States that the Special Rapporteur hopes and trusts could be made available in the same spirit of international solidarity and cooperation as that shown by the Government of the Russian Federation in inviting the Special Rapporteur.

**BIBLIOGRAPHY.** American Association for the Advancement of Science, Committee on Scientific Freedom and Responsibility. *Scientists Imprisoned in the Soviet Union in Violation of the Helsinki Final Act of 1975.* Washington, D.C.: 1987. NGO report, in English.

Amnesty International. *USSR: Review of Punitive Psychiatry since January 1987.* London: 1988. NGO report, in English.

Artz, Donna E. *Denial of Due Process: Soviet Failure to Provide for Appeal of Emigration Refusals.* Huntington, NY, USA: Soviet Jewry Law Project, 1988. NGO report, in English.

Barist, J., O. C. Pell, E. Oshman, and M. E. Hamel. *Who May Leave: A Review of Soviet Practice Restricting Emigration on Grounds of Knowledge of "State Secrets" in Comparison with Standards of International Law and the Policies of Other States.* New York: National Conference on Soviet Jewry and White & Case, 1987. NGO report, in English.

Bernhardt, Rudolf, et al. "Report on the Conformity of the Legal Order of the Russian Federation with Council of Europe Standards," *Human Rights Law Journal* 15, no. 7 (Oct. 1994): 249–300. Special issue, in English.

Chistyakova, Alexandra. "The Russian Bill of Rights: Implications," *Columbia Human Rights Law Review* 24, no. 2 (Summer 1993): 369–394. Scholarly article, in English.

Commission on Security and Cooperation in Europe. "Reform and Human Rights: The Gorbachev Record," in *Report Submitted to the Congress of the United States.* Washington, D.C.: U.S. Government Printing Office, 1988. Government report, in English.

Filatova, Irina. *Contested Domains: National Identity and Conflict in Russia and South Africa.* Johannesburg, South Africa: South African Institute of International Affairs, 1992. Scholarly article, in English.

Fitzpatrick, Catherine A. *Soviet Abuse of Psychiatry for Political Purposes.* New York: U.S. Helsinki Watch Committee, 1987. NGO report, in English.

Furtado, Charles F., and Henry R. Huttenbach, eds. "The Ex-Soviet Nationalities without Gorbachev," *Nationalities Papers* 20, no. 2 (Fall 1992). Special issue, in English.

Helsinki Watch. *By All Parties to the Conflict: Violations of the Laws of War in Afghanistan.* New York: Human Rights Watch, 1988. NGO report, in English.

——————. *New Citizenship Laws in the Republics of the Former USSR.* New York: Human Rights Watch, 1992. NGO report, in English.

——————. *Russia: War in Chechnya—New Report from the Field.* New York: 1995. NGO report, in English.

——————. *War or Peace?: Human Rights and Russian Military Involvement in the "Near Abroad."* New York: Human Rights Watch, 1993. NGO report, in English.

Hughes, Michael. "The Rise and Fall of Pamyat?" *Religion, State & Society* 20, no. 2 (1992): 213–229. Special issue, in English; bibliography, pp. 227–229.

Human Rights Watch. "Russia," in *Human Rights Watch World Report 1995,* pp. 219–223. New York: NGO report, in English.

Immigration and Refugee Board Documentation Centre. *CIS, Baltic States and Georgia: Nationality Legislation.* Ottawa, Ontario, Canada: 1992. Government briefing paper, in English and French; bibliography, pp. 20–23.

——————. *CIS, Baltic States and Georgia: Situation of the Jews.* Ottawa, Ontario, Canada: 1992. Government briefing paper, in English and French; bibliography, pp. 30–35.

Internationale Gesellschaft fur Menschenrechte (International Society for Human Rights). *CSCE and Human Rights: Divided Families and the Denial of Freedom of Movement,* vols. 1 and 2. Frankfurt, FRG: 1986. NGO report, in English.

Korey, William. "Helsinki, Human Rights and the Gorbachev Style," *Ethics and International Affairs* 1 (1987): 113–133. Scholarly article, in English.

Lawyers Committee for Human Rights. *Human Rights and Legal Reform in the Russian Federation.* New York: 1993. NGO report, in English.

Parchomenko, Walter. *Soviet Images of Dissidents and Nonconformists.* New York: Praeger, 1986. Monograph, in English.

U.S. Congress, Subcommittee on Human Rights and International Organizations and Subcommittee on Europe and the Middle East. *Religious Persecution in the Soviet Union, Part I: Soviet Jewry,* 99th cong., 1st sess., 1985. Government hearings, in English.

Wrobel, Brian. *Glasnost and Soviet Criminal Trials: A Report by the Parliamentary Human Rights Group.* London: Parliamentary Human Rights Group, 1987. NGO report, in English.

**RWANDA.** The Republic of Rwanda is a landlocked country in eastern Africa. It has borders with Burundi, Uganda, Tanzania, and Zaire. Formerly part of the UN trust territory of Rwanda–Urundi under Belgian administration, it became independent in 1962 and became a member of the United Nations the same year. Its population is estimated to be 7,573,000. Ethnic groups include the Batwa, the Bahutu, and the Batutsi; the first belongs to the pygmoid group; the second, to the Bantu group; and the third, to the Nilo–Hamitic group. The Batwa, Bahutu, and Batutsi intermarry, speak the same language, and share the same culture. Kinyarwanda is the only language spoken by all Rwandese; French is sometimes used in commerce and education. Religions practiced include Christianity (Roman Catholic, 56%; Protestant denominations, 12%), Islam (10%), and Animism and other beliefs (22%).

The government (1994) took the form of a republic. However, it was placed under military rule by a *coup d'etat* of 5 July 1973, at which time its elected president was replaced by an army officer Maj.-Gen. Juvenal Habyarimana. A new constitution, adopted in December 1978, provides for an elected Assembly and a single political party, the National Revolutionary Development Movement.

*END OF COLONIALISM.* In 1960 Belgium, the administering authority for Rwanda–Urundi, a former German colony which was a **LEAGUE OF NATIONS** mandate before becoming a United Nations trust territory, set up a provisional government there and announced its intention of holding elections for the purpose of constituting a national assembly. Belgium invited the United Nations to send a mission to observe the election, but the **GENERAL ASSEMBLY** decided that it should be held under UN supervision.

The election, held on 25 September 1960, produced a legislative body which proceeded to establish a constitutional democracy in the territory. The General Assembly set up a five-member commission in February 1962 to ensure the achievement of essential objectives before independence. After considering the report of the Commission, it decided to terminate the trusteeship agreement; and, on 1 July 1962, two independent and sovereign States emerged—Rwanda and Burundi.

Constitutional reforms were promulgated by President Habyarimana in June 1991, including separation of powers between the executive, legislative and judicial branches, a limit of two consecutive five-year terms for the president, creation of the position of Prime Minister and the right to strike for civil servants. Additionally, a law was passed regarding political parties and 15 had been registered by June 1992. President Habyarimana also resigned his military office and leadership of his political party.

*ETHNIC GROUPS.* Maintaining the peaceful co-existence of the Batwa, Bahutu, and Batutsi groups has been a primary concern of the Government of Rwanda, which does all it can to ensure that the members of those groups enjoy equality in law and in practice. Recently, special measures were taken on behalf of the Batwa, who had lived in cramped and rudimentary huts; the government granted subsidies for housing improvements and, in particular, made corrugated iron available to the Batwa for building purposes.

In a report presented to the **COMMITTEE ON THE ELIMINATION OF RACIAL DISCRIMINATION** on 22 April 1985, the government described its efforts to eliminate discrimination against, and between, minority groups as follows (UN Doc. CERD/C/115/Add. 2, paras. 11–13):

With a view to avoiding a preponderance of certain ethnic groups or of certain strata of the population, the Rwandese Government has for several years been pursuing a policy of equilibrium, consisting in the equitable allocation of jobs in the public and private sector and also in teaching, based on a representation of each ethnic group *pro rata* to the population as a whole. The three ethnic groups of which the Rwandese population is composed presumably each spoke their own language before becoming fully integrated; but it is difficult to determine at what point Kinyarwanda—the national language—became the one and only language in the country. The three ethnic groups can be recognized by their physical type. The Batutsi belong to the Nilo-Hamitic group, the Bahutu to the Bantu group and the Batwa to the pygmoid group. Interethnic marriages tend, however, to blur this distinction.

Special measures have been taken in the social, economic and cultural fields with a view to guaranteeing the proper development and protection of minority groups, particularly on behalf of the Batwa group who were very backward by comparison with the other groups. Special measures have been taken to assist the Batwa in the field of education, . . . and a major effort has been undertaken to alert them to the need to become more fully integrated in the national community. In addition, since Rwandans share the same culture, an endeavour has also been made to make this group play a more active part in the expression of this culture.

The feudal régime has been formally abolished by the Constitution, article 2 of which provides that "the monarchy is hereby abolished and cannot be reinstated". Furthermore, the Code of Civil and Commercial Procedure prohibits certain procedures in evidence, the use of which is a relic of feudal-colonialist bondage. For instance, the oath invoking the name of Mwami (the King, when there was a monarchy) and of the Kalinga (the sacred drum of the ancient royalty) is forbidden. It can be said that there are no longer any vestiges of feudalism in our country, particularly since the National Revolutionary Movement for Development (MRND) has adopted, among other aims, the elimination from the Rwandese mentality of the survival of such feudal attitudes as caste, the currying of favour, and intrigue, which act as an impediment to national development.

*THE HUTUS AND TUTSIS.* The 1990s brought unprecedented human suffering to Rwanda as millions of refugees lost their lives from genocide and disease epidemics brought on by fighting between the Hutus and Tutsis, 85% and 14% of the population, respectively. Beginning in October 1990 when the Tutsi-led rebel army, the Rwanda Patriotic Front, invaded northern Rwanda from Uganda, Rwandans began fleeing their country in huge numbers. In the first year of fighting, an estimated 80,000 had been displaced and it was estimated that by February 1993, one million had fled to Uganda and Tanzania.

Despite amnesty granted to Tutsis residing abroad and negotiations sponsored by the **ORGANIZATION OF AFRICAN UNITY,** fighting continued. The UN **SECURITY COUNCIL** approved the Observer Mission Uganda-Rwanda in June 1993 and a peace accord was signed in Arusha, Tanzania, in August, providing for a transitional government and multi-party elections, including the Patriotic Front, within 22 months.

Conflict between the government and the Patriotic Front continued, however, and the UN Security Council endorsed the creation of the 2,500-strong UN Assistance Mission to Rwanda in October 1993. The transitional government, including the Patriotic Front, was to be inaugurated in December 1993 but there were continued disagreements over its composition. Then in February 1994, the proposed Minister of Public Works from the Social Democratic Party was murdered, followed a few hours later by the apparent retaliatory murder of the leader of the Coalition for the Defense of the Republic. Riots broke out and a further 30 to 40 people were killed.

In April 1994, just three months after being installed as president of a transitional government, President Habyarimana was killed, along with the president and two cabinet officers of Burundi and the chief of staff of the Rwandan armed forces, when their plane was fired upon and crashed at Kigali airport. Speaker of the legislature, Dr. Theodore Sindikukbwabo assumed the presidency pursuant to the 1991 Constitution.

The Presidential Guard and Hutu militias immediately closed off the crash site, precluding a UN investigation, and began retaliatory executions of opposition political leaders, including the Tutsi prime minister, priests, nuns, relief workers and UN troops, including 10 Belgians who were disarmed before being executed. In the weeks and months following the president's death, the Hutus and Tutsis vied for control of the government and the city of Kigali. Both groups engaged in extreme violence against each other as well as moderates within their own groups, leaving at least 500,000 dead, mostly Tutsis. An estimated 250,000 refugees, mostly Hutus fearing reprisals, fled to Tanzania.

Emergency evacuations of foreign nationals were carried out by Belgium, France and the United States throughout April 1994 and all foreign embassies were closed. Refugees streamed out of the capital and out of the country over the next months as fighting was at its highest level.

Even as the Patriotic Front declared victory and announced a cease-fire in July, up to two million people, again mainly Hutu, fled to Zaire within days. An estimated 1.2 million refugees fled to the town of Goma at the northern end of Lake Kivu and another 600,000 to 800,000 to the area at the southern end of the lake near the town of Bukavu. Between one and two million had gone to the French safe-zone in southern Rwanda. Broadcasts seemed to encourage the exodus by instilling a fear of reprisals. Interim President Sindikukwabo urged Hutus in the French safe-zone to follow him to Zaire. On 18 July the Patriotic Front announced a ceasefire and the formation of a government comprised mainly of Hutu moderates.

The UN **WORLD FOOD COUNCIL,** the UN **HIGH COMMISSIONER FOR REFUGEES** and dozens of relief programs struggled to provide food and stem the spread of disease in the makeshift camps that were established in Zaire. Due to the remoteness of the area, a lack of equipment and the difficulty in drilling for clean water, cholera and dysentery spread quickly, killing 40,000 people in three weeks. **UNICEF** reported that there were 100,000 to 120,000 children whose parents were either dead or missing as a result of the events. Hundreds of millions of dollars in humanitarian aid was pledged over the following months by the European Union, the U.S. Government and the World Bank. There was widespread criticism that the world community had not acted swiftly enough to limit the human devastation.

In addition to the disease and increasing violence by extremist Hutu militias in the camps, the problems were exacerbated by the random closing of the border by Zaire officials, sometimes trapping Rwandan refugees fleeing their country or trying to return. The UN High Commissioner for Refugees resisted pressures to encourage the refugees home, arguing that it may not be safe to return. When the French peacekeepers withdrew from the southern safezone in August 1994, another group of refugees fled to Zaire.

In December 1994, the office of the UN High Commissioner for Refugees reversed its policy and began to assist refugees who wished to return to Rwanda after incidents in which refugees were killed in Zaire and thousands were ejected from makeshift camps by Zairean soldiers.

*WAR CRIMES TRIBUNAL.* UN human rights monitors were deployed throughout the country and UN Secretary-General Boutros-Ghali requested a report by October from the three African judges appointed to investigate the massacres in Rwanda. This panel reported in December 1994 that there was strong evidence of genocide by the Hutus against the Tutsis. The Rwandan Government had agreed in August to establishment of an international war crimes tribunal. In January 1995 the Security Council appointed as Chief Prosecutor Honore Rakotomana, former president of the Supreme Court of Madagascar, who was to work under Richard Goldstone, the Chief Prosecutor for the UN International War Crimes Tribunal in The

Hague. In February it selected Arusha, Tanzania, as the site of the tribunal.

It was estimated that 23,000 prisoners were being held in overcrowded Rwandan jails and in March 1995, 24 prisoners suffocated to death in a cell holding 74. That same month the moderate Hutu governor of the southern province of Butare was killed in yet more violence.

## RECOMMENDATIONS OF UN SPECIAL RAPPORTEUR.

In his discussions with members of the government, the Special Rapporteur made a number of suggestions or proposals which were favorably received. These proposals, some of which, it is true, already seemed to have been adopted, are designed essentially to encourage the return of the refugees and social peace in Rwanda. They relate to non-recourse to reprisals, additional measures of reassurance, and deployment of United Nations human rights experts in the field (paras. 30–47, 65–82):

### A. Non-Recourse to Reprisals

The main aim of the Special Rapporteur's approach to the new authorities in Kigali was to make sure that they would not engage in summary executions. The Special Rapporteur was satisfied by the reply that he received from the various personalities he met, a reply which was in fact completely unambiguous. It may be summarized as follows: the new Government pledges not only to refrain from taking measures or acts of reprisal but also to punish any persons engaging in such acts. The Prime Minister stated: "I undertake not to permit any summary executions, and any persons guilty of such executions will be punished. . . . Impunity cannot be tolerated in this country."

Impunity being one of the sources of serious human rights violations, including genocide, in Rwanda, the Government asserts its firm determination to eliminate it. To this end, a rapid reorganization of the judicial machinery is being undertaken by the Minister of Justice. It was also asserted no less firmly that non-recourse to reprisals and the prosecution of those guilty of genocide, a question which is inextricably linked with it, are essential conditions for the national reconciliation and unity that are vitally necessary. The Special Rapporteur took note with satisfaction of these views, which coincide with those he expressed in his preliminary report.

Non-recourse to reprisals, as referred to in the aforementioned statements by the three leading political figures of the State and which does not exclude prosecution of persons guilty of genocide, has a twofold objective. Firstly, in the immediate future, the aim is to reassure refugees that they can return to their land and homes in complete peace of mind and security. The second goal, over the longer term, is to prevent individuals from taking the law into their own hands and thus bring lasting social peace back to Rwanda.

In the immediate future, however, this position, praiseworthy and commendable though it is, is nevertheless limited. The Special Rapporteur therefore proposed additional measures.

### B. Additional Measures of Reassurance

The Special Rapporteur suggested that the political authorities should take a number of specific measures, in addition to those already adopted, in order to further reassure the refugees. Those suggestions concern both immediate and short-term measures.

*1. Immediate measures.* Immediate measures include:

(a) An information campaign aimed at the population within Rwanda, deploring and condemning the massacres, extending sympathy to victims and bereaved families, assuring them that the guilty will be tried and punished by the courts and urging them to refrain from taking the law into their own hands, on pain of severe penalties;

(b) Circulars, service notes and instructions addressed to all national or local authorities, calling on them not to tolerate any act of reprisal and to institute proceedings against any persons guilty of such acts;

(c) Regulations prohibiting and laying down heavy penalties for acts of incitement to ethnic hatred or violence. In this connection, the Special Rapporteur welcomed the fact that, according to members of the Government, the new identity cards no longer contain a reference to ethnic origin.

*2. Short-term measures.* The short-term measures recommended by the Special Rapporteur have to do mainly with education regarding human rights and strict respect for human dignity. This education would be provided both by schools and by radio broadcasts. It would be a matter simply of incorporating it into curricula and programmes. The short-term impact of such action can be gauged in terms of Rwanda's "radio culture" and its medium-term impact in terms of the school's role in educating future generations.

Long-term measures should be taken as soon as possible and supplemented by the deployment of United Nations human rights experts in the field.

### C. Deployment of United Nations Human Rights Experts

The Special Rapporteur finally secured the Rwandese authorities' acceptance of the idea of deploying United Nations human rights experts throughout the country. He emphasized the role of such experts and the plan of action for them.

*1. The role of United Nations Human Rights experts.* The presence of experts in the field presents definite advantages by virtue of the various roles which they can play: persuasion, deterrence, prevention and defence.

The first involves restoring the confidence of the refugees and displaced persons so that they can return with complete peace of mind; the presence of such experts is in itself reassuring in that it can provide them with a guarantee against further massacres. It is also a deterrent in that the new authorities will beware of carrying out reprisals in the presence of United Nations experts who, in addition, will ascertain the good faith of the authorities and their sincerity in not carrying out reprisals.

Deterrence leads to prevention in that it prevents further violations of human rights by virtue of the presence of United Nations experts who will monitor the return of the refugees, making sure of their safety and helping them to settle in again, with their rights being strictly observed. Finally, defence will purely and simply involve assisting with inquiries in the field in order to determine the facts regarding the various violations of human rights by the parties to the conflict and the perpetrators of massacres and genocide.

*2. Plan of action.* The action envisaged by the Special Rapporteur comprises three stages. Firstly, to take account of the limited resources of the Centre for Human Rights and the urgency of the matter, the number of United Nations experts would be restricted to 20 assigned as follows:

(a) Ten to monitor the refugees over the entire length of the "humanitarian routes" referred to above;

(b) Ten others, one in each of the following 10 major population centres: Kigali; Butare (136 km from Kigali); Byumba (75 km); Gitarama (53 km); Kibungo (108 km); Kibuye (139 km); Gisenyi (175 km); Gikongoro (165 km); Ruhengeri (116 km); Cyangugu (291 km). As the refugees and displaced persons reach their homes, the experts deployed along the "humanitarian routes" could reinforce those assigned to the above-mentioned locations.

In a second phase, as soon as resources allow, the United Nations should deploy between 150 and 200 experts throughout Rwanda for a period of not less than six months, in order to monitor not only the return, but also the reconstruction of Rwanda, and to conduct the necessary inquiries to ascertain the facts regarding the massacres. In this way, the plan will come into full operation during the difficult initial period of national reconstruction when human rights and fundamental freedoms could be open to serious violations.

Thirdly, at the end of the period of national reconstruction, the United Nations should begin to gradually withdraw its experts in the field, leaving only about 50 of them to conclude the inquiry by the end of the Special Rapporteur's mandate.

Collectively, these measures, if implemented, should overcome the reluctance of refugees and displaced persons, enable them to return en masse and guarantee their safety. At present, the United Nations escort operations have been interrupted in order to avoid importing the cholera epidemic into Rwanda. It is to be hoped that the epidemics will soon be halted and that the Rwandese refugees will be able to return to their lands and their homes without difficulty.

International assistance with the reconciliation and reconstruction efforts in Rwanda is vital. Accordingly, the Special Rapporteur associates himself with the urgent appeal made by the United Nations High Commissioner for Human Rights on 2 August 1994 to the international community for voluntary contributions to support the early deployment of human rights experts in the field, with the necessary logistical backup.

Inquiries are currently being conducted in south-western Rwanda by the team of human rights experts established by the High Commissioner for Human Rights. They will shortly be the subject of a report. . . .

### D. New Solutions

To cope with the situation in the camps for Rwandese refugees and displaced persons, the United Nations and its various partners have envisaged new solutions to supplement those which already exist. Among them, the two main solutions that should be adopted are the separation of refugees from politicians and their repatriation.

*1. The separation of refugees from politicians.* The policy of separating refugees or displaced persons from politicians is advocated by the United Nations Secretary-General in his report of 6 October 1994 (S/1994/1133). The final report of the United Nations Technical Mission on the state of security in the camps gives details of this operation. To sum up, two main points may be mentioned:

(a) The distinctions made in the Secretary-General's report between Rwandese refugees, particularly in Zaire:

(i) The former leaders, comprising some 50 families lodged in villas at Bukavu;

(ii) An estimated 16,000 military elements of the former RGF who, together with their families, form a group of 80,000 persons;

(iii) The militiamen, who are difficult to enumerate, since they have mingled with ordinary refugees; and

(iv) The ordinary refugees, estimated at more than 1 million.

(b) The aim of the operation is to separate the vast majority of refugees from those who yesterday masterminded or participated in the massacres and today are taking the Hutu survivors hostage. The latter fall into the first three categories. It is nevertheless difficult to identify the third category—the militiamen—in order to separate them from the general population. This operation will be conducted through the formation of an international isolation or interposition force estimated at some 2,000 to 3,000 policemen, the imminent establishment of which has been announced by the Secretary-General. However, this force will doubtless have to begin by exploring peaceful solutions and encouraging repatriation, force being used only in cases of extreme emergency.

*2. Repatriation.* Voluntary repatriation of refugees is covered by the relevant provisions of various United Nations conventions and the Protocol of Agreement concluded at Arusha on 9 June 1993 between the Government of the Rwandese Republic and the Rwandese Patriotic Front on the repatriation of Rwandese refugees and the resettlement of displaced persons. This was the basis for the tripartite Agreement on the repatriation of Rwandese refugees from Zaire which was concluded at Kinshasa, Zaire, on 24 October 1994 by the Government of the Rwandese Republic, the Government of the Republic of Zaire and the Office of the United Nations High Commissioner for Refugees.

The preamble to the Agreement defines "the procedures and specific modalities for the voluntary repatriation and definitive reintegration in Rwanda of Rwandese refugees at present in Zaire, with the assistance of the international community and through UNHCR and, if necessary, with the support of other United Nations agencies and intergovernmental and non-governmental organizations".

It imposes a number of obligations on the contracting parties, specifically:

(a) Zaire, the country of asylum, undertakes to respect the relevant clauses of various United Nations and OAU conventions on refugees and to take appropriate measures to ensure that the latter are not unduly influenced in their decisions;

(b) Rwanda, the country of origin, undertakes to adopt political, administrative and possibly customs measures to ensure and facilitate the return and reintegration of refugees in dignity and security, as well as social peace and national reconciliation;

(c) The Office of the United Nations High Commissioner for Refugees undertakes to monitor and supervise any repatriation operation from start to finish, placing particular emphasis on the voluntary nature of the returnees' decision, as well as on their security and dignity.

It is to be hoped that this Agreement, which refers to the communiqué of 26 July 1994 marking the meeting between the President of the Rwandese Republic and the President of the Republic of Zaire, will not experience the same fate as that communique and will be respected.

## Recommendations

The Special Rapporteur deplores the tendency to use the current insecurity in Rwanda as a pretext for suggesting that genocide is commonplace and justifying inaction. To do so is to confuse cause and effect. It overlooks the fact that genocide is to a great extent the cause of insecurity. A correct diagnosis is essential if the right medicine likely to heal the Rwandese sickness is to be found. Without in any way neglecting existing human rights violations, they must be viewed in context and their sources identified so that efforts can be made to eliminate them before it is too late. Rapid, indeed very rapid, action is required if we are not to be the powerless spectators of a second war and further massacres. It is in order to avoid a disaster of this nature that the following recommendations, addressed respectively to the Rwandese Government, the governments hosting refugees and the United Nations, are formulated.

### A. Cessation of Human Rights Violations

The United Nations should require the Rwandese Government to put an end to the serious violations of human rights which are being perpetrated in its territory and which comprise searches, arrests, arbitrary detentions, disappearances and summary executions.

The United Nations should recommend the following to the Rwandese Government:

(a) The organization of wide-ranging campaigns to make the population aware of the need to respect the physical integrity and property of others, as well as to prepare for a life in common and on good terms;

(b) The adoption, as advocated in the second report of the Special Rapporteur, of forceful administrative measures designed to deter acts of reprisal and at the same time to ensure respect for fundamental rights of anyone who may commit such acts;

(c) Observance of the prerogatives and decisions of the judicial authorities, which is an essential condition for the sound administration of justice.

### B. The Situation of Refugees

The United Nations should recommend that the Governments of countries hosting Rwandese refugees, and particularly the Zairian Government which has accepted the greatest number, take appropriate action to ensure that:

(a) The voluntary repatriation of refugees is effectively assured and facilitated;

(b) The refugees are not unduly influenced in one way or another—i.e., either to leave or to remain in the host country;

(c) Systematic information campaigns are organized for this purpose, so that the people concerned can take a fully informed decision;

(d) These Governments abide by their international commitments, particularly those deriving from the relevant provisions of international conventions on asylum and refugees;

(e) Their territories are not used as a base for destabilizing Rwanda or committing acts of aggression against that State.

The United Nations should assist in:

(a) Compensating those States for the losses they have suffered as a result of the installation of refugees and the deterioration of their crops and land;

(b) Financing refugee repatriation operations.

### C. International Assistance to Rwanda

The United Nations should formally appeal to Member States, particularly the great Powers and the African States, to provide substantial assistance for the reconstruction of the Rwandese State as a matter of urgency.

Such assistance, which should take various forms and be provided in all economic, political, social and cultural sectors, implies a prior overall assessment of needs.

In the immediate future, it appears especially urgent to provide the people concerned with food and health assistance designed to enable them to survive, as well as the means to save their crops, livestock and land and to produce the minimum needed to survive.

The United Nations should participate actively in this assistance operation and help to organize it. In particular, it should provide the Rwandese State with:

(a) Financial or material assistance in reconstituting the infrastructure of the administrative police, the criminal police, the gendarmerie and the judiciary;

(b) Assistance in judicial and law-enforcement personnel, including the training of policemen, gendarmes and judges, while helping local judges to render justice. In this connection, the United Nations might expand the Special Rapporteur's mandate to embrace technical assistance. Under this proposal, a specialized team of observers would be responsible for training policemen, judges, lawyers and court officers and establishing a Bar with a view to safeguarding the independence of the judiciary.

The United Nations should take the initiative in ensuring improved coordination of activities in Rwandese territory,—not only measures to promote human rights or humanitarian law but also other activities such as those involving food or military operations. Such coordination is essential in view of the large number and diversity of field activities. It would have the advantage of providing an integrated view of problems and avoiding overlapping, duplication of effort and aid waste.

The United Nations should, as soon as possible:

(a) Increase the number of human rights experts and their actual deployment in the field, some of them acting as observers, investigators and instructors at one and the same time;

(b) Launch the International Court which has just been set up, as well as the local courts that are to be established to try persons responsible for genocide, in order to stop, or at least reduce, acts of reprisal;

(c) Establish an appropriate legal framework to ensure the protection of widows and unaccompanied children and guarantee their fundamental rights. For this purpose, it would be appropriate to provide compensation for damage attributable to the perpetrators of massacres or their accomplices;

(d) Create an international force responsible for ensuring security in camps for refugees and displaced persons, as well as arrangements for their repatriation in appropriate conditions of security and dignity.

In cooperation with OAU, the United Nations should take steps to:

(a) Create conditions and a framework for a dialogue between various Rwandese political groups both inside and outside the country. This dialogue might lay the basis for a political settlement of the conflict in place of a military settlement;

(b) Convene an international conference on Rwanda designed, as initially recommended in the interim report, to induce the parties to the conflict to negotiate in good faith, taking due account of the Arusha Agreements of 4 August 1993, the conditions for peace, democratic transition, and national reconciliation and unity.

### UN OBSERVER MISSION TO UGANDA-RWANDA (UNOMUR).

In 1990, fighting between the armed forces of the Government of Rwanda and the Patriotic Front broke out across the border between Rwanda and its northern neighbor, Uganda. Despite a number of ceasefire agreements thereafter, hostilities resumed in the northern part of the country in early February 1993, which interrupted negotiations between the Government of Rwanda and the Patriotic Front. In separate letters to the president of the UN Security Council, both Rwanda and Uganda called for the deployment of UN military observers along the 150-km. common border to prevent the military use of the area, especially the transportation of military supplies. The mission was authorized on 22 June 1993 by the Security Council (resolution 846 [1993]). Initially, UNOMUR restricted its monitoring activities in Uganda along the area of the border with Rwanda controlled by the Patriotic Front. However, the resumption of civil war in Rwanda in April 1994 necessitated readjusting its tasks and reassigning UN military observers.

### UN ASSISTANCE MISSION FOR RWANDA (UNAMIR).

Once again, the fighting between the Government of Rwanda and the Patriotic Front was the cause of a UN mission. Talks on a comprehensive peace agreement between the two parties convened on 16 March 1993. The talks covered military issues, refugees and displaced persons, and political matters, including the amendment of the constitution. Early in the talks, the parties began to discuss an international neutral force to oversee the implementation of key aspects of the peace agreement. When the talks were successfully concluded on 4 August 1993, the parties called on the UN to send a reconnaissance mission to Rwanda to prepare for the quick deployment of the neutral international force. The reconnaissance mission recommended that UNAMIR be set up, and the assistance mission was established on 5 October 1993 by UN Security Council resolution 872 (1993). Initially UNAMIR was established for a period of six months with the proviso that it could be extended upon review by the Security Council. However, with the subsequent events in Rwanda and the civil war, humanitarian assistance was extended up to April 1994, amounting to $78 million to meet the needs of over 900,000 war-displaced people (approximately 13% of the population). Most of the displaced were living in and around thirty camps where serious malnutrition and disease

were prevalent. The situation was exacerbated by Rwanda's already precarious economic condition, overpopulation, and rapidly declining agricultural production. Then, in April 1994, with the deaths of President Habyarimana of Rwanda and President Ntaryamira of Burundi in an airplane crash near Kigali airport, the situation worsened considerably. Widespread killings, with both ethnic and political dimensions, spread across the country; within two weeks, the deaths were estimated to number in the tens of thousands.

In a report to the UN Security Council, on 20 April 1994, the Secretary-General reported that UNAMIR personnel "cannot be left at risk indefinitely when there is no possibility of their performing the tasks for which they were dispatched." On 21 April, the Security Council reduced UNAMIR to a total of 270 military personnel who would remain in Kigali to act as an intermediary between the warring factions. UNAMIR worked with a UN advance humanitarian team in Kigali, headed by Under-Secretary-General for Humanitarian Affairs Peter Hansen; and also coordinated activities with the **INTERNATIONAL COMMITTEE OF THE RED CROSS.**

On 13 May 1994, the Secretary-General recommended to the Security Council that a new mandate for UNAMIR II be established. UNAMIR II would include 5,500 troops, who would, *inter alia,* support and provide safe conditions for displaced persons and others in Rwanda and assist humanitarian organizations. UNAMIR II would also monitor border crossing points, although it would have no enforcement powers; it could only take action in self-defense against those who threatened protected sites and populations. On 17 May, the Security Council in resolution 918 (1994) authorized UNAMIR II and also imposed an arms embargo on the country.

**BIBLIOGRAPHY.** Amnesty International. *Rwanda: Mass Murder by Government Supporters and Troops in April and May 1994.* London: 1994. NGO report, in English.

ARTICLE 19. *Freedom of Information and Expression in Rwanda: A Commentary by ARTICLE 19 on the Report Submitted to the U.N. Human Rights Committee by the Government of Rwanda.* London: 1988. NGO report, in English.

Bruycker, Philippe. *Déclarations faites le 24 octobre 1990 par les délégués de la Ligue belge des droits de l'homme en collaboration avec la Fédération Internationale des Droits de l'Homme qui a organisé une visite d'observation au Rwanda du 18 au 23 octobre 1990* (Declaration made on October 24, 1990 by the Delegates of the Belgian League of Human Rights in Collaboration with the International Federation of Human Rights which Organized an Observer Mission to Rwanda from October 18–23, 1990). Brussels, Belgium: Ligue Belge des Droits de l'Homme, 1990. NGO factfinding report, in French.

# R

Burkhalter, Holly J. "The Question of Genocide: The Clinton Administration and Rwanda," *World Policy Journal* 11, no. 4 (Winter 1994–95): 44–54. Scholarly article, in English.

Chrétien, Jean-Pierre. "La Crise politique rwandaise," *Genève-Afrique/Geneva-Africa* 30, no. 2 (1992): 121–140. Scholarly article, in French.

Clark, Lance. "Post-Emergency Assistance for Refugees in Eastern and Southern Africa," *Migration News* no. 3–4 (July–Dec. 1987): 3–24. NGO research paper, in English.

Fédération Internationale des Ligues des Droits de l'Homme (International Federation of Human Rights Leagues). *Rwanda: Commission internationale d'enquête (7–21 janvier 1993): violations massives et systématiques des droits de l'homme depuis le 1er octobre 1990* (Rwanda: International Factfinding Mission [7–21 January 1993]: Massive and Systematic Human Rights Violations since October 1, 1990). Paris: 1993. NGO factfinding report, in French.

Human Rights Watch. "Rwanda," in *Human Rights Watch World Report 1995*, pp. 39–48. New York: 1995. NGO report, in English.

Human Rights Watch/Africa. *Genocide in Rwanda, April–May 1994.* New York: 1994. NGO report, in English.

————. *Rwanda: A New Catastrophe?—Increased International Efforts Required to Punish Genocide and Prevent further Bloodshed.* New York: 1994. NGO report, in English.

Human Rights Watch Arms Project. *Arming Rwanda: The Arms Trade and Human Rights Abuses in the Rwandan War.* New York: 1994. NGO report, in English.

Muwanga, Lance-Sera, and Henry Gombya. *The Pearl of Africa is Bleeding—"We Shall Massacre Them".* Vaxjo, Sweden: Program for Human Rights and Refugee Studies, 1991. Monograph, in English.

Rossel, Hubert. "Le Rwanda et le Burundi à la veille de leur 30e anniversaire d'indépendance" (Rwanda and Burundi on the Eve of Their 30th Anniversary of Independence), *Genève-Afrique* 30, no. 2 (1992): 11–74. Scholarly article, in French; bibliography, pp. 72–74.

Vassall-Adams, Guy. *Rwanda: An Agenda for International Action.* London: Oxfam, 1994. NGO report, in English.

Watson, Catharine. *Exile from Rwanda: Background to an Invasion.* Washington, D.C.: United States Committee for Refugees, 1991. NGO factfinding report, in English.

————. "Rwanda: War and Waiting," *Africa Report* 37, no. 6 (Nov.–Dec. 1992): 51–55. Article, in English.

# S

**SAAVEDRAS LAMAS, CARLOS (1878–1959).** In 1936, the **NOBEL PEACE PRIZE** was awarded to a South American for the first time. A member of the Argentinean aristocracy, Saavedras Lamas held a doctorate of law from the University of Buenos Aires and taught law and history at the University of La Plata, the University of Buenos Aires, and the University of Buenos Aires Law School, where he later served as president.

Saavedras Lamas served as minister of justice and education in 1915 and was appointed foreign minister in 1932. In this position, he profoundly influenced South American politics. He persuaded Argentina to rejoin the **LEAGUE OF NATIONS** after a hiatus of 13 years (he became president of the League's assembly in 1936), and negotiated an end to the Chaco War (1932–1935) between Bolivia and Paraguay. He was the author of the "Antiwar Pact," signed by eleven nations, which effectively allowed non-members of the League of Nations to work with the League to promote peace and prevent war.

**BIBLIOGRAPHY.** Gray, Tony. *Champions of Peace.* London: Paddington Press, 1976.

Schlessinger, Bernard S., and June H. Schlessinger, eds. *Who's Who of Nobel Prize Winners.* Phoenix, AZ, USA: Oryx Press, 1991.

**SADAT, ANWAR (1918–1981).** A military man who saw the necessity for peace, Egyptian President Anwar Sadat shared the 1978 **NOBEL PEACE PRIZE** with Israeli Prime Minister **MENACHEM BEGIN** for establishing accords between Egypt and Israel. Sadat is regarded as the initiator of the peace movement, going against most of the Arab world in his quest for a settlement to the hostilities in the Middle East. In the end, this great statesman paid for the peace with his own life.

Born in the Tala district of Cairo, Anwar Sadat was educated at the Royal Military Academy in Egypt. After graduation, he served in the Egyptian army and became a close ally of Gamal Abdel Nasser, himself later president of Egypt, in the overthrow of the corrupt regime of King Farouk in 1952. Under Nasser, Sadat fought for the nationalization of the Suez Canal and took part in the Six-Day War of 1967, which proved disastrous for Egypt. When Nasser died in 1970, Sadat assumed the presidency and continued Nasser's policies of Arab unity in the Middle East. However, after the 1973 October war, Sadat began to move closer toward reconciliation with Israel, even though the 1973 conflict proved advantageous for the Arabs. Through secret diplomacy, Sadat explored the options; when Menachem Begin, leader of the centrist Likud Party, became president of a coalition government in Israel in 1977, Sadat became the first Arab head of State to visit Jerusalem since the establishment of the Israeli State. For his courageous actions, he was named *Time* magazine's "Man of the Year" in 1977. In 1978, Sadat and Begin signed the Camp David Accords in the United States.

However, in much of the Arab world, Sadat's actions toward Israel were viewed as traitorous. In Egypt itself, opinion was divided between forces who saw themselves as somewhat Westernized and those who desired an Islamic government. Due to increasing violence, Sadat began a crackdown on Islamic extremists, although he was also criticized for restricting peaceful dissent. In 1981, while reviewing troops in Cairo, he was assassinated by Islamic militants.

**BIBLIOGRAPHY.** Sadat, Anwar. *In Search of Identity: An Autobiography.* New York: Harper and Row, 1978.

Schlessinger, Bernard S., and June H. Schlessinger, eds. *Who's Who of Nobel Prize Winners.* Phoenix, AZ, USA: Oryx Press, 1991.

**ST. KITTS AND NEVIS.** The Federation of St. Kitts and Nevis is a country occupying two of the Leeward Islands, in the eastern Caribbean Sea, separated by a narrow strait. St. Kitts and Nevis became a dependency of Great Britain under the 1713 Peace of Utrecht. The islands achieved independence from Great Britain in 1983 and became a member of the United Nations the same year. Their combined population is estimated to be 40,000. Ethnic groups include descendants of British and French settlers, African slaves, and Carib Indians. The language commonly used is English. Christianity (Anglican, 36%; Methodist, 32%; other

Protestant denominations, 8%; and Roman Catholic, 10%) is the predominant religion.

The government (1994) took the form of a parliamentary State. There is a unicameral legislature consisting of 11 elected members (eight from St. Kitts and three from Nevis), and three senators appointed by the governor-general. Nevis, in addition, has its own Island Assembly. Nevis also has the right of secession.

The judiciary is independent and modeled after the British court system. Political parties include the People's Action Movement, the Labor Party, and the Nevis Reformation Party.

On 12 October 1989, the UN **GENERAL ASSEMBLY** expressed distress (resolution 44/3) at the large number of afflicted persons and the destruction wrought by Hurricane Hugo, which, on 16 September 1989, devastated St. Kitts and Nevis, and urged all States to contribute generously to its relief, rehabilitation, and reconstruction efforts.

Rising political dissatisfaction by Labor Party supporters led to demonstrations and protests, and a 21-day state of emergency was enforced in December 1993. Troops from the Regional Security System were called in from Barbados and Labor Party members boycotted the opening of the National Assembly in January 1994.

**BIBLIOGRAPHY.** Organization of American States. *Annual Report of the Inter-American Commission on Human Rights.* Washington, D.C. IGO annual report, in English.

**ST. LUCIA.** A country which occupies one of the Windward Islands of the West Indies, located off the northern coast of South America, south of Martinique and between the Atlantic Ocean and the Caribbean Sea, St. Lucia achieved independence from Great Britain in 1979 and became a member of the United Nations the same year. Its population is estimated to be 153,000. Ethnic groups include Carib Indians, East Indians, and descendants of British and French settlers and their slaves. Languages commonly used include English and a local *patois*. Christianity (Roman Catholic, 92%; Church of England, 3%; and other Protestant denominations, 5%) is the predominant religion. Literacy is estimated at 78%.

The government (1994) took the form of a parliamentary State. Members of the 17-member House of Assembly are elected for a term of five years; members of the 11-member Senate are appointed by the governor-general, six on advice of the prime minister, three on advice of the leader of the opposition party, and two on nomination by appropriate non-governmental bodies. The judiciary is independent and modeled after the British system of justice. Political parties

include the United Workers' Party, the St. Lucia Labour Party, and the Progressive Labour Party.

The Regional Constituent Assembly issued a final report in 1992 in which an economic and political union under a federal system was predicted for St. Vincent, St. Lucia, Grenada, and Dominica.

**BIBLIOGRAPHY.** Organization of American States. *Annual Report of the Inter-American Commission on Human Rights.* Washington, D.C. IGO annual report, in English.

**ST. VINCENT AND THE GRENADINES.** A country which occupies one of the Windward Islands of the West Indies and a chain of nearly 600 small islets extending for 60 miles, all located 100 miles west of Barbados in the Caribbean Sea, St. Vincent and the Grenadines achieved independence from Great Britain in 1979 and became a member of the United Nations in 1980. Its population is estimated to be 116,000. Ethnic groups include Carib Indians and descendants of British and French settlers and their slaves, as well as a few Portuguese and East Indians. The language commonly used is English. Christianity (Anglican, 47%; Methodist, 28%; and Roman Catholic, 13%) is the predominant religion. Literacy is estimated at 78%.

The government (1994) took the form of a parliamentary State. The legislature includes 13 members elected by voters for five-year terms and six senators appointed by the governor-general, four on the advice of the prime minister, and two on the advice of the leader of the opposition. The judiciary is modeled after the British system. Political parties include the New Democrats and the St. Vincent Labor Party.

The Regional Constituent Assembly issued a final report in 1992 in which an economic and political union under a federal system was predicted for St. Vincent, St. Lucia, Grenada, and Dominica.

The St. Vincent Labor Party merged with the Movement for National Unity to create the Unity Labor Party. Dissatisfied over the minimum price set for their product, the Banana Salvation Committee led a series of protests. An obstruction of the ports created an estimated $2 million loss.

**BIBLIOGRAPHY.** Organization of American States. *Annual Report of the Inter-American Commission on Human Rights.* Washington, D.C. IGO annual report, in English.

**SAKHAROV, ANDREI DMITRIYEVICH (1921–1989).** The "father of the Soviet hydrogen bomb" who later became an advocate for international disarmament and democracy, Andrei Sakharov was the 1975 winner of the **NOBEL PEACE PRIZE,** the first Soviet citizen to be awarded this honor. In citing him for the Prize, the Peace Prize Committee stated, "Uncompromisingly and forcefully, . . . Sakharov has emphasized that the inviolable rights of man can serve as the only sure foundation for a genuine and long-lasting system of international cooperation."

Born in Moscow, Sakharov was educated at the Moscow State University, receiving a B.A. in 1942; and at the Lebedev Institute of Physics of the Soviet Academy of Sciences, from which he received his doctorate in 1947. He was admitted as a full member of the Soviet Academy of Sciences by the age of 32. From 1945 to 1968, he was a professor at the Lebedev Institute. During this time, he worked to develop a hydrogen bomb for the Soviet Union, viewing his work as necessary for a nuclear deterrent; but in 1961, he publicly denounced the Soviet plan to test a 100-megaton bomb in the atmosphere. From that time on, he was a thorn in the side of the Soviet Government. In 1968, Sakharov published *Progress, Coexistence and Intellectual Freedom,* a plea for disarmament by all nuclear powers. He was immediately removed from his professorship and became a spokesperson against Soviet political repression. In 1970, he founded the Committee for Human Rights within the Soviet Union. The Committee espoused the abolition of secret trials, the death penalty, and the use of psychiatric institutes for imprisoning political prisoners; many of these ideas were recognized in the Helsinki Accords of 1975.

Increasingly famous outside of the Soviet Union and infamous (in official quarters) within, Sakharov became the target of Soviet retaliation. He was denied a passport to visit Oslo to accept his Peace Prize, ostensibly because he possessed scientific secrets; Elena Bonner, his wife, accepted the Prize on his behalf and read his lecture, a scathing condemnation of political repression in the Soviet Union. In 1980, after he openly criticized the Soviet invasion of Afghanistan, Sakharov was banished to the city of Gorky, a "closed" center that was off-limits to foreigners because of its defense-related industries; during his confinement in Gorky, he underwent hunger strikes to protest the harassment of his relatives. He was released from internal exile in 1986, through the intervention of **MIKHAIL GORBACHEV,** then the Communist party secretary. He returned to Moscow and continued his campaign for reform, this time aided by forces within the Soviet Government itself. In 1989, he was elected to the newly formed Soviet Congress of People's Deputies.

While in exile in Gorky, Sakharov stated the following: "The ideology of human rights is probably the only one which can be combined with such diverse ideologies as communism, social democracy, religion, technocracy and those ideologies which may be described as national and indigenous. . . . The defense of human rights is a clear path toward the unification of people in our turbulent world, and a path toward the relief of suffering."

**BIBLIOGRAPHY.** Babyonyshev, Alexander. *On Sakharov.* New York: Knopf, 1982.
Gray, Tony. *Champions of Peace.* London: Paddington Press, 1976.
Schlessinger, Bernard S., and June H. Schlessinger, eds. *Who's Who of Nobel Prize Winners.* Phoenix, AZ, USA: Oryx Press, 1991.

**SAKHAROV AWARD FOR FREEDOM OF THOUGHT.** Sponsored by the European Parliament in honor of **ANDREI SAKHAROV,** this annual Award is given for study or research in the following areas: the application of the Helsinki Accords, freedom of scientific research, respect of human and international rights, or comparison between theory and practice of constitutional law concerning fundamental freedoms. The 1992 recipients were the Mothers of the Plaza de Mayo (Argentina).

For more information, contact: European Parliament, c/o Information Office, 2 Queen Ann's Gate, London SW1H 9AA, UK.

**SALVATION ARMY.** An international non-governmental organization in consultative status with the UN **ECONOMIC AND SOCIAL COUNCIL** (Category II) and with **UNESCO,** the Salvation Army has about 25,000 full-time ministers and "commissioned offices" and about 750,000 "soldiers" (members subscribing to its doctrines and providing voluntary support in religious service) in 95 countries and territories.

Founded in 1865 in London by Gen. William Booth and his wife Catherine as the Christian Mission, the Salvation Army works to relieve poverty and to carry out charitable activities throughout the world. The Salvation Army promotes a Christian evangelical ministry and provides social services for the needy of all ages and groups, irrespective of race or religion, through educational, medical, agricultural, and rehabilitation programs, especially in developing countries.

The Salvation Army has an extensive publication program, including the weeklies *The War Cry, The Salvationist,* and *The Young Soldier,* the bi-monthlies *All the World* and *The Deliverer,* and *The Salvation Army Year Book.*

Salvation Army. Address: 101 Queen Victoria Street, P.O. Box 249, London EC4P 4EP, UK. Telephone: (44-71) 236-5222. Fax: (44-71) 236-4981. Secretary-General: Eva Burrows.

**SAMOA.** The Independent State of Western Samoa is a Polynesian country occupying an island in the South Pacific Ocean 800 miles northeast of Fiji. Administered by New Zealand from 1914 to 1947 as a LEAGUE OF NATIONS mandate, and subsequently as a United Nations trust territory, it achieved independence on 1 January 1962. As Samoa, it became a member of the United Nations in 1976. Its population is estimated to be 197,000. Ethnic groups include Europeans, New Zealanders, Polynesians, and Euronesians (mixed). Languages commonly used include Samoan, Polynesian, and English. Christianity (Congregational, 50%; Roman Catholic, 22%; and Methodist, 16%) is the predominant religion; many adhere to local religions or beliefs or to none at all. Literacy is estimated at 95%.

The government (1994) took the form of a republic. Under the constitution approved in a plebescite held under United Nations supervision on 9 May 1961, the incumbent Head of State for Life will be succeeded by heads of State elected by the Legislative Assembly for terms of five years. The head of State appoints the prime minister and, on advice of the prime minister, eight ministers to form the cabinet; all executive authority is vested in these officials. Of the 49 members in the Legislative Assembly, 47 are elected by the titleholders (chiefs) of the largest family groups, and two are elected by universal adult suffrage to represent those not belonging to one of those groups. The judiciary includes the Supreme Court.

The legislative term was extended from three to five years in November 1991.

**SAN MARINO.** The Most Serene Republic of San Marino is a landlocked country in southern Europe, totally surrounded by Italy. It achieved independence, according to legend, in 301 A.D. and is a party to the statute of the INTERNATIONAL COURT OF JUSTICE. Its population is estimated to be 23,000. Ethnic groups include persons of Sammarinese and Italian origin. The language in common use is Italian. Christianity (Roman Catholic) is the predominant religion. Literacy is estimated at 97%.

The government (1990) took the form of a republic. Two coregents acts as heads of State. Executive authority is exercised by an 11-member Congress of State. Legislative functions are performed by the 60-member unicameral Grand and General Council. The judiciary is headed by the Council of Twelve, which is the court of final appeal. Political parties include the Christian Democratic Party, the Communist Party, the United Socialist Party, the Democratic Socialist Party, and the Republican Party.

San Marino is said to be the oldest republic in the world. Its citizens retain the right to vote regardless of residence abroad.

San Marino became a member of the COUNCIL OF EUROPE in 1988 and of the United Nations in 1992.

**SAO TOME AND PRINCIPE.** The Democratic Republic of Sao Tome and Principe is a country in middle Africa, occupying four islands in the Gulf of Guinea, about 150 miles off the coast of Africa. It achieved independence from Portugal in 1975 and became a member of the United Nations the same year. Its population is estimated to be 134,000. Ethnic groups include descendants of Portuguese settlers and their slaves. Portuguese is the only language commonly used. Christianity (Roman Catholic, 80%; Evangelical Protestant, Seventh Day Adventist, and other Protestant denominations, 20%) is the predominant religion. Literacy is estimated at 50%.

The government (1994) took the form of a republic. The president is elected by members of the People's Assembly from candidates nominated by the Movement for the Liberation of Sao Tome and Principe, the only legal political party. The People's Assembly, composed of members elected for terms of four years, is granted supreme power under the 1975 constitution.

The Portuguese used slave labor to develop extensive sugar and cocoa plantations on the islands of Sao Tome and Principe during the 17th century. It was the scene of labor riots in 1953, which ended with the killing of several hundred African laborers and the development of a liberation movement.

When the Portuguese departed from Sao Tome and Principe in 1975, they abandoned one of Africa's poorest countries. Because they had not trained the African population to maintain the roads and bridges or to manage the coffee and cocoa plantations, the economic situation deteriorated rapidly. In 1981, food riots erupted when the government could no longer afford to import dried fish. Since that time, however, governments and international organizations have provided massive assistance and the country has achieved food-sufficiency in coffee, sugar, and cooking oil. Much of the international aid was provided by the World Food Program.

A new constitution was approved by referendum in August 1990. It provided for direct election of a 55-member National Assembly, including multi-party and independent candidates, and direct election of a president who is limited to two five-year terms. The president appoints the prime minister, and other ministers, on the advice of the prime minister, and the National Assembly appoints the Supreme Court. Legislation

1316

governing formation of political parties came into effect in September 1990.

The first multi-party elections were held in 1991. In legislative elections in January the new Party for Democratic Convergence (PCD) obtained 33 seats in the National Assembly while the Movement for the Liberation of Sao Tome and Principe (MLSTP), previously the sole party, obtained only 21. A transitional government ruled until presidential elections were held in March, in which Miguel Trovoada, who had returned from exile a year before, stood as the sole candidate after two others had withdrawn. As an independent with the support of the PCD, Trovoada won and took office as president in April.

Economic reform proved difficult, with significant protests following a substantial depreciation in the currency coupled with large increases in prices, particularly for petroleum. The prime minister and Council of Ministers were dismissed by the president in April 1992.

By December 1992 and the first local elections since independence, there was disenchantment with the ruling party, which gained control of none of the local districts while the MLSTP gained control of five of the seven districts. Political unrest continued, with the government blamed for economic hardship and political authoritarianism. Legislation was passed in April 1994 strengthening the consultative role of the opposition in the National Assembly.

*BIBLIOGRAPHY.* Organization of American States. *Annual Report of the Inter-American Commission on Human Rights.* Washington, D.C. IGO annual report, in English.

**SATO, EISAKU (1901–1975).** Co-winner of the 1974 **NOBEL PEACE PRIZE,** along with **SEAN MACBRIDE,** Eisaku Sato was the first Japanese citizen, indeed the first Asian, to be so honored. The Prize Committee cited Sato for his determined antimilitarism and reconciliation policy that stabilized the Pacific area.

Sato was educated at the Imperial University, from which he received a law degree in 1924. Throughout his political career, he held various government posts until he rose to the prime ministership in 1964, a post he held until 1972. During his tenure as prime minister, Sato worked to establish Japan as an international political and economic power and was remarkably successful on both fronts. He accepted the 1947 Japanese constitution, which renounced war, as the basis for all political actions. His negotiations with the United States secured the return of Okinawa and the Ogasawara Islands to Japan and the promise that nuclear arms would not be maintained on American bases on Japanese soil. He also improved Japan's political and economic relations with South Korea, Myanmar (then Burma), Malaysia, Singapore, Thailand, Laos, Indonesia, Australia, New Zealand, the Philippines, and South Vietnam.

In accepting the Nobel Prize, Sato declared, "Japan is basically a difficult nation to understand because . . . our culture differs so much from those of the West and of other Asian countries. . . . I cannot but admit that at a time when international understanding was required, our efforts to promote . . . understanding were inadequate. . . . I therefore plan to use the prize I received to further the links between our country and the rest of the world."

*BIBLIOGRAPHY.* Gray, Tony. *Champions of Peace.* London: Paddington Press, 1976.

Schlessinger, Bernard S., and June H. Schlessinger, eds. *Who's Who of Nobel Prize Winners.* Phoenix, AZ, USA: Oryx Press, 1991.

**SAUDI ARABIA.** The Kingdom of Saudi Arabia is an Arab country occupying most of the Arabian Peninsula, on the Red Sea, the Gulf of Aqaba, and the Persian Gulf. It has borders with Iraq, Jordan, Kuwait, Oman, Qatar, the United Arab Emirates, and Yemen. It achieved independence in 1932 when King Ibn Saud united Hejaz and Nejd into a single kingdom, and it became a member of the United Nations in 1945. Its population is estimated to be 15,985,000. Ethnic groups include Arabs (90% of the population) and a variety of Afro–Asian mixtures. The language in common use is Arabic. Islam (Sunni, 85%; Shi'ite, 15%) is the predominant religion. Literacy is estimated at 80%.

The government (1994) took the form of a monarchy based on the *Sharia* (Islamic law). There is no formal constitution. King Fahd Ibn Abdul Aziz Al Saud is prime minister and head of State and government. There is a 21-member Council of Ministers to advise the king and to prepare legislation; all laws and regulations are promulgated in the form of royal or ministerial decrees. The religious law of Islam is the law of the land, and it is administered by religious courts headed by a chief judge who is also responsible for the Department of *Sharia* Affairs. There are no political parties.

*RELIGIOUS ISSUES.* In recent years, Saudi Arabia has periodically experienced difficulties with Iranian pilgrims to Mecca, who have numbered over 150,000 in some years and have caused severe damage to Muslim holy places. In 1988, Saudi Arabia limited the number of Iranians permitted to enter Mecca, and severed diplomatic relations with Teheran. It has since

S

supported Kuwait in what was considered to be Iranian-supported terrorism in the Arab Gulf.

Diplomatic relations with Iran were re-established and an accord reached in March 1991 by which a quota of 110,000 Iranians would be allowed to enter the country for the annual pilgrimage. In May 1994, 270 people died in a human stampede during the pilgrimage to Mecca.

During the 1990s issues of fundamentalism arose; and when petitions calling for increased Islamization were presented to the king, the Higher Judicial Council warned of the consequences of criticizing the king. Amidst allegations of suppression of dissent, the king denounced attempts of foreign nationals to foment dissatisfaction through the spread of Islamic fundamentalism. Six Islamic lawyers and scholars who formed a human rights organization in May 1993 were dismissed from their jobs and left the country, reorganizing in London. According to the NGO **HUMAN RIGHTS WATCH,** in 1994 arbitrary arrest, detention without trial, and ill-treatment of prisoners, especially of the Islamist government opponents, were rampant in Saudi Arabia. In addition, the ban on free speech was strictly enforced, and the government cracked down on peaceful dissent by Islamist groups. Between April and September 1994, several hundred religious opponents were arrested.

In March 1992 the king announced the creation of the 60-member advisory Consultative Council, appointed by the king every four years. The Council came into being in December 1993. However, almost all of the members of the Council are government loyalists, the majority of them longtime government employees. According to the Consultative Council Bylaws, issued in August 1994 by King Fahd, the Council's members retain their positions in the executive branch while serving their terms in the Consultative Council. King Fahd also issued a decree on the creation of a basic law of government, akin to a constitution, and the creation of regional authorities. In November 1992 the king also reorganized the 18-member Supreme Council.

In August 1994 the United States of America granted political asylum to the former first secretary to the Saudi UN mission who accused the Saudi Government of human rights abuses, corruption, and sponsorship of terrorism.

**BIBLIOGRAPHY.** Amnesty International. *Saudi Arabia: Religious Intolerance: the Arrest, Detention and Torture of Christian Worshippers and Shi'a Muslims.* London: 1993. NGO report, in English.
——. *Saudi Arabia: An Upsurge in Public Executions.* London: 1993. NGO report, in English.
Arab Organization for Human Rights. "Human Rights in the Arab World: Saudi Arabia," *AOHR Newsletter* no. 14–15 (February 1988): 7–8. NGO article, in English.
——. *Report: Human Rights in the Arab World.* Cairo, Egypt. NGO annual report, in Arabic or English.
Human Rights Watch. "Saudi Arabia," in *Human Rights Watch World Report 1995,* pp. 299–305. New York: 1995. NGO report, in English.
Middle East Watch. *Empty Reforms: Saudi Arabia's New Basic Laws.* New York: Human Rights Watch, 1992. NGO report, in English.
Minnesota Lawyers International Human Rights Committee. *Shame in the House of Saud: Contempt for Human Rights in the Kingdom of Saudi Arabia.* Minneapolis, MN, USA: 1992. NGO report, in English.
Peroncel-Huugoz, Jean-Pierre. "Arabie Seoudite: Les Travailleurs Immigres Devant l'Intolerance Religieuse" (Saudi Arabia: Migrant Workers Face Religious Intolerance), *Lettre de la FIDH* 257 (12 July 1988): 3–6. NGO article, in French.

**SAVE THE CHILDREN FUND.** An international non-governmental organization in consultative status (Category II) with the UN **ECONOMIC AND SOCIAL COUNCIL** and with the **WHO,** Save the Children is not a membership organization.

The Fund was founded in London in 1919 to fight for the rights of children throughout the world and to better the living conditions of children. Save the Children has medical and health programs in 35 countries, with its principal concern being education, nutrition, community development, and welfare programs. The organization publishes the bi-monthly *Branch-Out* and the quarterly *The World's Children.*

Save the Children Fund. Address: Central Information Section, Mary Datchelor House, 17 Grove Lane, London SE5 8RD, UK. Telephone: (44-71) 703-5400. Fax: (44-71) 703-2278.

**SCHELL (ORVILLE) CENTER FOR INTERNATIONAL HUMAN RIGHTS, YALE UNIVERSITY.** The Orville H. Schell, Jr., Center for International Human Rights is a univeristy-wide interdisciplinary human rights center, established at Yale Law School in 1989 in memory of the human rights advocate and lawyer of the same name. The Center's mission is to educate and train future human rights advocates and scholars; to bring theoretical insights to the study and practice of human rights; to increase the awareness of human rights concerns in the university and broader New Haven (CT, USA) community; and to provide direct assistance to the human rights community through scholarship, research, and advocacy.

The Schell Center, in collaboration with a consortium of human rights scholars, advocates, and librarians from around the world, also has undertaken work on **DIANA,** the internet-based human rights library. In addition, the Center provides ongoing support for the **ALLARD K. LOWENSTEIN INTERNATIONAL HUMAN RIGHTS LAW PROJECT,** a student-run organization at Yale Law School, and the **ALLARD K. LOWENSTEIN INTERNATIONAL HUMAN RIGHTS CLINIC,** a clinical class offered at Yale Law School.

***FELLOWSHIP PROGRAMS.*** The Center sponsors three fellowship programs: Senior and Junior Fellowships are open to established (senior) and aspiring (junior) human rights advocates and scholars, while Summer Fellowships are open to Yale University students.

*Senior Fellows.* Senior fellows spend up to a year in residence at the Center to provide them with the opportunity to focus on a particular area of human rights scholarship. In addition to research, a senior fellow may teach a class, give a major lecture, or join in discussions with other members of the Center and of the Yale faculty. Previous senior fellows included Gibson Kamau Kuria (Kenya), Margaret Popkin (El Salvador), Jacek Kuron (Poland), and Gisela von Muhlenbrock (Chile).

*Junior Fellows.* Junior fellows also focus on a particular human rights issue or problem and produce a scholarly article or book. They may give a lecture or informal talk, guest lecture in a class, present their research to the faculty of the law school, and work with students on human rights projects or research.

*Summer Fellows.* The Summer Fellowship program has a threefold purpose: to train future human rights advocates and scholars; to provide direct assistance to the human rights advocacy community; and to increase understanding and scholarship on a particular human rights problem. Yale summer fellows generally spend from six to twelve weeks working with a nongovernmental organization. In addition, summer fellows produce a written report or academic paper based on their experience. In the past, summer fellows have undertaken projects with the **INTER-AMERICAN COMMISSION ON HUMAN RIGHTS** in Washington, D.C., and with the UN **CENTER FOR HUMAN RIGHTS** in Geneva, Switzerland.

***HUMAN RIGHTS CURRICULUM.*** Through the Senior Fellowship program, the Center teaches at least one international human rights law class per year at the Yale Law School. At the undergraduate level, the Center collaborated with Yale's Center for International and Area Studies to develop an undergraduate major in international studies, a basic international human rights class being one of the core courses of this major.

***PUBLICATIONS.*** The Center supports a wide-ranging publication program for monographs on international human rights and has a human rights working paper series, consisting of final papers and works in progress that come out of Center-sponsored conferences or are produced by fellows. The series covers topics such as the establishment of a free press, transnational public law litigation, Islamic culture and universal human rights norms, the rights of women in South African prisons, and Argentina's transition to democracy. In addition, the Center produces videotapes of conferences, panel discussions, and lectures.

The Orville H. Schell, Jr., Center for International Human Rights. Address: Yale Law School, P.O. Box 208215, New Haven, CT 06520, USA. Telephone: (203) 432-7480. Fax: (203) 432-1040. Director: Harold Hongju Koh.

**SCHWEITZER, ALBERT (1875–1965).** This Alsatian medical missionary, theologian, and philosopher (and internationally renowned musician and musicologist) was awarded the 1952 **NOBEL PEACE PRIZE** for his humanitarian work, specifically the founding of a hospital in French Equitorial Africa. The Prize Committee cited Schweitzer's "altruism, reverence for life, and idea of brotherhood."

Born in Gunsbach, Alsace, when it was a part of the German empire, Schweitzer was the son of a Lutheran pastor. He studied theology and philosophy in Strasbourg, Paris, and Berlin, receiving his doctorate in philosophy in 1899 from the University of Strasbourg with a thesis on the philosophy of Immanuel Kant. After holding a number of posts at the Theological College of St. Thomas in Strasbourg, he entered medical school, qualifying as a medical doctor in 1913.

After graduation, Schweitzer left Europe for the mission station of Lambarene in French equatorial Africa. There, with his wife Helene Bresslau, he opened a hospital to serve the native population. However, with the outbreak of World War I, he was interned in France and released in 1918, staying in Europe until 1924. He returned to Africa in 1924 and lived there until his death. From his publications and lectures and from donations to his charitable institution, Schweitzer was able to expand his hospital to 70 buildings, able to accommodate 500 patients. With the money from his Nobel Peace Prize, he opened a special wing for lepers. After receiving the Prize, Schweitzer spoke out against atomic weapons testing.

***BIBLIOGRAPHY.*** Gray, Tony. *Champions of Peace.* London: Paddington Press, 1976.

Schlessinger, Bernard S., and June H. Schlessinger, eds. *Who's Who of Nobel Prize Winners.* Phoenix, AZ, USA: Oryx Press, 1991.

**SCHWEITZER (ALBERT) INSTITUTE FOR THE HUMANITIES.** The Albert Schweitzer Institute for the Humanities (ASIH) is a nonprofit, non-governmental, and nonpartisan organization affiliated with Quinnipiac College and the United Nations. Its mission is to foster Dr. Schweitzer's philosophy and promote individual responsibility and action on pressing social issues.

The Institute, established in 1984 by Harold Robles with the support of Dr. Schweitzer's daughter, Rhena Schweitzer Miller, carries out its mission through programs that reflect areas of Dr. Schweitzer's thought and work: health care and medical relief, music and arts, ecology and the environment, disarmament and demilitarization, human rights, animal issues, and theology and ethics. Each program is headed by an educator or social activist who works with volunteers to plan and carry out projects that range from community outreach to publications to international conferences. In 1993, the Institute airlifted medical equipment, clothing, school supplies, and toys to victims of the ethnic war in the former Yugoslavia; hosted an international environmental symposium at the United Nations; presented the first annual Albert Schweitzer Environmental Youth Award; and initiated an ongoing food and clothing drive at the local level, benefiting the homeless living in shelters in the Institute's resident state of Connecticut.

Albert Schweitzer Institute for the Humanities. Address: 515 Sherman Avenue, Hamden, CT 06514, USA. Telephone: (203) 281-8926. Fax: (203) 281-8929.

**SCIENCE AND TECHNOLOGY.** The impact of scientific and technological developments on the realization of human rights and fundamental freedoms was considered informally, but in some detail, at a seminar organized by the UN Division of Human Rights in cooperation with the Government of Austria and held in Vienna from 19 June to 1 July 1972. Expert participants and alternates, designated by 25 countries but serving in their capacity as individuals, took part in the seminar, together with observers from four additional countries and the representatives of a large number of intergovernmental and non-governmental organizations.

Those who attended the seminar realized that, whereas scientific and technological developments could improve the life of human beings in many spheres, they could at the same time, if applied without planning or built-in safeguards, lead to the violation of human rights in other spheres. They put forward a number of proposals and policies to ensure that all scientific discoveries and their technological applications are utilized in the interest of society as a whole but ultimately came to the conclusion that it was inappropriate for such an informal gathering to adopt common conclusions or recommendations.

The report of the seminar (UN Doc. ST/TAO/HR/45) reflects the extreme complexity of the problem and the wide diversity of views of the participants. The following extracts indicate the main trends of thinking, particularly as regards the impact of science and technology upon the right to privacy, the right to enjoy democratic government, the right to work, the right to rest and leisure, the right to health, the right to food, and the right to education and culture (*Ibid.,* paras. 21–61):

There was diversity of opinion as to what were the really important problems in relation to human rights and scientific and technological developments. Some speakers felt that the vital issues were not so much possible invasions of the right of privacy or questions arising from heart transplants as the use of modern science and technology to promote economic, social and cultural rights, including the rights to health, food and housing and threats to the rights to work posed by automation. It was noted that in the developing societies the concern to preserve respect for privacy was felt as strongly as in the industrialized societies; however, the need for specific local laws dealing with scientific and technological developments had not yet been felt with such urgency; all the more so in Islamic countries for instance where private life as well as public life was impregnated with religion, which was a balancing factor. It was remarked that one of the greatest dangers to the right to life itself were the advanced technologies of warfare. Attention was drawn also to the danger that science might be used to interfere with the integrity and sovereignty of nations, for instance through the use of observation satellites or devices used for espionage. Further, it was pointed out that until the basic rights of food, work and shelter had been realized, there ought to be a more careful use of resources by developing countries for the sophisticated technology. It was asserted by other speakers that the socialist form of government had led to very great developments in science and technology. Science and technology were also well developed in other countries which had other socio-economic bases.

Many participants wished to emphasize that science in general was a positive force in society for increasing production and improving the conditions of life of the citizens. Several participants felt that often scientific techniques had evolved for the benefit of an *élite* and that great sums of money were directed towards projects such as space research or sophisticated weaponry that did not necessarily benefit the pressing needs of humanity at large. It was said that the new phenomenon of the large multinational corporations which often pollute the air and water and disrupt the economic and social fabric of developing countries should be studied. Other speakers pointed to the need for technology assessment, since scientific and technological advances which appear to be an unmitigated good on a small or laboratory or pilot plant scale, might have unforeseen consequences when applied on a massive international scale. These were unexpected effects which occurred in the environment or in man, irrespective of the social system.

Participants in the seminar pointed out that contemporary scientific and technological progress had a very great influence on all aspects of social life in all societies. Advances in science and technology created vast opportunities for the development of the economy and culture of various countries, the improvement of the material welfare of peoples and the consolidation of peace, friendship and co-operation between peoples and States. Yet it would be a great mistake to view scientific and technological progress in the abstract or collectively, without taking account of the existence in the modern world of different social and political systems, or to disregard the major qualitative differences in the social consequences of the scientific and technological revolution in socialist, capitalist and developing countries. Scientific and technological progress could, of course, have negative effects too, but science itself and peoples were able to cope with them. There were therefore no grounds for pessimism, panic or fear.

Other participants doubted whether there was any fundamental difference between the disadvantages and possible dangers arising out of science and technology as between one system and another. The problems now arising from technological advance were the same in kind whenever they occurred, though they no doubt differed in degree. They could understand that solutions adopted might well differ according to the political, economic and social system, and that in some systems a given solution might be more readily accepted than in others.

Several speakers advocated the adoption of international instruments dealing with human rights and scientific and technological developments, as was envisaged by the preamble to General Assembly resolution 2450 (XXIII) and paragraph 10 of Commission on Human Rights resolution 10 (XXVII). Reference was made in this connexion to the possibility of adopting one or more conventions, declarations, model laws or regulations or minimum standards.

*(a) Right to Privacy (article 12 of the Universal Declaration of Human Rights).* The threats posed to the right of privacy due to surreptitious surveillance devices were pointed out by various participants. Whereas previously one could often detect intrusions, now the methods were more clandestine. Computers might be used for storing vast quantities of information on individuals and questions arose concerning invasion of privacy and the right to access to such information. Several participants described national computer systems used for health and social purposes and the measures being taken to prohibit or prevent the use of an individual's records for other than intended purposes. The use of drugs to obtain confessions was deplored. The importance of protecting a private sphere was emphasized by several speakers, but it was recognized that a specific right to privacy had not been explicitly defined in many countries. Moreover it was pointed out that the prevention of an assault on privacy by other individuals or private institutions was often more difficult to control than State intervention. Large data banks were being kept by commercial firms and personal information was published by newspapers and the electronic media to wide segments of the population. Some participants emphasized that the simple proclamation of a right was not enough; technological safeguards should also be sought, penal consequences for violations would be appropriate, but the real guarantees lay in a sensitive social and political system. Religious and legal attitudes of respect for inviolability of the person, family and home were also important bulwarks against invasion of privacy.

Attention was drawn to the invasion of privacy due to such features as new construction techniques, which result in the use of inferior materials such as thin walls in housing. An element of discrimination was pointed out; this type of housing was the only one that some could afford. Hence, an implied consent is given by the inhabitants to the violation of their right to privacy. The assault on this right caused by the noise, pollution and advertising present in advanced, industrialized countries was also recognized. The adverse effects of noise, pollution and advertising, especially in the industrially advanced countries, were also recognized. In particular, the conditioning of the consumer by television, radio and abusive advertising might sometimes constitute a veritable rape of the mind.

*(b) Right to Enjoy Democratic Government (article 21).* Several participants drew attention to the importance of radio and television and the other media of information for informing the electorate of political events and making better informed choices of their representatives. The advent of copying machines, an improved communication network, computers and other modern machines had resulted in better and more efficient public administrators. Many countries had voting machines which permitted a prompt and accurate calculation of the results of elections.

Other participants emphasized the danger of technocracy and the fear that computers would greatly influence many important decision-making functions. It was pointed out that if a computer made a determination and only one group had complete information, it would be very difficult to dispute the resulting decision. The inhibiting psychological impact of challenging the machine may often be a great danger to democratic participation in government. However, it had to be realized that many governmental decisions had in fact become highly technical and complex and beyond the ken of the average layman.

It was stated that the influencing of the electorate through the electronic media and use of sophisticated social science surveys and opinion polls can have a significant impact on the results of elections. It was pointed out that there were tendencies towards monopoly in the control of mass media. The cost of campaigning for office had risen in many countries due to the need for costly technology.

The use of surveillance devices and data banks, which violated the right to privacy, was also seen to threaten the rights to peaceful assembly, freedom of speech, thought and the press. The important question of access to computerized information kept by governments as well as private organizations was discussed. It was remarked that the use of tranquilizing drugs might render a whole population more docile.

Several participants told the seminar of positive social uses to which computers and other technological tools were being put in their respective countries, emphasizing that a stable economic and social environment was the best guarantee for democratic government. Towards this end participants from the developing world stresses the necessity of an increased transfer of technology.

*(c) Right to Work (article 23).* The increasing specialization necessary because of new technological requirements could, if remedial measures were not taken, exacerbate the employment situation for unskilled workers. Several speakers stated that the development of automation often displaced workers. Several participants spoke of the need for relatively frequent retraining. Because of the rapid advancement of technology, even technical, professional and managerial staff might be unemployed. Computer services intended to match vacancies with those looking for jobs had been adopted by one Government. Attention was drawn to the question

of the scientific workers' right to refuse to continue certain socially dangerous research; they should be protected against the possibility of losing their jobs or of any sort of persecution. The attention of participants in the seminar was directed to the need to guarantee for all people employment, democratic education and an improvement in its quality, and retraining for workers without reduction in salary; to establish public control of the introduction and use of new technology in the interests of the people; to prevent industrial accidents and to ensure real and effective participation by the workers in the management of the affairs of State and of society at all levels.

Attention was drawn to the use and abuse of psychological tests and personal data banks to assess a prospective employee's suitability for work and the use of secret surveillance methods and computer records to observe employees' performance and conduct.

Many participants described the care that their countries were taking to ensure safe and healthy working conditions when installing new technological processes. Female workers were given special protection in particular when working with potentially dangerous chemical substances.

Several participants mentioned the importance that computers and other scientific and technological developments had in the industries of their respective countries and in the stimulation of economic growth and therefore the creation of more jobs.

The need to provide everyone with a fair opportunity for decent employment was recognized by all participants. Attention was drawn to the dehumanizing tendency of automated industry, which often severely lowered the job satisfaction of the workers. However, the assumption that work itself was essential to the quality of life was challenged. Reference was made to shorter working weeks and earlier retirement, with the consequent need to stimulate education for the creative use of leisure.

Stress was laid upon the importance of continuing consultation and planning by government, employers and employees in anticipation of change so as to minimize disruption and redundancy when it came.

One participant suggested that article 23 of the Universal Declaration of Human Rights was itself offensive to human dignity in that it implied a subordination of the worker to his employer and reflected traditional conflicts which were now out of date. The emphasis now should be upon participation in productive processes on the basis of co-operation, not conflict.

*(d) Right to Rest and Leisure (article 24).* Many of the participants described the new facilities, being made available in their countries, for their citizens to enjoy the outdoors, take up sports, rest and pursue cultural activities. As the need for long hours of work declined, this sphere of human activity was becoming more important. Labour-saving devices abounded in the house to reduce the time necessary for household chores. Furthermore improved transportation made access to places of rest and recreation increasingly possible. Recreational equipment was mass-produced and increasingly available.

The destruction of the environment and the stresses caused by industrialization and urbanization were threats to the rights to rest and leisure. Better city planning was suggested to reverse adverse trends.

The social alienation characterized by the new technological age was mentioned. Better planning of man's social needs was suggested so that man might be able to fulfil himself creatively during his non-working hours.

*(e) Right to Health (article 25).* The term "technogenic" diseases was introduced to the seminar to characterize those diseases which were a direct result of technological advances. Occupational diseases and mental disorders caused by the urban environment were examples of such threats to the right to health posed by new technological developments. Science was continuously discovering the harmful effect which certain activities have on the health of man. Recent tests, for instance, had shown that cigarette smoke inhaled by non-smokers in the proximity of smokers in unventilated or poorly ventilated areas could be harmful to the non-smoker.

Several participants addressed themselves to the questions raised by organ transplantation, including the definition of death, attitudes to which were changing in the light of the possibility of maintaining heart and lung functioning after cessation of brain activity. Experimentation on human subjects also received considerable attention and participants discussed what constitutes "informed consent" for the purpose of such experiments. Several speakers drew attention to the psychological inferiority felt by patients entering modern hospitals. In some areas, patients had been abused for research or demonstration purposes and some feared that they might become involved in organ transplantation against their will.

The subjects of artificial fertilization, abortion, production of children in test tubes, compulsory sterilization and mutation of germinal cells were also touched upon. It was pointed out that it was possible to determine prior to birth that a foetus had Down's syndrome and it was asked whether the parents or society had a right to abort such a child.

Since the right to health and the application of science in these fields was involved, several participants stated that deontological codes should be more precise and should be constantly adjusted to discoveries and rapid changes.

It was pointed out that the effects of certain technological developments could have effects on later generations through production of mutations.

The dangers of air pollution were again referred to in the context of the right to health. The question of legal responsibility for the car exhaust which caused smog, and ultimately contributed to disability and death were referred to.

Several participants drew attention to the difficulties which inevitably arose in present conditions of scarcity in selecting beneficiaries of "iron lungs", the dialysis machines used by patients with kidney disease and other types of costly and scarce machinery, or costly surgical procedures, including organ transplantation and the "artificial" prolongation of life. It was also pointed out that sophisticated life-prolonging procedures were being used while many suffered a lack of basic medical attention. On the other hand, attention was drawn to certain dramatic recent events such as the development of a successful and inexpensive anti-polio vaccine.

It was observed that in numerous ways, technology was reducing the extent to which the individual must indulge in beneficial exercise.

*(f) Right to Food (article 25).* Several participants and observers referred to the importance of "the green revolution" in meeting food shortages in various countries. It was explained that this progress had come about through improved agricultural practices including improved seeds, synthetic fertilizers, pesticides and fungicides and better water and soil management. Certain pesticides and fungicides were recognized as being ecologically disruptive. Prudence was advocated in their use as well as in that of artificial growth stimulants for animals and chemical additives in

food, for which purpose adequate protective legislation might be necessary. It was also recognized that in order to improve methods of production, conservation and distribution of food, it was necessary in many countries to develop or reform the agrarian structure. The improvement of international trade practices in agricultural products was also deemed important.

DDT was recognized to have some long-range undesirable effects in the environment, but for many regions it was deemed necessary until a inexpensive substitute could be found. Since malnutrition was widespread in large areas of the world, the negative aspects of modern chemistry in the production of food should be kept in proper perspective.

The population growth rate stimulated by improved health services was recognized as having placed large demands on agriculturalists to ensure an adequate supply of food. The interdependence of fertility control and the right to food was noted.

*(g) Right to Education and Culture (articles 26 and 27).* The need for continuous education and even frequent retraining in the present era of rapid technological advances was stressed by several participants. The content of the educational curriculum must be regularly brought up to date and the demands placed on teachers were particularly great. Some participants in the seminar noted in their statements the democratic and advanced nature of education and the flowering of culture in socialist countries.

Others pointed out that in any case the freedom of research and of artistic creation should be safeguarded.

Modern audio-visual aids could make important contributions to education. Several participants referred to the importance of radio and television in educating their people, perhaps especially in rural areas. It was noted, however, that pictures and sound had to be augmented by high quality commentary in order to produce desirable results. Computers were playing an important part in the social sciences.

Reference was made to the phenomenon of cultural misrepresentation and interference being perpetuated against developing countries through certain types of advertising and commercial films and television shows.

It was said that violence portrayed on television had been shown to lead to anti-social behaviour in some children, who were unable fully to distinguish fact from fantasy, or who were otherwise susceptible to having their behaviour influenced through viewing television.

It was maintained that it should be possible to keep museums and libraries open free of charge in the evening and on weekends for the benefit of all.

Special emphasis was placed on the fact that the great technological advances should be used for progress in education and culture in developing countries.

One participant in the seminar stressed that the steps taken in some socialist countries to complete the transition to universal secondary education in condition of scientific and technological progress were of great social import.

**THE EFFECTS OF SCIENCE AND TECHNOLOGY ON HUMAN RIGHTS.** On 13 May 1968, the **TEHERAN INTERNATIONAL CONFERENCE ON HUMAN RIGHTS** adopted the Proclamation of Teheran, in which it pointed out (para. 18) that "while recent scientific discoveries and technological advances have opened vast prospects for economic, social and cultural progress, such developments may nevertheless endanger the rights and freedoms of individuals and will require continuing attention."

On proposal of the Conference, the **GENERAL ASSEMBLY** invited the Secretary-General (resolution 2450 [XXIII]) to study the problems in connection with human rights arising from developments in science and technology, in particular from the following standpoints: (a) respect for the privacy of individuals and the integrity and sovereignty of nations in the light of advances in recording and other techniques; (b) protection of the human personality and its physical and intellectual integrity in the light of advances in biology, medicine, and biochemistry; (c) uses of electronics which might affect the rights of the person and the limits which should be placed on such uses in a democratic society; and (d) more generally, the balance which should be established between scientific and technological progress and the intellectual, spiritual, cultural, and moral advancement of humanity.

In the following years, the Secretary-General prepared a number of studies on various aspects of the subject, including studies entitled "The impact of scientific and technological developments on economic, social and cultural rights" (UN Doc. E/CN.4/1084), "The impact of science and technology on the right to work and certain related rights" (UN Doc. E/CN.4/1115), "Respect for the privacy of individuals and the integrity and sovereignty of nations in the light of advances in recording and other techniques" (UN Doc. E/CN.4/1116 and Adds. 1–4), "The impact of science and technology on the right to rest and leisure and the right to social security" (UN Doc. E/CN.4/1141), and "Uses of electronics which might affect the rights of the person and the limits which should be placed on such uses in a democratic society" (UN Doc. E/CN.4/1142 and Add. 1). These studies—and a **UNESCO** report on the impact of scientific developments on the right to education, the right to culture, and authors' rights—were considered by the UN **COMMISSION ON HUMAN RIGHTS** at its 1974 session.

The Commission (resolution 2 [XXX]) called upon all States "to develop further international co-operation to ensure that the results of scientific and technological developments are used in the interests of strengthening international peace and security, realization of the peoples' right to self-determination and respect for national sovereignty, freedom and independence and for the purpose of economic and social development and improving the quality of life for the entire population." The Secretary-General was requested to bring the studies to the attention of governments and to seek their observations on the use to which science and technology can be put: (a) to strengthen international peace and security and the fundamental rights of peoples; (b) to promote and insure general respect for the human rights proclaimed in the UNIVERSAL DECLARATION OF HUMAN RIGHTS and the International Covenants on Human Rights; and (c) through raising their standard of living, to facilitate and protect the enjoyment by all peoples of their right to employment, education, food, health, and economic, social, and cultural well-being. He was further requested to prepare an analysis of the observations received in order to enable the Commission to consider possible guidelines or standards which could be included in appropriate international instruments.

The General Assembly, in 1975, examined a draft declaration on the use of scientific and technological progress in the interests of peace and for the benefit of mankind which had been submitted to it in 1974 by Bangladesh, Czechoslovakia, the German Democratic Republic, Mauritius, Poland, and the Union of Soviet Socialist Republics (UN Doc. A/C.3/L.2144). On 10 November 1975, it proclaimed the Declaration on the Use of Scientific and Technological Progress in the Interests of Peace and for the Benefit of Mankind. The Declaration emphasizes the incalculable potential of scientific and technological developments, but, at the same time, identifies the harmful consequences that might result from the improper use of technological advances; and it appeals to States to coordinate their actions by means of scientific and technological cooperation with a view to solving some of the problems that confront mankind.

The Commission on Human Rights has since devoted its efforts primarily to exploring ways and means of implementing the provisions of the Declaration. In 1977, it considered a number of relevant reports, including reports by the Secretary-General on the protection of the human personality and its physical and intellectual integrity in the light of biology, medicine, and biochemistry (UN Docs. E/CN.4/1172 and Adds. 1–3, and E/CN.4/1173); on the balance which should be established between scientific and technological progress and the intellectual, spiritual, cultural, and moral advancement of humanity (UN Doc. E/CN.4/1199 and Add. 1); on developments relating to science and technology elsewhere in the United Nations system (UN Doc. E/CN.4/1234); on national technological assessment machinery (UN Doc. E/CN.4/1235); and on human rights and international machinery for technological assessment (UN Doc. E/CN.4/1237). In addition, UNESCO submitted to it a report on the impact of scientific and technological developments on the right to education, the right to culture, and author's rights (UN Doc. E/CN.4/1196); and WHO submitted a report on the human rights implications of the genetic manipulation of microbes (UN Doc. E/CN.4/1236). The Commission noted (resolution 10 A

[XXXIII]) these reports and requested the SUB-COMMISSION ON PREVENTION OF DISCRIMINATION AND PROTECTION OF MINORITIES to study, with a view to formulating guidelines if possible, the question of the protection of those detained on the ground of mental ill-health against treatment that may adversely affect the human personality and its physical and intellectual capacity.

The Sub-Commission has since studied the problems of mentally ill persons. Meanwhile, the Commission has repeatedly called upon the Sub-Commission to initiate a study on the use of the achievements of scientific and technological progress to ensure the right to work and development (resolutions 38 [XXXVII], 1982/4, 1984/29, 1986/11, and 1988/61), a task which the Sub-Commission itself had not undertaken up to the end of 1989.

The General Assembly, at its 1988 session, invited the Commission (resolution 43/110) to take appropriate measures and to assist the Sub-Commission in preparing the study. Realizing that the science and technology of our times create possibilities for providing an abundance of material wealth on earth and establishing conditions for the prosperity of society as well as the all-around development of every person, the Assembly expressed serious concern that the results of scientific and technological progress could be used for the arms race and the development of new types of weapons to the detriment of international peace, security, and social progress; human rights and fundamental freedoms; and the dignity of the human person. It called upon all States to make every effort to use the achievements of science and technology in order to promote peaceful social, economic, and cultural development and progress and to put an end to the use of these achievements for military purposes; and to take all necessary measure to place the achievements of science and technology at the service of mankind and to ensure that they do not lead to the degradation of the natural environment.

***HUMAN EXPERIMENTATION.*** The UN Sub-Commission on Prevention of Discrimination and Protection of Minorities recommended, in resolution 1984/17 of 29 August 1984, that one of its members, Mr. Driss Dahak (Morocco), be authorized by the Commission on Human Rights and the ECONOMIC AND SOCIAL COUNCIL to prepare a study on the current dimensions and problems arising from unlawful human experimentation. However, in the absence of such authorization, the study was not completed.

***SEE ALSO*** *Privacy.*

***BIBLIOGRAPHY.*** Committee in Support of Solidarity. "In Defense of Academic Freedom: A Half Year's Struggle,"

*Committee in Support of Solidarity Reports* 36 (5 Oct. 1985): 19–26. NGO bulletin, in English.

Development Cooperation Information Department of the Ministry of Foreign Affairs. *Development Cooperation and the World Economy.* Cooperation between the Netherlands and Developing Countries No. 16. The Hague: n.d. Government report, in English.

Premont, D., M. Tom, and P. Mayenzet. *Essais sur le Concept de "Droits de Vivre"* (Essays on the Concept of a "Right to Live"). Brussels, Belgium: Bruylant, for the Association de Consultants Internation aux en Droits de l'Homme, 1988. Scholarly edited collection, in English and French.

Tinker, Jon. "AIDS in the Developing Countries," *Issues in Science and Technology* (Winter 1988): 43–48. Scholarly article, in English.

## SCIENCE AND TECHNOLOGY: DECLARATION ON THE USE OF SCIENTIFIC AND TECHNOLOGICAL PROGRESS IN THE INTERESTS OF PEACE AND FOR THE BENEFIT OF MANKIND, UN (1975).

The 1968 TEHERAN INTERNATIONAL CONFERENCE ON HUMAN RIGHTS warned that new scientific discoveries and technological advances might soon endanger the enjoyment of certain human rights. In 1975, the UN GENERAL ASSEMBLY studied the impact of certain developments upon the right to health and the right to a clean environment and adopted the Declaration reproduced below, calling upon all States to prevent the use of scientific and technological developments from limiting or interfering with the enjoyment of human rights and fundamental freedoms.

The Declaration was adopted by the General Assembly on 10 November 1975 (resolution 3384 [XXX]). The text, annexed to the resolution, is as follows:

The General Assembly,

Noting that scientific and technological progress has become one of the most important factors in the development of human society,

Taking into consideration that, while scientific and technological developments provide ever increasing opportunities to better the conditions of life of peoples and nations, in a number of instances they can give rise to social problems, as well as threaten the human rights and fundamental freedoms of the individual,

Noting with concern that scientific and technological achievements can be used to intensify the arms race, suppress national liberation movements and deprive individuals and peoples of their human rights and fundamental freedoms,

Also noting with concern that scientific and technological achievements can entail dangers for the civil and political rights of the individual or of the group and for human dignity,

Noting the urgent need to make full use of scientific and technological developments for the welfare of man and to neutralize the present and possible future harmful consequences of certain scientific and technological achievements,

Recognizing that scientific and technological progress is of great importance in accelerating the social and economic development of developing countries,

Aware that the transfer of science and technology is one of the principal ways of accelerating the economic development of developing countries,

Reaffirming the right of peoples to self-determination and the need to respect human rights and freedoms and the dignity of the human person in the conditions of scientific and technological progress, . . .

Solemnly proclaims that:

1. All States shall promote international cooperation to ensure that the results of scientific and technological developments are used in the interests of strengthening international peace and security, freedom and independence, and also for the purpose of the economic and social development of peoples and the realization of human rights and freedoms in accordance with the Charter of the United Nations.

2. All States shall take appropriate measures to prevent the use of scientific and technological developments, particularly by the State organs, to limit or interfere with the enjoyment of the human rights and fundamental freedoms of the individual as enshrined in the Universal Declaration of Human Rights, the International Covenants on Human Rights and other relevant international instruments.

3. All States shall take measures to ensure that scientific and technological achievements satisfy the material and spiritual needs of all sectors of the population.

4. All States shall refrain from any acts involving the use of scientific and technological achievements for the purposes of violating the sovereignty and territorial integrity of other States, interfering in their internal affairs, waging aggressive wars, suppressing national liberation movements or pursuing a policy of racial discrimination. Such acts are not only a flagrant violation of the Charter of the United Nations and principles of international law, but constitute an inadmissible distortion of the purposes that should guide scientific and technological developments for the benefit of mankind.

5. All States shall co-operate in the establishment, strengthening and development of the scientific and technological capacity of developing countries with a view to accelerating the realization of the social and economic rights of the peoples of those countries.

6. All States shall take measures to extend the benefits of science and technology to all strata of the population and to protect them, both socially and materially, from possible harmful effects of the misuse of scientific and technological developments, including their misuse to infringe upon the rights of the individual or of the group, particularly with regard to respect for privacy and the protection of the human personality and its physical and intellectual integrity.

7. All States shall take the necessary measures, including legislative measures, to ensure that the utilization of scientific and technological achievements promotes the fullest realization of human rights and fundamental freedoms without any discrimination whatsoever on grounds of race, sex, language or religious beliefs.

8. All States shall take effective measures, including legislative measures, to prevent and preclude the utilization of scientific and technological achievements to the detriment of human rights and fundamental freedoms and the dignity of the human person.

9. All States shall, whenever necessary, take action to ensure compliance with legislation guaranteeing human rights and freedoms in the conditions of scientific and technological developments.

**SECURITY COUNCIL, UN.** The Security Council of the United Nations was established in accordance with article 7 of the **UNITED NATIONS CHARTER**. Its principal functions and powers are (1) to investigate any disputes or situation which might give rise to a dispute in order to determine whether the continuance of the dispute or situation is likely to endanger the maintenance of international peace and security; (2) to decide on such procedures or recommend such terms of settlement as it may consider appropriate; (3) to make recommendations or decide to take enforcement measures in order to maintain or restore international peace and security; and (4) if it decides that these measures are, or have proved to be, inadequate, to take such action by air, sea, or land forces as may be necessary to restore international peace and security. The Council's enforcement action may take the form of measures not involving the use of armed force, such as complete or partial interruption of economic relations and of rail, sea, air, postal, telegraphic, radio, and other means of communication, and the severance of diplomatic relations; or "action by land, sea or land forces, including demonstrations, blockades, and other operations conducted by the armed forces of UN Member States."

The Council is so organized as to be able to function continuously; a representative of each of its members must be present at UN headquarters at all times. The Council meets in its own chamber at UN headquarters in New York; it has met elsewhere only occasionally, e.g., in Addis Ababa in 1972 and in Panama in 1973. It prepares annual and special reports for consideration by the **GENERAL ASSEMBLY**.

*MEMBERSHIP.* In accordance with article 23 of the UN Charter, as amended by resolution 1991 A (XVIII) of 17 December 1963, which entered into force on 31 August 1965, the Council consists of five permanent members (China, France, Union of Soviet Socialist Republics, United Kingdom of Great Britain and Northern Ireland, and the United States of America) and ten non-permanent members elected by the General Assembly. In 1963, the General Assembly decided that the non-permanent members of the Security Council should be elected according to the following pattern: five from African and Asian States, one from eastern European States, two from Latin American States, and two from western European and other States. The election is held by secret ballot, and there are no nominations. Non-permanent members are elected by a two-thirds' majority, and a retiring non-permanent member is not eligible for immediate re-election. For non-permanent members, the term of office is two years.

At its 40th plenary meeting, on 20 October 1994,

the General Assembly, in accordance with article 23 of the Charter of the United Nations and rule 142 of the rules of procedure of the Assembly, elected Botswana, Germany, Honduras, Indonesia, and Italy non-permanent to fill the vacancies occurring on the expiration of the terms of office of Brazil, Djibouti, New Zealand, Pakistan, and Spain.

As a result, the Security Council is composed of the following fifteen member States: Argentina, Botswana, China, the Czech Republic, France, Germany, Honduras, Indonesia, Italy, Nigeria, Oman, the Russian Federation, Rwanda, the United Kingdom, and the United States.

*COMMITTEES.* The Council has two standing committees: the Committee of Experts, which studies and advises on rules of procedure and other technical matters, and the Committee on the Admission of New Members. Each committee is composed of all members of the Council. In addition, the Military Staff Committee, composed of the chiefs of staff of the five permanent members or their representatives, was established under article 47 of the UN Charter to advise and assist the Council on such matters as its military requirements for maintaining peace, the strategic direction of armed forces placed at its disposal, the regulation of armaments, and possible disarmament.

**SELF-DETERMINATION.** The inalienable right of all peoples to self-determination was first proclaimed by the international community in the Declaration on the Granting of Independence to Colonial Countries and Peoples, adopted by the UN **GENERAL ASSEMBLY** on 14 December 1960 (resolution 1514 [XV]), in the following terms:

1. The subjection of peoples to alien subjugation, domination and exploitation constitutes a denial of fundamental human rights, is contrary to the Charter of the United Nations and is an impediment to the promotion of world peace and co-operation.
2. All peoples have the right to self-determination; by virtue of that right they freely determine their political status and freely pursue their economic, social and cultural development.
3. Inadequacy of political, economic, social or educational preparedness should never serve as a pretext for delaying independence. . . .

Both International Covenants on Human Rights contain an identical article 1 on the subject, which reads as follows:

*Article 1.* 1. All peoples have the right of self-determination. By virtue of that right they freely determine their political status and freely pursue their economic, social and cultural development.

2. All peoples may, for their own ends, freely dispose of their natural wealth and resources without prejudice to any obligations arising out of international economic co-operation, based upon the principle of mutual benefit, and international law. In no case may a people be deprived of its own means of subsistence.

3. The States Parties to the present Covenant, including those having responsibility for the administration of Non-Self-Governing and Trust Territories, shall promote the realization of the right of self-determination, and shall respect that right, in conformity with the provisions of the Charter of the United Nation.

In the Declaration on Principles of International Law Concerning Friendly Relations and Cooperation among States in Accordance with the Charter of the United Nations (see **INTERNATIONAL LAW**), adopted by the General Assembly in 1970 (resolution 2625 [XXV]), the Assembly proclaimed the following "principle of equal rights and self-determination of peoples":

By virtue of the principle of equal rights and self-determination of peoples enshrined in the Charter of the United Nations, all peoples have the right freely to determine, without external interference, their political status and to pursue their economic, social and cultural development, and every State has the duty to respect this right in accordance with the provisions of the Charter.

Every State has the duty to promote, through joint and separate action, realization of the principle of equal rights and self-determination of peoples, in accordance with the provisions of the Charter, and to render assistance to the United Nations in carrying out the responsibilities entrusted to it by the Charter regarding the implementation of the principle, in order:

(a) To promote friendly relations and co-operation among States; and

(b) To bring a speedy end to colonialism, having due regard to the freely expressed will of the peoples concerned; and bearing in mind that subjection of peoples to alien subjugation, domination and exploitation constitutes a violation of the principle, as well as a denial of fundamental human rights, and is contrary to the Charter.

Every State has the duty to promote through joint and separate action universal respect for and observance of human rights and fundamental freedoms in accordance with the Charter.

The establishment of a sovereign and independent State, the free association or integration with an independent State or the emergence into any other political status freely determined by a people constitute modes of implementing the right of self-determination by that people.

Every State has the duty to refrain from any forcible action which deprives peoples referred to above in the elaboration of the present principle of their right to self-determination and freedom and independence. In their actions against, and resistance to, such forcible action in pursuit of the exercise of their right to self-determination, such peoples are entitled to seek and to receive support in accordance with the purposes and principles of the Charter.

The territory of a colony or other Non-Self-Governing Territory has, under the Charter, a status separate and distinct from the territory of the State administering it; and such separate and distinct status under the Charter shall exist until the people of the colony or Non-Self-Governing Territory have exercised their right of self-determination in accordance with the Charter, and particularly its purposes and principles.

Nothing in the foregoing paragraphs shall be construed as authorizing or encouraging any action which would dismember or impair, totally or in part, the territorial integrity or political unity of sovereign and independent States conducting themselves in compliance with the principle of equal rights and self-determination of peoples as described above and thus possessed of a government representing the whole people belonging to the territory without distinction as to race, creed or colour.

Every State shall refrain from any action aimed at the partial or total disruption of the national unity and territorial integrity of any other State or country.

The **AFRICAN CHARTER ON HUMAN AND PEOPLES' RIGHTS,** open for acceptance by member States of the **ORGANIZATION OF AFRICAN UNITY,** contains the following provisions:

*Article 19.* All peoples shall be equal; they shall enjoy the same respect and shall have the same rights. Nothing shall justify the domination of a people by another.

*Article 20.* 1. All peoples shall have right to existence. They shall have the unquestionable and inalienable right to self-determination. They shall freely determine their political status and shall pursue their economic and social development according to the policy they have freely chosen.

2. Colonized or oppressed peoples shall have the right to free themselves from the bonds of domination by resorting to any means recognized by the international community.

3. All peoples shall have the right to the assistance of the States Parties to the present Charter in their liberation struggle against foreign domination, be it political, economic or cultural.

*Article 21.* 1. All peoples shall freely dispose of their wealth and natural resources. This right shall be exercise (sic) in the exclusive interest of the people. In no case shall a people be deprived of it.

2. In case of spoliation the dispossessed people shall have the right to the lawful recovery of its property as well as to an adequate compensation.

3. The free disposal of wealth and natural resources shall be exercised without prejudice to the obligation of promoting international economic cooperation based on mutual respect, equitable exchange and the principles of international law.

4. States parties to the present Charter shall individually and collectively exercise the right to free disposal of their wealth and natural resources with a view to strengthening African unity and solidarity.

5. States Parties to the present Charter shall undertake to eliminate all forms of foreign economic exploitation particularly that practised by international monopolies so as to enable their peoples to fully benefit from the advantages derived from their national resources.

After examining reports submitted by States parties to the **INTERNATIONAL COVENANT ON CIVIL AND POLITICAL RIGHTS** in accordance with article 40 of that Covenant, the UN **HUMAN RIGHTS COMMITTEE** adopted in 1984 a general comment on article 1 of that instrument. Although formulated by the Committee primarily to guide States in preparing the reports called for by the Covenant, such comments incidentally serve to throw light on the Committee's interpretation of certain provisions. The comments on article 1 are as follows (UN Doc. A/39/40, annex VI, paras. 1–8):

In accordance with the purposes and principles of the Charter of the United Nations, article 1 of the International Covenant on Civil and Political Rights recognizes that all peoples have the right of self-determination. The right of self-determination is of particular importance because its realization is an essential condition for the effective guarantee and observance of individual human rights and for the promotion and strengthening of those rights. It is for that reason that States set forth the right of self-determination in a provision of positive law in both Covenants and placed this provision as article 1 apart from and before all of the other rights in the two Covenants.

Article 1 enshrines an inalienable right of all peoples as described in its paragraphs 1 and 2. By virtue of that right they freely "determine their political status and freely pursue their economic, social and cultural development". The article imposes on all States parties corresponding obligations. This right and the corresponding obligations concerning its implementation are interrelated with other provisions of the Covenant and rules of international law.

Although the reporting obligations of all States parties include article 1, only some reports give detailed explanations regarding each of its paragraphs. The Committee has noted that many of them completely ignore article 1, provide inadequate information in regard to it or confine themselves to a reference to election laws. The Committee considers it highly desirable that States parties' reports should contain information on each paragraph of article 1.

With regard to paragraph 1 of article 1, States parties should describe the constitutional and political processes which in practice allow the exercise of this right.

Paragraph 2 affirms a particular aspect of the economic content of the right of self-determination; namely the right of peoples, for their own ends, freely to "dispose of their natural wealth and resources without prejudice to any obligations arising out of international economic co-operation, based upon the principle of mutual benefit, and international law. In no case may a people be deprived of its own means of subsistence". This right entails corresponding duties for all States and the international community. States should indicate any factors or difficulties which prevent the free disposal of their natural wealth and resources contrary to the provisions of this paragraph and to what extent that affects the enjoyment of other rights set forth in the Covenant.

Paragraph 3, in the Committee's opinion, is particularly important in that it imposes specific obligations on States parties, not only in relation to their own peoples but *vis-à-vis* all peoples which have not been able to exercise or have been deprived of the possibility of exercising their right to self-determination. The general nature of this paragraph is confirmed by its drafting history. It stipulates that "The States Parties to the present Covenant, including those having responsibility for the administration of Non-Self-Governing and Trust Territories, shall promote the realization of the right of self-determination, and shall respect that right, in conformity with the provisions of the Charter of the United

Nations". The obligations exist irrespective of whether a people entitled to self-determination depends on a State party to the Covenant or not. It follows that all States parties to the Covenant should take positive action to facilitate realization of and respect for the right of peoples to self-determination. Such positive action must be consistent with the States' obligations under the Charter of the United Nations and under international law: in particular, States must refrain from interfering in the internal affairs of other States and thereby adversely affecting the exercise of the right to self-determination. The reports should contain information on the performance of these obligations and the measures taken to that end.

In connection with article 1 of the Covenant the Committee refers to other international instruments concerning the right of all peoples to self-determination, in particular the Declaration on Principles of International Law concerning Friendly Relations and Co-operation among States in accordance with the Charter of the United Nations, adopted by the General Assembly on 24 October 1970 (General Assembly resolution 2625 (XXV)).

The Committee considers that history has proved that the realization of and respect for the right of self-determination of peoples contributes to the establishment of friendly relations and co-operation between States and to strengthening international peace and understanding.

**DEFINITION AND IMPLEMENTATION OF SELF-DETERMINATION.** The definition, scope, and legal nature of the right of peoples under colonial and alien domination to self-determination, and the means by which the implementation of that right has been promoted and monitored by the international community, are set out in the study entitled *The Right to Self-Determination: Implementation of United Nations Resolutions,* prepared by Mr. Hector Gros Espiell (Uruguay), Special Rapporteur of the UN **SUB-COMMISSION ON PREVENTION OF DISCRIMINATION AND PROTECTION OF MINORITIES.** The study was issued in 1979 (UN publication, Sales no. E/79.XIV.5).

As the Special Rapporteur points out, the right of peoples to self-determination is enshrined in the **UNITED NATIONS CHARTER,** both International Covenants on Human Rights, the Declaration on the Inadmissibility of Intervention and Interference in the Internal Affairs of States (see **STATES' RIGHTS**), the Declaration on the Strengthening of International Security, the Declaration on Principles of International Law Concerning Friendly Relations and Cooperation among States, the definition of **AGGRESSION,** the Charter of Economic Rights and Duties of States, the Declaration on Social Progress and Development (see **DEVELOPMENT**), and in numerous and repeated resolutions of the General Assembly, including the momentous and historic Declaration on the Granting of Independence to Colonial Countries and Peoples, which has been termed the Magna Carta of decolonization and which marks the beginning of the modern attitude to be found on the subject and the irreversible trend toward full decolonization.

This point of view was reiterated by the General Assembly in its resolution 49/148 of 23 December 1994.

As the Special Rapporteur points out (para. 50):

This is one of the spheres in which the Organization's achievements are unanimously acknowledged to be of outstanding value and of historic significance. The affirmation and implementation by the United Nations of the right of peoples to self-determination brought about the crisis of colonialism and set in motion the process of its universal elimination. What in the Covenant of the League of Nations and in the international law of that era was a principle, as is the case with nationalities, applicable preferentially or, rather, almost exclusively in Europe, which did not imply the rejection of colonialism in Africa, Asia and Latin America, what in the Charter of the United Nations was only the mention of a principle in Articles 1 (paragraph 2) and 73, was transformed, as a result of the work done by the Organization from 1952 onwards, but more particularly since 1960, into a basic principle, of universal applicability, into a right of all peoples and into a peremptory norm of international law which, with the end of the traditional colonialism—save for a few surviving remants—led to a complete change in international society.

In the study, the Special Rapporteur deals with questions relating to the definition, scope, and legal nature of the right to self-determination (chapter I), reviews the state of realization of United Nations decisions relating to that right (chapter II), refers to specific situations involving that right which have been dealt with by United Nations organs (chapter III), and puts forward his recommendations for further action to be taken by the international community (chapters IV and V).

As regards the question of definition, the Special Rapporteur presents the following views (paras. 56–63):

Self-determination is essentially a right of peoples. The divergence of opinion among legal theorists which existed on this point until a few years ago has been overcome; the Declaration adopted in resolution 1514 (XV) and the International Covenants on Human Rights have provided the basis for unquestioned acceptance in international law of the fact that self-determination is a right of peoples under colonial and alien domination. To characterize self-determination as a collective right possessed by peoples raises awkward theoretical problems, because of the difficulty of defining the concept of a people and drawing a clear distinction between that and other similar concepts. Self-determination of peoples is a right of peoples, in other words of a specific type of human community sharing a common desire to establish an entity capable of functioning to ensure a common future. It is Peoples as such which are entitled to the right to self-determination. Under contemporary international law minorities do not have this right. People and Nation are two closely related concepts; they may be one and the same, but they are not synonymous. Modern international law has deliberately attributed the right to Peoples,

and not to Nations and States. However, when the People and the Nation are one and the same, and when a People has established itself as a State, clearly that Nation and that State are, as forms or manifestations of the same People, implicitly entitled to the right to self-determination. There is no doubt that the theoretical and practical difficulties involved in these concepts are very great and the Special Rapporteur cannot possibly make a thorough and conclusive analysis of these concepts. All he can do is to make clear his ideas on the subject, even if they are only his first thoughts and presented in summarized form. Apart from such difficulties, however, it is evident that, both politically and practically, the right of peoples to self-determination is one of the major realities of the present day and that the invocation and recognition of this right have radically changed international society as it existed until a few years ago. In their replies, the Government of the Philippines stated that a minority or a foreign State cannot invoke the right of self-determination, and the Government of Iraq stressed the need to distinguish between peoples and minorities, since only peoples possess the right of self-determination. The reply of the Government of the German Democratic Republic gave a full analysis of the reasons why all peoples should be recognized as possessing it.

To assert that self-determination constitutes a collective right of peoples does not mean that an individual right, to which all human beings are entitled, cannot exist at the same time. A right can be simultaneously an individual right and a collective right. The presumed incompatibility between the two types of rights is inadmissible. This conclusion, already recognized, for instance, with respect to the right to development, the right to form trade unions and the right to freedom of information, is perfectly applicable to the case of the right to self-determination.

In the Special Rapporteur's judgement, it is important likewise to try to conceptualize the right to self-determination as a right of the individual. The Commission on Human Rights has repeatedly invoked it as such, without giving a precise reason for that conception and without distinguishing self-determination as a right of the individual from self-determination as a condition or prerequisite for the effective exercise of the other rights and freedoms. In the Special Rapporteur's view, self-determination may be regarded also, as a consequence or its initial recognition, as a right of peoples, as a right of the individual, in that it is every person's right that the people of which he is a member—if it is under colonial and alien domination—should be recognized as having the right to determine freely its own political, economic, social and cultural condition. The Special Rapporteur considers, moreover, that self-determination as a right of the human being is a consequence of the necessary recognition of the political rights of citizens and of the civil, economic, social and cultural rights of all individuals without any discrimination. The self-determination of citizens, individually, on the basis of the recognition of their political rights, is a prerequisite of the effective realization of self-determination as the people's collective right. This view is referred to in paragraph 284 of this study.

In addition, however, the effective exercise of a people's right to self-determination is an essential condition or prerequisite, although not necessarily excluding other conditions, for the genuine existence of the other human rights and freedoms. Only when self-determination has been achieved can a people take the measures necessary to ensure human dignity, the full enjoyment of all rights, and the political, economic, social and cultural progress of all human beings, without any form of discrimination. Consequently, human rights and fundamental freedoms can only exist truly and fully when self-determination also exists. Such is the fundamental importance of self-determination as a human right and a prerequisite for the enjoyment of all the other rights and freedoms. It is with awareness and appreciation of these characteristics of self-determination that the Special Rapporteur has approached the present study.

The United Nations has established the right of self-determination as a right of peoples under colonial and alien domination. The right does not apply to peoples already organized in the form of a State which are not under colonial and alien domination, since resolution 1514 (XV) and other United Nations instruments condemn any attempt aimed at the partial or total disruption of the national unity and the territorial integrity of a country. If, however, beneath the guise of ostensible national unity, colonial and alien domination does in fact exist, whatever legal formula may be used in an attempt to conceal it, the right of the subject people concerned cannot be disregarded without international law being violated. The Declaration on Principles of International Law concerning Friendly Relations and Co-operation among States in accordance with the Charter of the United Nations (General Assembly resolution 2625 (XXV)) uses particularly apt language in spelling out this idea: it reaffirms the need to reserve the territorial integrity of sovereign and independent States, but ties this concept to the requirement that the States must be "possessed of a government representing the whole people belonging to the territory without distinction as to race, creed or colour".

This right of peoples gives rise to the corresponding duty of all States to recognize it and to promote it. The international community and all States not only have a legal duty to refrain from opposing and impeding the exercise of the right to self-determination, but also are under a positive obligation to help in securing its realization, by promoting its exercise and by co-operating in every possible way to ensure that peoples under colonial and alien domination achieve their independence and that those peoples which have already become independent as a result of exercising their right to self-determination achieve their complete sovereignty and full development. These considerations have a particular bearing on the question of the legitimacy of the use of force to achieve self-determination, and the corresponding duty to display solidarity. The Special Rapporteur will pay special attention to this in paragraph 93.

The right of peoples under colonial and alien domination to self-determination is not contingent on any kind of condition or requirement. In particular, resolution 1514 (XV) precludes any opposition to the exercise of the right to self-determination on the pretext that a people has not reached a sufficiently high level of development to lead an independent existence.

Peoples under colonial and alien domination accordingly have rights and obligations conferred by contemporary international law. They therefore possess an international personality and as regards the exercise of their rights and the performance of their duties can be regarded as subjects of international law. Clearly, not all subjects of law have the same status, nor are their rights and duties identical. That is why the view that peoples are now, within the limits indicated above, subjects of law is tenable.

In examining the political, economic, social, and cultural aspects of the right of peoples to self-deter-mination, the Special Rapporteur emphasizes that each of these specific and necessary aspects of the general concept is closely and indissolubly linked to all the others, since they are interdependent and each can only be fully realized through the complete recognition and implementation of the others. His view on these aspects are as follows:

*Political Aspects (para. 114).* From the political point of view, the right of peoples under colonial and alien domination to self-determination has as its corollary their right to achieve independence, free association or integration with another independent State or the acquisition of any other freely determined status. The achievement of any of these objectives "in the effective exercise of national sovereignty against any hegemony and independence" must be the result of a free decision by the people concerned. Where the exercise of self-determination results in the establishment of a new, sovereign and independent State, the right to self-determination itself provides the basis for the right of the people of the new State freely to chose its political system. Thus the right to self-determination does not cease when independence or another possible status is achieved and recognized; it extends into the permanent defence and maintenance of the independence or other status achieved as a result of the initial exercise of the right to self-determination.

*Economic Aspects (para. 135–137).* The economic aspects of the right of peoples to self-determination are manifested, first, in the right of all peoples to determine in freedom and sovereignty, the economic system or régime under which they are to live. Where a people is still subject to colonial or alien domination this right already exists, even though the colonial Power may ignore it and violate it. Where the people has formed a free and sovereign State or has established some other political formula through the exercise of the right to self-determination, the people of that State naturally retains its right freely to determine the economic régime which is to exist in that State. This right will be of lasting efficacy and will continue to take effect in the future, which is of particular significance, in view of all the neo-colonialistic and neo-imperialistic schemes, whatever form they make take, to dominate the new States which have come into being as a result of the exercise of the right to political self-determination, through their power or unlawful intervention in the economic field.

Without prejudice to this general meaning of self-determination from the economic standpoint, it is necessary to specify that the economic content of the right of peoples to self-determination finds its expression in particular—without prejudice to many other different manifestations—in their right to permanent sovereignty over natural resources, a question which covers the problems raised by nationalizations and the harmful activities that may be undertaken in this area by transnational or multinational enterprises.

This right of peoples to self-determination exists, in its economic aspects, in all the above-mentioned manifestations, both in cases where the people concerned has not yet attained its political self-determination and is still struggling against colonial and alien domination, and where the people has formed a political entity or sovereign State as a result of the prior exercise of its right to self-determination.

*Social Aspects (para. 152–154).* Every people has the right to choose and determine the social system under which it is to live, in accordance with its free and sovereign will and with due respect for its traditions and special characteristics.

More specifically, it may be said that the social aspects of the right of peoples to self-determination are related, in particular, to the promotion of social justice, to which every people is entitled and which, in its broadest sense, implies the right to the effective enjoyment by all the individual members of a particular people of their economic and social rights without any discrimination whatsoever.

This aspect of self-determination is covered by various General Assembly resolutions, especially the Declaration on Social Progress and Development, which proclaims "national independence based on the right of peoples to self-determination" to be a primary condition of social progress and development. Other provisions of the Declaration are directly concerned with various aspects of the right of peoples to self-determination. The Declaration of Mexico on the Equality of Women and their Contribution to Development and Peace also refers to the question.

*Cultural Aspects (para. 158–160).* Every people, in the exercise of its right to self-determination, has the right to determine and establish the cultural régime or system under which it is to live; this implies recognition of its right to regain, enjoy and enrich its cultural heritage, and the affirmation of the right of all its members to education and culture.

A people subject to colonial and alien domination has the right to struggle to prevent its heritage, values and cultural identity from being destroyed or affected by the colonial or alien Power. Where that people, through the exercise of its right to self-determination, has formed a political entity or established a sovereign State, the cultural content of its right to self-determination remains in effect, even though it is now governed by the legal and political situation which this people has freely accepted.

The efficacy of the right of peoples to self-determination in its cultural aspects is essential in order that a people may be aware of its rights and consequently be fully capable of fighting for their recognition and implementation.

*Conclusions regarding the Work Done by the United Nations in This Field (para. 243–245).* This action taken by the entire United Nations system to secure recognition of the right of peoples under colonial and alien domination to self-determination has without doubt led to highly positive results as regards the final objective sought.

What has been achieved in this respect affords one of the most outstanding examples of the effectiveness and importance of the work done by the United Nations. The end of the great colonial empires and traditional colonialism and the creation of an international society based on effective recognition of the right of peoples to self-determination, with the result that 151 sovereign independent States are now Members of the United Nations, have to a large extent been achieved through United Nations efforts. These achievements and the problems raised by the right of peoples to self-determination, as well as future prospects, are summed up in paragraph 6 of the Declaration on the Occasion of the Twenty-Fifth Anniversary of the United Nations, adopted by the General Assembly in 1970 (resolution 2627 (XXV)). The terms of this paragraph deserve to be reproduced:

"We acclaim the role of the United Nations in the past twenty-five years in the process of the liberation of peoples of colonial, Trust and other Non-Self-Governing Territories. As a result of this welcome development, the number of sovereign States in the Organization has been greatly increased

and colonial empires have virtually disappeared. Despite these achievements, many Territories and peoples continue to be denied their right to self-determination and independence, particularly in Namibia, Southern Rhodesia, Angola, Mozambique and Guinea (Bissau), in deliberate and deplorable defiance of the United Nations and world opinion by certain recalcitrant States and by the illegal régime of Southern Rhodesia. We reaffirm the inalienable right of all colonial peoples to self-determination, freedom and independence and condemn all actions which deprive any people of these rights. In recognizing the legitimacy of the struggle of colonial peoples for their freedom by all appropriate means at their disposal, we call upon all Governments to comply in this respect with the provisions of the Charter, taking into account the Declaration on the Granting of Independence to Colonial Countries and Peoples adopted by the United Nations in 1960. We re-emphasize that these countries and peoples are entitled, in their just struggle, to seek and to receive all necessary moral and material help in accordance with the purposes and principles of the Charter."

However, despite the exceptional importance of what has been done, the problem has not yet been solved entirely, even from the political standpoint alone, nor has the right to self-determination become a reality everywhere. Many colonial situations still exist and there are still many United Nations resolutions on specific cases which have not yet been fully implemented. Hence the need to persevere, to maintain and, if possible, speed up the process of decolonization, and to consider, systematically and globally, the work done and the procedures employed, in order to determine what new measures are required and what approach should be taken with regard to the implementation of the resolutions already adopted.

*Recommendations (para. 247–250).* There can be no overlooking the difficulties which even today are seriously hampering the full achievement of the objectives of the Charter and General Assembly resolution 1514 (XV) with regard to the recognition of the right of peoples under colonial and alien domination to self-determination.

In addition to the negative influence exerted by undeniable political and military interests, there are the effects of other interests, particularly economic ones.

United Nations action to eliminate colonialism should take realistic account of the existence and impact of these adverse interests and should adopt a global, systematic and unified approach to the struggle for the recognition of the right to self-determination in every field, in all the competent organs and all the organizations of the United Nations system.

But while there is reason to think that this systematic and constant effort by the international community will shortly put an end to traditional colonialism, although there still remain some particularly serious problems inherent in that form of colonialism to be solved, inasmuch as the violation of the right to self-determination of peoples occurs openly, repeatedly, flagrantly and deliberately, it should not be forgotten that other problems continue to exist in this connexion and that new forms of violation of this right of peoples have appeared. Indeed, economic neo-imperialism and the new forms of colonialism, particularly serious for developing countries and especially for small States which have achieved independence in the last stage of the process of decolonization, constitute manifestations of the violation of the right to self-determination of peoples which may have the effect of cancelling out, to a large extent, the results achieved by the process of political decolonization. This is why it is essential for the United Nations to pay particular attention in the future to this question, which is directly related to the economic, social and cultural aspects of the right to self-determination.

The first of two general recommendations put forward by the Special Rapporteur is (para. 287):

... that all United Nations organizations and all organizations within the United Nations system should continue to take systematic and coordinated action to promote decolonization, in order that peoples under colonial and alien domination may enjoy the right to self-determination in all its political, economic, social and cultural aspects. The right of peoples to self-determination has been affirmed, recognized and accepted by the international community; its characteristics have been defined, and direct and indirect methods and procedures have been devised, to ensure that subject peoples may exercise it with the assistance and co-operation of the United Nations and of all States; the consequences of all this must be weighed with honesty and clarity for the time when recognition of principles must give way to effective action. Colonialism is doomed. The right of peoples to self-determination must now become fully realized, as the basis for a new international society in which international peace and security and human rights must be more effectively assured. The Special Rapporteur can only conceive of this new international society as being based on respect for all human rights and freedoms, including the right to self-determination, and on the international guarantee of their effective protection on the basis of non-discrimination.

The second recommendation is of a formal and juridical nature and is stated in the following terms:

Starting with the historic resolution 1514 (XV) of 14 December 1960, the General Assembly and other United Nations organs have put forth large numbers of resolutions covering political, military, legal, economic, social and cultural aspects of the right to self-determination. The novel and varied problems which have had to be confronted during this period have entailed the formulation of a long and complicated series of instruments which have now become a veritable maze of law. Nineteen years after the adoption of resolution 1514 (XV), which marked the beginning of a new stage in international law, the Special Rapporteur believes that a declaratory resolution should be drafted for adoption by the General Assembly to systematize, codify and update, in view of their progressive development, all the various matters relating to the right of peoples under colonial and alien domination to self-determination which have been the subject of the general resolutions adopted hitherto, and to deal with some new problems which contemporary international law must take up and resolve in this context, as stated in chapter IV of the resent study. This instrument, the drafting of which the Special Rapporteur believes should be started forthwith and which would be both an up-to-date representation of and a tribute to the principles set forth in resolution 1514(XV), would preside over the final stages in the implementation of the right of peoples to self-determination and over the end of colonialism, while being a further contribution to full and effective respect for human rights.

The Sub-Commission on Prevention of Discrimination and Protection of Minorities considered the Spe-

cial Rapporteur's final report (UN Doc. E/C.4/Sub.2/405) at its 1978 session and recommended (resolution 4 A [XXXI]) that it should be printed and given the widest possible distribution. It requested the Commission on Human Rights to entrust the Special Rapporteur, Mr. Hector Gros Espiell, with the preliminary draft of the international instrument proposed in his report. Further, in resolution 4 B (XXXI), it affirmed that the right to self-determination is a well-established principle of international law; recognized that the self-rule, home rule, or self-government formulae are entirely different from the principle of self-determination of peoples; and called upon all UN member States to observe faithfully their obligations under the Charter and relevant United Nations resolutions and to extend their support to the countries and peoples under colonial or alien domination or foreign occupation.

The General Assembly, later in 1978, noted (resolution 33/24) the study. The Commission on Human Rights, at its 1979 session, recommended (decision 3 [XXXV]) that the study should be published but took no decision on the Sub-Commission's request that Mr. Hector Gros Espiell be entrusted to prepare the preliminary draft of an international instrument dealing with the right to self-determination.

***DEVELOPMENT OF THE RIGHT TO SELF-DETERMINATION.*** The *Study of the Historical and Current Development of the Right to Self-Determination*, prepared by Mr. Aureliu Cristescu (Romania), Special Rapporteur of the UN Sub-Commission on Prevention of Discrimination and Protection of Minorities, was authorized by the ECONOMIC AND SOCIAL COUNCIL in 1974 (resolution 1865 [LVI]) and completed in 1978. It was issued in printed form in 1980 (UN publication, Sales no. E.80.XIV.3).

The opening chapters of the study trace the gradual development of the concept of the right of peoples and nations to self-determination through a number of major international instruments, including the United Nations Charter, the International Covenants on Human Rights, and the Declaration on Principles of International Law Concerning Friendly Relations and Cooperation among States in Accordance with the Charter of the United Nations. Chapters III to VIII deal with a number of legal and political aspects of the concept, including the related right of peoples freely to determine their political status and to pursue their economic, social, and cultural development.

The Special Rapporteur presents the conclusions of his study in chapter VIII, paras. 679–713, as follows:

The historical and current development of the right to self-determination shows that it has become one of the most important and dynamic concepts in contemporary international life and that it exercises a profound influence on the political, legal, economic, social and cultural planes, in the matter of fundamental human rights and on the life and fate of peoples and of individuals.

The proclamation in the Charter of the United Nations of the principle of equal rights and self-determination of peoples as one of the bases for friendly relations and co-operation among States constitutes a development of historic importance, in terms both of the recognition of that principle as a binding principle of international law and of its further elaboration and impact on various aspects of the life of peoples. The principle of equal rights and self-determination of peoples is a vital feature of the Charter; it is regarded as the basis for the development, on the one hand, of friendly relations among nations and the link between friendly relations and international co-operation and, on the other, of respect for the principle laid down by the provisions of Article 1, paragraph 2, and Article 55 of the Charter. The embodiment of that principle in the Charter of the United Nations is the culmination of a fairly long development. It marks not only the recognition of the concept as a legal principle and a principle of contemporary international law, but also the point of departure of a new process—the increasingly dynamic development of the principle and its legal content, its implementation, and its application to the most varied situation of international life. The importance of this principle is generally recognized, and the far-reaching changes which have occurred since the adoption of the Charter have brought out with ever-increasing force the importance which the principle has gained, on the one hand, from its role in achieving the purposes of the United Nations and, on the other, from its significant position in contemporary international law and in the legal system derived from the Charter of the United Nations.

The principle of equal rights and self-determination of peoples is the most important of the principles of International law concerning friendly relations and co-operation among States, and constitutes the basis for the other principles. Thus, the international co-operation which is the fundamental theme of United Nations activities is incompatible with any form of subjection or pressure exerted by the strong against the weak and must be based on the sovereign equality of States and the equal rights and self-determination of peoples has as its corollary sovereign equality, a fundamental principle of the United Nations which is closely bound up with the struggle to achieve equal rights, self-determination and independence and with the strengthening of national sovereignty. Non-intervention, another principle of International law concerning friendly relations and co-operation among States, should not be used as a cover for violations of self-determination: it should protect States and peoples struggling for their independence, since acts of intervention are violations of the principle of equal rights and self-determination of peoples. Though the principle of non-intervention of peoples is linked to the principle of non-resort to the threat or use of force, which protects the political independence and territorial integrity of States, aggression—the use or threat of force—is a violation not only of the principle of the non-use of force but also and more particularly, of the principle of equal rights and self-determination of peoples. Colonial domination and oppression, the practice of racism and foreign occupation, are clear cases of aggression against the peoples subjected to them.

The reaffirmation of the right of peoples to self-determination in the Declaration on the Granting of Independence to Colonial Countries and Peoples (General Assembly resolution 1514 (XV) of 14 December 1960) is of great importance, since, from the practical point of view, the principle was to constitute the driving force in the decolonization activities undertaken by the United Nations. The United Nations recognized the passionate yearning for freedom of all dependent peoples and the decisive role of those peoples in the attainment of their independence, expressed its conviction that all peoples had an inalienable right to complete freedom, the exercise of their sovereignty and the integrity of their national territory, and declared that all peoples had the right to self-determination and that, by virtue of that right, they freely determined their political status and freely pursued their economic, social and cultural development. By other special resolutions, the General Assembly has affirmed, *in concreto*, the right of particular peoples to self-determination. Thus the abolition of colonialism and the granting of independence to colonial countries and peoples have played a decisive role in the far-reaching development of the right of subject peoples to national independence and sovereignty. The various rules proclaimed by the United Nations, which define not only the content of the right of those peoples to political self-determination but also the measure to be adopted to that end, amount to a general law of decolonization. The decolonization activities of the United Nations, based on that law, have been of enormous scope and have led to profound changes on the international scene. Those activities must be resolutely pursued, and a determined effort must be made to ensure the full implementation of United Nations resolutions. The affront to human civilization constituted by colonial domination is now approaching its end, and the time when all peoples of the world will enjoy the benefits of independence and freedom is near.

Linked with colonial domination are racial discrimination and *apartheid*, which represent an affront to human conscience and dignity, a total negation of the purposes and principles of the Charter of the United Nations and a crime against humanity, based as they are on doctrines or exclusions on grounds of racial difference or ethnic or religious superiority, all of which are scientifically false, morally reprehensible and socially unjust. The United Nations must ensure the full implementation of the instruments which it has adopted with a view to eliminating these evils, which afflict peoples in a considerable part of the world. Firm support for such implementation from States and the discontinuance of all assistance to the racist régimes are essential to the success of this effort.

Universal respect for fundamental human rights and lasting world peace cannot be achieved so long as the unjust conditions recognized in resolutions of the United Nations General Assembly continue to exist and peoples under foreign occupation continue to be prevented from exercising their fundamental right to freedom, independence and self-determination. Accordingly, the United Nations must, as a matter of urgency, make fresh efforts to implement its resolutions concerning the cessation of foreign occupation and the right of peoples still under such occupation to self-determination.

The international community must persevere in its endeavours to eliminate all vestiges of colonialism, racism and foreign occupation and make a concerted effort to provide the peoples struggling against those evils with all the moral, political and material support they need. The national movements of peoples fighting for their liberation must be recognized as the authentic representatives of the peoples concerned.

The elimination of imperialism, colonialism, aggression, foreign occupation, all forms of discrimination and *apartheid* and threats against national sovereignty and territorial integrity is a prerequisite for the realization of the right of peoples to self-determination and for the social and economic advancement of peoples. The combined force of the movements for national and social liberation, which have shaken the old structures of our rapidly changing world to their very foundations, on the one hand, and the sustained impetus of the scientific and technological revolution, on the other, are paving the way for the full liberation of all mankind.

While colonialism, in the traditional sense, is nearing its end, imperialism and the policy of force and diktat continue to exist and may persist in the future, under the guise of neo-colonialism and power relationships. The exploitation by colonialist forces of the difficulties and problems confronting developing or recently liberated countries, interference in the internal affairs of those States and attempts to maintain, especially in the economic sector, a relationship based on inequality are serious threats to the new States. Colonialism, neo-colonialism and imperialism resort to various devices to impose their will on independent nations. Economic pressure and domination, interference, racial discrimination, subversion, intervention and the threat of force are neo-colonialist devices against which the newly independent nations must guard.

The countries which have acquired their national independence after years of struggle are reaffirming their determination, based in particular on the right of their peoples to self-determination, to resist, by any means available to them, any attempt to impair their sovereignty or to violate their territorial integrity. International relations are currently entering a phase characterized by increased interdependence and by the desire of States to pursue an independent policy. The democratization of international relations is therefore an imperative need at the present time. Some major Powers exhibit an unfortunate tendency to monopolize decision-making in regard to global problems which are of vital concern to all countries of the world. The true independence of States, as distinct from formal sovereignty, is incompatible with any form of interference in the internal affairs of States. Policies of interference are largely conducted through a wide variety of highly subtle and refined indirect techniques—economic aggression, subversion and the defamation of Governments—designed to break up States and their institutions.

For small and medium-sized States, interference in their internal affairs gives cause for deep concern. Although the decolonization process has made remarkable progress, there are some cases in which the independence of States has not been ensured. The policy of pressure and domination continues to pose a serious threat to the independence of States. Measures designed to sow division and disorder threaten internal security and create political confusion and economic chaos. Interference takes many forms—political, economic and military—and is also practised through the information media. One manifestation of such interference is the use of mercenaries to undermine the independence of sovereign States and the national liberation struggle against colonial domination.

International life has brought out the importance of ensuring that States enjoy full and genuine independence, as opposed to mere formal sovereignty. Unequal relations between States, accompanied as they often are by domination and even the extinction of States' hard-won freedoms, remain a matter for concern. The major issue of the present day is the fight against the unequal relations and domination deriving from colonialism and related forms of domination.

The right to self-determination is a collective right, a fundamental human right forming part of the legal system established by the Charter of the United Nations, the beneficiaries of which are peoples—whether or not constituted as independent States—nations and States. Individuals participate, both directly and through the realization of other human rights, in the exercise of this right. Similarly, national minorities exercise this right through the enjoyment of the rights granted to them by article 27 of the International Covenant on Civil and Political Rights and of other individual human rights, whether civil, political, economic, social or cultural. Since the principles of international law concerning friendly relations and co-operation among States are interrelated, the exercise of the right to self-determination must contribute to safeguarding the political independence and territorial integrity of States, ensuring non-interference in their internal affairs and promoting international co-operation. To respect the independence of peoples and their existence and personality is also to respect the sovereignty and integrity of their States, which are essential elements in the exercise of the right of peoples to independence, namely their right to determine their own future and to organize their national life as they please. Respect for the sovereign rights of nations and peoples makes it possible to establish international relations based on friendship and co-operation. The violation of the principle of equal rights and self-determination of peoples, on the other hand, constitutes a danger to the very existence of those peoples; it is an offence against international legality and a threat to world peace. The principle of equal rights and self-determination of peoples is therefore a fundamental element of the international order.

Although the principle of equal rights and self-determination of peoples constitutes a collective right, it nevertheless concerns each individual, since deprivation of that right would entail the loss of individual rights. The right to self-determination is a fundamental right without which other rights cannot be fully enjoyed. Consequently, the enjoyment of that right is essential to the exercise of all individual rights and freedoms. That is why it is accorded pride of place in the International Covenants on Human Rights. States therefore have an obligation to respect the right of peoples freely to determine their political status and to pursue their economic, social and cultural development. The right also implies that Governments owe their existence and powers to the assent of their people; the will of the people is the necessary basis of the Government's authority. It was with this in mind that the right to self-determination was incorporated in international instruments, and not with a view to encouraging secessionist or irredentist movements or foreign interference and aggression. By virtue of this principle, it is necessary to safeguard the political independence and territorial integrity of States which respect the equal rights of peoples and their right to self-determination and possess a Government representative of the population as a whole. Accordingly, the universal realization of the right to self-determination is of great importance for the effective guarantee and observance of fundamental human rights. At the same time, the promotion and protection of human rights and fundamental freedoms contributes to the implementation of the right to self-determination; the guarantee and observance of the various individual human rights and freedoms contribute, in the area of their exercise, to the realization of the different aspects—political, economic, social or cultural—of the right to self-determination.

The right to self-determination, which is a fundamental human right, plays an important part in the realization of the other human rights and freedoms, by creating the general framework and foundation for the implementation and promotion of human rights. At the same time, respect for each individual human right contributes to the exercise of the right to self-determination.

The political aspect of the right to self-determination continues to play a preponderant role, ensuring respect for the existence, sovereignty, independence and territorial integrity of nation States. However, the economic, social and cultural aspects of the right to self-determination are currently assuming increasing importance and are exercising a growing influence on the life of peoples, on the effort to establish a new international economic order, on balanced and integrated development and on the implementation and promotion of economic, social and cultural and civil and political human rights.

The recognition by the International Covenants on Human Rights and other important United Nations instruments of the economic, social and cultural aspects of the right to self-determination represented a milestone in the development of the content of that right. The interdependence of the various aspects of development, based on the right to self-determination, is now commonly recognized throughout the world and has led to the formulation of the concept of balanced and integrated development, which is playing an increasingly important part in the efforts to establish a new international economic order. At the same time, the elaboration of the various economic, social and cultural aspects of the right to self-determination has resulted in the adoption of new rule forming a veritable international law of development.

The right of peoples to self-determination has acquired importance as an essential pillar in the construction of the new international economic and political order, since the political, economic, social and cultural problems of mankind are intimately linked and call for concerted action and because economic emancipation is an essential factor for the elimination of political domination. It is undeniable that there is a close link between political and economic questions and it would be illogical to deal with economic problems separately from political problems. A complete change of political attitude and proof of political will are a first essential step in achieving the new international economic order. A feature of the present international situation is the intensification of the struggle of the peoples of the world for political and economic independence, for peace and progress and for an international political and economic order based on the principles of self-determination, justice, equality and peaceful coexistence among the peoples and nations of the world.

A new international economic order must put an end to the exploitation of the weak and the poor by the strong and the rich. The efforts of the developing countries to secure co-operation in the establishment of a new international economic order have not been successful and have not obtained a satisfactory response from the developed countries. The economic gap between developed and developing countries is still widening, the rich becoming richer and the poor becoming even poorer. The developing countries are being denied their right to equality and to effective participation in international progress. The technological revolution,

which is currently the monopoly of the wealthy countries, should constitute one of the main opportunities for the advancement of the developing countries. World solidarity is not only just a cause, it is a clear necessity. It is intolerable that some should today be enjoying a peaceful and comfortable existence at the expense of others condemned to poverty and misery.

A prerequisite for, and a vital component of, the new international economic order is a new political order for the system of inter-State relations, in other words, the construction of those relations on the basis of the fundamental principles and norms of international law in such a manner as to guarantee and ensure, in practice, full equality of rights for peoples, respect for their independence and national sovereignty, non-interference in their internal affairs and mutual advantage. Such a universal application of these principles and norms should, in practice, ensure the right of every people to be the master of its own affairs and a political order in which all States participate effectively in the preparation and adoption of decisions concerning the international community.

The permanent sovereignty of peoples over their wealth and natural resources, which is a component element of their right to self-determination and a new concept of international law deriving from the decolonization process and the formulation of human rights and freedoms, is giving rise to a review of the rules of traditional international law and, at the economic and social level, has become the cornerstone of development. Responsibility for development lies primarily with the developing countries themselves, which must mobilize to this end all their wealth and resources, but their permanent sovereignty over their wealth and resources must be respected and strengthened, permanent sovereignty being also a basic factor for their economic and social development and their political independence. Wealth and natural resources constitute the material basis which ensures for peoples the exercise of their right to self-determination and the exercise of the other fundamental human rights. Consequently, any action aimed at destroying the permanent sovereignty of peoples over their wealth and natural resources is a violation of international law and an attack on the international order.

The economic development of peoples poses many problems for the international community, which is seeking a new order that will be more just and more equitable. Industrialization is a prerequisite for economic development and for development in the areas of food and agriculture. The development and establishment of a new international economic order call for measures to stimulate an equitable expansion of international trade and economic co-operation among States that excludes all forms of pressure and interference in the internal affairs of States and makes international trade an effective instrument for economic development. Science and technology, which are genuine sources of civilization, power, well-being and progress, must be used for the general advancement of peoples, including that of the developing countries. New resources must be mobilized for financing the economic and social development of the developing countries. Economic development must be accompanied by social development and a just social order, which are prerequisites for the full satisfaction of the aspirations of mankind and for contributing to guaranteed international peace and solidarity.

The promotion of human, economic, social and cultural rights helps to strengthen the general development of peoples. A prerequisite for the observance, assurance and promotion of human, economic, social and cultural rights and the development of the human personality to the present level achieved by civilization is the achievement of the right of peoples to self-determination and to the exercise of permanent sovereignty over their wealth and natural resources, and their right to choose their own economic system and to ensure their economic, social and cultural development. In order to secure such a guarantee and the genuine promotion of fundamental human rights and such economic, social and cultural development, it is imperative to establish a new international economic order based on the sovereign equality of States and respect for the equal rights of all peoples, an order that also guarantees the integrated economic, social and cultural development of every people and every State, in accordance with its aspirations to progress and well-being. The members of the international community have a responsibility and a duty to create the necessary conditions for the full achievement of economic, social and cultural rights as an essential means of ensuring the effective enjoyment of civil and political rights and fundamental freedoms.

The right to development possessed by all peoples, whether they constitute sovereign States or not, is becoming vitally important for the progress of humanity as a whole. The affirmation, the observance and the promotion of this right must be a matter of major concern for the whole international community. The urgency of the question of this right is dictated by the imperative development needs felt throughout the world and particularly in the most backward areas, which constitute an affront to human dignity and to civilization. The international community cannot tolerate such an injustice, such an inequality and such an imbalance between levels of development and in the degree of participation of its various constituent parts in the progress and advances of modern civilization and culture, at a time when scientific progress has brought a hitherto unknown abundance within reach of a part of mankind.

The right to development is a means of attaining the noble purposes of the Charter of the United Nations, including the promotion of "social progress and better standards of life in larger freedom", the ending of the division of the world into zones of poverty and zones of abundance and the ensuring of prosperity for all.

The right to development is an instrument of peace, since it can help the peoples of the developing countries to achieve a higher standard of living and thus avoid the danger to international peace and security constituted by the widening gap between the levels of living of peoples, stemming from privileges, extremes of wealth and poverty and social injustice.

The right of peoples to ensure their economic, social and cultural development is becoming an essential factor in the context of the establishment of a new international economic order.

The realization of the right to development, which is a primary task of States and international organizations, calls for the elimination from society of all the evils and barriers to social progress, particularly inequality, exploitation, war, colonialism and racism.

The right to development is a means of ensuring social justice at the national and international levels, a better distribution of income, wealth and social services, the elimination of poverty and the improvement of living conditions for the whole population. In order to achieve a greater social justice, there must be an expansion of the national product, and specific social and economic policies that are oriented towards a distribution of income and wealth must be adop-

ted. In this connexion, the redistribution of income through transfers and the provision of social services without charge or at low cost are merely corrective measures; the initial organization of the distribution of income is a determining factor in its structure and the principal instrument for the achievement of greater equality, having a direct impact on the level of income and wealth of individuals and groups. It is an economic and social measure that has repercussions in all fields, particularly on employment and wages, investment, the democratization of wealth, fiscal policy and social welfare. However, public ownership of the means of production, which is practised by a steadily increasing number of countries, is still the determining factor for an equitable distribution of the national income, for economic and social democratization and for social justice. Thus, economic growth, social and cultural development and social justice are integrated and complementary objectives of the International Development Strategy, but social justice at the national level is clearly linked with international social justice, particularly in regard to trade, credits and financial assistance, prices and the marketing of products. The achievement of international social justice requires a new international economic order, since the existing order is in direct conflict with the contemporary international trends in political and economic relations, and there is a close correlation between the prosperity of the developed countries and the growth and development of the developing countries. The prosperity of the international community as a whole is linked with the prosperity of its constituent elements. Consequently, international co-operations for development is the goal and the common duty of all countries. In other words, the political, economic and social well-being of present and future generations depends, more than ever, on the existence among all the members of the international community of a spirit of co-operation based on sovereign equality and the elimination of the imbalance between them, on the realization of their aspirations and on the right of all peoples to ensure their political, economic, social and cultural development.

The real purpose of the new international economic order is not the material growth of nations, but the development of all men and women in every way, in a comprehensive cultural process involving profound values and embracing the national environment, social relations, education and welfare; in other words, the achievement of man's economic, social and cultural rights, or human development, for the benefit of man, must be the central factor in the development process. He is the key factor in economic and social development, which must be directed towards fulfiling the needs of an evolving and constantly diversifying human existence, and the unhampered affirmation, at all levels, of the human personality. The general goal of development must be to create equal social conditions for all individuals, in order that they may achieve their potential, as distinct personalities, in accordance with their capacities and aptitudes.

The fundamental element of the right to development and of the right of peoples to self-determination is permanent sovereignty over natural resources. Today, the right of peoples to self-determination can no longer be viewed from a purely political standpoint, but must also be seen increasingly from an economic social and cultural point of view, for development in all is forms creates a sound basis for political independence, and the first step in such development is achievement of the permanent sovereignty of peoples and States over their natural resources and wealth. Any action, whether direct or indirect, designed to prevent a people or a State from exercising permanent sovereignty over its wealth and natural resources undermines the development of the peoples concerned and violates their right to self-determination. Respect for and promotion of the right of peoples to permanent sovereignty over their wealth and natural resources are prerequisite for the achievement of the right to development and the right to self-determination of peoples, and are essential for the strengthening of co-operation and universal peace. The promotion of the right of peoples to permanent sovereignty over their wealth and natural resources must be reflected in concrete fashion by legal measures that will ensure respect for this right and by the development of principles and measures designed to prevent and combat speculative fluctuations in and imbalances between the prices of raw materials and those of industrial products, so as to ensure the normal development of international economic relations and thus to eliminate world economic insecurity, which is detrimental to the national planning of all countries and particularly of the developing countries, and to ensure the realization and promotion of the right of peoples to integrated and balanced economies and to social and cultural development.

The creation of suitable conditions at the international level is of vital importance for securing and promoting the right of peoples and individuals to development. Peaceful coexistence, friendly relations and active co-operation among States encourage the development of peoples. The success of international and national development activities will depend largely on improvement of that overall international situation and particularly on the concrete progress which must be made towards general disarmament, the elimination of colonialism, racial discrimination, *apartheid* and the foreign occupation of territories, and on promotion of equality of political, economic, social and cultural rights for all members of society. At the same time, the promotion of the right to development and the balanced economic and social development of peoples are prerequisite for ensuring the maintenance of peace and international security.

Development can be neither exported nor imported. On the contrary, it implies the taking into account of many economic, technical and social parameters and a choice of priorities and growth rates on the basis of a knowledge of specific needs, conditions and possibilities, and the participation of the whole community, animated by a common ideal and by individual and collective creativity, in the search for the solutions which are best adapted to the local conditions, needs and aspirations. The irreplaceable framework for such development, therefore, is State organization and the driving forces are the peoples and nations themselves, which have a direct interest in their own development. Peoples and States will be able to organize their development effectively only by ensuring the full exercise of their sovereignty, particularly in such matters as the choice of the form of social and political organization, control over natural resources, the choice of the development approach, the directions and pace of their economic and social development and the form of their participation in international trade. Rapid and economic social progress also requires structures and institutions that will ensure the creative participation of the people, fairness in the distribution of the fruits of development and the focusing of all efforts on the main directions of development. Bearing in mind that the national efforts of each people constitute the primary factor for development substantial and effective international assistance must be given to those efforts, for the elimination of under-development is not only a moral imperative and an essential requirement for equity, it is also the expression of the general interest of peoples at all levels. At a time when the economic interdependence of States is increasing and when no country can remain insulated from world economic processes, all States, whatever their social system, their territorial extent or their economic potential, must contribute actively to the solution of the world's present major economic problems and to the development of peoples.

The right to economic, social and cultural development and to political progress is based on respect for the dignity and value of the human person, on the immediate and complete elimination of all forms of inequality, exploitation of peoples and individuals, colonialism and racism, including Nazism, *apartheid* and all other principles of the United Nations concerning the recognition and effective observance of civil and political rights and economic, social and cultural rights, without any discrimination. At the same time, development also ensures the promotion of human rights and social justice.

*Realization of the Right to Development.* Development provides a vital contribution to the observance and promotion of human rights and fundamental freedoms. This most important idea has often been emphasized by the General Assembly, which stressed, in its resolution 2027 (XX) of 18 November 1965, the need, during the first United Nations Development Decade, to devote special attention at both the national and the international level to progress in the field of human rights, and to encourage the adoption of measures designed to accelerate the promotion of respect for and observance of human rights and fundamental freedoms. In its resolution 2586 (XXIV) of 15 December 1969, the General Assembly considered that, in the preparation of the strategy for the Second United Nations Development Decade, the final aim must be the attainment of a rapid and sustained rate of economic and social development, especially in developing countries, and also the well-being, freedom and dignity of all human beings, and the enjoyment of all the civil, political, economic, social and cultural rights recognized by the Universal Declaration of Human Rights and guaranteed by the two International Covenants on Human Rights. Since the right of peoples to self-determination forms the basis for the enjoyment and development of individual human rights and also has major implications for the political, economic, social and cultural advancement of every nation, it remains a corner-stone of the new international order. Promotion by the United Nations of the right of peoples to self-determination and the progressive development of this right will be an essential means of achieving a new international order and a better, more just and more equitable world.

The Special Rapporteur's recommendation for international action to ensure enjoyment of the right to self-determination are presented in chapter IX (paras. 714–729) of the study, as follows:

Respect for the right to self-determination—a right proclaimed by the United Nations as a fundamental principle of the Charter—must be the basis of any action taken by the United Nations itself or by the Member States. If this fundamental right of peoples is to be attained, it is essential that the action already initiated by the United Nations and its Members should be continued and that measures calculated to ensure, in particular, the execution and full realization of this right in the areas of greatest contemporary concern should be adopted. In this connexion, the elimination of colonialism, neo-colonialism, racism, *apartheid* and other forms of the violation of the right to self-determination, and the adoption of strong measures to establish truly democratic relations between States and peoples are an urgent necessity at the present time. The United Nations must continue to take vigorous and firm action to bring about the prompt eradication of the vestiges of colonialism, a shameful anachronism which is blatantly at variance with the international ethics and principles unanimously proclaimed by the peoples of the world. The United Nations and the Member States must take effective measures to ensure the immediate and complete liberation of all peoples from any form of foreign subjugation, to eliminate all manifestations of exploitation and discrimination, racism and *apartheid,* and to repress any action intended to revive such practices. With the same object, the United Nations must devise specific measures to end all support to the colonial and racist régimes that disregard the right to self-determination, and take practical action to support the movements for the liberation of peoples from colonialism, neo-colonialism, racism, *apartheid* and foreign occupation, and to ensure the adequate representation of such movements within the United Nations by establishing favourable conditions for the work of their observers and preparing, under United Nations auspices, detailed programmes of effective multilateral assistance for these movements.

The provisions of the Charter which are based on the concept of the recognition of the rights of some countries to administer and dominate other countries and peoples are totally inconsistent with the realities of the modern world. The Charter should proclaim with complete clarity the total and permanent abolition of colonialism, neo-colonialism and racism, and the determination of the States Members of the United Nations to eliminate all practices engendered thereby; it should prohibit any form of interference by one State in the internal affairs of other States, pressure by one State on another, the dependence of one State on another, and the subordination of one State to another. The Charter should clearly affirm the right to self-determination as a fundamental principle of contemporary international law, and the right of peoples to exercise permanent sovereignty over their natural wealth and resources and to develop their material and human potential, in accordance with their interests and aspirations. It should reflect the principles of law and justice which necessarily derive from the development of the right to self-determination and provide for the equalization of the levels of economic development of all countries, as a genuine basis for the democratization of international life. At the same time, it should affirm with the greatest possible clarity the need for the establishment of a new international economic order calculated to ensure the economic and social progress of all peoples and the unrestricted access of all peoples, in particular the least developed peoples, to the achievements of modern civilization and to open up the prospect of a better and more just world. The Charter of the United Nations should thus be the charter for the eradication of colonialism, neo-colonialism and racism, and of all forms of domination, oppression, inequity and inequality in international relations. It should be a charter of the rights of peoples, nations and States, and of fundamental human rights, and an international instrument such as to ensure full, multifaceted and unrestricted approval by every people and thereby open up the prospect of progress and peace for the whole world.

The political aspect of the right to self-determination, in other words the right of peoples to choose their political status, continues to be of particular importance, because this right will always ensure respect for the existence, sovereignty and territorial integrity of States. Consequently, the United Nations must always be capable of guaranteeing this right by combating any form of aggression, intervention or pressure against States and peoples, and of protecting their sovereignty and territorial integrity. The United Nations can no longer today permit the re-emergence, in any form whatsoever, of the domination of one State by another State or those forms of neo-colonialism which perpetuate the spoliation of peoples; it must combat any form of domination or subjugation which engenders international tension and conflict, wars with harmful and unforeseeable consequences, the arms race, the maintenance and accentuation of economic and social disparities between peoples and the phenomenon of economic crisis and instability.

*Apartheid,* all forms of racial discrimination, colonialism, foreign occupation, aggression and threats against national sovereignty, national unity or territorial integrity, and the refusal to recognize the fundamental rights of peoples to self-determination and of any nation to exercise its full sovereignty over its natural wealth and resources constitute factors which, by their very nature, are and engender, massive and flagrant violations of all the human rights and fundamental freedoms of peoples and individuals.

Consequently, the United Nations must continue forcefully to emphasize the harmful effect on the attainment of human rights, of the persistence of colonialism, aggression and threats against national sovereignty, national unity or territorial integrity, foreign occupation, discrimination in all its forms, *apartheid* and all forms of domination of one State by another.

At the same time, in connexion with the need to develop the right to self-determination, the United Nations must increase its contribution to the promotion, in international life, of new relations between peoples, nations and States. To this end, the preparation and adoption, within the context of the United Nations, of a universal code of conduct proclaiming the fundamental rights and duties of States will be of particular importance. Such a code will have to define standards to ensure rigorous respect for the right to self-determination, the incompatibiity of that right with all forms of domination or pressure, genuine equality of rights for peoples, full political independence, respect for the territorial integrity of peoples, the illegality of military occupation and of the acquisition of territory through the use of force, and the elimination from international life of the possibility of misusing self-determination for purposes of interference or to undermine the national unity of States.

The international economic situation, characterized as it is by major disparities in development, is having an unfavourable effect on the achievement of the right to self-determination and on the social situation within the various countries, especially the developing countries; social distress and poverty can be eliminated only if the preconditions are established for economic growth and balanced and generalized social development. It is therefore incumbent upon the United Nations to tackle those economic and social problems that are of vital importance for the peace, progress and prosperity of the peoples of mankind as a whole, to analyse them in depth and systematically, and to devise and adopt, for the purpose of establishing the new international economic order, precise standards calculated to commit all Member States and special action programmes aimed at the attainment of this new order.

If the right to self-determination is to be achieved, the efforts made at the national level must be continued, so as to promote progress and development in the economic, social, cultural and political sectors, in order to meet the fundamental needs of the peoples concerned. Particularly important measures include the promotion of a more equitable distribution of income and wealth at the national level, the elimination of hunger and malnutrition, the reduction of unemployment and under-employment, the improvement of the distribution of social services and the broad democratic participation of people in the management of the political, economic and social life of their country. The United Nations can contribute to such efforts as a centre for the harmonization of the activities of Member States and for the exchange of experience among them, and by furnishing advisory services and providing the necessary financial assistance to enable measures to be taken in these areas.

In the exercise of the right to self-determination, particular importance must be attached to the urgent need to ensure, at the international level, respect for the principles, and the implementation of the decisions, relating to the establishment of the new international economic order, and respect for the objectives and the implementation of the measures provided for in the International Development Strategy for the Second United Nations Development Decade—an essential condition for the success of the measures aimed at eliminating poverty and ensuring genuine social progress in the developing countries. To this same end, the developed countries which have so far failed to do so must act in a spirit of co-operation and interdependence, so as to ensure the social and economic development of the developing countries.

The ideal of the dignity and value of the individual, free and liberated from fear and poverty, can be achieved only if conditions are established to enable everyone to enjoy his economic, social and cultural rights, and his civil and political rights, and if all States fulfil the obligation to respect the purposes and principles of the Charter of the United Nations and to bring about international co-operation by resolving international problems of an economic, social, cultural or humanitarian nature, and by developing and encouraging respect for the human rights and fundamental freedoms of all, at the same time taking account of the varied nature of the problems which exist in the different societies and of the economic, social and cultural realities of each society. It is in this spirit that the United Nations must take due account, in its work concerning the execution and implementation of human rights, of the experience and over-all situation of the developing countries, and of the efforts made by these countries to give effect to human rights and fundamental freedoms. The United Nations must support these efforts through practical, far-reaching and long-term measures calculated to promote the economic, social and cultural progress of peoples and to create the international atmosphere of peace which is essential if progress is to be achieved in this area. In this context, too, more intensive efforts must be made within the United Nations to contribute to the execution and implementation of the economic, social and cultural rights of the individual, and to the affirmation, elaboration and implementation of the right to development as a fundamental human right.

To the same end, the United Nations must systematically and continuously support those efforts by States which are specifically reflected in structural measures aimed at ensuring the achievement of fundamental human rights, the elimination of social inequalities and all forms of discrimination, and the establishment of equal, genuine and effective rights to work, instruction, education, culture and the benefits of civilization.

The United Nations must take increasing account of the effect of mass information activities on international life and relations, and support national and international efforts to disseminate to the masses information which will promote the *rapprochement* of, and friendship among, peoples, the strengthening of respect for the traditions and culture of each people, and the dissemination of all of mankind's best achievements in all spheres of human activity and knowledge.

The United Nations must examine from an overall standpoint the progress achieved, firstly, in the establishment of a new international economic order, and secondly, in the implementation of the right to self-determination in all its aspects—political, economic, social and cultural—and in the execution and application of economic, social and cultural rights, and of civil and political rights. It would seem necessary to ensure co-ordination, within the international development strategy, between economic, social and cultural development, on the one hand, and human rights on the other, and to undertake a thorough examination of the progress achieved in this sphere. An over-all view of the achievement of the economic, social and cultural aspects of the right to self-determination and of its political aspect is necessary, because at present these different aspects come within the province of a variety of bodies within the United Nations and the specialized agencies. It is the responsibility of the Commission on Human Rights and the Sub-Commission on Prevention of Discrimination and Protection of Minorities to adopt this over-all approach to the achievement of the various aspects of the right to self-determination and the other fundamental human rights.

The progress achieved in social development must therefore be analysed in conjunction with the progress achieved in the sphere of human rights. This requires more effective co-ordination between the work of the United Nations bodies which deal with social questions and those which deal with fundamental human rights.

The United Nations must continue to study the relationship between the progress achieved in the implementation of economic, social and cultural rights, on the one hand, and civil and political rights, on the other, within the context of the realization of the right to self-determination. The attainment of the right to self-determination in all its aspects must constitute a continuing concern of the United Nations. In this connexion, on the basis of information received from Governments, the United Nations is able to publish reports on the attainment of this right. The violation of the right to self-determination and the right of peoples to free themselves from colonial domination, racism and *apartheid* constitutes an international crime. In specific cases of the violation of this right, the provisions of the international conventions relating to the prevention of genocide, racism and *apartheid* must be implemented.

The study of the most salient aspects of the achievement of the right to self-determination, as mentioned above, is the responsibility of the United Nations bodies and the specialized agencies, which must pay continuing attention to, and take an increasing interest in, that matter, acting both individually and jointly. At the same time, in order to assist the United Nations in carrying out its tasks in these areas, with all their complexity and contemporary relevance, conferences, debates, seminars, round tables, etc. might be organized, with the broad participation of States and international non-governmental organizations. Such discussions would make possible a broad and deep analysis serving as a basis for the new measures which might be recommended and for the realization by international public opinion of the urgent need for a solution to the major problems on which the full enjoyment by all peoples of their right to self-determination depends.

### UN SPECIAL COMMITTEE ON THE SITUATION WITH REGARD TO THE IMPLEMENTATION OF THE DECLARATION ON THE GRANTING OF INDEPENDENCE TO COLONIAL COUNTRIES AND PEOPLES.

Known informally as the Special Committee on Decolonization, the Special Committee was established by the UN General Assembly on 27 November 1961 (resolution 1654 [XVI]) to promote realization of the Declaration on the Granting of Independence to Colonial Countries and Peoples, which the Assembly had adopted and proclaimed on 14 December 1960 (resolution 1514 [XV]).

Originally, the Special Committee was authorized only to follow developments concerning the Declaration and to make suggestions and recommendations on the progress and extent of its implementation. Later, however, after the General Assembly dissolved other bodies which it had created to deal with decolonization questions—including the Special Committee on Territories under Portuguese Administration, the Committee on Information from Non-Self-Governing Territories, and the Special Committee on South West Africa—it called upon the new Special Committee to take over their tasks. A number of new functions was added to its mandate; these, as summarized in GA resolution 41/41 of 2 December 1986, include the request that the Special Committee continue to seek suitable means for the immediate and full granting of independence to all remaining colonies and territories and, in particular:

(a) to formulate specific proposals for the elimination of the remaining manifestations of colonialism and to report thereon to the General Assembly at its 42d session;

(b) to make concrete suggestions which could assist the Security Council in considering appropriate measures under the Charter with regard to developments in colonial Territories that are likely to pose a threat to international peace and security;

(c) to continue to examine the compliance of member states with resolution 1514 (XV) and other relevant resolutions on decolonization, particularly those relating to Namibia;

(d) to continue to pay special attention to the small territories, in particular through the dispatch of visiting missions to those territories whenever the Special Committee deems it appropriate, and to recommend to the General Assembly the most suitable steps to be taken to enable the populations of those territories to exercise their right to self-determination and independence; and

(e) to take all necessary steps to enlist world-wide support among governments, as well as national and international organizations having a special interest in decolonization, for the achievement of the objectives of the Declaration and the implementation of the relevant resolutions of the UN, particularly as concerns the people of Namibia.

The Special Committee originally was composed of 17 member States, nominated by the president of the General Assembly. It was enlarged to 24 in 1962 and to 25 in 1980. In 1985, one member State withdrew from the Committee. Thus, the Committee—popularly known as the "Committee of Twenty-Four" from 1962 to 1980—once again has 24 members. They are Afghanistan, Bulgaria, Chile, China, Congo, Cote d'Ivoire, Cuba, Czechoslovakia, Ethiopia, Fiji, India, Indonesia, Islamic Republic of Iran, Iraq, Mali, Norway, Sierra Leone, Syria, Trinidad and Tobago, Tunisia, Union of Soviet Socialist Republics, United Republic of Tanzania, Venezuela, and Yugoslavia. The term of office of members is indeterminate. Meetings of the Special Committee are held as required throughout the year. Its reports are considered by the General Assembly.

The Special Committee is assisted in its work by a working group and steering committee, consisting of its officers and three additional members; the Sub-Committee on Petitions, Information and Assistance, consisting of 13 of its members; and the Sub-Committee on Small Territories, consisting of 19 of its members.

***SEE ALSO*** States' Rights.

**BIBLIOGRAPHY.** Anaya, S. James. "The Capacity of International Law to Advance Ethnic or Nationality Rights Claims," *Human Rights Quarterly* 13, no (Aug. 1991): 403–411. Scholarly article, in English.

Ardant, Philippe. "Que reste-il du droit des peuples à disposer d'eux-mêmes?" (What's Left of the Rights to National Self-Determination?), *Nationalismes* (April 1991): 43–54. Scholarly article, in French.

Brölmann, Catherine, René Lefeber, and Marjoleine Zieck, eds. *Peoples and Minorities in International Law.* Dordrecht, the Netherlands: Martinus Nijhoff, 1993. Scholarly monograph, in English.

Cullen, Richard. "Mineral Revenues and Australian Aboriginal Self Determination," *University of British Columbia Law Review* no. 153 (1991): 153–170. Scholarly article, in English.

Dilton, Pamela. "Self Determination or Self Management?" *Australian International Law News* (1990): 3–13. Scholarly article, in English.

Dinstein, Yoram, ed. "Specific Problems of Minorities/ General Problems of Rights of Minorities," *Israel Yearbook on Human Rights* 21 (April 1993). Scholarly collection of articles, in English.

El Salhi, Abderachmen. "The Right to Self-Determination," Paper presented at the Second International Conference on Peoples Rights, Cairo, Egypt, Center for International Legal and Economic Studies, Zagazig University, 25–28 Nov. 1985. Unpublished conference paper, in Arabic.

Etzioni, Amitai. "The Evils of Self-Determination," *Foreign Policy* 89 (Winter 1992–1993): 21–35. Scholarly article, in English.

Gibson, Richard. *African Liberation Movements: Contempo-*

*rary Struggles against White Minority Rule.* London: Oxford University Press, for the Institute of Race Relations, 1972. Scholarly study, in English; bibliography, pp. 333–336.

Hannum, Hurst. *Autonomy, Sovereignty and Self-Determination: The Accommodation of Conflicting Rights.* Philadelphia, PA, USA: University of Pennsylvania Press, 1990. Scholarly study, in English.

————, ed. *Documents on Autonomy and Minority Rights.* Dordrecht, the Netherlands: Martinus Nijhoff, 1993. Scholarly monograph, in English.

Harvey, Richard J. "The Right of the People of the Whole of Ireland to Self-Determination, Unity, Sovereignty and Independence," *New York Law School Journal of International Comparative Law* 11, nos. 1 and 2 (1990): 167–206. Scholarly article, in English.

Heraclides, Alexis. "Secessionist Minorities and External Involvement," *International Organization* 44, no. 3 (Summer 1990): 341–378. Scholarly article, in English.

Institut interculturel de Montréal (Intercultural Institute of Montreal). "The Right of Conquest I," *INTER Culture* 25, no. 3 (no. 116) (Summer 1992). Special issue, in English and French.

————. "The Right of Conquest II," *INTER Culture* 25, no. 4 (no. 117) (Fall 1992). Special issue, in English and French.

Institute of Race Relations. "The Curse of Columbus," *Race and Class: A Journal for Black and Third World Liberation* 33, no. 3 (Jan.–March 1992). Special issue, in English.

Jayan Cortez, Dorindo, ed. *Quinientos Años de Conquista y de Resistencia Indígena* (Five-Hundred Years of Conquest and Indigenous Resistance). Panama City, Panama: Coordinadora Popular de Derechos Humanos de Panama (People's Coordinator for Human Rights in Panama), 1992. Monograph, in Spanish; bibliography, pp. 18–19.

Julien, Pierre. "Droits de l'Homme et Droit a l'Autodetermination" (Human Rights and the Right to Self-Determination). Paper presented at the Second International Conference on Peoples Rights, Cairo, Egypt, Center for International Legal and Economic Studies, Zagazig University, 25–28 Nov. 1985. Unpublished conference paper, in French.

Kiss, Alexandre. "The Peoples' Right to Self-Determination," *Human Rights Law Journal* 7, no. 2–4 (1986): 165–175. Scholarly article, in English.

Kutukdjian, Georges B., and Antonio Papisca, eds. *Rights of Peoples.* Padova, Italy: Center for Training and Research on Human Rights and the Rights of Peoples, University of Padua, 1991. Scholarly monograph, in English and French.

Lefeber, R., M. Fitzmaurice, and E. W. Vierdag, eds. *The Changing Political Structure of Europe: Aspects of International Law.* Dordrecht, the Netherlands: Martinus Nijhoff, 1991. Scholarly monograph, in English.

Mazzawi, Musa. "Self-Determination in International Law: A Study of the Rhodesian Case," *Poly Law Review* 1, no. 1 (Summer 1975): 15–23. Scholarly article, in English.

Mbemba, Jean-Martin. *L'autre mémoire du crime contre l'humanité* (The Other Memory of Crimes against Humanity). Dakar, Senegal: Présence Africaine, 1990. Monograph, in French.

Moquette, Marc. "Tibet, the Right to Self-Determination and Territorial Integrity," *Netherlands Quarterly of Human Rights* 8, no. 3 (1990): 261–274. Scholarly article, in English.

Nwosu, Humphrey N. "The Concepts of Nationalism and Right to Self-Determination: Cameroon as a Case Study," *Africa Quarterly* 2 (1976): 256–273. Scholarly article, in English.

Ortiz, R. D. *Indians of the Americas: Human Rights and Self-Determination.* London: Zed Books, 1984. Scholarly monograph, in English; bibliography, pp. 281–305.

Pearce, Elizabeth A. "Self-Determination for Native Americans: Land Rights and the Utility of Domestic and International Law," *Columbia Human Rights Law Review* 22, no. 2 (Spring 1991): 361–400. Scholarly article, in English.

Przetacznik, Frank. "The Basic Collective Human Right to Self-Determination of Peoples and Nations as a Prerequisite for Peace," *New York Law School Journal of Human Rights* 8, no. 1 (Fall 1990): 49–109. Scholarly article, in English.

Rigaux, François. *Pour une déclaration universelle des droits de peuples: identité nationale et coopération internationale* (For a Universal Declaration on Peoples' Rights: National Identity and International Cooperation). Brussels, Belgium, and Lyon, France: Vie ouvrière & Chronique sociale, 1990. Scholarly monograph, in French.

Tamir, Yael. "The Right to National Self-Determination," *Social Research* 58, no. 3 (Fall 1991): 565–590. Scholarly article, in English.

Thompson, Ruth, ed. *The Rights of Indigenous Peoples in International Law: Selected Essays on Self-Determination.* Saskatoon, Saskatchewan, Canada: Native Law Centre, University of Saskatchewan, 1987. NGO conference proceedings, in English.

Thornberry, Patrick. *International Law and the Rights of Minorities.* New York: Oxford University Press, 1991. Scholarly monograph, in English; bibliography, pp. 431–443.

Thurer, Daniel. "The Rights of Self-Determination," *Law and State* 35 (1987): 22–39. Scholarly article, in English.

Torres, Raidza. "The Rights of Indigenous Populations: The Emerging International Norm," *The Yale Journal of International Law* 16, no. 1 (Winter 1991): 127–175. Scholarly article, in English.

United Nations Commission on Human Rights. *The Right of Peoples to Self-Determination and its Application to Peoples under Colonial or Alien Domination or Foreign Occupation: Report of the Secretary-General.* E/CN.4/1987/12 and Add. 1. Geneva, Switzerland: 1986, 1987. IGO document, in English.

Vries, Gijs de. "Report: Broken Promises: Canada and Its Aboriginal Peoples," *Netherlands Quarterly of Human Rights* 10, no. 2 (1992): 166–183. Scholarly article, in English.

## SELF-DETERMINATION: DECLARATION ON THE GRANTING OF INDEPENDENCE TO COLONIAL COUNTRIES AND PEOPLES, UN (1960).

The proposal to adopt such a Declaration was put forward by Nikita Khrushchev, Chairman of the Council of Ministers of the Union of Soviet Socialist Republics, in a statement which he made to the UN **GENERAL ASSEMBLY** in 1960. His proposal was that, in keeping with the principles of its Charter, the United Nations should declare itself in favor of the "immediate and complete elimination of the colonial system in all its forms and manifestations." The Assembly considered draft declarations to this effect proposed by the USSR and by 43 African and Asian nations and adopted the latter by 89 to 0, with nine abstentions.

The Declaration was adopted by the UN General Assembly on 14 December 1960 (resolution 1514 [XV]). The text is as follows:

The General Assembly,

Mindful of the determination proclaimed by the peoples of the world in the Charter of the United Nations to reaffirm faith in fundamental human rights, in the dignity and worth of the human person, in the equal rights of men and women and of nations large and small and to promote social progress and better standards of life in larger freedom,

Conscious of the need for the creation of conditions of stability and well-being and peaceful and friendly relations based on respect for the principles of equal rights and self-determination of all peoples, and of universal respect for, and observance of, human rights and fundamental freedoms for all without distinction as to race, sex, language or religion,

Recognizing the passionate yearning for freedom in all dependent peoples and the decisive role of such peoples in the attainment of their independence,

Aware of the increasing conflicts resulting from the denial of or impediments in the way of the freedom of such peoples, which constitute a serious threat to world peace,

Considering the important role of the United Nations in assisting the movement for independence in Trust and Non-Self-Governing Territories,

Recognizing that the peoples of the world ardently desire the end of colonialism in all its manifestations,

Convinced that the continued existence of colonialism prevents the development of international economic co-operation, impedes the social, cultural and economic development of dependent peoples and militates against the United Nations ideal of universal peace,

Affirming that peoples may, for their own ends, freely dispose of their natural wealth and resources without prejudice to any obligations arising out of international economic co-operation, based upon the principle of mutual benefit, and international law,

Believing that the process of liberation is irresistible and irreversible and that, in order to avoid serious crises, an end must be put to colonialism and all practices of segregation and discrimination associated therewith,

Welcoming the emergence in recent years of a large number of dependent territories into freedom and independence, and recognizing the increasingly powerful trends towards freedom in such territories which have not yet attained independence,

Convinced that all peoples have an inalienable right to complete freedom, the exercise of their sovereignty and the integrity of their national territory,

Solemnly proclaims the necessity of bringing to a speedy and unconditional end colonialism in all its forms and manifestations;

And to this end

Declares that:

1. The subjection of peoples to alien subjugation, domination and exploitation constitutes a denial of fundamental human rights, is contrary to the Charter of the United Nations and is an impediment to the promotion of world peace and co-operation.

2. All peoples have the right to self-determination; by virtue of that right they freely determine their political status and freely pursue their economic, social and cultural development.

3. Inadequacy of political, economic, social or educational preparedness should never serve as a pretext for delaying independence.

4. All armed action or repressive measures of all kinds directed against dependent peoples shall cease in order to enable them to exercise peacefully and freely their right to complete independence, and the integrity of their national territory shall be respected.

5. Immediate steps shall be taken, in Trust and Non-Self-Governing Territories or all other territories which have not yet attained independence, to transfer all powers to the peoples of those territories, without any conditions or reservations, in accordance with their freely expressed will and desire, without any distinction as to race, creed or colour, in order to enable them to enjoy complete independence and freedom.

6. Any attempt aimed at the partial or total disruption of the national unity and the territorial integrity of a country is incompatible with the purposes and principles of the Charter of the United Nations.

7. All States shall observe faithfully and strictly the provisions of the Charter of the United Nations, the Universal Declaration of Human Rights and the present Declaration on the basis of equality, non-interference in the internal affairs of all States, and respect for the sovereign rights of all peoples and their territorial integrity.

**SENEGAL.** The Republic of Senegal is a country in western Africa, fronting on the Atlantic Ocean. It has borders with Gambia, Guinea, Guinea-Bissau, Mali, and Mauritania. It achieved independence from France in 1960 and became a member of the United Nations the same year. Its population is estimated to be 7,849,000. Its ethnic groups are classified by the government as (a) the Sahel-Sudanese group, which is 40% Wolof and 18% Serer, and lives mainly in the capital Dakar and the central regions; (b) the Al-Poular group, which is 15% Peul and 10% Tukulor, and lives in the Senegal River valley and in the Ferlo; (c) the Sub-Guinean group, which represents 13% of the population and is composed of Diolas, Balantes, Bassaris, and Sarakoles; and (d) the Mande group, which is numerically the smallest and lives in the southern part of the country. With regard to religion, the population is divided as follows: Islam, 90%; Christians, 5%, and others, 5%.

Senegal has provided refuge for more than 5,000 refugees from other parts of Africa, who receive assistance administered by the United Nations **HIGH COMMISSIONER FOR REFUGEES.** There are, in addition, nearly one million foreigners in Senegal, who are subject to the laws of the country and are granted equal protection with nationals in the enjoyment of human rights.

Literacy, estimated to be between 10 and 25%, has been below expectations for many years, and the government set up a National Literacy Department in the late 1970s to promote all types of activities and initiatives relating to the subject. The resulting literacy campaigns endeavor not only to teach people to read and write but also to encourage them to apply what they have learned to every aspect of their daily lives. These efforts are beginning to bear fruit and many of the country's workers are moving gradually away from the dependent situation to which they were confined by their lack of education.

The government (1994) took the form of a republic. Under the 1963 constitution, as amended, the president is head of State and of government; he is assisted by the Council of Ministers, which he himself appoints. Legislation is enacted by a 120-member National Assembly, members of which are elected for five-year terms: 60 by single-member constituencies and 60 by a form of proportional representation. Judges of the Supreme Court are appointed by the president. There are more than 15 political parties, including the Socialist Party, the Senegalese Democratic Party, and the *Rassemblement National Democratique.*

In 1980, the country's leader since independence, President Leopold Senghor, retired, turning over power to Abdou Diouf. President Diouf was elected with 83% of the votes in 1983 and re-elected to a second five-year term in 1988. As president of Senegal, Mr. Diouf also serves as president of the Confederation of Senegambia.

Substantial political changes took place in the early 1990s. Constitutional amendments in March 1991 restored the post of prime minister and provided for participation of the parliamentary opposition in government. In September 1991 the presidential term of office was extended from five to seven years and limited to two terms, the voting age reduced from 21 to 18 years, and the Supreme Court replaced by a Constitutional Court, the Council of State, and a Court of Cassation.

President Diouf was re-elected in February 1993 with 58% of the vote and the Socialist Party won 84 of the 120 Assembly seats in elections in May. The vice-president of the Constitutional Council was assassinated after the results were announced by the electoral commission, which was to submit the results to the Council for confirmation. In October 1993, Abdoulaye Wade, the leader of the opposition Senegalese Democratic Party who had challenged Diouf in presidential elections in 1983, 1988, and 1993, was charged with involvement in the assassination.

Stringent economic measures such as currency devaluation and wage reductions led to political unrest, general strikes, and violent demonstrations and rioting, including one incident in Dakar in February 1994 in which eight people, including six police officers, were killed. An Islamic youth movement was banned following allegations that it was involved in the violence.

Fighting between the government and the separatist rebels from the Movement of Democratic Forces of Casamance (MFDC) in the southern region of the country continued throughout the early 1990s, with estimates that between 500 and 1,000 people were killed in 1993 and between 25,000 and 30,000 people had fled to Gambia, Guinea-Bissau, or elsewhere in Senegal.

Diplomatic relations with Mauritania were restored in 1992 after several years of strained relations resulting from attacks on Senegalese and Mauritanians living in each others' country. An estimated 300,000 resident Mauritanians had traditionally dominated the retail trade in Senegal.

The Confederation of Senegambia, which came into existence in February 1982, was dissolved in September 1989, with President Diouf claiming that Gambia was not willing to move toward more complete political and economic integration. Senegal closed the border between the two nations in September 1993, adversely affecting Gambia's trade links.

***REPORT OF THE UN COMMITTEE ON ECONOMIC, SOCIAL AND CULTURAL RIGHTS.*** The **COMMITTEE ON ECONOMIC, SOCIAL AND CULTURAL RIGHTS** examined the initial report of Senegal at its 37th and 38th meetings on 1 and 2 December 1993; and, at its 49th meeting on 10 December 1993, adopted the following observations (paras. 257–268):

*Positive aspects.* The Committee notes with satisfaction the level of support accorded to International human rights activities by Senegal and, in general, the steps taken to fulfil its obligations under the various human rights instruments. In this regard, the Committee takes note of the information provided by the delegation, indicating that those instruments are applicable in domestic law and that they have been invoked in courts of law on a number of occasions.

The Committee welcomes indications by the delegation that the reports submitted to the human rights treaty bodies and the concluding observations adopted pursuant to those reports are made freely available to interested groups and individuals.

*Factors and difficulties impeding the implementation of the Covenant.* The Committee notes that economic factors, including difficulties caused by external debt servicing, have impeded the application of the Covenant. In this respect, the Committee notes with concern that short-term considerations applied in its structural adjustment policy have not adequately taken into account the long-term impact of reduced investment in the social sector.

*Principal subjects of concern.* The Committee is concerned that, in general, the State party has not provided satisfactory information concerning measures envisaged to improve the enjoyment of the rights covered under the Covenant, particularly with respect to the situation of women, youth and other vulnerable groups. The Committee is concerned about the extent to which women enjoy the rights contained in the Covenant, particularly with respect to articles 6 and 7. While noting that some progress has been achieved in this regard, there are continuing impediments to equality of access to employment. The Committee is particularly concerned that significantly lower literacy rates for women, as well as certain cultural practices, seriously compromise their opportunities for employment and advancement.

The Committee notes with alarm that budgetary cutbacks carried out in the educational sector under the programme of structural adjustment will have serious social and economic consequences for the future of the country. In this connection, the Committee is concerned about restrictions on school enrolment, which have been imposed with a view to reducing the number of qualified applicants to administrative posts in the public sector. The Committee is also concerned about the high proportion of drop-outs from general technical secondary education, which has reached the level of 35 per cent of total enrolment.

The Committee is concerned about the full enjoyment of trade union rights as provided for under article 8 of the Covenant. In this regard, the Committee notes that foreign workers are barred from holding trade union office and that authorities may unduly restrict the right to strike by imposing compulsory arbitration.

*Suggestions and recommendations.* The Committee recommends that the State party undertake a systematic and comprehensive review of the relevant legislation, administrative procedures and policies to give effect to economic, social and cultural rights in order to ensure that they conform to the requirements of the Covenant. Special attention should be paid to those areas concerning women and other vulnerable groups.

The Committee recommends that the State party, in its second periodic report, which is due in 1994, should provide focused information on the situation of women and other vulnerable groups and, in particular, measures taken and foreseen to facilitate the enjoyment of their rights under the Covenant. The State party should also provide the Committee with fuller information on the jurisprudence relating to the rights contained in the Covenant and measures envisaged to overcome the difficulties encountered in the implementation of the Covenant.

The Committee recommends that the State party undertake a thorough review of its policies with regard to education and vocational training with a view to expanding budgetary allocations for this section, expanding access to education and, in particular, reducing the number of student drop-outs. In this connection, the Committee underlines the importance of higher education and vocational training in developing a robust economy. The Committee suggests that the State party report more fully on this issue in its second periodic report.

The Committee recommends that the State party consider amending the relevant national legislation with a view to permitting foreign workers to hold trade union office and limiting the powers of authorities to restrict the right to strike by imposing compulsory arbitration.

In order to encourage and facilitate greater public involvement in the implementation of the Covenant, the State party should ensure that adequate publicity is given to the Covenant, that its provisions are translated into local languages and that its report to the Committee along with these concluding observations are made available to interested groups and individuals.

The Committee wishes to bring to the attention of the State party the need to ensure that structural adjustment programmes are so formulated and implemented as to provide adequate safety nets for the vulnerable sectors of society in order to avoid a deterioration of their enjoyment of the economic, social and cultural rights for which the Covenant provides protection.

***BIBLIOGRAPHY.*** Amnesty International. *Senegal: Mass Arrests and Torture—Most of the Detainees Appear to Be Prisoners of Conscience.* London: 1994. NGO report, in English.

————. *Senegal: Opposition Member of Parliament Tortured in Police Custody.* London: 1993. NGO report, in English.

Article 19. *Freedom of Information and Expression in Senegal: A Commentary by ARTICLE 19 on the Report Submitted to the U.N. Human Rights Committee by the Government of the Republic of Senegal.* London: 1987. NGO report, in English; bibliography of sources, p. 30.

Collin, François. "Les élections présidentielles du 21 février 1993 au Sénégal" (The 21 February 1993 Presidential Elections in Senegal), *Alternative Démocratique dans le Tiers Monde* no. 7 (Jan.–June 1993): 25–44. Article, in French.

Donnelly, J., and R. E. Howard, eds. *International Handbook on Human Rights.* Westport, CT, USA: Greenwood Press, 1987. Scholarly edited collection, in English.

Hayward, Fred M. *Elections in Independent Africa.* Boulder, CO, USA: Westview Press, 1987. Scholarly study, in English.

International Commission of Jurists. *Les Services Juridiques en Milieu Rural (Afrique de l'Ouest)* (Legal Services in Rural Areas [West Africa]). Geneva, Switzerland: 1987. NGO report, in French.

Kannyo, Edward. *Human Rights in Africa: Report of a Visit to Nigeria, Ghana, Ivory Coast, Senegal and Upper Volta.* New York: International League for Human Rights, 1981. NGO report, in English.

McLean, S., and S. E. Graham, eds. *Female Circumcision, Excision and Infibulation: The Facts and Proposals for Change,* 2nd rev. ed. London: Minority Rights Groups, 1985. NGO report, in English.

## SERVICE FOR PEACE AND JUSTICE IN LATIN AMERICA.

An international non-governmental organization in consultative status with the UN **ECONOMIC AND SOCIAL COUNCIL** (Category II) and with **UNESCO,** the organization endeavors to develop ways of freeing the poor from oppression and of creating a free, just, and humane society. It promotes education, based on Christian and humanitarian principles, for peace and human rights. It also supports and practices the principle of nonviolence.

Also known by its Spanish title, *Servicio Paz y Justicia en América Latina,* the service, founded in 1974, has national groups in 12 Latin American countries. The group was founded by **NOBEL PEACE PRIZE** recipient **ADOLFO PÉREZ ESQUIVEL.**

Service for Peace and Justice in Latin America. Address: P.O. 8867, Guayaqil, Ecuador. Telephone: (593-4) 201-451. Fax: (593-4) 203-600. Coordinator: Nelsa Corbelo.

## SEXUAL ORIENTATION.

In 1982, the UN **HUMAN RIGHTS COMMITTEE** examined a communication which it had received under article 5, para. 4, of the Optional Protocol of the **INTERNATIONAL COVENANT**

ON CIVIL AND POLITICAL RIGHTS, which contained allegations concerning discrimination on the ground of homosexuality. The action taken by the Committee is summarized in its 1982 report to the GENERAL ASSEMBLY as follows (UN Doc. A/37/40, annex XIV, paras. 18–24):

The authors of this communication claimed that the authorities of their country, including organs of the State-controlled broadcasting company, had interfered with their right of freedom of expression and information, as laid down in article 19 of the International Covenant on Civil and Political Rights, by imposing sanctions against participants in, or censuring, radio and television programmes dealing with homosexuality. According to the communication, it was extremely difficult, if not impossible, for a journalist to prepare a programme in which homosexuals were portrayed as anything other than sick, disturbed, criminal or wanting to change their sex.

The State party concerned, while rejecting the allegation that it was in breach of article 19 of the Covenant, stressed that the purpose of the prohibition of public encouragement to indecent behaviour between persons of the same sex was to reflect the prevailing moral conceptions in the country as interpreted by parliament and by large groups of the population. It further contended that discussions in the parliament indicated that the word "encouragement" was to be interpreted in a narrow sense. Moreover, the Legislation Committee of the parliament expressly provided that the law should not hinder the presentation of factual information on homosexuality. As to the decision of the broadcasting company concerning the programmes referred to by the authors, the State party contended that it did not involve the application of censorship but was based on "general considerations of programme policy in accordance with the internal rules of the company".

In an additional submission the authors argued that article 19 of the Covenant, when read in connection with article 2, paragraph 1, required the State party to ensure that its broadcasting company "not only deals with the subject of homosexuality in its programmes but also that it affords a reasonable and, in so far as is possible, an impartial coverage of information and ideas on the subject, in accordance with its own programme regulations."

In its examination of the communication, the Committee pointed out that its task was confined to clarifying whether the restrictions applied against the alleged victims, irrespective of the scope of penal prohibitions under the State party's penal law, revealed a breach of any of the rights under the Covenant. In addition, the Committee stressed that it was limited to examining whether an individual had suffered an actual violation of his rights. It could not review in the abstract whether national legislation contravened the Covenant. With regard to the claim of one of the authors, the Committee observed that the sole fact that he took a personal interest in the dissemination of information about homosexuality did not

make him a victim in the sense required by the Optional Protocol. The Committee accepted, however, the contention of two of the authors that their rights under article 19, paragraph 2, of the Covenant had been restricted. On the other hand, the Committee observed that article 19, paragraph 3, permitted certain restrictions on the exercise of the rights protected by article 19, paragraph 2, as were provided by law and were necessary for the protection of public order or of public health or morals. Concerning the communication under consideration, the government of the State party had specifically invoked public morals as justifying the actions complained of.

In formulating its views, the Committee emphasized that public morals differed widely. There was no universally applicable common standard. Consequently, in that respect, a certain margin of discretion had to be accorded to national authorities. The Committee found that it could not question the decision of those authorities that radio and television were not the appropriate forums to discuss issues related to homosexuality, as far as a programme could be judged as encouraging homosexual behaviour. According to article 19, paragraph 3, the exercise of the rights provided for in article 19, paragraph 2, carried with it special duties and responsibilities for those organs. As far as radio and television programmes were concerned, the audience could not be controlled, and, in particular, harmful effects on minors could not be excluded. Accordingly, the Committee was of the view that there had been no violation of the rights of the authors of the communication under article 19, paragraph 2, of the Covenant.

In an individual opinion appended to the Committee's views, one member of the Committee, although he agreed with the conclusion of the Committee, wished to clarify the following points:

This conclusion prejudges neither the right to be different and live accordingly, protected by article 17 of the Covenant, nor the right to have general freedom of expression in this respect, protected by article 19. Under article 19, paragraph 2, and subject to article 19, paragraph 3, everyone must in principle have the right to impart information and ideas—positive or negative—about homosexuality and discuss any problem relating to it freely, through any media of his choice and on his own responsibility.

Moreover, in my view the conception and contents of 'public morals' referred to in article 19, paragraph 3, are relative and changing. State-imposed restrictions on freedom of expression must allow for this fact and should not be applied so as to perpetuate prejudice or promote intolerance. It is of special importance to protect freedom of expression as regards minority views, including those that offend, shock or disturb the majority. Therefore, even if . . . laws . . . may reflect prevailing moral conceptions, this is in itself not sufficient to justify it under article 19, paragraph 3.

It must also be shown that the application of the restriction is 'necessary'.

However, as the Committee has noted, this law has not been directly applied to any of the alleged victims. The question remains whether they have been more indirectly affected by it in a way which can be said to interfere with their freedom of expression, and if so, whether the grounds were justifiable.

It is clear that nobody—and in particular no State—has any duty under the Covenant to promote publicity for information and ideas of all kinds. Access to media operated by others is always and necessarily more limited than the general freedom of expression. It follows that such access may be controlled on grounds which do not have to be justified under article 19, paragraph 3.

It is true that self-imposed restrictions on publishing, or the internal programme policy of the media, may threaten the spirit of freedom of expression. Nevertheless, it is a matter of common sense that such decisions either entirely escape control by the Committee or must be accepted to a larger extent than externally imposed restrictions such as enforcement of criminal law or official censorship, neither of which took place in the present case. Not even media controlled by the State can under the Covenant be under an obligation to publish all that may be published. It is not possible to apply the criteria of article 19, paragraph 3, to self-imposed restrictions: quite apart from the 'public morals' issue, one cannot require that they shall be only such as are 'provided by law and are necessary' for the particular purpose. Therefore I prefer not to express any opinion on the possible reasons for the decisions complained of in the present case.

The role of mass media in public debate depends on the relationship between journalists and their superiors who decide what to publish. I agree with the authors of the communication that the freedom of journalists is important, but the issues arising here can only partly be examined under article 19 of the Covenant.

Two other members of the Human Rights Committee associated themselves with the individual opinion expressed above.

***SEXUAL MINORITIES.*** In a resolution adopted on 26 May 1983, entitled "Suppression of the traffic in persons and of the exploitation of the prostitution of others," the UN **ECONOMIC AND SOCIAL COUNCIL** requested the **CENTER FOR HUMAN RIGHTS** to prepare, in liaison with the United Nations agencies and organs concerned and with the competent non-governmental organizations, two complementary studies: one on the sale of children and the other on the legal and social problems of sexual minorities, including male prostitution, and to submit those studies as soon as possible to the **SUB-COMMISSION ON PREVENTION OF DISCRIMINATION AND PROTECTION OF MINORITIES.** The study, entitled "The Legal and Social Problems of Sexual Minorities" (UN Doc. E/CN.4Sub.2/1988/31), prepared by Mr. Jean Fernand-Laurent at the invitation of the Secretary-General, was transmitted to the Sub-Commission at its 1988 session. It endeavored to answer

two questions in particular: (a) Are sexual minorities subjected to *de facto* or *de jure* discrimination and (b) if so, is such discrimination justified on any valid grounds?

The study deals, in the words of the author, "not with occasional and individual breaches of collective moral standards, but, rather, only with groups of persons who are, implicitly or explicitly, protesting against the established order, who refuse to play the role assigned to them as men or women and who, when possible, set up groups to demand the satisfaction of their particular needs and to help one another. This definition covers male and female homosexuals (lesbians), who set themselves apart by having a relationship with a partner of the same sex, and transsexuals, who refuse the legal sex assigned to them. They will henceforth be referred to as sexual minorities." It attempts to answer the question whether the **UNIVERSAL DECLARATION OF HUMAN RIGHTS** is compatible with legislation, regulations, and practices relating to sexual minorities, and to show whether discrimination which might have occurred is justified by valid reasons, such as the protection of the minorities themselves against economic exploitation, concern for public health, and the protection of children.

The study recalls that, in 1982, the UN Human Rights Committee adopted views under article 5 (4) of the Optional Protocol of the International Covenant on Civil and Political Rights with reference to a communication submitted by five Finnish journalists represented by the Organization for Sexual Equality of Finland. The authors of the communication contended that Finnish authorities, including organs of the State-controlled Finnish Broadcasting Company, had interfered with their right of freedom of expression and information, as laid down in article 19 of the Covenant, by imposing sanctions against participants in, or censuring, radio and television programs dealing with homosexuality. At the heart of the dispute was paragraph 9 of chapter 20 of the Finnish Penal Code, which reads:

If someone publicly engages in an act violating sexual morality, thereby giving offense, he shall be sentenced for publicly violating sexual morality to imprisonment for at most six months or to a fine.

Anyone who publicly encourages indecent behavior between persons of the same sex shall be sentenced for encouragement to indecent behavior between members of the same sex as decreed in sub-section 1.

The Finnish Government, while admitting that paragraph 9 of chapter 20 of the Penal Code constitutes a certain restriction on freedom of expression, referred to article 19 (3) of the Covenant, which states that the exercise of the rights provided for in article

19 (2) may be subject to certain restrictions, in so far as these are provided by law and are necessary for the protection of public order, or of public health or morals.

The Committee, after considering the merits of the communication, found (UN Doc. A/37/40, annex XIV)

that it cannot question the decision of the responsible organs of the Finnish Broadcasting Corporation that radio and TV are not the appropriate forums to discuss issues related to homosexuality, as far as a program could be judged as encouraging homosexual behavior. According to article 19 (3), the exercise of the rights provided for in article 19 (2) carries with it special duties and responsibilities for these organs. As far as radio and TV programs are concerned, the audience cannot be controlled. In particular, harmful effects on minors cannot be excluded. Accordingly, the Human Rights Committee is of the view that there has been no violation of the rights of the authors of the communication under article 19 (2) of the Covenant.

The study also recalls that between 1976 and 1981 the European Commission on Human Rights and the European Court of Human Rights considered a petition brought by a British subject against his government, complaining of the existence in Northern Ireland of laws which had the effect of establishing as offenses certain homosexual acts between consenting adults. The Court's judgment, dated 22 October 1981, led to an order by the British Government decriminalizing homosexual acts committed in private by two consenting adults aged 21 or more in Northern Ireland, thus bringing Northern Irish law on this issue into line with the law in force for the rest of the United Kingdom.

After examining in some detail the numerous problems, including those of prejudice and discrimination, encountered by male and female homosexuals, transsexuals, and male prostitutes, the study concludes with the following comments and proposals (paras. 95–106):

In considering three sexual minorities (homosexuals, lesbians and transsexuals), we have approached the depths of human nature and have come upon the most disturbing mysteries on which scholars have been unable to shed any light. These facts are very humbling and keep us from making any hard and fast judgements.

Our research brought us up against one of the basic structures of every society—the distinction between the sexes. It took us into the area of sexual activity which, together with power and money, forms one of the focal points of all private and social morality, and of all ethical thinking. However, the governing rules of morality, which have been widely challenged over the last 30 years in Western societies, no longer apply for young people, or even for some members of their parents' generation. They are no longer an insurmountable obstacle to the realization of any desires. Admittedly, this questioning attitude and trend towards permissiveness have

thus far affected only the industrialized market-economy countries, but neither the socialist countries nor the third world can consider themselves safe from such changes. Moreover, in so far as the law is determined to a large extent by social mores, some impact has begun to be seen in the Western countries, in both legislation and court decisions. Moral permissiveness, encouraged by the media, advertising and cultural industries and only tenuously reined in by the courts, may thus be approaching the point where a continuing deterioration would provoke a backlash in the form of a sudden return to traditional moral values and traditional sanctions, and thus the remarginalization of sexual minorities. The Commission for Social Development, in an effort to ensure the physical and mental equilibrium of the child, is already considering proposing to the Economic and Social Council a major United Nations effort on behalf of the family. It is perhaps for the Commission on Human Rights, without questioning the usefulness of such an initiative, to consider which rights of the human person are at stake in the situation experienced by individuals who, because of sexual proclivity, find themselves excluded from a society in which the family constitutes the basic unit.

In individual cases, we have seen a great deal of suffering engendered more often than not by the feeling of being confined in a ghetto. The members of sexual minorities, who are the victims rather than the instigators of this confinement, are asking not that we should pity them, but that we should respect their difference and that our behaviour should be based on fellowship. We must make every effort to eliminate the causes of their suffering and afford them the possibility of escaping from the ghetto and fitting into society.

It would be worthwhile drawing up a general strategy taking account, in particular, of the fact that many of the situations studied are encouraged, if not determined, by the attitude of society. It is likely that societies have emphasized the distinction between the sexes more than necessary to ensure a happy and fruitful family life, and has established excessively hard and fast male and female prototypes. It is more than likely that the assertion of a purported male supremacy has had a deeply disturbing effect on many women and that there would be fewer lesbians if men were able to be more affectionate, more attentive and more tactful. Also, the virility model presented to men, seeming unattainable to many of them, has caused them to drift towards alternative forms of sexual activity. There would be less impotence and homosexuality if men did not feel called on by the social model to achieve with their female partners an exceptionally high level of sexual performance. In short, a considerable effort would have to be made for the long term, through improved education and a thorough review of the conduct of the media, to eliminate the artificiality of the contrast between the sexes and promote more equality and reciprocity between them. This would bring closer that future time hoped for by Ranier Maria Rilke, when "love would no longer be a relationship between man and woman but a relationship between one human being with another. Being more human, it will be infinitely sensitive and considerate, good and clear in all things which it initiates and resolves. It will be that love for which we work so hard—two solitudes protecting one another, complementing one another, limiting one another and yielding to one another."

*In view of the foregoing observations, the Sub-Committee on Prevention of Discrimination and Protection of Minorities may wish to propose that the Commission on Human Rights should recommend to Member States the adoption of a set of coherent measures, first and foremost in the areas of education and communication, the preventive strategy suggested in the following two paragraphs.* [Italics found in study.]

The first preventive action will consist of a policy in support of the family unit and the educational capacity of the parents. At the same time, in formal education, and particularly as part of the moral education and civics training which should begin at nursery school, it would be as well to institute, instead of or in conjunction with simple sex education, education in respect for life, respect for feelings and for the body and mutual respect between the sexes, which would also provide an early preparation for parental responsibilities. These goals are already provided for in a number of ongoing UNESCO programmes (studies of the image presented of men and women in textbooks, research into the influence of the media on the image of women) encouraged by the Economic and Social Council (resolution 1983/30, para. 11).

With regard to the media (cinema, radio and television, the press, cartoon strips, video cassettes, telephone, telematics, etc.) and advertising in the press, on the screen and on hoardings, it would be worth establishing multidisciplinary advisory commissions on which both parents and teachers were represented, as is already the case with regard to the cinema in a number of countries. These commissions would encourage the media to adopt a deontology of respect for women and children and would formulate guidelines which could be approved by Governments, with a view to protecting children against the spread of pornography which could upset the psychological equilibrium of the most insecure individuals and turn them into sex maniacs.

In addition, in the area of positive law, we have noted that changes in moral values have resulted in the non-application of a number of existing laws, so that the public is no longer quite sure what is permitted and what is not; we have also noted that existing laws vary considerably from one country to another and even within countries with federal systems. There should therefore be greater coherence between the law and judicial practice and greater harmony between the laws of various countries. As for the guiding principles, these should of course be, first and foremost, freedom, equality and non-discrimination as embodied in the Universal Declaration of Human Rights (articles 2 and 7) and in the Covenants, together with the principle of respect for privacy (article 12 of the Universal Declaration) and of the "special safeguards" needed by the child (International Declaration of the Rights of the Child, adopted by the United Nations General Assembly on 20 November 1959).

*In the interests of non-discrimination and respect for privacy, the Sub-Commission on Prevention of Discrimination and Protection of Minorities may wish to propose to the Commission on Human Rights that it should recommend that Member States which have not already done so should take the legislative or regulatory measures described below as the second phase of an overall policy.* [Italics found in study.]

(a) As in the case of racism, any violence or discrimination practised against an individual because of sexual proclivity to be made punishable by law. Norwegian law already provides for this.

(b) All sexual practices to be tolerated between consenting adults, provided that they are practised in private and do not offend public decency.

(c) A genuine transsexual who has obtained a change of sex by medical means to be entitled to a change of civil status to conform to the new identity. This is already provided for by law in the Federal Republic of Germany and Sweden, among others.

(d) Sexual minorities to be authorized to form associations provided their activities do not contravene the law on associations or other laws.

However, as the guardian of the welfare of the community, the State has the right, and perhaps also the duty, to take, in respect of sexual minorities, precautions similar to those which it takes, without being reproached for it, with regard to any activity likely to present a danger to the natural environment, the human environment or the person engaging in the activity himself (as in the case of fishing, hunting, operation of powered equipment, possession and carrying of weapons, selling of alcoholic beverages and drugs, gambling, etc). In this respect, common sense coincides with the underlying ethics of the Universal Declaration of Human Rights in that, in order to make freedom and equality as accessible as possible to all, individuals and the State itself are called on, in a spirit of brotherhood, to protect the weakest and most vulnerable. This leads to the conclusion that, in addition to protecting sexual minorities . . . against any kind of persecution, the State can and must protect society against the potential dangers which such practices represent for "morality, public order and the general welfare" (article 29, 2, of the Universal Declaration). Furthermore, in the event of a conflict between the respective rights of men, women and children, the guiding principle should be to provide greater protection for the most vulnerable person—in many cases women, and in all cases the child.

*As part of their social defence responsibility, Governments and parliaments which feel unable to remain neutral with regard to such burning ethical and social issues could contemplate adopting (as the third element of an overall policy) the following legislation or regulations.* [Italics found in study.]

(a) *With regard to transsexuality,* protect:

The transsexual himself by imposing a period of reflection, requiring him to attend consultations before deciding to undergo an irreversible operation, and even establishing a minimum age for such operations;

The medical profession against the temptation of deriving profit from requests for unnecessary treatment, by making the administering of hormones and sex change operations subject to certain rules;

The spouse against the distortion, by a transsexual spouse, of the meaning and purpose of marriage by according the right to present any objections before an irreversible operation and affording him the possibility of a divorce on the basis of the decision taken.

(b) *With regard to homosexuality,* protect the health of the population and of homosexuals themselves by taking the precautions recommended by the World Health Organization, in so far as the male homosexual community is known . . . to be one of the groups exposed to a number of contagious diseases.

With regard to homosexuals in positions of authority over children (teachers, etc.), a frequently raised question . . . a choice must be made between the wish to avoid exposing children to the influence of a deviant model and the wish to eliminate any possible discrimination against a minority. Although no specific answer will be suggested here, attention is again drawn to the principle, recognized in the International Declaration of the Rights of the Child, of the special safeguards to be afforded to children by virtue of their vulnerability.

(c) *With regard to propaganda for any abnormal sexual practice,* to protect the mental and moral well-being of the population, and in particular of young people, by regulating freedom of expression to the extent authorized by article 19, paragraph 3, of the International Covenant on Civil and Political Rights, by imposing on propaganda for such practices "certain restrictions, but these shall only be such as are provided by law and are necessary: (a) for respect of the rights or reputations of others; (b) for the protection of national security or of public order (ordre publique) or of public health or morals". This power of the State was recognized by the Human Rights Committee when considering a complaint against Finland.

(d) *With regard to paedophilia,* since minors are unable to protect themselves against adults, prohibit and severely punish any sexual relations between minors and adults (active paedophilia), even if the minor declares himself to be consenting. In view of the opportunities afforded to paedophiles by international tourism, standardize the age of sexual majority (age of consent) in all countries and for both girls and boys. This recommendation has already been made by the Council of Europe Parliamentary Assembly.

(e) *Concerning male prostitution,* proceed as recommended for female prostitution in Economic and Social Council resolution 1983/30, and, in particular, protect:

Young people by prohibiting, among other things, active soliciting in public places and the access of minors to certain establishments;

Prostitutes themselves against exploitation, by punishing procuring and collectively or bilaterally combating international traffic by *inter alia,* prohibiting the residence of foreign prostitutes.

The foregoing three groups of suggestions . . . obviously call for numerous consultations and lengthy consideration in order to weigh the advantages and disadvantages of legislating on moral values which are in a state of transition, in the knowledge that the criminalization of an act generally forces it underground, whereas its decriminalization (as in the case of abortion) leads to its proliferation. Another question is whether the measures . . . designed to protect young people do not run the risk—which it is hoped to avoid—of placing the individuals concerned under surveillance, making their marginalization official and even, as those concerned fear, encouraging a witch hunt. Consequently, the question of the advisability of a measure which would clearly be legitimate under the Universal Declaration of Human Rights and the Covenants, must be considered in the cultural and political context of each State.

The Sub-Commission was not able to consider the study at its 1987 session because, although completed, it had not been issued as a Sub-Commission document. The Sub-Commission requested (resolution 1987/31) that it be made available in document form and made available to it at the 1988 session. At that session, the study (UN Doc. E/CN.4/Sub.2/1988/31) was examined in connection with item 14 A of the agenda, "Question of slavery and the slave trade in all their practices and manifestations, including the slavery-like practices of *apartheid* and colonialism."

**TRANSSEXUALISM.** On 29 September 1989, the Parliamentary Assembly of the **COUNCIL OF EUROPE** adopted a recommendation (1117 [1989]) that the Committee of Ministers of the Council should draw up a recommendation inviting member States to introduce legislation whereby, in the case of irreversible transsexualism: (a) the reference to the sex of the person concerned is to be rectified in the register of births and in the identity papers, (b) a change of forename is to be authorized, (c) the person's private life is to be protected, and (d) all discrimination in the enjoyment of fundamental rights and freedoms is prohibited in accordance with article 14 of the European Convention on Human Rights.

In the resolution, the Assembly pointed out that transsexualism is a syndrome characterized by a dual personality—one physical, the other psychological—together with such a profound conviction of belonging to the other sex that the transsexual person is prompted to ask for the corresponding bodily "correction" to be made. It noted that transsexualism raises relatively new and complex questions to which States are called upon to find answers compatible with respect for human rights, and observed that, in the absence of specific rules, transexuals are often the victims of discrimination and violation of their private life.

**SEE ALSO** *Minorities' Rights.*

**BIBLIOGRAPHY.** Amnesty International. *Violations of the Human Rights of Homosexuals: Extracts from Amnesty International Action Materials.* London: 1994. NGO report, in English

Anderson, Shelly. *Out in the World: International Lesbian Organizing.* Ithaca, NY, USA: Firebrand Books, 1991. Directory, in English.

Ben-Asher, David Ari. "Legal Discrimination against Homosexuals in America, and a Comparison with More Tolerant Societies," *New York Law School Journal of Human Rights* 7, no. 2 (Spring 1990): 157–178. Scholarly article, in English.

Dunne, Bruce W. "Homosexuality in the Middle East: An Agenda for Historical Research," *Arab Studies Quarterly* 12, nos. 3 and 4 (Summer/Fall 1990): 55–82. Scholarly article, in English.

"The Family in the 1990s: An Exploration of Lesbian and Gay Rights," *Law and Sexuality* 1 (Summer 1991): 1–96. Scholarly symposium contributions, in English.

Fisher, John W. *"Just Thoughts": Lesbian and Gay Equality under the International Bill of Rights.* Kingston, Canada: Queen's University, 1992. Master's thesis, in English.

Hayes, John Charles. "The Tradition of Prejudice Versus the Principle of Equality: Homosexuals and Heightened Equal Protection Scrutiny after Bowers v. Hardwick," *Boston College Law Review* 31 (1990): 375–475. Scholarly article, in English.

Helfer, Laurence R. "Lesbian and Gay Rights as Human Rights: Strategies for a United Europe," *Virginia Journal of International Law* 32, no. 1: 157–212. Scholarly article, in English.

Irish Council for Civil Liberties (ICCL). *Equality Now for Lesbians and Gay Men.* Dublin, Ireland: 1990. NGO report, in English.

"Legal Restrictions on Homophobic and Racist Speech: Collateral Consequences on the Lesbian and Gay Commu-

# S

nity," *Law and Sexuality* 2 (1992): 1–35. Scholarly symposium contributions, in English.

**SEYCHELLES.** The Republic of Seychelles is a country in eastern Africa occupying an archipelago consisting of 112 islands in the Indian Ocean north of Madagascar, the largest of which are Mahe, Praslin, and La Digue. It achieved independence from Great Britain in 1976 and became a member of the United Nations the same year. Its population is estimated to be 70,000. Ethnic groups include Asian, African, European, and Creole elements. Languages commonly used include Creole, spoken by 95% of the population; and English and French, both of which are official. Christianity (Roman Catholic, 90%; Anglican and other Protestant denominations, 10%) is the predominant religion. Literacy is estimated at 80%.

The government (1994) took the form of a republic. The president, elected for a term of five years, is head of State and government; he nominates and leads the Council of Ministers. There is a 25-member unicameral People's Assembly, of which 23 are elected for four-year terms and two are nominated by the president. However, both the constitution and the Assembly have been suspended since 1977; and the main political party is the Seychelles People's Progressive Front (SPPF).

President Rene, who had ruled by decree since 1977, invited dissidents to return to the country in 1991 to participate in the return to democracy. From 1992, political parties of more than 100 members were officially registered and took part in July 1992 multiparty elections to the constituent assembly, whose task was to draft constitutional reforms.

The SPPF won 11 of the Commission's 20 seats, with the Democratic Party (DP) winning 8 seats. The draft proposals from this first Commission, which had held closed sessions, failed to secure the 60% approval required in the referendum, receiving only 54% support. A second draft by a new Commission was approved by 74% in June 1993.

The new constitution calls for legislative and presidential elections every five years and limits a president to three terms. The president appoints the judiciary and the advisory Council of Ministers. The National Assembly comprises 22 directly elected members and 11 members based on proportional representation.

President Rene was re-elected in July 1993 with 60% of the vote and the SPPF won 21 of the 22 directly elected legislative seats and seven of the 11 proportionally allocated seats. The DP won a total of four seats and the Party Seychellois one seat.

***BIBLIOGRAPHY.*** Amnesty International. *Seychelles: Political Imprisonment and Allegations regarding the "Disappearance" or Extrajudicial Execution of Suspected Opponents of the Government.* London: 1985. NGO report, in English.

Immigration and Refugee Board Documentation Centre. *The Seychelles: Country Profile.* Ottawa, Canada: 1990. Government briefing paper, in English and French.

**SHELTER.** At its 1980 session, the UN **GENERAL ASSEMBLY** concluded (resolution 35/76) that a special year devoted to the problems of homeless people in urban and rural areas of the developing countries could be an appropriate occasion to focus the attention of the international community on their problems, and proclaimed 1987 International Year of Shelter for the Homeless. It decided that the objective of activities before and during the year would be to improve the shelter and neighborhoods of some of the poor and disadvantaged by 1987 and to demonstrate by the year 2000 ways and means of improving the shelter and neighborhoods of such people all over the world.

During the Year of Shelter for the Homeless, activities organized by the United Nations Centre for Human Settlements were undertaken in all parts of the world. In these activities, special attention was given to: (a) securing renewed political commitment by the international community to the improvement of the shelter and neighborhoods of the poor and disadvantaged and to the provision of shelter for the homeless; (b) consolidating and sharing relevant knowledge and experience in the field; (c) developing and demonstrating new approaches to the problem; and (d) exchanging experience and providing support among countries to meet the objectives of the Year.

At the close of the international year, the General Assembly received and noted (resolution 42/191) the reports of the executive director of the United Nations Centre for Human Settlements entitled *Shelter and services for the poor—a call to action* (UN Doc. HS/C/10/3) and *A new agenda for human settlements* (UN Doc. HS/C/10/2 and Corr. 1 and 4), and a summary of the comments made by governments at the tenth (commemorative) session of the Commission on Human Settlements (UN Doc. A/42/8).

Recognizing that adequate and secure shelter is a basic human right and is vital for the fulfilment of human aspirations and that a squalid residential environment is a constant threat to health and to life itself, thereby constituting a drain on human resources, a nation's most valuable asset, the Assembly expressed deep concern about the existing situation in which, despite the efforts of governments at the national and local levels and of international organizations, more than one billion people find themselves either completely without shelter or living in homes unfit for human habitation; and that, owing to prevailing demographic trends, the already formidable problems will escalate in the coming years unless concerted, determined efforts are taken immediately.

Encouraged by action which had been taken in many countries in order to prepare national shelter strategies and launch other measures to promote achievement of the goal of shelter for all, the Assembly decided that there shall be a Global Strategy for Shelter to the Year 2000, including a plan of action for its implementation, monitoring and evaluation, and that its objective would be to stimulate measures to facilitate adequate shelter for all by the year 2000. It requested the executive director of the Centre for Human Settlements to prepare a proposal for such a global strategy and called upon the Commission on Human Settlements to formulate the strategy for consideration by the Assembly in 1988.

On 20 December 1988, the General Assembly, bearing in mind the Vancouver Declaration on Human Settlements and noting that the Commission on Human Settlements had prepared a Global Strategy for Shelter to the Year 2000 as requested (UN Doc. A/43/8/Add. 1), adopted a series of guidelines for steps to be taken at the national and international levels, reproduced below, in support of the Global Strategy. The Assembly requested the Commission on Human Settlements, as the body designated to coordinate implementation of the strategy, to report biennially on the progress made.

## I. Guidelines for Steps to be Taken at the National Level

A. *Considerations for Governments When Formulating a National Shelter Strategy.* 1. A national shelter strategy must spell out clear operational objectives for the development of shelter conditions both in terms of the construction of new housing and the upgrading and maintenance of existing housing stock and infrastructure and services.

2. In the definition of those objectives, development of shelter should be seen as a process whereby conditions are gradually improved for both men and women. The objectives need to address the scale of the problem, while the "adequate" standard aimed at should be identified on the basis of an analysis of the standards and options affordable to the target population and society at large. The objectives should be based on a comprehensive view of the magnitude and nature of the problem and of the available resource base, including the potential contribution of men and women. In addition to finance, land, manpower and institutions, building materials and technology also have to be considered irrespective of whether they are held by the public or private, formal or informal sector.

3. The objectives of the shelter sector need to be linked to the goals of overall economic policy, social policy, settlement policy and environmental policy.

4. The strategy needs to outline the action through which the objectives can be met. In an enabling strategy actions such as the provision of infrastructure may mean the direct involvement of the public sector in shelter construction. The objective of "facilitating adequate shelter for all" also implies that direct government support should mainly be allocated to the most needy population groups.

5. The public sector is responsible for developing and implementing measures for national shelter policies and for the adoption of measures to stimulate the desired action by other sectors. This can happen through measures in areas such as the locally based small-scale building-materials industry, appropriate financial schemes or training programmes.

6. Another important component is the development of administrative, institutional and legislative tasks that are the direct responsibility of the Government, for example, land registration and regulation of construction.

7. An analysis of affordability will provide the criteria for defining the right priorities and appropriate approaches and standards for public sector involvement. Likewise, such an analysis gives the criteria for planning the indirect involvement of the public sector, that is, the type of activities to be promoted and the appropriate way of going about it.

8. The appropriate institutional framework for the implementation of a strategy must be identified, which may require much institutional reorganization. Each agency involved must have a clear understanding of its role within the overall organization framework and of the tasks expected of it. Mechanisms for the co-ordination of inter- and intra-agency activities need to be developed. Mechanism such as shelter coalitions are recommended and may be developed in partnership with the private and non-governmental sectors. Finally, arrangements for the continuous monitoring, review and revision of the strategy must be developed.

B. *Steps to be Taken by Governments When Implementing a National Strategy.* 9. Organize work for the preparation of the strategy. For instance, a task force may be appointed for the actual work and a steering committee ensuring high-level political commitment set up to guide its work. Alternately it may be possible to use existing mechanisms. Equal participation of women should be ensured at all levels.

10. Assess needs and resources. Estimates are required of the needs in housing construction and in upgrading and maintenance (including housing-related infrastructure), as well as of the resources that can be mobilized over the period to the year 2000 to cover those needs.

11. Analyse shelter options and standards that are affordable by the target groups and society at large, taking into account both the scale of need and all the resources available—finance, land, manpower and institutions, building materials and technology.

12. Set objectives for the construction of new housing and for the upgrading and maintenance of the existing housing stock in terms both of the scale of the activities and of the housing standards to be met.

13. Identify action through which those objectives can be realistically met. The estimated required resources for this action must not exceed those that can be made available by society. The action includes both direct government involvement and measures needed to encourage, facilitate and integrate active participation of other sectors in shelter delivery.

14. Prepare a plan of action in consultation and partnership with non-governmental organizations, people and their representatives, which:

(a) Lists the activities that are the direct responsibility of the public sector;

(b) Lists the activities to be taken to facilitate and encourage the other actors to carry out their part of the task;

(c) Outlines resource allocation to the aforementioned activities;

(d) Outlines the institutional arrangements for the implementation, co-ordination, monitoring and review of the strategy;

(e) Outlines a schedule for the activities of the various agencies.

### II. Guidelines for Steps to be Taken at the International Level

15. International action will be necessary to support the activities of countries in their endeavour to improve the housing situation of their poor and disadvantaged inhabitants. Such assistance should support national programmes and use know-how available locally and within the international community.

16. The goal of external assistance should be to enhance and support national capabilities to develop and implement national action components of the Global Strategy for Shelter to the Year 2000.

17. Mutual co-operation and exchange of information and expertise between developing countries in human settlement work stimulate and enrich national human settlement work.

18. The United Nations Centre for Human Settlements (Habitat) will act as the co-ordinating agency in the implementation of the Global Strategy for Shelter to the Year 2000, on the basis of biennial plans to be drawn up with the involvement of experts working with Governments and the Centre on a regional and subregional basis.

19. As the co-ordinating agency for the Strategy, the United Nations Centre for Human Settlements (Habitat) will stimulate international and national action by incorporating the Strategy in its future medium-term plans and biennial work programmes.

20. An inter-agency-level working arrangement will be made within the existing budget to provide continuous co-ordination of the Strategy.

21. The United Nations Centre for Human Settlements (Habitat) will prepare a reporting format to facilitate monitoring by the Commission on Human Settlements of progress achieved in the implementation of the Global Strategy.

**SEE ALSO** *Housing as a Human Right; Standard of Living.*

**SIERRA CLUB INTERNATIONAL.** This non-governmental organization has consultative status with the UN ECONOMIC AND SOCIAL COUNCIL (Roster). Established in 1972, the Sierra Club works to improve conditions in the ecosystem and to protect and restore the equality between natural resources and the human environment. Among its current projects is the reform of the World Bank and the clean-up of acid rain. It has members in 73 countries, the largest concentration of membership being in North America. The Sierra Club publishes the bi-monthly *Sierra Magazine.*

Sierra Club International: Address: 180 Montgomery Street, Suite 1400, San Francisco, CA 94104-4230, USA. Telephone: (415) 627-6700. Fax: (415) 627-6740. Executive Director: Douglas Wheeler.

**SIERRA LEONE.** The Republic of Sierra Leone is a country in western Africa, on the Atlantic Ocean. It has borders with Guinea and Liberia. It achieved independence from Great Britain in 1961 and became a member of the United Nations the same year. Its total population is estimated to be 4,424,000. Ethnic groups include Temnes (30%), Mendis (29%), and Creoles (2%). Languages commonly used include English (official), Krio (the *lingua franca*), Tenne, Menda, and other African languages. Religions practiced include Islam (39%), Animism and traditional tribal faiths (53%), and Christianity (Protestant, 6%; Roman Catholic, 2%). Literacy is estimated at 15%.

The government (1994) took the form of a transitional military government. Under the 1978 constitution, the All Peoples' Congress Party is the only legal political party. The president, elected unopposed in 1985, is head of State and government. Legislation is prepared by the 104-member parliament, which includes 85 members nominated by the All Peoples' Congress Party, 12 paramount chiefs, and 7 members appointed by the president. Judges of the Supreme Court are appointed by the president.

Founded in 1788 by British settlers as a home for runaway slaves who had sought refuge in London and for blacks discharged from the British armed forces, Sierra Leone was a British protectorate from 1896 to 1961. It declared itself a republic in 1971 after two coup attempts by army officers had failed; however, from April 1978 until early 1995, the only political party was the All Peoples' Congress.

The National Constitutional Review Commission drafted a new Constitution which was approved by the House of Representatives and by national referendum in August 1991. It provided for election of a president for a maximum of two five-year terms, a House of Representatives and a 22-member State Advisory Council comprising a Paramount Chief from each of the 12 districts and 10 members appointed by the president.

A military coup in April 1992 led by Capt. Valentine E. M. Strasser was followed by a proclamation dissolving the House of Representatives and all political parties and establishing the National Provisional Ruling Council, later renamed the Supreme Council of State.

During 1993 demands were made by the United Kingdom, the European Union and others that the government plan for a transition to civilian rule, ease severe press restrictions and provide information on the military trials of nine men accused of attempting a coup against Strasser and summarily executed in December 1992.

A two-year plan for return to civilian rule by January 1996 was revealed in November 1993, followed by formation in December of a five-member Interim National Electoral Commission headed by UN Assistant Secretary-General for Political Affairs, Dr. James Jonah. The 18-month state of emergency was ended and in January 1994 a 19-member National Advisory Council was established.

Its proposals included the election of a president for a maximum of two four-year terms (requiring 50% of the vote nationally and 25% of the vote from each of the four provinces), a popularly elected House of Representatives, and a 30-member Senate, including regional representatives and five presidential appointees.

Even after the military coup in 1992 the opposition Revolutionary United Front (RUF) continued fighting with the government. The UN World Food Program estimated that 900,000 people had been displaced from the beginning of the strife in 1991 to 1995.

On February 26, 1996, despite reports of widespread intimidation and mutilation of voters by RUF and Army personnel, elections were held to appoint a civilian government. The elections were reported to be largely fair, but neither of the two largest parties (the Sierra Leone Peoples Party or the United National Peoples Party, both newly formed in anticipation of the elections) achieved the majority required to take office. In a runoff election held March 16, the Sierra Leone Peoples Party achieved a 59.5% majority, and its leader, Ahmad Kabbah, was slated to assume the Presidency.

**BIBLIOGRAPHY**. Amnesty International. *Sierra Leone: The Extrajudicial Execution of Suspected Rebels and Collaborators.* London: 1992. NGO report, in English.
————. *Sierra Leone: Political Detainees at the Central Prison, Pademba Road, Freetown.* London: 1993. NGO report, in English.
————. *Sierra Leone: Prisoners of War? Children Detained in Barracks and Prison.* London: 1993. NGO report, in English.
Crisp, Jeff. "Sierra Leone: Nightmare Journey to a Land of Peace," *Refugees* 79 (Oct. 1990): 8–12. IGO article, in English and French.
U.S. Committee for Refugees. *"The Usual People": Refugees and Internally Displaced Persons from Sierra Leone.* Washington, D.C.: Immigration and Refugee Services of America, 1995. NGO report, in English.

**SIM NEWSLETTER.** See **NETHERLANDS QUARTERLY OF HUMAN RIGHTS.**

**SINGAPORE.** The Republic of Singapore is a country in southeastern Asia; it occupies Singapore Island, which lies off the southern tip of the Malay Peninsula between the South China Sea and the Indian Ocean, and 54 nearby islets. It achieved independence in 1965 upon withdrawing from the Federation of Malaysia and became a member of the United Nations the same year. Its population is estimated to be 2,812,000. Ethnic groups include Chinese (77%), Malays (15%), Indians (6%), and others (2%). Languages commonly used include English (the language of government and of higher education), Malay, Chinese, and Tamil; all are considered to be official languages. Religions practiced include Buddhism, Christianity, Confucianism, Hinduism, Islam, and Taoism. Literacy is estimated at 85%.

The government (1994) took the form of a republic. The president is head of State, and is assisted by a presidential council. The prime minister is head of government and represents the party or coalition given a majority in popular elections. There is a unicameral 79-member Parliament, members of which are elected for terms ranging up to five years from single-member constituencies. The judiciary is organized along British lines and includes the Supreme Court, the High Court, the Court of Appeal, and the Court of Criminal Appeal. The predominant political party is the People's Action Party; there are a number of opposition parties.

Lee Kuan Yew, who had ruled for nearly eight terms as prime minister since 1959, was replaced by his chosen successor, Goh Chok Tong, in November 1990.

Legislation and constitutional amendments in 1990 and 1991 provided for the government appointment of six unelected members of parliament and the election of a president with broad veto powers. The presidential candidates would be chosen by a committee and limited to those who had served as a government minister, chief justice, senior civil servant or head of a large corporation and would be reviewed by an election committee. Indeed, in the presidential election of August 1993, two prospective opposition candidates were rejected on the basis of alleged unsuitability of character and reputation.

The People's Action Party (PAP) remained strong with opposition parties facing obstacles such as the prohibition against legislators using offices within public housing, the government's announcement that it would prioritize public housing repairs based on the level of support for the government by its inhabitants and the government's authority over appointments and dismissals at the National University, the seat of prospective opposition candidates. Former PAP Deputy Prime Minister Ong Teng Cheong was elected president in August 1993 with 59% of the vote.

International attention was focused on Singapore's criminal justice system in 1994 and 1995. An American teenager was sentenced to six lashes with a rattan cane for vandalism in 1994. Following pressure from U.S.

President Bill Clinton and others, the sentence was reduced to four lashes. In March 1995 a Filipina maid was hanged for the 1991 murder of another Filipina maid and the four-year-old Singapore boy in her care. Thousands protested in the Philippines amid allegations that the maid had been framed by the boy's parents. Singapore refused to delay the execution despite international protests.

*BIBLIOGRAPHY.* Asia Watch. *Silencing All Critics: Human Rights Violations in Singapore.* New York: Human Rights Watch, 1989. NGO report, in English.

Muntarbhorn, Vitit. *The Status of Refugees in Asia.* Oxford, UK, and New York: Oxford University Press and Clarendon Press. Scholary monograph, in English; bibliography, pp. 201–212.

O'Grady, Ron. *Banished: The Expulsion of the Christian Conference of Asia from Singapore and Its Implications.* Hong Kong: Christian Conference of Asia, International Affairs Committee, 1900. NGO report, in English.

Scow, Francis. "The Tyranny of the Majority," *Index on Censorship* 19, no. 3 (March 1990): 3–8. NGO article, in English.

**SLAVERY AND THE SLAVE TRADE.** The UNIVERSAL DECLARATION OF HUMAN RIGHTS calls for the prohibition of these and similar violations of human rights in the following terms:

*Article 4.* No one shall be held in slavery or servitude; slavery and the slave trade shall be prohibited in all their forms.

International cooperation in endeavors to put an end to slavery, the slave trade, and similar practices, existed for many years prior to the proclamation of the Declaration. In 1890, signatories to the General Act of the Brussels Conference declared their intention to secure the complete suppression of slavery in all its forms, and of the slave trade by land and by sea, and established an elaborate international machinery which proved highly effective in diminishing the trade in slaves. Later, States parties to the Slavery Convention Signed at Geneva on 25 September 1926 (see SLAVERY) undertook (a) to prevent and suppress the slave trade and (b) to bring about, progressively and as soon as possible, the complete abolition of slavery in all its forms. To this end, they agreed to adopt all appropriate measures with a view to preventing and suppressing the embarkation, disembarkation, and transport of slaves in their territorial waters and upon all vessels flying their respective flags, to give one another every assistance with the objective of securing the abolition of slavery and the slave trade, and to take all necessary measures to prevent compulsory or forced labor from developing into conditions analogous to slavery. The Convention defined slavery as "the status or condition of a person over who any or all of the owners attaching to the right of ownership are exercised," and the slave trade as including "all acts involved in the capture, acquisition or disposal of a person with intent to reduce him to slavery; all acts involved in the acquisition of a slave with a view to selling or exchanging him; all acts of disposal by sale or exchange of a slave acquired with a view to being sold or exchanged, and, in general, every act of trade or transport of slaves."

The Convention of 1926 became a United Nations instrument when the Protocol Amending the Slavery Convention, adopted by the UN GENERAL ASSEMBLY in 1953, entered into force on 7 July 1955. However, studies undertaken by expert bodies of the United Nations and the INTERNATIONAL LABOR ORGANIZATION indicated that it had not effectively eliminated slavery or the slave trade in all parts of the world and that it needed to be augmented (a) to intensify national as well as international efforts to abolish these evils and (b) to make it clear that its definition of "slavery" includes not only literal slavery but also certain institutions and practices having the same effects as slavery, such as debt bondage, serfdom, and the exploitation of the labor of women and children.

Accordingly, the ECONOMIC AND SOCIAL COUNCIL convened (resolution 608 [XXI]) a Conference of Plenipotentiaries which met in Geneva and adopted, on 7 September 1956, the Supplementary Convention on the Abolition of Slavery, the Slave Trade and Institutions and Practices Similar to Slavery. The Convention entered into force on 30 April 1957.

With regard to institutions and practices similar to slavery, the supplementary Convention provides that:

*Article 1.* Each of the States Parties to this Convention shall take all practicable and necessary legislative and other measures to bring about progressively and as soon as possible the complete abolition or abandonment of the following institutions or practices, where they still exist and whether or not they are covered by the definition of slavery contained in article 1 of the Slavery Convention signed at Geneva on 25 September 1926:

(a) Debt bondage, that is to say, the status or condition arising from a pledge by a debtor of his personal services or of those of a person under his control as security for a debt, if the value of those services as reasonably assessed is not applied towards the liquidation of the debt or the length and nature of those services are not respectively limited and defined;

(b) Serfdom, that is to say, the condition or status of a tenant who is by law, custom or agreement bound to live and labour on land belonging to another person and to render some determinate service to such other person, whether for reward or not, and is not free to change his status;

(c) Any institution or practice whereby:

(i) A woman, without the right to refuse, is promised or given in marriage on payment of a consideration in money or in kind to her parents, guardian, family or any other person or group; or

(ii) The husband of a woman, his family, or his clan, has the right to transfer her to another person for value received or otherwise; or

(iii) A woman on the death of her husband is liable to be inherited by another person;

(d) Any institution or practice whereby a child or young person under the age of 18 years is delivered by either or both of his natural parents or by his guardian to another person, whether for reward or not, with a view to the exploitation of the child or young person or of his labour.

*Article 2.* With a view to bringing to an end the institutions and practices mentioned in article 1 (c) of this Convention, the States Parties undertake to prescribe, where appropriate, suitable minimum ages of marriage, to encourage the use of facilities whereby the consent of both parties to a marriage may be freely expressed in the presence of a competent civil or religious authority, and to encourage the registration of marriages.

With regard to the slave trade, the Supplementary Convention provides that:

*Article 3.* 1. The act of conveying or attempting to convey slaves from one country to another by whatever means of transport, or of being accessory thereto, shall be a criminal offence under the laws of the States Parties to this Convention and persons convicted thereof shall be liable to very severe penalties.

2. (a) The States Parties shall take all effective measures to prevent ships and aircraft authorized to fly their flags from conveying slaves and to punish persons guilty of such acts or of using national flags for that purpose.

(b) The States Parties shall take all effective measures to ensure that their ports, airfields and coasts are not used for the conveyance of slaves.

3. The States Parties to this Convention shall exchange information in order to ensure the practical co-ordination of the measures taken by them in combating the slave trade and shall inform each other of every case of the slave trade, and of every attempt to commit this criminal offence, which comes to their notice.

*Article 4.* Any slave who takes refuge on board any vessel of a State Party to this Convention shall *ipso facto* be free.

With regard to slavery and institutions and practices similar to slavery, the Supplementary Convention further provides that:

*Article 5.* In a country where the abolition or abandonment of slavery, or of the institutions or practices mentioned in article 1 of this Convention, is not yet complete, the act of mutilating, branding or otherwise marking a slave or a person of servile status in order to indicate his status, or as a punishment, or for any other reason, or of being accessory thereto, shall be a criminal offence under the laws of the States Parties to this Convention and persons convicted thereof shall be liable to punishment.

*Article 6.* 1. The act of enslaving another person or of inducing another person to give himself or a person dependent upon him into slavery, or of attempting these acts, or being accessory thereto, or being a part to a conspiracy to accomplish any such acts, shall be a criminal offence under the laws of the States Parties to this Convention and persons convicted thereof shall be liable to punishment.

2. Subject to the provisions of the introductory paragraph of article 1 of this Convention, the provisions of paragraph 1 of the present article shall also apply to the act of inducing another person to place himself or a person dependent upon him into the servile status resulting from any of the institutions or practices mentioned in article 1, to any attempt to perform such acts, to being accessory thereto, and to being a party to a conspiracy to accomplish any such acts.

The Supplementary Convention does not establish a special body to monitor the implementation of its provisions but calls for cooperation between the States parties to give effect to those provisions, as follows:

*Article 8.* 2. The Parties undertake to communicate to the Secretary-General of the United Nations copies of any laws, regulations and administrative measures enacted or put into effect to implement the provisions of this Convention.

3. The Secretary-General shall communicate the information received under paragraph 2 of this article to the other Parties and to the Economic and Social Council as part of the documentation for any discussion which the Council might undertake with a view to making further recommendations for the abolition of slavery, the slave trade or the institutions and practices which are the subject of this Convention.

Long before the promulgation of the Slavery Convention of 1926 and the Supplementary Convention of 1956, the international community had evidenced its concern with a particular practice resembling slavery in its effects—the traffic in women and children—and had prepared a series of instruments aimed at the suppression of such traffic, among them:

(a) The International Agreement of 18 May 1904 for the Suppression of the White Slave Traffic, as amended by the Protocol approved by the UN General Assembly on 3 December 1948;

(b) the International Convention of 4 May 1910 for the Suppression of the White Slave Traffic, as amended by the above-mentioned Protocol;

(c) the International Convention of 30 September 1921 for the Suppression of the Traffic in Women and Children, as amended by the Protocol as approved by the UN General Assembly on 20 October 1947; and

(d) the International Convention of 11 October 1933 for the Suppression of the Traffic in Women of Full Age, as amended by the above-mentioned Protocol.

The **LEAGUE OF NATIONS** had prepared, in 1937, a draft convention extending the scope of these instruments but had not been able to finalize or to adopt the text.

In 1949, the concerned United Nations bodies consolidated the proposed draft convention and the four instruments. The resulting Convention for the Suppression of the Traffic in Persons and of the Exploitation of the Prostitution of Others (see **SLAVERY**) was adopted by the General Assembly (resolution 317

[IV]) on 2 December 1949 and entered into force on 25 July 1951.

The Convention provides that:

*Article 1.* The Parties to the present Convention agree to punish any person who, to gratify the passions of another:

(1) Procures, entices or leads away, for purposes of prostitution, another person, even with the consent of that person;

(2) Exploits the prostitution of another person, even with the consent of that person.

*Article 2.* The Parties to the present Convention further agree to punish any person who:

(1) Keeps or manages, or knowingly finances or takes part in the financing of a brothel;

(2) Knowingly lets or rents a building or other place or any part thereof for the purpose of the prostitution of others.

*Article 3.* To the extent permitted by domestic law, attempts to commit any of the offences referred to in articles 1 and 2, and acts preparatory to the commission thereof, shall also be punished.

*Article 4.* To the extent permitted by domestic law, intentional participation in the acts referred to in articles 1 and 2 above shall also be punishable.

To the extent permitted by domestic law, acts of participation shall be treated as separate offences whenever this is necessary to prevent impunity.

The Convention does not provide for the establishment of special international machinery to monitor the implementation of its provisions. However, under article 21, the States parties undertake to communicate to the UN Secretary-General such laws and regulations as have already been promulgated in their countries and, thereafter, such laws and regulations as may be promulgated, relating to the subjects of the Convention, as well as measures taken by them concerning the application of the Convention. The information received is published by the Secretary-General, sent to member and non-member States of the United Nations, and examined by the Working Group on Contemporary Forms of Slavery.

In 1957, the General Conference of the International Labor Organization reviewed the provisions of the ILO Forced Labor Convention of 1930 and the ILO Protection of Wages Convention of 1949, and decided that further measures were required in order to put an end to certain forms of compulsory or forced labor. The General Conference accordingly adopted, on 25 June 1957, the ILO Abolition of Forced Labor Convention, which provides that:

*Article 1.* Each Member of the International Labour Organisation which ratifies this Convention undertakes to suppress and not to make use of any form of forced or compulsory labour:

(a) As means of political coercion or education or as a punishment for holding or expressing political views or views ideologically opposed to the established political, social or economic system;

(b) As a method of mobilising and using labour for purposes of economic development;

(c) As a means of labour discipline;

(d) As a punishment for having participated in strikes;

(e) As a means of racial, social, national or religious discrimination.

*Article 2.* Each member of the International Labour Organisation which ratifies this Convention undertakes to take effective measures to secure the immediate and complete abolition of forced or compulsory labour as specified in article 1 of this Convention.

The **INTERNATIONAL COVENANT ON CIVIL AND POLITICAL RIGHTS,** adopted by the UN General Assembly on 16 December 1966, includes the following provision relating to slavery and the slave trade:

*Article 8.* 1. No one shall be held in slavery; slavery and the slave-trade in all their forms shall be prohibited.

2. No one shall be held in servitude.

3. (a) No one shall be required to perform forced or compulsory labour;

(b) Paragraph 3 (a) shall not be held to preclude in countries where imprisonment with hard labour may be imposed as a punishment for a crime, the performance of hard labour in pursuance of a sentence to such punishment by a competent court;

(c) For the purpose of this paragraph the term "forced or compulsory labour" shall not include:

(i) Any work or service, not referred to in sub-paragraph (b), normally required of a person who is under detention in consequence of a lawful order of a court, or of a person during conditional release from such detention;

(ii) Any service of a military character and, in countries where conscientious objection is recognized, any national service required by law of conscientious objectors;

(iii) Any service exacted in cases of emergency or calamity threatening the life or well-being of the community;

(iv) Any work or service which forms part of normal civil obligations.

The United Nations Convention on the Law of the Sea, signed at Montego Bay, Jamaica, on 10 December 1982, contains the following provision:

*Article 9.* Every State shall take effective measure to prevent and punish the transport of slaves in ships authorized to fly its flag and to prevent the unlawful use of its flag for that purpose. Any slave taking refuge on board any ship, whatever its flag, shall *ipso facto* be free.

The **AMERICAN CONVENTION ON HUMAN RIGHTS,** open for acceptance by member States of the **ORGANIZATION OF AMERICAN STATES,** provides that:

*Article 6.* 1. No one shall be subject to slavery or to involuntary servitude, which are prohibited in all their forms, as are the slave trade and traffic in women.

2. No one shall be required to perform forced or compulsory labor. This provision shall not be interpreted to mean that, in those countries in which the penalty established for certain crimes is deprivation of liberty at forced labor, the carrying out of such a sentence imposed by a com-

petent court is prohibited. Forced labor shall not adversely affect the dignity or the physical or intellectual capacity of the prisoner.

3. For the purposes of this article, the following do not constitute forced or compulsory labor:

(a) work or service normally required of a person imprisoned in execution of a sentence or formal decision passed by the competent judicial authority. Such work or service shall be carried out under the supervision and control of public authorities, and any persons performing such work or service shall not be placed at the disposal of any private party, company, or juridical person;

(b) military service and, in countries in which conscientious objectors are recognized, national service that the law may provide for in lieu of military service;

(c) service exacted in time of danger or calamity that threatens the existence or the well-being of the community; or

(d) work or service that forms part of normal civic obligations.

The **African Charter on Human and Peoples' Rights,** open for acceptance by member States of the **Organization of African Unity,** provides that:

*Article 5.* Every individual shall have the right to the respect of the dignity inherent in a human being and to the recognition of his legal status. All forms of exploitation and degradation of man particularly slavery, slave trade, torture, cruel, inhuman or degrading punishment and treatment shall be prohibited.

The **European Convention on Human Rights,** open for acceptance by members of the **Council of Europe,** provides that:

*Article 4.* 1. No one shall be held in slavery or servitude.

2. No one shall be required to perform forced or compulsory labour.

3. For the purpose of this Article the term 'forced or compulsory labour' shall not include: (a) any work required to be done in the ordinary course of detention imposed according to the provisions of Article 5 of this Convention or during conditional release from such detention;

(b) any service of a military character or, in case of conscientious objectors in countries where they are recognised, service exacted instead of compulsory military service;

(c) any service exacted in case of an emergency or calamity threatening the life or well-being of the community;

(d) any work or service which forms part of normal civic obligations.

***INTERNATIONAL ACTION TO ABOLISH SLAVERY IN ALL ITS FORMS AND MANIFESTATIONS.*** In 1949, shortly after the proclamation of the Universal Declaration of Human Rights, the UN **Economic and Social Council** authorized the Secretary-General (resolution 238 [IX]) to select a committee of experts to survey the field of slavery and other institutions and customs resembling slavery, to assess the nature and extent of these problems, and to suggest ways of attacking them. The four-member committee reported in 1951 that, apart from slavery in its crudest form, a number of practices analogous to slavery, or resembling slavery in their effects, still existed in various parts of the world. It was on recommendation of the committee that the functions previously exercised by the League of Nations under the Slavery Convention of 1926 were transferred to the United Nations in 1953, and that the Supplementary Convention on the Abolition of Slavery, the Slave Trade, and Institutions and Practices Similar to Slavery was adopted by the General Assembly in 1956.

In 1963, the Council requested the Secretary-General (resolution 960 [XXXVI]) to appoint a Special Rapporteur to compile comprehensive and up-to-date information on the extent to which slavery persisted. The Special Rapporteur, Mr. Mohamed Awad, in his *Report on Slavery* (UN publication, Sales no. 67.XIV.2), clearly demonstrated that slavery, the slave trade, and similar institutions and practices continued to exist in some parts of the world and that women and children were among their victims.

After examining and noting the report, the Council referred the question of slavery and the slave trade in all their practices and manifestations, including the slavery-like practices of *apartheid* and colonialism, to the **Commission on Human Rights** (resolution 1126 [XLI]). The Commission, in turn, called upon its **Sub-Commission on Prevention of Discrimination and Protection of Minorities** (resolution 13 [XXIII]) to undertake regular consideration of the question, taking into account the *Report on Slavery* and other relevant materials, and to consider information submitted by States parties to the Supplementary Convention of 1956 in accordance with article 8 of that instrument.

In May 1968, the Council broadened the Sub-Commission's mandate in this field, authorizing it (resolution 1330 [XLIV]) "to undertake a study of the measures which might be taken to implement the International Slavery Convention of 1926 and the Supplementary Convention of 1956 on the Abolition of Slavery, the Slave Trade and Institutions and Practices Similar to Slavery and the various recommendations included in the resolutions of the General Assembly, the Economic and Social Council and the Commission on Human Rights relating to the slavery-like practices of *apartheid* and colonialism," and further authorizing it "to initiate a study of the possibilities of international police co-operation to interrupt and punish the transportation of persons in danger of being enslaved, taking into account, as appropriate, the view of the competent international organizations." These studies, completed in 1971 by the Sub-Commission's Special Rapporteur (UN Doc. E/CN.4/Sub.2/322), resulted in the adoption of a comprehensive resolution on slavery by the Council in 1972.

In the resolution (resolution 1695 [LII]), the Council called upon all eligible States which were not parties to the International Slavery Convention of 1926 and the Supplementary Convention of 1956 to become parties as soon as possible; drew attention to the close relationship between the effects of slavery, *apartheid,* and colonialism and to the need to take concrete measures to ensure the effective implementation of the relevant international conventions and decisions of the United Nations with a view to bringing about the complete elimination of these shameful phenomena; and called upon all States to enact any legislation necessary to prohibit slavery and the slave trade in all their practices and manifestations and to provide effective penal sanctions for persons committing, or ordering to be committed, any of the following acts: abduction, planning the abduction, or giving instructions for the abduction of any person by force, treachery, gifts, abuse of authority or power, or intimidation, which results in that person being placed in a status of slavery or servitude as defined in the International Slavery Convention of 1926 and the Supplementary Convention of 1956. The Council also called upon all States to search for persons alleged to have committed, or to have ordered to be committed, any such acts, and to bring such persons, regardless of their nationality, before its own courts, or to hand such persons over for trial to another State concerned.

The Secretary-General was requested to present a summary of the available information on slavery and the slave trade to the Sub-Commission at each session, to undertake a survey of national legislation for the purpose of eliminating practices similar to slavery and to prepare a plan of technical cooperation to contribute to the eradication of slavery and the slave trade.

The Sub-Commission was requested, by the same resolution, to examine the possibility of establishing some form of permanent machinery to give advice on the elimination of slavery and on the suppression of the traffic in persons and exploitation of the prostitution of others. Accordingly, the Sub-Commission initiated the practice of appointing a working group composed of five of its members to meet for not more than three working days before each Sub-Commission session "to review developments in the field of slavery and the slave trade in all their practices and manifestations, including the slavery-like practices of *apartheid* and colonialism, the traffic in persons and the exploitation of the prostitution of others as they are defined in the Slavery Convention of 1926, the Supplementary Convention of 1956, and the Convention for the Suppression of the Traffic in Persons and of the Exploitation of the Prostitution of Others of 1949." The mandate of the working group on slavery, the name of which in 1988 was changed to Working Group on Con-

temporary Forms of Slavery by the Commission on Human Rights (resolution 1988/42), has been progressively interpreted in such a way as to cover a growing number of additional relevant issues such as the sale of children, the exploitation of child labor, the sexual mutilation of female children, abuses against workers and indigenous populations, debt bondage, and the exploitation of the prostitution of others.

In 1980, the Sub-Commission appointed one of its members, Mr. Benjamin Whitaker (United Kingdom) as Special Rapporteur to update the *Report on Slavery.* The resulting report, entitled *Slavery,* was presented to the Sub-Commission in 1982 and published in 1984 (UN publication, Sales no. E.84/XIV.1). In it, the author described the contemporary manifestations of slavery and slavery-like practices and the action which had been taken to combat them by governments, the United Nations and other intergovernmental bodies, and non-governmental organizations, and presented his conclusions and recommendations. Among his conclusions were the following (paras. 187–188):

> The phenomenon of slavery manifests several of the gravest forms of the violation of human rights: often it combines coercion, severe discrimination and the most extreme form of economic exploitation. As Mr. Masud, a member of the Sub-Commission, pointed out, slavery-like practices have frequently been exploited by elites (initially, often by colonial invaders), and the long-term remedy lies in widening participation democracy and educating people about, and providing them with the means to safeguard, their human rights. Slavery is the ultimate structural abuse of human power; that any vestiges of it should remain in the 1980s is a disgrace to professed international standards.

> The cumulative evidence contained in this report substantiates *prima facie* that, although chattel slavery in the former traditional sense no longer persists in any significant degree, the prevalence of several forms of slavery-like practice continues unabated. Indeed, instances of new forms of servitude and gross exploitation have come to light only in recent years, as violators seek to circumvent laws or to take advantage of changing economic and social conditions. Some of the individual cases, although they may appear isolated, highlight wider and deeper problems that deserve attention. Hence the necessity to re-examine continuously both the nature of the problem and the manner in which the international community should deal with it.

The Sub-Commission on Prevention of Discrimination and Protection of Minorities and its working group have since, at each annual session, reviewed in some detail recent developments concerning slavery in its classical and contemporary forms. The 1989 review, prepared by the working group and set out in its report (UN Doc. E/CN.4 Sub.2/1989/39) deals (chap. IV) with prevention of the sale of children, of child prostitution and of child pornography and (chap. V) with other contemporary forms of slavery such as child labor, debt bondage, traffic in persons and exploitation of the prostitution of others, and the slavery-like practices of *apartheid* and colonialism.

The Commission on Human Rights, at its 1990 session, took note (resolution 1990/63) of the report of the working group but did not consider the measures proposed by the Sub-Commission in resolutions 1989/42 and 43. Expressing grave concern that slavery, the slave trade, slavery practices, and even modern manifestations of this phenomenon still exist, representing some of the gravest violations of human rights, the Commission requested the Secretary-General to invite States parties to the Slavery Convention Signed at Geneva on 25 September 1926, as amended, the Supplementary Convention on the Abolition of Slavery, the Slave Trade, and Institutions and Practices similar to Slavery, and the Convention for the Suppression of the Traffic in Persons and of the Exploitation of the Prostitution of Others to submit to the Sub-Commission regular reports on the situation in their countries as provided under the Conventions. It also called upon those eligible States which have not ratified the above-mentioned Conventions to consider doing so as soon as possible, and invited them to consider providing information regarding their national legislation and practices in this field. The Commission, further, invited intergovernmental organizations, the relevant United Nations agencies, and non-governmental organizations, including those interested in children's and women's rights, to attend sessions of the working group.

Finally, the Commission invited all member States to consider the possibility of taking appropriate action for the protection of children and migrant women against exploitation by prostitution and other slavery-like practices, including the possibility of establishing national bodies to achieve these objectives; and requested governments to pursue a policy of information, prevention, and rehabilitation of women victims of the exploitation of prostitution, and to take the appropriate economic and social measures deemed necessary to that effect.

***TRAFFIC IN PERSONS AND PROSTITUTION.*** This practice, which gives rise to effects similar to those of slavery and the slave trade, is characterized in the 1949 Convention for the Suppression of the Traffic in Persons and of the Exploitation of the Prostitution of Others as "incompatible with the dignity and worth of the human person."

A subject of international concern at the start of the 20th century, when governments cooperated to provide international protection against what was then known as the "white slave traffic," this practice retained in the late 1980s its high priority on the agenda of the Working Group on Contemporary Forms of

Slavery of the UN Sub-Commission on Prevention of Discrimination and Protection of Minorities.

In 1904, the parties to the International Agreement for the Suppression of the White Slave Traffic pledged themselves to establish in their respective countries "some authority charged with the co-ordination of all information relative to the procuring of women and girls for immoral purposes abroad" and to take concerted measures for securing to women of full age, who have suffered abuse or compulsion, as well as to girls under age, effective protection against that criminal traffic.

In 1910, the contracting parties to the International Convention for the Suppression of the White Slave Traffic undertook to punish any person who, to gratify the passions of others, hired, abducted, or enticed for immoral purposes, even with her consent, a woman or girl under 20 years of age, or over that age in case of violence, threats, fraud, or any compulsion, notwithstanding that the various acts which together constituted the offense were committed in different countries. The case of retention, against her will, of a woman or girl in a house of prostitution was excluded from the framework of this Convention because it was considered a question within the exclusive competence of national legislation.

In 1921, the International Convention for the Suppression of the Traffic in Women and Children, concluded under the auspices of the League of Nations, extended the protective measures provided for in the two earlier instruments to minors of either sex and raised the age limit for protection from 20 to 21 years of age.

In 1933, the International Convention for the Suppression of the Traffic in Women of Full Age declared as punishable offenses the acts of procuring, enticing, or leading away, even with her consent, a woman of full age, for immoral purposes to be carried out in another country. Attempts to commit, and acts preparatory to the commission of, these offenses were also made punishable.

None of the above-mentioned instruments dealt directly with the question of prostitution, which continued to be considered a domestic affair. However, special bodies of experts appointed by the League of Nations in 1927 and 1932, respectively, found that it was difficult, if not impossible, to isolate the international question entirely from various forms of commercialized vice where there was no transportation to a foreign country; and noted that a principal factor in the promotion of international traffic in women was the licensed house of prostitution.

For the purpose of securing international cooperation for the abolition of licensed houses and the prosecution and punishment of any person managing such a house or exploiting the prostitution of others, the League of Nations prepared, in 1937, a draft convention on the subject. Owing to the outbreak of the World War II, the draft convention was not adopted under the auspices of the League. It was, however, completed and adopted by the UN General Assembly in December 1949 as the Convention for the Suppression of the Traffic in Persons and of the Exploitation of the Prostitution of Others.

The 1949 Convention consolidates the earlier instruments and embodies the policy favored by the League of Nations' expert bodies: abolition of any form of regulation of prostitution. It binds the States parties "to take all necessary measures to repeal or abolish any law, regulation or administrative provision by virtue of which persons who engage in or are suspected of engaging in prostitution are subject either to special registration or to the possession of a special document or to any exceptional requirements for supervision or notification."

Advocates of this "abolitionist" system place emphasis upon effective legislation against illicit traffic and the exploitation of the traffic of others, drafted in such a way as to preclude traffickers and profiteers from circumventing them and escaping punishment; and point out that it is more effective than either the "regulationist" system, which legalizes prostitution and the existence of licensed brothels, or the "prohibitionist" system, which transforms prostitution into a criminal offense, giving rise to clandestine prostitution and often to a ruthless underworld organization conducting the illicit traffic in, and exploitation of, women and girls.

In 1982, the UN Economic and Social Council requested the Secretary-General (resolution 1982/20) to appoint a Special Rapporteur to prepare "a synthesis of the surveys and studies on the traffic in persons and the exploitation of the prostitution of others" and to propose "appropriate measures to prevent and suppress these practices that are contrary to the fundamental human rights of human beings."

Special Rapporteur Jean Fernand-Laurant (France) submitted his report in 1983. It was published in 1985 under the title *Activities for the Advancement of Women: Equality, Development and Peace* (UN publication, Sales no. E.85.IV.11). In it, he analyzed the problem of prostitution and its exploitation from the human rights point of view, considering it as a form of slavery, as follows (paras. 16–40):

## I. A Universal and Interdisciplinary Question

Although prostitution was and still is unknown in many so-called primitive societies, it is also true that it is found today to varying degrees in all States, in all cultures and in all parts of the world, especially where the population is dense and where money changes hands frequently.

The problem can be analysed from several angles, which is why it interests organizations with very different aims. It can be approached from the angle of ethnology, sociology or cultural history, for example; or from the angle of political economy, from which the world of prostitution can be seen as a closed economic system; or from the angle of criminology, as a branch of the criminal world because of the procuring involved. Prostitution can also be judged by the standards of public health, religion or mortality. Without overlooking any of these approaches, this report will take the human rights approach, as does the Economic and Social Council, in which prostitution is considered to be a form of slavery.

*A. A Three-way Trade.* Like slavery in the usual sense, prostitution has an economic aspect. While being a cultural phenomenon rooted in the image of man and woman given currency by society, it is a market and indeed a lucrative one. The merchandise offered is for men's pleasure, or the pleasure they enjoy in their imagination. This merchandise is unfortunately supplied by physical intimacy with women or children. Thus, the alienation of the person is here more far-reaching than in slavery in its usual sense, where what is alienated is working strength, not intimacy.

The market is created by demand, which is met by supply. The demand comes from the client, who could also be called the "prostitutor". The supply is provided by the prostitute. This is the simplest but also the rarest example. In most cases (8 or 9 times out of 10, according to observers, at least in Europe), a third person comes into the picture, perhaps the most important; this is the organizer and exploiter of the market, in other words, the procurer in his various guises: go-between or recruiter, pimp, owner of a house of prostitution, "massage parlour" or bar, or provider of a hotel room or studio. The procurer is usually a professional, involved to some extent in the world of crime. When it comes to children, it can be an older child who runs a "racket".

In the industrialized market-economy States, a concern not to hamper trade allows an overt market for eroticism and pornography to develop alongside the discreet prostitution market. The two complement and reinforce each other. The streets on which the sex shops are located are those where prostitution is heaviest.

Of the three partners in the three-way relationship: client, prostitute and procurer, least is known about the first mentioned. Since there are no laws or regulations that either punish or restrict the client, he can remain anonymous. There is so far no literature, to the Rapporteur's knowledge, in which the client has himself divulged his motivations. The reasons that prompt a bachelor or a married man to become a client have not as yet been analysed. Meanwhile, one can only suppose that his desires and his behaviour stem from the image that society gives him of his virility and from the conception that he has of women's duty being to serve his pleasure. Military service and the media no doubt play a decisive role here. Insufficient preparation for marriage among women, and also among men, might explain certain unsuccessful marriages that lead the husband to seek sexual satisfaction outside the home.

More is known about the prostitute because she is monitored by social workers and has often been described in literature. Moreover, in recent times, several former prostitutes have given autobiographical accounts of their prostitution experiences. Today, therefore, we know what brings a woman to the point of becoming a prostitute. Economic hardship is the main reason, but it is not enough; not all poor women become prostitutes. In addition to poverty, there must be a loss of respect for moral strictures, frustration or lack of affection (rejection of parents or by parents, desertion by a husband or lover), and a lack of outside assistance or a refusal to use it when it is available. Statistically, most prostitutes have been raised in broken families; a large number of them have been the victims of rape or incest. They therefore do not count on their families if they want to raise children they have had with men who have deserted them (many of them are unmarried mothers: 70 per cent according to the English Collective of Prostitutes, and they are very attached to their children). In the rare cases where the prostitute comes from an affluent family, she is motivated by a desire to challenge conventional morality combined with an excessive interest in money and the satisfaction it can provide. Does not, however, this need for money reflect the deeper need to use the external trappings of wealth to overcome the frustration of one whose personality fails to make a mark on those around her? More basically, a woman of any social level can fall into prostitution as she would fall into alcoholism or drug abuse, or as she would commit suicide: through grief, loneliness, boredom or despair. Then again it can happen in the case of addicts that prostitution seems to be the only means of obtaining drugs. In short, it could be said of most women prostitutes that they have moved from a marginal situation into another one even more marginal.

At any rate, even when prostitution seems to have been chosen freely, it is actually the result of coercion. That was the gist of the testimony given to the Congress of Nice on 8 September 1981 by three "collectives" of women prostitutes from two developed countries: "As prostitutes, we are well aware that *all* prostitution is forced prostitution. Whether we are forced to become prostitutes by lack of money or by housing or unemployment problems, or to escape from a family situation of rape or violence (which is often the case with very young prostitutes), or by a procurer, we would not lead the 'life' if we were in a position to leave it."

The rural exodus in the developing countries figures as a determining cause of prostitution. A survey published in 1978 by the Dakar magazine *Famille et Développement*, shows that employment in the cities is essentially male-oriented. Thus, the first victims in the cities are women. In the country, they have a role as producers; in the city their only role will be that of mothers and wives. Often illiterate and without professional qualifications, they have few alternatives: to be unskilled workers in the few factories where the work force is largely female, to work in domestic service, to ply a small trade or to become prostitutes. In recent years, this last option has been forced on many women as a condition of survival for themselves and their children. In addition, the supply of prostitutes has grown to meet the demand of large-scale tourism.

Emigration, which is often an extension of the rural exodus, produces comparable effects. Women immigrants are, as pointed out in the paper presented at Nice by three collectives, the most vulnerable to exploitation: "Women who have been raped, beaten, forced to work for a pimp (as a prostitute who works for a procurer or a domestic worker in a family), or for illegal wages on the black market, are too afraid of being deported and dare not complain to the police." Further comments will be made on the effects of workers migrations on prostitution.

Wherever foreign troops are present in large numbers, in both the country concerned and neighbouring countries where the soldiers spend their leave the appearance of a prostitution market or expansion of the existing market can be observed. Habits are established among the female population that, after that troops or bases are withdrawn, will be exploited by the tourist networks that take over. One organization of Asian women considers this yet another reason for opposing military alliances and use of the smallest countries in preparation for a new world war.

Occasional prostitution, the so-called "end-of-the-month" type, becomes permanent prostitution once the woman falls into the clutches of a procurer. The procurer is a character more often depicted in literature or in films than met with by the social workers. However, he is well known to the police who, sometimes, too often, use him as an informer. Contempt for women, congenital sloth and a total lack of morals are the characteristics that predispose a man to become a procurer. As a recruiter, he "sells" women to a house of prostitution or to a pimp. The pimps keep virtually all of women's daily earnings. All are involved in the world of crime. The considerable sums earned from procuring actually constitute, according to the police, the "working capital" of organized crime. These funds are sufficient to corrupt, when they are corruptible, those in political circles, the police and other State officials.

The naiveté of young people facilitates the task of the recruiters and pimps, who have several tricks for subjugating their victims without always having to resort to force. The procurer, who has hardly anything else to do, is adept at detecting the weaknesses of his future victims. Among the most frequently used tricks are seduction and a fraudulent promise of marriage or of lucrative employment, followed by a demand for "temporary" prostitution to repay a fictitious debt; sometimes the lure is a contract to join an artistic tour abroad, a tour that ends in a house of prostitution, or a restaurant or place of entertainment that is also used for prostitution; other times it is the offer of travel abroad as an *au pair* or a student in a language-training centre. When force is used, it involves drugs that facilitate kidnapping and sequestration, beating, torture, blackmail involving children and threats of mutilation or murder. Such threats are all the more to be feared since it is known that they are sometimes carried out.

Other tricks and constraints are practised on children. There is no doubt that in the slum belts of certain large cities, children sometimes have no other choice in order to survive but to pick through garbage, beg, steal or become prostitutes. But adults, paedophiles or procurers, often take the initiative by offering money or gifts. In depressed rural areas, where helpless peasant families are heavily in debt to a usurer, the children are sometimes bought or rented by a procurer from their parents, who may or may not be aware of their ultimate fate. If the child is an orphan, an abandoned child, a runaway or temporarily separated from his parents by some natural or man-made disaster, he or she is especially vulnerable and can simply be kidnapped. Paedophile tourists may be involved.

In some industrialized countries, child prostitution has recently been organized to benefit the pornography industry, which produces photograph albums, films and video cassettes. Children are photographed or filmed in indecent positions, and these pictures are sold for high prices through a clandestine network of persons interested in such things. This trade may be national or international.

Procuring does not stop at the activities of recruiter, go-between or pimp. Many laws consider as a procurer and prosecute as such any person who knowingly derives profit from the prostitution of others. This applies to a landlord or tenant who makes premises available, at rates above the average rent, to a prostitute for the pursuit of her activities: these are the offences of procuring through the provision of hotel or other premises. The owner or manager of a bar where waitresses are encouraged to act as prostitutes is also a procurer, although he is rarely prosecuted. An organizer of package tours ("sex tours") where the services of a prostitute are included in the package is also a procurer, although so far there have been no prosecutions. In this same category of procurers should be included the social clubs, or the so-called marriage bureaux, when such enterprises derive a profit from meetings where payment is made for sexual favours (some international marriages of convenience are concluded simply for the sake of prostitution). Should the publisher of a book or newspaper that encourages such practices also be considered a procurer? The human imagination is limitless where there is a profit to be made.

Certain intelligence services and capitalist firms act as procurers when, in order to corrupt or compromise a statesman or businessman, they arrange for him to meet women, styled as hostesses or secretaries, who are trained in this particular form of "high-class" prostitution.

Procurers usually conduct their activities with impunity. Perhaps because the police or the investigating officials are not sufficiently zealous (through negligence, fear or corruption), or because it is sometimes difficult to obtain proof of such offences (in court the victim, fearing reprisals, may withdraw charges made to the police and the investigating officials), or because the procurer is protected as an informer, or because the offender escapes prosecution by crossing the border, the fact remains that repression is ineffectual. In the Western European State that considers itself to be the strictest, repression affects about 1 procurer out of 10: the deterrent effect is very inadequate.

B. *A Form of Slavery.* A review of the various collective (remote) and individual (immediate) causes of prostitution: poverty, frustration or lack of affection, trickery and coercion on the part of procurers, makes it unnecessary to invoke any kind of mental weakness or supposed vicious inclination to explain why women fall into prostitution.

Once embarked on that course, they enter a state of servitude. Denied any independence, forced, in order to engage in their new activity, to abide by the rules imposed by the "old hands", exposed to the pressures, untempered by any competing influences, of the morality and law of the "underworld", which are neither the morality nor the law of lawful society, subjected by the procurer to a very effective discipline that metes out punishment with an infrequent admixture of reward, they immediately find themselves in a marginal situation and undergo a psychological conditioning such as may be experienced by someone living in a community within a sect. When able to judge objectively, those women who have been able to escape from this environment realize that they were deprived not only of their name, but of their very identity. A woman may also be sold by one procurer to another, as were slaves in the past and as is merchandise today. The relationship between prostitute and procurer, described by prostitutes in the West as "my husband" or "my man", is ambivalent: it is possible that the woman may find in the man, in spite of his brutality, both a husband and the father she never had in childhood. This does not alter the fact that the relationship is one of dominator and dominated, exploiter and exploited, master and slave. The restricted life of a house of prostitution, even

when christened "Turkish bath", "sauna", "massage parlour" or "Eros Centre", is even harsher than that of the street corner. The Director-General of the United Nations Educational, Scientific and Cultural Organization (UNESCO), through his spokesperson at the Mexico City World Conference in 1975, drew attention to the tortures sometimes inflicted on inmates. While it is true that not all are tortured, all are nevertheless subjected to the most degrading and destructive form of slavery.

It is easy to slide into prostitution; it is very difficult to escape from it. To free oneself from a procurer, it is usually necessary to pay him a substantial "fine", sometimes equivalent to a whole year's earnings from prostitution. If one has the courage to inform on him to the police, something which is forbidden by the law of the underworld, there is a risk of terrible reprisals: mutilation or even death. Those few prostitutes who are not controlled by a procurer do not find it much easier to break free of their environment, so profoundly have they been marked by it and so strongly do they feel themselves rejected, as in fact they often are, by the "normal" society to which they wish to return. It would not be an exaggeration to say that, if she is to be successfully reintegrated into that society, a prostitute requires heroic courage.

C. *International Networks.* The International Criminal Police Organization (ICPO or INTERPOL), an intergovernmental organization linked, through a special arrangement, with the Economic and Social Council and composed of the central criminal police bureaux of 134 States, prepared for its General Assembly of October 1975 in Buenos Aires a third report on the traffic in women. That report was published by Kathleen Barry as an annex to her book entitled *Female Sexual Slavery.* Parts of it were quoted by Whitaker in his report. Based on information received from the police in 69 States, the report identifies a number of international networks involved in this traffic: one flowing from Latin America to Puerto Rico and beyond, to southern Europe and the Middle East; one flowing from South-East Asia to the Middle East and central and northern Europe; a regional European market, in part supplied by Latin America and exporting French women to Luxembourg and the Federal Republic of Germany; one supplying some of the richer countries of West Africa from Europe; and a regional market in the Arab countries. The author of the report did not have access to information from East Africa and does not mention the existence, noted by travellers through that region, of slave markets supplying the Middle East. More recently, the migration of African refugees to Europe has involved women who have been found working as prostitutes only a few months later. Family group among migrant workers have also on occasion served as a cover for traffic networks. According to this incomplete information, few regions and few countries, with the possible exception of the centrally planned economy countries, are free of the international traffic in women, and that traffic is far from being confined to a flow from the less developed South to the more developed North: it would be more accurate to say that the movement involves the traffic of poor women towards rich men in all directions. Through these well-disguised networks, not only adult women but even under-age girls are moved from one country to another.

The replies to the annual questionnaire prepared by the Centre for Human Rights, although supplied by only a small minority of States, provide useful specific supplementary information concerning certain types of international traffic. For example, replies to question 10 were given, for the period 1979–1981, by three countries only: France, Singapore and Spain. These replies have been summarized in a report on slavery, provided by the Centre for Human Rights to the Working Group on Slavery for its eighth session in August 1982. They show that the traffic is often carried on under cover of what purport to be marriage bureaux or advertisements for jobs in touring stage shows. They give evidence of procuring networks supplying Geneva from Paris; Switzerland and the Federal Republic of Germany from Bangkok; Singapore from Malaysia and the Philippines; and Spain from France, Cape Verde, South America and the Philippines (109 young Philippine women aged between 16 and 28). Undoubtedly, if equally detailed replies were available from the other States, a clear picture would be established of the methods and routes used in the traffic in persons. In particular, it would be possible to verify and research in more detail the press reports cited by Whitaker (E/CN.4/Sub.2/ 1982/20, para. 17), indicating that South American prostitutes are shipped from Argentina to Melbourne, young Hawaiian and Californian women to Japan, and Swedish women from Singapore to the Far East.

More conspicuous, and therefore easier to trace, is the other type of traffic that, instead of transporting the prostitute, temporarily transplants the client. This is the channel of the sex tours, in which the services of a prostitute are included in the price the tourist pays for his ticket. This specialized kind of tourism is grafted onto an existing prostitution market and develops it. Several women's associations and the Churches have denounced this traffic, which is a flourishing movement from the developed countries of America, Europe and Asia towards the countries popular with tourists in Africa, Asia and the Caribbean. In September 1980, in Manila, an international workshop on tourism, meeting under the dual sponsorship of the Christian Conference of Asia and the Confederation of Asian Episcopal Conferences, adopted eight recommendations relating to prostitution. In July 1981, an international congress of theologians on "The Community of Men and Women in the Church", meeting in Sheffield, the United Kingdom of Great Britain and Northern Ireland, under the auspices of the World Council of Churches, denounced the phenomenon of sex tours in an "open letter to Christians". In Stockholm, in November 1981, the World Council of Churches organized an international conference on the theme "the Church and tourism", which heard evidence from all regions of the world and put forward a moral code for tourists. Together with this activity by the churches, joint action is being taken by the Asian Women's Association in Japan, the Philippines and the Republic of Korea: with the assistance of trade union organizations, demonstrations have been mounted in airports to coincide with the departure or arrival of sex tours; and a Third World Movement against the Exploitation of Women has been created among the countries of the Association of South-East Asian Nations. In addition, the Asian Confederation of Women's Organisations discussed prostitution at its July 1982 meeting and took cognizance of a document submitted by the Philippines containing recommendations that were studied at the government level at the meeting of the Programme for Women of ASEAN held at Bangkok in January 1983. All these activities have led to a perceptible reduction in organized sex tourism in that region; but will that reduction be lasting? And what of the situation in other regions of the world, such as the Caribbean, where local resistance has not yet become organized? In any event, it is advisable to view this issue in the general context of the cultural impact of tourism. That is the approach taken by the Holy See in its recommendations, virtually a code of ethics, on tourism drafted over several years,

while it continues to encourage the religious orders that are dedicated to the rescue of persons engaged in prostitution. It was also in the context of the cultural effects of tourism that prostitution was discussed by a group of experts that met at Vienna in September 1982 to discuss the issue "Women and the International Development Strategy". That group denounced the destructive effects on the local community and on the identity of women produced by the exploitation of prostitution for tourist purposes. In the view of the Special Rapporteur, such tourism is quite plainly the worst possible image of development that the industrialized countries could project. Together with erotic films, publications and advertising, it may, in the developing countries where it is prevalent, provoke hostile reactions to development itself and prompt a return to discriminatory moral strictures that could be an obstacle to the much-needed liberation of women.

The encouragement that the prostitution of young children receives from Western tourism has been highlighted by Tim Bond, a researcher with the "Terre des Hommes" association of Lausanne. In 1980 he carried out three surveys in two countries of South-East Asia, extending their scope to Europe, where he found publications on sale to the public providing information to paedophiles on the opportunities available to them among young boys from poor families in the big cities of South-East Asia and Africa. Bouhdiba referred to these facts in his report, mentioned above, to the Sub-Commission on Prevention of Discrimination and Protection of Minorities. UNICEF gave them wide publicity in *Ideas Forum*.

After examining the Special Rapporteur's report in 1983, the Economic and Social Council, recalling that the enslavement of women and children subjected to prostitution is incompatible with the dignity and rights of the human person, invited UN member States (resolution 1983/30) to sign, ratify, and implement the Convention for the Suppression of the Traffic in Persons and of the Exploitation of the Prostitution of Others and the International Convention for the Suppression of the Circulation of and Traffic in Obscene Publications; and recommended that they should draw up policies aimed, to the extent possible, at (a) preventing prostitution by moral education and civics training, in and out of school; (b) increasing the number of women among the State's personnel having direct contact with the populations concerned; (c) eliminating discrimination that ostracizes prostitutes and makes their reabsorption into society more difficult; (d) curbing the pornography industry and the trade in pornography and penalizing them very severely when minors are involved; (e) punishing all forms of procuring in such a way as to deter it, particularly when it exploits minors; and (f) facilitating occupational training for and the reabsorption into society of persons rescued from prostitution.

The Council, at the same time, invited member States to cooperate closely with one another in the research for missing persons and in the identification of international networks of procurers and, if they are members of INTERPOL to cooperate with that organization, requesting it to make the suppression of the traffic in persons one of its priorities. Later, the General Assembly invited the Council (resolution 40/103) to give further consideration to the whole question of the suppression of the traffic in persons and of the exploitation of the prostitution of others.

### RECENT DEVELOPMENTS RELATING TO THE TRAFFIC IN PERSONS AND THE EXPLOITATION OF THE PROSTITUTION OF OTHERS.

At its 1988 session, the UN Working Group on Contemporary Forms of Slavery reviewed recent developments relating to the traffic in persons and the exploitation of the prostitution of others. The discussion, as summarized in the working group's report to the 1988 session of the Sub-Commission on Prevention of Discrimination and Protection of Minorities (UN Doc. E/CN.4/Sub.2/1988/32, chap. III, E, paras. 65–73), was as follows:

The International Abolitionist Federation referred the Working Group to its Congress of 1984 held at Vienna which highlighted several factors which led, *inter alia*, to the traffic in persons and prostitution. An indifferent public opinion, irresponsible press, the inertia of Governments, fundamental inequality of men and women in many societies and economic crises were viewed as leading factors. The representative of the Federation also criticized the 1949 Convention for the Suppression of the Traffic in Persons and of the Exploitation of the Prostitution of Others on the grounds that its vague terminology and ineffective implementation machinery allowed States to ignore its application. The attention of the Working Group was drawn to resolution 1988/42 adopted by the Commission on Human Rights at its forty-fourth session calling on States and the Sub-Commission to draw up plans for the taking of concrete measures in the field of slavery. It was announced that an Asian regional conference in collaboration with the Federation would be held in November 1988 at New Delhi in India and that the Federation would hold a European Congress at Bern in 1989.

Another report presented by the International Abolitionist Federation concerned France. It pointed out that there were disparities between principles and declarations contained in the laws of France and what actually obtained in practice. It was pointed out, for instance, that although women and children were regarded as elements of society to be promoted and protected, their positions were constantly being undermined by the way in which they were projected in advertisements and pornography, as well as by their exploitation by prostitution. It was also pointed out that, although international and national standards in France opposed the exploitation of the prostitution of others, the Government profited from prostitution by taxing the earnings of prostitutes, as well as from the revenues it received from the operation of *Minitel Rose,* a communications system run by the Ministry of Posts and Communications and often used by those involved in prostitution. The report also indicated and analysed some inconsistencies within the texts of government policies themselves. The report criticized the ambiguities it had illustrated and emphasized the importance of good laws, conforming with established human rights standards, especially with the advent of greater harmoniza-

tion in Europe. The report referred to the Congress of the International Abolitionist Federation held in Stuttgart in 1987 which called for a study by the United Nations Educational, Scientific and Cultural Organization on the motivations of prostitutes, pimps and clients and indicated that the Federation itself would commence a publication concerning prostitution internationally. The report further indicated that the Federation called on the Secretary-General of the United Nations to press more States to sign the Convention of 1949 and to hold a diplomatic conference consisting of States parties to the Convention to establish means to ensure better implementation of its terms.

With reference to the report made by the International Abolitionist Federation concerning France, the Observer for France indicated that the Government of France was aware of the abuses of such new technology as *Minitel Rose* and was working on ways to prevent this. The Observer also stated that, although the earnings of prostitutes in France were taxed, this was simply because all income in France was taxable and that this in no way meant that the Government acknowledged prostitution as a legitimate profession. As an incentive for prostitutes to become rehabilitated, it was pointed out that they were sometimes exempted from tax whilst they were making such efforts. The Observer for France paid tribute to the role played by non-governmental organizations in the field of prevention and rehabilitation; he stressed the eagerness of his authorities to continue and to increase the co-operation with non-governmental organizations that was already taking place.

Regarding the statement by the Observer for France, the representative of the International Abolitionist Federation raised two issues concerning the taxation of the earnings of prostitutes. The representative questioned whether there was any difference between pimps and the State who both profited from the prostitution of others. The representative also questioned whether prostitutes would not simply have to work harder so that they could meet their payments to their ponces as well as pay their taxes.

The representative of the United Nations Educational, Scientific and Cultural Organization drew the attention of the Working Group to document E/CN.4/Sub.2/AC.2/1988/5, in which many of the organization's efforts in this field were detailed. Mention was made of the International Meeting of Experts held at Madrid in March 1987 during which the causes of prostitution were discussed. It was reported that the Meeting of Experts viewed prostitution as an economic phenomenon, involving the trade of a woman's body as an item of merchandise, as well as a phenomenon partly reflective of social structures and stereotypes. The document also highlighted the discovery of the United Nations Educational, Scientific and Cultural Organization of the contribution that international marriage markets made to the international traffic in persons and prostitution world-wide. The document further emphasized UNESCO's dissatisfaction with the terms of the 1949 Convention for the Suppression of the Traffic in Persons and of the Exploitation of the Prostitution of Others in that they raise a distinction between voluntary and enforced prostitution. UNESCO took the view that there were grounds in contemporary society for believing that such a distinction was unrealistic and that all prostitution violated international human rights standards.

The International Abolitionist Federation drew the attention of the Working Group to reports it had given to previous sessions of the Working Group concerning prostitution in Belgium. The representative of the Federation stated that the Belgian authorities had not only failed to take measures in support of prostitutes in the past but had increasingly commenced to act in a manner contrary to the spirit of the 1949 Convention. It was pointed out that a Belgian law of 1948 permitted the authorities to enact regulations concerning prostitution and that this power was being exercised contrary to the interests of prostitutes and the spirit of the 1949 Convention. It was reported that, in an effort to satisfy public opinion, the establishment of locations used for prostitution was being made more difficult. It was also reported that a regulation forcing prostitutes to work out of the view of passers-by had also been enacted. The representative of the Federation called for the abrogation of all such measures as they had the effect of further marginalizing people who were already the victims of prostitution.

With reference to the report by the International Abolitionist Federation concerning Belgium, the Observer for Belgium denied that the authorities in Belgium were neglecting the problem of prostitution. The Observer supported this by pointing out that Belgium was actively participating in the work of the Working Group and by reporting that the Minister of Justice of Belgium had spoken about prostitution at the Lisbon meeting of Ministers of Justice of the members of the Council of Europe. The Observer stated that the 1949 Convention was a problem in that its term were vague and that they lent themselves to a variety of interpretations.

A report by the International Abolitionist Federation concerning Japan stated that there were laws for the prosecution of those involved in prostitution but that they were largely ineffective as regards the prostitution of foreigners. This was illustrated by pointing out that although only 10 procurers of foreign prostitutes were indicted from 1986 to 1987 over 2,500 procurers in 1987 alone were indicted for employing Japanese prostitutes. The ineffectiveness of the laws regarding the prostitution of foreigners was explained on the basis that the foreigners had language difficulties, little money and that they were simply often deported as illegal immigrants. The report requested the Japanese Government to grant an amnesty to the foreign prostitutes so that they could seek relief from established shelters, find alternative employment and exercise their rights to bring law suits against those that had exploited them. It was requested that the Official Development Assistance from Japan to the rest of South-East Asia be reviewed to ensure that it created jobs in South-East Asian countries in an effort to combat the problem of prostitution. The report pointed out that a survey had been carried out in Japan which revealed that prostitution was viewed there as a problem of society rather than an issue in terms of the human rights of victimized people.

The representative of the Branch for the Advancement of Women from the United Nations Office in Vienna made a statement in which issues were raised concerning relevant international conventions. Mention was also made of possible links which might be established between that office and the Working Group regarding the reports of States parties particularly in the field of human trafficking.

On the basis of the discussion summarized above, the working group made a number of recommendations, as follows:

(a) That urgent consideration be given to the problems of the implementation of the 1949 Convention for the Suppression of the Traffic in Persons and of the Exploitation of the Prostitution of Others, with particular attention to the meaning and scope of its provisions in the light of new forms of prostitution and pornography imposed on children;

(b) That a study be undertaken of ways and means by which an effective implementation mechanism, including reporting systems, may be established for the 1949 Convention for the Suppression of the Traffic in Persons and of the Exploitation of the Prostitution of Others;

(c) That Governments be urged to pursue a policy of information, prevention and rehabilitation of women victims of the exploitation of prostitution and to take all economic and social measures deemed necessary to that effect;

(d) That United Nations institutions, in particular the United Nations Educational, Scientific and Cultural Organization, be encouraged to examine the possibility of organizing expert meetings on the international standards regarding the prevention of traffic in persons and exploitation of the prostitution of others;

(e) That at its future sessions the Working Group should give attention to the dissemination and proliferation of obscene publications and communications, particularly in the light of new technology;

(f) That resolution 1985/23 of the Sub-Commission, endorsed by resolution 1986/34 of the Commission on Human Rights, be submitted for approval to the Economic and Social Council and the General Assembly so that a world day for the abolition of slavery in all its forms can be proclaimed;

(g) That the receiving countries provide protection to migrant women against exploitation in the form of prostitution and other slavery-like practices;

(h) That the receiving and mother countries of migrant women should co-operate closely in protecting migrant women and preventing their exploitation by prostitution and other slavery-like practices;

(i) That all Member States be urged to consider the possibility of establishing national agencies or institutions for the protection of migrant women against exploitation by prostitution and other slavery-like practices.

***IMPLEMENTATION OF INTERNATIONAL CONVENTIONS.*** At its second session, in 1976, the UN Working Group on Contemporary Forms of Slavery (then known as the Working Group on Slavery and Slavery-Like Practices) noted that, although article 8 of the Supplementary Convention on the Abolition of Slavery, the Slave Trade and Institutions and Practices Similar to Slavery requires States parties to forward to the UN Secretary-General copies of new laws, regulations, and administrative measures enacted or put into effect to implement its provisions, no such reports had been received. At the same session, the working group noted that reports under article 21 of the Convention for the Suppression of the Traffic in Persons and of the Exploitation of the Prostitution of Others were no longer transmitted regularly by States parties, that the number of reporting governments had declined, and that information accumulated since 1958 had not been published. The working group accordingly recommended that the reporting procedures envisaged in the two Conventions should be set again in motion.

On recommendation of the Working Group and its Sub-Commission on Prevention of Discrimination and

Protection of Minorities, the UN Commission on Human Rights on 12 March 1984 requested the Secretary-General (resolution 1984/40) to call upon States parties to the Slavery Convention Signed at Geneva on 25 September 1926, the Supplementary Convention of 1956, and the Convention for the Suppression of the Traffic in Persons and of the Exploitation of the Prostitution of Others to submit regular reports on the situation in their countries, as provided for under the Convention; and to call upon other States, intergovernmental organizations, relevant agencies of the United Nations, and concerned non-governmental organizations, and the **INTERNATIONAL CRIMINAL POLICE ORGANIZATION** (INTERPOL) to supply relevant information to the working group.

### PROGRAM OF ACTION FOR PREVENTION OF SALE OF CHILDREN, CHILD PROSTITUTION AND CHILD PORNOGRAPHY.

In 1989, after examining the report of the working group, the Sub-Commission proposed (resolution 1989/42) that the Commission on Human Rights should appoint a Special Rapporteur to consider matters relating to the sale of children, child prostitution and child pornography, including the problem of adoption of children for commercial purposes; and (resolution 1989/43) that the Commission transmit to governments and to intergovernmental and non-governmental organizations, for their comments, the draft "Program of Action for Prevention of the Sale of Children, Child Prostitution and Child Pornography" prepared by the working group. The program follows:

**A. General.** 1. To prevent the sale of children, child prostitution and child pornography, concerted measures are called for at the national and international level, including information, education, assistance and rehabilitation, legislative measures and a strengthening of law enforcement in this field. Co-ordinating agencies should be appointed or established at the national, regional and global level.

2. At the global level, co-ordination of the Programme of Action should be carried out by the Centre for Human Rights in co-operation with other sections of the United Nations Secretariat including the Centre for the Advancement of Women, and with concerned intergovernmental agencies, in particular UNICEF and UNESCO. Co-operation should also be established with INTERPOL.

*Information and Education.* 3. An international information campaign to raise public awareness of these abuses should form part of the Programme. Religious and lay organizations should be encouraged to participate. The media should also be called upon in order to help break the practice of silence surrounding these issues, while avoiding sensationalism. Law enforcement agencies should be given a significant role in this campaign.

4. To improve the sources of information, studies and investigations of these abuses should be undertaken by public and private institutions. The outcomes should, wherever possible, be made public and exchanged between governmental and non-governmental organizations at the national and international level.

5. To provide a focus for the campaign, a World Day for the Abolition of Contemporary Forms of Slavery might be proclaimed. One possibility is to use the date of 2 December, the anniversary of the adoption of the Convention for the Suppression of the Traffic in Persons and of the Exploitation of the Prostitution of Others.

6. Special educational measures should be adopted, to be directed both at the general public and to specific groups. The education should be based on universally agreed ethical principles including the recognition of every child's fundamental right to the integrity of its own body. Emphasis should be placed on the damaging effects which these abuses have on children, ways in which the abuses can be prevented, discovered and exposed, and ways to assist children who have suffered from such abuse.

7. Preventive educational programmes at the primary and secondary level should make the children understand the dangers of these abuses, including the health dangers such as AIDS, and make them aware of their own right to the integrity of their body and thereby strengthen their defence against abuses.

8. Such education must avoid underplaying the issues but should also avoid sensationalizing it. Great care must be taken in developing educational programmes on these subjects. The age of the children concerned and the culture in which the children are living must be taken into account.

9. For street children, who are particularly affected by these practices, alternative educational programmes should be developed.

10. Social workers, health workers, members of law enforcement agencies and of the judiciary should also receive education on the occurrence of such abuses and the ways in which they can be counteracted.

*Social Measures, Development Assistance.* 11. It is recognized that these practices are often linked to poverty, and that long-range structural reforms in the social and economic fields will be required for their prevention. In the shorter run, development activities of the United Nations and other international as well as national agencies should have a substantive and positive impact on children. Priority should be given to policies aimed at improving the social, economic and working conditions of women in general and of the poorest women in particular. Local community projects, including collective self-help projects by vulnerable mothers, should also be encouraged.

12. The needs of children exposed to sexual exploitation should be taken into account in development plans and assistance. Special attention should be given to certain groups of street children and children whose mothers are engaged in prostitution. Governments and non-governmental organizations should be encouraged to initiate projects designed to protect street children from sexual abuse (e.g. small-scale enterprise projects for children, "safe houses", emergency centres, etc.). Efforts should also be made to reunite street children in cities with their families in rural areas.

*Legal Measures and Law Enforcement.* 13. Preventive legislation aimed at protecting children should be strengthened and better enforced. Police, courts and treatment and support systems should focus more on children. Legal aid should be easily available to those who claim to have been sexually violated and to parents or legal guardians in cases of sale of children. Methods should be developed to obtain evidence from the child without further traumatization, and witnesses should be afforded protection.

14. Sexual abuse and traffic in children are serious crimes and must be treated as such. More severe penalties should be imposed on consumers and procurers.

15. Effective legislative and enforcement measures must also be directed against the middlemen and others who encourage and make a profit from the sale and sexual exploitation of children: agents, dealers, brothel-owners, and others involved. The proceeds from such activities should be confiscated.

16. The draft Convention on the Rights of the Child, when adopted, provides protection against sale of children and sexual exploitation. States are encouraged to become parties to the Convention at the earliest possible moment. For its implementation within States, national institutions, with representatives of public agencies and private organizations, might be established to co-ordinate action and to protect children and their rights.

*Rehabilitation and Re-Integration.* 17. Programmes for rehabilitation and re-integration with an inter-disciplinary approach should be established to assist children who have been victims of sexual exploitation, and their families.

Agencies implementing such programmes, whether public or non-governmental, should be given the necessary support and funding.

*International Coordination.* 18. Bilateral and multilateral co-operation among law enforcement agencies is essential. States should establish their own data base, improve their reporting at all levels, and report to INTERPOL to allow for a special data bank on suspects involved in such abuses across borders. The experience gained in international police co-operation in combating drug traffic should be made use of to prevent international traffic involving the sale and sexual exploitation of children.

**B. Sale of Children.** 19. States should be encouraged to take effective legal and administrative measures to prevent the abduction and sale of children. Laws should be adopted or strengthened which impose penalties on parents and on all others knowingly involved in the traffic of children.

20. Measures should be taken to ensure that international adoptions do not involve the illicit removal of children from parents. Procedures for this purpose should be based on the 1986 United Nations Declaration on Social and Legal Principles relating to the Protection and Welfare of Children with Special Reference to Foster Placement and Adoption Nationally and Internationally, and the Convention on the Rights of the Child when adopted. Under no circumstances must adoption be allowed to involve financial gain for any of the parties involved.

21. States should adopt effective and urgent procedures at the national level and through international co-operation to find abducted, unlawfully removed or disappeared children and to reunite such children with their families.

**C. Child Prostitution.** 22. Legislative and other measures should be taken to prevent sex tourism. Such measures should be adopted both in the countries from which the customer comes (most often the industrialized countries) and the countries to which they go (often to developing countries). Marketing tourism through the enticement of sex with women and children should be penalized on the same level as procurement.

23. The World Tourist Organization should be encouraged to convene a world conference on ways in which to prevent such practices.

24. States having military bases or troops on foreign territories, as well as host States, should take all the necessary measures to prevent such military personnel from being involved in child prostitution. The same applies to other categories of persons who for professional reasons are posted abroad.

25. Legislation should be adopted to prevent new forms of technology from being used for soliciting prostitution.

**D. Child Pornography.** 26. Taking into account, as stated at the INTERPOL symposium in September 1988, that child pornography is the permanent visual depiction of the sexual molestation and exploitation of a child, and that there is an international market for this material, law enforcement agencies should place a higher priority on the investigation of child pornography with particular emphasis placed on the welfare of the child.

27. States are urged to enact legislation, where they have not yet done so, making it a crime to produce, distribute or possess pornographic material involving children.

28. Postal and custom services should be required to detect and prevent the transmission of material containing child pornography. Special attention has to be paid to new technology for producing pornography, including video films.

29. States should be encouraged to protect children from exposure to adult pornography through suitable legislation and appropriate measures of control.

**SEE ALSO** *Forced Labor.*

**BIBLIOGRAPHY.** Africa Watch. *Mauritania—Slavery: Alive and Well, Ten Years after It Was Last Abolished.* New York: Human Rights Watch, 1990. NGO factfinding report, in English.

Atchebro, Daniel, and Anthony Breaux. "'Child Slavery' Exposed at the United Nations Working Group on Contemporary Forms of Slavery" *Peoples for Human Rights: IMADR Yearbook* 3 (1991): 39–53. Article, in English.

Reanda, Laura. "Prostitution as a Human Rights Question: Problems and Prospects of United Nations Action," *Human Rights Quarterly* 13, no. 2 (May 1991): 202–228. Scholarly article, in English.

United Nations Sub-Commission on Prevention of Discrimination and Protection of Minorities. *Report of the Working Group on Contemporary Forms of Slavery on Its Sixteenth Session.* Chairman/Rapporteur: Mrs. F. Z. Ksentini. Geneva, Switzerland: 1991. IGO document, in English and French.

**SLAVERY: CONVENTION FOR THE SUPPRESSION OF THE TRAFFIC IN PERSONS AND OF THE EXPLOITATION OF THE PROSTITUTION OF OTHERS, UN (1949).** The Convention is based on a draft prepared by the UN Secretary-General in 1948, at the request of the **ECONOMIC AND SOCIAL COUNCIL**, which unified four existing instruments for the suppression of the traffic in women and children (the International Agreement of 18 May 1904 for the Suppression of the White Slave Traffic; the International Convention of 4 May 1910 for the Suppression of the White Slave Traffic; the International Convention of 30 September 1921 for the Suppression of the Traffic in Women and Children; and the International Convention of 11 October 1933 for the Suppression of the

Traffic in Women of Full Age) and also embodied the substance of a draft convention of the suppression of the exploitation of the prostitution of others prepared by the **LEAGUE OF NATIONS** in 1937. The Convention was adopted by the UN **GENERAL ASSEMBLY** on 2 December 1949 (resolution 317 [IV]) and entered into force on 25 July 1951. The text (United Nations, *Treaty Series*, vol. 96, p. 271) is as follows:

### Preamble

Whereas prostitution and the accompanying evil of the traffic in persons for the purpose of prostitution are incompatible with the dignity and worth of the human person and endanger the welfare of the individual, the family and the community,

Whereas, with respect to the suppression of the traffic in women and children, the following international instruments are in force:

1. International Agreement of 18 May 1904 for the Suppression of the White Slave Traffic, as amended by the Protocol approved by the General Assembly of the United Nations on 3 December 1948,

2. International Convention of 4 May 1910 for the Suppression of the White Slave Traffic, as amended by the above-mentioned Protocol,

3. International Convention of 30 September 1921 for the Suppression of the Traffic in Women and Children, as amended by the Protocol approved by the General Assembly of the United Nations of 20 October 1947,

4. International Convention of 11 October 1933 for the Suppression of the Traffic in Women of Full Age, as amended by the aforesaid Protocol,

Whereas the League of Nations in 1937 prepared a draft Convention extending the scope of the above-mentioned instruments, and

Whereas developments since 1937 make feasible the conclusion of a convention consolidating the above-mentioned instruments and embodying the substance of the 1937 draft convention as well as desirable alterations therein:

Now therefore

The Contracting Parties

Hereby agree as hereinafter provided:

*Article 1.* The Parties to the present Convention agree to punish any person who, to gratify the passions of another:

1. Procures, entices or leads away, for purposes of prostitution, another person, even with the consent of that person;

2. Exploits the prostitution of another person, even with the consent of that person.

*Article 2.* The Parties to the present Convention further agree to punish any person who:

1. Keeps or manages, or knowingly finances or takes part in the financing of a brothel;

2. Knowingly lets or rents a building or other place or any part thereof for the purpose of the prostitution of others.

*Article 3.* To the extent permitted by domestic law, attempts to commit any of the offences referred to in articles 1 and 2, and acts preparatory to the commission thereof, shall also be punished.

*Article 4.* To the extent permitted by domestic law, intentional participation in the acts referred to in articles 1 and 2 above shall also be punishable.

To the extent permitted by domestic law, acts of participation shall be treated as separate offences whenever this is necessary to prevent impunity.

*Article 5.* In cases where injured persons are entitled under domestic law to be parties to proceedings in respect of any of the offences referred to in the present Convention, aliens shall be so entitled upon the same terms as nationals.

*Article 6.* Each Party to the present Convention agrees to take all the necessary measures to repeal or abolish any existing law, regulation or administrative provision by virtue of which persons who engage in or are suspected of engaging in prostitution are subject either to special registration or to the possession of a special document or to any exceptional requirement for supervision or notification.

*Article 7.* Previous convictions pronounced in foreign States for offences referred to in the present Convention shall, to the extent permitted by domestic law, be taken into account for the purpose of:

1. Establishing recidivism;

2. Disqualifying the offender from the exercise of civil rights.

*Article 8.* The offences referred to in articles 1 and 2 of the present Convention shall be regarded as extraditable offences in any extradition treaty which has been or may hereafter be concluded between any of the Parties to this Convention.

The Parties to the present Convention which do not make extradition conditional on the existence of a treaty shall henceforward recognize the offences referred to in articles 1 and 2 of the present Convention as cases for extradition between themselves.

Extradition shall be granted in accordance with the law of the State to which the request is made.

*Article 9.* In States where the extradition of nationals is not permitted by law, nationals who have returned to their own State after the commission abroad of any of the offences referred to in articles 1 and 2 of the present Convention shall be prosecuted in and punished by the courts of their own State.

This provision shall not apply if, in a similar case between the Parties to the present Convention, the extradition of an alien cannot be granted.

*Article 10.* The provisions of article 9 shall not apply when the person charged with the offence has been tried in a foreign State and, if convicted, has served his sentence or had it remitted or reduced in conformity with the laws of that foreign State.

*Article 11.* Nothing in the present Convention shall be interpreted as determining the attitude of a Party towards the general question of the limits of criminal jurisdiction under international law.

*Article 12.* The present Convention does not affect the principle that the offences to which it refers shall in each State be defined, prosecuted and punished in conformity with its domestic law.

*Article 13.* The Parties to the present Convention shall be bound to execute letters of request relating to offences referred to in the Convention in accordance with their domestic law and practice.

The transmission of letters of request shall be effected:

1. By direct communication between the judicial authorities; or

2. By direct communication between the Ministers of Justice of the two States, or by direct communication from another competent authority of the State making the request to the Minister of Justice of the State to which the request is made; or

3. Through the diplomatic or consular representative of the State making the request in the State to which the request is made; this representative shall send the letters of request direct to the competent judicial authority or to the authority indicated by the Government of the State to which the request is made, and shall receive direct from such authority the papers constituting the execution of the letters of request.

In cases 1 and 3 a copy of the letters of request shall always be sent to the superior authority of the State to which application is made.

Unless otherwise agreed, the letters of request shall be drawn up in the language of the authority making the request, provided always that the State to which the request is made may require a translation in its own language, certified correct by the authority making the request.

Each Party to the present Convention shall notify to each of the other Parties to the Convention the method or methods of transmission mentioned above which it will recognize for the letters of request of the latter State.

Until such notification is made by a State, its existing procedure in regard to letters of request shall remain in force.

Execution of letters of request shall not give rise to a claim for reimbursement of charges or expenses of any nature whatever other than expenses of experts.

Nothing in the present article shall be construed as an undertaking on the part of the Parties to the present Convention to adopt in criminal matters any form or methods of proof contrary to their own domestic laws.

*Article 14.* Each Party to the present Convention shall establish or maintain a service charged with the coordination and centralization of the results of the investigation of offences referred to in the present Convention.

Such services should compile all information calculated to facilitate the prevention and punishment of the offences referred to in the present Convention and should be in close contact with the corresponding services in other States.

*Article 15.* To the extent permitted by the domestic law and to the extent to which the authorities responsible for the services referred to in article 14 may judge desirable, they shall furnish to the authorities responsible for the corresponding services in other States the following information:

1. Particulars of any offence referred to in the present Convention or any attempt to commit such offence;

2. Particulars of any search for and any prosecution, arrest, conviction, refusal of admission or expulsion of persons guilty of any of the offences referred to in the present Convention, the movements of such persons and any other useful information with regard to them.

The information so furnished shall include descriptions of the offenders, their fingerprints, photographs, methods of operation, police records and records of conviction.

*Article 16.* The Parties to the present Convention agree to take or to encourage, through their public and private educational, health, social, economic and other related services, measures for the prevention of prostitution and for the rehabilitation and social adjustment of the victims of prostitution and of the offences referred to in the present Convention.

*Article 17.* The Parties to the present Convention undertake, in connexion with immigration and emigration, to adopt or maintain such measures as are required, in terms of their obligations under the present Convention, to check the traffic in persons of either sex for the purpose of prostitution.

In particular they undertake:

1. To make such regulations as are necessary for the protection of immigrants or emigrants, and in particular, women and children, both at the place of arrival and departure and while en route;

2. To arrange for appropriate publicity warning the public of the dangers of the aforesaid traffic;

3. To take appropriate measures to ensure supervision of railway stations, airports, seaports and en route, and of other public places, in order to prevent international traffic in persons for the purpose of prostitution;

4. To take appropriate measures in order that the appropriate authorities be informed of the arrival of persons who appear, *prima facie*, to be the principals and accomplices in or victims of such traffic.

*Article 18.* The Parties to the present Convention undertake, in accordance with the conditions laid down by domestic law, to have declarations taken from aliens who are prostitutes, in order to establish their identity and civil status and to discover who has caused them to leave their State. The information obtained shall be communicated to the authorities of the State of origin of the said persons with a view to their eventual repatriation.

*Article 19.* The Parties to the present Convention undertake, in accordance with the conditions laid down by domestic law and without prejudice to prosecution or action for violations thereunder and so far as possible:

1. Pending the completion of arrangements for the repatriation of destitute victims of international traffic in persons for the purpose of prostitution, to make suitable provisions for their temporary care and maintenance;

2. To repatriate persons referred to in article 18 who desire to be repatriated or who may be claimed by persons exercising authority over them or whose expulsion is ordered in conformity with the law. Repatriation shall take place only after agreement is reached with the State of destination as to identity and nationality as well as to the place and date of arrival at frontiers. Each Party to the present Convention shall facilitate the passage of such persons through its territory.

Where the persons referred to in the preceding paragraph cannot themselves repay the cost of repatriation and have neither spouse, relatives nor guardian to pay for them, the cost of repatriation as far as the nearest frontier or port of embarkation or airport in the direction of the State of origin shall be borne by the State where they are in residence, and the cost of the remainder of the journey shall be borne by the State of origin.

*Article 20.* The Parties to the present Convention shall, if they have not already done so, take the necessary measures for the supervision of employment agencies in order to prevent persons seeking employment, in particular women and children, from being exposed to the danger of prostitution.

*Article 21.* The Parties to the present Convention shall communicate to the Secretary-General of the United Nations such laws and regulations as have already been promulgated in their States, and thereafter annually such laws and regulations as may be promulgated, relating to the subjects of the present Convention, a well as all measures taken by them concerning the application of the Convention. The information received shall be published periodically by the Secretary-General and sent to all Members of the United Nations and to non-member States to which the present Convention is officially communicated in accordance with article 23.

*Article 22.* If any dispute shall arise between the Parties to the present Convention relating to its interpretation or application and if such dispute cannot be settled by other means, the dispute shall, at the request of any one of the Parties to the dispute, be referred to the International Court of Justice.

*Article 23.* The present Convention shall be open for signature on behalf of any Member of the United Nations and also on behalf of any other State to which an invitation has been addressed by the Economic and Social Council.

The present Convention shall be ratified and the instruments of ratification shall be deposited with the Secretary-General of the United Nations.

The States mentioned in the first paragraph which have not signed the Convention may accede to it.

Accession shall be effected by deposit of an instrument of accession with the Secretary-General of the United Nations.

For the purposes of the present Convention the word "State" shall include all the colonies and Trust Territories of a State signatory or acceding to the Convention and all territories for which such State is internationally responsible.

*Article 24.* The present Convention shall come into force on the ninetieth day following the date of deposit of the second instrument of ratification or accession.

For each State ratifying or acceding to the Convention after the deposit of the second instrument of ratification or accession, the Convention shall enter into force ninety days after the deposit by such State of its instrument of ratification or accession.

*Article 25.* After the expiration of five years from the entry into force of the present Convention, any Party to the Convention may denounce it by a written notification addressed to the Secretary-General of the United Nations.

Such denunciation shall take effect for the Party making it one year from the date upon which it is received by the Secretary-General of the United Nations.

*Article 26.* The Secretary-General of the United Nations shall inform all Members of the United Nations and non-member States referred to in article 23:

(a) Of signatures, ratifications and accessions received in accordance with article 23;

(b) Of the date on which the present Convention will come into force in accordance with article 24;

(c) Of denunciations received in accordance with article 25.

*Article 27.* Each Party to the present Convention undertakes to adopt, in accordance with its Constitution, the legislative or other measures necessary to ensure the application of the Convention.

*Article 28.* The provisions of the present Convention shall supersede in the relations between the Parties thereto the provisions of the international instruments referred to in sub-paragraphs 1, 2, 3 and 4 of the second paragraph of the Preamble, each of which shall be deemed to be terminated when all the Parties thereto shall have become Parties to the present Convention.

### Final Protocol

Nothing in the present Convention shall be deemed to prejudice any legislation which ensures, for the enforcement of the provisions for securing the suppression of the traffic in persons and of the exploitation of others for purposes of prostitution, stricter conditions than those provided by the present Convention.

The provisions of articles 23 to 26 inclusive of the Convention shall apply to the present Protocol.

*RATIFICATIONS AND ACCESSIONS.* The following 70 UN member States have ratified or acceded to the Convention for the Suppression of the Traffic in Persons and of the Exploitation of the Prostitution of Others:

Afghanistan, Albania, Algeria, Argentina

Bangladesh, Belarus, Belgium, Bolivia, Bosnia Herzegovina, Brazil, Bulgaria, Burkina Faso

Cameroon, Central African Republic, Congo, Croatia, Cuba, Cyprus, Czech Republic

Djibouti

Ecuador, Egypt, Ethiopia

Finland, France

Germany, Guinea

Haiti, Honduras, Hungary

India, Iraq, Israel, Italy

Japan, Jordan

Kuwait

Laos, Latvia, Libya, Luxembourg

Macedonia, Malawi, Mali, Mauritania, Mexico, Morocco

Niger, Norway

Pakistan, Philippines, Poland, Portugal

Republic of Korea (South Korea), Romania, Russian Federation

Senegal, Seychelles, Singapore, Slovakia, Slovenia, South Africa, Spain, Sri Lanka, Syria

Togo

Ukraine

Venezuela

Yemen, Yugoslavia (Serbia and Montenegro)

*SIGNATURES.* Denmark, Iran, Liberia, and Myanmar have signed the Convention but have not yet ratified it.

## SLAVERY: PROTOCOL AMENDING THE SLAVERY CONVENTION, UN (1953).

The Protocol, which amends the Slavery Convention opened for signature under the auspices of the **LEAGUE OF NATIONS** on 25 September 1926 to place it under the auspices of the United Nations, was adopted by the UN **GENERAL ASSEMBLY** on 23 October 1953 and entered into force on 7 July 1955. As authorized in article 4 of the protocol, the Secretary-General subsequently published the Protocol and the Slavery Convention Signed at Geneva on 25 September 1926, as Amended.

The text of the Protocol (General Assembly resolution 794 [VIII], annex) is as follows:

The States Parties to the present Protocol,

Considering that under the Slavery Convention signed at Geneva on 25 September 1926 (hereinafter called "the Convention") the League of Nations was invested with certain duties and functions, and

Considering that it is expedient that these duties and functions should be continued by the United Nations,

Have agreed as follows:

*Article 1.* The State Parties to the present Protocol undertake that as between themselves they will, in accordance with the provisions of the Protocol, attribute full legal force and effect to and duly apply the amendments to the Convention set forth in the annex to the Protocol.

*Article 2.* 1. The present Protocol shall be open for signature or acceptance by any of the States Parties to the Convention to which the Secretary-General has communicated for this purpose a copy of the Protocol.

2. States may become Parties to the present Protocol by:

(a) Signature without reservation as to acceptance;

(b) Signature with reservation as to acceptance, followed by acceptance;

(c) Acceptance.

3. Acceptance shall be effected by the deposit of a formal instrument with the Secretary-General of the United Nations.

*Article 3.* 1. The present Protocol shall come into force on the date on which two States shall have become Parties thereto, and shall therefore come into force in respect of each State upon the date on which it becomes a Party to the Protocol.

2. The amendments set forth in the annex to the present Protocol shall come into force when twenty-three States shall have become Parties to the Protocol, and consequently any State becoming a Party to the Convention, after the amendments thereto have come into force, shall become a Party to the Convention as so amended.

*Article 4.* In accordance with paragraph I of Article 102 of the Charter of the United Nations and the regulations pursuant thereto adopted by the General Assembly, the Secretary-General of the United Nations is authorized to effect registration of the present Protocol and of the amendments made in the Convention by the Protocol on the respective dates of their entry into force and to publish the Protocol and the amended text of the Convention as soon as possible after registration.

*Article 5.* The present Protocol, of which the Chinese, English, French, Russian and Spanish texts are equally authentic, shall be deposited in the archives of the United Nations Secretariat. The texts of the Convention to be amended in accordance with the annex being authentic in the English and French languages only, the English and French texts of the annex shall be equally authentic, and the Chinese, Russian and Spanish texts shall be translations. The Secretary-General shall prepare certified copies of the Protocol, including the annex, for communication to State Parties to the Convention, as well as to all other States Members of the United Nations. He shall likewise prepare for communication to States including States not Members of the United Nations, upon the entry into force of the amendments as provided in article III, certified copies of the Convention as so amended.

In witness whereof the undersigned, being duly authorized thereto by their respective Governments, signed the present Protocol on the date appearing opposite their respective signatures.

Done at the Headquarters of the United Nations, New York, this seventh day of December one thousand nine hundred and fifty-three.

**Annex to the Protocol Amending the Slavery Convention Signed at Geneva on 25 September 1926**

In article 7 "the Secretary-General of the United Nations" shall be substituted for "the Secretary-General of the League of Nations".

In article 8 "the International Court of Justice" shall be substituted for the "Permanent Court of International Justice", and "the Statute of the International Court of Justice" shall be substituted for "the Protocol of December 16th, 1920, relating to the Permanent Court of International Justice".

In the first and second paragraphs of article 10 "the United Nations" shall be substituted for "the League of Nations".

The last three paragraphs of article 11 shall be deleted and the following substituted:

"The present Convention shall be open to accession by all States, including States which are not Members of the United Nations, to which the Secretary-General of the United Nations shall have communicated a certified copy of the Convention.

"Accession shall be effected by the deposit of a formal instrument with the Secretary-General of the United Nations, who shall give notice thereof to all States Parties to the Convention and to all other States contemplated in the present article, informing them of the date on which each such instrument of accession was received in deposit."

In article 12 "the United Nations" shall be substituted for "the League of Nations".

*RATIFICATIONS AND ACCESSIONS.* The following 56 UN member States have ratified or acceded to the Protocol amending the Slavery Convention of 1926:

Afghanistan, Antigua and Barbuda, Australia, Austria

Bahamas, Bangladesh, Barbados, Belgium, Bolivia, Bosnia Herzegovina

Cameroon, Canada, Chile, Croatia, Cuba

Denmark

Ecuador, Egypt

Fiji, Finland, France

Germany, Greece, Guatemala, Guinea

Hungary

India, Iraq, Ireland, Israel, Italy

Liberia

Mali, Malta, Mauritania, Mexico, Monaco, Morocco, Myanmar

Netherlands, New Zealand, Nicaragua, Niger, Norway

Romania

Saint Lucia, Saint Vincent and Grenadines, Solomon Islands, South Africa, Spain, Sweden, Syria

Turkey

United Kingdom, United States of America

Yugoslavia (Serbia and Montenegro)

Zambia

**SLAVERY: SLAVERY CONVENTION SIGNED AT GENEVA ON 25 SEPTEMBER 1926, AS AMENDED.** In the Slavery Convention prepared under the auspices of the **LEAGUE OF NATIONS,** opened for signature in Geneva on 25 September 1926, and entering into force on 9 March 1927 (League of Nations, *Treaty Series,* vol. 60, p. 253), States parties agreed upon a definition of slavery and undertook to prevent and suppress the slave trade and to bring about, progressively and as soon as possible, the complete abolition of slavery in all its forms. They further agreed that forced or compulsory labor should be exacted only for public purposes.

The Protocol Amending the Slavery Convention adopted by the UN **GENERAL ASSEMBLY** on 7 December 1953 (United Nations, *Treaty Series,* vol. 182, p. 51), replaced each reference to the League of Nations by a reference to the United Nations and each reference to the Permanent Court of International Justice by a reference to the **INTERNATIONAL COURT OF JUSTICE.** The amended text of the Convention thus reads as follows:

Whereas the signatories of the General Act of the Brussels Conference of 1889–90 declared that they were equally animated by the firm intention of putting an end to the traffic in African slaves,

Whereas the signatories of the Convention of Saint-Germain-en-Laye of 1919, to revise the General Act of Berlin of 1885, and the General Act and Declaration of Brussels of 1890, affirmed their intention of securing the complete suppression of slavery in all its forms and of the slave trade by land and sea,

Taking into consideration the report of the Temporary Slavery Commission appointed by the Council of the League of Nations on June 12th, 1924,

Desiring to complete and extend the work accomplished under the Brussels Act and to find a means of giving practical effect throughout the world to such intentions as were expressed in regard to slave trade and slavery by the signatories of the Convention of Saint-Germain-en-Laye, and recognising that it is necessary to conclude to that end more detailed arrangements than are contained in that Convention,

Considering, moreover, that it is necessary to prevent forced labour from developing into conditions analogous to slavery,

Have decided to conclude a Convention and have accordingly appointed as their Plenipotentiaries *[names omitted]*

. . . have agreed as follows:

*Article 1.* For the purpose of the present Convention, the following definitions are agreed upon:

(1) Slavery is the status or condition of a person over whom any or all of the powers attaching to the right of ownership are exercised.

(2) The slave trade includes all acts involved in the capture, acquisition or disposal of a person with intent to reduce him to slavery; all acts involved in the acquisition of a slave with a view to selling or exchanging him; all acts of disposal by sale or exchange of a slave acquired with a view to being sold or exchanged, and, in general, every act of trade or transport in slaves.

*Article 2.* The High Contracting Parties undertake, each in respect of the territories placed under its sovereignty, jurisdiction, protection, suzerainty or tutelage, so far as they have not already taken the necessary steps:

(a) To prevent and suppress the slave trade;

(b) To bring about, progressively and as soon as possible, the complete abolition of slavery in all its forms.

*Article 3.* The High Contracting Parties undertake to adopt all appropriate measures with a view to preventing and suppressing the embarkation, disembarkation and transport of slaves in their territorial waters and upon all vessels flying their respective flags.

The High Contracting Parties undertake to negotiate as soon as possible a general Convention with regard to the slave trade which will give them rights and impose upon them duties of the same nature as those provided for in the Convention of June 17th, 1925, relative to the International Trade in Arms (Articles 12, 20, 21, 22, 23, 24, and paragraphs 3, 4 and 5 of Section II of Annex II), with the necessary adaptations, it being understood that this general Convention will not place the ships (even of small tonnage) of any High Contracting Parties in a position different from that of the other High Contracting Parties.

It is also understood that, before or after the coming into force of this general Convention, the High Contracting Parties are entirely free to conclude between themselves, without, however, derogating from the principles laid down in the preceding paragraph, such special agreements as, by reason of their peculiar situation, might appear to be suitable in order to bring about as soon as possible the complete disappearance of the slave trade.

*Article 4.* The High Contracting Parties shall give to one another every assistance with the object of securing the abolition of slavery and the slave trade.

*Article 5.* The High Contracting Parties recognize that recourse to compulsory or forced labour may have grave consequences and undertake, each in respect of the territories placed under its sovereignty, jurisdiction, protection, suzerainty or tutelage, to take all necessary measure to prevent compulsory or forced labour from developing into conditions analogous to slavery.

It is agreed that:

(1) Subject to the transitional provisions laid down in paragraph (2) below, compulsory or forced labour may only be exacted for public purposes.

(2) In territories in which compulsory or forced labour for other than public purposes still survives, the High Contracting Parties shall endeavour progressively and as soon as possible to put an end to the practice. So long as such forced or compulsory labour exists, this labour shall invariably be of an exceptional character, shall always receive adequate remuneration, and shall not involve the removal of the labourers from their usual place of residence.

(3) In all cases, the responsibility for any recourse to compulsory or forced labour shall rest with the competent central authorities of the territory concerned.

*Article 6.* Those of the High Contracting Parties whose laws do not at present make adequate provision for the punishment of infractions of laws and regulations enacted with a view to giving effect to the purposes of the present Convention undertake to adopt the necessary measures in order that severe penalties may be imposed in respect of such infractions.

*Article 7.* The High Contracting Parties undertake to communicate to each other and to the Secretary-General of the United Nations any laws and regulations which they may enact with a view to the application of the provisions of the present Convention.

*Article 8.* The High Contracting Parties agree that disputes arising between them relating to the interpretation or application of this Convention shall, if they cannot be settled by direct negotiation, be referred for decision to the International Court of Justice. In case either or both of the States Parties to such a dispute should not be parties to the Statute of the International Court of Justice, the dispute shall be referred, at the choice of the Parties and in accordance with the constitutional procedure of each State, either to the International Court of Justice or to a court of arbitration constituted in accordance with the Convention of October 18th, 1907, for the Pacific Settlement of International Disputes, or to some other court of arbitration.

*Article 9.* At the time of signature or of ratification or of accession, any High Contracting Party may declare that its acceptance of the present Convention does not bind some or all of the territories placed under its sovereignty, jurisdiction, protection, suzerainty or tutelage in respect of all or any provisions of the Convention; it may subsequently accede separately on behalf of any one of them or in respect of any provision to which any one of them is not a party.

*Article 10.* In the event of a High Contracting Party wishing to denounce the present Convention, the denunciation shall be notified in writing to the Secretary-General of the United Nations, who will at once communicate a certified true copy of the notification to all the other High Contracting Parties, informing them of the date on which it was received.

The denunciation shall only have effect in regard to the notifying State, and one year after the notification has reached the Secretary-General of the United Nations.

Denunciation may also be made separately in respect of any territory placed under its sovereignty, jurisdiction, protection, suzerainty or tutelage.

*Article 11.* The present Convention, which will bear this day's date and of which the French and English texts are both authentic, will remain open for signature by the States Members of the United Nations.

The present Convention shall be open to accession by all States, including States which are not members of the United Nations, to which the Secretary-General of the United Nations shall have communicated a certified copy of the Convention.

Accession shall be effected by the deposit of a formal instrument with the Secretary-General of the United Nations, who shall give notice thereof to all States parties to the Convention and to all other States contemplated in the present article, informing them of the date on which each such instrument of accession was received in deposit.

The Secretary-General of the United Nations will subsequently bring the present Convention to the notice of States which have not signed it, including States which are not Members of the United Nations, and invite them to accede thereto.

A State desiring to accede to the Convention shall notify its intention in writing to the Secretary-General of the United Nations and transmit to him the instrument of accession, which shall be deposited in the archives of the organization.

The Secretary-General shall immediately transmit to all the other High Contracting Parties a certified true copy of the notification and of the instrument of accession, informing them of the date on which he received them.

*Article 12.* The present Convention will be ratified and the instruments of ratification shall be deposited in the office of the Secretary-General of the United Nations. The Secretary-General will inform all the High Contracting Parties of such deposit.

The Convention will come into operation for each State on the date of the deposit of its ratification or of its accession.

In faith whereof the Plenipotentiaries signed the present Convention.

Done at Geneva the twenty-fifth day of September, one thousand nine hundred and twenty-six, in one copy, which will be deposited in the archives of the United Nations. A certified copy shall be forwarded to each signatory State.

*RATIFICATIONS AND ACCESSIONS.* The following 91 UN member States have ratified or acceded to the Slavery Convention of 1926, as amended, as of 31 December 1994:

Afghanistan, Antigua and Barbuda, Australia, Austria

Bahamas, Bahrain, Bangladesh, Barbados, Belarus, Belgium, Bolivia, Bosnia Herzegovina, Brazil

Cameroon, Canada, Chile, Croatia, Cuba, Cyprus

Denmark, Djibouti, Dominica

Ecuador, Egypt, Ethiopia

Fiji, Finland, France

Germany, Greece, Guatemala, Guinea

Hungary

India, Iran, Iraq, Ireland, Israel, Italy

Jamaica, Jordan

Kuwait

Lesotho, Liberia, Libya

Madagascar, Malawi, Mali, Malta, Mauritania, Mauritius, Mexico, Monaco, Mongolia, Morocco, Myanmar

Nepal, Netherlands, New Zealand, Nicaragua, Niger, Nigeria, Norway

Pakistan, Papua New Guinea

Romania, Russian Federation

Saint Lucia, Saint Vincent and Grenadines, Saudi Arabia, Sierra Leone, Solomon Islands, South Africa, Spain, Sweden, Syria

Tanzania, Trinidad and Tobago, Tunisia, Turkey

Uganda, Ukraine, United Kingdom, United States of America

Yemen, Yugoslavia (Serbia and Montenegro)

Zambia

*SIGNATURE.* El Salvador has signed the Convention but has not yet ratified it.

## SLAVERY: SUPPLEMENTARY CONVENTION ON THE ABOLITION OF SLAVERY, THE SLAVE TRADE AND INSTITUTIONS AND PRACTICES SIMILAR TO SLAVERY (1956).

The Supplementary Convention adds to, but does not amend or supersede, the Slavery Convention signed at Geneva on 25 September 1926, as Amended. It provides for States parties to take all practicable and necessary legislative and other measures to bring about progressively and as soon as possible the complete abolition or abandonment of a number of institutions and practices—such as debt bondage, serfdom, and the sale or involuntary transfer of a woman or child from one person to another—whether or not they are covered by the definition of slavery contained in article 1 of the 1926 Convention as amended.

The Supplementary Convention was adopted at the European office of the United Nations, Geneva, on 7 September 1956 by a Conference of Plenipotentiaries which had been convened by the UN **ECONOMIC AND SOCIAL COUNCIL** on 30 April 1956 (resolution 608 [XXI]), and entered into force on 30 April 1957. The text of the Supplementary Convention (United Nations, *Treaty Series*, vol. 266, p. 3) is as follows:

### Preamble

The States Parties to the present Convention,

Considering that freedom is the birthright of every human being,

Mindful that the peoples of the United Nations reaffirmed in the Charter their faith in the dignity and worth of the human person,

Considering that the Universal Declaration of Human Rights, proclaimed by the General Assembly of the United Nations as a common standard of achievement for all peoples and all nations, states that no one shall be held in slavery or servitude and that slavery and the slave trade shall be prohibited in all their forms,

Recognizing that, since the conclusion of the Slavery Convention signed at Geneva on 25 September 1926, which was designed to secure the abolition of slavery and of the slave trade, further progress has been made towards this end,

Having regard to the Forced Labour Convention of 1930 and to subsequent action by the International Labour Organisation in regard to forced or compulsory labour,

Being aware, however, that slavery, the slave trade and institutions and practices similar to slavery have not yet been eliminated in all parts of the world,

Having decided, therefore, that the Convention of 1926, which remains operative, should now be augmented by the conclusion of a Supplementary Convention designed to intensify national as well as international efforts towards the abolition of slavery, the slave trade and institutions and practices similar to slavery,

Have agreed as follows:

### Section I: Institutions and Practices Similar to Slavery

*Article 1.* Each of the States Parties to this Convention shall take all practicable and necessary legislative and other measures to bring about progressively and as soon as possible the complete abolition or abandonment of the following institutions and practices, where they still exist and whether or not they are covered by the definition of slavery contained in article 1 of the Slavery Convention signed at Geneva on 25 September 1926:

(a) Debt bondage, that is to say, the status or condition arising from a pledge by a debtor of his personal services or of those of a person under his control as security for a debt, if the value of those services as reasonably assessed is not applied towards the liquidation of the debt or the length and nature of those services are not respectively limited and defined;

(b) Serfdom, that is to say, the condition or status of a tenant who is by law, custom or agreement bound to live and labour on land belonging to another person and to render some determinate service to such other person, whether for reward or not, and is not free to change his status;

(c) Any institution or practice whereby:

(i) A woman, without the right to refuse, is promised or given in marriage on payment of a consideration in money or in kind to her parents, guardian, family or any other person or group; or

(ii) The husband of a woman, his family, or his clan, has the right to transfer her to another person for value received or otherwise; or

(iii) A woman on the death of her husband is liable to be inherited by another person;

(d) Any institution or practice whereby a child or young person under the age of 18 years, is delivered by either or both of his natural parents or by his guardian to another person, whether for reward or not, with a view to the exploitation of the child or young person or of his labour.

*Article 2.* With a view to bringing to an end the institutions and practices mentioned in article 1 (c) of this Convention, the States Parties undertake to prescribe, where appropriate, suitable minimum ages of marriage, to encourage the use of facilities whereby the consent of both parties to a marriage may be freely expressed in the presence of a competent civil or religious authority, and to encourage the registration of marriages.

### Section II: The Slave Trade

*Article 3.* 1. The act of conveying or attempting to convey slaves from one country to another by whatever means of transport, or of being accessory thereto, shall be a criminal offence under the laws of the States Parties to this Convention and persons convicted thereof shall be liable to very severe penalties.

2. (a) The States Parties shall take all effective measures to prevent ships and aircraft authorized to fly their flags from conveying slaves and to punish persons guilty of such acts or of using national flags for that purpose.

(b) The States Parties shall take all effective measures to ensure that their ports, airfields and coasts are not used for the conveyance of slaves.

3. The States Parties to this Convention shall exchange information in order to ensure the practical co-ordination of the measures taken by them in combating the slave trade and shall inform each other of every case of the slave trade, and of every attempt to commit this criminal offence, which comes to their notice.

*Article 4.* Any slave who takes refuge on board any vessel of a State Party to this Convention shall *ipso facto* be free.

### Section III: Slavery and Institutions and Practices Similar to Slavery

*Article 5.* In a country where the abolition or abandonment of slavery, or of the institutions or practices mentioned in article 1 of this Convention, is not yet complete, the act of mutilating, branding or otherwise marking a slave or a person of servile status in order to indicate his status, or as a punishment, or for any other reason, or of being accessory thereto, shall be a criminal offence under the laws of the

States Parties to this Convention and persons convicted thereof shall be liable to punishment.

*Article 6.* 1. The act of enslaving another person or of inducing another person to give himself or a person dependent upon him into slavery, or of attempting these acts, or being accessory thereto, or being a party to a conspiracy to accomplish any such acts, shall be a criminal offence under the laws of the States Parties to this Convention and persons convicted thereof shall be liable to punishment.

2. Subject to the provisions of the introductory paragraph of article 1 of this Convention, the provisions of paragraph 1 of the present article shall also apply to the act of inducing another person to place himself or a person dependent upon him into the servile status resulting from any of the institutions or practices mentioned in article 1, to any attempt to perform such acts, to bring accessory thereto, and to being a part to a conspiracy to accomplish any such acts.

### Section IV: Definitions

*Article 7.* For the purposes of the present Convention:

(a) "Slavery" means, as defined in the Slavery Convention of 1926, the status or condition of a person over whom any or all of the powers attaching to the right of ownership are exercised, and "slave" means a person in such condition or status;

(b) "A person of servile status" means a person in the condition or status resulting from any of the institutions or practices mentioned in article 1 of this Convention;

(c) "Slave trade" means and includes all acts involved in the capture, acquisition or disposal of a person with intent to reduce him to slavery; all acts involved in the acquisition of a slave with a view to selling or exchanging him; all acts of disposal by sale or exchange of a person acquired with a view to being sold or exchanged; and, in general, every act of trade or transport in slaves by whatever means of conveyance.

### Section V: Co-operation Between States Parties and Communication of Information

*Article 8.* 1. The States Parties to this Convention undertake to co-operate with each other and with the United Nations to give effect to the foregoing provisions.

2. The Parties undertake to communicate to the Secretary-General of the United Nations copies of any laws, regulations and administrative measures enacted or put into effect to implement the provisions of this Convention.

3. The Secretary-General shall communicate the information received under paragraph 2 of this article to the other Parties and to the Economic and Social Council as part of the documentation for any discussion which the Council might undertake with a view to making further recommendations for the abolition of slavery, the slave trade or the institutions and practices which are the subject of this Convention.

### Section VI: Final Clauses

*Article 9.* No reservations may be made to this Convention.

*Article 10.* Any dispute between States Parties to this Convention relating to its interpretation or application, which is not settled by negotiation, shall be referred to the International Court of Justice at the request of any one of the parties to the dispute, unless the parties concerned agree on another mode of settlement.

*Article 11.* 1. This Convention shall be open until 1 July 1957 for signature by any State Member of the United Nations or of a specialized agency. It shall be subject to ratification by the signatory States, and the instruments of ratification shall be deposited with the Secretary-General of the United Nations, who shall inform each signatory and acceding State.

2. After 1 July 1957 this Convention shall be open for accession by any State Member of the United Nations or of a specialized agency, or by any other State to which an invitation to accede has been addressed by the General Assembly of the United Nations. Accession shall be effected by the deposit of a formal instrument with the Secretary-General of the United Nations, who shall inform each signatory and acceding State.

*Article 12.* 1. This Convention shall apply to all non-self-governing trust, colonial and other non-metropolitan territories for the international relations of which any State Party is responsible; the Party concerned shall, subject to the provisions of paragraph 2 of this article, at the time of signature, ratification or accession declare the non-metropolitan territory or territories to which the Convention shall apply *ipso facto* as a result of such signature, ratification or accession.

2. In any case in which the previous consent of a non-metropolitan territory is required by the constitutional laws or practices of the Party or of the non-metropolitan territory, the Party concerned shall endeavour to secure the needed consent of the non-metropolitan territory within the period of twelve months from the date of signature of the Convention by the metropolitan State, and when such consent has been obtained the Party shall notify the Secretary-General. This Convention shall apply to the territory or territories named in such notification from the date of its receipt by the Secretary-General.

3. After the expiry of the twelve-month period mentioned in the preceding paragraph, the States Parties concerned shall inform the Secretary-General of the results of the consultations with those non-metropolitan territories for whose international relations they are responsible and whose consent to the application of this Convention may have been withheld.

*Article 13.* 1. This Convention shall enter into force on the date on which two States have become Parties thereto.

2. It shall thereafter enter into force with respect to each State and territory on the date of deposit of the instrument of ratification or accession of that State or notification of application to that territory.

*Article 14.* 1. The application of this Convention shall be divided into successive periods of three years, of which the first shall begin on the date of entry into force of the Convention in accordance with paragraph 1 of article 13.

2. Any State Party may denounce this Convention by a notice addressed by that State to the Secretary-General not less than six months before the expiration of the current three-year period. The Secretary-General shall notify all other Parties of each such notice and the date of the receipt thereof.

3. Denunciations shall take effect at the expiration of the current three-year period.

4. In cases where, in accordance with the provisions of article 12, this Convention has become applicable to a non-metropolitan territory of a Party, that Party may at any time thereafter with the consent of the territory concerned, give notice to the Secretary-General of the United Nations denouncing this Convention separately in respect of that territory. The denunciation shall take effect one year after the

date of the receipt of such notice by the Secretary-General, who shall notify all other Parties of such notice and the date of the receipt thereof.

*Article 15.* This Convention, of which the Chinese, English, French, Russian and Spanish texts are equally authentic, shall be deposited in the archives of the United Nations Secretariat. The Secretary-General shall prepare a certified copy thereof for communication to States Parties to this Convention, as well as to all other States Members of the United Nations and of the specialized agencies.

In witness whereof the undersigned, being duly authorized thereto by their respective Governments, have signed this Convention on the date appearing opposite their respective signatures.

Done at the European Office of the United Nations at Geneva, this seventh day of September one thousand nine hundred and fifty-six.

***RATIFICATIONS AND ACCESSIONS.*** The following 114 UN member States have ratified or acceded to the Supplementary Convention on the Abolition of Slavery, the Slave Trade and Institutions and Practices Similar to Slavery:

Afghanistan, Albania, Algeria, Antigua and Barbuda, Argentina, Australia, Austria, Bahamas, Bahrain, Bangladesh, Barbados, Belarus, Belgium, Bolivia, Bosnia Herzegovina, Brazil, Cambodia, Cameroon, Canada, Central African Republic, Chile, Congo, Cote d'Ivoire (Ivory Coast), Croatia, Cuba, Cyprus, Czech Republic, Denmark, Djibouti, Dominica, Dominican Republic, Ecuador, Egypt, Ethiopia, Fiji, Finland, France, Germany, Ghana, Greece, Guatemala, Guinea, Haiti, Hungary, Iceland, India, Iran, Iraq, Ireland, Israel, Italy, Jamaica, Jordan, Kuwait, Laos, Latvia, Lesotho, Libya, Luxembourg, Macedonia, Madagascar, Malawi, Malaysia, Mali, Malta, Mauritania, Mauritius, Mexico, Mongolia, Morocco, Nepal, Netherlands, New Zealand, Nicaragua, Niger, Nigeria, Norway, Pakistan, Philippines, Poland, Portugal, Romania, Russian Federation, Saint Lucia, Saint Vincent and Grenadines, San Marino, Saudi Arabia, Senegal, Seychelles, Sierra Leone, Singapore, Slovakia, Slovenia, Solomon Islands, Spain, Sri Lanka, Sudan, Suriname, Sweden, Syria, Tanzania, Togo, Tunisia, Turkey, Uganda, Ukraine, United Kingdom, United States of America, Yugoslavia (Serbia and Montenegro), Zaire, Zambia.

***SIGNATURES.*** El Salvador and Peru have signed the Convention but have not yet ratified it.

**SLOVAKIA.** The Slovak Republic (formerly part of Czechoslovakia) is a landlocked country bordered by Austria to the west, the Czech Republic to the north and west, Poland to the north, Ukraine to the east, and Hungary to the south. Its population is estimated to be 5,287,000, comprising 86% Slovak, 11% Hungarian, 2% Gypsy, and 1 % Czech. The primary religion is Roman Catholicism (60%) while 10% of the populace proclaims atheism. Slovakia gained independence in 1993.

After brief unification with the Czechs in the 9th Century, the Slovaks were ruled by the Hungarians until the early 20th century. The result of both Slovakian and Czech nationalist movements was the formation of the Republic of Czechoslovakia after World War I in 1918.

Slovaks grew dissatisfied with their lack of autonomy, as reflected in the 1920 constitution, as well as a lack of economic development in their part of the Republic. Following a period of semi-autonomous Slovakian Government, ruled by a puppet Nazi regime from 1939 to 1945, Czechoslovakia reemerged after World War II. Limited autonomy was in effect in the form of a Slovak legislature and executive but they were dissolved in the constitution of 1960 by the Communists who had taken power in 1948.

The reform plans of Alexander Dubcek, a Slovak and First Secretary of the Communist Party of Czechoslovakia, were quashed by the invasion of 600,000 Soviet and Warsaw Pact troops in 1968. Two separate Socialist Republics were formed in 1969 but the organs of regional government had little power.

Despite repression of the Catholic Church and dissident groups such as Charter 77, public demonstrations continued throughout the 1980s and free elections to the Federal Assembly and two National Councils were held in June 1990. Vladimir Meciar became prime minister but was replaced in March 1991 for his strong support of Slovak autonomy. Elections in 1992 again resulted in Meciar's appointment as prime minister.

The Czech and Slovak Federative Republic, in existence since April 1990, dissolved with the Slovak declaration of sovereignty in July 1991. A Slovak constitution was approved by the Slovakian National Council but the vote on the dissolution of Czechoslovakia passed by only four votes in the Federal Assembly in November. The countries divided on 1 January 1993 and both countries were automatically admitted to the United Nations at that time.

The Slovak constitution went into effect in January 1993. It provides for the 150-member National Council, directly elected for a four-year term, to elect a president for a maximum of two four-year terms. The president appoints a prime minister and the cabinet. Presidential elections were held in January and Michal Kovac was elected. Following a year of strained relations, an approval rating of government leaders as low as 16% and an inflation rate of 25%, Prime Minister Meciar was forced to resign after an overwhelming vote of no confidence in March 1994. The new administration looked more to Europe and less to Russia for alliances.

An estimated 600,000 Hungarians living in Slovakia continue to press for a degree of autonomy and control. Slovakia became an associate partner of the Western European Union in May 1994 and its possible membership in the European Union by the year 2000 was discussed in December.

***BIBLIOGRAPHY.*** Butorova, Zora. "The Hard Birth of Democracy in Slovakia," *East European Reporter* 5, no. 1 (Jan.–Feb. 1992): 62–68. Article, in English.

Commission on Security and Cooperation in Europe. *Human Rights and Democratization in Slovakia.* Washington, D.C.: 1993. Government report, in English.

———. *Report on Slovakia.* Washington, D.C.: 1992. Government report, in English.

Human Rights Watch/Helsinki. *Slovak Republic: Restrictions on Press Freedom in the Slovak Republic.* New York: 1994. NGO report, in English.

Pehe, Jiri. "Growing Slovak Demands Seen as Threat to Federation," *Report on Eastern Europe* 2, no. 12 (22 March 1991): 1–10. Article, in English.

**SLOVENIA.** The Republic of Slovenia, formerly a republic within the Socialist Federal Republic of Yugoslavia, is bordered by the Adriatic Sea to the west, Italy and Austria to the north, Hungary to the north and east, and Croatia to the south and east. It declared its independence in 1991 and was admitted to the United Nations in 1992. It joined the **COUNCIL OF EUROPE** and was afforded observer status at the Western European Union in 1993 and joined NATO's "partnership for peace" program in 1994. Its population is estimated to be 1,965,000, comprising 91% Slovenes, 3% Croats, 2% Serbs, and 1% Muslim. The primary religion is Roman Catholicism.

Yugoslavia came into existence in 1929 when its name was changed from the Kingdom of the Serbs, Croats and Slovenes, which had been formed in 1918. The republic dissolved during World War II, being divided between Germany and Italy, but re-emerged after the war. Slovenia became the most prosperous of the Yugoslav republics.

In 1989 the Slovenian constitution was amended to allow for secession from the federal republic and the formation of political parties, both of which were alleged to contravene the federal constitution. Following a declaration of sovereignty for the republic's government in July 1990 and despite economic sanctions imposed by Serbia, 89% of voters in a national referendum held in December approved of the declaration of sovereignty. Following the declaration of independence in June 1991, federal troops bombed the capital of Ljubljana, killing 18 people, but began to withdraw the following day.

Pursuant to the 1991 constitution, presidential and legislative elections were held in December 1992 and Milan Kucan was elected president with 64% of the vote. A coalition government was formed under the premiership of Dr. Janez Drnovsek and including parties securing seats in the 90-member National Assembly, namely the Liberal Democratic Party, the Slovenian Christian Democrats, the Associated List of Social Democrats, the Greens of Slovenia, and the Social Democratic Party of Slovenia. The extreme right-wing Slovenian National Party also won 12 seats.

The Assembly comprises 38 directly elected members, fifty of whom are selected proportionally and two members representing the Italian and Hungarian minorities. The mainly advisory National Council was also formed, 22 members being directly elected and 18 members being appointed to represent assorted groups. The 1991 constitution grants the National Council the power to veto legislation from the National Assembly.

In the face of growing economic discontent, emergency legislation was introduced in 1993 prohibiting the police services from taking any strike action. Allegations of corruption in government and protection of former communist leaders prompted public demonstrations against the government.

The UN embargo on the sale of weapons to the former Yugoslav republics was found to have been violated by Slovenia when a shipment bound for Bosnia and Herzegovina was discovered. It was estimated that there were 60,000 refugees from Bosnia and Herzegovina in Slovenia by mid-1993 but the government rejected a UN proposal to allow them to stay permanently.

***REPORT OF THE UN HUMAN RIGHTS COMMITTEE.*** The Committee of Human Rights considered the initial report of Slovenia (CCPR/C/74/Add. 1) at its 1343rd and 1347th meetings, held on 20 and 22 July 1994, and adopted the following comments:

*Factors and difficulties affecting the implementation of the Covenant.* The Committee recognizes that Slovenia was created after the breakdown of the former Yugoslavia and declared its independence only in 1991. The Committee further recognizes that the remnants of the authoritarian rule have not yet been overcome and that several steps remain to be undertaken in consolidating and developing democratic institutions and strengthening the implementation of the covenant. Recognized obstacles stemming out of the continuing armed conflict close to Slovenia borders and the consequent influx of refugees as well as the intensity of the ethnic and religious conflicts in former Yugoslavia must be addressed in a manner compatible with respect for the Covenant.

*Positive aspects.* The Committee welcomes the fact that transition toward democracy and pluralism has started in Slovenia.

The Committee notes with appreciation the efforts undertaken to incorporate human rights in the Constitution and to harmonize the national laws with the Constitution, even though this process has not been completed.

The Committee notes with appreciation the attitude of Slovenia regarding its succession to the obligations of former Yugoslavia under the Covenant, in declaring that it succeeded as from the date of its independence. In this context, the Committee has also noted the statement of the delegation that victims of violations of human rights committed by the former regime are entitled to remedy by the new State. The Committee welcomes the fact that Slovenia also became party to a number of international human rights instruments, including the First and Second Optional Protocols to the Covenant.

The Committee also welcomes the abolition of the death penalty and the creation of the Office of the Ombudsman with authority to make recommendations to safeguard the observance of human rights.

*Principal subjects of concern.* The Committee is concerned that, while the Covenant may be given precedence over legislative acts, its status *vis-à-vis* the Constitution is not clearly defined. There appears to be little publicity given to the provisions of the Covenant and the Optional Protocols and the Covenant has yet not been invoked before the courts. The process of harmonization of national laws with the Constitution has not yet been completed and does not take into direct account provisions of the Covenant.

The Committee expresses its concern about remaining areas of discrimination against women, particularly regarding the extent of their participation in the conduct of public affairs, and the lack of information about violence against women.

The Committee notes with concern that the length or pre-trial detention, which may extend up to six months under certain circumstances, does not comply with the requirements of articles 9 and 14 of the Covenant.

The Committee is concerned by the provision in the Code of Criminal Procedure under which in specific cases accused juvenile persons are not separated from adults, which may raise issues under article 10 of the Covenant.

The Committee notes that the State party singles out Italians and Hungarians for special protection as minorities, including the right to political representation. Gypsies are also granted certain special protection as a minority. While this protection is welcome, all minorities are entitled to protection of their rights under article 27. Immigrant communities constituting minorities under the meaning of article 27 are entitled to the benefit of that article.

The Committee is concerned about the provisions of article 5 of the Constitution relating to the protection of only ethnic Slovene emigrants and migrant workers which, implicitly, tend to establish a privileged treatment in the Constitution for such Slovenes over other Slovene citizens living abroad.

*Suggestions and recommendations.* The Committee recommends that the legislative reforms presently under way in Slovenia be expanded and intensified in order to ensure that all relevant legislation be in conformity not only with the requirements of the Constitution but also with the Covenant.

The Committee emphasises that the text of the Covenant and the Optional Protocols should be translated into all languages spoken in Slovenia and widely publicized so that the general public be made fully aware of the rights enshrined in the provisions of these instruments.

With respect to the rights of women, the Committee believes that affirmative measures should be taken to strengthen their participation in the conduct of public affairs and in the economic and social life of the country as well as positive measures to ensure effective protection against violence of all kinds.

The Committee calls upon the State party to ensure that the maximum period of pre-trial detention be significantly shortened in order to comply with the requirements of articles 9 and 14 of the Covenant.

With reference to freedom of conscience and religion, including the issue of religious education, the Committee recommends the State party to take into account the Committee's general comment No. 22(48) on article 18 of the Covenant.

The Committee calls upon the State party to take appropriate measures to ensure to all persons belonging to minorities the full and equal enjoyment of their rights under article 27 of the Covenant. It must also ensure that all persons, including members of minorities, are entitled to receive the guarantees laid down in articles 25 and 26 of the Covenant. In this connection, the State party should take into account the recommendations contained in the Committee's general comment No. 23(50) on article 27 of the Covenant.

The Committee urges the Government to prepare its second periodic report in compliance with the Committee's guidelines for the preparation of State party reports (CCPR/C/20/Rev.1). The report should in particular include detailed information on the extent to which each right protected under the Covenant is enjoyed in practice, and refer to specific factors and difficulties that might impede its application.

**SOCIALIST INTERNATIONAL WOMEN.** This non-governmental organization has consultative status with the UN **ECONOMIC AND SOCIAL COUNCIL** (Category II), **UNESCO,** and the **ILO** (special list). It has members in 53 countries.

Founded in London in 1955, the group promotes socialist ideals and equality between the sexes. Among the themes in recent seminars have been disarmament; socialism and feminism; women and the new economic order; nuclear-free zones; and sexual mutilation of women. It publishes the quarterly *Women and Politics* in English.

Socialist International Women. Address: Maritime House, Old Town, Clapham, London SW4 OJW, UK. Telephone: (44-71) 627-4429. Fax: (44-71) 720-4448. Secretary-General: Maria Jones.

**SOCIAL SECURITY.** The right of everyone to social security is proclaimed in the **UNIVERSAL DECLARATION OF HUMAN RIGHTS** in the following terms:

*Article 25.* (1) Everyone has the right to a standard of living adequate for the health and well-being of himself and of his family, including ... the right to social security in the event of unemployment, sickness, disability, widowhood, old age or other lack of livelihood in circumstances beyond his control.

The INTERNATIONAL COVENANT ON ECONOMIC, SOCIAL AND CULTURAL RIGHTS contains the following provision:

*Article 9.* The States parties to the present Covenant recognize the right of everyone to social security, including social insurance.

Non-discrimination on racial grounds is ensured by the International Convention on the Elimination of Racial Discrimination (see RACIAL DISCRIMINATION) in the following provision:

*Article 5.* In compliance with the fundamental obligations laid down in article 2 of this Convention, States parties undertake to prohibit and to eliminate racial discrimination in all its forms and to guarantee the right of everyone, without distinction as to race, colour, or national or ethnic origin, to equality before the law, notably in the enjoyment of the following rights: . . .
(e) Economic, social and cultural rights, in particular: . . .
(iv) The right to public health, medical care, social security and social services. . . .

Non-discrimination on the ground of sex is ensured by the Convention on the Elimination of All Forms of Discrimination against Women (see WOMEN'S RIGHTS) in the following provisions:

*Article 11.* (1) States parties shall take all appropriate measures to eliminate discrimination against women in the field of employment in order to ensure, on a basis of equality of men and women, the same rights, in particular . . .
(e) The right to social security, particularly in cases of retirement, unemployment, sickness, invalidity and old age and other incapacity to work, as well as the right to paid leave; . . .
*Article 13.* States parties shall take all appropriate measures to eliminate discrimination against women in other areas of economic and social life in order to ensure, on a basis of equality of men and women, the same rights, in particular: . . .
(e) The right to family benefits . . .

*INSTRUMENTS OF THE INTERNATIONAL LABOR ORGANIZATION.* Within the United Nations system, primary responsibility for the preparation and supervision of international measures relating to the right to social security lies with the INTERNATIONAL LABOR ORGANIZATION. Its basic instruments in this endeavor are the ILO Social Security (Minimum Standards) Convention, adopted by the International Labor Conference in 1952, and the ILO Equality of Treatment (Social Security) Convention, adopted by the Conference in 1962.

The Social Security (Minimum Standards) Convention (1952) (ILO Convention No. 102) provides (article 7) that "each State party shall secure to the persons protected the provision of benefit in respect of a condition requiring medical care of a preventive or curative nature in accordance with the following articles of this Part. . . ." The "persons protected" include (article 9) prescribed classes of employees, of the economically active population and of residents and also their wives and children. Benefits are to be paid in the form of periodical payments in case of sickness, unemployment, old age, employment injury, maternity, or invalidity. Standards to be complied with, and methods of calculating the payments, are set out in detail.

The Equality of Treatment (Social Security) Convention (1962) (ILO Convention No. 118) provides (article 3) that each State party shall grant within its territory to the nationals of any other State party equality of treatment under its legislation with its own nationals, both as regards coverage and as regards the right to benefits, in respect of every branch of social security for which it has accepted the obligations of the Convention.

Both Conventions are supervised by the international machinery established by the International Labor Conference in 1926, consisting of two components: on the one hand, a committee of independent experts responsible for examining the reports received from governments on measures they have taken to give effect to the provisions of such instruments; and, on the other hand, the establishment, at each session of the conference, of a committee responsible for reviewing the application of conventions. Government reports are required, annually, under article 22 of the ILO constitution.

In addition to the Conventions mentioned above, two recommendations—the ILO Recommendation concerning Income Security (Recommendation No. 67), adopted by the International Labor Conference on 12 May 1944, and its Recommendation concerning Agreements relating to Social Security (Recommendation No. 75), adopted by the conference on 6 June 1946, provide guiding principles for action by all States in these particular fields.

*BIBLIOGRAPHY.* Bieback, Karl-Jürgen. "Harmonisation of Social Policy in the European Community," *Cahiers de droit* 32, no. 4 (Dec. 1991): 913–935. Scholarly article, in French.
Bok, Marcia. *Civil Rights and the Social Programs of the 1960s: The Social Justice Functions of Social Policy.* Westport, CT, USA: Praeger, 1992. Scholarly monograph, in English; bibliography, pp. 161–172.

**SOCIETY FOR THREATENED PEOPLES (GESELLSCHAFT FUR BEDROHTE VOLKER).** This non-governmental organization has consultative status with the UN ECONOMIC AND SOCIAL COUNCIL (Category II). Founded in 1970 in Hamburg, Germany, the Society works for international hearings for the plight

# S

and persecution of ethnic and religious minorities. It has members in eleven countries and publishes the bimonthly *Pogrom* in German.

Society for Threatened Peoples. Address: P.O. 2024, 37010, Göttingen, Germany. Telephone: (49-551) 49906. Fax: (49-551) 58028. Chair: Tilman Zuelch.

## SÖDERBLOM, NATHAN (1866–1931).

The recipient of the 1930 **NOBEL PEACE PRIZE,** Nathan Söderblom was the first clergyman to receive the Prize and also the minister who gave the last rites to Albert Nobel, who had been a member of Söderblom's congregation. On awarding the Prize, the Prize Committee cited his promotion of international understanding.

Born in Trönö, Sweden, Söderblom studied classical languages at Uppsala University and was ordained a Lutheran priest in 1893. From 1901 to 1914 he taught at the School of Theology at Uppsala and also taught at Leipzig University from 1912 to 1914. He was appointed archbishop of Uppsala in 1914 and primate of the Church of Sweden. As a churchman, Söderblom worked for ecumenism among denominations. His work culminated in 1925 when he organized the Universal Christian Conference on Life and Work, which brought together Anglican, Protestant, and Orthodox Christians. Although invited, the Vatican did not send a representative.

*BIBLIOGRAPHY.* Gray, Tony. *Champions of Peace.* London: Paddington Press, 1976.

Schlessinger, Bernard S., and June H. Schlessinger, eds. *Who's Who of Nobel Prize Winners.* Phoenix, AZ, USA: Oryx Press, 1991.

## SOLOMON ISLANDS.

The Solomon Islands comprise a country occupying an archipelago in the Coral Sea east of Papua New Guinea, including Guadalcanal, Malaita, San Cristobal, and New Georgia. Once a British protectorate, the islands achieved independence from Great Britain in 1978 and became a member of the United Nations the same year. The population is estimated to be 366,000. Ethnic groups include Melanesian (93%); Polynesian (4%); Micronesian (1.5%); Chinese (0.3%); Gilbertese, Europeans, and others (1.2%). Languages in common use include English (official), Melanesian Pidgin, and a large number of vernaculars. Christianity is the predominant religion (Anglican, 34%; South Seas Evangelical, 17%; Roman Catholic, 19%; United Church, 10%; and Seventh Day Adventist, 10%). Literacy is estimated at 15%.

The government (1994) took the form of a parliamentary State. The governor-general, a citizen of the Solomon Islands, represents the crown as head of State and serves for a term of five years. The prime minister is elected by and from members of Parliament, who themselves are elected by popular vote for four-year terms of office. The judiciary is modeled after the British system and includes a number of native and local courts which specialize in matters relating to customary land titles. Political parties include the United Party, the People's Alliance Party, and the National Democratic Party.

The unicameral National Parliament was enlarged to 47 seats in 1993.

## SOMALIA.

The Somali Democratic Republic is a country in eastern Africa, on the Indian Ocean and the Gulf of Aden. It has boundaries with Djibouti, Ethiopia, and Kenya. British Somaliland and Italian Somalia joined in 1960 to achieve independence as Somalia, which became a member of the United Nations the same year. Its total population is estimated to be 6,000,000; in addition, it has one of the largest refugee populations in the world. Ethnic groups include Somalis (98%) and Arabs and Asians (2%). Languages in common use include Arabic and Somali (both official), English, and Italian. Islam (Sunni) is the predominant religion. Literacy is estimated at 40%.

The government (1990) took the form of a republic. Under the 1979 constitution, the president is nominated by the Central Committee of the Somali Revolutionary Socialist Party and elected by the People's Assembly for a term of six years. The assembly consists of 121 members nominated by the party and elected by popular vote for terms of five years, and six members appointed by the president. The judiciary includes district courts, regional courts, courts of appeal, and the Supreme Court.

*PLIGHT OF REFUGEES FROM THE OGADEN DESERT REGION.* For many years, Somalia has claimed the Ogaden Desert, the easternmost territory of Ethiopia; and, in 1977, it backed rebels in that area, in which a large proportion of the people are Somalis. In eight months of fighting, Somalia lost most of its army and equipment. In 1978, the remaining Somali troops and rebels were decimated by Cuban units armed by the Soviet Union. Emergency food relief was provided by the United States of America at that time, but weapons sales were withheld because Somalia refused to give up its claims to the Ogaden area. However, in 1980, Somalia agreed to permit U.S. use of military bases in the country in return for $25 million in military aid in 1981 and more in later years.

Since 1980, the United Nations has provided assistance to Somalia in dealing with its refugee problem. At the beginning of 1982, the Somali Government and the United Nations agreed on a planning figure of 700,000 refugees; however, by 1986, 140,000 new refugees from the Ogaden region had entered the country. A large proportion of the refugees, all of whom are from Ethiopia, are women and children. They are accommodated in 44 centers located in four regions: 15 in the northeast, 12 in Gedo, 12 in Hiran, and 5 in Lower Shabelle.

A United Nations interagency mission visited Somalia in September 1987 and reported that 840,000 refugees continue to have a severe impact on Somalia's fragile economy. The report of the mission identified a number of priority areas requiring international assistance, such as water resources development, food and livestock production, health services, educational and vocational training, and the building of roads and ports. Concrete steps have since been taken to implement the mission's recommendations.

The UN GENERAL ASSEMBLY considered a report by the Secretary-General on the situation (UN Doc. A/44/462) at its 1989 session, and noted (resolution 44/152) that circumstances had made it necessary for the UN HIGH COMMISSIONER FOR REFUGEES and the World Food Program to suspend their food and other humanitarian assistance programs for refugees in the northwest districts of Somalia temporarily. It commended the measures taken by the Government of Somalia to provide assistance to refugees, in spite of its own limited resources and fragile economy, and called upon the High Commissioner and the World Food Program to resume their assistance programs for the refugees in the northwest districts as soon as possible.

*CIVIL WAR.* The circumstances referred to by the General Assembly included widespread fighting in a civil war that engulfed northern Somalia in mid-1989, in which government forces attacked members of the rebel Somali National Movement in a violent confrontation that caused more than 400,000 of Somali's refugees to flee to neighboring Ethiopia and displaced a like number of people in central and southern Somalia.

A new constitution came into effect in October 1990 under which opposition political parties were allowed to form. However, despite the government's attempt to reform the political process, insurgent groups remained determined to overthrow President Siad Barre who had assumed power in 1969. The United Somali Congress (USC) fought its way to power in January 1991 and took control of Mogadishu, at which time Siad Barre left the city for his native region near Kenya.

Ali Mahdi Mohammed was appointed president, but fighting within the USC and among the various clans broke out almost immediately, particularly between supporters of Ali Mahdi and those of the military commander, Gen. Mohamed Farah Aidid. It was estimated that by March 1992, 14,000 people had been killed in the fighting. The UN agreed to send a monitoring and peacekeeping mission, UNOSOM, in April 1992 following a ceasefire agreed to in New York by rival groups.

Siad Barre and his forces attempted to regain control of Mogadishu in April but were defeated, and he went into exile in Nigeria. He died of a heart attack in Lagos, Nigeria, in February 1995.

About 400,000 refugees from Somalia were in Kenya by the end of 1992, another 300,000 in Ethiopia, and 100,000 in Yemen. The Red Cross estimated that three quarters of the Somali population had been displaced by the fighting.

The United Nations authorized the deployment of 3,000 troops to protect humanitarian distribution of food to the millions of starving Somalis, but Gen. Aidid objected to having foreign troops on Somali soil. In a mission sanctioned by the UN SECURITY COUNCIL, U.S. troops landed in Mogadishu in December 1992 and were joined by troops from 21 nations for a total of 33,000 troops.

Ceasefire agreements continued to be signed and broken, and one such agreement was reached in Ethiopia in March 1993. A Transitional National Council, comprising 74 members representing the organizations attending the peace conference, as well as the administrative regions, was to rule the country until elections sometime in 1995.

*SECOND UNITED NATIONS OPERATION IN SOMALIA (UNOSOM II).* Early in 1993, the UN Secretary-General recommended to the Security Council that UNOSOM (mandated from April 1992 to April 1993) be expanded to UNOSOM II. UNOSOM had deployed 37,000 troops to southern and central Somalia, covering approximately 40% of the country's territory. UNOSOM II would be given the enforcement powers that the original mission lacked. The mandate of UNOSOM II covers all of Somalia and includes the following military tasks: (a) monitoring the cessation of hostilities and the peace agreements; (b) preventing the resumption of violence, if necessary by taking appropriate military against the violators; (c) maintaining control of the heavy weapons of the organized factions; (d) seizing small arms of unauthorized persons; (e) securing or maintaining the security of all ports, airports, and lines of communications necessary for humanitarian aid; (f) protecting all UN personnel and NGOs working in Somalia; (g) clearing minefields; and (h) assisting in the repatriation of refugees and displaced persons in Somalia. On 26 March 1993, the Security Council adopted resolution 814 (1993), by which it expanded the size and mandate of UNOSOM.

UNOSOM II became the largest peacekeeping mission in UN history and the first for which there had been no consent from within the country. Violent deaths of UNOSOM troops from several countries, including Pakistan, Italy, and the United States, and accidental deaths of Somali civilians by troops precipitated UN resolutions regarding the rehabilitation of Somali police forces and withdrawal of troops. The Security Council issued an arrest warrant for Aidid, which was never employed and was later suspended.

Another UN-brokered agreement between Gen. Aidid and Ali Mahdi Mohamed was signed in March 1994 with the understanding that a president, vice-president, and prime minister were to be elected in May of that year. However, through 1994, no government seemed completely in control of the country; and the administrative infrastructure, including a judicial system, was lacking. U.S. troops withdrew in March 1994, having successfully contained deaths from famine. They returned in March 1995 to aid in the withdrawal of all UN troops.

The territory of "Somaliland" had meanwhile declared its independence and maintained a relatively peaceful profile throughout the early 1990s. However, its independence was not recognized by other countries, the United Nations, or the ORGANIZATION OF AFRICAN UNITY.

BIBLIOGRAPHY. Africa Watch. *Somalia: Beyond the Warlords—The Need for a Verdict on Human Rights Abuses.* New York: Human Rights Watch, 1993. NGO report, in English.

———. *Somalia: Evading Reality—Government Announces Cosmetic Changes as Abuses Continue and Challenges to Regime Intensify.* New York: Human Rights Watch, 1990. NGO fact-finding report, in English.

———. *Somalia: A Fight to the Death?—Leaving Civilians at the Mercy of Terror and Starvation.* New York: Human Rights Watch, 1992. NGO factfinding report, in English.

———. *Somalia: A Government at War with its Own People: Testimonies about the Killings and the Conflict in the North.* New York: Human Rights Watch, 1990. NGO report, in English.

African Rights. *Somalia: Operation Restore Hope: A Preliminary Assessment.* London: 1993. NGO report, in English.

Amnesty International. *Somalia: Update on a Disaster—Proposals for Human Rights.* London: 1993. NGO report, in English.

Gejdenson, Sam. "Congress Makes US Foreign Policy—Somalia: A Case Study," *American University Journal of International Law and Policy* 5, no. 4 (Summer 1990): 1087–1107. Scholarly article, in English.

Gersony, Robert. "Why Somalis Flee: A Synthesis of Conflict Experience in Northern Somalia by Somali Refugees, Displaced Persons and Others," *International Journal of Refugee Law* 2, no. 1 (1990): 4–55. Scholarly article, in English.

Immigration Naturalization Service, Resource Information Center. *Somalia: Competing Political/Military Groups Since Barre's Fall.* Arlington, VA, USA: 1991. Government briefing paper, in English.

Immigration and Refugee Board. *Kenya, Ethiopia, Djibouti, Yemen, and Saudi Arabia: The Situation of Somali Refugees.* Ottawa, Canada: 1991. Government briefing paper, in English.

Physicians for Human Rights. *Hidden Enemies: Land Mines in Northern Somalia.* Boston, MA, USA: 1992. NGO report, in English; bibliography, p. 51.

Ramlogan, Rajendra. "Towards a New Vision of World Security: The United Nations Security Council and the Lessons of Somalia," *Houston Journal of International Law* 16, no. 2 (Winter 1993): 213–260. Scholarly article, in English.

Samatar, Abdi Ismail. "Destruction of State and Society in Somalia: Beyond the Tribal Convention," *Journal of Modern African Studies* 30, no. 4 (Dec. 1992): 625–641. Scholarly article, in English.

Samatar, Said S. *Somalia: A Nation in Turmoil.* London: Minority Rights Group, 1991. NGO report, in English; bibliography, p. 33.

Somali Committee for Peace. *The Role of the United Nations in Somalia: Present Crisis and Possible Solutions.* Gloucester, Canada: 1993. NGO conference proceedings, in English.

**SOROPTIMIST INTERNATIONAL.** An international non-governmental organization in consultative status with the UN ECONOMIC AND SOCIAL COUNCIL (Category I) and with UNESCO, SI is divided into four federations (the Americas; Europe; Great Britain and Ireland; and South West Pacific), consisting of approximately 2,700 "clubs" with approximately 91,000 members, in 85 countries and territories.

Founded in 1928 in Washington, D.C., as the "Soroptimist International Association," SI aims to maintain high ethical standards in business, the professions, and other aspects of life; to strive for human rights for all people and, in particular, to advance the status of women; to develop a spirit of friendship and unity among Soroptimists of all countries; to quicken the spirit of service and human understanding; and to contribute to international understanding and universal friendship. It sponsors a quadrennial convention.

Soroptimist International publishes *The International Soroptimist* quarterly. In addition, periodicals are issued by the regional federations.

Soroptimist International. Address: 87 Glisson Road, Cambridge CB1 2HG, UK. Telephone: (44-223) 311-833. Fax: (44-223) 467-951. Executive Office: Doreen Astley.

**SOUTH AFRICA.** The Republic of South Africa is a country in southern Africa, fronting on the Atlantic Ocean and the Indian Ocean. It has borders with Botswana, Mozambique, Swaziland, and Zimbabwe. The kingdom of Lesotho forms an enclave within its southeastern territory. Also lying within its southeastern territory are the "independent states" of Bophuthatswana, Transkei, Ciskei, and Venda, commonly known as "homelands" or "bantustans."

The union was formed by Great Britain over a period of years by joining territory that it had acquired after the Napoleonic Wars with Natal, Transvaal, and the Orange Free State, which it had acquired after the Boer War. It gained sovereignty as a member of the British Commonwealth of Nations in 1934 and became a member of the United Nations in 1945. On 31 May 1961, it became the independent Republic of South Africa.

The population of South Africa is estimated to be 33,040,000. It includes persons of black (70%), white (17%), colored or mixed (10%), and Asian (3%) descent. Languages in common use include English and Afrikaans (both official), Zulu, Xhosa, Sotho, Tswana, and other vernaculars. Christianity is the predominant religion (73%); Animism (13%), Hinduism (2%), and Islam (1%) are also widely practiced. Literacy is estimated at 99% among the white population, 50% among the non-white elements.

The government (1990) took the form of a republic. Under the 1984 constitution, the president—elected for a term of five years—is head of State and of government. Parliament is composed (since 1984) of three chambers: the House of Assembly (white) with 178 members, the House of Representatives for Coloureds (mixed races) with 85 members, and the House of Delegates for Indians, with 45 members. Although less than one person out of five in the country is white, black South Africans are not represented in the parliament.

The president is elected by an electoral college made up of the three houses of parliament; in that college, the House of Assembly has an automatic majority. The independent judiciary is headed by the Supreme Court. Each of the bantustans or homelands has its own unicameral legislature, to which members are elected by resident voters. National political parties, which are racially oriented, include the following: *White*: National Party, Progressive Federal Party, New Republic Party, Conservative Party, and Reconstituted National Party; *Mixed races*: Labor Party, Freedom Party, People's Congress Party, and New Convention People's Party; *Indian*: National People's Party.

**HISTORY OF COLONIALISM.** The first permanent white settlement in what is now the Republic of South Africa occurred at Capetown in 1652 and was organized by the Dutch East India Company. The indigenous black inhabitants were expelled from their own lands, while the settlers, known as Boers or Afrikaners,

established an economy based upon slavery and a government which sought to become an independent republic. But by 1814, at the end of the Napoleonic Wars, Great Britain took possession of the colony and brought in 5,000 settlers. Its action in 1833 to free the slaves so enraged the Afrikaners that most of them moved northward and founded the republics of Transvaal, the Orange Free State, and Natal. In doing so, they had to fight and defeat the indigenous inhabitants, including the fierce Zulu tribesmen, who were forced into small reservations and forbidden to hold land elsewhere.

Great Britain annexed Natal in 1843. After diamonds had been discovered in the Orange Free State and Transvaal, the influx of prospectors was so great that the Dutch authorities took steps to discourage them. By the end of 1899, the two sides were engaged in the South African War. The Boers were defeated in 1902; and, in 1910, the Union of South Africa was established with Louis Botha, a Boer, as its first prime minister. The union included the British colonies of the Cape and Natal, the Transvaal and the Orange Free State. Two main political parties developed: the Nationalists, who stood for Dutch superiority and restrictions on the non-white population, and the United South African Party which stood for cooperation between the national and racial groups.

Jan Christian Smuts, a statesman and soldier of Dutch stock and British nationality, headed the Unionists and served as prime minister from 1919 to 1924. He became prime minister again in 1939, when J. B. M. Hertzog, then prime minister, opposed South Africa's entry into World War II and was removed by parliament. Made a field marshal, he spent most of that war in England where he held a place in the British war councils and was active in organizing the United Nations. However, he was defeated in the 1948 elections, which were won by the Nationalist Party, and, under the new Prime Minister Daniel Malan, *apartheid* became South Africa's official policy.

**APARTHEID.** To establish and enforce the policy of *apartheid*, the South African Parliament adopted an incredible series of laws providing for the complete separation of racial groups in every walk of life, systematically depriving all non-whites of their human rights and fundamental freedoms and protecting the security forces from legal restraints. Millions of non-whites, including Indians, Pakistanis, and blacks, were forced to move out of "white" areas into segregated sections of South African cities. Many of the blacks were compelled to resettle in so-called "homelands"—undesirable enclaves within South Africa bearing such names as Bophuthatswana, Ciskei, Gazankulu, KwaZulu, Lebowa, Transkei, Venda, and QwaQwa. Four of these areas were declared "independent"—Bophutha-tswana, Ciskei, Transkei, and Venda—but their sovereignty is recognized only by South Africa. Blacks residing in "independent" areas were compelled to give up their South African citizenship, thus reducing the number and proportion of black South Africans.

The Nationalist Party's policies of *apartheid* were continued and intensified under Malan's successor, Prime Minister Hendrick F. Verwoerd. In 1961, the government broke with the British Commonwealth and declared the country to be the Republic of South Africa. In 1963, as racial tensions mounted, Verwoerd was assassinated.

Balthazar J. Vorster, also a Nationalist, succeeded Verwoerd but was forced by a scandal to resign in 1978. Pieter W. Botha replaced him and was inaugurated as president on 14 September 1984 after a new constitution had replaced parliamentary government by a strong presidency.

During his term of office, Botha took at least one important step towards ameliorating the effects of *apartheid.* In response to ever-increasing domestic and international appeals for change in a policy that had become notorious throughout the world, he offered freedom to **NELSON MANDELA,** leader of the **AFRICAN NATIONAL CONGRESS OF SOUTH AFRICA** who had served 18 years in jail on charges of sabotage and conspiracy to overthrow the government, if he would renounce violence. Mandela's reply was that he would not do so until the government assumes the initiative in dismantling *apartheid* and in ensuring full political rights to non-white South Africans.

**F. W. DE KLERK,** a descendant of Afrikaner politicians who realized that the white minority could not hold the reins in South Africa indefinitely, replaced Botha as president in August 1989. He also interviewed Nelson Mandela and, by the end of 1989, had legalized the ANC and 60 other organizations and ended restrictions on the movement of 374 persons. On 11 February 1990, Mandela was released from prison.

On 2 March 1990, the National Executive Committee of the ANC elected Mr. Mandela deputy president of the organization, enabling him to control the movement headed by Oliver N. Tambo, who had been hospitalized after suffering a stroke in August 1989. Mr. Mandela later led the ANC delegation, which met with Mr. de Klerk and other officials of the South African Government early in May 1990 to discuss such questions as the ending of the state of emergency, the repeal of repressive legislation, the halting of political trials, the removal of troops from black townships and the release of all political prisoners.

The text of the statement issued at the conclusion of the meeting, on 4 May 1990, is as follows:

The Government and the ANC agree on a common commitment toward the resolution of the existing climate of violence and intimidation from whatever quarter as well as a commitment to stability and to a peaceful process of negotiations. Flowing from this commitment, the following was agreed upon:

1. The establishment of a working group to make recommendations on a definition of political offenses in the South African situation; to discuss, in this regard, time scales; and to advise on norms and mechanisms for dealing with the release of political prisoners and the granting of immunity in respect of political offenses to those inside and outside South Africa. All persons who may be affected will be considered.

The working group will bear in mind experiences in Namibia and elsewhere. The working group will aim to complete its work before 21 May 1990. It is understood that the South African Government, in its discretion, may consult other political parties and movements and other relevant bodies. The proceedings of the working group will be confidential.

In the meantime the following offenses will receive attention immediately: (a) The leaving of the country without a valid travel document; (b) any offenses related merely to organizations which were previously prohibited.

2. In addition to the arrangements mentioned in Paragraph 1, temporary immunity from prosecution for political offenses committed before today will be considered on an urgent basis for members of the National Executive Committee and selected other members of the ANC from outside the country, to enable them to return and help with the establishment and management of political activities, to assist in bringing violence to an end and to take part in peaceful political negotiations.

3. The Government undertakes to review existing security legislation to bring it into line with the new dynamic situation developing in South Africa in order to insure normal and free political activities.

4. The Government reiterates its commitment to work toward the lifting of the state of emergency. In this context the ANC will exert itself to fulfill the objectives contained in the preamble.

5. Efficient channels of communication between the Government and the ANC will be established in order to curb violence and intimidation from whatever quarter effectively.

The Government and the ANC agree that the objectives contained in this minute should be achieved as early as possible.

*SOUTH AFRICA AFTER APARTHEID.* Laws of *apartheid* were repealed in 1990 and 1991, namely the Separate Amenities Act, the Land Acts of 1913 and 1936, the Group Areas Act, the Black Communities Act of 1984, and the Population Registration Act of 1950. The National Party was opened to all races and the ANC agreed to cease all terrorist activities. At the same time the government promised to release more political prisoners and to facilitate repatriation of approximately 40,000 exiles.

Violent clashes between supporters of the ANC and the renamed Inkatha Freedom Party (IFP) continued in the black townships in 1990 and 1991. It was discovered in 1991 that factions within the government had made secret payments to the Inkatha in 1989 and 1990 in order to destabilize the black communities and derail the planned reforms.

Nelson Mandela was elected president of the ANC in July 1991 and a government amnesty for all political exiles was announced in August, with plans for the UN to supervise their return. A peace agreement and code of conduct for the security forces was signed by the government, the ANC, the IFP, and 23 political organizations. In December 1991 the Convention for a Democratic South Africa met to plan the transition to majority rule. A referendum of white voters in March 1992 demonstrated strong support for de Klerk's reform measures. Violence continued, however, with reports of security forces killing ANC demonstrators and plotting the assassination of political leaders. The United Nations agreed to send personnel to monitor the situation.

The constitution was amended in October 1992 to allow blacks to serve in the Cabinet and by April 1993, one Indian and two Coloured Ministers were appointed. In that month, Chris Hani, General Secretary of the South African Communist Party, was assassinated, for which two members of the Conservative Party received the death penalty. Also that month, Oliver Tambo, Mandela's predecessor as president of the ANC, died. It was decided the following month that multi-party elections would be held no later than April 1994, and the date of 27 April 1994 was later set.

The President's Council was abolished in June 1993 and in September legislation established a multi-racial transitional executive council, an independent electoral commission, and independent media commission.

An Interim Constitution, to take effect in April 1994, was approved in December 1993. It provided that the 400-member National Assembly, elected by proportional representation, would elect a president from among its members. The president would appoint two deputy presidents, nominated by parties with a minimum of 80 seats in the Assembly, and a Constitutional Court from among nominees from an independent judicial commission. A 90-seat Senate would be elected by the nine provincial legislatures.

This interim constitution was to be in effect until ratification of a new constitution, which would be drafted by the Constitutional Assembly, comprising the National Assembly and the Senate, prior to elections to the legislature in 1999 and pursuant to principles contained in the Interim Constitution. These principles include multi-party democracy, an independent judiciary, basic human rights and limited autonomy of provincial legislatures.

Four independent homelands were again to become part of South Africa and citizenship restored to their people. An estimated 60 people were killed after 2,000 troops were sent to one such homeland, Bophuthatswana, which had demanded complete independence, to depose its leader and regain control so that voting could take place.

In December 1993 the Transitional Executive Council was installed and Parliament ratified the Interim Constitution, in effect dissolving itself. Amendments suggested by Mandela on a degree of regional autonomy were ratified by the Parliament which reconvened for that purpose in February 1994. Parliament was again reconvened in April to ratify amendments granting greater sovereignty over issues of traditional law and custom to the Monarch of KwaZulu/Natal (the renamed province of Natal). At that point the IFP agreed to take part in the elections. Pre-election violence and bomb attacks, mostly by right-wing extremists, claimed the lives of 21 people.

International organizations sent observers, including 2,800 from the United Nations alone, to monitor the April 26 and 27 elections, which were extended by one day in some areas because of the long lines of people waiting to vote. The Interim Constitution came into force on 27 April 1994. The ANC received 63% of the vote with the National Party receiving 20% and the IFP 11%. The National Assembly elected Nelson Mandela as president on 9 May 1994 and he appointed senior ANC official Thabo Mbeki as first deputy president and de Klerk as second deputy president. The presidential inauguration was attended by heads of State from around the world and was accompanied by celebrations throughout the country.

The 90-member Senate was elected in May by the provincial legislatures, with the ANC securing 60 seats, the National Party 17, and the IFP and Freedom Front each securing 5. The chairman of the Constitutional Assembly was the Secretary-General of the ANC. A 27-member cabinet comprised representatives of the ANC, the National Party, and Inkatha. Zulu Chief Mangosuthu Buthelezi became Minister of Home Affairs.

South Africa joined the Non-Aligned Movement in May 1994, became the 53rd member of the **ORGANIZATION OF AFRICAN UNITY** in June and resumed its 1961 ties with the British Commonwealth by becoming the 51st member.

Immediate programs were instituted to bring about education, health, social, and economic reforms. Immunity from prosecution for prior political offenses was offered to those who made successful application to a judicial commission. However, a temporary rift developed between President Mandela and Deputy Vice-President de Klerk in January 1995 when Mandela declared invalid a secret amnesty for 3500 police officers issued by de Klerk before the April 1994 elections. The two publicly reconciled and agreed to send the matter to a committee of cabinet ministers for resolution.

Winnie Mandela, the estranged wife of President Mandela, was dismissed from her post as Deputy Minister of Arts, Culture, Science and Technology in April 1995 for her repeated disagreements over government policy and her link to a financial scandal. (A 1991 conviction for assault had been reversed on appeal and a prison sentence for kidnaping suspended.) She maintained her seat in parliament and on the ANC executive committee. The ANC created a disciplinary committee in February to investigate any allegations of wrongdoing within the organization.

Joe Slovo, the former South African Communist Party leader, died in January 1995. He led the guerrilla military wing of the ANC in exile from 1963 to 1990 and became the first white man to sit on the ANC executive committee. He was Minister of Housing in President Mandela's cabinet.

The Inkatha staged a parliamentary walk out in February 1995, demanding that the ANC and National Party arrange international mediation of the political status of the Zulus in KwaZulu/Natal province under the permanent constitution. In April they then withdrew from the Constitutional Assembly which had convened in January to draft a permanent constitution for South Africa.

The first Constitutional Court was sworn in February 1995 and comprised seven Whites, three Blacks, and one Indian; three were women. They ruled that the interim constitution and bill of rights as interpreted by the court, rather than parliamentary law as previously, were sovereign. In June 1995 in its first decision the Court unanimously ruled the death penalty unconstitutional as inconsistent with the guarantees of human rights contained in the interim constitution. The death sentences of 450 prisoners were commuted to life imprisonment.

In President Mandela's second state of the nation address in February 1995, he focused on crime, corruption and fiscal responsibility as some of the country's most pressing problems.

*SEE ALSO* *African National Congress of South Africa; Apartheid entries; F. W. de Klerk; Nelson Mandela.*

**BIBLIOGRAPHY.** Adam, Heribert, and Kogila Moodley. "Political Violence, 'Tribalism' and Inkatha," *Journal of Modern African Studies* 30, no. 3 (Sept. 1992): 485–510. Scholarly article, in English.

Africa Watch. *The Killings in South Africa: The Role of the Security Forces and the Response of the State.* New York: Human Rights Watch, 1991. NGO factfinding report, in English.

———. *South Africa: Accounting for the Past—The Lessons for South Africa from Latin America.* New York: Human Rights Watch, 1992. NGO report, in English.

———. *South Africa: Ciskei—Ten Years on Human Rights and the Fiction of "Independence".* New York: Human Rights Watch, 1991. NGO report, in English.

———. *South Africa: "Traditional" Dictatorship: One Party State in KwaZulu Homeland Threatens Transition to Democracy.* New York: Human Rights Watch, 1993. NGO report, in English.

African Commission on Human And Peoples' Rights and UNESCO Division of Human Rights and Peace. *Human Rights Issues for a Post-Apartheid South Africa: Final Report of Banjul, The Gambia, Workshop 18–21 June 1991.* [s.l.]: 1991. Conference report, in English.

American Association for the Advancement of Science. *Apartheid Medicine: Health and Human Rights in South Africa: A Report to the American Association for the Advancement of Science, American Psychiatric Association, American Public Health Association, Institute of Medicine of the National Academy of Sciences.* Washington, D.C.: 1990. NGO factfinding report, in English.

Amnesty International. *South Africa: Detention and Torture of Trade Unionists.* London: 1986. NGO report, in English.

———. *South Africa—State of Fear: Security Force Complicity in Torture and Political Killings 1990–92.* London: 1992. NGO report, in English.

Asmal, Kader. "Victims, Survivors and Citizens: Human Rights, Reparations and Reconciliation in the South African Context," *East African Journal of Peace and Human Rights* 1, no. 1 (1993): 1–22. Scholarly article, in English.

Black Sash. *"Greenflies": Municipal Police in the Eastern Cape.* Mowbray, South Africa: 1987. NGO report, in English.

———. *Memorandum on the Suffering of Children in South Africa.* Johannesburg: 1986. NGO report, in English.

Budlender, Geoff, et al. "Debating the Land Issue," *South African Journal on Human Rights* 6, no. 2 (1990): 155–227. Scholarly article, in English.

Catholic Institute for International Relations. *Now Everyone is Afraid: The Changing Face of Policing in South Africa.* Cape Town: 1988. NGO report, in English.

Cole, Josette. *Crossroads: The Politics of Reform and Repression 1976–1986.* Johannesburg: Ravan Press, 1987. Scholarly monograph, in English; bibliography, pp. 165–169.

Cook, Helena. *The War against Children: South Africa's Younger Victims.* New York: Lawyers Committee for Human Rights, 1986. NGO mission report, in English.

Cowling, M. G. "Judges and the Protection of Human Rights in South Africa: Articulating the Inarticulate Premise," *South African Journal on Human Rights* 3 (July 1987): 177–201. Scholarly article, in English.

De Vos, Pierre. "A Bill of Rights in a Post-Apartheid South African Constitution: A Contextual International Human Rights Analysis," *Columbia Human Rights Law Review* (Summer 1993): 277–321. Scholarly article, in English.

Diar, Prakash. *The Sharpeville Six.* Toronto, Canada: McClelland & Stewart, 1990. Monograph, in English.

Egero, Bertil. *South Africa's Bantustans: From Dumping Grounds to Battlefronts.* Uppsala, Sweden: Scandinavian Institute of African Studies, 1991. Scholarly report, in English.

Foster, Don. *Detention and Torture in South Africa: Psychological, Legal and Historical Studies.* Cape Town: David Philip, 1987. Scholarly monograph, in English; bibliography, pp. 238–246.

Forsyth, Christopher. "Interpreting a Bill of Rights: the Future Task of a Reformed Judiciary," *South African Journal on Human Rights* 7, no. 1 (1991):1–23. Scholarly article, in English.

Frederikse, Julie. *The Unbreakable Thread: Non-Racialism in*

*South Africa*. Bloomington, IN, USA, and London: Indiana University Press and Zed Books, 1990. Scholarly monograph, in English.

Hale, Terrel, ed. *United States Sanctions and South Africa: A Selected Legal Bibliography*. Westport, CT, USA, and London: Greenwood Press, 1993. Bibliography, in English.

Hanlon, Joseph. *Beggar Your Neighbours: Apartheid Power in Southern Africa*. London: Catholic Institute for International Relations, 1986. NGO report, in English.

Haysom, Nicholas. "Licence to Kill, Part II: A Comparative Survey of the Law in the United Kingdom, United States of America and South Africa," *South African Journal on Human Rights* 3 (July 1987): 202–222. Scholarly article, in English.

————. *Mabangalala: The Rise of Right Wing Vigilantes in South Africa*. London: Catholic Institute for International Relations, 1986. NGO report, in English.

Haysom, N., and G. Marcus. "'Undesirability' and Criminal Liability under the Publications Act 42 of 1974," *South African Journal on Human Rights* 1 (May 1985). Scholarly article, in English.

Human Rights Commission. *Children and Repression: 1987–1989*. Johannesburg: 1990. NGO report, in English; bibliography, pp. 56–57.

Independent Board of Inquiry. *"To Protect and Serve?": A Special Report on Police Investigations into Politically Motivated Violence and Crimes*. Johannesburg, South Africa: 1992. NGO report, in English.

Keightley, Raylene. "International Human Rights Norms in a New South Africa," *South African Journal on Human Rights* 8, no. 2 (1992): 171–187. Scholarly article, in English.

Legal Education Action Project. *Back to the Laager: The Rise of White Right Wing Violence in South Africa*. Cape Town, South Africa: Institute of Criminology, University of Cape Town, 1991. NGO monograph, in English.

Moffett, M. R. *Government Restrictions on the Press in South Africa*. Washington, D.C.: International Human Rights Law Group, 1987. NGO report, in English.

Platzky, L., and C. Walker. *The Surplus People: Forced Removals in South Africa*. Johannesburg: Ravan Press, 1985. NGO report, in English.

Rayner, Mary. *Turning a Blind Eye: Medical Accountability and the Prevention of Torture in South Africa*. Washington, D.C.: American Association for the Advancement of Science and Committee on Scientific Freedom and Responsibility, 1987. NGO report, in English.

Sachs, Albie. "Towards a Bill of Rights in a Democratic South Africa," *South African Journal on Human Rights* 6, no. 1 (1990): 1–24. Scholarly article, in English.

Steenkamp, Anton J. "The South African Constitution of 1993 and the Bill of Rights: An Evaluation in Light of International Human Rights Norms," *Human Rights Quarterly* 17, no. 1 (Feb. 1995): 101–126. Scholarly article, in English.

Thompson, Leonard. *The Political Mythology of Apartheid*. New Haven, CT, USA: Yale University Press, 1985. Scholarly study, in English; extensive footnotes.

Truluck, Anne. *No Blood on Our Hands: Political Violence in the Natal Midlands; 1987 to mid-1992, and the Role of the State, "White" Political Parties and Business*. Pietermaritzburg, South Africa: Black Sash, Natal Midlands Region, 1992. Monograph, in English.

Tsotsi, W. M. *Human Rights in the Homelands of South Africa*. Roma, Lesotho: Institute of Southern African Studies, National University of Lesotho, 1992. Scholarly monograph, in English.

United Nations Economic and Social Council. *Violations of Human Rights in South Africa: Report of the Ad Hoc Working Group of Experts—Final Report of the Ad Hoc Working Group of Experts on Southern Africa Prepared in Accordance with Commission on Human Rights resolutions 1991/21 and 1992/19 and Economic and Social Council decision 1991/237*. New York: 1993. IGO document, in English.

United Nations Sub-Commission on Prevention of Discrimination and Protection of Minorities. *Adverse Consequences for the Enjoyment of Human Rights of Political, Military, Economic and other Forms of Assistance Given to the Racist and Colonialist Regime of South Africa*. Report of Special Rapporteur Mr. Ahmad M. Khalifa, E/CN.4/Sub.2/1987/8/Rev.1. 1987. IGO report, in English.

University of the Witwatersrand, Centre for Applied Legal Studies. "Focus on Socio-Economic Rights," *South African Journal on Human Rights* 8, no. 4 (1992): 451–490. Collection of articles, in English.

Van Es, A., and M. Van Grup. *Health Professionals and Human Rights in South Africa*. Leiden, the Netherlands: Johannes Wier Foundation/Dutch Foundation for Health and Human Rights, 1987. NGO mission report, in English.

Van Nieuwkerk, Anthoni. *Transitional Politics in South Africa: From Confrontation to Democracy*. Johannesburg: South African Institute of International Affairs, 1992. Scholarly report, in English.

Van Zyl Smit, Dirk. "'Normal' Prisons in an 'Abnormal' Society? A Comparative Perspective on South African Prison Law and Practice," *South African Journal on Human Rights* 3 (July 1987): 147–165. Scholarly article, in English.

**SOUTH WEST AFRICA.** See **NAMIBIA.**

**SOUTH WEST AFRICA PEOPLE'S ORGANIZATION (SWAPO).** A liberation movement of the people of **NAMIBIA,** recognized as such by the **ORGANIZATION OF AFRICAN UNITY** and by the UN **GENERAL ASSEMBLY,** SWAPO participated in the work of the General Assembly and of other United Nations bodies as an observer until Namibia achieved independence on 21 March 1990. Sam Nujoma, SWAPO's leader, was sworn in as Namibia's first president.

**SPAIN.** Spain is a country in southern Europe occupying 85% of the Iberian Peninsula, on the Atlantic Ocean, the Mediterranean Sea, and the Bay of Biscay; it also includes the Balearic Islands in the Mediterranean and the Canary Islands off the western coast of Africa. It has borders with France and Portugal. It achieved independence in 1492 and became a member of the United Nations in 1955. Its population is estimated to be 39,155,000. Ethnic groups include Gypsies, Basques, and Catalonians. Languages in common use include Castilian (official), Basque, Catalan, and Galician; Romany is the language of the Gypsy communities. Christianity (Roman Catholic, 82%) is the predominant religion. Literacy is estimated at 97%.

The government (1994) took the form of a monarchy, headed by the king as head of State. The prime minister, representing the party or coalition given the majority in a popular election, is elected by the Congress of Deputies; he exercises executive power as president of the government. The *Cortes* (parliament) consists of the Congress of Deputies and the Senate; members of both bodies are elected in popular vote. A proportional representation system is used in elections of members of the Congress of Deputies, which has not less than 300 members nor more than 400. In elections of members of the Senate, four senators are selected in each peninsular province, two each are selected by voters in the cities of Ceuta and Melilla, and each autonomous region chooses one or more depending upon the size of its population. The Senate thus has about 200 members. The judiciary includes territorial, provincial, regional and municipal courts, and is headed by the Supreme Tribunal. Judicial authorities are independent of the legislative and executive branches of the government. Political parties include the Spanish Socialist Workers' Party, the Popular Alliance, the Centre Democratic Union, the Social and Democratic Center, the Spanish Communist Party, the Catalonian Party, and the Nationalist Basque Independents.

In elections held in October 1989, Prime Minister Felipe Gonzalez Marquez of the Socialist Workers' Party won a renewed mandate to continue Spain's new democratic tradition and to modernize its economy.

***THE FRANCO REGIME.*** Neutral during World War I, Spain became a workers' republic in 1931 after King Alphonso XIII had been forced by anti-monarchists to leave the country. Its new constitution disestablished the Catholic Church and secularized the schools. However, in 1936 the army, led by Francisco Franco Bahamonde, mutinied, and its revolt soon developed into a civil war which was fiercely fought for three years and cost the lives of nearly a million people. With the aid of fascist Italy and Nazi Germany, Franco's forces finally seized Madrid in March 1939, and Franco was installed as head of State.

Nominally neutral during World War II, Spain maintained close ties with Italy and Germany and remained a totalitarian State after the war concluded. For this and other reasons, its admission to the United Nations was delayed until 1955.

Before he died of a heart attack in November 1975, Franco designated Prince Juan Carlos Alfonso Victor Maria de Bourbon as his successor. Sworn in as king, Juan Carlos quickly ended Spain's fascist institutions and presided over free elections in June 1977. Autonomy was granted to Catalonia and the Basque country in 1980, but the Basque campaign for independence has not ended. Nor has Spain's claim to Gibraltar, held by the British since 1704, been settled.

Prime Minister Felipe Gonzalez began his fourth term in July 1993 following the loss of an absolute majority for his Socialist Workers' Party in the general election in June. Gonzalez urged drastic measures to reform Spain's ailing economy but workers reacted to his policies by protesting in the streets and calling a 24-hour strike in January 1994.

Spain became one of seven countries in the European Union to implement the Schengen Agreement in March 1995 whereby border controls between the seven would be eradicated and external controls enhanced. The other countries are Belgium, France, Germany, Luxembourg, the Netherlands, and Portugal.

***RELIGIOUS AND ETHNIC DISCRIMINATION.*** In 1990, the government overturned the decree issued in 1492 by King Ferdinand and Queen Isabella ordering expulsion or conversion of Spain's Jewish population by signing an agreement granting the Jewish and Protestant faiths privileges comparable to those exercised by Roman Catholics. Under the agreement, Jews and Protestants may (a) negotiate with their employers on the observance of religious holidays, (b) receive religious instruction in their own faith in public schools and in the armed forces, (c) observe dietary laws, (d) receive tax and social security benefits, and (e) have their civil marriages recognized as such.

Because there are relatively few non-whites in Spain, racial discrimination is not considered a serious problem. However, Arabs from North Africa, illegal immigrants from Argentina and Chile, farm workers from West Africa, and Gypsies often complain of bias due to racist attitudes. The Arabs, numbering about 400,000, and the West Africans, numbering about 150,000, enter the country as migrant workers without visas or work permits, and are shamefully exploited by the farmers who employ them. The Gypsies, traditionally nomadic, suffer as a result of their instability and often need assistance in resolving social and legal problems and in improving their health and in replacing shanty towns by adequate housing units.

Basque separatist movements have operated in Spain for 20 years and are said to have killed about 500 people in their fight for a Basque nation in northern Spain and southern France. For the most part, terrorist attacks have been aimed at government and military targets. Violence by Basque separatists escalated in the early 1990s with a series of car bombs and abductions. Arrests were made in Spain and France.

Article 3 of the Spanish constitution states that the wealth of language variations in Spain is a cultural heritage which should be the object of special attention. To meet this goal, teaching in vernacular languages has been introduced in the public schools: Euskera is taught in the Basque country; Catalan, in Catalonia and the Balearic Islands; Galician, in Galicia; and Valencian, in Valencia. The Romany language of the Gypsy community is, however, not taught in the public educational system.

In a report presented to the **COMMITTEE ON THE ELIMINATION OF RACIAL DISCRIMINATION** on 17 July 1985 (UN Doc. CERD/C/118/Add. 29, paras. 13–40) the Government of Spain presented the following information concerning its Gypsies and the problems encountered with Romany and other vernacular languages:

*Gypsies.* Royal Decree 250/79 of 11 January established the Interministerial Commission to consider problems affecting the gypsy community, which is still in operation. Its Chairman is the Under-Secretary of the Ministry of Culture.

With regard to the gypsies, many activities have been carried out by special panels covering different fields. Thus, in the area of education, there have been many campaigns for the enrolment of children in school and for adult literacy programmes. Educational action has also been stepped up at the levels of pre-school education, general basic education and vocational training.

In the area of health, there are many provinces in which courses have been given on personal and family hygiene, vaccination campaigns have been conducted or welfare cards have been provided for those gypsies who lack social security.

In the area of housing, most of the activities are designed to eradicate shanty towns. To this end, many housing units have been built under State sponsorship, and used to accommodate members of this group. Campaigns have also been conducted to instruct them in how to use and care for a house so as to obtain maximum benefit from it and foster coexistence with neighbouring non-gypsy communities.

In the social and civic area, the census of the gypsy population in many provinces is significant. In some provinces, free centres for social and legal assistance were provided, and these made it possible to resolve an entire series of irregularities regarding documentation of the gypsies.

To conclude this section, it may be observed that in general, these panels try to undertake any activities which may result in improvements for this minority group.

Regarding the problems of the gypsies, the Spanish Government was asked questions on three points:

(a) Plans for improving the gypsies' situation;

(b) Contents of the report sent to the Council of Ministers by the Chairman of the Interministerial Commission set up to consider the problems of the gypsy community; and

(c) Special measures for increasing the representation of the gypsy population in the civil service.

Regarding the first question, it should be mentioned that the Interministerial Commission set up to consider problems affecting the gypsy community has established, within the Provincial Commissions in each Civil Governor's Office, a special panel for dealing with issues concerning the gypsy community.

The specific purpose of these panels is to carry out a series of actions designed to improve the situation of the gypsy community in the province in question.

Thus measures have been adopted concerning the most urgent problems of this group, such as the elimination of shanty towns through the construction of pre-fabricated housing and State-sponsored housing units where necessary, education through a school enrolment campaign, as a result of which many gypsy children have registered in national educational institutions. Large-scale literacy campaigns have also been carried out for adults and vocational training courses for young people.

In the area of health, there are now a larger number of welfare centres, at which gypsies receive proper medical assistance. Hygiene and sanitary campaigns have also been proposed for the purpose of attempting to improve the health of this group.

Finally, a study has been carried out on the sorts of conflicts gypsies get into for the purpose of discovering and possibly eliminating their causes.

Regarding the second question raised, the report sent to the Council of Ministers by the Chairman of the Interministerial Commission set up to consider problems affecting the gypsy community mentioned a series of actions which the Government is undertaking for the purpose of encouraging the development and promotion of the gypsy people. Among these actions, and by way of conclusion, we may mention the following:

The allocation of funds to the Ministry of Culture in the General State Budget Act of 1981 in order to promote the interests of ethnic minorities;

The public health and sanitary assistance programmes carried out by the Ministry of Labour, Health and Social Security, and the increase of subsidies from the National Social Welfare Fund to gypsy bodies and associations;

In the area of education, a significant agreement was reached between the Ministry of Education and Science and the Episcopal Commission on Emigrations, for the purpose of putting into operation "bridging schools" for gypsy children: the objective of these schools is to prepare gypsy children, through specialized teaching, for integration into ordinary national schools;

A study carried out by the Ministry of Public Works and Town Planning on the housing needs of this group;

Finally, and as part of the general policy for dealing with specific situations, each Ministry has adopted appropriate measures for gradually improving the situation of this group.

With reference to the last question raised, we should like to point out the Government's interest in increasing gypsy representation; to this end article 4 of Royal Decree 250/79, which set up the Interministerial Commission, established within the Commission one or more working groups whose members would include, where appropriate and with the prior agreement of the Commission, representatives of gypsy bodies or associations. The plenary Commission decided that the gypsies should participate in each of the working groups.

Gypsy associations are also being rigorously promoted. An increasing number of such associations are being formed to promote and undertake measures designed to achieve better integration of this ethnic minority into Spanish society.

*Romany.* The Romany language is not officially included in the educational system. However, the Directorate General of Secondary Education of the Ministry of Education and Science is working on the elimination of all forms of discrimination and paying particular attention to the gypsy race in order to avoid the discrimination situations, which still occur in our schools.

With regard to the Spanish gypsy community's own language, the Directorate General of Secondary Education reports that it has not been introduced at any secondary educational institution in any Self-Governing Community.

Among the reasons which have hindered and are still hindering the adoption of teaching in Romany, mention may be made of the following:

(a) There has not so far been enough demand to make society at large or the national and local authorities feel the need for it;

(b) The gypsy community is scattered in many small groups, which are perhaps not very highly motivated towards regular schooling in their language;

(c) In many cases, schools are far away from the places where members of the gypsy community live;

(d) Members of this community, at least in the past have tended to lead a wandering life;

(e) Properly trained teachers are not available to give instruction in the Romany language.

However, despite what has been said above about the Romany language of the gypsy community in Spain, it should be pointed out that regional languages are all included in the basic educational curriculum. The State lays down a minimum of basic instruction and each Self-Governing Community with its own language includes it in its programmes.

*Vernacular Languages.* Article 3 of the 1978 Spanish Constitution, after establishing that Castilian is the official language of the State and that the other languages of Spain are also official in the respective Self-Governing Communities, states that the wealth of the different language variations of Spain is a cultural heritage which shall be the object of special attention, respect and protection.

In order to meet this constitutional mandate, in the course of 1979 the nation's education administration, in collaboration with the not-yet self-governing authorities (constituted before approval of the Statutes of Self-Government) introduced teaching in their own languages for those communities which have them, through appropriate legal provisions. To this end, mixed commissions were appointed to supervise the introduction and conduct of such teaching.

Under these legal provisions, which rank as decrees, teaching in the vernacular language was introduced at non-university levels (as far as secondary education is concerned, in the baccalaureate first- and second-degree vocational training and the university preparation course), in the following Self-Governing Communities: Basque Country: Euskera; Catalonia: Catalan, with special attention to Aranés; Galicia: Galician; Valencia: Valencian; Balearic Islands: Catalan, with special attention to all the island variations.

These languages were included in the educational system under similar conditions to Castilian, with regard to their compulsory nature and place in the time-table. However, exemptions were permitted as an exception for those whose circumstances so warranted in the opinion of the local academic authorities.

The necessary material and staff were also supplied, university chairs and lectureships being established to promote better teaching of vernacular languages.

Once the above-mentioned Statutes of Self-Government were approved for these communities through Organizational Laws 3/1979 of 18 December, 4/1979 of 18 December, 1/1981 of 5 April, 5/1982 of 1 July and 2/1983 of 25 February, and the Communities received the services and budgetary allocations they needed in order to perform the functions laid down in their statutes, not just with respect to the teaching of their languages but with respect to all teaching, compliance with article 3 of the Constitution in relation to the teaching and use of vernacular languages has been the responsibility of the respective self-governing authorities.

With regard to the current situation of vernacular teaching, it may generally be stated that:

(a) In all the Self-Governing communities with a vernacular language teaching has been introduced in that language, under conditions similar to those for the Spanish language;

(b) This type of teaching is being expanded in the communities gradually, depending on the extent to which it existed at the outset, the degree of linguistic heterogeneity of the school population, the availability of appropriately trained teachers, etc;

(c) In all of these Self-Governing communities, the programmes have been drawn up in collaboration with the competent linguistic authorities;

(d) University chairs and lectureships have been created in the vernacular language;

(e) In all cases the possibility of exemptions has been provided for in order not to impose vernacular teaching indiscriminately and against their will on pupils whose stay in the Communities may be temporary;

(f) The teaching of historical variations of the same language, when they exist, is respected and encouraged by the local academic authorities;

(g) The Self-Governing Community of Aragon, entirely Castilian-speaking, has authorized teaching in Catalan in the north-eastern area since it is a zone with some remaining bilingualism.

Similarly, many educational institutions in Communities with a strong bilingual component provide secondary teaching in the vernacular language.

Finally, it should be pointed out that although racial discrimination as such is non-existent in our country, an attempt has been made to avoid any type of social discrimination, especially in the area of education, with the enactment of an important piece of legislation. The Royal Decree of 27 April 1983 on compensatory education is a regulation aimed at combating "the inequality of certain people with respect to the educational system owing to their economic capacity, social level or place of residence".

**REPORT BY THE UN COMMITTEE ON THE RIGHTS OF THE CHILD.** The Committee considered the initial report of Spain (CRC/C/8/Add. 6) at its 171st, 172nd, and 173rd meetings (CRC/C/SR.171–173), held on 6 and 7 October 1994, and adopted the following concluding observations on 14 October 1994:

*Positive factors.* The Committee notes with satisfaction the declaration made by Spain at the time of its ratification of the Convention with regard to the provisions of paragraphs 2 and 3 of article 38 and the commitment of the State party not to permit the recruitment and participation in armed conflict of persons below the age of 18 years.

The Committee also welcomes the open and self-critical approach taken by the Government of Spain in preparing its report.

The Committee welcomes the judgement of the Spanish Constitutional Court of 14 February 1991 declaring unconstitutional the procedure that juvenile courts followed in the past. The Committee notes with satisfaction the ruling of the Constitutional Court which explicitly takes up in full the terms of article 40, paragraph 2 (b), of the Convention and concludes, *inter alia,* that the fundamental rights brought together by the Spanish Constitution have to be respected also in criminal proceedings against minors.

The Committee further welcomes the fact that, in Spain, discriminatory acts committed by a public official are considered criminal offences under the law.

*Principal subjects of concern.* The Committee is concerned at the fact that effective coordination has not been fully developed between central authorities and regional and local authorities in the implementation of policies for the promotion and protection of the rights of the child. Coordination is also necessary for the purpose of monitoring in order to avoid disparities developing in the implementation of economic, social and cultural programmes relating to children.

The Committee is concerned at the impact on the rights of the child of the high rate of unemployment and the deterioration of the economic and social environment.

The Committee is worried about one aspect of the treatment of unaccompanied minors seeking refuge which may contradict the principle that each case be dealt with on an individual basis and on its own merits. The practice of automatically informing the authorities of their country of origin may lead to their persecution, or the persecution of their relatives, for political reasons.

Furthermore, the Committee expresses concern at the wording of article 154 of the Spanish Civil Code which provides that parents "may administer punishment to their children reasonably and in moderation", which may be interpreted to allow for actions in contradiction with article 19 of the Convention.

The Committee expresses its concern at the high percentage of single parent families and the need for special programmes and services to provide the necessary care for children from such families.

*Suggestions and recommendations.* The Committee recommends that the State party strengthen the coordination mechanisms existing in its constitutional and legislative framework and develop evaluation and monitoring at all levels of the administration, central, regional and local (including the *comunidades autónomas*), to ensure that the Convention on the Rights of the Child is fully respected and implemented.

The Committee further recommends that the Government of Spain gather all the necessary information in order to have an overall view of the situation in the country and to ensure a comprehensive and multidisciplinary evaluation of progress and difficulties in implementing the Convention. This evaluation should enable it to shape appropriate policies to combat disparities and lasting prejudices.

The State party is recommended to pay particular attention to the implementation of article 4 of the Convention and ensure a balanced distribution of resources at the central, regional and local levels. In establishing the budget allocated to the promotion and protection of economic, social and cultural rights, the best interests of the child should be taken as a primary consideration and available resources should be allocated to their maximum extent.

It is recommended that the State party consider reviewing its programme for international cooperation in order to assess the possibility of giving more emphasis to the social sectors and to direct the assistance to the most underprivileged children.

Measures should be taken to disseminate information and increase awareness about the Convention and to prevent discriminatory attitudes or prejudices towards vulnerable groups of children including migrant children and gypsies. To this effect, the Committee suggests that law enforcement officials, judges, other administration of justice officials and, more generally, members of professions concerned with the implementation of the Convention be provided with adequate training on the basic principles and norms contained in it.

The Committee suggests that the State party consider institutionalizing the existing relations with non-governmental organizations and research institutions in order to mobilize popular participation in activities and programmes relating to the promotion and protection of the rights of the child.

Furthermore, the Committee encourages the Spanish authorities to pursue the law reform to ensure full compliance of the domestic legislation with the provisions of the Convention. In this regard, the Committee recommends that the law reform include the review of the language used in legal provisions and, in particular, the revision of article 154 of the Spanish Civil Code stating that parents "may administer punishment to their children reasonably and in moderation", in order to bring it into full conformity with article 19.

The Committee recommends the State party to consider legal amendments in order to ensure the right to participation of children, including the right to freedom of association and to freedom of peaceful assembly as reflected in article 15 of the Convention.

The Committee also recommends that the Government of Spain improve the system of safeguards in the cases of intercountry adoption. In this connection, the Committee encourages Spain to consider ratifying the Hague Convention on Protection of Children and Cooperation in respect of Intercountry Adoption.

Further steps should be taken to strengthen the system of assistance to both parents in the performance of their child-rearing responsibilities, in particular in the light of article 18. It is further suggested that the problem of single parenthood be studied and that relevant programmes be established to meet their particular needs.

The Committee recommends that the Government of Spain take all the necessary measures to guarantee that refugee children, children who are asylum seekers and unaccompanied children enjoy the rights recognized by the Convention on the Rights of the Child and that, in accordance with its article 10, applications for asylum made for the purpose of family reunification be dealt with in a positive, humane and expeditious manner.

The Committee encourages the Government of Spain to consider signing and ratifying the International Convention on the Protection of the Rights of All Migrant Workers and Members of Their Families.

The State party should give particular attention to the implementation of the provisions of article 32 of the Convention aimed at protecting the child against economic exploitation as well as to the implementation of the relevant conventions of the International Labour Organisation that it has ratified.

Finally, the Committee recommends that the initial report of Spain, the summary records of the meetings of the Committee in which the report was considered and the concluding observations of the Committee on the report be published and disseminated as widely as possible in Spain.

**BIBLIOGRAPHY.** Amnesty International. *Spain: Torture and Ill-Treatment: Summary of Amnesty International's Concerns.* London: 1993. NGO report, in English.

Asociación Pro Derechos Humanos de España (Spanish Society for Human Rights). *Informe Anual: Derechos Humanos en España* (Annual Report: Human Rights). Madrid. NGO annual report, in Spanish.

————. *Informe Sobre la Carcel de Ocana I* (Report on the Ocana I Prison). Madrid: 1985. NGO mission report, in Spanish.

Donnelly, J., and R. E. Howard, eds. *International Handbook on Human Rights*. Westport, CT, USA: Greenwood Press, 1987. Scholarly edited collection, in English.

Escobar Hernandez, Concepción. "Asilo y Refugio en España" (Asylum and Refuge in Spain), *International Journal of Refugee Law* 3, no. 4 (Oct. 1991): 692–708. Scholarly article, in Spanish.

Helsinki Watch. *Prison Conditions in Spain*. New York: Human Rights Watch, 1992. NGO report, in English.

Jacoby, Daniel M. *Espane: Proces d'Un Militant Basque* (Spain: Trial of a Basque Militant). Paris: Federation Internationale des Droits de l'Homme, 1985. NGO mission report, in French.

Jurgies, Wolfgang. "Gernika 1937 and 1987" (Guernica 1937 and 1987), *Pogrom* 133 (June 1987): 14–16. NGO article, in German.

Korn, David. "State Terrorism: A Spanish Watergate?" *Freedom at Issue* 105 (Nov.–Dec. 1988). Scholarly article, in English.

Pulver, Bernhad. "Els Paisos Catalans" (The Catalonian Countries), *Pogrom* 133 (June 1987): 17–21. NGO article, in German.

Rodriguez Guerrero, L. F. "La Ley Antiterrorista Rompe el Sistema Constitucional" (Antiterrorist Law Breaks the Constitutional System), *Derechos Humanos* 9 (Feb.–March 1985): 9–11. NGO article, in Spanish.

## SPANISH ASSOCIATION FOR HUMAN RIGHTS (ASOCIACIÓN PRO DERECHOS HUMANOS DE ESPAÑA).

This non-governmental organization was established in 1975 to inform Spanish-speaking peoples throughout the world of the purpose of the UNIVERSAL DECLARATION OF HUMAN RIGHTS and to lobby for the establishment of human rights standards. The Association publishes the monthly *Derechos Humanos* and the yearly *Informe Anual* in Spanish.

Since 1982, the Association has awarded annually three human rights awards in the categories of International, National, and Journalism. The awards are open to individuals or organizations. The international and national winners receive a commemorative sculpture; the journalism award is honorary.

The 1991 recipients were: Movimento Nacional de Meninos e Meninas de Rua, Brazil (International); Asociacion de Solidaridad con Trabajadores Immigrantes (National); and Eduardo Haro Tecglen (Journalism).

Spanish Association for Human Rights. Address: Jose Ortega y Gasset 77, 2A, E-28006 Madrid, Spain. Telephone: (34-91) 402-3204; Fax: (34-91) 402-8499. President: Jose Antonio Gimbernat.

## SRI LANKA.

The Democratic Socialist Republic of Sri Lanka is a country in southern Asia occupying a large island in the Indian Ocean off the southeastern tip of the Indian subcontinent. It achieved independence in 1948 as the British Dominion then known as Ceylon and became an independent republic on 22 May 1972.

Sri Lanka became a member of the United Nations in 1955. Its population is estimated to be 17,740,000. Ethnic groups include Sinhala (74%), Sri Lanka Tamils (12.7%), Sri Lanka Moors (7%), Indian Tamils (5.5%), Malays (0.29%), Burghers (0.26%), and others (0.2%). The Sinhalese use Sinhala (official), a language of Indo–Aryan origin. The Tamils use Tamil (also official), the national language which is also the language of the Dravidians of southern India. Some Moors use Tamil, others Sinhala. Descendants of European peoples generally use English. Religions practiced include Buddhism, Christianity (Roman Catholic and a number of Protestant denominations), Hinduism, and Islam. Literacy is estimated at 87%.

The government (1994) took the form of a socialist republic. Under the 1978 constitution, the president is elected by popular vote for a six-year term and must receive at least 50% of all votes cast. He serves as head of State, head of the executive and of the government, and commander-in-chief of the armed forces. The prime minister and other ministers, who must be members of parliament, are appointed by the president. Legislation is prepared by the 168-member unicameral Parliament, the members of which normally serve for a period of six years; however, in 1982, the electorate voted to extend the term of the existing parliament for a further six years. The president has no veto over decisions made by the parliament. Political parties include the United National Party, the Tamil United Liberation Front, the Sri Lanka Freedom Party, and the Sri Lanka Mahajaua Party.

*TAMIL INSURGENCY.* The long tradition of amity, cordiality, and mutual cooperation that had characterized relationships between ethnic and religious groups in multiracial and multireligious Sri Lanka over many generations was broken in 1983 by open conflict between the Tamil minority and the Sinhalese majority. The aim of the Tamils was to establish a separate homeland in northern Sri Lanka which would have close ties with the Tamil-speaking peoples of nearby southern India.

The guerrilla insurgency waged by the Tamils in the northern and eastern provinces of Sri Lanka, and the efforts of the government to crush that insurgency by attacks on the city of Jaffna and other portions of the Jaffna Peninsula, resulted in more than 6,000 casualties up to July 1987. At that time, Indian forces entered the country as a peacekeeping force in accordance with an agreement signed by Ceylonese President J. R. Jayewardene and Indian Prime Minister Rajiv Gandhi and began to disarm the Tamil fighters. However, some separatist groups who opposed the peace accord, including the Liberation Tigers of Tamil Eelam, went underground and continued to attack rival Tamil groups and to wreck their offices and the villages in which they lived.

The Indian peacekeeping force, which at one time numbered as many as 50,000 men, spent nearly three years in Sri Lanka but was not able to disarm the Tamil Liberation Tigers, a group of fighters whose goal is a separate Tamil homeland. The force was withdrawn in March 1990 by India's new Prime Minister V. P. Singh at the request of Sri Lanka's new President Ranasinghe Premadasa. Both had won elections in 1989, the latter with a pledge to get the Indians out of the country and with the confidence and cooperation of the People's Front of Liberation Tigers, who hope to become the elected government of a Tamil homeland.

After the withdrawal of the peacekeeping force, thousands of Tamils who had cooperated with it fled to India in ships, hoping to settle in Tamil Nadu, the Indian State of which Madras is capital. India, however, refused to allow them to disembark on the ground that many did not fit the international definition of the term "refugee."

Although in March 1990 the government lifted the ban on political rallies and other emergency restrictions and hoped that the Liberation Tigers of Tamil Ealam (LTTE) would take part in elections for the northeastern provincial council as agreed, fighting between the government and the LTTE continued. The central Indian Government decided in January 1991 to dismiss the State government in Tamil Nadu because of its support for the LTTE. The group was then suspected of assassinating the Sri Lankan Minister of Defense in March and Indian Prime Minister Rajiv Gandhi in May 1991, and of murdering 170 Muslim villagers in October 1992 as well as various governmental and military officials.

Despite crucial success for his United National Party (UNP) in local elections in May 1991, an impeachment motion alleging 24 abuses of power was filed against Premadasa in August. Although it was rejected by the Speaker of the House, there followed the creation of an opposition party by former UNP legislators who had been expelled from the UNP for supporting the motion.

When this new Democratic United National Front (DUNF) party's leader was assassinated in April 1993 and Premadasa's government was accused, it blamed the LTTE which denied all responsibility. Finally, President Premadasa himself was killed in a bomb explosion in May 1993. Again the LTTE denied all responsibility. Prime Minister Dingiri Banda Wijetunga was elected to serve the remaining term.

In legislative elections in August 1994, the leftist coalition of nine parties called the People's Alliance won 125 of the 225 seats. Campaign violence claimed 24 lives and it was the first election that the UNP had lost in 17 years. Chandrika Bandaranaike Kumaratunga became prime minister and was elected the country's first female president in November. Another 50 people died in an attack on an opposition candidate at a rally in October.

President Kumaratunga vowed to eliminate the presidency and transfer the power to the prime minister and parliament. She also campaigned on the promise of ending the fighting with the LTTE and had brokered a temporary ceasefire and promised $800 million in economic aid to the site of the strife, the Jaffna peninsula.

**BIBLIOGRAPHY.** Amnesty International. *Sri Lanka: An Assessment of the Human Rights Situation.* London: 1993. NGO report, in English.

———. *Sri Lanka: Balancing Human Rights and Security: Abuse of Arrest & Detention Powers in Colombo.* London: 1994. NGO report, in English.

———. *Sri Lanka: The "Disappearances" from Eastern University Refugee Camp on 5 September 1990.* London: 1993. NGO report, in English.

———. *Sri Lanka: Extrajudicial Executions, 'Disappearances' and Torture, 1987 to 1990.* New York: 1990. NGO factfinding report, in English and French.

———. *Sri Lanka: New Emergency Regulations.* London: 1994. NGO report, in English.

———. *Sri Lanka: Proposed Amendments to the Constitution Affecting Fundamental Rights.* London: 1991. NGO report, in English.

———. *Sri Lanka: What Has Happened to the "Disappeared"?* London: 1988. NGO report, in English.

———. *Sri Lanka: When Will Justice Be Done?* London: 1994. NGO report, in English.

———. *States of Emergency: Torture and Violations of the Right to Life under States of Emergency.* London: 1988. NGO report, in English.

Article 19. *Freedom of Expression and Information in Sri Lanka.* London: 1991. NGO factfinding report, in English.

Asia Watch. *Human Rights Accountability in Sri Lanka.* New York: Human Rights Watch, 1992. NGO factfinding report, in English.

———. *Human Rights in Sri Lanka: An Update.* New York: Human Rights Watch, 1991. NGO factfinding report, in English.

Civil Rights Movement of Sri Lanka. *Death in Custody.* Colombo, Sri Lanka: 1988. NGO report, in English.

Forsythe, David P. *Human Rights and Peace: International and National Dimensions.* Lincoln, NE, USA: University of Nebraska Press, 1993. Scholarly monograph, in English.

Hyndman, Patricia. "Human Rights, the Rule of Law and the Situation in Sri Lanka," *University of New South Wales Law Journal* 8, no. 2 (1985): 337–361. Scholarly article, in English.

———. "The 1951 Convention Definition of Refugee: An Appraisal with Particular Reference to the Case of Sri Lanka Tamil Applicants," *Human Rights Quarterly* 9, no. 1 (Feb. 1987): 49–73. Scholarly article, in English.

# S

Jayawardena, K., and J. Uyangoda, eds. "Special Issue on the National Question in Sri Lanka," *South Asia Bulletin* 6, no. 2 (Fall 1986). Scholarly special issue, in English.

Law and Society Trust. "The 1994 Parliamentary Elections," *Law and Society Trust Fortnightly Review* 5, no. 82 (Sept. 1994). NGO special issue, in English.

Perera, Jayantha. "Political Development and Ethnic Conflict in Sri Lanka," *Journal of Refugee Studies* 5, no. 2 (1992): 136–148. Scholarly article, in English; bibliography, pp. 147–148.

Rajanayagam, P. *Sri Lanka: Human Rights Violations—Extra-judicial and Arbitrary Killings.* London: Human Rights Council and Tamil Information Centre, 1987. NGO monograph, in English.

Rubin, Barnett R. *Cycles of Violence: Human Rights in Sri Lanka since the Indo-Sri Lanka Agreement.* Washington, D.C.: Asia Watch, 1987. NGO report, in English.

Rupesinghe, Kumar, Berth Verstappen, and Anton Philip. *Ethnic Conflict and Human Rights in Sri Lanka: An Annotated Bibliography, Volume 2: 1989–1992.* London: Hans Zeller 1993. NGO bibliography, in English.

Social Scientists Association. *Ethnicity and Social Change in Sri Lanka.* Colombo, Sri Lanka: 1985. Scholarly edited collection, in English.

Vije, Mayan. *Where Serfdom Thrives: The Plantation Tamils of Sri Lanka.* Madras, India: Tamil Information and Research Unit, 1987. NGO report, in English.

Wynne, Alison. *Lament for Lanka.* Kowloon, Hong Kong: Christian Conference of Asia, 1988. NGO mission report, in English.

**STANDARD MINIMUM RULES FOR THE TREATMENT OF PRISONERS.** See **PRISONERS.**

**STANDARD OF LIVING.** The right of everyone to a standard of living adequate for the health and well-being of himself and of his family is proclaimed in the **UNIVERSAL DECLARATION OF HUMAN RIGHTS** in the following terms:

*Article 25.* 1. Everyone has the right to a standard of living adequate for the health and well-being of himself and of his family, including food, clothing, housing and medical care and necessary social services, and the right to security in the event of unemployment, sickness, disability, widowhood, old age or other lack of livelihood in circumstances beyond his control.

2. Motherhood and childhood are entitled to special care and assistance. All children, whether born in or out of wedlock, shall enjoy the same social protection.

The **INTERNATIONAL COVENANT ON ECONOMIC, SOCIAL AND CULTURAL RIGHTS** contains the following provision:

*Article 11.* 1. The States Parties to the present Covenant recognize the right of everyone to an adequate standard of living for himself and his family, including adequate food, clothing and housing, and to the continuous improvement of living conditions. The States Parties will take appropriate steps to ensure the realization of this right, recognizing to this effect the essential importance of international co-operation based on free consent.

2. The States Parties to the present Covenant, recognizing the fundamental right of everyone to be free from hunger, shall take, individually and through international co-operation, the measures, including specific programmes, which are needed:

(a) To improve methods of production, conservation and distribution of food by making full use of technical and scientific knowledge, by disseminating knowledge of the principles of nutrition and by developing or reforming agrarian systems in such a way as to achieve the most efficient development and utilization of natural resources;

(b) Taking into account the problems of both food-importing and food-exporting countries, to ensure an equitable distribution of world food supplies in relation to need.

Neither document contains a definition of an "adequate standard of living." However, principles to be applied in particular areas which have a bearing upon the provision of an adequate standard of living are set out in articles 22, 23, 24, 26, and 27 of the Declaration and articles 6, 7, 8, 10, 11, 12, 13, and 15 of the Covenant. These principles are dealt with individually in terms of separate rights and freedoms (right to work, right to education, etc.) and collectively in terms of the right to development.

**VANCOUVER DECLARATION ON HUMAN SETTLEMENTS (1976).** The Declaration was adopted on 11 June 1976 by HABITAT, the United Nations Conference on Human Settlements, convened at Vancouver, BC, Canada, from 31 May to 11 June 1976 with the mandate (a) to stimulate innovation, serve as a means for the exchange of experience, and ensure the widest possible dissemination of new ideas and technologies in the field of human settlements; (b) to formulate and make recommendations for an international program in this field which will assist governments; and (c) to stimulate interest in developing appropriate financial systems and institutions for human settlements among those making financial resources available and those in a position to use such resources, considering that the most appropriate and effective action for dealing with human settlements problems is action at the national level, but that such action will require assistance and cooperation between and among all states. The basic theme is to raise the standard of living for all people, no matter what their economic or social status.

The UN General Assembly on 16 December 1976 took note (resolution 31/109) of the report of the conference (United Nations publication, Sales No. E.76. IV.7), including the Vancouver Declaration (chap. I), and urged all governments to take the recommendations contained therein into account when reviewing their existing policies and strategies in the field of human settlements. The text of the Declaration is as follows:

HABITAT: United Nations Conference on Human Settlements,

Aware that the Conference was convened following recommendation of the United Nations Conference on the Human Environment and subsequent resolutions of the General Assembly, particularly resolution 3128 (XXVIII) by which the nations of the world expressed their concern over the extremely serious condition of human settlements, particularly that which prevails in developing countries,

Recognizing that international co-operation, based on the principles of the United Nations Charter, has to be developed and strengthened in order to provide solutions for world problems and to create an international community based on equity, justice and solidarity,

Recalling the decisions of the United Nations Conference on the Human Environment, as well as the recommendations of the World Population Conference, the United Nations World Food Conference, the Second General Conference of the United Nations Industrial Development Organization, the World Conference of the International Women's Year, the Declaration and Programme of Action adopted by the sixth special session of the General Assembly of the United Nations and the Charter of Economic Rights and Duties of States that establish the basis of the New International Economic Order,

Noting that the condition of human settlements largely determines the quality of life, the improvement of which is a prerequisite for the full satisfaction of basic needs, such as employment, housing, health services, education and recreation,

Recognizing that the problems of human settlements are not isolated from the social and economic development of countries and that they cannot be set apart from existing unjust international economic relations,

Being deeply concerned with the increasing difficulties facing the world in satisfying the basic needs and aspirations of peoples consistent with principles of human dignity,

Recognizing that the circumstances of life for vast numbers of people in human settlements are unacceptable, particularly in developing countries, and that, unless positive and concrete action is taken at national and international levels to find and implement solutions, these conditions are likely to be further aggravated, as a result of:

Inequitable economic growth, reflected in the wide disparities in wealth which now exist between countries and between human beings and which condemn millions of people to a life of poverty, without satisfying the basic requirements for food, educations, health services, shelter, environmental hygiene, water and energy;

Social, economic, ecological and environmental deterioration which are exemplified at the national and international levels by inequalities in living conditions, social segregation, racial discrimination, acute unemployment, illiteracy, disease and poverty, the breakdown of social relationships and traditional cultural values and the increasing degradation of life-supporting resources of air, water and land;

World population growth trends which indicate that numbers of mankind in the next 25 years would double, thereby more than doubling the need for food, shelter and all other requirements for life and human dignity which are at the present inadequately met;

Uncontrolled urbanization and consequent conditions of overcrowding, pollution, deterioration and psychological tensions in metropolitan regions;

Rural backwardness which compels a large majority of mankind to live at the lowest standards of living and contribute to uncontrolled urban growth;

Rural dispersion exemplified by small scattered settlements and isolated homesteads which inhibit the provision of infrastructure and services, particularly those relating to water, health and education;

Involuntary migration, politically, racially, and economically motivated, relocation and expulsion of people from their national homeland;

Recognizing also that the establishment of a just and equitable world economic order through necessary changes in the areas of international trade, monetary systems, industrialization, transfer of resources, transfer of technology, and the consumption of world resources, is essential for socioeconomic development and improvement of human settlement, particularly in developing countries,

Recognizing further that these problems pose a formidable challenge to human understanding, imagination, ingenuity and resolve, and that new priorities to promote the qualitative dimensions to economic development, as well as a new political commitment to find solutions resulting in the practical implementation of the New International Economic Order, become imperative:

*I. Opportunities and Solutions.* 1. Mankind must not be daunted by the scale of the task ahead. There is need for awareness of and responsibility for increased activity of the national Governments and international community, aimed at mobilization of economic resources, institutional changes and international solidarity by:

(a) Adopting bold, meaningful and effective human settlement policies and spatial planning strategies realistically adapted to local conditions;

(b) Creating more livable, attractive and efficient settlements which recognize human scale, the heritage and culture of people and the special needs of disadvantaged groups especially children, women and the infirm in order to ensure the provision of health, services, education, food and employment within a framework of social justice;

(c) Creating possibilities for effective participation by all people in the planning, building and management of their human settlements;

(d) Developing innovative approaches in formulating and implementing settlement programmes through more appropriate use of science and technology and adequate national and international financing;

(e) Utilizing the most effective means of communications for the exchange of knowledge and experience in the field of human settlements;

(f) Strengthening bonds of international co-operation both regionally and globally;

(g) Creating economic opportunities conducive to full employment where, under healthy, safe conditions, women and men will be fairly compensated for their labour in monetary, health and other personal benefits.

2. In meeting this challenge, human settlements must be seen as an instrument and object of development. The goals of settlement policies are inseparable from the goals of every sector of social and economic life. The solutions to the problems of human settlements must therefore be conceived as an integral part of the development process of individual nations and the world community.

3. With these opportunities and considerations in mind,

and being agreed on the necessity of finding common principles that will guide Governments and the world community in solving the problems of human settlements, the Conference proclaims the following general principles and guidelines for action.

*II. General Principles.* 1. The improvement of the quality of life of human beings is the first and most important objective of every human settlement policy. These policies must facilitate the rapid and continuous improvement in the quality of life of all people, beginning with the satisfaction of the basic needs of food, shelter, clean water, employment, health, education, training, social security without any discrimination as to race, colour, sex, language, religion, ideology, national or social origin or other cause, in a frame of freedom, dignity and social justice.

2. In striving to achieve this objective, priority must be given to the needs of the most disadvantaged people.

3. Economic development should lead to the satisfaction of human needs and is a necessary means towards achieving a better quality of life, provided that it contributes to a more equitable distribution of its benefits among people and nations. In this context particular attention should be paid to the accelerated transition in developing countries from primary development to secondary development activities, and particularly to industrial development.

4. Human dignity and the exercise of free choice consistent with over-all public welfare are basic rights which must be assured in every society. It is therefore the duty of all people and Governments to join the struggle against any form of colonialism, foreign aggression and occupation, domination, *apartheid* and all forms of racism and racial discrimination referred to in the resolutions as adopted by the General Assembly of the United Nations.

5. The establishment of settlements in territories occupied by force is illegal. It is condemned by the international community. However, action still remains to be taken against the establishment of such settlements.

6. The right of free movement and the right of each individual to choose the place of settlement within the domain of his own country should be recognized and safeguarded.

7. Every State has the sovereign and inalienable right to choose its economic system, as well as its political, social and cultural system, in accordance with the will of its people, without interference, coercion or external threat of any kind.

8. Every State has the right to exercise full and permanent sovereignty over its wealth, natural resources and economic activities, adopting the necessary measures for the planning and management of its resources, providing for the protection, preservation and enhancement of the environment.

9. Every country should have the right to be a sovereign inheritor of its own cultural values created throughout its history, and has the duty to preserve them as an integral part of the cultural heritage of mankind.

10. Land is one of the fundamental elements in human settlements. Every State has the right to take the necessary steps to maintain under public control the use, possession, disposal and reservation of land. Every State has the right to plan and regulate use of land, which is one of its most important resources, in such a way that the growth of population centres both urban and rural are based on a comprehensive land use plan. Such measures must assure the attainment of basic goals of social and economic reform for every country, in conformity with its national and land tenure system and legislation.

11. The nations must avoid the pollution of the biosphere and the oceans and should join in the effort to end irrational exploitation of all environmental resources, whether non-renewable or renewable in the long term. The environment is the common heritage of mankind and its protection is the responsibility of the whole international community. All acts by nations and people should therefore be inspired by a deep respect for the protection of the environmental resources upon which life itself depends.

12. The waste and misuse of resources in war and armaments should be prevented. All countries should make a firm commitment to promote general and complete disarmament under strict and effective international control, in particular in the field of nuclear disarmament. Part of the resources thus released should be utilized so as to achieve a better quality of life for humanity and particularly the peoples of developing countries.

13. All persons have the right and the duty to participate, individually and collectively in the elaboration and implementation of policies and programmes of their human settlements.

14. To achieve universal progress in the quality of life, a fair and balanced structure of the economic relations between States has to be promoted. It is therefore essential to implement urgently the New International Economic Order, based on the Declaration and Programme of Action approved by the General Assembly in its sixth special session, and on the Charter of Economic Rights and Duties of States.

15. The highest priority should be placed on the rehabilitation of expelled and homeless people who have been displaced by natural or man-made catastrophes, and especially by the act of foreign aggression. In the latter case, all countries have the duty to fully co-operate in order to guarantee that the parties involved allow the return of displaced persons to their homes and to give them the right to possess and enjoy their properties and belongings without interference.

16. Historical settlements, monuments and other items of national heritage, including religious heritage, should be safeguarded against any acts of aggression or abuse by the occupying Power.

17. Every State has the sovereign right to rule and exercise effective control over foreign investments, including the transnational corporations—within its national jurisdiction, which affect directly or indirectly the human settlements programmes.

18. All countries, particularly developing countries, must create conditions which make possible the full integration of women and youth in political, economic and social activities, particularly in the planning and implementation of human settlement proposals and in all the associated activities, on the basis of equal rights, in order to achieve an efficient and full utilization of available human resources, bearing in mind that women constitute half of the world population.

19. International co-operation is an objective and a common duty of all States, and necessary efforts must therefore be made to accelerate the social and economic development of developing countries, within the framework of favourable external conditions, which are compatible with their needs and aspirations and which contains the due respect for the sovereign equality of all States.

*III. Guidelines for Action.* 1. It is recommended that Governments and international organizations should make every effort to take urgent action as set out in the following guidelines:

2. It is the responsibility of Governments to prepare spatial strategy plans and adopt human settlement policies to

guide the socio-economic development efforts. Such policies must be an essential component of an over-all development strategy, linking and harmonizing them with policies on industrialization, agriculture, social welfare, and environmental and cultural preservation so that each supports the other in a progressive improvement in well-being of all mankind.

3. A human settlement policy must seek harmonious integration or co-ordination of a wide variety of components, including, for example, population growth and distribution, employment, shelter, land use, infrastructure and services. Governments must create mechanisms and institutions to develop and implement such a policy.

4. It is of paramount importance that national and international efforts give priority to improving the rural habitat. In this context, efforts should be made towards the reduction of disparities between rural and urban areas, as needed between regions and within urban areas themselves, for a harmonious development of human settlements.

5. The demographic, natural and economic characteristics of many countries, require policies on growth and distribution of population, land tenure and localization of productive activities to ensure orderly processes of urbanization and arrange for rational occupation of rural space.

6. Human settlement policies and programmes should define and strive for progressive minimum standards for an acceptable quality of life. These standards will vary within and between countries, as well as over periods of time, and therefore must be subject to change in accordance with conditions and possibilities. Some standards are most appropriately defined in quantitative terms, thus providing precisely defined targets at the local and national levels. Others must be qualitative, with their achievement subject to felt need. At the same time, social justice and a fair sharing of resources demand the discouragement of excessive consumptions.

7. Attention must also be drawn to the detrimental effects of transposing standards and criteria that can only be adopted by minorities and could heighten inequalities, the misuse of resources and the social, cultural and ecological deterioration of the developing countries.

8. Adequate shelter and services are a basic human right which places an obligation on Governments to ensure their attainment by all people, beginning with direct assistance to the least advantaged through guided programmes of self-help and community action. Governments should endeavour to remove all impediments hindering attainments of these goals. Of special importance is the elimination of social and racial segregation, *inter alia,* through the creation of better balanced communities, which blend different social groups, occupation, housing and amenities.

9. Health is an essential element in the development of the individual and one of the goals of human settlement policies should be to improve environmental health conditions and basic health services.

10. Basic human dignity is the right of people, individually and collectively, to participate directly in shaping the policies and programmes affecting their lives. The process of choosing and carrying out a given course of action for human settlement improvement should be designed expressly to fulfil that right. Effective human settlement policies require a continuous co-operative relationship between a Government and its people at all levels. It is recommended that national governments promote programmes that will encourage and assist local authorities to participate to a greater extent in national development.

11. Since a genuine human settlement policy requires the effective participation of the entire population, recourse must therefore be made at all times to technical arrangements permitting the use of all human resources, both skilled and unskilled. The equal participation of women must be guaranteed. These goals must be associated with a global training programme to facilitate the introduction and use of technologies that maximize productive employment.

12. International and national institutions should promote and institute education programmes and courses in the subject of "human settlements".

13. Land is an essential element in development of both urban and rural settlements. The use and tenure of land should be subject to public control because of its limited supply through appropriate measures and legislation including agrarian reform policies—as an essential basis for integrated rural development—that will facilitate the transfer of economic resources to the agricultural sector and the promotion of the agro-industrial effort, so as to improve the integration and organization of human settlements, in accordance with national development plans and programmes. The increase in the value of land as a result of public decision and investment should be recaptured for the benefit of society as a whole. Governments should also ensure that prime agricultural land is destined to its most vital use.

14. Human settlements are characterized by significant disparities in living standards and opportunities. Harmonious development of human settlements requires the reduction of disparities between rural and urban areas, between regions and within regions themselves. Governments should adopt policies which aim at decreasing the differences between living standards and opportunities in urban and non-urban areas. Such policies at the national level should be supplemented by policies designed to reduce disparities between countries within the framework of the New International Economic Order.

15. In achieving the socio-economic and environmental objectives of the development of human settlements, high priority should be given to the actual design and physical planning processes which have as their main tasks the synthesis of various planning approaches and the transformation of broad and general goals into specific design solutions. The sensitive and comprehensive design methodologies related to the particular circumstances of time and space, and based on consideration of the human scale should be pursued and encouraged.

16. The design of human settlements should aim at providing a living environment in which identities of individuals, families and societies are preserved and adequate means for maintaining privacy, the possibility of face-to-face interactions and public participation in the decision-making process are provided.

17. A human settlement is more than a grouping of people, shelter and work places. Diversity in the characteristics of human settlements reflecting cultural and aesthetic values must be respected and encouraged and areas of historical, religious or archaelogical importance and nature areas of special interest preserved for posterity. Places of worship, especially in areas of expanding human settlements, should be provided and recognized in order to satisfy the spiritual and religious needs of different groups in accordance with freedom of religious expression.

18. Governments and the international community should facilitate the transfer of relevant technology and experience and should encourage and assist the creation of endogenous technology better suited to the socio-cultural characteristics and patterns of population by means of bilat-

eral or multilateral agreements having regard to the sovereignty and interest of the participating States. The knowledge and experience accumulated on the subject of human settlements should be available to all countries. Research and academic institutions should contribute more fully to this effort by giving greater attention to human settlements problems.

19. Access should be granted, on more favourable terms, to modern technology, which should be adapted, as necessary, to the specific economic, social and ecological conditions and to the different stages of development of the developing countries. Efforts must be made to ensure that the commercial practices governing the transfer of technology are adapted to the needs of the developing countries and to ensure that buyers' rights are not abused.

20. International, technical and financial co-operation by the developed countries with the developing countries must be conducted on the basis of respect for national sovereignty and national development plans and programmes and designed to solve problems relating to projects, under human settlement programmes, aimed at enhancing the quality of life of the inhabitants.

21. Due attention should be given to implementation of conservation and recycling technologies.

22. In the planning and management of human settlements, Governments should take into consideration all pertinent recommendations on human settlements planning which have emerged from earlier conferences dealing with the quality of life and development problems which affect it, starting with the high global priority represented by the transformation of the economic order at the national and international levels (sixth and seventh special sessions), the environmental impact of human settlements (Stockholm Conference on the Human Environment), the housing and sanitary ramifications of population growth (World Population Conference, Bucharest), rural development and the need to increase food supply (World Food Conference, Rome) and the effect on women of housing and urban development (International Women's Conference, Mexico City).

23. While planning new human settlements or restructuring existing ones, a high priority should be given to the promotion of optimal and creative conditions of human co-existence. This implies the creation of a well-structured urban space on a human scale, the close interconnexion of the different urban functions, the relief of urban man from intolerable psychological tensions due to overcrowding and chaos, the creation of chances of human encounters and the elimination of urban concepts leading to human isolation.

24. Guided by the foregoing principles, the international community must exercise its responsibility to support national efforts to meet the human settlements challenges facing them. Since resources of Governments are inadequate to meet all needs, the international community should provide the necessary financial and technical assistance, evolve appropriate institutional arrangements and seek new effective ways to promote them. In the meantime, assistance to developing countries must at least reach the percentage targets set in the International Development Strategy for the Second United Nations Development Decade.

**SEE ALSO** *Environment; Food and Human Rights; Housing as a Human Right; Poverty; Shelter.*

**STATELESSNESS.** There are two categories of stateless persons: *de jure* and *de facto*. Stateless persons *de jure* are persons who are not nationals of any State, either because at birth or subsequently they were not given any nationality or because during their lifetime they lost their own nationality and did not acquire a new one. Stateless persons *de facto* are persons who, having left the country of which they were nationals, no longer enjoy the protection and assistance of their national authorities, either because these authorities refuse to grant them protection and assistance or because they themselves renounce the protection and assistance of the countries of which they were nationals. A stateless person, in short, is one who is unable or unwilling to avail himself of the protection of the government of his country of nationality or former nationality.

Statelessness is a recurrent source of difficulty for the country of reception, the country of origin, and the stateless person himself. These difficulties were described in the booklet entitled *A Study of Statelessness* (UN publication, Sales no. 1949. XIV.2), issued by the United Nations in 1949, as follows:

For the country of reception:

1. The stateless person does not fit smoothly into the legal administrative or social life of his country of sojourn. The provisions of international law which determine the status of foreigners are designed to apply to foreigners having a nationality. The stateless person is an anomaly and for reasons of principle or method it is often impossible to deal with him in accordance with the legal provisions designed to apply to foreigners who receive the assistance of their national authorities, and who must, in certain cases, be repatriated by the countries of which they are nationals.

2. Administrative authorities which have to deal with stateless persons, having no definite legal status and without protection, encounter very great and often insurmountable difficulties. Officials must possess rare professional and human qualities if they are to deal adequately with these defenceless beings, who have no clearly defined rights and live by virtue of good-will and tolerance.

3. The fact that large numbers of persons are obliged to live outside the law, as it were, that they are at the mercy of the administrative authorities and are led to adopt various extra-legal procedures to win the favour of those authorities, creates a state of affairs incompatible with a healthy conception of the law.

4. The uncertain status of stateless persons exposes the nationals of the reception countries to various risks. Because of this uncertainty, some abstain from dealing with stateless persons, others protect themselves from risk by imposing onerous conditions. As a consequence, relations between nationals and stateless persons are strained.

For the country of origin:

When the *de jure* or *de facto* stateless person is a political refugee, he often retains a very strong resentment against the regime of the country from which he has fled.

His hope is that sooner or later, thanks to a change of regime, he will be able to return to his own country. He looks forward to that day and in certain cases may seek by his activities and hostile propaganda to hasten its coming.

Once settled in a country where he can re-establish himself, and often set up a home by marrying a national whose nationality he will acquire, his attitude changes. He will become more or less assimilated in the reception country, and it is there that he will tend to focus his interests and affections; his children will feel fully at home there and will have no thought of returning. The process of peaceful re-settlement is complete.

For the stateless person:

Normally every individual belongs to a national community and feels himself a part of it. He enjoys the protection and assistance of the national authorities. When he is abroad, his own national authorities look after him and provide him with certain advantages. The organization of the entire legal and economic life of the individual residing in a foreign country depends upon his possession of a nationality.

The fact that the stateless person has no nationality places him in an abnormal and inferior position which reduces his social value and destroys his own self-confidence.

During the long period of peace and social stability at the end of the nineteenth and the beginning of the twentieth centuries, stateless persons were few and their situation was tolerable. Life was not highly organized as it is today and foreigners, whatever their status, enjoyed considerable freedom. The stateless person succeeded in making a place for himself in a country and finding a *milieu* to his liking. He was free to find employment as a wage-earner, to practice a craft or engage in trade. If his conduct was unobjectionable he was not troubled by the police, which exercised no special supervision over foreigners, and he could lead a more or less normal existence, without his legal disability causing him any serious difficulties.

Since the First World War, in Europe at any rate, the situation has completely changed. The re-establishment of the passport and visa system, the increased control over foreigners, the regulations governing all aspects of social life (work, exercise of professions, food, housing, movement within the country, and so on) bring the stateless person in constant contact with the authorities and make him conscious of his handicapped status.

A number of international problems resulting from statelessness were examined by the **INTERNATIONAL LAW COMMISSION** in 1953 and 1954, when it prepared a draft Convention on the Elimination of Future Statelessness and a draft Convention on the Reduction of Future Statelessness (UN Docs. A/2456 and A/2693). In April 1954, the **ECONOMIC AND SOCIAL COUNCIL** convened (resolution 526 A [XVII]) an International Conference of Plenipotentiaries to consider the two draft conventions. On 28 September of that year, the conference was able to adopt, and open for signature and ratification, one of the proposed instruments, the Convention relating to the Status of Stateless Persons.

A second instrument on the subject, the Convention on the Reduction of Statelessness, was adopted and opened for signature and ratification by another conference of plenipotentiaries, this one convened by the **GENERAL ASSEMBLY** (resolution 896 [IX]).

The Convention relating to the Status of Stateless Persons applies to "a person who is not considered as a national by any State under the operation of its law." The Convention calls for stateless persons to be given the same treatment as that accorded to refugees under the Convention relating to the Status of Refugees (see **REFUGEES**). However, the Convention places stateless persons in a position less favorable than that provided for refugees, in that they are not to be accorded the "most favored nation" treatment given refugees but only "treatment not less favorable than that accorded to aliens."

Under the Convention on the Reduction of Statelessness, a contracting State shall grant its nationality to a person born in its territory who would otherwise be stateless and shall not deprive a person of his nationality if such deprivation would render him stateless. Further, a contracting State may not deprive any person or group of persons of nationality on racial, ethnic, religious, or political grounds.

***SEE ALSO*** *Internally Displaced Persons; Nationality; Refugees.*

**BIBLIOGRAPHY**. Africa News Service. "Rwanda: The Right to Choose," *Africa News* 30, no. 3 (8 Aug. 1988): 6–7. NGO article, in English.

British Refugee Council. "Citizenship Crisis Solved for Plantation Tamils," *Sri Lanka Monitor* 8 (Oct. 1988). NGO article, in English.

Chan, Johannes M. M. "The Right to a Nationality as a Human Right: the Current Trend Towards Recognition," *Human Rights Law Journal* 12, nos. 1–2 (Feb. 1991): 1–14. Scholarly article, in English.

Touman, Khalil. "The Human Side of Family Reunification," *Al-Fajr* 8, no. 351 (6 Feb. 1987): 8. News article, in English.

Vije, Mayan. *Where Serfdom Thrives: The Plantation Tamils of Sri Lanka.* Madras, India: Tamil Information and Research Unit, 1987. NGO report, in English.

**STATELESSNESS: CONVENTION ON THE RE-DUCTION OF STATELESSNESS (1961).** The Convention was adopted and opened for signature by the United Nations Conference on the Elimination or Reduction of Future Statelessness, convened by the Secretary-General pursuant to **GENERAL ASSEMBLY** resolution 896 (IX) of 4 December 1954. The conference met at the UN European office in Geneva from 24 March–18 April 1959 and reconvened at UN headquarters in New York from 15–28 August 1961. The Convention provides for the establishment, within the United Nations system, of a body to which a person claiming the benefit of the Convention's provisions may apply for assistance. Since 1974, such assistance has been provided by the UN **HIGH COMMISSIONER FOR REFUGEES.**

The text of the Convention (A/Conf.9/15, 1961, annex) is as follows:

The Contracting States,

Acting in pursuance of resolution 896 (IX), adopted by the General Assembly of the United Nations on 4 December 1954,

Considering it desirable to reduce statelessness by international agreement,

Have agreed as follows:

*Article 1.* 1. A Contracting State shall grant its nationality to a person born in its territory who would otherwise be stateless. Such nationality shall be granted:

(*a*) At birth, by operation of law, or

(*b*) Upon an application being lodged with the appropriate authority, by or on behalf of the person concerned, in the manner prescribed by the national law. Subject to the provisions of paragraph 2 of this article, no such application may be rejected.

A Contracting State which provides for the grant of its nationality in accordance with sub-paragraph (*b*) of this paragraph may also provide for the grant of its nationality by operation of law at such age and subject to such conditions as may be prescribed by the national law.

2. A Contracting State may make the grant of its nationality in accordance with sub-paragraph (*b*) of paragraph 1 of this article subject to one or more of the following conditions:

(*a*) That the application is lodged during a period, fixed by the Contracting State, beginning not later than at the age of eighteen years and ending not earlier than at the age of twenty-one years, so, however, that the person concerned shall be allowed at least one year during which he may himself make the application without having to obtain legal authorization to do so;

(*b*) That the person concerned has habitually resided in the territory of the Contracting State for such period as may be fixed by that State, not exceeding five years immediately preceding the lodging of the application nor ten years in all;

(*c*) That the person concerned has neither been convicted of an offence against national security nor has been sentenced to imprisonment for a term of five years or more on a criminal charge,

(*d*) That the person concerned has always been stateless.

3. Notwithstanding the provisions of paragraphs 1 (*b*) and 2 of this article, a child born in wedlock in the territory of a Contracting State, whose mother has the nationality of that State, shall acquire at birth that nationality if it otherwise would be stateless.

4. A Contracting State shall grant its nationality to a person who would otherwise be stateless and who is unable to acquire the nationality of the Contracting State in whose territory he was born because he has passed the age for lodging his application or has not fulfilled the required residence conditions, if the nationality of one of his parents at the time of the person's birth was that of the Contracting State first above mentioned. If his parents did not possess the same nationality at the time of his birth, the question whether the nationality of the person concerned should follow that of the father or that of the mother shall be determined by the national law of such Contracting State. If application for such nationality is required, the application shall be made to the appropriate authority by or on behalf of the applicant in the manner prescribed by the national law. Subject to the provisions of paragraph 5 of this article, such application shall not be refused.

5. The Contracting State may make the grant of its nationality in accordance with the provisions of paragraph 4 of this article subject to one or more of the following conditions:

(*a*) That the application is lodged before the applicant reaches an age, being not less than twenty-three years, fixed by the Contracting State;

(*b*) That the person concerned has habitually resided in the territory of the Contracting State for such period immediately preceding the lodging of the application, not exceeding three years, as may be fixed by that State;

(*c*) That the person concerned has always been stateless.

*Article 2.* A foundling found in the territory of a Contracting State shall, in the absence of proof to the contrary, be considered to have been born within that territory of parents possessing the nationality of that State.

*Article 3.* For the purpose of determining the obligations of Contracting States under this Convention, birth on a ship or in an aircraft shall be deemed to have taken place in the territory of the State whose flag the ship flies or in the territory of the State in which the aircraft is registered, as the case may be.

*Article 4.* 1. A Contracting State shall grant its nationality to a person, not born in the territory of a Contracting State, who would otherwise be stateless, if the nationality of one of his parents at the time of the person's birth was that of that State. If his parents did not possess the same nationality at the time of his birth, the question whether the nationality of the person concerned should follow that of the father or that of the mother shall be determined by the national law of such Contracting State. Nationality granted in accordance with the provisions of this paragraph shall be granted:

(*a*) At birth, by operation of law, or

(*b*) Upon an application being lodged with the appropriate authority, by or on behalf of the person concerned, in the manner prescribed by the national law. Subject to the provisions of paragraph 2 of this article, no such application may be rejected.

2. A Contracting State may make the grant of its nationality in accordance with the provisions of paragraph 1 of this article subject to one or more of the following conditions:

(*a*) That the application is lodged before the applicant reaches an age, being not less than twenty-three years, fixed by the Contracting State;

(*b*) That the person concerned has habitually resided in the territory of the Contracting State for such period immediately preceding the lodging of the application, not exceeding three years, as may be fixed by that State;

(*c*) That the person concerned has not been convicted of an offence against national security;

(*d*) That the person concerned has always been stateless.

*Article 5.* 1. If the law of a Contracting State entails loss of nationality as a consequence of any change in the personal status of a person such as marriage, termination of marriage, legitimation, recognition or adoption, such loss shall be conditional upon possession or acquisition of another nationality.

2. If, under the law of a Contracting State, a child born out of wedlock loses the nationality of that State in consequence of a recognition of affiliation, he shall be given an opportunity to recover that nationality by written application to the appropriate authority, and the conditions governing such application shall not be more rigorous than those laid down in paragraph 2 of article 1 of this Convention.

*Article 6.* If the law of a Contracting State provides for loss of its nationality by a person's spouse or children as a consequence of that person losing or being deprived of that nationality, such loss shall be conditional upon their possession or acquisition of another nationality.

*Article 7.* 1. (*a*) If the law of a Contracting State entails loss or renunciation of nationality, such renunciation shall not result in loss of nationality unless the person concerned possesses or acquires another nationality.

(*b*) The provisions of sub-paragraph (*a*) of this paragraph shall not apply where their application would be inconsistent with the principles stated in articles 13 and 14 of the Universal Declaration of Human Rights approved on 10 December 1948 by the General Assembly of the United Nations.

2. A national of a Contracting State who seeks naturalization in a foreign country shall not lose his nationality unless he acquires or has been accorded assurance of acquiring the nationality of that foreign country.

3. Subject to the provisions of paragraphs 4 and 5 of this article, a national of a Contracting State shall not lose his nationality, so as to become stateless, on the ground of departure, residence abroad, failure to register or on any similar ground.

4. A naturalized person may lose his nationality on account of residence abroad for a period, not less than seven consecutive years, specified by the law of the Contracting State concerned if he fails to declare to the appropriate authority his intention to retain his nationality.

5. In the case of a national of a Contracting State, born outside its territory, the law of that State may make the retention of its nationality after the expiry of one year from his attaining his majority conditional upon residence at that time in the territory of the State or registration with the appropriate authority.

6. Except in the circumstances mentioned in this article, a person shall not lose the nationality of a Contracting State, if such loss would render him stateless, notwithstanding that such loss is not expressly prohibited by any other provision of this Convention.

*Article 8.* 1. A Contracting State shall not deprive a person of his nationality if such deprivation would render him stateless.

2. Notwithstanding the provisions of paragraph 1 of this article, a person may be deprived of the nationality of a Contracting State:

(*a*) In the circumstances in which, under paragraphs 4 and 5 of article 7, it is permissible that a person should lose his nationality;

(*b*) Where the nationality has been obtained by misrepresentation or fraud.

3. Notwithstanding the provisions of paragraph 1 of this article, a Contracting State may retain the right to deprive a person of his nationality, if at the time of signature, ratification or accession it specifies its retention of such right on one or more of the following grounds, being grounds existing in its national law at that time:

(*a*) That, inconsistently with his duty of loyalty to the Contracting State, the person:

(i) Has, in disregard of an express prohibition by the Contracting State rendered or continued to render services to, or received or continued to receive emoluments from, another State, or

(ii) Has conducted himself in a manner seriously prejudicial to the vital interests of the State;

(*b*) That the person has taken an oath, or made a formal declaration, of allegiance to another State, or given definite evidence of his determination to repudiate his allegiance to the Contracting State.

4. A Contracting State shall not exercise a power of deprivation permitted by paragraphs 2 or 3 of this article except in accordance with law, which shall provide for the person concerned the right to a fair hearing by a court or other independent body.

*Article 9.* A Contracting State may not deprive any person or group of persons of their nationality on racial, ethnic, religious or political grounds.

*Article 10.* 1. Every treaty between Contracting States providing for the transfer of territory shall include provisions designed to secure that no person shall become stateless as a result of the transfer. A Contracting State shall use its best endeavours to secure that any such treaty made by it with a State which is not a party to this Convention includes such provisions.

2. In the absence of such provisions a Contracting State to which territory is transferred or which otherwise acquires territory shall confer its nationality on such persons as would otherwise become stateless as a result of the transfer or acquisition.

*Article 11.* The Contracting States shall promote the establishment within the framework of the United Nations, as soon as may be after the deposit of the sixth instrument of ratification or accession, of a body to which a person claiming the benefit of this Convention may apply for the examination of his claim and for assistance in presenting it to the appropriate authority.

*Article 12.* 1. In relation to a Contracting State which does not, in accordance with the provisions of paragraph 1 of article 1 or of article 4 of this Convention, grant its nationality at birth by operation of law, the provisions of paragraph 1 of article 1 or of article 4, as the case may be, shall apply to persons born before as well as to persons born after the entry into force of this Convention.

2. The provisions of paragraph 4 of article 1 of this Convention shall apply to persons born before as well as to persons born after its entry into force.

3. The provisions of article 2 of this Convention shall apply only to foundlings found in the territory of a Contracting State after the entry into force of the Convention for that State.

*Article 13.* This Convention shall not be construed as affecting any provisions more conducive to the reduction of statelessness which may be contained in the law of any Contracting State now or hereafter in force, or may be contained in any other convention, treaty or agreement now or hereafter in force between two or more Contracting States.

*Article 14.* Any dispute between Contracting States concerning the interpretation or application of this Convention which cannot be settled by other means shall be submitted to the International Court of Justice at the request of any one of the parties to the dispute.

*Article 15.* 1. This Convention shall apply to all non-self-governing, trust, colonial and other non-metropolitan territories for the international relations of which any Contracting State is responsible; the Contracting State concerned shall, subject to the provisions of paragraph 2 of this article, at the time of signature, ratification or accession, declare the non-metropolitan territory or territories to which the Convention shall apply *ipso facto* as a result of such signature, ratification or accession.

2. In any case in which, for the purpose of nationality, a non-metropolitan territory is not treated as one with the metropolitan territory, or in any case in which the previous consent of a non-metropolitan territory is required by the constitutional laws or practices of the Contracting State or of the non-metropolitan territory for the application of the Convention to that territory, that Contracting State shall endeavour to secure the needed consent of the non-metropolitan territory within the period of twelve months from the date of signature of the Convention by that Contracting State, and when such consent has been obtained the Contracting State shall notify the Secretary-General of the United Nations. This Convention shall apply to the territory or territories named in such notification from the date of its receipt by the Secretary-General.

3. After the expiry of the twelve-month period mentioned in paragraph 2 of this article, the Contracting States concerned shall inform the Secretary-General of the results of the consultations with those non-metropolitan territories for whose international relations they are responsible and whose consent to the application of this Convention may have been withheld.

*Article 16.* 1. This Convention shall be open for signature at the Headquarters of the United Nations from 30 August 1961 to 31 May 1962.

2. This Convention shall be open for signature on behalf of:

(*a*) Any State Member of the United Nations;

(*b*) Any other State invited to attend the United Nations Conference on the Elimination or Reduction of Future Statelessness;

(*c*) Any State to which an invitation to sign or to accede may be addressed by the General Assembly of the United Nations.

3. This Convention shall be ratified and the instruments of ratification shall be deposited with the Secretary-General of the United Nations.

4. This Convention shall be open for accession by the States referred to in paragraph 2 of this article. Accession shall be effected by the deposit of an instrument of accession with the Secretary-General of the United Nations.

*Article 17.* 1. At the time of signature, ratification or accession any State may make a reservation in respect of articles 11, 14 or 15.

2. No other reservations to this Convention shall be admissible.

*Article 18.* 1. This Convention shall enter into force two years after the date of the deposit of the sixth instrument of ratification or accession.

2. For each State ratifying or acceding to this Convention after the deposit of the sixth instrument of ratification or accession, it shall enter into force on the ninetieth day after the deposit by such State of its instrument of ratification or accession or on the date on which this Convention enters into force in accordance with the provisions of paragraph 1 of this article, whichever is the later.

*Article 19.* 1. Any Contracting State may denounce this Convention at any time by a written notification addressed to the Secretary-General of the United Nations. Such denunciation shall take effect for the Contracting State concerned one year after the date of its receipt by the Secretary-General.

2. In cases where, in accordance with the provisions of article 15, this Convention has become applicable to a non-metropolitan territory of a Contracting State, that State may at any time thereafter, with the consent of the territory concerned, give notice to the Secretary-General of the United Nations denouncing this Convention separately in respect to that territory. The denunciation shall take effect one year after the date of the receipt of such notice by the Secretary-General, who shall notify all other Contracting States of such notice and the date of receipt thereof.

*Article 20.* 1. The Secretary-General of the United Nations shall notify all Members of the United Nations and the non-member States referred to in article 16 of the following particulars:

(*a*) Signatures, ratifications and accessions under article 16;

(*b*) Reservations under article 17;

(*c*) The date upon which this Convention enters into force in pursuance of article 18;

(*d*) Denunciations under article 19.

2. The Secretary-General of the United Nations shall, after the deposit of the sixth instrument of ratification or accession at the latest, bring to the attention of the General Assembly the question of the establishment, in accordance with article 11, of such a body as therein mentioned.

*Article 21.* This Convention shall be registered by the Secretary-General of the United Nations on the date of its entry into force.

In witness whereof the undersigned Plenipotentiaries have signed this Convention.

Done at New York, this thirtieth day of August, one thousand nine hundred and sixty-one, in a single copy, of which the Chinese, English, French, Russian and Spanish texts are equally authentic and which shall be deposited in the archives of the United Nations, and certified copies of which shall be delivered by the Secretary-General of the United Nations to all Members of the United Nations and to the non-member States referred to in article 16 of this Convention.

***RATIFICATIONS AND ACCESSIONS.*** The following 19 UN member States have acceded to or ratified the Convention on the Reduction of Statelessness as of 31 December 1994:

Armenia, Australia, Austria

Bolivia

Cameroon, Canada, Costa Rica, Croatia

Denmark

Germany

Ireland

Kiribati

Latvia, Libya

Netherlands, Niger, Norway

Sweden

United Kingdom

***SIGNATURES.*** The Dominican Republic, El Salvador, France, and Israel have signed the Convention but have not yet ratified it.

## STATELESSNESS: CONVENTION RELATING TO THE STATUS OF STATELESS PERSONS (1954).

The Convention was adopted on 28 September 1954

by a Conference of Plenipotentiaries convened at the headquarters of the United Nations, New York, by the **ECONOMIC AND SOCIAL COUNCIL** (resolution 526 A [XVII]). It entered into force on 6 June 1960. The Convention defines a stateless person as "a person who is not considered as a national by any State under the operation of its law." States that ratify or accede to it undertake to grant to stateless persons approximately the same standard of treatment as is granted to refugees.

The text of the Convention (United Nations, *Treaty Series,* vol. 360, p. 117) is as follows:

### Preamble

The High Contracting Parties,

Considering that the Charter of the United Nations and the Universal Declaration of Human Rights approved on 10 December 1948 by the General Assembly of the United Nations have affirmed the principle that human beings shall enjoy fundamental rights and freedoms without discrimination,

Considering that the United Nations has, on various occasions, manifested its profound concern for stateless persons and endeavoured to assure stateless persons the widest possible exercise of these fundamental rights and freedoms,

Considering that only those stateless persons who are also refugees are covered by the Convention relating to the Status of Refugees of 28 July 1951, and that there are many stateless persons who are not covered by that Convention,

Considering that it is desirable to regulate and improve the status of stateless persons by an international agreement,

Have agreed as follows:

### Chapter I: General Provisions

*Article 1. Definition of the Term "Stateless Person."* 1. For the purpose of this Convention, the term "stateless person" means a person who is not considered as a national by any State under the operation of its law.

2. This Convention shall not apply:

(i) To persons who are at present receiving from organs or agencies of the United Nations other than the United Nations High Commissioner for Refugees protection or assistance so long as they are receiving such protection or assistance;

(ii) To persons who are recognized by the competent authorities of the country in which they have taken residence as having the rights and obligations which are attached to the possession of the nationality of that country;

(iii) To persons with respect to whom there are serious reasons for considering that:

(*a*) They have committed a crime against peace, a war crime, or a crime against humanity, as defined in the international instruments drawn up to make provisions in respect of such crimes.

(*b*) They have committed a serious non-political crime outside the country of their residence prior to their admission to that country;

(*c*) They have been guilty of acts contrary to the purposes and principles of the United Nations.

*Article 2. General Obligations.* Every stateless person has duties to the country in which he finds himself, which require in particular that he conform to its laws and regulations as well as to measures taken for the maintenance of public order.

*Article 3. Non-discrimination.* The Contracting States shall apply the provisions of this Convention to stateless persons without discrimination as to race, religion or country of origin.

*Article 4. Religion.* The Contracting States shall accord to stateless persons within their territories treatment at least as favourable as that accorded to their nationals with respect to freedom to practise their religion and freedom as regards the religious education of their children.

*Article 5. Rights Granted Apart From This Convention.* Nothing in this Convention shall be deemed to impair any rights and benefits granted by a Contracting State to stateless persons apart from this Convention.

*Article 6. The Term "In the Same Circumstances."* For the purpose of this Convention, the term "in the same circumstances" implies that any requirements (including requirements as to length and conditions of sojourn or residence) which the particular individual would have to fulfil for the enjoyment of the right in question, if he were not a stateless person, must be fulfilled by him, with the exception of requirements which by their nature a stateless person is incapable of fulfilling.

*Article 7. Exemption From Reciprocity.* 1. Except where this Convention contains more favourable provisions, a Contracting State shall accord to stateless persons the same treatment as is accorded to aliens generally.

2. After a period of three years' residence, all stateless persons shall enjoy exemption from legislative reciprocity in the territory of the Contracting States.

3. Each Contracting State shall continue to accord to stateless persons the rights and benefits to which they were already entitled, in the absence of reciprocity, at the date of entry into force of this Convention for that State.

4. The Contracting States shall consider favourably the possibility of according to stateless persons, in the absence of reciprocity, rights and benefits beyond those to which they are entitled according to paragraphs 2 and 3, and to extending exemption from reciprocity to stateless persons who do not fulfil the conditions provided for in paragraphs 2 and 3.

5. The provisions of paragraphs 2 and 3 apply both to the rights and benefits referred to in articles 13, 18, 19, 21 and 22 of this Convention and to rights and benefits for which this Convention does not provide.

*Article 8. Exemption From Exceptional Measures.* With regard to exceptional measures which may be taken against the person, property or interests of nationals or former nationals of a foreign State, the Contracting States shall not apply such measures to a stateless person solely on account of his having previously possessed the nationality of the foreign State in question. Contracting States which, under their legislation, are prevented from applying the general principle expressed in this article shall, in appropriate cases, grant exemptions in favour of such stateless persons.

*Article 9. Provisional Measures.* Nothing in this Convention shall prevent a Contracting State, in time of war or other grave and exceptional circumstances, from taking provisionally measures which it considers to be essential to the national security in the case of a particular person, pending a determination by the Contracting State that that person is in fact a stateless person and that the continuance of such measures is necessary in his case in the interests of national security.

*Article 10. Continuity of Residence.* 1. Where a stateless person has been forcibly displaced during the Second World War and removed to the territory of a Contracting State, and is resident there, the period of such enforced sojourn shall be considered to have been lawful residence within that territory.

2. Where a stateless person has been forcibly displaced during the Second World War from the territory of a Contracting State and has, prior to the date of entry into force of this Convention, returned there for the purpose of taking up residence, the period of residence before and after such enforced displacement shall be regarded as one uninterrupted period for any purposes for which uninterrupted residence is required.

*Article 11. Stateless Seamen.* In the case of stateless persons regularly serving as crew members on board a ship flying the flag of a Contracting State, that State shall give sympathetic consideration to their establishment on its territory and the issue of travel documents to them or their temporary admission to its territory particularly with a view to facilitating their establishment in another country.

## Chapter II: Juridical Status

*Article 12. Personal Status.* 1. The personal status of a stateless person shall be governed by the law of the country of his domicile or, if he has no domicile, by the law of the country of his residence.

2. Rights previously acquired by a stateless person and dependent on personal status, more particularly rights attaching to marriage, shall be respected by a Contracting State, subject to compliance, if this be necessary, with the formalities required by the law of that State, provided that the right in question is one which would have been recognized by the law of that State had he not become stateless.

*Article 13. Movable and Immovable Property.* The Contracting States shall accord to a stateless person treatment as favourable as possible and, in any event, not less favourable than that accorded to aliens generally in the same circumstances, as regards the acquisition of movable and immovable property and other rights pertaining thereto, and to leases and other contracts relating to movable and immovable property.

*Article 14. Artistic Rights and Industrial Property.* In respect of the protection of industrial property, such as inventions, designs or models, trade marks, trade names, and of rights in literary, artistic and scientific works, a stateless person shall be accorded in the country in which he has his habitual residence the same protection as is accorded to nationals of that country. In the territory of any other Contracting State, he shall be accorded the same protection as is accorded in that territory to nationals of the country in which he has his habitual residence.

*Article 15. Right of Association.* As regards non-political and non-profit-making associations and trade unions the Contracting States shall accord to stateless persons lawfully staying in their territory treatment as favourable as possible, and in any event, not less favourable than that accorded to aliens generally in the same circumstances.

*Article 16. Access to Courts.* 1. A stateless person shall have free access to the courts of law on the territory of all Contracting States.

2. A stateless person shall enjoy in the Contracting State in which he has his habitual residence the same treatment as a national in matters pertaining to access to the courts, including legal assistance and exemption from *cautio judicatum solvi.*

3. A stateless person shall be accorded in the matters referred to in paragraph 2 in countries other than that in which he has his habitual residence the treatment granted to a national of the country of his habitual residence.

## Chapter III: Gainful Employment

*Article 17. Wage-earning Employment.* 1. The Contracting States shall accord to stateless persons lawfully staying in their territory treatment as favourable as possible and, in any event, not less favourable that that accorded to aliens generally in the same circumstances, as regards the right to engage in wage-earning employment.

2. The Contracting States shall give sympathetic consideration to assimilating the rights of all stateless persons with regard to wage-earning employment to those of nationals, and in particular of those stateless persons who have entered their territory pursuant to programmes of labour recruitment or under immigration schemes.

*Article 18. Self-employment.* The Contracting States shall accord to a stateless person lawfully in their territory treatment as favourable as possible and, in any event, not less favourable than that accorded to aliens generally in the same circumstances, as regards the right to engage on his own account in agriculture, industry, handicrafts and commerce and to establish commercial and industrial companies.

*Article 19. Liberal Professions.* Each Contracting State shall accord to stateless persons lawfully staying in their territory who hold diplomas recognized by the competent authorities of that State, and who are desirous of practising a liberal profession, treatment as favourable as possible and, in any event, not less favourable than that accorded to aliens generally in the same circumstances.

## Chapter IV: Welfare

*Article 20. Rationing.* Where a rationing system exists, which applies to the population at large and regulates the general distribution of products in short supply, stateless persons shall be accorded the same treatment as nationals.

*Article 21. Housing.* As regards housing, the Contracting States, in so far as the matter is regulated by laws or regulations or is subject to the control of public authorities, shall accord to stateless persons lawfully staying in their territory treatment as favourable as possible and, in any event, not less favourable than that accorded to aliens generally in the same circumstances.

*Article 22. Public Education.* 1. The Contracting States shall accord to stateless persons the same treatment as is accorded to nationals with respect to elementary education.

2. The Contracting States shall accord to stateless persons treatment as favourable as possible and, in any event, not less favourable than that accorded to aliens generally in the same circumstances, with respect to education other than elementary education and, in particular, as regards access to studies, the recognition of foreign school certificates, diplomas and degrees, the remission of fees and charges and the award of scholarships.

*Article 23. Public Relief.* The Contracting States shall accord to stateless persons lawfully staying in their territory the same treatment with respect to public relief and assistance as is accorded to their nationals.

*Article 24. Labour Legislation and Social Security.* 1. The Contracting States shall accord to stateless persons lawfully staying in their territory the same treatment as is accorded to nationals in respect of the following matters:

(*a*) In so far as such matters are governed by laws or regulations or are subject to the control of administrative authorities: remuneration, including family allowances where these form part of remuneration, hours of work, overtime arrangements, holidays with pay, restrictions on home work, minimum age of employment, apprenticeship and training, women's work and the work of young persons, and the enjoyment of the benefits of collective bargaining;

(*b*) Social security (legal provisions in respect of employment injury, occupational diseases, maternity, sickness, disability, old age, death, unemployment, family responsibilities and any other contingency which, according to national laws or regulations, is covered by a social security scheme), subject to the following limitations:

(i) There may be appropriate arrangements for the maintenance of acquired rights and rights in course of acquisition;

(ii) National laws or regulations of the country of residence may prescribe special arrangements concerning benefits or portions of benefits which are payable wholly out of public funds, and concerning allowances paid to persons who do not fulfil the contribution conditions prescribed for the award of a normal pension.

2. The right to compensation for the death of a stateless person resulting from employment injury or from occupational disease shall not be affected by the fact that the residence of the beneficiary is outside the territory of the Contracting State.

3. The Contracting States shall extend to stateless persons the benefits of agreements concluded between them, or which may be concluded between them in the future, concerning the maintenance of acquired rights and rights in the process of acquisition in regard to social security, subject only to the conditions which apply to nationals of the States signatory to the agreements in question.

4. The Contracting States will give sympathetic consideration to extending to stateless persons so far as possible the benefits of similar agreements which may at any time be in force between such Contracting States and non-contracting States.

### Chapter V: Administrative Measures

*Article 25. Administrative Assistance.* 1. When the exercise of a right by a stateless person would normally require the assistance of authorities of a foreign country to whom he cannot have recourse, the Contracting State in whose territory he is residing shall arrange that such assistance be afforded to him by their own authorities.

2. The authority or authorities mentioned in paragraph 1 shall deliver or cause to be delivered under their supervision to stateless persons such documents or certifications as would normally be delivered to aliens by or through their national authorities.

3. Documents or certifications so delivered shall stand in the stead of the official instruments delivered to aliens by or through their national authorities and shall be given credence in the absence of proof to the contrary.

4. Subject to such exceptional treatment as may be granted to indigent persons, fees may be charged for the services mentioned herein, but such fees shall be moderate and commensurate with those charged to nationals for similar services.

5. The provisions of this article shall be without prejudice to articles 27 and 28.

*Article 26. Freedom of Movement.* Each Contracting State shall accord to stateless persons lawfully in its territory the right to choose their place of residence and to move freely within its territory, subject to any regulations applicable to aliens generally in the same circumstances.

*Article 27. Identity Papers.* The Contracting States shall issue identity papers to any stateless person in their territory who does not possess a valid travel document.

*Article 28. Travel Documents.* The Contracting States shall issue to stateless persons lawfully staying in their territory travel documents for the purpose of travel outside their territory, unless compelling reasons of national security or public order otherwise require, and the provisions of the Schedule to this Convention shall apply with respect to such documents. The Contracting States may issue such a travel document to any other stateless person in their territory; they shall in particular give sympathetic consideration to the issue of such a travel document to stateless persons in their territory who are unable to obtain a travel document from the country of their lawful residence.

*Article 29. Fiscal Charges.* 1. The Contracting States shall not impose upon stateless persons duties, charges or taxes, of any description whatsoever, other or higher than those which are or may be levied on their nationals in similar situations.

2. Nothing in the above paragraph shall prevent the application to stateless persons of the laws and regulations concerning charges in respect of the issue to aliens of administrative documents including identity papers.

*Article 30. Transfer of Assets.* 1. A Contracting State shall, in conformity with its laws and regulations, permit stateless persons to transfer assets which they have brought into its territory, to another country where they have been admitted for the purposes of resettlement.

2. A Contracting State shall give sympathetic consideration to the application of stateless persons for permission to transfer assets wherever they may be and which are necessary for their resettlement in another country to which they have been admitted.

*Article 31. Expulsion.* 1. The Contracting States shall not expel a stateless person lawfully in their territory save on grounds of national security or public order.

2. The expulsion of such a stateless person shall be only in pursuance of a decision reached in accordance with due process of law. Except where compelling reasons of national security otherwise require, the stateless person shall be allowed to submit evidence to clear himself, and to appeal to and be represented for the purpose before competent authority or a person or persons specially designated by the competent authority.

3. The Contracting States shall allow such a stateless person a reasonable period within which to seek legal admission into another country. The Contracting States reserve the right to apply during that period such internal measures as they may deem necessary.

*Article 32. Naturalization.* The Contracting States shall as far as possible facilitate the assimilation and naturalization of stateless persons. They shall in particular make every effort to expedite naturalization proceedings and to reduce as far as possible the charges and costs of such proceedings.

### Chapter VI: Final Clauses

*Article 33. Information on National Legislation.* The Contracting States shall communicate to the Secretary-General of the

United Nations the laws and regulations which they may adopt to ensure the application of this Convention.

*Article 34. Settlement of Disputes.* Any dispute between parties to this Convention relating to its interpretation or application, which cannot be settled by other means, shall be referred to the International Court of Justice at the request of any one of the parties to the dispute.

*Article 35. Signature, Ratification and Accession.* 1. This Convention shall be open for signature at the Headquarters of the United Nations until 31 December 1955.

2. It shall be open for signature on behalf of:

(*a*) Any State Member of the United Nations;

(*b*) Any other State invited to attend the United Nations Conference on the Status of Stateless Persons; and

(*c*) Any State to which an invitation to sign or to accede may be addressed by the General Assembly of the United Nations.

3. It shall be ratified and the instruments of ratification shall be deposited with the Secretary-General of the United Nations.

4. It shall be open for accession by the States referred to in paragraph 2 of this article. Accession shall be effected by the deposit of an instrument of accession with the Secretary-General of the United Nations.

*Article 36. Territorial Application Clause.* 1. Any State may, at the time of signature, ratification or accession, declare that this Convention shall extend to all or any of the territories for the international relations of which it is responsible. Such a declaration shall take effect when the Convention enters into force for the State concerned.

2. At any time thereafter any such extension shall be made by notification addressed to the Secretary-General of the United Nations and shall take effect as from the ninetieth day after the day of receipt by the Secretary-General of the United Nations of this notification, or as from the date of entry into force of the Convention for the State concerned, whichever is the later.

3. With respect to those territories to which this Convention is not extended at the time of signature, ratification or accession, each State concerned shall consider the possibility of taking the necessary steps in order to extend the application of this Convention to such territories, subject, where necessary for constitutional reasons, to the consent of the Governments of such territories.

*Article 37. Federal Clause.* In the case of a Federal or non-unitary State, the following provisions shall apply:

(*a*) With respect to those articles of this Convention that come within the legislative jurisdiction of the federal legislative authority, the obligations of the Federal Government shall to this extent be the same as those of Parties which are not Federal States;

(*b*) With respect to those articles of this Convention that come within the legislative jurisdiction of constituent states, provinces or cantons which are not, under the constitutional system of the Federation, bound to take legislative action, the Federal Government shall bring such articles with a favourable recommendation to the notice of the appropriate authorities of states, provinces or cantons at the earliest possible moment.

(*c*) A Federal State Party to this Convention shall, at the request of any other Contracting State transmitted through the Secretary-General of the United Nations, supply a statement of the law and practice of the Federation and its constituent units in regard to any particular provision of the Convention showing the extent to which effect has been given to that provision by legislative or other action.

*Article 38. Reservations.* 1. At the time of signature, ratification or accession, any State may make reservations to articles of the Convention other than to articles 1, 3, 4, 16 (1) and 33 to 42 inclusive.

2. Any State making a reservation in accordance with paragraph 1 of this article may at any time withdraw the reservation by a communication to that effect addressed to the Secretary-General of the United Nations.

*Article 39. Entry Into Force.* 1. This Convention shall come into force on the ninetieth day following the day of deposit of the sixth instrument of ratification or accession.

2. For each State ratifying or acceding to the Convention after the deposit of the sixth instrument of ratification or accession, the Convention shall enter into force on the ninetieth day following the date of deposit by such State of its instrument of ratification or accession.

*Article 40. Denunciation.* 1. Any Contracting State may denounce this Convention at any time by a notification addressed to the Secretary-General of the United Nations.

2. Such denunciation shall take effect for the Contracting State concerned one year from the date upon which it is received by the Secretary-General of the United Nations.

3. Any State which has made a declaration or notification under article 36 may, at any time thereafter, by a notification to the Secretary-General of the United Nations, declare that the Convention shall cease to extend to such territory one year after the date of receipt of the notification by the Secretary-General.

*Article 41. Revision.* 1. Any Contracting State may request revision of this Convention at any time by a notification addressed to the Secretary-General of the United Nations.

2. The General Assembly of the United Nations shall recommend the steps, if any, to be taken in respect of such request.

*Article 42. Notifications by the Secretary-General of the United Nations.* The Secretary-General of the United Nations shall inform all Members of the United Nations and non-member States referred to in article 35:

(*a*) Of signatures, ratifications and accessions in accordance with article 35;

(*b*) Of declarations and notifications in accordance with article 36;

(*c*) Of reservations and withdrawals in accordance with article 38;

(*d*) Of the date on which this Convention will come into force in accordance with article 39;

(*e*) Of denunciations and notifications in accordance with article 40;

(*f*) Of requests for revision in accordance with article 41.

In faith whereof the undersigned, duly authorized, have signed this Convention on behalf of their respective Governments.

Done at New York, this twenty-eighth day of September, one thousand nine hundred and fifty-four, in a single copy, of which the English, French and Spanish texts are equally authentic and which shall remain deposited in the archives of the United Nations, and certified true copies of which shall be delivered to all Members of the United Nations and to the non-member States referred to in article 35.

***RATIFICATION OR ACCESSION.*** The following 42 UN member States have ratified or acceded to the Convention relating to the Status of Stateless Persons as of 31 December 1994:

Algeria, Antigua and Barbuda, Argentina, Armenia, Australia

Barbados, Belgium, Bolivia, Bosnia Herzegovina, Botswana

Costa Rica, Croatia

Denmark, Djibouti

Ecuador, El Salvador, Equitorial Guinea

Fiji, Finland, France

Germany, Greece, Guinea

Ireland, Israel, Italy

Kiribati

Lesotho, Liberia, Libya, Luxembourg

Netherlands, Norway

Republic of Korea (South Korea)

Sweden, Switzerland

Trinidad and Tobago, Tunisia

Uganda, United Kingdom

Yugoslavia (Serbia and Montenegro)

Zambia

*SIGNATURE.* Brazil, Colombia, Guatemala, the Holy See, Honduras, Liechtenstein, and the Philippines have signed the Convention but have not yet ratified it.

**STATE OF EMERGENCY.** Article 4 of the **INTERNATIONAL COVENANT ON CIVIL AND POLITICAL RIGHTS** sets out the circumstances in which an emergency may arise which would entitle a State to derogate from its obligations under the covenant, the condition under which measures derogating from those obligations may be taken, and the kind of notifications that are to be submitted thereon. It reads as follows:

*Article 4.* 1. In time of public emergency which threatens the life of the nation and the existence of which is officially proclaimed, the States Parties to the present Covenant may take measures derogating from their obligations under the present Covenant to the extent strictly required by the exigencies of the situation, provided that such measures are not inconsistent with their other obligations under international law and do not involve discrimination solely on the ground of race, colour, sex, language, religion or social origin.

2. No derogation from articles 6, 7, 8 (paragraphs 1 and 2) 11, 15, 16 and 18 may be made under this provision.

3. Any State Party to the present Covenant availing itself of the right of derogation shall immediately inform the other States Parties to the present Covenant, through the intermediary of the Secretary-General of the United Nations, of the provisions from which it has derogated and of the reasons by which it was actuated. A further communication shall be made, through the same intermediary, on the date on which it terminates such derogation.

The **INTERNATIONAL COVENANT ON ECONOMIC, SOCIAL AND CULTURAL RIGHTS** contains the following provisions relating to **DEROGATION** from the rights set out therein:

*Article 4.* The States Parties to the present Covenant recognize that, in the enjoyment of those rights provided by the State in conformity with the present Covenant, the State may subject such rights only to such limitations as are determined by law only in so far as this may be compatible with the nature of these rights and solely for the purpose of promoting the general welfare in a democratic society.

*Article 5.* 1. Nothing in the present Covenant may be interpreted as implying for any State, group or person any right to engage in any activity or to perform any act aimed at the destruction of any of the rights or freedoms recognized herein, or at their limitation to a greater extent than is provided for in the present Covenant.

2. No restriction upon or derogation from any of the fundamental human rights recognized or existing in any country in virtue of law, conventions, regulations or custom shall be admitted on the pretext that the present Covenant does not recognize such rights or that it recognizes them to a lesser extent.

The Convention against Torture and Other Cruel, Inhuman or Degrading Treatment or Punishment (see **TORTURE**) provides that:

*Article 2.* (1) No exceptional circumstances whatsoever, whether a state of war or a threat of war, internal political instability or any other public emergency, may be invoked as a justification of torture.

(2) An order from a superior officer or a public authority may not be invoked as a justification for torture.

The Inter-American Convention to Prevent and Punish Torture provides that:

*Article 5.* The existence of circumstances such as a state of war, threat of war, state of siege or of emergency, domestic disturbance or strife, suspension of constitutional guarantees, domestic political instability, or other public emergencies or disasters shall not be invoked or admitted as justification for the crime of torture.

The European Convention for the Prevention of Torture and Inhuman or Degrading Treatment or Punishment contains the following provision:

*Article 9.* (1) In exceptional circumstances, the competent authorities of the Party concerned may make representations to the Committee [European Committee for the Prevention of Torture and Inhuman or Degrading Treatment or Punishment] against a visit at the time or to the particular place proposed by the Committee. Such representations may only be made on grounds of national defense, public safety, serious disorder in places where persons are deprived of their liberty, the medical condition of a person or that an urgent interrogation relating to a serious crime is in progress.

(2) Following such representations, the Committee and the Party shall immediately enter into consultations in order to clarify the situation and seek agreement on arrangements

to enable the Committee to exercise its functions expeditiously. Such arrangements may include the transfer to another place of any person whom the Committee proposed to visit. Until the visit takes place, the Party shall provide information to the Committee about any person concerned.

### GENERAL COMMENTS BY THE UN HUMAN RIGHTS COMMITTEE.

After examining the reports submitted by States parties to the International Covenant on Civil and Political Rights in accordance with article 40 of that instrument, the **HUMAN RIGHTS COMMITTEE** adopted, in 1981, general comments on article 4, as follows (UN Doc. A/36/40, annex VII, paras. 1–5):

Article 4 of the Covenant has posed a number of problems for the Committee when considering reports from some States parties. When a public emergency which threatens the life of nation arises and it is officially proclaimed, a State party may derogate from a number of rights to the extent strictly required by the situation. The State party, however, may not derogate from certain specific rights and may not take discriminatory measures on a number of grounds. The State party is also under an obligation to inform the other State parties immediately, through the Secretary-General, of the derogations it has made including the reasons therefor and the date on which the derogations are terminated.

States parties have generally indicated the mechanism provided in their legal systems for the declaration of a state of emergency and the applicable provisions of the law governing derogations. However, in the case of a few States which had apparently derogated from Covenant rights, it was unclear not only whether a state of emergency had been officially declared but also whether rights from which the Covenant allows no derogation had in fact not been derogated from and further whether the other States parties had been informed of the derogations and of the reasons for the derogations.

The Committee holds the view that measures taken under article 4 are of an exceptional and temporary nature and may only last as long as the life of the nation concerned is threatened and that in times of emergency, the protection of human rights becomes all the more important, particularly those rights from which no derogations can be made. The Committee also considers that it is equally important for States parties, in times of public emergency, to inform the other States parties of the nature and extent of the derogations they have made and of the reasons therefor and, further, to fulfil their reporting obligations under article 40 of the Covenant by indicating the nature and extent of each right derogated from together with the relevant documentation.

The Committee, therefore, considers that it might assist States parties if special attention were given to a review by specially appointed bodies or institutions of laws or measures which inherently draw a distinction between men and women in so far as those laws or measures adversely affect the rights provided for in the Covenant and, secondly, that States parties should give specific information in their reports about all measures, legislative or otherwise, designed to implement their undertaking under this article.

The Committee considers that it might help the States parties in implementing this obligation, if more use could be made of existing means of international co-operation with a view to exchanging experience and organizing assistance in solving the practical problems connected with the ensurance of equal rights for men and women.

### REPORTS OF SPECIAL RAPPORTEURS.

In 1977, the UN **SUB-COMMISSION ON PREVENTION OF DISCRIMINATION AND PROTECTION OF MINORITIES** expressed concern (resolution 10 [XXX]) at the manner in which certain countries applied the provisions of article 4 of the International Covenant on Civil and Political Rights to situations known as state of siege or emergency, and proposed that a comprehensive study of the implications for human rights of developments in this sphere was justified. It appointed one of its members, Mrs. Nicole Questiaux (France) as Special Rapporteur for the study.

Mrs. Questiaux presented her final report (UN Doc. E/CN.4/Sub.2/1982/15) to the Sub-Commission at its 1982 session. In it, she recalled the basic rules of international law and domestic legislation which set out limitation of State power relating to emergency situations with a view to protecting human rights and analyzed the *de facto* impact of states of emergency upon the rule of law and respect for human rights. She observed that, too often, evidence showed that the model of guarantees provided by law was deviated from, and noted that States of emergency tended to become clandestine, permanent, or even institutionalized. The effects were particularly damaging for persons detained on political grounds. She, therefore, strongly recommended a series of measures to strengthen international monitoring of respect for human rights in such circumstances.

The Sub-Commission endorsed (resolution 1982/32) the Special Rapporteur's conclusions and recommendations and asked for the final report to be published and widely disseminated. At the same time, it requested the **COMMISSION ON HUMAN RIGHTS** to authorize it to undertake a closer study of the advisability of strengthening or extending the provisions of article 4, para. 2, of the International Covenant on Civil and Political Rights.

The Commission (resolution 1983/18) called upon the Sub-Commission to give further attention to Mrs. Questiaux's study and to propose concrete measures designed to ensure respect for human rights under states of siege or emergency. The Sub-Commission accordingly (resolution 1983/30) decided to include in its agenda an item entitled "Implementation of the right of derogation provided for under article 4 of the International Covenant on Civil and Political Rights and violations of human rights" for the purpose of requesting its UN Working Group on Detention to draw up and update a list of countries which proclaim or terminate a state of emergency each year and submit a special annual report to the Commission on the subject. One year later, it requested (resolution 1984/27) one of its members, Mr. Leandro Despouy (Argentina), to prepare an explanatory paper indicating how the task which it had envisaged could be carried out.

After examining Mr. Despouy's explanatory paper (UN Doc. E/CN.4/Sub.2/19), the Sub-Commission appointed him (resolution 1985/32) as its Special Rapporteur to prepare an annual report containing a list of States which, during the year, had proclaimed, extended or terminated a state of emergency.

Because the 1986 session of the Sub-Commission was postponed, the first annual report, in a revised version (UN Doc. E/CN.4/1987/19/Rev. 1), was considered only in 1987. It set out (annex I) information concerning the proclamation, extension, or termination of states of emergency by South Africa, Argentina, Bangladesh, Bolivia, Brunei Darussalem, Cameroon, Chile, Colombia, Egypt, El Salvador, Ecuador, Fiji, France, Malaysia, Nicaragua, Pakistan, Panama, Papua New Guinea, Paraguay, Peru, Syria, Sudan, Sri Lanka, Suriname, Turkey, and Zimbabwe. The Sub-Commission, after examining it, expressed (resolution 1987/25) its appreciation to the Special Rapporteur and to the governments and organizations which had provided him with information, and called upon him to continue to carry on the work.

The General Assembly, at its 1987, stressed on two separate occasions (resolutions 42/103 and 42/147) the importance of avoiding the erosion of human rights by derogation and observed that the maintenance of states of emergency constitutes the source of frequent violations of human rights and gives rise to the arbitrary intervention of the authorities in the free exercise of democratic activities.

The Special Rapporteur's 1988 report (UN Doc. E/CN.4/Sub.2/1988/18 and Add. 1) set out (annex I) information concerning the proclamation, extension, or termination of states of emergency, and the resulting impact on human rights, in Ecuador, Nicaragua, Peru, and Zimbabwe, and indicated that the Special Rapporteur was in the process of attempting to verify information relating to other countries received from non-governmental sources. The Sub-Commission (resolution 1988/24) expressed its satisfaction with that report, authorized him to update it so that the Commission on Human Rights would have before it the most recent and accurate information available at its session in January 1989, and invited him to continue to carry out his mandate. In addition, it requested him, in conjunction with the Special Rapporteur on detention without charge or trial, to submit to the Sub-Commission draft standard provisions on emergency situations, including situations of internal unrest or tensions.

The Commission on Human Rights examined, at its 1989 session, a revised and updated version of the Special Rapporteur's report, and approved (decision 1989/105) the Sub-Commission's request that he continue to prepare such reports for consideration by the Commission and the Sub-Commission.

The Special Rapporteur's third annual report (UN Doc. E/CN.4/Sub.2/1989/30 and Add. 1 and Add. 2/Rev. 1) indicated that, since November 1988, at least 25 States had proclaimed or extended a state of emergency, or had continued to take emergency measures, in respect of all or part of the territories under their jurisdiction or control. In addition, he indicated that he had received from non-governmental sources information, which he was endeavoring to verify, concerning such action in 11 other States.

On 1 September 1989, the Sub-Commission expressed (resolution 1989/28) its satisfaction with the report and with the accompanying list of States which have proclaimed, extended or terminated a state of emergency since 1 January 1985. It invited governments to limit the introduction of states of emergency exclusively to situations which are sufficiently serious and exceptional to justify them, particularly in the case of internal unrest, in order to avoid making the use of states of emergency commonplace and thus possibly perpetuating them. Further, it invited governments which have not yet done so to consider the adoption of internal legislation consistent with the requirements of international instruments concerning states of emergency.

In an addendum to his third report, the Special Rapporteur presented his views on model legal provisions applicable in emergency situations as follows (UN Doc. E/CN.4/Sub.2/1989/30/Rev. 1, paras. 28–34):

In his next report, the Special Rapporteur intends to present some model legal provisions that can serve as a reference for States so that their internal legislation on the state of emergency and its implementation will not have a negative impact on human rights and will meet the criteria of lawfulness deriving from relevant norms of public international law.

To this end, the Special Rapporteur would appreciate receiving the preliminary views of the Sub-Commission and the Commission on those of the criteria set out below which they consider to be the most important.

With respect to states of emergency, there clearly exists an international legal framework deriving from prevailing international norms, the practice of international organizations and the internal law of States, which provides a frame of reference for the lawfulness of states of emergency. However, on the basis of the information submitted to him, the Special Rapporteur believes that this legal framework is rarely respected.

The Special Rapporteur is of the opinion that, if, when it proclaims a state of emergency, a State satisfies the criteria of lawfulness derived from that legal framework, then the adverse consequences that the existence of that state of emergency entail for the enjoyment of human rights as a whole are necessarily limited.

Accordingly the Special Rapporteur proposes the establishment of standard criteria and legal provisions based on the following points, which were widely developed in his previous reports:

(a) The emergency situation capable of giving rise to the proclamation of a state of emergency should be clearly defined and delimited by the Constitution, the law or jurisprudence and, regardless of the phraseology employed, the existence of a real and imminent public danger should be clearly specified;

(b) It is essential that the *de facto* situation exhibiting these characteristics should be publicly announced and also reflected in the legal form of the state of emergency, in order to ensure that the population is informed of the restrictions imposed on its rights and freedoms;

(c) The emergency measures taken should be commensurate with the emergency situation for which they are intended;

(d) The part of the territory in which the emergency measures are to be applied should also be commensurate with the geographical extent of the emergency situation and should be officially specified;

(e) Domestic legislation should clearly specify which rights permit of derogation and which rights do not permit of derogation and must be respected in all circumstances; the Special Rapporteur proposes to draw up a list of those inviolable rights on the basis of the various international and regional instruments and international customary law concerning human rights, in order to provide States with a form of guideline to which they can refer;

(f) In all cases, there should be a monitoring mechanism, which could be either parliamentary, upon the proclamation or extension of a state of emergency, or judicial, for the assessment of measures taken against individuals;

(g) By providing for the legal liability of the State, it would be possible to compensate persons who have suffered under emergency measures. This would serve to prevent the misuse of the measures.

The Special Rapporteur believes that, in order to minimize the adverse effects of the existence of a state of emergency on the enjoyment of human rights, it is particularly important that States should endeavour:

(a) to avoid both a legal vacuum and conflicting legislation;

(b) to maintain the powers of the non-military courts and limit the competence of military courts to military crimes and offences;

(c) to maintain the procedural guarantees: in particular, *habeas corpus, amparo* and other remedies having the same purpose should in no circumstances be suspended;

(d) To avoid any *de facto* state of emergency (i.e., a situation in which emergency measures are taken without an official proclamation or in which, after a state of emergency has been officially repealed, exceptional measures are nevertheless maintained). *De facto* states of emergency, like the adoption of excessive measures during an emergency situation, have an extremely adverse effect, not only on the country's internal legal order but also in respect of the most fundamental human rights. Note should also be taken of another serious problem, which the Special Rapporteur proposes to analyse in depth, that exists in some countries, where persons can be arrested and detained, sometimes for very long periods, without a state of emergency having been proclaimed.

The establishment of standard legal provisions as a guideline is thus one way of encouraging States to respect human rights and fulfilling the mandate entrusted to the Special Rapporteur by the Commission on Human Rights, under which he is to propose to the Sub-Commission, for transmittal to the Commission, measures designed to ensure respect throughout the world of human rights and fundamental freedoms in situations where states of siege or emergency exist, especially of those rights referred to in article 4 (2) of the International Covenant on Civil and Political Rights, namely the inviolable rights not permitting of derogation in any circumstances whatsoever.

***ESSENTIAL JUDICIAL GUARANTEES DURING STATES OF EMERGENCY.*** At the request of the Government of Uruguay, the **INTER-AMERICAN COURT OF HUMAN RIGHTS,** on 6 October 1987, gave its advisory opinion (Opinion OG-9/7) on respect for judicial guarantees during states of emergency.

The Court met to deal with this question on 17 September 1986 and concerned itself mainly with the meaning and scope of the final sentence of article 27, para. 2, of the **AMERICAN CONVENTION ON HUMAN RIGHTS.** It considered, in particular, the following questions (E/CN.4/Sub.2/1988/18/Rev. 1):

(a) What judicial guarantees must remain in force during states of emergency?

(b) Do the guarantees mentioned in the last sentence of article 27, paragraph 2, relate only to the procedures for protecting the rights involved?

(c) Since states of emergency very often involve suspension of certain procedural guarantees, what is the situation regarding the principle of exhaustion of domestic remedies?

In its advisory opinion, the Court states that the issue raised by the request of the Uruguayan Government must be considered within a specific legal, historical and political framework, since states of exception or emergency and respect for human rights and for the essential judicial guarantees constitute a grave problem for human rights in America. The Court therefore considers that its opinion may be of practical value in a context where the basic principles involved have often been questioned.

The unanimous opinion of the members of the Court is as follows:

1. The following should be regarded as essential judicial guarantees which, according to article 27, paragraph 2, of the Convention, are not subject to suspension: the remedy of *habeas corpus* (art. 7, para. 6), the remedy of *amparo* and any other recourse to a judge or competent tribunal (art. 25, para.1) designed to guarantee respect for the rights and freedoms whose suspension is not authorized by the Convention.

2. Also to be considered as essential judicial guarantees which are not subject to suspension are those judicial procedures inherent in the representative, democratic form of government (art 29. para. (c)), provided by the States parties in their domestic law in order to guarantee the full exercise of the rights referred to in article 27, paragraph 2, of the Convention, suppression or restriction of which would result in the rights being left unprotected.

3. The above mentioned judicial guarantees must be ex-

ercised in the context and according to the principles of due process of law, enunciated in article 8 of the Convention.

## FREEDOM OF ASSOCIATION DURING STATE OF EMERGENCY.

With regard to possible effects of a state of emergency upon the full exercise of trade union rights, the ILO Freedom of Association Committee of the Governing Body has adopted the following principles (*ILO Digest of Decisions and Principles of the Freedom of Association Committee,* third edition, Geneva: 1985):

*Detentions During a State of Emergency.* The Committee, while refraining from expressing an opinion on the political aspects of a state of emergency, has always emphasized that measures involving detention must be accompanied by adequate judicial safeguards applied within a reasonable period and that all detained persons must receive a fair trial at the earliest possible moment.

Where circumstances approximate to a situation of civil war importance is attached to all detained persons receiving a fair trial at the earliest possible moment.

Due process would not appear to be ensured if, under the national law, the effect of a state of siege is that a court cannot examine, and does not examine the merits of the case. . . .

*State of Emergency.* Emergency legislation aimed at anti-social disruptive elements should not be applied against workers for exercising their legitimate trade union rights.

As regards countries which are in a state of political crisis or have just undergone grave disturbances (civil war, revolution, etc.), the Committee has considered it necessary, when examining the various measures taken by the governments, including some against trade union organizations, to take account of such exceptional circumstances when examining the merits of the allegations.

Where a state of siege exists, it is desirable that the government, in its relations with occupational organisations and their representatives, should rely, as far as possible, on the ordinary law rather than on emergency measure which are liable, by their very nature, to involve certain restrictions on fundamental rights.

Measures taken by the authorities in a state of emergency may constitute serious interference in trade union affairs, contrary to Article 3 of Convention No. 87, except where such measures are necessary because the organisations concerned have diverged from their trade union objectives and have defied the law. In any case, such measures should be subject to appropriate procedures for judicial review that may be invoked without delay.

The Committee has stressed that martial law is incompatible with the full exercise of trade union rights.

**SEE ALSO** *Derogation; Public Emergency.*

**BIBLIOGRAPHY.** Amnesty International. *Egypt: Recent Human Rights Violations under the State of Emergency.* London: 1990. NGO factfinding report, in English and French.

———. *Jordan: Human Rights Protection after the State of Emergency.* London: 1990. NGO report, in English.

———. *States of Emergency: Torture and Violations of the Right to Life under States of Emergency.* London: 1988. NGO report, in English.

Asia Watch. *Punishment Season: Human Rights in China after Martial Law.* New York: Human Rights Watch, 1990. NGO factfinding report, in English.

Asian Legal Resource Centre. *Use of Emergency Regulations in Peacetime in the Region, Workshop Papers, Kuala Lumpur, 5–8 Oct. 1987.* Kowloon, Hong Kong: 1987. NGO conference papers, in English.

Basson, Dion. "Judicial Activism in a State of Emergency: An Examination of Recent Decisions of the South African Courts," *South African Journal on Human Rights* 3, pt. 1 (March 1987): 28–43. Scholarly article, in English.

Corrigall, Jim, Elaine Unterhalter, and Gillian Slovo. *Subverting Apartheid: Education, Information and Culture under Emergency Rule.* London: IDAF Publications, 1990. Monograph, in English.

Funnemark, Bjorn Cato, and Arne Borg. *Irish Terrorism or British Colonialism? The Violation of Human Rights in Northern Ireland.* Oslo, Norway: International Helsinki Federation for Human Rights, 1990. NGO factfinding report, in English.

Garcia-Sayan, Diego. *Habeas Corpus y Estados de Emergencia* (Habeas Corpus and States of Emergency). Lima, Peru: Comision Andina de Juristas and the Friedrich Nauman Foundation, 1988. NGO report, in Spanish.

Hatchard, John. *Individual Freedoms and State Security in the African Context: The Case of Zimbabwe.* London and Athens, OH, USA: James Currey and Ohio University, 1993. Scholarly monograph, in English; bibliography, pp. 197–202.

Himwiingwa, Paulsen Afro. *Emergency Powers in Zambia.* Zambia: University of Zambia, 1984. LLM dissertation, in English.

Human Rights Commission. *State Violence: A Study of Repression and the Links between Security Legislation, Security Management, Vigilantes and Hit Squads.* Johannesburg, South Africa: 1990. NGO factfinding report, in English.

International Commission of Jurists. *States of Emergency: Their Impact on Human Rights.* Geneva, Switzerland: 1983. NGO report, in English.

Koshy, Ninan. "The Erosion of the Rule of Law in Asia," *Human Rights Forum* (March 1988): 1–8. NGO article, in English.

Linfield, Michael. *Freedom under Fire: U.S. Civil Liberties in Times of War.* Boston, MA, USA: South End Press, 1990. Scholarly monograph, in English; bibliography, pp. 259–268.

Luce, D., and R. Rumpf. *Martial Law in Taiwan.* Washington, D.C.: Asia Resource Center and Formosan Association for Human Rights, 1985. Monograph, in English; bibliography lists resources and organizations.

Melendez, Florentin. *La Suspension de los Derechos Fundamentales en El Derecho Internacional Convencional* (Suspension of Fundamental Rights in International Conventional Law). San Salvador, El Salvador: Instituto de Derechos Humanos, Universidad Centroamericana "Jose Simeon Canas," 1987. Scholarly monograph, in Spanish.

Pacheco, Allegra A. "Occupying an Uprising: The Geneva Convention and the Israeli Administrative Detention Policy during the First Year of the Palestinian General Uprising: December 1987-December 1988," *Columbia Human Rights Law Review* 21, no. 2 (Spring 1990): 515–563. Scholarly article, in English.

Regional Council on Human Rights in Asia. *The Law and Practice of Preventive Detention in the ASEAN Region.* Manila, the Philippines: 1988. NGO report, in English.

Shraga, Daphna. "Human Rights in Emergency Situations under the European Convention on Human Rights," in *Israel Yearbook on Human Rights,* pp. 217–242. Jerusalem, Israel: Alpha Press, 1986. Scholarly article, in English.

Stavros, Stephanos. "The Right to a Fair Trial in Emergency Situations," *International and Comparative Law Quarterly* 41 (April 1992): 343–365. Scholarly article, in English.

Sullivan, Kerry S. "Pre-Trial Detention of Suspects in Northern Ireland: A Violation of Fundamental Human Rights," *New York Law School, Journal of International Comparative Law* 11, nos. 1 and 2 (1990): 297–322. Scholarly article, in English.

Zovatto G., Daniel. *Los Estados de Excepción y los Derechos Humanos en América Latina* (States of Emergency and Human Rights in Latin America). Caracas, Venezuela: Instituto Interamericano de Derechos Humanos (Inter-American Institute of Human Rights) & Editorial Jurídica Venezolana, 1990. Scholarly monograph, in Spanish.

## STATES' RIGHTS: DECLARATION ON PERMANENT SOVEREIGNTY OVER NATURAL RESOURCES (1962).

On 12 December 1958, the UN **GENERAL ASSEMBLY** established (resolution 1314 [XIII]) a commission to conduct a full survey of the status of the right of peoples and nations to permanent sovereignty over their natural wealth and resources. On the basis of the work of the commission, the Assembly was able, on 14 December 1962, to adopt (resolution 1803 [XVII]) a declaration setting out its views on the subject. The text of the Declaration, annexed to the resolution, is as follows:

1. The right of peoples and nations to permanent sovereignty over their natural wealth and resources must be exercised in the interest of their national development and of the well-being of the people of the State concerned.

2. The exploration, development and disposition of such resources, as well as the import of the foreign capital required for these purposes, should be in conformity with the rules and conditions which the peoples and nations freely consider to be necessary or desirable with regard to the authorization, restriction or prohibition of such activities.

3. In cases where authorization is granted, the capital imported and the earnings on that capital shall be governed by the terms thereof, by the national legislation in force, and by international law. The profits derived must be shared in the proportions freely agreed upon, in each case, between the investors and the recipient State, due care being taken to ensure that there is no impairment, for any reason, of that State's sovereignty over its natural wealth and resources.

4. Nationalization, expropriation or requisitioning shall be based on grounds or reasons of public utility, security or the national interest which are recognized as overriding purely individual or private interests, both domestic and foreign. In such cases the owner shall be paid appropriate compensation, in accordance with the rules in force in the State taking such measures in the exercise of its sovereignty and in accordance with international law. In any case where the question of compensation gives rise to a controversy, the national jurisdiction of the State taking such measures shall be exhausted. However, upon agreement by sovereign States and other parties concerned, settlement of the dispute should be made through arbitration or international adjudication.

5. The free and beneficial exercise of the sovereignty of peoples and nations over their natural resources must be furthered by the mutual respect of States based on their sovereign equality.

6. International co-operation for the economic development of developing countries, whether in the form of public or private capital investments, exchange of goods and services, technical assistance, or exchange of scientific information, shall be such as to further their independent national development and shall be based upon respect for their sovereignty over their natural wealth and resources.

7. Violation of the rights of peoples and nations to sovereignty over their natural wealth and resources is contrary to the spirit and principles of the Charter of the United Nations and hinders the development of international co-operation and the maintenance of peace.

8. Foreign investment agreements freely entered into by or between sovereign States shall be observed in good faith; States and international organizations shall strictly and conscientiously respect the sovereignty of peoples and nations over their natural wealth and resources in accordance with the Charter and the principles set forth in the present resolution.

**SEE ALSO** *Self-determination.*

## STATES' RIGHTS: DECLARATION ON THE INADMISSIBILITY OF INTERVENTION AND INTERFERENCE IN THE INTERNAL AFFAIRS OF STATES, UN (1981).

In adopting the Declaration, the UN **GENERAL ASSEMBLY** expressed its deep concern at the gravity of the international situation and the increasing threat to international peace and security owing to frequent recourse to the threat or use of force, **AGGRESSION,** intimidation, military intervention and occupation, escalation of military presence, and all other forms of intervention or interference—direct or indirect, overt or covert—threatening the sovereignty and political independence of other States, with the aim of overthrowing their governments; and pointed out that such policies endanger the political independence of States, freedom of peoples, and permanent sovereignty over their natural resources, adversely affecting thereby the maintenance of international peace and security. In particular, it referred to "the imperative need for all foreign forces engaged in military occupation, intervention or interference to be completely withdrawn to their own territories, so that people under colonial domination, foreign occupation or racist regimes may freely and fully exercise their right to **SELF-DETERMINATION,** so as to enable the people of all States to administer their own affairs and determine their own political, economic and social system without external interference or control"; and also to "the imperative need for any threat of aggression, any recruitment, any use of armed bands, in particular mercenaries, against sovereign States to be completely ended, so as to enable the peoples of all States to determine their own political, economic and social systems without external interference or control."

The Declaration was approved by the UN General Assembly on 9 December 1981 (resolution 36/103). The text of the Declaration, annexed to that resolution, is as follows:

The General Assembly,

Reaffirming, in accordance with the Charter of the United Nations, that no State has the right to intervene directly or indirectly for any reason whatsoever in the internal and external affairs of any other State,

Reaffirming further the fundamental principle of the Charter that all States have the duty not to threaten or use force against the sovereignty, political independence or territorial integrity of other States,

Bearing in mind that the establishment, maintenance and strengthening of international peace and security are founded upon freedom, equality, self-determination and independence, respect for the sovereignty of States, as well as permanent sovereignty of States over their natural resources, irrespective of their political, economic or social systems or the levels of their development,

Considering that full observance of the principle of non-intervention and non-interference in the internal and external affairs of States if of the greatest importance for the maintenance of international peace and security and for the fulfilment of the purposes and principles of the Charter,

Reaffirming, in accordance with the Charter, the right to self-determination and independence of peoples under colonial domination, foreign occupation or racist régimes,

Stressing that the purposes of the United Nations can be achieved only under conditions where peoples enjoy freedom and States enjoy sovereign equality and comply fully with the requirements of these principles in their international relations,

Considering that any violation of the principle of non-intervention and non-interference in the internal and external affairs of States poses a threat to the freedom of peoples, the sovereignty, political independence and territorial integrity of States and to their political, economic, social and cultural development, and also endangers international peace and security,

Considering that a declaration on the inadmissibility of intervention and interference in the internal affairs of States will contribute towards the fulfilment of the purposes and principles of the Charter,

Considering the provisions of the Charter as a whole and taking into account the resolutions adopted by the United Nations relating to that principle, in particular those containing the Declaration on the Strengthening of International Security, the Declaration on the Inadmissibility of Intervention in the Domestic Affairs of States and the Protection of Their Independence and Sovereignty, the Declaration on Principles of International Law concerning Friendly Relations and Cooperation among States in accordance with the Charter of the United Nations and the Definition of Aggression,

Solemnly declares that:

1. No State or group of States has the right to intervene or interfere in any form or for any reason whatsoever in the internal and external affairs of other States.

2. The principle of nonintervention and noninterference in the internal and external affairs of States comprehends the following rights and duties:

*I.* (a) Sovereignty, political independence, territorial integrity, national unity and security of all States, as well as national identity and cultural heritage of their peoples;

(b) The sovereign and inalienable right of a State freely to determine its own political, economic, cultural and social systems, to develop its international relations and to exercise permanent sovereignty over its natural resources, in accordance with the will of its people, without outside intervention, interference, subversion, coercion or threat in any form whatsoever;

(c) The right of States and peoples to have free access to information and to develop fully, without interference, their system of information and mass media and to use their information media in order to promote their political, social, economic and cultural interests and aspirations, based, *inter alia,* on the relevant articles of the Universal Declaration of Human Rights and the principles of the new international information order;

*II.* (a) The duty of States to refrain in their international relations from the threat or use of force in any form whatsoever to violate the existing internationally recognized boundaries of another State, to disrupt the political, social or economic order of other States, to overthrow or change the political system of another State or its Government, to cause tension between or among States or to deprive peoples of their national identity and cultural heritage;

(b) The duty of a State to ensure that its territory is not used in any manner which would violate the sovereignty, political independence, territorial integrity and national unity or disrupt the political, economic and social stability of another State; this obligation applies also to States entrusted with responsibility for territories yet to attain self-determination and national independence;

(c) The duty of a State to refrain from armed intervention, subversion, military occupation or any other form of intervention and interference, overt or covert, directed at another State or group of States, or any act of military, political or economic interference in the internal affairs of another State, including acts of reprisal involving the use of force;

(d) The duty of a State to refrain from any forcible action which deprives peoples under colonial domination or foreign occupation of their right to self-determination, freedom and independence;

(e) The duty of a State to refrain from any action or attempt in whatever form or under whatever pretext to destabilize or to undermine the stability of another State or of any of its institutions;

(f) The duty of a State to refrain from the promotion, encouragement or support, direct or indirect, of rebellious or secessionist activities within other States, under any pretext whatsoever, or any action which seeks to disrupt the unity or to undermine or subvert the political order of other States;

(g) The duty of a State to prevent on its territory the training, financing and recruitment of mercenaries, or the sending of such mercenaries into the territory of another State, and to deny facilities, including financing, for the equipping and transit of mercenaries;

(h) The duty of a State to refrain from concluding agreements with other States designed to intervene or interfere in the internal and external affairs of third States;

(i) The duty of States to refrain from any measure which would lead to the strengthening of existing military blocs or the creation or strengthening of new military alliances, interlocking arrangements, the deployment of interventionist forces or military bases and other related military installations conceived in the context of great-Power confrontation;

(j) The duty of a State to abstain from any defamatory campaign, vilification or hostile propaganda for the purpose of intervening or interfering in the internal affairs of other States;

(k) The duty of a State, in the conduct of its international relations in the economic, social, technical and trade fields, to refrain from measures which would constitute interference or intervention in the internal or external affairs of another State, thus preventing it from determining freely its political, economic and social development; this includes, *inter alia,* the duty of a State not to use its external economic assistance programme or adopt any multilateral or unilateral economic reprisal or blockade and to prevent the use of transnational and multinational corporations under its jurisdiction and control as instruments of political pressure or coercion against another State, in violation of the Charter of the United Nations;

(l) The duty of a State to refrain from the exploitation and the distortion of human rights issues as a means of interference in the internal affairs of States, of exerting pressure on other States or creating distrust and disorder within and among States or groups of States;

(m) The duty of a State to refrain from using terrorist practices as state policy against another State or against peoples under colonial domination, foreign occupation or racist régimes and to prevent any assistance to or use of or tolerant of terrorist groups, saboteurs or subversive agents against third States;

(n) The duty of a State to refrain from organizing, training, financing and arming political and ethnic groups on their territories or the territories of other States for the purpose of creating subversion, disorder or unrest in other countries;

(o) The duty of a State to refrain from any economic, political or military activity in the territory of another State without its consent;

*III.* (a) The right and duty of States to participate actively on the basis of equality in solving outstanding international issues, thus actively contributing to the removal of causes of conflict and interference;

(b) The right and duty of States fully to support the right to self-determination, freedom and independence of peoples under colonial domination, foreign occupation or racist régimes, as well as the right of these peoples to wage both political and armed struggle to that end, in accordance with the purposes and principles of the Charter;

(c) The right and duty of States to observe, promote and defend all human rights and fundamental freedoms within their own national territories and to work for the elimination of massive and flagrant violations of the rights of nations and peoples, and, in particular, for the elimination of *apartheid* and all forms of racism and racial discrimination;

(d) The right and duty of States to combat, within their constitutional prerogatives, the dissemination of false or distorted news which can be interpreted as interference in the internal affairs of other States or as being harmful to the promotion of peace, co-operation and friendly relations among States and nations;

(e) The right and duty of States not to recognize situations brought about by the threat or use of force or acts undertaken in contravention of the principle of nonintervention and noninterference.

3. The rights and duties set out in this Declaration are interrelated and are in accordance with the Charter.

4. Nothing in this Declaration shall prejudice in any manner the right to self-determination, freedom and independence of peoples under colonial domination, foreign occupation or racist régimes, and the right to seek and receive support in accordance with the purposes and principles of the Charter.

5. Nothing in this Declaration shall prejudice in any manner the provisions of the Charter.

6. Nothing in this Declaration shall prejudice action taken by the United Nations under Chapters VI and VII of the Charter.

**SEE ALSO** *Self-determination.*

**BIBLIOGRAPHY.** Mapel, David R. "Military Intervention and Rights," *Millenium—Journal of International Studies* 20, no. 1 (1991): 41–55. Scholarly article, in English.

Niyugenko, Gérard. "The Implementation of International Humanitarian Law and the Principle of State Sovereignty," *International Review of the Red Cross* no. 281 (March–April 1991): 105–133. Scholarly article, in English and French.

**STRESEMANN, GUSTAV (1878–1929).** Co-winner of the 1926 **NOBEL PEACE PRIZE,** this former German chancellor was a pragmatist who was ardently pro-German during World War I, but who saw the need for conciliation after Germany's defeat.

Stresemann studied literature and history at Berlin University and economics at Leipzig; he received his Ph.D. in 1902. He worked in the commercial field, on a newspaper, and on the Dresden town council. He was elected to the Reichstag in 1908, the beginning of his successful public career. During World War I, he was an ardent and uncritical monarchist; but he accepted the republic as necessary to maintain peace after the war. He received the Prize largely for his role in the Locarno agreements; he also negotiated a treaty with Russia and was influential in having Germany join the **LEAGUE OF NATIONS.**

**BIBLIOGRAPHY.** Gray, Tony. *Champions of Peace.* London: Paddington Press, 1976.

Schlessinger, Bernard S., and June H. Schlessinger, eds. *Who's Who of Nobel Prize Winners.* Phoenix, AZ, USA: Oryx Press, 1991.

**SUB-COMMISSION ON PREVENTION OF DISCRIMINATION AND PROTECTION OF MINORITIES, UN.** Established by the UN **COMMISSION ON HUMAN RIGHTS** in 1947 under the authority of **ECONOMIC AND SOCIAL COUNCIL** resolution 9 (II), the Sub-Commission is a body of 26 experts in the field of human rights, and their alternates, which meets annually for a period of approximately four weeks during the month of August at the United Nations office in Geneva. It reports to the Commission and, through the Commission, to the Council and the General Assembly.

**MEMBERSHIP.** Originally established at 12, the membership of the Sub-Commission was increased to 13 in 1949, returned to 12 in 1950, and increased to 14 in 1959, to 18 in 1965, and to 26 in 1968. Each member may be assisted by an alternate who is also an expert in the field of human rights. Members and their alternates are elected by the Commission on Human Rights on nomination by their respective governments; the letters of nomination stress candidates' qualifications as experts.

In accordance with Council resolution 1334 (XLIV) and decision 1978/21, the geographical membership of the Sub-Commission is as follows: seven from African States, five from Asian States, six from western European and other States, five from Latin American States, and three from eastern European States. After the 26 members have been elected, the chairman of the Commission draws lots to select the 13 members, and their alternates, whose term will expire in two years in accordance with the following pattern: three from African States, three from Asian States, three from western European and other States, three from Latin American States, and one from an eastern European State. The remaining members, and their alternates, serve for terms of four years.

**SUB-COMMISSION WORKING GROUPS.** In May 1970, the Council authorized (resolution 1503 [XLVIII]) the Sub-Commission to establish the Working Group on Communications to consider all communications drawn to its attention "which appear to reveal a consistent pattern of gross and reliably-attested violations of human rights and fundamental freedoms within the Sub-Commission's terms of reference." The Sub-Commission examines the communications thus identified by the working group, together with relevant information supplied by the governments concerned, and decides whether or not to refer the cases to the Commission on Human Rights. The Commission may then decide what further consideration it should give to situations thus brought to its attention. The entire procedure is handled on a confidential basis. The working group consists of two members of the Sub-Commission from African States, two from Asian States, two from Latin American States, one from an eastern European State, and two from western European and other States. Members are designated by the chairman of the Sub-Commission after consultation with the regional groups and approved by the Sub-Commission.

The Sub-Commission has also established, on a continuing basis, the Working Group on Indigenous Pop-

ulations and the Working Group on Contemporary Forms of Slavery, each having a composition similar to that of the Working Group on Communications. These working groups meet annually, either before or during the annual session of the Sub-Commission.

In addition, the Sub-Commission has set up, on a sessional basis, the Working Group on Detention and the Working Group on the Question of Persons Detained on the Grounds of Mental Ill-Health or Suffering from Mental Disorder. These working groups are open to all members of the Sub-Commission; they meet as required during its annual session.

**FUNCTIONS OF THE SUB-COMMISSION.** The functions of the Sub-Commission and its subsidiary bodies, as formulated by the Commission on Human Rights at its first regular session, in 1947, are

(a) in the first instance, to examine what provisions should be adopted in defining the principles to be applied in the field of prevention of discrimination on grounds of race, sex, language or religion, and in the field of the protection of minorities, and to make recommendations to the Commission on urgent problems in these fields; and

(b) to perform any other functions which may be entrusted to it by the Economic and Social Council or the Commission on Human Rights.

These functions were clarified and extended in scope by the Commission at its fifth session, in 1949, by revision of the first paragraph to read

(a) to undertake studies, particularly in the light of the Universal Declaration of Human Rights, and to make recommendations to the Commission on Human Rights concerning the prevention of discrimination of any kind relating to human rights and fundamental freedoms and the protection of racial, national, religious and linguistic minorities.

At its 1988 session, the Commission on Human Rights expressed its appreciation (resolution 1988/43) for the positive contribution of the Sub-Commission to the promotion and protection of human rights, and in particular for its impartiality and objectivity which results from the independent status of its members and alternates. At the same time, however, it drew attention to some critical comments, as well as to some constructive suggestions, which had been made in the Commission, and requested the Sub-Commission to take them into account. It also set out, in the resolution, a series of guidelines designed to ensure the complementarity of the Sub-Commission's activities with those of the Commission and to maximize the effectiveness of its expert contributions to the Commission's work; and requested the chairman of the Sub-Commission to report to it on the implementation of those guidelines.

In the report which he presented to the 1989 session of the Commission (UN Doc. E/CN.4/1989/37), the chairman of the Sub-Commission's 1988 session stated that that body was endeavoring to apply the guidelines in the fulfillment of its functions and duties and that its members had agreed to review its program and methods of work, in future, on a biennial basis.

**SUDAN.** The Democratic Republic of Sudan is a country in northern Africa, on the Red Sea. It has borders with the Central African Republic, Chad, Egypt, Ethiopia, Kenya, Libya, Uganda, and Zaire. An Anglo–Egyptian condominium from 1899, Sudan achieved independence from Great Britain and Egypt in 1956 and became a member of the United Nations the same year. Its total population is estimated to be 28,760,000. Ethnic groups include Arabs, Africans, and Arab–Africans. Languages in common use include Arabic (official), English, and a number of tribal vernaculars. Religions practiced include Islam (73%), Animism (18%), and Christianity (9%). Literacy is estimated at 20%.

The government (1994) took the form of a provisional military government as was the case from October 1969 to April 1985 when a military regime was in control, headed by Maj. Gen. Gafaar Mohamed Nimeiri, who served first as president of the Council for the Revolution, then as prime minister, and finally, from 1971 onward, as the nation's first elected president.

At least three attempts to overthrow Nimeiri were unsuccessful but the fourth, staged while he was visiting the United States in 1985, stripped him of the presidency and replaced him by a military caretaker regime headed by his own defense minister, Gen. Abdel Rahman Siwar el-Dahab. This regime was immediately confronted with violent protests and strikes by public workers and supporters of President Nimeiri and, at the same time, challenged by rebels of the Sudan People's Liberation Movement, supported by neighboring Ethiopia. The rebel attacks, at first sporadic, soon developed into full-scale civil war.

A civilian government, headed by Prime Minister Sadiq al-Mahdi, took power in Khartoum in May 1986. But talks with rebel leaders were unsuccessful; the United Nations and the Red Cross were forced to end emergency foodlifts due to the mounting conflict, and the chaos in the south was worsened by an influx of ravaging former government soldiers from Uganda and a consequent rise in banditry.

On 25 July 1987, the chairman of the Supreme Council, Ahmed Ali al-Mirghani, announced the declaration of a year-long nationwide state of emergency "in view of the anarchy prevailing in the markets . . . the spread of smuggling in all its forms and the lack of security." Prime Minister Mahdi described the emergency decree as an evil meant to prevent a greater evil and said that the state of emergency would be lifted as soon as possible.

Since the Sudan achieved independence in 1956, it has been ruled by the military for more than 24 years. Its most recent civilian government, headed by Sadiq al-Mahdi, was overthrown in June 1989 by a military junta consisting of Lieut. General Omar Hassan al-Bashir and a 15-member council. In April 1988, that government announced that it had foiled an attempted coup and had executed 28 officers involved after summary court martials.

Since seizing power, General Bashir has declared a state of emergency, suspended the constitution, and dissolved parliament, political parties, and trade unions. The government has detained politicians, trade unionists, and human rights workers; and the press has been placed under strict State control.

*ISLAMIC FUNDAMENTALISM.* The government was increasingly influenced by Islamic fundamentalists, particularly the National Islamic Front, and the application of Shari'a law became a heated question, particularly as to whether it would apply in the south. Fighting between the government and the Sudan People's Liberation Movement (SPLM), and its armed factions, continued in the south despite international efforts at reconciliation and occasional ceasefires. The UN SECURITY COUNCIL adopted a resolution in December 1992 condemning human rights violations in the region, allegations the government denied.

In March 1994 the Sudan Justice Minister and Attorney General accused a UN human rights monitor of blasphemy for saying the punishment imposed under Islamic law violated UN agreements and treaties on human rights.

*DIVISION OF COUNTRY.* Continued attempts to reconfigure the government and political structure of the country were made, including the February 1991 division of the country into nine semiautonomous States, each with its own governor, 66 provinces and 281 local government entities; a gathering of 1600 delegates in April 1991 and creation of a 300-member National Assembly with legislative powers in March 1992. The National Assembly was appointed by al-Bashir and included members of the cabinet and Revolutionary Command Council (RCC) and governors of the nine States.

By October 1993, the RCC had been abolished and al-Bashir installed as president of a civilian government. Sudan was again divided in February 1994, this time into 26 States with increased legislative and executive autonomy.

***SOCIAL AND ECONOMIC CRISES.*** Before being deposed in 1989, in June 1988, with a view to securing international assistance in dealing with these difficulties, Prime Minister Mahdi requested the UN Secretary-General to alert the international community to the grave situation prevailing in the Sudan and to appeal for the emergency assistance needed to respond to the urgent requirements of the affected people. The government also requested the United Nations to support it in undertaking a comprehensive review of the situation; to update data on the number, condition, and background of the affected people; and to develop a comprehensive strategy leading to the early implementation of a program of immediate emergency assistance.

In response to the government's request, the Secretary-General, in July 1988, sent a high-level mission to the Sudan to set up a timetable and an operational framework to reach the above objectives. However, the advent of torrential rains and devastating floods in early August 1988 effectively paralyzed Khartoum until mid-September and wrought additional destruction in several parts of the country. The implementation of the program was thus delayed by two months.

A follow-up mission arrived in Khartoum in late September, travelled to all accessible parts of the country where large numbers of displaced persons had been reported. The findings of the mission were drawn to the attention of the General Assembly, which on 18 October 1988 requested the Secretary-General (resolution 43/8), in close cooperation with the Government of the Sudan, to coordinate efforts of the United Nations system to help the Sudan in its emergency, rehabilitation, and reconstruction efforts; to mobilize resources for the implementation of these programs; and to keep the international community informed of the situation.

On 27 October 1988, the Secretary-General, in a report to the General Assembly, described the crisis in the Sudan in the following terms (UN Doc. A/43/755, paras. 11–12, 22–24):

The immediate causes of the current deep-seated social and economic crisis affecting the Sudan include:
(a) Civil strife in the south;
(b) Heavy rains and flooding in the central and northern areas of the Nile basin that have devastated large parts of metropolitan Khartoum and the communities along the northern reaches of the Nile;
(c) Large numbers of refugees seeking extended asylum within its national territory;
(d) Pockets of drought and famine;
(e) Locust depredations.
As a result of the above, a significant portion of the national population is considered severely affected in terms of nutrition, health, water and shelter requirements. It is also

clear that the most affected are those who are least able to fend for themselves, i.e., those who have been displaced by war and low-income rural people who have been forced by drought to migrate to the Khartoum metropolitan area. Both groups have come to urban areas or to districts free from civil strife because they can no longer provide adequate food and shelter for their families in their areas of origin. Those who have only recently arrived in Khartoum, and are not yet integrated into the urban economy, have been doubly affected by the impact of the floods that struck the capital in August of this year. . . .

The current emergency is believed to affect over 2 million people who are in urgent need of assistance, although not all are accessible. . . .

In addition, a considerable number of people are reported to have lost their homes to flooding in small settlements along the Blue Nile and Atbara rivers. The extent of damage from locust depredation is not yet known, but this is likely to cause additional hardship for a significant portion of the rural people. Altogether, there may be as many as 2.5 million people in urgent need of food, shelter and/or medical attention.

Defining who must be served is often complicated by the unavailability of accurate statistical data about the various populations. In no case has this been more difficult than in enumerating the displaced. As part of the preparation for the present appeal, a review of data concerning the location and number of the displaced who are accessible to relief assistance was carried out by the government services concerned, in co-operation with the United Nations technical team and non-governmental organizations.

The General Assembly took note of the Secretary-General's report; and, on 8 December 1988, expressed its concern (resolution 43/52) about the serious plight of over two million Sudanese nationals displaced or seriously affected by civil strife, famine, and drought. It noted that these problems were in addition to those created in the country by the presence of over one million refugees and recognized the urgent need to take emergency action to alleviate the suffering of these victims and to improve the conditions of life of the displaced population.

The Assembly expressed its solidarity with the Government and the people of the Sudan in facing a grave and complex humanitarian and economic situation, and its gratitude and appreciation to governments and international and non-governmental organizations that had provided support and assistance to the Government of the Sudan in its relief and rehabilitation efforts. It took note of the interim assistance program outlined by the Secretary-General in his report and welcomed his decision to organize a meeting of bilateral donors and pertinent international institutions and organizations in order to mobilize resources needed to implement a follow-up emergency assistance program covering the rehabilitation and resettlement needs of the displaced persons.

The situation was no better when the Secretary-General again reported to the General Assembly at its 1989 session (UN Doc. A/44/426); on the contrary, it had been exacerbated by floods and infestations of insects and by the arrival of thousands of new refugees. Besides dealing with extremely difficult economic and social problems, the Sudan had the additional task, towards the end of 1989, of taking care of more than 1.5 million persons displaced by successive calamities and civil strife in countries to the south.

On 15 December 1989, the General Assembly recognized (resolution 44/151) the heavy burden shouldered by the people and the Government of the Sudan and the sacrifices they were making to host more than one million refugees, constituting approximately 7.5% of the total population of the country, and expressed deep concern that the great majority of the refugees had spontaneously settled in various urban and rural communities where they shared with the indigenous population the already meagre resources and services. It appealed to member States and intergovernmental and non-governmental organizations, and to the international financial institutions, to provide the Government of the Sudan with the necessary resources for the implementation of development assistance projects, and called upon the Secretary-General to mobilize the necessary financial and material assistance for the full implementation of ongoing projects in the areas affected by the presence of refugees.

In another resolution adopted at the same session, the General Assembly noted with appreciation (resolution 44/12) that the Khartoum Plan of Action on Operation Lifeline Sudan, endorsed by a high-level meeting organized jointly by Sudan and the United Nations and held at Khartoum on 8 and 9 March 1989, had been successfully and fully implemented, and that a plan was under preparation for the second phase of Operation Lifeline Sudan in order to meet the relief and rehabilitation requirements of the Sudan's displaced population.

Drought and famine continued to plague Sudan, exacerbated by the hundreds of thousands of refugees, primarily in the southern part of the country and from Chad and Ethiopia. It was estimated by the UN World Food Program that in 1994 three and a half million people would be in need of food assistance in Sudan.

**QUESTION OF SLAVERY.** In 1988, certain practices resembling slavery in their effects, which had been noted in the context of the armed conflict in Sudan, were drawn to the attention of the Working Group on Contemporary Forms of Slavery by the Anti-slavery Society for the Protection of Human Rights, a non-governmental organization in consultative status, as follows (UN Doc.E/CN.4/Sub.2/AC.2/1988/7/Add. 1):

Sudan is today experiencing a resurgence of chattel slavery.

The Anti-Slavery Society recently conducted an investigation into slavery in, mainly, the western provinces of Darfur and Kordofan, and in the capital, Khartoum.

The western region, populated largely by Baggara Arabs, borders on the province of Bahr el Ghazal, the home of the African people, the Dinka. The former are Sunni Muslims; the latter animists and Christian.

The present problem has a historical perspective, but it is more than a localized affair. It is a direct consequence of the five-year-old war between Khartoum and the Dinka-dominated Sudan People's Liberation Army (SPLA).

Armed tribal militias, used by Khartoum to counter the advance of the SPLA, are accused of raiding Dinka villages in northern Bahr el Ghazal, southern Darfur and Kordofan. The militia system is used as an offensive strategy to destabilize the Dinka in the countryside and to preclude Dinka support for the SPLA by depopulating the region. In practice this entails terrorism, and the reward for the militia is the booty that they seize—from goods and livestock to slaves.

In general, there is a link between Khartoum and the militia, which are organized along clan lines. Deputy Defence Minister Burma Nasir, who is credited with the military strategy, comes from Kordofan, where the link is particularly firm. There is strong support in the western area for Prime Minister Sadiq el Mahdi's Umma Party which according to its general-secretary, Dr Omar Nur el Daim, has 22,000 men under arms. There is also a connection between the militia and the army, which supplies them with ammunition. Automatic weapons are easily bought for £70 or £80 sterling. Several militia leaders are ex-soldiers who have personal ties with regional military commands.

The serious problem of insecurity in the west is attributable to an abundance of guns and to groups engaging in armed robbery. The make-up and role of the militia are imprecise, and where their actions merge into banditry is unclear. Young men, acting independently of local chiefs and the army, may also raid the Dinka, and it is common for these various armed bands to clash. The economic gain is the main priority, and the Dinka are easy targets. Despite the mixed ancestry of the Rezeigat, in particular Arab-Dinka, there is an ingrained psychology of racism or Arabism which deems the Dinka inferior.

The Society was informed that between 19 December 1986 until March 1988, over 600 Dinka had been killed in the Abyei area and 400 taken as slaves. This figure has been confirmed by Transport Minister Aldo Ajor, himself a Dinka. The captives are being held in Satep, Meram, Datelia, Kolek, Muglad and Tibum in southern Kordofan. They are sold for between about £18 and £36 or are kept by their militia kidnappers. They work as agricultural labourers or house servants. Males between the ages of 15 and 20 cultivate the fields in the rainy season and in the summer tend cattle. Children aged from 7 to 12 look after goats and other livestock or dig wells. Younger children are employed in the house along with the women that the militia captors "marry". Other women are also used as agricultural labour or water carriers.

The Society has been supplied with the names of 15 Dinkas taken from the Abyei area by Baggara militia at the end of February 1988. The militia are generally accused of murdering adult men out of fear that they may join the SPLA, or supply it with cattle. There have also been reports that slaves are killed after the harvest when their labour is no longer required.

The Society is also in possession of the names of 28 people

captured by Baggara militia on 2 December 1987 from around Aweil in northern Bahr el Ghazal. The militia had attacked on horseback, firing indiscriminately, houses and crops were burnt, and cattle and livestock seized. Those that failed to escape were roped together and marched into southern Darfur. In the same vicinity in March, a group of displaced Dinka travelling to Safaha on the Bahr el Ghazal-Darfur border were attacked by Baggara who abducted four members of the same family.

The Anti-Slavery Society is in possession of documents relating to the sale and ransom of Dinka captives. Children have been sold for the equivalent of between £30 and £50. The Baggara are also willing to release slaves on payment of a ransom (regarded as "compensation"). The detailed accounts appearing during 1987 in the Sudanese English language press suggest that this is common practice when relatives are able to raise the necessary amount.

Apart from direct capture by the militia, the war has created another avenue for slavery, which is the sale of children by their destitute parents. Since the beginning of the five-year-old conflict, an estimated two million southerners, predominantly Dinka, have been displaced. Militia attacks and the army's scorched earth policy have forced them off their land and deprived them of their cattle, the basis of the local economy and society. They head north, where they hope to find kinsmen and employment. But those who do arrive in Khartoum sink into one of a number of crowded, illegal and insanitary camps on the outskirts of the capital.

Since the beginning of April 20,000 Dinka, who walked from Aweil, have been camped in Safaha, a trading post on the banks of the Bahr el Arab, the riverine border between Darfur and Bahr el Ghazal. The refugees, mostly women and children and the old, are severely undernourished. The young men prefer the refugee camps in Ethiopia to the north of their own country.

Children are also sold to the Rezeigat. The euphemism commonly used is "pawning" or "renting". While in Safaha, the Anti-Slavery Society attempted to buy a seven-year-old boy, making it clear that he would be taken abroad, and was quoted a price of £40 by a merchant from Ed Daein who arranges the transactions. Apparently the system is that a prospective buyer pays the parents a fixed amount through the merchant who takes a £4 commission. During March the child-price was usually £30. To avoid the accusation of slavery, the merchant records the names of those involved, and the parents are theoretically able to buy back the child, but at double the original price.

But parents who had sold their children admitted during interviews conducted in Nyala that they did not know the names of the Arab owners, and had no expectation of seeing the children again. Certainly, Rezeigat at Safaha described the children for sale, who were mostly boys between the ages of 6 and 12, as "abid" (slave).

In February, the Society was informed, a child fetched £60; in April the price had fallen to £10. Despite the testimony of escaped slaves now living in Khartoum, and who have provided the locations and names of their abductors, the Government continues to deny the existence of slavery and refuses to set up an independent inquiry.

The Anti-Slavery Society notes: that the ruling Umma Party draws its support from the Baggara Arabs, whose militias are responsible for human rights violations, including slavery; that Khartoum, if not advocating racism, is effectively pursuing a racist policy in regard to its African population, in particular the Dinka; that the Dinka people as a whole are being treated as an internal enemy and are considered synonymous with the Sudan People's Liberation Army.

The Anti-Slavery Society urges the Government of Prime Minister Sadiq el Mahdi: to take all measures to stop the resurgence of chattel slavery; to seek out and punish military and other personnel involved in the practice; and to order regional authorities to end the "renting" of children, and it draws the attention of the Sudanese authorities to the fact that Sudan has ratified the 1956 Supplementary Convention on the Abolition of Slavery, the Slave Trade, and Institutions and Practices Similar to Slavery.

The Society urges the Sudanese authorities to be cognizant of their responsibilities under the Declaration of Human Rights, and the Supplementary Convention on the Abolition of Slavery.

The above information was not considered by the Working Group at its 1988 session because an understanding had been reached between the Society and the Government of Sudan for a factfinding visit to be made to that country in order to obtain more precise information on the subject.

***REPORTS OF EXTENSIVE HUMAN RIGHTS VIOLATIONS.*** After considering the question of human rights in Sudan in some detail at its 1994 session, the UN General Assembly adopted resolution 49/198 on the subject, which condemned the "summary executions, detentions without trial, forced displacement of persons and torture," as described reports submitted to the Commission on Human Rights at its 48th, 49th, and 50th sessions by Special Rapporteurs. The Assembly also expressed its deep concern over repeated attacks by Sudanese Government airplanes on civilian targets and reports of forced labor in southern Sudan; and its alarm over the number of internally displaced persons and Sudanese refugees in neighboring countries, caused by the continuing civil conflict.

In March 1995 the UN Human Rights Commission again condemned the country for its record of summary executions, improper detentions, forced displacements, slavery, torture, and abuses against women and children.

**BIBLIOGRAPHY.** Africa Watch. *Denying the "Honour of Living"—Sudan: A Human Rights Disaster.* New York: Human Rights Watch, 1990. NGO report, in English.

———. *Sudan: New Islamic Penal Code Violates Basic Human Rights.* New York: Human Rights Watch, 1991. NGO factfinding report, in English.

———. *Threat to Women's Status from Fundamentalist Regime.* New York: Human Rights Watch, 1990. NGO report, in English.

Amnesty International. *Religious Intolerance.* London: 1986. NGO report, in English.

———. *Sudan: The Military Government's First Year in Power—A Permanent Human Rights Crisis.* London: 1990. NGO factfinding report, in English and French.

———. *Sudan: Human Rights Developments since 1985.* London: 1988. NGO statement, in English.

———. *Sudan: The Ravages of War: Political Killings and Humanitarian Disaster.* London: 1993. NGO report, in English.

———. *Sudan: "The Tears of Orphans"—No Future without Human Rights.* London: 1995. NGO monograph, in English.

An-Na'im, A. A. "Detention without Trial in the Sudan: The Use and Abuse of Legal Powers," *Columbia Human Rights Law Review* 17, no. 2 (Spring–Summer 1986): 159–187. Scholarly article, in English.

An-Na'im, Abdullahi A., and Peter N. Kok. *Fundamentalism and Militarism: A Report on the Root Causes of Human Rights Violations in the Sudan.* New York: Fund for Peace, 1991. Research report, in English; bibliography, pp. 36–39.

Article 19. *Sudan: Press Freedom under Siege.* London: 1991. NGO factfinding report, in English.

Burr, Millard. *Sudan 1990–1992: Food Aid, Famine, and Failure.* Washington, D.C.: U.S. Committee for Refugees, 1993. NGO report, in English.

Davis, Joseph E. "The Islamization of the Sudan," *The First Freedom* 1, no. 3 (Oct. 1988): 3–5. NGO article, in English.

Dodge, Cole P., and Magne Raundalen. *Reaching Children in War: Sudan, Uganda and Mozambique.* Bergen, Norway, and Uppsala, Sweden: Nordiska Afrikainstitutet/Scandinavian Institute of African Studies, 1991. Collective works, in English.

Human Rights Watch. "Sudan," in *Human Rights Watch World Report 1995*, pp. 52–57. New York: 1995. NGO report, in English

Human Rights Watch, Africa. *Civilian Devastation: Abuses by All Parties in the War in Southern Sudan.* New York: 1994. NGO report, in English.

———. *Sudan: "In the Name of God"—Repression Continues in Northern Sudan.* New York: 1994. NGO report, in English.

International League for Human Rights. *Sudan's Human Rights Record: Comments on the First Report of Sudan to the Human Rights Committee July 1991.* New York: 1991. NGO report, in English.

Lesch, Ann. "Sudan," in *International Handbook on Race and Race Relations*, ed. J. Sigler, pp. 263–281. Westport, CT, USA: Greenwood Press, 1987. Scholarly book chapter, in English; bibliography, pp. 279–280.

Marchal, Roland. "Le Soudan entre islamisme et dictature militaire" (Sudan between Islamism and Military Dictatorship), *Monde arabe—Maghreb—Machrek* no. 137 (July–Sept. 1992): 56–79. Article, in French.

McLean, S., and S. Graham, eds. *Female Circumcision, Excision and Infibulation: The Facts and Proposals for Change*, 2nd rev. ed. London: Minority Rights Group, 1985. NGO report, in English.

Rogge, John R. *Too Many, Too Long: Sudan's Twenty-Year Refugee Dilemma.* Totowa, NJ, USA: Rowman and Allanheid, 1985. Scholarly monograph, in English; bibliography, pp. 185–190.

Survival International. "1,000 Massacred," *Survival International News* 19 (1988): 3. NGO article, in English.

———. "War Wastes Sudan Tribes," *Survival International News* 22 (1988): 1–2. NGO article, in English.

UN High Commissioner for Refugees. "Sudan under Stress," *Refugees* (April 1988): 15–35. IGO article, in English.

U.S. Committee for Refugees. *Khartoum's Displaced Persons: A Decade of Despair.* Washington, D.C.: 1990. NGO issue paper, in English.

**SURINAME.** The Republic of Suriname is a country in tropical South America, located on the northeastern coast of the continent, fronting on the Atlantic Ocean. It has borders with Brazil, French Guinea, and Guyana. Formerly known as Dutch Guiana, it achieved independence from the Netherlands in 1975 and became a member of the United Nations the same year. Its population is estimated to be 413,000. Ethnic groups include Hindi (37%), Creole (31%), Dutch and Indonesian (22%), and Bush Negro (10%). Languages commonly used include Dutch and English (both official), Surinamese (a *lingua franca*), Creole, and Hindi. Religions practiced include Christianity (Roman Catholic, Lutheran, Jehovah's Witnesses, and Seventh Day Adventists), Hinduism, and Islam. Literacy is estimated at 20%.

The government (1994) took the form of a republic. However, both the 1975 constitution and the elected assembly were suspended in 1980 when a 16-man military junta took over and installed a civilian premier. When the premier resigned in February 1987 because he no longer had the support of the junta, he was replaced by a deputy premier, also a civilian.

A prosperous British settlement on the banks of the Suriname River of northeast South America, Suriname was transferred to the Dutch in 1667 by the Treaty of Breda—the British receiving New York, New Jersey, and Delaware in return. Slaves imported from Africa furnished labor for the vast plantations; and, after slavery was abolished in 1863, indentured laborers were brought in from British India and the Dutch East Indies for this purpose. As a result, Suriname's population represents a mixture of indigenous Amerindians and Bush Negroes, descendents of slaves and migrant workers from Africa, India, and southeast Asia, and descendents of British, Dutch Indonesian, and Brazilian settlers. Surinamese of African descent, commonly known as Creoles, vie constantly with those of Asian descent for power within the State.

Self-governing since 1948 as a Dutch overseas territory, Suriname was given full independence in 1975 following a period of acute economic recession that triggered unemployment, inflation, and shortages which triggered riots between the completing ethnic groups. After a brief period of constitutional government, a coup d'etat in 1980 placed Lieut. Col. Desi Bouterse, leader of the so-called February 25 Movement, in control.

When, in 1982, 15 Surinamese civic leaders were arrested on suspicion of plotting a coup, then tortured, and summarily executed, charges of widespread human rights violations were made by several governments, including the United States, and by a number of non-governmental organizations, including **AM-**

NESTY INTERNATIONAL; and aid to Suriname was suspended by the Netherlands and the United States.

Similar charges were made between 1985 and 1987 as guerrilla warfare forced some 20,000 Bush people to flee from their homes into the forests in order to avoid harassment and attacks by Surinamese armed forces.

### REPORTS BY THE INTER-AMERICAN COMMISSION ON HUMAN RIGHTS.

The Commission on Human Rights of the ORGANIZATION OF AMERICAN STATES (OAS) prepared two special reports on the human rights situation in Suriname after investigating the death of the 15 Surinamese citizens in 1982, and a third as a follow-up on the further development of events relating to human rights.

In the first of these reports, issued on 5 October 1983, the OAS Commission concluded that high government officials were responsible for the deaths of the 15 persons. In the second, issued on 2 October 1985, the Commission "again reiterated to the Government of Suriname the fact that despite the recommendation stated in the first Report, to investigate the tragic events of 8 December 1982, the investigation had not been done and the high government officials responsible for those acts had not been sanctioned."

In the third report, issued on 25 September 1986, the Commission noted that the Government of Suriname had taken several political measures which might represent steps toward the country's democratization. Among the developments noted were the following (*Annual Report of the Inter-American Commission on Human Rights,* 1985–1986, OAS publication OEA/Ser. L/II,68, Doc. 8, Rev. 1, pp. 186–188):

In the first place, on November 23, 1985, representatives of the Government and of the three principal political parties of the country—NPS (National Party of Suriname), VHP (Progressive Reform Party) and Kaum Tani Persuatan Indonesia (KTPI)—reached an agreement by which those parties would integrate the country's highest political organ, that is, the Supreme Council (Topberaad).

Subsequently, on February 25, 1986, the Government of Suriname, by decree A-21, put an end to the state of emergency in force throughout the country since September 1980. The Commission, which had recommended such a measure in its 1985 Report, notes this change because it represents a positive step towards reestablishing the rule of law and the civil rights of the Surinamese people.

In May 1986 the three principal political parties the NPS, the KTPI and the VHP accepted the invitation of Colonel Bouterse to participate in the top deliberating council as agreed to in the November 1985 accord. Their participation was limited to political and administrative affairs. The political parties continued to demand general and secret elections before the transitional phase is completed.

On July 16, 1986, Colonel Bouterse named a new government led by Prime Minister Pretapnaarian Radhakishun, a businessman and member of the Progressive Reform Party (VHP). The new government under Radhakishun will remain in office until March 31, 1987, when the transitional phase which began with the appointment of Udenhout's cabinet in 1985 will end. The Government program presented by the new Prime Minister on July 24 made no specific mention of elections and gave few details on the planned April 1987 return to civilian rule. According to the program, further discussions will take place concerning the substance of the political and administrative order. It does not indicate if the military will continue to play a preponderant role in the executive branch of the government....

In compliance with a United Nations recommendation that the member countries establish institutions which warrant the protection of human rights, the Government of Suriname also created the National Institute for Human Rights by Decree A-18 of March 24, 1986. This official institution, staffed with personnel with direct links both to the Government and the military, has among its functions those of investigating and determining responsibility for violations of human rights; submitting the results of its investigations to the pertinent juridical authorities; promoting the teaching of human rights and adapting national legislation so as to conform it to international human rights instruments....

Furthermore, and in compliance with a program for full transition to a civilian government expected to take place in April 1987, the Government of Suriname has pledged that the transition will bring about a democratic and just society; that the rule of law will be guaranteed; that the National Assembly will meet its goal of concluding the transition phase towards a full democracy no later than next April; and a Constitution and the composition of the organ representative of the people be established in accordance with the principles of a true democracy.

However, in spite of this progress, the Commission considers that the right to freedom of opinion, expression and thought dissemination is still severely limited in Suriname. Decree No. 310 of May 7, 1984, mentioned in the Commission's 1983 and 1985 reports, is still in force; it prohibits importation, transportation, distribution, sale, possession, production or reproductions of certain written material.

Although the Commission has no knowledge of arrests being made for political reasons during the period in which this Report has been written, it does know of a case in which a person was arrested for possession of reports on human rights of the United Nations and the Inter-American Commission on Human Rights. Indeed, Dr. Linus Rensch was arrested with his family on February 3, 1986, at the Zanderij airport in Suriname after having found in his baggage a copy of the OAS 1985 Report on Suriname and a UN report on summary executions. Dr. Rensch was taken to Fort Zeelandia, military police central command, where he was interrogated. After having remained in detention for one day without being given anything to eat he was permitted to leave but instructed to report daily to Major Aalspeer of the Military Intelligence Service. Although Mr. Rensch was not permitted to leave the country he now lives abroad.

### RETURN TO CIVILIAN RULE.

After several delays, elections were held in Suriname in January 1988, and Ramshewak Shankar, an agricultural expert, was chosen by a 48-to-0 vote of the National Assembly to serve as the first civilian president of the country since the military takeover of 25 February 1980. The military leader, Col. Desi Bouterse, attended the voting procedure, and the army retained a mild oversight role in the government, as had been provided in the constitution approved in September 1987. Shankar's election marked a crucial step in the return to civilian rule in Suriname.

In July 1989 the Kouron Accord was signed by representatives of the government and the Suriname Liberation Army (SLA), which had been staging guerrilla attacks against the government since 1986 at which time a state of emergency had been declared. The Accord provided for an end to the state of emergency, an amnesty, and inclusion of SLA members in an interior police force. Further guerrilla activity by Amerindians in western Suriname followed the accord.

Following Bouterse's resignation as commander-in-chief in December 1990, the acting commander-in-chief staged a coup and placed former government and military officials in charge in a transitional government. However, a general election, which was monitored by the OAS, was held in May 1991. The alliance group, the Nieuw Front, won 30 of 51 seats in the National Assembly; but, despite not having won the two thirds majority required, refused to form a coalition and insisted upon naming its presidential candidate. After the United People's Assembly gathered, Ronald Venetiaan was elected with 79% of the votes.

President Venetiaan proceeded to reduce the size and budget of the military and its influence over politics, abolishing the Military Council. Bouterse again resigned as commander-in-chief in November 1992 but refused to hand over power to his named successor. When the military high command supported his position, they were also asked to resign by the National Assembly. Bouterse remained politically active in opposition to the government.

**BIBLIOGRAPHY.** Americas Watch and Caribbean Rights. *Suriname: Human Rights Conditions on the Eve of the Election.* New York: Human Rights Watch, 1991. NGO factfinding report, in English.

Amnesty International. *Suriname: Violations of Human Rights.* London: 1987. NGO report, in English.

Caribbean Rights. *The Old Shoe, It Fits?: Report of General Election in Suriname, November 25, 1987.* Georgetown, Guyana: 1988. NGO report, in English.

Council on Hemispheric Affairs. "Brunswijk Brings Battle to Bouterse: Surinamese Government Accused of Civilian Killings," *Washington Report on the Hemisphere* 7, no. 7 (24 December 1986): 1, 7. NGO article, in English.

Inter-American Commission on Human Rights. *Second Report on the Human Rights Situation in Suriname.* Washington, D.C.: 1985. IGO report, in English.

International Alert. *Suriname: An International Alert Report.* London: 1988. NGO report, in English; bibliography, pp. 37–38.

International Work Group for Indigenous Affairs. "Suriname—Call for Support for Indian Peoples," *IWGIA Newsletter* 49 (April 1987): 105–112. NGO article, in English.

Moiwana'86. *Human Rights in Suriname, 1992–1994.* Utrecht, the Netherlands: Netherlands Institute of Human Rights, 1994. (SIM Special, 14) NGO report, in English.

Organization of American States. *Annual Report of the Inter-American Commission on Human Rights.* Washington, D.C. IGO annual report, in English.

U.S. Committee for Refugees. *Flight from Suriname: Refugees in French Guiana.* Washington, D.C.: 1987. NGO report, in English.

Zwart, T. "Consideration of Human Rights Violations by International Organs: The Case of Suriname," *SIM Newsletter* 12 (Oct. 1985): 34–43. NGO article, in English.

**SURVIVAL INTERNATIONAL.** An international non-governmental organization in consultative status with the UN **ECONOMIC AND SOCIAL COUNCIL** (Roster), **UNESCO,** and the **ILO** (special list), Survival International was founded in London in 1969 to help tribal peoples protect their rights. The group campaigns for justice and an end to genocide and educates others about the value of tribal cultures. SI publishes *Urgent Action Bulletin* six to ten times a year in English, French, German, Italian, Japanese, Portuguese, and Spanish; *Survival International News* twice a year in English and French; and *Survival International Annual Review* in English.

Survival International. Address: 310 Edgware Road, London W2 1DY, UK. Telephone: (44-71) 723-5535. Fax: (44-71) 723-4059. Director General: Stephen Corry.

**SUTTNER, BERTHA VON (1843–1914).** This Austrian pacifist was awarded the 1905 **NOBEL PEACE PRIZE,** the first woman to achieve this recognition. Bertha von Suttner had worked as Alfred Nobel's secretary for a year and has been credited with influencing him to provide money for the Peace Prize in his will.

Born Countess von Kinsky in Prague, Hungary, she married Baron Arthur Gundaccar von Suttner in 1876. Despite her aristocratic background, she believed that new social standards would evolve that would lead to a greater understanding not only among people but among nations. Her 1884 novel *Die Waffen Nieder* (Lay Down Your Arms) was an international success. In 1891, Suttner founded the Austrian Peace Organization; from 1892 to 1899, she edited the journal *Die Waffen Nieder,* the title of which had been taken from her novel. Throughout the rest of her life (she died on the eve of World War I), she worked unceasingly for peace, disarmament, and European unification and against imperialism.

**BIBLIOGRAPHY.** Gray, Tony. *Champions of Peace.* London: Paddington Press, 1976.

Schlessinger, Bernard S., and June Schlessinger, eds. *Who's Who of Nobel Prize Winners*. Phoenix, AZ, USA: Oryx Press, 1991.

**SWAZILAND.** The Kingdom of Swaziland is a land-locked country in southern Africa. It has borders with Mozambique and South Africa. Constituted a British protectorate in 1963, it achieved independence in 1968 and became a member of the United Nations the same year. Its population is estimated to be 925,000. Ethnic groups include Swazis, Zulus, and persons of non-African descent. Languages commonly used include Siswati and English (both official). Religions practiced include Christianity (77%) and Animism and other indigenous faiths (27%). Literacy is estimated to be 65%.

The government (1994) took the form of a monarchy and member of the Commonwealth of Nations, of which the British monarch is the symbolic head. Swaziland's King Mswati III is ruler and head of State. The prime minister, appointed by the king, is head of government.

The former king, in 1973, suspended the constitution and political parties and assumed total power for himself. After his death in 1982, a general election was held in 1983 at which 40 members of the National Assembly were elected. The new king, installed in 1986, abolished the Supreme Council that had exercised State power since 1982. The judiciary includes national courts, traditional courts, the High Court, and the Court of Appeal.

*DEMOCRATIC CHANGES.* Electoral changes in October 1992 resulted in the National Assembly expanding to 65 deputies, 10 appointed by the king and 55 elected from among candidates nominated by the *Tinkhundla,* or local regional councils. The Senate was comprised of 20 members appointed by the king and 10 selected by the National Assembly. Elections were held in September and October 1993. Despite the reforms and contrary to law, opposition parties were formed, some of which comprised the alliance of organizations called the Convention for a Full Democratic Swaziland, established in December 1992 with the aim of demanding the full freedom of opposition political activity.

A new constitution, encompassing 92 electoral reforms is forecast to be drafted by a five-member committee appointed by the country's king.

In 1993 Swaziland, Mozambique and the UN **HIGH COMMISSIONER FOR REFUGEES** agreed to a plan to repatriate 24,000 Mozambicans from Swaziland.

**BIBLIOGRAPHY.** Amnesty International. *Swaziland: Detentions under the 60-Day Law.* London: 1985. NGO report, in English.

Amoah, P.K.A. "Independence of the Judiciary in Botswana, Lesotho and Swaziland," *CIJL Bulletin* nos. 10 and 11 (April–October 1987): 16–32. NGO article, in English.

———. "Swaziland: Human Rights Situation since May 1982." September 1985. Unpublished conference paper, in English.

Armstrong, Alice, ed. *Women and Law in Southern Africa.* Harare, Zimbabwe: Zimbabwe Publishing House, 1987. Scholarly edited collection, in English.

Maope, K. A. *Human Rights in Botswana, Lesotho and Swaziland: A Survey of the BOLESWA Countries.* Roma, Lesotho: Institute of Southern African Studies, 1986. NGO report, in English.

Neff, Stephen C. "Human Rights in Africa: Thoughts on the African Charter on Human and Peoples' Rights in the Light of Case Law from Botswana, Lesotho, and Swaziland," *International and Comparative Law Quarterly* 33 (1984): 331–347. Scholarly article, in English.

———. *Human Rights in Botswana, Lesotho and Swaziland: Implications of Adherence to International Human Rights Treaties.* Roma, Lesotho: Institute of Southern Africa Studies, 1986. Scholarly study, in English.

**SWEDEN.** The Kingdom of Sweden is a country occupying the eastern part of the Scandinavian Peninsula in northern Europe, on the Baltic Sea and the Gulf of Bothnia. It has borders with Denmark, Finland, and Norway. It was never other than independent and became a member of the United Nations in 1946. Its total population is estimated to be 8,619,000. The Finnish people living in Sweden, in areas close to Finland, comprise a national minority of about 30,000 persons. Ethnic groups include the Sami, about 17,000; Jews, about 16,000; and three distinct Gypsy groups: descendents of immigrants during the 19th century, about 1,400; postwar immigrants from Finland, about 3,000; and other postwar immigrants, about 1,700. Languages commonly used include Swedish (official), Finnish, English, Catalan, Lithuanian, Punjabi, Tamil, and Telegu; in 1982–1983, instruction was given in 55 languages to 55,000 students by 4,300 teachers. Christianity (Swedish Lutheran, the established national Church, 95%; Pentecost Movement, Mission Covenant Church of Sweden, Swedish Baptist Church, and other Protestant denominations, 2%; Roman Catholic and Orthodox Catholic, 2%) is the predominant religion; Judaism is the faith of about 1%. Literacy is estimated at 99%.

The government (1994) took the form of a monarchy. King Carl XVI Gustaf is sovereign and head of State but does not participate in the government. The prime minister, Ingvar Carlsson, elected by the *Riksdag,* exercises executive authority as head of government. Under the 1975 constitution, the unicameral *Riksdag,* composed of 349 members chosen in general elections for terms of three years, is the central organ or government. In the elections, 310 members are picked by voters in the 28 constituencies; the remaining 29 seats constitute a nationwide pool intended to provide proportionality to political parties that receive at least 4% of the vote. The administration of justice is entirely independent of the remainder of the government. The judiciary includes an "Equal Opportunities Ombudsman" to assist in the resolution of disputes or claims of discrimination. Political parties include the Social Democratic Party, the Conservative Party, the Center Party, the Liberal Party, and the Communist Party.

Partly because it averted involvement in both world wars, making neutrality the basis of its foreign policy, Sweden was able to achieve great prosperity and social progress during the 20th century. This enabled it to pioneer actions to ensure all its citizens the right to health, the right to housing, the right to job security, and the elimination of discrimination, particularly on the ground of sex. Supervision of the application of such measures is in the hands of the Equal Opportunities Ombudsman.

### INDIGENOUS SAMI POPULATION.

Like Norway and Finland, Sweden has a sizable indigenous Sami population living in its northern areas, engaged largely in the breeding of reindeer. Tourism, forestry, and the construction of hydroelectric power plants have intruded on the activities of the Samis; and a government commission to deal with their problems was established in 1982. The main functions of the commission are (a) to give a clear indication of the special needs of the Samis as an indigenous population, (b) to examine the need to strengthen the legal position of the Samis in matters related to reindeer breeding, (c) to consider the need for a new popularly elected Sami body to represent the Samis on various occasions, and (d) to investigate the legislation and practice of the courts as regards the balancing of the interests of the Sami reindeer breeders and those of companies engaged in forestry, municipal development, and mining.

Under the Sami School Ordinance, Sami children have the right to fulfil their compulsory school attendance at a Sami school instead of an ordinary primary school. They are taught in the Sami language as well as in Swedish; they may also be taught the Sami language if they have not learned it at home.

Since 1751, Sweden and Norway have entered into agreements periodically to regulate the right of Swedish and Norwegian Samis to cross the frontier with their reindeer on their way to traditional summer pastures in Norway and winter pastures in Sweden. The latest convention was concluded in 1972.

As regards aliens, immigrants, and other non-nationals, guidelines issued by the Swedish parliament in 1975 provide that all such persons should be treated with the aim of achieving equality. In accordance with this principle, all immigrants are entitled to virtually the same social benefits as native Swedes, non-Swedish persons have the right to vote and to stand for office in local and regional elections if they have been residents of the country for the three preceding years, and all children with a mother tongue other than Swedish are entitled to training and instruction in their "home language," as well as in Swedish, subject to decision by their parents. The aim of this arrangement is to develop bilingualism.

### SOCIAL WELFARE CHANGES.

The 1990s brought reductions in social welfare provisions, privatization of many State-owned companies and reduction in personal income taxes.

When the Social Democrats failed to win a majority in the Riksdag in general elections in September 1991, although they retained the largest number of seats, and the leader of the Moderates, Carl Bildt, formed a coalition and became the new prime minister. His government hastened the move towards privatization and reduction in welfare provisions. However, following proposals to allow private hospitals and medical practices, which were defeated, the coalition lost the support of the right-wing New Democracy Party.

In August 1994 the Social Democratic Labor Party won 162 of the 349 seats in the Riksdag and formed a government which was to create coalitions on the basis of individual issues. Ingvar Carlsson again became prime minister. The New Democracy Party lost all 25 of its seats because it did not receive 4% of the overall vote as required by the constitution.

Sweden became a full member of the European Union on January 1, 1995. A national referendum in November 1994 had shown 52% support for the move among the 82% of voters who participated. The turnout was the highest recorded for a referendum.

**BIBLIOGRAPHY.** Amnesty International. *Conscientious Objection to Military Service.* London: 1988. NGO report, in English.

Article 19. *Freedom of Expression and Information in Sweden.* London: 1991. NGO factfinding report, in English.

Beach, Hugh. *The Saami of Lapland.* London: Minority Rights Groups, 1988. NGO report, in English.

Brostad, J., J. Dahl, A. Gray, et al., eds. *Native Power: The Quest for Autonomy and Nationhood of Indigenous Peoples.* Oslo, Norway: International Work Group for Indigenous Affairs and Universitetsforlaget, 1985. Scholarly edited collection, in English.

Davey, Sheila. *Children and Pornography: A Survey of the Protection of Minors against Pornography.* Geneva, Switzerland: International Catholic Child Bureau, 1988. NGO report, in English.

International Work Group for Indigenous Affairs. *Self-Determination and Indigenous Peoples: Saami Rights and Northern*

*Perspectives.* Copenhagen, Denmark: 1987. NGO conference proceedings, in English.

Korsmo, Fae L. "Nordic Security and the Saami Minority: Territorial Rights in Northern Fennoscandia," *Human Rights Quarterly* 10, no. 4 (Nov. 1988): 509–524. Scholarly article, in English.

Minority Rights Group. *Co-existence in Some Plural European Societies.* London: 1986. NGO report, in English.

Nobel, Peter. "What Happened with Sweden's Refugee Policies?" *International Journal of Refugee Law* 2, no. 2 (April 1990): 265–273. Scholarly article, in English.

Robert, Jacques, ed. "Colloque franco-suédois sur 'les nouveaux enjeux des droits de l'homme' (Stockholm, 20–21 avril 1989)" (Franco-Swedish Colloquium on 'New Implications for Human Rights' [Stockholm, April 20–21, 1989]), *Revue du droit public* 106, no. 5 (Sept.–Oct. 1990): 1229–1402. Scholarly conference papers, in French.

Whitaker, Alan. "Radiation in Lappland," *Anti-Slavery Newsletter* 2, no. 7 (1986): 1. NGO article, in English.

Zentrale Dokumentationsstelle der Freien Wohlfahrtspflege fur Fluchtlinge and European Legal Network on Asylum. *European Lawyers Workshop on Detention, Choice of Residence and Freedom of Movement of Asylum Seekers and Refugees.* Bonn, Germany 1987. NGO conference report, in English.

**SWITZERLAND.** The Swiss Confederation is a country in western Europe consisting of 23 sovereign cantons. It has borders with Austria, France, Italy, Liechtenstein, and Germany. It achieved independence from the Holy Roman Empire in 1648, and its independence and neutrality were recognized and guaranteed by the Congress of Vienna in 1815. Although not a member of the United Nations, Switzerland has observer status there.

Switzerland's population is estimated to be 6,848,000. Ethnic groups include persons of Gypsy descent and temporary migrant workers from southern European countries; national groups include German, French, and Italian. Languages in common use include German (65%), French (19%), Italian (8%), and Romansch and others (8%). Christianity (Roman Catholic, 47%; Protestant denominations, 45%; others, 8%) is the predominant religion. Literacy is estimated at 99%.

The government (1994) took the form of a federal republic. The main organ of government is the bicameral legislature, consisting of the 46-member *Standerat,* or State Council, and the 200-member *Nationalrat,* or National Council. All members are elected for terms of four years. Members of the *Standerat* are elected by the cantons by whatever methods they themselves adopt and are paid by the cantons which they represent. Because two of the 23 cantons are politically divided, each half-canton elects one member. Members of the *Nationalrat* are elected directly by a system of proportional representation; the number of members elected in each canton corresponds to the population

of that canton. They are paid out of federal funds. Executive authority is exercised by the *Bundesrat,* or Federal Council, which consists of seven members elected by joint sessions of the two parliamentary bodies. The president of the Federal Council is called president of the confederation; he serves in this post for one year and is not immediately eligible for re-election. The vice president, elected by the same procedure, also serves for one year. He is not eligible for re-election to this post but may, and usually is, elected to succeed the outgoing president. The judiciary is headed by the *Bundesgericht,* or Federal Tribunal, members of which are appointed by the federal assembly for terms of six years. This court deals primarily with suits between the federation and the cantons and between one canton and another. It is also a court of appeal against decisions of other federal authorities.

In national elections held on 18 October 1987, the four-party coalition government—composed of the Social Democratic Party, the Radical Democratic Party, the Christian-Democratic Party, and the People's Party—retained its overwhelming parliamentary majority. Other political parties include the Liberals, the Independents, the National Campaign/Vigilance, the Evangelical Party, the Progressive Organizations Party, and two environmentalist groups—the Green Party and the Auto Party.

Switzerland has prospered because of its strategic location in central Europe and because of its strict neutrality, maintained through World Wars I and II. Geneva was the seat of the **LEAGUE OF NATIONS** and now houses the European office of the **UNITED NATIONS** and the headquarters of many intergovernmental organizations, including the **INTERNATIONAL LABOR ORGANIZATION** and the **WORLD HEALTH ORGANIZATION.**

In November 1989, the people of Switzerland voted to keep the Swiss army of 625,000 men, although it has not fought in a foreign war since 1915, as the best way of maintaining Swiss neutrality. The vote was taken as a result of an initiative, signed by 111,300 Swiss citizens, to adopt a constitutional amendment which stated that "Switzerland has no army." More than 35% of those who voted—over a million people—favored the amendment, while about 65%—nearly two million—opposed it.

The four-party coalition continued to see a decline in support in the elections to the National Council in October 1991 when it won only 149 of 200 seats, a decrease of ten seats. The Green Party increased its seats to 14 and the Automobile Party increased from two to eight seats, campaigning on a platform urging restrictions on immigration.

In national referenda in 1992 Swiss voters approved membership in the IMF and the World Bank but rejected membership in the European Economic Area, a free trade zone encompassing the EFTA and EU member States.

Following disclosure in February 1990 of the existence of over 900,000 secret files on 200,000 Swiss and foreign nationals, rioting occurred. The government opened most of the files to the public and initiated an investigation. It was disclosed in the report, published in June 1993, that the surveillance had focused on left-wing organizations since 1945.

**BIBLIOGRAPHY.** Amnesty International. *Conscientious Objection to Military Service.* London: 1988. NGO report, in English.

———. *Switzerland: Allegations of Ill-Treatment in Police Custody.* London: 1994. NGO report, in English.

———. "Switzerland: Refoulement," 2 January 1987. NGO urgent action bulletin, in English.

Caloz-Tscopp, Marie-Claire, and Jean-François Paroz. "La politique étrangère de la Suisse et les droits de l'homme: entretien avec Jean-Daniel Vigny, chef du service des droits de l'homme au département fédéral des affaires étrangères" (Swiss Foreign Policy and Human Rights: Interview with Jean-Daniel Vigny, Head of the Human Rights Division, Federal Department of Foreign Affairs), *Equinoxe—Revue romande des sciences humaines* no. 4 (Fall 1990): 151–159. Interview, in French.

Kalin, Walter. "The Legal Condition of Refugees in Switzerland," *Journal of Refugee Studies* 7, no. 1 (1994): 82–95. Scholarly article, in English.

Minority Rights Group. *Co-existence in Some Plural European Societies.* London: 1986. NGO report, in English.

Sigler, Jay A., ed. *International Handbook on Race and Race Relations.* Westport, CT, USA: Greenwood Press, 1987. Scholarly edited collection, in English; bibliography, pp. 449–454.

**SYRIA.** The Syrian Arab Republic is a country in western Asia, on the Mediterranean Sea. It has borders with Iraq, Israel, Jordan, Lebanon, and Turkey. Once part of the Ottoman Empire, Syria was made part of the Levant States mandate by the **LEAGUE OF NATIONS** after World War I; Lebanon was also included in that mandate. The French Government proclaimed Syria an independent republic in 1941 after Free French forces had invaded it and routed Vichy forces stationed there during World War II. Complete independence was achieved on 1 January 1944, and Syria became a member of the United Nations in 1945. However, in 1958, Syria joined Egypt to form the United Arab Republic. This arrangement ended, and Syria resumed its independence in 1961. Its population is estimated to be 14,070,000. Ethnic groups include Arabs (90%), Kurds, Armenians, Circassians, and Turks. Languages commonly used include Arabic (official) (89%), Kurdish (6%), Armenian (3%), and English and French (2%). Religions practiced include Islam (Sunni, Shi'ite, and Ismaili), 90%; Christianity (Greek Orthodox, Greek Catholic, Armenian Ortho-

dox, Syrian Orthodox, Armenian Catholic, and some Protestant denominations), 10%. Literacy is estimated at 78%.

The government (1994) took the form of a socialist republic. Under the 1973 constitution, the Arab Socialist Renaissance (Ba'ath) Party is the leading party in the State and in society. That party, running on a unified ticket with the Syrian Communist and Socialist Parties, won 70% of the seats in the People's Assembly in 1973, 1977, and 1981; its chairman is president of the republic and head of State. The premier, appointed by the president, exercises executive authority as head of government. Legislation is prepared by the 195-member People's Council, members of which are elected by universal suffrage for terms of four years. The judicial system, headed by the Supreme Court, is based on French and Islamic jurisprudence. Political parties, in addition to the Arab Socialist Renaissance (Ba'ath) Party, include the Syrian Arab Socialist Union, the Union Socialist Party, and the Communist Party of Syria. In May 1990 the People's Assembly was expanded to 250 members.

*SYRIAN ARAB GOLAN.* As regards the Syrian Arab Golan, occupied by Israel since 1967, the UN **SECURITY COUNCIL,** in resolution 487 (1981) of 17 December 1981, unanimously reaffirmed the principle that the acquisition of territory by force is inadmissible and decided that Israel's decision to impose its laws, jurisdiction, and administration in the occupied area was null and void and without international effect. The council demanded that Israel rescind its decision forthwith and decided unanimously that, if Israel did not comply, the council would meet urgently to consider taking appropriate measures in accordance with the **UN CHARTER.**

The UN **GENERAL ASSEMBLY** later considered the situation in the occupied Syrian Arab Golan at each regular session and at a special session in 1982. It determined, in resolution 44/40 B of 4 December 1989—as it had done on several earlier occasions—that the continued occupation of that territory since 1967 and its annexation by Israel on 14 December 1981 constitute a continuing threat to international peace and security. In particular, it strongly deplored the negative vote by a permanent member of the Security Council (the United States of America) which had prevented the council from adopting against Israel, under chapter 7 of the UN Charter, the "appropriate measures" to which the council had referred in its resolution; and it called upon all member States (a) to refrain from supplying Israel with any weapons and related equipment and to suspend any military assistance that Israel receives from them; (b) to refrain from acquiring any weapons or military equipment from Israel; (c) to suspend economic, financial and technological assistance to and cooperation with Israel; and (d) to sever diplomatic, trade and cultural relations with Israel.

The UN **COMMISSION ON HUMAN RIGHTS** also considered the situation in the occupied Syrian Arab Golan at its annual sessions and was disturbed in particular by its human rights implications. On 17 February 1989, for example, the Commission deplored (resolution 1989/1)

the inhuman treatment, terror and practices contrary to human rights which the Israeli occupation authorities continue to apply against Syrian citizens in the occupied Syrian Arab Golan by reason of their refusal of Israeli citizenship and in order to force them to carry Israeli identity cards, which practices constitute a flagrant violation of the Universal Declaration of Human Rights, the Geneva Convention Relative to the Protection of Civilian Persons in Time of War of 12 August 1949, and the relevant resolutions adopted by the Security Council, the General Assembly and other international bodies and also constitute a threat to international peace and security.

The Commission condemned Israel for persisting in its policies and practices of annexation in the occupied Syrian Arab Golan, *inter alia*, appropriating land, establishing settlements thereon and moving Israeli settlers into them, diverting water to those settlements, thus depriving the Golan population of its sources of livelihood, and in particular imposing a boycott on agricultural products, depriving that population of the right to export them. It called upon all States to urge Israel to cease such practices, including boycott measures, and to facilitate the marketing of the agricultural produce of the Golan population.

Finally, the Commission emphasized that Israel must allow the evacuees from among the Golan population to return to their homes and to recover their property and places of residence occupied by Israel since 1967, and firmly emphasized the overriding necessity of the total and unconditional withdrawal by Israel from all Syrian and other Arab territories occupied since 1967, including Jerusalem, which is an essential prerequisite for the establishment of peace in the Middle East.

In the early 1990s, Syria for the first time took part in negotiations with Israel aimed at a comprehensive Middle East peace settlement in general and Israel's return of the Golan Heights in particular. The official newspaper rejected the Israeli-PLO plan requiring only limited withdrawal of Israel from the occupied territories.

**SYRIAN JEWS.** A number of non-governmental organizations, including the Co-ordinating Board of Jewish Organizations, the World Jewish Congress, and the World Union for Progressive Judaism, drew the attention of the UN Commission on Human Rights to the plight of Syria's small Jewish population (estimated to total about 4,500) at the Commission's 1987 session (UN Doc. E/CN.4/1987/NGO 73). While recognizing that Syrian Jews are allowed to maintain their religious customs and Jewish education, that their economic situation has improved in recent years, and that they enjoy the possibility of travelling abroad for tourism, business, or medical purposes, the organizations maintain that, nevertheless, they live in continuous fear of the future and as virtual hostages. Among the difficulties reported by them to face Syrian Jews are the following:

1. Emigration from the Syrian Arab Republic is prohibited;

2. Whole families are not allowed to leave the Syrian Arab Republic for visits abroad. An individual who wishes to travel must leave a monetary deposit and his family must remain behind as a guarantee of his return;

3. The sale of property and the purchase of other property in exchange must be approved by Syrian authorities;

4. Jews cannot be employed in public posts;

5. The Jewish community is kept under close surveillance by security officials who are fully informed of any movement or disappearance of Jews from the Syrian Arab Republic. The authorities know of any Jew who does not return from an approved visit abroad and maintain close surveillance of any foreigner who visits the Jewish quarter;

6. Unlike other citizens, Syrian Jews alone are identified in their identity documents and passports by a stamp stating that they are "of the Mosaic faith";

7. Jewish girls of marriageable age, of whom there are approximately 300, who are unable to marry in the absence of Jewish single men, are denied exit visas to contract marriages abroad, despite the awareness of the authorities of this acute social problem;

8. Under government orders, the Jewish schools in Damascus and Haleb are run by Moslem principals.

Syrian troops withdrew from Beirut in 1992 but continued to have strong influence over Lebanese politics and also appeared to continue to support groups operating against Israel from within Syria. Three such groups, as well as their leaders, were subject to a 1995 order by the U.S. Government, freezing all of their assets held within the United States.

President Assad's son, Basel, who was often cited as his successor, was killed in an accident in January 1994.

**BIBLIOGRAPHY.** Amnesty International. *Arrests in Syria and Lebanon by Syrian Forces.* London: 1986. NGO report, in English.

————. *Syria: Long-term Detention and Torture of Political Prisoners.* London: 1992. NGO report, in English.

Centre for the Independence of Judges and Lawyers. "Syria: Continued Detention of Lawyers," *CIJL Bulletin* 15 (April 1985): 6–8. NGO bulletin article, in English.

Comité de Défense des Libertés Démocratiques et des Droits de l'Homme en Syrie (Committee for the Defence of Human Rights and Democratic Freedoms in Syria), in *Rapport annuel, 1994* (Annual Report, 1994). Paris: Fédération Internationale des Ligues des Droits de l'Homme (International Federation of Human Rights Leagues), 1995. (La lettre hebdomadaire de la FIDH, Horssérie, 193) Annual report, in Arabic and French.

Federation Internationale des Droits de l'Homme (International Federation of Human Rights). "Le Martyr du Peuple Kurde" (The Martyrdom of the Kurdish People), *Lettre de la FIDH* 241 (22 March 1988). NGO article, in French.

Human Rights Watch. "Syria," in *Human Rights Watch World Report 1995*, pp. 305–310. New York: 1995. NGO report, in English.

International Commission for the Defence of Human Rights in Syria. *Bulletin of the International Commission for the Defence of Human Rights in Syria* (January 1988). NGO newsletter, in English.

McDowall, David. *The Kurds,* 4th rev. ed. London: Minority Rights Group: 1985. NGO report, in English.

Middle East Watch. *Syria: European Parliament Should Condition EC Aid on Human Rights Improvements.* New York: Human Rights Watch, 1993. NGO report, in English.

———. *Throwing Away the Key: Indefinite Political Detention in Syria.* New York: Human Rights Watch, 1992. NGO report, in English.

National Academy of Sciences, Committee on Human Rights. *Scientists and Human Rights in Syria.* Washington, D.C.: National Academy Press, n.d. NGO report, in English.

Reporters sans frontières. "Dossier Syrie—Le Despotisme d'Hafez El Assad: Les médias syriens sont soumis au joug implacable d'un seul homme" (Syria File: The Despotism of Hafez El Assad—The Syrian Media Under One Man's Relentless Yoke), *La Lettre de Reporters sans Frontières* no. 22 (Feb. 1991): 9–12. NGO article, in French.

# T

**TAIWAN.** The Republic of China is a country consisting of the island of Taiwan, formerly known as Formosa, which lies in the Pacific about 100 miles off mainland Asia; two islands closer to the Chinese coast known as Quemoy and Matsu; and a string of smaller islands between Taiwan and the mainland known as Pescadores. Over the years, Taiwan was administered successively by the Dutch, the Spanish, the Chinese, the Japanese, and again—after World War II—the Chinese.

Taiwan's population is estimated to be 20,985,000. Ethnic groups include, in addition to Formosans, a small number of aborigines of Malaysian and Indonesian descent and a large population of Han Chinese from the mainland.

The Government of Taiwan (1994) took the form of a republic. There is a National Assembly and five major governing *Yuans*: the executive, legislative, judicial, control, and examination governing bodies. The president and vice president are elected by the Assembly for terms of five years. The Nationalist Party (*Kuomintang*) and the Democratic Progressive Party (DPP) are the leading political groups.

The Chinese arrived for the most part in 1949 when the Nationalist government headed by Generalissimo Chiang Kai-shek was overthrown on mainland China. For many years, the general maintained a government-in-exile and a powerful army in Taiwan in the hope of returning to the mainland. Although the United States of America supported his efforts, his one serious attempt to return to China was blocked, in 1953, by the stationing of the American Pacific fleet in the Strait of Formosa.

For more than twenty years, Taiwan, with the assistance of the United States of America and other powers, occupied the seat designated for "China" in various organs of the United Nations. This ended when the United Nations recognized the People's Republic of China as the legitimate representative of the Chinese people in 1971. Taiwan was never admitted separately to UN membership.

Both the Taipei and the Beijing Governments consider Taiwan as constituting an integral part of China, but Taiwan has rejected all efforts at reunification. However, travel and trade between the two countries increased gradually after the death of Chiang Kai-shek in 1975. Chiang Ching-kuo, who succeeded him as president, died in January 1988 and was, in turn, succeeded by Lee Teng-hui, the first native of Taiwan to serve simultaneously as president and chairman of the Nationalist Party.

In July 1988, 1,209 delegates to the party congress elected a new central committee of 180 members; in the process many elderly party officials were replaced by young, liberal Taiwanese. At the same time, the congress took steps to liberalize relations with mainland China, authorizing increases in trade, the resumption of mail service, visits by Taiwanese to family members on the mainland, and exchanges of certain categories of students.

A large influx of tourists from Taiwan was welcomed by Chinese authorities in the latter half of 1989, compensating in part for the losses suffered by the Chinese tourist industry after the military crackdown in June of that year. More than 500,000 Taiwan citizens visited China during the six-month period, ending a forced separation that had lasted nearly 40 years.

In mid-March 1990, more than 10,000 protesters, organized by the opposition Democratic Progressive Party, gathered in a park in Taipei to demand democratic changes and to call for replacement of 668 deputies in the 752-seat parliament who were elected on the Chinese mainland before 1949. However, in an election held a few days later, the Nationalists prevailed, and President Lee Teng-hui—the only candidate—was again selected to serve as president and party chairman. He continues to be under pressure to dissolve the electoral college and to allow general presidential elections; and he is not fully supported by some elderly assemblymen because, as a native of Taiwan, he does not share their dream of a victorious return to China. In May 1990, President Lee Teng-hui selected Defense Minister Hau Pei-tsun, the country's only four-star general, to be prime minister—a move denounced as a "backward step" by the Democratic Progressive Party.

Constitutional reform was begun in June 1990 with 150 delegates meeting at the National Affairs Conference and the formation of a Constitutional Reform Planning Group. The Democratic Progressive Party boycotted a session of the National Assembly in April 1991 in which constitutional amendments were approved, arguing that a new constitution should be drafted. Amendments included the direct election of a new, smaller 405-member National Assembly in 1991, retirement of the elderly, mainland-elected legislators and repeal of the Temporary Provisions, adopted in 1949, aimed at suppressing the Communist rebellion. President Lee officially recognized the existence of the People's Republic of China.

Both the Tawainese and Chinese Governments continue to reiterate official policies on the others' lack of legitimacy, but representatives of the two governments have held repeated talks aimed at establishing economic and other links. Taiwan passed several measures aimed at loosening restrictions on trade and travel between the two; and in January 1995 the cabinet approved a proposal for transportation links with China. However, airplane hijackings from Taiwan to the People's Republic have put additional strains on relations. Despite all the political problems, Taiwan ranked among the top investors in China in 1994.

In national and local elections in December 1991, December 1992, and November 1993, the Nationalist Party (KMT) retained its majorities amid harsh treatment of dissidents, including convictions and prison terms for sedition. (The sedition law was amended in May 1992 so that nonviolent acts could no longer be prosecuted.) Further political reform was evidenced by the National Assembly's approval in July 1994 of Taiwan's first direct presidential elections set for 1996. In December 1994 the DPP won the office of the mayor of Taipei.

**BIBLIOGRAPHY.** Amnesty International. *Republic of China (Taiwan): Political Imprisonment in Taiwan*. London: 1986. NGO report, in English.

———. *Taiwan: The Death Penalty*. London: 1988. NGO report, in English.

———. *Taiwan: Ill-Treatment on "Death Row"*. London: 1993. NGO report, in English.

———. *Trial of Two Prisoners of Conscience*. London: 1988. NGO report, in English.

Asia Resource Center and Formosan Association for Human Rights. *Martial Law in Taiwan*. Washington, D.C.: 1985. NGO report, in English.

Christian Conference of Asia. "Aboriginal Minorities in Taiwan and the Philippines," *CCA News* 22, no. 1 (15 Jan. 1987): 6. NGO article, in English.

Committee to Protect Journalists. "New Measures Taken against Taiwan's Opposition Press," 5 June 1986. NGO press release, in English.

Formosan Association for Public Affairs and Formosan Association for Human Rights. *The Taiwan Confrontation Crisis*. Washington, D.C.: 1985. NGO report, in English.

Ho Shuet-ying. *Taiwan: After a Long Silence: The Emerging New Unions of Taiwan*. Hong Kong: Asia Monitor Resource Center, 1990. NGO report, in English.

Hsiung, James. C. *Human Rights in East Asia: A Cultural Perspective*. New York: Pergamon House Publishers, 1985. Scholarly edited collection, in English.

Index on Censorship. "Publishers and Editors Jailed in Taiwan," 19 June 1986. NGO briefing paper, in English.

International Committee for Human Rights in Taiwan. "Eight Political Prisoners Remain Imprisoned," *Taiwan Communique* 34 (28 May 1988): 16–19. NGO article, in English.

———. "Freedom of the Press?" *Taiwan Communique* 26 (15 Aug. 1986): 15–21. NGO article, in English.

———. "December Election Victory for DPP," *Taiwan Communique* no. 43 (Jan. 1990): 2–14. NGO article, in English.

———. "Imprisoned Taiwanese Opposition Leaders on Hunger Strike," *Taiwan Communique* 20 (18 June 1985): 1–5. NGO article, in English.

———. "Taiwan Ends Martial Law after 38 Years," *Taiwan Communique* 31 (10 Sept. 1987): 1, 6. NGO article, in English.

———. "Taiwan's New National Security Law Still Highly Restrictive," 26 January 1987. NGO press release, in English.

Luce, D., and R. Rumpf. *Martial Law in Taiwan*. Washington, D.C.: Asia Resource Center and Formosan Association for Human Rights, 1985. NGO monograph, in English.

Morgan, S. M., and E. Colson, eds. *People in Upheaval*. Staten Island, NY, USA: Center for Migration Studies of New York, 1987. NGO document collection, in English.

Taiwan Church News. "Issues of Taiwan's Aborigines," *Occasional Bulletin* 5, no. 1 (Dec. 1987–Jan. 1988): 7–12. NGO article, in English.

World Council of Churches. *Behind the Mask: Human Rights in Asia and Latin America, An Inter-Regional Encounter*. Geneva, Switzerland: 1988. NGO report, in English.

**TAJIKISTAN.** The Republic of Tajikistan, formerly the Tajik Soviet Socialist Republic, is bordered by China to the east, Afghanistan to the south, Uzbekistan to the north and west, and Kyrgyzstan to the northeast. It declared its independence from the Soviet Union in 1991 and became a founding member of the Commonwealth of Independent States in December 1991. It was admitted to the United Nations in 1992. Its population is estimated to be 5,765,000, comprising approximately 65% Tajik, 25% Uzbek, 3.5% Russian, and 6.5% other. Of the people professing a religion, 80% are Sunni Muslims and 5% Shi'a Muslims. Tajik, similar to Farsi or Persian, replaced Russian as the official language in 1989.

Part of Tajikistan was ruled by the Russian Empire in the 19th century and incorporated into the Turkestan Autonomous Soviet Socialist Republic (ASSR) after the Bolshevik Revolution in 1918. Control over all of Tajikistan in 1924 led to the creation of the Tajik ASSR and the Tajik SSR, connoting full USSR control, in 1929. Russians were sent to replace Tajiks in the government in the 1930s.

**INDEPENDENCE.** Islamic awareness and interest in Iranian culture increased from the 1970s, culminating in anti-Soviet riots and the formation of opposition political parties. A state of emergency was declared in 1990 and opposition political parties were refused permission to register or take part in elections to the Tajik Supreme Soviet. A declaration of sovereignty was made by the Supreme Soviet but 90% of voters chose to maintain the USSR in a March 1991 referendum. Many Europeans and educated Tajiks left the country in the face of increasing Islamic and Iranian influence.

After the failed coup against the Soviet government in August 1991, the Tajik Supreme Soviet declared independence, and the name of the country was changed to the Republic of Tajikistan. In the presidential election in November 1991, the Communist leader Rakhmon Nabiyev won 57% of the votes, primarily with the strong support of the rural population.

**CIVIL WAR.** A month-long demonstration in the center of the capital in March 1992 grew into a civil war that resulted in a truce in May and an agreement to form a Government of National Reconciliation in which a third of the ministers would be from opposition parties. Conflict continued in outlying regions, however; and in August 1992 anti-government demonstrations in the capital led to the resignation of President Nabiyev and the installation of the chairman of the Supreme Soviet as temporary president. He resigned in November and the office of president was abolished. The chairman of the Supreme Soviet was to act as head of State.

The ensuing civil war between the pro-communist government forces and a coalition of Islamic and democratic groups claimed the lives of an estimated 20,00 to 50,000 people before the government reclaimed control of most of the country by March 1993. Another 600,000 people were displaced and 80,000 fled to Afghanistan. In early 1993 opposition parties were outlawed and press freedom suspended. However, in early 1994 Chairman Rahmonov stated his preference for a presidential system and commitment to enactment of a new constitution by the end of the year. Both a constitutional referendum and Tajikistan's first presidential elections were held in November 1994. An estimated 90% approved the new constitution, and Rahmonov was elected president with 60% of the vote.

Despite high-level talks in 1994 under the auspices of the United Nations and including representatives of Russia, Iran, Pakistan, and the United States and a resulting protocol on refugees, fighting continued along the border with Afghanistan, and assassinations occurred in the capital and in other regions. In April 1995, in some of the most intense fighting since the civil war, Russian and CIS troops fired rockets on border towns, allegedly killing hundreds of civilians and Tajik rebels.

**BIBLIOGRAPHY.** Benifand, Alexander. "The Russian Policy and the Intensification of Civil Wars in Georgia, Tajikistan and Moldova," *Refuge* 12, no. 7 (Feb. 1993): 12–15. Scholarly article, in English.

Critchlow, James. "Islam in Soviet Central Asia: Renaissance or Revolution?" *Religion in Communist Lands* 18, no. 3 (Autumn 1990): 196–211. Article, in English.

Doroszewska, Urszula. "The Forgotten War: What Really Happened in Tajikistan," *Uncaptive Minds* 6, no. 3(24) (Fall 1993): 25–35. Article, in English.

Helsinki Watch. *Conflict in the Soviet Union: Tadzhikistan.* New York: Human Rights Watch, 1991. NGO factfinding report, in English.

————. *Human Rights Watch in Tajikistan: In the Wake of Civil War.* New York: Human Rights Watch, 1993. NGO report, in English.

————. *Political Prisoners in Tajikistan.* New York: Human Rights Watch, 1995. NGO report, in English.

————. *Return to Tajikistan: Continued Regional and Ethnic Tensions.* New York: Human Rights Watch, 1995. NGO report, in English.

————. *Tajikistan: Human Rights in Tajikistan on the Eve of Presidential Elections.* New York: Human Rights Watch, 1994. NGO report, in English.

Human Rights Watch. "Tajikistan," in *Human Rights Watch World Report 1995*, pp. 225–229. New York: 1995. NGO report, in English.

Kuvaldin, Viktor B. "Post-Soviet Moslems at the Crossroads," *Security Dialogue* 24, no. 1 (March 1993): 37–48. Scholarly article, in English.

**TANZANIA.** The United Republic of Tanzania is a country in eastern Africa, fronting on the Indian Ocean, and including the offshore islands of Zanzibar and Pemba. Mainland Tanzania has borders with Burundi, Kenya, Malawi, Mozambique, Rwanda, Uganda, Zaire, and Zambia. The Protectorate of Tanganyika achieved independence from Great Britain in 1961 as Tanzania; Zanzibar achieved independence in 1963; and they were united in 1964. Tanzania became a member of the United Nations in 1961. The population of the United Republic of Tanzania is estimated by the UN to be 27,791,000, including about 700,000 residents of Zanzibar. More than 130 ethnic groups are said to exist in the United Republic, but statistics concerning them are not available because of the government's policy of treating the entire population as a single community. Languages commonly used include Kiswahili (official) and English. Religions practiced in mainland Tanzania include Islam (35%), Animism (35%), and Christianity (30%); in Zanzibar, Islam (96%) and Hinduism (4%). Literacy is estimated at 80%.

The government (1994) took the form of a republic. Under the constitution, the Tanganyikan African National Union and the Afro-Shirazi Party of Zanzibar were merged into the *Chama Cha Mapinduzi* (Revolutionary Party), which became an organ of State policy. On its nomination, the president, prime minister, first vice president, second vice president (also president of Zanzibar), and deputy prime minister are elected by universal suffrage. Legislation for the United Republic is prepared by the unicameral National Assembly and for Zanzibar alone by the House of Representatives, all members of which are nominated by the single political party. The judiciary is independent. In some Zanzibar courts, the rules of Islamic law prevail.

The single political party, *Chama Cha Mapinduzi*, functioned in Tanzania for 25 years after being installed by the country's first president, Julius K. Nyerere. Since his voluntary retirement in 1986, there has been some interest shown in the possibility of replacing it with a multi-party system, and even Mr. Nyerere has not ruled out such a possibility. However, this would require a change in the constitution, which would take some time. Meanwhile, Mr. Nyerere retains his position as chairman of the Revolutionary Party, while the new president, Ali Hassan Mwinyi, functions as head of State. By 1992, following pressure to move toward a multi-party system, some political parties were registered but unauthorized political meetings continued to be prohibited and opposition leaders were arrested.

The constitution of Tanzania, adopted in 1977, states (art. 1 [5]) that "the principal aims and objects of the Party shall be: . . . 2. to build socialism on the basis of self-reliance; . . . 11. to safeguard the inherent dignity of human beings in accordance with the Universal Declaration of Human Rights." An amendment which entered into force in 1984 added a bill of rights to the constitution, under which any person who suffers a violation of his rights may invoke its provisions in seeking redress from the courts of law.

**ZANZIBAR.** Following a tumultuous period in Zanzibar, which included numerous large-scale riots and the resulting dispatch of 4,000 Tanzanian troops to the island as well as a number of political scandals and dismissals within the island government, parliamentary and presidential elections were held in Zanzibar in October 1990. Dr. Salmin Amour, the sole candidate, was elected as president and chairman of the Supreme Revolutionary Council with 98% of the vote. Tanzanian general elections were also held for the 216 parliamentary seats and the presidency. Again, President Mwinyi was the sole candidate and was re-elected to a second term.

In December 1992 the question of Tanzanian unity again arose as a result of Zanzibar's unilateral admission into the **ORGANIZATION OF THE ISLAMIC CONFERENCE** (OIC), a move which a commission found violated the terms of the Tanzanian Constitution. Zanzibar withdrew from the OIC in 1993. Islamic fundamentalists and security forces clashed in April 1993 and in October of that year approximately 30,000 protested against the prohibition on unauthorized public meetings. President Amour then abolished the right of political parties to form security forces. Despite the turmoil, multi-party legislative and presidential elections were set for 1995.

**REFUGEES.** Refugees flooded into Tanzania from neighboring Burundi and Rwanda throughout the early 1990s. In August 1991, 300,000 refugees—170,000 from Burundi—were on Tanzanian soil. By October 1993 and following the assassination of the Burundi president, 420,000 refugees had fled to Tanzania, 317,00 of whom are estimated to have later returned home. Following the assassination of the president of Rwanda in April 1994, another 250,000 people came across the border in a 24-hour period. While some refugees returned home, further migrations occurred throughout 1994 and into 1995. By the end of 1994 more UN troops were sought to protect the 550,000 Rwandans in camps throughout Tanzania from escalating violence from Hutus. There were also an estimated 18,500 Mozambican refugees in Tanzania in 1994.

The city of Arusha in Tanzania was chosen as the site for the Rwandan War Crimes Tribunal, where individuals accused of genocide and additional war crimes would be prosecuted.

**BIBLIOGRAPHY.** Andreassen, B. A., and E. Asbjorn, eds. "Tanzania," in *Human Rights in Developing Countries 1987/88: A Yearbook on Human Rights in Countries Receiving Nordic Aid*, pp. 90–109. Copenhagen: Christian Michelsen Institute, 1988. NGO report in English; bibliography, pp. 361–362.

Daley, Patricia. "Gender, Displacement and Social Reproduction: Settling Burundian Refugees in Tanzania," *Journal of Refugee Studies* 4, no. 3 (1991): 248–266. Scholarly article, in English.

International Labour Office. *Child Labour in Tanzania: Conditions of Work and Welfare Facilities Branch, Working Conditions and Environment Department.* Geneva, Switzerland: 1992. IGO report, in English.

Kumar, Umesh. "Some Preliminary Observations on the Administration of Justice in a One-Party State: The Tanzanian Experience," *Lesotho Law Journal* 2, no. 1 (1986): 119–154. Scholarly article, in English.

Norwegian Human Rights Project, Christian Michelsen Institute. *Human Rights in Developing Countries 1986.* Oslo: Universitetsforlaget, 1986. Government annual report, in English; bibliography, classified by country.

Nyange, Herbert. *An Independent Judiciary and the Protection of Human Rights: An Examination of the Attitude of the Executive in the Phase One Government of Tanzania toward the Judiciary in Situations of its Complicity to Violations of Human Rights.* Toronto, Canada: AHRA, 1986. NGO report, in English.

———. "Legislative and Judicial Implementation of the Norm against Torture: The Case of Tanzania," *Indian Journal of International Law* 27, no. 2–3 (April—Sept. 1987): 208–227. Scholarly article, in English.

Peter, Chris Maina. *Human Rights in Africa: A Comparative*

*Study of the African Human and People's Rights Charter and the New Tanzanian Bill of Rights.* New York; Westport, CT, USA; and London: Greenwood Press for the Consortium on Human Rights Development, 1990. Scholarly monograph, in English.

Skelton, James W., Jr. "Standards of Procedural Due Process under International Law vs. Preventive Detention in Selected African States," *Houston Journal of International Law* 2 (Spring 1980): 307–331. Scholarly article, in English.

# TEHERAN INTERNATIONAL CONFERENCE ON HUMAN RIGHTS (1968).

The Conference, which met in Teheran from 22 April to 13 May 1968, was the first worldwide meeting of government representatives to deal with the entire range of human rights and fundamental freedoms. It was attended by representatives of 84 States and a large number of United Nations organs, specialized agencies, and governmental and non-governmental organizations.

Convened by the UN **GENERAL ASSEMBLY** in a resolution adopted on 20 December 1965 (resolution 2081 [XX]), the Conference aimed "to promote further the principles contained in the Universal Declaration of Human Rights, to develop and guarantee political, civil, economic, social and cultural rights and to end all discrimination and denial of human rights and fundamental freedoms on grounds of race, color, sex, language or religion; and, in particular, to permit the elimination of *apartheid*." Its specific purposes were: (a) to review the progress which had been made in the field of human rights since the adoption of the **UNIVERSAL DECLARATION OF HUMAN RIGHTS**; (b) to evaluate the effectiveness of the methods used by the United Nations in the field of human rights, especially with regard to the elimination of all forms of racial discrimination and the practice of the policy of *apartheid*; and (c) to formulate and prepare a program of further measures to be taken subsequent to the celebration of the International Year for Human Rights. The Assembly earlier had designated 1968 as the "International Year for Human Rights."

A major product of the conference was the Proclamation of Teheran, which set forth a consensus on the major human rights problems considered by the Conference. In its resolutions, the Conference addressed many recommendations to various United Nations bodies, specialized agencies, and member States. Later in 1968, the General Assembly noted the Final Act of the Conference (UN publication, Sales no. E.68.XIV.2) with approval and called upon all States and organizations to act in accordance with the Conference's recommendations.

Paragraph 2 of the Proclamation recognizes that "the Universal Declaration of Human Rights states a common understanding of the peoples of the world concerning the inalienable and inviolable rights of all members of the human family and constitutes an obligation for the members of the international community." This evaluation of the significance of the Universal Declaration went beyond any that had been made previously by a worldwide international organ.

***PROCLAMATION OF TEHERAN.*** The Proclamation was adopted by the Conference on 13 May 1968. The text (*Final Act of the International Conference on Human Rights*, United Nations publication, Sales no. E.68.XIV.2, chap. II) is as follows:

The International Conference on Human Rights,

Having met at Teheran from April 22 to May 13, 1968 to review the progress made in the twenty years since the adoption of the Universal Declaration of Human Rights and to formulate a programme for the future,

Having considered the problems relating to the activities of the United Nations for the promotion and encouragement of respect for human rights and fundamental freedoms,

Bearing in mind the resolutions adopted by the Conference,

Noting that the observance of the International Year for Human Rights takes place at a time when the world is undergoing a process of unprecedented change,

Having regard to the new opportunities made available by the rapid progress of science and technology,

Believing that, in an age when conflict and violence prevail in many parts of the world, the fact of human interdependence and the need for human solidarity are more evident than ever before,

Recognizing that peace is the universal aspiration of mankind and that peace and justice are indispensable to the full realization of human rights and fundamental freedoms,

Solemnly proclaims that:

1. It is imperative that the members of the international community fulfil their solemn obligations to promote and encourage respect for human rights and fundamental freedoms for all without distinctions of any kind such as race, colour, sex, language, religion, political or other opinions;

2. The Universal Declaration of Human Rights states a common understanding of the peoples of the world concerning the inalienable and inviolable rights of all members of the human family and constitutes an obligation for the members of the international community;

3. The International Covenant on Civil and Political Rights, the International Covenant on Economic, Social and Cultural Rights, the Declaration on the Granting of Independence to Colonial Countries and Peoples, the International Convention on the Elimination of All Forms of Racial Discrimination as well as other conventions and declarations in the field of human rights adopted under the auspices of the United Nations, the specialized agencies and the regional intergovernmental organizations, have created new standards and obligations to which States should conform;

4. Since the adoption of the Universal Declaration of Human Rights the United Nations has made substantial progress in defining standards for the enjoyment and protection of human rights and fundamental freedoms. During this period many important international instruments were adop-

ted but much remains to be done in regard to the implementation of those rights and freedoms;

5. The primary aim of the United Nations in the sphere of human rights is the achievement by each individual of the maximum freedom and dignity. For the realization of this objective, the laws of every country should grant each individual, irrespective of race, language, religion or political belief, freedom of expression, of information, of conscience and of religion, as well as the right to participate in the political, economic, cultural and social life of his country;

6. States should reaffirm their determination effectively to enforce the principles enshrined in the Charter of the United Nations and in other international instruments that concern human rights and fundamental freedoms;

7. Gross denials of human rights under the repugnant policy of *apartheid* is a matter of the gravest concern to the international community. This policy of *apartheid,* condemned as a crime against humanity, continues seriously to disturb international peace and security. It is therefore imperative for the international community to use every possible means to eradicate this evil. The struggle against *apartheid* is recognized as legitimate;

8. The peoples of the world must be made fully aware of the evils of racial discrimination and must join in combating them. The implementation of this principle of non-discrimination, embodied in the Charter of the United Nations, the Universal Declaration of Human Rights, and other international instruments in the field of human rights, constitutes a most urgent task of mankind at the international as well as at the national level. All ideologies based on racial superiority and intolerance must be condemned and resisted;

9. Eight years after the General Assembly's Declaration on the Granting of Independence to Colonial Countries and Peoples the problems of colonialism continue to preoccupy the international community. It is a matter of urgency that all Member States should co-operate with the appropriate organs of the United Nations so that effective measures can be taken to ensure that the Declaration is fully implemented;

10. Massive denials of human rights, arising out of aggression or any armed conflict with their tragic consequences, and resulting in untold human misery, engender reactions which could engulf the world in ever growing hostilities. It is the obligation of the international community to co-operate in eradicating such scourges;

11. Gross denials of human rights arising from discrimination on grounds of race, religion, belief or expressions of opinion outrage the conscience of mankind and endanger the foundations of freedom, justice and peace in the world;

12. The widening gap between the economically developed and developing countries impedes the realization of human rights in the international community. The failure of the Development Decade to reach its modest objectives makes it all the more imperative for every nation, according to its capacities, to make the maximum possible effort to close this gap;

13. Since human rights and fundamental freedoms are indivisible, the full realization of civil and political rights without the enjoyment of economic, social and cultural rights is impossible. The achievement of lasting progress in the implementation of human rights is dependent upon the sound and effective national and international policies of economic and social development;

14. The existence of over seven hundred million illiterates throughout the world is an enormous obstacle to all efforts at realizing the aims and purposes of the Charter of the United Nations and the provisions of the Universal Declaration of Human Rights. International action aimed at eradicating illiteracy from the face of the earth and promoting education at all levels requires urgent attention;

15. The discrimination of which women are still victims in various regions of the world must be eliminated. An inferior status for women is contrary to the Charter of the United Nations as well as the provisions of the Universal Declaration of Human Rights. The full implementation of the Declaration on the Elimination of Discrimination against Women is a necessity for the progress of mankind;

16. The protection of the family and of the child remains the concern of the international community. Parents have a basic human right to determine freely and responsibly the number and the spacing of their children;

17. The aspirations of the younger generation for a better world, in which human rights and fundamental freedoms are fully implemented, must be given the highest encouragement. It is imperative that youth participate in shaping the future of mankind;

18. While recent scientific discoveries and technological advances have opened vast prospects for economic, social and cultural progress, such developments may nevertheless endanger the rights and freedoms of individuals and will require continuing attention;

19. Disarmament would release immense human and material resources now devoted to military purposes. These resources should be used for the promotion of human rights and fundamental freedoms. General and complete disarmament is one of the highest aspirations of all peoples;

Therefore,

The International Conference on Human Rights,

1. Affirming its faith in the principles of the Universal Declaration of Human Rights and other international instruments in this field,

2. Urges all peoples and governments to dedicate themselves to the principles enshrined in the Universal Declaration of Human Rights and to redouble their efforts to provide for all human beings a life consonant with freedom and dignity and conducive to physical, mental, social and spiritual welfare.

**TERESA, MOTHER (1910–).** Agnes Gonxha Bojaxhiu, known to the world as Mother Teresa, was awarded the 1979 **NOBEL PEACE PRIZE.** Cited by the Prize Committee for her tireless work for children and refugees, this Roman Catholic nun has often been called a living saint.

Born in Skopje, Yugoslavia, Mother Teresa is now a citizen of India. At 18 years old, she entered the religious life, joining the Sisters of Loretto, a group of primarily Irish nuns with a vocation for missionary work; she took her first vows in 1928 and her final vows in 1937. She taught at and served as principal of St. Mary's High School in Calcutta, India, from 1928 until 1948. As she told Malcolm Muggeridge in his book *Something Beautiful for God,* in 1946 she felt a special spiritual calling: "The message was clear. I was to leave the convent and help the poor, while living among them." The Vatican released her from her vows with the Sisters of Loretto and gave her permission to pursue her calling under the guidance of the archbishop of Calcutta. In that city, in 1950, she founded the Congregation of the Missionaries of Charity, a Roman Catholic religious order dedicated to relieving the misery of slum dwellers. Members of the Congregation take the traditional religious vows of poverty, chastity, and obedience, with a fourth vow to give "wholehearted free service to the poorest of the poor—to Christ in his distressing disguise."

Mother Teresa opened her first refuge in Calcutta in 1952, the *Nirmal Hriday* (Pure Heart) Home for Dying Destitutes. In 1957, the Congregation dedicated special work to lepers. Because of growing numbers in the order, the sisters expanded their range of activities; the Congregation's work has spread to fifty Indian cities and more than twenty-five countries, operating schools, hospitals, youth centers, and orphanges. Her Nobel Peace Prize money (and, indeed, any donations she receives, including a Lincoln Continental limousine from Pope Paul VI) was used entirely to fund the Congregation's charitable work.

This humble woman may be the most honored human being on earth. Among her numerous accolades are the Padma Shri Lotus Order; the Magsaysay Prize; the Good Samaritan Prize; the Pope John XXIII Peace Prize; the Jawaharlal Nehru Award of India; the Templeton Prize for Progress in Religion; the St. Louise de Marillac Award; the Albert Schweitzer Award; and the Bharat Ratna Award.

***BIBLIOGRAPHY.*** *Current Biography Yearbook 1973*, pp. 403–406. New York: W.H. Wilson.

Muggeridge, Malcolm. *Something Beautiful for God.* New York: Walker, 1984.

Schlessinger, Bernard S., and June Schlessinger, eds. *Who's Who of Nobel Prize Winners.* Phoenix, AZ, USA: Oryx Press, 1991.

Spink, Kathryn. *The Miracle of Love: Mother Teresa of Calcutta, Her Missionaries of Charity and Her Co-Workers.* New York: Harper and Row, 1982.

Teresa, Mother. *Life in the Spirit: Reflections, Meditations, Prayers.* New York: Harper and Row, 1983.

———. *A Simple Path,* comp. Lucinda Vardey. New York: Ballantine Books, 1995.

**TERRORISM.** The Seventh United Nations Congress on the Prevention of Crime and the Treatment of Offenders, which met in Milan from 26 August to 6 September 1985, was deeply disturbed by the prevalence of actual or threatened violent attacks and other concerted acts of violence against innocent persons and agreed that terrorist activities—including kidnaping, murder, hijacking, the taking of **HOSTAGES,** and the destruction of property—seriously impair freedom and the political stability of communities.

The Congress noted that these acts had occurred in spite of being addressed in a number of accepted international instruments, including the Convention on Offences and Certain Other Acts Committed on Board Aircraft; the Convention for the Suppression of Unlawful Seizure of Aircraft; the Convention for the Suppression of Unlawful Acts Against the Safety of Civil Aviation; the Convention on the Prevention and Punishment of Crimes Against Internationally Protected Persons, Including Diplomatic Agents; and the International Convention against the Taking of Hostages (see **HOSTAGES**).

Gravely concerned at the human, social, and economic cost of such attacks, and the threat they posed to normal international intercourse—particularly in the areas of travel, commerce, and diplomatic relations—and bearing in mind the importance of safeguards and maintenance of basic rights under ordinary legal procedures and in conformity with international human rights standards, the Congress called upon all States to take the necessary measures to ensure the full observance of the obligations contained in the relevant conventions to which they are parties, in particular the application of appropriate law enforcement measures under ordinary legal procedures, in conformity with international human rights standards.

The Congress, further, invited all States that had not become parties to the above-mentioned conventions to consider taking the necessary steps to do so in an expeditious fashion; urged all States to adopt legislation that, whenever necessary, will strengthen legal measures against those who commit violent acts of terrorism and to facilitate the exchange of information between States in order to improve the abilities of governments to prevent violence, to safeguard their citizens and to respond more effectively in cases of offenses contemplated in the conventions; and also urged them to facilitate, to the fullest extent possible, the effective application of law enforcement measures with respect to those who commit violent acts of terrorism, to rationalize their extradition procedures and practices and other cooperative arrangements with their respective legal processes and to avoid inappropriate exceptions.

Terrorist acts have been condemned numerous times by various UN bodies. Most recently, the **COMMISSION ON HUMAN RIGHTS** (resolution 1994/46), the **SUB-COMMISSION ON PREVENTION OF DISCRIMINATION AND PROTECTION OF MINORITIES** (resolution 1994/18), and the UN **GENERAL ASSEMBLY** (resolutions 48/122 and 49/185) expressed their condemnation of terrorism. In resolution 49/185, the General Assembly noted the growing connection between the terrorist groups and the illegal traffic in arms and drugs, as well as the consequent commission of serious crimes such as murder, kidnaping, assault, and robbery. The Assembly decided to consider once again the problem of terrorism at its fiftieth session.

**SEE ALSO** *Hostages.*

**BIBLIOGRAPHY.** Americas Watch Committee. *The Continuing Terror: Seventh Supplement to the Report on Human Rights in El Salvador.* New York: 1985. NGO report, in English.

Aspen Institute for Humanistic Studies. *State Crimes: Punishment or Pardon.* Aspen, CO, USA: 1986. NGO conference papers, in English.

Baunach, P. J. "The U.S.-U.K. Supplementary Extradition Treaty: Justice for Terrorists or Terror for Justice?" *Connecticut Journal of International Law* 2, no. 2 (Spring 1987): 463—498. Scholarly article, in English.

Camargo, Eduardo Matyas. "Narco Paramilitarismo y Derechos Humanos en Colombia" (Narco-Paramilitarism and Human Rights in Colombia), *Boletín—Comisión Andina de Juristas* no. 25 (June 1990): 9–15. Scholarly article, in Spanish.

Charters, David A., ed. *The Deadly Sin of Terrorism: Its Effect on Democracy and Civil Liberties in Six Countries.* Westport, CT, USA: Greenwood Press, 1994. Collection of scholarly contributions, in English.

Comision Andina de Juristas (Andean Commission of Jurists). "Peru: Tribunales Especiales y Terrorismo" (Peru: Specialized Tribunals and Terrorism), *Boletin Comision Andina de Juristas* 13 (Dec. 1986): 12–14. NGO bulletin article, in Spanish.

Dinstein, Yoram, and Mala Tabory, eds. "Terrorism as an International Crime," *Israel Yearbook on Human Rights* 19 (1989): 1–412. Scholarly collective works, in English; bibliography, pp. 405–412.

Fisler, Lori, and David J. Scheffer, eds. *Law and Force in the New International Order.* Boulder, CO, USA: Westview Press for the American Society of International Law, 1991. Scholarly collection of articles, in English.

Funnemark, Bjorn Cato, and Arne Borg. *Irish Terrorism or British Colonialism? The Violation of Human Rights in Northern Ireland.* Oslo, Norway: International Helsinki Federation for Human Rights, 1990. NGO factfinding report, in English.

Gersony, Robert. *Summary of Mozambican Refugee Accounts of Principally Conflict-Related Experience in Mozambique.* Washington, D.C.: U.S. Department of State, 1988. Government report, in English.

Giraldo, Javier. *Algunos Rasgos de la Situation de Violencia que Vive Hoy Colombia* (Some Features of Violence in Colombia Today). Bogota, Colombia: Centro de Investigacion y Educacion Popular, 1987. NGO report, in Spanish.

Hillyard, Paddy. *Suspect Community: People's Experience of the Prevention of Terrorism Acts in Britain.* Boulder, CO, USA: Westview Press, 1993. Scholarly monograph, in English.

Institut des Etudes Palestiniennes (Institute of Palestine Studies). "Le Terrorisme d'Etat Israelien en Mer" (Israeli State Terrorism at Sea,. *Revue d'Etudes Palestiniennes* 26 (Winter 1988): 71–88. Scholarly article, in French.

Media Analysis Center. "Kuwait: Facing Terrorist Challenges and Internal Entanglements," *Contemporary Mideast Backgrounder* 246 (May 1988). NGO paper, in English.

National Lawyers Guild and Lawyers Committee against U.S. Intervention in Central America. *Counterinsurgency as Terrorism: Human Rights Violations in Guatemala.* Boston, MA, USA: National Immigration Project, 1983. NGO report in English.

North American Congress on Latin America. "Fatal Attraction: Peru's Shining Path," *Report on the Americas* 24, no. 4 (Dec.–Jan. 1990/1991): 9–39. NGO article, in English.

Patrnogic, J., and Z. Meriboute. *Terrorism and International Law.* San Remo, Italy: International Institute of Humanitarian Law, 1987. Scholarly article, in English.

People's Union for Democratic Rights. *Communal Terrorism in Punjab.* New Delhi, India: 1987. NGO report, in English.

Pyle, C. H. "Defining Terrorism," *Foreign Policy* 64 (Fall 1986): 63–78. Scholarly article, in English.

Rubin, B. R. *Cycles of Violence: Human Rights in Sri Lanka since the Indo-Sri Lanka Agreement.* Washington, D.C.: Asia Watch, 1987. NGO report, in English.

Schmid, A. P. *Political Terrorism: A Research Guide to Concepts, Theories, Data Bases and Literature.* New Brunswick, NJ, USA: Transaction Books, 1986. Research guide, in English.

Schmid, A. P., A. J. Jongman, et al. *Political Terrorism: A New Guide to Actors, Authors, Concepts, Data Bases, Theories and Literature,* 2nd ed. New Brunswick, NJ, USA: Transaction Books, 1988. Handbook/directory/bibliography, in English.

Singh, D. *Sikhs, Arms and Terrorism.* Cambridge, UK: Cambridge University Sikh Society, 1986. Scholarly monograph, in English.

Tarazona-Sevillano, Gabriella, and John B. Reuter. *Sendero Luminoso and the Threat of Narcoterrorism.* Washington, D.C.: Praeger Publishers with the Center for Strategic and International Studies, 1990. Monograph, in English.

## TERRORISM: CONVENTION ON THE SUPPRESSION OF TERRORISM, COUNCIL OF EUROPE (1977).

Under the Convention, contracting States undertake to extradite persons who have committed serious terrorist offenses, such as the taking of **HOSTAGES,** the hijacking of an aircraft, or the use of explosives, even though they seek to justify those actions on political grounds. However, the State may refuse to extradite a person if it has reasonable grounds to believe that the request for extradition has been made for the purpose of prosecuting or punishing a person on account of his race, religion, nationality, or political opinion.

The Convention was concluded by the Committee of Ministers of the **COUNCIL OF EUROPE,** convened in Strasbourg on 27 January 1977 and entered into force on 4 August 1978. The text (*European Treaty Series* 90) is as follows:

The member States of the Council of Europe, signatory hereto,

Considering that the aim of the Council of Europe is to achieve a greater unity between its Members;

Aware of the growing concern caused by the increase in acts of terrorism;

Wishing to take effective measures to ensure that the perpetrators of such acts do not escape prosecution and punishment;

Convinced that extradition is a particularly effective measure for achieving this result,

Have agreed as follows:

*Article 1.* For the purposes of extradition between Contracting States, none of the following offences shall be regarded as a political offence or as an offence connected with a political offence or as an offence inspired by political motives:

(a) an offence within the scope of the Convention for the Suppression of Unlawful Seizure of Aircraft, signed at The Hague on 16 December 1970;

(b) an offence within the scope of the Convention for the Suppression of Unlawful Acts against the Safety of Civil Aviation, signed at Montreal on 23 September 1971;

(c) a serious offence involving an attack against the life, physical integrity or liberty of internationally protected persons, including diplomatic agents;

(d) an offence involving kidnapping, the taking of a hostage or serious unlawful detention;

(e) an offence involving the use of a bomb, grenade, rocket, automatic firearm or letter or parcel bomb if this use endangers persons;

(f) an attempt to commit any of the foregoing offences or participation as an accomplice of a person who commits or attempts to commit such an offence.

*Article 2.* 1. For the purposes of extradition between Contracting States, a Contracting State may decide not to regard as a political offence or as an offence connected with a political offence or as an offence inspired by political motives a serious offence involving an act of violence, other than one covered by Article 1, against the life, physical integrity or liberty of a person.

2. The same shall apply to a serious offence involving an act against property, other than one covered by Article 1, if the act created a collective danger for persons.

3. The same shall apply to an attempt to commit any of the foregoing offences or participation as an accomplice of a person who commits or attempts to commit such an offence.

*Article 3.* The provisions of all extradition treaties and arrangements applicable between Contracting States, including the European Convention on Extradition, are modified as between Contracting States to the extent that they are incompatible with this Convention.

*Article 4.* For the purposes of this Convention and to the extent that any offence mentioned in Article 1 or 2 is not listed as an extraditable offence in any extradition convention or treaty existing between Contracting States, it shall be deemed to be included as such therein.

*Article 5.* Nothing in this Convention shall be interpreted as imposing an obligation to extradite if the requested State has substantial grounds for believing that the request for extradition for an offence mentioned in Article 1 or 2 has been made for the purpose of prosecuting or punishing a person on account of his race, religion, nationality or political opinion, or that that person's position may be prejudiced for any of these reasons.

*Article 6.* 1. Each Contracting State shall take such measures as may be necessary to establish its jurisdiction over an offence mentioned in Article 1 in the case where the suspected offender is present in its territory and it does not extradite him after receiving a request for extradition from a Contracting State whose jurisdiction is based on a rule of jurisdiction existing equally in the law of the requested State.

2. This Convention does not exclude any criminal jurisdiction exercised in accordance with national law.

*Article 7.* A Contracting State in whose territory a person suspected to have committed an offence mentioned in Article 1 is found and which has received a request for extradition under the conditions mentioned in Article 6, para-

graph 1, shall, if it does not extradite that person, submit the case, without exception whatsoever and without undue delay, to its competent authorities for the purpose of prosecution. Those authorities shall take their decision in the same manner as in the case of any offence of a serious nature under the law of that State.

*Article 8.* 1. Contracting States shall afford one another the widest measure of mutual assistance in criminal matters in connection with proceedings brought in respect of the offences mentioned in Article 1 or 2. The law of the requested State concerning mutual assistance in criminal matters shall apply in all cases. Nevertheless this assistance may not be refused on the sole ground that it concerns a political offence or an offence connected with a political offence or an offence inspired by political motives.

2. Nothing in this Convention shall be interpreted as imposing an obligation to afford mutual assistance if the requested State has substantial grounds for believing that the request for mutual assistance in respect of an offence mentioned in Article 1 or 2 has been made for the purpose of prosecuting or punishing a person on account of his race, religion, nationality or political opinion or that that person's position may be prejudiced for any of these reasons.

3. The provisions of all treaties and arrangements concerning mutual assistance in criminal matters applicable between Contracting States, including the European Convention on Mutual Assistance in Criminal Matters, are modified as between Contracting States to the extent that they are incompatible with this Convention.

*Article 9.* 1. The European Committee on Crime Problems of the Council of Europe shall be kept informed regarding the application of this Convention.

2. It shall do whatever is needful to facilitate a friendly settlement of any difficulty which may arise out of its execution.

*Article 10.* 1. Any dispute between Contracting States concerning the interpretation or application of this Convention, which has not been settled in the framework of Article 9, paragraph 2, shall, at the request of any Party to the dispute, be referred to arbitration. Each Party shall nominate an arbitrator and the two arbitrators shall nominate a referee. If any Party has not nominated its arbitrator within the three months following the request for arbitration, he shall be nominated at the request of the other Party by the President of the European Court of Human Rights. If the latter should be a national of one of the Parties to the dispute, this duty shall be carried out by the Vice-President of the Court or, if the Vice-President is a national of one of the Parties to the dispute, by the most senior judge of the Court not being a national of one of the Parties to the dispute. The same procedure shall be observed if the arbitrators cannot agree on the choice of referee.

2. The arbitration tribunal shall lay down its own procedure. Its decisions shall be taken by majority vote. Its award shall be final.

*Article 11.* 1. This Convention shall be open to signature by the member States of the Council of Europe. It shall be subject to ratification, acceptance or approval. Instruments of ratification, acceptance or approval shall be deposited with the Secretary General of the Council of Europe.

2. The Convention shall enter into force three months after the date of the deposit of the third instrument of ratification, acceptance or approval.

3. In respect of a signatory State ratifying, accepting or approving subsequently, the Convention shall come into

force three months after the date of the deposit of its instrument of ratification, acceptance or approval.

*Article 12.* 1. Any State may, at the time of signature or when depositing its instrument of ratification, acceptance or approval, specify the territory or territories to which this Convention shall apply.

2. Any State may, when depositing its instrument of ratification, acceptance or approval or at any later date, by declaration addressed to the Secretary General of the Council of Europe, extend this Convention to any other territory or territories specified in the declaration and for whose international relations it is responsible or on whose behalf it is authorised to give undertakings.

3. Any declaration made in pursuance of the preceding paragraph may, in respect of any territory mentioned in such declaration, be withdrawn by means of a notification addressed to the Secretary General of the Council of Europe. Such withdrawal shall take effect immediately or at such later date as may be specified in the notification.

*Article 13.* 1. Any State may, at the time of signature or when depositing its instrument of ratification, acceptance or approval, declare that it reserves the right to refuse extradition in respect of any offence mentioned in Article 1 which it considers to be a political offence, an offence connected with a political offence or an offence inspired by political motives, provided that it undertakes to take into due consideration, when evaluating the character of the offence, any particularly serious aspects of the offence, including:

(a) that it created a collective danger to the life, physical integrity or liberty of persons; or

(b) that it affected persons foreign to the motives behind it; or

(c) that cruel or vicious means have been used in the commission of the offence.

2. Any State may wholly or partly withdraw a reservation it has made in accordance with the foregoing paragraph by means of a declaration addressed to the Secretary General of the Council of Europe which shall become effective as from the date of its receipt.

3. A State which has made a reservation in accordance with paragraph 1 of this Article may not claim the application of Article 1 by any other State; it may, however, if its reservation is partial or conditional, claim the application of that article in so far as it has itself accepted it.

*Article 14.* Any Contracting State may denounce this Convention by means of a written notification addressed to the Secretary General of the Council of Europe. Any such denunciation shall take effect immediately or at such later date as may be specified in the notification.

*Article 15.* This Convention ceases to have effect in respect of any Contracting State which withdraws from or ceases to be a Member of the Council of Europe.

*Article 16.* The Secretary General of the Council of Europe shall notify the member States of the Council of:

(a) any signature;

(b) any deposit of an instrument of ratification, acceptance or approval;

(c) any date of entry into force of this Convention in accordance with Article 11 thereof;

(d) any declaration or notification received in pursuance of the provisions of Article 12;

(e) any reservation made in pursuance of the provisions of Article 13, paragraph 1;

(f) the withdrawal of any reservation effected in pursuance of the provisions of Article 13, paragraph 2;

(g) any notification received in pursuance of Article 14 and the date on which denunciation takes effect.

(h) any cessation of the effects of the Convention pursuant to Article 15.

In witness whereof, the undersigned, being duly authorised thereto, have signed this Convention.

Done at Strasbourg, this 27th day of January 1977, in English and in French, both texts being equally authoritative, in a single copy which shall remain deposited in the archives of the Council of Europe. The Secretary General of the Council of Europe shall transmit certified copies to each of the signatory States.

## TERRORISM: RECOMMENDATION CONCERNING INTERNATIONAL COOPERATION IN THE PROSECUTION AND PUNISHMENT OF TERRORISM, COUNCIL OF EUROPE (1982).

The Recommendation, directed to all States members of the **COUNCIL OF EUROPE,** proposes measures to improve cooperation between those States when acts of **TERRORISM** occur, including measures for expediting exchanges of information concerning suspects and measures for the prosecution of international offenders by a single competent State best suited for conducting such proceedings. The Recommendation was adopted by the Committee of Ministers of the Council of Europe at the 342nd meeting of the Ministers' Deputies, convened at Strasbourg, on 15 January 1982. The text is as follows:

The Committee of Ministers, under the terms of Article 15 (b) of the Statute of the Council of Europe.

Considering that the aim of the Council of Europe is to achieve greater unity among its members;

Concerned at the increased number of acts of terrorism committed in certain member States;

Considering the prevention and suppression of such acts to be indispensable to the maintenance of the democratic institutions of member States;

Having regard to Council of Europe initiatives in the past aimed at the suppression of terrorism, which represent important contributions to the fight against this threat to society;

Convinced that it is necessary to develop further and to strengthen international co-operation in this field;

Desirous of rendering existing procedures of international judicial co-operation simpler and more expeditious, of improving the exchange of information between the competent authorities of member States, particularly between those with a common border, and of facilitating the prosecution and punishment of acts of terrorism;

Having regard to existing co-operation and channels of communications between the police forces of member States;

Recalling the Declaration on Terrorism adopted by the Committee of Ministers on 23 November 1978;

Emphasising that any measure of international co-operation must be fully compatible with the protection of human rights and particularly with the principles contained in the Convention for the Protection of Human Rights and Fundamental Freedoms signed in Rome on 4 November 1950,

Recommends the Governments of member States to give effect, by the most appropriate means, to the following measures aimed at improving international co-operation in the prosecution and punishment of acts of terrorism directed against the life, physical integrity or liberty of persons, or against property where they create a collective danger for persons, including, in accordance with domestic law, attempts of or threats of or participation as an accomplice in these acts (referred to as "acts of terrorism" in the present recommendation).

## I. Channels of Communication for Mutual Judicial Assistance in Criminal Matters

1. Direct communication between the authorities concerned in the requesting and requested State, of requests for judicial assistance and the replies thereto should be encouraged in all cases where it is permitted by the law of these States or by any treaty to which these States are Party, if it is likely to render mutual judicial assistance more expeditious.

2. Where direct transmission is permitted, cases involving acts of terrorism should be treated with urgency according to the procedure provided by Article 15 (2) of the European Convention on Mutual Assistance in Criminal Matters or by other treaties in force between member States or by the law of these States, so that letters rogatory may be addressed by the authority concerned in the requesting State, it being understood that the requested State may require a copy to be sent to its Ministry of Justice or other competent ministry.

3. Where requests for assistance and the replies thereto may be communicated directly between the authorities concerned in the requesting and the requested State, their transmission should be effected as rapidly as possible, either through Interpol National Central Bureau, insofar as this is not contrary to Interpol's Constitution, or by other existing ways of transmission.

4. Where communication is effected between Ministries of Justice or other competent ministries, the authority concerned in the requesting State should be allowed directly to provide the authority concerned in the requested State with an advance copy of the request. The authority concerned in the requested State should be advised that the sole purpose of transmitting the copy is to enable it to prepare for the execution of the request.

## II. Exchange of Information

5. Exchanges of information between member States should be improved and reinforced. To that end, the competent authorities should, insofar as this is not contrary to domestic law, be enabled to furnish, of their own accord, information in their possession on such matters as:

(i) measures concerning the prosecution of the alleged offender (e.g. arrest, indictment)

(ii) the outcome of any judicial or administrative proceedings (e.g. conviction, decision on extradition)

(iii) the enforcement of any sentence (including pardon, conditional release)

(iv) other relevant information relating to the whereabouts of the person concerned (e.g. expulsion, escape, execution of an extradition decision) to the authorities of any member State concerned, as for instance, the State where the act of terrorism was committed, the State which has jurisdiction over the offence, the State of which the offender is a national, the State where the offender has his habitual residence, or any other State likely to have an interest in the particular element of information.

6. The exchange of this information should be effected with all necessary expediency either through Interpol National Central Bureaux, insofar as this is not contrary to Interpol's Constitution, or by other existing ways of transmission.

## III. Prosecution and Trial of Offences of an International Character

7. Where one or several acts of terrorism have been committed in the territory of two or several member States and there is a link between those acts or their authors, the member States concerned should examine the possibility of having the prosecution and the trial conducted in only one State. To that end, the States concerned should agree on the competent State, in accordance with existing international treaties and their internal law. The same should apply, if possible, where one or several acts of terrorism of an international character have been committed in the territory of a single State by several persons acting in unison who have been apprehended in various States. In negotiating such agreements on the competent State, the States concerned should, with a view to ensuring that prosecution and trial take place in the State best suited for conducting the proceedings, take into account the number of offences committed in each State, the seriousness of the offences, the availability of evidence, the personal circumstances of the alleged offender, in particular his nationality and residence, and the prospects of rehabilitation.

**THAILAND.** The Kingdom of Thailand is a country in southeastern Asia occupying the western half of the Indochinese Peninsula and the northern two-thirds of the Malayan Peninsula. It has borders with Cambodia, Laos, Malaysia, and Myanmar. It was never other than independent, although occupied by Japanese troops during World War II, and became a member of the United Nations in 1946. Its population is estimated to be 58,030,000. Ethnic groups include Thai (75%), Chinese (14%), and others (11%). Languages commonly used include Thai (Siamese), English, French, and several regional vernaculars. Religions practiced include Buddhism (85%), Islam (4%), Christianity (5%), Hinduism (2%), and others (4%). Literacy is estimated at 86%.

The government (1994) took the form of a monarchy. Under the 1978 constitution, King Bhumibol Adulyadej is head of State. A premier, representing the majority party or coalition, is appointed by the king and acts as head of government. The National Assembly, which exercises legislative authority, includes the House of Representatives, whose members are elected by universal suffrage, and the Senate, whose members are appointed by the king. The judiciary includes three levels of courts. Judges, appointed by the king, are independent in conducting trials and pronouncing judgments according to the law. Political

# T

parties include the Democrat Party, the Thai Nation Party, the Social Action Party, and the United Democratic Party. The Communist Party is prohibited.

A military coup in February 1991 resulted in the fall of the government of Chatichai Choonhavan, the dissolution of the House of Representatives and the Senate, abrogation of the constitution, and imposition of martial law. An interim constitution was in place by the following month as well as a primarily civilian interim Council of Ministers and a military-dominated, appointed 292-member National Legislative Assembly. Martial law was repealed in most places; and in December 1991 the National Legislative Assembly approved a new constitution. This provided for an elected 360-member House of Representatives, an appointed 270-member Senate, and a prime minister.

After a general election in March 1992, General Suchinda, formerly supreme commander of the armed forces and commander-in-chief of the army, was named as prime minister and 154 army or police officers were appointed to the 270-member Senate. In May the king had to intervene following violent demonstrations against the government and harsh retaliation by the government. He ordered the release of an opposition leader and Suchinda resigned. The constitution was amended to require that the prime minister be appointed from among the members of the House of Representatives. General elections were held again in September 1992; the leader of the largest party in the House of Representatives, the Democratic Party, Chuan Leekpai, became prime minister and formed a coalition government.

Coalitions shifted in December 1994 when former Prime Minister Chatichai agreed to join his 60-seat National Development Party delegation with the established coalition government of Prime Minister Chuan Leekpai, giving the government a parliamentary majority.

Once known officially in English-speaking countries as Siam, Thailand was dominated by Portuguese traders and missionaries after 1511 and was closed to all foreigners in the 17th century after the British, Dutch, and French broke the Portuguese monopoly.

***RELATIONS WITH NEIGHBORING COUNTRIES.*** Because trade is chiefly in the hands of the large Chinese minority, tension between Thais and Chinese has existed for many years. In recent years, Thai fishermen were accused of beating and robbing Vietnamese refugees attempting to reach Malaysia by sea, after Thailand had blocked a safer land route through Cambodia. The Thai Government considers most Vietnamese reaching its territory to be economic migrants rather than genuine refugees.

Between 1991 and 1993, the UN HIGH COMMIS-

SIONER FOR REFUGEES and the Governments of Thailand and Cambodia successfully orchestrated the return of over 300,000 Cambodian refugees from Thailand. However, another 20,000 entered the country in March 1994 when strife between the Cambodian Government and the Kmer Rouge intensified. Relations between the two countries continued to be strained by the location of the rebel Kmer Rouge troops on the border and the arrest of 14 Thais in connection with the June 1995 attempted coup against the Cambodian Government.

Separatist groups engaged in acts of terrorism in 1993 and 1994, including arson attacks on dozens of schools.

***BIBLIOGRAPHY.*** Amnesty International. "Slum Dwellers: The Less Privileged Segment of Urban Population: A Case of Bangkok Slum and Squatter Settlements," *Human Rights Forum* 1, no. 4 (Oct.–Dec. 1985): 9–16. NGO article, in English.

————. *Thailand: Extrajudicial Executions of Kampuchean Refugees.* London: 1988. NGO report, in English.

Cerquone, J., and V. Hamilton. *Uncertain Harbors: The Plight of Vietnamese Boat People.* Washington, D.C.: U.S. Committee for Refugees, 1987. NGO issue paper, in English.

Child Workers in Asia. "Say No! to Child Prostitution," *Child Workers in Asia* 6, no. 2 (April–June 1990). Special issue, in English.

Coordinating Group for Religion in Society. "Facing up to Child Labor Abuse," *Human Rights in Thailand Report* 9, no. 1 (Jan.–March 1985): 12–13. NGO conference report, in English.

Ekachai, Sanitsuda. *Behind the Smile: Voices of Thailand.* Bangkok, Thailand: Thai Development Support Committee, 1990. Monograph, in English.

Gallagher, Dennis. *The Refugee Situation in Thailand.* Washington, D.C.: Refugee Policy Group, 1985. NGO report, in English.

Lawyers Committee for Human Rights. *Seeking Shelter: Cambodians in Thailand.* New York: 1987. NGO mission report, in English.

O'Grady, Ron. *The Child and the Tourist: The Story behind the Escalation of Child Prostitution in Asia.* Bangkok, Thailand: End Child Prostitution in Asian Tourism, 1992. NGO monograph, in English.

Oomen, Joep. "Hill Tribes in Thailand: Victims of Development," *IWGIA Newsletter* no. 4 (Fall 1992): 38–40. Article, in English.

Physicians for Human Rights and Asia Watch. *Thailand: Bloody May—Excessive Use of Lethal Force in Bangkok, The Events of May 17–20, 1992.* Boston, MA, USA: 1992. NGO report, in Asia.

Pruksakasemsuk, Somyot. "Thai Workers' Struggle Continues," *UCL Newsletter* (Oct. 1988): 27–29. NGO article, in English.

Robinson, Court. "Buying Time: Refugee Repatriation from Thailand," in *World Refugee Survey—1992.* Washington, D.C.: U.S. Committee for Refugees, 1992. NGO article in a collection, in English.

————. "Refugees in Thailand: 'Is the Glass Half Full or Half Empty?'" *Refugee Reports* 8, no. 9 (11 Sept. 1987): 1–8. NGO article, in English.

————. "Vietnamese Refugees in Thailand Face First-

Asylum Crisis," *Refugee Reports* 9, no. 2 (26 Feb. 1988): 1–7. NGO article, in English.

————. *"The War is Growing Worse and Worse": Refugees and Displaced Persons on the Thai-Burmese Border*. Washington, D.C.: U.S. Committee for Refugees, 1990. NGO issue paper, in English; bibliography, pp. 23–24.

Robinson, C., and A. Wallenstein. *Unfulfilled Hopes: The Humanitarian Parole/Immigrant Visa Program for Border Cambodians*. Washington, D.C.: U.S. Committee for Refugees, 1988. NGO issue paper, in English.

Sigler, Jay A., ed. *International Handbook on Race and Race Relations*. Westport, CT, USA: Greenwood Press, 1987. Scholarly edited collection, in English; bibliography, pp. 449–454.

Soontorn, J. B., S. Kaiyoorawongs, and S. Chaykert. "Hill Tribes and Human Rights," *UCL Newsletter* (Oct. 1988): 16–19. NGO report, in English.

Survival International. "Thailand: Tribal Villages Torched," *Survival International News* 19 (1988): 2. NGO article, in English.

Tanchainan, Sucheela. "Sexual Violence against Women and the Women's Movement in Thailand," *Thai Development Newsletter* 3, no. 4 (1st quarter 1986): 3–5. NGO article, in English.

Tapp, Nicholas. *The Hmong of Thailand: Opium People of the Golden Triangle*. London: Anti-Slavery Society for the Protection of Human Rights and Cultural Survival, 1986. NGO monograph, in English.

Tarr, Shane P. "The Nature of Military Intervention in the Countryside of Surat Thani, Southern Thailand," *Bulletin of Concerned Asian Scholars* 23, no. 3 (July 1991): 34–50. Scholarly article, in English.

Taswell, Ruth, ed. *Southeast Asian Tribal Groups and Ethnic Minorities*. Cambridge, MA, USA: Cultural Survival, 1987. NGO conference proceedings, in English.

Thai Development Support Committee. "Background to Human Rights Situation in Thailand," *Thai Development Newsletter* 12 (Dec. 1986): 13–19. NGO article, in English.

————. "Environmental Problems in Thailand: Their Impact on the Rural Poor," *Thai Development Newsletter* no. 18 (Dec. 1990). Special issue, in English.

————. "Tourism Promotion and its Effects on Thai Women," *Thai Development Newsletter* 4, no. 1 (June 1986): 10–14. NGO article, in English.

Thongpao, Thongbai. "The State of Human Rights in Thailand in 1985," *Thai Development Newsletter* 3, no. 4 (1st quarter 1986): 11–14. NGO article, in English.

Union for Civil Liberty. "Thailand: The State of Human Rights Campaign," *UCL Newsletter* (1990). Special issue, in English.

U.S. Committee for Refugees. *Refugees from Laos: In Harm's Way*. Washington, D.C.: 1986. NGO issue paper, in English.

## THIRD WORLD MOVEMENT AGAINST THE EXPLOITATION OF WOMEN.

An international nongovernmental organization in consultative status (Roster) with the UN **ECONOMIC AND SOCIAL COUNCIL,** the Movement initiates or supports protests and other activities directed against the exploitation of women, giving special attention to those activities or attitudes which oppress, or constitute assaults upon, women and girls. It focuses on unethical activities of employment and marriage bureaus, international beauty contests, nudist resorts, etc., and operates a crisis center for sexual assault. It publishes the *TW-MAE-W Action Bulletin* every two months.

Founded in Manila in 1980, originally to oppose organized "sex tours" from Japan, the organization now functions in more than 68 countries, mainly through the efforts of its individual members.

Third World Movement against the Exploitation of Women. Address: 41 Rajah Matanda Project 4, Quezon City, 1109, Philippines. Telephone: (63-2) 78-6469. Fax: (63-2) 921-4093. Coordinator: Sr. Mary Soledad Perpinan.

## THOUGHT, CONSCIENCE AND RELIGION. See FREEDOM OF THOUGHT, CONSCIENCE AND RELIGION.

**TOGO.** The Republic of Togo is a country in western Africa, on the Gulf of Guinea. It has borders with Benin, Burkina Faso, and Ghana. A United Nations trust territory under French administration, it achieved independence in 1960 and became a member of the United Nations the same year. Its population is estimated to be 4,030,000. There are some 40 ethnic groups, including (1) a southern group, formed by the Ewe, Ouatchi, and Mina communities; (2) the central group, composed of the Akposo; and (3) the northern group, consisting of the Kabye, Cotocoli, and Lamba. Scattered about the country are members of the Fons, Adja, and Yoruba communities. The Ewe constitute 22% of the total population; the Kabye, 13%; the Ouatchi, 11%; the Cotocoli, 6%; and the Mina, 6%. In addition, persons of German, American, French, Lebanese, and Syrian descent live in the country. Languages commonly used include French (official), Ewe, Mina, Kabye, Akposa, Adja, Moba, and many regional vernaculars. Religions practiced include Animism (56%), Christianity (Catholic, 21%; Protestant, 6%), and Islam (17%). Togo is a secular State and gives all religions equal recognition. Literacy is estimated at 18%.

The government (1994) took the form of a republic. Under the constitution of 1980, the executive president is directly elected for a term of seven years. Legislative authority is exercised by a National Assembly of 77 delegates, elected for five-year terms. All candidates are approved by the *Rassemblement du Peuple Togolais,* the only legal political party. The head of the party is president of the country and head of State.

*FORMER TERRORITY.* Togoland became a German colony in 1884, and, for many years, it served as a major source of slaves. After World War II, Togoland was divided into two trust territories: Togoland under British administration and Togoland under French administration. Plebiscites were held in both territories under United Nations supervision to determine whether the people desired union with the neighboring Gold Coast, which was on the point of attaining independence, or wished to remain in the trusteeship system. A majority of residents of Togoland under British administration voted in favor of union with an independent Gold Coast, while a majority of residents of Togoland under French administration voted in favor of independence. The Governments of France and Togoland agreed that the latter should attain independence on 27 April 1960, and the UN **GENERAL ASSEMBLY** terminated the trusteeship agreement as of that date.

*THE EYADEMA REGIME.* President Gnassingbe Eyadema, who had led Togo since taking power in a bloodless coup in 1967, survived several coup attempts against his government throughout the 1970s and 1980s. Following allegations of torture and mistreatment of political detainees, the official National Commission on Human Rights was formed in 1987. It investigated allegations of torture of 13 detainees in 1990 and affirmed the allegations in four of the cases. Violent demonstrations of support of two men sentenced to five years for possession of subversive material were followed by presidential pardons for the two and clemency for participants in the demonstrations.

In the March 1990 elections to the National Assembly, 230 candidates loyal to the ruling party stood for the 77 seats. Following violent protests, repeated clashes with security forces, the closure of all educational establishments, and imposition of a night time curfew, political parties were finally permitted in April 1991. At that time, opposition groups alleged that the bodies of 26 people found in a lagoon in the capital of Lome had been left by security forces.

Political parties were officially registered and a conference to plan the move to a multi-party system convened in July 1991. A transitional legislature and prime minister were installed and presidential powers limited. However, armed forces loyal to Eyadema twice attempted to overthrow the transitional prime minister and two opposition political leaders were murdered in 1992.

A new constitution was approved by 98% of the voters in a national referendum in September 1992. The constitution provided for the direct election of a president and an 81-seat National Assembly (both for five-year terms), the presidential appointment of a prime minister and a Constitutional Court. It also outlines the rights and duties of citizens.

Elections were repeatedly postponed by Eyadema;

and the United States, France, and Germany canceled aid in February 1993 in response to renewed and fatal suppression of opposition to the Eyadema government. While the opposition nominated a parallel prime minister and serious conflict continued, an estimated 250,000 Togolese sought refuge in Benin and Ghana.

When the presidential election finally took place in August 1993 amid allegations of irregularities, including that the electoral register contained thousands of fictitious names, Eyadema won with 96% of the votes cast by 36% of eligible voters. Violence continued after the elections; it was reported that, during an armed attack on the presidential residence in January 1994, 67 people were killed.

Legislative elections followed in February 1994 in which the opposition CAR (Comite d'action pour le renouveau) won a narrow victory, capturing 36 of the 81 seats. However, President Eyadema nominated a prime minister over the protests of the CAR, who boycotted the National Assembly until May.

*REPORT BY THE UN HUMAN RIGHTS COMMITTEE.* The **HUMAN RIGHTS COMMITTEE** considered the second periodic report of Togo (CCPR/C/63/Add. 2) at its 1325th to 1327th meetings, held on 7 and 8 July 1994, and adopted the following comments on 27 July 1994:

*Factors and difficulties affecting the implementation of the covenant.* The Committee notes that Togo is only now emerging from a long and devastating period of internal disturbances during which grave human rights violations have occurred and that it is still in the process of recovery and transition to democracy. The lack of awareness of individuals of their rights under the Covenant and the Optional Protocol impedes the enjoyment thereof and further contributes to the failure to provide remedies for violations of those rights. The remnants of certain traditions and customs also constitute an obstacle to the effective implementation of the Covenant, particularly with regard to equality between men and women.

*Positive aspects.* The Committee welcomes the adoption of a new Constitution and related legislation which incorporate a number of provisions of the Covenant and purport to institute a legal environment favourable to the promotion and protection of human rights as well as the enactment of the new Electoral Code. It also takes note of the establishment of the Ministry of Human Rights which could play an important role in coordinating the Government's human rights policy.

*Principal subjects of concern.* The Committee notes with concern the internal disturbances which occurred in Togo during the period under review and which resulted in serious and systematic violations of the rights guaranteed by the Covenant, particularly its articles 4, 6, 7, 9, 10 and 14. It is particularly concerned with the fact that despite initiation of the democratic process, the rule of law has not yet been re-established in Togo and violations of human rights continue to occur. Consequently, a significant gap persists between constitutional and legal norms and their application in practice. The Committee also notes with concern in that context the manifold obstacles faced by the National Human Rights Commission which, unfortunately, is no longer operative and which is unable to contribute to the promotion of respect for human rights.

The Committee deplores the large number of cases of summary and arbitrary executions, enforced or involuntary disappearances, torture and arbitrary or unlawful detention committed by members of the army, security or other forces during the period under review. It is deeply concerned that those violations were not followed by any inquiries or investigations, that the perpetrators of such acts were neither brought to justice nor punished, and that the victims were not compensated. It notes that failure to exclude violators of human rights from service in the military or the security forces seriously undermine the transition to democracy.

The Committee is disturbed by the composition of the army, whose members are almost exclusively recruited from only one of the ethnic groups in Togo, depriving other groups of the opportunity for equitable participation. Such composition, whatever its historical background, together with the apparent lack of full and effective control by civilian authorities over the military and security forces, is a particular cause of anxiety.

The Committee regrets that the State party has not yet embarked on all the necessary reforms to cope with the factors and difficulties impeding equality of men and women in order to fully implement article 3 of the Covenant. The reported cases of traffic of women, the effect of certain customs and traditions, as well as the lack of effective Government measures aiming at promoting equality of the sexes constitute matters of grave concern.

The Committee regrets the fact that derogations from some of the rights provided for in the Covenant through proclamation of curfews during the transitional period have not been notified to the Secretary-General in accordance with article 4 of the Covenant.

The Committee is concerned with the excessive number of offences punishable by the death penalty in the Togolese legislation which contravenes the provisions of article 6 of the Covenant.

The Committee notes that freedom of expression is not yet fully guaranteed in Togo owing to censorship and control exercised by the authorities over the press, radio and television.

The Committee notes with concern the restrictive conditions in which the rights provided for in articles 21 and 22 of the Covenant are to be exercised, and deplores the severe repression of peaceful demonstrations during the period under review involving loss of life which has not been fully investigated.

The Committee has serious doubts and concerns about the existing electoral system as well as the conditions under which the presidential and legislative elections have recently taken place, which preclude the full guarantee of free choice by all voters and the participation of all citizens in the conduct of public affairs, as provided for in article 25 of the Covenant.

A number of additional concerns remain, including the failure to ensure full and effective application of the Covenant in matters pertaining to the enjoyment of the right to a fair trial and the rights of persons deprived of their liberty.

*Suggestions and recommendations.* The Committee urges the Government to proceed with national reconciliation and to restore the confidence of all ethnic groups.

The Committee recommends that the State party take appropriate measures to translate and disseminate the Covenant, so that all people in Togo become aware of their rights guaranteed under the Covenant.

The Committee urges that the Government take all necessary measures to prevent summary or arbitrary executions, enforced or involuntary disappearances, torture and ill-treatment and illegal or arbitrary detention; that all such cases be systematically investigated in order to bring those suspected of having committed such acts before the courts; and that those found guilty be punished and that the victims be compensated.

The Committee deems it necessary that specific measures be taken to ensure that human rights are respected by the military and security forces. Vigorous action should be taken to ensure that persons closely associated with human rights abuses do not re-enter the police, army or security forces. Urgent steps should be undertaken to ensure that the composition of the army equitably represents various ethnic groups of the Togolese population, including currently under-represented minority groups, and that the army remains subject to the control of the elected civil government.

The Committee exhorts the Government to take appropriate action in order to ensure the effective application of article 3 of the Covenant, in particular by adopting administrative and educational measures designed to break away with customs and traditional practices detrimental to the well-being and status of women in the Togolese society.

The Committee urges the authorities of Togo to revise the Criminal Code with a view to diminishing the number of offences carrying the death penalty, in conformity with article 6 of the Covenant.

The Committee emphasizes that measures should be taken to ensure the implementation in prisons and detention centres of all provisions of article 10 of the Covenant together with the United Nations Standard Minimum Rules for the Treatment of Prisoners. They should be more widely disseminated and observed, particularly among the personnel of armed forces, the security and police officers involved in arrest and detention matters, as well as members of the judiciary.

The Committee recommends that necessary measures be taken by the Government to ensure the independence and the proper functioning of the judiciary and to provide proper and adequate staffing of courts in accordance with the provisions or article 14 of the Covenant.

Measures should be taken to allow for a proper resuming of the activities of the National Human Rights Commission under its statutes, including the guarantee of safety of its members as well as proper funding.

The Committee recommends that the censorship and control exercised by the authorities over the press, radio and television should be brought in line with article 19 of the Covenant.

Measures should be taken to ensure that elections be organized in full conformity with the requirements of article 25 of the Covenant.

The Committee recommends that the Government of Togo avail itself of the advisory and technical assistance services of the United Nations Centre for Human Rights in order to overcome some technical difficulties in implementing the Covenant, including the preparation of the third periodic report in accordance with the Committee's guidelines.

**BIBLIOGRAPHY**. Action des Chretiens pour l'Abolition de la Torture (Christian Action for the Abolition of Torture). "Regard sur le Togo" (Focus on Togo), *Courrier de l'ACAT* 77 (July–Aug. 1987): 2–4. NGO article, in French.

Africa News Service. "Togo: Rights Spotlighted," *African News* 30, no. 12 (13 Dec. 1988): 6–7. NGO article, in English.

Agboyibo, Yawo. "Les Droits de l'Homme au Togo" (Human Rights in Togo), *Etudes* 375, no. 3 (May 1991): 609–613. Scholarly article, in French.

Amnesty International. *Togo: Impunity for Human Rights Violators at a Time of Reform.* London: 1991. NGO factfinding report, in English.

———. *Togo: Impunity for Killings by the Military.* London: 1993. NGO report, in English.

———. *Togo: Summary of Amnesty International's Concerns in 1990.* London: 1991. NGO factfinding report, in English.

Beaudoin, Patrick. *Rapport de mission—Togo: la situation des droits de l'homme* (Mission Report—The Situation of Human Rights in Togo). Paris: Fédération Internationale des Droits de l'Homme (International Federation for Human Rights), 1991. NGO factfinding report, in French.

Fédération Internationale des Ligues des Droits de l'Homme (International Federation of Human Rights Leagues). *Mission d'enquête internationale au Togo, 8 au 13 juin 1992—à propos des événements de Soudou survenus le 5 mai 1992* (International Fact-finding Mission in Togo, 8–13 May, 1992—Concerning the Soudou Events [5 May 1992]). Paris: 1992. (Rapport de la FIDH, 155) NGO factfinding report, in French.

International Commission of Jurists. *Les Services Juridiques en Milieu Rural (Afrique d l'Ouest)* (Legal Services in Rural Areas [West Africa]). Geneva, Switzerland: 1987. NGO report, in French.

**TONGA.** The Kingdom of Tonga is a country situated on a group of 169 islands in the South Pacific Ocean, the largest of which are Tongatabu, Vavau, and Haabi. Formerly known as the Friendly Islands, they were a British-protected State from 1900 to 1959, when they were granted self-rule within the British Commonwealth. They achieved complete independence on 4 June 1970. The population of the islands is estimated to be 103,000. Ethnic groups include Tongan (98%), European (.5%), part European (.7%), and others (.8%). Languages commonly used include Tongan and English. Christianity (Free Wesleyan, Roman Catholic, Free Church of Tonga, Church of Tonga, Latter Day Saints, Seventh Day Adventists, Anglicans, and members of the Assemblies of God) is the predominant religion. Literacy is estimated at 35% in Tongan only, .04% in English only, and 41% in Tongan and English.

The government (1994) took the form of a monarchy. Executive authority is exercised by the king with the assistance of a prime minister and cabinet appointed by himself. Legislation is prepared by a unicameral Legislative Assembly. The judicial system includes magistrates courts, the Land Court, the Supreme Court, and the Court of Appeals. There is no political party.

Demands for democratic reform led to the forma-

tion of the Pro-Democracy Movement in 1992. Despite the government's refusal to sanction or participate in or admit overseas visitors to a constitutional convention organized by the group, the Movement won six of the nine People's Representative seats in the legislative elections of February 1993.

The vast majority of the population of Tonga is indigenous; the remainder includes foreign workers in the country on a temporary basis. A person from another country who marries a Tongan is required to show that he has a return ticket for the Tongan husband or wife to the non-Tongan's homeland; this provision is intended to protect the rights of Tongan women who, in the past, often were subjected to desertion by their non-Tongan husbands after a marriage of very short duration.

**TORTURE.** Freedom from torture and other cruel, inhuman or degrading treatment or punishment is proclaimed as a fundamental right of all human beings in the **UNIVERSAL DECLARATION OF HUMAN RIGHTS,** in the following provision:

*Article 5.* No one shall be subjected to torture or to cruel, inhuman or degrading treatment or punishment.

The **INTERNATIONAL COVENANT ON CIVIL AND POLITICAL RIGHTS** contains the following provisions:

*Article 7.* No one shall be subjected to torture or to cruel, inhuman or degrading treatment or punishment. In particular, no one shall be subjected without his free consent to medical or scientific experimentation. . . .

*Article 10.* (1) All persons deprived of their liberty shall be treated with humanity and with respect for the inherent dignity of the human person.

(2) (a) Accused persons shall, save in exceptional circumstances, be segregated from convicted persons and shall be subject to separate treatment appropriate to their status as unconvicted persons;

(b) Accused juvenile persons shall be separated from adults and brought as speedily as possible for adjudication.

(3) The penitentiary system shall comprise treatment of prisoners, the essential aim of which shall be their reformation and social rehabilitation. Juvenile offenders shall be segregated from adults and be accorded treatment appropriate to their age and legal status.

Article 4, para. 2, of the Covenant provides against any **DEROGATION** from article 7.

The Convention on the Prevention and Punishment of the Crime of Genocide (see **GENOCIDE**) defines "genocide" as meaning "any of the following acts committed with intent to destroy, in whole or in part, a national, ethnical, racial, or religious group, as such: . . . (b) causing serious bodily or mental harm to members of the group; (c) deliberately inflicting on the group conditions of life calculated to bring about its physical destruction in whole or in part. . . ."

Similarly, the International Convention on the Suppression and Punishment of the Crime of Apartheid (see **APARTHEID**) defines ''the crime of *apartheid*'' as applying

to the following inhuman acts committed for the purpose of establishing and maintaining domination by one racial group of persons over any other racial group of persons and systematically oppressing them: (a) Denial to a member of a racial group or groups of the right to life and liberty of person: (i) by murder of members of a racial group or groups; (ii) by the infliction upon the members of a racial group or groups of serious bodily or mental harm, by the infringement of their freedom or dignity, or by subjecting them to torture or to cruel, inhuman or degrading treatment or punishment; (b) Deliberate imposition on a racial group or groups of living conditions calculated to cause its or their physical destruction in whole or in part.

The Supplementary Convention on the Abolition of Slavery, the Slave Trade and Institutions and Practices Similar to Slavery (see **SLAVERY**) provides that:

*Article 5.* In a country where the abolition or abandonment of slavery, or of the institutions or practices mentioned in article 1 of this Convention, is not yet complete, the act of mutilating, branding or otherwise marking a slave or a person of servile status in order to indicate his status, or as a punishment, or for any other reason, or of being accessory thereto, shall be a criminal offence under the laws of the States Parties to this Convention and persons convicted thereof shall be liable to punishment.

The definition and prohibition of torture is further elaborated in the Convention against Torture and Other Cruel, Inhuman or Degrading Treatment or Punishment, as follows:

*Article 1.* 1. For the purposes of this Convention, the term "torture" means any act by which severe pain or suffering, whether physical or mental, is intentionally inflicted on a person for such purposes as obtaining from him or a third person information or a confession, punishing him for an act he or a third person has committed or is suspected of having committed, or intimidating or coercing him or a third person, or for any reason based on discrimination of any kind, when such pain or suffering is inflicted by or at the instigation of or with the consent or acquiescence of a public official or other person acting in an official capacity. It does not include pain or suffering arising only from, inherent in or incidental to lawful sanctions.

2. This article is without prejudice to any international instrument or national legislation which does or may contain provisions of wider application. . . .

*Article 16.* 1. Each State Party shall undertake to prevent in any territory under its jurisdiction other acts of cruel, inhuman or degrading treatment or punishment which do not amount to torture as defined in article 1, when such acts are committed by or at the instigation of or with the consent or acquiescence of a public official or other person acting in

an official capacity. In particular, the obligations contained in articles 10, 11, 12 and 13 shall apply with the substitution for references to torture of references to other forms of cruel, inhuman or degrading treatment or punishment.

2. The provisions of this Convention are without prejudice to the provisions of any other international instrument or national law which prohibits cruel, inhuman or degrading treatment or punishment or which relates to extradition or expulsion.

The **AMERICAN CONVENTION ON HUMAN RIGHTS,** open for acceptance by member States of the **ORGANIZATION OF AMERICAN STATES,** provides that:

*Article 5.* 1. Every person has the right to have his physical, mental, and moral integrity respected.

2. No one shall be subjected to torture or to cruel, inhuman, or degrading punishment or treatment. All persons deprived of their liberty shall be treated with respect for the inherent dignity of the human person.

3. Punishment shall not be extended to any person other than the criminal.

4. Accused persons shall, save in exceptional circumstances, be segregated from convicted persons, and shall be subject to separate treatment appropriate to their status as unconvicted persons.

5. Minors while subject to criminal proceedings shall be separated from adults and brought before specialized tribunals, as speedily as possible, so that they may be treated in accordance with their status as minors.

6. Punishments consisting of deprivation of liberty shall have as an essential aim the reform and social readaptation of the prisoners.

The Inter-American Convention to Prevent and Punish Torture, also open for acceptance by OAS member States, provides (articles 6–14) that each State party shall take effective measures to prevent and punish torture and other cruel, inhuman, or degrading treatment or punishment, within their jurisdiction.

The **EUROPEAN CONVENTION ON HUMAN RIGHTS,** open for acceptance by **COUNCIL OF EUROPE** member States, provides that:

*Article 3.* No one shall be subjected to torture or to inhuman or degrading treatment or punishment.

The European Convention for the Prevention of Torture and Inhuman or Degrading Treatment or Punishment, also open for acceptance by Council of Europe member States, provides (paras. 7–14) for implementation by States parties within their jurisdiction.

**GENERAL COMMENTS BY THE UN HUMAN RIGHTS COMMITTEE.** After examining reports submitted by States parties to the International Covenant on Civil and Political Rights in accordance with article 40 of that instrument, the UN **HUMAN RIGHTS COMMITTEE**

adopted, in 1982, the following general comments on article 7 of the Covenant (UN Doc. A/37/40, annex V, paras. 1–3):

In examining the reports of States parties, members of the Committee have often asked for further information under article 7 which prohibits, in the first place, torture or cruel, inhuman or degrading treatment or punishment. The Committee recalls that even in situations of public emergency such as are envisaged by article 4 (1) this provision is non-derogable under article 4 (2). Its purpose is to protect the integrity and dignity of the individual. The Committee notes that it is not sufficient for the implementation of this article to prohibit such treatment or punishment or to make it a crime. Most States have penal provisions which are applicable to cases of torture or similar practices. Because such cases nevertheless occur, it follows from article 7, read together with article 2 of the Covenant, that States must ensure an effective protection through some machinery of control. Complaints about ill-treatment must be investigated effectively by competent authorities. Those found guilty must be held responsible, and the alleged victims must themselves have effective remedies at their disposal, including the right to obtain compensation. Among the safeguards which may make control effective are provisions against detention incommunicado, granting, without prejudice to the investigation, persons such as doctors, lawyers and family members access to the detainees; provisions requiring that detainees should be held in places that are publicly recognized and that their names and places of detention should be entered in a central register available to persons concerned, such as relatives; provisions making confessions or other evidence obtained through torture or other treatment contrary to article 7 inadmissible in court; and measures of training and instruction of law enforcement officials not to apply such treatment.

As appears from the terms of this article, the scope of protection required goes far beyond torture as normally understood. It may not be necessary to draw sharp distinctions between the various prohibited forms of treatment or punishment. These distinctions depend on the kind, purpose and severity of the particular treatment. In the view of the Committee the prohibition must extend to corporal punishment, including excessive chastisement as an educational or disciplinary measure. Even such a measure as solitary confinement may, according to the circumstances, and especially when the person is kept incommunicado, be contrary to this article. Moreover, the article clearly protects not only persons arrested or imprisoned, but also pupils and patients in educational and medical institutions. Finally, it is also the duty of public authorities to ensure protection by the law against such treatment even when committed by persons acting outside or without any official authority. For all persons deprived of their liberty, the prohibition of treatment contrary to article 7 is supplemented by the positive requirement of article 10 (1) of the Covenant that they shall be treated with humanity and with respect for the inherent dignity of the human person.

In particular, the prohibition extends to medical or scientific experimentation without the free consent of the person concerned (article 7, second sentence). The Committee notes that the reports of States parties have generally given little or no information on this point. It takes the view that at least in countries where science and medicine are highly developed, and even for peoples and areas outside their borders if affected by their experiments, more attention should be give to the possible need and means to ensure the observance of this provision. Special protection in regard to such experiments is necessary in the case of persons not capable of giving their consent.

***IMPLEMENTATION OF THE UN CONVENTION AGAINST TORTURE.*** The Convention against Torture and other Cruel, Inhuman or Degrading Treatment or Punishment, adopted by the UN **GENERAL ASSEMBLY** on 10 December 1984 (resolution 39/46), entered into force on 26 June 1987. In addition to defining "torture," as mentioned above, the Convention requires States parties to take effective measures to prevent acts of torture in any territory under their jurisdiction. No exceptional circumstances, such as war or public emergency, can be invoked to justify torture; nor can obedience to an order from a superior officer or a public authority be invoked as justification.

States parties undertake not to expel, return, or extradite a person to another State where there are substantial grounds for believing that he would be in danger of being subjected to torture and to ensure that all acts of torture, attempts to commit torture, complicity, or participation in torture are offenses punishable under their criminal law.

The Convention also provides for prosecution or extradition of persons alleged to have committed acts of torture, and States parties are called upon to afford one another judicial assistance in connection with criminal proceedings concerning acts of torture. It calls for education on the prohibition of torture to be part of the training of law enforcement personnel and other persons involved in the custody, interrogation, or treatment of prisoners or detainees; and it provides that States parties shall ensure legal measures for protection and compensation for victims of torture. Other forms of cruel, inhuman or degrading treatment or punishment, as defined in the Convention, which may be committed by persons acting in an official capacity, are also prohibited.

The implementation of the Convention is monitored by the **COMMITTEE AGAINST TORTURE,** consisting of 10 experts, elected by States parties to the Convention and serving in their personal capacity. The Committee held its first session at the United Nations office in Geneva from 18 to 22 April 1988. States parties to the Convention are required to report regularly to the Committee on the measures they have taken to give effect to the provisions of the Convention. The Committee considers such reports, makes general comments on them, and informs the other States parties and the General Assembly of its activity.

Under Article 20 of the Convention, if the Committee receives reliable information which appears to it to contain well-founded indications that torture is being systematically practised in the territory of a State party, the Committee invites that State party to co-operate in the examination of the information and to this end to submit observations with regard to the information concerned. The Committee may decide to make an inquiry, including a visit to the territory of the State party concerned, with its agreement. The proceedings of the Committee when it undertakes such an inquiry are confidential, but the Committee may decide to include a summary account of the results of the proceedings in its annual report to the State parties and to the General Assembly. In ratifying the Convention, States may express a reservation with regard to the competence of the Committee under Article 20. Of the initial 20 States which have ratified or acceded to the Convention, the Governments of Afghanistan, Bulgaria, Byelorussian SSR, Hungary, Ukrainian SSR, and the Soviet Union have declared that they do not recognize the competence of the Committee as defined by Article 20 of the Convention.

Under Article 21, a State party to the Convention may at any time declare that it recognizes the competence of the Committee against Torture to receive and consider communications to the effect that a State party claims that another State party is not fulfilling its obligations under the Convention. Under Article 22, a State party to the Convention may at any time declare that it recognizes the competence of the Committee to receive and consider communications from or on behalf of individuals subject to its jurisdiction who claim to be victims of a violation by a State party of the provisions of the Convention.

***REPORTS OF SPECIAL RAPPORTEUR.*** At its 1985 session, the UN Commission on Human Rights welcomed (resolution 1985/33) the adoption by the General Assembly on 9 December 1984 of the Convention against Torture and Other Cruel, Inhuman or Degrading Treatment or Punishment and decided to appoint a Special Rapporteur to examine various aspects of the question of torture. Mr. Peter H. Kooijmans (the Netherlands) was designated as Special Rapporteur and instructed to seek and receive credible and reliable information concerning torture from governments, specialized agencies, and intergovernmental and non-governmental organizations and to "respond effectively" to such information.

In his first report (UN Doc. E/CN.4/1986/15), the Special Rapporteur drew attention to the "grey area" between torture proper and other harsh treatment or punishment and pointed out that he had to take certain practices into account—such as corporal punishment, prolonged stays on death row, detention of minors along with adults, etc.—since they could, in a further analysis, constitute acts of torture. He also presented a preliminary analysis of the information he had received on the practice of torture and put forward some suggestions for preventative measures.

In his second report, the Special Rapporteur presented a full analysis of the information he had received on the practice of torture, as follows (UN Doc. E/CN.4/1987/13, chap. VI, paras. 72–79):

Torture is still a widespread phenomenon in today's world. From the information he has received the Special Rapporteur has been confirmed in his conviction that no society, whatever its political system or ideological colour, is totally immune to torture. Of particular concern to the international community, however, are situations where torture has become a more or less normal element of daily life. In such situations the authorities have either lost control over the security or law-enforcement personnel and condone the practice of torture, seemingly for the sake of more important goals, such as "national unity" or "national security", or cast a benevolent eye on such practices, as they help to create an atmosphere of fear or terror where opposition may be fairly easily stamped out.

The first is usually the case in situations of civil strife, where there is a confrontation of hostile groups. Violence, fed by mutual hatred, becomes the predominant feature of everyday life. Especially where civil strife has taken the form of guerrilla tactics, military and security personnel feel threatened and may gradually fall into the practice of physical abuse and torture to extract information about their opponents. Every person living within the guerrilla area may be seen as a potential enemy who withholds information and may, therefore, be forced to disclose it by all available means. Although in many cases the victims of such abuse are completely innocent, the inevitable effect of such practices is that mutual hatred increases and life becomes ever more violent. Torture breeds hatred and the increased hatred leads to more atrocities which in themselves seem to justify the practice of more severe torture. The Government may genuinely condemn the practice of torture, but feels that, in view of the need to maintain and uphold national integrity and security, it cannot do anything against it. It, therefore, usually closes its eyes to reality and either flatly denies that torture takes place or contends that it is a reaction to the commission of terrorists acts. Governments should realize, however, that the vicious circle in which they seemingly find themselves may well have started with the abuses and the arrogant practices of the representatives of the official authorities. The prohibition and suppression of such practices are not only an obligation under international law but may also be a matter of sound policy.

The Special Rapporteur has received many allegations about the practice of torture in countries where the whole or parts of the country are the scene of civil strife or civil war. In some of these countries the climate of violence has indeed led to a disheartening loss of respect for the physical and mental integrity of the human person and for his dignity. In this respect the Special Rapporteur wishes to mention the situation in Afghanistan. The situation in Sri Lanka, which finds itself caught in a spiral of violence and where civilians are allegedly tortured in order to extract information from them about planned acts of violence by the insurgents is also of great concern. Serious allegations continue to come in about torture practices in El Salvador. In spite of the fact that the Government has once again committed itself to respect and guarantee fundamental human rights, certain parts of the State apparatus have obviously been successful in evading those commitments.

In other countries torture is practised to deter civil strike and to stifle opposition. It is used as a means not only to extract information but also to enforce behaviour in conformity with the prevalent rules. In this respect mention may be made of the situation in Chile and in South Africa. The Special Rapporteur has also received alarming reports about the practice of torture in the Islamic Republic of Iran where behaviour or even opinions that deviate from the norm are not tolerated.

It is significant that in many of the situations referred to above, either a state of emergency is declared for the whole or parts of the country, under which enjoyment of certain basic human rights has been curtailed or suspended, or special security legislation is in force, under which persons may be arrested without warrant and kept incommunicado for a considerable period. It is well known that such situations easily lend themselves to the practice of torture, as torturers may find it quite simple to avoid criminal responsibility for their acts. It is particularly disquieting that torture becomes so endemic in such a society that even a return to normality does not bring an end to the practice. In various cases the Special Rapporteur has continued to receive allegations from countries where either the previous régime has been replaced or a transfer to a civilian (elected) government has taken place. A firm and unrelenting attitude by the new incumbent is, therefore, required, as well as strict rules and retraining programmes for law-enforcement personnel.

With regard to some countries the Special Rapporteur has received allegations of torture with regard to certain ethnic or religious groups in particular. In these cases torture usually took the form of gross physical abuses, such as beatings, rape, etc., often combined with robbery, testifying to a serious lack of respect for the dignity of these citizens. In such cases it should come as no surprise if eventually such a situation leads to insurgency of the group concerned, which in its turn will lead to the civil strife described above. Here again, the Government must adopt a firm position.

The Special Rapporteur has also received information concerning maltreatment in places of detention (irrespective of whether these were penal institutions) which amounted to torture as the effect was severe mental or physical pain. Such maltreatment can take the form of acts but also of omissions. In these cases the Special Rapporteur intends to start consultations with the Governments concerned and in one particular case has already done so. In such cases, the detained person, because he feels that his detention is the result of his divergent political views and that he is therefore unjustly detained frequently considers himself justified in resisting detention. This in turn leads to abusive treatment by security personnel which, however, is unacceptable if the detainee's physical or mental integrity is injured.

There are also cases where a specific type of punishment irreparably damages the integrity of the human person. Here also the Special Rapporteur feels that it is most appropriate to enter into consultation with the Governments involved and, in fact, he has tried to do so.

In his conclusions and recommendations, the special rapporteur advised the commission that (*Ibid.*, chap. VII, paras. 80–87):

Torture is an extremely complex phenomenon. It takes many forms and occurs in widely divergent situations. Its occurrence is often determined by specific political conditions; and at the same time in spite of the varying circumstances it occurs in a strikingly monotonous pattern.

Therefore, torture may be the derivative of certain political conditions, its source is invariably the same: contempt for the personality of the other individual which has to be destroyed and annihilated. It is for that reason that torture is one of the most heinous violations of human rights as it is the very denial of the essence of human rights, namely the

recognition that each living being has a personality of his own which has to be respected.

Therefore, a society that tolerates torture can never claim to respect other human rights; the duty to eradicate torture is thus a primordial obligation. Efforts to realize that goal should first and foremost be concentrated on the prevention of torture. It goes without saying that repressive measures are called for whenever torture has been practised. Those who have committed this offence should be brought to justice; but it is more important to go to the roots of the evil itself and to take away the causes which make torture possible. The Special Rapporteur can, therefore, only repeat the recommendations he made in his first report. In particular he wishes to stress the importance of limiting the period of incommunicado detention under national law, since many of the allegations he has received refer to torture in countries where a detainee may be kept incommunicado for a prolonged period. He also wishes to emphasize the importance of training programmes for law enforcement and security personnel, especially in countries where torture was regularly practised under a previous régime. The United Nations programme of advisory services should be particularly geared to respond favourably to requests made by Governments in this field. In view of the multitude of norms for the conduct of medical personnel, enumerated in chapter III, and the crucial role medical personnel allegedly often play in the practice of torture, the Special Rapporteur recommends that Governments and medical associations take strict measures against all persons belonging to the medical profession who have in that capacity had a function in the practice of torture. He also recommends that the role that the medical profession may play in the practice of torture should be highlighted in all courses on medical ethics.

A measure which may have an important preventive effect is the introduction of a system of periodic visits by a Committee of experts to places of detention or imprisonment. On 6 March 1980, the Government of Costa Rica submitted to the Commission on Human Rights a draft optional protocol to the draft Convention against torture and other cruel, inhuman or degrading treatment or punishment which provided for such a system of periodic visits. In resolution 1986/56 the Commission noting that the draft European Convention against torture was based on similar ideas, recommended that other interested regions where a consensus existed should consider the possibility of preparing draft conventions based on the concept of a system of visits. In this context, it may be mentioned that the Inter-American Convention to Prevent and Punish Torture (concluded on 9 December 1985) does not establish such a system of periodic visits nor any other comparable machinery.

The introduction of systems of periodic visits should be seen as a preventive rather than a repressive measure. Although the determination of actual acts of torture as a result of such visits could lead to repressive action against the offenders, the main emphasis should be on the advice which experts may give after such a visit with regard to steps to be taken to correct and improve the existing régime in places of detention and imprisonment in the country visited. The element of periodicity is designed to ensure that a system of visits is seen as a means of co-operating with Governments rather than as an instrument for denouncing them. The fact that the idea of periodic visits would eventually form part of regional systems for protection of human rights (of which there are currently three, established in the context of the Organization of African Unity, the Organization of American States and the Council of Europe) would not necessarily stand in the way of the conclusion of a world-wide convention to which States which were subject to such a system of visits under a regional instrument could become party. However, the implementation of the world-wide system could be suspended for States subject to a regional system.

Such a system of visits is no more an intrusion in the internal jurisdiction of a State than the visits of staff members of the International Atomic Energy Agency to nuclear plants which may also lead to recommendations for the improvement of existing standards. In both cases such visits would serve a purpose which is recognized by the international community as being of vital importance for the well-being of mankind as they would ensure respect for human dignity and the maintenance of international peace and security, respectively.

Until such systems of periodic visits have been established, the granting of admission to ICRC teams to places of detention and imprisonment must be recommended, as such visits by ICRC may contribute to the prevention of torture and—in fact—in some cases have ostensibly done so.

In this context, the Special Rapporteur may recall his readiness to visit countries with the consent or at the invitation of the Government, not only on account of allegations of torture he has received, but also on any other occasion for which such a visit may be deemed useful by the Government concerned, for instance, when a power has been transferred to a new Government which wishes to take effective measures to eradicate torture practices which occurred under the previous régime.

In 1987, the Special Rapporteur held consultations in Geneva with the Governments of Argentina, Colombia, Peru, and Uruguay with a view to exploring the possibility of carrying out on-the-site consultations on measures to prevent the phenomenon of torture. Having received a favorable reaction, he proposed to visit those countries from 9 to 18 December 1987. All agreed to the proposed dates, except Peru which preferred to postpone the visit to a later stage.

The Special Rapporteur visited Colombia from 9 to 13 December 1987, Argentina from 13 to 16 December 1987, and Uruguay from 16 to 18 December, and reported on these visits to the Commission on Human Rights at its 1988 session (UN Doc. E/CN.4/1988/17/ Add. 1). In the concluding paragraphs of that report, he wrote (paras. 21–23):

The visits paid to Colombia, Argentina and Uruguay have greatly expanded the Special Rapporteur's insight into the roots and causes of torture. Both in Uruguay and in Argentina, he was told that the widespread practice of torture during the military régime was facilitated by the already existing tradition of brutal treatment of detainees by the police; the important role of confession in criminal procedure had been instrumental in this tradition. In both countries it was stressed that the use of torture as a means of extortion and terror was passed from the police to the military not the other way round as is sometimes believed.

Common criminal procedures and the means by which evidence is collected therefore deserve much more attention than they usually get. Torture is very often seen mainly in the context of political controversies as a means of suppressing political opponents—and correctly so. But this focus on situations of political strife may lead us to close our eyes to the fact that the seeds of the use of torture for this particular end are often sown elsewhere and that, therefore, practical measures to prevent torture should also be taken elsewhere.

Another element which seems to be extremely relevant is that, although mentality training is undoubtedly very important, it is clearly not sufficient. The existence of technical expertise and technical equipment is also of vital significance. It is noteworthy that in two of the three countries visited members of the Government made an explicit appeal for assistance by the international community. In the whole concept of international co-operation economic and social development until now have played a preponderant role. This is logical and to the point since in large areas of the world economic and social human rights cannot be guaranteed without the combined efforts of the international community as a whole. The international community has been much less aware that the realization of political and civil rights may also be dependent upon international co-operation. This may be partly due to the fact that political and civil rights are usually seen as obligations for the State to abstain from interfering in the private sphere of the individual. However, for the full enjoyment of those rights, a certain infrastructure is essential. Up till now, hardly any funds have been set aside to comply with requests for assistance in this field. The programme of advisory services of the Centre for Human Rights—useful as it may be, in particular for the near future—will clearly be insufficient if awareness of the possibilities of international co-operation and assistance for the realization of civil and political human rights increases. The Special Rapporteur is of the opinion that the implications of requests for assistance from individual governments better to guarantee civil and political rights should be a matter for reflection in the Commission on Human Rights. Condemnation of systematic violations of human rights are certainly called for in quite a few cases. However, the commission, whose task it is to promote respect for human rights, would only be doing half its work if it turned a deaf ear to a government which asked the international community to help it better to fulfil its commitment to guarantee respect for human rights.

The Commission on Human Rights reviewed the Special Rapporteur's report at its 1988 session and, in resolution 1988/33, commended him for it and endorsed its conclusions and recommendations. It extended his mandate for two years in order to enable him to submit further conclusions and recommendations for its consideration.

In the course of 1988, the Special Rapporteur corresponded with the governments of a number of countries, transmitting to them reports of torture having occurred in territories under their jurisdiction without taking a position as to whether or not those reports were well-founded. Countries to which such communications were addressed included Afghanistan, Bahrain, Benin, Brazil, Burma, China, Colombia, Czechoslovakia, El Salvador, France, Greece, Grenada, Guatemala, Haiti, Honduras, India, Indonesia, Islamic Republic of Iran, Israel, Kenya, Mexico, Morocco, Panama, Paraguay, Peru, Philippines, Republic of Korea,

Sao Tome and Principe, Saudi Arabia, Singapore, Somalia, Spain, Sri Lanka, Sudan, Syrian Arab Republic, Turkey, the United Kingdom of Great Britain and Northern Ireland, and Vietnam.

In addition, he brought 42 appeals for urgent action, received during 1988, to the immediate attention of the respective governments on a purely humanitarian basis, to ensure that the right to physical and mental integrity of the individual was protected, and requested information on the remedial measures taken in case the allegations were proved correct. Most of the allegations concerned persons subjected to torture during interrogation while being held incommunicado by security police. Countries to which such urgent appeals were addressed included Benin, Burkina Faso, Myanmar, China, Colombia, El Salvador, Guatemala, Haiti, Honduras, Islamic Republic of Iran, Israel, Liberia, Mauritania, Panama, Peru, Philippines, Somalia, South Africa, Syrian Arab Republic, Turkey, United Arab Emirates, and Zaire.

Further, the Special Rapporteur, on invitation of the governments concerned, visited Peru, the Republic of Korea, and Turkey in the course of 1988. Such investigations were consultative in nature, rather than for the purpose of investigating specific allegations.

In his report to the UN Commission on Human Rights on his 1988 activities, the Special Rapporteur included the following general recommendations (UN Doc. E/CN.4/1989/15, chap. V, paras. 239–247):

The great majority of allegations received by the Special Rapporteur refer to torture practised during incommunicado detention. It seems, therefore, that a formal prohibition of incommunicado detention would greatly reduce the number of reported cases of torture.

In this context, the following recommendations are made, which are in conformity with the Declaration of Basic Principles of Justice for Victims of Crime and Abuse of Power, adopted by the General Assembly in resolution 40/34.

Legal provisions prescribing that a person shall be given access to a lawyer not later than 24 hours after he has been arrested usually function as an effective remedy against torture, provided compliance with such provisions is strictly monitored. Security personnel who violate such provisions should, therefore, be severely disciplined. A useful supplementary provision would be the obligation to inform the relatives of an arrested person within 24 hours of both the arrest and the place where the detainee is being held.

At the time of his arrest, a person should undergo a medical inspection; such an inspection should be repeated regularly, but in any case should be compulsory whenever a detainee is transferred from one place of detention to another.

Since many allegations refer to situations in which the victim of torture was blindfolded or the interrogators were made unrecognizable, each interrogation should be initiated with indentification of all the persons present.

Interrogation of detainees should only take place at official interrogation centres. Evidence obtained from the detainee in other places and not confirmed by him during interrogation at official locations should not be admitted as evidence in court.

Independent bodies should be established which may regularly inspect places of detention and may speak confidentially with the detainees. Such bodies should report publicly on their findings.

Each detainee should be able to initiate proceedings before a court on the lawfulness of his detention, in conformity with article 9, paragraph 4, of the International Covenant on Civil and Political Rights. It is recommended that this right should also be recognized under a state of siege or emergency. The right of *habeas corpus* should be strictly respected in all circumstances and should never be suspended.

The Code of Conduct for Law Enforcement Officials and the Standard Minimum Rules for the Treatment of Prisoners should be translated into the national language and used as teaching material during training courses for law enforcement personnel. In particular, such personnel should be instructed on their duty to disobey orders received from a superior to practice torture.

In the same report, the Special Rapporteur presented to the Commission his views on the handling of appeals from governments for direct assistance or for advisory services to assist them in the promotion and protection of human rights, as follows (UN Doc. E/CN.4/1989/15, paras. 235–238):

In the course of all his visits, without exception the Special Rapporteur received repeated appeals for assistance and advisory services.

Taking into account different situations, the Special Rapporteur is of the view that the Centre for Human Rights could assist Governments either to correct a given situation or to prevent the recurrence of past errors.

In countries where civil strife prevails, every effort should be made by the international community to spare the physical and mental integrity of the individual and to help newly elected Governments to correct a situation which may lead to a state of lawlessness. Therefore the following programmes are recommended:

(a) Courses in international humanitarian law on situations related to internal conflicts;

(b) Prototype regulations to safeguard human rights under states of emergency;

(c) Courses for medical associations on norms for the conduct of medical personnel, having regard to the role that the medical profession may play in the practice of torture;

(d) Courses for magistrates and law enforcement officials on *amparo* and *habeas corpus* procedures.

In countries where the military authorities have taken power in the recent past, courses on preventive measures may be envisaged. In fact, instruction programmes for security personnel, with emphasis on training for the correct approach to respect for the human rights of the individual, have already been requested by some countries. The Special Rapporteur considers that courses related to provisions contained in international intruments, specifically those contained in the new Convention against Torture, are indispensable.

In the course of 1988, the Special Rapporteur received invitations to visit Peru, the Republic of Korea, and Turkey from the governments of those countries.

He accepted them, feeling that consultations with the authorities *in situ* are an extremely effective instrument for carrying out his mandate. In his report to the Commission, he wrote (para. 7):

It should be pointed out that such visits have a consultative character and that the Special Rapporteur does not carry out investigations into specific allegations during such visits. It has been suggested from time to time to the Special Rapporteur that a Government, by extending an invitation to him, would admit that torture is actually practised in that country. The Special Rapporteur wishes to emphasize in this respect that, irrespective of the question whether torture did occur or still occurs in countries visited by him, such a visit should be seen mainly in the light of prevention of torture.

In his report to the Commission on Human Rights, the Special Rapporteur described his visits to Peru, the Republic of Korea, and Turkey and presented in the case of each country his evaluation and recommendations.

In the course of 1989, the Special Rapporteur continued his correspondence with the governments concerned and visited Guatemala and Honduras, describing these activities in his report to the 1990 session of the Commission on Human Rights (UN Doc. E/CN.4/1990/17). The conclusions and recommendations set out in that report were as follows (chap. V, paras. 259–272):

Though the fight against torture has considerably intensified during the last decade, torture still remains a common phenomenon in today's world. Over the past few years there have been hopeful developments in a considerable number of countries; in other countries, however, there has been a clear deterioration. The number of countries where torture is systematically applied may have decreased during that period, but at the same time it has become apparent that torture is far from exceptional in situations where it does not form part of a system. The sad conclusion must be drawn that respect for the inherent dignity of all human beings, irrespective of their race, creed and, most of all, their political conviction is still painfully underdeveloped. This should inspire the international community with renewed energy to continue the fight for the eradication of the horrendous crime of torture. All hopes for a stable, just and peaceful world—hopes which have been greatly nourished over the past year—will turn out to be idle if we do not succeed in instilling in mankind the basic requirement for a stable, just and peaceful world: the respect for the inherent dignity of the fellow human being.

The Special Rapporteur was in particular alarmed by the fact that he received a number of allegations referring to torture of children and juveniles. Torture is horrifying in all its forms and emanations, but the idea of children, who are still in their formative stage, being tortured is mind-boggling indeed. The fact that these alleged events took place at about the same time as the adoption by the international community of the Convention on the Rights of the Child glaringly illustrates how far this world is still removed from practising the standards it sets itself.

Education in the field of human rights, therefore, seems one of the most urgent tasks the international community has to tackle. The fact that the United Nations has launched a World Public Information Campaign for Human Rights is an important step in that direction. The primary responsibility for human rights education lies with Governments, who may be assisted in this vast task by private organizations. The world, however, cannot wait until this educational process takes effect; those in particular who are in a position that makes it possible for them to violate their fellow human beings' right to human dignity and physical and mental integrity must receive training how to deal with persons who have been brought under their control. In this respect the adoption by the General Assembly, by its resolution 43/173 of 9 December 1988, of the Body of Principles for the Protection of All Persons under Any Form of Detention or Imprisonment must be highlighted.

This document contains principles which, in part, had already been recognized in human rights conventions and resolutions of the organs of the United Nations—sometimes in even stronger form—such as, for example, the Standard Minimum Rules for the Treatment of Prisoners. The importance of this new Body of Principles lies in the fact that they are now contained in a document which can function as a check-list for Governments to see whether their legal provisions and administrative practices are in conformity with these principles, and to take corrective measures if this is not the case. In the covering resolution the General Assembly "urges that every effort be made so that the Body of Principles becomes generally known and respected", a recommendation which is addressed to all States. Another important aspect is that the Body of Principles applies to all forms of detention or imprisonment, whatever the form of deprivation of liberty may be. Everybody who is deprived of his liberty is entitled to the protection provided by the document. A third element which has to be noted is that no exception is made for times of emergency. Since an earlier draft contained a reference to such situations, it has to be assumed that the principles must be applied under all circumstances. The Body of Principles contains many elements which are of direct relevance to the prevention of torture and actually echo a number of recommendations the Special Rapporteur has made in previous reports; some of these may be referred to here.

Principle 11 states that a person shall not be kept in detention without being given an effective opportunity to be heard *promptly* by a judicial or other authority. Since torture is often practised immediately after arrest, this prompt hearing by a judge may be a guarantee for the arrested person's physical integrity. The legality of his detention can be considered and his right of access to legal counsel can be secured.

Of no less importance are principles 12 and 23, which prescribe the duty to record the circumstances at the time of arrest and of interrogation. Especially relevant is the duty to record the identity of the officials who are responsible for the arrest and the interrogation. Torture usually takes place under conditions which make it impossible for the victim to recognize his interrogators and torturers. Complaints filed afterwards are therefore often unsubstantiated as regards the alleged perpetrators.

Other elements which have relevance to the prevention of torture are the duty to give the detainee access to legal counsel (principles 17 and 18), the duty to inform his relatives promptly about the arrest (principle 19) and to provide him with medical care and have him medically examined (principles 24 and 25). With regard to the latter issue the

Special Rapporteur would have preferred a stronger wording in line with the recommendation made by him in last year's report and repeated in paragraph 272 (d) of the present report.

Of similar importance is principle 27, which states that non-compliance with the provisions contained in the Body of Principles in obtaining evidence shall be taken into account in determining the admissibility of such evidence against a detained or imprisoned person. Next to the rule that evidence which itself is obtained by torture is not admissible in court, this provision contributes to reducing the incidence of torture.

Another principle which deserves mention is principle 29, which prescribes regular inspection of all places of detention by an independent inspection team. The significance of such a system of visits, preferably by international teams, as a preventive measure can hardly be overestimated.

Principle 34 states that each death occurring during detention or imprisonment or shortly afterwards must be investigated by a judicial or other impartial authority. This principle is similar to a recommendation the Special Rapporteur made in one of his previous reports.

Finally, principles 7 and 33 are of great importance for the prevention and repression of torture. Principle 33 lays down the right of a detained or imprisoned person to file a complaint about torture or other maltreatment to which he has been subjected. Principle 7 states that any act contrary to the rights and duties contained in the Body of Principles should be prohibited by law and that such acts should be made subject to appropriate sanctions. Highly relevant for the prevention of torture is paragraph 3, which gives any person who has grounds to believe that a violation of the principles has occurred, the right to report the matter to the authorities in order to have it investigated.

Compliance with the Body of Principles, as urged by the General Assembly, would make torture during detention or imprisonment virtually impossible. This will only be the case, however, if the international community responds to requests by Governments for assistance in the field of training and provision of modern equipment which offers better guarantees for the physical and mental integrity of detained persons. Respect for human rights does not come by itself; nor is it merely dependent upon the political will of the authorities, indispensable though this political will may be. Respect for human rights often also calls for costly investments. The Voluntary Fund for Advisory Services and Technical Assistance in the Field of Human Rights is of vital importance in this respect and States should enable it to carry out its task by providing it with the necessary financial means.

In many allegations the practising of torture is ascribed to members of the security forces. In most countries it is a long-established rule that people belonging to the military who are suspected of having committted an offence have to stand trial before a military tribunal. This rule may be explained by the fact that from time immemorial the military have had their own *esprit de corps,* which is still appropriate in the case of offences that have a typically military character, such as desertion or mutiny. The rule, however, makes no sense at all in cases where members of the security forces have seriously violated a civilian's basic human rights. Such an act is an offence against the public civil order and, consequently, should be tried by a civilian court. Torture is forbidden under all circumstances and this prohibition applies to all officials, whether military or civilian. It therefore cannot be seen as having any relationship to the specific functions of the military. As the civilian courts are responsible for the administration of justice in general with a view to protecting the civil public order, the civilian courts should be competent to try all offences against the civil public order, whoever may have committed them.

In the light of the foregoing, the Special Rapporteur wishes to make the following recommendations, most of which will follow the general pattern of the Body of Principles for the Protection of All Persons under Any Form of Detention or Imprisonment:

(a) Since a great number of the allegations received by the Special Rapporteur referred to torture practised during incommunicado detention, incommunicado detention should be prohibited;

(b) Other allegations referred to torture practised during illegal detention before a detainee was presented to a judge. Those who act contrary to the rules prescribed for a lawful arrest should be subjected to appropriate sanctions;

(c) Any person who is arrested should be given access to legal counsel no later than 24 hours after his arrest; his relatives should be informed promptly of his arrest and the place where he is detained;

(d) Any person who is arrested should be medically examined immediately after his arrest. Such examination should take place regularly, and in any case should be compulsory whenever the detainee is transferred to another place of detention;

(e) All interrogation sessions should be recorded; the identity of all persons present should be included in the records. Evidence obtained from the detainee during non-recorded interrogations should not be admitted in court;

(f) All places of detention should be regularly inspected by independent inspection teams. Such teams should be allowed to speak with detainees in private;

(g) In every case of death of a person during his detention or shortly after his release, an inquiry into the cause of death and the circumstances surrounding it should be held by a judicial or other impartial authority;

(h) Everyone should be entitled to file a complaint about torture or severe maltreatment with an indepedent authority; the official in charge of the investigation of the detainee's case cannot be considered to be an independent authority;

(i) Whenever a person is found to be responsible for acts of torture or severe maltreatment he should be brought to trial; if found guilty, be should be severely punished;

(j) The Body of Principles for the Protection of All Persons under Any Form of Detention or Imprisonment, the Code of Conduct for Law Enforcement Officials and the Standard Minimum Rules for the Treatment of Prisoners should be translated into national languages and used as teaching material during training courses for law enforcement personnel and members of the security forces entrusted with the task of protecting internal law and order. In particular, such personnel should be instructed on their duty to disobey orders received from a superior to practise torture.

The Commission on Human Rights examined the 1987 and 1988 reports of the Special Rapporteur at its 1988 session and, on 8 March 1988 (resolution 1988/32), expressed its serious concern about the alarming number of cases of torture and other cruel, inhuman, or degrading treatment or punishment reported to be taking place in various parts of the world. It recognized that torture constitutes a criminal obliteration of the human personality which can never be justified under any circumstances, by any ideology, or overriding interest and indicated its determination to promote the full implementation of the prohibition under international and national law of the practice of torture.

The Commission endorsed most of the Special Rapporteur's conclusions and recommendations, in particular the conclusion stressing the importance of limiting, and eventually declaring illegal, incommunicado detention under national law, since many alleged cases of torture had been reported to have taken place during incommunicado detention; and the recommendation that governments and medical associations should take strict measures against all persons belonging to the medical profession who have in that capacity had a function in the practice of torture.

The Commission extended the mandate of the Special Rapporteur for two years and called upon him, in carrying out that mandate, to seek and receive credible and reliable information from governments as well as specialized agencies, intergovernmental organizations, and non-governmental organizations.

Further conclusions and recommendations were submitted by the Special Rapporteur at the 1994 session, as follows (E/CN.4/1994/31, paras. 666–671):

As in previous years, it must be concluded that torture occurs, lamentably, in a significant number of countries. It is virtually axiomatic that situations where torture is systematically practiced are characterized by one or both of the following phenomena:

(a) The legal system does not provide the institutional safeguards needed to restrain law enforcement officials and members of security forces from resorting to abusive and illegal behaviour to achieve their aims. In particular, persons suspected of crimes or of possessing information relevant to the detection of crime are left in the hands of their interrogators without access to the outside world or other authoritative external supervision. In effect, they are detained incommunicado. They cannot call the outside world to their aid and their captors and interrogators presume they are insulated from external interference. Indeed, in this sense, this element is connected with the second one.

(b) Those conducting the torture enjoy *de jure* or *de facto* impunity. *De jure* impunity generally arises where legislation provides indemnity from legal process in respect of acts to be committed in a particular context or exemption from legal responsibility in respect of acts that have in the past been committed, for example, by way of amnesty or pardon. *De facto* impunity occurs where those committing the acts in question are in practice insulated from the normal operation of the legal system. Such immunity may begin with the absence of safeguards of the sort mentioned in (a) above. Sometimes the safeguards may be formally in place and applicable, but those charged with maintaining public order are allowed to become "a law unto themselves" or, more accurately, the law is prevented from reaching their acts. Legality and the rule of law are dispensed with. In the case of torture, grave crimes are committed in the name of main-

taining public order. Nothing can be more corrosive of general respect for law, without which no organized society can in the long term be secure.

The United Nations is aware of these phenomena. It was in the context of its efforts to combat torture that the General Assembly, in its resolutions 3218 (XXIX) and 3453 (XXX), set in motion the drafting of the instrument that was to become the Body of Principles for the Protection of All Persons under Any Form of Detention or Imprisonment. This instrument constitutes a compilation of safeguards, respect for which would radically inhibit the incidence of torture in the world. Of crucial importance in this respect are Principles 15, 16, 18, 19, 24, 25, 29, 32 and 33. In this context, the Special Rapporteur recalls the words of Principle 15 whereby "communication of the detained or imprisoned person with the outside world, and in particular his family or counsel, shall not be denied for more than a matter of days."

As regards impunity, the World Conference on Human Rights evinced a general concern with the problem in the Vienna Declaration and Programme of Action, part II, paragraph 91 of which states:

"The World Conference on Human Rights views with concern the issue of impunity of perpetrators of human rights violations, and supports the efforts of the Commission on Human Rights and the Sub-Commission on Prevention of Discrimination and Protection of Minorities to examine all aspects of the issue."

In addition, concerning the specific issue of torture, part II, paragraph 60 states: "States should abrogate legislation leading to impunity for those responsible for grave violations of human rights such as torture and prosecute such violations, thereby providing a firm basis for the rule of law."

Furthermore, in resolution 1993/40, under which the Special Rapporteur was appointed, the Commission on Human Rights endorsed the recommendation of his predecessor that whenever a complaint of torture is found to be justified, the perpetrators should be severely punished, especially the official in charge of the place of detention where the torture is found to have taken place. (E/CN.4/1992/17, para. 294 (i)).

In the final analysis, the elimination of torture is a matter of political will. Its persistence is testimony to the failure of political will. Where it occurs the absence of safeguards and the prevalence of impunity is the measure of the gap between the commitment to its eradication and the political will required to enforce the commitment.

The Special Rapporteur appreciates the spirit of cooperation shown by those Governments that have responded to information he has transmitted to them. Yet he cannot conceal his disappointment at the incidence of responses that seem more designed to camouflage rather than deal with serious situations characterized by torture, such as flat denials, references to unspecified or unsubstantiated investigations, references to legal procedures that have already been so compromised as to be incapable of affording the inquiry or information or remedy they are alleged to be able to afford. There is no dearth of recommendations that may be made to Governments seriously committed to ending torture. Most of them have been made by the previous Special Rapporteur and endorsed by the Commission. The Special Rapporteur confirms his own view as to their value and commends them for serious action by Governments.

**SEE ALSO** *Committee against Torture, UN; Impunity; Law Enforcement; Prisoners; Victims' Rights.*

**BIBLIOGRAPHY.** American Association for the Advancement of Science. *Health Services for the Treatment of Torture and Trauma Survivors: From Symposia Sponsored by the AAAS Committee on Scientific Freedom and Responsibility*. Washington, D.C.: 1990. Conference papers, in English.

American Association for the Advancement of Science, Committee on Scientific Freedom and Responsibility. *The Open Secret: Torture and the Medical Profession in Chile*. Washington, D.C.: 1987. NGO report, in English.

Amnesty International. *File on Torture*. London: 1984. NGO report, in English.

———. *Human Rights in Chile: The Role of the Medical Profession*. London: 1986. NGO report, in English.

———. *States of Emergency: Torture and Violations of the Right to Life under States of Emergency*. London: 1988. NGO report, in English.

———. *Torture in the Eighties*. London: 1984. NGO report, in English.

Boulesbaa, Ahcene. "The Nature of the Obligations Incurred by States under Article 2 of the UN Convention against Torture," *Human Rights Quarterly* 12, no. 1 (Feb. 1990): 53–93. Scholarly article, in English.

Christensen, Jan. "Amnesty International's Work for Children," *International Treatment and Rehabilitation of Torture Victims* 1, no. 2–3 (Jan. 1989): 3–5. NGO article, in English.

Claude, R., E. Stover, and J. Lopez. *Health Professionals and Human Rights in the Philippines*. Washington, D.C.: American Association for the Advancement of Science, Clearinghouse on Science and Human Rights: 1987. NGO report, in English.

"Doctors, Ethics, and Torture," *Danish Medical Bulletin* (Aug. 1987): 185–216. Conference proceedings, in English.

Fischmann, Yael, and Jaime Ross. "Group Treatment of Exiled Survivors of Torture," *American Journal of Orthopsychiatry* 60, no. 1 (Jan. 1990): 135–142. Scholarly article, in English.

Huggins, Martha K., ed. *Vigilantism and the State in Modern Latin America: Essays on Extralegal Violence*. New York: Praeger, 1991. Scholarly collective works, in English; bibliography, pp. 243–248.

Jacobson, Lone, and Peter Vesti. *Torture Survivors—A New Group of Patients*. Copenhagen, Denmark: Danish Nurses' Organizations, 1990. Educational material, in English.

Lifton, Robert J. *The Nazi Doctors: Medical Killing and the Psychology of Genocide*. New York: Basic Books, 1986. Scholarly monograph, in English.

Marzouki, Moncef. *L'Arrache Corps* (The Broken Body). Paris: Editions Alternative et Paralleles, 1979. Scholarly monograph, in French; bibliography, pp. 255–257.

Matscher, Franz, ed. *The Prohibition of Torture and Freedom of Religion and Conscience: Comparative Aspects*. Kehl am Rhein, Germany: N.P. Engel Verlag, 1991. Scholarly monograph, in English and German.

Miranda, M. J. "Torture and the Right to Human Dignity," *The Lawyers* 5, no. 1 (Jan. 1990): 15–18. Scholarly article, in English.

National Academy of Sciences. *Science and Human Rights*. Washington, D.C.: National Academy Press, 1988. NGO conference papers, in English.

Physicians for Human Rights. *Medical Testimony on Victims of Torture: A Physician's Guide to Political Asylum Cases*. Boston, MA, USA: 1991. NGO guidelines, in English.

———. *Sowing Fear: The Uses of Torture and Psychological Abuse in Chile*. Somerville, MA, USA: 1988. NGO report, in English.

Ramshaw, P., and T. Steers. *Intervention on Trial: The New York War Crimes Tribunal on Central America and the Caribbean*. New York: Praeger Publishers and National Lawyers Guild, 1987. NGO report, in English.

Rasmusen, Ole Vede. "Medical Aspects of Torture," *Danish Medical Bulletin* 37, suppl. 1 (Jan. 1990). Special issue, in English; bibliography, pp. 62–67.

Rayner, Mary. *Turning a Blind Eye: Medical Accountability and the Prevention of Torture in South Africa*. Washington, D.C.: American Association for the Advancement of Science, Committee on Scientific Freedom and Responsibility, 1987. NGO report, in English.

Rehabiliterings Center for Torturofre (Rehabilitation Centre for Torture Victims). *Annual Report 19–*. Copenhagen, Denmark. NGO annual report, in English.

SOS Torture. *Practical Guide to the International Procedures Relative to Complaint and Appeals against Acts of Torture, Disappearances and Other Inhuman or Degrading Treatment*. Geneva, Switzerland: 1988. Manual, in English.

———. "The Role of NGOs in the Defence and Promotion of Human Rights, Especially in Relation to the Question of Torture," *SOS Torture* 6 (Jan. 1987): 28–35. NGO editorial, in English and French.

Stover, E., and E. Nightingale, eds. *The Breaking of Bodies and Minds: Torture, Psychiatric Abuse, and the Health Professionals*. New York: American Association for the Advancement of Science, 1985. Collection of essays, in English.

Sunga, Lyal S. *Individual Responsibility in International Law for Serious Human Rights Violations*. Dordrecht, the Netherlands: Martinus Nijhoff, 1992. Scholarly monograph, in English.

*Trabajamos para la Vida: Consecuencias de la Represion en el Cono Sur, el Medico y los Derechos Humanos* (We Work for Life: Consequences of Repression in the Southern Cone, Physicians and Human Rights). Montevideo, Uruguay: Universidad de la Republica, Facultad de Medicina, 1987. Conference proceedings, in Spanish.

UN Commission on Human Rights. *Question of the Human Rights of All Persons Subjected to Any Form of Detention or Imprisonment, Torture and Other Cruel, Inhuman or Degrading Treatment or Punishment*. Report by Special Rapporteur P. Kooijmans, E/CN.4/1987/13, 43rd sess. Geneva, Switzerland: 1987. IGO report, in English.

## TORTURE: CONVENTION AGAINST TORTURE AND OTHER CRUEL, INHUMAN OR DEGRADING TREATMENT OR PUNISHMENT, UN (1984).

The Convention defines "torture" and obliges every State party to take effective legislative, administrative, judicial, and other measures to prevent acts of torture in any territory under its jurisdiction. It authorizes (article 17) the establishment of the **COMMITTEE AGAINST TORTURE,** consisting of ten experts elected by the States parties but serving in their personal capacity. The States parties undertake to submit to the Committee every four years reports on the measures they have taken to give effect to the Convention, and the Committee is authorized to examine the reports and to make general comments on them.

The Convention provides (article 20) for the handling by the Committee of "reliable information which appears to contain well-founded indications that torture is being systematically practiced in the territory of a State Party." Under article 21, a State party may at any time declare that it recognizes the competence of the Committee to receive and consider communications to the effect that a State party claims that another State party is not fulfilling its obligations under the Convention. Special procedures are provided for the handling of such communications. Further, under article 22, a State party may at any time declare that it recognizes the competence of the Committee to receive and consider communications from or on behalf of individuals subject to its jurisdiction who claim to be victims of a violation by a State party of the provisions of the Convention, and special procedures are provided for the handling of those communications.

The Convention was preceded by the UN Declaration on the Protection of All Persons from Being Subjected to Torture and Other Cruel, Inhuman or Degrading Treatment or Punishment, which had been adopted by the UN **GENERAL ASSEMBLY** on 9 December 1975 (resolution 3452 [XXX]). The Convention, adopted by the General Assembly on 10 December 1984 (resolution 39/46), entered into force on 26 June 1987. The Committee against Torture was organized at a meeting of the States parties held on 26 June 1987.

The text of the Convention, annexed to resolution 39/46, is as follows:

The States Parties to this Convention,

Considering that, in accordance with the principles proclaimed in the Charter of the United Nations, recognition of the equal and inalienable rights of all members of the human family is the foundation of freedom, justice and peace in the world,

Recognizing that those rights derive from the inherent dignity of the human person,

Considering the obligation of States under the Charter, in particular Article 55, to promote universal respect for, and observance of, human rights and fundamental freedoms,

Having regard to article 5 of the Universal Declaration of Human Rights and article 7 of the International Covenant on Civil and Political Rights, both of which provide that no one shall be subjected to torture or to cruel, inhuman or degrading treatment or punishment,

Having regard also to the Declaration on the Protection of All Persons from Being Subjected to Torture and Other Cruel, Inhuman or Degrading Treatment or Punishment, adopted by the General Assembly on 9 December 1975,

Desiring to make more effective the struggle against torture and other cruel, inhuman or degrading treatment or punishment throughout the world,

Have agreed as follows:

## Part I

*Article 1.* 1. For the purposes of this Convention, the term "torture" means any act by which severe pain or suffering, whether physical or mental, is intentionally inflicted on a person for such purposes as obtaining from him or a third person information or a confession, punishing him for an act he or a third person has committed or is suspected of having committed, or intimidating or coercing him or a third person, or for any reason based on discrimination of any kind, when such pain or suffering is inflicted by or at the instigation of or with the consent or acquiescence of a public official or other person acting in an official capacity. It does not include pain or suffering arising only from, inherent in or incidental to lawful sanctions.

2. This article is without prejudice to any international instrument or national legislation which does or may contain provisions of wider application.

*Article 2.* 1. Each State Party shall take effective legislative, administrative, judicial or other measures to prevent acts of torture in any territory under its jurisdiction.

2. No exceptional circumstances whatsoever, whether a state of war or a threat of war, internal political instability or any other public emergency, may be invoked as a justification of torture.

3. An order from a superior officer or a public authority may not be invoked as a justification of torture.

*Article 3.* 1. No State Party shall expel, return (*"refouler"*) or extradite a person to another State where there are substantial grounds for believing that he would be in danger of being subjected to torture.

2. For the purpose of determining whether there are such grounds, the competent authorities shall take into account all relevant considerations including, where applicable, the existence in the State concerned of a consistent pattern of gross, flagrant or mass violations of human rights.

*Article 4.* 1. Each State Party shall ensure that all acts of torture are offences under its criminal law. The same shall apply to an attempt to commit torture and to an act by any person which constitutes complicity or participation in torture.

2. Each State Party shall make these offences punishable by appropriate penalties which take into account their grave nature.

*Article 5.* 1. Each State Party shall take such measures as may be necessary to establish its jurisdiction over the offences referred to in article 4 in the following cases:

(a) When the offences are committed in any territory under its jurisdiction or on board a ship or aircraft registered in that State;

(b) When the alleged offender is a national of that State;

(c) When the victim is a national of that State if that State considers it appropriate.

2. Each State Party shall likewise take such measures as may be necessary to establish its jurisdiction over such offences in cases where the alleged offender is present in any territory under its jurisdiction and it does not extradite him pursuant to article 8 to any of the States mentioned in paragraph 1 of this article.

3. This Convention does not exclude any criminal jurisdiction exercised in accordance with internal law.

*Article 6.* 1. Upon being satisfied, after an examination of information available to it, that the circumstances so warrant, any State Party in whose territory a person alleged to have committed any offence referred to in article 4 is present shall take him into custody or take other legal measures to ensure his presence. The custody and other legal measures shall be as provided in the law of that State but may be continued only for such time as is necessary to enable any criminal or extradition proceedings to be instituted.

2. Such State shall immediately make a preliminary inquiry into the facts.

3. Any person in custody pursuant to paragraph 1 of this article shall be assisted in communicating immediately with the nearest appropriate representative of the State of which he is a national, or, if he is a stateless person, with the representative of the State where he usually resides.

4. When a State, pursuant to this article, has taken a person into custody, it shall immediately notify the States referred to in article 5, paragraph 1, of the fact that such person is in custody and of the circumstances which warrant his detention. The State which makes the preliminary inquiry contemplated in paragraph 2 of this article shall promptly report its findings to the said States and shall indicate whether it intends to exercise jurisdiction.

*Article 7.* 1. The State Party in the territory under whose jurisdiction a person alleged to have committed any offence referred to in article 4 is found shall in the cases contemplated in article 5, if it does not extradite him, submit the case to its competent authorities for the purpose of prosecution.

2. These authorities shall take their decision in the same manner as in the case of any ordinary offence of a serious nature under the law of that State. In the cases referred to in article 5, paragraph 2, the standards of evidence required for prosecution and conviction shall in no way be less stringent than those which apply in the cases referred to in article 5, paragraph 1.

3. Any person regarding whom proceedings are brought in connection with any of the offences referred to in article 4 shall be guaranteed fair treatment at all stages of the proceedings.

*Article 8.* 1. The offences referred to in article 4 shall be deemed to be included as extraditable offences in any extradition treaty existing between States Parties. States Parties undertake to include such offences as extraditable offences in every extradition treaty to be concluded between them.

2. If a State Party which makes extradition conditional on the existence of a treaty receives a request for extradition from another State Party with which it has no extradition treaty, it may consider this Convention as the legal basis for extradition in respect of such offences. Extradition shall be subject to the other conditions provided by the law of the requested State.

3. States Parties which do not make extradition conditional on the existence of a treaty shall recognize such offences as extraditable offences between themselves subject to the conditions provided by the law of the requested State.

4. Such offences shall be treated, for the purpose of extradition between States Parties, as if they had been committed not only in the place in which they occurred but also in the territories of the States required to establish their jurisdiction in accordance with article 5, paragraph 1.

*Article 9.* 1. States Parties shall afford one another the greatest measure of assistance in connection with criminal proceedings brought in respect of any of the offences referred to in article 4, including the supply of all evidence at their disposal necessary for the proceedings.

2. States Parties shall carry out their obligations under paragraph 1 of this article in conformity with any treaties on mutual judicial assistance that may exist between them.

*Article 10.* 1. Each State Party shall ensure that education and information regarding the prohibition against torture are fully included in the training of law enforcement personnel, civil or military, medical personnel, public officials and other persons who may be involved in the custody, interrogation or treatment of any individual subjected to any form of arrest, detention or imprisonment.

2. Each State Party shall include this prohibition in the rules or instructions issued in regard to the duties and functions of any such persons.

*Article 11.* Each State Party shall keep under systematic review interrogation rules, instructions, methods and practices as well as arrangements for the custody and treatment of persons subjected to any form of arrest, detention or imprisonment in any territory under its jurisdiction, with a view to preventing any cases of torture.

*Article 12.* Each State Party shall ensure that its competent authorities proceed to a prompt and impartial investigation, wherever there is reasonable ground to believe that an act of torture has been committed in any territory under its jurisdiction.

*Article 13.* Each State Party shall ensure that any individual who alleges he has been subjected to torture in any territory under its jurisdiction has the right to complain to, and to have his case promptly and impartially examined by, its competent authorities. Steps shall be taken to ensure that the complainant and witnesses are protected against all ill-treatment or intimidation as a consequence of his complaint or any evidence given.

*Article 14.* 1. Each State Party shall ensure in its legal system that the victim of an act of torture obtains redress and has an enforceable right to fair and adequate compensation, including the means for as full rehabilitation as possible. In the event of the death of the victim as a result of an act of torture, his dependants shall be entitled to compensation.

2. Nothing in this article shall affect any right of the victim or other persons to compensation which may exist under national law.

*Article 15.* Each State Party shall ensure that any statement which is established to have been made as a result of torture shall not be invoked as evidence in any proceedings, except against a person accused of torture as evidence that the statement was made.

*Article 16.* 1. Each State Party shall undertake to prevent in any territory under its jurisdiction other acts of cruel, inhuman or degrading treatment or punishment which do not amount to torture as defined in article 1, when such acts are committed by or at the instigation of or with the consent or acquiescence of a public official or other person acting in an official capacity. In particular, the obligations contained in articles 10, 11, 12 and 13 shall apply with the substitution for references to torture of references to other forms of cruel, inhuman or degrading treatment or punishment.

2. The provisions of this Convention are without prejudice to the provisions of any other international instrument or national law which prohibits cruel, inhuman or degrading treatment or punishment or which relates to extradition or expulsion.

## Part II

*Article 17.* 1. There shall be established a Committee against Torture (hereinafter referred to as the Committee) which shall carry out the functions hereinafter provided. The Committee shall consist of ten experts of high moral standing and recognized competence in the field of human rights, who shall serve in their personal capacity. The experts shall be elected by the States Parties, consideration being given to equitable geographical distribution and to the usefulness of the participation of some persons having legal experience.

2. The members of the Committee shall be elected by secret ballot from a list of persons nominated by States Parties. Each State Party may nominate one person from among its own nationals. States Parties shall bear in mind the usefulness of nominating persons who are also members of the Human Rights Committee established under the International Covenant on Civil and Political Rights and who are willing to serve on the Committee against Torture.

3. Elections of the members of the Committee shall be held at biennial meetings of States Parties convened by the Secretary-General of the United Nations. At those meetings, for which two thirds of the States Parties shall constitute a quorum, the persons elected to the Committee shall be those who obtain the largest number of votes and an absolute majority of the votes of the representatives of States Parties present and voting.

4. The initial election shall be held no later than six months after the date of the entry into force of this Convention. At least four months before the date of each election, the Secretary-General of the United Nations shall address a letter to the States Parties inviting them to submit their nominations within three months. The Secretary-General shall prepare a list in alphabetical order of all persons thus nominated, indicating the States Parties which have nominated them, and shall submit it to the States Parties.

5. The members of the Committee shall be elected for a term of four years. They shall be eligible for re-election if renominated. However, the term of five of the members elected at the first election shall expire at the end of two years; immediately after the first election the names of these five members shall be chosen by lot by the chairman of the meeting referred to in paragraph 3 of this article.

6. If a member of the Committee dies or resigns or for any other cause can no longer perform his Committee duties, the State Party which nominated him shall appoint another expert from among its nationals to serve for the remainder of his term, subject to the approval of the majority of the States Parties. The approval shall be considered given unless half or more of the States Parties respond negatively within six weeks after having been informed by the Secretary-General of the United Nations of the proposed appointment.

7. States Parties shall be responsible for the expenses of the members of the Committee while they are in performance of Committee duties.

*Article 18.* 1. The Committee shall elect its officers for a term of two years. They may be re-elected.

2. The Committee shall establish its own rules of procedure, but these rules shall provide, *inter alia,* that:

(a) Six members shall constitute a quorum;

(b) Decisions of the Committee shall be made by a majority vote of the members present.

3. The Secretary-General of the United Nations shall provide the necessary staff and facilities for the effective performance of the functions of the Committee under this Convention.

4. The Secretary-General of the United Nations shall convene the initial meeting of the Committee. After its initial meeting, the Committee shall meet at such times as shall be provided in its rules of procedure.

5. The States Parties shall be responsible for expenses incurred in connection with the holding of meetings of the States Parties and of the Committee, including reimbursement to the United Nations for any expenses, such as the cost of staff and facilities, incurred by the United Nations pursuant to paragraph 3 of this article.

*Article 19.* 1. The States Parties shall submit to the Committee, through the Secretary-General of the United Nations, reports on the measures they have taken to give effect to their undertakings under this Convention, within one year after the entry into force of the Convention for the State Party concerned. Thereafter, the States Parties shall submit supplementary reports every four years on any new measures taken and such other reports as the Committee may request.

2. The Secretary-General of the United Nations shall transmit the reports to all States Parties.

3. Each report shall be considered by the Committee which may make such general comments on the report as it may consider appropriate and shall forward these to the State Party concerned. That State Party may respond with any observations it chooses to the Committee.

4. The Committee may, at its discretion, decide to include any comments made by it in accordance with paragraph 3 of this article, together with the observations thereon received from the State Party concerned, in its annual report made in accordance with article 24. If so requested by the State Party concerned, the Committee may also include a copy of the report submitted under paragraph 1 of this article.

*Article 20.* 1. If the Committee receives reliable information which appears to it to contain well-founded indications that torture is being systematically practised in the territory of a State Party, the Committee shall invite that State Party to co-operate in the examination of the information and to this end to submit observations with regard to the information concerned.

2. Taking into account any observations which may have been submitted by the State Party concerned, as well as any other relevant information available to it, the Committee may, if it decides that this is warranted, designate one or more of its members to make a confidential inquiry and to report to the Committee urgently.

3. If an inquiry is made in accordance with paragraph 2 of this article, the Committee shall seek the co-operation of the State Party concerned. In agreement with that State Party, such an inquiry may include a visit to its territory.

4. After examining the findings of its member or members submitted in accordance with paragraph 2 of this article, the Committee shall transmit these findings to the State Party concerned together with any comments or suggestions which seem appropriate in view of the situation.

5. All the proceedings of the Committee referred to in paragraphs 1 to 4 of this article shall be confidential, and at all stages of the proceedings the co-operation of the State Party shall be sought. After such proceedings have been completed with regard to an inquiry made in accordance with paragraph 2, the Committee may, after consultations with the State Party concerned, decide to include a summary account of the results of the proceedings in its annual report made in accordance with article 24.

*Article 21.* 1. A State Party to this Convention may at any time declare under this article that it recognizes the competence of the Committee to receive and consider communications to the effect that a State Party claims that another State Party is not fulfilling its obligations under this Convention. Such communications may be received and considered according to the procedures laid down in this article only if submitted by a State Party which has made a declaration recognizing in regard to itself the competence of the Committee. No communication shall be dealt with by the Committee under this article if it concerns a State Party which has not made such a declaration. Communications received under this article shall be dealt with in accordance with the following procedure:

(a) If a State Party considers that another State Party is not giving effect to the provisions of this Convention, it may, by written communication, bring the matter to the attention of that State Party. Within three months after the receipt of the communication the receiving State shall afford the State which sent the communication an explanation or any other statement in writing clarifying the matter, which should include, to the extent possible and pertinent, reference to domestic procedures and remedies taken, pending or available in the matter;

(b) If the matter is not adjusted to the satisfaction of both States Parties concerned within six months after the receipt by the receiving State of the initial communication, either State shall have the right to refer the matter to the Committee, by notice given to the Committee and to the other State;

(c) The Committee shall deal with a matter referred to it under this article only after it has ascertained that all domestic remedies have been invoked and exhausted in the matter, in conformity with the generally recognized principles of international law. This shall not be the rule where the application of the remedies is unreasonably prolonged or is unlikely to bring effective relief to the person who is the victim of the violation of this Convention;

(d) The Committee shall hold closed meetings when examining communications under this article;

(e) Subject to the provisions of subparagraph (c), the Committee shall make available its good offices to the States Parties concerned with a view to a friendly solution of the matter on the basis of respect for the obligations provided for in this Convention. For this purpose, the Committee may, when appropriate, set up an *ad hoc* conciliation commission;

(f) In any matter referred to it under this article, the Committee may call upon the States Parties concerned, referred to in subparagraph (b), to supply any relevant information;

(g) The States Parties concerned, referred to in subparagraph (b), shall have the right to be represented when the matter is being considered by the Committee and to make submissions orally and/or in writing;

(h) The Committee shall, within twelve months after the date of receipt of notice under subparagraph (b), submit a report:

(i) If a solution within the terms of subparagraph (e) is reached, the Committee shall confine its report to a brief statement of the facts and of the solution reached;

(ii) If a solution within the terms of subparagraph (e) is not reached, the Committee shall confine its report to a brief statement of the facts; the written submissions and record of the oral submissions made by the States Parties concerned shall be attached to the report.

In every matter, the report shall be communicated to the States Parties concerned.

2. The provisions of this article shall come into force when five States Parties to this Convention have made declarations under paragraph 1 of this article. Such declarations shall be deposited by the States Parties with the Secretary-General of the United Nations, who shall transmit copies thereof to the other States Parties. A declaration may be withdrawn at any time by notification to the Secretary-General. Such a withdrawal shall not prejudice the consideration of any matter which is the subject of a communication already transmitted under this article; no further communication by any State Party shall be received under this article after the

notification of withdrawal of the declaration has been received by the Secretary-General, unless the State Party concerned has made a new declaration.

*Article 22.* 1. A State Party to this Convention may at any time declare under this article that it recognizes the competence of the Committee to receive and consider communications from or on behalf of individuals subject to its jurisdiction who claim to be victims of a violation by a State Party of the provisions of the Convention. No communication shall be received by the Committee if it concerns a State Party which has not made such a declaration.

2. The Committee shall consider inadmissible any communication under this article which is anonymous or which it considers to be an abuse of the right of submission of such communications or to be incompatible with the provisions of this Convention.

3. Subject to the provisions of paragraph 2, the Committee shall bring any communications submitted to it under this article to the attention of the State Party to this Convention which has made a declaration under paragraph 1 and is alleged to be violating any provisions of the Convention. Within six months, the receiving State shall submit to the Committee written explanations or statements clarifying the matter and the remedy, if any, that may have been taken by that State.

4. The Committee shall consider communications received under this article in the light of all information made available to it by or on behalf of the individual and by the State Party concerned.

5. The Committee shall not consider any communications from an individual under this article unless it has ascertained that:

(a) The same matter has not been, and is not being, examined under another procedure of international investigation or settlement;

(b) The individual has exhausted all available domestic remedies; this shall not be the rule where the application of the remedies is unreasonably prolonged or is unlikely to bring effective relief to the person who is the victim of the violation of this Convention.

6. The Committee shall hold closed meetings when examining communications under this article.

7. The Committee shall forward its views to the State Party concerned and to the individual.

8. The provisions of this article shall come into force when five States Parties to this Convention have made declarations under paragraph 1 of this article. Such declarations shall be deposited by the States Parties with the Secretary-General of the United Nations, who shall transmit copies thereof to the other States Parties. A declaration may be withdrawn at any time by notification to the Secretary-General. Such a withdrawal shall not prejudice the consideration of any matter which is the subject of a communication already transmitted under this article; no further communication by or on behalf of an individual shall be received under this article after the notification of withdrawal of the declaration has been received by the Secretary-General, unless the State Party has made a new declaration.

*Article 23.* The members of the Committee and of the *ad hoc* conciliation commissions which may be appointed under article 21, paragraph 1 (e), shall be entitled to the facilities, privileges and immunities of experts on mission for the United Nations as laid down in the relevant sections of the Convention on the Privileges and Immunities of the United Nations.

*Article 24.* The Committee shall submit an annual report

on its activities under this Convention to the States Parties and to the General Assembly of the United Nations.

## Part III

*Article 25.* 1. This Convention is open for signature by all States.

2. This Convention is subject to ratification. Instruments of ratification shall be deposited with the Secretary-General of the United Nations.

*Article 26.* This Convention is open to accession by all States. Accession shall be effected by the deposit of an instrument of accession with the Secretary-General of the United Nations.

*Article 27.* 1. This Convention shall enter into force on the thirtieth day after the date of the deposit with the Secretary-General of the United Nations of the twentieth instrument of ratification or accession.

2. For each State ratifying this Convention or acceding to it after the deposit of the twentieth instrument of ratification or accession, the Convention shall enter into force on the thirtieth day after the date of the deposit of its own instrument of ratification or accession.

*Article 28.* 1. Each State may, at the time of signature or ratification of this Convention or accession thereto, declare that it does not recognize the competence of the Committee provided for in article 20.

2. Any State Party having made a reservation in accordance with paragraph 1 of this article may, at any time, withdraw this reservation by notification to the Secretary-General of the United Nations.

*Article 29.* 1. Any State Party to this Convention may propose an amendment and file it with the Secretary-General of the United Nations. The Secretary-General shall thereupon communicate the proposed amendment to the States Parties with a request that they notify him whether they favour a conference of States Parties for the purpose of considering and voting upon the proposal. In the event that within four months from the date of such communication at least one third of the States Parties favours such a conference, the Secretary-General shall convene the conference under the auspices of the United Nations. Any amendment adopted by a majority of the States Parties present and voting at the conference shall be submitted by the Secretary-General to all the States Parties for acceptance.

2. An amendment adopted in accordance with paragraph 1 of this article shall enter into force when two thirds of the States Parties to this Convention have notified the Secretary-General of the United Nations that they have accepted it in accordance with their respective constitutional processes.

3. When amendments enter into force, they shall be binding on those States Parties which have accepted them, other States Parties still being bound by the provisions of this Convention and any earlier amendments which they have accepted.

*Article 30.* 1. Any dispute between two or more States Parties concerning the interpretation or application of this Convention which cannot be settled through negotiation shall, at the request of one of them, be submitted to arbitration. If within six months from the date of the request for arbitration the Parties are unable to agree on the organization of the arbitration, any one of those Parties may refer the dispute to the International Court of Justice by request in conformity with the Statute of the Court.

2. Each State may, at the time of signature or ratification of this Convention or accession thereto, declare that it does not consider itself bound by paragraph 1 of this article. The other States Parties shall not be bound by paragraph 1 of this article with respect to any State Party having made such a reservation.

3. Any State Party having made a reservation in accordance with paragraph 2 of this article may at any time withdraw this reservation by notification to the Secretary-General of the United Nations.

*Article 31.* 1. A State Party may denounce this Convention by written notification to the Secretary-General of the United Nations. Denunciation becomes effective one year after the date of receipt of the notification by the Secretary-General.

2. Such a denunciation shall not have the effect of releasing the State Party from its obligations under this Convention in regard to any act or omission which occurs prior to the date at which the denunciation becomes effective, nor shall denunciation prejudice in any way the continued consideration of any matter which is already under consideration by the Committee prior to the date at which the denunciation becomes effective.

3. Following the date at which the denunciation of a State Party becomes effective, the Committee shall not commence consideration of any new matter regarding that State.

*Article 32.* The Secretary-General of the United Nations shall inform all States Members of the United Nations and all States which have signed this Convention or acceded to it of the following:

(a) Signatures, ratifications and accessions under articles 25 and 26;

(b) The date of entry into force of this Convention under article 27 and the date of the entry into force of any amendments under article 29;

(c) Denunciations under article 31.

*Article 33.* 1. This Convention, of which the Arabic, Chinese, English, French, Russian and Spanish texts are equally authentic, shall be deposited with the Secretary-General of the United Nations.

2. The Secretary-General of the United Nations shall transmit certified copies of this Convention to all States.

*RATIFICATIONS AND ACCESSIONS.* The following 85 UN member States have ratified or acceded to the Convention as of 31 December 1994:

Afghanistan, Albania, Algeria, Antigua and Barbuda, Argentina, Armenia, Australia, Austria, Azerbaijan

Belarus, Belize, Benin, Bosnia Herzegovina, Brazil, Bulgaria, Burkina Faso, Burundi

Cambodia, Cameroon, Canada, Cape Verde, Chile, China, Colombia, Comoros, Croatia, Czech Republic

Denmark

Ecuador, Egypt, Estonia, Ethiopia

Finland, France

Georgia, Germany, Greece, Guatemala, Guinea, Guyana

Hungary

Israel, Italy

Jordan

Latvia, Libya, Liechtenstein, Luxembourg

Malta, Mauritius, Mexico, Monaco, Morocco

Namibia, Nepal, Netherlands, New Zealand, Norway

Panama, Paraguay, Peru, Philippines, Poland, Portugal

Romania, Russian Federation

Senegal, Seychelles, Slovakia, Slovenia, Somalia, Spain, Sri Lanka, Sweden

Tunisia, Turkey

Uganda, Ukraine, United Kingdom, United States of America, Uruguay

Venezuela

Yemen, Yugoslavia (Serbia and Montenegro)

**SIGNATURES.** The following 14 UN Member States have signed the Convention but had not ratified it as of 31 December 1994:

Belgium, Bolivia

Cuba

Dominican Republic

Gabon, Gambia

Iceland, Indonesia, Ireland

Nicaragua, Nigeria

Sierra Leone, South Africa, Sudan

**BIBLIOGRAPHY.** Sottas, Eric. "Some Salient Features of the Convention against Torture and Other Cruel, Inhuman or Degrading Treatment or Punishment," *SOS Torture* 4 (Sept. 1986): 35–39. NGO journal article, in English and French.

## TORTURE: EUROPEAN CONVENTION FOR THE PREVENTION OF TORTURE AND INHUMAN OR DEGRADING TREATMENT OR PUNISHMENT

**(1987).** The Convention was concluded by the Committee of Ministers of the **COUNCIL OF EUROPE** on 26 June 1987 and entered into force on 1 February 1989. The text of the Convention (*European Treaty Series* 126) is as follows:

### Preamble

The member States of the Council of Europe, signatory hereto,

Having regard to the provisions of the Convention for the Protection of Human Rights and Fundamental Freedoms,

Recalling that, under Article 3 of the same Convention, "no one shall be subjected to torture or to inhuman or degrading treatment or punishment";

Noting that the machinery provided for in that Convention operates in relation to persons who allege that they are victims of violations of Article 3;

Convinced that the protection of persons deprived of their liberty against torture and inhuman or degrading treatment or punishment could be strengthened by non-judicial means of a preventive character based on visits,

Have agreed as follows:

### Section I

*Article 1.* There shall be established a European Committee for the Prevention of Torture and Inhuman or Degrading Treatment or Punishment (hereinafter referred to as "the Committee"). The Committee shall, by means of visits, examine the treatment of persons deprived of their liberty with a view to strengthening, if necessary, the protection of such persons from torture and from inhuman or degrading treatment or punishment.

*Article 2.* Each Party shall permit visits, in accordance with this Convention, to any place within its jurisdiction where persons are deprived of their liberty by a public authority.

*Article 3.* In the application of this Convention, the Committee and the competent national authorities of the Party concerned shall co-operate with each other.

### Section II

*Article 4.* 1. The Committee shall consist of a number of members equal to that of the Parties.

2. The members of the Committee shall be chosen from among persons of high moral character, known for their competence in the field of human rights or having professional experience in the areas covered by this Convention.

3. No two members of the Committee may be nationals of the same State.

4. The members shall serve in their individual capacity, shall be independent and impartial, and shall be available to serve the Committee effectively.

*Article 5.* 1. The members of the Committee shall be elected by the Committee of Ministers by an absolute majority of votes, from a list of names drawn up by the Bureau of the Consultative Assembly; each national delegation of the Parties in the Consultative Assembly shall put forward three candidates, of whom two at least shall be its nationals.

2. The same procedure shall be followed in filling casual vacancies.

3. The members of the Committee shall be elected for a period of four years. They may only be re-elected once. However, among the members elected at the first election, the terms of three members shall expire at the end of two years. The members whose terms are to expire at the end of the initial period of two years shall be chosen by lot by the Secretary General of the Council of Europe immediately after the first election has been completed.

*Article 6.* 1. The Committee shall meet in camera. A quorum shall be equal to the majority of its members. The decisions of the Committee shall be taken by a majority of the members present, subject to Article 10, paragraph 2.

2. The Committee shall draw up its own rules of procedure.

3. The Secretariat of the Committee shall be provided by the Secretary General of the Council of Europe.

### Section III

*Article 7.* 1. The Committee shall organise visits to places referred to in Article 2. Apart from periodic visits, the Committee may organise such other visits as appear to it to be required in the circumstances.

2. As a general rule, the visits shall be carried out by at least two members of the Committee. The Committee may, if it considers it necessary, be assisted by experts and interpreters.

*Article 8.* 1. The Committee shall notify the Government of the Party concerned of its intention to carry out a visit. After such notification, it may at any time visit any place referred to in Article 2.

2. A Party shall provide the Committee with the following facilities to carry out its task:

(a) access to its territory and the right to travel without restriction;

(b) full information on the places where persons deprived of their liberty are being held;

(c) unlimited access to any place where persons are deprived of their liberty, including the right to move inside such places without restriction;

(d) other information available to the Party which is necessary for the Committee to carry out its task. In seeking such information, the Committee shall have regard to applicable rules of national law and professional ethics.

3. The Committee may interview in private persons deprived of their liberty.

4. The Committee may communicate freely with any person whom it believes can supply relevant information.

5. If necessary, the Committee may immediately communicate observations to the competent authorities of the Party concerned.

*Article 9.* 1. In exceptional circumstances, the competent authorities of the Party concerned may make representations to the Committee against a visit at the time or to the particular place proposed by the Committee. Such representations may only be made on grounds of national defence, public safety, serious disorder in places where persons are deprived of their liberty, the medical condition of a person or that an urgent interrogation relating to a serious crime is in progress.

2. Following such representations, the Committee and the Party shall immediately enter into consultations in order to clarify the situation and seek agreement on arrangements to enable the Committee to exercise its functions expeditiously. Such arrangements may include the transfer to another place of any person whom the Committee proposed to visit. Until the visit takes place, the Party shall provide information to the Committee about any person concerned.

*Article 10.* 1. After each visit, the Committee shall draw up a report on the facts found during the visit, taking account of any observations which may have been submitted by the Party concerned. It shall transmit to the latter its report containing any recommendations it considers necessary. The Committee may consult with the Party with a view to suggesting, if necessary, improvements in the protection of persons deprived of their liberty.

2. If the Party fails to co-operate or refuses to improve the situation in the light of the Committee's recommendations, the Committee may decide, after the Party has had an opportunity to make known its views, by a majority of two-thirds of its members to make a public statement on the matter.

*Article 11.* 1. The information gathered by the Committee in relation to a visit, its report and its consultations with the Party concerned shall be confidential.

2. The Committee shall publish its report, together with any comments of the Party concerned, whenever requested to do so by that Party.

3. However, no personal data shall be published without the express consent of the person concerned.

*Article 12.* Subject to the rules of confidentiality in Article 11, the Committee shall every year submit to the Committee of Ministers a general report on its activities which shall be transmitted to the Consultative Assembly and made public.

*Article 13.* The members of the Committee, experts and other persons assisting the Committee are required, during and after their terms of office, to maintain the confidentiality of the facts or information of which they have become aware during the discharge of their functions.

*Article 14.* 1. The names of persons assisting the Committee shall be specified in the notification under Article 8, paragraph 1.

2. Experts shall act on the instructions and under the authority of the Committee. They shall have particular knowledge and experience in the areas covered by this Convention and shall be bound by the same duties of independence, impartiality and availability as the members of the Committee.

3. A Party may exceptionally declare that an expert or other person assisting the Committee may not be allowed to take part in a visit to a place within its jurisdiction.

**Section IV**

*Article 15.* Each Party shall inform the Committee of the name and address of the authority competent to receive notifications to its Government, and of any liaison officer it may appoint.

*Article 16.* The Committee, its members and experts referred to in Article 7, paragraph 2 shall enjoy the privileges and immunities set out in the Annex to this Convention.

*Article 17.* 1. This Convention shall not prejudice the provisions of domestic law or any international agreement which provide greater protection for persons deprived of their liberty.

2. Nothing in this Convention shall be construed as limiting or derogating from the competence of the organs of the European Convention on Human Rights or from the obligations assumed by the Parties under that Convention.

3. The Committee shall not visit places which representatives or delegates of Protecting Powers or the International Committee of the Red Cross effectively visit on a regular basis by virtue of the Geneva Conventions of 12 August 1949 and the Additional Protocols of 8 June 1977 thereto.

**Section V**

*Article 18.* This Convention shall be open for signature by the member States of the Council of Europe. It is subject to ratification, acceptance or approval. Instruments of ratification, acceptance or approval shall be deposited with the Secretary General of the Council of Europe.

*Article 19.* 1. This Convention shall enter into force on the first day of the month following the expiration of a period of three months after the date on which seven member States of the Council of Europe have expressed their consent to be bound by the Convention in accordance with the provisions of Article 18.

2. In respect of any member State which subsequently expresses its consent to be bound by it, the Convention shall enter into force on the first day of the month following the expiration of a period of three months after the date of the deposit of the instrument of ratification, acceptance or approval.

*Article 20.* 1. Any State may at the time of signature or when depositing its instrument of ratification, acceptance or approval, specify the territory or territories to which this Convention shall apply.

2. Any State may at any later date, by a declaration addressed to the Secretary General of the Council of Europe,

extend the application of this Convention to any other territory specified in the declaration. In respect of such territory the Convention shall enter into force on the first day of the month following the expiration of a period of three months after the date of receipt of such declaration by the Secretary General.

3. Any declaration made under the two preceding paragraphs may, in respect of any territory specified in such declaration, be withdrawn by a notification addressed to the Secretary General. The withdrawal shall become effective on the first day of the month following the expiration of a period of three months after the date of receipt of such notification by the Secretary General.

*Article 21.* No reservation may be made in respect of the provisions of this Convention.

*Article 22.* 1. Any Party may, at any time, denounce this Convention by means of a notification addressed to the Secretary General of the Council of Europe.

2. Such denunciation shall become effective on the first day of the month following the expiration of a period of twelve months after the date of receipt of the notification by the Secretary General.

*Article 23.* The Secretary General of the Council of Europe shall notify the member States of the Council of Europe of:

    (a) any signature;

    (b) the deposit of any instrument of ratification, acceptance or approval;

    (c) any date of entry into force of this Convention in accordance with Articles 19 and 20;

    (d) any other act, notification or communication relating to this Convention, except for action taken in pursuance of Articles 8 and 10.

In witness whereof, the undersigned, being duly authorised thereto, have signed this Convention.

Done at Strasbourg, this 26th day of November, 1987, in English and French, both texts being equally authentic, in a single copy which shall be deposited in the archives of the Council of Europe. The Secretary General of the Council of Europe shall transmit certified copies to each member State of the Council of Europe.

### Annex: Privileges and Immunities

*(Article 16)* 1. For the purpose of this annex, references to members of the Committee shall be deemed to include references to experts mentioned in Article 7, paragraph 2.

2. The members of the Committee shall, while exercising their functions and during journeys made in the exercise of their functions, enjoy the following privileges and immunities:

    (a) immunity from personal arrest or detention and from seizure of their personal baggage and, in respect of words spoken or written and all acts done by them in their official capacity, immunity from legal process of every kind;

    (b) exemption from any restrictions on their freedom of movement on exit from and return to their country of residence, and entry into and exit from the country in which they exercise their functions, and from alien registration in the country which they are visiting or through which they are passing in the exercise of their functions.

3. In the course of journeys undertaken in the exercise of their functions, the members of the Committee shall, in the matter of customs and exchange control, be accorded:

    (a) by their own Government, the same facilities as those accorded to senior officials travelling abroad on temporary official duty;

    (b) by the Governments of other Parties, the same facilities as those accorded to representatives of foreign Governments on temporary official duty.

4. Documents and papers of the Committee, in so far as they relate to the business of the Committee, shall be inviolable.

The official correspondence and other official communications of the Committee may not be held up or subjected to censorship.

5. In order to secure for the members of the Committee complete freedom of speech and complete independence in the discharge of their duties, the immunity from legal process in respect of words spoken or written and all acts done by them in discharging their duties shall continue to be accorded, notwithstanding that the persons concerned are no longer engaged in the discharge of such duties.

6. Privileges and immunities are accorded to the members of the Committee, not for the personal benefit of the individuals themselves but in order to safeguard the independent exercise of their functions. The Committee alone shall be competent to waive the immunity of its members; it has not only the right, but is under a duty, to waive the immunity of one of its members in any case where, in its opinion, the immunity would impede the course of justice, and where it can be waived without prejudice to the purpose for which the immunity is accorded.

## TORTURE: INTER-AMERICAN CONVENTION TO PREVENT AND PUNISH TORTURE (1985).

Under the Convention, open for acceptance by States members of the **ORGANIZATION OF AMERICAN STATES,** the States parties undertake to take effective measures to prevent and punish **TORTURE,** which is defined in article 2, and other cruel, inhuman, or degrading treatment or punishment within their jurisdiction. They agree to make torture, and attempts to commit it, offenses under their penal law punishable by severe penalties. They also undertake to prohibit public servants or employees from using torture at any stage of interrogation, detention, or arrest; to guarantee that every victim of torture shall have the right to an impartial examination of his case; to provide adequate compensation for the victims of torture; and to extradite anyone accused of having committed the crime of torture or sentenced for the commission of that crime.

States parties also agree to inform the **INTER-AMERICAN COMMISSION ON HUMAN RIGHTS** of the measures taken to apply the provisions of the Convention and of the results achieved. The Commission is authorized to monitor and analyze in its annual reports the situation existing in the OAS member States as regards the prevention and elimination of torture.

The Convention was drafted at the request of the OAS General Assembly by the Inter-American Juridical Committee in coordination with the Inter-American Commission on Human Rights. It was examined and revised by the OAS Permanent Council in the light of observations and comments on the draft submitted by the governments of member States. On the basis of the revised draft, the OAS General Assembly adopted the Convention and opened it for signature on 9 December 1985 (AG/RES. 783 [XV–0/85]). The text of the Convention, annexed to the Assembly's resolution, is as follows:

The American States signatory to the present Convention,

Aware of the provision of the American Convention on Human Rights that no one shall be subjected to torture or to cruel, inhuman, or degrading punishment or treatment;

Reaffirming that all acts of torture or any other cruel, inhuman, or degrading treatment or punishment constitute an offense against human dignity and a denial of the principles set forth in the Charter of the Organization of American States and in the Charter of the United Nations and are violations of the fundamental human rights and freedoms proclaimed in the American Declaration of the Rights and Duties of Man and the Universal Declaration of Human Rights;

Noting that, in order for the pertinent rules contained in the aforementioned global and regional instruments to take effect, it is necessary to draft an Inter-American Convention that prevents and punishes torture;

Reaffirming their purpose of consolidating in this hemisphere the conditions that allow for recognition of and respect for the inherent dignity of man, and ensure the full exercise of his fundamental rights and freedoms,

Have agreed upon the following:

*Article 1.* The States Parties shall prevent and punish torture in accordance with the terms of this Convention.

*Article 2.* For the purposes of this Convention, torture shall be understood to be any act intentionally performed whereby physical or mental pain or suffering is inflicted on a person for purposes of criminal investigation, as a means of intimidation, as personal punishment, as a preventive measure, as a penalty, or for any other purpose. Torture shall also be understood to be the use of methods upon a person intended to obliterate the personality of the victim or to diminish his physical or mental capacities, even if they do not cause physical pain or mental anguish.

The concept of torture shall not include physical or mental pain or suffering that is inherent in or solely the consequence of lawful measures, provided that they do not include the performance of the acts or use of the methods referred to in this article.

*Article 3.* The following shall be held guilty of the crime of torture:

(a) A public servant or employee who acting in that capacity orders, instigates or induces the use of torture, or who directly commits it or who, being able to prevent it, fails to do so.

(b) A person who at the instigation of a public servant or employee mentioned in subparagraph (a) orders, instigates or induces the use of torture, directly commits it or is an accomplice thereto.

*Article 4.* The fact of having acted under orders of a superior shall not provide exemption from the corresponding criminal liability.

*Article 5.* The existence of circumstances such as a state of war, threat of war, state of siege or of emergency, domestic disturbance or strife, suspension of constitutional guaran-tees, domestic political instability, or other public emergencies or disasters shall not be invoked or admitted as justification for the crime of torture.

Neither the dangerous character of the detainee or prisoner, nor the lack of security of the prison establishment or penitentiary shall justify torture.

*Article 6.* In accordance with the terms of Article 1, the States Parties shall take effective measures to prevent and punish torture within their jurisdiction.

The States Parties shall ensure that all acts of torture and attempts to commit torture are offenses under their criminal law and shall make such acts punishable by severe penalties that take into account their serious nature.

The States Parties likewise shall take effective measures to prevent and punish other cruel, inhuman, or degrading treatment or punishment within their jurisdiction.

*Article 7.* The States Parties shall take measures so that, in the training of police officers and other public officials responsible for the custody of persons temporarily or definitively deprived of their freedom, special emphasis shall be put on the prohibition of the use of torture in interrogation, detention, or arrest.

The States Parties likewise shall take similar measures to prevent other cruel, inhuman, or degrading treatment or punishment.

*Article 8.* The States Parties shall guarantee that any person making an accusation of having been subjected to torture within their jurisdiction shall have the right to an impartial examination of his case.

Likewise, if there is an accusation or well-grounded reason to believe that an act of torture has been committed within their jurisdiction, the States Parties shall guarantee that their respective authorities will proceed ex officio and immediately to conduct an investigation into the case and to initiate, whenever appropriate, the corresponding criminal process.

After all the domestic legal procedures of the respective State and the corresponding appeals have been exhausted, the case may be submitted to the international fora whose competence has been recognized by that State.

*Article 9.* The State Parties undertake to incorporate into their national laws regulations guaranteeing adequate compensation for victims of torture.

None of the provisions of this article shall affect the right to receive compensation that the victim or other persons may have by virtue of existing national legislation.

*Article 10.* No statement that is verified as having been obtained through torture shall be admissible as evidence in a legal proceeding, except in a legal action taken against a person or persons accused of having elicited it through acts of torture, and only as evidence that the accused obtained such statement by such means.

*Article 11.* The States Parties shall take the necessary steps to extradite anyone accused of having committed the crime of torture or sentenced for commission of that crime, in accordance with their respective national laws on extradition and their international commitments on this matter.

*Article 12.* Every State Party shall take the necessary measures to establish its jurisdiction over the crime described in this Convention in the following cases:

(a) When torture has been committed within its jurisdiction;

(b) When the alleged criminal is a national of that State; or

(c) When the victim is a national of that State and it so deems appropriate.

Every State Party shall also take the necessary measures to

establish its jurisdiction over the crime described in this Convention when the alleged criminal is within the area under its jurisdiction and it does not proceed to extradite him in accordance with Article 11.

This Convention does not exclude criminal jurisdiction exercised in accordance with domestic law.

*Article 13.* The crime referred to in Article 2 shall be deemed to be included among the extraditable crimes in every extradition treaty entered into between States Parties. The States Parties undertake to include the crime of torture as an extraditable offence in every extradition treaty to be concluded between them.

Every State Party that makes extradition conditional on the existence of a treaty may, if it receives a request for extradition from another State Party with which it has no extradition treaty, consider this Convention as the legal basis for extradition in respect of the crime of torture. Extradition shall be subject to the other conditions that may be required by the law of the requested State.

States Parties which do not make extradition conditional on the existence of a treaty shall recognize such crimes as extraditable offences between themselves, subject to the conditions required by the law of the requested State.

Extradition shall not be granted nor shall the person sought be returned when there are grounds to believe that his life is in danger, that he will be subjected to torture or to cruel, inhuman or degrading treatment, or that he will be tried by special or ad hoc courts in the requesting State.

*Article 14.* When a State Party does not grant the extradition, the case shall be submitted to its competent authorities as if the crime had been committed within its jurisdiction, for the purposes of investigation, and when appropriate, for criminal action, in accordance with its national law. Any decision adopted by these authorities shall be communicated to the State that has requested the extradition.

*Article 15.* No provision of this Convention may be interpreted as limiting the right of asylum, when appropriate, nor as altering the obligations of the States Parties in the matter of extradition.

*Article 16.* This Convention shall not affect the provisions of the American Convention on Human Rights, other Conventions on the subject, or the Statues of the Inter-American Commission on Human Rights, with respect to the crime of torture.

*Article 17.* The States Parties shall inform the Inter-American Commission on Human Rights of any legislative, judicial, administrative, or other measures they adopt in application of this Convention.

In keeping with its duties and responsibilities, the Inter-American Commission on Human Rights will endeavor in its annual report to analyze the existing situation in the member states of the Organization of American States in regard to the prevention and elimination of torture.

*Article 18.* This Convention is open to signature by the member states of the Organization of American States.

*Article 19.* This Convention is subject to ratification. The instruments of ratification shall be deposited with the General Secretariat of the Organization of American States.

*Article 20.* This Convention is open to accession by any other American state. The instruments of accession shall be deposited with the General Secretariat of the Organization of American States.

*Article 21.* The States Parties may, at the time of approval, signature, ratification, or accession, make reservations to this Convention, provided that such reservations are not incompatible with the object and purpose of the Convention and concern one or more specific provisions.

*Article 22.* This Convention shall enter into force on the thirtieth day following the date on which the second instrument of ratification is deposited. For each State ratifying or acceding to the Convention after the second instrument of ratification has been deposited, the Convention shall enter into force on the thirtieth day following the date on which that State deposits its instrument of ratification or accession.

*Article 23.* This Convention shall remain in force indefinitely, but may be denounced by any State Party. The instrument of denunciation shall be deposited with the General Secretariat of the Organization of American States. After one year from the date of deposit of the instrument of denunciation, this Convention shall cease to be in effect for the denouncing State but shall remain in force for the remaining States Parties.

*Article 24.* The original instrument of this Convention, the English, French, Portuguese, and Spanish texts of which are equally authentic, shall be deposited with the General Secretariat of the Organization of American States, which shall send a certified copy to the Secretariat of the United Nations for registration and publication, in accordance with the provisions of Article 102 of the United Nations Charter. The General Secretariat of the Organization of American States shall notify the member states of the Organization and the states that have acceded to the Convention of signatures and of deposits of instruments of ratification, accession, and denunciation, as well as reservations, if any.

**TORTURE: PRINCIPLES OF MEDICAL ETHICS RELEVANT TO THE ROLE OF HEALTH PERSONNEL, PARTICULARLY PHYSICIANS, IN THE PROTECTION OF PRISONERS AND DETAINEES AGAINST TORTURE AND OTHER CRUEL, INHUMAN OR DEGRADING TREATMENT OR PUNISHMENT, UN (1982).** In 1976, the UN **GENERAL ASSEMBLY** invited the **WORLD HEALTH ORGANIZATION** to prepare "a draft code of medical ethics relevant to the protection of persons subjected to any form of detention or imprisonment against torture and other cruel, inhuman or degrading treatment or punishment." The Executive Board of WHO decided, in 1979, to endorse the general principles on this subject which had been prepared by the Council for International Organisations of the Medical Sciences, entitled "Principles of Medical Ethics Relevant to the Role of Health Personnel in the Protection of Persons Against Torture and other Cruel, Inhuman or Degrading Treatment or Punishment." On the basis of these principles, the General Assembly adopted a more restricted set of principles directed in particular at the protection of prisoners and detainees.

The Principles of Medical Ethics was adopted by the General Assembly on 18 December 1982 (resolution 37/194). The text, annexed to that resolution, is as follows:

*Principle 1*. Health personnel, particularly physicians, charged with the medical care of prisoners and detainees have a duty to provide them with protection of their physical and mental health and treatment of disease of the same quality and standard as is afforded to those who are not imprisoned or detained.

*Principle 2*. It is a gross contravention of medical ethics, as well as an offence under applicable international instruments, for health personnel, particularly physicians, to engage, actively or passively, in acts which constitute participation in, complicity in, incitement to or attempts to commit torture or other cruel, inhuman or degrading treatment or punishment.

*Principle 3*. It is a contravention of medical ethics for health personnel, particularly physicians, to be involved in any professional relationship with prisoners or detainees the purpose of which is not solely to evaluate, protect or improve their physical and mental health.

*Principle 4*. It is a contravention of medical ethics for health personnel, particularly physicians:

(a) To apply their knowledge and skills in order to assist in the interrogation of prisoners and detainees in a manner that may adversely affect the physical or mental health or condition of such prisoners or detainees and which is not in accordance with the relevant international instruments;

(b) To certify, or to participate in the certification of, the fitness of prisoners or detainees for any form of treatment or punishment that may adversely affect their physical or mental health and which is not in accordance with the relevant international instruments, or to participate in any way in the infliction of any such treatment or punishment which is not in accordance with the relevant international instruments.

*Principle 5*. It is a contravention of medical ethics for health personnel, particularly physicians, to participate in any procedure for restraining a prisoner or detainee unless such a procedure is determined in accordance with purely medical criteria as being necessary for the protection of the physical or mental health or the safety of the prisoner or detainee himself, of his fellow prisoners or detainees, or of his guardians, and presents no hazard to his physical or mental health.

*Principle 6*. There may be no derogation from the foregoing principles on any ground whatsoever, including public emergency.

## TOTALITARIAN IDEOLOGIES.

An item concerning "Measures to be taken against Nazi, Fascist, and neo-Fascist activities and all other forms of totalitarian ideologies and practices based on apartheid, racial discrimination and racism, and the systematic denial of human rights and fundamental freedoms" has appeared under this or similar titles on the agenda of the UN GENERAL ASSEMBLY since 1967, and on that of the UN COMMISSION ON HUMAN RIGHTS since 1972.

Both organs have periodically noted with regret, as did the General Assembly at its 1988 session (resolution 43/150), that

in the contemporary world there continue to exist various forms of totalitarian ideologies and practices which entail contempt for the individual or a denial of the intrinsic dignity and equality of all human beings and of equality of opportunity in the civil, political, economic, social and cultural spheres, including the practices of *apartheid,* racial discrimination and racism; [and both have emphasized] that the doctrines of political, racial or ethnic superiority on which the totalitarian entities and régimes are based contradict the spirit and principles of the United Nations and that the application of such doctrines in practice leads to wars, mass and flagrant violations of human rights and crimes against humanity, such as genocide, and creates serious obstacles to friendly relations among nations and the development of all countries.

Both the Commission, in resolution 1988/63, and the General Assembly, in resolution 43/150 of 8 December 1988, repeated their earlier condemnations of all totalitarian or other ideologies and practices, including the Nazi, Fascist, and neo-Fascist, that are based on APARTHEID, racial discrimination, and racism, or which have such consequences; and both expressed their determination to resist all totalitarian ideologies, and especially their practices, which deprive people of basic human rights and fundamental freedoms and of equality of opportunity. Both called upon all governments to pay constant attention to educating the young in the spirit of respect for international law and fundamental human rights and freedoms and against Fascist, neo-Fascist, and other totalitarian ideologies and practices based on terror, hatred, and violence.

Both bodies also called upon all States to take the necessary measures to ensure the thorough investigation, detection, arrest, extradition, and punishment of all war criminals and persons guilty of crimes against humanity who have not yet been brought before a court and appropriately punished.

The Commission expressed the view that the pursuit of totalitarian ideologies and practices represents a serious threat to the exercise of the fundamental human rights, including the right to life, liberty, and security of person; and that the free and widespread participation by all levels of the population in democratic institutions based on respect for human rights is one of the most effective forms of defense against all totalitarian ideologies. Accordingly, it called upon all governments and the appropriate intergovernmental and non-governmental organizations to intensify measures against such ideologies and practices.

The General Assembly called upon all States, in accordance with the basic principles of international law, to refrain from practices aimed at the violation of basic human rights, particularly the right to SELF-DETERMINATION; and appealed to States that had not done so to consider becoming parties to the International Covenants on Human Rights, the Convention on the Prevention and Punishment of the Crime of Genocide (see GENOCIDE), the International Convention on the

Elimination of All Forms of Racial Discrimination (see **RACIAL DISCRIMINATION**), the Convention on the Non-applicability of Statutory Limitations to War Crimes and Crimes against Humanity (see **WAR CRIMES**), and the International Convention on the Suppression and Punishment of the Crime of Apartheid (see **APARTHEID**).

## TRAFFIC IN PERSONS AND EXPLOITATION OF THE PROSTITUTION OF OTHERS. See **SLAVERY**.

**TRINIDAD AND TOBAGO.** The Republic of Trinidad and Tobago is a country in tropical South America, occupying two islands off the northeast coast of Venezuela. It achieved independence from Great Britain in 1962 and became a member of the United Nations the same year. Its population is estimated to be 1,307,000. Ethnic groups include persons of African (40.8%), East Indian (40.7%), and mixed (18.5%) descent. Languages commonly used include English (official), Hindi, French, and Spanish. Religions practiced include Christianity (Roman Catholic, 33.6%; Anglican, 15%), Hinduism (25%), Islam (6%), and others (20.4%). Literacy is estimated at 95%.

The government (1994) took the form of a republic. Under the 1976 constitution, the president is elected by universal suffrage and acts as head of State. The prime minister, representing the party or coalition given the majority in an election, exercises executive authority as head of government. There is a bicameral parliament consisting of a 36-member House of Representatives and a 24-member Senate. The island of Tobago also has its own 15-member House of Assembly. The judiciary includes a Supreme Court, consisting of the High Court and the Court of Appeal. Political parities include the National Alliance for Reconstruction and the People's National Movement.

Section 91 of the constitution of Trinidad and Tobago creates the office of **OMBUDSMAN.** It is the function of the ombudsman to investigate complaints by persons of injustice arising from the exercise of administrative functions of government and quasi-governmental agencies. He may investigate any such matter, under section 93 (2), in any of the following circumstances:

(a) Where a complaint is duly made to the *Ombudsman* by any person alleging that the complainant has sustained an injustice as a result of a fault in the administration;

(b) Where a member of the House of Representatives requests the *Ombudsman* to investigate the matter on the ground that a person or body of persons specified in the request has or may have sustained such injustice;

(c) In any other circumstances in which the *Ombudsman* considers that he ought to investigate the matter on the ground that some body of persons has or may have sustained such injustice.

In July 1990 a small Islamic group launched an attack on the government attempting to seize power. The *Jamaat al Muslimeen* stormed the police headquarters, parliament, and the state television station. The prime minister and cabinet members were taken hostage and a **STATE OF EMERGENCY** was declared, as well as a curfew imposed. Thirty people were killed and 500 injured in the five days of conflict. The rebels surrendered pursuant to an agreement of amnesty. Although the government argued that the agreement was made under duress and therefore invalid, the High Court upheld the agreement, and those who had been arrested on capital crimes were ordered released.

Labor unrest continued unabated in the early 1990s, and the country's trade unions agreed to form a single union, the National Trade Union Centre. This unrest was reflected in the defeat of the ruling party and its strict economic measures in general elections held in December 1991 where the People's National Movement won 21 seats in the 36-seat House of Representatives. Labor unrest continued into 1994 and increasing crime rates precipitated a steady demand in the restoration of capital punishment. In July a convicted murderer was killed by hanging while the highest court of appeal, the British Privy Council, was still reviewing the merits of the death sentence.

**BIBLIOGRAPHY.** Amnesty International. *Trinidad and Tobago: Trying to Execute Regardless.* . . . London: 1994. NGO report, in English.

Article 19. *Freedom of Information and Expression in Trinidad and Tobago.* London: 1988. NGO report, in English.

Byre, Angela D., and Beverley Y. Byfield, eds. *International Human Rights Law in the Commonwealth Caribbean.* Dordrecht, the Netherlands: Martinus Nijhoff, 1991. Scholarly conference papers, in English.

Organization of American States. *Annual Report of the Inter-American Commission on Human Rights.* Washington, D.C. IGO annual report, in English.

Searle, Chris. "The Muslimeen Insurrection in Trinidad," *Race & Class* 33, no. 2 (Oct.–Dec. 1991): 29–44. Scholarly article, in English.

Sigler, Jay A., ed. *International Handbook on Race and Race Relations.* Westport, CT, USA: Greenwood Press, 1987. Scholarly edited collection, in English; bibliography, pp. 449–454.

Stern, Vivien. *Deprived of their Liberty.* Belleville, Barbados: Caribbean Rights, 1990. NGO report, in English.

Trinidad and Tobago Bureau on Human Rights. *Issue between the Government of Trinidad and the Jamaat-Al-Muslimeen.* San Fernando, Trinidad and Tobago: 1991. NGO appeal, in English.

———. *Report on Human Rights in Trinidad and Tobago.* San Fernando, Trinidad and Tobago. NGO annual report, in English.

———. *Report on the Administration of Justice in Trinidad and Tobago.* San Fernando, Trinidad and Tobago: 1987. NGO report, in English.

**TRUSTEESHIP COUNCIL, UN.** Established in accordance with the **UNITED NATIONS CHARTER** (article

7) as a principal organ of the United Nations, the Council supervises the administration of trust territories by considering reports of the administering authorities, accepting and examining petitions, arranging for periodic visits to the territories, and taking any other action called for by trusteeship agreements. With regard to "strategic" areas, the Trusteeship Council assists the **SECURITY COUNCIL** in exercising the functions assigned to the United Nations. Since 1977, only one of the original 11 trust territories remains within the trusteeship system, the Trust Territory of the Pacific Islands under United States' Territory administration. The Trusteeship Council receives and considers reports on political, economic, social, and other developments in the territory submitted by the administering authority. Because the territory has been designated as a "strategic area," the Trusteeship Council's report on it is directed to the Security Council. Conditions in the territory are also considered by the Special Committee on the Situation with Regard to the Implementation of the Declaration on the Granting of Independence to Colonial Countries and Peoples.

In accordance with article 86 of the UN Charter, the Council is composed of UN members administering trust territories and permanent members of the Security Council not administering trust territories. The United States is a Trusteeship Council member because it administers the Pacific Islands; and China France, the Russian Federation, and the United Kingdom are also Council members because they are permanent members of the Security Council and do not administer trust territories. Except for permanent members of the Security Council, members of the Trusteeship Council cease to be members when the territories administered by them become independent.

The Trusteeship Council meets as required to perform its functions, normally the headquarters of the United Nations in New York, and has no subsidiary bodies.

**TUNISIA.** The Republic of Tunisia is a country in northern Africa. It has borders with Algeria and Libya. It achieved independence from France in 1956 and became a member of the United Nations in 1957. Its population is estimated to be 8,495,000. Ethnically, the population is homogeneous, consisting mainly of Arab Malekite Moslems. The Berbers, who were the first inhabitants of the country, are scattered, few in number, and integrated into the Arab/Moslem civilization; they do not form a special, geographically located, autonomous community demanding special status. Languages commonly used include Arabic (of-

ficial) and French. Islam is the predominant religion (98%); Christianity (1.5%) and Judaism (.5%) are also practiced. Literacy is estimated at 64%.

The government (1990) took the form of a republic. Under the constitution of 1959, the president is elected by universal suffrage for a term of five years and is eligible for re-election for two additional terms; however, President Habib Bourguiba was made "President for Life" in 1975 after re-election to a fourth five-year term, the National Assembly amending the constitution for this purpose. The prime minister, representing the party or coalition winning an election, is head of government. The legislature consists of a unicameral 136-member National Assembly, elected by universal suffrage. The judiciary is independent of other branches of government. Political parties include the Socialist Destourian, the Social Democratic Movement, the Popular Unity Party, and the Community Party. After problems with Muslim fundamentalists in 1987, Bourguiba, at 84, was confined to a presidential residence south of Tunis, where he continued to receive the respect due the first president of Tunisia. Under his leadership Tunisia had developed into a modern secular State held together and controlled by the ruling Destourian Socialist Party, of which he was the head.

The Destourian Socialist Party was renamed the Democratic Constitutional Rally in 1988; and President Zine el-Albidene Ben Ali, its candidate, ran unopposed in national popular elections held in 1989, winning over 99% of the vote. Despite passage of electoral reform by the National Assembly in 1990, introducing a system of partial proportional representation, opposition groups boycotted the municipal elections in June, leaving the governing party with control of all of the 245 municipal councils except one.

President Ben Ali was reelected with 99% of the vote in March 1994. In simultaneous legislative elections, a new proportional representation system guaranteed opposition candidates 19 of the 163 seats. The President of the Tunisian League of Human Rights, who had resigned in order to oppose President Ben Ali in the election, failed to gain sufficient support in the National Assembly and was arrested and detained following the elections on charges of defaming the judiciary. Detentions of other political leaders continued after the elections, most notably the leader of the Communist Party who was sentenced to nine years imprisonment for formation of an illegal organization.

*ISLAMIC FUNDAMENTALISTS.* On 27 September 1987 seven members of the Movement for Islamic Tendencies, Tunisia's largest fundamentalist group, were sentenced to death after having been found guilty by the Tunisian Court for State Security of involvement in four hotel bombing incidents that killed 13 persons. Sixty-nine of the defendants, found guilty of lesser crimes, were sentenced to prison terms, while 14 were found not guilty. The government maintained that the trial was aimed at discouraging Iran-backed terrorists whose aim was to turn Tunisia into an Islamic revolutionary State.

After two of the death penalties had been carried out, President Bourguiba ordered a further crackdown on Islamic fundamentalists—a proposal that most government officials feared would plunge the country into turmoil and religious strife. At this point, Prime Minister and former Minister of Security Zine el-Albidene Ben Ali, with the concurrence of government and opposition leaders, deposed the aging "president for life" Bourguiba on the ground of mental deterioration, appointed himself president, and promised to abolish the post of president for life.

During the period leading up to and including the Persian Gulf War in 1990 and early 1991, popular and political support for Iraq, and Arabic and Islamic causes in general, mounted and demonstrations and attacks by Islamic activists were met with violent suppression by the government. A government human rights commission, which had been formed in 1990, was ordered to investigate allegations of torture of political detainees in mid-1991. By the end of the year, 1,070 detainees had either been released or had their sentences reduced.

Despite censorship, allegations of continued mistreatment of detainees, and suppression of Islamic fundamentalists, the government announced the formation of human rights units within the Ministries of Justice, Interior and Foreign Affairs in March 1992. In mid-1992 hundreds of members of the fundamentalist group, an-Nahdah, were tried, convicted and sentenced to terms up to and including life imprisonment on charges of conspiracy to overthrow the government.

Growing concern over right-wing Islamic fundamentalist groups prompted the governments of Germany, France, Spain Italy, Algeria and Tunisia to meet in Tunis in January 1995 in order to enact a policy of cooperation between their security forces in combating Muslim militancy.

### REPORT BY THE UN HUMAN RIGHTS COMMITTEE.
The **HUMAN RIGHTS COMMITTEE** considered the fourth periodic report of Tunisia (CCPR/C/84/Add. 1) at its 1360th to 1362nd meetings, held on 18 and 19 October 1994, and adopted the following comments on 2 November 1994:

*Positive aspects.* The Committee notes with satisfaction the attempt to build a comprehensive constitutional and legal framework for the promotion and protection on human rights. The Committee welcomes recent progress in enhancing and strengthening that framework, notably the establishment of a number of human rights posts, offices and units within the executive branch with a view to ensuring greater conformity of Tunisian law and practice with the Covenant and other international human rights instruments.

The Committee also notes with satisfaction recent legislative reforms aimed at bringing Tunisian law into closer harmony with the requirements of the Covenant. In this connection, the Committee welcomes changes in the Penal Code which have reduced the duration of preventive detention, and strengthened sanctions in cases of family violence directed against women. The Committee also welcomes recent reforms in the Personal Status Code and other laws aiming to guarantee and reinforce the equal rights of women in a number of areas, including divorce, custody and maintenance and to strengthen the protection of women against violence.

*Principal subjects of concern.* The Committee cannot conceal its disappointment with the deterioration in the protection of human rights in Tunisia in the period under review. It is concerned, in particular, with the growing gap between law and actual practice with regard to guarantees and safeguards for the protection of human rights. Although there is now in place an impressive array of State organs for the promotion and protection of human rights at various levels, the Committee notes that they have been concentrated exclusively within the executive branch of the Government. Consequently, it is not clear whether there are sufficiently independent mechanisms within the public administration and the judiciary to effectively monitor and enforce the implementation of existing human rights standards, including the investigation of abuses.

The Committee is particularly concerned with continuing reports of the abuse, ill-treatment and torture of detainees, including deaths in custody under suspicious circumstances. In this connection, it appears that Tunisian regulations are not strictly adhered to with respect to the prompt registration of persons arrested, the immediate notification to family members, the limitation of pre-trial detention to the 10-day maximum, the requirement of medical examinations whenever allegations of torture or other abuse and the carrying out of autopsies in all cases of death in custody. It is also not clear whether these and other requirements are being systematically monitored and whether investigations are automatically undertaken in all cases where there are either allegations or suspicious circumstances indicating that torture may have taken place. The Committee is also concerned that present laws overly protect Government officials, particularly those concerned with security matters; it is particularly concerned that those government officials who have been found guilty of wrong doing remain anonymous to the general public, becoming immune from effective scrutiny.

The Committee is concerned about the independence of the judiciary. It is also concerned by the reports on harassment of lawyers who have represented clients accused of having committed political offences and of the wives and families of suspects. With respect to article 6 of the Covenant, the Committee is concerned over the large number of crimes in Tunisia for which the death penalty may be imposed.

The Committee is concerned that, despite the significant progress which has been achieved regarding the equal rights of women, there remain a number of outdated legal provisions that are contrary to the Covenant. Those provisions concern the status of married women and their equal rights in matters of child custody, the transmission of nationality and parental consent for the marriage of minor children. The Committee is also concerned with legal discrimination against non-Muslims with respect to eligibility for public office.

The Committee is concerned that dissent and criticism of the Government are not fully tolerated in Tunisia and that, as a result, a number of fundamental freedoms guaranteed by the Covenant are not fully enjoyed in practice. In particular, it regrets the ban on the publication of certain foreign newspapers. The Committee is concerned that those sections of the Press Code dealing with defamation, insult and false information unduly limit the exercise of freedom of opinion and expression as provided for under article 19 of the Covenant. In this connection, the Committee is concerned that those offences carry particularly severe penalties when criticism is directed against official bodies as well as the army or the administration, a situation which inevitably results in self-censorship by the media when reporting on public affairs. The Committee also notes with concern that it is not clear how procedures ensure independent review on the merits, including judicial appeal, in cases where those provisions of the Press Code have been invoked.

The Committee is concerned that the Associations Act may seriously undermine the enjoyment of the freedom of association under article 22, particularly with respect to the independence of human rights non-governmental organizations. In this connection, the Committee notes that the act has already had an adverse impact on the Tunisian League for Human Rights. The Committee believes that the Political Parties Act and the conditions imposed on the activities of political parties, do not appear to be in conformity with articles 22 and 25 of the Covenant. The Committee is also concerned that, under the Passport Act, the grounds for refusing a passport are not clearly specified by law in a way that complies with article 12 of the Covenant, leaving open the possibility of refusal on political or other unacceptable grounds.

The Committee is concerned that, while generally there is a well protected freedom to practice and manifest one's religion, this right is not made available in respect of all beliefs.

*Suggestions and recommendations.* The Committee recommends that steps be taken to strengthen the independence of human rights institutions in Tunisia and thereby close the gap between law and practice and enhance the confidence of the public in those institutions. The Committee emphasizes that the work of the "mediateur administratif", the Presidential Human Rights Commissioner and any Commission investigating reports of human rights abuses should be transparent and the results should be made public. The Committee notes that a better balance is needed between State and private institutions concerned with human rights and, in that connection, suggests that steps be taken to provide more encouragement to human rights non-governmental organizations in Tunisia. The Committee also recommends that steps are taken to strengthen the independence of the judiciary, particularly from the executive branch.

The Committee strongly recommends that the State party consider ratifying or acceding to the first Optional Protocol to the International Covenant on Civil and Political Rights. Acceptance of the first Optional Protocol would strengthen the capacity of the Government with respect to inquiries into allegations of human rights abuses and also in regard to further elaborating jurisprudence relating to human rights matters.

With respect to reports of torture and abuse of detainees, the Committee strongly recommends closer monitoring of the arrest and detention process; systematic, prompt and open investigation into allegations; prosecution and punishment of offenders; and the provision of legal remedies for victims. There should be strict enforcement of registration procedures, including prompt notification of family members of persons taken into custody, and the 10-day limit to preventive detention. Steps should also be taken to ensure that medical examinations are automatically provided following allegations of abuse and that thorough autopsies are performed following any death in custody. In all cases where investigations are undertaken, the findings should be made public.

The Committee also recommends that the State party take steps to reduce the number of crimes for which the death penalty may be imposed and envisage acceding to the Second Optional Protocol to the Covenant.

With respect to discrimination, the Committee recommends that a further review of relevant legislation be undertaken with a view to amending the law where necessary in order to bring it into conformity with the requirements of the Covenant. Such a review should focus on the equal rights of women, particularly in regard to their parental and custodial rights and the transmission of nationality, as well as on existing legal impediments to the equal participation of non-Muslims in Presidential elections.

The Committee recommends that measures be taken to ensure the exercise of the freedom of opinion and expression in accordance with article 19 of the Covenant. In particular, there should be a review and, where appropriate, amendment of those provisions of the Press Code which unduly protect Government policy and officials from criticism. Provision should also be made for independent judicial review of all sanctions imposed under the act.

The Committee also recommends that a review be undertaken of the Associations Act, the Passport Act and the Political Parties Act to ensure that they are in full conformity with the requirements of the Covenant. With respect to freedom of religion, the Committee recommends that there be close and independent monitoring of the exercise of that right by all groups in Tunisia. The Committee emphasizes that its General Comment on article 18 should be reflected in Government policy and practice.

***REPORT BY THE UN COMMITTEE ON THE RIGHTS OF THE CHILD.*** The **COMMITTEE ON THE RIGHTS OF THE CHILD** considered the initial report of Tunisia (CRC/C/11/Add. 2) at its 225th, 226th, and 227th meetings, held on 1 and 2 June 1995 (CRC/C/SR.225–227), and adopted the following concluding observations on June 1995:

*Positive aspects.* The Committee welcomes the efforts made by the Government in bringing domestic law into line with the Convention, through the enactment of the draft Code for the Protection of the Child. Satisfaction is expressed at the fact that various national legislative provisions are more conducive to the realization of the rights of the child than those contained in the Convention. The Committee also notes with appreciation the adoption, following the World Summit for Children in 1990, of the National Plan of Action for the Survival, Protection and Development of Children, as well as the adoption of various programmes, specifically aimed at promoting and protecting the rights of the child, such as programmes for disabled children, and programmes aiming at sensitizing teachers to the philosophy of the Convention. The Committee notes with particular appreciation the sustained policies with a view to protecting children against the negative effects of structural adjustment.

*Factors and difficulties impeding the implementation of the Convention.* The Committee notes that there are still practices which impede the full enjoyment of certain rights of the child.

*Principal subjects of concern.* The Committee is concerned about the extent of the reservations and declarations made to the Convention by the State party. In particular, the reservation relating to the application of article 2 raises concern as to its compatibility with the object and purpose of the Convention.

The Committee notes that measures taken to ensure the implementation of the provisions of the Convention, particularly articles 2, 3, 12, 13 and 19, are still insufficient. The Committee is concerned at practices of discrimination against children born out of wedlock.

The Committee notes that the system of collecting data relevant for the monitoring of the implementation of the Convention needs to be improved and extended. It is concerned whether sufficient consideration has been given to the reinforcement of mechanisms, including of an independent nature, to follow up and evaluate the implementation of the Convention at the national and local levels.

The Committee is concerned that the legislative discrepancy between the age for completion of mandatory education and the minimum age for admission to employment may lead to encourage adolescents to drop out from the school system.

*Suggestions and recommendations.* In the spirit of the final document of the World Conference on Human Rights, the Committee wishes to encourage the State party to consider reviewing its reservations and declarations to the Convention with a view to withdrawing them, including particularly the reservation relating to article 2 of the Convention.

The Committee encourages the Government to pursue its efforts aiming at creating awareness of the Convention and having its basic principles grasped by the general public, and to continue training relevant professional groups such as teachers, judges, law-enforcement officials, social workers, the personnel in care and detention institutions, as well as military personnel.

The data collection on matters relating to the Convention should be systematized and amplified, with a view to covering all areas addressed by the Convention.

The Committee would like to suggest that the State party consider reinforcing the mechanisms for monitoring and evaluating the implementation of the Convention. A more efficient coordination between the central Government and the governorates is also recommended.

The State party is encouraged to pursue legislative reforms and to adopt measures translating into practice the general principles of the Convention, in particular the principle of non-discrimination against children born out of wedlock, the principle of the best interests of the child and the right of the child to express his or her views freely.

The Committee recommends to the State party to give further thought to possible ratification of ILO Convention No. 138 on the minimum age for admission to employment. Campaigns to prevent entry of adolescents into the labour force, including in the informal sector and agriculture, should be reinforced. In this regard, the Committee would like to encourage the State party to consider seeking technical assistance from the International Labour Organization.

Regarding the rights of the refugee and asylum-seeking child, the Committee recommends that the State party consider as a preventive measure adopting relevant legislative provisions, in consultation with the United Nations High Commissioner for Refugees.

As far as protection from ill-treatment is concerned, the Committee recommends that the social preventive approach be strengthened and that further measures be undertaken to educate parents about their responsibilities towards their children, including through the provision of family education which should emphasize the equal responsibilities of both parents and contribute to the prevention of the use of corporal punishment.

The Committee welcomes the invitation addressed by the delegation to the Committee to visit Tunisia. The Committee also recommends that the initial report, the summary records of the discussion between the delegation and the Committee and the present concluding observations be widely disseminated in order to deepen the debate on the rights of the child in Tunisia. The Committee would like to suggest that these documents be brought to the attention of the parliament and that the suggestions and recommendations for action contained therein be followed up.

**BIBLIOGRAPHY.** Amnesty International. *Tunisia: Heavy Sentences after Unfair Trials.* London: 1992. NGO report, in English.

————. *Tunisia: Prolonged Incommunicado Detention and Torture.* London: 1992. NGO report, in English.

————. *Tunisia: Rhetoric Versus Reality: The Failure of a Human Rights Bureaucracy.* London: 1994. NGO report, in English.

————. *Tunisia: Summary of Amnesty International's Concerns.* London: 1990. NGO factfinding report, in English and French.

Arab Organization for Human Rights. *Report: Human Rights in the Arab World.* Cairo, Egypt: 1987. NGO report, in Arabic or English.

Fédération Internationale des Droits de l'Homme (International Federation of Human Rights). *Rapport de mission: procès de Moncif Ben Salem* (Mission Report: Moncif Ben Salem Trial). Paris: 1990. NGO factfinding report, in French.

————. "Tunisia: Judicial Observation Mission," *FIDH Letter* (7–10 July 1986). NGO article, in French.

————. *Tunisie: Proces d'Islamiste Tunisiens devant la Cour de Surete de l'Etat* (Tunisia: Trial of Islamic Tunisians before the State Security Court). Paris: 1987. NGO report, in French.

*Freedom of Information and Expression in Tunisia: A Commentary by ARTICLE 19 on the Report Submitted to the U.N. Human Rights Committee by the Government of the Republic of Tunisia.* London: ARTICLE 19, 1987. NGO report, in English.

Institute for Women's Studies in the Arab World. "Tunisian Women Speak," *Al-Raida* 8, no. 33 (1 Aug. 1985). NGO article, in English.

International League for Human Rights. *Tunisia's Human Rights Record: A Critique of the Government's Official Report to the U.N. Human Rights Committee.* New York: 1986. NGO report, in English.

Lawyers Committee for Human Rights. *The Mass Trial of Islamists before Military Courts in Tunisia.* New York: 1992. NGO factfinding report, in English.

————. *Promise Unfulfilled: Human Rights in Tunisia Since 1987.* New York: 1993. NGO factfinding report, in English.

———. *Tunisia: Spreading the Net of Persecution.* New York: 1994. NGO report, in English.

Ligue tunisienne pour la defense des Droits de l'Homme (Tunisian League for the Defense of Human Rights). *Dossier: Plaidoyer pour la Ligue* (Documents: The Case for the League). Tunisia: 1987. NGO document collection, in French or Arabic.

Marzouki, Moncef. *L'Arrache Corps* (The Body Broken). Paris: Editions Alternative et Paralleles, 1979. Scholarly monograph, in French; bibliography, pp. 255–257.

———. "Winning Freedom," *Index on Censorship* 18, no. 1 (Jan. 1989): 23–35. NGO article, in English.

Middle East Watch and International Human Rights Law Group. *Tunisia: Military Courts That Sentenced Islamist Leaders Violated Basic Fair-Trial Norms.* New York: Human Rights Watch, 1992. NGO report, in English.

Minnesota Lawyers International Human Rights Committee. *Tunisia: Human Rights Crisis of 1987.* Minneapolis, MN, USA: 1988. NGO report, in English, bibliography, pp. 69—70.

———. *Tunisia: Human Rights Report of 1989.* Minneapolis, MN, USA: 1990. NGO factfinding report, in English.

Sidem-Poulain, Odile. "Proces de M. Ahmed Mestiri—Secretaire General du Movement des Democrates Socialistes" (The Trial of Mr. Ahmed Mestiri—General Secretary of the Socialist Democrat Movement), *La Lettre de la FIDH* 70 (4 June 1986). NGO mission report, in French.

———. *Rapport de Mission: Tunisie* (Mission Report: Tunisia). Paris: Federation Internationale des Droits de l'Homme, 1987. NGO report, in French.

# TURKEY

**TURKEY.** The Republic of Turkey is a country in western Asia, on the Black Sea and the Aegean Sea. It has borders with Bulgaria, Greece, Iraq, Iran, Syria, and the former Union of Soviet Socialist Republics. It achieved independence in 1923, when the Ottoman Empire was broken up, and became a member of the United Nations in 1945. Its population is estimated to be 58,620,000. Ethnic groups include Turks and about 10 million Kurds, who live in the mountaneous eastern part of the country. Turkish is in common use throughout the country; Kurdish is not recognized as a distinct language and its public use is banned. Islam (Sunni) is the predominant religion, with 98.2% of all believers; Christianity and Judaism (Sephardim) account for the remainder. The State is secular; there is no official religion. Literacy is estimated at 80%.

The government (1994) took the form of a republic. Under the 1982 constitution, the main legislative body is the 399-member Grand National Assembly, members of which are elected by universal suffrage. The Grand National Assembly elects the president, who serves for a term of seven years, acting as head of State. The prime minister, representing the party or coalition which was given the majority in the election, is head of government. The judiciary includes the Council of State, which is the highest administration tribunal. There is also the Constitutional Court, empowered to review and annul legislation and, if necessary,

to try the president of the republic. There are no religious courts, and religious law is not applied. There is, however, a Department of Religious Affairs, which, under article 136 of the constitution, "shall carry out its duties defined by law, in accordance with the principles of secularism, detached from political views and ideas and making national solidarity and integrity its objective." Political parties include the Motherland Party, the Populist Party, and the National Democracy Party.

In April 1993, short of his selection to lead a new party-derivative of the ANAP, President Ozal died of heart failure. Prime Minister Demirel was elected as Ozal's successor with a simple majority in the National Assembly, and Tansu Ciller became Turkey's first female prime minister. In municipal elections held in March 1993, the Islamic fundamentalist party, Refah Partisi, gained control of Ankara, Istanbul and 20 additional mayoral offices, with 18% of the overall vote.

***THE KURDS.*** Turkey's Kurdish minority has suffered discrimination on the ground of language since the founding of the modern Turkish State in 1923; and its continuous fight for recognition of its language, for autonomy, and eventually for independence, has been checked systematically and continuously by Turkish armed forces garrisoned in Kurdistan. Besides outlawing the use of Kurdish, Turkey has refused any recognition whatsoever to Kurds as a distinct people having a history and culture of their own. Kurds are sometimes disdainfully referred to as "mountain Turks" and characterized as "bandits."

For many years Turkish Kurds based their insurgent activities in neighboring Iran, Iraq, and Syria, all of which have Kurdish minorities of their own. However, in recent years, they have begun to operate openly within Turkey with some aid and support from the Kurdish Workers' Party, based in Syria and aligned with the territory of the former Soviet Union, which also has a Kurdish minority. The goal of that party is the establishment of an independent Marxist Kurdish State in what is now eastern Turkey.

In 1988, more than 60,000 Kurdish guerillas and their families, fleeing from northern Iraq to escape what was described, over Iraqi denials, as chemical warfare directed against them, were received and sheltered by Turkey on humanitarian grounds. Although the Turkish Government announced that it was prepared to offer them sanctuary indefinitely, most of them later returned to Iraq.

Following the Persian Gulf War in early 1991, more than 500,000 refugees from Iraq, most of them Kurds, fled toward the Turkish border and encamped in the mountains. International humanitarian aid was flown into the mountainous region, and Turkey agreed to allow its territory to be used for the deployment of patrols to protect the Kurds from further aggression by Iraq.

Following a period of attempting to balance the interests of the liberals and Islamic fundamentalists in the government, a general election was held in October 1991. A new coalition government was formed between the True Path Party (DYP) and Social Democratic Populist Party (SHP) which initiated a reform plan aimed at a new constitution, antiterrorist legislation, increased autonomy for local government, and increased cultural recognition for Kurds. Shortly thereafter, a separate Ministry of Human Rights was created, to be headed by a Kurd. However, political and armed strife between the government and the Kurdish separatists has continued throughout the early 1990s. The government closed a pro-Kurdish newspaper in 1993 and intensified the military strikes against Kurdish Workers' Party (PKK) camps in the south, with air strikes encroaching upon northern Iraqi territory. The government estimated that the conflict had cost 10,000 lives between 1984 and 1993. Turkish property abroad was also the target of Kurdish terrorist attacks, resulting in France and Germany banning all activity of the Kurdish Workers' Party within their borders.

In 1993, faced with increasing hostilities between Kurdish separatists and the armed forces and stiff political opposition, Prime Minister Ciller withdrew all plans to award cultural and educational rights to the Kurds. Eight Kurdish members of parliament had their parliamentary immunity revoked and were arrested, charged and convicted for their association with the illegal PKK. They were sentenced to prison terms ranging from three and one half to 15 years amidst international criticism.

Rioting broke out in Istanbul and Ankara in March 1995 following the murder in Istanbul of two Alawate or Shiite Muslims, allegedly by Sunni or fundamentalist Muslim gunmen. Many of the Alawate Muslims are part of the Kurdish minority as well as the religious faction. Thirty people were killed in three days of rioting.

In Turkey's largest deployment ever against the Kurds, 50,000 troops were sent to eradicate PKK strongholds in southern Turkey and northern Iraq in March 1995. Turkey claimed it was an act of self-defense in response to an ambush of a 40-vehicle army convoy, in which 18 Turkish soldiers were killed. Hundreds of civilians, 500 PKK rebels and 58 Turkish soldiers were killed before Prime Minister Ciller recalled the troops after five weeks of fighting.

Relations with European countries were further strained when Germany suspended all military aid as a result of the conflict with the Kurds; meanwhile, Hol-

land allowed the formation of a 65-delegate Kurdish government in exile in the Hague in April 1995. The **COUNCIL OF EUROPE** suspended Turkey until improvements in the treatment of Kurds could be achieved.

Following Turkey's formal application for membership to the European Union in 1987, the EU repeatedly cited human rights problems as a barrier to membership. However, in March 1995 Greece gave up its longstanding veto of agreements with Turkey and conceded to a trade agreement between Turkey and the EU.

***BIBLIOGRAPHY.*** Amnesty International. *Iraq/Turkey: Iraqi Kurds: At Risk of Forcible Repatriation from Turkey and Human Rights Violations in Iraq.* London: 1990. NGO factfinding report, in English.

———. *Turkey: Brutal and Systematic Abuse of Human Rights.* London: 1989. NGO report, in English.

———. *Turkey: Continuing Violations of Human Rights.* London: 1990. NGO report, in English.

———. *Turkey: The Death Penalty—Recent Developments and Some Examples.* London: 1988. NGO report, in English.

———. *Turkey: Escalation in Human Rights Abuses against Kurdish Villagers.* London: 1993. NGO report, in English.

———. *Turkey: Torture and Medical Neglect of Prisoners.* London: 1988. NGO report, in English.

———. *Turkey: Torture, Extrajudicial Executions, "Disappearances."* London: 1992. NGO report, in English.

———. *Turkey: An Unsafe Country of Waiting for Iranian Refugees.* London: 1988. NGO report, in English.

Article 19. *Violations of Freedom of Expression and Information in Turkey.* London: 1990. NGO factfinding report, in English.

Balian, Hrair. *Turkey: Continued Violations of International Human Rights and Humanitarian Law.* Berkeley, CA, USA: Human Rights Advocates, 1987. NGO report, in English.

Commission on Security and Cooperation in Europe. *Human Rights Abuses in Cyprus.* Washington, D.C.: 1985. Government hearing, in English.

———. *The State of Human Rights in Turkey (An Update): Report Submitted to the Congress of the United States.* Washington, D.C.: 1988. Government report, in English.

Committee for Defence of Democratic Rights in Turkey. "Kurdistan Refugees—Out of the Frying Pan into the Fire," *Turkey Newsletter* 84 (Nov.–Dec. 1988): 8–9. NGO article, in English.

Defence for Children International. *Children in Prison in Turkey.* Geneva, Switzerland: 1988. NGO report, in English.

Dikerdem, Mehmet Ali. "A Turkish Tug-of-War," *Index on Censorship* 16, no. 6 (June 1987): 15–19. NGO article, in English.

Fédération Internationale des Droits de l'Homme (International Federation of Human Rights). *Rapport de mission: Kurdistan Turc—14 au 24 Février 1991* (Mission Report: Turkish Kurdistan—14–24 February 1991). Paris: 1991. NGO factfinding report, in French.

———. "Le Martyr du Peuple Kurde" (The Martyrdom of the Kurdish People), *Lettre de la FIDH* 241 (22 March 1988). NGO article, in French.

———. "Turquie: Depuis 1981, 33 Morts dans la Prison de Diyarbakir" (Turkey: Since 1981, 33 Deaths in the Diyarbakir Prison), *Lettre de la FIDH* 158 (3 June 1986): 3. NGO article, in French.

Helsinki Watch. *Broken Promises: Torture and Killings Continue in Turkey*. New York: Human Rights Watch, 1992. NGO factfinding report, in English.

————. *Denying Human Rights and Ethnic Identity: The Greeks of Turkey*. New York: Human Rights Watch, 1992. NGO factfinding report, in English.

————. *The Kurds of Turkey: Killings, Disappearances and Torture*. New York: Human Rights Watch, 1993. NGO report, in English.

————. *"Nothing Unusual": The Torture of Children in Turkey*. New York: Human Rights Watch, 1992. NGO factfinding report, in English.

Human Rights Watch. "Turkey," in *Human Rights Watch World Report 1995*, pp. 229–234. New York: 1995. NGO report, in English.

Laber, J., and L. Whitman. *State of Flux: Human Rights in Turkey*. New York: U.S. Helsinki Watch Committee, 1987. NGO report, in English.

Lang, D. M., and C. J. Walker. *The Armenians*. London: Minority Rights Group, 1987. NGO report, in English.

McDowall, David. *The Kurds*, 4th rev. ed. London: Minority Rights Group, 1985. NGO report, in English.

Peeters, Yvo J. D. "The Rights of Minorities in Present-day Turkey," *Europa Ethnica* 44, no. 3 (1987): 131–137. News article, in English.

Picard, Elizabeth. *La Question Kurde* (The Kurdish Question). Brussels, Belgium: Editions Complexe, 1991. Monograph, in French.

Rumpf, Christian. "The Protection of Human Rights in Turkey and the Significance of International Human Rights Instruments," *Human Rights Law Journal* 14, no. 11–12 (Dec. 1993): 394–408. Scholarly article, in English.

Salmon, Mireille. *Rapport de Mission en Turquie 3/8* (Report of the Human Rights Mission to Turkey). Brussels, Belgium: International Association of Democratic Lawyers, 1986. NGO mission report, in French.

Siesby, Erik. *The Framework for Democracy and Human Rights in Turkish Law*. Vienna, Austria: International Helsinki Federation for Human Rights, 1988. NGO report, in English.

**TURKMENISTAN.** The Republic of Turkmenistan, formerly the Turkmen Soviet Socialist Republic, is bordered by the Caspian Sea to the east, Kazakhstan to the north-west, Uzbekistan to the north and east, Afghanistan to the southeast and Iran to the south. It declared its independence from the Soviet Union in 1991 and became a founder member of the Commonwealth of Independent States in December. It was admitted to the United Nations in 1992. Its population is estimated to be 3,884,000, comprising 73% Turkmen, 10% Russian, 9% Uzbek, 2% Kazakh, and 6% other. The two most common religions are Islam (87%) and Eastern Orthodox (11%). Turkmen replaced Russian as the official language in 1989.

Turkmenistan was ruled in part by the Persians from the 15th to the 17th centuries, then by the Bukharans, and finally by the Russians at the end of the 19th century. An estimated 20,000 Turkmen died in the final battle for Russian control in 1881. After the Bolshevik Revolution and the creation of the Turkestan Autonomous Soviet Socialist Republic in 1918, nationalist and British forces overthrew the government and established an independent government until the Red Army once again gained control in 1920. The Turkmen Soviet Socialist Republic was established in 1924 and became a constituent republic of the USSR in 1925.

The agricultural collectivization program enforced upon people who were traditionally nomadic as well as the the anti-religion program, which closed Islamic courts, mosques, and schools, ensured a continuation of the armed struggle against Soviet rule until 1936. Russians migrated to the republic and replaced Turkmen in many positions in the government.

The Turkmen resented the diminution of the importance of their religious and cultural heritage and the environmental and other problems resulting from the fact that the republic was used as a provider of natural gas and cotton to the other Soviet republics. However, lacking the communication ability and cohesion of some of the other republics in the late 1980s, they were late to challenge the Soviet authority and were the last to replace Russian as the official language in 1990.

In August the Turkmen Supreme Soviet adopted a declaration of sovereignty and presidential elections were held in October. The new president was Saparmurat Niyazov, former first secretary of the Communist Party of Turkmenistan and chairman of the Turkmen Supreme Soviet, winning 98% of the vote. Turkmen voted overwhelmingly (96%) for preserving the USSR, but following the failed coup attempt against the Soviet government in August 1991, 94% voted for independence, which was declared in October. The name of the country was changed to the Republic of Turkmenistan. The Communist Party remained in power but changed its name to the Democratic Party. Turkmenistan signed the Alma-Ata Declaration in December to become a founder member of the Commonwealth of Independent States.

A new constitution in May 1992 provided for direct election of a president for a maximum of two five-year terms, that person also being prime minister in the Council of Ministers, whom he appoints, and commander of the Armed Forces. A unicameral 50-seat Majlis elected every five years would replace the Supreme Soviet, although the 175-member Supreme Soviet elected for five years in 1990 would constitute the first Majlis.

Serving an oversight and advisory role, particularly on constitutional matters, is the People's Council (*Khalk Maslakhaty*), which includes the Majlis deputies as well as a further fifty elected and ten appointed representatives, the Council of Ministers, chairmen of the Supreme Court and the Supreme Economic Court, the procurator general, and the heads of local councils. The constitution also guarantees basic human rights, the equality of all ethnic minorities, the independence of the judiciary, and state secularism. It states that only ethnic Turkmen may hold state employment, but there have been few of the ethnic clashes characterizing other former Soviet republics despite the large percentage of ethnic minorities. At the end of 1993 ethnic Russians were granted the right to hold dual citizenship.

President Niyazov was reelected in June 1992 with 99% of the vote; in November 1993, the Mailis voted to extend his term until 2002, cancelling the election set for 1997. Despite some criticism of his style of governing, the move was supported by 99% of the people in a national referendum in January 1994.

**BIBLIOGRAPHY.** Amnesty International. *Turkmenistan: A Summary of Concerns about Prisoners of Conscience, Ill-Treatment and the Death Penalty.* London: 1993. NGO report, in English.

Human Rights Watch. "Turkmenistan," in *Human Rights Watch World Report 1995*, pp. 234–235. New York: 1995. NGO report, in English.

**TUTU, DESMOND MPILO (1931–).** In 1984, the NOBEL PEACE PRIZE Committee selected Bishop Desmond Tutu as the Peace Prize winner for "his role as a unifying leader . . . in the campaign to resolve the problem of apartheid in South Africa." But the citation also stressed that the award was given, in spirit, to the freedom fighters in that country who steadfastly stood against the racist system: "It is the committee's wish that the Peace Prize now awarded to Desmond Tutu should be regarded not only as a gesture of support to him and to the South African Council of Churches of which he is leader, but also to all individuals and groups in South Africa who, with their concern for human dignity, fraternity and democracy, incite the admiration of the world."

Desmond Mpilo Tutu was born in Klerksdorp, Witwatersrand, in the Transvaal section of South Africa.

His father was a schoolteacher and member of the Xhosas tribe; his mother, a domestic servant, of the Tswana tribe. When he was twelve, the family moved to Johannesburg. Tutu received a diploma at the Bantu Normal College, a B.A. degree at the University of Johannesburg, a licentiate in theology at St. Peter's Theological College in Johannesburg, becoming an Anglican deacon in 1960 and an ordained priest in 1961. He also holds a B.D. and an M.Th. from the University of London. From 1957 to 1975, he served as a teacher and pastor in various posts in South Africa and England.

In 1975, Tutu became bishop of Lesotho; and, in 1978, he was named the first black secretary general of the interdenominational South African Council of Churches. It was in this post that he was to make his greatest contribution to the struggle in his homeland. With most of the black political movements officially banned, the Council of Churches became the voice of the black movement. Throughout the late 1970s and the 1980s, Tutu advocated the withdrawal of foreign investments from South Africa as a peaceful and legitimate way of displaying international disapproval of **APARTHEID.** For his actions, his passport was revoked twice. Throughout the 1980s, he used his position as Peace Prize recipient and as the Anglican bishop of Johannesburg (the first black to hold that post) to urge governments and corporations to employ policies of "constructive engagement" that would cause economic hardship to the South African Government. Through his efforts, and the efforts of thousands of other South Africans, the South African government officially ended its policy of apartheid in 1992.

**BIBLIOGRAPHY.** *Current Biography Yearbook 1985*, pp. 418–421. New York: W. H. Wilson, 1985.

Schlessinger, Bernard S., and June Schlessinger, eds. *Who's Who of Nobel Prize Winners.* Phoenix, AZ, USA: Oryx Press, 1991.

Tutu, Desmond. *Crying in the Wilderness: The Struggle for Justice in South Africa.* London: A.R. Mowbray & Co., 1982.

———. *Hope and Suffering.* London: A.R. Mowbray & Co., 1984.

# U

**UGANDA.** The Republic of Uganda is a country in eastern Africa, on the equator. It has borders with Kenya, Rwanda, Sudan, Tanzania, and Zaire. It achieved independence from Great Britain in 1962 and became a member of the United Nations in 1963. Its population is estimated to be 17,410,000. Ethnic groups include the Baganda, from which the country derived its name; Africans of the Hamitic, Milotic, and Sudanese groups; and Congo Pygmies. Languages commonly used include English (official), Swahili, Lugando, Ateso, Luo, and many regional vernaculars. Religions practiced include Christianity (63%), Islam (6%), Animism and other indigenous beliefs (31%). Literacy is estimated at 52%.

The government (1994) took the form of a republic and member of the Commonwealth of Nations, of which the British monarch is the symbolic head. Under the constitution, embodied in the Uganda (Independence) Order in Council (1962), the crown-appointed governor-general was replaced by a popularly elected president as head of State. Sir Edward Mutesa, the first president, appointed Milton Obote as prime minister; but, four years later, in 1966, Obote seized control of the government with the help of an army officer, Col. Idi Amin. Col. Amin, in turn, deposed President Obote on 25 January 1971.

Idi Amin, a ruthless dictator who in 1976 had himself proclaimed "President for Life," conducted a systematic reign of terror and torture against his opponents in Uganda, resulting in an estimated 300,000 deaths. He was forced into exile in 1979 by troops from neighboring Tanzania, aided by Ugandans loyal to former President Obote, who successfully invaded the country.

Obote, who had sought refuge in Tanzania, returned to Uganda and led his People's Congress Party to victory in elections held in December 1980. His government announced its commitment to the restoration of constitutionality, the rule and due process of law, and the observance and guarantee of human rights and fundamental freedoms.

However, as time passed, the Obote regime gradually resumed, and even intensified, the massive abuses that had occurred under Amin, including massacres reported by the U.S. Government in 1984 to be "among the most grave in the world." The massacres, denied by Obote, were not widely reported in the information media and did not arouse international outrage at the time.

Obote was deposed by army troops on 27 July 1985, at which time Lieut.-Gen. Tito Okello assumed the presidency. However, the Okello regime proved unable to exercise control over its own troops, including elements of Idi Amin's armed forces, who continued to terrorize Ugandan citizens in an orgy of killing, arson, rape, and looting.

The National Resistance Army, composed of some 10,000 teenaged guerrillas, had taken control of the southwestern third of Uganda over the previous six months of fighting; and its 41-year-old leader, Yoweri Museveni, refused to accept a post in the Okello regime unless the behavior of the government troops was curbed. A ceasefire agreement was arranged between the Resistance Army and the government troops but never came into effect. Late in January 1986, the Resistance guerrillas moved northward and seized control of Kampala after heavy street fighting, winning praise and respect for its disciplined and humane behavior, particularly as contrasted with the brutality which had resulted in the death of more than half a million Ugandan citizens in the preceding two decades.

Museveni, installed as president after the collapse of the Okello regime, characterized the seizure of power not as "a mere change of guards" but rather as "a fundamental change in the politics of our Government." He vowed to strive for a unified government, free of tribal rivalries, stressed that "no regime has the right to kill any citizen of Uganda," and referred to the military officers he had overthrown as "criminals." Claiming to have modeled his guerrilla campaign after that of Cuba's Fidel Castro, he insisted that he was a nationalist and not a communist. Admitting that he had been "compelled by circumstances" to accept arms aid from Libya, he denied that he was a "tool" of Libyan leader Col. Muammar el-Qaddafi.

The government expanded the National Resistance Council, which had been acting in place of a legislature since 1986, to include 210 elected members; elections were held in February 1989. A constitutional commission was established that year and the government extended its term in office another five years in order to have time to bring about constitutional change. The 1986 ban on party political activity was also extended for another five years in 1990. A 288-member Constituent Assembly was elected in March 1994 to draft a new constitution.

The government stood its ground against an attempted coup in April 1991 and intense guerrilla fighting in the north and east of the country. Uganda also faced increasing problems of displaced persons. An estimated 130,000 Sudanese fled to Uganda to escape fighting in the Sudan in 1992 and 1993 and a further 100,000 arrived in early 1994.

Ugandans themselves were displaced by fighting on the Rwandan border, approximately 64,000 in 1992 alone. Following the deposit on the shores of Lake Victoria of approximately 40,000 mutilated bodies from Rwanda, the shores were declared a disaster area in May 1994. The decay of corpses raised alarm of a potential cholera outbreak and contamination of drinking water. The Ugandan Government was accused of supporting the Tutsis in their battle with the governing Hutus in Rwanda.

*ETHNIC TENSIONS.* The period between January 1971 and April 1979, during which Uganda was under military rule, witnessed a dramatic deterioration in race and ethnic relations. The most notable manifestation of discrimination during that period was the expulsion of the people of Asian origin, many of whom were citizens of Uganda, and the expropriation of their properties without due compensation. A drastic reduction of the American and European populations occurred during the same period. Furthermore, the military regime, by its policy of divide and rule, engendered deep ethnic divisions within the country. Apart from the effects of general destruction of the economy, ethnicity became a major factor in determining economic benefits and the provision of social services. In 1991, Ugandan Asians expelled in 1973 by former President Idi Amin were invited to return to seek property restitution.

**BIBLIOGRAPHY.** Amnesty International. *Administrative Detention.* London: 1988. NGO report, in English.

————. *Aide-Memoire: Summary of Amnesty International's Concerns in the Republic of Uganda.* London: 1987. NGO report, in English.

————. *Uganda: Criminal Charges against Critical Journalists.* London: 1988. NGO report, in English.

————. *Uganda: Evidence of Torture.* New York: 1985. NGO report, in English.

————. *Uganda: The Failure to Safeguard Human Rights.* London: 1992. NGO report, in English.

————. *Violations of Human Rights in the Republic of Uganda.* London: 1985. NGO report, in English.

Bazaara, Nyangabyaki. *The Struggle for Democracy at Makerere University 1986–1989: An Assessment.* Dakar, Senegal: Council for the Development of Economic and Social Research in Africa, 1990. Scholarly paper, in English.

Center on War and the Child. *Uganda: Land of the Child Soldier, a Summary Report.* Eureka Springs, AK, USA: 1987. NGO report, in English.

Clark, Lance. "Post-Emergency Assistance for Refugees in Eastern and Southern Africa," *Migration News* no. 3–4 (July–Dec. 1987): 3–24. NGO research paper, in English.

Dickens Mushemeza, Elijah. *The University and the State in Eastern Africa: A Case of Uganda.* Dakar, Senegal: Council for the Development of Economic and Social Research in Africa, 1990. Scholarly paper, in English.

Dodge, Cole P., and Magne Raundalen. *Reaching Children in War: Sudan, Uganda and Mozambique.* Bergen, Norway, and Uppsala, Sweden: Scandinavian Institute of African Studies, 1991. Collective works, in English.

Donnelly, J., and R. E. Howard, eds. *International Handbook on Human Rights.* Westport, CT, USA: Greenwood Press, 1987. Scholarly edited collection, in English.

Hansen, H. B., and M. Twaddle, eds. *Changing Uganda: The Dilemmas of Structural Adjustment and Revolutionary Change.* London: James Currey, 1991. Collection of scholarly contributions, in English.

Harries, Catherine. "Daughters of Our Peoples: International Feminism Meets Ugandan Law and Custom," *Columbia Human Rights Law Review* 25, no. 2 (Spring 1994): 493–539. Scholarly article, in English.

Heinz, Wolfgang S. *Ursachen und Folgen von Menschenrechtsverletzungen in der Dritten Weit* (Causes and Consequences of Human Rights Violations in Third World Countries). Saarbrucken, FGR: Verlag Breitenbach, 1986. Scholarly monograph, in German; bibliography on Uganda, pp. 315–318.

Ibingira, Grace, Joan Kakwenzire, and Roger P. Winter. *Three Papers Presented before the Commission of Inquiry into Violations of Human Rights, February 15–16, 1990, Kampala, Uganda.* Washington, D.C.: United States Committee for Refugees, 1990. Conference papers, in English.

International Alert. *Uganda: International Seminar on Internal Conflict.* London: 1987. NGO conference report, in English.

International League for Human Rights. *Uganda after Amin: A Case of Displacement and Discrimination against the Banyarwanda Population.* New York: 1985. NGO report, in English.

Magezi, Marble Gillianne. "Against a Sea of Troubles: AIDS Control in Uganda," *World Health Forum* 12, no. 3 (1991): 302–306. Scholarly article, in English.

Muwanga, Lance-Sera, and Henry Gombya. *The Pearl of Africa is Bleeding—"We Shall Massacre Them."* Vaxjo, Sweden: Program for Human Rights and Refugee Studies, 1991. Monograph, in English.

NGO Committee on UNICEF and UNICEF. "Child Soldiers of Uganda," *Action for Children* 1, no. 5 (1986): 6. IGO article, in English.

Oloka-Onyango, J. "The Dynamics of Corruption Control and Human Rights Enforcement in Uganda: The Case of the Inspector General of Government," *East African Journal of Peace and Human Rights* 1, no. 1 (1993): 23–51. Scholarly article, in English.

Otunnu, Ogenga. "Socio-Economic and Political Crises in Uganda: Reasons for Human Rights Violations and Refugees," *Refuge* 11, no. 3 (March 1992): 23–33. Article, in English.

Ovonji, Irene C. "Constitutional Government and Human

Rights in Uganda," in *Constitutional Government and Human Rights in Africa,* eds. E. S. Remble and E. Kalula. n.p.: n.d. Scholarly article, in English.

Radda Barnen, International Commission of Jurists (Swedish Section). *U.N. Assistance for Human Rights.* Stockholm, Sweden: 1988. NGO report, in English.

Rusk, John D. "Uganda: Breaking Out of the Mold?" *Africa Today* no. 2–3 (15 June 1987): 91–101. News article, in English.

Tamale, Sylvia. "Law Reform and Women's Rights in Uganda," *East African Journal of Peace and Human Rights* 1, no. 2 (1993): 164–194. Scholarly article, in English.

Uganda Human Rights Activists. *Report on Human Rights in Uganda.* Kampala, Uganda: 1987. NGO report, in English.

U.S. Committee for Refugees. *Human Rights in Uganda: The Reasons for Refugees.* Washington, D.C.: 1985. NGO report, in English.

**UKRAINE.** The Republic of Ukraine, formerly the Ukrainian Soviet Socialist Republic, is bordered to the south by the Black Sea and Sea of Asov; to the east and northeast by the Russian Federation; to the north by Belarus; and to the west by Moldova, Romania, Hungary, Slovakia, and Poland. Its population is estimated to be 51,846,958, comprising 73% Ukrainian, 22% Russian, 1% Jewish, and 4% other. The people professing a religious faith are predominantly Ukrainian Orthodox, Ukrainian Catholic, Protestant, and Jewish. The official language is Ukrainian. The Ukraine is a member of the United Nations pursuant to an agreement reached before the preparation of the **UNITED NATIONS CHARTER** in which the Ukrainian Soviet Socialist Republic and one other Soviet republic were admitted in 1945. It was a founding member of the Commonwealth of Independent States in 1991 after declaring its independence from the Soviet Union.

Ukraine has been ruled by Poland, Lithuania, and Russia throughout its history. Immediately after the Bolshevik revolution in 1917 it demanded autonomy and established its own legislature. Ukraine became part of Germany pursuant to a treaty in 1918 but again came under Soviet rule when the Ukrainian Soviet Socialist Republic was formed. Western Ukraine was ceded to Poland, Czechoslovakia, and Romania in 1921 and was not united with the rest of the country until after World War II. Ukrainian nationalism developed in the 1920s with an emphasis on language and economic prosperity; but famine from the Soviet policy of agricultural collectivization, the Stalin years, and World War II were all particularly hard on the peoples of Ukraine, many of whom lost their lives.

The government secrecy surrounding the nuclear accident at Chernobyl in 1986 and the reformist government of **MIKHAIL GORBACHEV** in the USSR were catalysts for the development of opposition movements including the Ukrainian People's Movement for Restructuring, or *Rukh,* miners and other workers, and religious groups, particularly Ukrainian Catholics. In elections to the Ukrainian Supreme Soviet in March 1990, opposition and independent candidates won 108 of the 450 seats, compared with 280 seats to the Communist Party. The legislature declared sovereignty in June 1990; and, although 70% of the voters supported the preservation of the USSR in a referendum in 1991 (90% of western Ukrainian voters supported independence), the Ukrainian Supreme Soviet declared independence following the failed coup attempt against the Soviet Government in August 1991. The name of the country was changed to the Republic of Ukraine and the legislature became the Supreme Council. The Communist Party was banned. The leaders of Ukraine, Belarus, and the Russian Federation agreed to form the Commonwealth of Independent States (CIS) in December 1991, established through the Alma-Ata Declaration and signed by eleven former Soviet republics.

The previous chairman of the Supreme Soviet, Leonid Kravchuk, won the direct presidential elections in December 1991 with 62% of the vote. The government was faced with economic decline, demonstrations by student groups, and strikes by miners and other workers who were opposed to the economic reforms, which included privatization and severe restrictions on government spending. Prime Minister Leonid Kuchma was given special powers to rule by decree. Leftist groups were particularly active, and the Communist Party was legalized again in late 1993.

Legislative elections were held in March and again in April 1994, in which the best performers were the left-wing parties, including the Communist Party, the Peasants' Party, and the Socialist Party, which won a total of 118 of the 450 seats; and independent candidates who won 170 seats. *Rukh* won only 20 seats. International observers were concerned with the loss of democratic conditions surrounding the elections, particularly in the rural areas where people had allegedly been enticed to vote. A remaining 113 seats were unfilled and contested in a third round of voting. The Supreme Council elected the leader of the Socialist Party as its chairman in June 1994. In presidential elections in July 1994, former Prime Minister Leonid Kuchma defeated President Kravchuk with 52% of the vote. President Kuchma faced a variety of problems including a mounting debt to Russia, international concern over Ukraine's nuclear capability, and increased crime including the smuggling of uranium to Europe.

*CRIMEA.* One of the most pressing problems was the continuing constitutional crisis with the pro-Russian secessionists in Crimea, violently opposed by the

Crimean Tatars who had been forcibly exiled from their country in 1944. Formerly part of the Russian Federation, Crimea came under Ukrainian rule in 1954. However, in 1992 its legislature declared independence and adopted its own constitution. Crimea's first president, Yury Meshkov, was elected in January 1994 with 73% of the vote and repeatedly voiced his secessionist ideas. An opinion poll taken in March 1994, which Ukrainian President Kravchuk declared illegal and in contravention of the Ukrainian constitution, indicated that as many as 70% of the voters were in favor of increased autonomy and independence from Ukraine.

The Crimean constitution was suspended and reinstated by the legislature until, under threat from Ukraine, the measures were rescinded and ruled invalid by the Ukraine Supreme Council. The two countries signed an agreement in June 1994 confirming Crimea's obligation to follow Ukrainian law. But internal conflict continued and in September Crimean President Meshkov took control of the media and announced that he would rule by decree until a constitutional referendum in April 1995. However, in March 1995 the Ukrainian legislature approved a bill which, while it did not revoke Crimean autonomy, dissolved the Crimean constitution, ousted President Meshkov, and granted the right to the Ukrainian Government to abolish the Crimean legislature.

**BIBLIOGRAPHY.** Commission on Security and Cooperation in Europe. *Report on the Supreme Soviet Elections in Ukraine.* Kiev, Ukraine: 1990. Government report, in English.

Immigration and Refugee Board Documentation Centre. *Ukraine: The Situation of Ethnic Minorities.* Ottawa, Canada: 1993. Government briefing paper, in English.

Naboka, Serhiy. "Nationalities Issues in Ukraine," *Uncaptive Minds* 5, no. 1 (Spring 1992): 75–80. Article, in English.

Seytmuratova, Ayshe. "New Legislation of the USSR, RSFSR and Ukraine concerning the Crimean Tatar People," *RCDA* 30, nos. 3 and 4 (1992): 52–55. Article, in English.

**UNEMPLOYMENT.** In a report to the 1986 session of the UN **GENERAL ASSEMBLY** (UN Doc. A/41/472), transmitting the views of governments regarding the proposal to promote a new international humanitarian order, the Secretary-General included a "Survey on Specific Humanitarian Issues in the Contemporary World" based on information solicited or collected from specialized agencies and other bodies within the United Nations system. The survey was prepared at the request of the assembly (resolution 40/126) within the United Nations Secretariat and, in appropriate instances, in consultation with the organizations directly concerned.

Section D of the survey (paras. 23–27), entitled "Massive Unemployment," reads as follows:

Unemployment across the world has grown enormously in recent years. In many low-income countries much of what had been underemployment of one kind or another has turned into open unemployment, in some countries rising to well over 20 per cent of the economically active population. In many industrialized countries the era of "full employment" of the 1950s and 1960s has passed, with seemingly chronically high levels being reached in large parts of Western Europe. Only in South-East Asia has unemployment remained low and in a very few countries it has fallen steadily in recent years.

As for the unemployed themselves, youths have attracted most attention; in some countries the unemployment rates for teenagers have exceeded 40 per cent. Even harder hit have been minority groups, such as coloured ethnic groups and immigrants. In southern Africa the majority group has borne the brunt of unemployment, but that is a special case.

Evidence on the incidence of unemployment among men and women is mixed, for in some countries employment of women has been growing, while employment of men has been shrinking. Nevertheless, taking due account of "discouraged workers", unemployment of women in many economies has been chronically high, and many unemployed women have had no other regular source of income to meet their own needs, or those of their children or other relatives.

Finally, there has been the growing phenomenon of older-worker unemployment. Already a majority of the world's population aged over 55 are in low-income countries; there and in many industrialized countries unemployment among older workers has grown massively in recent years, and in many cases workers in their 50s, once unemployed, become permanent rejects from the labour force, demoralized, increasingly prone to acute poverty, ill health and early death.

Coordinated international action is required to tackle global unemployment. Most countries that have tried to stimulate their economies in order to boost employment have found it impossible to sustain such efforts in the face of worsening import penetration and balance-of-payments crises. Coordinated actions by groups of trading partners are needed, coupled with measures to control inflation that do not place the burden of price changes on the unemployed. A more humanitarian method must be found of checking inflation and maintaining economic growth than the costly and tragic recipe of mass unemployment. It is a matter of human will and a matter of recognizing that the social malaise represented by unemployment deserves to be given very high priority in policy formulation. It is precisely because the unemployed have no effective lobby group working to protect their interest that national politicians and the international community have a special responsibility to work on their behalf.

**SEE ALSO** Work.

**UNESCO.** See **UNITED NATIONS EDUCATIONAL, SCIENTIFIC AND CULTURAL ORGANIZATION.**

**UNICEF.** See **UNITED NATIONS CHILDREN'S FUND.**

**UNION OF ARAB JURISTS.** An international non-governmental organization in consultative status with the UN **Economic and Social Council** (Category II) and with **UNESCO,** the Union consists of associations of jurists' associations in 15 countries. Founded in 1975 in Baghdad, its main function is to work for the political and economic liberation of the Arab homeland, to care for the Arab legal heritage, to formulate constitutional and legal frameworks for progressive political and social principles to be applied in the Arab homeland, and to defend human rights by providing legal measures for their realization. The Union has also been involved in the preparation of the draft of an "Arab Agreement for Human Rights and Fundamental Freedoms."

UAJ published the bi-annual journal *Al-Huqoqi Al-Arabi.*

Union of Arab Jurists. Address: Almansor P.O.B. 6026, Baghdad, Iraq. Telephone: (964-1) 537-5820. Fax: (964-1) 537-5238. Secretary-General: Abdul Latif Al-Saadoun.

**UNITED ARAB EMIRATES.** A federation of seven coastal States located in western Asia on the Gulf of Oman: Abu Dhabi, Dubai, Sharjah, Ajman, Fujairah, Umm al-Qaiwain, and Ras al-Khaimah, the United Arab Emirates have borders with Oman, Qatar, and Saudi Arabia. It was formed in 1971 and became a member of the United Nations in 1972. Its population is estimated to be 2,590,000. Ethnic groups include persons of Arab, Indian, Iranian, and Pakistani descent. Languages commonly used include Arabic (official), Farsi, and English. Religions practiced include Islam (Sunni and Shi'ite) (90%), Christianity (4%), Hinduism (4%), and others (2%). Literacy is estimated at 57%.

The government (1994) took the form of a federation of monarchies, each headed by an emir. Joint policies are adopted only in respect of foreign relations, defense, and development; otherwise, each emirate maintains its own system of government. The Supreme Council of Rulers, made up of the emirs or their representatives, elects the president and prime minister, who act as head of State and of government, respectively. It also appoints a Council of Ministers, which drafts legislation, based primarily upon the Islamic Shar'ia. Drafts of laws are considered by an elected 40-member National Council, which has consultative functions only, consisting of eight members each from Abu Dhabi and Dubai, six members each from Ras al Khaimah and Sharjah, and four each from the other emirates. The jurisdiction of local courts, where rules of Islamic law prevail, extends to all citizens of the

United Arab Emirates and to nationals of other Arab and Islamic States. There are no political parties.

**UNITED KINGDOM.** The United Kingdom of Great Britain and Northern Ireland is a country occupying a large portion of the British Isles, in the Atlantic Ocean and the North Sea off the northwest coast of Europe. It comprises a union of England, Northern Ireland, Scotland, and Wales. England occupies the southeastern part of the island of Great Britain; Wales occupies the western portion, and Scotland, the northern portion. Northern Ireland occupies the northeastern tip of the second largest of the British Isles, the larger southern portion being occupied by Ireland. The United Kingdom includes, in addition, a number of colonies and dependencies, among them Anguilla, Bermuda, the British Antarctic Territory, the British Indian Ocean Territory, the British Virgin Islands, the Cayman Islands, the Channel Islands, the Falkland Islands and dependencies, Gibraltar, Hong Kong, the Isle of Man, the Leeward Islands, Montserrat, Pitcairn Island, St. Helena, and the Turks and Caicos Islands.

Created in 1707 when Scotland, England, and Wales were united, the United Kingdom gained a fourth member after a rebellion in Ireland (1916–1921) had divided that country into the Irish Free State and Northern Ireland. It became a member of the United Nations in 1945. Its population is estimated to be 57,890,000. Ethnic groups include English, Scottish, Welsh, and Irish, joined in recent years by immigrants from the West Indian islands and Asian and African countries. Languages commonly used include English (official), Irish, Welsh, and Gaelic. The predominant religion is Christianity; Judaism and Islam are also practiced. The Church of England (Protestant Episcopal) is the established church of England; the monarch is its temporal head, with the right to appoint to various Church offices. The Church of Scotland (Presbyterian) is the established church of Scotland. Literacy is estimated at 99%.

The government (1994) took the form of a monarchy. Under the unwritten constitution, which consists primarily of statutes, common law, and practice, the monarch is head of State. The prime minister, representing the party or coalition given a majority in election of members of the House of Commons, is appointed by the monarch and serves as head of government. The supreme legislative authority, Parliament, consists of the 635-member House of Commons, composed of members (516 for England, 36 for Wales, 71 for Scotland, and 12 for Northern Ireland) elected by popular vote for terms of five years, unless Parliament is dissolved earlier; and the House of Lords, which includes more than 1,000 members (hereditary peers, life peers and peeresses, certain judges, and the bishops and archbishops of the Church of England). Executive power is exercised by the cabinet, headed by the prime minister; all members of the cabinet are members of one of the two houses of Parliament. The main activity of the House of Commons is to consider legislation proposed by the cabinet; the House of Lords may delay certain bills—but not "money bills"— for a maximum of one year. The judiciary includes magistrate's courts, county courts, high courts, and appellate courts and, in certain circumstances, the House of Lords. Political parties include the Conservative Party, the Labour Party, the Social Democrats, the Liberal Party, the Ulster Nationalists and other Northern Irish parties, the Scottish Nationalist Party, and the Welsh Nationalist Party.

Great Britain was the only member nation to opt out of the Social Chapter of the 1991 Maastricht Treaty, which sought greater integration of the twelve (fifteen as of January 1995) nations within the European Union. In April 1992 the Conservative Party won its fourth consecutive general election, the first party to do so since 1826.

*ETHNIC RELATIONS.* Discord between ethnic groups residing in the United Kingdom was first brought to world attention by the Notting Hill riots of 1958, aimed, in part, at ending discrimination against immigrant workers in employment and housing. Legislation aimed at reducing the flow of immigration was adopted in 1962, 1968, and 1971 but did not resolve the problem. After 1964, large numbers of foreign workers began to arrive from former British colonies in Asia, Africa, and the Caribbean, sometimes with the help and encouragement of British industry. Unable to accommodate themselves to British ways of life or to find suitable employment or accommodations, they complained bitterly of discrimination.

The Race Relations Act of 1968 established the Race Relations Board, with little authority, and the Community Relations Commission, which could only coordinate voluntary efforts at reducing racial tensions. It was replaced by the Race Relations Act of 1976, which made direct or indirect racial discrimination unlawful in fields of employment, education, and the provision of goods, services, facilities, and premises; and gave individuals a right of direct access to the civil courts and industrial tribunals for legal remedies for unlawful discrimination. The 1976 act also established the independent Commission for Racial Equality, vested with wide powers and the duty to work toward the elimination of discrimination, to promote equality of opportunity and good race relations, and to keep the operation of the act under review. The commis-

sion also has discretion to assist individuals who believe that they have been the subject of unlawful discrimination.

In addition, section 5A of the Public Order Act 1936 (which was inserted in the Race Relations Act of 1976) makes it an offense for any person to publish or distribute written matter, or to use words in any public place or at any public meeting, where the matter or words are threatening, abusive, or insulting and likely to stir up hatred against any racial group in Great Britain.

*NORTHERN IRELAND.* Intolerance and discrimination based on religion or belief have plagued Northern Ireland for many centuries. After numerous rebellions and a threat of civil war, the British Parliament in 1920 separated Catholic southern Ireland from predominantly Protestant northern Ireland, leaving each with its own government and parliament. When Ireland became a dominion in 1921 and gained sovereignty as the Republic of Ireland, Northern Ireland chose to remain as part of the United Kingdom.

From 1921 to 1972, Northern Ireland had a directly elected subordinate parliament and government. In 1972, responsibility for its administration was assumed by the United Kingdom Government and Parliament. This constitutional arrangement is, however, considered temporary, although it has been in force for approximately 20 years. In the meantime, the British Government has preserved Northern Ireland's separate statute book.

The Catholics of Northern Ireland, who make up about one-third of its population, staged massive demonstrations in 1968 and 1969, charging discrimination in housing, employment, and political rights. Elements of the Irish Republican Army (IRA)—a faction committed to ending the partition of the country but which had been outlawed in the Irish Republic—directed acts of violence and terrorism against members of the Protestant majority, against the police, and eventually against the British troops sent in to quell the disturbances.

Between 1969 and 1989, more than 2,750 persons were killed in Northern Ireland in sporadic waves of violence, and the religious communities came to resemble hostile armed camps. A considerable body of legislation was enacted to deal with the specific problems of religious, cultural, and political discrimination, including the Northern Ireland Constitution Act 1973, making it illegal for any public authority to discriminate on grounds of religious belief or political opinion and establishing the Standing Advisory Committee on Human Rights to advise the government on the effectiveness of the law; the Fair Employment Act

(Northern Ireland) 1976, outlawing discrimination in employment on ground of religious or political belief and setting up the Fair Employment Agency to enforce and promote equality of opportunity in employment; and the Prevention of Incitement to Hatred Act (Northern Ireland) 1970, prohibiting the use of written matter or words likely to provoke hatred based on religious belief, color, race, or ethnic or national origin, against any section of the public.

*TERRORISM.* In addition to anti-discrimination laws, Great Britain has enacted legislation in response to terrorism, particularly on the part of the IRA, which has resulted in curtailing civil liberties in Northern Ireland.

Among these statutes are the 1974 Prevention of Terrorism Act, as amended in 1976, 1984, and 1985; and the 1973 Northern Ireland Emergency Provisions Act, amended in 1978 and 1987. These acts restrict the activities of organizations connected with terrorism; expand the British criminal code to include terrorism and related activities; curtail the due process protection of suspected terrorists; authorize searches, seizures, and arrests without warrants for suspected terrorists; and allow the Secretary of State of Northern Ireland to detain a suspected terrorist for an unlimited period of time, *inter alia.*

Following the celebrated release of people apparently wrongly convicted for bombings in Britain in the mid-1970s, and the concern expressed by international human rights organizations regarding the treatment in custody of people suspected of terrorist offenses, peace in Northern Ireland came one step closer in December 1993 with the publication of the "Downing Street Declaration" by Prime Ministers John Major of Great Britain and Albert Reynolds of Ireland. The document mentioned **SELF-DETERMINATION** by the people of Northern Ireland and the possibility of a united Ireland. This was followed by an IRA ceasefire in August 1994 and the beginning of negotiations for a settlement in December.

In February 1995 came the publication of a plan drawn up by Prime Minister Major and Irish Prime Minister John Bruton. The plan called for a directly elected, 90-seat Ulster Assembly with legislative responsibility for most issues except security and taxation. This would mark the first "home-rule" for the province since the British Government took direct legislative responsibility in 1974. The plan also called for a "cross-border" group of representatives from the Irish Republic and Northern Ireland who would focus on mutual interests such as the environment, tourism, economic development, and culture.

Within the document the Irish Republic rescinded its constitutional claim to Northern Ireland. Those who wish the North to stay as part of the British monarchy responded with a document of their own, claiming that Britain was conceding union of the north with the Irish Republic. Following British troop reduction in Northern Ireland from 30,000 in 1992 to 17,500 in 1995 and an end to daytime patrols in the province, the peace plan proceeded with the first meeting since 1974 between a British Government minister and *Sinn Fein,* the political wing of the IRA.

*TERRITORIES.* The Government of Great Britain administers a number of territories, including Anguilla, Bermuda, the British Antarctic Territory, the British Indian Ocean Territory, the British Virgin Islands, the Cayman Islands, the Channel Islands, the Falkland Islands and dependencies, Gibraltar, Hong Kong, the Isle of Man, the Leeward Islands, Montserrat, Pitcairn Island, St. Helena, and the Turks and Caicos Islands.

Of these, the UN **GENERAL ASSEMBLY** has repeatedly, in recent years, affirmed the inalienable right of the people of certain of those territories—Anguilla, the Cayman Islands, Montserrat, Bermuda, the Turks and Caicos Islands, and the British Virgin Islands—to self-determination and independence, and has called upon the United Kingdom Government to expedite the process of decolonization in accordance with the expressed wishes of the people of each territory.

In the case of each of these territories, the General Assembly has pointed out that it is the responsibility of the United Kingdom, as the administering power, to create such conditions in the territories as would enable their peoples to exercise freely and without interference, from a well-informed standpoint as to the available options, their inalienable right to self-determination and independence. At the same time, it has made it clear that it is ultimately for the peoples of the territories themselves to determine freely their future political status.

As regards Gibraltar, which was turned over to Great Britain in accordance with the Treaty of Utrecht in 1713, Spain has never ceased to call for its return. A referendum on the question was held in 1967, but the residents of Gibraltar—nearly all of Spanish, Italian, or Maltese descent—voted overwhelming to remain a British territory. Although Spain blocked Gibraltar's land border from 1969 to 1980, the situation did not change. In 1980, however, the two governments indicated that they would settle the dispute in keeping with a UN resolution which called for the restoration of the territory to Spain at an unspecified future date; and the border was re-opened.

As regards Hong Kong, the United Kingdom reached a unique understanding with the People's Republic of China in 1984 under which the crown colony would return to Chinese sovereignty on 30 June 1997 as a special administrative region of the People's Republic but would retain its western social, economic, and legal system as well as its status as a free port. Under the agreement, Hong Kong's basic lifestyle would remain unchanged, its laws would continue in effect, and basic human rights—including freedom of speech, freedom of assembly and association, and freedom of religion or belief—would be guaranteed by the Government of China. However, after the events in China in June 1989, when the Chinese Government crushed a growing liberal movement toward democratization, residents of Hong Kong are said in media reports to be fearful of the future of their rights.

The territory moved toward its status as a "special administrative region" (SAR) by adopting a Basic Law, approved by China, making changes to the Legislative and Executive Councils, and determining the future of the Court of Appeal. A bill of rights, modeled on the UN **INTERNATIONAL COVENANT ON CIVIL AND POLITICAL RIGHTS**, came into effect in mid-1991.

### *CRIMINAL JUSTICE AND PUBLIC ORDER BILL.*

The controversial Criminal Justice and Public Order Bill, enacted in November 1994, formally did away with the right to silence in criminal proceedings. In addition to allowing courts to infer guilt from a suspect's silence, the law authorizes the police to take a sample of DNA without permission and to disband outdoor concerts and take equipment without a warrant. It also creates stiffer penalties, particularly for 12- to 14-year-olds who would be sent to secure training centers. The authority to infer guilt from one's silence was first employed in 1988 in Northern Ireland in trials of suspected terrorists.

**BIBLIOGRAPHY.** Addo, Michael K. "The Legal Condition of Refugees in the United Kingdom," *Journal of Refugee Studies* 7, no. 1 (1994): 96–110. Scholarly article, in English.

American Protestants for Truth about Ireland. *Documents concerning Summary Executions by the British Army and the Royal Ulster Constabulary.* Gwynedd, PA, USA: 1988. NGO brief, in English.

Amin, Kaushika, and Robin Richardson. *Politics for All: Equality, Culture and the General Election 1992.* London: Runnymede Trust, 1992. NGO report, in English; bibliography, pp. 66–67.

Amnesty International. *United Kingdom: Fair Trial Concerns in Northern Ireland: The Right of Silence.* London: 1992. NGO report, in English.

————. *United Kingdom: Killings by Security Forces in Northern Ireland Update.* London: 1990. NGO report, in English.

Bailey, Sidney, ed. *Human Rights and Responsibilities in Britain and Ireland: A Christian Perspective.* London: Macmillan, 1988. Scholarly study, in English.

Bonnechere, Michele. *Rapport Preliminaire sur la Mission d'Observation du Proces Concernant Gerard Kelly et Brendan McFarlane* (Preliminary Report on the Observer Mission to the Trial of Gerard Kelly and Brendan McFarlane). Brussels, Belgium: International Association of Democratic Lawyers, 1987. NGO report, in French.

Committee on the Administration of Justice. *Cause for Complaint: The System for Dealing with Complaints against the Police in Northern Ireland.* Belfast, Northern Ireland: 1990. NGO report, in English.

Feldman, David. *Civil Liberties and Human Rights in England and Wales.* Oxford, UK: Clarendon Press, 1993. Scholarly monograph, in English.

Gordon, P., and A. Newnham. *Different Worlds: Racism and Discrimination in Britain,* 2nd rev. ed. London: Runnymede Trust, 1986. NGO report, in English.

Haysom, Nicholas. "Licence to Kill, Part II: A Comparative Survey of the Law in the United Kingdom, United States of America and South Africa," *South African Journal on Human Rights* 3, pt. 2 (July 1987): 202–222. Scholarly article, in English.

Human Rights Watch. *Children in Northern Ireland: Abused by Security Forces and Paramilitaries.* New York: 1992. NGO report, in English.

————. *Freedom of Expression in the UK: Recent Developments.* New York: 1993. NGO report, in English.

————. *Human Rights in Northern Ireland.* New York: 1991. NGO report, in English.

————. *Prison conditions in the United Kingdom.* New York: 1992. NGO report, in English.

————. "United Kingdom and Northern Ireland," in *Human Rights Watch World Report 1994,* pp. 235–238. New York: 1995. NGO report, in English.

*Index on Censorship* 17, no. 8 (Sept. 1988). NGO special issue on the United Kingdom, in English.

Irish American Unity Conference, Human Rights Committee. *Report on Human Rights in Northern Ireland.* Whitestone, NY, USA: 1985. NGO report, in English.

National Council for Civil Liberties. *Identity Cards and the Threat to Civil Liberties.* London: 1988. NGO briefing paper, in English.

Pettman, Ralph. *Incitement to Racial Hatred: The International Experience.* Canberra, Australia: Human Rights Commission, 1982. Government monograph, in English.

Sieghart, Paul, ed. *Human Rights in the United Kingdom.* London: Human Rights Network, 1988. NGO monograph, in English; footnotes to article contain substantial bibliographic references.

Sigler, Jay A., ed. *International Handbook on Race and Race Relations.* Westport, CT, USA: Greenwood Press, 1987. Scholarly edited collection, in English; bibliography, pp. 449–454.

Tarnopolsky, Walter S. "Race Relations Commissions in Canada, Australia, New Zealand, the United Kingdom and the United States," *Human Rights Law Journal* 6, pt. 2–4 (1985): 145—178. Scholarly article, in English.

**UNITED NATIONS (UN).** The United Nations was established on 24 October 1945, when 51 original member countries ratified the **UNITED NATIONS CHARTER**; since 1947, October 24 has been annually commemorated as "United Nations Day." As stated in article 1 of the Charter, its principal mission is to "develop friendly relations among nations based on respect for the principle of equal rights and self-determination of peoples and to take other appropriate measures to strengthen universal peace" and "to achieve international co-operation in solving international problems of an economic, social, cultural, or humanitarian character, and in promoting and encouraging respect for human rights and for fundamental freedoms for all without distinction as to race, sex, language, or religion." There are six principal organs: the **GENERAL ASSEMBLY**, the **SECURITY COUNCIL**, the **SECRETARIAT** (described below), the **INTERNATIONAL COURT OF JUSTICE**, the **ECONOMIC AND SOCIAL COUNCIL**, and the **TRUSTEESHIP COUNCIL**.

*ESTABLISHMENT.* The **LEAGUE OF NATIONS** was the precursor of the United Nations. However, the League lost its authority when it was unable to prevent the outbreak of World War II. In 1946, the League dissolved itself; and its assets, property, and functions were transferred to the United Nations.

The first step that led to the establishment of the United Nations was the Inter-Allied Declaration of 12 June 1944, signed in London by representatives of Australia, Canada, New Zealand, South Africa, and the United Kingdom; and by representatives of the exiled Governments of Belgium, Czechoslovakia, France, Greece, Luxembourg, the Netherlands, Norway, Poland, and Yugoslavia, States that were under Nazi domination at the time. The Declaration stated the signers' intention "to work together, and with other free peoples, both in war and peace, to this end."

On 14 August 1941, President Franklin D. Roosevelt of the United States of America and Prime Minister Winston Churchill of the United Kingdom secretly met at sea and issued the Atlantic Charter, which called for an end to the use of force and disarmament. The Charter also stated that, after the final destruction of the Nazi tyranny, a peace would be established that would ensure all peoples the freedom to live their lives in security.

On New Year's Day 1942, representatives of 26 Allied nations signed the **DECLARATION BY UNITED NATIONS** proclaimed their support of the Atlantic Charter and their determination to overcome "savage and brutal forces seeking to subjugate the world." The Declaration was left open for signature by other nations that agreed with its purposes. In addition to the original 26 signatories, another 21 States signed the document, forming the core of the 51 States that were the original UN members.

Plans for the establishment of the United Nations were discussed at Dumbarton Oaks in Washington, D.C., in the summer of 1944. At the Dumbarton Oaks Conference, representatives of the United States, the United Kingdom, the Union of Soviet Socialist Republics, and China agreed on proposals for the aims, structure, and functioning of the world organization. On

11 February 1945, President Roosevelt, Prime Minister Churchill, and USSR Premier Josef Stalin conferred at Yalta, in the USSR, and announced their agreement that the establishment of a general international organization to maintain peace and security was essential; they called for a Conference of United Nations to be held in San Francisco, CA, on 25 April 1945, to prepare the charter of such an organization.

On the appointed date, delegates of 50 nations met in San Francisco for the conference known officially as the United Nations Conference on International Organization. The representatives unanimously adopted the Charter.

*MEMBERSHIP.* UN membership is open to all peace-loving countries that accept the obligations of the Charter. A country applies for membership through the Security Council. If the Council approves the application, it passes the application on to the General Assembly, which must accept by a two-thirds majority. Membership becomes effective on the date the Assembly accepts the application. A member may voluntary withdraw from the organization and may be expelled by the Security Council for violations of the principles of the Charter. Once expelled, there is no provision for readmission.

The original 51 members of the UN were States that took part in the San Francisco Conference or had signed the Declaration by United Nations. The original members were Argentina, Australia, Belgium, Bolivia, Brazil, Byelorussian Soviet Socialist Republic, Canada, Chile, China, Colombia, Costa Rica, Cuba, Czechoslovakia, Denmark, Dominican Republic, Ecuador, Egypt, El Salvador, Ethiopia, France, Greece, Guatemala, Haiti, Honduras, India, Iran, Iraq, Lebanon, Liberia, Luxembourg, Mexico, Netherlands, New Zealand, Nicaragua, Norway, Panama, Paraguay, Peru, Philippines, Poland, Saudi Arabia, South Africa, Syria, Turkey, Ukrainian Soviet Socialist Republic, Union of Soviet Socialist Republics, United Kingdom of Great Britain and Northern Ireland, United States of America, Uruguay, Venezuela, and Yugoslavia.

As of 31 December 1995, the following 185 countries are member States of the United Nations:

Afghanistan, Albania, Algeria, Angola, Antigua and Barbuda, Argentina, Armenia, Australia, Austria, Azerbaijan

Bahamas, Bahrain, Bangladesh, Barbados, Belarus, Belgium, Belize, Benin, Bhutan, Bolivia, Bosnia Herzegovina, Botswana, Brazil, Brunei Darussalam, Bulgaria, Burkina Faso, Burundi

Cambodia, Cameroon, Canada, Cape Verde, Central African Republic, Chad, Chile, China, Colombia, Comoros, Congo, Costa Rica, Cote d'Ivoire (Ivory Coast), Croatia, Cuba, Cyprus, Czech Republic

Democratic People's Republic of Korea (North Korea), Denmark, Djibouti, Dominica, Dominican Republic

Ecuador, Egypt, El Salvador, Equatorial Guinea, Eritrea, Estonia, Ethiopia

Fiji, Finland, France

Gabon, Gambia, Georgia, Germany, Ghana, Greece, Grenada, Guatemala, Guinea, Guinea-Bissau, Guyana

Haiti, Honduras, Hungary

Iceland, India, Indonesia, Iran, Iraq, Ireland, Israel, Italy

Jamaica, Japan, Jordan

Kazakhstan, Kenya, Kuwait, Kyrgyzstan

Laos, Latvia, Lebanon, Lesotho, Liberia, Libya, Liechtenstein, Lithuania, Luxembourg

Macedonia, Madagascar, Malawi, Malaysia, Maldives, Mali, Malta, Marshall Islands, Mauritania, Mauritius, Mexico, Micronesia, Moldova, Monaco, Mongolia, Morocco, Mozambique, Myanmar

Namibia, Nepal, Netherlands, New Zealand, Nicaragua, Niger, Nigeria, Norway

Oman

Pakistan, Palau, Panama, Papua New Guinea, Paraguay, Peru, Philippines, Poland, Portugal

Qatar

Republic of Korea (South Korea), Romania, Russian Federation, Rwanda

St. Kitts and Nevis, St. Lucia, St. Vincent and Grenadines, Samoa, San Marino, Sao Tome and Principe, Saudi Arabia, Senegal, Seychelles, Sierra Leone, Singapore, Slovakia, Slovenia, Solomon Islands, Somalia, South Africa, Spain, Sri Lanka, Sudan, Suriname, Swaziland, Sweden, Syria

Tajikistan, Tanzania, Thailand, Togo, Tonga, Trinidad and Tobago, Tunisia, Turkey, Turkmenistan

Uganda, Ukraine, United Arab Emirates, United Kingdom, United States of America, Uruguay, Uzbekistan

Vanuatu, Venezuela, Vietnam

Yemen, Yugoslavia (Serbia and Montenegro)

Zaire, Zambia, Zimbabwe.

In addition, the Holy See and Switzerland are nonmember States that maintain permanent observer missions.

**UN ADVISORY SERVICES FOR HUMAN RIGHTS.** In 1953 and 1954, the General Assembly of the United Nations first authorized the Secretary-General to assist governments, at their request, in promoting and safeguarding the rights of women, in eliminating racial discrimination, in protecting minorities, and in promoting freedom of information. In 1955, the Assembly incorporated these provisions in a single program of advisory services in the field of human rights. Several forms of assistance are authorized under the program:

seminars, regional training courses, fellowships, and the advisory services of experts. Such assistance may relate to any human rights question, provided that help is not otherwise available through a specialized agency or other organization. The program is designed to give governments an opportunity to share experiences and to exchange knowledge about the promotion and protection of human rights.

*Seminars.* As the program developed, emphasis was first placed on the holding of seminars for the discussion of various human rights problems and their possible solutions. The seminars, by bringing together for short periods of time key people nominated by their respective governments, are intended to stimulate thinking, provoke fresh ideas, elicit constructive suggestions, and make it possible to explore informally ways and means of dealing with matters relating to human rights that are of concern to the world community.

The first step in the organization of a seminar is the receipt of an invitation from a government offering to act as host. The Secretary-General consults with that government, usually through its permanent mission, with regard to the subject matter to be considered, the date and place of the seminar, and the list of governments to be invited to nominate participants. When these questions have been settled, an agreement is drawn up setting forth the responsibilities and services to be provided by the United Nations and by the host government. Generally speaking, the United Nations pays for the travel and subsistence of one participant from each country invited, for the preparation of background papers by expert consultants, and for assigning a team of officials from the United Nations Secretariat to organize and run the seminar. The host government is responsible for certain local costs and services, including the furnishing of appropriate conference facilities and personnel.

Invitations are then issued. In the case of worldwide seminars, 32 governments, in addition to the host government, are invited on the basis of the geographical distribution of countries in the COMMISSION ON HUMAN RIGHTS: eight from western Europe and other States, four from eastern European States, six from Asian States, eight from African States, and six from Latin American States. For regional seminars, all member States of the region concerned are invited. Each invited government is asked to nominate a participant and up to three alternates to attend the seminar. The host government is invited to nominate up to five participants and five alternates or observers. Participants, although nominated by their governments, attend the seminar in their personal capacity at the invitation of the Secretary-General and subject to confirmation by him, and do not speak on behalf of their government.

Specialized agencies and other intergovernmental organizations having an interest in the subject of the seminar are also invited to be represented. Non-governmental organizations in consultative status, whose aims and purposes are related to the subject of the seminar, are asked to send observers.

Expert consultants are called upon by the United Nations to prepare basic background papers to elucidate the topics on the agenda and to highlight problems with a view to stimulating their discussion at the seminar. These papers are translated, reproduced, and sent to those who will attend the seminar in advance of the opening date.

The United Nations pays for the air travel of one participant from each country invited, as well as a subsistence allowance for the duration of the seminar. Discussions at the seminar are conducted in an informal manner, no votes are taken, and no resolutions are adopted. There are no official records of the discussion; experience has shown that this results in a frank, friendly, and constructive exchange of opinions and experience. The report of the seminar, adopted at the last meeting, reflects the points of view expressed and summarizes the discussion. It may also include conclusions and recommendations if a consensus is achieved among participants as to their substance and formulation. Seminar reports are brought to the attention of competent United Nations organs, such as the General Assembly, the Commission on Human Rights, or the **Commission on the Status of Women,** in connection with their consideration of corresponding agenda items.

*Training Courses.* Training courses on various aspects of human rights were held in 1976 and 1977, respectively, the first at the Australian Institute of Criminology, Canberra, and the second at the United Nations Institute in Fuchu, Japan. Both were for candidates from countries that were members of the Economic and Social Commission for Asia and the Pacific.

Budgetary and administrative restraints reduced the number of training courses held in the following years. However, a sharp upturn occurred in 1987 after the Commission on Human Rights (resolution 1987/37) cited a course held in 1986 in La Paz, Bolivia, for persons involved in the preparation of reports under international human rights conventions as constituting "a particularly commendable example for future activities under the advisory services program" and requested the Secretary-General to establish and administer a voluntary trust fund to provide additional financial support for practical activities focused on the implementation of international conventions and other international instruments on human rights

promulgated by the United Nations, its specialized agencies, or regional organizations.

A training course on teaching human rights, for participants from the Asian Pacific region, was held at the headquarters of the Economic and Social Commission for Asia and the Pacific, Bangkok, from 12 to 23 October 1987. A course on the preparation of national reports under United Nations human rights conventions, for government officials from English-speaking African countries, was held at Lusaka from 9 to 20 November 1987. And a course on the latter subject, for participants from Spanish-speaking countries in Central America and the Caribbean, was held at San José, Costa Rica, from 23 November to 4 December 1987. The African course was organized jointly by the UN **Center for Human Rights,** the UN **Institute for Training and Research** (described below), and the **Organization of African Unity.** The Latin American course was organized by the UN Center for Human Rights, the **Inter-American Institute of Human Rights,** and the Latin-American Institute for the Prevention of Crime and Treatment of Offenders.

*Fellowships.* Under the advisory services program, the Secretary-General awards each year from 25 to 50 human rights fellowships to candidates nominated by their governments. The fellowships are intended to give persons entrusted with functions important to the promotion and protection of human rights in their respective countries an opportunity to broaden their professional knowledge and experience by acquainting themselves with advanced knowledge and techniques in this field already in use in other countries, so that their ability to understand and solve practical problems of human rights will be increased by the time they return to their own countries.

Most of the candidates nominated by governments are officials of high standing in national administration and have included judges, prosecutors, senior police officials, and officials responsible for drafting of national legislation. The greatest number of requests received has been for the study and observation of existing procedures of various aspects of the administration of justice, such as the use of writs of **habeas corpus,** techniques for ensuring the right of the accused to a speedy trial, and methods of interrogation of suspected or accused persons and their right to communicate with lawyers, family members, and friends. Fellowships have also been granted for the study of human rights questions which affect children and the family and for observation of the working of judicial and other remedies against the abuse of administrative authority.

The Center for Human Rights is responsible for the selection of fellows, for their placement—with the help of the host government concerned—with national institutions capable of providing the observation and training facilities required, and for evaluation of the success of each fellowship.

There is a continuing demand for fellowship awards from States at all stages of development, and the level of candidates proposed for such awards has been consistently high.

*Advisory Services of Experts.* Under the advisory services program, governments may request the services of an expert, or team of experts, to perform a specific task, such as drafting national legislation to promote and protect human rights or setting up national institutions for that purpose. However, only a few governments have so far availed themselves of such services; and, in 1987, the Commission on Human Rights (resolution 1987/38) encouraged them to do so, suggesting that they might use experts to draft basic legal texts in conformity with international human rights conventions.

*Voluntary Trust Fund.* The Commission on Human Rights, in the same resolution, requested the Secretary-General "to establish and administer . . . a voluntary fund for advisory services and technical assistance in the field of human rights." The United Nations Voluntary Fund for Victims of Torture was, accordingly, established on 16 November 1987, and appeals for funds were sent to the governments and the intergovernmental and non-governmental organizations concerned. Resources pledged to the voluntary fund are expected to permit a wider, fuller, and more consistent implementation of United Nations' international human rights instruments through practical assistance.

*Review of the Advisory Services Program.* In 1988, the Secretary-General presented to the Commission on Human Rights a comprehensive report (UN Doc. E/CN.4/1988/40 and Add. 1) on activities carried out within the framework of the advisory services program and on the establishment of the Voluntary Fund for Advisory Services and Technical Assistance in the Field of Human Rights. In the report, he outlined a new plan of activities for the program.

Under the proposed plan, the objectives of the program are (a) furthering knowledge and understanding of international human rights standards and their normative contents, with a view to promoting their widest application; (b) facilitating the implementation of international instruments (application of substantive provisions); and (c) practical assistance in the creation and development of national infrastructures for the promotion and protection of internationally recognized human rights norms and assistance to governments in this respect.

The developed program would include:

(1) regional seminars in those regions which could most benefit from such assistance, i.e., where a large number of States are not parties to human rights instruments;

(2) regional training courses, mainly for States parties to major human rights instruments, for government officials directly involved in the implementation of those instruments—legislators, judges, police and prison officials, and others responsible for the administration of justice;

(3) advisory services of experts and technical assistance in the field of human rights, with the aim of assisting governments in the development of the necessary infrastructures to meet international human rights standards;

(4) fellowships, to be awarded annually to official government nominees directly involved in functions affecting human rights, as well as members of national commissions on human rights and national non-governmental organizations involved;

(5) the establishment of regional arrangements for the promotion and protection of human rights in regions lacking them, including the establishment of regional depository centers for United Nations human rights materials and the establishment of regional institutes for training purposes; and

(6) the holding of regional seminars or training courses with a view to developing effective national institutions, including non-governmental organizations, for the promotion and protection of human rights in accordance with national legislation.

The Commission on Human Rights took note (resolution 1988/54) of the Secretary-General's report, reaffirmed that the program of advisory services in the field of human rights should continue to provide practical assistance in the implementation of international conventions on human rights to those States which indicate a need for such assistance, and requested the Secretary-General to pursue his efforts for an expanded program in which increasing emphasis would be placed on expert assistance and activities to assist governments in the development of the infrastructures necessary to meet international human rights standards.

The Commission further called upon the Secretary-General to ensure that the Center for Human Rights becomes a focal point to coordinate all UN advisory services activities and to ensure close cooperation between the activities of the regular program of advisory services and the activities undertaken by the voluntary fund.

In his 1990 report to the Commission (UN Doc. E/CN.4/1990/43), the Secretary-General summarized the steps taken to expand the program with increased emphasis on expert assistance and other activities to assist governments in developing the infrastructures necessary to meet international human rights standards. Highlights of the 1989 program included activities financed from the regular UN budget—such as an international seminar in Greece; a training course in the Union of Soviet Socialist Republics; advisory missions of experts to Equatorial Guinea, Guatemala, and Haiti; the awarding of fellowships; and activities financed under the Voluntary Fund for Advisory Services and Technical Assistance in the Field of Human Rights, such as assistance to the **AFRICAN COMMISSION ON HUMAN AND PEOPLES' RIGHTS**; country programs in Colombia, Guatemala, and the Gambia (including the provision of 21 fellowships and the advisory services of 17 experts); and the holding of training courses or workshops in Guinea, the Gambia, Ecuador, the Philippines, Italy, Peru, Argentina, and Guatemala.

After examining the report, the Commission noted (resolution 1990/58) the Secretary-General's enhanced efforts to coordinate system-wide advisory services and technical assistance in the field of human rights and to create a flexible interagency mechanism for human rights activities and supported the general thrust of the plan of future activities set out in the report. The operative paragraphs of the resolution were as follows (paras. 1–18):

[The Commission on Human Rights]

1. Welcomes the increasing number of requests from governments for support and technical assistance in the field of human rights;

2. Reaffirms that the programme of advisory services in the field of human rights should continue to provide practical assistance in the implementation of international conventions on human rights to those States which indicate a need for such assistance;

3. Requests the Secretary-General to provide urgently more human and financial resources for the enlargement of advisory services, particularly from section 24 of the regular budget concerning technical co-operation, in order to meet the increased demand on this important instrument intended to invigorate the human rights spirit in the world;

4. Also requests the Secretary-General to pursue his efforts for a medium-term plan for advisory services and technical assistance in the field of human rights, taking into account the comments and views expressed by Governments at the forty-sixth session of the Commission on Human Rights;

5. Recommends to the Secretary-General that the provision of expert assistance and activities to assist Governments in the development of the necessary infrastructures to meet international human rights standards should continue to increase;

6. Welcomes the setting-up of an advisory group in the Centre for Human Rights to assist the Under-Secretary General for Human Rights in the identification and evaluation of projects, and requests the Secretary-General to further restructure the secretariat in this area aiming at even more effective management of these activities;

7. Requests the Secretary-General to enable the Centre for Human Rights to intensify co-ordination within the United Nations system of the activities for the provision of advisory services and technical assistance in the field of human rights in all their aspects;

8. Notes with appreciation the co-operation between the Centre for Human Rights and the United Nations Development Programme and encourages the leadership of both organizations to further enhance co-ordination and co-operation between them;

9. Requests the Secretary-General to explore yet further the possibilities offered by co-operation between the Centre for Human Rights and specialized bodies of the United Nations system, such as the United Nations Development Programme and the Office of the United Nations High Commissioner for Refugees, as well as the International Committee of the Red Cross, in the development of strategies for the setting up or the strengthening of national and regional infrastructures for the promotion and protection of human rights and fundamental freedoms and the planning, execution and evaluation of specific projects;

10. Also requests the Secretary-General to ensure close co-ordination between the activities of the regular programme of advisory services and those of the Voluntary Fund for Advisory Services and Technical Assistance in the Field of Human Rights;

11. Further requests the Secretary-General to bring the need for further technical assistance in the legal field that has been indicated by a number of States to the attention of the United Nations bodies and agencies that are active in providing assistance in the field of development with a view to promoting human rights in the development strategies and policies of the United Nations;

12. Invites competent United Nations bodies, such as the committees set up under the International Covenants on Human Rights, the Committee on the Elimination of Racial Discrimination and the Committee against Torture, to make suggestions and proposals for the implementation of advisory services;

13. Requests its special rapporteurs and representatives, as well as the Working Group on Enforced or Involuntary Disappearances, to inform Governments, whenever appropriate, of the possibility of availing themselves of the services provided for under the programme of advisory services and to include in their recommendations, whenever appropriate, proposals for specific projects to be realized under the programme of advisory services;

14. Also requests the Secretary-General to give special attention to such proposals of special rapporteurs and representatives;

15. Appeals to all Governments to consider making use of the possibility offered by the United Nations of organizing, under the programme of advisory services in the field of human rights, information and/or training courses at the national level for appropriate government personnel on the application of international human rights standards and the experience of relevant international organs;

16. Encourages Governments in need of technical assistance in the field of human rights to avail themselves of the advisory services of experts in the field of human rights, for example, for drafting basic legal texts in conformity with international conventions on human rights;

17. Expresses its appreciation to all Governments and intergovernmental and non-governmental organizations which have responded to the Secretary-General's call to provide assistance to States that indicated their need for technical assistance in the field of human rights, and requests

the Secretary-General to pursue his efforts to co-ordinate and facilitate the flow of bilateral assistance in such cases;

18. Requests the Secretary-General to report to the Commission at its forty-seventh session on the progress made in the implementation of the programme of advisory services in the field of human rights.

**BIBLIOGRAPHY.** Bernard-Maugiron, Nathalie, and Eric Schneider. "38th Session of the Human Rights Committee," *Human Rights Monitor* no. 9 (June 1990): 4–8 (English); 24–28 (French). Report, in English and French.

Brody, Reed, Maureen Convery, and David Weissbrodt. "The 42nd Session of the Sub-Commission on Prevention of Discrimination and Protection of Minorities," *Human Rights Quarterly* 13, no. 2 (May 1991): 260–290. Scholarly report, in English.

Burgess, Jan. "New UNHCR Guidelines for Protection of Women," *Refugees* no. 87 (Oct. 1991): 40–41. Article, in English and French.

Capotorti, Francesco. *Study on the Rights of Persons Belonging to Ethnic, Religious and Linguistic Minorities.* New York: United Nations Centre for Human Rights, 1991. UN document, in English.

Cohen, Roberta. *Human Rights and Humanitarian Emergencies: New Roles for UN Human Rights Bodies.* Washington, D.C.: Center for Policy Analysis and Research on Refugee Issues, Refugee Policy Group, 1992. NGO discussion paper, in English.

Cohn, Cindy A. "The Early Harvest: Domestic Legal Changes Related to the Human Rights Committee and the Covenant on Civil and Political Rights," *Human Rights Quarterly* 13, no. 3 (Aug. 1991): 295–321. Scholarly article, in English.

Dewey, Arthur E. "UNHCR and the New World Order," *Refugees* no. 87 (Oct. 1991): 27–29. Article, in English and French.

———. "New Mandate? What New Mandate?" *Refugees* no. 88 (Jan. 1992): 38–40. Article, in English and French.

Goodwin-Gill, Guy S., ed. "Human Rights and Refugees in Crisis: An Overview and Introduction," *International Journal of Refugee Law* (Sept. 1990). Special issue, in English.

Gowlland, Vera, and Klaus Samson, eds. *Problems and Prospects of Refugee Law: Papers Presented at the Colloquium Organized by the Graduate Institute of International Studies in Collaboration with the Office of the United Nations High Commissioner for Refugees, Geneva, 23 and 24 May, 1991.* Geneva, Switzerland: Graduate Institute of International Studies, 1992. Conference paper, in English.

Human Rights Watch. *The Lost Agenda: Human Rights and the UN Field Operations.* New York: 1993. NGO report, in English.

Kamarotos, Alexander S. *A View into NGO Networks in Human Rights Activities: NGO Action with Special Reference to the UN Commission on Human Rights and its Sub-Commission.* Geneva, Switzerland: Graduate Institute of International Studies, 1990. Scholarly paper, in English.

Lawyers Committee for Human Rights. *The UNHCR at 40: Refugee Protection at the Crossroads.* New York: 1991. NGO report, in English.

Ramcharan, B. G. "The Security Council: Maturing of International Protection of Human Rights," *The Review* no. 48 (June 1992): 24–37. Scholarly article, in English.

———. "The Security Council and Humanitarian Emergencies," *Netherlands Quarterly of Human Rights* 9, no. 1 (1991): 19–35. Scholarly article, in English.

———. "Security Council Patterns for Dealing with Ethnic Conflicts and Minority Problems," in *Broadening the Frontiers of Human Rights: Essays in Honour of Asbjørn Eide,* pp. 27–40. New York: Scandinavian University Press, 1993. Scholarly article, in English.

Ramlogan, Rajendra. "Towards a New Vision of World Security: The United Nations Security Council and the Lessons of Somalia," *Houston Journal of International Law* 16, no. 2 (Winter 1993): 213–260. Scholarly article, in English.

Reierson, Karen, and David Weissbrodt. "The Forty-Third Session of the UN Sub-Commission on Prevention of Discrimination and Protection of Minorities: The Sub-Commission Under Scrutiny," *Human Rights Quarterly* 14, no. 2 (May 1992): 232–277. Scholarly report, in English.

Schmidt, Markus G. "Achieving Much With Little: The Work of the United Nations Centre for Human Rights," *Netherlands Quarterly of Human Rights* 8, no. 4 (1990): 371–380. Scholarly article, in English.

Thornberry, Patrick. *International Law and the Rights of Minorities.* Oxford, UK, and New York: Oxford University Press, 1991. Scholarly monograph, in English; bibliography, pp. 431–443.

Van Baarda, Th. A. "The Involvement of the Security Council in Maintaining International Humanitarian Law," *Netherlands Quarterly of Human Rights* 12, no. 2 (1994): 137–152. Scholarly article, in English.

van Boven, Theo. "Runaway Train or Re-orient Express? An Answer to U.S. Criticism of the UN Sub-Committee on the Prevention of Discrimination and the Protection of Minorities," in *Broadening The Frontiers of Human Rights: Essays in Honour of Asbjørn Eide,* pp. 13–15. New York: Scandinavian University Press, 1993. Scholarly article, in English.

———. "The Security Council: The New Frontier," *The Review* no. 48 (June 1992): 12–23. Scholarly article, in English.

Weiss, T. G., D. P. Forsythe, and R. A. Coate. *The United Nations and Changing World Politics.* Boulder, CO, USA: Westview Press, 1994. Scholarly monograph, in English; bibliography, pp. 268–276.

Zayas, Alfred de. "Les procédures de communications individuelles devant le Comité des Droits de l'Homme des Nations Unies" (Petitioning the United Nations Human Rights Committee), *Revue trimestrielle des droits de l'homme* 1, no. 4 (Oct. 1990): 339–351. Article, in French.

## UNITED NATIONS: CHARTER (1945).

The Charter of the United Nations was signed on 26 June 1945 at the conclusion of the United Nations Conference on International Organization, San Francisco, and entered into force on 24 October 1945. The **INTERNATIONAL COURT OF JUSTICE** is an integral part of the Charter.

The Charter defines the purposes of the United Nations, among them:

*Article 1.* (2) To develop friendly relations among nations based on respect for the principle of equal rights and self-determination of peoples, and to take other appropriate measures to strengthen universal peace;

(3) To achieve international co-operation in solving international problems of an economic, social, cultural, or humanitarian character, and in promoting and encouraging

respect for human rights and for fundamental freedoms for all without distinction as to race, sex, language, or religion.

It establishes the obligation of member States to co-operate for the advancement of these purposes in articles 55 and 56. Other provisions which have a direct bearing upon the promotion and protection of human rights are to be found in articles 8, 13, 24, 55, 56, 62, 73, 76, and 87.

Amendments to articles 23, 27, and 61 of the Charter were adopted by the UN GENERAL ASSEMBLY on 17 December 1963 and entered into force on 31 August 1965. A further amendment to article 61 was adopted on 20 December 1971 and entered into force on 24 September 1973. An amendment to article 109, adopted on 20 December 1965, entered into force on 12 June 1968.

The amendment to article 23 enlarged the membership of the SECURITY COUNCIL from 11 to 15. Article 27, as amended, provides that decisions of the Security Council on procedural matters shall be made by an affirmative vote of nine members (formerly seven) and on all other matters by an affirmative vote of nine members (formerly seven), including the concurring votes of the five permanent members of the Council. The amendment to article 61, which entered into force on 31 August 1965, enlarged the membership of the ECONOMIC AND SOCIAL COUNCIL from 18 to 27. The subsequent amendment to that article, which entered into force on 24 September 1973, further increased the membership of the Council to 54. The amendment to article 109, which relates to the first paragraph of that article, provides that a general conference of member States for the purpose of reviewing the Charter may be held at a date and place to be fixed by a two-thirds' vote of the members of the General Assembly and by a vote of any nine (formerly seven) members of the Security Council.

The text of the United Nations Charter, as amended, is as follows:

We the peoples of the United Nations, determined

to save succeeding generations from the scourge of war, which twice in our lifetime has brought untold sorrow to mankind, and

to reaffirm faith in fundamental human rights, in the dignity and worth of the human person, in the equal rights of men and women and of nations large and small, and

to establish conditions under which justice and respect for the obligations arising from treaties and other sources of international law can be maintained, and

to promote social progress and better standards of life in larger freedom, and for these ends

to practice tolerance and live together in peace with one another as good neighbours, and

to unite our strength to maintain international peace and security, and

to ensure, by the acceptance of principles and the insti-

tution of methods, that armed force shall not be used, save in the common interest, and

to employ international machinery for the promotion of the economic and social advancement of all peoples, have resolved to combine our efforts to accomplish these aims.

Accordingly, our respective Governments, through representatives assembled in the city of San Francisco, who have exhibited their full powers found to be in good and due form, have agreed to the present Charter of the United Nations and do hereby establish an international organization to be known as the United Nations.

### Chapter I: Purposes and Principles

*Article 1.* The Purposes of the United Nations are:

1. To maintain international peace and security, and to that end: to take effective collective measures for the prevention and removal of threats to the peace, and for the suppression of acts of aggression or other breaches of the peace, and to bring about by peaceful means, and in conformity with the principles of justice and international law, adjustment or settlement of international disputes or situations which might lead to a breach of the peace;

2. To develop friendly relations among nations based on respect for the principle of equal rights and self-determination of peoples, and to take other appropriate measures to strengthen universal peace;

3. To achieve international co-operation in solving international problems of an economic, social, cultural, or humanitarian character, and in promoting and encouraging respect for human rights and for fundamental freedoms for all without distinction as to race, sex, language, or religion; and

4. To be a centre for harmonizing the actions of nations in the attainment of these common ends.

*Article 2.* The Organization and its Members, in pursuit of the Purposes stated in Article 1, shall act in accordance with the following Principles.

1. The Organization is based on the principle of the sovereign equality of all its Members.

2. All Members, in order to ensure to all of them the rights and benefits resulting from membership, shall fulfil in good faith the obligations assumed by them in accordance with the present Charter.

3. All Members shall settle their international disputes by peaceful means in such a manner that international peace and security, and justice, are not endangered.

4. All Members shall refrain in their international relations from the threat or use of force against the territorial integrity or political independence of any state, or in any other manner inconsistent with the Purposes of the United Nations.

5. All Members shall give the United Nations every assistance in any action it takes in accordance with the present Charter, and shall refrain from giving assistance to any state against which the United Nations is taking preventive or enforcement action.

6. The Organization shall ensure that states which are not Members of the United Nations act in accordance with these Principles so far as may be necessary for the maintenance of international peace and security.

7. Nothing contained in the present Charter shall authorize the United Nations to intervene in matters which are essentially within the domestic jurisdiction of any state or shall require the Members to submit such matters to settle-

ment under the present Charter; but this principle shall not prejudice the application of enforcement measures under Chapter VII.

## Chapter II: Membership

*Article 3.* The original Members of the United Nations shall be the states which, having participated in the United Nations Conference on International Organization at San Francisco, or having previously signed the Declaration by United Nations of 1 January 1942, sign the present Charter and ratify it in accordance with Article 110.

*Article 4.* 1. Membership in the United Nations is open to all other peace-loving states which accept the obligations contained in the present Charter and, in the judgment of the Organization, are able and willing to carry out these obligations.

2. The admission of any such state to membership in the United Nations will be effected by a decision of the General Assembly upon the recommendation of the Security Council.

*Article 5.* A Member of the United Nations against which preventive or enforcement action has been taken by the Security Council may be suspended from the exercise of the rights and privileges of membership by the General Assembly upon the recommendation of the Security Council. The exercise of these rights and privileges may be restored by the Security Council.

*Article 6.* A Member of the United Nations which has persistently violated the Principles contained in the present Charter may be expelled from the Organization by the General Assembly upon the recommendation of the Security Council.

## Chapter III: Organs

*Article 7.* 1. There are established as the principal organs of the United Nations: a General Assembly, a Security Council, an Economic and Social Council, a Trusteeship Council, an International Court of Justice, and a Secretariat.

2. Such subsidiary organs as may be found necessary may be established in accordance with the present Charter.

*Article 8.* The United Nations shall place no restrictions on the eligibility of men and women to participate in any capacity and under conditions of equality in its principal and subsidiary organs.

## Chapter IV: The General Assembly

### Composition

*Article 9.* 1. The General Assembly shall consist of all the Members of the United Nations.

2. Each Member shall have not more than five representatives in the General Assembly.

### Functions and Powers

*Article 10.* The General Assembly may discuss any questions or any matters within the scope of the present Charter or relating to the powers and functions of any organs provided for in the present Charter, and, except as provided in Article 12, may make recommendations to the Members of the United Nations or to the Security Council or to both on any such questions or matters.

*Article 11.* 1. The General Assembly may consider the general principles of co-operation in the maintenance of international peace and security, including the principles governing disarmament and the regulation of armaments, and may make recommendations with regard to such principles to the Members or to the Security Council or to both.

2. The General Assembly may discuss any questions relating to the maintenance of international peace and security brought before it by any Member of the United Nations, or by the Security Council, or by a state which is not a Member of the United Nations in accordance with Article 35, paragraph 2, and, except as provided in Article 12, may make recommendations with regard to any such questions to the state or states concerned or to the Security Council or to both. Any such question on which action is necessary shall be referred to the Security Council by the General Assembly either before or after discussion.

3. The General Assembly may call the attention of the Security Council to situations which are likely to endanger international peace and security.

4. The powers of the General Assembly set forth in this Article shall not limit the general scope of Article 10.

*Article 12.* 1. While the Security Council is exercising in respect of any dispute or situation the functions assigned to it in the present Charter, the General Assembly shall not make any recommendation with regard to that dispute or situation unless the Security Council so requests.

2. The Security-General, with the consent of the Security Council, shall notify the General Assembly at each session of any matters relative to the maintenance of international peace and security which are being dealt with by the Security Council and shall similarly notify the General Assembly, or the Members of the United Nations if the General Assembly is not in session, immediately the Security Council ceases to deal with such matters.

*Article 13.* 1. The General Assembly shall initiate studies and make recommendations for the purpose of:

(a) promoting international co-operation in the political field and encouraging the progressive development of international law and its codification;

(b) promoting international co-operation in the economic, social, cultural, educational, and health fields, and assisting in the realization of human rights and fundamental freedoms for all without distinction as to race, sex, language, or religion.

2. The further responsibilities, functions and powers of the General Assembly with respect to matters mentioned in paragraph 1(b) above are set forth in Chapters IX and X.

*Article 14.* Subject to the provisions of Article 12, the General Assembly may recommend measures for the peaceful adjustment of any situation, regardless of origin, which it deems likely to impair the general welfare or friendly relations among nations, including situations resulting from a violation of the provisions of the present Charter setting forth the Purposes and Principles of the United Nations.

*Article 15.* 1. The General Assembly shall receive and consider annual and special reports from the Security Council; these reports shall include an account of the measures that the Security Council has decided upon or taken to maintain international peace and security.

2. The General Assembly shall receive and consider reports from the other organs of the United Nations.

*Article 16.* The General Assembly shall perform such functions with respect to the international trusteeship system as are assigned to it under Chapters XII and XIII, including the approval of the trusteeship agreements for areas not designated as strategic.

*Article 17.* 1. The General Assembly shall consider and approve the budget of the Organization.

2. The expenses of the Organization shall be borne by the Members as apportioned by the General Assembly.

3. The General Assembly shall consider and approve any financial and budgetary arrangements with specialized agencies referred to in Article 57 and shall examine the administrative budgets of such specialized agencies with a view to making recommendations to the agencies concerned.

### Voting

*Article 18.* 1. Each member of the General Assembly shall have one vote.

2. Decisions of the General Assembly on important questions shall be made by a two-thirds majority of the members present and voting. These questions shall include: recommendations with respect to the maintenance of international peace and security, the election of the non-permanent members of the Security Council, the election of the members of the Economic and Social Council, the election of members of the Trusteeship Council in accordance with paragraph 1(c) of Article 86, the admission of new Members to the United Nations, the suspension of the rights and privileges of membership, the expulsion of Members, questions relating to the operation of the trusteeship system, and budgetary questions.

3. Decisions on other questions, including the determination of additional categories of questions to be decided by a two-thirds majority, shall be made by a majority of the members present and voting.

*Article 19.* A Member of the United Nations which is in arrears in the payment of its financial contributions to the Organization shall have no vote in the General Assembly if the amount of its arrears equals or exceeds the amount of the contributions due from it for the preceding two full years. The General Assembly may, nevertheless, permit such a Member to vote if it is satisfied that the failure to pay is due to conditions beyond the control of the Member.

### Procedure

*Article 20.* The General Assembly shall meet in regular annual sessions and in such special sessions as occasion may require. Special sessions shall be convoked by the Secretary-General at the request of the Security Council or of a majority of the Members of the United Nations.

*Article 21.* The General Assembly shall adopt its own rules of procedure. It shall elect its President for each session.

*Article 22.* The General Assembly may establish such subsidiary organs as it deems necessary for the performance of its functions.

### Chapter V: The Security Council

### Composition

*Article 23.* 1. The Security Council shall consist of fifteen Members of the United Nations. The Republic of China, France, the Union of Soviet Socialist Republics, the United Kingdom of Great Britain and Northern Ireland, and the United States of America shall be permanent members of the Security Council. The General Assembly shall elect ten

other Members of the United Nations to be non-permanent members of the Security Council, due regard being specially paid, in the first instance to the contribution of Members of the United Nations to the maintenance of international peace and security and to the other purposes of the Organization, and also to equitable geographical distribution.

2. The non-permanent members of the Security Council shall be elected for a term of two years. In the first election of the non-permanent members after the increase of the membership of the Security Council from eleven to fifteen, two of the four additional members shall be chosen for a term of one year. A retiring member shall not be eligible for immediate re-election.

3. Each member of the Security Council shall have one representative.

### Functions and Powers

*Article 24.* 1. In order to ensure prompt and effective action by the United Nations, its Members confer on the Security Council primary responsibility for the maintenance of international peace and security, and agree that in carrying out its duties under this responsibility the Security Council acts on their behalf.

2. In discharging these duties the Security Council shall act in accordance with the Purposes and Principles of the United Nations. The specific powers granted to the Security Council for the discharge of these duties are laid down in Chapters VI, VII, VIII, and XII.

3. The Security Council shall submit annual and, when necessary, special reports to the General Assembly for its consideration.

*Article 25.* The Members of the United Nations agree to accept and carry out the decisions of the Security Council in accordance with the present Charter.

*Article 26.* In order to promote the establishment and maintenance of international peace and security with the least diversion for armaments of the world's human and economic resources, the Security Council shall be responsible for formulating, with the assistance of the Military Staff Committee referred to in Article 47, plans to be submitted to the Members of the United Nations for the establishment of a system for the regulation of armaments.

### Voting

*Article 27.* 1. Each member of the Security Council shall have one vote.

2. Decisions of the Security Council on procedural matters shall be made by an affirmative vote of nine members.

3. Decisions of the Security Council on all other matters shall be made by an affirmative vote of nine members including the concurring votes of the permanent members; provided that, in decisions under Chapter VI, and under paragraph 3 of Article 52, a party to a dispute shall abstain from voting.

### Procedure

*Article 28.* 1. The Security Council shall be so organized as to be able to function continuously. Each member of the Security Council shall for this purpose be represented at all times at the seat of the Organization.

2. The Security Council shall hold periodic meetings at which each of its members may, if it so desires, be repre-

sented by a member of the government or by some other specially designated representative.

3. The Security Council may hold meetings at such places other than the seat of the Organization as in its judgment will best facilitate its work.

*Article 29.* The Security Council may establish such subsidiary organs as it deems necessary for the performance of its functions.

*Article 30.* The Security Council shall adopt its own rules of procedure, including the method of selecting its President.

*Article 31.* Any Member of the United Nations which is not a member of the Security Council may participate, without vote, in the discussion of any question brought before the Security Council whenever the latter considers that the interests of that Member are specially affected.

*Article 32.* Any Member of the United Nations which is not a member of the Security Council or any state which is not a Member of the United Nations, if it is a party to a dispute under consideration by the Security Council, shall be invited to participate, without vote, in the discussion relating to the dispute. The Security Council shall lay down such conditions as it deems just for the participation of a state which is not a Member of the United Nations.

### Chapter VI: Pacific Settlement of Disputes

*Article 33.* 1. The parties to any dispute, the continuance of which is likely to endanger the maintenance of international peace and security, shall, first of all, seek a solution by negotiation, enquiry, mediation, conciliation, arbitration, judicial settlement, resort to regional agencies or arrangements, or other peaceful means of their own choice.

2. The Security Council shall, when it deems necessary, call upon the parties to settle their dispute by such means.

*Article 34.* The Security Council may investigate any dispute, or any situation which might lead to international friction or give rise to a dispute, in order to determine whether the continuance of the dispute or situation is likely to endanger the maintenance of international peace and security.

*Article 35.* 1. Any Member of the United Nations may bring any dispute, or any situation of the nature referred to in Article 34, to the attention of the Security Council or of the General Assembly.

2. A state which is not a Member of the United Nations may bring to the attention of the Security Council or of the General Assembly any dispute to which it is a party if it accepts in advance, for the purposes of the dispute, the obligations of pacific settlement provided in the present Charter.

3. The proceedings of the General Assembly in respect of matters brought to its attention under this Article will be subject to the provisions of Articles 11 and 12.

*Article 36.* 1. The Security Council may, at any stage of a dispute of the nature referred to in Article 33 or of a situation of like nature, recommend appropriate procedures or methods of adjustment.

2. The Security Council should take into consideration any procedures for the settlement of the dispute which have already been adopted by the parties.

3. In making recommendations under this Article the Security Council should also take into consideration that legal disputes should as a general rule be referred by the parties to the International Court of Justice in accordance with the provisions of the Statute of the Court.

*Article 37.* 1. Should the parties to a dispute of the nature

referred to in Article 33 fail to settle it by the means indicated in that Article, they shall refer it to the Security Council.

2. If the Security Council deems that the continuance of the dispute is in fact likely to endanger the maintenance of international peace and security, it shall decide whether to take action under Article 36 or to recommend such terms of settlement as it may consider appropriate.

*Article 38.* Without prejudice to the provisions of Articles 33 to 37, the Security Council may, if all the parties to any dispute so request, make recommendations to the parties with a view to a pacific settlement of the dispute.

### Chapter VII: Action with Respect to Threats to the Peace, Breaches of the Peace, and Acts of Aggression

*Article 39.* The Security Council shall determine the existence of any threat to the peace, breach of the peace, or act of aggression and shall make recommendations, or decide what measures shall be taken in accordance with Articles 41 and 42, to maintain or restore international peace and security.

*Article 40.* In order to prevent an aggravation of the situation, the Security Council may, before making the recommendations or deciding upon the measures provided for in Article 39, call upon the parties concerned to comply with such provisional measures as it deems necessary or desirable. Such provisional measures shall be without prejudice to the rights, claims, or position of the parties concerned. The Security Council shall duly take account of failure to comply with such provisional measures.

*Article 41.* The Security Council may decide what measures not involving the use of armed force are to be employed to give effect to its decisions, and it may call upon the Members of the United Nations to apply such measures. These may include complete or partial interruption of economic relations and of rail, sea, air, postal, telegraphic, radio, and other means of communication, and the severance of diplomatic relations.

*Article 42.* Should the Security Council consider that measures provided for in Article 41 would be inadequate or have proved to be inadequate, it may take such action by air, sea, or land forces as may be necessary to maintain or restore international peace and security. Such action may include demonstrations, blockade, and other operations by air, sea, or land forces of Members of the United Nations.

*Article 43.* 1. All Members of the United Nations, in order to contribute to the maintenance of international peace and security, undertake to make available to the Security Council, on its call and in accordance with a special agreement or agreements, armed forces, assistance, and facilities, including rights of passage, necessary for the purpose of maintaining international peace and security.

2. Such agreement or agreements shall govern the numbers and types of forces, their degree of readiness and general location, and the nature of the facilities and assistance to be provided.

3. The agreement or agreements shall be negotiated as soon as possible on the initiative of the Security Council. They shall be concluded between the Security Council and Members or between the Security Council and groups of Members and shall be subject to ratification by the signatory states in accordance with their respective constitutional processes.

*Article 44.* When the Security Council has decided to use force it shall, before calling upon a Member not represented on it to provide armed forces in fulfilment of the obligations assumed under Article 43, invite that Member, if the Member so desires, to participate in the decisions of the Security Council concerning the employment of contingents of that Member's armed forces.

*Article 45.* In order to enable the United Nations to take urgent military measures, Members shall hold immediately available national air-force contingents for combined international enforcement action. The strength and degree of readiness of these contingents and plans for their combined action shall be determined, within the limits laid down in the special agreement or agreements referred to in Article 43, by the Security Council with the assistance of the Military Staff Committee.

*Article 46.* Plans for the application of armed force shall be made by the Security Council with the assistance of the Military Staff Committee.

*Article 47.* 1. There shall be established a Military Staff Committee to advise and assist the Security Council on all questions relating to the Security Council's military requirements for the maintenance of international peace and security, the employment and command of forces placed at its disposal, the regulation of armaments, and possible disarmament.

2. The Military Staff Committee shall consist of the Chiefs of Staff of the permanent members of the Security Council or their representatives. Any Member of the United Nations not permanently represented on the Committee shall be invited by the Committee to be associated with it when the efficient discharge of the Committee's responsibilities requires the participation of that Member in its work.

3. The Military Staff Committee shall be responsible under the Security Council for the strategic direction of any armed forces placed at the disposal of the Security Council. Questions relating to the command of such forces shall be worked out subsequently.

4. The Military Staff Committee, with the authorization of the Security Council and after consultation with appropriate regional agencies, may establish regional sub-committees.

*Article 48.* 1. The action required to carry out the decisions of the Security Council for the maintenance of international peace and security shall be taken by all the Members of the United Nations or by some of them, as the Security Council may determine.

2. Such decisions shall be carried out by the Members of the United Nations directly and through their action in the appropriate international agencies of which they are members.

*Article 49.* The Members of the United Nations shall join in affording mutual assistance in carrying out the measures decided upon by the Security Council.

*Article 50.* If preventive or enforcement measures against any state are taken by the Security Council, any other state, whether a Member of the United Nations or not, which finds itself confronted with special economic problems arising from the carrying out of those measures shall have the right to consult the Security Council with regard to a solution of those problems.

*Article 51.* Nothing in the present Chapter shall impair the inherent right of individual or collective self-defence if an armed attack occurs against a Member of the United Nations, until the Security Council has taken measures necessary to maintain international peace and security. Measures taken by Members in the exercise of this right to self-defence shall be immediately reported to the Security Council and shall not in any way affect the authority and responsibility of the Security Council under the present Charter to take at any time such action as it deems necessary in order to maintain or restore international peace and security.

## Chapter VIII: Regional Arrangements

*Article 52.* 1. Nothing in the present Charter precludes the existence of regional arrangements or agencies for dealing with such matters relating to the maintenance of international peace and security as are appropriate for regional action, provided that such arrangements or agencies and their activities are consistent with the Purposes and Principles of the United Nations.

2. The Members of the United Nations entering into such arrangements or constituting such agencies shall make every effort to achieve pacific settlement of local disputes through such regional arrangements or by such regional agencies before referring them to the Security Council.

3. The Security Council shall encourage the development of pacific settlement of local disputes through such regional arrangements or by such regional agencies either on the initiative of the states concerned or by reference from the Security Council.

4. This Article in no way impairs the application of Articles 34 and 35.

*Article 53.* 1. The Security Council shall, where appropriate, utilize such regional arrangements or agencies for enforcement action under its authority. But no enforcement action shall be taken under regional arrangements or by regional agencies without the authorization of the Security Council, with the exception of measures against any enemy state, as defined in paragraph 2 of this Article, provided for pursuant to Article 107 or in regional arrangements directed against renewal of aggressive policy on the part of any such state, until such time as the Organization may, on request of the Governments concerned, be charged with the responsibility for preventing further aggression by such a state.

2. The term enemy state as used in paragraph 1 of this Article applies to any state which during the Second World War has been an enemy of any signatory of the present Charter.

*Article 54.* The Security Council shall at all times be kept fully informed of activities undertaken or in contemplation under regional arrangements or by regional agencies for the maintenance of international peace and security.

## Chapter IX: International Economic and Social Co-operation

*Article 55.* With a view to the creation of conditions of stability and well-being which are necessary for peaceful and friendly relations among nations based on respect for the principle of equal rights and self-determination of peoples, the United Nations shall promote:

(a) higher standards of living, full employment, and conditions of economic and social progress and development;

(b) solutions of international economic, social, health, and related problems; and international cultural and educational co-operation; and

(c) universal respect for, and observance of, human rights and fundamental freedoms for all without distinction as to race, sex, language, or religion.

*Article 56.* All Members pledge themselves to take joint and separate action in co-operation with the Organization for the achievement of the purposes set forth in Article 55.

*Article 57.* 1. The various specialized agencies, established by intergovernmental agreement and having wide international responsibilities, as defined in their basic instruments, in economic, social, cultural, educational, health, and related fields, shall be brought into relationship with the United Nations in accordance with the provisions of Article 63.

2. Such agencies thus brought into relationship with the United Nations are hereinafter referred to as specialized agencies.

*Article 58.* The Organization shall make recommendations for the co-ordination of the policies and activities of the specialized agencies.

*Article 59.* The Organization shall, where appropriate, initiate negotiations among the states concerned for the creation of any new specialized agencies required for the accomplishment of the purposes set forth in Article 55.

*Article 60.* Responsibility for the discharge of the functions of the Organization set forth in this Chapter shall be vested in the General Assembly and, under the authority of the General Assembly, in the Economic and Social Council, which shall have for this purpose the powers set forth in Chapter X.

### Chapter X: The Economic and Social Council

#### Composition

*Article 61.* 1. The Economic and Social Council shall consist of fifty-four Members of the United Nations elected by the General Assembly.

2. Subject to the provisions of paragraph 3, eighteen members of the Economic and Social Council shall be elected each year for a term of three years. A retiring member shall be eligible for immediate re-election.

3. At the first election after the increase in the membership of the Economic and Social Council from twenty-seven to fifty-four members, in addition to the members elected in place of the nine members whose term of office expires at the end of that year, twenty-seven additional members shall be elected. Of these twenty-seven additional members, the term of office of nine members so elected shall expire at the end of one year, and of nine other members at the end of two years, in accordance with arrangements made by the General Assembly.

4. Each member of the Economic and Social Council shall have one representative.

#### Functions and Powers

*Article 62.* 1. The Economic and Social Council may make or initiate studies and reports with respect to international economic, social, cultural, educational, health, and related matters and may make recommendations with respect to any such matters to the General Assembly, to the Members of the United Nations, and to the specialized agencies concerned.

2. It may make recommendations for the purpose of promoting respect for, and observance of, human rights and fundamental freedoms for all.

3. It may prepare draft conventions for submission to the General Assembly, with respect to matters falling within its competence.

4. It may call, in accordance with the rules prescribed by the United Nations, international conferences on matters falling within its competence.

*Article 63.* 1. The Economic and Social Council may enter into agreements with any of the agencies referred to in Article 57, defining the terms on which the agency concerned shall be brought into relationship with the United Nations. Such agreements shall be subject to approval by the General Assembly.

2. It may co-ordinate the activities of the specialized agencies through consultation with and recommendations to such agencies and through recommendations to the General Assembly and to the Members of the United Nations.

*Article 64.* 1. The Economic and Social Council may take appropriate steps to obtain regular reports from the specialized agencies. It may make arrangements with the Members of the United Nations and with the specialized agencies to obtain reports on the steps taken to give effect to its own recommendations and to recommendations on matters falling within its competence made by the General Assembly.

2. It may communicate its observations on these reports to the General Assembly.

*Article 65.* The Economic and Social Council may furnish information to the Security Council and shall assist the Security Council upon its request.

*Article 66.* 1. The Economic and Social Council shall perform such functions as fall within its competence in connexion with the carrying out of the recommendations of the General Assembly.

2. It may, with the approval of the General Assembly, perform services at the request of Members of the United Nations and at the request of specialized agencies.

3. It shall perform such other functions as are specified elsewhere in the present Charter or as may be assigned to it by the General Assembly.

#### Voting

*Article 67.* 1. Each member of the Economic and Social Council shall have one vote.

2. Decisions of the Economic and Social Council shall be made by a majority of the members present and voting.

#### Procedure

*Article 68.* The Economic and Social Council shall set up Commissions in economic and social fields and for the promotion of human rights, and such other Commissions as may be required for the performance of its functions.

*Article 69.* The Economic and Social Council shall invite any Member of the United Nations to participate, without vote, in its deliberations on any matter of particular concern to that Member.

*Article 70.* The Economic and Social Council may make arrangements for representatives of the specialized agencies to participate, without vote, in its deliberations and in those of the Commissions established by it, and for its representatives to participate in the deliberations of the specialized agencies.

*Article 71.* The Economic and Social Council may make suitable arrangements for consultation with non-governmental organizations which are concerned with matters within its competence. Such arrangements may be made with international organizations and, where appropriate, with national organizations after consultation with the Member of the United Nations concerned.

*Article 72.* 1. The Economic and Social Council shall adopt its own rules of procedure, including the method of selecting its President.

2. The Economic and Social Council shall meet as re-

quired in accordance with its rules, which shall include provision for the convening of meetings on the request of a majority of its members.

## Chapter XI: Declaration Regarding Non-Self-Governing Territories

*Article 73.* Members of the United Nations which have or assume responsibilities for the administration of territories whose peoples have not yet attained a full measure of self-government recognize the principle that the interests of the inhabitants of these territories are paramount, and accept as a sacred trust the obligation to promote to the utmost, within the system of international peace and security established by the present Charter, the well-being of the inhabitants of these territories, and, to this end:

(a) to ensure, with due respect for the culture of the peoples concerned, their political, economic, social, and educational advancement, their just treatment, and their protection against abuses;

(b) to develop self-government, to take due account of the political aspirations of the peoples, and to assist them in the progressive development of their free political institutions, according to the particular circumstances of each territory and its peoples and their varying stages of advancement;

(c) to further international peace and security;

(d) to promote constructive measures of development, to encourage research, and to co-operate with one another and, when and where appropriate, with specialized international bodies with a view to the practical achievement of the social, economic, and scientific purposes set forth in this Article; and

(e) to transmit regularly to the Secretary-General for information purposes, subject to such limitation as security and constitutional considerations may require, statistical and other information of a technical nature relating to economic, social, and educational conditions in the territories for which they are respectively responsible other than those territories to which Chapters XII and XIII apply.

*Article 74.* Members of the United Nations also agree that their policy in respect of the territories to which this Chapter applies, no less than in respect of their metropolitan areas, must be based on the general principle of good-neighbourliness, due account being taken of the interests and well-being of the rest of the world, in social, economic, and commercial matters.

## Chapter XII: International Trusteeship System

*Article 75.* The United Nations shall establish under its authority an international trusteeship system for the administration and supervision of such territories as may be placed there-under by subsequent individual agreements. These territories are hereinafter referred to as trust territories.

*Article 76.* The basic objectives of the trusteeship system, in accordance with the Purposes of the United Nations laid down in Article 1 of the present Charter, shall be:

(a) to further international peace and security;

(b) to promote the political, economic, social, and educational advancement of the inhabitants of the trust territories, and their progressive development towards self-government or independence as may be appropriate to the particular circumstances of each territory and its peoples and the freely expressed wishes of the peoples concerned,

and as may be provided by the terms of each trusteeship agreement;

(c) to encourage respect for human rights and for fundamental freedoms for all without distinction as to race, sex, language, or religion, and to encourage recognition of the interdependence of the peoples of the world; and

(d) to ensure equal treatment in social, economic, and commercial matters for all Members of the United Nations and their nationals, and also equal treatment for the latter in the administration of justice, without prejudice to the attainment of the foregoing objectives and subject to the provisions of Article 80.

*Article 77.* 1. The trusteeship system shall apply to such territories in the following categories as may be placed thereunder by means of trusteeship agreements:

(a) territories now held under mandate;

(b) territories which may be detached from enemy states as a result of the Second World War; and

(c) territories voluntarily placed under the system by states responsible for their administration.

2. It will be a matter for subsequent agreement as to which territories in the foregoing categories will be brought under the trusteeship system and upon what terms.

*Article 78.* The trusteeship system shall not apply to territories which have become Members of the United Nations, relationship among which shall be based on respect for the principle of sovereign equality.

*Article 79.* The terms of trusteeship for each territory to be placed under the trusteeship system, including any alteration or amendment, shall be agreed upon by the states directly concerned, including the mandatory power in the case of territories held under mandate by a Member of the United Nations, and shall be approved as provided for in Articles 83 and 85.

*Article 80.* 1. Except as may be agreed upon in individual trusteeship agreements, made under Articles 77, 79, and 81, placing each territory under the trusteeship system, and until such agreements have been concluded, nothing in this Chapter shall be construed in or of itself to alter in any manner the rights whatsoever of any states or any peoples or the terms of existing international instruments to which Members of the United Nations may respectively be parties.

2. Paragraph 1 of this Article shall not be interpreted as giving grounds for delay or postponement of the negotiation and conclusion of agreements for placing mandated and other territories under the trusteeship system as provided for in Article 77.

*Article 81.* The trusteeship agreement shall in each case include the terms under which the trust territory will be administered and designate the authority which will exercise the administration of the trust territory. Such authority, hereinafter called the administering authority, may be one or more states or the Organization itself.

*Article 82.* There may be designated, in any trusteeship agreement, a strategic area or areas which may include part or all of the trust territory to which the agreement applies, without prejudice to any special agreement or agreements made under Article 43.

*Article 83.* 1. All functions of the United Nations relating to strategic areas, including the approval of the terms of the trusteeship agreements and of their alteration or amendment, shall be exercised by the Security Council.

2. The basic objectives set forth in Article 76 shall be applicable to the people of each strategic area.

3. The Security Council shall, subject to the provisions of the trusteeship agreements and without prejudice to security

considerations, avail itself of the assistance of the Trusteeship Council to perform those functions of the United Nations under the trusteeship system relating to political, economic, social, and educational matters in the strategic areas.

*Article 84.* It shall be the duty of the administering authority to ensure that the trust territory shall play its part in the maintenance of international peace and security. To this end the administering authority may make use of volunteer forces, facilities, and assistance from the trust territory in carrying out the obligations towards the Security Council undertaken in this regard by the administering authority, as well as for local defence and the maintenance of law and order within the trust territory.

*Article 85.* 1. The functions of the United Nations with regard to trusteeship agreements for all areas not designated as strategic, including the approval of the terms of the trusteeship agreements and of their alteration or amendment, shall be exercised by the General Assembly.

2. The Trusteeship Council, operating under the authority of the General Assembly, shall assist the General Assembly in carrying out these functions.

## Chapter XIII: The Trusteeship Council

### Composition

*Article 86.* 1. The Trusteeship Council shall consist of the following Members of the United Nations:

(a) those Members administering trust territories;

(b) such of those Members mentioned by name in Article 23 as are not administering trust territories; and

(c) as many other Members elected for three-year terms by the General Assembly as may be necessary to ensure that the total number of members of the Trusteeship Council is equally divided between those Members of the United Nations which administer trust territories and those which do not.

2. Each member of the Trusteeship Council shall designate one specially qualified person to represent it therein.

### Functions and Powers

*Article 87.* The General Assembly and, under its authority, the Trusteeship Council, in carrying out their functions, may:

(a) consider reports submitted by the administering authority;

(b) accept petitions and examine them in consultation with the administering authority;

(c) provide for periodic visits to the respective trust territories at times agreed upon with the administering authority; and

(d) take these and other actions in conformity with the terms of the trusteeship agreements.

*Article 88.* The Trusteeship Council shall formulate a questionnaire on the political, economic, social, and educational advancement of the inhabitants of each trust territory, and the administering authority for each trust territory within the competence of the General Assembly shall make an annual report to the General Assembly upon the basis of such questionnaire.

### Voting

*Article 89.* 1. Each member of the Trusteeship Council shall have one vote.

2. Decisions of the Trusteeship Council shall be made by a majority of the members present and voting.

### Procedure

*Article 90.* 1. The Trusteeship Council shall adopt its own rules of procedure, including the method of selecting its President.

2. The Trusteeship Council shall meet as required in accordance with its rules, which shall include provision for the convening of meetings on the request of a majority of its members.

*Article 91.* The Trusteeship Council shall, when appropriate, avail itself of the assistance of the Economic and Social Council and of the specialized agencies in regard to matters with which they are respectively concerned.

## Chapter XIV: The International Court of Justice

*Article 92.* The International Court of Justice shall be the principal judicial organ of the United Nations. It shall function in accordance with the annexed Statute, which is based upon the Statute of the Permanent Court of International Justice and forms an integral part of the present Charter.

*Article 93.* 1. All Members of the United Nations are *ipso facto* parties to the Statute of the International Court of Justice.

2. A state which is not a Member of the United Nations may become a party to the Statute of the International Court of Justice on conditions to be determined in each case by the General Assembly upon the recommendation of the Security Council.

*Article 94.* 1. Each Member of the United Nations undertakes to comply with the decision of the International Court of Justice in any case to which it is a party.

2. If any party to a case fails to perform the obligations incumbent upon it under a judgment rendered by the Court, the other party may have recourse to the Security Council, which may, if it deems necessary, make recommendations or decide upon measures to be taken to give effect to the judgment.

*Article 95.* Nothing in the present Charter shall prevent Members of the United Nations from entrusting the solution of their differences to other tribunals by virtue of agreements already in existence or which may be concluded in the future.

*Article 96.* 1. The General Assembly or the Security Council may request the International Court of Justice to give an advisory opinion on any legal question.

2. Other organs of the United Nations and specialized agencies, which may at any time be so authorized by the General Assembly, may also request advisory opinions of the Court on legal questions arising within the scope of their activities.

## Chapter XV: The Secretariat

*Article 97.* The Secretariat shall comprise a Secretary-General and such staff as the Organization may require. The Secretary-General shall be appointed by the General Assembly upon the recommendation of the Security Council. He shall be the chief administrative officer of the Organization.

*Article 98.* The Secretary-General shall act in that capacity in all meetings of the General Assembly, of the Security Council, of the Economic and Social Council, and of the

Trusteeship Council, and shall perform such other functions as are entrusted to him by these organs. The Secretary-General shall make an annual report to the General Assembly on the work of the Organization.

*Article 99.* The Secretary-General may bring to the attention of the Security Council any matter which in his opinion may threaten the maintenance of international peace and security.

*Article 100.* 1. In the performance of their duties the Secretary-General and the staff shall not seek or receive instructions from any government or from any other authority external to the Organization. They shall refrain from any action which might reflect on their position as international officials responsible only to the Organization.

2. Each Member of the United Nations undertakes to respect the exclusively international character of the responsibilities of the Secretary-General and the staff and not to seek to influence them in the discharge of their responsibilities.

*Article 101.* 1. The staff shall be appointed by the Secretary-General under regulations established by the General Assembly.

2. Appropriate staffs shall be permanently assigned to the Economic and Social Council, the Trusteeship Council, and, as required, to other organs of the United Nations. These staffs shall form a part of the Secretariat.

3. The paramount consideration in the employment of the staff and in the determination of the conditions of service shall be the necessity of securing the highest standards of efficiency, competence, and integrity. Due regard shall be paid to the importance of recruiting the staff on as wide a geographical basis as possible.

### Chapter XVI: Miscellaneous Provisions

*Article 102.* 1. Every treaty and every international agreement entered into by any Member of the United Nations after the present Charter comes into force shall as soon as possible be registered with the Secretariat and published by it.

2. No party to any such treaty or international agreement which has not been registered in accordance with the provisions of paragraph 1 of this Article may invoked that treaty or agreement before any organ of the United Nations.

*Article 103.* In the event of a conflict between the obligations of the Members of the United Nations under the present Charter and their obligations under any other international agreement, their obligations under the present Charter shall prevail.

*Article 104.* The Organization shall enjoy in the territory of each of its Members such legal capacity as may be necessary for the exercise of its functions and the fulfilment of its purposes.

*Article 105.* 1. The Organization shall enjoy in the territory of each of its Members such privileges and immunities as are necessary for the fulfilment of its purposes.

2. Representatives of the Members of the United Nations and officials of the Organization shall similarly enjoy such privileges and immunities as are necessary for the independent exercise of their functions in connexion with the Organization.

3. The General Assembly may make recommendations with a view to determining the details of the application of paragraphs 1 and 2 of this Article or may propose conventions to the Members of the United Nations for this purpose.

### Chapter XVII: Transitional Security Arrangements

*Article 106.* Pending the coming into force of such special agreements referred to in Article 43 as in the opinion of the Security Council enable it to begin the exercise of its responsibilities under Article 42, the parties to the Four-Nation Declaration, signed at Moscow, 30 October 1943, and France, shall, in accordance with the provisions of paragraph 5 of that Declaration, consult with one another and as occasion requires with other Members of the United Nations with a view to such joint action on behalf of the Organization as may be necessary for the purpose of maintaining international peace and security.

*Article 107.* Nothing in the present Charter shall invalidate or preclude action, in relation to any state which during the Second World War has been an enemy of any signatory to the present Charter, taken or authorized as a result of that war by the Governments having responsibility for such action.

### Chapter XVIII: Amendments

*Article 108.* Amendments to the present Charter shall come into force for all Members of the United Nations when they have been adopted by a vote of two thirds of the members of the General Assembly and ratified in accordance with their respective constitutional processes by two thirds of the Members of the United Nations, including all the permanent members of the Security Council.

*Article 109.* 1. A General Conference of the Members of the United Nations for the purpose of reviewing the present Charter may be held at a date and place to be fixed by a two-thirds vote of the members of the General Assembly and by a vote of any nine members of the Security Council. Each Member of the United Nations shall have one vote in the conference.

2. Any alteration of the present Charter recommended by a two-thirds vote of the conference shall take effect when ratified in accordance with their respective constitutional processes by two thirds of the Members of the United Nations including all the permanent members of the Security Council.

3. If such a conference has not been held before the tenth annual session of the General Assembly following the coming into force of the present Charter, the proposal to call such a conference shall be placed on the agenda of that session of the General Assembly, and the conference shall be held if so decided by a majority vote of the members of the General Assembly and by a vote of any seven members of the Security Council.

### Chapter XIX: Ratification and Signature

*Article 110.* 1. The present Charter shall be ratified by the signatory states in accordance with their respective constitutional processes.

2. The ratifications shall be deposited with the Government of the United States of America, which shall notify all the signatory states of each deposit as well as the Secretary-General of the Organization when he has been appointed.

3. The present Charter shall come into force upon the deposit of ratifications by the Republic of China, France, the Union of Soviet Socialist Republics, the United Kingdom of Great Britain and Northern Ireland, and the United States of America, and by a majority of the other signatory states. A protocol of the ratifications deposited shall thereupon be

drawn up by the Government of the United States of America which shall communicate copies thereof to all the signatory states.

4. The states signatory to the present Charter which ratify it after it has come into force will become original Members of the United Nations on the date of the deposit of their respective ratifications.

*Article 111.* The present Charter, of which the Chinese, French, Russian, English, and Spanish texts are equally authentic, shall remain deposited in the archives of the Government of the United States of America. Duly certified copies thereof shall be transmitted by that Government to the Governments of the other signatory states.

In faith whereof the representatives of the Governments of the United Nations have signed the present Charter.

Done at the city of San Francisco the twenty-sixth day of June, one thousand nine hundred and forty-five.

## UNITED NATIONS: FUNDS.

The following are among the special funds set up by the United Nations:

*UN DEVELOPMENT FUND FOR WOMEN.* Originally established by the **GENERAL ASSEMBLY** on 16 December 1976 as the Voluntary Fund for the United Nations Decade for Women (resolution 31/133), the name and mandate of the fund were changed in 1984 when the General Assembly made it "a separate and identifiable entity in autonomous association with the United Nations Development Programme" (UNDP) and re-titled it the United Nations Development Fund for Women. The fund is used primarily to serve as a catalyst with the goal of ensuring the appropriate involvement of women in mainstream development activities, as often as possible at the pre-investment stages, and secondarily to support innovative and experimental activities benefitting women in line with national and regional priorities.

Whereas the UNDP administrator is accountable for all operations of the fund, he is advised by a consultative committee on all matters of policy. The committee is composed of five member States designated by the president of the General Assembly with due regard for equitable geographical distribution. Members are appointed for a term of three years. The board determines the time and place of its meetings. The board reports to the governing body of the UNDP; its report is also provided to the General Assembly and to the **COMMISSION ON THE STATUS OF WOMEN.**

At its 1988 session, the General Assembly took note (decision 43/325) of the appointments, by its president, of the German Democratic Republic, India, Mexico, the Netherlands, and Senegal as members of the consultative committee for a three-year term of office beginning on 1 January 1989.

The General Assembly, on 8 December 1988, took note of the report of the administrator of the United Nations Development Program on the activities of the United Nations Development Fund for Women (UN Doc. A/43/643, annex) and reaffirmed the dual priorities of the fund. It expressed its appreciation to governments, non-governmental organizations, and individuals contributing to the fund but noted that the fund's resources had been insufficient to enable it to respond adequately to the increasing requests received.

*UN VOLUNTARY FUND FOR ADVISORY SERVICES AND TECHNICAL ASSISTANCE IN THE FIELD OF HUMAN RIGHTS.* The fund was established by the Secretary-General of the United Nations in 1987 in accordance with a request by the UN **COMMISSION ON HUMAN RIGHTS** (resolution 1987/38), in which the Commission authorized the Secretary-General to receive voluntary contributions to the fund from governments, intergovernmental and non-governmental organizations, and individuals in a position to make such contributions and to solicit contributions or to make such representations or appeals for contributions as he deems appropriate. The objective of the trust fund is to provide additional financial support for practical activities focused on the implementation of international conventions and other international instruments on human rights promulgated by the United Nations, its specialized agencies, and regional organizations.

The Commission, in its resolution, requested the Secretary-General to bring regularly to the attention of all governments and of the competent human rights organs possibilities that exist under the trust fund to provide advisory services and technical assistance to governments at their request and encouraged governments in need of technical assistance in the field of human rights to avail themselves of the advisory services of experts.

In his report on the fund, presented to the 1990 session of the Commission on Human Rights (UN Doc. E/CN.4/1990/43, annex I), the Secretary-General indicated that contributions amounting to $US 1,035,404 had been received as of 31 December 1989, and that an additional $US 361,730 had been pledged. Expenditures and commitments entered into in 1988–1989 totaled $US 883,700, leaving an estimated balance of $US 135,000. The balance had been earmarked for previously approved and ongoing projects scheduled for 1990. Actual expenditures included: advisory services of experts, $164,500; provision of reference libraries, $16,500; fellowships, $126,800; training courses and workshops, $568,000; and publications, $7,900.

*UN VOLUNTARY FUND FOR INDIGENOUS POPULA-TIONS.* The fund was established by the UN General Assembly on 13 December 1985 (resolution 40/130). Its sole purpose is to assist representatives of indigenous communities and organizations to participate in the deliberations of the Educational and Training Program for Southern Africa. The fund, made up of voluntary contributions, was established by the UN General Assembly in 1967, when earlier special programs to assist persons from Namibia, South Africa, Southern Rhodesia (now Zimbabwe), and territories formerly under Portuguese administration in Africa were combined in a single operation by Assembly resolution 2349 (XXII). The program is administered by the Secretary-General in consultation with an advisory committee established in 1968, and is financed from a trust fund to which States, organizations, and individuals may contribute.

Students from South Africa are now the main recipients of the program; before 1991 they were obliged to study outside their country, but since that year they may attend educational or training programs within that country as well.

*UN VOLUNTARY FUND FOR VICTIMS OF TORTURE.* The fund was established in accordance with a decision taken by the UN General Assembly in 1981 (resolution 36/151) by which what was formerly known as the United Nations Trust Fund for Chile was given a broader mandate under a new name and charged with "receiving voluntary contributions for distribution, through established channels of assistance, as humanitarian, legal and financial aid to individuals whose human rights have been severely violated as a result of torture and to relatives of such victims, priority being given to aid to victims of violations by States in which the human rights situation has been the subject of resolutions or decisions adopted either by the Assembly, the Economic and Social Council or the Commission on Human Rights."

The voluntary fund is administered by the Secretary-General, with the advice of a board of trustees composed of a chairman and four members with wide experience in the field of human rights who act in their personal capacity. They are appointed by the Secretary-General with due regard for equitable geographical distribution and in consultation with their governments. The term of office is indeterminate. Members of the board are Mr. Jaap Walkate (Chairman) (Netherlands); Mrs. Elizabeth Odio Benito (Costa Rica); Mr. Waleed Sadi (Jordan); Mr. Ivan Tosevski (Yugoslavia); and Mr. S. Amos Wako (Kenya).

Between 1983 and 1988, the voluntary fund made 131 grants, totaling $3,688,894. The grants went to 67 projects in 32 countries in Africa, America, Asia, and Europe. Many of the projects were implemented in countries such as Argentina, the Philippines, Uganda, and Uruguay, where there have been important political changes in recent years and where persons tortured in the past, under different political conditions, are still urgently in need of help. The focus of the grants is on therapy and rehabilitation projects.

On 15 December 1989, the UN General Assembly took note of the report of the Secretary-General on the work of the board (UN Doc. A/44/708) and expressed (resolution 44/145) its gratitude and appreciation to all who had contributed to the fund, to the board of trustees for their work, and to the Secretary-General for the support given to the board.

*BIBLIOGRAPHY.* Danelius, Hans. "United Nations Voluntary Funds," *Nordic Journal of International Law* (1989): 185–187. Scholarly article, in English.

**UNITED NATIONS: SECRETARIAT.** Established in accordance with the **UNITED NATIONS CHARTER** (article 7) as a principal organ of the United Nations, the UN Secretariat consists of the Secretary-General and his staff. As chief administrative officer, the Secretary-General performs the functions entrusted to him by the Charter and by UN organs and reports annually to the **GENERAL ASSEMBLY** on the work of the organization as a whole. In addition, he may, on his own initiative, bring to the attention of the **SECURITY COUNCIL** any matter which, in his opinion, threatens the maintenance of international peace and security.

The Secretary-General appoints all other members of the UN Secretariat under regulations established by the General Assembly. The Charter forbids him (article 100) from seeking or receiving instructions from any government or from any other authority external to the organization; and each member State undertakes to respect the exclusively international character of the Secretariat's responsibilities and not to seek to influence its members in the discharge of their duties. The Charter stipulates (article 101) that the paramount consideration in the employment of the staff and in the determination of conditions of service is the necessity of securing the highest standards of efficiency, competence, and integrity. The staff is recruited on as wide a geographical basis as possible.

The main Secretariat units having responsibilities in the field of human rights are the **CENTER FOR HUMAN RIGHTS** and the **ADVANCEMENT OF WOMEN DIVISION** of the **CENTER FOR SOCIAL DEVELOPMENT AND HUMANITARIAN AFFAIRS.** Other units dealing with particular human rights questions when they arise include the Department of Political and Security Council Affairs; the Department of Political Affairs, Trusteeship and Decolonization; the Department of International Economic and Social Affairs; the Department of Public Information; the Office of Legal Affairs; the Office of the United Nations Children's Fund; the Office of the Special Representative of the Secretary-General for Namibia; and the Secretariat of the UN Committee and Congresses on Crime Prevention and Control, all located in New York; as well as the Office of the United Nations HIGH COMMISSIONER FOR REFUGEES, located in Geneva; the Office of the UNITED NATIONS ENVIRONMENT PROGRAM and the Center for Human Settlements, located in Nairobi; and the Office of the World Food Program, located in Rome.

In accordance with the United Nations Charter (article 97), the Secretary-General is appointed by the General Assembly upon the recommendation of the Security Council. The rules of procedure of the General Assembly provide (rule 141) that, when the Council has submitted its recommendation on the appointment of the Secretary-General, the Assembly shall consider the recommendation and vote upon it by secret ballot in private meeting. In practice, however, the Assembly has never held a private meeting; and, on four occasions, it did not take a vote by secret ballot.

The following persons served as Secretary-General in the past: Mr. Trygve Lie (Norway), 1 February 1946 to 10 April 1953; Mr. Dag Hammarskjold (Sweden), 11 April 1953 to 17 September 1962; Mr. U Thant (Burma), 3 November 1961 to 31 December 1971; Mr. Kurt Waldheim (Austria), 1 January 1972 to 31 December 1981; Mr. Javier Pérez de Cuéllar (Peru), 1 January 1982 to 31 December 1991. From 1 January 1992 to the present, Mr. Boutros Boutros-Ghali (Egypt) has served as Secretary-General.

The General Assembly has established two subsidiary bodies to deal with matters relating to the employment of UN staff:

(1) The United Nations Administrative Tribunal, established on 9 December 1949 (resolution 351 [IV]) is competent to hear and pass judgment upon applications alleging non-observance of employment contracts of Secretariat staff members or of the terms of appointment of such staff members. The Tribunal is composed of seven members, no two of whom may be nationals of the same country. Only three sit in a particular case. The Tribunal establishes its own rules and its schedule of meetings. Its decisions are taken by majority vote, and its judgments are final and without appeal. Its competence has been extended to a number of specialized agencies, which have agreed to be bound by its judgments and to pay any compensation awarded by the Tribunal in respect of a staff member of the agency.

(2) The International Civil Service Commission, es-

tablished on 18 December 1974 (resolution 3357 [XXIX]), deals with matters affecting the salary and personnel system of the UN and its related agencies. It is composed of 15 members appointed by the General Assembly "in their personal capacity as individuals of recognized competence who have had substantial experience of executive responsibility in public administration or related fields, particularly in personnel management." The term of office is four years. Recommendations of the Commission are communicated to the UN Secretary-General and, through him, to the executive heads of other organizations. Decisions taken thereon by the General Assembly are communicated by the Secretary-General to the executive heads of the other organizations for action under their constitutional procedures.

*WOMEN IN THE UN SECRETARIAT.* At a time when the United Nations faces an expanding role in world affairs, it becomes increasingly important that both men and women participate actively and visibly at all levels in the work of the organization, under conditions of full equality, in accordance with article 8 of the Charter of the United Nations.

In 1985, the General Assembly approved (resolution 40/258 B) a detailed action program (UN Doc. A/C.5/40/30) designed to address the obstacles to the improvement of the status of women in the United Nations Secretariat. In a progress report to the Assembly, dated 12 October 1988 (UN Doc. A/C.5/43/14), the Secretary-General indicated that, within the Secretariat, the Office of Human Resources Management is responsible for implementing the action program, while the Steering Committee for the Improvement of the Status of Women in the Secretariat—a high-level advisory group of senior women and men appointed by the Secretary-General, monitors the progress made and provides guidance through regular reports to the Secretary-General.

During the first months of 1988, according to the progress report, the steering committee identified a number of major achievements of the action program, including the following:

(a) The percentage of women in posts subject to geographical distribution had risen from 22.9 per cent in March 1985 to 26.2 per cent at 31 March 1988;

(b) Since March 1985, several women had been appointed to high-level posts, including three to the post of Under-Secretary-General;

(c) Nine women who had served on a succession of short-term contracts had been subsequently recruited, after a special review;

(d) The guidelines on cumulative seniority had contributed to the women's rate of advancement in the Professional category;

(e) In recruiting at entry levels for Professional staff, the percentage of women had risen, particularly through increased publicity on the principle of equality in Member States participating in national examinations;

(f) An effort was being made to redress inconsistencies in the classification standards for the secretarial occupation;

(g) Supervisory training had been strengthened and inter-agency co-operation in that area had been initiated;

(h) Inequities adversely affecting former General Service staff from other duty stations had been removed from the recruitment standards for that category for New York;

(i) Conditions for maternity leave had been improved;

(j) Inter-agency consultations had started on improved arrangements for child-care and adoption leave;

(k) The structure of the appeals process had been strengthened;

(l) Training modules had been prepared that addressed sexual harassment and gender discrimination.

The steering committee identified a number of priorities for the improvement of the status of women in the Secretariat, including further recruitment, assignment, and promotion of women at senior levels; the establishment of a career development system for the general service and related categories; and the strengthening of training programs and human resources planning systems within the organization. The Secretary-General accepted these recommendations and indicated that implementation of the action program will be pursued to the extent possible, taking into account the prevailing restraints on recruitment.

In October 1989, the Secretary-General submitted a report on the subject to the General Assembly (UN Doc. A/44/604), in which he stated that, of the 24 undersecretary-general positions, 22 were held by men and only 2 were held by women (8.3%); that 17 assistant-secretary-general positions were held by men and none by women; that, of the 85 D-2 positions, 78 were held by men and 7 by women (8.2%); and that, of the 235 D-1 positions, 220 were held by men and 15 by women (6.4%).

Noting the report, and noting also that a senior-level officer had been deployed as the focal point for women, in the Office of the Assistant Secretary-General for Human Resources Management of the Secretariat responsible for all aspects of the action program for the improvement of the status of women in the Secretariat, the Assembly requested the Secretary-General (resolution 44/75) to intensify his efforts to increase the number of women employed throughout the United Nations system, particularly in senior policy-level and decision-making posts, in order to achieve an overall participation rate by women of 30% by 1990. It also requested him to make renewed efforts to ensure more equitable representation of women from developing countries in posts subject to geographical distribution, subject to article 101 of the United Nations Charter.

In 1994 the General Assembly (resolution 49/167)

recalled the goal set in its resolutions 45/125, 45/239 C, 46/100, 47/93, and 48/106 of a 35% overall participation rate of women in posts subject to geographical distribution by 1995, and reaffirmed those resolutions as follows:

The General Assembly . . .

1. Welcomes the report of the Secretary-General on the improvement of the status of women in the Secretariat;

2. Takes note of the strategic plan of action for the improvement of the status of women in the Secretariat (1995–2000) contained in the report, and the goals and objectives of the strategic plan as proposed by the Secretary-General;

3. Urges the Secretary-General to implement fully the strategic plan of action for the improvement of the status of women in the Secretariat (1995–2000), noting that his visible commitment is essential to the achievement of the targets set by the General Assembly and the goals and objectives contained in the strategic plan;

4. Welcomes the Secretary-General's intention to ensure implementation of the strategic plan through, *inter alia*, the issuance of clear and specific instructions as to the authority and responsibility of all managers to implement the plan and the criteria by which performance will be appraised;

5. Urges the Secretary-General, in accordance with the Charter of the United Nations and consistent with the strategic plan, to accord greater priority to the recruitment and promotion of women in posts subject to geographical distribution, particularly in senior policy-level and decision-making posts and within those parts of the United Nations system and its specialized agencies where representation of women is considerably below the average, in order to achieve the goals set in its resolutions 45/125 and 45/239 C of an overall participation rate of 35 per cent by 1995 and 25 per cent in posts at the D-1 level and above by 1995;

6. Also urges the Secretary-General to examine further existing work practices within the United Nations system with a view to increasing flexibility so as to remove direct or indirect discrimination against staff members with family responsibilities, including consideration of such issues as spouse employment, job-sharing, flexible working hours, child-care arrangements, career-break schemes and access to training;

7. Further urges the Secretary-General to increase the number of women employed in the Secretariat from developing countries, particularly those which are unrepresented or under-represented, and from other countries that have a low representation of women, including countries in transition;

8. Requests the Secretary-General to ensure that equal employment opportunities exist for all staff;

9. Also requests the Secretary-General to enable, from within existing resources, the Focal Point for Women within the Secretariat effectively to monitor and facilitate progress in the implementation of the strategic plan;

10. Strongly encourages Member States to support the strategic plan and the efforts of the United Nations and the specialized agencies to increase the percentage of women in Professional posts, especially at the D-1 level and above, by identifying and submitting more women candidates, encouraging women to apply for vacant posts and creating national rosters of women candidates to be shared with the Secretariat, specialized agencies and regional commissions;

11. Requests the Secretary-General further to develop

comprehensive policy measures aimed at the prevention of sexual harassment in the Secretariat;

12. Also requests the Secretary-General to ensure that a progress report on the status of women in the Secretariat containing, *inter alia,* information on activities undertaken towards the achievement of the goals and objectives contained in the strategic plan and policy measures aimed at the prevention of sexual harassment in the Secretariat, is presented to the Commission on the Status of Women at its thirty-ninth session, in accordance with the relevant rules on the delivery timetable for documentation, and to the General Assembly at its fiftieth session.

## UNITED NATIONS: TREATY-MONITORING BOD-IES.

The supervision, investigation, and monitoring of the implementation of the treaty obligations entered into by States in regard to human rights and of the existing international standards in this regard are complicated, involving a large number of United Nations bodies dealing on a day-to-day basis with an ever-increasing body of international human rights standards. The functioning of these mechanisms is clarified in a report prepared by the UN Secretary-General and made available to the **COMMISSION ON HUMAN RIGHTS** at its 1994 session (UN Doc. E/CN.4/1994/42):

### Introduction

1. By its resolution 1993/58, adopted on 9 March 1993, the Commission on Human Rights requested the Secretary-General to submit to its fiftieth session a report on the various treaty based and non-treaty based mechanisms which have been established "for the supervision, investigation and monitoring of the implementation of the provisions of international legal instruments and standards" in the field of human rights. In particular, the Commission wished to be informed of the following:

(a) Original mandates assigned to the various treaty and non-treaty mechanisms;

(b) International legal norms and standards on which existing non-treaty mechanisms now base their activities;

(c) Conceptual framework, methods of work and procedural rules applied by each non-treaty mechanism in the discharge of its mandate;

(d) Various norms, criteria and practices established by each existing mechanism in regard to the admissibility of communications;

(e) Preliminary consideration and evaluation of communications, their referral to the interested parties and subsequent course of action;

(f) Criteria used in practice by the Centre for Human Rights for channelling communications either to an existing public machinery or into the confidential procedure governed by Economic and Social Council resolution 1503 (XLVIII), together with the legal foundation for such criteria.

2. The above issues will be briefly dealt with in the following paragraphs, with appropriate references to the primary source. Part A refers to treaty mechanisms, part B to non-treaty mechanisms.

### I. Treaty Mechanisms

### A. Reporting Procedures Under the Various Human Rights Instruments

3. At the present time, there are seven treaty bodies which have a mandate under the respective international instruments to consider reports submitted by States parties, as follows: (i) the Committee on Economic, Social and Cultural Rights, (ii) the Human Rights Committee, (iii) the Committee on the Elimination of Racial Discrimination, (iv) the Committee on the Elimination of Discrimination against Women, (v) the Committee against Torture, (vi) the Committee on the Rights of the Child and (vii) the Group of Three established under the International Convention on the Suppression and Punishment of the Crime of Apartheid.

*1. Committee on Economic, Social and Cultural Rights.* 4. In accordance with article 16 of the International Covenant on Economic, Social and Cultural Rights, the States parties to the Covenant undertake to submit reports on the measures which they have adopted and the progress made in achieving the observance of the rights recognized in the Covenant. All reports are submitted to the Secretary-General of the United Nations who transmits copies to the Economic and Social Council for its consideration.

5. In accordance with article 17 of the Covenant, the Council, in 1976, shortly after the Covenant entered into force, instituted, by its resolution 1988 (LX) a three phase reporting cycle according to which States parties were required to report, initially at two-yearly intervals, on different clusters of rights (arts. 6-9, 10-12 and 13-15). Subsequently, States parties were required to report on different clusters of rights every three years.

6. In accordance with article 18 of the Covenant, the Council also made arrangements with the specialized agencies in respect of their reporting on progress made in achieving the observance of the provisions of the Covenant falling within the scope of their activities.

7. By its resolution 1978/10, the Economic and Social Council established a 15-member sessional working group to assist it in considering the reports submitted by States parties. The working group was composed of representatives of States members of the Council which were also States parties to the Covenant.

8. By its resolution 1985/17, the working group was transformed by the Economic and Social Council into the Committee on Economic, Social and Cultural Rights, consisting of 18 experts who serve in their personal capacity.

9. The reporting system currently in force—proposed by the Committee on Economic, Social and Cultural Rights and endorsed by the Economic and Social Council in its resolution 1988/4—provides for the submission of initial reports on the implementation of articles 1 to 15 of the Covenant within two years of ratification or accession to the Covenant, and thereafter for report at five-year intervals.

10. The committee makes general recommendations to the Economic and Social Council based on its study of State reports and reports received from United Nations specialized agencies, in accordance with Economic and Social Council resolution 1987/5 and General Assembly resolution 42/102.

*2. Human Rights Committee.* 11. In accordance with article 40, paragraph 1, of the International Covenant on Civil and Political Rights, States parties undertake to submit reports to the Committee on the measures they have adopted to give effect to the rights recognized in the Covenant and on the progress made in the enjoyment of those rights. The first report is due within one year of the entry into force of the Covenant for the State party concerned; thereafter, whenever the Committee so requests. In accordance with the decision on periodicity adopted by the Committee on 22 July 1981, subsequent reports of States parties are due every five years.

12. In accordance with article 40, paragraph 4, of the Covenant, the committee began, in 1981, the practice of preparing general comments on substantive articles of the Covenant and, since 1992, concluding observations on State party reports.

13. In light of events indicating that human rights protected under the International Covenant on Civil and Political Rights had been seriously affected in certain States parties, the Human Rights Committee in 1991 adopted the practice of requesting States parties concerned urgently to submit reports on the human rights situation, generally within three months.

*3. Committee on the Elimination of Racial Discrimination.* 14. Under article 9, paragraph 1, of the International Convention on the Elimination of All Forms of Racial Discrimination, States parties undertake to submit to the Committee a report on the legislative, judicial, administrative or other measures which they have adopted and which give effect to the provisions of this Convention: (a) within one year after the entry into force of the Convention for the State concerned; and (b) thereafter every two years and whenever the Committee so requests.

15. In 1988, the Committee endorsed a proposal made at the eleventh meeting of the States parties providing for submission by States parties of comprehensive reports to the Committee every four years, with brief updating reports at intervening two-year periods.

16. In accordance with article 9, paragraph 2, of the Convention, the Committee makes suggestions and general recommendations based on the examination of the reports and information received from the States parties.

17. Under article 15 of the Convention, the Committee is entrusted with the task of giving opinions and making recommendations on petitions to United Nations bodies from individuals and groups in United Nations Trust Territories and Non-Self-Governing Territories who allege racial discrimination. The Committee also gives its views and recommendations on reports provided by other United Nations bodies of legislative, judicial, administrative and other measures to combat racial discrimination in these Territories.

*4. Committee on the Elimination of Discrimination against Women.* 18. Under article 18, paragraph 1, of the Convention on the Elimination of All Forms of Discrimination against Women, States parties undertake to submit for consideration by the Committee a report on the legislative, judicial, administrative or other measures which they have adopted to give effect to the provisions of the Convention and on the progress made in this respect: (a) within one year after the entry into force for the State concerned; (b) thereafter, at least every four years and further whenever the Committee so requests.

19. In accordance with article 21, paragraph 1, of the Convention, the Committee makes suggestions and general recommendations based on the examination of reports and information received from States parties.

*5. Committee against Torture.* 20. In accordance with article 19, paragraph 1, of the Convention against Torture and Other Cruel, Inhuman or Degrading Treatment or Punishment, the States parties submit for consideration by the Committee against Torture reports on the measures they have taken to give effect to their undertakings under the Convention, within one year after the entry into force of the Convention for the State party concerned. Thereafter, the States parties submit supplementary reports every four years on any new measures taken and such other reports as the Committee may request.

21. In accordance with paragraph 3 of the same article, the Committee may make such general comments on the report of a State party as it may consider appropriate and shall forward these to the State party concerned which, on its part, may respond to the Committee with any observations it chooses to make.

*6. Committee on the Rights of the Child.* 22. Under article 44, paragraph 1, of the Convention on the Rights of the Child, States parties undertake to submit for consideration by the Committee reports on the measures they have adopted which give effect to the rights recognized in the Convention and on the progress made on the enjoyment of those rights: (a) within two years of the entry into force of the Convention for the State party concerned; (b) thereafter, every five years. Under paragraph 3 of the same article, a State party which has submitted a comprehensive initial report to the Committee need not repeat basic information previously provided. Under paragraph 4 of the same article, the Committee may request from States parties further information relevant to the implementation of the Convention.

23. In accordance with article 45 of the Convention, the Committee may invite the specialized agencies, the United Nations Children's Fund and other competent bodies as it may consider appropriate to provide expert advice on the implementation of the Convention in areas falling within the scope of their respective mandates. The Committee may also invite the specialized agencies, the United Nations Children's Fund, and other United Nations organs to submit reports on the implementation of the Convention in areas falling within the scope of their activities.

24. According to the same article, the committee is empowered to transmit, as it may consider appropriate, to the specialized agencies, the United Nations Children's Fund and other competent bodies, any reports from States parties that contain a request, or indicate a need, for technical advice or assistance, along with the Committee's observations and suggestions, if any, on these requests or indications. In addition, the Committee may recommend to the General Assembly to request the Secretary-General to undertake on its behalf studies on specific issues relating to the rights of the child, and may make suggestions and general recommendations based on information received pursuant to articles 44 and 45 of the Convention.

*7. Group of Three under the Apartheid Convention.* 25. Under article VII of the International Convention on the Suppression and Punishment of the Crime of Apartheid, the States parties undertake to submit periodic reports to a group of three members of the Commission on Human Rights, established in accordance with article IX of the Convention, on the legislative, judicial, administrative or other measures that they have adopted to give effect to the provisions of the Convention.

26. The Commission on Human Rights, in its resolution 7 (XXXIV) of 1978, called upon States parties to submit their first report not later than two years after the entry into force of the Convention. The Commission established that subsequent reports should be submitted at two-year intervals.

27. In 1989, the Commission on Human Rights adopted resolution 1989/8 in which, upon recommendation by the

Group of Three, the Commission requested States parties to the Convention to continue to submit initial reports not later than two years after the entry into force of the Convention, and to submit their periodic reports at four-year intervals, on the understanding that States parties may submit additional information to the Group at any time in the intervening period. Periodic reports need not repeat information already included in previous reports.

## B. Inquiry Procedures

28. One of the human rights instruments, namely, the Convention against Torture and Other Cruel, Inhuman or Degrading Treatment or Punishment, also provides for an inquiry procedure under its article 20. Such a procedure is established by article 20 of the Convention. At the time of signature and ratification of, or accession to, the Convention, a State may declare that it does not recognize the competence of the Committee provided for in article 20. This reservation is permitted by the provisions of article 28, paragraph 1, of the Convention.

29. In respect of all the States which have accepted the procedure set out in article 20, the Committee is empowered to receive information concerning allegations of torture. If it appears to the Committee that the information received is reliable and contains well-founded indications that torture is being systematically practised in the territory of a State party to the Convention, the Committee invites that State to cooperate in its examination of the information and, to this end, to submit observations with regard to that information. It may also decide to request additional information either from the representatives of the State concerned or from governmental and non-governmental organizations as well as individuals, for the purpose of obtaining further elements on which to form an opinion.

30. If it considers that the information gathered warrants it, the Committee may designate one or more of its members to make a confidential inquiry. In that case, it invites the State party concerned to cooperate with it in the conduct of the inquiry. The inquiry may include, with the agreement of the State party, a visit to its territory by the designated members, who may then conduct hearings of witnesses.

31. The designated members submit their findings to the Committee, which transmits them, together with its own comments or suggestions, to the State party. It invites that State to inform the Committee of the action it has taken with regard to the Committee's findings.

32. After all the proceedings regarding an inquiry have been completed, the committee may decide to include a summary account of the results of the proceedings in its annual report. Only at that stage is the work of the Committee made public.

## C. Inter-State Complaints

33. Three of the international human rights instruments provide for a procedure according to which States parties to the instruments recognize the competence of the monitoring bodies established thereunder to receive and consider communications from a State party claiming that another State party is not fulfilling its obligations under the instrument concerned:

(a) The International Covenant on Civil and Political Rights, article 41 (optional); competent organ: Human Rights Committee;

(b) The International Convention on the Elimination of All Forms of Racial Discrimination, articles 11, 12 and 13 (obligatory); competent organ: Committee on the Elimination of Racial Discrimination;

(c) The Convention against Torture and Other Cruel, Inhuman or Degrading Treatment or Punishment, article 21 (optional); competent organ: Committee against Torture.

34. To date, this procedure has not yet been resorted to.

## D. Communications Procedures Under Treaty Mechanisms

35. At present, three treaty mechanisms provide for a procedure for dealing with communications (complaints about alleged violations of the provisions of the respective international human rights treaties). These are (i) the procedure governed by the first Optional Protocol to the International Covenant on Civil and Political Rights (hereinafter referred to as the Optional Protocol procedure); (ii) the procedure governed by article 22 of the Convention against Torture and other Cruel, Inhuman or Degrading Treatment or Punishment (hereinafter referred to as the CAT article 22 procedure); and (iii) the procedure governed by article 14 of the International Convention on the Elimination of All Forms of Racial Discrimination (hereinafter referred to as the CERD article 14 procedure). A fourth procedure for dealing with communications is envisaged under article 77 of the International Convention on the Protection of the Rights of All Migrant Workers and Members of Their Families (MWC). That convention is not yet in force and will not be dealt with in the present report.

1. *Original mandate.*

(a) *The Optional Protocol procedure.* 36. The Optional Protocol to the International Covenant on Civil and Political Rights was adopted and opened for signature, ratification and accession by General Assembly resolution 2200 A (XXI) of 16 December 1966. The Optional Protocol, which entered into force on 23 March 1976, lays down a procedure for the examination of individual complaints about alleged violations of the Covenant. Sventy-four of the 125 States parties to the Covenant have become parties to the Optional Protocol.

(b) *The CAT article 22 procedure.* 37. Article 22 of the Convention against Torture and Other Cruel, Inhuman or Degrading Treatment or Punishment (General Assembly resolution 39/46 of 10 December 1984), which entered into force on 26 June 1987, lays down a procedure for dealing with individual complaints about alleged violations of the Convention. Thirty-four out of the 80 States parties to the Convention have recognized the competence of the Committee against Torture to deal with individual complaints under the article 22 procedure.

(c) *The CERD article 14 procedure.* 38. Article 14 of the International Convention on the Elimination of All Forms of Racial Discrimination (General Assembly resolution 2106 A (XX) of 21 December 1965), which Convention entered into force on 4 January 1969, lays down a procedure for the handling of complaints from individuals or groups of individuals claiming to be victims of a violation by a State party of any of the rights set forth in the Convention. The competence of the Committee on the Elimination of Racial Discrimination (CERD) became effective on 3 December 1982, pursuant to article 14, paragraph 9, of the Convention. So far, only 19 out of the 137 States parties to the Convention have recognized the competence of CERD to deal with complaints under the article 14 procedure.

*2. International legal norms and standards on which existing non-treaty mechanisms now base their activities [not applicable to treaty-based procedures].*

*3. Conceptual framework, methods of work and procedural rules applied by each non-treaty mechanism in the discharge of its mandate [not applicable to treaty-based procedures].*

*4. The various norms, criteria and practices established by each existing mechanism in regard to the admissibility of communications.*

(a) *The Optional Protocol procedure.* 39. The norms and criteria governing the admissibility of communications are set out in articles 1, 2, 3 and 5, paragraph 2, of the Optional Protocol. These have been further elaborated in rules 87 to 92 of the rules of procedure of the Human Rights Committee (CCPR/C/3/Rev.2). The application of these norms and criteria is amply reflected in the Committee's case law, as reproduced in its annual report to the General Assembly. (See also CCPR/C/OP/1 and 2, Selected Decisions under the Optional Protocol, volume 1 and 2.)

(b) *The CAT article 22 procedure.* 40. The norms, criteria and practices regarding the admissibility of communications are set out in article 22 of the Convention and in the corresponding rules in the rules of procedure of the Committee against Torture. The application of these norms and criteria is reflected in the committee's case law, as reproduced in its annual reports to the General Assembly.

(c) *The CERD article 14 procedure.* 41. The norms, criteria and practices regarding the admissibility of communications are set out in article 14 of the Convention and in the corresponding rules in the rules of procedure of CERD (rules 91 and 92). The application of these norms and criteria is reflected in the Committee's case law, as reproduced in its annual reports to the General Assembly.

*5. Preliminary consideration and evaluation of communications, their referral to the interested parties and subsequent course of action.*

(a) *The Optional Protocol procedure.* 42. Pursuant to rules 89, paragraph 3, and 91, paragraph 1, of the Human Rights Committee's rules of procedure, preliminary consideration and evaluation of communications submitted under the Optional Protocol may be entrusted to one Committee member, acting as Special Rapporteur for new communications. The Special Rapporteur determines whether a new communication should be referred to the State party concerned on questions of admissibility, or whether to recommend to the Committee that a communication should be declared inadmissible, without prior referral to the State party. The latter course of action is followed if there is a clear ground for declaring a communication inadmissible. If a communication is referred to the State party, subsequent course of action consists of two stages: (a) determination of admissibility; (b) examination of the merits of the claim. The Committee's Working Group on Communications can declare a communication admissible (rule 87, para. 2, of the rules of procedure), but it cannot declare a communication inadmissible. A decision to declare a communication admissible requires the support of all five members of the Working Group. Failing that, the working Group places a recommendation before plenary for action. The Committee in plenary also acts on recommendations from the Working Group to declare a communication inadmissible.

43. After a communication has been declared admissible, the Working Group proceeds to consider the merits of the claim and prepares draft views for consideration by the ple-

nary. Final Views are then adopted by the Committee as a whole, stating whether the acts or omissions complained of reveal a breach of the Covenant, or not. Any member of the Committee can append an individual opinion to the Committee's Views.

(b) *The CAT article 22 procedure.* 44. Pursuant to rule 106 of the rules of procedure of the Committee against Torture (CAT), preliminary consideration and evaluation of communications submitted under article 22 of the Convention may be entrusted to a Working Group of five of its members. The Working Group makes recommendations to the Committee concerning the admissibility of communications submitted under article 22 of the Convention. Pursuant to rule 108 of the rules of procedure, the Working Group may solicit information from the State party on questions of admissibility before making its recommendation to CAT. In any case, no communication can be declared admissible by the Committee unless it has been transmitted to the State party and unless the State party has been given an opportunity to make its observations on questions of admissibility.

45. Pursuant to rules 110 and 111 of the rules of procedure, consideration of the merits of the claims takes place in plenary. The Committee formulates its views, as to whether the act or omission complained about constitutes a breach of the Convention, or not. Decisions of a final nature (Views on the merits, or decisions declaring a communication inadmissible under article 22) are made public in the Committee's annual report to the General Assembly.

(c) *The CERD article 14 procedure.* 46. Pursuant to rule 87 of CERD's rules of procedure (as amended at the Committee's forty-third session in 1993; see document A/48/18, annex V), preliminary consideration and evaluation of communications submitted under article 14 of the Convention may be entrusted either to a working group consisting of five Committee members or to a single member acting as Special Rapporteur. The Working Group or the Special Rapporteur make recommendations to CERD concerning the admissibility of communications. According to rule 92 of the rules of procedure, they may also decide on the transmittal of communications to States parties, seeking information on questions of admissibility before making recommendations to the Committee. No communication can be declared admissible without prior transmittal to the State party.

47. Pursuant to rules 94 and 95 of the rules of procedure, consideration of the merits of the claims takes place in plenary. The Committee formulates its Opinion, as to whether the act or omission complained about constitutes a breach of the Convention, or not. Decisions of a final nature (opinions on the merits, or decisions declaring a communication inadmissible) are made public in the Committee's annual report to the General Assembly.

*6. Criteria used in practice by the Centre for Human Rights for channelling communications either to an existing public machinery or into the confidential procedure governed by Council resolution 1503 (XLVIII)—Legal foundation for such criteria.*

(a) *The Optional Protocol procedure.* 48. The procedure governed by the Optional Protocol is normally seen as a confidential procedure, although the Views of the Human Rights Committee and other decisions of a final nature (decisions declaring communications inadmissible) are made public, after they have been communicated to the parties under article 5, paragraph 4, of the Optional Protocol. However, the issue as to whether a communication is channelled into the Optional Protocol procedure or the confidential procedure governed by Council resolution 1503 (XLVIII) may be relevant in the context of the present report. The criteria used in practice by the Secretariat in determining whether a communication is channelled into the Optional Protocol procedure or the 1503 procedure are set out in some detail in the Secretary-General's report on existing United Nations procedures for dealing with communications placed before the thirty-fifth session of the Commission on Human Rights in 1979, pursuant to Commission resolution 16 (XXXIV) of 7 March 1978 (document E/CN.4/1317). No objections were raised by the Commission in respect of the suggested criteria. While not explicitly spelt out in a resolution or decision, the Commission's tacit approval has been regarded as a legal basis, since 1979, for the Secretariat's working methods in this respect.

49. The same criteria are applied, *mutatis mutandis,* when it has to be determined whether a communication should be channelled into another treaty based complaints procedure or the 1503 procedure.

*(b) The CAT article 22 procedure.* [See paragraphs 48 and 49 above.]

*(c) The CERD article 14 procedure.* [See paragraphs 48 and 49 above.]

## II. Non-Treaty Mechanisms

### A. The Original Mandates Assigned to the Various Non-treaty Mechanisms

*1. Procedure for dealing with communications, governed by Economic and Social Council resolution 1503 (XLVIII).* 50. By resolution 8 (XXIII) of 16 March 1967, the Commission on Human Rights decided to place an item on the question of violations of human rights on its annual agenda. In that context, the Commission requested authority from the Economic and Social Council, *inter alia,* to examine information relevant to gross violations of human rights contained in the communications listed in the annual confidential list of communications pursuant to Council resolution 728 F (XXVIII) of 30 July 1959. These lists had their origin in Council resolution 75 (V) of 5 August 1947, when the Council for the first time approved the self-denying statement adopted by the Commission at its first session to the effect that it recognized that it had no power to take any action in regard to any complaints concerning human rights. The Secretary-General was nevertheless requested to compile before each session of the Commission a confidential list containing summaries of such complaints, and to furnish this list to the members of the Commission, in private meeting, without divulging the identity of the authors, unless they had no objection to the disclosure of their names. A number of minor modifications were made through the years in respect of Council resolution 75 (V). These modifications were consolidated in 1959 with the adoption of Council resolution 728 F (XXVIII). The "no power" doctrine still prevailed, but communications containing allegations of violations of human rights continued to be summarized in an annual confidential list of communications. This was the situation when the Commission in 1967 requested authority to examine communications concerning alleged gross violations of human rights, listed in the annual confidential list, and to take action thereon as it deemed appropriate.

51. By resolution 1235 (XLII) of 6 June 1967, the Economic and Social Council granted the requested authority and empowered the Commission, in appropriate cases, and after careful consideration of the information thus made available to it, to make a thorough study of situations which reveal a consistent pattern of violations of human rights.

52. It hampered the exercise of the authority to deal with communications relating to violations of human rights, that no specific procedure had been devised for that purpose. The Sub-Commission, the Commission and the Council set about devising such a procedure, which was finally established on 27 May 1970 with the adoption of Council resolution 1503 (XLVIII). Before the procedure, however, could start to function, the Council requested the Sub-Commission to devise appropriate procedures for dealing with the question of admissibility of communications. On 13 August 1971, the Sub-Commission adopted resolution 1 (XXIV) setting out "provisional procedures" for dealing with the question of admissibility of communications, and on 16 August 1971 the Sub-Commission adopted resolution 2 (XXIV), establishing the Working Group on Communications, the screening body envisaged by paragraph 1 of Council resolution 1503 (XLVIII). The procedure started to function the following year when the Working Group on Communications met for the first time.

53. In short, the 1503 procedure lays down a three-stage mandate involving the Working Group on communications, the sub-Commission and the Commission. As early as 1974, the commission added a further stage to the procedure, by establishing the Working Group on Situations. That Working Group was set up annually on an ad hoc basis, until the Council made it a permanent feature in the implementation machinery of the procedure in 1990 (Council resolution 1990/41 of 25 May 1990).

54. The role of the Working Group on Communications is to consider all communications received by the Secretary-General under Council resolution 728 F (XXVIII), together with all replies received from Governments thereon, with a view to bringing to the attention of the Sub-Commission those communications, together with corresponding government replies, as received, which appear to reveal a consistent pattern of gross and reliably attested violations of human rights and fundamental freedoms (Council resolution 1503 (XLVIII), para. 1).

55. The role of the Sub-Commission is to consider the communications and the government replies brought before it by a decision of a majority of the members of the Working Group on Communications and other relevant information, with a view to determining whether to refer to the Commission particular situations which appear to reveal a consistent pattern of gross and reliably attested violations of human rights requiring consideration by the Commission (Council resolution 1503 (XLVIII), para. 5).

56. The role of the Working Group on Situations is to examine the material referred to the Commission by the Sub-Commission under the 1503 procedure, any written government observations relating thereto and any particular situation kept pending before the Commission under the procedure, and to make recommendations to the Commission on what course of action to take in respect of each particular situation (Council resolution 1990/41).

57. Pursuant to paragraph 6 of Council resolution 1503 (XLVIII) the commission is called on to determine (a) whether a particular situation referred to it requires a thorough study and a report and recommendations thereon to the Council in accordance with paragraph 3 of Council resolution 1235 (XLII), or (b) whether a particular situation referred to it may be a subject of an investigation by an ad hoc committee. The latter course of action, which can only be embarked upon with the consent of the State concerned, has never been taken.

58. Paragraph 8 of Council resolution 1503 (XLVIII) lays

down a general rule of confidentiality and provides that all actions envisaged in the implementation of the resolution by the Sub-Commission or the Commission shall remain confidential until such time as the Commission may decide to make recommendations to the Economic and Social Council. The rule of confidentiality applies also to actions taken by the Working Group on Communications and the Working Group on Situations.

2. *Special procedures.* 59. During the past 25 years the Commission on Human Rights and ECOSOC have established a number of extra-conventional procedures and mechanisms which have been entrusted to either working groups composed of experts acting in their individual capacity or to independent individuals variously designated special rapporteurs/representatives or experts. The mandates given to such procedures and mechanisms are to examine and publicly report on human rights situations in specific countries or territories or on major phenomena of human rights violations worldwide. These procedures and mechanisms are collectively referred to as the special procedures of the Commission on Human Rights.

60. Each of the said special procedures has its own specific mandate which in certain cases has evolved in accordance with circumstances and needs, mostly upon specific directives given by the Commission. Equally, each procedure and mechanism has developed its own methods of work and adapted them to the mandates as they evolved and to the specificities of the situations to be examined. Although certain basic principles and criteria are common to all special procedures, the complexities and peculiarities of each individual mandate have often required unique approaches which have been described in the reports submitted by special rapporteurs/representatives/experts or working groups to the Commission on Human Rights.

61. It should also be noted that two working groups, i.e. the Working Group on Enforced or Involuntary Disappearances and the Working Group on Arbitrary Detention, have developed and placed before the Commission coherent sets of their methods of work. These methods of work are also continuously reviewed and refined so as to respond to the requirements of the mechanisms in question.

62. In an effort to respond adequately to the question put, and yet to accommodate the wide range of specificities and peculiarities among the procedures, and further taking into consideration the page limitations applicable to reports of the Secretary-General, an effort has been made to present the various applicable mandates, criteria and methods of work as succinctly and completely as possible. Thus, tables have been composed for both the "thematic" and "country-oriented" procedures under each question.

63. The first two tables reproduced below contain references to the original mandates as well as to the current mandates of the special procedures. The subsequent tables are explained in the corresponding introductory paragraphs. . . .

### B. The International Legal Norms and Standards On Which Existing Non-Treaty Mechanisms Now Base their Activities

1. *Procedure for dealing with communications, governed by Economic and Social Council resolution 1503 (XLVIII).* 64. The basic norms and standards applied under the 1503 procedure are those set out in the Universal Declaration of Human Rights. The implementing bodies are also guided by the rec-

ognized rules of international human rights law, as they have found expression in international human rights treaties.

2. *Special procedures.* 65. The special rapporteurs/representatives/experts and working groups of the special procedures of the Commission on Human Rights base their activities on those conventional and customary legal norms and standards applicable to the respective situations they monitor. Several have made specific references to these norms and standards in their reports to the Commission on Human Rights. The following table lists, to the extent the above-mentioned procedures they pronounced themselves, the most pertinent references. . . .

### C. The Conceptual Framework, Methods of Work and Procedural Rules Applied by Each Non-Treaty Mechanism in the Discharge of its Mandate

1. *Procedure for dealing with communications, governed by Economic and Social Council resolution 1503 (XLVIII).* 66. The conceptual framework of the 1503 procedure represents a mechanism permitting the Commission on Human Rights, and the other bodies involved in its implementation, to consider in a meaningful manner allegations of gross violations of human rights wherever they are said to occur. In so doing, the bodies involved rely on the cooperation of the Governments concerned. The receipt of government replies and written observations on the allegations made, as well as the active participation by the Governments concerned in the closed meetings of the Commission, are considered essential.

67. The rules of procedure of the functional commissions of the Economic and Social Council are relevant to the work of the Commission on Human Rights under the 1503 procedure. In accordance with rule 24 of these rules, they also apply to the work of the other bodies involved, in so far as they are applicable.

68. At the first stage in the implementation of the procedure, the Working Group on Communications screens the communications which have been processed by the Secretariat under Council resolution 728 F (XXVIII) during a 12-month period ending 12 weeks prior to its meeting (Sub-Commission decision 1990/112 of 28 August 1990). All Government replies received under Council resolution 728 F (XXVIII) in response to these communications are duly taken into account. Because of the volume of work, a certain division of labour is agreed on by the members for pre-screening purposes. The preselections are then discussed by the Working Group as a whole and, unless there is consensus, a vote is taken as to whether a communication should be brought to the attention of the Sub-Commission. No communication can be referred to the Sub-Commission unless a decision to do so has the support of at least three of the five members. The Working Group may also decide to defer a decision in respect of a communication to its following session. The working Group reports confidentially to the Sub-Commission.

69. At the second stage in the implementation of the procedure the sub-Commission considers the communications and government replies brought to its attention by the working Group on Communications and determines which particular situations to refer to the Commission on Human Rights for consideration. In so doing, the Sub-Commission may also take into account "other relevant information" (Council resolution 1503 (XLVIII), para. 5). In recent years, the Sub-Commission has taken its decisions by secret ballot,

as authorized by Council resolution 1991/32. It may also decide to defer taking a decision until its next session. The Sub-Commission reports confidentially to the Commission under the 1503 procedure.

70. Once a decision has been taken to refer a particular situation to the Commission, the Sub-Commission must so inform the Government directly concerned and invite it to submit written observations to be taken into account when the Commission examines the situation (Commission decision 3 (XXX) of 6 March 1974).

71. The third stage is entrusted to the Working Group on Situations, which examines the new and pending material to be considered by a given session of the Commission under the 1503 procedure and makes recommendations to the Commission on what course of action to take in respect of each particular situation. The Working Group cannot defer a decision until its next session. It reports confidentially to the Commission. However, to facilitate subsequent participation by the Governments directly concerned at the level of the Commission itself, the Working Group communicates to them in advance the text of the relevant recommendations (Commission decision 14 (XXXV) of 12 March 1979).

72. The fourth and the final stage in the implementation of the 1503 procedure takes place in the Commission on Human Rights. In the light of the recommendations placed before it by the Working Group on Situations, the Commission considers the particular situations referred to it by the Sub-Commission and any particular situation which it had decided (at the previous session) to keep under review. It takes into account all relevant government replies received under Council resolution 728 F (XXVIII) and government observations received under Commission decision 3 (XXX) of 6 March 1974. At this stage in the procedure, the Governments directly concerned are invited to attend the respective closed meetings of the Commission, to address the Commission and to reply to any oral questions put by the members (Commission decision 5 (XXXIV) of 3 March 1978). The representatives of the Governments concerned have the right to attend and to participate in the entire discussion concerning their country and to be present when the Commission decides what course of action to take (Commission decision 9 (XXXVI) of 7 March 1980).

73. While Council resolution 1503 (XLVIII) envisages that the Commission would determine either (a) whether a thorough study is warranted in respect of a given particular situation, or (b) whether a particular situation should be investigated by an ad hoc committee, the Commission has, through the years, developed its own mechanism of implementation within the spirit of the resolution. A thorough study under paragraph 6 (a) of the resolution has only been embarked upon once, since the Commission started to apply the resolution 20 years ago, and an investigation under paragraph 6 (b) has never been resorted to.

74. Instead of the alternatives spelled out in paragraph 6 of Council resolution 1503 (XLVIII), the Commission has devised the following four alternatives in the application of the procedure:

(a) To discontinue consideration of the matter, when further consideration or action is not warranted;

(b) To keep the situation under review, in the light of any further information received from the Government concerned and any further information which may reach the commission under the 1503 procedure;

(c) To keep the situation under review and to appoint an independent expert to enter into direct contacts with the Government and the people of the country concerned and to report back to the Commission at its following session. (Alternatively, the Commission has requested the Secretary-General to appoint a special representative for the same purpose.);

(d) To discontinue consideration of the matter under the confidential procedure governed by Council resolution 1503 (XLVIII), in order to take up consideration of the same matter under the public procedure governed by Council resolution 1235 (XLII).

75. Common to all stages in the implementation of the 1503 procedure is that all meetings of the bodies involved are closed. Confidential summary records are issued for the closed meetings of the Sub-Commission and the Commission, but not for the two working groups involved.

76. No publicity is given to the decisions taken by the Working Group on Communications, the Sub-Commission or the working Group on Situations. However, after the commission has concluded its work under the 1503 item each year, the Chairman makes a public statement, indicating which countries have been the subject of discussion. This practice has been followed since 1978. In the interest of equity, the Chairman also indicates which countries, if any, are no longer under consideration within the procedure.

*2. Special procedures.* 77. To the extent that the special rapporteurs/representatives/experts and working groups of the special procedures of the Commission on Human Rights have described the framework of their reporting, reference is made to the following documents of the Commission on Human Rights. (In this regard, it should be noted that the Working Groups on Enforced or Involuntary Disappearances and Arbitrary Detention have elaborated comprehensive methods of work which were placed before, and endorsed by, the Commission on Human Rights. . . .)

### D. The Various Norms, Criteria and Practices Established by Each Existing Mechanism in Regard to the Admissibility of Communications

*1. Procedure for dealing with communications, governed by Economic and Social Council resolution 1503 (XLVIII).* 78. The criteria for determining the admissibility of communications are established by Council resolution 1503 (XLVIII) itself ("consistent pattern of gross and reliably attested violations") and by the provisions of Sub-Commission resolution 1 (XXIV) of 13 August 1971. The latter resolution lays down basic criteria in respect of the object of the communication, the source of communications, the contents of communications and the nature of the allegations, existence of other remedies and timeliness of submission. These criteria, while mainly the concern of the Working Group on Communications and the Sub-Commission, are also taken into account by the Working Group on Situations and by the Commission itself.

*2. Special procedures.* 79. Information on this question may be found in the resolutions establishing the specific mandates as referred to above. To the extent that the following special rapporteurs/representatives/experts and working groups of the special procedures of the Commission on Human Rights have described the information received, and/or the treatment thereof, reference is made to the following documents of the Commission on Human Rights. . . .

### E. The Preliminary Consideration and Evaluation of Communications, Their Referral to the Interested Parties and Subsequent Course of Action

*1. Procedure for dealing with communications, governed by Economic and Social Council resolution 1503 (XLVIII).* 80. Once a communication has been summarized by the Secretariat under Council resolution 728 F (XXVIII), it automatically constitutes part of the information channelled into the 1503 procedure. Before the 1503 procedure starts to function a copy of the communication has been transmitted to the Government concerned, to permit that Government to reply to the allegations made. Thus, government replies received under Council resolution 728 F (XXVIII) constitute an integral part of the material considered under the 1503 procedure. As explained above, preliminary consideration and evaluation of communications under the 1503 procedure are entrusted to the Sub-Commission's Working Group on Communications. Subsequent course of action has already been explained above.

*2. Special procedures.* 81. The special rapporteurs/representatives/experts and working groups of the special Procedures of the Commission on Human Rights seek to receive the widest range of information from the most direct sources, within the limits of existing possibilities, and to obtain the views of the relevant Governments on allegations received. In this connection, reference is made to more specific descriptions given under various procedures as referred to in the tables under sections C and D above.

## F. Criteria used in Practice by the Centre for Human Rights for Channelling Communications into a Public Machinery or into the 1503 Procedure—Legal Foundation for Such Criteria

82. Communications are not "received" per se under Council resolution 1503 (XLVIII). The resolution envisages that communications "received" under Council resolution 728 F (XXVIII) would be channelled into the 1503 procedure. This was logical, at the time in question, since resolution 728 F (XXVIII) was the only global resolution applicable to Secretariat handling of communications concerning alleged violations of human rights. Subsequently, upon the entry into force of the International Covenant on Civil and Political Rights and the optional Protocol thereto, which sets out a procedure for dealing with individual complaints, the question arose whether there would be a duplication or overlapping of work between the 1503 procedure, on the one hand, and the communications procedure under the optional Protocol, on the other hand. It was no longer considered valid that the Secretariat would handle all communications under Council resolution 728 F (XXVIII). Practical suggestions were placed before the Commission at its thirty-fifth session in 1979, as to which communications would be channelled into the 1503 procedure, through Council resolution 728 F (XXVIII), and which communications would be channelled into the optional Protocol procedure (see E/CN.4/1317, paras. 30 to 36). The working methods proposed by the Secretary-General have been followed, uncontested, for the last 15 years (see para. 48 above).

83. Since 1979, it has been the practice of the Commission not to take any action under the 1503 procedure, if the country concerned is being dealt with under a public procedure. In line with that approach, no material has been referred to the Commission by the Sub-Commission under the 1503 procedure since 1982 in respect of country situations considered under a public procedure within the Commission's agenda item on the question of violations of human rights. Normally, the resolutions establishing such mandates provide that information may be solicited and received from various sources. Further, the Commission has

on a number of occasions decided to discontinue consideration of a country situation under the 1503 procedure, in order to take up consideration of the same matter under a public country mandate. In the circumstances, the Secretariat has adapted its working practices to be in line with the Commission's policy. This also applies in respect of the thematic mandates established by the Commission as public procedures since 1980. In short, communications relevant to established public procedures, country-oriented or thematic, are brought to the attention of the respective special rapporteurs or working groups. The above approach has been developed in consultation with the special rapporteurs and working groups concerned. In particular, thematic special procedures which concentrate their attention primarily on concrete individual cases need to be informed about all such cases brought to the attention of the Secretariat.

84. Furthermore, it should be noted that thousands of communications are each year addressed specifically to an established public mandate, thematic or country-oriented. In these cases the communications are routed to the procedure specifically indicated by the authors.

## G. Procedure for Dealing with Communications Concerning the Status of Women

85. By resolution 76 (V) of 5 August 1947, as amended by resolution 304 I (XI) of 14 and 17 July 1950 and resolution 1983/27 of 26 May 1983, the Economic and Social Council asked the Secretary-General to compile non-confidential lists of communications dealing with the principles relating to the promotion of women's rights in the political, economic, civil, social and educational fields, and confidential lists of other communications concerning the status of women. Both lists have to be made available to the members of the Commission on the Status of Women, the confidential ones in private meeting, without divulging the identity of the authors of the communications. The communications mechanism gives individuals or organizations the possibility to bring to the attention of the Commission on the Status of Women situations dealing with the violation of the principles relating to the promotion of women's rights in political, economic, civil, social and educational fields.

86. Upon receipt of a communication concerning the status of women, its content is communicated by the Secretary-General to the Government concerned without divulging the identity of the author, thus inviting the Government to comment on it.

87. The amendment contained in resolution 1983/27 requested the Secretary-General also to include in the lists of confidential and non-confidential communications received by the specialized agencies, regional commissions and other United Nations bodies and to solicit the cooperation of the United Nations system.

88. The lists contain summaries of the communications received by the Division for the Advancement of Women of the United Nations Secretariat, New York, including comments of Governments thereon, if any, as well as of communications concerning the status of women received by other units of the United Nations Secretariat, including the regional commissions, other United Nations bodies and the specialized agencies.

89. Resolution 1983/27 also authorized the Commission to appoint a working group of not more than five of its members, selected with due regard for geographical distribution, to meet in closed meetings during each session of the com-

mission in order to consider all communications and bring to the attention of the Commission those which appeared to reveal a consistent pattern of reliably attested injustice and discriminatory practices against women. Pursuant to that resolution, the working Group would prepare a report, based on its analysis of all the communications, indicating the categories in which communications were most frequently submitted to the Commission.

90. By resolution 1993/11 the Economic and Social Council invited each regional group to appoint, one week before each session of the Commission, a member of the Working Group on Communications. It also requested the Secretary-General to ensure proper coordination of the activities of the Commission on the Status of Women with those of other bodies of the Council.

91. The Commission on the Status of Women has the mandate, through Council resolution 1983/27, as reiterated by resolution 1993/11, to examine the report of the working group and to make recommendations to the Economic and Social Council on what action should be taken on emerging trends and patterns of discrimination against women as revealed by such communications.

## UNITED NATIONS: WORKING GROUPS.

Working groups are temporary bodies established by UN commissions and committees, such as the COMMISSION ON HUMAN RIGHTS or the SUB-COMMISSION ON PREVENTION OF DISCRIMINATION AND PROTECTION OF MINORITIES, to study a specific problem and to report to the parent commission on its work. A working group may be established to study an ongoing problem (such as contemporary forms of slavery) or to draft a specific set of rules for the parent commission to consider and eventually recommend to the GENERAL ASSEMBLY (such as the Working Group on the Draft Body of Principles and Guarantees for the Protection of Mentally-Ill Persons and for the Improvement of Mental Health Care). A working group is typically given a mandate for a two- to-three-year period, with renewals of its mandate being given as necessary to complete its work. A working group may be originally established for one purpose, but, at the end of its mandate and the completion of its initial task, it may be reconstituted for continuing purposes, as happened with the Working Group on the Right to Development. The working groups described below are those concerned with aspects of human rights and in operation as of 31 December 1995.

### WORKING GROUP ON COMMUNICATIONS.

This working group was established in accordance with resolution 1503 (XLVIII) of the UN ECONOMIC AND SOCIAL COUNCIL, which authorized the Sub-Commission on Prevention of Discrimination and Protection of Minorities "to consider all communications, including replies of governments thereon, received by the Secretary-General under Council resolution 728 F

(XXVIII) of 30 July 1959, with a view to bringing to the attention of the Sub-Commission those communications, together with the replies of governments if any, which appear to reveal a consistent pattern of gross and reliably-attested violations of human rights and fundamental freedoms within the terms of reference of the Sub-Commission."

The Working Group consists of five members of the Sub-Commission, one from each of the following regional groups: Africa, Asia, Latin America, eastern Europe, and western Europe and others. At each annual session, the Sub-Commission approves the composition of the Working Group for the following year.

The Working Group meets in closed sessions, generally for a period of two weeks prior to each session of the Sub-Commission. The results of its work are communicated to the Sub-Commission confidentially. The Sub-Commission, after examining its report and deciding to refer particular situations to the UN Commission on Human Rights, invites the governments concerned to submit written observations on those situations directly to the Commission. The Commission, after studying the situations and the comments of the government concerned thereon and after hearing from the chairman/rapporteur of the Working Group if he wishes to take the floor, reaches a decision as to the action required to deal with the situation.

### WORKING GROUP ON CONTEMPORARY FORMS OF SLAVERY.

This Working Group, originally established as the Working Group on Slavery by the Sub-Commission on Prevention of Discrimination and Protection of Minorities on 17 May 1974 (decisions 16 and 17 [LVI]), was renamed the Working Group on Contemporary Forms of Slavery by the UN Commission on Human Rights in 1988 (resolution 1988/42). The Working Group meets at the European office of the United Nations in Geneva for a period of three working days immediately prior to each annual session of the Sub-Commission and reviews developments in the field of slavery and the slave trade as defined in the Slavery Convention, the Supplementary Convention on the Abolition of Slavery, the Slave Trade and Institutions and Practices Similar to Slavery, and the Convention for the Suppression of the Traffic in Persons and of the Exploitation of the Prostitution of Others (see SLAVERY).

The Working Group consists of five members of the Sub-Commission, one from each of the following regional groups: Africa, Asia, Latin America, eastern Europe, and western Europe and others.

At its 1988 session, the Working Group reviewed recent developments relating to contemporary forms of slavery and the slave trade, including the exploitation of child labor and the sale of children, debt bondage, traffic in persons and exploitation of the prostitution of others, and certain slavery-like practices of apartheid and colonialism; and formulated a program of work for the period 1989 to 1991.

At its 1989 session, it again reviewed developments in those fields, concentrating on those relating to the sale of children, child prostitution, and child pornography. In its report, it included (UN Doc. E/CN.4/Sub.2/1989/39, chap. VII) a number of proposals for dealing with these problems for consideration by its parent bodies. It also included the draft of a "Program of Action for Prevention of Sale of Children, Child Prostitution and Child Pornography."

At its twentieth session, the Working Group on Contemporary Forms of Slavery welcomed the holding of the World Congress on Commercial Sexual Exploitation of Children at Stockholm in 1996; emphasized the revised draft program of action for the prevention of trafficking in persons and exploitation of the prostitution of others (E/CN.4/Sub.2/1995/28/Add. 1); noted the increase in trafficking in organs by industralized countries and that the COUNCIL OF EUROPE was considering a protocol on organ transplantation; and also considered the questions of bonded labor, child labor, and forced labor. It also considered a report (A/49/478) submitted by Mr. Vitit Muntarbhorn, the former Special Rapporteur on the sale of children, child prostitution and child pornography. The Working Group also decided to consider at its twenty-first session ways to combat incest and sexual abuse of children inside the family, which it considers a form of slavery, and emphasized the urgent need for adequate help to be offered to victims of such practices.

***WORKING GROUP ON DETENTION.*** In 1974, the UN Sub-Commission on Prevention of Discrimination and Protection of Minorities decided (resolution 7 [XXVII]) to review annually developments concerning the human rights of persons subjected to any form of detention or imprisonment. At its 1981 session, the Sub-Commission set up a sessional working group to assist it in this task. Similar working groups have been established at each subsequent session of the Sub-Commission.

The Working Group meets for five or six days each year immediately before the Sub-Commission's session, normally at the United Nations office in Geneva. It consists of one member of the Sub-Commission from each of five regional groups: Africa, Asia, Latin America, eastern Europe, and western Europe and others. Members are nominated by the regional groups and appointed by the Sub-Commission.

At its 1989 session, the Working Group on Detention conducted its annual review of developments concerning the human rights of persons subjected to any

form of detention or imprisonment and devoted particular attention to questions relating to such matters as the privatization of prisons and the execution of young offenders. In addition, it made progress in preparing a draft declaration on the protection of all persons against enforced or involuntary disappearances and authorized its chairman to prepare a revised draft, on the basis of informal discussions in the Working Group, for consideration at its 1990 session.

***WORKING GROUP ON A DRAFT DECLARATION ON THE RIGHT AND RESPONSIBILITY TO PROMOTE AND PROTECT HUMAN RIGHTS.*** On 16 March 1984, the UN Commission on Human Rights established (decision 1984/116) the Working Group to Draft a Declaration on the Right and Responsibility of Individuals, Groups, and Organs of Society to Promote and Protect Universally Recognized Human Rights and Fundamental Freedoms. The sessional Working Group, open to all members of the Commission, held its first meeting prior to the 1985 session of the Commission and was later convened annually for periods of from six to eight days prior to subsequent sessions of the Commission.

On 1 March 1990, the Working Group reported to the Commission (UN Doc. E/CN.4/1990/47) that it had not been able to complete the drafting of the Declaration and asked that it be authorized to meet for eight working days prior to the Commission's 1991 session. The report included an account of the discussions in the Working Group and a series of "Texts Provisionally Adopted by the Working Group at First Reading" (annex 1 of the report), reproduced below:

### Chapter I

*A.* No one shall participate in violating the [universally recognized] human rights and fundamental freedoms of others, and no one shall be subject to punishment or adverse action of any kind for refusing, [individually or in association with others], to violate or otherwise be associated with violations of [universally recognized] human rights and fundamental freedoms.

*B.* Each State has a prime responsibility and duty to promote and protect [universally recognized] human rights and fundamental freedoms, *inter alia,* by adopting such legislative, administrative and other steps as may be necessary to create the social and political conditions and legal guarantees required to ensure that all persons, individually and in association with others, are able to enjoy these rights and freedoms in practice.

Everyone has the right, individually and in association with others, to promote and to strive for the protection and realization of [universally recognized] human rights and fundamental freedoms at the national and international levels. Each State shall adopt such legislative, administrative and other steps as may be necessary to give effect to this right.

[Language to be added reflecting the role of national and

international law as well as other modalities, to be formulated when discussing issues assigned to Chapter V.]

**Chapter II**

*Title.* The rights to know, to be informed about, and to impart to others knowledge of universally recognized human rights and fundamental freedoms.

*Paragraph 1.* All persons have the right to know, and, individually as well as together with others, to be informed about, and to make known [their] universally recognized human rights and fundamental freedoms.

*Paragraph 2.* Everyone has the right, individually as well as together with others

(a) to seek, obtain, receive and hold information about these rights and freedoms, [including access to information on the means by which these rights and freedoms are given effect in domestic legislative, judicial or administrative systems];

(b) to publish, impart or disseminate freely to others views, information and knowledge of universally recognized human rights and fundamental freedoms....

*Paragraph 5.* Everyone has the right to develop and discuss new human rights ideas and principles, and to advocate their universal acceptance.

*Paragraph 6.* 1. The State has the responsibility to take legislative, judicial, administrative or other appropriate measures to promote the understanding by all persons under its jurisdiction of their civil, political, economic, social and cultural rights.

2. Such measures shall include:

(a) the publication and widespread distribution of national laws and regulations and of basic international human rights instruments;

(b) full and equal access to international documents in the field of human rights, including the State's periodic reports to the bodies established by the international human rights treaties to which it is a party, as well as the official report of these bodies.

3. The State has the responsibility to promote and improve the teaching of human rights and fundamental freedoms at all levels of education, and to encourage all those responsible for training lawyers, law enforcement officers, the personnel of the armed forces and public officials to include appropriate elements of human rights teaching in their training programmes.

**Chapter III**

*Article 1.* For the purpose of promoting and protecting [universally recognized] human rights and fundamental freedoms, everyone has the right, individually and in association with others, at the national and international levels:

(a) to meet or assemble peacefully;

(b) to form, join, and participate in non-governmental organizations, associations, or where relevant groups;

(c) to communicate with non-governmental or intergovernmental organizations.

*Article 2.* Everyone has the right, individually and in association with others, to have effective access, on a non-discriminatory basis, to participation in the government of his country and in the conduct of public affairs. This includes, *inter alia,* the right, individually and in association with others, to submit to governmental bodies and agencies and organizations concerned with public affairs criticism and pro-

posals for improving their functioning and to draw attention to any aspect of their work which may hinder or impede the promotion, protection and realization of human rights and fundamental freedoms.

*Article 3.* Everyone has the right, individually and in association with others, to participate in peaceful activities directed against violations of human rights and fundamental freedoms.

**Chapter IV**

*Article 1.* In the exercise of the right to promote and protect the human rights referred to in the present declaration, as well as in the exercise of other [universally recognized] human rights and fundamental freedoms, everyone has the right to protection and recourse to effective remedies in the event of violations of those rights.

*Article 2.* To this end, everyone has the right, *inter alia,* to:

(a) draw public attention to violations of human rights and to complain about the policies and actions of individual officials and governmental bodies by petitions or other means to competent national judicial, administrative, legislative authorities or any other competent authority provided for by the legal system of the State, as well as to any relevant competent international bodies;

(b) complain to and have that complaint promptly reviewed in a public hearing and decided by an independent, impartial and competent judicial or other authority established by law;

(c) obtain a just decision and award providing redress, including any compensation due as well as enforcement of the decision and award, all without undue delay;

(d) attend such relevant hearings or proceedings or, as the case may be, trials to assess their fairness and compliance with national and international standards;

(e) offer and provide assistance, including professionally qualified legal assistance, in defending [universally recognized] human rights and fundamental freedoms;

(f) seek and accept such assistance of his own free choice in order to enjoy effectively the measures of protection referred to in this Chapter;

(g) unhindered access to and communication with international bodies with general or special competence to receive and consider communications on matters of human rights in accordance with applicable international instruments and procedures.

*Article 3.* To the same end, each State shall, *inter alia*:

(a) ensure the protection by the competent authorities of everyone, individually or in association with others, against any violence, threats, retaliation, *de facto* or *de jure* adverse discrimination, pressure or any other arbitrary action as a consequence of their legitimate exercise of the rights referred to in this declaration.

**WORKING GROUP ON ENFORCED OR INVOLUNTARY DISAPPEARANCES.** This working group of the UN Commission on Human Rights was first established by the Commission on 29 February 1980 (resolution 20 [XXXVI]). Its mandate was extended annually until 1986. In 1986, and again in 1988 (resolutions 1986/55 and 1988/34), its mandate was extended for two years so as to enable the group to take into consideration all information communicated to it on the cases brought to its attention, while maintaining its annual reporting cycle.

The Working Group is composed of five members of the Commission, serving as experts in their individual capacities. They are appointed by the chairman of the Commission and serve for indeterminate terms.

The 1993 report of the Working Group can be found under the heading **DISAPPEARANCES.** Its methods of work, as described by the Working Group in the report, which it presented to the 1988 session of the Commission on Human Rights, are as follows (UN Doc. E/CN.4/1988/19, paras. 16–30):

The Working Group's methods of work are based on its mandate as stipulated in Commission on Human Rights resolution 20 (XXXVI) and are specifically geared to its main objective. That objective is to assist families in determining the fate and whereabouts of their missing relatives who, having disappeared, are placed outside the protective precinct of the law. To this end, the Working Group endeavours to establish a channel of communication between the families and the Governments concerned, with a view to ensuring that sufficiently documented and clearly identified individual cases which the families, directly or indirectly, have brought to the Group's attention, are investigated and the whereabouts of the missing person clarified. The Group's role ends when the fate and whereabouts of the missing person have been clearly established as a result of investigations by the Government or the search by the family, irrespective of whether that person is alive or dead. The Group's approach is strictly non-accusatory. It does not concern itself with the question of determining responsibility for specific cases of disappearance or for other human rights violations which may have occurred in the course of disappearances. In sum, the Group's activity is humanitarian in nature.

A typical example of enforced or involuntary disappearance may be described in general terms as follows: a clearly identified person is detained against his will by officials of any branch or level of government or by organized groups or private individuals allegedly acting on behalf or with the support, permission or acquiescence of the Government. These forces then conceal the whereabouts of that person or refuse to disclose his fate or to acknowledge that the person was detained.

The Working Group does not deal with situations of international armed conflict, in view of the competence of the International Committee of the Red Cross (ICRC) in such situations, as established by the Geneva Conventions of 12 August 1949 and the Protocols additional thereto.

In transmitting cases of disappearances, the Working Group deals exclusively with Governments, basing itself on the principle that Governments must assume responsibility for any violation of human rights on their territory. If, however, disappearances are attributed to terrorist or insurgent movements fighting the Government on its own territory, the Working Group has refrained from processing them. The Group considers that, as a matter of principle, such groups may not be approached with a view to investigating or clarifying disappearances for which they are held responsible.

Reports on disappearances are considered admissible by the Working Group when they originate from the family or friends of the missing person. Such reports may, however, be channelled to the Working Group through representatives of the family, Governments, intergovernmental organizations, humanitarian organizations and other reliable sources. They must be submitted in writing with a clear indication of the identity of the sender.

In order to enable Governments to carry out meaningful investigations, the Working Group provides them with information containing at least a minimum of basic data. In addition, the Working Group constantly urges the sources of reports to furnish as many details as possible on the identity of the missing person (if available, identity card numbers) and the circumstances of the disappearance. The Group requires the following minimum elements:

(a) Full name of the missing person;

(b) Date of disappearance, i.e., day, month and year of arrest or abduction or day, month and year when the missing person was last seen. When the missing person was last seen in a detention centre, an approximate indication is sufficient (i.e. March or spring 1980);

(c) Place of arrest or abduction or where the missing person was last seen (at least indication of town or village);

(d) Parties presumed to have carried out the arrest or abduction or to hold the missing person in unacknowledged detention;

(e) Steps taken to determine the fate or whereabouts of the missing person or at least an indication that efforts to resort to domestic remedies were frustrated or have otherwise been inconclusive.

Reported cases of disappearances are placed before the Working Group for detailed examination during its sessions. Those which fulfil the requirements as outlined above are transmitted, upon the Group's specific authorization, to the Governments concerned requesting them to carry out investigations and to inform the Group about their results. The reported cases are communicated by letter from the Group's Chairman to the Government concerned through the Permanent Representative to the United Nations.

Cases that occurred within the three months preceding receipt of the report by the Group are transmitted directly to the Ministers for Foreign Affairs by means of a cable. Their transmission can be authorized by the Chairman on the basis of a specific delegation of power given to him by the Group. Cases which occurred prior to the three-month limit but not more than one year before the date of their receipt by the Secretariat, provided that they had some connection with a case which occurred within the three-month period, can be transmitted between sessions by letter upon authorization by the Chairman.

At least once a year the Working Group reminds every Government concerned of the cases which have not yet been clarified. Furthermore, at any time during the year, any Government may request the summaries of the outstanding and/or clarified cases which the Working Group has transmitted to it.

All replies received from Governments on reports of disappearances are examined by the Working Group and summarized in the Group's annual report to the Commission on Human Rights. The number of cases on which a Government has provided one or several specific replies are listed in the statistical summary concerning each country in the annual report. Any information given on specific cases is forwarded to the sources of those reports who are invited to make observations thereon or to provide additional details on the cases.

If the reply clearly indicates where the missing person is (whether alive or dead) and if that information is sufficiently definite for the family to be reasonably expected to accept it, the Working Group considers the case clarified at the session following the receipt of that information. The case is accordingly listed under the heading "Cases clarified by the Government's responses" in the statistical summary of the annual report.

If the reply provides definite information on the missing person's fate after the reported date of disappearance, but does not unambiguously specify the person's present whereabouts (for instance that the person was released from prison some time ago or that he is free without stating where), a reply from the source has to be awaited. If the source does not respond within six months of the date on which the Government's reply was communicated to it, the case is considered clarified. If the source contests the Government's information on reasonable grounds, the Government is so informed and invited to comment.

If the sources provide well-documented information that a case has erroneously been considered clarified, because the Government's reply referred to a different person, does not correspond to the reported situation or has not reached the source within the six-month period described above, the Working Group transmits the case to the Government anew requesting it to comment. In such instances the respective case is again listed among the outstanding cases and a specific explanation is given in the Group's report to the Commission on Human Rights, describing the above-mentioned errors or discrepancies.

Any substantive additional information which the sources submit on an outstanding case is placed before the Working Group and, following its approval, transmitted to the Government concerned. If the additional information received amounts to a clarification of the case, the Government is informed immediately without awaiting the Group's next session. Clarifications by the sources are summarized in the Group's annual report and listed in the statistical summary under the heading "Cases clarified by non-governmental sources."

The Working Group retains cases on its files as long as the exact whereabouts of the missing persons have not been determined, in accordance with the criteria outlined in paras. 16, 26 and 27. This principle is not affected by changes of Government in a given country. However, the Working Group accepts the closure of a case on its files when the competent authority specified in the relevant national law pronounces, with the concurrence of the relatives and other interested parties, on the presumption of death of a person reported missing.

The following supplementary rules were added by the Working Group in the course of its meetings in 1988 (UN Doc. E/CN.4/1989/18, para 23):

(a) Reports on a disappearance indicating that officials from more than one country were directly responsible for or involved in a disappearance would be communicated to both the Government of the country where the disappearance occurred and the Government of the country whose officials or agents were alleged to have participated in the arrest or the abduction of the missing person. However, the case would only be counted in the statistics of the country in which the person was reportedly held in detention or last seen;

(b) In the case of the disappearance of a pregnant woman, the child presumed to have been born during the mother's captivity would be mentioned in the description of the case of the mother. The child would be treated as a separate case when witnesses reported that the mother had actually given birth to a child during detention.

In its report to the 1990 session of the Commission on Human Rights, the Working Group included the following observations on its work during the ten-year period from February 1980 to February 1990 (UN Doc. E/CN.4/1990/13, chap. V, paras. 337–365):

Already a full decade ago, numerous reports of widespread disappearances had been perturbing world public opinion. In 1980—at the prompting of the General Assembly, the Economic and Social Council and the Sub-Commission—the Commission on Human Rights responded to these reports by setting up the Working Group on Enforced or Involuntary Disappearances. The present report to the Commission is therefore the Group's tenth. At this juncture, a brief review of its activities to date seems warranted. Such an examination will permit the Commission to remind itself of the Group's evolution over the years, and it may help to indicate new directions for the Group to take. The Group has chosen to do this by highlighting a number of aspects of disappearances, both as regards the problem itself, and as regards the approach taken by the Group. Some of these have already been discussed in previous reports to the Commission.

In different terms, the Working Group has consistently expressed the view that enforced or involuntary disappearances constitute the most comprehensive denial of human rights of our time. They are a gruesome form of human rights violation which, the Group believes, continue to warrant the unstinting attention of the international community and in particular that of the Commission on Human Rights.

In its first two reports, the Working Group specifically dwelt on the question of which human rights and fundamental freedoms are violated as a result of a disappearance. It pointed out that practically all basic human rights of a disappeared person are infringed in one way or another following an abduction. The same holds true, in a greater or lesser extent, for all economic, social and cultural rights guaranteed by the various international instruments. Likewise, the Working Group has drawn attention to the wide circle of victims caused by a disappearance. Family members and other relatives or dependents suffer the immediate consequences of a disappearance. Not only are they subjected to agonizing uncertainty about what happened to their parent, child or spouse, but in many cases economic hardship and social alienation may be part of their sorry lot. The psychological effects on children are found to be severe, even devastating at times. Children born during the captivity of their disappeared mothers constitute a category all by themselves.

Making people disappear seems to be a convenient tactic for suppressing insurgence or stifling dissent, for it takes the victim out of the protective precinct of the law. People regarded as too militant in their quest for social justice or political reform may not be easily silenced by the process of law. The same may be true for people suspected of subversive activities. Yet, regardless of how sophisticated the protection of the individual citizen against abuse by his own Government provided by the law, all legal guarantees and procedural safeguards come to grinding halt once a person is reported missing. Disappearances continue to manifest themselves in may ways. Yet, whatever form they take, the result is almost invariably the same: once the authorities disclaim any responsibility or knowledge of a particular case, prospects for finding the person alive become increasiingly grim.

Several features may be emphasized which, in the Working Group's experience, are either contributing factors or corollaries to the incidence of disappearances. One striking relationship is that between states of emergency and serious social or political turmoil or subversive activity. Situations such as these are common and often lead to human rights violations, including disappearances. One of the reasons is that the powers of the civil authorities are being curtailed and the military operations are no longer or too little subject to ordinary democratic control or political guidance. This may be the result of the prevailing balance of power among the various branches of government, or of a deliberate policy of *laissez-aller*. In the most extreme form, of course, the military and security personnel can be consciously used by civilian or military Government as a instrument of repression.

In many cases, paramilitary groups carry out disappearances. It is difficult in some situations to identify a direct link between those groups and certain military authorities or other branches of the executive; whilst in other situations the relationship may be all too clear, as evidenced by the absence of any real obstacles to or consequences of their operations.

Harassment of witnesses and of relatives is a profoundly disturbing consequence of disappearances. The increasing number of reports on incidents of this nature have prompted the Working Group to draw the Commission's attention to this issue. It is a practice which essentially adds insult to injury because it is directed at a group which is already vulnerable. The Working Group intends to intensify its contacts with Governments on this matter. The Commission, for its part, should continue to keep a close eye on developments in this regard.

Perhaps the single most important factor contributing to the phenomenon of disappearances may be that of impunity. The Working Group's experience over the past 10 years has confirmed the age-old adage that impunity breeds contempt for the law. Perpetrators of human rights violations, whether civilian or military, will become all the more brazen when they are not held to account before a court of law. Impunity can also induce victims of these practices to resort to a form of self-help and take the law into their own hands, which in turn exacerbates the spiral of violence.

Military courts contribute significantly to impunity, in the Working Group's experience. A recurrent theme in times of internal crisis or under the doctrine of national security is that military personnel attested to have engaged in gross misconduct are almost invariably acquitted or given sentences that are disproportionate to the crime committed. Subsequent promotions are even commonplace.

One other cause of impunity, apart from the conduct induced by the State, is often institutional paralysis of the judicial system, in particular, the virtual or total lack of implementation of *habeas corpus*. Paralysis may be due either to overburdening of the judicial system on top of a longstanding lack of resources, or to assassination or systematic intimidation of judicial officers and other magistrates. Paralysis may also occur through lack of co-operation by the executive branch. *Habeas corpus,* for instance, is potentially one of the most powerful legal tools for unearthing the fate or whereabouts of a disappeared person. The most sophisticated rules governing this institution, however, are rendered inoperative in a situation where co-operation stops at the barrack's gate. In certain countries, *habeas corpus* laws have purposefully been subjected to severe restrictions.

On the question of impunity and responsibility, the Working Group's position, though clear and consistent from the very beginning, seems worth restating. In line with its non-accusatory approach, the Group does not engage in the attribution of responsibility of individual officers or agents of the State for individual cases of disappearances. More generally, the Group remains of the view that those responsible for disappearances should be prosecuted to the full extent of the law, a task that falls on the State. This concern was shared very early on by the General Assembly in resolution 33/173, which is one of the bases for the Group's mandate. The Group is primarily interested in the matter of responsibility from the perspective of prevention of disappearances.

Essentially, the mandate of the Working Group as described in Commission on Human Rights resolution 20 (XXXVI) is "to examine questions enforced or involuntary disappearances". (The distinction between enforced and involuntary, incidentally, is one of historical value only and no longer plays any role in practice.) On the basis of its terms of reference, the Working Group has from its early days operated on three different levels. First of all, and for the most part, the Group has been concerned with individual cases, trying to assist relatives to ascertain the fate and wherabouts of their loved ones. On a second level, the Group has studied situations of disappearances in individual countries; it has recorded its observations in its general reports as in special reports following visits to certain countries. Thirdly, it has devoted attention to the phenomenon of disappearances *per se*, its dynamics and dimensions. This is evident from the conclusions and recommendations in each of its reports to the Commission, as well as from chapters on specific aspects of the problem.

It has been argued that the Working Group's approach to individual cases represents at the same time the strongest and the weakest point in its endeavors. Strong, in the sense that the Group opened a window—unique at the time—into the United Nations system, allowing private individuals whose rights have been violated to address the pertinent human rights body swiftly and directly. Weak, in the sense that the Group seeks to clarify cases of disappearanes through co-operation with Governments which probably were responsible for them in the first place and who have little, if anything, to gain by strenous investigations. Be that as it may, the Working Group has insisted repeatedly that its humanitarian approach, perhaps imperfect, is the only real option available to it, and that only through co-operation and dialogue with States can its primary objective—the elimination of disappearances—be achieved. That is still the Group's view today.

It is a matter of satisfaction to the Working Group that, through patient and persistent efforts over the years, it has been able increasingly to move Governments towards a more responsive attitude. Indeed, there are only a few countries that have never given substantive replies to the Group's communications. On the other hand, when examining the substantive content of the co-operation received, one is struck by significant differences. Whereas some Governments have made efforts to comply with the Group's request by providing as much information as possible—Colombia is a case in point—others have, through written submissions and oral presentations and often by high-level delegations, tried to inform the Working Group about the political and other circumstances affecting the phenomenon in their countries or of the various problems encountered in the process of

**U**

investigation. In the past year, this was the case for Argentina, Mexico, the Philippines, and Sri Lanka. Although it is difficult to establish clear categories in this regard, the Working Group has attempted to reflect in each country subsection the degree of co-operation it is currently receiving from the government concerned.

Very soon after its creation, the Working Group began to develop a mechanism to deal with the influx of a great many cases of disappearances in a matter that would allow a dynamic response to the needs of people looking for missing relatives and friends. Part of that mechanism was the so-called urgent action procedure, which requires the Chairman in between sessions of the Group to process cases submitted within three months after their alleged disappearance. Even though the overall clarification rate against all outstanding cases is not considerable—it hovers around 7 per cent—clarifications under the urgent action procedure are as high as 25 per cent. This suggests that when acting swiftly, the Group may in effect help to prevent irreparable damage. The urgent procedure was subsequently emulated by other thematic mechanisms of the Commission.

Almost from the beginning, the Working Group has relied on visits as a preferred option for assessing the overall situation of disappearances in a given country. Not only does a visit provide an opportunity to obtain first-hand information on the matter, it also puts the Group in direct contact with family members, witnesses and non-governmental groups, as well as with the competent authorities at different levels. Working relationships established in the course of a visit usually continue afterwards. A visit also enables the Group to get the views of people from different segments of society, in order to analyse properly the context of disappearances. In 1982, visits were made to Mexico and Cyprus. In 1984, the Group addressed a letter to eight Governments, requesting them to consider the possibility of such a visit. A similar request to five Governments was sent in 1988. The Group's first visit to a country where the phenomenon was still developing occurred in 1985, when two members of the Group went to Peru, following an invitation of the Government. Similar visits took place to Peru in 1986, Guatemala in 1987 and Colombia in 1988. At the moment, the Group has three invitations outstanding to visit El Salvador, Sri Lanka and the Philippines.

Since 1985, following reports on its various visits, the Working Group has been able to make headway in the further development of its methods of work. Two features are worth mentioning. The first one relates to the format of its reports: its account of the visit was published as a separate addendum to the main report, so that it might circulate independently. The second more important one, had to do with the manner in which the Working Group expresses a position. As a rule, the Group never submits an evaluation of any given situation of disappearances. Under the various country sections of its general reports, the Group describes to the Commission what action it has taken, and gives a brief summary of the viewpoints submitted by both governmental and non-governmental sources. The conclusions and recommendations in its 10 general reports do not pertain to the situation in any country in particular, at least not explicitly so. In the four reports on its various countries, however, the Group felt it was in a better position to offer its own analysis of the situation and provide specific recommendations.

On the question of country-specific recommendations, the Commission, in resolution 1989/27, asked Governments to give all necessary attention to them. Unfortunately, the Working Group has no information to present on the extent to which any follow-up is indeed being given to these recommendations. This is all the more disturbing as most recommendations are geared to such issues as guaranteeing the right to *habeas corpus*, setting up tracing mechanisms, strengthening the judicial system and improving the security of non-governmental organizations and human rights activists. Perhaps the Commission should henceforth take a more critical look at this matter and accord it due priority at its forty-sixth session.

As to the format of its reports, the Group soon found a form of presentation which seemed to command the approval of the Commission. The introduction of statistical summaries, further refined in successive reports, as well as graphs, not only provided possibilities for easy reference, but also constituted unique features in human rights reporting. Of course, these cannot take away a basic drawback, namely that the figures presented by the Group are based entirely on submissions from external sources, processed according to the Group's criteria. Consequently, they do not necessarily reflect the true dimensions of a given situation of disappearances, which in many cases may be considerably larger; nor do they allow for any comparison between countries or geographical regions.

Over the past 10 years, the Working Group has transmitted some 19,000 cases to a total of 41 Governments. It must be remembered that only those cases are being forwarded which conform to the criteria established by the Group. Therefore, the total number of cases examined by the Group, including the ones that did not qualify for transmission, is at least 50,000. Most Governments to which cases had been sent, have made oral presentations to the Group at one time or another. Scores of non-governmental organizations, *ad-hoc* groups as well as individual witnesses have provided the group with pertinent information during its 29 meetings and its several missions. Some 20 Governments maintain more or less regular contact with the Group. A list of the non-governmental organizations that have addressed themselves to the Group over the years, is contained in annex I of the report.

In 1989, the Working Group dealt with some 700 cases said to have occurred in that very same year. This represents an alarming increase since 1988, when the corresponding number of cases totalled some 400. The Group is concerned about this development, in particular over the sharp rise in disappearances in certain countries, as reflected by the statistical summaries in the preceding pages.

For a number of years the Group has been stressing the importance of greater awareness of its aims and purpose as well as its *modus operandi*. Such awareness could, in its view, avoid erroneus ideas about what the Group was set up to do, prevent false expectations about what it could reasonably achieve and dispel misgivings about how it pursues its mandate. In the light of this, the Centre for Human Rights has recently published an information leaflet on the Working Group in its fact sheet series. Also, and more important for the Commission itself, the Working Group, in 1988, presented for the first time a comprehensive account of the methods of work it had developed over the previous eight years of operation. Since then it has continued to reflect on the development of its methods of work and kept the Commission informed accordingly.

The Working Group hopes that enhanced publicity may prompt organizations that have hitherto been unaware of the Group's existence to seek a working relationship with it. This, in turn, may lead to a more diversified flow of information, particularly from those corners of the world where human rights infrastructure—in terms of grass-root organizations, national commissions and the like—is as yet rather frail.

In 1988, for the first time in history, an international judicial body rendered a judgement on cases of disappearances. The Inter-American Court of Human Rights, in deciding three cases that took place in Honduras, made a number of important observations which have a direct bearing on the Working Group's activities and methods of work. First, the Court made a detailed analysis of the internationally recognized principle of the State's responsibility for the human rights violations committed within its territory and its obligations to prevent such violations or to investigate them where they have occurred. It declared that such responsibility continued to exist, for as long as uncertainty remained concerning the ultimate fate of the disappeared person.

These considerations have in different words been retained also by the Human Rights Committee in recent views expressed on cases brought before it under the Optional Protocol. These views are of direct relevance for the Working Group and reinforce the positions it has consistently taken. For in its dialogue with certain Governments arguments had been advanced first of all that cases stemming from a previous political period should not be ascribed to the Government in office and, hence, dropped from the Group's dossier. Secondly, it had been suggested rather strongly that the Working Group should declare inadmissable cases reported to it long after the alleged date of occurrence.

The Group, for its part, has always taken the view that a situation of disappearance does not come to an end once no new cases have been reported over a certain period of time. Under its terms of reference, the Group will continue to deal with cases as long as they have not been clarified. It believes that the need to insist on investigation of all cases of disappearances lies at the heart of its mandate. It does so bearing in mind the interest of those who will suffer anguish and bitterness as long as they cannot be assured of the fate or whereabouts of their loved ones. Furthermore, the Group has repeatedly stated that the advent of democracy or civil Government does not, in itself, imply that no new cases of disappearance will occur.

On three different occaisions, the Working Group has recommended that the Commission on Human Rights, in one form or another, take action on the idea of an international instrument against disappearances. The Group feels gratified that the Sub-Commission is now in the process of elaborating a draft declaration on the subject, generously supported by a number of non-governmental organizations, and has offered some constructive comments. Hopefully, the Sub-Commission will pursue this exercise with all the necessary vigour.

The Working Group would like to commend the members of the Secretariat, whose unwavering dedication has allowed the Group to develop its methods of work and to deal with its case load. Particularly in the initial period, when the Group had to find its way through uncharted territory under sometimes trying circumstances, but also up to the present, innovative thinking as well as common sense have been the hallmarks of the Centre's support unit. Sifting through the thousands of communications, entering them into the computer, cross-checking data, correspondence with sources and governments, preparing documentation, all of this is so labour-intensive that without the Secretariat, the Group would have been utterly helpless. Unfortunately, the Centre for Human Rights has, for several years already, been contending with a chronic shortage in financial and human resources.

If immediate remedies are not applied, the level of service to the Working Group will no longer be sustainable. This will inevitably result in backlogs that would not be fair to the families concerned, nor to the respective Governments, for that matter. The Commission would be well-advised to give this question its most serious consideration; its agenda gives it ample occasion to do so.

Finally, the Working Group wishes to reiterate that the advisory services system, would be of considerable benefit for many countries where the problem of disappearances has been epidemic. It hopes that more and more Governments will avail themselves of the possibilities offered by the United Nations in this regard. As it is in the minds of people that human rights violations are conceived, it is in their minds, and hearts, that consciousness about the inherent dignity of the human person must be instilled. Failing that, it will be quite impossible to end disappearances for all time. In any event, given the difficulties, the road ahead will be long and arduous.

The Commission extended for two years the term of the mandate of the Working Group, while maintaining its annual reporting procedure.

***WORKING GROUP ON INDIGENOUS POPULATIONS.*** Creation of the Working Group was first proposed by the UN Sub-Commission on Prevention of Discrimination and Protection of Minorities in 1982 (resolution 2 [XXXIV]). The proposal was endorsed by the Commission on Human Rights (resolution 1982/19) and the Economic and Social Council (resolution 1982/34). The Council thereby authorized the Sub-Commission to establish annually a Working Group on Indigenous Populations to meet for up to five working days before the Sub-Commission's sessions in order to (a) review developments pertaining to the promotion and protection of human rights and fundamental freedoms of indigenous populations, including information obtained by the Secretary-General from governments, specialized agencies, regional intergovernmental organizations, and non-governmental organizations in consultative status, particularly those of indigenous peoples, and to analyze such materials and to submit its conclusions to the Sub-Commission; and (b) give special attention to the evolution of standards concerning the rights of indigenous populations, taking account of both the similarities and the differences in the situations and aspirations of indigenous populations throughout the world.

The Working Group meets for five working days each year immediately before each annual session of the Sub-Commission, normally at the United Nations office in Geneva. It consists of one member of the Sub-Commission from each of five regional groups: Africa, Asia, Latin America, eastern Europe, and western Europe and others. Before the close of each Sub-Commission session, its chairman, after consulting with the regional groups, designates five members to constitute the Working Group for the next year.

More than 350 experts took part in the 1989 session of the Working Group, including observers from more than 32 UN member States and the Holy See, representatives of the **ILO,** observers from more than 30 non-governmental organizations in consultative status, and representatives of several hundred indigenous peoples' organizations and other interested groups.

The Working Group, at that session, held a general review of the situation and developments pertaining to the promotion and protection of the human rights and fundamental freedoms of indigenous peoples and heard reports highlighting some of the most important issues confronting them. In the course of the discussion, a number of proposals and recommendations were put forward, including general calls for greater consultation between governments and indigenous peoples, for the demilitarization of areas occupied by indigenous peoples, and for the resettlement of people brought into indigenous areas to change artificially the ethnic consistency of the area. There were also specific calls for:

(a) a Special Rapporteur or member of the Working Group to be mandated to witness and investigate human rights abuses to indigenous people;

(b) an international recourse procedure to be established for the use of indigenous people who had suffered human rights violations, e.g., a high commissioner or an international **OMBUDSMAN**;

(c) a permanent institution to be set up to monitor the deaths of indigenous people while in the custody of government authorities;

(d) a special committee of 24 to investigate the situation of indigenous peoples, as far as their decolonization mandate allows;

(e) elections for indigenous peoples to be conducted under the aegis of the United Nations;

(f) debt relief for economically disadvantaged countries, when provided, to be allocated to the assistance of indigenous peoples;

(g) the forthcoming United Nations Global Consultation on Development to take into account indigenous peoples and an international conference to be convened to examine the experience of indigenous peoples in their attempts at self-development;

(h) the United Nations to extend technical assistance to indigenous peoples and communities in their attempts at self-development;

(i) the United Nations Center on Transnational Corporations to monitor the work of transnational corporations and international institutions on projects which may affect the life and conditions of indigenous peoples; and

(j) a proclamation by the United Nations of an "International Year for Indigenous Rights," with an explicit focus on the development process for indigenous peoples.

The Working Group also considered the first revised text of a proposed draft "Universal Declaration on the Rights of Indigenous Peoples" (the draft declaration can be found under the entry **INDIGENOUS PEOPLES**), which had been prepared at its requests by its Chairman-Rapporteur, Mrs. Erica-Irene A. Daes (Greece) (UN Doc. E/CN.4/Sub.2/1989/33) and suggested amendments and additions to it. It recommended that Mrs. Daes be entrusted with the task of preparing a second revised text of the draft declaration based on the comments received in writing by members of the group as well as those made at sessions of the group. The Sub-Commission later endorsed (resolution 1989/34) the recommendations of the Working Group and requested the Secretary-General to transmit the working group's report to governments, indigenous peoples, and intergovernmental and non-governmental organizations for specific comments and proposals for the further elaboration of the revised text of the draft declaration.

***WORKING GROUP ON THE DRAFT BODY OF PRINCIPLES AND GUARANTEES FOR THE PROTECTION OF MENTALLY-ILL PERSONS AND FOR THE IMPROVEMENT OF MENTAL HEALTH CARE.*** At its 1989 session, the UN Commission on Human Rights established an open-ended working group to examine, revise, and simplify as necessary the "Draft Body of Principles and Guarantees for the Protection of Mentally-Ill Persons and for the Improvement of Mental Health Care" (the draft body of principles can be found under the entry **MENTAL HEALTH**), which had been prepared by the Sub-Commission on Prevention of Discrimination and Protection of Minorities after consideration of a report on the subject (UN Doc. E/CN.4/Sub.2/1984/16) prepared by the Sub-Commission's Special Rapporteur, Mrs. Erica-Irene A. Daes (Greece).

The Working Group, open to all members of the Commission, held its first session at the United Nations office in Geneva from 8 to 19 January 1990. The Working Group resumed its work at a second session held in January 1991 and the principles were adopted by the General Assembly 17 December 1991 (resolution 46/109).

***WORKING GROUP ON THE RIGHTS OF PERSONS BELONGING TO NATIONAL, ETHNIC, RELIGIOUS AND LINGUISTIC MINORITIES.*** At its 1978 session, the Commission on Human Rights set up a working group, open to all members of the Commission, to consider the drafting of a declaration on the rights of members of minorities, within the framework of the principles set forth in article 27 of the **International Covenant on Civil and Political Rights.** A draft declaration on the rights of persons belonging to national, ethnic, religious, and linguistic minorities was submitted by Yugoslavia (UN Doc. E/CN.4/L.1367/Rev. 1) and submitted to the Working Group to serve as a basis for discussion.

Open-ended working groups have been established at each subsequent session of the Commission to continue the drafting of the declaration. In 1981, a revised and consolidated text was prepared by the Working Group's chairman/rapporteur.

The Commission decided (resolution 1989/61) that it would establish another open-ended Working Group at its 1990 session to continue consideration of the revised draft declaration proposed by Yugoslavia.

For the text of the Declaration adopted by the General Assembly, see the entry **Minorities' Rights: Declaration on the Rights of Persons belonging to National or Ethnic, Religious and Linguistic Minorities.**

*WORKING GROUP ON THE RIGHT TO DEVELOPMENT.* The Working Group was established by the UN Commission on Human Rights on 11 March 1981 (resolution 35 [XXXVII]), originally to study the scope and contents of the right to **development** and the most effective means to ensure the realization, in all countries, of the economic, social, and cultural rights set out in various international instruments, paying particular attention to the obstacles encountered by developing countries in their efforts to ensure the enjoyment of those rights.

The Working Group consists of fifteen experts nominated by their governments and appointed by the chairman of the Commission on Human Rights for an indeterminate term of office. It normally convenes for a session of approximately three weeks, before or during the annual session of the Commission, at the United Nations office in Geneva.

For several years after its establishment, the Working Group concentrated on the preparation of the Declaration on the Right to Development. This phase of its work culminated in the adoption and proclamation of the Declaration by the UN General Assembly on 4 December 1986 (resolution 41/128). At that time, the Assembly and the Commission were in agreement that the Working Group should be continued to consider matters relating to the implementation of the provisions of the Declaration. Under this new mandate, the group has since held annual open-ended sessions in which all members of the Commission may participate.

By its resolution 1993/22, the Commission on Human Rights decided to establish, initially for a three-year period, a new Working Group on the Right to Development, composed of fifteen experts nominated by governments to be appointed by the Chairman of the Commission on Human Rights at its forty-ninth session, on the basis of equitable geographical representation and in consultation with the regional groups in the Commission, with the following mandate:

(a) To identify obstacles to the implementation and realization of the Declaration on the Right to Development, on the basis of information furnished by Member States and other appropriate sources;

(b) To recommend ways and means towards the realization of the right to development by all States.

The **Vienna World Conference on Human Rights,** which adopted the Vienna Declaration and Programme of Action on 16 June 1993, urged the Working Group to formulate promptly, for early consideration by the United Nations General Assembly, comprehensive and effective measures to eliminate obstacles to the implementation and realization of the Declaration on the Right to Development and to recommend ways and means toward the realization of the right to development by all States.

The newly reconstituted Working Group, which held its first session from 8 to 19 November 1993, submitted its report on its first session to the fiftieth session of the Commission on Human Rights (E/CN.4/1994/21 and Corr.1 and 2). By its resolution 1994/11, the Commission on Human Rights requested the Working Group to pay particular attention in its deliberations to the social repercussions of the policies adopted to face situations of external debt on the effective enjoyment of economic, social, and cultural rights.

In a recent report (E/CN.4/1995/11, paras. 77–94), the Working Group on the Right to Development recommended that the international community continue its efforts toward making the right to development operational, taking into account the variety of obstacles listed in the corresponding chapter of its report, particularly in the light of some of the grave consequences caused by recent changes in the world economy. It also recommended that the process of consultations with international agencies, programs, and bodies of the United Nations system, governments, and other concerned agents continue on the basis of the guidelines and checklists set out in the first report of the Working Group, and that agencies which have not responded in those terms be encouraged to do so. The following paragraphs are the conclusions and recommendations from that report (paras. 79–94):

The right to development highlights the indivisibility and universality of human rights, be they civil and political, or economic, social and cultural. In its implementation, one should therefore avoid making sharp distinctions between different categories of internationally recognized human rights.

The Working Group has noted that international agencies have not incorporated in their mandates the principles set out in the Declaration on the Right to Development. The Group recommends that the United Nations system take the necessary measures for the Declaration on the Right to Development to be incorporated in all their programmes.

In giving emphasis to the human rights aspect of development, and to make this right operational, there is a need, among other things, to encourage Governments to establish indicators by which to evaluate progress made in the realization of this right with, eventually, ways in which remedies can be sought in the event of lack of progress for particular groups. That these indicators must take into account the different conditions within individual countries, as well as differences between countries at a given stage of their development, are issues to be taken up in discussions with, among others, the treaty bodies.

The Working Group took note of the World Plan of Action on Education for Human Rights and Democracy adopted by the UNESCO International Congress on Education for Human Rights and Democracy (Montreal, Canada, 8–11 March 1993), and proposed that more information be requested with a view to studying the possibilities offered by the Plan of Action for the implementation of the right to development by the specialized agencies.

While the questions of development are approached either sectorally or thematically by a wide variety of agencies and programmes, only the Committees established under the two Covenants hold States responsible for the implementation of the rights to which they have subscribed by adhering to international treaties.

These international implementation procedures should be strengthened. In this context, particular attention should be paid to the International Covenant on Economic, Social and Cultural Rights. Any progress in implementing economic, social and cultural rights, and any step taken by the international community to make those rights more effective, would help to further the implementation of the Declaration on the Right to Development. The Working Group considers that greater political will should be demonstrated for the better implementation of economic, social and cultural rights.

The Working Group expects the High Commissioner for Human Rights to multiply efforts in order to ensure that all international agencies and bodies within the system pay the most serious attention to the need to make the right to development operational.

The implementation of the Declaration on the Right to Development is a collective responsibility of the United Nations system as a whole, implying greater coordination of strategies and programmes, more effective cooperation in the field, permanent consultation among the specialized agencies, and improved circulation of information between them.

In order to facilitate the coordination needed for concerted implementation of the Declaration on the Right to Development, it would be desirable for each agency to establish, assign special responsibility to or develop an administrative unit for that purpose.

Since the right to development implies an integrated approach to political, social, economic and cultural rights as a whole, care should be taken to avoid dissociating the eco-nomic and monetary aspects of development from its social aspects and to enhance the dialogue between international social and humanitarian agencies and international institutions responsible for financial and trade questions.

The Governments of Member States have a contribution to make to strengthening the role of the United Nations system in implementing the Declaration on the Right to Development, for which purpose they should see to it that the resolutions they have adopted in the United Nations General Assembly and the Economic and Social Council set objectives for the various specialized agencies which are at the same time global, precise and achievable.

It would be desirable for international financing for development to encourage the implementation of the right to development, bearing in mind the indivisibility and interdependence of its component elements. Hence the need for criteria taking account of that indivisibility and interdependence of human rights and for greater transparency in the distribution of development support funds.

The globalization of the economy increases the responsibility of the international community in regard to the implementation of the Declaration on the Right to Development. Ways and means of strengthening international cooperation and solidarity need to be explored. The establishment of new rules governing international trade relations cannot by itself protect the interests of the developing countries, and it is therefore necessary to enhance international dialogue to this effect. In particular, efforts should be made to ensure that developing countries do not lag behind as a result of new rules governing international trade relations.

The Working Group intends to pursue its exchanges of views with the Chairpersons of the various human rights treaty bodies, in order to envisage common methods for the evaluation of progress made by local, national, regional and international institutions in the implementation of the right to development.

The economic aspects of development seem to receive preference from funding bodies and donors over social aspects. Development assistance is not apportioned among specialized international agencies according to objective criteria related to the basic needs of individuals and population groups; the requirements of growth, production and productivity seem to win out over considerations that would make the human person "the central subject of development" as called for in article 2 of the Declaration on the Right to Development.

The consideration of the programmes and activities of the international institutions and specialized agencies show how far the globalization of the economy seems to be the most important change of our era, one in whose light the application of the Declaration on the Right to Development today needs to be studied. The increasingly clear consequences of this globalization of the economy are a reduction in States' room to manoeuvre and the ever more relative nature of their influence on the enjoyment of the right to development. At the same time, international cooperation seems more and more essential to the universal enjoyment of this right. The corollary to the globalization of the economy, then, is a strengthening of solid, productive international fellow-feeling; otherwise the application of the Declaration on the Right to Development will be, if not in vain, then at least an inadequate exercise.

***WORKING GROUP TO EXAMINE SITUATIONS WHICH APPEAR TO REVEAL A CONSISTENT PATTERN OF GROSS VIOLATIONS OF HUMAN RIGHTS.*** The Working

Group, established by the Commission on Human Rights at its 1974 session (decision 3 [XXX]), examines the particular situations referred to the Commission under resolution 1503 (XLVIII) of the UN Economic and Social Council, including those transmitted by confidential resolution of the Sub-Commission on Prevention of Discrimination and Protection of Minorities.

The Working Group first met prior to the Commission's 1975 session and submitted its recommendations confidentially to the Commission. A similar working group was set up each year since then. Meetings of the Working Group are closed to the public. They are normally held during the one-week period immediately prior to the Commission's annual session. The Working Group's reports are communicated confidentially to the Commission.

In 1974, the Commission decided (decision 3 [XXX]) that the governments concerned should thenceforth be invited to submit written observations relating to the particular situations which had been referred to the Commission. In 1978, it decided (decision 5 [XXXIV]) to issue invitations, during the first week of each session, to the States directly concerned, asking them to send representatives to address the Commission and to answer any questions put to them by its members. In 1979, it decided (decision 14 [XXXV]) to authorize its working groups in the future to communicate the text of the relevant recommendations as soon as possible to the governments directly concerned in order to facilitate their participation in the examination of the situations concerning their countries. In 1980, it decided (decision 9 [XXXVI]) that the States invited to attend the closed meetings of the Commission under Council resolution 1503 (XLVIII) should have the right to attend and to participate in the entire discussion of the situation concerning them and to be present during the adoption of the final decision taken in regard to that situation.

The Working Group consists of five members of the Commission, one from each of five regions: Africa, Asia, Latin America, eastern Europe, and western Europe and others. Before the end of each session of the Commission, its chairman announces, after consultations with the regional groups, the names of the members designated to serve in their personal capacity on the Working Group at the forthcoming session.

**BIBLIOGRAPHY.** Atchebro, Daniel, and Anthony Breaux. " 'Child Slavery' Exposed at the United Nations Working Group on Contemporary Forms of Slavery," *Peoples for Human Rights: IMADR Yearbook* 3 (1991): 39–53. Article, in English.

Barsh, Russel Lawrence. "The Right to Development as a Human Right: Results of the Global Consultation," *Human Rights Quarterly* 13, no. 3 (Aug. 1991): 322–338. Scholarly article, in English.

Brody, Reed. "The UN Working Group on Enforced or Involuntary Disappearances," *Peoples for Human Rights: IMADR Yearbook* 3 (1991): 30–38. Article, in English.

Gromacki, Joseph P. "The Protection of Language Rights in International Human Rights Law: A Proposed Draft Declaration of Linguistic Rights," *Virginia Journal of International Law* 32, no. 2 (Winter 1992): 515–579. Scholarly article, in English.

Newman, Frank, and David Weissbrodt. *International Human Rights: Law, Policy, and Process.* Cincinnati, OH, USA: Anderson Publishing, 1990. Educational material, in English; bibliography, pp. 733–762.

Sill, Marc A., and Glenn T. Morris. *Indigenous Peoples' Politics: An Introduction.* Denver, CO, USA: Fourth World Center for the Study of Indigenous Law and Politics, University of Colorado at Denver, 1993. Textbook, in English.

Torres, Raidza. "The Rights of Indigenous Populations: The Emerging International Norm," *The Yale Journal of International Law* 16, no. 1 (Winter 1991): 127–175. Scholarly article, in English.

## UNITED NATIONS CHILDREN'S FUND (UNICEF).

The United Nations International Children's Emergency Fund, established by the **GENERAL ASSEMBLY** on 11 December 1946 (resolution 57 [I]), has since been utilized for the benefit of children and adolescents of countries and territories which were victims of aggression. Its assistance is provided on the basis of need, without discrimination on the ground of race, creed, national status, or political belief. In 1953, the Assembly decided to continue the Fund indefinitely; it changed its title to the United Nations Children's Fund but retained the acronym UNICEF. In 1965, UNICEF was awarded the **NOBEL PEACE PRIZE.**

From 1956 to 1982, UNICEF was governed by an executive board consisting of 30 members elected by the **ECONOMIC AND SOCIAL COUNCIL.** In April 1982, the General Assembly enlarged the board to 41 members selected with the following geographic distribution: (1) nine seats for African States; (2) nine seats for Asian States; (3) four seats for eastern European States; (4) six seats for Latin American States; (5) 12 seats for western European and other States; and (6) one seat to be rotated among the five regional groups in the following order: (a) African States, (b) Latin American States, (c) Asian States, (d) western European and other States, and (e) eastern European States.

The UNICEF board usually meets once a year, in New York, for approximately ten days. At each session, the board establishes a "Programmer Committee" and a "Committee on Administration and Finance." Its reports are directed through the Economic and Social Council to the General Assembly.

UNICEF. Address: UNICEF House, 3 UN Plaza, New York, NY 10017, USA. Telephone: (212) 326-7000. Executive Director: James P. Grant.

# U

**UNITED NATIONS EDUCATIONAL, SCIENTIFIC AND CULTURAL ORGANIZATION (UNESCO).** By its constitution, which entered into force on 4 November 1946, UNESCO was established as an autonomous permanent intergovernmental organization with the basic purpose of contributing to peace and security "by promoting collaboration among the nations through education, science and culture in order to further universal respect for justice, for the rule of law and for the human rights and fundamental freedoms which are affirmed for the peoples of the world, without distinction of race, sex, language or religion, by the Charter of the United Nations."

To realize this goal, UNESCO is mandated to:

(a) collaborate in the work of advancing the mutual knowledge and understanding or peoples, through all means of mass communication and to that end recommend such international agreements as may be necessary to promote the free flow of ideas by word and image;

(b) give fresh impulse to popular education and to the spread of culture:

by collaborating with Members, at their request, in the development of educational activities;

by instituting collaboration among the nations to advance the ideal of equality of educational opportunity without regard to race, sex or any distinctions, economic or social;

by suggesting educational methods best suited to prepare the children of the world for the responsibilities of freedom;

(c) maintain, increase and diffuse knowledge:

by assuring the conservation and protection of the world's inheritance of books, works of art and monuments of history and science, and recommending to the nations concerned the necessary international conventions;

by encouraging co-operation among the nations in all branches of intellectual activity, including the international exchange of persons active in the fields of education, science and culture and the exchange of publications, objects of artistic and scientific interest and other materials of information;

by initiating methods of international co-operation calculated to give the people of all countries access to the printed and published materials produced by any of them....

Under the terms of the agreement between the United Nations and UNESCO, which entered into force on 14 December 1946, UNESCO transmits to the UN regular reports on its activities and complies to the fullest extent practicable with any request which the UN may make for the furnishing of special reports, studies, or information.

A total of 161 States are members of UNESCO; they include all UN member States with the exception of Djibouti, Solomon Islands, South Africa, the United States of America (which withdrew from membership on 31 December 1984), and Vanuatu; and seven non-member States of the UN—the Democratic People's Republic of Korea, the Republic of Korea, Monaco, Namibia (represented by the UN Council for Namibia), San Marino, Switzerland, and Tonga.

All States members of UNESCO are represented in the UNESCO General Conference, which determines policies and establishes programs of work for the organization. The UNESCO Executive Board, which is responsible for the execution of the programs, consists of 51 members elected by the conference from among the delegates appointed by the member States, together with the president of the conference who sits *ex officio* in an advisory capacity. The UNESCO Secretariat is headed by the Director-General, who in his capacity as chief executive officer of the organization appoints and directs its staff.

The ultimate aim in all sectors of UNESCO's activities—education, science, culture, and communication—is to safeguard human rights and peace. Even those activities which are not explicitly designed to develop respect for human rights in general, or to secure the implementation of specific rights or freedoms, serve, nevertheless, to create the material, intellectual, moral, and cultural conditions necessary if human rights are to become a living reality—rather than an aspiration—for everyone.

*UNESCO EXECUTIVE BOARD.* Established in accordance with article 3 of its constitution, the Executive Board currently consists of 51 members, each representing the government of the State of which he is a national, elected by the General Conference from among the delegates appointed by the member States. The president of the General Conference sits on the board *ex officio* in an advisory capacity. The board's composition and functions are set out in detail in the constitution (article 5).

*UNESCO SECRETARIAT.* Established in accordance with article 3 of the UNESCO constitution, the Secretariat consists of the Director-General and the staff which he appoints and directs. The responsibilities of the Director-General and of the staff are exclusively international in character and are set out in the constitution (article 6).

*UNESCO GENERAL CONFERENCE.* Established in accordance with article 3 of the UNESCO constitution, the Conference consists of representatives of the States members of the organization. Its main task is to determine the policies and program of work of the organization. Its composition, functions, and procedures are set out in detail in the constitution (article 4).

*UNESCO INTERNATIONAL LITERACY PRIZES.* There are currently five prizes, awarded annually, designed to intensify the fight for literacy through lifelong education and to reward the service of institutions, organizations, and individuals who have achieved results in fighting illiteracy. The five prizes are the Nadezhda

K. Krupskaya Prize, the International Reading Association Literacy Award, the Noma Prize, the Iraq Literacy Prize, and the King Sejong Literacy Prize.

Governments of UNESCO member States and nongovernmental organizations whose primary concern is education and who have consultative status with UNESCO may each nominate one candidate. Selection is made by the UNESCO Director-General.

Among past recipients are the following:

*Nadezhda K. Krupskaya Prize.* Adult Basic Education Society, Quranwala of Pakistan (1991); and People's Government of Xiping County, Henan Province of the Peoples's Republic of China (1990).

*International Reading Association Literacy Award.* UNESCO Co-Action Learning Centre Movement, Japan (1991); and Universidad Central del Este, Dominican Republic (1990).

*Noma Prize.* State Government of West Bengal, India (1991); and Institute of the Brothers of the Christian Schools (1990).

*Iraq Literacy Prize.* Accion Popular, Venezuela (1991); and General Directorate of Non-Formal Education, Cape Verde (1990).

*King Sejong Literacy Prize.* University of Ghana (1991); and Kerala Sastra Sahithya Parishad Trivandrum, India (1990).

For more information, contact: UNESCO, 7 Place de Fontenoy, 75700 Paris, France. Telephone: (33-1) 45-68-10-00.

**UNESCO PRIZE FOR PEACE EDUCATION.** Established in 1978, the UNESCO Prize is awarded biennially to educational institutions, organizations, or individuals who have worked to develop the teaching of human rights. The nominees must be nationals of, or institutions or organizations having their headquarters in, member States of UNESCO. The honoree receives $10,000. Among recent recipients were Vaclav Havel, president of Czechoslovakia and playwright (1990); Ms. Madeleine De Vits of Belgium and the Graduate Institute for Peace Studies of the Republic of Korea (1993); and the Venerable Prayudh Payutto of Thailand (1994).

For more information, contact: UNESCO, 7 Place de Fontenoy, 75700, Paris, France, 07-SP. Telephone: (33-1) 45-68-38-14. Fax: (33-1) 40-65-98-71.

**BIBLIOGRAPHY.** World Federation of UNESCO Clubs, Centres and Associations. *UNESCO and Human Rights.* Paris: UNESCO, 1989. IGO edited collection, in English.

# UNITED NATIONS EDUCATIONAL, SCIENTIFIC AND CULTURAL ORGANIZATION: CONSTITUTION (1945).

The constitution of UNESCO was adopted on 16 November 1945 by the Conference for the Establishment of an Educational, Scientific and Cultural Organization of the United Nations, convened in London by the Governments of France and Great Britain, and entered into force on 4 November 1946.

The purpose of UNESCO, a specialized agency of the United Nations, as stated in the constitution (article 1), is "to contribute to peace and security by promoting collaboration among the nations through education, science and culture in order to further universal respect for justice, for the rule of law and for human rights and fundamental freedoms which are affirmed for the peoples of the world, without distinction of race, sex, language or religion, by the Charter of the United Nations."

UNESCO's functions include collaboration in the work of advancing the mutual knowledge and understanding of peoples through all means of mass communication; giving fresh impulse to popular education and to the spread of culture; and maintaining, increasing, and diffusing knowledge through international cooperation.

The text of the constitution (United Nations, *Treaty Series,* vol. 4, p. 275), as amended by the UNESCO General Conference at its 2nd–10th, 12th, 15th, 17th, and 19th–21st sessions, is as follows:

The Governments of the States Parties to this Constitution on behalf of their peoples declare:

That since wars begin in the minds of men, it is in the minds of men that the defences of peace must be constructed;

That ignorance of each other's ways and lives has been a common cause, throughout the history of mankind, of that suspicion and mistrust between the peoples of the world through which their differences have all too often broken into war;

That the great and terrible war which has now ended was a war made possible by the denial of the democratic principles of the dignity, equality and mutual respect of men, and by the propagation, in their place, through ignorance and prejudice, of the doctrine of the inequality of men and races;

That the wide diffusion of culture, and the education of humanity for justice and liberty and peace are indispensable to the dignity of man and constitute a sacred duty which all the nations must fulfill in a spirit of mutual assistance and concern;

That a peace based exclusively upon the political and economic arrangements of governments would not be a peace which could secure the unanimous, lasting and sincere support of the peoples of the world, and that the peace must therefore be founded, if it is not to fail, upon the intellectual and moral solidarity of mankind.

For these reasons, the States Parties to this Constitution, believing in full and equal opportunities for education for all, in the unrestricted pursuit of objective truth, and in the free exchange of ideas and knowledge, are agreed and determined to develop and to increase the means of communication between their peoples and to employ these means for the purposes of mutual understanding and a truer and more perfect knowledge of each other's lives;

In consequence whereof they do hereby create the United

Nations Educational, Scientific and Cultural Organization for the purpose of advancing, through the educational and scientific and cultural relations of the peoples of the world, the objectives of international peace and of the common welfare of mankind for which the United Nations Organization was established and which its Charter proclaims.

*Article 1. Purposes and Functions.* 1. The purpose of the Organization is to contribute to peace and security by promoting collaboration among the nations through education, science and culture in order to further universal respect for justice, for the rule of law and for the human rights and fundamental freedoms which are affirmed for the peoples of the world, without distinction of race, sex, language or religion, by the Charter of the United Nations.

2. To realize this purpose the Organization will:

(a) Collaborate in the work of advancing the mutual knowledge and understanding of peoples, through all means of mass communication and to that end recommend such international agreements as may be necessary to promote the free flow of ideas by word and image;

(b) Give fresh impulse to popular education and to the spread of culture by collaborating with Members, at their request in the development of educational activities; by instituting collaboration among the nations to advance the ideal of equality of educational opportunity without regard to race, sex or any distinctions, economic or social; [and] by suggesting educational methods best suited to prepare the children of the world for the responsibilities of freedom;

(c) Maintain, increase and diffuse knowledge by assuring the conservation and protection of the world's inheritance of books, works of art and monuments of history and science, and recommending to the nations concerned the necessary international conventions; by encouraging co-operation among the nations in all branches of intellectual activity, including the international exchange of persons active in the fields of education, science and culture and the exchange of publications, objects of artistic and scientific interest and other materials of information; [and] by initiating methods of international co-operation calculated to give the people of all countries access to the printed and published materials produced by any of them.

3. With a view to preserving the independence, integrity and fruitful diversity of the cultures and educational systems of the States Members of the Organization, the Organization is prohibited from intervening in matters which are essentially within their domestic jurisdiction.

*Article 2. Membership.* 1. Membership of the United Nations Organization shall carry with it the right to membership of the United Nations Educational, Scientific and Cultural Organization.

2. Subject to the conditions of the Agreement between this Organization and the United Nations Organization, approved pursuant to Article 10 of this Constitution, States not Members of the United Nations Organization may be admitted to membership of the Organization, upon recommendation of the Executive Board, by a two-thirds majority vote of the General Conference.

3. Territories or groups of territories which are not responsible for the conduct of their international relations may be admitted as Associate Members by the General Conference by a two-thirds majority of Members present and voting, upon application made on behalf of such territory or group of territories by the Member or other authority having responsibility for their international relations. The nature and extent of the rights and obligations of Associate Members shall be determined by the General Conference.

4. Members of the Organization which are suspended from the exercise of the rights and privileges of membership of the United Nations Organization shall, upon the request of the latter, be suspended from the rights and privileges of this Organization.

5. Members of the Organization which are expelled from the United Nations Organization shall automatically cease to be Members of this Organization.

6. Any Member State or Associate Member of the Organization may withdraw from the Organization by notice addressed to the Director-General. Such notice shall take effect on 31 December of the year following that during which the notice was given. No such withdrawal shall affect the financial obligations owed to the Organization on the date the withdrawal takes effect. Notice of withdrawal by an Associate Member shall be given on its behalf by the Member State or other authority having responsibility for its international relations.

*Article 3. Organs.* The Organization shall include a General Conference, an Executive Board and a Secretariat.

*Article 4. The General Conference: A. Composition.* 1. The General Conference shall consist of the representatives of the States Members of the Organization. The Government of each Member State shall appoint not more than five delegates, who shall be selected after consultation with the National Commission, if established, or with educational, scientific and cultural bodies.

*B. Functions.* 2. The General Conference shall determine the policies and the main lines of work of the Organization. It shall take decisions on programmes submitted to it by the Executive Board.

3. The General Conference shall, when it deems desirable and in accordance with the regulations to be made by it, summon international conferences of States on education, the sciences and humanities or the dissemination of knowledge; non-governmental conferences on the same subjects may be summoned by the General Conference or by the Executive Board in accordance with such regulations.

4. The General Conference shall, in adopting proposals for submission to the Member States, distinguish between recommendations and international conventions submitted for their approval. In the former case a majority vote shall suffice; in the latter case a two-thirds majority shall be required. Each of the Member States shall submit recommendations or conventions to its competent authorities within a period of one year from the close of the session of the General Conference at which they were adopted.

5. Subject to the provisions of Article 5, paragraph 5 (c), the General Conference shall advise the United Nations Organization on the educational, scientific and cultural aspects of matters of concern to the latter; in accordance with terms and procedure agreed upon between the appropriate authorities of the two Organizations.

6. The General Conference shall receive and consider the reports sent to the Organization by Member States on the action taken upon the recommendations and conventions referred to in paragraph 4 above or, if it so decides, analytical summaries of these reports.

7. The General Conference shall elect the members of the Executive Board and, on the recommendation of the Board, shall appoint the Director-General.

*C. Voting.* 8. (a) Each Member State shall have one vote in the General Conference. Decisions shall be made by a simple majority except in cases in which a two-thirds majority is required by the provisions of this Constitution, or the

Rules of Procedure of the General Conference. A majority shall be a majority of the Members present and voting.

(b) A Member State shall have no vote in the General Conference if the total amount of contributions due from it exceeds the total amount of contributions payable by it for the current year and the immediately preceding calendar year.

(c) The General Conference may nevertheless permit such a Member State to vote, if it is satisfied that failure to pay is due to conditions beyond the control of the Member Nation.

*D. Procedure.* 9. (a) The General Conference shall meet in ordinary session every two years. It may meet in extraordinary session if it decides to do so itself or if summoned by the Executive Board, or on the demand of at least one-third of the Member States.

(b) At each session the location of its next ordinary session shall be designated by the General Conference. The location of an extraordinary session shall be decided by the General Conference if the session is summoned by it, or otherwise by the Executive Board.

10. The General Conference shall adopt its own rules of procedure. It shall at each session elect a President and other officers.

11. The General Conference shall set up special and technical committees and such other subordinate bodies as may be necessary for its purposes.

12. The General Conference shall cause arrangements to be made for public access to meetings, subject to such regulations as it shall prescribe.

*E. Observers.* 13. The General Conference, on the recommendation of the Executive Board and by a two-thirds majority may, subject to its rules of procedure, invite as observers at specified sessions of the Conference or of its Commissions representatives of international organizations, such as those referred to in Article 11, paragraph 4.

14. When consultative arrangements have been approved by the Executive Board for such international non-governmental or semi-governmental organizations in the manner provided in Article 11, paragraph 4, those organizations shall be invited to send observers to sessions of the General Conference and its Commissions.

*F. Transitional Provision.* 15. Notwithstanding the provisions of paragraph 9 (a) of this Article, the General Conference shall hold its twenty-second session in the third year following its twenty-first session.

*Article 5. Executive Board: A. Composition.* 1. The Executive Board shall be elected by the General Conference from among the delegates appointed by the Member States and shall consist of fifty-one members each of whom shall represent the Government of the State of which he is a national. The President of the General Conference shall sit *ex officio* in an advisory capacity on the Executive Board.

2. In electing the members of the Executive Board the General Conference shall endeavour to include persons competent in the arts, the humanities, the sciences, education and the diffusion of ideas, and qualified by their experience and capacity to fulfil the administrative and executive duties of the Board. It shall also have regard to the diversity of cultures and a balanced geographical distribution. Not more than one national of any Member State shall serve on the Board at any one time, the President of the Conference excepted.

3. Members of the Board shall serve from the close of the session of the General Conference which elected them until the close of the second ordinary session of the General Con-

ference following that election. They shall not be immediately eligible for a second term. The General Conference shall, at each of its ordinary sessions, elect the number of members required to fill vacancies occurring at the end of the session.

4. (a) In the event of the death or resignation of a member of the Executive Board, his replacement for the remainder of his term shall be appointed by the Executive Board on the nomination of the Government of the State the former member represented.

(b) The Government making the nomination and the Executive Board shall have regard to the factors set forth in paragraph 2 of this Article.

(c) When exceptional circumstances arise, which, in the considered opinion of the represented State, make it indispensable for its representative to be replaced, even if he does not tender his resignation, measures shall be taken in accordance with the provisions of sub-paragraph (a) above.

*B. Functions.* 5. (a) The Executive Board shall prepare the agenda for the General Conference. It shall examine the programme of work for the Organization and corresponding budget estimates submitted to it by the Director-General in accordance with paragraph 3 of Article 6 and shall submit them with such recommendations as it considers desirable to the General Conference.

(b) The Executive Board, acting under the authority of the General Conference, shall be responsible for the execution of the programme adopted by the Conference. In accordance with the decisions of the General Conference and having regard to circumstances arising between two ordinary sessions, the Executive Board shall take all necessary measures to ensure the effective and rational execution of the programme by the Director-General.

(c) Between ordinary sessions of the General Conference, the Board may discharge the functions of adviser to the United Nations, set forth in Article 4, paragraph 5, whenever the problem upon which advice is sought has already been dealt with in principle by the Conference, or when the solution is implicit in decisions of the Conference.

6. The Executive Board shall recommend to the General Conference the admission of new Members to the Organization.

7. Subject to decisions of the General Conference, the Executive Board shall adopt its own rules of procedure. It shall elect its officers from among its members.

8. The Executive Board shall meet in regular session at least twice a year and may meet in special session if convoked by the Chairman on his own initiative or upon the request of six members of the Board.

9. The Chairman of the Executive Board shall present, on behalf of the Board, to each ordinary session of the General Conference, with or without comments, the reports on the activities of the Organization which the Director-General is required to prepare in accordance with the provisions of Article 6.3(b).

10. The Executive Board shall make all necessary arrangements to consult the representatives of international organizations or qualified persons concerned with questions within its competence.

11. Between sessions of the General Conference, the Executive Board may request advisory opinions from the International Court of Justice on legal questions arising within the field of the Organization's activities.

12. Although the members of the Executive Board are representative of their respective Governments they shall ex-

ercise the powers delegated to them by the General Conference on behalf of the Conference as a whole.

*C. Transitional Provisions.* 13. Notwithstanding the provisions of paragraph 3 of this Article,

(a) Members of the Executive Board elected prior to the seventeenth session of the General Conference shall serve until the end of the term for which they were elected.

(b) Members of the Executive Board appointed, prior to the seventeenth session of the General Conference, by the Board in accordance with the provisions of paragraph 4 of this Article to replace members with a four-year term shall be eligible for a second term of four years.

*Article 6. Secretariat.* 1. The Secretariat shall consist of a Director-General and such staff as may be required.

2. The Director-General shall be nominated by the Executive Board and appointed by the General Conference for a period of six years, under such conditions as the Conference may approve, and shall be eligible for reappointment. He shall be the chief administrative officer of the Organization.

3. (a) The Director-General, or a deputy designated by him, shall participate, without the right to vote, in all meetings of the General Conference, of the Executive Board, and of the Committees of the Organization. He shall formulate proposals for appropriate action by the Conference and the Board, and shall prepare for submission to the Board a draft programme of work for the Organization with corresponding budget estimates.

(b) The Director-General shall prepare and communicate to Member States and to the Executive Board periodical reports on the activities of the Organization. The General Conference shall determine the periods to be covered by these reports.

4. The Director-General shall appoint the staff of the Secretariat in accordance with staff regulations to be approved by the General Conference. Subject to the paramount consideration of securing the highest standards of integrity, efficiency and technical competence, appointment to the staff shall be on as wide a geographical basis as possible.

5. The responsibilities of the Director-General and of the staff shall be exclusively international in character. In the discharge of their duties they shall not seek or receive instructions from any Government or from any authority external to the Organization. They shall refrain from any action which might prejudice their positions as international officials. Each State Member of the Organization undertakes to respect the international character of the responsibilities of the Director-General and the staff, and not to seek to influence them in the discharge of their duties.

6. Nothing in this Article shall preclude the Organization from entering into special arrangements within the United Nations Organization for common services and staff and for the interchange of personnel.

*Transitional Provision.* 7. Notwithstanding the provisions of paragraph 2 of this Article, the Director-General nominated by the Executive Board and appointed by the General Conference in 1980 shall serve for a term of seven years.

*Article 7. National Co-operating Bodies.* 1. Each Member State shall make such arrangements as suit its particular conditions for the purpose of associating its principal bodies interested in educational, scientific and cultural matters with the work of the Organization, preferably by the formation of a National Commission broadly representative of the Government and such bodies.

2. National Commission or National Co-operating Bodies, where they exist, shall act in an advisory capacity to their respective delegations to the General Conference and to their Governments in matters relating to the Organization and shall function as agencies of liaison in all matters of interest to it.

3. The Organization may, on the request of a Member State, delegate, either temporarily or permanently, a member of its Secretariat to serve on the National Commission of that State, in order to assist in the development of its work.

*Article 8. Reports by Member States.* Each Member State shall submit to the Organization, at such times and in such manner as shall be determined by the General Conference, reports on the laws, regulations and statistics relating to its educational, scientific and cultural institutions and activities, and on the action taken upon the recommendations and conventions referred to in Article 4, paragraph 4.

*Article 9. Budget.* 1. The Budget shall be administered by the Organization.

2. The General Conference shall approve and give final effect to the budget and to the appointment of financial responsibility among the States Members of the Organization subject to such arrangement with the United Nations as may be provided in the agreement to be entered into pursuant to Article 10.

3. The Director-General, with the approval of the Executive Board, may receive gifts, bequests, and subventions directly from Governments, public and private institutions, associations and private persons.

*Article 10. Relations with the United Nations Organization.* This Organization shall be brought into relation with the United Nations Organization, as soon as practicable, as one of the Specialized Agencies referred to in Article 57 of the Charter of the United Nations. This relationship shall be effected through an agreement with the United Nations Organization under Article 63 of the Charter, which agreement shall be subject to the approval of the General Conference of this Organization. The agreement shall provide for effective co-operation between the two Organizations in the pursuit of their common purposes, and at the same time shall recognize the autonomy of this Organization, within the fields of its competence as defined in this Constitution. Such agreement may, among other matters, provide for the approval and financing of the budget of the Organization by the General Assembly of the United Nations.

*Article 11. Relations with Other Specialized International Organizations and Agencies.* 1. This Organization may co-operate with other specialized intergovernmental organizations and agencies whose interests and activities are related to its purposes. To this end the Director-General, acting under the general authority of the Executive Board, may establish effective working relationships with such organizations and agencies and establish such joint committees as may be necessary to assure effective co-operation. Any formal arrangements entered into with such organizations or agencies shall be subject to the approval of the Executive Board.

2. Whenever the General Conference of this Organization and the competent authorities of any other specialized intergovernmental organizations or agencies whose purpose and functions lie within the competence of this Organization deem it desirable to effect a transfer of their resources and activities to this Organization, the Director-General, subject to the approval of the Conference, may enter into mutually acceptable arrangements for this purpose.

3. This Organization may make appropriate arrangements with other intergovernmental organizations for reciprocal representation at meetings.

4. The United National Educational, Scientific and Cul-

tural Organization may make suitable arrangements for consultation and co-operation with non-governmental international organizations concerned with matters within its competence, and may invite them to undertake specific tasks. Such co-operation may also include appropriate participation by representatives of such organizations on advisory committees set up by the General Conference.

*Article 12. Legal Status of the Organization.* The provisions of Articles 104 and 105 of the Charter of the United Nations Organization concerning the legal status of that Organization, its privileges and immunities, shall apply in the same way to this Organization.

*Article 13. Amendments.* 1. Proposals for amendments to this Constitution shall become effective upon receiving the approval of the General Conference by a two-thirds majority; provided, however, that those amendments which involve fundamental alterations in the aims of the Organization or new obligations for the Member States shall require subsequent acceptance on the part of two-thirds of the Member States before they come into force. The draft texts of proposed amendments shall be communicated by the Director-General to the Member States at least six months in advance of their consideration by the General Conference.

2. The General Conference shall have power to adopt by a two-thirds majority rules of procedure for carrying out the provisions of this Article.

*Article 14. Interpretation.* 1. The English and French texts of this Constitution shall be regarded as equally authoritative.

2. Any question or dispute concerning the interpretation of this Constitution shall be referred for determination to the International Court of Justice or to an arbitral tribunal, as the General Conference may determine under its rules of procedure.

*Article 15. Entry into Force.* 1. This constitution shall be subject to acceptance. The instrument of acceptance shall be deposited with the Government of the United Kingdom.

2. This Constitution shall remain open for signature in the archives of the Government of the United Kingdom. Signature may take place either before or after the deposit of the instrument of acceptance. No acceptance shall be valid unless preceded or followed by signature.

3. This Constitution shall come into force when it has been accepted by twenty of its signatories. Subsequent acceptances shall take effect immediately.

4. The Government of the United Kingdom will inform all Members of the United Nations of the receipt of all instruments of acceptance and of the date on which the Constitution comes into force in accordance with the preceding paragraph. In faith whereof, the undersigned, duly authorized to that effect, have signed this Constitution in the English and French languages, both texts being equally authentic.

Done in London the sixteenth day of November, one thousand nine hundred and forty-five, in a single copy, in the English and French languages, of which certified copies will be communicated by the Government of the United Kingdom to the Governments of all the Members of the United Nations.

# UNITED NATIONS ENVIRONMENT PROGRAM (UNEP).

An intergovernmental organization established in 1972 by the UN GENERAL ASSEMBLY (resolution 2997 [XXVII]) as an outgrowth of the United Nations Conference on the Human Environment, held in Stockholm earlier that year.

UNEP is directed by a Governing Body composed of 58 UN member States, elected by the General Assembly for a three-year term of office. With the assistance of a network of more than 100 stations for monitoring pollution of the atmosphere and at least 10 for recording daily changes in the environment, the program identifies, assesses, and monitors major environmental problems and provides warnings of significant environmental problems, risks, and opportunities to all concerned. Its particular concern is the impact of national and international environmental policies and measures on the developing countries. Among its main areas of activity are desertification, the disposal of potentially toxic wastes, protection of the right of every human being to a clean environment, and the conservation of nature and wildlife in all parts of the world. Among UNEP's priorities is "Earthwatch," a program to identify relevant environmental issues and provide data as a basis for effective environmental management. The three main components of Earthwatch are the Global Environmental Monitoring System (which monitors, measures, and interprets selected environmental variables, such as climate and health), the International Referral System (a worldwide register of sources of environment information), and the International Register of Potentially Toxic Chemicals (which supplies background information on the scientific, socioeconomic, and regulatory aspects of such chemicals).

The program is financed entirely by the voluntary contributions of UN member States. The governing body, which administers the UNEP fund, allocates the available funds on a regional basis. That body also administers smaller trust funds established to protect the environment of particular areas, such as the Regional Trust Fund for the Protection of the Mediterranean Sea and the Regional Trust Fund for the Protection of West and Central Africa.

UNEP. Address: P.O. Box 30552, Gigiri, Nairobi, Kenya. Telephone: (254-2) 333930. Cable: UNITERRA NAIROBI. Telex: 22068-22173. Executive Director: Dr. Mostafa K. Tolba.

# UNITED NATIONS HUMAN RIGHTS PRIZES.

At its seventy-fourth plenary meeting, held on 10 December 1993, the UN GENERAL ASSEMBLY, in accordance with its resolution 2217 (XVI) of 19 December 1966 and Assembly decisions 47/429 of 18 December 1992 and 48/410A of 7 December 1993, awarded prizes to Bassib Ben Ammer (Tunisia), Erica Daes (Greece), James Grant (U.S.A.), International Commission of Jurists, Medical Personnel of the Central Hospital of Sarajevo (Bosnia and Herzegovina), Sonia Picado Sotela (Costa Rica), Ganesh Man Singh (Nepal), Sudanese Women's Union (Sudan), and Father Julio Tumiri Javier (Bolivia), for outstanding contributions to the promotion and protection of human rights.

## UNITED NATIONS INDUSTRIAL DEVELOPMENT ORGANIZATION (UNIDO).

Based in Vienna, Austria, UNIDO is the UN agency that specializes in promoting and accelerating industrialization in developing countries. Through technical cooperation, policy advice, investment promotion, and technical support, UNIDO assists both governments and the public and private sector. Its services are avilable to developing countries and to countries in transition to a market economy wishing to strengthen their industrial base.

Established on 1 January 1967 by the UN **GENERAL ASSEMBLY** (resolution 2152 [XXI] of 17 November 1966), UNIDO became the UN's 16th specialized agency in 1985, with the mandate to act as the central coordinating body for industrial activities within the UN system and to promote industrial development and cooperation at global, regional, national, and sectoral levels.

Although it responds to industrial development needs and support requirements in all developing regions, UNIDO places special emphasis upon the industrialization of the developing countries in Africa, the majority of which are far behind those of the rest of the developing world in their economic and social advancement.

*WOMEN AND DEVELOPMENT.* As regards women in industrial development, UNIDO's main efforts are directed at helping women to meet the challenges of industrial restructuring, technological changes, and economic reforms by procedures that recognize women as full actors and equal partners in the target groups of UNIDO's own activities and programs, which are oriented to address the needs of women as well as men.

Developing women's skills facilitates their access and mobility within systems of education, training, and technology; and within occupations in industry itself. UNIDO promotes multi-skill training in higher management and technology fields to enable women to keep pace with changes in the industrialization process. It develops training programs to enhance the nature and extent of participation of women at decision-making and middle-management levels in development finance institutions and industrial companies. These programs feature industrial project preparation, evaluation, financing, and investment promotion. Other training packages support entrepreneurship programs for women running small and micro-enterprises in different industrial subsectors. A new program featuring training of women entrepreneurs and managers, and training of trainers, in the context of industrial modernization aims to increase participation of women in the industrial SME sector of countries making the transition to market economies.

UNIDO. Address: Vienna International Centre, P.O. Box 300, A-1400 Vienna, Austria. Telephone: (43-1) 211-310. Fax: (43-1) 232-156. Acting Director-General: Louis Alexandrenne.

## UNITED NATIONS INSTITUTE FOR TRAINING AND RESEARCH (UNITAR).

UNITAR was established in 1965 pursuant to a decision taken by the UN **GENERAL ASSEMBLY** at its 1963 session (resolution 1934 [XVIII]) as an autonomous institution within the framework of the United Nations system. Its basic purpose is to enhance the effectiveness of the United Nations in achieving its major objectives—in particular, the maintenance of peace and security and the promotion of economic and social development—through appropriate training and research programs. Its activities include the preparation of studies of UN problems, function, and structures and the organization of training courses for senior officials of the United Nations system and of governments. Although the Institute has dealt with human rights problems only occasionally, it participated actively in the observance of the Decade for Action to Combat Racism and Racial Discrimination and published a comprehensive study entitled *Racism and its Elimination,* prepared by one of its special fellows, Sir Rupert John (St. Vincent and the Grenadines) (UN publication, Sales no. E.81.15.ST/18).

An international board of trustees, appointed by the UN Secretary-General in consultation with the president of the General Assembly and the president of the **ECONOMIC AND SOCIAL COUNCIL,** is the policymaking organ for the Institute. The executive director is appointed by the Secretary-General after consultation with the board of trustees. Mr. Michel Doo Kingué has served as UNITAR's executive director since 1 January 1983.

In recent years, the Institute has experienced difficulty in determining its future role and in establishing long-term financing arrangements. In December 1988, the General Assembly noted with concern (resolution 43/201) that the 1988 UN Pledging Conference for Development Activities had not provided the Institute with the level of resources required to maintain a minimum training program and institutional structure. In the resolution, the Assembly reaffirmed the continuing validity of the Institute's mandate and requested the Secretary-General to present to it, in 1990, his recommendations on the future of the Institute, together with detailed financial information.

UNITAR. Address: 801 UN Plaza, Rm. U-212, New York, NY 10017, USA. Telephone: (212) 754-8621. Fax: (212) 697-8660. Executive Director: Michel Doo Kingué.

## UNITED NATIONS STANDARD MINIMUM RULES FOR THE ADMINISTRATION OF JUVENILE JUSTICE ("BEIJING RULES") (1985). See JUVENILE JUSTICE: STANDARD MINIMUM RULES FOR THE ADMINISTRATION OF JUVENILE JUSTICE, UN.

**UNITED NATIONS UNIVERSITY.** A system of academic institutions established by the UN **GENERAL ASSEMBLY** on 11 December 1972 (resolution 2951 [XXVII]), consisting of a programming and coordinating central organ and a decentralized system of affiliated institutions, integrated into the world University economy and devoted to action-oriented research into the pressing global problems of human survival, development, and welfare, as well as to the postgraduate training of young scholars and research workers for the benefit of the world community.

The University center is located in Tokyo, Japan. It unites a global network of institutions and scholars and has established its own research and training centers in various parts of the world. Capital and recurrent costs are met entirely from voluntary contributions by governmental and non-governmental sources and are allocated by the University Council, which is composed of 24 members appointed jointly by the UN Secretary-General and the Director-General of UNESCO for terms of six years. The rector of the University is a member of the Council, appointed for a term of five years by the UN Secretary-General in consultation with the Director-General of UNESCO. He is assisted by a university center in planning, coordinating, and administering the overall program.

Between 1977 and 1981, the University focused its attention on problems of global significance: world hunger, human and social development, and the use and management of natural resources. From 1982 onwards, five priority themes have predominated: (1) peace security, conflict resolution, and global transformation; (2) global economy; (3) hunger, poverty, resources, and environment; (4) human and social development and co-existence of peoples, cultures, and social systems; and (5) science and technology and their social and ethical implications. Under the Human Development Project, which examines the impact of development change on the welfare and rights of individuals, families, groups, and communities, the

following activities relating to the realization of human rights are under way (UN Doc. A/43/31, paras. 90–97):

*Perceptions of Desirable Societies in Different Religious and Ethical Systems.* The view of religious thinkers on contemporary issues is increasingly influential, and often may provide insights on how development might proceed in harmony with the values deeply held in a society. Three sections of this project dealing with Christianity, Islam and Buddhism have been completed and the resulting collections of papers are being edited for publication. Participants in the study on Hinduism met in Delhi in March to discuss the specific approaches of Hinduism to social issues, including its critique of modernity and the practical idealism represented in such movements as Sarvodaya and Svadhyay. A number of papers were Commissioned following the meeting.

Two conferences were held at Tokyo on subjects relating to the project in 1987. In April, a symposium on "The future of mankind and co-operation among religions" discussed the forms and possibilities of inter-religious co-operation. A seminar on "Science, technology and spiritual values: an Asian approach to modernization" took place in May. It provided a reflection on the contribution of religions to the critique of modern societies, from an Asian perspective.

*Economic Aspects of Human Development.* Research continued on five topics: alternative development experiences; development paradigms and the economy-culture interface; alternative epistemologies and methodologies; foundations of economics and alternative development; and obstacles to development: the case of Argentina (1945–1985). A meeting was held at Geneva in June, where papers on the first three topics were presented and discussed. The project's main ideas and conclusions were presented at the North-South Round-table on "Managing human development" which was sponsored by the United Nations Development Programme (UNDP) at Bucharest in September.

*The Global Impact of Human Migration.* Data gathered from 400–500 migrant workers from seven Asian countries to the Arab world form the empirical base for this study. The data base has been computerized at the Marga Institute in Sri Lanka, where it is available for further research and retrieval. Country studies derived from this collection were edited and reviewed for publication in 1987. Further analytical and conceptual papers on the political and socio-cultural aspects of migration were completed, along with a case study of immigration to France. A survey of research on migration by the United Nations and other international agencies was also prepared, covering three topics: the formulation of international policies, conventions and regulations governing migration; technical assistance for problems of migration, including refugees; and other issues relating to migration.

The United Nations University also acted as an associate executing agency, in co-operation with the International Labour Organisation (ILO), of a research programme on the "Enhancement of household capacity in the post-migration phase". This is a subprogramme of the Asian Regional Programme on International Labour Migration, which is funded by UNDP. A workshop in Bangkok in December brought together researchers from Bangladesh, India, the Republic of Korea, Pakistan, the Philippines, Sri Lanka and Thailand to review final reports of data from each country on approximately 50 households of returned migrant workers. Several manuscripts are also being prepared for publication.

*Ethnic Minorities and Human and Social Development.* The products of this project include a computerized World Guide to Ethnic Minorities, which is being centralized at El Colegio de México in Mexico City. Data have been collected thus far on more than 800 ethnic groups. Co-operating institutions around the world have provided inputs in return for access to the data bank. The Guide includes items on the principal social, economic and cultural characteristics of each minority, as well as information on major economic and political problems arising from relations with other ethnic groups or with the state. Reference is also included to international dimensions where they exist.

An international seminar on the "New faces of racism", held at Amsterdam in October, dealt with tensions among different ethnic groups in the industrialized countries of Western Europe. It was co-sponsored by the United Nations University, International Alert, the Swedish Ombudsman for Race Relations, and the Mayor of Amsterdam. A second seminar, held at Kampala in September, scrutinized "Ethnic conflicts and human rights in East Africa" and was co-sponsored by International Alert and the Makerere Institute of Social Research with the participation of the United Nations University. Several manuscripts are also being prepared for publication.

*Human Rights and Scientific and Technological Development.* In 1986, the United Nations Commission on Human Rights invited the United Nations University to conduct a study on the positive and negative effects of scientific and technological developments on human rights and fundamental freedoms. A proposal was drawn up, and research papers were Commissioned.

A workshop was convened in July 1989 to agree on a research plan. The final report was expected to be ready in February 1991. The University stated (E/CN.4/1990/29) that it would not, therefore, be possible to provide a report for consideration by the COMMISSION ON HUMAN RIGHTS at its 46th session, held in February 1990.

United Nations University. Address: Toho Seimei Building, 15-1 Shibuya-ku, Tokyo 150, Japan. Telephone: (03) 499-2811. Cable: CUNATUNIV TOKYO. Telex: J 25442 UNATUNIV. Rector: Prof. Soedjatmoko.

**UNITED NATIONS VOLUNTEERS.** This non-governmental organization was established in 1970. Its members are adult volunteer-specialists from 110 countries who work for economic and social progress in 116 different countries. The volunteers work within a community for two years as middle- and upper-level specialists in such fields as agriculture, forestry, education, and economic development planning and administration. The group implements the "Domestic Development Service Program," which supports economic and social development at the grassroots level. United Nations Volunteers publishes the semi-annual *UNV Spectrum* in English, French, and Spanish; the annual *Serving Abroad* in English, French, and Spanish;

and the quarterly *International Volunteer Day News* in English and French.

United Nations Volunteers. Address: Palais des Nations, Ch-1211, Geneva 10, Switzerland. Telephone: (22) 788-2455. Fax: (22) 788-2501. Executive Coordinator: Brenda Gael McSweeney.

**UNITED STATES OF AMERICA.** A country of the North American continent, lying between the Atlantic Ocean on the east and the Pacific Ocean on the west, the United States includes, in addition to its continental area, the states of Alaska and Hawaii and has borders with Canada to the north and Mexico to the south. It declared its independence from Great Britain on 4 July 1776. In 1945, it became a member of the United Nations and has since acted as host to UN headquarters in New York City.

The population of the United States is estimated to be 256,420,000. In addition to the English-speaking, white Christian majority, there are more than 25 million black Americans, many descended from slaves transported involuntarily from Africa and the Caribbean before—and even after—the slave trade was prohibited by law in 1807; 7 million Jews; 2 million Puerto Ricans; 2 million indigenous American Indians; and several million immigrants or refugees from such countries as Austria, China, Germany, Ireland, Italy, Japan, Mexico, the Philippines, Poland, and the Soviet Union. The language in common use is English; however, recent immigrants tend to adhere to their national language within their own communities. Christianity (more than 50 million Catholics and 73 million Protestants) and Judaism (more than 7 million) are the predominant religions. Literacy is estimated at 99%.

The government (1994) took the form of a federal republic. Under the constitution, there are three coordinate branches of government: the executive, the legislative, and the judicial. The powers allocated to each branch are so interlinked that none can function entirely independently of the others. The legislature makes the law, the executive branch enforces it, and the judiciary interprets it through cases and controversies that it is called upon to settle. It is this interrelationship that ensures the enjoyment of the rights laid down in the constitution but also extends them to meet the changing demands of a modern, complex society.

*BRANCHES OF GOVERNMENT.* The legislative branch, which makes the law, consists of a bicameral congress composed of a 435-member House of Representatives and a 100-member Senate. The number of members from each state in the House of Representatives is proportionate to the population of that state; members are elected by the state's voters for two-year terms of office. The number of members from each state in the Senate is two, regardless of the population of the state; members are elected by the state's voters for six-year terms of office, one-third of the total membership retiring every two years unless re-elected.

The judicial branch, which interprets the law, is independent and its members, appointed by the president with the advice and consent of the Senate, serve for life and cannot be removed except for treason, bribery, or other high crimes. The Supreme Court reviews cases from the lower federal courts and certain cases originating in state courts involving questions of federal law. It has the power to invalidate any federal or state law or executive action which it finds contrary to provisions of the constitution.

There are 12 federal courts of appeal and 89 federal trial courts, each with from 1 to 27 judgeships. There are also special federal courts, such as the U.S. Claims Court, to deal with specialized problems arising under federal statutes. The courts handle civil as well as criminal cases. Persons convicted of penal offenses may be confined in prison or in an institution, fined, or both, or in the case of drug addicts may be committed to hospitals for treatment.

The executive branch, which enforces the law, is headed by the president who functions both as head of State and of government, and also as commander-in-chief of the armed forces. The vice president has no established function other than to serve *ex officio* as president of the Senate but may succeed the president in office if the latter dies or is seriously disabled. The president is limited to two four-year terms of office.

*GOVERNMENTAL AGENCIES DEVOTED TO CIVIL RIGHTS.* Within the executive branch, the Civil Rights Division of the Department of Justice is responsible for enforcing federal civil rights laws that prohibit discrimination on the basis of race, national origin, religion, and, in some cases, sex or handicap, in the areas of voting, education, employment, housing, credit, the use of public facilities and public accommodations, and in the administration of federally assisted programs. Among the congressional standards which it enforces are the Civil Rights Acts of 1957, 1960, 1964, and 1968; the Voting Rights Act of 1965; the Equal Educational Opportunities Act of 1974; the Equal Credit Opportunity Act of 1976; and the Civil Rights of Institutionalized Persons Act of 1980. It also has the obligation to enforce specific criminal statutes, including those concerning willful deprivation of constitutional rights under color of law or through conspiracy, involuntary servitude, and violent interference with federally protected activities. A special section of the division concentrates on protecting the rights of indigenous American Indians while another, the Sex

Discrimination Task Force, reviews all federal policies, programs, and procedures with a view to eliminating discrimination against women and obtaining appropriate corrective action.

An independent agency, the Equal Employment Opportunity Commission, established in accordance with the Civil Rights Act of 1964, enforces that act by examining charges and complaints of job discrimination based on race, color, religion, sex, or national origin by private employers, state and local governments, and educational institutions with 15 or more employees, or by the federal government, private and public employment agencies, labor organizations, and joint labor-management committees for apprenticeship and training. The commission first endeavors to remedy the unlawful practices through informal methods of conciliation, conference, and persuasion. If it concludes that judicial action is necessary to carry out the purposes of the act, the commission—or the attorney-general in a case involving a governmental agency or political subdivision—may bring an action for appropriate relief pending final disposition of a charge.

A second independent agency, the Commission on Civil Rights, established by the Civil Rights Act of 1957 and re-established by the United States Commission on Civil Rights Act of 1983, collects and studies information on discrimination or denials of equal protection of the laws because of race, color, religion, sex, age, handicap, national origin, or in the administration of justice in such areas as voting rights, enforcement of federal civil rights laws, and equality of opportunity in education, employment, and housing. It makes findings of fact but has no enforcement authority. Its findings and recommendations are submitted to the president and to Congress, and many of its recommendations have been enacted either by statute, executive order, or regulation. The commission also evaluates federal laws and the effectiveness of government equal opportunity programs and serves as a clearinghouse for information on civil rights.

Within the Department of State, the Bureau of Human Rights and Humanitarian Affairs is responsible for the formulation and development and—in cooperation with other bureaus—the implementation of U.S. policy relating to the observance of human rights throughout the world. The bureau maintains liaison with non-governmental organizations active in the field of human rights and is principally responsible for the preparation of the annual State Department report on human rights practices in countries that are members of the United Nations or receive U.S. economic or military assistance. In addition, the bureau provides the department's advice to the Immigration and Naturalization Service regarding applications for political asylum by foreign nationals.

These safeguards notwithstanding, human rights and fundamental freedoms are not always enjoyed by everyone residing in the United States of America. For example, during World War II, more than 112,000 Americans of Japanese descent were interned or relocated from their homes in the western part of the country; and it was only in 1988 that the government acknowledged the wrongful act and awarded reparations to those who had suffered from it. Implementation of section 105 of the Civil Liberties Act of 1988, which provides restitution, is in the hands of the Civil Rights Division.

During the "McCarthy era" of the 1950s, so-called after Sen. Joseph McCarthy of Wisconsin, then chair of the Senate Committee on Un-American Activities, thousands of Americans suspected of having ties to the Communist Party were harassed by congressional investigative committees and federal "loyalty boards," and denied employment, the right to leave the country, and other rights on the spurious ground of "guilt by association."

More recently, the U.S. Supreme Court has upheld the use of the death penalty, even against the mentally retarded and immature juveniles, and has moved to review decades of political decisions aimed at protecting freedom of speech, separation of Church and State, and the rights of women including the right to choose an abortion in certain circumstances. However, as indicated above, none of the three coordinate branches of government can function entirely independent of the others; and actions by the judiciary are subject to concurrence or reversal by the executive or the legislative branches, or by both. Thus, for example, the U.S. Congress in mid-1990 took up a proposed Civil Rights Act of 1990 designed specifically to overturn five 1989 Supreme Court decisions that had made it harder for workers to bring and win employment discrimination cases and easier for employers to challenge court-ordered civil rights actions.

***RECENT LAWS.*** The early 1990s saw the ratification by the United States of several international treaties on human rights such as the **INTERNATIONAL COVENANT ON CIVIL AND POLITICAL RIGHTS** and Convention on the Prevention and Punishment of the Crime of Genocide (see **GENOCIDE**), and passage of legislation protecting people's rights, including the Americans with Disabilities Act, the Violence against Women Act, the Civil Rights Act, and the Freedom of Access to Clinic Entrances Act, the latter following the murder of several doctors and abortion clinic employees by abortion opponents.

However, laws were also passed that diminished people's rights. One such example was the anti-terrorism legislation passed shortly after a bomb killed 167 people in a federal building in April 1995. One such provision expanded authority to wiretap, with only one warrant, multiple telephone lines allegedly used by a suspect. Sentences of imprisonment were lengthened in both the federal and state criminal justice systems and mandatory minimum prison sentences were applied more broadly and more frequently.

Although the Supreme Court reversed some protection for minorities and women under rules of **AFFIRMATIVE ACTION,** making it more difficult to uphold such programs, its opinions were generally protective of **FREEDOM OF OPINION AND EXPRESSION** and **FREEDOM OF THOUGHT, CONSCIENCE AND RELIGION.** And although hate-filled expression alone was considered protected speech, physical harm accompanied by hateful words against women or minorities, so-called "hate crimes," were allowed to carry enhanced penalties.

***TERRITORIES.*** The Government of the United States of America retained, or assumed, responsibility for the administration of several non-self-governing territories shortly after the establishment of the United Nations, including the trust territory of the Pacific Islands, American Samoa, Guam, and the U.S. Virgin Islands. In accordance with the **UNITED NATIONS CHARTER,** it is now in the process of establishing the independence of those territories.

The trust territory of the Pacific Islands consists of three archipelagos: the Marshall Islands, the Carolines, and the Marianas. Although in the Marianas, the island of Guam is not a part of the trust territory.

On 28 May 1986, the UN **TRUSTEESHIP COUNCIL** adopted resolution 2183 (LIII), by which it noted that the peoples of the Northern Mariana Islands, the Marshall Islands, the Federated States of Micronesia, and Paulau had freely exercised their right to **SELF-DETERMINATION** in plebescites observed by visiting missions of the Council. They had chosen free association with the United States in the case of the Marshall Islands, the Federated States of Micronesia, and Paulau, and commonwealth status in the case of the Northern Marianas. The Council concluded that the United States Government had satisfactorily discharged its obligations under the trusteeship agreement and that the agreement should be terminated.

With regard to Guam, the UN **GENERAL ASSEMBLY** on 22 November 1988 reaffirmed (resolution 43/42), as it had on earlier occasions, the inalienable right of its people to self-determination and independence and called upon the U.S. Government to expedite the process of decolonization in accordance with the expressed wishes of the people of the territory.

With regard to American Samoa, the assembly likewise reaffirmed (resolution 43/43) the inalienable right of the people to self-determination and independence and called upon the U.S. Government to expedite the process of decolonization. It also reaffirmed the responsibility of the administering power, under the Charter, to promote the economic and social development of American Samoa and called upon it to intensify its efforts to strengthen and diversify the economy of the territory. In particular, it urged the administering power and the territorial government to take effective measures to safeguard and guarantee the inalienable right of the people of American Samoa to own and dispose of the natural resources of the territory, including marine resources, and to establish and maintain control over the future development of those resources.

With regard to the question of the U.S. Virgin Islands, the UN General Assembly on 22 November 1988 welcomed (resolution 43/44) the enactment of legislation, in March 1988, providing for a referendum to be held in November 1989 on options available for the territory's future status, i.e., statehood, independence, free association, incorporated territory, *status quo,* commonwealth, or compact of federal relations. The Assembly reaffirmed that it is ultimately for the people of the U.S. Virgin Islands themselves to determine their future political status in accordance with the relevant provisions of the Charter of the United Nations and the relevant resolutions of the General Assembly; and, in that connection, called upon the administering power, in cooperation with the territorial government, to facilitate programs of political education in the territory in order to foster an awareness among the people of the possibilities open to them in the exercise of their right of self-determination.

Guam, American Samoa, and the U.S. Virgin Islands each has a local legislature, acts of which are subject to modification or annulment by the U.S. Congress.

Puerto Rico has enjoyed limited self-government since 1952, when it attained the status of a commonwealth and its people began to elect their governor and other officials. However, the federal government remains responsible for its foreign relations, and a number of federal agencies continue to operate there.

The right of the people of Puerto Rico to self-determination and independence was considered by the UN Special Committee on the Situation with Regard to the Implementation of the Declaration on the Granting of Independence to Colonial Countries and Peoples (see **SELF-DETERMINATION**) in February 1989, on the basis of a report prepared by its rapporteur (UN Doc. A/AC.109/L.1703). After examining the report and devoting several meetings to hearing delegations, observers, and representatives of more than 50 interested organizations, the Special Committee on 17 August 1989 adopted a resolution in which

it reaffirmed (UN Doc. A/AC.109/L.1703) the inalienable right of the people of Puerto Rico to self-determination and independence, in conformity with General Assembly resolution 1514 (XV), and the full applicability of the fundamental principles of that resolution with respect to Puerto Rico.

The Special Committee expressed its hope, and that of the international community, that, in any consultations, Puerto Rico may exercise without hindrance its right to self-determination and independence, with the express recognition of the people's sovereignty and full political equality, in accordance with para. 5 of General Assembly resolution 1514 (XV). It requested its rapporteur to report in 1990 on the implementation of this and other resolutions concerning Puerto Rico and decided to retain the question on its agenda for further consideration.

Later in the year, the UN General Assembly considered the question of the U.S. Virgin Islands. On 11 December 1989, it took note (resolution 44/99) of the statement of the representative of the United States of America, as the administering power, that the participation of the people of the territory in the electoral process demonstrated that they exercised responsibility for local government and local political affairs, and that the policy of the United States was to respond to the wishes of the people regarding their future political status whenever they indicated the direction in which they wished to proceed.

In the resolution, the Assembly reaffirmed the inalienable right of the people of the U.S. Virgin Islands to self-determination and independence in conformity with the Declaration on the Granting of Independence to Colonial Countries and Peoples, and pointed out that it is the responsibility of the United States of America, as the administering power, to continue to create such conditions in the U.S. Virgin Islands as will enable the people of the territory to exercise that right freely and without interference. It called upon the United States to continue to take all necessary measures, in cooperation with the territorial government, to counter problems related to drug trafficking and to facilitate participation in various international and regional organizations. And it urged member States and organizations of the United Nations system to extend all assistance with a view to rehabilitating and reconstructing the territory devastated by hurricane Hugo.

*SPECIAL RAPPORTEUR ON RACISM AND RACIAL DISCRIMINATION.* The following are conclusions and recommendations (paras. 111–112) on the existence of racism and racial discrimination in the United States from a special report to the UN **HUMAN RIGHTS COMMITTEE:**

As he comes to the end of his investigation, the Special Rapporteur believes he can say that racism and racial discrimination persist in American society, even if not as a result of a deliberate policy on the part of the United States Government.

The Special Rapporteur found sociological inertia, structural obstacles and individual resistance hindering the emergence of an integrated society based on the equal dignity of the members of the American nation and willing to accept ethnic and cultural pluralism. Vested interests, competing influences and the power struggle between the various political and social components of American society also provide opportunities for residual racism and racial discrimination to linger on. Accordingly, the Special Rapporteur makes the following recommendations to the United States Government:

(a) It should be explicitly acknowledged that 30 years of intense struggle against racism and racial discrimination have not yet made it possible to eliminate the consequences of over 300 years of slavery and racial discrimination, particularly where African Americans are concerned.

(b) It should be recognized that when persons from ethnic minorities aspire to equal treatment, they are not asking for favours, but seeking to enjoy the rights guaranteed by the United States Constitution in their daily lives by virtue of their status as full citizens or lawful residents.

(c) Affirmative action programmes should be revitalized in order to offset the negative consequences of the policy pursued during the fields of health, housing, education and employment.

(d) Measures should be taken to prohibit the establishment of racist organizations and ban racist propaganda.

(e) Measures should be taken to abolish the death penalty, or failing that, to eliminate discriminatory application of the penalty.

(f) The Government, in conjunction with the State authorities, should ensure that the police do not use violence against persons belonging to ethnic or racial minorities; Congress should adopt laws to permit the criminal prosecution of police officers who use excessive force under the guise of enforcing the law.

(g) Effective, and in particular financial, support should be provided for organizations which combat racism and racial discrimination and which work for and contribute to peaceful coexistence between the different communities.

(h) Measures should be taken to eliminate racial discrimination against women from ethnic minorities, particularly in terms of employment, wages and access to health care.

(i) In the sphere of education, measures should be taken to increase funding for public schools and to ensure the equitable distribution of funds.

(j) The media should be encouraged to refrain from propagating stereotypes and to devote themselves to educating the public by disseminating the principles of human rights.

(k) Everyone must be persuaded to accept the existence of the indissoluble link between civil and political rights and the economic, social and cultural rights which are their natural corollary. Consequently, the Special Rapporteur urges the United States Government to ratify all the international human rights conventions, as a means of strengthening its foreign policy credibility.

(l) In addition, there should be more vigorous action on behalf of human rights education, in particular for law-enforcement officials. Such a step would promote greater acceptance of one another by the members of the different communities who live in the United States and would encourage sharing between them in the economic and social or even the cultural spheres. To assume fully, and in a genuine democracy, the cultural pluralism which characterizes the American nation is a challenge which the United States is undoubtedly capable of taking up.

*EXECUTION OF JUVENILE OFFENDERS.* The **INTER-AMERICAN COMMISSION ON HUMAN RIGHTS,** in its annual report for 1986–1987 (OAS Doc. OEA/Ser.L/V/II.71, Doc. 9, Rev. 1, chap. III), set out a series of resolutions regarding specific cases presented to it which the Commission had processed in accordance with the applicable legal provisions.

Resolution 3/87 relates to case 9647 (United States), in which the Government of the United States of America is alleged to have denied the internationally protected right to life to James Terry Roach and Jay Pinkerton by condemning them to death and executing them for crimes committed while they were under the age of eighteen. The issue presented by the case was the following: Does the absence of a federal prohibition on the execution of juvenile offenders within U.S. domestic law violate the human rights standards applicable to the United States under the Inter-American system?

The Commission's conclusion was—by five votes to one—that the United States Government had violated article 1 (right to life) and article 2 (right to equality before the law) of the **AMERICAN DECLARATION OF THE RIGHTS AND DUTIES OF MAN** in executing James Terry Roach and Jay Pinkerton.

Resolution 3/87 and the dissenting opinion of one member of the Commission are as follows (*Ibid.,* pp. 148–183):

### I. Introduction

*A. Summary of the Facts and the Petitioners' Complaint.* 1. The Petitioners are James Terry Roach and Jay Pinkerton who were sentenced to death and executed in the United States for crimes which they were adjudged to have committed, and which they perpetrated before their eighteenth birthdays.

2. The Petitioners are represented by David Weissbrodt and Mary McClymont. The American Civil Liberties Union and the International Human Rights Law Group have co-sponsored the complaint. Amnesty International also filed a petition with the Commission alleging that the imminent execution of James Terry Roach, while lawful in the United States, is a violation of international law. Eighteen organizations have communicated to the Commission their support of the complaint.

3. James Terry Roach was convicted of the rape and murder of a fourteen-year-old girl and the murder of her seventeen-year-old boyfriend. Roach committed these crimes at the age of seventeen and was sentenced to death in the General Session Court, Richland County, South Carolina on 16 December 1977. Roach petitioned the United States Supreme Court for a writ of certiorari on three separate occa-

sions. All petitions were denied. Roach also exhausted all appeals to the state and federal courts, and on 10 January 1986 he was executed.

4. Jay Pinkerton was convicted of murder and attempted rape which he committed at the age of seventeen. The death sentence was appealed to the Texas Supreme Court which affirmed the trial court's decision. The United States Supreme Court denied Pinkerton's writ of certiorari on 7 October 1985. Pinkerton was executed on 15 May 1986.

5. On 23 February 1987, the U.S. Supreme Court announced that it would decide in its next term the case of *Thompson v. Oklahoma,* thereby, for the first time, taking up the issue of the execution of juvenile offenders. The constitutional issue presented is whether the execution of a juvenile offender violates the U.S. Constitution's prohibition on cruel and unusual punishment.

6. In their complaint to the Commission, the petitioners allege that the United States has violated Article I (right to life), Article VII (special protection of children), and Article XXVI (prohibition against cruel, infamous or unusual punishment) of the American Declaration of the Rights and Duties of Man by executing persons for crimes committed before their eighteenth birthday. The Petitioners allege a violation of their right to life guaranteed under the American Declaration, as informed by customary international law, which prohibits the execution of persons who committed crimes under the age of eighteen.

*B. Proceedings Before the Commission.* 7. The petition on behalf of James Terry Roach was filed with the Commission on 4 December 1985 and registered as Case No. 9647 (United States). Jay Pinkerton's petition was registered with the Commission on 8 May 1986 following the setting of the date for his execution.

8. In both the case of Roach and of Pinkerton, the Commission cabled the United States Secretary of State, George P. Shultz, and the respective Governor of the Petitioner's state, requesting a stay of execution pending the Commission's examination and decision of Case No. 9647. The Commission stated in each telegram that its request for information did not prejudge the admissibility of the case in accordance with Article 34 of the Commission's Regulations.

9. Petitioner Roach had sought provisional relief measures under Article 29 of the Commission's Regulations. On 12 December 1985, the Chairman of the Commission cabled Secretary of State, George P. Shultz, and South Carolina Governor, Richard W. Riley, requesting a stay of execution pending the Commission's examination of the case. The Chairman stated that granting such a stay of execution would "be in the spirit of major human rights instruments and the universal trend favorable to the abolition of the death penalty." The Commission also requested that the U.S. Government provide information concerning the Petitioner's complaint.

10. On 23 December 1985 the Executive Secretary of the Commission cabled the United States Government with additional information relating to the date of Roach's execution scheduled for 10 January 1986 and stressed the necessity of receiving a response by that date. The Commission also reiterated its previous request to stay the execution of the Petitioner. Another cable was sent to the Secretary of State with a stay of execution request on 6 January 1986.

11. On 9 January 1986 the U.S. State Department replied. It stated that: "Under the circumstances, with respect to the Commission's request that the execution be stayed pending consideration of the case, the United States is constrained to reply that the matter is now in the hands of authorities for the State of South Carolina and, under the U.S. federal

system, there are no domestic legal grounds for executive intervention in the implementation of the sentence."

12. On 9 January 1986 the Secretary General of the Organization of American States cabled an appeal to the Governor of South Carolina to "follow the current tendency of almost all the countries in this hemisphere and to stay the execution."

13. On 9 January 1986, Governor Riley of South Carolina responded to the cables requesting a stay of execution by informing the Executive Secretary of his decision not to intervene in the case of James Terry Roach. The Governor stated that he had reviewed the case thoroughly and believed that the case had been "fairly litigated at the trial level and that all of his appeals in the courts have been given full and fair consideration." As a result, he found "no reason to intervene in the judicial process or to grant a request for clemency."

14. On 20 February 1986, the lawyers for the Petitioners filed a brief on Case No. 9647 with the Commission, setting forth their legal arguments pertaining to the case.

15. On 8 April 1986, the Petitioners requested that additional information compiled by Amnesty International on comparative national laws which proscribe the execution of persons under the age of eighteen around the world be incorporated by reference into the Petitioners' brief.

16. On 26 March 1986, the United States requested an extension of time until 28 August 1986 in order to respond fully to the issues raised by the Petitioners. The Commission at its 67th Session granted the U.S. Government an extension until 1 July 1986 in order to have a draft decision on the case before its next regular session.

17. On 9 May 1986, after having been informed by the Petitioners that Jay Pinkerton was to be executed on 15 May 1986, the Commission cabled the Secretary of State and Governor Mark White of Texas requesting a stay of execution in the case of Jay Pinkerton pending the Commission's examination and decision on Case 9647.

18. The U.S. Government responded on 14 May 1986. It stated that, as in the case of James Terry Roach, "the United States considers that U.S. domestic standards with respect to application of the death penalty are fully consistent with the principles stated in the Declaration," and given the U.S. federal system "there are no domestic legal grounds ( . . . ) for executive intervention in the implementation of Mr. Pinkerton's sentence." The Governor of Texas did not respond to the Commission's request for a stay of execution.

19. On 15 July 1986, the U.S. Government submitted its brief in response to petitioners' brief.

*C. The Final Decision.* 20. This final decision was drawn up by the Commission in accordance with Article 53 of the Regulations of the Inter-American Commission on Human Rights. The text of this final decision was adopted by the Commission on 27 March 1987. The following members were present: Gilda Russomano, President; Marco Tulio Bruni Celli; Oliver H. Jackman; Elsa Kelly; and Luis Adolfo Siles.

This final decision is now transmitted to the parties.

Bruce McColm, a U.S. national, chose not to participate in this decision, pursuant to Article 19 of the Commission's Regulations.

Marco Gerardo Monroy Cabra was not present at the Commission on that date.

## II. The Facts

21. The facts of the present case are not in dispute between the parties.

22. In the present case, the Petitioners allege that the

United States has denied them the internationally protected right to life by condemning them to death and executing them for crimes committed while under the age of eighteen. The issue presented is: Does the absence of a federal prohibition on the execution of juvenile offenders within U.S. domestic law violate the human rights standards applicable to the United States under the Inter-American system?

A. *James Terry Roach.* 23. Petitioner Roach was seventeen years old when he committed the rape and the murder of a fourteen-year-old girl and the murder of her seventeen-year-old boyfriend. Evidence revealed that Roach was borderline mentally retarded, with an I.Q. of between 75 and 80 and that he apparently suffered from Huntington's Chorea, an incurable brain disease. The psychological and medical evidence presented at the April 1980 postconviction proceedings suggest Roach actually functioned at the mental age of twelve when the offense was committed. Roach had two co-defendants. One was another youth of 16 who turned state's evidence and received life imprisonment. The other was J.C. Shaw, a twenty-two-year-old adult, who received the death sentence on 11 January 1985. Evidence showed Roach had been under the adult's influence when the offenses were committed.

24. Jurisdiction of the juvenile court in South Carolina is limited to those under seventeen years of age. Therefore, Roach was sentenced to death in adult criminal court in pursuance of South Carolina's death penalty statute which follows the Georgia statute upheld by the Supreme Court in *Gregg v. Georgia,* 428 U.S. 153 (1976). The South Carolina death penalty statute provides for a bifurcated trial which first considers the guilt or innocence of the defendant, and then upon conviction, a separate sentencing proceeding is conducted to determine whether the defendant is to be sentenced to life imprisonment or death. Roach pleaded guilty to the charges. At the sentencing hearing, the judge heard additional mitigating and aggravating evidence. At least one aggravating circumstance must be found beyond a reasonable doubt before the death sentence may be imposed. South Carolina law has seven statutory aggravating circumstances and nine statutory mitigating circumstances. Among the mitigating factors is that, "The defendant was below the age of 18 at the time of the crime." S.C. Code, 16-3-20 (C)(b)(9).

25. In considering the mitigating factors in the Roach case, the sentencing judge found that Roach had been under the domination of an adult during the commission of the crime. The judge also found that Roach's capacity to conform his conduct to the requirements of the law was substantially impaired, and that he was under the influence of extreme mental or emotional disturbance as he and his co-defendants were "shooting up" drugs and drinking beer before the offense. Another mitigating factor was that Roach had no significant history of prior criminal activity involving the use of violence against another. Roach's mental retardation, anti-social personality disorder, and the fact that he was below the age of 18 at the time of the crime, were also considered by the judge in Roach's sentencing. *Roach v. Martin,* 757 F.2d 1463, 1468-69 (1985).

26. Nevertheless, the sentencing judge also found beyond a reasonable doubt three statutory aggravating circumstances: murder committed while in the commission of rape, murder committed while in the commission of kidnapping, and murder committed while in the commission of robbery. S.C. Code 16-3-20 (C)(a)(1)(a), (c), (e). The judge found the evidence in the case warranted the imposition of the death penalty after weighing both mitigating and aggravating circumstances.

27. This sentence was upheld on direct appeal by the South Carolina Supreme Court. *State v. Shaw (and Roach),* 255 S.E. 2d 799, (1979). (First capital case reviewed under the current death penalty statutes) South Carolina law provides for a mandatory review in the imposition of the death penalty. Roach was later denied post conviction relief by the state trial court and the appeal of this was denied by the State Supreme Court of South Carolina. *Roach v. State,* Memo Op. N 81-MO-197 (S.C. July 17, 1981).

28. Petitioner also sought review of his case from the United States Supreme Court. He challenged as unconstitutional, among other issues, the imposition of the death penalty as being grossly disproportionate and offensive to contemporary standards of decency due to, among other factors, his age when the crime was committed. However, the Supreme Court denied the writ of certiorari. *Roach v. State,* 444 U.S. 1026, *reh'g denied* 444 U.S. 1104 (1980). He again raised the same issue of his age, as being one factor which resulted in the unconstitutionality of the imposition of the death penalty, in another petition for certiorari. This was denied on 25 January 1982. *Roach v. South Carolina,* 455 U.S. 927 (1982).

29. Roach brought a petition for a writ of habeas corpus in the U.S. District Court of South Carolina. This request was also denied. *Roach v. Martin,* Civil Action N 81-1907-14 (May 11, 1984). He appealed this denial, raising again the issue of his age as being a factor prohibiting the imposition of the death penalty. The U.S. Court of Appeals for the Fourth Circuit affirmed the district court's denial of the writ. *Roach v. Martin,* 757 F.2d 1463 (4th Cir. 1983). His final appeal to the United States Supreme Court was denied on 7 October 1985, and the petition for rehearing was denied on 2 December 1985. See, *Roach v. Aiken,* N 85-6155 (A-531). Petitioner Roach was executed in Columbia, South Carolina on 10 January 1986.

B. *Jay Pinkerton.* 30. Petitioner Pinkerton was found guilty of murder in the course of burglary with the intent to commit rape. The crime was committed when he was seventeen years old. Petitioner at seventeen was also beyond the age limit of the jurisdiction of Texas juvenile courts (age 17) and was tried as an adult. He was sentenced to death in accordance with the Texas capital punishment statute which had been upheld by the Supreme Court. *Jurek v. Texas,* 428 U.S. 262 (1976).

31. The Texas death penalty statute currently provides for the imposition of the death sentence only for capital murders. A capital murder is the intentional or knowing killing of a person accompanied by one of five listed aggravating factors. These factors focus on the identity of the victim and the dangerousness of the actor's conduct. Pinkerton was convicted of intentionally committing murder in the course of committing burglary which is one of the statutory aggravating factors defining capital murder. Tex. Code Crim. Proc. Ann., art. 19.03 (a)(2).

32. Conviction of capital murder results in either a mandatory death sentence or life imprisonment. The jury at the sentencing hearing must find beyond a reasonable doubt that (1) the actor killed intentionally or knowingly; (2) he will probably commit other crimes of violence if not executed; and (3) the killing was unreasonable in response to the provocation, if any, of the deceased. To warrant the death sentence all twelve jury members must answer each of these issues affirmatively. The Supreme Court of the United States upheld this Texas statute in *Jurek v. Texas,* 428 U.S. 262 (1976), finding that the second question is interpreted to allow the defendant to bring to the jury's attention what-

ever mitigating circumstances he may be able to show. *Id.* at 272. Therefore, although the statute does not specify age, this may be taken into consideration at the sentencing hearing. Texas law prohibits the imposition of the death penalty on anyone younger than seventeen when the capital felony was committed. Texas C.C.P., 8.07(e).

33. Pinkerton's statutorily provided review was taken to the Court of Criminal Appeals where his conviction and sentence were affirmed. Subsequent federal and state appeals were denied. The United States Supreme Court denied certiorari on 7 October 1985. *Pinkerton v. McCotter,* 88 L.Ed. 2d 158 (1985). Jay Pinkerton was executed by the State of Texas on 15 May 1986.

### III. Submissions of the Parties

*A. The Petitioners.* 34. The Petitioners allege that the imposition of the death penalty on James Terry Roach and Jay Pinkerton by United States courts for crimes committed before their eighteenth birthday violated the American Declaration of the Rights and Duties of Man. Specifically, Petitioners allege violations of Article I (right to life), Article VII (special protection of children), and Article XXVI (cruel, infamous or unusual punishment) of the American Declaration as informed by customary international law which prohibits the imposition of the death penalty for crimes committed by juveniles under eighteen.

35. The Petitioners state that the United States is subject to the jurisdiction of the Commission as a member State of the Organization of American States and is obligated, therefore, to observe the enumerated rights in the American Declaration.

36. The Petitioners' case meets the admissibility requirements of Article 37 of the Commission's Regulations as the Petitioners have exhausted all domestic remedies. United States courts, both federal and state, have failed to address Petitioners' claims that the imposition of the death penalty on juvenile offenders is constitutionally prohibited.

37. The Petitioners' complaint may be summarized as follows:

(a) Imposition of the death penalty on juveniles violates the American Declaration as informed by customary international law.

(b) The United States is legally bound by the American Declaration of the Rights and Duties of Man. The American Declaration should be interpreted according to the canons of the Vienna Convention on the Law of Treaties because the Convention represents a world-wide consensus on how international instruments should be construed.

(c) Articles 31 and 32 of the Vienna Convention set out the principal interpretative norms for treaties and other international instruments. According to Article 31 of the Vienna Convention, the terms of the American Declaration should be interpreted in accordance with their ordinary meaning and in light of the object and purpose of the instrument. Construing Articles I, VII and XXVI together and in accordance with their ordinary meaning, and in light of the object and purpose of the Declaration, these articles should be interpreted to prohibit the execution of persons who committed offenses under the age of 18.

(d) The U.S. Government is incorrect in asserting that the rights in the Declaration "must be interpreted in terms of the intentions of the member states at the time of the adoption of the Declaration, not in terms of changing norms of customary international law." This rigid and static approach to the interpretation of the Declaration is in conflict with the terms of the Declaration, the norms of the Vienna Convention, the normal approach which international bodies take to human rights instruments, the practice of the Commission, and the practice of the United States in its own domestic cases. The preamble to the American Declaration states, "The international protection of the rights of man should be the principal guide of an *evolving* American law. . . ." [Emphasis added].

(e) In construing the terms of the American Declaration in light of its object and purpose, the Commission should pay particular attention to Article XXVI which forbids "cruel, infamous or unusual punishment." This is broader than the United States constitutional prohibition against cruel *and* unusual punishment. Juveniles are recognized as lacking in maturity and are most susceptible to various influences and psychological pressure. Killing a young person who has not had the chance to mature to adulthood is the "ultimate cruel punishment," therefore, Article XXVI should be interpreted as a prohibition against the execution of juveniles. Then, on its ordinary meaning and in light of the object and purpose of these articles, the United States is violating the American Declaration by executing juveniles.

(f) Article 31 of the Vienna Convention also looks to "relevant rules of international law" to help interpret treaties. Therefore, the Commission should take into account the customary international law norm prohibiting the execution of juvenile offenders. This prohibition has obtained the status of customary international law. Pursuant to Article 38(1)(b) of the Statute of the International Court of Justice, "international custom, as evidence of a general practice accepted as law" is one of the sources of international law. Treaties are clearly evidence of State practice, especially if accompanied by *opinio juris,* or claims in the treaty or the *travaux préparatoires* indicating that a treaty provision is a restatement of pre-existing customary laws.

(g) The major human rights instruments such as the American Convention on Human Rights (Article 4(5)), the International Covenant on Civil and Political Rights (Article 6(5)), and the Fourth Geneva Convention prohibit the imposition of the death penalty on persons under eighteen years of age.

Article 4(5) of the American Convention reads: "Capital punishment shall not be imposed upon persons who, at the time the crime was committed, were under 18 years of age or over 70 years of age; nor shall it be applied to pregnant women." The fourth Geneva Convention states in Article 68, in relevant part: "In any case, the death penalty may not be pronounced on a protected person who was under eighteen years of age at the time of the offence."

As of January 1, 1986 there are 162 states parties to this Convention, including the United States. This Convention applies to periods of international armed conflict and Article 68 forbids the execution of civilians and military personnel no longer in combat, who committed offenses prior to the age of 18. If nearly all the nations of the world, including the United States, have agreed to such a norm for periods of international armed conflict, the norm protecting juvenile offenders from execution ought to apply with even greater force for periods of peace.

(h) In addition, approximately two-thirds of the nations of the world have either abolished the death penalty or have prohibited it for juveniles by adhering to these human rights instruments. Whereas the European "Convention for the Protection of Human Rights and Fundamental Freedoms" (1950), in Article 2 allowed the death penalty, an evolving abolitionist philosophy is reflected in Protocol N 6 which states "the death penalty shall be abolished. No one shall be condemned to such penalty or executed."

Petitioners point out that the *travaux préparatoires* of these Conventions demonstrate that these prohibitions against juvenile executions are in fact codifications of customary international law as can be derived from the debates during the drafting of the provisions of these Conventions.

(i) As further evidence of State practice, in terms of actually carrying out the death sentence, Petitioners submit evidence, compiled by Amnesty International, to the effect that since 1979, although 80 nations of the world have executed over 11,000 persons, only six persons who committed offenses under 18 were executed by four nations, including the United States.

In the United States, the laws of various jurisdictions which permit the use of the death penalty nonetheless recognize the uniqueness of juvenile offenders and at least 21 states set a minimum age for imposition of the death penalty. Therefore, although the data is incomplete, available information shows that national laws, as well as the practice of states not to execute minors, further demonstrate the existence of a customary law norm prohibiting execution of offenders who committed capital crimes as juveniles.

(j) The Commission should not rely on the *travaux préparatoires* of the American Declaration as the U.S. Government argues. The United States relies for support on the deletion of language pertaining to capital punishment from the Inter American Juridical Committee's draft. The original Article I reads as follows: "Every person has the right to life, including the fetus (*'los que están por nacer'*) and the terminally ill, the insane, and mentally retarded. Capital punishment shall only be applied in cases in which pre-existing law has established it for exceptionally grave crimes."

The original second sentence of Article I concerning capital punishment was dropped in the subsequent and final drafts. Like the capital punishment language, the latter half of the first sentence was also deleted in subsequent and final drafts. The present version of Article I reads: "Every human being has the right to life, liberty and the security of his person."

The deletion of the capital punishment language can no more by interpreted to infer that the drafters necessarily meant to authorize widely its use than can the deletion of the clause in the first sentence be interpreted to mean that the insane, terminally ill, or mentally retarded were no longer afforded the right to life. Instead, the deletion of the capital punishment language could be read to mean that the drafters were simply unable or unwilling to delineate each and every instance when capital punishment would be prohibited as they did not want to authorize it necessarily in every context.

(k) Finally, there is a limit on any State's ability to regulate a matter, such as capital punishment, if the result will violate international law. Domestic legislation of member states cannot validate conflict with international obligations; a state cannot invoke its contrary domestic law as justification for its failure to abide by an agreement. The United States argument that at the time of the drafting of the Declaration the death penalty was widely practiced and could not generally be considered cruel or unusual is irrelevant. Petitioners argue that "[H]uman rights instruments . . . are drafted to improve the human rights situation and not certainly to reconfirm any alleged right of nature to continue violating human rights."

(1) The petitioners request that the Commission find that the United States has violated the American Declaration, as interpreted in the light of customary international law, by having executed Petitioners Roach and Pinkerton for offenses they committed while under the age of eighteen. Petitioners also request the Commission to recommend that a moratorium be imposed on the execution of other juvenile offenders in the United States.

*B. The Government.* 38. The U.S. Government considers that the absence of a prohibition on the execution of juvenile offenders within United States domestic law is not inconsistent with human rights standards applicable to the United States. The Commission must look to the American Declaration for the relevant standards as the United States is not a party to the American Convention. The argument may be summarized as follows:

(a) The American Declaration is *silent* on the issue of capital punishment as Article I simply states, "Every human being has the right to life, liberty and the security of his person." From the drafting history of the Declaration, there is evidence that Article I was not meant to affect the legislative discretion of the American states with respect to capital punishment. A Declaration that does not expressly limit the circumstances under which the death penalty may be imposed may not be interpreted as foreclosing the reasonable discretion of the American states to determine for themselves the minimum age at which imposition of the death penalty is appropriate.

(b) The drafters considered and declined to adopt any specific standards on the issue of capital punishment. The reference to capital punishment prohibiting it except for exceptional crimes was deleted in the final draft. The debate surrounding Article I demonstrates that a standard on capital punishment could not be devised due to the diversity of State legislation in the hemisphere. Therefore, the States are able to legislate within their own discretion on the issue of capital punishment.

(c) Only Article I is at issue because if no standard on capital punishment was incorporated into the American Declaration, then a prohibition against the execution of juveniles could not be "silently subsumed" within the other rights. Article VII on the special protection and care of women and children was not contemplated to extend to juveniles convicted of serious crimes. There is no official record of the drafters' intentions but the use of the word "children" was not meant to refer to juveniles nearing their eighteenth year.

There is also no official record of the drafters' intentions with regard to the prohibition against "cruel, infamous or unusual punishment" of Article XXVI. However, at the time of the drafting the death penalty was widely practiced and therefore, could not be considered cruel or unusual.

None of the three articles of the Declaration cited by petitioners addresses the death penalty or establishes any particular age of majority. The U.S. Government believes that the Declaration is deliberately silent on the issue of capital punishment. Therefore, there purposely is no limitation on the legislative prerogative of the American States regarding the imposition of the death sentence.

(d) The Vienna Convention should not be relied on to interpret the American Declaration as the Declaration is not a treaty and it is not binding on the United States. The U.S. Government does not agree with the Commission's holding in Case No. 2141 (United States) that the Declaration acquired binding force with the adoption of the revised OAS Charter. Res. 23/81, OAS/Ser. L/V/II.52, Doc. 48., Mar. 6, 1981. The Declaration was not drafted with the intent to create legal obligations, therefore the Commission should take special care "where the intentions of the drafters are manifest with respect to any particular article," not to overturn that meaning.

Even assuming the Vienna Convention could be applied to the Declaration, the Petitioners have not shown the "clear meaning" of Articles I, VII, or XXVI. Each is "ambiguous" with respect to the prohibition of the death penalty on juveniles. Therefore, recourse to the *travaux préparatoires* is necessary.

(e) The petitioners request that the Commission look to the American Convention and other international instruments to "interpret" the Declaration as encompassing the standard of Article 4(5). This requires the Commission to go far beyond its interpretive powers. Specific standards in the American Convention, such as the prohibition against the execution of those who committed crimes under eighteen years of age, are binding only on those parties to the Convention. These standards were not accepted by the United States.

(f) The three human rights instruments mentioned by petitioners are irrelevant to the Commission's consideration of the case. The United States is not a party to the International Covenant nor the American Convention, and standards cannot be imposed by "interpretation" on a State which is not a party. See, Case No. 2141 (United States). In addition, the United States delegate at the drafting of the American Convention pointed out that the United States had problems with Article 4(5)'s arbitrary age limit of 18 conflicting with its federal structure.

(g) Petitioners are also incorrect in stating that Article 4(5) of the American Convention is declaratory of customary international law. The age of majority for purposes of imposing the death penalty is not a matter of uniform state practice. Some countries desired a specific age limit while others wanted reference only to "minors" or "juveniles" during the drafting of the International Covenant's Article 6(5), demonstrating that they were not codifying an already existing binding norm. Instead, this was a specific standard intended to create uniformity where none existed.

At the same time, there is no evidence of *opinio juris*. Even the states which have enacted prohibitions against the execution of those who committed crimes before their eighteenth birthday did not do so out of any sense of legal obligation. Since the American Convention and the International Covenant have been enacted, any changes in state legislation cannot be viewed as evidence of a generally applicable customary rule of law. "Relevant rules of law" must exist apart from any conventional or treaty standards. "Simply because states in the U.S. or other nations have chosen eighteen as the age of majority does not impose an obligation that other states must choose the exact same age."

(h) The U.S. Government does not acknowledge the existence of a customary international law norm which prohibits the execution of juveniles. To establish a norm of customary law there must be "extensive and virtually uniform" state practice and second, evidence of a belief that this practice is rendered obligatory by the existence of a rule of law requiring it. The rule must be recognized as a legal obligation based on the custom or practice of states. In this case, there is neither the uniformity of state practice, nor the required *opinio juris* to regard the standard as a binding norm of customary international law.

(i) The U.S. Government further maintains that it has dissented from such a standard. It abstained from participating in the debate and vote on the draft International Covenant, and submitted it to the U.S. Senate with reservations. The United States also opposed Article 4(5) of the

American Convention, and when President Carter signed the American Convention he proposed the Senate advice and consent to ratification of the treaty be accompanied by a reservation stating that "United States adherence to Article 4 is subject to the Constitution and other law of the United States." *Four Treaties Pertaining to Human Rights, Message from the President of the United States,* S. Doc. N Exec. C, D, E, 8F, at xii, 95th Cong., 2d Sess (1978).

The U.S. Government concludes its brief by stating that "There is no basis in international law for applying to the United States a standard taken from treaties to which it is not a party and which it has indicated it will not accept when it becomes a treaty."

(j) The U.S. Government requests the Commission to hold that the recent executions are not inconsistent with the American Declaration.

## IV. Admissibility

39. In denying Roach's and Pinkerton's appeals for a writ of certiorari, the U.S. Supreme Court deliberately decided not to review the issue of the constitutionality of the execution of juvenile offenders. As pointed out in Petitioners' brief, Justice Brennan in his dissent stated that the Roach case afforded "an opportunity to address the important question whether an accused may . . . be sentenced to death for a capital offense he committed while a juvenile." Since the U.S. Supreme Court chose not to address the question the Commission finds that the Petitioners had no further domestic remedies to exhaust.

40. In spite of the fact that the U.S. Supreme Court has not addressed the issue of the constitutionality of applying the death penalty to juvenile offenders, it has established certain trial and sentencing standards for state death penalty cases. A review of the evolution of these Supreme Court standards is relevant here.

*A. The United States Supreme Court and the Death Penalty.*
41. In the United States, since the 19th century the courts have moved away from mandatory death sentences, as such a system fails to take into account the individual and his circumstances. However, by 1972 the United States Supreme Court found that the courts had moved so far from a mandatory system that unlimited discretion had been given to the judge or jury to decide who received the death penalty. In *Furman v. Georgia*, 408 U.S. 238 (1972), the Court held that such unguided discretion created arbitrary and capricious imposition of the death penalty in violation of the Eighth Amendment's prohibition against cruel and unusual punishment. While the *Furman* decision did not hold that the death penalty, *per se*, violates the Eighth Amendment, it, in effect, suspended executions and made federal and state death penalty statutes inoperative until new laws were drafted which would comply with the Constitution in light of *Furman v. Georgia*. The execution of Gary Gilmore on January 17, 1977 was the first execution since June 2, 1967. In the decade since Gilmore there have been more than 60 executions. In the decade 1976–1986 over 3,000 people have been sentenced to death in the United States. Between 1963 and 1985 the U.S. did not execute a criminal who was under the age of 18 at the time of the crime. Since then three have been executed.

After *Furman* many states enacted new death penalty statutes. In 1976, the Court began to examine the post-*Furman* statutes and in *Gregg v. Georgia*, 428 U.S. 153 (1976), it addresses the question avoided in *Furman*, namely, is the imposition of the death penalty *per se* unconstitutional? The Court in *Gregg* stated that it was not unconstitutional, and began to set out guidelines for imposition of the death penalty.

(a) The U.S. Supreme Court held in *Gregg v. Georgia* that the Eighth Amendment, which has been interpreted in a flexible manner to accord with "evolving standards of decency," prohibits the death penalty if it is grossly disproportionate to the crime or if it is imposed arbitrarily or capriciously. The Court, however, upheld the Georgia statute in *Gregg* because it was carefully drafted to ensure that the sentencing authority was given adequate information and guidance. The Georgia statute provides for a bifurcated trial in which the jury first determines the defendant's guilt or innocence. At the sentencing hearing, the jury then considers any mitigating and/or aggravating circumstances in the case. Before the death penalty could be imposed the jury had to find that one or more statutory aggravating factors existed beyond a reasonable doubt and that such factors were not outweighed by mitigating factors.

(b) In two companion cases, the Court upheld the death penalty statutes of Florida and Texas which provide that the judge or the jury is given specific and detailed guidance to assist them in deciding whether to impose the death sentence or life imprisonment. *Proffit v. Florida,* 428 U.S. 242 (1976); *Jurek v. Texas,* 428 U.S. 262 (1976). Each statute guides and focuses the sentencing authority's objective consideration of the particular circumstances of the offense and the offender.

(c) The standards necessary to guide the jury or judge in sentencing have focused on the nature and circumstances of the crime and the character and record of the defendant. Aggravating circumstances may include such issues as whether the murder was committed by a convict or if the murder was atrocious or heinous. Special attention has been given by the Supreme Court to the mitigating factors. In *Lockett v. Ohio,* 438 U.S. 586 (1978), the Court struck down the Ohio death penalty statute which only specified three factors to be considered in the mitigation of the defendant's sentence. The Court found that the Eighth and Fourteenth Amendments require that the sentencer, "not be precluded from considering as a mitigating factor, any aspect of the defendant's record or character and any of the circumstances of the offense. . . ." *Id.* at 604. In that case, the sentencing judge had been precluded by the Ohio statute from considering as mitigating factors: the defendant's lack of a prior criminal record; the fact that she was twenty-one; her lack of specific intent to cause death; and her relatively minor part in the crime.

(d) In *Eddings v. Oklahoma,* 455 U.S. 104 (1982), the Court added that the states must consider the background and mental and emotional development of the defendant as mitigating factors. The defendant in *Eddings* had committed a murder at the age of sixteen. The Court had granted the writ of certiorari on the question of whether, in the light of contemporary standards, the Eighth Amendment forbids the execution of a defendant who was under eighteen at the time of the offense. The Court, however, declined to address that issue. It decided the case instead in light of *Lockett v. Ohio,* vacating the death sentence because it had been imposed without the type of individualized consideration of mitigating factors required by the Constitution. The Court's reversal of the death sentence evidences the importance the Court attaches to mitigating evidence in determining fair and just sentencing. The trial judge had refused to take into account the defendant's unhappy childhood and unique emotional disturbances. The Court's consideration of the mitigating evidence in the case emphasized the defendant's youth, his "serious emotional problems," his severe lack of the "care, concern and paternal attention that children deserve," and his "neglectful, sometimes even violent, family background."

*B. The Juvenile Justice System in the United States.* 42. The U.S. criminal justice system, since the beginning of the twentieth century, has treated children differently than adults. Reformers in the U.S. wished to abolish the harsh adult procedures and sentences applied to children who had committed crimes. The belief was that children should be treated and rehabilitated and therefore should not be subjected to the "harshness" and "rigidity" of the adult criminal law. (See, *In re Gault,* 387 U.S. 1, 15—16 (1967).)

(a) Every state in the United States has juvenile courts. The maximum age over which a juvenile court has jurisdiction is set by the state legislature. The age limits vary for juvenile jurisdiction, but most states set the limit between sixteen and eighteen. The focus in juvenile court is on the child's condition, not his guilt. Therefore, the purpose of a separate juvenile justice system is to rehabilitate children and to make social services available to help them. Punishment in juvenile court is not stressed; the maximum sentence which can be imposed is institutional confinement until the child reaches twenty-one years of age.

(b) Sometimes a juvenile court may have jurisdiction but it may waive its right to hear a case. The case is then brought before an adult criminal court. In some states the prosecutor may have the discretion of choosing which court to file in, but in most states the juvenile judge has the discretion of deciding whether to transfer a case or not. In some cases the juvenile may benefit from being transferred to criminal court. He is entitled to all the constitutional protections of an adult, such as the right to a jury trial and perhaps the ability to post bond if the jurisdiction provides such measures. Juries may be more sympathetic to a youth in criminal court. Nevertheless, because transfer to criminal court subjects the accused juvenile to adult punishments, the transfer process has been recognized as a critically important stage in juvenile court proceedings. (See, *Kent v. United States,* 383 U.S. 541 (1966).)

(c) There is little statutory guidance as to which children should be transferred for trial in adult criminal court. The juvenile court judge is given a great deal of discretion in determining who stays within the family court's jurisdiction. Since *Kent,* many states have adopted objective criteria by statute to be used in waiving juvenile jurisdiction. The two most common criteria used are the age of the youth and the nature of the offense.

(d) Many states set a minimum age at which a child cannot be transferred out of juvenile court jurisdiction. The exact age limit varies from state to state, from 13 years of age in Mississippi to 16 years in California.

(e) The nature of the alleged offense and the accused's prior history of criminal activity are also often used at a transfer hearing. For extremely serious crimes such as murder, rape and aggravated assault, states will rarely retain juvenile court jurisdiction. Such crimes are often used as objective criteria to determine that the child is not amenable to treatment within the juvenile system. Some states allow only for discretionary transfer if the juvenile is accused of a felony (e.g., Colorado). Other states such as Pennsylvania and Massachusetts have mandatory transfer provisions which are triggered if a child over fourteen years has allegedly committed murder.

(f) Some U.S. states have no death penalty laws in force, others prohibit the death penalty for juveniles. Fourteen states as of 1985, specifically mention age as a mitigating factor in their death penalty statutes. Indiana, however, allows for the transfer of a 10 year old in certain cases to adult criminal court. Indiana does not specify age as a mitigating factor in its death penalty statute, but it may be considered under "any other circumstances appropriate for consideration." Ind. Code Ann. 35-50-2-9. Therefore, in Indiana it is possible that a ten year old could receive the death penalty and be executed.

## V. Opinion of the Commission

*A. Point at Issue.* 43. The question presented by the petitioners in the present case is whether the absence of a federal prohibition within U.S. domestic law on the execution of persons who committed serious crimes under the age of 18 is inconsistent with human rights standards applicable to the United States under the Inter-American system.

Crimes in the United States fall under either state or federal jurisdiction. A defendant may be tried in federal court if he is charged with the commission of a crime under federal law, or he may appeal to a federal court from a state court under certain circumstances. A great deal of autonomy has been left to the states in prescribing the appropriate punishment for criminal conduct. However, all punishment must be in conformity with the United States Constitution as interpreted by the Supreme Court.

*B. The International Obligation of the United States Under the American Declaration.* 44. The American Declaration is silent on the issue of capital punishment. Article I of the American Declaration reads as follows: "Every human being has the right to life, liberty and the security of his person."

45. The American Convention on Human Rights, on the other hand, refers specifically to capital punishment in five of its provisions. Article 4 of the American Convention, which protects the right to life, reads as follows: "*Article 4. Right to Life.* 1. Every person has the right to have his life respected. This right shall be protected by law and, in general, from the moment of conception. No one shall be arbitrarily deprived of his life."

2. In countries that have not abolished the death penalty, it may be imposed only for the most serious crimes and pursuant to a final judgment rendered by a competent court and in accordance with a law establishing such punishment, enacted prior to the commission of the crime. The application of such punishment shall not be extended to crimes to which it does not presently apply.

3. The death penalty shall not be reestablished in states that have abolished it.

4. In no case shall capital punishment be inflicted for political offenses or related common crimes.

5. Capital punishment shall not be imposed upon persons who, at the time the crime was committed, were under 18 years of age or over 70 years of age; nor shall it be applied to pregnant women.

6. Every person condemned to death shall have the right to apply for amnesty, pardon, or commutation of sentence, which may be granted in all cases. Capital punishment shall not be imposed while such a petition is pending decision by the competent authority.

46. The international obligation of the United States of America, as a member of the Organization of American States (OAS), under the jurisdiction of the Inter-American Commission on Human Rights is governed by the Charter of the OAS (Bogotá, 1948), as amended by the Protocol of Buenos Aires on 27 February 1967, ratified by the United States on 23 April 1968.

47. The United States is a member State of the Organization of American States, but is not a State party to the American Convention on Human Rights, and, therefore, cannot be found to be in violation of Article 4(5) of the Convention, since as the Commission stated in *Case 2141* (United States), para. 31: "it would be impossible to impose upon the United States Government or that of any other State member of the OAS, by means of 'interpretation,' an international obligation based upon a treaty that such State has not duly accepted or ratified."

48. As a consequence of articles 3 *j*, 16, 51 *e*, 112 and 150 of the Charter, the provisions of other instruments of the OAS on human rights acquired binding force. Those instruments, approved with the vote of the U.S. Government, are the following: American Declaration of the Rights and Duties of Man (Bogotá, 1948) and the Statute and Regulations of the IACHR

49. The Statute provides that, for the purpose of such instruments, the IACHR is the organ of the OAS entrusted with the competence to promote the observance of and respect for human rights. For the purpose of the Statute, human rights are understood to be the rights set forth in the American Declaration in relation to States not parties to the American Convention on Human Rights (San José, 1969).

*C. The Petitioners' Argument.* 50. The central violation denounced in the petition concerns a violation of the right to life, Article I of the Declaration, which states: "Every human being has the right to life . . ." Since the Declaration is silent on the issue of capital punishment, Petitioners, in connection with Article I, seek an affirmative response to the question: Is there a norm of customary international law which prohibits the imposition of the death penalty on persons who committed capital crimes before completing eighteen years of age?

51. The elements of a norm of customary international law are the following:

(a) a concordant practice by a number of states with reference to a type of situation falling within the domain of international relations;

(b) a continuation or repetition of the practice over a considerable period of time;

(c) a conception that the practice is required by or consistent with prevailing international law; and

(d) general acquiescence in the practice by other states.

52. The evidence of a customary rule of international law requires evidence of widespread state practice. Article 38 of the Statute of the International Court of Justice (I.C.J.) defines "international custom, as evidence of a general practice accepted as law." The customary rule, however, does not bind States which protest the norm.

In the *Fisheries Case* (United Kingdom v. Norway) the I.C.J. found that although the ". . . ten-mile rule has been adopted by certain States both in their national law and in their treaties and conventions, and although certain arbitral decisions have applied it as between these States, other States have adopted a different limit. Consequently, the ten-mile rule has not acquired the authority of a general rule of law."

How many states need to engage in the state practice for it to acquire the authority of a customary norm has never been definitively established, but it is clear that while a universal practice is not necessary, the practice must be common and widespread.

53. The U.S. Government, in December 1977, transmitted the American Convention on Human Rights, *inter alia,* to the U.S. Senate for advice and consent to ratification subject to specified reservations. As regards the issue in question, the U.S. Government proposed reservations to Articles 4 and 5 which were presented as follows:

Article 4 deals with the right to life generally, and includes provisions on capital punishment. Many of the provisions of Article 4 are not in accord with United States law and policy, or deal with matters in which the law is unsettled. The Senate may wish to enter a reservation as follows: "United States adherence to Article 4 is subject to the Constitution and other law of the United States."

[Article (5)], [p]aragraph 5 requires that minors subject to criminal proceedings are to be separated from adults and brought before specialized tribunals as speedily as possible. ( . . . ) With respect to paragraph (5), the law reserves the right to try minors as adults in certain cases and there is no present intent to revise these laws. The following statement is recommended: "The United States ( . . . ) with respect to paragraph (5), reserves the right in appropriate cases to subject minors to procedures and penalties applicable to adults."

54. Since the United States has protested the norm, it would not be applicable to the United States should it be held to exist. For a norm of customary international law to be binding on a State which has protested the norm, it must have acquired the status of *jus cogens.* Petitioners do not argue that a rule prohibiting the execution of juvenile offenders has acquired the authority of *jus cogens,* a peremptory norm of international law from which no derogation is permitted. The Commission, however, is not a judicial body and is not limited to considering only the submissions presented by the parties to a dispute.

*D. General Principles applicable to the Present Case.* 55. The concept of *jus cogens* is derived from ancient law concepts of a "superior order" of legal norms, which the laws of man or nations may not contravene. The norms of *jus cogens* have been described by publicists as comprising "international public policy." They are "rules which have been accepted, either expressly by treaty or tacitly by custom, as being necessary to protect the public interest of the society of States or to maintain the standards of public morality recognized by them."

According to Ian Brownlie, the major distinguishing feature of rules of *jus cogens* is their "relative indelibility." Brownlie suggests certain examples of *jus cogens* such as: "the prohibition of aggressive war, the law of genocide, the principle of racial non-discrimination, crimes against humanity, and the rules prohibiting trade in slaves and piracy."

Since the acceptance of norms of *jus cogens* is still subject to some debate in some sectors, it might be argued that the International Court of Justice did not consider the prohibition against genocide, for example, to be a norm of *jus cogens.* It has been argued, however, that the World Court has made "indirect references" to the concept of *jus cogens,* without actually calling it such by name, in the advisory opinion on the *Reservations to the Genocide Convention* case, in which the Court stated: " . . . that the principles underlying the Convention are principles which are recognized by civilized nations as binding on States, even without any conventional obligation."

The rule prohibiting genocide would be binding on States not parties to the Genocide Convention, even if derived only from customary international law, without having acquired the status of *jus cogens,* but it achieves the status of *jus cogens*

precisely because it is the kind of rule that it would shock the conscience of mankind and the standards of public morality for a State to protest.

The International Court of Justice, in a later case, categorized the prohibition of genocide as an obligation *erga omnes.* Whereas the ICJ does not make reference to the concept *jus cogens,* it has been suggested that the examples given of obligations *erga omnes* are examples of what the ICJ would consider to be norms of *jus cogens.* The following distinction between obligations of a State vis-à-vis the international community *(erga omnes)* and vis-à-vis another State is taken from the judgment in the *Barcelona Traction* case:

"In these circumstances it is logical that the Court should first address itself to what was originally presented as the subject-matter of the third preliminary objection: namely the question of the right of Belgium to exercise diplomatic protection of Belgian shareholders in a company which is a juristic entity incorporated in Canada, the measures complained of having been taken in relation not to any Belgian national but to the company itself.

"When a State admits into its territory foreign investments or foreign nationals, whether natural or juristic persons, it is bound to extend to them the protection of the law and assumes obligations concerning the treatment to be afforded them. These obligations, however, are neither absolute nor unqualified. In particular, an essential distinction should be drawn between the obligations of a State towards the international community as a whole, and those arising vis-à-vis another State in the field of diplomatic protection. By their very nature the former are the concern of all States. In view of the importance of the rights involved, all States can be held to have a legal interest in their protection; they are obligations *erga omnes.*

"Such obligations derive, for example, in contemporary international law, from the outlawing of acts of aggression, and of genocide, as also from the principles and rules concerning the basic rights of the human person, including protection from slavery and racial discrimination. Some of the corresponding rights of protection have entered into the body of general international law (*Reservations to the Convention on the Prevention and Punishment of the Crime of Genocide,* Advisory Opinion, I.C.J. Reports 1951, p. 23); others are conferred by international instruments of a universal or quasi-universal character.

"Obligations the performance of which is the subject of diplomatic protection are not of the same category."

As to whether "the principles and rules concerning the basic rights of the human person" is intended to mean that all codified human rights provisions contained in international treaties are embraced by the concept of *jus cogens* is an issue that is both controversial and beyond the scope of the matter presented for the Commission to decide.

56. The Commission finds that in the member States of the OAS there is recognized a norm of *jus cogens* which prohibits the State execution of children. This norm is accepted by all the States of the Inter-American system, including the United States. The response of the U.S. Government to the petition in this case affirms that "[A]ll states, moreover, have juvenile justice systems; none permits its juvenile courts to impose the death penalty."

57. The Commission finds that this case arises, not because of doubt concerning the existence of an international norm as to the prohibition of the execution of children but because the United States disputes the allegation that there exists consensus as regards the age of majority. Specifically, what needs to be examined is the United States law and prac-

tice, as adopted by different states, to transfer adolescents charged with heinous crimes to adult criminal courts where they are tried and may be sentenced as adults.

58. Since the federal Government of the United States has not preempted this issue, under the U.S. constitutional system the individual states are free to exercise their discretion as to whether or not to allow capital punishment in their states and to determine the minimum age at which a juvenile may be transferred to an adult criminal court where the death penalty may be imposed. Thirteen states and the U.S. capital have abolished the death penalty entirely. As regards the other states which have enacted death penalty statutes since the *Furman* decision, these states have adopted death penalty statutes which either 1) prohibit the execution of persons who committed capital crimes under the age of eighteen, or 2) allow for juveniles to be transferred to adult criminal courts where they may be sentenced to the death penalty. It is the discretion and practice of this second group of states which has become the subject of our analysis. Whereas approximately ten retentionist states have now enacted legislation barring the execution of under-18 offenders, a hodge-podge of legislation characterizes the other states which allow transfer of juvenile offenders to adult courts from age 17 to as young as age 10, and some states have no specific minimum age. The Indiana state statute *(supra)* which allows a ten year old to be judged before an adult criminal court and potentially sentenced to death shocks this Commission.

59. The juvenile justice system was established in the United States at the turn of the century as a result of reformist efforts to mitigate the harshness of the adult criminal justice system. Under common law, children under the age of seven were conclusively presumed to have no criminal capacity and for children from age seven to fourteen, the presumption was rebuttable and the child could be convicted of a crime and executed. By a long series of statutory changes this age has been steadily increased, and the age of criminal incapacity is now set at 14 in most states. Consequently a child below the statutory age may be prosecuted by an adult criminal court but would not be adjudged responsible for a crime, the child would be adjudged a juvenile delinquent.

60. The Commission is convinced by the U.S. Government's argument that there does not now exist a norm of customary international law establishing 18 to be the minimum age for imposition of the death penalty. Nonetheless, in light of the increasing numbers of States which are ratifying the American Convention on Human Rights and the United Nations Covenant on Civil and Political Rights, and modifying their domestic legislation in conformity with these instruments, the norm is emerging. As mentioned above, thirteen states and the U.S. capital have abolished the death penalty entirely and nine retentionist states have abolished it for offenders under the age of 18.

61. The Commission, however, does not find the age question dispositive of the issue before it, which is whether the absence of a federal prohibition within U.S. domestic law on the execution of juveniles, who committed serious crimes under the age of 18, is in violation of the American Declaration.

62. The Commission finds that the diversity of state practice in the U.S.—reflected in the fact that some states have abolished the death penalty, while others allow a potential threshold limit of applicability as low as 10 years of age—results in very different sentences for the commission of the same crime. The deprivation by the State of an offender's life should not be made subject to the fortuitous element of

where the crime took place. Under the present system of laws in the United States, a hypothetical sixteen year old who commits a capital offense in Virginia may potentially be subject to the death penalty, whereas if the same individual commits the same offense on the other side of the Memorial Bridge, in Washington, D.C., where the death penalty has been abolished for adults as well as for juveniles, the sentence will not be death.

63. For the federal Government of the United States to leave the issue of the application of the death penalty to juveniles to the discretion of state officials results in a patchwork scheme of legislation which makes the severity of the punishment dependent not, primarily, on the nature of the crime committed, but on the location where it was committed. Ceding to state legislatures the determination of whether a juvenile may be executed is not of the same category as granting states the discretion to determine the age of majority for purposes of purchasing alcoholic beverages or consenting to matrimony. The failure of the federal government to preempt the states as regards this most fundamental right—the right to life—results in a pattern of legislative arbitrariness throughout the United States which results in the arbitrary deprivation of life and inequality before the law, contrary to Articles I and II of the American Declaration of the Rights and Duties of Man, respectively.

## Conclusion

64. The Commission concludes, by *5* votes to *1,* that the United States Government violated Article I (right to life) of the American Declaration of the Rights and Duties of Man in executing James Terry Roach and Jay Pinkerton.

65. The Commission concludes, by *5* votes to *1* that the United States Government violated Article II (right to equality before the law) of the American Declaration of the Rights and Duties of Man in executing James Terry Roach and Jay Pinkerton.

## Dissenting Opinion of Dr. Marco Gerardo Monroy Cabra, Member of the Inter-American Commission on Human Rights

Before explaining the reasons for my dissenting opinion, I must first make some general observations. In this Case No. 9647, there is no discussion as regards the facts that are accepted by the United States Government, and which are that James Terry Roach and Jay Pinkerton were sentenced to death and executed in the United States for crimes for which they were tried and which they committed before the age of 18. However, since the United States is not a State Party to the American Convention on Human Rights, Article 20 of the Statute of the Inter-American Commission on Human Rights, approved through Resolution N 447, applies. That resolution, which was adopted by the OAS General Assembly on October 31, 1979, establishes the following as falling within the competence of the Commission: "b) to examine communications submitted to it and any other available information, to address the government of any member state not a Party to the Convention for information deemed pertinent by this Commission, and to make recommendations to it, when it finds this appropriate, in order to bring about more effective observance of fundamental human rights." With regard to the principle of human rights that should be applied: "2. For the purposes of the present Statute, human rights are understood to be: (a) The rights set forth in the American Convention on Human Rights, in relation to the

States parties thereto; (b) *The rights set forth in the American Declaration of the Rights and Duties of Man,* in relation to the other member states." This means that since the United States is not a State Party to the American Convention, the question of whether or not a human rights violation has occurred with respect to the petitioners must be examined in the light of the American Declaration of the Rights and Duties of Man. I should also note that this case was processed in accordance with Chapter III "Petitions concerning States that are not Parties to the American Convention on Human Rights" (Art. 48 through 50) of the current Regulations of the Inter-American Commission on Human Rights, approved by the Commission at its meeting on April 8, 1980 during the 49th regular session.

The task therefore is to determine whether the sentences handed down by the United States courts violated articles 1 and 2 of the American Declaration of the Rights and Duties of Man by imposing the death penalty on persons who committed capital crimes while under 18 years of age. To interpret the 1948 American Declaration of the Rights and Duties of Man, the Inter-American Commission on Human Rights referred, in its majority decision, to customary international law and to *jus cogens.* I must therefore refer to these aspects.

It must, however, be made clear that the aim is not to use this case to determine generally whether or not U.S. laws on the death penalty violate customary international law, since the Commission is not empowered to issue advisory opinions; rather it must only interpret the American Declaration of the Rights and Duties of Man, for which it can refer to general international law. The Commission has said that in this case "the only point at issue is whether the absence of a federal prohibition within U.S. domestic law on the execution of juveniles who committed serious crimes under the age of 18 is inconsistent with human rights standards applicable to the United States under the Inter-American system"?. In my view, this is not the problem. The case consists of examining whether or not the human rights of petitioners James Terry Roach and Jay Pinkerton were violated, under the terms of the 1948 American Declaration of the Rights and Duties of Man. This is an individual case that was processed by the Commission according to the Regulations in effect for States not Parties to the American Convention on Human Rights, and therefore, there is no reason to address the matter of compatibility between U.S. federal or state legislation and general international law. This aspect does not lie within the sphere of competence of the Commission, which could not make general observations and recommendations when ruling on a case, especially since it does not have judicial functions.

In light of the foregoing, I wish to explain the legal reasons that influenced my decision not to join in the Commission's majority decision:

*1. The U.S. Application of the Death Penalty to Juveniles Does Not Violate the American Declaration of the Rights and Duties of Man.* Article 1 of the American Declaration of the Rights and Duties of Man approved by the IX International Conference of American States held in Bogota from March 30 through May 2, 1948, and included in the Final Act of the Conference states: "Every human being has the right to life, liberty and the security of his person." This article makes no reference, either explicitly or implicitly, to prohibition of the death penalty with respect to minors. The draft of the Inter-American Juridical Committee included the following as Article 1: "Every person has the right to life. This right extends to the right to life of incurables, imbeciles and the insane."

"Capital punishment may only be applied in cases in

which it has been prescribed by pre-existing law for crimes of exceptional gravity." After discussion, the IX Conference decided to omit any reference to the death penalty and to change the wording proposed by the Inter-American Juridical Committee. Article 1, therefore, was drafted in its present form, making no reference to the death penalty. A close look at the preparatory work leads to the unmistakable conclusion that the States participating in the IX International Conference of American States in Bogota in 1948 did not wish to preclude the death penalty since, otherwise, they would have agreed on its prohibition and, consequently, approved the text by the Inter-American Juridical Committee, which confined its application to crimes of exceptional gravity. An interpretation of Article 1 in the light of its current meaning, while taking into account the preparatory work recorded in the Proceedings of the Conference, the specific deletion of the provision concerning the death penalty would allow one to conclude that the American Declaration of the Rights and Duties of Man did not regulate the matter of the death penalty, and of course, far less did it include any provision on the general or specific proscription of its application in the case of juveniles. One might therefore conclude, with regard to this first aspect, that if the American Declaration of the Rights and Duties of Man remained silent on the death penalty and did not approve the draft that included it, the United States can establish the death penalty without violating Article 1 or any other standard in the aforecited American Declaration of the Rights and Duties of Man.

*2. In This Case, It Is Not Possible to Apply Treaties Not in Effect for the United States.* The United States is a member of the Organization of American States (OAS) since it ratified the OAS Charter amended by the 1967 Protocol of Buenos Aires when it deposited the instrument of ratification on April 23, 1968. As the Charter establishes, the Inter-American Commission on Human Rights is an organ of the OAS. The United States is bound by the Statute and the Regulations of the Inter-American Commission on Human Rights. The United States is also bound by the American Declaration of the Rights and Duties of Man, which as has been seen, does not prohibit the death penalty and remains silent on this matter. But the United States has not ratified the 1969 American Convention on Human Rights, "Pact of San José, Costa Rica", and therefore, is not bound by Article 4.5, which states: "Capital punishment shall not be imposed upon persons who, at the time the crime was committed, were under 18 years of age or over 70 years of age; nor shall it be applied to pregnant women."

In December of 1977, the United States Government sent the American Convention on Human Rights to the Senate for its approval and subsequent ratification. At the same time, it suggested making certain "reservations". With regard to Articles 4 and 5, it proposed the following reservations. "Article 4 deals with the right to life generally, and includes provisions on capital punishment. Many of the provisions of Article 4 are not in accord with United States law and policy, or deal with matters in which the law is still unsettled. The Senate may wish to enter a reservation as follows: 'United States adherence to Article 4 is subject to the Constitution and other law of the United States.' "

Article 5, "[P]aragraph (5) requires that minors subject to criminal proceedings are to be separated from adults and brought before specialized tribunals as speedily as possible." "With respect to paragraph 5, the law reserves the right to try minors as adults in certain cases and there is no present intent to revise these laws. The following statement is recommended: 'The United States ... with respect to paragraph 5, reserves the right in appropriate cases to subject minors to procedures and penalties applicable to adults' " (United States State Department, publication 8961, General Foreign Policy Series 310, November 1978). This means that articles 4 and 5 cannot be applied to the United States, since it has stated specifically that even if it ratified the Convention, it would make reservations on those provisions.

Treaties do not engender obligations for third states without their consent. The United States Government is therefore not obliged to comply with the provisions of Article 4.5 of the American Convention on Human Rights. Also, the United States has not ratified the International Covenant on Civil and Political Rights, adopted and opened for signature, ratification and accession by the United Nations General Assembly on December 16, 1966 in its resolution 2200 A (XXI), and which entered into effect on March 23, 1976. Under these conditions, the United States is not obliged to comply with the provisions of Article 6.5 of that Covenant, which states: "Sentence of death shall not be imposed for crimes committed by persons below eighteen years of age and shall not be carried out on pregnant women."

The United States is only bound by the Fourth Geneva Convention, which states in its Article 68: "In any case, the death penalty may not be pronounced on a protected person who was under eighteen years of age at the time of the offence." However, this treaty applies only in international conflicts, and therefore, cannot be applied for the execution of juveniles in the United States in times of normalcy and in the absence of an international conflict.

In conclusion, Neither the American Convention on Human Rights (Article 4 [5]), nor the International Covenant on Civil and Political Rights (Art 6 [5]), nor the Fourth Geneva Convention (Art. 68) is applicable to the pronouncement of the death penalty with respect to minors under 18 in the United States.

*3. There Is No Existing Rule in Customary International Law Prohibiting the Imposition of the Death Penalty with Respect to Juveniles.* Article 38 of the Statute of the International Court of Justice lists as a source of international law: "(b) international custom, as evidence of a general practice accepted as law". Max Sorensen states the following (Manual of Public International Law, St. Martin's Press, New York, 1968, page 130): "This formula has been criticized often because it reverses the logical order of events; in practice, in order to prove the existence of a customary rule, it is necessary to show that there exists a 'general practice' which conforms to the rule and which is 'accepted as law'. Custom is the direct product of the necessities of international life. It arises when states acquire the habit of adopting, with respect to a given situation, and whenever that situation recurs, a given attitude to which legal significance is attributed."

Ch. Rousseau, Professor of international law (Derecho Internacional Público Profundizado, La Ley, Buenos Aires, 1966, pages 96–97) lists three characteristics of custom:

"a) It is above all the expression of a common practice, resulting from precedents, in other words, from the repetition of conclusive acts; b) Second, custom presents itself as an obligatory practice, that is to say, it must be accepted as law, as corresponding to a legal need. In the absence of this psychological element, there would be no customary rule but rather a purely nonbinding custom or practice of international courtesy; c) Finally, international custom is a practice that evolves".

A generalized and uniform practice does not suffice; of vital importance is the *opinio juris*. In the judgment on the North Sea Continental Shelf Case, the International Court of Justice said the following on the requirement of the subjective element and *opinio juris*: "Not only must the acts concerned amount to a settled practice, but they must also be such, or be carried out in such a way, as to be evidence of a belief that this practice is rendered obligatory by the existence of a rule of law requiring it. The need for such a belief, i.e., the existence of a subjective element, is implicit in the very notion of the *opinio juris sive necessitatis*. The States concerned must therefore feel that they are conforming to what amounts to a legal obligation. The frequency, or even habitual character of the acts is not in itself enough. There are many international acts, e.g., in the field of ceremonial and protocol, which are performed almost invariably, but which are motivated only by considerations of courtesy, convenience or tradition, and not by any sense of legal duty." (I.C.J. Reports, 1969, page 44). According to Professor of international law, Eduardo Jiménez de Arechaga, (El Derecho Internacional Contemporáneo, Publishers: Tecnos, Madrid, 1980, pages 19 et seq), customary law, which finds its expression in treaties, can operate in three different ways: the text of the treaty can simply declare a customary rule that existed previously; it can give concrete expression to a rule that is developing in *statu nascendi*; or, the provision of a treaty can convert *de lege ferenda* to a subsequent state practice after a process of consolidation whereupon it converts to custom. In other cases, the custom can derive from the consensus of states in adopting United Nations General Assembly resolutions, as in the case of the 1970 Declaration on Principles of International Law concerning Friendly Relations and Cooperation among States in accordance with the Charter of the United Nations, or the 1963 Declaration of Legal Principles Governing the Activities of States in the Exploration and Use of Outer Space, or Resolution 1514 on the Granting of Independence to Colonial Countries and Peoples, etc.

According to Sorensen (op cit. p. 133), it is not possible to speak of a custom as general if its observance is confined to a particular group of states. This means that an essential requirement concerning custom is that it should derive from the community of States as a whole. Sorensen notes that: "A custom cannot be transformed into a rule of law if it encounters opposition of a proportion of the states comprising the international community or, as the case may be, the region or group within which it is in operation. For in such a case the requisite is not forthcoming" (op cit p. 135). This implies that the opposition of a number of states thwarts the formation of a general customary rule.

The application of the foregoing principles to Case 9647 shows, in my view, the nonexistence of a general rule of customary law prohibiting the application of the death penalty on persons who committed capital crimes under 18 years of age. This conclusion is drawn from the following analysis:

The fact that prohibition of the death penalty with respect to juveniles under 18 years of age appears in the American Convention on Human Rights (Article 4.5), in the International Covenant on Civil and Political Rights (Article 6.5) and in the Fourth Geneva Convention (Art. 68) does not mean that these treaties have declared an existing custom or have crystalized or reflected a custom. The only thing that can be accepted is the generating effect *de lege ferenda*, which can lead to the development of the custom if state practice in the matter is consolidated. With regard to the prohibition of the death penalty, there is no uniformity in the laws of states, since some allow it and others prohibit it; further, some prohibit the death penalty in the case of minors, and others accept it or remain silent on the subject. It is possible that with time, the practice of States will lead to the emergence of the custom in the instant case, but at present, it is not an international custom.

The practice and the laws of states with regard to the death penalty in general and in relation to minors show variations and discrepancies. Ultimately, one sees a lack of continuity, and contrary to the Commission's mistaken view, it is not possible to find standard and constant application of it practiced with the intent of producing legal effects. There is no proof to the effect that all states worldwide feel bound by an obligatory rule of customary law prohibiting the death penalty with respect to juveniles under 18 years of age given the fact that the laws of the states are not even uniform as regards the age at which an individual is punishable.

In fact, there is no evidence of *opinio juris,* that is to say, demonstration of state practice that has led to nonapplication of the death penalty with respect to minors under 18 years of age, or that this has been a practice for a long time.

Moreover, one must bear in mind that not only has the United States not given its consent to the development of the so-called custom; but rather it has not been proven that uniformity exists, not even with respect to the abolition of the death penalty. In the matter of the Barcelona Traction case, the International Court of Justice said that "a body of rules could only have developed with the consent of the parties concerned. The difficulties encountered have been reflected in the evolution of the law on the subject." (I.C.J. Reports, 1970, page 48, par. 89). Nor can one speak in terms of local American custom, since the American Convention on Human Rights has only been ratified by 19 of the 32 states in the Americas, an indication that there is no standard practice in the Americas regarding the prohibition of the death penalty, and even less so with regard to juveniles. The International Covenant on Civil and Political Rights has not yet been ratified by all states worldwide, and the Fourth Geneva Convention (art. 68), which has received 162 ratifications, only applies to international armed conflicts, and consequently, cannot be considered to be a demonstration of a custom in time of peace.

In conclusion, it was not proven that a widespread and uniform practice exists on the part of states, or the *opinio juris* or conviction that that practice has become obligatory because of the existence of a norm prohibiting the death penalty with respect to minors under 18 years of age. This custom does not derive from state practice, or from the provisions of public treaties that have not been ratified by all states. One cannot therefore consider that there is consensus on this matter.

*4. Prohibition of the Death Penalty With Respect to Minors Under 18 Years of Age Is Not a Norm of Jus Cogens.* Article 53 of the Vienna Convention on the Law of Treaties defines *jus cogens* as a "norm accepted and recognized by the international community of States as a whole as a norm from which no derogation is permitted and which can be modified only by a subsequent norm of general international law having the same character."

In its reference to reservations on genocide (May 28, 1951), the I.C.J. said that "the principles underlying the Convention are principles which are recognized by civilized nations as binding on States, even without any conventional obligation." The Shucking opinion in 1934 relies on *jus cogens* (C.D.L. Report, 80).

The following appeared as examples of *jus cogens* at the Vienna Conference on the Law of Treaties: a) Treaty concerning a case of the illegitimate use of force in violation of the principles of the Charter; b) Treaty concerning the perpetration of any other criminal act in international law; and c) Treaty to prohibit the perpetration or tolerance of such acts as the slave trade, piracy and genocide in the suppression of which every State is obliged to cooperate. While human rights standards constitute principles of *jus cogens,* as we have said in our publication on human rights (*Los Derechos Humanos,* Marco Gerardo Monroy Cabra, Edit. Temis, 1980), the prohibition of the death penalty with respect to juveniles under 18 years of age is not in the nature of a norm of *jus cogens.* Indeed, it has not been proven that uniformity exists, since not all states prohibit the death penalty and not all States prohibit the pronouncement of it with respect to minors under 18 years of age. While there is undoubtedly a tendency towards abolishing the death penalty, it cannot be said that the prohibition of the death penalty for minors under 18 years of age is a norm that has been accepted by the international community as a whole, and consequently, a norm of *jus cogens* has not been created. The prohibition of the death penalty with respect to minors under 18 years of age cannot be compared with the cases cited at the Vienna Conference, such as the prohibition of piracy or slavery or the white slave trade or racial discrimination or the prohibition of genocide, since in all these cases, all states prohibit them. Such is not the case here. The death penalty is still recognized by a considerable number of States. One cannot speak in terms of the existence of a norm of *jus cogens* in effect for the OAS member States since the American Convention on Human Rights, which prohibits the execution of minors under 18 years of age, has only been ratified by 19 States. Also, there are reservations on the matter of the death penalty and it is not a norm that has been accepted by the 32 American states, and far less by all states worldwide. By virtue of this fact, it is therefore not a general imperative norm. One need hardly point out that there can be no "American *jus cogens*" or "Africani *jus cogens,*" etc. Rather, one must be in the presence of an imperative norm that has gained acceptance in the international community "as a whole", as the Vienna Convention on the Law of Treaties states in its Article 53.

Not even in the United States is there a rule setting age 18 as the minimum age for imposition of the death penalty, and to date, the Supreme Court of Justice has not declared such application unconstitutional. The punishable age is not uniform among states since some set it at age 16, others at 17, and others at 18. This means that there is no standard legislation among states as regards the minimum punishable age or the minimum age for imposition of the death penalty.

In conclusion, it cannot be inferred from either the practice of states, or from international jurisprudence, or from doctrine, or from the laws of the states that a norm of *jus cogens* prohibiting the imposition of the death penalty with respect to minors under 18 years age of age has come into existence. While human rights standards are of *jus cogens,* specifically the prohibition of the death penalty and its application to minors under 18 years of age do not constitute an imperative norm of general international law since it has not been accepted by all states that make up the international legal community.

*5. There Has Been No Violation of Article 2 of the American Declaration of the Rights and Duties of Man.* Article 2 of the American Declaration of the Rights and Duties of Man states: "All persons are equal before the law and have the rights and duties established in this Declaration, without distinction as to race, sex, language, creed or any other factor."

I do not consider the imposition of the death penalty with

respect to minors under 18 years of age to constitute a violation of Article 2 of the American Declaration of the Rights and Duties of Man, because there is no federal law in the United States establishing such a prohibition and the laws of the States are not uniform in this matter. We are not discussing here the arbitrary deprivation of life because there is no federal law in the United States setting the death penalty for minors under 18 years of age; neither is there any prohibition in conventional international law applicable to the United States, nor in customary international law either, as previously demonstrated.

6. *Interpretation of the American Declaration of the Rights and Duties of Man done by the Inter-American Commission on Human Rights.* The Commission used the Vienna Convention on the Law of Treaties in order to interpret the American Declaration of the Rights and Duties of Man, which is a mistake since the Declaration is not a public treaty, not having gone through the necessary stages for the adoption, authentication, manifestation of consent to abide by the treaty, entry into force, registry and publication of any international treaty. Also, in interpreting the Declaration, the Commission did not attribute any value to the preparatory work leading up to the American Declaration of the Rights and Duties of Man contained in the Proceedings of the IX International Conference of American States held in Bogota in 1948. If this background had been taken into account, it would have concluded that there was a consensus to delete any reference to the death penalty from Article 1 in view of the differences that existed among the States on this matter.

The Commission interpreted Article XXVI of the Declaration prohibiting the imposition of "cruel, infamous or unusual punishment," as though this provision prohibited the execution of minors, when this conclusion cannot be drawn from the background and discussions concerning the American Declaration of the Rights and Duties of Man recorded in the Proceedings of the IX International Conference of American States in Bogota. Furthermore, given the fact that some American states applied the death penalty in 1948, it cannot be said that at that time it was considered cruel, infamous or unusual punishment.

To interpret the 1948 American Declaration of the Rights and Duties of Man, the Commission resorted to an analysis of customary international law, but it has already been ascertained that the petitioners have not proven that such a custom exists.

The American Declaration of the Rights and Duties of Man cannot be interpreted in the light of the provisions of the American Convention on Human Rights, the International Covenant on Civil and Political Rights and other treaties on human rights because these treaties are subsequent to the aforecited Declaration and are only binding for States Parties to them.

The erroneous interpretation of the 1948 American Declaration of the Rights and Duties of Man led the Commission to conclude that the Declaration prohibits the death penalty with respect to minors under 18 years of age when this conclusion cannot be drawn from either the letter or spirit of the Declaration.

In interpreting the American Declaration of the Rights and Duties of Man issued in 1948, the Commission could hardly use the practice of states as it stands in 1987, customary international law in effect today, the current notion of *jus cogens,* when the truth is that when drafting that Declaration, the States were not in agreement on prohibiting the death penalty as is apparent from the fact that the pertinent reference was deleted from the Inter-American Juridical Committee's draft. The only point that the Commission should have studied was whether the rights of James Terry Roach and Jay Pinkerton had been disregarded, under the terms of the American Declaration of the Rights and Duties of Man. It was not relevant to analyze whether or not the absence of a federal law in the United States establishing that prohibition of the death penalty with respect to minors violated customary international law, because the Commission is not an international tribunal, or whether U.S. legislation is in conflict with *jus cogens,* because this was not requested by the petitioners and is beyond the purview of the Commission. In this case, it could only apply the American Declaration of the Rights and Duties of Man because it is the sole international human rights instrument that is binding on the United States.

But even if one were to accept that the Commission could resort to customary international law or to *jus cogens* to interpret the Declaration, one cannot conclude that the United States violated articles 1 and 2 of that Declaration or any norm of general customary international law, since no violation in this regard has been proven in this case.

7. *Conclusions.* The following conclusions can be drawn from the foregoing: a) the imposition of the death penalty by state courts in the United States with respect to minors under 18 years of age does not violate articles 1 and 2 of the American Declaration of the Rights and Duties of Man; b) the imposition of the death penalty with respect to minors under 18 years of age does not violate customary international law since there is no custom in this matte; and c) the prohibition of the death penalty with respect to minors under 18 years of age is not a norm of *jus cogens* since it has not been accepted by the international community as a whole.

In accordance with the foregoing, the Inter-American Commission on Human Rights should have exonerated the United States from the charges levied against it by the petitioners.

It is thus that I substantiate my dissenting vote as regards the decision adopted by the Inter-American Commission on Human Rights.

The United States requested reconsideration of Case No. 9647. During the 71st period of sessions, the Commission received the request for reconsideration, which it granted, and by a majority vote, decided not to modify its decision. In a separate publication, the Commission presented the text of the U.S. Government's request for reconsideration, the observations of the petitioners, the reasons of the Commission for not modifying its decision, and the separate opinion of Dr. Monroy Cabra. Ambassador Elsa D. Kelly did not participate at this meeting. Mr. Bruce McColm, pursuant to article 19 of the Commission's regulations, did not participate in this matter.

The Special Rapporteur of the UN Commission on Human Rights on contemporary forms of racism, racial discrimination, xenophobia, and related intolerance, Mr. M. Ghele-Ahanhanzo, submitted to the Commission at its 1995 session a report on the mission to the United States of America which he had undertaken from 9 to 22 October 1994 (E/CN.4/1995/78/ and Add.1).

On that mission, he had talked to and collected information from a wide variety of sources on contemporary forms and expressions of racial discrimination existing there in a number of fields, including health, education, housing, employment, political participation, criminal justice and the application of the dealth penalty, police violence, incitement to racial hatred and racist violence, antisemitism, immigration and the right of asylum, women and racism, and racism about the environment. He had also learned much about measures taken by the Government, and the action taken by society at large, to correct these problems.

In the conclusions and recommendations outlined in Part V of his report, the Special Rapporteur set out his belief that racism and racial discrimination persist in American society, "even if not as a deliberate policy on the part of the United States Government." He added that on his mission he had found "sociological inertia, structural obstacles, and individual resistence hindering the emergence of an integrated society based on the equal dignity of everyone living in America and willing to accept its cultural pluralism. Vested interests, competing influences, and the power struggle between the various political and social components of American society also provide opportunities for residual racism and racial discrimination to linger on."

On the basis of these considerations, the Special Rapporteur submitted the following recommendations:

It should be explicitly acknowledged that 30 years of intense struggle against racism and racial discrimination have not yet made it possible to eliminate the consequences of over 300 years of slavery and racial discrimination, particularly where African Americans are concerned.

It should be recognized that when persons from ethnic minorities aspire to equal treatment, they are not asking for favours, but seeking to enjoy the rights guaranteed by the United States Constitution in their daily lives by virtue of their status as full citizens or lawful residents.

Affirmative action programmes should be revitalized in order to offset the negative consequences of the policy pursued during the 1980s in the fields of health, housing, education, and employment.

Measures should be taken to prohibit the establishment of racist organizations and ban racist propaganda.

Measures should be taken to abolish the death penalty, or failing that, to eliminate discriminatory application of the penalty.

The Government, in conjunction with the State authorities, should ensure that the police do not use violence against persons belonging to ethnic or racial monorities; Congress should adopt laws to permit the criminal prosecution of police officers who use excessive force under the guise of enforcing the law.

Effective, and in particular financial, support should be provided for organizations which combat racism and racial discrinination and which work for and contribute to peaceful coexistence between the different communities.

Measures should be taken to eliminate racial discrimination against women from ethnic minorities, particularly in terms of employment, wages, and access to health care.

In the sphere of education, measures should be taken to increase funding for public schools and to ensure the equitable distribution of funds.

The media shoud be encouraged to refrain from propagating stereotypes and to devote themselves to educating the public by disseminating the principles of human rights.

Everyone must be persuaded to accept the existence of the indissoluble link between civil and political rights and the economic, social, and cultural rights which are their natural corollary. Consequently, the Special Rapporteur urges the United States Government to ratify all the international human rights conventions, as a means of strengthening its foreign policy on behalf of peace and democracy.

In addition, there should be more vigorous action on behalf of human rights education, in particular for law-enforcement officials. Such a step would promote greater acceptance of one another by the members of the different communities who live in the United States and would encourage sharing between them in the economic and social or even the cultural spheres. To assume fully, and in a genuine democracy, the cultural pluralism which characterizes the American nation is a challenge which the United States is undoubtedly capable of taking up.

On 20 February 1995, a draft resolution entitled "Racism and racial discrimination as the utmost violations of human rights in the United States of America" (E/CN/4/1995/L.26) was submitted to the Commission by Cuba. After some discussion, it was withdrawn and a revised draft resolution, also sponsired by Cuba, replaced it. The revised draft resolution (E/CN.4/1995/L.26/Rev.1) was rejected by 32 votes to 3, with 18 abstentions, and a second revised draft resolution (E/CN.4/1995/L.26/Rev. 2) was rejected by a roll call vote of 32 to 3, with 18 abstentions.

**BIBLIOGRAPHY.** Adelman, Howard, ed. *Refugee Policy: Canada and the United States.* North York, Canada, and Staten Island, NY, USA: York Lanes Press for the Centre for Refugee Studies, York University, and Center for Migration Studies of New York, 1991. Conference papers, in English.

Aldrich, George H. "Prospects for United States Ratification of Additional Protocol I to the 1949 Geneva Conventions," *American Journal of International Law* 85, no. 1 (Jan. 1991): 1–20. Scholarly article, in English.

Aleinidoff, T. Alexander. "The Meaning of 'Persecution' in United States Asylum Law," *International Journal of Refugee Law* 3, no. 1 (Jan. 1991): 5–29. Scholarly article, in English.

American Friends Service Committee, Criminal Justice Program. *The Lessons of Marion: The Failure of a Maximum Security Prison—A History and Analysis, with Voices of Prisoners.* Philadelphia, PA, USA: 1985. NGO report, in English.

Americas Watch. *Brutality Unchecked: Human Rights Abuses along the U.S. Border with Mexico.* New York: Human Rights Watch, 1992. NGO report, in English.

Amnesty International. *Reasonable Fear: Human Rights and United States Refugee Policy.* London: 1990. NGO report, in English.

———. *USA: The Death Penalty.* London: 1987. NGO report, in English.

————. *USA: The Death Penalty in the United States of America: Developments from 1 September 1989 to 31 December 1990.* London: 1991. NGO factfinding report, in English.

————. *USA: Developments on the Death Penalty During 1994.* London: 1995. NGO report, in English.

Anti-Defamation League of B'nai B'rith. *1987 Audit of Anti-Semitic Incidents.* New York: 1987. NGO report, in English.

————. *Hate Groups in America: A Record of Bigotry and Violence,* rev. ed. New York: 1988. NGO report, in English; bibliography, pp. 91–96.

Barber, Benjamin R. "Global Multiculturalism and the American Experiment," *World Policy Journal* 10, no. 1 (Spring 1993): 47–55. Scholarly article, in English.

Bermann, Karl. *Under the Big Stick.* Boston, MA, USA: South End Press, 1986. Scholarly monograph, in English.

Bok, Marcia. *Civil Rights and the Social Programs of the 1960s: The Social Justice Functions of Social Policy.* Westport, CT, USA, and London: Praeger, 1992. Scholarly monograph, in English; bibliography, pp. 161–172.

Brandit, James R. "Reconciling Free Speech and Equality: What Justifies Censorship?" *Harvard Journal of Law and Public Policy* 9, no. 2 (Spring 1986): 429–460. Scholarly article, in English.

Breum, M., and A. Hendriks, eds. *AIDS and Human Rights: An International Perspective.* Copenhagen: Danish Center of Human Rights, 1988. Edited collection, in English.

Brostad, J., J. Dahl, A. Gray, et al. *Native Power: The Quest for Autonomy and Nationhood of Indigenous Peoples.* Oslo, Norway: International Work Group for Indigenous Affairs and Universitetsforlaget, 1985. Scholarly edited collection, in English.

Carleton, D., and M. Stohl. "The Foreign Policy of Human Rights: Rhetoric and Reality from Jimmy Carter to Ronald Reagan," *Human Rights Quarterly* 7, no. 2 (May 1985): 205–229. Scholarly article, in English.

Champagne, Duane. *Strategies and Conditions of Political and Cultural Survival in American Indian Societies.* Cambridge, MA, USA: Cultural Survival, 1985. NGO occasional paper, in English.

Cohen, Cynthia Price, and Howard A Davidson, eds. *Children's Rights in America: U.N. Convention on the Rights of the Child Compared with United States Law.* Washington, D.C.: American Bar Association, Center on Children and the Law, and Defense for Children International—USA, 1990. Scholarly monograph, in English.

Commission on Security and Cooperation in Europe. *Staff Report on Homelessness in the United States.* Washington, D.C.: U.S. Government Printing Office, 1990. Government report, in English.

Donnelly, J., and R. E. Howard, eds. *International Handbook on Human Rights.* Westport, CT, USA: Greenwood Press, 1987. Scholarly edited collection, in English.

Edelman, M. W., and J. D. Weill. "Status of Children in the 1980s," *Columbia Human Rights Law Review* 17, no. 2 (Spring–Summer 1986): 139–158. Scholarly article, in English.

Fanelli, Vincent. *The Human Face of Poverty: A Chronicle of Urban America.* New York: Bootstrap Press for NEW/Fourth World Movement, 1990. Scholarly monograph, in English.

Fawcett, J. T., and B. V. Carino, eds. *Pacific Bridges: The New Migration from Asia and the Pacific Islands.* Staten Island, NY: Center for Migration Studies of New York, 1987. NGO document collection, in English.

Finn, J., and L. R. Sussman, eds. *Today's American: How Free?* New York: Freedom House, 1986. Edited collection, in English.

Forbes, Susan S. *Adaptation and Integration of Recent Refugees to the United States.* Washington, D.C.: Refugee Policy Group, 1985. NGO report, in English.

Forsythe, David P. "Congress and Human Rights in U.S. Foreign Policy: The Fate of General Legislation," *Human Rights Quarterly* 9, no. 3 (Aug. 1987): 382–404. Scholarly article, in English.

————. *Human Rights and U.S. Foreign Policy: Congress Reconsidered.* Gainesville, FL, USA: University Presses of Florida, 1988. Scholarly study, in English.

Fund for Free Expression. *Freedom of Expression and the War: Press and Speech Restrictions in the Gulf and F.B.I. Activity in U.S. Raise First Amendment Issues.* New York: Human Rights Watch, 1991. NGO factfinding report, in English.

Gibney, Mark. "A 'Well-founded Fear' of Persecution," *Human Rights Quarterly* 10, no. 1 (Feb. 1988): 109–121. Scholarly article, in English.

————, ed. *World Justice? U.S. Courts and International Human Rights.* Boulder, CO, USA: Westview Press, 1991. Scholarly collective works, in English.

Harvard Law School Human Rights Program. "Human Rights Issues in United States Foreign Policy," *Harvard Human Rights Journal* 3 (Spring 1990): 157–224. Scholarly articles, in English.

"Human Rights Issues in United States Foreign Policy," *Harvard Human Rights Journal* 4 (Spring 1991): 1–222. Collection of scholarly articles, in English.

Human Rights Watch. *Crossing the Line: Human Rights along the U.S. border with Mexico Persist amid Climate of Impunity.* New York: 1995. NGO report, in English.

————. *Dangerous Dialogue Revisited: Threats to Freedom of Expression Continue in Miami's Cuban Exile Community.* New York: 1994. NGO report, in English.

————. *Human Rights Violations in the U.S.* New York: 1994. NGO monograph, in English.

————. *Prison Conditions in the United States.* New York: 1991. NGO monograph, in English.

————. "United States," in *Human Rights Watch World Report 1995,* p . 318. New York: 1995. NGO report, in English. The annual *Human Rights Watch World Report* also features a section on "U.S. Policy" for each country.

————. *A World Leader in Executing Juveniles.* New York: 1995. NGO report, in English.

Kozol, Jonathan. *Rachel and her Children: Homeless Families in America.* New York: Crown Publishers, 1988. Scholarly monograph, in English; bibliography, pp. 249–252.

Lawyers Committee for Human Rights. *Refugee Refoulement: The Forced Return of Haitians under the U.S.-Haitian Interdiction Agreement.* New York: 1990. NGO factfinding report, in English.

LeBlanc, Lawrence J. *The United States and the Genocide Convention.* Durham, NC, USA, and London: Duke University Press, 1991. Scholarly monograph, in English.

Leibowitz, Arnold H. "Comparative Analysis of Immigration in Key Developed Countries in Relation to Immigration Reforms and Control Legislation in the United States," *Human Rights Law Journal* 7, no. 1 (1986): 1–73. Scholarly article, in English.

Lillich, Richard B. "The United States Constitution and International Human Rights Law," *Harvard Human Rights Journal* 3 (Spring 1990): 53–81. Scholarly article, in English.

Linfield, Michael. *Freedom under Fire: US Civil Liberties in Times of War.* Boston, MA, USA: South End Press, 1990. Scholarly monograph, in English; bibliography, pp. 259–268.

Lowery, Charles D., and John F. Marszalek. *Encyclopedia of African-American Civil Rights: From Emancipation to the Present.*

New York and London: Greenwood, 1992. Encyclopedia, in English; bibliography, pp. 611–615.

Lutz, Chris, comp. *They Don't All Wear Sheets: A Chronology of Racist and Far Right Violence—1980–1986*. New York: Center for Democratic Renewal and National Council of Churches, 1987. NGO report, in English.

Minow, Martha. *Making All the Difference: Inclusion, Exclusion, and American Law*. New York: Cornell University Press, 1990. Monograph, in English.

Mower, A. Glenn, Jr. *Human Rights and American Foreign Policy: The Carter and Reagan Experiences*. Westport, CT, USA: Greenwood Press, 1987. Scholarly monograph, in English; bibliography, pp. 159–163.

Pacific Northwest Research Center, Africa Fund. *Unified List of U.S. Companies with Investments or Loans in South Africa and Namibia*. New York: Updated periodically. NGO report, in English.

Pearce, Elizabeth A. "Self-Determination for Native Americans: Land Rights and the Utility of Domestic and International Law," *Columbia Human Rights Law Review* 22, no. 2 (Spring 1991): 361–400. Scholarly article, in English.

Pettman, Ralph. *Incitement to Racial Hatred: The International Experience*. Canberra, Australia: Human Rights Commission, 1982. Government monograph, in English.

Poe, Steven C. "Human Rights and U.S. Foreign Aid: A Review of Quantitative Studies and Suggestions for Future Research," *Human Rights Quarterly* 12, no. 4 (Nov. 1990): 499–512. Scholarly article, in English.

Presidential Commission on the Human Immunodeficiency Virus Epidemic. *Report of the Commission*. Washington, D.C.: 1988. Government report, in English.

"Roundtable—The United States Constitution and the Adoption of International Human Rights Instruments: Freeing the Political Logjam," *Georgia Journal of International and Comparative Law* 20, no. 2 (1990): 253–459. Scholarly article, in English.

Rowles, James P. "Nicaragua vs. the United States: Issues of Law and Policy," *The International Lawyer* 20, no. 4 (Fall 1986): 1245–1288. Scholarly article, in English.

Shilts, Randy. *And the Band Played On: Politics, People and the AIDS Epidemic*. New York: St. Martin's Press, 1987. Journalistic monograph, in English.

Sigler, Jay, A., ed. *International Handbook on Race and Race Relations*. Westport, CT, USA: Greenwood Press, 1987. Scholarly edited collection, in English; bibliography, pp. 449–454.

Streib, Victor L. *Death Penalty for Juveniles*. Bloomington, IN, USA: Indiana University Press, 1987. Scholarly report, in English; bibliography, pp. 237–250.

Swift, Jeannine. *Dream and Reality: The Modern Black Struggle for Freedom and Equality*. New York and London: Greenwood Press, 1991. Monograph, in English.

Tarnopolsky, Walter S. "Race Relations Commissions in Canada, Australia, New Zealand, the United Kingdom and the United States," *Human Rights Law Journal* 6, pt. 2–4 (1985): 145—178. Scholarly article, in English.

Walker, Samuel. *In Defense of American Liberties: A History of the ACLU*. New York and Oxford, UK: Oxford University Press, 1990. Scholarly monograph, in English; bibliography, pp. 449–452.

## UNITED STATES OF AMERICA: DECLARATION OF INDEPENDENCE (1776).

Adopted unanimously by the representatives of the United States of America, assembled in Congress on 4 July 1776, the Declaration inspired many national and international human rights instruments adopted since that date. The text is as follows:

When in the course of human events, it becomes necessary for one people to dissolve the political bands which have connected them with another, and to assume among the powers of the earth the separate and equal station to which the Laws of Nature and of Nature's God entitle them, a decent respect to the opinions of mankind requires that they should declare the causes which impel them to the separation.

We hold these truths to be self-evident, that all men are created equal, that they are endowed by their Creator with certain unalienable Rights, that among these are Life, Liberty, and the pursuit of Happiness. That to secure these rights, Governments are instituted among Men, deriving their just powers from the consent of the governed. That whenever any Form of Government becomes destructive of these ends, it is the Right of the People to alter or to abolish it, and to institute new Government, laying its foundation on such principles and organizing its powers in such form, as to them shall seem most likely to effect their Safety and Happiness. Prudence, indeed, will dictate that Governments long established should not be changed for light and transient causes; and accordingly all experience hath shown, that mankind are more disposed to suffer, while evils are sufferable, than to right themselves by abolishing the forms to which they are accustomed. But when a long train of abuses and usurpations, pursuing invariably the same Object evinces a design to reduce them under absolute Despotism, it is their right, it is their duty, to throw off such Government, and to provide new Guards for their future security. Such has been the patient sufferance of these Colonies; and such is now the necessity which constrains them to alter their former systems of government. The history of the present King of Great Britain is a history of repeated injuries and usurpations, all having in direct object the establishment of an absolute tyranny over these States. To prove this, let facts be submitted to a candid world.

He has refused his assent to laws, the most wholesome and necessary for the public good.

He has forbidden his Governors to pass laws of immediate and pressing importance, unless suspended in their operation till his assent should be obtained; and when so suspended, he has utterly neglected o attend to them.

He has refused to pass other laws for the accommodation of large districts of people, unless those people would relinquish the right of representation in the legislature, a right inestimable to them and formidable to tyrants only.

He has called together legislative bodies at places unusual, uncomfortable, and distant from the depository of their public records, for the sole purpose of fatiguing them into compliance with his measures.

He has dissolved representative houses repeatedly, for opposing with manly firmness his invasion on the rights of the people.

He has refused for a long time, after such dissolutions, to cause others to be elected; whereby the legislative powers, incapable of annihilation, have returned to the people at large for their exercise; the State remaining in the meantime exposed to all the dangers of invasion from without and convulsions within.

He has endeavoured to prevent the population of these States, for that purpose obstructing the laws for naturalization of foreigners; refusing to pass others to encourage their migration hither, and raising the conditions of new appropriations of lands.

He has obstructed the administration of justice, by refusing his assent to laws for establishing judiciary powers.

He has made judges dependent on his will alone, for the tenure of their offices, and the amount and payment of their salaries.

He has erected a multitude of new offices, and sent hither swarms of officers to harass our people, and eat out their substance.

He has kept among us, in times of peace, standing armies without the consent of our legislatures.

He has affected to render the military independent of and superior to the civil power.

He has combined with others to subject us to a jurisdiction foreign to our constitution, and unacknowledged by our laws; giving his assent to their acts of pretended legislation:

For quartering large bodies of armed troops among us:

For protecting them, by a mock trial, from punishment for any murders which they should commit on the inhabitants of these States:

For cutting off our trade with all parts of the world:

For imposing taxes on us without our consent:

For depriving us in many cases of the benefits of trial by jury:

For transporting us beyond seas to be tried for pretended offences:

For abolishing the free system of English laws in a neighbouring Province, establishing therein an arbitrary government, and enlarging its boundaries so as to render it at once an example and fit instrument for introducing the same absolute rule into these Colonies:

For taking away our Charters, abolishing our most valuable laws, and altering fundamentally the forms of our governments:

For suspending our own Legislatures, and declaring themselves invested with power to legislate for us in all cases whatsoever.

He has abdicated government here, by declaring us out of his protection and waging war against us.

He has plundered our seas, ravaged our coasts, burnt our towns, and destroyed the lives of our people.

He is at this time transporting large armies of foreign mercenaries to compleat the works of death, desolation, and tyranny, already begun with circumstances of cruelty and perfidy scarcely paralleled in the most barbarous ages, and totally unworthy the head of a civilized nation.

He has constrained our fellow citizens taken captive on the high seas to bear arms against their country, to become the executioners of their friends and brethren, or to fall themselves by their hands.

He has excited domestic insurrections amongst us, and had endeavoured to bring on the inhabitants of our frontiers the merciless Indian savages, whose known rule of warfare is an undistinguished destruction of all ages, sexes, and conditions.

In every stage of these oppressions we have petitioned for redress in the most humble terms: our repeated petitions have been answered only by repeated injury. A prince whose character is thus marked by every act which may define a tyrant, is unfit to be the ruler of a free people.

Nor have we been wanting in attention to our British brethren. We have warned them from time to time of attempts by their Legislature to extend an unwarrantable jurisdiction over us. We have reminded them of the circumstances of our emigration and settlement here. We have

appealed to their native justice and magnanimity, and we have conjured them by the ties of our common kindred to disavow these usurpations, which would inevitably interrupt our connections and correspondence. They too have been deaf to the voice of justice and of consanguinity. We must, therefore, acquiesce in the necessity, which denounces our separation, and hold them, as we hold the rest of mankind, enemies in war, in peace friends.

We, therefore, the Representatives of the United States of America, in General Congress assembled, appealing to the Supreme Judge of the world for the rectitude of our intentions, do, in the name, and by authority of the good people of these Colonies, solemnly publish and declare, That these United Colonies are, and of right ought to be Free and Independent States; that they are absolved from all allegiance to the British Crown, and that all political connection between them and the State of Great Britain is and ought to be totally dissolved; and that as Free and Independent States they have full power to levy war, conclude peace, contract alliances, establish commerce, and to do all other acts and things which independent States may of right do. And for the support of this declaration, with a firm reliance on the protection of Divine Providence, we mutually pledge to each other our lives, our fortunes and our sacred honor.

## UNIVERSAL DECLARATION OF HUMAN RIGHTS

**(1948).** The Declaration, universally accepted as establishing "a common standard of achievement for all peoples and all nations," sets out the basic principles upon which the human rights activities of the United Nations system are based. Since its adoption, it has exercised incalculable influence upon governments and peoples everywhere; has made the men and women of every land conscious of the rights and freedoms to which they are entitled and inspired them to have these rights and freedoms recognized and respected; and promoted and protected not only the rights of individuals but also of peoples of different races, cultures, languages, religions, and social backgrounds. Fittingly, its anniversary is observed each year in nearly every country and territory of the world on 10 December: Human Rights Day.

The Declaration was adopted and proclaimed on 10 December 1948 by the UN **GENERAL ASSEMBLY** (resolution 217 [III]). The text, annexed to that resolution, is as follows:

### Preamble

Whereas recognition of the inherent dignity and of the equal and inalienable rights of all members of the human family is the foundation of freedom, justice and peace in the world,

Whereas disregard and contempt for human rights have resulted in barbarous acts which have outraged the conscience of mankind, and the advent of a world in which human beings shall enjoy freedom of speech and belief and freedom from fear and want has been proclaimed as the highest aspiration of the common people,

Whereas it is essential, if man is not to be compelled to have recourse, as a last resort, to rebellion against tyranny and oppression, that human rights should be protected by the rule of law,

Whereas it is essential to promote the development of friendly relations between nations,

Whereas the peoples of the United Nations have in the Charter reaffirmed their faith in fundamental human rights, in the dignity and worth of the human person and in the equal rights of men and women and have determined to promote social progress and better standards of life in larger freedom,

Whereas Member States have pledged themselves to achieve, in co-operation with the United Nations, the promotion of universal respect for and observance of human rights and fundamental freedoms,

Whereas a common understanding of these rights and freedoms is of the greatest importance for the full realization of this pledge,

Now, therefore,

The General Assembly

Proclaims this Universal Declaration of Human Rights as a common standard of achievement for all peoples and all nations, to the end that every individual and every organ of society, keeping this Declaration constantly in mind, shall strive by teaching and education to promote respect for these rights and freedoms and by progressive measures, national and international, to secure their universal and effective recognition and observance, both among the peoples of Member States themselves and among the peoples of territories under their jurisdiction.

*Article 1.* All human beings are born free and equal in dignity and rights. They are endowed with reason and conscience and should act towards one another in a spirit of brotherhood.

*Article 2.* Everyone is entitled to all the rights and freedoms set forth in this Declaration, without distinction of any kind, such as race, colour, sex, language, religion, political or other opinion, national or social origin, property, birth or other status.

Furthermore, no distinction shall be made on the basis of the political, jurisdictional or international status of the country or territory to which a person belongs, whether it be independent, trust, non-self-governing or under any other limitation of sovereignty.

*Article 3.* Everyone has the right to life, liberty and security of person.

*Article 4.* No one shall be held in slavery or servitude; slaver and the slave trade shall be prohibited in all their forms.

*Article 5.* No one shall be subjected to torture or to cruel, inhuman or degrading treatment or punishment.

*Article 6.* Everyone has the right to recognition everywhere as a person before the law.

*Article 7.* All are equal before the law and are entitled without any discrimination to equal protection of the law.

All are entitled to equal protections against any discrimination in violation of this Declaration and against any incitement to such discrimination.

*Article 8.* Everyone has the right to an effective remedy by the competent national tribunals for acts violating the fundamental rights granted him by the constitution or by law.

*Article 9.* No one shall be subjected to arbitrary arrest, detention or exile.

*Article 10.* Everyone is entitled in full equality to a fair and public hearing by an independent and impartial tribunal, in the determination of his rights and obligations and of any criminal charge against him.

*Article 11.* 1. Everyone charged with a penal offence has the right to be presumed innocent until proven guilty according to law in a public trial at which he has had all the guarantees necessary for his defence.

2. No one shall be held guilty of any penal offence on account of any act or omission which did not constitute a penal offence, under national or international law, at the time when it was committed. Nor shall a heavier penalty be imposed than the one that was applicable at the time the penal offence was committed.

*Article 12.* No one shall be subjected to arbitrary interference with his privacy, family, home, or correspondence, nor to attacks upon his honour and reputation. Everyone has the right to the protection of the law against such interference or attacks.

*Article 13.* 1. Everyone has the right to freedom of movement and residence within the borders of each State.

2. Everyone has the right to leave any country, including his own, and to return to his country.

*Article 14.* 1. Everyone has the right to seek and to enjoy in other countries asylum from persecution.

2. This right may not be invoked in the case of prosecutions genuinely arising from non-political crimes or from acts contrary to the purposes and principles of the United Nations.

*Article 15.* 1. Everyone has the right to a nationality.

2. No one shall be arbitrarily deprived of his nationality nor denied the right to change his nationality.

*Article 16.* 1. Men and women of full age, without any limitation due to race, nationality or religion, have the right to marry and to found a family. They are entitled to equal rights as to marriage, during marriage and at its dissolution.

2. Marriage shall be entered into only with the free and full consent of the intending spouses.

3. The family is the natural and fundamental group unit of society and is entitled to protection by society and the State.

*Article 17.* 1. Everyone has the right to own property alone as well as in association with others.

2. No one shall be arbitrarily deprived of his property.

*Article 18.* Everyone has the right to freedom of thought, conscience and religion; this right includes freedom to change his religion or belief, and freedom, either alone or in community with others and in public or private, to manifest his religion or belief in teaching, practice, worship and observance.

*Article 19.* Everyone has the right to freedom of opinion and expression; this right includes freedom to hold opinions without interference and to seek, receive and impart information and ideas through any media and regardless of frontiers.

*Article 20.* 1. Everyone has the right to freedom of peaceful assembly and association.

2. No one may be compelled to belong to an association.

*Article 21.* 1. Everyone has the right to take part in the government of his country, directly of through freely chosen representatives.

2. Everyone has the right of equal access to public service in his country.

3. The will of the people shall be the basis of the authority of government; this will shall be expressed in periodic and genuine elections which shall be by universal and equal suffrage and shall be held by secret vote or by equivalent free voting procedures.

*Article 22.* Everyone, as a member of society, has the right to social security and is entitled to realization, through national effort and international co-operation and in accordance with the organization and resources of each State, of the economic, social and cultural rights indispensable for his dignity and the free development of his personality.

*Article 23.* 1. Everyone has the right to work, to free choice of employment, to just and favourable conditions of work and to protection against unemployment.

2. Everyone, without any discrimination, has the right to equal pay for equal work.

3. Everyone who works has the right to just and favourable remuneration ensuring for himself and his family an existence worthy of human dignity, and supplemented, if necessary, by other means of social protection.

4. Everyone has the right to form and to join trade unions for the protection of his interests.

*Article 24.* Everyone has the right to rest and leisure, including reasonable limitation of working hours and periodic holidays with pay.

*Article 25.* 1. Everyone has the right to a standard of living adequate for the health and well-being of himself and of his family, including food, clothing, housing and medical care and necessary social services, and the right to security in the event of unemployment, sickness, disability, widowhood, old age or other lack of livelihood in circumstances beyond his control.

2. Motherhood and childhood are entitled to special care and assistance. All children, whether born in or out of wedlock, shall enjoy the same social protection.

*Article 26.* 1. Everyone has the right to education. Education shall be free, at least in the elementary and fundamental stages. Elementary education shall be compulsory. Technical and professional education shall be made generally available and higher education shall be equally accessible to all on the basis of merit.

2. Education shall be directed to the full development of human personality and to the strengthening of respect for human rights and fundamental freedoms. It shall promote understanding, tolerance and friendship among all nations, racial or religious groups, and shall further the activities of the United Nations for the maintenance of peace.

3. Parents have a prior right to choose the kind of education that shall be given to their children.

*Article 27.* 1. Everyone has the right freely to participate in the cultural life of the community, to enjoy the arts and to share in scientific advancement and its benefits.

2. Everyone has the right to the protection of the moral and material interests resulting from any scientific, literary or artistic production of which he is the author.

*Article 28.* Everyone is entitled to a social and international order in which the rights and freedoms set forth in this Declaration can be fully realized.

*Article 29.* 1. Everyone has duties to the community in which alone the free and full development of his personality is possible.

2. In the exercise of his rights and freedoms, everyone shall be subject only to such limitations as are determined by law solely for the purpose of securing due recognition and respect for the rights and freedoms of others and of meeting the just requirements of morality, public order and the general welfare in a democratic society.

3. These rights and freedoms may in no case be exercised contrary to the purposes and principles of the United Nations.

*Article 30.* Nothing in this Declaration may be interpreted as implying for any State, group or person any right to engage in any activity or to perform any act aimed at the destruction of any of the rights and freedoms set forth herein.

*SEE ALSO* *African Charter on Human and Peoples' Rights; American Convention on Human Rights and Protocols; American Declaration on the Rights and Duties of Man; European Convention on Human Rights and Protocols I–VIII; Inter-American Charter of Social Guarantees; International Bill of Human Rights; International Covenant on Civil and Political Rights and Optional Protocols; International Covenant on Economic, Social and Cultural Rights; United Nations Charter.*

## UNIVERSITY OF CALIFORNIA, HUMAN RIGHTS PROGRAM.

Established in 1994 to address academic and community needs for independent, interdisciplinary human rights education and research, the California Human Rights Program encourages both theoretical and applied scholarship on civil, political, economic, social, and cultural rights at the national and international levels. Visiting scholars present public lectures, conduct seminars; and have informal discussions with faculty, students, and community members. In addition to undergraduate programs, the program also offers graduate-level courses in association with the U.C. Berkeley School of Public Health and U.C. San Francisco.

Human Rights Program. Address: University of California Berkeley, Townsend Center for Humanities, 460 Stephens Hall, Berkeley, CA 94720, USA. Telephone: (510) 643-9670. Fax: (510) 643-5284. Associate Director: Prof. Rita Maran.

## UNIVERSITY OF DENVER, CENTER ON RIGHTS DEVELOPMENT.

Established in 1989 with a Ford Foundation grant, the Center on Rights Development prepares human rights monitors for work in the United States and abroad, documents and disseminates human rights information, and seeks compliance with the UNIVERSAL DECLARATION OF HUMAN RIGHTS.

Center on Rights Development. Address: Graduate School of International Studies, University of Denver, Denver, CO 80208, USA. Telephone: (303) 871-2523.

## UNIVERSITY OF ILLINOIS, PROGRAM IN ARMS CONTROL, DISARMAMENT, AND INTERNATIONAL SECURITY (ACDIS).

Founded in 1978 at the University of Illinois at Urbana-Champaign to support interdisciplinary research, teaching, and public service on the issues of peace and war, ACDIS is open to all faculty and students, regardless of discipline. The program does not offer an academic degree but does maintain a working research library; organizes seminars, workshops, and conferences; and produces and distributes publications featuring faculty and student research, in such outlets as *Swords and Ploughshares,* a quarterly journal, and *ACDIS Occasional Papers.*

Among the projects offered are the Politics, Ethics, and Technology of Peacekeeping Project; the South Asian Security Project; the European Security Project; the Unit for Cultural, Moral, and Legal Elements of International Relations; the War and Society in History Project; and the Ireland Seminar.

ACDIS Program, University of Illinois at Urbana-Champaign. Address: 607 S. Mathews Street, Urbana, IL 61801, USA. Telephone: (217) 244-0219. Director: Dr. Stephen P. Cohen.

## UNIVERSITY OF MARYLAND, GRADUATE PROGRAM IN HUMAN RIGHTS.

The International Graduate Studies Program in Human Rights Education and Training (HRET) at the University of Maryland provides formal education, training, and research opportunities to human rights activists and educators from around the world. The HRET program brings together some 20 internationally recruited participants with a strong background in human rights for 18 to 36 months of training. Key features of the program include specialized short-term workshops; multidisciplinary coursework and research leading to a master's degree in Political Science with a concentration in human rights; pedagogic training; study tours of U.S.-based human rights organizations; and internships in international and governmental agencies or non-governmental organizations.

International Graduate Studies Program in Human Rights Education and Training, University of Maryland. Address: Dept. of Government and Politics, College Park, MD 20742, USA. Telephone: (301) 405-4156. Directors: Dr. Edy Kaufman and Dr. Richard Claude.

## UNIVERSITY OF MINNESOTA, HUMAN RIGHTS CENTER.

Established in 1988, the Minnesota Human Rights Center supports public events and outreach, offers internship grants and fellowships to University of Minnesota students, and is developing a model human rights curriculum to be used in the state's public schools. In addition, the Center offers law students an opportunity to undertake the supervised representation of clients who might benefit from the application of international human rights law, and supervises the students in preparing applications for political asylum or in preparing oral and written interventions, as well as draft resolutions for UN and regional human rights bodies. Its Human Rights Documentation Center provides resources to lawyers, students, teachers, and others in the community.

Minnesota Human Rights Center. Address: University of Minnesota Law School, Room 437, 229 19th Avenue South, Minneapolis, MN 55455, USA. Telephone: (612) 626-0041. Fax: (612) 625-3478.

Directors: Prof. David Weissbrodt and Prof. Kristi Rudelius-Palmer.

## UNIVERSITY OF NEW SOUTH WALES, HUMAN RIGHTS CENTER.

The Human Rights Center was established within the University's Faculty of Law to coordinate and develop multidisciplinary human rights teaching and research at the international, regional, and national levels. The Center undertakes a broad range of activities: (1) it facilitates research, including postgraduate programs; (2) it coordinates and develops undergraduate subjects in the field and conducts specialized human rights courses of a continuing-education nature for professionals such as lawyers, judges, police, and doctors; and (3) it organizes conferences.

Human Rights Center. Address: University of New South Wales, Faculty of Law, P.O. Box 1, Kensington 2033, NSW, Australia. Telephone: (61-49) 697-2293. Telex: AA26054. Chairman: Garth Nettheim.

## UNIVERSITY OF PADUA, CENTER FOR HUMAN AND PEOPLES' RIGHTS.

Established in 1989, the Center for Human and Peoples' Rights is the only specialized international human rights program in Italy. The programs supports teaching and research in human rights and provides assistance to non-governmental organizations in all areas. The Center offers a master's degree in the field of human rights; conducts research in human rights and democracy; and publishes monographs, conferences proceedings, and a journal, *Pace, Diritti dell'Uomo, Diritti dei Popoli* three times a year in Italian.

Center for Human and Peoples' Rights. Address: University of Padua, Department of International Studies, Via Del Sevcovado 66, 35141 Padua, Italy. Telephone: (39-49) 875-1044. Fax: (39-49) 875-2951. Director: Prof. Antonio Papisca.

## UNIVERSITY OF SASKATCHEWAN, NATIVE LAW CENTER.

Founded in 1975, the Native Law Center undertakes and supports independent research into topics concerning native peoples in Canada and other countries. The Center aims to increase the involvement of native people in the legal profession and to promote a greater understanding of aboriginal rights issues in Canada.

To foster research, the Center maintains a publishing program, sponsors a summer pre-law program for native students, and has a collection of materials on native law.

Native Law Center. Address: University of Saskatchewan, 141 Diefenbaker Center, Saskatoon, Saskatchewan S7N 0W0, Canada. Telephone: (306) 966-6189. Director: Donald J. Purich.

## UNIVERSITY OF SRI LANKA, CENTRE FOR THE STUDY OF HUMAN RIGHTS.

Established in 1991, the Centre for the Study of Human Rights is the first such center at an institution of higher learning in Sri Lanka. The Centre promotes human rights teaching, research, and support programs. Participants study international law at the undergraduate and graduate levels. Projects include a diploma program on human rights for field workers and NGO personnel, the Pilot Project on Human Rights Education for the Armed Forces and Police, and an internship program. Research projects include a review of the emergency regulations in Sri Lanka, review of censorship of the arts, and a socio-legal study on the status of remanded prisoners.

Centre for the Study of Human Rights. Address: University of Sri Lanka, Faculty of Law Building, P.O. Box 1490, Colombo 3, Sri Lanka. Telephone: (94-1) 500-942. Fax: (94-1) 583-810. Director: Dr. Deepika Udagama.

## UNIVERSITY OF ULSTER, PEACE AND CONFLICT STUDIES PROGRAM.

Established in 1983 as a full-time academic department, the Peace and Conflict Studies Program includes the study of human rights as an integral part of its curriculum. The university's library contains a wide range of material on human rights in general and on the human rights situation in Northern Ireland in particular.

Peace and Conflict Studies Program. Address: Mager College, Londonderry BT48 73L, UK. Telephone: (44-504) 265-621. Telex: UNIULSTER. Director: Prof. T. M. Duffy.

## URBAN MORGAN INSTITUTE FOR HUMAN RIGHTS, UNIVERSITY OF CINCINNATI.

Established in 1979 by a grant by William J. Butler, trustee of the Urban Morgan Educational Fund, the Urban Morgan Institute for Human Rights is the first endowed institute at an American law school devoted to the study of international human rights law. The Institute recognizes that private organizations acting in domestic and transnational arenas are often the greatest contributors of new ideas and strategies in the international human rights field.

*ARTHUR RUSSELL MORGAN FELLOWSHIPS.* Each year, the Institute awards between ten and twelve fellowships to University of Cincinnati law students. The fellowships carry a stipend of $3,600 for the academic year ($6,000 for students possessing a doctorate or foreign law degree). Fellows in the law program study international human rights law over a three-year period. First-year fellows attend weekly seminars on human rights and work on the **HUMAN RIGHTS QUARTERLY** (edited by the Institute, although published by The Johns Hopkins University) and the **PENNSYLVANIA STUDIES IN HUMAN RIGHTS.** Second- and third-year fellows engage in human rights research and participate on the editorial staff of the *Human Rights Quarterly,* the Pennsylvania Studies in Human Rights, and the **AMNESTY INTERNATIONAL** USA *Legal Support Network Newsletter.*

*HUMAN RIGHTS EXTERNSHIPS.* The Institute attempts to place a number of its fellows in summer externships with human rights organizations in the United States and abroad. Fellows have been placed with the UN **CENTER FOR HUMAN RIGHTS** in Geneva, Switzerland; the European Court of Human Rights in Strasbourg, France; the **INTER-AMERICAN COURT OF HUMAN RIGHTS** in Costa Rica; the Chilean Human Rights Commission and the Netherlands Institute for Human Rights; in law firms in South Africa, Botswana, and Nepal; with NGOs such as Interrights, **ARTICLE 19,** Rights and Humanity, the Human Rights Law Group, the Lawyers Committee for Human Rights, and Amnesty International USA.

*URBAN MORGAN COLLECTION.* The Institute for Human Rights maintains an extensive collection of human rights literature and documents. The collection includes works on both the theoretical and practical aspects of the international protection of human rights, reports on the development of human rights case law abroad and before international tribunals, human rights journals, reports of international organizations, and significant works of fiction. In addition, the Institute contains a prototype database of **DIANA** on the Internet on a World Wide Web server. The prototype database contains a small sampling of some basic human rights documents from the United Nations, related U.S. State Department reports, cases from the Inter-American Court of Human Rights, and Diana Vincent-Daviss' bibliography on women's rights.

Urban Morgan Institute for Human Rights. Address: University of Cincinnati College of Law, Mail Location 40, Cincinnati, OH 45221, USA. Telephone: (513) 556-0068. Fax: (513) 556-6265. Program Director: Bert B. Lockwood, Jr.

## URUGUAY.

The Oriental Republic of Uruguay is a country in temperate South America, on the Atlantic Ocean. It has borders with Argentina and Brazil and achieved independence in 1828 as a buffer between those two countries. It became a member of the

United Nations in 1945. Its population is estimated to be 3,151,000. Ethnic groups include persons of European (mainly Spanish, Italian, and Portuguese) descent and mestizos (descendants of Amerindians absorbed into the Spanish and Portuguese populations). The language commonly used is Spanish (official). Christianity (Roman Catholic, 66%; Protestant denominations, 2%) is the predominant religion; Judaism is the religion of about 3%; and the remainder profess other faiths or none at all. Literacy is estimated at 94%.

The government (1994) took the form of a republic. Under the 1967 constitution, the president, elected by universal suffrage for a term of five years, is head of State and of government. Legislation is prepared by a bicameral General Assembly, consisting of a 99-member Chamber of Deputies and a 30-member Senate, all elected by popular vote. The independent judiciary is headed by the Supreme Court of Justice. Political parties include the Colorado Party, the Blanco Party, and the Broad Front Coalition.

*DISAPPEARANCE OF PERSONS.* The military regime which governed the country between 1973 and 1985 was accused of gross violations of human rights while in office, including widespread torture, "disappearances," and mistreatment of tens of thousands of persons. In turning the government over to civilian rule in March 1985, it demanded total amnesty for all such abuses. The amnesty was approved after acrimonious debate in both houses of the General Assembly, and signed on 22 December 1986 by President Julio Maria Sanguinetti as a step necessary to attain national reconciliation. The amnesty law barred judicial prosecution of military and police officials accused of human rights violations that took place prior to 1985. The office of the president retained the power to investigate cases of persons who "disappeared" during the period of military rule.

The Working Group on Enforced or Involuntary Disappearances of the UN **COMMISSION ON HUMAN RIGHTS** informed the Commission at its 1987 session that it had transmitted 64 cases to the government and that seven of those cases had been clarified by the government's responses and one by a non-governmental source, leaving 56 cases outstanding.

In this connection, the Working Group was informed by the permanent representative of Uruguay to the United Nations Office at Geneva that, since a new democratic government had come into power in Uruguay, disappearances had ceased and would not occur in the future provided democracy was preserved. The new government had taken several measures to put an end to human rights violations, such as an amnesty law covering all political offenses, which

had permitted the release of political prisoners, the return of exiles, and the reintegration of former officials to their posts. Concerning cases of disappearances, a parliamentary commission had been established in which all Uruguayan political parties participated. According to the findings of the commission, a total of 164 Uruguayan nationals had disappeared while military governments were in power.

Of the cases of disappeared persons, only 32 of them had disappeared in Uruguay, whereas 127 had disappeared in Argentina, three in Chile, and two in Paraguay. The report of the Commission had been transmitted to the judiciary to initiate proceedings.

*RECENT ELECTIONS.* In November 1989, Luis Alberto Lacalle, of the centrist National Party, was elected president of Uruguay, replacing President Sanguinetti of the Colorado Party, who was not eligible to stand for re-election. Lacalle promised an efficient, productive government that would substitute private enterprise for state control and reduce inflation, which had been running at more than 80% per year.

Resistance and opposition to the privatization plan and other stringent economic reforms were evidenced by the withdrawal of support for the government of former President Sanguinetti and a series of general strikes throughout the early 1990s.

In November 1994 former President Sanguinetti of the opposition Colorado Party was re-elected in Uruguay's closest elections in history. His centrist party won 32% of the vote versus 31% to the conservative National Party and 30% to the leftist Broad Front.

*REPORT OF THE UN COMMITTEE ON ECONOMIC, SOCIAL AND CULTURAL RIGHTS.* This Committee considered the initial report of Uruguay (E/1990/5/Add. 7) at its 3rd, 4th, 6th, and 13th meetings on 3, 4, and 10 May and, at its 25th meeting on 19 May 1994, adopted the following concluding observations (paras. 66–82):

*Positive aspects.* The Committee notes with satisfaction that a number of rights guaranteed by the Covenant have been incorporated in Uruguay's legislation, and in particular its Constitution. It also takes note of the concrete measures taken to comply with the obligations laid down in the Covenant. In that connection, it welcomes the progress made by the State party in ensuring free primary education for all and in making secondary and higher education free of charge and more accessible to all. In addition, the Committee notes with satisfaction that the State party has adopted social security measures aimed at offsetting the adverse consequences for the enjoyment of economic, social and cultural rights of the economic recession and the structural adjustments entailed by Uruguay's accession to the MERCOSUR economic agreement.

The Committee also regards the steps taken by the State

party to provide further training to unemployed persons as a positive development.

*Factors and difficulties impeding the implementation of the Covenant.* The Committee notes the economic difficulties encountered by State party, particularly the high rate of inflation, which impede the full implementation of economic, social and cultural rights.

*Principal subjects of concern.* The Committee is concerned about the apparent lack of measures to enable workers' and employers' organizations to participate in the discussions on the determination of minimum wages for public-sector employees and agricultural workers for the period 1990–1994.

The Committee would welcome clarification of the restrictions on the right to strike introduced by Act No. 13,720 of December 1968, as amended by Decree-Law No. 14,781 of 8 June 1978, and would appreciate receiving further details of the application of those provisions between the return to democracy and 1994. It would also wish to be informed of any bill regulating the exercise of the right to strike, since paragraph 104 of the State party's report indicated that such a bill would be submitted shortly.

The Committee would appreciate additional information on the measures taken to raise the minimum working age and to prevent or combat the exploitation of child labour. To that end, it would welcome information on the actual situation regarding the distribution of free school meals and the concrete measures taken to reduce truancy.

With regard to the implementation of article 11 of the Covenant, and more particularly the right to housing, the Committee is concerned about the shortage of housing in relation to demand and the high level of rents, particularly affecting the most vulnerable groups of society. It would appreciate having additional information on these two points.

The Committee is concerned about the standard of living of persons in rural areas, particularly those close to borders with neighbouring countries, and would welcome further information on their full access to economic, social and cultural rights.

The Committee is concerned about the impact of inflation on the enjoyment of an adequate standard of living. It would appreciate receiving specific information on the evaluation of average wage rates in relation to the cost of living since 1990.

The Committee considers that it has not been given enough information on access to health, drinking water, care and education by minority groups living in Uruguay, as well as access by such groups to various types of employment, *inter alia* in the public service.

The Committee is greatly concerned about the serious deterioration of teachers' salaries in terms of purchasing power, by the conflictual nature of relations between teachers and the State and by the apparent ineffectiveness of the measures taken to remedy that situation.

*Suggestions and recommendations.* In the light of the information submitted by the delegation and of other available sources, the Committee considers that Uruguay is making appreciable efforts to observe the economic, social and cultural rights provided for in the Covenant. However, the report submitted by the State party is not sufficiently precise or complete to give a comprehensive account of those efforts. Consequently, the Committee would wish to receive supplementary replies to the questions raised in part D above.

In addition, the Committee asks the State party to consider the possibility of ratifying the Protocol of San Salvador additional to the American Convention on Human Rights.

The Committee urges the State party to take measures to eliminate all forms of discrimination. In this connection it draws the Government's attention to its General Comment No. 3 (1990) dealing with the nature and scope of States parties' obligations under the Covenant.

With respect to the implementation of article 7 of the Covenant, and in the light of the comments made by the ILO on compliance with the requirements of the Minimum Wage Fixing Convention, No. 131, the Committee calls upon the State party to take steps with a view to establishing the national minimum wage for agricultural workers and public-sector employees in consultation with employers' and workers' representatives.

The Committee recommends that the State party should adopt urgent measures to increase the purchasing power of teachers' salaries and take that recommendation into account in the next budget of the national five-year plan.

The Committee urges the State party to take steps to improve health care for people living in areas distant from the capital, in particular by extending its primary health-care programme.

***BIBLIOGRAPHY.*** Artucio, Alejandro. "La Comunidad Internacional Frente a la Impunidad por los Crímenes de la Dictadura: Ley 15.848" (The International Community's Opposition to the Impunity over the Crimes of the Dictatorship. Law 15.848), *Revista de IELSUR* 6 (July 1990): 24–32. Scholarly article, in Spanish.

Bloche, Maxwell Gregg. *Uruguay's Military Physicians: Cogs in a System of State Terror.* Washington, D.C.: American Association for the Advancement of Science, Committee on Scientific Freedom and Responsibility, 1987. NGO report, in English.

Centro de Informacion, Investigacion y Documentacion del Uruguay (Center for Information, Research and Documentation of Uruguay). "La Mujer en Uruguay" (Women in Uruguay), *Boletin Sercom* 2 (1985): 2–15. NGO article, in Spanish.

Díaz Serra, Juan Carlos. "Los Derechos Humanos en el Sístema Penitenciario" (Human Rights in the Penitentiary System), *Revista de IELSUR* 7 (Dec. 1990): 11–20. Scholarly article, in Spanish.

Fernández, Gonzalo. "La Represión Penal de la Tortura en el Marco de la Convención de las Naciones Unidas," *Revista de IELSUR* 6 (July 1990): 13–23. Article, in Spanish; bibliography, pp. 22–23.

Fruhling, Hugo, ed. *Represion Politica y Defensa de los Derechos Humanos* (Political Repression and the Defense of Human Rights). Santiago, Chile: Academia de Humanismo Cristiano and Ediciones Chile y America, 1986. NGO edited collection, in Spanish.

Gros Espiell, Héctor. *La Corte Electoral del Uruguay* (The Uruguayan Electoral Court). San José, Costa Rica: Instituto Interamericano de Derechos Humanos Centro de Asesoría y Promoción Electoral (Inter-American Institute of Human Rights, Centre for Electoral Counselling and Promotion), 1990. Scholarly monograph, in Spanish.

Heinz, Wolfgang S. *Ursachen und Folgen von Menschenrechtsverletzungen in der Dritten Welt* (Causes and Consequences of Human Rights Violations in Third World Countries). Saarbrucken, Germany: Verlag Breitenbach, 1986. Scholarly monograph, in German; bibliography on Uruguay, pp. 571–572.

Madres y Familiares de Detenidos y Desaparecidos (Mothers and Relatives of the Detained-Disappeared). *Situation con-*

*cerning the Investigation of Prisoners and Disappeared in Uruguay.* Montevideo, Uruguay: 1985. NGO report, in Spanish.

Perez Aquirre, Luis. *Derechos Humanos: Un Relato Militante de Su Defensa y Promocion en el Uruguay* (Human Rights: A Participatory Account of their Defense and Promotion in Uruguay). Montevideo: Servicio Paz y Justicia, 1986. NGO report, in Spanish.

Secretariat International des Juristes pour l'Amnistie en Uruguay (International Secretariat of Lawyers for Amnesty in Uruguay). *Situacion de las Personas Desaparecidas y los Hechos que la Motivaron* (Situation of the Disappeared Persons and the Motivation behind It). Paris: 1985. NGO report, in Spanish.

Semino, Miguel Angel. "Comentarios Sobre la Acción de Amparo en el Derecho Uruguayo" (Commentaries on Amparo in Uruguayan Law), *Boletín—Comisión Andina de Juristas* 27 (Dec. 1990): 16–24. Scholarly article, in Spanish.

Servicio Paz y Justicia (Service for Peace and Justice). *Informe: Derechos Humanos en Uruguay/1988* (Report: Human Rights in Uruguay 1988). Montevideo, Uruguay: 1988. NGO annual report, in Spanish.

———. "La Condicion de la Mujer" (The Condition of Women), *Paz y Justicia* 1, no. 6 (June–July 1986): 20–41. NGO article, in Spanish.

———. "Uruguay: Paz vs. Crisis" (Uruguay: Peace vs. Crisis), *Pax y Justicia* 1, no. 7 (Aug.–Sept. 1986): 29–34. NGO article, in Spanish.

Varela, Carlos. "The Referendum Campaign in Uruguay: An Unprecedented Challenge to Impunity," *Human Rights Internet* 13, no. 1 (Spring 1989). Commentary, in English.

Weinstein, Martin. *Consolidating Democracy in Uruguay: The Sea Change of 1989 Elections.* New York: Bildner Center for Western Hemisphere Studies, 1990. Scholarly study, in English.

Westerveen, Gert. "Return to Democracy in Argentina and Uruguay: Some Outstanding Human Rights Problems," *SIM Newsletter* 11 (July 1985): 9–16. NGO article, in English.

**UZBEKISTAN.** The Republic of Uzbekistan, formerly the Uzbek Soviet Socialist Republic and now a member of the Commonwealth of Independent States, is bordered by Turkmenistan and Afghanistan to the south, Tajikistan to the southeast, Kyrgyzstan to the east, and Kazakhstan to the north. It declared its independence from the Soviet Union in 1991 and became a co-founder of the Commonwealth of Independent States in December 1991. It became a member of the United Nations in 1992.

Its population is estimated (1994) to be 22,608,866, comprising 71% Uzbek, 8% Russian, 5% Tajik, 4% Kazakh, 2% Tatar, 2% Karakalpak, and 7% other. The main languages are the official language of Uzbek (74%), Russian (14%), and Tajik (4%). The primary religions are Sunni Muslim (88%) and Eastern Orthodox (9%).

Uzbekistan came fully within the Russian Empire in the late 19th century and came under Soviet control after the Bolshevik revolution in 1917, first as part of the Turkestan Autonomous Soviet Socialist Republic and, from 1924, as the Uzbek Soviet Socialist Republic, which became a constituent member of the USSR in 1925. Although they raised significantly the rate of literacy, the Soviets harshly repressed the Muslim faith.

In the late 1980s, consistent with the opposition to the communist monopoly on power seen throughout the republics of the Soviet Union, an opposition political group was formed. Although the group (*Birlik,* "Unity") was not allowed to register as a political party and was later banned altogether, its campaign led to Uzbek being declared the official language in 1989.

Following an attempted coup against the reformist Soviet government in Moscow in August 1991, the Uzbek Supreme Soviet declared the country independent and changed its name to the Republic of Uzbekistan. The move was supported by 98% of voters in a referendum in December which coincided with direct presidential elections. The leader of the former Communist Party, now called the People's Democratic Party of Uzbekistan, was re-elected with 86% of the votes.

A new constitution was adopted in December 1992. The president, who is directly elected for a maximum of two five-year terms, appoints, with the approval of the legislature a prime minister and other ministers, as well as judges for the Constitutional Court, the Supreme Court, and the High Economic Court. Replacing the 500-seat Supreme Soviet as of December 1994 is the 250-seat *Oly Majlis* (Supreme Assembly), which is elected for a five-year term.

Although the new constitution contained guarantees of freedom of expression, opposition was strictly suppressed, members of *Birlik* were arrested, and newspapers and periodicals had to be registered with the State Committee for the Press. However, Uzbekistan did hold its first multiparty elections for its 250-seat assembly in December 1994. The People's Democratic Party won 30% of the vote and 179 seats, making it the largest party, followed by the Fatherland Progress Party.

**BIBLIOGRAPHY.** Amnesty International. *Uzbekistan: Clampdown on Dissent.* London: 1993. NGO report, in English.

Helsinki Watch. *Human Rights in Uzbekistan.* New York: Human Rights Watch, 1993. NGO report, in English.

Human Rights Watch. "Uzbekistan," in *Human Rights Watch World Report 1995,* pp. 238–242. New York: 1995. NGO report, in English.

# V

**VANUATU.** The Republic of Vanuatu is a country occupying an archipelago consisting of about 80 islands in the South Pacific Ocean, between New Caledonia and Fiji. The largest islands are Efate, Espiritu Santo, Malekula, Malo, Pentecost, and Tanna. Formerly known as the New Hebrides, an Anglo–French condominium, Vanuatu achieved independence from Great Britain and France in 1980 and became a member of the United Nations in 1981. Its population is estimated by the UN to be 226,000. The people are predominantly of Melanesian descent. Languages used commonly include Malaysian, French, and English. Religions practiced include Christianity (Presbyterian, 37%; Anglican, 15%; other Protestant denominations, 24%; Roman Catholic, 15%) and Animism (9%).

The government (1994) took the form of a republic and member of the Commonwealth, of which the British monarch is the symbolic head. Under the 1980 constitution, the president, elected by an electoral college for a term of five years, is head of State. The prime minister, representing the party or coalition given an elective majority, is head of government. Legislation is prepared by a 39-member Parliament, elected by popular vote. The Vanuaaku Party is the predominant political group.

Labor unrest and a strike by public servants at the end of 1993 led to a government ban on trade unions and dismissal of some of the strikers. The presidential election was boycotted in 14 February 1994. When no candidate received the requisite majority, another was held in March. Jean-Marie Leye of the Union of Moderate Parties was elected. Prime Minister Maxime Carlot continued in that post in a coalition government. Vanuatu resumed diplomatic relations with France in 1992 following a period of tension from 1981. Legislation introduced in May 1994 began a process of local government reorganization.

***BIBLIOGRAPHY.*** International Confederation of Free Trade Unions. "Strikes on Vanuatu," *Free Labour World* 8/88 (31 May 1988): 3. NGO article, in English.

Scott-Murphy, J., D. Dunstan, and N. Khan. *Human Rights in Melanesia: The Report of the Evatt Foundation Delegation.* Sydney, Australia: H.V. Evatt Memorial Foundation, 1988. NGO report, in English.

**VENEZUELA.** The Republic of Venezuela is a country in tropical South America, on the Caribbean Sea; it includes 72 offshore islands. It has borders with Brazil, Colombia, and Guyana. It achieved independence from Spain in 1821 and became a member of the United Nations in 1945. Its population is estimated by the UN to be 20,722,000. Although Venezuela does not classify or characterize its population by ethnic origin, it can be said that most of its people are of mestizo (mixed white and Amerindian) descent. There is an indigenous population of some 140,645 persons in rural, forest, and frontier areas: more than 20,000 families organized into some 1,595 indigenous communities, forming culturally and linguistically coherent, stable, and cohesive communities representing more than 30 distinctive ethnic minorities. Languages commonly used include Spanish, Portuguese, Arabic, German, and a number of Amerindian vernaculars. Christianity (Roman Catholic, 96%; Protestant denominations, 1%) is the predominant religion; others total 3%. Literacy is estimated at 86%.

The government (1994) took the form of a federal republic, with 20 states, two federal territories, and a dependency (the offshore islands). Each state is autonomous and has its own governor and legislature. The president is elected by universal and compulsory suffrage for a term of four years; he is not eligible for re-election until ten years after the end of his term. Assisted by a 24-member Council of Ministers, he serves as head of State and of government. There is a bicameral Congress, including the 200-member Chamber of Deputies and the 47-member Senate, all members of which are elected by popular vote for terms of five years. The judiciary is independent and headed by a Supreme Court of 18 members. Political parties include the Democratic Action Party, the Social Christian Party, the People's Electoral Movement, and the Democratic Republican Union.

Carlos Andres Perez, who stepped down in 1979 after serving four years as president of Venezuela, was re-elected in January 1988—the first Venezuelan president to win re-election. He succeeded President Jaime Lusinchi on 2 February 1989.

Following a tumultuous incumbency, including violent public demonstrations against the government's economic policies and two attempted coups, President Perez was permanently suspended from office in mid-1993 and charged with large-scale embezzlement from a government fund. Former President Dr. Rafael Caldera Rodriguez was elected president in December 1993 with 30% of the vote; he had previously served as president from 1963 to 1974. Economic woes continued with the collapse of numerous banks.

**INDIGENOUS POPULATION.** As regards Venezuela's indigenous populations, the government stated, in a report presented to the UN **COMMITTEE ON THE ELIMINATION OF RACIAL DISCRIMINATION** on 25 September 1986, that (UN Doc. CERD/C/148/Add. 18, paras. 19–20):

Article 77 of the Constitution prescribes that the law shall establish the special régime required for the protection of the indigenous communities and for their gradual incorporation into national life. In other words, in regulating matters of concern to the indigenous communities, the Venezuelan State must be guided by the fact that they need special and more extensive protection than that enjoyed by the other inhabitants of the country and that the indigenous peoples must be incorporated gradually into national life, as far as the various institutions and mechanisms are concerned that regulate the life or circumstances of the other inhabitants of Venezuela.

In conformity with the provisions of article 61 of the Constitution, the Venezuelan State assumes the obligation not to permit discrimination based on race, sex, creed or social status. It follows that the members of indigenous communities have the individual, social, economic and political rights which the Venezuelan State recognizes to all inhabitants of the Republic, including the right to life; liberty and security of person; inviolability of the home and correspondence; freedom of movement throughout the national territory; to profess one's religious faith and to worship, in private or public; to express one's opinion, either orally or in writing; to address petitions to any public entity or official; to use the organs for the administration of justice for the defence of one's rights and interests; to freedom of association, for lawful ends; to meet, either in public or private, without prior permission; to protection of health and to education; to work and to social security; to engage freely in a remunerative activity of one's choice; to vote or to hold public office and, finally, all those rights granted or bestowed by the Constitution and the laws, treaties or conventions on the protection of human rights, to most of which Venezuela is a party.

Racial tension erupted in January 1994 when a prison riot resulted in at least 100 deaths, highlighting the problem of extreme overcrowding in the country's prison system.

**BIBLIOGRAPHY.** Americas Watch. *Human Rights in Venezuela.* New York: Human Rights Watch, 1993. NGO report, in English.

———. *Venezuela: Prison Massacre in Maracaibo.* New York: Human Rights Watch, 1994. NGO report, in English.

Amnesty International. *Venezuela: Arbitrary Killings in February/March 1989: Victims Exhumed from Mass Graves.* London: 1991. NGO report, in English.

———. *Venezuela: The Eclipse of Human Rights.* London: 1993. NGO report, in English.

———. *Venezuela: Torture and Other Human Rights Violations.* London: 1992. NGO report, in English.

Branch, Hilary. "Death Well Revelations, Muzzle on Press Shocks Venezuelans," *Latinamerica Press* 16, no. 21 (5 June 1986): 1–2. News service article, in English.

Colchester, Marcus, ed. *The Health and Survival of the Venezuelan Yanoama.* London: Anthropology Resource Center, Survival International, and International Work Group for Indigenous Affairs. Scholarly articles, in English.

Comisión Andina de Juristas (Andean Commission of Jurists). *Venezuela: Administración de Justicia y Crisis Institucional* (Venezuela: Administration of Justice and Institutional Crisis). Lima, Peru: 1992. NGO report, in Spanish.

Fédération Internationale des Droits de l'Homme (International Federation of Human Rights). *Rapport de mission: mission d'observation judiciaire sur la situation des droits de l'homme au Vénézuéla, 15 au 21 septembre 1990* (Mission Report: Judicial Observer Mission on the Human Rights Situation in Venezuela, September 15–21, 1990). Paris: 1991. NGO fact-finding report, in French.

———. "Venezuela: Un Nouvel Etat Concerne par les Disparitions Forcees des Personnes?" (Venezuela: A New State Affected by Forced Disappearances of People?), *Lettre de la FIDH* 164 (16 Sept. 1986): 1–21. NGO bulletin article, in French.

Fernández, Fernando F. "Los Derechos Humanos frente a la Legislación y la Política Penitenciaria en Venezuela" (Human Rights with Respect to Prison Law and Policy in Venezuela), *Boletín—Comisión Andina de Juristas* no. 28 (March 1991): 28–34. Scholarly article, in Spanish.

Gonzalez, Jesus. "Statement from the Commission of the National Indian Council of Venezuela," *IWGIA Newsletter* no. 62 (Dec. 1990): 124–127. NGO article, in English.

Human Rights Watch. "Venezuela," in *Human Rights Watch World Report 1995*, pp. 119–123. New York: 1995. NGO report, in English.

Latin American Documentation. *The Church and Native Peoples.* Lima, Peru: 1986. NGO document collection, in English.

Molina, Jose Enrique. *Democracia Representative y Participacion Politica en Venezuela* (Representative Democracy and Political Participation in Venezuela). San Jose, Costa Rica: Instituto Interamericano de Derechos Humanos and Centro de Asesoria y Promocion Electoral, 1986. IGO monograph, in Spanish.

Pocaterra, Noeli. "Venezuela: Education and Indigenous Women," *IWGIA Newsletter* 55–56 (Oct.–Dec. 1988): 105–115. NGO article, in English.

Programa Venezolano de Educación-Acción en Derechos Humanos (Venezuelan Program on Human Rights Education and Action). *Situación de los Derechos Humanos en Venezuela: Informe Anual, Octubre 1989–Septiembre 1990* (Human Rights Situation in Venezuela: Annual Report, October 1989–September 1990). Caracas, Venezuela: 1990–. NGO annual report, in Spanish.

———. *Los Detenidos de Agosto (Resumen Cronologico de la Informacion de Prensa)* (August Detainees [Chronological Summary of Press Information]). Caracas, Venezuela: 1988. NGO report, in Spanish.

Survival International. *An End to Laughter? Tribal Peoples and Economic Development.* London: 1985. NGO report, in English.

**VICTIMS' RIGHTS.** International standards of compensation for those who are the victims of gross violations of human rights are clearly set out in several instruments.

The **UNIVERSAL DECLARATION OF HUMAN RIGHTS** proclaims that

*Article 8.* Everyone has the right to an effective remedy by the competent national tribunals for acts violating the fundamental rights granted him by the constitution or by law.

The **INTERNATIONAL COVENANT ON CIVIL AND POLITICAL RIGHTS** provides, in article 14, that

6. When a person has by a final decision been convicted of a criminal offence and when subsequently his conviction has been reversed or he has been pardoned on the ground that a new or newly discovered fact shows conclusively that there has been a miscarriage of justice, the person who has suffered punishment as a result of such conviction shall be compensated according to law, unless it is proved that the non-disclosure of the unknown fact in time is wholly or partly attributable to him.

Article 14 of the Convention against Torture and Other Cruel, Inhuman or Degrading Treatment or Punishment (see **TORTURE**) reads as follows:

1. Each State Party shall ensure in its legal system that the victim of an act of torture obtains redress and has an enforceable right to fair and adequate compensation, including the means for as full rehabilitation as possible. In the event of the death of the victim as a result of an act of torture, his dependants shall be entitled to compensation.
2. Nothing in this article shall affect any right of the victim or other persons to compensation which may exist under national law.

Articles 8 to 21 of the Declaration of Basic Principles of Justice for Victims of Crime and Abuse of Power (see next entry) provide that

*[A. Victims of Crime.] Restitution.* 8. Offenders or third parties responsible for their behaviour should, where appropriate, make fair restitution to victims, their families or dependants. Such restitution should include the return of property or payment for the harm or loss suffered, reimbursement of expenses incurred as a result of the victimization, the provision of services and the restoration of rights.
9. Governments should review their practices, regulations and laws to consider restitution as an available sentencing option in criminal cases, in addition to other criminal sanctions.
10. In cases of substantial harm to the environment, restitution, if ordered, should include, as far as possible, restoration of the environment, reconstruction of the infrastructure, replacement of community facilities and reimbursement of the expenses of relocation, whenever such harm results in the dislocation of a community.
11. Where public officials or other agents acting in an official or quasi-official capacity have violated national criminal laws, the victims should receive restitution from the State whose officials or agents were responsible for the harm inflicted. In cases where the Government under whose authority the victimizing act or omission occurred is no longer in existence, the State or Government successor in title should provide restitution to the victims.

*Compensation.* 12. When compensation is not fully available from the offender or other sources, States should endeavour to provide financial compensation to:

    (a) Victims who have sustained significant bodily injury or impairment of physical or mental health as a result of serious crimes;

    (b) The family, in particular dependants of persons who have died or become physically or mentally incapacitated as a result of such victimization.

13. The establishment, strengthening and expansion of national funds for compensation to victims should be encouraged. Where appropriate, other funds may also be established for this purpose, including in those cases where the State of which the victim is a national is not in a position to compensate the victim for the harm.

*Assistance.* 14. Victims should receive the necessary material, medical, psychological and social assistance through governmental, voluntary, community-based and indigenous means.
15. Victims should be informed of the availability of health and social services and other relevant assistance and be readily afforded access to them.
16. Police, justice, health, social service and other personnel concerned should receive training to sensitize them to the needs of victims, and guidelines to ensure proper and prompt aid.
17. In providing services and assistance to victims, attention should be given to those who have special needs because of the nature of the harm inflicted. . . .

*[B. Victims of Abuse of Power.]* 18. "Victims" means persons who, individually or collectively, have suffered harm, including physical or mental injury, emotional suffering, economic loss or substantial impairment of their fundamental rights, through acts or omissions that do not yet constitute violations of national criminal laws but of internationally recognized norms relating to human rights.
19. States should consider incorporating into the national law norms proscribing abuses of power and providing remedies to victims of such abuses. In particular, such remedies should include restitution and/or compensation, and necessary material, medical, psychological and social assistance and support.
20. States should consider negotiating multilateral international treaties relating to victims, as defined in paragraph 18.
21. States should periodically review existing legislation and practices to ensure their responsiveness to changing circumstances, should enact and enforce, if necessary, legislation proscribing acts that constitute serious abuses of political or economic power, as well as promoting policies and mechanisms for the prevention of such acts, and should develop and make readily available appropriate rights and remedies for victims of such acts.

Bearing these standards in mind, the UN **SUB-COMMISSION ON PREVENTION OF DISCRIMINATION AND PROTECTION OF MINORITIES** at its 1988 session recognized (resolution 1988/11) that all victims of gross violations of human rights and fundamental freedoms should be entitled to restitution; a fair and just compensation; and the means for as full a rehabilitation as possible for any damage suffered by them, either individually or collectively; and that, in the event of death of the victims as a result of such acts, their dependents should be entitled to fair and just compensation.

The Sub-Commission decided to examine the question further at its 1989 session with a view to considering the possibility of developing further basic principles and guidelines in this respect. At the 1989 session, the Sub-Commission decided (resolution 1989/13) to entrust one of its members, Mr. Theo van Boven (Netherlands) with the task of undertaking a study concerning the right to restitution, compensation, and rehabilitation for victims of gross violations of human rights and fundamental freedoms, taking into account relevant existing international human rights norms on compensation and relevant decisions and views of international human rights organs, with a view to exploring the possibility of developing some basic principles and guidelines in this respect. Mr. van Boven was requested to submit a preliminary report to the Sub-Commission at its 1990 session.

*COMPLAINTS AND OTHER COMMUNICATIONS CONCERNING HUMAN RIGHTS.* Many thousands of complaints and other communications concerning human rights reach the international organizations within the United Nations system every year, posted by individuals and groups in all parts of the world who appeal for help in realizing their human rights and fundamental freedoms or in obtaining redress for violations of those rights and freedoms.

A number of procedures have been established for dealing with different categories of complaints and communications, and their discreet handling has become a major function of several international organs, including the UN **COMMISSION ON HUMAN RIGHTS,** its Sub-Commission on Prevention of Discrimination and Protection of Minorities, and the **COMMISSION ON THE STATUS OF WOMEN.** These procedures are summarized below. Procedures established by treaty-based monitoring bodies are summarized under the respective titles of such bodies: the **COMMITTEE AGAINST TORTURE;** the **COMMITTEE ON ECONOMIC, SOCIAL AND CULTURAL RIGHTS;** the **COMMITTEE ON THE ELIMINATION OF DISCRIMINATION AGAINST WOMEN;** the **COMMITTEE ON THE ELIMINATION OF RACIAL DISCRIMINATION;** the Group of Three; and the **HUMAN RIGHTS COMMITTEE.**

*Procedures Provided by the UN Economic and Social Council.* (a) *Resolutions 75 (V) and 76 (V).* In resolution 75 (V), adopted on 5 August 1947, the Council approved a statement which had been adopted by the Commission on Human Rights at its first session, that "the Commission recognizes that it has no power to take any action in regard to any complaints concerning human rights," and requested the Secretary-General (i) to compile a confidential list of communications received concerning human rights, before each session of the Commission, with a brief indication of the substance of each; (ii) to furnish this confidential list to the Commission, in private meeting, without divulging the identity of the authors of the communications; (iii) to enable the members of the Commission, upon request, to consult the originals of communications dealing with the principles involved in the promotion of universal respect for and observance of human rights; (iv) to inform the writers of all communications concerning human rights, however addressed, that their communications have been received and duly noted for consideration in accordance with the procedure laid down by the United Nations (where necessary, the Secretary-General should indicate that the Commission has no power to take any action in regard to any complaint concerning human rights); and (v) to furnish each member State not represented on the Commission with a brief indication of the substance of any communication concerning human rights which refers explicitly to that State or to territories under its jurisdiction, without divulging the name of the author. The Council suggested to the Commission that it should at each session appoint an ad hoc committee to meet shortly before its next session for the purpose of reviewing the confidential list of communications prepared by the Secretary-General and recommending which of these communications, in original, should, in accordance with (iii) above, be made available to members of the Commission upon request.

In resolution 76 (V), the **ECONOMIC AND SOCIAL COUNCIL** recognized that the Commission on the Status of Women, as in the case of the Commission on Human Rights, had no power to take any action in regard to any complaints concerning the status of women and requested the Secretary-General to follow a procedure identical to that which it had established in resolution 75 (V).

(b) *Resolution 728 F (XXVIII).* In this resolution, adopted on 30 July 1959, the Council gave members of the Sub-Commission on Prevention of Discrimination and Protection of Minorities the same facilities, with respect to communications dealing with discrimination and minorities, as are enjoyed by members of the Commission on Human Rights.

(c) *Resolution 1235 (XLII).* In 1966, the **GENERAL ASSEMBLY,** now considerably enlarged by the admission of new member States, invited the Economic and Social Council and the Commission on Human Rights "to give urgent consideration to ways and means of improving the capacity of the United Nations to put an end to violations of human rights wherever they might occur." The Council, on 6 June 1967 (resolution 1235 [XLII]), granted the Commission and the Sub-Commission the authority "to examine information relevant to gross violations of human rights and fundamental freedoms ... contained in the communications listed by the Secretary-General pursuant to Council resolution 728 F (XXVIII)," and decided that the Commission might, in appropriate cases and after careful consideration of the information made available to it, "make a thorough study of situations which reveal a consistent pattern of violations of human rights ... and report, with recommendations thereon, to the Economic and Social Council."

*(d) Resolution 1503 (XLVIII).* By this resolution, entitled "Procedure for Dealing with Communications relating to Violations of Human Rights and Fundamental Freedoms," the Economic and Social Council on 27 May 1970 authorized the Sub-Commission on Prevention of Discrimination and Protection of Minorities to appoint a working group "to consider all communications, including replies of Governments thereon, received by the Secretary-General under Council resolution 728 F (XXVIII) of 30 July 1959 with a view to bringing to the attention of the Sub-Commission those communications, together with replies of Governments, if any, which appear to reveal a consistent pattern of gross and reliably attested violations of human rights and fundamental freedoms within the terms of reference of the Sub-Commission." Communications received under Council resolution 728 F (XXVIII) are those concerning human rights (and also women's rights) "however addressed," that is, irrespective of the form or of the addressee of the communication. They may be addressed to the United Nations, the Secretary-General, or to any office within the United Nations Secretariat.

On 13 August 1971, the Sub-Commission adopted (resolution 1 [XXIV])

provisional criteria for determining whether a communication is admissible under the procedure outlined in resolution 1503 (XLVIII). Those criteria have served during the 10 years of application of the procedure without change. They stipulate, *inter alia,* that the contents of the communication may not be in contradiction to the United Nations Charter, the Universal Declaration of Human Rights or other instruments on human rights; the examination of communications and replies by the Governments concerned must show that there are reasonable grounds to believe that they may reveal a consistent pattern of gross and reliably attested violations of human rights and fundamental freedoms. Such situations are considered not to be the exclusive internal affairs of a State and entitle United Nations organs to take action.

Resolution 1503 (XLVIII) sets the stage for a three-step procedure involving consideration of complaints by three bodies: a special working group of the Sub-Commission; the Sub-Commission itself; and the Commission on Human Rights. The working group, consisting of no more than five members, meets once a year in private meetings to consider all communications, including replies from Governments on them, received by the Secretary-General under Council resolution 728 F (XXVIII), in order to select by a majority vote those communications which appear to reveal a consistent pattern of gross and reliably attested violations of human rights and fundamental freedoms, in order to bring them to the attention of the Sub-Commission, together with the replies from Governments, if any.

The second stage of the procedure takes place in the Sub-Commission as a whole, which considers in private meetings the communications brought before it and any replies of Governments and other relevant information, in order to determine if particular situations which appear to reveal a consistent pattern of gross and reliably attested violations of human rights should be referred to the Commission on Human Rights.

The third step in the implementation of Council resolution 1503 (XLVIII) takes place at the Commission level. The Commission is called upon to determine whether a situation which has been referred to it by the Sub-Commission requires a thorough study by the Commission and a report and recommendations thereon to the Council in accordance with paragraph 3 of Council resolution 1235 (XLII), or whether it may be the subject of an investigation by an *ad hoc* committee, with the proviso that such an investigation can only be undertaken with the express consent of the State concerned, in constant co-operation with that State and under conditions agreed upon by it.

Paragraph 4 of Council resolution 1503 (XLVIII) contains specific instructions for the Secretary-General. The confidential lists of communications are to be prepared on a monthly basis for submission to the members of the Sub-Commission, together with the text of replies received from Governments. The Secretary-General is requested to make available to the members of the working group at their annual meetings the originals of such communications as they may request, and to circulate to the members of the Sub-Commission, in the working languages, the "originals" of those communications that have been referred to them by the working group.

At its 1989 session, the Sub-Commission adopted in closed meetings two decisions relating to the handling of communications. On 25 August 1989, it decided (decision 1989/101) to suspend rule 59 of the rules of procedure of the functional commissions of the Council so as to allow for voting by secret ballot for decisions adopted at the 1989 session under resolution 1503 (XLVIII). On the same day, it decided (decision 1989/102) that thenceforth its Working Group on Communications should not consider a communication until the government concerned had been allowed five months in which to submit a reply, from the date on which the communication was transmitted to the government under Council resolution 728 F (XXVIII).

*(e) Resolutions 277 (X) and 474 A (XV), on Trade Union Rights.* In accordance with these resolutions of 17 February 1950 and 9 April 1953, respectively, communications containing

allegations of infringements of trade union rights received from Governments or trade union or employers' organizations against States members of the International Labour Organisation (ILO) are forwarded to the Governing Body of the International Labour Office for its consideration as to referral to the Fact-Finding and Conciliation Commission on Freedom of Association. In regard to any Member of the United Nations which is not a member of the ILO, the Secretary-General, on behalf of the Council, will seek the consent of the Government concerned for the transmittal of a communication to the ILO. In the event that such consent is not forthcoming, the Council will decide on any appropriate alternative action designed to safeguard the rights relating to freedom of association involved in the case.

*(f) Resolution 607 (XXI), on Forced Labor.* In accordance with this resolution of 1 May 1956, the

Secretary-General transmits any information received on forced labour to the Director-General of the International Labour Office, notwithstanding the provisions of Council resolution 75 (V), as amended in resolutions 116 A (V), 192 A (VIII), and 275 (X). The independent *Ad Hoc* Committee on Forced Labour of the International Labour Organisation seeks to obtain relevant information on the alleged existence of forced labour. The Council invited the International Labour Organisation, in resolution 607 (XXI), to include in its annual report to the Council an account of action taken in that field.

### Procedures Adopted by Other United Nations Organs

*(a) The General Assembly.* The General Assembly does not as a rule deal with communications concerning human rights. However, a brief indication of communications from nongovernmental organizations which relate to items on the agenda of the Assembly appears in lists distributed under the A/INF series. Communications relating to human rights in non-self-governing territories are received and considered by the Special Committee on the Situation With Regard to the Implementation of the Declaration on the Granting of Independence to Colonial Countries and Peoples, and are issued in the A/AC.109 . . . series. The Special Committee has established a Sub-Committee which screens such communications. Communications relating to the racial policies of the Government of South Africa are received and considered by the Special Committee on *Apartheid.* That Committee has established a Sub-Committee which screens such communications and reports to the Special Committee with recommendations for appropriate action.

*(b) The Security Council.* A brief indication of communications which relate to matters of which the Security Council is seized appears in lists which are issued in the S/NC/ . . . series, and are circulated to the members of the Council. Copies are furnished, on request, to members of the Council.

*(c) The Trusteeship Council.* By article 87 (b) of the UN Charter, the Trusteeship Council is empowered to accept petitions and to examine them in consultation with the administering authority. Communications relating to human rights in trust territories are issued in document series T/PET . . . and T/COM. . . . The Economic and Social Council and the Trusteeship Council have agreed that those parts of the communications, dealt with by the latter, which are of concern to the Commission on Human Rights or the Commission on the Status of Women should be communicated to them. The Trusteeship Council may ask the Commission for such assistance as it may desire under article 91 of the Charter.

### Procedures Adopted by Specialized Agencies

*The International Labour Organisation.* The procedures on communications established by the International Labour Organisation (ILO) relate to problems in particular fields of social policy and legislation. None of them are confined to problems of particular categories of persons.

Articles 24 and 25 of the ILO constitution provide for the examination of representations by employers' and workers' organizations concerning the observance of ratified ILO Conventions.

Under the Standing Orders (ILO Doc. GB 212/14/21) concerning procedures for the examination of representations under articles 24 and 25 of the ILO constitution, the director-general shall acknowledge receipt when a representation is made to the International Labour Office under article 24 of the ILO constitution and inform the government against which the representation is made. The director-general shall immediately bring the representation before the officers of the governing body. If the governing body decides, on the basis of the report of its officers, that a representation is receivable (the communication must be in written form, emanate from an industrial association of employers or workers, must concern a member of the ILO, . . .), it shall set up a committee for its examination, composed of members of the governing body chosen in equal numbers from the government, employers' groups, and workers' groups.

According to article 6 of the Standing Orders, the committee, when it has completed its examination of the representation as regards substance, shall present a report to the governing body in which it shall describe the steps taken by it to examine the representation, present its conclusions on the issues raised therein, and formulate its recommendations as to the decisions to be taken by the governing body.

The meetings of the governing body at which questions relating to a representation are considered are to be held in private. The governments concerned shall be invited to participate, without the right to vote.

Articles 26 to 34 of the ILO constitution relate to complaints on the nonobservance of ratified Conventions and the examination of such complaints by a Commission of Inquiry.

The procedures followed by Commissions of Inquiry are indicated in paragraph 85 of the Manual on Procedures relating to International Labour Conventions and Recommendations (D.31.1965, Rev. 1980).

Paragraph 85 states that "there are no standing orders concerning the procedure of Commissions of Inquiry. In all cases in which complaints have been referred to a Commission of Inquiry, the governing body has left it to the Commission to determine its own procedures in accordance with the Constitution."

A special procedure for the examination of complaints of violations of trade union rights is provided in paragraphs 87 to 90 of the manual. At the present time, there are three bodies which are competent to hear complaints lodged with the ILO alleging infringements of trade union rights: the Committee on Freedom of Association set up by the governing body, the governing body itself, and the Factfinding and Conciliation Commission on Freedom of Association.

Complaints lodged with ILO directly or via the United Nations must come either from organizations of workers or employers or from governments. Allegations are receivable only if they are submitted by a national organization directly interested in the matter, by international organisations of employers or workers in consultative status with ILO, or other international organisations of employers or workers where the allegations relate to matters directly affecting their affiliated organisations.

Complaints must be presented in writing, duly signed by a representative of a body entitled to present them, and must be as fully supported as possible by proof of allegations relating to specific infringements of trade union rights.

Complaints originating from assemblies or gatherings which are not permanent bodies, or even definitive entities with which it is impossible to correspond (either because they have only a temporary existence or because the complaints do not contain any addresses of the complainants), are not receivable.

The Committee does not take cognizance of complaints presented by persons who, through fear of reprisals, request that their names or the place and origin of the complaints should not be disclosed. An exception is made in cases where the director-general, after examining the complaint in question, informs the committee that it contains allegations of some degree of gravity which have not previously been examined by the committee. The committee can then decide what action, if any, should be taken with regard to such complaints.

Complaints which do not relate to specific infringements of trade union rights are referred by the director-general to the Committee on Freedom of Association for an opinion, and the Committee decides whether any action should be taken.

The Committee consists of nine regular and nine substitute members, chosen from among the Government Group, the Employers' Group, and the Workers' Group of the governing body, that is, three regular and three substitute members from each group. Each member sits in a personal capacity.

The Committee always endeavours to reach unanimous decisions. In the event of a vote, substitutes do not vote when all the regular members of the group are voting.

The responsibilities of the Committee are essentially to consider, for recommendation to the governing body, whether cases are worthy of examination.

It is open to the governing body to refer to the Factfinding and Conciliation Commission, for impartial examination, any allegation of infringements of trade union rights which the governing body, on the report of the Committee on Freedom of Association, or the Conference, acting on the report of its Credentials Committee, considers it appropriate to refer to the Commission for investigation. Any government against which an allegation of infringements of trade union rights is made can refer such an allegation to the Commission for investigation.

The Factfinding and Conciliation Commission on Freedom of Association is appointed by the governing body and works in panels of not less than three nor more than five members. Its members are independent persons.

The Commission is essentially a factfinding body, but it is authorized to discuss situations referred to it for investigation with the government concerned, with a view to securing the adjustment of difficulties by agreement.

At its 191st session (November 1973) the governing body adopted a procedure for the examination of requests for "special surveys" which governments or organizations of employers or workers may submit on questions concerning the elimination of discrimination in employment.

The possibility of undertaking such special surveys, with a view to evaluating facts and seeking solutions in certain situations, was provided for by the governing body at its 188th session (November 1972), on the proposal of its Committee on Discrimination.

It was understood that such special surveys might be based on criteria such as those laid down in the Discrimination (Employment and Occupation) Convention (1958) (No. 111). However, this possibility is more general in scope and is not limited to countries which have ratified the Convention.

The questions raised should concern the situation of groups of people defined, for example, according to race, religion, national extraction, social origin, member of a minority group, sex, or age, but should not deal with individual cases unrelated to broader issues of policy.

The director-general was entrusted with "examining the effect to be given to any request for a special survey submitted by a member State, or a workers' or employers' organisation, on specific questions of concern to them, and, if the Government concerned agreed to such a survey, to settle the arrangements for carrying it out in agreement with the Government."

Provision is thus made for two different types of cases: those in which the request is directly submitted by the government of a member State in connection with questions arising in its own country, and those in which the request comes from an employers' or workers' organisation or another member State.

### Requests Submitted by the Government Concerned

The examination of the effect to be given to a request made in this circumstance raises no special procedural problems. The request may, for example, be aimed at obtaining a form of technical cooperation on question of evaluation or method in this field. In addition, recourse to outside observers, whose action would have an objective and impartial character, can help a government to overcome difficulties arising inside the country in connection with certain questions. In other circumstances, a government may wish to clear up certain doubts to which its action in this field may have given rise at the international level. A special survey on the national situation can, in particular, help a government to reach more precise conclusions regarding uncertainties which may have prevented it from ratifying the Discrimination (Employment and Occupation) Convention (1958) (No. 111). The governing body felt that this possibility should be drawn to the special attention of governments.

### Requests Submitted by an Employers' or Workers' Organization or by Another Government

*Receivability of Requests.* As regards requests submitted by employers' or workers' organisations, the governing body laid down principles similar to those which apply in regard to freedom of association: the request must come either from a national organisation directly concerned, or from international organisations in consultative status with ILO, or from other international or regional employers' or workers' organisations, provided the questions raised directly concern organisations affiliated to them.

In the case of a request submitted by the government of a member State in connection with questions arising in another country, the receivability of the request is strictly governed by the condition that the request must relate to "specific questions of concern to it." This presupposes a sufficiently close link between the interests of that government and the questions raised; the governing body considered that this could be the case, for example, when such questions concerned the situation of its own nationals working in another country.

*Communications with the Authors of Requests.* The director-general may, if necessary, ask the authors of requests to provide further details on the specific questions which they propose to raise, and to communicate additional information within a specified time-limit.

*Communications with the Government of the Country in regard to which the Survey Would Be Requested.* The director-general will inform the government concerned as soon as possible of any receivable and substantiated request, and will request the government to communicate, within an appropriate time-limit, its observations on this question and its views concerning the possibility of carrying out a special survey under the auspices of ILO on the questions raised.

In cases where the government requests or accepts such a survey, the director-general will settle the arrangements for carrying it out in agreement with the government, subject to the necessary safeguards, and in particular as regards the consultation of employers' and workers' circles concerned.

*Reports to the Governing Body Committee on Discrimination.* The director-general will report to the Committee on requests received, replies from governments, special surveys undertaken or planned, and on cases in which surveys could not be organized, including cases in which they have been refused or no replies have been communicated within a reasonable time-limit. On such questions, the Committee will, as necessary, be called upon regularly to make such recommendations as it deems appropriate.

*List of Experts Who Might Be Called upon to Participate in Special Surveys.* The director-general was entrusted with examining the possibility of drawing up a list of experts and persons of acknowledged competence, selected from the different regions of the world, whose services could be called upon in appropriate cases. It was further understood that, depending on the circumstances, surveys could also be carried out directly by the International Labour Office.

The governing body considered that the guidelines set out above should be applied on an experimental basis, on the understanding that they could be re-examined or redefined at a later stage, in the light of their practical application. . . .

*The United Nations Educational, Scientific and Cultural Organization.* UNESCO's Committee on Conventions and Recommendations examines in private session communications received. It decides on their admissibility in accordance with the following conditions:

(i) the communication must not be anonymous;

(ii) the communication must originate from a person or a group of persons who, it can be reasonably presumed, are victims of an alleged violation of any of the human rights referred to in paragraph (iii) below. It may also originate from any person, group of persons, or non-governmental organisation having reliable knowledge of those violations;

(iii) the communications must concern violations of human rights (women and men alike) falling within UNESCO's competence in the fields of education, science, culture, and information and must not be motivated exclusively by other considerations;

(iv) the communication must be compatible with the principles of the Organisation, the Charter of the United Nations, the Universal Declaration of Human Rights, the international covenants on human rights and other international instruments in the field of human rights;

(v) the communication must not be manifestly ill-founded and must appear to contain relevant evidence;

(vi) the communication must be neither offensive nor an abuse of the right to submit communications. However, such a communication may be considered if it meets all other criteria or admissibility, after the exclusion of the offensive or abusive parts;

(vii) the communication must not be based exclusively on information disseminated through the mass media;

(viii) the communication must be submitted within a reasonable time-limit following the facts which constitute its subject matter or within a reasonable time-limit after the facts have become known;

(ix) the communication must indicate whether an attempt has been made to exhaust available domestic remedies with regard to the facts which constitute the subject matter of the communication and the result of such an attempt, if any;

(x) communications relating to matters already settled by the States concerned in accordance with the human rights principles set forth in the Universal Declaration of Human Rights and the international covenants on human rights shall not be considered;

Under the procedures contained in decision 104 EX/3.3: . . .

(e) representatives of the governments concerned may attend meetings of the Committee in order to provide additional information or to answer questions from members of the Committee on either admissibility or the merits of the communication;

(f) The Committee may avail itself of the relevant information at the disposal of the director-general;

(g) Communications which warrant further consideration shall be acted upon by the Committee with a view to helping to bring about a friendly solution designed to advance the promotion of the human rights falling within UNESCO's fields of competence.

Under paragraph 15 of decision 104 EX/3.3 the Committee is requested to submit confidential reports to the Executive Board at each session on the carrying out of its mandate under the present decision. These reports shall contain appropriate information arising from its examination of the communications which the Committee considers it useful to bring to the notice of the Executive Board. The reports shall also contain recommendations which the Committee may wish to make either generally or regarding the disposition of a communication under consideration.

Paragraph 18 of decision 104 EX/3.3 refers to questions of massive, systematic, or flagrant violations of human rights and fundamental freedoms—including, for example, those perpetrated as a result of policies of aggression, interference in the internal affairs of States, occupation of foreign territory, and implementation of a policy of colonialism, genocide, apartheid, racialism, or national and social oppression—falling within UNESCO fields of competence which should be considered by the Executive Board and the General Conference in public meetings.

*SEE ALSO* Hostages; Impunity; Terrorism; Torture.

**BIBLIOGRAPHY.** Adzoxornu, Isaacs Komla. "Access to the Personal Grievance Procedures in New Zealand: The Human Rights Dimension," *University of Tasmania Law Review* 10 (1990): 40–58. Scholarly article, in English.

Association européenne contre les violences faites aux femmes au travail. *De l'abus de pouvoir sexuel: le harcèlement sexuel au travail* (Abuse of Gender Power: Sexual Harassment in the Workplace). Paris: Éditions La Découverte, 1990. Conference report, in French.

Bassiouni, M. Cherif. *Crimes against Humanity in International Criminal Law.* Dordrecht, the Netherlands: Martinus Nijhoff, 1992. Scholarly monograph, in English.

Carver, Richard. "Called to Account: How African Governments Investigate Human Rights Violations," *African Affairs* 89, no. 356 (July 1990): 391–415. Scholarly article, in English.

Committee on the Administration of Justice. *Cause for Complaint: The System for Dealing with Complaints against the Police in Northern Ireland.* Belfast, Northern Ireland: 1990. NGO report, in English.

Filice, Carlo. "On the Obligation to Keep Informed about Distant Atrocities," *Human Rights Quarterly* 12, no. 3 (Aug. 1990): 397–414. Scholarly article, in English.

Gibney, Mark. "Suing for Death, Suffering, and Peace," *Human Rights Quarterly* 12, no. 3 (Aug. 1990): 415–425. Scholarly article, in English.

Lester, Anthony. "Preparing and Presenting a Human Rights Brief," *Commonwealth Law Bulletin* 17, no. 3 (July 1991): 1055–1071. Conference paper, in English.

Zayas, Alfred de. "Les procédures de communications individuelles devant le Comité des Droits de l'Homme des Nations Unies" (Petitioning the United Nations Human Rights Committee), *Revue trimestrielle des droits de l'homme* 1, no. 4 (1990): 339–351. Scholarly article, in French.

# VICTIMS' RIGHTS: DECLARATION OF BASIC PRINCIPLES OF JUSTICE FOR VICTIMS OF CRIME AND ABUSE OF POWER, UN (1985).

The UN **GENERAL ASSEMBLY** formulated these Basic Principles on recommendation of the Sixth United Nations Congress on the Prevention of Crime and Treatment of Offenders because it realized that millions of people throughout the world suffer harm as a result of crime or the abuse of power and that the rights of these victims are not adequately recognized or protected: these victims, and also their families, witnesses, and others who have aided them, are unjustly subjected to loss, damage, or injury, and may, in addition, suffer hardship when assisting in the prosecution of offenders. The Declaration is designed to assist governments and the international community in their efforts to secure justice and assistance for victims of crime or of abuse of power.

The Declaration was adopted by the General Assembly on 29 November 1985 (resolution 40/34). The text is as follows:

## A. Victims of Crime

1. "Victims" means persons who, individually or collectively, have suffered harm, including physical or mental injury, emotional suffering, economic loss or substantial impairment of their fundamental rights, through acts or omissions that are in violation of criminal laws operative within Member States, including those laws proscribing criminal abuse of power.

2. A person may be considered a victim, under this Declaration, regardless of whether the perpetrator is identified, apprehended, prosecuted or convicted and regardless of the familial relationship between the perpetrator and the victim. The term "victim" also includes, where appropriate, the immediate family or dependants of the direct victim and persons who have suffered harm in intervening to assist victims in distress or to prevent victimization.

3. The provisions contained herein shall be applicable to all, without distinction of any kind, such as race, colour, sex, age, language, religion, nationality, political or other opinion, cultural beliefs or practices, property, birth or family status, ethnic or social origin, and disability.

*Access to Justice and Fair Treatment.* 4. Victims should be treated with compassion and respect for their dignity. They are entitled to access to the mechanisms of justice and to prompt redress, as provided for by national legislation, for the harm that they have suffered.

5. Judicial and administrative mechanisms should be established and strengthened where necessary to enable victims to obtain redress through formal or informal procedures that are expeditious, fair, inexpensive and accessible. Victims should be informed of their rights in seeking redress through such mechanisms.

6. The responsiveness of judicial and administrative processes to the needs of victims should be facilitated by:

*(a)* Informing victims of their role and the scope, timing and progress of the proceedings and of the disposition of their cases, especially where serious crimes are involved and where they have requested such information;

*(b)* Allowing the views and concerns of victims to be presented and considered at appropriate stages of the proceedings where their personal interests are affected, without prejudice to the accused and consistent with the relevant national criminal justice system;

*(c)* Providing proper assistance to victims throughout the legal process.

*(d)* Taking measures to minimize inconvenience to victims, protect their privacy, when necessary, and ensure their safety, as well as that of their families and witnesses on their behalf, from intimidation and retaliation;

*(e)* Avoiding unnecessary delay in the disposition of cases and the execution of orders or decrees granting awards to victims.

7. Informal mechanisms for the resolution of disputes, including mediation, arbitration and customary justice or indigenous practices, should be utilized where appropriate to facilitate conciliation and redress for victims.

*Restitution.* 8. Offenders or third parties responsible for their behaviour should, where appropriate, make fair restitution to victims, their families or dependants. Such restitution should include the return of property or payment for the harm or loss suffered, reimbursement of expenses incurred as a result of the victimization, the provision of services and the restoration of rights.

9. Governments should review their practices, regulations and laws to consider restitution as an available sentencing

option in criminal cases, in addition to other criminal sanctions.

10. In cases of substantial harm to the environment, restitution, if ordered, should include, as far as possible, restoration of the environment, reconstruction of the infrastructure, replacement of community facilities and reimbursement of the expenses of relocation, whenever such harm results in the dislocation of a community.

11. Where public officials or other agents acting in an official or quasi-official capacity have violated national criminal laws, the victims should receive restitution from the State whose officials or agents were responsible for the harm inflicted. In cases where the Government under whose authority the victimizing act or omission occurred is no longer in existence, the State or Government successor in title should provide restitution to the victims.

*Compensation.* 12. When compensation is not fully available from the offender or other sources, States should endeavour to provide financial compensation to:

(a) Victims who have sustained significant bodily injury or impairment of physical or mental health as a result of serious crimes;

(b) The family, in particular dependants of persons who have died or become physically or mentally incapacitated as a result of such victimization.

13. The establishment, strengthening and expansion of national funds for compensation to victims should be encouraged. Where appropriate, other funds may also be established for this purpose, including in those cases where the State of which the victim is a national is not in a position to compensate the victim for the harm.

*Assistance.* 14. Victims should receive the necessary material, medical, psychological and social assistance through governmental, voluntary, community-based and indigenous means.

15. Victims should be informed of the availability of health and social services and other relevant assistance and be readily afforded access to them.

16. Police, justice, health, social service and other personnel concerned should receive training to sensitize them to the needs of victims, and guidelines to ensure proper and prompt aid.

17. In providing services and assistance to victims, attention should be given to those who have special needs because of the nature of the harm inflicted or because of factors such as those mentioned in paragraph 3 above.

### B. Victims of Abuse of Power

18. "Victims" means persons who, individually or collectively, have suffered harm, including physical or mental injury, emotional suffering, economic loss or substantial impairment of their fundamental rights, through acts or omissions that do not yet constitute violations of national criminal laws but of internationally recognized norms relating to human rights.

19. States should consider incorporating into the national law norms proscribing abuses of power and providing remedies to victims of such abuses. In particular, such remedies should include restitution and/or compensation, and necessary material, medical, psychological and social assistance and support.

20. States should consider negotiating multilateral international treaties relating to victims, as defined in paragraph 18.

21. States should periodically review existing legislation and practices to ensure their responsiveness to changing circumstances, should enact and enforce, if necessary, legislation proscribing acts that constitute serious abuses of political or economic power, as well as promoting policies and mechanisms for the prevention of such acts, and should develop and make readily available appropriate rights and remedies for victims of such acts.

**VIENNA WORLD CONFERENCE ON HUMAN RIGHTS (1993).** The conclusions and recommendations of the World Conference on Human Rights were set out in the Vienna Declaration and Program of Action, adopted by acclamation at its 22nd plenary meeting, on 22 June 1993, as follows (UN Doc. A/CONF.157/24):

The World Conference on Human Rights,

Considering the promotion and protection of human rights is a matter of priority for the international community, and that the Conference affords a unique opportunity to carry out a comprehensive analysis of the international human rights system and of the machinery for the protection of human rights, in order to enhance and thus promote a fuller observance of those rights, in a just and balanced manner,

Recognizing and affirming that all human rights derive from the dignity and worth inherent in the human person, and that the human person is the central subject of human rights and fundamental freedoms, and consequently should be the principal beneficiary and should participate actively in the realization of these rights and freedoms,

Reaffirming their commitment to the purposes and principles contained in the Charter of the United Nations and the Universal Declaration of Human Rights,

Reaffirming the commitment contained in Article 56 of the Charter of the United Nations to take joint and separate action, placing proper emphasis on developing effective international cooperation for the realization of the purposes set out in Article 55, including universal respect for, and observance of, human rights and fundamental freedoms for all,

Emphasizing the responsibilities of all States, in conformity with the Charter of the United Nations, to develop and encourage respect for human rights and fundamental freedoms for all, without distinction as to race, sex, language or religion,

Recalling the Preamble to the Charter of the United Nations, in particular the determination to reaffirm faith in fundamental human rights, in the dignity and worth of the human person, and in the equal rights of men and women and of nations large and small,

Recalling also the determination expressed in the Preamble of the Charter of the United Nations to save succeeding generations from the scourge of war, to establish conditions under which justice and respect for obligations arising from treaties and other sources of international law can be maintained, to promote social progress and better standards of life in larger freedom, to practice tolerance and good neighborliness, and to employ international machinery for the promotion of the economic and social advancement of all peoples,

Emphasizing that the Universal Declaration of Human Rights, which constitutes a common standard of achievement for all peoples and all nations, is the source of inspiration and has been the basis for the United Nations in making advances in standard setting as contained in the existing international human rights instruments, in particular the International Covenant on Civil and Political Rights and the International Covenant on Economic, Social and Cultural Rights,

Considering the major changes taking place on the international scene and the aspirations of all the peoples for an international order based on the principles enshrined in the Charter of the United Nations, including promoting and encouraging respect for human rights and fundamental freedoms for all and respect for the principle of equal rights and self-determination of peoples, peace, democracy, justice, equality, rule of law, pluralism, development, better standards of living and solidarity,

Deeply concerned by various forms of discrimination and violence, to which women continue to be exposed all over the world,

Recognizing that the activities of the United Nations in the field of human rights should be rationalized and enhanced in order to strengthen the United Nations machinery in the field and to further the objectives of universal respect for observance of international human rights standards,

Having taken into account the Declarations adopted by the three regional meetings at Tunis, San José and Bangkok and the contributions made by Governments, and bearing in mind the suggestions made by intergovernmental and non-governmental organizations, as well as the studies prepared by independent experts during the preparatory process leading to the World Conference on Human Rights,

Welcoming the International Year of the World's Indigenous People (1993) as a reaffirmation of the commitment of the international community to ensure their enjoyment of all human rights and fundamental freedoms and to respect the value and diversity of their cultures and identities,

Recognizing also that the international community should devise ways and means to remove the current obstacles and meet challenges to the full realization of all human rights and to prevent the continuation of human rights violations resulting thereof throughout the world,

Invoking the spirit of outrage and the realities of our time which call upon the peoples of the world and all States Members of the United Nations to rededicate themselves to the global task of promoting and protecting all human rights and fundamental freedoms so as to secure full and universal enjoyment of these rights,

Determined to take new steps forward in the commitment of the international community with a view to achieving substantial progress in human rights endeavors by an increased and sustained effort of international cooperation and solidarity,

Solemnly adopts the Vienna Declaration and Programme of Action.

### Part I

1. The World Conference on Human Rights reaffirms the solemn commitment of all States to fulfill their obligations to promote universal respect for, and observance and protection of, all human rights and fundamental freedoms for all in accordance with the Charter of the United Nations, other instruments relating to human rights, and international law. The universal nature of these rights and freedoms is beyond question.

In this framework, enhancement of international cooperation in the field of human rights is essential for the full achievement of the purposes of the United Nations. Human rights and fundamental freedoms are the birthright of all human beings; their protection and promotion is the first responsibility of Governments.

2. All peoples have the right of self-determination. By virtue of that right they freely determine their political status, and freely pursue their economic, social and cultural development. Taking into account the particular situation of peoples under colonial or other forms of alien domination or foreign occupation, the World Conference on Human Rights recognizes the right of peoples to take any legitimate action, in accordance with the Charter of the United Nations, to realize their inalienable right of self-determination. The World Conference on Human Rights considers the denial of the right of self-determination as a violation of human rights and underlines the importance of the effective realization of this right. In accordance with the Declaration on Principles of International Law concerning Friendly Relations and Cooperation among States in accordance with the Charter of the United Nations, this shall not be construed as authorizing or encouraging any action which would dismember or impair, totally or in part, the territorial integrity or political unity of sovereign and independent States conducting themselves in compliance with the principle of equal rights and self-determination of peoples and thus possessed of a Government representing the whole people belonging to the territory without distinction of any kind.

3. Effective international measures to guarantee and monitor the implementation of human rights standards should be taken in respect of people under foreign occupation, and effective legal protection against the violation of their human rights should be provided, in accordance with human rights norms and international law, particularly the Geneva Convention relative to the Protection of Civilian Persons in Time of War, of 14 August 1949, and other applicable norms of humanitarian law.

4. The promotion and protection of all human rights and fundamental freedoms must be considered as a priority objective of the United Nations in accordance with its purposes and principles, in particular the purpose of international cooperation. In the framework of these purposes and principles, the promotion and protection of all human rights is a legitimate concern of the international community. The organs and specialized agencies related to human rights should, therefore, further enhance the coordination of their activities based on the consistent and objective application of international human rights instruments.

5. All human rights are universal, indivisible and interdependent and interrelated. The international community must treat human rights globally in a fair and equal manner, on the same footing, and with the same emphasis. While the significance of national and regional particularities and various historical, cultural and religious backgrounds must be borne in mind, it is the duty of States, regardless of their political, economic and cultural systems, to promote and protect all human rights and fundamental freedoms.

6. The efforts of the United Nations system towards the universal respect for, and observance of, human rights and fundamental freedoms for all, contribute to the stability and well-being necessary for peaceful and friendly relations among nations, and to improved conditions for peace and security as well as social and economic development, in conformity with the Charter of the United Nations.

7. The processes of promoting and protecting human rights should be conducted in conformity with the purposes and principles of the Charter of the United Nations, and international law.

8. Democracy, development and respect for human rights and fundamental freedoms are interdependent and mutually reinforcing. Democracy is based on the freely expressed will of the people to determine their own political, economic, social and cultural systems and their full participation in all aspects of their lives. In the context of the above, the promotion and protection of human rights and fundamental freedoms at the national and international levels should be universal and conducted without conditions attached. The international community should support the strengthening and promoting of democracy, development and respect for human rights and fundamental freedoms in the entire world.

9. The World Conference on Human Rights reaffirms that least developed countries committed to the process of democratization and economic reforms, many of which are in Africa, should be supported by the international community in order to succeed in their transition to democracy and economic development.

10. The World Conference on Human Rights reaffirms the right to development, as established in the Declaration on the Right to Development, as a universal and inalienable right and an integral part of fundamental human rights. As stated in the Declaration on the Right to Development, the human person is the central subject of development.

While development facilitates the enjoyment of all human rights, the lack of development may not be invoked to justify the abridgement of internationally recognized human rights.

States should cooperate with each other in ensuring development and eliminating obstacles to development. The international community should promote an effective international cooperation for the realization of the right to development and the elimination of obstacles to development.

Lasting progress towards the implementation of the right to development requires effective development policies at the national level, as well as equitable economic relations and a favorable economic environment at the international level.

11. The right to development should be fulfilled so as to meet equitably the developmental and environmental needs of present and future generations. The World Conference on Human Rights recognizes that illicit dumping of toxic and dangerous substances and waste potentially constitutes a serious threat to the human rights to life and health of everyone.

Consequently, the World Conference on Human Rights calls on all States to adopt and vigorously implement existing conventions relating to the dumping of toxic and dangerous products and waste and to cooperate in the prevention of illicit dumping.

Everyone has the right to enjoy the benefits of scientific progress and its applications. The World Conference on Human Rights notes that certain advances, notable in the biomedical and life sciences as well as in information technology, may have potentially adverse consequences for the integrity, dignity and human rights of the individual, and calls for international cooperation to ensure that human rights and dignity are fully respected in this area of universal concern.

12. The World Conference on Human Rights calls upon the international community to make all efforts to help alleviate the external debt burden of developing countries, in order to supplement the efforts of the Governments of such countries to attain the full realization of the economic, social and cultural rights of their people.

13. There is a need for States and international organizations, in cooperation with non-governmental organiza-

tions, to create favorable conditions at the national, regional and international levels to ensure the full and effective enjoyment of human rights. States should eliminate all violations of human rights and their causes, as well as obstacles to the enjoyment of these rights.

14. The existence of widespread extreme poverty inhibits the full and effective enjoyment of human rights; its immediate alleviation and eventual elimination must remain a high priority for the international community.

15. Respect for human rights and for fundamental freedoms without distinction of any kind is a fundamental rule of international human rights law. The speedy and comprehensive elimination of all forms of racism and racial discrimination, xenophobia and related intolerance is a priority task for the international community. Governments should take effective measures to prevent and combat them. Groups, institutions, intergovernmental and non-governmental organizations and individuals are urged to intensify their efforts in cooperating and coordinating their activities against these evils.

16. The World Conference on Human Rights welcomes the progress made in dismantling apartheid and calls upon the international community and the United Nations system to assist in this process.

The World Conference on Human Rights also deplores the continuing acts of violence aimed at undermining the quest for a peaceful dismantling of apartheid.

17. The acts, methods and practices of terrorism in all its forms and manifestations as well as linkage in some countries to drug trafficking are activities aimed at the destruction of human rights, fundamental freedoms and democracy, threatening territorial integrity, security of States and destabilizing legitimately constituted Governments. The international community should take the necessary steps to enhance cooperation to prevent and combat terrorism.

18. The human rights of women and of the girl-child are an inalienable, integral and indivisible part of universal human rights. The full and equal participation of women in political, civil, economic, social and cultural life, at the national, regional and international levels, and the eradication of all forms of discrimination on grounds of sex are priority objectives of the international community.

Gender-based violence and all forms of sexual harassment and exploitation, including those resulting from cultural prejudice and international trafficking, are incompatible with the dignity and worth of the human person, and must be eliminated. This can be achieved by legal measures and through national action and international cooperation in such fields as economic and social development, education, safe maternity and health care, and social support.

The human rights of women should form an integral part of the United Nations human rights activities, including the promotion of all human rights instruments relating to women.

The World Conference on Human Rights urges Governments, institutions, intergovernmental and non-governmental organizations to intensify their efforts for the protection and promotion of human rights of women and the girl-child.

19. Considering the importance of the promotion and protection of the rights of persons belonging to minorities and the contribution of such promotion and protection to the political and social stability of the States in which such persons live, the World Conference on Human Rights reaffirms the obligation of States to ensure that persons belonging to minorities may exercise fully and effectively all human rights and fundamental freedoms without any discrimina-

tion and in full equality before the law in accordance with the Declaration on the Rights of Persons Belonging to National or Ethnic, Religious and Linguistic Minorities.

The persons belonging to minorities have the right to enjoy their own culture, to profess and practice their own religion and to use their own language in private and in public, freely and without interference or any form of discrimination.

20. The World Conference on Human Rights recognizes the inherent dignity and the unique contribution of indigenous people to the development and plurality of society and strongly reaffirms the commitment of the international community to their economic, social and cultural well-being and their enjoyment of the fruits of sustainable development. States should ensure the full and free participation of indigenous people in all aspects of society, in particular in matters of concern to them. Considering the importance of the promotion and protection of the rights of indigenous people, and the contribution of such promotion and protection to the political and social stability of the States in which such people live, States should, in accordance with international law, take concerted positive steps to ensure respect for all human rights and fundamental freedoms of indigenous people, on the basis of equality and non-discrimination, and recognize the value and diversity of their distinct identities, cultures and social organization.

21. The World Conference on Human Rights, welcoming the early ratification of the Convention on the Rights of the Child by a large number of States and noting the recognition of the human rights of children in the World Declaration on the Survival, Protection and Development of Children and Plan of Action adopted by the World Summit for Children, urges universal ratification of the Convention by 1995 and its effective implementation by States parties through the adoption of all the necessary legislative, administrative and other measures and the allocation to the maximum extent of the available resources. In all actions concerning children, non-discrimination and the best interest of the child should be primary considerations and the views of the child given due weight. National and international mechanisms and programmes should be strengthened for the defense and protection of children, in particular, the girl-child, abandoned children, street children, economically and sexually exploited children, including through child pornography, child prostitution or sale of organs, children victims of diseases including acquired immunodeficiency syndrome, refugee and displaced children, children in detention, children in armed conflict, as well as children victims of famine and drought and other emergencies. International cooperation and solidarity should be promoted to support the implementation of the Convention and the rights of the child should be a priority in the United Nations system-wide action on human rights.

The World Conference on Human Rights also stresses that the child for the full and harmonious development of his or her personality should grow up in a family environment which accordingly merits broader protection.

22. Special attention needs to be paid to ensuring non-discrimination, and the equal enjoyment of all human rights and fundamental freedoms by disabled persons, including their active participation in all aspects of society.

23. The World Conference on Human Rights reaffirms that everyone, without distinction of any kind, is entitled to the right to seek and to enjoy in other countries asylum from persecution, as well as the right to return to one's own country. In this respect, it stresses the importance of the Universal Declaration of Human Rights, the 1951 Convention relating to the Status of Refugees, its 1967 Protocol and regional instruments. It expresses its appreciation to States that continue to admit and host large numbers of refugees in their territories, and to the Office of the United Nations High Commissioner for Refugees for its dedication to its task. It also expresses its appreciation to the United Nations Relief and Works Agency for Palestine Refugees in the Near East.

The World Conference on Human Rights recognizes that gross violations of human rights, including in armed conflicts, are among the multiple and complex factors leading to displacement of people.

The World Conference on Human Rights recognizes that, in view of the complexities of the global refugee crisis and in accordance with the Charter of the United Nations, relevant international instruments and international solidarity and in the spirit of burden-sharing, a comprehensive approach by the international community is needed in coordination and cooperation with the countries concerned and relevant organizations, bearing in mind the mandate of the United Nations High Commissioner for Refugees. This should include the development of strategies to address the root causes and effects of movements of refugees and other displaced persons, the strengthening of emergency preparedness and response mechanisms, the provision of effective protection and assistance, bearing in mind the special needs of women and children, as well as the achievement of durable solutions, primarily through the preferred solution of dignified and safe voluntary repatriation, including solutions such as those adopted by the international refugee conferences. The World Conference on Human Rights underlines the responsibilities of States, particularly as they relate to the countries of origin.

In the light of the comprehensive approach, the World Conference on Human Rights emphasizes the importance of giving special attention including through intergovernmental and humanitarian organizations and finding lasting solutions to questions related to internally displaced persons including their voluntary and safe return and rehabilitation.

In accordance with the Charter of the United Nations and the principles of humanitarian law, the World Conference on Human Rights further emphasizes the importance of and the need for humanitarian assistance to victims of all natural and man-made disasters.

24. Great importance must be given to the promotion and protection of the human rights of persons belonging to groups which have been rendered vulnerable, including migrant workers, the elimination of all forms of discrimination against them, and the strengthening and more effective implementation of existing human rights instruments. States have an obligation to create and maintain adequate measures at the national level, in particular in the fields of education, health and social support, for the promotion and protection of the rights of persons in vulnerable sectors of their populations and to ensure the participation of those among them who are interested in finding a solution to their own problems.

25. The World Conference on Human Rights affirms that extreme poverty and social exclusion constitute a violation of human dignity and that urgent steps are necessary to achieve better knowledge of extreme poverty and its causes, including those related to the problem of development, in order to promote the human rights of the poorest, and to put an end to extreme poverty and social exclusion and to promote the enjoyment of the fruits of social progress. It is

essential for States to foster participation by the poorest people in the decision-making process by the community in which they live, the promotion of human rights and efforts to combat extreme poverty.

26. The World Conference on Human Rights welcomes the progress made in the codification of human rights instruments, which is a dynamic and evolving process, and urges the universal ratification of human rights treaties. All States are encouraged to accede to these international instruments; all States are encouraged to avoid, as far as possible, the resort to reservations.

27. Every State should provide an effective framework of remedies to redress human rights grievances or violations. The administration of justice, including law enforcement and prosecutorial agencies and, especially, an independent judiciary and legal profession in full conformity with applicable standards contained in international human rights instruments, are essential to the full and non-discriminatory realization of human rights and indispensable to the processes of democracy and sustainable development. In this context, institutions concerned with the administration of justice should be properly funded, and an increased level of both technical and financial assistance should be provided by the international community. It is incumbent upon the United Nations to make use of special programmes of advisory services on a priority basis for the achievement of a strong and independent administration of justice.

28. The World Conference on Human Rights expresses its dismay at massive violations of human rights especially in the form of genocide, "ethnic cleansing" and systematic rape of women in war situations, creating mass exodus of refugees and displaced persons. While strongly condemning such abhorrent practices, it reiterates the call that perpetrators of such crimes be punished and such practices immediately stopped.

29. The World Conference on Human Rights expresses grave concern about continuing human rights violations in all parts of the world in disregard of standards as contained in international human rights instruments and international humanitarian law and about the lack of sufficient and effective remedies for the victims.

The World Conference on Human Rights is deeply concerned about violations of human rights during armed conflicts, affecting the civilian population, especially women, children, the elderly and the disabled. The Conference therefore calls upon States and all parties to armed conflicts strictly to observe international humanitarian law, as set forth in the Geneva Conventions of 1949 and other rules and principles of international law, as well as minimum standards for protection of human rights, as laid down in international conventions.

The World Conference on Human Rights reaffirms the right of the victims to be assisted by humanitarian organizations, as set forth in the Geneva Conventions of 1949 and other relevant instruments of international humanitarian law, and calls for the safe and timely access for such assistance.

30. The World Conference on Human Rights also expresses its dismay and condemnation that gross and systematic violations and situations that constitute serious obstacles to the full enjoyment of all human rights continue to occur in different parts of the world. Such violations and obstacles include, as well as torture and cruel, inhuman and degrading treatment or punishment, summary and arbitrary executions, disappearances, arbitrary detentions, all forms of racism, racial discrimination and apartheid, foreign occupation and alien domination, xenophobia, poverty, hunger and other denials of economic, social and cultural rights, religious intolerance, terrorism, discrimination against women and lack of the rule of law.

31. The World Conference on Human Rights calls upon States to refrain from any unilateral measure not in accordance with international law and the Charter of the United Nations that creates obstacles to trade relations among States and impedes the full realization of the human rights set forth in the Universal Declaration of Human Rights and international human rights instruments, in particular the rights of everyone to a standard of living adequate for their health and well-being, including food and medical care, housing and the necessary social services. The World Conference on Human Rights affirms that food should not be used as a tool for political pressure.

32. The World Conference on Human Rights reaffirms the importance of ensuring the universality, objectivity and non-selectivity of the consideration of human rights issues.

33. The World Conference on Human Rights reaffirms that States are duty-bound, as stipulated in the Universal Declaration of Human Rights and the International Covenant on Economic, Social and Cultural Rights and in other international human rights instruments, to ensure that education is aimed at strengthening the respect of human rights and fundamental freedoms. The World Conference on Human Rights emphasizes the importance of incorporating the subject of human rights education programmes and calls upon States to do so. Education should promote understanding, tolerance, peace and friendly relations between the nations and all racial or religious groups and encourage the development of United Nations activities in pursuance of these objectives. Therefore, education on human rights and the dissemination of proper information, both theoretical and practical, play an important role in the promotion and respect of human rights with regard to all individuals without distinction of any kind such as race, sex, language or religion, and this should be integrated in the education policies at the national as well as international levels. The World Conference on Human Rights notes that resource constraints and institutional inadequacies may impede the immediate realization of these objectives.

34. Increased efforts should be made to assist countries which so request to create the conditions whereby each individual can enjoy universal human rights and fundamental freedoms. Governments, the United Nations system as well as other multilateral organizations are urged to increase considerably the resources allocated to programmes aiming at the establishment and strengthening of national legislation, national institutions and related infrastructures which uphold the rule of law and democracy, electoral assistance, human rights awareness through training, teaching and education, popular participation and civil society.

The programmes of advisory services and technical cooperation under the Centre for Human Rights should be strengthened as well as made more efficient and transparent and thus become a major contribution to improving respect for human rights. States are called upon to increase their contributions to these programmes, both through promoting a larger allocation for the United Nations regular budget, and through voluntary contributions.

35. The full and effective implementation of United Nations activities to promote and protect human rights must reflect the high importance accorded to human rights by the Charter of the United Nations and the demands of the United Nations human rights activities, as mandated by Member States. To this end, United Nations human rights activities should be provided with increased resources.

36. The World Conference on Human Rights reaffirms the important and constructive role played by national institutions for the promotion and protection of human rights, in particular in their advisory capacity to the competent authorities, their role in remedying human rights violations, in the dissemination of human rights information, and education in human rights.

The World Conference on Human Rights encourages the establishment and strengthening of national institutions, having regard to the "Principles relating to the status of national institutions" and recognizing that it is the right of each State to choose the framework which is best suited to its particular needs at the national level.

37. Regional arrangements play a fundamental role in promoting and protecting human rights. They should reinforce universal human rights standards, as contained in international human rights instruments, and their protection. The World Conference on Human Rights endorses efforts under way to strengthen these arrangements and to increase their effectiveness, while at the same time stressing the importance of cooperation with the United Nations human rights activities.

The World Conference on Human Rights reiterates the need to consider the possibility of establishing regional and subregional arrangements for the promotion and protection of human rights where they do not already exist.

38. The World Conference on Human Rights recognizes the important role of non-governmental organizations in the promotion of all human rights and in humanitarian activities at national, regional and international levels. The World Conference on Human Rights appreciates their contribution to increasing public awareness of human rights issues, to the conduct of education, training and research in this field, and to the promotion and protection of all human rights and fundamental freedoms. While recognizing that the primary responsibility for standard-setting lies with States, the conference also appreciates the contribution of non-governmental organizations to this process. In this respect, the World Conference on Human Rights emphasizes the importance of continued dialogue and cooperation between Governments and non-governmental organizations. Non-governmental organizations and their members genuinely involved in the field of human rights should enjoy the rights and freedoms recognized in the Universal Declaration of Human Rights, and the protection of the national law. These rights and freedoms may not be exercised contrary to the purposes and principles of the United Nations. Non-governmental organizations should be free to carry out their human rights activities, without interference, within the framework of national law and the Universal Declaration of Human Rights.

39. Underlining the importance of objective, responsible and impartial information about human rights and humanitarian issues, the World Conference on Human Rights encourages the increased involvement of the media, for whom freedom and protection should be guaranteed within the framework of national law.

## Part II

### A. Increased Coordination on Human Rights within the United Nations System

1. The World Conference on Human Rights recommends increased coordination in support of human rights and fundamental freedoms within the United Nations system. To this end, the World Conference on Human Rights urges all United Nations organs, bodies and the specialized agencies whose activities deal with human rights to cooperate in order to strengthen, rationalize and streamline their activities, taking into account the need to avoid unnecessary duplication. The World Conference on Human Rights also recommends to the Secretary-General that high-level officials of relevant United Nations bodies and specialized agencies at their annual meeting, besides coordinating their activities, also assess the impact of their strategies and policies on the enjoyment of all human rights.

2. Furthermore, the World Conference on Human Rights calls on regional organizations and prominent international and regional finance and development institutions to assess also the impact of their policies and programmes on the enjoyment of human rights.

3. The World Conference on Human Rights recognizes that relevant specialized agencies and bodies and institutions of the United Nations system as well as other relevant intergovernmental organizations whose activities deal with human rights play a vital role in the formulation, promotion and implementation of human rights standards, within their respective mandates, and should take into account the outcome of the World Conference on Human Rights within their field of competence.

4. The World Conference on Human Rights strongly recommends that a concerted effort be made to encourage and facilitate the ratification of and accession or succession to international human rights treaties and protocols adopted within the framework of the United Nations system with the aim of universal acceptance. The Secretary–General, in consultation with treaty bodies, should consider opening a dialogue with States not having acceded to these human rights treaties, in order to identify obstacles and to seek ways of overcoming them.

5. The World Conference on Human Rights encourages States to consider limiting the extent of any reservations they lodge to international human rights instruments, formulate any reservations as precisely and narrowly as possible, ensure that none is incompatible with the object and purpose of the relevant treaty and regularly review any reservations with a view to withdrawing them.

6. The World Conference on Human Rights, recognizing the need to maintain consistency with the high quality of existing international standards and to avoid proliferation of human rights instruments, reaffirms the guidelines relating to the elaboration of new international instruments contained in General Assembly resolution 41/120 of 4 December 1986 and calls on the United Nations human rights bodies, when considering the elaboration of new international standards, to keep those guidelines in mind, to consult with human rights treaty bodies on the necessity for drafting new standards and to request the Secretariat to carry out technical reviews of proposed new instruments.

7. The World Conference on Human Rights recommends that human rights officers be assigned if and when necessary to regional offices of the United Nations Organization with the purpose of disseminating information and offering training and other technical assistance in the field of human rights upon the request of concerned Member States. Human rights training for international civil servants who are assigned to work relating to human rights should be organized.

8. The World Conference on Human Rights welcomes the convening of emergency sessions of the Commission on Human Rights as a positive initiative and that other ways of

responding to acute violations of human rights be considered by the relevant organs of the United Nations system.

*Resources.* 9. The World Conference on Human Rights, concerned by the growing disparity between the activities of the Centre for Human Rights and the human, financial and other resources available to carry them out, and bearing in mind the resources needed for other important United Nations programmes, requests the Secretary-General and the General Assembly to take immediate steps to increase substantially the resources for the human rights programme from within the existing and future regular budgets of the United Nations, and to take urgent steps to seek increased extrabudgetary resources.

10. Within this framework, an increased proportion of the regular budget should be allocated directly to the Centre for Human Rights to cover its costs and all other costs borne by the Centre for Human Rights, including those related to the United Nations human rights bodies. Voluntary funding of the Centre's technical cooperation activities should reinforce this enhanced budget; the World Conference on Human Rights calls for generous contributions to the existing trust funds.

11. The World Conference on Human Rights requests the Secretary-General and the General Assembly to provide sufficient human, financial and other resources to the Centre for Human Rights to enable it effectively, efficiently and expeditiously to carry out its activities.

12. The World Conference on Human Rights, noting the need to ensure that human and financial resources are available to carry out the human rights activities, as mandated by intergovernmental bodies, urges the Secretary-General, in accordance with Article 101 of the Charter of the United Nations, and Member States to adopt a coherent approach aimed at securing that resources commensurate to the increased mandates are allocated to the Secretariat. The World Conference on Human Rights invites the Secretary-General to consider whether adjustments to procedures in the programme budget cycle would be necessary or helpful to ensure the timely and effective implementation of human rights activities as mandated by Member States.

*Centre for Human Rights.* 13. The World Conference on Human Rights stresses the importance of strengthening the United Nations Centre for Human Rights.

14. The Centre for Human Rights should play an important role in coordinating system-wide attention for human rights. The focal role of the Centre can best be realized if it is enabled to cooperate fully with other United Nations bodies and organs. The coordinating role of the Centre for Human Rights also implies that the office of the Centre for Human Rights in New York is strengthened.

15. The Centre for Human Rights should be assured adequate means for the system of thematic and country rapporteurs, experts, working groups and treaty bodies. Follow-up on recommendations should become a priority matter for consideration by the Commission on Human Rights.

16. The Centre for Human Rights should assume a larger role in the promotion of human rights. This role could be given shape through cooperation with Member States and by an enhanced programme of advisory services and technical assistance. The existing voluntary funds will have to be expanded substantially for these purposes and should be managed in a more efficient and coordinated way. All activities should follow strict and transparent project management rules and regular programme and project evaluations should be held periodically. To this end, the results of such evaluation exercises and other relevant information should

be made available regularly. The Centre should, in particular, organize at least once a year information meetings open to all Member States and organizations directly involved in these projects and programmes.

*Adaptation and strengthening of the United Nations machinery for human rights, including the question of the establishment of a United Nations High Commissioner for Human Rights.* 17. The World Conference on Human Rights recognizes the necessity for a continuing adaptation of the United Nations human rights machinery to the current and future needs in the promotion and protection of human rights, as reflected in the present Declaration and within the framework of a balanced and sustainable development for all people. In particular, the United Nations human rights organs should improve their coordination, efficiency and effectiveness.

18. The World Conference on Human Rights recommends to the General Assembly that when examining the report of the Conference at its forty-eighth session, it begin, as a matter of priority, consideration of the question of the establishment of a High Commissioner for Human Rights for the promotion and protection of all human rights.

### B. Equality, Dignity and Tolerance

#### 1. Racism, Racial Discrimination, Xenophobia and Other Forms of Intolerance

19. The World Conference on Human Rights considers the elimination of racism and racial discrimination, in particular in their institutionalized forms such as apartheid or resulting from doctrines of racial superiority or exclusivity or contemporary forms and manifestations of racism, as a primary objective for the international community and a worldwide promotion programme in the field of human rights. United Nations organs and agencies should strengthen their efforts to implement such a programme of action related to the third decade to combat racism and racial discrimination as well as subsequent mandates to the same end. The World Conference on Human Rights strongly appeals to the international community to contribute generously to the Trust Fund for the Programme for the Decade for Action to Combat Racism and Racial Discrimination.

20. The World Conference on Human Rights urges all Governments to take immediate measures and to develop strong policies to prevent and combat all forms and manifestations of racism, xenophobia or related intolerance, where necessary by enactment of appropriate legislation, including penal measures, and by the establishment of national institutions to combat such phenomena.

21. The World Conference on Human Rights welcomes the decision of the Commission on Human Rights to appoint a Special Rapporteur on contemporary forms of racism, racial discrimination, xenophobia and related intolerance. The World Conference on Human Rights also appeals to all States parties to the International Convention on the Elimination of All Forms of Racial Discrimination to consider making the declaration under article 14 of the Convention.

22. The World Conference on Human Rights calls upon all Governments to take all appropriate measures in compliance with their international obligations and with due regard to their respective legal systems to counter intolerance and related violence based on religion or belief, including practices of discrimination against women and including the desecration of religious sites, recognizing that every individual has the right to freedom of thought, conscience, expression and religion. The Conference also invites all States to

put into practice the provisions of the Declaration on the Elimination of All Forms of Intolerance and of Discrimination Based on Religion or Belief.

23. The World Conference on Human Rights stresses that all persons who perpetrate or authorize criminal acts associated with ethnic cleansing are individually responsible and accountable for such human rights violations, and that the international community should exert every effort to bring those legally responsible for such violations to justice.

24. The World Conference on Human Rights calls on all States to take immediate measures, individually and collectively, to combat the practice of ethnic cleansing to bring it quickly to an end. Victims of the abhorrent practice of ethnic cleansing are entitled to appropriate and effective remedies.

## 2. Persons Belonging to National or Ethnic, Religious and Linguistic Minorities

25. The World Conference on Human Rights calls on the Commission on Human Rights to examine ways and means to promote and protect effectively the rights of persons belonging to minorities as set out in the Declaration on the Rights of Persons belonging to National or Ethnic, Religious and Linguistic Minorities. In this context, the World Conference on Human Rights calls upon the Centre for Human Rights to provide, at the request of governments concerned and as part of its programme of advisory services and technical assistance, qualified expertise on minority issues and human rights, as well as on the prevention and resolution of disputes, to assist in existing or potential situations involving minorities.

26. The World Conference on Human Rights urges States and the international community to promote and protect the rights of persons belonging to national or ethnic, religious and linguistic minorities in accordance with the Declaration on the Rights of Persons belonging to National or Ethnic, Religious and Linguistic Minorities.

27. Measures to be taken, where appropriate, should include facilitation of their full participation in all aspects of the political, economic, social, religious and cultural life of society and in the economic progress and development in their country.

*Indigenous People.* 28. The World Conference on Human Rights calls on the Working Group on Indigenous Populations of the Sub-Commission on Prevention of Discrimination and Protection of Minorities to complete the drafting of a declaration on the rights of indigenous people at its eleventh session.

29. The World Conference on Human Rights recommends that the Commission on Human Rights consider the renewal and updating of the mandate of the Working Group on Indigenous Populations upon completion of the drafting of a declaration on the rights of indigenous people.

30. The World Conference on Human Rights also recommends that advisory services and technical assistance programmes within the United Nations system respond positively to requests by States for assistance which would be of direct benefit to indigenous people. The World Conference on Human Rights further recommends that adequate human and financial resources be made available to the Centre for Human Rights within the overall framework of strengthening the Centre's activities as envisaged by this document.

31. The World Conference on Human Rights urges States to ensure the full and free participation of indigenous people in all aspects of society, in particular in matters of concern to them.

32. The World Conference on Human Rights recommends that the General Assembly proclaim an international decade of the world's indigenous people, to begin from January 1994, including action-orientated programmes, to be decided upon in partnership with indigenous people. An appropriate voluntary trust fund should be set up for this purpose. In the framework of such a decade, the establishment of a permanent forum for indigenous people in the United Nations system should be considered.

*Migrant Workers.* 33. The World Conference on Human Rights urges all States to guarantee the protection of the human rights of all migrant workers and their families.

34. The World Conference on Human Rights considers that the creation of conditions to foster greater harmony and tolerance between migrant workers and the rest of the society of the State in which they reside is of particular importance.

35. The World Conference on Human Rights invites States to consider the possibility of signing and ratifying, at the earliest possible time, the International Convention on the rights of All Migrant Workers and Members of Their Families.

## 3. The Equal Status and Human Rights of Women

36. The World Conference on Human Rights urges the full and equal enjoyment by women of all human rights and that this be a priority for Governments and for the United Nations. The World Conference on Human Rights also underlines the importance of the integration and full participation of women as both agents and beneficiaries in the development process, and reiterates the objectives established on global action for women towards sustainable and equitable development set forth in the Rio Declaration on Environment and Development and chapter 24 of Agenda 21, adopted by the United Nations Conference on Environment and Development (Rio de Janeiro, Brazil, 3–14 June 1992).

37. The equal status of women and the human rights of women should be integrated into the mainstream of United Nations system-wide activity. These issues should be regularly and systematically addressed throughout relevant United Nations bodies and mechanisms. In particular, steps should be taken to increase cooperation and promote further integration of objectives and goals between the Commission on the Status of Women, the Commission on Human Rights, the Committee for the Elimination of Discrimination against Women, the United Nations Development Fund for Women, the United Nations Development Programme and other United Nations agencies. In this context, cooperation and coordination should be strengthened between the Centre for Human Rights and the Division for the Advancement of Women.

38. In particular, the World Conference on Human Rights stresses the importance of working towards the elimination of violence against women in public and private life, the elimination of all forms of sexual harassment, exploitation and trafficking in women, the elimination of gender bias in the administration of justice and the eradication of any conflicts which may arise between the rights of women and the harmful effects of certain traditional or customary practices, cultural prejudices and religious extremism. The World Conference on Human Rights calls upon the General Assembly to adopt the draft against women in accordance with its provisions. Violations of the human rights of women in situations of armed conflict are violations of the funda-

mental principles of international human rights and humanitarian law. All violations of this kind, including in particular murder, systematic rape, sexual slavery, and forced pregnancy, require a particularly effective response.

39. The World Conference on Human Rights urges the eradication of all forms of discrimination against women, both hidden and overt. The United Nations should encourage the goal of universal ratification by all States of the Convention on the Elimination of All Forms of Discrimination against Women by the year 2000. Ways and means of addressing the particularly large number of reservations to the Convention should be encourage.

40. Treaty monitoring bodies should disseminate necessary information to enable women to make more effective use of existing implementation procedures in their pursuits of full and equal enjoyment of human rights and non-discrimination. New procedures should also be adopted to strengthen implementation of the commitment to women's equality and the human rights of women. The Commission on the Status of Women and the Committee on the Elimination of Discrimination against Women should quickly examine the possibility of introducing the right of petition through the preparation of an optional protocol to the Convention on the Elimination of All Forms of Discrimination against Women. The World Conference on Human Rights welcomes the decision of the Commission on Human Rights to consider the appointment of a special rapporteur on violence against women at its fiftieth session.

41. The World Conference on Human Rights recognizes the importance of the enjoyment by women of the highest standard of physical and mental health throughout their life span. In the context of the World Conference on Women and the Convention on the Elimination of All Forms of Discrimination against Women, as well as the Proclamation of Teheran of 1968, the World Conference on Human Rights reaffirms, on the basis of equality between women and men, a woman's right to accessible and adequate health care and the widest range of family planning services, as well as equal access to education at all levels.

42. Treaty monitoring bodies should include the status of women and the human rights of women in their deliberations and findings, making use of gender-specific data. States should be encouraged to supply information on the situation of women *de jure* and de facto in their reports to treaty monitoring bodies. The World Conference on Human Rights notes with satisfaction that the Commission on Human Rights adopted at its forty-ninth session resolution 1993/46 of 8 March 1993 stating that rapporteurs and working groups in the field of human rights should also be encouraged to do so. Steps should also be taken by the Division for the Advancement of Women in cooperation with other United Nations bodies, specifically the Centre for Human Rights, to ensure that the human rights activities of the United Nations regularly address violations of women's human rights, including gender-specific abuses. Training for United Nations human rights and humanitarian relief personnel to assist them to recognize and deal with human rights abuses particular to women and to carry out their work without gender bias should be encouraged.

43. The World Conference on Human Rights urges Governments and regional and international organizations to facilitate the access of women to decision-making posts and their greater participation in the decision-making process. It encourages further steps within the United Nations Secretariat to appoint and promote women staff members in accordance with the Charter of the United Nations, and encourages other principal and subsidiary organs of the United Nations to guarantee the participation of women under conditions of equality.

44. The World Conference on Human Rights welcomes the World Conference on Women to be held in Beijing in 1995 and urges that human rights of women should play an important role in its deliberations, in accordance with the priority themes of the World Conference on Women of equality, development and peace.

### 4. The Rights of the Child

45. The World Conference on Human Rights reiterates the principle of "First Call for Children" and, in this respect, underlines the importance of major national and international efforts, especially those of the United Nations Children's Fund, for promoting respect for the rights of the child to survival, protection, development and participation.

46. Measures should be taken to achieve universal ratification of the Convention on the Rights of the Child by 1995 and the universal signing of the World Declaration on the Survival, Protection and Development of Children and Plan of Action adopted by the World Summit for Children, as well as their effective implementation. The World Conference on Human Rights urges States to withdraw reservations to the Convention on the Rights of the Child contrary to the object and purpose of the Convention or otherwise contrary to international treaty law.

47. The World Conference on Human Rights urges all nations to undertake measures to the maximum extent of their available resources, with the support of international cooperation, to achieve the goals in the World Summit Plan of Action. The Conference calls on States to integrate the Convention on the Rights of the Child into their national action plans. By means of these national action plans and through international efforts, particular priority should be placed on reducing infant and maternal mortality rates, reducing malnutrition and illiteracy rates and providing access to safe drinking water and to basic education. Whenever so called for, national plans of action should be devised to combat devastating emergencies resulting from natural disasters and armed conflicts and the equally grave problem of children in extreme poverty.

48. The World Conference on Human Rights urges all States, with the support of international cooperation, to address the acute problem of children under especially difficult circumstances. Exploitation and abuse of children should be actively combated, including by addressing their root causes. Effective measures are required against female infanticide, harmful child labour, sale of children and organs, child prostitution, child pornography, as well as other forms of sexual abuse.

49. The World Conference on Human Rights supports all measures by the United Nations and its specialized agencies to ensure the effective protection and promotion of human rights of the girl child. The World Conference on Human Rights urges States to repeal existing laws and regulations and remove customs and practices which discriminate against and cause harm to the girl child.

50. The World Conference on Human Rights strongly supports the proposal that the Secretary-General initiate a study into means of improving the protection of children in armed conflicts. Humanitarian norms should be implemented and measures taken in order to protect and facilitate

assistance to children in war zones. Measures should include protection for children against indiscriminate use of all weapons of war, especially anti-personnel mines. The need for aftercare and rehabilitation of children traumatized by war must be addressed urgently. The Conference calls on the Committee on the Rights of the Child to study the question of raising the minimum age of recruitment into armed forces.

51. The World Conference on Human Rights recommends that matters relating to human rights and the situation of children be regularly reviewed and monitored by all relevant organs and mechanisms of the United Nations system and by the supervisory bodies of the specialized agencies in accordance with their mandates.

52. The World Conference on Human Rights recognizes the important role played by non-governmental organizations in the effective implementation of all human rights instruments and, in particular, the Convention on the Rights of the Child.

53. The World Conference on Human Rights recommends that the Committee on the Rights of the Child, with the assistance of the Centre for Human Rights, be enabled expeditiously and effectively to meet its mandate, especially in view of the unprecedented extent of ratification and subsequent submission of country reports.

### 5. Freedom from Torture

54. The World Conference on Human Rights welcomes the ratification by many Member States of the Convention against Torture and Other Cruel, Inhuman or Degrading Treatment or Punishment and encourages its speedy ratification by all other Member States.

55. The World Conference on Human Rights emphasizes that one of the most atrocious violations against human dignity is the act of torture, the result of which destroys the dignity and impairs the capability of victims to continue their lives and their activities.

56. The World Conference on Human Rights reaffirms that under human rights law and international humanitarian law, freedom from torture is a right which must be protected under all circumstances, including in times of internal or international disturbance or armed conflicts.

57. The World Conference on Human Rights, therefore, urges all States to put an immediate end to the practice of torture and eradicate this evil forever through full implementation of the Universal Declaration of Human Rights as well as the relevant conventions and, where necessary, strengthening of existing mechanisms. The World Conference on Human Rights calls on all States to cooperate fully with the Special Rapporteur on the question of torture in the fulfilment of his mandate.

58. Special attention should be given to ensure universal respect for, and effective implementation of, the Principles of Medical Ethics relevant to the Role of Health Personnel, particularly Physicians, in the Protection of Prisoners and Detainees against Torture and other Cruel, Inhuman or Degrading Treatment or Punishment adopted by the General Assembly of the United Nations.

59. The World Conference on Human Rights stresses the importance of further concrete action within the framework of the United Nations with the view to providing assistance to victims of torture and ensure more effective remedies for their physical, psychological and social rehabilitation. Providing the necessary resources for this purpose should be given high priority, *inter alia,* by additional contributions to the United Nations Voluntary Fund for the Victims of Torture.

60. States should abrogate legislation leading to impunity for those responsible for grave violations of human rights such as torture and prosecute such violations, thereby providing a firm basis for the rule of law.

61. The World Conference on Human Rights reaffirms that efforts to eradicate torture should, first and foremost, be concentrated on prevention and, therefore, calls for the early adoption of an optional protocol to the Convention against Torture and Other Cruel, Inhuman and Degrading Treatment or Punishment, which is intended to establish a preventive system of regular visits to places of detention.

### 6. Enforced Disappearances

62. The World Conference on Human Rights, welcoming the adoption by the General Assembly of the Declaration on the Protection of All Persons from Enforced Disappearance, calls upon all States to take effective legislative, administrative, judicial or other measures to prevent, terminate and punish acts of enforced disappearances. The World Conference on Human Rights reaffirms that it is the duty of all States, under any circumstances, to make investigations whenever there is reason to believe that an enforced disappearance has taken place on a territory under their jurisdiction and, if allegations are confirmed, to prosecute its perpetrators.

### 7. The Rights of the Disabled Person

63. The World Conference on Human Rights reaffirms that all human rights and fundamental freedoms are universal and thus unreservedly include persons with disabilities. Every person is born equal and has the same rights to life and welfare, education and work, living independently and active participation in all aspects of society. Any direct discrimination or other negative discriminatory treatment of a disabled person is therefore a violation of his or her rights. The World Conference on Human Rights calls on Governments, where necessary, to adopt or adjust legislation to assure access to these and other rights for disabled persons.

64. The place of disabled persons is everywhere. Persons with disabilities should be guaranteed equal opportunity through the elimination of all socially determined barriers, be they physical, financial, social or psychological, which exclude or restrict full participation in society.

65. Recalling the World Programme of Action concerning Disabled Persons, adopted by the General Assembly at its 37th session, the World Conference on Human Rights calls upon the General Assembly and the Economic and Social Council to adopt the draft standard rules on the equalization of opportunities for persons with disabilities, at their meetings in 1993.

### C. Cooperation, Development and Strengthening of Human Rights

66. The World Conference on Human Rights recommends that priority be given to national and international action to promote democracy, development and human rights.

67. Special emphasis should be given to measures to assist in the strengthening and building of institutions relating to

human rights, strengthening of a pluralistic civil society and the protection of groups which have been rendered vulnerable. In this context, assistance provided upon the request of Governments for the conduct of free and fair elections, including assistance in the human rights aspects of elections and public information about elections, is of particular importance. Equally important is the assistance to be given to the strengthening of the rule of law, the promotion of freedom of expression and the administration of justice, and to the real and effective participation of the people in the decision-making processes.

68. The World Conference on Human Rights stresses the need for the implementation of strengthened advisory services and technical assistance activities by the Centre for Human Rights. The Centre should make available to States upon request assistance on specific human rights issues, including the preparation of reports under human rights treaties as well as for the implementation of coherent and comprehensive plans of action for the promotion and protection of human rights. Strengthening the institutions of human rights and democracy, the legal protection of human rights, training of officials and others, broad-based education and public information aimed at promoting respect for human rights should all be available as components of these programmes.

69. The World Conference on Human Rights strongly recommends that a comprehensive programme be established within the United Nations in order to help States in the task of building and strengthening adequate national structures which have a direct impact on the overall observance of human rights and the maintenance of the rule of law. Such a programme, to be coordinated by the Centre for Human Rights, should be able to provide, upon the request of the interested Government, technical and financial assistance to national projects in reforming penal and correctional establishments, education and training of lawyers, judges and security forces in human rights, and any other sphere of activity relevant to the good functioning of the rule of law. That programme should make available to States assistance for the implementation of plans of action for the promotion and protection of human rights.

70. The World Conference on Human Rights requests the Secretary-General of the United Nations to submit proposals to the United Nations General Assembly containing alternatives for the establishment, structure, operational modalities and funding of the proposed programme.

71. The World Conference on Human Rights recommends that each State consider the desirability of drawing up a national action plan identifying steps whereby that State would improve the promotion and protection of human rights.

72. The World Conference on Human Rights reaffirms that the universal and inalienable right to development, as established in the Declaration on the Right to Development, must be implemented and realized. In this context, the World Conference on Human Rights welcomes the appointment by the Commission on Human Rights of a thematic working group on the right to development and urges that the Working Group, in consultation and cooperation with other organs and agencies of the United Nations system, promptly formulate, for early consideration by the United Nations General Assembly, comprehensive and effective measures to eliminate obstacles to the implementation and realization of the Declaration on the Right to Development and recommend ways and means towards the realization of the right to development by all States.

73. The World Conference on Human Rights recommends that non-governmental and other grass-roots organizations active in development and/or human rights should be enabled to play a major role on the national and international levels in the debate, activities and implementation relating to the right to development and, in cooperation with Governments, in all relevant aspects of development cooperation.

74. The World Conference on Human Rights appeals to Governments, competent agencies and institutions to increase considerably the resources devoted to building well-functioning legal systems able to protect human rights, and to national institutions working in this area. Actors in the field of development cooperation should bear in mind the mutually reinforcing interrelationship between development, democracy and human rights. Cooperation should be based on dialogue and transparency. The World Conference on Human Rights also calls for the establishment of comprehensive programmes, including resource banks of information and personnel with expertise relating to the strengthening of the rule of law and of democratic institutions.

75. The World Conference on Human Rights encourages the Commission on Human Rights, in cooperation with the Committee on Economic, Social and Cultural Rights, to continue the examination of optional protocols to the International Covenant on Economic, Social and Cultural Rights.

76. The World Conference on Human Rights recommends that more resources be made available for the strengthening or the establishment of regional arrangements for the promotion and protection of human rights under the programmes of advisory services and technical assistance of the Centre for Human Rights. States are encouraged to request assistance for such purposes as regional and subregional workshops, seminars and information exchanges designed to strengthen regional arrangements for the promotion and protection of human rights in accord with universal human rights standards as contained in international human rights instruments.

77. The World Conference on Human Rights supports all measures by the United Nations and its relevant specialized agencies to ensure the effective promotion and protection of trade union rights, as stipulated in the International Covenant on Economic, Social and Cultural Rights and other relevant international instruments. It calls on all States to abide fully by their obligations in this regard contained in international instruments.

### D. Human Rights Education

78. The World Conference on Human Rights considers human rights education, training and public information essential for the promotion and achievement of stable and harmonious relations among communities and for fostering mutual understanding, tolerance and peace.

79. States should strive to eradicate illiteracy and should direct education towards the full development of the human personality and to the strengthening of respect for human rights and fundamental freedoms. The World Conference on Human Rights calls on all States and institutions to include human rights, humanitarian law, democracy and rule of law as subjects in the curricula of all learning institutions in formal and non-formal settings.

80. Human rights education should include peace, democracy, development and social justice, as set forth in in-

ternational and regional human rights instruments in order to achieve common understanding and awareness with a view to strengthening universal commitment to human rights.

81. Taking into account the World Plan of Action on Education for Human Rights and Democracy, adopted in March 1993 by the International Congress on Education for Human Rights and Democracy of the United Nations Educational, Scientific and Cultural Organization, and other human rights instruments, the World Conference on Human Rights recommends that States develop specific programmes and strategies for ensuring the widest human rights education and the dissemination of public information, taking particular account of the human rights needs of women.

82. Governments, with the assistance of intergovernmental organizations, national institutions and non-governmental organizations, should promote an increased awareness of human rights and mutual tolerance. The World Conference on Human Rights underlines the importance of strengthening the World Public Information Campaign for Human Rights carried out by the United Nations. They should initiate and support education in human rights and undertake effective dissemination of public information in this field. The advisory services and technical assistance programmes of the United Nations system should be able to respond immediately to requests from States for educational and training activities in the field of human rights as well as for special education concerning standards as contained in international human rights instruments and in humanitarian law and their application to special groups such as military forces, law enforcement personnel, police and the health profession. The proclamation of a United Nations decade for human rights education in order to promote, encourage and focus these educational activities should be considered.

### E. Implementation and Monitoring Methods

83. The World Conference on Human Rights urges Governments to incorporate standards as contained in international human rights instruments in domestic legislation and to strengthen national structures, institutions and organs of society which play a role in promoting and safeguarding human rights.

84. The World Conference on Human Rights recommends the strengthening of United Nations activities and programmes to meet requests for assistance by States which want to establish or strengthen their own national institutions for the promotion and protection of human rights.

85. The World Conference on Human Rights also encourages the strengthening of cooperation between national institutions for the promotion and protection of human rights, particularly through exchanges of information and experience, as well as cooperation with regional organizations and the United Nations.

86. The World Conference on Human Rights strongly recommends in this regard that representatives of national institutions for the promotion and protection of human rights convene periodic meetings under the auspices of the Centre for Human Rights to examine ways and means of improving their mechanisms and sharing experiences.

87. The World Conference on Human Rights recommends to the human rights treaty bodies, to the meetings of chairpersons of the treaty bodies and to the meetings of States parties that they continue to take steps aimed at co-ordinating the multiple reporting requirements and guidelines for preparing State reports under the respective human rights conventions and study the suggestion that the submission of one overall report on treaty obligations undertaken by each State would make these procedures more effective and increase their impact.

88. The World Conference on Human Rights recommends that the State parties to international human rights instruments, the General Assembly and the Economic and Social Council should consider studying the existing human rights treaty bodies and the various thematic mechanisms and procedures with a view to promoting greater efficiency and effectiveness through better coordination of the various bodies, mechanisms and procedures, taking into account the need to avoid unnecessary duplication and overlapping of their mandates and tasks.

89. The World Conference on Human Rights recommends continued work on the improvement of the functioning, including the monitoring tasks, of the treaty bodies, taking into account multiple proposals made in this respect, in particular those made by the treaty bodies themselves and by the meetings of the chairpersons of the treaty bodies. The comprehensive national approach taken by the Committee on the Rights of the Child should also be encouraged.

90. The World Conference on Human Rights recommends that States parties to human rights treaties consider accepting all the available optional communication procedures.

91. The World Conference on Human Rights views with concern the issue of impunity of perpetrators of human rights violations, and supports the efforts of the Commission on Human Rights and the Sub-Commission on Prevention of Discrimination and Protection of Minorities to examine all aspects of the issue.

92. The World Conference on Human Rights recommends that the Commission on Human Rights examine the possibility for better implementation of existing human rights instruments at the international and regional levels and encourage the International Law Commission to continue its work on an international criminal court.

93. The World Conference on Human Rights appeals to States which have not yet done so to accede to the Geneva Conventions of 12 August 1949 and the Protocols thereto, and to take all appropriate national measures, including legislative ones, for their full implementation.

94. The World Conference on Human Rights recommends the speedy completion and adoption of the draft declaration on the right and responsibility of individuals, groups and organs of society to promote and protect universally recognized human rights and fundamental freedoms.

95. The World Conference on Human Rights underlines the importance of preserving and strengthening the system of special procedures, rapporteurs, representatives, experts and working groups of the Commission on Human Rights and the Sub-Commission on the Prevention of Discrimination and Protection of Minorities, in order to enable them to carry out their mandates in all countries throughout the world, providing them with the necessary human and financial resources. The procedures and mechanisms should be enabled to harmonize and rationalize their work through periodic meetings. All States are asked to cooperate fully with these procedures and mechanisms.

96. The World Conference on Human Rights recommends that the United Nations assume a more active role in the promotion and protection of human rights in ensuring full respect for international humanitarian law in all situa-

tions of armed conflict, in accordance with the purposes and principles of the Charter of the United Nations.

97. The World Conference on Human Rights, recognizing the important role of human rights components in specific arrangements concerning some peace-keeping operations by the United Nations, recommends that the Secretary-General take into account the reporting, experience and capabilities of the Centre for Human Rights and human rights mechanisms, in conformity with the Charter of the United Nations.

98. To strengthen the enjoyment of economic, social and cultural rights, additional approaches should be examined, such as a system of indicators to measure progress in the realization of the rights set forth in the International Covenant on Economic, Social and Cultural Rights. There must be a concerted effort to ensure recognition of economic, social and cultural rights at the national, regional and international levels.

### F. Follow-up to the World Conference on Human Rights

99. The World Conference on Human Rights recommends that the General Assembly, the Commission on Human Rights and other organs and agencies of the United Nations system related to human rights consider ways and means for the full implementation, without delay, of the recommendations contained in the present Declaration, including the possibility of proclaiming a United Nations decade for human rights. The World Conference on Human Rights further recommends that the Commission on Human Rights annually review the progress towards this end.

100. The World Conference on Human Rights requests the Secretary-General of the United Nations to invite on the occasion of the 50th anniversary of the Universal Declaration of Human Rights all States, all organs and agencies of the United Nations system related to human rights to report to him on the progress made in the implementation of the present Declaration and to submit a report to the General Assembly at its 53rd session, through the Commission on Human Rights and the Economic and Social Council. Likewise, regional and, as appropriate, national human rights institutions, as well as non-governmental organizations, may present their views to the Secretary-General on the progress made in the implementation of the present Declaration. Special attention should be paid to assessing the progress towards the goal of universal ratification of international human rights treaties and protocols adopted within the framework of the United Nations system.

**BIBLIOGRAPHY.** Boerifijin, I., and K. Davidse. "Every Cloud . . . ? The World Conference on Human Rights and Supervision of Implementation of Human Rights," *Netherlands Quarterly of Human Rights* 11 (1993): 457–468. Article, in English.

**VIETNAM.** The Socialist Republic of Vietnam is a country in southeastern Asia, occupying the eastern and southern part of the Indochinese Peninsula, on the South China Sea. It achieved independence in 1976 through the formal unification of North and South Vietnam after the capitulation of the former Republic of Vietnam and became a member of the United Nations in 1977. Its population is estimated by the UN to be 68,893,000. Apart from the majority Vietnamese (Kinh), who comprise more than 84% of the population, there are more than 50 ethnic minorities, including Tay, Thai, Muong, Nung, Kho-me, Gia-rai, Ede, Cham, and Coho. Each of these communities has its own written and spoken language and its own manners and customs. Languages commonly used include Vietnamese (official), French, Chinese, Khmer, and the minority vernaculars. Religions practiced include Buddhism, Christianity, Animism, Islam, and Taoism. Literacy is estimated at 78%.

The government (1994) took the form of a socialist republic. Under the 1980 constitution, the Communist Party is the ruling political party. Executive authority is exercised by the State Council and Council of Ministers, with "people's committees" governing in local jurisdictions. National legislation is prepared by the National Assembly; local legislation, by people's councils. The judiciary is headed by the Supreme People's Court. In an election held in April 1981, 829 candidates participated after being nominated at public meetings and 496 were elected. In addition to the Communist Party, two political parties—the Socialist Party and the Democratic Party—participated.

A new constitution took effect after a general election in July 1992, in which the Communist Party contributed 90% of the 601 candidates for the 395-seat National Assembly. General Le Duc Anh was elected president. The constitution states that the Communist Party is central to society and provides for a president to replace the Council of State. It also guarantees freedom of travel and investment abroad for Vietnamese.

*AFTERMATH OF THE VIETNAM WAR.* Between April 1975 and August 1984 more than 550,000 "boat people" from Vietnam found refuge abroad; and, in 1985, it was estimated that they continued to leave at the rate of 1,000 per month. Arrangements introduced by the UN **HIGH COMMISSIONER FOR REFUGEES** increased significantly the rescue of asylum-seekers in distress at sea, and international preventive measures resulted in a sharp decline in the number of refugee boats attacked by pirates.

Vietnamese refugees continue to be repatriated from Hong Kong. In addition, Germany agreed to provide economic incentives and aid to Vietnam in exchange for the repatriation of 60,000 Vietnamese immigrants who fled to Germany in the mid-1970s.

Following the revocation of the United States trade embargo against Vietnam by U.S. President Bill Clinton in February 1994, Vietnam returned the remains of dozens of soldiers missing in action since the war 20 years before. The United States resumed diplomatic relations with Vietnam in July 1995.

***ETHNIC MINORITIES.*** As regards the treatment of its ethnic minorities, the Government of Vietnam, in a report submitted on 22 December 1983 to the UN **COMMITTEE ON THE ELIMINATION OF RACIAL DISCRIMINATION,** indicated that the basic laws of the Vietnamese state stipulate, *inter alia,* the following principles: (a) solidarity, unity, and equality among the nationalities; elimination of national divisiveness and marks of contempt; and removal of the discrepancy in economic, cultural, and social development levels among the various ethnic groups; and (b) guaranteeing the rights and fundamental freedoms of citizens without any discrimination. In order to implement these principles, the government took steps to ensure the development of the minorities, among them "encouraging the development of production in the highlands, encouraging the ethnic groups to make use of their own spoken and written languages, establishing communal dispensaries in the highlands, establishing five universities and training colleges essentially for the children of the ethnic minorities, and granting priority access for young people from the ethnic minorities to the country's other universities."

The Commission on Ethnic Affairs was established in 1955 to monitor the application of the minorities policies. The Commission was converted in 1958 into the Central Committee of Nationalities, an organ with ministerial powers whose chairman is a member of the Council of Ministers.

Vietnamese military expansion into Laos and Cambodia has given rise to allegations of violations of the human rights of the peoples of those countries and to charges that their right to **SELF-DETERMINATION** has been denied.

**BIBLIOGRAPHY.** Amnesty International. *Memorandum to the Governments of Hong Kong and the United Kingdom Regarding the Protection of Vietnamese Asylum Seekers in Hong Kong.* London: 1990. NGO report, in English.
———. *Viet Nam: Arrests of Political Prisoners, 1990–1991.* London: 1992. NGO report, in English.
———. *Viet Nam: Long-Term Political Prisoners.* London: 1991. NGO factfinding report, in English and French.
———. *Socialist Republic of Viet Nam: Buddhist Monks in Detention.* London: 1994. NGO report, in English.
Asia Watch. *Viet Nam: The Case of Doan Viet Hoat and Freedom Forum.* New York: Human Rights Watch, 1993. NGO report, in English.
———. *Viet Nam: Human Rights in U.S.-Vietnam Relations.* New York: Human Rights Watch, 1993. NGO report, in English.
———. *Viet Nam: Repression of Dissent.* New York: Human Rights Watch, 1991. NGO factfinding report, in English.
———. *Viet Nam: Suppression of the Unified Buddhist Church.* New York: Human Rights Watch, 1995. NGO report, in English.
Canh, Nguyen Van. "Democracy and Human Rights in the Socialist Republic of Vietnam," *Indochina Journal* 4, no. 2 (1990): 11–16 . Speech, in English.
Chan Kwok Bun, ed. "Indochinese Refugees 15 Years Later," *Southeast Asian Journal of Social Science* 18, no. 1 (1990). Special issue, in English.
Chanda, Nayan. *Brother Enemy: The War after the War.* New York: Harcourt Brace Jovanovich, 1986. Scholarly monograph, in English.
Helton, Arthur C. "The Comprehensive Plan of Action for Indo-Chinese Refugees: An Experiment in Refugee Protection and Control," *New York Law School Journal of Human Rights* 8, no. 1 (Fall 1990): 111–148. Scholarly article, in English.
Human Rights Watch. "Vietnam," in *Human Rights Watch World Report 1995,* pp. 172–176. New York: 1995. NGO report, in English.
International League for Human Rights. *Vietnam's Human Rights Record: Examining the Government of Vietnam's First Official Report to the Human Rights Committee.* New York: 1990. NGO report, in English.
Nichols, Alan, and Paul White. *Refugee Dilemmas: Reviewing the Comprehensive Plan for Action for Vietnamese Asylum Seekers.* Manila, the Philippines: LAWASIA Human Rights Committee, 1993. NGO report, in English; bibliography, pp. 111–112.
Que Me, Vietnam Committee on Human Rights. *Vietnam 1987: Human Rights Revelations by Top C.P.V. Officials and Hanoi Press.* Gennevilliers, France: 1987. NGO report, in English.
Robinson, Court. "Southeast Asian Refugees: Critical Mass?" *Indochina Issues* 77 (Dec. 1987): 1–7. NGO article, in English.
Vietnam Committee on Human Rights. *Vietnam: Violations of Religious Freedom and Freedom of Conscience.* Gennevilliers, France: 1993. NGO report, in English.
Zentrale Dokumentationsstelle der Freien Wohlfahrtspflege fur Fluchtlinge. *Arbeitsmaterialien fur den Unterricht: Die Weltfluchtlingsproblematik und ihre Auswirkungen in der Bundesrepublik Deutschland* (Study Materials: The World Refugee Problem and its Consequences in the Federal Republic of Germany). Bonn, FRG: 1987. NGO edited collection, in German.

# W

**WALESA, LECH (1943– ).** Born in Popowo, Poland, on 29 September 1943, this former electrician was awarded the 1984 **NOBEL PEACE PRIZE** for leading protests by Polish workers for the right to organize. After imprisonment for his work with the Solidarity and the downfall of the Communist government, Walesa became president of a democratic Poland.

In 1976, Walesa served as a member of the strike committee at the Gdansk shipyard, and he was fired from his job for his union activities. He rose to international prominence in 1980, when tensions increased at the shipyard and the government announced increases in prices. Although no longer a worker at the plant, Walesa joined the workers inside the shipyard and took charge of a strike committee that demanded the right to unionization. Walesa became a symbol of Polish workers laboring under the Communist system. Fearing a national revolt as the strike grew to involve more than 300,000 workers, the government, represented by Deputy Prime Minister Mieczyslaw Jagielski, began negotiations that resulted in the Gdansk Agreement, which granted workers the right to strike and form independent unions, the first such agreement in any Communist country. In addition, the government agreed to grant wage increases and social benefits, relax censorship, open the state-controlled media, and broadcast Roman Catholic mass on Sundays. The unions, in turn, acknowledged the Communist party supremacy.

Following the 1980 success, millions of Polish workers formed unions; Walesa became head of Solidarity, a national federation that united the individual unions. But problems soon arose between the unions and the government; in 1981, Gen. Wojciech Jaruzelski became Polish Communist Party leader and premier and began to take action against the unions. Responding to a public call for a referendum on the government and its ties with the Soviet Union, the government imposed martial law, and Walesa was imprisoned for 11 months. When he emerged, Solidarity was in disarray. However, Walesa persevered in his efforts to bring down the Communist government. In 1989, in the first free elections in Poland in more than 40 years, Solidarity candidates swept into office and ousted the Communist Party. Walesa became president in 1990.

However, in elections held in 1995, Walesa lost the presidency in a run-off vote to an ex-Communist.

The Nobel Prize Committee cited Walesa for his "defense of human rights and his determination to solve his country's problems through negotiation and cooperation without resorting to violence." The Polish Government did not permit Walesa to travel to Oslo to receive his Prize; his wife Danuta went in his place.

*BIBLIOGRAPHY.* Ascherson, Neal. *The Book of Lech Walesa.* New York: Simon and Schuster, 1982.
*Current Biography Yearbook 1981,* pp. 418–421. New York: W. H. Wilson, 1985.
Schlessinger, Bernard S., and June Schlessinger, eds. *Who's Who of Nobel Prize Winners.* Phoenix, AZ, USA: Oryx Press, 1991.

**WALLENBERG (RAOUL) INSTITUTE OF HUMAN RIGHTS AND HUMANITARIAN LAW.** The Institute, located at Lund University, Stockholm, Sweden, promotes research on human rights and humanitarian law and initiates, develops, and supports scholarly/scientific education in these fields.

The Institute offers annually a month-long program that focuses on civil and political rights; economic, social, and cultural rights; the right to development; human rights monitoring systems; human rights in armed conflict; humanitarian law; and refugee policy. The program is interdisciplinary, involving aspects of law, the social sciences, and philosophy.

The program accepts 24 participants, primarily senior civil servants in public service and lecturers at universities and institutes. The program is conducted in English only. Applications are available from Swedish embassies and must be received by January 1.

The Raoul Wallenberg Institute of Human Rights and Humanitarian Law. Address: Sankt Annegatan 4, S-223 50 Lund, Sweden. Telephone: (46-46) 10-43-10. Fax: (46-46) 10-44-45.

**WAR CRIMES.** In one of its earliest decisions, the UN **GENERAL ASSEMBLY** on 13 February 1946 called (resolution 3 [I]) for the development of international cooperation to secure the punishment, in the countries where their deeds were committed, of war criminals and persons who had committed crimes against mankind.

At its 1987 session, the **Sub-Commission on Prevention of Discrimination and Protection of Minorities** noted that such cooperation had been established and was continuing but that, nevertheless, a large number of war criminals and persons guilty of crimes against mankind continued to live in territories of UN member States. It called for further international cooperation in this field to prosecute and punish them.

The UN **Commission on Human Rights,** at its 1988 session, commended (resolution 1988/47) the cooperation among various UN member States which had resulted in the fair trial and just punishment of important war criminals, including the Nazi war criminal Klaus Barbie, for their crimes against humanity; and noted the spirit of cooperation shown by several member States in facilitating the extradition of war criminals, who, in the aftermath of World War II, had attempted to elude responsibility for their deeds by taking refuge in other countries. At the same time, it recognized that, according to consistent and well-documented reports, a large number of persons alleged to have committed war crimes and crimes against humanity live in the territories of member States. It urged all States to take the necessary measures, in accordance with their national constitutional systems, to ensure full international cooperation for the purpose of securing, preferably in the place where they committed their deeds, the prosecution and punishment of all those who have committed war crimes and crimes against humanity.

**WAR CRIMES FILES.** On 31 August 1987, the Sub-Commission on Prevention of Discrimination and Protection of Minorities pointed out (resolution 1987/2) that the files of the War Crimes Commission, of which the United Nations is the custodian, were at that time accessible only to UN member States by virtue of rules which had been established by the **UN Secretariat.** Considering that these files might contain important sources of information concerning violations of human rights and fundamental freedoms during the Nazi regime, the Sub-Commission welcomed the prospect of a decision to broaden access to them.

Having been informed that the Secretary-General had determined that at least a majority of the 17 States that had been members of the War Crimes Commission were willing for the rules of access to be relaxed, under considerations to be determined jointly, the Sub-Commission recommended that the Commission on Human Rights encourage the Secretary-General to pursue these efforts and to suggest to him that the Sub-Commission advise him with regard to the drafting of guidelines concerning who, other than member States, should have access to the files and under what circumstances.

Before the Commission met for its 1988 session, however, access to the files of the War Crimes Commission had been broadened by the Secretary-General, in agreement with the States which had been members of the Commission, as a result of a meeting convened by the Secretary-General in September 1987.

**SEE ALSO** *Crimes against the Peace and Security of Mankind.*

**BIBLIOGRAPHY.** Amnesty International. *Memorandum to the United Nations: The Question of Justice and Fairness in the International War Crimes Tribunal for the Former Yugoslavia.* London: 1993. NGO memorandum, in English.

———. *Moving Forward to Set up the War Crimes Tribunal for the Former Yugoslavia.* London: 1993. NGO report, in English.

Aspen Institute for Humanistic Studies. *State Crimes: Punishment or Pardon.* Aspen, CO, USA: 1988. NGO conference papers, in English.

Bassiouni, M. Cherif. *Crimes against Humanity in International Criminal Law.* Dordrecht, the Netherlands: Martinus Nijhoff, 1992. Scholarly monograph, in English.

———. "Nuremberg Forty Years After: An Introduction," *Case Western Reserve Journal of International Law* 18, no. 2 (Spring 1986): 261–266. Scholarly article, in English.

Commission on Security and Cooperation in Europe. *Proposal for an International War Crimes Tribunal for the Former Yugoslavia.* Washington, D.C.: U.S. Government Printing Office, 1993. Government proposal, in English.

Cotler, Irwin. "Nazi War Crimes—An International Legal Responsibility," *Patterns of Prejudice* 20, no. 4 (Oct. 1986): 31–41. NGO journal article, in English.

Hamalengwa, Munyonzwe. *The Case for the Prosecution of Apartheid Criminals in Canada.* North York, Canada: 1988. NGO report, in English.

"Health Protection and Medical Assistance in Disaster Situations," *International Review of the Red Cross* 284 (English); 791 (French) (Sept.–Oct. 1991): 435–532 (English); 459–566 (French). Scholarly article, in English and French.

Helsinki Watch. *Procedural and Evidentiary Issues for the Yugoslav War Crimes Tribunal: Resource Allocation, Evidentiary Questions and Protection of Witnesses.* New York: Human Rights Watch, 1993. NGO report, in English.

———. *War Crimes in Bosnia-Hercegovina.* 2 vols. New York: Human Rights Watch, 1992–1993. NGO factfinding report, in English.

International Human Rights Law Group. *No Justice, No Peace: Accountability for Rape and Gender-Based Violence in the Former Yugoslavia.* Washington, D.C.: 1993. NGO factfinding report, in English.

Lippman, Matthew. "The Denaturalization of Nazi War Criminals in the United States: Is Justice Being Served?" *Houston Journal of International Law* 7, no. 2 (Spring 1985): 169—214. Scholarly article, in English.

Max Planck Institute for Comparative Public and International Law. *Encyclopedia of Public International, Vol. 8: Human Rights and the Individual in International Law—Interna-*

*tional Economic Relations.* New York: North-Holland, 1985. Encyclopedia, in English; bibliography after each article.

Meron, Theodor. "The Case for War Crime Trials in Yugoslavia," *Foreign Affairs* 72, no. 3 (Summer 1993): 122–135. Scholarly article, in English.

Middle East Watch. *Needless Deaths in the Gulf War: Civilian Casualties during the Air Campaign and Violations of the Laws of War.* New York: Human Rights Watch, 1991. NGO monograph, in English.

Pérez Esquivel, Adolfo. "El Juicio Debe Ir Mas Alla de las Juntas y Alcanzar a los Represores" (The Judgment Must Go beyond the Juntas and Reach Those Who Carried out the Repression), *Reencuentro* 1, no. 5 (June 1985): 11. NGO bulletin article, in Spanish.

Prévost, Ann Marie. "Race and War Crimes: The 1945 War Crimes Trial of General Tomoyuki Yamashita," *Human Rights Quarterly* 14, no. 3 (Aug. 1992): 303–338. Scholarly article, in English.

Ramshaw, P., and T. Steers. *Intervention on Trial: The New York War Crimes Tribunal on Central America and the Caribbean.* New York: Praeger Publishers and the National Lawyers Guild, 1987. NGO study, in English.

Rosenbaum, Alan S. *Prosecuting Nazi War Criminals.* Boulder, CO, USA: Westview Press, 1993. Scholarly monograph, in English.

Ruzie, Davie. "Klaus Barbie and the French Legal Process," *Patterns of Prejudice* 20, no. 3 (July 1986): 27–33. NGO article, in English.

Steiner, Eva. "Prosecuting War Criminals in England and in France," *Criminal Law Review* 33 (March 1991): 180–188. Scholarly article, in English.

Sunga, Lyal S. *Individual Responsibility in International Law for Serious Human Rights Violations.* Dordrecht, the Netherlands: Martinus Nijhoff, 1992. Scholarly monograph, in English.

Swinarski, Christophe. *Principales Nociones e Institutos del Derecho Internacional Humanitario como Sistema Internacional de Protección de la Persona Humana* (Primary Notions and Principles of International Humanitarian Law as an International System for the Protection of the Person). San José, Costa Rica: Instituto Interamericano de Derechos Humanos (Inter-American Institute of Human Rights), 1990. Scholarly monograph, in Spanish; bibliography, pp. 91–102.

Van Baarda, Th. A. "Is It Expedient to Let the World Court Clarify, in an Advisory Opinion, the Applicability of the Fourth Geneva Convention in the Occupied Territories?" *Netherlands Quarterly of Human Rights* 10, no. 1 (1992): 4–28. Scholarly article, in English.

Von Hebel, Herman. "An International Tribunal for the Former Yugoslavia: An Act of Powerlessness or a New Challenge for the International Community?" *Netherlands Quarterly of Human Rights* 11, no. 4 (1993): 437–456. Scholarly article, in English.

Wieland, G. "40th Anniversary of the Nuremberg Trial of German Major War Criminals: The GDR's Contribution to Punishing Nazi Crimes," *GDR Committee for Human Rights Bulletin* 11, no. 3 (1985): 167–179. NGO bulletin article, in English.

World Jewish Congress, Commission on the Holocaust and Crimes of the Nazis. *Waldheim's Nazi Past: The Dossier.* Geneva, Switzerland: 1988. NGO report, in English.

## WAR CRIMES: CONVENTION ON THE NON-APPLICABILITY OF STATUTORY LIMITATIONS

**TO CRIMES AGAINST HUMANITY AND WAR CRIMES, COUNCIL OF EUROPE (1974).** The Convention follows the general lines of the Convention on the Non-Applicability of Statutory Limitations to War Crimes and Crimes against Humanity (see next entry) adopted by the UN **GENERAL ASSEMBLY** on 26 November 1968. Under the European Convention, member States of the **COUNCIL OF EUROPE** undertake to adopt any measures necessary to ensure that no statutory limitation shall apply to crimes against humanity or war crimes or to the enforcement of sentences imposed for such offenses insofar as they are punishable under its domestic law.

The Convention was concluded by the Committee of Ministers of the Council of Europe, convened in Strasbourg, on 25 January 1974. The text of the Convention (*European Treaty Series,* 82) is as follows:

The member States of the Council of Europe, signatory hereto,

Considering the necessity to safeguard human dignity in time of war and in time of peace;

Considering that crimes against humanity and the most serious violations of the laws and customs of war constitute a serious infraction of human dignity;

Concerned in consequence to ensure that the punishment of those crimes is not prevented by statutory limitations whether in relation to prosecution or to the enforcement of the punishment;

Considering the essential interest in promoting a common criminal policy in this field, the aim of the Council of Europe being to achieve a greater unity between its Members,

Have agreed as follows:

*Article 1.* Each Contracting State undertakes to adopt any necessary measures to secure that statutory limitations shall not apply to the prosecution of the following offences, or to the enforcement of the sentences imposed for such offences, in so far as they are punishable under its domestic law:

1. the crimes against humanity specified in the Convention on the Prevention and Punishment of the Crime of Genocide adopted on 9 December 1948 by the General Assembly of the United Nations;

2. (a) the violations specified in Article 50 of the 1949 Geneva Convention for the Amelioration of the Condition of the Wounded and Sick in Armed Forces in the Field, Article 51 of the 1949 Geneva Convention for the Amelioration of the Condition of Wounded, Sick and Shipwrecked Members of Armed Forces at Sea, Article 130 of the 1949 Geneva Convention relative to the Treatment of Prisoners of War and Article 147 of the 1949 Geneva Convention relative to the Protection of Civilian Persons in Time of War,

(b) any comparable violations of the laws of war having effect at the time when this Convention enters into force and of customs of war existing at that time, which are not already provided for in the above-mentioned provisions of the Geneva Conventions, when the specific violation under consideration is of a particularly grave character by reason either of its factual and intentional elements or of the extent of its foreseeable consequences;

3. any other violation of a rule or custom of international law which may hereafter be established and which the Contracting State concerned considers according to a declara-

tion under Article 6 as being of a comparable nature to those referred to in paragraph 1 or 2 of this article.

*Article 2.* 1. The present Convention applies to offences committed after its entry into force in respect of the Contracting State concerned.

2. It applies also to offences committed before such entry into force in those cases where the statutory limitation period had not expired at that time.

*Article 3.* 1. This Convention shall be open to signature by the member States of the Council of Europe. It shall be subject to ratification or acceptance. Instruments of ratification or acceptance shall be deposited with the Secretary General of the Council of Europe.

2. The Convention shall enter into force three months after the date of deposit of the third instrument of ratification or acceptance.

3. In respect of a signatory State ratifying or accepting subsequently, the Convention shall come into force three months after the date of the deposit of its instrument of ratification or acceptance.

*Article 4.* 1. After the entry into force of this Convention, the Committee of Ministers of the Council of Europe may invite any non-member State to accede thereto, provided that the resolution containing such invitation receives the unanimous agreement of the Members of the Council who have ratified the Convention.

2. Such accession shall be effected by depositing with the Secretary General of the Council of Europe an instrument of accession which shall take effect three months after the date of its deposit.

*Article 5.* 1. Any State may, at the time of signature or when depositing its instrument of ratification, acceptance or accession, specify the territory or territories to which this Convention shall apply.

2. Any State may, when depositing its instrument of ratification, acceptance or accession or at any later date, be declaration addressed to the Secretary General of the Council of Europe, extend this Convention to any other territory or territories specified in the declaration and for whose international relations it is responsible or on whose behalf it is authorised to give undertakings.

3. Any declaration made in pursuance of the preceding paragraph may, in respect of any territory mentioned in such declaration, be withdrawn according to the procedure laid down in Article 7 of this Convention.

*Article 6.* 1. Any Contracting State may, at any time, by declaration addressed to the Secretary General of the Council of Europe, extend this Convention to any violations provided for in Article 1, paragraph 3, of this Convention.

2. Any declaration made in pursuance of the preceding paragraph may be withdrawn according to the procedure laid down in Article 7 of this Convention.

*Article 7.* 1. This Convention shall remain in force indefinitely.

2. Any Contracting State may, in so far as it is concerned, denounce this Convention by means of a notification addressed to the Secretary General of the Council of Europe.

3. Such denunciation shall take effect six months after the date of receipt by the Secretary General of such notification.

*Article 8.* The Secretary General of the Council of Europe shall notify the member States of the Council and any State which has acceded to this Convention of:

(a) any signature;

(b) any deposit of an instrument of ratification, acceptance or accession;

(c) any date of entry into force of this Convention in accordance with Article 3 thereof;

(d) any declaration received in pursuance of the provisions of Article 5 or Article 6;

(e) any notification received in pursuance of the provisions of Article 7 and the date on which the denunciation takes effect.

In witness whereof the undersigned, being duly authorised thereto, have signed this Convention.

Done at Strasbourg, this 25th day of January 1974, in the English and French languages, both texts being equally authoritative, in a single copy which shall remain deposited in the archives of the Council of Europe. The Secretary General of the Council of Europe shall transmit certified copies to each of the signatory and acceding States.

## WAR CRIMES: CONVENTION ON THE NON-APPLICABILITY OF STATUTORY LIMITATIONS TO WAR CRIMES AND CRIMES AGAINST HUMANITY, UN (1968).

The Convention was prepared after studies by the UN Secretary-General revealed that, in a number of countries, there were statutory limitations which would prevent the trial or punishment of certain war criminals after a specified date or period. The Convention affirms in international law the principle that there is not, and cannot be, any period of limitation for the prosecution of perpetrators of war crimes or crimes against humanity.

The Convention was adopted by the UN **GENERAL ASSEMBLY** on 26 November 1968 (resolution 2391 [XXIII]) and entered into force on 11 November 1970. The text (United Nations, *Treaty Series*, vol. 754, p.73) is as follows:

The States Parties to the present Convention,

Recalling resolutions of the General Assembly of the United Nations 3 (I) of 13 February 1946 and 170 (II) of 31 October 1947 on the extradition and punishment of war criminals, resolution 95 (I) of 11 December 1946 affirming the principles of international law recognized by the Charter of the International Military Tribunal, Nürnberg, and the judgement of the Tribunal, and resolutions 2184 (XXI) of 12 December 1966 and 2202 (XXI) of 16 December 1966 which expressly condemned as crimes against humanity the violation of the economic and political rights of the indigenous population on the one hand and the policies of *apartheid* on the other,

Recalling resolutions of the Economic and Social Council of the United Nations 1074 D (XXXIX) of 28 July 1965 and 1158 (XLI) of 5 August 1966 on the punishment of war criminals and of persons who have committed crimes against humanity,

Noting that none of the solemn declarations, instruments or conventions relating to the prosecution and punishment of war crimes and crimes against humanity made provision for a period of limitation,

Considering that war crimes and crimes against humanity are among the gravest crimes in international law,

Convinced that the effective punishment of war crimes and crimes against humanity is an important element in the prevention of such crimes, the protection of human rights and fundamental freedoms, the encouragement of confidence, the furtherance of co-operation among peoples and the promotion of international peace and security,

Noting that the application to war crimes and crimes against humanity of the rules of municipal law relating to the period of limitation for ordinary crimes is a matter of serious concern to world public opinion, since it prevents the prosecution and punishment of persons responsible for those crimes,

Recognizing that it is necessary and timely to affirm in international law, through this Convention, the principle that there is no period of limitation for war crimes and crimes against humanity, and to secure its universal application,

Have agreed as follows:

*Article 1.* No statutory limitation shall apply to the following crimes, irrespective of the date of their commission:

(*a*) War crimes as they are defined in the Charter of the International Military Tribunal, Nürnberg, of 8 August 1945 and confirmed by resolutions 3 (I) of 13 February 1946 and 95 (I) of 11 December 1946 of the General Assembly of the United Nations, particularly the "grave breaches" enumerated in the Geneva Conventions of 12 August 1949 for the protection of war victims;

(*b*) Crimes against humanity whether committed in time of war or in time of peace as they are defined in the Charter of the International Military Tribunal, Nürnberg, of 8 August 1945 and confirmed by resolutions 3 (I) of 13 February 1946 and 95 (I) of 11 December 1946 of the General Assembly of the United Nations, eviction by armed attack or occupation and inhuman acts resulting from the policy of *apartheid,* and the crime of genocide as defined in the 1948 Convention on the Prevention and Punishment of the Crime of Genocide, even if such acts do not constitute a violation of the domestic law of the country in which they were committed.

*Article 2.* If any of the crimes mentioned in article 1 is committed, the provisions of this Convention shall apply to representatives of the State authority and private individuals who, as principals or accomplices, participate in or who directly incite others to the commission of any of those crimes, or who conspire to commit them, irrespective of the degree of completion, and to representatives of the State authority who tolerate their commission.

*Article 3.* The States Parties to the present Convention undertake to adopt all necessary domestic measures, legislative or otherwise, with a view to making possible the extradition, in accordance with international law, of the persons referred to in article 2 of this Convention.

*Article 4.* The States Parties to the present Convention undertake to adopt, in accordance with their respective constitutional processes, any legislative or other measures necessary to ensure that statutory or other limitations shall not apply to the prosecution and punishment of the crimes referred to in articles 1 and 2 of this Convention and that, where they exist, such limitations shall be abolished.

*Article 5.* This Convention shall, until 31 December 1969, be open for signature by any State Member of the United Nations or member of any of its specialized agencies or of the International Atomic Energy Agency, by any State Party to the Statute of the International Court of Justice, and by any other State which has been invited by the General Assembly of the United Nations to become a Party to this Convention.

*Article 6.* This Convention is subject to ratification. Instruments of ratification shall be deposited with the Secretary-General of the United Nations.

*Article 7.* This Convention shall be open to accession by any State referred to in article 5. Instruments of accession shall be deposited with the Secretary-General of the United Nations.

*Article 8.* 1. This Convention shall enter into force on the ninetieth day after the date of the deposit with the Secretary-General of the United Nations of the tenth instrument of ratification or accession.

2. For each State ratifying this Convention or acceding to it after the deposit of the tenth instrument of ratification or accession, the Convention shall enter into force on the ninetieth day after the date of the deposit of its own instrument of ratification or accession.

*Article 9.* 1. After the expiry of a period of ten years from the date on which this Convention enters into force, a request for the revision of the Convention may be made at any time by any Contracting Party by means of a notification in writing addressed to the Secretary-General of the United Nations.

2. The General Assembly of the United Nations shall decide upon the steps, if any, to be taken in respect of such a request.

*Article 10.* 1. This Convention shall be deposited with the Secretary-General of the United Nations.

2. The Secretary-General of the United Nations shall transmit certified copies of this Convention to all States referred to in article 5.

3. The Secretary-General of the United Nations shall inform all States referred to in article 5 of the following particulars:

(*a*) Signatures of this Convention, and instruments of ratification and accession deposited under articles 5, 6 and 7;

(*b*) The date of entry into force of this Convention in accordance with article 8;

(*c*) Communications received under article 9.

*Article 11.* This Convention, of which the Chinese, English, French, Russian and Spanish texts are equally authentic, shall bear the date of 26 November 1968.

In witness whereof the undersigned, being duly authorized for that purpose, having signed this Convention.

## WAR CRIMES: PRINCIPLES OF INTERNATIONAL CO-OPERATION IN THE DETECTION, ARREST, EXTRADITION AND PUNISHMENT OF PERSONS GUILTY OF WAR CRIMES AND CRIMES AGAINST HUMANITY, UN (1973).

Finding it appropriate to stimulate the prosecution and punishment of persons guilty of war crimes and crimes against humanity, the UN **GENERAL ASSEMBLY** formulated nine principles to be observed universally and adopted and proclaimed them on 3 December 1973 (resolution 3074 [XXVIII]). The text of the Principles, annexed to that resolution, is as follows:

The General Assembly

Declares that the United Nations, in pursuance of the principles and purposes set forth in the Charter concerning the promotion of co-operation between peoples and the maintenance of international peace and security, proclaims the following principles of international co-operation in the detection, arrest, extradition and punishment of persons guilty of war crimes and crimes against humanity:

1. War crimes and crimes against humanity, wherever they are committed, shall be subject to investigation and the persons against whom there is evidence that they have committed such crimes shall be subject to tracing, arrest, trial and, if found guilty, to punishment.

2. Every State has the right to try its own nationals for war crimes or crimes against humanity.

3. States shall co-operate with each other on a bilateral and multilateral basis with a view to halting and preventing war crimes and crimes against humanity, and shall take the domestic and international measures necessary for that purpose.

4. States shall assist each other in detecting, arresting and bringing to trial persons suspected of having committed such crimes and, if they are found guilty, in punishing them.

5. Persons against whom there is evidence that they have committed war crimes and crimes against humanity shall be subject to trial and, if found guilty, to punishment, as a general rule in the countries in which they committed those crimes. In that connexion, States shall co-operate on questions of extraditing such persons.

6. States shall co-operate with each other in the collection of information and evidence which would help bring to trial the persons indicated in paragraph 5 above and shall exchange such information.

7. In accordance with article 1 of the Declaration on Territorial Asylum of 14 December 1967, States shall not grant asylum to any person with respect to whom there are serious reasons for considering that he has committed a crime against peace, a war crime or a crime against humanity.

8. States shall not take any legislative or other measures which may be prejudicial to the international obligations they have assumed in regard to the detection, arrest, extradition and punishment of persons guilty of war crimes and crimes against humanity.

9. In co-operating with a view to the detection, arrest and extradition of persons against whom there is evidence that they have committed war crimes and crimes against humanity and, if found guilty, their punishment, States shall act in conformity with the provisions of the Charter of the United Nations and of the Declaration of Principles of International Law concerning Friendly Relations and Co-operation among States in accordance with the Charter of the United Nations.

## WAR CRIMES: PRINCIPLES OF INTERNATIONAL LAW RECOGNIZED IN THE CHARTER OF THE NÜRNBERG TRIBUNAL AND IN THE JUDGMENT OF THE TRIBUNAL (1950).

The Principles, formulated by the **INTERNATIONAL LAW COMMISSION** as requested by the **GENERAL ASSEMBLY** on 21 November 1947 (resolution 177 [II]), and completed by the Commission at its 1950 session, are as follows:

*Principle 1.* Any person who commits an act which constitutes a crime under international law is responsible therefor and liable to punishment.

*Principle 2.* The fact that internal law does not impose a penalty for an act which constitutes a crime under international law does not relieve the person who committed the act from responsibility under international law.

*Principle 3.* The fact that a person who committed an act which constitutes a crime under international law acted as Head of state or responsible Government official does not relieve him from responsibility under international law.

*Principle 4.* The fact that a person acted pursuant to order of his Government or of a superior does not relieve him from responsibility under international law, provided a moral choice was in fact possible to him.

*Principle 5.* Any person charged with a crime under international law has the right to a fair trial on the facts and law.

*Principle 6.* The crimes hereinafter set out are punishable as crimes under international law:

(a) Crimes against peace:

(i) Planning, preparation, initiation or waging of war of aggression or a war in violation of international treaties, agreements or assurances;

(ii) Participation in a common plan or conspiracy for the accomplishment of any of the acts mentioned under (i).

(b) War crimes: Violations of the laws or customs of war which include, but are not limited to, murder, ill-treatment or deportation to slave-labour or for any other purpose of civilian population of or in occupied territory; murder or ill-treatment of prisoners of war, of persons on the seas, killing of hostages, plunder of public or private property, wanton destruction of cities, towns, or villages, or devastation not justified by military necessity.

(c) Crimes against humanity: Murder, extermination, enslavement, deportation and other inhuman acts done against any civilian population, or persecutions on political, racial or religious grounds, when such acts are done or such persecutions are carried on in execution of or in connexion with any crime against peace or any war crime.

*Principle 7.* Complicity in the Commission of a crime against peace, a war crime, or a crime against humanity as set forth in Principle 6 is a crime under international law.

## WAR CRIMES TRIBUNAL: FORMER YUGOSLAVIA (INTERNATIONAL TRIBUNAL FOR THE PROSECUTION OF PERSONS RESPONSIBLE FOR SERIOUS VIOLATIONS OF INTERNATIONAL HUMANITARIAN LAW COMMITTED IN THE TERRITORY OF THE FORMER YUGOSLAVIA SINCE 1991).

The Yugoslav Federation broke apart in 1991 and 1992 when Slovenia, Croatia, Bosnia and Herzegovina, and the Former Yugoslav Republic of Macedonia each declared their independence. From 1991 the intense fighting in both Croatia and Bosnia and Herzegovina caused massive loss of life and displacement of millions of people from their homes. Bosnian Serbs declared their own republic within Bosnia and engaged in what the international community initially termed "ethnic cleansing" or "demographic restructuring."

In 1992 the United Nations **SECURITY COUNCIL** passed Resolution 780 (1992) establishing a Commission of Experts to investigate alleged crimes against humanity committed in the war within the territories of the former Yugoslavia. While their investigations were continuing, the Security Council passed Resolution 808 (1993) proposing the establishment of an International Tribunal for the prosecution of serious violations of international humanitarian law from January 1, 1991. Resolution (827), passed in May 1993, offically established the tribunal and in June nations were invited to nominate two judges for four-year terms. Judges were to be elected by the **GENERAL ASSEMBLY** to sit in The Hague, as well as elsewhere, if it was in the interest of justice to do so.

The International Tribunal adopted a nine-part Rules of Procedure and Evidence in February 1994 which came into effect in March. Some of its provisions included the primacy of the Tribunal's concurrent jurisdiction with national courts, the rotation of judges between the trial and appellate chambers, the establishment of the Victims and Witnesses Unit to protect and counsel witnesses and victims, a statement on Investigations and the Rights of Suspects, the obligations of states to execute Tribunal arrest warrants and transfer the accused to the Tribunal, the authority of the Trial Chamber to order restitution, and sentences up to and including life imprisonment.

Sir Richard Goldstone of South Africa was appointed Chief Prosecutor and the Tribunal issued its first indictments and arrest warrants against Bosnian Serb military personnel and leaders in 1995. The first indictments against Bosnian Muslims came in 1996. Germany was holding a Bosnian Serb charged with war crimes with the intent of prosecuting him in domestic courts.

**WAR CRIMES TRIBUNAL: RWANDA (INTERNATIONAL CRIMINAL TRIBUNAL FOR THE PROSECUTION OF PERSONS RESPONSIBLE FOR GENOCIDE AND OTHER SERIOUS VIOLATIONS OF INTERNATIONAL HUMANITARIAN LAW COMMITTED IN THE TERRITORY OF RWANDA AND RWANDAN CITIZENS RESPONSIBLE FOR GENOCIDE AND OTHER SUCH VIOLATIONS COMMITTED IN THE TERRITORY OF NEIGHBORING STATES BETWEEN 1 JANUARY 1994 AND 31 DECEMBER 1994).** In April 1994, Rwandan President Habyarimana was killed, along with the President and two Cabinet members of Burundi, and the Chief of Staff of the Rwandan armed forces, when their plane was fired upon and crashed at Kigali airport. The Presidential Guard and Hutu militias immediately closed off the crash site, precluding a UN investigation, and began retaliatory executions of opposition political leaders, including the Tutsi Prime Minister, priests, nuns, relief workers, and UN troops, including 10 Belgians who were disarmed before being executed.

In the weeks and months following the President's death, the Hutus and Tutsis vied for control of the government and the city of Kigali. Both groups engaged in extreme violence against each other as well as moderates within their own groups, leaving at least 500,000 dead, mostly Tutsis. UN human rights monitors were deployed throughout the country and a Commission of Experts was authorized by the **SECURITY COUNCIL** in July 1994 to investigate the massacres. Its preliminary report was that there was strong evidence of genocide by the Hutus against the Tutsis.

The Rwandan government had agreed in August to the establishment of an international war crimes tribunal. The UN Security Council voted in November 1994 [S/Res/955(1994)] to establish such a Tribunal to prosecute three classes of crimes: genocide, crimes against humanity, and violations of the Geneva Conventions. In January 1995, the Security Council appointed as Chief Prosecutor Honore Rakotomana, former President of the Supreme Court of Madagascar, who was to work under Richard Goldstone, the Chief Prosecutor for the UN International War Crimes Tribunal in The Hague. In February it selected Arusha, Tanzania as the site of the tribunal.

It was estimated that 23,000 prisoners were being held in overcrowded Rwandan jails and, in March 1995, 24 prisoners suffocated to death in a cell holding 74.

**WAR RESISTERS INTERNATIONAL.** An international non-governmental organization in consultative status with the UN **ECONOMIC AND SOCIAL COUNCIL** (Category II) and **UNESCO,** War Resisters International has sections in 20 countries.

Founded in 1921 in the Netherlands as *Paco,* the organization moved to London and changed its name in 1923. It endeavors to help pacifists and their national organizations to wage the struggle for peace on a worldwide scale, to provide legal and financial assistance to conscientious objectors, and to work for disarmament and the abolition of conscription. It provides a link between peace organizations in all parts of the world and actively seeks legal recognition of conscientious objection to military service. It offers training sessions in nonviolent direct action and promotes this form of social change.

WRI publishes *The Broken Rifle* five times a year, in French, German, and Spanish; and the monthly *Peace News.*

War Resisters International. Address: 55 Dawes Street, London SE17 1EL, UK. Telephone: (44-71) 703-7189. Fax: (44-71) 708-2545. Chairperson: Jergen Johansen.

**WEBSTER UNIVERSITY, HUMAN RIGHTS EDUCATION PROJECT.** Established in 1993, the Human Rights Education Project offers an undergraduate certificate in international human rights. The Project is also devoted to developing a library collection on international human rights and to organizing community education programs.

Human Rights Education Project. Address: Webster University, 470 E. Lockwood Avenue, St. Louis, MO 63119, USA. Telephone: (314) 968-7055. Fax: (314) 968-7119. Director: Prof. Art Sandler.

**WIESEL, ELIE(ZER) (1928–).** The 1986 **Nobel Peace Prize** was awarded to one of the most distinguished survivors of the Holocaust, Elie Wiesel—writer, teacher, and philosopher. The Nobel Committee recognized Wiesel for his "message . . . of peace, atonement, and human dignity."

Elie Wiesel was born in Sighet, Romania, into a devout Jewish family, which upheld the values of the Torah, the Talmud, and humanism. His values were tested early in his life: in 1944, when he was 16, his family and the 15,000 Jews of Sighet were deported to concentration camps. The Wiesels were sent to Auschwitz in Poland; there, his mother, father, and youngest sister died. Elie and two sisters survived, although it was years after the end of World War II that he learned that his sisters were alive.

After liberation in 1945, Wiesel went to France, where, having mastered French, he studied literature and philosophy at the Sorbonne. He became a journalist, working for the French newspaper *L'Arche* and later, after emigrating to the United States, for the *Jewish Daily* in New York. It was as a writer of novels, however, that he was to make his mark on the international scene.

In 1958, after years of silence about the atrocities in the concentration camps, Wiesel published his first novel in French, *La Nuit* (The Night), about the experience of a young Jewish man in a concentration camp. Later novels, such as *L'Aube* (Dawn) (1961), *Le Jour* (The Accident) (1962), and *Le Ville de la Chance* (The Town beyond the Wall) (1964), also have as the main protagonist a holocaust survivor. As his career advanced, while still exploring themes of trial, survival, and rebirth, Wiesel broadened his scope to examine persecution in various forms. His work *Le Mendiant de Jerusalem* (A Beggar in Jerusalem) was the winner of the prestigious *Prix Médicis* in 1968. *The Jews of Silence: A Personal Report on Soviet Jewry* (1966) alerted the world to revived anti-Semitism in the Soviet Union. In his 1978 work *Un Juif, Aujourd'hui* (A Jew Today), he also looked at the suffering of peoples in South Africa, Vietnam, and Bangladesh. To date, he has written more than 30 works, including two plays: *Zalman: ou La Folie de Dieu* (Zalman: or, the Madness of God) and *Le Procès de Shamgorod tel qu'il se déroula le 25 Février 1649* (The Trial of God, as It Was Held on February 25, 1649, in Shamgorod), both of which examine human and divine indifference to atrocities. In his autobiography *All Rivers Run to the Sea* (1995), he describes his attitude toward his literary calling: "I don't believe in art for art's sake. For me literature must have an ethical dimension. The aim of the literature I call testimony is to disturb. . . . If I have learned anything in my life, it is to distrust intellectual comfort." In addition to the *Prix Médicis,* he has received the Jewish Book Council Literary Award (1965 and 1973), the *Prix Livre-Inter* (1980), the *Prix des Bibliothequaires* (1981), and the *Grand Prix de la Littérature de la Ville de Paris* (1983).

A United States citizen since 1963, Wiesel taught Judaic studies at the City University of New York from 1972 to 1976. Since 1976 he has served as the Andrew Mellon Professor in the Humanities at Boston University.

**BIBLIOGRAPHY.** Brown, Robert. *Elie Wiesel.* South Bend, IN, USA: University of Notre Dame Press, 1984.

*Current Biography Yearbook 1986.* New York: W. H. Wilson, 1986.

Schlessinger, Bernard S., and June Schlessinger, eds. *Who's Who of Nobel Prize Winners.* Phoenix, AZ, USA: Oryx Press, 1991.

Wiesel, Elie. *All Rivers Run to the Sea: A Memoir.* New York: Alfred A. Knopf, 1995.

**WILBERFORCE COUNCIL FOR HUMAN RIGHTS.** This non-governmental organization was established in 1980, based on the philosophy of the English philanthropist and antislavery crusader William Wilberforce (1759–1833). It supports prisoners of conscience, promotes governmental awareness of human rights violations, and coordinates campaigns to alert the public to cases of human rights abuse.

The Council publishes the semi-annual *Freedom Call* and the quarterly *Freedom Call—Stop the Press.*

Wilberforce Council for Human Rights. Address: Salisbury Hall, Park Road, Hull, Humberside HU3 1TD, UK. Telephone: (44) (482) 26848. Fax: (44) (482) 568756. Executive Director: Jack Lennard.

**WILLIAMS, BETTY (1943–).** On 10 August 1976, Betty Williams, a Catholic married to a Protestant in Northern Ireland, witnessed a car accident in Belfast. In 1977, she and **Mairead Corrigan** were belatedly awarded the 1976 **Nobel Peace Prize** for their "strong resistance against violence and misuse of power." As a result of that fatal accident, Williams and Corrigan launched the "Community of Peace People," an organization devoted to ending the sectarian violence in Northern Ireland.

The car accident that Betty Williams witnessed involved a Ford that had been driven by an IRA gunman. Pursued by British soldiers, the young gunman was shot dead, while still behind the wheel. His car veered into the path of a young mother, Anne Maguire, who was out walking with her children: eight-year-old Joanne, two-year-old John, and six-month-old Andrew, whom Joanne was wheeling in a baby carriage. The children died instantly; Mrs. Maguire survived, only to commit suicide in grief months later. Mairead Corrigan was Anne Maguire's sister and the aunt of the dead children.

After the accident, Williams, who had not yet met Corrigan, began organizing Catholic women in Andersontown, an IRA stronghold. First, she circulated a petition calling for an end to all violence and then organized a rally at the sight of the fatal crash. On hearing about the rally, Corrigan called Williams and invited her to the children's funeral. The two quickly organized more rallies for peace, achieving worldwide praise but local notoriety in many circles. Although thousands of women, both Protestant and Catholic, joined the marches, many IRA supporters and Protestant partisans attacked their credibility and sometimes physically attacked the two leaders themselves.

On accepting the Peace Prize, Williams stated, "We are for life and creation and we are against war and destruction, and in our rage in that terrible week [of the deaths of the Maguire children], we screamed that the violence had to stop."

**BIBLIOGRAPHY.** *Current Biography Yearbook 1979.* New York: W. H. Wilson, 1979.

Opfell, Olga S. *Lady Laureates: Women Who Have Won the Nobel Prize.* Metuchen, NJ, USA: Scarecrow Press, 1978.

Schlessinger, Bernard S., and June Schlessinger, eds. *Who's Who of Nobel Prize Winners.* Phoenix, AZ, USA: Oryx Press, 1991.

## WILSON, THOMAS WOODROW (1856–1924).

The 1919 **Nobel Peace Prize** was awarded to the 28th President of the United States of America, Woodrow Wilson. Wilson, an academic and intellectual, former president of Princeton University, was awarded the Prize for his efforts in ending World War I and for his concept of a "League of Nations" that would ensure peace through diplomacy.

Born in Staunton, Virginia, Wilson was a lawyer and university professor before being elected to the governorship of the state of New Jersey in 1910. His reputation as a reformist led to the Democratic Party's nomination for presidency: he served two terms as president (1913–1921). In American history, Wilson's presidency was a landmark one, witnessing the passage of the 19th amendment to the constitution, which guaranteed women's suffrage, and the passage of child

labor laws. His years as president also saw the late entrance of the United States into the European battlefield of World War I. Wilson had maintained a policy of neutrality throughout most of the war, particularly because American troops were busy in their own hemisphere in Latin America, handling problems in Haiti and Mexico. However, German submarine aggression on neutral targets led to an American declaration of war on 6 April 1917.

In January 1918, Wilson proposed peace in his "Fourteen Points" speech, which included an outline for a League of Nations. The speech stressed a "peace without victory" theme, intending an honorable and fair, even a magnanimous, armistice. Other nations, however, insisted on German reparations, so many points of Wilson's peace plan—and certainly its spirit—were abandoned. The Treaty of Versailles was signed on 28 June 1919, and Wilson returned to the United States to work for American entrance into the newly created **LEAGUE OF NATIONS.** During his strenuous campaign for acceptance of the League, Wilson collapsed. The U.S. Senate rejected his bid, based on a fear that American soldiers would be called upon to fight in foreign wars. Wilson died in 1924, never witnessing his dream of a strong international organization that would prevent war.

**BIBLIOGRAPHY.** Gray, Tony. *Champions of Peace.* London: Paddington Press, 1976.

Schlessinger, Bernard S., and June Schlessinger, eds. *Who's Who of Nobel Prize Winners.* Phoenix, AZ, USA: Oryx Press, 1991.

## WOMEN LIVING UNDER MUSLIM LAW (FEMMES SOUS LOIS MUSULMANES).

This non-governmental organization has associates in 34 countries. It links women and women's groups (including those prevented from organizing or who face repression if they attempt to organize) with Muslim countries and communities. The organization builds a network of information and solidarity and disseminates information through dossiers. It maintains a special coordinating office for Asia.

Women Living under Muslim Law. Address: P.O. 23, F-34790 Grabels, France.

## WOMEN'S INTERNATIONAL DEMOCRATIC FEDERATION.

An international non-governmental organization in consultative status with the UN **ECONOMIC AND SOCIAL COUNCIL** (Category I) and with **ILO, UNESCO, UNIDO,** and **UNICEF,** the Federation brings together 144 affiliates located in 113 countries and territories.

Founded at the International Congress of Women in Paris in 1945, WIDF has worked since that time to unite women regardless of race, nationality, religion, or political opinion with a view to implementing and defending their rights as mothers, workers, and citizens. It devotes particular attention to the rights of women in society and the family, including the right to work, the right to equal pay for equal work, and the right to education at all levels. It also has a special concern for the rights of children, including their right to education, health care, and adequate nutrition and their right to a happy childhood in a harmonious family.

WIDF was active in initiating the observance of International Women's Year (1975) and contributed to the drafting of the Declaration of the Rights of the Child (see **CHILDREN'S RIGHTS**). From time to time, it has joined with other organizations in publicizing gross violations of the human rights of women and children under foreign domination or occupation or under repressive regimes.

WIDF publishes the quarterly review *Women of the Whole World* in English and Russian, and issues numerous brochures, leaflets, and reports.

Women's International Democratic Federation. Address: rue du Faubourg Poissonnière, F-75010 Paris, France.

## WOMEN'S INTERNATIONAL LEAGUE FOR PEACE AND FREEDOM.

An international non-governmental organization in consultative status with the UN **ECONOMIC AND SOCIAL COUNCIL** (Category II) and with **ILO, UNESCO, FAO,** UNCTAD, and **UNICEF**; and links with the UN **HIGH COMMISSIONER FOR REFUGEES.**

Since it was founded by the International Women's Congress, convened at The Hague in 1915 under the chairmanship of Jane Addams, the League has endeavored to unite women of all countries to oppose war, exploitation, and oppression. It stands for the equality of all people in a world free of racism and sexism, for the building of a constructive peace through world disarmament, and for the changing of government priorities with a view to meeting human needs. It promotes and defends civil and political rights and is particularly interested in the elimination of all forms of discrimination, the protection of minorities, the elimination of slavery in all its forms, the abolition of capital punishment, and the advancement of women.

The League's principal publications are the quarterlies *Pax et Libertas* and *International News.*

Women's International League for Peace and Freedom. Address: 1 rue de Varembé, P.O. 28, CH-1211, Geneva 20, Switzerland. Telephone: (41-22) 733-6175.

Fax: (41-22) 740-1063. Secretary-General: Barbara Lochbihler.

## WOMEN'S INTERNATIONAL NETWORK.

A nonprofit participatory network founded in 1975 to provide a worldwide communication system by, for, and about women of all ages, national or social origins, backgrounds, and beliefs, the Network, with the assistance of organizations and individuals in many countries, collects and disseminates information concerning problems facing women in all parts of the world, concentrating on areas of prejudice and discrimination on the ground of sex and various forms of cruel, inhuman, or degrading treatment. It publishes the *Women's International Network News* periodically and the "CBPB Programme Series" by Fran P. Hosken and illustrated by Marcia L. Williams, which includes *Childbirth Picture Book* and the *Universal Childbirth Picture Book* in Arabic, English, French, and Spanish.

Women's International Network. Address: 187 Grant Street, Lexington, MA 02173, USA. Telephone: (617) 862-9431. Coordinator: Fran P. Hosken.

## WOMEN'S INTERNATIONAL ZIONIST ORGANIZATION.

An international non-governmental organization in consultative status with the UN **ECONOMIC AND SOCIAL COUNCIL** (Category II) and **UNICEF,** WIZO's affiliated federations, in 52 countries and territories, include about 260,000 individual members.

Founded in 1920, in London, WIZO provides constructive social welfare and educational facilities to women, senior citizens, and children in Israel and conducts educational research and programs on the status of women, child welfare, citizenship, education, and professional training. It maintains 650 institutions and services in Israel, serving all segments of the population.

WIZO publishes *Inside WIZO* (five times a year), *WIZO Review* (quarterly), and *Bamat Haisha* (quarterly).

Women's International Zionist Organization. Address: Blvd. David Hamelech 38, P.O. Box 33159, Tel Aviv 61331, Israel. Telephone: (972-3) 542-1717. Fax: (972-3) 695-8267. Director General: Arieh Shur.

## WOMEN'S RIGHTS.

The preamble to the **UNITED NATIONS CHARTER** declares that the organization will reaffirm the equal rights of men and women. In 1946, the UN **ECONOMIC AND SOCIAL COUNCIL** established the **COMMISSION ON THE STATUS OF WOMEN** to recommend and report on the promotion of women's rights in the political, economic, social, and education fields. Among the Commission's first achievements was its work on the Convention on the Political Rights of Women, adopted by the UN GENERAL ASSEMBLY in 1952; and the later conventions on the nationality of married women and on the consent to marriage. To date, the culmination of the Commission's work is the Convention on the Elimination of All Forms of Discrimination against Women (see next entry) adopted by the General Assembly in 1979, This six-part, thirty-article convention covers measures to be taken by ratifying States to eliminate discrimination against women in various fields, including political and public life, nationality, education, employment, health, marriage, and family life.

### INTERNATIONAL WOMEN'S YEAR (1975) AND INTERNATIONAL WOMEN'S DECADE (1976–1985).

On 18 December 1972, the UN General Assembly proclaimed (resolution 3010 [XXVII]) the year 1975 as International Women's Year. The highlight of the year was the World Conference of the International Women's Year, convened in Mexico City from 19 June to 2 July 1975 by the United Nations at the invitation of the Government of Mexico. Since the first conference in Mexico, there have been three other women's conferences held.

The Mexican conference, which was attended by 6,000 delegates, adopted as its principal decisions the Declaration of Mexico on the Equality of Women and Their Contribution to Development and Peace and the World Plan of Action for the Implementation of the Objectives of the International Women's Year. Acting on recommendations of the conference, the General Assembly on 15 December 1975 proclaimed (resolution 3520 [XXX]) the period from 1976 to 1985 as the "United Nations Decade for Women: Equality, Development and Peace," and decided to convene, in 1980, at the mid-point of the decade, a world conference to review progress made in implementing the objectives specified by the Mexico City conference. The second world conference was held at Copenhagen from 14 to 30 July 1980 and was attended by 8,000 delegates. The conference in Denmark was followed by the World Conference to Review and Appraise the Achievements of the United Nations Decade for Women: Equality, Development and Peace, convened in Nairobi from 15 to 26 July 1985. The latter conference prepared and adopted the Nairobi Forward-Looking Strategies for the Advancement of Women. This conference was attended by 14,000 delegates.

### NAIROBI FORWARD-LOOKING STRATEGIES FOR THE ADVANCEMENT OF WOMEN.

Adopted by consensus by the World Conference to Review and Appraise the Achievements of the United Nations Decade for Women: Equality, Development and Peace, which met in Nairobi, Kenya, from 15 to 26 July 1985, the Nairobi Forward-Looking Strategies for the Advancement of Women was endorsed by the UN General Assembly on 13 December 1985 (resolution 40/108). In the resolution, the General Assembly pointed out that implementation of the forward-looking strategies should result in the elimination of all forms of inequality between men and women and in the complete integration of women into the development process, achievements which should guarantee broad participation by women in efforts to strengthen peace and security in the world.

The Assembly called upon governments to allocate adequate resources and to take effective appropriate measures to implement the forward-looking strategies as a matter of high priority, including the establishment or reinforcement, as appropriate, of national machineries to promote the advancement of women and to monitor the implementation of these strategies with a view to ensuring the full integration of women in the political, economic, social, and cultural life of their countries. In particular, it called upon all governments of member States to appoint women to decision-making positions, bearing in mind their contribution to national development.

The Assembly emphasized the central role of the Commission on the Status of Women in matters related to the advancement of women and called upon it to promote the implementation of the forward-looking strategies to the year 2000 based on the goals of the United Nations Decade for Women: Equality, Development and Peace and the subthemes of employment, health, and education. It urged all organizations of the United Nations system to cooperate with the Commission in this task.

The Forward-Looking Strategies presented a series of commitments intended to establish, modify, expand, or enforce a comprehensive legal base for the equality of women and men, calling for governments to promote equality by ensuring "equality before the law, the provision of facilities for equality of educational opportunities and training, health services, equality in conditions and opportunities of employment, including remuneration, and adequate social security" (section B, para. 54). The document further outlined measures for implementation of the basic strategies at the national level in the areas of development and peace. In the area of development, the strategies examined goals for employment; health; education; food, water, and agriculture; industry; trade and commercial services; science and technology; communications; housing, settlement, community development and transport; energy; the environment; and social services. In the area of peace, the document examined, in particular, the situation of women and children under *apartheid,* Palestinian women and children, and women in areas affected by armed conflicts. In a final chapter, the document examined the problems of women worldwide with areas of special concern (section 4, paras. 277–304):

There is an increasing number of categories of women who, because of their special characteristics, are experiencing not only the common problems indicated under the separate themes but also specific difficulties due to their socio-economic and health condition, age, minority status or a combination of these factors. Moreover, in many countries increasing demographic pressure, deteriorating political conditions have been exacerbated by the current economic recession, leading to the dislocation of large sections of populations. In this process women experience particular difficulties and are often the more vulnerable because of their traditional lack of access to development opportunities.

The special groups of women identified below are extremely diverse, and their problems vary tremendously from one country to another. No single strategy or set of measures can apply adequately to all cases, and the present document is therefore limited to highlighting their special circumstances and the need for each country, as well as the international community, to give these issues the necessary attention. The basic strategy must remain one of fundamentally changing the economic conditions that produce such deprivation and of upgrading women's low status in society, which accounts for their extreme vulnerability to such conditions, especially to poverty. This is aggravated by the increase in drug-dependence, which adversely affects all sectors of society, including women. Building an organizational base for such change is a crucial strategy that can provide a rallying point for solidarity among women. Measures needed to provide immediate emergency assistance should be supplemented by longer-term efforts to enable women to break out of these situations. In many cases, permanent solutions to these issues can only be found through the broader efforts directed towards the reallocation of resources and decision-making power and towards the elimination of inequality and injustice.

There is a need to recognize the survival mechanisms already developed by these women as basic strategies in their own right and to build on them. A first priority would be to strengthen their organization capabilities by providing physical, financial and human resources, as well as education and training. Also of extreme importance is the need to revitalize these women's aspirations in order to eliminate the chronic despair that characterizes their daily lives.

The economic, social, cultural and political conditions of those groups of women should be improved basically by the implementation of the measures proposed for the attainment of equality, development and peace for women in general. Additional efforts should be directed towards ensuring the gainful and productive inclusion of these women in mainstream development and in political activities. Priority emphasis should be placed upon income-generating opportunities and for the independent and sustained improvement of their condition and by the full integration and active participation of women as agents and beneficiaries of development.

Policies, programmes and projects aimed at or incorporating especially vulnerable and underprivileged groups of women should recognize the particular difficulties of removing the multiple obstacles facing such groups and should place equal emphasis on addressing the social, economic and human dimensions of their vulnerability and their underprivileged positions. Measures needed to provide them with immediate assistance should be supplemented by comprehensive long-term plans to achieve lasting solutions to their problems. These will usually necessitate global efforts in resolving the special problems of vulnerable groups, of which women are a significant part.

Basic to all efforts to improve the condition of these women should be the identification of their needs and hence the gathering of gender-specific data and economic indicators sensitive to conditions of extreme poverty and oppression. Such data should contain spatial, socio-economic and longitudinal characteristics and should be designed specifically for use in policy, programme and project formulation and implementation. Monitoring efforts at national, subregional, regional and international levels should be intensified.

*A. Women in Areas Affected by Drought.* During the Decade, the phenomenon of drought and desertification grew and developed incessantly, no longer affecting merely some localities in a single country but several entire countries. The scale and persistence of drought constitutes a grave threat, particularly for the countries of the Sahel, in which famine and a far-reaching deterioration of the environment set in as a result of the desertification process. Hence, despite the considerable efforts of the international community, the living conditions of the peoples, particularly those of women and children, which were already precarious, have become particularly miserable.

In view of that situation steps should be taken to promote concerted programmes between the countries concerned for combating drought and desertification. Efforts should be intensified for the formulation and implementation of programmes aimed at food security and self-sufficiency, in particular by the optimum control and exploitation of hydrogeological resources.

A distinction should be made between emergency aid and productive activities. Emergency aid should be intensified when necessary and as far as ever possible directed towards development aid.

Measures should be adopted to take into account women's contribution to production, involve them more closely in the design, implementation and evaluation of the programmes envisaged and ensure ample access for them to the means of production and processing and preservation techniques.

*B. Urban Poor Women.* Urbanization has been one of the major socio-economic trends over the past few decades and is expected to continue at an accelerating rate. Although the situation varies considerably from one region to another, it can generally be expected that by the year 2000 close to half the number of women in the world will be living in urban areas. In developing countries, the number of urban women could nearly double by the year 2000, and it is envisaged that there could be a considerable increase in the number of poor women among them.

To deal effectively with the issue, Governments should organize multi-sectoral programmes with emphasis on economic activities, elimination of discrimination and the provision of supportive services and, *inter alia,* adequate child-care facilities and, where necessary, workplace canteens to enable women to gain access to economic, social and educational opportunities on an equal basis with men. Particular attention should be devoted to the informal sector, which constitutes a major outlet for employment of a considerable number of urban poor women.

*C. Elderly Women.* The International Plan of Action on Aging adopted by the World Assembly on Aging in 1982 emphasized both the humanitarian and developmental aspects of aging. The recommendations of the Plan of Action are applicable to women and men with a view to providing them with protection and care, and ensuring their involvement and participation in social life and development. However, the Plan of Action recognizes a number of specific areas of concern for elderly women since their longer life expectancy frequently means an old age aggravated by economic need for isolation for both unmarried women and widows, possibly with little or no prospect of paid employment. This applies particularly to those women whose lifetimes were spent in unpaid and unrecognized work in the home with little or no access to a pension. If women have an income, it is generally lower than men's, partly because their former employment status has in the majority of cases been broken by maternity and family responsibilities. For this reason, the Plan of Action also noted the need for long-term policies directed towards providing social insurance for women in their own right. Governments and non-governmental organizations should, in addition to the measures recommended, explore the possibilities of employing elderly women in productive and creative ways and encouraging their participation in social and recreational activities.

It is also recommended that the care of elderly persons, including women, should go beyond disease orientation and should include their total well-being. Further efforts, in particular primary health care, health services and suitable accommodation and housing as strategies should be directed at enabling elderly women to lead a meaningful life as long as possible, in their own home and family and in the community.

Women should be prepared early in life, both psychologically and socially, to face the consequences of longer life expectancy. Although, while getting older, professional and family roles of women are undergoing fundamental changes, aging, as a stage of development, is a challenge for women. In this period of life, women should be enabled to cope in a creative way with new opportunities. The social consequences arising from the stereotyping of elderly women should be recognized and eliminated. The media should assist by presenting positive images of women, particularly emphasizing the need for respect because of their past and continuing contributions to society.

Attention should be given to studying and treating the health problems of aging, particularly in women. Research should also be directed towards the investigation and slowing down of the process of premature aging due to a lifetime of stress, excessive work-load, malnutrition and repeated pregnancy.

*D. Young Women.* Initiatives begun for the 1985 International Youth Year should be extended and expanded so that young women are protected from abuse and exploitation and assisted to develop their full potential. Girls and boys must be provided with equal access to health, education and employment to equip them for adult life. Both girls and boys should be educated to accept equal responsibilities for parenthood.

Urgent attention should be paid to the educational and vocational training of young women in all fields of occupation, giving particular emphasis to those who are socially and economically disadvantaged. Self-employed young women and girls should be assisted to organize co-operatives and ongoing training programmes to improve their skills in pro-

duction, marketing and management techniques. Special retraining programmes should also be developed for teenage mothers and girls who have dropped out of school and are ill equipped to enter productive employment.

Steps should be taken to eliminate exploitative treatment of young women at work in line with ILO Convention No. 111 concerning discrimination in respect of employment and occupation, 1958 and ILO Convention No. 122 concerning employment policy, 1964. Legislative measures guaranteeing young women their rights should be enforced.

Governments should recognize and enforce the rights of young women to be free from sexual violence, sexual harassment and sexual exploitation. In particular, Governments should recognize that many young women are victims of incest and sexual abuse in the family, and should take steps to assist the victims and to prevent such abuse by education, by improving the status of women and by appropriate action against offenders. Young women should be educated to assert their rights. Particular attention should also be given to sexual harassment and exploitation in employment, especially those areas of employment such as domestic service, where sexual harassment and exploitation are more prevalent.

Governments must also recognize their obligation to provide housing for young women who because of unemployment and low incomes suffer special problems in obtaining housing. Homeless young women are particularly vulnerable to sexual exploitation.

In the year 2000 women aged 15–24 will constitute over 8 per cent of both rural and urban populations in developing countries. The great majority of these women will be out of school and in search of jobs. For those employed, frequent exploitation, long working hours and stress have serious implications for their health. Low nutritional levels and unplanned and repeated pregnancies are also aggravating factors.

*E. Abused Women.* Gender-specific violence is increasing and Governments must affirm the dignity of women, as a priority action.

Governments should therefore intensify efforts to establish or strengthen forms of assistance to victims of such violence through the provision of shelter, support, legal and other services.

In addition to immediate assistance to victims of violence against women in the family and in society, Governments should undertake to increase public awareness of violence against women as a societal problem, establish policies and legislative measures to ascertain its causes and prevent and eliminate such violence, in particular by suppressing degrading images and representations of women in society, and finally encourage the development of educational and re-educational measures for offenders.

*F. Destitute Women.* Destitution is an extreme form of poverty. It is estimated that its effects on large segments of the population in developing and developed countries are on the increase. Forward-looking Strategies to promote the objectives of the United Nations Decade for Women: Equality, Development and Peace at the national and international levels are the basis for dealing with this problem. In addition strategies already specified for the implementation of the International Development Strategy for the Third United Nations Development Decade and the new international economic order are suggested in these recommendations. Governments should therefore ensure that the special needs and concerns of destitute women are given priority in the above-mentioned strategies. Moreover, efforts being undertaken for the International Year of Shelter for the Homeless

(1987) should focus attention on the particular situation of women commensurate with their relative needs.

*G. Women Victims of Trafficking and Involuntary Prostitution.* Forced prostitution is a form of slavery imposed on women by procurers. It is, *inter alia,* a result of economic degradation that alienates women's labour through processes of rapid urbanization and migration resulting in underemployment and unemployment. It also stems from women's dependence on men. Social and political pressures produce refugees and missing persons. Often these include vulnerable groups of women who are victimized by procurers. Sex tourism, forced prostitution and pornography reduce women to mere sex objects and marketable commodities.

States Parties to the United Nations Convention for the Suppression of the Traffic in Persons and of the Exploitation of the Prostitution of Others should implement the provisions dealing with the exploitation of women as prostitutes. Urgent consideration should also be given to the improvement of international measures to combat trafficking in women for the purposes of prostitution. Resources for the prevention of prostitution and assistance in the professional, personal and social reintegration of prostitutes should be directed towards providing economic opportunities, including training, employment, self-employment and health facilities for women and children. Governments should also endeavour to co-operate with non-governmental organizations to create wider employment possibilities for women. Strict enforcement provisions must also be taken at all levels to stem the rising tide of violence, drug abuse and crime related to prostitution. The complex and serious problems of the exploitation of and violence against women associated with prostitution call for increased and co-ordinated efforts by police agencies internationally.

*H. Women Deprived of Their Traditional Means of Livelihood.* The excessive and inappropriate exploitation of land by any party for any purpose, *inter alia,* by transnational corporations, as well as natural and man-made disasters are among the predominant causes of deprivation of traditional means of livelihood. Droughts, floods, hurricanes and other forms of environmental hazards, such as erosion, desertification and deforestation, have already pushed poor women into marginal environments. At present the pressures are greatest in drought-afflicted arid and semi-arid areas. Urban slums and squatter settlements are also seriously affected. Critically low levels of water supplies, shortage of fuel, over-utilization of grazing and arable lands, and population density are all factors that deprive women of their livelihood.

National and international emphasis on ecosystem management should be strengthened, environmental degradation should be controlled and options provided for alternative means of livelihood. Measures should be established to draw up national conservation strategies aimed at incorporating women's development programmes, among which are irrigation and tree planting and also orientation in the area of agriculture, with women constituting a substantial part of the wage-earning labour force for those programmes.

*I. Women who are the Sole Supporters of Families.* Recent studies have shown that the number of families in which women are the sole supporters is on the increase. Owing to the particular difficulties (social, economic and legal) which they face, many such women are among the poorest people concentrated in urban informal labour markets and they constitute large numbers of the rural unemployed and marginally employed. Those with very little economic, social and moral support face serious difficulties in supporting themselves as well as in bringing up their children alone. This has

serious repercussions for society in terms of the quality, character, productivity and human resource capabilities of its present and future citizenry.

The assumptions that underlie a large part of the relevant legislation, regulations and household surveys that confine the role of supporter and head of household to men hinder women's access to credit, loans and material and non-material resources. Changes are needed in these areas to secure for women equal access to resources. There is a need to eliminate terms such as "head of household" and introduce others that are comprehensive enough to reflect women's role appropriately in legal documents and household surveys to guarantee the rights of these women. In the provision of social services, special attention has to be given to the needs of these women. Governments are urged to ensure that women with sole responsibility for their families receive a level of income and social support sufficient to enable them to attain or maintain economic independence and to participate effectively in society. To this end, the assumptions that underlie policies, including research used in policy development, and legislation that confines the role of supporter or head of household to men should be identified and eliminated. Special attention, such as accessible, quality child care, should be given to assisting those women in discharging their domestic responsibilities and to enabling them to participate in and benefit from education, training programmes and employment. The putative father should be made to assist in the maintenance and education of those children born out of wedlock.

*J. Women with Physical and Mental Disabilities.* It is generally accepted that women constitute a significant number of the estimated 500 million people who are disabled as a consequence of mental, physical or sensory impairment. Many factors contribute to the rising numbers of disabled persons, including war and other forms of violence, poverty, hunger, nutritional deficiencies, epidemics and work-related accidents. The recognition of their human dignity and human rights and the full participation by disabled persons in society is still limited, and this presents additional problems for women who may have domestic and other responsibilities. It is recommended that Governments should adopt the Declaration on the Rights of Disabled Persons (1975) and the World Programme of Action concerning Disabled Persons (1982) which provide an overall framework for action and also refer to problems specific to women that have not been fully appreciated by society because they are still not well known or understood. Community-based occupational and social rehabilitation measures, support services to help them with their domestic responsibilities, as well as opportunities for the participation of such women in all aspects of life should be provided. The rights of intellectually disabled women to obtain health information and advice and to consent to or refuse medical treatment should be respected; similarly, the rights of intellectually disabled minors should be respected.

*K. Women in Detention and Subject to Penal Law.* One of the major areas of current concern in the field of crime prevention and criminal justice is the need for equal treatment of women by the criminal justice system. In the context of changing socio-economic and cultural conditions some improvements have taken place but more need to be made. The number of women in detention has increased over the Decade and this trend is expected to continue. Women deprived of freedom are exposed to various forms of physical violence, sexual and moral harassment. The conditions of their detention are often below acceptable hygienic standards and their children are deprived of maternal care. The recommendations of the Sixth United Nations Congress on the Prevention of Crime and the Treatment of Offenders, held at Caracas, in 1980, and the principles of the Caracas Declaration with special reference to the "fair and equal treatment of women", should be taken into account in designing and implementing concrete measures at the national and international levels. The proportions of indigenous women imprisoned in some countries is a matter of concern.

*L. Refugee and Displaced Women and Children.* The international community recognizes a humanitarian responsibility to protect and assist refugees and displaced persons. In many cases refugee and displaced women are exposed to a variety of difficult situations affecting their physical and legal protection as well as their psychological and material well-being. Problems of physical debility, physical safety, emotional stress and socio-psychological effects of separation or death in the family, as well as changes in women's roles, together with limitations often found in the new environment including lack of adequate food, shelter, health care and social services call for specialized and enlarged assistance. Special attention has to be offered to women with special needs. Furthermore, the potential and capacities of refugee and displaced women should be recognized and enhanced.

It is recognized that a lasting solution to the problems of refugees and displaced women and children should be sought in the elimination of the root causes of the flow of refugees and durable solutions should be found leading to their voluntary return to their homes in conditions of safety and honour and their full integration in the economic, social and cultural life of their country of origin in the immediate future. Until such solutions are achieved, the international community, in an expression of international solidarity and burden-sharing, should continue providing relief assistance and also launching special relief programmes taking into account the specific needs of refugee women and children in countries of first asylum. Similarly, relief assistance and special relief programmes should also continue to be provided to returnees and displaced women and children. Legal, educational, social, humanitarian and moral assistance should be offered as well as opportunities for their voluntary repatriation, return or resettlement. Steps should also be taken to promote accession by Governments to the 1951 Convention relating to the Status of Refugees and to implement, on a basis of equity for all refugees, provisions contained in this Convention and its 1967 Protocol.

*M. Migrant Women.* The Decade has witnessed the increasing involvement of women in all forms of migration, including rural-rural, rural-urban and international movements of a temporary, seasonal or permanent nature. In addition to their lack of adequate education, skills and resources, migrant women may also face severe adjustment problems due to differences in religion, language, nationality, and socialization as well as separation from their original families. Such problems are often accentuated for international migrants as a result of the openly-expressed prejudices and hostilities, including violation of human rights in host countries. Thus recommendations of the World Population Plan of Action and the Programme of Action for the Second Half of the United Nations Decade for Women pertaining to migrant women should be implemented and expanded in view of the anticipated increase in the scope of the problem. It is also urgent to conclude the elaboration of the draft International Convention on the Protection of the Rights of All Migrant Workers and their Families, as agreed by the General Assembly in the relevant resolutions.

The situation of migrant women, who are subject to double discrimination as women and as migrants, should be given special attention by the Governments of host countries, particularly with respect to protection and maintenance of family unity, employment opportunities and equal pay, equal conditions of work, health care, benefits to be provided in accordance with the existing social security rights in the host country, and racial and other forms of discrimination. Particular attention should also be given to the second generation of migrant women, especially with regard to education and professional training, to allow them to integrate themselves in their countries of adoption and to work according to their education and skills. In this process, loss of cultural values of their countries of origin should be avoided.

*N. Minority and "Indigenous" Women.* Some women are oppressed as a result of belonging to minority groups or populations which have historically been subjected to domination and suffered dispossession and dispersal. These women suffer the full burden of discrimination based on race, colour, descent, ethnic and national origin and the majority experienced serious economic deprivation. As women, they are therefore doubly disadvantaged. Measures should be taken by Governments in countries in which there are minority and indigenous populations to respect, preserve and promote all of their human rights, their dignity, ethnic, religious, cultural and linguistic identity and their full participation in societal change.

Governments should ensure that the fundamental human rights and freedoms as enshrined in relevant international instruments are fully guaranteed also to women belonging to minority groups and indigenous populations. Governments in countries in which there are indigenous and minority populations should ensure respect for the economic, social and cultural rights of these women and assist them in the fulfilment of their family and parental responsibilities. Specific measures should address dietary deficiencies, high levels of infant and maternal mortality and other health problems, lack of education, housing and child care. Vocational, technical, professional and other training should be provided to enable these women to secure employment or to participate in income-generating activities and projects, and to secure adequate wages, occupational health and safety and their other rights as workers. As far as possible, Governments should ensure that these women have access to all services in their own languages.

Women belonging to minority groups or indigenous populations should be fully consulted and should participate in the development and implementation of programmes affecting them. The Governments of countries where minorities and indigenous populations exist should take proper account of the work of bodies such as the Committee on the Elimination of Racial Discrimination and the Sub-Commission on Prevention of Discrimination and Protection of Minorities, in particular its Working Group which is developing a set of international standards to protect the rights of indigenous populations. The General Assembly should consider the advisability of designating an international year of indigenous and traditional cultures in order to promote international understanding and to emphasize the distinctive role of women in sustaining the identity of their people.

***UNITED NATIONS FOURTH WORLD CONFERENCE ON WOMEN (1995).*** The fourth Women's Conference was held in Beijing, China, from 4–15 September 1995.

This Conference was attended by some 30,000 people, which included 24,000 delegates at the NGO Forum, which opened prior to the UN Conference (30 August–8 September). Over 180 UN member States sent delegates, with another eight countries participating as observers. The Conference's secretary-general was Gertrude Mongella (Tanzania); the executive director of the NGO Forum was Irene Santiago (Philippines).

The Beijing Conference was called to assess how women's lives have changed since the Nairobi Conference and to accelerate the implementation of the Nairobi Forward-Looking Strategies. The Platform for Action that emerged from the Conference is intended not to replace the Forward-Looking Strategies but to pursue new partnerships between men and women into the 21st century.

The UN **COMMISSION ON THE STATUS OF WOMEN** was the preparatory body for the four conferences. For the Beijing Conference, the Commission adopted five goals:

(1) sharing power in private, public, political, and economic life;

(2) providing full access to the means of development (education, employment, and health);

(3) overcoming poverty;

(4) promoting peace and defending women's human rights;

(5) inspiring a new generation of women and men to work together for equality.

In a draft Program of Action, intended as a globally relevant "how-to" book, the Commission outlined critical areas that need immediate action:

(1) The persistent and growing burden of poverty on women;

(2) Inequality in access to education, health, and related services and means of maximizing the use of women's capacities;

(3) Violence against women;

(4) Effects of armed or other kinds of conflict on women;

(5) Inequality in women's access to and participation in the definition of economic structures and policies and the productive process itself;

(6) Inequality between men and women in the sharing of power and decision-making at all levels;

(7) Insufficient mechanisms at all levels to promote the advancement of women;

(8) Lack of awareness of, and commitment to, internationally and nationally recognized women's human rights;

(9) Insufficient use of mass media to promote women's positive contributions to society;

(10) Lack of adequate recognition and support for women's contribution to managing natural resources and safeguarding the environment.

The Beijing Conference opened in controversy due to the Chinese Government's relocation of the NGO Forum and its refusal to let groups representing Taiwan or Tibet participate. It also ended in dissent when delegates from the Vatican and 37 countries registered reservations over the proposed Platform for Action. The contested portions of the Program of Action referred to women's sexual and reproductive rights, to abortion, and to the rights of adolescents to privacy and confidentiality in obtaining birth-control counseling or devices. The dissenting delegates were predominately from countries with strong Islamic or Roman Catholic traditions. Overt language calling for a ban on discrimination against lesbians was removed from the Platform in response to objections. The final document urges governments to put a stop to violence against women, female genital mutilation, the killing of baby girls and prenatal sex selection, and equal education and health opportunities for boys and girls.

The following is the text of the "Declaration of Beijing," which, along with the Platform for Action, is a core document of the Conference:

1. We, the Governments, participating in the Fourth World Conference on Women,

2. Gathered here in Beijing, in September 1995, the year of the fiftieth anniversary of the founding of the United Nations,

3. Determined to advance the goals of equality, development and peace for all women everywhere in the interest of all humanity,

4. Acknowledging the voices of all women everywhere and taking note of the diversity of women and their roles and circumstances, honouring the women who paved the way and inspired by the hope present in the world's youth,

5. Recognize that the status of women has advanced in some important respects in the past decade but that progress has been uneven, inequalities between women and men have persisted and major obstacles remain, with serious consequences for the well-being of all people,

6. Also recognize that this situation is exacerbated by the increasing poverty that is affecting the lives of the majority of the world's people, in particular women and children, with origins in both the national and international domains,

7. Dedicate ourselves unreservedly to addressing these constraints and obstacles and thus enhancing further the advancement and empowerment of women all over the world, and agree that this requires urgent action in the spirit of determination, hope, cooperation and solidarity, now and to carry us forward into the next century.

*We reaffirm our commitment to:*

8. The equal rights and inherent human dignity of women and men and other purposes and principles enshrined in the Charter of the United Nations, the Universal Declaration of Human Rights and other international human rights instruments, in particular the Convention on the Elimination of All Forms of Discrimination against Women and the Convention on the Rights of the Child, as well as the Declaration on the Elimination of Violence against Women and the Declaration on the Right to Development;

9. Ensure the full implementation of the human rights of

women and of the girl child as an inalienable, integral and indivisible part of all human rights and fundamental freedoms;

10. Build on consensus and progress made at previous United Nations conferences and summits—on women in Nairobi in 1985, on children in New York in 1990, on environment and development in Rio de Janeiro in 1992, on human rights in Vienna in 1993, on population and development in Cairo in 1994 and on social development in Copenhagen in 1995 with the objectives of achieving equality, development and peace;

11. Achieve the full and effective implementation of the Nairobi Forward-looking Strategies for the Advancement of Women;

12. The empowerment and advancement of women, including the right to freedom of thought, conscience, religion and belief, thus contributing to the moral, ethical, spiritual and intellectual needs of women and men, individually or in community with others and thereby guaranteeing them the possibility of realizing their full potential in society and shaping their lives in accordance with their own aspirations.

*We are convinced that:*

13. Women's empowerment and their full participation on the basis of equality in all spheres of society, including participation in the decision-making process and access to power, are fundamental for the achievement of equality, development and peace;

14. Women's rights are human rights;

15. Equal rights, opportunities and access to resources, equal sharing of responsibilities for the family by men and women, and a harmonious partnership between them are critical to their well-being and that of their families as well as to the consolidation of democracy;

16. Eradication of poverty based on sustained economic growth, social development, environmental protection and social justice requires the involvement of women in economic and social development and equal opportunities and the full and equal participation of women and men as agents and beneficiaries of people-centered sustainable development;

17. The explicit recognition and reaffirmation of the right of all women to control all aspects of their health, in particular their own fertility, is basic to their empowerment;

18. Local, national, regional and global peace is attainable and is inextricably linked with the advancement of women, who are a fundamental force for leadership, conflict resolution and the promotion of lasting peace at all levels;

19. It is essential to design, implement and monitor, with the full participation of women, effective, efficient and mutually reinforcing gender-sensitive policies and programmes, including development policies and programmes, at all levels that will foster the empowerment and advancement of women;

20. The participation and contribution of all actors of civil society, particularly women's groups and networks and other non-governmental organizations and community-based organizations, with full respect for their autonomy, in cooperation with Governments, are important to the effective implementation and follow-up of the Platform for Action;

21. The implementation of the Platform for Action requires commitment from Governments and the international community. By making national and international commitments for action, including those made at the Conference, Governments and the international community recognize the need to take priority action for the empowerment and advancement of women.

*We are determined to:*

22. Intensify efforts and actions to achieve the goals of the Nairobi Forward-looking Strategies for the Advancement of Women by the end of this century;

23. Ensure the full enjoyment by women and the girl child of all human rights and fundamental freedoms, and take effective action against violations of these rights and freedoms;

24. Take all necessary measures to eliminate all forms of discrimination against women and the girl child and remove all obstacles to gender equality and the advancement and empowerment of women;

25. Encourage men to participate fully in all actions towards equality;

26. Promote women's economic independence, including employment, and eradicate the persistent and increasing burden of poverty on women by addressing the structural causes of poverty through changes in economic structures, ensuring equal access for all women, including those in rural areas, as vital development agents, to productive resources, opportunities and public services;

27. Promote people-centered sustainable development, including sustained economic growth through the provision of basic education, life-long education, literacy and training, and primary health care for girls and women;

28. Take positive steps to ensure peace for the advance of women and recognizing the leading role that women have played in the peace movement, work actively towards general and complete disarmament under strict and effective international control, and support negotiations on the conclusion, without delay, of a universal and multilaterally and effectively verifiable comprehensive nuclear-test-ban treaty which contributes to nuclear disarmament and the prevention of the proliferation of nuclear weapons in all its aspects;

29. Prevent and eliminate all forms of violence against women and girls;

30. Ensure equal access to and equal treatment of women and men in education and health care and enhance women's sexual and reproductive health as well as education;

31. Promote and protect all human rights of women and girls;

32. Intensify efforts to ensure equal enjoyment of all human rights and fundamental freedoms for all women and girls who face multiple barriers to their empowerment and advancement because of such factors as their race, age, language, ethnicity, culture, religion, or disability, or because they are indigenous people;

33. Ensure respect for international law, including humanitarian law, in order to protect women and girls in particular;

34. Develop the fullest potential of girls and women of all ages, ensure their full and equal participation in building a better world for all and enhance their role in the development process.

*We are determined to:*

35. Ensure women's equal access to economic resources including land, credit, science and technology, vocational training, information, communication and markets, as a means to further the advancement and empowerment of women and girls, including through the enhancement of their capacities to enjoy the benefits of equal access to these resources, *inter alia*, by means of international cooperation;

36. Ensure the success of the Platform for Action which will require a strong commitment on the part of Governments, international organizations and institutions at all levels. We are deeply convinced that economic development, social development and environmental protection are interdependent and mutually reinforcing components of sustain-

able development, which is the framework for our efforts to achieve a higher quality of life for all people. Equitable social development that recognizes empowering the poor, particularly women living in poverty, to utilize environmental resources sustainably is a necessary foundation for sustainable development. We also recognize that broad-based and sustained economic growth in the context of sustainable development is necessary to sustain social development and social justice. The success of the Platform for Action will also require adequate mobilization of resources at the national and international levels as well as new and additional resources to the developing countries from all available funding mechanisms, including multilateral, bilateral and private sources for the advancement of women; financial resources to strengthen the capacity of national, subregional, regional and international institutions; a commitment to equal rights, equal responsibilities and equal opportunities and to the equal participation of women and men in all national, regional and international bodies and policy-making processes; the establishment or strengthening of mechanisms at all levels for accountability to the world's women.

37. Ensure also the success of the Platform for Action in countries with economies in transition, which will require continued international cooperation and assistance;

38. We hereby adopt and commit ourselves as Governments to implement the following Platform for Action, ensuring that a gender perspective is reflected in all our policies and programmes. We urge the United Nations system, regional and international financial institutions, other relevant regional and international institutions and all women and men, as well as non-governmental organizations, with full respect for their autonomy, and all sectors of civil society, in cooperation with Governments, to fully commit themselves and contribute to the implementation of this Platform for Action.

**SEE ALSO** *Advancement of Women Division, UN; Commission on the Status of Women, UN; Committee on the Elimination of Discrimination against Women, UN; Domestic Violence; Equality; Marriage and the Family.*

**BIBLIOGRAPHY.** Asociation européenne contre les violences faites aux femmes au travail. *De l'abus de pouvoir sexuel: le harcèlement sexuel au travail* (Abuse of Gender Power: Sexual Harassment in the Workplace). Paris: La Découverte, 1990. Conference report, in French. Collection of scholarly articles, in English; bibliography, pp. 217–231.

Bunch, Charlotte. "Women's Rights as Human Rights: Toward a Revision of Human Rights," *Human Rights Quarterly* 12, no. 4 (Nov. 1990): 486–498. Scholarly article, in English.

Change. *Thinkbook.* A series of reports and handbooks, including G. Ashworth, *Of Violence and Violation: Women and Human Rights.* London: 1986.

Clark, Belinda. "The Vienna Convention Reservations Regime and the Convention on Discrimination against Women," *American Journal of International Law* 85, no. 2 (April 1991): 281–321. Scholarly article, in English.

Commonwealth Secretariat. *The Convention on the Elimination of All Forms of Discrimination against Women: The Reporting Process—A Manual for Commonwealth Jurisdictions.* London: 1988. IGO briefing paper, in English.

Cook, Rebecca J. "Bibliography: The International Right to Nondiscrimination on the Basis of Sex," *Yale Journal of International Law* 14, no. 1 (1989): 161–181. Bibliography, in English.

―――――. "International Human Rights Law concerning Women: Case Notes and Comments," *Vanderbilt Journal of Transnational Law* 23, no. 4 (1990): 779–818. Scholarly article, in English.

Femmes sous Lois Musulmanes (Women Living under Muslim Laws). *Dossier.* Journal published quarterly. Montpellier, France.

Flanz, Gisbert H. *Comparative Women's Rights and Political Participation in Europe.* Transnational Publishers, 1983. Scholarly study, in English.

Fraser, Arvonne S. *The UN Decade for Women: Documents and Dialog.* Boulder, CO, USA: Westview Press, 1987. Collection, in English.

Hevener, N. K. *International Law and the Status of Women.* Boulder, CO, USA: Westview Press, 1983. Scholarly study, in English.

Human Rights Watch, The Women's Rights Project. A special project, established in 1990, to work with Human Rights Watch regional divisions. Publishes periodic reports on individual countries.

International Women's Rights Action Watch. *Assessing the Status of Women: A Guide to Reporting Using the Convention on the Elimination of All Forms of Discrimination against Women.* New York: 1988. NGO report, in English.

―――――. *The Women's Watch.* Quarterly newsletter, in English; published in Minneapolis, MN, USA, and New York.

International Women's Tribune Centre. *Rights of Women: A Workbook of International Conventions relating to Women's Issues and Concerns.* New York: 1983. NGO workbook, in English.

―――――. *The Tribune: A Women and Development Quarterly.* Newsletter, in English; published in New York.

Isis International. *Powerful Images: A Women's Guide to Audiovisual Resources.* Rome: 1986. Resource, in English.

―――――. *Rural Women in Latin America: Experiences from Ecuador, Peru and Chile.* Santiago, Chile: 1987. NGO study, in English and Spanish.

―――――. *Women and Media: Analysis, Alternatives and Action.* Rome: 1984. NGO study, in English.

―――――. *Women in Action.* Quarterly journal, in English; also published in Spanish as *Mujeres en Accion.*

Isis: Women's International Cross-Cultural Exchange. *Women's World.* Quarterly newsletter, in English. Geneva, Switzerland.

Khushalani, Y. *Dignity and Honour of Women as Basic and Fundamental Human Rights.* Ultrecht, the Netherlands: Kluwer Academic, 1983. Scholarly study, in English; special focus on widespread rape of Bangladeshi women by Pakistanis in 1971.

Liddle, J., and R. Joshi. *Daughters of Independence: Gender, Caste and Class in India.* London: Zed Books, 1986. Scholarly study, in English.

Rehof, Lars Adam. *Guide to the Travaux Préparatoires of the United Nations Convention on the Elimination of All Forms of Discrimination against Women.* Dordrecht, the Netherlands: Martinus Nijhoff, 1993. Scholarly monograph, in English. Also in *International Studies on Human Rights,* 29.

Shreir, Sally, ed. *Women's Movements of the World: An International Directory.* London: Longman Group, 1988. Directory, in English.

Tomasevski, Katarina. *Women and Human Rights.* London: Zed Books, 1993. Monograph, in English; bibliography, pp. 151–155.

United Nations. *Report of the World Conference to Review and Appraise the Achievements of the United Nations Decade for Women:*

*Equality, Development and Peace, Nairobi, 15–26 July 1985.* New York: 1986. IGO conference report, in English.

Women's International Network. *Female Sexual Mutilations: The Facts and Proposals for Action.* Lexington, MA, USA: 1980.

————. *WIN News.* Quarterly journal, in English. Lexington, MA, USA.

## WOMEN'S RIGHTS: CONVENTION ON THE ELIMINATION OF ALL FORMS OF DISCRIMINATION AGAINST WOMEN, UN (1979).

The Convention elaborates and puts into the form of a multilateral treaty the substantive provisions of the Declaration on the Elimination of Discrimination against Women (see next entry). It establishes international machinery for the implementation of its provisions along the lines of those established for implementation of the **INTERNATIONAL COVENANT ON CIVIL AND POLITICAL RIGHTS,** i.e., an 18-member **COMMITTEE ON THE ELIMINATION OF DISCRIMINATION AGAINST WOMEN** empowered to settle disputes between States parties concerning observance of the Convention and to receive and examine information from them on measures taken to achieve its goals. The Convention's underlying philosophy is that discrimination against women is incompatible with human dignity and constitutes an obstacle to the full realization of the potentialities of women; therefore, the right of women to share equally in improved conditions of life must be promoted and protected.

The Convention was adopted by the UN **GENERAL ASSEMBLY** on 18 December 1979 (resolution 34/180) and entered into force on 3 September 1981. The text, annexed to the resolution, is as follows:

The States Parties to the present Convention,

Noting that the Charter of the United Nations reaffirms faith in fundamental human rights, in the dignity and worth of the human person and in the equal rights of men and women,

Noting that the Universal Declaration of Human Rights affirms the principle of the inadmissibility of discrimination and proclaims that all human beings are born free and equal in dignity and rights and that everyone is entitled to all the rights and freedoms set forth therein, without distinction of any kind, including distinction based on sex,

Noting that the States parties to the International Covenants on Human Rights have the obligation to ensure the equal right of men and women to enjoy all economic, social, cultural, civil and political rights,

Considering the international conventions concluded under the auspices of the United Nations and the specialized agencies promoting equality of rights of men and women,

Noting also the resolutions, declarations and recommendations adopted by the United Nations and the specialized agencies promoting equality of rights of men and women,

Concerned, however, that despite these various instruments extensive discrimination against women continues to exist,

Recalling that discrimination against women violates the principles of equality of rights and respect for human dignity, is an obstacle to the participation of women, on equal terms with men, in the political, social, economic and cultural life of their countries, hampers the growth of the prosperity of society and the family and makes more difficult the full development of the potentialities of women in the service of their countries and of humanity,

Concerned that in situations of poverty women have the least access to food, health, education, training and opportunities for employment and other needs,

Convinced that the establishment of the new international economic order based on equity and justice will contribute significantly towards the promotion of equality between men and women,

Emphasizing that the eradication of *apartheid*, all forms of racism, racial discrimination, colonialism, neo-colonialism, aggression, foreign occupation and domination and interference in the internal affairs of States is essential to the full enjoyment of the rights of men and women,

Affirming that the strengthening of international peace and security, the relaxation of international tension, mutual co-operation among all States irrespective of their social and economic systems, general and complete disarmament, in particular nuclear disarmament under strict and effective international control, the affirmation of the principles of justice, equality and mutual benefit in relations among countries and the realization of the right of peoples under alien and colonial domination and foreign occupation to self-determination and independence, as well as respect for national sovereignty and territorial integrity, will promote social progress and development and as a consequence will contribute to the attainment of full equality between men and women,

Convinced that the full and complete development of a country, the welfare of the world and the cause of peace require the maximum participation of women on equal terms with men in all fields,

Bearing in mind the great contribution of women to the welfare of the family and to the development of society, so far not fully recognized, the social significance of maternity and the role of both parents in the family and in the upbringing of children, and aware that the role of women in procreation should not be a basis for discrimination but that the upbringing of children requires a sharing of responsibility between men and women and society as a whole,

Aware that a change in the traditional role of men as well as the role of women in society and in the family is needed to achieve full equality between men and women,

Determined to implement the principles set forth in the Declaration on the Elimination of Discrimination against Women and, for that purpose, to adopt the measures required for the elimination of such discrimination in all its forms and manifestations,

Have agreed on the following:

### Part I

*Article 1.* For the purposes of the present Convention, the term "discrimination against women" shall mean any distinction, exclusion or restriction made on the basis of sex which has the effect or purpose of impairing or nullifying the recognition, enjoyment or exercise by women, irrespective of their marital status, on a basis of equality of men and women, of human rights and fundamental freedoms in the political, economic, social, cultural, civil or any other field.

*Article 2.* States Parties condemn discrimination against women in all its forms, agree to pursue by all appropriate means and without delay a policy of eliminating discrimination against women and, to this end, undertake:

(a) To embody the principle of the equality of men and women in their national constitutions or other appropriate legislation if not yet incorporated therein and to ensure, through law and other appropriate means, the practical realization of this principle;

(b) To adopt appropriate legislative and other measures, including sanctions where appropriate, prohibiting all discrimination against women;

(c) To establish legal protection of the rights of women on an equal basis with men and to ensure through competent national tribunals and other public institutions the effective protection of women against any act of discrimination;

(d) To refrain from engaging in any act or practice of discrimination against women and to ensure that public authorities and institutions shall act in conformity with this obligation;

(e) To take all appropriate measures to eliminate discrimination against women by any person, organization or enterprise;

(f) To take all appropriate measures, including legislation, to modify or abolish existing laws, regulations, customs and practices which constitute discrimination against women;

(g) To repeal all national penal provisions which constitute discrimination against women.

*Article 3.* States Parties shall take in all fields, in particular in the political, social, economic and cultural fields, all appropriate measures, including legislation, to ensure the full development and advancement of women, for the purpose of guaranteeing them the exercise and enjoyment of human rights and fundamental freedoms on a basis of equality with men.

*Article 4.* 1. Adoption by States Parties of temporary special measures aimed at accelerating *de facto* equality between men and women shall not be considered discrimination as defined in the present Convention, but shall in no way entail as a consequence the maintenance of unequal or separate standards; these measures shall be discontinued when the objectives of equality of opportunity and treatment have been achieved.

2. Adoption by States Parties of special measures, including those measures contained in the present Convention, aimed at protecting maternity shall not be considered discriminatory.

*Article 5.* States Parties shall take all appropriate measures:

(a) To modify the social and cultural patterns of conduct of men and women, with a view to achieving the elimination of prejudices and customary and all other practices which are based on the idea of the inferiority or the superiority of either of the sexes or on stereotyped roles for men and women;

(b) To ensure that family education includes a proper understanding of maternity as a social function and the recognition of the common responsibility of men and women in the upbringing and development of their children, it being understood that the interest of the children is the primordial consideration in all cases.

*Article 6.* States Parties shall take all appropriate measures, including legislation, to suppress all forms of traffic in women and exploitation of prostitution of women.

**Part II**

*Article 7.* States Parties shall take all appropriate measures to eliminate discrimination against women in the political and public life of the country and, in particular, shall ensure to women, on equal terms with men, the right:

(a) To vote in all elections and public referenda and to be eligible for election to all publicly elected bodies;

(b) To participate in the formulation of government policy and the implementation thereof and to hold public office and perform all public functions at all levels of government;

(c) To participate in non-governmental organizations and associations concerned with the public and political life of the country.

*Article 8.* States Parties shall take all appropriate measures to ensure to women, on equal terms with men and without any discrimination, the opportunity to represent their Governments at the international level and to participate in the work of international organizations.

*Article 9.* 1. States Parties shall grant women equal rights with men to acquire, change or retain their nationality. They shall ensure in particular that neither marriage to an alien nor change of nationality by the husband during marriage shall automatically change the nationality of the wife, render her stateless or force upon her the nationality of the husband.

2. States Parties shall grant women equal rights with men with respect to the nationality of their children.

**Part III**

*Article 10.* States Parties shall take all appropriate measures to eliminate discrimination against women in order to ensure to them equal rights with men in the field of education and in particular to ensure, on a basis of equality of men and women:

(a) The same conditions for career and vocational guidance, for access to studies and for the achievement of diplomas in educational establishments of all categories in rural as well as in urban areas; this equality shall be ensured in pre-school, general, technical, professional and higher technical education, as well as in all types of vocational training;

(b) Access to the same curricula, the same examinations, teaching staff with qualifications of the same standard and school premises and equipment of the same quality;

(c) The elimination of any stereotyped concept of the roles of men and women at all levels and in all forms of education by encouraging coeducation and other types of education which will help to achieve this aim and, in particular, by the revision of textbooks and school programmes and the adaptation of teaching methods;

(d) The same opportunities to benefit from scholarships and other study grants;

(e) The same opportunities for access to programmes of continuing education, including adult and functional literacy programmes, particularly those aimed at reducing, at the earliest possible time, any gap in education existing between men and women;

(f) The reduction of female student drop-out rates and the organization of programmes for girls and women who have left school prematurely;

(g) The same opportunities to participate actively in sports and physical education;

(h) Access to specific educational information to help

to ensure the health and well-being of families, including information and advice on family planning.

*Article 11.* 1. States Parties shall take all appropriate measures to eliminate discrimination against women in the field of employment in order to ensure, on a basis of equality of men and women, the same rights, in particular:

(a) The right to work as an inalienable right of all human beings;

(b) The right to the same employment opportunities, including the application of the same criteria for selection in matters of employment;

(c) The right to free choice of profession and employment, the right to promotion, job security and all benefits and conditions of service and the right to receive vocational training and retraining, including apprenticeships, advanced vocational training and recurrent training;

(d) The right to equal remuneration, including benefits, and to equal treatment in respect of work of equal value, as well as equality of treatment in the evaluation of the quality of work;

(e) The right to social security, particularly in cases of retirement, unemployment, sickness, invalidity and old age and other incapacity to work, as well as the right to paid leave;

(f) The right to protection of health and to safety in working conditions, including the safeguarding of the function of reproduction.

2. In order to prevent discrimination against women on the grounds of marriage or maternity and to ensure their effective right to work, States Parties shall take appropriate measures:

(a) To prohibit, subject to the imposition of sanctions, dismissal on the grounds of pregnancy or of maternity leave and discrimination in dismissals on the basis of marital status;

(b) To introduce maternity leave with pay or with comparable social benefits without loss of former employment, seniority or social allowances;

(c) To encourage the provision of the necessary supporting social services to enable parents to combine family obligations with work responsibilities and participation in public life, in particular through promoting the establishment and development of a network of child-care facilities;

(d) To provide special protection to women during pregnancy in types of work proved to be harmful to them.

3. Protective legislation relating to matters covered in this article shall be reviewed periodically in the light of scientific and technological knowledge and shall be revised, repealed or extended as necessary.

*Article 12.* 1. States Parties shall take all appropriate measures to eliminate discrimination against women in the field of health care in order to ensure, on a basis of equality of men and women, access to health care services, including those related to family planning.

2. Notwithstanding the provisions of paragraph of this article, States Parties shall ensure to women appropriate services in connexion with pregnancy, confinement and the post-natal period, granting free services where necessary, as well as adequate nutrition during pregnancy and lactation.

*Article 13.* States Parties shall take all appropriate measures to eliminate discrimination against women in other areas of economic and social life in order to ensure, on a basis of equality of men and women, the same rights, in particular:

(a) The right to family benefits;

(b) The right to bank loans, mortgages and other forms of financial credit;

(c) The right to participate in recreational activities, sports and all aspects of cultural life.

*Article 14.* 1. States Parties shall take into account the particular problems faced by rural women and the significant roles which rural women play in the economic survival of their families, including their work in the non-monetized sectors of the economy, and shall take all appropriate measures to ensure the application of the provisions of the present Convention to women in rural areas.

2. States Parties shall take all appropriate measures to eliminate discrimination against women in rural areas in order to ensure, on a basis of equality of men and women, that they participate in and benefit from rural development and, in particular, shall ensure to such women the right:

(a) To participate in the elaboration and implementation of development planning at all levels;

(b) To have access to adequate health care facilities, including information, counselling and services in family planning;

(c) To benefit directly from social security programmes;

(d) To obtain all types of training and education, formal and non-formal, including that relating to functional literacy, as well as, *inter alia,* the benefit of all community and extension services, in order to increase their technical proficiency;

(e) To organize self-help groups and co-operatives in order to obtain equal access to economic opportunities through employment or self-employment;

(f) To participate in all community activities;

(g) To have access to agricultural credit and loans, marketing facilities, appropriate technology and equal treatment in land and agrarian reform as well as in land resettlement schemes;

(h) To enjoy adequate living conditions, particularly in relation to housing, sanitation, electricity and water supply, transport and communications.

**Part IV**

*Article 15.* 1. States Parties shall accord to women equality with men before the law.

2. State Parties shall accord to women, in civil matters, a legal capacity identical to that of men and the same opportunities to exercise that capacity. In particular, they shall give women equal rights to conclude contracts and to administer property and shall treat them equally in all stages of procedure in courts and tribunals.

3. States Parties agree that all contracts and all other private instruments of any kind with a legal effect which is directed at restricting the legal capacity of women shall be deemed null and void.

4. States Parties shall accord to men and women the same rights with regard to the law relating to the movement of persons and the freedom to choose their residence and domicile.

*Article 16.* 1. States Parties shall take all appropriate measures to eliminate discrimination against women in all matters relating to marriage and family relations and in particular shall ensure, on a basis of equality of men and women:

(a) The same right to enter into marriage;

(b) The same right freely to choose a spouse and to enter into marriage only with their free and full consent;

(c) The same rights and responsibilities during marriage and at its dissolution;

(d) The same rights and responsibilities as parents, irrespective of their marital status, in matters relating to their children; in all cases the interests of the children shall be paramount;

(e) The same rights to decide freely and responsibly on the number and spacing of their children and to have access to the information, education and means to enable them to exercise these rights;

(f) The same rights and responsibilities with regard to guardianship, wardship, trusteeship and adoption of children, or similar institutions where these concepts exist in national legislation; in all cases the interests of the children shall be paramount;

(g) The same personal rights as husband and wife, including the right to choose a family name, a profession and an occupation;

(h) The same rights for both spouses in respect of the ownership, acquisition, management, administration, enjoyment and disposition of property, whether free of charge or for a valuable consideration.

2. The betrothal and the marriage of a child shall have no legal effect, and all necessary action, including legislation, shall be taken to specify a minimum age for marriage and to make the registration of marriages in an official registry compulsory.

### Part V

*Article 17.* 1. For the purpose of considering the progress made in the implementation of the present Convention, there shall be established a Committee on the Elimination of Discrimination against Women (hereinafter referred to as the Committee) consisting, at the time of entry into force of the Convention, of eighteen and, after ratification of or accession to the Convention by the thirty-fifth State Party, of twenty-three experts of high moral standing and competence in the field covered by the Convention. The experts shall be elected by States Parties from among their nationals and shall serve in their personal capacity, consideration being given to equitable geographical distribution and to the representation of the different forms of civilization as well as the principal legal systems.

2. The members of the Committee shall be elected by secret ballot from a list of persons nominated by States Parties. Each State Party may nominate one person from among its own nationals.

3. The initial election shall be held six months after the date of the entry into force of the present Convention. At least three months before the date of each election the Secretary-General of the United Nations shall address a letter to the States Parties inviting them to submit their nominations within two months. The Secretary-General shall prepare a list in alphabetical order of all persons thus nominated, indicating the States Parties which have nominated them, and shall submit it to the States Parties.

4. Elections of the members of the Committee shall be held at a meeting of States Parties convened by the Secretary-General at United Nations Headquarters. At that meeting, for which two thirds of the States Parties shall constitute a quorum, the persons elected to the Committee shall be those nominees who obtain the largest number of votes and an absolute majority of the votes of the representatives of States Parties present and voting.

5. The members of the Committee shall be elected for a term of four years. However, the terms of nine of the members elected at the first election shall expire at the end of two years; immediately after the first election the names of these nine members shall be chosen by lot by the Chairman of the Committee.

6. The election of the five additional members of the Committee shall be held in accordance with the provisions of paragraphs , 3 and 4 of this article, following the thirty-fifth ratification or accession. The terms of two of the additional members elected on this occasion shall expire at the end of two years, the names of these two members having been chosen by lot by the Chairman of the Committee.

7. For the filling of casual vacancies, the State Party whose expert has ceased to function as a member of the Committee shall appoint another expert from among its nationals, subject to the approval of the Committee.

8. The members of the Committee shall, with the approval of the General Assembly, receive emoluments from United Nations resources on such terms and conditions as the Assembly may decide, having regard to the importance of the Committee's responsibilities.

9. The Secretary-General of the United Nations shall provide the necessary staff and facilities for the effective performance of the functions of the Committee under the present Convention.

*Article 18.* 1. States Parties undertake to submit to the Secretary-General of the United Nations, for consideration by the Committee, a report on the legislative, judicial, administrative or other measures which they have adopted to give effect to the provisions of the present Convention and on the progress made in this respect:

(a) Within one year after the entry into force for the State concerned;

(b) Thereafter at least every four years and further whenever the Committee so requests.

2. Reports may indicate factors and difficulties affecting the degree of fulfilment of obligations under the present Convention.

*Article 19.* 1. The Committee shall adopt its own rules of procedure.

2. The Committee shall elect its officers for a term of two years.

*Article 20.* 1. The Committee shall normally meet for a period of not more than two weeks annually in order to consider the reports submitted in accordance with article 8 of the present Convention.

2. The meetings of the Committee shall normally be held at United Nations Headquarters or at any other convenient place as determined by the Committee.

*Article 21.* 1. The Committee shall, through the Economic and Social Council, report annually to the General Assembly of the United Nations on its activities and may make suggestions and general recommendations based on the examination of reports and information received from the States Parties. Such suggestions and general recommendations shall be included in the report of the Committee together with comments, if any, from States Parties.

2. The Secretary-General of the United Nations shall transmit the reports of the Committee to the Commission on the Status of Women for its information.

*Article 22.* The specialized agencies shall be entitled to be represented at the consideration of the implementation of such provisions of the present Convention as fall within the scope of their activities. The Committee may invite the specialized agencies to submit reports on the implementation of the Convention in areas falling within the scope of their activities.

### Part VI

*Article 23.* Nothing in the present Convention shall affect any provisions that are more conducive to the achievement of equality between men and women which may be contained:

(a) In the legislation of a State Party; or

(b) In any other international convention, treaty or agreement in force for that State.

*Article 24.* States Parties undertake to adopt all necessary measures at the national level aimed at achieving the full realization of the rights recognized in the present Convention.

*Article 25.* 1. The present Convention shall be open for signature by all States.

2. The Secretary-General of the United Nations is designated as the depositary of the present Convention.

3. The present Convention is subject to ratification. Instruments of ratification shall be deposited with the Secretary-General of the United Nations.

4. The present Convention shall be open to accession by all States. Accession shall be effected by the deposit of an instrument of accession with the Secretary-General of the United Nations.

*Article 26.* 1. A request for the revision of the present Convention may be made at any time by any State Party by means of a notification in writing addressed to the Secretary-General of the United Nations.

2. The General Assembly of the United Nations shall decide upon the steps, if any, to be taken in respect of such a request.

*Article 27.* 1. The present Convention shall enter into force on the thirtieth day after the date of deposit with the Secretary-General of the United Nations of the twentieth instrument of ratification or accession.

2. For each State ratifying the present Convention or acceding to it after the deposit of the twentieth instrument of ratification or accession, the Convention shall enter into force on the thirtieth day after the date of the deposit of its own instrument of ratification or accession.

*Article 28.* 1. The Secretary-General of the United Nations shall receive and circulate to all States the text of reservations made by States at the time of ratification or accession.

2. A reservation incompatible with the object and purpose of the present Convention shall not be permitted.

3. Reservations may be withdrawn at any time by notification to this effect addressed to the Secretary-General of the United Nations, who shall then inform all States thereof. Such notification shall take effect on the date on which it is received.

*Article 29.* 1. Any dispute between two or more States Parties concerning the interpretation or application of the present Convention which is not settled by negotiation shall, at the request of one of them, be submitted to arbitration. If within six months from the date of the request for arbitration the parties are unable to agree on the organization of the arbitration, any one of those parties may refer the dispute to the International Court of Justice by request in conformity with the Statute of the Court.

2. Each State Party may at the time of signature or ratification of the present Convention or accession thereto declare that it does not consider itself bound by paragraph of

this article. The other States Parties shall not be bound by that paragraph with respect to any State Party which has made such a reservation.

3. Any State Party which has made a reservation in accordance with paragraph of this article may at any time withdraw that reservation by notification to the Secretary-General of the United Nations.

*Article 30.* The present Convention, the Arabic, Chinese, English, French, Russian and Spanish texts of which are equally authentic, shall be deposited with the Secretary-General of the United Nations.

In witness whereof the undersigned, duly authorized, have signed the present Convention.

**BIBLIOGRAPHY.** Clark, Belinda. "The Vienna Convention Reservations Regime and the Convention on Discrimination against Women," *American Journal of International Law* 85, no. 2 (April 1991): 281–321. Scholarly article, in English.

Goldfarb, Alan. "A Kenyan Wife's Right to Bury Her Husband: Applying the Convention on the Elimination of All Forms of Discrimination against Women," *ILSA Journal of International Law* 14 (1990): 1–21. Scholarly article, in English.

International Women's Rights Action Watch. *Dreaming a Different Reality—Challenge and Change: Creating New Traditions.* Minneapolis, MN, USA: Humphrey Institute of Public Affairs, University of Minnesota, 1990. Conference report, in English.

Plata, María Isabel. "La Convención de la ONU y la Mujer" (The UN Convention and Women), *El Otro Derecho* 8 (June 1991): 25–37. Scholarly article, in Spanish.

Rahman, Anika. "Religious Rights Versus Women's Rights in India: A Test Case for International Human Rights Law," *Columbia Journal of Transnational Law* 28, no. 2 (1990): 473–498. Scholarly article, in English.

Rehof, Lars Adam. *Guide to the Travaux Préparatoires of the United Nations Convention on the Elimination of All Forms of Discrimination against Women.* Dordrecht, the Netherlands: Martinus Nijhoff, 1993. Scholarly monograph, in English.

## WOMEN'S RIGHTS: DECLARATION ON THE ELIMINATION OF DISCRIMINATION AGAINST WOMEN, UN (1967).

The Declaration represents an important milestone in the work of the United Nations for the advancement of women. It terms discrimination against women "fundamentally unjust and . . . an offence against human dignity" and calls for measures to be taken to ensure universal recognition of the principle of equality between men and women.

The Declaration was adopted by the UN **GENERAL ASSEMBLY** on 7 November 1967 (resolution 2263 [XXII]).

The text, annexed to that resolution, is as follows:

The General Assembly,

Considering that the peoples of the United Nations have, in the Charter, reaffirmed their faith in fundamental human rights, in the dignity and worth of the human person and in the equal rights of men and women,

Considering that the Universal Declaration of Human Rights asserts the principle of non-discrimination and proclaims that all human beings are born free and equal in dignity and rights and that everyone is entitled to all the rights and freedoms set forth therein without distinction of any kind, including any distinction as to sex,

Taking into account the resolutions, declarations, conventions and recommendations of the United Nations and the specialized agencies designed to eliminate all forms of discrimination and to promote equal rights for men and women,

Concerned that, despite the Charter of the United Nations, the Universal Declaration of Human Rights, the International Covenants on Human Rights and other instruments of the United Nations and the specialized agencies and despite the progress made in the matter of equality of rights, there continues to exist considerable discrimination against women,

Considering that discrimination against women is incompatible with human dignity and with the welfare of the family and of society, prevents their participation, on equal terms with men, in the political, social, economic and cultural life of their countries and is an obstacle to the full development of the potentialities of women in the service of their countries and of humanity,

Bearing in mind the great contribution made by women to social, political, economic and cultural life and the part they play in the family and particularly in the rearing of children,

Convinced that the full and complete development of a country, the welfare of the world and the cause of peace require the maximum participation of women as well as men in all fields,

Considering that it is necessary to ensure the universal recognition in law and in fact of the principle of equality of men and women,

Solemnly proclaims this Declaration:

*Article 1.* Discrimination against women, denying or limiting as it does their equality of rights with men, is fundamentally unjust and constitutes an offence against human dignity.

*Article 2.* All appropriate measures shall be taken to abolish existing laws, customs, regulations and practices which are discriminatory against women, and to establish adequate legal protection for equal rights of men and women, in particular:

(a) The principle of equality of rights shall be embodied in the constitution or otherwise guaranteed by law;

(b) The international instruments of the United Nations and the specialized agencies relating to the elimination of discrimination against women shall be ratified or acceded to and fully implemented as soon as practicable.

*Article 3.* All appropriate measures shall be taken to educate public opinion and to direct national aspirations towards the eradication of prejudice and the abolition of customary and all other practices which are based on the idea of the inferiority of women.

*Article 4.* All appropriate measures shall be taken to ensure to women on equal terms with men, without any discrimination:

(a) The right to vote in all elections and be eligible for election to all publicly elected bodies;

(b) The right to vote in all public referenda;

(c) The right to hold public office and to exercise all public functions.

Such rights shall be guaranteed by legislation.

*Article 5.* Women shall have the same rights as men to acquire, change or retain their nationality. Marriage to an alien shall not automatically affect the nationality of the wife either by rendering her stateless or by forcing upon her the nationality of her husband.

*Article 6.* 1. Without prejudice to the safeguarding of the unity and the harmony of the family, which remains the basic unit of any society, all appropriate measures, particularly legislative measures, shall be taken to ensure to women, married or unmarried, equal rights with men in the field of civil law, and in particular:

(a) The right to acquire, administer, enjoy, dispose of and inherit property, including property acquired during marriage;

(b) The right to equality in legal capacity and the exercise thereof;

(c) The same rights as men with regard to the law on the movement of persons.

2. All appropriate measures shall be taken to ensure the principle of equality of status of the husband and wife, and in particular:

(a) Women shall have the same right as men to free choice of a spouse and to enter into marriage only with their free and full consent;

(b) Women shall have equal rights with men during marriage and at its dissolution. In all cases the interest of the children shall be paramount;

(c) Parents shall have equal rights and duties in matters relating to their children. In all cases the interest of the children shall be paramount.

3. Child marriage and the betrothal of young girls before puberty shall be prohibited, and effective action, including legislation, shall be taken to specify a minimum age for marriage and to make the registration of marriages in an official registry compulsory.

*Article 7.* All provisions of penal codes which constitute discrimination against women shall be repealed.

*Article 8.* All appropriate measures, including legislation, shall be taken to combat all forms of traffic in women and exploitation of prostitution of women.

*Article 9.* All appropriate measures shall be taken to ensure to girls and women, married or unmarried, equal rights with men in education at all levels, and in particular:

(a) Equal conditions of access to, and study in, educational institutions of all types, including universities and vocational, technical and professional schools;

(b) The same choice of curricula, the same examinations, teaching staff with qualifications of the same standard, and school premises and equipment of the same quality, whether the institutions are co-educational or not;

(c) Equal opportunities to benefit from scholarships and other study grants;

(d) Equal opportunities for access to programmes of continuing education, including adult literacy programmes;

(e) Access to educational information to help in ensuring the health and well-being of families.

*Article 10.* 1. All appropriate measures shall be taken to ensure to women, married or unmarried, equal rights with men in the field of economic and social life, and in particular:

(a) The right, without discrimination on grounds of marital status or any other grounds, to receive vocational training, to work, to free choice of profession and employment, and to professional and vocational advancement;

(b) The right to equal remuneration with men and to equality of treatment in respect of work of equal value;

(c) The right to leave with pay, retirement privileges and provision for security in respect of unemployment, sickness, old age or other incapacity to work;

(d) The right to receive family allowances on equal terms with men.

2. In order to prevent discrimination against women on account of marriage or maternity and to ensure their effective right to work, measures shall be taken to prevent their dismissal in the event of marriage or maternity and to provide paid maternity leave, with the guarantee of returning to former employment, and to provide the necessary social services, including childcare facilities.

3. Measures taken to protect women in certain types of work, for reasons inherent in their physical nature, shall not be regarded as discriminatory.

*Article 11.* 1. The principle of equality of rights of men and women demands implementation in all States in accordance with the principles of the Charter of the United Nations and of the Universal Declaration of Human Rights.

2. Governments, non-governmental organizations and individuals are urged, therefore, to do all in their power to promote the implementation of the principles contained in this declaration.

## WOMEN'S RIGHTS: DECLARATION ON THE ELIMINATION OF VIOLENCE AGAINST WOMEN, UN (1993).

On 20 December 1993, the UN **GENERAL ASSEMBLY** adopted unanimously (resolution 48/104) this Declaration. In doing so, the Assembly recognized "that violence against women is a manifestation of historically unequal power relations between men and women which have led to domination over and discrimination against women and to the prevention of their full advancement, and that it is one of the crucial social mechanisms by which women are forced into a subordinate position compared to men." Further, it expressed concern "that some groups of women—such as women belonging to minority groups, indigenous women, refugee women, women in institutions or in detention, female children, women with disabilities, elderly women, and women in situations of armed conflict—are especially vulnerable to violence."

In later action, in a preliminary report, the Special Rapporteur on violence against women, Ms. Radhika Coomaraswarry, submitted to the **COMMISSION ON HUMAN RIGHTS** the following conclusions and preliminary recommendations (E/CN.4/1995/42, chap. 5, paras. 314–317):

The Special Rapporteur has intended in this first report to provide a general overview of the issues relating to violence against women, including its causes and consequences. Subsequent reports will deal more specifically with the areas of violence in the family, violence in the community and violence by the State. These reports will contain detailed recommendations with regard to eliminating violence against women in these spheres.

As a preliminary measure at the national level, however, States could be called upon to meet their responsibilities contained in the Declaration on the Elimination of Violence against Women. More specifically, States should be called upon:

(a) To condemn violence against women and not invoke custom, tradition or religion to avoid their obligations to eliminate such violence;

(b) To ratify the Convention on the Elimination of All Forms of Discrimination against Women without reservation;

(c) To formulate national plans of action to combat violence against women;

(d) To initiate strategies to develop legal and administrative mechanisms to ensure effective justice for women victims of violence;

(e) To ensure the provision of specialized assistance for the support and rehabilitation of women victims of violence;

(f) To train and sensitize judicial and police officials with regard to issues concerning violence against women;

(g) To reform educational curricula so as to instil values which will prevent violence against women;

(h) To promote research with regard to the issues concerning violence against women;

(i) To ensure proper reporting of the problem of violence against women to international human rights mechanisms.

At the international level, the Special Rapporteur reiterates the call contained in the Vienna Declaration and Programme of Action to incorporate human rights and the equal status of women into the mainstream of United Nations action in the field of human rights and requests the Commission on Human Rights to make available the present report to the Fourth World Conference on Women, to be held in Beijing in 1995.

Finally, the Special Rapporteur encourages the formulation of an optional protocol to the Convention on the Elimination of All Forms of Discrimination against Women allowing for an individual right of petition once local remedies are exhausted. This will ensure that women victims of violence will have a final recourse under an international human rights instrument to have their rights established and vindicated.

The text of the 1993 Declaration is as follows:

*Article 1.* For the purpose of this Declaration, the term "violence against women" means any act of gender-based violence that results in, or is likely to result in, physical, sexual, or psychological harm or suffering to women, including threats of such acts, coercion or arbitrary deprivation of liberty, whether occurring in public or in private life.

*Article 2.* Violence against women shall be understood to encompass, but not be limited to, the following:

(a) Physical, sexual, and psychological violence occurring in the family, including battering, sexual abuse of female children in the household, dowry-related violence, marital rape, female genital mutilation, and other traditional practices harmful to women, nonspousal violence, and violence related to exploitation;

(b) Physical, sexual, and psychological violence occurring within the general community, including rape, sexual abuse, sexual harassment, and intimidation at work, in education institutions and elsewhere, trafficking in women and forced prostitution;

(c) Physical, sexual, and psychological violence perpetrated or condoned by the State, wherever it occurs.

*Article 3.* Women are entitled to the equal enjoyment and protection of all human rights and fundamental freedoms in the political, economic, social, cultural, civil, or any other field. These rights include,*inter alia,*

(a) The right to life (Universal Declaration of Human Rights, art. 3; and International Covenant on Civil and Political Rights, art. 6);

(b) The right to equality (International Covenant on Civil and Political Rights, art. 26);

(c) The right to liberty and security of person (Universal Declaration of Human Rights, art. 3; and International Covenant on Civil and Political Rights, art. 9);

(d) The right to equal protection under the law (International Covenant on Civil and Political Rights, art. 26);

(e) The right to be free from all forms of discrimination (International Covenant on Civil and Political Rights, art. 26);

(f) The right to the highest standard attainable of physical and mental health (International Covenant on Economic, Social and Cultural Rights, art. 12);

(g) The right to just and favourable conditions of work (Universal Declaration of Human Rights, art. 23; and International Covenant on Economic, Social and Cultural Rights, art. 6 and 7);

(h) The right not to be subjected to torture, or other cruel, inhuman, or degrading treatment or punishment (Universal Declaration of Human Rights, art. 5; International Covenant on Civil and Political Rights, art. 7; and Convention against Torture and Other Cruel, Inhuman or Degrading Treatment or Punishment).

*Article 4.* States should condemn violence against women and should not invoke any custom, tradition, or religious consideration to avoid their obligations with respect to its elimination. States should pursue by all appropriate means and without delay eliminating violence against women and, to this end, should:

(a) Consider, where they have not yet done so, ratifying or acceding to the Convention on the Elimination of All Forms of Discrimination against Women or withdrawing reservations to that Convention;

(b) Refrain from engaging in violence against women;

(c) Exercise due diligence to prevent, investigate, and, in accordance with national legislation, punish acts of violence against women, whether those acts are perpetrated by the State or by private persons;

(d) Develop penal, civil, labour, and administrative sanctions in domestic legislation to punish and redress the wrongs caused to women who are subjected to violence; women who are subjected to violence should be provided with access to the mechanisms of justice and, as provided for by national legislation, to just and effective remedies for the harm that they have suffered; States should also inform women of their rights in seeking redress through such mechanisms;

(e) Consider the possibility of developing national plans of action to promote the protection of women against any form of violence, or to include provisions for this purpose in plans already existing, taking into account, as appropriate, such cooperation as can be provided by nongovernmental organizations, particularly those concerned with this subject;

(f) Develop, in a comprehensive way, preventive approaches and all those measures of a legal, political, administrative, and cultural nature that promote the protection of women against any form of violence, and ensure that the revictimization of women does not occur because of gender-insensitive laws, enforcement practices, or other interventions;

(g) Work to ensure, to the maximum extent feasible in the light of their available resources and, where needed,

within the framework of international cooperation, that women subjected to violence and, where appropriate, their children have specialized assistance, such as rehabilitation, assistance in child care and maintenance, treatment, counselling, health and social services, facilities and programmes, as well as support structures, and should take all other appropriate measure to promote their safety and physical and psychological rehabilitation;

(h) Include in government budgets adequate resources for their activities related to the elimination of violence against women;

(i) Take measures to ensure that law-enforcement officers and public officials responsible for implementing policies to prevent, investigate, and punish violence against women receive training to sensitize them to the needs of women;

(j) Adopt all appropriate measures, especially in the field of education, to modify the social and cultural patterns of conduct of men and women and to eliminate prejudices, customary practices and all other practices based on the idea of the inferiority or superiority of either of the sexes and on stereotyped roles of men and women;

(k) Promote research, collect data, and compile statistics, especially concerning domestic violence, relating to the prevalence of different forms of violence against women, and encourage research on the causes, nature, seriousness, and consequences of violence against women and on the effectiveness of measures implemented to prevent and redress violence against women; those statistics and findings of the research will be made public;

(l) Adopt measures directed to the elimination of violence against women who are especially vulnerable to violence;

(m) Include, in submitting reports as required under relevant human rights instruments of the United Nations, information pertaining to violence against women and measures taken to implement the present Declaration;

(n) Encourage the development of appropriate guidelines to assist in the implementation of the principles set forth in the present Declaration;

(o) Recognize the important role of the women's movement and nongovernmental organizations worldwide in raising awareness and alleviating the problem of violence against women;

(p) Facilitate and enhance the work of the women's movement and nongovernmental organizations and cooperate with them at local, national, and regional levels;

(q) Encourage intergovernmental regional organizations of which they are members to include the elimination of violence against women in their programmes, as appropriate.

*Article 5.* The organs and specialized agencies of the United Nations system should, within their respective fields of competence, contribute to the recognition and realization of the rights and the principles set forth in the present Declaration, and to this end should, *inter alia,*

(a) foster international and regional cooperation with a view to defining regional strategies for combating violence, exchanging experiences, and financing programmes relating to the elimination of violence against women;

(b) Promote meetings and seminars with the aim of creating and raising awareness among all persons of the issue of the elimination of violence against women;

(c) Foster coordination and exchange within the UN system between human rights treaty bodies to address the matter effectively;

(d) Include in analyses prepared by organizations and

bodies of the UN system of social trends and problems, such as the periodic reports on the world social situation [and] examination of trends in violence against women;

(e) Encourage coordination between organizations and bodies of the UN system to incorporate the issue of violence against women into ongoing programmes, especially with reference to groups of women particularly vulnerable to violence;

(f) Promote the formulation of guidelines or manuals relating to violence against women, taking into account the measures mentioned herein;

(g) Consider the issue of the elimination of violence against women, as appropriate, in fulfilling their mandates with respect to the implementation of human rights instruments;

(h) Cooperate with nongovernmental organizations in addressing violence against women.

*Article 6.* Nothing in the present Declaration shall affect any provision that is more conducive to the elimination of violence against women that may be contained in the legislation of a State or in any international convention, treaty, or other instrument in force in a State.

BIBLIOGRAPHY. Bunch, Charlotte. "Women's Rights as Human Rights: Toward a Re-Vision of Human Rights," *Human Rights Quarterly* 12, no. 4 (Nov. 1990): 486–498. Scholarly article, in English.

Bunch, Charlotte, and Roxanna Carrillo. *Gender Violence: A Development and Human Right Issue.* New Brunswick, NJ, USA: Center for Women's Global Leadership, Douglass College, Rutgers University, 1990. Scholarly monograph, in English.

Cook, Rebecca J. "State Responsibility for Violations of Women's Human Rights," *Harvard Human Rights Journal* 7 (Spring 1994): 125–175. Scholarly article, in English.

Copelon, Rhonda. "Recognizing the Egregious in the Everyday: Domestic Violence as Torture," *Columbia Human Rights Law Review* 25, no. 2 (Spring 1994): 291–367. Scholarly article, in English.

Duque, Isabel, Teresa Rodriguez, and M. Soledad Weinstein. *Violence Against Women: Definitions and Strategies.* New Delhi, India, and Santiago, Chile: Huriter School of International Studies, Jawaharlal Nehru University, 1990. NGO conference paper, in English.

U.S. Congress, House of Representatives, Committee on Foreign Affairs. *International Human Rights Abuses against Women: Hearings before the Subcommittee on Human Rights and International Organizations of the Committee on Foreign Affairs, House of Representatives, One Hundred and First Congress, Second Session, March 21 and July 26, 1990.* Washington, D.C.: U.S. Government Printing Office, 1991. Government report, in English.

## WOMEN'S RIGHTS: DECLARATION ON THE PARTICIPATION OF WOMEN IN PROMOTING INTERNATIONAL PEACE AND CO-OPERATION, UN (1982).

The Declaration originated in a text (resolution 29) adopted by the World Conference of the International Women's Year (1975), which called upon women to intensify their forces in order to strengthen peace and to promote international co-operation. A draft declaration on the subject was dis-

cussed extensively in the Third Committee of the UN **GENERAL ASSEMBLY** in 1980 and 1981, and the Declaration was adopted unanimously by the Assembly on 3 December 1982 (resolution 37/63).

In May 1988, the **ECONOMIC AND SOCIAL COUNCIL,** wishing to encourage the active participation of women in promoting international peace, security, and cooperation and the elimination of violence against women within the family and society, appealed (resolution 1988/28) to all governments to take practical institutional, educational, and organizational measures to facilitate women's participation on an equal footing with men in activities related to peace, disarmament negotiations, and the resolution of conflicts and to inform the Secretary-General of the activities undertaken.

The text of the Declaration on the Participation of Women in Promoting International Peace and Co-operation, annexed to resolution 29, is as follows:

### Part I

*Article 1.* Women and men have an equal and vital interest in contributing to international peace and cooperation. To this end women must be enabled to exercise their right to participate in the economic, social, cultural, civil and political affairs of society on an equal footing with men.

*Article 2.* The full participation of women in the economic, social, cultural, civil and political affairs of society and in the endeavor to promote international peace and cooperation is dependent on a balanced and equitable distribution of roles between men and women in the family and in society as a whole.

*Article 3.* The increasing participation of women in the economic, social, cultural, civil and political affairs of society will contribute to international peace and cooperation.

*Article 4.* The full enjoyment of the rights of women and men and the full participation of women in promoting international peace and co-operation will contribute to the eradication of apartheid, of all forms of racism, racial discrimination, colonialism, neo-colonialism, aggression, foreign occupation and domination and interference in the internal affairs of States.

*Article 5.* Special national and international measures are necessary to increase the level of women's participation in the sphere of international relations so that women can contribute, on an equal basis, with men to national and international efforts to secure world peace and economic and social progress and to promote international cooperation.

### Part II

*Article 6.* All appropriate measures shall be taken to intensify national and international efforts in respect of the participation of women in promoting international peace and cooperation by ensuring the equal participation of women in the economic, social, cultural, civil and political affairs of society through a balanced and equitable distribution of roles between men and women in the domestic sphere and in society as a whole, as well as by providing an equal opportunity for women to participate in the decisionmaking.

*Article 7.* All appropriate measures shall be taken to promote the exchange of experience at the national and international levels for the purpose of furthering the involvement of women in promoting international peace and cooperation and in solving other vital national and international problems.

*Article 8.* All appropriate measures shall be taken at the national and international levels to give effective publicity to the responsibility and active participation of women in promoting international peace and cooperation and in solving other vital national and international problems.

*Article 9.* All appropriate measures shall be taken to render solidarity and support to those women who are victims of mass and flagrant violations of human rights such as *apartheid*, all forms of racism, racial discrimination, colonialism, neo-colonialism, aggression, foreign occupation and domination and of all other violations of human rights.

*Article 10.* All appropriate measures shall be taken to pay tribute to the participation of women in promoting international peace and co-operation.

*Article 11.* All appropriate measures shall be taken to encourage women to participate in nongovernmental and intergovernmental organizations aimed at the strengthening of international peace and security, the development of friendly relations among nations and the promotion of cooperation among States and, to that end, freedom of thought, conscience, expression, assembly, association, communication and movement, without distinction as to race, political or religious belief, language or ethnic origin, shall be effectively guaranteed.

*Article 12.* All appropriate measures shall be taken to provide practical opportunities for the effective participation of women in promoting international peace and cooperation, economic development and social progress and, to that end:

(a) To promote an equitable representation of women in governmental and non-governmental functions,

(b) To promote equality of opportunities for women to enter diplomatic service,

(c) To appoint or nominate women, on an equal basis with men, as members of delegations to national, regional or international meetings,

(d) To support increased employment of women at all levels in the secretariats of the United Nations and the specialized agencies, in conformity with Article 101 of the Charter of the United Nations.

*Article 13.* All appropriate measures shall be taken to establish adequate legal protection of the rights of women on an equal basis with men in order to ensure effective participation of women in the activities referred to above.

*Article 14.* Governments, nongovernmental and international organizations, including the United Nations and the specialized agencies and individuals, are urged to do all in their power to promote the implementation of the principles contained in the present Declaration.

## WOMEN'S RIGHTS: INTER-AMERICAN CONVENTION ON THE GRANTING OF CIVIL RIGHTS TO WOMEN, OAS (1948).

This Convention, and the Inter-American Convention on the Granting of Political Rights to Women (see next entry), emerged from a single draft, on the granting of civil and political rights to women, prepared by the Inter-American Commission of Women.

The Inter-American Convention on the Granting of Civil Rights to Women sets out in terms of an international legal commitment the agreement of the governments of the American States that women shall enjoy the same civil rights as men. It was adopted by the Ninth International Conference of American States, convened at Bogota, on 2 May 1948 and entered into force on 22 April 1949. The text (*OAS Treaty Series* 23) is as follows:

The Governments represented at the Ninth International Conference of American States,

Considering:

That the majority of the American Republics, inspired by lofty principles of justice, have granted civil rights to women;

That it has been a constant aspiration of the American Community of nations to equalize the status of men and women in the enjoyment and exercise of civil rights;

That Resolution XX of the Eighth International Conference of American States expressly declares:

"That women have the right to the enjoyment of equality as to civil status";

That long before the women of America demanded their rights they were able to carry out nobly all their responsibilities side by side with men;

That the principle of equality of human rights for men and women is contained in the Charter of the United Nations,

Have resolved:

To authorize their respective representatives, whose full powers have been found to be in good and due form, to sign the following articles:

*Article 1.* The American States agree to grant to women the same civil rights that men enjoy.

*Article 2.* The present Convention shall be open for signature by the American States and shall be ratified in accordance with their respective constitutional procedures. The original instrument, the English, French, Portuguese and Spanish texts of which are equally authentic, shall be deposited with the General Secretariat of the Organization of American States, which shall transmit certified copies to the Governments for the purpose of ratification. The instruments of ratification shall be deposited with the General Secretariat of the Organization of American States, which shall notify the signatory Governments of the said deposit. Such notification shall serve as an exchange of ratifications.

## WOMEN'S RIGHTS: INTER-AMERICAN CONVENTION ON THE GRANTING OF POLITICAL RIGHTS TO WOMEN, OAS (1948).

This Convention, and the Inter-American Convention on the Granting of Civil Rights to Women (see previous entry), emerged from a single draft, on the granting of civil and political rights to women, prepared by the Inter-American Commission of Women.

The Inter-American Convention on the Granting of Political Rights to Women sets out in terms of an international legal commitment the agreement of the governments of American States that women shall enjoy the same political rights enjoyed by men. It was adopted by the Ninth International Conference of American States, convened at Bogota, on 2 May 1948 and entered into force on 22 April 1949. The text (*OAS Treaty Series* 3) is as follows:

The Governments represented at the Ninth International Conference of American States,
Considering:
That the majority of the American Republics, inspired by lofty principles of justice, have granted political rights to women;
That it has been a constant aspiration of the American community of nations to equalize the status of men and women in the enjoyment and exercise of political rights;
That Resolution XX of the Eighth International Conference of American States expressly declares:
"That women have the right to political treatment on the basis of equality with men";
That long before the women of America demanded their rights they were able to carry out nobly all their responsibilities side by side with men;
That the principle of equality of human rights for men and women is contained in the Charter of the United Nations;
Have resolved:
To authorize their respective representatives, whose full powers have been found to be in good and due form, to sign the following articles:
*Article 1.* The High Contracting Parties agree that the right to vote and to be elected to national office shall not be denied or abridged by reason of sex.
*Article 2.* The present Convention shall be open for signature by the American States and shall be ratified in accordance with their respective constitutional procedures. The original instrument, the English, French, Portuguese and Spanish texts of which are equally authentic, shall be deposited with the General Secretariat of the Organization of American States, which shall transmit certified copies to the Governments for the purpose of ratification. The instruments of ratification shall be deposited with the General Secretariat of the Organization of American States, which shall notify the signatory Governments of the said deposit. Such notification shall serve as an exchange of ratifications.

**WORK.** The right of everyone to work is proclaimed in the **UNIVERSAL DECLARATION OF HUMAN RIGHTS** in the following terms:

*Article 23.* 1. Everyone has the right to work, to free choice of employment, to just and favourable conditions of work and to protection against unemployment.
2. Everyone, without any discrimination, has the right to equal pay for equal work.
3. Everyone who works has the right to just and favourable remuneration ensuring for himself and his family an existence worthy of human dignity, and supplemented, if necessary, by other means of social protection.
4. Everyone has the right to form and to join trade unions for the protection of his interests.

The **INTERNATIONAL COVENANT ON ECONOMIC, SOCIAL AND CULTURAL RIGHTS** contains the following provisions:

*Article 6.* 1. The States Parties to the present Covenant recognize the right to work, which includes the right of ev-

eryone to the opportunity to gain his living by work which he freely chooses or accepts, and will take appropriate steps to safeguard this right.
2. The steps to be taken by a State Party to the present Covenant to achieve the full realization of this right shall include technical and vocational guidance and training programmes, policies and techniques to achieve steady economic, social and cultural development and full and productive employment under conditions safeguarding fundamental political and economic freedoms to the individual.
*Article 7.* The States Parties to the present Covenant recognize the right of everyone to the enjoyment of just and favourable conditions of work which ensure, in particular:
(a) Remuneration which provides all workers, as a minimum, with:
(i) Fair wages and equal remuneration for work of equal value without distinction of any kind, in particular women being guaranteed conditions of work not inferior to those enjoyed by men, with equal pay for equal work;
(ii) A decent living for themselves and their families in accordance with the provisions of the present Covenant;
(b) Safe and healthy working conditions;
(c) Equal opportunity for everyone to be promoted in his employment to an appropriate higher level, subject to no considerations other than those of seniority and competence;
(d) Rest, leisure and reasonable limitation of working hours and periodic holidays with pay, as well as remuneration for public holidays.

The International Convention on the Elimination of All Forms of Racial Discrimination (see **RACIAL DISCRIMINATION**) provides for non-discrimination on racial grounds in respect of the right, as follows:

*Article 5.* In compliance with the fundamental obligations laid down in article 2 of this Convention, States Parties undertake to prohibit and to eliminate racial discrimination in all its forms and to guarantee the right of everyone, without distinction as to race, colour, or national or ethnic origin, to equality before the law, notably in the enjoyment of the following rights: . . .
(e) Economic, social and cultural rights, in particular:
(i) the rights to work, free choice of employment, just and favourable conditions of work, protection against unemployment, equal pay for equal work, just and favourable remuneration. . . .

The Convention on the Elimination of All Forms of Discrimination against Women (see **WOMEN'S RIGHTS**) provides for non-discrimination on the ground of sex in respect of the right, as follows:

*Article 11.* 1. States Parties shall take all appropriate measures to eliminate discrimination against women in the field of employment in order to ensure, on a basis of equality of men and women, the same rights, in particular:
(a) The right to work as an inalienable right of all human beings;
(b) The right to the same employment opportunities, including the application of the same criteria for selection in matters of employment;

(c) The right to free choice of profession and employment, the right to promotion, job security and all benefits and conditions of service and the right to receive vocational training and retraining, including apprenticeships, advanced vocational training and recurrent training;

(d) The right to equal remuneration, including benefits, and to equal treatment in respect of work of equal value, as well as equality of treatment in the evaluation of the quality of work;

(e) The right to social security, particularly in cases of retirement, unemployment, sickness, invalidity and old age and other incapacity to work, as well as the right to paid leave;

(f) The right to protection of health and to safety in working conditions, including the safeguarding of the function of reproduction.

2. In order to prevent discrimination against women on the grounds of marriage or maternity and to ensure their effective right to work, States Parties shall take appropriate measures:

(a) To prohibit, subject to the imposition of sanctions, dismissal on the grounds of pregnancy or of maternity leave and discrimination in dismissals on the basis of marital status;

(b) To introduce maternity leave with pay or with comparable social benefits without loss of former employment, seniority or social allowances;

(c) To encourage the provision of the necessary supporting social services to enable parents to combine family obligations with work responsibilities and participation in public life, in particular through promoting the establishment and development of a network of child-care facilities;

(d) To provide special protection to women during pregnancy in types of work proved to be harmful to them.

3. Protective legislation relating to matters covered in this article shall be reviewed periodically in the light of scientific and technological knowledge and shall be revised, repealed or extended as necessary.

The **African Charter on Human and Peoples' Rights,** open for acceptance by member States of the **Organization of African Unity,** contains the following provision:

*Article 15.* Every individual shall have the right to work under equitable and satisfactory conditions and shall receive equal pay for equal work.

Article 6 of the International Covenant on Economic, Social and Cultural Rights is unique in that its second paragraph, rather than providing that all States parties shall "ensure" or "guarantee" enjoyment of the right, instead prescribes a series of specific steps to be taken by them for this purpose. Paragraph 1 of the article is so worded as not to permit the introduction of forced labor by a State party, and paragraph 2 appears to cover both the right to be provided with work and the right not to be prevented from working.

*THE ILO.* Within the United Nations system, primary responsibility for the preparation and supervision of international measures relating to the right to work lies with the **International Labor Organization** (ILO). Its basic instruments in this endeavor are the ILO Discrimination (Employment and Occupation) Convention, adopted by the International Labor Conference in 1958, and the ILO Employment Convention, adopted by the Conference in 1964.

The ILO Convention concerning Discrimination in Respect of Employment and Occupation, also known as the Discrimination (Employment and Occupation) Convention (1958) (No. 111), provides that States parties undertake "to declare and pursue a national policy designed to promote, by methods appropriate to national conditions and practice, equality of opportunity and treatment in respect of employment and occupation, with a view to eliminating any discrimination in respect thereof." They further undertake "to seek the co-operation of employers' and workers' organizations and other appropriate bodies in promoting the acceptance and observance of this policy" and "to repeal any statutory provisions and to modify any administrative instructions or practices which are inconsistent with the policy." In respect of employment under the direct control of the national authority, States parties undertake to pursue the policy of equality of opportunity and treatment.

The ILO Convention concerning Employment Policy, also known as the Employment Policy Convention (1964) (No. 122) provides, in article 1, that:

1. With a view to stimulating economic growth and development, raising levels of living, meeting manpower requirements and overcoming unemployment and under-employment, each Member shall declare and pursue, as a major goal, an active policy designed to promote full, productive and freely chosen employment.

2. The said policy should aim at ensuring that:

(a) There is work for all who are available for and seeking work;

(b) Such work is as productive as possible;

(c) There is freedom of choice of employment and the fullest possible opportunity for each worker to qualify for, and to use his skills and endowments in, a job for which he is well suited, irrespective of race, color, sex, religion, political opinion, national extraction or social origin.

3. The said policy shall take due account of the stage and level of economic development and the mutual relationships between employment objectives and other economic and social objectives, and shall be pursued by methods that are appropriate to national conditions and practices.

Both Conventions are supervised by international machinery established by the International Labor Conference in 1926, consisting of two components: on the one hand, a committee of independent experts responsible for examining the reports received from governments on measures they have taken to give effect to such instruments, and, on the other hand, the establishment, at each session of the Conference, of a committee responsible for examining the question of the application of the Conventions. The government reports are required, annually, under article 22 of the ILO constitution.

In accordance with the procedures for the implementation of the International Covenant on Economic, Social and Cultural Rights, adopted by the **ECONOMIC AND SOCIAL COUNCIL** on 11 May 1976 (resolution 1988 [LX]), the ILO submits to the Council at regular intervals reports on the progress made in achieving the observance of the provisions of that document falling within the scope of its activities, as provided under article 18 of the Covenant.

Preparation of such reports is entrusted to the ILO Committee of Experts on the Application of Conventions and Recommendations. In the ninth such report, in 1987, the Committee of Experts noted that the Economic and Social Council had decided (resolution 1985/17) to set up a Committee on Economic, Social and Cultural Rights. Following the creation of the new committee, the Committee of Experts re-examined the manner in which the ILO could best submit its reports in accordance with article 18 of the Covenant. The ILO Committee recommended that the ILO should no longer seek to evaluate separately the extent to which the Covenant was implemented, but that it should inform the new committee of the results of the operation of the various ILO supervisory procedures in the fields covered by the Covenant. It would remain open to the Committee of Experts to report on particular situations whenever it deemed this desirable or when specifically requested to do so by the new committee. The ILO Governing Body, in May 1987, approved this recommendation.

The tenth report accordingly had been drawn up in accordance with the arrangements approved by the ILO Governing Body. In addition to information on the situation concerning articles 6 to 9 of the Covenant in a number of countries and the list of relevant ILO Conventions mentioned above, it included the following general considerations (E/1988/6, paras. 7–12):

In previous reports, the Committee of Experts has commented on several occasions on the relationship between the provisions of the Covenant and the standards laid down in international labour Conventions, the nature of the obligations resulting from them and the way in which the Committee of Experts consequently presented its comments on the implementation of the Covenant. Upon the completion of the first cycle of the reporting programme on the Covenant, the Committee of Experts, in its sixth report (E/1983/40), recalled these general observations which it hoped could be of use to the States Parties and would be of interest to the Economic and Social Council and its Sessional Working Group responsible for examining the implementation of the Covenant. It would therefore appear appropriate to recall briefly the main points of these observations.

The Committee of Experts noted that the provisions of Article 2, paragraph 1, of the Covenant, and the nature of a number of the rights recognized in the Covenant, rather than implying an immediate obligation to achieve a fixed standard, require continuing action for the mobilization of available resources in order to progressively implement and improve the exercise of these rights. This is the case, for example, with the right to work, the right to the enjoyment of just and favourable conditions of work and the right to social security, which the States Parties undertake to recognize in accordance with Articles 6, 7 and 9 respectively of the Covenant. However, in respect of trade union rights, the States Parties undertake in accordance with Article 8 of the Covenant, not only to recognize, but also to ensure the rights in question. The nature of obligations under Article 8 of the Covenant is therefore similar to those under corresponding ILO Conventions. The Committee of Experts also noted that the achievement of union rights is not dependent on the availability of resources, but should represent an important contribution not only to a basic freedom but also to the effective participation of the productive forces in society in the development process.

With regard to the subjects dealt with in the various Articles of the Covenant, those covered by Articles 6–9 are all within the competence of the ILO. In respect of Articles 10–12, only two questions dealt with in paragraphs 2 and 3 of Article 10 fall directly within the scope of the ILO, namely maternity protection and the protection of children and young persons in relation to employment and work. However, of the matters dealt with within the framework of the application of Articles 6–9 of the Covenant, those in the fields of training and employment, remuneration and social security, affect the right to an adequate standard of living, within the meaning of Article 11. Similarly, questions concerning occupational safety and health and the provision of health care within the framework of social security also affect the right to health within the meaning of Article 12. Articles 13–15 deal with questions which fall principally within the scope of organizations other than the ILO.

Article 23 of the Covenant includes among the methods of international action for the achievement of the rights recognized in the Pact, the conclusion of Conventions and the adoption of Recommendations. In this respect, ILO standards that are relevant to Articles 6–10 of the Covenant, even if they have not been ratified, may provide a useful source of reference and guidance in the fields under consideration.

Mention may be made in this connection of the general surveys of the Committee of Experts that are undertaken each year on the application of instruments selected by the Governing Body of the ILO as the subject of reports on unratified Conventions and Recommendations and under article 19 of the Constitution of the International Labour Organisation. These general surveys in recent years have dealt with questions directly linked to the rights provided for under Articles 6–10 of the Covenant: abolition of forced labour (1979), minimum age (1981), freedom of association and collective bargaining (1983), working time (1984), equal remuneration (1986), protection of the working environment (1987). In 1988, the general survey of the Committee of Experts will be on the Discrimination (Employment and Occupation) Convention (No. 111) and Recommendation (No. 111), 1958. In 1989, the survey will deal with social security standards concerning old-age benefits.

In addition to standard-setting activities, other ILO activities may be of interest in view of their relevance to questions having a general influence on the recognition and achievement of the human rights provided for in the Covenant. Reference may be made by way of illustration to the High-Level Meeting on Employment and Structural Adjustment (Geneva, 23–25 November 1987), attended by representatives of the principal international institutions concerned, which examined the consequences of international trade and financial and monetary practices on employment and poverty. These questions are closely related to issues of the current international economic situation in respect of which the Committee on Economic, Social and Cultural Rights has expressed its deep concern (Report on the First Session of the Committee, paragraph 302). Similarly, a number of the subjects discussed at the International Labour Conference or examined by the various bodies of the Governing Body of the ILO would be of interest within the framework of the international measures likely to contribute to the effective implementation of the Covenant referred to under its Articles 22 and 23.

*Principal ILO Conventions relevant to Articles 6–10 of the Covenant.* The following is a list, for each of articles 6–10 of the International Covenant on Economic, Social and Cultural Rights, of the principal relevant ILO Conventions.

**Article 6 of the Covenant.** Unemployment Convention, 1919 (No. 2); Forced Labour Convention, 1930 (No. 29); Fee-Charging Employment Agencies Convention, 1933 (No. 34); Employment Service Convention, 1948 (No. 88); Fee-Charging Employment Agencies Convention (Revised), 1949 (No. 96); Abolition of Forced Labour Convention, 1957 (No. 105); Discrimination (Employment and Occupation) Convention, 1958 (No. 111); Social Policy (Basic Aims and Standards) Convention, 1962 (No. 117); Employment Policy Convention, 1964 (No. 122); Paid Educational Leave Convention, 1974 (No. 140); Human Resources Development Convention, 1975 (No. 142); Workers with Family Responsibilities Convention, 1981 (No. 156); Termination of Employment Convention, 1982 (No. 158); Vocational Rehabilitation and Employment (Disabled Persons) Convention, 1983 (No. 159).

**Article 7 of the Covenant.** *Remuneration.* Minimum Wage-Fixing Machinery Convention, 1928 (No. 26); Minimum Wage-Fixing Machinery (Agriculture) Convention, 1951 (No. 99); Minimum Wage-Fixing Convention, 1970 (No. 131).

*Equal Remuneration.* Equal Remuneration Convention, 1951 (No. 100).

*Rest, Limitation of Working Hours and Holidays with Pay.* Hours of Work (Industry) Convention, 1919 (No. 1); Weekly Rest (Industry) Convention, 1921 (No. 14); Hours of Work (Commerce and Offices) Convention, 1930 (No. 30); Forty-Hour Week Convention, 1935 (No. 47); Holidays with Pay Convention, 1936 (No. 52); Holidays with Pay (Agriculture) Convention, 1952 (No. 101); Weekly Rest (Commerce and Offices) Convention, 1957 (No. 106); Holidays with Pay Convention (Revised), 1970 (No. 132).

*Safe and Healthy Working Conditions.* White Lead (Painting) Convention, 1921 (No. 13); Marking of Weight (Packages Transported by Vessels) Convention, 1929 (No. 27); Protection against Accidents (Dockers) Convention, 1929 (No. 28); Protection against Accidents (Dockers) Convention (Revised), 1932 (No. 32); Safety Provisions (Building) Convention, 1937 (No. 62); Labour Inspection Convention, 1947

(No. 81); Radiation Protection Convention, 1960 (No. 115); Guarding of Machinery Convention, 1963 (No. 119); Hygiene (Commerce and Offices) Convention, 1964 (No. 120); Maximum Weight Convention, 1967 (No. 127); Labour Inspection (Agriculture) Convention, 1969 (No. 129); Benzene Convention, 1971 (No. 136); Occupational Cancer Convention, 1974 (No. 139); Working Environment (Air Pollution, Noise and Vibration) Convention, 1977 (No. 148); Occupational Safety and Health (Dock Work) Convention, 1979 (No. 152); Occupational Safety and Health Convention, 1981 (No. 155); Occupational Health Services Convention, 1985 (No. 161); Asbestos Convention, 1986 (No. 162).

**Article 8 of the Covenant.** Right of Association (Agriculture) Convention, 1921 (No. 11); Freedom of Association and Protection of the Right to Organise Convention, 1948 (No. 87); Right to Organise and Collective Bargaining Convention, 1949 (No. 98); Workers' Representatives Convention, 1971 (No. 135); Rural Workers' Organisations Convention, 1975 (No. 141); Labour Relations (Public Service) Convention, 1978 (No. 151); Collective Bargaining Convention, 1981 (No. 154).

**Article 9 of the Covenant.** Workmen's Compensation (Agriculture) Convention, 1921 (No. 12); Workmen's Compensation (Accidents) Convention, 1925 (No. 17); Workmen's Compensation (Occupational Diseases) Convention, 1925 (No. 18); Equality of Treatment (Accident Compensation) Convention, 1925 (No. 19); Sickness Insurance (Industry) Convention, 1927 (No. 24); Sickness Insurance (Agriculture) Convention, 1927 (No. 25); Old-Age Insurance (Industry, etc.) Convention, 1933 (No. 35); Old-Age Insurance (Agriculture) Convention, 1933 (No. 36); Invalidity Insurance (Industry, etc.) Convention, 1933 (No. 37); Invalidity Insurance (Agriculture) Convention, 1933 (No. 38); Survivors' Insurance (Industry, etc.) Convention, 1933 (No. 39); Survivors' Insurance (Agriculture) Convention, 1933 (No. 40); Workmen's Compensation (Occupational Diseases) Convention (Revised), 1934 (No. 42); Unemployment Provisions Convention, 1934 (No. 44); Maintenance of Migrants' Pension Rights Convention, 1935 (No. 48); Social Security (Minimum Standards) Convention, 1952 (No. 102); Equality of Treatment (Social Security) Convention, 1962 (No. 118); Employment Injury Benefits Convention, 1964 (No. 121); Invalidity, Old-Age and Survivors' Benefits Convention, 1967 (No. 128); Medical Care and Sickness Benefits Convention, 1969 (No. 130); Maintenance of Social Security Rights Convention, 1982 (No. 157).

**Article 10 of the Covenant.** *Maternity Protection.* Maternity Protection Convention, 1919 (No. 3); Maternity Protection Convention (Revised), 1952 (No. 103).

*Protection of Children and Young Persons in Relation to Employment and Work.* Minimum Age (Industry) Convention, 1919 (No. 5); Minimum Age (Sea) Convention, 1920 (No. 7); Minimum Age (Agriculture) Convention, 1921 (No. 10); Minimum Age (Trimmers and Stokers) Convention, 1921 (No. 15); Minimum Age (Non-Industrial Employment) Convention, 1932 (No. 33); Minimum Age (Sea) Convention (Revised), 1936 (No. 58); Minimum Age (Industry) Convention (Revised), 1937 (No. 59); Minimum Age (Non-Industrial Employment) Convention (Revised), 1937 (No. 60); Minimum Age (Fishermen) Convention, 1959 (No. 112); Social Policy (Basic Aims and Standards) Convention, 1952 (No. 117); Minimum Age (Underground Work) Convention, 1965 (No. 123); Minimum Age Convention, 1973 (No. 138); Night Work of Young Persons (Industry) Convention, 1919 (No. 6); Night Work (Bakeries) Convention, 1925 (No. 20); Night Work of Young Persons (Non-Industrial Occupations) Convention, 1946 (No. 79); Night Work of Young Persons (Industry) Convention (Revised), 1948 (No. 90); White Lead (Painting) Convention, 1921 (No. 13) (Article 3); Radiation Protection Convention, 1960 (No. 115) (Article 7); Maximum Weight Convention, 1967 (No. 127) (Article 7); Benzene Convention, 1971 (No. 136) (Article 11); Medical Examination of Young Persons (Sea) Convention, 1921 (No. 16); Medical Examination (Seafarers) Convention, 1946 (No. 73); Medical Examination of Young Persons (Industry) Convention, 1946 (No. 77); Medical Examination of Young Persons (Non-Industrial Occupations) Convention, 1946 (No. 78); Medical Examination (Fishermen) Convention, 1959 (No. 113); Medical Examination of Young Persons (Underground Work) Convention, 1965 (No. 124).

**ANTI-DISCRIMINATION AGENCIES.** Established by national or local governments with a view to eliminating discrimination in employment based on any ground such as race, sex, language, or religion, the role and functions of such agencies are described in the Secretary-General's report entitled *National Institutions for the Protection and Promotion of Human Rights* (UN Doc. E/CN.4/1987/37), prepared at the request of the **GENERAL ASSEMBLY** (resolution 40/123), in the following terms (paras. 91–98):

The importance of fair labour practices and the availability of adequate redress for discrimination in the area of employment has been generally recognized throughout the world as an essential part of any comprehensive human rights protection programme. While Governments frequently include Ministers of Labour in their cabinets to deal with the many issues and problems which characterize the area of employment, an ever-increasing number of States consider that resources of a local and specialized nature are required to address the needs and demands of workers adequately. For instance, labour courts and tribunals, which conciliate, mediate and adjudicate disputes arising under labour agreements, or between workers' unions and employers, have been established in many countries.

States have also created administrative commissions or agencies, responsible for addressing specific problems in the labour market that may infringe on the rights of some groups and individuals in the community to equal work for fair and equal compensation and adequate working conditions. These commissions frequently operate under the Ministry of Labour. For example, to assist in eradicating unemployment, the Government of Zimbabwe created the Department of Employment and Employment Promotion, which functions under the Ministry of Labour and Social Services. The primary purpose of this body is to match persons seeking work with existing employment vacancies as quickly as possible, and to work closely with other governmental bodies in an attempt to create productive employment opportunities.

Many of the organizations created by States are established to deal primarily with sexual and racial discrimination in employment. The powers and duties of these commissions and agencies differ from country to country. Sometimes, they exist solely on the national level, but they are often organized on both the national and local level. For instance, in Australia National and Local Employment Discrimination Committees were established in 1973 to deal with cases of discrimination covered by the International Labour Organisation (ILO) Discrimination (Employment and Occupation) Convention (No. 111), 1958. Basically, the Australian Employment Discrimination Committees consider questions concerning possible discrimination in the remuneration of employees. The National Committee's primary functions are to:

". . . consider allegations of discrimination referred by the State (Local) Committees; consider allegations which involve the Federal Government as an employer and those which are of national significance; to advise the Federal Government on relevant matters of policy; and to develop and promote a community education programme."

The six State (Local) Committees investigate charges of discrimination against employers, and attempt to arrive at amicable settlements through conciliation. The membership of Australia's Employment Discrimination Committees is comprised of representatives of Government, national employers' organizations and the trade-union movement, as well as individuals with special expertise in the problems of employment regarding Aboriginals, migrants and women.

With some modifications, similar powers and duties characterize the United States Equal Employment Opportunity Commission (EEOC). Established by the Civil Rights Act of 1964, EEOC was created to hear and investigate claims of discrimination in employment practices and procedures. When EEOC receives a complaint, it transfers that complaint to the competent State or local agency, which is required to act on the complaint within 60 days. If no such action takes place, EEOC then takes up the claim, investigates the complaint and attempts to arrive at an amicable settlement. If no settlement can be reached, EEOC is empowered to seize the United States District Court (federal court) for adjudication of the matter. This seizure of the court by EEOC does not preclude the victim in the case from initiating his own judicial action as well. Decisions or rulings by the court constitute legally binding precedents, which affect employment policy throughout the nation. Finally, State and local agencies of EEOC which investigate claims of discrimination in employment, are also empowered to investigate charges of unequal access to public facilities and housing as a result of discrimination.

Some equal employment agencies function as "watchdogs" to ensure that particular pieces of legislation concerning employment and labour are fully complied with. As an example of such an agency, mention may be made of the Vigilance Committees in India. These Committees were created under the Bonded Labour Systems Abolition Act of 1976. Vigilance Committees are comprised of officials, representatives of the locality, social workers and financial and credit institutions. Their basic functions are to advise the district authorities on the implementation of the Act forbidding the practice of bonded labour, to monitor offences under the Act, and to make recommendations on whether action should be taken regarding these offences. The Committee also defends suits instituted against bonded debts.

Often equal employment commissions and agencies also perform advisory services. As previously stated, the Australian National Employment Discrimination Committee advises the Federal Government on employment and labour policy. Similarly, the Tripartite Advisory Committees in India, comprised of government, employer and employee representatives, were established to advise the Government on the formulation of labour policy and to ensure the implementation of labour laws. The French Supreme Council for Professional Equality Between Men and Women, established in 1983 is also an advisory body. The Supreme Council is consulted by the Government on bills and draft decrees designed to ensure professional equality between men and women, as well as on texts dealing with the particular working conditions of the different sexes. The Council may also make proposals designed to improve professional equality between the sexes.

Equal employment agencies are also required, in most cases, to include activities aimed at promoting equality in the employment area as part of their basic functions. For example, both the Danish Equality Council and the Portuguese Commission on Women's Conditions are charged with promoting equality between the sexes in employment and vocational training. The United States EEOC proposes affirmative action hiring plans to employers and industries for voluntary undertaking. Once employers accept such plans, they become binding. In many countries, however, the promotion of equality in employment is the responsibility of human rights and civil rights commissions.

The role of equal employment commissions in safeguarding the workplace from discrimination is clearly an important factor in protecting the human and civil rights of the individual. Although it is often the responsibility of human rights commissions to address issues concerning discrimination in employment, the existence of widespread discrimination in the field of labour relations seems to corroborate the idea that separate agencies, designed to deal solely with employment and labour issues are needed to protect the individual's right to work in an environment free from discrimination. Moreover, agencies comprised of employers and workers play an important role in advising Governments on the needs of the working community. Discrimination in employment is one of the most pernicious violations of human rights, since it undercuts the very livelihood of the individual and frequently triggers a chain reaction of financial and social circumstances which often expose the individual to further exploitation. Therefore, agencies which can address the problem of discrimination in the workplace exclusively, provide an essential service in the protection of human rights.

**SEE ALSO** *Children's Rights; Debt Bondage; Forced Labor; Migrant Workers (all entries); Social Security; Unemployment.*

**BIBLIOGRAPHY.** American Federation of Labour-Congress of Industrial Organizations, International Affairs Department. *Worker Rights and the Generalized System of Preferences: The AFL-CIO Petition to the Office of the U.S. Trade Representative.* Washington, D.C.: AFL-CIO, 1990. Report, in English.

Asia Watch. *Chinese Workers Receive Harsh Sentences: ILO Reports on 91 Cases.* New York: Human Rights Watch, 1991. NGO report, in English.

————. *Retreat from Reform: Labor Rights and Freedom of Expression in South Korea.* New York: Human Rights Watch, 1990. NGO factfinding report, in English.

Barr, Michael S., Robert Honeywell, and Scott A. Stofel. "Labor and Environmental Rights in the Proposed Mexico-United States Free Trade Agreement," *Houston Journal of International Law* 14, no. 1 (Fall 1991): 1–84. Scholarly article, in English.

Ewing, Keith. "Citizenship and Employment," in *Rights of Citizenship*, ed. Robert Blackburn, pp. 99–123. London: Mansell, 1993. Scholarly article, in English.

Hong Kong Trade Union Education Centre. *A Moment of Truth: Workers' Participation in China's 1989 Democracy Move-ment and the Emergence of Independent Unions.* Hong Kong: Asia Monitor Resource Center, 1991. Monograph, in English.

International Labour Office. *International Labour Standards: A Workers' Education Manual.* Geneva, Switzerland: 1990. Educational material, in English.

Mullick, Pranab. "Right to Work as a Fundamental Right," *The Lawyers* 5, no. 8 (Aug. 1990): 15–20. Article, in English.

Tomuschat, Christian. "The Right to Work," in *Human Rights in a Changing East-West Perspective*, eds. A. Rosas, J. Helgesen, and D. Gomien, pp. 174–201. London: Pinter Publishers, 1991. Scholarly article, in English; bibliography, pp. 199–201.

## WORLD ALLIANCE OF REFORMED CHURCHES.

An international non-governmental organization in consultative status (Roster) with the UN ECONOMIC AND SOCIAL COUNCIL, WARC has 166 affiliated member churches in 92 countries.

The current World Alliance of Reformed Churches emerged in 1970 from the merger of the World Presbyterian Alliance and International Congregational Council. WARC seeks to foster an ecumenical movement among Christian churches and to further the work of evangelism, mission, and stewardship. It is also committed to helping member churches which are weak or persecuted and to promoting and defending religious and civil liberties wherever they are threatened. WARC has undertaken the causes of individual member churches in Korea, Taiwan, South Africa, and Romania, among others. In 1976, it issued a booklet, "Theological Basis of Human Rights," which concluded that Christian churches, congregations, and ecumenical organizations should represent the unassailable dignity of human beings and the unity of their human rights and duties and should press for the restoration of particular rights which have become neglected, weakened, or repressed.

WARC publishes the quarterly journal *Reformed World* in English and the quarterly newsletter *Update* in English, French, German, and Spanish.

World Alliance of Reformed Churches. Address: 150 route de Ferney, 1211 Geneva 20, Switzerland. Telephone: (41-22) 791-6237. Fax: (41-22) 791-6505. Secretary-General: Dr. Milan Opocensky.

## WORLD ASSOCIATION FOR THE SCHOOL AS AN INSTRUMENT OF PEACE.

An international non-governmental organization in consultative status with the UN ECONOMIC AND SOCIAL COUNCIL (Roster), UNESCO, the ILO, and the COUNCIL OF EUROPE, the Association includes national sections in 19 countries and organizations, individuals, and schools in more than 70 countries.

Founded in Geneva in 1967, the World Association promotes universal principles of civic education and endeavors to unite mankind through the teaching of human rights and peace to children in school. It also works to open the door to mutual understanding for children throughout the world, to teach respect for life and for man, and to help children to understand that progress requires the active collaboration of all. The Association publishes the quarterly *Ecole et paix* as well as a simplified version of the **UNIVERSAL DECLARATION OF HUMAN RIGHTS** in English, French, Hindi, Spanish, Thai, and Urdu.

World Association for the School as an Instrument of Peace. Address: Rue du Simplon 5-7, CH-1207 Geneva, Switzerland. Telephone: (41-22) 735-2422. Fax: (41-22) 736-4863.

## WORLD ASSOCIATION OF GIRL GUIDES AND GIRL SCOUTS.

This non-governmental organization was founded in Budapest, Hungary, in 1928. It has consultative status with the UN **ECONOMIC AND SOCIAL COUNCIL** (Category II), **UNESCO, FAO, ILO, WHO, UNICEF,** and the **COUNCIL OF EUROPE.** It has full members in 88 countries, with a total membership of approximately 8 million individuals.

The Association promotes unity of purpose and common understanding based on the fundamental principles of the Girl Guide/Girl Scout movement and encourages friendship among girls and young women of all nations. It stresses self-training and the development of character, responsible citizenship, and service in one's own and the world community. The organization conducts training sessions and gatherings at its World Centers in the United Kingdom, Switzerland, Mexico, and India. It also operates a "Mutual Aid Scheme," coordinated by the World Bureau, whereby national organizations financially assist one another.

Among the Association's many publications are the bi-monthly *Our World News* in English, French, and Spanish and the monograph *Girl Guiding/Girl Scouting: A Challenging Movement* in English, French, and Spanish.

World Association of Girl Guides and Girl Scouts. Address: World Bureau, Olave Centre, 12c Lyndhurst Road, London N3 5PQ, UK. Telephone: (44-71) 794-1181. Fax: (44-71) 431-3761. Director: Jan Holt.

## WORLD ASSOCIATION OF WORLD FEDERALISTS.

An international non-governmental organization in consultative status with the UN **ECONOMIC AND SOCIAL COUNCIL** (Category II) and with **UNESCO,** the Association brings together 40 national and associated organizations, with a total membership of more than 25,000.

Founded in Luxembourg in 1946, WAWF coordinates policies and activities directed toward the creation of a world federation having a defined sphere of jurisdiction, functioning through a legislature to make world law, a judiciary to interpret that law, and an executive with adequate powers to enforce it upon individuals, associations, and states. In this connection, it studies the possibilities for revision of the **UNITED NATIONS CHARTER** that would give the UN limited powers to prevent war and to increase the well being of people everywhere, without interfering with internal sovereignties of member States. It assists in the establishment of new national organizations to achieve these purposes, organizes conferences on peace action, and promotes the exchange of relevant political and educational information.

WAWF publishes two quarterlies, *Transnational Perspectives* and *World Federalist News,* and issues special reports from time to time.

World Association of World Federalists. Address: Leliegracht 21, 1016 GR Amsterdam, the Netherlands. Telephone: (31-20) 227502. Executive Director: Ron J. Rutherglen.

## WORLD CONFEDERATION OF LABOR.

An international non-governmental organization in consultative status with the UN **ECONOMIC AND SOCIAL COUNCIL** (Category I) and with **ILO, UNESCO,** and **FAO,** WCL's membership includes national organizations and professional federations in 97 countries and territories, representing a total individual membership of about 15 million workers.

Founded at the Hague in 1920 as the International Federation of Christian Trade Unions, the organization changed its name to World Confederation of Labor in 1968 and revised its organizational structure in 1969 to reflect the increasing role of third world workers' organizations. WCL's current principal functions are to promote human and trade union rights, to ensure the exercise of those rights by all workers, to give moral and material support to its affiliated organizations, and to promote the exchange of information between them. In a larger sense, it works for peace, disarmament, and the solidarity of workers and peoples.

WCL publishes the fortnightly bulletin *Flash,* the bi-monthly review *Labor,* and the bi-annual journal *Events,* in Dutch, English, French, German, and Spanish.

World Confederation of Labor. Address: Rue de Trèves 33, B-1040 Brussels, Belgium. Telephone: (32-2) 230-62-95. Fax: (32-2) 230-87-22. Secretary-General: Carlos Luis Custer.

## WORLD CONFEDERATION OF ORGANIZATIONS OF THE TEACHING PROFESSION.

An international non-governmental organization in consultative status with the UN ECONOMIC AND SOCIAL COUNCIL (Category II), and with ILO, UNESCO, UNICEF, the ORGANIZATION OF AMERICAN STATES and the COUNCIL OF EUROPE, the Confederation includes members in 120 countries and territories, with a total membership of approximately 13.5 million individuals.

The Confederation was founded in 1952 by a merger of three major international federations: the World Organization of the Teaching Profession (WOTP), the International Federation of Teachers' Associations (IFTA), and the International Federation of Secondary Teachers (known by its French acronym FIPESO). IFTA and FIPESO remain in being as constituent federations of WCOTP.

The World Confederation exerts independent political influence on behalf of teachers and works for equality of opportunity through education and for improvement of the quality of education. It asserts and defends the individual and collective rights of teachers and strives for the advancement of their status and the improvement of their working conditions. It maintains that the professional and trade union interests of teachers are inseparable and has worked in the preparation and promotion of the ILO/UNESCO Recommendation concerning the Status of Teachers.

WCOTP publishes *echo,* a quarterly newsletter (in English, French, Spanish, Chinese, German, and Japanese); a biennial report on activities and programs (in English, French, and Spanish); a handbook; reports of conferences, seminars, studies, and investigations; and service publications on various aspects of education, trade union operations, welfare services, and international affairs.

World Confederation of Organizations of the Teaching Profession. Address: 5 avenue du Moulin, CH-1110 Morges, Switzerland. Telephone: (41-21) 801-7467. Fax: (41-21) 801-7469. Secretary-General: Robert Harris.

## WORLD CONFERENCE ON RELIGION AND PEACE INTERNATIONAL.

An international non-governmental organization in consultative status with the UN ECONOMIC AND SOCIAL COUNCIL (Category II) and with UNESCO and UNICEF, the World Conference has regional offices in eight countries and individual members in 73 countries.

In 1968, the World Conference on Religion and Peace International was founded to promote common actions for peace and justice by believers of all traditional world religions. The first World Conference on Religion and Peace was convened in Kyoto on the initiative of American and Japanese religious leaders. World assemblies have since been held in Louvain, Belgium (1974), Princeton, New Jersey, USA (1979), and Nairobi, Kenya (1984).

WCRP's main function is to promote interreligious cooperation and understanding. It works for the establishment of world peace and the realization by everyone of human rights and fundamental freedoms and consistently champions the rights of members of religious and ethnic minorities. In addition, it conducts humanitarian projects on an interreligious basis.

The Conference publishes the proceedings of its conferences and the quarterly newsletter *Religion for Peace.*

World Conference on Religion and Peace International. Address: 777 UN Plaza, New York, NY 10017, USA. Telephone: (212) 687-2163. Fax: (212) 983-0566. Secretary-General: William Vendley.

## WORLD COUNCIL OF INDIGENOUS PEOPLES.

An international non-governmental organization in consultative status with the UN ECONOMIC AND SOCIAL COUNCIL (Category II) and with UNESCO and the ILO, the Council was founded in 1975 at the International Conference of Indian Peoples held in Port Alberni, Canada, a conference which brought together 52 delegates from indigenous organizations in 19 countries; it has since grown to include individuals and organizations in 29 countries.

Under the WCIP charter, the Council's main functions are to protect the rights, further the interests, and ensure unity of indigenous peoples in accordance with their own cultures; to contribute in all ways to abolish the possibility of physical and cultural genocide and ethnocide; to participate in combating racism; to ensure political, economic, and social justice to indigenous peoples; and to promote and support the principle of equality among indigenous peoples and the people of nations who may surround them. It supports and finances indigenous organizations and encourages them to work together to achieve common goals.

The Council issues the WCIP *Newsletter* from time to time.

World Council of Indigenous Peoples. Address: 555 King Edward Avenue, K1N 6N5 Ottawa, Canada. Telephone: (613) 230-9030. Fax: (613) 230-9340. President: Clem Chartier.

## WORLD FEDERATION FOR MENTAL HEALTH.

An international non-governmental organization in consultative status with the UN ECONOMIC AND SOCIAL COUNCIL (Category II) and with UNESCO, ILO, UNICEF, and WHO, the Federation has approximately 135 member associations (national and international organizations working to enhance and maintain mental health resources) and approximately 100 national affiliates (organizations supporting WFMH's goals but not directly involved in its work).

The Federation was founded in London in 1948, during the Third International Congress on Mental Health, as the successor to the *Comite international d'hygiene mentale,* which had been established in 1931. It endeavors to promote among peoples and nations everywhere the highest possible standard of mental health, as defined in the broadest biological, medical, educational, social, and cultural terms. It collaborates with the United Nations and other international agencies to improve mental health services in their member States. Through international, regional, and national projects, WFMH works to overcome the stigma attached to mental illness, to increase the number and effectiveness of trained mental health workers, to protect the rights of patients suffering from mental ill-health, and to stimulate the creation of national and regional mental health associations. It also serves as an international clearinghouse for information on mental health issues.

WFMH publishes the *WFMH Newsletter* five times a year and issues the proceedings of its World Conferences on Mental Health (held every two years). In addition, it produces monographs on particular aspects of its work.

World Federation for Mental Health. Address: 1021 Prince Street, Alexandria, VA 22314-2971, USA. Telephone: (703) 684-7722. Fax: (703) 684-5968. Secretary-General: Eugene B. Brody.

## WORLD FEDERATION OF DEMOCRATIC YOUTH.

An international non-governmental organization in consultative status with the UN Economic and Social Council (Category I) and with ILO, UNESCO, and FAO, WFDY has more than 270 affiliated and observer organizations in 110 countries and territories.

The World Federation of Democratic Youth was founded in London in 1945. It works to promote the active participation of youth in economic, social, cultural, and political life by acting against all restriction and discrimination connected with age, sex, methods of education, domicile, property, social status, religion, political convictions, color, and race. The Federation supports the struggle of world youth for higher living standards; better conditions of education, work, and leisure; and the development of cultural, educational, and sports activities for young people to ensure optimal human development. To accomplish these goals, WFDY conducts seminars and establishes voluntary work camps. It also has established a voluntary international aid fund.

The Federation publishes *WFDY News* and *World Youth* monthly in English, French, and Spanish.

World Federation of Democratic Youth. Address: P.O. Box 147, H-1389 Budapest, Hungary. Telephone: (36-1) 129-5226. Fax: (36-1) 129-5226. Secretary-General: Andjle Yawa.

## WORLD FEDERATION OF METHODIST WOMEN.

An international non-governmental organization in consultative status (Category II) with the UN Economic and Social Council and UNICEF, WFMW has national units in 86 countries.

Founded in 1939 in Pasadena, California (USA), the Federation works to build a Christian community through evangelism, ministries, education, and social services. Its work is carried out in eight main areas: social justice; health; family life; the changing role of women; instability in the home; child abuse; drug and alcohol abuse; and cross-cultural programs. WFMW conducts local and regional seminars for leadership training and Bible study and holds a quinquennial assembly.

The Federation publishes the quarterly *Tree of Life* and the *WFMW Newsletter,* as well as the *WFMW Handbook* and *Methodist Women: A World Sisterhood.*

World Federation of Methodist Women. Address: Inglenook, Royal Terrace Lane, Dun Laoghaire (County Dublin), Ireland. President: Edith M. Loane.

## WORLD FEDERATION OF TRADE UNIONS.

An international non-governmental organization in consultative status with the UN Economic and Social Council (Category I) and with ILO, UNESCO, UNICEF, UNIDO, UNCTAD, and FAO, WFTU has members in 85 countries, with approximately 175 million individual members.

Established in 1945 as an international trade union organization affiliating national trade union centers, the World Federation of Trade Unions has as one of its aims, as stated in its constitution, "the achievement of economic and political democracy, the development of workers' rights and freedoms, respect for human rights and the implementation of the Universal Declaration of Trade Union Rights." Its principle concern is to coordinate the activities of affiliated national centers in promoting international solidarity in defense of trade union rights and human rights and to organize support for these struggles in various countries.

Among WFTU's regular publications are the biweekly *Flashes* (in English, French, Russian, and Spanish) and the monthly *World Trade Union Movement* (in English, French, Russian, and Spanish).

World Federation of Trade Unions. Address: Branická 112, Branik, CS-14999 Prague 4, Czech Republic. Telephone: (42-2) 46-2140. Fax: (42-2) 46-1378. Secretary-General: Alexander Zharikov.

**WORLD FEDERATION OF UNITED NATIONS AS-SOCIATIONS.** An international non-governmental organization in consultative status with the UN **ECO-NOMIC AND SOCIAL COUNCIL** (Category I) and with **ILO, UNESCO,** UNCTAD, **UNICEF, WHO,** and **FAO,** the Federation has 76 national affiliates.

WFUNA was founded in 1946, in Luxembourg, to mobilize support for the purposes and principles set out in the **UNITED NATIONS CHARTER** and to stimulate public awareness and understanding of the activities of the United Nations and its agencies. It conducts worldwide educational programs, projects, conferences, and seminars and uses all media of information to disseminate knowledge of the United Nations. It issues periodic reports on its projects and the quarterly *WFUNA Bulletin*.

World Federation of United Nations Associations. Address: Palais des Nations, CH-1211 Geneva 10, Switzerland. Telephone: (41-22) 733-0730. Fax: (41-22) 733-4838. Secretary-General: Marek Hagmajer.

**WORLD FOOD COUNCIL.** The Council, established by the UN **GENERAL ASSEMBLY** on 17 December 1974 (resolution 3348 [XXIX]), was set up "at the ministerial or plenipotentiary level to function as an organ of the United Nations." Its mandate, as had been proposed to the Assembly by the World Food Conference on 16 November 1974 (resolution XXII), includes the following tasks:

(c) The Council should review periodically major problems and policy issues affecting the world food situation, and the steps being proposed or taken to resolve them by Governments, by the United Nations system and by its regional organizations, and should further recommend remedial action as appropriate. The scope of the Council's review should extend to all aspects of world food problems in order to adopt an integrated approach towards their solution;

(d) The Council should establish its own programme of action for co-ordination of relevant United Nations bodies and agencies. While doing so, it should give special attention to the problems of the least developed countries and the countries most seriously affected;

(e) The Council should maintain contacts with, receive reports from, give advice to, and make recommendations to United Nations bodies and agencies with regard to the formulation and follow-up of world food policies;

(f) The Council should work in full co-operation with regional bodies to formulate and follow up policies approved by the Council. Committees to be established by these regional bodies should be serviced by existing United Nations or FAO bodies in the region concerned.

The Council consists of 36 members nominated by the **ECONOMIC AND SOCIAL COUNCIL** and elected by the General Assembly "taking into consideration balanced geographical distribution, with one-third of the members retiring every year and the retiring members being eligible for re-election." The members of the Council are elected according to the following pattern: nine members from African States, eight members from Asian States, seven members from Latin American States, four members from socialist States of eastern Europe, and eight members from western European and other States. The term of office is three years.

The Council normally meets in ministerial sessions once a year; special sessions are held when the need arises. Sessions are usually held in Rome, but the Council has also met in other places, including the Philippines, Mexico, and Canada. The Council reports to the General Assembly through the Economic and Social Council.

**WORLD HEALTH ORGANIZATION (WHO).** By its constitution of 1946, the World Health Organization was established as an autonomous permanent intergovernmental organization dedicated to the premise that the enjoyment of the highest attainable standard of health is one of the fundamental rights of every human being without distinction as to race, religion, political belief, or economic or social condition. Over the years, WHO has specialized in carrying out worldwide campaigns to combat communicable diseases. In developing countries, in particular, it has wiped out smallpox, checked the spread of cholera, and immunized millions of children against the diseases of childhood: diphtheria, tetanus, whooping cough, poliomyelitis, measles, and tuberculosis. It has also developed, through biomedical research, efficient techniques to combat tropical diseases such as malaria, schistosomiasis, filariasis, trypanosomiasis, leprosy, and leishmaniasis. Its international health regulations provide for epidemiological disease surveillance on a worldwide scale, promote the development of national surveillance services, and improve cooperation among countries in this field. WHO also carries out an extensive technical assistance program covering many aspects of public health, in which the teaching and training of health personnel are emphasized.

A total of 189 States are members of the World Health Organization. WHO's main organs are the World Health Assembly, composed of representatives of each member State; the executive board, consisting of 30 persons technically qualified in the field of health who are elected by the Assembly on the basis of nominations by member States; and the Secretariat, headed by the director-general, who is appointed by the Assembly on the nomination of the executive board.

The World Health Assembly meets annually for a period of about two weeks, usually at ILO headquarters in Geneva, during the month of May. The executive board meets twice a year, one session of about three weeks' duration in January and a second of about two days' duration in May, also at WHO headquarters in Geneva.

Many of the activities of WHO have been decentralized to six regional organizations, each maintaining a regional office and a regional committee composed of States within the region. These offices are in New Delhi, for southeast Asia; Alexandria, for the eastern Mediterranean; Manila, for the western Pacific; Washington, D.C., for the Americas (Pan American Sanitary Bureau); Brazzaville, for Africa; and Copenhagen, for Europe. The International Agency for Cancer Research, located in Lyon, France, is an autonomous body within the framework of WHO.

Under the terms of its agreement with the United Nations, the World Health Organization transmits reports to UN organs on its activities and complies with requests from those organs for special reports, studies, or information. For example, WHO was represented on the Working Group on Traditional Practices affecting the Health of Women and Children, which prepared a comprehensive report on this subject at the request of the UN ECONOMIC AND SOCIAL COUNCIL.

*CONSTITUTION.* The constitution of WHO was adopted on 22 July 1946 by the World Health Conference, convened in New York by the United Nations, and entered into force on 7 April 1948.

The objective of WHO, a specialized agency of the United Nations, as stated in the constitution (article 1), is "the attainment by all peoples of the highest possible level of health." WHO is authorized to take all necessary action to attain that objective. The long list of its functions, set out in article 2 of the constitution, is supplemented from time to time by new mandates added by the UN GENERAL ASSEMBLY.The text of the constitution (United Nations, *Treaty Series,* vol. 14, p. 185), as amended by the 20th, 26th, and 29th World Health Assemblies, is as follows:

The States parties to this Constitution declare, in conformity with the Charter of the United Nations, that the following principles are basic to the happiness, harmonious relations and security of all peoples:

Health is a state of complete physical, mental and social well-being and not merely the absence of disease or infirmity.

The enjoyment of the highest attainable standard of health is one of the fundamental rights of every human being without distinction of race, religion, political belief, economic or social condition.

The health of all peoples is fundamental to the attainment of peace and security and is dependent upon the fullest co-operation of individuals and States.

The achievement of any State in the promotion and protection of health is of value to all.

Unequal development in different countries in the promotion of health and control of disease, especially communicable disease, is a common danger.

Healthy development of the child is of basic importance; the ability to live harmoniously in a changing total environment is essential to such development.

The extension to all peoples of the benefits of medical, psychological and related knowledge is essential to the fullest attainment of health.

Informed opinion and active co-operation on the part of the public are of the utmost importance in the improvement of the health of the people.

Governments have a responsibility for the health of their peoples which can be fulfilled only by the provision of adequate health and social measures.

Accepting these principles, and for the purpose of co-operation among themselves and with others to promote and protect the health of all peoples, the Contracting Parties agree to the present Constitution and hereby establish the World Health Organization as a specialized agency within the terms of Article 57 of the Charter of the United Nations.

### Chapter I: Objective

*Article 1.* The objective of the World Health Organization (hereinafter called the Organization) shall be the attainment by all peoples of the highest possible level of health.

### Chapter II: Functions

*Article 2.* In order to achieve its objective, the functions of the Organization shall be:

(a) to act as the directing and co-ordinating authority on international health work;

(b) to establish and maintain effective collaboration with the United Nations, specialized agencies, governmental health administrations, professional groups and such other organizations as may be deemed appropriate;

(c) to assist Governments, upon request, in strengthening health services;

(d) to furnish appropriate technical assistance and, in emergencies, necessary aid upon the request or acceptance of Governments;

(e) to provide or assist in providing, upon the request of the United Nations, health services and facilities to special groups, such as the peoples of trust territories;

(f) to establish and maintain such administrative and technical services as may be required, including epidemiological and statistical services;

(g) to stimulate and advance work to eradicate epidemic, endemic and other diseases;

(h) to promote, in co-operation with other specialized agencies where necessary, the prevention of accidental injuries;

(i) to promote, in co-operation with other specialized agencies where necessary, the improvement of nutrition, housing, sanitation, recreation, economic or working conditions and other aspects of environmental hygiene;

(j) to promote co-operation among scientific and professional groups which contribute to the advancement of health;

(k) to propose Conventions, agreements and regulations, and make recommendations with respect to international health matters and to perform such duties as may be assigned thereby to the Organization and are consistent with its objective;

(l) to promote maternal and child health and welfare and to foster the ability to live harmoniously in a changing total environment;

(m) to foster activities in the field of mental health, especially those affecting the harmony of human relations;

(n) to promote and conduct research in the field of health;

(o) to promote improved standards of teaching and training in the health, medical and related professions;

(p) to study and report on, in co-operation with other specialized agencies where necessary, administrative and social techniques affecting public health and medical care from preventive and curative points of view, including hospital services and social security;

(q) to provide information, counsel and assistance in the field of health;

(r) to assist in developing an informed public opinion among all peoples on matters of health;

(s) to establish and revise as necessary international nomenclatures of diseases, of causes of death and of public health practices;

(t) to standardize diagnostic procedures as necessary;

(u) to develop, establish and promote international standards with respect to food, biological, pharmaceutical and similar products;

(v) generally to take all necessary action to attain the objective of the Organization.

### Chapter III: Membership and Associate Membership

*Article 3.* Membership in the Organization shall be open to all States.

*Article 4.* Members of the United Nations may become Members of the Organization by signing or otherwise accepting this Constitution in accordance with the provisions of Chapter XIX and in accordance with their constitutional processes.

*Article 5.* The States whose Governments have been invited to send observers to the International Health Conference held in New York, 1946, may become Members by signing or otherwise accepting this Constitution in accordance with the provisions of Chapter XIX and in accordance with their constitutional processes provided that such signature or acceptance shall be completed before the first session of the Health Assembly.

*Article 6.* Subject to the conditions of any agreement between the United Nations and the Organization, approved pursuant to Chapter XVI, States which do not become Members in accordance with Articles 4 and 5 may apply to become Members and shall be admitted as Members when their application has been approved by a simple majority vote of the Health Assembly.

*Article 7.* If a Member fails to meet its financial obligations to the Organization or in other exceptional circumstances, the Health Assembly may, on such conditions as it thinks proper, suspend the voting privileges and services to which a Member is entitled. The Health Assembly shall have the authority to restore such voting privileges and services.

*Article 8.* Territories or groups of territories which are not responsible for the conduct of their international relations may be admitted as Associate Members by the Health Assembly upon application made on behalf of such territory or group of territories by the Member or other authority having responsibility for their international relations. Representatives of Associate Members to the Health Assembly should be qualified by their technical competence in the field of health and should be chosen from the native population. The nature and extent of the rights and obligations of Associate Members shall be determined by the Health Assembly.

### Chapter IV: Organs

*Article 9.* The work of the Organization shall be carried out by:

(a) The World Health Assembly (herein called the Health Assembly);

(b) The Executive Board (hereinafter called the Board);

(c) The Secretariat.

### Chapter V: The World Health Assembly

*Article 10.* The Health Assembly shall be composed of delegates representing Members.

*Article 11.* Each Member shall be represented by not more than three delegates, one of whom shall be designated by the Member as chief delegate. These delegates should be chosen from among persons most qualified by their technical competence in the field of health, preferably representing the national health administration of the Member.

*Article 12.* Alternates and advisers may accompany delegates.

*Article 13.* The Health Assembly shall meet in regular annual session and in such special sessions as may be necessary. Special sessions shall be convened at the request of the Board or of a majority of the Members.

*Article 14.* The Health Assembly, at each annual session, shall select the country or region in which the next annual session shall be held, the Board subsequently fixing the place. The Board shall determine the place where a special session shall be held.

*Article 15.* The Board, after consultation with the Secretary-General of the United Nations, shall determine the date of each annual and special session.

*Article 16.* The Health Assembly shall elect its President and other officers at the beginning of each annual session. They shall hold office until their successors are elected.

*Article 17.* The Health Assembly shall adopt its own rules of procedure.

*Article 18.* The functions of the Health Assembly shall be:

(a) to determine the policies of the Organization;

(b) to name the Members entitled to designate a person to serve on the Board;

(c) to appoint the Director-General;

(d) to review and approve reports and activities of the Board and of the Director-General and to instruct the Board in regard to matters upon which action, study, investigation or report may be considered desirable;

(e) to establish such committees as may be considered necessary for the work of the Organization;

(f) to supervise the financial policies of the Organization and to review and approve the budget;

(g) to instruct the Board and the Director-General to bring to the attention of Members and of international organizations, governmental or non-governmental, any matter with regard to health which the Health Assembly may consider appropriate;

(h) to invite any organization, international or national, governmental or non-governmental, which has responsibilities related to those of the Organization, to appoint representatives to participate, without right of vote, in its meetings or in those of the committees and conferences convened under its authority, on conditions prescribed by the Health Assembly; but in the case of national organizations, invitations shall be issued only with the consent of the Government concerned;

(i) to consider recommendations bearing on health made by the General Assembly, the Economic and Social Council, the Security Council or Trusteeship Council of the United Nations, and to report to them on the steps taken by the Organization to give effect to such recommendations;

(j) to report to the Economic and Social Council in accordance with any agreement between the Organization and the United Nations;

(k) to promote and conduct research in the field of health by the personnel of the Organization, by the establishment of its own institutions or by co-operation with official or non-official institutions of any Member with the consent of its Government;

(l) to establish such other institutions as it may consider desirable;

(m) to take any other appropriate action to further the objective of the Organization.

*Article 19.* The Health Assembly shall have authority to adopt Conventions or agreements with respect to any matter within the competence of the Organization. A two-thirds vote of the Health Assembly shall be required for the adoption of such Conventions or agreements, which shall come into force for each Member when accepted by it in accordance with its constitutional processes.

*Article 20.* Each Member undertakes that it will, within eighteen months after the adoption by the Health Assembly of a Convention or agreement, take action relative to the acceptance of such Convention or agreement. Each Member shall notify the Director-General of the action taken, and if it does not accept such Convention or agreement within the time limit, it will furnish a statement of the reasons for non-acceptance. In case of acceptance, each Member agrees to make an annual report to the Director-General in accordance with Chapter XIV.

*Article 21.* The Health Assembly shall have authority to adopt regulations concerning:

(a) sanitary and quarantine requirements and other procedures designed to prevent the international spread of disease;

(b) nomenclatures with respect to diseases, causes of death and public health practices;

(c) standards with respect to diagnostic procedures for international use;

(d) standards with respect to the safety, purity and potency of biological, pharmaceutical and similar products moving in international commerce;

(e) advertising and labelling of biological, pharmaceutical and similar products moving in international commerce.

*Article 22.* Regulations adopted pursuant to Article 21 shall come into force for all Members after due notice has been given of their adoption by the Health Assembly except for such Members as may notify the Director-General of rejection or reservations within the period stated in the notice.

*Article 23.* The Health Assembly shall have authority to make recommendations to Members with respect to any matter within the competence of the Organization.

### Chapter VI: The Executive Board

*Article 24.* The Board shall consist of thirty-one persons designated by as many Members. The Health Assembly, taking into account an equitable geographical distribution, shall elect the Members entitled to designate a person to serve on the Board, provided that, of such Members, not less than three shall be elected from each of the regional organizations established pursuant to Article 44. Each of these Members should appoint to the Board a person technically qualified in the field of health, who may be accompanied by alternates and advisers.

*Article 25.* These Members shall be elected for three years and may be reelected, provided that of the eleven members elected at the first session of the Health Assembly held after the coming into force of the amendment to this Constitution increasing the membership of the Board from thirty to thirty-one the term of office of the additional Member elected shall, insofar as may be necessary, be of such lesser duration as shall facilitate the election of at least one Member from each regional organization in each year.

*Article 26.* The Board shall meet at least twice a year and shall determine the place of each meeting.

*Article 27.* The Board shall elect its Chairman from among its members and shall adopt its own rules of procedure.

*Article 28.* The functions of the Board shall be:

(a) to give effect to the decisions and policies of the Health Assembly;

(b) to act as the executive organ of the Health Assembly;

(c) to perform any other functions entrusted to it by the Health Assembly;

(d) to advise the Health Assembly on questions referred to it by that body and on matters assigned to the Organization by Conventions, agreements and regulations;

(e) to submit advice or proposals to the Health Assembly on its own initiative;

(f) to prepare the agenda of meetings of the Health Assembly;

(g) to submit to the Health Assembly for consideration and approval a general programme of work covering a specific period;

(h) to study all questions within its competence;

(i) to take emergency measures within the functions and financial resources of the Organization to deal with events requiring immediate action. In particular it may authorize the Director-General to take the necessary steps to combat epidemics, to participate in the organization of health relief to victims of a calamity and to undertake studies and research the urgency of which has been drawn to the attention of the Board by any Member or by the Director-General.

*Article 29.* The Board shall exercise on behalf of the whole Health Assembly the powers delegated to it by that body.

### Chapter VII: The Secretariat

*Article 30.* The Secretariat shall comprise the Director-General and such technical and administrative staff as the Organization may require.

*Article 31.* The Director-General shall be appointed by the Health Assembly on the nomination of the Board on such terms as the Health Assembly may determine. The Director-General, subject to the authority of the Board, shall be the chief technical and administrative officer of the Organization.

*Article 32.* The Director-General shall be *ex-officio* Secretary of the Health Assembly, of the Board, of all commissions and committees of the Organization and of conferences convened by it. He may delegate these functions.

*Article 33.* The Director-General or his representative may establish a procedure by agreement with Members, permitting him, for the purpose of discharging his duties, to have direct access to their various departments, especially to their health administrations and to national health organizations, governmental or non-governmental. He may also establish direct relations with international organizations whose activities come within the competence of the Organization. He shall keep regional offices informed on all matters involving their respective areas.

*Article 34.* The Director-General shall prepare and submit to the Board the financial statements and budget estimates of the Organization.

*Article 35.* The Director-General shall appoint the staff of the Secretariat in accordance with staff regulations established by the Health Assembly. The paramount consideration in the employment of the staff shall be to assure that the efficiency, integrity and internationally representative character of the Secretariat shall be maintained at the highest level. Due regard shall be paid also to the importance of recruiting the staff on as wide a geographical basis as possible.

*Article 36.* The conditions of service of the staff of the Organization shall conform as far as possible with those of other United Nations organizations.

*Article 37.* In the performance of their duties the Director-General and the staff shall not seek or receive instructions from any government or from any authority external to the Organization. They shall refrain from any action which might reflect o their position as international officers. Each member of the Organization on its part undertakes to respect the exclusively international character of the Director-General and the staff and not to seek to influence them.

## Chapter VIII: Committees

*Article 38.* The Board shall establish such committees as the Health Assembly may direct and, on its own initiative or on the proposal of the Director-General, may establish any other committees considered desirable to serve any purpose within the competence of the Organization.

*Article 39.* The Board, from time to time and in any event annually, shall review the necessity for continuing each committee.

*Article 40.* The Board may provide for the creation of or the participation by the Organization in joint or mixed committees with other organizations and for the representation of the Organization in committees established by such other organizations.

## Chapter IX: Conferences

*Article 41.* The Health Assembly or the Board may convene local, general, technical or other special conferences to consider any matter within the competence of the Organization and may provide for the representation at such conferences of international organizations and, with the consent of the Government concerned, of national organizations, governmental or non-governmental. The manner of such representation shall be determined by the Health Assembly or the Board.

*Article 42.* The Board may provide for representation of the Organization at conferences in which the Board considers that the Organization has an interest.

## Chapter X: Headquarters

*Article 43.* The location of the headquarters of the Organization shall be determined by the Health Assembly after consultation with the United Nations.

## Chapter XI: Regional Arrangements

*Article 44.* (a) The Health Assembly shall from time to time define the geographical areas in which it is desirable to establish a regional organization.

(b) The Health Assembly may, with the consent of a majority of the Members situated within each area so defined, establish a regional organization to meet the special needs of such area. There shall not be more than one regional organization in each area.

*Article 45.* Each regional organization shall be an integral part of the Organization in accordance with this Constitution.

*Article 46.* Each regional organization shall consist of a regional committee and a regional office.

*Article 47.* Regional committees shall be composed of representatives of the Member States and Associate Members in the region concerned. Territories or groups of territories within the region, which are not responsible for the conduct of their international relations and which are not Associate Members, shall have the right to be represented and to participate in regional committees. The nature and extent of the rights and obligations of these territories or groups of territories in regional committees shall be determined by the Health Assembly in consultation with the Member or other authority having responsibility for the international relations of these territories and with the Member States in the region.

*Article 48.* Regional committees shall meet as often as necessary and shall determine the place of each meeting.

*Article 49.* Regional committees shall adopt their own rules of procedure.

*Article 50.* The functions of the regional committee shall be:

(a) to formulate policies governing matters of an exclusively regional character;

(b) to supervise the activities of the regional office;

(c) to suggest to the regional office the calling of technical conferences and such additional work or investigation in health matters as in the opinion of the regional committee would promote the objective of the Organization within the region;

(d) to co-operate with the respective regional committees of the United Nations and with those of other specialized agencies and with other regional international organizations having interests in common with the Organization;

(e) to tender advice, through the Director-General, to the Organization on international health matters which have wider than regional significance;

(f) to recommend additional regional appropriations by the Governments of the respective regions if the proportion of the central budget of the Organization allotted to that region is insufficient for the carrying-out of the regional functions;

(g) such other functions as may be delegated to the regional committee by the Health Assembly, the Board or the Director-General.

*Article 51.* Subject to the general authority of the Director-General of the Organization, the regional office shall be the administrative organ of the regional committee. It shall, in addition, carry out within the region the decisions of the Health Assembly and of the Board.

*Article 52.* The head of the regional office shall be the Regional Director appointed by the Board in agreement with the regional committee.

*Article 53.* The staff of the regional office shall be appointed in a manner to be determined by agreement between the Director-General and the Regional Director.

*Article 54.* The Pan American Sanitary Organization [renamed Pan American Health Organization in 1958] represented by the Pan American Sanitary Bureau and the Pan American Sanitary Conferences, and all other inter-governmental regional health organizations in existence prior to the date of signature of this Constitution, shall in due course be integrated with the Organization. This integration shall be effected as soon as practicable through common action based on mutual consent of the competent authorities expressed through the organizations concerned.

## Chapter XII: Budget and Expenses

*Article 55.* The Director-General shall prepare and submit to the Board the budget estimates of the Organization. The Board shall consider and submit to the Health Assembly such budget estimates together with any recommendations the Board may deem advisable.

*Article 56.* Subject to any agreement between the Organization and the United Nations, the Health Assembly shall review and approve the budget estimates and shall apportion the expenses among the Members in accordance with a scale to be fixed by the Health Assembly.

*Article 57.* The Health Assembly or the Board acting on behalf of the Health Assembly may accept and administer gifts and bequests made to the Organization provided that the conditions attached to such gifts or bequests are acceptable to the Health Assembly or the Board and are consistent with the objective and policies of the Organization.

*Article 58.* A special fund to be used at the discretion of the Board shall be established to meet emergencies and unforeseen contingencies.

## Chapter XIII: Voting

*Article 59.* Each Member shall have one vote in the Health Assembly.

*Article 60.* (a) Decisions of the Health Assembly on important questions shall be made by a two-thirds majority of the Members present and voting. These questions shall include: the adoption of Conventions or agreements; the approval of agreements bringing the Organization into relation with the United Nations and inter-governmental organizations and agencies in accordance with Articles 69, 70 and 72; amendments to this Constitution.

(b) Decisions on other questions, including the determination of additional categories of questions to be decided by a two-thirds majority, shall be made by a majority of the Members present and voting.

(c) Voting on analogous matters in the Board and in committees of the Organization shall be made in accordance with paragraphs (a) and (b) of this Article.

## Chapter XIV: Reports Submitted by States

*Article 61.* Each Member shall report annually to the Organization on the action taken and progress achieved in improving the health of its people.

*Article 62.* Each Member shall report annually on the action taken with respect to recommendations made to it by the Organization and with respect to Convention, agreements and regulations.

*Article 63.* Each Member shall communicate promptly to the Organization important laws, regulations, official reports and statistics pertaining to health which have been published in the State concerned.

*Article 64.* Each Member shall provide statistical and epidemiological reports in a manner to be determined by the Health Assembly.

*Article 65.* Each Member shall transmit upon the request of the Board such additional information pertaining to health as may be practicable.

## Chapter XV: Legal Capacity, Privileges and Immunities

*Article 66.* The Organization shall enjoy in the territory of each Member such legal capacity as may be necessary for the fulfilment of its objective and for the exercise of its functions.

*Article 67.* (a) The Organization shall enjoy in the territory of each Member such privileges and immunities as may be necessary for the fulfilment of its objective and for the exercise of its functions.

(b) Representatives of Members, persons designated to serve on the Board and technical and administrative personnel of the Organization shall similarly enjoy such privileges and immunities as are necessary for the independent exercise of their functions in connexion with the Organization.

*Article 68.* Such legal capacity, privileges and immunities shall be defined in a separate agreement to be prepared by the Organization in consultation with the Secretary-General of the United Nations and concluded between the Members.

## Chapter XVI: Relations With Other Organizations

*Article 69.* The Organization shall be brought into relation with the United Nations as one of the specialized agencies referred to in Article 57 of the Charter of the United Nations. The agreement or agreements bringing the Organization into relation with the United Nations shall be subject to approval by a two-thirds vote of the Health Assembly.

*Article 70.* The Organization shall establish effective relations and co-operate closely with such other inter-governmental organizations as may be desirable. Any formal agreement entered into with such organizations shall be subject to approval by a two-thirds vote of the Health Assembly.

*Article 71.* The Organization may, on matters within its competence, make suitable arrangements for consultation and co-operation with non-governmental international organizations and, with the consent of the Government concerned, with national organizations, governmental or nongovernmental.

*Article 72.* Subject to the approval by a two-thirds vote of the Health Assembly, the Organization may take over from any other international organization or agency whose purpose and activities lie within the field of competence of the Organization such functions, resources and obligations as may be conferred upon the Organization by international agreement or by mutually acceptable arrangements entered into between the competent authorities of the respective organizations.

## Chapter XVII: Amendments

*Article 73.* Texts of proposed amendments to this Constitution shall be communicated by the Director-General to Members at least six months in advance of their consideration by the Health Assembly. Amendments shall come into force for all Members when adopted by a two-thirds vote of the Health Assembly and accepted by two-thirds of the Members in accordance with their respective constitutional processes.

### Chapter XVIII: Interpretation

*Article 74.* The Chinese, English, French, Russian and Spanish texts of this Constitution shall be regarded as equally authentic.

*Article 75.* Any question or dispute concerning the interpretation or application of this Constitution which is not settled by negotiation or by the Health Assembly shall be referred to the International Court of Justice in conformity with the Statute of the Court, unless the parties concerned agree on another mode of settlement.

*Article 76.* Upon authorization by the General Assembly of the United Nations or upon authorization in accordance with any agreement between the Organization and the United Nations, the Organization may request the International Court of Justice for an advisory opinion on any legal question arising within the competence of the Organization.

*Article 77.* The Director-General may appear before the Court on behalf of the Organization in connexion with any proceedings arising out of any such request for an advisory opinion. He shall make arrangements for the presentation of the case before the Court, including arrangements for the argument of different views on the question.

### Chapter XIX: Entry into Force

*Article 78.* Subject to the provisions of Chapter III, this Constitution shall remain open to all States for signature or acceptance.

*Article 79.* (a) States may become parties to this Constitution by

(i) signature without reservation as to approval;

(ii) signature subject to approval followed by acceptance; or

(iii) acceptance.

(b) Acceptance shall be effected by the deposit of a formal instrument with the Secretary-General of the United Nations.

*Article 80.* This Constitution shall come into force when twenty-six Members of the United Nations have become parties to it in accordance with the provisions of Article 79.

*Article 81.* In accordance with Article 102 of the Charter of the United Nations, the Secretary-General of the United Nations will register this Constitution when it has been signed without reservation as to approval on behalf of one State or upon deposit of the first instrument of acceptance.

*Article 82.* The Secretary-General of the United Nations will inform States parties to this Constitution of the date when it has come into force. He will also inform them of the dates when other States have become parties to this Constitution.

In faith whereof the undersigned representatives, having been duly authorized for that purpose, sign this Constitution.

Done in the City of New York this twenty-second day of July 1946, in a single copy in the Chinese, English, French, Russian and Spanish languages, each text being equally authentic. The original texts shall be deposited in the archives of the United Nations. The Secretary-General of the United Nations will send certified copies to each of the Governments represented at the Conference.

WHO. Address: CH-1211 Geneva 27, Switzerland. Telephone: (41-22) 791-2111. Fax: (41-22) 791-0746. Director-General: Dr. Hiroshi Nakajima.

**WORLD INTELLECTUAL PROPERTY ORGANIZATION (WIPO).** Established in accordance with the Convention Establishing the World Intellectual Property Organization, signed at Stockholm on 14 July 1967, WIPO became a specialized agency of the United Nations in December 1974. Its basic function is to promote the protection of intellectual property, including patented inventions and copyrighted artistic works, and to administer a number of international treaties for this purpose.

WIPO, which has its headquarters in Geneva and a membership of more than 125 States, is governed by a general assembly and a conference, each consisting of all its member States. Its activities are coordinated by the International Bureau, which centralizes information of all kinds relating to the protection of intellectual property and maintains international registers of patents, trademarks, industrial designs, and appellations of origin.

The term "intellectual property" is defined in the Convention (art. 2) as including the rights relating to "literary, artistic and scientific works; performances of performing artists, phonograms, and broadcasts; inventions in all fields of human endeavor; scientific discoveries; industrial designs; trademarks, service marks, and commercial names and designations; protection against unfair competition; and all other rights resulting from intellectual activity in the industrial, scientific, literary or artistic fields."

The objectives of the organization are (art. 3) "(1) to promote the protection of intellectual property throughout the world through cooperation among States and, where appropriate, in collaboration with any other international organization; and (2) to ensure administrative cooperation among the Unions." The term "Unions" in this context refers to the Paris Union, established by the Convention for the Protection of Industrial Property, signed in Paris on 20 March 1883; the Berne Union, established by the Convention for the Protection of Literary and Artistic Works, signed in Berne on 9 September 1886; and similar groups established by any other international agreement the administration of which is assumed by WIPO.

WIPO. Address: 34 chemin des Colojbettes, P.O. 18, CH-1211, Geneva 20, Switzerland. Telephone: (41-22) 730-9111. Fax: (41-22) 733-5428. Director-General: Dr. Arpad Bogsch.

**WORLD JEWISH CONGRESS.** An international non-governmental organization in consultative status with the UN **Economic and Social Council** (Category II) and with **UNESCO, UNICEF,** and the **ILO,** WJC is affiliated with Jewish communities and representative organizations in approximately 70 countries.

Founded in Geneva in 1936 as the successor to the Committee of Jewish Delegations, the Congress fosters the unity of Jewish people and seeks to ensure the continuity and development of Jewish religious, spiritual, cultural, and social heritage. In addition to supporting Jewish solidarity throughout the world and intensifying the bonds of world Jewry with the State of Israel, WJC works to secure the rights, status, and interest of Jews and Jewish communities and defends these rights wherever they are denied, violated, or threatened.

WJC has an international publication program. The Congress publishes *WJC Report* (New York), *Gesher* (Jerusalem), *Boletin Informativo OJI* (Buenos Aires), *Patterns of Prejudice* and *Christian Jewish Relations* (London), and *Batfutsot* (Jerusalem).

World Jewish Congress. Address: 501 Madison Avenue, New York, NY 10022, USA. Telephone: (212) 775-5770. Fax: (212) 755-5883. Secretary-Treasurer: Israel Singer.

## WORLD MOVEMENT OF MOTHERS.
An international non-governmental organization in consultative status with the UN ECONOMIC AND SOCIAL COUNCIL (Category II) and with UNESCO, UNICEF, and FAO, also known by its French title, *Mouvement Mondial des Mères* (MMM), the organization has members in 36 countries.

Founded in 1947, in Paris, as an apolitical organization devoted to defining and defending the principal role of the mother in the life of the family, as well as in the educational development of the child, the World Movement prepares surveys and studies and organizes symposia and conferences to promote national, regional, and international recognition of the rights of mothers and their children and of families in distress. It has conducted research on such subjects as slavery, fetus commerce, respect for specific cultures, philosophic and religious liberty, and the rights of children.

MMM publishes bulletins and reports on its work and issues the periodical *Nouvelles et documents du MMM*.

World Movement of Mothers. Address: 56 rue de Passy, 75016 Paris, France. Telephone: (33-1) 45-20-55-80. President: Marie-Laure Beck.

## WORLD MUSLIM CONGRESS.
An international non-governmental organization in consultative status (Category I) with the UN ECONOMIC AND SOCIAL COUNCIL and UNICEF, WMC has branches and affiliates in 67 countries.

Founded in 1926, in Mecca, the Congress works for greater fellowship, unity, and cooperation among Muslims and for the social and cultural solidarity of all mankind. It conducts study groups, public seminars, symposia, and cultural exhibitions. It also publishes the weekly *Muslim World* in English and the *World Muslim Gazetter*.

World Muslim Congress. Address: 9/A Block 7, Gulshan-E-Iqbal, University Road, Karachi 47000, Pakistan. Telephone: (92-21) 410057. Fax: (92-21) 466878. Secretary-General: Raja Mohummed Zafar-ul-Haq.

## WORLD PEACE COUNCIL.
An international non-governmental organization in consultative status with the UN ECONOMIC AND SOCIAL COUNCIL (Roster) and with UNESCO, ILO, and UNCTAD, WPC has national committees in 137 countries and territories.

Founded in Warsaw in 1950, the Council works for the prohibition of all weapons of mass destruction and the end of the arms race; for the abolition of foreign military bases; for disarmament; for the elimination of all forms of colonialism and racial discrimination; for the right of peoples to sovereignty and independence; for noninterference in the internal affairs of nations; and for peaceful coexistence between States. WPC has standing commissions devoted to disarmament, development, human rights, racial discrimination, and environmental issues. It also campaigns for nuclear weapon-free zones.

WPC publishes the monthly *Peace Courier* and the bi-monthly journals *Disarmament Forum* and *New Perspectives,* all in English, French, German, and Spanish. It also publishes the quarterly *International Mobilization Against Apartheid and for the Liberation of Southern Africa* in English and French and periodically publishes *Indo-China Newsletter*.

World Peace Council. Address: Lönnrotinkatu 25A/V1, SF-00180 Helsinki, Finland. Telephone: (358-0) 693-1044. Fax: (358-0) 693-3703. Secretary-General: Romesh Chandra.

## WORLD SOCIETY OF VICTIMOLOGY.
This non-governmental organization has consultative status with the UN ECONOMIC AND SOCIAL COUNCIL (Category II). It was established in 1979 in Münster, Germany, at the Fifth International Symposium on Victimology. The Society works to advance victimological research and practices throughout the world and encourages interdisciplinary and comparative work and research in this field. The Society has members in 43 countries and territories. It publishes the bi-annual *World Society for Victimology Newsletter*. It has also published the following scholarly works and reports: Hans J. Schneider, *The Victim in International Perspectives,* 2 vols. (1982);

Koichi Miyazawa and Minoru Ohya, *Victimology in Comparative Perspectives* (1986); and Zvonimir P. Separovich, *Victimology: International Action and Study of Victims,* 2 vols. (1988–1989).

World Society of Victimology. Address: Fachochschule Niederrhein, School of Social Work, Richard Wagner-Strasse, 101, D-4050, Mönchengladbach 1, Germany. Fax: (49-2161) 186-327. Secretary-General: Dr. Gerd Ferdinand Kirchhoff.

## WORLD STUDENT CHRISTIAN FEDERATION.

This non-governmental organization is in consultative status with the UN Economic and Social Council (Category II) and UNESCO. It was founded in 1895 in Vadstena, Sweden, as "World Federation" comprising national student Christian movements and student sections of the YMCA and the YWCA. The Federation works to bring together Christian students to strive for peace and justice among nations; it has members in 86 countries. It publishes the quarterlies *Federation News* and *WSCF Journal.*

World Student Christian Federation. Address: Ecumenical Centre, 5 route des Morillons, Grand-Saconnex, CH-1218 Geneva, Switzerland. Telephone: (41-22) 798-8953. Fax: (41-22) 798-2370.

## WORLD UNION FOR PROGRESSIVE JUDAISM.

An international non-governmental organization in consultative status with the UN Economic and Social Council (Roster) and with UNESCO and UNICEF, WUPJ has more than 1.5 million constituent, associate, and honorary members in 27 countries.

The World Union for Progressive Judaism encourages the formation of progressive Jewish religious communities or congregations in different countries and stimulates and encourages the study of Judaism and its adaptation to modern life.

The Union issues reports of its annual conferences and has published *The First Twenty-Five Years 1925–1951,* reviewing its activities since it was established in London.

World Union for Progressive Judaism. Address: 838 Fifth Avenue, New York, NY 10021, USA. Telephone: (212) 249-0100. Fax: (212) 517-3940. Executive Director: Rabbi Richard G. Hirsch.

## WORLD UNION OF CATHOLIC WOMEN'S OR-GANIZATIONS.

An international non-governmental organization in consultative status with the UN Economic and Social Council (Category II) and with ILO, UNESCO, FAO, and the Council of Europe, WUCWO has 91 affiliated and corresponding organizations in 40 countries.

Founded in Brussels in 1910 and originally called the "International Union of Catholic Women's Leagues," the Union supports the building of a more just and fraternal human community, fosters the advancement of women, and promotes the collaboration of women in fashioning society and in the mission of the Church. It has developed educational activities on all continents and holds a quadrennial Congress. It publishes the quarterly *WUCWO Newsletter* in English, French, German, and Spanish.

World Union of Catholic Women's Organizations. Address: 20 rue Notre-Dame des Champs, F-75006 Paris, France. Telephone: (33-1) 45-44-27-65. Fax: (33-1) 42-84-04-80.

## WORLD UNIVERSITY SERVICE.

An international non-governmental organization in consultative status with the UN Economic and Social Council (Category II) and with UNESCO and FAO, WUS has national committees in 44 countries.

Founded in 1920—as an outgrowth of the World Student Christian Federation and under the name of "European Student Relief"—to publicize and relieve the needs of students and academies who suffered from the effects of World War I, the programs and self-help projects of the World University Service were extended during the 1930s into the fields of student health, cooperative work, and research into problems of higher education. In 1970, following a decision of its general assembly, WUS moved away from its university welfare role into its present role of promoting social welfare through university action. WUS' programs are action-oriented and fall into six broad categories: (1) defense of human rights; (2) development education; (3) anti-discrimination programs; (4) scholarships; (5) social action; and (6) community development. National WUS chapters are actively engaged in similar programs financed out of resources available in the individual countries.

WUS irregularly publishes the *WUS News* and has published *WUS and Human Rights.*

World University Service. Address: Chemin des Iris 5, CH-1216 Geneva COINTRIN, Switzerland. Telephone: (41-22) 798-8711. Fax: (41-22) 798-0829. Secretary-General: Nigel Hartley.

## WORLD VETERANS FEDERATION.

An international non-governmental organization in consultative status with the UN Economic and Social Council (Category I), UNESCO, ILO, WHO, FAO, UNCTAD, UNICEF, and the Council of Europe, WVF is composed of associations of war veterans, former resistants, deportees, prisoners of war, and war victims, totaling approximately 27 million members in 61 countries.

Founded in 1950, in Paris, as the "International Federation of War Veterans' Organizations," the Federation works for international peace and security by application, in letter and spirit, of the UN CHARTER and the implementation of the UNIVERSAL DECLARATION OF HUMAN RIGHTS and defends the spiritual and material interests of war veterans and victims by legal and constitutional means. It sponsors and encourages surveys and research on rehabilitation of handicapped persons and legislation concerning war veterans and protection of human rights. It also supports disarmament and peacekeeping missions. The creation of the International Sports Organization for the Disabled in 1961 was a WVF initiative. Of particular concern to the Federation is the problem of accessibility of the manmade environment—housing, public transportation, streets, and workplaces. In 1986, the WVF International Socio-Medical Information Centre was set up in Oslo, Norway, in cooperation with the University of Oslo, to collect, analyze, and disseminate information dealing with diagnosis, etiology, treatment, rehabilitation, and prevention relative to psycho-social effects of war and similar situations including post-traumatic stress disorders.

WVF publishes periodicals and reports on international cooperation in areas such as rehabilitation, veterans legislation, economic development, disarmament, and human rights.

World Veterans Federation. Address: Rue Hamelin 16, F-75116 Paris, France. Telephone: (33-1) 47-04-33-00. Fax: (33-1) 47-04-20-84. Secretary-General: Serge Wourgaft.

**WORLD VISION INTERNATIONAL.** This non-governmental organization was founded in 1950 in Monrovia, California (USA) to serve as a nondenominational Christian humanitarian agency dedicated to ministering to people spiritually and physically. Its five basic ministries are ministering to children and families (more than 5,000 projects); providing emergency relief and rehabilitation (81 projects); developing community relations (more than 400 projects); developing evangelical leadership (more than 100 projects); and challenging to mission. World Vision International is in consultative status with the UN ECONOMIC AND SOCIAL COUNCIL (Category II), UNICEF, and WHO. It has field offices in 51 countries. World Vision International publishes the quarterly *Together Magazine* and the annual *Unreached Peoples.*

World Vision International. Address: 919 W. Huntington Drive, Monrovia, CA 91016, USA. Telephone: (818) 303-8811. Contact: James Newton.

**WORLD YOUNG WOMEN'S CHRISTIAN ASSOCIATION.** An international non-governmental organization in consultative status with the UN ECONOMIC AND SOCIAL COUNCIL (Category II) and with UNESCO, ILO, FAO, and UNICEF, the Young Women's Christian Association is an international voluntary women's organization which began as a prayer and service circle in Great Britain in 1894. At present, the World YWCA unites women and girls in 77 national YWCAs. Current issues of concern in the YWCA movement include the problems of women and youth in a changing world; problems of development; education; job creation; family life education; political education; participation in national development; health; and human rights education and development.

The World YWCA issues the quarterly *Common Concern,* the bi-annual *Energy and Environment Newsletter,* and the biennial *World YWCA Directory,* as well as annual reports and special reports.

World Young Women's Christian Association. Address: 37 Quai Wilson, CH-1201 Geneva, Switzerland. Telephone: (41-22) 372-3100. Fax: (41-22) 731-7938.

# X

**XENOPHOBIA.** Xenophobia is an unreasonable hatred of foreigners, which often results in the aggrandizement of one's own national or ethnic affiliation and discrimination against others. Hostility against foreigners can result in physical assaults and deaths. In 1960, both the **SUB-COMMISSION ON PREVENTION OF DISCRIMINATION AND PROTECTION OF MINORITIES** (resolution 3 B [XII]) and the UN **COMMISSION ON HUMAN RIGHTS** (resolution 1510 [XV]) took note of "the manifestations of anti-Semitism and other forms of racial and national hatred and religious and racial prejudices of a similar character which have occurred in various countries, reminiscent of the crimes and outrages committed by the Nazis prior to and during the Second World War" and expressed their gratification that governments, peoples, and private organizations had spontaneously reacted in opposition to those manifestations.

On recommendation of the Commission and Sub-Commission, the UN **GENERAL ASSEMBLY** on 12 December 1960 expressed the principle (resolution 1510 [XV]) "that the United Nations is duty bound to combat these manifestations, to establish the facts and the causes of their origin, and to recommend resolute and effective measures which can be taken against them." The Assembly, further, resolutely condemned all manifestations and practices of racial, religious, and national hatred in the political, economic, social, educational, and cultural spheres of the life of society as violations of the **UNITED NATIONS CHARTER** and the **UNIVERSAL DECLARATION OF HUMAN RIGHTS**; it called upon the governments of all States to take all necessary measures to prevent all manifestations of such hatred.

In 1993, the UN **HUMAN RIGHTS COMMITTEE** issued General Recommendation XI on Non-citizens (42nd session) in regard to the International Convention on the Elimination of All Forms of Racial Discrimination (see **RACIAL DISCRIMINATION**):

Article 1, paragraph 1, of the International Convention on the Elimination of All Forms of Racial Discrimination defines racial discrimination. Article 1, paragraph 2, excepts from this definition actions by a State party which differentiate between citizens and non-citizens. Article 1, paragraph 3, qualifies article 1, paragraph 2, by declaring that, among non-citizens, States parties may not discriminate against any particular nationality.

The Committee has noted that article 1, paragraph 2, has on occasion been interpreted as absolving States parties from any obligation to report on matters relating to legislation on foreigners. The Committee therefore affirms that States parties are under an obligation to report fully upon legislation on foreigners and its implementation.

The Committee further affirms that article 1, paragraph 2, must not be interpreted to detract in any way from the rights and freedoms recognized and enunciated in other instruments, especially the Universal Declaration of Human Rights, the International Covenant on Economic, Social and Cultural Rights and the International Covenant on Civil and Political Rights.

In 1993, the World Conference for Human Rights, meeting in Vienna, Austria, adopted the Vienna Declaration and Programme of Action, which contained the following articles concerning xenophobia:

*Article 15.* Respect for human rights and for fundamental freedoms without distinction of any kind is a fundamental rule of international human rights law. The speedy and comprehensive elimination of all forms of racism and racial discrimination, xenophobia and related intolerance is a priority task for the international community. Governments should take effective measures to prevent and combat them. Groups, institutions, intergovernmental and non-governmental organizations and individuals are urged to intensify their efforts in cooperating and coordinating their activities against these evils. . . .

*Article 30.* The World Conference on Human Rights also expresses its dismay and condemnation that gross and systematic violations and situations that constitute serious obstacles to the full enjoyment of all human rights continue to occur in different parts of the world. Such violations and obstacles include, as well as torture and cruel, inhuman and degrading treatment or punishment, summary and arbitrary executions, disappearances, arbitrary detentions, all forms of racism, racial discrimination and apartheid, foreign occupation and alien domination, xenophobia, poverty, hunger and other denials of economic, social and cultural rights, religious intolerance, terrorism, discrimination against women and lack of the rule of law.

Concerning the coordination of human rights programs within the UN system, the World Conference urged all governments to take immediate measures and to develop strong policies to prevent and combat all forms and manifestations of racism, xenophobia, or related intolerance, where necessary by enactment of appropriate legislation, including penal measures, and by the establishment of national institutions to combat such phenomena. The World Conference welcomed the decision of the UN Commission on Human Rights to appoint a Special Rapporteur to report on contemporary forms of racism, racial discrimination, xenophobia, and related intolerance.

**SEE ALSO** *Anti-Semitism; Race; Racial Discrimination.*

**BIBLIOGRAPHY.** Batselé, Didier, Michel Hanotiau, and Odile Daurmont. "La lutte contre le racisme et la xénophobie: mythe ou réalité?" (Fighting Back Racism and Xenophobia: A Myth or Reality?), *Revue trimestrielle des droits de l'homme* 2, no. 7 and 8 (July 1991): 319–346, 435–471. Scholarly article, in French.

European Parliament. *Commission d'enquête sur le racisme et la xénophobie: rapport sur les résultats des travaux* (Commission of Inquiry on Racism and Xenophobia: Report on the Inquiry Findings). Luxembourg: Office of Official Publications of the European Community, 1991. IGO report, in French.

France, Commission Nationale Consultative des Droits de l'Homme (National Consultative Committee on Human Rights). *1990: La lutte contre le racisme et la xénophobie* (1990: The Fight against Racism and Xenophobia). Paris: Documentation française, 1991. Research report, in French.

Human Rights Watch. *"Germany for Germans": Xenophobia and Racist Violence in Germany.* New York: 1995. NGO report, in English.

————. *Playing the "Communal Card": Communal Violence and Human Rights.* New York: 1995. NGO monograph, in English.

*L'Intolérance et le droit de l'autre* (Intolerance and the Rights of Others). Geneva, Switzerland: Labor et Fides, 1992. Scholarly monograph, in French.

Perotti, Antonio. *Action to Combat Intolerance and Xenophobia in the Activities of the Council of Europe's Council for Cultural Co-Operation, 1969–1989.* Strasbourg, France: Council of Europe, 1991. Scholarly paper, in English; bibliography, pp. 45–47.

Sivanandan, A., ed. "Europe: Variations on a Theme of Racism," *Race & Class* 32, no. 3 (Jan.–March 1991). Special issue, in English; bibliography, pp. 153–160.

United Nations Centre for Human Rights. *Implementation of the Programme of Action for the Second Decade to Combat Racism and Racial Discrimination: Report of the Seminar on the Political, Historical, Economic, Social and Cultural Factors Contributing to Racism, Racial Discrimination and Apartheid, Geneva 10–14 December 1990.* Geneva, Switzerland: 1991. IGO document, in English.

van Boven, Theo. "Combating Racial Discrimination in the World and in Europe," *Netherlands Quarterly of Human Rights* 11, no. 2 (1993): 163–172. Scholarly article, in English.

# Y

**YEMEN.** The Yemeni Republic is an Arab country occupying the southwestern portion of the Arabian Peninsula, established on 22 May 1990 by the merger of the countries formerly known as the Yemen Arab Republic (North Yemen) and the People's Democratic Republic of Yemen (South Yemen). It has borders with Oman and Saudi Arabia and fronts on the Red Sea and the Gulf of Aden. North Yemen achieved independence from Turkey in 1934 and became a member of the United Nations in 1947. South Yemen achieved independence from Great Britain in 1967 and became a member of the United Nations the same year. The combined population of the unified country is estimated to be 12,215,000, almost all of Arab origin. Arabic is the only language in common use; English and Mahri are used in some business transactions. The predominant religion is Islam. Literacy is estimated at 20%.

The government (1994) took the form of a republic. Its capital is Aden, formerly the capital of South Yemen. In May 1991 a draft constitution was approved in a referendum and political parties formed in anticipation of legislative elections. Political and economic unrest continued throughout the early 1990s, however, with demonstrations and political assassinations. Approximately 850,000 Yemenis returned from working in Saudi Arabia when their privileges were withdrawn in response to Yemen's opposition to foreign troops in the Gulf in 1990. Unemployment rose as a result of the large influx. Elections to the 301-seat House of Representatives were held in early 1993 with 4,730 challengers, 70% of whom were independents. The two former ruling parties comprised the majority bloc in the legislature. President Saleh and Vice-President al-Baidh were re-elected by the Presidential Council for another four-year term in October 1993.

*CIVIL WAR.* Opposing army units began fighting in early 1994, primarily along the former border between north and south, and by May a state of emergency was declared. Later that month, on the fourth anniversary of the unification of the country, al-Baidh announced the independence of the Democratic Republic of Yemen in the south and pronounced himself president. Fighting lasted until Saleh's troops captured Aden in July. Thousands, including Somali refugees, were said to have died in the nine-week civil war. Yemen had also received tens of thousands of refugees from the conflict in Somalia in 1992.

*BIBLIOGRAPHY.* Amnesty International. *Yemen: Human Rights Concerns Following Recent Armed Conflict.* London: 1994. NGO report, in English.
————. *Yemen: Incommunicado Detention and Unfair Trial.* London: 1988. NGO report, in English.
————. *Yemen: Unlawful Detention and Unfair Trials of Members of the Former National Democratic Front.* London: 1993. NGO report, in English.
Arab Organization for Human Rights. *Report: Human Rights in the Arab World.* Cairo, Egypt. NGO annual report, in English or Arabic.
Middle East Watch. *Yemen: Human Rights in Yemen during and after the 1994 War.* New York: Human Rights Watch, 1994. NGO report, in English.
————. *Yemen: Steps toward Civil Society.* New York: Human Rights Watch, 1992. NGO report, in English.

**YOUTH AND HUMAN RIGHTS.** At its 1985 session, the UN **COMMISSION ON HUMAN RIGHTS** emphasized (resolution 1985/13) the necessity to ensure full enjoyment by youth of the rights stipulated in all relevant international instruments as indispensable for human dignity and for the free development of the human personality, and requested its **SUB-COMMISSION ON PREVENTION OF DISCRIMINATION AND PROTECTION OF MINORITIES** to pay due attention to the role of youth in the field of human rights, particularly in achieving the objectives of the International Youth Year (1985).

In response the Sub-Commission, later in 1985, requested one of its members, Mr. Dumitru Mazilu (Romania), to prepare a report on human rights and youth analyzing the efforts and measures for securing the implementation and enjoyment by youth of human rights, particularly the right to life, the right to education, and the right to work. This decision was later endorsed by the Commission on Human Rights and the **ECONOMIC AND SOCIAL COUNCIL.**

The Secretary-General issued the report on 10 July 1989 in two parts: (1) the report entitled "Human Rights and Youth" (UN Doc. E/CN.4/Sub.2/1989/41) and (2) the addendum to that report sub-titled "A

Special View on the Romanian case" (UN Doc. E/CN.4/Sub.2/1989/41/Add. 1), the latter of which can be found under **ROMANIA**. The Sub-Commission considered the report at its 1989 session, and decided (resolution 1989/45) to request Mr. Mazilu to update it and to present his updated report in person to the Sub-Commission at its 1990 session. The tentative conclusions and recommendations of the Special Rapporteur—which are to be updated in his final report to the Sub-Commission—are as follows (UN Doc. E/CN.4/Sub.2/1989/41, chap. VIII, paras. 371–387):

*A. Conclusions.* Developments in the contemporary world convincingly demonstrate that young people have a more and more important role to play in attaining the objectives of progress and development set by all peoples. Their right to life, to education and to work and their freedoms are of particular importance and significance.

Consideration of these rights and freedoms in a special report is a mark of the real interest taken by the United Nations in alerting Governments and world public opinion and in giving impetus to concern already felt in this respect.

Millions of young people continue to be exposed to great sufferings caused by lack of the resources needed for their informal physical and intellectual development, as is happening in Romania. In some countries, governed by tyrannical regimes, young people endure unimagined forms of coercion, a veritable aggression against their rights and freedoms. Through starvation, terror and cold, the rulers of those countries strive to reduce them to silence, to prevent them from concerning themselves with the major problems of their respective societies, and to transform them into an amorphous, easily manipulated mass. Many young people gain an education by great efforts, and when the teaching process is over they are disappointed not to find jobs in which to apply their knowledge, talent and characteristic enthusiasm. In other countries, the process of instruction and education is passing through an especially critical period owing to the absence of professionalism and the presence of a superfluity of doctrinaire, politicizing elements of no practical utility. The jobs young people get in those countries do not allow their skills to be encouraged or use to be made of their intelligence and characteristic energy, so that they lapse into indifference and uniformity.

Again, there are countries—including Romania—in which the lives of millions of young people are in jeopardy. The absence of the most elementary rights and freedoms, their arrest, conviction and execution on political grounds, bring to mind the darkest years of the oppression practised by maniacal despotic régimes. Threats of every kind, daily dangers directed against young people who have the courage to express critical opinions, maintain an atmosphere of tension and terror that is hard to bear.

The positive changes of recent years have rekindled the torch of freedom and dignity. The hopes of millions upon millions of young people for the elimination of repressive anachronisms and the possibility of a real restructuring of society on the principles of democracy and freedom have been reborn.

"No" is being said, with increasing determination, to policies of economic and cultural stagnation, of oppression and repression of ethnic and religious discrimination. There is a demand for the institution of political and economic structures which are consistently democratic and which preclude the monopoly of power of life and the imposition of maniacal despots. The fixing of precise terms of office in all public posts and election by secret ballot of all those who are to occupy them are major guarantees of democracy and freedom. The separation of powers in a State is the surest way to the normal conduct of legislative, judicial and executive business and to the elimination of abuses of power. The closing down of the concentration camps and the final elimination of ethnic and social genocide are priority objectives of the reinstatement of right and justice in human society.

The experiences of the past few decades have furnished compelling proof of the importance that attaches to economic and political pluralism and to diversity of opinion as prerequisites for effective progress in all spheres and as the expression of the level of culture and civilization attained in the development of human communities.

The young people of the world, including the young people of Romania, regard the refusal of reforms, the rejection of the process of democratic restructuring of society, as a reactionary attitude, as confirmation of the contempt for the human being, the disdain for human rights and freedoms, shown by some dictatorial cliques that have difficulty in parting with the regal privileges conferred by doctrinaire ideas and structures of government which have long since fallen into disuse and been roundly condemned by the entire civilized world.

The young generation insistently demands the abandonment of out-of-date doctrines, the elimination of dogmas that run counter to human progress and to the happiness and well-being of man, and the removal of the oppressors, of the dictators who in the name of a few reactionary slogans oppose the increasingly powerful trend towards democracy and freedom. The voice of reason must carry the day. "Peoples are not herds of subjects that despots can drive where they choose with a whip!" "The people is the true sovereign and the maker of its own history!" "Any leader must subordinate himself to the will and interests of the people!" "The peoples are not in the service of the rulers; the rulers are the servants of human communities, which must be given an accounting of their actions and must be asked for approval regarding all government measures!" "Truth and right sometimes come tardily, but they come surely!"

Youth is the fiercest fighter for the rebuilding of the world on criteria of progress, well-being, democracy and freedom.

Orders based on terror, dictatorship and tyranny are repudiated and condemned by history.

The dark age of terror, dictatorship and tyranny is gradually passing away. A new age of freedom and human dignity can be glimpsed on the horizon. We are drawing closer as quickly as possible to giving back to young people the confidence they need in order to build a future of enlightenment and freedom.

*B. Recommendations.* Recognizing that young people have an important role in the life of society for the achievement of social justice and the attainment of the objectives of economic and social progress and the maintenance of international peace and security, and mindful of the grave political, economic, social and cultural problems facing youth and the need to ensure the full exercise of youth's fundamental rights to life, education, vocational training, work, social assistance, the elimination of all forms of social and racial discrimination, so that youth can participate actively in the decision-making process, we consider the following necessary:

(a) At the national and international levels, effective measures should be taken to put an immediate end to the flagrant violations of the fundamental right to life of young people. The right to life is sacrosanct. Deprivation of life is irrevocable. Respect for the right to life transcends all social, national, racial, political, religious, ethnic and other differences. Summary or arbitrary executions of young people opposed to, or perceived or imagined to be opposed to those who wield political or economic power in the State or government, or perceived to be opposed to certain aspects of their political, economic, social and cultural policies, as well as enforced or involuntary disappearances, torture and mistreatment of prisoners and detainees, are continuing on a large scale throughout the international community. These flagrant violations of the fundamental right to life of young people show a serious erosion in the level of acknowledgement of and respect for the right to life of young people.

(b) The international community must, as a matter of extreme urgency, act collectively to halt this erosion by adopting effective measures and means through which to react speedily to threatened or imminent summary or arbitrary executions, enforced or involuntary disappearances.

(c) All States should adopt effective measures for a healthier environment of young people and the containment and reduction of such afflictions as disease, famine, war, corruption, criminality and social breakdown.

(d) All States should attack on a priority basis every aspect of the illicit drug business, including the production, possession, trafficking, demand, consumption, and financing of illicit drugs, which must be recognized as a crime against humanity, and launch objective informational, educational and orientation programmes to make young people aware of the risks to health, security and other implications of illicit drug use, thus eliminating the demand for illicit drugs.

(e) At the national and international levels, effective measures should be taken for the elimination of illiteracy and for the promotion of education and vocational training for youth based upon both formal and informal learning and designed to link theoretical learning and practical training, on the one hand, with productive and creative work, on the other.

(f) Young people shall be brought up in a spirit of peace, justice, freedom, mutual respect and understanding in order to promote equal rights for all human beings and all nations, economic and social progress, and the maintenance of international peace and security. All means of education, including as of major importance the guidance given by parents or family, instruction and information intended for young people should foster the ideals of peace, humanity, liberty and international solidarity and all other ideals which help to bring peoples closer together, and acquaint young people with the role entrusted to the United Nations as a means of preserving and maintaining peace and promoting international understanding and co-operation.

(g) Young people should be brought up in the knowledge of the dignity and equality of all men, without distinction as to race, colour, ethnic origins or beliefs, and in respect for fundamental rights and for the right of peoples to self-determination. All States shall take the necessary measures, including legislative measures, to ensure that the utilization of scientific and technological achievements promotes the fullest realization of rights and fundamental freedoms of young people without any discrimination whatsoever on grounds of race, sex, language or religious beliefs.

(h) All States should take the necessary measures to implement large-scale national employment programmes, in conformity with the actual situation and priorities of every country, which would include legislative, educational, economic and social measures designed to eliminate all forms of discrimination, guarantee that young people participate actively in economic and social development and in the process of drawing up and taking decisions, and encourage adequate representation of youth in Parliament, in government, and in other decision-making bodies. All Government shall take every possible step to ensure appropriate education and employment opportunities for children of refugees, foreign nationals and peoples displaced from their country of origin.

(i) All States should take the necessary measures to ensure that, in the pursuit of balanced economic growth, industrialization and highest productivity, the application of new technologies will enhance the situation of young people in order to provide them with a productive, satisfying and secure future. All Governments shall give special attention to the problem of rapid demographic growth, especially in developing countries, and give high priority to achieving an appropriate relationship between resources, productivity, population levels and population distribution.

(j) Taking into account the fact that the relatively weak position of young workers in the labour market may at times render them vulnerable to exploitation and may oblige them to accept substandard wages and jobs, Governments, employers and workers should take action when necessary to prevent these situations from arising. Working conditions should be such as not to discriminate between various categories of workers. It should be recognized, at the same time, that young people in their formative years require clearly determined and defined hours and conditions, taking into account the need to limit working time in order to allow for sufficient time for education, rest and leisure activities. This policy is to aim at ensuring the fullest possible opportunity for each young worker to qualify for, and to use his skills and endowments in, a job for which he is well suited.

(k) At the national and international levels, encouragement and facilities should be given for exchanges, travel, tourism, meetings, the study of foreign languages, the twinning of towns and universities without discrimination and similar activities, to be organized for young people of all countries in order to bring them together in educational, cultural and sporting activities in a spirit of mutual respect, understanding and co-operation.

(l) All States, the United Nations, the specialized agencies, international intergovernmental and non-governmental organizations, as well as youth organizations, shall stimulate debates and convene seminars and conferences which could serve to mobilize efforts to promote the best educational, professional and living conditions for young people, to ensure their active participation in the overall development of society and to encourage the preparation of new local, national and international programmes in accordance with the ideals of peace, security, justice and dignity of human person.

Taking into account the fact that massive and flagrant violations of the rights and fundamental freedoms of young people and, in general, of every human being are continuing on a large scale throughout the international community, on the grounds that the individuals concerned are in opposition to, or are perceived or imagined to be in opposition to, those who wield political, economic, or social power in the State or Government, or to certain aspects of their political, economic, social or cultural policies, and because life, liberty, justice, well-being and the dignity of the human person, human rights and fundamental freedoms, are universally recognized values transcending all social, national, racial, political, religious, ethnic and other differences, the international community must, as a matter of extreme urgency, act collectively to halt such massive and flagrant violations of the rights and fundamental freedoms of young people and, in general, of every human being, by adopting effective means such as setting up a mechanism that will react speedily to threatened or imminent flagrant violations of human rights. This mechanism should monitor this phenomenon and suggest ways and means of eliminating it altogether. High priority shall be given to the preventive measures and the involvement of Governments in this process.

Words of deploration and condemnation are by far not enough. Young people have asked us to give them real guarantees that massive and flagrant violations of human rights will be eliminated forever.

There are no international rules or principles that could be invoked by those who are violating human rights and fundamental freedoms. No one who really respects life, liberty and the dignity of human beings could ever oppose such urgent measures.

Taking into account the tragic experience of Romania and of other countries, I strongly suggest the setting up of a special body of the United Nations with full powers to supervise the situation of human rights in every country and to adopt recommendations and efficient measures in order to restore the liberty and dignity of man, where and when they are violated.

The final report on Human Rights and Youth (E/CN.4/Sub.2/1992/36) was presented by Mr. Mazilu to the Sub-Commission at its 1992 session under an agenda item entitled "Promotion, protection and restoration of human rights at the national, regional and international levels: (a) Prevention of discrimination and protection of children: human rights and youth: (b) Prevention of discrimination and protection of women." In his introductory remarks, made at the sixth meeting of that session held at 7 August 1992, the Special Rapporteur warmly thanked members of the Sub-Commission who had helped him during his years of detention and pointed out that the recommendations made in his report should help not only policy-makers but also youth organizations to identify ways and means of promoting the rights and freedoms of young people in various societies.

Several members of the Sub-Commission, while congratulating the author on his work, pointed out that the report failed to deal with a key question: whether "young people" should be considered as a special category for the purposes of human rights. They recognized that certain rights, in particular those set out in the Convention on the Rights of the Child, related only to young people; but they were not certain up to what age a young person should be entitled to such special protection or from what age one should be treated as a fully autonomous adult.

***EDUCATION AND WORK.*** At its 1981 session, the UN **GENERAL ASSEMBLY,** in the course of preparing for the observance of 1985 as International Youth Year: Participation, Development, Peace, recognized (resolution 36/29) the profound importance of the role of youth for all-around development of each country and expressed its view that further action was needed to codify and implement the rights of youth, with special regard for the right to work, stipulated as a fundamental human right in article 6 of the **INTERNATIONAL COVENANT ON ECONOMIC, SOCIAL AND CULTURAL RIGHTS.**

In the resolution, the Assembly indicated its awareness of the fact that the unemployment of youth is a hindrance to the full participation of young people in the socio-economic life of their country, limits their ability to participate in the development process, and is, furthermore, a source of increased social ills; and, in this regard, emphasized the importance of the secondary and higher education of youth as well as of its access to appropriate technical, vocational guidance, and training programs. It considered it necessary that States and international organizations should examine in a more comprehensive, systematic, and effective manner, ways and means to secure human rights, particularly the right to education and to work, aimed at solving the problem of youth unemployment.

Accordingly the Assembly called upon all States to adopt appropriate legislative, administrative, and other measures for the implementation and the enjoyment by youth of human rights and appealed to governmental and non-governmental organizations to pay increased attention to the securing and realization of the basic right of young people to education and vocational training and to work.

At its 1988 session, the Assembly, after considering again the question of youth, expressed its conviction (resolution 43/94) that it is necessary to ensure full enjoyment by youth of the rights stipulated in the **UNIVERSAL DECLARATION OF HUMAN RIGHTS,** the International Covenant on Economic, Social and Cultural Rights and the **INTERNATIONAL COVENANT ON CIVIL AND POLITICAL RIGHTS**; invited national coordinating bodies and bodies implementing policies and programs in the field of youth to give priority to human rights activities to be undertaken after 1985, particularly the right of young people to education and to work; stressed the importance for youth and youth organizations of the freedom of association so as to enable their active and direct participation in policies, projects, and activities organized on their behalf; and stressed the need to intensify the efforts for educating youth in accordance with national experience, conditions, and priorities and to act effectively as channels of communication.

Finally, the Assembly emphasized that providing education and employment to each young person is a worthy goal for all States and should serve the full development of the human being, which can best be ensured by countries that respect the fundamental rights and freedoms of everyone.

**SEE ALSO** *Children's Rights.*

**BIBLIOGRAPHY.** Asamblea Permanente de Derechos Humanos de Bolivia (Permanent Assembly for Human Rights in Bolivia). "Los Derechos Humanos y Juventud (sic)" (Human Rights and Youth), *Boletin* 1, no. 3 (June 1985): 1–2. NGO bulletin, in Spanish.

Centre for Socio-Legal Research and Documentation Service. "Young Persons Harmful Publications Act No. 93 of 1956," *Socio-Legal Concern Newsletter* 2, no. 5 (May 1986): 9–11. NGO bulletin article, in English.

Collins, Frank. *Non-Violence and Death at Bir Zeit University: An Investigative Report.* Jerusalem: Database Project on Palestinian Human Rights, 1987. NGO report, in English.

Human Rights Watch. *The Lost Boys: Child Soldiers and Unaccompanied Boys in Southern Sudan.* New York: 1994. NGO report, in English.

———. *The United States of America: A World Leader in Executing Juveniles.* New York: 1995. NGO report, in English.

North American Coalition for Human Rights in Korea. "Concentration Camps for Students Threatened in New 'Campus Stabilization Law,'" *Korea Update* 74 (15 Aug. 1985): 1–2. NGO newsletter article, in English.

"Problems of Contemporary Soviet Youth: Interview with Vasily Semenov, Former Sailor in the Soviet Fishing Fleet," *Samizdat Bulletin* 146 (June 1985). NGO bulletin, in English.

Radio Free Europe/Radio Liberty. "Independent Students' Association Demands Legalization," *Radio Free Europe Research* 13, no. 8 (26 Feb. 1988). Government article, in English.

Shehadeh, Raja. *Occupier's Law: Israel and the West Bank.* Washington, D.C.: Institute for Palestine Studies and Law in the Service of Man, 1985. NGO report, in English.

## YOUTH: DECLARATION ON THE PROMOTION AMONG YOUTH OF THE IDEALS OF PEACE, MUTUAL RESPECT AND UNDERSTANDING AMONG PEOPLES, UN (1965).

The Declaration echoes the conviction of the UN **GENERAL ASSEMBLY** that the education of the young—and exchanges of young people and ideas in a spirit of peace, mutual respect, and understanding—can help to improve international relations and to strengthen peace and security.

The Declaration was adopted by the General Assembly on 7 December 1965 (resolution 2037 [XX]). The text, annexed to that resolution, is as follows:

The General Assembly, . . .
Proclaims this Declaration on the Promotion among Youth of the Ideals of Peace, Mutual Respect and Understanding between Peoples and calls upon Governments, nongovernmental organizations and youth movements to recognize the principles set forth therein and to ensure their observance by means of appropriate measures:
*Principle 1.* Young people shall be brought up in the spirit of peace, justice, freedom, mutual respect and understanding in order to promote equal rights for all human beings and all nations, economic and social progress, disarmament and the maintenance of international peace and security.
*Principle 2.* All means of education, including as of major importance the guidance given by parents or family, instruction and information intended for the young should foster among them the ideals of peace, humanity, liberty and international solidarity and all other ideals which help to bring peoples closer together, and acquaint them with the role entrusted to the United Nations as a means of preserving and maintaining peace and promoting international understanding and cooperation.
*Principle 3.* Young people shall be brought up in the knowledge of the dignity and equality of all men, without distinction as to race, colour, ethnic origins or beliefs, and in respect for fundamental human rights and for the right of peoples to self-determination.
*Principle 4.* Exchanges, travel, tourism, meetings, the study of foreign languages, the twinning of towns and universities without discrimination and similar activities should be encouraged and facilitated among young people of all countries in order to bring them together in educational, cultural and sporting activities in the spirit of this Declaration.
*Principle 5.* National and international associations of young people should be encouraged to promote the purposes of the United Nations, particularly international peace and security, friendly relations among nations based on respect for the equal sovereignty of States, the final abolition of colonialism and of racial discrimination and other violations of human rights.
Youth organizations in accordance with this Declaration should take all appropriate measures within their respective fields of activity in order to make their contribution without any discrimination to the work of educating the young generation in accordance with these ideals.
Such organizations, in conformity with the principle of freedom of association, should promote the free exchange of ideas in the spirit of the principles of this Declaration and of the purposes of the United Nations set forth in the Charter.
All youth organizations should conform to the principles set forth in this Declaration.
*Principle 6.* A major aim in educating the young shall be to develop all their faculties and to train them to acquire higher moral qualities, to be deeply attached to the noble ideals of peace, liberty, the dignity and equality of all men, and imbued with respect and love for humanity and its creative achievements. To this end the family has an important role to play.
Young people must become conscious of their responsibilities in the world they will be called upon to manage and should be inspired with confidence in a future of happiness for mankind.

## YOUTH FOR DEVELOPMENT AND COOPERATION.

This non-governmental organization has consultative status (Roster) with the UN **ECONOMIC AND SOCIAL COUNCIL,** the **COUNCIL OF EUROPE,** UNCTAD, and **UNICEF.** It works to bring together youth from European countries and around the world for mutual understanding, protection of the environment, and third-world development. Founded in Montreaux, Switzerland, in 1947, the organization serves as an international network for youth organizations and pressure groups concerned with the problems of people living in developing countries; eleven international organizations cooperate in its operation. It also has member chapters in 28 countries. The group publishes the quarterly journal *Impact* and the quarterly *Least-Development Countries Newsletter*.

Youth for Development and Cooperation. Address: Overschietstraat 9, NL-1062 HN Amsterdam, the Netherlands. Telephone: (31-20) 614-2510. Fax: (31-20) 617-5545. Secretary-General: Jan Pakulski.

**YUGOSLAVIA.** The Federal Republic of Yugoslavia, consisting of the Republics of Serbia and Montenegro, is a country in south-eastern Europe with borders with Hungary to the north; Romania and Bulgaria to the east; the former Yugoslav republic of Macedonia and Albania to the south; and Bosnia and Herzegovina, Croatia, and the Adriatic Sea to the west. Its population is estimated to be 10,670,000. Orthodox Christianity is the primary religion and the primary language is Serbian-Croat. It was admitted to the United Nations in 1945.

From 1945 to 1991, the Federation consisted of six Socialist Republics (Bosnia and Herzegovina, Croatia, Macedonia, Montenegro, Serbia, and Slovenia); it broke apart in 1991 and 1992 when Slovenia, Croatia, Bosnia and Herzegovina, and Macedonia (officially named "the Former Yugoslav Republic of Macedonia" by the UN) each declared independence. Following the declaration of independence by Slovenia in 1991, federal troops bombed the capital of Ljubljana, killing 18 people, but the troops began to withdraw the following day. Serbia and Montenegro agreed to remain under the name of Yugoslavia; and a new constitution was adopted in 1992, under which each of the republics elects their own president and assembly. A directly elected federal president nominates the federal prime minister. The Federal Assembly consists of the directly elected 138-seat Chamber of Citizens and the 40-seat Chamber of Republics. Human rights and equality under the law are guaranteed by the constitution.

Parliamentary and presidential elections took place at both the federal and republican levels in December 1992. Federal President Dobrica Cosic, who was reelected with 85% of the vote, was removed from office six months later, accused of trying to overthrow Serbian President Slobodan Milosevic. Yugoslavia closed its border with Bosnian in 1994.

Since 1991 the intense fighting in both Croatia and Bosnia and Herzegovina has caused massive loss of life and displacement of millions of people from their homes. A 1991 UN **SECURITY COUNCIL** resolution imposing an arms embargo on Yugoslavia remained in effect and was coupled with economic sanctions in 1992. The United Nations Protection Force (UNPROFOR) arrived in March 1992. "Safe havens" were established in Bosnia and Herzegovina; but even some of these came under Serb attack and, in 1995, under Serb control, causing massive displacement of people and an extraordinarily complicated and difficult refugee problem in the midst of the war.

*YUGOSLAVIA AS A SOCIALIST STATE.* Invaded on 6 April 1941 by the German Army assisted by forces from Bulgaria, Hungary, and Italy, Yugoslavia was divided among the invading powers; and, for a long period, fearful atrocities were committed by the occupation forces. However, contingents of Yugoslav troops resisted fiercely from their mountain strongholds under the leadership of Draja Mikhailovich; and, in 1942, a separate "Army of National Liberation," organized by Josip Broz Tito with the support of the Soviet Union, entered the struggle. For a short time, the two liberation forces fought each other, but eventually they turned against the common foe. Helped by the surrender of Italy in 1943, they expelled the invaders from Yugoslavia.

By November 1944, Tito's Council of Liberation had become the only effective governing force in the country. It was merged with the remnants of the monarchy headed by Peter II; but, in national elections held in 1945, Tito won broad support—the monarchists boycotted the election—and emerged as premier. Under his guidance, Yugoslavia remained in harmony with other eastern European countries for some years, pursuing a vigorous policy of socialization, reconstruction, and industrialization. In 1946, the trial and conviction of Archbishop Stepinac and the execution of Mikhailovich—who was charged with collaboration with the Axis and treason because his guerrillas had fought Tito's forces—provoked great indignation throughout the non-communist world.

In 1948, a breach developed between Russia and Yugoslavia. Tito announced that Yugoslavia intended to pursue its "independent way to socialism" and charged that the Soviet Union was seeking to control his country; and was, in turn, accused of being hostile to the Soviet Union and of deviating from the program of the Communist Party. After 1948, Yugoslavia maintained its independence only with economic and military assistance supplied by the United States and its western allies. An eastern economic blockade which lasted from 1949 to 1953 forced Yugoslavia to seek new contacts in the West. It identified itself as a leader of the non-aligned nations.

Intermittant strife between the six republics, and between ethnic groups as such, escalated in 1989 when other European countries moved more rapidly towards pluralism. Fierce arguments developed on the pace of political change but went unresolved because the system of rotating presidencies and chairmanships limited the ability of local and national governments to make decisions and to act upon them.

However, in January 1990, the Yugoslav Communist Party, after a long and bitter debate, renounced its constitutionally guaranteed "leading role in society" and called upon Parliament to enact "political pluralism, including a multi-party system." And in April, the first free multi-party elections since Tito assumed power were held in Croatia after its Communist Party had expressed readiness "to compete in elections with other political programs." In those elections, the conservative and nationalist Croatian Democratic Union won a solid majority and called upon its leader, Franjo Tudjman—a former communist who had been jailed in 1972 for supporting Croatian nationalism and in 1981 for criticizing Yugoslavia's one-party system—to form a government that would guarantee the enjoyment of human rights to everyone in Croatia, including members of minorities, while contributing to the unity and stability of Yugoslavia.

***ETHNIC DIVISIONS.*** Before the breakup of Yugoslavia, the people tended to regard themselves not as Yugoslavians but as Serbians, Croatians, Montenegrins, Bosnians, Slovenians, or ethnic Albanians; and tension between these groups has erupted into violence from time to time. Serbia, for example, has experienced great difficulty in controlling the population of its autonomous province of Kosovo, in which ethnic Albanians constitute more than 80% of the population. Ethnic Albanians have also provoked confrontations in Montenegro and Macedonia, which, like Kosovo, share borders with Albania. And in central Bosnia-Herzegovina, where the Islamic faith is widely practiced, waves of religious nationalism have periodically produced intolerance and discrimination. Since the breakup, the feelings of ethnicity have had a devastating effect on the territory.

***REPORT BY THE UN COMMITTEE ON THE ELIMINATION OF RACIAL DISCRIMINATION.*** At its 984th meeting, held on 19 March 1993, the Committee expressed its grave concern over the ongoing ethnic conflict taking place in the territory of the former Yugoslavia and requested the Government of the Federal Republic of Yugoslavia (Serbia and Montenegro), as well as other successor governments, in accordance with article 9, paragraph 1, of the Convention, to submit further information on the implementation of the Convention, not later than 31 July 1993.

The report (CERD/C/248) submitted by the Federal Republic of Yugoslavia (Serbia and Montenegro) pursuant to the aforementioned decision was considered by the Committee at its 1003rd, 1004th, 1005th, and 1006th meetings, held on 13 and 16 August 1993 (see CERD/C/SR.1003–1006). The main aspects of the report (paras. 511–529, 533–547) are as follows:

The report was introduced by the representative of the State party, who said that disrespect for and denial of the right to self-determination to all peoples in the territory of the former Yugoslavia had led to the tragic conflict there with its resulting destruction, ethnic cleansing, mass exoduses and population displacements.

The representative stated that the crisis had been compounded by international interference and, in particular, the imposition of sanctions against the Federal Republic of Yugoslavia (Serbia and Montenegro) which had led to a collective condemnation of a people and which was contrary to the spirit of the International Convention on the Elimination of All Forms of Racial Discrimination. Those sanctions threatened not only the rights of the citizens of the Federal Republic of Yugoslavia (Serbia and Montenegro) but also those of the more than 600,000 refugees who had fled to the country regardless of their national or religious background. The resulting political, economic and social climate had eroded public security and the rule of law and had strengthened extremist forces pressing for intolerance and prejudice.

With respect to national minorities in the Federal Republic of Yugoslavia (Serbia and Montenegro), the representative stated that the legal system guaranteed minorities even greater rights than those provided for in international norms, including those agreed upon by the Conference on Security and Cooperation in Europe (CSCE). Additionally, work on the Federal Law on Minorities was in its final phase and would provide a further guarantee concerning the rights of members of minorities both as individuals and as a collectivity.

The issue of minority rights in the Federal Republic of Yugoslavia (Serbia and Montenegro) had been politicized and abused. In that connection, the Albanian national minority in Kosmet (Kosovo) and Metohija had clearly secessionist objectives and had tried to promote the "Kosovo Republic" idea in the Working Group on Ethnic and National Minorities of the International Conference on the Former Yugoslavia. That was being done despite the fact than constitutional provisions guaranteed Kosmet territorial and cultural autonomy, as well as the right to regulate questions in the fields of development, health, social protection and culture, including the use of the national minority language. Unfortunately, members of the Albanian national minority had almost completely boycotted school curricula in their own language. Similarly, there had been a decrease in the number of Albanians in the judiciary, police force and health institutions, which was due not to discrimination or expulsion from work but to their refusal to recognize the legitimate authorities of the State.

The situation in Vojvodina and Sandzak had also been politicized as part of the pressure being applied to the Federal Republic of Yugoslavia (Serbia and Montenegro). In Vojvodina, there were about 344,000 members of the Hungarian national minority whose ethnic, cultural, linguistic and religious identity was completely guaranteed. In places where there was a greater number of Hungarians, they held a majority in all the institutions of authority, including education, the economy and social life. With respect to the Raska (Sandzak) region, it was no more than a geographic area and the problems of the rights and status of Muslims living there had been politically imposed and artificially construed.

Members of the Committee expressed satisfaction that the State party had submitted further information as had been requested and that a delegation had been sent from the capital to respond to the questions posed by the Committee. Members noted that although the report contained useful information on the legal framework for the protection of national and ethnic minorities, there was little information on the actual situation of the various minorities and the extent to which their rights were protected in reality. There was also little information on the tense situation prevailing in certain regions of the State where there had been serious violations of the Convention and where ethnic tensions threatened to escalate into armed conflict.

Members of the Committee referred to information from other sources on the situation in the Federal Republic of Yugoslavia (Serbia and Montenegro), in particular the report of the Special Rapporteur on the situation of human rights in the territory of the former Yugoslavia (E/CN.4/1993/50). In that regard, members of the Committee wished to have further information on restrictions on the media in Kosovo and on problems that had arisen in the educational sector there following the reported changes in the school curricula which suppressed Albanian culture. Members also requested clarification on a number of laws listed in the report of the Special Rapporteur which were reported to be discriminatory in nature (see E/CN.4/1993/50, para. 156).

Members expressed their concern over the deterioration of the situation in Kosovo and wished to know why the autonomous status of that province had been revoked and the provincial courts there had been abolished. Regret was expressed over the fact that the Albanians there had chosen not to participate in social and public life. Emphasizing the need to foster a dialogue between the Government and the local minority leaders in Kosovo, members wished to know what active steps the Government was undertaking with a view to reducing tension and normalizing the situation there.

Members were particularly concerned over reports of police brutality, arbitrary arrests, disappearances and mass dismissals of the Albanian national minority in Kosovo and wished to know what had been done to investigate those reports and punish those responsible for such acts. Members also wished to know to what extent Albanian language newspapers, radio broadcasts and television programmes were still available in Kosovo.

Members expressed their concern over reports of verbal and physical threats and other acts of intimidation directed against the minorities living in Vojvodina, including the destruction of homes and cultural and religious monuments. According to those reports, the police and judiciary had not provided effective protection to the victims of such abuse. Members were particularly disturbed over reports of complacency on the part of law enforcement officials regarding the campaigns of terror and intimidation directed against minorities by paramilitary groups, and requested further clarification of the situation in that regard.

Members noted with concern that a similar situation prevailed in Sandzak, where there had been reports of a campaign of terror carried out by paramilitary organizations with the aim of intimidating the Muslim population into abandoning their homes. In that connection, members wished to receive further information on the steps being taken to investigate allegations of such ethnically motivated campaigns, whether there had been any punishment of the guilty in that regard and what steps had been taken to avoid recurrences.

Stressing the need for ongoing monitoring of ethnic tensions in the State party, members wished to know why the Government had so far declined to renew the mandate of the CSCE monitoring missions in Kosovo, Vojvodina and Sandzak.

Members also wished to have further information on the role of government officials in inciting the public to ethnic intolerance and violence; on discriminatory practices concerning employment, education and housing; on reported frequent harassment of gypsies by the police; and on the number of ethnic Bulgarians in the Federal Republic of Yugoslavia (Serbia and Montenegro), their participation in government and measures taken to facilitate the use of their language. Members also requested clarification on the extent to which the Federal army was linked to activities in neighbouring States where massive human rights violations and ethnic cleansing had been occurring.

Members wished to know whether the Federal Republic of Yugoslavia (Serbia and Montenegro) was considering making the declaration under article 14 of the Convention recognizing the competence of the Committee to receive individual complaints alleging violations of the Convention.

Replying to the questions, the representative of the State party stated that there was significant representation of minority groups at all levels of government and he provided detailed figures to that effect. With reference to problems concerning education in Kosovo, the representative stated that the ethnic Albanians were the only minority in the Federal Republic of Yugoslavia (Serbia and Montenegro) who refused to exercise their rights and had chosen to boycott the schools. As a result, there were 466 schools for ethnic Albanians in Kosovo that were not used. There was a large number of schools that had been provided for the use of other minorities in Kosovo as well as in Vojvodina and Sandzak and which were used.

With regard to the mass media, the representative stated that public information facilities were controlled by minority groups and that special resources were made available to them in order to support their operation. Specific information was given indicating that there were many newspapers and weeklies as well as radio and television programmes in minority languages throughout the country. In particular, such facilities were provided in the Hungarian, Slovak, Albanian, Russian, Romanian, Ukrainian and Bulgarian languages.

With respect to the war crimes tribunal that was to be established pursuant to the decision of the Security Council, cooperation with that body would depend on decisions taken by Parliament, particularly concerning amnesty and extradition laws.

Concerning the CSCE monitoring missions in certain areas of the country, the Government had no objection to those missions and there had been cooperation in that regard. The agreement had not been extended beyond the original six-month mandate, however, because the participation of the Federal Republic of Yugoslavia (Serbia and Montenegro) in CSCE had not been clarified. The Federal Republic of Yugoslavia (Serbia and Montenegro) sought only to participate as a member of that body and, thereby, in the decisions affecting its own future.

The representative stressed that the Government was open to dialogue with all minorities in the country. He stated that international criticism of the Federal Republic of Yugoslavia (Serbia and Montenegro) had not been objective and that there had been mistakes and shortcomings on all sides that had contributed to the problems which the region was currently experiencing. He declared his Government's willingness to fulfil its obligations under the Convention and to cooperate with the Committee as well as other international bodies in the search for constructive solutions. . . .

At its 1012th meeting, held on 20 August 1993, the Committee adopted the following concluding observations:

*Positive aspects.* The Committee welcomed the timely submission of the requested information and the presence of a delegation as an indication of the State party's willingness to continue the dialogue with the Committee.

The Committee took note of information made available to it regarding the Federal Ministry for Human and Minority Rights and of measures under consideration to provide a legal framework for the protection of the rights of members of minorities.

The Committee welcomed the interest shown by the delegation of the Federal Republic of Yugoslavia (Serbia and Montenegro) in an active role for the Committee with respect to re-establishing a dialogue between the interested parties in Kosovo within the framework of the early warning measures and urgent procedures devised by the Committee in its working paper of March 1993 (annex III).

*Principal subjects of concern.* The Committee expressed deep concern over reports of serious and systematic violations of the Convention occurring in the territory of the Federal Republic of Yugoslavia (Serbia and Montenegro). In that regard, the Committee considered that by not opposing extremism and ultranationalism on ethnic grounds, State authorities and political leaders incurred serious responsibility.

The Committee also noted with great concern that links existed between the Federal Republic of Yugoslavia (Serbia and Montenegro) and Serbian militias and paramilitary groups responsible for massive, gross and systematic violations of human rights in Bosnia and Herzegovina and in Croatian territories controlled by Serbs.

The Committee expressed alarm over the deteriorating situation in Kosovo. A number of measures had been implemented there which were in violation of the provisions of the Convention, including the enactment of discriminatory laws, the closing of minority schools, the mass dismissal of Albanians from their jobs and the imposition of restrictions on the use of the Albanian language. Such measures had resulted in the increasing marginalization of the Albanians in Kosovo. In that regard, the Committee noted that Albanians in Kosovo did not participate in public life.

The Committee was deeply concerned by reports indicating that in Kosovo, as well as in Vojvodina and Sandzak, members of national minorities had been subject to a campaign of terror carried out by paramilitary organizations with the aim of intimidating or forcing them into abandoning their homes. The Committee also noted that information provided by the Government referred to such practices directed against Serbs in Kosovo. The Committee was particularly concerned that the Government of the Federal Republic of Yugoslavia (Serbia and Montenegro) had not ensured that public security and law enforcement officials took steps effectively to prohibit such criminal activities, punish the perpetrators and compensate the victims, as required

under article 6 of the Convention. The Committee was also concerned that other minorities in other regions of the Federal Republic of Yugoslavia (Serbia and Montenegro) were suffering from various forms of discrimination.

The Committee regretted the absence of a dialogue between the Government and the leaders of the Albanians in Kosovo aimed at reducing tension and helping to prevent further massive human rights violations in the region. In that connection, the Committee regretted the recent lapse of the CSCE mission that was monitoring ethnic tension and human rights violations in Kosovo, as well as in Vojvodina and Sandzak.

The Committee was also concerned that Serbs in Bosnia and Herzegovina were hindering the attempts of the Government of that State to implement the Convention.

*Suggestions and recommendations.* The Committee underlined that non-discrimination in the enjoyment of fundamental, civil, political, economic, social and cultural rights must be effectively guaranteed in law and actively protected in practice if further ethnic unrest was to be avoided. The Committee in no way encouraged unilateral trends towards separatism or secession. In that connection, the Committee noted that separatism could best be discouraged by the active promotion and protection of minority rights and interethnic tolerance.

The Committee recommended that, in conformity with articles 2 and 4 of the Convention, the Government should prohibit racial discrimination and should urgently take vigorous steps to ban racist activities and propaganda. In that connection it was vital that paramilitary groups be disbanded, reports of ethnically motivated attacks, including allegations of arbitrary arrests, disappearance and torture, promptly investigated and those responsible punished. The Committee emphasized the importance of providing proper training in human rights norms for law enforcement officials in accordance with its general recommendation XIII and of ensuring the equitable representation among their ranks of national minorities.

The Committee strongly emphasized the need for urgent measures in respect of the situation in Kosovo in order to prevent persisting ethnic problems there from escalating into violence and armed conflict. The Committee recommended, in particular, that all possible measures be taken by both sides to foster dialogue between the Government and the leaders of Albanians in Kosovo. The Committee recommended that the Government of the Federal Republic of Yugoslavia (Serbia and Montenegro) strengthen the territorial integrity of the State by considering ways of assuring autonomy in Kosovo with a view to ensuring the effective representation of the Albanians in political and judicial institutions and their participation in democratic processes.

The Committee urged the Federal Republic of Yugoslavia (Serbia and Montenegro) to undertake all measures at its disposal with a view to bringing to an end the massive, gross and systematic human rights violations currently occurring in those areas of Croatia and Bosnia and Herzegovina controlled by Serbs. The Committee also urged the State party to assist efforts to arrest, bring to trial and punish all those responsible for crimes which would be covered by the terms of reference of the international tribunal established pursuant to Security Council resolution 808 (1993). The Committee further urge the Federal Republic of Yugoslavia (Serbia and Montenegro) to give effect to the International Court of Justice's Order of Provisional Measures of 8 April 1993.

*Further action.* Taking into account the wish expressed by

the representative of the Government and the need to promote a dialogue between the Albanians in Kosovo and the Government, the Committee offered its good offices in the form of a mission of its members. The purpose of the mission would be to help promote a dialogue for a peaceful solution of issues concerning respect for human rights in Kosovo, in particular the elimination of all forms of racial discrimination and, whenever possible, to help parties concerned to arrive at such a solution. It was understood that such a mission should have every opportunity to inform itself of the situation directly, including full discussion with central and local authorities, as well as with individuals and organizations. In that connection, no one should be victimized for, or in any way have their rights or security impaired as a result of, cooperating with the mission. The Committee requested the State party to respond by 1 October 1993 if it wished to accept that offer, in which case the Chairman, after due consultations, would designate members of the Committee for such a mission.

In accordance with article 9, paragraph 1, of the Convention, the Committee requested further information from the State party on measures taken to implement the provisions of the Convention, particularly in view of the concluding observations adopted by the Committee at its forty-third session. The State party was requested to provide that information by 1 January 1994 so that it might be considered by the Committee at its forty-fourth session.

*REACTION BY YUGOSLAV GOVERNMENT.* In 1995, the Government of Yugoslavia reported once again to the UN Committee on the Elimination of Racial Discrimination on measures it has enacted to give effect to the provisions of the Convention, i.e., measures to protect human and minority rights. The foremost task facing the federal government is to take measures to ensure a subsistence level for all citizens of Yugoslavia given that the grave economic crisis and hyperinflation have led to a dramatic fall in living standards throughout the country. The government has adopted the Programme of Economic Recovery, launched on 24 January 1994 and designed to break the neck of inflation and impose financial and monetary discipline. The report proceeds as follows (paras. 87–116):

The wartime operations in Yugoslavia's immediate neighbourhood, the effects of the war and the sanctions in evidence throughout the Federal Republic of Yugoslavia have led to a rise in the crime rate. In certain parts of the country, such as the Autonomous Province of Vojvodina in Serbia and the town of Pljevlja in the Republic of Montenegro for example, cases have been reported of pressure on persons belonging to national minorities, particularly Croats and Muslims, in the form of threats, assaults, threatening phone calls and also, in some places in the form of serious crimes.

In the Republic of Montenegro, and in the town of Pljevlja in particular, the security situation was destabilized especially in 1992, which led to the cooling of ethnic relations, a number of terrorist raids, and to the throwing of explosive devices and grenades on facilities owned by Muslims.

The small town of Pljevlja (with a population of 45,000) is located in the part of the Republic of Montenegro bordering on the war-torn areas of Bosnia-Herzegovina. It has a mixed Serb, Montenegrin and Muslim population. The war conflagration in neighbouring Bosnia has provoked not only ethnic intolerance and hatred but also terrorist raids against persons belonging to other nationalities, primarily involving the planting of explosives in shops and residential buildings. (According to the data of the Interior Ministry of the Republic of Montenegro, during 1992, over 80 such blasts were registered, of which 30 were in Pljevlja, 25 in Bijelo Polje and 13 in the capital of Podgorica.) However, the situation was the worst in Pljevlja, as testified by the larger number of planted explosive devices. Apart from the planted explosives and arson, the population was also prompted into action against the Muslims by the activities of individual national parties with ultra-nationalist programmes, i.e. by extreme pressure applied by such parties which resorted to verbal threats and openly called on the Muslims to move out. According to the data of the Interior Ministry of the Republic of Montenegro, in the course of this year several hundred Muslims moved out of this commune, which also includes a number of villages around Pljevlja, and left mainly for Turkey, Macedonia and Germany. Mention should however be also made of some one hundred persons of Serb or Montenegrin nationality who moved out of Rozaje in the same period. The National Assembly of the Republic of Montenegro has discussed this situation on a number of occasions so far and instructed the competent local authorities to take resolute action to defuse tension. To that end, the authorities have taken the following measures:

(a) Thirteen cases of planting of explosives in buildings owned by the Muslims have been elucidated, the suspects arrested and investigation undertaken by the competent court of law;

(b) Indictments have been served against a total of 21 residents of Pljevlja and of Bijelo Polje nearby (which is also the seat of the State Prosecutor in charge of the district as a whole) who stand accused of acts of terrorism against Muslims. Nine of the accused are suspected of occasionally crossing over into Bosnia-Herzegovina, so the court will also assess their activity across the border. All persons against whom investigation has been undertaken belong to the Serb or the Montenegrin nationality;

(c) Police reinforcements have been sent to Pljevlja, particularly since September, thus consolidating the overall civil security, so there have been no further threats nor pressure applied nor explosives planted against the Muslims;

(d) Throughout Montenegro resolute measures have been taken since August to seize illegally owned weaponry from civilians. As a result, 500 items of different armaments, ammunition and explosives have been seized;

(e) The Interior Ministry of the Republic of Montenegro has undertaken an inquiry against 11 police officers in places where public security has come under threat and initiated an investigation to establish whether any mistakes were made in efforts to maintain public law and order. According to the preliminary analyses, this was due to negligence, but, to find out more, the findings of the official enquiry which is under way are needed.

We also wish to point out that the Higher Public Prosecutor in Podgorica has submitted a request for an inquiry to be conducted against four persons suspected of having committed homicide in Bistričko Naselje, Nikšić and, simultaneously, provoked ethnic and religious hatred, discord and intolerance. The said persons are currently held in detention.

According to the data of the Federal Government, the pressures and displacement along nationalist lines have ceased. It is quite clear in this case as well that the authorities of the Republic of Montenegro have neither provoked nor encouraged ethnic cleansing, so that speaking about an "official policy" would here be out of the question.

The civil war in the former Yugoslav Republic of Bosnia-Herzegovina, as well as the surge of Muslim fundamentalism, have also led to tension mounting in the Raška district, a border area inhabited by an ethnically mixed population identical in composition to that of its war-afflicted neighbourhood. A number of Muslims from this area joined the war effort in Bosnia-Herzegovina, i.e. the Muslim military units and police formations in Sarajevo, which has led to the further worsening of the overall situation.

The economic conditions in the Raška district, which was an economically underdeveloped region in the former Socialist Federal Republic of Yugoslavia, have deteriorated significantly in the past two years. This has been due especially to the United Nations Security Council sanctions.

The Federal Government received in August 1993 the so-called Memorandum on the Establishment of Special Status for Sandžak from the Muslim National Council of Sandžak, i.e. a demand for territorial and political autonomy to be established in the Raška district. The purpose of this act is to form a national Muslim state with legislative, executive and judicial powers. The Federal Government decided that this act called into question the territorial integrity of the Federal Republic of Yugoslavia, or rather of its constituent republics, their sovereignty and constitutional order.

We wish in particular to point to the facts relating to the arrest and judicial proceedings against 25 Muslims from the Raška district, namely: Hajriz Kolašinac, Fadil Ugljanin, Hajro Aljković, Džemail Etemović, Šefčet Gračanin, Mustava Alič, Hode Jakupović, Ibrahim Fahović, Alija Halilović, Jonuz Škrijelj, Adem Hasić, Sefkija Rašljanin, Safet Zilkić, Rifat Dupljak, Nedžib Hodžic, Hajriz Fejzović, Zekrija Hajrović, Asim Sećierović, Mersat Plojović, Nasuf Halilović, Murat Mušić, Zubdija Hodžić, Jakub Hodžić, Mirsad Hodžić, and Šemsudin Kučević.

The District Public Prosecutor in Novi Pazar indicted the above-mentioned persons on 18 October 1993 on suspicion of having committed the criminal offence of violating the territorial integrity of the Federal Republic of Yugoslavia, and 17 persons of those 25 suspects have also been accused of procuring without permission, keeping, wearing, manufacture, exchange or selling of firearms or explosive substances.

According to the bill of indictment, in the period from May 1991 to May 1993 the suspects formed military and police formations and units and the Main Headquarters for Sandžak and main municipal HQs. They trained sabotage groups in handling infantry weapons and explosives, the so-called "black threesomes" were formed for quiet liquidation of individuals, and sabotage raid plans were developed (targeting military barracks, particular railway sections, bridges, municipal water supply, radio stations, etc.). Apart from training in the country, a certain number of persons have also received training in Turkey.

There are plans, drawings, maps, lists and documents testifying to the preparation of terrorist raids. Thus, for example, a plan for Sjenica has been developed dividing this commune up into regions, setting up HQs for each, determining strategic thrust of action, peak elevation markings and facilities to be captured. The plan further envisages the required manpower to carry out the above tasks and included lists of names of Muslim men fit for military service.

A certain quantity of weapons, ammunition and explosive materials was seized from arrested persons who were unable to produce the required licences. There is also other evidence (written orders) testifying to the distribution of armaments and ammunition, as well as to the collection of medical supplies. Thirteen persons stand accused of having taken part in a drive to steal a total of 260 kg of explosives from a warehouse near the quarry at Tutin.

Apart from wartime plans for the Raška district, maps and drawings of terrain required for conducting combat operations in this area, a decision was also taken to set up a corridor in between Bosnia and the so-called Sandžak to connect the following towns: Foča, Goražde, Čajuiče, Rudo, Višegrad, Pljevlja and Priboj.

Without prejudice to the court ruling on this case, we have only wished to appraise you of the facts and evidence collected in the course of investigation on the basis of which the bill of indictment has been served in order to show that this is by no means a political process, let alone a judicial process taken because of a person's belonging to a minority community or a political organization.

Ethnic intolerance between Hungarians, Croats and Serbs has been registered in the following towns and villages: Nikinci, Ruma, Ruski Krstur, Golubinci, Kukujevci, Novi Slankamen and Beška. Particular problems have arisen at Hrtkovci where some 500 Serb refugee families have taken refuge after fleeing Croatia, including 350 veterans. Some 200 families or around 600 persons have moved out of the village of Hrtkovc into Croatia mostly after having swapped their real estate in a legal procedure. A large number of Croat youths have signed up for the National Guard (ZNG) and villagers belonging to the Croat nationality have raised considerable funds in aid of Croatia's struggle, for which they have been particularly commended by President Tudjman. The "Hrtkovci case" was bloated mostly by foreign mass media, which went about the whole problem in an inadequate manner, passing in silence over the ethnic cleansing which occurred at the same time in Croatia, which resulted in the exodus of 350 Serb veterans with their families to Hrtkovci alone.

The joint drive of the Federal Ministry of Justice, the Interior Ministry and the Ministry of Justice and the Interior Ministery of the Republic of Serbia and the visit by the Federal Minister for Human and Minority Rights have brought the whole matter to an end. Peace and order have been restored and the personal and material safety of all citizens have been guaranteed without distinction as to national affiliation. To that end, the following measures have been taken:

(a) Reinforcement of the police force and patrols in villages where there are no police stations;

(b) Twenty cases of planted explosive devices and use of hand grenades have been elucidated and investigated and 12 persons have been taken into custody;

(c) Eight complaints have been filed for criminal offences and eight persons arrested and accused of the criminal offences of violation of the freedom and rights of persons belonging to another nationality and judicial proceedings against such persons have been completed or are continuing;

(d) One hundred and forty-five persons have been identified and handed over to the courts for wearing weapons without licence and the haul of the raids in question included a large quantity of weapons and ammunition.

Although, generally speaking, "disappearances" are not frequent in the territory of the Federal Republic of Yugoslavia, it has to be noted with regret that on two occasions citizens of the Federal Republic of Yugoslavia, mainly Muslims, have been abducted and that unfortunately the abductions have remained unresolved so far. The two cases of disappearance—the first on 22 October 1992 when 17 persons belonging to the Muslim nationality were abducted and the second on 27 February 1993 when 19 persons were abducted of whom 18 were Muslims and one was a Croat—have remained unresolved although certain arrests have been made on their account. The main obstacle in the investigation is the fact that both kidnappings (one at Sjeverin, and the other at Žegča) took place outside the territory of the Federal Republic of Yugoslavia, namely in the Republic of Srpska.

As for the armed clashes going on in the territory of the former Bosnia-Herzegovina, the Federal Government wishes to remind the esteemed Committee members that in the civil war being waged in the territory of the former Bosnia-Herzegovina, the human rights of members of all three constituent peoples (Serbs, Croats and Muslims), as well as of other citizens living in that region, are being grossly and repeatedly violated.

The Federal Republic of Yugoslavia has explicitly called for the immediate cessation of wartime operations and for the signing of a peace accord.

Accordingly, the Federal Government condemns, and urges the punishment of, perpetrators of war crimes, crimes against peace, crimes against humanity and other forms of gross violation of human rights without distinction as to their national affiliation.

In that connection, the Government of the Federal Republic of Yugoslavia and the competent agencies have taken and are taking measures to expose and punish the perpetrators of such criminal offences, as well as to remove the causes of massive and gross human rights violations in the territory of this former Yugoslav republic.

The Federal Government points out that with the pull-out of the former Yugoslav People's Army (JNA) from the territory of the former Bosnia-Herzegovina there are no longer any members of the Yugoslav Army in that former Yugoslav republic.

The competent agencies of the Federal Republic of Yugoslavia have recently launched a resolute drive to disarm all unlawfully armed persons. Thus, action has been taken at the District Court of Leskovac against four persons accused of committing the criminal offence of procuring without authorization, wearing, manufacturing, exchange or sale of firearms, ammunition and explosive devices under article 33 of the Law on Weaponry and Ammunition of the Republic of Serbia. The said persons are also being prosecuted for committing the criminal offence of attempted homicide. All four defendants, citizens of the Republic of Serbia and Serbs by nationality, sought in June 1993 to put to death the refugees in the village hospital at Veliki Grabovci in the commune of Leskovac. Some 90 persons were being treated at the hospital of whom 75 were Muslims, 14 were Croats and one was a Serb woman. The defendants committed the criminal offence by throwing a bomb and by activating a mobile missile-launcher. Thus, they inflicted light bodily harm on a Serb woman and a Muslim woman and deliberately threatened the lives of other persons, mostly children and women. The defendants have been ordered to remain in custody.

The District Public Prosecutor in Šabac (Republic of Serbia) has filed a request for inquiry to be made with regard to a person of Serbian nationality, a citizen of the Federal Republic of Yugoslavia on suspicion of having committed a war crime against civilians under article 142 of the Criminal Code of the Federal Republic of Yugoslavia. There is reason to believe that on 10 June 1992 the defendant shot down 17 persons of Muslim nationality at the Cultural Centre at Čelopek near Zvornik (in the territory of the former Bosnia-Herzegovina) where a large number of civilians of Muslim nationality from Divač had gathered, and then transported the bodies to the nearby gravel plant where he killed another 4 persons also of Muslim nationality. He is further suspected of having shot down 19 persons at the same place with an automatic rifle and wounded another 13 on 27 June 1992. All victims were Muslims by nationality. The defendant is charged with having taken for questioning another 34 persons from the Cultural Centre at Čelopek. He reportedly took them in an unknown direction and their fate remains unknown. An inquiry has also been undertaken against the same defendant for raping a Muslim woman at Radaje by Mali Zvornik (Republic of Serbia) on 21 July 1993 and robbing her of DEM 1,000.

The Higher Court of Podgorica (Republic of Montenegro) sentenced four persons to 20 years in prison each (the maximum sentence) for the criminal offence of homicide under article 39 of the relevant law of the Republic of Montenegro. The convicts, who belonged to the special territorial defence units of the Republic of Srpska, put to death under a previous agreement a three-member Muslim family from the former Bosnia-Herzegovina. The crime took place in the territory of the Republic of Montenegro, to which the family had fled for shelter.

Proceedings are under way at the Military Tribunal in Niš against a person who has put to death seven persons of Croat nationality at Kijev Do in the commune of Trebinje.

Investigation is under way at the District Court of Šabac to establish the responsibility of two persons who stand accused of war crimes against the civilian population, under article 142 of the Criminal Code of Yugoslavia, perpetrated in an area of the former Bosnia-Herzegovina.

Criminal proceedings are under way at the Military Court of Belgrade against a person who has put to death two prisoners-of-war belonging to the enemy formations.

The Government of the Federal Republic of Yugoslavia wishes, in conclusion, once more to underline its willingness to establish open cooperation with the Committee, as well as to reiterate that ensuring efficient and effective protection of human rights and minority rights in the territory of the Federal Republic of Yugoslavia is its primary concern.

The UN Commission on Human Rights, in resolution 1995/89 of 8 March 1995, expressed its dismay that a wide variety of international actions taken by itself, the General Assembly, the Security Council and the International Court of Justice, had failed to put an end to massive systematic violations of human rights occurring in the States on the territory of the former Yugoslavia, especially in Bosnia and Herzegovina. At the same time, it noted with appreciation the establishment of the Federation of Bosnia and Herzegovina by the Washington Agreements of 1 March 1994, which had tangibly improved the human rights situation and facilitated the delivery of humanitarian supplies in the territory.

Noting with anguish the reports of the Special Rapporteur, and in particular his seventh, eighth, ninth and tenth periodic reports (E.CN.4/1995/4, E/CN.4/

1995/10, A/49/641-S/1994/1252, E/CN.4/1995/57) and his special report on the media (E/CN.4/1995/54), the Commission adopted, on 8 March 1995, resolution 1995/89 containing *inter alia* 44 conclusions and recommendations, as follows:

Commends and thanks the Special Rapporteur for his continued tenacity in fulfilling his mandate under the most trying circumstances, and for the light shed by his important reports, in particular his latest reports, and notes that his continuing activity can be a force to reduce human rights violations in the region;

Again deplores and strongly condemns the continual refusal of the Federal Republic of Yugoslavia (Serbia and Montenegro) and the self-proclaimed Bosnian Serb authorities, as described in the reports of the Special Rapporteur, to permit the Special Rapporteur to conduct investigations in territories under their control, as mandated by the Commission;

Strongly condemns the specific violations identified by the Special Rapporteur in his reports, most of which are committed in connection with the systematic policy of "ethnic cleansing" and genocidal acts in the areas of the former Yugoslavia under the control of the self-proclaimed Serb authorities, and which include mass killing, torture, disappearances, rape, and other sexual abuses against women and children, the use of civilians as human shields on confrontation lines and as mine clearers, arbitrary executions, the destruction of houses, religious objects and cultural and historical heritage, forced and illegal evictions, detentions, arbitrary searches and other acts of violence;

Also condemns the systematic impediments by the self-proclaimed Bosnian Serb authorities and the self-proclaimed Serb authorities in the occupied part of Croatia of humanitarian operations, and particularly the obstruction of humanitarian relief convoys forwarded to besieged areas and towns;

Further condemns the indiscriminate shelling and besieging of cities and civilian areas, the systematic terrorization and murder of non-combatants, the destruction of vital services and the use of military force against civilian populations and relief operations, including the use of cluster and napalm bombs against civilian targets by Bosnian and Croatian Serb forces;

Again denounces the continued deliberate and unlawful attacks and use of military force against civilians and other protected persons by all sides, recognizing that the primary, though not the sole, responsibility lies with the Serbian forces;

Reaffirms the responsibility of all parties to the conflict to find peaceful solutions through negotiations and to protect fully human rights at all times;

Strongly reaffirms that in order to achieve a peaceful and lasting solution and to improve the human rights situation in Bosnia and Herzegovina, the right of return to their homes in safety and dignity of all refugees and displaced persons victims of the "ethnic cleansing" must be protected.

Strongly condemns the continued refusal of the Federal Republic of Yugoslavia (Serbia and Montenegro) and the self-proclaimed Bosnian Serb authorities to permit the Special Rapporteur to conduct investigations in territories under their control;

Condemns categorically all violations of human rights and international humanitarian law, as established by the Special Rapporteur in his reports, recognizing that primary responsibility for most of these violations is borne by the leadership in territory under Serb control and political and military leaders in Yugoslavia (Serbia and Montenegro);

Strongly condemns the self-proclaimed Bosnian Serb authorities for gravely violating the Agreement on Complete Cessation of Hostilities, concluded on 31 December 1994, as exemplified in the safe area of Bihac;

Strongly urges the international community to continue to support the ongoing peace process through acceptance by all sides of the Contact Group peace plan on Bosnia and Herzegovina, and to exert all pressure on the self-proclaimed Bosnian Serb authorities to accept that peace plan;

Demands immediate, firm and resolute action by all concerned parties and the international community to put an end to all human rights violations and breaches of international law, to secure a just and lasting peace in Bosnia and Herzegovina, and to bring those responsible to trial;

Expresses its alarm at the conclusions of the Special Rapporteur that nationalistic rhetoric and sweeping attacks and slurs against other national groups have been a dominant feature of reports propagated by some media in Croatia and in Bosnia and Herzegovina, but especially in a systematic way by most media of the Federal Republic of Yugoslavia (Serbia and Montenegro), and particularly by media under the control of the self-proclaimed Bosnian Serb authorities as described in the reports of the Special Rapporteur, and of the self-proclaimed Bosnian Serb authorities in parts of Croatia, and that this phenomenon has led directly to the commission of fearful atrocities on the battlefields and throughout the territory, underlines in this regard the importance of ensuring the existence of independent media, and calls for immediate action by each Government to implement the recommendations of the Special Rapporteur in this regard (E/CN.4/1995/54, paras. 211-216);

Stresses in this context the importance of the closure of the international border between the Federal Republic of Yugoslavia (Serbia and Montenegro) and Bosnia and Herzegovina, and the sealing of border crossing points in accordance with the expressed desire of the international community in support of the acceptance of the Contact Group's territorial proposal;

Condemns the continuation, particularly in the areas of Banja Luka, Prijedor and Bijelina, of the heinous and illegitimate acts identified by the Special Rapporteur as elements of "ethnic cleansing", while commending the courage and sacrifice of the many Serbs who continue to refuse to take part in such violations, and urge the international community to use all its influence on the parties, in particular the authorities in parts of Croatia and Bosnia and Herzegovina under Serbian control and occupation, to end them immediately and to reverse their effects;

Also condemns all deliberate and arbitrary impeding of the delivery of food, medical and other supplies essential for the civilian population, in particular of the Bihac area, which can constitute a serious violation of international law, and of medical evacuations, as well as attacks on and continued harassment of the United Nations Protection Force and personnel working with the Office of the United Nations High Commissioner for Refugees and other humanitarian organizations, which have caused injuries to and the death of those who seek to protect civilians and to deliver humanitarian assistance, and demands that all parties ensure that all persons under their control cease all such attacks and acts of harassment;

Renews its expression of outrage at the systematic practice

of rape as a weapon of war against women and children and as an instrument of "ethnic cleansing" in the areas of armed conflict in the territory of the former Yugoslavia, and again recognizes that rape in these circumstances constitutes a war crime;

Reaffirms that all persons who perpetrate or authorize violations of international law are individually responsible and accountable, and should be brought to justice in accordance with internationally recognized principles of due process;

Welcomes in this connection the expanding activities of the International Tribunal established by the Security Council in its resolution 827 (1993) of 25 May 1993, and in this context requests States, as a matter of urgency, to make available to the International Tribunal resources, services and expert personnel, including experts in the prosecution of crimes of sexual violence, as recommended by the General Assembly, and encourages as well voluntary contributions from intergovernmental and non-governmental organizations so that the Tribunal may conduct without any further delay its stipulated functions of trying those accused of and punishing those responsible for violations of international law;

Also welcomes the progress made by the Prosecutor of the International Tribunal, as shown by the series of indictments announced by the Tribunal, and expresses its support for this crucial effort to investigate and prosecute persons suspected of having committed serious violations of international humanitarian law;

Reaffirms that States are to be held accountable for violations of human rights, that they have the obligation to enforce respect for human rights and that they should ensure that those responsible for violations are brought to trial;

Requests all states, as required under Security Council resolution 827 (1993), to cooperate with the International Tribunal in providing information and evidence for investigation and trials and in the apprehension and surrender of persons accused of crimes within the jurisdiction of the Tribunal;

Again urges the Special Rapporteur, all United Nations bodies, including the United Nations Protection Force and the United Nations human rights treaty bodies, specialized agencies, Governments and informed intergovernmental and non-governmental organizations to cooperate fully with the Prosecutor of the International Tribunal and provide him on a continuing basis with all relevant and accurate information in their possession related to his task;

Demands the immediate internationally supervised release of all persons arbitrarily or otherwise illegally detained and the immediate closure of all places of detention not authorized by or in compliance with the Geneva Conventions of 12 August 1949 and the Additional Protocols thereto;

Reiterates its demand that all parties immediately notify the International Committee of the Red Cross of the locations of all camps, prisons and other places of detention, and that there be immediate, unimpeded and continued access to such places by the International Committee of the Red Cross, the Special Rapporteur and other relevant international and regional organizations;

Commends and thanks the expert member of the Working Group on Enforced and Involuntary Disappearances for his first report on the special process on missing persons in the territory of the former Yugoslavia (E/CN.4/1995/37);

Recalls its resolution 1995/35 of 3 March 1995, in which the Commission expressed its appreciation to the Governments of Bosnia and Herzegovina and Croatia and requested them to continue and expand their cooperation with the special process and urged the Government of the Federal Republic of Yugoslavia (Serbia and Montenegro) to undertake maximum efforts to cooperate by disclosing all relevant available information and documentation, and again urges all parties to cooperate with the special process;

Strongly condemns the discriminatory measures and practices, as well as the violations of human rights, carried out by the authorities of the Federal Republic of Yugoslavia (Serbia and Montenegro) against ethnic Albanians in Kosovo;

Again demands that the Federal Republic of Yugoslavia (Serbia and Montenegro) respect the human rights and fundamental freedoms of ethnic Albanians in Kosovo, recalling that the best means to prevent the possible escalation of the conflict is to safeguard human rights and establish democratic institutions in Kosovo;

Urgently demands that the authorities of the Federal Republic of Yugoslavia (Serbia and Montenegro):

(a) Cease all human rights violations, discriminatory measures and practices against ethnic Albanians in Kosovo, in particular arbitrary detention and violation of the right to a fair trial and the practice of torture and other cruel, inhuman and degrading treatment;

(b) Release all political prisoners and cease the persecution of political leaders and members of local human rights organizations;

(c) Respect the will of the inhabitants of Kosovo, allowing its expression by democratic means as the best way of preventing the escalation of the conflict there;

(d) Guarantee the freedom of the media throughout the country, and in particular in Kosova, and cease the obstruction of the Albanian-language media in Kosovo;

(e) Abrogate the official settlement policy of the Government of the Federal Republic of Yugoslavia (Serbia and Montenegro), which is conducive to the heightening of the ethnic tensions;

(f) Allow the Special Rapporteur to visit Kosovo in order to prepare comprehensive reports on the human rights situation there;

(g) Cooperate with the Organization on Security and Cooperation in Europe to enable the long-term mission to resume its activities immediately, iinter alia/I by permitting its return to Kosovo;

Urges the Secretary-General to explore ways and means to establish an adequate international monitoring presence in Kosovo;

Express its serious concern at a new escalation of violence and harassment mainly directed against members of the Muslim community in Sandjak, especially in the regions at the border with the Republic of Bosnia and Herzegovina, as reported by the Special Rapporteur in his ninth report (A/49/641-S/1994/1252, para. 188), and demands that the Government of the Federal Republic of Yugoslavia (Serbia and Montenegro), as well as the Governments of Serbia and Montenegro, end these violations and respect the human rights and fundamental freedoms of the local population in Sandjak;

Also expresses its grave concern at renewed reports of violations of human rights in Vojvodina and, as noted by the Special Rapporteur, concerning members of the Bulgarian minority and the Croatian minority, while commending the courage and sacrifice of the many Serbs who continue to refuse to take part in such violations;

Urges all parties in Serbia and Montenegro, particularly in Kosovo, Sandjak, and Vojvodina, to engage in a substantive dialogue, under the auspices of, *inter alia*, the International Conference in the Former Yugoslavia and the Organization on Cooperation and Security in Europe, to act with the utmost restraint and to settle disputes peacefully and with respect for human rights;

Demands that the Federal Republic of Yugoslavia (Serbia and Montenegro) permit entry into Kosovo, Sandjak, and Vojvodina of United Nations observer missions and field officers of the Special Rapporteur and resumption of the missions of long duration of the Organization on Security and Cooperation in Europe;

Expresses its serious concern at the prevalence of lawlessness in the Serb-controlled territories of Croatia and the lack of adequate protection for Croatian and other non-Serb populations remaining in the Serb-controlled municipalities where these populations continue to experience physical violence and insecurity, as reported by the Special Rapporteur;

Welcomes the efforts by the Governments of Croatia and of Bosnia and Herzegovina to uphold human rights in their territories, urges them to fulfill the human rights commitments they have made, and in particular asks the Government of Croatia to eliminate the arbitrary practices on the part of the Croation authorities, as reported by the Special Rapporteur;

Condemns the continuation of "ethnic cleansing" in areas under the control of the self-proclaimed Serb authorities in the United Nations Protected Areas;

Notes with concern that many of the Special Rapporteur's past recommendations have not been fully implemented, in some cases because of resistance by the parties on the ground, and again strongly urges the parties, all States and relevant organizations to give immediate consideration to them;

Recommends that there be a human rights component in any internationally negotiated arrangement for Bosnia and Herzegovina and that implementation of such a component be conducted in close cooperation with the High Commissioner for Human Rights, the Special Rapporteur, and the Centre for Human Rights;

Decides to extend for one year the mandate of the Special Rapporteur as defined in its resolution 1994/72, and requests that he continue his vital efforts, especially by carrying out all such additional missions as he deems necessary, in particular to the Federal Republic of Yugoslavia (Serbia and Montenegro), and that he continue to submit periodic reports, as appropriate, to the Commission and the General Assembly, and to request the Secretary-General to continue to make the Special Rapporteur's reports available to the Security Council and to the International Conference on the Former Yugoslavia;

Requests the Secretary-General to take steps to assist in obtaining the active cooperation of all United Nations bodies in implementing the present resolution and, pursuant to paragraph 28 of the General Assembly resolution 49/196, to make available, from within the overall budgetary framework of the United Nations, all necessary resources requested by the Special Rapporteur, including for his field staff, to enable him to fulfill his mandate and, in particular, to provide for the appointment of field staff in the countries under his mandate in order to provide first-hand, timely reports on the situation of human rights there and to ensure coordination with other United Nations bodies involved, including the United Nations Protection Force;

Decides to remain seized of the matter and to consider the reports of the Special Rapporteur at its fifty-second session under the relevant agenda item.

**BIBLIOGRAPHY.** Amnesty International. *Yugoslavia: Ethnic Albanians—Trials by Truncheon.* London: 1994. NGO report, in English.

————. *Yugoslavia: Ethnic Albanians—Victims of Torture and Ill-Treatment by Police in Kosovo Province.* London: 1992. NGO report, in English.

————. *Yugoslavia: Further Reports of Torture and Deliberate and Arbitrary Killings in War Zones.* London: 1992. NGO report, in English.

————. *Yugoslavia: Police Violence Against Ethnic Albanians in Kosovo Province.* London: 1994. NGO report, in English.

————. *Yugoslavia: Torture and Deliberate and Arbitrary Killings in War Zones.* London: 1991. NGO report, in English.

Commission on Security and Cooperation in Europe. *The Conflict in Yugoslavia. Hearings before the Commission on Security and Cooperation in Europe, 102nd Congress, 1st Session, October 31, 1991.* Washington, D.C.: U.S. Government Printing Office (GPO), 1991. Government report, in English.

————. *Proposal for an International War Crimes Tribunal for the Former Yugoslavia.* Washington, D.C.: U.S. GPO, 1993. Government report, in English.

————. *Report on the April and May 1990 Elections in the Yugoslav Republics of Slovenia and Croatia.* Washington, DC: U.S. GPO, 1990. Government report/election-observer mission report, in English.

————. *The Yugoslav Republics: Prospects for Peace and Human Rights. Hearings before the Commission on Security and Cooperation in Europe, 102nd Congress, 2nd Session, February 5, 1992.* Washington, D.C.: U.S. GPO, 1992. Government report, in English.

Femmes sous lois musulmanes—Réseau international de solidarité (Women Living under Muslim Laws—International Solidarity Network). *Dossier d'information sur les crimes de guerre contre les femmes en ex-Yougoslavie: actions et initiatives pour les défendre* (Information File on War Crimes against Women In Ex-Yugoslavia: Actions and Initiatives to Defend Them). Montpellier, France: 1992. NGO report, in English and French.

Hebel, Herman von. "An International Tribunal for the Former Yugoslavia: An Act of Powerlesness or a New Challenge for the International Community," *Netherlands Quarterly of Human Rights* 11 (1993): 437–456. Article, in English.

Helsinki Watch. "Abuses Continue in the Former Yugoslavia: Serbia, Montenegro and Bosnia-Hercegovina," *Helsinki Watch* 5, no. 11 (July 1993): NGO report, in English.

————. *Open Wounds: Human Rights Abuses in Kosovo.* New York: Human Rights Watch, 1993. NGO report, in English.

————. *War Crimes in Bosnia-Hercegovina: Volume I.* New York: Human Rights Watch, 1992. NGO factfinding report, in English.

————. *War Crimes in Bosnia-Herzegovina: Vol. II.* New York: Human Rights Watch, 1993. NGO report, in English.

————. *Yugoslavia: Human Rights Abuses in Kosovo 1990–1992.* New York: Human Rights Watch, 1992. NGO factfinding report, in English.

Helsinki Watch and International Helsinki Federation for Human Rights. *Yugoslavia: Crisis in Kosovo.* New York: Human Rights Watch, 1990. NGO report, in English.

Human Rights Watch. "Federal Republic of Yugoslavia," in *Human Rights World Report 1995,* pp. 242–245. New York: 1995. NGO report, in English.

International Confederation of Free Trade Unions. *Dismissals and Ethnic Cleansing in Kosovo.* Brussels, Belgium: 1992. NGO factfinding report, in English and French.

International Court of Justice. *Reports of Judgments, Advisory Opinions and Orders: Case Concerning Application of the Convention on the Prevention and Punishment of the Crime of Genocide:*

*(Bosnia and Herzegovina v. Yugoslavia): Further Requests for the Indication of Provisional Measures: Order of 13 September 1993.* 13 September 1993. IGO court decision, in English and French.

International Human Rights Law Group. *No Justice, No Peace: Accountability for Rape and Gender-Based Violence in the Former Yugoslavia.* Washington, D.C.: 1993. NGO factfinding report, in English.

Jambrek, Peter. "Human Rights in a Multiethnic State: The Case of Yugoslavia," in *Human Rights and Security: Europe on the Eve of a New Era,* eds. Vojtech Mastny and Jan Zielonka, pp. 177–201. Boulder, CO, USA: Westview Press, 1991. Scholarly article, in English.

Johannes Wier Foundation for Health and Human Rights; Physicians for Human Rights. *Yugoslavia Mistreatment of Ethnic Albanians: A Case Study.* The Hague, the Netherlands: 1991. NGO factfinding report, in English.

U.S. Committee for Refugees. *Yugoslavia Torn Asunder: Lessons for Protecting Refugees from Civil War.* Washington, D.C.: American Council for Nationalities Service, 1992. NGO report, in English.

# Z

**ZAIRE.** The Republic of Zaire is a country in middle Africa, on the Atlantic Ocean. It has borders with Angola, Burundi, the Central African Republic, Congo, Rwanda, Sudan, Uganda, and Zambia. Formerly known as the Belgian Congo, it achieved independence from Belgium in 1960 as the Democratic Republic of the Congo and became a member of the United Nations the same year. Its name was changed to Zaire in 1971. Its population is estimated to be 39,750,000. Ethnic groups include the Bantu, who comprise the majority, and minorities of Sudanese, Nilotes, Pygmies, and Hamites. In addition, 329,000 refugees were living in Zaire in 1985, including 265,000 from Angola. Languages commonly used include French (official), Lingala (a *lingua franca*), Kiswahili, Tshiluba, Kikongo, and about 200 regional vernaculars. Religions practiced include Christianity (Roman Catholic, 50%; Protestant denominations, 20%), Islam (10%), Animism (10%), and Kimbanguist (10%). Literacy is estimated at 55%.

The government (1994) took the form of a republic. Under the 1978 constitution, as amended in 1980, supreme power is vested in the sole political party, the *Mouvement Populaire de la Revolution* (MPR), whose leader is automatically president and head of State, although this is confirmed in a popular election. Members of the unicameral National Legislative Council are elected (one per 100,000 inhabitants) from a list prepared by the MPR and serve for five-year terms. The judiciary includes the Justice Department, the Supreme Court, nine courts of appeal, and 32 courts of first instance.

***INDEPENDENCE AND CIVIL WAR.*** Belgium recognized the Republic of the Congo as an independent nation on 30 June 1960; but, within a week, a mutiny broke out in the Congolese army and grave acts of violence were committed against Belgian officers and civilians. On 10 July, Belgian troops intervened and occupied the principal cities. These disorders led to a mass exodus of Belgians, resulting in the breakdown of essential services in many parts of the country.

On 12 July 1960, Joseph Kasavubu and Patrice Lumumba, president and prime minister, respectively, of the new republic, called upon the United Nations to protect the national territory against external aggression by Belgium. The UN **SECURITY COUNCIL** on 14 July called upon Belgium to withdraw its troops and arranged for them to be replaced by contingents from neutral countries under United Nations command. These contingents were initially ordered to use force only in self-defense; later they were permitted to use force as a last resort if necessary to prevent civil war.

The United Nations force restored order as the Belgian troops withdrew and eventually reached a maximum strength of about 20,000. However, serious differences about their functions soon arose between Prime Minister Lumumba and UN Secretary-General **DAG HAMMARSKJÖLD.** Lumumba maintained that they should be used to subdue the rebel government of Katanga Province, headed by Moishe Tshombe, while Hammarskjöld stated that this was outside the mandate given them by the Security Council.

In September 1960, President Kasavubu dismissed Lumumba. Later that year, Lumumba, after several months of confinement to his residence under United Nations guard, left the house and was apprehended with several colleagues by Congolese troops. Taken to Katanga Province, he was killed on 17 January 1961. Later, on 17 September 1961, UN Secretary-General Dag Hammarskjöld died in a plane crash en route to a peace conference in Katanga Province.

After long negotiations punctuated by sporadic outbreaks of violence, the Katangese secession ended on 14 January 1963. However, the United Nations force remained in the country to assist in maintaining law and order. The United Nations also provided the government with the technical assistance necessary to ensure the continued operation of essential services and to supply necessary food and medical supplies. Both the military and the civilian operations were discontinued in June 1964.

In 1965, Col. Joseph Mobutu, chief of staff of the army, seized power from President Kasavubu. After a period of military rule, Mobutu was elected president for a seven-year term in 1970 and re-elected in 1977. Mobutu's policy of soliciting international investment to replace Belgian interests won wide support abroad. However, his arrangement, which permitted Zairians—including army officers and government officials—to take over and operate businesses which had been established by some 40,000 expatriate Portuguese, Greeks, Belgians, French, and Pakistanis, created havoc in trade circles and disrupted the flow of many necessities of life.

***RELATIONS WITH ANGOLA.*** Invaders from neighboring Angola attacked Katanga (now known as Shaba) Province in 1977 and again in 1978. They were turned back in 1977 by 1,500 Moroccan troops airlifted from France and, in 1978, by 1,750 Belgian soldiers and Foreign Legion paratroopers flown to the area by the U.S. Air Force. Later Zaire and Angola signed an agreement not to support rebels in each other's country.

Non-governmental organizations, including **AMNESTY INTERNATIONAL** and the **INTERNATIONAL LEAGUE FOR THE RIGHTS AND LIBERATION OF PEOPLES,** have repeatedly drawn the attention of the UN **COMMISSION ON HUMAN RIGHTS** to the situation prevailing in Zaire. In particular, they have pointed out that the country, once self-sufficient in food, has become almost wholly dependent upon outside sources to feed its population; that more than 50% of the population suffers from the effects of bacteriological, viral, and parasitical diseases; and that infant mortality is catastrophic.

A representative of Zaire, Mr. Lwamba-Katansi, provided information concerning the human rights situation in his country at a meeting of the UN **HUMAN RIGHTS COMMITTEE** held at Geneva on 10 July 1987. He referred in particular to the Department of Rights and Freedoms of the Citizen, which had been established on 31 October 1986, to which he was personally attached. The department's function, he said (UN Doc. CCPR/C/Sr. 738, para. 20),

was to receive complaints from all citizens who considered that they had been wronged by judicial or administrative decisions, acts of violence, etc. It was headed by a Political Office, composed of the Minister in charge of the Department and his advisers. Below there were several legal services specializing in various kinds of cases: a service dealing with judicial proceedings, another with administrative actions, another with political matters and another for international issues (he was personally attached to the last named service). At the bottom level, there were offices, each composed of three persons including a principal delegate, chosen in the commune or neighbourhood for his high reputation, and not necessarily a lawyer, and was therefore assisted by two lawyers. In Kinshasa, there was an office for each commune, 24 in all, and also two offices which dealt specifically with complaints from firms, one for the west side of the town and the other for the east side. When a complaint was submitted to an office, the latter examined it and if it considered the complainant to be justified, it transmitted the complaint to the central administration of the Department. If, however, the delegation considered that the complaint did not fulfil

the necessary conditions, it advised the complainant about other remedies, for example, through official channels. When a complaint was referred to the central administration, the latter considered it and on the basis of that examination, the Minister took the decision he deemed appropriate to restore the rights of the complainant. In the event a decision thus taken not being implemented by any body or individual, the Department could make representation to the Permanent Disciplinary Commission appointed by the Central Committee of the People's Movement for the Revolution or to the President of the Republic himself.

The Committee had handled about 500 complaints, he added, and its functions had been widely publicized through the information media.

***VISIT OF SPECIAL RAPPORTEUR TO ZAIRE.*** From 13 to 20 January 1990, Mr. Peter Koojmans (Netherlands), Special Rapporteur of the UN **COMMISSION ON HUMAN RIGHTS** on the question of the human rights of all persons subjected to any form of detention or imprisonment, torture, or other cruel, inhuman, or degrading treatment or punishment, visited Zaire on invitation of the government. Prepared and organized by the Department of Rights and Freedoms of the Citizen, the visit enabled the Special Rapporteur to hold discussions with many high officials and to visit two offices of the department. His evaluation of the human rights situation in Zaire, and his recommendations, were set out in his report to the Commission as follows (UN Doc. E/CN.4/1990/17Add. 1, paras. 33–51):

As stated before, the human rights situation in Zaire has considerably improved during the recent years. The Government has taken some meaningful steps to strengthen the existing mechanisms guaranteeing the respect of human rights by introducing new ones. The creation of a separate Department of Rights and Freedoms of the Citizen is, in itself, quite unique and has undoubtedly contributed to a greater awareness of the importance of human rights both with the population and with the authorities. The department has only been operational for two and a half years and to a certain extent is still in the formation period; it is therefore too early to give a conclusive evaluation of its efficiency. Informing the people about their rights by the dissemination of material which is understandable to everyone is one of the most important requisites for the rule of law. The President of the Bar Association told the Special Rapporteur that although detained persons were entitled to legal assistance as from the moment of their arrest, in actual practice, and due to lack of information, people hardly ever resorted to a lawyer until the moment their case came before a court. Nor was it generally known that a person who did not have the necessary means to employ a lawyer could address the judge or the President of the Bar Association who then had to ask the Bar to designate a lawyer.

It is equally important to inform the law-enforcing authorities about the detainee's rights and to instruct them to respect the detainee's inherent dignity. The introduction of training courses for the personnel of the law-enforcement forces is, therefore, of great significance. Such courses should not only be focused on mentality training but also on the teaching of how to conduct interrogations in a manner which recognizes and respects the detainee's rights and dignity.

The competence of the Department of Rights and Freedoms of the Citizen to visit and inspect all places of detention concurrently with the legally prescribed periodic visits by magistrates of the Public Prosecutor's office may be an effective preventive measure against illegal arrests and detention. These, in turn, may—and in fact often did in the past—lead to torture and maltreatment. The Special Rapporteur was informed that in all cases when a detainee was not duly registered with the Public Prosecutor's office, the Department could have him released immediately. He was also informed that in all other cases where the legal provisions had seemingly not been complied with, it was left to the Public Prosecutor's office to decide on the lawfulness of the detention. Moreover, the Department itself could, on its own initiative, table such cases during the meetings with the Judicial Council which were provided for on a monthly basis in the protocol of co-ordination concluded with that body.

In view of the fact that the number of alleged cases of illegal or arbitrary arrest or detention is still relatively high, the Special Rapporteur feels that the Public Prosecutor's office should thoroughly scrutinize the legality of all arrests, not only at the moment when they are registered (after the 48-hour term), but also when requests for the renewal of a remand order are made.

Of equal importance for the strict compliance with the legal rules is the presentation of the detainee *in persona* to the competent judge within five days after his arrest since this enables the detainee to inform the judge about the circumstances under which he was arrested and to provide him with all other relevant information. There again, the Special Rapporteur feels that the prevalent rules should be applied more strictly. It has come to his knowledge that in numerous cases detainees were not presented to a judge within the period prescribed by the law, or were not presented to a judge at all, although a remand order was issued.

Useful as the competences of the Department are, in essence they are corrective measures which—apart from cases of manifestly illegal detention—would not have been necessary if the Public Prosecutor's office and the judiciary had carried out their mandate satisfactorily.

Article 9, paragraph 4, of the International Covenant on Civil and Political Rights states that anyone who is deprived of his liberty by arrest or detention shall be entitled to take proceedings before a court, in order that that court may decide without delay on the lawfulness of his detention and order his release if the detention is not lawful. It has not become clear to the Special Rapporteur whether the Code of Criminal Procedure explicitly gives a detained person such right to take, on his own initiative or through his lawyer, such proceedings before a court. In view of the fact that the report submitted by the Government of Zaire under article 40 of the International Covenant on Civil and Political Rights makes no mention of such legal provisions (while being very elaborate on other issues), the Special Rapporteur feels entitled to assume that such a provision does not exist. An amendment to the Code of Criminal Procedure to bring it in conformity with article 9, paragraph 4, of the International Covenant on Civil and Political Rights would be an important step to suppress and prevent illegal or arbitrary arrest or detention.

All law-enforcement forces have their own places of detention (*cachots*). As stated before, in the case of common crimes, the suspect is usually transferred to a general prison relatively soon after his arrest. Persons, however, who are suspected of having committed offences against the security of the State or of the armed forces are usually kept in the detention place of the security agency concerned until the investigation has been completed. The Administrateur-Général of Agence Nationale de Documentation told the Special Rapporteur that in such cases it was impossible to transfer the suspect to the place where accused persons awaiting trial were normally kept in view of the fact that such places of detention were relatively open and the régime for visitors was relatively liberal. In sensitive cases, therefore, the suspect had to be detained at the agency's detention place until the investigation was finalized. The magistrates of the Public Prosecutor's office were, nevertheless, informed and once the inquiry was finished, the suspect was transferred to the Judiciary.

In general, the Special Rapporteur feels that it is rather undesirable if suspects are held in places run by the agency which is at the same time the investigating authority. Such a situation may easily lead to undue influence or even duress since living conditions and conditions of detention may be made subservient to the course of the investigation.

The Special Rapporteur feels that it would be useful to establish central detention facilities in the main cities for persons suspected of having committed security offences and who would consequently be tried by the Cour de Sûreté de l'Etat. Such detention centres should be placed under the supervision of the Judicial Council just like ordinary prisons. The various detention places of the law-enforcement and security agencies should only be used as a provisional lock-up until the arrest has been legalized. Evidence obtained from the suspect outside such central detention facilities and not confirmed by him during his stay there should not be admitted in court.

The Special Rapporteur was informed that a number of secret places of detention which had not been registered with the President of the Judicial Council, as required by the law, had recently been closed, and that those who had run these places of detention would be prosecuted. The Special Rapporteur is of the opinion that severe punishment of persons who exploit illegal places of detention is a highly effective preventive measure. Evidence collected in such places should not be accepted as legally obtained evidence.

During his mission, the Special Rapporteur visited the Central Prison of Kinshasa (Makala Prison) and two detention places (*cachots*) of the Service d'Action et de Renseignements Militaires and of the Agence Nationale de Documentation respectively. He was able to talk to a number of detainees in private. None of them claimed to have been subjected to torture or maltreatment in the places where they were presently kept, although a number of persons who were serving prison sentences in Makala Prison after having been tried by the Cour de Sûreté de l'Etat said they had been tortured during their preventive detention in 1984–85. The two persons kept in the AND detention place were both foreigners awaiting a decision to expel or extradite them. One of them had been kept there for about eight months, the other for about two months. Although according to the papers shown, they had been registered with the Public Prosecutor's office, they said they had never been presented to a judge. The eight persons kept in the SARM detention place had all been arrested or kept in custody (four Angolan soldiers awaiting a decision on their return to Angola) quite recently.

Those parts of Makala Prison shown to the Special Rapporteur were clean and well-kept. Living conditions seemed to be acceptable and medical care to be adequate. There is one pavilion for female detainees which is not separated from the other pavilions. Accused persons were not separated from convicted persons, as required by article 10, paragraph 2 (a), of the International Covenant on Civil and Political Rights. They, however, are not required to work whereas for convicted prisoners work is obligatory. According to the prison authorities, juveniles were kept in other detention places. The Special Rapporteur feels that the establishment of a separate detention centre for accused persons, part of which could be reserved, as a separate unit, for persons suspected of having committed security-related offences, as recommended in paragraph 42, above, would be a commendable measure.

As regards the question of administrative detention, the Special Rapporteur feels that the Government should clarify its position on this issue. As long as it is practised, the conditions under which a person may be temporarily detained should be laid down and should be subjected to judicial control by the Supreme Court.

The fact that the Department of Rights and Freedoms of the Citizen is authorized to receive complaints from citizens who claim that their fundamental rights have been violated is another indication that meaningful steps have been taken to strengthen the rule of law in Zaire. The Special Rapporteur visited two of the Department's local offices in Kinshasa and talked with the main delegates of these offices. The main delegate is a person who is chosen from people who have a good reputation and authority in society and is assisted by two lawyers and an administrative staff. The local offices are easily accessible to the public. The Special Rapporteur was impressed by the commitment of the persons he met. He was informed that sometimes the authorities to whom the complaint referred were unco-operative and were obviously not yet used to the new developments; he was also informed that members of some of the law-enforcement forces still tended to be rather indifferent to the rights of the citizens who often fell victims to harassment. It could, therefore, be recommendable to strengthen the position of the local offices in order to enable them to take corrective measures on the spot.

The Special Rapporteur could not avoid noting that the resources of the local offices were minimal. No means of transport was available and there was no telephone. Under such circumstances, work was extremely difficult and was certainly less effective than if it was done in more adequate conditions. In view of the priority given to human rights issues by the Government, it may be recommended that the local offices be provided with appropriate equipment in order to enable them to carry out satisfactorily their highly important task.

In conclusion, it can be said that until recent years, the legal and institutional framework in principle guaranteed the respect for human rights quite satisfactorily, but that in actual practice the system did not work properly. The result was that in a considerable number of cases even the most basic human rights, like the right to physical and mental integrity, were violated. The creation of DDLC can be seen as a remarkably bold effort to revitalize the long-neglected system of checks and balances. The Zairian Government must be commended since it decided to approach the question in a comprehensive way, reflected in the Department's work programme: consciousness-building, training and formation, co-ordination between the various Government organs and redress. It is precisely this comprehensive character which makes the creation of the DDLC a unique experi-

ment. As stated earlier, it is still too early to evaluate the outcome of the experiment. But it can only be successful if all branches of Government are fully prepared to strictly comply with the rules.

It has to be recognized that the authorities are hampered in carrying out their programme by the fact that the existing infrastructure is badly deficient and as a developing country Zaire will face tremendous difficulties in improving this infrastructure. As the Special Rapporteur said in previous reports: everyone should be aware of the fact that respect for civil and political rights depends not only on political will—indispensable as that may be—but often also requires costly investments. It is in particular with regard to this second element that international solidarity can play a decisive role.

The phenomenon of torture has considerably decreased in Zaire. Satisfactory as this may be, no government should be content with that statement of fact. It is as important to strengthen the structure which may prevent its recurrence. It is a well-known fact that illegal or arbitrary arrests and detentions may easily lead to situations where torture is likely to be practised. It is therefore only logical that the DDLC has made the extinction of such illegal arrests one of its main objectives. The following recommendations should be seen in that context:

(a) The procedure for the ratification of the United Nations Convention against Torture and Other Cruel, Inhuman or Degrading Treatment or Punishment should be completed at the earliest possible date;

(b) The training of law-enforcement personnel on human rights issues should get high priority;

(c) The provisions of the law with regard to arrest or deprivation of liberty should be strictly complied with. The Public Prosecutor's office should in each case carefully scrutinize the conditions under which the arrest is made and the grounds on which it is made. No person should be remanded in custody until he is seen by the competent judge;

(d) As long as administrative detention is still practised, it should only be applied under independent judicial control by the Supreme Court;

(e) The Code of Criminal Procedure should be amended to give a detained person the right to bring proceedings before a court in order to have the lawfulness of his detention decided upon without delay;

(f) All officials who have not complied with the legal provisions for arrest or detention should be either disciplined or prosecuted, without delay; if they have abused their authority by seriously violating basic human rights, including torture, they should be severely punished;

(g) Special detention centres under the supervision of the Judicial Council should be established for people who are accused of having committed crimes against the security of the State or the armed forces;

(h) Only evidence obtained under interrogation in such detention centres should be admitted in court;

(i) All possible efforts should be made to provide the local offices of the DDLC with the equipment necessary for the effective exercise of their tasks;

(j) The competences of the officials of the DDLC to take corrective measures in cases of abuse of authority by law-enforcement personnel against individuals should be strengthened.

President Mobutu faced considerable political opposition in the early 1990s which included violent demonstrations, general strikes, and formation of an alliance of opposition groups. Head of state since 1965, Mobutu remained in office beyond the expiration of his term in December 1991. The National Conference, charged with drafting a new constitution, declared itself to have sovereign powers and installed a new transitional government in August 1992. Mobutu attempted to dissolve the Conference's successor, the High Council of the Republic, and failed to recognize its leader, Etienne Tshisekedi, as head of State. In early 1993 fighting ensued in which 65 died, including the French Ambassador. In March 1994, a United Nations Special Envoy was sent to Zaire to mediate in the crisis. In September the two sides agreed to a transitional constitution, subject to a referendum, and, in January 1994, agreed to a government of national reconciliation. However, Mobutu's dissolution of the High Council and the National Legislative Council, their replacement with a new, unicameral legislature, and its election of a moderate opposition leader as prime minister were all declared illegitimate by the radical opposition.

**REFUGEES.** As well as the repatriation of some 30,000 Zaireans from the Congo in 1991, Zaire saw a huge influx of refugees from the neighboring conflicts in Rwanda and Burundi—two million from Rwanda made their way toward Zaire in July 1994 alone. An epidemic of cholera and extreme violence, including lynchings and mutilations, in the refugee camps led the office of the UN **HIGH COMMISSIONER FOR REFUGEES** to eventually reverse its policy and seek repatriation for these refugees. An estimated 40,000 Rwandans lost their lives to cholera in July and August alone. Waves of refugees continued to arrive, prompting Zaire to temporarily close its border, trapping refugees with nowhere to go. By November 1994 the UN estimated that there were 1.3 million Rwandan refugees in Zaire. UN **PEACEKEEPING FORCES** arrived to monitor the camps and the distribution of food, which had been taken over by Hutu militias from Rwanda. Both the refugee influx and violence in the camps continued into 1995. In 1995, the Zaire government threatened to expel the refugees forcibly if the United Nations did not repatriate the 1.2 million refugees. Zaire suspended the forced expulsion after the High Commission reinstituted a policy of voluntary repatriation.

The deadly Ebola virus, first discovered in 1976, again arose in May 1995 in the town of Kikwit, which was placed under a quarantine by the **WORLD HEALTH ORGANIZATION.** The death toll had reached 150 by mid-1995.

**BIBLIOGRAPHY.** Africa Watch. *Zaire: Inciting Hatred—Violence against Kasaiens in Shaba.* New York: Human Rights Watch, 1993. NGO report, in English.

———. *Zaire: Two Years without Transition* New York: Human Rights Watch, 1992. NGO report, in English.

Amnesty International. *Prisoners of Conscience Restricted under the Terms of Administrative Banishment Orders in the Republic of Zaire.* London: 1985. NGO report, in English.

———. *Republic of Zaire: Amnesty International's Concerns between January 1987 and January 1988.* London: 1988. NGO report, in English.

———. *The Republic of Zaire: Outside the Law—Security Force Repression of Government Opponents, 1988–90.* London: 1990. NGO factfinding report, in English and French.

———. *Torture in Zaire—The Pattern and Individual Cases.* London: 1986. NGO report, in English.

———. *Zaire: Collapsing under Crisis.* London: 1994. NGO report, in English.

———. *Zaire: Violence against Democracy.* London: 1993. NGO report, in English.

*Crisis in Zaire: Myths and Realities.* Trenton, NJ, USA: Africa World Press, 1986. Scholarly collection, in English.

Federation Internationale des Droits de l'Homme (International Federation of Human Rights). "Zaire: Le Comite des Droits de l'Homme de l'ONU Constate les Violations Dont ont ete Victims des Parlementaires de l'Opposition" (Zaire: The United Nations Committee on Human Rights Verifies Violations against Opposition Members of Parliament). *La Lettre de la FIDH* 159 (17 June 1986): 3. NGO article, in French.

*Freedom of Information and Expression in Zaire: Commentary by ARTICLE 19 on the Report Submitted to the U.N. Human Rights Committee by the Government of Zaire.* London: ARTICLE 19, 1987. NGO report, in English; bibliography of sources, pp. 44–45.

Giantonio, Patrick. "A 2-Million-Acre Headache in Zaire," *Cultural Survival Quarterly* 14, no. 1 (1990): 58–61. Article, in English.

International Human Rights Law Group. *Human Rights and the Transition to Democracy in Zaire.* Washington, D.C.: 1991. NGO factfinding report, in English.

International League for Human Rights. *Zaire's Human Rights Record: Comments on the Government of Zaire's Official Report to the Human Rights Committee.* New York: 1987. NGO report, in English.

Lawyers Committee for Human Rights. *Zaire: Massacre of Students at Lubumbashi.* New York: 1991. NGO factfinding report, in English.

———. *Zaire: Repression as Policy: A Human Rights Report.* New York: 1990. NGO report, in English.

"Les enfants d'abord: un défi et une mission" (Children First: A Challenge and a Mission Call"), *Zaïre-Afrique* 32, no. 270 (Nov. 1992): 515–575. Article, in French.

Ligue Zaïroise des Droits de l'Homme (Human Rights League of Zaire). *Rapport sur l'état des libertés au Zaïre* (Freedom Status Report in Zaire). Kinshasa, Zaire: 1990. NGO factfinding report, in French.

Otemikongo Mandefu Yarisule. "Le Multipartisme au Zaïre: mythe et réalité" (The Multi-Party System in Zaire: Myth and Reality), *Zaïre-Afrique* 31, no. 260 (Dec. 1991): 541–548. Article, in French.

Posner, Michael. "Zaire under Mobutu," *Index on Censorship* 16, no. 9 (Oct. 1987): 24–25, 40. NGO article/testimony, in English.

Saint-Moulin, Léon de. "Brève histoire des constitutions du Zaïre" (A Short Constitutional History of Zaire), *Zaïre-Afrique* 31, no. 256 (June–July 1991): 291–316. Article, in French.

U.S. Committee for Refugees. *Inducing the Deluge: Zaïre's*

*Internally Displaced People.* Washington, D.C.: American Council for Nationalities Services, 1993. NGO factfinding report, in English.

Voix des sans voix pour les droits de l'homme (Voice of the Voiceless for Human Rights). *Rapport: check up sur l'état de la démocratisation au Zaïre du 24 avril 1990 au 31 décembre 1991* (Report: The State of Democracy in Zaire, April 24, 1990–December 31, 1991). Kinshasa, Zaire: 1991. NGO factfinding report, in French.

Wamba-dia-Wamba, Ernest. "Democracy, Multipartyism and Emancipative Politics in Africa: The Case of Zaire," *Afrique et Développement/Africa Development* 18, no. 4 (1993): 95–118. Scholarly article, in English; bibliography, p. 118.

**ZAMBIA.** The Republic of Zambia is a landlocked country in eastern Africa. It has borders with Angola, Botswana, Malawi, Mozambique, Namibia, Tanzania, Zaire, and Zimbabwe. Formerly known as Northern Rhodesia, it achieved independence from Great Britain in 1964 and became a member of the United Nations the same year. Its population is estimated to be 8,475,000. Ethnic groups include numerous Bantu and other tribal communities. Languages in common use include English (official) and about 70 tribal vernaculars. Religions practiced include Christianity, Animism, Hinduism, and Islam. Literacy is estimated at 54%.

The government (1994) took the form of a republic. The 1991 constitution provides for a president elected through multi-party elections, with some presidential powers reduced from those in previous constitutions, and a 150-member National Assembly to prepare legislation.

There is also an advisory House of Chiefs, on which the country's traditional tribal authorities are represented.

The area in south central Africa occupied by Zambia was not penetrated by Europeans until the latter half of the 19th century, when David Livingstone reached Victoria Falls (1855) and Cecil Rhodes obtained the first mineral concessions from local chiefs (1888). Northern Rhodesia was proclaimed a British sphere of influence and became a protectorate administered by the British Colonial Office. In 1953, it joined with Southern Rhodesia (now Zimbabwe) and Nyasaland (now Malawi) to form the Federation of Rhodesia and Nyasaland. The Federation, however, was dissolved ten years later, its unity destroyed by inability to reconcile African demands for greater participation in government and Europeans' fears for their future under an African majority regime.

*INDEPENDENCE.* On 24 October 1964, Northern Rhodesia achieved independence as the Republic of Zambia, and a new nation comprising 73 ethnic tribes found itself at the center of the liberation struggle in southern Africa. After some indecision, the 1964 con-

stitution was abrogated in 1973 for a new one designed to achieve a "one-party participatory democracy."

Under the 1973 constitution, the sole candidate for the presidency of Zambia was the person selected to be the president of the United National Independence Party (UNIP)—the only legal political party—by that party's General Conference; voters would say "yes" or "no" to his candidacy. Dr. Kenneth Kaunda, first elected for a five-year term in 1973, was re-elected in 1978 and 1983. The second-ranking government official was the secretary-general of the UNIP, appointed by the president of that party from the membership of the party's Central Committee.

As the arms struggles in its neighboring countries intensified, Zambia became host to thousands of refugees from those countries who were fighting for independence. Because some of them were suspected of being enemy agents sent to destabilize Zambia, a "state of emergency" was maintained for several years, under which the government could detain people, seize their property, and amend or suspend any law by administrative fiat.

In April 1990, Zambia experienced its second cholera epidemic in three months, reflecting the deep poverty of most of its township-dwelling population and the disintegration of such public services as garbage collection, water purification, and sanitation.

In 1991, Dr. Kaunda, head of state since 1964, was defeated by Frederick Chiluba, leader of the new Movement for Multi-party Democracy. Stringent economic measures and a refusal to re-examine the constitutional powers of the presidency led even Chiluba's previous supporters to become disenchanted. Kaunda's three sons were arrested and a state of emergency declared in March 1993 when Chiluba discovered an alleged plot to destabilize his government.

*REPORT OF THE UN COMMITTEE ON THE ELIMINATION OF RACIAL DISCRIMINATION.* In a 1994 report, the Committee noted with satisfaction that Zambia had entered no reservations. The main points of the report are as follows (paras. 359–369):

*Positive aspects.* The Committee expressed its appreciation of the fact that some legal measures had been put in place to eliminate discrimination against women. It also appreciated the fact that after the enactment of the 1991 Constitution, a constitutional review committee which included women's non-governmental organizations had been put in place to further review all discriminatory laws and practices.

It expressed its appreciation for the establishment of women's desks in all ministries, the extensive educational efforts concerning women and the emergence of new women's organizations.

*Principal subjects of concern.* The Committee was very concerned about the persistence of traditional sex roles, which were deeply embedded in the cultural life of the Zambians and which generally seemed to impede equality. Great concern was also expressed regarding the violation of women's rights in general, particularly the rights of those women under customary marriage laws.

The Committee also noted with concern the lack of women's access to formal employment and the difficulties encountered by women working in the informal sector in general and from governmental officials.

The Committee was also concerned about acts of violence against women in their private sphere. It also noted the high fertility rate and its negative impact on the status of women in addition to the difficulty caused by the current adjustment programmes.

*Suggestions and recommendations.* The Committee suggested that the Government of Zambia study the possibility of codifying the customary laws so that those found to be in violation of the Convention could be reformed or abolished. It recommended that the customary marriage law be reformed so that customary marriages were registered, in order to give women married under that law equal rights and benefits with men.

The Committee also recommended that in future reports a much more detailed description be given of the customs and traditions affecting women's rights in all areas of the Convention in a positive or negative way. It suggested further review of existing legislation and expected in the subsequent report to be informed about the practical results of the constitutional review committee and their implementation.

It recommended that, although structural adjustment programmes posed difficulties to the State party, women's issues should remain at centre stage even in times of economic distress. The Committee therefore recommended that women have access to budgetary and policy decision-making positions to mitigate some of the negative effects of the structural adjustment on women's lives.

The Committee urged the State party, women's non-governmental organizations and all concerned to engage in a nationwide awareness campaign to change the attitudes of men and women in order to achieve de facto equality in all spheres of life. The Committee also wished to be informed in subsequent reports about the situation of women in female-headed households.

It was the wish of the Committee that Zambia's next report provide all the information with the necessary sex-segregated statistics in accordance with the articles of the Convention and in closer compliance with the guidelines for submitting reports to the Committee.

**BIBLIOGRAPHY.** Amnesty International. *Amnesty International's Concerns in the Republic of Zambia.* London: 1987. NGO report, in English.

Andreassen, B. A., and A. Eide, eds. "Zambia," in *Human Rights in Developing Countries 1987/88: A Yearbook on Human Rights in Countries Receiving Nordic Aid,* pp. 110—127. Copenhagen, Denmark: Christian Michelsen Institute, 1988. NGO report, in English; bibliography on Zambia, pp. 362–363.

Armstrong, Alice, ed. *Women and Law in Southern Africa.* Harare, Zimbabwe: Zimbabwe Publishing House, 1987. Scholarly edited collection, in English.

Chan, Stephen. *Prospects for the 1991 Elections in Zambia.* Johannesburg, South Africa: South African Institute of International Affairs, 1991. Speech, in English.

Defense for Children International—USA. *The Effects of Maternal Mortality on Children in Africa: An Exploratory Report on Kenya, Namibia, Tanzania, Zambia, and Zimbabwe.* New York: 1991. NGO research report, in English; bibliography, appendix III.

*Freedom of Information and Expression in Zambia.* London: ARTICLE 19, 1988. NGO report, in English.

Freund, P. J., and K. Kalumba. "Spontaneously Settled Refugees in Northwestern Province, Zambia," *International Migration Review* 20, no. 2 (Summer 1986): 299–312. NGO article, in English.

Hamalengwa, Munyonzwe. "The Legal System of Zambia," *AHRA Working Paper* 19 (1986). Research paper, in English.

Mubako, S. V. "Fundamental Rights and Judicial Review: The Zambian Experience," *Zimbabwe Law Review* 1–2 (1983–1984): 97–132. Scholarly article, in English.

Mwaba, Lameck. "The Refugee Control Act of Zambia," *RPN—Refugee Participation Network* no. 9 (Aug. 1990): 30–32. NGO article, in English.

Mwalimu, Charles. "Police, State Security Forces and Constitutionalism of Human Rights in Zambia," *Georgia Journal of International and Comparative Law* 21, no. 2 (1991): 217–243. Scholarly article, in English.

Ndulo, M., and K. Turner. *Civil Liberties Cases in Zambia.* Oxford, UK: African Law Reports, 1984. Legal monograph/collection, in English.

Parker, Collins. "Control of Executive Discretion and Preventive Detention in Zambia." *Comparative and International Law Journal of Southern Africa* 13, no. 2 (July 1980): 159—176. Scholarly article, in English.

Tramberg Hanson, Karen. "Urban Women and Work in Africa: A Zambian Case," *TransAfrica Forum* 4, no. 3 (Spring 1987): 9–23. NGO article, in English.

U.N. High Commissioner for Refugees. "Zambia under Threat," *Refugees* 31 (July 1986): 11–13. IGO journal article, in English.

Zimba, L. S. *The Zambian Bill of Rights: An Historical and Comparative Study of Human Rights in Commonwealth Africa.* Nairobi, Kenya: East African Publishing House, 1984. Scholarly study, in English.

**ZIMBABWE.** A landlocked country in eastern Africa, Zimbabwe has borders with Botswana, Mozambique, South Africa, and Zambia. Formerly known as Southern Rhodesia, it achieved independence from Great Britain in 1980 and became a member of the United Nations the same year. Its population is estimated to be 10,000,000. Ethnic groups include descendants of the Mashona, Matabele, and other indigenous tribes; Asians; Europeans; and persons of mixed ancestry. Languages commonly used include English (official), Shona, Sindebele, and many regional vernaculars. Religions practiced include Syncretism (mixtures of Christianity and traditional African faiths), 49%; Christianity (Anglicans, Presbyterians, Methodists, Roman Catholics, and others), 25%; Animism, 24%; Hinduism, 1%; and Islam, 1%. Literacy is estimated at 55%.

The government (1994) took the form of a republic. Under the 1979 constitution, the president was to be elected by Parliament for a term of six years and to serve as head of State. However, the constitution was amended in 1987 to create the position of executive president: a president who is also prime minister. As the sole candidate, Prime Minister Robert Mugabe, president of the Zimbabwe African National Union (ZANU) Party, was elected to this post.

Up to late 1987, Parliament consisted of a 100-member House of Assembly and a 40-member Senate. The House of Assembly is composed of 80 members elected by the country's 8.5 million blacks and 20 elected by the white population of about 100,000, and the Senate consists of 30 members elected by the black members of the House of Assembly and 10 by the white members of that House. However, on 21 August 1987, Parliament abolished the practice of reserving seats for the white minority.

Zimbabwe's judicial system is independent of other branches of the government and, in appropriate cases, applies African customary law. Village courts and community courts have been established to replace the tribal courts and district commissioner's courts of colonial days.

***RHODESIA.*** A British colony from 1890 until 1980, Zimbabwe (then Southern Rhodesia) was never directly administered from London; it was, rather, internally self-governing with its own legislature, civil service, armed forces, and police. From 1953 to 1963, it was joined in the Federation of Northern Rhodesia and Nyasaland (now Zambia and Malawi). When the Federation was dissolved, the United Kingdom refused to grant independence to Southern Rhodesia until it demonstrated its intention to move toward eventual majority rule. White Rhodesians, led by Prime Minister Ian Smith, would not take this step. Instead Smith issued a Unilateral Declaration of Independence from the United Kingdom on 11 November 1965.

Although the British Government considered the declaration to be illegal, it did not use force to end the rebellion; instead, it imposed unilateral economic sanctions on Rhodesia and requested other countries to do the same. The United Nations **SECURITY COUNCIL,** on 16 December 1966, imposed mandatory economic sanctions for the first time on a State. On 29 May 1968, the Security Council broadened these sanctions by imposing an almost total embargo on all trade with the country.

***INSURGENCY.*** During the early 1970s, Southern Rhodesia was the target of frequent guerrilla activity which resulted in widespread destruction and economic dislocation, as well as a sharp drop in white morale. The pressure intensified in 1974 after shifts in power in Mozambique and Angola occurred as a result of the change of government in Portugal, and by the formation of a "patriotic front" by the two major African groups, the Zimbabwe African National Union

(ZANU), led by Robert Mugabe, and the Zimbabwe African People's Union (ZAPU), led by Joshua Nkomo.

In 1976, the Ian Smith government met with these and other black leaders in Geneva but failed to reach agreement on steps to be taken to resolve the situation. However, in 1977, an "interim settlement" was signed in Salisbury calling for qualified majority rule and elections with universal suffrage. Elections held in April 1979 returned Bishop Abel Muzorewa, chairman of the United National African Council, as the country's first black prime minister. However, unrest in the country and conflict between various factions continued in many areas.

A new round of consultations between the parties and other black-ruled States was initiated by the British Government at Lancaster House, London, on 10 September 1979, and resulted after three months of bargaining with an agreement signed on 21 December calling for a ceasefire, new elections, a transition period under British rule, and a new constitution which would implement majority rule while protecting minority rights.

Under the agreement, Rhodesia reverted temporarily to the status of a British colony. A new constitution was adopted and elections were held. Robert Mugabe, leader of the victorious ZANU Party, formed the first government of the new country, called Zimbabwe, which was granted independence by the British government on 18 April 1980.

Since independence, the government has sought national reconciliation but has refused to share power with the minority political party, ZAPU. Emphasis has been placed upon reconstruction, integration of the armed forces, re-establishment of education and social services, and resettlement of approximately one million refugees and displaced persons. Some progress has also been achieved in reversing past discriminatory practices in employment, wages, and land distribution.

However, destabilizing guerrilla activity has continued in some parts of the country, blamed sometimes on neighboring South Africa and sometimes on the Ndebele tribesmen who are the main followers of ZAPU's Joshua Nkomo. In 1983 and 1984, the government sent troops into parts of Matabeleland to suppress such guerrilla activity; these "security forces" were widely reported to have used undue violence in accomplishing their assignment. More recently, dissident guerrillas have been charged with the murder of a number of white farmers and of tourists and with attacks upon government installations and personnel. In addition, the Mozambique National Resistance, which is fighting the Marxist government of neighboring Mozambique, has declared war against Zimbabwe because of its military support for Mozambique and has conducted hit-and-run raids across the frontier.

In the 1985 election, the Zimbabwe African National Union increased its majority in the House of Assembly but failed to win the 70 seats Mugabe had sought with a view to ensuring eventual one-party rule. In the 1990 election, the Zimbabwe Unity Movement (ZUM) won considerable support for its stand in favor of capitalism and multi-party democracy and against increasing unemployment and disintegration of the transport services. But, although his calls for a one-party State won him few supporters, President Robert Mugabe was re-elected by wide margins on both occasions.

The elections, on 31 March–1 April 1990, involved five political parties, contesting 119 parliamentary seats. All parties campaigned freely, held rallies throughout the country, and had access to the news media. The voting was by secret ballot. Mr. Mugabe won 78% of the total vote, and his party won 116 of the 119 seats in the parliament.

Mr. Mugabe's party again won nearly all the contested seats in parliamentary elections in April 1995.

Opposition groups continued to form, however, and the Zimbabwean Supreme Court ruled in 1994 that the statutory prohibition on peaceful public demonstrations was contrary to the country's Bill of Rights.

Zimbabwe received its share of refugees with 250,000 Mozambicans in the country in 1992. A plan by the UN **High Commissioner for Refugees** to repatriate them was underway.

**BIBLIOGRAPHY.** Africa Watch. *Zimbabwe: Government Moves to Curb Academic Freedom—Constitutional Rights Under Threat.* New York: Human Rights Watch, 1990. NGO report, in English.

Amnesty International. *Detention without Trial of Political Prisoners in Zimbabwe.* London: 1985. NGO report, in English.

————. *Zimbabwe: Detention without Trial of Seven Opposition Politicians.* London: 1985. NGO report, in English.

Andreassen, B. A., and A. Eide, eds. "Zimbabwe," in *Human Rights in Developing Countries 1987/88: A Yearbook on Human Rights in Countries Receiving Nordic Aid,* pp. 128—160. Copenhagen, Denmark: Christian Michelsen Institute, 1988. NGO report, in English; bibliography on Zimbabwe, pp. 363–365.

Armstrong, Alice, ed. *Women and Law in Southern Africa.* Harare, Zimbabwe: Zimbabwe Publishing House, 1987. Scholarly edited collection, in English.

Arnold, M. W., L. Garber, and B. Wrobel. *Zimbabwe: Report on the 1985 General Elections: Based on a Mission of the Election Observer Project of the International Human Rights Law Group.* Washington, D.C.: International Human Rights Law Group, 1986. NGO mission report, in English.

Berkeley, B., and E. Schrage. *Zimbabwe: Wages of War—A Report on Human Rights.* New York: Lawyers Committee for Human Rights, 1986. NGO mission report, in English.

Catholic Commission for Justice and Peace in Zimbabwe. "The Labour Relations Act," *Catholic Commission for Justice and Peace in Zimbabwe Bulletin* 7 (April 1986): 2—3. NGO article, in English.

Defense for Children International—USA. *The Effects of Maternal Mortality on Children in Africa: An Exploratory Report on Kenya, Namibia, Tanzania, Zambia, and Zimbabwe.* New York: 1991. NGO research report, in English; bibliography, appendix III.

Hatchard, John. *Individual Freedoms and State Security in the African Context: The Case of Zimbabwe.* London and Athens, OH, USA: James Currey and Ohio University, 1993. Scholarly monograph, in English; bibliography, pp. 197–202.

————. "The Institution of the Ombudsman in Africa with Special Reference to Zimbabwe," *International and Comparative Law Quarterly* 35, pt. 2 (April 1986): 255–270. Scholarly article, in English.

Women's Action Group. *Speak Out/Taurai/Khulumani.* Harare, Zimbabwe: 1989. NGO articles, in English and African languages.

**ZONTA INTERNATIONAL.** An international non-governmental organization in consultative status with the UN **Economic and Social Council** (Category I) and with **UNESCO, UNICEF,** and the **Council of Europe,** Zonta International unites about 1000 clubs, totaling 35,000 individual members, in 59 countries.

Founded in 1919 in Buffalo, New York (USA), and formally entitled Zonta International—International Service Organization of Executive and Professional Women, ZI endeavors to improve the legal, political, economic, and professional status of women and to encourage their entry into business and the professions. In the United States, it annually awards 6,000 Amelia Earhart fellowships to women for graduate work in aerospace sciences. It sponsors programs to improve international relations and supports projects for the advancement of women. It publishes the quarterly magazine *The Zontian.*

Zonta International. Address: 557 W. Randolph St., Suite 2040, Chicago, IL 60606-2284, USA. Telephone: (312) 930-5848. Fax: (312) 930-0951. Executive Director: Bonnie L. Koenig.

# Glossary

**ABROGATION.** Annulment, cancellation, or repeal of a law or rule by legislative or other constitutional authority or by usage that invalidates it.

**ABUSE OF RIGHTS.** Excessive or unreasonable invocation of rights contrary to limitations or restrictions legitimately placed upon them.

**ACCEPTANCE.** The act by which a State establishes definitively its consent to be bound by the terms of a particular treaty or other bilateral or multilateral agreement. Acceptance may be by ratification, by accession, or by succession. Signature of a treaty or agreement normally constitutes only a preliminary to acceptance.

**AD HOC.** (L). "For a special purpose." In the international community, an *ad hoc* committee or commission is one created to perform a single mandate and ceases to exist after it has fulfilled its mandate.

**ALIEN.** An individual who is not a national of the State in which he or she is present.

**AMNESTY.** The abolition or overlooking an offence of a political nature, such as treason or rebellion—by a government, frequently on condition that the offender resume his duties as a citizen within a prescribed time.

**APARTHEID.** A system of institutionalized racial segregation and discrimination for the purpose of establishing and maintaining domination by one racial group of persons over another racial group of persons and systematically oppressing them, such as that pursued in South Africa.

**APARTHEID IN SPORTS.** Application of the policies and practices of *apartheid* in sports activities, whether organized on a professional or an amateur basis.

**ASYLUM.** The principle that everyone has the right to seek and enjoy freedom from persecution in other countries, embodied in the Universal Declaration of Human Rights. Territorial asylum refers to the right of States to admit into their territory, or to refuse to extradite, persons persecuted elsewhere for political reasons. Diplomatic asylum refers to the right of States to offer refuge in their legations to persons persecuted for political reasons in countries where the legations are located.

**BIOLOGICAL WEAPONS.** Living organisms—whatever their nature or the infective material derived from them—which are intended to cause disease or death in man, animals, or plants; and which depend for their effects on their ability to multiply in the person, animal, or plant attacked.

**CHEMICAL WEAPONS.** Weapons which employ chemical sustances, whether gaseous, liquid, or solid, because of their direct toxic effects on man, animals, or plants.

**COLLECTIVE BARGAINING.** All negotiations which take place between an employer, a group of employers or one or more employers' organizations, on the one hand, and one or more workers' organizations, on the other, for (1) determining working conditions and terms of employment; and/or (2) regulating relations between employers and workers; and/or (3) regulating relations between employers or their organizations and a workers' organization.

**CONCILIATION.** Settlement of a dispute between two parties by a third party acting as mediator, with a view to reaching an amicable settlement.

**CONSENT.** Agreement of the parties legally concerned.

**CONTRACTING STATE.** One which has consented to be bound by a treaty, whether or not the treaty has entered into force.

**CONVENTION.** A term, in UN usuage, which indicates a treaty concluded between two or among more States. Human rights conventions are international agreements containing provisions to promote or protect one or more human rights or fundamental freedoms. Such conventions are normally prepared by a body within the UN system or by a special conference convened for that purpose and are open for signature and ratification by the States specified in the convention. A convention enters into force only after it has been ratified by the number of States specified in one of its articles and is legally binding only upon those States which have ratified it.

**CONVENTIONAL WEAPONS.** Military armament or all kinds, except nuclear, chemical, or biological weapons.

**COPYRIGHT.** The exclusive legal right to reproduce, publish, and sell the matter and form of any produced work. Under various conventions, copyright protection extends to the rights of authors, organizations, and other proprietors in literary, scientific, and artistic works, including writings; musical, dramatic, and cinematographic works; paintings, engravings, and sculpture; published and unpublished works; and translations, among others.

*CORPUS JURIS CIVILIS.* (L) The body of civil law.

*COUP D'ETAT.* (Fr) A sudden, decisive exercise of force in politics, usually involving the violent overthrow of a government by a group of conspirators.

**COVENANT.** A treaty of exceptional importance, concluded between two or more States.

**CRIMES AGAINST HUMANITY.** Actions punishable as crimes under international law and encompassing murder, extermination, enslavement, deportation and other inhuman acts done against any civilian population, or persecutions on political, racial, or religious grounds, when such acts are done or such persecutions are carried on or in execution of or in connection with any crime against peace or any war crime.

**CRIMES AGAINST PEACE.** Actions punishable as crimes under international law and encompassing (1) the planning, preparation, initiation, or waging of a war of aggression or a war in violation of international treaties, agreements, or assurances; or (2) participation in a common plan or conspiracy for the accomplishment of any of the acts mentioned in (1).

**DECLARATION.** A formal and solemn instrument, setting our principles of great and lasting importance. As contrasted with conventions, declarations adopted by United Nations organs are morally but not legally binding upon all member States; they set out international principles and standards with which all States are expected to comply.

**DECOLONIZATION.** The process by which a trust or non-self-governing territory or a territory subjected to alien subjugation, domination, or exploitation achieves independence and self-government.

**DEROGATION.** Refusal or failure of a State party to a treaty to fulfill an obligation that it has accepted under the treaty.

**DEVELOPMENT.** Participation in, contribution to, and enjoyment by every human being and all peoples of cultural, social, economic, and political objectives.

**DISABLED PERSON.** A person unable to ensure by him- or herself, wholly or partly, the necessities of a normal individual and/or social life, as a result of deficiency, either congenital or not, in his or her physical or mental capabilities.

**DISCRIMINATION.** Any distinction, exclusion, limitation, or preference which, being based on race, color, sex, language, religion, political or other opinion, national or social origin, economic condition, property, or birth, has the purpose or effect of nullifying or impairing equality of treatment.

**DISINFORMATION.** Purposeful release and dissemination of false or distorted information.

**DISINVESTMENT.** Withdrawal of assets or invested funds, or cancellation of financial aid or subsidies, as a protest against a national public policy which is internationally unacceptable.

**EQUALITY OF STATES.** The principle that every independent State enjoys full equality with all other independent States, regardless of discrepancies of power.

**EXTRADITION.** The delivery of a suspected or convicted person by the State in which the person is located to the State in the jurisdiction of which the offense was committed or the person convicted.

**FORCED OR COMPULSORY LABOR.** Work or service which is exacted from any person for any penalty and for which the person has not offered himself voluntarily.

**GENOCIDE.** Any of the following acts committed with intent to destroy, in whole or in part, a national, ethnical, racial, or religious group as such: (1) killing members of the group; (2) causing serious bodily or mental harm to members of the group; (3) deliberately inflicting on the group conditions of life calculated to bring about its physical destruction in whole or in part; (4) imposing measures intended to prevent births within the group; and (5) forcibly transferring children of the group to another group.

**GOOD OFFICES.** An endeavor by an impartial third party (usually a high-ranking national or international official or a commission composed of such officials) to bring together States involved in a dispute with a view to persuading them to reach an amicable settlement.

*HABEAS CORPUS.* (L) An order requiring that a detained person be brought before a judge or court within a specified time for investigation of the legality of his detention.

**HEGEMONY.** Predominant political, economic, or other influence exercised by one State over another, or over a group of States.

**HOSTAGE.** A person seized, detained, or threatened with death or injury in order to compel a third party—such as a State, an intergovernmental organization, a natural or juridical person, or a group of persons—to do or abstain from doing any act as an explicit or implicit condition for his release.

**INCENDIARY WEAPON.** A shell, bomb, or grenade containing a substance that burns with an intense heat.

**INDIGENOUS PEOPLES.** A term applied to (a) tribal peoples in independent countries whose social, cultural and economic conditions distinguish them from other sections of the national community, and whose status is regulated wholly or partially by their own traditions or by special laws or regulations; (b) peoples in independent countries who are descendents of the populations which inhabited the country, or a geographical region to which the country belongs, at the time of conquest or colonization or the establishment of present State boundaries and who, irrespective of their legal status, retain some or all of their own social, economic, cultural, and political institutions. Self-identification as tribal or native is regarded as a fundamental criterion for determining whether a people is to be regarded as indigenous.

**INTERNATIONAL ORGANIZATION.** An organization composed of States.

*JUS COGENS.* (L) A peremptory norm of general international law, i.e., a standard accepted and recognized by the international community of States as a whole as one from which no derogation is permitted and one which can be modified only by a subsequent norm of general international law having the same character. If a new peremptory norm of general international law should emerge, any existing treaty in conflict with that norm becomes void and ends.

**LAW ENFORCEMENT OFFICIALS.** All officers of the law, whether appointed or elected, who exercise police powers, especially the powers of arrest or detention. In countries where police powers are exercised by military authorities, whether uniformed or not, or by State security forces, officers of such services are regarded as law enforcement officials.

**LIMITATIONS.** Restrictions on the exercise or full enjoyment of rights or freedoms.

**MARTIAL LAW.** Government or control by military forces over civilians or civilian authorities in domestic territory. Also a wartime system of government or control established or administered in hostile territory under which existing civil laws and the normal administration of justice are replaced by a system dependent solely on the will of the military commander.

**MERCENARY.** Any person who (a) is specially recruited locally or abroad to fight in an armed conflict; (b) is motivated to take part in the hostilities essentially by the desire for private gain and, in fact, is promised, by or on behalf of a party to the conflict, material compensation substantially in excess of that promised or paid to combatants of similar rank and functions in the armed forces of that party; (c) is neither a national of a party to the conflict nor a resident of territory controlled by a party to the conflict; (d) is not a member of the armed forces of a party to the conflict; and (e) has not been sent by a State which is not a party to the conflict on official duty as a member of its armed forces. Also any person who, in any other situation, (a) is specially recruited locally or abroad for the purpose of participating in a concerted act of violence aimed at: (i) overthrowing a government or otherwise undermining the constitutional order of a State; or (ii) undermining the territorial integrity of a State; (b) is motivated to take part therein essentially by the desire for significant private gain and is prompted by the promise or payment of material compensation; (c) is neither a national nor a resident of the State against which such an act is directed; (d) has not been sent by a State on official duty; and (e) is not a member of the armed forces of the State on whose territory the act is undertaken.

**MIGRANT WORKER.** Any person who leaves a country in which he is a citizen and travels to another country, otherwise than on his own account, with a view to being employed. The term *excludes* frontier workers; artists and members of liberal professions who have entered the country on a short-term basis; seamen; persons coming specifically for training or education; and employees of organizations and States who have travelled to that country at the request of their employer to undertake specific duties or assignments, for a limited and defined period of time, and who are required to leave that country on the completion of their assigment.

**NEGOTIATING STATE.** A State that participated in the drawing up of a treaty.

**NEO-COLONIALISM.** The *de facto* exercise of economic or political dominance by a strong nation over a weak nation or group of nations without reducing them *de jure* to colonial status.

*NON BIS IN IDEM.* (L) The principle that no one should be tried twice for the same crime.

**NON-INTERVENTION.** The principle that no State or group of States has the right to interfere, directly or indirectly, for any reason, in matters that are essentially within the domestic jurisdiction of another State. This principle does not however, prejudice the application by the United Nations of enforcement measures under article 7 of the UN Charter.

*NON-REFOULEMENT.* (Fr) The principle that no one should be rejected at a frontier, expelled, or returned to a country where he will be subject to persecution.

*NULLUM POENA SINE LEGE.* (L) The principle that no act is punishable without a pre-existing legal prohibition.

*PACTA SUNT SERVANDA.* (L) The principle that every treaty in force is binding upon all parties to it and must be performed by them in good faith.

**PROTOCOL.** A treaty revising or adding to the provisions of an earlier treaty.

**RATIFICATION.** The international act by which a State establishes its consent to be bound by the terms of a treaty.

**REMEDY.** The means by which a right is enforced or its violation is prevented, redressed, or compensated.

**REPATRIATION.** The right of any refugee, if he so wishes, to leave his country of asylum and to return to the country of his nationality. The Statute of the United Nations High Commissioner for Refugees requires the High Commissioner to facilitate and promote the voluntary repatriation of refugees. For such an action to be "voluntary" presupposes the elimination, or at least the substantial removal, of the cause of the fear or danger which had led the refugee to depart from the country of his nationality; it also presupposes, in many cases, the willingness of the country of origin to re-admit the refugee and to cooperate with the country of asylum in arranging for his safe return.

**RESERVATION.** A unilateral statement, however phrased or named, made by a State when ratifying or otherwise consenting to be bound by the terms of a treaty, purporting to exclude or to modify the legal effect of certain provisions of the treaty in their application to that State.

*RES NULLIUS.* (L) A territory not claimed by any State.

**SELF-DETERMINATION.** The right of all peoples freely to determine their political status and freely to pursue their economic, social, and cultural development. They may, for their own ends, freely dispose of their natural wealth and resources without prejudice to any obligations arising out of international economic cooperation, based upon the principle of mutual benefit, and international law. In no case may a people be deprived of its own means of subsistence.

**SOVEREIGNTY.** The absolute power of an independent State to do whatever may be necessary to maintain its independence and to regulate its internal affairs without interference from, or accountability to, any external authority.

**STATE.** A body of people occupying a fixed territory, politically organized under one government, exercising sovereignty over all persons and things within its boundaries, capable of making war and peace and of entering into international relations with other such entities.

**STATELESS PERSON.** A person who is not considered a national by any State under the operation of its law.

**STATE PARTY.** A State which has expressed, on the international plane, by an act of ratification (acceptance, approval, or accession) or by a notification of succession, its consent to be bound by the terms of a treaty, and for which the treaty is in force.

**STATE TERRORISM.** Government recognition of and support to terrorist groups. Support may be given by supplying arms, aiding and abetting in the terrorists' plans, providing financial aid, assisting in training or supplying training facilities, providing housing, and any other means that provides succor to a terrorist group.

**STATUTORY LIMITATION.** A legal provision to the effect that no suit shall be maintained, nor any criminal charge be made, unless initiated within a specified period of time.

**SUCCESSION OF STATES.** Replacement of one State by another in the responsibility for the international relations of a country or territory.

**TREATY.** An international agreement concluded between two or more States in written form and governed by international law, whether embodied in a single instrument or in two or more instruments, and whatever its particular designation (agreement, convention, covenant, etc.).

**VICTIMS OF ABUSE OF POWER.** Persons who, individually or collectively, have suffered harm, including physical or mental injury, emotional suffering, economic loss, or substantial impairment of their fundamental rights, through acts or omissions that do not yet constitute violations of national criminal laws but of internationally recognized norms relating to human rights.

**WAR CRIMES.** Actions punishable as crimes under international law, including violations of the law of customs of war, which include—but are not limited to—murder, ill-treatment, or deportation to slave-labor or for any other purpose of the civilian population of or in occupied territory; murder or ill-treatment of prisoners of war or persons on the seas; killing of hostages; plunder of public or private property; and wanton destruction of cities, towns, or villages, or devastation not justified by military necessity.

# APPENDIX A

# CHRONOLOGICAL LIST OF INTERNATIONAL INSTRUMENTS CONCERNED WITH HUMAN RIGHTS

The following is a listing in chronological order of the international instruments concerning the realization of human rights that can be found in this encyclopedia:

| Document Title | Date of Adoption |
|---|---|
| ILO Right of Association (Agriculture) Convention | 12 November 1921 |
| Protocol for the Prohibition of the Use in War of Asphyxiating, Poisonous or Other Gases, or of Bacteriological Methods of Warfare | 17 June 1925 |
| Slavery Convention signed at Geneva, as Amended | 25 September 1926 |
| ILO Forced Labor Convention | 28 June 1930 |
| Atlantic Charter | 14 August 1941 |
| Declaration by United Nations | 1 January 1942 |
| International Labor Organization Constitution | 10 May 1944 |
| United Nations Charter | 26 June 1945 |
| United Nations Educational, Scientific and Cultural Organization Charter | 16 November 1945 |
| World Health Organization Charter | 22 July 1946 |
| ILO Labor Inspection Convention | 11 July 1947 |
| Organization of American States Charter | 30 April 1948 |
| Inter-American Charter of Social Guarantees | 2 May 1948 |
| Inter-American Convention on the Granting of Political Rights to Women | 2 May 1948 |
| Inter-American Convention on the Granting of Civil Rights to Women | 2 May 1948 |
| American Declaration on the Rights and Duties of Man | 2 May 1948 |
| ILO Freedom of Association and Protection of the Right to Organize Convention | 9 July 1948 |
| ILO Night Work (Women) Convention, revised | 9 July 1948 |
| Convention on the Prevention and Punishment of the Crime of Genocide | 9 December 1948 |
| Universal Declaration of Human Rights | 10 December 1948 |
| Council of Europe Statute | 5 May 1949 |
| ILO Migration for Employment Convention, revised | 1 July 1949 |
| ILO Protection of Wages Convention | 1 July 1949 |
| ILO Right to Organize and Collective Bargaining Convention | 1 July 1949 |
| Geneva Convention Relative to the Treatment of Prisoners of War | 12 August 1949 |
| Geneva Convention Relative to the Protection of Civilian Persons in Time of War | 12 August 1949 |
| Declaration concerning the Essentials of Peace | 1 December 1949 |
| Convention for the Suppression of the Traffic in Persons and of the Exploitation of the Prostitution of Others | 2 December 1949 |
| European Convention on Human Rights | 4 November 1950 |
| UNESCO Agreement on the Importation of Educational, Scientific and Cultural Materials, and annexed Protocol | 22 November 1950 |

| *Document Title* | *Date of Adoption* |
|---|---|
| ILO Equal Remuneration Convention | 29 June 1951 |
| Convention relating to the Status of Refugees | 28 July 1951 |
| European Convention on Human Rights: Protocol I | 20 March 1952 |
| ILO Maternity Protection Convention, revised | 28 June 1952 |
| ILO Social Security (Minimum Standards) Convention | 28 June 1952 |
| Universal Copyright Convention, revised, and Protocols | 6 September 1952 |
| Convention on the International Right of Correction | 16 December 1952 |
| Convention on the Political Rights of Women | 20 December 1952 |
| Protocol amending the Slavery Convention Signed at Geneva on 25 September 1926 | 23 October 1953 |
| Inter-American Convention on Diplomatic Asylum | 28 March 1954 |
| Inter-American Convention on Territorial Asylum | 28 March 1954 |
| UNESCO Convention for the Protection of Cultural Property in the Event of Armed Conflict | 14 May 1954 |
| Convention relating to the Status of Stateless Persons | 28 September 1954 |
| Standard Minimum Rules for the Treatment of Prisoners | 30 August 1955 |
| European Convention on Establishment and Protocol | 13 December 1955 |
| Supplementary Convention on the Abolition of Slavery, the Slave Trade, and Institutions and Practices Similar to Slavery | 13 December 1956 |
| Convention on the Nationality of Married Women | 29 January 1957 |
| ILO Abolition of Forced Labor Convention | 25 June 1957 |
| European Agreement on Regulations governing the Movement of Persons between Member States of the Council of Europe | 13 December 1957 |
| European Convention on Extradition | 13 December 1957 |
| Convention on the High Seas | 28 April 1958 |
| ILO Discrimination (Employment and Occupation) Convention | 25 June 1958 |
| Declaration of the Rights of the Child | 20 November 1959 |
| UNESCO Convention against Discrimination in Education | 14 December 1960 |
| Declaration on the Granting of Independence to Colonial Countries and Peoples | 14 December 1960 |
| Convention on the Reduction of Statelessness | 30 August 1961 |
| European Social Charter | 18 October 1961 |
| UNESCO International Convention for the Protection of Performers, Producers of Phonograms and Broadcasting Organizations | 26 October 1961 |
| ILO Social Policy (Basic Aims and Standards) Convention | 23 June 1962 |
| ILO Equality of Treatment (Social Security) Convention | 28 June 1962 |
| Convention on Consent to Marriage, Minimum Age for Marriage and Registration of Marriages | 7 November 1962 |
| UNESCO Convention against Discrimination in Education: Protocol | 10 December 1962 |
| Declaration on Permanent Sovereignty over Natural Resources | 14 December 1962 |
| European Convention on Human Rights: Protocol II | 6 May 1963 |
| European Convention on Human Rights: Protocol II | 16 May 1963 |
| European Convention on Human Rights: Protocol IV | 6 May 1963 |
| Organization of African Unity Charter | 25 May 1963 |
| Declaration on the Elimination of All Forms of Racial Discrimination | 20 November 1963 |
| European Code on Social Security and Protocol | 16 April 1964 |
| ILO Employment Policy Convention | 9 July 1964 |
| Protocol to the Charter of the Organization of African Unity, Establishing the Commission of Mediation, Conciliation and Arbitration | 21 July 1964 |
| Cairo Declaration: Program for Peace and International Cooperation | 10 October 1964 |
| Recommendation on Consent to Marriage, Minimum Age for Marriage and Registration of Marriages | 1 November 1965 |

| *Document Title* | *Date of Adoption* |
|---|---|
| Inter-American Declaration on Racial Integration in the Americas | 30 November 1965 |
| Declaration on the Promotion among Youth of the Ideals of Peace, Mutual Respect and Understanding among Peoples | 7 December 1965 |
| International Convention on the Elimination of All Forms of Racial Discrimination | 21 December 1965 |
| European Convention on Human Rights: Protocol V | 20 January 1966 |
| UNESCO Declaration on the Principles of International Cultural Co-operation | 4 November 1966 |
| UNESCO Recommendation concerning the Status of Teachers | 5 November 1966 |
| European Convention on the Adoption of Children | 24 April 1967 |
| Declaration on the Elimination of All Forms of Discrimination against Women | 7 November 1967 |
| Declaration on Territorial Asylum | 14 December 1967 |
| Proclamation of Teheran | 13 May 1968 |
| Convention on the Non-Applicability of Statutory Limitations to War Crimes and Crimes against Humanity | 26 November 1968 |
| European Agreement relating to Persons Participating in Proceedings of the European Commission and Court of Human Rights | 6 May 1969 |
| ILO Medical Care and Sickness Benefits Convention | 25 June 1969 |
| African Convention governing the Specific Aspects of Refugee Problems in Africa | 10 September 1969 |
| American Convention on Human Rights | 22 November 1969 |
| Declaration on Social Progress and Development | 11 December 1969 |
| European Declaration on Mass Communication Media and Human Rights | 23 January 1970 |
| European Convention on the Repatriation of Minors | 28 May 1970 |
| ILO Minimum Wage Fixing Convention | 22 June 1970 |
| ILO Holidays with Pay Convention, revised | 24 June 1970 |
| Declaration on Principles of International law concerning Friendly Relations and Cooperation among States in Accordance with the Charter of the United Nations | 24 October 1970 |
| Declaration on the Occasion of the 25th Anniversary of the United Nations | 24 October 1970 |
| Convention on the Means of Prohibiting and Preventing the Illicit Import, Export and Transfer of Ownership of Cultural Property | 14 November 1970 |
| Basic Principles for the Protection of Civilian Populations in Armed Conflicts | 9 December 1970 |
| Convention for the Suppression of Unlawful Seizure of Aircraft | 16 December 1970 |
| ILO Workers' Representatives Convention | 23 June 1971 |
| Universal Copyright Convention and Protocols I and II, revised | 24 July 1971 |
| Convention for the Suppression of Unlawful Acts against the Safety of Civil Aviation | 23 September 1971 |
| Convention on the Prohibition of the Development, Production and Stockpiling of Bacteriological (Biological) and Toxic Weapons and on their Destruction | 10 April 1972 |
| European Convention on the Transfer of Proceedings in Criminal Matters | 15 May 1972 |
| Declaration of the United Nations Conference on the Human Environment | 16 June 1972 |
| UNESCO Declaration of Guiding Principles on the Use of Satellite Broadcasting for the Free Flow of Information, the Spread of Education and Greater Cultural Exchange | 15 November 1972 |
| UNESCO Convention concerning the Protection of the World Cultural Heritage | 16 November 1972 |

| Document Title | Date of Adoption |
|---|---|
| European Convention on Social Security | 14 December 1972 |
| ILO Minimum Age Convention | 26 June 1973 |
| International Convention on the Suppression and Punishment of the Crime of Apartheid | 30 November 1972 |
| Principles of International Cooperation in the Detection, Arrest, Extradition and Punishment of Persons Guilty of War Crimes and Crimes against Humanity | 3 December 1973 |
| Basic Principles of the Legal Status of the Combatants struggling against Colonial and Alien Domination and Racist Regimes | 12 December 1972 |
| Convention on the Prevention and Punishment of Crimes against Internationally Protected Persons, including Diplomatic Agents | 14 December 1973 |
| European Convention on the Non-Applicability of Statutory Limitation to Crimes against Humanity and War Crimes | 25 January 1974 |
| ILO Paid Educational Leave Convention | 24 June 1974 |
| Universal Declaration on the Eradication of Hunger and Malnutrition | 16 November 1974 |
| UNESCO Recommendation concerning Education for International Understanding, Cooperation and Peace and Education relating to Human Rights and Fundamental Freedoms | 19 November 1974 |
| UNESCO Recommendation concerning Technical and Vocational Education, revised | 19 November 1974 |
| UNESCO Recommendation on the Status of Scientific Researchers | 20 November 1974 |
| Declaration on the Protection of Women and Children in Emergency and Armed Conflict | 11 December 1974 |
| ILO Human Resources Development Convention | 23 June 1975 |
| ILO Rural Workers' Organizations Conventions | 23 June 1975 |
| ILO Migrant Workers (Supplementary Provisions) Convention | 23 June 1975 |
| Declaration of Mexico on the Equality of Women and Their Contribution to Development and Peace | 2 July 1975 |
| Helsinki Accord: Final Act of the Conference on Security and Cooperation in Europe | 1 August 1975 |
| European Convention on Extradition | 15 October 1975 |
| European Agreement on the Legal Status of Children Born Out of Wedlock | 15 October 1975 |
| Declaration on the Use of Scientific and Technological Progress in the Interests of Peace and for the Benefit of Mankind | 10 November 1975 |
| Declaration on the Protection of All Persons from Being Subjected to Torture and Other Cruel, Inhuman or Degrading Treatment or Punishment | 9 December 1975 |
| Declaration on the Rights of Disabled Persons | 9 December 1975 |
| Vancouver Declaration on Human Settlements | 11 June 1976 |
| Declaration of Principles and Program of Action of the Tripartite World Conference on Employment | 14 June 1976 |
| Declaration of Abijan | 9 July 1976 |
| UNESCO Agreement on the Importation of Educational, Scientific and Cultural Materials: Protocol | 26 November 1976 |
| UNESCO Recommendation on the Development of Adult Education | 26 November 1976 |
| UNESCO Recommendation on Participation by the People at Large in Cultural Life and Their Contribution to It | 26 November 1976 |
| European Convention on the Suppression of Terrorism | 27 January 1977 |
| Geneva Conventions: Protocols I and II | 9 June 1977 |
| ILO Working Environment (Air Pollution, Noise and Vibration) Convention | 20 June 1977 |
| Lagos Declaration against Apartheid | 2 August 1977 |
| Declaration on the Rights of Deaf-Blind Persons | 16 September 1977 |

| *Document Title* | *Date of Adoption* |
|---|---|
| European Convention on the Legal Status of Migrant Workers | 24 November 1977 |
| International Declaration against Apartheid in Sports | 14 December 1977 |
| European Convention on Extradition: Second Additional Protocol | 17 March 1978 |
| Charter of Rights for Migrant Workers in Southern Africa | 7 April 1978 |
| ILO Labor Relations (Public Service) Convention | 27 June 1978 |
| Declaration of Alma Ata | 12 September 1978 |
| UNESCO International Charter of Physical Education and Sport | 21 November 1978 |
| UNESCO Declaration on Race and Racial Prejudice | 27 November 1978 |
| UNESCO Declaration on Fundamental Principles concerning the Contribution of the Mass Media to Strengthening Peace and International Understanding, to the Promotion of Human Rights and to Countering Racialism, Apartheid, and Incitement to War | 28 November 1978 |
| Declaration on the Preparation of Societies for Life in Peace | 15 December 1978 |
| Code of Conduct for Law Enforcement Officials | 17 December 1979 |
| International Convention against the Taking of Hostages | 17 December 1979 |
| Convention on the Elimination of all Forms of Discrimination against Women | 18 December 1979 |
| European Convention on Recognition and Enforcement of Decisions concerning Custody of Children and on Restoration of Custody of Children | 28 May 1980 |
| European Convention for the Protection of Individuals with Regard to Automatic Processing of Personal Data | 28 January 1981 |
| Inter-American Convention on Extradition | 25 February 1981 |
| Convention on Prohibitions or Restrictions on the Use of Certain Conventional Weapons Which May Be Deemed Excessively Injurious or to Have Indiscriminate Effects, and Protocols | 10 April 1981 |
| ILO Collective Bargaining Convention | 19 June 1981 |
| ILO Occupational Safety and Health Convention | 22 June 1981 |
| ILO Workers with Family Responsibilities Convention | 23 June 1981 |
| African Charter on Human and Peoples' Rights | 28 June 1981 |
| Declaration on the Elimination of All Forms of Intolerance and of Discrimination Based on Religion or Belief | 25 November 1981 |
| Declaration on the Inadmissibility of Intervention and Interference in the Internal Affairs of States | 9 December 1981 |
| Declaration on the Prevention of Nuclear Catastrophe | 9 December 1981 |
| European Recommendation concerning International Co-operation in the Prosecution and Punishment of Terrorism | 15 January 1982 |
| European Declaration on Freedom of Expression and Information | 29 April 1982 |
| Declaration on the Participation of Women in Promoting International Peace and Co-operation | 3 December 1982 |
| Principles governing the Use by States of Artificial Earth Satellites for International Direct Television Broadcasting | 10 December 1982 |
| Principles of Medical Ethics Relevant to the Role of Health Personnel, particularly Physicians, in the Protection of Prisoners and Detainees against Torture and Other Cruel, Inhuman or Degrading Treatment or Punishment | 18 December 1982 |
| European Convention on Human Rights: Protocol VI | 28 April 1983 |
| Declaration of the Second World Conference to Combat Racism and Racial Discrimination | 12 August 1983 |
| Geneva Declaration on Palestine | 7 September 1983 |
| Convention on International Civil Aircraft | 10 May 1984 |
| Inter-American Convention on Conflict of Laws concerning the Adoption of Minors | 24 May 1984 |

| *Document Title* | *Date of Adoption* |
|---|---|
| Safeguards Guaranteeing the Protection of the Rights of Those Facing the Death Penalty | 25 May 1984 |
| Nairobi Forward-looking Strategies for the Advancement of Women | 26 July 1984 |
| Declaration on the Right of Peoples to Peace | 12 November 1984 |
| European Convention on Human Rights: Protocol VII | 22 November 1984 |
| Convention against Torture and Other Cruel, Inhuman or Degrading Treatment or Punishment | 10 December 1984 |
| Declaration on the Control of Drug Trafficking and Drug Abuse | 14 December 1984 |
| European Convention on Human Rights: Protocol VIII | 19 March 1985 |
| Proclamation of the International Year of Peace | 24 October 1985 |
| Basic Principles of the Independence of the Judiciary | 29 November 1985 |
| Declaration of Basic Principles for Victims of Crime and Abuse of Power | 29 November 1985 |
| United Nations Standard Minimum Rules for the Administration of Juvenile Justice (Beijing Rules) | 29 November 1985 |
| Inter-American Convention to Prevent and Punish Torture | 9 December 1985 |
| International Convention against Apartheid in Sports | 10 December 1985 |
| Declaration on the Human Rights of Individuals who are not Nationals of the Country in Which They Live | 13 December 1985 |
| Declaration on Social and Legal Principles relating to the Protection and Welfare of Children, with Special Reference to Foster Placement and Adoption Nationally and Internationally | 3 December 1986 |
| Declaration on the Right to Development | 4 December 1986 |
| European Convention for the Prevention of Torture and Inhuman or Degrading Treatment or Punishment | 26 June 1987 |
| European Social Charter: Protocol | 26 November 1987 |
| Khartoum Declaration | 8 March 1988 |
| Apartheid: ILO Declaration and Program of Action | 16 June 1988 |
| American Convention on Human Rights: Additional Protocol with Regard to Economic, Social and Cultural Rights | 17 November 1988 |
| Body of Principles for the Protection of All Persons under any Form of Detention or Imprisonment | 9 December 1988 |
| European Convention on Transfrontier Television | 5 May 1989 |
| Principles on the Effective Prevention and Investigation of Extra-legal, Arbitrary and Summary Executions | 24 May 1989 |
| ILO Indigenous and Tribal Peoples Convention | 27 June 1989 |
| Tallinn Guidelines for Action on Human Resources Development in the Field of Disability | 22 August 1989 |
| Convention on the Rights of the Child | 20 November 1989 |
| International Convention against the Recruitment, Use, Financing and Training of Mercenaries | 4 December 1989 |
| Declaration on Apartheid and its Destructive Consequences in South Africa | 14 December 1989 |
| International Covenant on Civil and Political Rights: Second Optional Protocol, Aiming at Abolition of the Death Penalty | 15 December 1989 |
| Declaration on the Protection of all Persons from Enforced Disappearance | 18 December 1992 |
| Declaration on the Rights of Persons belonging to International or Ethnic Religious and Linguistic Minorities | 18 December 1992 |
| Vienna Declaration and Programme of Action | 25 June 1993 |

# APPENDIX B

# STATUS OF INTERNATIONAL HUMAN RIGHTS CONVENTIONS

The status of a number of important human rights conventions, as of the date mentioned in each case, is indicated in the paragraphs below. For this purpose, the conventions are divided into (1) those concluded under the auspices of the United Nations, (2) those concluded by diplomatic conferences, (3) those concluded under the auspices of the International Labor Organization, (4) those concluded under the auspices of the United Nations Educational, Scientific and Cultural Organization, (5) those concluded under the auspices of the Council of Europe, (6) those concluded under the auspices of the Organization of African Unity and (7) those concluded under the auspices of the Organization of American States.

Within each grouping, the conventions on which information is available are arranged in alphabetical order.

## 1. Conventions Concluded under the Auspices of the United Nations

### A. Convention against Torture and Other Cruel, Inhuman or Degrading Treatment or Punishment

Up to 30 June 1995, the following States have become parties to the convention by ratification or accession: Afghanistan, Albania, Algeria, Antigua and Barbuda, Argentina, Armenia, Australia, Austria, Belarus, Belize, Benin, Bosnia Hezegovina, Brazil, Bulgaria, Burundi, Cambodia, Cameroon, Canada, Cape Verde, Chad, Chile, China, Colombia, Costa Rica, Croatia, Cuba, Cyprus, Czech Republic, Denmark, Ecuador, Egypt, Estonia, Ethiopia, Finland, France, Georgia, Germany, Greece, Guatemala, Guinea, Guyana, Hungary, Israel, Italy, Jordan, Latvia, Libya, Liechtenstein, Luxembourg, Malta, Mauritius, Mexico, Monaco, Morocco, Namibia, Nepal, Netherlands, New Zealand, Norway, Panama, Paraguay, Peru, Philippines, Poland, Portugal, Qatar, Romania, Russian Federation, Senegal, Seychelles, Slovakia, Slovenia, Somalia, Spain, Sri Lanka, Sweden, Switzerland, Tajikistan, The Former Yugoslav Republic of Macedonia, Togo, Tunisia, Turkey, Uganda, Ukraine, United Kingdom of Great Britain and Northern Ireland, United States of America, Uruguay, Venezuela, Yemen, and Yugoslavia.

The following States have signed the convention: Belgium, Bolivia, Dominican Republic, Gabon, Gambia, Iceland, Indonesia, Ireland, Nicaragua, Nigeria, Sierra Leone, South Africa, and Sudan.

The following States have made the declaration recognizing the competence of the Committee Against Torture under articles 21 and 22 of the Convention: Algeria, Antigua and Barbuda, Argentina, Australia, Austria, Bulgaria, Canada, Croatia, Ecuador, Finland, France, Greece, Hungary, Italy, Liechtenstein, Luxembourg, Malta, Monaco, Netherlands, New Zealand, Norway, Poland, Portugal, Russian Federation, Slovakia, Slovenia, Spain, Sweden, Switzerland, Togo, Tunisia, Turkey, Uruguay, Venezuela, and Yugoslavia. The provisions of articles 21 and 22 entered into force on 26 June 1987 in accordance with article 21 (para. 2) and article 22 (para. 8).

### B. Convention for the Suppression of the Traffic in Persons and of the Exploitation of the Prostitution of Others

Up to 30 June 1995, the following States have become parties to the Convention by ratification or accession: Afghanistan, Albania, Algeria, Argentina, Bangladesh, Belarus, Belgium, Bolivia, Bosnia Herzegovina, Brazil, Bulgaria, Burkina Faso, Cameroon, Central African Republic, Congo, Croatia, Cuba, Cyprus, Czech Republic, Djibouti, Ecuador, Egypt, Ethiopia, Finland, France, Germany, Guinea, Haiti, Honduras, Hungary, India, Iraq, Israel, Italy, Japan, Jordan, Kuwait, Lao People's Democratic Republic, Latvia, Libya, Luxembourg, Malawi, Mali, Mauritania, Mexico, Morocco, Niger, Norway, Pakistan, Philippines, Poland, Portugal, Republic of Korea, Romania, Russian Federation, Senegal, Seychelles, Singapore, Slovakia, Slovenia, South Africa, Spain, Sri Lanka, Syria, The Former Yugoslav Republic of Macedonia, Togo, Ukraine, Venezuela, Yemen, and Yugoslavia.

The convention has been signed by Denmark, Iran, Liberia, and Myanmar.

### C. Convention on Consent to Marriage, Minimum Age for Marriage, and Registration of Marriages

Up to 30 June 1995, the following States have become parties to the convention by ratification or accession:

Antigua and Barbuda, Argentina, Austria, Barbados, Benin, Bosnia Herzegovina, Brazil, Burkina Faso, Croatia, Cuba, Czech Republic, Denmark, Dominican Republic, Fiji, Finland, Germany, Guatemala, Guinea, Hungary, Iceland, Jordan, Mali, Mexico, Mongolia, Netherlands, New Zealand, Niger, Norway, Philippines, Poland, Romania, Samoa, South Africa, Spain, Sweden, Trinidad and Tobago,Tunisia, United Kingdom of Great Britain and Northern

Ireland, Venezuela, Yemen, and Yugoslavia.

The Convention has been signed by Chile, France, Greece, Israel, Italy, Romania, Sri Lanka, and the United States of America.

### D. Convention on the Elimination of All Forms of Discrimination against Women

Up to 30 June 1995, the following States have become parties to the convention by ratification or accession: Albania, Angola, Antigua and Barbuda, Argentina, Armenia, Australia, Austria, Bahamas, Bangladesh, Barbados, Belarus, Belgium, Belize, Benin, Bhutan, Bolivia, Bosnia Herzegovina, Brazil, Bulgaria, Burkina Faso, Burundi, Cambodia, Cameroon, Canada, Cape Verde, Central African Republic, Chad, Chile, China, Colombia, Comoros, Congo, Costa Rica, Croatia, Cuba, Cyprus, Czech Republic, Denmark, Dominica, Dominican Republic, Ecuador, Egypt, El Salvador, Equatorial Guinea, Estonia, Ethiopia, Finland, France, Gabon, Gambia, Georgia, Germany, Ghana, Greece, Grenada, Guatemala, Guinea, Guinea Bissau, Guyana, Haiti, Honduras, Hungary, Iceland, India, Indonesia, Iraq, Ireland, Israel, Italy, Jamaica, Japan, Jordan, Kenya, Kyrgyzstan, Lao People's Democratic Republic, Latvia, Liberia, Libya, Lithuania, Luxembourg, Madagascar, Malawi, Maldives, Mali, Malta, Mauritius, Mexico, Mongolia, Morocco, Namibia, Nepal, Netherlands, New Zealand, Nicaragua, Nigeria, Norway, Panama, Paraguay, Peru, Philippines, Poland, Portugal, Republic of Korea, Republic of Moldova, Romania, Russian Federation, Rwanda, St. Kitts and Nevis, St. Lucia, St. Vincent and the Grenadines, Samoa, Senegal, Seychelles, Sierra Leone, Slovakia, Slovenia, Spain, Sri Lanka, Suriname, Sweden, Tajikistan, Thailand, The Former Yugoslav Republic of Macedonia, Togo, Trinidad and Tobago, Tunisia, Turkey, Uganda, Ukraine, United Kingdom of Great Britain and Northern Ireland, United Republic of Tanzania, Uruguay, Venezuela, Viet Nam, Yemen, Yugoslavia, Zaire, Zambia, and Zimbabwe.

The convention has been signed by Afghanistan, Côte d'Ivoire (Ivory Coast), Lesotho, South Africa, Switzerland and the United States of America.

### E. Convention on the Nationality of Married Women

Up to 30 June 1995, the following States have become parties to the convention by ratification or accession: Albania, Antigua and Barbuda, Argentina, Australia, Austria, Bahamas, Barbados, Belarus, Bosnia Herzegovina, Brazil, Bulgaria, Canada, Croatia, Cuba, Cyprus, Czech Republic, Denmark, Dominican Republic, Ecuador, Fiji, Finland, Germany, Ghana, Guatemala, Hungary, Iceland, Ireland, Israel, Jamaica, Jordan, Latvia, Lesotho, Libya, Luxembourg, Malawi, Malaysia, Mali, Malta, Mauritius, Mexico, Netherlands, New Zealand, Nicaragua, Norway, Poland, Romania, Russian Federation, Saint Lucia, Sierra Leone, Singapore, Sri Lanka, Swaziland, Sweden, The Former Yugoslav Republic of Macedonia, Trinidad and Tobago, Tunisia, Uganda, Ukraine United Republic of Tanzania, Venezuela,Yugoslavia, and Zambia.

The convention has been signed by Belgium, Chile, Colombia, Guinea, India, Pakistan, Portugal, South Africa, and Uruguay.

### F. Convention on the Non-Applicability of Statutory Limitations to War Crimes and Crimes against Humanity

Up to 30 June 1995, the following States have become parties to the convention by ratification or accession: Afganistan, Albania, Armenia, Belarus, Bolivia, Bosnia Herzegovina, Bulgaria, Cameroon, Croatia, Cuba, Czech Republic, Democratic People's Republic of Korea, Estonia, Gambia, Georgia, Germany, Guinea, Hungary, India, Kenya, Kuwait, Lao People's Democratic Republic, Latvia, Libya, Mongolia, Nicaragua, Nigeria, Philippines, Poland, Republic of Moldova, Romania, Russian Federation, Rwanda, St. Vincent and the Grenadines, Slovakia, Slovenia, Tunisia, Ukraine, Viet Nam, Yemen, and Yugoslavia.

The convention has been signed by Mexico.

### G. Convention on the Political Rights of Women

Up to 30 June 1995, the following States have become parties to the convention by ratification or accession: Afghanistan, Albania, Angola, Antigua and Barbuda, Argentina, Australia, Austria, Bahamas, Barbados, Belarus, Belgium, Bolivia, Bosnia Herzegovina, Brazil, Bulgaria, Burundi, Canada, Central African Republic, Chile, Colombia, Congo, Costa Rica, Croatia, Cuba, Cyprus, Czech Republic, Denmark, Dominican Republic, Ecuador, Egypt, Ethiopia, Fiji, Finland, France, Gabon, Germany, Ghana, Greece, Guatemala, Guinea, Haiti, Hungary, Iceland, India, Indonesia, Ireland, Israel, Italy, Jamaica, Japan, Jordan, Lao People's Democratic Republic, Latvia, Lebanon, Lesotho, Libya,

Luxembourg, Madagascar, Malawi, Mali, Malta, Mauritius, Mauritius, Mexico, Mongolia, Morocco, Nepal, Netherlands, New Zealand, Nicaragua, Niger, Nigeria, Norway, Pakistan, Papua New Guinea, Paraguay, Peru, Philippines, Poland, Republic of Korea, Republic of Moldava, Romania, Russian Federation, Senegal, Sierra Leone, Slovakia, Slovenia, Solomon Islands, Spain, Swaziland, Sweden, Thailand, Trinidad and Tobago, Tunisia, Turkey, Ukraine, United Kingdom of Great Britain and Northern Ireland, United Republic of Tanzania, United States of America, Venezuela, Yemen, Yugoslavia, Zaire, and Zambia.

The convention has been signed by El Salvador, Liberia, Myanmar, South Africa, and Uruguay.

## H. *Convention on the Prevention and Punishment of the Crime of Genocide*

Up to 30 June 1995, the following States have become parties to the convention by ratification or accession: Afghanistan, Albania, Algeria, Antigua and Barbuda, Argentina, Armenia, Australia, Austria, Bahamas, Bahrain, Barbados, Belarus, Belgium, Bosnia Herzegovina, Brazil, Bulgaria, Burkina Faso, Cambodia, Canada, Chile, China, Colombia, Costa Rica, Croatia, Cuba, Cyprus, Czech Republic, Democratic People's Republic of Korea, Denmark, Ecuador, Egypt, El Salvador, Estonia, Ethiopia, Fiji, Finland, France, Gabon, Gambia, Georgia, Germany, Ghana, Greece, Guatemala, Haiti, Honduras, Hungary, Iceland, India, Iran, Iraq, Ireland, Israel, Italy, Jamaica, Jordan, Kuwait, Lao Democratic People's Republic, Latvia, Lebanon, Lesotho, Liberia, Libya, Liechtenstein, Luxembourg, Malaysia, Maldives, Mali, Mexico, Monaco, Mongolia, Morocco, Mozambique, Myanmar, Namibia, Nepal, Netherlands, New Zealand, Nicaragua, Norway, Pakistan, Panama, Papua New Guinea, Peru, Philippines, Poland, Republic of Korea, Republic of Modova, Romania, Russian Federation, Rwanda, St. Vincent and the Grenadines, Saudi Arabia, Senegal, Seychelles, Slovakia, Slovenia, Spain, Sri Lanka, Sweden, Syria, Togo, Tonga, Tunisia, Turkey, Ukraine, United Kingdom of Great Britain and Northern Ireland, United Republic of Tanzania, United States of America, Uruguay, Venezuela, Viet Nam, Yemen, Yugoslavia, Zaire, and Zimbabwe.

The convention has been signed by Bolivia, Dominican Republic, and Paraguay.

## I. *International Convention Against Apartheid in Sports*

Up to 30 June 1995, the following States have become parties to the convention by ratification or accession: Algeria, Angola, Antigua and Barbuda, Bahamas, Barbados, Belarus, Bolivia, Bosnia Herzegovina, Bulgaria,

Burkina Faso, Croatia, Cuba, Czech Republic, Ecuador, Egypt, Equatorial Guinea, Estonia, Ethiopia, Germany, Ghana, Guinea, Guyana, India, Indonesia, Iran, Iraq, Jamaica, Jordan, Latvia, Libya, Mali, Mauritania, Mauritius, Mexico, Mongolia, Nepal, Niger, Nigeria, Peru, Philippines, Poland, Qatar, Russian Federation, St. Kitts and Nevis, Senegal, Sudan, Syria, Togo, Trinidad and Tobago, Tunisia, Uganda, Ukraine, United Republic of Tanzania, Uruguay, Venezuela, Yugoslavia, Zambia, and Zimbabwe.

The convention has been signed by Benin, Burundi, Cameroon, Cape Verde, Central African Republic, China, Colombia, Cuba, Cyprus, Gabon, Guinea-Bissau, Haiti, Kenya, Lebanon, Liberia, Madagascar, Malaysia, Maldives, Morocco, Nicaragua, Panama, Rwanda, Saint Lucia, Sierra Leone, Somalia, Yemen, and Zaire.

## J. *International Convention against the Taking of Hostages*

Up to 1 June 1995, the following States have become parties to the convention by ratification or accession: Antigua and Barbuda, Austria, Bahamas, Barbados, Bhutan, Brunei Darussalam, Bulgaria, Byelorussian S.S.R., Cameroon, Canada, Chile, Czechoslovakia, Denmark, Dominica, Ecuador, Egypt, El Salvador, Federal Republic of Germany, Finland, German Democratic Republic, Ghana, Greece, Guatemala, Honduras, Hungary, Iceland, Italy, Japan, Jordan, Kenya, Kuwait, Lesotho, Malawi, Mauritius, Mexico, Netherlands, New Zealand, Norway, Oman, Panama, Philippines, Portugal, Republic of Korea, Senegal, Spain, Suriname, Sweden, Switzerland, Trinidad and Tobago, Ukrainian S.S.R., Union of Soviet Socialist Republics, United Kingdom of Great Britain and Northern Ireland, Venezuela, and Yugoslavia.

The following States have signed the convention: Belgium, Bolivia, Canada, Dominican Republic, Gabon, Greece, Haiti, Iraq, Israel, Jamaica, Liberia, Luxembourg, New Zealand, Uganda, and Zaire.

## K. *International Convention on the Elimination of All Forms of Racial Discrimination*

Up to 30 June 1995, the following States have become parties to the convention by ratification or accession: Afghanistan, Albania, Algeria, Antigua and Barbuda, Argentina, Armenia, Australia, Austria, Bahamas, Bahrain, Bangladesh, Barbados, Belarus, Belgium, Bolivia, Bosnia Herzegovina, Botswana, Brazil, Bulgaria, Burkina Faso, Burundi, Cambodia, Cameroon, Canada, Cape Verde, Central African Republic, Chad, Chile, China, Colombia, Congo, Costa Rica, Côte d'Ivoire (Ivory Coast), Croatia, Cuba, Cyprus, Czech Republic,

Denmark, Dominican Republic, Ecuador, Egypt, El Salvador, Estonia, Ethiopia, Fiji, Finland, France, Gabon, Gambia, Germany, Ghana, Greece, Guatemala, Guinea, Guyana, Haiti, Holy See, Hungary, Iceland, India, Iran, Iraq, Israel, Italy, Jamaica, Jordan, Kuwait, Lao People's Democratic Republic, Latvia, Lebanon, Lesotho, Liberia, Libya, Luxembourg, Madagascar, Maldives, Mali, Malta, Mauritania, Mauritius, Mexico, Mongolia, Morocco, Mozambique, Namibia, Nepal, Netherlands, New Zealand, Nicaragua, Niger, Nigeria, Norway, Pakistan, Panama, Papua New Guinea, Peru, Philippines, Poland, Portugal, Qatar, Republic of Korea, Republic of Moldava, Romania, Russian Federation, Rwanda, Saint Lucia, St. Vincent and the Grenadines, Senegal, Seychelles, Sierra Leone, Slovakia, Slovenia, Solomon Islands, Somalia, Spain, Sri Lanka, Sudan, Suriname, Swaziland, Sweden, Switzerland, Syria, Tajikistan, The Former Yugoslav Republic of Macedonia, Togo, Tonga, Trinidad and Tobago, Tunisia, Turkmenistan, Uganda, Ukraine, United Arab Emirates, United Kingdom of Great Britain and Northern Ireland, United Republic of Tanzania, United States of America, Uruguay, Venezuela, Viet Nam, Yemen, Yugoslavia, Zaire, Zambia and Zimbabwe.

The convention has been signed by Benin, Bhutan, Grenada, Ireland, South Africa, and Turkey.

The following States have made the declaration recognizing the competence of the Committee on the Elimination of Racial Discrimination under article 14 of the convention: Algeria, Australia, Bulgaria, Costa Rica, Cyprus, Denmark, Ecuador, France, Hungary, Iceland, Italy, Netherlands, Norway, Peru, Russian Federation, Senegal, Slovakia, Sweden, Ukraine and Uruguay.

### L. International Convention on the Suppression and Punishment of the Crime of Apartheid

Up to 30 June 1995, the following States have become parties to the convention by ratification or accession: Afghanistan, Algeria, Antigua and Barbuda, Argentina, Armenia, Bahamas, Bahrain, Bangladesh, Barbados, Belarus, Benin, Bolivia, Bosnia Herzegovina, Bulgaria, Burkina Faso, Burundi, Cambodia, Cameroon, Cape Verde, Central African Republic, Chad, China, Colombia, Congo, Costa Rica, Croatia, Cuba, Czech Republic, Ecuador, Egypt, El Salvador, Estonia, Ethiopia, Gabon, Gambia, German Democratic Republic, Ghana, Guinea, Guyana, Haiti, Hungary, India, Iran, Iraq, Jamaica, Jordan, Kuwait, Lao People's Democratic Republic, Latvia, Lesotho, Liberia, Libya, Madagascar, Maldives, Mali, Mauritania, Mexico, Mongolia, Mozambique, Namibia, Nepal, Nicaragua, Niger, Nigeria, Oman, Pakistan, Panama, Peru, Philippines, Poland, Qatar, Romania, Russian Federation,

Rwanda, St. Vincent and the Grenadines, Sao Tome and Principe, Senegal, Seychelles, Slovakia, Slovenia, Somalia, Sri Lanka, Sudan, Suriname, Syria the Former Yugoslav Republic of Macedonia, Togo, Trinidad and Tobago, Tunisia, Uganda, Ukraine, United Arab Emirates, United Republic of Tanzania, Venezuela, Viet Nam, Yemen, Yugoslavia, Zaire, Zambia and Zimbabwe.

The convention has been signed by Kenya.

### M. International Covenant on Civil and Political Rights

Up to 30 June 1995, the following States have become parties to the covenant by ratification or accession: Afghanistan, Albania, Algeria, Angola, Argentina, Armenia, Australia, Austria, Azerbaijan, Barbados, Belarus, Belgium, Benin, Bolivia, Bosnia Herzegovina, Brazil, Bulgaria, Burundi, Cambodia, Cameroon, Canada, Cape Verde, Central African Republic, Chad, Chile, Colombia, Congo, Costa Rica, Côte d'Ivoire, Croatia, Cyprus, Czech Republic, Democratic People's Republic of Korea, Denmark, Dominica, Dominican Republic, Ecuador, Egypt, El Salvador, Equatorial Guinea, Estonia, Ethiopia, Finland, France, Gabon, Gambia, Georgia, Germany, Grenada, Guatemala, Guinea, Guyana, Haiti, Hungary, Iceland, India, Iran, Iraq, Ireland, Israel, Italy, Jamaica, Japan, Jordan, Kenya, Kyrgyzstan, Lebanon, Libya, Luxembourg, Madagascar, Mali, Mauritius, Mexico, Mongolia, Morocco, Netherlands, New Zealand, Nicaragua, Niger, Norway, Panama, Peru, Philippines, Poland, Portugal, Republic of Korea, Romania, Rwanda, St. Vincent and the Grenadines, San Marino, Senegal, Somalia, Spain, Sri Lanka, Sudan, Suriname, Sweden, Syria, Tanzania, Togo, Trinidad and Tobago, Tunisia, Ukrainian S.S.R., Union of Soviet Socialist Republics, United Kingdom of Great Britain and Northern Ireland, Uruguay, Venezuela, Viet Nam, Yemen, Yugoslavia, Zaire, and Zambia.

The covenant has been signed by Cambodia, Honduras, Israel, Liberia, and the United States of America.

The following States have made the declaration recognizing the competence of the Human Rights Committee under article 41 of the covenant: Argentina, Austria, Belgium, Canada, Congo, Denmark, Ecuador, Federal Republic of Germany, Finland, Gambia, Hungary, Iceland, Italy, Luxembourg, Netherlands, New Zealand, Norway, Peru, Philippines, Senegal, Spain, Sri Lanka, Sweden, and the United Kingdom of Great Britain and Northern Ireland.

### N. International Covenant on Civil and Political Rights: Optional Protocol

Up to 30 June 1995, the following States have become parties to the optional protocol by ratification or accession: Algeria, Angola, Argentina, Armenia, Australia, Austria, Barbados, Belarus, Belgium, Benin, Bolivia, Bosnia Herzegovina, Bulgaria, Cameroon, Canada, Central African Republic, Chad, Chile, Colombia, Congo, Costa Rica, Cyprus, Czech Republic, Denmark, Dominican Republic, Ecuador, El Salvador, Equatorial Guinea, Estonia, Finland, France, Gambia, Georgia, Germany, Guinea, Guyana, Hungary, Iceland, Ireland, Italy, Jamaica, Kyrgyzstan, Latvia, Libya, Lithuania, Luxembourg, Madagascar, Malta, Mauritius, Mongolia, Namibia, Nepal, Netherlands, New Zealand, Nicaragua, Niger, Norway, Panama, Paraguay, Peru, Philippines, Poland, Portugal, Republic of Korea, Romania, Russian Federation, St. Vincent and the Grenadines, San Marino, Senegal, Seychelles, Slovakia, Slovenia, Somalia, Spain, Suriname, Sweden, Togo, Trinidad and Tobago, Ukraine, Uruguay, Venezuela, Zaire, and Zambia.

The optional protocol has been signed by Honduras and Yugoslavia.

## O. International Covenant on Economic, Social and Cultural Rights

Up to 30 June 1995, the following States have become parties to the covenant by ratification or accession: Afghanistan, Albania, Algeria, Angola, Argentina, Armenia, Australia, Austria, Azerbaijan, Barbados, Belarus, Belgium, Benin, Bolivia, Bosnia Herzegovina, Brazil, Bulgaria, Burundi, Cambodia, Cameroon, Canada, Cape Verde, Central African Republic, Chad, Chile, Colombia, Congo, Costa Rica, Côte d'Ivoire, Croatia, Cyprus, Czech Republic, Democratic People's Republic of Korea, Denmark, Dominica, Dominican Republic, Ecuador, Egypt, El Salvador, Equatorial Guinea, Estonia, Ethiopia, Finland, France, Gabon, Gambia, Georgia, Germany, Greece, Grenada, Guatemala, Guinea, Guinea-Bissau, Guyana, Honduras, Hungary, Iceland, India, Iran, Iraq, Ireland, Israel, Italy, Jamaica, Japan, Jordan, Kenya, Kyrgyzstan, Latvia, Lebanon, Lesotho, Libya, Lithuania, Luxembourg, Madagascar, Malawi, Mali, Malta, Mauritius, Mexico, Mongolia, Morocco, Namibia, Nepal, Netherlands, New Zealand, Nicaragua, Niger, Nigeria, Norway, Panama, Paraguay, Peru, Philippines, Poland, Portugal, Republic of Korea, Republic of Moldova, Russian Federation, Romania, Rwanda, St. Vincent and the Grenadines, San Marino, Senegal, Seychelles, Slovakia, Slovenia, Solomon Islands, Somalia, Spain, Sri Lanka, Sudan, Suriname, Sweden, Switzerland, Syria, The Former Republic of Macedonia, Togo, Trinidad and Tobago, Tunisia, Uganda, Ukraine, United Kingdom of Great Britain and Northern Ireland, United Republic of Tanzania, Uruguay, Venezuela, Viet Nam, Yemen, Yugoslavia, Zaire, Zambia and Zimbabwe.

The covenant has been signed by Liberia, South Africa and the United States of America.

## P. Slavery Convention Signed at Geneva on 25 September 1926, as amended

Up to 30 June 1995, the following States have become parties to the convention, as amended, by ratification or accession: Afghanistan, Albania, Algeria, Antigua and Barbuda, Australia, Austria, Bahamas, Bahrain, Bangladesh, Barbados, Belarus, Belgium, Bolivia, Bosnia Herzegovina, Brazil, Cameroon, Canada, Chile, Croatia, Cuba, Cyprus, Denmark, Djibouti, Dominica, Ecuador, Egypt, Ethiopia, Fiji, Finland, France, Germany, Greece, Guatemala, Guinea, Hungary, India, Iraq, Ireland, Israel, Italy, Jamaica, Jordan, Kuwait, Lesotho, Liberia, Libya, Madagascar, Malawi, Mali, Malta, Mauritania, Mauritius, Mexico, Monaco, Mongolia, Morocco, Myanmar, Nepal, Netherlands, New Zealand, Nicaragua, Niger, Nigeria, Norway, Pakistan, Papua New Guinea, Philippines, Romania, Saint Lucia, St.Vincent and the Grenadines, Saudi Arabia, Sierra Leone, Solomon Islands, South Africa, Spain, Sri Lanka, Sudan, Sweden, Switzerland, Syria, Trinidad and Tobago, Tunisia, Turkey, Uganda, Ukraine, United Kingdom of Great Britain and Northern Ireland, United Republic of Tanzania, United States of America, Yemen, Zambia and Yugoslavia.

## Q. Convention on the Rights of the Child

Up to 30 June 1995, the following States have become parties to the convention, as amended, by ratification or accession: Afghanistan, Albania, Algeria, Angola, Antigua and Barbuda, Argentina, Armenia, Australia, Austria, Azerbaijan, Bahamas, Bahrain, Bangladesh, Barbados, Belarus, Belgium, Belize, Benin, Bhutan, Bolivia, Bosnia Herzegovina, Botswana, Brazil, Bulgaria, Burkina Faso, Burundi, Cambodia, Cameroon, Canada, Cape Verde, Central African Republic, Chad, Chile, China, Colombia, Comoros, Congo, Costa Rica, Côte d'Ivoire (Ivory Coast), Croatia, Cuba, Cyprus, Czech Republic, Democratic Republic of Korea, Denmark, Djibouti, Dominica, Dominican Republic, Ecuador, Egypt, El Salvador, Equatorial Guinea, Eritrea, Estonia, Ethiopia, Federated States of Micronesia, Fiji, Finland, France, Gabon, Gambia, Georgia, Germany, Ghana, Greece, Grenada, Guatemala, Guinea, Guinea-Bissau, Guyana, Haiti, Holy See, Honduras, Hungary, Iceland, India, Indonesia, Iran, Iraq, Ireland, Israel, Italy, Jamaica, Japan, Jordan, Kazakhstan, Kenya, Kuwait, Kyrgyzstan, Lao People's Democratic Republic, Latvia, Lebanon, Lesotho, Liberia, Libya, Lithuania, Luxembourg, Madagascar, Malawi, Malaysia, Maldives, Mali, Malta, Marshall Islands, Mauritania, Mauritius, Mexico, Monaco, Mongolia, Morocco, Mozambique,

Myanmar, Namibia, Nauru, Nepal, Netherlands, New Zealand, Nicaragua, Niger, Nigeria, Norway, Pakistan, Panama, Papua New Guinea, Paraguay, Peru, Philippines, Poland, Portugal, Qatar, Republic of Korea, Republic of Moldova, Romania, Russian Federation, Rwanda, Saint Kitts and Nevis, Saint Lucia, Saint Vincent & the Grenadines, Samoa, San Marino, Sao Tome and Principe, Senegal, Seychelles, Sierra Leone, Slovakia, Slovenia, Solomon Islands, South Africa, Spain, Sri Lanka, Sudan, Suriname, Sweden, Syria, Tajikistan, Thailand, The Former Yugoslav Republic of Macedonia, Togo, Trinidad and Tobago, Tunisia, Turkey, Turkmenistan, Uganda, Ukraine, United Kingdom of Great Britain and Northern Ireland, United Republic of Tanzania, Uruguay, Uzbekistan, Vanuatu, Venezuela, Viet Nam, Yemen, Yugoslavia, Zaire, Zambia and Zimbabwe.

The convention has been signed by Liechtenstein, Swaziland, Switzerland and United States of America.

### R. *Convention on the Rights of the Migrant Workers and the Members of their Families*

Up to 30 June 1995, the following States have become parties to the convention, as amended, by ratification or accession: Colombia, Egypt, Morocco and the Seychelles.

The convention has been signed by Chile, Mexico and Monaco.

## 2. Conventions Concluded by Special Diplomatic Conferences

### A. *Convention on the Reduction of Statelessness*

Up to 30 June 1995, the following States have become parties to the Convention on the Reduction of Statelessness by ratification or accession: Armenia, Australia, Austria, Bolivia, Cameroon, Canada, Costa Rica, Denmark, Germany, Ireland, Kiribati, Latvia, Libya, Netherlands, Niger, Norway, Sweden and the United Kingdom of Great Britain and Northern Ireland.

The convention has been signed by the Dominican Republic, El Salvador, France, and Israel.

### B. *Convention relating to the Status of Refugees*

Up to 30 June 1995, the following 124 States have become parties to the convention by ratification or accession: Albania, Algeria, Angola, Argentina, Armenia, Australia, Austria, Azerbaijan, Bahamas, Belgium, Belize, Benin, Bolivia, Bosnia Herzegovina, Botswana, Brazil, Bulgaria, Burkina Faso, Burundi, Cambodia, Cameroon, Canada, Central African Republic, Chad, Chile, China, Colombia, Congo, Costa Rica, Côte d'Ivoire (Ivory Coast), Croatia, Cyprus, Czech Republic, Denmark, Djibouti, Dominica, Dominican Repub-

lic, Ecuador, Egypt, El Salvador, Equatorial Guinea, Ethiopia, Fiji, Finland, France, Gabon, Gambia, Germany, Ghana, Greece, Guatemala, Guinea, Guinea-Bissau, Haiti, Holy See, Honduras, Hungary, Iceland, Iran, Ireland, Israel, Italy, Jamaica, Japan, Kenya, Lesotho, Liberia, Liechtenstein, Luxembourg, Madagascar, Malawi, Mali, Malta, Mauritania, Monaco, Morocco, Mozambique, Netherlands, New Zealand, Nicaragua, Niger, Nigeria, Norway, Panama, Papua New Guinea, Paraguay, Peru, Philippines, Poland, Portugal, Republic of Korea, Romania, Russian Federation, Rwanda, Saint Vincent & the Grenadines, Samoa, Sao Tome and Principe, Senegal, Seychelles, Sierra Leone, Singapore, Slovakia, Slovenia, Somalia, Spain, Sudan, Suriname, Sweden, Switzerland, Tajikistan, Togo, Tunisia, Turkey, Tuvalu, Uganda, United Kingdom of Great Britain and Northern Ireland, United Republic of Tanzania, Uruguay, Yemen, Yugoslavia, Zaire, Zambia, and Zimbabwe.

### C. *Convention relating to the Status of Refugees: Protocol*

Up to 30 June 1995, the following States have become parties to the protocol by ratification or accession: Albania, Algeria, Angola, Argentina, Armenia, Australia, Austria, Azerbaijan, Bahamas, Belgium, Belize, Benin, Bolivia, Bosnia Herzegovina, Botswana, Brazil, Bulgaria, Burkina Faso, Burundi, Cambodia, Cameroon, Canada, Cape Verde, Central African Republic, Chad, Chile, China, Colombia, Congo, Costa Rica, Côte d'Ivoire (Ivory Coast), Croatia, Cyprus, Czech Republic, Denmark, Dominica, Dominican Republic, Ecuador, Egypt, Ethiopia, Fiji, Finland, France, Gabon, Gambia, Germany, Ghana, Greece, Guatemala, Guinea, Guinea-Bissau, Haiti, Holy See, Honduras, Hungary, Iceland, Iran, Ireland, Israel, Italy, Jamaica, Japan, Kenya, Lesotho, Liberia, Liechtenstein, Luxembourg, Madagascar, Malawi, Mali, Malta, Mauritania, Monaco, Morocco, Mozambique, Netherlands, New Zealand, Nicaragua, Niger, Nigeria, Norway, Panama, Papua New Guinea, Paraguay, Peru, Philippines, Poland, Portugal, Republic of Korea, Romania, Russian Federation, Rwanda, Samao, Sao Tome and Principe, Senegal, Seychelles, Sierra Leone, Singapore, Slovakia, Slovenia, Somalia, Spain, Sudan, Suriname, Swaziland, Sweden, Switzerland, Tjikistan, Togo, Tunisia, Turkey, Tuvalu, Uganda, United Kingdom of Great Britain and Northern Ireland, United Republic of Tanzania, United States of America, Uruguay, Venezuela, Yemen, Yugoslavia, Zaire, Zambia, and Zimbabwe.

### D. *Convention relating to the Status of Stateless Persons*

Up to 30 June 1995, the following States have become parties to the convention by ratification or accession:

Algeria, Antigua and Barbuda, Argentina, Armenia, Australia, Barbados, Belgium, Bolivia, Bosnia Herzegovina, Botswana, Costa Rica, Croatia, Denmark, Djibouti, Ecuador, El Salvador, Equatorial Guinea, Fiji, Finland, France, Germany, Greece, Guinea, Ireland, Israel, Italy, Kiribati, Lesotho, Liberia, Libya, Luxembourg, Netherlands, Norway, Republic of Korea, Sweden, Switzerland, Trinidad and Tobago, Tunisia, Uganda, United Kingdom of Great Britain and Northern Ireland, Yugoslavia, and Zambia.

The convention has been signed by Brazil, Colombia, Guatemala, Holy See, Honduras, Liechtenstein, and the Philippines.

### E. Geneva Conventions: Protocols I and II

Up to 1 June 1995, the following States have become parties to the protocols by ratification or accession: Algeria, Angola (Protocol I only), Antigua and Barbuda, Argentina, Austria, Bahamas, Bangladesh, Bahrain, Barbados, Belgium, Belize, Benin, Bolivia, Botswana, Bulgaria, Burkina Faso, Byelorussian S.S.R., Cameroon, Central African Republic, China, Comoros, Congo, Costa Rica, Côte d'Ivoire (Ivory Coast), Cuba (Protocol I only), Cyprus, Czech and Slovak Federal Republic, Democratic People's Republic of Korea, Denmark, Ecuador, El Salvador, Equatorial Guinea, Finland, France (Protocol II only), Gabon, Gambia, Ghana, Greece, Guatemala, Guyana, Guinea, Guinea-Bissau, Holy See, Hungary, Iceland, Italy, Jamaica, Jordan, Kuwait, Laos, Libya, Liberia, Liechtenstein, Luxembourg, Mali, Malta, Mauritania, Maritius, Mexico (Protocol I only), Mozambique (Protocol I only), Namibia, Netherlands, New Zealand, Niger, Nigeria, Norway, Oman, Peru, Philippines (Protocol II only), Qatar (Protocol I only), Republic of Korea, Rwanda, St. Kitts and Nevis, Saint Lucia, Saint Vincent and the Grenadines, Samoa, Saudi Arabia (Protocol I only), Senegal, Seychelles, Sierra Leone, Solomon Islands, Spain, Suriname, Sweden, Switzerland, Syria, (Protocol I only), Tanzania, Togo, Tunisia, Ukrainian S.S.R., Union of Soviet Socialist Republics, United Arab Emirates, Uruguay, Vanuatu, Viet Nam (Protocol I only), Yemen, Yugoslavia, and Zaire (Protocol I only).

### F. Supplementary Convention on the Abolition of Slavery, the Slave Trade, and Institutions and Practices Similar to Slavery

Up to 30 June 1995, the following States have become parties to the supplementary convention by ratification or accession: Afghanistan, Albania, Algeria, Antigua and Barbuda, Argentina, Australia, Austria, Bahamas, Bahrain, Bangladesh, Barbados, Belarus, Belgium, Bolivia, Bosnia Herzegovina, Brazil, Bulgaria, Cambodia, Cameroon, Canada, Central African

Republic, Chile, Congo, Côte d'Ivoire (Ivory Coast), Croatia, Cuba, Cyprus, Czech Republic, Denmark, Djibouti, Dominica, Dominican Republic, Ecuador, Egypt, Ethiopia, Fiji, Finland, France, Germany, Ghana, Greece, Guatemala, Guinea, Haiti, Hungary, Iceland, India, Iran, Iraq, Ireland, Israel, Italy, Jamaica, Jordan, Kuwait, Lao People's Democratic Republic, Latvia, Lesotho, Libya, Luxembourg, Madagascar, Malawi, Malaysia, Mali, Malta, Mauritania, Mauritius, Mexico, Mongolia, Morocco, Nepal, Netherlands, New Zealand, Nicargua, Niger, Nigeria, Norway, Pakistan, Philippines, Poland, Portugal, Romania, Russian Federation, Saint Lucia, Saint Vincent and the Grenadines, San Marino, Saudi Arabia, Senegal, Seychelles, Sierra Leone, Singapore, Slovakia, Slovenia, Solomon Islands, Spain, Sri Lanka, Sudan, Suriname, Sweden, Switzerland, Syria, The Former Yugoslav Republic of Macedonia, Togo, Trinidad and Tobago, Tunisia, Turkey, Uganda, Ukraine, United Kingdom of Great Britain and Northern Ireland, United Republic of Tanzania, United States of America, Yugoslavia, Zaire, and Zambia.

The supplementary convention has been signed by El Salvador, Liberia, and Peru.

### G. Universal Copyright Convention (Revised)

Up to 1 January 1995, the following States have become parties, by ratification or accession, to the convention as revised: Algeria, Andorra, Argentina, Australia, Austria, Bahamas, Bangladesh, Barbados, Belgium, Belize, Brazil, Bulgaria, Cameroon, Canada, Chile, Colombia, Costa Rica, Cuba, Czechoslovakia, Denmark, Dominican Republic, Ecuador, El Salvador, Federal Republic of Germany, Fiji, Finland, France, German Democratic Republic, Ghana, Greece, Guatemala, Guinea, Haiti, Holy See, Hungary, Iceland, India, Ireland, Israel, Italy, Japan, Kenya, Laos, Lebanon, Liberia, Liechtenstein, Luxembourg, Malawi, Malta, Mauritius, Mexico, Monaco, Morocco, Netherlands, New Zealand, Nicaragua, Nigeria, Pakistan, Panama, Paraguay, Peru, Poland, Portugal, Republic of Korea, St. Vincent and the Grenadines, Senegal, Spain, Sri Lanka, Sweden, Switzerland, Trinidad and Tobago, Tunisia, Union of Soviet Socialist Republics, Venezuela, Yugoslavia, and Zambia.

The following States have signed the convention: Honduras, San Marino, and Uruguay.

### 3. Conventions Prepared Under the Auspices of the International Labor Organization

### A. ILO Abolition of Forced Labor Convention, 1957 (No. 105)

Up to 1 June 1995, the convention had been ratified or acceded to by the following States: Afghanistan, Algeria, Angola, Antigua and Barbuda, Argentina, Australia, Austria, Bahamas, Bangladesh, Barbados, Belgium, Belize, Benin, Brazil, Burundi, Cameroon, Canada, Cape Verde, Central African Republic, Chad, Colombia, Comoros, Costa Rica, Côte d'Ivoire (Ivory Coast), Cuba, Cyprus, Denmark, Djibouti, Dominica, Dominican Republic, Ecuador, Egypt, El Salvador, Federal Republic of Germany, Fiji, Finland, France, Ghana, Greece, Grenada, Guatemala, Guinea, Guinea-Bissau, Guyana, Haiti, Honduras, Iceland, Iran, Iraq, Israel, Italy, Jamaica, Jordan, Kenya, Kuwait, Lebanon, Liberia, Libya, Luxembourg, Malaysia, Mali, Malta, Mauritius, Mexico, Morocco, Mozambique, Netherlands, New Zealand, Nicaragua, Niger, Nigeria, Norway, Pakistan, Panama, Papua New Guinea, Paraguay, Peru, Philippines, Poland, Portugal, Rwanda, Saint Lucia, Saudi Arabia, Senegal, Seychelles, Sierra Leone, Somalia, Spain, Sudan, Suriname, Swaziland, Sweden, Switzerland, Syria, Tanzania, Thailand, Tunisia, Turkey, Uganda, United Kingdom, Uruguay, Venezuela, Yemen, and Zimbabwe.

### B. ILO Collective Bargaining Convention, 1981 (No. 154)

Up to 1 June 1995, the convention has been ratified or acceded to by the following States: Belgium, Cyprus, Finland, Gabon, Niger, Nigeria, Spain, Sweden, Switzerland, Uganda, Uruguay, and Zambia.

### C. ILO Discrimination (Employment and Occupation) Convention, 1958 (No. 111)

Up to 1 June 1995, the convention has been ratified or acceded to by the following States: Afghanistan, Algeria, Angola, Antigua and Barbuda, Argentina, Australia, Austria, Bangladesh, Barbados, Belgium, Benin, Bolivia, Brazil, Bulgaria, Burkina Faso, Cameroon, Canada, Cape Verde, Central African Republic, Chad, Chile, Colombia, Costa Rica, Côte d'Ivoire (Ivory Coast), Cuba, Cyprus, Czechoslovakia, Denmark, Dominica, Dominican Republic, Ecuador, Egypt, Ethiopia, Federal Republic of Germany, Finland, France, Gabon, German Democratic Republic, Ghana Greece, Guatemala, Guinea, Guinea-Bissau, Guyana, Haiti, Honduras, Hungary, Iceland, India, Iran, Iraq, Israel, Italy, Jamaica, Jordan, Kuwait, Lebanon, Lesotho, Liberia, Madagascar, Malawi, Mali, Mata, Mauritania, Mexico, Mongolia, Morocco, Mozambique, Nepal, Netherlands, New Zealand, Nicaragua, Niger, Norway, Pakistan, Panama, Paraguay, Peru, Philippines, Poland, Portugal, Qatar, Romania, Rwanda, Saint Lucia, San Marino, Sao Tome and Principe, Saudi Arabia, Senegal, Sierra Leone, Somalia, Spain, Sudan, Swaziland, Sweden, Switzerland, Syria, Togo, Trinidad and Tobago, Tunisia, Turkey, Ukrainian S.S.R., Union of Soviet Socialist Republics, Uruguay, Venezuela, Viet Nam, Yemen, Yugoslavia, and Zambia.

### D. ILO Equal Remuneration Convention, 1951 (No.100)

Up to 1 June 1995, the convention has been ratified or acceded to by the following states: Afghanistan, Albania, Algeria, Angola, Argentina, Australia, Austria, Barbados, Belgium, Benin, Bolivia, Brazil, Bulgaria, Burkina Faso, Byelorussian S.S.R., Cameroon, Canada, Cape Verde, Central African Republic, Chad, Chile, Colombia, Comoros, Costa Rica, Côte d'Ivoire (Ivory Coast), Cuba, Cyprus, Czechoslovakia, Denmark, Djibouti, Dominica, Dominican Republic, Ecuador, Egypt, Equatorial Guinea, Federal Republic of Germany, Finland, France, Gabon, German Democratic Republic, Ghana, Greece, Guatemala, Guinea, Guinea-Bissau, Guyana, Haiti, Honduras, Hungary, Iceland, India, Indonesia, Iran, Iraq, Ireland, Israel, Italy, Jamaica, Japan, Jordan, Lebanon, Libya, Luxembourg, Madagascar, Malawi, Mali, Malta, Mexico, Mongolia, Morocco, Mozambique, Nepal, Netherlands, New Zealand, Nicaragua, Niger, Nigeria, Norway, Panama, Paraguay, Peru, Philippines, Poland, Portugal, Romania, Rwanda, Saint Lucia, San Marino, Sao Tome and Principe, Saudi Arabia, Senegal, Sierra Leone, Spain, Sudan, Swaziland, Sweden, Switzerland, Syria, Togo, Tunisia, Turkey, Ukrainian S.S.R., Union of Soviet Socialist Republics, United Kingdom, Venezuela, Yemen, Yugoslavia, Zaire, Zambia, and Zimbabwe.

### E. ILO Equality of Treatment (Social Security) Convention, 1962 (No. 118)

Up to 1 June 1995, the convention has been ratified or acceded to by the following States: Bangladesh, Barbados, Bolivia, Brazil, Cape Verde, Central African Republic, Denmark, Ecuador, Federal Republic of Germany, Finland, France, Guatemala, Guinea, India, Iran, Iraq, Ireland, Israel, Italy, Jordan, Kenya, Libya, Madagascar, Mauritania, Mexico, Netherlands, Norway, Pakistan, Rwanda, Suriname, Sweden, Syria, Tunisia, Turkey, Uruguay, Venezuela, Viet Nam, and Zaire.

### F. ILO Right to Organize and Collective Bargaining Convention, 1949 (No. 98)

Up to 1 June 1995, the convention has been ratified or acceded to by the following States: Afghanistan, Albania, Algeria, Angola, Antigua and Barbuda, Argentina, Australia, Austria, Bahamas, Bangladesh, Barbados, Belgium, Belize, Benin, Bolivia, Botswana, Brazil, Bulgaria, Burkina Faso, Byelorussian S.S.R., Cameroon, Cape Verde, Central African Republic, Chad, Colombia, Comoros, Costa Rica, Cote d'Ivoire (Ivory

Coast), Cuba, Cyprus, Czechoslovakia, Denmark, Djibouti, Dominica, Dominican Republic, Ecuador, Egypt, Ethiopia, Federal Republic of Germany, Fiji, Finland, France, Gabon, German Democratic Republic, Ghana, Greece, Grenada, Guatemala, Guinea, Guinea-Bissau, Guyana, Haiti, Honduras, Hungary, Iceland, Indonesia, Iran, Iraq, Ireland, Israel, Italy, Jamaica, Jordan, Kenya, Lebanon, Lesotho, Liberia, Libya, Luxembourg, Malawi, Malaysia, Mali, Malta, Mauritius, Mongolia, Morocco, Nigeria, Norway, Pakistan, Panama, Papua New Guinea, Paraguay, Peru, Philippines, Poland, Portugal, Romania, Rwanda, Saint Lucia, San Marino, Senegal, Sierra Leone, Singapore, Spain, Sri Lanka, Sudan, Swaziland, Sweden, Syria, Tanzania, Togo, Trinidad and Tobago, Tunisia, Turkey, Uganda, Ukrainian S.S.R., Union of Soviet Socialist Republics, United Arab Emirates, United Kingdom, Uruguay, Venezuela, Viet Nam, Yemen, Yugoslavia, and Zaire.

### G. ILO Social Security (Minimum Standards) Convention, 1952 (No. 102)

Up to 1 June 1995, the convention has been ratified or acceded to by the following States: Bahamas, Barbados, Belgium, Bolivia, Costa Rica, Czechoslovakia, Denmark, Ecuador, Federal Republic of Germany, France, Greece, Iceland, Ireland, Israel, Italy, Japan, Libya, Luxembourg, Mauritania, Mexico, Netherlands, Niger, Norway, Peru, Senegal, Spain, Sweden, Switzerland, Tanzania, Turkey, United Kingdom, Venezuela, Yugoslavia, and Zaire.

### H. ILO Working Environment (Air Pollution, Noise and Vibration) Convention, 1977 (No. 148)

Up to 1 June 1995, the convention has been ratified or acceded to by the following states: Brazil, Costa Rica, Cuba, Czechoslovakia, Denmark, Ecuador, Egypt, Finland, France, Ghana, Guinea, Iraq, Italy, Malta, Norway, Portugal, San Marino, Spain, Sweden, Tanzania, Union of Soviet Socialist Republics, United Kingdom, Uruguay, Yugoslavia, and Zambia.

### 4. Conventions Prepared under the Auspices of UNESCO

### A. UNESCO Convention against Discrimination in Education

Up to 1 January 1995, the following States have become parties to the convention by ratification or accession: Albania, Algeria, Argentina, Australia, Barbados, Belize, Benin, Brazil, Brunei Darussalam, Bulgaria, Byelorussian S.S.R., Central African Republic, Chile, Congo, Costa Rica, Cuba, Cyprus, Czecho-

slovakia, Denmark, Dominica, Dominican Republic, Ecuador, Egypt, Federal Republic of Germany, Finland, France, German Democratic Republic, Guatemala, Guinea, Hungary, Indonesia, Iran, Iraq, Israel, Italy, Jordan, Kuwait, Lebanon, Liberia, Libya, Luxembourg, Madagascar, Malta, Mauritius, Mongolia, Morocco, Netherlands, New Zealand, Nicaragua, Niger, Nigeria, Norway, Panama, Peru, Philippines, Poland, Portugal, Romania, St.Vincent and the Grenadines, Saudi Arabia, Senegal, Sierra Leone, Solomon Islands, Spain, Sri Lanka, Swaziland, Sweden, Tanzania, Tunisia, Uganda, Ukrainian S.S.R., Union of Soviet Socialist Republics, United Kingdom of Great Britain and Northern Ireland, Venezuela, Viet Nam, and Yugoslavia.

The following States have also become parties to the 1962 protocol instituting a Conciliation and Good Offices Commission to be responsible for seeking a settlement of any disputes which may arise between States parties to the Convention against Discrimination in Education: Argentina, Australia, Brunei Darussalam, Costa Rica, Cyprus, Denmark, Dominica, Egypt, Federal Republic of Germany, France, Guatemala, Israel, Italy, Libya, Madagascar, Malta, Morocco, Niger, Norway, Panama, Philippines, Portugal, St. Vincent and the Grenadines, Senegal, Solomon Islands, United Kingdom of Great Britain and Northern Ireland, and Viet Nam.

### B. UNESCO Convention for the Protection of Cultural Property in the Event of Armed Conflict

Up to 1 January 1995, the following States have become parties to the convention by ratification or accession: Albania, Australia, Austria, Belgium, Brazil, Bulgaria, Burkina Faso, Byelorussian S.S.R., Cameroon, Côte d'Ivoire (Ivory Coast), Cuba, Cyprus, Czechoslovakia, Dominican Republic, Ecuador, Egypt, Federal Republic of Germany, France, Gabon, German Democratic Republic, Ghana, Greece, Guatemala, Guinea, Holy See, Hungary, India, Indonesia, Iran, Iraq, Israel, Italy, Jordan, Kuwait, Lebanon, Libya, Liechtenstein, Luxembourg, Madagascar, Malaysia, Mali, Mexico, Monaco, Mongolia, Morocco, Myanmar, Netherlands, Nicaragua, Niger, Nigeria, Norway, Oman, Pakistan, Panama, Poland, Qatar, Romania, San Marino, Saudi Arabia, Senegal, Spain, Sudan, Sweden, Switzerland, Syria, Tanzania, Thailand, Tunisia, Turkey, Ukrainian S.S.R., Union of Soviet Socialist Republics, Yemen, Yugoslavia, and Zaire.

The following States have signed the convention: Andorra, Denmark, El Salvador, Japan, New Zealand, Philippines, Portugal, United Kingdom of Great Britain and Northern Ireland, United States of America, and Uruguay.

### C. UNESCO Convention on the Means of Prohibiting and Preventing the Illicit Import, Export and Transfer of Ownership of Cultural Property

Up to 1 January 1995, the convention has been ratified or acceded to by the following States: Algeria, Argentina, Bangladesh, Bolivia, Brazil, Bulgaria, Burkina Faso, Byelorussian S.S.R., Cambodia, Cameroon, Canada, Central African Republic, Colombia, Cuba, Cyprus, Czechoslovakia, Democratic People's Republic of Korea, Dominican Republic, Ecuador, Egypt, El Salvador, German Democratic Republic, Greece, Guatemala, Guinea, Honduras, Hungary, India, Iran, Iraq, Italy, Jordan, Kuwait, Libya, Madagascar, Mali, Mauritania, Mauritius, Mexico, Nepal, Nicaragua, Niger, Nigeria, Oman, Pakistan, Panama, Peru, Poland, Portugal, Qatar, Republic of Korea, Saudi Arabia, Senegal, Spain, Sri Lanka, Syria, Tanzania, Tunisia, Turkey, Ukrainian S.S.R., United States of America, Uruguay, Union of Soviet Socialist Republics, Yugoslavia, Zaire, and Zambia.

### D. UNESCO International Convention for the Protection of Performers, Producers of Phonograms and Broadcasting Organizations

Up to 1 January 1995, the following States have become parties to the convention by ratification or accession: Austria, Barbados, Brazil, Burkina Faso, Chile, Colombia, Congo, Costa Rica, Czechoslovakia, Denmark, Dominican Republic, Ecuador, El Salvador, Federal Republic of Germany, Fiji, Finland, France, Guatemala, Ireland, Italy, Luxembourg, Mexico, Monaco, Niger, Norway, Panama, Paraguay, Peru, Philippines, Sweden, United Kingdom of Great Britain and Northern Ireland, and Uruguay.

The following States have signed the convention: Belgium, Cambodia, Iceland, India, Israel, Lebanon, Spain, and Yugoslavia.

### 5. Conventions Prepared under the Auspices of the Council of Europe

### A. European Agreement relating to Persons Participating in Proceedings of the European Commission and of the Court of Human Rights

Up to 1 February 1995, the agreement has been ratified by the following States: Austria, Belgium, Cyprus, Denmark, Federal Republic of Germany, France, Ireland, Italy, Liechtenstein, Luxembourg, Malta, Netherlands, Norway, Portugal, San Marino, Spain, Sweden, Switzerland, and the United Kingdom of Great Britain and Northern Ireland.

### B. European Convention for the Prevention of Torture

Up to 1 February 1995, the convention has been ratified by the following States: Austria, Cyprus, Denmark, France, Ireland, Italy, Luxembourg, Malta, Netherlands, Norway, Spain, Sweden, Switzerland, Turkey, and the United Kingdom of Great Britain and Northern Ireland.

### C. European Convention on Human Rights

Up to 1 February 1995, the following States have become parties to the European Convention on Human Rights by ratification or accession: Austria, Belgium, Cyprus, Denmark, Federal Republic of Germany, France, Greece, Iceland, Ireland, Italy, Liechtenstein, Luxembourg, Malta, Netherlands, Norway, Portugal, San Marino, Spain, Sweden, Switzerland, Turkey, and the United Kingdom of Great Britain and Northern Ireland. Finland, which acceded to the council on 5 May 1989, has not become a party to the Convention.

All of the States parties to the convention have made a declaration under article 25 thereof recognizing for three years the competence of the European Commission on Human Rights to receive individual petitions.

All of the States parties to the convention, except Turkey, have made a declaration under article 46 thereof recognizing the compulsory jurisdiction of the European Court of Human Rights.

### D. European Convention on Human Rights: Protocols

Up to 1 February 1995, Protocol I has been ratified by all the States parties to the convention except Liechtenstein, Spain, and Switzerland.

Protocol II has been ratified by all the States parties to the convention.

Protocol IV is in force among the following States: Austria, Belgium, Denmark, Federal Republic of Germany, France, Iceland, Ireland, Italy, Luxembourg, Netherlands, Norway, Portugal, San Marino, and Sweden.

Protocol VI has been ratified by the following States: Austria, Denmark, Federal Republic of Germany, France, Iceland, Italy, Luxembourg, Netherlands, Norway, Portugal, San Marino, Spain, Sweden, and Switzerland. It entered into force on 1 March 1985.

Protocol VII has been ratified by the following States: Austria, Denmark, France, Greece, Iceland, Luxembourg, Norway, San Marino, Spain, Sweden, and Switzerland. It entered into force on 1 November 1988.

Protocol VIII has been ratified by all States parties to the convention. It entered into force on 1 January 1995.

*E. European Convention on Social Security*

Up to 1 January 1995, the following States have become parties to the convention by ratification or accession: Austria, Luxembourg, Netherlands, Portugal, and Turkey.

The following States have signed the convention: Belgium, France, Greece, Ireland, and Italy.

*F. European Convention on the Suppression of Terrorism*

Up to 1 January 1995, the following States have become parties to the convention by ratification or accession: Austria, Belgium, Cyprus, Denmark, Federal Republic of Germany, France, Greece, Iceland, Italy, Liechtenstein, Luxembourg, Netherlands, Norway, Portugal, Spain, Sweden, Switzerland, Turkey, and the United Kingdom of Great Britain and Northern Ireland.

Ireland and Malta have signed the convention.

*G. European Social Charter*

Up to 1 January 1995, the following States have become parties to the charter by ratification or accession: Austria, Cyprus, Denmark, Federal Republic of Germany, France, Greece, Iceland, Ireland, Italy, Malta, Netherlands, Norway, Spain, Sweden, and United Kingdom of Great Britain and Northern Ireland.

The following States have signed the charter: Belgium, Luxembourg, Portugal, Switzerland, and Turkey.

## 6. Conventions Prepared under the Auspices of the Organization of African Unity

*A. African Charter on Human and Peoples' Rights*

Up to 1 January 1995, the following States have become parties to the African Convention on Human and People's Rights by ratification or accession: Algeria, Benin, Botswana, Burkina Faso, Cape Verde, Central African Republic, Chad, Congo, Comoros, Egypt, Equatorial Guinea, Gabon, Gambia, Ghana, Guinea, Guinea-Bissau, Liberia, Libya, Mali, Mauritania, Niger, Nigeria, Rwanda, Sao Tome and Principe, Senegal, Sierra Leone, Somalia, Sudan, Tanzania, Togo, Tunisia, Uganda, Zaire, Zambia, and Zimbabwe.

*B. African Convention governing the Specific Aspects of Refugee Problems in Africa*

Up to 1 January 1995, the following States have become parties to the convention by ratification or accession: Algeria, Angola, Benin, Burkina Faso, Burundi, Cameroon, Cape Verde, Central African Republic, Chad, Congo, Egypt, Equatorial Guinea, Ethiopia, Gabon, Gambia, Ghana, Guinea, Lesotho, Liberia, Libya, Malawi, Mali, Mauritania, Morocco, Niger, Nigeria, Rwanda, Senegal, Seychelles, Sierra Leone, Sudan, Swaziland, Tanzania, Togo, Uganda, Zaire, Zambia, and Zimbabwe.

## 7. Conventions Prepared under the Auspices of the Organization of American States

*A. American Convention on Human Rights*

Up to 1 January 1995, the following States have become parties to the convention by ratification or accession: Argentina, Barbados, Bolivia, Colombia, Costa Rica, Dominican Republic, Ecuador, El Salvador, Grenada, Guatemala, Haiti, Honduras, Jamaica, Mexico, Nicaragua, Panama, Peru, Suriname, Uruguay, and Venezuela.

The following States have signed the convention: Chile and Paraguay.

The following States have accepted the competence of the Inter-American Commission on Human Rights to hear petitions brought by one State party against another: Argentina, Colombia, Costa Rica, Ecuador, Jamaica, Peru, Uruguay, and Venezuela.

The following States have accepted the competence of the Inter-American Court of Human Rights: Argentina, Colombia, Costa Rica, Ecuador, Guatemala, Honduras, Peru, Suriname, Uruguay, and Venezuela.

*B. Inter-American Convention on Conflict of Laws concerning the Adoption of Minors*

Up to 1 June 1995, the following countries have become parties to the convention by ratification or accession: Colombia and Mexico.

The convention has been signed by Bolivia, Brazil, Chile, Dominican Republic, Ecuador, Haiti, Uruguay, and Venezuela.

# SUBJECT INDEX